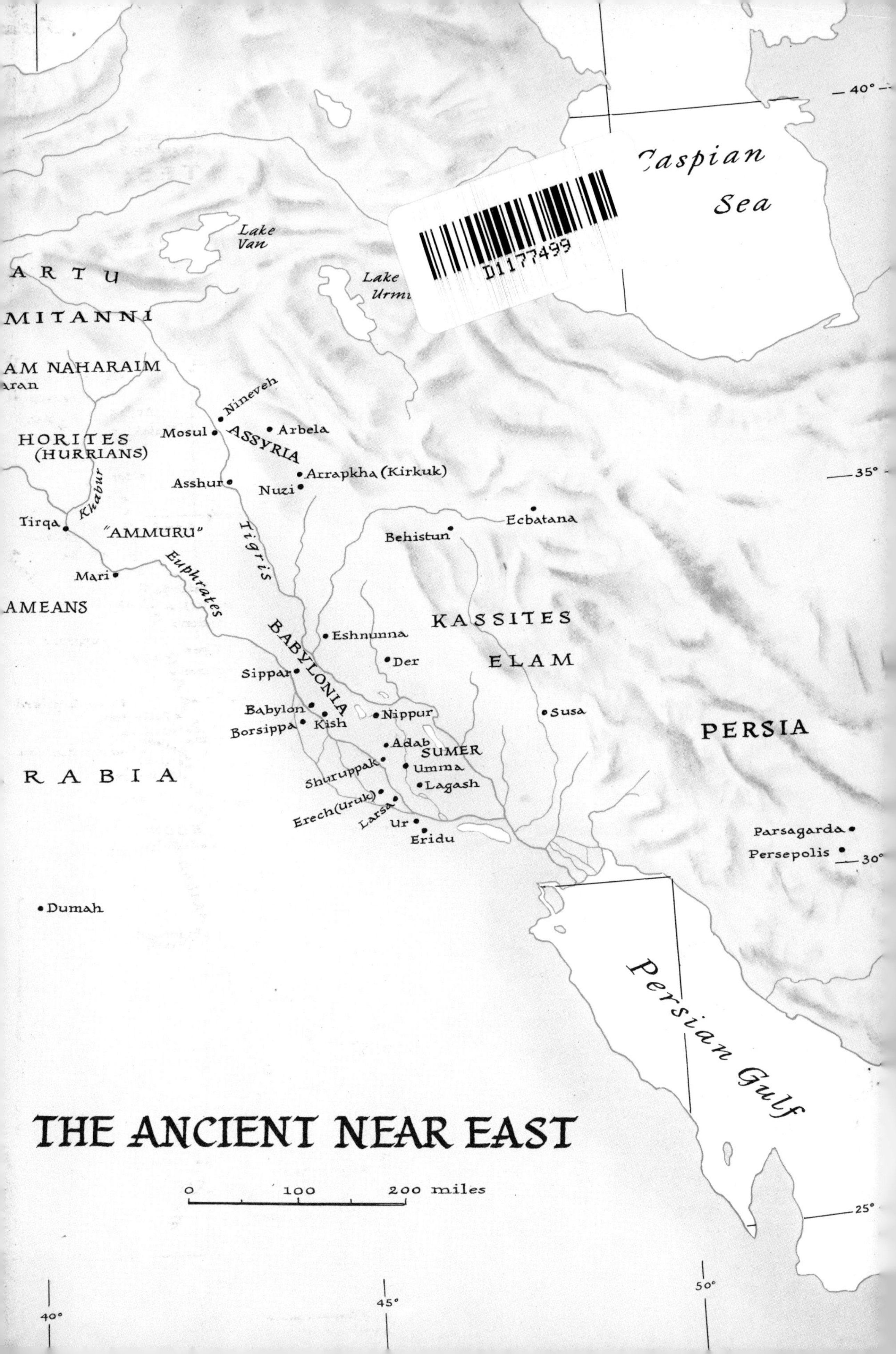
THE ANCIENT NEAR EAST
0
100
200 miles
Caspian
Sea
Lake
Van
Lake
Urmi
ARTU
MITANNI
AM NAHARAIM
aran
Nineveh
Mosul
Arbela
ASSYRIA
HORITES
(HURRIANS)
Khabur
Asshur
Arrapkha (Kirkuk)
Nuzi
Tirqa
"AMMURU"
Tigris
Euphrates
Mari
AMEANS
Ecbatana
Behistun
KASSITES
ELAM
BABYLONIA
Eshnunna
Der
Sippar
Babylon
Kish
Borsippa
Nippur
Susa
PERSIA
Adab
SUMER
Shuruppak
Umma
Lagash
Erech (Uruk)
Larsa
Ur
Eridu
RABIA
Parsagarda
Persepolis
Dumah
Persian Gulf
40°
35°
30°
25°
40°
45°
50°

THE JEROME BIBLICAL COMMENTARY

Edited by

RAYMOND E. BROWN, S.S.
Union Theological Seminary, New York
Woodstock College, New York

JOSEPH A. FITZMYER, S.J.
Weston College School of Theology
Cambridge, Mass.

ROLAND E. MURPHY, O.CARM.
The Divinity School
Duke University, Durham, N. C.

With a Foreword by
His Eminence Augustin Cardinal Bea, S. J.

Volume I

THE OLD TESTAMENT

Volume II

THE NEW TESTAMENT
AND TOPICAL ARTICLES

THE JEROME BIBLICAL COMMENTARY

PRENTICE-HALL, INC. *Englewood Cliffs, New Jersey*

Nihil Obstat

Raymond E. Brown, S.S.
Joseph A. Fitzmyer, S.J.
Roland E. Murphy, O.Carm.
Censores Deputati

Imprimatur

✠ Lawrence Cardinal Shehan
Archbishop of Baltimore
June 6, 1968

THE JEROME BIBLICAL COMMENTARY—*Two Volumes*
Editors
Raymond E. Brown, S.S.
Joseph A. Fitzmyer, S.J.
Roland E. Murphy, O.Carm.

19 18 17 16 15 14 13

Library of Congress Catalog Card No.: 68-9140
Printed in the United States of America

PRENTICE-HALL INTERNATIONAL, INC., *London*
PRENTICE-HALL OF AUSTRALIA, PTY. LTD., *Sydney*
PRENTICE-HALL OF CANADA, LTD., *Toronto*
PRENTICE-HALL OF INDIA PRIVATE LTD., *New Delhi*
PRENTICE-HALL OF JAPAN, INC., *Tokyo*

To the Memory of
POPE PIUS XII
Whose Promotion of Biblical Studies
Bore Fruit in the Second Vatican Council

"In the sacred books the Father who is in heaven meets his children with great love and speaks with them; and the force and power in the word of God is so great that it remains the support and energy of the Church, the strength of faith for her sons, the food of the soul, the pure and perennial source of spiritual life."

Dei Verbum (Constitution on Divine Revelation of Vatican II) #21

FOREWORD

I have repeatedly stated that in many ways the Second Vatican Council would not have been possible without the long and fruitful doctrinal preparation provided by Pope Pius XII. To give only one example, we may recall how three great encyclicals of Pope Pius prepared the way for the three central documents of the Council—the encyclicals *Mystici Corporis, Divino Afflante Spiritu,* and *Mediator Dei* related respectively to the constitutions on the Church, on Divine Revelation, and on the Sacred Liturgy. Moreover, the Council would not have been able to meet successfully so many problems of modern life if beforehand the truly indefatigable teaching ministry of Pius XII had not thrown light little by little on so many pressing difficulties. In the biblical field it is certain that the flourishing development of Catholic biblical studies, due in large part to the encyclical *Divino Afflante Spiritu,* was what made possible the truly biblical orientation of the conciliar documents, based, as they were, on scriptural foundations. It was precisely for this reason that the documents of Vatican II were rightly appreciated even by our non-Catholic brethren.

This development and the fruits that it has borne have fully confirmed what I wrote years ago, namely, that the encyclical *Divino Afflante Spiritu* of Pope Pius XII "is no less important than the encyclical *Providentissimus Deus* of Pope Leo XIII, which has been called the Magna Carta of biblical studies." (See "Pio XII e le scienze bibliche," *Pio XII Pont. Max. postridie calendas martias* MDCCCLXXVI–MDCCCCLVI [Milan, 1956] 72.) I have often had occasion to note with great pleasure that the Catholics of the United States have had a large share in this development of biblical studies. It suffices to mention the Catholic Biblical Association and its magazine *The Catholic Biblical Quarterly,* along with various other initiatives undertaken by it to make Sacred Scripture better known, studied, and loved.

The present commentary on the whole Bible is another instance of this spirit, and that is why I greet it with particular pleasure. Its great value is that it is not only *about* the Bible, but that it also, as it were, brings the reader to the Word of God itself—to read it, to study it, and to meditate on it. Indeed, we can never insist enough on the advice of Pius XII that emphasizes the power and the spiritual fruitfulness of the words of Scripture: "The Word of God . . . needs no artificial devices nor human adaptation to move hearts and arouse souls. For the Sacred Pages inspired by God are in themselves rich in original meaning; endowed with a divine power, they have their own value; adorned with heavenly beauty, of themselves they radiate light and splendor, provided only that they are so fully and accurately explained by the interpreter that all the treasures of wisdom and prudence contained therein are brought to light" (*EB* 553; *RSS*, p. 94).

The present commentary makes it possible for the Word of God to act on man in this religious and spiritual way, since it is concerned principally with expounding "the theological doctrine of the individual books and texts in relation to faith and morals" (as the encyclical directs: *EB* 551; *RSS*, p. 93). In this way the exegesis found in the commentary will not only be of use to professors of theology, but will "also be of assistance to priests in their presentation of Christian doctrine to the people and thus help all the faithful to lead a life that is holy and worthy of a Christian" (*Ibid.*).

Thus, by putting the reader himself in contact with the Written Word of God, *The Jerome Biblical Commentary* makes a real contribution toward realizing the goal firmly insisted upon in the constitution on Divine Revelation of Vatican II (#22): "It is necessary that the faithful have full access to Sacred Scripture." Nor can there be any doubt that this work will also be a fruitful contribution to the great cause of ecumenism; for as the conciliar decree on Ecumenism (#21) has said: "In the dialogue [with our non-Catholic brethren] Sacred Scripture makes an excellent tool in the powerful hand of God for the attainment of that unity which the Savior offers to all men."

I hope therefore that this work will enjoy a wide distribution. May it realize the desire with which the constitution on Divine Revelation (#26) closes: "Through the reading and study of the sacred books, let 'the word of the Lord run its course and be glorified' (2 Thes 3:1), and let the treasure of revelation entrusted to the Church increasingly fill the hearts of men."

+ Aug Card Bea

AUGUSTIN CARDINAL BEA, S.J.
Member of the Pontifical Biblical Commission
President of the Secretariat for Promoting Christian Unity

CONTENTS

Volume I

THE OLD TESTAMENT

Volume II

THE NEW TESTAMENT AND TOPICAL ARTICLES

EDITORS' PREFACE

This work is a compact commentary on the whole Bible written by Roman Catholic scholars according to the principles of modern biblical criticism. It is no secret that the last fifteen or twenty years have seen almost a revolution in Catholic biblical studies—a revolution encouraged by authority, for its Magna Carta was the encyclical *Divino Afflante Spiritu* (1943) of Pope Pius XII. The principles of literary and historical criticism, so long regarded with suspicion, are now, at last, accepted and applied by Catholic exegetes. The results have been many: a new and vital interest in the Bible throughout the Church; a greater contribution of biblical studies to modern theology; a community of effort and understanding among Catholic and non-Catholic scholars. But there has remained a need to gather the fruits of these insights into one place where they will be conveniently available to all who are interested.

A great number of Catholic introductions to the Bible have appeared in recent years and have performed the useful task of explaining the new attitudes. But inevitably the readers, once instructed in how to approach Scripture, have looked for help in working through the biblical books themselves—in short, they have needed a commentary. Useful pamphlet commentaries have multiplied, but their very simplicity is limiting. The *JBC* is intended to aid those who find pamphlets inadequate.

In this work, which is primarily and emphatically a commentary, the editors have envisioned an audience of educated readers who wish *to study* the Scriptures. Hopefully this will include a large number of the laity, for Bible courses have now become significant in Catholic religion and theology programs. Not only students but also teachers of religion and theology on all levels feel the need of an adequate background in Scripture, since the Bible is playing such an important part in modern religious education. Special attention has been paid to seminarians and priests who require a commentary on the Scriptures both for their study of theology and for preaching. For them the present work may well serve both as a basic text in the seminary and as a reference book throughout the ministry—as a foundation and a *vade mecum*. Some of the readers may ultimately progress to deeper Scripture study, wanting to consult scientific articles and even commentary series where a whole volume is dedicated to a particular book of the Bible. With this in mind, a deliberate attempt has been made to supply ample bibliographical guides in several languages and to introduce the reader to the technical terminology necessary for more detailed research.

When this volume was being planned, the editors gave serious thought to its ecumenical implications. The most obvious solution would have been to invite non-Catholic contributors; but a more careful consideration convinced the editors that they could best serve the ecumenical needs of the times by producing a truly modern commentary by Roman Catholics. Everyone now knows that generally Catholic and non-Catholic biblical scholars work very well together and have the same approach to and interpretation of most biblical passages. But there remains a feeling or suspicion both within and without the Roman Catholic Church that such cooperation represents a private endeavor of only a few and that it is without any official backing in the Church. The question of *the* Catholic interpretation of the Bible constantly reappears. It seemed to the editors that the best way to expose the misunderstanding implicit in this question was to produce a commentary written entirely by Catholics. This would allow readers of all persuasions to see a representative group of Catholic scholars at work—not the isolated and allegedly liberal mavericks, but some fifty contributors teaching in Catholic colleges and seminaries in the United States, Canada, and abroad. Naturally some are more critical than others in their approach to the Bible and thus exemplify the variation to be found in any community of scholars. But this variation itself should destroy once and for all the myth of *the* Catholic position, as if there were a series of biblical interpretations or positions that all must profess. We hope that our non-Catholic brethren can find in this commentary the same scientific method and love for objectivity that characterize the best commentaries written by scholars of their own denominations. The heavy dependence of our contributors on non-Catholic research is cheerfully and gratefully acknowledged on almost every page, laying to rest the image of a parochial mentality in Roman Catholic biblical studies. This does not mean that our Catholic contributors are indifferent either to religious implications or to theology. They profess the one faith; yet they are convinced that it is a disservice to that faith to seek anachronistically to read the Scriptures in the light of later religious problems and disputes. Rather their duty is to interpret the Scriptures as accurately as possible according to the mind of the men who wrote them. And while a serious effort has been made to bring out the theological import of the Bible, biblical theology has been conceived in thought patterns and terminology that often do not provide decisive solutions for the problems of subsequent centuries.

The large number of contributors, necessary both to the purpose and success of the commentary, has presented problems to the editors. The initial request for contributions was sent out in 1962. Inevitably some contributors missed their deadlines; in addition, death and sickness took a toll. This meant that some articles had to be reassigned to generous eleventh-hour workers; others had to be supplied by the editors themselves, beyond the articles for which they had originally contracted. Only in early 1967 were all the contributions in the editors' hands. They then had the difficult task of correlating and revising the eighty articles, so that the whole work would truly represent scholarship as of the date of publication. Moreover, although the editors wished to accord to each contributor as much independence of view and method as possible, they had to achieve a certain overall unity that at times necessitated additions and subtractions, minor alterations of style, and insertions of bibliography. The contributors have shown themselves most cooperative; and all in all the commentary is a common production wherein, nonetheless, the contributors are honestly responsible for their own articles. This, of course, does not mean that the editors have any illusion that the articles are all of equal value.

A few practical guides will be helpful to the reader. Because of the length of the work, a frequent use of abbreviations was necessary. A quarter-hour's perusal of the table of abbreviations used for the biblical books, for the apocrypha, for the biblical languages, etc., will forestall too frequent recourse to these tables. The biblical books bear the titles now common in English, as exemplified in the RSV version, with the exceptions that we use Sirach for Ecclesiasticus (to avoid confusion with Ecclesiastes) and Apocalpyse for Revelation (to avoid the misunderstanding common in the use of the latter). Proper names are given in the common English (RSV) spelling. Chapter and verse enumeration follows the original language patterns even in those books where the versions differ (thus, Hebrew numbering, rather than Greek or Latin, for the Psalms). The order of the commentary articles is normally chronological (→ 67:22, 57).

Frequent cross references to other *JBC* articles have been supplied by means of an arrow, followed by the abbreviated title of the article to which reference is made. To facilitate this, all eighty articles have been numbered and broken down into sections (indicated by boldface marginal numbers); and both article and section numbers are given in references. Thus → Exodus, 3:29 means to consult *JBC* article 3 (article on Exodus), section 29. (No confusion with references to biblical books, chapters and verses, is possible, since the presence of the arrow always indicates a cross reference to a *JBC* article.) The index will be a help to the reader in finding additional information.

There are two types of articles: topical and commentary. Knowing that many would need background before beginning a verse-by-verse study of the Bible, the editors planned for twenty-five articles of a topical, introductory nature. Acquaintance with some of these can be very helpful to the reader in understanding the more technical details in the commentary articles. For instance, the article on Hermeneutics (Art. 71) supplies a basic treatment of attitudes in approaching the Bible. The article on Canonicity (Art. 67) gives a survey of the composition of biblical literature that is essential for any reader. A generous amount of space has been devoted to articles on biblical theology. Old Testament themes are traced through their different historical stages of development; and a careful distinction is made in the New Testament section among the differing theologies of the various authors. Students and teachers would do well to look over the topical articles carefully before starting the commentaries.

The structure and paragraphing of the commentary articles are determined by the outlines of the respective biblical books. The commentary generally proceeds verse by verse, and lemmata (the words of Scripture being commented upon) are supplied in italics for easy reference. The editors made the difficult decision of not requiring the contributors to comment on any one English translation of the Bible. They recognized that there are in current usage many excellent translations, for instance, the RSV, the new CCD, the American or "Chicago" Bible, the Jerusalem Bible, the new Jewish *Torah,* the NEB; and they wished that this commentary might be used with any of them. (Moreover, they did not wish to countenance the extravagant claims of advertising for the universal superiority of one translation, since part of the serious study of the Bible is the recognition of the limitations inherent in all translations.) The editors did insist that the lemmata faithfully represent the biblical original, whether Hebrew, Aramaic, or Greek, so that the reader using a standard translation from the original languages would be able to recognize the biblical phrases without difficulty. (Note that the *JBC* is *not* a commentary on an English translation of the Latin Vulgate; in this it differs from previous Catholic commentaries.)

We close our preface with a word of thanks. Besides acknowledging our obvious debt to the contributors, we wish to express our appreciation to His Eminence

Augustin Cardinal Bea for his Foreword—it is a source of pride that the man who has embodied so much of the spirit of change in Catholic biblical studies should extend his blessing upon our work. In the matter of ecclesiastical approbation we have had the most understanding cooperation of the Baltimore Archdiocese (in which two of the editors reside), and we are deeply grateful to His Eminence Lawrence Cardinal Shehan.

The index was prepared by Messrs. Joseph Tiernan, Lawrence Plutko, and students at St. Mary's Seminary, Baltimore; and we are appreciative of the care expended on it. Thanks are also due to Reverend James B. Donnelly, S.J., who translated Article 64. If the work of so many contributors offered difficulty to the editors, it presented even greater problems to the publishers. Paul E. O'Connell, Assistant Vice President of Prentice-Hall, has shown a personal interest in the project since its inception and was most generous in the time he gave to the editors. Without the much-tried patience of Mary F. Sherwood, Supervisory Editor, our commentary would never have seen the light of day. We are deeply grateful too for the meticulous artistic work of the cartographer, Louis M. Kobbé, for the painstaking editing done by Claire Jones, Natalie Krivanek, and Mary Jane Rutsch, and for the careful proofreading by Margaret G. McNeily. All that remains now is to entrust our work to the reader.

Raymond E. Brown, S.S.
Editor of Topical Articles (Volume II)

Joseph A. Fitzmyer, S.J.
Editor of NT Commentary Articles (Volume II)

Roland E. Murphy, O.Carm.
Editor of OT Articles (Volume I)

This commentary is named after St. Jerome,
the foremost Scripture scholar among the Church Fathers,
a pioneer in biblical criticism.

CONTRIBUTORS

Blenkinsopp, Joseph, D.Phil., Associate Professor of Old Testament, University of Notre Dame, Notre Dame, Ind.
Deuteronomy

Bourke, Myles M., S.S.L., S.T.D., Pastor, Corpus Christi Church, New York, N. Y.; Adjunct Professor, Fordham University, Bronx, N. Y.
Hebrews

Brown, Raymond E., S.S., S.S.L., S.T.D., Ph.D., Professor of Biblical Studies, Union Theological Seminary, New York and Woodstock College, New York, N. Y.
Canonicity; Apocrypha; Texts and Versions; Hermeneutics; Church Pronouncements; Biblical Geography; Aspects NT Thought

Castelot, John J., S.S., S.S.L., S.T.D., Professor of Scripture, St. John's Provincial Seminary, Plymouth, Mich.
Religious Institutions

Collins, Thomas A., O.P., S.S.B., S.T.D., Professor, Department of Religious Studies, Providence College, Providence, R. I.
Church Pronouncements

Couturier, Guy P., C.S.C., S.S.L., S.T.L., Elève diplômé de l'Ecole Biblique de Jérusalem, Professor of Scripture, Faculté de Théologie, Université de Montréal, Montreal, Canada.
Jeremiah

Crossan, John Dominic, S.S.L., S.T.D., Associate Professor of Theology, De Paul University, Chicago, Ill.
Judges

D'Aragon, Jean-Louis, S.J., S.S.L., S.T.L., Professor of New Testament, Faculté de Théologie, Université de Montréal, Montreal, Canada.
Apocalypse

Denzer, George A., S.T.D., Professor of Scripture, Seminary of the Immaculate Conception, Huntington, N. Y.
Pastorals

Dillon, Richard J., S.S.L., S.T.L., Professor of New Testament, St. Joseph's Seminary, Dunwoodie, Yonkers, N. Y.; Adjunct Professor, Fordham University, Bronx, N. Y.
Acts of the Apostles

Dumm, Demetrius R., O.S.B., S.S.L., S.T.D., Professor of Scripture, St. Vincent Archabbey, Latrobe, Pa.
Tobit, Judith, Esther

Ellis, Peter F., C.SS.R., S.S.L., S.T.D., Assistant Professor, Graduate Institute of Religious Education, Fordham University, Bronx, N. Y.
1–2 Kings

Faley, Roland J., T.O.R., S.S.L., S.T.D., Professor of Old Testament, Our Lady of Loretto Seminary, Loretto, Pa.
Leviticus

Fitzgerald, Aloysius, F.S.C., S.S.L., S.T.D., Assistant Professor of Semitics, Catholic University of America, Washington, D. C.
Hebrew Poetry; Baruch

Fitzmyer, Joseph A., S.J., S.S.L., S.T.L., Ph.D., Professor of New Testament and Biblical Languages, Fordham University, Bronx, N. Y.
Acts of the Apostles; Life of Paul; NT Epistles; Galatians; Philippians; Romans; Philemon; 1 Peter; History of Israel; Pauline Theology.

Forestell, J. Terence, C.S.B., S.S.L., S.T.L., Professor of Scripture, St. Basil's Seminary, Toronto, Canada.
Proverbs; 1–2 Thessalonians

Gast, Frederick T., O.C.D., S.S.L., S.T.L., Associate Professor of Scripture, St. Paul's College and Dunbarton College, Washington, D. C.
Synoptic Problem

Grassi, Joseph A., S.S.L., S.T.L., Associate Professor, Department of Theology, Marquette University, Milwaukee, Wisc.
Colossians; Ephesians

Hartman, Louis F., C.SS.R., S.S.L., Ling.Or.L., Late Professor of Semitics, Catholic University of America, Washington, D. C.
Daniel

Huesman, John E., S.J., S.S.L., S.T.L., Ph.D., Professor of Old Testament, Jesuit School of Theology at Berkeley, Berkeley, Calif.
Exodus

Hunt, Joseph Ignatius, S.S.L., S.T.D., Professor of Old Testament and Semitic Languages, Nashotah House, Nashotah, Wisc.
Israel and Her Neighbors

Kearney, Peter J., S.S.L., S.T.L., Assistant Professor of Scripture, Catholic University of America, Washington, D. C.
Joshua

King, Philip J., S.S.L., S.T.D., Professor of Scripture, St. John Seminary, Brighton, Mass.
Amos; Micah

Kselman, John S., S.S., S.T.L., Ph.D., Professor of Old Testament, St. Mary's Seminary, Roland Park, Baltimore, Md.
Modern NT Criticism

Kugelman, Richard, C.P., S.S.L., S.T.L., Professor of New Testament and Chairman, Theology Department, St. John's University, Jamaica, N. Y.
1 Corinthians

Leahy, Thomas W., S.J., S.S.L., S.T.L., Ph.D., Professor of New Testament, Jesuit School of Theology at Berkeley, Berkeley, Calif.
James; Jude; 2 Peter

McCarthy, Dennis J., S.J., S.S.L., S.T.D., Professor of Old Testament, Pontifical Biblical Institute, Rome, Italy.
Hosea

McEleney, Neil J., C.S.P., S.S.L., S.T.L., Professor of Scripture, St. Paul's College, Washington, D. C.
1–2 Maccabees

McGowan, Jean Carroll, R.S.C.J., Ph.D., Associate Professor, Religion Department, Manhattanville College of the Sacred Heart, Purchase, N.Y.
Jonah

McKenzie, John L., S.T.D., Professor of Theology, De Paul University, Chicago, Ill.
Matthew; Aspects OT Thought

MacKenzie, Roderick A. F., S.J., S.S.D., Professor of Old Testament and former Rector, Pontifical Biblical Institute, Rome, Italy.
Job

MacRae, George S., S.J., S.T.L., Ph.D., Associate Professor of New Testament, Weston College School of Theology, Cambridge, Mass.
Texts and Versions

Maly, Eugene H., S.T.D., S.S.D., Professor of Scripture, Mt. St. Mary's of the West Seminary, Cincinnati, Ohio.
Introduction to Pentateuch; Genesis

Mally, Edward J., S.J., S.S.L., S.T.L., Assistant Professor of New Testament, Woodstock College, New York, N. Y.
Mark

Moriarty, Frederick L., S.J., S.S.L., S.T.D., Professor of Old Testament, Weston College, Weston, Mass., and Gregorian University, Rome, Italy.
Numbers; Isaiah 1–39

Murphy, Richard T. A., O.P., S.T.D., S.S.D., Professor of the Science of Religion, King's College, London, Ont., Canada.
Zephaniah, Nahum, Habakkuk

Murphy, Roland E., O.Carm., S.S.L., S.T.D., Professor of Old Testament, The Divinity School, Duke University, Durham, N. C.
Introduction to Wisdom Literature; Canticle; Qoheleth; Psalms; History of Israel

North, Robert, S.J., S.T.L., S.S.D., Professor of Archaeology, Marquette University, Milwaukee, Wisc. and Pontifical Biblical Institute, Rome, Italy.
1–2 Chronicles, Ezra, Nehemiah; Biblical Geography; Biblical Archaeology

O'Rourke, John J., S.S.L., S.T.L., Professor of Scripture, St. Charles Seminary, Overbrook, Philadelphia, Pa.
2 Corinthians

Skehan, Patrick W., S.T.D., LL.D., Professor of Semitics, Catholic University of America, Washington, D. C.
Text and Versions

Smith, Richard F., S.J., S.T.L., S.T.D., Professor of Historical Theology, School of Divinity, St. Louis University, St. Louis, Mo.
Inspiration

Stanley, David M., S.J., S.T.L., S.S.D., Professor of New Testament, Regis College, Willowdale, Ontario, Canada.
Aspects NT Thought

Stuhlmueller, Carroll, C.P., S.T.L., S.S.D., Professor of Scripture, Catholic Theological Union at Chicago, Chicago, Ill.; St. John's University, Jamaica, N. Y.
Post-Exilic Period: Spirit, Apocalyptic; Deutero-Isaiah; Haggai, Zechariah, Malachi; Luke

Suelzer, Alexa, S.P., Ph.D., Visiting Associate Professor, Catholic University of America, Washington, D. C.
Modern OT Criticism

Tkacik, Arnold J., O.S.B., S.S.L., S.T.L., Professor of Scripture, St. Benedict's College and Seminary, Atchinson, Kan.
Ezekiel

Turro, James C., S.S.L., S.T.L., Professor of Scripture, Darlington Seminary, Ramsey, N. J.
1–2 Samuel; Canonicity

Vawter, Bruce, C. M., S.T.L., S.S.D., Professor of Scripture, De Paul University, Chicago, Ill.
Introduction to Prophetic Literature; 1–3 John; John; Johannine Theology

Weber, Thomas H., S.S.L., S.T.L., Professor of Scripture, St. Mary Seminary, Cleveland, Ohio.
Sirach

Wood, Geoffrey E., S.S.L., S.T.D., Associate Professor of Theology, Loyola College, Baltimore, Md.
Joel, Obadiah; Ruth, Lamentations

Wright, Addison G., S.S., M.A., S.S.L., S.T.D., Professor of Scripture, St. Mary's Seminary, Roland Park, Baltimore, Md.
Wisdom; History of Israel

ABBREVIATIONS

PROTOCANONICAL AND DEUTEROCANONICAL BOOKS OF THE BIBLE

Old Testament

Gn	Genesis	Wis	Wisdom
Ex	Exodus	Sir	Sirach (Ecclesiasticus)
Lv	Leviticus	Is	Isaiah
Nm	Numbers	Dt-Is	Deutero-Isaiah
Dt	Deuteronomy	Jer	Jeremiah
Jos	Joshua	Lam	Lamentations
Jgs	Judges	Bar	Baruch
Ru	Ruth	Ez	Ezekiel
1 Sm	1 Samuel	Dn	Daniel
2 Sm	2 Samuel	Hos	Hosea
1 Kgs	1 Kings	Jl	Joel
2 Kgs	2 Kings	Am	Amos
1 Chr	1 Chronicles	Ob	Obadiah
2 Chr	2 Chronicles	Jon	Jonah
Ezr	Ezra	Mi	Micah
Neh	Nehemiah	Na	Nahum
Tb	Tobit	Hab	Habakkuk
Jdt	Judith	Zeph	Zephaniah
Est	Esther	Hag	Haggai
Jb	Job	Zech	Zechariah
Ps(s)	Psalms	Dt-Zech	Deutero-Zechariah
Prv	Proverbs	Mal	Malachi
Eccl	Ecclesiastes (Qoheleth)	1 Mc	1 Maccabees
Ct	Canticle of Canticles	2 Mc	2 Maccabees

New Testament

Mt	Matthew	1 Tm	1 Timothy
Mk	Mark	2 Tm	2 Timothy
Lk	Luke	Ti	Titus
Jn	John	Phlm	Philemon
Acts	Acts of the Apostles	Heb	Hebrews
Rom	Romans	Jas	James
1 Cor	1 Corinthians	1 Pt	1 Peter
2 Cor	2 Corinthians	2 Pt	2 Peter
Gal	Galatians	1 Jn	1 John
Eph	Ephesians	2 Jn	2 John
Phil	Philippians	3 Jn	3 John
Col	Colossians	Jude	Jude
1 Thes	1 Thessalonians	Ap	Apocalypse
2 Thes	2 Thessalonians		

APOCRYPHA OF THE OT

Apoc. Bar.	*Apocalypse of Baruch*
Apoc. Mos.	*Apocalypse of Moses*
Aristeas	*(Letter of) Aristeas to Philocrates* (→ 68:32–33)
2 Baruch	*Syriac Apocalypse of Baruch* (→ 68:43)
3 Baruch	*Greek Apocalypse of Baruch* (→ 68:44)
Enoch	*First Enoch* (in Ethiopic) (→ 68:9–15)
2 Enoch	*Second Enoch* (in Slavonic; = *Book of the Secrets of Enoch*) (→ 68:8)
1 Esdras	Esdras A of the LXX; III Esdras of the Latin versions (→ 68:38–41)
2 Esdras	IV Esdras of the Vg (→ 68:40)
4 Ezra	*Apocalypse of Ezra* (= chs. 3–14 of *2 Esdras*) (→ 68:41)
Jub	*Book of Jubilees* (→ 68:16–24)
3 Mc	*Third Maccabees* (= *Ptolemaica*) (→ 68:35)
4 Mc	*Fourth Maccabees* (= *On the Supremacy of Reason*) (→ 68:36)
Pss Sol	*Psalms of Solomon* (→ 68:45–47)
QL	Qumran Literature (see "Dead Sea Scrolls and Related Texts")
SibOr	*Sibylline Oracles* (→ 68:48)
Test.	*Testaments of the Twelve Patriarchs* (→ 68:25–31)
T. Asher, T. Levi, etc.	*Testament of Asher, Testament of Levi,* etc. (= one of the individual testaments in *Test.*)

DEAD SEA SCROLLS AND RELATED TEXTS (QL)

CD	Cairo (Geniza text of the) Damascus (Document) (→ 68:75)
DSS	Dead Sea Scrolls
Hev	Nahal Hever caves (→ 68:108)
Mas	Masada (→ 68:110)
Mird	Khirbet Mird (→ 68:105)
Mur	Wadi Murabba'at caves (→ 68:106)
p	Pesher (commentary; → 68:77)
Q	Qumran
1Q, 2Q, 3Q, etc.	Numbered caves of Qumran, yielding written material; followed by abbreviation of biblical or apocryphal book
1QapGn	Genesis Apocryphon of Qumran Cave 1 (→ 68:81)
1QH	*Hôdāyôt* (Hymns of Thanksgiving) (→ 68:74)
1QIs [a, b]	First or second copy of Isaiah from Qumran Cave 1 (→ 69:23)
1QpHab	Pesher on Habakkuk from Qumran Cave 1 (→ 68:77)
1QM	*Milḥāmâ* (War Scroll) (→ 68:76)
1QS	*Serek ha-Yaḥad* (Rule of the Community, Manual of Discipline) (→ 68:71)
1QSa	Appendix A (Rule of the Congregation) to 1QS (→ 68:72)
1QSb	Appendix B (Blessings) to 1QS (→ 68:73)
3Q*15*	Copper Scroll of Qumran Cave 3 (→ 68:82)
4QFlor	Florilegium (or Eschatological Midrashim) of Qumran Cave (→ 68:80)
4QMess ar	Aramaic "Messianic" text from Qumran Cave 4
4QPrNab	Prayer of Nabonidus from Qumran Cave 4 (→ 26:20)
4QTest	Testimonia text from Qumran Cave 4 (→ 68:79)
4QTLevi	*Testament of Levi* from Qumran Cave 4 (→ 68:25)
11QMelch	Melchizedek text from Qumran Cave 11 (→ 68:69)
11QtgJob	Targum of Job from Qumran Cave 11 (→ 69:83)

(For the system used in referring to biblical mss. from Qumran, → Texts, 69:20)

ANCIENT AND MODERN PUBLICATIONS, SERIALS, INSTITUTIONS

AAS	*Acta apostolicae sedis*
AASOR	*Annual of the American Schools of Oriental Research*
AB	Anchor Bible (Garden City)
Abel, *GP*	F.-M. Abel, *Géographie de la Palestine* (2 vols.; 2nd ed., Paris, 1933–38)
AbhTANT	Abhandlungen zur Theologie des Alten und Neuen Testaments (Zurich)
AC	*L'antiquité classique*
AcOr	*Acta orientalia*
ACW	Ancient Christian Writers (Westminster, Md.)
AER	*American Ecclesiastical Review*
AfO	*Archiv für Orientforschung*
AG	W. F. Arndt and F. W. Gingrich, *A Greek-English Lexicon of the New Testament* (Chicago, 1957)
AgAp	Josephus, *Against Apion*
AHDL	*Archives d'histoire doctrinale et littéraire*
AJA	*American Journal of Archaeology*
AJP	*American Journal of Philology*
AJSL	*American Journal of Semitic Languages and Literatures*
AJT	*American Journal of Theology*
ALBO	Analecta lovaniensia biblica et orientalia (Louvain)
Albright, *AP*	W. F. Albright, *The Archaeology of Palestine* (Harmondsworth, 1960)
Albright, *ARI*	W. F. Albright, *Archaeology and the Religion of Israel* (Baltimore, 1953)
Albright, *BP*	W. F. Albright, *The Biblical Period from Abraham to Ezra* (Harper Torchbook; N.Y., 1963)
Albright, *FSAC*	W. F. Albright, *From the Stone Age to Christianity* (Garden City, 1957)
AmiCl	*L'ami du clergé*
AnalBib	Analecta biblica (Rome)
AnalGreg	Analecta gregoriana (Rome)
ANE	J. B. Pritchard, ed., *Ancient Near East* (Princeton, 1965)
ANEP	J. B. Pritchard, ed., *Ancient Near East in Pictures* (Princeton, 1955)
ANET	J. B. Pritchard, ed., *Ancient Near Eastern Texts* (rev. ed.; Princeton, 1955)
Ang	*Angelicum*
AnglTR	*Anglican Theological Review*
Ant.	Josephus, *Antiquities of the Jews*
Anton	*Antonianum*
AOS	American Oriental Series (New Haven)
APOT	R. H. Charles, *Apocrypha and Pseudepigrapha of the Old Testament* (2 vols.; Oxford, 191
Arch	*Archaeology*
ARM	A. Parrot and G. Dossin, eds., *Archives royales de Mari* (Paris, 1950—)
ArOr	*Archiv Orientální*
ASNU	Acta seminarii neotestamentici upsaliensis (Uppsala)
ASOR	American Schools of Oriental Research
ASTI	*Annual of the Swedish Theological Institute*
AtBib	H. Grollenberg, *Atlas of the Bible* (London, 1956)
ATD	Das Alte Testament deutsch (Göttingen)
AusBR	*Australian Biblical Review*
AusCRec	*Australian Catholic Record*
BA	*Biblical Archaeologist*
BAC	Biblioteca de autores cristianos (Madrid)
BAL	*Berichte über die Verhandlungen der sächsischen Akademie der Wissenschaften zu Leipzig* (Berlin)
BANE	G. E. Wright, ed., *The Bible and the Ancient Near East* (Fest. W. F. Albright; N.Y., 1961)
BAR	*Biblical Archaeologist Reader* (2 vols.; N.Y., 1961, 1964)
BASOR	*Bulletin of the American Schools of Oriental Research*
BB	Bonner-Bibel (Bonn)
BBB	Bonner biblische Beiträge (Bonn)
BBLAK	Beiträge zur biblischen Landes- und Altertumskunde
BCCT	J. L. McKenzie, ed., *The Bible in Current Catholic Thought* (N.Y., 1962)

BDB	F. Brown, S. R. Driver, and C. A. Briggs, *A Hebrew and English Lexicon of the Old Testament* (Oxford, 1952)
Beginnings	F. J. Foakes Jackson and K. Lake, eds., *Beginnings of Christianity* (5 vols.; London, 1920–33)
Benoit, *Exégèse*	P. Benoit, *Exégèse et théologie* (2 vols.; Paris, 1961)
Bentzen, *IOT*	A. Bentzen, *Introduction to the Old Testament* (2 vols.; Copenhagen, 1952)
BeO	*Bibbia e oriente*
BG	W. Barclay and F. F. Bruce, eds., Bible Guides (London, 1961—)
Bib	*Biblica*
BibArch	G. E. Wright, *Biblical Archaeology* (rev. ed.; Phila., 1963)
BibLex	H. Haag, *Bibel-Lexikon* (Einsiedeln, 1951). German version of *EDB*
BibSt	Biblische Studien (Neukirchen, 1951—)
BIES	*Bulletin of the Israel Exploration Society*
BIFAO	*Bulletin de l'institut français d'archéologie orientale*
Bijdr	*Bijdragen*
BiKi	*Bibel und Kirche*
BiViChr	*Bible et vie chrétienne*
BJPES	*Bulletin of the Jewish Palestine Exploration Society* (Jerusalem, Israel)
BJRylL	*Bulletin of the John Rylands Library*
BKAT	Biblischer Kommentar: Altes Testament (Neukirchen)
BKW	J. R. Coates, ed., Bible Key Words (London)
Black, *AAGA*	M. Black, *Aramaic Approach to the Gospels and Acts* (2nd ed.; Oxford, 1954)
Bl-Deb-F	F. Blass and A. Debrunner, *A Greek Grammar of the New Testament,* tr. R. W. Funk (Chicago, 1961)
BLitE	*Bulletin de littérature ecclésiastique*
BndM	*Benediktinische Monatsschrift*
BNTC	Black's New Testament Commentaries (London). British printing of HNTC
BNTE	W. D. Davies and D. Daube, eds., *The Background of the New Testament and Its Eschatology* (Fest. C. H. Dodd; Cambridge, 1954)
BO	*Bibliotheca orientalis*
BPl	E. Dhorme, ed., *Bible de la Pléiade* (Paris, 1956, 1959)
Bright, *Hist.*	J. Bright, *A History of Israel* (Phila., 1959)
BS	*Bibliotheca sacra*
BSt	Biblische Studien (Freiburg, 1895—)
BT	*The Bible Today*
BTS	*La Bible et terre sainte*
BTW	J. B. Bauer, ed., *Bibeltheologisches Wörterbuch* (2 vols.; Graz, 1962)
BulComEt	*Bulletin du comité d'étudès*
BulSNTS	*Bulletin of the Studiorum Novi Testamenti Societas*
Bultmann, *HST*	R. Bultmann, *The History of the Synoptic Tradition* (N.Y., 1963)
Bultmann, *TNT*	R. Bultmann, *The Theology of the New Testament* (2 vols.; N.Y., 1952–55)
BWANT	Beiträge zur Wissenschaft vom Alten und Neuen Testament (Stuttgart)
BWL	W. Lambert, *Babylonian Wisdom Literature* (Oxford, 1961)
BZ	*Biblische Zeitschrift*
BZAW	Beihefte zur *ZAW* (Berlin)
BZNW	Beihefte zur *ZNW* (Berlin)
CAH	*Cambridge Ancient History* (12 vols.; 5 vols. of plates; Cambridge, 1924–56)
CanJT	*Canadian Journal of Theology*
CAT	Commentaire de l'Ancien Testament (Neuchâtel)
CB	*Cultura bíblica*
CBL	Collectanea biblica latina (Rome, 1912—)
CBLAA	A. J. Mattill and M. B. Mattill, *A Classified Bibliography of Literature on the Acts of the Apostles* (NTTS 7; Leiden, 1966)
CBQ	*Catholic Biblical Quarterly*
CBSC	Cambridge Bible for Schools and Colleges (Cambridge)
CC	*Civiltà cattolica*
CCHS	B. Orchard *et al.*, eds., *A Catholic Commentary on Holy Scripture* (London, 1953)
CCL	Corpus christianorum latinorum
Cerfaux, *Christ*	L. Cerfaux, *Christ in the Theology of St. Paul* (N.Y., 1959)
Cerfaux, *Church*	L. Cerfaux, *The Church in the Theology of St. Paul* (N.Y., 1959)
CGTC	Cambridge Greek Testament Commentary (Cambridge)
CGTSC	Cambridge Greek Testament for Schools and Colleges (Cambridge)

ChQR	*Church Quarterly Review*
CIG	*Corpus inscriptionum graecarum* (Berlin, 1828—)
CIL	*Corpus inscriptionum latinarum* (Berlin, 1862—)
CINTI	W. Klassen and G. F. Snyder, eds., *Current Issues in New Testament Interpretation* (Fest. O. Piper; N.Y., 1962)
CIS	*Corpus inscriptionum semiticarum* (Paris, 1881—)
CiTom	*Ciencia tomista*
CJ	*Classical Journal*
ClBull	*Classical Bulletin*
ClMthly	*Clergy Monthly*
ClR	*Clergy Review*
CNEB	Cambridge Bible Commentary: New English Bible (Cambridge)
CNT	Commentaire du Nouveau Testament (Neuchâtel)
ColBG	*Collationes brugenses et gandavenses*
ColFranc	*Collectanea franciscana*
ColMech	*Collectanea mechlinensia*
ComViat	*Communio viatorum*
ConNeot	*Coniectanea Neotestamentica*
Conzelmann, *Theology*	H. Conzelmann, *The Theology of St. Luke* (N.Y., 1960)
CP	*Classical Philology*
CQ	*Classical Quarterly*
CR	*Classical Review*
CSCO	Corpus scriptorum christianorum orientalium (Louvain)
CSEL	Corpus scriptorum ecclesiasticorum latinorum (Vienna)
CSS	Cursus sacrae scripturae (Paris)
CST	Contemporary Studies in Theology (London)
CTM	*Concordia Theological Monthly*
CW	*Classical Weekly*
DACL	*Dictionnaire d'archéologie chrétienne et de liturgie* (15 vols.; Paris, 1924–53)
DAFC	*Dictionnaire apologétique de la foi catholique* (4th ed.; Paris, 1925)
DanTTs	*Dansk teologisk tidsskrift*
DB	H. Denzinger and C. Bannwart, *Enchiridion symbolorum* (31st or earlier ed.; Freiburg, 1957). Cf. DS
De Vaux, *AI*	R. de Vaux, *Ancient Israel* (London and N.Y., 1961)
DictB	J. Hastings, ed., *Dictionary of the Bible* (N.Y., 1963)
DJD	Discoveries in the Judaean Desert of Jordan (Oxford, 1955—)
DocC	*Documentation catholique*
DOTT	D. W. Thomas, *Documents from Old Testament Times* (London, 1958)
DowR	*Downside Review*
Driver, *Introd.*	S. R. Driver, *Introduction to the Literature of the Old Testament* (new ed.; N.Y., 1913, repr. 1957)
DS	H. Denzinger and A. Schönmetzer, *Enchiridion symbolorum* (32nd and later ed.; Freiburg, 1963). Cf. DB
DSSHU	E. L. Sukenik, ed., *The Dead Sea Scrolls of the Hebrew University* (Jerusalem, Israel, 1955)
DSSMM	M. Burrows, ed., *The Dead Sea Scrolls of St. Mark's Monastery* (vols. 1 and 2/2; New Haven, 1950–51)
DTC	*Dictionnaire de théologie catholique* (16 vols.; Paris, 1903–65)
DThomP	*Divus Thomas (Piacenza)*
DublinRev	*Dublin Review*
DunR	*The Dunwoodie Review*
EB	*Enchiridion biblicum* (4th ed:; Naples and Rome, 1961)
EBib	Études bibliques (Paris)
Echter-B	Echter-Bibel (Würzburg)
EDB	L. F. Hartman, ed., *Encyclopedic Dictionary of the Bible* (N.Y., 1963). English version of *BibLex*
EHAT	Exegetisches Handbuch zum Alten Testament (Münster)
Eichrodt, *Theology*	W. Eichrodt, *Theology of the Old Testament*, tr. J. Baker (2 vols.; London and Phila., 1961, 1967)
Eissfeldt, *Einl.*	O. Eissfeldt, *Einleitung in das Alte Testament* (3rd ed.; Tübingen, 1964)
Eissfeldt, *OTI*	O. Eissfeldt, *The Old Testament: An Introduction* (N.Y., 1965)
EncyclBrit	*Encyclopaedia Britannica* (Chicago)

EstBib	*Estudios bíblicos*
EstEc	*Estudios eclesiásticos*
ETL	*Ephemerides theologicae lovanienses*
EvQ	*Evangelical Quarterly*
EvT	*Evangelische Theologie*
ExpT	*Expository Times*
F-B	P. Feine and J. Behm, *Introduction to the New Testament,* rev. by W. G. Kümmel; tr. A. J. Mattill (Nashville, 1965)
FrancLA	*Studii biblici franciscani liber annuus*
FrancP	Publications of the Studium biblicum franciscanum (Jerusalem)
FrancSt	*Franciscan Studies*
FreibZ	*Freiburger Zeitschrift für Philosophie und Theologie*
FRLANT	Forschungen zur Religion und Literatur des Alten und Neuen Testaments (Göttingen)
GCS	Griechische christliche Schriftsteller (Berlin)
GKC	Gesenius-Kautzsch-Cowley, *Hebrew Grammar* (Oxford, 1946)
Gl	*Glotta*
Gnom	*Gnomon*
GrBib	M. Zerwick, *Graecitas biblica* (4th ed.; Rome, 1960). Numbers correspond to English tr., *Biblical Greek* (Rome, 1963)
Greg	*Gregorianum*
Guthrie, *NTI*	D. Guthrie, *New Testament Introduction* (3 vols.; London, 1961, 1962, 1965)
HarvTR	*Harvard Theological Review*
HAT	Handbuch zum Alten Testament (Tübingen)
HBk	Herders Bibelkommentar: Die hl. Schrift für das Leben erklärt (Freiburg)
HDSB	*Harvard Divinity School Bulletin*
HE	Eusebius, *Historia ecclesiastica*
Hennecke, *NTA*	E. Hennecke and W. Schneemelcher, *New Testament Apocrypha,* ed. R. McL. Wilson (2 vols.; London, 1963, 1965)
HeythJ	*Heythrop Journal*
HibbJ	*Hibbert Journal*
HJPTJC	E. Schürer, *A History of the Jewish People in the Time of Jesus Christ* (6 vols.; Edinburgh, 1905)
HKAT	Handkommentar zum Alten Testament (Göttingen)
HKNT	Handkommentar zum Neuen Testament (Göttingen)
HL	A. Huck and H. Lietzmann, *Synopsis of the First Three Gospels* (Oxford, 1951)
HNT	Handbuch zum Neuen Testament (Tübingen)
HNTC	Harper's New Testament Commentaries (N.Y.). American printing of BNTC
HPR	*Homiletic and Pastoral Review*
HTKNT	Herders theologischer Kommentar zum Neuen Testament (Freiburg)
HTS	Harvard Theological Studies (Cambridge, Mass.)
HUCA	*Hebrew Union College Annual*
HUzT	Hermeneutische Untersuchungen zur Theologie (Tübingen)
IB	*Interpreter's Bible* (12 vols.; Nashville, 1952–57)
ICC	International Critical Commentary (N.Y.)
IDB	G. A. Buttrick, ed., *Interpreter's Dictionary of the Bible* (4 vols.; Nashville, 1963)
Interpr	*Interpretation*
ILN	*Illustrated London News*
IPLAP	B. M. Metzger, *Index to Periodical Literature on the Apostle Paul* (NTTS 1; Leiden, 1960)
IPLCG	B. M. Metzger, *Index to Periodical Literature on Christ and the Gospels* (NTTS 6; Leiden, 1966)
IrER	*Irish Ecclesiastical Record*
IrTQ	*Irish Theological Quarterly*
IsrEJ	*Israel Exploration Journal*
IZBG	*Internationale Zeitschriftenschau für Bibelwissenschaft und Grenzgebiete*
JA	*Journal asiatique*
JAL	S. Zeitlin, ed., Jewish Apocryphal Literature (N.Y.)
JAOS	*Journal of the American Oriental Society*
JBL	*Journal of Biblical Literature*
JBR	*Journal of Bible and Religion*

JCS	*Journal of Cuneiform Studies*
JE	I. Singer, ed., *Jewish Encyclopedia* (12 vols.; N.Y.; 1901–6)
JEA	*Journal of Egyptian Archeology*
JEOL	*Jaarbericht . . . ex oriente lux*
Jeremias, *EWJ*	J. Jeremias, *Eucharistic Words of Jesus* (2nd English ed.; London, 1966)
JES	*Journal of Ecumenical Studies*
JHS	*Journal of Hellenic Studies*
JJS	*Journal of Jewish Studies*
JNES	*Journal of Near Eastern Studies*
Joüon, *Grammaire*	P. Joüon, *Grammaire de l'hébreu biblique* (Rome, 1947)
JPOS	*Journal of the Palestine Oriental Society* (Jerusalem, 1921–37)
JQR	*Jewish Quarterly Review*
JRAS	*Journal of the Royal Asiatic Society*
JRel	*Journal of Religion*
JRS	*Journal of Roman Studies*
JSemS	*Journal of Semitic Studies*
JTS	*Journal of Theological Studies*
Jud	*Judaica*
JW	Josephus, *Jewish War*
KAT	E. Sellin and W. Rudolph, eds., Kommentar zum Alten Testament (Leipzig and Gütersloh)
KB	L. Koehler and W. Baumgartner, *Lexicon in veteris testamenti libros* (Leiden, 1953)
Kittel-Kahle, *BH* ³	R. Kittel and P. Kahle, eds., *Biblia hebraica* (3rd ed., rev. by A. Alt and O. Eissfeldt; Stuttgart, 1937)
KL	J. A. Kleist and J. L. Lilly, *The New Testament: Rendered from the Original Greek with Explanatory Notes* (Milwaukee, 1954)
KS	*Kirjath-Sepher*
LAE	A. Deissmann, *Light from the Ancient East* (London, 1927)
LCL	Loeb Classical Library (London and Cambridge, Mass.)
LCQ	*Lutheran Church Quarterly*
LD	Lectio divina (Paris)
Life	Josephus, *Life*
LS	H. G. Liddell and R. Scott, *A Greek-English Lexicon* (9th ed., rev. by H. S. Jones and R. McKenzie; Oxford, 1925–40)
LSB	La sacra Bibbia
LTK	*Lexikon für Theologie und Kirche* (2nd ed.; 11 vols.; Freiburg, 1957–67)
LUA	Lunds universitets årsskrift (Lund)
Luckenbill, *ARAB*	D. D. Luckenbill, *Ancient Records of Assyria and Babylonia* (2 vols.; Chicago, 1926–27)
LumenV	*Lumen vitae*
LumVi	*Lumière et vie*
LumViSup	*Lumière et vie, Supplément biblique*
Meyer	H. A. W. Meyer, Kritisch-exegetischer Kommentar über das Neue Testament (Göttingen)
M-G, *Kings*	J. A. Montgomery, *Kings,* ed. H. S. Gehman (ICC; N.Y., 1951)
MGWJ	*Monatsschrift für Geschichte und Wissenschaft des Judentums*
MNTC	Moffatt New Testament Commentaries (N.Y. and London)
MR	J. L. McKenzie, *Myths and Realities* (Milwaukee, 1963)
MScRel	*Mélanges de science religieuse*
Mus	*Muséon*
MUSJ	*Mélanges de l'université Saint-Joseph*
MüTZ	*Münchener theologische Zeitschrift*
MVAG	*Mitteilungen der vorderasiatisch-ägyptischen Gesellschaft* (Leipzig)
NatGeog	*National Geographic*
NCE	*New Catholic Encyclopedia* (15 vols.; N.Y., 1967)
NFT	New Frontiers in Theology (N.Y. and London)
NICNT	New International Commentary on the New Testament (Grand Rapids)
NKZ	*Neue kirchliche Zeitschrift*
Noth, *Hist.*	M. Noth, *History of Israel,* rev. tr. P. R. Ackroyd (N.Y., 1960)
Noth, *UP*	M. Noth, *Uberlieferungsgeschichte des Pentateuchs* (Darmstadt, 1960)
Noth, *US*	M. Noth, *Überlieferungsgeschichtliche Studien* (Darmstadt, 1957)
NovT	*Novum Testamentum*

NovTSup	Novum Testamentum Supplements (Leiden)
NRT	*Nouvelle revue théologique*
NTA	*New Testament Abstracts*
NTAbh	Neutestamentliche Abhandlungen (Münster)
NTB	C. K. Barrett, *New Testament Background: Selected Documents* (N.Y., 1961)
NTD	Das Neue Testament deutsch (Göttingen)
NThSt	*Nieuwe theologische Studiën*
NThTij	*Nederlands theologisch Tijdschrift*
NTRG	New Testament Reading Guide (Collegeville, Minn.)
NTS	*New Testament Studies*
NTTS	New Testament Tools and Studies (Leiden)
NuSup	Numen Supplement (Leiden)
OAB	Oxford Annotated Bible (N.Y., 1962)
OCD	M. Cary *et al.*, eds., *The Oxford Classical Dictionary* (Oxford, 1949)
OCP	*Orientalia christiana periodica*
Oesterley-Robinson, *History*	W. O. E. Oesterley and T. H. Robinson, *A History of Israel* (2 vols.; Oxford, 1932)
Oesterley-Robinson, *Introd.*	W. O. E. Oesterley and T. H. Robinson, *Introduction to the Books of the Old Testament* (N.Y. and London, 1934)
Or	*Orientalia*
OssRom	*Osservatore romano*
OSTGU	Oriental Society Transactions, Glasgow University (Glasgow)
OTMS	H. H. Rowley, ed., *The Old Testament and Modern Study* (Oxford, 1951)
OTRG	Old Testament Reading Guide (Collegeville, Minn.)
OTS	*Oudtestamentische Studiën*
PAAJR	*Proceedings of American Academy for Jewish Research*
PBC	Pontifical Biblical Commission
PCB	M. Black and H. H. Rowley, eds., *Peake's Commentary on the Bible* (rev. ed.; London, 1962)
PEQ	*Palestine Exploration Quarterly*
Pfeiffer, *Introd.*	R. H. Pfeiffer, *Introduction to the Old Testament* (N.Y., 1941)
PG	J. Migne, *Patrologia graeca* (Paris)
PGC	Pelican Gospel Commentaries (Harmondsworth)
Ph	*Philologus*
PJB	*Palästina-Jahrbuch*
PL	J. Migne, *Patrologia latina* (Paris)
PPBS	Paulist Pamphlet Bible Series (Glen Rock, N.J.)
ProcCTSA	*Proceedings of the Catholic Theological Society of America*
PSB	L. Pirot, *La sainte Bible,* rev. by A. Clamer (12 vols.; Paris, 1935—)
PW	Pauly-Wissowa, *Realencyclopädie der classischen Altertumswissenschaft* (Stuttgart, 1893—)
PWSup	Supplement for PW, *Realencyclopädie* . . .
QD	Quaestiones disputatae (English series; N.Y.)
QDAP	*Quarterly of the Department of Antiquities in Palestine*
RA	*Revue d'assyriologie et d'archéologie orientale*
RAC	*Reallexikon für Antike und Christentum* (Stuttgart, 1950—)
RAscMys	*Revue d'ascétique et mystique*
RB	*Revue biblique*
RBibIt	*Rivista biblica italiana*
REA	*Revue des études anciennes*
REBras	*Revista eclesiastica brasileira*
RechBib	Recherches bibliques (Bruges)
REg	*Revue d'égyptologie*
REGr	*Revue des études grecques*
REL	*Revue des études latines*
RELiège	*Revue ecclésiastique de Liège*
RenBib	Recontres bibliques
RES	*Revue des études sémitiques*
RevArch	*Revue archéologique*
RevBén	*Revue bénédictine*
RevDTour	*Revue diocésaine de Tournai*
RevExp	*Review and Expositor*
RevQum	*Revue de Qumran*
R-F	A. Robert and A. Feuillet, *Introduction à la Bible* (2 vols.; Paris, 1957–59)

R-F, *INT* — A. Robert and A. Feuillet, *Introduction to the New Testament,* tr. P. W. Skehan *et al.* (N.Y., 1965). English version of R-F, vol. 2
RFIC — *Rivista di filologia e d'istruzione classica*
RGG — K. Galling, ed., *Die Religion in Geschichte und Gegenwart* (3rd ed.; 7 vols.; Tübingen, 1957–65)
RHPR — *Revue d'histoire et de philosophie religieuses*
RHR — *Revue de l'histoire des religions*
Richardson, *ITNT* — A. Richardson, *Introduction to the Theology of the New Testament* (London, 1958)
RIDA — *Revue internationale des droits de l'antiquité*
RNT — Regensburger Neues Testament (Regensburg)
RPh — *Revue de philologie*
RRel — *Review for Religious*
RScRel — *Revue des sciences religieuses*
RSO — *Rivista degli studi orientali*
RSPT — *Revue des sciences philosophiques et théologiques*
RSR — *Recherches de science religieuse*
RSS — *Rome and the Study of Scripture* (7th ed.; St. Meinrad, Ind., 1962)
RstaB — *Revista biblica*
R-T — A. Robert and A. Tricot, *Guide to the Bible* (vol. 1; 2nd ed.; N.Y.)
RTAM — *Recherches de théologie ancienne et médiévale*
RTh — *Revue thomiste*
RTP — *Revue de théologie et de philosophie*
RUnLav — *Revue de l'université Laval*
RUnOtt — *Revue de l'université d'Ottawa*
RyF — *Razón y fe*
SAns — *Studia anselmiana*
SB — Sources bibliques (Paris, 1964—)
SBA — A. Parrot, ed., Studies in Biblical Archaeology (London)
SBB — Soncino Books of the Bible (London)
SBS — Stuttgarter Bibelstudien (Stuttgart)
SBT — Studies in Biblical Theology (London and Naperville, Ill.)
SBU — *Symbolae biblicae upsalienses*
SC — Sources chrétiennes (Paris)
ScEccl — *Sciences ecclésiastiques*
ScotJT — *Scottish Journal of Theology*
Scr — *Scripture*
ScuolC — *Scuola cattolica*
SE — F. L. Cross, ed., *Studia evangelica* (*SE* 1 = TU 73 [Berlin, 1959]; *SE* 2 = TU 87 [Berlin, 1964]; *SE* 3 = TU 88 [Berlin, 1964])
SEA — *Svensk exegetisk årsbok*
SGL — D. E. Nineham, ed., *Studies in the Gospels* (Fest. R. H. Lightfoot; Oxford, 1957)
SHAW — *Sitzungsberichte der Heidelberger Akademie der Wissenschaften*
Simons, *JOT* — J. Simons, *Jerusalem in the Old Testament* (Leiden, 1952)
SLOE — H. H. Rowley, *The Servant of the Lord and Other Essays* (London, 1952)
Smith, *Hist Geog* — G. A. Smith, *The Historical Geography of the Holy Land* (26th ed.; London, 1935)
SP — J. Coppens *et al.*, eds., *Sacra pagina* (2 vols.; Gembloux, 1959)
SPB — Studia postbiblica (Leiden)
SPC — *Studiorum paulinorum congressus* (= AnalBib 17–18)
SPSS — R. E. Brown, *Sensus plenior of Sacred Scripture* (Baltimore, 1955)
ST — *Studia theologica*
StANT — Studien zum Alten und Neuen Testament (Munich)
StJud — Studia judaica: Forschungen zur Wissenschaft des Judentums (Berlin)
Str-B — H. L. Strack and P. Billerbeck, *Kommentar zum Neuen Testament* (6 vols.; Munich, 1922–61)
StudCath — *Studia catholica*
StudNeot, Stud — Studia Neotestamentica, Studia (Paris and Bruges)
Summa — Thomas Aquinas, *Summa theologica*
SZ — *Stimmen der Zeit*
TAPA — *Transactions of the American Philological Association*
Taylor, *FGT* — V. Taylor, *Formation of the Gospel Tradition* (2nd ed.; London, 1935)
TBC — Torch Bible Commentaries (N.Y. and London)

TD	*Theology Digest*
TGl	*Theologie und Glaube*
ThDNT	G. Kittel, ed., *Theological Dictionary of the New Testament* (Grand Rapids, 1964—). English version of *ThWNT*
ThHk	Theologischer Handkommentar (Berlin)
ThHkNT	Theologischer Handkommentar zum Neuen Testament (Berlin)
ThStKr	Theologische Studien und Kritiken (Hamburg; now Berlin)
ThWNT	G. Kittel, ed., *Theologisches Wörterbuch zum Neuen Testament* (8 vols.; Stuttgart, 1933—). German version of *ThDNT*
TLZ	*Theologische Literaturzeitung*
TPQ	*Theologisch-Praktische Quartalschrift*
TQ	*Theologische Quartalschrift*
TR	*Theologische Revue*
TRu	*Theologische Rundschau*
TS	*Theological Studies*
TT	*Tijdschrift voor Theologie*
TTod	*Theology Today*
TTZ	*Trierer theologische Zeitschrift*
TU	Texte und Untersuchungen (Berlin)
TynNTC	Tyndale New Testament Commentary (Grand Rapids)
TZ	*Theologische Zeitschrift*
UM	C. H. Gordon, *Ugaritic Manual* (Rome, 1955)
UT	C. H. Gordon, *Ugaritic Textbook* (Rome, 1965)
UUA	*Uppsala universitets årsskrift*
Van Imschoot, *Théologie*	P. van Imschoot, *Théologie de l'Ancien Testament* (2 vols.; Tournai, 1954–56)
VBW	B. Mazar *et al.*, eds., *Views of the Biblical World*, tr. M. Dagut (5 vols.; N.Y., 1961)
VD	*Verbum domini*
VDBS	F. Vigouroux, *Dictionnaire de la Bible, Supplément* (7 vols.; Paris, 1928—)
VerbC	*Verbum caro*
VieInt	*Vie intellectuelle*
VieSp	*Vie spirituelle*
VigChr	*Vigiliae christianae*
Von Rad, *OT Theology*	G. von Rad, *Old Testament Theology* (2 vols.; Edinburgh, 1962, 1965)
VP	*Vivre et penser* (= *RB* 1941–44)
Vriezen, *Outline*	T. Vriezen, *An Outline of Old Testament Theology* (Oxford, 1958)
VS	Verbum salutis (Paris)
VT	*Vetus Testamentum*
VTSup	Vetus Testamentum Supplements (Leiden)
WC	Westminster Commentaries (London, 1904—)
Weiser, *OT*	A. Weiser, *The Old Testament: Its Formation and Development* (N.Y., 1961)
WHAB	G. E. Wright and F. V. Filson, eds., *The Westminster Historical Atlas to the Bible* (rev. ed.; Phila., 1956)
Wik, *NTI*	A. Wikenhauser, *New Testament Introduction* (N.Y., 1958)
WMzANT	Wissenschaftliche Monographien zum Alten und Neuen Testament (Neukirchen)
WO	*Die Welt des Orients*
WVDOG	Wissenschaftliche Veröffentlichungen der deutschen Orientgesellschaft (Berlin and Leipzig)
WZdUR	*Wissenschaftliche Zeitschrift der Universität Rostock* (Rostock)
WZKM	*Wiener Zeitschrift für die Kunde des Morgenlandes*
ZA	*Zeitschrift für Assyriologie*
ZAW	*Zeitschrift für die alttestamentliche Wissenschaft*
ZDMG	*Zeitschrift der deutschen morgenländischen Gesellschaft*
ZDPV	*Zeitschrift des deutschen Palästina-Vereins*
Zerwick, *Analysis*	M. Zerwick, *Analysis philologica novi testamenti graeci* (2nd ed.; Rome, 1960)
ZKG	*Zeitschrift für Kirchengeschichte*
ZKT	*Zeitschrift für katholische Theologie*
ZNW	*Zeitschrift für die neutestamentliche Wissenschaft*
ZSystTh	*Zeitschrift für systematische Theologie*
ZThK	*Zeitschrift für Theologie und Kirche*

TRANSLITERATION OF HEBREW AND ARAMAIC

Consonants

'	=	א	*z*	=	ז	*m*	=	מ	*q*	=	ק
b	=	ב	*ḥ*	=	ח	*n*	=	נ	*r*	=	ר
g	=	ג	*ṭ*	=	ט	*s*	=	ס	*ś*	=	שׂ
d	=	ד	*y*	=	י	*'*	=	ע	*š*	=	שׁ
h	=	ה	*k*	=	כ	*p*	=	פ	*t*	=	ת
w	=	ו	*l*	=	ל	*ṣ*	=	צ			

Note: The presence or absence of *dageš lene* in the *begadkepat* letters is not shown. Consonants with *dageš forte* are written double.

Vowels (shown as preceded by *b*)

With *matres lectionis*			Without *matres lectionis*						With *vocal šewa*		
bâ	=	בָה	*bā*	=	בָ	*ba*	=	בַ	*bă*	=	בֲ
bô	=	בוֹ	*bō*	=	בֹ	*bo*	=	בָ	*bŏ*	=	בֳ
bû	=	בוּ	*bū*	=	בֻ	*bu*	=	בֻ			
bê	=	בֵי	*bē*	=	בֵ	*be*	=	בֶ	*bĕ*	=	בֱ
bî	=	בִי	*bī*	=	בִ	*bi*	=	בִ	*bᵉ*	=	בְ

bāh = בָהּ or בָה. *bā'* = בָא (even where א is merely a *mater lectionis*).
bēh = בֵהּ, and *beh* = בֶה (although *h* is merely a *mater lectionis here*).
pataḥ furtivum: rûaḥ = רוּחַ.

TRANSLITERATION OF GREEK

ē	=	η	*h*	=	ʽ	*ph*	=	φ
ou	=	ου	*th*	=	ϑ	*ch*	=	χ
ō	=	ω	*y*	=	υ	*ps*	=	ψ

MISCELLANEOUS ABBREVIATIONS

aeth	Ethiopic version of the Bible
app. crit.	Critical apparatus (in a Greek NT text)
Aq	Aquila (Greek translation of the OT)
Aram	Aramaic
AUC	*Ab urbe condita* (from the founding of the City [Rome])
AV	Authorized Version
b	Babylonian Talmud (followed by the name of a specific tractate)
BJ	La sainte Bible [de Jérusalem] (fascicle edition; Paris)
bo	Bohairic (Coptic) version of the Bible
CCD	Confraternity of Christian Doctrine translation of the Bible
Eng	English
Ep.	*Epistula* or Epistle
Fest.	Festschrift (generic name for *any* publication honoring a person)
Fr	French
Ger	German
GesSt	*Gesammelte Studien*
Gk	Greek
Hebr	Hebrew

it	*Vetus itala* (part of the Old Latin translation of the Bible)
Ital	Italian
j	Jerusalem Talmud (followed by the name of a specific tractate)
KJ	King James Version of the Bible
KlSchr	*Kleine Schriften* (e.g., of A. Alt, O. Eissfeldt, etc.)
Lat	Latin
lat	Latin versions of the Bible (in general)
l.v.	*Lectio varia* (variant reading [in textual criticism])
LXX	Septuagint (Greek translation of the OT)
Midr.	Midrash
ms(s).	Manuscript(s)
MT	Masoretic Text (of the Hebrew Bible)
NEB	New English Bible (Oxford and Cambridge version)
NF, NS	Neue Folge, New Series (in serial listings)
NT	New Testament
OT	Old Testament
par.	Parallel passage(s) in the Synoptic Gospels
Pesh	Peshitta (Syriac) version of the Bible
RSV	Revised Standard Version of the Bible
RSV CE	Revised Standard Version, Catholic Edition
sa *or* sah	Sahidic (Coptic) version of the Bible
syh	Syriac version of the Bible, called Harclean
Sym	Symmachus (Greek translation of the OT)
Syn	Synoptic Gospels *or* Synoptic writers
syp	Syriac version of the Bible, in the Peshitta
Syr	Syriac
Tg.	Targum (Aramaic version of the OT)
Vg	Vulgate (common Latin version of the Bible)
VL	*Vetus latina* (pre-Vulgate Old Latin version of the Bible)
WV	Westminster Version of the Bible
*	*Prima manus* (reading of the first copyist of a biblical ms.)
→	Arrow indicates a cross reference to an article in this commentary; it is normally followed by a shortened title of the article, its number, and a marginal paragraph number (e.g., → Gospel Jn, 63:20)

Volume I

THE OLD TESTAMENT

Edited by

ROLAND E. MURPHY, O.CARM.

I

INTRODUCTION TO THE PENTATEUCH

Eugene H. Maly

BIBLIOGRAPHY

1 Bright, J., "Modern Study of Old Testament Literature," *The Bible and the Ancient Near East* (Fest W. F. Albright; N.Y., 1961) 13–31. Cazelles, H., "La Torah ou Pentateuque," R–F 1, 278–382; "Pentateuque," *VDBS* 7, 736–858. Coppens, J., *The Old Testament and the Critics* (Paterson, N.J., 1942). De Vaux, R., "A propos du second centenaire d'Astruc réflexions sur l'état actuel de la critique du Pentateuque," VTSup 1 (1953) 182–98. Freedman, D. N., "Pentateuch," *IDB* 3, 711–27. Hahn, H. F., *Old Testament in Modern Research* (2nd ed.; Phila., 1966). North, C. R., "Pentateuchal Criticism," *OTMS* 48–83. Noth, M., *UP*. Pfeiffer, R. H., *Introd.* 129–289. Robert, A., "The Law (Pentateuch)," R–T 1, 157–282. Suelzer, A., *The Pentateuch* (N.Y., 1964). Von Rad, G., *Das formgeschichtliche Problem des Hexateuchs* (BWANT 4; Stuttgart, 1938).

2 OUTLINE

ANALYSIS OF THE PENTATEUCH

3 **(I) Content of the Pentateuch.** The Pentateuch, from the Greek meaning "five rolls" or "books," is the title given early in the Christian era to the first five books of the OT. It was referred to by the Jews as the Torah, or Law, the term by which it is found in the NT. It contains the books of Gn, Ex, Lv, Nm, and Dt, titles given by the Greeks to indicate their contents as clearly as possible in one word. The Jews designated the same books by the first word(s) of the sacred text.

4 The framework that gives unity to this collection is the historical narrative, which takes the reader from the creation, through the early story of mankind, the history of the patriarchs and the descent into Egypt, the Exodus and the covenant of Sinai, the wandering in the wilderness, and finally to the arrival at the eastern side of the Jordan. The account of Moses' death and burial in Moab appropriately closes this first section of the OT. Despite this narrative framework, the greater portion of the Pentateuch is made up of laws (hence the Jewish designation) that have been conceived as the emergent of the divine revelation made to Moses and accordingly inserted into the narrative.

Because these books contain all the legal collections of Israel (no other OT book has a legal corpus that bound the historical Israel), it is understandable that they have been considered a unity. From a literary viewpoint, however, it is possible to speak of a "Tetrateuch" (the first four books), since the canonical book of Dt was composed as an introduction to the history of Israel from the time of Joshua to the fall of the southern kingdom. Again, it is possible to speak of a "Hexateuch" (six books) or even an "Octateuch" (eight books), etc., since Jos–Kgs are considered by some to continue the traditions found in the preceding books. Although these distinctions are helpful for understanding the development of the inspired text, they cannot displace the concept of the

Pentateuch as the legal basis of Israel's constitution as the people of God.

5 The relationship between law and history in the Pentateuch is significant. Israel's theology of law was determined by her theology of history. Unlike her neighbors she had no legal code or collection of rubrics that enjoyed separate existence. These were always conceived and presented as part of her salvation history. The legal obligations binding her represented her response to the historical intervention of a moral Lord on her behalf. Since that historical intervention was repeated, the legal prescriptions, by being placed within this historical framework, take on a dynamic character; they become a part of her national life. Despite the quantitatively lesser role, therefore, that the narrative sections of the Pentateuch play, and despite their episodic character, they lie at the basis of Israel's conception of herself in her relationship to God. History provided the fact of God's choice of his people, a theocratic nation whose charter is the Law.

6 A brief analysis of the five books will show this intimate connection between law and history and, consequently, the basic unity that the Pentateuch enjoys. As a prologue to the whole work, the story of mankind from creation to the introductory drama of salvation history is presented first (Gn 1–11). The divine preparation for the choice of a people is evident in the story of the individual patriarchs (Gn 12–50: Abraham, 12–25; Isaac, 25–26; Jacob, 26–36; Joseph, 37–50). The divine initiative in delivering the oppressed Hebrews from Egypt (Ex 1–18) is climaxed by the solemn proclamation of the covenant at Sinai, with its consequent obligations for the new people of God (Ex 19–23) and also by its solemn ratification (Ex 24). In the remainder of Ex and throughout Lv, the ordinances guiding this new people's cultic life are presented. First appear the instructions for the construction of a sanctuary and of its appointments and for the consecration of priests (Ex 25–31). A narrative section intervenes describing the violation of the covenant by the people and the renewal of the tablets (Ex 32–34). The completion and erection of the sanctuary conclude this second book (Ex 35–40).

Various laws dealing with sacrifices (Lv 1–7), legal purity (Lv 11–15), legal holiness (Lv 17–26), and vows and tithes (Lv 27) constitute the whole of the third book, except for two narrative sections—one describing the ordination of Aaron and his sons (Lv 8–10) and the other the solemn Day of Atonement (Lv 16). The fourth book opens with a census of the people and is followed by prescriptions concerning the arrangement of the 12 tribes and by other laws (Nm 1–10:10). The journey from Sinai to Moab (Nm 10:11–22:1) and the events in Moab, which are interspersed with more cultic regulations (Nm 22:2–36), complete this book. The fifth and last book presents Moses in Moab reviewing the events of the past (Dt 1–4:43) and explaining to the people the significance of the covenant (Dt 4:44–11). This forms an exhortatory introduction to the deuteronomic code of laws (Dt 12–26), the sanctions of which are described in a series of curses and blessings (Dt 27–30). Moses' commission of Joshua (Dt 31), his victory song (Dt 32), his blessing of the 12 tribes (Dt 33), and the account of his death and burial (Dt 34) conclude the book and the Pentateuch.

7 **(II) Composition of the Pentateuch.** If the general conclusions regarding the composition of the Pentateuch are less assured today than ever before, it is not so much from the inadequacy of the scientific principles as from a better understanding of the inherent complexity of the problem. The science of pentateuchal criticism is more than 200 years old. Its beginnings are commonly traced to the French physician, Jean Astruc, whose literary analysis of Gn was published in 1753, although others before him, notably the Oratorian Richard Simon (1678), had paved the way for his work. After Astruc the science developed rapidly, principally along the lines of documentary hypotheses. These were based on a literary analysis of the text and argued for the existence of independent literary documents that had been conflated to form the present Pentateuch. Eichhorn (1780) and Ilgen (1798) concentrated on the "Elohistic" documents, one of which would later be called the "Priestly Code." Vater (1802) and others were struck by the disparate character of the narratives and rejected the documentary hypothesis in favor of a fragment hypothesis, according to which many unconnected passages were simply collected and put together. A partial return to the earlier theory was marked by Ewald's (1831) supplement hypothesis, which argued for a basic document to which other sources, or excerpts from them, were added. Hupfeld (1853) then showed, more clearly than his predecessors, the existence of three documents in Genesis, two Elohistic (E and P) and one Yahwistic (J). When Riehm, a year later, distinguished the deuteronomic document (D), a solid basis was laid for the later classical theory of the four sources.

8 It was the determination of the relative chronology of the documents that provided the necessary framework of the theory. The formulation of this chronology was principally done by Reuss (1833), Graf (1866), Kuenen (1869), and Wellhausen (1878). Document D was identified with the book found in the temple in Josiah's time (622 BC), and the others were dated on the basis of a comparison with it. Documents J and E, which presumed a plurality of cult places against which D fought, were clearly early; P, which presumed the unity of the sanctuary, was just as clearly late. These relative chronological positions were confirmed by other criteria, which also helped to establish the absolute chronology: J, a 9th-cent. Judean document; E, an 8th-cent. document from the northern kingdom; D, the 7th-cent. work of a Judean author; and P, the post-exilic work of the priests of Jerusalem. Called the "Wellhausen Hypothesis" because of that scholar's great work in synthesizing the findings, the theory quickly gained the ascendancy among the majority of scholars and has maintained it, with important modifications, ever since (→ Modern OT Criticism, 70:23–25).

9 The modifications were introduced by further scholarly work in three distinct directions. First, a more intense literary analysis revealed that the documents were not composed *ex nihilo* by one author at a fixed time in history. Each document was, instead, a composite literary work, and attempts were made to separate the underlying sources. The multiplication of sigla (e.g., J1, J2, Pa, Pb, L, K, etc.) pointed to the complexity of the investigation. Although few of the resulting individual theories gained wide acceptance, the analysis did show the need for other approaches to the problem.

10 The second approach began, not with the document as a whole, but with the individual units (stories, poems, legends, etc.) within the documents and sought to determine the life situation in ancient Israel that gave rise to the unit and accordingly helped give it its literary structure. The commentary by H. Gunkel on Gn (1902) was the trail-blazing work in this regard, and today almost all scholars use the form-critical approach to some extent (→ Modern OT Criticism, 70:37–40). Outstanding instances of its application to the legal content of the Pentateuch, for example, are A. Alt's *Die Ursprünge des israelitischen Rechts* (1934) and G. E. Mendenhall's *Law and Covenant in Israel and the Ancient Near East* (1955). Although this approach is not opposed to the documentary hypothesis, its conclusions will affect the latter's formulation.

11 A radically new approach, with devastating effects on the classical documentary hypothesis, was introduced by the so-called Uppsala school of Sweden. Its scholars, notably I. Engnell, denied any extensive literary activity in Israel until post-exilic times, at least with regard to narrative traditions. Prior to this the material was transmitted orally and was gradually gathered into two cycles of traditions, the "P-work" (the Tetrateuch) and the "D-work" (Dt and Jos–Kgs). The school's emphasis on the importance of oral transmission and of its faithfulness, with a consequent higher regard for the antiquity of much of the material, was a welcome reaction to the premature conclusions of the Wellhausen school, which had posited such late dates for most of the material's creation. At the same time its general disregard for earlier literary activity in Israel precluded the need, or even the possibility, of an extensive literary analysis. This disregard is shared by few scholars today.

12 Modern scholars are extremely hesitant about formulating rigid conclusions concerning the genesis, development, and final literary form of the traditions and of their material. Despite this fluid state of scholarly opinion, some firm conclusions can be made regarding particular points. The existence of doublets, or parallel forms of legal and narrative material, is an established fact. Moreover, criteria of style, vocabulary, and theological thought (which can be called "constants") show a relationship existing between blocks of material. These point, in turn, to separate traditions (the precise extent of which, however, is still much debated) that developed within Israel and which can be conveniently identified by the fourfold sigla: J, E, D, and P. By comparing the traditions, a relative chronology can be established regarding their final redaction as separate traditions. This chronology will agree, in general, with that supposed by Wellhausen for the four documents. Finally, their gradual amalgamation into the canonical Pentateuch can be traced in general lines.

13 **(III) The Four Traditions.** Independent stories (e.g., Gn 26:6–11), cult narratives (e.g., Gn 28:10–22), primitive songs (e.g., Gn 4:23–24), oracles (e.g., Nm 23–24), etymological explanations (e.g., Gn 25:22–26), and legends (e.g., Gn 6:1–4) all provided material for the earliest history of Israel. Supposedly some such collection of historical material, perhaps in poetic form, was being orally transmitted already in the period of the Judges, since the later separate histories (J and E) show dependence on some common source. The sanctuaries of Israel would have been the more usual depositories for the material.

14 **(A) Yahwist Tradition.** The earliest discernible tradition in the Pentateuch, called "Yahwist" (or "J" from the German form) because of its anachronistic use of "Yahweh" in the Gn material, is more commonly dated about the 10th cent. in the southern kingdom. This date, however, represents only that period which seems to have had the most decisive influence on the selection, arrangement, and redaction of the material; it precludes neither earlier nor later editorial work. The constants distinguishing the tradition include a characteristic vocabulary, a stylistic elegance reflected in its colorful presentation of scenes, especially the dialogues, a perceptive psychology, deep theological insights, and a bold use of anthropomorphisms.

The J tradition presents a remarkably wide sweep of history, beginning with the first man and showing the relevance of all early history to God's specific plan for the chosen people as evidenced first in the patriarchal narratives and more immediately in the events of the Exodus. It is this plan as conceived by J that gives coherence and meaning to the disparate material. Moved by the glorious eminence to which God had brought the tribe of Judah in the period of David and Solomon, J can present the divine communion with men with a boldness of conviction that is at times disconcerting (cf. Gn 3:8,21; 4:15; 18–19). For the same reason he betrays an optimism that, despite the continuing prevalence of sin, can foresee victory in the moment of defeat (cf. Gn 3:15; 4:7). Moreover, his emphasis of the "younger son" theme (Isaac chosen in preference to Ishmael, Jacob to Esau, Judah to his older brothers in the Joseph stories, Israel itself to the superior Egyptians) can be partly explained by the tribe of Judah's ascendancy over the other tribes in the amphictyony and by the divine choice of David over his older brothers and over Saul (cf. J. L. McKenzie, *The Bible and Modern Science* [Cincinnati, 1961] 2–5). And the unconditioned Davidic covenant described in the Nathan oracle (2 Sm 7:4–17) is paralleled, not by the conditioned covenant of Sinai (Ex 19; J's theology of this covenant is difficult to assess), but by the similarly unconditioned covenant with Abraham (cf. Gn 12:2).

15 **(B) Elohist Tradition.** The sister tradition of J is called "Elohist" (E) because of its careful use of "Elohim" in the pre-Sinai material. It is a northern document probably edited in a definitive form some time after the schism of 922. The reform of the northern kingdom, initiated by the prophet Elijah, probably supplied the background for E's reconstruction of Israel's history. The scope is more restricted than that of J; it begins only with Abraham who is presented, anachronistically, as a prophet (Gn 20:7). With Elijah's zeal for the divine transcendence, E avoids the more striking anthropomorphisms; God speaks to man generally in dreams or from clouds or the midst of fire or, finally, through the medium of angels. It is E, with experience of pagan practices in the north, who tells of Jacob's command to remove the foreign gods (Gn 35:2). Similarly, his morality is stricter than J's (cf. Gn 20; cf. J's 26:6–11) reflecting his reaction to the degrading Canaanite practices that flourished in the north. And his more didactic style lacks the color and spontaneity of J.

For E, the great climax of history was the covenant of God with Israel (→ Aspects OT Thought, 77:74–85). Conceived in terms of an overlord-vassal treaty, the covenant and its stipulations are stressed as a strictly religious event that determined Israel's life irrevocably (J's emphasis is on the divine initiative that made Israel what she was, which was manifested in the mighty saving acts of the Exodus). Without J's political interests, which were conditioned by the divine approval of the dynastic principle in David, E, in reaction to the surrounding pagan civilization, shows a preference for an idealized desert existence. These ideas and ideals are reflected even in E's patriarchal stories to some extent, which are centered understandably around the northern sanctuaries.

The conflation of J and E, to the advantage of the former, was effected in the south, probably after the collapse of Israel in 721. It may be connected with Hezekiah's attempt to win over "all Israel" to the worship of Yahweh as practiced in the Jerusalem sanctuary.

16 **(C) Deuteronomic Tradition.** The third tradition is somewhat more easily distinguished and dated. In its pentateuchal form it is restricted, with possibly small exceptions, to the book of Dt, whence its name and abbreviation (D). The marked hortatory style, expressed in a distinctive vocabulary, points to a period of religious crisis for its composition. One such period was that following the collapse of Israel when the Assyrian threat to Judah continued and a number of evil kings endangered the Yahwistic religion. Salvation could be had, in D's outlook, only by a loyal response to Yahweh's covenant laws and by a return to the pure worship of God at the one sanctuary of Jerusalem. The book was probably put in a definitive form some time during the first half of the 7th cent., and it is commonly identified, at least in part, with the book found by Josiah in the temple in 621 (cf. 2 Kgs 22:8–10). The identification is supported by the fact that Josiah's reforms closely parallel the reforms inculcated by D.

But D had a long prehistory. The nucleus of its laws and customs is traced to the northern kingdom; its emphases are similar to those found in E. Brought to the south by the refugees in 721, these laws and customs would have been gradually codified. It also underwent a later evolution until it reached its present canonical form. As such it forms the preface to the so-called deuteronomic history (Jos–Kgs), which evaluates Israel's history by deuteronomic principles (cf. Jgs 2 for a good example of D's capsule evaluation). This entire complex was probably given its final form some time during the Exile (cf. 2 Kgs 25:27–30).

The basic theological contribution of D is the conception of the covenant (an E emphasis) as God's loving election of Israel (based on a J idea) and of law as Israel's loyal response to election. But the response must be personal; it must be made by every individual of every generation (cf. Dt 6:20–25; 26:5–11). The urgency of D's appeal is marked by the constant reference to "you" and to the "now" or "today" of their decision. On this decision and its implementation will depend the final judgment of God (cf. Dt 28).

17 **(D) Priestly Tradition.** The attribution of the fourth tradition, with its obvious concern for liturgy, to the priests of Jerusalem accounts for its title, "Priestly" (P). Like D it can be easily distinguished in the Pentateuch. Its style is abstract and redundant; it is fond of genealogies, chronological precision, and minute descriptions of ritual elements; it avoids anthropomorphisms even more carefully than E. Most of the latter half of Ex, all of Lv, and most of Nm belong to P. Occasional narrative passages in these books and in Gn provide a framework for the predominantly legal and ritual sections. Like the other traditions, P had a long prehistory and contains much ancient material, but its final form as an independent document was probably given in the exilic period. It was later incorporated into the other pentateuchal material.

Israel's faith was under siege during the Exile. The crisis provided the background for P's history. As Yahweh is holy, so must Israel remain holy, i.e., separated from, and uncontaminated by, any man-made morality or cult. This view explains the concern for the many prescriptions of ritual and legal cleanness. Moreover, she must look forward to celebrating the liturgy of the temple of Jerusalem on her return. To inculcate this, P has presented the history of Israel with strong liturgical overtones. The creation story (Gn 1:1–2:4a) has ritual and liturgical allusions and applications. The precise dates given in all the narratives are liturgically meaningful in P's calendar. The feasts as celebrated in later Israel are placed in the historical context of the Exodus to emphasize their ritual significance. The Exodus itself, the march through the desert and the encampments, appear as parts of a grand liturgical procession climaxed by the Sinai theophany. Moreover, the whole of the history is divided into four periods, each marked by a special covenant of God with man, and each showing the gradual development of man's sacrificial worship of his creator and of God's revelation of himself to man. Through the climactic paschal deliverance in Egypt, Israel became a liturgical people (*'ădat yiśrā'ēl*, used in Ex 12:3 for the first time, but over 100 times afterward), a new creation of God's. This new creation of a holy people through liturgical celebration is the ideal held up by P to the forlorn exiles in Babylon.

The final contribution to the formation of the Pentateuch was P. Perhaps around the time of Ezra the historical books, Jos–Kgs, were separated from the rest of this history, thus isolating the Pentateuch, which became the basic Law or Torah for later Judaism.

18 **(IV) Meaning of the Pentateuch.** The literary analysis of the four traditions, as just presented, affords a rich insight into the gradual development of revelation throughout much of the OT period. Because of its intimate connection with history, Israel's theology remained constantly alive and adaptable to the new situations that marked God's continuing direction of his people to the eschatological goal. The theologies of the four histories preserved in the Pentateuch and contributed to by a long line of Israel's sacred writers bear witness to this living dialogue between God and man in the OT.

Despite the Pentateuch's varying theologies, each with its distinctive emphases, there is also an emerging unity to the whole that could justify its later conception as a single block of inspired material. This unity is apparent in what R. de Vaux refers to as the golden threads of promise, election, covenant, and law, which tie the Pentateuch together (*La Genèse*, [BJ; Paris, 1951] 23).

19 Israel's history was interpreted and written in the light of the contemporary situation. It offered a theological explanation of that situation in which Israel enjoyed the divine favor in preference to all other nations. Its people could boast of no glorious past because they had none. The ancient credos preserved a vivid reminder of their past abject condition; on the purely natural level they were the descendants of slaves in Egypt (Dt 6:21) and, before that, of a wandering Aramean (Dt 26:5). Nor did the prepatriarchal period bear the seeds of any human greatness; relying solely on himself, man fell further and further away from God (Gn 3–11). Nevertheless, from the beginning Israel was convinced there was always the hope based on the divine promise. God promised an ultimate victory for mankind after the first fall from grace (Gn 3:15). He promised a new order in the universe after the catastrophe of the flood (Gn 9:8–17). In Abraham the promise becomes more specific; it envisages a single land and a single people (Gn 12:1–3). Throughout the rest of Gn, that promise, renewed in each generation, is the one great binding force that brings coherence and unity to the individual stories.

20 The promise was both ordained to election and expressed in election. Election is one of the more profound religious notions in the Scriptures; it is conceivable only by a people that has belief in a personal lord with a moral will. On the part of God it is the act of sovereign free choice; on the part of man it indicates the choice of one from among all others. The ultimate goal of the promise was the election of the one people, Israel. Its expression in the classical vocabulary of election (*bāḥar*) is relatively late, appearing frequently in Dt: "For you are a people sacred to the Lord, your God; he has chosen you from all the nations on the face of the earth to be a people peculiarly his own" (Dt 7:6). But the notion is already implied in the earlier passages where the divine initiative is clearly stated (e.g., Ex 3:7–10). The divine free choice of Israel was the goal and fulfillment of the promises made to the patriarchs.

21 But the patriarchal promises themselves were necessarily accompanied by an act of election. Abraham was chosen by God, for no apparent natural reason, to be the instrument of the divine plan. His story begins with an absolute act of divine initiative (Gn 12:1–2f). The succeeding heirs of the promise, Isaac and Jacob, can similarly find no natural reason for their choice; they are the objects of election. In a more subtle fashion, the opening chapters of Gn reveal the divine process at work in the gradual elimination of those who will have no active role in the fulfillment of the divine plan. This is especially evident in the genealogies, which list all the descendants, but ultimately center their attention on the individuals who are the object of the divine choice.

22 Election was almost invariably accompanied by covenant, which expressed the relationship resulting from election and guaranteed its validity. Covenants were a common part of the social order of the ancient Near East. By them man defined the nature of the relationship existing between himself and his covenant partner. Examples in the OT are the friendship pact between David and Jonathan (1 Sm 23:18) and the peace treaty between Abraham and Abimelech (Gn 21:22–33); both were covenants between equals. Examples of covenants between superior and inferior have come to light in fairly recent times with the discovery of the Hittite literature, which speaks of a special treaty drawn up between the Hittite emperor and his vassal kings in outlying territories. The literature has contributed to a fuller understanding of the OT covenant form (cf. D. J. McCarthy, *CBQ* 27 [1965] 217–40).

The covenants between God and man in the Pentateuch necessarily involve, like election itself, the divine initiative; the covenant partners are not equals. Although all the traditions speak of the covenants, it is P who has systematically divided history into four periods, each marked by its distinctive covenant. The first, only implied in Gn 1:26–2:4a, is with Adam. The second is with Noah (Gn 9:8–17) and is unconditioned. The third, also unconditioned, is with Abraham (Gn 17). The last is the covenant of Sinai between God and his people (Ex 19:1–5). This covenant, the reason for which all the preceding ones are seen to have been formed, is the climactic point not only of the Pentateuch but also of the entire OT.

23 The Law, the fourth of the binding threads, is what provides instruction for Israel in the manner of its way of life with Yahweh. Although formulated at various times throughout much of Israel's history in response to varying historical conditions, the Law was always seen as flowing from the Sinai covenant, as stipulations of the divine overlord, and hence these stipulations were always brought into relationship with the covenant.

Promise, election, covenant, and Law, therefore, make the Pentateuch a coherent unity. But this unity is ordained to something more. Israel's concept of her God was such that she could not conceive of his choice of her as the final goal of all his activity. The promises made to the patriarchs had yet to be fulfilled in large measure. No doubt the tribes that wandered many years in the desert looked forward to the conquest and possession of the land of promise as the realization of that goal, but the reality of the conquest proved different. The story of Joshua is not the fulfillment of the pentateuchal hope any more than the book of Joshua is the Pentateuch's literary conclusion. In fact, the succeeding history shows that the hope was never completely fulfilled in Israel's lifetime; the Pentateuch remained always open, allowing Christ to say that he came to fulfill it, not to destroy it (Mt 5:17).

24 **(V) The Pentateuch and Moses.** The four traditions, which as we have seen go to make up the canonical Pentateuch, received definitive shape in varying periods, ranging from the 10th to the 6th cents. Therefore, even the earliest of these is much later in time than the Moses of the 13th cent., to whom the Pentateuch has been traditionally ascribed. The resulting problem cannot be solved by simply denying the assured results of literary and historical criticism. The solution, rather, involves a more nuanced approach both to the origin of the contents of the traditions and to the concept of authorship as understood by the Israelites and the early Christians.

It has already been pointed out that the material contained in the four traditions was not created by the later authors. They depended to a great extent on both oral and written traditions formed long before them. Recent scholarship has emphasized the fidelity of even oral transmission among these peoples (one of the contributions of the Uppsala school). Research, especially archaeological, has also shown that both the historical and legal contents are much older than are the periods of their later formulation. The later authors, or editors, were more concerned with interpreting older history in the light of the contemporary situation or with adapting the older laws to the new social conditions. Thus, the history of the patriarchs and of the Hebrews in Egypt and in the desert, as related in the Pentateuch, has been shown to tally remarkably with what is known from other sciences to have been the social, political, and historical conditions at those times. No later author could possibly have invented that history. Moreover, the two traditions that are more strictly historical in content, J and E, suppose a common tradition antecedent to both. The same is to be said, *mutatis mutandis*, for the legal sections. Despite the variations in formulation, all the codes rest on the same juridical principles flowing from the same religious convictions and regulating the same basic cult and religious life. All unanimously trace their origin and *raison d'être* to the events of Sinai.

These findings presume the reality of some extraordinary religious event(s) at a determined time in the past, which radically affected Israel's conception of herself and of her relationship to God. One may also presume, at least with great probability, the existence of a religious leader who could give directing force to the event's significance, making it concrete and applicable to the lives of his contemporaries. Moses plays this role in the story of the Exodus and wandering, and no amount of literary or historical criticism has succeeded in denying this basic role. Moses is a perfectly understandable figure of the 13th cent. His supervisory office as presented in the Pentateuch gives meaning both to the united actions of the freed Hebrews of his day and to the homogeneous development of the traditions in the later periods. Without Moses, or someone similar to him, these facts would remain without adequate explanation. Moses, therefore, is at the heart of the Pentateuch and can, in accord with the common acceptance of the ancient period, correctly be called its author.

25 This common acceptance of the ancient period was already analyzed by Lagrange in 1897 in a lecture at the Catholic Congress in Fribourg (cf. Lagrange, *RB* 7 [1898] 10–32). The modern world has a rigid concept of the inviolability of an author and hence a repugnance to successive and extensive redactions of material over a long period of time, especially in the case of the inspired word. This concept was not shared by the peoples of the ancient Near East, who practiced community in thought and in the written word. The conscious editorial work that was going on even in a very late period is shown by a comparison of the MT with that of the LXX (Lagrange, *op. cit.*, 14–18). Moreover, the formula "God said to Moses" (which is applied, incidentally, relatively rarely and then to specific passages) is a literary fiction justified by the need to bring the changing aspect of law into harmony with its eternal aspect. The latter is the divine authority speaking either immediately or mediately through Moses, the first legislator. The formula, therefore, emphasizes the stable element in law; laws must be passed "forever" (Lagrange, *op. cit.*, 20–21). The use of similar formulas in other pseudepigraphical works of the OT confirms this explanation (Lagrange, *op. cit.*, 22–23).

Finally, Lagrange answered the objection based on the Christian tradition concerning Moses' role by distinguishing between his historical and literary role. The former, which is clearly primary, concerns his role as legislator of Israel and Mosaicism as the heart of Israel's history. But Moses' literary role flowed from, and was dependent on, the historical. It would be false to conclude, therefore, that Moses wrote the Pentateuch because Israel cannot be adequately explained without him (Lagrange, *op. cit.*, 24–27). In sum, the historical tradition is completely valid; the literary tradition is conditioned. This viewpoint coincides basically with that expressed in the "Reply of the Biblical Commission to Cardinal Suhard," 1948 (text in *RSS* 577–80; → Church Pronouncements, 72:31).

2

GENESIS

Eugene H. Maly

BIBLIOGRAPHY

1 Many of the older commentaries, such as those of H. Gunkel, O. Procksch, J. Skinner, E. Ryle, and S. R. Driver, are still useful; we list here only the more recent general works. Fuller bibliographical references will appear throughout the commentary. Chaine, J., *Le Livre de la Genèse* (LD 3; Paris, 1948). Clamer, A., *La Genèse* (La Sainte Bible, Pirot-Clamer; Paris, 1953). De Vaux, R., *La Genèse* (BJ; Paris, 1951). Heinisch, P., *Das Buch Genesis* (Bonn, 1930). Junker, H., *Genesis* (Würzburg, 1949). Speiser, E. A., *Genesis* (AB; N.Y., 1964). Vawter, B., *A Path Through Genesis* (N.Y., 1956). Von Rad, G., *Genesis* (tr. J. H. Marks; Phila., 1961).

INTRODUCTION

2 **(I) Composition.** The criteria for distinguishing the various traditions are particularly clear in Gn, which helps to explain why the literary analysis of this book set the stage for the documentary hypothesis concerning the composition of the Pentateuch. Therefore, we can apply what has been said about that composition, with proper qualifications, to the composition of Gn. Three of the traditions (J, E, and P) are generally accepted as being represented here (for a strong position for another source, cf. O. Eissfeldt, *IDB* 2, 368–74). The J and P traditions alone are represented in the primitive history (chs. 1–11). It is obvious that of the two, J provides the narrative framework for this section as well as for the rest of the book. On the other hand, P introduces a chronological backbone to the narratives, and there is some reason for supposing that, at least in Gn, it presupposes the narratives of J and E. Whether E ever did contain any prepatriarchal narratives cannot be known with certainty. At any rate, its patriarchal history has been preserved in only a shortened form, since its conflation with J was made to the latter's benefit; the value of E lies not in contributing a consecutive narrative but in theological insights.

The prehistory of the material preserved by the three traditions is extremely complex. In the commentary, we shall attempt to trace the origin of the various literary units wherever possible. In general, we can say that Israel's historians made use of material of all kinds, including ancient creation stories, genealogical lists, songs, proverbs, etiological tales, legends, etc. All contributed to the authors' purposes and must, of course, be interpreted ultimately in the light of those purposes.

3 **(II) The "History" of Gn and Its Meaning.** Are these literary units reflections of actual historical realities and events? The answer requires some explanation. No scholar today would hold that Gn presents history in the modern sense of that term. The sacred authors' conception of history as a linear movement of events determined by divine interventions and tending to a divinely conceived goal militates against such a presentation. They were interested in the "facts" of history only inasmuch as they illustrated the divine plan. This interest was the overriding factor in their choice of material.

With regard to the patriarchal history, the basic "facts" included such items as the movements of the patriarchs, their occupations, their relations with their neighbors, and their marriages and deaths. There is every reason for the modern scientific historian to accept this basic family history, which served as the foundation for the authors' religious history. The sciences of ancient Near Eastern history and especially of archaeology have shown that the underlying social, juridical, political, geographical, and religious conditions in Gn are precisely those of the 2nd millennium and could not have been invented by an author living in a much later period. Consequently, strictly on historical grounds, we can admit the existence of these seminomadic shepherds who originated, at least proximately, in Upper Mesopotamia, migrated to Canaan, lived out their lives much as described in Gn, and at least some of whom descended into Egypt.

These basic "facts," however, were primitively recorded and preserved in a popular form. Personal names were given etymological explanations to stress the character either of the person or of his descendants. Family incidents were "dressed up" to serve as material for ballads and sagas sung or recounted for the entertainment and edification of the local inhabitants. Some events could be given a framework based on local cult legends or cultic practices to illustrate their religious significance.

4 This was the type of material that came down, in individual units or, in some cases, in cycles of traditions, to the sacred historians of later Israel. They, in turn, made their own literary contributions to clarify their own purpose, which was, above all, religious. They wished to show the divine plan successively revealed in the events of history, and they therefore stressed the divine initiative throughout. Abraham's migration to the land of Canaan is not a haphazard incident conditioned solely by the circumstances of the period, but is primarily the result of a divine call he could not ignore. The patriarch's adventures in Canaan, his successful transactions with others, his escapes from harm, the birth of his children—all are introduced and explained in the light of God's plan to form for himself a people who would ultimately possess the land and worship him alone. The plan is concretized in the form of a promise made to Abraham and renewed in those of his descendants who are the object of the divine choice (Isaac and Jacob). This unifying divine plan, expressed in the successive promises, similarly explains the adventures of these descendants. The patriarchal history, therefore, has an absolute unity by reason of the absolute divine purpose. Because it is supernatural, the purpose is beyond the effective control of modern scientific history. Therefore, the ultimate meaning of Gn, like that of the other books of the Bible, will always elude the historian who works outside its religious postulates.

5 What was said of the religious nature of the patriarchal history can also be said of the primitive history; however, in the latter case the groundwork for the religious history is quite different. Here the basic "facts" are not incidents in the lives of individuals racially related, but events of a cosmic order that affected universal man. Some of these events are unique by their very nature, such as creation and a first fall from grace. The others are frequently occurring events, such as fratricide, acts of vengeance, floods, destructions of cities, etc. These "facts" of history, then, become the material of the inspired prehistorian who, within his religious postulates, is concerned with the gradual drift of man away from God. The authors of the primitive history in Gn, therefore, are much like the scientific prehistorian who "cannot for lack of documentation, produce a biography, a name, a single situation; he treats of the typical event, the long-term trend, the ecology of a whole population" (R. A. F. MacKenzie, "Before Abraham Was...," *CBQ* 15 [1953] 139–40). This statement does not mean, however, that his material is not historical.

6 The first 11 chapters of Gn present truths based on historical facts. There was a creation by God in the beginning of time, a special divine intervention in the creation of man, the existence of the first man in a condition of friendship with God, a fall from that condition, an increasing separation between man and God brought about by man's sins, and a succession of natural catastrophes by which man suffered the consequences of his sins. Whereas these are religious explanations that in most cases transcend the competence of modern science, they are at the same time historical in that they explain historical events.

Therefore, these chapters contain history, if only analogously, the nature of which is threefold. First, as we already explained, they deal with history in the same way as the modern science of prehistory; both are concerned with the "typical," and not the individual, event. Second, the need to popularize the presentation and make it comprehensible to an unsophisticated audience has resulted in an individualization of the "typical events." In most cases, one man is presented as doing what many men did; the story of one particular catastrophe is used to illustrate and explain all such catastrophes. Third, the religious purpose of the sacred author has further conditioned his treatment of the material. This purpose is the most important factor in the evaluation of the history of chs. 1–11. In Israel, the theology of creation (ktisiology) was secondary to, and dependent on, the theology of salvation (soteriology). Cosmic and human origins, therefore, are related to the origins of the chosen people; the former were conceived in the light of the latter. This relationship of dependence of theological notions will explain the lack of strictly cosmological or anthropological concern. The burden of the author's presentation is soteriological in essence.

7 The most recent directive of the Pontifical Biblical Commission concerning these chapters confirms the analogous nature of the history they contain. In his letter of January 16, 1948, to Cardinal Suhard of Paris, the Secretary of the Commission wrote that "...they relate in simple and figurative language, adapted to the understanding of a less developed people, the fundamental truths presupposed for the economy of salvation, as well as the popular description of the origin of the human race and of the Chosen People" (*CBQ* 10 [1948] 318–23 = *RSS* 581).

8 We can add here a word concerning the origin of the material in these opening chapters. Although the possibility of a direct revelation of the events with their details to the inspired authors cannot be denied a priori, neither can it be presupposed. In fact, the manner of God's acting in history would argue against such a supposition. Moreover, the literary analysis of the narratives points to a natural and much more complex origin and development. The possibility of a faithful transmission of the narratives from the primitive individuals featured in them to the historians of Israel is even more fantastic. The many millennia between the time of the first man and that of Israel would preclude, on natural grounds, the possibility of a faithful transmission. If miraculous intervention be supposed, then a series of miracles greater than a single act of revelation would be required. The supposition has no basis in the biblical record itself. Furthermore, Israel testifies of herself that her fathers came from "beyond the River, and worshiped other gods..." (Jos 24:2). These polytheistic "fathers" could not have been bearers of a monotheistic tradition.

Therefore, because the narrative material antedates Israel herself, it must have originated outside Israel. The most likely place would be northern Mesopotamia, whence Israel's ancestors came. Literary comparison of the Gn narratives with similar stories of Mesopotamia confirms this supposition but does not imply Israel's direct dependence on her pagan neighbors for the contents of these chapters, which have been affected radically by Israel's theology. Although the framework and imagery common to non-Israelite stories have been retained, it is the theology that gives the fullest meaning to the stories, and the theology is uniquely Israel's.

9 **(III) The Teaching of Gn.** To explain God's intervention at the time of the patriarchs and ultimately his election of the people Israel, the book presents a brief survey of the religious condition of mankind from the beginning to the time of Abraham. The one God is the sole author of all that exists (1:1), and his creative activity is unopposed (1:2). His omnipotence is reflected in the total efficacy of his word, which achieves its effect in the absolute correspondence of the created object to the creating will (1:3ff.). Man surpasses all other created beings by reason of his special relationship to God (1:26–30). By divine ordinance, woman is man's proper companion, sharing his dignity (1:27; 2:18–23) and united to him in the indissoluble bond of marriage (2:24).

Man's original state was one of innocence (2:25) and friendship with God (3:8a). Tempted to achieve a state beyond his created nature, man sinned (3:1–6). The effects of this first sin became the common lot of all his descendants. They included loss of divine friendship (3:23–24), lack of mutual esteem (3:7), physical evils in accord with the nature of man (3:17–19) and of woman (3:16), and a constant struggle against the power of evil (3:15a). But the promise of ultimate victory in the struggle (3:15b) is demanded of the God whose saving will was manifested so clearly in Israel's regard. The promise is the first message of the good news of final victory.

The continuing struggle resulted at first in continuing defeat for man (chs. 4–11). Having rebelled against his God, man rebelled against his neighbor. Murder (4:1–8), vengeance (4:24), polygamy (4:19), and concupiscence of the flesh (6:5) marked the history of man and of civilization (4:17–22). The offended divine justice is expressed in the natural catastrophes that overtook man (6:6–7,11–13); his mercy and will to save is expressed in the salvation of the just (6:8–9). But God's covenant with the just man, symbolized in nature (9:8–17), was followed by man's continuing moral perversity (9:20–27), which resulted in the alienation of human society from God and of men from one another (11:1–9).

10 God now intervened in this world in a special way. He called Abraham to his service (12:1–3), and Abraham responded in faith (12:4a; 15:6). God became the personal God of the fathers (31:5,29,42,53,etc.), and this personal relationship became determinative of the patriarchal history. As a result of this relationship, initiated by the free choice of God, the promise of a great posterity and of the land was made to Abraham (12:1–2; 13:14–16; 15:5; etc.), renewed to his descendants (26:2–5; 28:13–15), and was to be fulfilled in the people Israel (15:13–14,18–21).

The special divine concern for the patriarchs can only be explained by the divine plan. Whereas his power is not limited (cf. 12:17; 14:19–20; 19:24–29), it was exercised in a special way in the patriarchs' regard and in the land he had promised to them. The examples of his justice (cf. 12:17; 19:20–21; 38:7) and mercy (cf. 18:22–32; 19:29) are all relevant to the overriding plan. Even the varying use of the divine names must be understood in its light. The occurrence of "Yahweh" (Lord) signals the identification of the God of the patriarchs with the God of Israel, and the occurrences of "Elohim" (God), "El Shaddai" (God Almighty), "El Elyon" (God Most High), and "El Olam" (God Eternal) show that the gradual revelation of God's plan involved a gradual revelation of his person. Throughout, he is the one and only God (cf. 35:2) whose one plan embraces one people in one land.

11 Genesis provides a number of teachings subsidiary to the development of God's plan. Among these are the necessity of worshiping God in sacrifice and of calling on his name (12:7–8; 13:4,18; 26:25; 31:54; 33:20; 35:1,7; 46:1), concern for sexual morality (12:17; 19; 20; 38:24; 39:7–12), abhorrence of human sacrifice (ch. 22) and of murder (37:21–22f.), charity to strangers (18:1–8; 24:17–20), obligation of justice (31:36–42; 38:8–10,26), forgiveness of offences (50:15–21), and respect for the dead (23; 25:8–10; 35:19–20f.,29; 50:1–14). Finally, in a succession of scenes, at times the divine condescension is emphasized (e.g., ch. 18) and at times the divine transcendence (the intervention of God through the medium of an angel, or in a dream).

The basic importance of Gn for the development of revelation is evident in the frequent allusions to it in the NT and in the Fathers and in its use in the liturgy of the Church. From its teachings regarding the first man flows the Pauline doctrine of original sin and of the new Adam. The Fourth Gospel contains many allusions to the opening chapters of Gn. In 1 Pt, the figure of Noah's ark is applied to the sacrament of baptism. The faith of Abraham plays a dominant role in Paul's development of the doctrine of justification. The symbolism of the figure of Melchizedek in its teaching on the priesthood of Christ is developed in Heb 7:1–17. All these and other figures and passages of Gn are taken up in turn by the Fathers in bringing out the fullness of revelation in the NT teaching (cf. *Abraham, père des croyants* [Cahiers Sioniens; Paris, 1952]).

12 **(IV) Texts and Versions.** The MT is remarkably well preserved in Gn. Its fidelity to the original, generally accepted, has been confirmed by the recent discoveries in the Dead Sea area; the Gn passages represented in the QL vary in only a few cases from the MT. On the other hand, the Sam agrees more with the LXX, which, while the best of the versions, is inferior to the MT. The tendency of the LXX to soften the Hebr anthropomorphisms is one indication. Among the other Gk versions, that of Aquila is extemely literal and that of Symmachus is extremely free. The Pesh is of some value because of its general fidelity. The other ancient versions are not extremely significant for the reconstruction of the text. Among the modern English versions, the CCD, RSV, the "American Translation" (Smith-Goodspeed, U. of Chicago), and the AB can be recommended as critical translations from the original Hebrew. The RSV adheres more closely to the Hebrew, the "American Translation" tries to clarify the meaning and hence is more free in its rendering, and the CCD strikes a middle ground.

13 **(V) Outline.** Within the context of the Pentateuch, Gn provides the introduction to the story of Israel. As such, it describes the origin, or beginning, of salvation history revealed in its fullness in the election of Israel. Conceptually, therefore, the contents of the book were interpreted only by what happened in the later period. The interpretation involved two principal blocks of material—the patriarchal narratives, which were seen as the immediate preparation for, or introduction to, the story of Israel, and the primitive history that preceded and explained the divine intervention at the time of Abraham. This primitive history was thus the general introduction to the whole. The book is accordingly divided into two main parts: primitive history (1:1–11:32) and patriarchal history (12:1–50:26). In the detailed outline that follows, we have subdivided the patriarchal history into three sections. There are indications that such a subdivision was intended by the final author or editor. After each section, the tradition (i.e., J, E, or P) to which it is attributed is noted in parentheses; these attributions are, in some cases, only tentative.

(I) Primitive History (1–11)
- (A) Creation of World and Man (1:1–2:4a) (P)
- (B) Creation of Man and Woman (2:4b–25) (J)
- (C) The Fall (3:1–24) (J)
- (D) Cain and Abel (4:1–16) (J)
- (E) Genealogy of Cain (4:17–26) (J)
- (F) Genealogy of Adam to Noah (5:1–32) (P)
- (G) Prologue to the Flood (6:1–22) (J and P)
- (H) The Flood (7:1–8:22) (J and P)
- (I) The Covenant with Noah (9:1–17) (P)
- (J) The Sons of Noah (9:18–27) (J)
- (K) The Peopling of the Earth (10:1–32) (P and J)
- (L) The Tower of Babel (11:1–9) (J)
- (M) Concluding Genealogies (11:10–32) (P and J)

(II) The Patriarch Abraham (12:1–25:18)
(A) The Call of Abram (12:1–9) (J, P)
(B) Abram and Sarai in Egypt (12:10–20) (J)
(C) The Separation of Abram and Lot (13:1–18) (J, P)
(D) Abram and the Four Kings (14:1–24) (?)
(E) Promises Renewed (15:1–20) (J, E?)
(F) Hagar's Flight (16:1–16) (J, P)
(G) The Covenant of Circumcision (17:1–27) (P)
(H) Promise of a Son; Sodom and Gomorrah (18:1–19:38) (J)
(I) Abraham and Sarah in Gerar (20:1–18) (E)
(J) Isaac and Ishmael (21:1–21) (J and P)
(K) Abraham and Abimelech (21:22–34) (E)
(L) The Sacrifice of Isaac (22:1–24) (E, J)
(M) The Purchase of the Cave of Machpelah (23:1–20) (P)
(N) The Wife of Isaac (24:1–67) (J)
(O) Abraham's Descendants (25:1–18) (P and J)
(III) The Patriarchs Isaac and Jacob (25:19–36:43)
(A) The Birth of Esau and Jacob (25:19–34) (J, P)
(B) Isaac in Gerar and Beer-sheba (26:1–35) (J, P)
(C) Isaac's Blessing of Jacob (27:1–45) (J)
(D) Jacob's Departure for Paddan-aram (27:46–28:9) (P)
(E) Vision at Bethel (28:10–22) (J and E)
(F) Jacob's Marriages (29:1–30) (J, E?)
(G) Jacob's Children (29:31–30:24) (J and E)
(H) Jacob Outwits Laban (30:25–43) (J, E)
(I) Jacob's Departure (31:1–21) (E, J)
(J) Laban's Pursuit (31:22–42) (E, J)
(K) The Contract Between Jacob and Laban (31:43–32:3) (J and E)
(L) Preparation for the Meeting with Esau (32:4–22) (J and E)
(M) Jacob's Struggle with God (32:23–33) (J)
(N) Jacob's Meeting with Esau (33:1–20) (J, E?)
(O) The Rape of Dinah (34:1–31) (J and E)
(P) Jacob at Bethel (35:1–29) (E and P)
(Q) The Descendants of Esau (36:1–43) (P?)
(IV) The History of Joseph (37:1–50:26)
(A) Joseph Sold into Egypt (37:1–36) (J and E)
(B) Judah and Tamar (38:1–30) (J)
(C) Joseph's Temptations (39:1–23) (J)
(D) Joseph Interprets the Prisoners' Dreams (40:1–23) (E)
(E) Joseph Interprets Pharaoh's Dreams (41:1–57) (E, J)
(F) First Encounter of Joseph with His Brothers (42:1–38) (E, J)
(G) Second Journey to Egypt (43:1–34) (J, E)
(H) Judah's Plea for Benjamin (44:1–34) (J)
(I) The Recognition of Joseph (45:1–28) (J and E)
(J) Jacob's Journey to Egypt (46:1–34) (J, E, and P)
(K) The Hebrews in Egypt (47:1–31) (J and P)
(L) Jacob Adopts Joseph's Sons (48:1–22) (J and E, P)
(M) Jacob's Blessings (49:1–33) (J?)
(N) The Burial of Jacob and the Final Acts of Joseph (50:1–26) (J, E, and P)

COMMENTARY

14 **(I) Primitive History (1–11).** These chapters form a necessary introduction to the story of the patriarchs, which in turn introduces the pivotal point of all OT history, the Exodus and covenant. It is almost universally agreed that the two traditions, J and P, are represented here and that their distinction is, in general, assured. Whereas the primeval history in J is a complete narrative in itself, P seems to suppose some of the events narrated by J. Other than the stories of creation and the flood, P has no narrative material here; instead, it provides with its genealogical lists the chronological and ethnological framework to J's story. The historical character of these stories and their provenance are discussed in individual introductions and commentaries.

The relevance of Gn 1–11 to salvation history (also true of the patriarchal narratives) is based on the climactic events that marked the beginning of Israel's history as the chosen people. The God of Israel was seen, in the light of those events, to be the God of all nature and of all history. Consequently, this primeval history is the theological interpretation of those events significant for the later development of Israel's own story. As such it is not, and was not intended to be, a complete record of all that transpired from the beginning of the world; rather it is selective to the extreme. Creation (the necessarily initial act of salvation history) and the fall are the determining acts of what follows, i.e., of the gradual *aversio a Deo* on the part of man that will lead to the definitive intervention of God in a new creation—that of his people.

(Arbez, E. P., "Genesis I–XI and Prehistory," *AER* 123 [1950] 81–92, 202–13, 284–94. Cramer, K., *Genesis 1–11: Urgeschichte* [Tübingen, 1959]. Hauret, C., *Beginnings: Genesis and Modern Science* [tr. E. P. Emmans; Dubuque, 1955]. MacKenzie, R. A. F., "Before Abraham Was...," *CBQ* 15 [1953] 131–40. Renckens, H., *Israel's Concept of the Beginning* [N.Y., 1964].)

15 **(A) Creation of World and Man (P).** The most majestic of the contributions of P, this creation hymn gives evidence of a prehistory. For example, the liturgical (or mnemonic) device "God saw that it was good," marking each great creation event, was seemingly added primitively at the end of each work. Its double application to distinct works of the third and sixth days can be explained by the author's compression of the original narrative into six days, thereby wishing to teach the divine approval of Israel's traditional six-day work week. The days, therefore, are understood as normal 24 hour periods; as such they form the literary framework of the hymn and have no other significance.

The primitive cosmology of the author's time is used to teach the creation of all things by God. The absolute power of the transcendent God is emphasized. Whereas the pagan epics depict creation as the result of a struggle between the gods and the forces of chaos, the biblical account stresses the effortless activity of the one God. The imagery borrowed from these other accounts becomes material for the author's polemic against the myths; it also helps to make the picture live for his readers. The final editor of Gn has given prominence to the teachings of P by placing the story at the beginning.

16 (a) (1:1–2). **1.** Forming an inclusion with 2:4a, the verse is an absolute statement: the whole visible world (the Gk cosmos) came into being as the result of sovereign divine activity (cf. V. Hamp, *Lex Tua Veritas* [Fest. H. Junker; Trier, 1961] 113–26; taken as temporal clause by others: cf. W. F. Albright, *Mélanges A. Robert* [Paris, 1957] 23; S. Herrmann, *TLZ* 86 [1961] 413ff.). The vb., *bārā'*, used exclusively of God, makes no suggestion here of pre-existing material. **2.** In the pagan myths, many of these terms depict the primitive chaos from which the gods emerged and against which they struggled for mastery: *Tōhûwābōhû*, the "formless void" (Phoenician Baau, the nocturnal mother goddess [Von Rad, *op. cit.*, 48]); *ḥōšek*, "primeval darkness" (allied with Tiamat against the creating god in *Enuma Elish*); *tehôm*, the "watery abyss" (Tiamat, the principal antagonist in *Enuma Elish*); *rûaḥ 'ĕlōhîm*, the "mighty storm-wind" (part of the picture of the primeval chaos). Together these are a concrete image of the formlessness essentially opposed to the order of creation (see H. Junker, *Mélanges A. Robert* [Paris, 1957] 27–37). Their primitive pagan connotations have been nullified in P's theology of the absolute Lord (cf. v. 1). If *rûaḥ 'ĕlōhîm* is to be translated the "wind of God" (cf. H. Orlinsky, *JQR* 48 [1957–58] 174–82), the concept of impotence is contrasted with the vivifying power of God.

17 (b) (1:3–5). God's personal will, expressed in his word, which bridges the chasm between God and formlessness, first produces light, the most sublime of the elements. It stands in marked contrast to the darksome chaos and, by reason of its perfect correspondence to the divine ordering will, is found to be "good" (on the basis of Northwest-Semitic parallels, Albright translates the refrain: "God saw how good it was"; cf. Albright, *Mélanges A. Robert* [Paris, 1957] 22–26). The basis is given for the first and principal division into "Day" and "Night," here conceived as realities that can be given names, according to the Semitic mentality, only by one who has absolute control over them.

(c) (1:6–8). The firmament is regarded as a huge inverted bowl of hammered metal that retains the waters above it (cf. 7:11b). Because the division of the waters is not perfectly realized until the third day, the divine approbation formula is not yet applied. The vestige of a more primitive and more direct creation account is found in the statement that God "made" (*wayya'aś*) the firmament (v. 7).

18 (d) (1:9–10). The work of the third day, a continuation of the created order brought to the primeval chaos, provides the basis for the division into "Earth" and "Seas." The work of the second day is now completed; the chaotic waters are effectively delimited, as was the primeval darkness on the first day.

(e) (1:11–13). Vegetation is created mediately (a new concept in the story) through the agency of the mother earth. But the productive power of the earth (evident to ancient man) is not self-given; it comes from God and thus is not a proper object of worship (cf. Canaanite religions). P implies here that plants and trees do not have life in the same way as animals and man. The first triduum, basically the *opus distinctionis* (separation), is now terminated.

19 (f) (1:14–19). The *opus ornatus* (equipment) begins with the creation of the heavenly lights. Of the three functions of the sun, moon, and stars, the second emphasizes their cultic purpose (v. 14b). This emphasis is expected in P, in which salvation history is reconstructed throughout as a liturgical history. The sun and moon are not named, because their Semitic names would recall pagan gods worshiped at times by Israel herself (cf. 2 Kgs 23:11), and the Babylonian cult of these gods was a special danger to the exiles. The personification of the lights (they "rule" the day and night) is perhaps an indication of an earlier form of the hymn but is not foreign to Semitic mentality. The notion of service to man is deliberately stressed.

(g) (1:20–23). The description of the fifth day's work is distinguished by two expressions: *nepeš ḥayyāh* (living being) and *bārā'* (create). According to the ancients, animals were superior to plants inasmuch as they were living beings and able to transmit life. Therefore they were created by God, not simply made. The word *bārā'*, applied here for the first time to a specific creature, connotes a special and uniquely divine act. Included with the fish and birds are the legendary monsters of the deep (cf. Is 27:1; Jb 40:15–16f.), inimical to the gods in Canaanite and other mythologies, but here creatures of the one God and therefore good. Their procreative power is the result of a divine blessing, because all life comes from God. The direct creation of these creatures by God and the special blessing given them (cf. vv. 24–25f.) may be explained by the fact that primitive man did not consider the sea and air to have the productive power of the land.

20 (h) (1:24–25). We note again the occasional unevenness of the story, attesting to several redactions. The land animals, though *nepeš ḥayyāh* like the sea creatures, are produced by the earth—perhaps a literary reminiscence of the ancient mother-earth concept. But for P, whatever power the earth possesses comes from God. In v. 25, a later addition, God makes these creatures directly; the special word *bārā'* is not used here, perhaps to note the contrast between animals and man, who is also the work of the sixth day. The divine blessing is omitted because their procreative power was conceived as coming indirectly from God through the earth.

(i) (1:26–27). **26.** The P tradition notes the climax of creation reached in man by mentioning the divine consultation with the heavenly court. This reference softens the strong anthropomorphism implied in the more primitive poem in v. 27, where man is to be created in God's image alone. *Ṣelem* (image) means, ordinarily, an exact copy or reproduction. Again, the harshness of the implication is softened by the addition of *d^e^mût* (likeness), ordinarily meaning resemblance or similarity. The Semites knew of no dichotomy in man in our terms; the whole man, as a complete personality, had God's image, manifested especially in the resulting ability to rule over other creatures (cf. H. Gross, *Lex Tua Veritas* [Fest. H. Junker; Trier, 1961], 89–100). Man, as God's image, is his representative on earth (statues represented the ancient kings in those regions of the empire where they could not be present personally). **27.** The poetic version adds the conviction that the distinction of the sexes is of divine origin and therefore good. The full meaning of "mankind" (*'ādām*) is realized only when there is man and woman. (For an inspired commentary on the passage, cf. Ps 8.)

21 (j) (1:28–31). **28.** To offset a possible confusion with pagan notions, P carefully shows man's procreative power to be not an indication of his divine likeness (achieving a kind of immortality), but the result of a special divine blessing. By using this power, man does not enter into the mythical world of the gods, as in the pagan rite of sacred prostitution, but he fulfills a divine precept. Dominion over the animals is expressed in strong verbs (*rādāh*, "trample" [v. 26]; *kābaš*, "tread down" [v. 28]); man's rule is not as effortless as God's, for he is only God's ambassador. **29–30.** A hint of the peace that existed in the beginning by God's will is given in the reference to the food of man and animals. This harmony, which will also characterize the eschatological age (cf. Is 11:6–8), is later disrupted (Gn 9:2–4), presumably as the result of sin. **31.** The perfection of all creation is expressed by a superlative form, unusual for the ordinarily laconic author. The order and harmony of the cosmos, which P has expressed by the orderly arrangement, are totally in keeping with the divine ordering will.

(k) (2:1–4a). **1–2.** God completed his work on the "seventh" day (thus in the MT, not the "sixth" day as in the LXX and the CCD), implying activity of a different kind (cf. v. 3); the Sabbath rest of God is not something negative. **3.** Between the ordered cosmos and the creator in majestic repose, a special relationship is set up, expressed in the blessing (endowing with vital powers) and making holy (setting apart) of the day. By observing the Sabbath, P implies, Israel imitates the divine repose and is saved (blessed) and set apart (made holy); she enters into the special relationship. The relationship, on God's part, never ceases; there is no reference to the evening and morning of the seventh day. **4a.** *Tôl^e^dôt* (story) usually refers to a genealogical account (cf. 5:1; 6:9; etc.). In P, it marks important stages in salvation history. Similar statements are otherwise found at the beginning of an account; it is placed here (perhaps by a later editor) to preserve the majestic beginning (v. 1).

(Duncker, P. G., "L'Immagine di Dio nell' uomo (Gen. 1,26–27)," *Bib* 40, part 1 [1959] 384–92. Ridderbos, N. H., "Genesis I, 1 und 2," *OTS* 12 [1958] 214–66. Stamm, J. J., *Die Gottebenbildlichkeit des Menschen im Alten Testament* [Theologische Studien 54; Zollikon, 1959]. Westermann, C., *The Genesis Accounts of Creation* [Facet Books 7; Phila., 1964]. Whitley, C. F., "The Pattern of Creation in Genesis, Chapter 1," *JNES* 17 [1958] 32–40.)

22 **(B) Creation of Man and Woman (2:4b–25) (J).** The Yahwist's story differs greatly from P's. The literary genre is a popular story with elements having a closer dependence on extrabiblical sources. The style is more vivid and concrete; the presentation of God is more anthropomorphic; the perspective is earthly and human rather than cosmic and divine. The didactic aim, although profound at times, is subordinate to the narrative itself and is not as marked as in P.

Analysis can disengage various strands of traditions indicating primitive independent contexts, but they probably had been united before J gave the final literary form to the whole. The original stories can no longer be reconstructed from the present text (see J. L. McKenzie, *TS* 15 [1954] 541–72 = *MR* 146–81). In the context of J the story of creation is a prelude to the story of the fall and the consequent story of man's gradual estrangement from God, all of which is introductory to the patriarchal narratives and, ultimately, to the saving acts of the Exodus. Therefore, the story of creation in J, as in P, is the beginning of salvation history.

23 (a) (2:4b–7). Stylistically the opening words can be compared with the opening line of *Enuma Elish* (cf. *ANET* 60). The fusion of Yahweh Elohim (Lord God) is to be attributed to the final editor. What P describes in ten majestic verses J describes in one subordinate clause; his interest is in the condition of the earth already created. **5.** It is a barren earth bereft of the blessing of water. For P, the chaos of floodwaters would be replaced by an organized cosmos; for J, the chaos of barrenness would be replaced by a fruitful garden. The reference to man as tiller of the soil reflects a sedentary interest. **6.** Only water from the ground was available. **7.** The center of interest and the first object of divine activity is man (*'ādām*, in a collective sense), who has a relationship to the earth (*'ădāmāh*): The earth is destined for man's use (v. 5b), and he will return to it (3:19). But man also has a special kind of life distinguishing him from all earthly beings, a life that comes from God (*nišmat ḥayyîm* "breath of life"). These truths are expressed in an imagery partly paralleled in nonbiblical literature (*ANET* 68a, 99d).

24 (b) (2:8–9). **8.** The scene is set for the story in ch. 3. The garden, symbol of divine blessings, is located in "Eden," an Akkadian loanword meaning "steppe," but in the Bible an unspecified geographical term; it is "to the east" (Mesopotamia). The author probably intended that his readers recall the similar Hebr word *'ēden* (pleasure). **9.** Among the trees of the garden, two are given special mention: the tree of life, a common ancient symbol of immortality (cf. *ANET* 96), and the tree of knowledge of good and evil (explained later; cf. 3:4–5). For irregularities in the text, indicating a pre-Yahwist conflation of several traditions, cf. 2:8b and 2:15, and 2:9c and 3:3a.

(c) (2:10–14). This colorless passage, added later, has no essential connection with the story. Apparently it establishes a connection between the blessings of the contemporary world (the four rivers and the territory embraced by them) and the original world of Eden. The first two rivers cannot be located with certainty (cf. Speiser, *Genesis*, 19–20). The last two agree with v. 8 in placing the garden in the east, seemingly in northern Mesopotamia.

25 (d) (2:15–17). **15.** The narrative is resumed after the interruption (cf. v. 8). Man's enjoyment of the garden is a gift from God. Work itself is not evil (cf. 3:17b–18). **16–17.** Man's happiness (v. 16) is consequent upon his remaining subject to God. In this concept lies the whole meaning of the garden. The possibility of questioning the divine command does not occur to J; that itself would imply rebellion (cf. 3:4–5f.; Jb 9:12). *the tree of knowledge of good and evil:* For the Semites, "to know" means to experience in any way. "Good" and "evil" are terms of polarity and can signify totality (cf. Nm 24:13), hence a total experience, not necessarily in a moral sense.

(e) (2:18–25). **18.** "A helper like himself" expresses two profound ideas: Woman complements man, a social being by nature, but she is not a mere service appendage; she "corresponds to him," i.e., has a similar nature. **19–20.** In these verses, J introduces the creation of the animals to emphasize, by contrast, the true role of woman. Animals, named by man and hence under his control (cf. 1:26b,28b), are not fit companions for his total being; they have no nature corresponding to his (an indirect polemic against bestiality?). **21–23.** The "deep sleep" of man (*tardēmāh*) suggests the mysterious and highly significant nature of the divine activity (cf. Gn 15:12). The description of woman's formation is, like that of man's, etiological. All the expressions—the "rib" (of uncertain meaning; perhaps connected with the Sumerian word meaning "rib" and "life"), "bone of my bone and flesh of my flesh" (cf. Gn 29:14; 2 Sm 19:12,13), "woman" (*'iššāh*) and "man" (*'îš*)—indicate the unity of nature of man and wife (see L. Arnaldich, *SP* 1, 346–57). The thrice-repeated "this one" ("she" in the CCD; *zō't* in the MT) marks the contrast with v. 20b; woman, unlike animal, is the "helper like himself." But woman's existence, psychologically and in the social order, is dependent on man. **24.** The author concludes this first part of his narrative with a general principle—a theological conviction that had prompted and conditioned the story of woman's formation. The unity of marriage and its monogamous nature are God-willed. **25.** This transitional verse, implying the state of innocence of the first man (but not primarily the lack of sexual disorder; rather, "mutual trust and esteem"; cf. A. M. Dubarle, *DowR* 76 [1958] 242 = *The Biblical Doctrine of Original Sin* [London, 1964] 74), introduces the story of the first sin.

26 **(C) The Fall (3:1–24) (J).** The connection of this story with the preceding is apparent from the vocabulary, the style, the imagery, and the movement of the narrative. The truths contained here required no special revelation; they result from the author's convictions concerning man's present condition and God's actions in Israel's history (see MacKenzie, "Before Abraham Was...," *CBQ* 15 [1953] 131–40).

(a) (3:1–3). **1.** The serpent is one of the "beasts of the field" and hence a creature of God. It is introduced here to symbolize the power hostile to man and to give movement to the story; later revelation will go far beyond this (cf. Wis 2:24; Jn 8:44; Ap 12:9). The serpent was chosen by J particularly because of its role in the idolatrous fertility rites of Canaan (see F. Hvidberg, *VT* 10 [1960] 285–94). A polemical motif is suggested. (For a possible sexual interpretation of the whole story, see L. Hartman, *CBQ* 20 [1958] 26–40, with bibliography.) The serpent's question, a distortion of the divine command, insinuates the possibility of an unwarranted restriction by God and provokes the reply necessary if the conversation is to be maintained. **2–3.** The woman corrects the serpent's distortion, but she adds her own ("...neither shall you touch it"). Sin begins with some distortion of the truth.

27 (b) (3:4–13). **4–5.** The serpent first denies the inevitability of the punishment and then offers likeness to God as the result of eating of the tree. This likeness to God ("knowing good and evil") could be the quasi-immortality through offspring achieved by sexual intercourse (see Hartman, *op. cit.*, 25–36f.), moral autonomy—i.e., the right to decide for oneself what is good and evil (De Vaux, *La Genèse*, 45)—and reliance on self rather than on God, the Gk *hybris* (Von Rad, *op. cit.*, 87). All these explanations presume the correctness of the serpent's statement (seemingly confirmed in 3:22a). But if likeness to God is not the result of the act, "knowing good and evil" may simply refer to a total experience, i.e., of physical and moral happiness before the fall and of physical and moral evil after the fall (see J. de Fraine, *Mélanges A. Robert* [Paris, 1957] 47–65). **6.** Without sensationalism, the threefold stage of temptation is presented in an ascending order (cf. 1 Jn 2:16). The woman is tempted and falls first; she then tempts man. Behind the story may lie a conviction about woman's curiosity and her ability to lure man; it does not concern the basic truths of the account. **7.** Their nakedness becomes an occasion of shame, something impossible before the sin. Note the play on words: *'êrummîm*, "naked," and *'ārûm*, "cunning" (3:1). **8–13.** In the garden, man enjoyed an intimacy with God. It is disrupted by sin (cf. 11:5, where God must "come down"). Compare man's fear of meeting God because of his nakedness with Ex 20:26, where the cultic encounter with God demands proper dress. As head of the family, man is the responsible member and hence is questioned first; this is the order of creation. His response, an implicit accusation of God ("the woman you gave me"), is the result of sin.

28 (c) (14–15). **14.** In J, the natural characteristics of the serpent are used to symbolize the punishment of the power of evil. Though directed to the serpent, the curse involves man also (v. 15). Man loathes this power, which is thereby humiliated (cf. Is 49:23; Mi 7:17). **15.** The relationship between the power of evil and man is more precisely stated. It is one of enmity that will continue throughout all generations ("your seed and her seed"). In the ensuing struggle, man (i.e., the woman's seed) will gain the clearer victory ("your head" and "his heel"). The optimism of J, a constant of his history and based on his conviction of the saving acts of God in Israel's behalf, conditions his composition throughout (cf. 3:21; 4:7c). Later revelation will confirm this first vague message of victory and specify the manner in which the victory will be attained.

(d) (3:16–19). **16.** The present condition of woman as wife and mother is seen as a punishment of the first sin. The punishment is threefold: Woman bears children in pain; her desire for her husband, despite its consequences, is controlled with difficulty; man dominates woman in the domestic and social order. Man's domination, although part of the order of creation (cf. 2:21–23), is intensified by sin beyond the divinely willed measure. **17–19.** Unlike the serpent, the man is not cursed directly, but through the earth. (Nature's involvement in salvation history, a constant biblical theme [cf. Ps 28; Is 11:6–9; etc.], is a religious, not a scientific, concept.) Between man's labor and its results exists no proportion (cf. 2:15). The passage may reflect the conditions of two types of life: that of the sedentary farmer (vv. 17c and 19ab) and that of the seminomad (vv. 18 and 19c). In the conflated form, the emphasis is on the former (Von Rad, *op. cit.*, 91–92; cf. also 3:23). In the ancient poem adopted by the author, death is seen as man's natural lot (v. 19bc); in the context, it results from sin. Death is not seen here to follow immediately upon the sin, but not too much is to be made of this contrast with 2:17b; the author's use of his sources at times conditions the clarity.

29 (e) (3:20–24). **20.** "Woman," called *'iššāh* (2:23b) because of her relation to "man" (*'îš*), is now called *ḥawwāh* (Eve) because of her relation to "all the living (*ḥāy*). Though it breaks the context of punishment, the statement is not foreign to J's thought. Sin has introduced death, but life will continue. **21.** Like the preceding verse, it clashes somewhat with the context of punishment and is difficult to reconcile with 3:7. But, as often in J, it serves to introduce a note of hope: God still provides for fallen man. **22.** The interpretation depends on the understanding of "knowing good and evil." If it refers to moral autonomy or to rejection of dependence as a creature, the statement causes no difficulty. If the reference is to total experience of good and evil, both physical and moral (cf. vv. 4–5), then God speaks ironically (compatible with J's mentality; cf. 11:5). The mention of the tree of life (immortality) is demanded by 3:19bc. **23–24.** The actual expulsion is related twice (perhaps an indication of two traditions). In Babylonian mythologies, the *k*[e]*rubîm*, creatures that are half-man and half-animal, guard the gates of the temples and palaces. The imagery was borrowed by the Hebrews (cf. also Ex 37:7–9; Ez 1:10; etc.) to express their belief in sacred ministers of Yahweh. The flaming sword, another mythological figure, probably seen here as a flash of lightning zigzagging back and forth, symbolizes the divine anger.

(Coppens, J., *La connaissance du bien et du mal et le péché du Paradis* [Louvain, 1948]. Haag, H., "Die Themata der Sündenfall-geschichte," *Lex Tua Veritas* [Fest. H. Junker; Trier, 1961] 101–11. Lambert, G., "Le drame du Jardin d'Eden," *NRT* 76, part 2 [1954] 917–48. Rigaux, B., "La femme et son lignage dans Genèse III, 14–15," *RB* 61 [1954] 321–48.)

30 **(D) Cain and Abel (4:1–16) (J).** This story perhaps originally explained the origin of the Kenites (cf. Jgs 4:11,17; Von Rad, *op. cit.*, 104). It may also have been an exaltation of the seminomadic life (Abel) in contrast to the sedentary (Cain before the crime) and the strictly nomadic (Cain after the crime). Conflicts with the sedentary Canaanites and with the wild desert tribes, such as the Midianites (cf. Jgs 6ff.), could have conditioned the attitude (De Vaux, *La Genèse*, 13–14f.). The story receives a more universal meaning from J; it concerns all mankind, not the eponymous ancestors of specific tribes.

Without its proper historical roots, the story contains anachronisms. Civilization is well developed (v. 2b); sacrifice has been instituted (vv. 3–4f.); the existence of other peoples is supposed (v. 14–15f.). But these inconsistencies fade before the religious truths: Man's revolt against God leads to his revolt against his fellow man; the crime of murder confirms the fallen state of man; God is just in the punishment of sin, but merciful in its application (cf. v. 15); sacrifice must be offered in the proper spirit; sin must be, and therefore can be, mastered by man (v. 7).

31 (a) (4:1–7). **1.** The story has been connected with that of the first parents. The name of Cain (*qayin*) is derived, by popular etymology, from the words of Eve, "I have given birth" (*qānîtî*, lit., "I have gotten"). **2.** Abel's name (*hebel*) is not explained (perhaps suggesting the same Hebr word meaning "breath," and thus the transitory nature of Abel's life). As farmer and shepherd, they represent two of the principal ancient ways of life. **3–5.** In J, no reason is given for God's acceptance of Abel's sacrifice and his rejection of Cain's. It is the Lord's concern (cf. Ex 33:19b); J is probably more interested in the "younger son" motif (cf. Gn 25:23). Like Isaac with regard to Ishmael, Jacob to Esau, and Judah to his older brothers, Abel is preferred to Cain. **6–7.** The text and precise meaning are obscure. Sin, or temptation, is pictured as a continually present animal (*rōbēṣ*, "crouching"; in Assyro-Babylonian documents, a demon called *rabîṣu* is mentioned, which awaits its prey along the roadside [cf. also *ANET* 103cd]) which man must master.

32 (b) (4:8–16). **8–10.** As in 3:6, the sin is described simply and without dramatization. (In the MT the words "Let us go out into the field" are missing; they are supplied by the Sam, the LXX, the Tg., and the Vg.) The progress of evil is confirmed by Cain's insolent reply to God (cf. 3:10). For the ancients, life was in the blood (cf. Lv 17:11–14). Since human life originates from God in a special way (Gn 2:7), human blood spilled by a creature will cry out to its rightful lord. **11–12.** The "earth" (*'ădāmāh*) plays a large role in J's theology of the beginnings (cf. 2:5–7,19a; 3:17b–19,23). The relationship of man to the earth is intimate, a concept conditioned by man's dependence on its fruits. Here the earth is personified; the relationship is shattered by the ground itself, which refuses altogether to respond to man's toil (cf. 3:17b–18). Cain is thereby forced to the strict nomadic life. For the first time man is directly cursed. **13–14.** By metonymy, the "crime" (*'āwōn*) becomes the punishment. Banishment from the soil meant banishment to the desert places, the refuge of demons and outlaws. By the same token, it meant banishment from the presence of Yahweh, who was considered to dwell in a special way among his people (the author has Canaan, land of promise, in mind). Without God's presence and (implied) protection, Cain's life will be endangered. **15.** The social institution implied here is that of tribal blood-vengeance. Desert tribes were restrained from indiscriminate killing only by fear of vengeance from the tribe or clan of the murdered one. The mark ("token") would indicate the tribe. The tribe of Cain is here presented as exacting especially severe vengeance. Our author gives a religious significance to this mark; it is a sign of divine protection. **16.** Cain dwelt in the land of Nod, a symbolic name referring to Cain the "wanderer" (*nād*; cf. vv. 12b and 14b).

33 **(E) Genealogy of Cain (4:17–26) (J).** This list has been taken by J from a separate tradition. Originally, the Cain of v. 17, who founds a city, could not be Cain the wanderer (cf. also Abel the shepherd in 4:2 and Jabal the forerunner of shepherds in 4:20). The author has fused the two sources. The common element in both, which justifies the fusion, is the increase of evil in the world. In the genealogy, this evil is represented in the development of material civilization, which J and other inspired authors see as harmful to religious life. As we shall discuss, this list parallels another from a separate tradition (Gn 5:12–28).

(a) (4:17–24). **17.** The first city is named after Cain's son, Enoch (*ḥănôk*, possibly a punning reference to the root *ḥānak* meaning "to dedicate" or "to initiate"). **18–22.** Although no explicit judgment is made on the polygamy of Lamech (v. 19), the context (the line of Cain) implies a condemnation. Hebrew names are given to the inventors of the various occupations in accord with the Hebr names of the occupations. Jabal is from the root *yābal*, "to lead," as flocks. Jubal is from *yôbēl*, "trumpet." Tubal is the name of a people dealing in metals (cf. Ez 27:13). To this last is added "Cain" (meaning "forger" in other Semitic languages) as an explanation of Tubal. The significance of Naamah (*na'ămāh*, "lovely," "gracious") is unexplained. **23–24.** This ancient war chant, in typical Semitic parallelism, seems originally to have been a "boasting song"; J gives it a new meaning by adding v. 24 and placing it in the present context. The spirit of vengeance has increased; it is no longer satisfied with the divine vengeance (cf. 4:15).

34 (b) (4:25–26). These two verses are a remnant of an ancient genealogy of which 5:29 originally may have been a part. Therefore, J showed two lines descending from the first man, but P's list (ch. 5) prevailed in the final redaction. The line of Cain issued in a terrible cry of vengeance (vv. 23–24f.); the line of Seth (*šēt*, here connected with *šāt*, "he has placed") issued in an attitude of prayer. Man is not yet completely estranged from God. The name Yahweh (Lord) was only revealed later (cf. Ex 3:14), but J uses the name from the beginning (cf. 2:4b), thereby explicitly identifying the God of Israel with the creator. Perhaps J implies here (v. 26b) that "man" (*'ĕnôš*, "Enosh") was capable of worshiping the one God from the beginning.

(Gabriel, J., "Die Kainitengenealogie," *Bib* 40, part 1 [1959] 409–27. Lussier, E., " *'adam* in Genesis 1, 1–4, 24," *CBQ* 18 [1956] 137–39.)

35 **(F) Genealogy of Adam to Noah (5:1–32) (P).** This genealogy, linking the first man with the flood, is continued in chs. 10–11, which, in turn, provide the link between the flood and Abraham. The salvation history of the later period is thus shown to be intimately connected with that of the beginnings—not cyclic but linear in its movement. The literary form of genealogy, here used for a distinct religious purpose, was known to other peoples. A list of Babylonian kings shows ten names before the flood, as here, the last the hero of the flood, as here. The seventh king was carried off to the gods, as was Enoch. All have extraordinary ages, in the thousands, which differ in the various lists of the Babylonian kings as they do for the patriarchs in the MT, the LXX, and the Sam (for full discussion, see Clamer, *op. cit.*, 172–75).

A definite connection exists between J's Cain list and P's Seth list: *qayin* (J) and *qênān* (P); *ḥănôk* (J) and *ḥănôk* (P); *'îrād* (J) and *yered* (P); *m^{e}ḥûyā'ēl* (J) and *mahăl'ēl* (P); *m^{e}tûšā'ēl* (J) and *m^{e}tûšelaḥ* (P); *lemek* (J) and *lemek* (P); and *nōaḥ* (J) and *nōaḥ* (P). The striking similarities show that the list in P is also ancient. In both lists, the Hebr names show that they have been adapted for the authors' purpose. The exact source of either list cannot be determined.

The precise significance of the ages given by P is not certain. The general decrease in ages probably indicates the further estrangement from God, since long life is attributed to "fear of the Lord" (cf. Prv 10:27). What J expresses in story form, P expresses more subtly; he has no story of the fall or of man's progress in evil.

36 (a) (5:1–11). **1–5.** Note the connection with 2:4a: There was presented the "story" (*tôl^{e}dôt*) of creation; here are the "descendants" (*tôl^{e}dôt*) of Adam, which is now used as a proper name (as in 4:25). There God created man in his image and likeness (1:26–27; cf. 5:1b); here Adam begets a son in his own image and likeness. Seth here corresponds with the Seth in J's list (4:25). **6–8.** As in J (4:26), Seth begets Enosh. **9–11.** In P, Cain becomes Kenan (same Hebr root), but is part of the genealogy of Seth; in J, Cain constitutes a line distinct from Seth.

(b) (5:18–32). **18–24.** Enoch, the seventh in the line, is of special but mysterious significance. He lived 365 years, a number corresponding perfectly to the number of days in the solar calendar. He "walked with God" (an unusual phrase for P; cf. Gn 17:1), signifying intimacy with the divine. "God took [*lāqaḥ*] him"; the expression is a technical one indicating a metahistorical event (cf. Elijah in 2 Kgs 2:3,5,9,10,16; the psalmist in Pss 48:16; 73:24). Utnapishtim in the Gilgamesh Epic is also "taken" by the gods into their world (cf. *ANET* 99). Later writers develop the legend of Enoch and explain its significance (cf. Sir 44:16; Heb 11:5; Jude 14–15, where the apocryphal work of Enoch is quoted). **28–32.** The rhythm of P's list is disrupted by v. 29, which originally belonged to J (reference to cursing of ground [cf. 3:17b] and use of name Yahweh). The name of Noah (*nōaḥ*) is connected phonetically with the word "to console" (*nāḥam*). How the author understood this is uncertain (a reference to Gn 9:8–17?).

37 **(G) Prologue to the Flood (6:1–22) (J and P).**

(a) THE SONS OF GOD AND THE DAUGHTERS OF MEN (6:1–4) (J). The lack of any narrative connection with the preceding accounts (P or J) shows that this ancient legend has been adapted only in a most general way to the theology of prehistory. Details cannot be pressed. The inspired author's contribution (mainly the introduction of Yahweh in v. 3) stresses the growing estrangement of man from God. Whatever the precise meaning of the primitive story (a common mythological theme), it is unlikely that the author intended any special meaning for the sons of God (e.g., angels, men in general, line of Seth), the daughters of men (e.g., women in general, line of Cain), or for the Nephilim (referred to in Nm 13:33?).

(b) JUDGMENT ON MANKIND (6:5–8) (J). Unlike the previous sections, J is here independent of traditions. In characteristic style and terminology, J gives an inspired personal analysis and judgment of what has happened (Von Rad, *op. cit.* 112–13f.; cf. R. A. F. MacKenzie, *CBQ* 17 [1955] 277–86). The anthropomorphisms are strong, emphasizing the personal element of the divine justice and mercy. The passage provides the theological connection between man's sin and the natural catastrophe of the flood.

38 PROLOGUE TO THE FLOOD (6:9–22) (P). The prologue of P is in theological agreement with J (cf. 6:11–13 and 6:5–8) but is expressed less anthropomorphistically. In P the ancient sources are already introduced. **9–10.** The story (or "genealogy," *tôlᵉdôt*; cf. 2:4a; 5:1) of Noah includes a reference to the reason for his finding favor with God (cf. 6:8); he was "just" (*ṣaddîq*, conforming to the divine norm for man) and "blameless" (*tāmîm*, "whole"—i.e., "without blemish"). Like Enoch (cf. 5:22–24), Noah "walked with God." **11–13.** "Violence" (*ḥāmās*, used frequently by the prophets and implying violation of [divine] rights) marks the Priestly description of the situation. Note the contrast between the divine reaction in 6:12 and that in 1:4,10, etc. **14–16.** The author here depends on his ancient source. The "ark" (*tēbāh*, cf. also Ex 2:3) is pitch-covered (typically Mesopotamian) and about 450 ft. long, 75 ft. wide, and 45 ft. high. The "opening" (*ṣōhar*, an hapaxlegomenon) is a window, or perhaps the roof (Von Rad, *op. cit.*, 123). The extraordinarily large boat has three decks. **17–18.** The reference to the "covenant" (*bᵉrît*, used here for first time) is anticipatory (cf. 9:8ff.). **19–22.** A pair of each kind of animal is to be taken for preservation, not for food (cf. 1:29 and 6:21).

39 **(H) The Flood (7:1–8:22) (J and P).** Beginning with ch. 7, the two traditions, J and P, are not simply juxtaposed but are at times interwoven. The division of the two stories, as generally proposed, follows: J, 7:1–5,7–10,12,16b,17b,22–23; 8:2b,3a,6–12,13b,20–22; and P, 7:6,11,13–16a,17a,18–21,24; 8:1–2a,3b–5,13a,14–19. (There are slight differences of opinion regarding some of the verses.) The final form favors P which provides the framework. There are obvious doublets: 6:13,17 and 7:4; 7:7–9 and 7:13–16a; 7:21 and 7:22–23; etc. The differences are just as obvious: 6:19–20 and 7:2–3; 7:4,12 and 7:24; 8:5 and 8:9; etc. (For details, see Clamer, *op. cit.*, 178–79f.)

The biblical recensions of the flood story can both be traced, directly or indirectly, to a Mesopotamian original now unknown. Several nonbiblical accounts survive, showing marked similarities to the younger Hebr accounts. In a Sumerian version (largely a corrupt text; cf. *ANET* 42–44), the divine assembly apparently decides to destroy mankind, contrary to the will of some of the gods. Ziusudra, a pious king, is informed of the decision by one of the gods (Enki?). The flood rages for seven days and nights. Afterward, Ziusudra offers sacrifices. In the more extensive Babylonian version (part of the Gilgamesh Epic; cf. *ANET* 93–95), the gods decree a flood. Ea, one of the gods, warns Utnapishtim, who builds a ship according to the god's direction—about 180 ft. high, 180 ft. wide, and 180 ft. long, and with 7 stories. It is completed on the seventh day, and filled with provisions. Besides Utnapishtim's family and kind, "the beasts of the field, the wild creatures of the field" and all the craftsmen board the ship. A storm arises and lasts for six days and nights. On the seventh day the storm subsides, and the hero notes that "all of mankind had returned to clay." The ship grounds on Mt. Nisir, and, on the seventh day, a dove and then a swallow are sent out, but both return. Finally a raven is sent and does not return. Utnapishtim then offers sacrifice to the gods, who "smelled the sweet odor" and "crowded like flies about the sacrificer."

Which flood (of many) in the Mesopotamian Valley gave rise to these accounts is not known. The nonbiblical versions reflect pagan mythology; there are many gods who decree the flood for no apparent reason. The hero is warned by one of them, again for no apparent moral reason. In the biblical story, the one God, supreme lord of the situation, decrees the flood because of man's sin. Noah is saved because of his justice. The basic difference, therefore, between the biblical and pagan accounts is in the religious interpretation of this natural catastrophe, and in this the former is infinitely superior.

(Lambert, G., "Il n'y aura plus jamais de déluge," *NRT* 77, part 2 [1955] 581–601, 693–724.)

40 (a) (7:1–5). The account of the building of the ark has not been preserved by J. It begins immediately with God's command to Noah to enter the ark. Noah is found "just" in God's sight, as P had noted (6:9). The ritual distinction between clean and unclean animals was already a feature of Israel's religion at the time J was written. As in other cases (e.g., 4:2–4), J introduces an anachronism by placing the distinction in the past (vv. 2–3); P is more careful in this regard (cf. 6:19–20). As in the Gilgamesh Epic, the storm will begin on the seventh day (v. 4a). Except for the name of God (here Yahweh), v. 5 is almost identical with 6:22 (Elohim); in both cases, Noah's obedience is stressed.

41 (b) (7:6–24). **6.** The chronological concern marks an insertion from P. **7–10.** Basically J, this passage has been edited in the light of P; "your [Noah's] sons, your wife, and your sons' wives" is characteristic of P (6:18); J uses "all your household" (7:1). In vv. 8–9, the distinction between clean and unclean (J) is combined with the reference (P) to a pair of each animal (cf. 6:19–20 and 7:2–3). God (Elohim) is also characteristic of P.

11. Besides the chronological note, the description of the flood's cause is also distinctly P. The cosmic nature of the flood is stressed, just as creation had involved a cosmic ordering. Man's sin has destroyed this order and chaos (1:2) results. **12.** The viewpoint of J is less transcendent; "rain" causes the deluge. **13–16a.** This is the original version in P of the entrance into the ark (cf. 7:7–9). **16b.** "And the Lord shut him in." This bold anthropomorphism of J (note also "Yahweh") underscores God's decisive role in salvation history. **17.** The first part of the verse, attributed to P, is probably an editorial addition based on J (7:4). **18–21.** With typical concern for figures (cf. v. 20), P notes the extent of the flood. The waters are almost personified here; they "rose higher and higher" (lit., "they grew very very strong"). They are the forces of chaos. Note again the cosmic viewpoint. **22–23.** In J the effects of the flood are more detailed; his viewpoint is more earthly. **24.** In P, the chronology is precise and in accord with 7:11 and 8:4. The flood lasts 5 months, or 150 days (cf. 8:3b).

42 (c) (8:1–5). **1–2a.** An unusual descent to anthropomorphism for P, God's "remembering" Noah is necessary for the continuation of salvation history. The "wind" (*rûaḥ*) here has a salvific effect (cf. 1:2). (For v. 2a, cf. 7:11.) **2b–3a.** In J, the rain is withheld, and the waters recede (cf. 7:12). **3b–5.** Again, we note the precise chronology of P. According to the perpetual solar calendar, apparently adopted by the post-exilic priestly school (cf. A. Jaubert, *La date de la Cène* [Paris, 1957]), the first ebbing of the waters takes place on a Wednesday (v. 3b) and the first appearance of the mountains on a Wednesday (v. 5b). These are "liberation" events (cf. Ex 12:40–51 and Nm 33:3, where Exodus from Egypt and departure from Rameses occur on a Wednesday; both are also from P). The ark "rested" (*nûaḥ*, pun on Noah's name) on the mountains of Ararat (in modern Armenia) on a Friday, P's day of "arrivals" (cf. Jos 4:19; Ezr 7:9b).

(d) (8:6–22). **6–12.** The scene recalls the story of Utnapishtim. Birds were frequently used by ancients for similar purposes. Note the details and vividness of J: suspense; Noah's humaneness (v. 9c); climax (v. 11); and anticlimax (v. 12). Salvation history shares these characteristics. **13–19.** Except for v. 13b, the passage is from P. Chronological concern, the divine name, repetition, and no distinction of animals are all characteristic. The days indicated in 8:13a,14 are both Wednesday, the day of "liberation" according to P (cf. 8:3b–5); the first date (v. 13a) shares by anticipation in the Exodus event, which also took place on the first day of the new year (cf. Ex 12:40–42). In P, the initiative is always God's (v. 15); a new epoch begins, a new creation (cf. 8:17 and 1:28). The eschatological "world judgment of the flood hangs like an iron curtain between this world age and that of the first splendor of creation" (Von Rad, *op. cit.*, 126). **20–22.** In J, the flood story ends with an emphasis on man and the restoration of his life with God. The distinction of animals (v. 20), the offering of sacrifice (here "altar" and "holocausts" are used for the first time), and the anthropomorphisms are familiar. The expression "the Lord smelled the sweet odor" (v. 21) can be compared with "the gods smelled the sweet savor" of the Babylonian story; the phrase is a persistent element of the ancient flood tradition. Compare man's inclination to evil in v. 21 with 6:5–6f.; man has not changed, but God's firm salvific will now dictates mercy and the continuation of salvation history. As usual in J, this mercy is symbolized in nature (v. 22; cf. 3:17–19); the rhythm of the days and seasons will not be disturbed again.

43 **(I) The Covenant with Noah (9:1–17) (P).** The first epoch in division of world history according to P ended with the flood. The ideal conditions of that epoch, marked by an implicit covenant with the first man (cf. 1:28–30), no longer obtained. The second epoch, marked by the covenant with Noah, supposes the theological disorder caused by sin and introduces as normal those adverse conditions of life that every man encounters. Highly reflective and profoundly religious, the passage presents an important stage in the P theology of history. **1.** The new epoch, despite its inherent deficiencies caused by sin, requires the divine blessing for continuance as much as did the first (cf. 1:28). **2–4.** What would have been abnormal before now becomes normal. Man's kingship is exercised, not in peace, but through fear. The slaughter and eating of animals is a recognized part of the new era. However, because of the Semitic concept of blood as the seat of life, P sees in the later Israelite regulations forbidding the eating of blood (cf. Lv 17:10–14; Dt 12:23) a basic law binding all men (cf. Acts 15:29). **5–7.** Verse 5, affirming God's ultimate authority, is a necessary introduction to the ancient *māšāl* in v. 6, in which man's right and duty to execute sentence is succinctly asserted; because of the connection of the two verses, it is clearly seen as a delegated authority. Verse 7 forms an inclusion with v. 1, stressing the positive theology of this passage. **8–10.** In fulfillment of his promise (cf. 6:18; note the completely thought-out presentation in P), God makes a covenant with Noah, the first explicitly mentioned. For P, covenants mark the succession of world epochs. This covenant with Noah requires nothing on man's part (unilateral), is extended to all creation (vv. 9–10), and its sign is a natural phenomenon (vv. 13–16). The covenant with Abraham presupposes his personal commitment to God, is extended only to his descendants, and its sign is circumcision (Gn 17). The covenant with Israel requires continuing loyalty (Ex 24:7–8), is restricted to the nation, and its sign is the Sabbath observance (Ex 31:16–17). For P, therefore, the meaning of history is greatly determined by a covenant theology describing the varying and successively more intimate relationships between God and man. **11.** The content of the covenant is God's merciful permission of history's continuance. There will never again be a flood that has the theological significance of indicating the end of a world epoch. **12–17.** The visible sign of this covenant, for both man and God, is the rainbow. For the ancient pagans, this natural phenomenon was considered a divine bow used by the gods to inflict punishment on man. Its appearance in the sky signified the divine appeasement. This ancient concept has been taken by P and given new meaning in the context of his theology. The anthropomorphisms (cf. v. 15, God "remembers"; v. 16, God "sees and recalls") are unusual for P and reveal profound convictions.

44 **(J) The Sons of Noah (9:18–27) (J).** A primitive story, explaining the origin of the vine and its product, was later taken over to explain an historical situation in Palestine—i.e., the peaceful domination of the Canaanites by the immigrating Semites (Shem) who were accompanied by other peoples from Asia Minor (Japheth). In its final and present form, the story is given a more universal orientation by the introduction of Ham (vv. 18,22), who is made the father of Canaan. As such, it serves as a preface to the genealogy of ch. 10. For J, the story also explains the privileged status of Shem, father of the chosen people, and the continuing moral disorder. Inconsistencies resulting from the editorial work are still apparent. **18–19.** These introductory verses connect the story of the flood with the later description of the peopling of the earth. **20–23.** Noah is *'îš hā'ădāmāh* (man of the soil [MT, v. 20]). The theology of J is earth-oriented (cf. 2:5,7; 3:17–19); the renewed tilling of the soil is a necessary condition of man's life. A moral judgment is passed, not on Noah's but on Ham's (Canaan's) action. The filial piety of Shem and Japheth is emphasized. **24–27.** Cursings and blessings in the Semitic mentality are not mere wishes, but efficacious "words" that share the power of the pronouncer. Canaan is the "youngest son" in the older story (v. 24). The curse indicates that he will be slave to (i.e., overcome by) the invading Semites and Japhetites. Shem's blessing is transformed by J to a blessing of Shem's God, Yahweh, a deliberate anachronism (contrast with "elohim" in v. 27, where Japheth's God is not identified with Yahweh) to emphasize the unity of salvation history. Among the ancients, a people's power depended on the power of its god. Hence, Shem is effectively blessed. A pun explains Japheth's destiny: God will "expand" (*yapt*) Japheth (l^{e}*yepet*). He will share Shem's (Israel's) land (?). The precise meaning intended by J is uncertain. **28–29.** An insertion of P's resumes the genealogy of ch. 5 (cf. 5:32) and introduces that of ch. 10.

45 **(K) The Peopling of the Earth (10:1–32) (P and J).** This genealogy is basically P's (vv. 1–7, 20, 22–23, and 31–32) with insertions from J. The apparent contradictions show that such genealogies indicated not strictly ethnic but historical and geographical relations that could vary. Composed during Israel's monarchical period, the list reflects a complex historical situation. Theologically it affirms the unity of the human race and sees the peopling of the earth as the result of the divine blessing (cf. 9:1); it is a new creation, but now of the nations of the earth. The transcendence of P is evident in his emphasis of the divine role (cf. 9:1 and contrast with J's man-oriented explanation of the peopling of the earth in 11:1–9) and in his remarkable restraint regarding Israel; pre-Abrahamic "Israel" is not distinguished here at all (cf. Von Rad, *op. cit.*, 140–41f.).

46 (a) (10:1–12). **1.** We note P's stereotyped formula (cf. 5:1). Here, "descendants" for the most part are national groups. The names cannot all be identified (see *BPl* 1, 30ff., for details). **2–5.** Most of the Japhetites are located in Asia Minor and the Mediterranean islands. Possible identifications include: Gomer, Cimmerians; Magog, Lydia; Madai, Medes; Javan, Greece (properly, Ionia); Tubal and Meshech, residents of Black Sea area; Ashkenaz, Scythia; Elishah, Cyprus; Tarshish, Tartessus (in southern Spain); Kittim, Cypriotes; and Dodanim, people of Rhodes. **6–7.** The Hamites populate the southern regions. Possible identifications include: Cush, Ethiopia; Mizraim, Egypt; and Put, Libya. Note that Canaan is associated with Ham, although Canaanites were ethnically Semites. The "sons" of Cush are all SW and NW Arabian peoples. **8–12.** P's genealogy provided the framework into which the redactor worked part of J's. Characteristically J has preserved fragments of ancient legends. The origins of the Nimrod story may be Egyptian (he is a son of Cush, therefore a Hamite, and Egyptian power extended at times to the Euphrates [cf. v. 10]) or Mesopotamian (cf. v. 10). The cities "founded" by him are all in Babylonia (Shinar) and Assyria (Asshur), two countries historically inimical to Israel, which explains their grouping under Ham (Canaan). (On Nimrod, see Speiser, *Genesis*, 67–68, 72.)

47 (b) (10:13–20). **13–14.** As in P (cf. v. 6), Egypt (Mizraim) is a descendant of Ham. Egypt's "children" inhabit the neighboring lands and are associated by J with the hated Egyptians who enslaved Israel. In particular, mention is made of the Caphtorim (Cretans) as the "fathers" of the equally detested Philistines. History has shaped much of J's genealogy. **15–19.** The third son of Ham in the J list produced more enemies of Israel, especially Canaan. The territory peopled by these groups is principally the ancient land of Canaan (v. 19). Most of the names are familiar from other biblical lists (e.g., Ex 3:8; Dt 7:1), but their precise ethnic reference is not always certain (cf. *BPl* 1, 32–33, for details). **20.** The verse is P's stereotyped conclusion to the Ham list (cf. v. 5).

48 (c) (10:21–32). **21.** A fragment from J is used to introduce the line of Shem. In J, the Hebr people have been attached to Shem by the introduction of the eponymous Eber. **22–23.** In P, the Semites include the Elamites (ethnically non-Semites), Assyrians (Asshur; cf. v. 11 where they are Hamites in J), Lydians (Lud; cf. v. 13 where these are also Hamites in J), and Arameans. Of the others little is known. P was aware of the Mesopotamian origin of Israel, hence the connection of Assyria with Shem. **24–25.** The J document resumes the genealogy of Shem. The eponymous Eber is again featured. He produces two sons, one of whom, Peleg, P will later emphasize (cf. 11:16ff.). **26–30.** Here, J is interested only in Joktan, the father of Arabian tribes that were truly Semites (cf. v. 7, where they are Japhetites). **31–32.** With characteristic precision, P adds the conclusion first to the particular genealogy of Shem, then to the general one of Noah.

49 **(L) The Tower of Babel (11:1–9) (J).** An ancient story (or stories) is used by J to give the theological reason for the division of mankind described more prosaically in ch. 10. Primitively only an etiological explanation of the origin of different languages (or of the city of Babel), it now serves to climax the whole prehistory of mankind and introduce the story of the patriarchs. The sin of the first man resulted in the alienation of man from God (3:22–24) and from his fellow man (4:1–16). From sin now results the alienation of all human society from God and men from one another. The prophets will announce the future reversal of this movement (cf. Is 2:1–5), fulfilled on Pentecost (cf. Acts 2:5–12). **1–4.** Babylonia (Shinar) is the scene of the story, confirmed by the reference to bricks and bitumen, the common building material of Mesopotamia. The Palestinian redaction is revealed in the reference to stone and mortar. The evil is in their desire to "make a name" for themselves (cf. 12:2) rather than in the attempt to build a tower "with its top in the heavens." The latter reference is to the ziggurat, a staged tower common in ancient Babylonia. **5–7.** Human smallness, not divine impotence, is emphasized in the Lord's descent. We have noted before J's irony (3:22). The plural in v. 7 may reflect the concept of God's royal court, an early idea in Israel. The punishment had been anticipated in v. 4. **8–9.** The name of the city, Babel, is here associated with the Hebr root *bll*, "to confound." The great city and its (implied) defeat thus becomes synonymous with man's revolt against God and its consequences.

50 **(M) Concluding Genealogies (11:10–32) (P and J).** A predominantly P genealogy (only vv. 28–30 are from J) brings the prehistory of salvation to its climax in the call of Abram. The method of P here follows that of ch. 5, except that the total age of the patriarchs is not given. The list parallels J's (10:21,24–30) to Eber, where P concentrates on his son Peleg (cf. 11:18ff. and 10:25ff.). With ch. 5, this passage presents an unbroken line from Adam to Abram, indicating the unity of salvation history. The symbolic ages are lower here, however, stressing the result of sin. We should also note P's process of gradual elimination of lateral branches and increasing emphasis of the Abramic line. Recent discoveries in Mesopotamia confirm the great age of this list (Speiser, *Genesis*, 78–79). **10–26.** Some of the names are identifiable with place names in NW Mesopotamia: e.g., Serug (Sarug, a Syrian village); Nahor (Nakhur, a

Mesopotamian village mentioned in the Mari tablets, etc.); Terah (a Mesopotamian village). The name Abram, meaning "the Father [God] is exalted," occurs in Babylonian texts. The entire list confirms both the northwestern Mesopotamian origin of Israel's ancestors and the mixed ethnic background (note the non-Semitic Arpachshad) suggested by later Israelite traditions (cf. Albright, *FSAC* 238–39f.). **27–32.** The *tôl*^{e}*dôt* of v. 27 indicates the beginning of a new story. This conflated section (vv. 28–30 are from J) bridges prehistory and Abram's call. According to P, Abram was born and was married in Ur (southern Mesopotamia) and was taken to Haran by his father (cf. v. 31). The "Ur of the Chaldeans" in v. 28 (J) may be a harmonizing gloss. At any rate, later Israelite tradition will stress only the NW Mesopotamian origin (cf., e.g., Gn 24:1–10; 28:2; 29:4; Dt 26:5). The names Sarai (princess) and Milcah (queen) indicate that the bearers of these names were devotees of Ningal, consort of the moon-god Sin, worshiped in Ur and Haran. Emphasis on Sarai's barrenness by J (v. 30; note the Semitic parallelism) is a subtle preparation for future events.

51 **(II) The Patriarch Abraham (12:1–25:18).** With the appearance of Abraham, the story of Gn takes on a completely new form. From the viewpoint of salvation history a new period begins, marked by a divine intervention destined to reshape history's course. An obscure Semite is called by God, and, through his response in faith, there begins the unfolding of God's plan which will reach its climax in the events of the Exodus and Sinai. The mounting *aversio a Deo* that characterized the first 11 chapters now gives way to a *conversio ad Deum*. The sacred writer shows that all the stories collected here have this new orientation and were written, in their present form, for this purpose. Genesis 12–50 is the introduction to the story of Israel. We discussed the historical character of the patriarchal stories in the introduction. (For further details, see R. de Vaux, *RB* 53 [1946] 321–48; *RB* 55 [1948] 321–47; *RB* 56 [1949] 5–36; *TD* 12 [1964] 227–40; J. C. L. Gibson, *JSems* 7 [1962] 44–62; H. Cazelles, *VDBS* 36, 81–156.)

52 **(A) The Call of Abram (12:1–9) (J, P).** This passage is the first in the Abraham cycle. Almost completely J, it portrays a movement generally consonant with that of a seminomad in the central hill country of Canaan and in the Negeb area. Around ancient cult centers traditions tended to develop (Shechem in v. 6; Bethel in v. 8) which J has collected and loosely presented as the background of the divine movement. **1–3.** Abram's call is dramatically presented. The initiative is Yahweh's, not Abram's. The first requirement is complete disassociation from the pagan past, represented in a mounting personal disinvolvement (v. 1b). The second is migration to a land of God's choice (v. 1c). The reward is divine blessing affecting Abram himself and his descendants. This promise will become a dominant theme of Gn (cf. J. Hoftijzer, *Die Verheissungen an die drei Erzväter* [Leiden, 1956]). The Niphal of v. 3b is usually translated as a reflexive: Abram will be an accepted formula of blessing. But the passive sense—i.e., "all... will be blessed through you" (LXX; Acts 3:25; Gal 3:8)—is in keeping with the universalist context of this transitional passage (cf. 11:9). **4–9.** Abram's response was factual, not verbal. In vv. 4b–5, P underscores the divine power by giving Abram the symbolic age of 75. Shechem, an ancient Canaanite city and pagan shrine, is the scene of the first theophany. Emphasized by J, as here in v. 7, will be the connection between theophany and the land of promise. The altars erected at pagan Shechem and Bethel represent the special claim of Yahweh to this land, initiated through his representative, Abram. The term of the patriarch's journey is the Negeb, in the south, where the tradition was preserved.

53 **(B) Abram and Sarai in Egypt (12:10–20) (J).** In the primitive tradition, 12:9 was probably followed by 13:2. The intervening story is J's attribution to Abram of an incident that he will later record of Isaac (26:6–11). The religious implications justified the fiction. The preservation of Rebekah was considered a divine confirmation of the promise of 12:2. The story here illustrates Abram's greater claim to the promise. It is more stylized than 26:6–11: Abram is aware of what will happen before the event (vv. 11–13); the great Pharaoh of Egypt himself is involved, adding to the story's effect; and the issue is resolved through the direct action of Yahweh (v. 17; cf. E. H. Maly, *CBQ* 18 [1956] 255–62; Speiser, *Genesis*, xxxi–xxxii, xl–xli). J placed the story close to the beginning of the Abram cycle to emphasize the validity of the divine promise made in 12:2–3 (E also has a version, which we shall consider later; cf. 20:1–18).

54 **(C) The Separation of Abram and Lot (13:1–18) (J, P).** **1–13.** This passage, principally J's (vv. 6, 11b, and 12a are from P), presents an authentic picture of shepherd nomads grazing their flocks in the hill areas between the great cities. The area indicated is N of Jerusalem in the territory of Benjamin, from which the Jordan Valley is visible (v. 10). The strifes were accentuated by the presence of Canaanites and Perizzites (v. 7b), the latter probably ancient Hurrian inhabitants of Canaan (cf. Gn 34:20; Jgs 1:4–5, where the two are also associated). As in Gn 26:20, the dispute may have been over the use of wells (cf. v. 10, where the "well-watered" Jordan region is a motive for Lot's choice); P's insertion in v. 6 attributes it to the "great possessions." The story is connected (perhaps originally) with an ancient tradition found in Gn 19 (cf. 13:13). The inspired author uses it as an introduction to the renewal of the promise in vv. 14–18. Lot's free decision, although inspired by human wisdom (cf. v. 10), will work ultimately for the fulfillment of the divine plan. **14–18.** J has provided the climax to the story of Lot's choice—the renewal, in greatly expanded form, of the promise of 12:7. Abram settles in the southern area near the "terebinths of Mamre," an ancient shrine about 20 mi. S of Jerusalem. Hebron, 2 mi. S of Mamre, was founded about 1700, therefore after Abram's time; it is an explanatory addition (v. 18).

55 **(D) Abram and the Four Kings (14:1–24) (?).** This chapter is the most likely to provide the key needed to solve the enigma of the patriarchal narratives' precise historical background. It contains more historical and geographical allusions than any other chapter, but the tentative identifications lead to no conclusions as yet. Belonging to none of the three accepted traditions, it relates, in a manner somewhat analogous to the Zakir stela (*ANET* 501–502), the expedition of four kings from the north against a rebel coalition of five kings of the Dead Sea Plain. Abram is mentioned only late in the narrative and almost incidentally. The Melchizedek episode (vv. 18–20) has been inserted from a separate tradition. The original connection of the Abram-Lot story (vv. 12–17 and 21–24) with the Elamite victory is more puzzling. The connection is loose (v. 12 betrays the redactor's hand; vv. 13ff. take up the shift of interest), but the story of Abram's exploits is not as fantastic as is sometimes suggested; the reference to Abram "the Hebrew" (v. 13), unique in the Abram saga, may indicate an ancient (perhaps non-Israelite) tradition. It is not impossible, therefore, that the Abram-Lot story reflects an authentic memory of an incident connected with the invasion, but preserved independently. The redactor would have rejoined the two and inserted the passage concerning Melchizedek.

The meaning of the chapter in context is clearer. Intrigued by the ancient tradition of Abram's "victory" over four "world" powers, and having the account of their invasion, the author has prefixed the latter to emphasize the irresistible nature of the divine plan, which the military exploits of the great pagan world only serve to further. Ultimately, therefore, the chapter extols the power of God. The Melchizedek scene has a religious meaning of its own, but it was added here because it provided the interpretation of the whole chapter (cf. v. 20)

56 (a) (14:1–13). **1.** Amraphel is a Babylonian (Shinar) king as yet unidentified. Arioch is a Hurrian name instanced in the N Syrian Mari tablets (Arriwuk.) If the two are the same, then "Ellasar" cannot refer to Larsa, a S Babylonian city. Ched-or-laomer is correctly identified in the document as an Elamite, but no extra-biblical record has yet revealed more information about him. Tidal may be Tudhalia, one of several Hittite kings of that name. Just when such an alliance, under Elamite leadership, was historically probable cannot be determined with certainty. Estimates range from the 19th to the 17th cent. **2.** Four of the five rebel kings are given names that may be symbolic, although the absence of a name for the fifth king is striking. The Pentapolis is referred to elsewhere (cf. 10:19). **3.** The "Valley of Siddim" is otherwise unattested; we may infer that it was located where the Salt Sea now lies. A later extension of the Salt Sea S may explain the reference. **4–6.** The conquerors' route followed in general the trade route from Ashteroth-karnaim in southern Syria to El-paran, near the Gulf of Aqabah. The peoples mentioned here are traditionally associated, in the Bible, with Transjordan (cf. Dt 2:10–12, 20–22). Archaeology has demonstrated the existence of communities in this area before 1900 (cf. N. Glueck, *BASOR* 152 [1958] 18–38). **7–9.** The route then turned N to Kadesh, about 60 mi. S of Beer-sheba. Hazazon-tamar is near the Dead Sea. Amalekites would be expected in the area; the presence of the Amorites is puzzling. The direction of the march could be explained by the need to protect the vital trade route of the south. **10–12.** The presence of bitumen pits in the area is credible. **13.** The Ḫabiru are referred to in numerous texts throughout the whole of the 2nd millennium; their presence is noted in almost every Near Eastern land. Not an ethnic designation, the name was applied to a social class. It could well fit the seminomadic Abram. The names of his "allies" are otherwise place names (cf. 13:18 [Mamre]; Nm 13:23–24f. [Eshcol]).

57 (b) (14:14–24). **14–17.** Palestinian chieftains are known to have had "retainers" ("trained men" in CCD; *ḥănîkîm* in MT, seemingly of Egyptian origin; cf. *ANET* 328d; T. Lambdin, *JAOS* 73 [1953] 150). "Dan" is an anachronism (cf. Jgs 19:27–29). "Hobah" is unknown. The "victory" is not incredible if we understand it as nocturnal harassing activity by less encumbered men on the rear guard. The armies would have gladly relinquished a few prisoners and some loot to escape the annoyance. On his return, Abram was met by the king of Lot's Sodom in a valley near Jerusalem (cf. 2 Sm 18:18). **18.** The geographical reference (the valley near Jerusalem) justified the insertion here of the originally independent Melchizedek tradition. *Malkî ṣedeq* (My king is Justice) is an ancient Canaanite name, similar to Adonizedek in Jos 10:1. Salem (*šālēm*) is almost certainly Jerusalem (Uru-salim in the Tell el-Amarna tablets, but cf. W. F. Albright, *BASOR* 163 [1961] 52). The mention of bread and wine may indicate a covenant meal. Priest kings were not unknown; *'ēl 'elyôn*, Melchizedek's god, is a name attested among the Arameans and Phoenicians. That Melchizedek was a monotheist is most unlikely, but that the author intended this name as a reference to the one God of Israel is almost certain (cf. v. 22). **19–20.** Melchizedek's blessing extols the power of God who gained the victory. Abram's tithe may originally have been part of the covenant between the two. The author intends it as a recognition of Melchizedek's (typical) role in salvation history; the King of Jerusalem rightly receives the spoils of victory. Whereas the general meaning of the whole episode in context seems clear, a more precise knowledge of the time and circumstances of its composition would throw more light on the passage (cf. Von Rad, *op. cit.*, 175). Apparently it is a justification of the later role of Jerusalem as God's dwelling place and of Jerusalem's king as a priest, not according to the Levitical order but to that of Melchizedek (cf. Ps 110:4). The later messianic figure has conditioned the interpretation. The author of Heb exploited the typology (cf. Heb 7; J. A. Fitzmyer, *CBQ* 25 [1963] 305–21). **21–24.** The scene reverts to the meeting with the king of Sodom dealing with a discussion over the splitting of the booty. It has an authentic ring. Significant is the identification of Yahweh (omitted by the LXX and other vss.!) with El Elyon of v. 19. The author thus makes clear the previously implied identification.

(Cornelius, F., "Genesis XIV," *ZAW* 72 [1960] 1–7. Hunt, I., "Recent Melkizedek Study," *BCCT* 21–33.)

58 **(E) Promises Renewed (15:1–20) (J, E?).** The chapter contains two stories originally independent—one (1–6) describing a prophetic vision in which Abram is promised a great posterity, and the other (7–20) centering on the promise of the land and the covenant ritual. Joined and placed here, they form a fitting introduction to the following stories of tension. Moreover, literary criticism has revealed, for many authors, the presence of a third tradition here, especially in the first story. It would be E's first appearance in Gn, but no satisfactory analysis has yet been proposed.

(Kaiser, O., "Traditionsgeschichtliche Untersuchung von Genesis 15," *ZAW* 70 [1958] 107–26. Snijders, L. A., "Genesis XV. The Covenant with Abram," *OTS* 12 [1958] 261–79.)

(a) (15:1–6). **1.** We note the prophetic phrase "the word of the Lord came"; in 20:7 Abraham is called a prophet. The "reward," God's free gift, is associated with Abram's faith (v. 6). **2.** No satisfactory explanation has been given for the *ben mešeq* and *dammešeq*; the text is corrupt. There is an allusion here to the custom, known from Nuzi, whereby an adopted slave could become an heir. If this verse is from E, it may parallel J's 12:1–3 and refer to Abram's call in his homeland. **3.** This verse repeats the idea of v. 2 and is probably from a different source. **4.** The Nuzi tablets stipulate that an adopted heir must yield to a true son born later. **5–6.** Abram's trust in the realization of a promise that could not ordinarily be realized makes him agreeable to God. "To believe" (*'mn*) is to stand firm in, to accept with assurance, God's plan. *Ṣᵉdāqāh* is that conformity to the proper relationship between God and man that faith expresses.

59 (b) (15:7–20). **7–8.** The Lord's identification of himself indicates an introduction to a separate narrative. The land of promise is contrasted, as frequently (cf. 12:1; 13:12; etc.), with other lands. Abram's request for a sign here contrasts with his absolute faith mentioned previously. **9–12.** In answer to Abram's request, God seals a covenant with him. The larger animals are cut in two and laid side by side. From Jer 34:18 we know that the contracting parties passed between the two halves, symbolizing their willingness to suffer the fate of the animals if they broke the covenant. The "birds of prey" are symbolic of the dangers that will threaten the covenant (they are, as it were, driven off by Abram's faith). Verse 12 contains all the elements expressing the awesomeness of the supernatural intervention: the setting sun, the deep sleep (*tardēmāh*, as in 2:21), terror, and darkness. **13–16.** An insertion, breaking the continuity between vv. 12 and 17, explains the long delay in the fulfillment of the promise. The redactor perhaps saw the later oppression of the people and the "wickedness of the Amorites" as evidences of the "birds of prey," which might explain the insertion. The author's sense of salvation history is profound; even 400 years do not really interrupt the plan of God, who is seen to direct all history toward his appointed goal. **17.** God is frequently symbolized by fiery figures (cf. Ex 3:2; 13:21; 19:18). He alone passes through because the covenant is unilateral, unconditioned on Abram's part. **18.** The concluded covenant assures later Israel of the possession of the land (the vb. is in the proph. pf.). The borders were traditional in Solomon's time (1 Kgs 4:21). **19–20.** An explicative insertion presents the peoples "dispossessed" in favor of God's people. Such lists are frequent; their variations show there was no attempt at historical accuracy. New here are the Kenites (gentilic of Cain, cf. Jgs 1:16), the Kenizzites (seemingly Hurrians), and the Kadmonites ("Easterners," from *qedem*).

60 **(F) Hagar's Flight (16:1–16) (J, P).** The story is an ancient one reflecting the connection between the Ishmaelites and the southern area of Canaan (cf. H. Cazelles, *VDBS* 7, 123–24f.). In E's version (21:8ff.), the child is already born. In both accounts, the glory of the Ishmaelites is extolled without reference (originally) to the Abrahamic promise. Here J has used it to stress the growing tension in Abram's soul over the lack of an heir. **1–3.** The brief statement in v. 1a speaks volumes in the whole context. Several Mesopotamian texts record the custom referred to here. The maid's child would be considered the legal wife's child. **4–6.** Hagar's attitude (v. 4b) justifies, according to Mesopotamian law, Abram's (v. 6a) and Sarai's (v. 6b) actions; Hagar is reduced to slave status. Unsympathetic with polygamous practices, J depicts the scene at its worst. **7–10.** Hagar's flight takes her to the road to Shur, which extended from Beer-sheba to Egypt. If we assume Mamre is the point of departure, it would have been a great distance for a pregnant woman to travel, an indication of an originally independent tradition. The "angel of the Lord" is, etymologically, a "messenger" (*mal'āk*). From v. 13, it is evident that the story originally depicted an appearance of God himself. The "angel" seems a later attempt (repeated in other appearances in Gn) to soften the anthropomorphism. The angel's promise (v. 10, in the first person!) is similar to that made to Abram (13:16; 15:5). **11–12.** The name of Hagar's child will be a justification of the slave wife, "El hears" (*yišmāʿʾēl*); but J has interpreted it as *Yahweh* (the Lord). The future son is vividly described as an independent, warlike nomad (v. 12); he personifies his descendants. **13–14.** An explanation of the Ishmaelites seems to underlie the preceding verses; here a cultic concern seems to predominate. God is called *'ēl rŏ'î* ("God of seeing" or "God of vision") by Hagar, but the explanation of the name is obscure; it stresses the fact that Hagar did not die after seeing God (cf. Ex 33:20). The name of the "well" (*beʾēr*) is *laḥay rō'î*, i.e., dedicated "to the living one who sees me." It is located in the deep southern area of Canaan. **15–16.** Either J did not relate the birth of Ishmael or it was not preserved. The present conclusion, in the stereotyped style of P, presumes Hagar's return to Abram's house (already anticipated in v. 9, where the passage shows signs of reworking).

61 **(G) The Covenant of Circumcision (17:1–27) (P).** This chapter contains two P narratives. One (1–4) corresponds to J's account of the covenant in 15:1–20, and the other (15ff.) to J's announcement of Isaac's birth in 18:1–15. Both J and P agree in the basic facts, but P's theology is much more profound. The scene is centered wholly on God, minimizing the human element (cf. v. 3). The solemnity, ritual concern, style, and vocabulary echo Gn 1.

This covenant marks, for P, the third great stage in salvation history, after those of Adam and Noah. Each introduces a new ritual institution (cf. 2:1–3; 9:4–7), here circumcision. A new divine name is revealed (v. 1); the revelation of "Yahweh" will mark the final period (Ex 6:3–6). For P, human history partakes of the solemnity and rigidity of a liturgical procession.

62 (a) (17:1–14). **1–2.** God reveals himself now as *'ēl šadday*, etymologically probably "God of the mountain," a Mesopotamian name. Always emphasized by P is the religious and moral response that man must make to God (cf. Lv 11:44–45). Note that God does not "cut" (*kārat*) a covenant here as in 15:18, but "gives" (*nātan*) it. **3–6.** Abram's gesture signifies his acceptance. The content of the unilateral pact is the divine promise of a great seed. The change in name indicates the change effected in the patriarch by the promise. Abram (*'abrām*, "the father [God] is exalted") becomes Abraham (*'abrāhām*), etymologically similar to Abram, but by assonance indicating "father of a multitude" (*'ab hămôn*). The "multitude of nations" implies an extra-Israelite extension of God's kingdom. **7–8.** The new item here (v. 7) is the extension of the covenant to succeeding generations. The promise of the land (v. 8) parallels 15:18 but is stated more solemnly. **9–14.** Circumcision becomes the sign of the covenant on the part of God, inasmuch as he will recognize the circumcised as a covenant partner, and on the part of the circumcised, inasmuch as he thus indicates his acquiescence to the divine will (cf. 9:12–17, where the latter element has no place). Although an ancient practice among the Hebrews, circumcision received the full religious significance indicated here only at the time of the Exile. The precise stipulations of vv. 12–13f. indicate later development (cf. Lv 12:3). Refusal to be circumcised was tantamount to rejecting the covenant and warranted excommunication.

63 (b) (17:15–27). **15–16.** Sarai shares in the covenant blessing and so merits a change in name to "Sarah." No explanation of the new name is given; etymologically there is no difference. As in v. 5, P simply theologizes an ordinary linguistic change. Note how P has connected the two narratives (cf. vv. 6 and 16), which J has separated (chs. 15 and 18). **17.** The laughter motif is connected with Isaac's birth several times (cf. 18:12–15; 21:6); what was originally a play on words (*yiṣḥāq*, "Isaac"; *ṣḥq*, "to laugh"), P has used to express the extraordinary character of the event. Because the birth is a necessary factor in the divine plan, it shares in the wonder of any divine intervention. **18–19.** Abraham asks, but in vain, that the divine favor be granted to Ishmael, who is already born, rather than reserved for one whose birth seems problematical. **20–22.** God hears the plea for Ishmael (again a play on the root *šmʿ*; cf. 16:11) by granting him fecundity. (For the "twelve princes," see 25:12–16.) **23–27.** This careful and precise description of the carrying out of the prescription contained in vv. 11–14 indicates both the importance of the rite for P and Abraham's total compliance. Since P had noted Ishmael's birth in Abram's 86th year (16:16), he now carefully notes that he is 13 years old in his father's 99th year.

64 **(H) Promise of a Son; Sodom and Gomorrah (18:1–19:38) (J).** These two chapters contain several traditions (18:1–16; 19:1–29,30–38), originally independent but now united by J in a literary composition of exquisite artistry. The reworking of the traditions appears most clearly in the uncertainty surrounding the number of guests and their identity ("the Lord," 18:1; "three men," 18:2; "two angels," 19:1). At any rate, J has stressed the presence of the Lord in ch. 18 and the agency of the two "messengers" in ch. 19. These are all southern traditions (cf. Cazelles, *VDBS* 7, 125 for discussion). Contrasted by J are the idyllic scene of the opening incident (18:1–15) with the ugly picture of the Sodomites (19:1–11) and, similarly, the mercy of God (18:16–33) with the fate of sinners (19:12–28). The religious motifs are paramount here and have been emphasized by the literary elaboration.

(a) (18:1–15). **1–5.** The scene is vividly described. The principal visitor is immediately identified by J for his readers' sake. In much of the rest of the story, he allows the ancient tradition to speak (e.g., "three men" in v. 2). According to the story, it is no longer possible to determine just when Abraham first recognized his visitor; Oriental hospitality demanded his act of obeisance in v. 2 and his address, "my Lord," (*'ădonāy*) in v. 3. **6–8.** The implied anthropomorphism (God eating with men) is in the style of J. **9–15.** The story comes to its intended point with the question about Sarah. The abrupt change from the plural in v. 9 to the singular in v. 10 betrays the overriding interest in the Lord's words (cf. v. 1). Sarah's reaction to the announcement of the birth is similar to Abraham's in P (17:17), but J enlarges on it and makes the theological point explicit. The Lord (again "Yahweh") is able to effect it. The other visitors have been temporarily forgotten in the dramatic climax of the scene.

65 (b) (18:16–33). **16.** This verse forms the link between the preceding story and the following. It appears now that the original goal of the three visitors was the city of Lot. **17–19.** Through a divine soliloquy, this passage relates all that follows to salvation history. The fate of the two cities is presumably sealed (v. 17). However, Abraham's role in God's total plan (vv. 18–19) is such that he must be privy to the Lord's purposes. The personification of Israel, hinted at in v. 18, is clearer in v. 19. **20–21.** The soliloquy continues, but the theology is more primitive. The Lord must descend to see what fate the cities deserve (cf. 11:5). **22.** Again the thread of the narrative, interrupted by the soliloquy, is taken up. But another interruption is anticipated in the remark concerning Abraham remaining with the Lord. **23–33.** This passage reflects J's grappling with a theological problem that runs throughout much of the OT—that of divine retribution. Collective responsibility for a crime, and therefore collective punishment, was an accepted principle in early Israel (cf. Jos 7:16–26). Here also, the collective, not the individual, note is pressed, but J now asks whether the justice of a few men cannot win God's mercy for the whole group. It is the same picture of community responsibility now viewed from the other side. The question basically, therefore, proceeds, not from a concern for the just who will be punished but from a consideration of what norm will be used by God in deciding a guilty or not guilty verdict on the city (cf. Von Rad, *op. cit.* 207–208). Although no final and precise norm is arrived at, the extremes of the divine mercy are emphasized.

66 (c) (19:1–11). **1.** The two men, now called *mal'ākîm* (messengers) to indicate their task as divine agents, come to Sodom; the link is established with the preceding narrative. The reference to Lot and the emphasis on his fate throughout the story connect these ancient traditions with that contained in 13:5–13. Originally they all formed a unit. **2–11.** Lot's hospitality is comparable to Abraham's, but the present scene has an entirely different sequel. The men of Sodom desire the two visitors for unnatural purposes (whence the modern term, "sodomy"). Lot's offer of his two daughters, although less reprehensible in the light of ancient morality and in view of the ancients' emphasis on protecting guests, is not necessarily condoned by J (his reaction is perhaps reflected in vv. 30–38). The reference to Lot as a "stranger" (v. 9) links the story with 13:5–13. The divine judgment on the city is anticipated in v. 11.

67 (d) (19:12–29). **12–14.** The divine mercy, theoretically presented in 18:23–33, is now illustrated in practice (v. 12). The "outcry" against the city (*ṣeʿāqāh*) is a demand for justice (cf. 18:21), usually made by the oppressed (e.g., Ex 3:7). The ambiguity as to who will destroy the city ("we" in v. 13; "the Lord" in v. 14) is only superficial; ultimately it is only the Lord (cf. vv. 21–24,29). The reaction of Lot's relatives to the warning (v. 14c) adds a tragic note. **15–23.** This passage is more immediately concerned with the divine mercy shown to Lot and his family. The etiological explanation of Zoar (*ṣôʿar* in v. 22; cf. *miṣʿār*, "a little one," in v. 20) may have been added later to the original story, although it is a natural part of J's narrative. We again note the abrupt shift in Lot's address from the plural in v. 18 to the singular in vv. 19–22; J makes it clear that the climactic decisions are the Lord's. **24–25.** The destruction is described briefly and soberly, in contrast to the preceding narratives. The sporadic mention of Gomorrah (here and in 18:20; 19:28) is disconcerting; but all later traditions link the two (cf. Am 4:11; Is 1:9–10f.; Jer 49:18; etc.). The geographical allusions, geological considerations, and local traditions indicate the southern part of the present Dead Sea as the most likely site of a natural catastrophe (cf. 14:3). **26.** Whatever the origin of this piece (perhaps a popular interpretation of the humanlike rock formations of the area), J intends more than an etiological explanation. It is the divine judgment on indecision (cf. v. 17). **27–28.** The narrative of these verses has been masterfully woven with the preceding by J (cf. 18:16,22,33). **29.** Whereas the preceding verses provided an excellent conclusion, P has added a summary of the whole story, emphasizing the theological aspect. For P, the Lot traditions have no interest in themselves; they are told only because God "remembered Abraham."

68 (e) (19:30–38). The actors in this narrative are the main link joining it and the preceding; a literary addition has forged it (v. 30). The story probably had several meanings in its long prehistory. Possibly it is of Moabite-Ammonite origin, people who may well have gloried in the zeal of their ancestors enough to preserve racial purity by any means. Israel, although aware of a racial connection with them (as the retention of the Lot tradition itself indicates), could see the story as a derogatory reference to the origins of their traditional enemies. For J, it is just the godless conclusion to the story of a man who had freely chosen a way that lay beyond the pale of God's immediate plan (cf. 13:11a). The names "Moabites" (*mô'āb* is perhaps understood as coming from *mē'āb*, "from the father") and "Ammonites" (*benê ʿammôn*; cf. *ben ʿammî*, "son of my parent") would have provided the material for the etiology.

69 **(I) Abraham and Sarah in Gerar (20:1–18) (E).** This story, like that of 12:10–20, is connected with a set of traditions different from that of the preceding stories. It was probably preserved at Beer-sheba among the Simeonites (cf. Cazelles, *VDBS* 7, 125–26f.). The use of "Elohim," the more effusive style, the vocabulary, and the more sophisticated theology lead scholars to attribute it to E. It is the first complete narrative preserved from this tradition (cf. ch. 15). Like 12:10–20, this passage attributes to Abraham an incident originally experienced by Isaac (cf. 26:6–11). The theological motive is the same—the divine protection of Sarah in view of the promise. It is placed before the birth of Isaac to emphasize the protection despite the resulting inconsistency (cf. 18:11–12). **1.** The point of departure ("from there") is not specified; in the present context, it would be the Dead Sea area. The Negeb is the general area in southern Palestine, S of Hebron. Gerar probably lay SE of Gaza. **2–8.** The story differs from 12:10–20 in several respects: God appears to Abimelech in a dream (as generally in E); it is specifically mentioned that Abimelech had not approached Sarah (a more refined moral sense); Abraham is called a prophet (*nābî'*) in the sense of one who intercedes for another; the long dialogue betrays a greater theological consciousness. **9–13.** Unlike in 12:10–20, Abraham is allowed to justify his action, thus making it less reprehensible in the eyes of the readers. The same concern for morality is seen in his explanation of Sarah's relationship to him, not mentioned in J's story. Verse 13 recalls 12:1–3 and suggests that E had, originally, a similar account. **14–18.** Again, Abimelech's actions are designed to vindicate Abraham and his wife. Abraham's intercession is in accord with the statement in v. 7b. Verse 18 is an explanatory gloss (note "Yahweh").

70 **(J) Isaac and Ishmael (21:1–21) (J and P).** The account of Isaac's birth is conflated from P (vv. 2b–6a, a sequel to ch. 17) and J (vv. 1–2a, 6b–7, a sequel to 18:1–15). The precise division of the verses is not certain; probably all three traditions recorded the birth. Although the promise had been described several times in elaborated passages (cf. 15:1–6; 17:15–22; 18:1–15) to heighten the tension, the fulfillment is presented briefly and soberly; the wonder of the divine action is sufficiently apparent in the very fulfillment.

The story of the expulsion of Hagar and Ishmael (vv. 8–21) is a parallel account (E) of 16:1–14 (J). From 17:25 and 21:8 we can deduce that Ishmael would be about 16 years old, which clashes with the present account (cf. vv. 14–17). But the differences in the two accounts justify the inclusion of both. Here Abraham's obedience to God is accented (cf. vv. 11–13) in preparation for ch. 22, and the definitive expulsion of Ishmael (cf. 16:9) leaves the arena of salvation history free for Isaac. **1–7.** The connection between promise and fulfillment is emphasized (vv. 1–2). The chronological concerns are due to P (vv. 4–5; cf. 17:1,21). Two more explanations are given for Isaac's name (cf. 17:17; 18:12–15). *Yiṣḥāq* is probably the shortened form of *yiṣḥāq'ēl*, i.e., "may God smile [on the child]." In v. 6a, the name expresses Sarah's joyful laughter at the event; in v. 6b, it expresses either the joy of others who hear of it (will laugh with me) or their mockery (will laugh at me). **8.** A child's weaning, when about three years old, was the occasion of a (religious) feast (cf. 1 Sm 1:22–28). **9–13.** Ishmael is not mentioned by name throughout the story; he is only "the son of the slave girl," which emphasizes his lesser position in God's plan in relation to Isaac's. The reference to his "playing" (*m*^{e}*ṣaḥēq*) with Isaac is another pun on the latter's name. Rabbinic tradition interpreted this reference in an evil sense, and it was on this tradition that Paul based his "persecution" of Isaac by Ishmael (cf. Gal 4:29). Ancient law ordinarily forbade the expulsion of a slave wife and her child, and no justification for it is indicated here as in 16:4; Abraham accordingly hesitates (v. 11). In vv. 12–13, E expatiates on the divine plan as illustrated in the incident (cf. 16:5–6). **14–18.** The "desert of Beer-sheba" agrees in general with 16:7. In v. 16c, the MT has "and she raised her voice and wept"; a redactor wished to avoid the inconsistency with 17:25. The versions have the correct reading, as in the CCD. "God heard" is a play on the child's name (cf. 16:11), but, to avoid the anthropomorphism (see comment on 16:7–10), E has "the angel of God" speak to Hagar. An incipient universalism is present (v. 18), as also in J (cf. 4:15; 12:3b); salvation history touches others, if only indirectly. **19–21.** The presence of a well agrees with 16:7,14, but E has omitted the etiologies. Where Ishmael lives ("the desert of Paran," between Egypt and Edom), his way of life (a nomadic "bowman"), and his racial connections (his wife, like his mother, is an Egyptian) emphasize his exclusion from God's specific plan. This exclusion of Abraham's beloved son centers attention on Isaac and heightens the tension of ch. 22.

71 **(K) Abraham and Abimelech (21:22–34) (E).** Two originally independent stories explaining the name Beer-sheba have been conflated by E. The one (vv. 22–24, 27, and 31) traces the name to an oath sworn by Abraham and Abimelech. The other (vv. 25–26, 28–30, and 32) traces it to the seven lambs given by Abraham to Abimelech. The birth of Isaac had emphasized the fulfillment of the promise of an heir; this story stresses the initial fulfillment of the promise of the land. Ancient tradition has provided the material for the theology. **22–24.** The initiative of Abimelech is explained by 20:1–18. The pagan king acknowledges the divine origin of Abraham's material success and wants to establish an alliance. The inspired writer considered this a confirmation by the pagan world of Abraham's privileged status. Phicol, mentioned here and in 26:26, may be a Hurrian (cf. Cazelles, *VDBS* 7, 126). **25–26.** In the dispute over the well, Abraham takes the initiative. The loftier tone of the preceding passage is no longer present; we have to do with a common incident which provided the occasion for many such disputes. **27.** This is the conclusion of the first incident. The number of animals given by Abraham is not specified; it plays no role in this story. **28–30.** In the development of the second story, the number of lambs ("seven," *šeba'*) is significant; it is repeated three times. Abimelech's acceptance of the lambs indicates his recognition of Abraham's right to the well. **31.** The etiology contained in the first story is explained. The place is called Beer-sheba (*b*^{e}*'ēr šeba'*, "well of the oath") because an oath (*nišb*^{e}*'û*) was taken there. **32–34.** The etiological explanation of the second story has been dropped in favor of the first, but it is implied, since Beer-sheba can also mean "well of the seven." The reference to the Philistines is anachronistic. The planting of the tamarisk tree would signify Abraham's right to ownership. Because of the association with the invocation of the deity, it may also be a religious rite, similar to the erection of an altar (cf. 12:8). The God named here is *'ēl 'ôlām*, "the Everlasting God," an hapaxlegomenon in the Pentateuch. He is the "God of the indefinite past and future," worshiped by Abraham as the true God and identified by the later author with Yahweh (for discussion, cf. Cazelles, *VDBS* 7, 127–28).

72 **(L) The Sacrifice of Isaac (22:1–24) (E, J).** The story has been linked artificially with the Beer-sheba traditions (v. 19). There are no clear chronological or geographical indications; the mount is a "three-day journey" from no determined place (cf. vv. 3–4; for a "three-day journey" cf. also Ex 3:18; 5:3; 8:27; 15:22; Nm 10:33; 33:8; Jos 1:11). The theological character has been intensified by this spatial and temporal disinvolvement.

Principally E, with some evidences of J (vv. 11, 14, and 15–18, and the reference to Moriah in v. 2), the story has gone through various stages of religious interpretation. The motif of Abraham's faith, added from J by the redactor, is stressed in vv. 15–18 and represents the final and "canonical" interpretation. There may have been a sanctuary motif, similar to 28:11–22, but the connection of its name with the incident narrated seems very loose and not original. The motif of substitution for human sacrifice, a fairly persistent concern in Israel (cf. 2 Kgs 16:3; 17:17; 21:6; Jer 7:31; 19:5; Ez 23:37), could explain its origin, based on ancient traditions (for discussion, cf. J. L. McKenzie, *Scr* 9 [1957] 79–84).

The story of Ishmael's expulsion is preparation for this story. Isaac, the reward of faith, becomes the test of that same faith. Paradoxically there is demanded of Abraham's faith the surrender of that faith's only basis, since it is through Isaac the promise must be fulfilled (cf. 21:12b). The absolute gratuity of the divine choice and man's (Israel's) acceptance of that gratuitousness are at the basis of this moving story. It is rightly considered one of the most artistic of the patriarchal narratives.

73 (a) (22:1–4). **1–2.** The momentous character of what is to follow is emphasized by the simplicity of the introduction and by the burden of the divine command; they recall 12:1–3. The author's mention of a "test" gives the reader a psychological advantage that Abraham did not enjoy. In v. 2a there is a masterful emphasis, in the Hebrew, of what is required of Abraham: lit., "take your son, your only son, whom you love, Isaac...." The "district of Moriah" (*'ereṣ hammōriyyāh*) is unknown. The name occurs elsewhere only in 2 Chr 3:1, where Moriah is the mount of the temple. The Gn occurrence may be a later insertion to connect the sacrifice with the temple site, but the *'ereṣ*, instead of *hār*, is difficult to explain. The Chronicler may have been influenced by the Gn story. The textual tradition is fluid: the Pesh has *'ereṣ hā'ĕmōrî* (land of the Amorites); the LXX has *tēn gēn tēn hypsēlēn* (the high land); the Vg has *in terram visionis* (the land of vision). The Pesh reading seems preferable (cf. Clamer, *op. cit.*, 312–13). The holocaust was a whole burnt sacrifice, hence the wood of v. 3; it was the perfect and irrevocable offering. **3–8.** Abraham's perfect obedience is expressed in action, as in 12:4. The early morning departure suggests that the command was given in a dream at night, as frequent in E. The "place" (*hammāqôm*) in vv. 3–4 is a sacred place, as in 12:6. The Fathers saw in Isaac's carrying the wood (v. 6) a figure of Christ carrying the cross. The conversation between father and son adds tension to the drama. Abraham's reply in v. 8 is an unconscious preparation for v. 14. **9–14.** Commentators note the detailed description of individual actions as the story reaches its climax. The "angel of the Lord" is identified with Yahweh himself, as the end of v 12 makes clear (see comment on 16:7–10). The "fear of God" is here perfect obedience. The substituted ram of v. 13 was a usual victim for holocausts (cf. Lv 1:10–13). The name given to the site by Moses (*yahweh yir'eh*, "Yahweh will see" or "Yahweh will provide") is not the usual type of topographical denomination; it is simply a play on words to express a theological notion. Nor does it agree with the explanation given in the latter part of the verse, where the Niphal form is used (*yērā'eh*, "it shall be provided"). This form can also mean "he [Yahweh] will appear"; it has been suggested (McKenzie, *Scr* 9, 81) that this latter was the original name of the site of a theophany, and from this was derived the later name to explain the patriarch's sacrifice. The vagueness of the present geographical reference may be intended to underline the note of mystery in the whole story. (The "Moriah" of v. 2, whose final element, *yāh*, is the usual abbreviation of Yahweh in personal and place names, may have been connected with the name in v. 14 by assonance.)

74 (b) (22:15–24). **15–19.** This addition to the primitive narrative, which had explained the substitution motif or the site of a theophany, agrees with the present orientation of the story and with the general theme of promise running through the patriarchal narratives. The extraordinary faith of Abraham justifies a much more solemn form (God "swears by himself"; cf. Ex 32:13). Paul has taken a phrase from v. 16 to indicate the fullness of revelation in the sacrifice of God's Son (Rom 8:32). The promise in v. 17c is new; it strikes a nationalistic note, perhaps influenced by 24:60 where such would be more in place. Also more nationalistic than 12:3c is the promise of v. 18. Here the Hithpael (*hitbārăkû*), instead of the Niphal, is used, and the reflexive meaning is intended: "in your seed all the nations of the earth will bless themselves," i.e., Abraham's descendants will be a formula of blessing for others (see comment on 12:3c). **20–24.** This J addition (cf. P's parallel list in 10:23) prepares the way for Isaac's marriage in ch. 24, as the gloss in v. 23a indicates. Like Ishmael (cf. 25:13–16) and Jacob-Israel, Nahor has 12 sons, and, like those of Jacob-Israel (cf. 35:23–26), 8 are by his wife (wives) and 4 by his concubine(s). As frequent in J, the names are generally those of tribes or cities whose relations with Israel explain their presence. Uz, Buz, and Hazo are located in the confines of the Syro-Arabian desert. The Kemuel of this list is unknown, as are Pildash, Jidlaph, and Gaham. Aram and Chesed (or "Chaldeans" in 11:28) were Semitic peoples related to the Hebrews (cf. 24:10; 28:2,5–7). Bethuel is a personal Aramean name (cf. 25:20). Tebah (cf. 2 Sm 8:8 in Pesh), Tahash, and Maacah are names of places in the region E of Lebanon.

75 **(M) The Purchase of the Cave of Machpelah (23:1–20) (P).** The chronological and geographical details of vv. 1, 2, and 19, the reference to the Hittites as "the sons of Heth," and the general precision of the account indicate the P tradition; however, the nature of the story with its earthy and slightly humorous details suggests that P has used an ancient narrative for his higher purpose. The discovery of the Hittite code of laws in the ancient Hittite capital has thrown some light on the transaction described here. According to that code, one who buys the entire property of another must render certain (unspecified) feudal services. Understandably, then, Ephron wishes to sell all his property, "the field and the cave that is in it" (v. 11). Just as understandably, Abraham, who would not be anxious to provide feudal services, desires only the cave (v. 9), but is forced, under the circumstances, to buy the field as well (v.12; cf. M. R. Lehmann, *BASOR* 125 [1953] 15–18).

The field would become the burial place, not only of Sarah, but also of Abraham (25:9–10, from P), Isaac, Rebekah, Leah, and Jacob (49:29–32, also from P); this condition would partially justify the preservation of the story. More importantly, the story is connected with the promise of the land (cf. 17:8). This small piece of land is the "first installment," juridically acquired, on that promise. The incipient realization of the promise in Abraham's lifetime would have appealed to P. Also, it may be that P wished to contrast this strictly legal purchase, on the human level, of a small piece of property with the later gift, on the divine level, of the entire land. The story is conveniently placed at the end of the narratives centering on Abraham.

76 (a) (23:1–6). **1–2.** The age of Sarah at her death is consistent with 17:17. As elsewhere (cf. 35:27), P gives the ancient name of Hebron—Kiriath-arba, "the city of four" (cf. 13:18). The mourning for the dead involved much ceremony (cf. 2 Sm 1:11–12; 3:31; 13:31; Mi 1:8). **3.** The "Hittites" of this narrative may be only a later designation for non-Semitic peoples in Canaan and not the now famous inhabitants of Asia Minor. However, legal elements implied in the narrative can be explained by recently discovered Hittite laws, and the presence of Hittites in this part of Canaan is not impossible at this period (cf. Nm 13:29; O. Gurney, *The Hittites* [London, 1952] 59–62). **4–6.** Abraham is a "stranger and resident," probably a reference to his seminomadic status in which he may reside in the land but without proprietary rights. This point is important in P's story. The Hittites identify Abraham as a "prince of God" (*nᵉśîʾ ʾĕlōhîm*), correctly translated in the CCD as "a mighty prince" (*ʾĕlōhîm*, used as a superlative as in Gn 1:2 and Is 9:5b). The title is a subtle preparation for the bargaining to follow.

77 (b) (23:7–20). **7–9.** Abraham, responding with typical Oriental courtesy, specifies his request. He wishes the "cave of Machpelah" (meaning, perhaps, the "double" cave), at one end of the property of Ephron. A mosque covers the traditional site of this cave at Hebron. **10–11.** Ephron indicates, obliquely as is usual in such transactions, his desire to sell the whole field. The witnesses, frequently referred to, will guarantee the legality of the transaction. The "fellow citizens" of v. 10 are, lit., "all who come to the gate of the city," i.e., who can juridically act as witnesses (cf. E. A. Speiser, *BASOR* 144 [1956] 20–23). **12–15.** Abraham accepts, necessarily, the condition to buy the whole field and inquires, in the accepted form, about the price. Ephron's reply is similarly phrased courteously. He asks 400 shekels of silver, the value of which is unknown. **16.** Abraham understands the meaning of Ephron's statement and weighs out the money in the presence of the legal witnesses. The phrase "commercial standard" (*ʿōbēr lassōḥēr*, "current with the merchant") refers to the practice among such peoples of having the merchants determine the value of silver at any given period. **17–18.** The precise legal formulation, familiar from ancient commercial texts, would have delighted the tidy soul of the editor of P. At the end of v. 18, the repeated reference to the "fellow citizens" (cf. v. 10) serves as a legal seal to the transaction. **19–20.** The conclusion of the story contains a gloss ("that is, Hebron") identifying Mamre with the later city of Hebron, which is actually about 2 mi. S.

78 **(N) The Wife of Isaac (24:1–67) (J).** This story, the longest and one of the most artistic compositions in Gn, is attributed to J. The tradition was seemingly connected with that of Ishmael in the southern Negeb district (cf. 16:7–14), since Abraham's servant brings Rebekah directly to Isaac in Beer-lahai-roi (cf. vv. 62–63f.). No connection with the Mamre tradition is indicated. One could only be deduced from the fact that the story follows immediately the P narrative of the burial of Sarah at Mamre, but this link is artificial. Moreover, J has no record of Abraham's death at Mamre. We would be led to suppose, from the evidence available, that the last acts of Abraham, in both J and E, are connected with the south (cf. Cazelles, *VDBS* 7, 129–30f.). It may be that J had reported the death of Abraham in the course of the story, which would explain the servant's going directly to Isaac, but the report would have been omitted to allow the insertion of ch. 25 (De Vaux, *La Genèse*, 110).

The present form of the story is greatly elaborated. The artificial nature of the speeches, the parallels (cf. vv. 1–9 and 34–41; 12–14 and 16–20; 12–27 and 42–48), the delicate balancing of the scenes connected by short narrative passages, and the absence of overt divine interventions distinguish it from other patriarchal stories. It is composed of a series of dialogues between Abraham and his servant (1–9), the servant and God (10–14), the servant and Rebekah (15–27), the servant and Laban (28–49), and the servant and Rebekah's family (50–57). While the basic elements of the story are true to the patriarchal milieu, the present form is highly artificial and bespeaks a complete reworking of the primitive tradition. We can note certain harmonizing efforts in the references to Rebekah's family.

In its present context, the narrative is transitional, linking the Abraham stories with the continuation of patriarchal history in Rebekah's offspring. The theological emphasis is quite marked; all is under the guiding hand of God (cf. vv. 7, 12–14, 21, 27, 40, 48, 50, and 56). His invisible arrangement of events, rather than direct intervention, indicates the more sophisticated theology. Isaac's wife must be one designated by God himself, thus fit to transmit the promises, and she must come back to the land of promise. (The first theme is basically the same found in the story of Sarah's bearing of Isaac at an advanced age; the divine choice and the divine action to implement the choice are present in both stories.)

79 (a) (24:1–9). There is no indication of the place where the scene unfolds. The preceding narratives point to Mamre, but the author may have omitted the specific reference to avoid an inconsistency (→ 78 above). Abraham's initiative in arranging the marriage is in accord with the customs of the time. The servant (perhaps Eliezer—cf. 15:2 where, however, the text is corrupt) is obviously an important personage who enjoys Abraham's complete confidence. Swearing by the genital organs, considered the transmitters of life, added solemnity to the oath (cf. 47:29). Also, the epithet applied to Yahweh, "the God of heaven and the God of earth," not used elsewhere in Gn, adds a formal and universal note. The first charge to the servant is a negative one; Isaac must not marry a Canaanite woman. On the profane level, this prohibition could be explained by the custom of endogamy among seminomadic tribes. On the theological level, as here, its purpose is to avoid contact with the religiously depraved inhabitants of Canaan (cf. Ex 34:16). The second charge is positive; he must seek a wife for Isaac among Abraham's kindred, who, although also pagans (cf. 31:19), were presumably more open to the divine action. These two charges are related to the promise of a progeny. The third and fourth, anticipated by the servant's reply in v. 5, concern the promise of the land. Isaac is not to return to Mesopotamia (i.e., to settle there), and the servant is to return if the woman refuses to come with him. But the faith of Abraham in the certainty of God's promise assures him of the success of the mission (v. 7). The reference to the angel is an indication of an antianthropomorphistic tendency and hence implies a late composition date.

This opening scene resembles a deathbed instruction. The solemn oath required of the servant supposes that Abraham will not be able to oversee the arrangements. Commentators suggest that the recording of the patriarch's death may have been placed at the end of v. 9, which would explain the servant's statement in v. 36 that Isaac had already inherited "all his property," and his reference to Isaac as "my master" (v. 65). The passage would have been deleted when ch. 25 was added (cf. Von Rad, *op. cit.*, 250).

80 (b) (24:10–27). **10–14.** The servant journeys to Aram-naharaim (lit., "Syria of the two rivers"), a district in northern Mesopotamia. According to 11:31, Abraham's family lived in Haran, an ancient city on the Balikh River, a tributary of the Euphrates. The picture evoked in v. 11 is true to Oriental life. The sign asked of God by the servant is one dictated by common sense. It is the linking of this very obvious sign, one that the servant could have recognized without divine help, with the supernatural that gives the scene its deeply theological tenor. **15–27.** A harmonizing touch appears in the brief genealogy of Rebekah. According to one tradition, she is the daughter of Nahor, Abraham's brother (cf. 29:5 where Laban, Rebekah's brother, is called Nahor's son). This genealogy would also agree with 24:48, if the word *'āḥ* is taken in the strict sense of "brother" (the CCD has "kinsman"). The P tradition, however, identifies her as the daughter of Bethuel, son of Nahor by Milcah (cf. 25:20; 28:2,5). The redactor has harmonized the two by introducing into the text the name of Bethuel (vv. 15, 24, and 47), who plays no role in the story. After the mention of the lineage, the author describes Rebekah. She corresponds to the ideal sought in a wife—beautiful and a virgin (*bᵉtûlāh*), the last followed by the parallel expression "undefiled" (lit., "man did not know her"). The theological motif is emphasized again in v. 21. The bestowal of gifts is in view of the marriage which, in the author's view, is now expected because God has given the sign. The girl would hardly have understood it, hence the repetition in v. 53. The gold ring is a nose ring. The series of questions and answers in vv. 23–26 is awkward, suggesting reworking of the material. The "constant favor" of v. 27 includes the two basic attitudes that God has toward man: "steadfast love and constancy" (*ḥesed wᵉ'ĕmet*).

81 (c) (24:28–57). **28–49.** The mention of the "mother's" household indicates that the father (Bethuel or Nahor) is dead. In the MT, the phrase "Laban hastened to the man at the spring" occurs as part of v. 29. The context demands its transposition to its present place (as in the CCD). The transposition emphasizes the character of Laban, who appears venal throughout the traditions. The expression "blessed of the Lord" (v. 31) is an anomaly coming from Laban, a polytheist. The servant's desire to speak before he eats stresses the urgency of his mission. In the speech, which to us seems a tedious repetition of all that has preceded, the inspired author shows an artistic touch by having the servant emphasize Abraham's wealth, now the property of Isaac; its mention gives insight into the character of Laban, whom the servant is trying to impress. The details of the speech correspond with what has occurred, except that no mention is made of Abraham's charge to return if the woman refuses to accompany him (its inclusion would have been offensive to the Oriental courtesy) and that the gifts were given, according to the servant, after his questioning of Rebekah (cf. vv. 47 and 22–23; possibly another indication of reworking). The theological note of God's direction of events is continued throughout; God has "prospered the road" (*hiṣlîaḥ derek*; vv. 21, 40, 42, and 56). In v. 49, the same attributes spoken of God in v. 27 (i.e., *ḥesed wᵉ 'ĕmĕt*, translated simply as "favor" in the CCD) are now sought in Laban. **50–57.** In v. 50, the MT has "Laban and Bethuel." The Hebr *bᵉtû'ēl* is generally corrected, as in the CCD, to read *bêtô* (his family). Some such correction is demanded, since Bethuel's presence is not presumed throughout the story (cf. vv. 28, 29, 53b, and 55). Whatever may have been Laban's true motives for accepting the offer (for his sister), his remark that "this comes from the Lord" is certainly in accord with the author's convictions. The giving of gifts to the girl and her family on the occasion of the betrothal is a custom attested to in Assyrian and Babylonian literature. The gifts here may also be in lieu of the actual marriage, because no dowry is mentioned later (vv. 66–67). The servant's desire to leave, contrary to Oriental custom on such occasions, adds tension to the story and stresses the whole purpose of the mission, which is now completed. The Lord has "prospered his journey"; there is no reason for remaining. The girl's permission is sought, not for the marriage, but for the journey to Canaan; according to ancient law, the married woman could remain at her paternal home (cf. De Vaux, *RB* 56, 29–30).

82 (d) (24:58–67). **58–61.** The family's blessing of Rebekah recalls the general theme of a great progeny found in all the patriarchal stories but expressed in a more martial spirit, as we would expect of these people (see comment on 22:17). **62–67.** The story reaches its conclusion at Beer-lahai-roi, where the tradition would have deen preserved. The expression in v. 63 *lāśûaḥ* is uncertain ("to walk" in the CCD; "to meditate" in the RSV). More likely is a more recent suggestion, based on the reading of a rule in the DSS (cf. G. R. Driver, *Mélanges A. Robert* [Paris, 1957] 66–68), that the word means "to dig a hole" and is a euphemism for relieving nature. Rebekah veils her face in accord with custom which forbade a man to see his wife's face before the marriage. Some authors would put the original account of Abraham's death after v. 61, which would explain the servant's otherwise unaccountable journey to the Negeb and his address of Isaac as "my master." In this case, v. 67 would have referred to "his father" instead of "his mother." These final verses are a brief and sober account of what the preceding elaborated story had anticipated. This method is in accord with the biblical style in which the antecedents of the divine action in history are carefully drawn and long pondered over and the fulfillment is described briskly and succinctly (cf. 19:23–28; 21:1–7).

83 **(O) Abraham's Descendants (25:1–18) (P and J).** This "postscript" to the Abraham stories contains three sections representing both J and P. The first (1–6) is a genealogy supplied by J and listing hitherto unreported descendants of the patriarch. The second (7–11), almost exclusively P's, reports his death. The third (12–18), again principally P's, concludes the history of Ishmael with a list of his descendants. The two genealogies are ancient and attest to the sacred authors' respect for their sources; in spite of occasional inconsistencies, they allow both their full place in sacred history.

(a) (25:1–6). We have some insight into the deeply theological character of the narratives relating the conception and birth of Isaac (17:15–19; 18:1–15; 20; 21:1–7) from this prosaic account of Abraham's other children. The final redactor, at least, felt no embarrassment in saying that Abraham took another wife, even after a passage such as 18:11–15. Keturah's "sons" are, for the most part, Arabian peoples who had relations with Israel at various times in her history. Among the better known are the Midianites, who later constantly cross Israel's path in her early history (cf. Gn 37:28,36; Ex 2:15–22; 3:1; 18; Jgs 6–8); the people of Sheba, who lived in the southwestern section of the Arabian peninsula and were noted for their caravans of spices and other goods (cf. 1 Kgs 10:1–13; Jer 6:20); and the Dedanites, linked with the Sabeans in 10:7, who lived further N in the peninsula and whose caravans were also known to Israel (cf. Is 21:13). Of the others little is known. The descendants of Dedan may have been added later from another list; they do not occur in the parallel list of 1 Chr 1:32–33f., and their plural forms contrast with the other names. That all of them, however, refer to Arabian peoples (including the Asshurim, who are not Assyrians despite the similarity) is confirmed by the association of Ephah with Midian and Sheba in Is 60:6. These historical associations do not affect the transmission of the promise through Isaac, which J emphasizes by his insistence on Isaac's inheritance (v. 5) and on the separation of the others from Isaac (v. 6). Given a token of the father's love, they can no longer claim a share in the inheritance.

84 (b) (25:7–11). The account of Abraham's death in P's stereotyped style is the formal conclusion to the Abraham stories. Consistent in his chronological references, P notes, implicitly, that Abraham had spent

100 years in Canaan in his new life with God (cf. 12:4). These years had been marked by divine blessings and by divine promises of a great posterity. He had lived to see the initial realization of these promises; hence, he died "after a full life." The expression "gathered to his kinsmen" probably refers to the shadowy existence in Sheol. The reference in vv. 8–9 to his burial place accords with all that was said by P in ch. 23. Remarkable only is the mention of Ishmael, whose expulsion had been related earlier by both J and E (cf. 16:6–14; 21:9–21). Probably he is added here to prepare for the inclusion of his genealogy in the following verses. In v. 11a, we have another example of P's more transcendent theology in contrast to J's in vv. 5–6; v. 11b is J's addition.

85 (c) (25:12–18). P has found this list in the *tôlᵉdôt* (genealogies) source that he has used throughout. As in 22:20–24, 12 sons are listed, an indication of another 12-tribe system outside of Israel (cf. Noth, *Hist.* 85–89). Partly nomadic and partly sedentary (cf. v. 16, "their villages and encampments"), the Ishmaelites inhabit the northwestern area of the Arabian peninsula, consistent with the Ishmael traditions previously reported (cf. 16:1–14; 21:9–21). Nebaioth may be equated with the later Nabateans of the Transjordan area. Kedar is associated with Nebaioth in Is 60:7, and, like Nebaioth, is mentioned in Assyrian texts which bear witness to the military prowess of the people (cf. also Is 21:17). Tema is known as a desert people from Is 21:4 and Jer 25:23. These 12 "princes" (*nᵉśî'îm*, the religio-political leaders in the 12-tribe systems; cf. E. A. Speiser, *CBQ* 25 [1963] 111–17) fulfill the promise recorded by P in 17:20. Verse 17 concludes the story of Ishmael and is similar in form to vv. 7–8 above. The significance of Ishmael's age is unknown. Verse 18, from J, fixes the limits of the Ishmaelites' territory, from Havilah in northwest Arabia to Shur near Egypt. The final remark (v. 18b) is a reference to 16:12.

86 **(III) The Patriarchs Isaac and Jacob (25:19–36:43).** Very little has been preserved of the traditions concerning Isaac, and what does concern him alone (ch. 26), is a series of accounts found also in the Abraham cycle. For the rest, the Isaac traditions have been absorbed by either Abraham or Jacob. Nevertheless, P, or the final redactor who inserted the P tradition, has given greater prominence to Isaac by making a great many of the Jacob stories part of the "family history" (*tôlᵉdôt*) of Isaac. He has done this by beginning the narratives with the remark, "this is the family history of Isaac" (25:19) and closing them with the account of Isaac's death (35:29). Similarly, the history of Joseph (chs. 37–50) is seen by this same author as the history (*tôlᵉdôt*) of Jacob (cf. 37:2 and 49:33; Von Rad, *op. cit.*, 258).

87 **(A) The Birth of Esau and Jacob (25:19–34) (J, P).** The stories contained here come from the J tradition with a few insertions from P (vv. 19, 20, and 26b). They serve as a transition and introduction to the history of Jacob. In both these popular stories, etymologies abound, providing the material for both the historical and theological implications. The historical picture is the ascendancy of Israel over her Edomite neighbors to the S. The theological picture, made predominant by the context, is the divine choice of the more unlikely candidate, Jacob, as the heir of the patriarchal promises. Esau—the first-born, the one loved by the father, and the stronger of the two sons—is, despite these evident qualifying characteristics, rejected in favor of Jacob. The absolute gratuity of God's choice is a constant theme of J, as is illustrated in the stories of Isaac, Joseph, and Israel herself. This divine element in Jacob's case has been masterfully brought out in this brief section recording his birth and early life.

88 (a) (25:19–26). **19–20.** These verses from P introduce, as mentioned, all that follows to the death of Isaac (35:29). P consistently refers to Rebekah as the daughter of Bethuel (28:2,5; see comment on 24:15) and is the only one to refer to the place of origin as Paddan-aram (the "plain of Aram"; cf. 24:10). **21–23.** What had been described of Abraham in several chapters is said of Isaac in a few brief verses: His children are the fruit of faith. Rebekah conceives as an answer to Isaac's prayer The precise meaning of Rebekah's remark in v. 22 is uncertain; the general meaning is that something occurred during her pregnancy that occasioned the consultation of the Lord. The place of consultation would have been a sanctuary such as Beer-lahai-roi or Beer-sheba. The response, given in oracular form (the means of transmission is not mentioned; cf. 1 Sm 9:9), presents in anticipation two of the anomalies that will mark the following stories: The older and stronger brother will be servant to the younger and weaker. **24–26.** The account of the delivery shows the Semitic delight in etymologies. The mention that the first child was "red" (*'admônî*) is evidently linked with the name "Edom," not mentioned here. The statement may be a gloss (Clamer, *op. cit.*, 345), or it may be that J, knowing his readers would make the association with the dark-skinned Edomites, did not want to stress this etymology because of the other he would introduce later (v. 30). Also, the connection of Esau (*'ēśāw*) with the "hairy garment" (*kᵉ'aderet śē'ār*) is not clear; however, the *śē'ār* may be an allusion, easily recognized by the Hebrews, to Seir (*śē'îr*), the ancient name of Edom, where Esau's descendants dwelled (cf. 32:4; 36:8; Jgs 5:4). The etymology of "Jacob" (*ya'ăqōb*) is clearer; it is conceived as derived from *'āqēb*, "heel" (cf. 27:36). The name actually is a shortened theophoric name, found in its full form as *y'qb'l* in an 18th cent. Upper-Mesopotamian text, which probably means "may God protect" (cf. De Vaux, *RB* 53, 323–24; Cazelles, *VDBS* 7, 132). In this reference to Jacob, J sees an initial fulfillment of the oracle. Verse 26b, P's insertion, is a typical chronological detail that stresses the divine element (after 20 years of barrenness; cf. v. 20).

89 (b) (25:27–34). **27–28.** The frequently tense relationships between the nomadic hunter and the sedentary shepherd are reflected here. That Isaac preferred Esau is one more natural reason for supposing that the latter would receive the inheritance. Rebekah's preference for Jacob anticipates the story of ch. 27. **29–34.** The reasons for attributing these verses to E (cf. Chaine, *op. cit.*, 299) seem insufficient; the story has all the detailed allure of J. Another popular etymology is behind Esau's request for the "red food" (*hā'ādōm hā'ādōm;* the repetition of the word, idiomatically translated "that red stuff there," indicates Esau's eagerness); the *'ādōm* justifies the name of *'ĕdôm.* The birthright, desired by Jacob, would assure him a double portion of the inheritance (cf. Dt 21:15–17). It has been argued with some conviction (D. Daube, *Studies in Biblical Law* [Cambridge, 1947] 193–200) that, after exacting an oath from Esau, Jacob gave him "bread and lentils" instead of the "red dish," the latter perhaps a blood soup. This possibility would explain why the lentils were not mentioned before, why Jacob required an oath (which would be binding despite his dishonest substitution), and why Esau later referred to a double deception by Jacob (27:36). Verse 34b is J's judgment on Esau, a greedy man whose only thought is for the present. Jacob's role, though hardly commendable, fits into the divine plan and receives no adverse judgment.

90 **(B) Isaac in Gerar and Beer-sheba (26:1–35) (J, P).** We have remarked that this chapter is the only one containing stories dealing with Isaac alone, and that they are doublets of stories in the Abraham cycle. Their relation to that cycle rather than to that of Jacob is confirmed by the fact that the stories do not mention Isaac's children (vv. 34–35 are from P) and presume that the husband and wife are still young (cf. v. 7). Originally separate, the accounts have been interwoven by J. His purpose in uniting these stories, their theological import paralleling that of their counterparts in the Abraham cycle, is to assure his readers of the continuation of the divine plan in Isaac. Inaugurated with Abraham and reaching a climax in Jacob and his descendants, that plan must also be realized in Isaac, the link between the two.

91 (a) (26:1–11). **1–5.** The first unit is explicitly theological and gives the tone to the rest. It contains inconsistencies which indicate reworking of the material. The first verse was originally connected with v. 6, perhaps without the reference to the earlier famine (i.e., that of 12:10). When vv. 2–3 were added, v. 1 was retouched to provide an occasion for the Lord's words. The addition caused the discrepancy between vv. 1 and 2. The divine address is a mosaic of texts recalling and renewing the promises made to Abraham. Verses 3b–5 are an editorial expansion of the simple blessing of v. 3a. **6–11.** This passage is the third occurrence of the same story continuing the motif of danger to the patriarch's wife (cf. 12:10–20; 20:1–18). Compared with the other two, the complete naturalness and absence of artificial development of the present account argue for its originality. In the course of its preliterary history, it could have been told for various motives, even secular. In the present context (cf. especially vv. 2–5), the religious motive prevails, i.e., the divine protection of the wife of the patriarch to whom the promise has been made. This motive was enlarged and made more explicit when applied to Abraham.

92 (b) (26:12–22). A similar incident is narrated of Abraham (21:22–34). The redactor, aware of the similarities, has reconciled the two accounts by adding vv. 15 and 18, which contribute nothing to the present story. The mention of a crop (v. 12) is in accord with seminomadic custom, whereby, residing with their flocks for a period in one place, the shepherds would engage in limited agricultural activity. The enmity of the "Philistines" (an anachronism, as in 21:32,34; 26:1) was seemingly occasioned by Isaac's prosperity (vv. 13,14,16). The enmity increases because of the dispute over the ownership of the wells (vv. 19–21), whence their names: Esek (*ʿēśeq*, "contention") and Sitnah (*śitnāh*, "enmity"). Isaac's third attempt is more successful (v. 22); there is no contention, and the well is accordingly named Rehoboth (*reḥōbôt*, "wide spaces") because the Lord has "made room" (*hirḥib*, same root as *reḥōbôt*). Again, these ancient etymological traditions became the vehicle for the theological emphasis on the promise of the land.

93 (c) (26:23–35). **23–33.** The parallel account of this incident at Beer-sheba is found in 21:22–34, where the theological note is much more prominent. The promises are renewed in a theophany (v. 24) which explains the erection of the altar and the cultic act (v. 25; cf. 21:33). The appearance of Abimelech and Phicol agrees with 21:22, but that of Ahuzzath, the king's friend or adviser, is new. The king's recognition of Isaac's favored position (v. 28; cf. 21:22b) is, for the sacred author, an anticipated fulfillment of the promise that all nations would be blessed in his descendants (cf. v. 4b)—i.e., they would find in them, because of their greatness, a formula of blessing (the Hithpael is used, as in 22:18; cf. the Niphal in 12:3c). Isaac's agreement to the covenant is implied in the covenant meal that follows (v. 30); the partaking of the same food creates a bond between them. The finding of a well and the giving of a name to it in commemoration of the covenant concludes the story. The name "Shibah" (*šibʿāh*, "seven") in the MT has been influenced by 21:28–31; the LXX reads *šebûʿāh* (oath), which agrees with the context. These various etymologies of the name Beer-sheba attest to its importance as a cult center. **34–35.** An addition from P, mentioning the two Hittite wives of Esau, is to be joined to 27:46–28:9. The names vary somewhat from those given in 36:1–3, and the implied basis of the contention between Esau and Jacob (made explicit in P's remarks in 28:1–9) differs from that of J in ch. 27. Despite their "Hittite" origin, the wives have Semitic names. Note that Esau, like Isaac (25:20), marries at the age of 40.

94 **(C) Isaac's Blessing of Jacob (27:1–45) (J).** The present story, which connects the traditions of the youths Esau and Jacob with those of Jacob in the Transjordan area, is attributed to J. Certain inconsistencies (e.g., the means of Isaac's recognition of his son in vv. 22 and 27) have led some authors (Chaine, *op. cit.*, 311; Clamer, *op. cit.*, 355) to suppose a fusion of J and E. But the inconsistencies are not great, and the artistic flow of the narrative argues against an editorial conflation (De Vaux, *La Genèse*, 125).

Much more complex is the history of this tradition and its connection with the remainder of the Jacob-Esau stories. We can only indicate here the existence of the problem. The localization of the present chapter is admittedly loose; only in its present context is it associated with Beer-sheba (cf. 26:33 and 28:10). The Jacob stories, in general, are connected with the central Palestinian area (Bethel, Shechem) and with Penuel in Transjordan. The Esau stories would naturally be thought to be associated with the southern Palestinian area because of the Esau-Edom identification, but Esau is also connected with the E Jordan area (see 33; 32–34f.). On the bases of these and other considerations, various solutions have been offered which, however, have not met with general agreement by all scholars (cf. Noth, *UP* 103–11; Cazelles, *VDBS* 7, 133).

While the ultimate solution of the problem will give us a deeper insight into the methodology of the inspired writers, and consequently into the manner of the divine revelation, the theology of the chapter as it stands is clear. Jacob, despite the odds against him and his own unworthiness, is the object of the divine free choice (cf. Mal 1:3; Rom 9:13); in that choice, the people of Israel, whom Jacob personified, came to understand better their own choice by the same God. In the earlier history of these Esau-Jacob stories, there may have been a grosser presentation of the actions and motives of the two and the stories would have been told to belittle Israel's enemies, the Edomites. J has refined them somewhat, removing some of the opprobrium from Jacob (e.g., 27:11–13) and describing Esau more compassionately (cf. 27:34–38). But he has not denied altogether the slyness and treachery of Jacob, and it is through this man—in fact, through the acts of treachery themselves—that the divine plan operates (cf. v. 20b). There is only one plan, already devised and initiated; therefore, there can be only one effective blessing (cf. vv. 33b and 38). Like ch. 24, this chapter is artistically developed in five scenes presenting five dialogues between the various actors.

95 (a) (27:1–4). The story opens with the dialogue between Isaac and Esau. It was customary for a dying man to bless those in his charge (cf. 48:9–20; Dt 33; for the Hurrian background of 27:1ff., see Speiser, *Genesis*, 211–13). This special blessing of the first-born is not otherwise recorded in Gn, but it might be presumed that such a blessing was given to indicate the right of inheritance (perhaps implied in 24:36b). At least Isaac intended it as such (vv. 28–29). Just as Esau had sold his birthright in coming from the hunt (25:29–34), so would he lose his blessing in returning to the hunt (Michaeli, *Le Livre de la Genèse* [Paris, 1957–60] 86).

96 (b) (27:5–17). The dialogue between Rebekah and Jacob reveals the former's cunningness which would explain the trait in her son (it is also characteristic of her brother, Laban; cf. 24:29–32). Isaac's blessing, as reported by Rebekah, is a religious act (v. 7, "in the sight of the Lord"), making the mother's willingness to accept the curse (v. 13) all the more reprehensible. It would not be consonant with the character of the story, in either its earlier or final form, to inquire too closely into the effectiveness of the strategem described; the author had a different purpose in mind. Jacob's objections (vv. 11–12), while decreasing his guilt somewhat, are not highly motivated.

97 (c) (27:18–29). The meeting between Isaac and Jacob is recorded simply, with just those details needed to give tension to the narrative. Jacob's deception of the blind man was serious enough (cf. Lv 19:14); it is compounded by his statement that Yahweh had guided him (v. 20). Many consider v. 23 an explanatory gloss, anticipating the blessing of vv. 28–29. The distinction of sources here (e.g., vv. 18b–23 to J; vv. 24–28 to E) raises more questions than it answers; the suspense would be weakened, and several details in both stories would have to be presumed omitted by the editor. The blessing is given in oracular form (vv. 27b–29). It is unlike the other patriarchal blessings and is directly applied to the "nation" descended from Jacob (cf. 25:23). The Israelites will be blessed with fertility of the soil (v. 28). The incongruity of the supposed Esau, a hunter, receiving a blessing fitting for a sedentary farming people did not bother the author, if it occurred to him. They will also be masters of their enemies (v. 29), a theme that runs through the Jacob-Esau stories and reflects later historical relations between Israel and Edom. Here the plural ("nations," "brothers," "sons") would include all the neighboring peoples, such as the Moabites and Ammonites. The final phrase (v. 29c) is a usual concluding formula (cf. 12:3).

98 (d) (27:30–40). Again, the narrator's art is evident throughout this passage describing the dialogue between Isaac and Esau. The scene opens just as the preceding one (cf. vv. 31–32 and 18–19a). Isaac's disturbed statement that he had already blessed another, "and he shall be blessed," indicates the irrevocable nature of patriarchal blessings. (In v. 33, the MT has *wā'ōkal mikkōl*, "and I ate from all of it"; it is commonly corrected to *wā'ōkal 'ākōl*, "and I ate heartily." In either case, the connection of the substantial meal with the blessing, as in v. 4, seems inescapable.) This conception of an irrevocable blessing is confirmed by Esau's anguished cry; in desperation he asks for a blessing. Esau's etymology of Jacob's name differs from that of 25:26, although derived from the same root (*'āqab*, "to supplant"). The first supplanting had been the taking of his birthright (*bᵉkōrātî*); the second is the taking of his blessing (*birkātî*). Esau's triple request finally brings a response, but hardly a blessing. The words describe the barren territory of Edom and the warlike character of its inhabitants (vv. 39–40a) in the same oracular style as the blessing of Jacob. Verse 40b may be a reference by J to Edom's initial attempt at rebellion against Judah in the time of Solomon (cf. 1 Kgs 11:14–22,25), or it may be a later gloss referring to Edom's successful rebellion in the time of Jehoram of Judah (cf. 2 Kgs 8:22–24). The latter is suggested by the different style.

99 (e) (27:41–45). The final scene, between Rebekah and Jacob, prepares the way for 28:10, where J has continued his narrative. Esau's remark in v. 41 indicates, as did the whole story, that Isaac is on his deathbed. Thus problems arise concerning the conflation of all these traditions, since Isaac, according to 35:29, apparently does not die until after Jacob's 20-year stay in Haran. Rebekah had apparently overlooked the possibility of Esau's revenge, and she must now devise a scheme to save not only Jacob but also Esau (v. 45b), for the murder of his brother would necessarily make him a fugitive. J has added a tragic note in Rebekah's remark that she would send for Jacob after Esau's fury subsided; she would never see him again. Perhaps the author intended to suggest here the mother's unfulfilled longing for her son in the years that followed, and so implied her punishment. If so, it is a master stroke. (Verse 46 is part of the following story.)

100 **(D) Jacob's Departure for Paddan-aram (27:46–28:9) (P).** That this passage comes from a tradition different from the one preceding is apparent from its wholly different tone. Jacob's departure is not a flight but a mission given by Isaac. There is no indication of the strained relations between Isaac and Jacob and, more especially, between Jacob and Esau. The author of the passage expresses no awareness of the stories in 25:21–34 and 27. The vocabulary (e.g., *bᵉnôt ḥēt* in 27:46; *bᵉnôt kᵉnā'an* in 28:1; *'ēl šadday* and *qᵉhal 'ammîm* in 28:3), the designation of the homeland as Paddan-aram (cf. 25:20), and the theological concerns point to P as the author. These concerns deal primarily with the continuation of the patriarchal blessings in the Jacob line and with the avoidance of religious contamination through mixed marriages. While this latter was a problem throughout Israel's history, it was especially noted in the post-exilic period (cf. Ezr 9–10; Neh 13:23–31). Neither of these concerns is foreign to the other, more ancient traditions, but their presence here, to the exclusion of the more earthly motivations in ch. 27, is typical of P's usual procedure. **27:46.** The verse follows directly on 26:34–35 and introduces the mission of Isaac to Jacob. **28:1–4.** This version of the blessing given to Jacob by his father is P's, recorded earlier by J (27:27–29). Bethuel, the father of Rebekah, figures constantly in P's genealogy (see comment on 24:15). Whereas the blessing in J had fixed solely on the descendants of Jacob, P emphasizes the connection of the blessing with that given to Abraham (v. 4). The expression *qᵉhal 'ammîm* ("an assembly of peoples"; the CCD has "many nations"), used here for the first time, may have liturgical overtones; *qāhāl* is used frequently by P in this sense. "Should one think of a universal eschatological cultic community of nations when reading this rather rudimentary prophecy...?" (Von Rad, *op. cit.*, 277). The *'ereṣ mᵉgurèkā* (land in which you are immigrants) is, for P, the land already bequeathed by divine promise to Abraham; the promise is yet to be fulfilled (→ 75 above). **5.** The departure of Jacob is related without details. The repetitious genealogical reference is characteristic (cf. v. 2). **6–9.** We note P's emphasis on the evils of mixed marriages; even Esau is aware of the prohibition, which provides the occasion for noting the marriage of Esau to Mahalath, daughter of Nebaioth, an Ishmaelite (cf. 25:13). Behind this union may be an alliance between Edom (Esau) and the Ishmaelites, confirmed by other indications (De Vaux, *La Genèse*, 131). The reference to Jacob's journey being motivated by obedience (v. 7) illustrates P's tendency to stress the theology of events.

101 **(E) Vision at Bethel (28:10–22) (J and E).** The presence of two traditions, J and E, is generally recognized. The distinction of the divine names "Elohim" and "Yahweh," the manner of presenting the theophany, and the presence of parallel passages are the bases for the distinction. Verses 10–12, 17–18, and 20–22 are attributed to E and vv. 13–16 and 19 to J. The conflation has been skillfully executed.

The character of these traditions is connected with the history of the Bethel sanctuary, a 2nd millennium Canaanite shrine where the god "Bethel" was probably worshiped ("Bethel," as the name of a deity, is frequently attested); the patriarchs would have known of it. It continued as an Israelite shrine after the conquest (cf. Jgs 20:18,26–28; 21:2). After the schism of 922, it became one of the chief shrines of northern Israel (1 Kgs 12:26–33), and an occasion of religious syncretism (cf. Am 4:4; etc.), justifying its destruction by Josiah (2 Kgs 23:15). Much of this history would have been known to the authors of our passage, who are concerned to preserve this ancient tradition of Bethel's origin as a sanctuary of the God of Israel.

In its present context, the passage presents a divine confirmation of the blessing given by Isaac to Jacob. The latter's human character, realistically portrayed in the preceding stories, is lost in the universal scope of the divine plan. Jacob becomes, at least in part, the historical Israel (cf. v. 14b). The human element is insignificant in this overriding plan; God's personal protection of the patriarch is demanded solely by virtue of the promise (v. 15).

102 (a) (28:10–15). **10.** The author has connected the story with the Isaac traditions by mentioning the point of departure as Beer-sheba. **11.** The word "place" (*māqôm*), occurring five times in the passage, has a cultic significance here; Jacob came to a Canaanite sanctuary. Theophanies frequently take place at night (cf. 15:12,17), and, especially for E, in dreams (cf. 20:3,6). **12.** It is consonant with E's theology that God should not appear directly to men; messengers (here, "angels") are the instruments of his contact with man (cf. 21:17). This use of messengers is combined with the symbol of a ladder (*sullām*, an hapaxlegomenon in the OT), possibly occasioned by the staged towers of Babylonia (ziggurats), the summits of which represented the gods' true dwelling place. As used by E, it is a representation, with the divine messengers descending and ascending, of the continuing contact between God and Israel. **13–15.** The presence of a separate tradition is apparent in the fact of the immediate presence of God (the "angels" are forgotten) and confirmed by the reference to "Yahweh." As generally in J, the Lord identifies himself as the God of the patriarchs, and especially of Abraham (cf. 24:12; 26:23); he is not, therefore, the god of the pagan sanctuary, to be identified by a place name. As the God of the individual patriarchs, he is not limited spatially in his power. The first two parts of the promise (vv. 13b–14a) renew the promises of the land and of a great posterity, the latter expressed here in terms that recall later Israel. The third part is the same as 12:3b. The final part of the message is intended for Jacob personally, but in view of the larger promise.

103 (b) (28:16–22). **16.** Jacob's reaction is expressed in words that imply some kind of localization of the deity (cf. Chaine, *op. cit.*, 316–17). **17–18.** In E, Jacob's reaction is similar, but the awesomeness of the vision is emphasized (*wayyîrā' . . . māh nôrā'*). The vision explains Bethel's name (here "house of God"). The "gate of heaven" probably refers to the ladder which led up to heaven and may have been added to avoid the suggestion that God is "confined" here. The acts of Jacob in v. 18 have a cultic significance. The stone is a *maṣṣēbāh*, or "memorial pillar," used also by the Canaanites to indicate the presence of the deity. The later prohibition of the stones' use in Israel is explained by the ease with which pagan ideas could be attached to them (cf. Hos 3:4; Mi 5:12). The anointing with oil was an act of consecration (cf. Ex 30:22–33). Whatever Canaanite elements may have been present in these acts, any possible pagan significance has been avoided by their attachment to Jacob's vision of the "God of his fathers." **19.** This verse is J's conclusion to the story and explains the name of the place (cf. v. 17). The second part of the verse is a gloss. According to Jos 16:2, Luz was near, but distinct from Bethel. By the author's time, only the name Bethel was used. **20–22.** The account by E continues with another religious act, Jacob's vow. It contains certain conditions (usual in such vows; cf. Jgs 11:30–31; 1 Sm 1:11) which obligate the person making the vow. Here, they are essentially what was promised in vv. 14c–15 (J), but elaborated. The conclusion of the condition as presented, "the Lord shall be my God," is hardly correct; it is better to take it as part of the condition, i.e., "and if the Lord shows himself to be my God . . ." (the presence of "Yahweh" here and in v. 20 is due to the redactor). Jacob's obligation will be the offering of the tithe (an explanation of the origin of a later custom; cf. Am 4:4).

(Delorme, J., "A propos du songe de Jacob," *A la rencontre de Dieu* [Fest. A. Gelin; LePuy, 1961] 47–54. Keller, C. A., "Über einige alttestamentliche Heiligtumslegende, I, C. Die Legende von Bethel," *ZAW* 67 [1955] 162–68.)

104 **(F) Jacob's Marriages (29:1–30) (J, E?).** Two scenes are presented here: the first is the arrival of Jacob at Laban's house and the latter's recognition of his kinsman (1–14); the second recounts Jacob's marriages to Leah and Rachel (15–30). The first is attributed to J; the style and vocabulary recall the similar account by J of Isaac's adventure in Aram-naharaim (cf. ch. 24). The attribution of the second to E is much less certain; the statement in v. 16 seems to suppose an account that had not referred to Rachel previously. It is almost certain that both traditional circles would have preserved the story of the marriages (the presence of E in chs. 29 and 31 would demand an E account); the redactor has chosen those parts of each which best suited his purpose. Although God is not referred to throughout the narrative, the larger context supplies the theology. God works through the ordinary events to accomplish his will. Jacob's marriages, natural enough in themselves, will be the necessary condition for the fulfillment of the divine promises.

105 (a) (29:1–14). **1.** The "people of the East" is a general reference to the nomadic tribes living E of Canaan (cf. 25:6). Since this designation of Laban's homeland is not usual in J some would attribute the verse to E (Clamer, *op. cit.*, 368–69). **2–3.** Wells are frequently the scenes of encounters among seminomadic groups. These verses indicate that the well was used by various groups and that certain formalities were observed in its use. The RSV conveys the sense more precisely. **4–6.** The term "brothers" (*'aḥay*) is used in a wide sense for kinsmen, or even for friends, as frequently in the Bible. Rachel (*rāḥēl*, "ewe lamb") is presented here as the daughter of Laban and granddaughter of Nahor (see comment on 24:15). **7–8.** Jacob's suggestion is perhaps occasioned by his desire to be alone with Rachel, but the shepherds must observe the formalities. **9–10.** Jacob's act, motivated by gallantry, emphasizes his extraordinary physical strength (perhaps a preparation for 32:25–29). **11–14.** The family reunion is very similar to that in 24:22–33. Jacob is the "relative" (*'āḥ*; cf. note on v. 4) of Rachel's father, i.e., his nephew. The expression "my flesh and bone" indicates close relationship (cf. 2:23).

106 (b) (29:15–30). **15.** Jacob's situation as Laban's relative was not covered by the regular customs governing the payment of workers; he was neither a slave nor an ordinary hired hand (Von Rad, *op. cit.*, 285). According to another suggestion, both parts should be translated as questions: "Are you my brother? Should you serve me for nothing?" It is implied that Jacob is not his brother and therefore should not serve him for nothing. Jacob loses his status in the family and becomes a hireling; Laban repudiates him (cf. D. Daube and R. Yaron, *JSemS* 1 [1956] 60–62). **16–17.** Leah (*lē'āh*, perhaps "cow") has weak or pale eyes, unattractive to Orientals. **18–19.** For the *mohar*, or "bride price," paid by the bridegroom, see De Vaux, *AI* 26–29. Seven years of service is a large price, indicating the intensity of Jacob's love. Laban's acceptance is ostensibly motivated by the desire, common in the ancient Near East, to have his daughter marry a kinsman; however, his future actions will betray other motives. **20–21.** Again Jacob's intense love is emphasized. After the seven years he claims his right. **22–23.** The custom of keeping the bride veiled (cf. 24:65) would be a sufficient reason for Jacob's failure to recognize Leah; the feast would have contributed to it. The author probably saw Laban's treachery as retribution for Jacob's similar treachery in 27:1–29. **24.** This verse disrupts the narrative and is considered an addition (perhaps by P) to prepare for 30:9ff. **25–28.** Laban's explanation of his act is reasonable but does not excuse his failure to tell Jacob of the custom beforehand. The nuptial celebrations last a week (cf. Jgs 14:10–17). **29.** Like v. 24, this verse is an addition. **30.** Leviticus 18:18 forbids the marriage to two sisters; this later law was unknown in patriarchal times. Ezekiel (ch. 23) portrays Judah and Israel as two sisters married to Yahweh, elaborating the figure in Jer 3:6–10; the prophets were aware of the ancient practice.

107 **(G) Jacob's Children (29:31–30:24) (J and E).** This section is also a composite of both J and E, but, unlike the one preceding, the two traditions are interwoven and not juxtaposed. The commentary will indicate the attribution of the verses. The birth of the 11 sons and one daughter is presented in a series of incidents which occasion the names given to the children. The etymologies, as usual, are popular ones; unlike others in Gn (e.g., 25:25–26), however, they do not refer to the tribes later descended from these sons, but rather to the individual situations narrated. These 11 sons, with Benjamin (cf. 35:16–18), will provide the connection between the patriarchs and the 12 tribes of Israel. This insistence on the number 12, persistent in all the accounts of the tribes, reflects the period when the 12 tribes formed the sacral amphictyony based on their common allegiance to Yahweh (cf. Noth, *Hist.* 85–108). The less evident insistence on 6 (the Leah group; cf. also 25:2) may reflect an earlier 6-tribe league to which others were later joined to make up 12. At any rate, the fact that the number 12 was rigorously adhered to despite the absorption of smaller tribes into larger ones, the substitution of one for another, and other historical occurrences indicate that 12 was sacrosanct (cf. Bright, *Hist.* 142ff.). Although the present composite passage reflects this later historical situation, the names are not necessarily purely eponymous. Sufficient evidence exists that the names of individuals could become the names of tribes (De Vaux, *RB* 53 [1946] 326).

That the sacred author does not intend a description of the tribes (the case in Gn 49) is evident both from the manner of the descriptions and from the actual irrelevance of the etymological explanations to the later tribal histories. The emphasis here is on the very human personalities and situations God uses to achieve his purposes. Very ancient incidents, passed down over the years, have been used to present this rather subtle but profound theology.

(Mowinckel, S., "'Rahelstämme' und 'Leahstämme,'" *Von Ugarit nach Qumrân* [Fest. O. Eissfeldt; Berlin, 1958] 129–50.)

108 (a) (29:31–35). **31.** This verse, as well as the remaining verses of the chapter, are from J, who sees the Lord's (Yahweh's) hand in the exaltation of the lowly and despised; Leah, rejected for the more favored Rachel, becomes the object of the divine mercy. The text states literally that Leah was hated; in the context, this language is legal terminology similar to that found in Dt 21:15–17. **32.** Reuben's name (*r*^{e}*'ûbēn*, "behold, a son") is explained, seemingly, as composed of *rā'āh b*^{e}*'onyî*, "he has looked on my affliction." The popular etymology is, in this case, rather farfetched. (For possible other earlier interpretations, cf. Clamer, *op. cit.*, 373–74.) **33.** Simeon (*šim'ôn*) is properly derived from the vb. *šāma'*, "to hear." God's "hearing" is again connected with Leah's rejection. **34.** Levi (*lēwî*) is connected with the vb. *lāwāh*, "to cleave to." **35.** The true etymology of Judah (*y*^{e}*hûdāh*) is unknown. It is here explained as coming from the vb. *yādāh*, "to praise" (*'ôdeh*, "I will praise").

109 (b) (30:1–13). **1–3.** The first eight verses of this chapter seem to derive from E (note "Elohim"), but with some mixture of J. Rachel's expedient (giving her slave girl to Jacob) has been noted before (16:1–2). The expression "bear on my knees" refers to the rite of adoption whereby the newly born child is placed on the lap of the adopting woman to indicate that she had legally borne the child. **4–6.** The fact that Rachel gives the name, instead of Bilhah, indicates her legal rights. The name "Dan" (*dān*) is connected with the first part of Rachel's statement, "God has pronounced judgment in my favor" (*dānannî*). The second part of the statement may indicate the remnant of another tradition explaining Simeon's name ("he has heard," *šāma'*; *BPl* 1, 96). **7–8.** The name of Naphtali (*naptālî*) is derived from the verb *pātal* (in Niphal, "to wrestle"). The text reads, lit., "I have wrestled great wrestlings (or "wrestlings of God," with *Elohim* used as a superlative; cf. 1:2) with my sister." **9–11.** Verses 9–13 seem to come, for the most part, from J. Zilpah, Leah's maid, is also given to Jacob. Her first son is called Gad (*gād*, "good fortune"; the Syrians worshiped a god of good fortune called Gad; cf. Is 65:11) because of Leah's exclamation, "What good fortune!" (*b*^{e}*gād*; *bāgād* in the MT has been interpreted by some variants as *bā' gād*, i.e., "good fortune has come"). **12–13.** The name of Zilpah's second son, Asher (*'āšēr*), is derived from the word for happiness (*'ešer*; only in pl.). This name, too, may be that of a Syrian god (cf. Clamer, *op. cit.*, 375–76f.).

110 (c) (30:14–24). **14–15.** It is not always possible to distinguish clearly the two traditions in the remainder of this section (vv. 14–24), but vv. 14–16 belong to J. The reference to the wheat harvest, one of the rare agricultural notes in Gn (De Vaux, *La Genèse*, 138), suggests a different provenance for this story. Mandrakes (*dûdā'îm*, from the same root as *dôd*, "loved one") were considered aphrodisiacs by the ancients. **16.** Leah's statement that she has "bargained" (*śākōr ś*^{e}*kartîkā*) for Jacob is an implicit explanation of Issachar's name. **17–18.** The E tradition explains the name of Issachar (*yiśśākār* or *yiśśākār*) as Leah's reward (*ś*^{e}*kārî*) from God. The more theological explanation is typical of E; there is no connection with the rather profane story of the mandrakes. **19–20.** Both J and E provide explanations for the name of Zebulun (*z*^{e}*bulûn*). According to E, God has bestowed a gift (*zābad*) on Leah; according to J, Leah's husband will now "dwell with" or "honor" her (*zābal*). **21.** The daughter's name, Dinah (*dînāh*, from the same root as Dan), is not explained. The author is concerned solely with the sons. **22–24.** Rachel, who had bargained for the mandrakes with the view to using every possible means to obtain a child, finally does conceive.

But the incident of the mandrakes is forgotten; it is God who remembers and makes her fruitful. The child's name is given a double etymology. According to E, God (Elohim) has taken away (*'āsap*) Rachel's reproach; thus, the child is called Joseph (*yôsēp*). According to J, Rachel prays that the Lord (Yahweh) will add (*yōsēp*) another son, an anticipation of the birth of Benjamin (35:16–18).

111 **(H) Jacob Outwits Laban (30:25–43) (J, E).** The literary analysis of this story is even more difficult than that of the preceding. Apparently J provided the basic narrative to which the redactor added portions of E. The resulting conflation presented certain inconsistencies which later copyists compounded. Twice Jacob asks permission to leave (vv. 25 and 26); twice he refers to his service (vv. 26 and 29); twice Laban asks what he should pay (vv. 28 and 31). Moreover, it is difficult to know just precisely what agreement was made between the two concerning the division of the flocks. (For a tentative division of the traditions, see Clamer, *op. cit.*, 378.)

Despite these and other difficulties (which also illustrate how the ancient authors used their sources), the general meaning of the story is clear. It is this meaning which the author wished to emphasize. The fertility of Jacob's wives is paralleled by the fertility of his flocks. Although in both cases the most natural means were employed, the larger context of both J and E, and especially of the redactor, declares that God's promises were being fulfilled. The historical circumstances which reveal his action are not the artificially contrived ones of a mythical world but the ordinary ones of the real world.

112 (a) (30:25–34). **25–28.** The doublets in these verses have already been mentioned. The conversation between Jacob and Laban presupposes certain legal issues. Jacob's wives and children still belong to Laban (cf. 31:43); Jacob, although not a slave (in which case, see Ex 21:4–6), is not in his own homeland and thus has no legal claims in this community. While Laban could rightfully send Jacob home empty-handed, he is aware of an obligation that is beyond the ordinary level of law. He has "surmised" (*niḥaštî*, lit., "I have divined," or "I have ascertained by divination," perhaps used here in a broad sense) that God (Yahweh in the MT) blessed him because of Jacob. Laban's superstitious fear of offending such a divinity urges him to show his gratitude; his Oriental craftiness cautions him not to be too hasty. **29–31.** Aware of Laban's superstitious fear, Jacob elaborates on the blessings that the Lord has poured on him ever since his arrival. Asked what the price would be, Jacob answers that he wants nothing of all that he has already obtained for Laban. He proposes, rather, to continue tending the flocks, but under new conditions. **32–34.** Behind the conditions is the fact that most lambs were white and most goats dark-colored. Jacob proposes that the speckled goats and black lambs be separated from the flock, thereby greatly increasing the odds against the birth of such animals from the regular flock. He would take as his wages only those "irregulars" born of the regular flock. Not only would this be greatly advantageous to Laban, but it would be a simple matter to check Jacob's honesty (v. 33; the verse reads, lit., "my honesty [or 'conformity to the agreement'] will answer for me").

113 (b) (30:35–43). **35–36.** Laban, having accepted the agreement, shows his extremely cautious nature by giving the "irregulars" to the care of his sons and separating them, by a three-day journey, from the "regulars." **37–39.** Jacob's actions presuppose the popular belief that the nature of the offspring is at least partially determined by external influences on the mother at the time of conception. Therefore the female lambs watching the striped boughs at the time of conception would conceive striped offspring. **40.** This difficult verse reads, lit., "And Jacob set apart the lambs (and he set the faces of the flock toward the striped and all the black in Laban's flock) and constituted a flock for himself alone and did not place them with Laban's flock." By omitting the words in parentheses, apparently those of a copyist, the verse follows a bit more clearly from what preceded. **41–43.** Not only did Jacob manage to acquire a large flock, but also, by employing his stratagem only with the best of the flock, he obtained a hardy breed of "irregulars." The concluding verse is a typical expression of a seminomad's wealth (cf. 12:16; 24:35). Without impairing his honesty, a point that would have delighted the ancient narrators of this story, Jacob has succeeded in outwitting his wily opponent. For the inspired author, it is all part of the divine plan.

114 **(I) Jacob's Departure (31:1–21) (E, J).** Both J and E would have preserved an account of Jacob's departure. In the present passage, J is represented only by a few verses (1, 3, and 21); the remainder, except for a few touches, is from E. This delineation is clear from the repeated use of *Elohim*, the reference to dreams as the medium of divine communication, the use of the "angel of God" to bring the divine message, and other considerations. The whole content of this section is intimately connected with the preceding story and must have formed an original unit with it in the E document.

The theology is much more explicitly stated than in the preceding J narrative, E generally being more scrupulous in this regard than J, who frequently lets his readers discover the divine plan. Perhaps it was to provide a more explicit theology for all that went before that the redactor chose to emphasize the E account here.

115 (a) (31:1–13). **1–5.** In vv. 1 and 3, J presents two reasons for Jacob's departure: the attitude of Laban's sons toward him because of his newly acquired riches (v. 1); the Lord's (Yahweh's) express command (v. 3). E presents here only the first reason (vv. 2 and 5); he develops the second (cf. v. 13b) by an extended narrative. J is more concerned with the future divine protection of Jacob (v. 3b); E, with his greater moral sensitivity, is concerned to justify Jacob's past actions ("God... *has been* with me," v. 5b). **6–9.** That Jacob should justify himself before his wives is understandable because of their continuing relationship to Laban (cf. v. 43). He must persuade them that God has acted through him if he wants them to accompany him; the later reaction of Laban's "family" to the flight (cf. vv. 23, 31, and 43) shows that the wives could, and normally even would, have remained at home. In his speech, Jacob first points out Laban's trickery (v. 7; from the evidence available in chs. 29–30, this version is somewhat exaggerated by Jacob) and then recounts God's reversal of Laban's plans in Jacob's favor. Verse 8 is considered by some to be a gloss explaining the change in pay mentioned in v. 7; it does not agree with 30:32–42. However, it may refer to a development of E not preserved in ch. 30. **10–12.** Jacob had dreamed that the he-goats were all speckled; in other words, the majority of the offspring would be of this same color. The following verses show that this dream was of divine provenance and hence a certain indication of its veracity. (Verses 10 and 12 do not follow clearly in the story and could be omitted without difficulty. They were probably added by a redactor who wished to make the point quite clear [De Vaux, *La Genèse*, 143]. Moreover, it is unusual that a message should be delivered in v. 12 before the identification in v. 13.) As usual in E, God does not himself appear, but an angel (v. 13, however, shows that the angel is a literary device). **13.** The words "who appeared to you at" are from the LXX and are not in the MT. Some feel that it is easier to explain their omission than their later insertion and so consider them original. The allusion is to 28:10–22. The condition of Jacob's vow (cf. 28:20–21) has been fulfilled; he is to return home (cf. v. 3).

116 (b) (31:14–21). **14–16.** The wives reply in a series of questions. They are, for all practical purposes, strangers in this community. By not giving his daughters at least part of the bride price (he had "used up" all the money received through Jacob's services), Laban treated them as slaves who could only be sold outright (cf. De Vaux, *AI* 27). They see God's actions in favor of Jacob as a divine confirmation of their complaint. **17–18.** Verse 18 has characteristics of P, especially the mention of Paddan-aram (cf. 25:20; 28:2–7). **19.** The fact that Laban was busy shearing his flock was an extra advantage foreseen by Jacob. The household idols (*tᵉrāpîm*) were small cult objects that served, in this case at least, as family gods. Their theft will be a major source of Laban's indignation (cf. vv. 30–35). **20–21.** The expression "Jacob outwitted Laban" reads, lit., "Jacob stole [*wayyignōb*] the heart of Laban." It is probably intended as a parallel to Rachel's act of theft (*wattignōb*) in v. 19b. The rather unusual reference to Laban as "the Aramean" here and in v. 24 is a preparation for the contract between Jacob and Laban that would affect both peoples—Israelites and Arameans. The "river" is the Euphrates; Gilead is in the Transjordan highlands.

117 **(J) Laban's Pursuit (31:22–42) (E, J).** Again, E provides the major part of this passage which is a continuation of the preceding. The highly elaborate speeches betray the narrator's art; their final purpose is to highlight the innocence of Jacob and the protection accorded him by God. Thus, E has made his theology quite explicit; in the scene in Rachel's tent (vv. 33–35), he has presented his attitude toward pagan gods more subtly.

(a) (31:22–32). **22–23.** The "third day" may be a reference to 30:36. If Laban was able to reach Gilead in seven days, he could not have lived in Haran, which is associated with the Hebrews' ancestors in J and P (cf. 11:31–32; 12:4–5; 27:43; 28:10; 29:4). It would seem E places Laban's homeland further W, between Canaan and Mesopotamia, thus making Laban a nomadic shepherd of the area NE of Canaan (cf. 29:1). **24.** As usual, E has the message presented in a dream (cf. 31:10–11). "Anything at all" is, lit., "from good to evil," an expression of polarity similar to that found in 24:50 (cf. also 2:9,17). **25.** It is generally supposed that the name of the "hill country" in v. 25a has been omitted from the text. If the encounter took place on the modern Mt. Gilead (*Jebel Gelʿad*), it would have been S of the Jabbok, which does not seem to agree with 31:43–32:3 (cf. Clamer, *op. cit.*, 385). **26–30.** Laban's harangue is in accord with his character as depicted throughout the story. He begins with the condemnation of Jacob for having taken his daughters, legally still part of Laban's household. (Verse 27 is probably a remnant of the J tradition.) The superior number of his kinsmen (cf. v. 23) would give him a definite advantage in a struggle with a cob, but, because of the dream, he will do nothing about this complaint. He is still concerned, however, about the theft of his gods, which indicates the gravity of the matter. According to an Akkadian text from Nuzi, an adopted son could not have the father's gods if the latter has a son of his own (cf. *ANET* 219–20, but also M. Greenberg, *JBL* 81 [1962] 239–48). Seemingly the possession of the gods indicated legitimate inheritance. While Laban was willing to forfeit his daughters by reason of the divine command, he did not want Jacob to be his sole heir. **31.** Jacob's reply in this verse breaks the train of thought. Laban had already indicated that he would do nothing about his daughters; therefore, the verse is probably another remnant of J. **32.** Jacob is aware of the seriousness of the crime, but is ignorant of the theft.

118 (b) (31:33–42). **33–35.** All commentators point out the incisive irony of this scene which is narrated with consummate skill. On the surface, Laban alone is the victim of this ruse, but the ancient readers would not have missed the underlying ironical attack on the pagan idols. Not only are they unable to avoid this indignity (cf. Is 44:9–20), but they are in danger of being soiled because of Rachel's condition. The sacred idols become unclean (cf. Lv 15:19–20)! If Albright's contention that camels were not generally domesticated until the end of the 12th cent. is correct (cf. Albright, *AP* 206–207), then this scene would have been added to the ancient Jacob tradition. (Similarly, it would suggest that other references to camels in Gn are anachronistic.) **36–37.** Jacob's relief in Laban's inability to find the idols gives rise to a speech filled with indignation. It is Laban's turn to listen to accusations. **38–40.** The difficult life of a shepherd depicted here is authentic. According to Ex 22:12 and similar laws of ancient Near Eastern codes, if the custodian of the owner's animal could produce evidence that the animal was killed by a wild beast, he was exempted from making restitution (cf. also Am 3:12). Jacob did not even claim this right (v. 39). If these verses are from J, as some suppose, the humor of this statement is emphasized by Jacob's conduct in 30:25ff. **41.** Jacob sums up his charges. For the "change in pay," cf. 31:7–8. **42.** The personal God of Jacob's ancestors has intervened in his favor and kept him from being despoiled of everything (cf. v. 24). "The God whom Isaac fears" is, lit., "the fear [or 'terror'] of Isaac" (*paḥad yiṣḥāq*), a primitive name for God that occurs only here and in v. 53; in the context, it refers to the appearances of God that produced terror in those affected by them (cf. 28:17; 31:24,29; 35:5). Parallel forms are "the Mighty One of Jacob" (*'ăbîr yaʿăqōb*) and "the rock of Israel" (*'eben yiśrā'ēl*) in 49:24.

119 **(K) The Contract Between Jacob and Laban (31:43–32:3) (J and E).** The content of this passage concerns a pact made between Jacob and Laban. The literary analysis, however, reveals that the elements of two pacts have been conflated. The essence of the covenant in v. 50 concerns Laban's daughters, but in v. 52, it concerns the borders of the two contracting parties. There are two signs of the covenant: a memorial pillar in vv. 45, 51, and 52, and a heap of stones in vv. 46, 48, 51, and 52. A covenant meal is twice referred to (vv. 46 and 53). Finally, the two signs of the covenant result in two place names: Galeed (v. 48b) and Mizpah (v. 49a). Presumably the two traditions, J and E, have contributed to the present passage.

As a covenant between the two individuals, Jacob and Laban (cf. v. 50), it is part of the whole context of the relations between the two as described in the preceding chapters. The covenant referring to the boundaries (v. 52) can best be explained by a pact made between Israelite elements living in the Transjordan area in a later era and certain Aramean tribes living in the north. The frequent clashes between Aram and Israel in the later historical period are sufficient evidence for the likelihood of such an agreement.

In the theology of the inspired editor, both these covenants are part of the one divine plan for the eventual fulfillment of the promises made to Jacob. For this reason, the actions of both the individual patriarch and his descendants can be combined legitimately.

120 (a) (31:43–49). **43.** Throughout the story, there has seemed to be a conviction that, in some way, the daughters of Laban still belonged to him (cf. 30:26; 31:26; and see comment on 31:6–9,26–30). By what title Laban could make this claim is disputed. Von Rad considers it a *Ṣadiqa* marriage in which "the husband is released from his paternal confederation, while the wife remains in her father's family" (Von Rad, *op. cit.*, 306). Such would seem to be true in the case of Gideon (Jgs 8:31), but Rachel and Leah are more than concubines. **44.** Laban's proposal comes strangely after the preceding remark, an indication of editorial work. "The Lord" (Yahweh) does not appear in the MT. Possibly some words have been omitted. **45–46.** The two verses represent the two traditions, one referring to a memorial stela, the other to a heap of stones. Since in v. 49 it is Laban who gives the name to the place because of the monuments, and in v. 51 it is he who claims to have erected them, it is possible that a later copyist changed the name of Laban here to Jacob to attribute the initiative to Israel's ancestor. The eating in v. 46 refers to a covenant meal. **47.** The verse is considered a gloss by many commentators; it is more likely that the following verses (48–49) were part of the original text. The name Jegar-sahadutha (*yᵉgar śāhădûtā'*) is Aramaic for "heap of witness." Galeed (*gal'ēd*) is a Hebr term with the same meaning. **48–49.** The name Mizpah (*miṣpāh*) is connected by the author with the verb *yiṣep* ("he will watch"). There was probably a place named Mizpah in the area (it is a very common place name), and the popular etymology of the name found its way into one of the traditions; it is unexpected here. The identification is uncertain.

121 (b) (31:50–32:3). **50.** The verse contains the essence of the contract according to the one tradition. The Nuzi text referred to (see comment on 31:26) contains the stipulation that the adopted son will forfeit the inheritance if he marries another woman (*ANET* 220). This condition would serve to strengthen the position of the first wife. **51–52.** The fusion of the two traditions is evident, but the essence of the covenant here (v. 52b) concerns the transgression of the boundary lines between Aram and Israel. **53.** The word "judge" is plural in the MT, but singular in the LXX. The latter wished to avoid the semblance of polytheism and identified the god of Nahor with the God of Jacob. Similarly "the god [not "gods" as in the CCD] of their fathers" is a gloss added here for the same reason. The more primitive texts were less careful about these references to the gods of other peoples (cf. Jgs 24:11). The God of Jacob is here again given the name "the fear of Isaac" (cf. v. 42). **54.** The sacrificial meal was partaken of by the two to represent their unity in covenant. **32:1.** The LXX and the Vg have this verse as v. 55 of the preceding chapter and are thus one verse behind the MT throughout ch. 32. **2–3.** These two verses can be read as either the conclusion to the preceding story or the introduction to the one following. The short passage, the remnant of a longer piece describing the origin of the place name Mahanaim, was an originally independent narrative used by E to indicate that Jacob had once again returned to the land specially blessed by God's presence. The place is called Mahanaim (*maḥănāyim*, "the two camps," or "the place of the camp") because God's "army" (i.e., the "angels"; cf. Jos 5:13–15) was encamped (*maḥăneh*, "encampment") there.

122 **(L) Preparation for the Meeting with Esau (32:4–22) (J and E).** Unlike many of the preceding sections, the present one contains the two traditions, J and E, placed side by side. In v. 14a, we have a reference to Jacob's spending the night at the camp; the same reference occurs in v. 22b. What precedes these two references belongs to the corresponding tradition: vv. 4–14a to J; vv. 14b–22 to E. The mention of "Lord" (Yahweh) in v. 10 and the use of other words sufficiently identify J; the presence of E is mainly inferred.

The story of Jacob's preparations for the meeting with his presumably still angry brother has great significance for the inspired author of the whole account. The pact with Laban had successfully concluded one phase of Jacob's life that had been marked with some danger to him. The meeting with God's angels in the land of promise would seem to have augured well for the future, but the impending meeting with Esau could have disastrous results. The author has emphasized the tension in conflating the two traditions to prepare for the climactic scene of the struggle with the angel (32:23–31). Throughout the patriarchal narratives, we find this seemingly paradoxical mixture of contingent human events and the supernatural. It is the latter that gives the significance to all human history.

123 (a) (32:4–11). **4.** To prepare for a meeting that he knows must take place eventually, Jacob sends messengers to Esau. Seir is another name for Edom, the territory S of the Dead Sea and the traditional land of the Edomites, descendants of Esau. **5–6.** Jacob's message indicates his desire to appease his brother, whom he would naturally believe to be still angry over the affair of the birthright and blessing. He refers to Esau as "lord" and to himself as "your servant." The mention of his many possessions is probably intended to arouse the expectation of some recompense, which Jacob would be happy to make. **7–9.** The presence of Esau (Edom) in this area far to the N presents a problem in the history of the Jacob-Esau traditions (→ 94 above). The present text would presume that Esau's coming with 400 men was the result of his hearing of Jacob's arrival from the messengers. But this journey would have been close to 200 mi. (round trip) over very rough terrain. The whole context, therefore, supposes that Esau was in the neighborhood. Jacob reacts in fear. The division of his entourage into two camps (*maḥănôt*) another reference, here by J, to the place name Mahanaim) contrasts Jacob's shrewdness with Esau's superior strength, a constant juxtaposition in the traditions. **10–11.** Commentators point out the noncultic and nonpoetic nature of the prayer; it is "the free prayer of a layman" (Von Rad, *op. cit.*, 313). Addressing the personal God of his fathers—i.e., Yahweh—Jacob reminds him of the divine command to return and the promise of divine protection. He follows his statements with a prayer of thanksgiving in which he refers to his departure from Canaan with only a staff and his return with "two camps" (cf. v. 8). The reference to the Jordan suggests that the prayer is a later development of J's story; in the context, the reference would have been to the Jabbok River (cf. v. 23). By this prayer, J has artfully united all the traditions concerning Jacob's earlier and later life.

124 (b) (32:12–22). **12–14a.** The prayer reaches its climax in the explicit request for help and in the expression of the petitioner's anxiety. It is concluded with another reference to the divine promise—not the promise of personal salvation but rather that of a great posterity which would be nullified by the death of Jacob and all his family. In this prayer, J has beautifully woven the general patriarchal promise into the particular incident recorded. **14b–16.** Whereas in J the presentation of gifts was only suggested by Jacob's message, in E it is actually made. The word here used for "gift" (*minḥāh*) may be a punning reference to the place name, Mahanaim. For the wisdom of Jacob's strategy, see Prv 18:16; 19:6; 21:14. **17–20.** The details of the strategy are in keeping with the Oriental manner and, in particular, with Jacob's shrewdness. The successive appearance of each gift, instead of the expected Jacob himself, is designed to wear away gradually every trace of possible resentment, effecting a much greater psychological effect than would the outright single gift of the whole. **21–22.** Jacob explicitly mentions his purpose; it is to "appease" Esau, or, lit., "cover his face." The term (*kāpar*) is a technical one in Lv for the expiation of sin. As in the J account (v. 14a), Jacob spends the night in the camp.

125 **(M) Jacob's Struggle with God (32:23–33) (J).** While the presence of doublets in vv. 23–24 (a double crossing of the river) and again in vv. 31, 32–33 (the two names "Peniel" and "Penuel" and the double etiology) might argue for two separate traditions, many scholars insist on the unity of the account which they attribute to J. The unevenness could well result from the long prehistory.

This long history of the story in its precanonical form and the various interpretations given it in the successive stages are important for an appreciation of the author's use. The struggle of mysterious (divine) beings with man is a very common theme of ancient folklore. Frequently, these beings are presented as guarding the passage of a river, as being effective only during the night, and as being forced to reveal something to the human antagonist. The presence of all these elements and the extremely mysterious character of the entire story suggest that the later inspired author took over a very ancient piece of folklore that had already been subjected to several interpretations. One of the earliest would have been the etiological explanation of the place name, "Penuel." Traces of this and of the later etiological explanation found in vv. 32–33 have been preserved in the final form. But also quite early, and already in the patriarchal period, the story would have been applied to Jacob, since the issue of the combat revolves around his name. The Israelites would have known only this form of the story.

This tradition history can help us to determine the meaning intended by the author. Certainly the etiological explanations, while of some antiquarian interest to him, are by no means primary. Jacob's struggle with God (and there is no doubt that J thus identified the mysterious being) and the consequent change of his name are the dominant motifs. In the context of J's whole story, the incident takes on extreme importance in indicating a new era in the life of Israel's ancestor. Its place here, before his crossing over to Canaan, suggests a contrast with the theophany at Bethel (28:10–22) which had given meaning to his sojourn with Laban. This new theophany, with its particularly awesome character and significant result, will give meaning to his future life. His change of name implies a change of mission in life. The cunning Jacob becomes the divinely commissioned Israel, father of the chosen people and the special object of God's protection. The final author would also have seen in this story references to the destiny of the people who went by the name of their ancestor. The people Israel would have a constant reminder of their own "struggle with God," as well as of their mission as God's people in the total plan of salvation history.

(McKenzie, J. L., "Jacob at Peniel: Gn 32, 24–32," *CBQ* 25 [1963] 71–76. Schildenberger, J., "Jakobs nächtlicher Kampf mit dem Elohim am Jabok (Gn 32, 23–33)," *Miscellanea Biblica B. Ubach* [Fest. B. Ubach; Barcelona, 1953] 69–96. Van Trigt, F., "La signification de la lutte de Jacob près du Yabboq Gen xxxii 23–33," *OTS* 12 [1958] 280–309.)

126 (a) (32:23–29). **23–25.** Despite some unevenness in the account, the meaning is clear: The supernatural event can have no witnesses. The mysterious being (*'îš*, "a man") is identified only later. The word for "wrestled" (*'ābaq*) is used only in this passage, probably a play on the name of the river (*yabbōq*). **26–27.** The incident of the touching of the socket of the thigh seems to be an addition, with vv. 32b–33, to the primitive story; it disturbs the order of the account. The sacred author used it because he did not wish to imply a complete victory by Jacob. Jacob's request for a blessing indicates his identification of the person. **28–29.** In the popular etymology given here of "Israel" (*yiśrā'ēl*), the theophoric element is the object of the verb, most unusual for such names. The verb is here (and in Hos 12:4b) popularly derived from *śārāh*, "contend with." The name is given an enlarged interpretation ("and men") to indicate the struggles of Jacob (and, implicitly, of the people Israel) that will result in victory. Only in view of this new mission is Jacob's request for a blessing (cf. v. 27) granted.

127 (b) (32:30–33). **30–31.** Since the name is indicative of the bearer's nature or mission, as Jacob's changed name implies, the patriarch now wishes to know his antagonist's name. The latter's refusal to reveal it heightens his mysterious character, but Jacob realizes that it is God and names the place Peniel (*p*[e]*nî'ēl*), i.e., "face of God." Behind Jacob's statement is the conviction that man cannot see God and live. **32–33.** The form of the name given here, Penuel (*p*[e]*nû'ēl*), is the usual one; the other form (v. 31) was given to make the etymology clearer. The dietary proscription is a very ancient one the origins of which are now lost. An ancient author had found in the story an explanation of a taboo which Israel no longer observed.

128 **(N) Jacob's Meeting with Esau (33:1–20) (J, E?).** The passage is almost entirely from J, with possible traces of E (vv. 5 and 11). For the final author, the story illustrates, through the happy outcome of the feared encounter, the divine protection of the new Jacob. Jacob's meeting with God has influenced the meeting with Esau (v. 10). Just as Lot's departure for the Jordan Valley had prepared the way for Abram's unhampered possession of the land of promise (cf. 13:1–13), so Esau's departure for Edom prepares for the fulfillment of the promise made to Jacob.

(a) (33:1–11). **1–2.** The story in 32:4–22 is presumed; the transition from 32:23–33 is awkward. The division of the wives and children indicates their closeness in affection for Jacob; the less loved ones are placed in the front. **3–4.** The sevenfold prostration is known from the Amarna letters; it is a form of extreme reverence. The meeting, so greatly feared, is vividly described; it is a climactic moment for the author. The impulsive Esau (cf. 25:29–34) forgets the past in the emotion of the moment. **5–7.** Jacob's family is presented to Esau in the same order in which they had been deployed before the meeting. The reference to "God" (Elohim) in v. 5 points to E. **8–11.** The remonstrations over the gifts that Jacob presents to Esau are in the usual Oriental style. Note that Jacob calls Esau "my lord" in accord with his subservient attitude, but Esau uses the more laconic "my brother." Jacob likens the meeting to a meeting with God because of the pleasure it affords him and because of its happy outcome. The author intends an allusion to 32:23–33.

129 (b) (33:12–20). **12–16.** Jacob has not lost all his astuteness. Afraid of what might develop from too lengthy a stay with his brother, he finds an excuse for not accompanying Esau. Promising to follow him to Seir, Jacob goes W to Canaan instead. Nothing more in Gn is related to Esau. Salvation history is no longer concerned with him as an individual. **17.** The verse contains an etiological explanation of the same Succoth (*sukkôt*, "booths" or "sheds"), situated in the Jordan Valley near the Jabbok. **18.** The reference to Paddan-aram is an insertion from P. **19.** Jacob's purchase of land is similar in significance to Abram's (cf. ch. 23). The value of the sum mentioned is unknown. (On Shechem and the sons of Hamor, see ch. 34.) **20.** Instead of "altar" (*mizbēaḥ*), some read "memorial pillar" (*maṣṣēbāh*). It is erected in the name of the God of Israel, not, as among the pagans, in honor of a local god.

130 **(O) The Rape of Dinah (34:1–31) (J and E).** The literary analysis is most difficult. Most authors would argue for the presence of two traditions, J and E, with possible influences of P in the latter. In the presumed J tradition, Shechem pleads his own cause (v. 11), while in E, it is his father, Hamor (vv. 6 and 8–10). In J, Dinah's full brothers, Simeon and Levi, are the only avengers of the crime (vv. 25b–26 and 30–31); in E, all Jacob's sons take part (vv. 27–29a). In J, Shechem alone is circumcised (vv. 14 and 19); In E, all the males are circumcised (vv. 15, 22, and 24). In general, J stresses the individuals involved, while E stresses the relations between the two peoples (cf. vv. 9–10, 15–17, and 20–24). Therefore, the supposition of a double source is likely.

More significant is the tradition history of the narrative. Now linked to the preceding account by 33:18–20, and to that following by 35:2–4, the story was originally independent. The more common suggestion is that it reflects a treacherous attack on Shechem in the Tell el-Amarna period when Khapiru elements (here represented by the tribes of Simeon and Levi) took over the area (cf. *ANET* 489, letter 289). This theory would explain the later peaceful settlement of Israel in Shechem (cf. Jos 24, where no mention is made of a capture of the city; presumably it is occupied by friendly elements who now accept the covenant), the absence of archaeological evidence for the destruction of the city at the time of the conquest, and the presumed greatness of the tribes of Simeon and Levi in an earlier period. We would thus suppose, and it is commonly admitted, that not all the tribes descended into Egypt with Jacob at the time of the Hyksos control. Another view, accepting the same general interpretation of the story as an account of a conflict between ethnic groups, would refer it to an earlier period. Hamor is considered a Horite, or Hurrian (the word "Hivite" in v. 2 is rendered "Horite" in the LXX), a people probably connected with the Hyksos movement. The story would concern a conflict between this Hurrian-Hyksos group at Shechem and Semitic invaders, Jacob and his family (cf. E. Campbell, *BA* 26 [1963] 7–8). In either case, the incident provided an explanation for the later destinies of the tribes of Simeon and Levi—the absorption of the former into the tribe of Judah and the latter's failure to acquire a portion of the land (cf. Gn 49:5–7). Jacob's role is secondary throughout the passage, suggesting its later incorporation into the Jacob cycle.

(Lehming, S., "Zur Überlieferungsgeschichte von Gen 34," *ZAW* 70 [1958] 228–50.)

For the later inspired author of Gn, the story has its place in the theology of the patriarchal narratives. The promise of the land is gradually fulfilled, at times through purely natural circumstances (cf. 33:19–20), but the fulfillment is not without its dangers to Israel's faith. It will involve some contact with indigenous pagan elements. While this is unavoidable, Israel must guard against compromise to her faith.

131 (a) (34:1–12). **1–5.** As in 33:19, Shechem is here the name of an individual, although elsewhere in the OT it is the name of the city strategically located in central Canaan between Mt. Ebal and Mt. Gerizim. Its history as a local political and military power began around 1800 (cf. Campbell, *op. cit.*, 4–5), and is known from both biblical and extrabiblical sources (cf. B. W. Anderson, *BA* 20 [1957] 10–19; W. Harrelson, *BA* 20 [1957] 2–10 = *BAR* 2, 258–74) to have exerted considerable influence during much of Israel's history. The name of Hamor, here Shechem's father, is a Semitic word for "ass." Mari documents reveal an Amorite covenant ritual in which an ass was slaughtered. The "sons of Hamor," therefore, are probably members of such an "ass-covenant" (cf. Campbell, *op. cit.*, 7–8; cf. Jgs 9:4,46). **6–12.** The word used in v. 7 for the violation of Dinah is an especially strong one (*n*ᵉ*bālāh*; cf. Jgs 19:22–24; 20:6), suggesting a sacrilege that involved the whole covenant community (Von Rad, *op. cit.*, 327). The later demand of Jacob's sons that the Shechemites be circumcised, a religious practice in Israel, strengthens this suggestion. "Israel" is here anachronistically depicted (v. 7) as already constituting the covenant people. Note that in the E account (vv. 6 and 8–10), the bargaining is done by Hamor, who suggests a general *connubium* between the two peoples, while in the J account (vv. 7 and 11–12), Shechem alone is involved in both the bargaining and in the proposed marriage.

132 (b) (34:13–24). **13–19.** The word "deceitfully" in v. 13 implies a moral judgment (Von Rad, *op. cit.*, 328) by the author who is uneasy about the tactics of Jacob's sons. The uncircumcised Shechemites are not part of the Semitic Canaanite population, which partially confirms their Hurrian (non-Semitic) origin. The acceptance of circumcision, a religious rite, may have involved an acceptance of Israel's faith if the expression "one people" (v. 16) is understood in a religious sense. The reference to "our daughter" in v. 17 is strange in the mouths of Dinah's brothers, but it may have been influenced by the same expression in v. 16 where it is more intelligible. In v. 19, Shechem is said to carry out the proposal, i.e., to be circumcised, without delay; it is part of J (with v. 14). In E (vv. 13 and 15–18), the whole community is involved. **20–24.** The passage is attributed to E and supposes that the proposal of circumcision must still be approved by the community. Hamor plays the dominant role (some consider "and his son Shechem" in vv. 20,24 an addition by the later editor who fused the two traditions). The speech makes no mention of the actual occasion of the proposal; it stresses, rather, the advantages to the Shechemites of having the sons of Jacob with all their cattle as members of the community.

133 (c) (34:25–31). **25–29.** The story in J reached its climax with the attack on the city by Dinah's two full brothers, Simeon and Levi (vv. 25–26). The circumcision would have produced the greatest discomfort for the adult males on the third day. Hamor and Shechem are slain and Dinah rescued, which reveals the original intent of the brothers in making the proposal. In vv. 27–29, E adds the sacking of the city by all the sons of Jacob. Archaeology has discovered the remnants of an ancient wall of the Hyksos period (Campbell, *op. cit.*, 4–5), suggesting that a military campaign, at least on a small scale, would have been required. **30–31.** Jacob's remonstrance, based on the possible subsequent danger to him and his family, reflects a mild disapproval of the sons' actions. But the final verse shows that the author's sympathy is with Jacob's sons, who avenged, in a manner not unusual for seminomadic tribes, a crime against Israel. Jacob's statement can also be seen as a reason for his leaving the area, and, therefore, as a preparation for the following story.

134 **(P) Jacob at Bethel (35:1–29) (E and P).** This chapter concludes the Jacob cycle. It is a collection of stories from the three traditions represented in Gn.

The incidents related have little connection with one another; some joyful, some sorrowful, they tie up the loose ends of the Jacob story and prepare for the Joseph cycle in ch. 37.

The first section can be generally divided into two blocks: 1–8 from the E tradition; 9–15 from P (with the possible exception of 14–15). The final editor here stresses the religious concerns of the "new" Jacob (1–8) and his prominent place in salvation history (9–15).

135 (a) (35:1–8). **1–4.** The departure for Bethel is here attributed to a direct command from God. Jacob is to build an altar at the place of the theophany (cf. 28:10–22). Before the departure, an act of purification takes place in which the people hand over pagan cult objects, such as household idols (cf. 31:19,30–35) and earrings used as amulets, and change their clothes to symbolize their interior renewal. The whole symbolizes the renunciation of all that is profane, and, positively, is an act of faith in the one God (cf. Jos 24:9–24). Behind this description, many commentators (cf. especially A. Alt, *KS* 1, 79–88) see a reference to a regular pilgrimage by ancient Israel from Shechem to Bethel in the period of the Judges. The origin of the pilgrimage may be the transference of the ark from the central sanctuary at Shechem (Jos 24) to Bethel (cf. Jgs 20:26–28; cf. also J. A. Soggin, *ZAW* 73 [1961] 78–87). **5.** This verse serves as the link between E's story of the departure and the preceding narrative (cf. especially 34:30), according to which some reprisal by the local inhabitants would have been expected. The "great fear" is literally "a terror of [from] God," perhaps suggesting some extraordinary phenomenon. For the author, it is a sign of the divine protection of the patriarch who has constantly been with Jacob (cf. v. 3b). **6–7.** (For Luz, see comment on 28:19.) The origin of Bethel as an Israelite shrine is here attributed to Jacob who builds an altar, just as Abram once had (12:8). This attribution of the origin of the sanctuary to the two great patriarchs indicates its later importance. The Hebr text (corrected by the versions) has the vb. "appeared" in the plural; the "elohim" would then refer to the heavenly beings of 28:12. **8.** This brief notice is entirely unexpected. Rebekah's nurse (cf. 24:59) would hardly be associated with Jacob. Perhaps an independent tradition, connected with the area, was inserted here because of the geographical proximity. Some suggest a connection between the prophetess Deborah's palm tree of Jgs 4:5, situated between Ramah and Bethel, and the oak tree of this verse.

136 (b) (35:9–15). **9–13.** We recognize P by "Paddan-aram" in v. 9, "God Almighty" (*'ēl šadday*) in v. 11, and the overtly theological nature of the passage. The only other fairly extensive passage that has been preserved of the story of Jacob in P is 27:46–28:9, with which we might compare this. The change of name in v. 10, without explanation, contrasts strongly with the version in 32:22–31, although P is not adverse to explaining such changes (cf. 17:5). The twofold promise of the land and posterity is couched in terminology typical of P (cf. 17:4–8). An incongruity is noted in the command to "be fruitful and multiply"; Jacob is already the father of 11 sons! **14–15.** Verse 14 is generally recognized as the original conclusion of E's story, now placed here by the editor to form a conclusion to the conflated passages. There is an evident similarity to 28:18 which may have influenced its addition to the story of the pilgrimage account. Others think it follows on 35:8 and describes a funerary rite, parallel examples of which are found in Assyro-Babylonia, Egypt, Greece, and among the Arabs (Chaine, *op. cit.*, 363–64). In this case, the words "where God has spoken with him" would be a gloss influenced by the same words in v. 15. The statement in v. 15, more commonly considered P's conclusion (Von Rad, *op. cit.*, 332, attaches it to E, confirming the opinion that the whole is a parallel narrative to 28:10–22), is the third mention of the naming of Bethel (cf. 28:19; 35:7), each linked to a separate incident. It is another indication of the shrine's importance to Israel's national memory. The final editor, who has preserved all these traditions, clearly accepts this importance.

137 (c) (35:16–29). **16–20.** The present scene (the passage is attributed to E) takes place at Ephratha, situated near Ramah in Benjaminite territory according to 1 Sm 10:2 and Jer 31:15. This location agrees with the context (Benjaminite Ephratha is not too far from Bethel) and with the presumption that the mother's tomb would be venerated in the territory of the tribe descended from her (cf. J. A. Soggin, *VT* 11 [1961] 432–40). The presence of an Ephrathite clan in Bethlehem of Judah (cf. Ru 1:2; 2 Chr 2:50–51) would explain the later tradition of Rachel's tomb being located there, and also the gloss in Gn 35:19 and 48:7. The son born to the dying Rachel is a fulfillment of her wish expressed on the occasion of the birth of her first-born, Joseph (cf. 30:24). The child's name as given by Rachel is hardly auspicious (*ben'ōnî*, "son of my affliction") and is quickly changed by Jacob to the more auspicious *binyāmîn*, i.e., "son of my right hand," since the right side was considered the place of honor. The erection of the memorial pillar may have been accompanied by other funerary rites (cf. v. 14). Such rites, widely practiced, were later discouraged because of possible pagan connotations; Israelite law makes no provision for the practices (Dt 26:14 implies some repugnance to them). **21–22a.** The location of Migdal-eder (tower of the flock) is not known. The account of Reuben's incest is incomplete; the mention of Jacob's reaction would be expected at least. But the editor would have included it, even if incomplete, because of its bearing on 49:3–4. The reference to Jacob as "Israel" indicates that the primitive story had already taken on tribal proportions. **22b–26.** P's list of the 12 sons of Jacob is in general accord with chs. 29–30. Verse 26b would seem to suppose that Benjamin was also born in Paddan-aram, but it may be just a generalization. **27–29.** P, who has preserved very little of the Jacob story (cf. 27:46; 28:1–9; 35:9–13), here concludes the cycle with the accounts of Jacob's return to Hebron, the death of Isaac (cf. 27:1–5!), and his burial by his two sons. This oversimplification of the complex events stresses the transcendent simplicity of salvation history in P; human history takes on an unsuspected unity by reason of the divine plan.

138 **(Q) The Descendants of Esau (36:1–43) (P?).** As in 25:12–18, where the descendants of Ishmael are given after the account of Abraham's death to prepare for the history of Isaac and Jacob, so here the final author has summed up the descendants of Esau to prepare for the history of Joseph. This chapter, however, is much more complex. It contains six distinct lists (vv. 1–8, 9–14, 15–19, 20–30, 31–39, and 40–43) attributable, for the most part, to P (Von Rad considers the first three and the last as P; Von Rad, *op. cit.*, 339), but all reflecting originally distinct and ancient sources. Their great age is confirmed by the divergences.

The very completeness of the lists attests to the interest of Israel in her "brother" nation. Throughout her history Israel had relations with Edom, at times peaceful but more often warlike, which considerably affected salvation history. The author, not unaware of this, presents these lists with the names of all Esau's descendants to suggest Edom's importance from the human viewpoint. But despite this importance, the Lord "loved Jacob, but hated Esau" (Mal 1:3). Many commentators, therefore, see an ironical note contained here.

139 (a) (36:1–19). **1–8.** The word "descendants" (*tōlᵉdôt*) is characteristic of P. The names of Esau's wives and their daughters differ considerably from 26:34 and 28:9, even though all are attributed to P. The differences simply reflect separate tradition histories; the similarities point to a common origin. Their historical accuracy did not concern P. The account of the separation of Esau and Jacob (vv. 6–7), while not in agreement with the J and E story of the two brothers, recalls the separation of Lot from Abraham (13:5–12). The land of promise belongs to Jacob by divine right as it did to Abraham. Esau settles in Seir, an ancient name (it appears in the Amarna letters; cf. *ANET* 488) for the territory S of Canaan, inhabited by the Edomites (see comment on 25:25). **9–14.** This list contains the same names of Esau's wives and children as the first. It differs in calling Esau the "father of Edom" (v. 9; cf. v. 1), and in naming the grandchildren of Adah and Basemath. The first difference is explained by the fact that in v. 1 Esau is considered the eponymous ancestor of the Edomites, and the second, by the fact that the list originally described a 12-tribe amphictyony (there are twelve names, excluding the illegitimate Amalek, as in 25:12–16 [Ishmael] and 35:22b–26 [Jacob-Israel]). "Reuel" appears later as the name of Moses' father-in-law (Ex 2:18). Timna is a place in Edom (Am 1:12; etc.). Kenaz is the eponymous ancestor of the Kenizzites (Gn 15:19). Amalek is the father of the Amalekites, who inhabited the general area between Canaan and Egypt and are prominent in the story of the Exodus (cf., e.g., Ex 17:8–16). **15–19.** This list parallels the preceding, with only slight variations (Timna is here the son of Adah). Attributed to P, its primitive origin is possibly Edomite. The Hebr word used here for "chiefs" (*'allûp*) is applied only to Edomite (and Hurrian) leaders (cf. vv. 29–30 and 40–43; Ex 15:15).

140 (b) (36:20–43). **20–30.** This list is almost completely different from the preceding. It gives the genealogy of Seir, the eponymous ancestor of the inhabitants of Seir, the ancient name of Edom. He is identified here as a Horite, or Hurrian. The presence of this non-Semitic group in Canaan and to the S is attested to by several Egyptian texts (see also Bright, *Hist.* 55–56, 106–107). Although Dt 2:12,22 supposes that they were dispossessed by the Edomites, the evidence suggests a mixture of the races, confirmed by this list (De Vaux, *La Genèse*, 163). The reoccurrence of Timna (v. 22) and Oholibamah (v. 25) can be noted. The "hot springs" of v. 24, if a correct translation of the hapaxlegomenon, reflect the area of the Dead Sea and give an authentic note to the whole. **31–39.** This ancient list of Edomite kings existed at least as early as the Israelite monarchy (cf. v. 31), and attests to an elective kingship in early Edom (the kings are not of the same dynasty and their capitals correspond to the cities of their origin). Israel may have been influenced by Edom in this regard in initiating her own kingship. Verse 31 can be translated to mean that these kings ruled before Israel had a king (therefore before Saul), or before an Israelite king ruled over Edom (i.e., David; cf. 2 Sm 8:14). Some commentators suggest that the first king, Bela (v. 32) is the same as Moses' contemporary, the diviner Balaam (cf. Nm 22:5). The last king, Hadar ("Hadad" according to the parallel list in 1 Chr 1:43–50), would conceivably be the one conquered by David, which could explain the more complete information concerning his family (v. 39). Among the theophoric elements contained in the names can be mentioned the Syrian god Hadad, the Phoenician Baal, and the Canaanite El ("Mehetabel," v. 39). **40–43.** Some of the names contained here are the same as those in vv. 15–30; the rest are seemingly place names, in accord with the remark in v. 40. Clamer (*op. cit.*, 417) suggests that the mixture of place names and clan names corresponds to political or administrative divisions, rather than to the earlier tribal divisions. This later division would have been inaugurated after the fall of the Edomite monarchy. The designation of Esau as the "father of the Edomites" (v. 43) is the same as in the second list (cf. v. 9) and may indicate the same compiler.

141 **(IV) The History of Joseph (37:1–50:26).** The final section of Gn, while it presents a logical continuation of the preceding patriarchal history, is at the same time remarkably different in style and content. Its literary genre has been likened to that of the wisdom literature (Egypt was noted for this genre and had early developed an extensive literature): Joseph is a typical wise man, whose humility in the exercise of power, forgiving spirit, and fear of God reflect the ideal of all Israel. Also, the development of the story without the direct intervention of God and without the revelation of new truths contrasts with the preceding sections; here the message is contained in the story itself and is seen as a profound teaching on the ways of divine providence which brings seemingly ill-fated events to a happy conclusion (cf. 50:19–20). Accordingly, the section cannot be broken down into originally independent narratives; each scene develops logically from the one preceding (only chs. 38 and 49 are intrusive).

Joseph's history has been preserved by both J and E (P is noted in only a relatively few places). The presence of doublets and occasional breaks, however, does not detract notably from the flow of the narrative which has been artfully developed to present a connected series of dramatic scenes involving true-to-life persons.

By content also, this section differs from the preceding sections. Etiological explanations of names and customs, eponymic reflections of later Israelite history, and concern for the origins of sanctuaries and cultic practices have all given way to a continuous narrative about an individual and his fortunes in a foreign land. While some development of the narrative in the course of its tradition history is likely, there is no reason to question the basic historical framework. The picture of Egyptian life and customs in the 2nd millennium is authentic. That it is the Egypt of the Hyksos period has been frequently suggested, which would explain many of the details, but the evidence is not conclusive (cf. Bright, *Hist.* 77–78).

Despite the contrasts with the stories of Abraham, Isaac, and Jacob, the history of Joseph is not independent of the former on the level of salvation history. It presents the divine plan's concluding stage for preparing the constitution of the chosen people. The same God as before is at work directing the fortunes of the patriarch. The theme of the promised land is emphasized, even though the story itself takes place in Egypt (cf. 47:29–31; 48:21; 50:4ff.). The inclusion by the final editor of the two "intrusive" chs. 38 and especially 49 underlines the common patriarchal themes.

(Kaiser, O., "Stammesgeschichtliche Hintergründe der Josephsgeschichte," *VT* 10 [1960] 1–15. Montet, P., *L'Égypte et la Bible* [Cahiers d'Archéologie biblique 11; Neuchâtel, 1959]. Vergote, J., *Joseph en Égypte* [Orientalia et biblica Lovaniensia 3; Louvain, 1959].)

142 **(A) Joseph Sold into Egypt (37:1–36) (J and E).** The presence of repetitions and doublets attests to the twofold tradition used by the author, but the conflation has been so skillfully done that, except for a few passages, there is no universal agreement as to the precise division of the sources. Seemingly J is the basic tradition. Theologically, this incident takes up a theme noted before, especially in the story of Jacob: The youngest son, contrary to expectations, becomes the instrument of divine providence for the execution of the plan. Moreover, the connection of Jacob's deception by his sons with Isaac's deception by Jacob was not unintended by the author. These human elements bring out more clearly the providential disposition of the events.

(a) (37:1–4). **1–2.** The first verse is attached by many to the preceding chapter and is seen as a contrast to Esau's dwelling in the land of Edom (cf. 36:8). The place is not mentioned, but according to P in 35:29, it would be Hebron. The second verse, also from P, contains the formula frequently used to introduce a new section, *tōl*ᵉ*dôt*, i.e., "family history" (the obvious use of the term here in a much wider sense than "generations" would give added significance to its use in 2:4a). What follows is called the "family history" of Jacob, although the center of the entire narrative is Joseph. However, the history of the sons is conceived as the history of the father, as long as he lives (see comment on 25:19). The rest of the verse contains a truncated account of P's version of what happened. Joseph, pasturing the flocks with his half-brothers, Dan, Naphtali, Gad, and Asher (cf. 35:25–26), brought home an evil report concerning them. This account seems the better understanding of *dibbātām* (which could mean "their report" or a "report about them"), for whatever P's original meaning may have been, the final author used this remnant to introduce the note of strained relations between Joseph and his brothers. **3–4.** These lines from J (cf. "Israel" as in 35:21, also from J) mark the true beginning of the story. Here the cause of the brothers' hatred is Jacob's preferential love for Joseph, the son of his old age. The love was expressed in the gift of a special tunic of a length that characterised it as a robe worn by royalty (cf. 2 Sm 13:18). The LXX and the Vg translated the difficult *passim* as "many colored"; the CCD version is better.

143 (b) (37:5–17). **5–11.** The immediate cause of the brothers' hatred is given as Joseph's dreams and their interpretation (vv. 8 and 11), indicating another source, E. The dreams, which always appear in double form in the Joseph story (cf. chs. 40–41), probably to emphasize their import, are seen as divine manifestations of the future. Unlike other dreams reported by E (cf. 20:3; 28:10ff.; 31:10–13,22–24), there is no direct address from God. The theological element is thus more subtly introduced. The reference to the sheaves of wheat agrees with seminomadic customs (see comment on 26:12). The first dream foretells Joseph's elevation over his brothers in Egypt, although later Israel may have seen an allusion to the hegemony of the house of Joseph in the period of the amphictyony. The second dream includes Joseph's parents (the "sun" and "moon") in the act of worship. The implied references to Rachel do not agree with 35:16–20, which may indicate an independent origin of the stories, a later arrangement of them producing an anachronism, or, simply, an adaptation of the facts to the elements of the dream. Jacob's reprimand of Joseph (v. 10) and his "pondering" of the matter emphasize the theological significance of the dreams. **12–17.** The geographical references complicate the analysis. Apparently dwelling in Hebron (cf. v. 14b), the brothers pasture their flock in Dothan, close to 100 mi. distant over very rough terrain. Also, the reference to Shechem seems to ignore the story of ch. 34 and the resulting enmity of the Shechemites (cf. 34:30; 35:5). It is an indication of the complex nature of the history of these various traditions. The present passage gives no indication of Jacob's awareness of the danger in Joseph's rendezvous with his brothers, which might argue for a source (J) different from that of the preceding. The aimless wandering of Joseph, minutely described, suggests "the dangers which beset Joseph from the beginning" (Von Rad, *op. cit.*, 347–48). Dothan is located about 20 mi. N of Shechem.

144 (c) (37:18–27). **18–20.** From this point, the two traditions are interwoven in such a way as to make their identification most difficult. These verses (except possibly v. 18b) are evidently connected with vv. 5–11 and assigned to E. Joseph is called a *ba'al haḥălōmôt*, which implies more than "man of dreams." Because of the divine significance attributed to dreams by the ancients, the brothers would consider them effective so long as the one who pronounced them was alive (Von Rad, *op. cit.*, 348). The use of cisterns as prisons is known from Jer 38; they were usually dry toward the end of summer. **21–24.** In the section that follows, both Reuben and Judah are credited with the attempt to save Joseph, a witness to the two traditions, J and E. Many commentators prefer to read "Judah" in v. 21 (J) instead of "Reuben," who would be the speaker in v. 22 (E). A redactor, or possibly the final author, would have made the changes to avoid the too evident confusion arising from the conflation. Also, v. 23 is attributed to J because of the reference to the tunic (cf. vv. 3–4), and v. 24 to E because of the mention of the cistern (cf. v. 20). **25–27.** These verses are attributed to J. The mention of the brothers sitting down to eat does not, then, appear too strange if it follows directly on v. 23. In the J account, it is a caravan of Ishmaelites that appears. Descendants of Abraham by Hagar (cf. 16:11–12; 25:12–18), the Ishmaelites were desert nomads who frequently engaged in transporting goods from the east to Egypt. The caravan route would have passed near Dothan and continued on to the coast. That Judah is also represented as attempting to save Joseph is now clear from the text (v. 26). His motive is to avoid bloodguilt; concealing the blood by covering it over is useless, for it cries out for vengeance (cf. 4:10).

145 (d) (37:28–36). **28–30.** The presence of two traditions conflated in v. 28 is clear. The Midianites and the cistern of the first part of the verse point to E, while the Ishmaelites (J) are referred to in the second part. The Midianites were also nomadic tribesmen and were related to Abraham through Keturah (cf. 25:2). Seemingly, they also engaged in slave trade (cf. v. 36). Verse 28c is also attributed to E, since it forms the transition from v. 28a to v. 36. Verses 29–30 are also clearly from E, because it is now Reuben who is the would-be savior of Joseph from the cistern (cf. vv. 22 and 24). Reuben's motives had not been indicated; from his cry of anguish it would seem that he considered himself, as the oldest son, the one responsible for the youth's safety. **31–36.** In vv. 31–33, the tunic motif, a constant of J in the narrative, reappears. The bloody robe would be considered evidence of the accidental death for which the brothers would not be held responsible (see a somewhat parallel case in Ex 22:12). The second phrase in v. 33 is considered an insertion from E because of its relation to v. 20. As his son Reuben, Jacob rends his garments as a sign of his grief (v. 34a belongs to E), dons sackcloth and mourns his son (v. 34b belongs to J). Jacob's cry that he would "go down to his son mourning to Sheol" implies an eventual reunion in the shadowly region of the underworld (cf. 2 Sm 12:23). The final verse, clearly from E (cf. v. 28a and c), retains the suspense in a story that would otherwise have come to a natural conclusion, and prepares the way for the incidents in chs. 39ff. The Pharaoh's officer (literally a "eunuch," but here understood in a general sense of a royal official) is Poti-phar (a shortened form of Potiphera; cf. 41:45,50), meaning "the one whom Re [the sun god] has given."

146 **(B) Judah and Tamar (38:1–30) (J).** This ancient tradition, preserved by J, is generally interpreted as an explanation of the origin of the Judah tribe. The three surviving sons of the patriarch mentioned here, Shelah, Perez, and Zerah, become the ancestors of the principal clans of later Judah (cf. Nm 26:19–22; 1 Chr 2:1ff.). More difficult to explain is its present place in the narrative. It clearly breaks the sequence of the Joseph story and is not in accord with the general context, because the later chapters give no indication of Judah's separation from the rest of the family (cf. 38:1). It does, however, agree with the psychological context; Joseph's temptation by the Egyptian woman (ch. 39) provided a parallel to Judah's temptation. Moreover, the disappearance of Joseph focuses the interest on Judah, who will become the principal object of the divine blessing because of the older sons' failure to merit it (cf. 49:3–7). The rest of salvation history, therefore, will center on the tribes of Joseph and Judah. It is this more universal historical outlook that prompted the author to place the narrative here.

Besides the general theological theme mentioned above, there is also present the common patriarchal theme of the promise of a great posterity. That this promise should be realized through such extraordinary means as suggested here only emphasizes the divine action in history. Just as Isaac and Jacob had become the heirs of the promise in unexpected ways, so the descendants of Judah will not be able to point to the human merits of their ancestors as the reason for their providential place in history.

147 (a) (38:1–14). **1.** The verse is important for the early history of the tribe of Judah. It states that Judah separated (reading *wayyārād* for *wayyārēd*, with Gunkel and others) from his brothers. Judah's early isolation from the other tribes is attested to by Jgs 5, where the tribe is not mentioned at all, and by Dt 33:7, where God is asked to bring Judah back to his people. On the basis of these and other indications, many think that Judah did not participate in the events of the Exodus. Here Judah is presented as settling in Adullam, in the hill country SW of Jerusalem, and mixing with the local Canaanites. **2–7.** Judah's marriage to the Canaanite woman is reported without moral judgment, contrary to the practice in other passages (cf. 24:3–4). It is a *fait accompli* that J is reporting, and these verses are only an introduction to the main story. The oldest of Judah's three sons is given in marriage to Tamar, a Canaanite. What Er's wickedness consisted in is not indicated. **8–10.** Judah's second son, Onan, is required by ancient custom (practiced by other people [cf. Clamer, *op. cit.*, 428] and formulated in Dt 25:5–10) to take Tamar as wife. The first-born of the union would be considered the son of the dead brother, would inherit his property, and would continue the "name" of his legal father. Onan's act of wasting the seed (whence the term onanism) is explicitly stated as motivated by the unwillingness to raise up descendants to his brother. It is for this violation of the law of the levirate marriage that he is struck dead. **11.** According to law, the third son, Shelah, must undertake the levirate obligations. Judah, however, fears that his only remaining son will meet the fate of his two brothers (for a similar fear, cf. Tb 3; 8). If Shelah is really under-age, then Tamar is considered a widow and can return to her father's house (cf. Lv 22:13). But Judah's fear for his son's life and the events that follow suggest that he had no intention now of giving his son to Tamar (cf. v. 26). **12–14.** After the prescribed mourning rites for his dead wife, Judah goes to Timnah (in the Judean hills W of Bethlehem) with his friend Hirah. Tamar's actions, i.e., changing from a widow's garb (cf. Jdt 8:6; 10:2) to that of a sacred prostitute, are dictated by her interpretation of Judah's delay in giving Shelah to her in marriage.

148 (b) (38:15–30). **15–19.** Judah thinks her a sacred prostitute (here *zônāh*, an ordinary harlot, but cf. v. 21) and wishes to have intercourse with her. Sacred prostitution, a pagan religious act honoring the goddess of fertility, was practiced in Canaan and condemned by the prophets (cf. Hos 4:14). Tamar's motives are neither lust nor religious commitment, but the desire for offspring, for which she is later praised. Her demand for a pledge of later payment is a necessary part of the plot; the pledge demanded, Judah's ornate staff and his signet or incised seal used in "signing" clay tablet documents would be the best means of identifying him later. **20–23.** Judah's desire to recover the pledge is understandable, as is his desire to discontinue the search for the woman; too much publicity would result and cast dishonor on him. The same motive lies behind his use of Hirah as an intermediary. The term used in vv. 21–22 for Tamar is *q*e*dēšāh*, the technical term for the temple prostitute (cf. v. 15 and note; cf. also G. R. Driver, *op. cit.*, 70–72). **24–26.** As the legal wife of Shelah according to the levirate practice, Tamar can be punished for adultery. As the head of the family, Judah was responsible for the execution of the punishment, ordinarily stoning (cf. Dt 22:22–24) except in the case of the daughter of a priest when burning was prescribed (cf. Lv 21:9). The present text may reflect an older custom. Tamar's action in producing the identifying pledge is the climax of the narrative and brings the desired results; Judah recognizes his guilt as much greater than that of his daughter-in-law. The final remark about Judah not having further relations with Tamar emphasizes his guilt. **27–30.** This epilogue contains an etiological explanation of the predominance of the Perez clan, from which David would be descended (cf. Ru 4:18–22), over that of Zerah. The name "Perez" (*pereṣ*) is associated with the Hebr word for "make a breach" (*pāraṣ*). Zerah (*zāraḥ*) is so called, as the context indicates, because of the scarlet thread, but there is no explicit connection made by the author; the etymology of the word is unknown.

149 **(C) Joseph's Temptation (39:1–23) (J).** The present chapter continues the narrative interrupted at the end of ch. 37. It is from the J tradition, which explains the reference to the Ishmaelites in v. 1 (cf. 37:36). The literary genre of the wisdom literature is especially noted here: Joseph fears the Lord who continues to be with him in all his adventures; he is the wise man who counsels others and runs the household efficiently; he is strong in the face of temptation; he is humble in the face of adversity. All these qualities are emphasized in the sapiential books; here they are illustrated in the Joseph narrative.

The story of the temptation by the Egyptian's wife contains a motif found in many popular stories of the day, notably in "The Story of Two Brothers" (*ANET* 23–25), found in a 19th-Dynasty Egyptian manuscript (cf. Vergote *op. cit.*, 22–24). The "wisdom" theology contained here accords well with the theology of J, who has made it a part of his patriarchal history. Yahweh's presence with Joseph, though not as anthropomorphistically presented as in the earlier chapters, is a necessary condition for the eventual unfolding of the divine plan.

150 (a) (39:1–9). **1.** The verse has been edited to make it agree with the information contained in 37:36, although J's mention of the Ishmaelites has been retained. The rest of the chapter (except for v. 20 which has also been edited) gives no indication that Joseph's master was a royal official. **2–6.** Two themes are elaborated here. The first is the modesty and industriousness of Joseph, which is subordinated to the second, Yahweh's continued presence with him. The position attained by Joseph is that of superintendent of all his master's possessions, not only of the house (cf. Vergote, *op. cit.*, 24–25). The remark about the food (v. 6) can be explained simply as suggesting that the master had to concern himself with nothing but eating his meals, or it may refer to ritual prescriptions which the Egyptian would not leave to a foreigner. **7–9.** The woman's suggestion and Joseph's response present a concrete example of what is found in Prv 5–7. In his refusal, Joseph enlarges on the trust placed in him by his master, which would indicate a purely human motive. But this human motive only strengthens the religious motive with which Joseph's speech comes to its climax. The use of "Elohim" for the expected "Yahweh" is explained by the fact that the one addressed is a foreigner in whose presence the sacred name would not be pronounced.

151 (b) (39:10–23). **10–19.** The scene of the attempted seduction is artfully composed. The garment left behind by Joseph is used as false evidence by the jilted woman whose lust has turned to hatred. She summons the servants to be able to use them as witnesses. Her reference to Joseph as a Hebrew (vv. 14 and 17) could be intended as opprobrious; it is always a term used by foreigners of the Hebrews, or by the biblical authors to contrast Israelites with foreigners (cf. 14:13). **20–23.** Why Joseph is said to be imprisoned instead of being put to death, the expected punishment, can be satisfactorily explained only as a necessary feature of the entire story. The phrase "where the king's prisoners were kept" (v. 20) is an editorial insertion to harmonize the story with E's narrative in ch. 40. (For the hapaxlegomenon *bêt hassōhar*, "prison," in v. 20, see Vergote, *op. cit.*, 25–28.) The parallel between Joseph's fortunes in the prison (vv. 21–23) and in the Egyptian's house (vv. 2–6) is striking and emphasizes the dominant theme of the whole story: The Lord is with those who fear him.

152 **(D) Joseph Interprets the Prisoners' Dreams (40:1–23) (E).** It is generally agreed that ch. 40 represents the E tradition with some harmonizing glosses. The emphasis on dreams and the use of "Elohim" are characteristic; inconsistencies with the date in ch. 39 confirm the attribution. According to E, Joseph was sold by the Midianites to Poti-phar, the captain of the guard (cf. 37:36 and the edited 39:1), who assigns him to the task of serving the imprisoned royal officials (40:4). The narrative seems unaware of the high position Joseph had attained in the prison as related by J (cf. 39:21–23) Conflation of the traditions resulted in some unevenness (39:1,20; 40:3,7,15).

The theology is more subtle than in J. Joseph's ability to interpret dreams is God-given (cf. v. 8). This first feat is a God-willed preparation for a later act that will catapult him into a high position (ch. 41). The divine plan is unfolding as surely as in ch. 39, if less explicitly stated.

153 (a) (40:1–8). **1–4.** These verses prepare for the drama to follow. Intrigue was common in bureaucratic Egypt and is reflected in the imprisonment of the royal officials who, despite their plebeian titles, could exercise great influence. (For an explanation of the various offices mentioned here, see Vergote, *op. cit.*, 31–37.) The phrase "in the prison where Joseph was confined" is an editorial gloss from J. **5–8.** Because of the great importance attached to dreams in Egypt, their interpretation had developed into a science (cf. an ancient Egyptian key for interpreting dreams, dated in the 19th Dynasty, in *ANET* 495). The imprisoned officials are sorrowful because they have no access to the interpreters. Joseph's rejoinder (v. 8b) is a theological polemic against the superstitious practice of the Egyptians. (The phrase in v. 7, "in custody with him in his master's house," is a harmonizing gloss, omitted in the Vg.)

154 (b) (40:9–23). **9–15.** The description of the dream is highly stylized, and not in accord with the manner of dreams. Only those details have been mentioned which would give color to the story and meaning to the interpretation. As in all the dreams in these chapters, the numbers have a chronological significance. The expression in v. 13, "will take up your case," is, lit., "will lift up your head (*yiśśā'* . . . *'et rō'šekā*) and refers here to his eventual liberation (cf. 2 Kgs 25:27); the CCD translation is acceptable in view of v. 20, but does not convey the pun intended in the Hebrew. The final remark in v. 15 is another harmonizing gloss. **16–19.** As in the case of the butler, the baker's dream is compatible with his office. Here the two lower baskets are present only for their chronological significance. The unfavorable nature of the dream is evident from the theft of the Pharaoh's food, as well as from the presence of the birds, a frequently used symbol of evil (cf. 15:11). In v. 19, the text reads, lit., "will lift up your head from you" (*yiśśā'* . . . *'et rō'šekā mē'ālèkā*). While *mē'ālèkā* may be a gloss influenced by the same word at the end of the verse, it emphasizes the unfavorable significance of the whole expression, in contrast with v. 13; decapitation is implied. **20–23.** The fulfillment of the dreams is precisely as Joseph had predicted. Again, the expression "lifted up the head" is featured as in vv. 13 and 19. The mention of the chief butler's failure to "think of Joseph" adds suspense to the story and prepares for the following incident.

155 **(E) Joseph Interprets Pharaoh's Dreams (41:1–57) (E, J).** The present chapter is unintelligible without the preceding and comes, for the most part, from the same tradition (E). Only in the latter part have insertions from J been made. The story is told with typical Semitic love of repetition (cf. ch. 24), and reveals an intimate acquaintance with Egyptian life and customs.

The exaltation of Joseph is the climax of the first episode in his history and prepares for the next episode, the confrontation with his brothers. While, as noted before, the theology is less obtrusive than in the preceding patriarchal narratives, it is clear enough from the frequent references to God who is directing "from behind the scenes."

156 (a) (41:1–24). **1–7.** The dreams of Pharaoh (lit., "the great house," applied originally to the royal palace and later to the king) are generally similar in number, nature and stylistic form to those of ch. 40. In v. 1, there is the first mention of the Nile (lit., "the river"). The importance of the Nile for the fertility of the land justifies its inclusion, however forced, in the dream. The double dream, as in ch. 40, emphasizes the certainty of the event symbolized. The "east wind" (v. 6) is the hot, dry *sirocco* well known in the Mediterranean area. The statement in v. 7b (lit., "and Pharaoh awoke, and behold [it was] a dream") stresses the reality of the dream. **8–13.** Unlike the two royal prisoners in ch. 40, Pharaoh has access to the official interpreters (the term "magicians," *ḥarṭummîm*, is Egyptian and seemingly has ritual implications; the term "wise men" is more general; cf. Vergote, *op. cit.*, 66–73). But their availability is of no help. The butler now becomes an official accuser (*ḥăṭā'ay...mazkîr;* cf. Von Rad, *op. cit.*, 370–71), recalling his failure to remember Joseph's plea (cf. 40:14). **14–24.** Joseph shaves before presenting himself to the Pharaoh in accord with Egyptian, and in contrast to Semitic, custom (cf. *ANEP* 1–20). Pharaoh tells Joseph he has heard that he need only "hear a dream to interpret it" (MT), implying that Joseph is even greater than Pharaoh's magicians. As in 40:8, Joseph rejects any claims to this "science." The slight elaborations in Pharaoh's repetition of the dreams (especially in vv. 19–21) add color to the story and anticipate the interpretation (cf. vv. 21 and 31).

157 (b) (41:25–36). **25–32.** Joseph's interpretation is somewhat repetitious but clear. The reference to a seven-year famine was probably not intended to be understood literally, despite the finding of a text from the Ptolemaic period describing a seven-year famine (*ANET* 31–32). The importance of this document is literary, in referring to precisely seven years, and historical, in referring to long periods of famine in Egypt. The historical background of the biblical narrative is assured by many other texts. **33–36.** In advising Pharaoh to appoint an "intelligent and prudent man," Joseph gives a (unintentional) description of himself; his further counsels are intelligent and prudent (note the wisdom theme again). In v. 34, "prepare the land" in the CCD does not clearly express *ḥimmēš*, "take the fifth part [of the produce]" in the MT (cf. 47:24). The practice of storing a fifth part for future use was probably an Egyptian custom reflected here. The use of granaries as early as the 6th Dynasty is attested (cf. *ANEP* 90). The unevenness of these verses suggests some conflation of the traditions (De Vaux, *La Genèse*, 182).

158 (c) (41:37–44). **37–41.** Pharaoh recognizes a divine origin of the interpretation and counsel and, because Joseph has the characteristics recommended by himself (cf. v. 33), he is made, effectively, the vizier of the king (cf. *ANET* 213–14 for a text from the 18th Dynasty describing the office of the vizier; cf. Vergote *op. cit.*, 98–114 for full discussion of the office, or offices, implied here). The expression "in charge of my palace" (*'al bêtî*) recalls that of 2 Kgs 18:18,37; Is 22:20–24. The phrase "all of my people shall obey your commands" is, lit., "on your mouth [i.e., 'at your order'] all my people will kiss [the ground]" (*'al pîkā yiššaq kol 'ammî*); it is the Hebr form of an Egyptian expression for a profound bow (Vergote, *op. cit.*, 96–97). Verse 41 (with pf. tense) may contain the appointment of the office promised in v. 40 (with impf. tense), which would exclude a conflation of traditions. **42–44.** The investiture in the office includes the handing over of the royal seal with which the vizier authenticated the royal decrees. The linen clothes (*šēš* is an Egyptian word) were possibly distinctive ones worn by the vizier. The chain of gold (with def. art.) was also distinctive. Chariots were introduced into Egypt by the Hyksos; Joseph's is "second" only to the Pharaoh's, an indication of his high office. The word *'abrēk* has been variously translated, as Egyptian for "Attention!" or as Hebrew for "bow down!" Verse 44 seems to be an insertion from J.

159 (d) (41:45–57). **45–46.** The new office demands a change of name. The Hebraized Egyptian form is obscure; it is commonly interpreted as "God speaks: he is living!" (but see Vergote, *op. cit.*, 141–46). The name of Joseph's wife means "she belongs to Neith," the goddess of Sais. If v. 45 is from J, the name of Joseph's father-in-law may not indicate the royal officer of 37:36. On (Heliopolis) was from ancient times the center of worship of the sun-god. Verse 45b is a gloss (missing in the LXX) from v. 46b. The reference to Joseph's age is an insertion from P. **47–52.** Joseph's interpretation of the dream having been proven correct, the author now emphasizes his administrative ability. The names of Joseph's sons, who become living symbols of their father's prosperous state, are given popular etymologies, as usual. "Manasseh" (*m^enaššeh*) is derived from *nāšāh*, "to forget," whence "he made me forget" (*naššanî*); "Ephraim" (*'eprāyim*) is derived from *pārāh*, "to be fruitful," whence "he made me fruitful" (*hiprani*). The statement that Joseph forgot his sufferings and his family is best understood as a hendiadys for the sufferings connected with his family. **53–57.** These verses are the climax to the story of Joseph's rise to power and the preparation for what follows (cf. vv. 54 and 57). There is a bit of stylistic unevenness in the passage (cf. vv. 54b and 55; 56b and 57), probably caused by the author's attempt to stress both the complete authority of Joseph (the Egyptians had to go to him for food) and the reason why Jacob's sons would have come to Egypt (there was abundance of grain there).

160 (F) First Encounter of Joseph with His Brothers (42:1–38) (E, J). The interest is no longer on Joseph's relationship to Egypt and the Pharaoh but on that to his family, a theme prepared for in 41:53–57. Here again the chapter is basically E, but insertions from J, intended to make the transition to ch. 43 (mainly J) easier, have produced some inconsistencies. The theology, evident to the readers of the events, is explicitly formulated only later (cf. 45:5–8).

(a) (42:1–17). **1–5.** Famines were frequent and widespread in the Mediterranean area; Egypt was known to provide relief (cf. 12:10; *ANET* 251c). Jacob's sons join other caravans that are going on the same mission. Benjamin, like Joseph, the son of the beloved Rachel, is kept behind. The repetitious nature of v. 5 and the reference to Jacob as Israel suggest an insertion from J. **6–8.** Joseph is here given the title of "governor" (*šallîṭ*), which corresponds to his office of vizier (cf. Sir 8:8; 10:5). The author seems unaware of the difficulty implied in a direct meeting between the great vizier and ten Hebrews, unless a large caravan is supposed which would have been brought to Joseph's attention. The prostration is in accord with custom (cf. *ANEP* 5), but the author probably sees it as a fulfillment of Joseph's dream (37:5–10). Their failure to recognize their brother, shaven, in distinctive garments and wielding such power, is understandable. **9–13.** Joseph's charge of spying is consonant with Egypt's traditional fear of enemy infiltration from the more vulnerable northeastern frontier. The "weak spots" (lit., "nakedness") presumably refer to the less-guarded areas. The brothers' reply that they are from one family suggests that their large number may have occasioned the Egyptians' anxiety. **14–17.** Joseph's "test" of his brothers has a purpose beyond that suspected by them, as the events will show. Joseph's oath, "as Pharaoh lives," implying the divinity of the king, may be an authentic Egyptian form (cf. Vergote *op. cit.*, 162–67). Its attribution to Joseph without comment reflects an early period of composition when such oaths were not looked upon with special horror.

161 (b) (42:18–38). **18–24.** Joseph's new condition (cf. vv. 15–16) that only one should stay behind until Benjamin is brought before him is agreed upon. The brothers' anguish recalls the anguish they had once caused Joseph and makes them aware of their guilt. This is the first sign of the change that Joseph was trying to effect in them. The reference to the interpreter (v. 23) indicates another reason why they failed to recognize their brother. The author's observation that Joseph withdrew and wept heightens the drama of the whole scene. By binding Simeon ("before their eyes" in order to impress them) instead of the expected Reuben, the oldest son, Joseph would give the others the occasion to suspect that God had spared the one who had tried to save him (cf. v. 22). **25–28.** Joseph secretly returns the money paid for the grain, a gesture that betrays, like v. 24a, his deep love despite his external harshness. Verses 27 and 28 are generally considered intrusions from J, since they patently clash with the statement in v. 35. The brothers' conviction of a divine intervention causes religious awe. **29–34.** Returning to Canaan, the brothers repeat their experiences to Jacob. The impression that Joseph, "lord of the land," made on them is evident from their account. **35–38.** On v. 35, cf. vv. 27–28. Jacob's anguish is even greater than that of his sons (cf. v. 21). Just as Reuben in the E account had tried to save Joseph (37:21), so now he offers his own sons as pledge for the safety of Benjamin (in J it is Judah who makes the offer; cf. 43:8–9). But Jacob can seemingly resign himself more easily to the loss of Simeon than to the possible loss of his youngest son. The final remark of Jacob is explained by the belief that the dead remained in the state of soul in which they died; he, therefore, would be in perpetual mourning for Benjamin.

162 **(G) Second Journey to Egypt (43:1–34) (J, E).** The indications of a tradition different from that of ch. 42 are plentiful. Here Judah is the spokesman and guarantor instead of Reuben (see 43:3–10; cf. 42:37). In Judah's speech there is no reference to the imprisonment of Simeon; when the latter is mentioned (vv. 14 and 23b), editorial work can be strongly suspected. Also, Jacob is called "Israel" as usual in J. Most commentators agree that the present chapter, therefore, is from J, with occasional insertions from E to provide a link with the preceding narrative. The author is master of his material and presents a moving story of the encounter between Joseph and his brothers. The theology, which will be fully disclosed only at the close of the entire narrative, is only slightly more explicit in J than in E (cf., e.g., v. 23).

163 (a) (43:1–14). **1–2.** Since, according to many commentators, v. 38 of the preceding chapter is from J, the statement in 43:1–2 is difficult to explain; has Jacob forgotten about his decision? Some would, therefore, consider 42:38 an original part of ch. 43, situated directly after v. 2. Its present position in ch. 42 would have been dictated by the editorial need for a response to Reuben's proposal. The severity of the famine, however, may have been such as to prompt the patriarch's new decision. **3–7.** Judah's speech and Israel's response have all the signs of being given for the first time, pointing to a separate tradition. Israel seems unaware of the condition imposed by "the man," i.e., Joseph (his presence dominates the scene here just as in 42:29–34). Also, Judah's explanation does not refer to the spying charge as the occasion of Joseph's minute questioning about the family. Here no motive is given, and no mention is made of Simeon. **8–14.** Judah's willingness to accept responsibility (v. 10; the formulation of the vow would have been extremely impressive to the ancients) parallels Reuben's in 42:37, and is in accord with the role played by Judah in the J account. Once convinced, Jacob-Israel assumes his more familiar role of a shrewd man of business. The customary gifts for the political rulers are recommended (v. 11), and, to impress the Egyptian with their honesty, they are to return the money put in their sacks. Finally, the patriarch freely tells them to take Benjamin along. Verse 14 is difficult. The name "Almighty God" (*'ēl šadday*) is P's usage, but there is no evidence that P had such a story. Many feel that the verse has been reworked by the final editor of the Pentateuch in order to include an allusion to Simeon; this editor would have taken the divine name from P.

164 (b) (43:15–34). **15–23.** The second scene, the encounter with Joseph's steward, is now introduced and presented. It is masterfully done. All details not necessary for heightening the drama are omitted. The fright of the brothers, their self-questioning, and their explanations to the steward give us a vivid and dramatic picture. The steward's reply, prompted by Joseph, heightens the mystery by introducing a religious theme. The final statement in v. 23 is too laconic for J, who would surely have described the reunion in joyful terms; it is an editorial link with ch. 42. **24–34.** The final scene is as vividly presented as the preceding, but the climax adds to the interest. The humble conduct of the brothers, obsequious by our standards, is evident in the presentation of their gift, their prostration and the reference to Jacob as "your servant." This and their amazement at Joseph's treatment of them (v. 33) are what would be expected of relatively uncultured Hebrews in the home of a vizier. Similarly Joseph's gracious, even paternal, regard for them cannot but impress the reader; however, his princely conduct conceals only with difficulty his inner emotions (vv. 30–31). Eating at separate tables (cf. v. 32) is in accord with Egyptian custom. As later (cf. 45:22), Benjamin receives five times the share of his brothers, a symbolic number frequently used by the Egyptians. This emphasis of the role of Benjamin prepares for the following narrative.

165 **(H) Judah's Plea for Benjamin (44:1–34) (J).** The perfect consistency of all that is said and done in this passage with the preceding chapter is sufficient evidence of the presence of the same tradition (J). Again, the storyteller's art is present to a marked degree. Joseph and Judah appear as the two principal protagonists: one has the power to execute a cruel fate for the brothers; the other has a penitential spirit occasioned by what has occurred which forces him to reach into the depths of his conscience and pour forth his confession. In the background are the innocent Benjamin (throughout portrayed as a young boy to emphasize his innocence, although various chronological references would suppose an age in the thirties at least) and the aged father awaiting his son's return. The author clearly sees these dramatic events and the passions of the men involved as the instruments of God's providence.

166 (a) (44:1–10). **1–5.** Joseph's final test of his brothers involves a plan with consequences which could easily be seen as fatal by the ancient readers. The whole interest is here on Joseph's silver cup (the reference to the money in vv. 1–2 is read by many as a later addition influenced by 42:25ff.). The cup here referred to is a sacred object used in divination. Objects thrown into it formed patterns or disturbed the liquid content in a manner that revealed the future (for details, see Vergote, *op. cit.*, 172–76; for the legal implications of the theft, see Daube, *op. cit.*, 235–57). Verse 5 in the MT reads, lit., "Is not this [the cup] from which my master drinks and this by which he indeed divines...?" The narrative throughout supposes Joseph's practice of the art, but no moral judgment is made. **6–10.** The absolute conviction of their innocence prompts the brothers to pronounce a curse on themselves if any one of them is found guilty; all will suffer in accord with the principle of collective responsibility. Joseph's steward, aware of his master's stratagem, changes the penalty to slavery for the guilty one; he knows that Benjamin alone will be involved.

167 (b) (44:11–34). **11–17.** Throughout this section, the brothers' reaction is significant. Instead of surrendering Benjamin in accord with the steward's statement (v. 10) and as they had once done with Joseph, they now recognize God's hand in the whole affair and declare themselves all guilty (v. 16). Joseph's seemingly gracious refusal of such collective punishment is, of course, intended as one final test of their complete change of heart. **18–34.** Judah's speech is universally recognized as one of the most beautiful and moving passages in ancient literature. While the forms of address used are within the bonds of propriety, there is a wildness of eloquence in the speech itself that no courtly considerations could restrain. In the first and longest part, Judah gives the arguments for the proposal that he will make. They are entirely emotional and presumably would have great effect on an ancient audience. The reader, of course, recognizes what effect they would have on Joseph. An aged father and his beloved youngest son are the center of interest. With a natural art, the past events are detailed in a crescendo of emotional appeal. (No reference is made to the imprisonment of Simeon, of which J seems unaware.) The appeal culminates (vv. 33–34) in the proposal that Judah himself be permitted to take the place of Benjamin as a slave in Egypt. By this proposal, Judah shows himself willing to expiate a crime committed against Joseph by which the latter had himself been made a slave in Egypt.

168 **(I) The Recognition of Joseph (45:1–28) (J and E).** It is clear that this chapter does not proceed as smoothly as the preceding one. The conflation of the two traditions is evident from the several doublets, inconsistencies, and varying vocabulary. The editorial work detracts somewhat from the effect that this climactic scene probably had in the separate traditions.

The theology is clearly stated for the first time, and at some length (vv. 5–8). Salvation history has given a unity to the preceding events that they could not have had in themselves, for it shows them to have meaning also for the future. "Together with 50:20, these verses provide the key to the story of Joseph" (De Vaux, *La Genèse*, 197).

169 (a) (45:1–8). **1–4.** Because the reunion with his brothers is a purely personal matter, Joseph has his courtiers leave the room, but his emotional outburst is such that they can hear his weeping. (Both J and E emphasize the emotional element in the whole history of Joseph. It is a characteristic of the ancient narrative art.) The question about his father in v. 3, immediately following Judah's long speech, reveals the presence of E. The double identification of Joseph is similarly considered an evidence of conflation, although it does add to the psychological effect; in the context of ch. 44, the brothers' slowness to comprehend is understandable. **5–8.** In this passage (its unevenness betraying editorial work), the providence of God in the whole affair is emphasized. Although his brothers had sold him into Egypt, Joseph was really sent by God. Verse 7, which records the divine purpose of the events, contains a theology that shares by anticipation in the theology of the Exodus. While Joseph's meaning is, of course, restricted to his own generation, the canonical author would have seen the further implications. The notion of the remnant (*š^e'ērît*) will be especially developed in later, prophetic theology. Among the titles that Joseph applies to himself in v. 8 is the new one, "father to Pharaoh." Similarly, the vizier Ptahhotep calls himself "God's [i.e., the Pharaoh's] Father" (*ANET* 412). The term is used in the same sense of Eliakim in Is 22:21 and of the messianic prince in Is 9:5.

170 (b) (45:9–28). **9–15.** Joseph's message to Jacob, with its recommendation of haste (vv. 9a and d and 13b), is dictated as much by his desire to see his father as soon as possible as by the fact of Jacob's advanced age. Benjamin is especially urged to bear witness to his identity, since the father had been deceived before by the others. The entire family is invited to settle in the land of Goshen, a fertile area in the NE Delta region. Joseph says that thus they will be "near" him (v. 10). Whereas this by itself could simply be a literary element (Von Rad, *op. cit.*, 394–95), the following chapters imply the presence of the royal court in lower Egypt, a fact verified only in the Hyksos period and in that of the later 19th Dynasty. If this context has historical validity, it would indicate the Hyksos period for the whole history of Joseph. **16–20.** The Pharaoh's gracious invitation to the brothers to bring their families to Egypt (a doublet, repeating the invitation of Joseph) is considered by some as another indication of the period of the Hyksos, who would be favorably inclined to fellow Asiatics. The double order to bring the families to Egypt (vv. 18 and 19), the differing means of transporation ("animals" in v. 17; "carts" in v. 20), and the double reference to the "best of the land" (vv. 18 and 20) are all evidence of the conflation of two traditions. **21–28.** The brothers' departure is marked by another show of munificence on the part of Joseph (cf. 42:25; 44:1–2), but this time openly and with no ulterior motives. Benjamin, a prominent if silent character in the whole story, receives special attention as usual. The final enigmatic injunction of Joseph (v. 24b) has not been satisfactorily explained. The brothers' return to Canaan and their report to Jacob is anticlimactic. An attempt is made to add a note of reality (v. 26b), but the author is now seemingly more concerned with the account of Jacob's departure for Egypt. The happy ending, better told in concise form, is somewhat overdrawn by the presence of the two traditions, indicated by the use of the two names "Israel" (vv. 21 and 28) and "Jacob" (vv. 25 and 27).

171 **(J) Jacob's Journey to Egypt (46:1–34) (J, E, and P).** The closing chapters are now centered on Jacob-Israel; Joseph's position in Egypt is only the necessary background for what follows. The present chapter contains all three traditions with J and E providing the narrative framework. The first five verses are a mixture of the two, with E predominating ("Elohim," "Jacob," the dream motif). Verses 6–27 are clearly P; J concludes the chapter. The theology is enunciated in the vision at Beer-sheba, where the patriarchal promise is renewed for the last time. The genealogical list in P adds significance to the promise, for from these tribes will be formed the people Israel.

172 (a) (46:1–5). **1.** The point of departure, according to the last indication (37:14), would be Hebron. The road to Egypt would pass Beer-sheba where, according to J (26:25), Isaac had erected an altar. **2–5.** In this passage, principally E, Jacob's decision to go to Egypt is confirmed by God in a vision. (J had revealed no hesitation on Jacob's part.) In E's theology, the departure from the land of promise to settle in a foreign land can be justified only by the final purpose of God, to make of Jacob in Egypt "a great people." The statement that God would bring him up again is intended on a twofold level: Not only would Jacob himself be buried in Canaan (50:10–13), but also—and this especially—would Israel, the people of God, come up again. Verse 5a concludes the E account. J is recognized in v. 5b by the reference to "Israel" and to the carts (cf. 45:19–21). Originally followed by the events in vv. 28ff., J's account has been interrupted by an insertion from P which enhances E's theology, just indicated.

173 (b) (46:6–34). **6–27.** The difficulties raised by this list are numerous, indicating the reworking needed to make it conform to the context. Originally a list of the descendants of Jacob, it had comprised 70 persons (33 descendants from Leah, 16 from Zilpah, 14 from Rachel, and 7 from Bilhah). The number 66 (v. 26) was arrived at by the exclusion of the already dead Er and Onan (v. 12b) and Joseph and his two sons, already in Egypt, and the inclusion of Dinah (v. 15). By including Jacob himself, Joseph, and his two sons, the total of 70 was reached. As Dt 10:22 indicates, this number had become traditional (see also Ex 1:5). The present list, therefore, represents a concerted effort to retain the number despite the resulting inconsistencies (see Clamer, *op. cit.*, 475–77 for details). **28–30.** The text of v. 28 is uncertain. Judah (J tradition) is sent ahead to prepare for the reunion between Joseph and his father. The importance of the occasion is noted: Joseph arrives by chariot and "appears" to Jacob (*wayyērā'*, used before this by J only for theophanies). As expected, the scene is highly emotional. Jacob's remark (v. 30) can be contrasted with the statement in 42:38 (cf. also Lk 2:29–31). **31–34.** Joseph's practical counsel is intended to pave the way for a favorable decision by the Pharaoh regarding the family's place of sojourn. The text supposes that the Pharaoh had not yet decided on this matter (cf. 45:16–20). The passage is variously interpreted. Joseph's purpose is clearly to have them settled in Goshen. Is the Pharaoh to choose this area because they are shepherds who must not be brought into close contact with Egyptians (v. 34c), or because they are a stable element ("keepers of cattle") who can be trusted in a frontier province, or simply because Goshen is an ideal place for shepherds (cf. 47:3–6)? The interpretation is complicated by the final remark (v. 34c), which may be an anachronistic addition reflecting the later hatred of Egyptians for the Hyksos, considered a shepherd people like the Hebrews.

174 **(K) The Hebrews in Egypt (47:1–31) (J and P).** The tradition history of this chapter is somewhat complex. Verses 1–5a are a continuation of the preceding account and attributed to J. Verses 5b–11 are from P. The long passage in vv. 13–26 has some characteristics of J but may be a later addition. The final verses are from J, except for vv. 27b–28 (P). Again, by gathering these heterogeneous traditions with their varying emphases, the final author stresses the relevance of all events to the divine plan.

(a) (47:1–12). **1–4.** The audience with the Pharaoh is arranged by Joseph and proceeds according to plan. Joseph's diplomacy is noted in his offhand reference to Goshen. The brothers are more to the point and ask bluntly for permission to settle there. The mention of "five" brothers may be another indication of an Egyptian attachment to the number (cf. 43:34; 45:6,11,22; Clamer, *op. cit.*, 463). **5–6.** The LXX changes the order of the verses and adds a phrase (cf. note in the CCD with the reading). The LXX preserves the original traditions more clearly and shows that there were two parallel accounts (J and P) of the audience with the Pharaoh. The MT represents an attempt to harmonize the two accounts. **7–12.** The presentation of Jacob to the Pharaoh is narrated by P with a sobriety that gives it a touch of grandeur. For P, the patriarchs are "immigrants" or "sojourners" in the land; the promise of the land will only be fulfilled later. Also consonant with P's theology is the gradual increase of evil and the consequent decrease in age. The anachronistic reference to Rameses, named after Ramses II (period of the Exodus), is intended to indicate the same area as Goshen in the other traditions. The geography is not precise; P has the events of the Exodus more in mind (cf. Ex 1:11; 12:37). Verse 12, by reason of its resemblance to 45:10b–11, is attributed to E.

175 (b) (47:13–31). **13–26.** If not a later addition, this long passage (perhaps J) originally belonged after ch. 41. It extols the wisdom of Joseph in his government of the land (cf. v. 25). Its present place can best be explained as presenting a contrast between the fate of the Egyptians and that of the family of Jacob, whose story it interrupts (cf. vv. 11–12 and 27). Despite the obvious oversimplifications indicated by the universal statements ("all the money," v. 14; "all the Egyptians," v. 15; "all their cattle," v. 17 [MT]; "all the land," v. 20), the general background is historically accurate. The process of centralization in Egypt, from which the priests' holdings were exempt (cf. vv. 22 and 26), gained momentum in the new kingdom (*ca.* 1570) and was fostered by the belief that the Pharaoh, as a divinity, was absolute master of both land and people. It is not impossible that the ancient Israelite author, interested in the origin of (to him) curious customs, traced this peculiar Egyptian practice to the agrarian policy of Joseph. In v. 17, the horse is mentioned for the first time in Gn; it was introduced into Egypt by the Hyksos. **27–28.** The interrupted story of Israel's settlement in Goshen is now continued. The text mentions, and the context emphasizes, their prosperity. The chronological data in v. 28 agree with the statement in v. 9. **29–31.** These lines begin J's account of Jacob's death. His insistence on burial in Canaan is underlined by the gesture demanded of Joseph ("put your hand under my thigh"; see comment on 24:2) and by the oath (v. 31). Jacob wishes to be buried in "their sepulchre"—i.e., of his fathers Isaac and Abraham, which would be the cave of Mach-pelah (cf. 49:30–31 [P]—but J seems to think that Jacob had dug his own sepulcher (cf. 50:5). It may be that a redactor changed the original "my sepulchre" to "their sepulchre" (Clamer, *op. cit.*, 487). The final statement in v. 31 remains enigmatic.

176 **(L) Jacob Adopts Joseph's Sons (48:1–22) (J and E, P).** All three traditions are represented in this chapter, attesting to the importance of its content. As some guide to the reader, we give Clamer's division (*op. cit.*, 488), though it is not intended as conclusive: vv. 1–2a, E; 2b, J; 3–6, P; 7–9a, E; 9b–10a, J; 10b–12, E; 13–14, J; 15–16, E; 17–19, J; and 20–22, E.

In this chapter, as in the following, the interest of the author(s) is more in the later tribes of Israel than in the actual sons of Jacob. Here the tribes of Ephraim and Manasseh are the chief concern. It is their adoption and blessing by the patriarch that is seen as the reason for their later tribal prominence, something that demanded an explanation, since they were not strictly sons of Jacob. Moreover, the later pre-eminence of Ephraim over Manasseh is also explained. The P account, inserted at the beginning, casts its theological light over the whole and so "canonizes" the tribes of Ephraim and Manasseh by bringing them within the framework of the patriarchal promises.

177 (a) (48:1–7). **1–2.** The opening verse evidently jars with the end of ch. 47, and indicates thereby the presence of another tradition (E). The editor has used it to introduce the entire narrative because of the mention of Ephraim and Manasseh. Their presence gives immediacy and concreteness to the otherwise abstract blessing formula of P. **3–6.** The divine name "Almighty God" signals the presence of P. Jacob mentions the theophany at Bethel (35:11–12), where the twofold promise of the land and a great progeny had been made, thus giving meaning to his adoption of Joseph's sons; they will share the same promises by legal right. The order of their naming in v. 5 reverses that of v. 1; it is a subtle indication of the later pre-eminence of Ephraim. Reuben and Simeon are named because they are the two oldest sons; it may also imply their later decline (cf. 49:3–7). Any other children of Joseph will not share in these same promises (v. 6). **7.** The verse comes strangely here. Rachel, of course, was the beloved wife of Jacob, who suffered much for her. The presence of Joseph, Rachel's son, may have occasioned the reminiscence. Some commentators think the verse originally may have contained a wish to be buried with Rachel, similar to the wish in J's account (47:30). This part would then have been omitted because it did not harmonize with J's.

178 (b) (48:8–16). **8–12.** The beginning of this section clearly shows how the insertion of P (vv. 3–6) has disturbed the context. On the surface, the scene appears as a first meeting between Jacob and Joseph's sons, at which the grandfather fondles and rejoices over his grandsons. (The setting here is shortly after the entrance of Jacob into Egypt, and not 17 years later, if the context of P in 47:28 is followed.) But there are indications of something more momentous. Joseph took the children "from his knees" (v. 12), which indicates a rite of adoption (cf. 30:3). Also, Joseph's prostration indicates something more solemn than a simple family gathering. **13–14.** Because of the privileges of the first-born, Joseph understandably puts Manasseh at Jacob's right (the position of honor). Jacob's deliberate crossing of his hands (the Hebr *śikkēl* has not been explained, but the meaning is clear from the context and from the versions) makes more significant his blessing of Ephraim with his right hand. **15–16.** Though directed to Joseph, the blessing is obviously intended for his sons, as the text (v. 16a) and the context (vv. 13–14) indicate. It has been noted that, while the pagans invoked all the gods in the pantheon, Israel invoked the various attributes of the one God (cf. Clamer, *op. cit.*, 491). Here God is first invoked as one before whom Abraham and Isaac "walked" (cf. 17:1). This first invocation establishes the contact with the "God of the fathers," and marks the solidarity of Jacob's blessing with that given to his fathers by God. The second (v. 15b) makes use of a term, "shepherd," that will characterize God's relationship with later Israel (cf. Pss 23; 80:1–2). The third invocation (v. 16a) characterizes God as he reveals himself on earth to man (cf. 16:7–14). The content of the blessing is that the boys be considered full sons of the patriarchs despite their birth from an Egyptian mother (v. 16b) and hence have equal rights among the tribes of Israel.

179 (c) (48:17–22). **17–19.** The continuation of the narrative (J; cf. vv. 13–14) stresses the greater blessing given to the younger son. Two ancient convictions underlie this section: patriarchal blessings are irrevocable (which explains Joseph's concern); the right hand is more powerful in blessing than the left. It is characteristic of J's theology that the natural rights of primogeniture have no inviolable standing in God's eyes. Ephraim will become a greater tribe than Manasseh (cf. Dt 33:17 and the actual prominence of Ephraim in the history of the northern kingdom). **20.** Generally attributed to E, the verse would be a continuation of vv. 15–16. Ephraim and Manasseh will become a formula of blessing for all Israel. "Israel" is here used clearly in the tribal sense as in 34:7; the historical perspective is that of the later period. (Note the sing. *b^ekā* in the MT, corrected to the pl. *b^ekem* in the LXX.) **21–22.** The reference to the Amorites is characteristic of E. The word translated "portion" (*š^ekem*) in the CCD is an allusion to Shechem, an important city in the later history of Ephraim. The ancient tradition contained here has no obvious connection either with 33:18–19 (where Jacob is said to have bought the land), or with ch. 34 (where it was recorded that Jacob's sons destroyed the city, an act disapproved by the patriarch). Whatever the primitive meaning of the tradition may have been, it is added here to emphasize the continuity between the patriarchal history and the events following the conquest.

180 **(M) Jacob's Blessings (49:1–33) (J?).** Traditionally called a blessing because of v. 28, the poem is rather a description of the historical fortunes of the 12 tribes (cf. v. 1). The references to precise political (e.g., v. 10) and geographical details (e.g., v. 13) indicate its composition in the postconquest period. It is probably a collection of ancient aphorisms composed on Canaanite models (cf. B. Vawter, *CBQ* 17 [1955] 1–18) in the period of the Judges, to which the section on Judah was added in the period of David. While this addition may be attributed to J, the other passages cannot be assigned with certainty to any of the major traditions.

The insertion of the whole in the canonical book of Gn would have been much later (post-exilic) and provided the present theological significance: The later history of the 12 tribes cannot be conceived independently of the patriarchal history. The divine plan, including especially the hegemony of Judah (vv. 8–12) and the important role played by the Joseph tribes (vv. 22–26), is already revealed in the "creative" word of the patriarch (Von Rad, *op. cit.*, 417). Essentially, therefore, the poem has the same function, but on a much grander scale, as the two transitional verses that conclude the preceding chapter.

(Coppens, J., "La bénédiction de Jacob, son cadre historique à la lumière des parallèles ougaritiques," VTSup 4 [1957] 97–115.)

181 (a) (49:1–7). **1–2.** A redactor (perhaps J) has added this introduction. The expression "in days to come" is often eschatological in the prophetic literature (cf. Es 38:16), and may have been so intended here by the post-exilic editor because of v. 10; its original reference would be simply to the distant future. The prose form of v. 1 is followed by a poetic form in v. 2. **3–4.** According to the Semitic mentality, the first-born should have all the qualities of the father; therefore, Reuben would have been expected to achieve prominence. His failure to do so is attributed to his incestuous act (cf. 35:22). The tribe of Reuben, settled in the Transjordan area between Moab and Ammon (Jos 13:15–23), could not displace its more powerful neighbors. It is censured for not rallying to the aid of the northern tribes (Jgs 5:15b–16) and in Dt 33:6 is pictured as greatly reduced in numbers. (The text of ch. 49 is uncertain and probably corrupt; cf. Clamer, *op. cit.*, 495–505; Vawter, *CBQ* 17 [1955] 3–17 for suggested readings.) **5–7.** Simeon and Levi are jointly condemned because of their attack on the Shechemites (ch. 34). The passage is ancient and shows no awareness of the later prominence of the tribe of Levi in the priestly office (cf. Dt 33:8–11); its dispersion in Israel occurred while it was still a nonpriestly tribe. The tribe of Simeon disappeared early; it is not mentioned either in Jgs 5 or in Dt 33. The cities listed in Jos 19:1–9 as belonging to Simeon are considered Judahite in Jos 15:20–32. It is likely that Simeon was early absorbed by the more vigorous Judah (cf. Jos 19:9). The passage has the form of a divine oracle and could not have been pronounced originally by Jacob (cf. v. 7b). (The difficult *m^ekērōtêhem* in v. 5 has been translated "circumcision blades," from the root *krt*, by M. Dahood, *CBQ* 23 [1961] 54–56.)

182 (b) (49:8–18). **8–12.** Judah, the only son actually praised in the poem, is described in terms that can only reflect the Davidic period. The lion image (v. 9) may have been influenced by the Davidic conquest of a Canaanite shrine of a lion-goddess (Vawter, *CBQ* 17 [1955] 5–6). The difficult v. 10 asserts, in general, the permanence of David's hegemony. The CCD, and many other translations, reads the MT *šîlōh* in v. 10c as *šellô* (lit., "which [i.e., the scepter] is to him"); this derivation is difficult to confirm grammatically. A better suggestion is the two words, *šay* and *lôh*, "tribute to him"; hence, we have "until tribute is brought to him, and his is the obedience of the peoples" (W. Moran, *Bib* 39 [1958] 405–25). David remains the center of interest. Verses 11–12 depict the abundance of the period in terms which will take on messianic significance (cf. Am 9:13–15). The messianism of the whole passage, while possibly envisioned typically by the ancient Judahite author, would have been strengthened by the later prophetic oracles and perhaps directly intended by the post-exilic editor. **13.** Zebulun's position by the seashore is a curiosity for the inland-dwelling Israelites. Sidon represents all of Phoenicia. **14–15.** The reference to Issachar is probably derisive (Von Rad, *op. cit.*, 421), suggesting its later subjection to the surrounding Canaanites. Deborah praises both Zebulun (Jgs 5:14,18) and Issachar (Jgs 5:15) for their part in the struggle against Sisera, showing that they had not yet lost their independence. **16–18.** That

Dan (*dān*) will "achieve justice" (*yādîn*) is a circumlocution, dictated by the play on words, to express its continuation as an independent tribe capable of administering justice to its people. It is like a serpent inasmuch as it is victorious despite its size (cf. Jgs 18). The enigmatic v. 18 may be an editorial refrain occasioned by Dan's "salvation" (Clamer, *op. cit.*, 502), or it may simply mark the approximate middle of the poem (De Vaux, *La Genèse*, 214).

183 (c) (49:19–33). **19.** The tribe of Gad, situated in the Transjordan area, was subject to hostile raids by the nomadic desert tribes. The CCD reproduces the alliteration of the Hebrew, where a triple pun on the name of Gad is made. **20.** Asher's territory in western Galilee was fertile land (cf. Dt 33:24). **21.** Naphtali was situated near the Lake of Tiberias. The text here is uncertain; no clear meaning emerges. **22–26.** Joseph is the only son truly blessed by Jacob. The text is most uncertain, and, for the most part, only generalities can be deduced from it. The first part (v. 22) suggests the prosperity of the tribe, represented by Ephraim and Manasseh. The second part (vv. 23–24) depicts Joseph's victory over his enemies (the historical allusion is not clear; perhaps Jgs 6–8). The epithets applied to God in v. 24b are bold anthropomorphisms (Vawter, *CBQ* 17 [1955] 10–12). The blessing proper follows naturally in vv. 25–26. Although God is the only true source of the blessings, they have been given a particularly concrete formulation in v. 25b; "each of the elements which figure in Gn and Dt (33:13–16) as sources of blessings is personified as a deity in the Ugaritic pantheon, or is used as a surrogate for deity" (Vawter, *CBQ* 17 [1955] 13). Verse 26a stresses the permanence of the blessings. In v. 26b Joseph is called a *nāzîr*, i.e., "one consecrated" or "one set apart" by the special election of God, another reference to the pre-eminence of the Joseph tribes in historical Israel. **27.** Only the history of the tribe of Benjamin could justify this description (cf. Jgs 3:15–30; 19–21). As in almost all the other cases, the very early history of the tribe is intended, attesting to the antiquity of the individual poems. **28a.** The conclusion reflects the editor's awareness that the "blessings" concerned the tribes of Israel, not Jacob's sons. **29b–33.** The section parallels J's account in 47:29–31. The terminology (cf. ch. 23), precise details, and insistence on the legal possession of the piece of land reveal P's hand. As in the other traditions, the theology of the one land and the one people is emphasized. Verse 33a is an insertion from J, originally concluding Jacob's blessing of Ephraim and Manasseh in ch. 48 (cf. 48:2).

184 **(N) The Burial of Jacob and the Final Acts of Joseph (50:1–26) (J, E, and P).** The final chapter resumes the three traditions. The burial of Jacob is related by both J (vv. 1–11 and 14) and P (vv. 12–13). The last acts of Joseph (vv. 15–26) are related principally by E. Both sections form a fitting conclusion to the book and provide a summary of its theology in narrative form. The second stage of the divine plan, expressed in the patriarchal promises, will be worked out in Egypt, but the transference of Jacob's remains to Canaan already prefigures the later deliverance of his people from Egypt. God will save his people (v. 20) and will fulfill the promise of the land (v. 24).

185 (a) (50:1–14). **1–3.** The Egyptians' highly developed views on the afterlife explain the practice of embalming. Joseph would have had his father embalmed because of the long journey to Canaan. Egyptian records frequently mention 70 days (with some variations) as the period of mummification (cf. v. 3b; Vergote, *op. cit.*, 199–200). The number of days mentioned by J (40, v. 3a) can only be a round number. **4–6.** Mourning ritual may have forbidden Joseph's appearance in court, or it may be that Joseph wanted the backing of other court officials. J seems to be aware of a special burial place dug by Jacob himself (v. 5; see comment on 47:30). **7–9.** With typical love for colorful details, J describes the funeral procession. The chariots, besides adding to the pomp, would have also afforded protection along the way. **10–11.** Neither "Goren-Atad" (the "threshing floor of Atad") nor Abel-mizraim are known. As noted (cf. v. 5), J seems to suppose a special burial place for Jacob which, according to our passage, would be in the Transjordan area (vv. 10a,11b). J's account of the actual burial there would have been omitted to make room for P's account (vv. 12–13). The name "Abel-mizraim" (*'ābēl miṣrayim*, "the plain of the Egyptians") is explained by the "mourning" (*'ēbel*) of the Egyptians. **12–13.** These verses belong to P, as a conclusion to the narrative in 49:28bff. Despite the inconsistencies resulting from this conflation of traditions, the editor wishes to preserve the theology inherent in P. **14.** With this verse, J concludes (with the possible exception of v. 22). As usual, the Yahwist theology must be deduced from the events themselves. On the contrary, the conclusion of E, which follows, makes the theology explicit.

186 (b) (50:15–26). **15–17.** The repeated mention of the fear of Joseph's brothers (cf. 42:21; 43:18; 44:13) underscores the forgiving nature of Joseph. Here the fear is occasioned by the death of Jacob who, while alive, would have kept peace among them. In the first scene (vv. 16–17), the brothers send a message recalling Jacob's charge to Joseph to forgive them. Such a charge, though not recorded, is not unlikely. The explicit reference to "the God of your father" stresses the religious motive, the bond of common worship. **18–21.** In this second scene, the theology of all the preceding events is made clear. The turn of events has manifested the divine plan and, implicitly, the divine judgment. The brothers' evil deed, like all history, is used by God for his purposes, and in this sense, that deed is part of salvation history. By punishing them Joseph would, in effect, be reversing the divine judgment and so would "take the place of God." "To save the lives of many people" (v. 20) would, in the context, refer to preservation from the famine (cf. 45:5–8). The sacred author doubtless envisioned a larger context (cf. v. 24). **22–23.** Abundant records from Egypt show that 110 years were considered an ideal lifetime (cf. Vergote, *op. cit.*, 200–201; *ANET* 414d). Machir was an important clan in later Israel (cf. Nm 32:39–40; Jos 17:1; Jgs 5:14c), possibly at one time a tribal member of the amphictyony, which would explain the ethnic etiology here ("born on Joseph's knees," i.e., adopted by him; cf. 30:3; 48:12). **24–26.** The last words of Joseph (and of Gn) transcend the particular history of the sons of Jacob and recall the original promise made to Abraham (cf. 12:7), repeated frequently throughout the patriarchal narrative. At the same time, they anticipate the Exodus and the fulfillment of the promise (cf. Heb 11:22). The mention of Joseph's age in v. 26 suggests that v. 22b is a doublet (perhaps from J). The final statement (v. 26b) is at once a fitting conclusion to the patriarchal story, and, because Joseph is not buried as would be expected by Hebr custom, a vivid suggestion that the story has not ended.

3

EXODUS

John E. Huesman, S.J.

BIBLIOGRAPHY

1 Auerbach, E., *Moses* (Amsterdam, 1953). Auzou, G., *De la servitude au service: Étude du Livre de l'Exode* (Paris, 1961). Barsotti, D., *Spiritualité de l'Exode* (Bruges, 1959). Buber, M., *Moses* (N.Y., 1958). Cassuto, U., *A Commentary on the Book of Exodus* (in Hebrew; Jerusalem, 1959). Cazelles, H. *et al.*, *Moïse, l'homme de l'alliance* (Cahiers Sioniens; Paris, 1954). Clamer, A., *L'Exode* (Paris, 1956). Driver, S. R., *The Book of Exodus* (Cambridge, 1911). Finegan, J., *Let My People Go* (N.Y., 1963). Fortier, P. and H. de Lubac (eds.), *Origène: homélies sur l'Exode* (Paris, 1947). Galbiati, E., *La Struttura letteraria dell' Esodo* (Rome, 1956). Mallon, A., *La géographie de l'Exode* (Cairo, 1926). Neher, A., *Moses and the Vocation of the Jewish People* (London, 1959). Noth, M., *Exodus* (Phila., 1962). Rabbinowitz, J., *Exodus* (Soncino; London, 1947). Wright G. E., "Exodus" *IDB*, 2, 189–99.

INTRODUCTION

2 The Exodus, viewed as a complexus of choice, deliverance, and covenant, has long been hailed by biblical scholars as the cardinal dogma of OT religion. What the incarnation is to Christianity the Exodus is to the OT; without it, we cannot understand the history and religion of the Hebrews. Genesis constitutes an introduction, in two stages (prehistory, chs. 1–11, and the history of the patriarchs, chs. 12–50), to this key event.

Exodus has received its Lat and Eng title from the LXX. Inasmuch as only chs. 1–15 concern the departure from Egypt, its title does not do full justice to its content. The Hebr title is *wᵉʾēlleh šᵉmôt* (and these are the names), which constitutes the opening words of the book.

The literary form of Ex has been aptly designated as a religious epic. It contains sound historical facts, facts which form the groundwork of Israelite religion but which are frequently embellished with an epic tone. Such a mode of writing served a twofold end: It enhanced the greatness of the God of Israel, and it put in singular relief the people of his choice.

3 **(I) Composition.** Any adequate discussion of the composition of Ex would involve a thorough analysis of the entire pentateuchal problem and the documentary hypothesis (→ Pentateuch, 1:6–16). Yahwist, Elohist, and Priestly sources are prominent in this book, with touches as well of the Deuteronomist. Where pertinent, individual sources will be discussed in the commentary. The final redaction, or the form of the book as we have it today, probably dates from the 5th cent. BC.

4 **(II) The Date.** Unfortunately, our sources do not name the Egyptian Pharaoh or Pharaohs under whom the events transpired. The reference in 1 Kgs 6:1 to 480 years from the Exodus to the Solomonic temple has led some scholars to maintain a 15th-cent. date. With Solomon's accession set rather firmly at 960 BC, the Exodus would be *ca.* 1440 BC. Against this date is the biblical evidence that the Hebrews were employed on royal building projects in the delta area, projects prominent in the 19th Dynasty but unknown to the 18th Dynasty, which flourished in the 15th cent. Because archaeological evidence leans toward a 13th cent. date, it is perhaps safer to take the 480 years of 1 Kgs as a round number indicating 12 generations.

From Ex 1:11 (the Israelites built for Pharaoh store cities), we arrive at the era of Seti I (1309–1290) as the period of the oppression, an era continued by his successor Ramses II (1290–24). Shortly after the accession of the latter, the actual Exodus from Egypt took place. After the 40 years (again, a generation) of desert wandering, the conquest of Palestine began (*ca.* 1250). The destruction of numerous Palestinian towns (e.g., Hazor, Lachish, and Tell Beit Mirsim) in the second half of the 13th cent.—a fact noted by modern scientific archaeology—confirms this dating. Thus we shall assume throughout the present commentary the approximate date 1280 for the actual Exodus. (For more thorough discussions of this problem, see H. H. Rowley, *From Joseph to Joshua* [London, 1948]; and Albright, *FSAC*.)

5 **(III) Exodus and Typology.** Evidences of Ex typology are scattered throughout the OT, the NT,

and patristic literature; a few references to Mt serve as illustration.

It has often been remarked that Matthew saw in Christ the new Israel and the new Moses. Hosea's reference to the first Exodus (Hos 11:1) is applied in Mt to Christ's return from Egypt (Mt 2:15), "Out of Egypt have I called my son." The first Israel was "baptized" in the Reed Sea (Ex 14); Christ, the new Israel, was baptized in the waters of the Jordan (Mt 3:13–17). Christ was to spend 40 days in the desert (Mt 4:1–11) to recall the 40 years of Israel's testing in the Exodus (Ex and Nm) and the 40 days of Moses' sojourn on Sinai (Ex 24:18).

The first Moses, Israel's great lawgiver, presented his people with the law promulgated on Mt. Sinai (24:3–8). Christ, the new Moses, proposed his law in the Sermon on the Mount (Mt 5–6). Matthew is the only evangelist to stress the mount imagery for the site of this event. In his narrative of the transfiguration (Mt 17:1–8), he relates Moses and Christ. The bright cloud that once enveloped the first Moses (Ex 24:15–18) now descends upon Christ, the new Moses, as well (Mt 17:5). (For further treatment of this topic, see J. Daniélou, *From Shadows to Reality* [London, 1960] 153–226; B. M. Ahern, *The Bridge* [vol. 1; N.Y., 1955] 53–74.)

6 **(IV) Outline.** Exodus can be divided into six sections. The first section (1:1–12:36) tells the story of Israel in Egypt: the oppression of the Israelites; the birth and adoption of Moses; his flight to, and sojourn in, Midian; and his call by Yahweh. After his choice, Moses returns to confront Pharaoh with the divine command, "Let my people go." The obduracy of Pharaoh and the crescendo of plagues occupy most of the remaining material of this section. With the death of the first-born of the Egyptians, the Israelites win their freedom and prepare to depart from the land of slavery.

The second section (12:37–18:27) treats the Exodus and the wandering. Avoiding the Way of the Land of the Philistines, Moses leads his people across the Sea of Reeds onto the rugged terrain of the Sinai Peninsula. Throughout the narrative, special emphasis is laid on the divine assistance accorded the Israelites. The victory paean of ch. 15 constitutes a glorious and joyful hymn of praise and simultaneously provides us with one of our oldest pieces of Hebr poetry. To the subsequent complaints of the people, Yahweh responds with manna, quail, and water from the rock. Through Moses' intercession, he also grants them victory over the Amalekites, and the section closes with the institution of judges.

The third and most important section (19:1–24:18) deals with the covenant. Yahweh summons his chosen leader to Sinai's mount and through him proposes a unique union with Israel—the Israelites will be his people and he will be their God. The Decalogue and Book of the Covenant announce the stipulations incumbent upon Israel as a result of this union.

The fourth section (25:1–31:18) enumerates the detailed instructions for the Tabernacle: e.g., the size, construction materials, and adornments. Also in this section occurs the divine institution of the priesthood, with specific instructions regarding consecration and priestly vestments. Further injunctions concern sacrifices.

The brief fifth section (32:1–34:35) tells of the sorry apostasy of the chosen people and their worship of the golden calf. The further mediation of Moses averts the destruction of his people and wins a renewal of the covenant with Yahweh. The sixth and final section (35:1–40:38) describes the fulfillment of the commands in chs. 25–31.

(I) Israel in Egypt (1:1–12:36)
- (A) Growth of the Israelites (1:1–7)
- (B) Oppression of the Israelites (1:8–22)
- (C) Birth and Adoption of Moses (2:1–10)
- (D) Moses' Flight and Sojourn in Midian (2:11–22)
- (E) The Call of Moses (2:23–4:9)
- (F) Aaron as Assistant (4:10–17)
- (G) The Return of Moses and Pharaoh's Obduracy (4:18–5:13)
- (H) Complaint of the Israelites and Renewal of God's Promise (5:14–6:13)
- (I) The Genealogy of Moses (6:14–27)
- (J) The Commission to Moses and Aaron (6:28–7:13
- (K) The Plagues (7:14–11:10)
  - (a) The First Plague: Water Turned to Blood (7:14–24)
  - (b) The Second Plague: Frogs (7:25–8:11)
  - (c) The Third Plague: Gnats (8:12–14)
  - (d) The Fourth Plague: Flies (8:16–28)
  - (e) The Fifth Plague: Pestilence (9:1–7)
  - (f) The Sixth Plague: Boils (9:8–12)
  - (g) The Seventh Plague: Hail (9:13–35)
  - (h) The Eighth Plague: Locusts (10:1–20)
  - (i) The Ninth Plague: Darkness (10:21–29)
  - (j) The Tenth Plague: Death of the First-Born (11:1–10)
- (L) The Pasch and Azymes (12:1–20)
- (M) The Passover: Death and Deliverance (12:21–36)

(II) The Exodus and Wandering (12:37–18:27)
- (A) The Departure from Egypt (12:37–51)
- (B) Azymes and the Consecration of the First-born (13:1–16)
- (C) Israel Leaves Its Place of Bondage (13:17–22)
- (D) The Crossing of the Reed Sea (14:1–22)
- (E) Destruction of the Egyptians (14:23–31)
- (F) A Paean of Victory (15:1–21)
- (G) Marah and Elim (15:22–27)
- (H) Manna and Quail (16:1–36)
- (I) Water from the Rock (17:1–7)
- (J) A Challenge from Amalek (17:8–16)
- (K) Moses Meets Jethro (18:1–12)
- (L) The Institution of Judges (18:13–27)

(III) The Covenant (19:1–24:18)
- (A) Israel Comes to Sinai (19:1–3)
- (B) A Divine Promise (19:4–8)
- (C) The Theophany of Sinai (19:9–25)
- (D) The Decalogue (20:1–17)
  - (a) The First Commandment (20:2–6)
  - (b) Commandments Two Through Ten (20:7–17)
- (E) The Mediation of Moses (20:18–21)
- (F) The Book of the Covenant (20:22–23:19)
  - (a) Laws of Worship (20:22–26)
  - (b) Laws Regarding Slaves (21:1–11)
  - (c) Laws Regarding Homicide (21:12–17)
  - (d) Laws Regarding Bodily Injuries (21:18–32)
  - (e) Laws Regarding Property Damages (21:33–22:14)
  - (f) Social Laws (22:15–30)
  - (g) Justice and Duties to One's Neighbors (23:1–9)
  - (h) Religious Laws (23:10–19)
- (G) Warnings and Promises (23:20–33)
- (H) Ratification of the Covenant (24:1–11
- (I) Moses on Sinai (24:12–18)

(IV) The Tabernacle (25:1–31:18)
- (A) Collection of Materials (25:1–9)
- (B) The Ark (25:10–22)
- (C) The Table of Showbread (25:23–30)
- (D) The Lampstand (25:31–40)
- (E) The Tent Cloth (26:1–14)
- (F) The Framework (26:15–30)
- (G) The Veils (26:31–37)
- (H) The Altar of Sacrifice (27:1–8)
- (I) The Tabernacle Court (27:9–21)
- (J) The Priesthood (28:1–5)
- (K) The Ephod and the Breastpiece (28:6–30)
- (L) Other Vestments (28:31–43)
- (M) Consecration of the Priests (29:1–9)
- (N) Ordination Sacrifices (29:10–37)
- (O) Daily Sacrifices (29:38–46)
- (P) The Altar of Incense (30:1–10)
- (Q) Census Tax (30:11–16)

COMMENTARY

(I) Israel in Egypt (1:1–12:36)

7 **(A) Growth of the Israelites (1:1–7).** The chronological setting of the opening verses of Ex is the era *ca.* 1710 BC. At this time, the sons of Jacob moved to Egypt in the wake of the Hyksos rule (*ca.* 1720–1550). The inspired author shows little concern for secular history, however, and contents himself with the fate of the family of Jacob. **5.** According to the MT, the total number of Jacob's direct descendants was 70; they are named in Gn 46:8–27. In the LXX, as well as in Acts 7:14, the number given is 75, a figure justified by the inclusion of two sons and a grandson of Ephraim and a son and a grandson of Manasseh. The LXX, then, includes all the descendants of Jacob, not merely (as in the MT) those who accompanied Jacob to Egypt. **7.** The language used to describe the growth of the Israelites in Egypt is reminiscent of ch. 1 of Gn (1:20,28). This flowering of the Israelites marks the fulfillment of God's promises, to Abraham in Gn 12:2 and 17:6 and to Jacob in Gn 35:11. The land in this verse may be the area of Goshen of Gn 47:1, but the Pharaoh's concern with the sweeping growth of these foreigners would seem to indicate that they have spread throughout his kingdom. Goshen itself was a valley 30 to 40 mi. long, centering in the Wadi Tumilat area of NE Egypt and extending from Lake Timsah to the Nile.

8 **(B) Oppression of the Israelites (1:8–22).** The new Pharaoh, who knew nothing of Joseph, was—in our reckoning—Seti I. With his successor in the 19th Dynasty, Ramses II, this monarch moved the royal throne from Thebes in Upper Egypt to the delta area and inaugurated a vast building program. The excavations at Tell er-Retabeh (ancient Pithom) and Tanis indicate the plausibility of the slave labor imposed upon the Israelites. The story of the midwives serves to emphasize God's providential care of his people, a theme that pervades the whole book. **19.** The "robust" of this verse may also be read "animals," alluding to the speed and ease with which the women gave birth. According to Josephus (*Ant.* 2. 9, 2), the midwives were themselves Egyptians. The MT, however, calls them Israelites, a stand strengthened by modern research establishing their names to be of NW Semitic, not Egyptian, origin.

9 **(C) Birth and Adoption of Moses (2:1–10).** These colorful details about Moses' origin have been amplified in later Jewish tradition, where we learn, e.g. that Pharaoh's daughter fetched the child from the water herself because her handmaids refused to disobey their monarch's edict. This tradition is depicted on a mural in the ancient synagogue at Dura-Europos in eastern Syria. Further legendary rabbinical tradition tells us that as a result of her charity, Pharaoh's daughter—at her first touch of the basket—was cured of leprosy. There is no historical justification for such traditions, but they proved very popular with the people and led to the formulation of a specific literary form known as haggadic midrash, i.e., a pious tale told to edify. **10.** Here we have a popular etymology for the name Moses, based on the Hebr root *mšh*, "to draw up." Such popular etymologies are common throughout the OT; the word "Hebrew," e.g., means "the people from across the river." Modern authorities are convinced of the Egyptian origin of Moses and assure us it is only a part of his whole name. The Egyptian *Mose* means "is born." Egyptologists point to other examples, such as Ah-mose (Ah is born) and Tut-mose (Tut is born). Jewish tradition has removed the first part of Moses' distinctively Egyptian name.

The OT makes no mention of Moses' education, although Josephus and Philo speak quite freely on this matter (cf. Acts 7:22). Egypt at this time still controlled a far-flung empire. To assure her dominance, she trained enterprising young courtiers in the intricacies of her own hieroglyphic and hieratic scripts as well as in the Assyro-Babylonian, Hittite, and Ugaritic cuneiform of the neighboring nations. Amidst such an atmosphere, there is no reason to suppose gratuitously, as did 19th-cent. scholars, that Moses must have been illiterate.

10 **(D) Moses' Flight and Sojourn in Midian (2:11–22).** Despite his privileged status at court, Moses remembered his ethnic background and rose to take vengeance against an oppressor of his people. The attitude of his fellow Hebrew (v. 14) gives evidence of the dispirited condition to which the oppression had dragged the Israelites and with which, as future leader of the people Moses would have frequent occasion to contend. Josephus (*Ant.* 2. 10, 11) provides a different motive for Moses' flight. It was occasioned, he tells us, by the jealousy of the Pharaoh himself. In this story, Moses had led a successful military campaign in Ethiopia and had returned to Egypt with a daughter of the king as his bride. Once again we know nothing of Josephus' sources. Because Canaan belonged to Egypt at this time, Moses chose the Sinai Peninsula as a safer destination for his flight. The Midianites, among whom he spent this exile, are not new to biblical readers (cf. Gn 25:2). There remains some controversy regarding the precise locality of the Midianites. W. Phythian-Adams maintains that they inhabited what is now the northern Hejaz, the area E of the Gulf of Aqabah and the mountains of ancient Edom. W. F. Albright (Albright, *FSAC* 257) and others favor the Sinai Peninsula itself, which accords better with the traditional site of Mt. Sinai. Hence, Moses picked a kindred Semitic people among whom to hide. Once again, he undertakes the cause of the oppressed, driving off the shepherds who were abusing the daughters of Reuel.

18. Albright suggests the following reading: "And they [the daughters of the priest of Midian, v. 16] came to ⟨Jethro, son of⟩ Reuel their father" (W. F. Albright, *CBQ* 25 [1963] 6–11). Our sources give us three names for the patron and father-in-law of Moses: Reuel, Jethro, and Hobab. To solve this problem and to harmonize the varied characteristics assigned to Jethro (Ex 3:1) and Hobab (Nm 10:29 and Jgs 4:11), Albright proposes first that Reuel is merely a clan name. Jethro, the aged father with seven daughters who later advises Moses from the wealth of his experience, was Moses' father-in-law. Hobab, the vigorous younger man whom Moses wishes to employ as their guide in the desert, was actually Moses' son-in-law. We are told simply that Moses spent a long time among this Bedouin folk and took a wife from among them. That he did not consider himself a member of their clan is clear from the name he gave his newborn son; for Gershom simply means "a stranger there."

We have already mentioned that the author of Ex employed various sources. These early verses clearly illustrate a composite character. In ch. 1, P contributes a genealogy (1–5). The following verses (6–14) provide J's account of the persecution of the Israelites by the Pharaoh, "who knew nothing of Joseph" (v. 8). Verses 15–22, as well as the description of the birth of Moses (2:1–10), show E's imprint. The author relies once again on J to relate Moses' flight to Midian (2:11–22). This combinative process constitutes a phenomenon that recurs throughout the book.

11 **(E) The Call of Moses (2:23–4:9).** The Egyptian monarch whose death is heralded in v. 23 would be Seti I; the year would be 1290. Typical of Near Eastern peoples, the subject nations took the occasion of the death of an unpopular monarch as a signal for rebellion. Hence, we may be sure that the enslaved Hebrews were ripe for the leadership to free them from their yoke. Moreover, the new Pharaoh would soon prove a much more energetic builder than his predecessor, a fact that would bring little comfort to the Hebr corvée.

Horeb of 3:1 is E's designation of the mountain which J terms Sinai. Such instances of dual designation are common in the Pentateuch. The angel of the Lord (3:2) in OT literature may represent God himself or his angel. Here we are more probably confronted with a theophany in which God somehow makes himself known to his chosen human instrument. To Moses he reveals his relationship to Abraham, Isaac, and Jacob, his fixed resolve to deliver the descendants of the patriarchs from their oppressors, and that Moses is to be his chosen instrument of deliverance. To Moses' consternation at his selection, God replies "I will be with you" (3:12). The present text marks the first OT occurrence of this formula, one that will find frequent use throughout the OT (e.g., Gideon and Jeremiah), reaching its climax in the mission of the apostles (Mt 28:20). It constitutes a divine assurance of success accorded a chosen human instrument in carrying out a mission far beyond his natural powers.

12 In answer to Moses' question regarding his name, God replies with the celebrated "I am who I am" (3:14). This statement is certainly the occasion for the divine title *Yahweh*. Of the many suggestions on the meaning of Yahweh, the most satisfactory is Albright's "He causes to be." The form can only be a causative Hiphil. On our present text, Albright writes: "The enigmatic formula in Ex 3:14 which in biblical Hebrew means 'I am what I am,' if transposed into the form in the third person required by the causative *Yahweh*, can only become *Yahweh asher yihweh* (later *yihyeh*), 'He Causes to be what Comes into Existence' " (Albright, *FSAC* 261). To object that such an interpretation involves too abstract a meaning for the period is to overlook numerous Egyptian and Akkadian texts of the pre-Mosaic period that provide similar illustrations of this idea.

Some authorities (e.g., BJ) propose a completely different understanding of the mysterious "I am who I am." Among the ancient Semites, one who knew a name supposedly had power over the being so titled. Hence, to know God's name—as Moses requested—was tantamount to seeking power over God. Our present formula, they contend, constitutes a refusal on God's part to betray his name to man, consequently reaffirming his transcendent otherness.

In later times, a deep reverence for the name Yahweh led to the use of the term *Adonai* (my lord) as its substitute. The LXX uses *Kyrios*, the Vg, *Dominus*, and both the CCD and the RSV, "Lord," to represent the sacred tetragrammaton *YHWH*. The oft-heard Jehovah has resulted from a misreading of the name in the pointed Hebr text; therefore, no justification exists for its use. According to J, God was worshiped under the title Yahweh even before the flood (Gn 4:26). According to P, God made himself known to the patriarchs under the title El Shaddai (Gn 17:1; Ex 6:2–3). Our present text (from E) maintains that it was to Moses, in these specific circumstances, that God revealed the divine name Yahweh. In contrast to J, which stresses continuity, these sources underline the specific revelation made at Sinai. The theory that Yahweh was the God of the Kenites and that it was from this source that Moses learned of him (Rowley, *op. cit.*) is unlikely. The sacred author assures us it is no new God being revealed to Moses, but the God of Abraham, Isaac, and Jacob.

After the revelation of his name, God elaborates the mission of his newly chosen instrument (vv. 16–22): Moses is to lead his fellow Hebrews to the land of the Canaanites, and his invitation will be heeded by the people. The Pharaoh's reaction will not be favorable; loathe to lose these valuable slaves, he will loudly protest their departure. Only the tempering hand of Yahweh will eventually urge him to free them. Nor are Yahweh's people to leave the land empty-handed. Their long years of slavery are to be repaid in a spoliation of the Egyptians before their departure. To Moses' doubt about his reception among his people—he might well remember the incident of Ex 2:14—God gives the answer of physical signs as assurance of the divine protection.

13 **(F) Aaron as Assistant (4:10–17).** Despite the signs already given him, Moses continues to doubt his fitness as a leader. Now it is his slowness of speech that troubles him. The patient Yahweh assigns Moses' brother Aaron to be his spokesman, or, lit., his "mouth," but Aaron must utter only the message given him by Moses or by Yahweh himself.

14 **(G) The Return of Moses and Pharaoh's Obduracy (4:18–5:13).** With the blessing of his father-in-law, Jethro, Moses sets off with his wife and children. En route, he hears the celebrated reminder that Yahweh will harden Pharaoh's heart (4:21). The ancient Hebr writers very frequently bypassed all secondary causality to attribute everything to the First Cause, i.e., God. Their interest in thus safeguarding Yahweh's influence and the working out of his providence never led them to forget about man's responsibility and his guilt for sin. At least three times, the sacred author will point to Pharaoh's responsibility in this matter—8:15; 8:28; 9:34. We note this same Semitic approach in Is 6:10 and in Christ's reference to this verse in Mt 13:10–15.

Verses 24–26 remain very mysterious. Moses has probably become ill and lies helpless. Just what is his guilt? Perhaps it is his own lack of circumcision or his failure to circumcise his sons. Or, it could be his adoption of the Midianite practice of circumcision at the time of marriage. In Gn, God's command regarding circumcision (Gn 17:9–12) is clearly stated. As the leader of God's people, Moses should heed every divine prescription. It is clear that Zipporah herself circumcised her son. She then most probably simulated a circumcision of her husband by touching him with his son's foreskin. The mention of feet is no doubt a euphemism. Some suggest that vv. 24–26 represent a later effort on the part of a fervent traditionalist to connect the practice of circumcision with Moses himself.

15 We next learn of the meeting of Moses and his brother Aaron, which took place near Sinai (4:27). Moses informs his brother of God's designs for his people and of Aaron's role in this work. In the subsequent gathering of the elders of Israel, Aaron fulfills his task as spokesman for his brother for the first time. When Moses performs the signs enjoined him by Yahweh, the elders are convinced. They profess their belief and express their gratitude to the God who has remembered his suffering people.

The next scene (5:1) is Moses and Aaron's initial confrontation with Pharaoh. The item uppermost in the monarch's mind is the accomplishment of his great building projects. The very suggestion that this prize labor force be set free to worship their God in leisure is an affront to his goals. Hence, he adds to their already heavy burden the chore of collecting the straw so essential to provide consistency to their clay bricks. The Pharaoh's proud attitude sets in bolder relief the drama wherein the unknown Yahweh gradually strips him of the trappings of his glory.

16 **(H) Complaint of the Israelites and Renewal of God's Promise (5:14–6:13).** The taskmasters were probably the Egyptian officials in charge of building operations. In dealing with subject peoples, the controlling power generally used their more promising leaders as foremen. In their new plight, these foremen petition Pharaoh for a more righteous consideration of their situation. Pharaoh tells them that it is the request of Moses and Aaron that has brought about the deterioration of their working conditions. For the first time since his appointment, Moses experiences the wrath of his own people, an occurrence that was to become commonplace for him in effecting their deliverance. Inextricably trapped between the divine command and the anger of the people, Moses pleads with Yahweh for help. Once more he is assured that the power of Israel's God will force Pharaoh to his knees.

The present material comes from P and parallels for us the account of Moses' call as found in chs. 3–4. Because P has structured Gn by the Noachic and Abrahamic covenants, it is not surprising to find here the covenant formula, "I will take you as my own people, and you shall have me as your God" (6:7). This covenant concept will be discussed at greater length in the commentary on ch. 20.

17 **(I) The Genealogy of Moses (6:14–27).** This tradition derives from P. Although Moses and his brother are of the Levitical line, Reuben and Simeon are mentioned first because they are Levi's older brothers. According to the present enumeration, Moses is a fourth-generation descendant of Jacob. How may we correlate this fact with the length of the Egyptian sojourn? This list nowhere claims to mention all the generations of Jacob, and the term son referred quite loosely to anyone in the direct line, whether son, grandson, great-grandson, etc. The type of marriage between Amram and his aunt (cousin in the LXX) would be forbidden by later legislation. The progeny of Moses go unmentioned, whereas Eleazar and Korah, the descendants of Aaron, are noted, the former for his priestly role and the latter for his connection with the temple ritual. Although late in origin, the authenticity of the present list is strengthened by the faithful retention of such distinctively Egyptian names as Putiel and Phinehas.

18 **(J) The Commission to Moses and Aaron (6:28–7:13).** This account is the P version of the mandate described in 3:1–4:17 (J, E). The role of Aaron fulfills the prophetic office perfectly, because it consists primarily in his being spokesman for another. The ages assigned to Moses and Aaron are very probably too high, resulting from both the common Hebr practice of counting 40 years to a generation and P's own peculiar system of years. Albright and other authorities more realistically figure 25 years to a generation.

The final part of this section again reflects P's predilection for Aaron. Whereas ch. 4 emphasized that Moses was to use his own rod in performing signs for Pharaoh, we here learn that his lieutenant, Aaron, assumes the role of thaumaturge for him.

19 **(K) The Plagues (7:14–11:10).** At the start we note two distinctive approaches to this lengthy section. The first, predominant until relatively modern times, viewed the events as strictly supernatural—clear and direct interventions by Almighty God to effect the release of his people. The second, which today wins the assent of most Catholic exegetes, points out that the plagues have bases in natural phenomena occurring annually, or at least frequently, in Egypt between July, when the Nile begins to overflow its banks, and the following April. Adherents of this second approach are quick to emphasize the providential character of these phenomena—e.g., in their intensity—in effecting the release of the Hebrews; on the other hand, the biblical narrative interprets all the happenings as God's will.

What does the sacred author mean by the wondrous character of these events? For us, owing to our acquaintance with the natural sciences, nature itself has come to mean a compact system, governed by rigid laws. The clear-cut interference with these laws we term a miracle. Such an idea was unknown to the ancient Semite, for whom the elements of nature not only were personalized, but also very frequently were even given a divine personality. To the pagan neighbors of Israel, these nature deities were friendly or hostile insofar as they benefited or harmed their earthly subjects. Through divine revelation, the Hebrew realized that the omnipotent Yahweh controlled these forces himself, using them for his own designs. Indeed, the forces of nature manifested Yahweh. Hence the Hebrew could, and frequently did, look upon natural phenomena as wondrous signs of Yahweh that did not involve simultaneously any suspension of our technically conceived laws of nature.

No single source lists all the plagues for us; J gives eight (1–2, 4–5, 7–10); E, five (1, 7–10); and P, five (1–3, 6, 10). All agree on the first and last. As is usual, the sources vary in their approach. In J, God intervenes directly at the word of Moses. In E, God is at work when Moses stretches forth his rod. In P, the effective intervention of Aaron, who wields the rod, receives emphasis, and we have the Egyptian magicians creating a contest between Yahweh and their own deities. The redactor who gathered these sources has interwoven them with great skill to heighten the dramatic effect. He, too, views the events as a contest between Yahweh and the pagan deities, one that will prove the omnipotence of Yahweh.

The first four plagues provide little more than a source of annoyance; some, in fact, even the Egyptian magicians can perform. The next four are more serious, causing damage to persons and property. The ninth is a source of terror and the tenth brings utter consternation to the Egyptians, resulting in Pharaoh's resolve to let this people go. The epic coloring of the events is not restricted to the Ex account. It is evident in Pss as well (Pss 78 and 105) and in the distinctively midrashic approach of Wis (Wis 11:14–20; 16:1–18).

(See Hort, G., "The Plagues of Egypt," *ZAW* 69 [1957] 84–103; *ZAW* 70 [1958] 48–59. McCarthy, D. J., "Moses' Dealings with Pharaoh: Ex 7, 8–10, 27," *CBQ* 27 [1965] 336–47.)

20 (a) The First Plague: Water Turned to Blood (7:14–24). This section shows evidence of J, E, and P. Shortly before the annual inundation, as it sweeps through the mountainous region of Africa the Nile picks up red deposits that transform its color; it is thus known to the natives as the Red Nile. It remains red for a short time before it assumes a greenish shade. Epic embellishments are the work of P: e.g., the importance of Aaron's role and the coloration not only of the Nile, but of all the waters of Egypt.

(b) The Second Plague: Frogs (7:25–8:11). (J and P are evident.) The phenomenon of swarms of frogs is a second sequel to the Nile's inundation. Here, the sign element consists in the intensity of numbers and Moses' ability to halt the plague. Once again, P alludes to the influence of Aaron, underscoring the uniquitous character of the plague and the challenge of the magicians. The Pharaoh's change of heart is short-lived.

(c) The Third Plague: Gnats (8:12–14). This plague is the work of P only. There is some controversy as to whether the term *kinnîm* should be translated "gnats" or "mosquitoes." Once again, the flooding of the Nile provides ideal circumstances for the genesis of such a plague.

21 (d) The Fourth Plague: Flies (8:16–28). This plague which we attribute to J, seems to be a doublet of the previous plague. Once again, there is some doubt regarding the plague's nature, i.e., whether it consisted of ordinary flies, so common to all Near Eastern countries, or whether we have here swarms of dogflies (in the LXX). The element of sign appears in the intensity of their presence, their absence from the Hebr territory in Goshen, and their disappearance at the prayer of Moses. Here, too, occurs Pharaoh's first concession: The Hebrews may have time off to sacrifice to their God, but within the confines of Egypt. Moses disdainfully rejects this offer, for the sacrifices in vogue among Semites would have incurred the wrath of the Egyptian people, who had deified the animals commonly employed for sacrifice by their Semitic neighbors. Pharaoh then yields to the demands of Moses, only to renege once again on his promise.

22 (e) The Fifth Plague: Pestilence (9:1–7). This plague is the work of J. The obvious discrepancy between 9:6–7 and 9:9,11 results from the different traditions being utilized. Among the animals mentioned in v. 3 are the horse, introduced into Egypt at the time of Hyksos invasion (*ca.* 1710), and the camel, not domesticated until the period of the Judges (cf. the Midianite incursions in Jgs 6:1–6). Mention of the camel here, as well as earlier references (Gn 12:16; 24:11), must be regarded as anachronisms.

(f) The Sixth Plague: Boils (9:8–12). The source of the sixth plague is P. Just what type of malady is involved in the present section is not known. Because animals are also afflicted, some scholars think that this plague is P's version of the fifth. Others suggest that we are dealing here with the "Nile-scab," an irritating but relatively harmless skin eruption that occurs at the time of the Nile inundation.

23 (g) The Seventh Plague: Hail (9:13–35). With barley in ear and flax in bud in the early months of the year (9:31–32—perhaps a preparation for 10:5), January or February would be indicated as the time of the seventh plague. Although hailstorms are rare in Egypt, they do occur occasionally during these months with unusual severity. Even in modern times, 2-lb. hailstones have been found which have killed cattle in the field. Verses 14–16 (possibly an editorial redaction) inform us why God allowed Pharaoh so many chances despite his short-lived good will; the very ill will of Pharaoh enables Yahweh to exhibit his power before the world. Paul refers to this passage in Rom 9:17.

(h) The Eighth Plague: Locusts (10:1–20). Once again Moses threatens the Pharaoh with a disaster that has been known to strike the Near East (cf. Jl 1:2–10). In modern times, clouds of locusts have been swept into an area only to be blown out again by a sudden change in wind direction. To Moses' threat, Pharaoh makes a concession: The Hebr men can join Moses in the sacrificial expedition. To Moses' insistence that all the Hebrews must be allowed to share the sacrificial rite, the monarch turns a deaf ear. The concession for the men (v. 11) and the admission of sin (v. 16) serve to heighten the conflict between Yahweh and the Pharaoh; the latter is yielding. After the chastising hand of Yahweh visits the Egyptians once again, the Pharaoh reacts as previously, with no results for the Hebr people (v. 20).

24 (i) The Ninth Plague: Darkness (10:21–29). Veteran travelers to the Near East are familiar with the *khamsin*, a hot wind that blows off the desert during March and April and brings with it darkness and a very oppressive atmosphere. As recently as 1959, the present writer can testify to this phenomenon in Cairo. Generally such winds last about three days, and their end occasions joyous response from the people. The ensuing darkness suggests a numinous fear; events are building to a climax. **28–29.** These lines are more suitable at 11:8.

25 (j) The Tenth Plague: Death of the First-born (11:1–10). This plague may represent J, E, and P. The final catastrophe is merely announced in this chapter. Moses' alleged prestige (v. 3) seems to belong to a particular tradition (possibly J). The purpose (v. 9) contrasts slightly with the strong affirmations in 7:17; 8:6,18; and 9:14,16,29.

26 **(L) The Pasch and Azymes (12:1–20).** The Hebr term for the Passover is *pesaḥ*, the etymology of which is disputed. In popular biblical etymology, it is connected with the Hebr vb. *psḥ*, "to limp," "to hobble," or "to jump." Concretely, then, it would refer to the fact that in the tenth plague Yahweh "jumped over" the houses where this rite had been properly observed. Others see in this word a cognate of the Akkadian vb. *pašâḫu*, "to appease"; still others look to the Egyptian language for a solution, where we find a variety of suggestions. Some see in it a Semitic transcription of an Egyptian word meaning "a blow." In this analysis, the tenth plague would be "the blow" in which Yahweh struck down the first-born of the Egyptians. Finally, another group wishes to connect it with the Egyptian *pa sha*, "a souvenir"; thus, the event of the tenth plague would be "the souvenir" marking the definitive deliverance of Yahweh's people. It is unlikely, however, that the Hebrews would give an Egyptian name to a custom of Semitic origin. Furthermore, these efforts seek to find in the tenth plague an explanation of the Passover, but this plague was a later feature of the feast.

Whatever its etymology, it seems that this feast is very ancient, long antedating the Exodus itself. In early times, it was a nomadic or seminomadic spring rite in which the priest and altar were unimportant but the use of blood was most important. It insured the fecundity of the flock, and, through the blood smeared on tentpoles, it warded off hostile or evil powers.

Maṣṣôt, or the Feast of Unleavened Bread, or Azymes, was an ancient feast that reflected an agricultural background. It was borrowed from the Canaanites and marked the beginning of the barley harvest. During this feast, the people ate unleavened bread for seven days, and, of course, they made an offering—a contribution of the first fruits of the harvest.

These two feasts, then, very primitive in character and reflecting nomadic or seminomadic and agricultural backgrounds, have been "historicized," i.e., charged with the great event of the deliverance of God's people from Egypt and thus given a fresh, salvific significance (see De Vaux, *AI* 484–93).

27 **12:1–14.** This section is generally attributed to P; vv. 15–20, although reflecting the same tradition, represent a later addition, because the Exodus is here considered to be already accomplished (v. 17). Detailed instructions are given regarding the time of the feast, the age and condition of the sacrificial animal, the size of the group to share the sacrificial meal, the sprinkling of the sacrificial blood on the doorposts and lintel, the accompanying unleavened bread and herbs, and the distinctly religious and memorial character of the feast. These stipulations reflect the later practice of Israel.

28 **(M) The Passover: Death and Deliverance (12:21–36).** Verses 21–28 are somewhat parallel to vv. 1–14. The importance of oral tradition in ancient Israel is illustrated by vv. 24–27, and the historicization of the ritual is clear: What was originally a ritual for deliverance (vv. 21–23) became later a commemorative rite of Israel's salvation. The death of the first-born is usually understood to result from a deadly pestilence, from which the Israelites were spared. The designation of the first-born would be another instance of epic embellishment. Whatever the case, the Pharaoh quickly allows the Hebrews—husbands, wives, children, and flocks—to set forth. The willingness of the Egyptians to provide gold, silver, and clothing to the departing slaves is easily explained. To the Egyptian mentality, Yahweh, the God of the Israelites, had proved his strength; to allow his people to leave empty-handed would be an affront. A similar mentality is reflected in the action of the Philistines in later times (I Sm 6:3ff.).

29 **(II) The Exodus and Wandering (12:37–18:27).** The biblical text excludes the relatively easy Way of the Land of the Philistines (13:17) for the route of the Exodus. Also avoided were the Way of the Wilderness of Shur, which provided access to Beer-sheba, and the trade route between Egypt and Arabia, which cut directly E from the northern tip of the Gulf of Suez to Ezion-geber. All these routes were well-traveled and patrolled by government troops. Once these three routes are excluded, unanimity ceases among modern authorities.

Except for Succoth, the identification of the other sites mentioned in the text is uncertain. Succoth itself, modern Tell el-Mashkuteh, lies 32 mi. SE of Raamses in the Nile Delta. At one time it was erroneously identified with Pithom, which authorities now locate 8.5 mi. W of Succoth. Etham in Egyptian means "fortress"; it probably lay at the northern tip of the Bitter Lakes, bordering the desert. Pi-ha-hiroth is in the vicinity of Qantir, which in turn lies almost directly S of Raamses. As for Migdol, which also means "fortification," several sites bear this title. One is modern Tell el-Her, about 10 mi. S of Pelusium, most frequently identified with the Migdol of Jer 44:1; 46:14; and Ez 29:10; 30:6. The other Migdol lies S of the Bitter Lakes region. Baal-zephon was known in later biblical times as Tahpanhes. To the Greeks it was Daphne, and today it is known as Tell Defneh. It lies SE of Tanis, and it was here that Jeremiah was taken after the destruction of Jerusalem and the subsequent murder of Gedaliah. Work on the Suez Canal has clearly changed the area between the Gulf of Suez and Lake Menzaleh on the Mediterranean: e.g., Lake Balah has disappeared.

Mention of the Red Sea in the Ex context is a mistranslation, found in both the LXX and the Vg. A glance at a map reveals the complete irrelevance of the Red Sea to the Ex narrative. The Hebr term *yām sûp* signifies "Reed Sea." Ancient texts inform us that two bodies of water lay near Raamses-Tanis; one is "the water of Horus," the Shihor of Is 23:3 and Jer 2:18 (cf. the MT); the other is "the Papyrus Marsh," which is probably our "Reed Sea." The very position of this Reed Sea is moot. For some researchers, it lies N of the Bitter Lakes—in fact, N of Lake Timsah as well; the crossing would then have been N of these lakes. For others, this marshy area lies W of the southerly section of the Bitter Lakes, in which case Moses would have crossed S of the Bitter Lakes. The Reed Sea could thus be regarded as a northern extension of the Red Sea. (See G. E. Wright, "Exodus, Route of," *IDB* 2, 197–99; Biblical Geography, 73:27–29.)

30 **(A) The Departure from Egypt (12:37–51).** Moses led his people S from the capital city of Raamses to Succoth, a prudent choice. The coastal route to Canaan, later to be known as the Way of the Land of the Philistines (Ex 13:17), or the more central routes across the Sinai Peninsula would have been shorter and easier but would also have provided possible opposition from Egyptian forces garrisoned along the way. Hence the roundabout way had its advantages.

Various solutions have been proffered regarding the number of Israelites who left Egypt with Moses. The text lists 600,000 men, which would imply about 3 million persons including women and children. Some authors are sure we have here merely the phenomenon of gross exaggeration, so well known in ancient Semitic documents. Others claim that this figure is the work of a later editor who has taken the results of the census under David in the 10th cent. (2 Sm 24) and anachronistically applied them to the time of Moses. Still a third group prefers to see in the Hebr term *'elep*, generally rendered "thousand," a "subsection of a tribe" or "a family" (cf. G. E. Mendenhall, *JBL* 77 [1958] 52ff.). Such an understanding of the term would provide a realistic total of about 5000 or 6000.

At any rate, the figure in v. 37 is impossible. Such a host could never have forded the Reed Sea in one night. Then again we are told that the Hebrews were insufficient in numbers to take over Canaan at once (Ex 23:29–30), a simple task had this figure been realistic. Furthermore, when we learn that Ramses II could only muster a force of 20,000 fighting men for the most important battle of his career—against the Hittites at Kadesh on the Orontes—we can see how completely out of proportion the given number is.

31 **40.** If we set the date of the Exodus shortly after the accession of Ramses II (1290), the 430-year stay of the Israelites in Egypt indicates an entry date *ca.* 1720–10, which, of course, coincides with the conquering thrust of their fellow Semites, the Hyksos. The 430 years of our present text, apparently an effort at rather exact reckoning, should provide no contradiction to the round number of 400 years given in Gn 15:13.

42–49. Once again mention is made of Passover regulations. (The vigil element, in v. 42, has been restored to the liturgy of the Lat rite Easter vigil service.) The regulations obviously reflect a later period when Israel had settled in Canaan (vv. 44–46,48–49). The prescription in v. 47 serves as the type for the scene on Golgotha (Jn 19:36; cf. 1 Cor 5:7). This section determines with greater precision those who may participate in the Passover. Excluded are those whose stay among the Hebrews is temporary, whether as guest or hired servant. Servants purchased for lasting service as well as resident aliens may participate, provided they are first circumcised, a requisite for the observance of this feast.

32 **(B) Azymes and the Consecration of the First-born (13:1–16).** In contrast to 12:14–20 (the P account of the unleavened bread regulations) is the more primitive J version presented here. It makes use of the old Canaanite name of the month, Abib (v. 5), whereas P simply designates the first month. The latter calls for special solemnities on the first and seventh days (12:16), whereas J proposes solely the seventh day (13:6). The relationship of the practice to the deliverance from Egypt is expressly stated (13:8). The "sign" on the hand would resemble the signet ring so commonly employed for identification purposes; the "reminder" on the forehead would recall to the Israelites the special tattoos or ritual marks employed by their neighbors. It is probably because of this prescription that later generations of Jews made such prominent use of phylacteries, the tiny parchment scrolls worn around the brow which contain the teachings about the one God and his deliverance of his people from Egypt.

The legislation about the first-born is to be supplemented by Ex 22:28–29; Nm 3:11–13,40–41 (the Levites as first-born), and Dt 15:19–20. Humans were not to be sacrificed, but redeemed by a vicarious offering (34:19–20; cf. Gn 22). The ass was specifically excluded as an offering because it was considered unclean. In its stead a sheep should be sacrificed; otherwise a first-born ass was to die. **15.** The practice is explained by reference to the Exodus and the tenth plague; cf. 12:24–27.

33 **(C) Israel Leaves Its Place of Bondage (13:17–22).** The route follows the safe way S. Before the departure, however, E states (v. 19) that the bones of the patriarch Joseph were disinterred for subsequent burial in the land of his fathers, according to his demands (Gn 50:25). On abandoning their camp at Succoth, the Israelites moved toward Etham, which the text merely identifies as bordering the desert. From the start of the march, the special presence of God with his people is underlined: J speaks of the cloud by day and the column of fire by night; E mentions the cloud in 20:21; and P speaks of the cloud and the glory of God as a consuming fire (24:16–17). Mystics and ascetical writers have made wide use of such Ex imagery.

34 **(D) The Crossing of the Reed Sea (14:1–22).** The order to "turn about" (v. 1) indicates that the Hebrews headed toward the marshy area N of the Bitter Lakes. **4.** See also v. 17; as in the plague episodes, the sovereign purpose of the Lord is emphasized. The narrative has definite epic tones: "all the other chariots of Egypt" (7); the Lord fights for Israel (14); his mere "glance" panics the Egyptians (24). The various sources agree on the fundamental historical fact of Israel's deliverance, but there are several embellishments to the basic elements. For example, the walls of water stand to the right and left of the fleeing Israelites (14:29). Interesting, too, is the manner in which our redactor has interwoven his sources, appealing to the "angel of God" in v. 19 (E), the staff of Moses in v. 16 (P), and the direct intervention of God in v. 21 (J). Authors today generally agree that natural phenomena were employed by divine providence in the crossing. The occurrence is not isolated in history. From classical sources we learn of the winds that drove back the waters of the lagoon and thus enabled Scipio to capture New Carthage. The text itself informs us of the part the wind played in facilitating this crossing for the Hebrews through the shallow waters of the Sea of Reeds.

Many commentators today approve the suggestion of the great Danish scholar J. Pedersen (*Israel* [Copenhagen, 1940] vol. 3, 384–415; vol. 4, 728–37), who maintained that the account of the Exodus was primarily employed as a cult narrative to be read during the Passover liturgy, which commemorated the actual historical deliverance of the Hebr people. The purpose of such a liturgical feast was, of course, the glorification of God; hence the literary embellishments are intelligible. The theme is developed in the rest of the OT (Ps 114; Wis 19), and continues into the NT (1 Cor 10: 1ff.).

35 **(E) Destruction of the Egyptians (14:23–31).** The Egyptian pursuit is motivated by a sudden change of heart (14:5); the release of Israel involved a substantial loss for them. Balanced against it is the purpose of the Lord (14:4,17,30–31). Once again we may postulate the providential use of natural phenomena as the reason for the destruction of the Egyptian forces. As the wind which caused the movement of the tide (v. 21) in turn subsided, the waters of the Reed Sea flowed back and effectively mired the chariots of the Egyptians. The phrase, "Not a single one of them escaped" (28) has the typical flavor of Hebr epic embellishment; however, we must not maintain that the Pharaoh himself perished in the engagement, despite the poetic allusion in Ps 136:15.

The Reed Sea incident was to achieve the divinely intended result of making the people conscious of God's special intervention on their behalf. Numerous passages in the OT testify to this purpose: e.g., Dt 26:5–8; Solomon's famous prayer in 1 Kgs 8:16,21,51,53; in the prophets—Jer 2:6, Hos 2:15 and 11:1, Am 2:10 and 3:1, Mi 6:4; and in Pss—Pss 78:11–14 and 136:10–15. Among the prophets, this particular proof of God's concern for Israel was to serve also as assurance of future deliverance for the people of his choice; see e.g., Is 43: 1–7,16–19 and 51:9–11. For the earliest literary monument to this great event, we now turn to the Song of Moses, or, as it is sometimes called, the Song of Miriam.

36 **(F) A Paean of Victory (15:1–21).** Some authors suggest that vv. 1–18 constitute the Song of Moses, whereas vv. 19–21 make up the more ancient Song of Miriam. Others see in the whole a literary unity and appeal to the well-known Semitic practice of literary attribution to a person of note. The work of modern Ugaritic scholars, such as W. F. Albright, has undermined the late date of composition proposed by writers like H. Holzinger and R. Pfeiffer. Literary affinity with Canaanite (Ugaritic) triumphal poems has led Albright to insist on a 13th-cent. date for the present piece. Hence this chant and the Song of Deborah (Jgs 5) constitute our oldest pieces of Hebr poetry. The mention of Philistia (v. 14) should provide no problem, because it was a common anachronism employed by pentateuchal redactors. And, of course, the conquest of Canaan (vv. 15–17) was largely effected before the close of the 13th cent. There is solid probability in A. Weiser's thesis that this poem was employed in Israelite cult, most logically in the Passover celebration itself.

The spirit of the song is clearly set forth in the hymnic beginning: "I will sing to the Lord, for he is gloriously triumphant." To the primitive Semite, any military activity was a sacred function. By the present deliverance, then, Yahweh has clearly proved his dominion over all gods (v. 11) and shown himself the singular savior of Israel (v. 2).

Verses 13–17 concern facts subsequent to the Reed Sea incident. However, as previously noted, references to the wilderness wandering (v. 15) and the era of conquest (v. 16), do not necessarily indicate authorship later than the 13th cent. The phrase, "The mountain of your inheritance" (v. 17) is a clear instance of a Hebr adaptation of Ugaritic reference to Baal's seat. The "sanctuary" of the same verse need not refer to the Temple of Solomon; in pre-Solomonic times, the people who sheltered the Ark received God's sanctuary. Some authors also see a definite antiphonal character in v. 21. This refrain, they tell us, would be frequently repeated in the course of the song.

(Cross, F. M. and D. N. Freedman, "The Song of Miriam," *JNES* 14 [1955] 237–50. Rozelaar, M., "The Song of the Sea," *VT* 2 [1952] 221–28, J. D. W. Watts, "The Song of the Sea," *VT* 7 [1957] 371–80.)

37 **(G) Marah and Elim (15:22–27).** Once across the Reed Sea, the Israelites found themselves on the Sinai Peninsula, triangular in shape and 260 mi. long and 150 mi. wide at its north. A sandy belt about 15 mi. deep lies along the Mediterranean shore, to the S of which a high plateau stretches out for 150 mi. At the apex of the Sinai Peninsula are mountains, some of which reach 8000 ft. Here lay the copper and turquoise mines so diligently worked by the Egyptians, and here stood Mt. Sinai toward which Moses led his refugees.

From the Reed Sea area itself we are told that Moses led the people to the desert of Shur, called the wilderness of Etham in Nm 33:8. The Hebr word *šûr* signifies a wall; the desert was so-called for the steppelike formation in the northern area of the peninsula. A three-day march brought the people to a spring with the etiological name Marah (bitterness). Two sites have been proposed for this spring. One is Ain Hawarah, a series of wells about 41 mi. S of the crossing point. The second and more probable site is Ain Musa (the well of Moses), approx. 25 mi. S of the crossing point. Encumbered as the refugees were with "numerous flocks and herds" (12:38), they would be fortunate to cover 25 mi. in three days.

The identity of the "wood" (v. 25; cf. Sir 38:4–6) which sweetened the waters is unknown. Arabs speak of a special thorn with this quality, but it is unknown to us. Verse 25b appears out of context here. For this reason many prefer to place it with 17:1–7. The Hebr word *nissāhu* (25b), "put them to the test," is the same basic root as *massāh* of 17:7 (but cf. M. Greenberg, *JBL* 79 [1960] 273–76) and fits well as a varying explanation of the events there; v. 26 seems to be a later deuteronomic addition.

Much more unanimity exists regarding the identification of Elim (v. 27) than that accorded Marah. Most contend that it is the oasis of Wadi Gharandel, which lies 63 mi. from Suez and just 20 mi. S of Ain Musa (Marah) where the first Sinai stop was made.

38 **(H) Manna and Quail (16:1–36).** The events of this chapter take place in the wilderness of Sin, the desert area between Elim and Mt. Sinai known today as Debbet er-Ramleh. It should not be confused with the "Wilderness of Zin," which lies W of the mountains of Seir. Even a cursory reading of this section provides difficulties concerning the coherent development here and the variance it affords the account in Nm 11. The internal difficulties are best explained by a rather awkward combination of P and J materials: verses 4, 13b–15, 21b, 31, and 35a belong to J; the remainder is the work of P. According to Nm 11:21–23, quail were provided only because the people were dissatisfied with the manna; in all likelihood, this account is the older narrative which was later reworked by P to place greater emphasis on the manna.

To the people's complaint—the murmuring in the desert is a constant motif—Yahweh promises prompt relief. Manna and quail are to be their nourishment, and for both items we may look to phenomena common to the Sinai Peninsula. The manna is a honeydew excretion produced by two species of scale insect that infest the tamarisk thickets of the area, which, in fact, have gained the technical name *tamarix mannifera.* From the leaves of the thicket the substance drops to the ground where it becomes somewhat firm in the cool night air of the desert. It has, however, a low melting point (70° F) and hence must be gathered by 8:30 A.M. before the sun causes it to melt. To the Bedouins who still roam the area, it remains a delicacy because of its sweet taste (see F. S. Bodenheimer, "The Manna of Sinai," *BA* 10 [1947] 2–6).

The quail fly S annually from their northern European and Scandinavian quarters in September and October to winter in African warmth. Then in May and June they take up their homeward journey. Their long flights over water cause them to land exhausted on the Sinai Peninsula, where they may be captured easily.

9. The phrase "before the Lord" is most probably the work of a redactor. It implies a sanctuary, or tent of meeting, neither of which has yet come into existence.

39 Our Eng term manna is adopted from the *manna* of the LXX editor in Nm 11:6–7. In Ex 16:15, we find a popular etymology, for when the Israelites first spotted this substance, their query was: "What is this?" The use of *mān* in the Hebr text raises an issue, because the interrogative in Aramaic is *man*, but in Hebrew it is *māh*. Some think that we do not have an interrogative here, but rather an Egyptian term used to describe this substance. In this case, the Israelite reaction would have been: It is man. In the famous Johannine section on the bread of life (6:31–59), the Evangelist notes that the desert manna was a type of the Eucharist itself.

16–22. Only fixed quantities of this manna were to be collected. On five days of the week, an omer (or gomor) per person was to be the quantity (approx. 4 bu. in modern measure). On the Sabbath eve a double measure was to be gathered. **23–31.** The P tradition describes the incident of the manna with a view to inculcating the Sabbath rest.

32–34. There is a memorial aspect to the manna. One omer was to be set aside in a special urn to remind subsequent generations of God's provident care for his people.

40 **(I) Water from the Rock (17:1–7).** From the wilderness of Sin the Israelites moved on to Rephidim, which most authors today locate in the Wadi Refayid, 8 mi. NW of Jebel Musa. Once again the lack of water brings on murmuring by the people. The Hebr term, *rîb* (quarrel) in v. 2 prepares us for the later designation of the place as "Meribah." A later source introduces Massah (a testing) into the story.

Besides our present narrative, two other water stories are to be connected with the wandering of the Israelites: the Marah incident of Ex 15:22–27, already discussed; and the Meribah crisis of Nm 20:2–13, regarded by some as Moses' celebrated fault, for which he was later forbidden entry into the promised land. These versions may possibly be variants of a single incident, but we have no definitive answer. Dt 33:8 seems to favor different sites.

All agree that the Horeb of v. 6 is the addition of a later editor. From this incident, later rabbis were to build a legend that the rock source of this providential water followed the Israelites through the desert. Still later, St. Paul interpreted this Exodus event and the rabbinical accretions as a type of Christ (1 Cor 10:4).

41 **(J) A Challenge from Amalek (17:8–16).** Our text next tells us of the first military activity of the newly freed Hebrews. Victory, however, was to depend largely on the intercessory powers of Moses. It is an incident that establishes him as a sort of mediator Christ figure. The Amalekites controlled the caravan routes between Arabia and Egypt and hence resented the intrusion of these Hebrews. The incident is mentioned in Dt 25:17–19, with one notable omission. True to his usual theme of one place of worship, D overlooks the mention (v. 16) that Moses erected an altar on the spot. For the first time, Joshua enters the sacred text, in the role of military leader. He will be mentioned frequently later in Ex (e.g., 24:13; 32:17; 33:11), in Nm (e.g., 11:28; 13:16; 27:18), and, of course, throughout Jos. **15.** The title *Yahweh-nissî*, which Moses assigned to the altar he built at Rephidim, means "Yahweh is my banner."

42 **(K) Moses Meets Jethro (18:1–12).** Chapter 18 is generally considered to be out of place. In 17:1, we hear of the encampment at Rephidim, and in 19:1, of the departure from Rephidim for Sinai. Again the appointment of judges in this chapter conflicts with the testimony of Dt 1, where we learn that such appointments followed the covenant at Sinai. In an effort to explain the position of this chapter, it has been suggested that a later editor took offense at the idea of a Midianite priest sacrificing to Yahweh at Sinai after God had revealed himself to Israel. To avoid the issue, the editor moved these postcovenant happenings to the present position. **2.** The E source names two sons of Moses by Zipporah: Gershom and Eliezer; J (2:22) knew only the former.

6. The events of this section take place near "the mountain of God." The OT assures us that Yahweh has only two holy mountains: Sinai, where he manifested himself to Israel; and Zion, where he dwelt. Since Zion is out of the question here, Sinai is evidently intended. Again, Dt 1:6 clearly relates the site of the institution of judges to Horeb (Sinai).

43 **(L) The Institution of Judges (18:13–27).** What was just said about the time and place of the meeting with Jethro holds true as well for the present section. A clear dichotomy of authority is here set forth. Moses is and remains the special agent of Yahweh, God's prophet to his people. From his converse with God, he is to relate to the people the proclamation of divine statutes and decisions and the promulgation of the right way to live. In the more difficult cases raised by individuals (v. 22), it is Moses who is to give judgment; in the ordinary exercise of civil justice, however, representatives of the people were to handle the cases. (See Dt 1:15.)

44 **(III) The Covenant (19:1–24:18).** We have already stated that the Exodus—precisely as complexus of choice, deliverance, and covenant—constituted the cardinal dogma of OT religion. In this section, we shall discuss the final element of those essential constituents. Two items of special importance are found in these chapters: the Decalogue (or Ten Commandments) and the Book of the Covenant, which marks the legal expression and development of the relationship arising from the covenant. We are dealing with a basic historical fact—the unique treaty made by Almighty God with the people of Israel. It is a datum upon which all subsequent Israelite religion depends.

We would be incorrect, however, in presuming that the present chapters provide a scientific report of the Sinai events. Modern authors agree that these great events, which set off Israel as unique, became the basis of special liturgical representation. In fact, through this liturgical re-enactment, the very events themselves were relived by the people. Much of the description here, then, constitutes not an historical report, but rather a theological interpretation of the events as they were subsequently liturgically re-enacted for the people of Israel. However, we must not forget that a real confrontation between Yahweh and Israel is the basis for these descriptions.

The notion of covenant has been considerably enriched in recent OT research. The basic idea that covenant involves a treaty in which rights and duties are exchanged has long been known. Now, however, Israel's covenant with Yahweh has been placed in the background of contemporary Near Eastern culture, thanks to the basic study of G. E. Mendenhall (*Law and Covenant in Israel and the Ancient Near East* [Pittsburgh, 1955]), which points out the similarities to the Hittite suzerainty treaties. The import of these discoveries has been summarized elsewhere (→ Aspects OT Thought, 77:76–92, especially 79–80,86). Here, we shall merely indicate the essential characteristics of the suzerainty treaty relevant to the text of Ex: the preamble, which identifies the great king (Ex 20:2); the historical prologue (I-thou address), which summarizes the benefits bestowed upon the vassal in the past by the great king; the stipulations (in particular, the prohibition of any treaties with other nations); the public reading; a list of the gods as witnesses; and a formula of curses and blessings. (See the survey of the question by D. J. McCarthy, *CBQ* 23 [1965] 217–40.)

45 **(A) Israel Comes to Sinai (19:1–3).** After the journey from Rephidim to the desert of Sinai, Moses ascends the mountain of God (v. 3). Some scholars still attempt to locate Mt. Sinai at Kadesh, or Petra, or somewhere else E of the Sinai Peninsula, their most pressing reason being the seeming presence of volcanic activity in the narrative (e.g., 19:18). Because no volcanic activity has been known to exist on the Sinai Peninsula itself, they are led to these new conjectures. However, the data causing them concern need not be considered evidence of such volcanic conditions, but only typical Semitic descriptions of a great mountain storm. For further instances of such writing, we may mention the majestic verses of Ps 29, wherein God reveals himself in a mountain storm, or Ps 18:8–15, another description of a theophany, many of the elements of which parallel our present section.

Therefore, most modern authorities identify the mountain of God with Jebel Musa on the Sinai Peninsula. This particular peak rises to a height of 7467 ft. and can be scaled in approximately one and one-half hours. Even loftier peaks lie S of Jebel Musa, but they would require about five hours to scale and lack open areas at their bases. The Jebel Musa location is further confirmed by the adjacent plain of er-Raha, which coincides with the encampment area at the base of the mountain of God (19:2).

46 **(B) A Divine Promise (19:4–8).** To his chosen mediator, Almighty God here makes an astounding offer: If the Israelites will choose to abide by his special covenant, they will in turn become something very special—God's own people, his special possession, a kingdom of priests, a holy nation (5–6). In this, one of the classic OT sections, the mystery of the divine choice is once again set forth. In the working out of salvation history, the people Israel were to enjoy a special place and a unique intimacy with God. In turn, much would be required of them—to be holy as their very God is holy, and to fulfill their role of priesthood to the nations. This special vocation was not to be forced on the people, but left to their free choice. In v. 8, they readily accept the covenant.

47 **(C) The Theophany of Sinai (19:9–25).** Moses receives instructions about the impending theophany. The divine presence is to confirm Moses in his role of prophet, the special spokesman of Yahweh. Prescriptions for sanctification follow, and certain ritual purificatory observances are named. Anyone having sexual intercourse was rendered ritually unclean and was thus barred from sacred activities (cf. Lv 15:18; 22:3–7).

In the description of the theophany, Yahweh's role as lord of nature is very evident. Some authors consider the trumpet blast (16, 19) to represent figuratively a mighty wind, thus becoming another storm element like the thunder and lightning of v. 16.

48 **(D) The Decalogue (20:1–17).** The text of our Ten Commandments has evolved in two forms: Ex 20 and Dt 5:6–21. A harmonization of the two appears in the Nash Papyrus of the 2nd cent. BC, found in the Fayyum area of Egypt in 1902. A third form is the so-called Ritual Decalogue in Ex 34:11–26 (J).

In this section on the Decalogue, the Bible presents us with Israel's distinctive contribution to legal lore. Numerous law codes antedate the Decalogue: e.g., the Code of Lipit-Ishtar, the Code of Eshnunna, the Code of Hammurabi, and the Hittite codes. The basis of these codes is casuistic law: If so-and-so does this, then the following penalty is operative. In the Decalogue, however, we meet the characteristic apodictic law: Thou shalt or thou shalt not do such-and-such, with no introductory conditional element.

Many authors maintain that the formula of the Decalogue found in Commandments Four through Ten represents the original. In the first three, the original pithy statements have been supplemented by later traditions. This change must have taken place at an early period, because the added formulas are found also in the Deuteronomic Code.

The division of the Ten Commandments provides further variation. In accordance with rabbinical tradition, modern Jews divide them thus: the first, 20:2; the second, 20:3–6; and the third through the tenth, 20:7–17. Following Philo, Josephus, and the Greek Fathers, the modern Greek and Reformed Churches (except the Lutherans) divide them thus: the first, 20:2–3; the second, 20:4–6; the third, 20:7; the fourth, 20:8–11; and the fifth through the tenth, 20:12–17. In the tradition of the Latin Fathers, Roman Catholics and Lutherans divide them thus: the first, 20:2–6; the second, 20:7; the third, 20:8–11; the fourth through the eighth, 20:12–16; the ninth, 20:17a; and the tenth, 20:17b.

The chief discrepancies between Ex and Dt consist in the humanitarian motivation added in the latter for the observance of the Sabbath precept, and in the reversal of order in Ex 20:17 and Dt 5:21. In Ex, "house" is named first and then "wife."

Commandments Four through Ten constitute essential elements of the natural law; therefore, we also find them in earlier law codes. Even here, however, we can note a major difference: In the codes of other Near Eastern peoples, violation of these precepts constitutes a crime against one's fellow man; in the Bible, their violation marks a crime against God himself. Hence we note an entirely new orientation. For further details, see W. Harrelson, "Ten Commandments," *IDB* 4, 569–73.

49 (a) The First Commandment (20:2–6). The recognition of one God was intended to distinguish Israel from her Near Eastern neighbors, who all boasted a host of heavenly deities. In this precept, we note the clear, practical monotheism which would culminate later in the speculative monotheism of the prophets. A verse such as Ex 15:11, "Who is like to you among the gods, O Lord?" clearly indicates that the early Israelites had not as yet learned of speculative monotheism. Many evidently accorded reality to the deities of other nations. In the practical monotheism of this commandment, the Israelites were warned that they were to worship only Yahweh. As a corollary came the definitive proscription of Yahweh images, which served again to differentiate Israel from her neighbors, to whom images of the national deity were commonplace. In Dt 4:15–16, we find an apt commentary on this prohibition: "You saw no form at all on the day the Lord spoke to you...."

Modern archaeology confirms that the Israelites proved faithful at least to this aspect of the First Commandment. Amidst the numerous scientifically excavated biblical sites, no images of Yahweh have been found. Similar searches in the neighboring countries, however, have unearthed great quantities of material representations of pagan deities.

Most scholars agree that the present text of the First Commandment includes later accretions. Originally, it most likely read: "I the Lord am your God. You shall have no other gods besides me."

We can identify the borrowings from the Hittite suzerainty covenant by pointing to 20:2, where Yahweh identifies himself in the first person. Then, in line with the Hittite historical prologue, Yahweh recalls how he benefited Israel: "I... who brought you out of the land of Egypt, that place of slavery" (v. 2). This section also begins to set down the stipulations of the covenant, the third element of the Hittite pattern, for Israel shall have no gods but Yahweh, who jealously covets their exclusive adoration. Throughout the remainder of the Decalogue, as well as in its subsequent Mosaic applications in the Book of the Covenant (20:22–23:19), further stipulations are established to bind Israel. We also note the I-Thou formula.

50 (b) Commandments Two Through Ten (20:7–17). The Second Commandment concerns use of the divine name. The phrase "in vain" (v. 7) seems to mean here: "You shall not make evil use of the name of the Lord your God." Thus were forbidden the perjured use of the divine name and the appeal to Yahweh's name to support curses or magical formulas. Again, the common use of divine names for such purposes among Israel's neighbors is evident from the execration texts of early Egypt. The pagans believed the invocation of the divine name an effective weapon. Although such usage was forbidden to Israel, the taking of oaths was not proscribed. Later, Yahweh's name was completely avoided. Whenever the name occurred in text, the reader pronounced it *Adonai*, "Lord."

From Ex 16:23, it is clear that the Sabbath probably existed long before its expression in the Decalogue. In its present form, it prescribes no special ritual for the Israelites, but rather consecrates a period of time to God. The formulas of the Decalogue in Ex and Dt provide different motivation for this precept. In Ex, man is reminded of his need to imitate God, whose creative activity left the Sabbath free from work (Gn 2:2–3); however, in Dt, a distinctively humanitarian motive is ascribed to this precept (5:12–15).

The First, Second, and Third Commandments provide specific regulations involving man's relations with God. With the Fourth Commandment, the Decalogue takes up man's relations with his fellow man. First is stressed the obligation to one's parents. This commandment is not restricted to children, but is a universal precept. (For the penalty for its violation, see Ex 21:17; Lv 20:9; Dt 21:18–21.) Paul notes that it is "the first commandment with a promise" (Eph 6:2).

The Fifth Commandment seeks to protect the very sacredness of human life by forbidding murder. Killing in battle or by capital punishment is not an issue here. The Pentateuch fully approves both in Dt 20:1–14 (where vv. 10–13 seem to reflect contemporaneous views on the *ḥerem* rather than divine legislation) and in Ex 21:12–17.

The sanctity of marriage is safeguarded by the Sixth Commandment, as is that of private property by the Seventh Commandment. In the latter case, some recent exegetes maintain that the issue here also includes loss of freedom. Hence they tell us that Commandment Seven forbids the enslavement of free Israelites by force, whether for personal use or for trade.

The Eighth Commandment forbids perjured testimony. This precept is not limited to formal legal action but excludes as well any false statement damaging to one's neighbor. By "neighbor" the law envisions anyone with whom an Israelite has contact.

We have already mentioned the reversed order in Commandments Nine and Ten as they appear in Ex and Dt. Both precepts reprimand illicit desires, desires that may well lead to actions already forbidden by the Sixth and Seventh Commandments. Appearance of the term "house" has led some commentators to suggest that it reflects a later addition. The same Hebr word, however, may signify the tent dwelling of the nomad or semi-nomad. Hence, the term is not anachronistic. Moreover, in addition to the dwelling itself, the word includes everything in the house.

51 **(E) The Mediation of Moses (20:18–21).** This section (the work of E) returns us to the context of ch. 19 and provides further evidence of the fear engendered by the theophany. The two features most common to E are evident here: the utter transcendence of God, and his practice of communicating with man indirectly through an intermediary.

52 **(F) The Book of the Covenant (20:22–23:19).** In the 19th cent., it was usual to read that pentateuchal legislation was actually the work of 1st millennium authors and bore no sound relationship to the life in the 2nd millennium. Archaeology has proved otherwise. Prominent among the results of exacting excavation has been the previously mentioned discovery of numerous law codes of the ancient Near East indicating a 2nd millennium background for the Book of the Covenant. Numerous codes are now at the scholar's disposal, at least three of which antedate the well-known Code of Hammurabi. They present a broad spectrum of Near Eastern peoples, and directly or indirectly, they have influenced Israel.

Perhaps the earliest code is that of Ur-Nammu, written in Sumerian *ca.* 2050, and named for Ur-Nammu, ruler of the small city-state of Ur in southern Mesopotamia. (On this law, see S. N. Kramer and A. Falkenstein, "Ur-Nammu Law Code," *Or* 23 [1954] 40–51.)

The Code of Eshnunna was found at Abu Harmal. This site constituted part of the kingdom of Eshnunna, which lay E of modern Baghdad and reached its peak in the 20th cent. Authorities therefore project a date *ca.* 1925 for these laws. (For a version of 59 extant formulas from this early cuneiform code, see *ANET* 161–63.)

The Code of Lipit-Ishtar, fifth monarch of the Isin Dynasty, who ruled in the first half of the 19th cent., antedates Hammurabi's work by more than 150 years. (For the surviving contents of this Sumerian code—prologue, epilogue, and 37 precepts—see *ANET* 159–61.)

Most famous of ancient Near Eastern cuneiform codes is that of Hammurabi. As a member of the Old Babylonian (Amorite) Dynasty, Hammurabi ruled from 1728–1686 (the low chronology advocated by Albright). Near the beginning of his reign, he promulgated the code that bears his name. Our copy, written on a diorite stele (now in the Louvre), is topped by a bas-relief showing Hammurabi receiving a mandate to compose his code from the sun-god and god of justice, Shamash. (For a version of the prologue, epilogue, and 282 laws of the work, see *ANET* 164–80.)

The Hittite code was found amid the ruins of Boghazkoy and dates to *ca.* 1450. Two tablets have preserved 200 laws. (For the translation, see *ANET* 189–97.)

Like the Hittite code, the Assyrian code also lacks the name of the lawgiver. These tenets were inscribed on clay tablets unearthed during the excavation of Ashur in northern Mesopotamia. They originated in the Middle Assyrian period *ca.* 1350. (A version appears in *ANET* 180–88.)

53 The title for the present code, the Book of the Covenant, originates from Ex 24:7. H. Cazelles, in an important study (*Études sur le code de l'alliance* [Paris, 1946]), argues that the code dates to the Reuben and Gad settlement of Transjordan. This view accounts for the agricultural background so evident in much of the code. Noth observes many of the same problems as Cazelles but refuses to be more specific than to maintain a predeuteronomic date (Noth, *op. cit.*) Albright remarks: "The Book of the Covenant represents the form which the more-or-less common corpus of older customary laws and court decisions took under the special conditions existing in Canaan, and it may have passed into Israelite hands during the period of the Judges. In the form that it takes in the Book of the Covenant, it can hardly be dated before the 9th century" (Albright, *FSAC* 268). Therefore, we are safe in asserting that much of this code's material originated well into the 2nd millennium. The actual Hebr written formulation, however, would be placed somewhat later.

Although many similarities exist between the early codes and the Book of the Covenant, the biblical form clearly portrays a cruder, more primitive culture than those revealed in the others. The cultural superiority of the Canaanites is apparent elsewhere; however, despite this shortcoming, the biblical code evidences a higher standard of religion and morality.

In general, the Book of the Covenant treats civil and penal laws (21:1–22:14), laws of worship (20:22–26; 22:28–30; 23:10–19), and laws controlling morality (22:16–27; 23:1–9). The obvious disarrangement of materials makes it clear that either the original order was disrupted or subsequent additions disregarded logical connections; note, e.g., the widely separated laws of worship.

The combination of casuistic and apodictic materials is also noteworthy. The latter is not characteristic in the codes of the neighboring peoples.

54 (a) Laws of Worship (20:22–26). The superscription in 21:1 indicates that this verse marked the original opening of the Book of the Covenant; therefore, this short section was most probably withdrawn from later worship legislation to assign it a place commensurate with its importance.

At the very beginning, we learn that God speaks from heaven, which indicates a break with the J and E sources that precede this section. According to J, (19:18,20), Yahweh has actually descended on Sinai, whereas E (20:21) depicts God's presence on the mountain as in the cloud. The unique character of the God of Israel is once more proclaimed. The making of images is prohibited. If images of silver and gold are forbidden, a fortiori would it hold for inferior materials.

Immediately following the statement of monotheism comes the altar legislation, testifying to the importance of cult. A plurality of altars may exist, but only in the places chosen by Yahweh himself (contrast Dt 12–26), who would indicate such sites by theophanies or dreams (cf. Gn 35:7; Ex 17:15; Jos 8:30–31; Jgs 6:23–24; 13:18–20; 21:4; 1 Sm 7:5–9).

Simplicity was to be the mark of Yahweh's altar; piled-up earth was to be the regular form. If stones were used, they were to remain in the unhewn state; for man-made tools would rob them of their primitive integrity.

Two types of sacrifice are mentioned: "holocausts and peace offerings" (v. 24). Subsequent legislation in Lv will greatly expand the list. In the holocaust, the entire sacrificial animal was offered to Yahweh. In the peace offering, a choice part of the victim was offered; the remainder provided a sacrificial banquet for the offerer and his family and friends, thus stressing the aspect of divine communion. No mention is made as yet of the priesthood's role; in earliest times, the father of the family or the patriarch of the clan fulfilled this function.

A final note forbids an elevated altar that might involve immodest disclosure of the sacrificer. This danger was removed by subsequent legislation dealing with the garb of the priesthood (Ex 28:40–42).

55 (b) Laws Regarding Slaves (21:1–11). The ways whereby an Israelite might become a slave were numerous. He (or she) might be sold by a father (Ex 21:7; Neh 5:5), or a captured thief unable to make restitution could be purchased (Ex 22:2). In difficult times, a man could become so impoverished that he would sell himself into servitude (Lv 25:39). The widow and children of a debtor could be taken in slavery (2 Kgs 4:1). Some authors maintain that the use of the term "Hebrew" in v. 2 has the primitive connotation of ʿApiru, or Habiru—i.e., a landless group whose situation caused them to hire themselves out to others. In the present historical situation, however, it is preferable to use the term merely as a synonym for Israelite.

After six years of service, an Israelite slave became free to return to his exact status at the time of his enslavement. If single, he was to depart single; if married, his wife joined him in freedom. If, however, his wife was a gift from his master, she remained with their owner. Any children of such a union remained with their mother, their relationship to her was considered closer than that to their father. Here, as elsewhere in the OT, women were considered more as possessions than as persons, which reflected the customary law of the Semitic ancient Near East. Should a slave endowed with a wife by his master prefer to remain with her, he could do so by pledging himself to lasting service.

6. The piercing of the ear lobe symbolized the slave's obedience to his master (cf. Ps 40:7). **7.** A young girl could be sold outright, or she might be sold under certain conditions (8–11). Should the buyer violate these conditions, the girl received her freedom absolutely, without cost to herself.

56 (c) Laws Regarding Homicide (21:12–17). **12.** This verse sets down the general principle for this section and reiterates the teaching of Gn 9:6. The same basic legislation occurs also in Lv 24:17 and Nm 35:30–33. Although the text does not name the executioner, we know that in early Israel it was the *gōʾēl*, or "avenger of blood"—the man nearest of kin to the slain.

Unpremeditated homicide, or accidental manslaughter, did not involve the same punishment. Such a slayer could take refuge until the wrath of the avenger of blood should subside and his innocence could be cleared by judgment. For the malicious murderer, however, no sanctuary was to be granted.

The Book of the Covenant presents sterner legislation for deliberate homicide than do other Near Eastern codes. The Code of Hammurabi treats solely—in the matter of homicide—of a wife who murders her husband; she must be impaled (law 153; *ANET* 172); it says nothing about other cases of homicide. In the OT, however, the sacredness of life could be safeguarded only by destroying the life of the murderer.

15. The reverence due to parents brought serious consequences on the son who failed to bestow it. The Deuteronomic Code goes into greater detail on the same issue but is equally stern (Dt 21:18–32); in fact, even a curse merited the same penalty, implying the primitive belief that such curses were effective. On this subject, too, the Israelite code is more severe than those of her neighbors. The Sumerian code prescribed that the offending son be thrown out of the house, sold, or disinherited, and the Code of Hammurabi maintained that a son who raised a hand against his parents should have his hands cut off (law 195; *ANET* 175).

Kidnapping is punishable by death, but the Deuteronomic Code restricts this penalty to one who kidnaps and then sells a fellow Israelite (Dt. 24:7).

57 (d) Laws Regarding Bodily Injuries (21:18–32). **18–19.** The law prescribes compensation for both medical costs and the enforced idleness of one injured in a quarrel. The Code of Hammurabi requires compensation only for the former, and the Hittite code demands a further payment of fine.

20. If a slave dies under the rod, the Bible prescribes punishment for the offending master, the nature of which is disputed among exegetes. To some, death under the rod could be termed accidental; hence, the offender would compensate by fine. To others, blood-vengeance, carrying the death penalty, would be in order. **21.** When the slave dies some time after the incident, there seems to be no issue made of a direct causal relation between the beating and the death; the owner is apparently sufficiently penalized by the loss of his property.

22. If a pregnant woman should suffer a miscarriage as a result of a blow, the guilty party need only make the monetary compensation demanded by her husband; however, should the woman die, capital punishment is prescribed for the offender. In vv. 23–25 we have the first biblical enunciation of the renowned *lex talionis* (law of talion) which was intended to limit revenge (proportionate compensation). Further pentateuchal evidence for this law occurs in Lv 24:17–20 and Dt 19:21. Later legislation indicates that in many instances money could compensate for damages. For the false accuser, however, no such possibility existed; the *lex talionis* was to operate with full rigor (Dt 19:21).

26–27. These verses make clear that the *lex talionis* was applicable to free men only. Slaves did have some rights, for they received freedom for the bodily harm done them.

28. The prescription of Gn 9:5 is in force regarding an ox that has gored a man to death. Not only must the beast die, but he must also not be eaten, for by his action he has become a taboo to the community. The animal's owner must pay the *lex talionis* only if he has been culpably negligent, and even then he may buy off the avenger of blood. Once again we note separate legislation for a slave involved in such a death. In this case also, the ox must die, but the offending owner need only pay the owner of the slave the current market price for a slave.

58 (e) Laws Regarding Property Damages (21:33–22:14). **33–34.** Negligence of a landowner resulting in the death of a neighbor's ox or ass requires payment for the animal, but the guilty party retains the right to the carcass. If two oxen clash and one dies from the goring, both the live ox and the carcass are sold and the price is divided between the owners. If one owner is negligent, however, he must make full restitution for the dead animal.

Stern restitution is legislated for stolen animals (21:37–22:3); the thief unable to comply may be sold into slavery. The case of the nocturnal thief is interesting (22:1). To kill a thief in the dark involved the killer in no bloodguilt, perhaps because under the circumstances the victim did not know whether the intruder's purpose was murder or merely theft. By day, however, the intruder could be identified. In Assyrian law, death or frequently mutilation is prescribed for the thief (Tablet F, 1–2; *ANET* 187–88). Hittite law resembles the Israelite code in the present matter, but enjoins higher restitution (Tablet I, 57–64; *ANET* 192).

59 **22:4.** A negligent landowner must recompense his neighbor for any damages done to his field or vineyard. The deposit of money or valuables with a trusted friend was a normal procedure for a shepherd whose work kept him months from home. If such a deposit were stolen and the thief apprehended, twofold restitution was in order. If the thief went unfound, the holder of the borrowed goods was obliged to swear a solemn oath regarding his innocence. There is no indication that an ordeal was imposed on him, such as that required of a wife accused of infidelity (Nm 5:11–28). In the case of disputed misappropriation, the parties had to seek divine adjudication. Just how this was carried out in practice is unknown, but probably some primitive practice was employed, such as the Urim and the Thummim. The form of this law seems either to have been borrowed directly from some neighboring code or to reflect pre-Mosaic Israelite customary law, for we are told in v. 8 that whosoever "the gods" (CCD, "God") convict must make twofold restitution. The Hebr *'ĕlohîm* is a plural form frequently used for the one God, in which case it always appears with a singular verb. Here, however, the verb is plural.

Similar laws applied to animals. Again, the oath of innocence was required of one who lost an animal entrusted to his keeping. When an animal was borrowed by a gratis loan, the recipient was required to make restitution for any harm done to the beast; however, if the animal were hired out, the owner could receive no restitution for such harm.

60 (f) SOCIAL LAWS (22:15–30). **15–16.** An unbetrothed virgin was regarded as the property of her father. Her seduction involved serious financial loss to him; winning a respectable *mohar* (bride price) from a prospective suitor was difficult in the case of a deflowered maiden. Other evidences for the *mohar* appear in Gn 34:12 and 1 Sm 18:25. Assyrian law required such a seducer to pay three times the normal *mohar*, and even after payment, the father need not give him his daughter in marriage. This law concerns only the unbetrothed virgin; Dt 22:23–39 treats, at greater length, the case of the betrothed virgin.

17. Common in antiquity was the effort to control superhuman powers by magic, and thus penetrate the secrets of the future, work havoc on enemies, and bring benediction on friends. From the present prohibition, we gather it was principally a feminine preoccupation (see also 1 Sm 28:7; Ez 13:18). Further OT denunciations of this practice are found in Lv 20:6,27 and Dt 18:9–14. Nonreligious sorcery was also proscribed in the Code of Hammurabi and by Assyrian law, both of which considered it harmful to one's fellow man.

18–19. Bestiality and sacrifice to false gods also merited the death penalty. That the former vice was well known in the Near East is attested by Herodotus (2. 46), with regard to the Egyptians, and by Lv 18:23–25, with regard to the Canaanites. The punishment of the *ḥerem* was prescribed for anyone who dared sacrifice to false gods. It involved the total destruction of the person and his belongings; he is "devoted" to God.

61 **20.** The Israelites' relationship to the underprivileged is specified. The alien (*ger*) is one who, because of war, plague, famine, or bloodguilt, was forced to leave his home. In his new abode, of course, his civic rights are less than those of his neighbors. As assurance that the Israelites would be hospitable to these unfortunates, the code reminds them of their former status as aliens in Egypt. This concern with the alien is a familiar theme throughout the OT (cf. Lv 19:33–34; Dt 1:16; 10:17–19; 14:28–29; 16:11–14; Jer 7:6). Any wrong done the unprotected widow and the orphan would incur a wrathful Yahweh as their avenging kinsman.

24. Extortion of interest on a loan to a fellow Israelite, particularly if he were needy, was sharply prohibited. However, the OT does not proscribe all interest. From both Lv 25:35–38 and Dt 23:20–21, the injunction clearly regarded only a loan to one's countryman. The Deuteronomic Code clearly allows interest to be demanded of a foreigner. The Code of Hammurabi permitted interest on all loans, but sought to safeguard the needs of the debtor.

27. Blasphemy brought capital punishment to the offender. The same legislation appears in Lv 24:15–16. Of interest here is the juxtaposition of God and the Hebr *nāśî'*, meaning "chief," "deputy," or "spokesman" (rather ineptly rendered "prince" in the CCD; the monarchy did not yet exist, so there was no concern with a king or prince; cf. E. A. Speiser, *CBQ* 25 [1963] 111–17). The *nāśî'* was probably the representative of each of the 12 tribes on those occasions when all Israel congregated. Cursing this legitimate authority likewise merited death.

62 **28–29.** The sacred duty of providing cultic offerings is enjoined. Verse 28 may be more literally rendered, "Your fullness and your overflowing you shall not delay; the first-born of your sons you will give to me." Some authors connect the "fullness" with wine, in view of Nm 18:27, and the "overflowing" with oil. No quantities were legislated at this time, and the designation of the eighth day for the consecration of the first-born did not determine it as the only occasion possible. In Lv 22:27, it is clear that this oblation could be made from the eighth day onward. That child sacrifice was not enjoined was well understood in Israel (see Ex 13:11–13).

30. The final prescription of this chapter deals with the eating of torn flesh and is regarded by many as a later addition from the legislation in Lv 17:15. It was impossible to drain the blood properly from an animal so slain, and the Hebrews considered the eating of the blood a major taboo.

63 (g) JUSTICE AND DUTIES TO ONE'S NEIGHBORS (23:1–9). In the opening verses of this section, general directions regarding judicial procedure are enjoined on all Israelites. False witnesses are condemned as is also the joining of a group who may seek a gain by the perversion of justice. **3.** Many commentators amend *dāl*, "poor man," to *gādōl*, "great man." They argue that the present reading makes little sense, i.e., favoritism to the underprivileged party would be most unlikely.

4–5. The Book of the Covenant next takes up the practical charity due even to one's enemy (see also Lv 19:17–18). **9.** See comment on 22:20.

64 (h) RELIGIOUS LAWS (23:10–19). **10–11.** Legislation on the Sabbath year is found also in Lv 25:2–7 and Dt 15:1–3. The Lv 25:4 passage assigns a religious motivation to this legislation, whereas that of Ex 23:11 is basically humanitarian. The rich could readily store needed supplies for this Sabbath year; the slaves under their jurisdiction would also receive provisions. Hence, the law takes special note of the poor (also undomesticated animals), who could make no such adjustments. The OT provides little evidence of the enforcement of this law, but several instances are mentioned briefly in Neh 10:31 and 1 Mc 6:49,53. We do not know whether the Sabbath year was observed simultaneously throughout the land or whether fields were rotated in some systematic pattern.

12. This Sabbath legislation recalls Ex 20:8–11; once again the humanitarian motive is stressed. Slaves, aliens, and even beasts are to take advantage of this day of rest. **13a.** This injunction would come more logically at the end of the code. **13b.** Here is stressed the exclusiveness of the God of Israel—a God who does not even tolerate mention of other gods. Legislation such as this explains the revulsion of later authors at the adoption of Baal names by their fellow Israelites. The scribes changed several names: e.g., Eshbaal, "man of Baal," the fourth son of Saul (1 Chr 8:33), was changed to Ishbosheth (2 Sm 3:14), "man of shame."

65 Following the Sabbath legislation is a mandate for triannual pilgrimages to the sanctuary (i.e., "before the Lord God," v. 17). We are reminded of the stipulation of the Hittite treaties, whereby the vassal was to appear before his suzerain at stated intervals. Pasch, Pentecost, and Tabernacles are here listed according to their agricultural character—i.e., the Feast of Unleavened Bread (*Maṣṣôt*), the Feast of Harvest, and the Feast of Gathering. The joint feast of Azymes and Pasch was already treated in Ex 12:1–27. During the seven days of Azymes, bread made from the first produce of the new crop was to be eaten in its pristine state, i.e., untouched by leaven. No mention is made here of the Passover sacrifice that would also occur with this celebration. The Feast of Harvest occurred *ca.* 50 days (hence the title, Pentecost) after the Feast of Unleavened Bread, thus coinciding with the wheat and barley harvests. The final gathering of God's people (Tabernacles) was to take place in the fall, in the seventh month of the year (our September–October period); it marked the close of the grape and olive harvests.

18–19. No "leavened bread" could be used in the sacrifices. Perhaps the basis of this injunction is the idea that leaven constituted a change in the bread from its original condition. In like manner, we noted earlier that hewn stones (i.e., their original character changed) were not allowed in the construction of an altar (20:25). The "fat" of the sacrificial victim was regarded as its most precious part, which, if retained overnight, might spoil.

The legislation in 19b (and in Dt 14:21) puzzled commentators for centuries; however, the discovery and publication of the Ras Shamra literature (*UM* 52:14, "Birth of the Gods") have eliminated this conundrum. It is now clear that this practice was a cultic one among the Canaanite neighbors of the Hebrews. Hence, the Israelites were to refrain from it, lest they also adopt some of the Canaanite cultic inferences.

66 **(G) Warnings and Promises (23:20–33).** The exhortation which immediately follows the Book of the Covenant is a parallel to the hortatory epilogues following the Holiness Code (Lv 26) and the Deuteronomic Code (Dt 28). Three times during this section Yahweh promises to send someone before Israel, if they are faithful to their God. First, his "angel" will safeguard them; this angel will be Yahweh's own emissary, for God's authority resides in him (v. 21). Second, he will send "fear" among other nations which will cause them to flee before the Israelites. Third, he will send "hornets" (possibly a plague) before them.

24. The pillars are the *maṣṣēbôt* connected with the Canaanite shrines of Baal. Their offensive character, so clearly stated here, was not understood by later Israel; Solomon himself set up the famous bronze pillars, Jachin and Boaz, before Yahweh's Temple. These pillars had lost their crude pagan connotations for the Solomonic builders. Their precise symbolic meaning remains a matter of conjecture, e.g., sun and moon, or winter and summer, etc.

30. Yahweh will drive out the Canaanites gradually, lest the land become desolate because of insufficient laborers to work it. An entirely different motivation is assigned in the midrash of Wis 12:3–10, where we are told that God drove the Canaanites out gradually to give them an opportunity to repent. **31.** The boundaries of the promised land are described. The "sea of the Philistines" is the Mediterranean and the "River" is the Euphrates. Only in the era of David and Solomon did the Israelites control such an area (cf. 1 Kgs 4:24).

67 **(H) Ratification of the Covenant (24:1–11).** Two sources appear in this section: J (vv. 1–2 and 9–11) and E (vv. 3–8). In the former's account, the action takes place on the mountain; Moses ascends to the top and his associates remain below; in the latter's account, the action takes place at the foot of the mountain. The covenant is ratified by the sacrificial meal in J and by the sprinkling of the blood in E. Both versions testify to the special covenant accorded Israel and its solemn acceptance by the people.

The 70 elders (v. 1) accompany Moses as representatives of the people. The presence of Aaron is justified by his status as Moses' prophet, and that of Nadab and Abihu by their positions as sons of Aaron and future priests. **10.** Although the text tells us that they "beheld" God, we are immediately informed only of the appearance "Under his feet." The OT notion that seeing God is lethal may be excepted here, for we read, "he did not smite these chosen Israelites." Moses and his deputation participate in the sacrificial meal in J.

In E, Moses serves as the direct and sole mediator between God and the people. He alone writes down the ordinances of the Lord and erects a special altar at the foot of the mountain with the pillars symbolic of the 12 tribes. **5–6.** Before the institution of the priesthood, any man could offer sacrifice legitimately. Moses' enactment of the rite of the blood marks the most solemn ratification of the covenant. **7.** The people have heard the conditions and stated their willingness to abide by them. Half the blood Moses then splashed on the altar—here representing Yahweh—and half he splashed upon the people themselves. The covenant between Yahweh and Israel was now a reality. References to this solemn ratification in blood appear in Zech 9:11 and Heb 9:18–20. Likewise was the New Covenant to be ratified in blood, i.e., Christ's blood (cf. Mt 26:28; Mk 14:24; Lk 22:20; 1 Cor 11:25).

68 **(I) Moses on Sinai (24:12–18).** Moses is once more summoned to ascend the mountain; this time, he receives the stone tablets and instructions regarding cultic legislation. That stone was a usual substance on which to inscribe such ordinance is clear from the Code of Hammurabi and the stele on which the Decree of Harem-hab was incised (cf. *ANEP* 246). **12.** The CCD obviates a problem by failing to translate "the law," which precedes "the commandments" in the Hebr text. Most are in agreement that the former is a later addition to this section because it is never stated in the OT that Yahweh gave Moses anything in writing other than the Ten Commandments (31:18; 32:15; 34:1).

For part of the ascent, Joshua accompanied Moses. The people were left under the authority of Aaron and Hur. Moses spent six days in preparation. On the seventh, God summoned him from the cloud atop Sinai. Moses passed into the cloud, and the text informs us that he spent 40 days and 40 nights on the mountain. The numbers 7 and 40—appearing so frequently throughout the OT—need not be taken literally; they probably refer to periods of lesser or greater extension.

69 **(IV) The Tabernacle (25:1–31:18).** This section is the work of P. It dates from the post-exilic period in its present form, but it also preserves early material. What Yahweh orders (chs. 25–31) is executed (chs. 35–40). In these chapters, very ancient cultic elements are fused with additions from a growing Israelite community, the purpose being to show the foundation of Israel's liturgical life in Mosaic tradition, which consequently represents God's express will for his people. Therefore, the liturgy of the Temple of Solomon, of the sanctuary of Shiloh, and of the desert Tabernacle are represented as one and the same—a divine institution accorded Israel (→ Religious Institutions, 76:44–48).

70 **(A) Collection of Materials (25:1–9).** Yahweh intends (v. 8) to "tabernacle" with his people; he outlines both the "Dwelling" (*miškān*) he desires and its furnishings. **3.** Gold, silver, and bronze will find their way into the casting of sanctuary vessels. The fabric dyes were processed from shellfish living in Phoenician coastal waters. The goats' hair would later be woven by the women into a first covering for the Tabernacle (26:7); the other skins would rest over it (26:14). **5.** The "thahas skins" may be from a species of dolphin found in the Red Sea. The "acacia" provided the framework of the Tabernacle (26:15).

71 **(B) The Ark (25:10–22).** The Ark was a rectangular cabinet, 2.5 by 2.5 by 1.5 cubits. (The Hebr cubit—i.e., the measure from the elbow to the tip of the middle finger—was approx. 17 in., or approx. .5 yd.) It was to be made of acacia wood and plated inside and out with gold. Four golden rings were set on top through which gold-plated acacia poles were inserted to facilitate carrying.

The cover of the Ark was known as the "propitiatory." Whether or not the appellation was the original title for this slab of solid gold is unknown. Some claim it received the name later because of its use on the Day of the Atonement (Lv 16:15–16), when the blood of the sacrificial victims was sprinkled on the top of the Ark. In Pauline literature, Christ receives this title, *hilastērion* (Rom 3:25).

Some critics challenge the statement that the Ark was to house the tablets of the Decalogue (Ex 16:21). Their reasons for doubt hardly seem valid—e.g., the improbability that tablets of law would be hidden in a chest. Indeed, the tablets were not precisely hidden, and recent research has emphasized that Near Eastern covenants were frequently written down and then carefully deposited, to be brought forth from time to time for the ratification of the covenant.

From either end of the Ark, two golden cherubim spread their wings over the propitiatory. It is now certain that the Hebrews borrowed the visible representation of these cherubim from their pagan neighbors, among whom they served as minor deities who protected the palace or temple. In biblical literature, they find frequent use as visible manifestations of the spirits ministering to Yahweh (Gn 3:24; Ps 17:11; Ez 10:1–21). For the form of these cherubim, the Hebrews probably imitated their Phoenician neighbors rather than the distant Assyrians. In the latter case, the cherubim would have been winged lions with human heads.

The Ark and its winged cherubim were hailed as the throne of Yahweh (cf. 1 Sm 4:4). Thus the ark served a twofold purpose: a depository for the Decalogue, and hence a constant reminder of the covenant of Sinai; and the throne of Yahweh, whence he manifested himself to his people and consoled them by his lasting presence.

(For further discussion on the presence of Yahweh and the Ark, see Congar, M. J., *The Mystery of the Temple* [Westminster, 1962]. Daniélou, J., *The Presence of God* [Baltimore, 1959].)

72 **(C) The Table of Showbread (25:23–30).** Like the Ark, the table was to be constructed of acacia and gold-plated. It was also almost of the same proportions. On its top, there was always to be kept the showbread. On the Sabbath eve, 12 loaves of unleavened bread were set upon this table where they remained until replaced the following Sabbath eve. Various titles are used for this showbread throughout the OT, e.g., "bread of the presence" (1 Sm 21:6), "holy bread" (1 Sm 21:4,6), and "continual bread" (Nm 4:7). Its most probable symbolism was as acknowledgment of Yahweh's continuing bounty to his people. The antiquity of the practice is attested by the David and Ahimelech incident in 1 Sm 21:3–6.

73 **(D) The Lampstand (25:31–40).** This confusing description has long bothered scholars. (A study of the lampstand of Herod's temple, portrayed on the Arch of Titus, may help us understand this account [*At Bib* 138, fig. 407].) The lampstand was to be made of beaten gold and weigh one talent (approx. 70 lb.). From the large, central stem, three branches swept outward and upward on each side. Both central stem and side branches were adorned with cups shaped like almond blossoms. Seven lamps, probably pottery, stood atop the main stem and branches. In the excavations at Tell Beit Mirsim, Albright discovered pottery lamps with niches for seven wicks, dating from *ca.* 900 BC. The text does not explain the purpose of the lampstand. It may have been a highly ornate creation with a strictly functional use, or it may have been rich in symbolism for the Hebrews.

74 **(E) The Tent Cloth (26:1–14).** These verses describe the Tabernacle. Four coverings were used. The first (approximately 56.5 by 40 ft.) was made of ten linen panels fastened together with loops and clasps of gold (4–6) and adorned with the figures of cherubim. The second (approx. 62 by 42.5 ft.) was of goats' hair; bronze clasps and loops joined its smaller sections into a whole. Over these were placed the third and fourth coverings—one of rams' skins dyed red and the other of thahas skins.

75 **(F) The Framework (26:15–30).** Individual panels, approx. 14 ft. high and 2 ft. wide, were to form the framework of the Tabernacle. Twenty of these panels were to stand on the S side and 20 on the N. side. In the back stood eight more frames of similar size. Hence the whole measured approx. 42 ft. long, 16 ft. wide, and 14 ft. high. The panels were connected by gold-plated acacia bars inserted through rings affixed to each board. Two projections under each panel slipped into silver sockets (in the CCD "pedestals"), giving added stability.

(G) The Veils (26:31–37). The chamber enclosed by this paneling was in turn to be divided. The smaller section was to be known as the Holy of Holies, comprising an area approx. 14 by 14 ft., in which rested the Ark of the Covenant and the Ten Commandments. Verse 34 makes it clear that the propitiatory or "mercy seat" was an addition to the Ark, not merely its gold top. The most sacred spot was to be separated from the sanctuary's second chamber, or Holy Place, by a veil of both violet, purple, and scarlet yarn, and embroidered linen, which was supported by four gold-plated acacia poles set into silver sockets. In the area of the Holy Place, on opposite sides, stood the table of showbread and the lampstand. This section of the sanctuary was also cut off from public view. Another veil, similar to the one described and supported by five acacia poles, was to provide this privacy.

76 **(H) The Altar of Sacrifice (27:1–8).** The present section deals with the construction of a single altar for the ritual immolation of animals (the altar of incense [30:1ff.] is another matter). It was to be constructed of acacia wood, approx. 7 by 7 by 4 ft. From each corner projected a horn, and together they constituted the most sacred part of the altar. On them, the blood of the sacrificial victims was smeared (29:12); fugitives clung to them to gain the right of sanctuary (1 Kgs 1:50; 2:28). Similar horns are found in Assyrian, Canaanite, and early Greek altars. Their precise symbolism is unknown, but most scholars agree that they signify power, inasmuch as the bull generally characterized great strength throughout the Near East. Bronze plating covered the acacia wood, and the sacrificial tools were to be of bronze. A bronze grating, half the height of the altar, surrounded it.

8. The altar was basically a hollow acacia wood box; therefore, any attempt to burn the victim within this hollow space would also destroy the altar. The bronze plating atop the altar would hardly withstand the heat of sacrificial fires. Perhaps heaped-up stones provided a burning zone (the grating of v. 4 was most probably intended to protect the altar). Possibly stones were placed atop the altar itself for the actual burning (cf. Ex 29:18, which speaks of burning on the altar). Before the burning, of course, the victim's blood was smeared on the horns of the altar, symbolizing the victim's life. Like the other items in the sanctuary, the altar was also equipped with rings through which carrying poles were inserted.

77 **(I) The Tabernacle Court (27:9–21).** The final site described by the sacred author is the court itself. It measured approx. 142 by 71 ft. It was set apart from the adjoining area by acacia poles at 7-ft. intervals. These bars had hooks at their tops; beneath each was a projection which fitted into a bronze socket. Linen veils or curtains hung from a height of approx. 7 ft. set off the court from any area devoted to profane uses. Here, then, was the great sacred area of Israel—Yahweh himself resided above the cherubim within the Holy of Holies; in the Holy Place, he met his priestly ministers and received their special ministrations and intercession; in the surrounding court, the God of Israel partook of the homage of his people.

20–21. The final verses of the chapter deal with the pure olive oil to be used in the Holy Place. It is to come from the people, but the sons of Aaron are to see to its liturgical use before the Lord. (For a succinct historical and theological evaluation of the Tabernacle, see F. M. Cross, *BAR* 1, 201–28.)

78 **(J) The Priesthood (28:1–5).** Here the divine institution of the priesthood is proclaimed (→ Religious Institutions, 76:11–32). **3.** Special vestments are prescribed to set the priests apart for their sacred service: breastpiece, ephod, robe, brocaded tunic, miter, and sash.

79 **(K) The Ephod and the Breastpiece (28:6–30).** In the 19th cent., critical writers maintained that the ephod was a post-exilic creation; today, scholars place its origin in antiquity. First used as a loincloth, it kept its place among priestly robes even after fuller garb came into use. The description of David in 1 Sm 6:14,20 substantiates this early characteristic of the ephod. The ephod of P, however, reflects a much later and more sophisticated era. At this time, no doubt, the ephod was a mark of the high priesthood and no longer a simple loincloth. Onyx stones bearing the names of the sons of Jacob were set in the shoulder straps, and filigree rosettes of gold and two chains of pure gold adorned it.

The so-called breastpiece of decision was likewise of linen, embroidered with gold and violet thread. Twelve precious stones representing the tribes of Israel were mounted into it. Gold clasps enabled twisted gold cords to join it to the shoulder straps of the ephod. Similarly, two more gold clasps attached it to the ephod proper below. To visualize these two sacred garments, we might compare the ephod with a short apron, worn below the waist and tied not only in the back, but also over the shoulders. The breastpiece was attached at its top to the two shoulder straps and at its bottom to the waist-level ephod.

The breastpiece contained the Urim and Thummim. (See v. 30; → Religious Institutions, 76:7–8).

80 **(L) Other Vestments (28:31–43).** The high priest also wore a one-piece violet robe fitted with an opening for the head and the arms. It extended to the knees and was adorned at its bottom with woven pomegranates and golden bells. He also wore a miter and a golden diadem inscribed with the awesome phrase, "Sacred to the Lord." Of the priest's tunic we learn only that it was brocaded, and of his sash, that it was of variegated work. **41.** *ordain them:* Literally, "fill their hand" (→ Religious Institutions, 76:11). **42–43.** A final injunction warns that the priest must beware of any immodesty as he approaches the altar or ministers in the sanctuary.

(M) Consecration of the Priests (29:1–9). A fuller account of the actual ordination of Aaron and his sons occurs in Lv 8:1–38 (→ Leviticus, 4:20–21). Exodus prescribes that a bull (for a sin offering), two rams (one for a holocaust, the other for the consecration rite), unleavened cakes mixed with oil, and unleavened wafers covered with oil (for a meal offering) be brought to the Tabernacle. Then, after bathing and investment, Aaron and his sons are anointed.

81 **(N) Ordination Sacrifices (29:10–37).** The first sacrifice is a sin offering (cf. Lv 4:1–12). Aaron and his sons lay their hands upon the head of a young bull to signify that this animal is their substitute. Moses smears some of the sacrificial blood upon the horns of the altar and pours out the rest at its base. Flesh, hide, and offal were to be burned outside the camp. In a normal sin offering, the priest also shared in the victim (Lv 5:13; 6:22). In this instance he does not, for the victim was slain for the sins of the priests themselves.

15. There follows the holocaust (cf. Lv 1) of one of the rams. As in the case of the young bull, once again occurs the ritual imposition of hands. After the slaughtering, the blood is splashed upon the altar with the same significance as before. The beast is then butchered and burnt in its entirety upon the altar. **19–20.** The second ram is led up to undergo the imposition of hands. After its slaughter, Moses smears some of its blood on the right ear, right thumb, and right great toe of Aaron and each of his sons to indicate their total consecration.

22. From this ram, Moses takes its outer fat, the fatty tail (still a delicacy in Arab lands), the fat covering the inner organs, the lobe of the liver, the kidneys, and the right thigh; from the basket, he takes one loaf of bread, one cake, and one wafer. These Aaron and his sons take as a wave offering before the Lord. In this distinctive offering, the priest first elevated the parts so chosen toward the altar—indicating that they were given to God—and then lowered them to himself—indicating that God returned them to the priests for their sustenance. In this particular rite of ordination, however, because investiture is incomplete, Moses burns these parts upon the altar. Moses received the breast of the victim as a wave offering.

82 **27–30.** Verses 27–30 interrupt the ordination ceremony to point out that the Israelites must grant part of their offerings to the priest and that the sacred vestments of Aaron must pass to his descendants for use in their own ordination ceremonies.

31–35. The ordination ceremonies continue with notice to cook the remaining flesh of the ordination ram. This flesh and the bread remaining in the basket are to provide a meal for Aaron and his sons. Because this ram and unleavened bread were parts of a sacred rite, no layman could participate in this meal. Whatever remained of the flesh or bread could not be kept overnight; it was to be burned immediately upon the meal's conclusion.

36–37. The ordination ceremony took seven days, and on each day a young bull was offered as a sin offering. There is question not of the sanctification of the priests, but of the altar itself, which, because of these sin offerings, takes on a singularly sacred character. In the future, whatever touches it becomes sacred. (Note, e.g., Lv 6:20, where the victim thus rendered sacred in turn makes sacred anyone who touches it.) Many authors consider these verses a later addition. Chapter 29 deals with the consecration of persons, not things. Furthermore, in the preceding narrative the altar has already been employed for sacrifices. In the Lv account, Moses purifies the altar before the actual rite of ordination.

83 **(O) Daily Sacrifices (29:38–46).** Two lambs per day were to be offered on the altar: one in the morning and the second at evening twilight. To each lamb sacrifice were added one-tenth of an ephah of fine flour (one ephah equals .6 bu.), one-quarter hin of olive oil (one hin is approx. 1 gal.), and one-quarter hin (approx. 1 qt.) of wine. Here, too (vv. 38–42), many authors maintain we are dealing with a later edition. The practice of daily sacrifices is definitely ancient (cf., e.g., 1 Kgs 18:29) but generally seemed to involve a holocaust only in the morning, with a meal offering in the evening (2 Kgs 16:15). Ezekiel (46:13–15) makes mention only of a morning holocaust, as does Lv 6:5. Hence, the practice of morning and evening holocausts and the insertion of this legislation here appear to be later additions.

43–46. Chapter 29 ends in a fitting manner. Yahweh will consecrate Tabernacle, altar, and priests to his service, and, as the special mark of his affection for Israel, he will dwell in their midst. In fact, Israel is to realize that her providential deliverance from slavery in Egypt was directed to this end, i.e., that God might dwell with his people.

84 **(P) The Altar of Incense (30:1–10).** (→ Religious Institutions, 76:73–74.)

85 **(Q) Census Tax (30:11–16).** This section presupposes a census, an event which occurs first in Nm 1. The ancients had a dread superstition regarding such a census, as though it automatically incurred the anger of God (cf. 2 Sm 24). By the payment of "a forfeit for his life" (v. 12), however, a person so enrolled hoped to escape any ill fate. The present legislation encouraged this hope of deliverance. Rich and poor were to pay the same, inasmuch as the question was one of a common cultic right. **13.** The gerah indicates another Israelite borrowing from the Babylonian monetary system. The Ex system reckons 20 gerahs to the shekel; the original Babylonian table, however, called for 24 gerahs to the shekel. That the Israelite change was definitive is clear from Lv 27:25; Nm 3:47; 18:16; and Ez 45:12. The funds from this collection were used for the upkeep of the sanctuary.

Again, it is possible that the census tax is a later addition. In fact, some writers maintain that it occurs first in Neh, when the people consent to pay one-third of a shekel for this purpose (Neh 10:32). Others contend that some such tax is of Mosaic provenance, but that its formulation followed the census ordered in Nm 1.

86 **(R) The Laver, Anointing Oil, and Incense (30:17–38).** Before their ministrations in the sanctuary, the priests are enjoined to wash hands and feet (note the similar statute imposed on all Moslems even today before prayer in the mosque). Unlike all the other elements involved in Israelite cult, no description or measurements are set down for the laver. There is no allusion to it in 38:29–31, where the amount of bronze collected from the people, as well as the various appurtenances made from this bronze, are listed. Again, if of Mosaic origin, it would more logically have followed the description of the altar itself (ch. 27). Thus, there is general agreement that this passage is a later addition.

22–33. Strict instructions are set down for the constituents of the sacred oil. Imported spices were to be added to the native olive oil in fixed quantities. Myrrh is a gumlike substance from Arabia; cinnamon and cassia were spices most probably imported from the Far East; the fragrant cane may have been indigenous to India. The varying estimates for a shekel (anywhere from 11.03 to 12.25 g.) and for a hin render it impossible today to duplicate the oil exactly. The sacred character of the oil is stressed. Its profane use brought excommunication to the offender.

This section also shows evidence of a later addition. In the earliest ordination ceremonies, only Aaron or the high priest was anointed with the sacred oil (29:7–9); by the time this passage was added, all priests were so anointed (v. 30).

34–38. The ingredients for ceremonial incense were stacte, onycha, galbanum, and frankincense in equal parts. Stacte, a fragrant balsam taken from tree bark, is the CCD version of the MT *sammîm*, which most lexicographers will only identify as "perfume." Onycha came from a Red Sea shellfish. Galbanum was a resin indigenous to Palestine, and frankincense was another fragrant resin. To these elements salt was added, and the whole was then crushed to powder for use in a censer or on the altar of incense. Like the anointing oil, it was reserved for cultic use; other uses brought excommunication.

87 **(S) Choice of Artisans (31:1–11).** Providential assistance is promised the artisans entrusted with the construction of all sacred objects. Throughout the OT (Jgs 3:10; 1 Sm 11:6ff.; Is 42:1, etc.), there is frequent mention that the spirit of God has singularly endowed a human instrument for a specific mission. The text lists all the items that Bezalel and Oholiab are to construct. Because it includes objects from ch. 30 as well, this catalogue is believed to be a later addition. Of the artisans here mentioned, Bezalel, whose name means "in the shadow of God," is assigned to the tribe of Judah. In 1 Chr 2:18–20, he is a descendant of Caleb, hence a Calebite. The Calebite clan was eventually absorbed into the tribe of Judah, so there is no conflict. Oholiab, "father's tent," is mentioned only in Ex.

88 **(T) The Sabbath (31:12–18).** This section presents the most solemn OT statement regarding the Sabbath. The Sabbath constitutes a token of the special covenant between Yahweh and Israel which makes Israel holy. It also recalls the divine plan of creation. Desecration of this solemn day would therefore bring death to the offender.

18. After the lengthy insertion on the Tabernacle, this verse serves to introduce ch. 32; Moses had been promised the "tablets" in 24:12. Some commentators attach this verse to Ex 28:43 and regard all intervening material as a later addition.

(V) Apostasy and Renewal of the Covenant (32:1–34:35). Chapters 32–34 continue the theme begun in ch. 24 (24:14–18). Most of the material is ascribed to J, especially ch. 34, which parallels the text of chs. 20–24.

89 **(A) The Golden Calf (32:1–29).** The confusion in ch. 32 has led scholars to maintain that the narrative of the apostasy is an addition to J, introduced to explain the condemnation of the cult of Jeroboam at Dan and Bethel (1 Kgs 12:28). Among the problems in ch. 32 are the role of Aaron and the punishment that is meted out. In v. 4 it is Aaron himself who fashions the golden calf, whereas in v. 24b, his part is definitely mitigated. In v. 20, Moses punishes the revelers by making them drink the water into which the powdered calf has been mixed. Verses 26–29 describe the vengeance of the Levites (a P addition, which would explain the later role of the Levites). Finally, in v. 34, no specific punishment is named, but we are told that Yahweh will punish the people in his own good time.

1–6. The MT specifically mentions the request to Aaron (v. 1) that he make "gods who will go before us" (contrary to the CCD, both noun and verb are in pl.; the import of the pl. form is indicated in v. 8). Aaron compromises and fashions a single gold figure for the people. The bull image would have been well known to the Israelites, either in the 13th cent. or in the time of the monarchy, for it represented Apis in the Egyptian pantheon and Baal among the Canaanites. Before this image the Israelites bowed in worship proclaiming, "These [pl. in the MT] are your gods, O Israel, who brought [pl. in the MT] you out of the land of Egypt" (v. 4). Only one image was fashioned by Aaron, so the plural here seems clearly to be a polemic against the two calves installed by Jeroboam (1 Kgs 12:28). The LXX reads "and he said," thus attributing this statement to Aaron rather than to the people. The LXX emendation, however, is out of context with vv. 5–6. Aaron proceeds to make an altar before this image and proclaim a feast to Yahweh.

90 **7–14.** Yahweh informs Moses of the people's sin; these verses must originate from a source other than that of v. 18, where Moses appears ignorant of what is happening in the camp. Yahweh has divorced himself from this sinful people, for he refers to them as "your people." He intends to destroy the wicked and form a new nation. Moses now assumes the role of mediator and appeals to God's honor for his own name before the pagan nations as a motive to prevent the destruction of his people. As a second motive, Moses recalls the promises accorded to Abraham. We note, however, the subsequent conflicting elements of the punishments invoked by Moses (32:20,25–29) and the testimony of Yahweh (32:34).

15–24. The discovery of the calf (vv. 18–19) leads to the smashing of the tablets, which symbolizes the breaking of the covenant. Moses melts the golden calf, grinds it into powder, and casts it into the Israelites' drinking water, thus creating an ordeal whereby the guilty would be punished and the innocent would be unharmed (cf. Nm 5:11–28). (In Dt 9:21, we have a different version of the incident.) **21.** Against Moses' reproach for his activity, Aaron weakly attempts to justify himself. Note the marked contrast between v. 4, which expressly states that Aaron molded the golden calf, and v. 24b, where he simply throws the collected gold into the fire and the calf comes wondrously forth.

25–29. The number slain by the Levites is 3000; the Vg gives 23,000 (which seems to have been influenced by 1 Cor. 10:7). We have already noted the etiological character of vv. 25–29; the episode served to justify the Levites' privileged position in Israelite cult.

91 **(B) The Further Mediation of Moses (32:30–35).** In vv. 30–34, Moses intercedes with the Lord ("to make atonement for your sin," v. 30) and appears to obtain a postponement; however, in v. 35 occurs the abrupt statement that the Lord "smote the people," which is probably the continuation of the ordeal in v. 20. The intercession of Moses, already emphasized in vv. 11–14, will figure again in ch. 33. His request to be stricken from the "book" (v. 32) presupposes that the Lord has a list of the living and that he strikes from it those who are to die (cf. Ps 69:29). This figure may derive from the official list of the names of citizens found in certain areas (Ez 13:9; Jer 22:30).

92 **(C) The Order to Depart (33:1–6).** According to 19:1, the people had arrived at Sinai in the third month of their journey, and in Nm 10:11–12, they leave Sinai in the second month of the second year. Their sojourn, then, lasted almost a year. **2.** As in 23:20, an angel will lead them, but now the motive is lest God's anger lead him to destroy the fickle Israelites. As Noth remarks (*op. cit.*, 253), the theme of God's presence is central to ch. 33. **4.** At this announcement, the people stop using the ornaments that had played a part in the golden calf incident. Simply refraining, however, does not satisfy Yahweh; they must strip themselves of them completely as a token of their repentance.

93 **(D) The Tent of Meeting (33:7–11).** These five verses mark a break in the context, with no relevance to either the golden calf incident, which they follow, or Moses' request to see God, which they precede. The tent here described (*'ōhel mô'ēd*) is not the Tabernacle of chs. 25–26. The latter was to be in the middle of the camp (25:8), whereas this tent of meeting was to be pitched outside the camp (v. 7). For the Tabernacle, the Levites were to be the ministers (Nm 3:5–7); for the present meeting tent, Joshua, an Ephraimite, was the minister. It was simple and small, for Moses pitched it himself; the Tabernacle and its paraphernalia of the earlier account required numerous porters. Missing also is the liturgical ceremony associated with the Tabernacle. This tent seems to function more as an oracle place (Nm 17:7–9)—i.e., a meeting place and not a dwelling place like the Tabernacle. When Moses sought divine guidance, he would enter this tent and await the presence of Yahweh, signaled by the descent of the cloud upon the tent. The Israelites witnessed these meetings of Yahweh and Moses with great awe and from the distance of their own tents (vv. 8 and 10). This particular tent, then, constituted a unique means whereby Moses alone could contact Yahweh (Nm 10:4–8). The face-to-face experience of God's presence represents a different source from that of Ex 33:20, where it is specifically stated that no one can see God and live.

94 **(E) The Prayer of Moses (33:12–23).** This section continues the narrative of 33:6 and plays on the theme of God's presence. **12.** In light of vv. 1–3 (cf. 32:34!), Moses questions Yahweh regarding whom or what God will send with him as a sign of his presence. Obviously Moses is not satisfied with the angel of v. 3. Furthermore, Moses seeks to know the "ways" of God, i.e., his intentions for Israel and how Moses may deal with him. Before the crisis of the golden calf, God dwelled with his people, who enjoyed his personal leadership. Now there is a sense of loss of God.

14. In this situation, Yahweh relents and once again promises Moses his guidance. **15.** Moses will go only with the presence of God. **16.** It is Yahweh's presence with his people that distinguishes Israel from all other nations.

Emboldened by the success of his initial prayer, Moses petitions a more intimate knowledge of God—to see his very glory. A frequent OT motif (v. 20) makes this request impossible; the sight of God is too much for mortal man to bear (Gn 32:30; Dt 4:33; Jgs 6:22–23, etc.). The obscure and enigmatic description of vv. 21–23 most probably indicates that although his request was refused, Moses was granted a knowledge of God superior to that accorded ordinary men or even other charismatics. The language and thought of these verses evoke also the description of Elijah's divine confrontation in 1 Kgs 19:9–13.

95 **(F) Renewal of the Tablets (34:1–9).** Verses 1–5 and 9–28 of ch. 34 are the work of J; vv. 6–8 are attributed to a later redactor. This section is J's version of the making of the covenant, and is a parallel to chs. 19–20; it may have been intended, after the breaking of the tablets (32:19), to show that the covenant would continue. **3.** The earlier warning of 19:12 is repeated, but unlike the previous occasion (19:24), Aaron is not to accompany his brother. **5.** Concealed by the cloud, Yahweh reveals his name (cf. 33:19). **6–8.** The redaction reflects elements from Ex 20:5–6, Nm 14:18, and Dt 5:9–10. **9.** Once more, Moses asks God to accompany the people (cf. 33:15–16).

96 **(G) The Covenant (34:10–28).** **10.** The "marvels" most probably refer to the divine assistance to Israel in settling Canaan, but the covenant and prodigies depend, in turn, on the observance of the commandments that Yahweh will give his people.

There follows the so-called Ritual Decalogue. Although not all scholars agree regarding a tenfold division, the cultic aspect stands out clearly. Most of the legislation can be paralleled to the Book of the Covenant (Ex 20:22–23:19).

13–16. The account begins with strong warnings about the peoples of Canaan. So acute is the danger of syncretism that the Israelites are to make no agreements with them; in fact, they must destroy all signs of

Canaanite cult. Altars, sacred pillars (*maṣṣēbôt*), and sacred poles (*'ăšērîm*) are specifically named. The sacred pillars were special stones that symbolized the male deity in Canaanite worship, numerous examples of which were unearthed during the excavations at Gezer. The sacred poles were symbols of Asherah, goddess of love and fecundity. Worship and intermarriage with these pagans are likewise proscribed.

17. Metal images of the deity are forbidden (cf. 20:4). The command to observe the Feast of Unleavened Bread recalls the earlier legislation in 12:15ff., 13:3–4, and 23:15. Yahweh's right to the first-born of man and beast (vv. 19–20) was heralded earlier in 13:12–13 and 22:28–29. **20.** At the appointed seasonal visits, the Israelites are again reminded not to appear empty-handed (cf. 23:15). **21.** The law of the Sabbath refers to 20:8–11. **22.** As in 23:16, the Israelites are told to keep both the Feast of Weeks (Pentecost) at the time of the first wheat harvest and a final feast at the time of the fall fruit harvest. **23.** Three times a year they are to appear before the Lord (23:17), a prescription that presupposes a single sanctuary for all Israel. The legislation against the use of leavened bread in sacrifice and against the saving of sacrificial material has precedence in 23:18. **26.** As in 23:19, the best of their fruits are to be an offering to Yahweh, and, again, they are forbidden to boil a kid in its mother's milk. **28.** See 24:18.

97 **(H) Moses Returns to the People (34:29–35).** **29–33.** These verses belong to P, and resume the narrative of 31:18. The radiance of Moses' face marks a reflection of the divine glory he has in some way confronted on the mountain. To convey the brilliant rays of light emanating from the countenance of Moses, the MT uses the term *qeren*. Because the first meaning of this word is "horn," St. Jerome translated it as such. Michelangelo was following the Vg when he adorned his heroic Moses with horns projecting from his forehead. For a Pauline consideration of this passage and its relation to the New Covenant, see 2 Cor 3:7–4:6.

(VI) Fulfillment of the Divine Mandate (35:1–40:38). This final section, ascribed to P, enunciates the execution of the orders given in chs. 25–31. For the most part, the earlier commands are repeated literally. Some of the materials added later to chs. 25–31, particularly elements in chs. 30–31, have been systematically worked into the narrative of chs. 35–40. Either the LXX has followed a different Hebr MS. from that followed by the MT, or the LXX translator has freely changed the order; however, only the omission of the incense altar (37:25–28) is of real importance.

98 **(A) The Assembly of Israel (35:1–39:43).** **35:2–3.** See 31:13–17; the proscription of lighting a fire on the Sabbath is added here. **35:4–9.** See comment on 25:2–7. **35:10.** Artisans are summoned to fashion "all that the Lord has commanded."

99 **36:1.** To Moses' words, the people respond with a generous outpouring of all necessary materials. With them, Bezalel and Oholiab join forces with other "experts." So magnanimous were the Israelites in their contributions that Moses is represented as calling a halt to their giving.

36:8–38:20. This section duplicates the instructions in chs. 26–30. For the tent cloth (36:8–19), cf. 26:1–11,14. For the boards (36:20–34), cf. 26:15–29. For the veil (36:35–38), cf. 26:31–32,36–37. For the ark (37:1–9), cf. 25:10–14,17–20. For the table (37:10–16), cf. 25:23–29. For the lampstand (37:17–24), cf. 25:31–39. For the altar of incense (37:25–28), cf. 30:1–5. For the oil and incense (37:29), cf. 30:22–25,34–35. For the altar of holocausts (38:1–7), cf. 27:1–8. For the laver (38:8), cf. 30:17–18. For the court (38:9–20), cf. 27:9–19.

There follows a section (38:21–31) concerning the amount of metal used. That this is a later redaction is clear from the facts that the Levites mentioned in v. 21 were instituted later (Nm 3:5ff.), and that Ithamar becomes their head still later (Nm 4:33). Furthermore, from v. 26 we gather that the precious metals came from the sanctuary tax; correspondingly, reference is made in v. 26 to the subsequent census of the people (Nm 1:45–46). Thus the evidence of 35:21 and 36:3 regarding the voluntary character of the people's gifts is ignored. The numbers involved seem to be greatly exaggerated (see comment on 12:37).

39:1–31. See comment on ch. 28. **32–43.** The completion of the work is an occasion for a catalogue of all the items.

100 **(B) The Erection of the Dwelling (40:1–38).** Orders are given for the setting up and the anointing of the tabernacle and for the robing and anointing of the priests. With great meticulousness it is noted that Moses did "as the Lord commanded him" (vv. 16, 19, 21, 23, 25, 27, 29, and 32). **17.** The time would be about nine months after the arrival at Sinai. **34–38.** Cf. 25:8; 29:43–46. Again emphasized is the presence of the Lord among his people—described in imagery characteristic of P—which foreshadows Nm 9:15ff., where the cloud is the signal for breaking camp. It is on the consoling note of the Lord's presence (cf. 33:1–34:9) that Ex ends.

4

LEVITICUS

Roland J. Faley, T.O.R.

BIBLIOGRAPHY

1 Auzou, G., *Connaissance du Levitique* (Paris, 1953). Cazelles, H., *Le Levitique* (BJ; Paris, 1958). Davies, G. H., "Leviticus," *IDB* 3, 117–22. Herbert, A. S., *Worship in Ancient Israel* (London, 1959). Micklem, N., *Leviticus* (*IB* 2; Nashville, 1953) 3–134. North, C. R., *Leviticus* (Abingdon Commentary; N.Y., 1929). Noth, M., *Das dritte Buch Mose* (ATD; Göttingen, 1962) (ET: *Leviticus* [London, 1965]). Schneider, H. and H. Junker, *Zweites bis fünftes Buch Moses* (Echter-B; Würzburg, 1958). Snaith, N. H., *Leviticus* (*PCB*; London, 1962) 241–53.

INTRODUCTION

2 **(I) Title.** Called in Hebrew by its opening word, *Wayyiqrā'* (And he called), Lv derives its English title from the Vg translation of the LXX *Leuitikon.* The name is appropriate, for Lv served as the liturgical handbook of the levitical priesthood, and at the same time it taught the Israelites the necessity of an untainted holiness in every aspect of their lives. Being almost wholly concerned with laws and rubrics, the book advances but slightly the pentateuchal narrative.

(II) Authorship. As in the case of the entire Pentateuch, it is impossible to speak of the author of Lv in any restricted sense. Certainly, no single figure is more responsible for it than Moses, who, as the great lawgiver, undoubtedly regulated Israel's earliest expressions of cult. Yet the finished form of Lv is centuries removed from the primitive worship of the wilderness. Its detailed code of sacrifice, rite of priestly investiture, and town-life considerations clearly place it within a well-structured sedentary society with its Temple the center of public worship. Leviticus is, then, the work of many hands engaged through the centuries in adapting Mosaic statutes to the needs of a later time. Permeated throughout with the spirit of Sinai, it can be termed a book of Moses inasmuch as he is its font, its ultimate source.

3 **(III) Origin, History.** The more proximate origin of Lv must be sought among the major strands or traditions that constitute the Pentateuch. Unlike Gn, Ex, and Nm, wherein different sources are combined, Lv belongs entirely to the P tradition, representing the major work of the P school. However, its history is more complex and is protracted over a period of many years. It has some decidedly primitive features, which are best explained as legislation preserved by the priests at local sanctuaries during the early centuries of Israelite occupation. The book itself began to take form with the editing of the Holiness Code (chs. 17–26), edited by members of the Jerusalem clergy at the end of the 7th, or the beginning of the 6th cent. BC. This early compendium greatly influenced the later work of the P school, including the composition of the Book of Ezekiel.

In its present form, Lv is post-exilic, the work of the Priestly school during the period of cultic reorganization after the Exile's termination (538). The Holiness Code, which had taken on some additions during the Exile, was once more re-edited and became the nucleus of Lv. To it were added the sacrificial code (chs. 1–7), the ordination rite (chs. 8–10), and the legal purity code (chs. 11–16). Chapter 27, dealing with the commutation of vows, comes from a still later edition. The purpose of Lv was to supply directives on all aspects of religious observance for the post-exilic community, especially as they related to the Temple liturgy.

4 **(IV) Outline.** Although it is true that the diversity of the material in certain parts of Lv prohibits detailed schematization, the general structure of the book is not difficult to determine. The commentary will adhere to the following outline:

(I) The Law of Sacrifice (1:1–7:38)
- (A) Types of Sacrifice (1:1–5:26)
  - (a) Holocausts (1:1–17)
  - (b) Cereal Offerings (2:1–16)
  - (c) Peace Offerings (3:1–17)
  - (d) Sin Offerings (4:1–5:13)
  - (e) Guilt Offerings (5:14–26)
- (B) The Priest and Sacrifice (6:1–7:38)
  - (a) The Daily Holocaust (6:1–6)

(b) The Daily Cereal Offering (6:7–16)
(c) Sin Offerings (6:17–23)
(d) Guilt Offerings (7:1–10)
(e) Peace Offerings (7:11–21,28–34)
(f) Blood and Fat Prohibitions (7:22–27)
(g) Conclusion (7:35–38)
(II) The Ceremony of Ordination (8:1–10:20)
(A) Ordination of Aaron and His Sons (8:1–13)
(B) Ordination Sacrifices (8:14–36)
(C) Octave of the Ordination (9:1–24)
(D) Sin of Aaron's Sons (10:1–20)
(III) Legal Purity (11:1–15:33)
(A) Clean and Unclean Animals (11:1–47)
(B) Childbirth (12:1–8)
(C) Leprosy (13:1–14:57)
(a) In Humans (13:1–46)
(b) In Clothing (13:47–59)
(c) Purification (14:1–32)
(d) In Buildings (14:33–57)
(D) Sexual Uncleanness (15:1–33)
(IV) The Day of Atonement (16:1–34)
(V) The Law of Holiness (17:1–26:46)
(A) Sacredness of Blood (17:1–16)
(B) Sacredness of Sex (18:1–30)
(C) Various Rules of Conduct (19:1–37)
(D) Penalties (20:1–27)
(E) Priestly Sanctity (21:1–24)
(F) Rules on Sacrifice (22:1–33)
(G) The Liturgical Year (23:1–44)
(a) Passover and Unleavened Bread (23:4–14)
(b) Pentecost (23:15–21)
(c) New Year's Day (23:23–25)
(d) Day of Atonement (23:26–32)
(e) Feast of Booths (23:33–36,39–43)
(H) Additional Legislation (24:1–23)
(I) The Holy Years (25:1–55)
(a) Sabbatical Year (25:2–7)
(b) Jubilee Year (25:8–55)
(J) Sanctions (26:1–46)
(VI) Redemption of Votive Offerings (27:1–34)

COMMENTARY

5 **(I) The Law of Sacrifice (1:1–7:38).** The sacrificial ritual inaugurating the book of Lv, because of its importance in Israel's cultic life, interrupts the P tradition account of the construction and furnishing of the Lord's dwelling (Ex 25–40) and its logical sequel, the installation of the priests (Lv 8–10). This sacrificial code, edited by the Priestly school in the post-exilic period and representing the flourishing liturgy of the rebuilt Temple, is actually the final stage in a history of Israelite sacrifice, which was protracted over many centuries.

(A) Types of Sacrifice (1:1–5:26). Sacrificial terminology is more complex than an initial reading of these chapters would indicate. Here, as elsewhere in the OT, the Eng word "sacrifice" is used to render a number of Hebr words, some of them indistinguishable. Moreover, in the course of centuries, certain ideas, originally connected with one or another sacrifice, were evidently lost; others merged with rites that were closely akin. In many respects, the division of sacrifice into the five main types in the Lv ritual is less a matter of etymology than a reflection of custom and common usage.

6 (a) HOLOCAUSTS (1:1–17). The Eng term is derived from the Vg and LXX translation of the Hebr *ʿôlāh*, signifying something that ascends or rises. Whether this notion of ascent referred to the victim's ascent to the altar, or from the altar to God, or a combination of both, cannot be determined with certainty. The Gk *ʿolokautôma*, meaning something wholly destroyed by fire, aptly expresses the essential characteristic of the sacrifice—the victim's being placed on the altar and its complete consummation.

1. *the Meeting Tent* (*'ōhel môʿēd*): Here the Lord confronts Moses and presents his legislation. The P tradition account of the dwelling's plan and execution is found mainly in Ex 25–27,35–40. The tent was primarily a place of revelation from which Yahweh as head of the covenant assembly directed the activity of his people (Ex 25:22; 29:42–43; 30:36). Moses does not enter the tent at this time, covered as it is by the cloud and filled with the Lord's glory (Ex 40:34–38). (F. M. Cross, "The Priestly Tabernacle," *BAR* 1, 201–28. M. Haran, "The Nature of the *'ōhel môʿēdh* in Pentateuchal Sources," *JSemS* 5 [1960] 50–65.) The Lord immediately enunciates the first principle regarding animal sacrifice in restricting the offering to domestic animals of the bovine (bulls, cows, calves) and ovine (sheep, lambs, goats) classes. **2.** *offering* (*qorbān*): That which a man "brings near" to God. The same root *qrb* is found in Ugaritic with the causative equivalent, "to offer in sacrifice." It is applied to various types of sacrifice in Lv, Nm, and Ez, as well as to nonsacrificial offerings made to God (Neh 10:35; 13:31). The victim must be of superior condition and devoid of any physical defect.

The ritual itself (3–9) is comprised of six steps: the presentation of the victim, the slaughter, the aspersion of the altar, the removal of skin and dissection of the victim, the washing of certain parts, and the burning. The imposition of hands in v. 4 is not a rite of substitution or sin transfer since a sin-ridden victim would never have been an acceptable offering. The action denotes solidarity, closer identification between the offerer with his personal dispositions and the gift being offered. The slaughtering is done by the offerer, not the priests. In relatively few sacrifices—e.g., those offered in their own name (4:4) or in the name of the whole community (2 Chr 29:22,24, 34)—did the priests slay the victim themselves. The contact between the blood, equated by the Hebrew with life itself (17:14), and the altar, which was a sign of the divine presence, brought about the victim's transition from the earthly sphere to the divine realm. The altar upon which the blood was sprinkled was located before the entrance to the tent, just as the altar of holocausts was located in front of the Solomonic Temple (2 Kgs 16:14). The piecing of the victim suggests a sacred repast—all of which, in this instance, is given to the Lord. The lighting of the fire was proper only to the first sacrifice offered; thereafter it was never extinguished (6:5–6). The prepared pieces, together with the head, the fat, and the washed intestines and extremities, were placed on the altar and consumed. **9.** *sweet smelling oblation:* The term for oblation here is *'iššeh*, which appears also in vv. 13 and 17. Still much discussed regarding etymology, it is used with reference to any offering partly or totally consumed by fire (*'ēš*), and, as indicated by L. Moraldi (*RSO* 32 [1957] 329–30), in Lv it is an equivalent expression for the victim itself. The sacrifice's pleasant odor is an anthropomorphic expression indicating divine acceptance (Gn 8:21).

The ritual for sheep or goat holocausts (10–13) differs little from the preceding. The absence of any mention of the imposition of hands or its religious value may be either that it is presupposed (the skinning of the animal is also omitted) or that it may be reflective of the holocaust's more primitive ritual (Jgs 6:19–22; 13:16–20). **11.** *north* *side of the altar:* The specification is lacking in 1–9. The Temple's north entrance was known as the Sheep Gate (Neh 3:1).

The ceremony for the bird holocaust (14–17) is carried out entirely by the priest at the altar. The head is detached, as opposed to 5:8 where it is snapped loose but not severed. Owing to the limited amount of blood, aspersion is made on only one side of the altar. This type of holocaust is not envisioned in the instructions of v. 2; it is quite likely an addition to the holocaust legislation inserted at the time of the sacrificial ritual's final edition. As the customary offering of the poorer class (5:7; 12:8; 14:22,30), it represents an accommodation of the sacrificial ideal in admitting the use of animals upon which man had no real dependence for his sustenance.

7 (b) Cereal Offerings (2:1–16). Much debate still surrounds the etymology of the Hebr *minḥāh*. Most probably its basic meaning is "gift, tribute," and it is so used in a noncultic context at least 37 times in the OT. Outside the Pentateuch and Ez, it is applied to any type of sacrifice (1 Sm 2:17; Mal 2:13; 3:3ff.; 2 Chr 32:23), whereas in the former it has the more restricted meaning of an unbloody offering of vegetable products cultivated by man (→ Religious Institutions, 76:89–90).

The present chapter treats various forms of cereal offering. The first (1–3) is of pure unbaked wheat mixed with oil to which frankincense was added. Part of the offering was burned; the remainder was given to the priests. **2.** *frankincense:* A powder of fine spices (Ex 30:34–35) added as a supplement to the cereal offering. *token offering ('azkārāh):* Moraldi (*op. cit.*, 330) links this word with the causative form of the Hebr root *zkr* meaning "to make remember." Hence, it may signify either a memorial, i.e., a means of focusing God's attention on the offerer, or a pledge, i.e., the small part offered serving as a token of the whole (see G. R. Driver, *JSemS* 1 [1956] 97–105). It is used only with reference to cereal or incense (24:7) offerings.

The baked cereal offering is next considered (4–13). Cakes, whether fried or baked, had to be unleavened and mixed with oil. Part was burned and part was given to the priests. Leaven, because it produced fermentation, was viewed as an agent of decomposition and could not be used in sacrificial offerings. Israelite transgressions of this regulation (Am 4:5) no doubt resulted from the influence of the Canaanites, who looked upon fermentation as a symbol of fertility. Honey, too, despite its extensive use by the ancients, was seen as a corrupting agent, and, perhaps because of its animal origins, was also considered unfit for sacred use. **13.** *salt of the covenant:* The esteem for the purifying and preservative virtue of salt (Ez 16:4; 2 Kgs 2:20–22; Mt 5:13; Mk 9:49; Col 4:6) is akin to that still found among the Arabs. Moreover, it was a sign of friendship and solidarity binding participants at a banquet (see M.-J. Lagrange, *Études sur les religions sémitique* [Paris, 1905] 251). The sacrificial salt, within the framework of a sacred repast, strongly underscored the permanence of the covenant relationship between Yahweh and his people. See Nm 18:19 where the "inviolable covenant" renders the Hebr "covenant of salt."

Finally, specifications are given for the cereal sacrifices as part of the first-fruits offering (14–16). The rather ambiguous phrasing of the MT seems to depict a process by which freshly cut ears of grain were roasted and then ground to obtain the grits. Oil and frankincense were added, and the offering concluded in the same manner as the cereal offering seen above.

(Haran, M., "The Use of Incense in the Ancient Israelite Ritual," *VT* 10 [1960] 113–29. Snaith, N. H., "Sacrifices in the O.T.," *VT* 7 [1957] 308–17.)

8 (c) Peace Offerings (3:1–17). Although the ritual for the peace offering (Hebr, *zebaḥ šᵉlāmîm*) is clearly defined, the meaning of the Hebr term remains obscure. *Zebaḥ* means something "slain" or "slaughtered," hence, a slain sacrificial victim (Am 5:25; Hos 3:4); *šᵉlāmîm* is derived from the root *šlm* meaning "to be complete," "to be whole," or "to be in harmony." Separately, the terms *zebaḥ* and *šᵉlāmîm* refer to sacrifices only partly destroyed, with part of the victim eaten by the offerers or priests (Dt 12:27; 18:3; 27:7; Gn 31:54?). Thus, either term could be contrasted with the completely consumed holocaust (1 Sm 15:22; Hos 6:6; Ex 20:24; Jgs 20:26). This common denominator, coupled with the fluidity of sacrificial terminology, enabled the Priestly authors of Lv to interchange the terms or even unite them when speaking of those sacrifices in which the offerer shared the victim with God as in the thanksgiving (7:12–15; 22:29–30), the free will, and the votive (7:16–17; 22:21–23) offerings. The designation "peace offering" is derived from the LXX and, for most authorities, falls short of the idea. Suggested alternatives are fulfillment offering, offering of completeness, and final offering. Although the precise meaning of *šᵉlāmîm* remains uncertain, the common translation as peace offering does serve to underscore one important aspect of the sacrifice: the preservation of harmonious relations between the participants and Yahweh as portrayed especially in the common meal. Some authors, as H. Cazelles and R. de Vaux, term the offering a communion sacrifice because one of its key elements is the notion of life sharing between God and his faithful (→ Religious Institutions, 76:79–81).

The ritual itself allows ox, sheep, or goat offerings, either male or female. For the herd offering (1–5), initial steps include the imposition of hands, the slaughter, and aspersion. Considerable discussion has centered around the purpose of the blood ritual. Does the blood here have the expiatory value found in the sin and guilt offerings? If so, how is it to be reconciled with the offerer's innocent state? According to A. Charbel (*SP* 1, 366–76), there is no atoning value connected with the blood ritual in the peace offering. Consumption of the sacred food is here an essential feature, an action clearly prohibited for anyone in a state of uncleanness (7:20–21). Since the shedding of blood is necessary to the sacrifice itself, its aspersion on the sides of the altar simply points up the sacredness of blood (life) as belonging solely to the Lord. Fat, too, was sacred to the Lord as linked with life itself and could not be eaten as sacrificial food (3:16–17; 7:22–24). Thus, the internal organs, connected with the more vital life processes—i.e., the intestines, liver, and kidneys, and all the fat attached thereto—were burned on the altar where the customary daily holocaust was offered.

The procedure for the sheep offering (6–11) is the same. The only addition is the animal's tail, which in some Palestinian species is laden with fat. **11.** *food of the Lord's oblation:* "Food" is suppressed in the LXX and supplanted by "pleasing scent." Such efforts to emphasize God's transcendent nature by the avoidance of anthropomorphisms are frequent in the Greek. However, the idea of a communal banquet is basic to the *zebaḥ šᵉlāmîm*, and the problem of the Lord's eating resolves itself symbolically with the burning of his portion.

The goat ritual (12–17) is identical with that of the herd offering. Verse 17 is an emphatic statement on the ritual's binding character and a final prohibition regarding blood and fat. The law against eating fat was concerned only with those animals ordinarily offered in sacrifice (7:22–24); the fat of other animals could be eaten.

Chapter 3 must be studied in conjunction with 7:11–38.

The laws given there regulate consumption of the sacrificial food.

9 (d) Sin Offerings (4:1–5:13). The sin offering or *ḥaṭṭā't*, centered in the idea of expiation, could be offered for the high priest (1–12), the entire community (13–21), the prince (22–26), and private persons (4:27–5:13). Parallel legislation with certain variations and in abbreviated form is found in Nm 15:22–31. The Hebr *ḥaṭṭā't* signifies both sin and its consequences (Nm 32:23) as well as the offering for sin; see Snaith, *VT* 7 (1957) 316–17. This sacrifice looked to a re-establishment of the covenant relationship between God and man destroyed by sin. Its two most distinctive features were the generous aspersion of the blood and the disposal of the slaughtered victim (→ Religious Institutions, 76:83–90).

As regards the high priest (1–12), the proper offering was an untainted bull. As a result of his authoritative status in the community, the high priest's sin was considered to affect the people as a whole. **2.** *a person inadvertently commits a sin:* Sin was a positive violation of the covenant relationship, whether voluntary or involuntary. Israel's responsibilities were clearly enunciated in the Law, and any departure therefrom disturbed the right order of things. The presence or absence of volition did not alter the objective situation. The wrong had to be righted, and even the unwitting party (with whom ch. 4 is wholly concerned) had to offer atoning sacrifice. The community shares the priest's guilt not through personal culpability as we interpret it but because the people, closely identified with their leader, were enveloped in the wide ambit of the fault's consequences (see B. Vawter, "Scriptural Meaning of Sin," *TD* 10 [1962] 223–26). **3.** *the anointed priest:* See comment on 8:1–13. On the imposition of hands, see comment on 1:4. After the slaughter, the blood was brought into the meeting tent. Only in the cases of the sin offering for the priest and for the community was part of the animal victim brought into the Holy Place of the Temple. The blood was then sprinkled against the Temple veil, an act that looked to the consecration of the blood itself (see T. C. Vriezen, *OTS* 7 [1950] 201–35). The central expiatory act was the blood aspersion, which was performed on the horned corners of the altar of incense, likewise located within the meeting tent. The remainder was deposited outside at the base of the holocaust altar. The usual organs and fatty parts were then consumed on the altar, and the animal's remains were taken to the ash heap and burned. The priest offerer did not partake of the food, a communal privilege prohibited in view of his sinful condition.

When the community as a whole was guilty of an inadvertent violation of the Law, the ritual (13–21) was the same as that for the high priest; however, the imposition of hands was performed by the elders representing the people. The parallel legislation in Nm 15:22–26 specifies two victims: a young bull as a holocaust and a he-goat as a sin offering. This directive may well be even later than that in Lv.

Next in importance is the sin offering for the prince, the lay leader of the community (22–26). The term *nāśî'* is both premonarchical and postmonarchical in biblical usage, ending with Jos and recommencing with Ez, with only rare occurrences in the intervening period. Ezekiel applies the term not only to Israel's post-exilic lay leader but also to lesser foreign rulers. He thereby makes clear to the restored Jews the importance of a modest temporal outlook within the reborn community, which is to be marked by spiritual excellence. In a study (*CBQ* 25 [1963] 111–17), E. A. Speiser, arguing from the point of etymology and usage, sees *nāśî'* as a passive derivative from *nāśā* (to raise up, elevate). It thus refers to a duly elected chieftain (LXX, *archōn*), which, in the case of Ez, would refer to one elected not only by the assembly but by God, hence, a "leader." After laying his hands on the victim, a male goat, and slaughtering it on the N side of the altar of holocausts, the leader leaves the atoning blood distribution to the priest (not the high priest), who places the blood on the hornlike protrusions of the holocaust altar and pours the remainder at its base. None of the blood is taken into the Holy Place. The fat is burned on the altar, the remaining parts going to the priest, who, not personally involved in the sin, may eat of the sacred food (6:19).

The only significant difference between the sin offering of a private person (27–35) and that of the leader of the community is indicative of its lesser stature: The victim could be a female goat or lamb. **35.** *with the other oblations:* The phrase signifies sacrifices regularly offered, e.g., the morning holocaust (6:1–6).

10 The first half of ch. 5 is casuistic, containing a number of "special cases" regarding the offerer and his offering. The initial section (1–6) envisions certain offenses that would necessitate an atoning sacrifice. These include the conscious withholding of evidence by a witness under oath (Ex 23:1–3; Dt 19:15–20) and the inadvertent actions (with subsequent awareness) of contracting legal uncleanness or of swearing publicly to do something. Anyone guilty of such violations had first to confess his sin by a solemn and public attestation of guilt (known also from Assyrian and Babylonian sources) and then to offer the atoning sacrifice. The rite and victim are the same as for the private expiatory sacrifice (4:27–35). The term for the sacrifice in v. 6 is not *ḥaṭṭā't* but *'āšām* (guilt offering); see vv. 14–26.

Verses 7–13 look to the guilty poor man, who in the aforementioned circumstances is unable to supply the animal victim. The substitute offering (*'āšām*) was a pair of turtledoves or pigeons. In either case, one of the birds was offered as a sin offering (*ḥaṭṭā't*) and the other as a holocaust. The ritual for the sin offering was a simplified version of the animal offering: The head was snapped loose but not detached, and the blood was sprinkled on one side of the altar and the rest deposited at the altar's base. The holocaust was offered in the manner prescribed in 1:14–17. Finally, an added concession was made for those even more indigent in the form of a cereal offering, consisting of one-tenth of an ephah of flour (one ephah equals about 1 bu.). Devoid of either incense or oil, part of the flour was burned with the regular daily sacrifices as a "token offering" (*'azkārāh;* see 2:2), the remainder going to the priest.

11 (e) Guilt Offerings (5:14–26). The Hebr *'āšām* means both "guilt" and "guilt offering"; the verbal form *'āšēm* means "to be guilty" or "to transgress." Although this expression is clearly an oblation that seeks to right a wrong or repair an injury, the etymology of the word affords scant help in determining the distinction between the sin and guilt offerings. Equally disconcerting is the casual interchange of the two terms in the Lv ritual (see vv. 7–13). Attempts to distinguish adequately between the two terms dates at least to the time of Josephus (*Ant.* 3.9, 3; cf. P. Saydon, *CBQ* 7 [1946] 393–99). The one fundamental idea, proper to *'āšām* in every instance, is an offense or an offering for an offense, which is imputable regardless of personal awareness. In this regard, it is identical with the sin offering. Whatever may have been the historical distinction between the two, it is obviously lost on the redactors of the Lv ritual. That the terms are even used synonymously (5:6–7) is indication of the evident lack of precision in the matter. Moreover, despite the casuistic breakdown in ch. 5, either type was capable of being offered for a violation of any of the Lord's commands (4:2; 5:17).

Since for private persons the guilt-offering rite does not differ from that of the sin offering, the blood was not taken into the Holy Place and the priests were permitted to partake of the victim, an unblemished ram, valued at two shekels according to the standard established by the Temple authorities. The present pericope passes over the question of procedure and is solely concerned with certain offenses demanding this type of reparation. The first category treats of inadvertent action: failure to pay Temple tithes in the full amount (14–16) (requiring restitution to the Temple, plus an added 20 per cent) or, in general, any violation of the Lord's commands (17–18). The final case (20–26), implying full awareness, deals with the fraudulent retention of another's material property, whether securities, stolen goods, or discovered articles. In matters of injustice, restitution had to be made before the offering was acceptable; this included not only the restoration of the other's property but an additional one-fifth of the object's value as compensation.

12 **(B) The Priest and Sacrifice (6:1–7:38).** Much of the material here presented is concerned with sacrifices already treated in the previous section. In the main, this additional legislation concerns the rights and duties of the priests in their sacrificial role. Thus, Moses is told (6:1) to address his words not to the Israelites as previously (1:2; 4:1) but to Aaron and his sons.

13 (a) The Daily Holocaust (6:1–6). Two daily holocausts are prescribed, one in the evening (2) and one in the morning (5), paralleling the directives of Ex 29:38–42 and Nm 28:2–8. This post-exilic ritual differs from that of the monarchical period with its single holocaust in the morning, clearly distinguished from the evening cereal offering (2 Kgs 16:15). Even as late as the Torah of Ezekiel, there is mention of only one daily holocaust (Ez 46:13–15). Performed on the holocaust altar where the perpetual fire burned, the evening offering was left on the hearth through the night with the ashes removed in the morning and laid at the side of the altar. The priest performed this latter action wearing his sacred ceremonial garb, and only after changing to other clothes did he leave the holy confines to carry the ashes outside of the camp to a clean place worthy to serve as a depository for the sacred relics. The final verses indicate that the continuation of the fire on the altar was the priests' responsibility. Each morning firewood was added prior to the early holocaust and the other offerings of the day. The perpetual fire, a characteristic trait of Persian cult (E. Dhorme, *RB* 10 [1913] 19), served as an uninterrupted prayer of the Hebr community to the Lord.

14 (b) The Daily Cereal Offering (6:7–16). Closely allied to ch. 2, this section serves as an adjunct to the daily holocaust legislation. Comprised of two parts, it first deals with the daily *minḥāh* offered by any priest (7–11), and then with the daily offering of the high priest (12–16 [especially 13 and 15]). The rite for the first (unbaked flour with oil and incense) is identical with that of the customary unbaked cereal offering (2:1–3), with the added specification that the part left over, the priestly portion, must be eaten as unleavened cakes within the court of the meeting tent. Since the Lord deigned to share with his priests the sanctified gift, its sacredness had to be respected and safeguarded. It was eaten only by cult personnel (male descendants of Aaron) in a clearly designated place. Similar restrictions obtained for the sin offering (6:22) and the guilt offering (7:6). **11.** *whatever touches the oblations becomes sacred:* Both cleanness and uncleanness were contagious. Sacred objects, e.g., the altar and other Temple appurtenances (Ex 30:29), could communicate their sanctity; this holiness could be contracted by a person (even without his volition) or by other objects. Through such contact the sphere of the deity was extended, and the person (or object) could no longer be considered profane. Verses 12–16, not found in the Codex Alexandrinus of the LXX, contain a reference to the cereal offering proper to the day of the high priest's investiture (v. 13; cf. 8:26), which, by the time of the present Lv ritual, had become a daily sacrifice (called in v. 13 of the MT a "regular" [*tāmîd*] cereal offering; cf. Nm 4:16). Offered in the high priest's name and that of the other priests, the twice-a-day *minḥāh* was first fried and then broken into pieces and burned as a whole offering, no part being consumed by the priest.

15 (c) Sin Offerings (6:17–23). As a complement to ch. 4, this added legislation emphasizes the sin offering's special sacredness, which, since it could be easily transmitted, demanded special directives regulating the use and disposal of the victim's remains. A garment stained by its blood was washed in a sacred place (20); the vessel in which it was cooked before eating was either destroyed or thoroughly cleansed (21). In this way, holiness was removed in much the same manner that impurity was, to avoid its being diffused in any way (see De Vaux, *AI* 460–61). Both the priest offerer (19) and his fellow priests (22) could eat of the sacrifice in the court of the meeting tent; this custom, of course, did not apply to the sin offerings of the high priest (4:1–12) or of the whole community (4:13–21), in which instances the entire victim was burned.

16 (d) Guilt Offerings (7:1–10). The ritual for these, not specified previously, was, as has been indicated, basically the same as that for the sin offering of private individuals (4:27–31). The meat could be eaten by the priests under the usual conditions. Verses 7–10 delineate in summary fashion the distribution of the sacred portions for the various types of sacrifice. To the priest offerer belongs the meat of the sin and guilt offering, the animal hide of the holocaust, and the remains of the baked or fried cereal offerings. These in turn could be shared with the other priests (cf. 7:6). The ordinary flour offering, with its almost casual ritual demanding so little of the priest (2:1–2), is given to the priestly group as a whole.

17 (e) Peace Offerings (7:11–21,28–34). Taken in conjunction with the legislation in ch. 3, the section deals with a supplementary cereal offering as well as with the distribution and consumption of the peace offering. Three distinct species of peace offering are cited: the *tôdāh* or thanksgiving offering (12–15), offered as an expression of gratitude for benefits received (Ps 107:22); the *nēder* or votive offering (16–17), an obligatory oblation rising from a vow or promise made to the Lord; and the *n^e^dābāh* or free-will offering (16–17), a spontaneous gift, devotional in character, required neither by law nor personal indebtedness. Although each of these has its own particular characteristics, the distinction among them is often imprecise. For the thanksgiving offering, together with the animal victim, an assortment of unleavened and leavened baked products are prescribed as a *minḥāh*. A portion of these was burned on the altar with the animal, exclusive of the leavened cakes that were prohibited (2:11; see comment on 2:4). The remainder of the cereal offering was divided between the officiating priest and the offerer. Because of its sacred character, the meat of the victim was to be eaten on the day of the sacrifice to avoid any contamination or spoiling. The votive and free-will offerings, otherwise identical in ritual with the preceding, prescribed more lenient ruling regarding the leftover meat: What was not eaten on the day itself could be finished on the following day; if any meat remained after that, it had to be burned. This latter regulation sought to avoid the abuses that could easily arise in a sacrificial repast permitting a rather extensive lay participation. Thus, the meat became refuse, an "abominable thing" (*piggûl*) after the second day, and if the law were

violated, not only would the violator be guilty of sacrilegious conduct (cf. also 19:5–8) but also the whole offering would be deemed worthless. Because the peace offering meat lost its sacredness through contact with anything unclean between the time of offering and consumption, it was to be burned if such occurred. Finally, a state of legal purity was required of all participants in the sacred repast. To partake of the victim in a state of uncleanness from whatever cause—e.g., disease or contact with some species of unclean animal—was to incur serious guilt. **20.** *shall be cut off from his people:* The phrase does not necessarily mean the death penalty, although such is the meaning in certain instances. The offender could be socially ostracized, forbidden free access and participation in cult, and, as a result, be separated from the divine favor that fell upon the community of God's people. The particulars regarding the penalty's nature and duration are not stated.

Verses 28–34 summarize the priest's action in the peace offering. The fatty portions and designated organs (3:3–4) were burned; the choice parts, the breast, and right leg, reverted to Aaron and his sons. **30–32.** *wave offering* (t^{e}*nûpāh*).... *raised offering* (t^{e}*rûmāh*)*:* Many commentators connect the two terms with the manner of offering the victim. The former was moved to and fro before the altar (*nûp*, "to swing," "to wave"); the latter, raised aloft (*rûm*, "to be high," "to be elevated"). However, Driver (*op. cit.*, 100–105) claims that such a conclusion is not supported by the evidence. Their repeated use together (7:34; 10:14,15; Nm 6:20) is indicative of their mutual affinity, but Driver notes that the motion idea is completely absent in certain instances of use, e.g., Ex 25:2; Nm 8:11,13,15. Moreover, none of the ancient versions attests to any special rite in their rendering of the term. Thus, postulating a Hebr root *nwp*, meaning "to be supereminent," he sees t^{e}*nûpāh* as derived ultimately from the Babylonian and to be rendered "special contribution" or "additional gift." T^{e}*rûmāh*, best associated with the Assyrian *tarāmu*, takes its Hebr origin from the root *trm* meaning "to levy" (despite its repeated use with the causative form of *rûm*). The substantive refers to something levied or assessed. Either term, then, can be translated as "contribution," being virtually interchangeable in use and identical in application. Driver argues that what were originally Assyro-Babylonian commercial terms were primitively taken over by Israelite cult and are used without precise understanding by the Priestly editors, whose sacrificial terminology on more than one occasion has lacked clarity and consistency.

18 (f) Blood and Fat Prohibitions (7:22–27). This section represents an interruption in the peace-offering ritual; thus it is treated separately. The fatty parts of the ox, sheep, or goat, specified in 3:3,9,14, could be eaten under no circumstances whatsoever (see comment on 3:1–5). This prohibition applied even if their death proceeded from natural or violent causes, although the law allowed the use of such fat for other purposes. Moreover, it did not extend to the fat of other species of clean animals or even to the fat from other parts of the specified animals. The law forbidding blood is universal and is emphatically enunciated three times elsewhere in Lv (3:17; 17:10–14; 19:26). The sanction is separation from the community (see 7:20).

(g) Conclusion (7:35–38). Verse 35 loosely connects the sacrificial code with the ordination of Aaron and his sons, announced in Ex 29 and executed in Lv 8:1ff. The final verses, enumerating the various sacrifices, link them with the historical focal point of all Israelite law: Mt. Sinai. The purpose is for emphasis, for the discussion between Moses and Yahweh has thus far been centered around the meeting tent, situated at the base of Sinai. (→ Religious Institutions, 76:77–107.)

(De Vaux, *AI* 424–56. Gray, G. B., *Sacrifice in the O.T.* [Oxford, 1925]. Oesterley, W., *Sacrifices in Ancient Israel* [London, 1937]. Rowley, H. H., "The Meaning of Sacrifice in the O.T.," *BJRyL* 33 [1950–51] 74–110.)

19 **(II) The Ceremony of Ordination (8:1–10:20).** The solemn rite of ordination prescribed for Aaron and his sons is carried out according to the directives of Ex 28:1–29:35; 39:1–31; 40:12–15. Anything but primitive in character, this detailed account draws upon the ordination ceremony of the high priest with its investiture and anointing (8:7–13), three sacrifices (8:14–36), and octave-day observance (9). Chapter 10 contains the only piece of fairly continuous narrative in the book, but even there a careful reading betrays its purpose—the story serves as a vehicle to present added ritual requirements.

20 **(A) Ordination of Aaron and His Sons (8:1–13).** The place of worship and its official attendants were inseparable in ancient Israel. Thus, the directives for the Lord's dwelling (Ex 25–27) are followed by those for the priests (Ex 28–29); by the same token, the present chapters form a sequel to the actual construction of the dwelling completed at the close of Ex. Yahweh first orders Moses to assemble the entire community at the entrance to the meeting tent together with Aaron and his four sons (see Ex 28:1). There follows a tripartite ceremony consisting of lustration, investiture, and anointing. A detailed description of the high priest's vestments is given in Ex 28–29. Worthy of special note is the regal character of his attire, e.g., the miter or turban (*miṣnepet*) (see Ez 21:31 and the $ṣ^{e}$*nîp* of Is 62:3), the diadem (*nēzer*; see 2 Sm 1:10; 2 Kgs 11:12)—symbols of royal authority given the high priest in postmonarchical times. **8.** *Urim and Thummim:* (→ Religious Institutions, 76:8.) Given only passing mention in the P tradition, they serve at most as a symbolic relic of the past, although perhaps the reference to them is no more than an archaic one made long after they became obsolete (see De Vaux, *AI* 352–53). The anointing of the high priest is joined with that of the dwelling, the altar and its furnishings, and the basin, which served as a blood receptacle. (For the post-exilic origins of priestly anointing, → Religious Institutions, 76:12,30; see also R. Tournay, *RB* 67 [1960] 5–42.) After Aaron's anointing, his sons, representative of the whole priestly class, were invested in a simpler ceremony wherein no mention is made of the ephod, breastplate, or golden diadem; the turban (*migbā'āh*) they received was the regular head-dress of the priests, not the royal *miṣnepet*.

21 **(B) Ordination Sacrifices (8:14–36).** Three sacrifices, all offered by Moses, were part of the ordination rite: a sin offering (14–17), a holocaust (18–21), and a special ordination sacrifice (22–36). The sin offering was made in atonement for the holocaust altar, to erase any uncleanness connected with it and thus make it suitable to serve as the place of sacred encounter between the divine and the human. It was identical in procedure with the sin offering for the lay leader or private persons (4:22–35), with one difference: like the oblation for the high priest or the whole community (4:1–21), the victim was a young bull whose remains were burned and not eaten. Consumption was denied even the priests because of their intimate connection with the altar. The ordination holocaust followed the sin offering with a ram specified as victim; the procedure was that prescribed in the sacrificial code (1:10–13). The final offering, that of investiture or *millu'îm* (see v. 33), climaxed the ceremony and marked the formal assumption of office.

It was likely viewed as an act of thanksgiving, following the main lines of the peace offering: imposition of hands, slaughter, blood aspersion, burning of the usual parts, accompanying cereal offering, and sacred meal. However, the blood was applied by Moses to the right ear, thumb, and large toe of Aaron and his sons. The same was done with both blood and oil on the occasion of a leper's purification (14:14,17,25,28). The exact significance of this ceremony is hard to determine, but the signing of the extremities may well have symbolized the sanctification of the whole man just as the altar was sanctified by spreading blood on its outermost parts (8:15). H. Cazelles (BJ, note on Lv 14:14) links it with the idea of service: The ears receive instruction, which the hands and feet execute. Moses, having taken the designated organs of the ram plus the right leg, together with a single sample of each type of unleavened cereal offering (7:12), handed them to Aaron and his sons, directing them to make the act of presentation (i.e., wave offering; see comment on 7:30). He then took the offering back to burn it on the altar with the holocaust. The breast was reserved for Moses as his personal portion. The final blood and oil aspersion of the priests and their vestments is viewed by some commentators as an interpolation. It disturbs the continuity of the passage (M. Noth in ATD places it after v. 24), and the exact purpose of a second consecration of Aaron (even though including the vestments) is not clear. This problem is connected with the more basic question of the extent to which Aaron's sons were included in the earlier redactions of the Lv ritual, which was originally concerned principally with the high priest; in several instances the obviously intrusive mention of the other priests in connection with certain rites evidences the work of a later hand.

The cooked meat and the bread offering of this final sacrifice were to be eaten by the priests as sacred food, i.e., within the sacred confines the same day (7:15). The ordination observance was to extend over a seven-day period during which time at least the sin offering was to be repeated daily (Ex 29:36–37). During this time the newly ordained were forbidden to leave the forecourt of the meeting tent under penalty of death. **33.** *your ordination is to last seven days:* The literal translation is "for seven days he will fill your hands," *y^e^mallē' 'et yed^e^kem.* (For the idea of "filling the hands," → Religious Institutions, 76:11.)

22 **(C) Octave of the Ordination (9:1–24).** The eighth day after the initial ceremony was marked by a series of concluding sacrifices (1–21) and a theophany (22–24). Moses orders Aaron to prepare a sin offering and a holocaust to be offered on the priests' behalf, whereas the senior members of the community were to make ready a sin offering, a holocaust, a peace offering, and a cereal oblation. With the community assembled, Aaron, in his sin offering, followed the same ritual previously employed by Moses (8:14–17); no blood was sprinkled within the meeting tent (4:5–7) inasmuch as he had not yet formally entered the Holy Place. Unable to be eaten by the priests, the remains were burned outside the camp. The holocaust that followed was offered in the usual way. The sacrifices for the community were then executed by Aaron with his sons' assistance; the sin offering and holocaust were carried out as before. **16.** *other than the morning holocaust:* An anachronism showing the liturgical rather than historical concern of the editor is evident. The daily holocaust was offered only after the priests had undertaken their duties (6:1–6). The people's cereal and peace offerings were the last offered.

The ceremony is solemnly concluded in vv. 22–24 with the high priest's blessing (Nm 6:23–26) and his initial entrance into the meeting tent with Moses, pointing up his singular right of access to the dwelling of Yahweh. The second blessing (23) may arise from fusion with another tradition, wherein both Moses and Aaron blessed the people as opposed to the blessing of Aaron alone in v. 22. The Lord's stamp of approbation upon the proceedings takes the form of a theophany similar to that marking the completion of the dwelling (Ex 40:34–38). **23.** *the glory of the Lord:* The *k^e^bôd Yahweh* was particularly manifest in unusual signs and phenomena, clearly indicative of might and transcendence: e.g., the desert cloud (Ex 16:10), the cloud and fire on Sinai (Ex 24:15–17), and the cloud encircling the dwelling (Ex 40:34–35). (See "Herrlichkeit," *BibLex* 699). In the present instance, his glory takes the form of fire issuing from the meeting tent and consuming the already burning offerings on the altar to the awe of the onlookers. The meaning of the theophany is clear: The ordination proceedings and the sacrifices of the priest are approved as sacred and acceptable to the Lord.

23 **(D) Sin of Aaron's Sons (10:1–20).** The tragic episode of the death of Aaron's two sons, Nadab and Abihu (1–7), transcends the interests of mere narration and emphasizes the importance of strict adherence to ritual legislation. Tucked appropriately within ch. 10 is an added body of laws for the priests (8–15), and the chapter closes with the puzzling dialogue between Moses and Aaron (16–20).

During the time of the octave-day celebration, Nadab and Abihu offered an illicit incense offering for which they suffered a fiery death in the Lord's presence. It is difficult to determine the exact nature of their sin. The suggestion that their sacrifice was offered outside of the prescribed times lacks sufficient evidence. Cazelles (BJ, note on 10:1) proposes that the account follows an earlier tradition of chs. 8–9 in which only Aaron had received priestly consecration; thus, the sons were performing these ceremonial acts without being priests. On the other hand, Ḥaran (*VT* 10 [1960] 115) sees the key to the solution in the "strange" or "profane" fire (*'ēš zārāh*) of v. 1. The sons had taken their fire from a place outside the altar area, whereas the censer fire was to be taken from the altar itself (16:12). It is only in connection with this "profane fire" that their sin is elsewhere recalled (Nm 3:4; 26:61). (See the similar view of W. von Baudissin, *Geschichte des alttestament. Priesterthums* [Leipzig 1889] 22.)

Moses' commentary on the event takes the form of a short distich in which words of the Lord, otherwise unknown, are quoted. Its rather loose connection with the context and its poetic character argue strongly for an independent source, possibly an encomium on the priesthood. Both Yahweh's sacredness (*qōdeš*) and his glory (*kābôd*) seek external manifestation: the latter in signs and wonders as exemplified in the theophany of 9:23–24; the former in similar marvels (Nm 20:13; 27:14), in the people themselves (19:2), and, in a special way, in his priests—"those who approach me"—whose holiness should be unsurpassed (Ex 19:22; Lv 21:17,21; Ez 42:13–15). In the present context, however, the verse is being used reproachfully, explaining the severe punishment that has been meted out. God's sacredness is manifest through the swift and definitive removal of evil from his midst, i.e., the death of the two priests; his glory, so often restricted to loving signs of his power and might, is here revealed in a frightening and awesome manner (cf. Ez 28:22). In the face of the tragedy, Aaron remained silent while Mishael and Elzaphan, Aaron's cousins (Ex 6:18,22), were summoned to remove the bodies in the tunics in which they died, without funeral solemnities, to a spot outside the camp. The priests were strictly prohibited to indulge in customary mourning observances; i.e., letting the hair hang loose and tearing one's garments as a sign of grief. These tokens of mourning also indicated a state of uncleanness (13:45), which would arise in this instance from contact with the dead. By reason of their sacred position, the priests were not to become unclean through contact with a corpse, the only exception being death in the immediate family of the ordinary priest (21:1–4), an exception not extended to the head priest (21:10–11). In the present case, because of the seriousness of the violation, not even Aaron's remaining sons were permitted to participate even remotely in the burial rites of Nadab and Abihu, although such was not forbidden the other Israelites. This whole episode underscores the importance of observing even the minutiae of ritual detail.

The legal material in vv. 8–15 is unrelated to the untimely death of the two priests. So that they would be able to exercise their duties responsibly, especially in distinguishing the multiple categories of the clean and unclean, and be fit to instruct the people in the Law, the priests were forbidden the use of any alcoholic beverage prior to the exercise of their office. The prohibition is presented as given by the Lord himself. The following passage on the sacrificial repast resumes the octave-day ritual abruptly terminated in 9:21, allowance being made for the intervening data by the reference to Aaron's "surviving sons" in 10:12. The cereal offering, as most sacred, was to be eaten by the priests alone, near the altar. The contributed portions of the community's peace offering, the leg and breast, however, could be eaten by male or female members of the priests' families in any place not tainted by uncleanness; regulations regarding this participation are given in 22:10–16.

In the concluding pericope, Moses' anger is aroused upon learning that the people's sin offering (9:15) had been burned and not eaten. Yet, this was the very procedure that was demanded for such a sin offering (4:21), since neither the priests nor the community could eat of it. The key to the solution lies in 6:23. One could not partake of any sacrifice in which some of the blood had been brought into the sanctuary, a requisite for the sin offering of the priests and the community. Thus, the priests were forbidden to eat the sin offering of the people, not because it was offered in their own name (as, e.g., in 9:8ff.), but because its blood had been sprinkled before the sanctuary veil. It was precisely this action that was lacking in Aaron's sacrifice prior to the formal entry into the meeting tent, which is indicated as having taken place after the octave-day sacrifices. Therefore, the meat should have been eaten by the priests; in fact, it was considered part of the rite of expiation. Aaron's response is a plea of moral uncleanness; he lacked the necessary integrity required of anyone partaking of such a sacrifice. Affected by his dead sons' sinful deed and, in Hebr thought, a sharer in their guilt, he did not enjoy a state of holiness compatible with the sin-offering repast. The response appeases Moses' anger. (→ Religious Institutions, 76:5–38.)

(De Vaux, *AI* 345–405. Gray, *op. cit.*, 179–270. Lohse, E., *Die Ordination im Spätjudentum und im Neuen Testament* [Göttingen, 1951]. Noth, M., *Amt und Berufung im Alten Testament* [Bonn, 1958].)

24 **(III) Legal Purity (11:1–15:33).** The third major division of Lv is concerned with the various ways in which a state of uncleanness could arise and the means of regaining the state of purity. The purity code treats of four major categories: clean and unclean animals (11:1–47), childbirth (12:1–8), leprosy (13:1–14:57), and sexual uncleanness (15:1–33). Each, except the second, has its own conclusion. The laws, although edited in post-exilic Israel, have a distinctly archaic ring.

Basically, the distinction between the clean and unclean was related to cult, for it was in terms of service to Yahweh, either in active worship or simply in being his covenanted people, that integrity was demanded. To be unclean was to lack holiness, and such was viewed not as a moral condition but as a state of being, incompatible with the holiness of Yahweh and hence prohibitive of any contact with him. Parallel legislation on legal cleanness is found in Dt 14:3–20.

25 **(A) Clean and Unclean Animals (11:1–47).** The list is concerned with large land animals (1–8), sea life (9–12), winged creatures (13–23), and small animals (29–38). The classification is popular rather than scientific and sheds no real light on the ultimate reasons for the clean and unclean distinction. Extensive discussion has centered on the reasons for the distinctions made, a summary of which is given by W. H. Gispen (*OTS* 5 [1948] 193–94). Since the definitive answer lies in a past so remote that it was probably known not even by the Lv editors whose classification give no indication, we are probably on safest ground to view the distinction primarily along cultic lines (see Noth, ATD 77). The animals immediately excluded from the Hebr diet were those hallowed in pagan worship as enjoying a role in sacrifice, magic, or superstitious practice—e.g., the pig used in sacrifice to the Babylonian god, Tammuz. By the same token, despite the dearth of information, it is not unlikely that other reasons, such as hygiene and natural abhorrence, also affected Hebr custom and legislation.

The dietary legislation is directed to both Moses and Aaron, the latter now enjoying added prestige after his ordination. With regard to the larger animals (1–8), the law is first stated positively: Only those animals that were split-hoofed and cud chewing could be eaten. This law excluded such species as the horse and the ass, as well as hoofless quadrupeds like the dog, cat, and bear (cf. v. 27). As the subsequent classification indicates, the distinction was based solely on external similarities. The rock badger and the hare, although excluded on one count, could actually have been eliminated on two because they are not ruminants, despite the fact that their mastication process suggests the action of chewing the cud. That the list is by no means exhaustive gives credence to the view that the exclusion of these animals rested ultimately on some other basis. The prohibition extended to consumption as well as to contact with the dead animals, but simple contact with them while living was not forbidden.

Only aquatic animals having both fins and scales could be eaten (9–12); although no examples are given, such forms as the eel would be excluded. Contact with their dead bodies was also prohibited.

Unlike in the preceding classifications, there is no general norm governing the prohibition of birds in vv. 13–19, only an enumeration of the unclean species. The identification of some of these remains uncertain, since the exact meaning of the Hebr terms, so rare in their appearance, cannot be determined. We are at a loss to determine why they were rejected, the only possible clue being that they are preponderantly carnivorous.

26 The section on insects (20–23) begins and concludes with an unqualified rejection of all winged quadrupeds (the "other" of v. 23 is not present in the Hebrew). The interpolation in vv. 21–22 was introduced as an exception in favor of certain members of the grasshopper family, classified popularly in terms of the strong hind legs on which they leap. This exception may have arisen from the general respect that prevailed for their skill and ingenuity, reflected in their rather frequent appearance in Oriental art.

The brief excursus on uncleanness through contact in vv. 24–28 is abruptly inserted and only indirectly connected with the main theme. The central thought here is not with eating the animals but with the distinction between touching and lifting the animals previously treated. Contact with any of these lifeless forms resulted in uncleanness for the entire day, cleanness being restored, it would seem, by the day's termination, despite the mention of a sin offering required in such circumstances in 5:2,6. If one picked up the corpse or any part thereof, his clothing became unclean through contact and was to be washed. This law reflects the ancients' dread of contact with the dead, which implied some form of undesired communication.

Legislation on contact rather than consumption is continued in the following pericope (29–38) treating of rodents and lizards, which were never eaten. The identification of the various species in v. 30 remains largely uncertain: e.g., "mole" renders the Hebr *tinšemet*, also used for one of the bird species (owl?) in v. 18. Anyone touching the corpse was unclean until evening. Moreover, uncleanness was communicated to anything on which or into which the dead body fell, examples of which are given along casuistic lines: man's personal effects (clothing, etc.), household furnishings (pottery, ovens), and moistened grain. To remove impurity, pottery and earthenware utensils were destroyed; personal articles were washed and considered unclean for the day. Liquid was considered a carrier of impurity; for this reason everything in the water-filled vessel was contaminated (34), as was all cultivated grain that had been moistened before the mishap (38). Fresh water (36), however, whether earth water or rain water, removed all impurities (Nm 19:17ff.; Zech 13:1). Thus, springs and cisterns remained clean despite the accident.

Another digression appears in vv. 39–40 with legislation regarding animals ordinarily edible. Such were forbidden if they died a natural death; a touch resulted in day-long uncleanness, and any closer contact (carrying, eating) made one's clothing unclean as well.

Another popular dietary classification resumes the discussion of reptiles in vv. 41–45, going beyond the species of vv. 29–30 in its all-embracing character. This abhorrence of reptiles, no doubt, derived at least partially from the Hebr attitude toward the snake (Gn 3:14) and the cultic role it played in pagan fertility rites. Motivation for avoidance of such creatures is strongly positive: The holiness of Yahweh himself demands it.

The chapter closes with a recapitulation like that closing the sacrifice ritual (7:37ff.), extending to all the creature categories that have been treated.

27 **(B) Childbirth (12:1–8).** The remainder of the material on legal purity is concerned with cases of temporary uncleanness (→ Religious Institutions, 76:113–19), beginning with the most important, childbirth. Viewed as a cause of impurity by numerous ancient peoples, this state of uncleanness arose neither from the act of conception nor from the delivery as such, but rather from the loss of blood connected with the latter (vv. 4a, 5b, and 7b). The woman's vitality, linked with her blood, was diminished by childbirth, and by that token she was objectively separated from Yahweh, the source of life, until her former integrity was restored. The uncleanness was more pronounced during the period immediately following birth—i.e., the first 7 days after a male birth, the first 14 after a female—during which time her impurity was as contagious as during the time of menstruation (15:19–24). After this initial period, a general lack of integrity, prohibiting any contact with the sacred, continued for an additional 33 days after the birth of a boy, and 66 after the birth of a girl. Male childbirth was considered the greater blessing probably because of the greater strength and vitality connected with the male.

At the end of the designated period, the woman effected her own purification through the offering of atoning sacrifices in the form of a holocaust (lamb) and a sin offering (pigeon or turtledove). The offering was the same for a male or female birth. A bird offering (either a turtledove or pigeon) was permitted for both sacrifices if the woman belonged to the poorer class. The oblation of the Virgin Mary on the occasion of her purification was this simple offering of the poor (Lk 2:22–24).

28 **(C) Leprosy (13:1–14:57).** The references to leprosy in the OT are numerous, e.g., Ex 4:6; Nm 12:10–15; 2 Sm 3:29; 2 Kgs 5:1,27; 7:3; 15:5. Although leprosy as we know it today was certainly not unknown to the ancient man, the Hebr *ṣāraʿat* (Vg *lepra*) is not so restricted in its use, including various forms of skin disease. This section of Lv is not concerned with Hansen's disease but with temporary disorders, the symptoms of which are given in 13:1–44, and all of which are curable. Primitive hygiene considered such maladies highly contagious and demanded the stricken person's isolation; in Lv, however, although hygienic concerns cannot be excluded, it was the lack of bodily integrity necessary for the worship of Yahweh that resulted in religious and social ostracism. Corrupting agents present in clothing and buildings—e.g., mildew, mold, and moss—because of their apparent likeness to skin diseases, likewise rendered such objects "leprous" and unclean. In all such cases, it was the presence of the evil force of corruption that necessitated protective legislation. Because so much of the material on legal purity and the means to regain it is absent from the pre-exilic literature, De Vaux sees here a mass borrowing and incorporation of material from various sources, rooted in archaic beliefs and superstitions, by the purity-conscious writers of the P code (De Vaux, *AI* 463–64).

29 (a) IN HUMANS (13:1–46). The popular character of the described disorders makes it impossible to determine the exact nature of the illness cited. Not every skin disease made one unclean, but only those considered active and, therefore, infectious. Such malignancy manifested itself in different ways: through spreading (vv. 7, 22, 27, and 35); through sores, which penetrated the skin with discoloring of the surrounding hair (vv. 3, 20, 25, and 30); and through an open sore ("raw flesh") (vv. 10, 15, and 42). Ordinary skin blotches, scabs resulting from boils or burns, scalp disorders, face eruptions, and baldness were not signs of impurity so long as they were devoid of infectious symptoms. Whiteness of the skin, the aftermath of a skin disease, was a sign of healing and indicated cleanness (vv. 13, 16–17, and 38–39).

The determination of the disease's active or inactive state belonged to the priest, who exercised his function not as a physician (no treatment is prescribed) but as a judge and interpreter of the Law, whose favorable decision was required before purification rites permitting re-entry into the community could be initiated. When a case was doubtful, a period of quarantine was imposed, lasting in some cases a week (21 and 26) or at most a fortnight (4ff. and 31ff.). During the time of his uncleanness the diseased person had to remain outside the city, giving notice of his condition to the unsuspecting through the customary signs indicative of his state: torn garments, long, flowing hair (see comment on 10:6), covered beard (Ez 24:17), and the repeated cry of "Unclean!"

30 (b) IN CLOTHING (13:47–59). The evil force of corruption was also seen to be present in mildewed clothing, textiles, or leather goods, rendering them unclean. After the priest's initial inspection, the object was isolated for seven days (47–50); if during that time the corruption spread, it was to be burned; if not, it was washed and quarantined for another week (51–54). If with the next inspection the infection had not at least diminished, the object was destroyed; if the growth seemed to be vanishing, it was excised, and the article could be used again providing the growth did not reappear. If there were no sign of the mildew left at all, the article was declared clean and restored to former use after a second washing (55–58).

31 (c) PURIFICATION (14:1–32). The treatment of the various forms of uncleanness, to be resumed in 14:33–57, is here interrupted by the purification ritual for a leprous person. It was actually composed of two ceremonies: an archaic rite symbolizing liberation from the evil spirit (vv. 2–9) followed by sacrifical rites, common in spirit and form to those of the Priestly code (chs. 1–7).

The unusual ceremony in 14:2–9 reflects a primitive idea that linked physical illness with a winged evil demon, which had to be exorcised for health to be restored. The priest, as sole arbiter in the matter, met the person outside the camp. If he appeared to be healed, the priest ordered him to slay one of two clean birds and mix its blood with spring water (see comment on 11:36). Taking the other bird, a piece of cedar, some red yarn, and a sprig of hyssop, the priest immersed them all in the water and blood, sprinkled the man seven times to purify him, and then released the living bird. The lustral waters drew their purifying powers from being both fresh and reddened by the bird's blood. Since the color red had an inherent power to frighten evil spirits, this was likely the significance of the crimson yarn, colored by dyestuffs derived from insects (see also the red-heifer rites, Nm 19). Both the cedar and hyssop (the latter actually a form of caper, true hyssop not being found in Palestine) were used for sacred aspersions (Nm 19:18; Ps 51:9). It is possible that the yarn bound the hyssop sprig to the cedar to form an aspergillum (H. Cazelles) although the text is not so explicit and they are evidently not so arranged in Nm 19:6. The release of the bird symbolized the departure of the evil spirit. The liberated sufferer completed this initial phase of his purification by washing his garments and shaving all his hair, in which the relics of the disease might still be concealed. Although readmitted to the community, complete reintegration was delayed for a week, during which time he remained out-of-doors for fear of contaminating his dwelling, which would require added purification rites. At the end of the seven days, he shaved, washed his body and clothing once again, and thereby regained his former state of purity.

Verses 10–32 represent a later complementary feature of purification, linked historically with the sacrificial liturgy of the Second Temple. On the eighth day after the inauguration of purification, official cultic readmittance was gained by the formerly diseased person whose state of objective separation from the Lord had not yet been completely overcome. The offerings consisted of a male lamb as a guilt offering, an ewe as a sin offering, and another male lamb as a holocaust, plus a cereal offering (flour mixed with oil) and a separate log of oil (about 1 pt.). The priest took the guilt offering and the oil and presented them as a "contribution" to the Lord (see comment on wave offering, 7:30). Because of its sacred character, the lamb was slaughtered in the sanctuary court where the holocaust and sin offering victims were killed. Then, taking some of the victim's blood, the priest anointed the man's right ear, thumb, and big toe, doing the same with the oil after he first consecrated it by sprinkling it toward the Lord's dwelling. The remainder of the oil in his hand was placed on the man's head. The marked similarities here with the ceremonies for the ordination of the priests (8:12,23–24; Ex 29:20) has led some authors (e.g., Cazelles, BJ, note on 14:14) to view this action as a rededication rite by which the leper is reintegrated into the holy community in terms of service. De Vaux, on the other hand, sees the anointing in Lv 14 solely in terms of purification (De Vaux, *AI* 463). Blood had axiomatic expiatory value (17:11; 8:15; Ex 30:10), and the oil-anointing had its counterpart in rites for the liberation of slaves, known to us from Mesopotamian and Ugaritic contracts. With the offering of the prescribed sacrifices, cleanness was finally attained.

A commutation was granted in favor of the poor leper (21–32); his offering consisted of a male lamb as a guilt offering, a smaller portion of flour mixed with oil, a log of oil, and either two turtledoves or two pigeons for the sin offering and holocaust. With the exception of these modifications, the ceremonial procedure was the same as that of a man in ordinary circumstances.

32 (d) IN BUILDINGS (14:33–57). Because of their external resemblance to human skin disease, certain forms of fungus, such as moss, when found on buildings were believed to have made them "leprous." **34.** *if I put a leprous infection:* The phrase reflects the Hebr attitude of overlooking secondary causes in attributing all things to God as the ultimate cause. Uncleanness was present only when the fungus was active, a factor determined by the priest's inspection; however, even before judgment was passed, the house was completely emptied of its furnishings if it even bore the appearance of contagious infection (33–36). If in the priest's judgment the growth gave evidence of penetrating the surface of the wall or its color strongly suggested malignancy, a seven-day quarantine was imposed on the dwelling to allow time for greater certainty in the matter (37–38). To enter the house during quarantine was to incur uncleanness for the day; more intimate contact, e.g., eating or sleeping therein, resulted in impurity of both person and clothing (46–47; cf. 11:24–28). If at the end of the week the priest's reinspection verified the active character of the leprosy, the affected stones were removed and, together with all the plaster scraped from the walls, carried to an unclean place beyond the city (39–41). The house could be repaired but had to be demolished completely if the growth reappeared (a procedure paralleling the treatment of clothing, 13:55–57). If the corrosive condition did not recur, the house was declared clean (42–48).

The house was purified (49–53) in the same way as the leprous man (14:1–9), the ancient "bird" ritual alone sufficing with no accompanying sacrifice required. Chapter 14 closes with a general summary of the disorders treated and the purpose of the preceding casuistry—i.e., the discernment of legal purity (54–57).

33 **(D) Sexual Uncleanness (15:1–33).** Not only was there a certain aura of mystery surrounding the faculty of generation, but also a loss of vitality, a diminution of the life principle, was indicated in the loss of seed by a man or blood by a woman. Either resulted in a state of unworthiness precluding any active role in Israel's cultic life. The concern here is not with moral culpability. Moreover, the isolation demanded was not a punitive measure; it prevented the spread of impurity through contact. Although hygienic reasons, known from Babylonian and Egyptian sources, underlie much of the legislation, the emphasis in Lv is clearly cultic (31); therefore, its rather primitive medical outlook, often based on popular assumption, should not be surprising.

Uncleanness in men, treated in vv. 2–17, could arise in various ways. The abnormal flow (Hebr *zob*) of 2–15 is, in all probability, a reference to genital excretions resulting from gonorrhea. The sufferer communicated his impurity to other people contacted, furniture on which he lay or sat, saddles on which he rode, and household articles that he touched. Anyone brought into contact with the man himself or any object he had infected had to wash himself and his garments and remain unclean until evening; clay vessels were destroyed and wooden articles were rinsed. At the termination of his illness, he waited seven days before effecting his purification with the usual lustrations. His social reintegration was gained on the eighth day with the public offering of the two turtle doves or pigeons as an atoning sin offering and holocaust. The second cause of male impurity (16–17) was the loss of semen, whether voluntary or not. His unclean state lasted the day and demanded only that he wash himself and any piece of cloth or leather stained by the seed. In Dt 23:11 is the added directive of absenting oneself from the community.

Verse 18 is transitional, linking the two sections on impurity in men and women. Legal impurity resulted from sexual relations between man and woman whether the act was licit or illicit. The law was concerned with the male's loss of vitality and with the woman's uncleanness springing from contact with the male semen. The resultant state was short-lived—of one day's duration—and the only ritual required was the bath. This cultic unworthiness arising from sexual intercourse was common among the ancients, and its antiquity in Israel is reflected in 1 Sm 21:4–5.

Female impurity (19–30) arose from either menstruation (19–24) or an abnormal flow of blood outside the customary time or beyond the usual length of the period (25–30). At the time of menstruation the impurity lasted for seven days, during which time uncleanness could be communicated to persons and objects in much the same way as in the case of the man with a chronic flow. The exact sense of v. 23 in both the MT and LXX is difficult to determine, but the following is recommended as the closest rendering of the Hebr: "If there be an object on the bed or seat where she lies, in touching it, one makes himself unclean until evening." A man approaching a menstruating woman sexually contracted her uncleanness, remained in it for a week, and was capable of transmitting it during that time. The stricter penalty imposed for the same act in 20:18 proceeds from an independent tradition more concerned (as the context indicates) with the moral aspects of the case. In menstrual irregularity, the woman remained unclean and in a contagious condition during the time of the flow of blood. Since this was a true illness and not a purely natural phenomenon, its more serious character demanded cultic purification on the eighth day after its cessation with the bird oblations as sin offering and holocaust. Verse 31 is significant for the chapter as well as the entire section on legal purity: The interests of cult lay at the heart of the clean and unclean legislation, any defilement of the Lord's dwelling being punishable by death. A complete summary of all categories treated is given in v. 32. (→ Religious Institutions, 76:118–19).

34 **(IV) The Day of Atonement (16:1–34).** The detailed treatment of Yom Kippur in Lv is appropriately situated after the sacrificial ritual and the code of legal purity, both of which serve as background material for an understanding of the feast itself (→ Religious Institutions, 76:156–57). The ritual is given first (1–28), followed by directives on certain peripheral features of the feast, e.g., fast and rest (29–34). This annual observance, so important in post-exilic Israel, is never mentioned in the pre-exilic literature, and, as it is presented in Lv, the ceremonies of the day represent a combination of distinct rites, brought together in a rather loosely edited chapter (note the doublets in vv. 6 and 11, 9b and 15, and 3b and 32b).

In outlining the ritual (1–28), the Lord addresses Moses alone who is, in turn, to convey the message to Aaron. The reference to the death of Aaron's sons in v. 1 has no chronological value, serving only as an artificial link for the incorporation of the Yom Kippur material. The feast's solemnity is immediately underscored by the announcement that only with the celebration of this feast each year could the high priest pass behind the veil screening the Holy of Holies and enter the Holy Place. **2.** *in front of the propitiatory (kappōret):* The golden cover over the Ark (Ex 25:17–22) is indicated. Since the Ark itself was never recovered after the Exile, the propitiatory alone remained in the Holy of Holies, which accounts for the emphasis given it in ch. 16. Because the glory of Yahweh was there made manifest (Ex 40:34; Nm 7:89), entrance at any other time would result in death because of man's inability to stand before the resplendent divine presence.

The first of the combined rites was the sin offering of a bull for the priests' transgressions and a goat for the sins of the people (3a and 5). Bathed and clothed in sacred linen, the high priest took the blood of the slaughtered bull together with the glowing censer and incense into the Holy of Holies, where he incensed the propitiatory to obscure the divine presence and sprinkled it with the bull's blood to signify its consecration to the Lord (3b–4, 6, and 11–14). The same procedure was followed for the people's sin offering (9 and 15). In this way, the sins of priests and people were expiated.

Verse 16, however, introduces another theme: atonement for ritual transgressions that had affected the Lord's dwelling itself (Ez 45:18–20). It was accomplished by a blood aspersion within the sanctuary (here identified with the aspersions of the sin offering) and a second sprinkling and blood application at the altar (probably of holocausts) outside. This rite (16–19), which has been joined to the Kippur ceremony, was clearly an act of atonement for the sacred places. However, the question has been posed as to whether the blood action within the Holy of Holies, after the two rites were joined, was then expiatory or consecrating, for the sprinkling before the propitiatory (14b), like the customary sprinkling before the veil (cf. 4:6), although it looked to atonement for the priests or the people, was in itself a consecrative act. Moreover, according to Vriezen (*op. cit.*, 232), the aspersion of the propitiatory itself (14a) was actually the highest form of blood dedication and so, too, was originally a consecration act, reaching to the very place where Yahweh was enthroned. Hence, it retains the same sense here as in other passages where blood was sprinkled toward the Lord. Although this sense seems to have been lost early in favor of the expiatory idea of cleansing the sacred place (see v. 16), its original purpose was to dedicate the atoning blood to God in a most special way.

Still another rite (20–26), of unquestionably ancient vintage, was blended into the Day of Atonement liturgy. Its earliest reference is found in the mention of the two male goats (5 and 7–10). One of these, "for the Lord," became the people's sin offering, whereas the latter, "for Azazel," became the bearer of the community's guilt. With the purification of the sanctuary completed (20), the priest imposed hands on the remaining goat and confessed the people's sins, thus bringing about a transmission of the sins to the goat. Carrying its evil burden, it was led off to a desert place by an attendant, who became unclean in the execution of his task. The evil was thus removed from the people's midst. The name Azazel occurs only in ch. 16. Driver (*op. cit.*, 97–98) identifies it with a place name meaning "rugged rocks" or "precipice," from the root *'zz* (Arabic *'azâzu(n)*, "rough ground"). De Vaux finds the argument unconvincing in terms of the personal parallelism demanded by the context: one goat for Yahweh and one for Azazel. With most modern commentators, he explains the term as the name of a supernatural being, a devil whose customary haunt was the desert (Is 34:14) (De Vaux, *AI* 509). The Vg, following the LXX, refers to it as "the goat sent out" (*caper emissarius*), whence the Eng escape goat or scapegoat. The idea of sin transference to animals is found among the primitive customs of various peoples even today (see J. G. Frazer, *The Golden Bough* [N.Y., 1951] 626–27), and certain ancient Babylonian and Hittite parallels have been the object of a comparative study by S. Landersdorfer (*BZ* 19 [1931] 20–28). The most evident biblical parallel is the liberated bird of the leper's purification (14:7).

To conclude the ceremony (23–38), before offering the two holocausts the high priest removed his linen vestments, infected by contact with the sinful animal, and vested in his ordinary ceremonial attire after bathing in a sacred place. The fat of the bull and goat offered earlier was burned with the holocaust; the remaining parts were destroyed outside the camp. No part of the common sin offering was eaten. Unlike the man in v. 26 whose lustrations were for impurity contracted, the person's washing in v. 28 was to prevent the diffusion of holiness received from the sacred sacrificial victims.

The conclusion (29–34), still addressed to Moses, sets the date of the annual observance of Kippur for the tenth day of the seventh month, Tishri (our September-October period). Both Israelite and non-Israelite residents were to fast (Hebr "afflict oneself," Is 58:3–5) and desist from any form of work on this "most solemn sabbath," or day of rest. This fast is the only one prescribed in the entire Torah. Verse 34 mentions only personal atonement as the purpose of the feast, whereas v. 33 gives pre-eminence to expiation of the Temple. (→ Religious Institutions, 76:155–58.)

(Auerbach, E., "Neujahrs- und Versöhnungs-Fest. in den biblischen Quellen," *VT* 8 [1958] 337–43. Frazer, J. G., *The Scapegoat* [London, 1913]. Kaupel, H., *Die Dämonen im Alten Testament* [Augsburg, 1930] 81–91. Landersdorfer, S., *Studien zum biblischen Versöhnungstag* [Münster, 1924]. Löhr, M., *Das Ritual von Lev. 16* [Berlin, 1925].)

35 **(V) The Law of Holiness (17:1–26:46).** (→ 3 above.) The earliest part of Lv, this originally independent collection of laws inspired much of the later Priestly teaching and legislation. It represents a compilation of the pre-exilic Jerusalem clergy. Collected and edited before 586, most of the laws proceed from an earlier period, with some added at a time of later editing during and after the Exile itself.

Like the Deuteronomic Code (Dt 12–26), the Holiness Code has its own literary unity, beginning with regulations regarding the sanctuary and sacrifice and concluding with "blessings and curses." But the collection itself is marked by an almost disconcerting diversity of material, its sole unifying feature lying in its emphasis on the holiness of Yahweh. This consideration serves as the springboard for its demands of the Israelites who, in every aspect of their lives, are to be holy as their Lord (19:2; 20:26). It was this prominent feature of Lv 17–26 that led A. Klostermann in 1877 to name it the Law of Holiness. It must be noted, however, that the holiness solicited here exceeds mere legal purity and embraces moral rectitude as well, without which holiness is incomplete. It is this characteristic underscoring of the transcendent sanctity of Yahweh that will have such a marked effect on the entire P tradition.

36 **(A) Sacredness of Blood (17:1–16).** Originally, the slaughter of clean animals, even for profane use, was considered a sacrificial act. The shedding of blood, as an act of dominion over life itself, was the exercise of a divine prerogative and could not be viewed as legitimate unless the life was first restored to God. For this reason, all such killings were reserved for a place of cult (1 Sm 14:32–35). This requirement apparently presented no great difficulty as long as local sanctuaries were allowed, but with the centralization of cult under Josiah (621), such a law became impossible. It was mitigated in Dt 12:15–16,20–25 to a simple act of reverence for the slaughtered animal's blood.

It is suprising that the older law should be resurrected in 17:3–7 at a time after the Josian reform. Twofold motivation is given: The sacredness of blood (4) and the avoidance of idolatrous practices (7); the interests of both were best served by regulating the slaughtering procedure. Verse 5 indicates that the animals were first to be brought to the meeting tent and there offered to the Lord; otherwise, there resulted the guilt of bloodshed and consequent separation from the community (see 7:20). **7.** *satyrs* (*se'îrîm*): The word denotes demons popularly identified with wild goats making their haunts in ruins and desert places, as Azazel (16:8). Because of the historical situation in the post-Josian period, the place designated for the killing could only have been the Jerusalem Temple. The law would have been so totally impractical in the post-exilic period that it must be dated with the Holiness Code itself in the period of Jerusalem's last days. Since it would hardly have been included simply as a relic of the past with no practical import, it may represent a hopeful ideal of the Jerusalem clergy opposed to the deuteronomic freedom in the matter, or, as Noth suggests (ATD 112), an actual revival of the custom because of continued idolatrous practices in Jerusalem of the type Josiah had once attempted to correct (2 Kgs 23:8). In addressing itself most explicitly to the ordinary killing of edible animals, the law included, of course, all forms of properly cultic sacrifices as well.

The following pericope in vv. 8–12 repeats the same directives of 3–7 with two additional features. The prohibition against all local sacrifices included the holocaust also (8b), and the law was directed to both Israelites and non-Israelite residents of the country who as part of the community were bound by such regulations. Blood had a special sacredness as a means of atonement (11), divine forgiveness being more readily attained through the oblation of that which was most precious in the eyes of man and God alike, life itself. The law forbidding the Hebrew to partake of blood was safeguarded by sacrificial centralization.

Two remaining possibilities, directed to Israelites and all other residents, are treated in vv. 13–16 and concern the animal caught during a hunt and the animal dying of natural or violent causes. In the former instance, the animal could be eaten only after the blood was carefully disposed of in a manner similar to that prescribed for general slaughter in Dt 12. In the second case, the animal was unclean and was therefore prohibited; anyone eating thereof contracted uncleanness and had to undergo a purification rite to be free of his guilt (11:39–40).

37 **(B) Sacredness of Sex (18:1–30).** The chapter, chiefly concerned with sexual matters, is formed around a series of apodictic laws, which prohibit relations within determined degrees of consanguinity and affinity (6–18) and outlaw certain other forms of abnormal behavior (19–23). This material is introduced by an exhortation addressed to all the Israelites (1–5) and is concluded with similar injunctions (24–30). The sacredness surrounding the act that communicates human life prohibited sexual contact with those already allied by blood, or any close relationship, since such, especially in the former case, would be tantamount to union with one's own flesh. Moreover, these laws were safeguards against those inroads of carnal promiscuity that so marked the culture of the Canaanites. As the laws themselves indicate, it was also a time when polygamy was an accepted fact in Hebr life.

The introduction (1–5) carries a tone of exceptional seriousness with emphasis on the necessity of an observance that was to be the very antithesis of Canaanite practice. The reference to the Egyptians in v. 3 (not mentioned in the conclusion) was included to lend authenticity to the law's purported historical setting in the desert when the only culture known to Israel would have been that of Egypt. The life to which observance leads in v. 5 is the "good life," that sign of Yahweh's favor identified with the possession of the promised land.

The laws for sexual conduct within the clan (6–18) are introduced in v. 6 by a general prohibition regarding relations and a fortiori marriage with blood kin, although certain cases of affinity also form part of the code. Specifically, the forbidden degrees, which are not necessarily all inclusive as here listed, embraced: son and mother (7); father and granddaughter (10), in the direct line; and brother and sister (9), in the collateral line. The "sister" in this latter verse refers either to a full sister, one "born in your own household," or to a half sister from a previous marriage of the mother, one "born elsewhere," which clearly distinguishes the sense from that of v. 11. More remotely, union was forbidden between brother and half sister (11), and nephew and aunt (12–13). Restricted by reason of affinity were son and stepmother (8), father-in-law and daughter-in-law (15), nephew and aunt by marriage (14), and brother-in-law and sister-in-law (16). Verse 17 forbade union or marriage with the daughter or granddaughter of a woman with whom one had had relations, and v. 18 outlawed simultaneous marriage with two sisters.

A number of sexual abuses, frequently seen as repugnant to the Hebr mind in the OT, are excluded by the apodictic decrees of vv. 19–23. These include intercourse during the uncleanness of menstruation (19; cf. 15:24), sodomy among men (22), and bestiality indulged in by man or woman (23; cf. Ex 22:18). An extraneous law in v. 21 (perhaps suggested by the term seed [offspring] in the Hebr of v. 20) forbade the pagan practice of child sacrifice, directed by the Canaanites to the worship of Molech (cf. 20:2–5), and adopted also by the Hebrews at certain sad moments in their cultic history (2 Kgs 16:3; 21:6; Ez 16:20ff.; 20:26,31; 23:37).

Removal from the land, the same punishment meted out to the Canaanites for their sexual wantonness, serves as the threatening sanction of the Lord for native Israelites as well as for resident aliens in the community (24–30). Since the sacred land, which had been defiled, could never digest such abuses, it is depicted here as itself discharging the Canaanite evil, to be repeated if necessary in the case of an unfaithful Israel. Personal sanction in v. 29 takes the form of the offender's severance from the community without the specific delineations given elsewhere, e.g., death for sodomy (20:13), bestiality (20:15), and child sacrifice (20:2).

38 **(C) Various Rules of Conduct (19:1–37).** This miscellaneous collection of laws on worship, justice, charity, and chastity, with its clearly primitive character, is of particular interest as a mirror of pre-exilic cultic and social life. In its dependence upon the Decalogue and its own subsequent influence upon post-exilic legislation, it serves as an important link between the earlier and later stages of Israelite law. The chapter forms a unit with its own introduction (1–2) and conclusion (36b–37), which anchor the diversified contents in respect for the holiness of Yahweh.

Priority is given reverence for parents, observance of the Sabbath, and avoidance of idolatry (3–4), all represented in the Decalogue (Ex 20:2–6,8,12; Dt 5:6–10,12–16). The rules regarding the peace offering (5–8) are substantially the same as in 7:15–19; this passage, however, points up the intimate connection between oblations and consumption, the eating of the offering after the set time limit making the whole sacrifice a profanation.

The law regarding the harvest (9–10) forbade such thoroughness in gleaning as would leave nothing in the fields or vineyards for the needy (23:22; Dt 24:19–22; Ru 2). The charitable motivation given this procedure is an early Hebr adaptation of a pre-Israelite custom of leaving something of the harvest to honor the deity responsible for the soil's fertility, a motive clearly excluded by the concluding affirmation in 10b.

Verses 11–18 are centered mainly upon man's responsibility to practice justice and charity in his social dealings. The influence of the Decalogue is again pronounced: the prohibition in v. 12 against profaning the divine name by perjury (more restricted than the Decalogue's general law of respect for God's name, Ex 20:7; Dt 5:11); and the law against any form of lying and deception in v. 11b (broader than that of the Decalogue, which looks to court testimony, Ex 20:16; Dt 5:20). The precept regarding theft (11a), as in Ex 20:15 and Dt 5:19, was concerned with the deprivation of another's personal liberty—i.e., kidnaping (cf. Ex 21:16, Hebr "anyone stealing a man..."; Dt 24:7)—and was thus clearly distinguished from the law regarding another's goods in 13a (see A. Alt, *KlSchr* 1, 333–40). The strong were not to take advantage of the weak by cheating or stealing (13a), withholding wages (13b; cf. Dt 24:14–15), or other forms of unkind treatment (14). **14.** *you shall not curse the deaf:* The curse, once uttered, was irrevocable and effective whether heard by the accursed or not.

Court proceedings (15–16), presided over by the elders or senior members of the clan, were to be marked by strict adherence to the interests of justice, which forbade either favoring the mighty or showing compassion to the weak. In a negative way, the individual Israelite was to uphold justice by refraining from any falsification about a person made to members of the judicial body, and in a positive way, he was bound to bring to light evidence that might save the life of the one accused.

The demands of charity (17–18) precluded a spirit of enmity, revenge, and grudge-bearing and required that fraternal correction be made when necessary. **17b.** *do not incur sin because of him:* Sin would lie in the failure to correct in terms of the seriousness of the responsibility to do so (Ez 3:18–19; 33:8–9; cf. also Mt 18:15). The most celebrated passage in Lv (18b) proposes self-love as the measure of charity toward a fellow countryman. According to the teaching of Christ (Mt 22:37–39; Mk 12:30–31; wherein "neighbor" is taken in its widest possible extension), this lofty precept, taken together with Dt 6:5, sums up the whole of the Law and the Prophets (see A. Fernandez, *VD* 1 [1921] 27–28).

39 The law against crossbreeding and cross-semination in v. 19 (cf. Dt 22:9) is seen by Noth (ATD 123) as a very ancient, probably pre-Israelite, regulation. Heterogeneous coupling was evidently considered a perversion of the divinely established order, and the prohibition was gradually extended to the use of different fibers in sewing, the yoking of different animals, and even transvestism (cf. Dt 22:11,10,5).

An interesting sidelight on the question of adultery and its attendant death penalty occurs in the case (20–22) wherein the woman with whom one had relations was still unmarried although cohabiting with another man, her state of slavery making marriage impossible before freedom was granted (cf. Ex 21:7–11). Since the primary evil of adultery lay in the violation of a husband's rights, and since the sinning couple were not guilty of such a crime, an unspecified punishment, but not death, was to be administered. The offended party was the slave girl's master, whose property she was and whose claim to her continued services had to be respected. The presentation of a guilt offering was prescribed for the male offender.

Just as the male child did not properly belong to Yahweh until the time of his circumcision (Gn 17:9–14), so by analogy the fruit of a tree produced prior to the first-fruits offering was termed uncircumcised (23–25). Not before the fourth year, when the fruit was truly well developed and worth eating, could it be offered to the Lord as a token of thanks. Hence, the people were forbidden to eat the fruit any time prior to the fifth year.

The older laws of 26–31 were prompted mainly by the dangers arising from the cultic practices of Israel's neighbors. Besides the oft-mentioned prohibition of blood (17:10–12), likewise prohibited were the following: divination and magic arts as attempts to plumb divine secrets or to control events; the mourning customs of the Canaanites—cutting of hair, body lacerations, tattooing—probably viewed as means of warding off the departed spirit by changing the appearance to avoid recognition; the abandonment of a daughter to cult prostitution, which, because of its link with the pagan fertility rites, would degrade the sacredness of the land itself; and consultation with mediums or fortune-tellers to commune with the dead or foresee the future (Ex 22:17; Dt 18:11; 1 Sm 28:1–25). In a positive way, faithful observance included respect for the Sabbath and the sacredness of the sanctuary wherein religious syncretism often led to profanation (Dt 23:18–19; Hos 4:14).

In regard to charity and justice (32–36a), respect was to be shown the senior members of the community, and all attitudes of economic superiority were to be avoided in dealing with dependent strangers. The given motive for this charity, recalling the days of Egyptian bondage, has a deuteronomic ring (Dt 10:19; 5:15) and is probably a secondary addition. Correct scales, weights, and measuring containers (the ephah, approx. 1 bu.; the hin, approx. 1 gal.) were to be used in all commercial transactions (Dt 25:13–16; Ez 45:10).

40 **(D) Penalties (20:1–27).** There is a marked affinity between ch. 20 and ch. 18, the present concern being the sanctions attached to many of the aforementioned crimes. The attraction between the two chapters in Lv results from their common material rather than from any direct literary dependence, since ch. 20, like chs. 18 and 19, forms a complete unit introduced originally by the exhortation in vv. 7–8, followed by the list of crimes and penalties, and concluded in vv. 22–26. Thus, vv. 2–6 and 27 should be considered secondary additions.

Child sacrifice to Molech (2–5; cf. 18:21) was punished by death (stoning), executed by the community or, with their failure to do so, by the Lord himself. Note the solidarity concept of the family's sharing in the man's guilt (5a), an idea to be greatly altered in post-exilic religious thought. Also in the line of cult, v. 6 sanctions with death the previous mandate (19:31) against consulting diviners.

After the customary paraenesis in vv. 7–8 (wherein Yahweh is both the reason and cause of holiness), the kernel of the chapter in 9–21 imposes sanctions for the sexual abuses of ch. 18. Prior to this, however, first place is given to the matter of uttering maledictions against one's parents (9), a precept included implicitly within the general scope of the law in 19:3. In the sexual sphere, death for both offenders was prescribed in the following cases: adultery (10; 18:20; Dt 22:22); relations between son and stepmother (11; 18:8) and father-in-law and daughter-in-law (12; 18:15); sodomy (13; 18:22); simultaneous marriage with a mother and daughter (14; 18:17; Dt 27:23), in which case the three offenders were burned; bestiality (15–16; 18:23; Ex 22:18; Dt 27:21), wherein the animal also bears objective guilt in the wrongdoing; and relations between brother and sister (17; 18:9; Dt 27:22), with a menstruating woman (18; 18:19), and between nephew and aunt (19; 18:12–13). In the case of sexual misbehavior with an aunt by marriage (20; 18:14) or marriage with a sister-in-law (21; 18:16; Mk 6:18), a substitute for the humanly executed death penalty took the form of a childless marriage, divinely decreed, depriving a man of the all important continuance of his life and name through his progeny. Verse 21 does not contradict the levirate law (Dt 25:5ff.), since the latter looked to marriage with a sister-in-law only after the death of a brother who had died childless.

The conclusion (22–26) closely parallels 18:24–30 with its admonitions and promises centered around observance of the Lord's decrees. Verse 25, ill fitting the context, seems to be an addition suggested by the "separation" idea in v. 24; on the subject of clean and unclean animals, see ch. 11. Equally problematic is the abrupt addition in v. 27, which complements v. 6. The meaning, however, is clear. Not only were those consulting diviners reprobate, but also to be stoned were those who professionally practiced such arts and thus induced others to idolatrous conduct (cf. Dt 13:7ff.; 17:2ff.).

41 **(E) Priestly Sanctity (21:1–24).** Chapters 21–22 are concerned mainly with cultic regulations directed principally to the priests. Chapter 21 can be divided, according to content, into directives concerning all the priests (1–9) and the main priest of the community (10–15) in the first part, and sacerdotal impediments (16–23) in the second part.

Contact with the dead (e.g., in preparing and moving the corpse) rendered any Israelite unclean (Nm 19:11–19; 31:19,24). Although it was permitted for the people to contract such uncleanness with good reason, such was not the case for the priests, impurity being ordinarily incompatible with their lofty office. As vv. 2–4 indicate, however, exception was made in the case of a death in the priest's immediate family (see comment on 10:6–7; Ex 44:25–27). The sense of v. 4 is extremely obscure in both the MT and the LXX. The MT reads: "A husband shall not make himself unclean among his people"; "the people" perhaps refers to the priest's in-laws. The CCD emends the text so that it is elaborative of v. 3; a married sister, now "one flesh" with her husband, was no longer joined to the family of her birth. Certain funeral customs (5–6), derived from pagan sources and prohibited for all Israelites (19:27–28), were especially outlawed for the priests. **6.** *the food of their God:* See comment on 3:11.

As to marriage (7–8), the priest was required to marry a virgin, widows not being explicitly excluded. The latter is allowed by Ez 44:22 only when it is the widow of a priest. The case in v. 9 has only a loose connection with the preceding, imposing the death penalty upon the sinning daughter of a priest; the principal evil resided in the sacrilegious nature of the act, since, by reason of family solidarity, the priest would share in his daughter's guilt.

Verses 10–15 contain special directives for the main priest of the community. The Hebr phrase, "the priest most exalted among his brothers," is a descriptive designation and not the same as the title high priest, arising in the post-exilic period (Hag 1:1; Zech 3:1; and common in the later P tradition). However, the phrase does indicate a unified priesthood, hierarchically structured, at a time after the cultic reform of Josiah (621), thus paving the way for the later title. The mention of the anointing in v. 10 provides no definitive argument for the pre-exilic existence of such a custom, because we lack information on the present passage's time of final editing (see comment on 8:12). The community's main priest was prohibited any contact with the dead whatsoever, even close relatives, and so would never be in a position to practice accepted forms of mourning: the loosening of the hair (not "baring the head," cf. 10:6) and tearing of the garments—neither of which is to be confused with the totally prohibited practices of v. 5. The danger to his holiness, moreover, forbade his leaving the precincts of the Temple area wherein he resided (cf. 10:7), since his sacredness would be profaned by any sallying forth into the world. In selecting a spouse, he was to choose only a virgin, with widows excluded, and his wife was to be "from his own people"—i.e., the tribe of Levi (LXX: *ek tou genous autou*)—lest the purity of the Levitical strain be in any way debased in this most important family.

Integrity of the whole man was demanded of cultic functionaries. Physical imperfection was, then, an impediment to the exercise of the priestly office in a descendant of Aaron (16–23). Inasmuch as the animals offered to Yahweh were to be flawless (1:3,10; 22:22–25), the same was required of priests, physical defect being irreconcilable with the perfection of God. The list of impediments in 18–20 contains a number of rare terms, only the general meaning of which can be determined. Since a priest was not unclean because of such a defect, he was permitted to partake of the various sacrificial repasts, but, as long as his impediment remained, he could approach neither the sanctuary veil nor the altar of holocausts, i.e., act in any priestly capacity. Finally, in v. 24, Moses relays the message to the priests and, as a matter of concern (cf. v. 8), to all the Israelites as well.

42 **(F) Rules on Sacrifice (22:1–33).** The first section (1–16) deals with the right of participation in the sacrificial food, with v. 2 serving as its introduction; the second part (17–30) treats of acceptable victims; vv. 31–33 serve as a general conclusion.

Disregard for the sacred character of an offering was disregard for the very person of Yahweh (2). Therefore, the eating of those parts of the victim designated for the priests (6:19–23; 7:7–10; 7:28–34) was to follow prescribed procedure and to be carried out only when the participants were in a state of cleanness under the usual penalty of extirpation. The same rule applied equally to all Israelites in those instances where they were participants (7:20–21), but the priests' rights in the matter were, of course, more extensive. In vv. 4–8, priests were excluded who suffered from "leprosy" (see comment on chs. 13–14), who had abnormal genital excretions (see comment on 15:2–15), who had experienced an emission of semen (see 15:16), or who had come in contact with any unclean person or thing. The more transient nature of the last category (uncleanness lasting only the day) conceded the restoration of rights with the usual lustration, probably equally true for the emission of seed (15:16). Disqualified also were those who ate an animal not properly slain (7:24; 11:39–40; 17:15; Ez 4:14). Disregard of these precepts would result in death (9), the manner (whether by divine or human intervention) remaining undetermined.

Only members of the priest's family were allowed to eat the victim (10:14). Excluded in vv. 10–14 are the following: any ordinary layman (*zār*, "a stranger"), i.e., one in no way affiliated with the sacerdotal family; a priest's tenant (*tôšāb*), i.e., a resident alien or settler economically dependent on an Israelite landowner, similar to, but not the social equal of, the more common type of alien, the *gēr*, who was more integrated into Israelite life; and a hired servant (*śākîr*), a wage earner employed for a definite job. Slaves, however, were part of the household, whether purchased or born to slaves in the house (although the latter category, *y^{e}lîdê bayt*, may be broader in scope, embracing all personnel attached to a house as slaves, who, without necessarily living therein, had certain responsibilities to their lord; cf. Gn 14:14). The priest's daughter, married to a layman, belonged to the lay, not the clerical, household and was therefore excluded. If she returned to her paternal home widowed or divorced and childless, her rights were restored. A layman inadvertently eating the sacrificial food incurred objective guilt and was held to make restitution according to the estimated value plus an added one-fifth as a penalty for his oversight. Verses 15–16 enjoin the priests both to prevent any profanation by allowing abuses in these matters and not to incur punishable guilt by allowing prohibited parties to eat the sacrifice.

The section on unacceptable victims (17–30) presents a classification of sacrifices proper to the Holiness Code, more primitive than that found in the initial chapters of Lv. The main distinction is between holocausts (18) and peace offerings (*š^{e}lāmîm*, v. 21), either of which could be offered under the title of a votive offering—arising from a vow or promise—or a free-will offering—spontaneous and independent of any previous commitment. As in the sacrifical code (chs. 1–7), the animal victims destined for such oblations had to be unblemished. An exception is introduced in v. 23 (which when compared with the universal tone of the preceding verses would seem to be a secondary addition) in allowing certain defects in the free-will offering, since such was offered purely from motives of devotion. The special reference to the animal's genitals in v. 24 portrays Semitic reverence for the procreative faculty.

The offering from the herd or the flock was unacceptable before the eighth day after birth (27), the same law being found in the Book of the Covenant (Ex 22:29) with reference to the first-born animal. This prohibition is accounted for in terms of the young's complete dependence on its parent during this time, and because like the undeveloped fruit (19:23–24), such offspring, not yet ready for human consumption, were not fit offerings for the Lord. The prohibition against the simultaneous slaughter of the ox or sheep with its young (28) is enigmatic but may well carry a polemic note against Canaanite practices of honoring the fertility deity by sacrificing the offspring together with its parent, the source of its life. The third form of peace offering, the thanksgiving sacrifice, heretofore unmentioned in the chapter but found together with the votive and free-will offerings in the sacrificial code (see comment on 7:11–21), must be eaten on the day of the sacrifice itself (30), a rule stated with equal force in 7:15.

43 **(G) The Liturgical Year (23:1–44).** In its more primitive form as part of the original code, the chapter treated solely of the three main annual feasts—Passover and Unleavened Bread (4–8), Pentecost (16–21), and Booths (34–36)—and had its own conclusion (37–38).

Compare Ex 23:14–17; 34:18,22–23; Dt 16:1–17. Later editors of the Holiness Code have added the Sabbath precept (3), the rubrics of 10–15, the Day of Acclamation (23–25), the Day of Atonement (26–32), the added directives for Booths (39–43), and a new conclusion (44). For the Sabbath observance, see comment on Ex 20:8–11.

44 (a) PASSOVER AND UNLEAVENED BREAD (23:4–14). Celebrated on the evening of the 14th of the first month, Nisan (March–April), this most solemn commemoration of the Exodus is found in its historical setting in Ex 12. There, as here, Passover is joined to the Feast of Unleavened Bread (*maṣṣôt*). The latter commenced the day after the Pasch and continued for seven days, with a solemn gathering and complete abstention from work on the first and last days and determined sacrifices offered each day within the week (Nm 28:16–25). It was an agricultural feast, likely taken over from the Canaanites by the Hebrews, to honor Yahweh, Lord of the harvest, at the time of the spring ingathering of the barley. Originally Passover and Unleavened Bread were completely distinct feasts, but their celebration at approximately the same time, and the making of Passover, like Unleavened Bread, a pilgrimage feast (Dt 16:5ff.) at the time of the deuteronomic reform (621), resulted in a merger of the two. As stated in v. 6b, the bread of *maṣṣôt* was devoid of leaven, i.e., without any admixture of remains from the previous year's harvest. Thus, with bread made entirely from the fresh grain, the feast marked a new beginning as, during the first week, the initial gleanings were eaten and special daily sacrifices were offered.

Prior to its merger with Passover, the Feast of Unleavened Bread had no fixed date, beginning at the time of the ripened harvest. This situation is reflected in vv. 9–14, which present the ritual procedure for first-fruit offerings. The feast began on a Sabbath with the observances mentioned in v. 7. On the day following the Sabbath, the beginning of the work week, the landowner gave a sheaf of grain to the priest, which was in turn "waved" (see comment on 7:30) as an offering before the Lord. Moreover, a community oblation was made, consisting of a lamb holocaust plus a cereal-and-drink offering. Before this presentation to the Lord, it was forbidden to use any of the grain for the ordinary purposes of the harvest produce (14). This first sheaf ritual is a post-exilic addition of earlier material to the Holiness Code. Since by the time of its insertion the date of Unleavened Bread was no longer variable, long since joined to Passover and this falling always on 15 Nisan, the Sabbath reference in v. 11, although the cause of much discussion in later Judaism, is probably converted into a reference to the day of the feast itself, a day of sabbath (complete rest) although not the Sabbath.

45 (b) PENTECOST (23:15–21). Known also as the Feast of Weeks, this second of the three great feasts of pilgrimage (*ḥāg*) was celebrated seven weeks after Unleavened Bread (Gk *pentēkostos*, "fiftieth"; see comment on 25:10) and marked the conclusion of the wheat harvest. The lack of unanimity in later Judaism on the exact date of the feast arose from the diverse interpretations of the Sabbath reference in vv. 11 and 15. Also of pre-Israelite origin, the feast lasted only one day, with a religious assembly and the presentation of offerings. The latter consisted of two loaves of bread from the harvester (the only instance of leaven being prescribed for ritual use) and from the community as a whole, first a holocaust of seven lambs, one bull, and two rams, with cereal offerings and libation, and then a goat as a sin offering and two lambs as a peace offering. **20.** *the priest shall wave:* See comment on 7:30. The loaves and designated portions of the peace offering were given to the priest (cf. 7:32–34). The offerings prescribed in Nm 28:26–31, from a later ritual, are slightly different. Subsequent tradition made this feast a commemoration of the giving of the law on Sinai 50 days after the Exodus (Ex 19:1).

The precept in v. 22, providing for the needs of the poor and the alien, suggested perhaps by the harvest context, is an addition to the primitive text, which treated wholly of festive observance; see comment on 19:9–10.

46 (c) NEW YEAR'S DAY (23:23–25). This name for the feast (*rô'š haššānāh*) was unknown before the beginning of the Christian era; it is not so called in Josephus or Philo but was common by the time of the Mishnah. Such a designation is found neither in the present verses nor elsewhere in the OT. Moreover, with the adoption of the Babylonian calendar before the Exile (which is clearly the one followed in this chapter), the year's beginning was in the spring, Nisan, not in Tishri (September-October), the seventh month and the date indicated in v. 24. An account of festive observance on this day in Neh 8:1–12 makes no mention of it as a New Year's celebration; in Nm 29:1–6 it is called the Day of Acclamation (or Trumpets). Nevertheless, since the seventh month was a most important one for feasts, its solemn inauguration in this manner may well have been the relic of a former feast when, according to the earlier calendar, the year began in the autumn. Cazelles admits the distinct possibility of such a fall feast honoring Yahweh as creator and king and dating from the monarchical period ("Nouvel An en Israel," *VDBS* 6, 620–45). It is on this feast that S. Mowinckel places his much discussed annual celebration of the "enthronement" of Yahweh (*He That Cometh* [Oxford, 1956] 21–95). According to the directives here given, the day was marked by complete rest and a solemn convocation (Neh 8:1–12), announced by blasts of the silver trumpets (Nm 10:1–10) as a formal reminder. The sacrifices ordered for the day are listed in Nm 29:2–5.

47 (d) DAY OF ATONEMENT (23:26–32). This was the second autumn feast, celebrated nine days later. For the detailed ritual, see ch. 16. This, too, is a post-exilic addition to the chapter, emphasizing the fast and abstention from work connected with the observance (16:29–31). The reckoning of a day from one evening to the next (32) was a result of Mesopotamian influence and became an Israelite commonplace from about the time of the Exile.

48 (e) FEAST OF BOOTHS (23:33–36,39–43). Called also Tabernacles, Tents, Ingathering, or simply the Hebr *sukkôt*, this was the last of the three major and most ancient Israelite feasts. Like The Feasts of Unleavened Bread and Pentecost, it was a pilgrimage feast made annually to central sanctuaries but, by the time of the final edition of Lv, celebrated only in Jerusalem. With this agricultural feast of Canaanite origin, the Israelites thankfully closed the grape and olive harvest in the fall on the 15th day of the seventh month (Tishri), five days after the Day of Atonement. It lasted one week with solemn assembly and abstention from work on the opening day and on the concluding (eighth) day after the week-long observance. Special sacrifices were carefully delineated for each day of the octave (Nm 29:12–38). Verses 39–43, deriving from a later hand and inserted after the original conclusion in 37–38, present slight variations, especially regarding the gathering of fruit and branches (40), for a purpose not clearly specified. According to later rabbinical, and evidently correct, interpretation, these were used for joyful processions (cf. 2 Mc 10:6–8) and not, in the present case, as materials for constructing booths (see G. W. MacRae "Meaning and Evolution of Feast of Tabernacles," *CBQ* 22 [1960] 271–72). Verses 42–43 point up the feast's significance; the building of huts, undoubtedly an ancient fruit-harvest custom, was incorporated by the Israelites into the framework of their sacred history, commemorating the time they dwelt in such constructions during their desert sojourn. Thus the Feast of Booths, like the other two major feasts, relived one of the important events of the Exodus.

Verses 37–38 point out that the observances and offerings for these occasions supplement and do not supplant other laws and directives. **38.** *in addition to those of the Lord's Sabbaths:* Read instead "In addition to the Lord's Sabbaths." (→ Religious Institutions, 76:132–34; 140–50.)

(Cazelles, "Nouvel An en Israel," *VDBS* 6, 620–645. De Vaux, *AI* 484–517. Gaster, T., *Passover: Its History and Traditions* [N.Y., 1949]. Haag, H., "Pâque," *VDBS* 6, 1120–49. MacRae, G. W., "Meaning and Evolution of Feast of Tabernacles," *CBQ* 22 [1960] 251–76. Maertens, T., *A Feast in Honor of Yahweh* [Notre Dame, 1965].)

49 **(H) Additional Legislation (24:1–23).** The material treated here is rubrical (1–9) and moral (10–23) in content and clearly interrupts the calendar theme of chs. 23 and 25. For the detailed description of the Temple lampstand (1–4) see Ex 25:31–40. The injunction given to Moses in vv. 2–3 repeats Ex 27:20–21.

The Temple showbread or *leḥem happānîm* (bread of the countenance or divine presence), treated in 5–9, consisted of 12 cakes made of pure wheat, which were placed in two rows on the goldplated wooden table before the Holy of Holies (Ex 25:23–30). An incense offering, placed on the table with the bread, was burned on the altar when the loaves were replaced each Sabbath; this practice gave the bread offering a certain sacrificial character, the incense actually being a token oblation (*'azkārāh*) for the bread itself (see comment on 2:2). Unlike the setting in pagan cult where such was simply a meal for the deity, the communal character of the act, symbolized by the sharing of food with Yahweh, served to remind the Israelites of the perpetuity of the covenant he had made with the 12 tribes (8). As something sacred and received by the Lord, the bread was eaten only by the priests under circumscribed conditions (cf. 1 Sm 21:3–6).

The blasphemy incident (10–16,23), the only piece of narrative in the Holiness Code, actually serves as a backdrop for the law enunciated in 15–16. This casuistic setting (see also Nm 15:32–36) is presented as a precedent in the light of which similar cases were to be judged. The case is centered around the sacredness of God's name (Ex 20:7; 22:27), which was never pronounced and, at certain periods, not written without grave cause (e.g., the Hebrew of v. 11, [*he*] *blasphemed the Name*). The chief concern here is with the punishment for blasphemy, especially in the case of a foreigner. Despite his Israelite mother, the man in question was still considered an alien, a fact that would give this law considerable exilic and post-exilic relevance. Moses receives the Lord's decision: death by stoning for any blasphemer, native or alien. The imposition of hands in v. 14 is the same as the scapegoat ritual in ch. 16. All who had heard the blasphemy shared in its objective malice; here it is recommunicated to the offender. The entire community, Israelite and foreigner alike, participate in the malefactor's execution apart from the sacred confines of the camp (23).

Verses 17–22 treat of the law of retaliation (*lex talionis*), which, based on the principle of like for like, was the common procedure in ancient criminal cases—e.g., in the Code of Hammurabi (J. Pritchard, *ANET* 163–80; cf. also laws 200, 210, 219, 245, and 263). The law formerly stated in Ex 21:23–25 here includes foreigners as well as Israelites, a factor that may account for its insertion within the blasphemy pericope.

50 **(I) The Holy Years (25:1–55).** In addition to the rest for man and beast provided by the weekly Sabbath (Ex 20:8–11; Dt 5:12–15), the land itself was to have a year of reprieve at stated intervals. Ancient Oriental custom left the land uncultivated to assure its future fertility; in Israelite hands, the practice took on added meaning in focusing attention on the sole proprietorship of Yahweh, an idea central to the sabbatical (1–7) and jubilee (8–55) years.

51 (a) Sabbatical Year (25:2–7). Cultivation of field and vineyard was to be terminated after the sixth year; they were to be left untouched for the year following. **4.** *during the seventh year:* Neither here nor in Ex 23:10–11 does the text indicate whether the date was fixed and universal or variable depending on the beginning of a man's land tenure. Correlative legislation required the freeing of slaves after six years of service, "in the seventh year" (Ex 21:2–6). However, Dt 15, wherein the sabbatical legislation includes both the liberation of slaves and the relaxation of debts, leaves no doubt that the seventh year of remission was fixed (cf. 15:7–11). During the year, planting, pruning, and harvesting for storage were forbidden; the spontaneous growth was taken as needed by the owner and all his dependants without discrimination. The sabbatical law was evidently not well observed (26:34–35; Jer 34:14), being later restated (Neh 10:31) and carried out, at least in part, in Hellenistic times (1 Mc 6:49,53).

52 (b) Jubilee Year (25:8–55). The grand sabbatical derives its name from the trumpet (Hebr *yôbēl*, "ram," "ram's horn") sounded to inaugurate the year (9). It, too, had a fixed date (15–16), coinciding with the seventh sabbatical. **10.** *in this fiftieth year:* The reference is a *crux interpretum*. Some authors (M. Noth, R. North, A. Jirku) see here a broad reference to the 49th year; others (R. de Vaux), the 50th year, or year after the seventh sabbatical, hence a two-year fallow. The text's obscurity occasioned equal diversity of interpretation in antiquity (cf. J. T. Milik, "De vicissitudinibus notionis et vocabuli jubilaei," *VD* 28 [1950] 165–66). Since Hebr enumeration often included the first number and last number in a series, it is quite likely that the number 50 stands for an actual count of 49. Thus, there is no need to posit a jubilee envisioned immediately after a sabbatical; the seventh sabbatical was itself a jubilee, a special year of remission (see R. North, *Sociology of the Biblical Jubilee* [Rome, 1954] 109–34). The year was to begin on the Day of Atonement (the tenth day of Tishri) and was a period of emancipation (*d^erôr*) in which, in addition to the usual sabbatical observance (11–12), all alienated property was returned to its original owner (10).

The specific stipulations of vv. 13–17 point to the fixed jubilee date. Since in any property transaction there was prime concern with the number of years the field would yield crops to the investor's benefit, the years remaining before the next jubilee with its reversion of property determined the sale price. The law of land return strongly emphasizes the inalienable character of family holdings.

A reassuring note is struck in vv. 18–22 in response to an understandable concern about survival during sabbatical (or jubilee) years. The promise of sufficient provisions is linked with the oft-repeated assurance of abundance in return for fidelity (18–19). So copious would be the produce of the sixth year that it would suffice for the seventh, as well as the eighth (replanting) and ninth (new harvest) years.

53 General precepts related to the ideal set forth in the jubilee legislation (23–55) constitute the remainder of ch. 25, with the basic principle set forth in v. 23: The land belongs to the Lord and is entrusted to the Israelites as a result of the covenant. Strictly speaking, they were not owners but tenants with the right of use and usufruct, and any permanent sale of land was in excess of the tenant's right. Therefore, an impoverished Israelite forced to sell was faced with three possibilities (24–28); reacquisition of the family land in the name of the poor man by a relative acting as a *gô'ēl;* reacquisition by the poor man himself on the occasion of later good fortune (with proportionate reduction made from the original sale price); or reversion at the time of the jubilee.

The transition from clan settlements to town life weakened family ties with landholdings. In addition, such walled towns, originally Canaanite in many instances, were further from the Israelite ideal. Thus, privileges were restricted (29–31). The possibility of redemption lasted only one year, and the home was not repossessed at the jubilee. The village settlements (without walls) were more closely allied to the adjoining farmland; alienated property therein did not have the one-year restriction and enjoyed the jubilee benefits.

The special property rights of the Levites were to be respected (32–34). In their cities (not exclusively theirs, but places where they had their own holdings; cf. Jos 21) they had the unrestricted right of house redemption at any time prior to the jubilee release. Any attached land, allotted to the Levites and therefore appropriated by the Lord in a special way, could never be sold.

Deference was to be shown an indigent fellow Israelite (35–38); he was to receive the same courtesy extended to non-Israelite inhabitants, i.e., residence without landed property. To demand interest from him in any form was prohibited, although such was allowed in the case of a non-Israelite debtor (Dt 23:21).

It was likewise forbidden for Israelites to make slaves of their fellow countrymen (39–43), since the people, like the land, were properly Yahweh's own possession and could not become the property of another. The needy man, remaining free, could become an economic dependent (*tôšāb*)—e.g., by working the land for his keep—or he could become a wage earner (*śākîr*), but only until the time of the jubilee in either case. This law is a modification of earlier legislation, which permitted Israelites to become slaves of their own people, at least for a limited length of time (Ex 21:2–11; Dt 15:12–18). According to vv. 44–46, the Hebrews were allowed slaves of foreign origin procured either outside the country or from among the resident aliens. Such individuals lost their freedom and became personal property to the extent that they could be willed to one's heirs. Since Lv forbade the enslavement of one Israelite to another, there remained the question of a Hebrew who "sold" himself to a resident foreigner (47–55). In such a case, the former was to be treated respectfully as a wage earner (53) and not as a slave. During his time as such, he could be redeemed by either a relative or himself. In the latter case the payment was determined in terms of the years of service left before the next jubilee by a distribution of the original sale price over the years, with proportionate deductions made for past years' services. The cost of redemption depended on the years (many or few) before the next jubilee. If he and his offspring were not liberated beforehand, they were released at the jubilee.

The question arises how these jubilee directives (land return, resolution of debts, liberation of slaves) could have been practically carried out in any advanced state of social development. In truth, the OT records no historical observance of the jubilee. The reference to it in Ez 46:17 (and possibly in Is 61:1–2) is in a future ideal context, which is probably the key to the jubilee itself. Although we cannot exclude the possibility of its being observed in the early years of the land's occupation, its presence in Lv is best explained as a social blueprint, founded on the deeply religious concepts of justice and equality, which strove to apply the simple sabbatical principle to a society that had become more economically complex. It was drawn up and added to the Holiness Code in the period after the Exile. Although not realized in the letter, its spirit of appreciation for personal rights and human dignity synthesizes much of OT teaching and serves as a proximate forerunner of the true equality of the Christian era (Gal 3:26–29).

De Vaux, *AI* 173–77. Gordon, C. H., "Parallèles nouziens aux lois et coutumes de l'Ancien Testament," *RB* 44 [1935] 38–41. Milik, J. T., "De vicissitudinibus notionis et vocabuli jubilaei," *VD* 28 [1950] 162–67. North, R. *Sociology of the Biblical Jubilee* [Rome, 1954].)

54 **(J) Sanctions (26:1–46).** The Code of Holiness terminates with the promise of blessings for fidelity to its precepts (3–13) and punishment for their disregard (14–39), sharing this type of conclusion with the Deuteronomic Code (Dt 28) and the Book of the Covenant (Ex 23:20–33); however, the latter contains only blessings. In this respect the law codes follow the vassal treaty form of the 2nd millennium in which a superior political power concluded the terms of his written agreement with curses and blessings. The apparent dependence in certain ideas and expressions on Ez strongly suggests a later edited form.

A final admonition precedes the benedictions in vv. 1–2, negatively by enjoining avoidance of idolatry in any form and positively by urging recognition of Yahweh's sole dominion through Sabbath observance and respect for his presence among them (19:1–4). The blessings (2–13) center chiefly around fertility of the soil (3–5 and 10), with the abundant yield of the harvest presented in vivid, if exaggerated, imagery (cf. Am 9:13). The people's future is described as a life of peace and accord with the forces of nature and easy victory over their foes (6–8), abundant offspring (9), and crowned with the inestimable blessing of the Lord's presence (12). Such favor is viewed wholly in terms of the Sinai alliance (9b), the outcome of their deliverance from Egyptian bondage (13).

The sanctions for disregard of the law (14–39), more numerous and detailed than the blessings, clearly reflect the chapter's period of composition during Judah's critical last years. The predicted chastisements are set forth in a rising crescendo, in a style similar to that of the Egyptian plagues (Ex 7:14–11:10). A reverse in many ways of the promised blessings, the threats include disease, the destruction of crops by overrunning hordes (16–17), and agricultural failure from lack of rain (18–20). **18.** *sevenfold:* Seven was the perfect number; hence, complete and comprehensive destruction is indicated. There would be also the return of wild beasts to decimate the population and its livestock (21–22). The ominous pace is stepped up with the threatened simultaneous attack of enemy, disease, and famine (23–26). **25.** *the sword, the avenger of my covenant:* We have here the reverse of 9b. Punishment, like favor, was not arbitrary but demanded by the very terms of the covenant. **26.** *ten women will need but one oven:* Ordinarily each family had its own oven; during the catastrophe there would be but one-tenth the normal supply of bread.

Obstinacy in sin launches the final measure (27–35). Famine will reduce them to cannibalism, the consumption of their own offspring (29; Dt 28:53; Jer 19:9; Ez 5:10; 2 Kgs 6:28ff.), and they will suffer a destruction of their sites of pagan cult (30), their cities, and their sanctuaries (31) so frightening as to appal even their invaders (32). Dispersion and exile will be their lot (33). In the actual historical context of the chapter's composition, the disregard of the more primitive sabbatical legislation is noteworthy (34–35; see comment on 25:1–7). The defenseless lot of those dispersed in foreign lands will be one of constant apprehension and terror; finally they will be lost in their pagan surroundings (36–39). Just as their unity as a people hinges on the presence of Yahweh in their midst (cf. 11–13), when he turns his back on them they quickly lose their national identity.

Yet, the punishment will not be terminal but medicinal (40–45). Despite Israel's infidelity, Yahweh will, in the last analysis, remain always true to the covenant made with the patriarchs and faithful to the land, an integral part of the promise (42). Moreover, the abandonment of the land would not be viewed as a chastisement of the sacred soil; this was to be its opportunity for a renewal of its life-giving forces, formerly precluded through disregard of the sabbatical (43). The notion of survival, for at least part of the population, in view of the covenant, is a most important OT theme; its expression here is strikingly similar to Ez 16:53–63. Like the vassal treaties, the Holiness Code closes with this final mention of the covenant and the brief summary of v. 46 (cf. also Dt 28:69).

55 **(VI) Redemption of Votive Offerings (27:1–34).** This appendix modifies a number of its laws in the light of later practice. Any vow carried with it a solemn obligation of fulfillment (Nm 30:2–3; Dt 23:22–24), but gradually in post-exilic times the tendency grew to convert personal and real property commitments into their monetary equivalents. Regulations regarding such commutation are given detailed treatment here.

From early times it was possible to vow a person to the Lord, i.e., to the sanctuary where his services would be used for liturgical ceremonies (1 Sm 1:11). Since, after the Exile, such functions were performed solely by the Levites, it seems to have been customary to redeem persons so dedicated. Such was the normal procedure for the consecrated first-born (Ex 13:2,12–13). Verses 1–8 specify the amount to be paid, and the sum was determined by the person's capacity to work. Thus the highest figure was for a man between 20 and 60 with proportionately descending values placed on a woman, a young man, a young girl, the elderly, and male and female children. The exact worth of a shekel cannot be determined accurately, but the price of a slave was 30 shekels. These determined sums were not invariable; in extenuating circumstances the priest could arrive at a satisfactory figure.

In the case of animal offerings (9–13), a distinction is made between the clean—i.e., fit for sacrifice (see comment on 1:2)—and the unclean animal. In the former case (9–10), the offering made the animal sacred, and no form of exchange or commutation was permitted. If substitution with another animal were attempted, the offerer would suffer the loss of both. In the latter case (11–13), since such were presented simply as a nonsacrificial gift, the priest determined the animal's value to which a 20 per cent tax was affixed if redemption were sought later.

Real property in the form of buildings or land could also be vowed (14–24). The priest determined a house's worth, which served as the exchange price with the added 20 per cent (14–15). In the case of land (16–24), hereditary property was distinguished from that acquired by purchase. Should a man vow part of his patrimony, the field's monetary value would be put at 50 shekels for each portion of the land capable of yielding one homor (about 11 bu.) of barley. The Hebrew of v. 16 reads: "Your valuation shall be in accord with the amount of its seed [crop]; the seed [crop] of a homor of barley at 50 silver shekels." De Vaux contends that if this verse were to be interpreted as a reference to the seed sown, the price of the field would be absurdly low (De Vaux, *AI* 198–99). The customary valuation was in terms of the harvest (cf. 25:16b). Since the consecration was temporary, expiring at the time of the jubilee, the land was assessed at full value only when donated at the beginning of a jubilee period; if donated sometime later the value was determined solely by the prejubilee years remaining (17–18). With the price thus established, the field could be redeemed prior to the jubilee by paying the fixed sum plus an additional one-fifth (19). Priestly rights were protected against transfer of ownership in the interim; if such occurred, all rights of redemption ceased, and at the time of the jubilee the field became the property of the priests (20–21). **21.** *doomed (ḥērem):* It may be read "to separate," "to set aside," "to leave exclusively for the Lord." In its earliest OT use, it was applied to the fruits of war, set aside for the Lord by being destined for doom and destruction. By extension, anything vowed to the Lord could be said to be "doomed." In the case of property acquired (22–24), another man's patrimony could be vowed, with payment made at once to the sanctuary based on the field's estimated value in terms of the remaining prejubilee years. At the time of the jubilee it reverted to the original owner. All monetary transactions were to follow the official Temple standard (25).

Every first-born male animal belonged to the Lord by right (Ex 13:2,12; 34:19; Nm 18:15) and thus could not become the object of a vow (26–27). The clean animals were sacrificed (Nm 18:17), whereas the unclean could be redeemed or sold by the priests. Money is the only term of exchange here, no mention being made of the animal substitution elsewhere allowed in certain cases (Ex 13:13; 34:20).

Likewise the exclusive property of the Lord (in the adverse sense of "doomed," see comment on v. 21) were those persons or things under one's domain with which contact was forbidden, especially idolaters and their goods (Ex 22:19; Dt 13:13–19). Because such evil was worthy of extinction, the malefactors and their goods were to be set aside for the Lord (doomed) and could be neither sold nor redeemed (28–29).

The practice of tithing (30–33) provided for the needs of the Levites (Nm 18:21,24) as well as of the poor (Dt 26:12); this 10 per cent of all farm produce was not considered a voluntary offering. Redemption, however, was permitted for grain and fruit tithes at determined value plus 20 per cent. Only clean animals were taken as tithes. They were chosen by a process of impartial selection, and attempted substitution resulted in the loss of the original and its substitute. Verse 34 is the book's second conclusion (cf. 26:46), an addendum to the appendix linking its material with the Sinai legislation.

5

NUMBERS

Frederick L. Moriarty, S.J.

BIBLIOGRAPHY

1 Binns, L. E., *The Book of Numbers* (WC; London, 1927). Cazelles, H., *Les Nombres* (BJ; 2nd ed.; Paris, 1958). Clamer, A., *Les Nombres* (*PSB;* Paris, 1946) 211–481. Flack, E. E., "Recent Study and the Book of Numbers," *Interpr* 13 (1959) 3–23. Harrelson, W., "The Theology of Numbers," *Interpr* 13 (1959) 24–36. Krämer, K. F., *Numeri* (HBk; Freiburg, 1955). Marsh, J., *The Book of Numbers* (*IB;* N.Y., 1953) 2, 135–308. Moriarty, F. L., *The Book of Numbers*, parts 1 and 2 (PPBS; N.Y., 1960); *Foreword to the Old Testament Books* (Weston, 1954) 21–24. R–T, 207–41. Saydon, P. P., *Numbers* (*CCHS;* N.Y., 1953) 245–60. Schneider, H., *Numeri* (Echter-B; 2nd ed.; Würzburg, 1955); "The Law," *VBW* 1, 201–44. Sullivan, K., "The Book of Numbers," *Worship* 31 (1957) 592–600. Toombs, L., *Nation Making* (BG 4; N.Y., 1962).

INTRODUCTION

2 **(I) Title and Authorship.** The Book of Numbers is the fourth book of the Pentateuch or Law (Torah). Its title in our English Bibles is a direct translation of the Vg "Numeri," which in turn is derived from the LXX *Arithmoi.* In the MT, Nm is called *B^{e}midbar*, "in the wilderness," from the fourth word of the opening verse. Neither the Eng nor the Hebr title gives a wholly adequate idea of the contents of Nm, but each indicates a characteristic of the work. Nm is interested in the census of God's people and shows a concern for arithmetical precision in the matter of sacrificial offerings, the spoils of war, the days required for purification, and the division of territory around the Levitical cities (we name only the most important items). In general, the picture of Israel in Nm leaves us with the impression of a carefully structured and organized religious society moving through history under the sustaining and guiding hand of God.

The Hebr title calls to mind the traditional 40 years of wandering between the Exodus and the entrance into the promised land, the time of testing when God prepared his people, by the rugged discipline of the desert, for entrance into their inheritance. Nm is obviously a transitional work, a connecting link in the epic of Israel's redemption from Egypt and her settlement in Canaan. The Pentateuch is a unified work, dominated by the theme of promise and fulfillment; Nm fits within that general structure, and it can be neither understood nor interpreted apart from what precedes and follows it.

3 Like the other books of the Pentateuch (→ Pentateuch 1:11–16), which both Jewish and Christian traditions attach to the name of Moses, Nm is a compilation of several sources embodying material from different stages of Israel's history. It is even misleading and anachronistic to call Nm a "book" as we understand the term today; we should rather speak of a very complex assemblage of historical, legal, and liturgical traditions spanning a period of approximately 1000 years. Analysis of Nm reveals that the J, E, and P traditions predominate, the last impressing on Nm its own peculiar spirit and character. The J and E traditions in Nm cannot be separated easily; they were probably drawn together, or conflated, shortly after the destruction of Samaria in 721. Both traditions were subject to the editorial control of P, and it is generally agreed that the P tradition has given Nm its final form.

Given the complex character of this collection of traditions, we would be out of place to speak of one man, Moses, as the author of the book, understanding the word "author" in our modern, individualistic sense. Rather, this account is Israel's cherished memory of her past, the recollected traditions of the community that experienced these awesome and saving events. The historical books preserve the living memory of that experience, articulated by a very complex process of divine inspiration.

4 **(II) Historical Value.** Two extremes are to be avoided in any assessment of the historical value of Nm. In the first place, this compilation of ancient traditions does not pretend to give us an accurate, literal record of events exactly as they happened. It was not written according to the standards and ideals of

modern historical scholarship. Therefore, he who hopes to learn in precise detail what happened to the Israelite tribes from the time they encamped about Sinai until they arrived in Canaan approaches the work from a false viewpoint. The Israelites were not capable of writing this kind of history; even if they were, such a documentary account would have been of little interest to them. What mattered to them most was the significance of that history, the disclosure of God's active intervention in time for a supernatural purpose best described by the word "redemption." To the Israelites, history was important because God had acted in it, was acting here and now, and would, in a time known only to him, intervene decisively once again. Since the Israelite could never accept the view that the preservation and development of his people were just simple, natural facts instead of undeserved gifts from God, he could never understand a purely secular viewpoint in history.

On the other hand, we would be incorrect to conclude that the Israelite considered the historical event irrelevant and that only God's message was important. The theological element neither cancels nor distorts the solid foundation of historical fact underlying the biblical traditions. God has saved men by entering into man's history, and it is in the theater of time and space that both Israelite and Christian meet God. Beyond the guarantees accompanying biblical inerrancy, when understood correctly (→ Inspiration, 66:79ff), historical and archaeological results have only enhanced our respect for the substantial historicity of the biblical tradition. Some examples of these results are indicated in the commentary.

5 **(III) Religious Value.** This subject has already been stated broadly in the preceding section. Numbers is primarily concerned with the theological significance of the events narrated. The events focus, not on a heterogeneous grouping of tribes, but on a holy community in whose midst God dwelt. He was the center of these people's lives, despite their persistent infidelities. Here his sanctuary was erected, and the camp was made holy by the divine presence. During the wilderness wanderings God exercised a special care over his people even as he demanded from them absolute obedience to his will as it had been revealed in the sacred Law. God both cared for and tested his people. Many liturgical regulations, cherished by the P tradition, are included in Nm. Most of these prescriptions undoubtedly come from a later period when the people settled in Canaan. An exacting religious calendar and an elaborate sacrificial system scarcely suit a people on the move.

6 We might wonder why this large amount of later legislation was set within the framework of events that had taken place centuries before. The answer is that one could scarcely find a better way of showing that these regulations, although coming centuries after Moses and reflecting conditions in a settled rather than a seminomadic society, were a normal and legitimate extension of the Law given to Israel through Moses. Besides underscoring the continuity of this community, the sacred writer could thereby give divine and Mosaic authority to laws promulgated long after Moses, and meant for the new conditions of life in Canaan. The Law of Moses was to stamp the authentic Israelite life at all periods of her history.

7 **(IV) Outline.** It is difficult to set down a clear and coherent plan for a book that is such a composite. The historical sequence is frequently interrupted by various laws and regulations pertaining to the community. Any outline can only be approximate, but there is general agreement on the following triple division. The sojourn at Sinai (1:1–10:10) covers the last 19 days the Israelites spent at Sinai. Just one month before the date given in Nm 1:1 the people had finished making and setting up the Tabernacle (Ex 40:1,17). The whole section belongs to the P tradition. The second section deals with the travels from Sinai to Moab (10:11–22:1) and covers a span of about 38 years. The bulk of the material, however, concerns the opening and closing months of the period. This is the traditional "forty years" in the wilderness. The third part, events in Moab (22:2–36:13), takes up about five months. Apart from the Balaam cycle, the material is very heterogeneous. The section ends with the Israelites poised on the plains of Moab for the assault on Canaan.

(I) Sojourn at Sinai (1:1–10:10)
- (A) Census of the Tribes and Status of the Levites (1:1–4:49)
- (B) Miscellaneous Laws and Regulations (5:1–6:27)
- (C) Offerings of Princes and Rules for Levites (7:1–8:26)
- (D) Preparations for Departure (9:1–10:10)

(II) From Sinai to Moab (10:11–22:1)
- (A) From Departure to Defeat at Hormah (10:11–14:45)
- (B) Miscellaneous Rules, the Authority of Moses, March to Moab (15:1–22:1)

(III) Events in Moab (22:2–36:13)
- (A) The Story of Balaam (22:2–24:25)
- (B) Various Incidents and Laws (25:1–31:54)
- (C) Topographical Regulations and Miscellaneous Laws (32:1–36:13)

COMMENTARY

(I) Sojourn at Sinai (1:1–10:10).

(A) Census of the Tribes and Status of the Levites (1:1–4:49).

8 (a) All Tribes Except the Levites Are Numbered (1:1–54). **1.** *the second month:* Iyyar extended from mid-April to mid-May. *the Lord said to Moses:* This conventional phrase indicated the divine authority behind Mosaic legislation; God's act of revealing is dramatized through the literary form of a conversation between God and Moses. The "Meeting Tent" (*'ōhel mô'ēd*) appears in the Vg as "tabernacle." Both the meeting tent and the Ark of the Covenant go back to the nomadic period of Israel (see R. de Vaux, *A la rencontre de Dieu* [Fest. Gelin; Le Puy, 1961] 55–70). *the desert of Sinai:* For analysis and description of the three main regions of the Sinai area, see *VBW* 1, 201. **2.** The purpose of the *census* was mainly military. Although Israel had no standing army at this time, it must have had some military organization for self-defense. A census would provide a list of those eligible for service when the clans were summoned to war. There was no such thing as a scientific demographic survey in the ancient world. The inflated numbers reported in vv. 21ff. presuppose a population of several million living in the desert, an impossible figure, as all scholars recognize. Various solutions of the problem have been proposed. Some believe that the writer has incorporated here the list compiled by David's agents when they took the census of Israel and Judah (2 Sm 24). W. F. Albright believes that the two parallel census lists of Nm 1 and 26 are variants of one original list, which is certainly related in some way to the Davidic census of all Israel (see Albright,

ARI 123). There is nothing inherently improbable in such an interpolation; with his keen sense of solidarity, promoted by the liturgy, the Israelite of a much later date thought of himself as being present at Sinai at the decisive moments of Israel's history.

9 Another solution is based on new knowledge of military organization and recruitment practices in the ancient Near East. The key to the solution consists in taking the word *'elep*, translated throughout our text as "thousand," to mean a unit or subsection of the tribe. Our census list, beginning in v. 26, would then give the number of units or subsections into which the tribe was divided and would immediately add the number of men who were capable of bearing arms. This hypothesis may be clearer if we apply it to the text itself, paraphrasing where necessary to bring out the meaning. Numbers 1:26–29 would read as follows:

> Of the descendants of Judah, registered by lineage in clans and ancestral houses: when all the males of twenty years or more who were fit for military service were polled, seventy-four units or subsections of the tribe were recorded and from those units six hundred men were enrolled for military service.
>
> Of the descendants of Issachar, registered by lineage in clans and ancestral houses: when all the males of twenty years or more who were fit for military service were polled, fifty-four units or subsections were recorded and from those units four hundred men were enrolled for military service.

Totaling the census of Nm 1:21–43, we arrive at a figure of 598 units or subsections, contributing 5550 men capable of bearing arms. This explanation is one of several possible alternatives; the merit of this working hypothesis is that it provides a plausible number of warriors and that it resembles other census lists known to have existed in the ancient Near East. (See G. E. Mendenhall, "The Census Lists of Numbers 1 and 26," *JBL* 77 [1958] 52–66).

47. Because of their special status within the community, the Levites (→ Religious Institutions, 76:17, 34) were exempted from the census. Verses 50–51 give the reason, i.e., the sacred duty of caring for the Dwelling, symbol of Yahweh's presence. The wrath of God would be visited upon anyone who violated the sanctity of the divine presence by an act of irreverence. In 3:21–4:49, the duties of the Levites are given in detail.

10 (b) Ordering of the Tribes (2:1–34). According to 10:11–28, the Israelites observed this order when they broke camp and departed from Sinai. The camp was arranged in a huge square with the Tabernacle in the middle. For a similarly stylized description of a restored Jerusalem, see Ez 48:30–35. **2.** The division (*degel*) was a fighting unit occupying a specific position in the military order of the Israelite army. The *degel* comprised a larger number of men than the "company," which was made up of about 100 armed men. The "ensign" was an emblem or device mounted on a wooden staff and carried by a standard-bearer. From the 3rd millennium BC such standards were used for military or ceremonial purposes. They are mentioned in 1QM (see Y. Yadin, *The Scroll of the War of the Sons of Light Against the Sons of Darkness* [Oxford, 1962] 38–49). It would seem that the warriors changed the emblems with each new stage in the battle (see *VBW* 1, 202–203). Contemporary Egyptian reliefs found at Abu Simbel show that the armies of that time observed an order for encampment and marching that resembles the arrangement described in this chapter.

11 (c) Status of the Levites (3:1–51). **1-4.** See Lv 10:1–2; Nm 26:59–61. Since the two oldest sons, Nadab and Abihu, died without heirs in punishment for a crime against the cult, the two youngest sons, Eleazar and Ithamar, inherited their functions as priests. **3.** *the anointed priests:* In some texts, the P tradition restricts the anointing to the high priest; in others, all priests receive the anointing. **9.** *you shall give the Levites to Aaron and his sons:* The "given" ones (n^e*tînîm*) were originally public slaves, probably foreigners, assigned to work in the Temple. This system prevailed during the monarchy. De Vaux suggests that the institution was eventually abandoned and that the work was done by the Levites (De Vaux, *AI* 390). In a later period, reflected in our verse, the Levites were looked upon as "given" to the priests for service in the sanctuary. In 8:16 the Levites are said to be "given" to God rather than to Aaron. **12.** As the first fruits of marriage, the first child belonged to God. God accepted the consecration of the Levites as a substitute for what would be an abomination to him—the sacrifice of a child. **39.** *twenty-two thousand:* This high figure may be interpreted according to our earlier hypothesis to explain the general census. Here, as in the former case, the *'elep* would indicate some kind of population unit within the tribe rather than the "thousand" of our translation.

12 (d) Duties of the Levitical Clans (4:1–49). **2.** *the Kohathites:* They appear to have enjoyed a preeminence among the Levites, possibly because they numbered in their ranks the sons of Amram, father of Moses and Aaron (Ex 6:18,20).

(B) Miscellaneous Laws and Regulations (5:1–6:27). All these regulations are from P; they resemble some of the laws in the Holiness Code of Lv 17–26. But it is in the spirit of Lv 11–15, almost obsessively concerned with ritual purity, that this section has been redacted.

13 (a) Expulsion of the Unclean (5:1–4). The Israelites were enjoined to preserve the purity of their camp. The motive for this drastic action was religious and not merely hygienic. Underlying the rule was the belief that the Israelites might incur divine displeasure by any contact with unclean people. Their disability was considered infectious. The law of the camp in vv. 1–4 is matched by similar rules of purity in 1QM 7:3–7. The NT has its own rules of purity, but it has given them a new spiritual dimension (1 Cor 5:7–13; 2 Cor 6:16–18; Ap 21:27).

14 (b) Rule of Restitution (5:5–10). This rule supplements the law of Lv 5:14–26, the basic law on unjust possession. **8.** *next of kin:* This person was the "redeemer" (*gō'ēl*), a relative obliged to keep property within the family. After restitution was made, the offender was obliged to offer a sacrifice of reparation (*'āšām*). The additional fine, one-fifth the total value, which had to be paid either to the relative or to the priest, did not constitute a part of the sacrifice. *and shall fall to the priest:* An addition to the law in Lv, it stipulated that if there were no kinsman, the restitution would go to the priest as Yahweh's representative.

15 (c) Trial by Ordeal (5:11–31). Leviticus 20:10 decreed the sentence of death where both parties were proven guilty of adultery. Where legal proof was lacking, a way was sought to determine the guilt or innocence of a suspected wife. The priestly legislators have transformed an archaic practice into a ceremony consistent with the Yahwist faith. De Vaux observes that no exact parallel to this ordeal existed in the ancient Near East (De Vaux, *AI* 158). Conversely, we find no trace in Israel of the widely attested practice—in Assyria, Babylonia, and Nuzi—of throwing the suspected person in the river. This ordeal was judicial, mentioned in the Code of Hammurabi (*ANET* 166). The Israelite ritual ascribes punishment of the guilty woman to Yahweh and not to some magical effect of the water she was forced to drink. **15.** *a tenth of an ephah:* The ephah is a

dry measure; the amount here would be about 3.5 qt. **18.** *the bitter water that brings a curse:* If the woman were guilty, the potion would make her barren forever, a frightful punishment in a society placing such a high value on numerous offspring. The water was holy because dust from the floor of the Tabernacle had been sprinkled in it. Uncovering of the head was a sign of shame or mourning. **23.** *put these imprecations in writing:* Using some kind of ink, the priest is to write the curses on a scroll and then dissolve the writing in the water.

16 (d) Rules for the Nazirite (6:1–21). A *nāzîr* was any man or woman consecrated to God for a limited period of time. Nowhere else in the Pentateuch are the Nazirites even mentioned. During the period of consecration, the *nāzîr* could take neither wine nor any other fermented drink; his hair could not be cut, and all contact with a corpse was forbidden. The regulations in Nm codify a very ancient practice and adapt it to the Levitical ritual. Instead of a consecration for life, this set of rules reduced the commitment to a temporary vow. In the story of Samson (Jgs 13:2–7) the consecration was for life. As late as the NT period we hear of Christians taking the Nazirite vow for a limited period of time (Acts 21:23–26). Note that the laws in chs. 5 and 6 slow the narrative pace of Nm, but these insertions have been made for a purpose. The author, by sandwiching in a body of legislation, most of which is later than the time of Moses, gives these rules a special divine sanction by attaching them to the literature of the legislator par excellence, Moses. **3.** *wine and strong drink:* All intoxicating beverages are included. The text mentions "wine vinegar" because the Hebrews made a wine from grapes that had become sour. **5.** The hair was a sign of strength. Uncut hair became the characteristic sign of the Nazirite, and the untrimmed vine was known as a "Nazirite vine" (Lv 25:5,11). There may be some relation between this feature of the vow and the ritual of holy war in which the fighters let their hair grow (Jgs 5:2, in some translations). **10.** *two turtledoves or two pigeons:* This offering was the least expensive kind of animal sacrifice (Lv 12:8). **18.** *collect the hair, and put it in the fire:* It is very unlikely that this act was sacrificial, like the hair offerings of primitive peoples.

17 (e) The Priestly Blessing (6:22–27). This beautiful prayer was used by the priests when they blessed the people. **25.** *let his face shine upon you:* The act is a sign of the divine pleasure. The word for "be gracious" (*ḥānan*) occurs often in Pss. Psalm 66:2 closely resembles this blessing. (See L. J. Liebreich, "The Songs of Ascent and the Priestly Blessing," *JBL* 74 [1955] 33–36.)

(C) Offerings of Princes and Rules for Levites (7:1–8:26).

18 (a) Offerings of the Princes (7:1–89). This chapter is one of the longest in the Bible, and it would seem as if the priestly writers were attempting to stimulate the Israelites to make offerings to the Temple as their fathers of old had done for the Dwelling. **2.** "Prince" (*nāśî'*) was the title given the leaders of the Israelite tribes during the desert sojourn. Noth believes that the *nāśî'* was the tribal representative at the amphictyonic assembly of the 12 tribes. (Noth, *Hist.* 98). He suggests that the word means "speaker." Midianite leaders (Nm 25:8; Jos 13:21) used the same title. Genesis 17:20 speaks of Ishmael becoming the "father of twelve princes," a striking parallel to Israelite tribal organization. The office corresponds closely with that of the sheik among modern Arabs. **13.** *weighing a hundred and thirty shekels:* This amount would be about 60 oz. The shekel was the basic unit of weight, the noun being derived from the verb "to weigh" (*šāqal*). The shekel was common to all Semitic systems of weight and had to conform to some official standard, in this case the "sanctuary" standard (Ex 30:13; Lv 5:15). Verses 12–88 tabulate, in the manner of an official registration, what each of the tribal princes brought for an offering. **89.** Chapter 7 ends with an isolated fragment describing the entrance of Moses into the place where God had promised to speak to the people (Ex 25:22; 33:9–11). For the "propitiatory," see Ex 25:17–22.

19 (b) Miscellaneous Rules (8:1–26). **2.** *the seven lamps:* See the description in Ex 25:31–40 and Lv 24:2–4. Josephus (*Ant.* 3.6,7) says that the seven lamps represented the sun, moon, and planets, constantly reminding the Israelite of Yahweh's creative power. **7.** *the water of remission:* This "water of sin" was used for expiating guilt. The rules for purifying the Levites should be compared with those concerning the priests (Lv 8). Such comparison shows that the priests were superior to the Levites. Priests were sanctified; Levites were cleansed. Greater care was taken in preparing the priest for his functions. The Levites, however, were sharply distinguished from the Israelite laity just as the ordinary Israelite was distinguished from the non-Israelite.

20 **24.** In this section, the limits of Levitical service were fixed between the ages of 25 and 50, as against Nm 4:3, which sets the limits between 30 and 50. Both of these regulations resemble those of 1QS. The candidate for membership in the Qumran sect became a full-fledged member of the community at the age of 25. At 30, he could plead cases and serve in the militia. The "Manual of Discipline" (1QS) may help us to resolve the discrepancy between Nm 4:3 and 8:2. Numbers recognized that community service began at 25, but fully active service in the sanctuary and in the militia began only at 30. **25.** Despite a compulsory retirement age, the Levite "emeritus" could still volunteer his services to his younger colleagues, especially in lighter tasks.

(D) Preparations for Departure (9:1–10:10).

21 (a) A Second Passover (9:1–14). The general regulations for the celebration of Passover are given in Ex 12, which belongs to P. Ceremonial defilement through contact with a corpse disqualified some of the Israelites; they received permission to celebrate Passover one month later. The privilege was extended to those who were traveling and thus could not celebrate Passover at the same time as the others. Sharing in this rite was important, for it was the Israelite's way of participating in the historical event of deliverance through which Israel became the people of Yahweh. By its celebration, the Israelite established his own identity.

The concession of a later celebration was granted for two specific cases; the incident appears to reflect conditions after the Exile when a new situation was created by the constantly growing Diaspora. Jewish communities were now established in Babylon and elsewhere; a more liberal policy for celebrating the Passover was necessary for those who had to travel great distances. The resident alien enjoyed the same privilege and was bound by the same law as the native Israelite. **3.** *the evening twilight of the fourteenth day of this month:* See Lv 23:5. The priestly tradition required that the Passover lamb be slaughtered on the fourteenth of Nisan between the time that the sun went down and darkness fell. This twilight period is very short in the Near East. The meat of the sacrifice had to be roasted and eaten on this same night. **14.** As well as the free citizen and the foreign traveler, who could depend on the laws of hospitality, the "resident alien" (*gēr*) was also accepted by the community and protected by its laws. He was obliged to celebrate the Sabbath and the fast on Yom Kippur (Day of Atonement). He could offer sacrifices, participate in religious festivals, and above all, celebrate Passover with the rest of the Israelites.

22 (b) The Fiery Cloud (9:15–23). **15.** The P document prefers the name "Dwelling" (*miškān*) for the Tabernacle. The word originally described a nomad's tent. Thus, P expressed belief in God's presence on earth as well as in heaven. The *miškān* theology laid the groundwork for the later Jewish theology of the Shekinah, which is reflected in Jn 1:14. *but from evening until morning it took on the appearance of fire:* During the day it was a cloud, whereas it glowed at night, functioning as the pillar of fire (J tradition) that had guided the Israelites in their march through the wilderness. The cloud now directed the movements of the people; when it descended they encamped, and when it rose from the tent they marched. The impression is of a community under the constant guidance of its God.

23 (c) The Silver Trumpets (10:1–10). The last item in the Israelites' preparation for the departure from Sinai was the order to fashion two trumpets of hammered silver. Examples of such instruments appear on the memorial Arch of Titus at the entrance to the Roman Forum. The "trumpet" was a long, tubular instrument, flared at one end. It was useful for giving signals in war because its strident metallic tone could be heard above the din of battle. In the Egypt of the new kingdom, and elsewhere in the ancient Near East, trumpets were commonly used for ceremonial and military purposes. **5.** The "alarm" was a war cry that belonged to the ritual of the Ark of the Covenant, carried into battle by the Israelite warriors. It was a fierce shout, meant to encourage the fighters and throw the enemy into panic. **9.** *when in your own land you go to war against an enemy:* The 1QM cites this verse in its regulations about holy war, understood by the covenanters as the final, apocalyptic struggle between good and evil. The parallels between 1QM and the biblical material have been fully discussed by Y. Yadin (*op. cit.*).

(II) From Sinai to Moab (10:11–22:1).

(A) From Departure to Defeat at Hormah (10:11–14:45).

24 (a) Israel Leaves Sinai (10:11–36). **11.** *in the second year:* About 11 months after they arrived at Sinai the Israelites broke camp and set out on their journey to the promised land. The rising cloud was the signal for the departure. **12.** *the desert of Paran:* This area is the dry and forbidding wilderness to the S and SE of Kadesh. The tribes on the march observed the order described in Nm 2, but in this section the clans of Gershon and Merari were allowed to precede the Reubenites to prepare a place for the meeting at the new camping site. **29.** The Midianites were related to the Kenites, in whose land Moses received his call. They preserved some kind of relationship with the Israelites as late as the time of Saul (Jgs 1:16; 1 Sm 15:6). The invitation of Moses is one of the earliest examples of Israel's willingness to share the blessings promised by God with strangers. It was also true, of course, that Hobab was completely at home in this area and knew the desert tracks as did few others. Since there were very few oases in the Sinai region, and those known only to the nomads of that place, Hobab's service as a guide would have been virtually indispensable. With good reason it was said of him: "You will serve as eyes for us" (31). Even today, Bedouins often call a guide the "eye of the caravan." The conversation with Hobab breaks off and we do not know his answer to Moses' plea. Judges 1:16 would suggest that Hobab finally acceded to the request, but we are not certain. **35.** *arise, O Lord, that your enemies may be scattered:* This sentence is a fragment of an ancient poem connected with the liturgy of the Ark. It preserves the oldest tradition in the Pentateuch linking the Ark with the movements of Yahweh (→ Religious Institutions, 76:46–48). **36.** *return, O Lord:* This invocation is given after the victory. The image of Yahweh riding on the clouds is very similar to the Canaanite image of Baal, the cloud rider (cf. Ps 68:5).

25 (b) Complaints in the Wilderness (11:1–35). **1.** The motif of "murmuring" occurs frequently in the desert narratives. **3.** Taberah means "burning." The short account is meant to explain how the place got its name. The use of a story to explain an ancient name or place is called "etiology." (For a concise explanation and evaluation of the etiological principle, see Albright, *FSAC* 70–72.) The exact location of Taberah is unknown; Dt 9:22 places it in the region of Kadesh-barnea. **4.** *the foreign elements among them:* The Hebrews who left Egypt did not comprise a homogeneous body. The OT preserves a strong tradition on Israel's mixed origins. Here, the reference is to groups that associated themselves with the Mosaic movement without bringing to it the normative patriarchal tradition that other clans had brought. Being a missionary religion, Yahwism was ready to assimilate foreign elements without, however, tolerating the retention of pagan practices. **6.** The *manna* was probably that sweet and sticky substance excreted by insects sucking the sap from tamarisk bushes. This kind of edible material is still found in the central valleys of Sinai, especially in June and July. The Arabs spread it on bread. (Cf. F. S. Bodenheimer, "The Manna of Sinai," *BA* 10 [1947] 2–6; A. De Guglielmo, "What Was the Manna?" *CBQ* 2 [1940] 112–29.) **8.** *grind it between millstones:* In Palestine, flour was prepared from grain either by grinding or pounding. The miller used an upper and lower millstone for grinding, and the grain was worked until it became a powder that could be kneaded. Pounding meant the use of mortar and pestle. Many examples of millstones, mortars, and pestles have been found on excavated sites. These instruments were usually made of black basalt.

26 **12.** *was it I who conceived all this people?* The pronoun "I" is strongly emphasized by the syntax of the sentence. It was God who had brought about the Exodus, and his was the responsibility of caring for the people. The image of the *foster father* carrying the child is an especially tender one. Both BJ and RSV translate our "foster father" ('*ōmēn*) as "nurse." **17.** *I will also take some of the spirit that is on you:* The 70 will share Moses' authority. For a similar passing on of a great man's spirit to his successor, see 2 Kgs 2:9. **25.** *they prophesied:* The Hebrew *yitnabbeʾû* is the technical word for exercising the prophetic charism (→ Prophetic Lit, 12:8–14). The person endowed with the charism often manifested some abnormal state such as trance, frenzy, or rapture. **31.** Every autumn, great flocks of quail migrate from Europe to the warmer climate of Africa. After their long flight over the Mediterranean they often drop exhausted on the land and are easily captured. **34.** Kibroth-hattaavah means "graves of craving." In Dt 9:22 the incident is located near Kadesh-barnea. **35.** *Hazeroth:* It may be modern Ain Khudra, a small oasis NE of Sinai.

27 (c) Complaints of Aaron and Miriam (12:1–16). **1.** Cush usually refers to Ethiopia, but it may indicate a part of N Arabia (Hab 3:7); it is possible that the woman was Zipporah of Midian (Ex 2:21). **2.** The marriage to a foreign woman was only a pretext for grumbling, the real reason being Moses' position as unique mediator between Yahweh and the people. Miriam's claim was not totally unfounded, since she was called a "prophetess" in Ex 20:15. **3.** *the meekest man:* He was one of the "pious" ('*ănāwîm*) who lived a humble and God-fearing life. The term occurs frequently in Pss. It should not be confused with weakness. Moses' awareness of his own limitations is indicated in Ex 3:11;

4:10–13. **8.** *face to face:* Also "mouth to mouth," the metaphor suggests the directness and immediacy of God's dealing with Moses. He alone could "see the face of God" and not die (Ex 33:20). **14.** *spit in her face:* This act was not only a grave insult (Dt 25:9) but also a curse.

28 (d) RECONNOITERING THE LAND (13:1–33). The spies were to collect as much information as possible about the people and the land, its strength and weakness. This sort of military intelligence is always sought by army commanders on the eve of invasion. The priestly tradition carefully notes the selection of one "leader" (*nāśî'*) from each tribe, in accord with the priestly ideal of orderliness. **17.** *the Negeb:* The name applies generally to the wilderness S of Judah. Since 1952, it has been systematically mapped by the American archaeologist Nelson Glueck (see *Rivers in the Desert: A History of the Negeb* [N.Y., 1959]). **19.** *open or fortified?:* In this briefing of the spies, "open" refers to encampments outside the walls; such settlements were an easy prey for invaders. The term may also refer to the quarters in sites like those of Hazor and Carchemish, where a large lower quarter, surrounded by an earthen wall, spread out from the foot of the fortified citadel above. **20.** *is the soil fertile or barren, wooded or clean?:* The terrain of Palestine presents many contrasts. The soil of the coastal plain is fertile and there is little problem with water; the lowlands of the Shephelah have always been renowned for their vineyards and olive groves. In ancient times, the central mountain ridge was covered with trees and was interlaced with some of the richest valleys in the country. In contrast to this fertile territory were the arid lands of the Negeb, the wilderness of Judah, and much of the Jordan Valley. The spies set out during the second half of July, "the season for early grapes."

21. The spies proceeded directly N from Paran, crossed the desert of Zin, which is SW of the Dead Sea, and went to the extreme N of Palestine. This point was known as "the entrance to Hamath." It lies in the lush valley known today as the Beqaʿ and is due E of Byblos. Apparently the spies confined their attention chiefly to the central hill country, moving along the high road that followed the Palestinian watershed. **22.** Hebron is about 20 mi. S of Jerusalem, in good vine-producing country. The Anakim appear in the Egyptian execration texts as a rebel tribe that troubled the Egyptians around the 19th cent. BC (*ANET* 328). The parenthetical remark associates the founding of Hebron with that of Zoan, the Hyksos capital (Gk Tanis) in the eastern part of the Nile Delta. Both Hebron and Zoan were established *ca.* 1720 BC. **23.** Eshcol means "cluster [of grapes]"; the valley was located near Hebron. **27.** *flow with milk and honey:* In J and D, the phrase is a conventional expression for great fertility. **29.** The Amalekites, nomads of the desert S of Judah, were enemies of the Israelites (Ex 17:8–16). **31.** There is little wonder that the ill-trained and poorly equipped Israelites were terrified at the fortified cities of Canaan. Excavations show that these towns often had massive walls from 30 to 50 ft. high and 15 ft. or more thick. The effect upon seminomadic people can well be imagined. Caleb filed a minority report (30). **32.** *that consumes its inhabitants:* The land does not produce enough to sustain life. This report, from P, does not coincide with the report of J and E (27–30). Some scholars suggest that the report, with its reference to "consuming," implies cannibalism on the part of the natives, but there is no evidence to support this conjecture. **33.** Anthropology provides no evidence that men of unusual stature lived in Palestine during this period; however, the reason for the tradition is fairly clear. The existing dolmens and the size and strength of the Canaanite fortresses suggest that only giants could have built them. We find this same idea among the Greeks, who reported that the huge walls of their ancient cities had been built by the Cyclopes, giant artisans from Asia Minor. This tradition has led to the expression "Cyclopean" masonry, to describe the huge blocks used in constructing some ancient cities.

29 (e) THREATS OF REVOLT AND ANGER OF YAHWEH (14:1–45). **6.** *tore their garments:* This expression of grief is common in the Near East. **9.** "Food" (*leḥem*) is mentioned here possibly as a direct answer to the alarmist report of 13:32, couched in the same idiom; or, possibly Caleb means that the people of the land will be beaten as easily as one eats bread. *their defense:* The literal translation is "their shadow," suggesting the picture of rocks offering shade in a very hot country. Because their gods have deserted them, they have no defense. Yahweh is Israel's "rock" (Dt 32:4). **13.** Moses speaks as though the honor of God were at stake. Should Yahweh destroy the people as a punishment, the Canaanites, hearing the report, would conclude that he was an impotent God and could never drive them out of their land. **18.** *the Lord is slow to anger and rich in kindness:* For the same self-revelation of God's nature, see Ex 34:6–7. "Slow to anger, patient" is, lit., "long of face" (*'erek 'appayim*). See Prv 14:29, where it is contrasted with "quick-tempered." "Kindness" (*ḥesed*) is one of the most important theological terms in the OT; "covenant loyalty" is perhaps the best translation (A. R. Johnson in *Fest. S. Mowinckel* [Oslo, 1955] 100–112). *to the third and fourth generation:* Family solidarity, in both good and evil, is a fundamental OT concept. It was only later that a more individualistic approach to reward and punishment was taken. The children were conceived as extensions of the personality of the family head. The whole family made up a corporate personality, which was rewarded or punished as a group.

25. *set out in the desert on the Red Sea road:* Because they had grumbled against Yahweh, the Israelites were not allowed to enter Canaan by the direct route. They had to make a detour S as far as modern Eilat, at the head of the Gulf of Eilat, called "the Reed Sea" (*yam sûp*) in this verse. A glance at a map of the Exodus will show the direction of the march, although it should be remembered that modern scholars differ in detail in their reconstruction of the itinerary. (On this point, it is interesting to compare the Exodus maps of two excellent modern atlases: *WHAB* 41, plate 5; *AtBib* 44, map 9.) **33.** *must wander for forty years:* Only Joshua and Caleb would survive the long wilderness wanderings. They would lead the people into the land (26:65). **44.** *yet they dared to go up into the foothills:* The Israelites ignored the divine sentence and decided to enter Canaan the short way, through the Negeb to Arad, and finally into the hill country of southern Judah. The attempt to force an entrance into Canaan was thrown back by the natives who controlled the "foothills" that lie E of Beer-sheba and give access to Judah. For a parallel account of the same abortive invasion, see Dt 1:41–45. **45.** *as far as Hormah:* The Hebrews fell back to Hormah, "destruction," a royal Canaanite city (Jos 12:14) in southern Judah. Although its exact location is unknown, modern Tell Malḥata (el-Milḥ), between Arad and Beer-sheba, may be the site.

(B) Miscellaneous Rules, the Authority of Moses, March to Moab (15:1–22:1).

30 (a) OFFERINGS JOINED TO SACRIFICES (15:1–41). Again the narrative is interrupted by a series of regulations concerning sacrifice, the Sabbath-breaker, and the wearing of tassels on the corners of garments. The rules are to apply only after the people have entered the land. Three kinds of sacrifices should be distinguished in this passage: the animal sacrifice, the cereal offering, and the libation. These laws complement the legislation found in Lv 1–3. **5.** *fourth of a hin:* The quantity is about 1 qt. (For capacity measures, see De Vaux, *AI* 199–203.) **32.** *was discovered gathering wood:* It was forbidden to light a fire on the Sabbath. This sin was apparently not committed unwittingly. **34.** *there was no clear decision:* The statement is strange in view of the laws in Ex 31:12–17; 35:1–3, where the death penalty was decreed for a Sabbath violator. Later Jewish commentators saw the discrepancy and resolved the difficulty by claiming that Ex did not specify the way in which the capital sentence was to be carried out. **38.** "Tassels" were intended to aid remembrance (39). In the NT period, they were worn by all observant Jews, including Our Lord (Mt 9:20), but he condemned affectation connected with this custom (Mt 23:5).

31 (b) REBELLION WITHIN THE RANKS (16:1–17:28). Two revolts against the authority of Moses are combined here. A careful reading of the text permits us to discern the differences between the revolt of Korah (P) and the revolt of the Reubenites Dathan and Abiram (J and E). Most critics divide the narrative as follows: (a) Revolt of Korah, 1a, 2b–11, 16–24, 27a, 35; (b) revolt of Dathan and Abiram, 1b–2, 12–15, 25–34. In the first few verses of ch. 16, both stories have been fused. We shall consider them separately. **1.** Does this genealogy of Korah mean that there were only three generations between the patriarchal and Mosaic ages? It would seem not, for these and similar genealogies do not preserve accurate information regarding the ancestral line prior to the conquest of Canaan; they designate the clan and tribe to which the man belonged. In this case, we would simply have the information that a certain Korah ben-Isaar was a member of the Caath clan within the tribe of Levi. (See D. N. Freedman, "The Chronology of Israel," *The Bible and the Ancient Near East* [N.Y., 1961] 206–207.) **3.** *the whole community, all of them, are holy:* The malcontents appealed to a tradition based on Ex 19:6 and similar passages. Korah and his followers were, first of all, protesting the selection of certain leaders to approach Yahweh. Why could not everyone come near to Yahweh at his altar? Moses' answer to this first challenge is found in 5–7, inviting the rebels to a kind of trial by ordeal. The outcome is described in 16:35. **10.** *and yet you now seek the priesthood too:* This was the second challenge of Korah and his band; they claimed a share in the priesthood as distinct from Levitical duties. De Vaux observes that the Korahites "were always the same, full of intrigue, battling their way forward, first as doorkeepers, then as singers, and finally even usurping Priestly functions" (De Vaux, *AI* 393). **12.** *Dathan and Abiram:* The leaders of a second revolt, they complained that Moses had misled the people by bringing them out of Egypt, here described as a land "flowing with milk and honey." This revolt was of laymen, whereas that of Korah was a religious protest against the leadership of Moses. In both cases, the authority of the great lawgiver was jeopardized. **33.** *they went down alive to the nether world:* The "nether world," or Sheol was the subterranean dwelling place of the dead. It is difficult to determine precisely what happened on this occasion, but the narrative implies that death was sudden and extraordinary. The death of family and relatives along with Dathan and Abiram underscores the ancient Semitic principle of solidarity in guilt. All who were associated with the guilty one shared in the punishment. **35.** *and fire from the Lord came forth:* This statement concludes the priestly narrative of Korah's rebellion. The leader is not mentioned, but we may assume he died with his followers (26:10). (See G. Hort, "The Death of Qorah," *AusBR* 7 [1959] 2–26.)

32 17:2. *remove the censers:* Since they had been touched by the divine fire, these censers, or incense shovels, could no longer be put to profane use. Even the coals of fire had to be scattered. **3.** *plates to cover the altar:* Exodus 27:1–8 describes the altar of holocausts. Bronze plates were fastened over the planks from which the altar was made. It was therefore occasionally called the "bronze altar." The covering was a perpetual reminder and warning that no one but the priests should approach the altar of Yahweh. **10.** *that I may consume them at once:* Wisdom 18:20–25 comments, in midrashic form, on this episode, glorifying both the mercy of God and the intercessory power of Aaron. Usually atonement was made by means of blood; here Aaron atones by the same kind of instrument used in the ordeal, an incense shovel (16:35). **20.** "Staff" (*maṭṭeh*) means both "staff" and "tribe." The family of Aaron is symbolized by the staff, or rod. The incident was meant to teach the preeminence of the house of Aaron and tribe of Levi over the rest of the Israelites, and it is another indication of the persisting tension between the Levites and the secular tribes. **23.** *ripe almonds:* The overnight blossoming of the staff was characteristic of the almond branch, which could also symbolize the swift coming of divine judgment (Jer 1:12). The beautiful white and pink blossoms of the almond tree sometimes appeared even during winter, carrying the promise of a spring which could not be too far off. **27.** *we are perishing; we are lost:* The frightened people now realize that access to the Lord could bring them mortal danger.

33 (c) DUTIES AND DUES OF PRIESTS AND LEVITES (18:1–32). **1.** *the Lord said to Aaron:* Only here, in giving these instructions, and in Lv 10:8, does God address Aaron alone and directly. In almost all cases divine instructions came through Moses. *you and your sons:* To the hereditary priesthood went the care of altar and sanctuary. The Levites were to assist in this task, but they were not to touch the altar or sacred vessels under threat of death to both priests and Levites. **4.** *but no layman shall come near you:* This prohibition could be taken as an answer to the question raised in 17:28. **5.** *that wrath may not fall again upon Israelites:* Priests and Levites were responsible for seeing that no unauthorized people approached the altar. **9.** *oblations that are most sacred:* These offerings were not consumed upon the altar of sacrifice, but only the male members of the priestly families could eat them. **11.** *wave offering:* This offering could be eaten by the priests, their wives, or any members of their family, provided they had no ceremonial impurity, which would prevent them from partaking. **14.** *whatever is doomed:* Signified is anything that has been voluntarily "devoted" to God. What was devoted or dedicated was set aside from profane use, for it was sacred to Yahweh. **19.** *inviolable covenant:* The literal translation is "a covenant of salt." The use of salt as a symbol of inviolability comes either from the belief that men were mutually bound when they ate salt together or from the idea that salt was a preservative (Mt 5:13) and thus a sign of perpetuity. **21.** The Levites, like the priests, were obliged to obtain their livelihood from service at Yahweh's altar. A "tithe" is 10 per cent of a man's income. **26.** *a tithe of the tithes:* The Levites were obliged to give 10 per cent of what they had received to the priests. Levites were then free to use their income as they wished.

34 (d) RITE OF THE RED HEIFER, AND RULES FOR CLEANSING (19:1–22). **2.** *red heifer:* This animal had to be without blemish and one that had never been used for ordinary secular purposes. **3.** To safeguard the ritual purity of Aaron, the beast was handed over to Eleazar. A layman slaughtered the beast in his presence, and while the whole carcass was being burned, the priest threw cedar wood, hyssop, and scarlet yarn into the fire. **9.** The ashes were set aside until they were used in the preparation of lustral water. The holy water was prepared by putting the ashes in a jar and then pouring in water taken directly from a fresh stream or spring. Originally, this practice was undoubtedly a pagan rite with magical overtones. Red color was thought to be helpful in averting evil. The rite was taken over by the Israelites and assimilated into the priestly ritual. In Heb 9:13, this rite and the other rites of the Old Law are contrasted with the efficacy of the blood of Christ. **11.** The lustral water served to purify anyone who had contracted ritual impurity by touching a corpse, bones, or even a tomb. The house and furnishings of a dead man could also be purified by sprinkling this water on them. **15.** Were a vessel tightly closed, it would escape defilement. In the excavations at Hazor, a vessel was found with a lid held on tightly by cords passing through holes made in it and then through the loop handles of the jar. As far as we can judge from ancient texts (Gn 46:4; 50:1), the Hebrews did not originally believe that one was defiled by contact with a corpse. This archaic rite of the ashes of the red heifer appears, then, to have existed side by side with the official religion, which saw no impurity in contact with the dead. Eventually the rite was incorporated into priestly legislation and thus became normative for all Israelites (see De Vaux, *AI* 462).

35 (e) THE JOURNEY RESUMED (20:1–29). The narrative of the journey was interrupted at the end of ch. 14. According to Nm 13:26, the Israelites had reached Kadesh many years before. Very likely the events narrated in chs. 13–14 took place at the beginning of the settlement around Kadesh. The present chapter brings us to the end of that sojourn, about 40 years later. What is told now, therefore, probably pertains to the end of their long stay at Kadesh.

1. Numbers 34:3 and Jos 15:1 affirm that the desert of Zin reached as far as the border of Edom and formed the southern border of Canaan. It therefore cut across the entire Negeb and included a territory that archaeological evidence proves was heavily settled at the turn of the 2nd millennium. It would be along this terrain that the caravans of Abraham would have moved from Canaan to Egypt and back. After a long period of abandonment, this same territory was repopulated during the time of the dual monarchy in Israel-Judah. *the first month:* We have no information as to the day or year; therefore, the chronological indication remains uncertain. Part of the text may have been lost. **2.** *they held a council against Moses and Aaron:* This incident is paralleled in Ex 17:1–17. At the end of the story it adds an explanation, somewhat obscure, as to why Moses and Aaron were not allowed to lead the people into the promised land. **5.** *here there is not even water to drink:* During this period, the 13th cent., the region of Zin was only sparsely settled, and irrigation systems of an earlier day lay crumbled on the sand. An adequate water supply for themselves and their cattle would have been a constant problem for the Israelites. Moses and Aaron are, as usual, the scapegoats. **8.** *take the staff:* The staff was probably the "rod" of Aaron (17:25), which had miraculously budded. **12.** *because you were not faithful to me:* At this point, a puzzling incident took place. God suddenly became angry with Moses and Aaron. How did they offend God? Some commentators suggest that the story is incomplete and has omitted some serious offense out of deference to the lawgiver. But this solution is desperate and from silence. Others suggest that Moses showed a certain lack of faith by striking the rock twice, a conclusion hardly better than the first attempt at a solution. A way out of the difficulty may be found by setting the incident in the larger context of God's dealing with his people during the wilderness wandering.

36 We should recall that on many occasions God had gone to great lengths to manifest to his people his mastery over nature. This crisis in the desert provided another excellent opportunity to manifest that control. God would order Moses to strike the rock and water would gush forth. Once again the people would have proof of God's unfailing providence—in this case, by the timeliest of signs! Instead of carrying out this divine plan of mercy, Moses and Aaron used the occasion to upbraid the people. The address in 10 shows both anger and sarcasm. Still burning with anger, Moses struck the rock, and the water flowed out. But by that time the two leaders had changed the whole character of the event as it was intended by God. Instead of making the occasion a joyful manifestation of God's effortless control over nature, they had turned it into a scene of bitter denunciation. In the biblical phrase of 12, they had failed to "show forth my sanctity," i.e., to glorify and hallow God's name before the people. Under these circumstances we can better understand the severe punishment. (See E. Arden, "How Moses Failed God," *JBL* 76 [1957] 50–52.) **13.** Meribah means "strife" or "contention." The parallel account is Ex 17:1–7. **14.** *Moses sent men to the king of Edom:* The Israelites had already made an unsuccessful attempt to invade Canaan from the S (14:45). They now planned an assault from the E. They therefore needed to pass through the territory of Edom for which permission was now requested. In the Near East it is still customary for tribes to ask for passage through another's territory. *your brother Israel:* The Edomites were descended from Esau, so that they stood in some form of kinship with the Israelites. In this case, the ties were apparently not strong enough to dispel the suspicion that such a grant might be dangerous to the Edomites. **16.** The mention of an *angel* is characteristic of the E tradition (Ex 3:2; 14:19; 23:20; 33:2). **17.** *royal road:* This route was known as the King's Highway, a famous caravan route, which ran from N to S and bisected the land of Edom. **18.** *you shall not pass through:* Edom's answer was curt and final. To back up the refusal, they mobilized a considerable force, obliging Israel to make a detour around their land.

37 **22.** *the whole Israelite community came to Mount Hor:* Most modern commentators identify Mt. Hor with Jebel el Madra, an impressive limestone peak in the middle of the Nahal Zin (Wadi Fikra). But no trace of ancient remains has been found there, neither settlements nor graves. The selection of Jebel el Madra, aside from its prominence, has been made on the assumption that the Israelites, leaving Kadesh, headed toward the Arabah. But the biblical tradition, when closely studied, does not support this view. Rather, Mt. Hor is connected in some way with the journey from Kadesh to Arad. In both Nm 21:1 and 33:40, the battle with the king of Arad is mentioned immediately after Mt. Hor. The road from Kadesh to Arad ran N, and it is not out of place to mention the Israelite fortresses (of a later period) and watchtowers discovered by Nelson Glueck along this same route. Mount Hor is described in 20:23 as "on the border of the land of Edom," indicating that it was not too far from Kadesh, which, in 20:16, is said to be "at the edge of your [Edom's] territory." Glueck's expedition believes that it has located this sacred mountain, discernible from some distance in the plain between Bir Hafir and Beerotaim. Many years ago, Père Abel had proposed this same area as the site of Mt. Hor. (See B. Rothenberg, *God's Wilderness* [N.Y., 1962] 141.) **26.** *then strip Aaron of his garments:* This action symbolized the transfer of priestly power from Aaron to his son. The garments of the high priest are described in Lv 8:7–9. From the Semitic viewpoint, the clothes were really a part of a man's personality. In receiving them, Eleazar would be inheriting the priestly characteristics of Aaron. **28.** The sign of Aaron's death was the return of Moses and Eleazar, newly clad in the vestments of his father. **29.** *thirty days:* The mourning for Moses lasted the same length of time (Dt 34:8).

38 (f) VICTORIES ALONG THE WAY (21:1–22:1). Chapters 21–25 are a combination of J and E. **1.** The incident at Arad is an insertion, interrupting the sequence of events. Verse 21:4 follows naturally after 20:29. The name of Arad survives to this day in a very large tell or mound E of Beer-sheba. Pottery found at the site proves that it was first settled in the 4th millennium, or Chalcolithic Age. The site was occupied in the Canaanite period, as we would expect from our narrative, and habitation continued into the Israelite period. The king probably headed a coalition of several Canaanite towns in the region. **3.** The short notice of Arad's engaging Israel in battle and taking some captives is immediately followed by a description of Israel's victory over the Canaanites, after the vow to "consecrate" the spoils of war to Yahweh. It is very probable that a century intervened between the two skirmishes. For another version of Israel's victory, see Jgs 1:16–18. Note the significant phrase: "Later, when the Lord heeded Israel's prayer..." The close linking of defeat by, and victory over, the same enemy, with a telescoping of the time element, brings home very vividly the seesaw struggle that went on for many years between Canaanites and Israelites. The narrative of the journey from Kadesh to Moab resumes after the brief interruption, in v. 4. **6.** The serpents were venomous; because their bite caused inflammation, they were called "fiery" (*śārāp*). **9.** *Moses accordingly made a bronze serpent:* Archaeology has shown that the cult of the snake was widely practiced in Canaan, probably in connection with fertility rites. A bronze snake has been found in the excavations of Lachish; it dates from the Late Bronze Age, about the same time as the Exodus. Moses could easily have learned to make such an image from his Kenite relatives, metalsmiths by profession (the name "Kenite" means "smith"). It is also significant that the incident took place in the vicinity of Punon (33:42), one of the great copper sources in ancient times. The cure certainly looks like a case of sympathetic magic, but J takes care to inform the reader that it was Yahweh who healed. John 3:14–16 alludes to this incident as a prefigurement of Christ's own death. The bronze serpent never became a permanent feature of Israelite cult. Hezekiah broke it in pieces and extirpated a cult that was considered an abuse (2 Kgs 18:4).

39 **10.** *Oboth:* Its location is uncertain but was probably the modern Ain el-Weiba, SW of the Dead Sea. Iye-abarim is also unknown but is possibly the modern Mahay, S of Moab. The Wadi Zered is modern Wadi el-Hesa, the southernmost tributary of the Dead Sea on the eastern side. The name means "brook of the willows." Although few of these sites can be identified with certainty, the general direction of the Israelite itinerary is clear. They moved N through the Arabah and then crossed the valley at a point just S of the Dead Sea. Moving along the Wadi Zered, between Edom to the S and Moab to the N, the Israelites successfully avoided open conflict with the kingdoms. To avoid a military showdown with Moab, the tribes bypassed Moab on the E. After crossing the Arnon River they settled temporarily "in the plains of Moab on the other side of the Jericho stretch of the Jordan" (22:1). **13.** Formerly, the territory N of the Arnon had belonged to Moab, but at the time of the Exodus the river formed Moab's northern frontier facing the Amorite kingdom of Sihon. **14.** *Book of the Wars of the Lord:* Apparently a collection of popular war songs recalling the heroic past of the Israelite tribes, it is no longer extant. For a similar collection, see the allusion to the Book of Jashar in Jos 10:13. Waheb and Suphah have not been located. **15.** Ar was the capital of Moab. **16.** *Beer:* The name means "well," and although its location is uncertain, it was undoubtedly a place remembered for the well dug by the tribal leaders. **17–18.** This ancient Song of the Well, set down in writing not long after the event it commemorated, reflects the joy and thanksgiving of the nomad when he has found a source of water. Even today the Bedouin sings water songs by wells. The poem has an unmistakable rhythm with a very regular accentuation. Like all archaic Hebr poetry, the text has undergone, in the course of transmission, a considerable revision in spelling and grammar, which has obscured many of the archaic features of this kind of poetry. The telltale marks of ancient poetry can, however, be recovered by careful examination and the use of sound hypotheses. The restoration of these archaic forms, ordinarily without any change of the MT, is among the most significant tasks of modern textual studies. **19–20.** The sites have not been located with certainty, but the general area is clear. All are on or near the great plateau of Moab. Bamoth, meaning "high places," is most likely the Bamoth-Baal of 22:41. Jeshimon, meaning "desert," is the wilderness of Judah; according to 1 Sm 23:19, it is the forbidding desert region NW of the Dead Sea.

40 **21.** *now Israel sent men to Sihon:* For the second time Israel requested safe passage from a foreign nation whose territory lay in its line of march. Again the request was refused. Sihon even tried to check the northern advance of the tribes. **23.** *Jahaz:* The site is unknown but may possibly be modern Khirbet Umm-el Idham. Sihon was not only badly beaten, but he seems to have lost his country as well. This territory was the first E of the Jordan taken in battle by the Israelites. **25.** Heshbon, the capital of Sihon's kingdom, has preserved its name in modern Hisban, just a short distance off the King's Highway and about 20 mi. E of Jericho. "Dependencies" translates Hebr *bānôt* meaning "daughters," the name given to villages that surrounded a large city or the capital, which was sometimes called "mother" (2 Sm 20:19). **26.** Not long before the arrival of the Israelites, Sihon had succeeded in extending his southern border to the Arnon River, achieved at the expense of the kingdom of Moab. The following ballad preserves reminiscences of the clash between Sihon and Moab.

27–30. This work is a clear, and perhaps unique, example of a pure Amorite poem, probably dating from as early as the 13th cent. BC. Very likely only a short time elapsed between its oral composition and its setting down in writing. *fire went forth:* War is often compared to a raging fire. Chemosh was the national god of the Moabites. His name appears on the famous Moabite Stone of King Mesha (*ANE* 209, plate 74). *he let his sons become fugitives:* Note the use that Jer 48:46 has made of this poem. The idea is that the god was angry and so allowed his people to be defeated. A distance of about 20 mi. separates Heshbon from Dibon; Medeba (modern Madeba) lies between them. **33.** Bashan is N of the territories of Moab and Sihon. Known today as the Hauran, it reaches up to the slopes of Mt. Hermon. For centuries the area was renowned for the fertility of its soil and its dense forests. Og was more famous for his bedstead (sarcophagus?) of iron, 9 cubits long and 4 cubits wide (Dt 3:11). His capital, Edrei, was about 30 mi. E of the Sea of Galilee.

Again Moses was given the assurance that Israel would be victorious. As successes began to multiply, the Hebrews became more confident of their relatively untrained forces. Yahweh's intervention made the difference. **22:1.** While consolidating their gains, the Israelites took up positions on the plains of Moab E of the Jordan, overlooking Jericho. On this majestic plateau Moses would now put down the burden of leadership. The conquest was about to begin.

(III) Events in Moab (22:2–36:13).

41 **(A) The Story of Balaam (22:2–24:25).** Both J and E traditions have preserved this early and intriguing narrative, which consists of both prose and poetry. The problems of the literary critic are notorious; the narrative is not homogeneous and has many apparent contradictions and inconcinnities. It is not always possible to make a clear division between J and E, or to explain satisfactorily how the divergencies in the narrative arose. Literary analysis has done about all that can reasonably be asked of it, but doubts and questions remain. The four Oracles of Balaam are generally divided as follows: the first and second are E; the third and fourth are J. However, in the case of these poems, we lack hard and fast criteria for assigning them to the usual pentateuchal traditions. Analysis of their textual data, with what we now know about the evolution of Hebr spelling, has led Albright to conclude that the poems were first written in or about the 10th cent. Textual difficulties disregarded, few sections in the Pentateuch are more important theologically than this remarkable narrative. In a real sense the Balaam story may be said to summarize the revelation of God's purpose as it was communicated to Moses. (See G. Von Rad, *Moses* [London, 1960] 70–80; W. F. Albright, "The Oracles of Balaam," *JBL* 63 [1944] 207–33.)

42 (a) BALAK CALLS FOR BALAAM, THE DIVINER (22:2–14). **2.** Balak was a king of Moab; his name recurs in Jos 24:9; Jgs 11:25; and Mi 6:5. At this time, *ca.* 1300, the Semitic tribes in Transjordan had organized themselves into kingdoms, ending a long period in which nomadic tribes wandered at will through the territory. Archaeology as well as the biblical record bears witness to a gap in the sedentary, permanent settlement of Transjordan between the 19th and 13th cents. Had the Israelites entered Transjordan a century earlier, they would have had little or no trouble. As it was, they were forced to bypass, or engage in battle with, the entrenched kingdoms. **4.** Balak's apprehension was undoubtedly shared by the other kingdoms to whom land-hungry and migrating tribes were always a threat. **5.** Pethor lay on the W bank of the Euphrates, about 12 mi. S of Carchemish. The name appears in the Assyrian royal annals as Pitru, which was colonized by the Assyrians in the 11th cent. BC and was conquered a century later by the Aramaeans. In Dt 23:5, the town is located in the territory known as Aram-Naharaim, comprising northeastern Syria and northern Mesopotamia. There is no need to emend the text to read "sons of Ammon" instead of Amauites. The Idrimi inscription from the 15th cent. mentions *'amau* as part of the king's territory. It is located in the Sajur Valley between Aleppo and Carchemish. An inscription 200 years earlier than Balaam has thus established the location of his homeland (W. F. Albright, *BASOR* 118 [1950] 15, n. 13). **6.** *curse this people for us:* Ancient Semites greatly esteemed the spoken word. It was more than a symbol, for it released dynamic power capable of bringing blessing or misfortune. Provided the person speaking had the power and the right to utter a blessing or curse, the spoken word accomplished what it stated (J. L. McKenzie, *TS* 21 [1960] 187–91). In Mesopotamia, the best-known practitioners of the art were the seers (Akkadian, *bārû*), who were eagerly sought after once they had established a reputation for effectiveness. Underlying the word for "curse" (Hebr *'ārar*) is the basic idea of casting a supernatural spell. Balaam was hired by the Moabite king to immobilize Israel and render her powerless to resist (E. A. Speiser, *JAOS* 80 [1960] 198).

43 (b) THE SECOND SUMMONS (22:15–41). **18.** The name of Yahweh on the lips of Balaam is strange, but it is not necessary to hold that the pagan diviner was a worshiper of the true God. The sacred writer was teaching the reader that Balaam was completely dependent on the all-powerful God of Israel. His control of events extended beyond the borders of Israel; the will of Yahweh and not the spoken word of any prophet was the decisive factor. And the will of God could not be coerced by a fee! **22.** *the angel of the Lord stationed himself on the road:* At this point, a colorful and popular story interrupts the narrative, which is resumed in v. 35. The writer used this ancient bit of folklore for a theological purpose—i.e., to drive home the lesson of God's never failing providence over his people. God's control over nature was so complete and his word was so powerful that he could even use a dumb beast as the bearer of his word. The incident is not meant as a sober historical account of an ass who once complained to his owner. The narrator's purpose was doctrinal; he has inserted into his narrative, even at the risk of disrupting its smooth flow, a popular and somewhat humorous episode, because he saw in it the means to teach an important theological lesson. (See D. M. Stanley, "Balaam's Ass, or a Problem in New Testament Hermeneutics," *CBQ* 20 [1958] 50–56; H. Eising, "Balaams Eselin," *BiKi* 13 [1958] 45–46). **39.** Kiriath-huzoth is probably modern El Qerieh, about 10 mi. NE of Dibon. **41.** *Bamoth-Baal:* The name means "Heights of Baal." It was located on the western edge of the Transjordan plateau, from which the seer had a good view of the Israelite encampment.

44 (c) THE FIRST ORACLE (23:1–12). **5.** *when he had put an utterance in Balaam's mouth:* The essence of prophecy is to speak the word that has been received from the Lord (Jer 1:9). **7.** *eastern mountains:* An ancient Canaanite term for the Anti-Lebanon range and the surrounding regions. This reference, which parallels the geographical reference in the first half of the verse, proves that there is no justification for emending Aram to Edom. **8.** *how can I curse whom God has not cursed?:* It was futile to exercise the diviner's art against the people of God. Even the pagan seer was completely in God's hands and could utter only what he was allowed to utter. As Von Rad remarks: "Here the story of Balaam reaches its culmination. The hidden inner side of all these strange happenings is now brought out into the open. A prophetic word lays bare that will of God which is hidden from human eyes, that will that is continuously at work in and behind those projects that men may devise for themselves. The blessing of God sets limits to the effect of the darkest and bitterest curses" (Von Rad, *op. cit.*, 74). **9.** *here is a people that lives apart:* Throughout her history, Israel was aware of a special destiny under God. She was to be as different from other nations as Yahweh was different from their gods. The people of the covenant must carry the burden of singularity; it would often be used as a reproach against Israel. In our time we have seen this quality twisted into a pretext for persecution. **10.** *may I die the death of the just:* This wish is an oath formula; Balaam asserts that he is prepared to die if what he says does not come to pass.

45 (d) THE SECOND ORACLE (23:12–26). **14.** *the lookout field:* It was probably an observation post from which one could keep an eye on an enemy's moves. Balak did not realize that the defeat of his plans was not due to an unsuitable location but to the will of Yahweh. **18.** This time Balak was addressed directly. He not only refused to curse Israel but exulted in her invincibility. With the first oracle a word was set in motion, and nothing could frustrate it. Past blessings were recalled and future victories were promised. **19.** *is he one to speak and not act?:* The same doctrine is found in 1 Sm 15:29, Rom 11:29, and elsewhere. It has been observed (Albright, *JBL* 63 [1944] 224, n. 119) that similar statements were well known in Egypt during the 13th and 12th cents. In the Ramses II stele from Beth-shan it was said of the pharaoh: "What is spoken by his mouth is done by his hands." Of Ramses III it was said: "The things which he announces [promises], they come to pass." The early occurrence of these expressions obviously has some bearing on the dating of these poems. **21.** *with him is the triumph of his King:* The Hebrew for "triumph" (*trʿt*) should probably be vocalized as *tōraʿat*, meaning "terror-producing majesty." The same word possibly appears in Jb 33:26. In this verse we have one of the earliest expressions of belief in Yahweh as Israel's king. **22.** *a wild bull of towering might:* The second oracle contains a number of similes that emphasize Israel's great strength; she is compared to some of the strongest and fiercest animals known in the ancient Near East. Among his many titles, Hammurabi boasted of himself as the "fiery wild bull who gores the foe." In the Blessing of Moses, it is said of Joseph that his "horns are those of the wild ox" (Dt 33:17). (See *VBW* 1, 228.) **24.** *a people that springs up like a lioness:* Poets, painters, and sculptors of the ancient East were deeply impressed by the terrifying sight of the lion devouring its prey. A stronger figure of speech could not be found to express the might of Israel's army. See Gn 49:9 for the same image.

46 (e) THE THIRD ORACLE (23:27–24:13). The second oracle ended with the despairing cry of Balak. But the Moabite king tried for the third time to obtain an oracle that would bring disaster upon Israel. **28.** Peor is unidentified, but presumably it was a vantage point from which one enjoyed a clear view of Jeshimon, the wilderness of Judah (21:20). **24:1.** *did not go aside as before:* The same ritual was observed as in 23:1,14, but, instead of seeking a direct revelation, Balaam looked off to the distant wilderness. **2.** *the spirit of God came upon him:* It took hold of him in the same way as the spirit would later seize kings, prophets, and judges, endowing them with a special charism. **4.** "Almighty" (*šadday*) means "the one of the mountains." We now know from an Egyptian inscription that a name formed with *šadday*, the name for God used by the Patriarchs before the name "Yahweh" was adopted, was current among the Semites dwelling in Egypt before the Exodus. A slightly different form of the name was common among the Amorites of the Upper Euphrates Valley in the early 2nd millennium. **7.** *his king shall rise higher than....:* The word for "king" (Hebr *mlk*) should probably be rendered, with the LXX and Vg, as "kingdom" or "royalty." H. L. Ginsberg has pointed out that, in several northwestern Semitic dialects, we find *mulk* and *molk* meaning "kingdom" (W. F. Albright, *BASOR* 87 [1942] 35, n. 20). The word preceding *mlk*, left untranslated in the CCD, should probably be rendered "Agag," as it is in the Hebrew. There may be a play on words here, the proper name Agag suggesting the Hebrew *gag*, "roof." The first half of the line would then read: *His kingdom shall be higher than Agag.* The jussive form for both verbs is also possible. **8.** *he shall devour the nations like grass:* There is no need to emend the text. The Hebrew *gwym* should be read as a construct plural plus an enclitic *mem* (Hebr *gᵉwê* and *m*) of a word meaning "body" or "back." Read: "He shall consume the flesh of his enemies" (M. Dahood, *Bib* 43 [1962] 65). **9.** *who shall arouse him?:* For a similar expression, describing Judah as a lion's whelp, see Gn 49:9. The image is that of a well-fed beast taking his rest after devouring the prey. *blessed is he who blesses you:* An old patriarchal formula, it is found in Gn 12:3 and 27:29. **10.** For clapping of the hands as a sign of scorn, see Jb 27:23.

47 (f) THE FOURTH ORACLE (24:13–25). Before departing, Balaam gives a final and completely unsolicited oracle, predicting what Israel shall do to Moab in the days to come. **17.** *a star shall advance from Jacob, and a staff shall rise from Israel:* As the CCD stands, the reference is to David and his conquests. Against the CCD translation and other versions is the probability that both noun subjects are plural in form, each having an enclitic *mem* attached. The word for "advance" (Hebr *dārak*) is difficult, but on the basis of Canaanite *darkatu*, meaning "rule" or "dominion," the verb may be translated "have rule over" or "prevail." In keeping with the pl. subject, it should probably be vocalized *dārᵉkû*. Similarly, Hebr *qām* would be vocalized *qāmû*. We would then have the following translation: "The stars of Jacob shall prevail, and the tribes of Israel shall rise up." Although many of the Fathers have interpreted this passage as a messianic prophecy, it is not quoted in the NT. This text did play a role in the messianic hopes of the Qumran sect; cf. 1QM 11:5–7; CD 7:19–20. **17.** *and the skulls of all the Suthites:* The Suthites are the same group mentioned in the Egyptian execration texts of the 20th and 19th cents. as nomadic people dwelling in Palestine. We know nothing about the ethnic relation between the Suthites and Moabites of later centuries. **20.** It is not clear why the Amalekites are called "first"; it may be because they were the first to attack Israel after she had left Egypt (Ex 17:8). They were a nomadic people who moved between the Negeb and the Sinai Peninsula. It was not until the time of Saul that Israel was able to even her accounts with this redoubtable foe (1 Sm 15:2–8). Later, David struck them a crushing blow (1 Sm 30:1–20). **21.** *O smith:* "Smith" (*qyn*) is etymologically identical with "Kenite." The Kenites were famous as metalworkers in antiquity, and it is very likely that they introduced the early Hebrews to the art of metallurgy. Their nomadism is largely explained by their trade as itinerant metalsmiths. Balaam puns on their name when he says that their "nest" (*qen*) is set on a cliff, referring to the great Edomite center of Sela (modern Petra) on the E and high above the Wadi Arabah. **23.** *who shall survive of Ismael?:* The text is very uncertain. Preserving the same consonants, it is possible to read: "the isles shall be gathered from the north." By changing one consonant, the balancing half of the verse would read: "and ships from the farthest ends of the sea." This and the following verse, although extremely difficult and obscure, appear to reflect the 12th-cent. invasion of the Sea Peoples, but the full picture is still far from clear.

(B) Various Incidents and Laws (25:1–31:54).

48 (a) THE RITES OF BAAL-PEOR (25:1–18). The narrative pauses to relate two relapses of the Israelites prior to their entrance into Canaan. The infidelity of the people and their proneness to disobedience are a constant theme of the desert tradition. **1.** Shittim (acacia trees) was located E of the Jordan. It was the place from which Joshua sent the spies to reconnoiter the land (Jos 2:1). We do not know the exact nature of the false worship offered the Moabite gods, but it probably had some connection with the fertility cults, which were widely practiced in the ancient Near East. Once in Canaan, the Israelites would come into almost daily contact with this abhorrent perversion of religious practice. **4.** An order was given to execute the guilty, but the actual execution is not recorded. That the leaders were singled out does not mean that they were either the only or the worst offenders. In accordance with ancient ideas of tribal solidarity, they were obliged to bear chief responsibility for the crime.

6–15. This episode is distinct from what precedes; it comes from the P tradition. Its only point in common with 1–5 is that foreign women are made the source of trouble. It would seem that the introduction to the story is missing, for we are given no reason for the weeping at the entrance to the meeting tent. We are not told why the plague, checked by Phinehas' act, was sent. As a member of the priestly class, Phinehas felt a special obligation to preserve the purity of the Israelite camp. His zeal, which we would judge intemperate, became proverbial in Israel (Ps 106:30; Sir 45:23–26; 1 Mc 2:26,54). The "retreat" (v. 8, *qubbāh*) was a small tent for which the best parallels may be sought among the pre-Islamic desert tribes of the Arabian desert. It was a small sacred tent, usually made of red leather, where the idols of the tribe were kept. In religious processions the tent was carried on the back of a camel; it was also carried into battle. While in the camp, men came to the *qubbāh* seeking oracles. The tent was tended by women. This is the only occurrence of the word in the OT, and it is not clear what connection it had with the meeting tent mentioned in v. 6 (De Vaux, *AI* 296–97). In v. 9, "thousand" (*'elep*) should probably be understood as a subsection of a tribe rather than as a strict numerical designation (see comment on Nm 1:2). Phinehas was rewarded with the perpetual status of priesthood (10). The word for "pledge" (*b^erît*) is the same as that for "covenant" (Nm 3:4). The Zadokite priesthood traced its ancestry through Phinehas to Aaron (1 Chr 5:30–34). During the reign of Solomon, Zadok replaced Abiathar in the priesthood and became sole holder of the priestly office (1 Kgs 2:35). **17.** *treat the Midianites as enemies:* This command connects the two preceding incidents involving foreign women, and it serves as an advance notice of the action to be taken against the Midianites (Nm 31:1–12).

49 (b) ANOTHER CENSUS (26:1–65). The second census (see Nm 1:2–46) forms a prelude to military action about to be taken, proximately against the Midianites and ultimately against the Canaanites. It was a step toward the mobilization of the folk militia, which consisted of Israelites fighting under the command of their own tribal leaders. As remarked earlier, the census enumerated the number of "units" into which each tribe was divided, and it added the number of eligible fighting men to be taken from the tribe. The structure of the census and the results obtained are substantially the same for both lists, although the census of this chapter shows a tendency toward larger units than those of Nm 1. **53.** *the land shall be divided as their heritage:* Two principles seem to underlie the parceling out of the land: the population of the group; and the distribution by lot. To cast lots was to seek the divine will; apportionment by lot implied the divine sovereignty over the land (see J. Lindblom, "Lot-casting in the Old Testament," *VT* 12 [1962] 164–78). **54.** *to a large group you shall assign a large heritage:* Since a certain proportion had to be observed in the distribution of the land, it would seem that, besides the two-fold classification of large and small tribes, the lot-casting for each group must have been carried out by a rather complicated procedure. Lot-casting and strictly proportional allotment are not easily reconciled. **57.** Since the Levites held a special place in the community life of Israel they were not included in the regular census of the people (→ Religious Institutions, 76:17, 34). This section has preserved a clan division different from the traditional triple classification of Gershonites, Kohathites, and Merarites, enumerated here. To these were added five other clans (58). In the list of Ex 6:16–23, Libni, Hebron, Mahli and Mushi are listed together as sons of Gershon, Kohath, and Merari, respectively. De Vaux notes that the Nm list is very old, certainly premonarchic, and that it seems to place all the Levitical settlements in the territory of Judah. After the time of the Judges they fanned out into other areas. By the time the document listing the Levitical towns in Jos 21 was first edited, the Levites had expanded through all the tribes of Israel (see De Vaux, *AI* 370–71). **61.** *when they offered profane fire before the Lord:* The irregularity is described in greater detail in Lv 10:1–3. **65.** *not one of them was left except Caleb:* See 14:30 for the prediction. The writer used the census to indicate that a whole generation had perished between the two censuses. Only two survived, and they were to be the nucleus of the new community about to enter the land.

50 (c) LAWS OF INHERITANCE (27:1–11). The editor reports a human-interest story in which a precedent was established for laws governing inheritance according to degrees of kinship (27:6–11). The lot of women in the Near East has traditionally been hard. For example, in early times a woman had no right to inherit landed property. It was a law such as this that left the daughters of Zelophehad in such a desperate predicament. **1.** The names that appear in this section, both those of the daughters and their ancestors, also occur as place names in the area allotted to the tribe of Manasseh. They help us to form a somewhat better picture of the territorial situation of this region. In Jos 17:3–6, we learn that Zelophehad's daughters received territory on the western side of the Jordan, and in Transjordan Gilead and Bashan were allotted to the other children of Manasseh. In the Samaria ostraca of the 8th cent. BC, the names Noah and Hoglah turn up as place names. **2.** *they came forward:* The five girls brought the case before Moses and the whole "assembly." They were seeking an exception to the law, which, had it taken its course, would have eradicated their father's name from the clan. **3.** Like the rest of the Israelites who had grumbled and lost faith, Zelophehad had been denied the privilege of entering the land. But he had not joined Korah's rebellion; he had died a natural death in the desert. The rebellion of Korah must still have been a bitter memory to Moses and the other faithful leaders. **8.** The case was submitted to the adjudication of the Lord and the answer was phrased in the legal style common in the ancient Near East. As casuistic law, it began with a supposition or condition to which the ruling was immediately attached. The whole purpose of the legislation was to keep land in the family. The Levirate marriage, described in Dt 25:5–10, and the rules laid down in Nm 36:2–10, supplemented the decision in favor of Zelophehad's daughters. **11.** *as the Lord commanded Moses:* By making use of this formula, the legislation was put on the same footing as the rest of the Mosaic law.

51 (d) JOSHUA TAKES COMMAND (27:12–23). **12.** *the Abarim Mountains:* The name applies to the summits, including Mt. Nebo, which rise along the western slopes of Moab's plateau. From these high points one can enjoy a magnificent panorama of Palestine. **18.** The "spirit" of Yahweh had taken hold of Joshua, and he was endowed with the wisdom and courage required of a leader in Israel. Leadership was not hereditary but charismatic, and no one could assume its functions unless he had first received the gift of the spirit. The institution of charismatic leadership emphasized the providential guidance of Yahweh. **19.** The P tradition carefully notes the part played by Eleazar in the installation ritual. **21.** *the Urim:* These were the sacred lots, the use of which is described more fully in 1 Sm 14:41–42. After David's time, the ephod, with the Urim and Thummim, was no longer used for obtaining oracles. Joshua was never to have the full authority Moses possessed; nor was he to enjoy that peculiar intimacy with Yahweh, which set Moses apart as the man of God.

52 (e) LAWS PERTAINING TO SACRIFICE (28:1–29:39). The narrative is interrupted at this point by a long series of liturgical regulations, including a list of the feasts celebrated at the time this document was composed. The elaborate development of these regulations and the religious calendar indicate a relatively late date, long after the people had settled in Canaan. Such prescriptions do not fit the situation of a people on the move, as the Israelites were at this time. Only settled communities observe a very exacting religious calendar such as we find here. Numbers 28–29 is really a priestly commentary on the liturgical cycle described in Lv 23. These two chapters have preserved a complete list of the sacrifices offered in the Second Temple from the time of Ezra and later. **6.** *this is the established holocaust:* This daily ritual is more accurately called the "perpetual" (*tāmîd*) holocaust; see the parallel passage in Ex 29:38–42. **7.** *libation:* The drink offering, which accompanied the holocaust, was to consist of "strong drink" to be poured out at the base of the altar that stood in the Temple court (Sir 50:15). **9.** The Sabbath prescriptions were, in all details, the same as those for the daily sacrifice. It would seem, then, that the sacrifices were simply doubled on the Sabbath. **11.** The priestly tradition for the Feasts of Passover and Unleavened Bread, eventually combined into one, is found in Lv 23:5–8; Ex 12:1–20,40–51; and Nm 28:16–25. **26.** In Lv 23:15–21 is given the most detailed account of the Feast of Weeks. Here it is also called the feast of "first fruits." Like Passover, the Feast of Weeks was later "historicized," or related to a specific event in Israel's salvation history—namely, the Covenant. Its Christian counterpart is Pentecost.

53 **29:1.** *on the first day of the seventh month:* The month was Tishri, the September-October period. Although this is the date on which Judaism, in NT times and today, celebrates the Feast of New Year, De Vaux cautions us against assuming that it was regarded as a New Year feast in this passage (De Vaux, *AI* 503). In the religious calendar of Lv 23 and Nm 28–29, the religious year began with the Feast of Passover. It is possible that this feast kept alive the memory of the pre-exilic beginning of the religious and civil year in the autumn. *a day on which you sound the trumpet:* It would be more accurate to call this a day of "acclamation (*teruʿāh*). Originally, the *terûʿāh* was a battle cry meant to arouse the Israelite warriors and to throw the enemy into panic. It had strong religious overtones, and the cry or acclamation was later incorporated into the Temple liturgy (Lv 23:24; Nm 29:1). **7.** The "Day of Atonement" (*yôm kippur*) was introduced into Judaism during the last centuries of the OT period. It was always observed on the tenth of Tishri. Even before these Babylonian names for the months were adopted, it was celebrated on the same date, the tenth day of the seventh month. **12.** *on the fifteenth day of the seventh month:* This was the "Feast of Tents" (*sukkôt*), originally an agricultural feast celebrated by the native Canaanite population in thanksgiving for the harvest. The ceremony, as described in several OT passages, recalls a custom that still exists of erecting booths of tree branches. They were set up in the vineyards and orchards while the grapes, olives, and fruits were being gathered. The feast, Canaanite and pagan in origin, was taken over by the Israelites. Eventually, the feast was historicized, as were the other major feasts. The Feast of Tents commemorated the dwelling in tents after the Exodus from Egypt (Lv 23:43). It was thus a reminder of Yahweh's leading the Israelites through the desert to the promised land. **12.** The "Pilgrimage Feast" (Hebr *ḥāg*) was added by the Israelites to the original harvest festival without changing the basic meaning of the festival as an act of thanksgiving to Yahweh for the gifts sent in the annual harvest. The element of pilgrimage may be very old, reverting to an ancient and annual pilgrimage (and tent) festival celebrated by the nomads. This pilgrimage feature would also have been taken over, at an early date, by the Israelites. (See G. W. MacRae, "The Meaning and Evolution of the Feast of Tabernacles," *CBQ* 22 [1960] 251–76; L. Rost, "Zu den Festopfervorschriften von Numeri 28 und 29," *TLZ* 83 [1958] 329–34.)

54 (f) RULES CONCERNING VOWS (30:1–17). The taking of a "vow" or a pledge of "abstinence" was a very serious matter among the Hebrews. Once initiated, the person was obliged to stand by his action (Dt 23:22–24). It was thought better to make no vows at all than to make them and then violate them (Eccl 5:3–5). The present passage restricts its interest to the vows of women, and it is the only one in the OT which deals specifically with this aspect of vows.

A woman's right to inherit was laid down in a previous chapter (Nm 27); this section concerns her obligations. An unmarried woman's vow was valid only when ratified by her father. Similarly, a married woman needed her husband's consent to bind herself by vow. His disapproval meant nullification, provided he raised his objection and took action as soon as he learned she had taken the vow. A widow or divorced woman could validly pronounce vows. Interesting comparisons might be made in this matter between Hebrew, Greco-Roman, and Anglo-Saxon law.

55 (g) RULES CONCERNING WAR (31:1–54). Chapter 31 is the sequel to 25:18, where Moses was told to engage and crush the Midianites because of their hostility to Israel and their part in leading her astray in the matter of worship. **3.** The "vengeance" fell on both Israel and her enemies, more terribly even on the former. The anger of Yahweh was not simply a figure of speech but a dreadful reality, which could burst forth suddenly and fiercely. God would execute his vengeance on Midian because of the haughty pride with which Midian had humiliated God's people (see J. L. McKenzie, *Scr* 12 [1960] 33–39). **6.** *a thousand from each tribe:* The description of the assembly and dispatch of the troops is highly stylized in keeping with other accounts of holy war (see 1QM). Phinehas, the fiery zealot, was put in charge; he carried the "trumpet" that gave the signal for breaking camp and setting out for battle. Questions of interest to the modern reader are given little or no attention. Nothing is said about the time, place, or progress of the battle. Strictly historical interests were subordinated to other considerations, such as the distribution of booty and the purification of objects unclean because of the battle. Victory in war was the gift of Yahweh, and the spoils were his; laws for their distribution had to be observed strictly. The act of killing another man in combat defiled a man; he would have to be purified before he could once again take a full part in the sacred community of Israel. **7.** *and killed every male among them:* That this statement should not be understood in a mathematically literal sense is obvious. Within a generation, the Midianites, stronger than ever, would prove to be a very redoubtable foe of Israel (Jgs 6). **8.** *and they also executed Balaam:* In the Balaam cycle of chs. 22–24, the diviner was associated with Moab, and there was no reference to Midianite connections. He now appears in another tradition (cf. v. 16) as one of the casualties in the war against Midian. In the NT, Balaam appears as a type of the false prophet (Jude 11; 2 Pt 2:16; Ap 2:14).

15. Only the virgins were spared, because they could marry Israelites and thereby be assimilated into the Israelite community. The problem of mixed marriages does not emerge—a hint that we probably have here elements of a very old tradition; in the post-exilic period, mixed marriages were forbidden. **23.** After holy war all participants and even the spoils were "sanctified." The warriors had to be deconsecrated before returning to normal community life. This period of purification lasted seven days. The "lustral water" was prepared from the ashes of the red heifer (19:9). **27.** The spoils were divided equally between combatants and noncombatants; equality in sharing is common in a group where the sense of tribal unity is very strong. We find a similar arrangement in David's time (1 Sm 30:20–25). A small proportion of the booty was set aside for Yahweh and the Levites. The figures given in 32–46 are fantastic, and we do not know the principle underlying the exaggeration. The whole section illustrates well the priestly concern for tabulation; moreover, this interest in arithmetical details is characteristic of the whole book and, as already noted, accounts for its title in the LXX. **50.** The captured jewelry was put in the tent of meeting as a reserve fund. Jewelry was highly prized by Bedouins like the Midianites because it could be transported easily from place to place. Some of the articles mentioned have not yet been identified satisfactorily, although jewelry of this kind is constantly unearthed in excavations.

(C) Topographical Regulations and Miscellaneous Laws (32:1–36:13).

56 (a) DIVISION OF TRANSJORDAN (32:1–42). In the seminomadic society of the Hebrews no distinction was made between a standing army and the people in general. Wars were waged by a folk militia, signifying that everyone capable of bearing arms was called to do his part in carrying out raids and defending the tribal rights to property and possessions. Occasionally all the tribes were summoned to fight, as when a common peril faced the community or when some large objective, which could not be gained by a single tribe, was sought. But tribal independence was jealously guarded, and anything like regimentation under one military leader was usually resented. With tribal organization went almost inevitably that centrifugal force that eventually made kingship in Israel necessary. When we describe the Israelites as a people under arms, we should not picture them as the strictly disciplined units of an organized army. Chapter 32 deals with a crisis that arose when two of the tribes reasserted their traditional independence.

1. How Reuben and Gad, within a generation, managed to outstrip the others in the number of cattle they possessed is left unexplained. Possibly the conditions following a long sojourn in the rich pasture lands of Transjordan have been read back into the past. In any event, the two tribes had decided to settle in this area. Jazer is probably modern Khirbet es-Sireh, about 8 mi. W of modern Amman, capital of Jordan (G. M. Landes, *BASOR* 144 [1956] 30–37). In this verse, Gilead refers to the land S of the Jabbok River. Gad's northern boundary would later be on this river. The towns listed in v. 3 were situated in the region between the Jabbok and the Arnon. **7.** *why do you wish to discourage the Israelites?*: Moses recognized at once that the morale of the tribes would seriously be weakened if he acceded to the request of Reuben and Gad. He then read the two tribes a lesson in history to remind them how God treated a faltering fidelity. For a similar complaint by the prophetess Deborah, see Jgs 5:16–17. **16.** The Reubenites and Gadites protested that they had no intention of shirking their duties to the rest of the Israelites. They only wished to secure their own position before joining the others in the war of conquest. "Sheepfolds" served as protection for both shepherd and flock. Several examples have been discovered in Transjordan. They were rather spacious enclosures of roughhewn stones with a narrow opening; in times of danger from raiders or wild animals, the flocks could be herded quickly into the enclosures (*VBW* 1, 235). **20.** The compromise proposal was acceptable to Moses, who then ordered Eleazar and Joshua to make sure that the agreement was honored.

Chapter 32 ends with a list of towns rebuilt and fortified by the two tribes. The mention of the half-tribe of Manasseh (33) may refer to a later conquest by this tribe. By saying that Moses gave the half-tribe its territory, the writer was lending the prestige of a Mosaic grant to territory conquered and settled only at a later date.

57 (b) ROUTE FROM EGYPT TO CANAAN (33:1–56). Were we able to identify accurately the camping sites noted in this long and schematic itinerary from Egypt to Moab, we could determine with a high degree of certainty the route of the Exodus. Unfortunately, we cannot, but since the possibilities of such a long journey through the desert are limited, we have a general picture of the Israelites' route. Many of the places mentioned here were only temporary stopping places whose names have long since been lost. We are certain, however, that the primary object of the march was Kadesh-barnea, a well-known location that served as a rallying point for the Israelites during a whole generation (cf. J. Simons, *The Geographical and Topographical Texts of the Old Testament* [Brill; Leiden, 1959] 233–66). On the route of the Exodus →Biblical Geography, 73:27–31.

5–15. Here appears a condensed account of Ex 12:37–19:2. Only Dophkah and Alush are missing from Ex. The former has been identified with Serabit el Khadem in the turquoise mining area of the southern Sinai Peninsula, where the Proto-Sinaitic inscriptions were discovered. The identification of Alush with a site in the Wadi el ʿesh, SE of Dophkah, is only probable (for both places, see *AtBib* 44, map 9). **36.** Kadesh-barnea bordered on the wilderness of Zin and the wilderness of Paran. The biblical sources are unanimous on the sojourn of the Israelites at Kadesh, not surprising, because the area abounds in water and beautiful gardens. No greater contrast could be imagined than that for a traveler leaving the scorching desert to enter this lush, well-watered valley. The most abundant spring in the region is Ain el-Qudeirat, where in recent years have been discovered ancient remains from the Middle Bronze (Patriarchal) Age, the period of the Judean kings, the Nabatean, Roman, and Byzantine periods. It was undoubtedly the most heavily populated part of the area. About 12 mi. S of Ain el-Qudeirat is the oasis of Ain Qudeis, which has preserved the name Kadesh. That there were two centers of population in the Kadesh region is reflected in the name Kadesh-barnea, which probably represents a combination of two independent place names belonging to two different places several miles apart. As yet no evidence of the 13th-cent. settlement of the Israelites has come to light, although it is very likely that more intensive work at the site will turn up remains from this period.

37. For the location of Mt. Hor, see comment on 20:22. It was most likely a holy site, for it was chosen as a burial place for Aaron. Since the phrase *Har-el*, "mountain of God," is already attested in a document long before Moses' time (the list of Thutmoses III), an element is probably missing from the name Hor.

58 (c) Division of Canaan (34:1–29). The territory described in vv. 2–15 was not conquered by the invading Israelites under Joshua; it was only during the time of David and Solomon that Israelite rule extended over so vast an area. Some have considered this division of Canaan as an idealized picture with little relation to the situation in the 13th cent. However, it now appears that the "Canaan" herein described is simply the old Egyptian province of Syria-Palestine, long under the domination of Egyptian pharaohs until the time of Ramses II (1290–24). It was under Ramses II that a treaty was signed with the Hittite king, *ca.* 1270, freezing the status quo of Egyptian holdings in the Syria-Palestine area. The Israelites, roughly contemporaneous with these events, simply took over this term "Canaan" with the meaning and extension it had at that time. We would be dealing, therefore, not so much with an idealized picture as with a stereotyped understanding of "Canaan" (B. Mazar, *JBL* 80 [1961] 17).

3. The southern boundary cut directly across the Negeb from a point south of the Dead Sea, along the River of Egypt, and thence to the Mediterranean. This line very closely parallels that given in Jos 15:3–4 and Ez 47:19. Even today the River of Egypt (Wadi el-Arish) serves as a natural barrier between the Negeb and Sinai (*VBW* 1, 240–44). **6.** *western boundary:* The Mediterranean, often called in the OT simply "the sea" (*yām*), came to stand for "the west," since it was always the western boundary of the land. The coastline was without good harbors, thereby discouraging commercial activities in this part of the land. **7–9.** Some of the places mentioned have not been identified. In general, the northern border extended from the Mediterranean, slightly N of Byblos, directly E to the edge of the desert just beyond Damascus. The name of Zedad is preserved in the modern town of Sedad, NE of Mt. Hermon. **10–12.** Hazar-enan is probably Banias at the source of the Jordan. From there the eastern boundary followed the tortuous course of the Jordan until it emptied into the Dead Sea.

59 (d) Levitical Cities and Cities of Refuge (35:1–34). The Levitical cities are treated in three OT passages: Lv 25:32–34; Nm 35:1–8; and Jos 21:1–40. The last describes how the directions of Nm were implemented; a full list of the cities may be found there. A parallel list to the enumeration of towns in Jos may be found in 1 Chr 6:54–81. Forty-eight cities, including the six cities of refuge, were allotted to the Levites. In addition, the "pasture lands" were also given, and vv. 4–5 are instructions on how they were to be measured out. The account, here and in Jos, contains utopian elements, especially if we regard the systematization of the list, a characteristic of the whole P tradition. But the list is undoubtedly based on ancient traditions, which at some time reflected a real historical situation. There is no need to hold that these cities were inhabited exclusively by Levites; the population was undoubtedly mixed, with the Levitical families residing side-by-side with non-Levites. **6.** Included in the Levitical cities are all six cities of asylum. It was probably the priestly, sacred character of the Levitical cities that made them suitable as places of refuge from the fury of the blood avenger. Since all these Levitical cities had an altar or shrine, they were well suited to be places of asylum for the fugitive. See Ex 21:14 and 1 Kgs 1:51 for the traditional association of the altar with asylum. (See De Vaux, *AI* 366–67; M. Haran, "Studies in the Account of the Levitical Cities [Preliminary Considerations, I; Utopia and Historical Reality, II]," *JBL* 70 [1961] 45–54, 156–65; Albright, *ARI* 121–24.) **11.** The cities of refuge, "cities of intaking," were set aside for the protection of the accidental homicide. Three were in Canaan, and three were in Transjordan. Exodus 21:12–14 and Dt 19:1–13 also deal with the right of asylum, the humanitarian purpose of which is obvious. Private vengeance must be checked in any civilized society, and no society can last long where the blood feud is not restrained by law.

60 There is no reason to assume that this legislation in Nm is late, since there is nothing in these laws that does not dovetail perfectly with the conceptions and customs of Israel during the earliest period. The institution, which set public law between the slayer and the avenger, was intended to protect only the involuntary slayer. The one who committed premeditated murder could not be received, and blood vengeance, a solemn duty of the "kinsman" (*gō'ēl*), was allowed to run its course.

16–21. These verses contain a list, in the casuistic style of ancient Near Eastern legislation, of the various crimes for which capital punishment was decreed. In all these cases, murderous intent is presumed. **22.** The man who had killed without premeditation received protection, but he was obliged to expiate in some way for the homicide. The city of refuge offered him protection, but his forcible detention there was also a form of expiation. **25.** The title "high priest" does not occur before the Exile and is used only rarely after it. The reference is probably to that part of the slayer's expiation accomplished only by the death of the anointed priest. The death was, therefore, an expiatory act after which the involuntary homicide could quit the city of refuge. The penalty for the guilt incurred by the slaying had been paid in the atoning deal of the high priest (M. Greenberg, *JBL* 78 [1959] 125–32). **31.** *you shall not accept indemnity in place of the life of a murderer:* Life and money were not commensurable. The taking of life caused a guilt that could not be expiated by any means short of death. **33.** *you shall not desecrate the land where you live:* To leave murder unrequited would mean that Yahweh's land was polluted by innocent blood.

61 (e) Inheritance of Heiresses (36:1–13). **3.** *but if they marry into one of the other Israelite tribes:* These regulations supplement the decision taken in the case of Zelophehad's daughters (27:1–11). **6.** To forestall the alienation of family property, the law decreed that heiresses should marry within their father's clan. **13.** *these are the commandments and the decisions:* Numbers concludes with a brief notice that gives divine sanction to the laws enacted on the eastern side of the Jordan. The notice refers to all legislation in chs. 22–36. Note again how the sacred writer has taken pains to place this synthesis of law, ritual, and custom under the name and authority of Moses, the great lawgiver.

6

DEUTERONOMY

Joseph Blenkinsopp

BIBLIOGRAPHY

1 *General up-to-date surveys:* Eissfeldt, *OTI* 171–82, 219–33. R-F 1, 367–71. Weiser, *OT* 125–35.

Older commentaries (basis of later work): Driver, S. R. (1903), Robinson, H. W. (1907), Steuernagel, C., (2nd ed.; 1923), and others.

Recent commentaries: Brown, R. E., OTRG (Collegeville, 1965). Buis, P. and J. Leclercq, *Les sources bibliques* (Paris, 1963). Cazelles, H., BJ. Clamer, A., *PSB* (1946). Davies, G. H., *PCB*. Junker, H., Echter-B (Würzburg, 1952). Von Rad, G., *Deuteronomy* (London, 1966). Wright, G. E., *IB* 2, 311–537.

On the origins and date of the book: Bewer, J. A., G. Dahl and L. B. Paton, *JBL* 47 (1928) 305–79. Manley, G. T., *The Book of the Law. Studies in the Date of Deuteronomy* (London, 1957). Walker, N., *VT* 3 (1953) 413–14.

On the question of the Josian reform: Budde, K., "Das Deuteronomium und die Reform König Josias," *ZAW* 44 (1926) 177–224. Lohfink, N., "Die Bundesurkunde des Königs Josias," *Bib* 44 (1963) 261–88, 461–98.

On the relation with Jeremiah: Bright, J., "The Date of the Prose Sermons of Jeremiah," *JBL* 70 (1951) 15–35. Hyatt, J. P., "Jeremiah and Deuteronomy," *JNES* 1 (1942) 153–73. Robert, A., "Jérémie et la reforme deutéronomique d'après Jér XI, 1–14," *Science religieuse* (Paris, 1943) 5–16. Rowley, H. H., "The Prophet Jeremiah and the Book of Deuteronomy," *Studies in Old Testament Prophecy Presented to T. H. Robinson* (Edinburgh, 1950) 157–74.

On the "deuteronomic history": North, C. R., "The Deuteronomists," *The Old Testament Interpretation of History* (London, 1946). Noth, M., *GesSt* 34–40. Noth, *US* 1, 16ff. Plöger, O., "Reden und Gebete im deuteronomistischen und chronistischen Geschichtswerk," *Fest. G. Dehn* (Neukirchen, 1957) 35–49. Wolff, H. W., "Das Kerygma des deuteronomistischen Geschichtswerkes," *ZAW* 73 (1961) 171–86.

Recent studies on the theology of Dt: Bächli, O., *Israel und die Völker. Eine Studie zum Deuteronomium* (Zurich, 1962). Dummermuth, F., "Zur deuteronomistischen Kulttheologie und ihren Voraussetzungen," *ZAW* 70 (1958) 59–98. Kuyper, L. J., "The Book of Deuteronomy," *Interpr* 6 (1952) 321–40. Lohfink, N., *Das Hauptgebot. Eine Untersuchung literarischer Einleitungsfragen zu Dtn. 5–11* (AnalBib 20; Rome, 1963); summary in *VD* 41 (1963) 73–77. MacKenzie, R. A. F., "The Messianism of Deuteronomy," *CBQ* 19 (1957) 299–305. Moran, W. L., "The Ancient Near Eastern Background of the Love of God in Deuteronomy," *CBQ* 25 (1963) 77–87. Myers, J. M., "The Requisites for Response. On the Theology of Deuteronomy," *Interpr* 15 (1961) 14–31. Von Rad, G., *Studies in Deuteronomy* (London, 1953).

INTRODUCTION

2 **(I) Title.** The title comes from the Gk mistranslation of Dt 17:18, "a copy of this law," which, although an inaccurate translation, points to a basic problem of the book—the relation of the law promulgated in Moab to the original law of Sinai. The Hebr title is *ʾēlleh hadd^{e}bārîm*, "these are the words . . . ."

3 **(II) Origin and Literary History.** Since the celebrated dissertation of W. de Wette (1805), Dt or some part of it has generally been identified with "the book of the law" found in the Temple during the reign of Josiah (640–609), chiefly because of the close similarity between the deuteronomic legislation and the religious reform that followed, in particular the insistence on one central sanctuary (Dt 12:1–7; 2 Kgs 23:8ff.). De Wette, followed by J. Wellhausen, interpreted this finding as a pious fraud to authenticate the reform; thus the date of the book could be established with some precision. This view has not, however, won wide recognition, and most see Dt as containing a blueprint for an earlier reform during either the reign of Hezekiah (C. Steuernagel, H. Cazelles) or the dark days of Manasseh (S. R. Driver; A. R. Siebens, *L'origine du Code Deutéronomique* [Paris, 1929]; H. H. Rowley). A 7th-cent. date is confirmed by linguistic and stylistic affinities with Jeremiah and the Lachish letters (cf. Albright, *FSAC* 319–21; F. M. Cross and D. N. Freedman, "Josiah's Revolt Against Assyria," *JNES* 12 [1953] 56–59; Wright, *IB* 2, 318ff.).

The anchoring of Dt in the 7th cent. has not, however, gone unchallenged. Some have preferred to read it either as a utopian program for a future national state put together toward the end of the Exile (G. Hölscher, F. Horst, R. Kennett) or as a post-exilic composition

(J. Pedersen). Others, a large and growing number, have been struck by the genuinely archaic character of much of the material in the book and have thus placed its composition much earlier—either during the time of Samuel (T. Oestreicher), or during the period of the judges and early monarchy (A. C. Welch) or during the period of the great Shechem covenant meeting described in Jgs 24 (R. Brinker). E. Robertson considers Dt the codification of genuine Mosaic Law assembled by Samuel as a blueprint for the age of the monarchy.

In view of this wide spectrum of opinion and the actual variety of material in the book itself, we should treat Dt as the result of a long process of formation, from earliest times to the post-exilic period—i.e., part of the mainstream of the great canonical tradition passed on in the north and edited by a Judean hand some time after the fall of Samaria (721). This concept has been stressed in the form-critical studies of Von Rad and confirmed by recent enquiry into the question of covenant structure. In keeping with this, recent years have seen a decline of confidence in the possibility of arriving at the "Urdeuteronomium," the "law book" found by Hilkiah. No entirely satisfactory answer has been obtained from traditio-historical or stylistic analysis alone (e.g., the division into strata on the basis of sing. and pl. forms of address as proposed by C. Steuernagel and M. Noth; cf. G. Minette de Tillesse, *VT* 12 [1962] 29–87), although it is generally admitted that we cannot simply equate it with the legislative corpus in Dt 12–26 as Wellhausen did. We should regard it as the heir of the northern E tradition, between the writing prophets and the epoch of the written Law, as the result of successive "editions" (applying also to the laws, which are generally older than their framework). We thus arrive at least at the middle of the 6th cent., for deuteronomic history extends to the accession of Amel-marduk in 562 (2 Kgs 25:27).

4 **(III) Theological Relevance.** Composed as it is mainly of homiletic expansion of law, Dt is one of the most theological of the OT books. It gives a mature picture of the covenant and life under it, therefore also of the OT concept of revelation and the Word of God, which is at times practically hypostatized (e.g., 30:11–14). This Word is addressed liturgically to the community, *qᵉhāl* Yahweh (see especially ch. 23), which becomes the *ekklēsia tou theou* of the NT. The moral demand made on the covenant community is considered within this theology of encounter and as part of the total self-revelation and self-giving of the covenant God and the corresponding human response. It reaches its highest expression in the Shema (6:4–9), quoted by Jesus as the greatest and the first of the commandments (Mt 22:37).

Few OT books are quoted or alluded to so frequently in the NT as Dt; in Mt and Heb in particular, its influence is dominant. It not only provides the mandatory picture of the charismatic, liturgical community, but also is used to illuminate the mission of Jesus, who quoted from it three times in the temptation scene (Mt 4:4–10) and who is seen as the new Moses or the prophet like Moses of Dt 18:18 (see Jn 1:21; 3:14; Acts 3:22; Heb 3:1–11), especially during the Sermon on the Mount. The figure of Moses as eschatological prophet based on Dt plays a large part also in Samaritan theology and in QL (see J. Bowman, "The Samaritans and the Book of Deuteronomy," OSTGU 17 [1959] 9–18).

5 **(IV) Contents and Structure.** Dt can be characterized as a law book with appropriate introduction and conclusion expanded by homiletic and poetic material of different kinds. Its basic structure resembles closely that of Ex, without the long sections (Ex 25–31 and 35–40) containing specifications and rubrics of the post-exilic P editors:

Exodus	*Deuteronomy*
1–18 From Egypt to Sinai	1–4:43 From Sinai to Moab
19–20:21 Covenant and Ten Commandments	4:44–5:22 Covenant and Ten Commandments
20:22–23:33 Book of the Covenant	12–26 Deuteronomic Code
24 Concluding Ceremony	27–28 Concluding Ceremony
32–34 Aaronic Apostasy, Intercession of Moses, Renewal of Alliance	9:7–10:5 Aaronic Apostasy, Intercession of Moses, Tablets Rewritten

The most obvious difference is that divine discourse predominates in Ex, whereas Dt consists mainly of Moses' public address to the laity (1:1; 4:44; 5:1; 27:1; 29:1; 31:1; 31:30; 33:1). Although some passages are displaced (e.g., 9:7ff. and part of ch. 27), the basic similarity derives from a common pattern—that of the covenant and its liturgical renewal, which we can now study in the light of extrabiblical material, especially suzerainty treaties of the ancient Near East.

(Baltzer, K., *Das Bundesformular* [Neukirchen, 1960]. Brueggemann, W., *A Form-critical Study of the Cultic Material in Deuteronomy* [Dissertation of Union Theological Seminary; N.Y., 1951]. Kline, M. G., *Treaty of the Great King, the Covenant Structure of Deuteronomy* [Grand Rapids, 1961]. McCarthy, D. J., *Treaty and Covenant* [Rome, 1963]. Mendenhall, G., *Law and Covenant in Israel and in the Ancient Near East* [Pittsburgh, 1955]. Muilenburg, J., "Covenantal Formulations," *VT* 9 [1959] 347ff.)

6 **(V) Outline.** The book may be divided as follows:

(I) First Address of Moses: From Horeb to Moab (1:1–4:43)
- (A) Introduction to the Address (1:1–5)
- (B) Command to Possess the Land and Creation of Leaders (1:6–18)
- (C) The Stay at Kadesh-barnea (1:19–46)
- (D) Passage Through Edom, Moab, and Ammon (2:26–3:11)
- (E) Conquest of Heshbon and Bashan (2:26–3:11)
- (F) Settlement of the Tribes East of the Jordan (3:12–22)
- (G) Prayer of Moses (3:23–29)
- (H) Prologue to the Promulgation of the Law to All Israel (4:1–14)
- (I) A Commentary on the First Part of the Decalogue (4:15–31)
- (J) The Unique Vocation of Israel in the Covenant (4:32–40)
- (K) The Cities of Sanctuary (4:41–43)

(II) Second Address of Moses: Introduction to the Law Book (4:44–11:32)
- (A) Introduction to the Address (4:44–49)
- (B) The "Ten Words" (5:1–22)
- (C) Moses Delegated to Promulgate the Law (5:23–33)
- (D) Appeal to Covenant Fidelity in the Land (6:1–19)
- (E) The Passover Haggadah (6:20–25)
- (F) The *ḥerem* Must Be Applied to the Populations of Canaan (7:1–16)
- (G) Confidence in Yahweh Required for Success (7:17–26)
- (H) Appeal to Remembrance (8:1–20)
- (I) The Conquest of the Land Is the Work of Yahweh (9:1–7)
- (J) The Horeb Apostasy Recalled (9:8–29)
- (K) Renewal of the Covenant (10:1–11)
- (L) Living Within the Covenant (10:12–11:7)
- (M) Promise of the Land—Motive for Covenant Fulfillment (11:8–25)
- (N) Israel Must Decide Between Blessing and Curse (11:26–32)

(III) The Book of the Law (12:1–28:68)
- (A) The Place of Worship (12:1–14)
- (B) Rules for Sacred and Profane Meat (12:15–28)
- (C) Warning Against Idolatry in the Land (12:29–32)
- (D) Different Forms of Temptation to Idolatry (13:1–18)

(E) Laws Forbidding Pagan Customs and Foods Ritually Taboo (14:1–21)
(F) Tithes (14:22–29)
(G) The Sabbatical Release (15:1–18)
(H) The First-Born Reserved for Sacrifice (15:19–23)
(I) The Three Pilgrim Feasts (16:1–17)
(J) The Various Officers in the Theocratic Society (16:18–18:22)
(K) Rules Relating to Cult and Apostasy (16:21–17:7)
(L) Judges and Kings (17:8–20)
(M) The Levitical Priest (18:1–8)
(N) The Prophet (18:9–22)
(O) The Cities of Sanctuary (19:1–13)
(P) Rulings Regarding Boundary Marks and Witnesses (19:14–21)
(Q) Rules for the Holy War (20:1–20)
(R) The Case of Undetected Murder (21:1–9)
(S) Miscellaneous Laws (21:10–25:19)
  (a) Treatment of Women Captured in War (21:10–14)
  (b) Three Casuistic Laws (21:15–23)
  (c) A Series of Humanitarian and Ritual Laws (22:1–12)
  (d) Laws Concerning Sexual Mores (22:13–23:1)
  (e) Those Who Are To Be Excluded from the Plenary Assembly (23:1–8)
  (f) Purity in the Camp During the Holy War (23:9–14)
  (g) Various Laws (23:15–25)
  (h) Prohibition of Second Marriage with the Same Woman (24:1–4)
  (i) Measures in Favor of the Depressed Classes (24:5–25:4)
  (j) The Levirate Law (25:5–10)
  (k) Various Ordinances (25:11–19)
(T) Offering of the First Fruits (26:1–11)
(U) The Ceremony of the Triennial Tithing (26:12–15)
(V) Conclusion of the Covenant (26:16–19)
(W) A Conflation of Different Covenant Traditions (27:1–26)
(X) The Curses (27:15–26)
(Y) Concluding Blessings and Curses (28:1–68)
(Z) The Curses (28:15–68)

(IV) The Final Discourse of Moses; Traditions About His Last Days and Death (29:1–34:12)
(A) A Summary of the Covenant Ceremony (29:1–14)
(B) Homiletic Actualization of the Covenant Experience (29:15–29)
(C) Liturgical Address to the Exilic Community (30:1–20)
(D) Conclusion of the Ceremony and the Succession of Joshua (31:1–29)
(E) Introduction to the Song (31:16–29)
(F) The Song of Moses (31:30–32:44)
(G) Conclusion to the Giving of the Law and the Song (32:45–52)
(H) The Blessings of Moses on the Tribes (33:1–29)
(I) Death of Moses and Succession of Joshua (34:1–12)

COMMENTARY

7 **(I) First Address of Moses: From Horeb to Moab (1:1–4:43).** This first address gives an account of the vicissitudes of the Israelites in the various stages of their passage from Horeb to the promised land. It thus points to a fundamental theme of the whole book, namely, the land of Canaan as both object of divine promise and source of temptation. Noth (*GesSt* 34–40) sees this section as the prologue to his deuteronomic history (Jos–Kgs), a position which many scholars have accepted. (For the section as a whole, see also N. Lohfink, *Bib* 41 [1960] 105–34).

8 **(A) Introduction to the Address (1:1–5).** This rather expanded introductory note gives the circumstances of time and place (cf. 4:44–49). The address is part of a liturgical occasion, directed to *kŏl-yiśrā'ēl*, the plenary assembly of the tribes. It is important for determining the character of the book as a whole. **1b–2.** The verses are a topographical gloss; the region lies between the Dead Sea and the Red Sea (Hebr *yām sûp*, "sea of reeds"). (For Tophel, see H. Cazelles, *VT* 9 [1959] 412–15.) **2.** Horeb is the northern E term for Sinai, one of numerous contacts between Dt and this tradition. Kadesh-barnea in the Sinai Peninsula was an important stopping place and played a significant role in the formation of early traditions. **4.** Verse 4 summarizes the previous stages as told in Nm 21:21–35. **5.** We would expect the law to follow at once; the law of 5:1ff., or 9:8–10:11 according to Eissfeldt, may have been displaced when this introduction was added at a later stage.

9 **(B) Command to Possess the Land and Creation of Leaders (1:6–18).** **6.** The address begins here. Dt follows the prophets in attempting to solve the crisis of faith brought on by possession of the land of Canaan. **7.** Amorites, the term used in the E source, corresponds to Canaanites in J. The ideal boundaries of the land are given. **8.** Men of authority in the community are proposed from beneath and appointed by Moses; cf. Nm 11:16–30, of northern provenance, showing the charismatic nature of office in the community. Dt is the heir of this theology of the Spirit. **10.** The frequent occurrence of "today" and "this day," emphasizes the liturgical context of covenant renewal and the actuality and relevance of past events in sacred history (cf. Ps 95; Heb 3:7ff.). **15.** *officers:* The *šōṭēr* was a scribe (cf. Akkadian *šaṭāru*, "to write"), but in Dt his function was much wider (cf. 16:18; 20:5). **16.** The appointment of judges must be read in the light of Ex 18:13–27 (E), where again the application of the subsidiarity principle is clear, indicating how the casuistic law in Dt could have developed. *brethren:* The word *āḥ* (brother) denotes fellow Israelite; *gēr* (alien) denotes one ethnically different who had been incorporated into the social structure but without the rights of a full Israelite. **17.** These general moral principles reflect the influence of the great prophets, especially those of the north.

10 **(C) The Stay at Kadesh-barnea (1:19–46).** In recent years, the importance of the long period (1:46) that some of the tribes remained around this center, also a holy place, has been increasingly recognized (e.g., H. H. Rowley, *From Joseph to Joshua* [Oxford, 1948] 104–105; M. Newman, *The People of the Covenant* [N.Y., 1962] 72–101). The northern traditions contained in Nm 11–20 have a special link with Kadesh-barnea, as do also the Levites, who seem to be the agents of tradition for the deuteronomic law and covenant (see Dt 31:9; 33:8; Von Rad, *Studies in Deuteronomy*, 13–14, 66–67; G. E. Wright, "The Levites in Deuteronomy," *VT* 4 [1954] 325–30; J. A. Emerton, "Priest and Levites in Dt," *VT* 12 [1962] 129–38). **22.** The sending out of spies follows Nm 13–14 (cf. Jos 2:1–7). **26.** *but you refused to go up:* The refusing and the murmuring seem strange after the spies' good report; this oddity results from the Dt summary of the longer account in Nm 13—an illustration of the process of editing the older material. **28.** Cf. 2:10; the Anakim were a prehistoric population, remnants of whom were known to the Hebrews in the Philistine area and around Hebron (see L. G. Fonseca, *VD* 8 [1928] 145–47). **31a.** This verse may have been added later, because it is in the singular and intrusive syntactically. The appeal to

God's care for his people in the desert and the representation of Israel as Yahweh's son derive from Hosea and perhaps earlier (see Hos 11:1; cf. Dt 8:5; 14:1; 32:6; Ex 4:22). **32.** *trust:* It is derived from the root *'mn*, implying taking God at his word, the courage to commit oneself totally in accordance with his revealed will. For Dt this moral quality is basic. In vv. 30–33, we find the first signs of theological presentation of the holy war, a notion connected intimately with the Ark, which Dt inherited from the northern tradition (cf. Nm 10:33–36; Ex 40:36–38). (See especially Von Rad, *Studies in Deuteronomy*, 45–59.) **35.** *one man of this evil generation:* It is a good example of the stylized phrase and homiletic amplification of Dt (cf. Nm 14:31). **36.** *Caleb:* Eponymous founder of the southern tribe of Kenizzite (Kenite?) origin, forming part of the Hebron "amphictyony" (see Nm 13:30; 14:6–7; 32:12; Jos 14:6ff.; Jgs 1:12). **37.** *on your account:* Cf. 3:26; 4:21; the incident in Nm 20 is hardly adequate to explain the punishment inflicted. Here, the reason is the abandonment of the original invasion plan, and it is natural that in a law book ascribed to Moses the ultimate blame should be shifted to the people. **41–46.** The account of an abortive invasion from the south follows closely the Kadesh tradition of Nm 14:20ff. *Hormah:* It is a city in the Negeb (cf. Nm 21:3; Jgs 1:17).

11 **(D) Passage Through Edom, Moab, and Ammon (2:1–25).** The first stage in the displacement from Kadesh to Moab is one of peaceful infiltration that lasted a long generation (2:14). Dt has special interest in Yahweh's dealings with the "nations round about," seen within a scheme of providential history (cf. Bächli, *op. cit.*). The account may well reflect the situation in the latter part of the 7th cent., with the prospect of political independence from Assyria. **4.** *the descendants of Esau:* They are Edomites (see Gn 25:29ff.). This account diverges from Nm 20:13–22, in which Edom refuses the request for passage addressed from Kadesh. **7.** A sudden change to the singular breaks into the narrative and contradicts 2:14. **8b.** Comparison with Nm 21:10 provides another example of Dt editing and management of older material. **10–12.** The verses are a gloss dealing with the prehistoric populations of the Moab area. The Emim are classed as Rephaim (cf. Gn 14:5); the Horites are probably Hurrians (cf. Gn 14:6). **14.** The sinful generation had to disappear entirely before the sacred operation of the conquest of the land began (cf. the deuteronomic Ps 95:11). **15.** *the Lord's hand that was against them:* It marks a reversal of the holy war and of the Exodus (cf. W. L. Moran, "The End of the Unholy War and the Anti-Exodus," *Bib* 44 [1963] 333–42). **20–23.** Another long gloss appears on the prehistoric populations of Ammon. The Zamzummin and Avvim were non-Semitic groups, the latter ousted by the Caphtorim—i.e., the sea peoples (including the Philistines). **25.** *you:* in the singular, it was possibly added as peroration at a later stage of redaction.

12 **(E) Conquest of Heshbon and Bashan (2:26–3:11).** For the holy war with Heshbon, cf. Nm 21:21–32 and the speech of Jephthah to the Ammonite king, Jgs 11:18–22 (for the ideology of the holy war, see Von Rad, *Studies in Deuteronomy*, 45–59; C. H. Brekelmans, "Le ḥerem chez les Prophètes du royaume du nord et dans le Dt," *SP* 1, 377–83; De Vaux, *AI* 258–63). **26.** For the city of Kedemoth, see Jos 13:18; 21:37; others read "of the East" (Hebr *qedem*). **27.** *highway:* This road was the great caravan route, the kingsway, *derek hammelek*, of Nm 21:22. **30.** The motive behind this, to us, strange theological formulation (cf. Ex 4:21; Is 6:10) is God's absolute will for his people; all human agencies cooperate in this supreme purpose. **34.** The application of the *ḥerem*, although given a special theological sense in Dt, was not exclusively an Israelite practice (e.g., see the Moabite stele, *ANET* 320). **37.** *you:* See comment on 2:25. **3:1.** Bashan is the broad, fertile land in Transjordan N of Ammon. For this stage of the holy war, cf. Nm 21:33–35. In this case, the Dt account is somewhat expanded. **5.** *unwalled towns:* The analogy is with Jgs 5:7 where p^{e}*rāzôn* is translated "peasantry" (cf. 1 Sm 6:18; Est 9:19). **8.** A summary is given of the two campaigns. **9.** A gloss gives different local variations on the name Hermon (see A. Pohl, *VD* 21 [1941] 190). **11.** The gloss deals with folkloric interest in the semi-legendary Og and his preternaturally long bed (about 13 ft.) (see N. Glueck, *The River Jordan* [Phila., 1946] 117–18). The origin may have been some peculiarly shaped natural feature, or a basalt slab fallen from a prehistoric monument of the kind frequently found in the region.

13 **(F) Settlement of the Tribes East of the Jordan (3:12–22).** The passage is a very contracted form of Nm 32 (E) that takes the form of a dialogue between Moses and the tribes of Reuben and Gad. To it was added a town list and a summary account of the process of sedentarization. A much more complete list for the three Transjordan tribes appears in Jos 13:15–33. Reuben and Gad were the first to be sedentarized, but their existence was precarious and brief because of the encroachments of Moab and Ammon. From the Reuben taunt-song (Jgs 5:15b–16) and the absence of any mention of Gad in the Song of Deborah, they apparently did not keep their promise (see also Dt 33:6,21–22; Gn 49:3–4, 19). The insistence here and in Jos 1:12–18 on all the tribes participating in the conquest of the land follows from a theological premise. **13.** Manasseh was territorially the largest and originally the most important of the tribes. The relation of the two half-tribes is not clear; the division into halves shows the importance of keeping the number of tribes at 12. **13b–14.** The explanatory note entails Bashan and the capture of a group of villages near Argob by Jair, a Manassite clan; for Geshur, see Jos 13:13; 2 Sm 3:3; 13:37; 14:23; 32. **15.** *Machir:* This Manassite clan features in the Song of Deborah (Jgs 5:14; see Bright, *Hist.* 143). **16.** (For topography, see J. Simons, *PEQ* 79 [1947] 27–39.) **17.** Chinnereth is a place in Naphtali on the NW shore of the lake of the same name (i.e., Sea of Galilee). The sea of the Arabah or Salt Sea was, of course, the Dead Sea. **21.** The continuity between Moses and Joshua is stressed, and the description of the conquest under Joshua follows the same pattern as here. Sihon and Og are in line with the kings W of the Jordan, overcome by Joshua. The continuity is, above all, prophetic and charismatic (cf. 31:1–8; 34:9, and the account of the passing on of the Spirit in Nm 27:12–23; see N. Lohfink, "Die deuteronomistische Darstellung des Übergangs der Führung von Moses auf Josue," *Scholastik* 37 [1962] 32–44). **20.** *settled:* Lit., "given rest"; "rest" is a key theological expression in the deuteronomic literature (see Dt 12:9).

14 **(G) Prayer of Moses (3:23–29).** **24.** For the terminology, cf. Ex 6:21–22; 7:19; 9:26; 11:2–3; etc. Dt returns thematically to the Exodus as the revelation of the power of God, as the answer to national and religious crisis. *for what god . . . ?:* The oratorical question is part of the "high utterance" of Dt and confirms the impression of the book as a means toward a national revival based on Mosaic Yahwism as against other alternatives (cf. 4:7–8,33–34; 5:26). **26.** See 1:37. **27.** Pisgah is the E name corresponding to the prominence of Nebo in Moab (see also Dt 34:1; Nm 21:20; 23:14). **29.** Beth-peor is a locality in Reuben territory, N of Pisgah, where the *baʿal* of Peor was worshiped (see O. Henke, "Zur Lage von Beth Peor," *ZDPV* 75 [1959] 155–63).

15 **(H) Prologue to the Promulgation of the**

Law to All Israel (4:1–14). This promulgation is new because some had already heard the Law given at Horeb (1:3; 4:12–13). Moses undertakes to explain it (4:1; cf. 1:5). Because of displacements and successive editing, the place of this section in the overall structure of the work is not clear, but it is a prologue to the stipulations of the law, following the historical introduction, as evident from *w*^{e}*ʿattāh* (4:1) and the stylistic inclusion (4:1,14—same formula). We might surmise that the introduction to the deuteronomic history ends at 3:29 and that the original law book begins here, 1:1–5 being added when the two were joined. **1.** The Dt style is strongly exhortatory (see also vv. 9, 15, etc.); *š*^{e}*maʿ* (listen) indicates the opening of a liturgical address (cf. 5:1; 6:1; 6:3,4; 9:7). *statutes and decrees:* The word *ḥûq* means a positive decree of law; *mišpāṭ* indicates a judicial decision as a basis for case law from the root *špṭ*, "to judge." The giving of the Law is intimately connected with the promise of the land (cf. 4:1,5,14,21,25,38,40). Canaan is seen as a source of temptation—the great theme of the prophets, especially in the north—hence, the relevance at the time of Josiah's reform and in the years immediately preceding the return from the Exile. **2.** The prohibition to alter the wording of a treaty (covenant) or legal enactment usually occurs in the epilogue, as in the Hammurabi Code (see *ANET* 178). **3.** Only a passing reference is made to the incident of Nm 25:1–18. **4.** *Today:* The liturgical actualization of the covenant giving is repeated constantly throughout the discourses (see also Ps 95:7; Heb 3:7–11). **6.** *your wisdom and your intelligence: Ḥokmāh* often should be translated "prudence" rather than "wisdom" in the OT, but we may detect here the beginning of the process which eventually identified the Law with wisdom (see Prv 8:22–36; Sir 24). Also present, perhaps, is an appeal to the ruling classes of the writer's day. **7.** *what great nation . . .?:* This theology of "the God who is near" is connected with the older ideology of the Ark as the locus of Yahweh's active presence to his people; he comes near in theophany, which is intimately associated with the Ark that Dt calls "the ark of the covenant" (Dt 31:9,25,26; 10:18; Jos 3:8). We see here too Dt's role in a great national revival, for the Ark was also the political center—Israel is here "a great nation," *gôy gādôl*. God rescues his people when they call upon him, as is clear from the deuteronomic edition of Jgs. **9.** The role of memory and tradition, with reference to the Exodus-Horeb event, is often stressed in Dt (cf. B. S. Childs, *Memory and Tradition in Israel* [London, 1962]). Israel is addressed here in the singular. **10.** *assemble the people for me:* The verb *qhl* is used in Dt here and in 31:12,28 only, but the substantive *qāhāl*, "assembly" or "congregation," occurs often and has influenced the concept of the Church in the NT through the LXX translation, *ekklēsia* (see R. H. Kennett, *The Church of Israel* [Cambridge, 1933] 73–98; A. R. Hulst, "Het Woord kahal in Dt," *NThSt* 22 [1939] 159–66; K. L. Schmidt, *ThWNT* 3, 502–39). **11–12.** The fire of Horeb takes on an archetypal and symbolic character in Dt. It describes the numinous experience of encounter with the covenant God and his transcendent nature (cf. 4:33,36; 5:4,22,24ff.; 9:10). He is "a consuming fire" (4:24; cf. Heb 12:29), an image derived from the northern tradition. **13.** Cf. Ex 34:28. The original Dt seems to have implied two stages: the giving of the "ten words" on Horeb; statutes and provisions, based on the "words," for life in Canaan and promulgated just before the occupation.

16 **(I) A Commentary on the First Part of the Decalogue (4:15–31).** The rejection of idolatry is behind the first three imperatives of the Decalogue and the brief prologue preceding them (5:6–10; Ex 20:2–6). The enumeration of idols here follows that of the Decalogue. In both, the aniconic nature of the covenant God is stressed and possession of the land is the reward of observance of the law. This rejection of idolatry was basic to the Josian reform (2 Kgs 23:4; for the Assyrian worship of the heavenly bodies, 23:4,11; cf. Dt 4:19; 17:3) and to the exilic period. Here, the Exile is seen as caused by idolatry (for the addition of vv. 25–31, cf. Is 40ff.; Gn 1:14–15). **15.** (On the "spirituality" of the covenant God, see W. Eichrodt, *Theology of the OT* [London, 1961] 210–20.) In fact, archaeology has not turned up any representation of Yahweh. **16–18.** Different kinds of "idols" are meant: those of Canaanite cults, e.g., Baal and Astarte, the bull, and the snake; or those of Egyptian cults, e.g., Horus (the falcon). **19.** This verse does not necessarily deny that the objects mentioned are not objects of worship; it denies that they are such for the Hebrews (cf. Dt 29:25). **20.** *out of that iron foundry:* The same representation is found in Jer 11:4, one of many literary and theological parallels. As a result of the Exodus, Israel becomes "the people of inheritance" ("very own people") of Yahweh. The election and rejection of Israel is the leitmotiv of the deuteronomic history. **21.** See comment on 1:37; we are reminded that Dt is, in effect, the last will and testament of Moses to the people before his death, on the eve of their entering the land (cf. 32:48ff.; 34:1ff.). **24.** *a jealous God:* The title *'ēl qannā'* is used extensively throughout the OT but seems to have originated in the northern tradition (Ex 20:5; 34:14; Dt 5:9; 6:15). The adjective "jealous" is used with reference to deity also in Ugarit, and the Song of Moses refers twice to Yahweh being "jealous" (32:16,21). The context is always that of idolatry—i.e., as possible rivals for the allegiance of his people—suggesting that the northerner Hosea (Hos 1–3) may have developed a traditional motif in his own way. The word does not express the irrational or demonic in Yahweh, but rather his holiness and oneness (see Eichrodt, *op. cit.*, 209–10; S. Lyonnet, "De Zelotypia Yahve," *VD* 35 [1957] 83–87; B. Renaud, *Je suis un Dieu jaloux* [Paris, 1963]). **25.** Subject matter and comparison with Jgs 23:15–16 and 2 Kgs 17:7–23, both deuteronomic, suggest that vv. 25–31 are exilic (see Weiser, *OT* 129; cf. 30:1ff.). **26.** *I call heaven and earth to witness:* Cf. 32:1. The calling of witnesses was an essential feature of ancient covenants—either gods, deified natural elements, or mere humans (see G. Mendenhall, *BA* 17 [1954] 50ff., with reference to Hittite suzerainty treaties; also, Jos 24:27; 1 Sam 12:5–6). **27.** *handful of you:* This phrase is the prophetic *š*^{e}*'ērît*, or remnant. **29.** The phraseology is characteristic of Dt (cf. 6:5). **30** *finally:* "In the latter days," *b*^{e}*'aḥ*^{a}*rît hayyāmîm* (cf. 31:29), refers to the future, but one in which the situation will be different (cf. Gn 49:1; Nm 24:14; Is 2:2; Mi 4:1; Hos 3:5; and especially Jer 23:20; 30:24; 48:47). It will be the time for *šûb*, "return" or "conversion," when Yahweh will show in a special way his covenant qualities of mercy and fidelity.

17 **(J) The Unique Vocation of Israel in the Covenant (4:32–40).** We have here a magnificent homily on the election of Israel, one of the stylistic and theological high points of the book. It, too, may have descended in its present state from the exilic period (opinion of Robinson and others): the occurrence of *bārā'* (v. 32), rarely used of the creation of man before this time, is frequent in Dt and Is (see especially Is 45:12); the Exodus theme in relation to God's creation of the world is one of the basic motifs of Is 40ff.; the polemic against idolatry endorses Yahweh as the one God (cf. Is 45:5,6,18,22; Dt 4:35; see also Is 41:22–23; 43:10–12,25; 44:6). It is equally possible, however, that behind Dt, the prose passages in Jer, and parts of Dt–Is, there lies

a Levitical sermon style developed in Judah in the 7th cent. (see H. Breit, *Die Predigt des Deuteronomisten* [Munich, 1953]; Wright, *IB* 2, 318–19. For the pastoral viewpoint, cf. G. Von Rad ("The Preaching of Dt and Our Preaching," *Interpr* 15 [1961] 3–13). **33.** In the OT, it is axiomatic that one cannot see God and live (Jgs 6:22–23; 13:22, etc.). **34.** This way of speaking of the Exodus was already canonical, fixed by its repetition in the liturgy. **39.** Yahweh has superseded both the chthonian and uranian gods of Canaan and "the nations round about."

18 **(K) The Cities of Sanctuary (4:41–43).** It is difficult to see why this notice has been placed before Moses' second address. It is evidently intended to complete the description of the settlement E of the Jordan (see 3:12–22), but the question is brought up again in the Deuteronomic Code, 19:1–13, following the Book of the Covenant, Ex 21:13–14 (see also Jos 20:1–9, for the complete list of six cities, and Nm 35:9–34, for the exhaustive treatment of the post-exilic editors). **42.** Sanctuary did not cover deliberate homicide; its purpose was to mitigate the iron law of vendetta in the absence of a police force (cf. the custom in feudal Europe; see M. Greenberg, "The Biblical Concept of Asylum," *JBL* 78 [1959] 125–32).

(II) Second Address of Moses: Introduction to the Law Book (4:44–11:32).

19 **(A) Introduction to the Address (4:44–49).** These verses are a much expanded introductory note, parallel to 1:1–5 where redactional activity is clearly discernible—e.g., double title (vv. 44–45). **44.** *this is the law:* Torah (Law) refers to the complex of legislation, specified in the second introduction as "ordinances, statutes and decrees"; cf. 1:5, "Moses began to explain (*bē'ēr*) this torah"; this statement leaves room for homiletic expansion of the kind contained in these chapters (see G. Östborn, *Tōrā in the Old Testament* [Lund, 1945]). **46.** See comment on 3:29. The Torah is addressed to them on the point of entering the land, hence the intimate connection between Law and land. **47–49.** The note briefly summarizes the Transjordan conquests (see 2:26ff.). (For ch. 4, cf. A. C. Welch, *ExpT* 42 [1930–31] 227–31.)

20 **(B) The "Ten Words" (5:1–22).** **1.** *Moses summoned all Israel:* The repetition of the Ten Commandments and the homilies that follow are seen as taking place within the amphictyonic meeting. Many have understood the original Dt to begin here (H. Cazelles, R-F 1, 371; Davies, *op. cit.*, 269). *hear, O Israel:* The phrase is the usual introduction to the Dt kerygma (cf. 4:1; 6:1). What follows is the liturgical actualization of the covenant—hence the note of actuality: "not with our fathers... but with us, all of us who are alive here this day" (v. 3).

The Ten Commandments come to us also in the P recension (Ex 20:2–17), but both go back to a much earlier and doubtless briefer form normal for apodictic laws of this kind. They are called "the ten words" (Ex 34:28; Dt 4:13 [see comment on]; 10:4); it seems to have been common to arrange laws in decads, e.g., Ex 34:17–26 (see T. J. Meek, *Hebrew Origins* [N.Y., 1960] 37, 57–58). Although it is now difficult to reconstruct their original form and grouping (we have to compare with the text in the Nash papyrus and the Qumran phylacteries; for the latter, see H. Schneider in *BZ* 3 [1959] 18–31), we have no reason to doubt that the original form derives from the Mosaic age. We have no exact extrabiblical parallel from this or an earlier time, but certain ritual "negative confessions" in Akkadian and Egyptian texts (e.g., *ANET* 34–35) show the custom of listing vices or sins. **6.** The solemn declaration of identity is given by the lawgiver (as in the prologue to Hammurabi's Code, *ANET* 164–65)—i.e., the God who has revealed himself in the Exodus (cf. Ex 20:2; Hos 12:10; 13:4). **8.** See comment on 4:15–16. There is no sound reason for considering this commandment secondary. **9.** See comment on 4:24. Corporate responsibility, the solidarity of the blood-group, is stressed in Dt, both horizontally and, as here, vertically. This deep religious truth was corrected by stress on individual responsibility and guilt, mainly as a result of the national calamity of the Exile—see especially 7:10; 24:6; Ez 14:12; 18:1–32, where the vertical nexus is, in fact, broken. **10.** *steadfast love:* Intended is *ḥesed,* the supreme covenant love, implying benevolence and fidelity toward the other party (→ Aspects OT Thought, 77:95). Jn 13:15 shows the influence of this covenant formulation. **11.** *in vain:* It is from the LXX *epi mataiō.* The MT *laššāw'* means "falsely," abusively as in perjury, calling Yahweh to witness to a lie (cf. Lv 19:12; Dt 5:20). **12.** Sabbath observance here has a social and humanitarian motivation, as in the code of the covenant (Ex 23:12); rather than being a reference to creation as in P (Ex 20:8; cf. Gn 1), it is referred to the period of slavery in Egypt, thus associated with the deuteronomic theological theme of rest in the land. (On Dt's humanitarianism, see M. Weinfeld in *JBL* 80 [1961] 241–49). **17.** *kill:* The technical term for murder is *raṣaḥ* (cf. Jer 7:9; Hos 4:2). **21.** It is not clear whether two separate laws are intended here, but it is significant that "woman" (wife) comes before "house," possibly reflecting progress in social thinking (cf. Mi 2:2). **22.** The moral stipulations of the covenant are addressed directly to the *qāhāl,* "assembly" (LXX *synagōgē*). *nothing more:* He left it to Moses to expound the Ten Words in "statutes and ordinances." The act of writing the berit gave it juridical force (cf. Ex 24:4).

(Alt, A., *KlSchr* 1, 278–332. Cazelles, H., *VDBS* 5, 497–530. Kennett, R. H., *Deuteronomy and the Decalogue* [Cambridge, Eng., 1920]. Kessler, W., *VT* 7 [1957] 1–16. Rowley, H. H., *Moses and the Decalogue* [Manchester, 1951]. Welch, A. C., *ExpT* 41 [1929–30] 396–400.)

21 **(C) Moses Delegated to Promulgate the Law (5:23–33).** **23.** The numinous experience of Horeb was probably recreated from an early time in the liturgy of covenant renewal (see Ex 20:18–21). **24.** See comment on 4:33. **26.** *the living God:* This title, implying a rejection of false gods (who are dead), is especially associated with Dt (cf. 32:40; Jos 3:10 [deuteronomic]; Jer 10:10; 23:36; Hos 2:1). The same polemical note appears in its use in 1 Sm 17:26,36; 2 Kgs 19:4,16 (which may result from deuteronomic revision; cf. also Pss 42:3; 84:3). **27.** Thus, Moses' role of mediator is established and the Deuteronomic Code is prepared for. This function was essentially priestly, irrespective of a possible P origin (see C. Hauret, *Bib* 40 [1959] 509–21). **31.** Dt is at pains to separate the Ten Words from "all the commandment [sing. in the MT], the statutes and decrees"—i.e., the Deuteronomic Code, which regulated life in the land (cf. 4:5,14). **33.** *that you may live...:* We must situate the moral attitude of Dt within its total OT context. There then existed no idea of a reward in another world; sanctions for violation of law, especially for injustice, were entirely of this world, and no sharp division was made between moral and physical welfare (cf. 4:1,40; 5:16; 6:2; 17:20; Jos 1:7; see M. Weinfeld, *Tarbiz* 30 [1960–61] 8–15). (For the whole chapter, see Welch, *ExpT* 41, 396–400.)

22 **(D) Appeal to Covenant Fidelity in the Land (6:1–19).** Chs. 6–11 are continuous and divisions are to some extent arbitrary. Whether they result from several successive editions of the "Urdeuteronomium" (three, according to C. Steuernagel and F. Horst; four, according to R. Pfeiffer) or from a long paraenetic process (G. Von Rad, G. E. Wright), the lineaments of the liturgical encounter of covenant renewal are still, if faintly, perceptible (the cultic aspect is stressed by Weiser, *OT* 130; Brueggemann, *op. cit.*). Hölscher's view that Dt 6–11 is the original nucleus of the book is no longer popular, although some (e.g., Bächli) still adhere to it. Lohfink interprets the section as a development from 6:4–9 (*Das Hauptgebot*). It is difficult to ascribe, with J. Pedersen and I. Engnell, all or nearly all of this homiletic matter to the post-exilic period. **1.** See 5:31, which would appear to be the title of the code (cf. 12:1), although the lack of agreement may have arisen through conflating the *miṣwāh*, referring to 6:4, with the *ḥuqqîm wemišpāṭîm*, referring to 12:1ff. **3.** *hear:* See comment on 4:1. *a land flowing with milk and honey:* See Ex 3:8. The phrase is Canaanite; similar expressions appear in the Ugarit Baal cycle (49, III, 6–7, 12–13, etc.; *ANET* 140). The fertility of Canaan raised a sharp theological problem for the Hebrews entering from the infertile desert (Nm 13:17–27), for fertility is the divine blessing (Gn 27:28; see especially Dt 8:7–16). This problem is the basic one in the northern prophets, and in this sense Dt can be said to be "the spiritual heir of Hosea" (S. R. Driver). **4.** This abjuration refers to other gods, the Baal of Canaan in particular. We know that in Dt, Yahweh is the only real, the only living, God (4:35; 32:39; etc.). The one God for Israel is intimately linked with the law of one sanctuary (Dt 12:5). **5.** Dt emphasizes the love of both partners and adds to the basically juridical expression an emotive depth: "heart, soul, strength"—a characteristic deuteronomic phrase (e.g., 4:29; 10:12; 11:13; 13:4; 26:16; 30:2,6,10; Jos 22:5; 23:14). It is especially significant in its occurrence in 2 Kgs 23:3,25. Dt follows Hos (cf. Hos 2:19–20; 4:1; 6:6) in giving love this deeper and wider meaning (cf. Jer 31:31ff., where knowledge of Yahweh is equivalent to *ḥesed* in the Hosean sense). **8.** It is not certain whether here, and in Ex 13:16 and Dt 11:18, the "sign" was purely figurative, but later interpretation did result in the phylacteries (pouches containing the sacred text) worn on the left arm and on the forehead. Verses 4–9 came to be the great Jewish prayer, the Shema, and are referred to by Jesus as the greatest commandment of the Law (Mt 22:37). **12.** The call to remember points to the liturgical character of much of the material in Dt, for the chief purpose of the liturgy is *anamnēsis* or *zikkārôn*, recalling and actualizing the saving events of the Exodus and covenant. This is a "northern" prophetic theme (Elijah's journey to Horeb, 1 Kgs 19; the recollection of the desert period, Am 5:25; Hos 11:1ff.; see E. Blair, *Interpr* 15 [1961] 41–47; B. S. Childs, *op. cit.*, 68ff.). **13.** The stylistic inversion is for emphasis; "fear" refers to religious reverence expressed in worship (hence LXX [A], correctly *proskynēseis*; cf. Mt 4:10). **15.** See comment on 4:24. **16.** See Ex 17:1–17; Nm 20:2–13. This example was the standard one of "tempting" Yahweh—i.e., doubting his word and not having faith in him; Massah, at Kadesh-barnea, derives from *nāsāh*, "to tempt" (cf. Mt 4:7).

23 **(E) The Passover Haggadah (6:20–25).** Cf. Ex 12:26–27; 13:8–9. In this latter text, the Passover is called a *zikkārôn*, "memorial service," with the same injunction as Dt 6:9, showing the intimate connection between lawgiving and Passover (against G. Von Rad, *Genesis* [London, 1961] 15ff.; see Weiser, *OT* 83ff.). Both Passover and covenant have to be passed on from father to son (see Dt 4:9; 6:7). **21.** The words are certainly older than their context and are canonized by liturgical usage. They have the distinctive character of rhythmic recitative.

24 **(F) The *herem* Must Be Applied to the Populations of Canaan (7:1–16).** This section contains an injunction to apply the *ḥerem* followed by a paraenetic development giving reasons; it concludes with a repetition of the injunction (inclusion). It is a further development of 6:4—the worship of Yahweh alone, leading eventually to the unity of sanctuary law, 12:2–5. **1.** Yahweh is responsible for the conquest—a theological postulate of the holy war (see 1:30; 2:25). *many nations:* Dt shows special interest in the indigenous populations of Canaan and Transjordan (cf. 1:28; 1:44; 2:20–23; 3:11,13–14; 20:17). For the list of nations, see Ex 23:23 (E), Ex 34:10–17 (the "cultic decalogue" of J), and Gn 10:15ff.; 15:19ff. Dt adds the Girgashites and follows the former source rather closely. The Hittites (Gn 23:3) refer loosely to the non-Semitic element in Canaan; the Girgashites (Gn 10:16) are Canaanites (cf. Gn 15:21; Jos 3:10; 24:11). Amorite is the usual term in E corresponding to Canaanite in J, although they are separate in all the lists. The last three peoples mentioned are non-Semitic elements, the Hivvites probably referring to the Hurrian element (see Bright, *Hist.* 106–107). **2.** *doom:* See comment on 2:34; cf. Dt 13:13–18; 20:16–18. It is difficult, however, to know to what extent this wholesale slaughter was carried out in these early years owing to the theological coloring of the late redaction of Dt, and of Jgs in particular (see C. H. Brekelmans, *De herem in het Oude Testament* [Nijmegen, 1959]; De Vaux, *AI* 260–61). **5.** This program corresponds with the account of the Josian reform (2 Kgs 23:4–14), but it was implemented only sporadically and partially before then, and, in fact, many of the Canaanite altars and sanctuaries continued in use after the conquest. The pillar (*maṣṣēbāh*; see Gn 28:18; Ex 23:24; 34:13) was a commemorative stele, often a baalist and phallic symbol (2 Kgs 3:2; 10:26–27). The *'ăšērāh* (sacred pole) was the equivalent for the goddess of the same name, consort of El in the Ugaritic texts and of Baal in the OT. The "asherah" taken from the Temple and destroyed by Josiah (2 Kgs 23:6) was probably a genuine statue (cf. Ez 8:3). **6.** *a people sacred to the word:* They were separated for, therefore consecrated to, Yahweh in the etymological sense (cf. *ḥrm*—the same basic meaning!). Compare 14:2—again, to justify a command to dissociate from Canaanite religious practices (see also 26:19). This idea descends from the northern covenant theology that envisioned Israel as "a kingdom of priests, a holy people" (Ex 19:6); all took part in the cultic encounter and in it were united by an exclusive bond to the covenant God. *he has chosen you:* A dominant theme of Dt is Yahweh's search for a people among the nations (4:20,34; 26:7–8; etc.). **8.** His choice expressed in the covenant is the outcome of his "love" (*'ahabāh*). This attribution of love to God can be traced to Hos and is strong in Jer; in Dt (see also 7:14; 10:14–15), this prophetic insight is incorporated into covenant theology; "experience is transformed into dogma" (G. Quell; see also Eichrodt, *op. cit.*, 250–58). **9.** See comment on 5:10. **10.** We have here a strong statement on personal retribution; cf. 24:16, referred to in 2 Kgs 14:6 (Amaziah). Thus, both the traditional teaching on retribution (see comment on 5:9; cf. Ex 34:7) and the newer individual approach are represented in Dt. **12.** For this list of blessings, cf. the E list in Ex 23:22–26, on which it depends, and Dt 11:10–15 and 28:1–14. These blessings form an integral part of the structure of covenant making and renewal, acting as the ultimate sanction for compliance with the stipulations solemnly undertaken. Note how the blessings are concerned above all with fertility, that of the good land of Canaan (11:10–12!), thus solving the problem of faith that the land poses. Yahweh, not the Baals, is the ultimate source. This point had already been made by Hosea (2:5,8–9) (see comment on 6:3). **16.** *ensnared:* Cf. 7:25. This theme, frequent in E and D, appears in Ex 10:7; 23:33; 34:12; Jos 23:13; Jgs 2:3; 8:27.

25 **(G) Confidence in Yahweh Required for Success (7:17–26).** **17.** The Passover theme recurs, based on Ex 23:27ff. (see comment on 6:12,20). **20.** *hornets:* The verse is an excellent example of homogeneity in style and vocabulary between E and D (see Ex 23:28; Jos 24:12; on these affinities, cf. Wright, *IB* 2, 318ff., 320, n. 28). **21.** *in your midst:* The word b^{e}qirbekā is often used of the Ark; cf. m^{e}hûmāh g^{e}dolāh (v. 23), the divinely inspired panic which arises when the Ark is present (cf. 1 Sm 4:7; 5:9,11; 7:10). (For holy war terminology, see J. Blenkinsopp, *CBQ* 26 [1964] 427–31.) **22.** It is one of several reasons given to explain the gradual and incomplete nature of the settlement (cf. Ex 23:29–30; Jos 23:4–13; Jgs 2:22–23; 3:1–2). (For the chapter as a whole, see Welch, *ExpT* 41, 409–12.)

26 **(H) Appeal to Remembrance (8:1–20).** Chapter 8 deals with the *anamnēsis* of the Exodus and desert period. It marks the end of one stage in the history which had begun with the covenant at Horeb, and the commencement of another, which begins with the covenant in Moab. **1.** See comments on 4:1; 5:33. **2.** The remembrance of the desert period, the 40 years, is a prophetic theme (e.g., Am 5:25; Hos 2:14–15; etc.). This temptation (i.e., trial) theme by God of his people in the wilderness has influenced Matthew's story of the Temptation of Christ (4:1–11; Dt quoted three times). **3.** *fed you with manna:* See Ex 16; Nm 11:16–23. The conclusion of Dt, quoted by Jesus in Mt 4:4, that man lives authentically only from God's Word and Law, is already implied in these sources with their strong theological character. It is also prophetic teaching (e.g., Am 8:11). *every word that comes forth from the mouth of God:* See H. Brunner (*VT* 8 [1958] 428ff.). **5.** *as a man disciplines his son:* See comment on 1:31a. **7.** The theme of the fertile land is repeated—the fulfillment of the blessing to the fathers—but the description is followed by "Be careful!" (v. 11) (see comment on 6:3; cf. Am 4:9; 9:13–14; Hos 2:8–9,22; 10:1; 14:5–7). **9.** *iron and copper:* This statement could not have been true before the time of the united monarchy. Iron and bronze are not found in Palestine. **15.** The dangers of the desert period are recalled. *saraph serpents:* Cf. Nm 21:6–9. "Saraph" (Is 14:29; 30:6) is a substantive referring to a winged creature whose habitat is the desert (Is 30:6). For the view that it is the symbol of Aaron and the Levites, see Meek (*Hebrew Origins,* 122–24). *parched:* For the theme of the desert that is made to bloom, see the references in the two late poems, Is 35:7 and Ps 107:34, where the same rare word, *ṣimmā'ôn,* is used. For the water from the rock, see Ex 17:1ff. and Nm 20:1ff. **20.** In keeping with prophetic teaching, Dt stresses that the covenant is conditional and that nonobservance makes her "like the nations" (cf. Am 2:6ff.; 6:8ff.; 9:7–8; Hos 8:1ff.).

27 **(I) The Conquest of the Land Is the Work of Yahweh (9:1–7).** **1.** *hear, O Israel:* See comment on 4:1. **2.** *Anakim:* See comment on 1:28. **3.** This kind of language is associated with the Ark (cf. Jos 3:3, etc.) and can be taken as a theological blueprint for the D description of the conquest. For the expression "a consuming fire," see comment on 4:11. **4.** Cf. 8:17. The two theological reasons for the success of the conquest are given: the moral perversion of the native population; promise–fulfillment (cf. 7:22). **7.** *this place:* The place of meeting is meant (cf. 1:31; 11:5; 29:7). A liturgical origin, perhaps with reference to Shechem, may be surmised from the occurrence of the phrase in the "credal statement" of 26:9 (cf. "the place which Yahweh will choose," 12:5, etc.).

28 **(J) The Horeb Apostasy Recalled (9:8–29).** This account is clearly the D version of the incident described in Ex 32, but the unity of place has been broken by additions at 9:22–23 and 10:6–9. The narrative of Ex 32, which was not composed at one sitting, already reflects the reaction to later experience—possibly the bull cult of the north—and it is clear that D is here concerned more with a situation that he envisioned as archetypal for Israel than with an historical reconstruction in detail. For the view that the incident was originally connected with Bethel and the northern kingdom, see R. H. Kennett (*JTS* 6 [1905] 161ff.) and T. J. Meek (*Hebrew Origins,* 136–38). **9.** The verse begins a parallel tradition to that in 5:1–31; its present position would have been suggested by the context immediately preceding. Moses' 40-day fast is repeated in expiation of the apostasy and in preparation for the renewal of the covenant, 9:18 (cf. 1 Kgs 19:8; Mt 4:2). **10.** *on the day of the assembly:* The presence of "all Israel" at Horeb is interpreted as the prototype of the liturgical assembly on the occasion of covenant renewal (see comments on 4:10 and 5:22). **12.** The corrupt action consisted in making an image, a reminder of Jeroboam's initial act of apostasy, or at least syncretism (1 Kgs 12:23ff.; cf. Aaron's exclamation in Ex 32:4 with that of Jeroboam in 1 Kgs 12:28!). The statues set up by Jeroboam are called *massēkôt* (molten) in the deuteronomic meditation on the fall of Samaria (2 Kgs 17:16). **13.** *stiff-necked:* This expression is used only by Yahweh or Moses (Ex 32:9; 33:3,5; 34:9; Dt 9:6,13; 31:27). **16.** *a molten calf:* Cf. Ex 32:4. The *'ēgel* was the bull, worship of which in the northern kingdom is verified in both biblical texts and archaeological data. It implied a symbiosis between Yahweh and the Baal of Canaan (cf. 1 Kgs 12:23). **17.** *broke them before your eyes:* This juridical act signified that for Yahweh, the covenant was no longer binding. If the analogy of the suzerainty treaty is accepted, it would moreover be a form for initiating proceedings against a recalcitrant vassal; cf. the Egyptian practice of breaking sherds inscribed with the names of rebellious vassals before proceeding against them (*ANET* 328–29). **20.** The intercession for Aaron is absent from Ex 32 and may result from a separate tradition or recension. **21.** According to Ex 32:20, they had to drink it! Cf. Nm 5:16ff., the application of ordeal, a kind of preternatural truth drug. **22–24.** This section breaks into the narrative, referring to 1:26ff. Several scholars attach the preceding incident to Kadesh-barnea rather than to Horeb (e.g., Newman, *op. cit.,* 190). The place names are stopping places on the route from Horeb to Moab. For Taberah (burning), see Nm 11:3; Massah (trial or temptation) was probably at or near Kadesh; Kibroth-hattaavah (graves of craving) was NE of Horeb (see Nm 11:34; 33:16). **25.** This narrative is not continuous with the previous one, but takes up from v. 19 and amplifies the note of intercession in the form of a prayer. On Moses' priestly role of mediation and intercession, see comment on 5:27; he intercedes for the people at every stage of the covenant breaking in Ex 32–33. Intercession was the office of a king (2 Sm 24:17; 1 Kgs 8:30ff.), a prophet (Am 7:2ff.; Jer 10:23), and a priest (Jl 2:17). **26.** Moses' intercession takes on one of the "classical" forms of ancient prayer: address; petition; the appeal to remember; and motives for answering the prayer (cf. Ex 32:11ff.; 33:12ff.). *ransomed:* This term originally meant to get back, by paying a price, what had for some reason become the property of another. It is used in the OT principally of the ritual ransoming of the first-born, who belonged to God (Ex

13:11ff.; Lv 27:27; Nm 18:15–17), but it acquired a definite theological connotation first with regard to Yahweh's ransoming of his people in the Exodus (Hos 7:13; 13:14), and then principally in the following: Jer 15:21; 31:11; Dt 7:8; 9:26; 13:6; 15:15; 21:8; 24:18; 2 Sm 7:23 (D). Exilic or post-exilic texts refer the term to the return from Exile seen as a new Exodus (Is 29:22; 35:10; 51:11). **27.** For the memory motif, see comment on 6:12 and cf. Ex 32:13. **28.** This rather artless approach often occurs in the OT side by side with deep theological insight (cf. Jos 7:9—"What will become of your great name?").

29 **(K) Renewal of the Covenant (10:1–11).** **1.** The account of the renewal of the covenant was especially important within the framework of Dt because the book seems either to have come into existence, or to have been used, for a feast of covenant renewal. It is based on the J narrative in Ex 34, but the sequence—i.e., covenant making (E), Aaronic apostasy, and covenant renewal (J)—arises as much from theological as from historical preoccupations. *an ark of wood:* This phrase is added to the account in Ex 34. The term "the Ark of the covenant" is deuteronomic (10:8; 31:9,25,26; Jos 3:8,14,17; etc.), and is explained by this narrative. It is not clear whether this interpretation of the Ark as a box is entirely distinct from the Ark considered as a throne and whether this account is a retrojection of a liturgical ceremony of a later time, e.g., the covenant feast at Shechem, the "day of the assembly" (see De Vaux, *AI* 297–302). On the Ark of Shechem, see Jos 8:33 (of Dt provenance), denied by Albright (Albright, *ARI* 103–104) and Bright (Bright, *Hist.*, 147) and accepted by Noth (Noth, *Hist.*, 97) and Von Rad (*Studies in Deuteronomy*, 42–43; *GesSt* 128–29), on the basis of the covenant making in Jos 24, the use of Ark terminology, and the deuteronomic tradition. **6–9.** This section interrupts the Horeb narrative (cf. 9:22–24). It consists in a continuation of the series of stopping places in the journey from Horeb (cf. Nm 33:31–38). Moserah is Moseroth in Nm 33:30, the scene of Aaron's death; according to Nm 20:22ff. (P), he died on Mt. Hor near Kadesh. The order of the two places is reversed here. For Eleazar, son of Aaron, see Nm 3:32; 20:22ff. For Gudgodah, cf. Nm 33:32, Hor-haggidgad. **8.** The purpose of the intrusion of this section is explained—namely, to show that the Levites were not connected with Aaron's apostasy inasmuch as he was already dead before they came into existence (on the Levites as the agents of tradition, see the comments on 1:19; 33:8). Their origin is still extremely obscure (Gn 46:11; Ex 6:16; Nm 1:48ff.; 3:6,8; 4:1ff.). According to the genealogy in Chr (Chr 5:27ff.), Aaron is a descendant of Levi. **9.** There is no reason to doubt that Levi was originally a secular tribe like the others. **10–11.** This passage completes the narrative of vv. 1–5.

30 **(L) Living Within the Covenant (10:12–11:7).** This homiletic development is typically D, in which the influence of the prophetic teaching is easily seen. **12.** *and now:* The term *w^{e}ʿattāh* points to the moral conclusions drawn from the historical premises (see comment on 4:1; cf. the list of fundamental moral attitudes in Mi 6:8). It is possible that both derive from a more or less fixed form of covenant preaching. **14.** The preacher captures here the awe and wonder of the divine election, his dominant theme in this book. **16.** *circumcise your hearts:* It is difficult to know whether this forceful expression of an interiorized and fully committed attachment to the covenant is original to Dt (cf. also 30:6) or derives from Jer (4:4; 9:24–25; cf. the circumcision of the ears in 6:10, because one must listen to God's Word to take it into one's heart); perhaps both derive from common homiletic usage. This way of speaking is discussed in the NT with reference to the new covenant (Acts 7:51; Rom 2:25ff.). **17.** The genitives here are used as superlatives. **18.** Doing justice is the supreme royal prerogative, which is evident from both biblical and extrabiblical literature—e.g., Ugarit. On the resident alien (*gēr*), see comment on 1:16. For Dt, these three form the most needy classes, who are the object of the divine compassion and for whom provision must be made in the laws (cf. 16:11,14; 24:17,19; etc.). **20.** *by his name:* That of another god was not possible. **22.** The new thought sequence may begin here (rather than in 11:1)—i.e., the past experience of Israel as a motive for covenant observance, beginning with a contrast between the original nucleus of 70 and the great multitude present at the covenant renewal. **11:1.** Observance of covenant stipulations appear in the context of the love of the covenant god (cf. Jn 13:15). **2.** *now:* Intended is "this day" (cf. vv. 4, 8, 26, 28, 32; see comment on 4:4). The verb *yāsar*, from which *mûsār* (discipline) is derived, can mean "chastisement," but, following its usage in Jer (2:30; 17:23; 32:33; 35:13), it refers here to Yahweh's educative influence exerted through historical experience. **3.** Again, the reference is the Exodus story (see comment on 6:20–21). The narrative reaches the level of a rhymed recitative—e.g., v. 4: *'ăšer hēṣîp et-mê yam-sûp*, "how he made the water of the Sea of Reeds engulf [them]." **4.** *to this day:* If we infer it as during the reign of Josiah, it must refer to the time when Psammeticus was an Assyrian vassal before the campaigns of Neco. Alternatively, it may refer to the period after the Persian occupation of Egypt by Cambyses in 525. **6.** Cf. Nm 16.

31 **(M) Promise of the Land—Motive for Covenant Fulfillment (11:8–25).** See comment on 4:1; 5:33. **10.** The fertility of Egypt depended on a system of irrigation exploiting the annual Nile flood. The inundation was not necessary in Canaan, which depended on the regular occurrence of rain. The "early rain and the late rain" come, respectively, in the October-November and March-April periods. The nonoccurrence of these rains, vital for the fertility of the land, was interpreted as divine punishment (e.g., Am 4:7; 7:4ff.; Jer 14:1–6). (On 11:10–15, see W. Vischer, *RHPR* 44 [1964] 102–109.) **16.** *be careful:* See comment on 6:3, and cf. thought pattern in 8:11ff. (see also T. J. Meek, *JBL* 67 [1948] 235–36). **18.** The verse parallels 6:6ff. (see comment on 6:8). **24.** They are the ideal boundaries of the land (cf. 1:6–8; Jos 1:3–4). This picture did not become possible before the united monarchy.

32 **(N) Israel Must Decide Between Blessing and Curse (11:26–32).** In the covenant formulation, blessing and curse were ultimate sanctions, to be taken extremely seriously. The contracting partners, or the vassal in the case of a suzerainty treaty, recited them and took them upon themselves. In 27:11–28:46, we have what is probably an amplified form of the original D covenant blessings and curses, but there are traces elsewhere in the book—7:12–15 and here; cf. Jos 8:30–35 (D). **26.** *this day:* Emphasized is the existential nature of the covenant encounter—the need to make a final decision. We may have here the origin of the "two ways" category (cf. Dt 30:15–20; Ps 1; Didache 1:1; 1QS 4; Mt 7:13–14). **29.** This verse, which is in the singular, may have been added from 27:11ff. (cf. Jos 8:30ff.). The mention of this locality in connection with the covenant making strengthens the hypothesis of dependence on a Shechem liturgy (cf. Jos 23–24). **30.** The gloss explains the topography. Gilgal means a circle—usually of stones—and refers to a place near Shechem not the Gilgal of Jos 4:19). For "the oak of

Moreh" see Gn 12:6. On the incident as a whole, see comment on 27:12.

33 **(III) The Book of the Law (12:1–28:68).** This nucleus of Dt is first and foremost a law book. It contains different kinds of law covering every aspect of national life: cultic, criminal, and social. Its repetitions and homiletic developments make it improbable, as Wellhausen supposed, that chs. 12–26 were, in fact, the book found in the Temple by Hilkiah (2 Kgs 22:8). Whatever the form of that book, recent study of the structure of a covenant agreement and an attentive study of 2 Kgs 22–23 (especially the violent reaction of Josiah on hearing of the discovery of the book, 2 Kgs 22:11), as well as the inclusion of 28:69 (cf. 12:1), suggest that it would have included blessings and curses of the kind found in chs. 27–28 (with H. H. Rowley, A. Weiser, K. Baltzer, etc.). We might read it tentatively as a law book drawn up by Levites and based on old amphictyonic law for the "use" of a sanctuary such as Shechem and/or Mizpah—a revision of the E Book of the Covenant (Ex 20:22–24:18); the law would have been promulgated from the national capital with special reference to the northern provinces on the eve of their liberation from the Assyrian yoke. It was evidently intended as a program for a great religious and national revival.

(See Siebens, A. R., *L'origine du Code Deutéronomique* [Paris, 1929]. Simpson, C. A., "A Study of Dt 12–28," *AnglTR* 34 [1952] 247–51. Welch, A. C., *The Code of Deuteronomy* [London, 1924]. Wiener, H. M., "The Arrangement of Dt 12–26," *JPOS* 6 [1926] 185–95.)

34 **(A) The Place of Worship (12:1–14).** **1.** This heading applies to the whole Book of the Law (cf. 28:69). **2.** The sanctuary law appears first, as it does in the E code (Ex 20:24–26), because the law is preserved at the sanctuary and is intimately connected with worship, and because the sanctuary is the center of the covenant life of the community. The Deuteronomic Code, by insisting on one central sanctuary, abrogates the E presumption of many sanctuaries. This law is of primary importance in the deuteronomic scheme (against the views of Oestreicher and Welch in particular, the latter holding that 12:1–7 is a later addition). It provides a vital link with the Josian religious reform (cf. 2 Kgs 23:4ff.), which was concerned not only with purity but also with unity. Ch. 12 is probably a conflation of two, possibly three, versions of the law of one sanctuary and the provisions for sacrifice.

(See Dobbie, R., "Dt and the Prophetic Attitude to Sacrifice," *ScotJT* 12 [1959] 68–82. Dummermuth, *ZAW* 70, 59–98. Maag, V., "Erwägungen zur deuteronomistischen Kultzentralisation," *VT* 6 [1956] 10–18. Nicholson, E., "The Centralisation of the Cult in Dt," *VT* 13 [1963] 380–89. Steuernagel, C., *Deuteronomium und Joshua* [2nd ed.; Göttingen, 1923]. Welch, A. C., *The Code of Deuteronomy*; "The Two Descriptions of the Sanctuary in Deuteronomy," *ExpT* 36 [1924–25] 442–44; *ExpT* 37 [1925–26] 215–19.)

5. *the place:* Cf. Ex 20:24, "In every place where I cause my name to be remembered." Oestreicher's interpretation of the deuteronomic text as "any place" is grammatically inadmissible, but that does not mean that the "place" could only have been Jerusalem. The ideal of one central tribal sanctuary—Shechem, Shiloh, Mizpah—can be deduced safely from the history, and the Josian reform can be interpreted as a revival of this ideal, applied naturally to the national capital, although not, of course, for the first time. The word *māqôm*, "place," appears to be the technical term for a sanctuary in the E tradition (e.g., Gn 22:3–5; 28:11) and the deuteronomic history (2 Sm 7:10; 1 Kgs 8:29,30; etc.). The idea of one central sanctuary is, at any rate, clearly presumed, although not rigorously practiced, in the history of Samuel (note the book put in the sanctuary in 1 Sm 10:25!) and in the oracle of Nathan (2 Sm 7; see Junker, *op. cit.*). *designates:* Lit., "to put his name"; cf. the law of the altar, Ex 20:24 (on deuteronomic "name theology," see Von Rad, *Studies in Deuteronomy*, 37ff.). The idea of Yahweh's "dwelling" at the sanctuary, in the midst of his people, by means of his "name" is to be connected with the Ark (see 2 Sm 6:2) and has profoundly influenced the deuteronomic history (e.g., 1 Kgs 8:27–29). It has contributed not a little to NT incarnational formulations (e.g., Jn 1:14). **6.** For the different kinds of sacrifices and offerings, see De Vaux (*AI* 415ff.). **7.** Joyful participation in the liturgy, especially at the great feast of covenant renewal, is characteristic of Dt; cf. 14:26; 16:11,14,15; 26:11; 27:7; 28:8. **8.** Here the Israelites are evidently in Canaan! *what seems right:* Acting according to one's own good pleasure is meant, referring to the frequenting of local shrines, as is clear from Jgs 17:6; 21:25. **9.** *restingplace:* The term *m*ᵉ*nûḥāh*, is used by D for Canaan, the object of the divine promises (cf. 25:19; Ps 95:11); in earlier traditions, this term was also connected with the Ark (Nm 10:33; see G. Von Rad, *Zwischen den Zeiten* 12 [1932–33] 104–11). **10.** Here begins a more or less parallel formulation. **12.** *the Levite that is within your towns:* On the role of the Levites in Dt, see comments on 1:19 and 33:8. The situation of the Levite here is similar to that of the Bethlehemite Levite of Jgs 17:7ff.; they were also classified as "aliens."

35 **(B) Rules for Sacred and Profane Meat (12:15–28).** **15.** Primitively, all slaughter of livestock was considered a sacred act (*zābaḥ*, "to slaughter" or "to sacrifice"). According to Lv 17:3ff., the slaughter of all sacrificial animals was sacred, whereas in Dt, the sacral element is reduced to abstention from the life-giving blood, an ancient religious taboo (cf. 1 Sm 14:32ff.), and to those animals actually destined for sacrificial use. **19.** Levites, who were not then of settled domicile or independent means, are commended to the charity of the faithful whom they served (cf. 14:27,29; 16:14; 26:12). **20.** This legislation was brought about by the change from a seminomad to a settled farmer. Verses 20–28 seem to parallel the preceding prohibition.

(C) Warning Against Idolatry in the Land (12:29–32). The source of the danger was the commonly accepted belief that domicile in a certain land implied a special relationship with the god or gods of that land. In Canaan, the Baals were already in possession. **30.** See comment on 7:16. **31.** Cf. 18:10; see comment on Lv 18:21. The practice of child sacrifice is mentioned in the Josian reform (2 Kgs 23:10).

36 **(D) Different Forms of Temptation to Idolatry (13:1–18).** This section contains three stipulations in the form of casuistic law (beginning with *kî*. . . "If a prophet. . .," "If your brother. . .," "If you hear. . ."—see 17:2–7 for a fourth) against possible sources of temptation to practise idolatry in Canaan. In view of the presumed situation, and especially the similarity in form to the casuistic sections in Ez (14:13ff.; 14:21ff.; especially ch. 18), we may conjecture that these sections belong to the exilic recension of the book. **2.** In the MT, 12:32 is 13:1. As the heir of the E tradition, Dt gives importance to prophecy and dreams. According to 18:22, the test of a true prophet is the verification of his prediction, but it must be considered with his fidelity to Yahweh; cf. Jer 23:9–40, dealing in part with false prophecy at the time of Dt. For the deuteronomic attitude toward dreams, which played such a great part in Phoenician-Canaanite religion, see 13:2,4,6. **4.** Cf. God's testing his people in the desert (8:2). **6.** *he has*

preached apostasy: This phrase, which seems to suggest the kingship of Yahweh, is used only here and in Jer 28:16; 29:32; both deal with false prophets. **7.** Nothing human can stand in the way of the worship of the one true God (cf. Lk 14:20–27). **14.** *certain scoundrels:* Lit., "sons of Belial" (*b^{e}lî yaʿal*, "without profit," "useless"), it is used frequently in the deuteronomic history (e.g., Jgs 19:22; 20:13, of the men of Gibea; 1 Sm 2:12, of the sons of Eli; etc.). In Na 1:11; 2:1, it is a prophetic pseudonym for an Assyrian aggressor, and in Ps 18:5, a proper name signifying "death." Understood in this sense—as a demon or evil spirit—it occurs in QL and other apocalyptic literature of that period, sometimes in the form Beliar (cf. 2 Cor 6:15). **17.** *heap of ruins:* A *tēl* is a mound or hill, formed about a ruined and deserted site (cf. Jos 8:28). This verse betrays the ideology behind the deuteronomic history of the conquest in Jos. **17b–18.** A final, inclusive exhortation is given, showing the oral, liturgical life setting of the lawgiving.

37 **(E) Laws Forbidding Pagan Customs and Foods Ritually Taboo (14:1–21).** **1.** See comment on 1:31a. Whether this verse concludes the previous section or opens this one, it is an example of the homiletic context of the laws. The prohibition of incisions or tonsure as a sign of mourning the dead is found also in the Holiness Code, Lv 19:27. It seems to have been practiced also by the prophetic communities in Canaan (cf. 1 Kgs 20:41; 2 Kgs 2:23; cf. Aqhat I iv, 11). In Jer 16:6; 7:29; 41:5; etc., however, it seems to have been regarded as normal practice. **2.** For this homiletic conclusion to the enunciation of the law see comment on 7:6. **3.** There follows (vv. 3–21a) a series of *tôʿēbāh* (abomination) rules concerning ritually permissible and impermissible food, introduced by the original apodictic law (v. 3) and roughly parallel to the series in the Holiness Code (Lv 11). It represents a later redaction, but contains early material (R. K. Yerkes, *JQR* 14 [1923–24] 1–29). The rationale behind these food taboos is not stated in the texts; we may suppose either natural revulsion (e.g., birds of prey and certain insects), or sinister and ominous associations (e.g., raven, Lv 11:15), or the fact that certain foods were sacrificed in pagan rites (e.g., camel and swine) although much of the sacrificial material of Israel and Canaan was similar. This ritual part of the Law was abrogated by Christ (Mt 15:10–20; cf. 1 Cor 8, etc.). **6.** These criteria and the classification of fauna in general were established on the basis of ordinary unscientific observation. **9.** Water is a good, life-giving element; ocean-going mammals were known but only as mythical creatures, and crustaceans were approximated to reptiles, therefore taboo. But, in fact, the Hebrews had little acquaintance with the sea and its food. **19.** In Lv 11:21, an exception is made for locusts. **21.** Cf. Lv 17:15. The reason is that in these circumstances the warm blood, which belonged to God, could not be drained (cf. 12:23). The series ends with the formula, "For you are a people sacred"—the theological motivation of these rules (cf. Lv 11:45). **21b.** Cf. Ex 23:19; 34:26. This reference is to part of a religious ritual practiced in Canaan, the exact import of which escapes us. It occurs in an obscure Ugaritic text (cf. G. R. Driver, *Canaanite Myths and Legends* [Edinburgh, 1956] 121; see also A. Casey, *VD* 16 [1936] 142–48, 174–83).

38 **(F) Tithes (14:22–29).** The practice of paying tithes was evidently very ancient, although the P legislation (Nm 18:21–32; Lv 27:30–33) is not identical with that of Dt. In Am 4:4 is attested the custom in the north (cf. Jacob at Bethel pays tithes, Gn 28:22); Dt develops this law homiletically in the usual way. **22.** The tithe is levied on the produce of the soil and livestock. **23.** See comment on 12:5. For a good example of homiletic development which updates the original and pre-Josian law, see Von Rad (*Studies in Deuteronomy*, 17). The soil of Canaan now belongs to Yahweh and the tithe must be allocated for a sanctuary feast characterized by rejoicing (cf. Jgs 21:19ff.; 1 Sm 1:3,14). **24.** Provision is made to commute to money, thus solving the difficulty of transport. **26.** The sacrificial meal was always a joyful occasion; see comment on 12:7. (For the deuteronomic emphasis on joy in the festivals, see H. J. Elhorst, *ZAW* 42 [1924] 136–45.) **27.** See comment on 12:19. **28.** According to Nm 18:25ff., all the tithes were apparently allocated to the Levites, who handed over one tenth to the priests. Here, Levites are grouped, as usual, with other needy classes (see comments on 10:18 and 12:12). For the ceremony for this paying of tithes, see 26:12–15.

39 **(G) The Sabbatical Release (15:1–18).** This type of preaching seems to be addressed particularly to the landed classes, and it was these, conservative by nature, who were probably behind the Josian reform. The humanitarianism of Dt is very striking here (see comment on 5:12). **1.** This law was the basic, ancient law on the *š^{e}miṭṭāh*, "release" or "remittance." For the application to the land, see Ex 23:10–11; Lv 25:1–7; see also 1 Mc 6:49ff. What follows is a "modern" interpretation and application of the law to a sphere to which it had not originally applied, showing the influence of the stand of the 8th-cent. prophets against social injustice. (For form criticism of the passage, see Von Rad, *Studies in Deuteronomy*, 15–16.) **2.** On "what he has loaned," see S. Cavaletti (*Anton* 31 [1956] 301–304) and R. North (*VT* 4 [1954] 196–99). **2–6.** It is a homiletic expansion and application. It is difficult to say to what extent this law was observed (for the post-exilic period, see Neh 5:6ff.; cf. De Vaux, *AI* 173–75). **7.** The two following sections (vv.7–11), in the form of casuistic law familiar from extrabiblical codes, are more exhortations than laws in the strict sense. As such, they are unparalleled in ancient legislation. **11.** Cf. Mt 26:11, in contrast to Dt 15:4. **12.** The law of release applied to slavery following the Book of the Covenant (Ex 21:2–6). It is probably correct to read this verse with the previous section, because the slaves in question have sold themselves into slavery to pay their debts. In Jer 34:8–16, we see that the law was not observed; that there was need to protect the poor debtor can be seen in Amos' complaint (Am 2:6) that "they sell the righteous for silver, the pauper for a pair of sandals." (See M. David, *OTS* 5 [1948] 63–79; for possible extrabiblical parallels, see C. H. Gordon, *RB* 44 [1935] 38–41; O. Loretz, *Bib* 41 [1960] 167–75; in the Code of Hammurabi, see *ANET* 171.) **15.** For the motivation, cf. 5:15, the Sabbath. **17.** The religious significance is brought out more clearly in Ex 21:6–7. Piercing the ear signifies obedience (*šāmaʿ*, "to hear" or "to obey"). **18.** Inasmuch as, according to Ex 21:32, a slave costs 30 shekels, this reference may imply that annual wages were about 10 shekels (see De Vaux, *AI* 76).

(H) The First-Born Reserved for Sacrifice (15:19–23). This ruling modifies the stipulation of E (Ex 22:28–9), allowing the first-born of livestock to be kept until the annual Shrine Feast. In Ex 13:14–15 may well be preserved the credal statement made on this occasion parallel to that which accompanied the offering of the first sheaf, Dt 26:5–10. This ancient practice is also found in the parallel tradition of Ex 34:19–20 and the P traditions: Ex 13:2; Nm 18:15–19; Lv 27:26ff.

40 **(I) The Three Pilgrim Feasts (16:1–17).** The Code continues with cultic legislation, passing to the three pilgrim feasts of Passover, Weeks, and Booths.

The deuteronomic calendar is later than Ex 34:18–23 (J) and 23:14–17 (E), neither of which mentions the Passover. It can also be compared with Lv 23:5–8 (and the rules in Nm 28:16–29:39) and with the later Ez 45:18–25. The chief difference is the insistence in Dt on coming to the central shrine (vv. 2,6, and 7)—the feast is really a pilgrimage (*ḥag* means both)—and the prominence given to the Passover, secondarily fused with Azymes. On Feasts → Religious Institutions, 76:132–48.

(Atkinson, C. W., *AnglTR* 44 [1962] 70–85. Bauer, L., *NKZ* 37 [1926] 794–805. De Vaux, *AI* 470–74, 484–506.

1. *Abib:* The Canaanite name (meaning "ear of wheat") corresponds to the March-April period. After the Exile, it is replaced by the Babylonian "Nisan." *the Passover:* Cf. Ex 12:1. Significantly, Josiah's Passover, which crowned the whole work of reform, followed the deuteronomic prescriptions (2 Kgs 23:21–23; 2 Chr 35:1–18; cf. the description of a Passover under Hezekiah, 2 Chr 30:15–27; see Lohfink, *Bib* 44, 274) and constituted an innovation, insofar as previously the Passover was apparently celebrated in the family circle. **2.** Cf. Ex 12:5 where the choice of animal was limited to a sheep or goat; however, this prescription is later than that of Dt. **3.** Passover and Azymes happened to coincide in time and were eventually fused; originally, however, they were two separate feasts—the former, that of a seminomadic society and the latter, which was the more ancient, that of a sedentary population. **4b–7.** With v. 3, these vv. form a separate prescription. *the bread of affliction:* Cf. Ex 12:15ff.; 13:3ff. Unleavened bread is normal Bedouin fare, but the absence of yeast is referred to in the Exodus story (Ex 12:39) and in this explanatory note to the bread eaten in captivity in Egypt. **7.** This prescription to cook was later changed (see Ex 12:9). **8.** *a solemn assembly:* The great Passover assembly is meant (Jos 5:10–12; 2 Kgs 23:21–23; Ezr 6:19). **9.** The Feast of Weeks, *šābuʿôt*, corresponded with the wheat harvest. It was later known as Pentecost and was connected with the giving of the Torah. It was an occasion of great rejoicing. **13.** The Feast of Tents, *sukkôt*, known in the earlier calendars as "Ingathering" (Ex 23:16; 34:22), occurred "at the end of year"—i.e., in the autumn. It seems to have been the great feast of the tribal federation before the monarchy (see Jgs 21:19; 1 Sm 1:3) and may have become a new year feast of the kind known to be celebrated in other Near Eastern countries. It was also the feast of covenant renewal (see 31:10). **16.** The final summary is based on the rule in the E code (Ex 23:17) and reworded in accord with the principle of unity of sanctuary. *shall appear before:* This translation agrees with MT vocalization (*Niphal* or passive) and LXX; however, the construction suggests *Qal*, "shall see the face of Yahweh," a phrase that implies a visit to a sanctuary (cf. Ps 42:2; 2 Sm 21:1).

41 **(J) The Various Officers in the Theocratic Society (16:18–18:22).** This section deals mainly with the organs of government and judicature in the sacred community: judges, the king, Levites, and prophets. There is an interruption (16:21–17:7) containing rules relating to cult and apostasy. Although based on traditional forms and ideas, it reflects the conservative reform of Josiah. **18.** *judges and officials:* This verse has already been anticipated to some extent in 1:15–18; however, there the exceptional rulings are left to Moses and here they are left to the Levitical priests (17:9). The *šōpēṭ* (judge) and the Levitical priest combined continue the judiciary function of the amphictyonic priesthood; the former must be distinguished from the *šōpēṭ* as saviour hero (see O. Grether, *ZAW* 57 [1939] 110–21). For the *šōṭēr* (official), see comment on 1:15. Their function in the deuteronomic scheme, and perhaps in the Josian state, seems to extend beyond the function of scribe (cf. 29:9; 31:28, where they are placed after heads of tribes and elders). **19.** The verse contains a series of short, apodictic laws based on the E code (Ex 23:1–3,6–9). These old laws are made to apply to judges by placement in this new context (cf. also 1:16–17).

42 **(K) Rules Relating to Cult and Apostasy (16:21–17:7).** **21.** There follow three short cult prohibitions in the same apodictic form that can be classified as *tôʿēbāh* laws (cf. 14:3). They are intrusive here and would seem to belong better after 12:31. Quite likely they come from a time long before Josiah but will have been seen to have special reference to the impieties of Manasseh (2 Kgs 21:1ff.; 23:4ff.). For the "pole" and "pillar," see comment on 7:5. *beside the altar:* This phrase may refer to a statue of the goddess as consort of Yahweh, set up in the shrine; cf. 2 Kgs 21:7; 23:4, and the aberrant Jewish cult at Elephantine.

1. For 17:1, see the prohibition in Lv 22:20ff. **2.** The next section (2–7) is the fourth of a series beginning in 13:1. It would have been transferred here as a rule for judges (note the direct address in 4–7). **6.** In the absence of a system of crime detection, the role of witnesses was crucially important—hence the insistence on the number and the religious sanctions to discourage perjury (cf. 19:15–21; see Z. W. Falk, *VT* 11 [1961] 88).

43 **(L) Judges and Kings (17:8–20).** **8.** Verses 8–13 deal with exceptional cases of civic offenses that had to be settled at the central sanctuary. Ordinary matters were settled at the local level by the elders (see 21:19; 22:15; 22:18–19). The central court, the decision of which was beyond appeal, consisted of Levitical priests and a judge serving a term of office according to roster. This participation of the Levitical priesthood in the judiciary is found as early as Sm (1 Sm 7:16; 8:2) and during the reign of Josaphat according to 2 Chr 19:4ff., but the reign of Josiah probably saw a definite stage of reorganization. **14.** In view of the connection with the Josian reform, the question of monarchy would be bound to loom large. It lies at the center of the deuteronomic history that connects monarchy with apostasy, especially in the case of Solomon and Jeroboam, and justifies the institution only insofar as it retains its charismatic character. What follows (vv. 14–20) is not so much a law as a warning, although it may have some connection with the book containing "the rights and duties of the kingship" deposited by Samuel in the sanctuary of Mizpah (1 Sm 10:25). *like all the surrounding nations:* The phrase is typically deuteronomic (cf. 6:14; 13:8; Jgs 2:12; cf. especially 1 Sm 8:5). The danger in such a king was loss of the charismatic character guaranteed by prophetic anointing or some external manifestation of the divine complacence. **16.** For a people used to transport by ass and camel, the horse was the symbol of pride, the war engine *par excellence* (see Ex 15:1; 1 Sm 8:11ff.; 1 Kgs 10:26ff.). *go back again to Egypt:* Cf. 28:68. Egyptian contacts, particularly strong during the united monarchy, raised the old problem of the danger of idolatry and syncretism. At the time of Josiah, the question of relations with Egypt was particularly pressing. After Josiah's death in battle against the Egyptian army, Judah fell briefly into Egyptian hands (2 Kgs 23:29–35). **17.** This verse is strongly reminiscent of the judgment on Solomon (1 Kgs 10:14–11:8). **18.** *A copy of this law* (→ 3 above). *the Levitical priests:* The impression gained elsewhere of the special importance of the Levites or "country priests" as those responsible for Dt is confirmed (see comments on 1:19; 10:8). **20.** The intimate connection between monarchy and covenant from the beginning (e.g., 2 Sm 11, David's sin; 2 Sm

24:18ff., the purchase of a threshing floor from Arauna) excluded any full-scale application of the ideological pattern of kingship in the ancient Near East.

(Causse, A., "L'idéal politique et social de Deutéronome," *RHPR* 13 [1933] 289–321. Galling, K., "Das Königsgesetz im Dt," *TLZ* 76 [1951] 133–38.)

44 (M) The Levitical Priest (18:1–8). That Dt does not distinguish between Levite and priest is evident from the frequent use of the term "Levitical priests" (17:9,18; 21:5; 24:8; 34:9) and from the comparison between 31:9 and 31:25. It presumes a situation in which they are scattered throughout the towns (e.g., in 21:5), either in the manner of the Bethlehemite Levite of Jgs 17:7ff., or officiating at local sanctuaries like the sons of Eli (1 Sm 2:12ff.). This condition evidently gave rise to the economic inequality which necessitated recommending them to the charity of the laity (see 12:12). **1.** *portions due:* As listed (vv. 3–4), they accrued to the shrine priesthoods long before the Josian reform; meant also are the tithes payable to them by law (see 14:28). **2.** *heritage:* Cf. Jos 13:14,33, taken up in the P recension (Nm 18:20). Several of the psalms in which this *naḥalāh* terminology occurs (e.g., Ps 16:6) may well come from a Levitical hand. **3.** Cf. Lv 7:31; Nm 18:18 (later texts), where the portions are more generous; 1 Sm 2:27–36 traces the indigenous condition of the country priests to venality, exemplified in the sons of Eli. **6.** It is stated that all Levites could, on principal, minister at the central sanctuary and share in the material advantages connected with this service. This possibility was rendered impossible (clear from 2 Kgs 23:9), by the opposition of the temple (Zadokite) clergy, although the text may have referred originally only to the celebration of the Passover (*'ālāh* is a technical term for "going up" for a feast). **8.** The end of this verse is obscure. The CCD indicates that the Levite gets a full portion, in addition to his ancestral heritage.

45 (N) The Prophet (18:9–22). The question at issue here is the all-important one of the vital link with the deity. The fundamental opposition between a nature religion, the aim of which was control of and leverage on the deity, and that of the Hebrew, who was to live by obedience to God's saving word, is reflected in the differing means of approach. Ecstatic prophecy was common to Israel and Canaan, but the end that it served was in each case profoundly different. **10.** Cf. Lv 18:21; 20:2–5. This custom of child sacrifice was practiced, especially at times of crisis, and was associated in Israel with the Valley of Hinnom near Jerusalem; it is mentioned only during the later monarchy (2 Kgs 16:3; 21:6; 23:10, the site destroyed during the Josian reform; Jer 7:31; 19:5; 32:35; Ez 16:20–21; 20:31). Molech, to whom these sacrifices were presumed to be made, appears to be a Phoenician-Punic word for a type of sacrifice (see De Vaux, *AI* 444–46), although it may have been understood as offered to Melek, a divine appellative connected with the Jebusite city. There follow eight different forms of commerce with the divinity that are forbidden by law (also in Lv 19:31; 20:6,27), but practiced intermittently in Israel especially during a national or personal crisis. Saul banned these practices but relapsed into them himself (1 Sm 28:3ff.), and it was natural that they should be again alluded to at the time of Josiah's reform after their active encouragement under Manasseh (2 Kgs 21:6). **15.** *a prophet like me:* Prophecy is for Israel the great means of mediation with her God, in opposition to the surrogates mentioned above. In view of vv. 20–22, the reference must be to the prophetic office seen by Dt as founded at Horeb and as an office of mediation like that of Moses himself, who was, however, a unique prophet (cf. Ex 33:11; Nm 12:1ff.; Dt 34:10). The E tradition, followed by D, sees the prophets in a charismatic sequence descending from Moses and vitalizing the national history. **18.** This verse was interpreted in later Judaism as applying to an eschatological prophetic figure (see Jn 1:21; 6:14; 7:40; 1QS 9); the Christian Church saw it fulfilled in Christ (Acts 3:22ff.; 7:37ff.). **21.** It is a simple test for distinguishing false from true prophets (see also 1 Kgs 22:5ff., 28; 2 Kgs 1:10ff.; Aspects NT Thought, 78:14).

(See Peters, P., *Schrift und Bekenntnis* 7 [1926] 180–93; 8 [1927] 9–23, 47–66. Teeple, H. M., *The Mosaic Eschatological Prophet* Phila. 1957]. Vosté, J. M., *Bib* 30 [1949] 1–9.)

46 (O) The Cities of Sanctuary (19:1–13). See comment on 4:41 where the three cities E of Jordan are named to complete the account of the Transjordan settlement. Here the names of the sanctuary cities in Canaan are withheld as if they were to be decided on after the occupation, although, in fact, Jos 20, which mentions them (Kedesh, Shechem, Hebron), is earlier. **3.** The area in which sanctuary law pertained had to be clearly demarked and accessible. The sanctuary city simply extended the old idea of the inviolability of an altar or shrine (see 1 Kgs 1:51; 2:28–31). **4.** Here Dt follows the E code (Ex 21:13–14) in distinguishing between manslaughter and homicide with malice aforethought. This is significant as being one of the first cases of the "state" taking over and modifying the practice of private vendetta. **6.** *the avenger of blood:* This person is the nearest of kin, upon whom fell the duty of avenging a death in the family group (e.g., 2 Sm 14:11), or of "redeeming" the property of a deceased relative (Lv 25:25–26), or of making restitution (Nm 5:8). The word (*gō'ēl*) is first used in the OT of the relative as blood avenger, but in Is 40–66 it is applied to Yahweh as blood relative by covenant, and, therefore, redeemer of the Israelite. **8–9.** Provision is made for three more cities in the event of territorial expansion. It seems that the verses were added to the original text, possibly at some time of national revival that brought the hope of incorporating the irredentist parts of the Davidic empire. **12.** Both here and in Jos 20:4, the role of the elders of the city is emphasized.

47 (P) Rulings Regarding Boundary Marks and Witnesses (19:14–21). This passage is a typical Dt legal paragraph, based on old laws, both apodictic (14–15) and casuistic (16), and on traditional maxims for legal practice (21b) amplified and edited to fit a new situation—that of a theocratic state. **14.** The question of exact delimitation of boundaries plays a conspicuous part in Dt (see Von Rad, *Studies in Deuteronomy*, 59). Comparison with 27:17 enables us to distinguish the original apodictic law and the typical Dt addition. **15.** See comment on 17:6 and cf. the later rule in Nm 35:30. This ruling was adopted by the early Christian community (Mt 18:16; 1 Tim 5:19) and is used polemically by Jesus himself (Jn 8:16–18); cf. also Heb 10:28. **16.** *a defection:* This term indicates, in fact, apostasy (*sārāh*) (cf. 13:6; Jer 28:16; 29:32; Is 1:5; 31:6; 59:13). This ruling, therefore, covers the only exception to the law just annunciated—that of an accusation of apostasy, providing the necessary safeguard against the danger of abuse when only one witness is involved (already dealt with in 13:10–11; 17:4ff.). **17.** *before the Lord:* The central tribal sanctuary is intended, perhaps Shechem, then later Jerusalem. For the priests and judges, see 17:9. **21.** The so-called law of retaliation, evidently an ancient judicial maxim, is inserted here with reference to the judgment in v. 19 and perhaps also in association with "eye" in the concluding sentence of the judgment, v. 21a.

In the E code it is also introduced to give force to a particular case (Ex 21:24–25; see also Lv 24:20). Far from evincing a vindictive and barbaric mentality, as often alleged, it was an attempt to apply the principle of equity to the uncontrolled private vendetta then in vogue (cf. Gn 4:23!). At the same time, Christian morality was to make far higher demands (see Mt 5:38).

48 **(Q) Rules for the Holy War (20:1–20).** See comments on 1:30–33; Dt, here and elsewhere, (21:10–14; 23:10–14; 25:17–19), revives the old rules of the tribal holy war, theologizing them and putting them at the service of the national revival with which the book is connected. In many details, these rules presuppose a period long after the settlement. **1.** The presence of Yahweh with his armies, and especially in battle (e.g., 1 Sm 4:5ff.), is associated with the Ark (see comment on 9:3). The conquest is the work of Yahweh. **2.** The priest played an important part in the holy war, as did the Babylonian *bārû* (e.g., 1 Sm 2:28; 4:11). **5.** *the officials:* For the *šōṭᵉrîm*, usually translated "scribes" or "clerks," see comment on 1:15 (see also De Vaux, *AI* 155). Here, it is evidently a question of recruiting officers. What follows is a list of classes exempt from military service: those who are building a new house, or have bought one but not yet lived in it; those who own a vineyard that has not yet given fruit; those who are engaged but not yet married. These exemptions are based on old custom stemming from the beginning of the tribal organization in Canaan. They were still regarded as in force during the Maccabee period (1 Mc 3:56). (See W. Herrmann, *ZAW* 70 [1958] 215–20; S. B. Gurewicz, *AusBR* 6 [1958] 111–21.) **6.** *enjoyed its fruits:* Lit., "profaned it." According to the ritual rule in Lv 19:23–25, the fruit of a vineyard had to be desacralized after 3 years and could be eaten only in the fifth year after planting. **7.** Cf. the rule in 24:5, which gives the newlywed 1 year's grace before being liable to conscription. **8.** The addition of this verse may have been suggested by Gideon's reduction of his army, Jgs 7:3. **10.** This paragraph (10–18) deals with the conduct of the Israelites toward the conquered. While preserving the basic theological imperative of the ban (see comment on 7:2), its application here is greatly mitigated and the whole presentation is clearly more theological than practical. *offer it terms of peace:* This distinction is the first to be made; a surrender must be accepted in the case of a non-Canaanite city, one "very far from you," and the population is to be put to forced labor. The reference to such cities either presupposes a period of territorial expansion outside Canaan or perhaps reflects the relations of the Israelites with the Gibeonite tetrapolis (cf. Jos 9:6–27). **16.** In the case of Canaanite cities, the ban had to be applied in all its rigor. For the list of nations, see comment on 7:1. **19.** The practice of deforesting the land surrounding a besieged city in order to build siegeworks was common among the Assyrians and has been confirmed by the excavations at Lachish; the Israelites of the settlement period would not have been familiar with siege tactics (see Jos 6:5ff.; 8:4ff.). These stipulations humanize the indiscriminate destruction associated with total war.

49 **(R) The Case of Undetected Murder (21:1–9).** Undetected crime was considered to involve the scene of the crime and, in particular, the nearest population center, in divine retribution for bloodguilt, and possibly also retribution from the "blood avenger." In the Ugaritic tale of Aqhat, the murderer was unknown and Danel curses Qir-mayim, the Spring of Water, scene of his son's murder. The practice described may well be Canaanite in origin (Aqhat I iii, 46–49). There is no mention of compensation for next of kin, as in the Hammurabi Code (§ 24; *ANET* 167). **2.** For judges, see comment on 16:18. The elders formed a kind of town council and are the chief organ of local government in Dt. The Dt legislation is centered on the town (e.g., 21:18–19; 22:13–14; 25:5ff.), rather than, as in the E code that it supplanted, on the tribal federation as such. **3.** *a heifer that has never been put to work:* This animal, together with the unplowed and unsown valley, is a necessity of this type of ritual (cf. 1 Sm 6:7; Mk 11:2). It is not a sacrifice because the heifer's neck is broken—i.e., its throat is not cut (Vg) and its head is not struck off (Douai). (See R. Patai, *JQR* 30 [1939–40] 59–69.) **5.** For the religious and civic importance of the Levites in the Dt scheme, see comments on 1:19; 10:8; 17:8. **6.** It is possible that the breaking of the heifer's neck represents the will to bring the murderer to justice in the event of his being found; the washing of hands is the cleansing from blood-guilt. **8.** The land and the people, which belong to Yahweh, must not be stained with blood-guilt (cf. 21:23; 32:43). *forgive:* Lit., *kappēr* means "cover up" or "expiate." The latter sense becomes standard in the P writings but is attested earlier (see 2 Sm 21:3). For the idea of Yahweh redeeming Israel see comment on 10:26. (On the paragraph as a whole, see C. H. Gordon in *RA* 33 [1936] 1–6; H. Cazelles in *VT* 8 [1958] 105ff.)

50 **(S) Miscellaneous Laws (21:10–25:19).**

(a) Treatment of Women Captured in War (21:10–14). Women captured after battle became part of the spoils of war (see Jgs 5:30; Nm 31:35). Dt applies the same discrimination and even humanitarianism here as elsewhere, evident by comparison with practice among other peoples. **11.** Marriages with foreign women were forbidden on principle, but here it is a case of an exslave who has had to accept the faith of her master. **12.** These signs are symbolic at the same time of the end of her old life and the beginning of a new one in association with her master; they are also symbolic of the mourning for the parents who have "died" with that old life.

51 (b) Three Casuistic Laws (21:15–23). There follow three case laws, beginning, "If a man...." **15.** The first law, The right of primogeniture, is to be respected. In a society where polygamy was tolerated—although it never became the prevalent practice—the supplanting of the first-born on the grounds of aversion to one or other of the wives could easily happen and, in fact, did (e.g., Gn 21:10ff.; 1 Kgs 1:17ff.). This change often takes place on a theological principle, i.e., the election of Yahweh rather than the ordinary course of succession (e.g., Gn 48:13–14). Dt here legislates against the abuses inherent in this situation. **17.** *a double share:* This was the application of primogeniture in the Assyrian laws (see *ANET* 185) and in the Nuzu tablets (see I. Mendelsohn, *BASOR* 156 [1959] 38–40). It is applied metaphorically to Elisha in 2 Kgs 2:9. **18.** The second law deals with treatment of the incorrigible son. Great importance was always given in Israel to *pietas* toward parents (Dt 5:16), but this law again represents a mitigation of the almost absolute power of the *paterfamilias*, who must hand the son over to the town council composed of the elders. The death penalty, although imposed for a wide variety of crimes, was not so extensive as in other nations. Significantly, both parents have equal right to respect, and take proceedings against, the son together. **22.** The third law treats the disposal of the corpse of the executed criminal. *hung on a tree:* This is not the form of execution (hanging was, in fact, unknown in the OT), but rather the exposure of the corpse on a tree or stake as an example to others. Its correspondence to actual practice is evident (Jos 8:29;

10:27; 2 Sm 4:12). **23.** Any corpse is ritually impure, and if left until decomposition sets in, it was considered to pollute the land, which belonged to the living God (cf. 23:14). Paul makes accommodated use of this text in Gal 3:13.

52 (c) A Series of Humanitarian and Ritual Laws (22:1–12). This and the following sections contain a collection of laws most of which antedate the framework in which they now appear. The principle behind the grouping and editing of this mostly ancient material is partly subject matter—e.g., ritual prohibitions, 22:5,9,10,11; sexual mores, 22:13–30; community membership, 23:1–8—and partly category: apodictic, 22:1–5,9–11; 22:30–23:8; or casuistic, 22:6–8,13–29. The reason for the disturbance of an earlier order is not always easy to follow. **1–3.** Closely allied with Ex 23:4, it goes beyond the laws on theft (Ex 20:15; Dt 5:19). The E code (Ex 22:3) prescribes twofold restitution for a stolen animal in contrast to the tenfold demand of the Hammurabi Code (§ 8; see *ANET* 166). Dt, in keeping with its nationalistic character, obligates only toward a fellow Israelite—*'āḥ*, which is synonymous with *rēa'*, "neighbor"—whereas Ex (23:4) regards one's enemy. **4.** Cf. Ex 23:5—it required two to unload the pack and get the animal upright. **5.** This is the first of a short series of apodictic laws forbidding cultic irregularities that upset the natural order and could bring disaster to the offender (vv. 5–9 and 10–11; see Von Rad, *Studies in Deuteronomy*, 19). Transvestitism may have originated from the bad example of Caananite cult practices (cf. 23:17–18). The law consists in the old formulation with the Dt addition, classifying it as a *tō'ēbāh* law (see comment on 7:25). **6–7.** This casuist law gives a small case of the at times exquisite discrimination of the Dt corpus. **8.** The injunction to put up a roof parapet may reflect the sad experience of the first days of the settlement with the change from tents to the flat-roofed houses of Canaan. **9.** This verse follows from v. 5. *forfeit:* Lit., "sacred." According to 20:6, the produce of a vineyard could be desacralized only in the fifth year. If any crop was planted between the trees, its produce would accrue to sacred use—i.e., the sanctuary, together with the vine, either during the whole period or, following Lv 19:23–24, in the fourth year. **10.** Cf. Lv 19:19, where the coupling of animals of different species is prohibited. There is some magical idea here which escapes us now. **11.** Cf. Lv 19:19b. **12.** This law, which is not of the same apodictic category, has been placed here because of its association with the preceding. There is iconographic evidence for this practice to which the priests later attached a religious significance (Nm 15:37ff.; cf. Mt 9:20; 23:5).

53 (d) Laws Concerning Sexual Mores (22:13–23:1). There are here four casuistic laws in defense of the wronged wife, against adultery and seduction, to which we add the first (23:1) of a series of short apodictic laws that belong here. **13.** The first law appears. *spurns:* Lit., "hates," which appears to be a technical term for divorce as in the Elephantine papyri (*ANET* 222). **15.** *the evidence of her virginity:* This phrase presupposes the custom of handing to the woman's parents a stained garment or bed covering as an acknowledgment on the husband's part that the hymen was intact until the wedding night. **18.** The punishment for a false charge of this kind, a flogging and a fine of 100 silver shekels, can be compared with the much more severe Assyrian punishment for a similar offense (*ANET* 181). **21.** According to Gn 38:24, the penalty for this offense was burning alive, the punishment reserved for a priest's daughter in Lv 21:9. **22.** The second law, on adultery, forbidden in the "ten words" (Dt 5:18; Ex 20:14), carries the death penalty for both parties here and in Lv 20:10. According to the Hammurabi Code (§ 129; *ANET* 171, 181), both parties were drowned; the Assyrian laws also attached the death penalty to adultery, although both these laws and the Hammurabi Code granted wide discretionary power to the injured husband. **23.** The third law dictated that the rape of a young woman engaged but not yet married was punishable by death. It was considered more a crime against the neighbor than a sexual misdemeanor; cf. the Hammurabi Code (§ 130; *ANET* 171). The same distinction between "in the city" and "in the open fields," as a basis for judging the presumed complicity or innocence of the woman, lies behind the Assyrian legislation (*ANET* 181, 185) which also imposed the death penalty. **28.** The fourth law treated rape of an unbetrothed girl, for which the penalty was payment of 50 silver pieces and the obligation to marry the wronged girl with the complete exclusion of divorce. The law in the Book of the Covenant (Ex 22:15–16) enjoins payment of the marriage price, the *mōhār*, and obligation to marry. There is no provision for punishment in the case of a married man as in the Assyrian law, which is very similar on this point (*ANET* 185). **23:1.** In form, this verse belongs with the apodictic laws that follow; in subject matter, it belongs with the preceding material. The prohibition is directed not against incest but against possession of one of the father's concubines (cf. 27:20; Lv 18:8). It entailed, in the case of the royal son at least, a claim to succeed, as with Absalom (2 Sm 16:22), David (2 Sm 12:8), and Adoniah (1 Kgs 2:22). It was the fault for which Reuben was punished with loss of the rights of the first-born (Gn 35:22; 49:3–4).

54 (e) Those Who Are To Be Excluded from the Plenary Assembly (23:1–8). This short list of five apodictic rules, four of them dealing with ethnic disqualifications and amplified by a short commentary, is probably an excerpt from a longer list determining qualification for participation in the full amphictyonic assembly. **1.** Wholeness was necessary for participation in the cultic assembly, which was conceived as a meeting with God; cf. the exclusion from the priesthood of various classes including eunuchs in Lv 21:17–21 and the lame, paralyzed, and the like from the *qāhāl* in 1QSa 2: 4–9 (which refers to Dt 23:1 and which classifies these physical defects as human impurity). This and the following rules were dissolved, with the deeper realization of Israel's universal mission (see Is 56:3–5), and they are the contrary of Christian universality (cf. Lk 14:31). **3.** *Ammonite or Moabite:* The simple prohibition is expanded by means of a *pešer* (explanation) typical of the Dt approach to laws. Aliens of Ammonite or Moabite origin were excluded in perpetuity on historical grounds (cf. 2:9,19ff.) and the events related in Nm 22. This exclusivism is taken even further and interpreted even more strictly in the immediate post-exilic period (see Neh 13:1–3). **7.** *Edomite:* See 2:4ff.; Esau, brother of Jacob, was represented as the ancestor of the Edomites. This benevolence to Edom would have been out of the question after the fall of Jerusalem and is not mentioned in Neh 13:1ff. *Egyptian:* The memory of the years of bondage in Egypt plays a significant part in Dt (cf. 5:15; 6:21; 24:22). Here, again, it would have been out of the question after the incursion of Neco into Palestine in 609 (see K. Galling, "Das Gemeindegesetz in Dt 23," *Fest. A. Bertholet* [Tübingen, 1950] 176–91; and criticism in A. R. Hulst, *OTS* 9 [1951] 87–102).

55 (f) Purity in the Camp During the Holy War (23:9–14). The necessity of ritual purity in the camp derived from the Ark presence, represented here very materialistically in what are probably predeuteronomic cult laws. The holy war demanded sexual abstention (1 Sm 21:5–6) and the removal of those with physical defects involving cultic uncleanness (Nm 5:1–4). **10.** A nocturnal emission rendered one ritually impure (cf. Lv 15:16). **14.** *journeys along within your camp:* Here occurs the same popular presentation as in Gn 3:8 (nakedness was a grave cultic fault!) and in 2 Sm 5:24 (a holy war incident), spiritualized in the P idea of God who dwells in the midst of the camp (Nm 5:3). This idea of "holiness," while stressing the radical otherness of God, was to be profoundly modified by Jesus (see especially Mt 15:10–20).

(For the section, see Glueck, N., *M. M. Kaplan Jubilee Vol* [N.Y., 1953] 261ff.)

56 (g) Various Laws (23:15–25). There follows a small collection of laws without any thematic unity: four in the negative apodictic form and four regulations of the casuistic type, which are changed, however, into the second person as elsewhere in Dt (see Von Rad, *Studies in Deuteronomy*, 21). The same stylistic structure obtains in the Sermon on the Mount (Mt 6:2,5,16). **15.** Ancient legislation was usually strict on runaway slaves and on anyone conniving to prevent their return, e.g., Hammurabi Code (§§ 15–16,19; *ANET* 166–67). The slave here was evidently a foreigner (cf. 15:12, where Hebr slaves are referred to) who must not be extradited, but allowed to settle as an alien like the Moabites of Is 16:3–4. Like 23:20, it may exemplify the strong nationalism of Dt. **17.** The cultic prostitute, both female (*qᵉdēšāh*) and male (*qādēš*), had an integral part in the fertility rites of the ancient Near East, including (indeed, especially) Canaan; evidently the practice caught on in Israel (e.g., 1 Kgs 14:24; Am 2:7; Hos 4:14). The expulsion of these cult functionaries was an important element of reform movements (1 Kgs 15:12; 22:47), including that of Josiah (2 Kgs 23:7). **18.** *dog's price:* The term is one of contempt for a male temple prostitute. **19.** The prohibition of lending at interest to fellow Israelites also appears in the E code (Ex 22:24; cf. Lv 25:36–38), although there is evidence that this custom was not always observed. Dt adds the permission to lend at interest to foreigners (*nokrî* not *gēr*, "resident alien"). **21.** The solemn binding nature of the religious vow, usually made at the sanctuary in the presence of the priest, is stressed; the P editors developed this doctrine along their own casuistic lines (Nm 30:2ff.). **24.** The two rules which follow limit private property rights in the interests of the needy wayfarer but forestall abuses. **25.** Cf. Mt 12:1ff.

57 (h) Prohibition of Second Marriage with the Same Woman (24:1–4). Chs. 24–25 contain miscellaneous laws and ordinances: ten in the form of case law; six short apodictic laws; and two others. Verses 1–4 are not a divorce law enjoining the handing of a written document to the woman, as is supposed by the Vg mistranslation; there is a long protasis with four members and the apodosis begins only with "then her former husband" (4). The prohibition is ritual in character; the woman has been rendered impure for the former husband. **1.** *something indecent:* The same phrase occurs here as in 23:14, *ʿerwat dābār*. The sufficient reason for divorce was disputed at the time of Christ between the rigorist school of Shammai and the laxists, followers of Hillel, who allowed divorce "for any cause whatever" (Mt 19:3). *a bill of divorce:* We may suppose that this document would also deal with the question of indemnity for the woman where this was payable, as in the Hammurabi Code (§§ 137–41; *ANET* 172) and Assyrian laws (*ANET* 183). See B. N. Wambacq, *VD* 33 [1955] 331–35; S. B. Gurewicz, "Divorce in Jewish Law," *Res Judicatae* 7 [1956] 357–62.)

58 (i) Measures in Favor of the Depressed Classes (24:5–25:4). **5.** See the rules for exemption from military service (20:7); this was one of the ancient regulations governing the holy war and was practiced also in Ugarit (see Keret A ii, 101). **6.** The first of three rules (see also vv. 10 and 12) about surety taken for payment of debt, which gives a good example of the deuteronomic humanitarian concern for social justice and the mitigation of the strict letter of the law. Nothing might be taken in surety which was necessary for subsistence (cf. Jb 24:3). **7.** Cf. 23:15, which deals with foreign slaves. This rule modifies that in the E code (Ex 21:15–16), which is not restricted to Israelites, in a way similar to 22:1–3 (cf. Ex 23:4). Kidnapping a child in order to rear him as a slave is also punishable by death in the Hammurabi Code (§ 14; *ANET* 166). It is possible that, in view of the context in Dt, the reference is to enslavement for nonpayment of debt. **8.** Lv 13–14 contains priestly prescriptions for leprosy—a term which covered a wide variety of skin diseases—that must have been based on ancient cultic taboos. The injunction to "take care" introduces not a law but an exhortation typical of the Dt sermon style (cf. 4:1,9,15; 8:11; 11:16; 12:32). **9.** See Nm 12:9–15. The basic idea for Dt is the ritual purity of the state conceived as a camp within the ideology of the holy war (see 23:9ff. and cf. application of the leprosy law in CD 13). **10.** The second surety rule (cf. 24:6) dictates that the creditor was not to seize, but to request, the article given in pledge. **12.** The garment given in pledge could symbolize the person of the debtor himself, who would fall into the hands of his creditor in the event of nonpayment. This law, too, is the fruit of prophetic denunciation (see Am 2:8; Ez 22:25–26; 33:15). **14.** The laborer must be paid the same day before sunset. Occasional labor was paid daily (cf. Mt 20:2ff.). The abuse of nonpayment under some pretext, or truck payment, is also condemned in the Prophets; see Jer 22:13; Mal 2:5 (cf. the priestly rule in Lv 19:13). **16.** This principle is juridical, although we do not know what cases it covered. The deuteronomic historian sees an application in Amaziah's execution of the conspirators against his father (2 Kgs 14:6). By changing *yûmat*, "be put to death," to *yāmût*, "will die," it was evolved into a theological principle; see Jer 31:29–30; Ez 14; 18:4; 33:10ff., confirmed by the occurrence of the D type of case law presentation in Ez 14; 18:5ff. **17.** The fatherless, including particularly daughters who usually would not be provided for and the children of cult prostitutes (see comment on 10:18), widows, resident aliens and Levites—the last two composed to a considerable extent of immigrants from the northern kingdom—were the special concern of the Deuteronomic Code (see 10:18; 14:28–29; 16:11; 24:19; 26:12–13; etc.). This formulation is based on that in the Book of the Covenant (Ex 23:6) and is repeated in the concluding curses (Dt 27:19). **19.** These three humanitarian laws provide a means of assisting the economically depressed categories, based on the same principle as the E provision for leaving the fields fallow in the sabbatical year (Ex 23:10–11; cf. also Lv 19:9–10; 23:22). **1.** In 25:1, we have a law stipulating that the sentence must be carried out in the presence of the judge, and the number of strokes inflicted must not exceed 40—another example of the deuteronomic setting of limits and safeguards to the person, of applying equity. The number was later reduced to 39 out of scruple of exceeding the limit by inadvertence (2 Cor 11:24). **2.** For the LXX text of 1–3, see A. Allgeier (*Bib* 19 [1938] 1–18) and J. Hofbauer (*ZKT* 62 [1938] 385–89). **4.** The consideration of Dt extends even to the animal world (cf. 5:14; Ex 23:11). This text is applied typologically to Christian ministers in 1 Cor 9:9 and 1 Tim 5:18.

59 (j) THE LEVIRATE LAW (25:5–10). This law was so called from Latin *levir*, "brother-in-law." This ancient custom obtained among many Semitic peoples, among the Hittites of Asia Minor and the Arabs of the Yemen, and was based, apart from the practical necessity of preserving the family estate, primitively on the worship of ancestral spirits. It required a man to marry his brother's widow if she were childless, and any son born of this union to bear the name and be the heir of the dead brother. How serious was this obligation at an early period can be seen from the Onan story (Gn 38:6ff.). **5.** *brothers live together:* It applies if they are in business together or share the family estate. This modification of the old law, together with the provision for evading the obligation, shows a later stage of development; cf. the possibility of annulment in the parallel Assyrian law (§§ 30–31,33; *ANET* 182). (See C. H. Gordon, *JPOS* 15 [1935] 29–34.) The idea lingered to a late period (Mt 22:23ff.). **7.** Repudiation is made onerous by the necessity of a private and public refusal. **9.** The "levir" in Ru 4:7ff., who declines to perform this office, hands his sandal to Boaz as a sign of renunciation in his favor. It may have been the original significance of the action here.

60 (k) VARIOUS ORDINANCES (25:11–19). **11.** Severing the hand for this kind of intervention in a brawl is the only case of mutilation in Hebr law. It applies equivalently the law of retaliation, perhaps also since *yād*, "hand," is used for the male organ (for a parallel in the Assyrian code, § 8, see *ANET* 181). **13.** Two short apodictic laws are followed by two positive related injunctions and closed by the usual Dt homiletic amplification; cf. Lv 19:35–36 with its ending. They are forbidden to have different weights (lit., stones) and measures for buying and selling (for the "measure," *'ēpāh*, see De Vaux, *AI* 199). The insistence on social justice here also recurs frequently in the 8th-cent. prophets (Am 8:5; Hos 12:8–9; Mi 6:10–12). **17.** *bear in mind:* See comment on 6:12. The presence in Dt of this exhortation to take vengeance on the Amalekites for their war of attrition against Israel in their movements in the Sinai Peninsula may be explained by the special role of the Levites in Ex 17:8ff., and the prominence of campaigns against the Amalekites in the history of the holy war (Ex 17:15–16; Nm 24:20; 1 Sm 15:1ff.). It derives from a pre-Josian stage in the literary history of Dt. **19.** *rest from all your enemies:* See comment on 12:9.

61 **(T) Offering of the First Fruits (26:1–11).** This offering was already commanded in the E code (Ex 22:28; 23:19), and although the text does not mention a fixed occasion, this act probably took place on the spring festival of Azymes. In the two most ancient calendars, there is an injunction not to come into the presence of Yahweh on this occasion with empty hands (Ex 34:20; 23:15). Dt 16:8 prescribes a "solemn assembly" for Azymes and the P calendar provides for the offering of the first sheaf on this feast (Lv 23:10ff.). This historicization of what was originally a Canaanite spring festival (for its original character, cf. 2 Sm 21:9, "at the beginning of the barley harvest"; cf. Ex 22:28) derives from the first days of the settlement, opposing the fertility cult with radically historical faith. Von Rad views 5–10 as the festival legend of Gilgal recited at the Feast of Weeks, as distinct from the Shechem covenant renewal festival (see Von Rad, *Genesis*, 14–15; *GesSt*, 9–86; for criticism of this position, see Noth, *UP* 55; Weiser, OT 83–90; Eichrodt, *Theology* 512–20). Von Rad's designation of "cultic credo" is, however, apt, and it is notable that the sacred recital here and elsewhere in Dt (6:20–25; 21:7–8; 26:13–15) has a marked rhythmic and stylistically exalted character. **3.** This declaration strikes a keynote of deuteronomic faith: The possession of the land is the fulfillment of the divine promise. **5.** The father is Jacob, renamed Israel. The Hebrews were chiefly, but not exclusively, Aramean in origin (cf. Ez 16:3,45). The credo of Jos 24:2ff. goes back to Terah and Abraham and may, therefore, represent a later stage of the historical tradition (see D. D. Luckenbill, *AJSL* 36 [1919–20] 244ff.; M. A. Beek, *OTS* 8 [1950] 193–212; C. H. Brekelmans, *TT* 3 [1963] 1–11). **6.** For the deep Hebr feeling for participation in a common historical heritage and tradition, the change in person is significant; my father was Israel, therefore *I* am Israel! Although this represents an ancient liturgical form, it does so indirectly (against Von Rad), because the scheme and the stylistic presentation are clearly owing to Dt (cf. the pattern in Jgs 3:7–11; etc.). **8.** This "canonized" Passover terminology (cf. 4:34; 6:21) shows the close association between the two feasts that were later amalgamated. **11.** For the liturgical joy characteristic of Dt, see comment on 12:7.

62 **(U) The Ceremony of the Triennial Tithing (26:12–15).** On the tithes' law, see 14:22,28. The distribution of the triennial tithes was done at home, but here is prescribed a confession, somewhat similar to the "negative confession" of the Egyptian Book of the Dead, to be made at the amphictyonic sanctuary. It also took place at a harvest festival—hence reference to the land of Canaan (15; cf. v. 9), a joyful occasion with feasting and strong drink (14:26) and the abjuration of the Canaanite seasonal fertility rite (v. 14). **13.** *the sacred portion:* This tithe was reserved for the indigenous classes. **14.** Cf. Hos 9:4, referring to *leḥem 'ōnîm*, "bread of mourning" or "lamentation"; Ez 24:17 also refers to "bread of man" in the context of lamentation. Perhaps the lamentation referred to was for the fertility god, whose death, burial, and rising were mimed ritually (see H. Cazelles, *RB* 55 [1948] 54–71). *offered any of it to the dead:* The use of the singular again suggests a funerary meal in honor of the Canaanite fertility god (cf. 14:1 where the same possibility exists). In the Ugaritic Baal cycle, Lutpan and Anath mourn the dead *Ba'al* by lacerating their bodies (see J. Gray, *The Canaanites* [London, 1964] 132). **15.** Cf. the deuteronomic prayer at the dedication of the Temple (1 Kgs 8:43).

63 **(V) Conclusion of the Covenant (26:16–19).** In keeping with the general pattern of covenant making, we have here a final recapitulation followed in ch. 28 by the blessings and curses. **16.** *this day:* See comment on 4:4 and the cultic Ps 95:7–11. **17.** See G. Mercati (*Bib* 24 [1943] 201–204). The reciprocal assumption of the new bond brought into existence by the covenant relationship is expressed in the formula: "I am your God—you are my people" (Jer 31:33; Hos 2:23); cf. the formulary of marriage and divorce (Hos 1:9). **19.** *a people sacred to the Lord:* See comment on 7:6 and Ex 19:6. The holiness, that is, apartness, derives from the new bond created by the covenant.

64 **(W) A Conflation of Different Covenant Traditions (27:1–26).** All agree that this chapter is not in harmony with the rest of this last section of the book and bears many signs of successive edition. Thus, Moses and the elders speak in v. 1, Moses and the Levitical priests in v. 9, Moses alone in v. 11, and the Levites in v. 14. There are two commands to set up stones—immediately after crossing the Jordan (2) and at Ebal (4); the Levites are counted among the tribes on Gerizim (12) and act as heralds of the covenant ceremony (14). Inasmuch as 27:4–8,11–26, which immediately follow the Deuteronomic Code, and the corresponding 11:29–30, which immediately precede it, both refer to a ceremony at or near Shechem and are clearly to be read in association with Jos 8:30–35 and ch. 24, the conclusion suggests itself that at some stage of redaction the Deuteronomic Code was understood to have been derived from one in use at that sanctuary. Following 31:10–11, Von Rad sees the greater part of this chapter as faithful to the covenant pattern of Ex 19–24 and representing the festival of covenant renewal according to the "use" of Shechem. For covenant format → Aspects OT Thought, 77:79. (Bülow, S., "Der Berg des Fluches," *ZDPV* 73 [1957] 100–107. Lewy, I., "The Puzzle of Dt 27: Blessings announced but Curses noted," *VT* 12 [1962] 207–11. L'Hour, J., "L'Alliance de Sichem," *RB* 69 [1962] 161–84. Noth, *GesSt*, 155–71. Von Rad, *GesSt*, 23–37.)

1. Verse 26:19 is continued in 28:1; this opening verse is redactional and sutural. **2–3.** The command to set up plastered stones inscribed with the Law immediately upon entering the land is duplicated in 4–8, for Ebal (Shechem) was certainly not reached the first day of the entry into Canaan. This may be an elaboration of the tradition of the commemorative stones in Jos 4:19–20 and may derive from the sanctuary of Gilgal. **4.** It is widely held that 4–8 is the beginning of an older tradition closely associated with E, which has been touched up in the D fashion and inserted at this point. *Mount Ebal:* The mountain is N of Shechem and faces Gerizim. Sam has "on Mount Gerizim"—the holy mountain of the Samaritans (cf. 11:29; Jos 8:30,33). *coating them with plaster:* The phrase was added from v. 2 when the Shechem text was introduced; it involves an abrupt change from plural to singular. **5.** Building an altar, offering sacrifices and eating the sacrificial banquet, writing down the covenant law—all this fits into the structure of covenant making and shows affinities with the E code (Ex 24:4–11) and the Shechem ceremony described in Jos 8:30–35, which is, as Noth maintains, probably anterior to this text. **9.** Verses 9–10 continue 26:16–19 linking the passage to 28:1. Dt makes the Levites the custodians of the Ark and the Law placed in it (see 31:9). **11.** Here continues the account of a ceremony at Shechem although a hiatus occurs between 8 and 11 and between 11–13 and the curses. **12.** This introductory phrase is not deuteronomic; in fact, the blessings and curses proper to the Deuteronomic Code are in ch. 28. For the ceremony, cf. 11:29 and Jos 8:33–34. Gerizim is on the right of Shechem and Ebal on the left. This is the model for Luke's Sermon on the Plain (Lk 6:20–26).

65 **(X) The Curses (27:15–26).** **14.** *the Levites:* Here, they are the official promulgators of the Law, as in Neh 8:7–8, and not a secular tribe, as in v. 12. This change suggests that the connection between the situation in 12–13 and the curses may be artificial, but it has been observed that the latter would fit in well with the covenant meeting at Shechem described in Jos 24 (Mendenhall, *BA* 17 [1954] 67). **15.** The series of curses was certainly added at a later stage of the formation of Dt when it already contained the blessings and curses of ch. 28, although the individual curses themselves are mostly ancient. We do not know why the blessings announced in v. 12 do not follow; the redactor may have omitted them in view of 28:1–6. Whatever their origin, the curses are here brought into relationship with the observance of the Deuteronomic Code in chs. 12–26. If, as seems probable, the first and last form a redactional inclusion, we are left with a decalogue of curses on actions committed in secret, which, therefore, only the divine judgment can reach. The first curse (15) is directed against what is the essence of idolatry for Dt (cf. 4:15–20; 5:8; Ex 20:4). The language used betrays a late date. **16.** The next ten curses have an affinity with the E code (four are either identical with, or very close to, stipulations found there) but in an even more marked way with a decalogue in the Holiness Code dealing with sexual matters and preceded by a condemnation of those who curse their parents (Lv 20:9–21; five are identical, or nearly so). The question of dependence cannot be raised easily because the rules, prohibitions, or curses will often be older than the framework in which they are now arranged. *dishonors:* Ex 21:17 and Lv 20:9 have "curses." The opposite is commanded in the Decalogue (5:16; Ex 20:12). **17.** Cf. 19:14. **18.** Cf. Lv 19:14. **19.** Cf. Ex 22:20 and see comment on 10:18. **20.** See comment on 22:30 and cf. Lv 20:11 and the similar laws in the Hammurabi Code (§§ 154–58, *ANET* 172–73). **21.** Bestiality was practiced in Canaan as a means of promoting fertility by sympathetic magic; it is forbidden also in Ex 22:18 and Lv 18:23. **22.** Collateral incest is forbidden also in Lv 18:9 and 20:17. **23.** Cf. Lv 18:8; 20:14. **24.** This is a special case of the Seventh Commandment (see 5:17; Ex 20:13). It specifies "in secret," in keeping with the rest of the crimes which are the object of the curses. **25.** Cf. Ex 23:8. A hired assassin would presumably also work in secret. **26.** The verse is the conclusion of the public reading of "this law" (cf. 28:58). This kind of conclusion perseveres under a different form in Mt 7:36ff.

66 **(Y) Concluding Blessings and Curses (28:1–68).** After the curses which originally formed part of the Shechem covenant renewal feast (to which also it seems possible to attach the E code and the equivalent of blessings which follow it, Ex 23:20–33), we have the blessings and curses with which the Deuteronomic Code and covenant close in accordance with the pattern of covenant making in the ancient Near East (see E. Mørstad, *Wenn Du der Stimme des Herrn deines Gottes gehorchen wirst* [Oslo, 1960]). While there is a symmetrical order between the blessings of 1–6 and the curses of 15–19, and, to a much smaller extent, between 7ff. and 25ff., very much more space is given up to cursing than to blessing. Rather than indicating a preponderance in Dt of law over "gospel" (Von Rad, *Studies in Deuteronomy*, 72), this fact corresponded to the covenant pattern in which the curses, being the self-administered oaths that sanctioned the Law, played a more important part, as is clear from 29:14 (see comment on 29:14), the reaction of Josiah (2 Kgs 22:13), and the "deuteronomic" passage in Jer 11:1–12. There is, of course, much redactional expansion (see N. Lohfink, *BZ* 6 [1962] 32–56).

1. This verse continues the homiletic note of 26:16–19 and 27:9–10. **3.** The blessing, *beraḵāh*, derives from ancient forms fixed by custom, most of which deal with fertility, as here (e.g., Gn 24:60; 27:28–29). Dt is a law for life in the fertile land of Canaan. **4.** Cf. Lk 1:42. The "thou" addressed is Israel, both man and woman, the latter here and in v. 5. **7.** Reminiscent of the seven kings defeated during the preconquest and conquest campaigns. **9.** *a people sacred to himself:* See comment on 7:6; Dt stresses that the covenant is bilateral; Israel, in fact, broke the covenant, a fact which is the basis of the deuteronomic history.

67 **(Z) The Curses (28:15–68).** **15.** The curses here are in a homiletic setting, but were originally juridical forms recited aloud and accepted by the people (cf. 27:15, "Amen"). It is significant that none of them pursue the cursed after death—apart from that of remaining unburied (26)—but stay within the spiritual perspective of that age. **15–19.** Curses are presented as the exact antithesis of 1–6, with the exception of "the offspring of your livestock" (cf. v. 4), missing in the LXX. **20.** The different forms that judgment on covenant infidelity take reflect the oracles of doom of the pre-exilic prophets (e.g., Am 4:6ff.; 5:16ff.; 7:1ff.). **21.** The law is for life in the land; if it is violated, they will be driven out of the land—the leitmotiv of the deuteronomic history (see 2 Kgs

17:7ff.,23). The end of infidelity is the reversal of the Exodus—a (symbolical) return to Egypt, i.e., to servitude (68). **25.** It is the reverse of v. 7. **26–29.** The plagues of Egypt are turned against the Israelites. The prophetic theme of God's judgment on the nation is turned against Israel (Am 1:3–2:16; 9:7–8). **30.** This corresponds to 20:5–7; The threat also occurs frequently in the Prophets (e.g., Am 5:11; 7:17). **33.** The reference is to the Babylonians. **36.** This was the great crisis of faith brought on by exile—the apparent defeat of Yahweh at the hands of another god (see J. Blenkinsopp, *Scr* 14 [1962] 81–90, 109–118). **44.** Cf. 13. **47.** After 45–46, which concluded the curses at an earlier redactional stage, we have here an expansion in the sermon style, derived from the prophets of doom and painting a realistic picture of war, siege, and exile (see especially Is 5:26ff., following a list of curses; Jer 5:15–17, with the deuteronomic note added in 5:19; 16:10–13; 22:8; 1 Kgs 9:8–9 [D]). The preacher is speaking in concrete terms drawn from experience. **52–57.** This terrible description of a siege, written with rhythmic urgency and leading to a climax of horror, need not necessarily presuppose the experience of 587 BC (Jer 19:6–9; Ez 5:10; Lam 2:10; 4:10; but see Dt 29:28). We hear of cannibalism also during a siege of Samaria (2 Kgs 6:28–30). **58.** *the Law which is written in this book:* What follows is the conclusion of the whole ceremony of covenant renewal after the Law had been read from the "book of the law" (see 2 Kgs 22:8), which certainly contained curses (see v. 61 and 2 Kgs 22:11). The proclamation of the name of God was the climax of the covenant renewal festival; see Ex 20:24 (*zkr* meaning here "to name" rather than "to remember"), Nm 6:27; 2 Sm 6:2 (where the name is called out, *niqrā'*), etc. (see A. Weiser, *The Psalms* [London, 1962] 30–32). **60.** *all the diseases of Egypt:* See comment on 20:26. Through infidelity, Israel is back where she started, as slaves in Egypt "few in number" (26:5). This presentation is a theological parallel to the Exodus promise so frequently mentioned in Dt. As in Hos 8:13; 9:3; 11:5, Egypt is symbolic of any victorious and oppressive power. At the same time, v. 68 may refer to what happened after the battle of Megiddo in 609 (see 2 Kgs 23:33–35). **69.** Cf. 29:1.

68 **(IV) The Final Discourse of Moses; Traditions About His Last Days and Death (29:1–34:12).** The last section of Dt contains a covenant sermon attributed to Moses (29) followed by a homily for the exiled people (30). There follow the final dispositions of Moses before his death: the passing on of his authority to Joshua; the writing out of the Law, which is then confided to the Levitical priests and put near the Ark of the Covenant; and the command to keep a festival of covenant renewal. According to one tradition, the Law is to be a witness against the people, should they be unfaithful; according to another, the Song of Moses (which follows in 32) is the witness. From Mount Nebo, Moses pronounces the last blessing upon the tribes and there follows an account of his death and burial (34).

69 **(A) A Summary of the Covenant Ceremony (29:1–14).** **1.** The previous verse (28:69) is a typical introduction; cf. 1:1; 4:44–45; 6:1; 12:1 (yet cf. 5:22 and Lv 26:46). What follows is a summary of the Moab covenant presented as a new and revised edition of the Horeb covenant. **2.** The new meeting of "all Israel" opens with the holy recital, an essential element of covenant making. The theme is: You have seen but you have not perceived. It resumes themes already presented in 2:26–3:11 and 4:29–31. **3.** As in Is 19:14 and 29:9–10, perception and the lack of it are attributed to Yahweh. **5.** God's saving presence could be known through the provision of miraculous food. The speaker is no longer Moses but Yahweh, whose self-manifestation is the center of the covenant liturgy. **6–7.** The verses recapitulate 2:26–3:16. **9.** This language is liturgical; the plenary assembly is at the moment of covenant renewal. **10.** *hew wood and draw water:* These have a function similar to that of the *n^{e}tînîm*, or temple servants of the postexilic period (see Ezr 2:43; Neh 7:50; cf. Jos 9:21–23; 1 Kgs 9:20). **11.** *that you may enter into the covenant:* Since the *Sitz im Leben* is certainly covenant renewal, there would be no question of Israelites *entering* the covenant, i.e., the covenant community. We are therefore led to think of a covenant making at which others were incorporated into Israel, as with the Shechem and Gibeon covenant. The covenant is confirmed with an oath. **12.** The fundamental covenant formulation is presented (cf. Hos 2:23; Jer 31:33). **13.** The curse was an integral part of the ceremony (→ 67 above). **14.** "Those who are not here" may refer either to the descendants of those who are (22ff.) or to tribes not physically present at the ceremony that this text reflects.

70 **(B) Homiletic Actualization of the Covenant Experience (29:15–29).** Written from the viewpoint of the exiled community (v. 27), this strongly worded warning against idolatry is similar to those found in Is 40ff. **17.** This homiletic style is typical of Dt; cf. Heb 6:12, immediately after the quotation from the deuteronomic Ps 95. **21–23.** This question and answer form is one of the hallmarks of the deuteronomic style and a means of creating historical perspective (cf. 1 Kgs 9:8ff.; Jer 5:19ff.; 16:10ff.; 22:8–9). Within the thought pattern of Dt, it was natural that infidelity should be followed by infertility of the land, as in Hos. Admah and Zeboiim are the northern and Elohist equivalent of Sodom and Gomorrah (Hos 11:8; Is 1:9–10; Gn 10:19). **25.** Yahweh is represented here as allotting gods to other nations, e.g., Marduk to Babylon (cf. 4:19). **27.** *today:* This verse presupposes a redactional stage during the Exile; cf. Lv 26:39ff. **28.** An exalted idea of God's absolute freedom in his self-revelation is expressed in MT. The CCD (emended text) indicates that this verse is a gloss expressing the pertinence of the revelation for future generations.

71 **(C) Liturgical Address to the Exilic Community (30:1–20).** The cultic character of this sermon is clearly marked: by "today" (vv. 2, 8, 11, 15–16, 18–19); by God experienced as near through his proclaimed Word (11ff.); and by the strongly emphasized call to conversion. Probably 29:16–30:20 dates from the Exile (cf. 4:27–31 and the covenant sermon in Lv 26), and it may have been influenced by the promise of a "new covenant" in Jer 31:31ff. The relevance of a Mosaic covenant in Moab for those who hoped for an eventual reoccupation of the promised land would be obvious. **1.** *ponder them:* This was the first step toward reconstituted Israel: to see in the catastrophe of defeat and exile the fulfillment of the prophetic oracles of judgment and the result of covenant infidelity. The theme of return (i.e., conversion) is stressed even by means of assonance (vv. 1–3): *h^{a}šēbōtā. . .šabtā. . .šab et-š^{e}bût^{e}kā.* **3.** *change your lot:* For the phrase *šûb š^{e}bût*, see R. Borger, *ZAW* 66 (1954) 315–16. The reversal of captivity—i.e., the restoration of good fortune and prosperity—may have been represented in the covenant renewal festival (see Weiser, *The Psalms*, 47; for the role of this feast, see Pss 53:6; 85:1, 126:1; see also Jer 29:14; Am 9:14; Hos 6:11). **6.** *circumcise your hearts:* See comment on 10:16. This way of speaking emphasizes the necessity of a new covenant written on the heart, a radicalization and interiorization of the whole ancient covenant tradition, as in Jer 31:33; Ex 36:26–32 also speaks of a new covenant *in the land.* Verses 11–14 are a special case of the oratorical art of Dt written with a rhythmic power and cadence and a structured perfection of balance all its own. It illustrates a process of conceptualization—word, law, commandment, inheritance—which leads directly to the treatment of the Torah in the wisdom writings (e.g., Prv 8:1ff.; Sir 24). There is already in Dt the beginning of a conceptual treatment of revelation (e.g., 29:29) as manifesting God acting in freedom and power (e.g., 7:7–11; 10:14–22) and a strong insistence upon meditation of experience (4:39; 6:6; 30:1), the starting point of the wisdom writings. **15.** See comment on 11:26, a parallel. The liturgy of covenant renewal confronts the community with the necessity of committing itself to a binding decision. The "life" in question is further specified as fullness of life in the promised land. **19.** *I call heaven and earth today to witness:* See comment on 4:26. This passage leads to the covenant witnessing in ch. 31.

72 **(D) Conclusion of the Ceremony and the Succession of Joshua (31:1–29).** There is general agreement that this chapter is composite but great divergence exists in attempts at literary analysis (see Eissfeldt, *OTI* 229ff.). Chapters 31–34 are sometimes regarded as a series of appendices to the Book of the Covenant (e.g., Wright, *IB* 2, 314), but there remains the question of links with the earlier chapters. We distinguish three themes: provision for writing the law, confiding it to the Levites, and reading it on the occasion of a covenant renewal feast so that it should be a witness against the unfaithful people (9–13 and 24–27); the succession of Joshua (1–8, 14–15, and 23); the song as a witness against the people (16–22 and 28–30). This order is clearly that of the literary formation of the chapter, the succession of Joshua being the first link in the deuteronomic history and the introduction to the song being added as parallel to the law when the song itself was incorporated into the book. **2.** The age of Moses, three generations, is in accord with the schematic P computation that makes him 80 at the beginning of the Exodus (Ex 7:7). The inability of Moses to enter the land and the charismatic succession of Joshua play an important part at the beginning of the deuteronomic history (cf. 1:37–38; 3:21–22,25–29; 32:48–52; 34:9; Nm 27:15–23). **3.** *the Lord, your God, who will cross before you:* Cf. 3:22. The basic idea of the D account of the conquest is that the victorious presence of Yahweh, symbolized by the Ark, is responsible for success (see comment on 1:30). Thus, the defeat of the five Canaanite kings is seen as parallel to that of the two E of Jordan. **6.** *be brave and steadfast:* Cf. the deuteronomic passage in Jos 1:6–9. **9.** On the Levites and their relation to the Ark and the D tradition, see comment on 10:8; on the Ark itself, see comment on 10:1. As long as the written law remained in the sanctuary, it had juridical effect. **10.** Provision is made for public reading of the Law and renewal of the covenant at the amphictyonic center on the Feast of Tents (the September-October period) every seventh, or sabbatical, year (see 15:1). We read elsewhere of such covenant renewal feasts (2 Kgs 23; Neh 8), but without reference to this seven-year interval. In addition to an ancient custom of Law reading at this interval (see A. Alt, *Die Ursprünge des israelitischen Rechts* [Leipzig, 1934] 63ff.), there may also have been an annual covenant renewal festival that coincided with the Feast of Tents, although rabbinical tradition connects it rather with the Feast of Weeks. **11.** *to appear before the Lord:* Read: "to see the face of the Lord"; see comment on 16:16. **14.** The commissioning of Joshua in the tent would appear to fit better before 1–8. It must be read in conjunction with Nm 11:16–17,24–30, the charismatic "ordination" of the 70 elders, because Joshua was one of these. In fact, there were two traditions of Joshua's succession: that of E, in which the charismatic aspect is uppermost (cf. Dt 34:9); that of P, in which the presence of the priest Eleazar plays an important role (Nm 27:18–22; see Lohfink, *Scholastik* 37 [1962] 32–44).

73 **(E) Introduction to the Song (31:16–29).** **16.** Here begins the introduction to the song, added at the last stage of redaction. **19.** *write out this song:* In Ex 17:14 (E), Moses is also ordered to write down an epic poem about the battle with Amalek; cf. also 2 Sm 1:18, the command to teach the sons of Judah the Davidic elegy. The song must be a witness insofar as it will stir their memory and conscience, as the reading of the Law did for Josiah (2 Kgs 22:11). **23.** This verse continues 1–8 and 14–15. **24.** Since 28–30 certainly continue speaking of the song, the temptation is to alter *hattôrāh* (law) in v. 24 to *haššîrāh* (song), but this is hardly justified. Both the writing of the tablets of the Decalogue by God himself (5:22) and the placing of the Deuteronomic Code near the Ark—which is therefore called in Dt "the ark of the covenant"—express the divine authentication that the Law was considered to have. We recall that in treaty making in the ancient Near East there was generally provision for depositing the treaty in a temple and occasional public reading of it. **28.** This is the immediate introduction to the song considered the "last words" of Moses, as can be seen by the command to gather the people around him (cf. Gen 49:1; Jos 23:2). The vision is retrospective, as so often in Dt.

74 **(F) The Song of Moses (31:30–32:44).** There is considerable divergence between the MT and the versions in this poem; the 4Q fragments from QL support the LXX readings against the MT. The debate on the time of composition and insertion in Dt continues. The theme of the poem—Yahweh's choice of Israel as his son and the rejection by Israel of that choice, shown by infidelity to the covenant law—explains its insertion into the covenant book. According to Eissfeldt and Albright, this insertion took place as early as the 11th cent. (reasons: its origin within the E corpus; its genuine archaic language; its comparison with Ex 15, Jgs 5, Nm 23:7–24:25, 1 Sm 2:1–10, Ps 78), but the date is difficult to accept for the poem as a whole, owing to the at times mature theological presentation and kinship with the prophetic literature. That a strongly archaic impression could be given by late compositions can be seen in Hab 3, and we have to remember, in any case, that a composition such as this one would constantly have been readapted for liturgical use (7, the call to remember "days of old"; 15, direct address to a congregation, etc.). This didactic poem is basically in trimeter (cf. Gn 49 and Nm 23–24). (On the text, see P. W. Skehan, *CBQ* 13 [1951] 153–63; *BASOR* 136 [1954] 12–15; *JBL* 78 [1959] 22; E. Vogt, *Bib* 36 [1955] 264–65; on the date, see E. Sellin, *ZAW* 43 [1925] 161–73; M. Frank, *JJS* 1 [1948] 126; O. Eissfeldt, *ZAW* 67 [1955] 126; *Das Lied Moses und das Lehrgedicht Asaph* [Berlin, 1958]; W. F. Albright, *VT* 9 [1959] 339–46; Weiser, *OT*, 118–19; see also R. Gordis, *JTS* 34 [1933] 390–92; E. Henschke, *ZAW* 11 [1934] 279–82; A. J. Levy, *The Song of Moses* [Paris, 1934]; E. Baumann, *VT* 6 [1956] 414–24; W. L. Moran, *Bib* 43 [1962] 317–27; for the song's place in Dt, see Lohfink, *BZ* 6 [1962] 45ff.)

1. *give ear, O heavens:* The conjuration addressed to the heavens and the earth (cf. 4:26; 30:19; Jer 2:12; Ps 50:4–6) is a constant feature in the *rîb*, a forensic indictment leading to proceedings against the unfaithful covenant partner (see G. E. Wright, *Israel's Prophetic Heritage* [New York, 1962] 26–67; J. Harvey, *Bib* 43 [1962] 172–96). This feature is a valuable indication of the song's function in Dt. **4.** *the Rock:* Whether this term arose in connection with Horeb (see Ex 17:6; 33:21–22), it is used both here and in David's psalm (2 Sm 22:3,32,47) and often in the Pss as a metaphor for the strong covenant God, a God who can be relied upon. **5–6.** See 1:31 and

Hos 11:1. This representation of Yahweh as father, or perhaps, "ancestor," of the Israelites is apparently genuinely archaic. It expresses the intimate nature of the covenant bond. **7.** *think back on the days of old:* A deuteronomic theme recurs: the appeal to remembrance and the vital importance of a living tradition (see comment on 6:12). **8.** *the Most High:* The divine title Elyon stems from Canaan and probably from pre-Israelite Jerusalem (cf. Gn 14:18ff.); it is found in compositions dating from the time of the early monarchy (Nm 24:16; 2 Sm 24:14). *after the number of the sons of God:* This figure originates in the heavenly court and courtiers of Canaanite-Phoenician mythology; each nation has its guardian deity. Against this background, the author sees the unique vocation of Israel (see P. Winter, *ZAW* 67 [1955] 40–48; *ZAW* 75 [1963] 218–23; R. Meyer, *Fest. W. Rudolph* [Tübingen, 1961] 197–209, who dates the poem from the Persian period). **10.** This providence of Yahweh for his people in the desert is an ancient theme, worked over often by the prophets in different forms (e.g., Hos 9:10; Jer 2:6; on the text of v. 10, see G. Richter, *ZAW* 11 [1934] 77–78; also K. Marti, *ZAW* 39 [1921] 315–16; S. A. B. Mercer, *AnglTR* 3 [1920–21] 151–52). **13.** Here again we touch on a central theme of Dt—the temptation of the fertile land (see 6:3; 8:7). The text of the first stich is corrupt. Much of this poetical language of the earth and vegetation was certainly indigenous; e.g., "blood of the grape" (Gn 49:11); cf. *dm ʿṣm*, "blood of trees" in the Ugaritic Baal cycle (II ii, 43). **15.** *the darling:* *y*^{e}*šurûn* (33:5) is used ironically here. The etymology is uncertain; it either derives from *šôr*, "bull," or is to be connected with *yāšār*, "upright." **17.** This polemic against other (false) gods and the exclusive claim (jealousy) of Yahweh recur frequently in Dt (see comment on 4:24). The Hebrew *šed*, "demon," is the Akkadian minor deity, *šêdu*. **19.** Here begins the pronunciation of sentence. There is, as in other cases of judicial sentence for covenant violation, a correspondence between crime and punishment (cf. Hos 1:9; 2:1; Jer 2:11). **22.** *a fire is enkindled:* It reaches to the underworld, scorching the sources of fertility; cf. Jgs 9:15,20; Am 2:4ff., and especially 7:4ff., where fire means drought. **26.** From this point there is a change of perspective—the nation will not be destroyed because it would be represented as a victory for Yahweh's enemies (cf. Jos 7:9). In the prophets also we have the at times sudden transition from condemnation to blessing. (For vv. 26–34, see K. Fullerton, *ZAW* 5 [1928] 138–55.) **30.** This verse apparently refers to a definite historical setback for the Israelites. **31.** But Israel's enemies will not prevail against the Lord. **32.** It contrasts with v. 14. The metaphor of the vineyard and its produce is used frequently in the prophetic literature (Hos 10:1; Is 5:1–7). **34–35.** Yahweh has stored up his vengeance. **39.** The divine self-predication is at the heart of the covenant (cf. Ex 3:14; Is 41:4; etc.). It is Yahweh who gives death and life, who has absolute control over the sources of life, and not the gods to whom they are drawn (cf. 1 Sm 2:6; Hos 6:1–2). **40.** The attitude of oath taking is encountered. Yahweh swears by himself. The divine vengeance is described in terms familiar in Canaanite mythology (cf. Hab 3). **43.** See the textual analysis by F. M. Cross (*The Ancient Library of Qumran* [N.Y., 1961] 182–84) and by P. Skehan (*CBQ* 13 [1951] 156).

75 **(G) Conclusion to the Giving of the Law and the Song (32:45–52).** Verses 45–47 evidently follow 31:24–27, referring to the Law, and not to the song. There, Moses announces his death and prepares for what follows here. **47.** *your very life:* Although for Paul the Law became, in fact, an instrument of death (Rom 7:9; 10:5; Gal 3:10–12), when it is accepted as part of the self-giving of God in the covenant, it brings life (cf. Lv 18:5). **48.** The theme of Moses' exclusion from the land has already occurred, perhaps in a variant tradition (1:37–38; 3:26–28), where the mountain is Pisgah (also Nm 27:12–14 [P]). Both are in the Abarim (lit., mountain passes) range. **50.** For the death of Aaron, see Nm 20:22–29 (P). **51.** See Nm 20:10–13.

76 **(H) The Blessings of Moses on the Tribes (33:1–29).** It was customary to attribute memorable last words or oracular utterances, especially in the form of blessings, to the great men of the past; cf. Isaac (Gn 27), Jacob (Gn 49), and David (2 Sm 21:1–7). Whatever their origin, which is certainly ancient, these oracles became part of a processional liturgy, traces of which can be detected in the psalmic framework (vv. 2–5 and 26–29) as in other ancient hymnic compositions (e.g., Ps 68). The tendency today is to move away from the once popular late date, whether late in the 6th cent. (Mowinckel) or in the reign of Jeroboam II. Comparison with the oracles of Jacob (Gn 49) show that Dt 33 in its final form is later: Simeon has been absorbed, Dan has migrated, Levi is no longer a secular tribe. At the same time, the language is certainly archaic (which helps to explain the corrupt state of the text), so that a date sometime during the early monarchy is indicated. The insertion of this poem in Dt may well have resulted from its use in the central covenant festival of the tribes.

(Burkitt, F. C., *JTS* 35 [1934] 68. Cassuto, U., *RSO* 11 [1927–28] 233–53. Cross, F. M. and D. N. Freedman, *JBL* 67 [1948] 191–201. Pythian-Adams, W. J., *JPOS* 3 [1923] 158–66. Tournay, R. J., *RB* 65 [1958] 181–213. Van Hoonacker, A., *Mus* 42 [1929] 42–60.)

2. *the Lord came from Sinai:* The introduction begins with a theophany, as in Jgs 5:4 and Hab 3:3, in which Yahweh is represented as king of the tribes. This idea corresponds to the theology of the covenant renewal festival. The reference to Meribah-kadesh in the CCD is based upon conjecture; the MT speaks of "holy ones" accompanying the Lord. **3.** The interpretation of this verse remains uncertain. The CCD refers the "holy ones" to Israel. For points of detail, see O. Komlos (*VT* 6 [1956] 435ff.), and for general interpretation, see H. S. Nyberg (*ZDMG* 92 [1938] 320–44) and T. H. Gaster (*JBL* 66 [1947] 53–62). **4.** There is no need to excise 4a; it follows from what precedes, has a regular rhythm, and, given the cultic interpretation, the reference to the Law would be natural. The great tribal assembly is presupposed in what follows. **6.** The title of the oracle is missing. The Transjordan tribe of Reuben, still powerful in Gn 49:3–4 and the object of a taunt in the Song of Deborah (Jgs 5:15b–16), was evidently in danger of extinction as a result of pressure from neighboring states. It was probably not represented at the assembly. **7.** *Judah:* This prayer seems to presuppose that Judah was also absent from the assembly—which would be explicable if, as is likely, the blessings are from E. This individual unit is certainly older than Gn 49:8–12, unless it is taken to date from the divided monarchy (see E. Sellin, *ZAW* 60 [1944] 57–67). **8.** *Levi:* A purely secular tribe in Gn 49:5–7, Levi now has a sacred function. This oracle is later than most, if not all, of the others, and it may be the peculiar contribution of Dt for whom the Levites played a role of vital importance (see comment on 1:19). For Urim and Thummin as a means of divination, see Ex 28:30 and 1 Sm 14:41 (LXX and Vg). Ex 32:25–29 records the events at Kadesh-barnea referred to here. (See T. H. Gaster, *VT* 8 [1958] 217–19; for the controversial question of Levite origins, see Meek, *Hebrew Origins*, 121–32.) **12.** *Benjamin:* Benjamin was at first more orientated to the north than to the south, but with the gradual ascendancy of Judah and David, it was absorbed after a bitter struggle. This favorable oracle is northern, and probably earlier than Gn 49:27, which is Judean (see T. H. Gaster, *ExpT* 46 [1934–35] 334).

77 **13.** *Joseph:* In contrast with the predominance of Judah in Gn 49, here the Joseph tribes are preeminent; Joseph is "prince among his brothers." Because the oracle paints a picture of prosperity and political expansion, some read it as coming from a period such as the reign of Jeroboam I or II, but it can be read equally well as coming from the period preceding the ascendancy of Judah and therefore earlier than Gn 49:8–12. As in Gn 49:22–26, which it resembles quite closely, the language is markedly Canaanite. The great "abyss" below, the mass of waters under the earth, still mythologically personalized as "crouching," is the source of fertility. **15.** The "age-old mountains" are part of the mythological world image, as in Gn 49:26; Hab 3:6. **16.** *of him who dwells in the bush:* See Ex 33:16. *prince among his brothers:* In its primary sense, *nāzîr* (prince) means "one consecrated," and the consecration was with a view to the holy war. The nazirite obligation to leave the hair of the head uncut may be reflected in the previous stich. **17.** *the majestic bull:* Read, making a slight alteration with many versions, "The first-born of the Bull—glory to him!" This title applies to Baal, son of El, the Bull, in Canaanite mythology, and a symbiosis between bull worship and Yahwism was endemic in the northern tribes (see 1 Kgs 12:28ff.; Ex 32:3ff.). Horns are a symbol of strength. **18.** Zebulun settled along the Phoenician coast; Issachar settled in the rich plain of Esdraelon, where they were subject to the Canaanites, who were specially strong there. Whether they threw off the yoke as a result of their participation in the victory of Deborah (Jgs 5:14–15,18) it is difficult to say (cf. Gn 49:13–15). **19.** *the mountains:* An example is Mt. Carmel, which had been a cult center from remote times. **20.** With Reuben, Gad settled in Transjordan, which explains the absence of both from the list of tribes in Jgs 5:14ff. In their fight for survival against the inroads of tribes from the Syrian desert and the neighboring states, they acquired a reputation for fierceness (see Gn 49:19). **22.** *Dan:* The migration of Dan northward (Jgs 18:7ff.) has already taken place and they are settled in Laish (lion), renamed Dan, which was in Bashan. **23.** The "favors" and "blessings" refer to the fertile land around the Sea of Galilee, which Naphtali possessed. The reference to the "south" is obscure. **24.** Both here and in Gn 49:20, reference is made to the prosperity of Asher, no doubt largely because of the olive plantations in the coastal area of Galilee and the securely guarded cities. It was for this reason that she did not answer the tribal call to arms (Jgs 5:17). **26.** The conclusion, like vv. 2–5, is in the style of the Pss, with the same theophanous imagery. *darling:* See comment on 32:15. *who rides the heavens:* Read, perhaps more accurately, "the Rider of the Skies" (26b in parallelism is "clouds" rather than "skies"), a title used of Baal, the storm god in Canaanite literature, and of Yahweh in Ps 68:5 (cf. Ps 18:11–16; see F. M. Cross and D. N. Freedman, *BASOR* 108 [1947] 6–7; H. L. Ginsberg, *BASOR* 110 [1948] 26). **27.** The text is uncertain, and the CCD emends it in the light of Is 40:22. **29.** *upon their heights:* Cf. 2 Sm 1:19; but it may also be understood lit., "upon their backs."

78 **(I) Death of Moses and Succession of Joshua (34:1–12).** This chapter forms the conclusion not only of Dt but also of the entire Pentateuch, which explains the evident signs of retouching: Nebo and Pisgah are parallel names for the same mountain (see 3:27); the attribution of 120 years to Moses at his death (P; see comment on 31:2); the D finale of vv. 11–12 (ill-joined to 10); and possibly others. The account of the death, numinous as that event was held to have been, is intimately linked with the charismatic succession of Joshua (cf. 1:37–38; 3:25–28) in the same way as with Elijah and Elisha, both being the fruit of a prophetic "theology" of the Spirit. Verse 9 serves as a link with Jos and the history that follows (cf. Jos 1:1–2). **1.** *the Lord showed him all the land:* The panoramic vision of Canaan takes in an immense arc from N to S (cf. Mt 4:8). On a clear day, in fact, the Mediterranean can be seen from Nebo. **4.** This verse has been prepared for in Dt 1:37; 3:25–27; 4:21–22; 32:48–52, and it achieves a poignancy at the end. The narrative takes up from 32:52. **6.** The MT can be rendered: "he [Yahweh] buried him"; Sam and some LXX readings have the plural. The departure of the Prophet could not be less numinous than that of Elijah (see J. R. Harris, *BJRylL* 8 [1924] 404–405). A whole literature grew up around the ultimate fate of Moses and the location of his remains (cf. Jude 9). **7.** For the P editors, the career of Moses covered three generations: to the visit to his suffering brethren (presumed—see Acts 7:23), to the Exodus (Ex 7:7), to his death. He died in the full possession of his powers. On his "vigor" (*lēaḥ*, the "life principle"—cf. Ugaritic *lḥt*), see W. F. Albright (*BASOR* 94 [1944] 32–35). Statutory for mourning was evidently 30 days; cf. the 70 for Joseph according to the Egyptian practice (Gn 50:3). **9.** This statement is a summary of the charismatic succession of Joshua, which takes into account Dt 3:28 and Nm 27:18–23 (P). The laying on of hands signified the passing on of the spirit, the *mana* (Nm 27:20, *hôd*), and, at the same time, the commissioning—implying the authority in the sacred community is not separable from charism (see comment on 31:14). **10.** See comment on 18:15. **11.** The verse is an apt conclusion, bringing finally to the attention of the worshiping community, "all Israel," the great redemptive event wrought by God through his servant.

7

JOSHUA

Peter J. Kearney

BIBLIOGRAPHY

1 *Commentaries:* Bright, J., *The Book of Joshua* (*IB*; Nashville, 1953) 2, 539–673. Hertzberg, H. W., *Die Bücher Josua, Richter, Ruth* (ATD; 2nd ed.; Göttingen, 1959) 7–140. May, H. G., *Joshua* (*PCB*; N.Y., 1962) 289–303. Noth, M., *Das Buch Josua* (HAT; 2nd ed.; Tübingen, 1953).

Studies: L'Hour, J.,"L'Alliance de Sichem," *RB* 69 (1962) 5–36, 161–84, 350–68. McKenzie, J. L., *The World of the Judges* (Englewood Cliffs, N.J., 1966). Moran, W., *Adnotationes in Librum Josue* (private lecture notes). Rowley, H. H., *From Joseph to Joshua* (London, 1950).

For further bibliography, see Eissfeldt, *OTI* 248, 747–48.

INTRODUCTION

2 **(I) Literary History.** The book contains a very wide variety of literary materials; the history of their composition and combination covers most of the OT period. Naturally, theories of their history have differed; the following is based principally on those of Noth and Bright.

The oldest literary complex is chs. 2–11, excluding principally 8:30–35. It comprises a series of etiologies (2–9; 10:16–39) and battle narratives (10:1–15; 11:1–14) combined into a flowing account by an author called the "Compiler" (*Sammler*, M. Noth), *ca.* 900 BC (although Solomon rebuilt Hazor, 1 Kgs 9:15, the memory of its previous abandonment is preserved, 11:11). The etiologies (except ch. 7 and 10:16–39) take place within Benjamin territory and (except, perhaps, 10:16–39) had probably been preserved at Gilgal. Next, the editor (referred to as the Deuteronomist, the D editor, or sometimes simply as D) of the Deuteronomic, or D, History (Jos, Jgs, Sm, Kgs) edited this section and incorporated it into his great historical work. He added ch. 1 as an introduction and probably added 11:21–22 and 14:6–15 to the Compiler's conclusion, forming the sequence: 11:21–23a, 14:6–15, 11:23b. This new conclusion clarified several gaps in the conquest—a point of interest to D, because it is the presence of the Canaanites that will imperil Israelite fidelity to God. This same interest is reflected in 13:2–6, probably also added by D; the conclusion also told of Caleb's reward (14:6–15), another special interest of D (Dt 1:36). He added the list of conquered kings (12), noted the dismissal of the Transjordan tribes (22:1–6), and closed with Joshua's farewell address, again warning about the remaining Canaanites (23). The original D edition included, therefore, 1–12 (except 8:30–35), 13:2–6, 14:6–15, 22:1–6, and 23.

Sometime after the Compiler had composed his narrative of the conquests, another author called the "Editor" (*Bearbeiter*, M. Noth) composed a document of tribal possessions. It was a geographical survey rather than a narrative, composed principally of a boundary list dating from the early monarchy or premonarchical period, joined with a province list of Judah, dating from the divided monarchy (reflecting a more complex organization than Solomon's, 1 Kgs 4:19b). Here the Israelites, not Joshua, distributed the land, and Joshua was among the recipients (19:49–50); this document included chs. 14–21:42 (except 14:6–15; 15:13–19; 17:14–18; and 18:2–10), and also 13:16–21 and 25–27. It now underwent D editing, with a view to its incorporation into the Jos–Kgs history, which had already appeared without it. This second editor, working probably during the Exile, made the survey more like a narrative, in which Joshua allotted the territory. He removed 14:6–15 from its earlier setting (after 11:23a) and complemented it with another Caleb tradition, 15:13–19. He added also 17:14–18 and 18:2–10; all four of these narratives concern the initiative of the Judahite and Josephite tribes in taking possession of their territory. The inclusion of this new material probably accounts for these groups being treated first among the western tribes.

The Transjordan tribes now stand outside the original framework of the survey document, but most likely some eastern territory was in the original. Because of his special interest in these tribes, the editor has placed them in first position, in ch. 13. He has taken what appears to be a single block of territory (perhaps originally "Gad"; Reuben may have already practically vanished), one which does not even appear to contain genuine boundaries; this he divided between Reuben and Gad, then creating a kind of list for half Manasseh. This document (including 13:2–6 from the original edition) was now inserted into the D history by means of 13:1, anticipating 23:1. This procedure brought with it, however, the inconvenience of making the distribution appear to be the final words of Joshua; it also postponed the dismissal of the Transjordan tribes (22:1–6), even though they had already received their territory and the fighting was long since over. This long section was also given its own D conclusion in 21:43–45, constructed largely from earlier material in ch. 23. The large insertion demanded some editing in Dt, which originally spoke of only three asylum cities. Now, because of Jos 20:7–8, Dt 19:8–9 was added. The introduction of the Levitical cities in Jos 21, however, was given no preparatory text in Dt (there can be no doubt that Levitical cities were listed in the original survey document: the Israelites, not Joshua, designate them, 21:3).

The D editing accounts for other small changes throughout Jos, as does the next major stage, the work of the P school. The principal P contributions to the second half of the book are the introduction of Eleazar (14:1; 19:51; 21:1) and Shiloh (cf. 18:1–10), extensive reworking of ch. 21, and the insertion of 22:7–34. A final editor, heir of both the D and P schools, added 8:30–35 and concluded his new edition of the Hexateuch by adding ch. 24.

3 **(II) Historical Value.** It is undeniable that the Israelites did gain control of Canaan. It is likewise sure that memories of this accomplishment survived. Among those found in the Scriptures, there are so many allusions to victory in battle that a purely peaceful acquisition seems impossible. We can say in general that Jos must preserve genuine memories of the Israelite conquest. It would be oversimplification, therefore, to say that because so many traditions in Jos are etiologies, seeking to explain some local institution or landmark, they are consequently nothing but creations of popular imagination. Since some of the material is folklore, we may not be able to argue to a particular historical fact, but we can affirm at least in a general way that the traditions are founded on history.

Both the conquest and the allotment sections evince secondary aggrandizement of Joshua, but it would be a mistake to assign him a minor role in the conquest. His position as leader of the Josephites in 17:14–18 is not seriously challenged; although an Ephraimite, he is the leader in the Benjamin traditions (chs. 2–9); his role in the formation of the 12-tribe league at Shechem (ch. 24) is generally accepted as original. All factors point to a significant role in the conquest itself.

Portions of Jos describe the conquest as complete, but such statements are clearly idealistic schematizations or summaries. In details the authors show a desire to remain faithful to their sources; for example, 10:28–40 deliberately stretches out the narrative to give the impression of an extensive conquest through the south, although the source shows the conquest was not very extensive. The Compiler remains faithful to the meagerness of his material in ch. 11 when he describes the victories in the north. The central portion of Canaan is accounted for merely by the Benjamin traditions and several new names in the list of ch. 12. Never was the Philistine coast expressly claimed, nor the Plain of Esdraelon, nor Jerusalem. The D historian repeatedly referred to areas not yet conquered (11:21–22; 13:2–6; 23:4–5).

The evidence of archaeology must be used with caution in relation to the conquest, for which it does offer some support: Lachish, Debir, and Hazor were destroyed around the time of the Israelite conquest. But the connection between this destruction and the Israelite conquest is not fully clear; likewise, it would be hazardous to affirm that this destruction gave rise to the conquest narratives we now possess. The evidence at Ai and Jericho even militates against the historicity of these two victories.

4 **(III) Religious Value.** Although the different levels of tradition share religious values in common, each level adds a special emphasis of its own. The Compiler saw the conquest as the action of God; on man's part it was like an act of worship, closely associated with the sanctuary at Gilgal and the sacred rites performed there. This outlook, however, is linked with the primitive idea that total annihilation of the enemy was an act of worship, a view accented even more strongly by D, even though this ritual custom of "holy war" was no longer practiced in his time—undoubtedly D was reacting against the Canaanite influence that in his view was Israel's greatest danger. The Compiler also expresses the primitive idea that a community bears the guilt of an individual (ch. 7), a view still persisting in the P school (22:18). The D editor added his covenant themes to the narrative: possession of the land is conditional upon fidelity to God's Law; the covenant curses may yet be realized. Also, Israelite morality is a response to God's gifts; the Israelites have entered a close personal relationship with their God. The second D editor, who added chs. 13–21, professed his faith in God's continuing benefits: total possession of the land will be restored, even though the Exile makes such a dream seem distant.

The P editors reaffirmed this faith even more idealistically, picturing the future Israel as a worshiping community of 12 tribes gathered around the central sanctuary, each tribe making careful provision for the welfare of the priests. The final editor accents Israel's personal relationship with God: the choice is a free one (24:15). He strengthens the convictions of his predecessors still further; he reaffirms his faith in both God and Israel. The book no longer ends with Joshua's warning about the future (ch. 23); now the people repeatedly protest that they will serve God (24:24). The closing verses of the book (and the Hexateuch) emphasize the fidelity of Israel and the possession of the land (vv. 30–33).

5 **(IV) Outline.** The literary history should be consulted for a fuller understanding of the following general outline:

- (I) Introduction (1:1–18)
  - (A) The Divine Commission of Joshua (1:1–11)
  - (B) Loyalty of the Transjordan Tribes (1:12–18)
- (II) The Conquest of Canaan (2:1–11:23)
  - (A) The Spies in Jericho (2:1–24)
    - (a) Rahab Conceals the Spies and Deceives the King's Emissaries (2:1–7)
    - (b) Rahab's Pact with the Spies (2:8–24)
  - (B) The Crossing of the Jordan (3:1–5:1)
    - (a) Preparation for the Crossing (3:1–13)
    - (b) The Crossing (3:14–17)
    - (c) The Tradition of the Stones (4:1–9)
    - (d) Completion of the Crossing (4:10–14)
    - (e) The Waters Resume Their Course (4:15–18)
    - (f) The Placing of the Stones at Gilgal (4:19–5:1)
  - (C) The Rites at Gilgal (5:2–12)
    - (a) The Circumcision (5:2–9)
    - (b) The Passover (5:10–12)
  - (D) The Fall of Jericho (5:13–6:27)
    - (a) The Theophany (5:13–6:5)
    - (b) The Battle of Jericho (6:6–6:27)
  - (E) Defeat and Victory at Ai (7:1–8:29)
    - (a) The Initial Defeat and Its Cause (7:1–26)
    - (b) Victory at Ai (8:1–29)
  - (F) The Altar on Mt. Ebal (8:30–35)
  - (G) The Completion of the Conquest of Canaan (9:1–11:23)
    - (a) The Covenant with the Gibeonites (9:3–27)
    - (b) Defeat of the Anti-Gibeonite Coalition and Conquest of the South (10:1–43)

(c) The Conquest of the North (11:1–14)
(d) Summary of the Conquest (11:15–23)
(III) The List of Conquered Kings (12:1–24)
(IV) Allotment of the Promised Land (13:1–21:45)
(A) Introduction to the Allotment (13:1–33)
(B) Introduction to the Distribution of the Western Territory (14:1–5)
(C) The Calebites in Hebron (14:6–15)
(D) The Boundaries of Judah (15:1–12)
(E) The Territory of Caleb and Othniel (15:13–19)
(F) The Towns of Judah (15:20–63)
(G) The Territory of the Josephite Tribes (16:1–17:18)
(H) Introduction to the Remaining Allotment (18:1–10)
(I) The Allotment to Benjamin (18:11–28)
(J) The Allotment of Simeon (19:1–9)
(K) The Allotment of the Galilee Tribes (19:10–39)
(L) The Allotment of Dan (19:40–48)
(M) Conclusion of the Allotment (19:49–51)
(N) The Cities of Asylum (20:1–9)
(O) Levitical Cities (21:1–42)
(P) God's Faithfulness to His Word (21:43–45)
(V) Return of the Transjordan Tribes and the Construction of Their Altar (22:1–34)
(A) Dismissal of the Transjordan Tribes (22:1–6)
(B) The Altar Beside the Jordan (22:7–34)
(VI) Joshua's Farewell Address (23:1–16)
(VII) Epilogue: The Assembly at Shechem and the Burial Traditions (24:1–33)
(A) Assembly at Shechem (24:1–28)
(B) Burial Traditions (24:29–33)

COMMENTARY

6 **(I) Introduction (1:1–18).** For D, whose style pervades ch. 1, this introduction in dialogue form alludes to his favorite theological concerns. The unity of the people is accentuated through the position of Joshua, who is presented with repeated mention of his relationship to Moses, and who fully succeeds to Moses' office (vv. 3, 5, and 17). The Transjordan tribes, although they live outside the territory of the promised land and thus might appear to counter the author's perspective of unity, fully accept his authority and share in the conquest of the western territory. At the climax of God's message to Joshua is the D guarantee for the preservation of this unity, fidelity to God's Law (vv. 7–8).

7 **(A) The Divine Commission of Joshua (1:1–11).** **1.** The opening words link Jos with the death of Moses in Dt 34. Joshua's commission is a development of the divine mandate in Dt 31:14,15,23. *Moses' aide:* That this means a "military aide" can be inferred from the ancient tradition of Joshua's role in the battle with the Amalekites (Ex 17:9–14), whereas the personal devotion implied in Joshua's service is reflected in the tradition of Moses' changing his name from Hoshea to Joshua (Nm 13:16). Both names are in fact the same, Hoshea being an abbreviation of what is undoubtedly the original form "Joshua." Although this original form is certainly a combination of the divine name and some verb expressing the rule of God, its precise meaning is unknown (Moran, *op. cit.*). It has been understood as "Yahweh is salvation." Although he is still merely "Moses' aide," Joshua now receives God's word directly as Moses did (cf. Dt 31:23, where he receives his commission directly from God even before Moses' death). In 24:29, he merits Moses' title "servant of the Lord." **2.** The actual commission is cast in a rather flexible form comprising a statement of fact, a mandate grounded on this fact, a promise of divine help (v. 5, "I will be with you"), and an exhortation (v. 6, "be firm and steadfast"); cf. a similar pattern in David's mandate that Solomon build the temple (1 Chr 22:7–13) and also in Mt 28:18–20 (cf. N. Lohfink, *Scholastik* 37 [1962] 32–44; also Moran, *op. cit.*). *all the people:* D stresses the unity of the tribes in the conquest. **3.** *where you set foot:* These words probably express a judicial institution, whereby ownership of the land was expressed by marking off its boundaries on foot; cf. Gn 13:17. **4.** Verse 4 is a more detailed version of Dt 11:24–25; these boundaries were never attained; cf. also the rather late, idealized delineation of Solomon's domain in 1 Kgs 5:1,4 (Hebr) and 1 Chr 9:26. The Hebrew is difficult and there is disagreement over the precise meaning of these frontiers. Although Noth holds that Transjordan is included, it is more likely that the D editor tacitly supposes that the western bank of the Jordan is the eastern boundary of the promised land (cf. Dt 3:25) and describes only the remaining frontiers: the steppes ("desert") to the south (Noth holds that this includes also some of Transjordan); Lebanon as far east as the Euphrates to the north (see also Gn 15:18 and Dt 1:7 for the Euphrates as a northern boundary); and the Mediterranean Sea to the west (Moran, *op. cit.*). **5.** The Israelite conquest will be a holy war; God himself will fight for his people. **6.** *be firm and steadfast:* Addressed to a military leader, these words seem at first an exhortation to personal bravery in battle. In this holy war setting, however, they serve to focus on God as the leader; they are an exhortation to trust completely in him. It is then a short step to a favorite theme of the editor, as in vv. 7–8 he rises above the context of the approaching conquest to give voice to a principle that directs the whole history of Israel: it is only through fidelity to God's Law (expressed for D in the "Book of the Law," Dt), that the people can remain in possession of the promised land. **10.** *officers: šoṭ^{e}rîm* are in general officials of lower rank, whether foremen of a labor crew (Ex 5:6), or court clerks (Dt 16:18), or, as here, army officers (Dt 20:5). **11.** *provisions:* Battle rations are meant; in this holy war setting, no mention is made of the weapons used.

8 **(B) Loyalty of the Transjordan Tribes (1:12–18).** The union of these tribes with those in the west posed a special problem for D. How could they be members of the chosen people and still live outside the promised land? Ignoring ancient traditions of strife between the tribes on either side of the Jordan (Jgs 12:1–6; 21:5–14), he stressed the legitimacy of the Transjordan occupation. First, God himself will permit them to settle in this land (v. 13—sense of Hebr: They will be partakers of the "Repose," the tranquil enjoyment of the blessings of the promised land). Second, Moses gave them this land (v. 14). Third, they will share in the western conquest (v. 15). **14.** *armed:* More probably translated "in battle array," the word is related to the root meaning "five," and probably refers to a fivefold marching formation like that described in Nm 10:11–28 (De Vaux, *AI* 216). **16.** The three tribes solemnly bind themselves, as in a covenant (Ex 24:3). **17.** *but may the Lord your God be with you:* Since the author wishes to stress the participation of the Transjordan tribes, these words, as well as the final exhortation of v. 18, are most likely not a condition placed on Joshua's authority. They either express a wish (similar to that in 1 Chr 22:12) or are a strong affirmation of confidence in Joshua—"Indeed, the Lord your God will be with you"—and a consequent exhortation—"No matter what, be firm and steadfast"

(Moran, *op. cit.*). In any case, the D editor considers that the one essential attribute of a ruler is unshakable confidence in the God who is with him.

9 **(II) The Conquest of Canaan (2:1–11:23).**

(A) The Spies in Jericho (2:1–24). Recent archaeological investigations have found no trace of a Canaanite city on the site of Jericho later than the one destroyed by the Egyptians about 1550, some three centuries before the arrival of Joshua. It may be that the city remained in ruins throughout the first three centuries of the Israelite occupation, and could thus have become associated in popular tradition with the conquests of Joshua. The final verses of the Rahab story, as we have them in 6:17,22,23,25, indicate that it is an etiological narrative that seeks to explain the presence of a Canaanite settlement, known as the house of Rahab, still living in or near Jericho (Noth). By linking this group with the exploits of Joshua, the narrative explained they had perdured on this site because their ancestor, Rahab, had aided Joshua in the conquest of Jericho. There are still strong indications that this aid was originally described as a betrayal of the city. Capture of a city through betrayal (cf. Jgs 1:22–25) could be most conveniently arranged in a house such as Rahab's because of both the nature of her trade and the strategic location of the building (v. 15). Rahab's deliberation with the spies (v. 12), their insistence on absolute secrecy (vv. 14 and 20), and the sign of the scarlet cord (v. 18) all point to a probable earlier form involving a betrayal. If so, then the visit of the spies has been deprived of its strategic value, and the earlier outcome of the story has been neglected in favor of a miraculous conquest of Jericho through the collapse of its walls. (For the archaeological problem of Jericho's destruction, → Biblical Archaeology, 74:60–61.)

The Rahab incident, however, had more than merely etiological interest. Even at some stage of its earlier formulation (before it was incorporated into the Jos–Kgs history), it expressed the ancient faith that the conquest of Palestine was a holy war, that God was fighting for his people and spreading terror among the enemies of Israel (vv. 9, 10a, 11a, 24). The D editor supplemented Rahab's profession of faith with mention of the victories in Transjordan (v. 10b) and even with a formula of faith expressing profound Israelite piety (v. 11b; cf. Dt 4:39)! That Rahab's profession is really the most important element in the entire chapter is then made clear through the structure of the narrative. Through a series of flashbacks, action and dialogue are so ordered as to place her act of faith at the mid-point of the narrative (Moran). The story was most likely given its present structure before the D editor incorporated it, because this narrative technique is evident throughout the chapter, even where there are no signs of deuteronomic influence. This central position of Rahab's profession of faith even at an earlier stage of tradition most likely was arranged more to extol the action of God rather than the virtue of Rahab. For the editor, however, Rahab's words were meant to express his teaching that continued possession of the promised land depended on faith in God; she was allowed to share the blessings of the promised land only because she shared the Israelite faith.

10 (a) Rahab Conceals the Spies and Deceives the King's Emissaries (2:1–7). The episodes of this section follow in rapid-fire order. After the flurry of activity, as the closing of the gate closes also this first part of the narrative, the reader is left wondering why Rahab has protected the spies.

1. *Shittim:* Also called Abel-shittim (Nm 33:49) "Stream of the Acacia Trees," it is today Tell el-Hammam on the eastern side of the Jordan Valley, directly opposite Jericho. *Jericho:* Perhaps named for a cult of the moon goddess (*yārēaḥ*, "moon"), it is today Tell es-Sultan, on the western border of the Jordan Valley. *the land:* Territory outside the city but still within the city-state of Jericho is indicated (likewise in vv. 2–3). *Rahab:* Most likely a theophoric name from which the name of the god has been dropped: "...is great." *where they lodged:* The author passes over for the moment all the dialogue in vv. 9–14, 17–21 (to the words "...she replied"). **3.** *visitors who have entered your house:* The charge of the emissaries, as well as Rahab's answer in v. 4, imply a sexual relationship (Hebr), somewhat euphemized in v. 3 through a later addition that suggests mere lodging at the house. **4.** The Hebrew does not make clear whether she hid the spies before or after the emissaries came. **6.** This brief explanatory flashback prepares for the much longer one beginning in v. 8.

11 (b) Rahab's Pact with the Spies (2:8–24). The author now explains why Rahab has concealed the spies. This flashback is interrupted by vv. 15–16, which again pick up the narrative thread of v. 7 and explain the method of escape to be spoken of by the spies when the author reverts once more to the earlier conversation on the rooftop (vv. 17–18ff.). **9.** *I know:* The dramatic force of Rahab's profession of faith is heightened by her previous "I did not know" (v. 4)..."I do not know" (v. 5). **10.** *the Lord dried up the waters:* This description of God's action is unique to this tradition and argues for its independence of pentateuchal sources. *Sihon and Og:* Concerned with the legitimacy of the Transjordan inhabitation, the Deuteronomist is eager to associate these victories with God's saving plan. Total annihilation or "the ban" (*ḥerem*) was a characteristic rite of holy war and was conceived as an offering of the vanquished to God; any violation of the ban was thus considered a serious offense against him (7:11). **12.** *since I am showing kindness:* The Hebrew can also mean "if I show kindness," a translation clarifying that Rahab has not yet spoken to the king's messengers. *unmistakable token:* The author leaves us wondering what this token is. For the time being he concentrates on Rahab's faith, mentioning only in a general way the favorable response it evokes (v. 14) and leaving the condition of the oath and a clarification of the unmistakable token (the scarlet cord) until later. **15.** The author returns to his story, but still has not given us all the details of the original agreement; he will do so in vv. 18–21, in which the flashback is resumed. *house built into the city wall:* This may be an etiological element, occasioned by the remains of such a house in the ruins of Jericho (Noth). **18.** The window is built into the wall (cf. 2 Cor 11:33). **21.** Translate, rather, "through which you shall let us down." The Hebrew admits a fut. perfect. *the hill country:* While the pursuers have headed E in the direction of Joshua's camp, Rahab directs the spies toward the hills W of Jericho. **21.** The narrative is resumed from v. 17, as the scene shifts once again to the escape of the spies through the window. Before leaving this scene, the author notes that Rahab tied the cord in the window, without necessarily implying that she did so at once. The story now draws to a hurried finish. The spies report that the terror characteristic of holy war has seized the inhabitants and thus effectively announce that God has already begun the conquest.

12 **(B) The Crossing of the Jordan (3:1–5:1).** Although commentators may differ widely on the literary background of this section, they agree that the history of the text and the traditions it represents has been a complicated one; detailed explanations of the repetitions and inconsistencies in the text must repeatedly offer merely possible solutions. The general lines of the narrative, however, are fairly clear. The central event is the miraculous division of the waters, enabling the people to cross over into the promised land. Linked with this event is an etiology that explains the origin of the stones placed in the sanctuary at Gilgal (4:20). There is possibly another explaining stones amassed in the Jordan river bed (4:9). Intimately associated with these traditions, preserved most likely at Gilgal, is the Ark of the Covenant which was most probably the cultic center of that sanctuary. The association of these traditions with the Ark occasioned much of the later development emphasizing the Ark and the priests in the episode of the crossing. This development has caused the crossing to be described more as a liturgical procession than as a military tactic.

Efforts to solve problems in the text through a division of the narrative into multiple sources have resulted in fragmentary materials that do not represent a coherent tradition. Noth has keenly observed that despite all the repetitions in the text, the central event, the division of the waters, is narrated only once (3:16). By tracing connections between this material and that in ch. 2, and by searching for links between the verses of those chapters themselves, selecting as well that material which seems more ancient, we can discern an admittedly complex but single tradition which remains coherent when separated from the D material and those minimal retouches which reflect the P tradition. Such a method provides us with the following suggested division of the text: Compiler, 3:1,5,10a,11–17; 4:1–11(6–7 D?),13,15–20(21–22 D?),23; 5:1; Deuteronomist, 3:2,6–9,10b; 4:(6–7?)12,14,(21–22?),24; Priestly additions, expression "ark of the commandments" (4:16) and the date of the crossing (4:19).

13 (a) PREPARATION FOR THE CROSSING (3:1–13). **1.** The mention of Shittim (see 2:1) indicates that the author is continuing to follow his narrative source. **2–4.** *three days later:* The D editor now continues his own material, referring back to 1:10–11. The scene is still the camp at Shittim, and the journey described in vv. 2–6 is clearly the journey to the Jordan. The editor does not try to harmonize his chronology with that of the Compiler in ch. 2. There, the spies had journeyed approximately 11 mi. from Shittim to Jericho, lodged some time with Rahab, then hidden for three days in the hills, and finally returned to Joshua at Shittim. The three days of preparation would hardly allow time for all these episodes. **3.** *ark of the covenant:* The role of the Ark pervades chs. 3–4 and 6; no etiology seeks to explain its presence at Gilgal. Its association with the ancient rites of holy war during the desert wandering (Nm 10:33,35–36) also argues that the Ark in chs. 3–4 is not a later development in the tradition. **3.** *levitical priests:* The D tradition still attributed full priestly authority to all the Levites (Dt 18:6–7), although the gradual centralization of worship at the major sanctuaries was removing the livelihood of those at the smaller shrines. The centralizing reform of Josiah led to the gradual reduction of the status of the Levites. Ezekiel distinguishes the Levites who serve at the altar from those who are temple assistants, still calling both classes "priests" (Ez 40:45–46), whereas in the P tradition the distinction between "priests" and "Levites" is total (Nm 18:1–7). **4.** The space between the people and the Ark, equal to about 1000 yds., is meant to extol the sanctity of the Ark (cf. Mt. Sinai in Ex 19:21–24). This entire verse shows the author is speaking of the journey to, not across, the Jordan. **5.** This verse follows v. 1 very smoothly. If it does belong to the original source, its setting was originally in the camp by the Jordan, but the D editor places it in the camp at Shittim. *sanctify yourselves:* A ritual purity was required to engage in holy war; it included sexual abstinence (1 Sm 21:6) and several hygienic measures (Ex 19:10,14; Dt 23:9–14). **6.** The D editor now reaches the point already attained by the Compiler in v. 1. **7.** This verse is clearly linked to 1:5. **8–9.** These verses follow v. 7 smoothly and thus may be the work of D. **10.** *living God:* The title is not found otherwise in deuteronomic literature. Little is known about some of these pre-Israelite inhabitants of Canaan. The Hittite kingdom was centered in Asia Minor; the Amorites and Hivites are not clearly distinguished in the Scriptures; the Perizzites and Canaanites are linked in Jgs 1:5; the Jebusites had inhabited Jerusalem (15:63). **11.** *ark of the Lord of the whole earth:* It is probably the original expression, and may be very ancient. **12.** This verse appears to be out of context; it is surely to be related to 4:1–10a, but has probably been inserted here in order to affirm that Joshua included the building of the monument among his plans for the crossing; his role is thus exalted still more forcefully than in some of the earlier material of ch. 4. **13.** The expression "ark of the Lord" is apparently very ancient; this verse also follows v. 11 smoothly.

14 (b) THE CROSSING (3:14–17). The Compiler here begins the events of the day of the crossing; the D editor had already brought us to this day in v. 7. **14–15.** The Hebrew constructs these verses as five subordinate propositions, serving as a dramatic introduction to the principal clauses, in fact the principal theme of chs. 3–4, in v. 16, the disappearance of the waters. **15.** *season of the harvest:* The flow of the Jordan swells at harvest time (Sir 24:26), toward the end of April, when the snows of the northern mountains melt. This parenthetical note concerning the harvest season links this tradition with the Passover after the crossing (cf. 5:11). **16.** Adam has been identified as Tell ed-Damiyeh, near the Jabbok River, slightly over 1 mi. E of the Jordan, and about 16 mi. from Jericho. Similar blockings of the Jordan flow, caused by the collapse of her banks, have been recorded—one near Adam as recently as 1927. The distance of Adam from Jericho may indicate a tradition of a crossing made farther N of Jericho. Zarethan may be Tell es-Sa'idiyeh, about 11 mi. NE of Adam. The two cities are linked in 1 Kgs 7:46, and may have been associated here to distinguish this Adam from that of 19:36. The Arabah is the valley in which the Jordan River and Dead Sea are situated. **17.** The source links the role of the priest with the miracle; the waters remain motionless as long as the priests remain motionless (same Hebr vb. for both). (For this area, → Biblical Geography, 73:65–66.)

15 (c) THE TRADITION OF THE STONES (4:1–9). The Hebrew of 3:17 does not treat the crossing as a fully accomplished fact. The opening words of ch. 4, however, jump ahead to the completion of the crossing to juxtapose the traditions of the crossing and of the stones commemorating it. That part of the tradition explicitly mentioning Gilgal (4:20) is reserved until the narrative ends, when it is first stated that Gilgal was the place where Joshua camped on his first night in the promised land (4:19). This present section seems to contain two traditions: one explaining the stones at Gilgal (1b–8) and another the stones in the Jordan (9). The latter etiology is discernible in this one verse only. Noth has suggested that the stones may have originally marked the place of a ford.

However, it is not likely that the etiology of a miraculous crossing would fix on a place where it would have been easiest. If, on the other hand, the stones were in a deep spot in the river, it seems improbable that they would be seen often enough to arouse the popular imagination. That a tradition would be condensed to a single verse and be allowed to disturb the context also seems unlikely. A possible solution would be to understand *btwk hyrdn* of v. 9 not as "in the middle of the

Jordan," but "from the middle of the Jordan." For *b* meaning from, see 3:16, where *b'dm* means "from Adam," and 5:1, where *b'br hyrdn ymh* means "from across the Jordan to the sea"; (cf. *UM* 10:1; cf. also Ez 31:14, where *btwk bny'dm* most likely means "from among the sons of Adam"). If the text can be so understood, then v. 9 forms a perfect conclusion to the etiology contained in vv. 1–8, although only a temporary conclusion. That the etiology is not yet complete is clear because the site of the stones is yet unnamed. The author resumes the etiology in 4:20, using a vocabulary similar to that in 4:9 ("Joshua set up"), much as he had used similar vocabulary in 3:17 and 4:10 to indicate that in 4:10 he was once again taking up his narrative. As is clearer in the commentary below, vv. 2–8 show a gradual apotheosis of Joshua. If v. 9 is part of this pericope, it is an attempt to show that it was Joshua who set up the stones, and not the Israelites, as we might suppose from v. 8.

This interpretation has its difficulties, however. The absence of an article with *'bnym* (stones), makes it appear that these stones are not the ones mentioned in v. 8. To suppose a haplography of *h* in the Hebr text is perhaps too easy a solution. Also, the wording of the Hebrew would suppose a rather awkward ellipsis, reading: "And Joshua set up twelve (i.e., the stones) from the middle of the Jordan." However, perhaps the difficulties involved in affirming that v. 9 is a separate tradition are more serious.

16 **2.** *choose twelve men:* This injunction, given to Joshua as if 3:12 were not part of the text, is in the imper. plural, as is "instruct" of v. 3. These words are addressed to a group rather than to an individual. **3.** *carry them...place them:* Again in the plural, these verbs are addressed by God to the same group, or are perhaps a continuation of the instructions to be given to the 12. *where you are to stay tonight:* "You" is plural. Does it refer to the 12, or to the unidentified group which seems represented by Joshua, or to all the Israelites? **4.** *whom he had selected:* Unlike v. 2, clear reference is made to 3:12. **6.** Suddenly the words of Joshua seem no longer directed to the 12 but to all the Israelites. **8.** *the twelve Israelites:* "Twelve" is not in the Hebrew. Here it seems all the Israelites are carrying out the command, and yet the command is attributed to Joshua, although his directions were made to the 12. The words "according to the Lord's direction" in v. 9 are, lit., "as the Lord spoke to Joshua," and are placed in the Hebrew after the words "from the bed of the Jordan" in v. 8. Here again, Joshua's role in the setting up of the stones is emphasized.

In summary, this tradition contains a perceptible confusion between Joshua, a group of unnamed leaders, and the Israelites in general. Several verses seem ignorant of Joshua's role, while others are careful to emphasize it. The confusion seems best explained by affirming that the tradition bears traces of a very early history in which an undetermined number of leaders commanded that an undetermined number of stones be taken from the Jordan after the crossing and be carried to the Israelite camp (at Gilgal). That later period when Gilgal became a sanctuary of the federated tribes would then be reflected in the emphasis both on the number 12 and on the role of Joshua as leader of all the Israelites. **6–7.** Although this brief catechesis resembles Dt 6:20, it is not sure that it is deuteronomic in origin. Similar forms are found in non-deuteronomic texts, such as Ex 12:26–27; 13:14–15.

(d) Completion of the Crossing (4:10–14). **10.** The author again resumes the narrative from 3:17, using a vocabulary similar to that in 3:17, and finally notes the completion of the crossing. **11.** The D editor is careful again to note the participation of these three tribes. *armed:* Cf. 1:14. **13.** *forty thousand:* Rather than "thousand," *'elep* probably means a subsection of a tribe (Jgs 6:10), a term applied then also to the military unit belonging to that subsection (as in Jgs 4:6; 5:8; cf. G. E. Mendenhall, *JBL* 77 [1958] 52–66, esp. 60).

17 (e) The Waters Resume Their Course (4:15–18). Here it is difficult to detect the narrative source. It surely had some mention of the return to normal flow. The exit of the priests bearing the ark of the commandments (P) is mentioned again (cf. v. 11) to highlight the relationship between their action and the course of the river.

(f) The Placing of the Stones at Gilgal (4:19–5:1). **19.** *the first month:* Nisan, according to the Babylonian calendar adopted some time after the beginning of the Exile, is employed here by a P editor. The exact location of Gilgal remains doubtful; the original meaning of the name is likewise unknown, although "circle" (of stones) is usually accepted (Jos 5:9 is a folk etymology). **20.** The stones at this shrine originally may have been boundary markers, or perhaps they were Canaanite in origin, memorial pillars (*stelae*) either honoring the dead, such as the kind found at Hazor, or else commemorating a sacrifice. **21–24.** This brief catechesis, like that in vv. 6–7, employs the vocabulary of the narrative source in chs. 2–3 (cf. 3:16 and 4:7—lit., the waters "were cut off"; cf. also 2:10 and 4:23—the Lord "dried up" the waters). It is therefore not clear that the two catecheses represent different traditions, nor are there clear signs that either of them was ever part of a tradition about stones erected in the Jordan River. This present text shows an obvious effort to draw a parallel between the crossing of the Red Sea and that of the Jordan. Not only does the author explicitly mention both, but the action of God is the same ("dried up"), the Ex vocabulary is employed ("on dry ground," cf. Ex 14:16,22,29; "mighty hand," see Ex 13:9; 32:11), and the same terror results among the enemies (cf. Jos 2:11; 5:1). The D influence on this passage is difficult to determine; as noted (vv. 6–7), the instruction of children, although of interest to D (cf. also Dt 4:9–10), is not a theme peculiar to him. The transition from 22 to 23, awkward in the Hebrew, and the deuteronomic ring of v. 24 argue that D is responsible for the references to the pentateuchal account.

5:1. The division of the pagan inhabitants is greatly simplified (see Nm 13:29), the Amorites standing for all those living in the central mountain region and the Canaanites for all those along the coastal plain. *to the west of the Jordan:* Lit., it is from across the Jordan (i.e., on the W bank) to the sea (*b*, "from"; cf. *UM* 10:1).

18 **(C) The Rites at Gilgal (5:2–12).** The tradition of the circumcision (vv. 2–9) seems to have been originally an etiology of the names Gibeath-haaraloth ("Hill of the Foreskins") and Gilgal, although there is disagreement concerning the relationship of v. 9 (etymology of Gilgal) to the preceding verses dealing with circumcision. Some think this verse is the fragment of a separate tradition joined (or perhaps merely juxtaposed) to the preceding tradition, because it contains no clear location of the site and does not have the customary etiological conclusion. It seems more probable that vv. 2–3 and 8–9 represent a single tradition explaining the origin of the name Gibeath-haaraloth (undoubtedly a shrine located in or near Gilgal, and a place where circumcision was frequently performed), and especially the origin of the name Gilgal, both in relation to circumcision.

The original narrative incorporated the etiology at this point for theological rather than historical reasons. The convalescent period required after circumcision (v. 8; also Gn 34:24–25) could not have been permitted to Joshua's army in these dangerous circumstances; the tradition rather prepares for the Passover pericope (vv. 10–12): only the circumcised could celebrate the Passover (Ex 12:43–49). Together the traditions characterize as religious events both the entry into Canaan and the first conquests. The rites at Gilgal are the people's response to the providence of God, who has just given them the promised land.

The circumcision narrative had been developed in the original narrative to the point of affirming that the whole nation of Israelites had still to be circumcised after the crossing (v. 8). The D editor regarded this neglect of circumcision as an historical problem to be explained. His solution (vv. 4–7), however, does not solve the problem directly, but only recalls the faithlessness of the generation that died during the wandering, a generation already characterized by D as "evil" (Dt 1:35; cf. Nm 14:20–38). If the explanation of D seems to avoid the issue, it has the merit of presenting the entry into Canaan as a new beginning in the history of the Israelites; he probably added the expression "for the second time" in v. 2, intending to present the circumcision and Passover of Gilgal as a repetition of the rites of the Exodus (Ex 12:43–49)—a fresh start, a prototype of the restoration of Israel that D himself longed for.

The Passover tradition, by linking the local practices of Gilgal with the sacred history of the nation, seeks primarily to explain why unleavened cakes and parched grain are eaten at the Passover feast: these practices commemorate the cessation of the manna. The original narrative incorporates the tradition not only because it imparts a religious character to the occupation of Canaan, but also because it indicates that the promised land is truly the possession of the Israelites: although they have just entered Canaan, they have already begun to enjoy the produce of its fields.

19 (a) The Circumcision (5:2–9). **2.** *flint knives:* Such primitive instruments indicate the antiquity of the practice, performed according to the original ritual even in later periods when the use of metals was known. *circumcise:* Lit., "again circumcise... for the second time"; by reading "again" (*šûb*) without the *mater lectionis* (therefore, *šb*) we can obtain the more likely original: "sit, circumcise" ("for the second time" is most likely D's work); the one performing the operation was seated (cf. *ANEP* 629). **4–7.** The passage is readily attributable to D because of his vocabulary ("after the departure from Egypt"; "obeyed the command of the Lord"; "all the people"; "which he had promised their fathers he would give us"). **6.** *land flowing with milk and honey:* The original sense of this expression is probably that the land has an abundant rainfall, covering the fields with grass and flowers for the cattle and bees. Rain is a great blessing in Dt 11:10–17; also in the Ugaritic Baal and Anat cycle (*UM* 49:III:12–13), a fall of rain is described: "The heavens rain oil; the wadies run with honey."

9. *I have removed the reproach of Egypt from you:* "removed" is lit. rolled. Some have interpreted this reproach to be the state of noncircumcision, also called a reproach in Gn 34:14; however, there is no apparent reason why it should be called the reproach of Egypt. The D editor relates that those who went out from Egypt were circumcised (v. 4), and the Egyptians are also known to have practiced circumcision. Others prefer to interpret the reproach as slavery, which has now come to an end with the entry into the promised land; however, there is no clear connection between circumcision and the end of slavery or the possession of the land. Some then see a link between v. 9 and the following passage about the Passover, celebrating the entry into Canaan. Such a connection is doubtfully original, for v. 9 appears to be rather the conclusion than the beginning of an etiology, and the original meaning of the reproach still remains obscure. Noth even wonders whether there is any connection at all between this verse and the surrounding material, which is apparently composed of fragmentary traditions.

Perhaps another solution can be offered, based on a restudy of the consonantal text. The "reproach of Egypt" was probably written originally *ḥrpt mṣrm.* The enclitic *mem* of Ugaritic has been attested in Hebrew, even with nouns in the construct form (*UM* 11:7). If we may read the first *mem* of *mṣrm* as an enclitic, we obtain *ḥrpt (m) ṣrm,* strikingly close to the consonants for "flint knives" in v. 2, *ḥrbt ṣrm.* That *ḥrpt* could be a variant of *ḥrbt,* "knives," is suggested by the root meaning of *ḥrp,* "to be sharp," and by the Egyptian form for *hrb,* which is *hrp* (KB). If we can then read the first *mem* of *mʿlykm,* lit., "from upon you," as a dittography, and thus have *ʿlykm,* "upon you," we can obtain the following translation: Today I have rolled flint knives upon you. God thus says that he has performed this rite of circumcision; the name Gilgal is then imagined to have come from *gll,* the verb "to roll." If this reading may be accepted, v. 9 follows as a perfect conclusion to the etiology, ending with a variant on the theme with which it opened in v. 2. The meaning "shame" would have been given to *ḥrpt* rather early (perhaps under the influence of Gn 34:14)—i.e., early enough for the expression "Roll reproach from upon me" to have become acceptable Hebrew in Ps 119:22. Once the enclitic *mem* was no longer understood, and the meaning "reproach of Egypt" was consequently given to the text, v. 9 became and remained an enigma.

20 (b) The Passover (5:10–12). **10.** *the fourteenth of the month:* Possibly an addition made by the same P editor who added the date in 4:19; the date may be original because the Passover was a full moon feast, hence always occurring at this time of the month. **11.** *on the day after the Passover:* most likely an addition made after the Passover was joined to the Feast of Unleavened Bread some time after the reform of Josiah (cf. Nm 33:3; Lv 23:5–6). *parched grain:* It is not mentioned in the other traditions concerning the Passover and the Feast of Unleavened Bread. This rite was peculiar to the Passover at Gilgal; the P additions attempt to harmonize it with the national practice adopted after the cult was centralized in Jerusalem. *on that same day:* The Hebrew makes this phrase part of the preceding sentence; as such, it seems to contradict the expression, "on the day after the Passover," a puzzling contradiction inasmuch as both expressions are very likely P additions (cf. Ex 12:17,41; Lv 23:21,28–30). However, they need not be contradictory, because the expression "on that same day" often indicates the importance of the day rather than its chronological setting (cf. Ex 12:41; Lv 23:28–30). **12.** *after the Passover:* The Hebrew says simply "on the next day," again a P addition similar to "on the day after the Passover" in v. 11. *that year:* This indefinite phrase argues that the preceding expressions concerned with the precise time for eating the unleavened bread are not original.

21 **(D) The Fall of Jericho (5:13–6:27).** Jericho was apparently in ruins when the Israelites entered Canaan. It seems to have remained uninhabited or only sparsely settled up to the period of the monarchy. It was therefore quite natural that the popular imagination should link this ruined city with the memories of the heroic figure Joshua. If the conquest of Canaan was a work of God's power rather than man's, then surely such extensive destruction of this walled city must be attributed to a special divine act. Thus, the conquest of Jericho was conceived more as an act of ritual than an armed struggle—a series of symbolic actions that a primitive imagination portrayed as vehicles of divine power. (For a discussion and bibliography on the Jericho excavations, see J. Kelso in *IDB* 2, 835–39.)

The conquest is preceded by a theophany. Although it seems better to consider 5:13–6:5 as a literary unit, commentators disagree about the connection between the "captain of the host of the Lord" (5:13–15) and the directions given by the Lord to Joshua (6:1–5). For some, 5:13–15 is the fragment of an independent tradition. Since Gilgal is territorially linked with Jericho (4:13,19), perhaps this fragment has been associated with the other Gilgal traditions merely to show that a theophany has justified its being a center of worship. The journey of an angel from Gilgal to Bochim (Jgs 2:1–5) suggests a transfer of the Ark; so also this vision of an angel should perhaps be associated with the presence of the Ark at Gilgal. However, the mention of Jericho rather than Gilgal in this tradition greatly weakens the probability of this being one that grounds the sacred character of Gilgal. Others affirm that this theophany originally was associated with a shrine within Jericho, on the force of the expression "in Jericho" (5:13), and that it has been here artificially joined to the story of the conquest of Jericho, even though it originally supposed that the city was already under Israelite control. Certainly, however, the preposition *b* (in) need not be so restricted in meaning, especially since Jericho was a city-state with territory extending beyond its walls. Besides, the presence of an Israelite sanctuary within the ruins of Jericho, commemorating some theophany after the conquest, is an extremely weak hypothesis.

The fragmentary nature of this tradition is also very difficult to explain. The angel's announcement that he has now come seems to demand an explanation of the purpose of his visit, but the explanation appears to have been omitted and substituted with a stereotyped expression that signifies the holiness of the site (cf. Ex 3:5). However, if something of the angel's message has been omitted before Joshua's question, then this question is rendered meaningless. Nor need the injunction of this angel that Joshua remove his sandals be considered a substitute conclusion, for a similar command to Moses is merely the preface to a divine message (Ex 3:5–10). Thus, it is preferable to understand 6:2–5 as the angel's message, with the angel now being more openly identified as the Lord himself (cf. Gn 22:10–18; 31:11–16).

The setting of the theophany is somewhere near Jericho, where the Israelites have apparently already laid seige to the city. The inhabitants of Jericho are safe, however, within their strong walls (6:1). If ever the Israelites would need divine help, it was now, and it comes (5:14; note also the promise that an angel would help in the conquest of Canaan, Ex 23:23, a tradition perhaps related to this present text). As Joshua removes his sandals (5:15), there is sufficient pause for the author to note, humanly speaking, the hopelessness of the Israelite cause (6:1). Although 6:1 might seem more fitting as an introduction to the theophany, the author has saved it until now to highlight more effectively the divine power expressed in the verse immediately following, "I have delivered Jericho and its king into your power."

22 The interpretation of the divine instructions and their execution in the battle of Jericho has remained a constant source of difficulty and disagreement among commentators. Some believe that the present text is a combination of two traditions. One, more popular in origin, told of a march around the city once each day for seven days, conducted in absolute silence until the battle cry was finally given by Joshua. The other told rather of a march in which the priests and the Ark were prominent figures, the Ark circling the city seven times in one day, and finally the walls collapsing as the priests played their trumpets. The two stories were harmonized to some extent when they were combined, but inconsistencies remain. This two-source theory meets serious difficulties when we attempt to reconstruct the original texts; the most serious is that the central fact of the story, the collapse of the walls and the consequent capture, is narrated only once (6:20). Rather, this text is a single tradition which has experienced additions and modifications such as make it now impossible to detect with certainty an original form of the narrative.

It is possible, however, to establish several principles that enable us to understand partially the development of this tradition and guard us from unfounded reconstructions of an original form. First, inasmuch as this tradition does not date back to an actual battle of Jericho, but rather to a period somewhat later than the occupation of Canaan, there is no need to remove as later additions all reference to the priests and the Ark. In fact, attempts to do so must argue from mere assumption. The ritual character of the march would itself suggest the presence of the Ark, at least. Second, one inescapable source of doubt in any explanation of the text is its very structure. Imprecise references at times make it impossible to determine precisely which persons are performing the actions. Third, a certain tension in the tradition seems to have been caused by efforts to extol the position both of the priests and of Joshua, at the price of consistency and clear chronology. Fourth, the inconsistencies of the tradition cannot be attributed reliably to a plurality of sources. A striking parallel is Gideon's victory over the Midianites (Jgs 7:15–22). In this much simpler tradition, there is no reliable evidence for a plurality of sources, and yet it is not clear precisely how and in what order the rites were performed by the soldiers. Yet, even though we cannot reconstruct an exact chronology of the battle of Jericho, the principle value of any such reconstruction is not lost to us, for with some probability we can still discern in the tradition a growing emphasis on the roles of Joshua and the priests, against an ever-present background of the divine power.

23 (a) THE THEOPHANY (5:13–6:5). **14.** *the host of the Lord:* This is the army of angels (Ps 103:20–21), seen in a vision by Jacob (Gn 32:1–2) and Elisha (2 Kgs 6:17). **6:4.** *seven priests carrying rams' horns:* This reference may be a later expansion of the tradition made to emphasize both the role of the priests and the sacred character of the number seven (four times in v. 4). **5.** This verse is the core of the tradition and is repeated almost verbatim when the walls actually collapse (6:60). The signal blast from the ram's horn is certainly part of the original tradition, because no other signal for the loud shout has been given. However, it is not clear who gives this signal. It is possible that the mention of the priests in v. 4 is secondary, and that perhaps Joshua, either alone or with a group of soldiers, was originally understood as the one giving the signal on the horn (as in the case of Gideon, Jgs 7:18). The blast of the horn and the loud shout are typical of the ancient rites of holy war (Jgs 7:20; Nm 9:8–9); through them God spread terror among the enemy. The blowing of the horn as a signal has led some to argue that the horns were silent until that moment in an earlier form of the tradition; it is a possibility. *the wall of the city:* It has been argued that this is a metaphorical expression for the "garrison of the city," and that, therefore, "the wall collapsed" really means "the soldiers became helpless." The solution seems forced. It seeks to avoid historical and chronological problems that are nonexistent once the etiological origin of the story is understood. It is clear also from the Hebrew of 6:1 that Jericho was understood to be a walled city, and the sense of this verse is that the walls rather than the soldiers were the obstacle to the Israelite forces.

24 (b) THE BATTLE OF JERICHO (6:6–6:27). **6–11.** The primary concern of these verses seems to be the proper order to be followed in the procession; this concern for ritual detail has undoubtedly caused considerable expansion of the original tradition, through the influence of the priests at Gilgal. Despite the many difficulties these verses contain, they form a unity, summarizing the commands of Joshua (vv. 6–7) and then explaining in detail how they were carried out (vv. 8–11); even the vocabulary favors this unity. Joshua orders, Proceed (*'br*)...surround (*sbb*) the city in v. 7; the beginning of v. 8 seems better translated, "And the people acted according to Joshua's orders," The explanation follows: The people (or the priests?) proceeded (v. 8)... the ark surrounded the city (v. 11). This passage clarifies Joshua's plans, and is not the actual beginning of the assault; v. 12 confirms this opinion, for the expression "And Joshua rose early in the morning" is commonly used at the beginning of an enterprise (3:1; 7:16; 8:10). If this interpretation is correct, then "on this second day" (v. 14) is an insertion made once vv. 6–11 were understood as describing the first day's action.

These verses also contain further obscurities. According to the Hebrew of v. 7, we should read "And they ordered the people to proceed," with perhaps the priests rather than Joshua giving the orders. The opening words of v. 8 (translated above) may then be an attempt to emphasize that it was Joshua who gave the orders. The Hebrew also does not make clear the function of the seven priests in v. 8; perhaps it is actually the people rather than the priests who are said to be proceeding and blowing the horns. The Hebrew of v. 9, although difficult, may well have the picked troops playing on the trumpets, while the most natural sense of the Hebrew also attributes the continual blowing of the horns to the rear guard rather than to the priests. Thus, it seems that the entire group is blowing the horns, as was done by the entire group of Gideon's soldiers (Jgs 7:20). This development in the tradition may well explain the most difficult problem, the role of Joshua in v. 10. Some have argued that this verse is a residue of the original tradition that told of a procession carried out for seven days with an unnerving absolute silence until the command to give the battle cry and attack. This interpretation meets serious difficulties, however. It cannot be clearly inferred from this verse that the silence before Joshua's command was absolute, excluding even the playing of trumpets. Even more serious, it seems impossible to place this verse on the same level of antiquity as vv. 5 and 20, which contain the core of the tradition and clearly state that the sound of the trumpet rather than Joshua's voice was to be the signal for the shout. It seems we must place v. 10 on a late level of tradition. Now that vv. 6–11 present the playing of horns as a continuous feature of the procession, it becomes necessary to adopt a new signal for the shout; v. 10 thus makes it clear that Joshua will call out the signal, modifying somewhat inconsistently the more ancient provision of vv. 5 and 20.

25 **14–16.** The flow of the narrative here becomes simpler, but v. 16 seems to preserve the unresolved tension of a signal given both by the priests and by Joshua. An attempt has been made on the basis of Hebr grammar (absence of *waw apodoseos* before *tāqeʿû*) to remove the mention of the priests playing the trumpets as secondary. This cannot be done safely, because there is a similar sentence structure in the ancient stratum of v. 5 (although not in v. 20). **17–19.** Joshua certainly could not have spoken at this length in the original signal for the battle cry; the Compiler here inserts material relating to the preceding story of Rahab (v. 17) and to the next etiology, the story of Achan (vv. 18–19; see 7:1,21). **17.** *the Lord's ban:* "Ban" is here *ḥerem.* The climax of the rites of holy war was the annihilation of the conquered, carried out to varying degrees in different battles. This total destruction was considered a consecration of the victims to God. While it was surely an ancient practice, it is difficult to determine the extent to which it was actually performed, for the more ancient holy-war traditions in Jgs allude to it rarely (De Vaux, *AI* 260). **20.** The Hebrew opens with the words "And the people shouted," a clause which originally followed the end of v. 16, before vv. 17–19 were added; it is not clear, however, whether the following words "and they blow horns" should be understood as continuing these opening words, and thus mean that the people blew the horns or whether they are to be considered a return to the theme of the priests blowing the horns in v. 16a. Verse 20b, however ("when they heard the signal horn..."), returns to the original core of the tradition (v. 5). **21–24.** It seems that the opening words of v. 24 contain the original notice of the destruction of the city ("the city itself they burned with all that was in it"). Before this final stage of the destruction, the Compiler again asserts themes from the etiologies of Achan (v. 21; it is possible, however, that 21 was part of the original Jericho story with 24a; cf. Dt 13:15–16) and Rahab (vv. 22–23). The remainder of v. 24 also serves as a link with the Achan story (cf. 6:19; 7:21), whereas Joshua's final dispositions for the house of Rahab (v. 25) are also to be considered secondary. **26.** Jericho remained an unwalled city until Hiel of Bethel rebuilt the walls, possibly offering his sons as human sacrifices for the occasion, as is later noted in D history (1 Kgs 16:34). The humbled condition of Jericho as well as the shocking circumstances of its reconstruction are here attributed by D to a curse uttered by Joshua, in what appears to be the only D addition in this entire section (5:13–6:27). **27.** This conclusion is to be attributed to the Compiler, for it seems to ignore the Deuteronomist's comparisons of Joshua to Moses (1:5; 3:7; 4:14).

26 **(E) Defeat and Victory at Ai (7:1–8:29).** The Compiler weaves two originally separate traditions, one of which narrates an initial defeat at Ai, followed by the victory through the tactics of a feigned retreat and an ambush, while the other tells of Achan's violation of the ban and his consequent punishment in the Valley of Achor. The Achan story may have been a tradition proper to the tribe of Judah: Achan is a member of this tribe (7:1), and the Valley of Achor is within its boundaries (15:7). Of all the etiological stories within chs. 2–9, this is the only one localized outside Benjamin; it is therefore possible that its original context was not the battle of Jericho, but rather some battle the record of which we no longer possess. In any case, it is now linked with the battle of Jericho; Achan commits his crime at that battle (cf. 6:18 and 7:1) and the Valley of Achor is near the camp at Gilgal (7:24; also 15:7). It is therefore clear that the link between the Valley of Achor and Ai is secondary, for this town, situated near Bethel, was near the northern border of Benjamin in the hill country (18:12–13). The tradition of an unsuccessful attack upon Ai, begun without a divine mandate and based on an overconfident report of the spies (7:3–4), provided the Compiler with the opportunity to insert the tradition of Achan as another more theological explanation of the defeat.

If the tradition of Achan's crime was originally proper to the tribe of Judah, its union with the Benjaminite traditions of the conquest can be partially explained by the role of Gilgal as cult center for all the tribes, particularly during the reign of Saul (1 Sm 13:4; cf. "the twelve stones" in Jos 4:20). It may also be argued that the conquest of Jericho was considered a cooperative effort from the earliest times and that, therefore, the tradition of Achan never existed apart from the story of Jericho. However, the present location of the Achan tradition seems a result of a later intertribal rivalry rather than of an original intertribal cooperation. We can elsewhere detect signs of rivalry between the tribes of Benjamin and Judah, especially in the eclipse of Benjaminite Saul by Judahite David, and the rival claims of the two tribes to the city of Jerusalem (15:63 and 18:28). Because the Achan story is the only tradition in chs. 2–9 localized outside the territory of Benjamin, and because it also is uncomplimentary to the tribe of Judah, the rivalry of the two tribes may partially account for the joining of the traditions concerning Achan and Ai. In fact, it seems very likely that the native pride within Benjamin has partially shaped the Ai tradition. In Jgs 20, the near extermination of Benjamin was achieved through feigned retreat and ambush. The victory at Ai is achieved through this same tactic, with Benjamin, in the original form of the tradition, being this time the victor. Such a form could have been given to the story of Ai sometime during the later history of Benjamin, both to blot out the shame of the past and to foster the tribe's waning prestige (cf. W. Roth, *ZAW* 75 [1963] 296–303).

27 An attempt to explain with greater precision the origins of the Ai tradition must be concerned with the location of that site. It is generally agreed that Ai is present-day et-Tell, about 2 mi. SE of Bethel, because this site fits well with the geographical data of the story. Also, the name Ai is generally understood to mean "the heap of ruins," corresponding closely to the modern Arabic *et-Tell*, "the mound." The site of et-Tell raises an historical problem, however. Archaelogical investigations have shown that et-Tell was destroyed *ca.* 2000 BC, remained uninhabited except for a small settlement which lasted from *ca.* 1200 to 950, and was then abandoned once more. Thus, the city was in ruins long before the Israelites entered Canaan.

In the face of this historical problem, one study has attempted to prove on linguistic and geographical grounds that et-Tell could not possibly be Ai but is rather Beth-aven ("house of iniquity"), whereas Ai may possibly be the still unexcavated Khirbet Haiyan, S of et-Tell (J. Grintz, *Bib* 42 [1961] 201–16). Grintz argues that there can be no linguistic connection between Ai and et-Tell since Ai does not mean "the ruin," as is generally supposed, but rather "the heap of stones." The conclusion is too hastily drawn, because the Hebrew for "heap of stones" (*'iy*) is employed by the prophets to describe the future ruins of the city of Jerusalem (Jer 26:18; Mi 3:12; cf. Ps 79:1). Besides, it is not even important that there should be a linguistic connection between Ai and et-Tell in order to associate them. Some time after the total abandonment of the site, it was known as a "tell," even among the Israelites (8:28), and the Arabic name may merely express this word rather than Ai. Then, too, linguistic connection of names is itself an unsure method of identification; still less can arguments be drawn from linguistics to exclude positively an identification. Concerning the identification of et-Tell with Beth-aven, none of the arguments adduced by Grintz is able to eliminate the more likely hypothesis that Beth-aven is a prophetic term of opprobrium for the shrine at Bethel (Noth). That Ai is too close to Bethel for an ambush on Ai to have been carried out effectively remains an objection only when one thinks that the Ai story must be the account of an actual battle at that city. Our present state of knowledge urges rather that we accept et-Tell as the most likely site and then explain the origin of the Ai tradition in terms of the archaeological findings, the etiological and theological themes of the narrative, and, in this case, the theme of tribal honor.

It seems, therefore, that the Ai tradition is a concretization and glorification of Benjamin's share in the conquest of Canaan. The small 13th-cent. settlement at Ai corresponds to the period of Israel's entry into Canaan and was most likely Benjaminite. The name Ai probably dates from the period of this settlement (the use of the article is characteristic of Benjaminite names; cf. 18:26; also, no other name of this settlement has been preserved), although the origin of the name is not clear. It may have originally referred to the ruinous condition of the mound, or perhaps even to the heap of stones in 8:29. At some time during this period, the Benjaminites explained their possession of this site in terms of a conquest, one which they gave the form of a victory through ambush to offset the story of their own near destruction in Jgs 20. The exception to the rule of total destruction, whereby the conquerors were allowed to retain the spoil and livestock (8:2,27), is probably the explanation of how the Benjaminites were able to settle at Ai. The story was then concretized through the various geographical and etiological references scattered through the Ai tradition, although they apparently had secondary importance in the formation of the tradition; for example, "everlasting mound of ruins" (8:28) must have been added only some time after the final abandonment of Ai in the 10th cent. At a certain point in the tradition, Joshua of the tribe of Ephraim (24:30) assumed the role of the conquering leader, but we may still possess a remnant of the pre-Joshuan tradition in 8:11–13. The Compiler made the dominant theme of the Ai and Achan narratives theological: despite the human endeavor involved, greater than in the case of Jericho, the conquest still remains the work of God and is to be carried out with recognition of God's supremacy. Perhaps the Compiler is responsible for the obvious parallel drawn between the actions of Joshua and Moses in 8:18,26 (cf. Ex 18:11–12); as Joshua holds the javelin, God fights the battle. The insertion of the Achan story into the Ai tradition has specially emphasized the sacral character of Israel's beginnings. For a NT midrash on the Achan story, cf. Acts 5:1–11. For a summary of views on Ai, cf. G. E. Wright, *BibArch* 80–81.

28 (a) THE INITIAL DEFEAT AND ITS CAUSE (7:1–26). **1.** This verse is separated from the rest of the Achan story to serve as a transition from ch. 6 to chs. 7–8. Some argue that the name Achan has a popular origin, being merely a variation of Achor, the name of the valley. Achan's genealogy remains obscure in its origins, although it may argue that Achan is the name of a real person. **2.** A Hebr gloss had added that Ai is "beside Beth-aven," but it is omitted in the translation. **3.** *two or three thousand:* Cf. comment on 4:13. **5.** *till they broke ranks:* Some translate "as far as the quarries."

6–9. These verses fuse the Ai and Achan stories; it is impossible to assign them exclusively to one or the other tradition. Perhaps the Compiler composed them after the manner of Nm 11:11–15. **6.** For a similar lamentation ritual, cf. 1 Sm 4:12; 2 Sm 1:2. In Ugaritic literature, *Ltpn* puts dust on his head and sits on the earth as he mourns for Baal (*UM* 67:VI:15). **7.** *the Amorites:* The reference is probably as in 5:1; so also the Canaanites in v. 9.

11. *the covenant:* There is no other text in Dt or Jos that says that total annihilation of the vanquished and their property was given the stable form of covenant law. In Dt 20:16–18, only the people are to be destroyed; total annihilation is prescribed in Dt 13:13–18, but in the case of an Israelite city guilty of idolatrous practices. Perhaps the expression "covenant" results from the influence of legal terminology and practice pervading the Achan story; there is a technical ring to such expressions as: "shameful crime in Israel" (v. 15), i.e., a crime against the community; "give... glory and honor" (v. 19), a summons to testify under oath; and "truly thus, truly thus have I done" (v. 20, Hebr), an admission of guilt (for the emphatic use of *waw*, cf. KB; also Is 43:12; 44:8, where the context implies an oath).

12. By contact with the spoils, Achan had come under the ban himself, and through him, the entire community. **13.** *sanctify the people:* Cf. comment on 3:5. Here ritual purity is required for the ceremony of drawing lots. **14.** The exact nature of this ceremony is not known; cf. 1 Sm 10:20–21; 14:38–42. **15.** For burning as a penalty for profaning the sacred, cf. Lv 21:9. Here the burning is especially understood as a means of absolving the community from guilt. **21.** *shekel:* It is a unit of weight rather than a coin. **24.** *with the silver, the mantle, and the bar of gold:* It is unlikely that these spoils had an original place in the burning and stoning at the Valley of Achor. **25.** The words of Joshua serve to highlight the etiology of the name Achor. The Hebr root for "misery" and "afflicted" is *'kr*, similar in sound to Achor. The description of the punishment is difficult in the Hebrew: a stoning, then a burning, another stoning, and finally (v. 26) a piling of the stones. The translation omits, at the end of v. 25, "and they burned them with fire and they stoned them with stones," referring the punishment not only to Achan but also to his family and belongings. Perhaps one form of the tradition concerned only the punishment of Achan. The words omitted in the translation appear to have been added to extend the punishment beyond Achan himself. Even in this addition, the joining of the stoning and burning is strange, but these words are apparently also an attempt to reconcile the variants that told of the burning of "Achan with all that is his" (v. 15), and the stoning of Achan alone and the piling of the stones over his body (vv. 25–26). The heap of stones may originally have been a funeral pile serving also as a place of worship (Jb 27:15).

29 (b) Victory at Ai (8:1–29). **1–2.** Although the original tradition required some form of divine command to attack Ai, this command has been thoroughly reworked by D (cf. Dt 3:2,7). "I have delivered the king of Ai into your power" anticipates the more ancient "I will deliver it into your power" (v. 18). **3.** *thirty thousand:* Cf. comment on 4:13. This time, the entire fighting force participates; 30 units are chosen to set the ambush. **4.** *from the rear:* That is, from the west is meant; one determined direction by facing E. **8.** *in obedience to the Lord's command:* This phrase refers to v. 2: "set an ambush behind the city." The abrupt wording of v. 2 suggests that both these phrases are the result of later reworking. **9.** *in the plain* (*b^etôk hā'ēmeq*): This reading is a correction made on the basis of v. 13. The Hebrew of v. 9 reads "among the people" (*b^etôk hā'ām*)—i.e., the main body of warriors (as in v. 5).

11–13. These verses present a special difficulty, because they seem to delay the attack upon Ai another day, an impossible delay if the ambushing forces are to remain concealed. Also, the 5 units in v. 12 apparently contradict the 30 in v. 3. Some prefer to regard vv. 10–12 as a narrative parallel to vv. 3–9, with v. 13 attempting to interweave the two narratives (Bright). It seems preferable to consider v. 10 as continuing the narrative until the morning of the conquest, when the soldiers assume their attack positions. The author then breaks the flow of the narrative in v. 11 to give a variant account of the preceding day's preparations (vv. 11–13)—the Hebr structure of v. 11 shows that the chronology has been interrupted; the tense of all the verbs in vv. 11–13 is the pluperfect. This insertion seems to be a very early variant form of the Ai tradition, still bearing signs of a pre-Joshuan formation. "The people" are the subject of the actions in v. 11. Inasmuch as there is no expressed subject of the principal clauses in v. 12, the subject may be the people again, and not Joshua; the 5 units for the ambush would also represent a more ancient form of the story than the 30 in v. 3. Finally, the people are once again the subject of the action in v. 13a. The tradition is then closed with a reference to Joshua parallel to that contained in v. 9, and the narrative is resumed in v. 14. If we may correctly understand vv. 11–13 as an earlier variant of the day of preparations, there still remains the problem of explaining the reason for its inclusion here, despite the contradiction between vv. 3 and 12. Perhaps the author included it because of the geographical precision it contained, greater than that in the brief notice of v. 9 (the "ravine," v. 11; "north," vv. 11, 13; the "plain," Hebr of v. 13). **13.** *Joshua waited overnight with his troops:* The texts vary between "waited" (*yln*) and "went" (*ylk*). The Hebrew has "plain" (*'mq*) rather than "troops" (*'m*). Since a decision concerning the original form of the text seems impossible, it is likewise impossible to determine whether this clause furnishes information independently of v. 9, or whether it was originally identical to the close of v. 9 and was therefore merely repeated to take up the narrative again after the brief parenthesis formed by vv. 11–13.

14. *at the descent:* The text has been corrected according to 7:5; the Hebrew here reads "at the meeting place," perhaps retaining an item of local topography. **17.** *or Bethel:* It is undoubtedly a gloss, reflecting a supposition that Bethel, so close by, must have participated in the battle. The mention of Bethel may also point to a link between the Ai tradition and the sanctuary at Bethel (Hertzberg). **18.** Joshua gives the signal for the ambushers to attack, but this verse (with v. 26) is clearly a secondary development in the tradition, because the main force and those waiting in ambush could not see each other (cf. v. 21). **25.** *thousand:* Cf. comment on 4:13. **28.** *everlasting mound of ruins:* This epithet most likely dates from some time after the final abandonment of Ai, and may be the work of D (cf. Dt 13:17; also Jer 49:2). **29.** A criminal who was put to death and whose corpse was then hung from a tree could not be exposed overnight (Dt 21:22–23).

30 **(F) The Altar on Mt. Ebal (8:30–35).** This passage clearly interrupts the natural union between 8:29 and 9:1 and causes an abrupt transfer from Ai to the area of Shechem (about 18 mi. NE) and then back to the camp at Gilgal (9:6). Both in geography and in content it is more closely related to Jos 24 than to its present context, where it presents the fulfillment of Moses' command to erect an altar in the promised land after the crossing of the Jordan (Dt 27:1–8,11–13; 11:29–30). It is best explained (L'Hour, *op. cit.*) as the original composition of a postexilic editor who inserted it here in the final edition of Jos, which now formed the conclusion of the Hexateuch. This editor, schooled in both the D and P traditions, sought to unite the extant religious traditions under the shadow of the Sinai covenant. The ancient tradition of the covenant at Shechem presented a special problem, because the D legislation, already given a Mosaic character in the D history, had called for the centralization of cult at the sanctuary of Jerusalem. This editor was able to preserve the Shechem tradition (ch. 24) by removing from it elements offensive to the D reform, and by leaving it in its originally independent form, not woven into the Jos narrative, using it rather as a second conclusion to Jos, and even more, a conclusion to the entire Hexateuch. As much as possible, he sought to approximate the Shechem tradition to the orthodox covenants at Sinai and on the plains of Moab. To effect this harmonization, the editor drew from the Shechem tradition to compose Dt 11:29–30; 27:1–8,11–13 (command), and Jos 8:30–35 (fulfillment), using these insertions to associate this tradition with Dt (Dt 11:29–30 and 27:1–8,11–13 enclose the D legislation; Jos 8:30–35 associates Shechem with the Gilgal traditions, which were regarded by D as the fulfillment of the deuteronomic covenant in Moab), thus smoothing the way for Jos 24. The editor makes no clear mention of a covenant in these three preparatory texts, lest he detract from the deuteronomic covenant, even though their context clearly suggests a covenant. Likewise Shechem is not mentioned in Jos 8:30–35, so that this passage might more easily be associated with the Gilgal traditions (note a similar purpose in Dt. 11:30).

Why Jos 8:30–35 was inserted precisely here has received several explanations. Noth regards the destruction of Ai as Joshua's first opportunity to continue to Shechem, a possible explanation, especially since the editor may have wanted to mention the altar as soon as possible after the battle of Jericho, the last one clearly mentioned in ch. 24 (v. 11). One factor in the editing may have been the alliance with the Gibeonites in ch. 9: it would be fitting that the erection of the altar at Shechem, now considered a fulfillment of the deuteronomic alliance because of the insertions in Dt 11 and 27, should precede the less important alliance with the Gibeonites. Another factor may have been the opportunity to compare Moses and Joshua: Moses held a rod in his hand at the battle against Amalek and then built an altar (Ex 17:8–16); here Joshua extends his javelin over Ai (8:18,26) and then builds an altar.

31 **30.** *Mount Ebal:* It was perhaps originally Mt. Gerizim, the mountain of the blessings (Dt 27:12), changed to Ebal here and in Dt 27:4 in polemic against the Samaritan temple on Mt. Gerizim. **31.** *unhewn stones:* Such stones had not yet been removed from their natural, divine sphere by human industry. *as recorded in the Book of the Law:* This precept recalls the opening words of the Book of the Covenant (Ex 20:24–23:19), which is the original legal material of the Shechem covenant, now transposed to a Sinai context lest it seem to oppose the later D legislation (L'Hour, *op. cit.*, 350–64). *holocausts and peace offerings:* Such is the sacrifice made in Ex 24:3–8, which contains the original Shechem covenant ritual, (L'Hour, *op. cit.*). **32.** The stela erected at Shechem (Jos 24:26), reflecting a practice later condemned (Dt 16:22), is made as inoffensive as possible. It is changed from 1 stone to 12, to approximate the Gilgal tradition (4:20); the stones themselves are pictured not as cultic objects, but merely as tablets on which the Law (that is, Dt; cf. Dt 27:8) is written, like the tablets Moses used (Ex 34:27–28). These stones should not be understood as the same ones used to build the altar, despite Dt 27:8. In Dt 27:3–8, the editor desires to de-emphasize the altar at Ebal (vv. 5–7), especially inasmuch as he is dealing with deuteronomic legislation, and strives to associate this altar with the other stones used for the copying of the Law (L'Hour, *op. cit.*, 182–84). **33.** Although there is no mention of the Ark and the Levites in Dt 11:29; 27:12–13, the editor has borrowed them from Dt 31:9, apparently because of their predominance in the Gilgal traditions. *stranger and native:* The distinction is not clear. It appears to be of late P origin; the strangers are apparently of a lower social stratum, non-Israelite in origin (Dt 29:10). *facing:* More probably "in front of" is meant ("on Mount Gerizim...on Mount Ebal"; cf. Dt 27:12–13); for this grammatical construction, cf. Ex 34:3. **34–35.** The Levites proclaimed the curses in Dt 27:14–26; it is, however, doubtful whether this passage belongs to the Shechem tradition. In Dt 31:9–12, clearly a source for 8:30–35, it is the Levites who are commissioned to read the Law; however, Jos 8 has followed more closely the tradition of Jos 24. The late origin of Jos 8:30–35 is further revealed in the change from "Israel" (Dt 31:11) to the P expression "entire community" (Jos 8:35). (For the region of Shechem, → Biblical Geography, 73:101; Religious Institutions, 76:40.)

32 **(G) The Completion of the Conquest of Canaan (9:1–11:23).** **9:1–2.** These verses of the Deuteronomist introduce the exploits of the following three chapters, in which the conquests spread from Benjamin (ch. 9) through the south of Canaan (ch. 10) and finally to the north (ch. 11). **1.** *the news:* The conquest of Jericho and Ai is meant (6:1–8:29). Concerning these Canaanite peoples, cf. 3:10. The Girgashites are omitted from 9:1.

(a) The Covenant with the Gibeonites (9:3–27). Almost the entire remainder of the chapter was originally an etiology explaining the presence of the Gibeonites as slaves at some Israelite sanctuary. That the etiology is founded on an actual covenant made between Israel (the tribe of Benjamin) and Gibeon is supported both by 2 Sm 21:1–9 (where the entire context suggests that Saul's murder of the Gibeonites was a covenant violation) and by v. 17 of this chapter, which seems to express an independent tradition of a covenant between Benjamin and four Canaanite cities.

It is not clear to what sanctuary this etiology originally referred, whether to Gibeon or Gilgal. The former is more likely. If so, the tradition was later transferred to Gilgal, to which it most naturally refers in its present form (v. 6). Strains of a pre-Joshuan tradition in this chapter preclude an original reference to the Temple at Jerusalem, but a (post-exilic?) D editor may have applied the story to the Jerusalem Temple in v. 27 ("in the place of the Lord's choice"), either because he knew of Gibeonites at the Temple, or because he regarded the slaves there as descendants of the Gibeonites.

This etiology, although somewhat inconsistent in its present setting (Joshua would hardly provide for Temple slaves during the instability of an extended battle campaign), introduces the coalition against Gibeon (ch. 10), which was instrumental in furthering Joshua's conquests. **3.** This verse resumes the narrative interrupted at 8:29. Gibeon is el-Jîb, slightly over 5 mi. NW of Jerusalem. **4.** *a device of their own:* It corresponds to Joshua's craftiness at Ai. *chose provisions for a journey:* This reading, found in some texts, is a slight variation of the MT, which reads, "they assumed the role of ambassadors." **6–8.** The lack of coherence, as the position of authority alternates between Joshua and the "men of Israel," probably indicates a pre-Joshuan tradition. **7.** This verse reflects Dt 7:2, which demanded utter destruction of the seven pagan peoples in Canaan. **9–10.** The D editor paraphrases words he had placed in Rahab's mouth (2:10). **14.** *the Israelite princes:* The MT reads "the men," which can be emended slightly to read "princes," as the LXX does. Either reading could well belong to a pre-Joshuan stage of tradition. The antiquity of this verse is further indicated by its reference to a covenant meal (a reference made with some irony, considering the condition of the food the Israelites ate and its use as a means of deceiving them).

33 **16–21.** This pericope has retained its more ancient flavor, with no mention of Joshua. **17.** Apparently, the Israelites began a march to the cities in league with the Gibeonites after they had learned of the Gibeonite trick. More likely, however, this verse is a later addition made to explain how the Israelites discovered the trick "three days after the agreement" (v. 16). It is probably drawn from an independent tradition of a Benjaminite covenant with these four cities (they are counted among the cities of Benjamin in 18:25–28) and was added here to show Israel's control over the central portion of Canaan. Chephirah is Tell Kefireh and Kiriath-jearim is Deir el-Azhar. Both are roughly 5 mi. SW of Gibeon; Beeroth is possibly el-Bireh, roughly 5 mi. N of Gibeon. **21.** *hewers of wood and drawers of water:* It is perhaps a stereotyped expression for slave labor (cf. Dt 29:10), without designating any particular cultic function (for association of Gibeonites with cultic slave labor, see M. Haran, *VT* 11 [1961] 159–69). *and the community did:* This phrase is in some Gk texts, but not in the Hebrew. It supposes the Hebrew was omitted through haplography, because of similarity with the preceding phrase, a possibility. If we take the Hebrew as it stands, v. 21 reads, lit., "And the princes said to them 'Let them live.' And they became hewers of wood and drawers of water for the entire community, as the princes decreed to them." The principal difficulty with this reading is that there has been no such decree of the princes. Yet it is still possible that this is the correct translation, with the decree of the princes having been almost entirely omitted in order to have Joshua deliver the verdict in vv. 23 and 27.

24–25. This D addition excuses the Gibeonites to some degree for their trickery, but it especially shows that they truly partook of the Israelite faith and could thus be permitted to share the blessings of the promised land (as in the case of Rahab, 2:9–11).

34 (b) Defeat of the Anti-Gibeonite Coalition and Conquest of the South (10:1–43). This chapter divides quite readily into the defeat of the five Amorite kings at Gibeon (vv. 1–15), the execution of the five Amorite kings at Makkedah (vv. 16–27), and the conquest of the south (vv. 28–43). Commentators disagree, however, about the original relationship of these parts to each other. The Makkedah narrative has been called a local etiology, seeking to explain the meaning of five trees outside a walled-up cave near the city. Through several editorial adjustments (notably v. 15), it was artificially linked with the Gibeon tradition; finally, a separate listing of conquered cities was added to these sections to fill out the story of the conquest. From another point of view, however, it is possible that the unity of this chapter is more than artificial. (For pertinent geographical material, → Biblical Geography, 73:73–74.)

First, as Noth has pointed out, the list of the conquered cities (vv. 28–39) undoubtedly belongs originally to the Makkedah tradition; only five cities are mentioned (except for Makkedah itself, v. 28, and Gezer, v. 33, where it is the army rather than the city that is destroyed), corresponding to the five kings and five trees of the Makkedah story. The original form of this etiology most likely could point out the cities of the kings; the five cities listed in the third section (Libnah, Lachish, Eglon, Hebron, and Debir) were not far from Makkedah (located in the western hill country of Judah, cf. 15:41) and are most likely the original cities of the story, rather than the five cities now listed in v. 23.

The problem of the origin of v. 23, then, raises the more difficult question of the relationship of the Gibeon and Makkedah narratives. Each has the flavor of a story complete in itself, and each narrates the total rout of a Canaanite coalition—one near Gibeon, the other near Makkedah. The Compiler has joined them through the insertion of "and Makkedah" in v. 10, and, if our opinion is correct, through the insertion of the five cities mentioned in the Gibeon narrative (vv. 3,5) into the Makkedah narrative. It is probable, however, that a unity actually exists between the narratives on a deeper level, for the following reasons. First, it is very likely that the coalition of five Canaanite kings is original in both narratives—certainly in the version with its five trees; the Gibeon story is partially similar (cities of Hebron, Lachish, and Eglon) but has its own variant: the cities of Jerusalem and Jarmuth and the names of the individual kings. The precise details of the Gibeon list (the information in v. 3 is not found elsewhere in the Scriptures) argue both for its independence and for its authenticity, while its similarities to the Makkedah list argue for some relationship with that list. Second, both stories tell of victory over a Canaanite coalition, and it is likely that such a victory was obtained through an Israelite coalition. Involved in these stories are the neighboring territories of Benjamin (Gibeon) and Judah (Makkedah), and possibly Ephraim (Beth-horon, v. 10; cf. 21:22). Also, Joshua, himself an Ephraimite (Nm 13:8,16; Jgs 2:9), however much his role was exaggerated as tradition developed, was certainly a major force in the formation of the primitive Israelite 12-tribe league (cf. Jos 24). It is thus possible that his role in ch. 10 reflects historical fact.

Therefore, the two independent narratives of this chapter may well be founded on the same historical event, the defeat of a Canaanite coalition by an Israelite coalition including Benjaminites, Judahites, and, presumably, Ephraimites, under Joshua. Benjamin localized its memories at Gibeon, while the memory was preserved in Judah through association with the cave at Makkedah. If so, the work of the Compiler followed this pattern: he joined the two narratives, and, preferring the Gibeon king list to the Makkedah (perhaps because of the inclusion of Jerusalem in the former), used that list for both stories. He then used the other list as the basis for the victories he outlines in vv. 28–39, thus stretching the list of victories and preparing for the grand summary in vv. 40–43.

35 **1.** Zedek was perhaps the local god of Jerusalem. Adonizedek ("Zedek is my lord") is often identified with Adonibezek of Jgs 1:4–8; the LXX reads "Adonizedek" in both places. However, the difference of names in the Hebrew is not easily removed. *remaining among them:* Most likely the Gibeonites remained among the Israelites. **2.** *large enough for a royal city:* Probably it did not have its own king (9:11). **3.** Except for Jerusalem (in Benjamin), these cities are all in Judah (cf. 15: 13–15, 39,42). **8.** The words of the Lord are typical of the "holy war" pattern, as is the "disorder" (panic) which he causes in v. 10. **11.** The progress of the chase is from Gibeon to Upper Beth-horon (v. 10), then 2.5 mi. NW to Lower Beth-horon (v. 11), and then to Azekah (Tell ez-Zakariyeh), about 18 mi. S of Lower Beth-horon. Possibly Azekah (as well as Makkedah) is a later addition to the text, serving to bring the battle area closer to Makkedah.

12–13. The poetic excerpt from the Book of Jashar probably does not begin until the words "Stand still"; it may have originally concerned the same battle at Gibeon as has just been narrated. **12.** The textual variations in the prose introduction, as well as the form of the quotation, lend weight to the suspicion that the Lord and not Joshua is the original speaker of the poem. The last line of the citation can be translated, "And he [the Lord] took vengeance on the enemy nation." *stand still:* The original meaning of *dmm* in this context is, rather, "Stop shining," and refers to the darkening of the sun and moon that often is the setting for a great intervention by God. This darkening may refer to the storm in v. 11 (cf. also Hab 3:11) or to the darkness that accompanies the "day of the Lord," without any clear allusion to a storm (e.g., Is 13:9–10; Jl 4:15). In the latter case, the excerpt can be understood as a typically poetic expression of the fearsomeness of God's action, before which the powers of heaven are aghast, without implying an actual darkening of the sun. **13.** *the moon stayed:* The verb *ʿmd*, "to stand," is not contained in the first part of the citation, where *dmm* applies to both sun and moon. If it is not a later addition, it can nonetheless be understood, through parallelism, in the same sense as *dmm*. *Book of Jashar:* This book is apparently an ancient poetic anthology concerning Israelite heroes (cf. 2 Sm 1:18). *Jashar* (just) refers either to the heroes in the book, or perhaps to the artistry with which it was composed (see *yšr* in the latter sense in Eccl 12:10). *the sun halted:* The Compiler now adds his own prose commentary. Some hold that he understood the passage in the same sense as the original author of the poem (a storm), and that the apparent lengthening of the day resulted from the length of the storm, which lasted a whole day and ended with the sun reappearing at about the same place in the sky where it had last been seen. It is more likely that the Compiler understood the poem as the description of a miraculous prolonging of the day so that Joshua would have sufficient daylight to finish the battle (Sir 46:4 seems to express the same belief).

36 **15.** This verse interrupts the natural flow of the narrative. Joshua would hardly interrupt his pursuit of the enemy, make the full-day march back to Gilgal, and then continue the pursuit. It has been understood as a conclusion to an originally independent tradition, but left in place after the Gibeon and Makkedah traditions were joined. It duplicates v. 43. However, there is a slight possibility that it may be an addition made after the traditions were joined, to duplicate the sequence "God fights for Israel—Israel returns to camp" found in vv. 42–43.

16. This tradition originally concerned some battle near Makkedah; if the kings had truly been fleeing from Gibeon, we would expect them to seek refuge in their still-intact cities rather than in this cave. **18.** *roll large stones:* This strange command of Joshua may be the survival of a tradition according to which the kings were buried alive and starved to death in the cave. **20.** The Compiler explicitly mentions the escaped survivors to provide some opposing force when Joshua attacks these "fortified cities" in vv. 29–39. **24.** Placing one's foot on the neck of an enemy was a sign of his utter defeat (Ps 110:1). **25.** The verse is clearly a D addition. **26.** A corpse could not be left hanging overnight (Dt 21:23). **28.** The Hebrew does not run smoothly. *at that time:* Lit., it is "on that day," an expression which does not fit well with v. 27. *on its king:* The Hebrew adds "on them," apparently referring to the other five kings. Several attempts have apparently been made in this verse to bring the destruction of Makkedah into an earlier form of the tradition which did not mention it; the addition also links Makkedah with Jericho, although there was no mention of the King of Jericho in Jos 6.

37 **29–39.** The five cities that Joshua destroys in these verses are most likely the original five of the Makkedah tradition. The Compiler mentions explicitly the death of the kings of Libnah (v. 30) and Debir (v. 39) because he did not include them among the kings in the caves; he omits reference to the kings of Lachish (v. 32) and Eglon (v. 35) because they had been mentioned. The execution of the King of Hebron (v. 37) must be considered an inadvertent later addition, for he was one of the kings in the cave (the King of Hebron is noticeably absent from v. 39). **32.** Lachish is Tell ed-Duweir, actually destroyed in the late 13th cent. during the period of the Israelite invasions. **33.** There is no claim that the city was destroyed; cf. 16:10, which states that the Ephraimites could not drive the Canaanites out of Gezer. **34.** Eglon is Tell el-Hesi; the tell gives evidence of violent destruction around the same time as Lachish. **37–38.** Jos 15:13–19 and Jgs 1:10–15,20 present different traditions about the capture of Hebron and Debir; they may indicate an entrance of some Judahite tribes through the borders of southern Canaan. It is perhaps impossible to decide on the relative historical value of these traditions; we must at least beware of dismissing the Makkedah tradition too lightly (concerning the possibility of repeated conquests of these cities, as well as the superior value, in some respects, of Jos 10 to Jgs 1, cf. G. E. Wright *JNES* 5 [1946] 105–14). Debir is Tell Beit Mirsim; it was destroyed about the same time as Lachish and Eglon.

40. *the entire country:* The Compiler wishes to create the impression of a general conquest in the south, and yet his summary is roughly equivalent to the particular victories he has described. *the Negeb:* Cf. 15:19, where Debir is associated with this southern desert area (in 15:48, it is part of the mountain region). *the foothills:* Jarmuth, Lachish, Eglon, Makkedah, and Libnah are all in this area (cf. 15:39–42). *the mountain slopes:* It probably signifies from the Judean hills to the Dead Sea. The Compiler does not mention the coastal plain. **41.** These names may designate respectively the southern, western, eastern, and northern limits of the conquest (roughly equivalent to the area of the tribe of Judah). *Gaza:* This is the one area of the coastal plain mentioned by the Compiler, and reflects a later period when Gaza was part of Judah (15:47). Jos contains an earlier tradition reflecting the inability of the Israelites to capture Gaza (11:22; 13:2–3), as does also Jgs (1:8).

38 (c) THE CONQUEST OF THE NORTH (11:1–14). The structure of the battle at the waters of Merom (vv. 1–10) clearly parallels that of the battle at Gibeon in ch. 10. Ch. 11, however, bears no trace of a link with Gilgal; without any explanation, the camp of Joshua is now located in northern Canaan (v. 5). The geography of these 15 verses shows that they found their original home somewhere within the borders of the tribe Naphtali. To some, the place of Joshua in the battles at Merom and Hazor is not original; he has probably replaced some now unknown northern hero (Noth). Some also see this section as conflicting with Jgs 4–5. Despite all this, it seems we do not have sufficient justification to deny Joshua a leading role in these battles, and hence an original place in the tradition.

In the first place, ch. 11 (as also ch. 10) has several signs of antiquity of tradition and yet gives no textual evidence of Joshua having been a later introduction into the text, contrary to the case of several Benjaminite traditions in chs. 2–9 (note the details of the enemy coalition in 11:1, and also the instructions concerning the horses and chariots in v. 6, expressing without any theologizing the ancient belief that the Israelites did not need the might of chariots when the Lord was fighting for them; cf. the Song of Miriam, Ex 15:21, and the prophecy of Deborah, Jgs 4:13–14). Second, the archaeological evidence at Hazor testifies to destruction of both the upper and lower city in the 13th cent. The upper city (the heavily fortified "tell" area) shows two phases of small Israelite settlements before the city was rebuilt by Solomon (1 Kgs 9:15); the first phase had contained the temporary dwellings of seminomads (Y. Yadin, *BAR* 2, 191–224). Third, the traditions of Jgs 4–5 need not be a contradiction to Jos 11, since Jgs is concerned mostly with a single battle against the Canaanites' General Sisera (the waters of Merom are not mentioned), treats of King Jabin's final defeat only in very summary fashion (4:23–24), and, in fact, makes no explicit mention of the destruction of Hazor. Fourth, the Song of Deborah (Jgs 5) gives extremely ancient testimony to an Israelite coalition fighting against the northern Canaanites; among the Israelites are the princes of Ephraim (5:14). Because Joshua was an Ephraimite and an active unifying force among the tribes in ancient Israel, what the previous arguments have tended to show seems quite reasonable: his position as leader of a coalition in the north at this early period is an historical possibility, even in a Naphtali tradition.

1. *Hazor:* Tell el-Qedah, somewhat less than 10 mi. NW of the Sea of Galilee. **5.** *waters of Merom:* Probably meant is Wadi Meiron, which flows S into the NW part of the Sea of Galilee. **8.** The extent of the pursuit spreads the Israelites over the northern territory and thus magnifies the area under their control; "Greater Sidon" (probably including the outskirts of Sidon) is the northern limit, and Misrephoth the western. **10.** The great size of the tell, 170 acres, confirms its importance at the time of its destruction. It was the largest city in the holy land during the Canaanite period. (→ Biblical Archaeology, 74:21,63.)

39 (d) SUMMARY OF THE CONQUEST (11:15–23). This section was written largely by the Compiler and was probably augmented by D. In his opening statement (v. 16) and in the final verse, the Compiler strikes the major chord of his summary; "Joshua captured the whole country." The territorial extent of the conquest (v. 17) goes somewhat beyond the more usual "from Dan to Beer-sheba," but the limitations of the conquest are apparent: the Compiler omits explicit reference to the Plain of Jezreel and the coastal plain in v. 16. **15.** The Deuteronomist adds his own preface to the summary and refers to the commands in ch. 1. **16.** The Compiler seems to betray his southern origin, since he feels no need to specify which mountain regions and foothills, except when he mentions those of the north (Israel); it is not clear whether these two states were fully separated. **17.** Mt. Halak is Jebel Halak, about 25 mi. S of Beer-sheba and W of the Arabah. Seir is usually the Edomite territory E of the Arabah; here, however, it may include the land occupied by the Edomites W of the Arabah. If it does not, it just serves to indicate "the south." *Baal-gad:* It is perhaps Baalbek, if "Mount Hermon" can be understood as a general term for the Lebanon range (Noth) or for the direction north. **20.** The Compiler may be responsible for this speculation (of limited value theologically, and also historically inasmuch as the ban was not actually carried out to this extent). *but be exterminated, as the Lord commanded Moses:* This amplification is the work of D. **21.** The Anakim are described as giants in Dt 1:28; 2:10,21; Nm 13:33, perhaps because of the mysterious dolmens found by the Israelites in Canaan and Transjordan. *Anab:* This city is somewhat over 3 mi. SE of Debir. The combination of these two cities with Hebron is a unique and very likely authentic tradition. The role of Joshua jars slightly with traditions that the Calebites and Kenizzites were more closely involved in the capture of Hebron and Debir (Jos 14:13; 15:13–19; Jgs 1:10–15,20; there has been perhaps a harmonization of the roles of Joshua and Caleb in Jos 14:13; 15:13). We have already seen still another variant for the capture of Hebron and Debir in the Makkedah etiology (ch. 10). This new material is probably added from a source of the Deuteronomist, who explains that "the mountain regions" are those of Judah and Israel. **22.** This addition is probably still part of that of the Deuteronomist. The grouping of Philistine cities is as unexplained as the triad in the preceding verse. There may have been a tradition about giants living in these cities (Goliath was from Gath, 1 Sm 17:4). **23.** This conclusion was probably that of the Compiler. *and the land enjoyed peace:* This phrase is found in only one other place in the Scriptures, Jos 14:15, where it seems out of place because there is no explicit mention of any conflict and the whole context is distribution, rather than conquest of land. Noth is probably correct in saying the Deuteronomist had originally placed the Calebite tradition of Hebron (Jos 14:6–15, beginning with the Kenizzite Caleb) immediately before this concluding phrase, and that it was later transferred, with this phrase, to its present place in ch. 14. D placed it here originally as a qualification of the immediately preceding phrase ("apportioning it among the tribes"), thus explaining why the non-Israelite Calebites were living in territory from which Joshua had just expelled the Anakim (v. 21). The story also concluded his treatment of the Calebites (Dt 1:36). The second D editor transferred it to its present place when chs. 13–21 were added to the D history. There it is linked with the allotment of Judah (ch. 15), the tribe into which the Calebites had been assimilated. (→ Biblical Geography, 73:88.)

40 **(III) The List of Conquered Kings (12:1–24).** Although the material of this chapter varies in origin, it is now presented as a unity by D. His first list (vv. 1–6) concerns one of his special theological interests—the role of the Transjordan tribes—and is developed from Dt 3:8–17 and Jos 13:9–32. In contrast to the second list, this one contains a great deal of geographical material. Perhaps D himself included it so that he could more thoroughly associate the Transjordan territory with the promised land (the Hebr of v. 1 makes "the land" refer especially to the promised land). The list of the Canaanite conquests (vv. 7–24) is actually composed of two lists. The first (vv. 9–12, to Debir) follows the order of conquests in Jos 6–10; only Libnah is omitted, for it appears soon after in v. 15. The second (vv. 12–24, beginning with Geder) is of unknown origin; it proceeds through the Cisjordan territory from S to N, excepting Tirzah, which is S of several previously mentioned cities (a possible parallel is the pharaoh Shishak's list of conquered Israelite towns, which may follow geographical order; cf. *ANET* 264). This list need not mean that all these cities were captured, but merely that their kings were defeated in battle; it gives the impression of a total conquest of the land.

4. The Rephaim were also described as giants, like the Anakim; cf. 11:21. **7–8.** The geography draws upon 10:40 and 11:17; consequently, "the desert" probably is the Desert of Judah along the western side of the Dead Sea (cf. 10:40–41). **13.** Both Hormah and Arad are in the Negeb. **15–16.** Libnah, Adullam, and Makkedah are in the foothills of Judah. Bethel, Tappuah, Hepher, and Aphek are located in approximately an E to W direction across the Samarian hill country. **19–23.** Not all these cities are identified, but they seem to follow an E to W direction across Galilee (Noth). *the foreign king at Gilgal:* The text is difficult. The Greek reads "Galilee" for "Gilgal"; some would translate "the king of Goim in Galilee," considering this an alternate name for Harosheth-hagoiim (Jgs 4:2). If "Gilgal" is correct, it is probably modern Jaljúlya, near the eastern side of the Plain of Sharon.

(IV) Allotment of the Promised Land (13:1–21:45).

41 **(A) Introduction to the Allotment (13:1–33).** In a sense Jos here starts again. The second D editor has clearly structured this chapter to parallel ch. 1: a statement of fact (1:1–2 and 13:1) that grounds a command from God (1:2 and 13:7); the special promise of divine help and exhortation to courage are not needed in the context of ch. 13; and, finally, the participation of the Transjordan tribes (1:12–18 and 13:15–32). While the major theme of chs. 1–12 is conquest of the land, here the theme is settlement of the land. Both the logic and language of vv. 2–6 and 8–13 (beginning with "as Moses the servant of the Lord gave to them" in v. 8) show that they are not original to this text. The former section intends to enlarge still further upon the territory which was to be divided, although the Deuteronomist had intended it merely as a list of unconquered, potentially dangerous territory; the latter section provides a general view of the Transjordan territory before it is divided. The verses about the Levites resemble footnotes, concluding the two surveys of Transjordan territory (vv .14 and 33).

The D editor presents his material on the territory of the Transjordan tribes as a flashback to the activity of Moses. The origin of the territorial details has received different explanations. Noth has dealt the deathblow to the theory that a P document is the basis for chs. 13–21, because only a few phrases can with certainty be traced to a P editor. Noth himself says this entire section is a composition of two independent documents—one a town list of the kingdom of Judah dating from the time of King Josiah (since it includes territory not conquered by David or Solomon, and not possessed by Judah until Josiah's reign), and the other, a survey of the boundaries dating from the premonarchical period (the Transjordan holdings are still restricted), based both on ideal limits and on boundaries actually controlled (thus, very little of the Transjordan territory is included). According to this theory, the two lists were combined and adjusted in such a way as to allot boundaries and/or towns to all 12 tribes. As is apparent from 14:1,4,5 and 19:49, this entire section existed as a unit apart from Jos; in its original form, the Israelites themselves divided the land.

Noth's theory is persuasive, although not all points are generally accepted. Bright prefers to assign the boundary document to the monarchical rather than premonarchical period. There is also widespread hesitation at attributing to the province list a date as late as the reign of Josiah. It seems, too, that several other sources unknown to us were used by the editor in compiling his town lists. Explanations differ concerning the allotment of the Transjordan territory. Bright argues there is no genuine boundary list there, while Noth believes the boundaries of a rather small territory were originally described and then divided artificially between Reuben and Gad. He thinks the town list divided secondarily among the three Transjordan tribes represents the beginning of a 13th Judahite province, formed from the Transjordan conquests of Josiah. It is still possible, however, that the second D editor used sources unknown to us in his extensive reworking of the Transjordan area.

42 **1.** This verse anticipates 23:1 and permitted the insertion of chs. 13–21 (→ 2 above). **3.** Although the translation runs smoothly, the Hebrew is a group of disconnected phrases, probably revealing successive stages of addition to the text. *stream:* The Hebrew is actually an Egyptian word, meaning "the Waters of Horus." **4.** Rather than Afka in Lebanon, perhaps Aphek in Sharon (12:18) is meant; in effect, these verses would exclude the whole coastal area from the conquered territory. **8.** *the other half of the tribe of Manasseh:* This phrase is not in the Hebrew but must unquestionably be restored; it was dropped through confusion with the end of v. 7. **8.** The Hebrew shows that an introduction (omitted in the translation) was rather awkwardly attached to the end of this verse to provide for the insertion of the general survey that follows and which is based mostly on Dt 3, with some items drawn from this chapter, vv. 15–31. **14.** Cf. Dt 10:19; 18:1. **21.** *the other cities of the tableland:* This was probably a concluding formula. The remaining historical notes of vv. 21–22 may well be later additions. *generally:* The Hebrew reads "all," which conflicts with v. 27; here it is evident that a precise distinction between Reuben and Gad has not been made. *vassals:* This translation is confirmed by a Ugaritic text (cf. *UM* glossary, 1253). **25.** Gilead is apparently understood in its limited original sense, comprising the hill country S of the Jabbok. *half the land of the Ammonites:* In Jgs 11:21–23 it is clear that the territory of Ammon was to some degree under the control of Sihon; therefore, this phrase may be an authentic tradition of the early Israelite control of Ammon. It seems strange, however, that this territory is not explicitly mentioned in the previous general survey (v. 11) even if Gilead is to be taken there in a wider sense as including some of the Ammonite territory. The tradition of Ammon's inviolability (Dt 2:19) suggests rather that this phrase is a later addition, perhaps reflecting an acquisition of some Ammonite territory during the period of the Israelite kingdoms. **27.** *the other part of the kingdom of Sihon:* This territory is only vaguely distinguished from the share of Reuben (v. 21). **31.** Gilead seems to be understood in a later, wider sense, as including land both N and S of the Jabbok. This verse may, however, be an attempt to reconcile the data of v. 25 and Dt 3:15, understood as contradictory (these verses need not be so understood, however; it seems Gilead was also at one time applied to land exclusively above the Jabbok, as it is in Dt 3:15, which gives the third meaning of "Gilead"). *half the clans descended from Machir:* This obviously later addition seeks to modify the previous allusion to Machir in this verse. It may have been inserted because of the tradition that Machir also occupied territory W of the Jordan (Jg 5:14), or because only "half of Gilead" is the subject of this verse and Machir had obtained all Gilead (Dt 3:15; Jos 17:1). The various shifts in meaning given to Gilead have apparently caused some confusion in the transmission of the text. (→ Biblical Geography, 73:50.)

43 **(B) Introduction to the Distribution of the Western Territory (14:1–5).** In the oldest level of tradition, the Israelites themselves distribute the land (vv. 1, 5); the role of Joshua, Eleazar, and the heads of families (v. 1) is a modification introduced by a P editor, following Nm 34:17–18. **2.** *by lot:* The phrase is possibly a P modification (Nm 33:54; 34:13). **3–4.** These verses explain why there is distribution among 12 tribes, even though the Levites are not counted.

(C) The Calebites in Hebron (14:6–15). **1.** The opening clause has apparently nothing to do with the following story. Rather than the remnant of a lost tradition, it may be an editorial device to associate Caleb with the tribe of Judah. The Kenizzites are an Edomite people (Gn 36:11) who were finally incorporated into the Judahites (Nm 13:6; 34:19). *about you and me:* This phrase probably represents a later level of the tradition, in which Joshua is associated with Caleb in urging the attack from the south. A reading of Nm 13:30; 14:24 seems to indicate that the tradition originally concerned only Caleb. Jos 15:13–19 may also preserve a tradition of an independent attack by the Calebites in the south; cf. also 11:21. **9.** *Moses swore:* The tradition is slightly modified; the Lord swore in Dt 1:34. *you have set foot:* Cf. 1:3. **10.** *forty-five years:* Since the D tradition allowed for 38 years of wandering after Kadesh (Dt 2:14), this verse implies that the conquest was completed in 7 years. **11.** The Lord himself has shown that Caleb should occupy the land by wondrously preserving him in youth. **12.** *this mountain region:* The phrase becomes intelligible if we understand that the story formerly followed shortly after 11:21. The reference to the Anakim, their cities, and their expulsion by Caleb, was undoubtedly added to the story when it was placed here; the addition was intended to harmonize the story with 15:13–14, and is out of context, for Caleb merely receives the land from Joshua in vv. 13–14. The Anakim are no longer a concern (cf. again 11:21). **15.** Kiriath-arba may actually mean "tetrapolis." Arba stands for "four," but it came to be understood as the name of a giant. *and the land enjoyed peace:* See comment on 11:23.

44 **(D) The Boundaries of Judah (15:1–12).** This boundary list is clearly not of the same period as the Judahite province list (vv. 21–62). No matter which of the several theories one adopts in reconstructing the original province list, at least the following differences remain: Kadesh-barnea is notably absent from the southernmost province (vv. 21–32); the Philistine holdings (vv. 45–47) do not correspond to the total possession described in the boundary list. While the province list surely dates from the monarchical period, the boundary list may well antedate the kingdom and outline early tribal claims.

This Judahite boundary list is idealistic, including all the Philistine territory, some of which Israel never possessed, and extending far southward through territory in which Israel never actually settled. It includes the territory of Simeon, which had by this time already disappeared as a tribe (19:1).

The southern and especially the northern borders are given with particular detail. The southern border has its parallel in the southern boundary of the land given in Nm 34:3–5, whereas part of the northern is repeated, although in the opposite direction (W to E), as the southern border of Benjamin (18:15–19). A comparison of these texts offers strong support to the theory that the original boundary list was not conceived as a continuous boundary line, but rather as a series of outposts or frontier towns that in our text were secondarily strung together to form a boundary line. Even the boundary points themselves indicate that the border was not imagined as a continuous line ("below the pass of Akrabbim...a point south of Kadesh-barnea"). **7.** Gilgal should perhaps read Geliloth (18:17); the exact location of this place is not known. **9.** *fountain of waters of Nephtoah:* Without changing the Hebr consonants, we may read fountain of Merneptah, a pharaoh who attacked Israel in the 13th cent. (cf. *DOTT* 137–41).

(E) The Territory of Caleb and Othniel (15:13–19). The bulk of this section is an etiology explaining why certain water sources belong to the clan of Othniel. The background of this story may be that certain pools once used by the Calebites came to be used later by the neighboring clan of Othniel.

The acquisition of the Calebite territory (vv. 13–14) is a combination of Jgs 1:10,20 and stands as an introduction to the etiology. Together, these sections narrate the acquisition of territory by clans that had become associated with the tribe of Judah. (For varying traditions concerning the capture of Debir, cf. 10:38 and 11:21.)

45 **(F) The Towns of Judah (15:20–63).** This town list is generally regarded as an administrative catalogue of 12 provinces comprising the southern kingdom of Judah. The listing for each province includes the name of several towns plus a conlcuding phrase giving the total number of towns mentioned. The Hebr text presently lists only 11 such provinces, but the Gk text makes it clear that an entire province was accidentally omitted and should be reinserted after v. 59, thus giving us a division of Judah corresponding to Solomon's division of the northern territory into 12 provinces (1 Kgs 4:7–19). If this list does represent such an administrative division, however, a problem immediately arises. The territory delineated by these towns does not extend beyond the northern border of the tribe of Judah, and yet at least some territory of Benjamin was always part of the southern kingdom. Where is the Benjaminite territory? In 18:21–28 we find two provinces of Benjamin that closely resemble the town list of Judah in structure. Now various theories arise about how the two lists should be combined to round out the territory of the southern kingdom. (→ Biblical Geography, 73:89.)

The southern Benjaminite province (18:21–24) lists Beth-arabah (v. 22), as does the 12th Judahite province (15:61); the northern Benjaminite province (18:25–28) lists Kiriath (most likely to be read Kiriath-jearim—jearim was accidentally dropped because of its similarity to the following Hebr word), as does the 11th Judahite province (15:60). Noth has concluded that these Benjaminite provinces were originally listed under the 11th and 12th Judahite provinces, but were later removed and assigned to the tribe of Benjamin somewhat carelessly, as the duplication of city names shows. F. Cross and G. E. Wright (*JBL* 75 [1956] 202–26) should also be consulted for the location of towns in this list; they are unwilling to attribute such carelessness to an editor. Also, they cannot imagine that Judah should ever have contained such a province as results from the combination of 18:21–24 and 15:61–62, thus linking the mountains of Ephraim with the whole western coast of the Dead Sea. Instead, they consider 15:45–47 a later addition to the town list, totally atypical in construction and containing Philistine territory that surely was never a province of the southern kingdom. Since there are then only 11 provinces, they find the missing province in 18:21–24. Beth-arabah is mentioned both in 18:22 and 15:61 probably because it was a border between the two provinces and was added to 15:61 as a result of later Judahite expansion.

What, then, becomes of the northern Benjaminite province (18:25–28)? The 11th Judahite province (15:60) is clearly too small to have constituted a separate province; the northern Benjaminite province must have originally been part of this province, but was later assigned to Benjamin (R. De Vaux, *AI* 136, accepts this reconstruction). Here, their opinion is close to that of Noth, except that Cross and Wright do not explain the duplication of Kiriath in 18:28 and 15:60 as the result of careless division. They think that it was ascribed to Judah in 15:60 probably under the influence of 18:14 and 15:9–10; its original place in the town list was with the towns now attached to Benjamin, but an editor later ascribed it to Judah, thus harmonizing the town list with other Judahite material (18:14 and 15:9–10) and at the same time providing himself with a 12th Judahite province. Cross and Wright presumably hold that Rabbah in 15:60 is, like Kiriath-jearim, a secondary construction, taken from the original Benjaminite list (18:25–28). However, Rabbah is not contained in this list, so they hold it probable that it was dropped from 18:28 through a corruption of the text.

46 The solutions proposed thus far demand painstaking rearrangement of the text, but also raise problems of dating the list. If all the Benjaminite territory is to be considered originally a part of the Judahite list, at what period did Judah contain all this territory? During the reigns of Abijah (913–911) and Josiah (640–609), Judah extended its boundaries to include these cities (Abijah: 2 Chr 13:19; Josiah: 2 Kgs 23:8,15,19). Noth places the town list in the reign of Josiah. Indeed, Cross and Wright themselves acknowledge there are cities in the list which did not exist in the time of Abijah (cf. particularly 15:61–62). However, they do not think that Josiah, whose dream was to restore the united monarchy of David, would have concerned himself about an administrative organization limited to the kingdom of Judah; Noth admits this redistricting must have occurred early in Josiah's reign. Cross and Wright likewise notice the absence of Beth-shemesh in the first foothill province (15:33–36); it had been rebuilt by the time of Josiah and should have been included if the list dated from his reign (Noth has solved this problem by affirming that this

foothill province originally contained the towns now apportioned to Dan, 19:41–46; Irshemesh, 19:41, is the same as Beth-shemesh). Cross and Wright then opt for the reign of Jehoshaphat (870–848), arguing that he retained the conquests of Abijah, that his reign was sufficiently stable to permit a reorganization of the territory, and that Beth-shemesh had still not been rebuilt.

Y. Aharoni (*VT* 9 [1959] 225–46) presents several arguments against the conclusions of Cross and Wright. He charges that they have acted inconsistently in considering half the Benjaminite list as a new province (18:21–24) and combining the other half with a Judahite province (18:25–28 plus 15:60); he argues further that 15:60, despite its brevity, can well represent an entire province as it stands. Also, the biblical text gives us no clear indication that Jehoshaphat possessed territory any farther N than Mizpah, fortified by Jehoshaphat's predecessor Asa, who had lost much of Abijah's acquisitions (cf. 1 Kgs 15:16–22). Also, 18:21–24, extending from the mountains of Ephraim to the Dead Sea, can hardly be considered a province of Judah. Rather, this territory should be understood as a province of the northern kingdom of Israel. The original 12 provinces are those delineated in the province list, except for 15:45–47; the missing province is the southern province of Benjamin (18:25–28). The boundaries of the town list, inasmuch as they do not include the northern Benjaminite province, are more typical of those that obtained through most of the history of Judah. Thus, the repetition of Beth-arabah results from the fact that in one case the list is of northern origin (18:22), but in the other, southern (15:61). The repetition of Kiriath-jearim is only apparent. One province mentions this town (15:60), whereas the other refers to a place a slight distance away: Gibeath-Kiriath-jearim (18:28; cf. 1 Sm 7:1). Aharoni re-examines the archaeological data of Beth-shemesh and finds that its period of desertion fits closely with the reign of Uzziah (781–740); his choice of this reign as the date for the town list is confirmed by the size of the Negeb province (15:21–32): Uzziah carried out extensive construction there (2 Chr 26:10).

This solution, however, presents one serious difficulty, as noted by Z. Kallai-Kleinmann (*VT* 11 [1961] 223–27; cf. also *VT* 8 [1958] 134–60): although the Benjaminite list (18:21–28) appears to be unified, Aharoni must divide it, giving a separate origin to each half. If this list is to be assigned to some period after the division of the kingdom, as is generally agreed (the resettling of Jericho [v. 21] and the absence of Beth-shemesh from the list are strong indications for such a dating), then 18:21–28 must be assigned to one Judahite king, for the text gives no indication that the two Benjaminite provinces ever belonged to separate town lists.

47 The basic supposition of all the foregoing theories is that the Judahite town list is an administrative catalogue of the provinces in the southern kingdom, and therefore needs further enlargement, as it now stands. Since the proposed reconstructions are all to some extent unsatisfactory, Kallai-Kleinmann has denied this basic supposition, arguing that while the Benjaminite and Judahite town lists may give some knowledge about a "possible administrative set-up" (*VT* 11 [1961] 224), their main purpose is tribal—to list the territory belonging to each tribe. This theory grossly underplays the administrative origin of these lists. That they both form the provincial town list of the southern kingdom seems inescapable. Yet perhaps the two town lists did exist separately for some time before they formed part of chs. 13–21. Perhaps a spirit of tribal rivalry between Benjamin and Judah persisted even into the period of the divided kingdom and prompted a division of the list. Such a divided version would have been deprived of its administrative purpose and could thus undergo revisions that did not always correspond to the territory actually possessed, making recombination of the lists the unrewarding task it has become.

Concerning the date of the Judahite town list, the presence or absence of certain towns from the list has been used by the various authors as an argument against an origin during the reigns of either Abijah or Jehoshaphat (there is no clear proof against the Judahite control of all these towns in the time of Josiah). Kallai-Kleinmann (*VT* 8 [1958] 151–53) suggests the final form is traceable to the reign of Hezekiah (vv. 45–47 seem to reflect his activity in the Philistine territory; cf. 2 Kgs 18:8). But we would expect Beth-shemesh to be contained in the list because it was quite probably recaptured from the Philistines during Hezekiah's reign. He responds that it is probably one of the towns alluded to, but not specifically mentioned in 15:45–47—a very unconvincing suggestion, as Aharoni points out. Yet perhaps we cannot identify the list with the reign of any one ruler, but while placing its origin in the divided monarchy, must admit that it has suffered additions and subtractions through the reigns of several Judahite monarchs—changes made perhaps with some inconsistency, if the list was for a time removed from its original administrative setting.

25. There are several combinations with Hazor (meaning, roughly, "homestead") in this southern province. The number of towns has thus been greatly enlarged through the inclusion of rather small territories. **32.** *twenty-nine cities:* The number does not correspond to the previous catalogue, as in the case of several other provinces. Apparently, changes were made without the total being changed. **45.** Noth holds that Ekron is all that remains of the original province, which has been transferred to Dan (19:41–46; Ekron is repeated in v. 43). The remainder of this province (vv. 46–47), he holds, is the result of later attempts to make it appear more like a province. Cross and Wright regard vv. 45–47 as a later addition seeking to include the Philistine territory in the boundaries of Judah, thus making the town list conform more closely to the boundary list (cf. 15:12). Unless one is willing to accept Noth's premise that there is only one original (Judahite) town list, which was secondarily divided among the other tribes, it seems more likely that these verses are independent of the Danite list. **63.** This verse says of Judah what Jgs 1:21 says of Benjamin. It seems to be an addition made to promote the Judahite claim to Jerusalem; cf. possible further signs of tribal rivalry in 7:1–8:29.

48 **(G) The Territory of the Josephite Tribes (16:1–17:18).** This section presents an obvious contrast to the abundant detail of the Judahite lists. Here, there is no evidence of a town list at all. The borders are outlined in most summary fashion, except for the line between Ephraim and Manasseh (16:5–8). At least twice the description is made somewhat carelessly: in 17:10, both Ephraim and Manasseh are said to border on Asher and Issachar, whereas only Manasseh did; in 16:7, the eastern border of Ephraim is protracted to the Jordan, even though its eastern limit must have stopped at Jericho, which was the SE corner of the Josephite territory (16:1). It is also very likely that this section has been rearranged to describe Ephraim before Manasseh, although the original text probably presented Manasseh first (Noth). This theory is supported by the order of the tribes in 16:4, by the explanatory note accompanying Michmethath and Tappuah in 17:7–8 (as if these towns had not already been mentioned in 16:6,8), but most of all by the general sense of 17:1–6. More specifically, 16:1 treats the Josephite territory as a single block (as in Gn 49:22–26 and Dt

33:13–17); the editor understands that the entire territory is a unit belonging originally to Manasseh, but that in the boundary list a portion of this territory has been secondarily apportioned to Ephraim (thus, in 16:9 and 17:9 the territory of Ephraim is said to be actually part of Manasseh). The border list thus presents the editor with a repetition of the southern Josephite boundary; in one case it describes the entire territory (Manasseh, 16:2,3), whereas in the other case, it ascribes most to Ephraim (16:5). This situation, unique in the boundary list, seems to explain the unusual addition of 17:1–6 to the boundary material. By drawing on various traditions that describe the division of Manasseh territory, the editor seeks to offer at least a kind of explanation for the location of Ephraim within Manasseh. If this analysis is correct, then it seems more likely that 17:1–6 formed an introduction to the boundary description. The original order of this section thus seems to be as follows: 16:1–4 (literal Hebr of v. 4: "And the sons of Joseph, Manasseh and Ephraim, received their inheritance"); 17:1–13; 16:5–10; 17:14–18. The material was later rearranged to give preference to Ephraim, which actually surpassed Manasseh in importance; the new arrangement illustrated the traditional theme of the younger brother taking the position of the elder (the theme is applied to these tribes in Gn 48:1–20). (For the territory of Ephraim and Manasseh, → Biblical Geography, 73:96ff.)

The concluding verses, 17:14–18, treat of the expansion of Josephite territory, but it is not fully clear whether the Transjordan occupied by Manasseh is meant. This pericope is actually composed of two smaller sections, 14–15 and 16–18, now woven into a continuous narrative by an editor (perhaps the D editor). In the first, it seems that Joshua sends the Josephites into the Transjordan territory, while in the second he is urging them to clear the forest area in the western territory. Although Noth thinks that the editor made the whole pericope refer to the Transjordan, it seems rather that the reference to Transjordan was vague enough to allow the editor to combine both sections into a narrative culminating in a "blessing" (v. 18), analogous to those in Gn 49 and Dt 33, whereby Joshua foretells the gradual expansion of the Josephites on the western side, through the forested hill country, even onto the plain.

49 **16:1.** *to the waters of Jericho:* This phrase seems further clarification of the preceding "Jericho"; it places Jericho itself within the territory of Benjamin (18:21). **2.** Bethel and Luz are not the same place; it seems the name Bethel was later applied to Luz, as in 18:13 (Noth). **3.** *ending thence at the sea:* The protraction of the boundary to the sea, here as in vv. 5 and 8, may be an artificial construction of the editor, similar to his certainly artificial extension of Ephraim's eastern boundary to the Jordan (v. 7; → 48 above). In this verse, we might expect boundary indications farther W than Gezer, approximately 15 mi. from the sea, if such a boundary actually existed. The original boundary document may well have marked off a territory for Dan, some of which may have lain directly W of Ephraim. If so, the editor may have cut off at least part of the Danite territory in favor of Ephraim, since by this time Dan had migrated to the north. In 16:1–3, the editor gives only the southern boundary of the Josephite territory (used also as the northern boundary of Benjamin—18:12–13); he gives only a most fragmentary northern boundary in vv. 7 and 10. Perhaps Manasseh did not have a clearly defined northern boundary in the document; however, the editor may have made it very general because of a conflict in his sources: the boundary list (17:11) gave to Issachar and Asher cities that Jgs 1:27 attributed to Manasseh (Noth). **5.** *east:* It is surely to be omitted, since the boundary heads W. *Upper Beth-horon:* Noth argues convincingly that this city, omitted in v. 3 and yet surely on the same boundary line, is here mentioned because it had a special importance for Ephraim. It was here that the southern boundary curved N to form the western boundary. The editor, however, has suppressed this western boundary and extended the western border of Ephraim to the sea coast.

6–7. A description of the eastern border of Ephraim is given, from N to S. *Ataroth* (read Ataroth-addar, 18:13) cannot be the same as Ataroth in v. 3. **8.** The northern boundary of Ephraim is given, from E to W. It is repeated in 17:7 (in the original order, 17:7 appeared before 16:8) and should be understood as beginning with the NE border point, Michmethath, which has been omitted in 16:8 because of a previous mention in 16:6 (Noth). **10.** This addition was borrowed from Jgs 1:29; the text here adds that the Canaanites were "impressed as laborers," a fact verified by 1 Kgs 9:15–22.

50 **17:1.** *Machir:* This tribe receives mention, only to be then excused for its absence from the following verses. Why it was mentioned at all perhaps results from the fact that it was the original counterpart to Ephraim in this document, until the editor replaced it with the more familiar Manasseh. If so, then these chapters deal with a group originally known as the Josephites, later subdivided into Machir and Ephraim, and finally into Manasseh and Ephraim (Noth). The Hebrew seems to make Machir the recipient of territory allotted W of the Jordan; the Song of Deborah shows that Machir did, in fact, possess land there (Jgs 5:14). **2–3.** The substance of these verses is contained in Nm 26:30–33, with some slight variations in the list of male children; also, the six males are there sons of Gilead rather than of Manasseh. This latter change causes an obvious inconsistency in the text: Hepher is both the grandfather (v. 3) and great-great-granduncle of the five daughters. Apparently the editor was willing to allow this inconsistency to remove Machir and Gilead from a context that considers the division of the western Josephite territory. The names of these sons and daughters are probably administrative divisions of the northern kingdom; Abiezer, Helek, Shechem, Shemida, Noah, and Hoglah are all found mentioned in the Samarian ostraca. **4.** This verse refers to, and supposes as known, Nm 27:1–11; there, however, the daughters appear before Moses, not Joshua. **5.** The extensive division of Manasseh seems to be a preparation for the apportionment of part of Manasseh to Ephraim. **10.** *on the east:* This direction should be understood as northeast. The actual eastern border of Manasseh, the Jordan, is not mentioned.

11–13. These verses are undoubtedly drawn from Jgs 1:27–28; this text adds Endor to the list. Also, the Hebrew clarifies that the mention of Dor in Jos 17:11 is syntactically disconnected from the rest of the sentence. Perhaps an editor interpreted the Dor of Jgs 1:27 as Endor, but a later editor inserted the Jgs phrase about Dor, even though it did not fit in Jos grammatically; someone tried to clarify the situation by adding a further parenthesis on Dor at the end of the verse. **15.** *the forest:* Which forest is meant—the wooded areas in the western Josephite hill country or the forest of Ephraim in Transjordan (2 Sm 17:26; 18:6)? The Perizzites are usually in the western territory. The Rephaim are almost always associated with Transjordan, but cf. 15:8. *mountain regions of Ephraim:* This expression argues strongly that Joshua is directing the tribes to Transjordan; the same words are used to describe a district of Solomon that included the whole hill country of Samaria (1 Kgs 4:8). It seems arbitrary to limit this area merely to the lower half of the hill country, and thus make "the forest" (v. 15) refer merely to the northern Samaritan hill country. **16.** Although this verse originally was the start of a separate tradition, it now seems to continue the dialogue between Joshua and the Josephites; if, as is more likely, the preceding verses referred to a Transjordan expansion, this theme is now dropped, for the Josephites are concerned merely with opposition in Canaan.

17. Ephraim and Manasseh are omitted from the Greek and appear to be an addition in the Hebrew. *not merely one share:* That is, once they clear their territory, they will find it much larger than the other individual allotments. **18.** *the mountain region:* As in v. 15, the reference is to all the Samaritan hill region. *adjacent land:* It seems to refer to some of the plain area, as the mention of iron chariots suggests; this prophecy finds some fulfillment in v. 13. *if...you drive out the Canaanites:* If we can understand this final verse as a form of "blessing," it is better translated "you will certainly drive out the Canaanites."

51 **(H) Introduction to the Remaining Allotment (18:1–10).** Although this section introduces the allotments in chs. 18–19, it might seem more fitting in ch. 13, at the start of the distribution of the land. In fact, such a survey as Joshua here prescribes is logically presupposed in the Judahite and Josephite allotments of chs. 15–17. Yet this pericope is clearly in place here, and is presented at this point because it indicates the active cooperation of the remaining tribes in the settlement of the land. In 14:6–15 and 17:14–18, the D editor possessed traditions about the spontaneous measures initiated by the tribes concerned; lacking such tradition for the remaining tribes (cf. v. 3; in Jgs 1, Simeon does not initiate a plan), he wishes to indicate some particular cooperation on their part. The strong emphasis on a written description (Hebr, vv. 4, 6, 8–9) shows that the D editor wishes to attribute the document he has before him to the cooperative effort of the remaining tribes. In their boundary list we have at least some concrete sign of their cooperation!

1. *after they had subdued the land:* The Hebrew places this phrase at the end of the verse, where it seems to be merely a parenthetic reminder that the conquest ended in ch. 11. This verse is clearly a P construction ("community," "Meeting Tent"). A P editor has transferred the scene of operations from Joshua's headquarters at Gilgal (cf. geography in v. 5) to the Ephraimite city Shiloh, a change first made possible by the allotment in chs. 16–17. Historically, Shiloh was a successor to Gilgal as a national shrine, and apparently its memory lived dear in P tradition long after its destruction in the middle of the 11th cent. *Meeting Tent:* It was probably not set up in Shiloh, because the sanctuary was a temple, even before the monarchical period (1 Sm 3:15). **4–10.** Although the translation runs smoothly, the Hebrew contains apparently meaningless repetition, well explained by Noth. An original form of these verses contained an order from Joshua to the remaining Israelites to conduct a survey of the land. This order was made more specific by a later editor who introduced the three-man teams and repeated the directions of Joshua, addressing them this time to the smaller groups; the editor also noted their compliance with Joshua's orders alongside the older text that spoke of a compliance on the part of the Israelites in general. Thus, a later editor added v. 4 (including "when they return to me," v. 5), v. 8, and the conclusion of v. 10 ("casting lots..."). **7.** This verse, together with the note on Judah and Joseph in v. 5, is an explanation of the number seven in vv. 5–6; it parallels 14:3–4, where the number two and one-half is explained.

52 **(I) The Allotment to Benjamin (18:11–28).** **12.** Here begins the northern boundary, which appears, with several changes, as the southern boundary of Joseph (16:1–3). **13.** At several points, both the northern and southern boundary of Benjamin are described with reference to territory actually within either Joseph or Judah. The boundary list was originally a series of points that divided the tribes but did not specify to whom each town belonged (see comment on 15:1–12); thus, we find variations in the way the points are connected, according to which territory is being outlined. Apparently such a system could cause confusion over boundaries (cf. 17:8), but it is understandable in a more primitive society where tribal relationships were generally peaceful, and where waterholes and pasture areas were commonly shared among tribes. **12–13.** For Beth-aven, Luz, and Bethel, see comment on 7:2 and 16:2. **14.** The western boundary has only the northern and southern points. Noth believes that the boundaries of Benjamin actually extended to the Mediterranean, but that the editor drew his own western boundary to provide some area for the Danite towns he lists in 19:41–46. Noth discerns a more northern area for Dan in the original boundary document, but argues that the editor suppressed it in favor of the Philistine shore area. Cross and Wright (*op. cit.*) argue more convincingly that the western boundary of Benjamin in v. 14 is original, and that there is an area W of this boundary not described in the boundary list as we now have it. The boundary list probably traced out an area for Dan W of Benjamin, but the editor omitted these boundaries because Dan had migrated from this area to the north (see comment on 19:35–38,41–46). **15.** For the southern boundary, see comment on 15:6–9, where the border towns are listed in the opposite direction for Judah.

21–28. Although the matter is uncertain (see comment on 15:20–63), this town list may have been separated from the Judahite town list for some time before both were incorporated into chs. 13–21. In any case, the presence of the Ephraimite towns Ophrah (v. 23) and Ophni (v. 24) in the northern Benjaminite province reflects the reign of Abijah (Kallai-Kleinmann, *VT* 11 [1961] 226) or Josiah (Noth). **28.** *Jerusalem:* This city is expressly excluded from the boundaries of Judah (15:8) and included within the boundaries of Benjamin (18:16), although it was the Judahite David who conquered the Jebusite city (2 Sm 5:6–10). We can discern rival claims concerning the city (15:63; Jgs 1:8,21); perhaps Benjamin's claim to the city was a later attempt to restore the waning prestige of that tribe (see comment on 7:1–8:29).

53 **(J) The Allotment of Simeon (19:1–9).** This list gives no explicit treatment of the boundaries of Simeon, and the editor seems to be aware that he does not possess such a listing (vv. 1 and 9). Simeon was, in fact, absorbed very early into the tribe of Judah; by Saul's time, several of these Simeonite cities are said to belong to Judah (1 Sm 30:26–31); Simeon is also absent from the blessings in Dt 33, which probably date from the period of the judges. Although the tribal boundary list used in Joshua dates at least from the early monarchy (Bright) and quite possibly from the premonarchical period (Noth), the absence of Simeon's boundaries from such an early list is still possible. However, it is possible that the list contains boundary points (v. 8 seems to be a boundary fragment). Noth denies this. He points out the similarities between the Simeonite list and that part of the first Judahite province contained in 15:26–32. He argues that the Simeonite list has been simply adapted from the Judahite town list and attributed secondarily to Simeon—here, however, the editor did not remove the towns from the Judahite list, but let them remain in both places. Thus, Noth is able still to maintain one basic premise: The entire section on the distribution of the land (chs. 13–21) contains only one town list, Josiah's administrative list for Judah.

However, there are notable differences as well as similarities between 19:2–8 and 15:26–32. Also, both these lists are very similar to a third in 1 Chr 4:28–33. It is much more likely that the Simeonite list does not directly depend on the Judahite list; it is quite possible that all three of these lists are based on a single original Simeonite town list—possibly even a Simeonite boundary list (Cross and Wright). **7.** *thirteen:* One town is a later addition; 14 are listed. "Ain," and "Rimmon" are understood as one city in 15:32, but as two in 1 Chr 4:32. Ether and Ashan are listed in the 4th Judahite province (15:42)—a further argument that this Simeonite list is independent of the Judahite list in 15:26–32.

54 **(K) The Allotment of the Galilee Tribes (19:10–39).** The territory of Zebulun is described with a rather well-defined border, Naphtali and Asher with less detail, whereas Issachar has hardly any border description at all. Each tribe also seems to be provided with a town list; in the case of Issachar, it seems to comprise almost the entire allotment, while Asher apparently has it interspersed freely within the border towns.

However, from such an early document as the tribal boundary list (judges or early monarchy), we should expect rather detailed boundaries for all, or almost all, the tribes. Inasmuch as the boundary list was originally in the form of unconnected border points (see comment on 15:1–17 and 18:11–28), much of what appears to be town lists in these four tribes is actually the original border towns; through much of Asher, the connecting phrases are omitted, or are made in very elementary form (v. 27), while in Issachar, they have been almost entirely omitted because of a lack of knowledge or interest on the editor's part. This theory of the boundary lists in the Galilean tribes has been proposed by Noth, who also questions whether any genuine town lists exist in these tribes. He traces the formation of the text as follows: The primary element is the boundary document, filled out with numerous connecting phrases, or a few, or almost none, depending on the tribe. Then several towns were added from the Levitical cities in ch. 21; at this point, an editor, treating the entire matter as town lists, added the totals which appear near the end of each tribal territory (e.g., "twelve cities and their villages," v. 15). Later, the territories of Zebulun, Asher, and Naphtali were augmented further through the addition of town names from Jgs 1 (those towns that follow the word "thus" in 19:15,29; also "Beth-anath" and "Beth-shemesh" in v. 38). The material remaining is too sparse, Noth affirms, to have a genuine town list as its basis; therefore, there is no town list in Galilean territory.

That much of what appears to be town lists is actually from the boundary document is undoubtedly true. Also, as Noth points out, the final verses for Zebulun, Asher, and Naphtali (vv. 16, 31, and 39) are somewhat jarring after the numerical totals preceding them; these final verses should be understood as referring to the entire territory rather than to a number of towns. Undoubtedly, the totals are later additions. Also, the towns following "thus" in vv. 15, 29, and 30 were added still later. However, the removal of Beth-anath and Beth-shemesh from v. 38 still does not give us the total 19. It is highly doubtful that these cities can be considered an addition to the list in which they stand. In fact, differences in spelling and word order allow very little probability for direct dependence on Jgs 1 and Jos 21; only by very tenuous argument can we avoid the conclusion that there are actual town lists (of unknown origin) in v. 15, 29–30 ("Mahalab... Rehob"), and 35–38 (→ 56 below).

55 **11.** *went up west:* It appears that some of the text was lost; in fact, the remainder of the text contains no western boundary for Zebulun. However, perhaps the Hebrew for "west" (*yammāh*) was the name of a town; we get the desired number 12 (v. 15) if it is counted as a town. The absence of the western border may then have another explanation; v. 11 gives the southern border. **12–13.** These verses describe the eastern border. **14.** The northern border is given. The western points of the southern and northern borders ("wadi that is near Jokneam... valley of Iphtahel") are natural boundaries; perhaps they are to be understood as forming the western border (Noth). **15.** Noth argues that this list was borrowed from Jgs 1:30, which has only the forms "Kitron" and "Nahalol"; the other towns apparently have been lost. It is much more likely that v. 15 gives us a town list independent of Jgs 1. **20–21.** Noth states that Rabbith, Kishion, Remeth, and En-gannim were taken from Jos 21:28–29. The structure of the text in Jos 19, as well as the variations of word order and spelling in Jos 21, lend no support to this hypothesis.

25–26. This passage probably traces the southern border of Asher. It may have enclosed the entire Plain of Esdraelon (Noth), but there is disagreement about this. The remaining data do not permit us to trace a complete boundary; many of the border points are no doubt included in the other Galilean tribes, but the editor is content with a single hasty reference to Zebulun (v. 27; cf. v. 34). **28.** *Masal:* A slight emendation of the Hebrew, which reads "on the left," gives us this town, probably the same as Mishal in v. 26. Noth traces the origin of Masal, Abdon, Rehob to the names in 21:30–31. He must then say that Helkath was omitted from 19:28 because it appeared in 19:25, while Masal was retained even though it also appeared in 19:26. Rather, the dependence of 19:28 on 21:30–31 is very doubtful. *Greater Sidon:* The Hebrew may intend to include it as a boundary point; if so, both Sidon and Tyre (v. 29) should be considered later additions, because they bring the boundary line to the seacoast prematurely (Noth); cf. 11:8. The Israelites never occupied either city (Hiram of Tyre was a friend of David and Solomon, 1 Kgs 5:1–12). **30.** Ummah should perhaps be read as in the Greek, "Accho." Noth states that the five cities in this list were drawn from Jgs 1:31, but it is highly doubtful. **33–34.** It is possibly Naphtali's northern border. **34.** Naphtali also bordered on Issachar to the south, but the editor neglects to mention it.

56 **35.** *the fortified cities were:* This introduction is unique in chs. 13–19; we have undoubtedly a genuine town list in what follows. Besides eliminating Beth-anath and Beth-shemesh from the list (→ 54 above), Noth attributes Hammath, Rakkath (v. 35), and Kedesh (v. 37) to Jos 21:32. He further proposes that this list of fortified cities seems to form a line running from S to N, W of the Jordan; it was probably the western border of northern Dan, whose eastern border, E of the Jordan, is probably contained in Nm 34:7–12. Apart from the lack of solid textual evidence, this theory must contend with several serious difficulties. First, the proposed eastern boundary of northern Dan is very likely an idealistic enlarging of the Israelite territory; second, the theory must suppose that the editor suppressed an actual set of Danite boundaries and then artificially cut a section from the tribe of Benjamin where the Danite list could be located (see 18:14). Although the Danite town list was not originally part of the boundary document (Cross and Wright have attempted to trace a boundary in vv. 42–46, through Noth's highly dubious method of removing "additions" made from Jos 21 and Jgs 1, but their results are "only hypothetical"), the editor wanted to use it because it covered the area considered the earliest settlement of Dan. This theory, however, supposes that the editor felt a need to carve out borders for Dan, although he felt no such need for Simeon, even though he knew Dan as one of the northern tribes—a group for which he manifests a lesser interest. Even if he were trying to harmonize his list with the mention of southern Danite cities in Jos 21 and Jgs 1 (a very doubtful hypothesis), he could much more easily and reasonably have attributed these few cities to Dan, then mentioned the migration N (as he does, vv. 47–48), and finally have given the northern boundaries that he supposedly possessed in his boundary document. In short, it is more likely that the original boundary document contained the borders of only southern Dan, now omitted because of Dan's migration N.

57 **(L) The Allotment of Dan (19:40–48).** Noth points out that this list is in a more primitive state than the preceding Galilean material: there is no numerical total of towns in the conclusion; also, this list has not received additions from Jgs 1. Instead, it is precisely a similarity between this list and Jgs 1:35 that permitted the editor to remove the Danite list from its original position in the Judahite province list and to assign it to Dan (see comment on 15:20–63, esp. v. 45). Cross and Wright, however, argue convincingly that the Danite list cannot be reinserted into the Judahite list and should be considered independent of it. Kallai-Kleinmann (*VT* 8 [1958] 139) treats it as a separate source, based probably on Solomon's second Israelite district (1 Kgs 4:9). Noth also accepts this district as a basis for the Danite list (see comment on 18:14; 19:35–38). **41.** Because Noth considers this list originally part of the Judahite list, he must account for the presence of Zorah and Eshtaol also in 15:33. He argues that they were added secondarily to 19:42 because of their repeated association with Dan (e.g., Jgs 13:25). **47.** *was too small for them:* A slight emendation of the Hebrew gives this reading, also found in the Greek. The Hebrew as it stands, however, gives an acceptable reading: "was lost to them" (RSV). They migrated N, because they could not conquer the Canaanites on the coastal plain.

(M) Conclusion of the Allotment (19:49–51). **49–50.** These verses probably form the oldest conclusion to chs. 14–19; the Israelites, rather than Joshua, distribute the land (cf. 14:1,5). **50.** *the city which he requested:* That Joshua requested a particular city is told only here; perhaps this phrase is a later addition showing that he displayed the same initiative he demanded in 18:3 (the Hebr construction somewhat supports this opinion). **51.** Clearly a later P conclusion, it continues the thread of 14:1b and 18:1.

58 **(N) The Cities of Asylum (20:1–9).** This brief chapter combines ancient and recent materials. The most ancient part of all the material about the cities of asylum (cf. esp. Dt 19:1–13; Nm 35:9–34), is vv. 7–9 (only the first half of v. 9, reading lit., "These were the designated cities for any Israelite or stranger living among them"). Limitation of blood vengeance was surely an ancient need; the earliest asylum was a sanctuary (Ex 21:14); vv. 7–9 reflect the ancient form of the institution: Shechem and Hebron were famous sanctuaries; the name Kedesh ("holy") indicates it was also one; we can most probably say the same for the Transjordan cities. This list is surely not an invention; all these asylum cities are also in the list of Levitical cities (Jos 21); Bezer and Golan appear in the Bible only as one or the other kind of city. Also, although Golan has not been identified, its name has been preserved in the Hellenistic province Gaulanitis (roughly equivalent to the modern region of western Basan). The list dates most likely from Solomon (or possibly David) and not before, because geography rather than tribal boundaries is important for the selection of the sites, and not much after, because of Israel's losses in Transjordan (De Vaux, *AI* 162–63).

The remaining material (vv. 1–6, 9a) is definitely a later addition to the original group of cities. These verses are closely related to Dt 19:1–13 and Nm 35:9–34, although the exact relationship is not clear. Nm 35, because of its detailed legal procedure and post-exilic expressions ("community," "high priest"), is very likely the most recent of the three texts. Jos 20 seems to have a tradition very similar to that in Dt 19 as its basis. This tradition has a more ancient flavor than Nm 35; probably it is pre-exilic, although this is not sure (the "elders," Dt 19:12 and Jos 20:4, also appear in post-exilic texts; e.g., Ezr 10:8,14). However, Jos 20 has clearly undergone the influence of Nm 35 in vv. 6 and 9, and probably also in v. 3. The term "cities of asylum" (v. 2, Hebr) is not found in the older stratum of Jos 20 (see v. 9) nor in Dt 19, whereas it is frequent in Nm 35. Its origin remains obscure. If it originated in Nm 35, Jos 20:1–6 could no longer be said to have undergone some retouching from Nm 35; it would have to be a rather free combination of the traditions of Nm 35 and Dt 19, later than both of them. However, the expression may have originated here in Jos 20; if so, then vv. 1–6 are basically deuteronomic, with additions from Nm 35.

Whatever the precise relationship of the three texts, it is almost certain that they deal with a reform that was never put into effect. Dt 19 and Nm 35 preserve the memory of the ancient institution involving six cities (Dt 19:2 mentions only three at first, because the Transjordan territory was lost by this time); however, they do not name the cities for the revival of the institution. Also, the D and P traditions vary on legal procedure; Dt 19:12 and Jos 20:4, although sparse in detail, both indicate that the guilt or innocence of the refugee is decided in the asylum city, whereas Nm 35:24,25 makes it quite clear that he is to be tried before the congregation in his own town. Perhaps the greatest sign that we are dealing with pure theory is that these contradictory prescriptions could be inconsistently joined in Jos 20, so that the congregation is now that of the asylum city, where both the elders and the congregation must decide the case (vv. 4, 6, and 9).

2. *through Moses:* This phrase probably refers to Dt 19 rather than to Nm 35. **3.** *accidental:* The Hebr expression is found also in Nm 35:11; it was perhaps inserted here from that text. **4.** *the elders:* The D tradition secularizes the ancient custom. It is not said that the cities need be sanctuaries; the elders rather than the priests decide the case. **6.** This verse combines Nm 35:12 and 35:25. The P tradition restores somewhat the religious character of the institution through mention of the (religious) community and the high priest. **7.** The designation of the mountain regions seems to refer more to geographical areas than to tribes. Thus, the mountain region of Ephraim is the whole Samaritan mountain area comprising both Manasseh and Ephraim (see comment on 17:14–18). Mention of the tribes is a later addition, made in imitation of what seemed to be a reference to three tribes in v. 7. **9.** *designated cities:* In the Hebrew this term is clearly technical, more primitive than "cities of asylum."

59 **(O) Levitical Cities (21:1–42).** This section seems to be based on an ancient list of towns where Levitical families lived. Bright argues that the Israelites controlled these areas only during the 10th cent. Noth on the other hand argues that this theory fails to explain the striking gaps in the territory of the list. The central portion of Judah (including Jerusalem) and the entire hill country of Samaria (except for Shechem, a later addition) are omitted. Noth claims that this text reflects the unfinished reform of Josiah, who brought into Jerusalem the priests from the sanctuaries in Judah (2 Kgs 23:8; the presence of some Judahite towns in the list shows that this project was uncompleted) and put to death the priests of Samaria (2 Kgs 23:19–20). De Vaux (*AI* 367) questions the historicity of 2 Kgs 23:19–20, and wonders whether Noth is not acting arbitrarily in accepting this text fully, while placing a limitation on 2 Kgs 23:8. He tries to reconcile the positions of Bright and Noth through a very persuasive hypothesis: The list contains those cities where Levitical families lived, apart from those inhabiting the great sanctuaries of the period. The gap in Judah would be explained by the absorption of the Levites around Jerusalem into the Temple staff, while the gap in Samaria is analogously explained by the development of the official northern sanctuary at Bethel (cf. 1 Kgs 12:29–33).

Thus, this chapter may be based on a pre-exilic document, but it definitely manifests extensive post-exilic reworking. First, the territory is divided among those clans representing the three sons of Levi: the Kohathites, Gershonites, and Merarites (cf. also 1 Chr 6:1). Noth suspects that the division pertains to the ancient profane tribe of Levi; it seems, however, that this division of Levi is always the result of post-exilic composition or editing. Second, the clan of Kohathites is subdivided into the descendants of Aaron (the priests) and the other Kohathites (the lesser Levites). This distinction of the two groups is post-exilic. The two groups are still listed within the same clan; the distinction between them is still more thorough in Nm 3–4, where Aaron, although understood to be of Levitical origin, is not included in the genealogy of the Levites, all of whom, including all the Kohathites, are now his ministers. The assigning of these cities to the various Levitical clans was probably purely theoretical, especially since the functions of the Levites outside Jerusalem were by now greatly reduced. (→ Religious Institutions, 76:33–34.)

60 A further development is the mention of the other Israelite tribes by name. It more probably followed upon the division of the cities among the Levite clans, since the unusual grouping of the tribes in vv. 6–7 is understandable only if a later editor has already been limited by this previous division (there is a link between Gershom and Manasseh in Jgs 18:30; however, "Manasseh" is a Massoretic alteration of "Moses"). This development also seems to be theoretical to a large extent: the editor introduces the vanished tribes of Simeon and southern Dan; he does not hesitate to list noncontiguous tribes under the same clan (cf. summary in vv. 6–7); and, most of all, he assigns four cities to each tribe. Although it does not appear that every tribe has four cities, it is impossible to avoid the impression that an editor intended such a division, particularly when we also examine the parallel text in 1 Chr 6:39–66. It supplies us with a fourth city for Ephraim (since Shechem, v. 21, is a still later addition), and possibly also for Naphtali. If we regard Hebron as a later addition to the Judah-Simeon list, then we have the required eight cities for these two tribes.

The removal of Shechem and Hebron, both "cities of asylum," from the 48 cities originally divided among the 12 tribes raises a difficult question about the relationship of the asylum cities to the Levitical cities. Because the independent texts concerning the asylum cities do not link them with the Levitical cities, their association in this text seems to be a late development. It apparently followed upon the division of the original 48 cities among the Israelite tribes. This list could well have originally contained the names of the asylum cities, except for Hebron and Shechem. After the original list was divided among the 12 tribes listed in vv. 4–7, an editor added the notes identifying the asylum cities as such, and completed the list by adding Hebron and Shechem; this addition upset the original division of four cities per tribe. Meanwhile, the list appears to have undergone several changes, either through scribal errors, or, as Noth points out, through editorial attempts to identify sites the names of which had become unfamiliar (cf. numerous variants in 1 Chr 6:39–66). At a point when Jos 21 contained 48 city names, an editor noted the totals after the listing of each tribe; in the case of Judah–Simeon and Naphtali, the number was no longer four per tribe. To this final editorial stage belong vv. 4–8, which, besides summarizing the final editorial stage of the list, also expand upon v. 3 (repeated substantially in v. 8) and add emphasis to the distribution by lot. This final stage of the text is reflected in Nm 35:1–8; these latter verses refer to the six asylum cities (v. 6), the total 48 (v. 7), and apparently also to the unequal distribution of the cities among the tribes (v. 8). This text also further illustrates the theoretical character of the list by setting apart a pasture area outside each city without taking any account of the topography of each (vv. 4–5).

61 **1–2.** This part of the introduction is clearly a P notation (cf. 14:1 and 19:51). The late distinction between the "sons of Aaron" and the Levites is apparent in v. 1, since Eleazar was a descendant of Aaron (1 Chr 6:1–3). *cities be given us:* The original sense is, of course, not that the Levites be the only inhabitants, although such may be the later meaning (cf. v. 12). *pasture lands:* No doubt these were the common property of the town. **3.** This verse seems more ancient than vv. 1–2, for the Israelites distribute the territory (cf. also 14:1,5; 19:49). **4.** The priests receive the area closest to Jerusalem; this allotment is theoretical, for the place of the "descendants of Aaron" was only in Jerusalem. **11–12.** These verses attempt to reconcile the giving of the city both to the Levites and to Caleb (15:13). **21.** If Noth has correctly identified Michmethath as SE of Shechem (17:7), then Shechem was actually in Manasseh. Since it belongs to the Samaritan hill country, an area absent from the list, and since we can list four cities for Ephraim without it (taking Jokneam from 1 Chr 6:53), it can be safely regarded as a later addition, placed here because of "the mountain region of Ephraim" (cf. 20:7). **25.** Ibleam (or Jeblaam) is restored from 1 Chr 6:55 (Gk). The Hebrew here mistakenly repeats Gath-rimmon (v. 24). **32.** Hammath and Rakkath are corrections on the basis of 19:35; textual links between chs. 19 and 21 are, however, highly questionable. Perhaps a fourth city can be restored to this group from 1 Chr 6:61. If the cities there are merely variant forms for the ones here, a fourth city may have been lost at an earlier stage of the text's history (the totals for each tribe pertain to the final stage). **35.** Rimmon is a correction based on 1 Chr 6:62; the Hebrew here reads "Dimnah." Noth suspects that the appearance of Zebulun in this unusual grouping may result from a faulty identification of Rimmon by the editor who inserted the tribal names. The cities assigned to Zebulun may actually represent Transjordan territory, attributed, however, to Zebulun because of a Rimmon that existed there (19:13).

62 **(P) God's Faithfulness to His Word (21:43–45).** These verses are closely linked with the material which follows—they describe the peace that could permit the Transjordan tribes to depart (cf. 23:4; 1:15). However, they are probably a conclusion to chs. 13–21, and thus the work of the second D editor drawing upon themes in ch. 23 (cf. vv. 9 and 14). Even more, they form a summary of the entire book thus far. As is clearer from the Hebrew, the author surveys the stages of the history in reverse order: inhabitation of the land (v. 43); the "peace" that permitted the return of the Transjordan tribes (v. 44); complete victory in battle (v. 44); all finally traced back to the Word of God, his promise (v. 45). The power of God's Word is expressed in the frequent repetition (five times in the Hebr) of "all," and is also reflected in the simplicity and serenity of the passage—qualities reaching their fullest expression in the final brief clause (Moran, *op. cit.*).

The covenant literary form, so prominent in the D tradition, has influenced the construction of these verses. An examination of 23:14–16 shows that the promises (lit., "good word") are the blessings promised in the covenant. Here, the emphasis is on the fulfillment of the blessings; in ch. 23, the threats of the covenant are no less certain of fulfillment if the covenant is broken (23:14–16), as the Deuteronomist had already at least begun to experience.

63 **(V) Return of the Transjordan Tribes and the Construction of Their Altar (22:1–34).**

(A) Dismissal of the Transjordan Tribes (22:1–6). This section is clearly the counterpart of 1:12–18. But the Deuteronomist also draws on a theme from 1:7—just as the three tribes had exhorted Joshua to courage, the essential attribute of a leader (1:18), Joshua in turn points out the essential virtue needed to retain the land: fidelity to the Law (v. 5).

(B) The Altar Beside the Jordan (22:7–34). This narrative exhibits signs of an ancient tradition, an etiology that explained the origin of an altar on the western bank of the Jordan. Thus, it had some original similarity to the etiologies found in chs. 2–9; here, however, Joshua is not mentioned even once (the narrative begins in v. 9). The etiological character has also been very much reduced: the usual "to the present day" is absent from the conclusion, and the very center of the etiology, the name of the altar, has been omitted from v. 34, and perhaps also from vv. 11 and 26. The existence of an altar of worship outside Jerusalem was abhorrent to the later P editor, who so reworked the story that what was originally a place of worship became merely a memorial.

There are several further signs of P editorial work besides this most obvious one—i.e., the unique sanctuary for all the tribes (here it is Shiloh, v. 9): the whole (religious) congregation of Israel (e.g., vv. 12, 18); the various kinds of sacrifices (e.g., vv. 23, 27, 29). Also the sanctuary at Shiloh, the prominence of Phinehas, son of Eleazar, and the participation of the princes are typical of the P tradition, but they may possibly be based on elements original to the story: we know of another Phinehas at Shiloh (1 Sm 1:3), and the princes also appear in ancient texts (Gn 34:2; Ex 22:27). The "half-tribe" of Manasseh is also a latecomer to the tradition; in several places, only Reuben and Gad are mentioned (vv. 25, 32–34). This text is thus somewhat parallel to Nm 32:1–33, a tradition concerning only Reuben and Gad, yet containing the name of Manasseh in the final verse. This insertion is an attempt to bring the text more in line with the deuteronomic view that Manasseh's original settlement was on the eastern side of the Jordan. Reuben and Gad may be original to the text, but the tradition has been so thoroughly reworked that even this is not certain. Although the original form of the story has been lost, its general purpose for the P editor is clear enough: It stresses the unity of the tribes around a single sanctuary (Jerusalem). It possibly had particular application to a post-exilic settlement in Transjordan; we read of Jews living in Gilead in the time of Judas Maccabee (1 Mc 5).

64 **7–8.** These verses are a later introduction to the story. They refer entirely to the tribe of Manasseh and seek to explain why Manasseh was not mentioned in the following story ("the half-tribe of Manasseh" had not yet been inserted into the narrative). The reason for Manasseh's absence is their early dismissal, granted because of the great amount of wealth that had to be divided between the two halves of the tribe. **10.** The distinction between Canaan and Gilead in v. 9 makes it clear that the altar was built on the W bank of the Jordan; the tribes have not yet reached their destination, as is also clear in the Hebrew of v. 9. **11.** This verse has been regarded as a later addition that placed the altar on the eastern bank of the Jordan, but the Hebrew need not have this meaning. *facing the land of Canaan:* This phrase can mean "at the front of the land of Canaan," i.e., on the border (cf. 8:33; 9:1; 2 Sm 11:15, where *'elmûl* need not imply any separating distance). *across from them:* This phrase should be considered a further clarification of the preceding one and be translated "on the side of the Israelites" (cf. *'ēber* meaning "side" in 1 Sm 14:4; it is the only possible meaning in 1 Sm 31:7, which mentions the western and eastern sides of Mount Gilboa). *an altar:* Lit., "the altar," this strange use of the def. article perhaps indicates that the name of the altar was once contained here. **13.** *on Gilead:* cf. 13:31 and 17:1. Phinehas championed morality there also (Nm 25). **18.** *we are still not free of that:* Apparently the sense is that sacrifices must still be offered for this crime. These words of Phinehas have no parallel in other scriptural references to Peor. **19.** *unclean:* The sense is that it is not truly part of the promised land. For Phinehas and his company, the Transjordan tribes had built their own altar W of the Jordan so that they could have some claim to the western territory. Phinehas' words express a problem shared by the P, as well as the D, traditions: Do the Transjordan tribes share the blessings of the promised land? (See comment on 1:12–18.) The problem was made more acute, no doubt, by the fact that so much of Transjordan was either never under Israelite control or was lost to Israel even before the Assyrian invasions in the 8th cent. Ezekiel's idealistic boundaries omit the Transjordan area entirely (Ez 48). **20.** Cf. 7:10–26. **22.** The reply begins with an oath. The translation omits a clause at the end of the verse: "do not save us this day." Perhaps it should be understood as addressed to God. **26.** *this altar of our own:* As in v. 11, the Hebrew reads, simply, "the altar." Perhaps the name of the altar was contained here also. *sacrifices:* Unlike the holocaust, these offerings were eaten. **27–30.** "Sacrifices" and "peace offerings" are the same thing (De Vaux, *AI* 415–18). There is a similar use of "and" (*waw*) in v. 30, joining the "princes" and the "leaders," actually the same persons (v. 14). In these cases, *waw* means "that is" (cf. KB for other examples). **31.** *the Lord is with us:* The sense is that a sin of rebellion would have brought guilt on the whole community, but it was not committed. **34.** As Noth points out, the explanation of the altar as a witness provides no reliable indication of the original name, but may simply be based on vv. 27–28.

65 **(VI) Joshua's Farewell Address (23:1–16).** A great part of Dt seems to be a homiletic development of the covenant renewal ceremony held periodically at Shechem (Jos 24). Among the most important elements of this covenant form are: a narrative of sacred history; the stipulations of the covenant; the promises ("blessings") that observance of the covenant will see realized; and the threats ("curses") to be carried out in case of infidelity. These four elements, interwoven with a freedom permitted in homiletic style, explain the construction of ch. 23. The stipulations receive special emphasis by being placed at climactic positions in the progression: sacred history (vv. 3–4), blessings (v. 5), and stipulations (vv. 6–8); then, beginning again, history (v. 9), blessings (v. 10), and stipulation (v. 11). Throughout these three elements, the Deuteronomist employs imagery from the ancient institution of holy war: the battles of Israel are God's battles and he is their leader in battle. Now the threats are introduced (vv. 12–13), and receive such emphasis as to give the impression that the author's main purpose in this chapter is to forewarn about the possibility of their fulfillment. In v. 14, he begins afresh (note similarity to v. 1); now the history and also the blessings that the Israelites have already begun to enjoy are mentioned only to accent the certainty of punishment for infidelity. The chapter closes with a warning that makes it an apt immediate introduction to the deuteronomic history, which moves gradually to the fulfillment of the threats.

Repeated mention of the surviving nations is made, even though the Deuteronomist himself writes as though the conquest were completed (v. 14). Noth considers most of these references as later additions, but they may actually be traceable to the Deuteronomist, for it is precisely these surviving nations that will endanger the covenant, and whose influence on Israel will lead to the carrying out of the threats. This author has elsewhere highlighted the dangerous presence of these nations: Jgs 2:20–22 and Dt 7 (this latter text is a source for much of our chapter; it refers to intermarriage in v. 3, the pagan gods in v. 16, and the surviving nations in v. 22).

2. The "elders" formed a kind of senate; the "leaders" governed the tribes. *judges:* Cf. Dt 16:18. *officers:* Cf. 1:10. The reference to Joshua's age adds special solemnity to his words. **6.** The covenant form demanded that a written document of the covenant be retained; hence the mention of "the Book" (Dt). **7.** *mingling with these nations:* The Hebrew implies a sexual relationship (as in 2:3–4) further specified in v. 12. *serve them or worship them:* An expression of the Decalogue (Dt 5:9), it became a technical term for the worship of false gods. **8,12.** *remain loyal:* This Hebr expression is translated by "ally yourselves" in v. 12, where it connotes a marriage relationship. A similar relationship may well be intended in v. 8. **13.** *scourge...thorns:* The translation remains uncertain: "scourge" is found only here, and "thorns" here and in the same expression in Nm 33:55. If the translation is correct, perhaps the thorns are barbs on the end of a whip, striking the Israelites as they march into exile.

66 (VII) Epilogue: The Assembly at Shechem and the Burial Traditions (24:1–33).

(A) Assembly at Shechem (24:1–28). Chs. 23–24 are closely related, but it does not seem possible they were both joined to Jos at the same time; their presence argues for two D editions of Jos: the edition of the Deuteronomist, ending with ch. 23 and leading directly into Jgs 2:6, and a later post-exilic edition, with ch. 24 added as a conclusion to the Hexateuch (see comment on 8:30–35). Like 8:30–35, this chapter gives evidence of very ancient material, D retouchings, and also P vocabulary; unlike the former text, however, it underwent at Shechem a long history of transmission that has greatly complicated the task of discerning the original material and makes certainty at times impossible to obtain. The general history of the text can be clearly traced, however. It is based on a Shechem covenant ceremony which has given indication elsewhere in the Scriptures of having a very ancient background: in Jgs 9:46, the god of Shechem is called "El-berith" (God of the covenant); the citizens are called "men of Hemor"—i.e., in the original sense, "members of the covenant" (joined at a ceremony in which an ass ($h^emôr$) was slaughtered, according to the Amorite-Hurrite custom). Most striking evidence of all is the extrabiblical Hittite vassal treaties of the second millennium BC, which show undeniably the same basic form as Jos 24. (Cf. G. E. Mendenhall, *Law and Covenant in Israel and the Ancient Near East* [Biblical Colloquium; Pittsburgh, 1955], rep. from *BA* 17 [1954] 26–46, 49–76; for a general survey of covenant studies, cf. D. McCarthy *CBQ* 27 [1965] 217–40.) (For Shechem as a sanctuary, → Religious Institutions, 76:40; for covenant, → Aspects OT Thought, 77:74.)

Points of contact between these Hittite treaties and Jos 24 follow: the preamble, in which the suzerain gives his titles (v. 2); the historical prologue, which grounds the obligation of the vassal and indirectly assures him of future benefits (vv. 2–13); the stipulations (vv. 14, 25); the recording of the covenant in written form (v. 26); the invocation of witnesses, among them the gods of the suzerain and vassal in the Hittite form (vv. 22, 27); the formula of blessings for fidelity and curses for infidelity finds a counterpart only in a fleeting allusion to the curses in v. 20. Along with other elements of the Shechem tradition, they have been transferred to a Sinai context by the final editor (cf. 8:30–35).

The original covenant on which Jos 24 is based was probably a peaceful union of the Shechemites and the newly arrived Israelites; indeed, nowhere is Shechem listed among the cities conquered by Joshua and there is no evidence on the site for a destruction of the city from the end of the late bronze period (*ca.* 1200) to the period of the divided monarchy. Some hold that the population of Shechem included Josephites who did not go down into Egypt, an hypothesis which receives some support from the very fact of the covenant. However, the accounts of the patriarchal contacts with Shechem (Gn 12:6–8; 33:18–20; 35:1–5; 37:12–14) that would favor this theory may well be a reflection of a later Shechemite history. The peaceful union of both groups may be partially traceable to the presence of Simeonites and Levites, who occupied the city at a very early period (Gn 34).

As Dt shows, this original covenant was kept alive in the memory of Israel through periodic renewal at a covenant ceremony in Shechem. This liturgical history led to later changes in the text of ch. 24, but the text itself, containing traditions alien to the deuteronomic reform, was not incorporated into the deuteronomic history. Lest such a venerable tradition be lost, the final editor undertook the great task of neutralizing offensive elements in the tradition. The covenant ceremony is described only in a very general way in 8:30–35. Also, Jos 24 adds further detail but is not inserted into any historical context, and the greater emphasis is placed on the people's acknowledgement of God's role in their history (vv. 1–25). Thus, it stands as an epilogue, generally applicable to all periods of Israelite history. Finally, the particular stipulations and the ceremonial are neutralized by their insertion into a (predeuteronomic) Sinai context (see comment on 8:30–35). This grand plan, extending over the books of Ex, Dt and Jos, shows that ch. 24 was intended as an epilogue to an edition of the Hexateuch.

67 **1.** Shechem (Hebr *šekem*, "shoulders") was so named because of its position between the "shoulders" of Mt. Ebal to the NW and Mt. Gerizim to the SW. Possibly this shrine contained the Ark of the Covenant, but clear indications are lacking (8:33 is too recent to be a sure argument; however, the patriarchal journeys from Shechem to Bethel [Gn 12:6–8; 35:1–5] may reflect a transfer of the Ark to Bethel). *summoning their elders... officers:* It is most probably a gloss added because of 23:2. *stood in ranks before God:* An expression probably originating in the holy war ritual, it was later applied to other liturgical assemblies. **2.** The mention of Terah is awkward. It is probably an addition made to exclude the later patriarchs from the worship of other gods. Mention of such worship hinted at in Gn 28:21; 32:29; and 35:2–4 argues for the antiquity and independence of this chapter. **4.** Esau's role in this sacred history raises the question, "What happened to Jacob?" The question is not answered until v. 13.

5–6. The end of v. 5 and the beginning of v. 6 read (Hebr): "...I brought you out; and I brought your fathers out...." The former clause may be a later homiletic expansion originating in the renewal of the covenant (cf. vv. 16–18, parts of which seem to pertain to such a late development; cf. also 1 Sm 12:10–11). Other verses containing "you" forms may have undergone such a homiletic adaptation. Not all the following phrases using the "you" form can be called secondary—e.g., it is certainly original in v. 13; in others, it may also be original, emphasizing the unity of the nation through its history. **7.** The strange alteration of the Lord from the first to the third person has parallels in extrabiblical treaties and is therefore not an indication that this verse is secondary. *he put darkness:* This expression is peculiar to Jos 24. *between your people and the Egyptians:* It means between you and the Egyptians (Hebr). The Sinai covenant is not mentioned. One opinion holds that the Sinai traditions and Exodus traditions were originally separate; another argues that the events at Sinai are a ceremony commemorating the sacred history of the Exodus. Thus, the ceremony would not form part of an historical prologue (cf. McCarthy, *op. cit.*). Furthermore, the absence of Sinai may emphasize that there is no distinction between the covenant made with the ancestors and that now offered to those present.

68 **8.** *the two kings of the Amorites:* This phrase is actually found in v. 12, in apposition with "(which drove) them," and is thought to belong here instead. **9.** *prepared to war against Israel:* He actually warred against Israel (Hebr). This datum seems to contradict Dt 2:9 and Jgs 11:25. Since it presents a peculiar tradition, the material about Balaam may have been adapted later from Dt 23:5–6. **11.** *the men of Jericho fought against you:* The unique tradition contradicts ch. 6. **12.** *hornets:* Translate "panic" (KB), a typical feature of holy war. The seven nations are actually found in v. 11 (Hebr), in apposition with "(I delivered) them." They were surely added there, probably to explain "them" of v. 12, which now refers to the "two kings of the Amorites" (v. 8). If this last phrase really belongs in v. 12, it cannot mean the two Transjordan kings, Sihon and Og. Perhaps the Greek retains a better reading: "12 kings of the Amorites," meaning the Canaanite kings as a group, considered in league against Israel. Admittedly, "them" (v. 12) remains a problem, and the text has experienced some later confusion because of attempts to give the pronoun an antecedent. Possibly "them" originally meant the "men of Jericho" (v. 11). If so, then Jericho is the only battle W of the Jordan that is mentioned. **13.** Some mention of a giving of the land is necessarily original, to resolve the tension in v. 4. The entire verse may be original, Dt 6:10–11 being a later expansion of it. **14.** The final editor leaves intact only a very general stipulation, one in harmony with the Mosaic teaching. *and in Egypt:* Other gods in Egypt are not mentioned in vv. 2–13; this may be an addition to explain the continuing presence of these gods among the people (vv. 14, 23). **15.** Clearly, non-Israelites are being incorporated into the Yahwistic faith. This freedom of choice does not have a parallel in extrabiblical vassal treaties.

69 **16–18.** Much of these verses apparently dates from the covenant renewal; the vocabulary is largely deuteronomic. Verse 16 shows that the people are already Israelites. The decision to serve the Lord (v. 18) is part of the original form, however. **18.** *all the peoples, including:* It was added by one who understood "all the peoples" in v. 17 as referring to the nations W of the Jordan; or, perhaps it was added because of the seven nations in v. 12. **19–24.** After Joshua's exhortation in v. 14, vv. 19–20 sound strange. Some understand this section as a rhetorical construction, largely deuteronomic, composed by one who had already witnessed the Exile—thus the emphasis on failure to keep the covenant. Therefore, the people are named as witnesses, although the ancient form required that a witness not be one of the contracting parties. Perhaps vv. 19–24 are a later rhetorical expansion, but the date of origin remains very doubtful, for the emphasis on infidelity may be traced to the curses of the original form. Also, none of this section is clearly deuteronomic except "and obey his voice"(v.24). **25.** *made a covenant:* Lit., "cut a covenant," it probably refers to the slaughter of animals as part of the covenant ritual (Ex 24:3–8). Shechem corresponds to Shechem in v. 1. This "inclusion" marks off the section the final editor wished to stress. **26.** *Book of the Law of God:* A late expression, it is found only in Neh and 2 Chr (sometimes with a variation in the divine name) and therefore includes more than Dt; the original record was undoubtedly made on the large stone (a sacred pillar, as Ex 24:4 and Jgs 9:6 show). Read "sacred pillar" for "military station" in Jgs 9:6. The expression has been changed here in v. 26 because of Dt 16:22). **28.** Dependence on Jgs 2:6 is not likely.

70 **(B) Burial Traditions (24:29–33).** This section was probably constructed by the final editor who added the previous part of ch. 24 to Jos. He has drawn vv. 29–31 from Jgs 2:7–9, changing the order so that they now form a conclusion to Jos rather than a transition to Jgs. The notice concerning the bones of Joseph brings the Hexateuch to a close. The editor depends on Gn 33:19 and prepares for this notice through his previous additions (Gn 50:25 and Ex 13:19). The cycle is complete: Joseph had gone down to Egypt but is at last in his homeland. It was probably this same editor who added the closing note about Eleazar, whom a P editor had already placed at Joshua's side for the distribution of the land (14:1). This section makes a particularly apt conclusion, because Israelite burial sites were a sign that the land was now truly their own. **29.** *servant of the Lord:* In apotheosis, Joshua receives the title of Moses (1:10). *a hundred and ten:* Joseph also died at this age (Gn 50:22), an ideal age among the Egyptians. It seems Joseph and Joshua are intentionally paralleled: the former called his brothers down to Egypt, while the latter led the "Israelites" back into the land. Timnath-serah is Khirbet-tibneh, in the SW part of the Samaritan hill country (Noth). **32.** Hemor is personalized (but cf. introduction to vv. 1–28). **33.** *the hill:* It is "the hill of Phinehas" (Hebr), an unknown site.

8

JUDGES

John Dominic Crossan

BIBLIOGRAPHY

1 Alonso-Schökel, L., "Erzählkunst im Buche der Richter," *Bib* 42 (1961) 143–71. Eissfeldt, O., *Die Quellen des Richterbuches* (Leipzig, 1925). Garstang, J., *Joshua; Judges* (Foundations of Bible History; London, 1931). Hertzberg, H. W., *Die Bücher Joshua, Richter, Ruth übersetzt und erklärt* (ATD 9; 1953). McKenzie, J. L., *The World of the Judges* (Englewood Cliffs, N.J., 1966). Richter, W., *Die Bearbeitungen des "Retterbuches" in der deuteronomischen Epoche* (BBB 21; 1964). Robertson, E., "The Period of the Judges: A Mystery Period in the History of Israel," *BJRylL* 30 (1946) 91–114. Simpson, C. A., *Composition of the Book of Judges* (Oxford, 1957). Vincent, A., *Le Livre des Juges; Le Livre de Ruth* (BJ; 2nd ed. rev.; Paris, 1958).

For a fuller bibliographical survey, see Eissfeldt, *OTI* 241, 257, 749–50.

INTRODUCTION

2 **(I) Title.** The Hebr title of Jgs is *Šōpeṭîm*, which the LXX translated *Kritai*—hence the Vg name, *Liber Judicum*, "The Book of Judges." This Eng title does not adequately express the biblical resonance of the term *šōpēṭ*, which was most likely borrowed from the Canaanitic (cf. Am 2:3) where it meant "leader" or "prince." These men were not magistrates like today's judges, for they were not primarily administrators of judicial sentence according to either written law or oral tradition. They were charismatic leaders raised up at given times by the impulse of Yahweh's spirit, and their function was to deliver God's people from their pagan oppressors. By so doing, and especially by effecting it under divine assistance, they vindicated the salvific justice of Yahweh. Since oppression had only arisen because of the people's infidelity (Dt 28:15–68; Jgs 2:11–15), so deliverance could only come in their repentance and return to Yahweh (Dt 28:1–14; Jgs 2:18). It was guaranteed by Yahweh's fidelity to his ancient covenantal promises—i.e., because Yahweh was just. Accordingly, these charismatic leaders were the chosen instruments of vindication for his divine justice. As "judges" or as "deliverers" (Jgs 3:9,15,31), they were but instruments of Yahweh's salvific fidelity to his word.

(Grether, O., *ZAW* 16 [1939] 110–21. Noth, M., *Fest. A Bertholet* [Tübingen, 1950] 404–17. Van Imschoot, P., *ColBG* 21 [1934] 209–11.)

3 **(II) Composition.** Certain sutures are immediately evident in the book's plan. Jgs 1:1–2:5 forms a good introduction to Jgs, but so does 2:6–3:6; moreover, the latter passage connects directly with the conclusion of Jos, as Jos 24:28–31 = Jgs 2:6–9. Thus, Jgs 1:2–2:5 seems almost a diverging recapitulation of Jos itself. The central section in 2:6–3:6 appears as a carefully worked unity in which the theological thesis of the deuteronomic school (cf. W. Harrington, *IrTQ* 29 [1962] 207–22) is sketched in 2:6–3:6 and then used to interpret the history that follows in 3:7–16:31. The two appendices in 17:1–18:31 and 19:1–21:25, and their common preoccupation (17:6; 19:1; 21:25) with the sad state of premonarchical Israel, evidence a different theological outlook from either 1:1–2:5 or 2:6–16:31.

This narrative—the first introduction (1:1–2:5)—of the slow infiltration of certain tribes into their allotted territory shows that some could do no better than live alongside the indigenous population until becoming strong enough to subdue them. This narrative of "conquest" in 1:1–36 is judged theologically in 2:1–5, and the failure of the tribes to destroy the pagan inhabitants of Canaan is the sin the punishment for which will be detailed in 2:6–16:31. It is already a deuteronomic interpretation of the "conquest" period but not the polished theology of 2:6–3:6 for the later period.

Some epic stories of the settlement period had been preserved orally only in the northern traditions, while others were retained only in the southern kingdom; still others were remembered, but modified differently, in both traditions. All were combined sometime after the fall of the northern kingdom (721) in a first edition of Jgs that even then bore a deuteronomic interpretation in the presence of 10:6–16. Later, another edition of this material wished to make this interpretation even more explicit and rigid in terms of a repeated cycle of sin, oppression, repentance, and deliverance. The introduction in 2:11–3:6 was then added and the individual sagas were framed more precisely within this theology. Possibly at this same time, the D-interpreted (2:1–5) narrative of the conquest (1:1–2:5) was placed in preface to Jgs, an insertion necessitating the repetition of Jos 24:28–31 in Jgs 2:6–9. This redactor may also have deliberately omitted Jgs 9 and 16 as unedifying and irrelevant for his purpose. This complex of 1:1–16:31 (without chs. 9 and 16?) contained only six judges (Othniel, Ehud, Barak, Gideon, Jephthah, and Samson). A later redactor added six more, whose existence was recalled by the tradition but whose exploits had been long forgotten (Shamgar, Tola, Jair, Ibzan, Elon, and Abdon). The addition served to constitute a "Book of Twelve Judges," which was, presumably, this author's purpose. It was also this same redactor who replaced Jgs 9 and 16 in the framework.

Two separate narratives—that of the sanctuary of Dan in chs. 17–18 and that of the crime of Gibeah in chs. 19–21—show the interests of a later time and were added at the exilic period. They do not show the D preoccupations of chs. 1–16.

The present Jgs, then, is the result of long development within an inspired tradition (cf. R. A. F. MacKenzie, *CBQ* 20 [1958] 3; D. J. McCarthy, *TS* 24 [1963] 553–76) as chs. 1–16 came under successive waves of deuteronomic interpretation (10:6–16; 2:6–3:6; 2:1–5) before the addition of a later theology's (Chronicler's?) narration of the traditions in chs. 17–21.

(Manley, G. T., *EvQ* 31 [1959] 32–38. O'Doherty, E., *CBQ* 18 [1956] 1–7. Van Imschoot, P., *ColBG* 21, 153–60.)

4 **(III) Chronology.** If all the chronological data of Jgs were taken successively, the period would extend 410 years (3:8,11,14,30; 4:3; 5:31; 6:1; 8:28; 9:22; 10:2–3,8; 12:7,10–11,14; 13:1; 15:20–16:31). Even when we allow for a certain schematic use of the number 40 (3:11; 5:31; 8:28; 13:1), we still have much longer period than can be fitted between the ordinarily accepted time of the conquest (*ca.* 1200) and the inauguration of Saul (*ca.* 1040). Short of subjective changes in the given numbers, we must presume that much of Jgs took place simultaneously in different parts of Palestine. Israel is in strife throughout this entire period in one tribe or another and in one region or another with the indigenous Canaanites or the surrounding peoples (W. Vollborn, *Fest. B. Baumgärtel* [Erlangen, 1959] 192–96).

5 **(IV) Christian Relevance.** The OT has indirect relevance in that it was the necessary preparation for the ultimate presence of God to human history in the Christ-event. It also has direct relevance for the Christian in that the great historical crises of God's people are forever archetypal of his own life and his own Christian development. Jgs presents the crisis of idolatry as Israel encountered it in the period of the settlement—the acceptance of the God who had confronted them from without or the acceptance of the gods in their surroundings. This same crisis is basic for the existence of every Christian—the acceptance of the Absolute that meets him from without or the service of the absolute that his own hands have made.

6 **(V) Outline.** The general outline follows:

(I) First Introduction (1:1–2:5)
(II) Second Introduction (2:6–3:6)
(III) The Book of the Twelve Judges (3:7–16:31)
  (A) Othniel (3:7–11)
  (B) Ehud (3:12–30)
  (C) Shamgar (3:31)
  (D) Deborah and Barak (4:1–5:31)
  (E) Gideon (6:1–8:35)
  (F) Abimelech (9:1–57)
  (G) Tola (10:1–2)
  (H) Jair (10:3–16)
  (I) Jephthah (10:17–12:7)
  (J) Ibzan (12:8–10)
  (K) Elon (12:11–12)
  (L) Abdon (12:13–15)
  (M) Samson (13:1–16:31)
(IV) First Appendix (17:1–18:31)
(V) Second Appendix (19:1–21:25)

COMMENTARY

7 **(I) First Introduction (1:1–2:5).** This very ancient tradition tells of the conquest of Canaan by slow stages, with each tribe fighting alone or, at best, in coalition with other tribes. Compared to it, the conquest in Jos is idyllic and simplified, so that it combines in one onslaught the work of slow victory only finally accomplished under David and Solomon (cf. G. E. Wright, *JNES* 5 [1946] 105–14). The passage 1:1–2:5 is coincident with, and not successive to, the period of Jos. But the tradition whereby many of the tribes settled among the native population and were content to force them into service only with the passage of time is theologically interpreted as the primordial sin of the conquest period (2:1–5), so that the continued existence of these pagan peoples later became a divine punishment for Israel. From the historical viewpoint, it is necessary to retain both the swift strikes in the hill country, which initiated the conquest and gave the Israelites a foothold in these regions (Jos 1–12), and also the later slow infiltration that spread and consolidated these first victories (Jgs 1).

The invasion attacked first the southern hill country, where Judah and Simeon defeated Adonibezek, took Hebron, Debir, and Hormah, but could not gain control of the coastal plain (1–21). The house of Joseph invaded the central highlands and captured Bethel (22–26). To the north, the tribes of Manasseh, Ephraim, Zebulun, Asher, and Naphtali settled among the Canaanites, and, as they grew stronger, gradually forced them into slave labor (27–33). To the west, the tribe of Dan was hemmed in against the highlands and could not conquer the plains (34–36).

8 **1:1a.** The opening words stem from the final editor's attempt to show that the events of Jgs followed those of Jos; they are on the analogy of Jos 1:1a–1b. The narrative begins with the tribes that had crossed the Jordan encamped presumably at Jericho (1:16); the oracle may possibly have been consulted to the east at Gilgal (2:1; cf. 20:17–18,23,27–28). The term Canaanites is used here as a general name for the indigenous population. **2–3.** Were this mere southern bias in favor of Judah, Simeon's role would hardly have been mentioned. Judah and Simeon (cf. Gn 29:32–35) agree to attack together the territory allotted to each. **4.** The Perizzites are either a separate indigenous people of Canaan, or, more likely, the inhabitants who lived outside the walled cities (cf. Gn 13:7; 34:30). Bezek (*Ibẓiq*) does not seem a likely place for this battle, which must have occurred near Jerusalem. The text is redundant with vv. 5–6, possibly betraying editorial compression of a longer narrative (cf. Jos 10). In this case, Bezek as the location would be a conclusion from the title Adonibezek (Lord of Bezek), which is itself a punned corruption of Adonizedek (H. W. Hertzberg, *JPOS* 6 [1962] 213–21). **5.** This Adonizedek (Jos 10:1–3) led a coalition of Canaanite kings against Joshua and was defeated before Gibeon (Jos 10). **6–7.** The mutilation incapacitated the King as a warrior, and he may have been allowed to return to his city in the hope that it might then capitulate (Jos 10:1). **8.** This verse is a gloss (Jos 15:63; Jgs 1:21), because Jerusalem was captured much later under David (2 Sm 5:6–9).

9 **9.** These three sectors are the natural divisions into which Judah's territory was divided. Judah and Simeon are presumably still together in vv. 4, 9–10, and 18–19, but it is only mentioned specifically in vv. 3 and 17. **10.** There is a discrepancy between v. 10, where Judah defeats Sheshai, Ahiman, and Talmai, and v. 20, where Caleb evicts the three sons of Anak. In the light of Jos 15:13–19 (and cf. Jos 14:6–15), it seems necessary to reread Jgs in the following sequence: 1:10a; 1:20; 1:10b; 1:11–15. Therefore, Caleb is the subject from 1:10b onward. Judah and Simeon move first against Hebron in the mountain region (1:10b), but it is Caleb and not Joshua (despite Jos 10:36–37; 11:21) who takes it, and expels the three sons of Anak (1:20)—Sheshai, Ahiman, and Talmai (1:10b). (→ Biblical Geography, 73:88, 90.)

11–12. Accordingly, it is also Caleb (despite Jos 10:38–39; 11:21) who marches against Debir (Tell Beit Mirsim) on the descent toward the desert, and he promises the town and his daughter to its conqueror. **13–15.** Grammatically, Othniel can be either the nephew or the younger brother of Caleb 1:13 (Jos 15:17), but the latter is more likely; he is thus marrying his niece, Achsah. She instigated Othniel to request more land around Debir, probably as dowry (1:14a). Achsah then came to her father, "alighted from the ass" into the position of a suppliant (1 Sm 25:23), and asked that the dry land of her dowry be accorded water sources, which she obtained (1:15). Thus, Kenizzite Debir held rights to certain springs over Calebite Hebron. **16.** The Kenite, Moses' father-in-law, is called Reuel (Ex 2:18,21), Jethro (Ex 3:1), or Hobab (Nm 10:29), and, besides the term Kenite, is elsewhere called a Midianite. Possibly Reuel is to be considered a clan name, Jethro is the father-in-law, but Hobab the son-in-law; Kenite denotes function (smiths) while Midianite details origin (cf. W. F. Albright, *CBQ* 25 [1963] 1–11). The "city of palms" often means Jericho (3:13; Dt 34:3), but in this case, it must designate a city of the same name in Midian. These nomadic tribesmen had accompanied Moses as guides but refused to settle down with him after the conquest.

17. Simeon is mentioned in 1:17 because the two tribes now turn from Judah's territory (1:3–16) to his (1:17–19). They capture and devote to *ḥerem*, or sacrificial destruction (21:11; Nm 21:1–3; Dt 2:34; 1 Sm 15:3; cf. S. Gevirtz, *VT* 13 [1963] 52–62), the city of Zephath-Hormah. **18–19.** The more logical sequence would be: 1:18; 1:19b; 1:19a. Together, 1:18 and 19b give the fact and reason why Judah (and Simeon) could not conquer the three cities of the coastal plain. To the three sectors of territory in 1:9, it stands as an unconquered fourth, but their victories have also isolated Judah from the other tribes to the north. **20.** Cf. 1:10. The command was in reward for Caleb's fidelity to Yahweh after the incident of the spies in Nm 14:24; Dt 1:34–36; Jos 14:6–15; 15:13–14. The Anakim were "the giants," the predecessors of the people living in Canaan at the time of the conquest (Dt 2:10–12,20–21). **21.** Cf. 1:8. From Jos 15:63 it is likely that Benjaminites had replaced Judahites; therefore, 1:21 would not clash with the inserted 1:8 (Jos 18:28).

10 **22–26.** After the southern thrust of Judah-Simeon, Jgs narrates the attack of the "house of Joseph" (tribes of Ephraim and Manasseh) into the central highlands. They captured Bethel (Beitin); for this campaign, cf. Jos 7–8 against Ai (Bethel?). **27–28.** Because of these failures, the central foothold was separated from the tribes N of Esdraelon in Galilee by a line of Canaanite fortresses guarding the plain and the mountain passes; it was also cut off from Judah to the south by other unconquered fortress cities (1:35). The cities of Beth-shan (Beisan), Taanach (Tell Taʿannak), and Megiddo (Tell Mutesellim) enclosed them from the north. Only much later, under David and Solomon, were these cities subdued (1 Kgs 4:12) and their native inhabitants used as labor forces for the building activity of this latter monarch (1 Kgs 9:20–21). Part of these enforced labors involved the fortification of their own captured cities—e.g., Megiddo (1 Kgs 9:15). **29.** On the southern boundary of the house of Joseph's allotted territory, Ephraim could not take Gezer (Tell Djezer), and it remained as another wedge between the tribes of the center and those of the south. Eventually it also became Israelite (1 Kgs 9:15–17).

30–33. The third division of the attack was against the north, but here the tribes were unable to achieve even the partial victory of Judah-Simeon in the south (1:1–21) or the house of Joseph in the center (1:22–29). These latter had obtained some success in the mountain regions of Judah and Ephraim, respectively; scant success is mentioned concerning the north. On Hazor, not mentioned here (Jos 11), → Biblical Archaeology, 74:63. Once again it is stressed (1:30,33) that these cities were captured later under David and Solomon. **34–35.** At first the tribe of Dan had tried to establish itself S of Ephraim, but, having failed to hold the lowlands, it was forced back to the mountains around Zorah and Eshtaol (31:2,25; 18:2,8,11). The majority of the Danites later migrated to Laish (18:7), which they renamed Dan (18:29). The Amorites (Jos 10:5) designate the Canaanites, especially those in the mountains. But where Dan had failed, the house of Joseph succeeded even before the monarchy (1 Sm 6:12). **36.** For "Amorites," read Edomites as in other sources; the pass of Akrabbim was on the borders of Judah and Edom (Jos 15:1–4). The verse gives the southern boundaries between Israel and the Edomites.

11 **2:1.** The main encampment of Israel after the Jordan crossing was in the plain of Jericho at Gilgal (Jos 4:19–20), considered a holy place (H. J. Kraus, *VT* 1 [1951] 181–99; J. Mauchline, *VT* 6 [1956] 19–33). The transferral of the religious center to Bethel marks the end of the first stage of the conquest as outlined in Jgs 1. The "angel of the Lord" (Ex 23:20–22) designates the presence of Yahweh to his people as it manifests itself externally, especially by oracle. The original text had, most likely, Bethel instead of Bochim (Gn 35:8), and it was their new center for the tribal amphictyony (20:18,26; 21:2). The intrusion of vv. 1b–5a with its etymology of Bochim led to the change from Bethel in vv. 1a and 5. **1b–5a.** The summary of conquest in Jgs 1 had originally concluded with the transfer of the Ark from Gilgal to Bethel (2:1a,5b). But the editor, who wished to draw the theological lesson from Jgs 1, reinterpreted the initial failure to eradicate completely the pagan peoples of Canaan as the reason for Yahweh's refusal to assist Israel during the later stages of the conquest. The words of Yahweh in 2:1–3 explain the function of the first introduction in 1:1–2:5. The deuteronomic interpretation of the conquest in the first introduction serves as a prelude to the deuteronomic analysis (2:6–3:6) of the settlement period that follows from 3:7. **5b.** The sacrifice at Bethel would have ended the original text now summarized in 2:1a,5b (cf. Jgs 20:26). (On Bethel and Gilgal as sanctuaries, → Religious Institutions, 76:41,49.)

12 **(II) Second Introduction (2:6–3:6).** The fact that the indigenous people of Canaan had not been completely exterminated and their land given over totally to Israel, immediately formed a theological problem for their faith in Yahweh's action in history. From a simple explanation, such as that in Ex 23:29–30 and Dt 7:22, or that reflected in Jgs 2:22–23; 3:1,4, the answer grew in theological scope to the one outlined already in Jgs 2:1b–5a: The slowness of the conquest resulted from Israel's initial infidelities to God's command of total extermination, and the continuance of these peoples resulted from Israel's continuing infidelities (2:20–21). The author of 2:6–3:6 seeks to combine the lesson of the settlement period (2:6–19) with that of the conquest period (2:20–3:6): The nations were left alongside Israel, both as a punishment for past infidelities (2:1b–5a) and as a source of punishment for future sins (2:11–19). Traces of an older explanation of the conquest's failure appear in 3:2.

6–10. This passage repeats Jos 24:28–31 in the sequence 24:28,31,29–30. Since the insertion of 1:1–2:5, it is necessary to repeat Jos 24:28–31 as a conclusion to the conquest and as preparation for the account of the settlement to follow. These verses give the aftermath to the great covenant renewal at Shechem (Jos 24:1–27; cf. J. L'Hour, *RB* 69 [1962] 5–36, 161–84, 350–68). Joshua was buried at Timnath-serah (Jos 19:49–50; 24:30), or Timnath-heres (Jgs 2:9), with the former used most likely to avoid the latter's pagan name. **11–19.** There is evidence of two traditions combined in this statement of the deuteronomic thesis: 2:12,14b–15,18–19 (D) and 2:13,14a,16–17 (non-D). The rhythm of sin, punishment, repentance, and deliverance, in which the narratives of the individual judges are framed (3:7,12; 4:1; 6:1; 8:33; 10:6) and the history of the entire period is interpreted, becomes obscured in the process of combination. There are divergent traditions on the effect of the judges' actions: no avail (2:16–17); or temporary fidelity (2:18–20). Also, the "cry" of distress and repentance that would have been expected after 2:16 appears only obliquely in 2:18b (cf. 3:9,15; 4:3; 6:6; 10:10). Thus, the editor who is interpreting the epics of the judges is doing so according to traditions that preceded his own work.

13 The core of Israel's covenant obligations, based on Yahweh's gratuitous deliverance of them from Egypt, was fidelity to himself; all the other stipulations depended on this first commandment. Idolatry concretely meant allegiance to the local Baals of Canaan (2:11) or to the consorted couple of the male and female divinities of the fertility cults, the Baals and Ashtaroth of that land (2:13). These two names are used quite often in the OT as general appellations for the gods and goddesses of the Canaanites; more properly, Baal is the main deity of the Ras Shamra texts (W. F. Albright, *CBQ* 7 [1945] 5–31) and Ashtaroth (or Astarte), the mother goddess, is his consort and the goddess of fertility. The sin of idolatry begets punishment by oppression from the surrounding nations (2:10–15). The function of the charismatic judge as deliverer or savior (2:16,18) makes him the instrument whereby the covenantal justice of Yahweh is vindicated. The tradition that the people did not follow even the judges (2:16–17) is not that accepted by the redactor of Jgs; he writes 2:18–19 as his thesis and lets it stand beside this former statement. **20–21.** These words reflect the theology of 2:1b–5a rather than that of 2:11–19; they revert to the problem of the indigenous and unconquered peoples of Canaan, who continue to exist within the boundaries of the promised land because Yahweh keeps them there as a penalty for Israel's reiterated infidelity. **22–23.** This tradition differs from that in 2:20–21; here, the nations are left alongside Israel as a divine trial to test their fidelity. It represents another theological interpretation of the same facts; that will appear again in 3:1,4, and it seems to pertain to the non-D strand incorporated into 2:11–19 (compare 2:17 with 3:4).

3:1. This verse continues the "trial" explanation of 2:22–23. **2.** This obvious addition gives yet another explanation for the same facts: The nations were left to teach a new generation of Israelites the art of war. **3.** The catalogue of indigenous and unconquered inhabitants of Canaan follows. "The five" are of the cities of Gaza, Ashdod (Azotus), Ashkelon, Gath, and Ekron (Jos 13:3). The term "all the Canaanites" does not have the same extension as in Jgs 1; here, it refers only to the population that Israel had not subjugated, especially that of the plains (Jos 13:4). The Hivites (Jos 9:7) should read "Hittites" (1:26; Jos 11:3), whose southern border alone is indicated, and more exactly in Jos 13:5. Thus, the writer claims for Israel, but admits it does not yet possess, the entire coastal plain, the lowlands of the Philistines to the south, and the Lebanon possessions of the Hittites to the north. **4.** This verse expresses the theological view of 2:22–23; 3:1. **5–6.** A repetition, in general, of 3:1,3–4. It would fit well as the culmination of the deuteronomic interpretation in 2:12,14b–15,18–21 (cf. Dt 7:3–4; Jos 23:12). Most of these names have been mentioned already (1:4,21,26,34–35; 3:3), and this is the standard list (Ex 3:8; Dt 20:17).

14 **(III) The Book of the Twelve Judges (3:7–16:31).** In its present form, 3:7–16:31 contains six judges mentioned in some detail and six others who are merely mentioned in passing.

(A) Othniel (3:7–11). The author had little information on the exploits of Othniel (1:13–15; cf. H. Hänsler, *Bib* 11 [1930] 391–418; 12 [1931] 3–26,276–96). Apparently, he knew only of a victory of Othniel over Cushan-rishathaim and fleshed out the narrative with the deuteronomic theology of Jgs 2:11–19: sin (3:7), punishment (3:8), repentance (3:9), and deliverance (3:10–11). The sin was idolatry with "the Baals and the Asheroth"; this latter term is another name for Astarte (2:13), but was also used to denote the wooden cult symbols of that goddess that stood beside the altar (6:25,28,30). The punishment is oppression by Cushan-rishathaim (E. Taubler, *HUCA* 20 [1947] 137–42), an ironic name meaning "Cushan-of-double-evil." In Hab 3:7, Cushan is paralleled with the land of Midian, and it is argued that instead of Aram Naharaim (v. 8) and Aram (v. 10) we should read "Edom." Therefore, the text originally intended an invasion by the nomadic Edomites into the territory of Judah-Simeon. A judge from Judah thus opened the book, and the paucity of traditional information about him merely served the better to exemplify the deuteronomic thesis in 3:7–11.

15 **(B) Ehud (3:12–30).** The exploits of Ehud (E. Auerbach, *ZAW* 51 [1933] 47–51; E. G. H. Kraeling, *JBL* 54 [1935] 205–10) are framed in the usual interpretation of sin (3:12a), punishment (3:12b), repentance (3:15a), and deliverance (3:15b), but the details of the original narrative are left untouched in 3:13–14,16–30. **12–14.** Moab is allied with his northern neighbor, the Ammonites, and the southern nomads, the Amalekites (6:3). The allies capture Jericho, "the city of palms," in the territory of Benjamin. Thus, Ehud is of the clan of Gera (Gn 46:21) and of the tribe of Benjamin. He leads the bearers who carry the tribute to Eglon. **16.** The story unfolds slowly, "left-handed" (v. 15) prepares for "right thigh" (v. 16); "a foot long" (v. 16) prepares for "very fat" (v. 17). **19–20.** There are slight traces of two traditions combined in the narrative: one places the event E of the Jordan in Moab, so that Ehud passes Gilgal (E of Jericho) as he returns to Ephraim (3:19,26); the other places the event at the oasis of Jericho (3:14,28). The scene is most likely Moab, and it is the occupation troops within Israel's territory who are slain in 3:28–29. Gilgal was an ancient holy place, the cromlech stones of which were traditionally associated with the Jordan passage (Jos 4:19–24). For such a divine message from the holy place at Gilgal, private communication was necessary and the servants withdrew. The junction of the two narratives shows in the doublet nature of 3:19 and 20. Ehud's preceding tribute and subsequent return without retinue would disarm suspicion. The final words of the Hebr text (after "from his body") are textually corrupt, and all emendations are conjectural (P. Joüon, *Bib* 21 [1940] 56–59); they are best omitted (as in CCD; possibly a dittography from the start of 3:24). (For the territory of Moab, → Biblical Geography, 73:43–46.)

23–25. Ehud departs as he had entered, but he locks the door after him (cf. "Key" in *EDB*). The servants, seeing him depart, return (v. 19) to their master and, finding the door locked, presume he has gone to sleep (v. 24; cf. 1 Sm 24:3). **26–29.** Ehud escapes via Gilgal and gathers the Israelites. There are again traces of two different traditions in vv. 27–28, as previously in vv. 24–26. They hold the fords from Israel into Moab and thus cut off the retreat of the Moabites. **30.** This formula is the standard closing one of the theological framework (4:23; 8:28; 11:3), but Moab is defeated rather than conquered.

16 **(C) Shamgar (3:31).** Shamgar is one of the "minor" judges, but without their distinctive formulas (10:1–5; 12:8–15); also, 4:1 is connected directly with 3:30, so that their juxtaposition precedes the addition of 3:31. Many of the ancient versions place 3:31 after 16:31, so that both Samson and Shamgar would have been anti-Philistine heroes. Possibly a later scribe inserted the name here because of its mention in 5:6. There may also be some confusion between the anti-Philistine hero, Shammah, son of Agee (2 Sm 23:11–12), who was probably neither an Israelite nor a judge. The "oxgoad" could have been easily used as a spear; possibly it was tipped with iron, for it was a tool rather than a weapon (1 Sm 13:19–22).

(Danelius, E., *JNES* 22 [1963] 191–92. Hertzberg, H. W., *TLZ* 79 [1954] 285–90. Maisler, B., *PEQ* 66 [1934] 192–94.)

17 **(D) Deborah and Barak (4:1–5:31).** The prose narrative of Jgs 4 preludes the triumphal ode of Jgs 5, but this latter is itself almost contemporaneous with the events, as the hyperbolic vehemence of its contempt and the primitive poetry of its form indicate. The prose account mentions Jabin of Hazor (4:2; cf. S. Yeivin, *Mélanges A. Robert* [Paris, 1957] 95–104) and identifies Sisera, who alone is mentioned in the poetry account, as his general of chariotry. It is most likely that Jgs 4 is attempting to combine a tradition such as that of Jos 11:1–11 from an earlier period with the battle between Barak and the forces of Sisera (Jgs 4–5) at a later date. The author of Jgs 4 had not only the poem as a source but also an older prose account containing details not found in the poem (4:4,6,13), and the identification of the battle against Jabin with that of Sisera may already have taken place in this source. (For the Plain of Esdraelon, → Biblical Geography, 73:105–108.)

4:1. This verse is the standard statement of the sin theme (2:19), and it connects directly with 3:30. **2–3.** The punishment theme is composed of the combination of two traditions: that of the Jabin battle and that of the Sisera combat. The juncture was effected by making Sisera the leader of Jabin's forces, but it creates serious problems as the narrative proceeds. The chariotry held command of the Esdraelon Plain (Jos 17:16). **4–5.** Deborah was, like Miriam (Ex 15:20), a prophetess, but her function as judge resembles that of Samuel (1 Sm 7:16–17) rather than the other military leaders of Jgs. She interpreted the will of Yahweh to disputants who came to her for decision. Deborah's palm tree, between Ramah (Er-Ram) and Bethel (Beitin; cf. 1:23) would be between 5 and 12 mi. N of Jerusalem; this passage reflects a confusion with the oak of Deborah, nurse of Rebecca (Gn 35:8). No doubt the location of judgment was somewhere much farther N and close to the scene of Jgs 4–5. **6–7.** Barak lived at Kedesh, N of Hazor. He was summoned to Deborah, and a residence for her in the Zebulun-Naphtali region makes 4:6,9–10 more understandable. By divine command he is to attack the chariotry of Sisera from the wooded vantage of Mt. Tabor along with the forces of Naphtali and Zebulun. Sisera and Jabin are once again mentioned in passing. **8–10.** Barak and Deborah gather the tribal forces at Kedesh, requiring a march past Hazor to reach Mt. Tabor—an unlikely strategy if Jabin of Hazor really belonged to the narrative.

18 **11.** This verse serves as preparation for 4:17, so it will not have to interrupt the narrative there. Heber the Kenite had left the main body of his tribe in the south (1:16); on the "terebinth," cf. Jos 19:33. **12–13.** The Wadi Kishon (4:7; 5:21) drains the plain, and the northern tributaries to it are W of Mt. Tabor. **14–16.** The attack was launched at divine command, and the chariotry became mired in the plain flooded by the Wadi Kishon (5:20–22); thus, Sisera himself had to dismount and flee on foot. **17–22.** Once again it would be difficult to explain Sisera's flight directly past his master's city of Hazor and on to Kedesh, unless Jabin of Hazor did not really belong to the original narrative. The comment in v. 17 about peace is interpretative and renders the act quite heinous and unlikely. The nomadic women erected the tents, and Jael uses only a wooden tent peg to kill Sisera (cf. 5:25–26). **23–24.** Once again Jabin is introduced (4:2,7,17); the standard ending for the deliverance theme is begun in vv. 4 and 23–24, and completed in 5:31b. The author who placed the triumphal ode in Jgs considered Deborah herself as the source of the poem; but verses in the poem itself where Deborah speaks in the first person (5:7b) are uncertain. The addition of "and Barak" in 5:1 may be even later, and introduced in the light of 5:12. The general structure of the poem follows: 2–11, overture, with 2–5 reiterated in 9–11 so that 6–8 is the core of the exordium; 12–18, the muster of the amphictyonic league of tribes; 19–22, the battle and victory; 23–30, death of Sisera.

(Blenkinsopp, J., "Ballad Style and Psalm Style in the Song of Deborah: A Discussion," *Bib* 42 [1961] 61–76. Gerleman, G., "The Song of Deborah in the Light of Stylistics," *VT* 1 [1951] 168–80. Piatti, F., "Una nuova interpretazione metrica, testuale, esegetica del cantico di Debora," *Bib* 27 [1946] 65–106, 161–206 [cf. appended bibliog., 207–9]. Seale, M. S., "Deborah's Ode and the Ancient Arabian *Qasida*," *JBL* 81 [1962] 343–47. Weiser, A., "Das Deboralied. Eine gattungs- und traditionsgeschichtliche Studie," *ZAW* 71 [1959] 67–97.)

19 **5:2.** The subject of the poem is given; for the leaders (2a) and the warriors of the victory (2b), the audience is invited to bless the Lord (2c)—thus, the invitation (Bless the Lord!) rather than statement in both 5:2c and 9b (C. Rabin, *JJS* 6 [1955] 125–34). **3.** The verse uses standard, parallel word pairs (cf. Gn 4:23; Nm 23:18; Ps 2:2; Hab 1:10). The "I" could be Deborah or the collective Israel (Ex 15:1). **4–5.** The divine advance is here described as Yahweh comes to aid his people against Sisera. He comes from "Seir," in poetic parallel with "land of Edom" (Gn 32:3), which reflects the ancient belief in Sinai (Dt 33:2) as the special dwelling place of God (N. Glueck, *JAOS* 56 [1936] 462–71). The imagery is standard symbolism for divine presence since the great theophany of Sinai itself (Ex 19:16–18). This recollection of the Exodus convinced some scribe to add "This is Sinai" (but cf. W. F. Albright, *BASOR* 62 [1936] 26–31) in the margin as an explanation of "Mountains" (5:5); thence, it entered the text after "Lord." But the verses refer here to the divine presence in battle against Sisera (cf. Ps 68:7–10) and not directly to Sinai. **6–7a.** The state of Israel before the deliverance is depicted in 5:6–8. Shamgar is not the person in 3:31 but must be some Canaanite ruler associated with the oppression of Sisera. Possibly the reference is not only to the dangers of commerce and travel in this period but also to attempts to isolate and separate the Israelite groups from one another, rendering them easier to control. **7b.** Grammatically, either first or second person is possible; in view of 5:12,15 "you" is more likely. It is addressed to, not by, Deborah. **8.** The verse continues 5:6–7c, giving the background to 5:7b. The text of "new gods" is uncertain, and translations are hypothetical; as it stands, it would refer to the sin of Israel and the succeeding divine punishment, according to the deuteronomic thesis, but this reading was hardly the original. **9–11.** In general, the passage repeats vv. 2–5, thus binding the overture to the poem. The ideas of subject (vv. 2, 9), audience (vv. 3a, 10), and proclamation (vv. 3b, 11a) and of divine intervention (vv. 4–5, 11b) are again repeated (cf. Seale, *op. cit.*, 345; C. Goodwin, *JBL* 63 [1944] 257–62).

20 **12.** After the exordium (vv. 2–11), the muster of the tribes for battle is described (vv. 12–18). In context, this verse must be seen as a call to Deborah and Barak to gather the tribes—Deborah to incite the warriors to valor and Barak to lead them into battle (cf. A. Fernandez, *Bib* 2 [1921] 61–65). **13.** The gathering of the tribes is described in general in v. 13 and then in detail in vv. 14–15a and 19, for those who came, and in vv. 15b–17, for those who did not respond to Barak's call. The meaning of v. 13 is clear although the exact reading is doubtful: Israel, the people of God, went down to battle as brave warriors. The original plan presumed behind vv. 14–18 is that all the tribes, except Judah and Simeon, isolated to the south, were to converge to the assistance of Zebulun and Naphtali, the core of the revolt (4:6,10; 5:14–15,18). This plan would presumably have given three points of attack and convergence on the chariotry-held plain of Jezreel. But four of the tribes did not come to join the attack—Reuben, Gilead-Gad, Dan, and Asher—while six answered the amphictyonic muster—Ephraim, Benjamin, Machir-Manasseh, Zebulun, Issachar, and Naphtali; on the league of the tribes, cf. Bright, *Hist.* 142–60.

14–15a. The "house of Joseph" (1:22–29; 2 Sm 19:20) appears in three sections after the invasion: Ephraim, Benjamin, and Manasseh; Machir is here used for Manasseh (Nm 26:29; 32:39; Jos 17:1–13). After the mention of the three tribes from S of the plain come those from its northern flank: Zebulun and Issachar. Most likely we must read "Naphtali and Barak" (4:6) for "Barak"; thus, both Zebulun and Naphtali alone are mentioned twice (5:14–15,18; 4:6,10), for they were the heart of the attack by the six tribes. **15b–17.** Reuben is especially reproached for not joining the attack; the tribe would later be swallowed by Moab and lost to history (Dt 33:6). Gilead is also castigated; intended is the tribe of Gad, settled E of the Jordan in Gilead (Jos 13:24–28). Dan is now dwelling to the north (1:34; 17–18) and neither it nor adjacent Asher joined Barak. The phrase "in ships" refers to Dan's association by location with the Phoenicians (18:7). **18.** Zebulun and Naphtali are singled out for special praise again as the center of the revolt (4:6,10; 5:14–15).

21 **19–22.** After the muster of the amphictyonic tribes (vv. 12–18), the actual battle and victory is described (vv. 19–22). The gathering place in 4:6,12,14 was Mt. Tabor, where the boundaries of Zebulun, Issachar, and Naphtali met. It is not mentioned in Jgs 5, but the scene of the battle is "Taanach by the waters of Megiddo." The "waters" are the southern tributaries of the Kishon (4:7,13), which drains the plain of Jezreel to the Mediterranean N of Mt. Carmel. The phrase in 5:20 may be no more than poetic hyperbole, but it would seem that behind Jgs 4:7,15 and 5:20–22 lies the fact that a sudden storm trapped and bogged down the chariotry of Sisera between the swollen arms of the Kishon. They were then easily routed by Barak's tribes. This theory would also explain why Sisera fled on foot (4:15).

23–24. The poem hurries over the actual battle to linger with gleeful irony on the death of Sisera (5:23–30). The account is told in contrast between the actuality (vv. 25–27) and the possibility (vv. 28–30), and the balanced curse and blessing (vv. 23–24) appears as the overture. "Meroz" is possibly Khirbet Marus, S of Kedesh. It is cursed for not having slain the fleeing Sisera, in contrast with the act of the nomad Jael. **25–27.** The death of Sisera and the vicious irony of the counterpointed vv. 28–30 show the emotional intensity of the composition. The description of the murder is not that of Jgs 4:18–21; the latter account seems based on a misunderstanding of the poetic parallelism of 5:26a. The picture in 5:25 is of a man struck heavily from behind as he drains a heavy bowl of curdled milk. For "left hand" and "right," we must understand the standard parallelism (Is 48:13; Pss 21:9; 26:10; 74:11; 80:18; 91:7); the right hand is meant so that only one death instrument is actually mentioned in the poem: a heavy tent peg. It parallels a very vague and general word simply denoting an instrument for striking, rather than the specific "workman's mallet." Thus, 5:26a–b are in poetic parallelism and describe one single action of Jael. Sisera falls at her feet and the reiterated verbs of 5:27 gloat a savage chorus over his corpse. **28–30.** Sisera appears as a king in his own right and not only as a general of Jabin. The poem ends on a note of mocking irony for the mother's worry. **31a.** The concluding line summarizes the theology of the ode. **31b.** The standard deuteronomic "rest" terminates the narrative (4:23–24).

22 **(E) Gideon (6:1–8:35).** The narrative is framed in the usual deuteronomic formulas: "offended," "delivered" (6:1), "cried" (6:2), "save" (6:14). The problem of literary criticism is difficult. The events of 6:1–8:3 are not continuous. The opening in 6:1–6 shows traces of two traditions: the enemy is either Midian (6:1–2,5–6) or Midian, Amalek, and the Kedemites (6:3–4). The narrative in 6:7–40 has two complexes of the following: divine messenger, divine sign, and altar to Yahweh (6:7–10,25–32,36–40 and 6:11–18,22–24,19–21). It seems likely that there are two separate events behind chs. 6–8 and not just two differing traditions of the one happening: an attack by the Kedemites (only?) on Gideon's clan results in their pursuit under divine impulse and their eventual defeat beyond the Jordan (6:3–4,7–10,25–32,34,36–40; 7:2–8; 8:4–21; but actually 8:12 = 7:9–22a). Later, Gideon leads a confederation of the clans to a decisive victory over the Midianites near Jezreel (6:1–2,5–6,11–24,33,35; 7:1,22b,23–25; 8:1–3), but the details of this battle are not given.

(Alonso-Schökel, L., "Heros Gedeon: De genere litterario et historicitate Jdc 6–8," *VD* 32 [1954] 3–20, 65–76. Daube, D., "Gedeon's Few," *JJS* 7 [1956] 155–61. Kutsch, E., "Gedeons Berufung und Altarbau," *TLZ* 81 [1956] 75–84. Malamat, A. "The War of Gideon and Midian: A Military Approach," *PEQ* 85 [1953] 61–65. Penna, A., "Gedeone e Abimelec: Genere letterario e origine di Giudici 6–9," *BeO* 2 [1960] 86–89, 136–41. Whitley, C. F., "The Sources of the Gedeon Stories," *VT* 7 [1957] 157–64.)

6:1. It is clear from 6:25–32 that the sin was, as usual, idolatry with the Canaanite gods. Midian (Gn 25:2–6) was composed of camel-riding nomads of the Arabian desert whose novel method of swift travel and attack made their threat exceedingly dangerous. The settled Israelites were now in their own turn under nomadic attack. **2.** The annual devastations at harvest time necessitated special procedures for warning and refuge. **3–5.** The marauding bands are here amplified into Midian, Amalek, and the Kedemites; all are Bedouin, but the latter two are from the southern and eastern desert, respectively. Two traditions seem to merge at this point. **6.** Verse 6 is the standard deuteronomic phrase for repentance. **7–10.** The narrative proper opens with two divine messengers—a prophet in 6:7–10 and an angel in 6:11–18; the former message seems abbreviated by the lack of any concluding divine threat (2:1–3; 10:11–16). Presumably, the combination of a second tradition in 6:11–18 has caused this condition. On Amorites, see comment on 1:34. There is a separate strand of tradition on Gideon in 6:7–10,25–32,36–40, and it was possibly the missing conclusion of 6:7–10 that originally prepared the way for 6:25–32. **11–18.** The account of the divine message (vv. 11–18), sign (vv. 19–21), and altar to Yahweh (vv. 22–24) is older and more anthropomorphic than the parallel account of message (vv. 7–10), sign (vv. 36–40), and altar (vv. 25–32) in the other tradition. The divine message is brought to Gideon by an "angel" (6:11; but cf. 6:14,16,23) at the sacred tree in Ophrah (Et-Teiyibeh?). Abiezer was a clan of Manasseh settled W of Jordan (Jos 17:2). Gideon was working in a concealed place from fear of the Midianite bands. **19–24.** The divine sign guaranteeing the charismatic election has its parallel in the other tradition in 6:36–40 (D. R. Ap-Thomas, *JTS* 41 [1940] 175–77). In the narrative, an original offering of food (Gn 18:3–8) is converted into a communion sacrifice offered by Gideon and accepted in holocaust as a divine sign (cf. parallel sacrifice in 6:25–26). The fire from Yahweh consecrated the sanctuary as his (Lv 9:24; 1 Kgs 18:38) and Gideon erected an altar (cf. parallel in 6:26). The name given to it is "Yahweh-Šālôm" (God is peace), a reference to the divine assurance of peace ("calm") in 6:23.

23 **25–32.** In 6:11–24, Gideon's call is told in terms of his change of a Baal sanctuary (v. 11) into a Yahwistic one (v. 24) by the erection of a new altar (v. 24) and sacrifice (v. 21). This narrative is parallel, but it also adds the result. The Baal altar is replaced by one to Yahweh, and the sacred symbol ("pole") is burned in kindling for the sacrifice. As priest of Baal (6:11), the words of Joash save Gideon, but the irony may be that of the author and not Joash! Original names with Baal endings in Israel denoted admission that Yahweh was the lord (*baʿal*), but as Baal became the synonym for idolatry, these names were changed or reinterpreted. It is more likely that Gideon was originally Jerubbaal (lit., "the Lord will take action" [for, not against] the name bearer), which was changed to Gideon either after the charismatic call or in later tradition. **33.** The Midianites have crossed the Jordan and control the Jezreel plain (4:3). Possibly the addition of Kedemites (6:3–4; 8:10) is from a different incident in which Gideon fought against them. **34.** This verse continues the tradition in 6:3–4,7–10,25–32, and may refer only to Gideon's counterattack for the murder of his clansmen (8:4–21). **35.** The tribes to the immediate south (Manasseh) and north (Asher, Zebulun, Naphtali) of the plain are called to battle (4:6,10; 5:14–18). **36–40.** This divine sign parallels the other tradition in 6:19–21; but God addresses Gideon without any intermediary (S. Tolkowsky, *JPOS* 3 [1923] 197–99).

7:1. It continues the situation of 6:33. The opposing forces were encamped toward the southeastern end of the plain: Harod is ʿAin Tubaʿun and "the hill of Moreh" is Jebel Dahi (Vincent, *op. cit.*). **2–8.** The 300 men were possibly the forces Gideon led by forced marches to a night attack on the Kedemites (?) when they had withdrawn beyond the Jordan after an attack on his own clan (8:4–21). It would have been wiser to execute this fast pursuit and night attack with selected warriors and not a vast army. The large numbers (7:3) might refer to the tradition's recall of the numbers in the tribal muster later against Midian. In this case, "the water" would be the Jordan, which they are going to cross in pursuit of the Bedouin (8:4). The reason for the choice is not clear; possibly one who "laps up the water as a dog" retains his weapons and bespeaks the trained warrior; one who "kneels down to drink" would, in this interpretation, cup his hands and have to leave his weapons momentarily aside. The departure of the others left Gideon with an extra supply of horns, which prepares for the strategy to follow. The reference in 7:8b is in line with 6:33 and 7:1. **9–15.** The hypothesis is that the vengeance pursuit by Gideon, which is told in 8:4–21 but without the details on its concluding battle (8:11–12), is presented in full detail in 7:9–22a. The battle in which Gideon and the tribes routed Midian appears only in the account of the end of the battle in 7:23–8:3. The "dream" is taken symbolically: "barley bread" stands for the settled peasantry while the "tent" refers to the marauding nomads. If the name of Gideon is not an editorial amplification, it may support the idea that it was Gideon's clan the nomads had attacked, and thus they feared counterattack specifically from him (8:18–19). (For the region of the battle in 7:1–8, → Biblical Geography, 73:111.)

24 **16–22a.** This account of the night attack seems to embody two slightly different traditions: in one, the alarm is caused by the lamps and the battle cry and flight ensues; in the other, the sudden trumpets arouse the camp and they fight with one another in their panic. Horns and a battle cry were hardly simultaneous; nor were jars and horns handled at the same time. The battle cry should be the same in 7:18 and 20, but 7:14 has intruded the "sword" in 7:20. The distinction of the traditions shows in the two terminations in 7:21 and 22a. **22b.** A similar fusion of two traditions explains this double set of directions. Both agree that the enemy fled southward along the Jordan Valley, intending, no doubt, to cross as soon as possible S of Beth-shan. **23.** This verse repeats the muster mentioned in 6:35 but omits Zebulun; its present position is editorial expansion of 7:24–25. In the battle with the Midianites, these tribes were with Gideon, which so infuriated Ephraim. Hence, 7:23–8:3 must be the conclusion of the (unmentioned) battle between the northern confederacy and the Midianites, and not the vengeance raid by Gideon narrated in 8:4–21 and detailed in 7:2–22a. **24–25.** Ephraim is called to cut off the fleeing Midianites at Beth-barah—possibly Tell Farʿah (Vincent, *op. cit.*)—where the wadi enters the Jordan and the fleeing army would be caught between the streams. The two chiefs are slain, and an editorial comment in v. 25b seeks to join 7:24–25a and 8:4–21 by having the Ephraimites cross the Jordan to meet Gideon (F. Zimmermann, *JBL* 71 [1952] 111–14).

25 **8:1–3.** The Ephraimites considered themselves the leading tribe (12:1–6) and probably sought an excuse to relieve the tribal confederacy of some of their booty. Gideon's deferential reply placates their pride. **4–9.** This narrates the vengeful pursuit of Gideon across the Jordan with, in the hypothesis advocated above, 300 men of his own clan. Both Succoth and Penuel would be on an eastern route following the Jabbok River. The background presumes that Gideon is far from victorious. The territory is that of Gad (5:17). The threat of 8:7 is that he will crush them in beds of thorns and thistle, as grain is threshed. **10–12.** The statement in 10b is editorial harmonization of 10a with the preceding victory in 7:24–8:3; the numbers are certainly exaggerated. The nomads are heading on a southeastern route toward the desert and already believe themselves to be secure. The attack of 8:11–12 is that detailed already in 7:9–22a. Gideon brings the captive chiefs back to his home (Ophrah?) to revenge there the blood of his slain clansmen. **13–17.** Returning by a different route, Gideon punished first Succoth and then Penuel. **18–21.** Gideon brought back to his home the two captive chiefs and recalls to them their attack on his own clan near Mt. Tabor, which had started his pursuit of them across the Jordan. Jether was next in line of obligation for the performance of the blood vengeance, and it is offered to him as an honor as well as a further degradation of the captives.

22–23. Two separate traditions are used by the deuteronomic author in 8:22–23 and 8:30–9:57. Both agree that the victory of Gideon over the Midianites, whose termination was recounted in 7:22b,24–8:3, led to his assuming the function, even if not the title, of king over certain clans centered around Shechem and that eventually his family went down in ruin. However, one tradition explains it in terms of the golden ephod that led to idolatry (8:22–26), whereas the other explains it in terms of Abimelech and Jotham (9:56–57). Both accounts have received deuteronomic coloring (8:28,33) and have been integrated into the general plan of Jgs (10:1), but whereas the former account was specifically anti-idolatry, the latter narrative was originally directed primarily against the idea of hereditary monarchy (G. H. Davies, *VT* 13 [1963] 151–57). The offer of the monarchy in 8:22–23 is accepted, but the title of king is not, because of religious scruples; from the action in 8:24 and the narrative in 9:2, we must understand 8:22–23 as acceptance of power but not title (1 Sm 8:7; 10:19; 12:12). **24–27.** No doubt Gideon intended the golden ephod as a symbol of Yahweh's rule through him. The ephod is especially associated with oracles (8:22–23); it was made from rings (earrings?) taken as booty from Midian (Nm 31:50) and was thus a symbolic image plated with gold. It was placed at Ophrah (6:11,24) as the seat of Gideon's rule. The details of spoil in 8:26b refer to the booty that fell to Gideon as leader and not to what was accorded him for the ephod. The ruin of Gideon's house detailed in the other tradition in 8:30–9:57 is here attributed to eventual abuse of the ephod symbol as an idol.

26 **28.** The verse is the standard deuteronomic termination to the history of a judge (but cf. 10:1). **29.** Originally, the tradition in 7:24–8:3 may have concluded with this phrase (7:1; 8:29), but it was removed thence after 8:4–21 was combined with 8:3. **30–35.** It is very likely that the deuteronomic editor who worked the six "major" judges in the sin-oppression-cry-deliverance framework had omitted Jgs 9 from his materials as irrelevant to this theme and inserted in its place the synopsis of 9:1–57 found in 8:32–35. When the later editor expanded this work to "twelve" judges, he replaced Jgs 9 and presumably changed 10:1 accordingly, thus making Abimelech the conclusion of the deliverance of Gideon (8:28 and 10:1). He would also have inserted 8:30–32 as the introduction to the replaced 9:1–57. Here, then, the usual deuteronomic aftermath to the death of a judge (2:18–19) appears in 8:33–34, whereas 8:35 abstracts the events of 9:1–57. Baal-berith (8:33; 9:4) is a syncretistic combination of the covenantal God of Israel with the Canaanitic Baal at Shechem. Gideon must have originally ruled over both Israelites and Canaanites, for both would have had been prey to the nomadic Midianites (V. Vilar, *EstBib* 21 [1961] 65–67). The revolt of Abimelech is that of a half-Israelite, son of Gideon at Shechem (8:31), against the pure Israelite stock of Gideon at Ophrah. Even as the narrative stood in its predeuteronomic state, it had a religious moral (9:56–57), although its main value and the reason for its retention in the tradition may have been the antimonarchical tone of the narrative. This tone would be an example of the northern thinking whose southern counterpart appears in 1 Sm 8.

27 **(F) Abimelech (9:1–57).** Abimelech was the son of Gideon and a Canaanite woman (8:31); Shechem (Nablus) was on the southern border of the tribal territory of Manasseh. Probably at the death of Gideon, when the succession was in dispute, Abimelech appealed to the Shechemites to elect him, rather than a pure Israelite descendant of Gideon, as their king.

(Frühstorfer, K., "Abimelechs Königtum," *TPQ* 83 [1930] 87–106. Nielsen, E., *Schechem. A Traditio-Historical Investigation* [Copenhagen, 1955]. Van Imschoot, P., "Le règne d'Abimelek," *Col BG* 22 [1935] 3–13. Wright, G. E., *Shechem* [N.Y., 1965].)

9:1–6. *on one stone:* The murder of Gideon's sons was performed publicly, almost as a ritual act, to show openly the change of power (2 Kgs 10). Beth-millo is most likely another name for Migdol-Shechem (9:46,49); both designate the fortified section of Shechem, which would have contained the king's palace and important public edifices such as the temple of Baal-berith. For "military post," read "standing stone" (*maṣṣēbāh*). Abimelech is made king under the sacred tree at Shechem, mentioned also in Gn 12:6; 35:4; Dt 11:30; Jos 24:6. **7–15.** Shechem is in the valley between Mt. Ebal (N) and Mt. Gerizim (S). The parable poem is older than its use by Jotham and represents the nomadic disrespect for monarchy (M. Adinolfi, *RBibIt* 7 [1957] 322–42; E. H. Maly, *CBQ* 22 [1960] 299–305). The argument is that the best do not have time to be kings; therefore, it usually falls to the worthless to accept the role of the monarch. The "buckthorn" cannot even furnish shade—the minimum requirement of a tree in a hot country; furthermore, it is dangerous, for it easily catches fire and burns rapidly, thereby destroying even the stately "cedars of Lebanon." In choosing a king, one receives, in effect, a choice between the nonshade of the thornbush or, even worse, its fiery onslaught—i.e., either the useless or the dangerous. **16–21.** The way in which Jotham has to stretch the parable shows it was not created for his argument. In Jotham's use, it is their reactions to Gideon and his family (9:16b–19b) rather than their action in making Abimelech king that concerns him. In 9:48–49, 9:56–57 sees the fulfillment of the curse by fire (cf. 9:20–21). Jotham then flees to Beer (El Bireh) N of Beth-shan and outside the territory of Manasseh (J. Van der Meersch, *VD* 31 [1953] 335–43).

28 **22–25.** The narrative in 9:22–49 is composed of two traditions of the same event: the instigation to rebellion and its effects appear in vv. 22–25 and 26–29 in parallel; the attack by Abimelech is told in vv. 42–45 and again in vv. 30–41, following, respectively, the previously

mentioned accounts. God acts in 9:22 to effect 9:56–57. The "ambush" is "for him" (Abimelech) in that it robs him of the levies of passage paid by caravans passing through the crossroads of Shechem. **26–29.** This passage is a second and parallel account of the rebellion, in which the role of God is not mentioned but the historical circumstances through which he worked are described. Gaal, son of Ebed was most likely a pure Canaanite who appeals to his people against the half-Canaanite, Abimelech (9:26). He recalls to them their ancestral hegemony in the land where Abimelech now rules (R. G. Boling, *VT* 13 [1963] 479–82). **30–40.** This passage follows the narrative of 9:26–29. Zebul (9:28) betrays Gaal, then taunts him (v. 36), and finally provokes him (v. 38) into an open battle with Abimelech. **41.** This verse ends one tradition on the defeat of Shechem's revolt; the much fuller but parallel tradition of the rebellion's punishment occurs in 9:42–45. **42–44.** In this tradition, the city of Shechem is destroyed and the land salted to assure sterility (Dt 29:22; cf. A. M. Honeyman, *VT* 3 [1953] 192–95). **46–49.** The final stand of the Shechemites is made in the strongest part of their city and in a place possibly considered safe as being under the special protection of Baal-berith (8:33). Abimelech, however, does not shed their blood in the sacred place; he burns them to death instead. **50–55.** Thebez (Toubas) was to the northeast of Shechem and had presumably joined in the revolt. Abimelech was killed in the act of setting fire to the tower (9:20b). The movable upper stone of a handmill was a natural instrument for a woman defender. The army of Abimelech was composed of "Israelites" fighting a Canaanite uprising. **56–57.** The earlier religious moral of the story was that God revenges the blood of Gideon by fulfilling the curse of 9:20 in both its parts.

29 **(G) Tola (10:1–2).** The introduction of Shamgar (3:31), Tola, Jair (10:3–5), Ibzan, Elon, and Abdon (12:8–15) follows a standard pattern: name, origin, rule, death, burial, and family. This scheme is not the same as that used by the deuteronomic introduction to Othniel, Ehud, Barak, Gideon, Jephthah, and Samson. The author who inserted 10:1–5 also replaced 9:1–57 in the narrative and wrote 10:1 accordingly. These short notices, which bring the over-all number of judges to the symbolic fullness of 12, are of leaders whose epic remembrance was enshrined in the clans bearing their names; they are such as the unnamed of 5:2,9,15. Tola is a clan name of Issachar (Gn 46:13; Nm 26:23). Dodo appears also as the name of one of David's warriors (2 Sm 23:9) and may be the abbreviated form of a name with the suffix of a divinity. Some of the tribe of Issachar must have dwelt, or at least fallen in battle, in the territory of Ephraim, for the tomb of the clan hero was at Shamir in their lands.

30 **(H) Jair (10:3–16).** The initial "after him" (3:31; 10:1; 12:8,11,13) makes the entire work read like a succession of judges, but this concept is that of a later writer and does not reflect the actual simultaneity of much of the events in different tribal situations. Jair is one of the clan names of Manasseh, and the clan ancestor is associated with the capture of the northern section of Gilead E of the Jordan (Nm 32:41; Dt 3:14). The "cities" are nomadic encampments, in which different families of one clan would group themselves; the location is between the Jabbok and the Yarmuk Rivers. Jair, then, was a nomadic ancestor of eastern Manasseh. The burial place where his memory was recalled was Kamon (Qamn) E of the Jordan in Gilead.

31 **10:6–16.** The earlier work that the first deuteronomic editor had used already contained a faith-given interpretation of the past epic history. It appeared already in the predeuteronomic tradition united to the deuteronomic in 2:6–3:6. There are also two traditions carefully united in 10:6–16: the earlier one was most likely intended as a prelude to the oppression of Israel by the Philistines (10:6,7,12), and to the work of Samson (Jgs 13–16) and Samuel (1 Sm 1–12). The second evidences the characteristic deuteronomic themes as a prologue to the oppression of the Ammonites (10:6–7,9, 12) and to the deliverance of Jephthah (to follow in 10:17–12:7). In its present position and format, 10:6–16 recapitulates 2:6–3:6 and prepares for the stories of the Ammonites and Philistines. The insertion of Jgs 17–21 breaks the continuity of the Jgs 10–1 Sm 12 complex.

The general terms Baals and Ashtaroth (2:11–13) are specified in 10:6b, which represents a secondary amplification. An author, to whose mind Yahweh punished Israel for worshiping the gods of the surrounding countries by oppression specifically from those same countries, seems to have expanded the list in 10:6b and 10:11–12 to summarize Israel's infidelity in all the period before his time. Thus, there are traces of at least three hands in 10:6–16.

6. The usual deuteronomic opening in 10:6a (2:11–13; 3:7; 4:1; 6:1) is expanded by a later hand, as previously suggested. **7.** The deuteronomic preparation for the history of both Ammonite (10:17–12:7) and Philistine oppression (chs. 13–16; 1 Sm 1–12) contains the usual phrases (2:14,20; 3:8; 4:2; 6:1). **8–9.** These verses refer exclusively to the Ammonite invasion from which Jephthah was to be deliverer—part of the original preparation for the Jephthah saga. Bashan is a conjectural reading. The Ammonites occupied the territory of the Moabites (3:12–30) E of the Jordan; they not only harried the southern section of Gilead (territory of Gad; 5:17) but crossed over against the southern tribes W of the Jordan. **10–16.** The list of nations opposing Israel in the past (10:13) includes those two whose oppression is yet to be detailed in Jgs 11–16.

32 **(I) Jephthah (10:17–12:7).** It was argued that the first deuteronomic redactor of Jgs had omitted 9:1–57 from his source materials as irrelevant and/or unedifying, inserting in its place the summary comment of 8:33–35. Later, the final redactor had replaced 9:1–57 after 8:33–35. The same omission and later replacement has occurred in the Jephthah narrative. The original sources most likely contained 11:1–10,11a,29a,30–40; 12:1–6. The first redactor did not use 11:1–10 but summarized it briefly in 10:17–18 (compare 10:18b and 11:9). He used neither the vow story in 11:30–31,34–40 instead summarizing it discreetly in 11:11b, nor 12:1–6, for probably the same reason; it is much less edifying a narrative than 7:24–8:3 and not related to his theme. Thus, 11:33b terminated his narrative with typical deuteronomic comment. Doublets such as 10:17a and 11:4, 10:18b and 11:9, and 11:11b and 11:30–34 testify that the later redactor reinserted the omitted sections without, in his turn, displacing their own earlier summary replacements.

17–18. This summary of 11:1–10 promises post-bellum power to the leader against the Ammonites. They were encamped in the territory of Gilead, S of the Jabbok; Israel's camp was at Mizpah. These terse statements summarize the attack by the Ammonites, the call of Jephthah from exile, and the muster of 11:1–10,11a,29a. The "princes" of Gilead is probably a harmonizing gloss in view of 11:4–11; only "the people" was mentioned in the original summary. (For Gilead, → Biblical Geography, 73:50–51.)

33 **11:1–3.** Behind the narrative is the same problem as occurred with the half-Israelite, half-Canaanite, Abimelech in 9:1–6. Jephthah was also a half-Israelite born to an Israelite father in Gilead of a native woman

(8:31). Just as the full Canaanite Gaal managed to rouse his fellow Canaanites against Abimelech, so here the full Israelites (of Gad?) drive out the half-Israelite Jephthah, lest he cause them trouble. He became a nomadic plunderer living with his followers on the borders of the desert and the town. Tob is in the northeastern reaches of Gilead (9:4; 1 Sm 22:1–2). **4–10.** The fuller details behind 10:18b appear here. The risk of having Jephthah conspire against Israel was much lighter than the certainty of Ammon's attack. They swear solemnly that if he leads them successfully against Ammon he will become their chieftain thereafter; the commander becomes king. **11a.** This verse followed immediately upon 10:18 in the first redaction, before the restoration of 11:1–10 by the second editor. The original continuation of 11:11a would have been 11:29a,30–31. **11b.** This verse sums up the entire vow incident of 11:30–31,34–40, omitted by the first editor, just as 8:33–35 abstracted the excised 9:1–57 and 10:17–18, the excluded 11:1–10. The sanctuary at Mizpah (Gn 31:49) was the scene of Israel's assembly to obtain divine assistance for the campaign; thus, the vow was made there also.

34 **12–28.** The dialogue by messages is later than the source into which it has been inserted; it breaks the unity of narration in 11:11a,29a. The jurisdictional serenity of the document probably stems from a later vindication of Israel's rights to the lands E of the Jordan between Arnon and Jabbok. Ammon claimed this area as theirs. Most of the document discusses the territory E of the Jordan belonging to Moab (11:15,24–25) rather than Ammon. Possibly the background to the incident is a time when Ammon had conquered sections of Moab to the south and then claimed the lands which Sihon had conquered from Moab, and then Israel from him long before. The reply stresses the fact that on Israel's journey from Egypt they had asked permission to pass through Edom (Nm 20:14–21) and Moab. Transit refused them, they skirted the frontiers of Edom and Moab (Nm 20:22; 21:4) and did not turn W toward the promised land until they reached the Arnon (Nm 21:11,13), the boundary between Moab and the territory that Sihon had conquered earlier from Moab (Nm 21:26–30). Their request for passage was again refused, and instead Sihon attacked them (Nm 21:23; Dt 2:32). The cities of Heshbon and Jahaz were Moabite cities (Is 15:4) conquered by Sihon. All this territory was given by Yahweh in battle to Israel. Chemosh is the god of Moab, not of Ammon (Nm 21:29; 1 Kgs 11:5), which may indicate a scribal mistake. Possibly the argument is that the god of Moab and the king of Moab (Dt 22:2–3; Jos 24:9) did not stop Israel's taking possession of the territory, and, even if Ammon had now subdued Moab, it was too late to establish claim to the ancient Moabite territories long in Israelite possession (J. Obermann, *JBL* 58 [1939] 229–42).

29a. The sequel to 11:11a from the original source appears here. It would represent the muster of the tribes as in 4:10; 5:14–18; 6:33–35; and 7:23–24. The tribes involved were Gad, Manasseh, and Ephraim (12:1–6). It is possible that Mizpah-Gilead was actually the other Mizpah in Ephraim, and that 11:29b represents an indication of the unsuccessful muster call to Ephraim mentioned in 12:2. **29b.** In the hypothesis that the first editor deleted 11:30–31, he may also have added 29b, thereby preparing for the redundancy with 11:32a when the second redactor replaced 11:30–31. **30–31.** Jephthah is a Yahwist (A. von Hoonacker, *Le voeu de Jephte* [Louvain, 1903]), but his view of Yahweh shows contemporary contamination (2 Kgs 3:27; Mi 6:7). He vows human sacrifice (of a servant?) for victory. **32–33.** Aroer is not that on the Arnon in 11:26 but the city in Jos 13:25, E of Rabbah. Minnith and Abel-keramim are N of Heshbon (11:19,25) in the direction of Rabbah. **34–40.** Jephthah's only child is the one who meets him as she leads the group of those who greet the returning hero (1 Sm 18:6–7). The story is told with tragic dignity; the father offers his daughter in holocaust after a period in which she mourns the fact that she dies barren. The story of the vow perdured, no doubt, to explain the annual mourning in 11:40.

35 **12:1–3.** Presumably Ephraim now wants a share in the spoils of Ammon and crosses the Jordan under pretext of anger with Jephthah. Zaphon is on the E bank of the Jordan near Succoth (Jos 13:27). Ephraim still claims (8:1–3) hegemony over the tribes. **4–6.** Ephraim considered the territory E of the Jordan and opposite their own holdings to belong to them, just as Manasseh held possessions on both banks of the river to the north (8:4b). After an initial defeat of Ephraim's presumption, the victorious Gileadites cut off the straggling survivors at the Jordan "fords" by a trick of pronunciation. "Shibboleth" means "flood" or "current" in a river; the word is appropriate, but it was the failure to pronounce the "sh" sound that betrayed them (E. A. Speiser, *BASOR* 85 [1942] 10–13; F. Willsen, *VT* 8 [1958] 97–98). **7.** The original ending of the first redactor was most probably in 11:33b, as a standard deuteronomic ending to a judge's activity (3:30; 8:28). When the second editor added in again the vow fulfillment in 11:34–40 and the Ephraim narrative in 12:1–6, he terminated the full Jephthah saga with a new ending in 12:7 that is typical for the narrative of the "minor" judges in 10:2,5; 12:10,12,15.

36 **(J) Ibzan (12:8–10).** Bethlehem is not that in Judah but that in Zebulun near Nazareth (Jos 19:15). The marriages outside the family were for alliance purposes.

(K) Elon (12:11–12). Elon was another judge from the tribe of Zebulun, and is the best example of the schematic framework in which the "minor" judges are noted. The name is a Zebulun clan name (Gn 46:14; Nm 26:26).

(L) Abdon (12:13–15). Pirathon is SW of Shechem in the "mountains" of "Ephraim." The numerous progeny is a sign of the wealth and importance of the individual concerned. If "Amalekites" is not textually corrupt, the presumption would be that some of these southern nomads had settled in these regions at an earlier period.

37 **(M) Samson (13:1–16:31).** The existence of two endings to the saga of Samson in 15:20 and 16:31b, and the fact that the narrative in Jgs 16 is the least edifying of the entire complex, would point to the conclusion that, as previously with chs. 9 and 11–12, so here also the first redactor had omitted Jgs 16 as irrelevant to his own theological message and terminated the narrative with 15:20; then the second editor replaced it together with its own ending in 16:31. The cycle consists of the birth story (13:1–25), and the adventures of Samson with various women: at Timnah (14:1–15:20); at Gaza (16:1–3); and at the Wadi Sorek (16:4–31).

(Blenkinsopp, J., "Some Notes on the Saga of Samson and the Heroic Milieu," *Scr* 11 [1959] 81–89; "Structure and Style in Jdg 13–16," *JBL* 82 [1963] 65–76. Kalt, E., *Samson* [Breisgau, 1912]. Zapletal, V., *Der biblische Samson* [Fribourg, 1906].)

13:1. The traditional opening of the first deuteronomic redactor (3:12; 4:1; 10:6) reappears. The story of Samson is placed within this frame (15:20). "The Philistines" were a segment of the migrating sea peoples from the Aegean and Crete, who had been repulsed from Egypt by Ramses III soon after 1200. They had settled on the southern coastal plain of Palestine. Their encroachments forced the tribe of Dan to migrate from their allotted territory around Zorah and Eshtaol (Jos 19:47; Jgs 18; cf. 13:25) and settle instead in the region of Mt. Hermon at the northern extremities of Palestine. Possibly the activity of Samson dates from after this migration, and hence he never became the leader of the Danites against the Philistines. The emphasis on Samson's personal strength and unorthodox weaponry (15:15–16; 16:3) may reflect the Philistine monopoly on iron weapons until their final defeat under David (1 Sm 13:19–22). **2–5.** Zorah and Eshtaol (13:25; 18:2,11), were W of Jerusalem on the borders of the plain and the foothills. Thence Dan eventually migrated N. The birth (Gn 11:30; 1 Sm 1:2; Lk 1:7) is a special divine act and presages a unique mission for the child involved. The sequence of literary elements—divine message, offer of food, meal become sacrifice, fear, reassurance in 13:2–23—is the same as in 6:11–23. The rites of the Nazirite observance in Nm 6 are much more detailed and developed than here and refer only to the grown person who becomes a Nazirite. Here, Samson is marked for this special destiny from the womb; therefore, its rites applied to the mother as well. **6–8.** Samson is to be a perpetual Nazirite, like Samuel (1 Sm 1:11–28). **9–14.** The dynamics of the narrative serve to produce a triple statement of the extraordinary consecration of Samson from the womb itself: 13:4–5,7,13–14; but no fuller detail appears in 13:13–14 over 13:4–5, despite the question in 13:12. **15–21.** Manoah, like Gideon, suspects that he is dealing with the divine presence and makes an analogous offer that is somewhat ambiguous—either meal or sacrifice. The divine messenger refuses the meal but accepts the offering as a sacrifice for Yahweh. Manoah probes constantly for more information or possibly proofs of the messenger's assertions (13:12,17). He is still uncertain about the reality of the divine communication. Only after the sacrifice is he convinced that the messenger is from Yahweh, a manifestation of his presence (13:20–21). **24–25.** Mahaneh-dan means "Camp of Dan" and would be an unnecessary title within the actual territory of Dan. If this point were that from which the great migration of the Danites departed (13:25; 18:2), we might imagine Samson's decision to remain and conduct personal guerilla war with the Philistines as the background to 13:25.

38 **14:1–4.** Timnah belonged to Dan (Jos 19:43) and was situated near the border of Judah (Jos 15:10). From this sector, the Amorites had pushed the Danites back against the mountains (1:34–35). This passage begins three narratives (14:1–15:20; 16:1–3; 16:4–31) of Samson's exploits, all of which have the same basic structure: Samson becomes involved with some Philistine woman; the Philistines use her in an attempt to trap him; he foils their plans and then devastates them. In the first incident, this pattern is actually repeated twice with regard to the same woman—in 14:1–20 and 15:1–20 (A. van Selms, *JNES* 9 [1950] 65–75). Samson's father refuses to negotiate the marriage and allow the Philistine woman to be brought into the ancestral home. Unknowingly, Samson's demand and their refusal was part of the divine plan. In what follows, the presumption is that the marriage must then be exogamous—one in which the bride stays with her own family, no bride price is paid, the children belong to her family, and the groom must bring a present when he visits his wife (8:31; 9:1). **5–9.** A later scribal hand did not understand the special nature of the wedding, or did not consider it legitimate; thus were added certain insertions on the presumption that the father finally acquiesced to Samson's request, accompanying him to Timnah and assisting him in obtaining the girl. Therefore, the simple narrative of Samson's personal visit to close the exogamous marriage, on the way to which he killed a lion and on the return from which he found honey in the dried carcass, is confused by this author's attempt to include the parents on the journey. He tries to describe the exogamous marriage in terms of the ordinary Israelite wedding customs, where the bride was brought home to the groom's family—hence, the addition of "with his father and mother" in 14:5 and the resultant clash of "they" and "him" in 14:5. Thereafter, the insertion of 14:7b becomes necessary for, since the parents are now with Samson (14:5b), a contradiction would otherwise exist with 14:5b,16b. The translation seeks to make the text more comprehensible, only possible by the excision of 14:5b and 7b. The translation in 14:7–8 then reads as follows: "...a kid. (But he did not mention to his father or mother what he had done.) He continued his journey, spoke to the woman and she pleased him. As he returned from his visit with her he stepped aside...." The first visit to settle the exogamous marriage is preceded by the lion's slaying, on the return from which the honey is found and brought home without explanation. Nobody, then, could have known the answer to the future riddle except Samson himself (14:9).

39 **10–14.** The second visit is made for the marriage and takes place in 14:10 (not 14:8). Once again, the later scribe attempts to insert the father into the narrative as the negotiator of an ordinary endogamous marriage; thus, the clash between the "father went down" and "Samson gave a banquet" in 14:10. The parents have nothing to do with the wedding; they refused their assistance in 14:3–4. The "companions" of the groom in such a marriage are not Danites but Philistines (14:11,16–17). The later scribe seeks also to explain the fact that the "banquet" was given by the groom at the bride's home and not at his own by the simple statement that this "was customary!" But it was so only for exogamous marriages. The Philistines themselves supply the "friends of the bridegroom"; in an ordinary marriage, these men would have been the tribesmen of the groom. The riddle is proposed in poetic parallelism: eater parallel to strong; food parallel to sweetness (H. Torczyner, *HUCA* 1 [1924] 125–50). **15–17.** The feast lasted for 7 days but the marriage was consummated the first night (Gn 29:22). The chronological data in 14:15 ("three," "fourth") contradict 14:17 and possibly are to be omitted. The Philistines, then, do not attempt to solve the insoluble riddle; instead, they bring pressure to bear immediately on his wife so that she importunes him for the 7 days. He only gives in when he considers it safe to do so—"on the seventh day." **18–20.** There is still time, however, and the answer is returned to Samson "before the sun set." Ashkelon (or Ascalon) was a Philistine stronghold on the coast SW of Timnah. The betrayal is considered the excuse for the attack (14:4). He then left his wife, and her father, presuming Samson was repudiating her, remarried her to the "best man." **1–5.** The gift shows again the exogamous nature of the marriage; such a gift was presumably expected at each visit in lieu of the initial bride price of the endogamous relationship. For "foxes," one should possibly understand jackals, whose pack habits would make a large number easy to catch at one time. **6–8.** The Philistines retaliate fire by fire and each incident only goads Samson deeper into his personal war (14:19–20; 15:3–5,8). **9–13.** The Philistines campaigned against Samson in Judah. To rid themselves of these Philistines, the men of Judah campaigned against Samson. **14–16.** On "Lehi," cf. comment on 3:31. Samson puns on the word for "ass" and "heap" in celebrating his victory in this couplet. The name Ramath-lehi means the "Height of Lehi," but this popular etymology explains it in view of the supposed exploit of Samson as meaning the "throwing" of "the jawbone" (*l^e ḥi*). This meaning gives another interpretative etymology of a place associated with the saga of Samson. En-hakkore is interpreted as the "spring of the one who called" upon God for assistance; actually, it means the "spring of the partridge." But in a region where the memory of the epic deeds of Samson was recalled, it was inevitable that place names would tend to be given popular etymologies explaining them in terms of his great deeds, commemorating some and inventing more. **20.** Cf. 16:31. This ending to the narrative of Samson would be that of the first redactor replacing all of the omitted Jgs 16. It is based on 16:31.

40 **16:1–3.** Gaza is one of the five cities of the Philistines (E. G. H. Kraeling, *AJSL* 41 [1924–25] 174–78). The narrative, like that in 14:1–20, has been composed with some amplification by a later scribal hand; most of 16:2 is such an amplification. Knowing he was in the city and the gates locked upon him, they planned simply to take him at dawn. An all-night ambush at the gates would have been senseless and is contradicted by what happens. Samson leaves despite the locked gates by lifting them up and carrying them off quietly with him. Because Hebron was about 40 mi. away, it is possible that the text originally said "in the direction" of Hebron (1:10).

4–5. For the third time, a Philistine woman is the instrument that leads to Samson's eventual devastation of their forces. Wadi Sorek connects with the Wadi-es-Sarar and is located close to Zorah, the home of Samson (13:2). Delilah is most probably a descriptive term ("traitress") rather than a personal name. The Philistines believed that some magical or supernatural force gave Samson his power; once it was removed (charm, amulet, etc.), they would be able to conquer him. **6–9.** The first reply is that he must be bound with seven green bowstrings. Delilah then does so and wakes him with a cry which does not reveal her intentions. When he breaks the bonds, the Philistines remain in hiding and she passes off the treachery as a jest. All three stories in 16:6–9,10–12,13–14 are told with this same sequence of question, answer, action, warning, and breaking of the bonds. **10–12.** The second answer replaces green bowstrings with unused ropes and the tactic is the same. The presumption is that Samson knows only that Delilah is jesting; he knows nothing of the hidden Philistines. **13–14.** The third answer almost comes to the truth—the secret concerns his hair, as the symbol of his consecration to Yahweh, the source of his strength. As he sleeps near the loom imbedded in the ground, she works his long hair into the cloth at progress on the loom and pushes the strands tightly together with the pin. Once again Samson releases himself; he tears up the loom from the earth with his hair.

15–22. Samson finally breaks down and tells her the truth (F. C. Fensham, *EvQ* 31 [1959] 97–98). His admission has opened the way to disobedience to the command of God (13:5), and his consecration is thereby lost. This states on the personal level, and in a much more primitive manner, what has been the theme of Jgs on the tribal and national level: God's presence insures strength; God's departure opens the way for oppression. Blinded, he was forced to do menial work (Is 47:2) at Gaza (16:1), but 16:22 already looks forward to the conclusion of the saga. **23–25.** The verses in 23b and 25b have, respectively, three and five lines ending with a rhymed *ēnû*; unusual in Hebr poetry, it appears also in 14:18 (double *āthî*) and Gn 4:23 (double *āthî*). Dagon was the common god of the five (3:3) Philistine sectors (1 Sm 5). **26–30.** The rulers and people were gathered in the court of the temple of Dagon, presumably in front of the columned entrance to the interior of the temple. Samson pushes over the middle two of these columns and brings the entire edifice down on the audience and himself. **31.** On "between Zorah and Eshtaol," cf. comment on 13:2. The "burial" element is the usual note of the "minor" judges in 10:2,5; 12:10,12,15, but also of Jephthah (12:7), all presumably under the influence of the same redactor.

41 **(IV) First Appendix (17:1–18:31).** The narrative of the migration of Dan from their original location between Judah and Ephraim to a position near the sources of the Jordan as the northernmost tribe of Israel would fill out the information of 1:34. It must have taken place before the time of Barak (5:17) and most likely occurred early in the conquest period. Its present position would stem from the concern of the preceding narrative with a Danite hero (Samson) from the area from which the tribe departed for the north (13:2,25; 18:2). There is evidence of two accounts of this migration having been combined, which shows in certain recurring redundancies in the text and seems to indicate that the two accounts were originally similar in content.

(Bewer, J. A., "The Composition of Judges, chs. 17–18," *AJSL* 29 [1913–14] 261–83. Fernandez, A., "El santuario de Dan: Estudio critico exegetico sobra Jud. 17–18," *Bib* 15 [1934] 237–64. Murtonen, A., "Some Thoughts on Judges 17s," *VT* 1 [1951] 223–24. Noth, M., "The Background of Jdg 17–18," *Israel's Prophetic Heritage* [Fest. J. Muilenburg; N.Y., 1962] 68–85.)

17:1–6. Two narratives of the sanctuary of Micah are combined here: one appears in 17:2–4 and stresses the silver "idol"; the other is mentioned in 17:5 and speaks of "ephod" and "household idols." It is possible that 17:2–4 reflects a pejorative rendition of the account, wishing to show the unedifying origins of the idol of Micah. The text has become disarranged, probably by a later scribe seeking to clarify a text meaningless to himself. The original story would have been as follows: Micah takes money belonging to his mother; she curses the money in his presence by dedicating it to God for an idol; were he now to use it for himself the anger of the divinity might be expected; he is thus forced to return the money and his mother revokes the curse with a blessing. The text should be read in this order: 17:2a,4b (actual curse), 2b,4a,3. The idol is possibly a calf as symbol of Yahweh (1 Kgs 12:28). The second narrative appears in 17:5a where only "ephod and household idols" (Gn 31:19; 35:2–4) are mentioned; the detail in 17:5b may be another tradition of 17:11b. **6.** The comment (cf. 18:1; 19:1; 21:25) is by the editor, who included the appendices and intends to explain how such strange things happened at that time—no monarchy. The four statements appear as concluding comments to the story of Micah's idol (17:1–6), Micah's consecration of the Levite as priest (17:7–18:1a), the establishment of both idol and priest at Dan (18:1b–19:1a), and the crime of Benjamin (19:1b–21:25). **7–13.** Two narratives are again visible: in 17:7,11b–12a, the Levite had been accepted as one of Micah's sons and is now consecrated priest; in 17:8–11a, 12b–13, the wandering Levite is invited in specifically to be "father and priest" to Micah. **18:1a.** It concludes the narrative of 17:7–13; cf. 17:6 (H. H. Rowley, *ExpT* 51 [1939–40] 465–71).

42 **18:1b.** The tribe of Dan first sought territory on the maritime flank of the house of Joseph, but was forced back against the mountains by the Amorites (1:34–36). The great majority of the clan was thereupon forced to go N to seek a new home (Jos 19:40–48). **2–6.** The narrative is again redundant from the combination of two almost identical traditions. The mission (v. 2), arrival at Micah's home (v. 3a), question to the Levite (v. 3b), and his answer (v. 4) all show doublets, but the consultation of the oracle and its reply (vv. 5–6) is a single tradition. The Levite may have passed through their territory in his wanderings, for they recognize his accent (1 Sm 26:17). **7–10.** Laish is close to Caesarea Philippi at the sources of the Jordan; the place was separated from the Phoenician (W) and Aramean (E) states and hence invited attack. The narrative shows the usual redundance from source combination in vv. 7a and 7b; the mention of the Sidonians is for different reasons and from a different source. The report of the spies in vv. 8–10 is also combined: one source has them simply narrate that the land is good and they should attack it (8–9a), and the other has them persuade a reluctant people to attack (9b–10). **11–12.** The full migration consists of 600 fighting men with their families and possessions (18:21). They gathered from the region between Zorah and Eshtaol (13:25; 18:2) to a camp near Kiriath-jearim; this reason is offered to explain the name Mahaneh-dan (13:25).

13–21. The text reads with some difficulty, for later scribes have sought to explain in it discrepancies arising from the combination of sources. The first basic story would have had the 600 men staying outside the village and the original 5 going in and persuading the priest of Micah to come with them and bring the idol (18:14–15,16a,19–20). The other story sees the 600 as distracting the priest's attention while the idol is stolen; only afterward does he protest (18:16b,17–18). It is unlikely they would have planned to take the idol without the priest, so the first sequence is the better tradition. Discrepancies show clearly in 18:15,17, and again in 18:18,20. The "ephod, household idols and carved idol" (v. 20) result from the combination of sources in 17:4–5. Their action is performed in comparative secret, but they expect attack as soon as it is discovered—hence 18:21. **22–26.** No redundancy or combination occurs in this brilliant vignette, which may have been present in only one of the accounts. The pursuers do not know the numbers of the migrating group until they catch up with them. **27–31.** There is some repetition in 18:27 and 29b; vv. 30 and 31 are the two conclusions for the two separate sources that have been intertwined throughout the narrative (C. Hauret, *Mélanges A. Robert* [Paris, 1957] 105–13). Beth-rehob (cf. Nm 13:21) may possibly be an earlier name of Baniyas (Caesarea Philippi). The account of the sanctuary's establishment in 18:30 gives the name and genealogy of the priest, which was omitted from one earlier account in view of the geographic identification in the second (17:7). Jonathan is the "young Levite" (18:3). The sanctuary lasted until the first or the final captivity of the northern kingdom (either 733 or 721). The statement of the second source in 18:31 merely notes that the sanctuaries of Dan and Shiloh were originally contemporaneous. This latter was destroyed by the Philistines (1 Sm 4), but the former lasted much longer (2 Kgs 10:29; Am 18:4).

43 **(V) Second Appendix (19:1–21:25).** The events behind this narrative date from very early in the conquest period. The crime of Gibeah led to a savage reprisal to purge the guilt of covenant disobedience from Israel; however, the present form of the story dates from the early post-exilic period and is rewritten to show in ideal fashion how the ideal community of Israel should act in face of such a crime. The temporary submersion of Benjamin is reflected in Jgs 5:14, and the crime is mentioned in Hos 9:9; 10:9. The exaggerated numbers and the perfect unanimity of those involved in the punitive action, however, serve as warning that this is a didactic and idealistic retelling of the actual historical event.

(Eissfeldt, O., "Der geschichtliche Hintergrund der Erzählung von Gibeas Schandtat," *Schriften* 2 [Tübingen, 1963] 64–80. Fernandez, A., "El atentado de Gabaa," *Bib* 12 [1931] 297–315.)

19:1a. The verse refers to the events of 18:1b–31; cf. 7:6. **1b–9.** It is possible to argue for a combination of sources behind the protracted narration of 18:5–9, but it is more likely to be just a storyteller's device to increase the effect of the climax by delaying its advent. **10–15.** They travel N to Jerusalem, which a scribe glosses as being then called Jebus (Jos 15:8; 18:16,28). Actually, it was never so called; the earlier name was Urusalim, in the 15th cent., and the name Jerusalem appears in Jgs 1:7,21; Jos 15:63. The refusal to stay in a non-Israelite city heightens the irony of the events at Gibeah. This city was in the territory of Benjamin N of Jerusalem; Ramah was still further N. There are traces of sources in the repetitions of 19:10b,11a and 19:12,13. **16–28.** The inhabitants are already typed, because only a fellow stranger offers them hospitality for the night, indeed, more than they actually need. The resemblances between this narrative and that of Gn 19, the crime of Sodom, are deliberate literary parallels. It is quite likely that the words in 19:24 are intended as allusion to Gn 19:8; the narrative reads easily and continually from 19:23 into 19:25. The host refuses to allow the crime in the name of hospitality, and the visitor sacrifices his own wife to save himself and possibly his host as well (Gn 12:12–20; 20:1–18; 26:6–11). **29–30.** The action was intended to arouse the tribes against Gibeah (1 Sm 11:7) by forcing them to face the problem of what they had to do to exculpate the guilt of one of their members (G. Wallis, *ZAW* 64 [1952] 57–61). The words in 19:30 are most likely asked first by the messengers of the Levite before being repeated in agreement by the challenged tribes (in Gk version).

44 **20:1–2.** Verses 1–2 continue the story and show the interests of a post-exilic redactor imbued with the spirit of the Chronicler. It appears in the nature and action of the ideal assembly of the people of God (but recall 5:15b–17; 8:1–3; 12:1–6). Mizpah (Tell en-Nasbeh) of Benjamin, not that of Gilead (11:11,29,34) was an ancient sanctuary (1 Sm 7:5–14). The gathering is of all those W of the Jordan from Dan (N) to Beer-sheba (S), and those E of the Jordan (but cf. 21:8) as well. On Gilead, cf. 11:1. With the exaggerated numbers, cf. 18:11. **3–7.** The statement in 20:3 interrupts the narration to no purpose—Mizpah was in the center of Benjamin. It may have been more closely connected originally to the countermuster of Benjamin in 20:14. **8–10.** There is evidence of two traditions combined: One stemmed from the sanctuary at Mizpah, and the other centered around that of Bethel. The election of 10 per cent of the gigantic force for a supply corps belongs to the later didactic retelling of the original story and is inappropriate as preceding the demand for the surrender of the guilty parties at Gibeah in 17:11–13a. Were this fulfilled, the whole maneuver would be unnecessary. The "lot" of 20:9b is actually that of 20:17–18. **11–19.** The original request was rather modest—the death of those personally guilty for the crime is all that is demanded. Gibeah refuses and all Benjamin joins it to repel the other tribes. (For the sanctuaries of Bethel and Mizpah, → Religious Institutions, 76:41,51.)

20–28. The battle strategy is liturgical rather than military; the writer is interested in stressing the divine punishment involved and the divine guidance of the other tribes toward this end. Once again, the numbers are didactic rather than real; one-tenth of the tribal forces fall in the first two encounters. The base of the army is Bethel, an ancient sanctuary N of Gibeah. In such an idealistic assembly of the tribes, Judah would take precedence according to the principles of the Chronicler's theology. The purpose of 20:27b–28a is an attempt to explain why the ancient story mentioned Bethel; it does so by having the Ark there instead of at Shiloh (Jos 19:10; 1 Sm 1) and having Phinehas (Nm 25:7–13) present as a legitimate priest. **29–35.** Two separate but quite similar traditions of the attack on Gibeah are preserved in 20:29–35 and 20:36–42a. These are now coordinated, but the former tradition had been mostly concerned with the field tactics of the tribes, whereas the latter concentrated on the ambush. The tactical obscurities of 20:30–34 result from the attempt to add details from the earlier ambush account in 20:37–42a into the later field account of 20:29–35. The Benjaminites are drawn after the fleeing tribes along the route toward Bethel and Gibeon, N and NW of Gibeah. The tactical account in 20:33 is rather obscured. The details of the ambush in 20:29,33 were probably added to 20:30–35 from 20:36–42a by the redactor, who combined the two traditions. The regrouping of the fleeing warriors at Baal-tamar is to be understood in the light of 20:39–40. The end of the defeat in 20:35 closes the later of the two traditions. **36–42a.** The earlier and fuller account makes the battle much clearer (Jos 8). The Benjaminites are drawn from their unguarded city in pursuit of the others; when they have passed the men in ambush, these descend upon the city and then signal to their "fleeing" companions, who turn upon the pursuing Benjaminites and catch them between pincers; these are then forced in their turn to flee to the east. The difficult 20:42b most probably means that those who had devastated the city also came out against the defeated Benjaminites. **43–47.** The account of the pursuit has also been obscured in the combination. The original narrative told of the Benjaminites having been caught between the forces near Geba and of 18,000 having been slain there while 600 escaped and fled to Rimmon (20:43–44,47). The purpose of 20:45–46, in which 7000 more are killed on pursuit to Gidom (or Gibeah, Geba, or possibly not a place but the result of the pursuit itself), is an attempt to bring the 18,000 of 20:44 into agreement with the 25,000 of the second narrative in 20:35, so that 20:46 can reiterate it. Rimmon is E of Bethel and N of the battle and pursuit. **48.** The entire tribe, save the 600 at Rimmon, was wiped out; they received the same treatment as the captured cities of Canaan (1:7).

45 **21:1–5.** The decree of extermination against Benjamin had been total (20:48), and the tribes found themselves faced now with the possibility that one tribe would vanish from the Israelite amphictyony. All those who had congregated at Mizpah (20:1) had so sworn, and they therefore could not give their daughters to the 600 warriors, even to avoid the extinction of the tribe of Benjamin. There are two main accounts of the restoration of Benjamin: 21:6–14 and 21:15–23. These have been harmonized in the present redaction as partial solutions for the one problem (21:14b), rather than as separate traditions of the one solution; 21:1–5 serves as an explanatory preface to these accounts. In 21:1,5 the two vows of the tribes are recorded in preparation for the story to follow. In 20:2–4, the solution is placed under divine aegis and guidance. Mizpah (20:1) and Bethel (20:17) were the sanctuaries traditionally cited as bases for the attack on Benjamin (J. Dus, *ZAW* 75 [1963] 45–54).

6–14. The account in 21:8–13 was probably part of the aftermath of the Benjamin war. The retribution against Jabesh-gilead (1 Sm 11:1–10; 31:11–13) for nonparticipation spared the virgins of that city according to the law of Nm 31:17–18. This historical adjunct to the war against Benjamin could easily have become confused with the purpose of obtaining wives for Benjamin, as narrated in the tradition of 21:15–23; thus, 21:6–7,14 were added to the core story. The note about Shiloh (21:12b) is, like that in 20:27–28a, an attempt to erase the memory of the other sanctuaries of Mizpah and Bethel and the association of the action with them. Instead, the presence of the Ark at Shiloh is the center of the activity against Benjamin (21:19). The final statement in 21:14 (2:6–7) connects this narration with the restoration of Benjamin.

15–23. In this older account, 21:15 repeats 21:6 and 21:16 repeats 21:7; thus, the two traditions have been harmonized as much as possible. The background is one of the great annual feasts celebrated at Shiloh, N of Bethel, where the Ark was located. The account idealizes the collective seizure of the women, which can hardly have been advised in solemn assembly of the tribes unless the men of Shiloh were absent. Possibly Benjamin first stole the women of Shiloh and afterward it was decided that it was the best solution to the dilemma of either a tribe's extinction from Israel or the breaking of their oath on the part of the others involved. Hence, 21:22 explains what happened afterward; 21:22b harmonizes the tradition with that of Jabesh-gilead (21:12b,14b), and 21:22c gives the acquiescence of the tribes in the deed. **24.** The ideal war concludes with the members of the great solemn assembly, which has been theoretically in session since 20:1, dispersing finally to their homes. **25.** The final verse "explains" how such things could happen in Israel; cf. 17:6.

9

1-2 SAMUEL

James C. Turro

BIBLIOGRAPHY

1 Albright, *ARI.* Brockington, L., *I and II Samuel* (*PCB*; London, 1962). Carlson, R. A., *David, the Chosen King* (Stockholm, 1964). De Vaux, R., *Les Livres de Samuel* (BJ; Paris, 1961). Driver, S. R., *Notes on the Hebrew Text and the Topography of the Books of Samuel* (Oxford, 1913). Goldman, S., *Samuel* (Soncino; London, 1959). Hertzberg, H. W., *I & II Samuel* (Phila., 1964). Klostermann, A., *Die Bücher Samuelis* (Nordlingen, 1897). Leimbach, K., *Die Bücher Samuel* (BB; Bonn, 1936). Maly, E., *The World of David and Solomon* (Englewood Cliffs, N.J., 1966). McKane, W., *I & II Samuel* (London, 1963). McKenzie, J. L., "The Four Samuels," *Biblical Research* (vol. 7; 1962) 3–18. Noth, *US.* Smith, H. P., *The Books of Samuel* (ICC; N.Y., 1929). Weiser, A., *Samuel, seine geschichtliche Aufgabe und religiöse Bedeutung* (Göttingen, 1962). Wellhausen, J., *Der Text der Bücher Samuelis* (Göttingen, 1871).

INTRODUCTION

2 **(I) Title.** The Books of Samuel have varied in name and shape throughout their existence. Originally, to which Jerome and Eusebius stand witness, they formed a single book. The partition into two books seems first to have been made in the LXX where these books were termed 1 and 2 "Kingdoms" (*Basileiōn*); 1 and 2 Kgs were labeled 3 and 4 "Kingdoms." The Vg in the beginning also referred to them as 1, 2, 3, and 4 "Regnorum," which in time gave way to "Regum." This division was taken over by the Douai version, which called 1 and 2 Sm "1 and 2 Kgs." In this version, "3 and 4 Kgs" designates those books elsewhere known as 1 and 2 Kgs. Since the 15th cent., Hebr manuscripts and printed editions have followed the practice of presenting the original single unit as 1 and 2 Sm.

3 **(II) Date.** It is not possible to date with precision the origin of 1–2 Sm. In part, these books undoubtedly contain very old materials, some dating from the first years of the monarchy in Israel. The Narrative of Succession (2 Sm 9–20) is an example of such early documentation. It was probably fixed in written form soon after the events that it narrates took place. The entire work was probably given its definitive shape—allowance made for some later additions and retouching—shortly before, or during, the Exile. This final restyling was accomplished under D influence, reflected especially in 1 Sm 2:27–36 and 2 Sm 7.

4 **(III) Author.** The Talmud (*Baba Bathra* 15a) confidently maintains that Samuel is the author of the books that bear his name, but this hypothesis is at best a surmise growing out of 1 Chr 29:29–30. The attribution of these books to Samuel cannot be taken seriously, if only because Samuel's death is reported relatively early in the account (1 Sm 25). It is far more likely that Samuel's name became attached to the work because of his dominance in the events of the early part of 1 Sm. In time, an aura of prophetic greatness formed around his name and memory, which fostered the assumption of Samuel as author.

Even a hasty perusal must convince us that these books are not the work of one hand. They could hardly have been produced "from scratch" in one draft by a single author. The doublets, repetitions, and divergences throughout the text enforce the conclusion that it is rather a compilation of heterogeneous, literary pieces brought together and worked over by various men.

5 **(IV) Composition.** Very little can be said with certainty about the process that yielded the Books of Samuel in their present form. Did they grow out of earlier source documents? K. Budde thought so. He felt that the influence of the J and E documents was verifiable not only in the Heptateuch but in the Books of Samuel as well. O. Eissfeldt agrees, although he postulates a third source, L (the Lay Source), which he believes he had isolated in the Pentateuch (Eissfeldt, *OTI* 269ff.). On the other hand, A. Bentzen and A. Weiser have judged that there is simply not enough evidence to warrant a documentary hypothesis. In their view, 1–2 Sm took shape from a collection of disparate traditions, originating in different literary ambients.

Weiser (*OT* 157–70) ventures the following scheme as marking the significant stages in the development of the work: Individual traditions fashioned by the people and the court—e.g., 2 Sm 10ff.; comprehensive accounts resting on existing traditions—e.g., 1 Sm 9ff.; the collection and combination of these accounts and the welding of the same into one tradition; the prophetic formation and reshaping of this tradition into a complete history interpreted theologically; the Deuteronomistic revision of the work as a whole; and later expansions by interposing poetic pieces—e.g., 1 Sm 2:1–10.

Bentzen (*IOT* 2,91–96) has envisioned the compilation process differently. He believes that 1–2 Sm grew around the nucleus account, 2 Sm 9–20, the Narrative of Succession. This story recounts the incidents connected with finding a successor to David. Its preoccupation is to show the over-all durability of the Davidic dynasty. Around these central events the other narratives were grouped: the institution of the monarchy; the anointing of David; and so on—all set in relation to the Narrative of Succession.

The modern reader becomes quickly aware of a certain disjointedness and want of organization in the text, which he ought not to take amiss. The authors of 1–2 Sm were not guided by contemporary norms of style. Consequently, they did not strive in every case to forge a firm, logical connection among the various strips of material they were consolidating. Nor were they as sedulous in screening out discrepancies in the same degree that a present-day writer might. Rather, they practiced their craft as their reader expected, providing a comprehensive narrative including all the data at hand, even if at times these data did not agree among themselves on a specific point.

The disparate nature of the collections that make up 1 Sm is obvious in the following indications, which do not pretend to be exhaustive. Samuel is chosen by God at Shiloh, and recognized as a prophet by all Israel (chs. 1–3); he is a judge and military leader (ch. 7; chs. 4–6 concern the Ark, rather than Samuel). In a sympathetic view of the monarchy, we discover how Saul came to be king; he is searching for his father's donkeys, but finds a crown when he comes to Samuel at Ramah. The people accept him as king at Gilgal after his victory over the Ammonites (chs. 9; 10:1–16; 11:1ff.). On the other hand, there is an antimonarchist version of Saul, in which the people demand a king of Samuel. The Lord reluctantly concedes, and Saul is crowned at Mizpah (chs. 8; 10:17–27; 12:1ff.). Two traditions are relative to David's meeting with Saul. These seem to be introduced by the story of the consecration at Bethlehem (16:1–13). In chs. 16–17, the two traditions merge: David is a musician (16:14–23) hired to soothe Saul, and also a warrior, who volunteers to fight the Philistine giant; David is a boy, sent by his father to the battle front with food for his brothers (17:12–31), who, when he hears of the Philistine challenge and the reward, apparently expresses himself strongly and is brought to Saul. In addition, several doublets concern David's life at court and his period of exile, which we shall discuss later.

The account in 2 Sm is much more unified, thanks to the "court history" or Narrative of Succession in chs. 9–20. Chs. 1–5 sketch David's rise to power; chs. 6–8 deal with the transfer of the Ark to Jerusalem, the oracle of Nathan, and David's victories; chs. 21–24 are appendices.

6 **(V) Theology.** Although there is hardly one unified theme (perhaps, trials and tribulations of the monarchy?), 1–2 Sm raises many important theological considerations. They provide us with a vivid picture of early religious practice and they throw light on important religious institutions, such as prophetism (→ Prophetic Lit, 12:6–12), priesthood (→ Religious Institutions, 76:14) and messianism (→ Aspects OT Thought, 77:20).

7 **(VI) Text.** The Hebr text of 1–2 Sm has been preserved in a lamentable state, and at some points it defies the most persistent efforts to reconstruct and understand it. The LXX differs from it in many particulars, and it must have been translated from a Hebr original that was very different from the standard MT. The discoveries at Qumran have yielded several fragmentary manuscripts of a Hebr text that agree with the LXX; at times, these fragments give readings superior to both the LXX and the MT (see F. M. Cross, *The Ancient Library of Qumran* [N.Y., 1961] 179–81; → Texts, 69:22).

8 **(VII) Outline.** The outline for 1–2 Sm follows:

(I) The Role of Samuel (1 Sm 1:1–7:17)
- (A) Elkanah and His Family (1:1–8)
- (B) Hannah's Petition and Answer (1:9–21)
- (C) Samuel's Dedication (1:21–28)
- (D) Hannah's Hymn of Praise (2:1–11)
- (E) The Corruption of Eli's Sons; the Prophecy of Their Doom (2:12–36)
- (F) The Call of Samuel (3:1–18)
- (G) Samuel as Prophet (3:19–21)
- (H) The Capture of the Ark (4:1–22)
- (I) The Ark Among the Philistines (5:1–12)
- (J) The Return of the Ark to Israel (6:1–7:2)
- (K) Samuel as Judge (7:3–17)

(II) Samuel and Saul (1 Sm 8:1–15:35)
- (A) The Israelites Ask for a King (8:1–22)
- (B) Samuel Anoints Saul (9:1–10:16)
- (C) Saul Chosen and Acclaimed King at Mizpah (10:17–27)
- (D) Encounter at Jabesh-gilead (11:1–15)
- (E) Samuel's Farewell (12:1–25)
- (F) The Rejection of Saul (13:1–23)
- (G) Jonathan's Exploit (14:1–52)
- (H) The War with the Amalekites (15:1–35)

(III) Saul and David (1 Sm 16:1–31:13)
- (A) The Anointing of David (16:1–13)
- (B) David at Saul's Court (16:14–23)
- (C) David Slays Goliath (17:1–58)
- (D) David's Relationship to the Royal Family (18:1–30)
- (E) David's Flight (19:1–24)
- (F) David's Farewell to Jonathan (20:1–42)
- (G) David's Flight to Nob and Gath (21:1–15)
- (H) David's Life as an Outlaw (22:1–23)
- (I) Episodes in the Judean Desert (23:1–29)
- (J) David Spares Saul's Life (24:1–22)
- (K) David and Abigail (25:1–44)
- (L) David Spares Saul's Life (26:1–25)
- (M) David Among the Philistines (27:1–12)
- (N) Saul and the Witch of Endor (28:1–25)
- (O) The Philistines Dismiss David (29:1–11)
- (P) David and the Amalekites (30:1–31)
- (Q) Saul's Death at Gilboa (31:1–13)

(IV) David as King (2 Sm 1:1–8:18)
- (A) The Report of Saul's Death (1:1–16)
- (B) David's Dirge over Saul and Jonathan (1:17–27)
- (C) David, King of Judah at Hebron (2:1–7)
- (D) Civil War Between David and Ishbosheth (2:8–32)
- (E) The Murder of Abner (3:1–39)
- (F) The End of Ishbosheth (4:1–12)
- (G) David, King of Israel in Jerusalem (5:1–16) (= 1 Chr 11:1–9)
- (H) Wars with the Philistines (5:17–25) (= 1 Chr 14:8–16)
- (I) The Transfer of the Ark to Jerusalem (6:1–23) (= 1 Chr 13:1–16:43)
- (J) The Oracle of Nathan (7:1–29) (= 1 Chr 17:1–27)
- (K) David's Wars (8:1–18) (= 1 Chr 18:1–17)

(V) David's Court (2 Sm 9:1–20:26)
- (A) David and Mephibosheth (9:1–13)
- (B) David's Wars with the Ammonites and Arameans (10:1–19) (= 1 Chr 19:1–19)
- (C) David's Adultery with Bathsheba (11:1–27)
- (D) Nathan's Parable and David's Penitence (12:1–31)
- (E) Amnon's Crime and Absalom's Revenge (13:1–38)
- (F) Joab Effects Absalom's Return (14:1–33)

(G) Absalom's Revolt (15:1–37)
(H) Details of the Revolt (16:1–23)
(I) The Undoing of Ahithophel's Counsel (17:1–29)
(J) David's Victory and Absalom's Death (18:1–33)
(K) The Restoration (19:1–43)
(L) Sheba's Revolt (20:1–26)
(VI) Appendices (2 Sm 21:1–24:25)
(A) The Famine and the Hanging of Saul's Descendants (27:1–14)
(B) The Philistine Wars (21:15–22)
(C) A Song of Praise (22:1–51)
(D) "The Last Words of David" (23:1–7)
(E) David's Heroes (23:8–39) (= 1 Chr 11:11–41; 27:2–15)
(F) David's Census (24:1–25) (= 1 Chr 21:1–28)

COMMENTARY—1 SAMUEL

(I) The Role of Samuel (1 Sm 1:1–7:17).

9 **(A) Elkanah and His Family (1:1–8).** **1:1–2.** Samuel's identity is established in terms of people and places. His parentage is given to the fifth generation, a detail that hints at noble descent. The family seat appears to be Ramathaim-zophim (vv. 1–2,11,19), located by some at the present-day Er-Ram, about 5 mi. N of Jerusalem. Others identify it with the NT Arimathea (cf. Mt 27:57; Jn 19:38), known today as Rentis, lying NE of Lydda. The casual reference to polygamy would argue for its acceptance at the time, which possibly grew out of the fear of childlessness. It is an obvious parallel to the situation of Abraham (Gn 16:4–5) and Jacob (Gn 30:1ff.). The same rivalry exists between the two wives (cf. De Vaux, *AI* 25). **3–8.** The custom of an annual visit to the sanctuary may be taken as a favorable comment on the piety of Elkanah and his family. These pilgrimages may have been made on the Feast of Tabernacles, celebrated yearly at Shiloh since the time of the judges (Jgs 21:19). Shiloh is the present-day Seilun, 18 mi. S of Nablus between Shechem and Bethel. In v. 3 is found the first incidence in the OT of the expression "The Lord of hosts" (cf. B. N. Wambacq, *L'épithète divine Jahvé Sébaot* [Rome, 1947]; O. Eissfeldt, "Jahwe Zebaoth," *KlSchr*, 103–23). The meaning of this phrase is not altogether clear. It may refer to the armies of Israel or to the heavenly armies—i.e., angels or stars. Those who favor the meaning, "Lord of the armies of Israel," point out that allusion to the heavenly bodies is generally made by the word in the singular, whereas here the word "host" is in the plural. Furthermore, in the context of 1 Sm, where God is viewed as intimately associated with Israel in its battles, this meaning seems preferable. If so, then 17:45 would be a definition of the concept. Whatever their specific denotation, these words speak unmistakably of the might of God. (→ Aspects OT Thought, 7:14.)

The climax of the pilgrimage came with the sacrificial meal, the mood of which was one of gaiety and joy in God. Although such was not customary, Elkanah allows both the women and children to participate. The text is cloudy at this point but seems to say that a distribution of food was made that naturally favored Peninnah, Elkanah's other wife, because she received for herself and her offspring. This fact served as the occasion for her cruel taunts of Hannah.

10 **(B) Hannah's Petition and Answer (1:9–21).** **9–12.** Hannah stands at the entrance to the Temple ("before the Lord") and articulates her plea, which she fortifies with a vow. Given the Oriental milieu of the narrative, it is not surprising that she should pray not for a child but specifically for a son. Contrary to custom, Hannah prayed silently, moving only her lips, which Eli, the priest sitting before the Temple, construed as a sign of drunkenness. Intoxication was probably not a rare occurrence at such feasts, because drinking was part of the ritual (cf. v. 18; Is 22:13; Am 2:8). Speaking in her own behalf, Hannah expressed herself with moderation and refinement. As in the case of Isaac, Samson, and John the Baptist, Samuel would be vouchsafed by God to a sterile mother. Hannah dedicates the son to the service of the Temple, the outward sign of which would be his unshorn hair. The Hebr text does not show the word "Nazirite" used of Samson in a similar circumstance (Jgs 13:5; 16:17), but it is found in the LXX (cf. De Vaux, *AI* 467). Hannah's vow is rendered superfluous, it would seem, by the law that compels the dedication to God of every first-born. The force of the vow, however, could be the renunciation of her intention to redeem the child. **19–20.** Clearly, Hannah has not resorted in vain to the Lord of Hosts. The child is called Samuel (lit., "name of God"; more fully, "he over whom the name of God is pronounced"; the name could also mean "the name of God is El"). The connection between the name and the explanation, given in this text as the words of Hannah, is a matter for conjecture. It has been suggested that there is a transfer of traditions here from Saul (lit., "the one who was asked for") to Samuel. The grounds for this view, however, are not completely convincing. In any case, the name is entirely fitting for one who bears a special mission from God.

11 **(C) Samuel's Dedication (1:21–28).** The vow spoken of in v. 21 as Elkanah's is taken by some to be in reality Hannah's (v. 11), which Elkanah took over and made his responsibility; cf. Nm 20:14. Hannah may have refrained from making the pilgrimage on this occasion possibly out of a desire to prolong the time she would keep the child. The practice in the Near East, however, is to nurse a child for a considerably long time—3 years, according to 2 Mc 7:27. Eventually, when the child was weaned, he was brought to the Temple and presented with a very respectable offering.

12 **(D) Hannah's Hymn of Praise (2:1–11).** The Song of Hannah is a poem that originally appears to have celebrated the triumphs of some king. The very mention of a king (v. 10) serves to date it later than Hannah, for the kingship dates from a later time. It seems likely that the reference to "the barren" who bears (v. 5) suggested to the editor the ascription to Hannah. The hymn's particular theological viewpoint also agrees perfectly with Hannah's situation. God controls human destiny (v. 6), precisely the theological point made both in the story of Samuel and in that of Saul. God's omnipotence is here forcefully affirmed: "He brings down to Sheol and raises up" (v. 6), and "the pillars of the earth are his" (v. 8). The psalm bears a certain similarity to Pss 2 and 8; most striking, however, is its resemblance to the Magnificat, Lk 1:46ff. This latter obviously has drawn freely from the OT, but, more than any other section, the Song of Hannah is its model. The Magnificat, however, is much more sharply focused on a person. **11.** The MT speaks only of Elkanah's return to Ramah. The LXX reading, "they," indicating the return of both parents, seems preferable.

13 **(E) The Corruption of Eli's Sons; the Prophecy of Their Doom (2:12–36).** From here to the end of the chapter, two strands of narrative run side by side. One tells of the growth and progress of Samuel; the other reports the sins of Eli's sons and forecasts their punishment. This juxtaposition of accounts is apparently of set design. The author wants Samuel's success to be set off by the ruin of Eli's house. In this very way are told the stories of the houses of Saul and David (2 Sm 3:1). The same counterplay is found again in the account of Christ and the Baptist ("He must increase, but I must decrease," Jn 3:30). Under Eli's tutelage, Samuel is trained in the ministry.

Eli's sons are branded as unscrupulous, preferring their own interests to God. "They did not know the Lord," (v. 12) means they did not care about him. Two instances of their willfulness are mentioned. Not caring about the laws specifying the parts of meat that should go to the priests (Lv 7:30; Dt 18:3), they take what they please. Their greed is evident because they took the meat while it was still cooking. As further proof of their arrogance, they demanded the meat raw, unwilling to wait until God was honored by the rite of burning the fat before the meat was cooked (De Vaux, *AI* 379, 428). Samuel meanwhile continues in the service of the Lord. He invests a linen ephod (cf. De Vaux, *AI* 349–50), an apparel that marks him off as a priest. God repays his ministry with rich blessing, implied in the birth of five more children to Elkanah and Hannah.

22–26. The term "tent of meeting" is explained by assuming that the sentence is modeled on Ex 38:8, where the same expression occurs. By this time, the sanctuary was probably a regular building and no longer a tent. The sacred character of the duties of the servant women (v. 22) aggravates the sin of Eli's sons. They become ever more unpopular because of their misdemeanors, and, at the same time, Samuel's standing in the community improves constantly (v. 26).

27–36. This passage is a later insertion, which we may deduce from 3:1 affirming that prophets were rare in these times. In texts edited by the D school we occasionally find pieces similar to this one (cf. Jgs 6:8–10; 9:7–20). The force of these sections is to draw out the theological implications of what has preceded in the narrative. All the events recounted are interpreted as having transpired under God's plan and direction. These verses present some difficulty of interpretation. Clearly, they speak of the rejection of the house of Eli. Not so clear, however, is the replacement. We think immediately of Samuel; however, it is hinted that the priestly clan of Zadok will be the one to supplant Eli's family. It is explicitly recorded in 1 Kgs 2:27, where Abiathar, descendant of Eli, is displaced by the family of Zadok. The "faithful priest" of v. 35 seems to be rather a whole line of priests. The plea of Eli's descendants for some minor clerical offices (v. 36) seems to suggest the D reform, which did away with the priests serving at countryside shrines. These were superseded by the Zadokite priesthood. If this hypothesis is credited, we must view this material as having been reworked by a D editor to show the succession of the priestly house of Zadok to that of Eli. This is an instance of a *vaticinium ex eventu*, here employed to establish the legitimacy of the house of Zadok.

14 **(F) The Call of Samuel (3:1–18).** Ch. 3 forms around two themes: the downfall of the house of Eli, and the call of Samuel. **4.** Samuel is "called" as other men of God were "called" before him—e.g., Moses, Gideon, and Samson. He was dedicated to the service of God in the Temple, but this alone did not qualify him for the special task that lay before him, for which God issued a special call. **5.** Samuel slept in the Temple, perhaps to enable him to tend the lamp that burned there, or to serve as a watchman. The fact that "the lamp of God" had not yet gone out (v. 3) implies that it was not yet morning. According to Ex 27:20–21 and Lv 24:3, a lamp was to burn in the sanctuary throughout the night. **11–14.** Cf. 2:27–36. **16–18.** In questioning Samuel about his experience, Eli does not mention God by name. He may have done so either out of fear (Am 5:10), or so as not to suggest to Samuel who it was that spoke with him. Eli presses Samuel under threat of a curse to make known to him the substance of the message he has received. The editor has softened the brunt of the malediction by repeating it in general terms. In reality, such imprecations specified the evils that were called down upon the person.

(G) Samuel as Prophet (3:19–21). The expression "the Lord was with him" (v. 19) has more than its usual force here for Samuel. God brings to realization the words spoken by Samuel: "He let none of his words fall to the ground" (v. 19). They could only have the effect of solidifying Samuel's status as a man of God. His image as a prophet gains in the eyes of all the people from Dan to Beer-sheba (the northern and southern frontiers of the land in the period of the united kingdoms under David). Because of Samuel's presence, Shiloh becomes the place of God's revelation.

15 **(H) The Capture of the Ark (4:1–22).** The underlying intention of ch. 4 may be to show that, because of the crimes of Eli's sons, Israel was no longer worthy of the personal presence of God in the Ark. Although conflicts with the Philistines are reported earlier in the OT (Jgs 15ff.), they were apparently inconclusive. The impression given here is that now, for the first time, the Philistines and Israelites prepare for a decisive encounter to determine the destiny of Palestine. The site of the battle lay N of the Philistine territories. Aphek is today Ras el Ain, situated at the source of the Yarkon River. No positive identification can be made for Ebenezer (different from the town of the same name mentioned in 7:12); it must have been near Aphek.

The elders felt that the presence of the Ark among the troops would boost their morale. Although it played a significant role in Israel's military enterprises, it was not commonly carried to the front lines of battle. **4.** "Who is seated above the Cherubim" is an allusion to the divine presence that rested upon the Ark and its cherubim as upon a throne (cf. De Vaux, *AI* 297–302, 304). **5.** The Israelites' cry of acclaim as the Ark entered their camp seems eventually to have become part of the ritual of the Ark (cf. 2 Sm 6:15). **7.** In several places, the OT tells of other peoples who knew of the God of Israel and were in awe of him: Jos 2:9; 5:1; 1 Kgs 20:23; 2 Kgs 5:15. Here, the Philistines are pictured as anxious about the arrival of the Israelite "gods" in the enemy camp (the word "elohim" is construed as plural, for it is modified by plural adjectives), which may well mean to reflect the inaccurate way the Philistines would have conceived and spoken of the God of Israel. The same explanation may lie behind the inexact phrase in v. 8: "He it is who struck down the Egyptian in the desert." The plagues materialized in Egypt proper. The Philistines would not have known this precise detail, but it is possible, however, that the words "in the desert" are employed to describe generally the whole period of the Exodus.

12–13. Although the text says Eli sat "anxiously watching the road," the sense is rather that he sat "waiting," for he was blind. The courier bringing the news of defeat ran about 18 mi. to arrive on the same day; his disheveled appearance forebodes tragedy. **18.** Only here is Eli described as a judge. It is not entirely clear what justification exists for this assertion, and the "40 years" suggests deuteronomic editing (cf. Jgs 8:28). **19–22.** The shock of the news brought on a premature delivery in Phinehas' wife. Her remarks underscore the loss of the Ark more than personal grief. Some consider the mention of her father-in-law and husband a gloss.

The explanation of the name Ichabod ("where is the glory?") is a play on words and represents a popular etymology. The glory that has left Israel is the glory of God manifested in the Ark. Five allusions are made (vv. 11, 17, 19, 21, and 22) to the loss of the Ark, the main burden of ch. 4.

16 **(I) The Ark Among the Philistines (5:1–12).** The Philistines are pictured more as religious rivals than as political opponents. This conclusion is confirmed by the occasional reference elsewhere to the Philistines as "uncircumcised." They were one might say, the "classical" adversaries of Israel (→ Excursus Israel, 11:12). They bore the Ark as the chief prize of their victory to the temple of their god Dagon in Ashdod, one of their five chief cities, on some such principle as to the victorious god belong the spoils. The Philistines conceived their conflict with Israel as being the battle between divinities. Dagon was a god of fertility represented in human form. At one time, commentators supposed he was a "fish god," because the name was thought to have been built on the Hebr word for fish (*dāg*). The name seems rather to derive from *dagan*, a Semitic word for "grain." The Semitic cast of the word reveals that the Philistines, unlike the Hebrews, were willing to accept into their pantheon the local divinities (cf. F. Montalbano, *CBQ* 13 [1951] 381–97). **3–4.** The statue of Dagon is found prostrate before the Ark—i.e., in the posture of a slave before his master or a votary before his god—which serves to indicate the towering power and majesty of the God of Israel. The incident is alleged as the origin of the custom of leaping over the threshold of a temple rather than stepping on it. In fact, it was a religious usage of the ancient Near East, which derived from the belief that spirits inhabited the threshold. This custom seems to have been introduced even into Jerusalem and is reproved in Zeph 1:9.

6–7. The population is ravaged by an epidemic of "boils" (bubonic plague?). The LXX and Vg speak of a plague of mice as well. In light of what is described subsequently in 6:4, these readings merit some consideration. **8.** Gath (unidentified; perhaps Araq el-Manshiyeh) and Ekron guarded the Philistine frontier to the east. The name of Ekron is preserved by the hamlet Aqir, but its actual location is probably farther SW, at the present village of Qatra.

17 **(J) The Return of the Ark to Israel (6:1–7:2).** **3.** The reasoning of the priests and diviners as presented in the text is not as clear as we would wish; v. 3b seems to be an elliptical way of saying: you will find out that you were afflicted because you had not paid God the honor that is his due. **4–5.** The guilt offerings prescribed are images of the plague boils and golden mice. The inclusion of mice here would seem to justify the LXX reading in 5:6, which speaks of the land as plagued with mice, whereas the people were afflicted with boils. The reference in v. 5 ("images of your mice that ravage the land") would then fall into place. It is possible that two traditions lie behind the present account. According to one, the plague consisted in an epidemic of boils; according to the other, it was a plague of mice. The solution proposed by the priests and diviners was *similia similibus:* Since boils were the affliction, boils should be the votive offering. The number of objects offered is not clear; the number of golden mice given in v. 4 is five, but in v. 18 another figure is implied. Besides the guilt offering, the Philistines are counseled to "give glory to the God of Israel" (v. 5), which, in context, apparently means a repentant acknowledgement of their offense against God.

7–9. The preparations for the return of the Ark are to take the form of a test that will manifest God's will in the matter. Two milch cows, never before worked, were to be used, and their calves were to be kept at home. It would have been quite natural for these animals, unused to a yoke, to refuse to pull the cart and, following their natural instincts, return to their calves. Instead, they proceeded to Beth-shemesh. This outcome, beyond all normal expectations, suggests God's hand. **13–16.** The cows halted before a huge stone, the destination of the whole journey, for this was the first place inside the borders of Israel suitable for sacrifice. Beth-shemesh ("house of the sun") is SW of Ekron on the border of Philistine territory. The narrative is briefly suspended by v. 15, apparently the insertion of an editor appalled at the image of the Ark handled, and thus profaned by lay hands. Accordingly, the Levites are introduced. In v. 14, it had been noted that the cart was broken up. It is made to seem in v. 15 as though the large rock served only as a temporary resting place for the offerings. The sacrifice, we are left to infer, was conducted at a more legitimate place. The object of v. 15 seems to be to legitimize the report of the proceedings.

19–21. No less than for the Philistines it remains for some Israelites to discover how formidable is the Ark. The LXX indicates that the sons of Jeconiah (MT, "men of Beth-shemesh") were castigated for want of proper respect toward the Ark. The number in the MT is confused: "of the people 70 men, 50,000 men." Perhaps "70" is to be read. As previously among the Philistines, so now at Beth-shemesh the mighty acts of God strike a salutary fear in men: "Who is able to stand before the Lord, this holy God?" **7:1–2.** The Ark is brought deeper into Israelite territory to Kiriath-jearim ("city of forests") about 8 mi. N of Jerusalem. As one of the four cities of the Gibeonites (Jos 9:17), it was therefore Israelite by naturalization. No reason is given why the Ark was not returned to Shiloh. It must be assumed that it was destroyed, although its destruction is unmentioned in this context. Even if Shiloh were out of the question, why should the Ark not have been brought to one of the other established sanctuaries—e.g., Mizpah? Perhaps the Philistines, not wanting it within their own borders for obvious reasons, had it deposited safely in Israel but within eye range, as it were, so as to keep watch on it. The Ark remained in Kiriath until David eventually brought it to Jerusalem (2 Sm 6).

18 **(K) Samuel as Judge (7:3–17).** There are reasons for supposing that 7:3ff. are not in proper sequence. Although they continue to report on the same Philistines referred to in previous verses, the image of Samuel found here is surprisingly new. He enters the scene as the liberator of Israel in the struggle against the Philistines. Historically, however, the effective removal of the Philistine menace resulted not so much from his activity as from that of Saul, and, even more, that of David. It is not difficult to see why a later tradition, unsympathetic to the monarchy, would tend to stress Samuel's contribution by crediting him with the victory. He had, in fact, prepared for this victory by shoring up Israel's faith and hope in Yahweh.

If the foregoing assessment of this section is correct, then its purpose must be conceived as mainly theological: God is at work here, through Samuel, his chosen vessel. The figure of Samuel is reminiscent of the judges of an earlier period. He is shown as judging the people at the sanctuaries. He intercedes for them, and acts to bring them back to the service of Yahweh. He stands behind the birth of the monarchy and God stands behind him, so that the role of God in the origin of the monarchy is revealed. Elsewhere, Samuel is represented as a prophet (3:20), a seer (9:11), and as exercising priestly functions (7:9).

3–4. Samuel's call for the elimination of foreign gods is reminiscent of the deuteronomic version of Israel's history (Jgs 2:11–15; 3:17; etc.). Archaeology has turned up numerous statues of the fertility goddess, Astarte—an indication that devotion to her was fairly widespread. Mizpah ("the lookout") is placed by some in the territory of Benjamin, N of Jerusalem at Tell en-Nasbeh; others favor Nebi Samwil. **6.** The libation rite is nowhere else in the OT expressly spoken of. The context strongly implies that it is an expiatory rite, because it is referred to in the same verse with fasting and confession of sins. Samuel "judges" in the sense of handing down legal decisions (vv. 15–17). **7–11.** Samuel's intercession (like that of Moses, Ex 17:8–13) is sought. His quality as priest (v. 9) is intimated by his offering of sacrifice. It is not noted that the Israelites took any military action to meet the attack of the Philistines; faith and prayer were their only weapons. It is God's action that is decisive in routing the enemy. **12.** Ebenezer means "rock of help," and it is not the same Ebenezer as in 4:1, where the Israelites were defeated. The same name is introduced here where there is talk of military success, as it were, to cancel the earlier setback. **13.** See the concluding formulas in the accounts of the judges (Jgs 3:30; 8:28; 11:33). **14.** This territory had, in fact, not previously belonged to Israel. It was David who first brought them under Israelite rule. This treatment of the facts is to be understood in the light of what was already stated regarding the position and theologizing function of these verses. **15–17.** This section concludes with a reference to Samuel's activity (as judge) at three sanctuaries and at his native place, the point being to clarify that God took care of Israel through his chosen judge, Samuel.

19 **(II) Samuel and Saul (1 Sm 8:1–15:35).** The shift from judges to kings is represented as willed by God and the people, and eventually by Samuel as well, although at the outset he was opposed. By all this is emphasized the continuity governing the story of salvation. It is Samuel, the last of the judges, who sets up the king. He stands athwart two periods in the history of Israel. Most commentators recognize a fusion of two sources: 9:1–10:16; 11:1–15 (promonarchy); and 8:1–22; 10:17–27; 12:1–25 (antimonarchy).

(A) The Israelites Ask for a King (8:1–22). **1–5.** The self-seeking of Samuel's sons, auxiliary judges at the southern sanctuary of Beer-sheba, is reminiscent of the behavior of Eli's sons (Joel—"Yahweh is God"; Abijah—"Yahweh is my father"). The people's request for a king was not only a wish to emulate the other nations but also a desire for effective leadership to meet the challenge of other nations. **6–9.** The reaction of the people is construed as evil by the narrator. In the theocratic view, this action of the people is tantamount to a rejection of the rule of God in favor of a king: "They have rejected me from being a king over them" (cf. 12:12; Jgs 8:22–23). **10–18.** As a warning, Samuel details for the people the procedure of the king. The picture of the king that emerges is recognizable as typical in the Near East. This judgment is confirmed by texts found at Ugarit and Alakh. The easy commandeering of a man's private life—appropriating his flocks, his fields, even his children—was standard practice "such as all the nations had" (cf. I. Mendelsohn, *BASOR* 143 [1956] 17–22). The monarchy in Israel was not wielded in such an absolutist way owing to the prophets. The grasping behavior of the king as described here is faintly suggestive in content and form of the Tenth Commandment. **19–22.** The close of this section is so edited as to allow for the insertion of the account of Saul's anointing (9:1–10:16), which is favorable in its tone to the monarchy.

20 **(B) Samuel Anoints Saul (9:1–10:16).** The following account is probably pieced together from two earlier sources, each current in a different locale. Thus, 9:4–6 suggests that Saul, in quest of his father's animals, has traveled a fair distance from home when he meets the seer. On the other hand, Samuel seems to live quite near Saul in 10:17,26. **1–2.** Saul is here spoken of as David will be later (16:12)—as one who made a good impression from the outset. He is attractive in his build and bearing. **4–5.** The place names occurring in these verses have not been successfully identified. **6.** The city would be Ramah, already given as Samuel's home (7:17). Saul's preoccupation to provide an offering for the seer is understandable in light of the custom of those times; a prophet was remunerated for his services with a gift (Nm 22:7; 1 Kgs 14:3; 2 Kgs 4:42; 5:15). **9.** Seer is equated with prophet. This remark may derive from the editor who combined the two earlier traditions. This text gives us valuable insight into the dawn of prophecy. Originally, seers seem to have been distinct from prophets. They possessed the penetrating power of vision to perceive what others could not—e.g., the future. The prophets, on the other hand, were men taken over by God and charged by him (→ Prophetic Lit, 12:7). **12.** The "high place" served as a legitimate site for worship until the reforms of Hezekiah and Josiah. Because they were tainted with Canaanite practice, the danger persisted of adulterating the true worship with pagan elements. Against such syncretism the prophets inveighed (Hos 10:8; Am 7:9; Jer 7:31).

14. For the first time in this narrative, Samuel is mentioned by name. **15–16.** This action of God in the affair serves to make legitimate the choice and anointing of Saul. Throughout this section (9:1–10:16), Saul is consistently referred to as *nāgîd*, i.e., one who is designated by God to lead. Eventually, Saul's charismatic designation was acknowledged, and he was acclaimed king. The charismatic leader, the *nāgîd*, (v. 16) becomes the king, the *melek* (11:15). **18–21.** Samuel establishes himself as a genuine seer by telling Saul of the lost asses before Saul has had a chance to tell him his problem. **22–24.** Saul is ushered into the select company of the invited guests gathered in the sacred hall. The existence of such an edifice, as shelter from the elements, witnesses the sanctuary's importance. Saul is treated as the expected guest, for whom the choicest morsels are saved out of deference. **25–27.** Also indicative of the respect with which Saul is regarded is the provision made for him to spend the night. A bed is spread for him on the roof, a comfortable place to sleep in the hot climate of the Near East. Samuel seems anxious to anoint Saul in private; he thus rouses him from sleep early and has Saul send his servant on ahead.

10:1. Samuel's kiss ought to be viewed not as part of the ceremony but more likely as an earnest mark of his good will toward Saul. For the anointing of kings, see De Vaux, *AI* 103ff. **2–4.** To forestall any hesitations he might have, Saul is guaranteed signs by which he may know the authenticity of what has transpired. **5–7.** Gibeath-elohim, (4 mi. N of Jerusalem, the modern Tell el-Ful), "the hill of God," was probably a popular shrine—a fact that might explain the Philistine garrison there. The prophets Saul encountered are a group such as could be found frequently at a sanctuary. They represented a phenomenon found in Canaan and neighboring lands (→ Prophetic Lit, 12:5–7). These prophets often induced an ecstatic state in themselves artificially. Saul shares their exhilaration and ecstasy—a sign that he is "changed into another man" (v. 6). **8.** Saul is directed to Gilgal near Jericho, to await further instruction. The latter part of this verse may be an insertion to prepare for the account of Saul's meeting with Samuel at Gilgal, which is related in 11:14–15. **9–13.** Saul is apparently known at the sanctuary, for his enthusiastic outburst causes some surprise. The question about the father of the prophets may be a derogatory allusion to their detached, uprooted way of life. On the other hand, the question could possibly imply that a prophet's inspiration is not hereditary; therefore, Saul is as entitled as anyone to be among the prophets. **14–16.** These fragmentary lines hearken back to 9:1–3.

21 (C) Saul Chosen and Acclaimed King at Mizpah (10:17–27). Until now, the reference has been to Saul's anointing as "leader" (*nāgîd*). From here on, the references are to Saul's choice as "king." Saul's assumption of the kingship is variously described in various places, and the common denominator in these accounts is the agreement that God is the chief protagonist, who makes use of Samuel as his agent. (For Mizpah as a sanctuary, → Religious Institutions, 76:51.)

17. Samuel begins his address by reminding the people of God's beneficence during the Exodus. He interprets their clamor for a king as ingratitude toward God, who saved them from their calamities. **20–25.** The choice of Saul is determined by lot, and the proclamation of the procedure of the king (also committed to writing) comes as the final act of the drama (cf. Dt 17:14ff.). **26–27.** Saul returns to his home in Gibeah, but some cannot bring themselves to accept him as king. The author seems to hold these latter in contempt, as though in despising the king they are doubting God's decision.

22 (D) Encounter at Jabesh-gilead (11:1–11). If 10:17–27 represents a Mizpah tradition, this section (promonarchical in tone) may be attributed to Gilgal (vv. 12–15). **1.** Jabesh-gilead, in Transjordan, figured in the story of Jgs 21. Now, under pressure from the Ammonites, it faces surrender if it is not saved by the Israelites (vv. 2–4). **5.** Saul's inconspicuous role as a farmer is noteworthy. **6.** The tone of the story is suggestive of the activity of the "spirit of God" in the stories of Jgs (11:29; 14:19). **7.** The dismembering of the oxen recalls the incident of Jgs 19; the symbolic action is an effective call to arms. **8.** Bezek is opposite Jabesh-gilead, but on the W side of the Jordan; here Saul musters his army. The numbers are impossibly large for the troops of this period. **10.** The text carries a play on words: "tomorrow we will come out to you" can carry the overtones of "we will attack" as well as "we will surrender." **12–14.** These verses connect with 10:27, apparently an editorial link; Saul had already been proclaimed king at Mizpah (10:24), but had not received universal recognition. Once again Samuel is on the scene to "renew the kingdom" (in view of 10:24), and the ceremony takes place at Gilgal (v. 15).

23 (E) Samuel's Farewell (12:1–25). This section purports to be an address delivered by Samuel to the Israel of his day. As a matter of historical fact, it is probably an expression of the concerns and reflections of a D editor, directed by him to his contemporaries. This chapter continues the antimonarchical mood underlying 8:1–22 and 10:17–27.

1–5. It is the king who will from now on be subject to the scrutiny of the people, as Samuel has been these many years. The allusion to Samuel's sons as adults may be intended to underscore the length of time that Samuel served. The people are solemnly charged to come forward and, before God and his anointed (the king), to testify to Samuel's integrity. The paradox of this antagonistic attitude toward the kingship is once again evident. The king (God's anointed) is viewed as one endowed by God and called to an office so high and sacred that the community may swear by him. At this point, the concept of the sacred kingship intrudes; this notion was current only at a later period, following the development of the theology of the Davidic kingship. **6–8.** Here begins an historical retrospect that seeks to show the happy state of affairs when God was king of his people. The Exodus from Egypt, the decisive action of God in the people's behalf, is mentioned twice. **9–12.** Several expressions are reminiscent of the deuteronomic theology in Jgs: "to forget the Lord," "to be sold," "to cry out to the Lord," "to serve the Baals and Ashtaroth" (cf. Jgs 2:11–15; 4:2–3). **11.** In the MT, Samuel (LXX: "Samson") is said to be the last of the judges, which may be understood as an attempt to group Samuel with the whole line of judges shown here in a favorable light. **12.** Curiously, the people's demand for a king is presented here as the upshot of the Ammonite threat, not the impression we have earlier when mention is made (7:9–16) of the people's pressing for a king. There, it is ostensibly the Philistine peril that generates a desire for a king. It is problematical whether the D editor has drawn upon another source of the incident or whether he has given the event an original turn. **13–15.** Once again it is observed that God, far from rejecting the people's wish for a king, granted it. To preserve the ideal relationship between God and themselves, the people need only to obey his commands and serve him. The editor surveyed the situation from a period subsequent to the catastrophe of 587.

16–18. The wondrous aspect of the storm lies in the time of its occurrence. It was not usual to have a thunder and rain storm during the season of the wheat harvest (end of May). The purpose is to show that Samuel did indeed speak in the name of God. **20–25.** The "vain things" warned against in v. 21 must be idols (cf. Is 41:29). Avoiding strange gods is a constant D preoccupation (cf. Dt 6:14; 11:28; 28:14). **22.** "Because of his great name," need not be understood merely as a concern for God's reputation; the expression can also be taken to mean that God's purposes in the choice of Israel would not be frustrated.

24 (F) The Rejection of Saul (13:1–23). Saul's destiny and the significance of his reign were tied to the role of the Philistines. What follows is a connected account of the outbreak of hostilities between the Israelites and Philistines.

1. The opening formula, giving the king's age and the years of his rule, occurs elsewhere (e.g., 1 Kgs 14:21) and is the work of the D editor. The years of Saul's reign are given as "two," an impossible number that seems to result from textual corruption. The MT also fails to indicate Saul's age, and the LXX omits the verse. **2.** The account of Saul's rule opens significantly with the description of a military episode; his dominion is based on a military circumstance—the Philistine threat. Presumably, following the Ammonite war, a number of men are dismissed, but some 3000 are retained to begin a standing army. The phrase "every man to his tent" is a relic of Israel's nomadic past. Michmash was a Benjaminite city, some 7 mi. NE of Jerusalem. There is some question about Gibeah in this place. Some would emend it to Geba, whereas Geba in v. 3 would be made to read Gibeah. **3.** The word translated as "garrison" could also mean "pillar"—i.e., a marker set up as a token of Philistine domination. Thus far, the Philistines had had no occasion to be anxious about developments in Israel. As is recounted in 13:19–22, they had taken precautions to disarm the Israelites. The recent fighting between the Hebrews and Ammonites would have suggested that both Israelites and Ammonites were debilitated by the skirmish.

4–7a. Heading the list of Philistine war potential are the dreaded chariots before which the Hebrews had long been defenseless. However, on the hilly terrain where this military encounter was forming, foot soldiers would surely be more effective than chariots. Nonetheless, the demoralizing effect of the chariots ought not to be discounted. It must be assumed, although the text is not explicit, that Saul withdrew, leaving the area in the north to the Philistines, who proceeded to Michmash, the base of their operations. **7b–15a.** The Gilgal episode recounted here remains something of a puzzle. To all intents and purposes, it begins as a clarification of Saul's rejection. In the end, however, it fails to deliver a plausible reason for this rejection. Considering the broader context of this narrative, the episode can only be interpreted as an attempt, on the part of an editor unfriendly to Saul, to show that his rule was amiss from the beginning. Lurking behind these verses is an obvious conflict between the spirit of the source material used (it was favorable toward Saul) and the intention of the editor to make the account reflect poorly on Saul. Ch. 15 displays a similar situation: a coming to terms between Saul and Samuel. The physical setting is in both instances the same—Gilgal. In one place, however, the incident is linked with a military action against the Philistines; in the other, it is connected with an action against the Amalekites. The latter version (ch. 15) is more pointed in describing the rejection of Saul. Beneath the account one must see the tensions that developed between the king and the man of God—strains that grew from a certain obscurity regarding the spiritual and secular role of the king. **15b–18.** Saul's unduly long stay in Gilgal is a tactical error. Fear of the enemy had reduced the number of fighting men, and the unimpeded sallies of the Philistines throughout the land had a discouraging effect on Israel's morale. Ophrah was a Benjaminite city located in the hills NE of Jerusalem. Beth-horon was on the southern border of Ephraim. The valley of the Zeboim was in the territory of Benjamin SE of Michmash. **19–23.** The desperate situation of the Israelites is indicated by the Philistine iron monopoly. It was probably the Philistines who first introduced iron into Palestine, and it gave them a military advantage. **21.** Archaeological discovery has identified the "pim" as a small weight, about two-thirds of a shekel; the text should read: "The price was a pim for the plowshares and axes, and a third of a shekel for sharpening the adzes and setting the goads." The final verse (23) prepares for ch. 14.

25 **(G) Jonathan's Exploit (14:1–52).** This fascinating narrative (cf. J. Blenkinsopp, *CBQ* 26 [1964] 423–49) describes another step in Saul's gradual downfall and introduces the reader to David's strong friend. **1–3.** Jonathan's stratagem is portrayed more as a sudden impulse than as a carefully elaborated plan. He proposes a raid, while Saul remains behind at Gibeah. The mention of the ephod in v. 3 prepares for the consultation of Urim and Thummim in vv. 36–42. **4–7.** The inclines at the pass (the present-day Wadi Suweinit, 7 mi. NE of Jerusalem) are known by the formidable names "the slippery" (*Bôṣēṣ*) and "the thorny" (*Senneh*). **8–15.** Jonathan interprets the divine will by the reaction of the Philistines, as Eliezar interprets the concrete action in Gn 24, and Gideon in Jgs 6:36ff. The derisive attitude of the Philistines is illustrated by their comment in v. 11. **16–19.** Saul resorts to the ephod (thus in the LXX; MT: "Ark") for enlightenment (cf. vv. 36ff.). **20–23.** The epic formula, "on that day," rounds off the short account of the victory that the Lord achieves for Israel (v. 23). The time factor in the entire description is important (cf. vv. 24, 31, 37). **24.** Saul's curse is the center around which the whole theological structure of ch. 14 pivots. It is, of course, misconceived; even after he has been informed of it, Jonathan can see no point to it (vv. 29–30). It does, however, provide the climax described in vv. 36–46. **31–35.** After the great rout of the Philistines "from Michmash to Aijalon," Saul calls for a great stone for the ritual slaughtering, so that the divine law concerning partaking of blood (Lv 19:26; Dt 12:16) may be observed.

36–42. Saul wants to follow the opening success in the manner of "doom" war (Jos 10:30–39), but the failure in consulting the Lord indicates that a "sin" (v. 38) has been committed. It is characteristic of ancient Israelite thought to judge the action alone, apart from the motive. **43–46.** It is implied that Jonathan's victory was God's seal of approval, a clear sign that God would not desire his death, "for he has worked with God this day" (v. 45). Jonathan's ransom would have been effected by offering an animal, or perhaps by a payment of another kind. **47–48.** This summary is in the style of the notice concerning David in 2 Sm 8:1ff., but the whole tenor of Saul's reign hardly favors this notice. The Amalekites are dealt with in ch. 15. **49–51.** Another note provides information concerning his family. Ishvi is otherwise unknown, perhaps to be identified with Ishbaal or Ishbosheth (cf. 2 Sm 2:8). **52.** This note prepares for the story of David in 16:14.

26 **(H) The War with the Amalekites (15:1–35).** The rejection of Saul as king is motivated by his appropriation of the priestly office in 13:8–15. In the present account, he is rejected because he fails to carry out the ban, or "doom" war, against the Amalekites. **1–3.** The campaign against the Amalekites is represented as deriving from the will of God and Samuel, not from any particular contemporary event. The mention of the anointing of Saul at God's behest is designed to underscore the religious character of this military endeavor, a "holy" war (Dt 20:16–18). The Amalekites inhabited the southern desert and figured as enemies of Israel in Ex 17:7ff. **4–11.** Saul musters his forces in Telaim in the Judean desert and defeats the Amalekites. The consideration shown the Kenites (Nm 10:29; Jgs 1:16) demonstrates the kind of war this was—not an uncontrolled outburst but a reasoned action based on certain principles. With the capture of King Agag, the war ended, for all practical purposes. Saul violated the ban in two particulars: he spared Agag and permitted the soldiers to retain the better specimens among the flocks. From Carmel (cf. 25:2), where he set up a stele commemorating his victory, Saul returned to Gilgal. **13–21.** Curiously, it is only in the course of his conversation with Samuel that Saul appears to become aware of his sin. As he explains his action in withholding the best cattle for sacrifice, it seems as though he was persuaded that he had done something not only permissible but pious and commendable as well. To him, it seemed to make small difference whether he slaughtered the animals under the ban immediately or subsequently in sacrifice. The religious difference between the ban and the sacrifice lies in the fact that the victims of the ban, by being totally destroyed, were considered to be given over wholly to God, whereas in sacrifice, the people frequently shared the victim with God. **22.** Underlying this confrontation is the question of the relative value of ban over sacrifice. The ban is the outgrowth of obedience to God. In this sense, observance of the ban was higher service of God than sacrifice: "To obey is better than sacrifice" (cf. Is 1:11–17; Mi 6:5–8; Am 5:21–24; Hos 6:6). **23.** Disobedience is comparable to the sin of magic and divination. What was expected of Saul was his active obedience to God, not the passivity he showed in letting the people have their way. The man who works for God must be dependable, and Saul was not.

24–26. Saul construed his offense as a transgression that could be atoned for; accordingly he begged for indulgence. **27–28.** The MT reads, "As Samuel turned to go away he laid hold of the skirt of his robe and it tore." The pronoun "he" in this sentence should be understood as referring to Samuel. Then the remarks of Samuel in v. 28 would be prepared for by his symbolic act of tearing the robe in v. 27. The act would symbolize tearing away the kingship from Saul. "Your neighbor" (v. 28) is an allusion to David. **29.** Despite the assertions made in vv. 11 and 35 to the effect that God repented that he had made Saul king, the reader is here warned against having too human an image of God. It may be the attempt of a later hand to revise the anthropomorphism of vv. 11 and 35. **30-31.** Underlying the present text at this point may be two traditions: one that reported on the break between Saul and Samuel and another that told how both Samuel and Saul "stood before the Lord" in Gilgal. **32-35.** The full meaning of Agag's remark is not clear. The MT reads, "surely the bitterness of death is past." This interpretation would mean that Saul had done all the killing necessary; there was no need to resume the slaughter.

Samuel takes matters into his own hands and executes Agag. His action reflects upon Saul, who, in sparing Agag's life, had neglected his duty. Samuel's action also serves to consummate the ban left unfulfilled by Saul. With this, Saul and Samuel part company (cf. 28:3ff.).

27 **(III) Saul and David (1 Sm 16:1-31:13).** Because of its obvious link with ch. 15, the present account is also attributed to the Gilgal tradition. Most scholars hold that there are two versions of David's introduction to Saul. One depicts him as a musician brought in to pacify Saul (16:14-23); the other depicts him as a competent warrior, one who could be eminently useful to Saul (17:12-30). The account of David's anointing (16:1-13) serves to associate him, like Saul, with Samuel. It does not have any effect in the ensuing narrative, for David is anointed at Hebron (2 Sm 2:4; 5:3).

(A) The Anointing of David (16:1-13). The story is told with a certain suspense (vv. 2-3, the fear of Saul), and local color (vv. 4-5, the meeting with the elders). **6-13.** The choice of David before his brothers serves to underline the freedom of the divine election. The anointing of David before "all his brothers" does not agree with the attitude shown him by Eliab in 17:28.

28 **(B) David at Saul's Court (16:14-23).** According to this version, David has just the necessary qualifications to serve Saul (v. 18): He is a musician who can soothe the king in moods of despondency (which, apparently, are notable after the Amalekite episode and the rejection, ch. 15); he is a warrior (contrary to vv. 1-13). **14.** Saul's despondency is explained, in typical biblical fashion, in terms of divine causality: "An evil spirit from the Lord tormented him" (cf. 1 Kgs 22:19-23). **21.** The relationship between Saul and David becomes very close; David is a formidable enough warrior to become the king's armor bearer (in contrast to 17:31-39, 55-58). **22-23.** The description of David's success at court can be said to be explained, in a sense, by the anointing in vv. 1-13. Only one who possessed the "spirit of the Lord" (v. 13) could succeed in this manner.

29 **(C) David Slays Goliath (17:1-58).** This famous event is told with consummate artistry, but the identity of Goliath is questionable. The text usually refers to him as "the Philistine," and perhaps originally there was no identification. In 2 Sm 24:19, the victor over Goliath is said to be Elhanan of Bethlehem; in 1 Chr 20:5, Elhanan is said to have slain Lahmi, brother of Goliath. It seems likely that divergent traditions existed which no one succeeded in really harmonizing, but the presentation of David to Saul in ch. 17 clearly stems from a tradition that differs from 16:14ff. The following is a possible separation of the traditions: 16:14-23; 17:1-11 and 17:12-30; 17:55-18:2. Both seem to be intermingled in 17:31-54.

1-3. The setting for the encounter between David and Goliath was the hill country in the west, the frontier land between Israel and Philistia. Socoh was a town of the Shephelah, whose name has been preserved in modern Khirbet Shuweikeh. Azekah is identified with Tell ez-Zekariyeh, about 15 mi. NW of Hebron. The "valley of Elah" ("valley of the terebinth") is thought to be Wadi-es-Sant, about 15 mi. SW of Bethlehem. Ephes-dammim is unknown. Each army took its position on a hillside facing each other across the valley, probably a river bed that was dry in summer. **4-7.** It was not unheard of in OT times to decide an issue by a contest of individuals (2 Sm 2:14ff.). Neither the name Goliath (Gk Alyattes?) nor his weaponry are typical, but the description makes him a giant of about 10 ft. **8-11.** The dramatic tension of the narrative heightens, as discouragement grips Saul and the Israelites. **12-15.** This short biography of David proceeds as if he had not been mentioned before in the text! The LXX (B) omits vv. 12-31, perhaps in an attempt to soften the conflicts of the traditions. **16-31.** We note the skill with which the events are narrated: provisions for the brothers who are fighting at the front—and for the commander!—the timing of the Philistine's challenge with the arrival of David; the conversation in vv. 24-27 that prepares for David's action; the "smaller brother" treatment David receives from Eliab (vv. 28-29). **31-40.** A memorable scene is the encounter between the shepherd boy and King Saul (cf. 16:21). The role of the Lord (v. 37) prepares for the divine intervention in vv. 45-47. **41-47.** David's reply to the Philistine's taunts supplies the theological implications of the event; it is the Lord, and not material advantage, that prevails for Israel. **52-53.** This description of the rout of the Philistines seems almost incidental and unimportant in the whole narrative. **54.** Even if this verse is an addition, it is not easy to understand. Jerusalem was not taken until many years after this event, and David has no "tent" in the camp. **54-58.** This description of Saul's reaction agrees with the story of the shepherd lad's visit to the battlefield (vv. 12ff.).

30 **(D) David's Relationship to the Royal Family (18:1-30).** The story of David's rise to power is marked by many apparent doublets that will be discussed in the course of the commentary. **1-5.** David's friendship with Jonathan is immortalized in the dirge of 2 Sm 1:19ff. Jonathan's gift of garment and equipment is more than a gesture; it is a token of the covenanted friendship that now existed between them—David was Jonathan's alter ego (Hertzberg). **6-9.** Saul's jealousy is described against the background of David's exploits and popularity (cf. 21:12; 29:5). **10-11.** This incident is described again in 19:9-10, where it seems more in context. **12-16.** Cf. vv. 28-30. **17-27.** David fails to obtain Merab, Saul's daughter, as his wife, despite the fact that she is promised to him (cf. 17:25); his victories over the Philistines continue. Under similar circumstances (vv. 25-27), he succeeds in obtaining another daughter, Michal.

31 **(E) David's Flight (19:1-24).** **1-7.** This story of Jonathan's intercession in David's favor resembles 20:1-42, in that both envision David hiding in a secret place. The situation in v. 3 is not very clear; why should Jonathan have to relate secretly anything to David if he is speaking with his father in the very field where David is? Unlike ch. 20, however, Saul relents (v. 6). **9-10.** Cf. 18:10-11. **11-17.** Michal's successful ruse saves David, but it is not likely that this event could follow on the attempt by Saul narrated in vv. 9-10. The implication of the teraphim (v. 16) seems to be that it was a life-size image, although this fact has never been confirmed by any archaeological evidence (but cf. Albright, *ARI* 114, 207,

n. 63). **18–24.** The saying concerning Saul among the prophets was already explained in 10:9–13. Here, it figures in such a way as to explain how David escaped from Naioth in Ramah where he had taken refuge with Samuel (who is represented here as one of the band of prophets).

32 (F) David's Farewell to Jonathan (20:1–42). In the MT, 20:42 is 21:1. Even Saul's children defend David against him: Michal (19:11–17); Jonathan, in a story that has some similarity with his intercession in 19:1–7. **1.** There is no indication how David would have been able to communicate with Jonathan. **2.** In this version, Jonathan refuses to think that his father is opposed to David; obviously, this tradition is separate from 19:2. **5–8.** David's presence at the royal table on the Feast of the New Moon is to be used as a sort of test case; the fact that David is actually in flight from Saul is simply ignored. **11–17.** This section seems to be an addition; it presupposes that Jonathan can give David a direct answer, whereas the rest of the chapter makes an arrangement for a sign (vv. 19ff.). Moreover, Jonathan, not David, appears as a suppliant in the narrative. **24–34.** Saul quickly reveals to Jonathan his intense hatred of David. **34–41.** The elaborate sign that was set up seems useless. The words in v. 38, "Hurry..." seem destined for David, rather than for Jonathan's aide—a verbal confirmation of the arrow stratagem—but the reunion in the poignant scene of v. 41 makes the maneuvering with the arrows superfluous.

33 (G) David's Flight to Nob and Gath (21:1–15). In the MT, the passage is 21:2–16. The incident at Nob is related only here, but the episode with Achish of Gath seems to find an elaborate, if different, doublet in ch. 27. **1.** Nob was situated on the Mount of Olives E of Jerusalem. Ahimelech, a descendant of Eli, is the same person as Ahijah (14:3). His question is possibly prompted by a premonition of trouble. It could, however, be understood as a reaction of surprise that a man of David's importance would in normal circumstances be traveling alone. **2–3.** David encourages Ahimelech to think that he would be acting as a loyal subject of the king in providing David and his men with rations. **4.** The loaves in question were an oblation made to Yahweh (Ex 25:30; Lv 24:5–9). Ordinarily, this bread could be consumed only by priests. In an emergency situation such as this, exceptions could be made (cf Mt 12:3–4; Mk 2:25–26; Lk 6:3–4). **5.** The meaning of this verse is disputed. It may be that David was reassuring Ahimelech. His men kept themselves from women (as war seemed to demand) and were therefore ritually pure and able to partake of holy bread (Dt 23:10; 2 Sm 11:11). **6.** According to Lv 24, the bread was replaced with fresh loaves each Sabbath. **7.** No indication is given as to just why Doeg was detained. It might have been because of a vow or because he was awaiting an oracle from God. It is also possible that this is an oblique way of saying Doeg was prevented from performing a religious exercise because of a ritual impurity. Later, it becomes clear from David's remark that he felt uneasy about Doeg's presence at the sanctuary (22:22). The reference to Doeg prepares for the role he is to play in 22:9ff. **8–9.** Cf. 17:51ff. The ephod must have been large if the sword could be kept behind it.

10. David's flight to Achish of Gath resembles 27:1ff., although there are significant differences. It is somewhat ironic that this event should be placed here so as to follow upon David's regaining possession of Goliath's sword (vv. 8–9). **11–15.** David's feigned madness (and so, possession by a spirit) makes him untouchable.

34 (H) David's Life as an Outlaw (22:1–23). Although David's vagabond existence lasts until he is installed at Hebron, the text notes (v. 2) that he gathered around him a band of followers, and his life as a kind of desert sheik begins here. **3–4.** Through his ancestor, Ruth, David had ties with Moab, of which he took advantage to remove his family from Saul's rage. **5.** The advice of Gad (cf. 2 Sm 24) is not easy to understand because David is already within Judah. **6–29.** This murder of the priests of Nob sealed Saul's fate as far as orthodox Yahwists were concerned. Even his own followers refused to lay hands on the priests, and it was left to an Edomite, Doeg (21:7), to slay them. **20–23.** Abiathar, the only person to escape the slaughter, has a prominent role in the story of David, until he is removed finally by Solomon (1 Kgs 2:26–27).

35 (I) Episodes in the Judean Desert (23:1–29). The final verse corresponds to MT 24:1. **1–5.** The deliverance of Keilah from the Philistines is one of the many examples of David's loyalty to his own people. By such measures he was also guaranteed a certain measure of safety and sustenance. The "inquiring of the Lord" (v. 2) was done probably (v. 6) by means of the ephod of Abiathar; according to OT mentality, the Lord speaks by means of the casting of the lot (Prv 16:33). **6–14.** The intent of the story is to illustrate David's venturesome life, which is under the guidance and protection of God. Ziph (v. 14) is in the hill country S of Hebron and is the scene of Jonathan's visit (vv. 15–18) and the betrayal (vv. 19–29). **15–18.** This episode belongs to the traditions that tell of David's friendship with Jonathan (19:1–7; 20:1ff.). **19–29.** Cf. the doublet in 26:1–3. (For this area of the Judean desert, → Biblical Geography, 73:87.)

36 (J) David Spares Saul's Life (24:1–22). In the MT, the passage is 24:2–23. The doublet to this event is in 26:1–25, where the details differ. **1–7.** In the region of En-gedi on the shore of the Dead Sea, David surprises Saul in a cave. His action in cutting off part of the garment is itself symbolical, confirming the action of Samuel (15:27–28). His words in v. 6 testify to the reverence for the "anointed of the Lord," the sacral person of the king. **8–15.** When he reveals himself to Saul, from a safe distance, David reinterprets his action as one that proved his loyalty in a moment when he could have taken Saul's life (vv. 10–11). The proverb in v. 13 means: To touch a wicked person brings ill fortune; it may be a gloss here. A "dead dog" seems to be a term of humble abasement when used of oneself, but a term of opprobrium when hurled at another (2 Sm 16:9). **20–22.** In contrast to 26:22, Saul acknowledges that David will be king. Such an admission is unlikely, and the tenor of these lines is more in line with the attitude of Jonathan (20:12–17; 23:15–18).

37 (K) David and Abigail (25:1–44). This lively story illustrates well David's manner of life in the Judean desert. **1a.** Samuel's obituary (also in 28:3) may have been inserted here because of the admission of Saul in 24:20. The kingship of the man anointed by Samuel is assured. **2.** *Carmel:* It is in the Judean desert, S of Maon; the "wilderness of Paran" (1b) is too far S to be pertinent here. **3–8.** Nabal, whose name means fool (v. 25), belongs to the Calebites who merged with Judah (Jos 15:13ff.; Jgs 1:12ff.). It was customary to celebrate at the shearing time, and David asks for a "gift" (actually a shakedown) in turn for the very real protection he had provided Nabal's servants (vv. 14–17). **18–31.** Abigail proves herself to be a prudent manager and an engaging speaker. Her argument is cleverly developed: Her reaction to David's fierce and earthy oath (vv. 21–22) is to acknowledge her own "guilt" (v. 24). She then develops the theme of her husband's folly (v. 25), David's enemies (v. 26), and David's secure future (vv. 27–29) and ultimate role as king (v. 30). In view of all this, she is keeping him from vengeance (as David himself admits, vv. 33–34).

36–38. Nabal dies apparently as the result of a stroke. **39–42.** David's reaction is characteristic of OT mentality; the death is a sign of God's punishment of Nabal for his conduct toward David. **43–44.** The marriage of David to Abigail serves to introduce the mention of his marriage to Ahinoam, mother of Amnon (2 Sm 3:2), who came from Jezreel in this southern area (Jos 15:56). Michal and Palti (or Paltiel) will reappear in 2 Sm 3:13–16.

38 **(L) David Spares Saul's Life (26:1–25).** This passage is doubtless a doublet of ch. 24; in both cases, the event follows upon the report of the Ziphites (vv. 1–2; cf. 23:19ff.), but ch. 26 has more interesting details. **6–12.** Joab and Abishai, of whom more will be heard, were sons of David's sister (1 Chr 2:16). Abishai is a particularly volatile character (cf. 2 Sm 19:21). The same respect for the Lord's "anointed" appears here as in 24:6. The removal of the royal spear would have been a particularly daring act, possible only because in the OT view a "deep sleep from the Lord" (v. 16) had fallen upon Saul's party. **13–16.** The taunt hurled against Abner also underscores the sacral aspect of the king's person. **17–20.** David's remonstrations to Saul reflect the close association between the land and the divinity (v. 19). David interprets his exile from Israel as forced exile from Yahweh, equivalent to "serve other gods!" Similar, are the attitudes of Ruth (Ru 2:12) and Naaman (2 Kgs 5:17). **21–25.** Saul's kind words (which do not go as far as those of 24:20–22) have no effect on the situation.

39 **(M) David Among the Philistines (27:1–12).** See the other account of David's dealings with Achish of Gath in 21:10–16. Ch. 12 provides considerable detail, but it does not enable us to answer with certainty just what David's motives were. Union with the Philistines was not the best way to escape Saul, and it is only by treachery that David is able to succeed. **1–7.** No mention is made of doubts on the part of Achish, and he readily accedes to David's request for Ziklag, NE of Beer-sheba on the margin of Philistine territory. From this as a center, David would be expected to control the area to the best interests of Achish. **8–12.** David's strategy favors his future return to his people, because the desert tribes mentioned in v. 8 were natural enemies of the Israelites in the Negeb. At the same time, his report to Achish made him appear loyal to the Philistines (vv. 10–12).

40 **(N) Saul and the Witch of Endor (28:1–25).** This episode belongs after ch. 30, since v. 4 mentions Saul's presence at Gilboa, not far from Endor. **1–2.** These verses end David's relationship to Achish (except for 29:1–11), and prepare for the description of the military measures taken by the Philistines against Saul. David's reply to Achish (v. 2) is deliberately ambiguous. **3.** Cf. 25:1. Witchcraft and necromancy were forbidden in Israel (Lv 19:31; 20:6; Dt 18:11); nonetheless, such practices existed (2 Kgs 21:6; Is 8:19). **4–5.** The seriousness of the Philistine threat is revealed in their presence deep into the NE of Palestine. **6–7.** Saul is represented as being unable to learn the will of God by the casting of lots; the whole story intends to be a comment upon his downfall. **8–14.** In this vivid description, the events happen very quickly. Saul has to reassure the witch that there is nothing to fear, and he requests the presence of Samuel (which might have been enough to give away his own identity). At least, the witch concludes that she is dealing with Saul, once she sees Samuel! Her reply to Saul (v. 13) is particularly noteworthy. She says that she sees an *'ĕlōhîm* (a "god," or "elohim" being) coming up out of the earth; this term is frequently reserved for members of the heavenly court. **15.** Perhaps this line is what one would expect from someone who comes up from Sheol! **16–19.** Samuel confirms that the doom of Saul is certain. **20–25.** The industrious and practical activity of the witch is a somewhat surprising, if welcome, ending to this strange story.

41 **(O) The Philistines Dismiss David (29:1–11).** The scene is now in the north at Aphek, not yet as far E as Gilboa (ch. 31), and the moment of truth arrives for David. Fortunately, the Philistines themselves refuse to credit his loyalty (vv. 4–5; cf. 18:7; 21:11), despite the protestation of Achish (v. 3). Hence, David is given his leave, to return apparently to Ziklag, his city (ch. 30). **6–11.** Achish is represented as dismissing David very unwillingly, and David, while affirming his loyalty, does not press the matter too much. **9.** *an angel of God:* It is apparently a proverbial saying, at least among the Hebrews (2 Sm 14:20; 19:27), but Achish is already represented as speaking as an Israelite in the oath of v. 6.

42 **(P) David and the Amalekites (30:1–31).** During David's absence from Ziklag, the Amalekites raid his city, and David is faced with revolt (vv. 1–6). **7–10.** Recourse to the ephod to determine the divine will indicates that the Amalekites should be pursued. At the brook Besor (S of Gaza) a contingent remains behind—a situation that gives rise to the ruling expressed in vv. 21–25. **11–15.** There is a surprising amount of detail given to the episode with the abandoned Egyptian slave. "Cherethites" (v. 14) usually means Cretan; they came to be associated with the Philistines, and from them, David formed a personal bodyguard (2 Sm 8:18; 15:18). **26–31.** The towns of Judah mentioned here are all in the Negeb. We may surmise that David's generosity is calculated, in view of future developments (2 Sm 2:4).

43 **(Q) Saul's Death at Gilboa (31:1–13).** This event follows naturally upon ch. 28. **1–3.** Saul's army is utterly routed, and his wound seems to be mortal. **4–6.** The description of Saul's death by his own hand is dramatic; the motif of touching the Lord's anointed reappears. Saul chooses suicide, so infrequent among the Israelites, to avoid torture and shameful death. **7.** The mention of people from Transjordan seems questionable; it is lacking in 1 Chr 10:13. **8–10.** The brutal public display is in keeping with ancient Near Eastern practice. **11–13.** This action of the people of Jabesh-gilead is prompted by gratitude (ch. 11); cremation is not customary in the OT.

COMMENTARY—2 SAMUEL

(IV) David as King (2 Sm 1:1–8:18).

44 **(A) The Report of Saul's Death (1:1–16).** The following version of Saul's death differs from that of 1 Sm 31:1–13, and the veracity of the Amalekite is hardly to be trusted. But the narrative itself shows signs of a combination of two distinct traditions. According to one (vv. 1–4), a "man from Saul's camp" came to Ziklag to announce the death; according to the other (vv. 5–10), it was an Amalekite who brought the news, possibly in hope of obtaining a remuneration for his part in Saul's death. **10.** The "crown" (*nēzer*) was the royal emblem, and it is significantly offered to David. **11–12.** These are the usual signs of mourning, and there is no reason to question the mourners' sincerity. **13–16.** The messenger was the son of a sojourner (*gēr*), or resident alien. Such residents were guaranteed certain rights, but without full citizenship. David has him put to death on the basis of the sacred character of the "anointed of the Lord" (1 Sm 24:7; 26:9).

45 **(B) David's Dirge over Saul and Jonathan (1:17–27).** This famous poem has been poorly transmitted and is widely regarded as a Davidic composition: "That so perfect a poem as 2 Sm 1:17ff. appears at the beginning of the history of Israel demonstrates the greatness of the poetry of Israel at a very early age" (A. Bentzen, *IOT* 1, 136). **18.** The "Song of the Bow" results from a corrupt text in this verse. *book of Jashar:* This book was probably a collection of poems (cf. Jos 10:13). **19.** *how the mighty are fallen:* This type of expression is characteristic of the lamentation; note the refrain in v. 27. **20.** The prohibition forbids the telling of the disaster in the Philistine towns. **21.** A curse (of drought) is leveled against Gilboa; the text is corrupt, but a Ugaritic parallel suggests "upwelling of the deeps" in 21b (cf. H. Ginsberg, *BAR* 2, 49). **22–23.** David extols the bravery and courage of Saul and Jonathan (v. 22), and idealizes their union of spirit (cf. 1 Sm 22:8!). **24.** The apostrophe to the women reminds them of their debt to Saul. **25.** Cf. vv. 19 and 27. **26.** The poignant sincerity of the words about Jonathan is confirmed by the events of 1 Sm 19–20.

46 **(C) David, King of Judah at Hebron (2:1–7).** **1–4.** Hebron, about 19 mi. S of Jerusalem, is to become David's capital. It was only natural that he would receive the support from his own tribe of Judah, particularly in view of his previous overtures (1 Sm 30:26–31) and his military prowess that could be turned against the Philistines. **5–7.** His message to the people of Jabesh-gilead was sincere (v. 6) as well as political (v. 7).

47 **(D) Civil War Between David and Ishbosheth (2:8–32).** The "bosheth" in the name of Saul's son results from a deliberate change; the name was originally Ishbaal, but the unhappy associations around the word "baal" dictated the change. Ishbosheth is set up at Mahanaim in Transjordan as successor of Saul, but Abner is the power behind the throne. **9.** The MT has "Ashurites" (Assyrians), but probably "Asherites" should be read; the followers of Ishbosheth seem to be concentrated in Transjordan, although he is technically king of Israel. **10–11.** The "two years" of Ishbosheth's reign does not agree well with David's reign of seven years at Hebron (also 5:5). **12–17.** A sort of duel takes place at Gibeon and develops into a full scale combat. Gibeon (el-Jîb) is about 6 mi. NW of Jerusalem; a large rock-cut pool was excavated there in 1956 by J. Pritchard (*Archaeology and the Old Testament* [Princeton, 1958] 87–90), which is probably the landmark mentioned in v. 13. **18.** Two of this trio of brothers will figure largely in the reign of David. In the ensuing conflict (vv. 19–23), Asahel is killed by an unwilling Abner, who well knows that he will have to deal with blood vengeance from Joab (v. 22). **24–32.** The truce puts an end to this first conflict, in which David's men were the victors.

48 **(E) The Murder of Abner (3:1–39).** David's rise to power is aided by the death of Saul's old general, related here in great detail (vv. 6–39) after a preliminary notice about David (vv. 2–5). **2–5.** Of these sons, three are particularly important in the chapters that follow: Amnon, Absalom, and Adonijah. **6–11.** Abner's possession of a royal concubine had political overtones (cf. 16:21–22; 1 Kgs 2:22), which are not lost on Ishbosheth; it was a way of pressing a claim to the throne. Abner displays an air of injured loyalty (v. 8; on "dog" as a term of contempt, see D. W. Thomas, *VT* 10 [1960] 410–27) and then threatens to go over to David (vv. 9–10). **12–21.** The negotiations between Abner and David are certainly favorable to the latter. The demand for Michal is prompted by political motives rather than love (vv. 13–16; cf. 1 Sm 18:20–27), for David is asserting that he is, after all, the son-in-law of Saul. Abner speaks to important parties (the "elders," and especially Benjamin, the tribe of Saul) on behalf of David. **22–39.** This vivid scene will not be the only instance of Joab's murderous instincts (cf. 20:8–10). Joab is motivated by blood vengeance (cf 2:22–23) and also by the fact that Abner was a rival for his own position as general in the new order. **31–39.** David's dismay is doubtless genuine, but the bloody deed was likely to undo all the political moves toward full kingship. Hence, he spares no effort in disassociating himself from Joab's action: official mourning, with David as principal mourner (vv. 33–34); personal fasting; and a powerful curse upon Joab (whom he dares not punish or dismiss). **29.** *spindle:* The point of this metaphor is that Joab's descendants might be weak and effeminate.

49 **(F) The End of Ishbosheth (4:1–12).** One might almost have foreseen the fall of this weak king; again, David's measures against the murderers are calculated to win the goodwill of the northern tribes. **2–3.** Identified are the murderers, with details on their Benjaminite origins (although Beeroth was a Gibeonite town, Jos 9:17). **4.** The note on Mephibosheth fits in properly at 9:3. The name disguises the original form, Meribbaal, which was deliberately changed (see comment on 2:8). **5–8.** The murderers attempt a theological justification (v. 8) of their deed. **9–12.** David's reaction is swift and brutal, and at the same time shows his own innocence and his respect for the house of Saul; however, now the kingdom belongs to him.

50 **(G) David, King of Israel in Jerusalem (5:1–16) (= 1 Chr 11:1–9).** **1–5.** David had been anointed king of Judah (2:4). Now he is anointed by the elders of Israel. The two kingdoms did not thereupon coalesce, but remained distinct entities; David ruled over a twofold kingdom that eventually drew apart (1 Kgs 12). It has been called a personal union (A. Alt, *KlSchr* 2, 66–75) in which the government of the two states joined in the person of David. **6–8.** David's choice of Jerusalem as the capital was wise. It stood at the border of Judah and Israel, outside the sphere of influence of any one tribe, and was never before occupied by Israelites. These verses are obscure; perhaps the reference to the "blind" and the "lame" indicates the opinion that it could be adequately defended by anyone. The "water shaft" (*ṣinnôr*) has been taken by some to indicate the way in which Joab (1 Chr 11:6) entered the city, but this is doubtful. **9.** The "city of David" is Zion, the fortified city he captured from the Jebusites, and which is identified with the triangular hill bounded by the Tyropoeon and Kedron valleys. The Millo ("filling") refers to a rampart or earthwork, probably to the north of the city. **11.** Cf. 1 Kgs 9:11; the Phoenicians were able to supply personnel and material. There is no chronological sequence to these notices, which are interspersed with theological reflection (vv. 10, 12). **13–16.** Cf. 3:2–5 for the family born in Hebron. (On Jerusalem, → Biblical Geography, 73:92–94; Religious Institutions, 76:54.)

51 **(H) Wars with the Philistines (5:17–25) (= 1 Chr 14:8–16).** **17–21.** The first battle to be noted began in the valley of Rephaim SW of Jerusalem; David leaves the "stronghold" (probably Adullam; cf. 23:13) and defeats the Philistines at Baal-perazim ("Lord of breaking through"—hence, the play on words in v. 20). **22–25.** In a second battle, David drives the Philistines back to their coastal territory. The sound of marching in the balsam trees is interpreted as the presence of God with David's army (vv. 23–24). More information concerning the early part of David's reign, and especially his war with the Philistines, is available in the appendices chs. 21–23.

52 (I) The Transfer of the Ark to Jerusalem (6:1–23) (= 1 Chr 13:1–16:43). 1–15. This is one of David's most important deeds. He now made Jerusalem the religious center of the people; the Ark was the symbol of religious unity for the north and the south. The account of the Ark ceased in 1 Sm 7:1, where it was left in Kiriath-jearim (apparently called Baale-judah here). Although the MT is not clear, it appears that Uzzah paid with his life for presuming to touch the Ark (v. 7). This should be understood as a *post hoc, ergo propter hoc* conclusion; God is the direct cause of everything that happens, and the sudden death of Uzzah was associated with his touching the sacred Ark. It is only after the house of Obed-edom is blessed by the presence of the Ark that David dares to move it with dancing and celebration to Jerusalem. **16–23.** David, as king, is a sacred person, and can offer sacrifice (v. 18). Michal's biting remarks are answered with the simplicity that seems to have characterized David's religious outlook. Her sterility (v. 23) seems to result from the fact that David simply put her aside; the result is that Saul's line is not continued through David. Ps. 132 should be compared with this chapter.

53 (J) The Oracle of Nathan (7:1–29) (= 1 Chr 17:1–27). This oracle is the basis of (royal) messianism in the OT (→ Aspects OT Thought, 77:155). Nathan reverses his first word, that the king should build a temple; instead of David building a "house" (temple) for the Lord, the Lord will build a "house" (dynasty—an everlasting dynasty) for David.

(Amsler, S., *David, Roi et Messie* [Neuchâtel, 1963]. Gese, H., "Der Davidsbund und die Zionserwählung," *ZThK* 61 [1964] 10–26. McKenzie, J. L., *MR* 205ff.)

5–7. This passage reflects a somewhat hostile attitude (or, at least, indifference) toward the Temple, and a preference for the desert practice; a favorable attitude appears in v. 13, which may be a later addition. **8–12.** The promise to David is a personal one—the continuation of his line in an everlasting dynasty (vv. 12, 16)—but Israel, God's people (vv. 10–11), will enjoy peace and security. **13.** The reference is to Solomon's building the Temple (cf. 1 Chr 22:7–10), and the assurance of divine favor is extended to the dynasty (vv. 14–16). **18–29.** In reply, David offers this touching prayer of praise and thanksgiving before the Ark. **23.** Cf. Dt 4:7,34; Ps 44:2–3. Ps 89 should be compared with this chapter; in v. 35, the promise is called a covenant.

54 (K) David's Wars (8:1–18) (= 1 Chr 18:1–17). This summary may have been added by D, perhaps on the basis of royal annals. **1.** The text is uncertain; "Metheg-ammah" is unknown, and 1 Chr 18:1 reads "Gath and its villages." **2.** David's harshness to the Moabites (a slaughter of two-thirds) is related without any comment as to the reason; it is difficult to understand in view of 1 Sm 22:3–4. **3–8.** Cf. 10:6–19. The victory over the Arameans is achieved by defeating Hadadezer of Zobah (in the Antilebanon), who had the Arameans of Damascus as his allies. **4.** David's treatment of the chariot horses leads us to infer that his forces were still largely foot soldiers; otherwise he would have made use of the horses for his own army. **9–11.** The action of Toi of Hamath (N of Zobah) is that of a vassal ruler who pays tribute to a sovereign king. **13–14.** The Valley of Salt is in the vicinity of the Arabah, which continues the depression S of the Dead Sea (cf. 1 Kgs 11:15–17). **15.** In Israel itself the king actually administered justice (cf. 15:2–4); he governed the empire through governors and garrisons (vv. 6, 14) or vassal kings. **16–18.** This list is perhaps earlier than the one in 20:23–25. Joab is the general of the army and Benaiah is the head of David's personal soldiers, the Cherethites and Pelethites (Cretans and Philistines—mercenaries). Jehoshaphat was the "recorder" (*mazkîr*), an office derived from the Egyptian court and equivalent to "royal herald." (De Vaux, *AI* 132). The office of secretary or scribe (*sôpēr*) also corresponds to the Egyptian post. David's cabinet is completed by the two priests, Zadok and Abiathar (son of Ahimelech, not the reverse). Zadok is mentioned here for the first time, and is the forefather of the priestly line that eventually gained control of the Jerusalem sanctuary (on his origins, see De Vaux, *AI* 372–74). The mention of David's sons as priests (v. 18) is replaced in 20:26 and omitted in 1 Chr 18:17, but we must remember that royalty carried with it priestly prerogatives (6:18). (→ Religious Institutions, 76:20.)

55 (V) David's Court (9:1–20:26). There is general agreement that chs. 9–20 constitute a unique historical document in the OT, perhaps written by either a member of the court or, at least, a contemporary. It is often given the name "Succession Document," because L. Rost (*Die Überlieferung von der Thronnachfolge Davids* [BWANT 42; 1926]) first pointed out the basic question: Who shall succeed David? It was, of course, finally Solomon, and hence 1 Kgs 1–2 are included in this block of narrative (cf. Eissfeldt, *OTI* 137–39; G. von Rad, *GesSt* 159–88).

56 (A) David and Mephibosheth (9:1–13). 1. David remains faithful to his friendship with Jonathan (1 Sm 18:1–4; 20:15–17). His question about the "house of Saul" indicates that the event related in 21:14 had already occurred. **2–8.** Through Ziba, one of Saul's servants, he locates Jonathan's crippled son, Mephibosheth (see comment on 4:4), and keeps him as a retainer in his own household. It was also convenient for David to anticipate any revolt that might be raised in favor of Saul's family. **9–13.** Ziba is commissioned to manage Saul's property. Both men will figure in 16:1–4 and 19:24–30.

57 (B) David's Wars with the Ammonites and Arameans (10:1–19) (= 1 Chr 19:1–19). Ch. 10 leads into the Bathsheba affair (ch. 11). **2–5.** Nahash of Ammon had been hostile to Saul (1 Sm 11) and perhaps friendly to David; his successor now provokes war by his treatment of David's messengers. **6–8.** Cf. 8:3–8; two new Syrian principalities are added; both Tob and Maacah are in northern Transjordan. **9–19.** Joab's strategy brings victory (vv. 9–14), but the reinforcements of the Arameans induce a new campaign that is successfully conducted by David.

58 (C) David's Adultery with Bathsheba (11:1–27). 1. The Ammonite campaign continues (Rabbah, the capital, is present-day Amman, the capital of Jordan), but David remains in Jerusalem; even his own bodyguard is in the field with Joab. **2–5.** The sin with Bathsheba is forthrightly told. Uriah is mentioned in 23:39 as a "hero," and was probably one of the royal bodyguards; the designation "Hittite" describes him as a foreigner. The purpose of the parenthetical remark in v. 4 about purification is not clear. **5.** The succinctness of this message prepares for the various methods David will employ to unite husband and wife, so as to cover his own guilt. **6–13.** As a campaigning soldier, Uriah abstains from intercourse (cf. 1 Sm 21:4). **8.** *wash your feet:* Its broad meaning is indicated by Uriah's words in v. 11. Neither royal present nor banquet can induce Uriah to come to his wife; one wonders if he suspected something. **14–25.** David engineers the death of Uriah, and Joab correctly calculates David's reaction to the course of the battle—and to Uriah's death! **26–27.** There is some irony in the remark that the marriage follows the mourning, and the entire chapter culminates in the final remark of v. 27.

59 (D) Nathan's Parable and David's Penitence (12:1–31). 1–6. This simple and beautiful parable of the ewe lamb draws David into an untenable position (vv. 5–6). **7–15.** After David has risen to the bait, the words ring out: "you are the man." David had apparently taken over Saul's harem (v. 8), and now he has taken the wife of one of his soldiers. **10.** The rest of the court story (Amnon, Absalom) bears out the statement that the sword shall never depart from David's house. **11.** Cf. 16:21–22; it is so explicitly stated that we may suspect it is an editorial addition. **13–14.** David's frank confession is an acknowledgement of sin "against the Lord." The child will die, because "you have scorned the Lord" (not, as in the MT, "the enemies of the Lord"). **15–23.** The description of David's penitence is in line with his simplicity (cf. 6:21–22) and his sense of realism (vv. 20–23). He sought to ward off the death of the child, but he failed; he fully expects to go to Sheol (v. 23), but this is the "land of no return," as the ancients called it. **24–25.** The birth of Solomon (Jedidiah, "beloved of the Lord") is recorded as an indication of the Lord's pardon. We have the first inkling that Solomon will succeed to the throne at the end of a bloody and sad history (and against heirs with better rights to the throne). **26–31.** This section closes out the campaign against the Ammonites. Joab has captured the water supply (v. 27, "city of waters") of Rabbah and invites David to capture the capital and make it a royal city ("lest it be called by my name"). **30.** Instead of "their king," one should read "Milcom," the Ammonite divinity. **31.** The MT has suggested a bizarre massacre, effected with workmens' tools; a slight change in the text would indicate that David put the people to work at the kilns—i.e., forced labor.

60 **(E) Amnon's Crime and Absalom's Revenge (13:1–38).** David's son, Absalom, is a central figure in the events of chs. 13–20, which form a commentary on 12:11. **1.** Amnon is David's oldest son and presumptive heir to the throne. His half-sister Tamar is full sister of Absalom, next in the line of succession (since the second son, Chileab, is apparently dead). **2–14.** The plan suggested by an otherwise unknown Jonadab enables Amnon to force Tamar to yield to him; her words in v. 13 indicate that a marriage relationship would not have been forbidden (Lv 18:9 speaks for later legislation). **15–19.** This description is poignant and also true to life. **20–22.** Absalom's words to Tamar are not as indifferent as they sound, as the sequel shows. David's anger (v. 21) is meaningless; he never was able to control and discipline his family. **23–29.** On the festive occasion of sheepshearing (1 Sm 25:4ff.), Absalom sets a trap for Amnon; v. 26 would suggest that David suspected something. **30–36.** Jonadab corrects the report that Absalom had killed all the princes, and they return safely to the king. **37–38.** Absalom takes refuge in the home of his mother's family at Geshur (3:3), an Aramean principality under David's rule, E of the Sea of Galilee. **39.** This remark prepares for 14:1.

61 **(F) Joab Effects Absalom's Return (14:1–33).** **1–7.** The wily Joab persuades a wise woman from David's own home area of Tekoa to put on an "act" and speak a parable in the style of Nathan (12:1–7), which parallels David's situation. **8–11.** She is not satisfied with David's vague reply (v. 8); the guilt of which she speaks in v. 9 is the responsibility for not pursuing the murderer—she is ready to assume this "guilt." **12–17.** Now that the king has issued an opinion, she comes to the heart of the affair: the exiled Absalom. Her realistic philosophy appears in v. 14, which should read, "like water poured out upon the ground that cannot be gathered up again—nor can God take it up." **17.** *like the angel of God:* David has "divine" wisdom (cf. v. 20), knowing all things ("good and evil"; Gn 3:5). **18–20.** This remarkable conversation comes to an end as David surmises that Joab has put the woman up to this. **21–24.** Joab brings Absalom back, but the royal palace is out of bounds. **25–27.** This personal note interrupts the sequence; the mention of Absalom's long hair prepares for 18:9, and 18:18 conflicts with v. 27. **28–33.** Absalom is not satisfied with Joab's intercession; he is the type to whom all must yield, and he demands the return to the king's favor.

62 **(G) Absalom's Revolt (15:1–37).** Although Absalom would be heir to the throne on Amnon's death, he could not wait, and apparently thought that his own actions had put him in an unfavorable light. **1–6.** Absalom gives himself the air of a pretender to the throne, playing on the tribal feelings (the north, as against Judah), correcting injustice, and appearing as a prince (v. 1). **7–12.** For four years (v. 7), Absalom prepares his revolt. Hebron may have been chosen to set off the revolt, for in that city there may have been resentment over David's choice of Jerusalem as capital. The *coup d'état* occurs with surprising ease, and the 200 who participate in the religious feast (v. 11) apparently find themselves identified with the rebels. Giloh, the home of Ahithophel, may be identified with Khirbet Jala, 5 mi. NW of Hebron; he seems to have been the grandfather of Bathsheba (11:3; 23:34), which may explain his participation in the revolt.

13–37. The ensuing events in David's flight are described succinctly but vividly; it is not the first time that David has been the hunted one! His strategy is immediate flight; at the same time, he leaves some of his followers (the priests, Hushai) behind to remain in contact with him. The loyalty he inspired is quite evident in the stirring episode of Ittai the Gittite (vv. 19–22). Even though Ittai was probably a free-lance fighter from the Philistines and unable to return home, he wholeheartedly threw his support to David. The exit from Jerusalem is described in picturesque detail (vv. 23, 30). **24–29.** Although some commentators think of David's commission to Zadok and Abiathar as strategy (the desirability of having "spies" in Jerusalem), we should not overlook vv. 25–26. They testify to the simplicity and directness of David's religious attitude. **32–37.** Eminent strategy, on David's part, is shown by his plan for Hushai, who must have been a person of some standing in the community. His patronymic, "Archite," indicates that he belonged to a Canaanite group near Bethel (Jos 16:2). The meeting takes place "where God was worshiped," i.e., perhaps the sanctuary at Nob (1 Sm 21:2).

63 **(H) Details of the Revolt (16:1–23).** **1–4.** See 9:1–13. There are other instances of local inhabitants provisioning an army (17:27–29; 19:33). Ziba's version is contradicted by Mephibosheth in 19:27–28, and David himself refuses to determine who is at fault (19:30); his decision in Ziba's favor (v. 4), is precipitate. **5–14.** It is not to be expected that David would escape vilification at the hands of Saul's relatives. Shimei, son of Gera (one of the "sons" of Benjamin, 46:21; hence, a Benjaminite name), curses him. **8.** The allusion of the "blood of the house of Saul" may be to 21:1–14. **9–13.** David's reaction is quite considerate, and consonant with the resigned attitude that has characterized his conduct in the flight (v. 11). He restrains Abishai (cf. 1 Sm 26:8–9; 2 Sm 3:39) and hopes that the Lord will be moved to support him. **15–19.** Absalom is deceived by Hushai, who makes himself out to be the supporter of whomever the Lord and Israel have chosen as king. **20–23.** Ahithophel's advice is designed to make all Israel realize that the revolt is irrevocable. Absalom's appropriation of his father's harem is a final and definitive step (see comment on 3:7), which would have the effect of firming up his adherents' commitment to him.

64 **(I) The Undoing of Ahithophel's Counsel (17:1–29).** **1–4.** Ahithophel's advice rings true: immediate pursuit of David in his present circumstances. Moreover, only David is to be struck down (vv. 2–3); it is with him alone that the quarrel lies, not with the people. **5–14.** Hushai's objections are extremely well put: David would not be with the rest of his men; moreover, he was an extremely able warrior, so everyone ("from Dan to Beer-sheba") should first be gathered for the pursuit. The final comment (v. 14) is editorial, one of the few explicit indications (11:25) of the thread of divine providence running through this narrative. **15–23.** Apparently Hushai does not even wait for Absalom's decision (v. 14), because he merely relates both views to Zadok and Abiathar and counsels David to cross the Jordan. The tension is increased by the sparkling description of the narrow escape of the priests' sons, Jonathan and Ahimaaz. **23.** The starkness of this note concerning Ahithophel is clear, especially in view of the rarity of suicide in the Bible. **24–29.** David repairs to Mahanaim in Transjordan, once the residence of Ishbosheth (2:8), where he is cordially received and bountifully provisioned (vv. 28–29) by non-Israelites (Shobi, perhaps Barzillai) as well as by Israelites. Meantime Absalom comes to Gilead with his contingent. **25.** Amasa will play an important role in chs. 19–20. His genealogy here is doubtful; 1 Chr 2:17 reads "Jether" for Ithra, and "Jesse" for Nahash, which may have crept in here from v. 27.

65 **(J) David's Victory and Absalom's Death (18:1–33).** (In the MT, 18:33 is 19:1). **1–5.** The leaders of David's army are all experienced, loyal men. In v. 3, we should read, with the versions, "you are worth ten thousand of us." **5.** The Absalom motif pervades the entire chapter. **6–8.** This description of the battle is almost epigrammatic (v. 8); the "forest of Ephraim" is more jungle than forest, and is located in Transjordan. **9–14.** Absalom is somehow caught in a tree, and a traditional explanation has called on the data of 14:26 (his long hair) to explain this. The conversation (vv. 10–14) between Joab and the soldier reflects the Absalom motif and also serves to underline the fierce warlike qualities of David's general; the soldier's reasoning seems perfectly valid. The work of the armor bearers appears to be unnecessary (v. 15), but such an action was part of their function (cf. 1 Sm 14:13). **16–18.** In contrast with Absalom's sad end is the mention of the impressive monument he had already had built for himself in Jerusalem. The relatively late (Roman?) tomb that is pointed out in the Kedron Valley as the "tomb of Absalom" has nothing to do with Absalom's original monument. In fact, Absalom appears to have had three sons (14:27). **19–33.** It is a particularly vivid and dramatic description of the manner in which the news of Absalom's death was reported to David; the details are carefully noted (the Cushite bowing before Joab, v. 21; the two gates, v. 22; etc.). **19–23.** Joab opposes Ahimaaz, precisely because the news is bad; it should be left for the Cushite courier, but he finally relents and Ahimaaz outruns the Cushite. **24–33.** The final verse is 19:1 in the MT. In this remarkable description, the tension and anxiety of David and the watchman are well brought out. The fact that the messenger is alone is considered to be a good sign; bad news would have been indicated by a group of fugitives. In his reply, Ahimaaz holds back the news of Absalom's death, which is left for the Cushite to announce. David's grief over Absalom was doubtless genuine, but he had never succeeded in understanding him during his life.

66 **(K) The Restoration (19:1–43).** The versification of the MT reads one ahead of these numbers throughout ch. 19. David stays his return to Jerusalem, apparently because of his mourning for Absalom, and the slow process of reconciliation and restoration begins. **1–8.** When David allows his grief to go beyond bounds, Joab intervenes. He is a hard, tough soldier, but completely devoted to David. Joab evaluates the situation correctly (vv. 5–7), as David himself realizes (v. 8). **9–15.** The northern tribes seem ready to take David back (vv. 9–10), and he moves immediately to be invited back by the leaders of his own tribe of Judah. Blood proves thicker than water, and besides (as 20:1ff. indicate), David knew where the true loyalty was. Again, he shows his political astuteness; his forgiveness of the rebels extends even to Amasa, whom he appoints as his new commander in place of Joab (thus, he hoped to repay Joab for the slaying of Absalom). **16–23.** Cf. 16:5–14. David displays great forbearance toward Shimei, even overcoming the objections of the always hot-tempered Abishai (16:9); but later events show that he was far from forgetting Shimei (1 Kgs 2:8–9).

24–30. It is not completely clear who is lying, Ziba or Mephibosheth, but the attitude of the latter seems more honest. Ziba rushes to the Jordan (v. 17) to meet David before the crippled son of Jonathan arrives; he has been making the most of his new fortune, while Mephibosheth seems to have been distraught by events (v. 24). David clings to his decision, and Mephibosheth's generous statement (v. 30) makes him look rather niggardly. **31–40.** In return for Barzillai's loyal support (17:27–29), David offers to bring him to the court. Barzillai's description of old age is quite expressive. He pleads with David to take his "servant" Chimham (one cannot be sure that Jer 41:18 refers to this man), and David accepts. After a touching farewell to the old man (v. 39), David is accompanied to Gilgal by groups from the north and south who are far from being unified. **41–43.** The bickering between "Israel" and "Judah" ends in Judah's favor, but the seeds of discontent will flower into rebellion (ch. 20).

67 **(L) Sheba's Revolt (20:1–26).** This revolt does not merely reflect the old hostility between David and the house of Saul, but also the enmity between Israel and Judah (19:41–43). **1–2.** The rebel cry, "each man to his tents, O Israel" (proclaimed also at Shechem, 1 Kgs 12:16), reflects the independent, nomadic strain that never expired. **3.** David's sequestration of his harem was necessary after the action of Absalom (cf. 16:21–22). **4–10.** As he had promised (19:13), David makes Amasa his commander, but the latter's dilatoriness persuades David to rely upon Abishai and the royal bodyguard to quell the revolt. Joab is not to be outdone, however, and he slays Amasa deceitfully; the "great stone" may be a reference to the stone of an altar at the Gibeon high place where Solomon sacrificed (1 Kgs 8). **11–13.** Joab naturally takes over the leadership, and his cause is identified with David's (v. 11). **14–22.** The pursuit of Sheba leads to Abel-beth-maacah (Tell Abil, 12 mi. N of Lake Huleh). Joab's assault leads to the solution proposed by the "wise woman," and, in a gruesome scene, the head of Sheba is thrown over the wall, ending the revolt. The proverb in v. 18 suggests the town's reputation as a center of wisdom and judgment. The metaphor of mother and daughters (v. 19) indicates towns and dependent villages. **23–26.** See comment on 8:16–18. Adoram is the Adoniram who is also employed under Solomon (1 Kgs 4:6; 12:18). Sheva (v. 25) is variously named: Seraiah (8:17), Shavsha (1 Chr 18:16), and Shisha (1 Kgs 4:3). Ira, who derives from the clan of Jair (Nm 32:41), is identified by some with one of David's heroes, "Ira the Ithrite" (23:38). The "succession history," as Rost conceives it, is continued in 1 Kgs 1–2, since the basic question answered by the narrative is: "Who shall occupy the throne of David?" This is only resolved by Solomon's victory over Adonijah.

(VI) Appendices (2 Sm 21:1–24:25).

68 (A) The Famine and the Hanging of Saul's Descendants (21:1–14). This grisly episode must have occurred early in David's reign (cf. 9:1; 16:8). **1.** The famine is interpreted as punishment from the Lord because Saul violated the oath made to the Gibeonites—a slaying that is not recorded in the Bible. **3–6.** The bloodguilt must be eliminated, and David allows the Gibeonites to choose the manner, and accedes to their request for the hanging of seven descendants. **7–9.** David spares Jonathan's son, but he hands over Saul's two sons and five grandsons (sons of Merab, according to LXX). The time indicated by "the beginning of the barley harvest" is April-May, and v. 10 indicates that the bodies were exposed all summer, until the rainy period in autumn. **10–14.** The fierce devotion of Rizpah becomes known (vv. 10–11), and David doubtless won favor by burying the remnants of Saul and Jonathan with those who were hanged. Zela is one of the towns of Benjamin (Jos 18:28) between Jerusalem and Gibeon.

69 (B) The Philistine Wars (21:15–22). The following exploits against the Philistines fit into the beginning of David's reign (cf. 5:17–25). **15–17.** This story illustrates the loyalty and reverence that David's men had for him. Ishbibenob (v. 16) is a Philistine on the scale of Goliath (cf. 1 Sm 17:7), but is otherwise unknown. *lamp of Israel:* The phrase is a metaphor for the Davidic dynasty, which must not be endangered (cf. 1 Kgs 11:36; 2 Sm 14:7).

70 (C) A Song of Praise (22:1–51). The psalm inserted here is also preserved in the Psalter: Ps 18 (→ Psalms, 35:35). The differences between them are slight, and a full treatment of them is given by F. Cross and D. Freedman (*JBL* 72 [1963] 15–34).

71 (D) "The Last Words of David" (23:1–7). Another song of praise is inserted here as David's "last words," in the style of Jacob (Gn 49) and Moses (Dt 33). Although it purports to be an "oracle" (v. 1) spoken by the spirit (v. 2), it takes up a common theme of the wisdom literature (the just prosper; the wicked perish; cf. Ps 1). The Hebr text is uncertain at many points. **1.** *the sweet psalmist of Israel:* It is reasonable to think that David's reputation as a "psalmist" has a solid basis in tradition, although it was later made too specific. The Hebr phrase can also be understood to mean "the favorite of the songs of Israel." **3–5.** God's beneficence to a just ruler is climaxed in the "everlasting covenant" he has made with David; the reference is to the oracle of Nathan (2 Sm 7). **6–7.** In contrast to the just ruler stand the godless men.

72 (E) David's Heroes (23:8–39) (= 1 Chr 11:11–41; 27:2–15). The previous poems interrupted the sequence at 21:22. More information about the Philistine wars is now given. **8–12.** The "Three" form a special group. The name of the first (v. 8) is uncertain; he is called Jashobeam, a Hachmonite, in 1 Chr 11:11. Shammah's exploit (vv. 11–12) is attributed to Eleazar in 1 Chr 11:12–14; Lehi is the site of Samson's famous exploit against the Philistines (Jgs 15). **13–17.** The "three" may be those described in vv. 8–12, but the text seems to be in some disorder; the "thirty" are not mentioned until v. 18, where they introduce another group. The episode illustrates, once again, David's hold on his men, and his gesture in pouring out the water is worthy of their courage. **18–39.** The "thirty" were a select group of warriors. Most of them come from southern Judah and they doubtless represent the warriors of David's early band. Probably not all the names have been transmitted, and some have been corrupted (v. 32; cf. 1 Chr 11:34). **18–19.** Abishai is well known from 1 Sm 26:6; 2 Sm 2:18; 10:10; 16:9–10; 18:2; 19:21–22; 20:6. **20–23.** Benaiah appears already in 8:18 and 20:23. The two "ariels of Moab" attributed to him are an unknown quantity. **24–39.** Among the more notable figures are Asahel (2:18–23), Elhanan (21:19), Shammah (v. 33; cf. v. 11), Ira (v. 38, perhaps the Ira of 20:26), and Uriah (v. 39; cf. ch. 11). The number 37 does not tally with the names; even if we include the names in vv. 8–23, there are only 36.

73 (F) David's Census (24:1–25) (= 1 Chr 21: 1–28). **1–9.** A count of the men who are able for military service (v. 9) is viewed as lack of confidence in Yahweh; one relies upon human means instead of God. Even Joab tries to dissuade David from the census (v. 3), and ultimately David acknowledges that it was sinful (vv. 10–11). The text attributes the incident to God's anger; it is the Lord who "incites" David (v. 1). Two principles of Hebr mentality are shown here: the Lord causes everything, both good and evil; adversity (in this case, famine) results from the Lord's displeasure at man's wrongdoing. Later Israelite theology modified this simplist view, to the extent that the Chronicler deliberately changes "Lord" to "Satan" (cf. 1 Chr 21:1) **5–7.** The extent of David's kingdom is indicated: from Aroer near the Arnon in Moabite territory to Kadesh on the Orontes in the north (therefore, the census took place after the campaigns against the Syrians, 8:3–12; 10:15–19), and then south to Beer-sheba. The distinction between the census in Judah and in Israel (v. 10) is noteworthy; the two kindgoms retain their separate identities during the "united monarchy." **10–14.** David is given a choice of one of the three traditional punishments; the prophet Gad has already appeared in 1 Sm 22:5. **15–17.** In several other instances, an avenging angel is made the executor of God's justice (Ez 12:23; 2 Kgs 19:35). The fact that the plague stops at the threshing floor of Araunah is significant, because it is to become the site of the Temple. It seems that the sequence beginning at v. 10 is meant to explain how the threshing floor became the location of the Temple. In v. 16, God relents out of affection for Jerusalem; in v. 17 it seems as though David's humble confession of guilt and his prayer are instrumental in staying God's hand. **18–25.** This scene not only describes the buying of the threshing floor, but portrays David as inaugurating sacrifices there; this is the point of emphasis (and not the fact that the sacrifices induced God to put an end to the plague, because the end has already been given in v. 16). (→ Religious Institutions, 76:55.)

10

1-2 KINGS

Peter F. Ellis, C.SS.R.

BIBLIOGRAPHY

1 Albright, *ARI; BP*. De Vaux, R., *Les Livres des Rois* (BJ; Paris, 1949). Driver, *Introd.* Fohrer, G., *Elia* (*AbhTANT*; Zurich, 1957). Garofalo, S. *Il Libro dei Re* (Turin, 1951). Gray, J., *I–II Kings* (Phila., 1963). Médebielle, A., *Les Livres des Rois* (*PSB;* Paris, 1949). M–G, *Kings* (ICC; N.Y., 1951). Noth, *US*. Rehm, M., *Königsbücher* (Echter-B; Würzburg, 1949). Schulz, A., *Die Bücher der Könige* (Münster, 1911–12). Von Rad, G., *Old Testament Theology I* (N.Y., 1962); "Die deuteronomistische Geschichtstheologie in den Königsbüchern," *GesSt* 189–204; *Studies in Deuteronomy* (SBT; London, 1948) 74ff.

Additional references: Eissfeldt, *OTI* 281ff. 752ff. Jenni, E., "Zwei Jahrzehnte Forschung an den Büchern Josua bis Könige," *TRu* 27 (1961) 97–146.

INTRODUCTION

2 **(I) Occasion, Date, and Place of Composition.** A great crisis occasioned the writing of Kgs. In 587, the Babylonian armies of Nebuchadnezzar breached the walls of Jerusalem, destroyed the city, burnt the Temple to the ground, and deported to Babylonia the cream of the Judean citizenry. The protection of Israel promised by God in the Sinai covenant was not realized. The Temple where he had said "My name shall be there" lay in ruins. The 400-year-old rule of the Davidic dynasty, to which God had promised perpetuity, had come to a jarring halt, and for the believing Israelite fact had brought faith to a horrible impasse. How could God be said to be faithful to his covenant promises? How could Israel still believe the divine promise that the Davidic dynasty would perdure eternally? The Jewish exiles in Babylon asked these questions of themselves after the catastrophe of 587. The last event narrated in 2 Kgs—the preferential treatment accorded Jehoiachin by Evil-merodach—is dated to 562. It was some time after this date that the book was written. Since nothing is said about the return from the Exile, 1–2 Kgs in its present state must date from sometime between 562 and 539. Some authors argue for a pre-exilic edition in the period between 621 and 597 (cf. Pfeiffer, *Introd.* 377–80). Others, with better justification, place the first edition of the book in the exilic period, some time after 562 (cf. Von Rad, *Old Testament Theology I*, 335–36).

It is impossible to say where the book was written, whether in Palestine among the remnant left in the devastated land or in Babylonia among the exiles of 597 and 587. Far more important are the audience for whom the book was written and the purpose of the author.

3 **(II) Destination and Purpose.** The book was written for the Jews who had witnessed the catastrophe of 587 and for their children whose faith was wavering. It was intended to instruct and encourage them, to elicit from them acts of repentance for their past sins, and to renew their hopes for the future. It was written, in short, to answer the distressing questions raised by the events of 587. Thus, the author instructs the exiles by demonstrating that Israel through her kings had been unfaithful to the covenant, and that God, far from being unfaithful to his part of the covenant, had remained faithful and patient with erring Israel long after Israel's infidelity had released him from any covenant bonds. He writes, therefore, to convince his people that they and not God have been unfaithful. The author's purpose, however, is not only to instruct but also to encourage. Thus, he returns repeatedly to the promise of perpetuity made to the Davidic dynasty and to the eternal bond between the dynasty, the Temple, and Jerusalem. These promises have never been annulled and it is upon their fulfillment that Israel must place her hopes for the future.

4 **(III) Nature and Message of the Book.** It must be understood clearly that the author is not primarily an historian but a theologian who uses history to elucidate and inculcate a number of definite theological propositions essential to the fulfillment of his teaching purpose. That the author is not writing history for the sake of history is amply demonstrated by the fact that he gives to the reigns of Israel's two greatest kings, Omri and Jeroboam II (the latter reigned almost 50 years), a total of 15 verses! It is also demonstrated by the author's concern throughout for religious matters—the Temple,

observance of the covenant, reforms of religion, and the relations between the kings and the prophets. The author's referral of his readers to sources giving additional information about the kings is another way in which he shows that his principal interest is religious rather than historical (cf. 1 Kgs 14:23; 2 Kgs 20:20).

A full understanding of the author's message can be obtained only by a consideration of the place of Kgs in the Deuteronomic History (Jos–Kgs) as a whole and by some idea of how he used, connected, and interpreted his sources to give witness to the theological foundations basic to his narrative and, indeed, evocative of his work as a whole. His basic message, however, is not difficult to formulate. Three major theological propositions are advanced. Two are hammered home by means of cumulative, exemplary proof and repeated, formulated expression. The third is insinuated by direct and indirect expression and by deduction from the second proposition.

The first proposition follows: Catastrophe has overtaken Israel because of the infidelity of the kings to covenant and Temple, not because of any lack of covenant fidelity on God's part. This proposition is hammered into the consciousness of his readers by the author's judgments on the kings both of Israel and Judah. All, without exception of the northern kings and the majority of the southern, Davidic, kings (with a few notable exceptions), are adjudged unfaithful to covenant and Temple. The same proposition is even more clearly inculcated in the author's explanatory discourses in 1 Kgs 11 and 2 Kgs 17.

The second proposition may be stated thus: It was the Word of God through Moses that brought Israel into history at Sinai. It is the Word of God through his prophets, continuously intervening and infallibly fulfilled, that has shaped Israel's history through the centuries. This proposition is drilled into the consciousness of his readers by the author's use of sources from the prophetic school. From them he selects stories detailing prophetic predictions and their infallible fulfillment. A total of 45 different prophetic prediction-fulfillment stories are spread over the two books (25 in 1 Kgs; 20 in 2 Kgs), with 15 of the 22 chapters in 1 Kgs and 20 of the 25 chapters in 2 Kgs containing at least one prediction-fulfillment story. The cumulative effect of these stories is such that the reader cannot doubt that once the Word of the Lord has gone forth it will be fulfilled infallibly.

The third proposition may be stated as follows: The promise made to David in 2 Sm 7, that his dynasty would be eternal, is a promise and a prediction that by its nature must be fulfilled, all things to the contrary notwithstanding. Because of the historical circumstances in the time of the author (the nation destroyed, the citizens in exile, the king deposed), he cannot point, as he does in the case of the other promise predictions he records, to the fulfillment of this promise. For all Israelites, however, as for himself, the fulfillment of this promise must be a matter of faith (→ Aspects OT Thought, 77:155–60).

5 That there is a firm foundation for this faith the author makes clear in a number of ways. First, the series of 45 different examples of prophetic prediction-fulfillment stories spread over the length of his book provides for his readers a sound basis for the logical deduction that the promise made to David in 2 Sm 7 must be fulfilled. If the Word of God has run unerringly to fulfillment in so many prophecies of infinitely less importance than the Nathan prophecy, how can it be that the promise of Nathan to David concerning the perpetuity of his dynasty will not also be infallibly fulfilled?

Second, to further inculcate the importance and perdurance of the Nathan oracle, the author makes 40 different references to David, with seven direct and seven indirect references to Nathan's promise in 2 Sm 7 (cf. 1 Kgs 2:4,45; 3:6–7,14; 5:5; 6:12; 11:32,34,36,39; 15:4–5; 2 Kgs 8:19). Moreover, he is solicitous to highlight the special protection accorded the Davidic dynasty "for the sake of David" (cf. 1 Kgs 11:12,32,34, 36,39; 15:4; 2 Kgs 8:19; 11:1ff.; 19:34) and to preserve the credentials for the legitimacy of the Davidic dynasty by giving the name of the queen mother for 19 of the 21 Davidic kings and by attesting to the burial "in the city of David" of at least 12 of the 21 Davidic kings. In contrast, nothing is said about the burial place of the northern kings, nor is any mention made of the queen mothers in the north.

Third, subtle but significant in addition is another contrast between the northern kings and the Davidic kings. All the former are condemned because they follow "in the footsteps of Jeroboam, the son of Nebat," whose sin weighs, as the author seems to be at pains to point out, as an "original sin" upon all the kings of Israel (cf. 1 Kgs 14:7–16). The southern kings, on the contrary, are compared with David, and although the comparison is mainly unfavorable, there are nevertheless some notable and even glorious exceptions (e.g., Asa, Jehoshaphat, Hezekiah, and especially Josiah). It would appear thus that while the northern kings perish under the weight of the "original sin" of Jeroboam I, the Davidic kings draw protection and support as a group from the "original justice" of David.

Fourth, and finally, if endings are important, it is of no small significance that the author ends his book with the statement that Evil-merodach (Nebuchadnezzar's successor in 562) "spoke kindly to him [the Davidic king, Jehoiachin] and set his throne above the throne of the kings who were with him in Babylon" (2 Kgs 25:27–30).

The other propositions, less substantially supported and of lesser importance, are the author's teachings concerning Jerusalem, the Temple, and retribution. By his insistent association of Jerusalem and the Temple with Nathan's oracle, and by his repeated references to Jerusalem as the city chosen by God and the Temple as the place wherein God chose to dwell "forever," the author apparently insinuates that Jerusalem and the Temple share in some way in the promise of perpetuity made to the Davidic dynasty. The author supports this proposition in a number of explicit statements (cf. 1 Kgs 6:11–13; 8:12–13; 9:3–9; 11:13,32,36; 14:21; 15:5; 2 Kgs 19:34; 20:6; 21:7–8) as well as by his extensive description of the building of the Temple (cf. 1 Kgs 6–7), by his praise for those kings who paid special attention to the Temple (cf. 1 Kgs 3–10; 15:9–15; 2 Kgs 12:1–2; 18:1–3; 22:1–2; 23:25), and by his extensive descriptions of Temple reforms carried out by such kings as Asa (1 Kgs 15), Jehoash (1 Kgs 12), Hezekiah (2 Kgs 18), and Josiah (2 Kgs 22). Concerning retribution, the author is careful to point to God's punishment of the wicked kings and of both kingdoms as collective entities. But he is also solicitous to note that God relents or puts off punishment of wicked kings in return for some good they have done or in view of their repentance (cf. 1 Kgs 11:12; 21:29; 2 Kgs 20:17–19; 22:18–20). Inasmuch as these theological propositions are not immediately evident to the eye of the modern reader because of the Jewish author's Oriental mode of theologizing, it will be helpful to search out the author's method of inculcating his message.

6 **(IV) Author's Method.** To the modern theologian, the method of theologizing used by the theologian author of Kgs appears primitive. It is so, however, only in comparison with modern, scientific, theological method. In his own time, the author was hardly a pioneer, for his predecessors were the Yahwist, the Elohist, and the compiler theologian of Dt. A comparison would show that he had much in common with these earlier theologians and, indeed, that he followed in their footsteps. It will be of more value, however, to point out his methodology and then show how he established his basic theological propositions using this methodology.

As already stated, the author of 1–2 Kgs was not interested in history as history but in using it to serve his theological purposes. Thus, a basic element in his method was the selection from the source books of Israel's history of those episodes that supported his theological teaching. Because the narrative material did not always make clear to the uninitiated reader the presence of the hand of God in Israel's history, the author was compelled to intervene and clarify by selection, arrangement, and interpretation of the material what would otherwise be intelligible only to the sophisticated reader. This he did by means of explanatory asides (e.g., 1 Kgs 11; 2 Kgs 17), by explicit theological judgments (e.g., those made on each of the kings of Israel and Judah), and by interpretative discourses (e.g., 1 Kgs 8:23–53; 9:3–9; 11:11–13,31–39; 14:7–16; 2 Kgs 20:16–19; 21:11–15; 22:15–19; 23:26–27).

Once the reader is aware of these elementary steps in the author's methodology, he can proceed to an analysis of Kgs as follows. First, isolate as far as possible the sources used by the author and single out what is common to each. Next, isolate as far as possible those parts of the book that represent the author's personal contribution by way of explanatory asides, explicit theological judgments, and interpretative discourses. What is personal to the author as distinct from the sources used by him may be determined on the basis of stylistic criteria; an a priori presumption in favor of bridges or connecting passages as being the author's personal contribution, and the possibility and often the probability that discourses found in the book may be literary devices of the author, or at least original discourses expanded by him for didactic purposes. These latter may be sought in divine discourses, prophetic discourses, and sometimes in discourses given by kings (e.g., Solomon in 1 Kgs 8). Finally, one can cross check findings by comparing what is common to the sources with what is common to the author's contribution.

The procedure described will enable the reader to explain the major portion of the material compiled in Kgs. Extraneous elements will remain, however, which are not always easy to explain. In general, we may often account for them as proper to the sources used by the author but not thoroughly edited by him. At times, we may account for them as sources used by the author to provide the foundation for less important theses of his theology.

7 **(V) Sources.** Of the many sources (a minimum of ten) used and compiled by the author, only three are cited by name: "The Book of the Acts of Solomon" (1 Kgs 11:41), "The Book of the Acts of the Kings of Israel" (1 Kgs 14:19 and *passim*), and "The Book of the Acts of the Kings of Judah" (1 Kgs 15:17 and *passim*). Other sources not cited by name include: the conclusion of the Court History of David (1 Kgs 1–2); a priestly source dealing with the Temple (1 Kgs 6–7); the Elijah cycle (1 Kgs 17–19; 21; 2 Kgs 1:2–17); the Elisha cycle (2 Kgs 2–8:15; possibly 9–10; 13:14–21); two combined Judean sources concerning Athaliah (2 Kgs 11); a source concerning the prophet Isaiah from the disciples of Isaiah (2 Kgs 18:17–20:19); and a heterogeneous collection of stories, possibly from different sources, about prophets and their relations with different kings of Israel and Judah. This collection contains a story about: Shemaiah and Rehoboam (1 Kgs 12:21–24); two nameless prophets in relation to Jeroboam I and Josiah (1 Kgs 13; 2 Kgs 23:16–20); Ahijah and Jeroboam I (1 Kgs 14); two other nameless prophets and Ahab (1 Kgs 20); Jehu and Baasha (16:1–12); Micaiah and Ahab (1 Kgs 22); and Huldah, the prophetess, and Josiah (2 Kgs 22:11–20).

Although much has been done (cf. R-F 1, 441–55; M-G, *Kings* 30ff. Driver, *Introd.* 187ff.; Noth, *US* 66ff.), a definitive analysis of the sources used in Kgs—their precise provenance, date, and extent—has yet to be made. It is uncertain, for example, whether the three sources quoted by the author represent the official archives of the respective kingdoms or, more probably, are independent works by earlier authors who drew some of their material from the official archives and some from prophetic sources. The way in which the independent cycles of Elijah and Elisha have been merged and the sheer weight in numbers of the prophetic prediction-fulfillment stories dealing with the relations between kings and prophets in the northern kingdom would seem to indicate that these stories had already been gathered into an independent corpus before the time of the author of Kgs.

8 **(VI) Outline.** The general structure of the book is simple: Part I, the history of Solomon (1 Kgs 1–11); Part II, the synoptic history of the kings of Israel and Judah, from 922 to 722 (1 Kgs 12–2 Kgs 17); Part III, the history of the remaining kings of Judah, from 722 to 587 (2 Kgs 18–25). The books may be divided further as follows:

(I) Solomon the Magnificent (1 Kgs 1:1–11:41) (= 2 Chr 1–9)
- (A) Solomon Succeeds to the Throne of David (1:1–2:46)
  - (a) Adonijah and Solomon Vie for the Throne of David (1:1–53)
  - (b) David's Death and the Removal of the Opposition (2:1–46)
- (B) The Reign of Solomon (3:1–11:41)
  - (a) Solomon the Sage (3:1–4:34)
  - (b) Solomon the Builder (5:1–9:14)
    - (i) Solomon's building preparations (5:1–18)
    - (ii) Solomon's Temple (6:1–38)
    - (iii) Solomon's palaces (7:1–14)
    - (iv) The bronze work for the Temple (7:15–51)
    - (v) The dedication of the Temple (8:1–66)
    - (vi) Solomon's vision (9:1–9)
    - (vii) The episode of Cabul (9:10–14)
  - (c) Solomon the International Merchant Prince (9:15–10:29)
  - (d) Solomon the Sinner (11:1–41)

(II) The Synoptic History of the Kings (1 Kgs 12:1–2 Kgs 16:34)
- (A) The Division of Solomon's Kingdom (12:1–13:34)
  - (a) The Division of the Kingdom (12:1–20) (= 2 Chr 10)
  - (b) A Prophetic-Fulfillment Story (12:21–24) (= 2 Chr 11:1–4)
  - (c) The Deuteronomist's Explanation of Jeroboam's Sin (12:25–32)
  - (d) A Prophetic-Fulfillment Story (12:33–13:34)
- (B) Synoptic History to the Time of Elijah (14:1–16:34)
  - (a) Jeroboam I, 922–901 (14:1–20)
  - (b) Rehoboam, 922–915 (14:21–31) (= 2 Chr 11:5–12:16)
  - (c) Abijam, 915–913 (15:1–8) (= 2 Chr 13)
  - (d) Asa, 913–873 (15:9–24) (= 2 Chr 14–16)
  - (e) Nadab, 901–900 (15:25–31)
  - (f) Baasha, 900–877 (15:33–16:7)
  - (g) Elah, 877–876 (16:8–14)
  - (h) Zimri, 876 (16:15–20)
  - (i) Omri, 876–869 (16:21–28)
  - (j) Ahab, 869–850 (16:29–34; 22:39–40)

(C) The Elijah Cycle (1 Kgs 17:1–2 Kgs 1:18)
- (a) Elijah, Ahab, and the Three-Year Drought (17:1–18:46)
- (b) Elijah's Flight to Horeb (19:1–21)
- (c) Ahab and the Prophets During the War with Aram (20:1–43)
- (d) Jezebel's Murder of Naboth (21:1–29)
- (e) Ahab Opposed by Micaiah (22:1–40)
- (f) Jehoshaphat of Judah, 873–849 (22:41–50) (= 2 Chr 17:1–21:1)
- (g) Ahaziah of Israel, 850–849 (1 Kgs 22:51–2 Kgs 1:18)

(D) The Elisha Cycle (2:1–8:29)
- (a) Elisha Succeeds Elijah (2:1–25)
- (b) Jehoram of Israel (849–842) and the War with Moab (3:1–27)
- (c) The "Fioretti" of Elisha (4:1–8:15)
  - (i) The poor widow (4:1–7)
  - (ii) The rich woman of Shunem (4:8–37)
  - (iii) The poisoned stew (4:38–41)
  - (iv) Multiplication of the loaves (4:42–44)
  - (v) Naaman the leper and Gehazi (5:1–27)
  - (vi) The lost axe (6:1–7)
  - (vii) Syrian ambuscades foiled by Elisha's clairvoyance (6:8–23)
  - (viii) Ben-hadad's siege of Samaria (6:24–7:20)
  - (ix) The rich woman of Shunem (8:1–6)
  - (x) Elisha and Hazael (8:7–15)
- (d) Jehoram of Judah, 849–842 (8:16–24) (= 2 Chr 21)
- (e) Ahaziah of Judah, 842 (8:25–29)

(E) Synoptic History from Jehu to the Fall of Samaria (9:1–17:41)
- (a) Jehu, 842–815 (9:1–10:36)
- (b) Athaliah of Judah, 842–837 (11:1–20 (= 2 Chr 22:10–23:21)
- (c) Jehoash of Judah, 837–800 (12:1–21) (= 2 Chr 24)
- (d) Jehoahaz of Israel, 815–801 (13:1–9)
- (e) Jehoash of Israel, 801–786, and the Death of Elisha (13:10–25)
- (f) Amaziah of Judah, 800–783 (14:1–22) (= 2 Chr 25)
- (g) Jeroboam II of Israel, 786–746 (14:23–29)
- (h) Azariah (Uzziah), 783–742 (15:1–7) (= 2 Chr 26)
- (i) Zechariah and Shallum of Israel, 746–745 (15:8–15)
- (j) Menahem, 745–738 (15:16–22)
- (k) Pekahiah and Pekah of Israel, 738–732 (15:23–31)
- (l) Jotham of Judah, 750–735 (15:32–38) (= 2 Chr 27)
- (m) Ahaz of Judah, 735–715 (16:1–20) (= 2 Chr 28)
- (n) Hoshea (732–724) and the Fall of Samaria, 722 (17:1–41)

(III) The Last Kings of Judah (2 Kgs 18:1–25:30)

(A) Hezekiah, 715–687 (18:1–20:21) (= 2 Chr 29–32; Is 36–39)
- (a) Hezekiah's Reforms and the Invasion of Sennacherib, 701 (18:1–16)
- (b) Sennacherib's Invasion According to the Isaian Source (18:17–19:37)
- (c) Hezekiah's Sickness and Merodach-baladan (20:1–21)

(B) Manasseh (687–642) and Amon (642–640) (21:1–26) (= 2 Chr 33)

(C) Josiah, 640–609 (22:1–23:30) (= 2 Chr 34–35)

(D) Jehoahaz (609) and Jehoiakim (609–598) (23:31–24:7) (= 2 Chr 36:1–8)

(E) Jehoiachin (598–597) and Zedekiah (597–587) (24:8–25:30) (= 2 Chr 36:9–23)

COMMENTARY

9 **(I) Solomon the Magnificent (1 Kgs 1:1–11:41) (= 2 Chr 1–9).** At least three distinct sources have contributed to the composition of Part I: chs. 1–2, from the Court History of David; chs. 3–5 and 9:10–10:29, from the Acts of Solomon; and chs. 6:1–8:13, from a P source. The exilic author's hand is evident in 2:3–4,10–11,46b; 3:2–3; 4:24; 6:1; 8:14–66; 9:1–9; 11:11–13,29–39. By incorporating the praises of Solomon from the work entitled "The Acts of Solomon," the author has encouraged his exilic readers with a picture of the kingdom in its prime, thus demonstrating the "first fruits" flowing from the promise made to David concerning his dynasty and the Temple. By recording the downfall of Solomon (ch. 11), he has begun his history of the kings' infidelity by introducing Solomon as the first of the unfaithful monarchs, whose sins have been instrumental in bringing about the three great catastrophes in Israel's history: the division of the kingdom in 926; the destruction of Israel in 721; and the destruction of Judah in 587.

(A) Solomon Succeeds to the Throne of David (1:1–2:46). Detached from the court historian's account of Solomon's succession to the throne of David, chs. 1–2 serve the purposes of the exilic author in two ways: they emphasize the Nathan oracle (cf. 1:13,17,30; 2:4,15b,24,45); they introduce Solomon as the first of the unfaithful kings (see L. Waterman, "Some Historical and Literary Consequences of Probable Displacement in 1 Kings 1–2," *JAOS* 60 [1940] 383ff.).

10 (a) ADONIJAH AND SOLOMON VIE FOR THE THRONE OF DAVID (1:1–53). **1–4.** With his characteristic brilliance, the court historian paints a brief but colorful word picture of David's senility (David was about 70; cf. 2 Sm 5:5; 1 Kgs 2:11) and at the same time introduces Abishag, who will figure prominently in the ultimate downfall of Adonijah (cf. 2:13–25). The method for restoring the king's circulation was not unique, for it is mentioned by ancient physicians (e.g., Galen). That the maid from Shunem (modern Sholem), a town on the northern edge of the Plain of Jezreel, remained a virgin, is explained by the author in anticipation of Adonijah's request for her as wife (2:13ff.). **5–6.** With David almost in his dotage and with no clear policy stated concerning succession to the throne, Adonijah, who is not only the oldest of the living sons of David since the death of Absalom but also the popular choice for king (2:15), takes matters into his own hands. His first step is "to act the king," as Absalom had before him (2 Sm 15:1). **7–8.** Before detailing the court intrigues that led to Adonijah's downfall and to Solomon's triumph, the court historian quickly lines up the rival factions. Adonijah has on his side Joab, David's old commander in chief (2 Sm 8:16; 20:23), and Abiathar, the priest and sole survivor of Saul's massacre of the priests of Nob (1 Sm 22:20–23; 2 Sm 8:17); both were men of consequence in David's rise to power. Those opposed to Adonijah are as follows: Zadok the priest (cf. Ez 40:46; 1 Chr 6:38ff.); Benaiah, commander of David's mercenaries from Philistia (2 Sm 8:18; 20:23); the prophet Nathan, whose prophecy concerning David's dynasty (2 Sm 7:11ff.) and predilection for Solomon (2 Sm 12:24–25) laid the groundwork for the whole succession

account; Shimei, probably the future minister of Solomon (1 Kgs 4:18); Rei, otherwise unknown; and the as yet unmentioned Solomon and his mother Bathsheba (2 Sm 12:24–25).

9. *Adonijah sacrificed:* Adonijah's *coup d'état* involved a sacrificial ceremony at En-rogel (lit., "the pool of the stream"), a deep well tapping a subterranean stream from the drainage of the Kedron Valley, now known as Job's Pool (although the name Job is probably a corruption of an earlier "Joab's pool"), and also a sacred banquet (vv. 41ff.). It is not mentioned, but undoubtedly Adonijah was anointed king there by the priest Abiathar in the course of the ceremonies. Although excluded from the clandestine anointing, Nathan, Benaiah, and Solomon were aware of what was transpiring, as the sequel shows. **10.** "Solomon" is probably the king's throne name—a shortened form of "May Yahweh guard his welfare." His name before becoming king is given in 2 Sm 12:25 as Jedidiah, "beloved of Yahweh." He was the second son of Bathsheba (2 Sm 12:24).

11–27. Verses 11–27 deal with Nathan's counterplot. The masterful intrigue of Nathan would seem to indicate that David knew about Adonijah's attempt to present him with a *fait accompli* (cf. v. 6), but because of senility or indifference, he took no steps to frustrate it. Nathan's plan is to spur David to action by playing upon his pride and upon the safety of his beloved Bathsheba and her son Solomon. If Bathsheba needs encouragement as well, it is no accident that Nathan refers to Adonijah as "the son of Haggith," perhaps a rival wife, and that he reminds Bathsheba of the fate in store for both herself and her son if Adonijah is successful. His counsel to Bathsheba to insinuate in her words to David that Adonijah's plot has taken place behind his back is meant to arouse the king's pride. The appeal to David's honor regarding an oath he is reputed to have made that Solomon would be his successor may rest on a true promise (cf. 2 Sm 7:13; 12:25; 1 Kgs 1:17,30; 2:15,24). It and the insinuation that he could not possibly have wavered in fidelity to his promise is meant to be a further goad to David's pride. Sending Bathsheba to the king first and then following with the same story has the desired psychological effect—David is stirred from lethargy to action.

28–40. Acting decisively, if belatedly, David gives precise instructions as to the place and ceremony for the anointing of Solomon (see De Vaux, *AI* 100ff.). **38.** Preceded by the royal ministers and riding upon the royal "mule," a privilege symbolizing royalty (cf. Gn 41:43; Est 6:8), Solomon proceeds to "Gihon" (lit., "the gusher"; cf. 2 Chr 32:30; 33:14), identical with the well at the foot of the W slope of the hill of Zion, now known as the Well of the Lady Miriam (Mary). There he is anointed by Zadok and probably also by Nathan (cf. vv. 34 and 45; also 1 Sm 11:15; 15:13; 2 Kgs 9:1–6). **39.** *blew the trumpet:* The blowing of the trumpet was associated with the proclamation of the new king and was probably followed by the sending out of messengers to announce the coronation, which, in turn, was followed by the rejoicing of the people (cf. v. 40; 2 Kgs 11:12–20). Thus, Solomon, like Jotham at a later date (2 Kgs 15:5), reigns as coregent with David (see De Vaux, *AI* 101). **41.** Significantly, it is the old warrior, Joab, who above the noise of the festivities at En-rogel hears the blast of the trumpets half a mile away at Gihon and perhaps senses immediately the coup announced by Jonathan (vv. 42ff.).

49–53. The verses treat Adonijah's submission. **49.** In fear of his life, Adonijah flees for sanctuary to the tent housing the Ark and clings to the most sacred part of the altar, the horns to which the blood of the sacrifice was touched (see *ANE* 575; cf. Am 3:14; Ex 27:1ff.). The right of sanctuary was an ancient custom, later regulated by law (cf. Ex 21:13–14; Nm 35:9ff.), allowing a manslayer temporary protection from the avenger of blood (De Vaux, *AI* 160–61). Perhaps for political reasons, perhaps out of sympathy for a half brother, Solomon spares Adonijah, but only temporarily (cf. 2:13–25).

11 (b) DAVID'S DEATH AND THE REMOVAL OF THE OPPOSITION (2:1–46). **3–4.** Because of the deuteronomic phraseology, almost all authors consider vv. 3–4 to be an addition to the original narrative (on the authenticity of the whole passage, see M–G, *Kings* 87ff.). The insistence of the author on fidelity of the kings to the Law of Moses as a condition for the continuation of the dynasty and the Temple (e.g., 1 Kgs 3:14; 6:12–13; 11:34) should not be construed as doubt on the part of the author concerning the absolute perdurance of the dynasty promised by God. These texts should rather be interpreted in the light of the conditional part of the same promise (cf. 2 Sm 7:14b) and as the author's method of explaining the scandal caused by the destruction of the Temple and the apparent end of the Davidic dynasty. Indeed, as the author abundantly proves by his interpretative theological discourses (see 1 Kgs 8–9; 11; 2 Kgs 17; 20:16–18; 21:7–15; 22:15–20; 23:22–27; 24:3–4) and by his judgments on the kings (*passim*), the rulers were not faithful and were indeed punished—first by the division of the kingdom, then by the destruction of Israel, and finally by the destruction of the Temple and the captivity of the Davidic king and his people.

5–6. Many emend v. 5 to read: "...how he avenged in time of peace the blood of war and stained with innocent blood the girdle of my loins and the sandal of my feet...." David's advice to Solomon to liquidate Joab shocks us, but it must be understood in its cultural context. According to the belief of the time, bloodguilt had to be avenged (cf. Ex 21:12–14). David's point is that Joab's bloodguilt for the murders of Abner and Amasa (2 Sm 3:27ff.; 20:8ff.), if not avenged, would hang over and menace the Davidic house until it was removed (see De Vaux, *AI* 10ff.). It is for the welfare of the kingdom, therefore, that Joab be executed (cf. David's execution of Saul's grandchildren in expiation of Saul's murder of the Gibeonites, 2 Sm 21; also Herodotus' story of how Croesus paid the penalty for "the sin of his ancestor in the fifth degree, who had slain his master" [I, 91]). **7.** *Barzillai:* Barzillai's kindness to David is recounted in 2 Sm 17:27ff. *eat at your table:* To eat at the king's table meant to be pensioned (cf. 2 Sm 9:7; 19:29; 2 Kgs 18:19). **8.** Shimei must also be punished, not so much for what he had done to David—for which David had pardoned him (cf. 2 Sm 19:16ff.)—as for his curse (2 Sm 16:5ff.), which threatens the dynasty as long as he lives. **10–11.** Doubtlessly based on 2 Sm 5:4–5, this editorial note, so similar in format to the editorial notes on Solomon (11:41–43) and Jeroboam (14:19–20), is the first instance of the schematic formula so characteristic of the author (→ 6 above).

12 **12–46.** These verses take up the removal of the opposition. **12.** This verse is redactional (see M–G, *Kings* 91) to introduce the tragic end of Adonijah's ill-starred career. **13.** The court historian judges no one but lets events speak for themselves, leaving to the reader to divine whether Adonijah was truly attempting another coup, whether Bathsheba really suspected nothing or perhaps knew but decided to let Adonijah have enough rope to hang himself, and whether Solomon nipped in the bud a real plot against the throne or used the innocent request of Adonijah as a pretext for getting him out of the way. Adonijah's openness (vv. 13–17) argues for innocence if not simplicity, but the guilty flight of

Joab (v. 28) would argue for complicity, although it can be otherwise explained. Bathsheba's realization that Abishag had remained a virgin (cf. 1:4,15) might explain her apparent complaisance, although such naïveté is otherwise inexplicable in so experienced a woman (for Bathsheba as queen mother, see De Vaux, *AI* 117). On the other hand, Solomon cannot be blamed for suspecting a plot, because, according to the custom of the time, possession of a former king's wife could involve a claim to the throne (De Vaux, *AI* 116; 2 Sm 3:6–8; 16:21–22). **22.** *ask for him the kingdom as well:* Solomon's words indicate he knew full well the possible implications of Adonijah's request.

26. Solomon knows Abiathar is involved in the plot but does not make the political error of Saul, who killed the priests of Nob (1 Sm 22:13ff.) and thereby certainly alienated many who would otherwise have supported him. Abiathar is banished to Anathoth, 3 mi. NE of Jerusalem (cf. Jer 1:1). **27.** *in fulfillment* (On the significance of prophetic-fulfillment narratives, → 4–5 above). Abiathar's replacement by Zadok is recorded in v. 35.

28. Joab's flight implies, if it does not assure complicity, because he may well have known that Solomon was looking for a pretext to destroy his enemies. His hope that the right of sanctuary invoked earlier by Adonijah and honored by Solomon (1:50ff.) would save him avails nothing. Solomon applies the law strictly (Ex 21:14), appealing to David's deathbed instructions (2:5–6) for justification (vv. 31–34). **35.** In 1 Chr 6:11ff. and 24:3, we find an artificial genealogy for Zadok; literary criticism is unable to clarify his origin. For the opinions that he was high priest at Gibeon (1 Chr 16:39), or perhaps priest of the Jebusite sanctuary at Jerusalem and therefore heir of Melchizedek (Gn 14:18–20; Ps 110:4), see De Vaux, *AI* 373–74.

36. Spared but restricted to the environs of Jerusalem, Shimei, a member of Saul's family (2 Sm 16:5ff.), swears on pain of death to obey Solomon's restrictive stipulation. **39.** *slaves ran away:* The incident is mentioned because it occasions the breaking of Shimei's promise to Solomon. Shimei's successful quest for the slaves—one which evidently demanded his personal intervention—presupposes some kind of slave extradition clause in Israel's treaty with the king of Gath (cf. De Vaux, *AI* 87), an agreement probably imposed by David after his conquest of the Philistines (2 Sm 8:1). Whatever the reason for Shimei's action, whether carelessness or supposed security, Solomon seizes the occasion as an opportunity to execute him and thus carry out the last of David's deathbed injunctions (cf. vv. 44–45 and 2:8–9).

13 **(B) The Reign of Solomon (3:1–11:41).** Two main sources exist for the description of Solomon's reign: the Book of the Acts of Solomon (11:41), from which the author takes his material in chs. 3–5 and 9–11, and which was probably composed in the early 9th cent.; P source of unknown origin, from which the author takes his description of Solomon's Temple, chs. 6–7. To both of these sources the author has made his own additions: 3:3–4; 6:1; 8:14–9:9 *passim*; 11:1–43 *passim*. So much space given to a king who was ultimately unfaithful to the covenant is unusual for the author, who usually deals summarily with unfaithful kings. The extensive description of Solomon's reign is probably best explained as the author's way of reanimating the discouraged exiles for whom he wrote, first by showing them that the glory of Solomon's reign is in fulfillment of the promise to David in 2 Sm 7, and second by showing them what glory the kingdom could have retained had its kings been faithful (→ History of Israel, 75:61–62).

(a) Solomon the Sage (3:1–4:34). To those unacquainted with the ancient Near Eastern understanding of "wisdom" and "wise man," it may appear that only those pericopes expressly dealing with wisdom deal with Solomon as a sage. When we consider, however, that the ancients commonly equated wisdom with success in life, arts, politics, or in whatever else one was engaged, it becomes understandable that the two sections from the Acts of Solomon (3–4; 9:10–10:29) are dedicated to the same purpose—praise of Solomon the sage. Thus, the original author introduced his praise of Solomon the sage with the dream-given gift of wisdom (3:5–15) and then proceeded to illustrate his sagacity with the story of the two mothers (3:16–28), an account of Solomon as administrator (4:1ff.), builder (5–7), trader (9:15ff.), etc. Thus, the account of the visit of the Queen of Sheba in 10:1–13 is not out of context but is simply another story illustrating Solomon's fame as a sage. He is in every way eminently successful as befits a great sage. Whether the author of the Solomon source added the story of Solomon's downfall in ch. 11 is difficult to determine. More likely, it is from the hand of the exilic author of Kgs.

14 **3:1.** *a marriage alliance with Pharaoh:* The most important of many wives (11:1) and seemingly his favorite (7:8; 9:24), Pharaoh's daughter is probably the daughter of Psousennes II, one of the weak Pharaohs of the 21st dynasty. According to 9:16, she brought as dowry to Solomon the Philistine city of Gezer (but see Albright, *ARI* 136 and n. 29). The marriage indicates the political stature of Israel, third only to Assyria and Egypt, both in this period at a low ebb of power and influence (see E. Drioton and J. Vandier, *Les peuples de l'Orient méditerranéen, II Egypte* [Paris, 1962] 511, 524–25; Bright, *Hist.* 191). *city of David:* The early Jebusite city of Jerusalem was situated on the SE hillock above the Gihon Pool, so called because it was captured by David (2 Sm 5:6–9).

2–15. Verses 2–15 treat Solomon's dream. **2.** *high places:* Forbidden by Dt 12:2–3, the high places (Hebr *bāmôt*) were sacred knolls used for cultic worship, usually but not always on hilltops, legitimate in the early days of the monarchy but frequently, especially in later periods, associated with Israel's syncretistic Baal worship at the Canaanite fertility shrines (cf. Jer 2:20; 3:6; Is 57:5; see De Vaux, *AI* 284ff.). **3.** *burned incense:* Hosea (4:13) mentions incense as an element of the cult practiced on the high places. Verses 2–3 are probably glosses interpolated to excuse people and kings; they reflect the concerns of later writers for the deuteronomic law of a single sanctuary (Dt 12) and for Solomon's reputation. **4.** *Gibeon:* It is probably the same as Mizpah, located on the height now known as Nebi Samwil, 6 mi. NW of Jerusalem. Gibeon was an ancient shrine of the Gibeonites that had become a Yahwistic shrine perhaps as early as the conquest period (cf. Jos 9:23,27) and certainly by the time of the judges (cf. 1 Sm 7:5; 10:17). According to 1 Chr 16:39; 21:29; 2 Chr 1:3, the meeting tent was kept at Gibeon, perhaps indicating that after the destruction of Shiloh and before the building of the Temple, Gibeon may have been the central shrine of Israel. It is perhaps for this reason that the author speaks of it as "the great high place" and that Solomon offered sacrifices there even before offering them before the Ark in Jerusalem. On exceptional occasions, but not regularly, the earliest kings of Israel, as sacred persons with a special relation to Yahweh, acted as religious heads of the nation (cf. 1 Sm 13:9–10; 2 Sm 6; 1 Kgs 8; 9:25). They were not, however, strictly priests. **5.** *in a dream by night:* Revelation by dream has an extensive biblical and extrabiblical background and is mentioned in Gn

20:3; 28:12; 37; Jgs 7:13ff.; Jb 4:13, and in Zech, Jl, and Dn, *passim* (cf. 2 Chr 1:1–13; also T. Vriezen, *An Outline of Old Testament Theology* [Oxford, 1958] 243ff.; M–G, *Kings* 105ff.). **7.** *to go out or come in:* It is a Hebr phrase to express all that a man does (cf. 1 Sm 18:16). **9.** Solomon prays for judicial wisdom, i.e., the ability to judge well when cases are appealed to him as supreme arbiter of justice in the kingdom. Thus, it amounts to a prayer to govern well for the good of his people. It is for this reason that his prayer is so pleasing to God (vv. 10–11) and merits him in addition great gifts for himself (vv. 12–13).

16–28. The verses treat Solomon's judgment. **16.** *two women:* The story has widespread, although later, parallels in ancient literature and is used by the author to illustrate the judicial wisdom bestowed by God on Solomon (cf. v. 28 and M–G, *Kings* 108ff.). **17.** *in the same house:* Prostitution and hostelry were frequent companions in ancient times (cf. Jos 2; Code of Hammurabi, 108–11, *ANET* 170).

15 **4:1–28.** The organization of Solomon's kingdom is now described. Continuity exists between the bureaucracy of David and that of Solomon. Solomon employs the same herald as David, as well as the son of one of his priests, the two sons of his secretary, and two sons of the prophet Nathan. The lists in ch. 4 are from the royal archives but have been re-edited (note the stylistic similarity of the lists in Sm and Kgs, e.g., 1 Sm 7:15–17; 14:47–52; 2 Sm 8:16–18; 20:23–26; 1 Kgs 4:1–6).

2. Although the term *śārîm* sometimes means "princes" or "elders," it is here used in the sense of "officials," chiefs of the people, men of the official family, who enjoyed a privileged position among the people and sometimes received special land grants from the king (cf. 1 Sm 8:14; 22:7). **3.** *scribes:* The names of Elihoreph and his father, Shisha, are probably Egyptian and reflect the influence of the Egyptian bureaucracy which Israel imitated. The scribe or royal secretary was one of the three most important positions in the kingdom, so important that the names of royal secretaries are recorded to the end of the monarchy (cf. 2 Kgs 18:18, Shebna in 701; 2 Kgs 22:3, Shaphan in 621; Jer 37:15, Jonathan in 588). *recorder:* Royal herald (*mazkîr*) is meant; cf. 2 Sm 8:16ff. **5.** Azariah was the official who directed the work of the 12 prefects mentioned in 4:7–9. *the king's friend:* An honorary title, probably of Egyptian origin, it carried with it no known function (cf. 2 Sm 15:37). **6.** *over the house:* The phrase implies major-domo or the king's steward; Ahishar, as master of the palace and first minister of the king, had extensive administrative powers, which the text of Is 22:22 describes. *Adoniram:* The name is Phoenician; Adoniram was chief of the levy or forced-labor battalions (1 Kgs 5:13–17; 9:15–19; 12:18). **7.** *twelve prefects:* The governors of the 12 prefectures were expected to supply monthly, in turn, the provisions for the royal staff (cf. vv. 22–23, 27–28). With this obligation went the right to govern their respective districts and to collect taxes. A somewhat similar organization is known in the Neo-Babylonian Empire, and Herodotus records the same system in vogue under Cyrus the Great (I, 192).

8–19. The mention of Solomon's two sons-in-law (vv. 11, 15) dates the list to the second half of Solomon's reign. Five of the prefects are listed only under their patronymic, "son of X," which may mean that their personal names were lost, perhaps because of a damaged list. It may also signify that they belonged to certain families that served the king from father to son and were listed as a consequence only under their patronymic, as in certain Ugaritic administrative lists. The 12 prefectures fall into three groups: the territory of Ephraim and Manasseh, along with some captured Canaanite cities and some sections of Transjordan (vv. 8–14); the northern tribes (15–17); and Benjamin and Gad (18–19). Nothing is said about Judah (unless v. 19 is interpreted as "one prefect in the king's own land"—Judah), which presumably had its own administrative districts, perhaps the cities listed in Jos 15:21–62 (cf. De Vaux, *AI* 133–38; M–G, *Kings* 121ff.).

21. (For the order of verses in the LXX, see M–G, *Kings* 126ff.). The "river" is the Euphrates. The reference in 2 Chr 8:4 to Solomon's activities at Tadmor (Palmyra) would tend to substantiate the broad limits indicated here for the extent of the territory ruled by Solomon, even though he eventually lost control of Damascus (11:23–25) and perhaps part of Edom (11:14–22). *all the kingdoms:* The kingdoms are those conquered by David (2 Sm 8:1–14; 10:1–19). Solomon himself conquered no additional territory. **24.** *beyond the river:* The phrase derives from a late Assyrian expression that became common after the 7th cent. to designate the territories between the Euphrates and the Mediterranean (cf. Neh 2:7); it is equivalent to "Trans-Euphrates," and betrays the hand of the exilic author, who speaks from the topographical position of one in Babylon looking W. *over all the kings:* Assyria's weakness and Egypt's apathy in the 10th cent. made David's conquests and Solomon's hegemony possible (cf. Albright, *ARI* 130ff.). **26.** *horses ...chariots:* See comments on 9:15–19; 10:26,28–29.

4:29–34. Before describing the construction of the Temple, the author summarizes in hyperbolical language Solomon's reputation as a sage. **30.** *Arabs:* Both the Arabs and the Egyptians were famous for their wisdom teachers, and Israelite writers were well acquainted with these ancient sages (cf. Prv 22:17ff.; 30:1ff.; 31:1–9; J. Montgomery, *Arabia and the Bible* [Phila., 1934] 169ff.; → Wisdom Lit, 28:5–6). **32.** *proverbs:* The number is round and hyperbolical, but the fact of Solomon's prowess in the making of proverbs is attested to by at least two collections of his writings in Prv (10:1–22:16; 25:1–29:27).

16 (b) SOLOMON THE BUILDER (5:1–9:14). The account as a whole is made up of at least three literary strands: a section from the Book of the Acts of Solomon (5:1–18; 8:1–14; 9:10–25); a section from a P source (6:2–7:51); and the work of the author of Kgs himself (6:1; 8:15–66 *passim*; 9:1–9).

(i) *Solomon's building preparations* (5:1–18). **1.** *Hiram:* King of the Phoenician littoral from the Bay of Acre northward, Hiram (*ca.* 969–936) ruled from Tyre at the time of Phoenicia's great expansion W (Albright, *ARI* 131ff.; *BASOR* 83 [1941] 14–22). *sent his servants:* The reference is to an embassy sent to congratulate Solomon on his accession to the throne (cf. 2 Sm 10:1–3), and, no doubt, to renew the alliance made with David (5:12). **5.** *as the Lord spoke:* It is an allusion to 2 Sm 7:12–13, the prophecy to which the author constantly returns. **6.** Hiram had already supplied building materials for David's palace (2 Sm 5:11); he was known from Phoenician records to have built several temples at Tyre. Solomon enlists his help and experience for the building of the Temple and enters into a trading agreement with him (5:10–12). **8.** *cedar and cyprus timbers:* The stands of cedar and cyprus on Mt. Lebanon, one of the main sources of timber in the ancient Orient and consequently in great demand, are now almost depleted because of centuries of exploitation. The trees were felled in the mountains, dragged to the shore, brought by ship or raft to the port of Joppa (2 Chr 2:16), and transported from there to Jerusalem. **12.** *ratified a treaty:* Of this trading treaty, Montgomery says that it "presents an early picture of correct historical similitude, reporting diplomatic and commercial relations between two states of Syro-Palestine—actually in its extent a fairly unique report" (M–G, *Kings* 132; also W. Moran, "The Ancient Near Eastern Background of the Love of God in Deuteronomy," *CBQ* 26 [1963] 80).

13. Solomon's extensive building projects—Temple, palace, garrison towns, refineries and fleet at Ezion-geber—brought the levying of forced laborers to a fully developed institution, with a special minister for forced labor among the royal officials (4:6) and superintendents over the levies conscripted from the individual administrative districts (11:28). Although most of the forced labor was conscripted from subject nations, it is certain, despite 9:20–22 and 2 Chr 2:17–18; 8:7–9, that Israelites were conscripted as well, at least for work on the Temple and probably for other projects also, for the text explicitly says "out of all Israel." It is precisely because of the Israelite forced labor that Jeroboam rebels (cf. 11:26ff.; De Vaux, *AI* 141ff.). **15.** *stone cutters:* They are probably master masons from Phoenicia (cf. 7:9) employed in Jerusalem by Solomon just as he employed master woodsmen from Phoenicia for the wood cutting (5:6,18). **18.** The citizens of ancient Byblos (sometimes written Gebal; cf. R. Dussaud, "Byblos et la mention des Giblites. . . ." *Syria* 4 [1923] 300ff.) were among the skilled masons, carpenters, and artisans on loan from Hiram.

17 (ii) *Solomon's Temple* (6:1–38). (For the description, → Religious Institutions, 76:55–65.) Critics consider the account to be very old, probably of P provenance and contemporary with the Temple. It is not, however, the work of an architect and is consequently difficult at times to interpret (2 Chr 3–4 contains a summary, but with variations). The author of Kgs, or a glossator, has retouched the original lightly by adding 6:1,7,11–14.

6:1. The date of 480 years is artificial, based on 12 generations (a generation being 40 years) after the Exodus from Egypt and 12 generations before the Exile, if the dating is that of the Deuteronomist (= D), author of Kgs, or 12 generations before the building of the Second Temple, if the dating is the work of a post-exilic glossator. It could also be that the date is based on the 12 generations of priests (cf. 1 Chr 5:29–34) from Zadok, in the time of Solomon, to Joshua (Hag 1:1), the high priest at the time of the building of the Second Temple (cf. De Vaux, *AI* 193, 375; H. H. Rowley, "Israel's Sojourn in Egypt," *BJRylL* 22 [1938] 1ff.). **11.** In vv. 11–13, the author again uses his favorite literary device—the interpretative theological discourse (cf. 2:3–4)—to explain away the scandal that the destruction of the Temple in 587 gave to his exilic contemporaries. **37.** *fourth year:* The time is *ca.* 960. **38.** The names of the months are derived from Canaanite names connected with the seasons: Ziv is the month of flowers; Bul is the month of the great rains. The archaic names for the months, as well as the method of reckoning the date by the years of the king's reign—the usual method until the time of the Exile—inclines critics to accept this dating as original (cf. De Vaux, *AI* 183, 193, 498f.).

(iii) *Solomon's palaces* (7:1–14). **7:1.** *thirteen years:* In 9:10, the 13 years of 7:1 and the 7 years of 6:38 are summarized editorially as 20 years. However, it is probable that the 7 years for the Temple should be included in 13, which would represent the time it took Solomon to complete the whole complex of buildings: the Temple; the house of the forest of Lebanon (v. 2); the porch of pillars (v. 6); the porch of the throne (v. 7); Solomon's own palace (v. 8a); and a palace for Pharaoh's daughter (v. 8b). **2.** *House of the Forest of Lebanon:* The building received its name from the three rows of cedar columns (v. 3), 15 in a row, which supported the roof (cf. M–G, *Kings* 162ff.). It served as an armory (10:16–17; Is 22:8) and perhaps as a treasury (10:21). **6–7.** The "hall of pillars" was perhaps either a distinct building or a special chamber formed by a continuation of the rows of pillars in the house of Lebanon. The porch or Gate of Justice was used as a reception hall and judgment hall (v. 7) and housed the throne described in 10:18ff. **8.** *his own house:* Little is said about the king's own dwelling place, the harem, and the special palace built for his Egyptian wife (cf. 3:1; 9:24), except that they were separated from the judgment hall (v. 8a) and located in a second court distinct from the enclosure that surrounded the public buildings (v. 12b). **13.** *Hiram:* A skilled worker in bronze and son of a Phoenician father and an Israelite mother, Hiram is perhaps the most important of the artisans imported by Solomon for his building projects. Such importation of foreign artists was not uncommon (cf. Albright, *FSAC* 159).

(iv) *The bronze work for the Temple* (7:15–51). (→ Religious Institutions, 76:59; see G. E. Wright, *BibArch* 139–42.) **51b.** *things David had dedicated:* The Chronicler has significantly expanded this tradition (1 Chr 22–29). The "things" would refer to the booty, etc. (cf. 2 Sm 8:11–12).

18 (v) *The dedication of the Temple* (8:1–66). This passage is extensively expanded by the interpolation of D's interpretative theological discourses, and it is liberally glossed, as comparison with the LXX shows (cf. M–G, *Kings* 185ff.); hence it is difficult to determine the original material taken from the author's source, the Book of the Acts of Solomon, or perhaps the P source used in chs. 6–7. It would seem that only vv. 1–13 and perhaps vv. 14–21 and 62–66 (but not the glosses in vv. 1–4, 9, and 65) are original. The remainder would be the work of D and glossators during and after the Exile.

8:1. David had brought the Ark, the visible sign of Yahweh's presence, to Jerusalem, the old Jebusite city on the SE hillock, originally called Ophel and later called the city of David (2 Sm 5–6). Solomon now brings the Ark from the city of David—i.e., Zion, as a glossator explains, for the name "city of David" is archaic in his time—with a procession and festivities reminiscent of those described in 2 Sm 6 (cf. also Ezr 6:16–18). The entrance of the Ark into the new Temple, symbolic of Yahweh's taking possession of his house, is the principal ceremony of the dedication, because it is for Yahweh, dwelling above the Ark, that the Temple has been constructed, according to the wish of David (2 Sm 7:1ff.) and the doing of Solomon. **2.** *Ethanim:* If the gloss "which is the seventh month" correctly places the Canaanite month of Ethanim, and if the similar gloss in 6:38 correctly places the Canaanite month of Bul as the "eighth month," then it would appear that the Temple was dedicated 1 month before it was finished, or 11 months after it was finished. Either alternative seems embarrassing. Since the text explicitly speaks of "the feast in the month of Ethanim," which is almost certainly the autumn harvest feast, commonly known as the Feast of Tents or Tabernacles, it is likely that the dedication coincided with the Feast of Tents, celebrated when the harvest was gathered in (cf. v. 65). If the harvest were gathered early, the dedication of the Temple was probably celebrated early (in the seventh month), and in the following month of Bul, the eighth month, the Temple was finished as 6:38 says "in all its details and specifications" (cf. De Vaux, *AI* 498–99). **6.** *inner room:* This is the *Debir* or "Holy of Holies," where the Ark of the Covenant rested beneath the outstretched wings of the cherubim (v. 7; cf. Ex 25).

8. *poles were seen:* Made of acacia wood (Ex 25:12–15), the poles fitted through rings attached to the Ark and were used for carrying it in procession (cf. 1 Sm 4:3–4; 2 Sm 6). By prescription of Ex 25:15, they were never to be removed from the Ark. Thus, when the Ark rested in the *Debir* they would project out through the curtain that separated the *Debir* from the *Hekal*, or "Holy Place," and be the only element of the Ark visible from the Hekal. The curtain or veil is the *pārōket*, "separation" (cf. Ex 26:31–35; 27:21); it is nowhere described in 1 Kgs 6–7, although it is mentioned in 2 Chr 3:14 (cf. De Vaux, *AI* 314). The phrase "unto this day" indicates that the author of this source lived before the destruction of the Temple in 587. **10.** *a cloud:* It is the sensible manifestation of Yahweh taking up his abode in the Temple (cf. Ex 19:16; 33:9,40; 40:34–35; Ez 43:45). **12–13.** Perhaps only the first lines of a longer hymn, this brief snatch of poetry compares the darkness of the Holy of Holies, where God has chosen to dwell forever (v. 13), with the cloud which is the symbol of his presence (v. 10). Certain Gk versions (LXX 8:53) expand the text by introducing a contrast between the visibility of the sun in the sky and the hiddenness of God who has taken up his abode in the darkness of the Holy of Holies and by reporting the literary source of this snatch of poetry as from the Book of Jashar (cf. Jos 10:13; 2 Sm 1:18). The originality of the LXX additions is debatable (see M–G, *Kings* 189ff.).

19 **14–61.** Solomon's three discourses (vv. 15–21; 23–53; 56–61), attributed to him by the final author, are all interpretative theological discourses exhibiting strong affinities with Dt in phraseology and revealing throughout the basic theological teachings of the exilic author of Kgs (see comment on 9:1–3). In the first discourse (15–21), the author associates, as he does in many other passages (cf. 1 Kgs 6:12–13; 8:23–53 *passim*; 11:13,32,36; 14:21; 15:4; 2 Kgs 8:19; 19:34; 20:6–7; 21:7), the eternity of the Temple with the eternity promised to the Davidic dynasty in 2 Sm 7, an association of great significance for the exiles. In the second discourse (23–53), a litanylike prayer, the author stresses again the association of Temple and Davidic dynasty (23–26) and composes a prayer (which may have a pre-exilic core from the Temple liturgy, especially in vv. 31–40) with a number of allusions to the circumstances of the Jews in exile. It is transparently the author's attempt to express those sentiments of repentance and trust that he wishes the exiles to feel and manifest (cf. the expression "toward this place" in vv. 29–30, 35, 43–44, 48; cf. also the references to captivity and exile in vv. 33–34, 37, and especially 46–53). The third discourse is a prayer (56–61) composed to inspire confidence in the exiles by recalling God's infallible fulfillment of his promises when his people hear and obey him.

15. *with his own mouth:* The reference is to the Nathan oracle (2 Sm 7), one aspect of which is elaborated, namely: the relation between David's desire to build the Temple and Solomon's fulfillment of this desire—an aspect which would appear secondary in 2 Sm 7 and therefore certainly secondary here (note that vv. 22–26 refer to the more basic element of 2 Sm 7, i.e., the dynastic promise (see J. McKenzie, "The Dynastic Oracle: 2 Samuel 7," *TS* 8 [1947] 187ff.; Bright, *Hist.* 204). **16.** God's choice fell first on David and the dynasty, then only on Jerusalem and the Temple, which henceforward come to be associated with the destiny of the eternal dynasty (cf. 1 Kgs 8:13; 11:13,32,36; 14:21; 15:4; 2 Kgs 8:19; 19:34; 20:6; 21:7). *name might be there:* The name represents the person. Thus, where God's name is, there God is present (cf. 8:27ff.; Is 30:27). **19.** *you shall not build:* The reference is to 2 Sm 7:4ff. The reason given by the Chronicler is that David has "shed much blood" (1 Chr 22:7–8).

20. *has made good his word:* As in so many other places, the author of Kgs, adhering to his purpose to show that God's word directs Israel's history and is infallibly fulfilled, points to the fulfillment of a prophetic word (cf. Von Rad, *OT Theology I*, 340ff.). **23.** The deuteronomic teaching on reciprocity of fidelity (Dt 4:39; 7:9 and *passim*) is invoked to show that God has kept his promise in relation to the Temple and will do the same for the dynasty of David, providing the kings, like David, are faithful (v. 25).

20 **27.** *can God really dwell:* The question sets the stage for a resolution of the tension between God's transcendence—a theological notion much emphasized after the Exile, no doubt as a result of the destruction of the Temple—and his proximity to Israel in the Temple. Even the highest heavens cannot contain God, the author insists; nevertheless if the faithful pray at the Temple, God in his heavens will hear them because he has determined to hear the prayers of those who pray to him in that place of which he has said "my name shall be there" (8:17,28–30; Dt 12:5). Thus, the author disposes of the grossly restricted concept of God's presence in the Temple held by many pre-exilic Jews (cf. Jer 7:1ff.) and no doubt shared by many of his exilic compatriots (cf. De Vaux, *AI* 325ff.). **31.** *an oath:* It is a sort of an ordeal by oath by which a man could clear himself of guilt. The man accused was compelled to take an oath attesting his innocence of a particular crime. If he refused, he was considered guilty; if he perjured himself, the curses contained in the oath would overtake him. Otherwise, he was considered justified. Thus the prayer is that God punish the perjuror and deliver the innocent (cf. Ex 22:6–12; Lv 5:21–24; Nm 5:19–31; Jgs 17:1–2; Eccl 9:2). **33.** *turn and praise:* By acknowledging their guilt and praising God in the Temple, the guilty people can, according to sacral law, hope to bring to an end God's wrath and consequent punishment (cf. Jos 7:19; Ezr 10:7ff.; Von Rad, *OT Theology I*, 357–58). It is true of captivity (v. 34), according to Dt 30:1–4, and therefore the author, who is writing for the Jews in exile, has good reason to recall it.

41. The stranger or alien referred to (Hebr *nokrî*) is not the same as the resident alien (*gēr*), whose rights were determined by law (Nm 15:14ff.), but the foreigner who is attracted to Israel's God (e.g., Naaman, the Syrian, 2 Kgs 5). The universalist attitude behind this prayer is typical of exilic and post-exilic times (cf. Is 40–55 *passim*; Jon; Tb 13:6–11; Zech 8:18ff.) and reflects perhaps the first serious proselytizing undertaken by the exiles in Babylon. **44.** *in the direction of the city:* Prayer toward Jerusalem by those in exile or abroad is mentioned in Tb 3:11 and Dn 6:11. **46.** Israel knew deportation to Assyria as early as the time of Tiglath-pileser III (cf. 2 Kgs 15:29). In 597 and 587, Nebuchadnezzar deported large numbers of Jews to Babylon (2 Kgs 24–25). It is for these latter exiles that the author speaks in the prayer of vv. 47–53 (cf. Lam *passim*; Jer 29:5–8; Tb 13). **54.** *he arose:* The apparent contradiction between vv. 54 and 22 is clarified by 2 Chr 6:13, where it is clear that the verb *'āmad*, which ordinarily means "to stand erect," can also have the meaning "to be in front of," without implying that one is actually standing. Although the Israelites ordinarily took a standing position for prayer, especially in NT times, it is clear from this and other texts that they occasionally knelt and even prostrated themselves (cf. Neh 9:3–5; Is 45:23; Dn 6:11; Ps 99:5). **56.** The peroration of Solomon's prayer (vv. 56–61), in which he blesses the people, is omitted by the Chronicler (2 Chr 6:40), because blessing the people was a function he wished to reserve as a privilege of the priesthood (cf. Nm 6:22–23). The phraseology is deuteronomic (vv. 56, 58, 61) and the same universalist attitude is manifest (v. 60) as in vv. 41–43.

62. On special occasions, but not ordinarily, the king, by virtue of his anointing and adoption as son by Yahweh, personally offered sacrifices (cf. 1 Sm 13:9–10; 2 Sm 6:17–18; 24:25; 1 Kgs 9:25; Ps 110:4). **63.** *thank offerings:* Following the procedure of 2 Sm 6—procession, dedication, sacrifices—Solomon concludes the dedication of the Temple with the thanksgiving sacrifices customary on such occasions (cf. 2 Sm 6:17–19; Neh 12:27–43). The number of victims has been exaggerated in typical Oriental manner. **65.** *a feast:* It is undoubtedly the Feast of Tabernacles, which coincided with the dedication of the Temple (cf. 8:2). *Hamath to the brook of Egypt:* Hamath, a city at the opening of the great valley between the two Lebanons, is given as the northernmost boundary of the kingdom, and the Brook of Egypt, the Wadi el-Arish, SW of Philistia near the northern border of Egypt, is given as the southernmost (cf. Abel, *GP* 1, 78).

21 (vi) *Solomon's vision* (9:1–9). One of the clearest examples of the interpretative theological discourse so methodically used by the D author of Kgs (cf. also 1 Kgs 8:14–53; 11:11–13; 11:31–39; 14:6–16; 2 Kgs 19:15–19; 20:17–19; 21:7–9; 21:10–15; 22:15–20; 23:27), the dream revelation attributed to Yahweh expresses succinctly some of the basic theological positions of the author: God has chosen the Temple as his eternal abode (v. 3); God has conferred eternity on the Davidic dynasty (v. 5); neither Temple nor dynasty will be spared unless (vv. 6–9) Israel follows in Yahweh's paths—"therefore the Lord brought upon them all this evil" (v. 9). The discourse, at the same time that it establishes the divine promises, also explains apologetically the reasons for the catastrophe of 587. Implicit is the invitation to the exiles, reminiscent of Dt 30:1ff., to convert and once more "keep the commands and statutes" that Yahweh has set before them (see Von Rad, *OT Theology I*, 338–39). **2.** *in Gibeon:* In Solomon's first vision at Gibeon (3:5ff.), he had received the gift of wisdom for judging his people. The author builds on this ancient tradition to develop his interpretative discourse **3.** *the Lord said:* Thus, the author introduces an interpretative discourse attributed to God. As H. T. Fowler says in his article "Herodotus and the Early Hebrew Historians" (*JBL* 49 [1930] 236), "Both Herodotus and the Hebrew historians assume a knowledge of the ways of the unseen powers to which a modern historian would not lay claim." (On the interpretative discourse as a literary device, see C. H. Lohr, *CBQ* 23 [1961] 411ff.). **8.** *house shall become ruins:* The reference is the destruction of the Temple in 587 (cf. 2 Kgs 25:8–9). *shall hiss:* Hissing expressed mockery, hatred, and surprise (cf. Dt 28:37; Jer 18:16; 29:18).

22 (vii) *The episode of Cabul* (9:10–14). **10.** *twenty years:* The figure includes the 7 years of 6:38 and the 13 years of 7:1, covering the major period of Solomon's building activities. **11.** *twenty cities:* The implication is that Solomon gave Hiram these cities in payment for building materials. However, 5:11 states clearly the payments made by Solomon for building materials, and 9:14 gives the price paid by Hiram for the 20 cities. It would appear that Solomon's ambitious projects had brought him close to bankruptcy so that he found it necessary to sell Israelite territory to bail himself out. The towns ceded to Hiram lay along the frontier near the Bay of Acre. **13.** *Cabul:* Noth considers the whole account a later etiological explanation of the name of the city of Cabul (modern Kabul), a town in Asher mentioned in Jos 19:27 (Noth, *Hist.* 212; see however, M–G, *Kings* 204–5).

23 (c) Solomon the International Merchant Prince (9:15–10:29). Mainly archival data, the material is a miscellany compiled by the author from the Book of the Acts of Solomon. He attempts to give some idea of Solomon's magnificence as a king by listing disparate but significant events and accomplishments of his reign: 9:15–25, Solomon's labor battalions; 9:26–28, Solomon's international trading ventures; 10:1–13, the visit of the Queen of Sheba; 10:14–25, Solomon's wealth; 10:26–29, Solomon's chariot cities and chariotry.

15. *levy of forced labor:* See comment on 5:13 and De Vaux, *AI* 141–42. The archival items dealing with Solomon's construction gangs list first some of Solomon's projects (vv. 15b–19), then the subject peoples he pressed into service (vv. 20–21), next a note about the officials in charge of the labor gangs (vv. 22–23), and finally two small items concerning the palace of Pharaoh's daughter and the Temple (vv. 24–25). The list in vv. 15–18 gives the names of the key cities in Solomon's military establishment, indicating that Solomon's fabulous reign of peace was sustained by no mean security measures. From 11:27 it would appear that the Millo provided a defensive wall N of the old Jebusite city subsequently known as "the city of David" (see J. Simons, *Jerusalem in the Old Testament* [Leiden, 1952] 131–44). *wall of Jerusalem:* The lines of this wall are uncertain, but they probably surrounded the Ophel hill SE of the Temple area and perhaps included the Millo. *Hazor:* The largest city in Galilee, destroyed by Joshua two cents. before (Jos 11:1ff.), Hazor was rebuilt to serve as the key city in the defense line Solomon built facing his Aramean possessions in the north. Excavations in recent years under Y. Yadin have contributed much information concerning Hazor (cf. *BAR* 2, 191–224). *Megiddo:* It was the key city guarding the main pass through the Carmel range to the Mediterranean (cf. Albright, *AP* 124ff.). *Gezer:* Excavated by Macalister at the beginning of the century and identified as modern Tell Djezer, Gezer is W of Jerusalem on the hills above the maritime plain, well situated as a western defense for Israel. It is difficult to see (v. 16) how Pharaoh, probably Psousennes II, would have had to conquer it, because presumably David had done so before him (cf. Noth, *Hist.* 216; Albright, *ARI* 136, n. 29; *AASOR* 12, 74–75). **18.** *Beth-horon:* Not far from Gezer and commanding the pass leading W to Jerusalem, Beth-horon also provided a defense for Solomon in the west. *Baalat and Tamar:* Both are in the Negeb fronting on Edom (cf. Jos 15:29); they closed the circle of Solomon's garrison cities and at the same time protected his trade route to the Red Sea. **19.** *chariot cities:* See comment on 10:26. **21.** *made no slave of the Israelites:* Some reservation must be understood. It is clear from 5:13; 11:28; 12:4–16 that Israelites were pressed into service, at least temporarily (see De Vaux, *AI* 141–42). **24.** *Pharaoh's daughter:* See comment on 3:1.

26. Ezion-geber was Solomon's port city at the head of the Gulf of Aqabah in Edom; it provided access to the Red Sea and the Indian Ocean. *Elath:* A short distance E of Ezion-geber, Elath was the port city from which Solomon's fleet sailed to Ophir. With the help of Hiram of Tyre, Solomon equipped his fleet and bartered the products of his copper foundries for the exotic products of Arabia and East Africa (cf. 10:11,22). **28.** *Ophir:* It was probably located on the southwestern coast of Arabia or on the opposite Somali coast of Africa.

24 **10:1–13.** Assyrian records mention five Queens of Saba in the 8th and 7th cents. (*ANET* 283), and biblical authors bear witness to gold, spices, frankincense, and precious stones, for which Sabaean traders were famous (cf. Is 60:6; Ez 27:22; Jer 6:20; Ps 72:15). Recent excavations have shown that the kingdom of Saba or Sheba was situated in southern Arabia, in what is now Yemen. Its capital was Marib and it flourished from the 12th to the 1st cent. BC, principally as a result of its camel caravans that made it middleman by land trade routes between the Far East and Asia Minor until the 1st cent. when Phoenician sailors discovered a sea route from the Gulf of Suez to the East bringing an end to Saba's prosperity. The Queen's visit was primarily commercial (cf. vv. 2, 10, 13), but the author has used it as another illustration (cf. 1 Kgs 3–4) to enhance Solomon's reputation (cf. vv. 3–9) as a sage (see W. F. Albright, *BASOR* 119 [1950] 5–6; *BASOR* 129 [1953] 20–24; *BASOR* 143 [1956] 9–10; W. Phillips, *Qataban and Sheba* [N.Y., 1955]; M–G, *Kings* 215ff.).

14. *weights of gold:* Inasmuch as the talent weighed approximately 75 to 80 lb., the figure of 666 talents seems excessive. It may have been reached by adding the figures for gold mentioned in 9:14,28; 10:10 (see De Vaux, *AI* 203ff.). **16.** *shields:* There were two types: the large man-height covering shield known as the *ṣinnāh*; and the smaller circular buckler type known as the *māgēn* (cf. 2 Chr 14:7). The large shields plated with gold were no doubt used on parade; in battle, simpler, inexpensive shields made of leather stained red were used (De Vaux, *AI* 244–45). **18.** *throne:* Thrones discovered by archaeologists illustrate substantially the description of Solomon's fabulous throne (cf. *ANE* 332, 415–17, 458). **22.** *Tarshish ships:* The expression means "very large ships," ancient ocean liners. Tarshish (from the Phoenician word meaning "foundry") was the name of one or perhaps even several "foundry" settlements founded by the Phoenician mariners on the distant shores of the western Mediterranean (cf. 9:26–28; 10:11; Jon 1:3; 4:2; Is 66:19; Ps 72:10).

26. *chariots:* Unlike David, whose army was based on the foot soldier, Solomon concentrated on chariotry. The number 1400 seems high but it is known that King Ahab of Israel brought 2000 chariots to the battle of Qarqar in 853. Excavations have confirmed the extent of Solomon's chariot installations, showing stalls at Megiddo alone for 450 horses, with elaborate stables and drinking troughs. Other chariot cities are listed in 9:15–19 (cf. 5:8; Albright, *ARI* 136; *AP* 124–25; De Vaux, *AI* 222ff.; G. E. Wright, *BA* 13 [1950] 28–46). **28.** Solomon reaped a middleman's profits, monopolizing trade between Syria and Egypt. He imported horses from Cilicia (in some texts, "Kue"), famous for its stud farms, and he obtained the finest chariots from Egypt. Syria thus depended on Israel for chariots and Egypt depended on Israel for horses (cf. De Vaux, *AI* 78, 222–23).

25 (d) SOLOMON THE SINNER (11:1–41). The major part of ch. 11 is from the hand of the exilic author; some archival items from the Book of the Acts of Solomon are incorporated. It breaks down into five parts: vv. 1–10, the author's deuteronomic explanation of Solomon's downfall; vv. 11–13, an interpretative discourse attributed to God predicting the division of the kingdom; vv. 14–28 and 40, a number of archival items (probably from the Acts of Solomon) explaining how God prepared events for the division of the kingdom; vv. 29–39, a prophetic-fulfillment story concerning Ahijah and Solomon with an interpretative discourse attributed to the prophet Ahijah; vv. 41–43, the end of the reign of Solomon.

1. Marriage with foreigners was not uncommon in ancient Israel, despite later laws that sought to prevent it (cf. Ex 34:15–16; Dt 7:3–4; Ezr 9–10; Neh 10:31). David had a Calebite and an Aramean among his seven wives (2 Sm 3:3). Solomon, however, married foreign women primarily for political reasons—to seal alliances and to maintain amicable relations with other nations—and for prestige, for the possession of a large harem was a mark of wealth and power. The author judges Solomon on the basis of Dt 7:3–4 and his judgment is negative (v. 2; cf. Von Rad, *OT Theology I*, 336–37). **3.** *seven hundred wives... three hundred concubines:* David had at least seven wives and ten concubines (2 Sm 3:2–5; 15:16). When Pharaoh Amenophis III married a young princess from Mitanni, she brought with her 317 young maidens. Ct 6:8 refers to "sixty queens, eighty concubines, and maidens without number." The numbers given here are round and legendary, but there is no reason to doubt that Solomon had a well-populated harem inasmuch as the custom was prevalent and the king's concern for prestige, evidenced by his building projects, is more than obvious.

4. *when Solomon was old:* Although the introduction of foreign religions and shrines into Judah and Jerusalem was probably simultaneous with the introduction of foreign wives, and therefore early in Solomon's reign (vv. 5–8), the author intimates that the king himself did not apostatize or at least practice syncretistic worship until the later years of his reign. *as was the heart of David:* The emphasis on David, habitual with the exilic author, is found throughout his work but nowhere more so than in the passages proper to him as bridge passages or interpretative discourses (cf. vv. 6, 12–13, 32–34, 36, 38–39; see comment on 9:1). **5.** Widely venerated in the ancient Semitic world, Astarte (Hebr, Ashtoreth) was goddess of fertility in plants, animals, and man. Many places had their own special Astarte, so that in several texts the word is used in the plural (Jgs 2:13; 10:6). Excavations have turned up many amulets and statues of the "naked goddess" (*ANE* 464–74). *Milcom:* It is the god of the Ammonites, who is mentioned by Zephaniah (1:5) and Jeremiah (32:35) in the 7th cent. when idolatry was widespread in Judah. **7.** *high place:* See comment on 3:2. *Chemosh:* The chief god of the Moabites (Nm 21:29; Jer 48:46), he is mentioned on the Moabite Stone (cf. *ANET* 320) and is certainly the unnamed god in 2 Kgs 3:27 to whom the infant son of the King of Moab was offered. It is probable that Chemosh and Milcom are all variant names for Nergal, the Mesopotamian god of death and the underworld. **9.** *was angry:* The expression and its near equivalent, "to be provoked to jealousy," are typical of the author (cf. 1 Kgs 8:46; 14:9,22; 16:7; 21:22; 2 Kgs 17:17–18; 21:6,15; 23:26; 24:20) and reducible to the influence of Dt (cf. Dt 1:37; 4:21; 9:8,20; 4:25; 9:18; 31:29; 32:16,21). **11–13.** *the Lord said:* It is an interpretative discourse; see comment on 9:1.

26 **14.** *Hadad:* The archival item concerning the fugitive Edomite prince in vv. 14–22, and 24 is incomplete as it stands, because it does not explain how or to what extent Hadad troubled Solomon. The author, however, was not so much interested in Hadad as in showing the fulfillment of the prediction made in the preceding interpretative discourse, which is clear from his opening words: "Accordingly the Lord raised up...." **15.** The present episode is probably, although not certainly, related to David's conquest of Edom described in 2 Sm 8:13ff. It could be David's suppression of a later and otherwise unrecorded insurrection. The hospitality accorded the young Edomite prince (vv. 18–22) was neither purely gratuitous nor devoid of ulterior purposes, as the sequel shows (v. 25), and Pharaoh was following a fairly normal political course in harboring a potential troublemaker to be unleashed at the opportune time to embarrass an enemy (cf. v. 40; and Gn 36:31–39).

23. *Rezon:* To the trouble in the south caused by Hadad is added trouble in the north. The extent of the trouble caused by Rezon is unknown, but the capture of Damascus could have been no small loss to Solomon in view of the trade routes that passed through the city. Hadadezer of Zobah, Rezon's immediate overlord, had been conquered by David (2 Sm 8:10; 10:16ff.) and presumably governed the whole region until overthrown by Rezon, the first king of Damascus known to us by name. **26.** *Jeroboam:* The account concerning Jeroboam's unsuccessful revolt runs from vv. 26 to 40, but only vv. 26–28 and 40 come from the original source; vv. 29–39 is a prophetic story expanded into its present interpretative discourse form by the exilic author. The name Jeroboam, which probably means "may the people multiply," and possibly is in imitation of Rehoboam's name, which means "may the people expand," may be a throne name adopted by Jeroboam when he became king of Israel. An Ephraimite, Jeroboam had the long history of his tribe's distaste for domination to support his uprising. **27.** *reason:* Actually no reason is given unless it is either the encouragement of the prophet Ahijah recorded in vv. 29–39, or the same reason as that given in 12:3 for the later, successful revolt. *Millo:* See comment on 9:15. **28.** *charge of the forced labor:* Jeroboam's ability came to Solomon's attention in the course of the work on the Millo. As a result, he was made an official in the compulsory labor organization initiated by Solomon (cf. 4:6; 5:13–16; 9:15–23), a position that no doubt helped achieve prominence for him and made him the natural spokesman for the northern tribes when they later rebelled against Rehoboam's continuance of Solomon's labor *corvées* (cf. 12:3ff.). It is not certain when the revolt took place but it seems to be connected with the work on the Millo and therefore probably occurred early in Solomon's reign (cf. 11:29). The failure of the revolt and Jeroboam's flight for refuge to Egypt (cf. Hadad's flight to Egypt, 11:17ff.) is laconically recorded in v. 40 (see Noth, *Hist.* 206–207).

27 **29.** *Ahijah:* From Shiloh, once celebrated as the resting place of the Ark (Jos 18:1; Jgs 18:31; 1 Sm 1–4), Ahijah appears as a revolutionary committed to the overthrow of Solomon. It is probable that he was the spokesman for the antimonarchical faction, to which so many of the prophets belonged. Here, the exilic author is interested in explaining the impending division of the kingdom as the work of God in accordance with the interpretative discourse prediction of 11:11–13. **30.** *twelve pieces:* The prophets employed symbolic actions (cf. Is 20:2–3; Jer 13:1–11; 19:1–13; Ez 4:1ff.), not only because they were graphic and unforgettable but also because according to the ancient way of thinking they rendered their oracles more efficacious (cf. 22:10–11). The ten pieces represent the ten northern tribes of Israel (cf. 2 Sm 19:43). The remaining two pieces represent Judah alone, which by the time of David had incorporated the tribe of Simeon.

31. *says the Lord:* The exilic author's interpretative discourse, which is probably based on an early oracle of Ahijah, properly begins here. It complements the interpretative discourse of 11:11–13 and places the same emphasis on David and Jerusalem (cf. 11:13 and 11:32–39) according to the Nathan oracle of 2 Sm 7. The fulfillment of both interpretative discourses is recorded in 12:15. Thus, the author shows the lamp of messianic hope lit by the dynastic oracle of Nathan and fed by the faith of Israel shining brightly just before the darkness begins to gather over the messianic kingdom. **40.** *Shishak:* Cf. 14:25. **41.** The author concludes the reign of Solomon, as he concluded the reign of David—with a set formula (cf. 2:10–11), which he will continue to use with variations for all the succeeding kings of Israel and Judah (cf. 14:19–20,29–31). *book of the acts of Solomon:* The early source used by the final author appears to have been a simple compilation of archival data, rich in detail but poor in depth and perception, entirely unlike the brilliant Court History of David (see Noth, *Hist.* 204).

28 **(II) The Synoptic History of the Kings (1 Kgs 12:1–2 Kgs 16:34).** Many sources have contributed to the composition of Part II: "The Book of the Acts of the Kings of Israel" (*passim*); "The Book of the Acts of the Kings of Judah" (*passim*); the Elijah cycle (1 Kgs 17–2 Kgs 1 *passim*); the Elisha cycle (2 Kgs 2–13, 25 *passim*); a heterogeneous collection of prophetic-fulfillment stories. The exilic author-editor has cleverly combined his main sources to present a synoptic history of Israel and Judah from the time of the division in 922 to the destruction of Israel in 721. In addition, he has sandwiched into the synoptic history a large number of prophetic-fulfillment stories designed (and often tailored by the author) to highlight the hand of God in Israel's and Judah's history and to draw attention to the infallible fulfillment of the prophetically pronounced word. In the appropriate places, he has introduced his interpretative discourses (1 Kgs 14:6–16; 2 Kgs 17) to make doubly clear the lessons to be drawn from Israel's history. As in 1 Kgs 1–3, 8–9, and 11, the author continues to refer to David, thus keeping alive his reader's remembrance of the Nathan oracle of 2 Sm 7 (cf. 1 Kgs 15:4–5; 2 Kgs 8:19; 19:35; 20:6; 21:7–8, and the many comparisons of the Judean kings to their forefather, David).

Of particular note in Part II are the opening and closing formulas for each king's reign and the synchronizations used by D as a framework (not unlike the framework used in Jgs 3–16) for his synoptic narrative. His procedure is the juxtaposition of excerpts from the respective chronicles of Israel and Judah to present a synoptic view of both kingdoms, completing the narrative of each king's reign before dealing with the concurrent reign or reigns in the other kingdom. When he has overlapped reigns, he returns to the first series and continues. For each king, the author follows stereotyped opening and closing formulas. The former begins with a synchronization of the reign under consideration with the reign of the other kingdom; then follows the age of the king (only for the Judean kings), the length of his reign, the judgment on the king (containing quite often a comparison with David for the Judean kings, but a comparison with Jeroboam for the Israelite kings), and finally the name of his mother (only for the Judean kings). The judgment (always adverse for the kings of Israel) is usually quite simple (e.g., 1 Kgs 15:26), but occasionally fuller particulars are given (e.g., 1 Kgs 14:22–24). The closing formula contains a reference to the author's source, the death of the king, his burial, and the name of his successor (cf. 1 Kgs 15:7–8). Between the opening and closing formulas, the author occasionally gives additional information about the king's reign; however, more often than not, he introduces at least one, and sometimes several, prophetic-fulfillment stories (e.g., 1 Kgs 16:29–22:39–40).

29 **(A) The Division of Solomon's Kingdom (12:1–13:34).** The story of the division (12:1–20), probably taken from an early Judean source (cf. 12:15; cf. also 12:16 with 2 Sm 20:1), has been expanded by D for didactic purposes by the addition of prophetic-fulfillment stories and interpretative discourses. It breaks down into four parts: the division (12:1–20); a prophetic-fulfillment story (12:21–24); D's explanation of Jeroboam's sin (12:25–32); a prophetic-fulfillment story (12:33–13:34) (→ History of Israel, 75:63–64).

(a) The Division of the Kingdom (12:1–20) (= 2 Chr 10). **1.** *Shechem:* SE of modern Nablus, and already venerable as an early Israelite sanctuary (cf. Gn 12:6–7; 33:18–20; Jos 24:21–24), Shechem was the natural place for the elders of Israel to gather in assembly to acclaim the new king. **2–3.** It was to be expected that Jeroboam would return from exile in Egypt after the death of his enemy, Solomon (cf. 11:40). Nevertheless, there is disagreement between v. 3a and v. 20, and authors agree that at least v. 3a, if not also v. 2 and the reference to Jeroboam in v. 12, may have come either from 2 Chr 12:2,12 or from the hand of a glossator (see M–G, *Kings* 248–49). **4.** *hard service:* Solomon's heavy taxes (4:7–19) and forced-labor gangs (5:13–27) are meant. What the elders of Israel seek, unsuccessfully as the sequel shows (vv. 5–15), is to reach an agreement or covenant with Rehoboam concerning diminution of these burdens before accepting him as king. **11.** *scorpions:* A technical term, it was presumably used for a more severe type of whip. The advice of the young counselors would indicate that Solomon had nurtured an autocratic and even despotic type of courtier. **15.** *by the Lord:* Following the description of Rehoboam's tactless and imprudent behavior, D interpolates his personal comment (or makes his own the earlier author's sentiment) to stress the fact that behind the apparently all too human course of events there runs the purpose and the guiding hand of God. *to establish his word:* According to his custom, D signals the fulfillment of the prophetic word (cf. 11:11,31). **16.** *what portion:* The well-known watchword of rebellion (cf. 2 Sm 20:1) is raised again—for the last time. **18.** *Adoram:* Compounding his imprudence, Rehoboam sends Adoram, chief of the detested labor gangs (4:6), to negotiate with the rebels. His death by stoning seals the insurrection with violence. **20.** This verse implies, contrary to vv. 2 and 12, that Jeroboam had not been present at the original confrontation of the elders with Rehoboam.

(b) A Prophetic-Fulfillment Story (12:21–24) (= 2 Chr 11:1–4). The story of Shemaiah's prophecy is included by D to highlight, as in 12:15, the divine hand behind the division of the kingdom and to signal, as is his custom, the fulfillment of the Word of God (v. 24). **21.** The LXX has 120,000 troops instead of 180,000, but either figure is absurd, which does not mean, as some authors hold, that the story is unhistorical. Neither can one argue from 14:30 against the historicity of Shemaiah's prophecy, for 14:30 refers to sporadic warfare over a long time, but 12:24 refers to a specific campaign aimed at forcing the northern tribes to reunite with Judah. The story is found without change in 2 Chr 11:1–4. (On the Gk supplement to the history of Jeroboam following v. 24, see M–G, *Kings* 251ff.)

30 (c) The Deuteronomist's Explanation of Jeroboam's Sin (12:25–32). With the exception of the archival items in v. 25, the major portion of this pericope is probably D's hindsight explanation of the harm done Israel by Jeroboam's innovations in worship, which, although politically rather than religiously inspired at the time of their introduction, had dire consequences for Israel. **25.** Since Shechem was already old, the author probably means that Jeroboam organized and fortified it as his capital city. No reason is given for the transfer of the capital to Penuel, but some emergency—possibly the invasion of Pharaoh Shishak—must have occasioned this otherwise inexplicable transfer, if such it truly was (see M–G, *Kings* 254). Penuel, the modern Tulul ed-dahab (Abel, *GP* 2, 406), is in Transjordan in the deep valley of the Jabbok River. At a later date, Jeroboam transferred his capital to Tirzah (see 14:17; 15:33). **26.** *said to himself:* The monologue put in Jeroboam's mouth by D probably represents quite accurately the mind of this rebel king. David and Solomon had made Jerusalem not only the political but also the religious center of the nation. Moreover, they had associated Jerusalem and the Temple so intimately with their dynasty that to think of one was to call to mind the other as well. Jeroboam rightly deduced that the attraction of the Temple in Jerusalem might eventually have political repercussions. His ensuing moves in the religious sphere, therefore, are politically motivated, and, at least in the beginning, there is no valid reason to question his Yahwist orthodoxy.

28. *two golden calves:* These wooden statues are plated with gold like the Golden Calf in Ex 32; they were not originally meant to be representations of Yahweh. Like the Ark and the cherubim, which formed the throne of Yahweh in the Temple of Jerusalem, the young bulls formed either Yahweh's throne or its pedestal in Jeroboam's new temples (see De Vaux, *AI* 333ff.). If the golden calves had been representations of Yahweh, the northern prophets would certainly have spoken out against them. But neither Elijah, Elisha, nor Amos says a word against them. On the other hand, the young bull was the animal that symbolized the Canaanite god Baal. The danger of Jeroboam's innovation was that the calves would lead at least the simple Israelites to confuse Yahweh with Baal. Indeed, it happened in due course, certainly by the time of Elijah in the 9th cent. (1 Kgs 17–18) and probably even within the lifetime of Jeroboam (1 Kgs 14:7–16). Israel's eventual apostasy and destruction as a result are traced by D to Jeroboam's golden calves, repeatedly referred to as "the sin of Jeroboam" (15:34 and *passim*; → Religious Institutions, 76:66).

29. *Bethel:* Bethel was an ideal choice for a shrine city, not only because it would draw pilgrims going S to Jerusalem, but also because it had already been a sacred city for centuries as a result of its association with the patriarchs (Gn 12:8; 28:10–22; see also De Vaux, *AI* 335). Pilgrims, moreover, had journeyed to the sanctuary at Bethel for centuries before Jerusalem became an Israelite city (1 Sm 10:3; Jgs 20:18,26–28; 21:2). *Dan:* A shrine city since the time of the judges (Jgs 17–18), Dan lay at the northern extremity of the new kingdom at the headwaters of the Jordan. It was chosen by Jeroboam to cater to the isolated northern tribes. Nothing more is known about the shrine beyond that it was still functioning in the time of Amos (Am 8:14). **32.** *a feast:* The feast is undoubtedly the Feast of Tents, one of a pilgrimage. Since the people were accustomed to going in pilgrimage to Solomon's Temple for the Feast of Tents, Jeroboam supplies the same feast in his new temples to draw Israelites who might otherwise continue to travel to Jerusalem (see comment on 8:2; see De Vaux, *AI* 499). It was at this same feast that Solomon dedicated his temple (8:65).

31 (d) A Prophetic-Fulfillment Story (12:33–13:34). The story of the disobedient prophet from Judah serves D in three ways: First, it shows God's opposition to the Bethel cult instituted by Jeroboam against the legitimate cult of Solomon's Temple; second, it teaches by the punishment of the disobedient prophet the inviolate character of the Word of God; and third, it provides another example in the series of prophetic-fulfillment stories by means of which D wishes to focus attention on the as yet unfulfilled Nathan oracle (→ 5 above). Whereas the story speaks for itself in showing God's opposition to the Bethel cult and in teaching the inviolate character of the Word of God, D, to stress the prophetic-fulfillment aspect, expands the original in v. 2 by interpolating the name of Josiah. Later on, as is his custom, he will relate the fulfillment of this prophecy (cf. 2 Kgs 23:15–19). Some authors would claim the story of the disobedient prophet belongs to the literary form known as haggadic midrash (on this form, see A.

Wright in *CBQ* 28 [1966] 105-38). **33.** This verse, which is repetitious and obviously redactional, marks the seam by which D attached the midrashic story to the chronicle material of the previous verses. Although later authors (e.g., 2 Chr 26:18) protested the intrusion of the kings in the priestly sphere, there is no great protest here. It is the altar at Bethel, i.e., the worship at Bethel, with which D is concerned, and the story he incorporates begins with a condemnation of the altar (vv. 2-3). Thus, the historical core of the original story would appear to have been the prophetic protest against the new worship instituted by Jeroboam. It would seem from the reaction of Ahijah that prophetic circles supported the political, but not the religious, division of Solomon's kingdom (cf. 11:29-39 and 14:7-16; see also De Vaux, *AI* 113-14 and M-G, *Kings* 260ff.). **2.** *Josiah by name:* The explicit naming of a future individual, so contrary to prophetic practice, is obviously the interpolation either of a writer in the time of Josiah, when the midrashic story may have been composed, or of D himself (cf. 13:32 and 2 Kgs 23:15-19). *burn men's bones:* Contact with the dead would make the altar unclean, because both the corpse and the tomb containing it were considered unclean (Lv 21:1-4; 22:4; De Vaux, *AI* 57ff., 460-61). **22.** *grave of your fathers:* Not to be buried in the family tomb was considered a punishment from God. **33.** *priests:* The interpolator of the midrashic story closes his account of Jeroboam's religious innovations with another derisive remark about the northern priests (see De Vaux, *AI* 361-62).

32 **(B) Synoptic History to the Time of Elijah (14:1-16:34).** Properly speaking, D's synoptic history begins in ch. 12 with Rehoboam and Jeroboam, but the author's interest there is taken up with the story of the division of the kingdom, and it is not until ch. 14, with the death of Jeroboam, that he begins to use his stereotyped synoptic formulas (14:19-20; → 25 above). We shall treat briefly the reigns of Jeroboam, Rehoboam, Abijam, Asa, Nadab, Baasha, Elah, Zimri, Omri, and Ahab. Since it is generally agreed that D did not always work out the regnal dates in his synchronisms with complete success, we shall omit discussion of discrepancies in the synchronisms and follow the chronology worked out in "The Chronology of Israel and the Ancient Near East" by N. Freedman and E. F. Campbell, Jr. (*BANE* 203-28).

(a) JEROBOAM I, 922-901 (14:1-20). The midrashic story of Ahijah and the sick son of Jeroboam is incorporated by D not so much for its value as another prediction-fulfillment story (cf. vv. 12, 17-18) as for the opportunity it gives him to put into the mouth of the prophet an interpretative discourse spelling out the destruction not only of the dynasty of Jeroboam but also of the northern kingdom as a whole (vv. 7-16). **2.** *disguise yourself:* The statement presumes Jeroboam knows his erstwhile friend (11:29ff.) has turned against him. If the queen had come in royal garments, she would have been recognized immediately. **3.** *ten loaves:* It was customary to make an offering to a seer for his services (cf. Nm 22:17; 1 Sm 9:7-8; 2 Kgs 5:15). **7-8.** The interpretative discourse attributed to the prophet by D is a death sentence by hindsight laid upon the new kingdom even before the death of its first king (cf. vv. 15-16). Moreover, D predicts the destruction of Jeroboam's line by Baasha (v. 14) and at the appropriate time signals the fulfillment of this "prediction" (15:28-29). **9.** *any that were before you:* Either D has forgotten that Jeroboam is the first king of Israel or he is simply using a hackneyed phrase (cf. 16:25,30; 2 Kgs 23:25) or comparing him adversely even with Solomon! **11.** *him that dies...:* The formula may have been proverbial (cf. 16:4) or may have originated with Elijah (compare 21:24 and 2 Kgs 9:35-36) and have been appropriated by D as a formula. **14.** *shall cut off:* The reference is to Baasha, who assassinates Jeroboam's son Nadab (15:28-29). **15.** *beyond the river:* The river is the Euphrates, beyond which lay Assyria (cf. 2 Kgs 17:6,23). There is no evidence that Jeroboam introduced the Astarte cult (cf. 11:5) into Israel. The author speaks from the vantage point of 560 or later. **19.** After his closing formula (→ 28 above), the author turns now to the kings of Judah, who reigned concomitantly with Jeroboam. Only when he has finished the reign of Asa, the successor of Abijam and Rehoboam, which overlapped that of Jeroboam, will he turn again to the northern king, Nadab, the son of Jeroboam (15:25-31).

33 (b) REHOBOAM, 922-915 (14:21-31) (= 2 Chr 11:5-12:16). **21.** The age of the Davidic kings at the time of their accession is occasionally given; the age of the Israelite kings, however, is never given. *to put his name:* The phrase is not intrusive from the Chronicler (cf. 12:13), as some have thought (see M-G, *Kings* 268), but is characteristic of D, who wishes to emphasize the Temple and Jerusalem in relation to the Nathan oracle (cf. 1 Kgs 8:29; 9:3; 11:36; 2 Kgs 21:4; 21:7; cf. also 1 Kgs 6:12-13; 8:12-13; 11:13,32; 15:4; 2 Kgs 19:34; 20:6-7). **22.** The judgment on Rehoboam's reign, a regular item in D's synoptic opening formula, indicates that Rehoboam continued the syncretistic policies of his father. **23.** *high places:* See comment on 3:2. **24.** Male prostitution was practiced, after the manner of the depraved Canaanite cult (cf. Dt 23:18-19; see De Vaux, *AI* 385). **25.** *Shishak:* First Pharaoh of the 22nd dynasty, Shishak (*ca.* 935-914) invaded not only Judah but also Israel, as the numerous names of conquered Israelite cities in his Karnak Palestine list clearly show—e.g., Megiddo, Taanak, Beth-shan, and Shunem. Shishak, despite his earlier friendship with Jeroboam, evidently took advantage of the war-torn Hebr state to regain control of the commercial route that led up the Mediterranean coast and across the Plain of Esdraelon. The list of 15 fortified towns mentioned in 2 Chr 11:6-10 may represent Rehoboam's measures to ward off the threatening invasion of Shishak (see Albright, *BP* 58-59). **26.** It would seem that Shishak spared Jerusalem but demanded so heavy a tribute that both the Temple and palace treasuries were emptied. Among the art objects taken by Shishak were the famous gold shields of Solomon (cf. 10:16).

29. *acts of the Kings of Judah:* Mentioned 15 times by D in his closing synoptic formula, these Acts, like the Acts of the Kings of Israel (cf. 14:19), were probably a popular history of the Davidic kings that drew upon the royal archives for the basic biographical facts of each king's life. Since the reader is invited to consult this work, it was apparently readily available. The royal archives, on the other hand, would hardly have been available at any time to the general reader and not at all at the time of D, because they were probably destroyed in 587 when Jerusalem fell to the Babylonians. Both works, the Acts of the Kings of Israel and the Acts of the Kings of Judah, falter at the end of the respective kingdoms, the northern Acts about 725 and the southern about 590. **30.** The Shemaiah story in 12:21-24 would indicate that no major war took place, which does not mean that sporadic fighting did not break out over the years. Indeed, Rehoboam's successful retention of Benjamin almost certainly involved a certain amount of warfare (see Bright, *Hist.* 213).

34 (c) ABIJAM, 915-913 (15:1-8) (= 2 Chr 13). **2.** *Maacah:* Deposed as queen mother by Asa because of her rampant paganism (15:13), Maacah certainly contributed further to the spread of Canaanite religion begun under Solomon and Rehoboam (11:4-10; 14:22-24). As daughter of Absalom, who was born of a pagan

Geshurite princess and lived for a time in Geshur (2 Sm 3:3; 13:37–38), Maacah to a certain extent inherited her pagan background. It may be, as Albright opines, that she was mother of both Abijam and Asa (Albright, *ARI* 157–58; see also M–G, *Kings* 274). **4.** *a lamp:* The expression is metaphorical for a successor (cf. Ps 132:17; Jb 18:6; 21:17) and is characteristic of D's solicitude to highlight the import of the Nathan oracle (cf. 1 Kgs 11:32–39; 2 Kgs 8:19). **5.** *Uriah the Hittite:* Intrusive, the remark is probably the moralizing judgment of a scrupulous glossator. **7.** *war between Abijam and Jeroboam:* 2 Chr 13 tells the story of at least one encounter between the two kings. Although the account is exaggerated and liberally expanded, there is no reason to doubt its basic historicity (see Bright, *Hist.* 215).

35 (d) Asa, 913–873 (15:9–24) (= 2 Chr 14–16). **10.** *Maacah:* Either she was mother of both Abijam and Asa (see comment on 15:2) or as grandmother of Asa she continues in power as queen mother until death. **12.** Asa is the first of the Davidites to institute a reform of the Temple, which was undoubtedly only part of a general religious reform (cf. 2 Chr 14:2–4; 15:1–15). He is followed in reform work by Hezekiah (2 Kgs 18:3–4) and Josiah (2 Kgs 23). The externals of the reform consisted in removing from the Temple Canaanite practices and cult objects, some of which are mentioned here (see De Vaux, *AI* 322; Albright, *BP* 61). **13.** *queen mother:* By her title (*g^{e}bîrâ*, "powerful lady"), rather than by the normal influence of a mother upon a son, the king's mother enjoyed special privileges and powers that could be withdrawn, as in this instance, if she proved unworthy. The power of a queen mother is dramatically exemplified in Judah by Athaliah (2 Kgs 11:1ff.) and in Egypt by Hatshepsut. **15.** *dedicated things:* They are gifts made to the Temple (cf. 2 Kgs 12:18). **17–22.** Baasha's attempt to fortify Ramah, only 5 mi. N of Jerusalem and strategically located to govern the approach to the southern capital, posed a serious threat to Judah. Asa's energetic measures (vv. 18–23) show that he appreciated the situation. With the help of Ben-hadad of Damascus, he not only repulsed Baasha but also extended his defenses as far as Geba and Mizpah, fortifying these and other cities against not only Baasha but also Zerah, the Ethiopian, a garrison commander of Osorkon I, the successor of Shishak (cf. 2 Chr 14:9–15; see Albright, *BP* 61–62; M–G, *Kings* 275–78).

36 (e) Nadab, 901–900 (15:25–31). **25.** *two years:* His short reign, ended by assassination (v. 27), shows the difficulty of establishing dynastic stability in Israel. In the two centuries of her history, at least seven of Israel's kings fell by the sword. **27.** *Gibbethon:* A Philistine stronghold in Danite territory (cf. Jos 19:41–46; see Abel, *GP* 2, 333), Gibbethon was still a bone of contention between Israel and Philistia in the time of Elah (16:15). **29.** *Ahijah:* Presumably Ahijah was the prophet behind Baasha's insurrection (14:14). As usual, D records the fulfillment of the prophet's prediction. **32.** Absent in the Greek, this verse is an unnecessary repetition of v. 16.

(f) Baasha, 900–877 (15:33–16:7). **33.** *Tirzah:* Once a royal Canaanite city (Jos 12:24), Tirzah had become the capital of Israel under Jeroboam (cf. 14:17) and remained so until Omri founded a new capital at Samaria (16:24). It has been located at Tell el Far'ah, 7 mi. NE of Shechem (see R. de Vaux, *PEQ* 88 [1956] 125–40; *RB* 68 [1961] 557–92). **16:1.** *Jehu:* The prophet is again mentioned in the reign of Jehoshaphat (cf. 2 Chr 19:2–3; 20:34). His oracle against Baasha (vv. 2–3) is similar to Ahijah's oracle against Jeroboam (see comment on 14:11), and it is possible that he, not Ahijah, was the prophet who originally had backed Baasha's revolution (15:27–30), only to turn against him later as Ahijah had turned against Jeroboam (see Noth, *Hist.* 229). **7.** *because he smote it:* This unlikely reason for Baasha's condemnation, and the fact that the verse only repeats the substance of vv. 2–3, would indicate it is a gloss (see M–G, *Kings* 282).

(g) Elah, 877–876 (16:8–14). **9.** *half his chariots:* As commanding general of half Israel's chariot force, Zimri was an officer of some consequence. *over the house:* See comment on 4:6. **12.** *according to the word:* As usual, D cites fulfillment of the prophetic word (cf. 16:2). **13.** *sins of Baasha:* Attributing the downfall of the dynasty to Baasha's sins is somewhat unusual, for D almost always cites the sin of Jeroboam as the cause of all evil in Israel.

(h) Zimri, 876 (16:15–20). **15.** *Gibbethon:* See comment on 15:27. Like Jehu, another commander of the army who revolted in time of war (2 Kgs 9), Zimri takes advantage of the absence of Israel's army, occupied with the siege of Gibbethon, to carry out his *coup d'état.* **16.** The army supports Omri, another army commander, for king. In the ensuing civil war (vv. 17–19), his supporters make short work of Zimri. **18.** The "castle" or "citadel" (*'armôn*) is a heavily fortified part of the palace (cf. 2 Kgs 15:25; see De Vaux, *AI* 235).

37 (i) Omri, 876–69 (16:21–28). **21.** *Tibni:* nothing is known about Tibni, but, according to the dating in v. 23, the civil war between the factions of Omri and Tibni lasted four years; in view of the later renown of Omri, Tibni must have been no mean adversary to have held out so long. *Omri:* Neither "Omri" nor "Ahab" would seem to be Israelite names. It is possible that he was a foreign mercenary who rose through the ranks to become general of the militia (see Noth, *Hist.* 230). **24.** *Samaria:* The last and most important capital of the northern kingdom, Samaria (modern Sebaste) was ideally located on an easily defended hill at the northern end of a fertile valley that began at Shechem 7 mi. to the south. Through the valley and past Samaria ran the best road N to the Plain of Esdraelon. Excavations have shown that the fortifications of Samaria begun by Omri and completed by his son, Ahab, were not only unequaled in Palestine for excellence of workmanship but also so strong that even the mighty Assyrian armies required more than 2 years to breach them. *after the name of Shemer:* This is probably a folk etymology; the site showed some signs of occupancy before the time of Omri and most likely received its name from the fact that the hill had always served as a natural "watch post," from the Hebr vb. *šāmar*, "to watch."

(For archaeological data on Samaria, see: Abel, *GP* 2, 443–46. Crowfoot, J. W., *et al., The Buildings at Samaria* [London, 1942]; *The Objects from Samaria* [London, 1957]. Hartman, L., *EDB* 2075–78. Maisler, B., *JPOS* 22 [1948] 117–33. O'Doherty, E., *CBQ* 15 [1953] 24–29. Reisner, G. S. *et al., Harvard Excavations at Samaria* [Cambridge, 1924]. Wright, G. E., *BA* 22 [1959] 67–78; *BASOR* 155 [1959] 13–29.)

27. *his prowess:* D says little about Omri's well-deserved renown in the secular sphere because his interests are primarily religious. The evidence, however, shows that Omri not only built a great capital but also halted the disintegration of the kingdom and thus strengthened the nation militarily, politically, and economically. In fact, for generations Israel was known in Assyrian annals as "the land of Omri." Thus, he re-established good relations with Phoenicia and Judah by intermarriage between the royal houses (1 Kgs 16:31; 2 Kgs 8:18), he successfully staved off the rising might of Aram in the northeast, and he reconquered all of Transjordan except Ammon, making Moab a vassal state and settling Israelites in the territory N of the Arnon (cf. 2 Kgs 3:4; see *ANET* 320; Bright, *Hist.* 220–24; Albright, *BP* 63).

38 (j) AHAB, 869–850 (16:29–34; 22:39–40). Owing to D's incorporation of accounts from the Elijah cycle dealing with Ahab (chs. 17–22), which are sandwiched between his usual opening formula in 16:29–34 and his closing formula in 22:39–40, much more is known about Ahab than about his more illustrious father, Omri. **21.** *Jezebel:* Omri's arrangement of a marriage between his son and Jezebel sealed an alliance between Israel and Phoenicia that was to have dire consequences for Israel in the religious sphere. Daughter of Ittobaal, the Sidonian king of Tyre (887–856), who had previously been high priest of the Tyrian Baal temple, Jezebel spearheaded a crusade for the Baal conquest of Israel (cf. 1 Kgs 18:4; 19:1–2; 2 Kgs 9:22; see Bright, *Hist.* 225–26). **33.** *sacred pole:* Made of wood (Jos 6:26; Ex 34:16), the sacred pole (Hebr *'ăšērāh*) was a symbol of the female divinity in Baal religion, just as the upright stone pillar (Hebr *maṣṣēbāh*) was the symbol of the male divinity (see De Vaux, *AI* 285–86). **34.** *rebuilt Jericho:* D includes this insignificant archival item because it provides him with the fulfillment part of another prophetic-fulfillment story (for the prediction, see Jos 6:26). In ruins since its destruction in the time of Joshua, Jericho remained an unwalled village (Jgs 3:13; 2 Sm 10:5) until rebuilt by Hiel, who probably undertook the project under the auspices of Ahab as part of Israel's defenses against Moab (cf. 22:39). *his first-born:* It is difficult to say whether the author refers to a foundation sacrifice of children, a Canaanite practice (cf. 2 Kgs 3:27) that might have been adopted for a time in Israel under the Phoenician influence of Jezebel, or simply to the popular interpretation that looked upon the natural death of Hiel's children as a curse put upon him for rebuilding Jericho (see De Vaux, *AI* 442; M–G, *Kings* 288–89).

39 **(C) The Elijah Cycle (1 Kgs 17:1–2 Kgs 1:18).** The Elijah cycle, as it stands, is composite. In addition to the narratives taken from a cycle of stories about Elijah (chs. 17–19, 21, and 2 Kgs 1), the Deuteronomist (or perhaps an earlier compiler) has incorporated a number of prediction-fulfillment stories dealing with Ahab's Aramean wars—one about Ahab and a number of unnamed prophets (ch. 20) and another about Micaiah and Ahab (22:1–38). These stories, with the exception of the very popular accounts in 1 Kgs 20:35–43; 2 Kgs 1:1–18, are early and of historic value. The accounts about the reigns of Jehoshaphat and Ahaziah (22:41–53) are taken from the Acts of the Kings of Judah. The sudden appearance of Elijah, the abrupt termination in 19:18 with the insertion of the notice about the call of Elisha (19:19–21), and the placement of the Naboth incident (ch. 21, which in the LXX follows ch. 19) are all indications that D, whatever the amplitude of his original source, did not intend to give a biography of Elijah. All of the stories, both those about Elijah and Micaiah and those about the unnamed prophets, either enhance the authority of the prophetic word or show it infallibly fulfilled by prediction-fulfillment stories. In either case, in these different stories D finds support for his basic thesis concerning the fulfillment of the Word of God (→ 5 above; cf. R-F 1, 445–49).

40 (a) ELIJAH, AHAB, AND THE THREE-YEAR DROUGHT (17:1–18:46). **1.** *neither dew nor rain:* The great drought was long remembered and is recorded in Tyrian annals, as Menander of Ephesus testifies in writing about the reign of Ittobaal of Tyre (see Josephus, *Ant.* 8.13, 2; Noth, *Hist.* 242). **3.** *brook Cherith:* Probably it is the Wadi Yabis, N of Tishbe in Gilead; like Zarephath in Sidon (v. 9), it was outside Ahab's jurisdiction. **8–16.** This prediction-fulfillment story has the prediction in v. 14 and the fulfillment in v. 16. The episode is alluded to in Lk 4:24. **9.** *Zarephath:* Modern Sarafend is 9 mi. S of Sidon near the coast.

17–24. The story of the raising of the widow's son is told, like so many other miracle stories about the prophets (cf. the "fioretti" of Elisha in 2 Kgs 2:1–8:29; 20:1–11), to enhance the reputation of the Prophet and thereby help establish the authority of his word—a thesis of no small importance to D (see v. 24, "Now indeed I know that you are a man of God, and that the word of the Lord is really in your mouth"). Some authors see a literary dependence on the Elisha cycle (2 Kgs 4:18–37), citing not only the basic similarity of the stories but also the title "man of God" (17:18,24), one habitually given to Elisha, and the similar rite of resuscitation (cf. 1 Kgs 17:21 and 2 Kgs 4:34; see R-F 1, 447–48). **18.** The widow interprets her son's death, according to a mentality that prevailed even into NT times (cf. Jn 9:2), as a punishment for her sins, drawn to God's attention by the presence of the man of God in her home. **21.** *stretched himself:* In Acts 20:9–10, Paul follows the same procedure.

41 Chapter 18, as a whole, relates the fulfillment of two related prophecies: the actual length of the drought (cf. 17:1 and 18:1), and the end of the drought (cf. 18:1 and 18:45). **1.** *in the third year:* Perhaps three full years are meant, but possibly only parts of three different years reckoned as three. On this basis, a drought beginning with the failure of the spring rains of one year and the fall rains of the following year (the new year began in October) with no rain until after the fall following another new year could be reckoned as three years, although in actual extent the rainless period lasted only 18 months. **3.** The loyalty of so high an official as Obadiah to his Yahwistic faith and his clandestine efforts to save other loyal Yahwists testify eloquently both to the savageness of Jezebel's persecution (cf. v. 4 and 19:2) and to the underground resistance movement of those whom Elijah will later immortalize as "the 7000 who have not bent the knee to Baal" (19:18). That there were other loyal Yahwists in high places is clear from the whole tenor of Jehu's revolution (cf. 2 Kgs 9). **4.** *a hundred prophets:* They are not prophets in the full sense of the word but disciples, or, as the Hebr expression puts it, "sons of the prophets"—i.e., men of strong Yahwistic faith who lived a common life in loose associations or guilds (cf. 2 Kgs 4:38). They were, as Jerome calls them, the "monks" of the OT (see J. Lindblom, *Prophecy in Ancient Israel* [Oxford, 1962] 65ff.). *in a cave:* Palestine abounds in caves; Carmel alone is reckoned to have at least 2000.

9. *wherein have I sinned:* Obadiah's speech is a model of Oriental delicacy and indirection, whereby he warns Elijah and at the same time beseeches him not to disappoint Ahab. He asks wherein he has sinned because he fears that if he tells Ahab he has found Elijah and Elijah disappears again, as he has been wont to do, the king in his desperation and frustration might vent his anger upon him as scapegoat. **19.** *Carmel:* Called the Sacred Cape in Egyptian geographical lists from the 15th cent. BC, Carmel had a long history as a place of worship. With its highest hill about 1800 ft. above sea level, the small Carmel range extends 15 mi. SE to NW, ending as a promontory overlooking the Mediterranean. Tradition locates the place of Elijah's altar at el-Muhraqa on the SE side of Carmel (see Albright, *ARI* 156; Abel, *GP* 1, 350–53). *eat at Jezebel's table:* The prophets of Baal and Astarte were subsidized by Jezebel as officials.

20–40. Elijah confronts the prophets of Baal on Carmel. **21.** *limp:* Faced with the dilemma of choosing between the traditional worship of Yahweh and the Baal worship of Jezebel, the Israelites cannot make up their minds.

27. *limped about the altar:* A sacred dance as part of the cult is mentioned by a number of ancient authors (see M–G, *Kings* 301–2). **28.** *slash one another:* The purpose of the gashes and the blood was to make the prayer more urgent and more effective. It was forbidden in Israelite worship (cf. Dt 14:1; Lv 19:28), although occasionally practiced (cf. Jer 41:5), but was a common practice in ancient religion (see R. de Vaux, *Bulletin du Musée de Beyrouth* 5 [1944] 7–20). **29.** *offering of the oblation:* An evening oblation was offered after 3 P.M. Here, the reference is to the time of the day. **30.** *repaired the altar:* The text testifies to the existence on Mt. Carmel of a Yahwist shrine, which presumably had been destroyed by Jezebel. The reference in vv. 31–32a to the 12 stones is probably a gloss inspired by Ex 24:4; Jos 4:1–9 (but see M–G, *Kings* 304). **32.** *a trench:* The elaborate preparations are not so much magical rites as a means of enhancing the miracle of the fire from heaven. **38.** *fire of the Lord:* The reference is to lightning (cf. Nm 11:13; Lv 9:24; Jgs 6:21; on the miracle of the fire, see H. H. Rowley, "Elijah on Mount Carmel," *BJRylL* 43 [1960] 210–19).

41–46. The passage treats the end of the drought. **41.** *eat and drink:* Elijah no doubt had asked all, including the king, to fast as part of the supplication that God might end the drought. **42.** *top of Carmel:* From what follows, it is clear that the Prophet was seeking a vantage point from which to look out over the Mediterranean and see the first approach of the rain-bearing clouds. *crouched down:* The position is unusual and perhaps indicates a very intense form of prayer. **46.** *ran before Ahab:* With the enthusiastic response of the people and the massacre of the Baal prophets, Elijah has reason to believe he has triumphed. He runs therefore as a herald before the chariot of Ahab (who perhaps has had a temporary change of heart) to announce the news in Jezreel (modern Zerin, about 15 mi. from the traditional place of Elijah's sacrifice). The running of Elijah is a feat attributed by the author to "the hand of the Lord," i.e., divine impulse. As a gymnastic feat, it is rivaled by Arab runners who have been known to cover as much as 100 mi. in two days.

42 (b) ELIJAH'S FLIGHT TO HOREB (19:1–21). The narrative has close affinities with the story of Moses at Sinai. Its abrupt termination and the telescoping of Elijah's career in the program outlined in vv. 15–17 indicate that D is not interested in the biography of Elijah as such, but rather in the prophecies that biography supplied for him. **2.** *a messenger to Elijah:* It is doubtful that Jezebel would have warned Elijah if she intended to kill him. More likely she was warning him to get out of the kingdom. **3.** Discouraged and afraid, Elijah flees for his life to Beer-sheba, on the southern border of Judah. **4.** Since Jezebel has almost overnight turned his triumph to ashes and apparently canceled his long and arduous campaign to turn Israel back to Yahweh, Elijah is in despair and begs God to take him. God, however, will both comfort and strengthen his prophet. **5.** *an angel:* As in 17:6, Elijah receives miraculous rations. **8.** *Horeb:* In the pentateuchal sources E and D, the name Horeb is regularly used, whereas Sinai is found in the J and P sources. The distance to Horeb is roughly 300 mi. via Aqabah, a distance that Elijah could have traveled in much less than 40 days. The numbers are probably either round numbers or a transfer from the same numbers used in the Mosaic narrative (cf. Ex 24:18). The same can be said for Elijah's lodging in a cave (cf. Ex 33:21ff.).

9. *the word of the Lord:* Because vv. 9b–11a are repeated in vv. 13–14, and Elijah does not go out to the entrance of the cave until v. 13b, it is probable that 9b–11a are secondary (see M–G, *Kings* 314). **11.** *the Lord was passing by:* That the Lord is not in the mighty wind, the earthquake, or the fire, but rather in the gentle whisper of the breeze is a lesson for the fiery Prophet. God in his own way without great fanfare will work his will for Israel. **13.** The question "What are you doing here, Elijah?" is at the same time a word of rebuke (cf. Jer 12:5) and a word of comfort. Elijah's ready defense in v. 14 is ignored. The Lord in due time will bring about the overthrow of Jezebel's crusade (vv. 15–18). **15.** *go, return:* The interpretative discourse put into God's mouth is another example of the prediction-fulfillment story technique. The program to be initiated by Elijah and carried out by Elisha is summarized in the prophecies, all of which will be fulfilled in due time, although not in the order nor by the persons indicated. Even though D will include two more stories about Elijah (1 Kgs 21 and 2 Kgs 1:1–18), the interpretative discourse is a transition from the Elijah cycle to the Elisha cycle that is taken up, inchoatively at least, in the subsequent account of Elisha's call (vv. 19–21). Before he proceeds, however, to the Elisha cycle and the fulfillment in 2 Kgs 8–10 of the prophecies about Hazael (v. 15) and Jehu (v. 16), D will include several other prediction-fulfillment narratives (20; 22:1–38) and fill out his synoptic history of the kings (1 Kgs 22:39–2 Kgs 1:18).

19. *twelve yoke:* The number of oxen indicates Elisha came from a well-to-do family. *threw his mantle:* The mantle symbolized the personality and rights of the owner (cf. Ru 3:9). Since the hair-shirt mantle of the prophets was part of their official dress (cf. 2 Kgs 1:8; Zech 13:4), casting it upon another would indicate an investiture and initiation. **20.** *go back again:* The request of Elisha is normal. Elijah's answer is enigmatic; he appears affronted and without good reason, but perhaps his answer only means, "Go ahead. Have I done anything to stop you?" **21.** *sacrificed them:* The sacrificial meal on the spot, shared by his neighbors and accompanied by the destruction of his farming equipment, signifies Elisha's renunciation of his previous life for his new vocation as Elijah's disciple (cf. 1 Sm 6:14; 2 Sm 24:22–23). *attendant:* Moses had Joshua as attendant (Ex 24:13). Elijah already had an attendant in 18:43–44. Later, Elisha himself will have an attendant (2 Kgs 4:12). The position, although menial, may have enjoyed certain prerogatives, for both Joshua and Elisha succeeded in a sense to the place of their masters; however, Elisha's attendant Giezi seems to have been nothing more than a servant.

43 (c) AHAB AND THE PROPHETS DURING THE WAR WITH ARAM (20:1–43). The chapter contains several prediction-fulfillment stories that probably account for its inclusion by D, since it contributes nothing to the story of Elijah and serves no other perceptible purpose in the book. The style and tone differ from that of the Elijah cycle. Authors consequently attribute it to a separate source, perhaps an original "Acts of Ahab." In the LXX, ch. 21 precedes ch. 20 (see R-F 1, 447; M–G, *Kings* 318–19). 1 Kgs 20, 22 and 2 Kgs 6, 9 testify to the intermittent wars between Israel and Aram that lasted from the reign of Baasha (900–877) until the reign of Jehoash (801–786), although both states fought together at Qarqar in 853 against Shalmaneser III of Assyria (see Noth, *Hist.* 240ff.).

1. Ben-hadad is the successor of Ben-hadad I, the first king of Aram (cf. 15:18; see B. Mazar, *BA* 25 [1962] 106ff.). *thirty-two kings:* They are probably tribal princes and heads of small states subject to Ben-hadad II (cf. v. 24). **10.** In a boastful hyperbole, the Syrian king claims he can carry off the whole city by handfuls (cf. 2 Sm 17:13). **11.** This proverbial saying (only four words in Hebr) means that the time for boasting is after the battle has been won, not before.

13–21. These verses tell the first prediction-fulfillment story. **13.** *thus says the Lord:* For the fulfillment, see vv.

20–21. **14.** *the young men:* They form an elite corps of officers capable of inflicting a lightning attack on the overconfident besiegers (cf. vv. 19–21; see M–G, *Kings* 322–23).

22–27. The passage contains the second prediction-fulfillment story. **22.** *a prophet:* Nameless, like the prophets in vv. 13, 28, and 35, this man predicts another victory for Ahab (for fulfillment, see vv. 26–27). *return of spring:* Spring was the time when kings went to war (cf. 2 Sm 11:1). **23.** *mountain gods:* The polytheistic expression means that Israel is protected only as long as she fights in the hills where her God thus far has protected her (cf. v. 28). **24.** *take the kings away:* The text testifies to a political reorganization of the loosely organized Aramean kingdom by turning the satellite states into administrative districts headed by governors appointed directly by Ben-hadad himself (see B. Mazar, *BA* 25 [1962] 108–109). **26.** *Aphek:* Aphek is modern Fiq, the border fortress of Geshur E of the Lake of Galilee on the road to Damascus (cf. 2 Kgs 13:17).

28–34. The third prediction-fulfillment story is a follow-up on vv. 22–27 and involves the same cast of characters, although it has its distinct prediction. **28.** *man of God:* He is probably the same prophet as in v. 22 The fulfillment of the prediction is recorded in vv. 29–30. **29–30.** The numbers are certainly exaggerated and are typical of popular stories. At the battle of Qarqar, Ben-hadad had an army of 22,000 men. **34.** *the cities:* They are possibly the cities taken from Baasha by Ben-hadad I (cf. 15:18–20), or cities lost by Omri in an otherwise unrecorded war.

35–43. The fourth prediction-fulfillment story, the story of the man killed by the lion, is like that of the disobedient prophet in 13:24ff. Its purpose is to show that disobedience to the Word of God is severely punished. More particularly, however, D includes it as a prediction of Ahab's death. **35.** *son of a prophet:* He is a disciple of the prophets, or, more properly, a member of one of the prophetic guilds or associations (cf. 2 Kgs 2:3). Because he speaks "through the word of God," the man he asks to strike him is bound to obey. For his disobedience he is killed by a lion! **37.** *strike me:* The second man who is asked obeys, and the stage is set for an object lesson to be given the king after the manner of Nathan's parable in 2 Sm 12:1–12. **38.** The bandage covers not only the wound mentioned in v. 38—one perhaps intended to show that the prophet had done his part according to the Word of the Lord—but also distinctive markings or tattoos, worn by the members of the prophetic guilds (see v. 41 and cf. Zech 13:6; Ez 9:4; 1 Kgs 18:28), which would have given away the identity of the prophet and made the king suspicious of the story told in vv. 39–40. **40.** *such is your verdict:* Like David in 2 Sm 12, Ahab is made to condemn himself for releasing Ben-hadad. **42.** *thus says the Lord:* The prediction of Ahab's death is fulfilled in 22:34–38.

44 (d) JEZEBEL'S MURDER OF NABOTH (21:1–29). It seems that D includes this story because it occasioned Elijah's prediction of the downfall of the house of Omri (vv. 20–24,29), a prediction the fulfillment of which he records at length in 2 Kgs 9–10. **3.** *inheritance:* Naboth refuses, not because Ahab's offer is unreasonable or his price unjust, but because jealous retention of ancestral property in the family was the Israelite ideal, sealed by custom and protected by law; even a king could not force a man to give up or sell his family property (cf. Dt 19:14; Nm 27:7–11; Jer 32:6–9; Ru 4:9; see De Vaux, *AI* 124, 166–67). **8.** The "elders," i.e., heads of families, formed a sort of council that governed the village. The "nobles," i.e., men of good birth, were the rich and the powerful, who with the elders held administrative posts in local and national government. **9.** A fast was proclaimed to appease God in time of calamity, for presumably the calamity resulted from sin (cf. Jl 1–2; 1 Sm 7:6; 14:24ff.). **10.** *two unscrupulous men:* The law demanded at least two witnesses for a death sentence (cf. Nm 34:30; Dt 17:6). *cursed God:* The penalty for blasphemy was death by stoning (cf. Lv 24:14,23). **15.** *arise, take possession:* Presumably the property of men condemned to death was forfeit to the crown, which would explain Jezebel's infamous strategy (v. 7). **19.** *dogs lick up:* The fulfillment of this prophecy is recorded in 22:38. **21.** In vv. 21–26, the author repeats the prediction formulas used in the condemnation of Jeroboam (14:1–11) and Baasha (16:34), which presumably had become proverbial; but these verses may be redactional throughout (see M–G, *Kings* 332). **23.** *dogs shall eat Jezebel:* The literal fulfillment of this prophecy is recorded in 2 Kgs 9:35–36. **24.** For fulfillment, see 2 Kgs 9:25–26. **29.** *humbled himself:* In a number of places, D notes that God relents or puts off punishment of wicked kings either for some good they have done or because of their repentance (cf. 1 Kgs 11:12; 2 Kgs 20:17–19; 22:18–20). It is difficult to say whether such judgments are original or represent later attempts, after the manner of interpretative discourses, to account for the fact that the prophet's earlier prediction was not fulfilled exactly as expected. *in his son's days:* For fulfillment, see 2 Kgs 9–10.

45 (e) AHAB OPPOSED BY MICAIAH (22:1–40). Here D introduces a prediction-fulfillment story relating to the death of Ahab (vv. 1–38; the third such story—see 20:35–43 and 21:1–26), and rounds off the reign of Ahab (begun in 16:29–33) with his usual concluding formula (vv. 39–40). The story of Micaiah, like the stories about the prophets and Ahab in ch. 20, is probably from an original "Acts of Ahab" source. It deals with the Aramean wars and has nothing whatever to say about Elijah.

1. The "three years" of peace probably date from the treaty mentioned in 20:34, which, in turn, probably immediately preceded the alliance of Israel and Aram against Assyria at Qarqar in 853. **2.** Ramoth-gilead has been identified as Tell Ramith, an imposing mound of ruins in Transjordan about 10 mi. SW of Edrei, not far from the southern frontier of modern Syria (see N. Glueck, *BASOR* 92 [1943] 10–16). In Jos 21:38, it is listed as a Levitical city, and in 1 Kgs 4:13, as capital of Solomon's sixth administrative district. It is unknown when Aram captured the city from Israel, but only Jeroboam II (2 Kgs 14:25) was finally able to hold it. *Jehoshaphat:* See vv. 41–50. The alliance in this period of the Judean kings with the Israelite kings in their wars against Aram (1 Kgs 22:2–38), Moab (2 Kgs 3:4–27), and again against Aram (2 Kgs 9), shows that the two kingdoms had settled at least their outstanding disputes. In addition, the two kingdoms were united by marriage between Ahab's daughter, Athaliah, and Jehoshaphat's son, Jehoram (2 Kgs 8:18). **6.** *prophets:* For the number see 18:19. Apparently these men are prophets of Yahweh, but they are clearly representatives of the state religion, political prophets, devoted to the king, and probably deeply tainted with the syncretism introduced by Jezebel and Ahab. **7.** *prophet of the Lord:* Jehoshaphat rightly doubts the legitimacy of Ahab's court prophets.

8. *Micaiah:* He is not the minor prophet, a contemporary with Isaiah in the 8th cent., but a loyal Yahwist who had earned the hatred of Ahab because of his truthfulness. After the manner of Elijah, Micaiah fits the definition of a true prophet given by Jeremiah (Jer 28:8–9). Although the holy war concept had long ago deteriorated into the profane wars of the kings, prophets were nevertheless occasionally consulted (cf. 2 Kgs 3:11–19; 13:15;

see De Vaux, *AI* 263, 353). **10.** The antics of the false prophets are suspiciously similar to the exhibition put on by the Baal prophets of Jezebel on Mt. Carmel (18:26–29). **11.** *horns of iron:* Horns symbolized strength (Dt 33:17); here, they symbolize the conquering might of Ahab. Even the great prophets occasionally used such symbolic demonstrations (cf. Is 20:3; Jer 27:2; Ez 4:1–3). **15.** *go up and prosper:* As Ahab immediately perceives (v. 16), Micaiah is being ironic, and he deliberately imitates Zedekiah (v. 12). **17.** *all Israel scattered:* The kind of prediction Ahab both feared and expected from Micaiah is forthcoming (vv. 8, 18)—not only defeat but also apparently even his own death in the battle. **19–23.** The whole vision is a literary artifice to dramatize the dreadful message. God is pictured as surrounded by his heavenly court, the angels, or as they are also called, "sons of God" (cf. Jer 23:18; Am 3:7; see Lindblom, *op. cit.*, 56ff., 112ff.). **20–23.** The personification of the lying spirit of the false prophets as an angel is Micaiah's way of showing that God is in complete control of events and that even men's lies come under his causality. The prophets did not philosophize about the causality of evil in relation to a good God. They simply accepted God as the ultimate cause of all things, good and evil. *fall at Ramoth-gilead:* The fulfillment of this prediction of Ahab's death is recorded in vv. 34–37.

25. *into an inner chamber:* The reference is to Israel's defeat; the defeated will seek to hide from the vengeance of the conquerors (cf. 20:30). Unlike a similar prophecy in 2 Kgs 7:17ff., the fulfillment of this prophecy is unrecorded, although it is implicit in the account of Israel's defeat (vv. 35–37). **34.** *breastplate:* Of Hurrian origin, the breastplate was made of small bronze, and later iron, plates like scales that were sewn to cloth or leather (cf. 1 Sm 17:5; 2 Chr 26:14). **38.** *dogs licked:* The author is careful to record the fulfillment of Elijah's prediction in 21:19. He is apparently unconcerned, however, that the Prophet not only located the fulfillment of the prophecy in the vineyard of Naboth rather than on the battlefield at Ramoth-gilead, but also later on retracted it and transferred it to Ahab's sons (21:29). Either the text has been glossed or D has perhaps allowed his zeal for recording the fulfillment of prophecies to outrun the facts. *harlots:* Probably a gloss on the word "dog," which was the popular pejorative term for a male prostitute (cf. Dt 23:19).

46 (f) Jehoshaphat of Judah, 873–849 (22:41–50) (= 2 Chr 17:1–21:1). After finishing the record of Ahab's reign with his usual concluding formula (vv. 39–40), D continues with his synoptic history, treating first Jehoshaphat (vv. 41–50) and then Ahab's son, Ahaziah (1 Kgs 22:51–2 Kgs 1:18). **43.** This verse shows that D's judgment of Jehoshaphat is favorable but qualified. A more detailed account of his long and pious reign is given by the Chronicler (2 Chr 17–20). **48.** *no king in Edom:* Edom remained subject to Judah into the reign of Jehoshaphat's son Jehoram (cf. 2 Kgs 8:20ff.). Presumably at this time there was an interregnum in the kingdom and Jehoshaphat ruled directly. **49.** *ships of Tarshish:* See comments on 9:26 and 10:22. *ships were wrecked:* Jehoshaphat's attempt to emulate Solomon with the help of Ahaziah of Israel foundered, perhaps for lack of the skilled Phoenician mariners who manned Solomon's ships. For another view of the failure, see 2 Chr 20:35–37.

47 (g) Ahaziah of Israel, 850–849 (1 Kgs 22:51–2 Kgs 1:18). The division of the history into two parts, 1 and 2 Kgs, with the dividing point in the middle of Ahaziah's reign (v. 53) is the work of later editors. It is not that of the author, for whom the whole was one continuous book. **52.** *did that which was evil:* The opening formula contains an extremely grave indictment of Ahaziah, even though he reigned only one year. Before concluding the reign of Ahaziah in 2 Kgs 1:17–18, D recounts another prediction-fulfillment story dealing with Ahaziah and Elijah. **2 Kgs 1:1.** *Moab rebelled:* In his brief reign, Ahaziah was unable to prevent the revolt. Jehoram, however, succeeded against Moab (cf. 3:4ff.). **2.** *sent messengers:* The whole incident, bizarre and in parts revolting to modern sensibilities, is taken from the Elijah cycle to provide another prediction-fulfillment story and, at the same time, to supply a sequence to 1 Kgs 22:53, "he [Ahaziah] served the Baal and worshiped him and aroused the jealous anger of the Lord." The Israelite reader would understand the loss of Moab (v. 1) and the mortal injury incurred by the king (v. 2) as the punishments of a just and jealous Lord. The rest of the story is probably a mixture of fact and legend, which illustrates the effects of the "jealous anger of the Lord." *Baal-zebub:* The name means, literally, "Lord of the Flies"; however, "zebub" is probably a contemptuous alteration of an original "zebul" (meaning "prince"), so that originally the name was "Baal the Prince" (cf. Mt 10:25). Ekron, one of the five cities of the Philistine pentapolis, was situated in the northeastern part of Philistia about 40 mi. from Samaria. **3.** *is it becaues:* The question expresses the revulsion of loyal Yahwists for an Israelite king who would so shamelessly manifest his apostasy. It is against the background of this revulsion that the rest of the story is to be understood.

8. *a hairy man:* Jewish tradition interprets the words literally in the sense that Elijah was a man of abundant body hair. Most commentators understand the expression as "a man with a hairy garment," on the grounds that such was the traditional garb of the prophets (cf. Zech 13:4; Mt 3:4). Ahaziah's immediate recognition of Elijah on the basis of the description given would favor the Jewish interpretation, since the traditional garb of the prophets would have been worn by many in the prophetic guilds (cf. 2:3,7). **9.** *commander of fifty:* Units in the Israelite armies were composed of 1000, 100, 50, and 10 men (see De Vaux, *AI* 226). One may rightly suspect that Ahaziah has ordered Elijah's arrest. In such an event, both Elijah's reply, which is a refusal to submit to duress, and the religious fear of the three commanders, who do not dare to lay hands on the famous prophet, are understandable. **10–14.** It is not improbable that the whole bizarre sequence of events represents an early midrashic elaboration of Elijah's threatening reply to the first of the three commanders sent to arrest him. Like the midrashic episode in 2:23–34, the purpose of the elaboration would be to inculcate reverence for, and obedience to, the prophets sent by God. **17.** *so he died:* With his usual formulas—one for the conclusion of a prediction-fulfillment narrative and another for the conclusion of a king's reign—D closes his Ahaziah narrative.

48 **(D) The Elisha Cycle (2:1–8:29).** The Elisha cycle is usually reckoned to run from 2:1–13:21. However, since the verses between 8:15 and 13:21, with the exception of the account of Elisha's death in 13:14–21, are taken from other sources, we have restricted our treatment of the Elisha cycle to 2:1–8:29, including with it the synoptic history of Jehoram and Ahaziah of Judah found in 8:16–29.

Whatever the extent of the original Elisha cycle, it must be recognized that the Deuteronomist was no more interested in writing a biography of Elisha than he was of Elijah. His primary aim and interest is to establish the authority of the prophets and to show the fulfillment of their prophecies. It is on this basis that he makes his selection of matter from the sources at his disposal.

He is not particularly concerned about the chronological order of his stories nor even their intrinsic probability (many are obviously legendary after the manner of second nocturn lives of ancient saints). He is, in a word, uncritical about his sources. They serve his purpose and that is enough for him. In presenting his matter, he attempts to keep within the bounds of his synoptic history schema (cf. 3:1–3; 8:16–29), but it always takes second place to his prophetic material (for a more detailed discussion of the Elisha cycle, see *R-F* 1, 350–53; M–G, *Kings* 39–42; Pfeiffer, *Introd.* 406–9).

49 (a) Elisha Succeeds Elijah (2:1–25). **1–18.** These verses discuss the ascension of Elijah. **1.** *Gilgal:* The Gilgal is not that by the Jordan mentioned in Jos 4:19ff. but that near Bethel. **3.** For the "sons of the prophets," see comment on 1 Kgs 18:4; see also Bright, *Hist.* 229–30. **8.** *struck the waters:* Elijah reproduces the miracles of Moses at the Red Sea and of Joshua at the Jordan. **2.** *double share:* The eldest son in Israel generally received a double share of the paternal inheritance. Elisha's request is that he be recognized as the principal spiritual heir of Elijah. **12.** *my father:* The teacher-student relationship was expressed by the words "father" and "son" (cf. Prv *passim*). *chariots of Israel:* The same expression is used of Elisha himself in 13:14 by the king of Israel. It means that the Prophet's spiritual strength is of more value for Israel's defense than her chariots. *saw him no more:* Although it is not said, it is deduced that Elijah did not die, and he is ranked with Enoch (Gn 5:24) in Jewish tradition. Later writers speak of Elijah's return (cf. Mal 3:23–24; Mk 6:15; 8:28). **14.** *waters were divided:* The repetition of Elijah's miracle by means of the same miraculous mantle confirms Elisha as Elijah's successor, and the guild prophets immediately acknowledge him (v. 15). **19.** A second miracle is worked as confirmatory of Elisha's succession to Elijah. The spring has been identified as Ain es-Sultan, also popularly called "Elisha's Spring." **23.** *baldhead:* It is not certain whether the word refers to Elisha's actual baldness or to a tonsure used as a distinguishing mark by the prophets. **24.** Bears were not uncommon in ancient Palestine (cf. 1 Sm 17:34; Hos 13:7–8). The story is told to inculcate reverence for the prophets, and, like the two previous miracles, it is introduced as confirmation of Elisha's succession to Elijah's spiritual powers.

50 (b) Jehoram of Israel (849–842) and the War with Moab (3:1–27). **1.** The introductory formula makes clear what was only implicit in 1:17—namely, that Jehoram was "the son of Ahab," the brother, therefore, of Ahaziah, who, according to 1:17, had no son. Jehoram no doubt "put away the sacred pillar of Baal" as a token concession to the loyal Yahwists. **4.** *Mesha:* On a stele, the Moabite Stone found at Dibon in Transjordan in 1868, Mesha left an inscription on which he mentions his subjection to Omri and boasts of his later successful war of liberation against the son (grandson) of Omri (see *ANET* 320–21; *ANE* 209–10; R. E. Murphy, *CBQ* 15 [1953] 409–17). **7.** Jehoram continues the alliance between Israel and Judah begun under Jehoshaphat and Ahab (1 Kgs 22) and cemented by the marriage of his sister Athaliah to Crown Prince Jehoram of Judah (8:18). A special reason for the alliance with Judah and Edom is Jehoram's plan for an indirect attack on Moab, leading his armies through Judah and Edom around the end of the Dead Sea to attack Mesha from the south rather than at the common boundary of Israel and Moab N of the Arnon River (v. 8). **11.** *who poured water:* Elisha was servant and disciple to Elijah (1 Kgs 19:21), just as Gehazi is to Elisha (4:12). **15.** *a minstrel:* In making use of music to prepare himself for communion with God, Elisha shows himself a typical member of the prophetic guilds (cf. 1 Sm 10:5ff.). **20.** *suddenly water came:* If the armies of the three kings were camped at the Wadi el-Hesa, above the torrent of Zered that marked the boundary between Edom and Moab and was the logical place for an invasion of Moab from the south, then the sudden onrush of water probably resulted from a rainstorm falling in the uplands of Edom and pouring streams of water down the gullies and wadies leading into the Zered, thereby fulfilling Elisha's prediction (vv. 16–17). The Bedouin speak of this phenomenon as a *seil*. **23.** *this is blood:* Either the water, seen against the background of red sandstone and by the light of early morning, took on the appearance of a mirage, or the author is playing on the Hebr words for blood (*dām*) and Edom (*'ĕdōm*), insinuating that the Moabites mistakenly thought the Edomites had revolted against their allies from the north. **25.** *Kir-hareseth:* The capital of ancient Moab (cf. Is 16:7,11; Jer 48:31,36), it is the modern Kerak. **27.** *burnt offering:* The actual immolation of children was rare but not unknown in ancient times, especially in the lands where Baal was worshiped (cf. 1 Kgs 16:34; for the exceptional cases in Israel, see Jgs 11:29ff.; 2 Kgs 16:3). *wrath upon Israel:* Most likely the Israelites raised the siege because of a superstitious fear of the consequences of Mesha's oath to Chemosh, the god of Moab. Possibly, however, the sacrifice of the crown prince filled the defenders with such desperate courage that they repulsed the invaders (cf. Jos 9:20; see Albright, *ARI* 164; De Vaux, *AI* 442, 446; M–G, *Kings* 364).

51 (c) The "Fioretti" of Elisha (4:1–8:15). Similar to the naïve and delightful legends told about Francis and his little band at the Portiuncula and Carceri, the "fioretti" of Elisha testify to the momentous and lasting impression left by the great prophet upon his disciples. Where fact leaves off and fancy begins it is impossible to say.

(i) *The poor widow* (4:1–7). **1.** *wife:* The story indirectly shows that members of the prophetic guilds married despite the fact that they sometimes lived in community (cf. 4:38–41). *slaves:* The law did not permit one Israelite to enslave another permanently (Lv 25:46). Israelites could, however, be sold into slavery for a limited time to satisfy debts (Ex 21:7; Is 50:1), and in many cases Israelites were probably reduced to permanent slavery despite the law and the strong sentiment against it (cf. Neh 5:1–13; Jer 34:14; Ex 21:16; Dt 24:7; see De Vaux, *AI* 82–83).

(ii) *The rich woman of Shunem* (4:8–37). The account in 8:1–7 is a continuation of the present story and was probably separated from it because it dealt with the period after the seven-year famine mentioned in 4:38. **13–15.** Elisha's indirect conversation through Gehazi and the sequence of verbs show the delicacy of both the Prophet and his host, because it was not customary for a lady to visit a man in his private room. Elisha's intercession with the king might secure a reduction of her taxes or some such similar favor, but the woman replies with some pride that her "own people" can take care of her. **23.** *neither new moon nor sabbath:* They are the ordinary times for making a pilgrimage to see a holy man. **29.** *do not greet him:* Elaborate greetings were customary, omission of which indicated an urgent mission (cf. Lk 10:4). **34.** *mouth upon mouth:* Cf. 1 Kgs 17:17ff.; Acts 20:9ff.

(iii) *The poisoned stew* (4:38–41). **38.** *famine:* It is apparently the same famine mentioned in 2 Kgs 8:1–7. *sitting before him:* Elisha is preaching or giving instruction. Scholars customarily sat before the master and repeated his words; thus a school came to be called a Yeshivah, i.e., a sitting. **39.** *gourds:* The "coloquintida" is a creeper producing a small, yellow, melonlike fruit with a bitter taste and a violent purgative effect. **41.** *bring meal:* The mixture of meal counteracted the effect of the gourds.

(iv) *Multiplication of the loaves* (4:42–44). **42.** *Baal-shalishah:* It is modern Kefr Tilt, 15 mi. N of Lydda (cf. 1 Sm 9:4). *first fruits:* It constitutes bread milled from grain of the recent harvest. **43.** *thus says the Lord:* The common formula for the prediction in a prediction-fulfillment story is followed in v. 44 by the common formula for the fulfillment—"according to the word of the Lord."

52 (v) *Naaman the leper and Gehazi* (5:1–27). The account begins with Elisha's cure of Naaman's leprosy (vv. 1–19) and concludes with a related episode about Gehazi, Elisha's servant (vv. 20–27). **1.** *king of Syria:* He is probably Ben-hadad (cf. 2 Kgs 8:7). *leper:* The term covers, besides true leprosy, a variety of scabious diseases, some curable (cf. Lv 13) and others incurable. Ordinarily, the victim was quarantined but probably only in advanced stages of the malady (cf. 7:3ff.; Lv 15:5). Both Naaman and Gehazi (8:4ff.) remain in society despite their leprosy. **7.** *king of Israel:* Meant is probably Jehoram, a king for whom Elisha ordinarily has little liking (cf. 2:6–14; 6:30–33). **10.** *sent a message:* Elisha stands on his dignity. Naaman, the suppliant, does not deign to enter, and Elisha will not go out. **17.** *two mule-loads of earth:* Naaman acknowledges Yahweh as Lord of all the earth but realizes he is God of Israel in a special way. Therefore, he wishes to have some of the soil of Israel upon which to build his altar when he worships the true God in Damascus, his home city. **18.** *pardon your servant:* Custom demanded that Naaman accompany his royal master to the Baal temple. He wishes it to be known that what he does is not an act of worship of the Baal. *house of Rimmon:* The deity of Damascus was Hadad, worshiped under the title Rimmon. His temple, at present beneath the Omayyad Mosque, was famous until Roman times (cf. 16:10–13; Zech 12:11; see B. Mazar, *BA* 25 [1962] 110–11). **20.** *Gehazi:* He is Elisha's servant (4:12ff.; 8:4ff.) and perhaps his disciple, but not a very exemplary one as the story is at pains to point out. **26.** *present in spirit:* There is ample testimony to Elisha's clairvoyant powers (cf. 6:8–12; 8:7–15). **27.** *leprosy:* Gehazi is punished not only for his avarice but also for his controversion of his master's will, bringing disgrace on his name (cf. vv. 15–16; Mi 3:5).

(vi) *The lost axe* (6:1–7). **1.** *the place:* It is presumably Gilgal, N of Bethel (cf. 2:1–2; 4:38). **2.** *to the Jordan:* With its luxurious growth, the Jordan would provide abundant timber for economical building. **6.** *cut off a stick:* The wood floats, and so does the metal axe!

(vii) *Syrian ambuscades foiled by Elisha's clairvoyance* (6:8–23). The main purpose of the story is to arouse admiration for the Prophet's supernatural powers and to show that God protects his own. The remaining stories in the cycle deal with Elisha's part in contemporary politics. **9.** *the king:* If it is King Jehoash of 2 Kgs 13, the Prophet's sympathy is understandable; if it is Jehoram, Elisha's dislike for him (cf. 2:6–14; 6:30–33) does not dampen his patriotism. **12.** Elisha's reputation after the Naaman cure (5:1–19) is increased by reports of his powers of clairvoyance. **13.** *Dothan:* It is modern Tell Dotan, 10 mi. N of Samaria, a strategic point at the entrance into the Ephraim highlands. **16.** *they who are with us:* Elisha's words summarize the lesson inculcated by the story—God protects his prophets. **19.** *brought them to Samaria:* The irony of the event is in the ambushers themselves being ambushed. **22.** *you shall not slay:* Despite exceptional examples of cruelty in war (cf. Jos 10:24–26; 1 Sm 27:9,11; 2 Chr 25:12), Israelite kings had a reputation for clemency toward prisoners (1 Kgs 20:31), of which Elisha is jealous (see De Vaux, *AI* 256).

53 (viii) *Ben-hadad's siege of Samaria* (6:24–7:20). The story is the longest and most elaborate in the Elisha cycle and bears the same mark of reporting genius exhibited in the political narratives of 1 Kgs 20, 22. **24.** Neither the Syrian nor the Israelite king can be identified from the text. Presumably, the Syrian king is Ben-hadad II and the Israelite king is Jehoram, but the possibility should not be ruled out that the siege took place in the time of Ben-hadad III and Jehoahaz of Israel (cf. 13:1–7,24–25). **25.** *great famine:* The purpose of a siege was precisely to cut off supplies and wait until hunger and thirst forced the besieged to surrender (see De Vaux, *AI* 236–37). *dove's dung:* The text should be corrected to read "ornithogale," a bulbous plant common in Palestine and used as food by the very poor (see A. Vaccari, *Bib* 19 [1938] 198ff.). **28.** The eating of human flesh in time of siege was not uncommon (cf. Dt 28:56f.; Lam 2:20; 4:10; Ez 5:10; see Josephus, *JW* 6.3, 4). **31.** *head of Elisha:* The king is enraged at Elisha, possibly because he himself is doing penance and thinks the Prophet, who should be bringing divine help (v. 33), is doing nothing, or possibly because Elisha has counseled the war and encouraged the resistance, thereby leading the king to his present desperate position. **32.** *son of a murderer:* Not necessarily a reference to Ahab, the murderer of Naboth and the father of Jehoram, it is more likely simply the Hebr way of saying "assassin" (cf. 1 Sm 20:30).

7:1–2. Elisha makes two predictions. **1.** He predicts the end of the siege by foreseeing an incredible reduction in the price of food, a change which only the termination of the siege could effect. **2.** *on whose hand:* This refers to the king's squire, who was called the "third man" because he accompanied the king in his chariot along with the driver (the "second man"), and carried the king's weapons. As such he was an important officer. *windows in the heavens:* The expression, a forceful statement of disbelief in the Prophet's prediction, may refer to the rain that comes from the heavens (cf. Gn 7:11; 8:2) but more likely means that God will have to rain down grain direct from heaven to bring about such a drastic reduction in prices. *shall see... but... not eat:* The fulfillment of this prophecy and that preceding will be recounted with obvious relish at the end of the story (vv. 16–20).

3–15. The episode of the four lepers is told. **4.** *let us enter the city:* The lepers are forced to remain outside towns because of their malady (cf. Lv 13–14). With famine inside and outside, they have little choice. Their decision to desert to the enemy camp leads to the unexpected discovery that the Syrians have given up the siege (vv. 4–8). **6.** *kings of the Hittites:* The author supposes that the besiegers feared imminent attack by Hittite and Egyptian mercenaries hired by the king of Israel (for the hiring of mercenaries in time of war, see 2 Sm 10:6; Is 7:20; 1 Kgs 15:18–20; Hos 8:9). **12.** The king knows that no mercenaries have been hired and suspects a Syrian trick designed to lure the Israelites out, thus opening the city to the invaders. **17.** *third officer:* It is the fulfillment of 7:2. **18.** *measures of barley:* It is the fulfillment of 7:1.

54 (ix) *The rich woman of Shunem* (8:1–6). This story is a continuation of 4:8–37, which was interrupted by the accounts in 4:38–7:20, the first and last of which deal with famine, the key word connecting these stories. **3.** *appeal to the king:* The woman's property had been confiscated, perhaps by the Crown (see De Vaux, *AI* 124,

152). **5.** *just then:* By happy chance, the woman makes her appeal just as Gehazi is telling the king about Elisha's resuscitation of her son. As a result, the wish of the Prophet to do her a favor at court (4:13) is unexpectedly fulfilled.

(x) *Elisha and Hazael* (8:7–15). In these verses, D records the fulfillment of the prediction made in 1 Kgs 19:15 and thereby links the Elisha cycle with the Elijah cycle, at the end as he did at the beginning (cf. 2:1ff. and also 9:1ff.). **7.** *was sick:* The king, presumably Ben-hadad II, knows of Elisha's cure of Naaman (5:1ff.) and appeals to the Israelite prophet in the same way Ahaziah of Israel had appealed to Baal-zebub of Ekron (1:1–18). **11.** *fixed his gaze:* In an ecstatic trance, the Prophet sees that Ben-hadad will die, not of his disease, but at the hand of Hazael. What is worse, he foresees the destruction Hazael will bring on Israel when he becomes king of Syria (v. 12). **13.** *a dead dog:* The expression is one of humility (cf. 1 Sm 24:15; 2 Sm 9:8). Hazael protests that he is too insignificant a person to do such great things to Israel. Elisha then clearly tells him that he is to be king of Syria. **15.** *took the coverlet:* Hazael murdered his master and became king in his stead. According to the annals of Shalmaneser III, "Hadadezer [Ben-hadad II] perished. Hazael, a commoner [lit., "son of nobody"], seized the throne..." (*ANET* 280). That the king died was probably the story given out by his assassin and successor. Hazael's usurpation of the throne of Damascus took place before 842 (cf. 8:28).

55 (d) JEHORAM OF JUDAH, 849–842 (8:16–24) (= 2 Chr 21). **18.** *daughter of Ahab:* More likely, she is the daughter of Omri. Since Athaliah's son, according to 8:26, was born in 862, Athaliah was either the sister of Ahab or a daughter born to him before he became King in 869 (see Bright, *Hist.* 222). **19.** *a lamp:* See comment on 1 Kgs 11:36. **20.** *Edom revolted:* Edom had been subject to Judah since the time of David. Its loss, entailing the loss of the seaport and industries at Ezion-geber, was a serious blow to the Judean economy. **22.** *to this day:* A comparison with 14:7,22 and 16:6 shows that this expression is relative to the chronicle from which the data was taken rather than to the time of the author. *Libnah:* A town W of Judah on the Philistine border, it is probably Tell es-Safi.

(e) AHAZIAH OF JUDAH, 842 (8:25–29). **26.** *reigned one year:* Ahaziah reigns but one year, for shortly after he becomes king he is assassinated, along with Jehoram, by Jehu, the leader of the revolt that overthrows the Omrid dynasty in Israel (cf. 9:27–29). **28.** *went with Jehoram:* The alliance between Jehoshaphat and Ahab (cf. 1 Kgs 22; 2 Kgs 3) continues under their successors, Ahaziah and Jehoram. *Hazael:* Elisha's prediction that Hazael would ravage Israel (8:12) is quickly fulfilled. *Ramoth-gilead:* See comment on 1 Kgs 22:2. From 9:14 it is clear that the Israelites are defending, not attacking, Ramoth-gilead. **29.** The mention of Jezreel (see comment on 1 Kgs 18:46) turns D to a new source (chs. 9–10) for the continuation of his story. It also leads him to neglect the ordinary synoptic-formula conclusion for the reign of Ahaziah, perhaps because the king's death is so well described in the account of Jehu's revolt (cf. 9:27–29), or perhaps because Ahaziah's successor, Athaliah, is a usurper (11:1ff.).

56 **(E) Synoptic History from Jehu to the Fall of Samaria (9:1–17:41).** Under Jehu and his successors, Yahwism became again, at least nominally, the official religion of Israel. Jehu's dynasty ruled from 842 to 745, the most stable of the many dynasties in Israel during the 200 years she existed as an independent kingdom. It has seemed best, therefore, to begin a new division of D's history with the revolt of Jehu, even though it is also the natural climax of the Elijah and Elisha cycles (→ History of Israel, 75:72–79).

(a) JEHU, 842–815 (9:1–10:36). The account of Jehu's revolt has long been recognized as a masterpiece of historical narrative. The wealth of detail, the sure touch in the delineation of the various strong personalities involved, and the headlong pace of the narrative make it certain that the author is a contemporary and perhaps even an eyewitness. The similarity in tone and style to the dramatic accounts of the Aramean wars in 1 Kgs 20, 22 makes it likely that they came from the same school of writers—a member of one of the prophetic guilds. That the original author on the whole approves of Jehu's revolt is certain (10:30). That he approves of everything in particular that Jehu did is not nearly so clear, especially if the judgment on Jehu in 10:31 comes from him rather than from D. The narrative can be divided as follows: 9:1–13, the anointing of Jehu as king; 9:14–29, the assassination of the kings at Jezreel; 9:30–37, the execution of Jezebel; 10:1–11, the slaughter of the remaining members of the royal family along with their supporters; 10:12–14, the slaughter of the kinsmen of Ahaziah of Judah; 10:15–17, Jehu's meeting with Jehonadab, the son of Rechab, and the ride to Samaria; 10:18–28, the slaughter of the Baal worshipers in Samaria; 10:29–36, D's closing formula for Jehu.

57 **9:1–13.** Jehu is anointed. **1.** *Elisha:* In 1 Kgs 19:16, Elijah was commissioned to anoint both Hazael and Jehu. Either the author had two parallel accounts, which he incorporated despite their obvious inconsistencies, or the transfer of the commission from Elijah to Elisha was contained in a part of the Elijah cycle that D chose not to incorporate. **3.** The old custom of selection of kings by a prophet who spoke in the name of God is revived (cf. 1 Sm 10:1; 16:13; 1 Kgs 11:29ff.). **6.** *thus says the Lord:* The recurrence of expressions found in the oracles against previous kings (1 Kgs 14:10–11; 16:3–4; 21:21–24) makes it probable that the discourse given by Elisha's disciple is actually an interpretative discourse from D's hand. **11.** *mad man:* The peculiar life and habits of the ecstatic prophetic guilds would not readily command the respect of hardened military men. Nevertheless, they accept the Prophet's designation of Jehu as king (v. 13). **14–29.** The kings are assassinated at Jezreel. **15.** *let no one escape:* The first step in Jehu's *coup d'état* is to keep the revolt secret so that he can strike before the king discovers the uprising and calls upon loyal troops from Samaria to support him against the insurgents. **17.** The tower is a fortification (Hebr *migdāl*) or castle inside the walls of the city. Because Jezreel, on the southern edge of the Plain of Esdraelon, overlooks the road leading to the Jordan, the watchman could see for miles and would be able to spot the dust raised by a chariot long before he could pick out the chariot itself. **22.** *is it peace:* Until the last moment, the unsuspecting Jehoram is thinking only of the military situation at Ramoth-gilead. **26.** Jehu remembers well the prediction of Elijah and fulfills it literally (cf. 1 Kgs 21:19,29). The discrepancies between the quotation of Elijah's prediction in 1 Kgs 21 and 2 Kgs 9 result from the fact that D used parallel sources without attempting to harmonize their discrepancies. **27.** *Beth-haggan:* Probably Jenin is meant, 6 mi. S of Jezreel on the road to Jerusalem. *Ibleam:* Tell Belame, immediately S of Jenin, is indicated. *Megiddo:* It is 12 mi. NW of Jenin in the direction of Haifa. **28.** *buried him:* The statement is as near as D comes to giving Ahaziah the customary concluding synoptic formula. The chronological note in v. 29 is a gloss (cf. 8:25).

30–37. Jezebel is executed. **30.** Jezebel has no illusions about her fate. She makes up her face carefully and dresses royally, not to seduce Jehu, but because she is determined to die like a queen. When Jehu arrives, she insults him roundly before he can even get out of his chariot. **31.** *you Zimri:* The taunt hearkens back to Zimri, who, like Jehu, had been a commander in the Israelite army, and had betrayed and assassinated his royal master, King Elah (cf. 1 Kgs 16:9–10). **36.** *the word of the Lord:* The grisly details of Jezebel's death are a literal fulfillment of Elijah's prophecy (1 Kgs 21:23).

10:1–11. The remaining members of the royal family are slaughtered along with their supporters. **1.** *seventy:* It is a round number for the totality of one's descendants (cf. Gn 46:27; Jgs 8:30; 12:14). Usurpers habitually destroyed all who might have a legitimate right to the usurped throne (cf. 1 Kgs 15:29; 16:11; 2 Kgs 11:1). **9.** *who killed all these:* The craven capitulation of the authorities in Samaria and their execution of the direct descendants of Ahab's family have, as Jehu no doubt planned it, implicated them as much as himself in the overthrow of the reigning dynasty.

12–14. The kinsmen of Ahaziah of Judah are slaughtered. The incident should probably be placed earlier in the sequence of events precipitated by Jehu's ride to Jezreel. Since the visitors were on their way from Samaria to Jezreel, they would presumably know about the events narrated in 10:1–11. **12.** *Beth-eked:* The place cannot be identified but must have been on the road between Samaria and Jezreel inasmuch as Ahaziah's kinsmen were on their way to Jezreel. **13.** *queen mother:* The queen mother was an institution in Judah but not in Israel; Judeans, not Israelites, use the term. Jezebel is the person in question (see comment on 1 Kgs 15:13).

58 **15–17.** This incident, Jehu's meeting with Jehonadab, son of Rechab, and the ride to Samaria, like the preceding, is perhaps out of place, for the presence of Jehonadab, a fiery Yahwist, at the side of Jehu would otherwise have alerted the Baal priests to Jehu's true sentiments and prevented the successful outcome of the ruse subsequently perpetrated on them (vv. 18–28). **15.** *Jehonadab:* Little is said about Jehonadab here, but from Jer 35:1–19 it is known that he was the founder and legislator of an extremist sect of Yahwists who lived as nomads in opposition to the sedentary culture that the Israelites adopted from the Canaanites. They gloried in a "back to the desert" ideal in an attempt to emulate the fiery faith of Israel's early days in the desert, before she began to compromise her faith in the corrupt surroundings of Canaanite civilization (see De Vaux, *AI* 14–15). **16.** *see my zeal:* However morally unenlightened he was, Jehu probably believed sincerely that he was doing the will of God in slaughtering all the adherents of Baalism in Israel (cf. 9:22,25; 10:9–10,18–29). In his fanaticism, he certainly had the support of Jehonadab's sect and no doubt of many in the prophetic guilds, although later on a reaction set in against him (cf. Hos 1:4).

18–29. The Baal worshipers in Samaria are slaughtered. **19.** *sacrifice for the Baal:* Israelite and Canaanite sacrificial customs did not materially differ; thus, Jehu has no difficulty simulating the Baal ritual (see De Vaux, *AI* 438–39). **21.** *temple of Baal:* Probably the temple built by Ahab (1 Kgs 16:32) is meant. **22.** *garments:* Among the preliminary purifications performed before taking part in divine worship, was a change of garment (cf. Gn 35:2). **23.** *Jehonadab:* See comments on vv. 15–17. It is possible that Jehonadab has been intruded here because of his position in vv. 15–17. **24.** *eighty men:* Judging from the number of troops engaged in the slaughter, the number of Baal adherents could not have been very large (cf. 1 Kgs 18:40). **26.** *sacred pole:* See comment on 1 Kgs 16:33.

29–36. Here D gives the closing formula for Jehu. **30.** *the Lord said to Jehu:* The words constitute a brief interpretative discourse from D's hand after the manner of 1 Kgs 9:3–9; 11:11–13; 19:15; 2 Kgs 21:7–9,10–15. The fulfillment of the prediction concerning "sons to the fourth generation" is given in 15:12. **32.** *Hazael defeated them:* Internally paralyzed by revolution (while Phoenicia and Judah were alienated by the respective purges of Jezebel and Ahaziah of Judah), Jehu was an easy mark for Hazael. In short order, the Syrian king dominated most of Transjordan, perhaps even as far as the Bay of Elath (cf. 12:18–19; 13:22; Am 1:3; see B. Mazar, *BA* 25 [1962] 114–15; Albright, *BP* 68–69; Bright, *Hist.* 234).

59 (b) Athaliah of Judah, 842–837 (11:1–20) (= 2 Chr 22:10–23:21). For the story of Athaliah's usurpation of the throne of Judah and her subsequent execution by the army seven years later, D has harmonized two sources, each of which recounts Athaliah's death (vv. 16,20). The first source (1–12,18b–20) focused attention on the part taken by the priest Jehoiada and by the army in the uprising. The second (13–18a) recounted the part taken by the citizenry. Although the story completes the account of the destruction of the Omrid dynasty begun in ch. 9, it is taken from a different, southern source. Because Athaliah is not a legitimate ruler, D gives neither introductory nor concluding formulas for her. He probably included the story to show how God had protected the Davidic dynasty from extinction, the fate of so many northern dynasties.

1. *Athaliah:* The daughter of Ahab had married Jehoram, the son of Jehoshaphat (8:18). Jehoram died *ca.* 843 of a disease of the bowels, according to the Chronicler (2 Chr 21:19). When Athaliah's son, King Ahaziah, who succeeded Jehoram (8:26), was assassinated a year later by Jehu (9:27), the queen mother usurped the throne and attempted to purge all legitimate claimants. **2.** *Jehosheba:* Apart from her womanly instincts that prompted her to save her nephew, Joash, Jehosheba's part in the priestly coup is explained by the Chronicler, who shows her to have been the wife of the high priest Jehoiada (2 Chr 22:11). *nurse:* It was probably a slave who suckled the child in place of its mother. **3.** *in the house of the Lord:* As wife of Jehoiada, Jehosheba lived in the priests' quarters within the large Temple precincts. It was there, rather than in the Temple proper, that the child was hidden. **4.** *Carites:* Mercenaries, they are possibly the same as the Cherethites, recruited by David for his bodyguard (2 Sm 8:18; 20:23). **5.** *on the sabbath:* Jehoiada evidently took advantage of the extra guards, who were posted in the Temple for the Sabbath, to keep all the guards on duty. Thus, he was able to present the people and Athaliah with a solid show of force in support of the young king. (For the change of guard on the Sabbath, see M–G, *Kings* 419–20.) **12.** *diadem and armlets:* The diadem (*nēzer*) was the principal symbol of royalty. The armlets (read *ṣeʿādôt*) were also, according to 2 Sm 1:10, symbolic of royalty. If the original reading, *ʿēdût*, meaning "decree," "testimony," or "protocol," is retained instead of the above *ṣeʿādôt*, then the reference is to the decree or testimonial that the king presented as a title of legitimation. It probably contained the king's different names and titles and some affirmation of his power as coming from God after the manner of the decree in Ps 2:7–9. Its presentation was part of the coronation rites (see De Vaux, *AI* 102ff.; Von Rad, *OT Theology I*, 40–41).

13. *came to the people:* Athaliah, like Jezebel (9:30ff.), was an evil but courageous woman who preferred facing down her enemies to fleeing. **14.** *by the column:* In Egypt the Pharaohs had a special place reserved for them in the Temple. Here, it would appear, the special place reserved for the king was near one of the two great pillars that stood before the Temple (cf. 1 Kgs 7:15–22; 2 Kgs 23:3). *people of the land:* The expression, which recurs in vv. 18–20 and in 15:5; 16:15; 21:24; 23:30,35; 25:3,19, has political import and signals the rising power and influence of the free citizens of the land, who must, from this time on, be taken into account by both army and kings (see De Vaux, *AI* 70ff.). **17.** *covenant:* The covenant between the "Lord and the kings and the people," is religious, like the covenant in 23:1ff. The covenant between the king and "the people of the land" is political, and shows the political stature of the citizenry. **18.** *house of the Baal:* Like Jezebel, Athaliah had introduced into Judah the Baal religion replete with temple, priests, and worship. The people of the land, for religious and possibly also for nationalistic reasons, now destroy the foreign religion as Jehu's followers had done seven years before in Israel (10:25–27). *watchmen over the house of the Lord:* These were appointed probably to prevent a counterrevolt by the partisans of Athaliah and the Baal religion.

60 (c) Jehoash of Judah, 837–800 (12:1–21) (= 2 Chr 24). A comparison with the Chronicler's account of Jehoash's reign shows that D is far more tolerant of Jehoash (vv. 3–4) than the Chronicler and far less favorable to the priesthood (vv. 6–16). Consequently, there seems little reason to consider vv. 6–16 a separate source taken from a history of the Temple, as some authors claim (see *R-F* 1, 453). The rebuke of the priests by Jehoash (v. 7) would indicate the account is taken from D's regular source, the Chronicles of the Kings of Judah (v. 20), a source more prophetic and political than priestly. It should be noted that the MT 12:1 is 11:21 in the Vg and other versions (also RSV).

2. *seven years old:* Jehoash's reign, according to dynastic reckoning, should be dated from his infancy, but the author wishes to connect his account with the previous narrative concerning Athaliah (cf. 11:4). **3.** *priest instructed him:* This may be a gloss based on 2 Chr 24, which shows clearly that the early years of Jehoash were greatly influenced by the high priest Jehoiada. His part in the execution of Jehoiada's son, Zechariah (2 Chr 24:21–22), may very well have been his belated reaction to this domination. **5–6.** The orders of Jehoash show that the Temple was a state sanctuary, run by the king, who utilized the priests like civil servants. Jehoash does not diminish directly the ordinary offerings given to, and retained by, the priests as revenue, but by obliging them to use part of their revenue to defray the expenses of the repairs on the Temple, he indirectly diminishes their share of the offerings. The priests, as the sequel shows, do not contest the order; they simply ignore it (vv. 7–8). The king's second order (v. 7) seeks to remove part of the priestly revenues and consign them directly to payment for the Temple repairs. The priests (v. 9) agree to discontinue taking the money for themselves, but do not agree to be responsible for the repairs on the Temple (see De Vaux, *AI* 320, 376, 380). **10.** *a chest:* Inasmuch as the priests will not accept responsibility for the Temple repairs, a special collection box is placed near the Temple doors as a receptacle for offerings to finance the repairs (cf. 22:4). The money was not in the form of coins, but of pieces of silver that were melted down into ingots and then weighed to determine value. **16.** The mention of the honesty of the laymen contains an innuendo against the priests for their dubious dealings in the Temple repair program (vv. 7–9). **18.** *Hazael:* With Assyrian pressure lessened after 837, Hazael had begun to extend his influence (cf. 10:32–33). His attack on Gath and Jerusalem took place *ca.* 815, and Aramean domination of Palestine lasted until renewed pressure from a new Assyrian king, Adad-nirari III (13:3–5), forced Hazael's son, Ben-hadad III, to retire to Aram and its immediate dependencies (see B. Mazar, *BA* 25 [1960] 114ff.). **21.** *Millo:* See comment on 1 Kgs 9:15. **22.** The Chronicler (2 Chr 24:25) insinuates that Jehoash was assassinated in revenge for his part in the execution of Jehoiada's son, Zechariah.

61 (d) Jehoahaz of Israel, 815–801 (13:1–9). **5.** The nameless savior may be Jeroboam II, who reigned from 786 to 746 and restored Israel's boundaries as far N as Hamath (14:25–27). It is quite possible, however, that the author is referring to Adad-nirari, the new Assyrian king (811–783), whose military expeditions to Palestine after 805 (*ANET* 281–82) crushed the power of Aram under Hazael's son, Ben-hadad III (13:24–25). Hazael himself had died shortly before 805. **6.** Personal names on the ostraca from Samaria, dating from 738 to 736, show that approximately half the people even at that late date still formed their names with Baal instead of Yahweh. Baalism, therefore, continued to be the basic religion of many Israelites, despite Jehu's purge in the middle of the 9th cent. (see Albright, *BP* 70–71). **7.** The text, which details the extremities to which Hazael's domination had reduced Israel, is a commentary on the title "savior" in v. 5. In 853, against the Assyrians at Qarqar, Ahab had been able to field a force of 2000 chariots!

(e) Jehoash of Israel, 801–786, and the Death of Elisha (13:10–25). **12.** *now the rest:* The concluding formula is an addition duplicated from 14:15–16. **14.** *Elisha:* The prediction-fulfillment story (vv. 19,25) is told for the same purpose as the other prediction-fulfillment stories. The miracle (vv. 20–21) is recounted for its value in authenticating "the word of the Lord" through his prophets. Elisha was active before Jehu's rebellion in 845, and his prophetic career must have lasted at least 50 years. **15.** *my father:* See comment on 2:12. **16.** *hands upon the king's hands:* Elisha thus signifies the communication of divine power to Jehoash. **17.** *toward the east:* The direction, toward Aram, prefigures Jehoash's victory over Aram. **18.** *strike:* The number of times Jehoash struck would prefigure the number of victories. His lack of forcefulness presages the limited extent of his victories (for other examples of such prophetic actions, see Ex 17:8ff.; Jos 8:18ff.; Jer 18:1ff.; 1 Kgs 22:11). **21.** *he revived:* The miracle story, which is similar to the stories related in chs. 2–8, testifies to the power of Elisha even after death. **22.** The brief resumé (vv. 22–24) of Aram's oppression of Israel leads up to the fulfillment in v. 25 of Elisha's prediction (v. 19)—a fulfillment that D, as usual, is solicitous to note.

62 (f) Amaziah of Judah, 800–783 (14:1–22) (= 2 Chr 25). **2.** *reigned twenty-nine years:* It is suggested that Amaziah retired after 13 years and let his son, Uzziah, reign as regent. This possibility would account for the unusual statement in v. 17; the addition of the figures in vv. 2 and 17 would account for the 29-year reign. (For the synchronization and regnal term, see M–G, *Kings* 438–39.) **6.** *in the book of the law:* The citation is from Dt 24:16. Under the more primitive tribal law of Israel, the solidarity of the family involved the punishment not only of the guilty individual but also of his family (cf. Jos 7:24; 2 Sm 21:5). **7.** The valley of salt is the Arabah, the continuation of the Dead Sea gorge to the south. Sela is perhaps Petra, the Edomite city that later became the capital of the Nabatean kingdom, between 200 BC and AD 100. Edom had revolted against Jehoram (8:20–22). Amaziah was probably trying to reconquer the trade route that led to Elath and the Red Sea. *Joktheel:* The name given to the conquered city is otherwise unknown. **8.** *messengers to Jehoash:* Amaziah's declaration of war on Israel is without motivation in the text but is explained in 2 Chr 25:5–24, especially in vv. 6, 10, 13, which tell of Israelite mercenaries sent home by Amaziah who along the way vented their anger by pillaging Judean towns. In retaliation, Amaziah declared war on Israel. **9.** *thistle:* Jehoash's fable (cf. the similar fable in Jgs 9:8–15) is meant to show up the foolish presumption of Amaziah, who had conquered Edom and now thought himself capable of taking on Israel (v. 10). Subsequent events (vv. 11–14) show how correct Jehoash's judgment was (see Bright, *Hist.* 238–39). **11.** *Beth-shemesh of Judah:* It is modern Tell er-Rumeileh, about 15 mi. W of Jerusalem. **15.** *now the rest:* The concluding formula, which more properly should follow 13:25, is placed here because D has brought together both Jehoash and Amaziah in the story of their war. He follows immediately with the concluding formula for Amaziah. **19.** *conspiracy:* 2 Chr 25:27 attributes the conspiracy to opposition aroused by Amaziah's apostasy. *Lachish:* It is modern Tell ed-Duweir, 15 mi. W of Hebron (see W. F. Albright, *BASOR* 68 [1937] 22ff.). **21.** *Azariah:* He is known as Uzziah in 15:13 and regularly in Chr, Am, Hos, and Is. Azariah was probably his birth name (cf. 1 Chr 3:12) and Uzziah his coronation name. **22.** *Elath:* See comment on 1 Kgs 9:26. The city was probably reconquered by Amaziah (3:7), who may also have started the rebuilding finished by his son.

63 (g) JEROBOAM II OF ISRAEL, 786–746 (14:23–29). **25.** During his long reign, Jeroboam II restored Israel's ancient borders to what they had been in the time of David; he so administered the kingdom that it reached a peak of prosperity that rivaled that of Solomon. *Jonah:* The name of this Israelite prophet was used for the pseudonymous protagonist of the later midrashic Book of Jonah. *Gath-hepher:* It is modern Meshhed, about 13 mi. W of Tiberias. (For a more realistic evaluation of Jeroboam II, the greatest of Israel's kings, to whom D grudgingly allows but seven lines, see Bright, *Hist.* 238–39; Albright, *BP* 70–71). **28.** *how he fought:* The MT is corrupt; BJ suggests the reading, "and how he fought against Damascus and turned away from Israel the wrath of Yahweh."

(h) AZARIAH (UZZIAH), 783–742 (15:1–7) (= 2 Chr 26). **1.** *Azariah:* See comment on 14:21. **5.** *leper:* For details, see 2 Chr 26:16–21. Jotham carried out the administrative duties of his father and perhaps acted as coregent. **6.** Like Jeroboam II, his contemporary in the north, Azariah had a long and prosperous reign, which, however, D ignores (see Bright, *Hist.* 239ff.).

(i) ZECHARIAH AND SHALLUM OF ISRAEL, 746–745 (15:8–15). **8.** *Zechariah:* He is the last king of Jehu's line. His brief reign and subsequent assassination introduce a period of troubles for Israel in the course of which four of six kings (Zechariah, Shallum, Pekahiah, and Pekah) are assassinated, civil wars engulf the country, and Assyrian influence and domination increase until, under Shalmaneser V in 721, the kingdom is destroyed and the people are carried off into captivity. (On the complex events of the last 23 years of Israel, see Bright, *Hist.* 252–58; for Assyrian records throwing light on the period, see *ANET* 282–84). **10.** *Ibleam:* See comment on 9:27. **11.** *word of the Lord:* As is his custom, D solicitously records the fulfillment of the prophetic word given in 10:30. **13.** *Shallum:* The usurper's reign of one month is the second shortest in Israel; Zimri reigned only one week (1 Kgs 16:15). **14.** *Tirzah:* See comment on 15:33.

(j) MENAHEM, 745–738 (15:16–22). **16.** *Tappuah:* It is possibly modern Sheikh Abu Zarad, 10 mi. S of Nablus, but the text and identification are both disputed. *disemboweled:* Such barbarity was not uncommon (cf. 8:12; Am 1:13; Hos 14:1). **19.** *Pul:* Tiglath-pileser III (745–727) took this name (*Pulu*) as a throne name when he conquered Babylon in 729 (*ANET* 283). *a thousand talents:* Equivalent to 3 million shekels, the tribute was raised by taxing 60,000 landholders in Israel at 50 shekels each (v. 20). The incident, which probably occurred in 738 just before the death of Menahem, shows Israel is still wealthy; at the same time, it signals the Assyrian advance that will ultimately spell utter destruction for the northern kingdom. **20.** *withdrew:* Only temporarily absent, he returns in 733 (15:29).

64 (k) PEKAHIAH AND PEKAH OF ISRAEL, 738–732 (15:23–31). **23.** *Pekahiah:* His two-year reign (738–737), during which he remained subject to Assyria in accord with the policy of his father, was terminated by Pekah, leader of an anti-Assyrian faction in Israel (cf. vv. 25, 29–30; 16:5–7). **27.** *Pekah:* In Hebrew, his name is the same as that of his predecessor, but he is distinguished by the addition "son of Remaliah" (15:32; 16:5; Is 7:5). Presumably, he usurped both the throne and the throne name of his predecessor. *twenty years:* For the chronology, see H. J. Cook, "Pekah," *VT* 14 (1964) 121–35. **29.** *captured:* The invasion is dated 733 to 732. The Assyrian king occupied the better part of Israel and divided it into three Assyrian provinces: Gilead in Transjordan; Megiddo (including Galilee); and Dor (taking in the coastal plain). It is probable that Hoshea's assassination of Pekah and the subsequent submission to Tiglath-pileser saved Israel from complete destruction (v. 30). *Ijon, Abel-beth-maacah:* These towns are on the northern border of Israel (cf. 1 Kgs 15:30). *Janoah:* It is unidentified. *Kedesh:* It is NW of Lake Huleh. *Hazor:* Hazor is W of Lake Huleh. The first of the tribes go into captivity; the rest will follow in 722 (17:1ff.). **30.** *Hoshea:* Tiglath-pileser's inscription (*ANET* 284) mentions the conspiracy against Pekah. Tiglath-pileser boasts: "I placed Hoshea over them as king." **31.** This is the last time the Chronicles or Acts of the kings of Israel is quoted, perhaps because most of the records for the following turbulent years before the end were either not kept or destroyed, or perhaps for some reason the author of the Chronicles terminated his story of Israel at this point.

(l) JOTHAM OF JUDAH, 750–735 (15:32–38) (= 2 Chr 27). **33.** *reigned sixteen years:* Of these years, perhaps eight (750–742) were spent as coregent with his ailing father, King Uzziah (see W. F. Albright, *BASOR* 100 [1945] 22). **37.** *began to send:* Pekah and Rezin of Damascus sought to induce Jotham to join them in a coalition against Assyria. When he refused, they determined to conquer Judah, depose Jotham, and enthrone a puppet king who would be more cooperative. Jotham died before the arrival of the Israelite and Aramean armies. The blow fell instead on his son Ahaz (16:5ff.; Is 7:1ff.).

65 (m) AHAZ OF JUDAH, 735–715 (16:1–20) (= 2 Chr 28). **1.** *Ahaz:* The name is an abbreviated form of Jehoahaz, found in full in an Assyrian source as *Ia-u-ha-zi* (*ANET* 282). The author may have deliberately omitted the divine element of the name because of Ahaz's well-known apostasy. Ahaz is one of the few Davidic kings whose mother's name is not mentioned. **3.** *through the fire:* The infant sacrifice is like the Canaanite practice (cf. 21:6; 23:10; Mi 6:7; Jer 7:31; see comment on 3:27). **4.** *spreading tree:* Baal religious rites were frequently practiced in the open air (cf. 17:10; 1 Kgs 14:23; Dt 12:2; Jer 2:20; see comments on 3:2 and 1 Kgs 11:5). **5.** *Rezin:* He was the last king of Damascus, taken in 732 by Tiglath-pileser (v. 9). The coalition of Damascus and Israel aimed to replace Ahaz with the son of Tabeel (Is 7:6), presumably a non-Judean, thereby either gaining Judah as an ally against Assyria or at least neutralizing her. A land in northern Transjordan named *Bēt Ṭāb'el* is known from contemporary Assyrian records (see W. F. Albright, *BASOR* 140 [1955] 24–35). An exaggerated account of the effect of this invasion on Judah is given in 2 Chr 28:5–8. **6.** *Edom:* Judah's southern vassal (cf. 14:22) used the attacks on her overlord as an opportunity for revolt. According to 2 Chr 28:17, the Edomites then joined Israel and Damascus in their attack on Judah. **6.** *messengers:* Ahaz sought and received the help of Assyria (vv. 8–10) against his enemies, contrary to the advice of Isaiah (Is 7:1–8:18). Ahaz's tribute is mentioned in Tiglath-pileser's annals. **9.** *killed Rezin:* Tiglath-pileser's campaign in 732 ended Aram-Damascus as an independent kingdom. Rezin's territory was divided into four Assyrian provinces. Israel had been invaded in the previous year (15:29).

10. *altar:* It was probably the altar of the temple of Hadad-rimmon (spoken of as Beth-rimmon in Damascus in 5:18) that Uriah the priest (cf. Is 8:2) used as a model for his altar to Hadad-rimmon in the Temple of Jerusalem (cf. 2 Chr 28:23). Ahaz's political subservience to Assyria (cf. v. 18) involved as a lamentable consequence the recognition of Assyrian deities (see Von Rad, *OT Theology I*, 43; Bright, *Hist.* 259–60). Uriah's obedience to Ahaz shows that the king controlled the Temple as a state sanctuary (vv. 10–16). **14.** *bronze altar:* The old altar of holocausts (cf. 1 Kgs 8:64), replaced by the pagan altar modeled on the altar from Damascus, was moved and continued in use (see M–G, *Kings* 460–61). **17.** Presumably Ahaz had to strip the Temple to pay tribute to Tiglath-pileser. **18.** The meaning is uncertain; there was probably a dais set up in the court of the Temple for the King. The "entrance for the king" was a special royal entrance (cf. 1 Chr 9:18; Ez 46:1–3). The closing of this entrance "on account of the king of Assyria" may have been a way of making Ahaz acknowledge at least symbolically that he no longer controlled his own Temple.

66 (n) Hoshea (732–724) and the Fall of Samaria, 722 (17:1–41). Chapter 17 begins with a brief account of the fall of Samaria (vv. 1–6), continues with an interpretative discourse on the fall of Israel (vv. 7–23), and closes with a description of the origins of the Samaritans (vv. 24–41). **2.** For reasons unknown (perhaps archival material favorable to Hoshea but omitted by D) Hoshea, the last king of Israel, is judged more benignly than his predecessors. **3.** *servant:* The sequence of events in Hoshea's relations with Assyria is not clear. It would seem from 15:30 that Hoshea headed the pro-Assyrian faction in Israel in 733 and became a tributary to Tiglath-pileser. Possibly he ceased paying tribute to Assyria at the time of Tiglath-pileser's death in 727 but continued in 725 when Shalmaneser sent an army against Tyre and Israel, only to revolt again later. Since Shalmaneser's armies definitely besieged Samaria in 724, the difficulty is in finding time for two invasions between 727 and 724. A better solution is that Shalmaneser sent only one invading army in 724. The invaders came because of the conspiracy mentioned in v. 4 and Hoshea capitulated before the army's arrival, bringing the tribute to Shalmaneser mentioned in v. 3. Perhaps on this occasion, Shalmaneser convicted Hoshea of conspiracy with the king of Egypt, put him in prison, and sent his army to besiege Samaria as vv. 4b–6 describe (see Bright, *Hist.* 258). **4.** Read, with H. Goedicke (*BASOR* 171 [1963] 64–66): "to Sais, to the king of Egypt" (→ Excursus Israel, 11:13). **5.** Shalmaneser began the siege in 724 and completed it in the autumn of 722, just a few months before his death in the winter of 722–721 (see H. Tadmor, *JCS* 12 [1958] 22–40, 77–100). Because Samaria fell in his accession year, Sargon II (722–705) claimed for himself the conquest of Samaria and "the wide land of Beth-Omri" (*ANET* 284–85). **6.** Sargon II lists 22,290 Israelites deported to upper Mesopotamia and Medes. When compared with the 60,000 wealthy landowners mentioned in 15:19–20, the number would constitute approximately one-tenth, possibly one-twentieth, of the population (see H. G. May, *BA* 6 [1943] 57–58). This number would include the cream of Israel's citizenry, because the purpose of the deportations was to discourage rebellion by removing from the land the influential classes and those in general who might lead the people in a new insurrection against Assyria. *Halah:* It is a district on the Khabur, a tributary of the Euphrates in northern Mesopotamia not far from Harran. *Gozan:* It is probably Tell Halaf in eastern Mesopotamia.

67 **7.** The exilic author pauses to deliver a moralizing discourse on the fate of Israel (vv. 7–23), fully justifying the warnings contained in his previous interpretative discourses (cf. 1 Kgs 9:3–9; 14:7–16) and the tenor of his judgments against all the kings of Israel from Jeroboam to Hoshea. The discourse contains a good deal of the phraseology of Dt and Jer (see Driver, *Introd.* 200–204). **10.** *every high hill and under every spreading tree:* Cf. Dt. 12:2; Jer 3:6; 17:2. **11.** *provoking the Lord:* Cf. Dt 4:25; 9:18; 31:29; Jer 8:19; 11:17. **13.** *my servants the prophets:* Cf. Jer 7:25; 25:4; 29:19; 35:15; 44:4. **14.** *would not listen:* Cf. Jer 7:26; 11:7. **15.** *followed vanity:* Cf. Jer 2:5. **18.** *removed them out of his sight:* Cf. Jer 32:31; 7:15; 23:39. **19.** *also Judah:* The exilic author anticipates the fall of Jerusalem in 587 (note the reference to Judah in v. 13). Verses 19–20 have all the earmarks of a later addition, but the exilic author regularly looks ahead in his interpretative discourses to the fall of Jerusalem (cf. 1 Kgs 8:46–53; 9:6–9; 2 Kgs 20:16–19; 21:10–15; 22:15–20; 23:27). **20.** *rejected all the descendants of Israel:* Cf. Jer 31:27.

24. The Assyrian policy included the importation of other conquered peoples into Israel. In his records, Sargon II says he deported survivors from the tribes of Tammad, Ibadidi, Marsimanu, and Haiapa "and settled them in Samaria" (*ANET* 286). The deportations of aliens to Samarina, as the new Assyrian province was called, probably took place periodically over the years (cf. Ezr 4:2,9–10). *Cuthah:* Modern Tell Ibrahim, it is N of Babylon and E of the Euphrates. In rabbinical writings, "Cuthites" is a term of opprobrium for the Samaritans. *Avva:* Unidentified, it is probably in Syria near Hamath and Sibraim (cf. 18:34; 19:13). *Hamath:* A Syrian city on the Orontes, Hamath was defeated by Sargon II in 720; the deportation to Samaria probably followed upon the defeat. *Sepharvaim:* It is probably the Sibraim mentioned along with Hamath in Ez 47:16. **25.** *lions:* Lions were indigenous to the Middle East until the 12th cent. AD, and Asshurbanipal (668–633) records a similar plague of lions in Babylonia in his time. **27.** Albright suggests that the Assyrian king, for political reasons, sought to reorganize Bethel as a rival sanctuary to Jerusalem to keep the new Assyrian province of Samarina faithful to Assyria (*BP* 77; Albright, *ARI* 172). Rebellions in Palestine against Assyrian hegemony in 711 (Is 20:1) and 701 (Is 36–37) would support this explanation. **29.** *Samaritans:* The religious degeneration of the Samaritans, scored in vv. 24–41, is held by some to be a later legend incorporated into the text in late post-exilic times when the widening political and religious gulf between the Jews and the Samaritans had become impassable (see H. H. Rowley, "The Samaritan Schism in Legend and History," *Israel's Prophetic Heritage* [B. Anderson and W. Harrelson, eds.; N.Y. 1962] 208–22; L. Hartman, *EDB* 2112). The account is biased but no more so than the exilic author's attitude toward Israel throughout 1 and 2 Kgs. Moreover, the style is not significantly different from that of D in his other interpretative discourses (cf. 1 Kgs 14:7–16; 2 Kgs 17:7–23). **30.** *Succoth-benoth:* The name is possibly a combination of Sakkuth, the Babylonian name for the planet Saturn (cf. Am 5:26), and Banitu, a title of the goddess Ishtar (but see M–G, *Kings* 474). *Nergal:* Nergal was the god of the underworld and had a temple at Cuthah. *Ashima:* She is possibly the goddess consort of Eshmun, worshiped at Hamath. *Nibhaz and Tartak:* Unidentified deities, the former is possibly a variant of the Babylonian god, Nebo, and the latter, a variant of the Syrian goddess Artagatis. *Adrammelech:* He is probably the Syrian storm-god Adad-melek (see Albright, *ARI* 163). *Anammelech:* He is probably Anu, the consort of the Syrian goddess Anat.

68 **(III) The Last Kings of Judah (2 Kgs 18:1–25:30).** Now D turns all his attention to the last of the Judean kings and to the final catastrophe of 587. In his interpretative discourses in Part I, he had already discreetly pointed toward the downfall of Judah (cf. 1 Kgs 8:23–53; 9:3–9). In Part II, his discourses pointed to the fall of Samaria (cf. 1 Kgs 11:11–13,31–39; 14:7–16), with one brief reference to the fall of Judah (2 Kgs 17:19–20). In Part III, several interpretative discourses point directly to the fall of Jerusalem (cf. 20:16–19; 21:10–15; 22:15–19; 23:26–27). As in Part II, the author continues to provide introductory and concluding formulas for each of the kings and, where his sources allow, interpolates stories concerning the prophets (cf. 18:17–20:21; 22:14–20; 23:16–20). The Isaiah stories would seem to have come from a cycle about Isaiah not unlike the Elijah and the Elisha cycles and are probably the work of Isaiah's disciples (cf. Is 8:16). However, D, as is his custom, uses them for theological rather than biographical purposes. In 18:4, and especially in chs. 22–23 *passim*, the author has apparently borrowed, as in chs. 12 and 16, from some kind of source dealing with the history of the Temple (but see M-G, *Kings* 37–38; → History of Israel, 75:81–87).

(A) Hezekiah, 715–687 (18:1–20:21) (= 2 Chr 29–32; Is 36–39). The sequence and chronology of events in D's treatment of Hezekiah's reign are much disputed. Without attempting to solve all the problems, we shall divide the material into three parts—18:1–16, 18:17–19:37, and 20:1–21—and deal with the problems pertinent to each part.

69 (a) Hezekiah's Reforms and the Invasion of Sennacherib, 701 (18:1–16). Most of the material in this part would appear to be from the Chronicles of the Kings of Judah. **4.** The brief account of Hezekiah's reform is supplemented by 2 Chr 29–31. The need for reform was imperative after the irreligious reign of Ahaz (cf. 16:2–18). The timing, in view of Assyrian political and religious influence, must have been gradual; however, undoubtedly the fact that Sargon II was beset by rebellion in many of his subject states in the years following 721 favored Hezekiah's reform. It is likely that a combination of nationalism and Yahwistic zeal led to a beginning of reform early in Hezekiah's reign, but it is doubtful, despite the Chronicler's placement of the whole reform in the first year of Hezekiah (2 Chr 28:3), that the King would have eliminated all Assyrian influence from the Temple until he felt that such acts, tantamount to rebellion, could be indulged without fear of Assyrian retaliation (see Bright, *Hist.* 265ff.). *high places:* See comments on 1 Kgs 3:2; 11:5. *sacred poles:* See comment on 1 Kgs 16:33. *bronze serpent:* Called Nehushtan, this ancient cult object, reputed to date from the time of Moses (Nm 21:8–9), had become the object of idolatrous worship in Jerusalem. **8.** *conquered the Philistines:* Since Sargon II boasts a successful campaign against the Philistine cities in 711 (cf. Is 20:1; *ANET* 286–87), Hezekiah's attack almost certainly was part of a rebellion against Assyria (cf. vv. 7,13–16). It is probable, but by no means certain, that the attack took place in the years following Sargon's death in 705, when Hezekiah, in league with Merodach-baladan of Chaldea (cf. 20:12–19), Pharaoh Shabako of Egypt (710–696), and the kings of Tyre, Ashkelon, and Ekron, was preparing to revolt against Assyria. The attack may have been an attempt to force the remaining Philistine cities to join the coalition against Assyria.

9–12. The whole passage, a repetition of 17:5–6 with synchronisms based on 18:1, has the appearance of a later addition. **13.** *fourteenth year:* On the dating, see W. F. Albright, *BASOR* 100 [1945] 22. It is certain from the annals of Sennacherib (*ANET* 288) that he invaded Palestine in 701, sacked many cities, deported a large number of Jews, and compelled Hezekiah to pay a huge tribute. Sennacherib explicitly states that on this occasion he besieged Jerusalem (a statement notably in contradiction with the prophecy of Isaiah in 19:32–34) and made Hezekiah a prisoner in Jerusalem "like a bird in a cage," but he nowhere says that he actually captured Jerusalem. Thus, historians think that the account in vv. 13–16 agrees substantially with the account given in Sennacherib's annals. Whether the story that follows in 18:17–19:37 deals with the same invasion, however, is another question (see comment on 18:17ff.). **14.** *Lachish:* Identified with Tell ed-Duweir, Lachish, in the Shephelah about 15 mi. W of Hebron, was the chief fortress in a chain of strongholds protecting Judah. Sennacherib was so proud of his conquest of Lachish that he had the event commemorated in a bas-relief on stone (see *ANE* 371–74; *DOTT* 69–70; G. E. Wright, *BibArch* 110–11).

70 (b) Sennacherib's Invasion According to the Isaian Source (18:17–19:37). Whether the account in 18:17–19:37 (which may contain two parallel accounts of the same events, the first in 18:17–19:8 and the second in 19:9–37) relates to the invasion of Sennacherib in 701, laconically summarized in the archival data contained in 18:13–16, or to a second invasion of Sennacherib, to be dated ca. 689–688, is a matter of dispute among authors (see M–G, *Kings* 513–18). The two-campaign theory has been adopted here (see Bright, *Hist.* 282ff.). The account in Is 36–37 is identical, except for its omission of 18:14–16 (→ Isaiah, 16:61–64). **17.** *The Rab-saris* [chief of the eunuchs]*:* Probably one of the king's confidential advisers (see De Vaux, *AI* 121). *conduit of the upper pool:* The reference is to one of the pools fed by Gihon, S of the city and not far from the palace on the northern end of Zion hillock (cf. 1 Kgs 1:9,33; Is 7:3).

18. *Shebna the scribe:* See comment on 1 Kgs 4:3. In the context of Is 22:29ff., in which Isaiah predicts the disgrace and subsequent replacement of Shebna by Eliakim, son of Hilkiah, there is a reference to many "breaches in the city of David," a condition easily explained after the 701 invasion but not before. The whole context of Is 22:9ff., which deals with repairing the city walls and making a new reservoir "between the two walls for the water of the old pool," would imply that the city had already suffered one invasion and was preparing for a second—a situation that would support the two-campaign explanation of 18:13–16 and 18:17ff. **21.** *broken reed, Egypt:* It is unclear whether the field marshal is declaring that the aid promised by Egypt will be useless (see v. 24) or referring to the defeat of the Egyptian army that came to relieve the siege of Jerusalem (but see v. 19). If the latter, it would appear to refer to the defeat of the Egyptians at Elteqeh in 701 and would indicate, against the two-campaign theory, that the author is giving a fuller account of the campaign summarized in 18:13–16. **26.** *Aramaic:* By the time of Ben-hadad II, imperial

Aramaic had become the official language of the new Aramean empire. In the following centuries, especially the 8th cent., it spread beyond the borders of the Aramean empire to become the lingua franca of the Near East (see B. Mazar, *BA* 25 [1962] 111–12). *in Judean:* The Hebr language spoken in Judah is meant. The Jewish envoys are afraid the people on the wall (v. 27) will be influenced by the field marshal's propaganda. **34.** *Hamath:* See comment on 17:24. *Arpad:* It is Tell Ergad, N of Aleppo. *Hena:* The place is unidentified.

19:3. *children have come...:* The expression is proverbial for a desperate situation. **4.** *remnant:* It is one of Isaiah's favorite themes (cf. Is 7:3; 10:20–21). **7.** *spirit:* The power of God moves men to fulfill his designs in history. *certain rumor:* These words provided the juncture or seam for introducing the second and parallel account of the second campaign. Presumably the "rumor" was the news Sennacherib received from home (19:36–37), following which he departed for Nineveh and was subsequently assassinated. An early editor, or perhaps the exilic author of Kgs himself, interpreted the "rumor" to mean the news that the Egyptian army under Tirhakah was approaching (vv. 8–9), and he inserted at this point the parallel account that speaks clearly of the Egyptian intervention. The text says, "when he hears a certain rumor he shall return to his own land etc.," a prediction fulfilled by Sennacherib's return to Nineveh and subsequent assassination as told in 19:36–37. If the "rumor" was the news that Tirhakah's army was approaching, it might also explain Sennacherib's retreat, because he met, but did not conquer, the Egyptian army; however, the text implies that it was the "rumor" that led to his return to Nineveh, not the encounter with the Egyptians (see comment on 19:35).

71 **9.** *Tirhakah* is the non-Egyptian name of the third king of the 25th (Ethiopian) dynasty of Egypt (690–664). Since he was born in 710, those who follow the one-campaign explanation for 18:13–19:37 are obliged to hold either that Tirhakah led an army against Sennacherib in 701 when he was only nine years old or that the name has been mistakenly interpolated into the text (see W. F. Albright, *BASOR* 130 [1953] 8–11; J. M. Janssen, *Bib* 34 [1953] 23–43). It is more likely that Tirhakah was associated with a second rebellion of Hezekiah against Sennacherib in 689–688. **12.** *Rezeph:* It is modern Resafa, NE of Palmyra. *Edenites:* They are people from the territory of modern Tell Basher on the Euphrates, S of Harran. **14.** *spread it out before the Lord:* Hezekiah's action is a striking and touching demonstration of his belief in God's presence in the Temple (cf. Pss 42:5; 76:3; 84; 122:1–4). **15.** *seated upon the Cherubim:* Hezekiah has probably entered into the immediate presense of the Ark in the Holy of Holies. **20.** *Isaiah:* The Prophet's message is substantially the same as the parallel message in 19:6–7, but with the addition of a taunt song (vv. 21–38) that is similar to Isaiah's taunt against Assyria in Is 10:5ff. **29.** The sign, like the sign in Ex 3:12 and Is 7:14, is meant as later confirmatory testimony to the truth of the prediction as such, since the latter, as a matter of fact, was fulfilled before the sign (cf. v. 35). **32.** The annals of Sennacherib for the invasion of 701 (*ANET* 288) show that Sennacherib (contrary to the prophecy that declares "he shall not...shoot an arrow there, nor...cast up a mound against it") did, indeed, at least besiege Jerusalem in 701, although he did not capture it. It would appear, therefore, that either the prophecy is not to be taken literally or, what is more likely, it is to be understood as referring to a later invasion of Judah, perhaps in 689–688.

35. *angel:* The reference may be to a pestilence (cf. 2 Sm 24:15–17). Herodotus (II, 141) speaks of a battle between Sennacherib and Sethos at the border of Egypt, during which there came "a multitude of field mice, which devoured all the quivers and bow-strings of the enemy [the army of Sennacherib].... Next morning they commenced their flight, and great multitudes fell...." Herodotus' account, based on hearsay evidence, is obviously legendary, but both the biblical account and Herodotus' account could derive from the same historical event—a pestilence, perhaps the bubonic plague (cf. 1 Sm 5:6ff.; 6:1ff.), that decimated Sennacherib's army and compelled him to retreat to Assyria. **36.** The implication is that Sennacherib's return and subsequent assassination followed not too long after the debacle mentioned in v. 35. It is certain that Sennacherib was killed in 681 by his son (*ANET* 302, 309). If the deliverance of Jerusalem mentioned in v. 35 were that of 701, there would be 20 years between the events; if it were that of 689–688, there would be a much more reasonable 7 years.

37. *Nisroch:* The name is unknown. Perhaps it is a deformation of Marduk or Ninurta, both gods of the Babylonian pantheon. *Adrammelech:* The Babylonian chronicles that speak of the assassination of Sennacherib (*ANET* 302, 309) mention only that he was murdered by his son. Only one son is mentioned and no names are given. The name *Adadmilki-ila* occurs in a late Assyrian text and indicates that the correct Hebrew form should be *Hadad-melek* (cf. A. Pohl, *Bib* 22 [1941] 35). *Sharezer:* The reference is perhaps to an official named *Nabu-sar-usur*, who was eponym for 682–681. *Esarhaddon:* The youngest son and successor of Sennacherib, Esarhaddon (681–670) speaks of a conspiracy in 681 led by his older brothers but does not mention the assassination of his father (*ANET* 288–89; see H. Kraeling, *JPOS* 53 [1933] 335–46). That the murderers fled to Ararat (Armenia) is confirmed by Esarhaddon's statement that in the first year of his reign he pursued the leaders of the conspiracy into Hanigalbat, a country in Armenia.

72 (c) Hezekiah's Sickness and Merodach-Baladan (20:1–21). It is clear from internal evidence (vv. 6, 15–17) that the events in ch. 20 preceded the events in chs. 18–19. Some hold that Kgs originally contained the correct order of events (i.e., chs. 20, 18, 19) but that the editor of Is, in borrowing these chapters from Kgs (cf. Is 36–39; Kgs 18–20), changed the order to have Isaiah's prophecy concerning the Babylonian Captivity (20:16–19) immediately precede the section of Isaiah (ch. 40–55) that deals with the exiles in Babylon. Later, it is claimed, the original order in Kgs was corrected (wrongly, however) to conform with the order in Isaiah. Although this solution is possible, it is more likely that the author of Kgs, who habitually terminates his narratives with prophetic-fulfillment stories pointing to the next great catastrophe to overtake either Israel or Judah or their kings (cf. 1 Kgs 11:31–39; 14:6–16; 21:20–24; 22:28; 2 Kgs 10:30; 17:19–20; 20:16–18; 21:11–15; 23:26–27), purposely arranged the material from his Isaian source so that it would end with a prophecy concerning the downfall of Judah. His lack of concern for exact chronological order is more than evident in his handling of the Elijah and Elisha cycles. It should cause no surprise that he does the same with the Isaian cycle.

1. *set your house in order:* Before death, Israelites gave oral instructions about the distribution of their property (cf. 2 Sm 17:23). **4.** *middle courtyard:* It is between the palace and the Temple (cf. 1 Kgs 7:8,12). **6.** *fifteen years:* His sickness is usually dated to the years immediately preceding the invasion of Sennacherib in 701. He died in 687, approximately 15 years later. *I will deliver:* The text shows that originally the pericope preceded the events recounted in chs. 18–19. If it is not what it seems—a case of proleptic prophecy—then it would indicate that

Hezekiah's sickness occurred at a time when Sennacherib's invasion was already anticipated, perhaps 703. If the author of Kgs had left this prophecy in its original position in the Isaian cycle, he certainly, as was his wont, would have pointed out its fulfillment. **7.** *cake of figs:* The ancients used such a "plaster" to reduce inflammation. **11.** *ten steps:* The reference is to a stairway built by Ahaz, possibly in connection with the upper chamber mentioned in 23:12. According to De Vaux (*AI* 183) "the miracle in question is not that of a 'clock' going forward or backward, but of the sudden movement of a shadow on a stairway" (cf. S. Iwry, *BASOR* 147 [1957] 27ff.). **12.** *Merodach-baladan:* A continual thorn in the side of Assyria, Merodach-baladan was a Chaldean prince who seized power in Babylon after the death of Shalmaneser V and reigned there from 721 to 710. Dislodged by Sargon II in 710, he was back again in Babylon for nine months after the death of Sargon, and remained there until Sennacherib forced him out in 704. His ambassadors to the court of Hezekiah were no doubt sent to draw Hezekiah into an anti-Assyrian coalition (cf. vv. 1–17 and Isaiah's manifest displeasure).

17. *to Babylon:* The fulfillment of this prediction was well-known to the author's exilic readers. The prediction is the first of a series of prophecies and interpretative discourses pointing to the fall of Jerusalem (cf. 21:11–15; 22:15–20; 23:26–27). **19.** *peace:* Hezekiah is content that the catastrophe does not come in his time. For calamity postponed because of merit, see 22:18ff.; 1 Kgs 21:27ff. **20.** *water into the city:* In addition to the open conduit that brought water from the Gihon spring (see comment on 1 Kgs 1:38) to the southern end of the city, Hezekiah had a tunnel cut through the rock under the hill of Ophel to bring the water directly into the city to a pool in the Tyropoeon Valley, thus ensuring a water supply in time of siege (cf. 2 Chr 33:30; Sir 48:17). Is 22:9ff., which mentions the tunnel, suggests that it was dug after the 701 invasion in preparation for a new invasion. An inscription (see *ANET* 321) left in the tunnel by Hezekiah's engineers and found in 1880 gives a brief description of this remarkable engineering feat (cf. *VDBS* 4, 941–49).

73 **(B) Manasseh (687–642) and Amon (642–640) (21:1–26) (= 2 Chr 33).** In addition to the usual formulas dealing with the kings, the author introduces a brief interpretative discourse (vv. 9–15) attributing the approaching fall of Jerusalem in a special way (cf. 23:26–27; 24:3; Jer 15:1–4) to the "abominations" of Manasseh. Manasseh, as the author shows (vv. 2–7, 16), not only reversed all the reforms of Hezekiah but also plunged Judah into a long dark night for Yahwism (see Bright, *Hist.* 289ff.).

1. *fifty-five years:* The figure is approximately ten years too much. During his long reign, Manasseh remained subject to Assyria (but cf. 2 Chr 33:11–13), which during this time, under Sennacherib (705–681), Esarhaddon (681–670), and Asshurbanipal (669–633), reached a peak of prestige and power, controlling not only all the Fertile Crescent to Palestine but Egypt as well, after Esarhaddon's defeat of Tirhakah in 671. Manasseh is mentioned several times in Assyrian records, always as a subject king (*ANET* 291, 294). **3.** *host of heavens:* Indicated are astral deities worshiped in the Assyrian pantheon and adopted by Manasseh (cf. 17:16; Zeph 1:5; Jer 7:18; Dt 4:19; 17:3). **6.** Assyrian records for the period contain innumerable references to magic, divination, and astrology, practices no doubt imitated under Manasseh. **7.** *Asherah:* The Canaanite goddess of fertility, wife of Baal, widely worshiped in Palestine, her amulets and statuettes have been found in abundance by excavators not only in Canaanite remains but also in Israelite levels (cf. 1 Kgs 15:13; 16:33; 2 Kgs 13:16; see *ANEP* 464–79). **16.** *innocent blood:* Jewish legend attributes the martyrdom of Isaiah to Manasseh. **19.** *Jotbah:* The native city of Amon's grandfather, Haruz, is probably modern Khirbet Jefat, N of Sephoris in Galilee. **24.** *people of the land:* See comment on 11:13. Whatever the cause of the conspiracy against Amon, the people of the land remain faithful to the Davidic dynasty (cf. 23:30).

74 **(C) Josiah, 640–609 (22:1–23:30) (= 2 Chr 34–35).** Thanks to the rapid disintegration of the Assyrian empire after the death of Asshurbanipal in 633, Judah begins gradually to throw off Assyrian hegemony (see Bright, *Hist.* 291–95; Noth, *Hist.* 269–74). This political background is important for an understanding of Josiah's reform, described at length in chs. 22–23. Because of the detailed description of the finding of the "book of the law" (22:8ff.) and of Josiah's reform, it is sometimes said that the author must have been a contemporary of these events and subsequently wrote Kgs to spur on the reforms begun by Josiah. The opinion may be true, but it requires termination of Kgs at 23:25 and postulates so many interpolations by exilic editors that Kgs, for all practical purposes, becomes a new book. Nor does the opinion explain why an author so interested in the reform should begin his story of the reform with the year 621 instead of 629, the true beginning of the reform, in the course of which in 621 the Book of the Law was found in the Temple (cf. 2 Chr 34:3). It is more reasonable to expect that the author of Kgs wrote during the Exile (after 562) and chose from a source (perhaps the Chronicles of the Kings of Judah or a prophetic work) only that section dealing with the progress of the reform in 621, because it contained two prophetic-prediction-fulfillment stories (22:15–20 and 23:16–18). As is evident throughout Kgs, the author had a propensity for such stories.

3. *eighteenth year:* It would be 621; 2 Chr 34:3 shows the reform had begun as early as 629–628, not long after the death of Asshurbanipal in 633 and just about the time Josiah would have come of age to take over the government. *Shaphan:* He was Josiah's secretary of state (cf. Jer 36:11–12). **4.** *money:* The account reflects the same interests, sometimes in the same words (cf. 22:4–7; 12:12–16), as the account of the Temple repairs in the time of Jehoash (12:4ff.). **8.** *book of law:* Critics are agreed that this book was Dt, or some part thereof, perhaps Dt 12–26, 28. It is thought the book was written in the reign of Hezekiah from Levitical traditions brought to Jerusalem after the fall of Samaria in 721. Presumably it was a proscribed work during the irreligious reign of Manasseh and lay neglected in the Temple until found by Hilkiah (see De Vaux, *AI* 337–39; Von Rad, *Studies in Deuteronomy* [London, 1948]). **13.** *wrath of the Lord:* See the threats in Dt 28:15ff.; 29:21ff. **14.** *Huldah:* Otherwise unknown, she evidently enjoyed a reputation not yet shared by the canonical prophets, Jeremiah and Zephaniah. **15.** Huldah's discourse points to the coming fall of Jerusalem and is but one of many discourses used by the author for this purpose (cf. 1 Kgs 8:46–53; 9:3–9; 2 Kgs 17:19–20; 20:16–18; 21:10–15; 23:26–27). **20.** *in peace:* Josiah died in battle (23:29), which is considered a blessing for otherwise he might have lived to see the terrible catastrophe of 587.

75 **23:3.** *by the column:* See comment on 11:14. *the covenant:* See 11:17; Jos 24:2ff. **4.** *king commanded:* Josiah's reformation in Jerusalem and throughout the land, even in Samaria (vv. 15, 19), proceeds rapidly after the finding of the book; it is described in detail in vv. 4–20. *second priest:* A comparison with 25:18 would suggest that the high priest, the second priest, and the three keepers of the threshold were the highest priestly officials in the Temple (see De Vaux, *AI* 378–79). *Asherah:* See comment on 21:7. *fertility cult:* See comment on 1 Kgs 14:24. **8.** *brought all the priests:* The move was part of Josiah's centralization of cult in Jerusalem, following the prescription of Dt 12 (see De Vaux, *AI* 338–39, 362ff.). *high places:* Yahwistic sanctuaries were destroyed because they interfered with the policy of centralization. *Geba:* Geba was a city on the northern boundary of Judah (cf. 1 Kgs 15:22). *Beer-sheba:* The ancient city was on the southern boundary of Judah (cf. 1 Kgs 19:3). *satyrs:* These demons were represented as goats (cf. Lv 17:7; 2 Chr 11:15). **9.** *did not come up:* It is a way of saying these priests were deposed, because to "come up" to the altar was equivalent to exercising one's function as priest. *ate unleavened cakes:* The bread was eaten during the Passover festivities (cf. Ex 12:15; Dt 16:3–4). Probably the reference is to the great Passover of Josiah (vv. 21–23), at which the Jerusalem priests imposed the stricter prescriptions of Dt 12:11–12, rather than those of Dt 18:6–7 that would have allowed to the provincial priests the same privileges claimed by the Jerusalem priests.

10. *Topheth:* The Canaanite shrine is in the valley of the sons of Hinnom, S of Jerusalem; infant sacrifice was occasionally practiced there (cf. Jer 7:31–32; 19:1–13; 1 Kgs 16:3). **12.** *upper chamber:* Astral worship after the manner of the Assyrians and the Babylonians took place on rooftops (cf. 20:11; Zeph 1:5; Jer 32:29). **13.** *Solomon...built:* See comment on 1 Kgs 11:5–7. **14.** *human bones:* The intention was to desecrate the altars irrevocably. **15.** *altar at Bethel:* Josiah's extension of the reformation to the north would indicate that he had become bolder in his defiance of Assyria. Imposition of the reform on Bethel and upon the cities of Samaria (v. 19) shows that he had taken over what had formerly been the Assyrian province of Samaria, probably with the hope of eventually restoring the boundaries of Judah to what they had been in the time of David. His death at Megiddo (v. 29), which was the capital of the Assyrian district of lower Galilee, indicates the extent of his control by 609 (cf. 2 Chr 34:6–7). **16.** *according to the word:* As usual, the author of Kgs records the fulfillment of prophetic predictions, in this case that of 1 Kgs 13:2ff. **18.** *prophet:* Cf. 1 Kgs 13:31. **21.** The celebration of the Passover, which had acquired nationalistic overtones, provided a strategic climax to the great reform. **25.** *after him:* Presumably the author is comparing Josiah with the bad kings who followed him, particularly Jehoiakim and Zedekiah. **26.** *great anger:* The author keeps ever before his readers the approaching fall of Jerusalem (cf. the interpretative discourse here with those in 20:17–18; 21:10–15; 22:15–20). **29.** *Pharaoh Neco:* Neco was King of Egypt from 609 to 594; his campaign, ostensibly to help Assyria at Harran against Nabopolassar and Nebuchadnezzar, was really designed to extend his power, in view of the rapid disintegration of Assyria, as far as the Euphrates. The battle in 609 was indecisive, but Neco was decisively defeated at Carchemish in 605 by Nebuchadnezzar (cf. Jer 46:1–2). *went to meet him:* Josiah hoped to prevent Neco from assisting the Assyrians, whose Palestinian provinces he was in the process of annexing to Judah. *Neco slew him:* Cf. 2 Chr 35:20–24.

76 **(D) Jehoahaz (609) and Jehoiakim (609–598) (23:31–24:7) (= 2 Chr 36:1–8).** **31.** *three months:* This short reign was terminated when Pharaoh Neco returned from his Syrian campaign (v. 29) and asserted control over Judah. Jehoahaz probably attempted to continue his father's aggressive policies. Consequently, he was deposed (v. 34) and deported to Egypt as hostage royalty, and his erstwhile kingdom was laid under heavy tribute (v. 35). **34.** Jehoiakim is the throne name of Eliakim. Neco probably changed the name to signify his authority over Judah. Jehoiakim gets little attention from the author beyond an adverse judgment (v. 37), amply substantiated in Jer 22:18ff.; 36:30; 25–26; 35–36.

24:1. *Nebuchadnezzar:* Son and successor of Nabopolassar, and the greatest and most famous king of the Neo-Babylonian Empire, he became king following his victory over the Egyptians at Carchemish in 605 and reigned until 562. His reign has been amply documented in recent years by the British Museum's publication of the Babylonian Chronicle (see W. F. Albright, *BASOR* 143 [1956] 28–33; Hartman, *EDB* 1595–97). *three years:* Because Jehoiakim rebelled in 599–598, his submission to Nebuchadnezzar may be placed in 603–602. Sometime after 601, when the Babylonian army retreated after an indecisive battle with Egypt, Jehoiakim returned his allegiance to Pharaoh Neco, mistakenly believing Babylonian power in Palestine was at an end. **2.** The Syrians, Ammonites, and Moabites remained faithful to Babylon, and, with Babylonian troops, they conducted guerrilla raids on Judah that terminated with a full-scale invasion by Nebuchadnezzar in the winter of 598–597. **6.** *slept with his fathers:* Jehoiakim died or was assassinated (cf. Jer 22:19; 36:30) in December, 598 and was succeeded for three months by his son, Jehoiachin. **7.** After the battle of Carchemish in 605, Babylonian hegemony was extended in a few years to cover all of Syria and Palestine to the borders of Egypt.

77 **(E) Jehoiachin (598–597) and Zedekiah (597–587) (24:8–25:30) (= 2 Chr 36:9–23).** **8.** *three months:* The Babylonian armies breached the walls of Jerusalem on March 16, 597 (v. 10), thus terminating Jehoiachin's brief reign, begun after Jehoiakim's death in December, 598. In short order, Nebuchadnezzar took Jehoiachin to Babylon as a royal hostage (v. 12); he pillaged but did not destroy the Temple and palace (v. 13), and deported, after the manner of the Assyrians (see comment on 17:6), many of Judah's influential citizens (vv. 14–16). **17.** *Mattaniah:* The third son of Josiah to reign as king of Judah, he received from Nebuchadnezzar the throne name Zedekiah (cf. 23:34) and reigned from 597 to 587, although for most Judeans, Jehoiachin remained the only legitimate king. Additional information about Zedekiah and his reign is given in Jer 21; 27–29; 32–34; 37–39.

78 **25:1.** *Zedekiah rebelled:* As early as 593, Zedekiah conspired against Nebuchadnezzar (cf. Jer 27). The Babylonian armies opened the siege of Jerusalem January 15, 588, and on July 29, 587, when the inhabitants had been starved into submission (vv. 2–4), they took the city. **4.** *fled by night:* Zedekiah's ignominious end—capture, execution of his sons before his eyes followed by the putting out of his eyes, and his removal to Babylon in chains (vv. 4–7)—was a punishment for rebellion, compounded by the breaking of a solemn oath to Nebuchadnezzar (cf. Ez 17:11–21). *king's garden:* According to Neh 3:15, the garden lay "close by the wall of the pool of Siloam." *Arabah:* The Jordan Valley is meant. **5.** Zedekiah was caught in the plain near Jericho attempting to escape across the Jordan. **8.** *Nebuzaradan:* He is mentioned in Jer 39:13–14; 41:10; 43:6; his title *rab ṭabbāḥîm* (lit., "chief of the executioners") is equivalent to "head of the king's bodyguard." His work of destruction, pillage, and execution (vv. 9–21) took place in the fifth month—i.e., August, one month after the fall of Jerusalem. The land was completely devastated and the population reduced to a mere 10,000 or 15,000 people (for this figure, see Albright *BP* 86–87). **18.** *second priest:* See comment on 22:4. **21.** *carried captive:* Some consider this statement the original end of Kgs (see M–G, *Kings*

564). **22.** *Gedaliah:* Son of Ahikam, the friend of Jeremiah (cf. Jer 26:24) and perhaps grandson of Shaphan, he was secretary of state to Josiah (cf. 22:12); as a seal found at Lachish testifies, he had been master of the place in Zedekiah's cabinet before his appointment as governor by Nebuchadnezzar.

23. *Mizpah:* (→ Religious Institutions, 76:51); perhaps chosen because Jerusalem was not habitable. **26.** *Egypt:* Cf. Jer 40:7–41:18. The third deportation in 582, mentioned in Jer 52:30, may have been in reprisal for Ishmael's murder of Gedaliah and the Babylonian troops, although it would seem from the text that this slaughter took place in October, 587 (v. 25). **27.** *thirty-seventh year:* Reckoned from 597, the year is 562, the year Evil-merodach (562–560), son and successor of Nebuchadnezzar, came to the throne of Babylon. Recently published documents from the archives of Nebuchadnezzar, dating to the year 592, mention by name Jehoiachin and five of his sons. The documents give the name as *Ya-u-kinu*, refer to him as "king of Judah" (*Ya-u-du*), and specify the rations given to him and his entourage, Inasmuch as the documents were found in the royal palace, it seems likely Jehoiachin lived there as royal hostage (see *ANET* 308; W. F. Albright, *BA* 4 [1942] 49–55). The Deuteronomist ends his history on an optimistic note. Although Evil-merodach did not restore to Jehoiachin his kingdom, he admitted him to court and treated him as royalty—a presage, as the author no doubt wished to intimate, of better things to come and an added reason for all faithful Israelites to hope for the eventual fulfillment of the oracle of Nathan.

79 With the ending of Kgs, a reconsideration of the so-called Earlier Prophets is in order. Martin Noth (*US* 3–110) was the first scholar to recognize in Dt 1:1–4:43, Jos, Jgs, Sm and Kgs a "Deuteronomic History," and his understanding of this corpus has become widely accepted. The compiler of this history was supposedly active about 550 BC. He joined separate and independent works—to the Earlier Prophets, Noth would also add Dt 4:44–30:20 as a subsequent addition to the history. He was more than an editor, he was truly an author who made definite selections, followed a definite plan, and inserted his own guide-lines. Thus, he unified seven centuries of Israelite history according to the point of view of the Book of Deuteronomy: When Israel was faithful to the Lord, she prospered; when she was unfaithful, she met her downfall (e.g., Dt 11:26–32; Jgs 2:11–23). This survey of Israel's history is not motivated by an interest in the national history, but by a didactic purpose. It explained the catastrophe of 587 in the light of the Lord's constant action in Israel's past; the warning and punishment, so many times repeated in former centuries, finally gave way to utter destruction. A secondary, but important, theme in the work is the emphasis on centralization of worship. The deuteronomic point of view recognized that disaster had stemmed from the worship on the "high places" associated with Canaanite fertility cults. Hence the opposition to these sanctuaries and to the "sin of Jeroboam" (the sanctuaries of the northern kingdom at Dan and Bethel). Only in the Jerusalem Temple, where the "Name" of the Lord dwells (Dt 12:5 and *passim*) is worship to be carried out. In 1–2 Kgs one can detect a sequence of events that is fixed by the Word of God (→ 4–6 above and the prophecy fulfillments indicated in the commentary). As Von Rad remarks, this attempt to understand Israel's history from the point of view of the Lord's Word gives the deuteronomic history a particular theological pre-eminence—history is to be understood in the light of his Word, judging, saving, fulfilling (*OT Theology I*, 344).

11

EXCURSUS: ISRAEL AND HER NEIGHBORS

Joseph Ignatius Hunt

BIBLIOGRAPHY

1 Albright, *FSAC*. Bright, *Hist*. De Vaux, *AI*. Finegan, J., *Light from the Ancient Past* (2nd ed.; Princeton, 1959). Frankfort, H., *et al.*, *The Intellectual Adventure of Ancient Man* (Chicago, 1949). Gadd, C. J., *PCB* 96–101. Gray, J., *PCB* 109–14. Moscati, S., *The Semites in Ancient History* (Cardiff, 1959). Pritchard, J., *Archaeology and the Old Testament* (Princeton, 1958). R-T 2, 147–86. Thacker, T. W., *PCB* 102–08.

In addition to the appropriate entries in *EDB*, *IDB*, and *RGG*, see the ten essays on "Cities and Lands of Israel's Neighbors" in *BAR* 2, 3–188.

2 OUTLINE

Major Peoples (§ 3–23)
- (I) Assyrians (§ 4–7)
- (II) Babylonians (§ 8–9)
- (III) Arameans (§ 10)
- (IV) Ugarit (§ 11–12)
- (V) Phoenicians (§ 13)
- (VI) Ammonites (§ 14)
- (VII) Edomites (§ 15–16)
- (VIII) Moabites (§ 17–18)
- (IX) Philistines (§ 19–20)
- (X) Egyptians (§ 21–23)

Some Lesser Peoples (§ 24–32)
- (I) The Hittites (§ 24)
- (II) The Jebusites (§ 25)
- (III) The Midianites (§ 26)
- (IV) The Amorites (§ 27)
- (V) The Amalekites (§ 28)
- (VI) The Kenites (§ 29)
- (VII) The Jerahmeelites (§ 30)
- (VIII) The People of the East (§ 31)
- (IX) The Medes (§ 32)

MAJOR PEOPLES

3 During the more than 600 years that separated the first steps of the conquest (*ca.* 1200 BC) from the fall of Jerusalem (587 or 586; cf. E. Auerbach, *VT* 11 [1961] 128–36, who retains the 586 date, and D. N. Freedman, *BANE* 212–13), Israel's contacts with her neighbors were constant and had much to do with her own history and with what limited national unity she was able to achieve (cf. Albright, *FSAC* 286). Canaanite tribes, invading peoples, and perilous relationships with major world powers vitally affected this entire span of her history, making an orderly summary difficult. We are going to consider these "neighbors" both in themselves and especially in their relationship to Israel.

When the Israelites entered Canaan from Transjordan there is no positive proof that they had allies waiting for them there. According to Jgs 1:16, the Kenites "went up from the City of Palms with the sons of Judah...," but this is in a later and uncertain context; the help of these nomadic smiths would have been limited. There are other possibilities, however. Gn 50:7–14, even allowing for hyperbole, shows that relations with Canaan had not been broken off completely during the sparsely documented period of the Egyptian sojourn. Leaving aside certain names known from Gn 12–50 that possibly occur in Egyptian annals as being at that time represented in Canaan (e.g., Jacob-El; Joseph-El; Simeon; and Asaru

[Asher]; cf. A. Gelin, *Josué* [*PSB* 3, 2nd ed.;] 16–17), there is the possibility that certain groups related to the Israelites had never gone down to Egypt with the family of Jacob, and that these groups became the allies of the Israelites at some time during the Conquest. The events described in Jos 8:30–35 and 24:1–28 may serve as indirect indications along this line (cf. R. de Vaux, "Israel," *VDBS* 4, 738). Others have thought of an earlier and partial exodus from Egypt by some Israelites that would have put them in Canaan before the arrival of the main group (for discussion on this point, cf. R. North, *AER* 134 [1956] 161–82).

Trade routes as well as armies passed through Canaan, a factor that only aggravated the task that lay before Israel. "An impartial observer of the early twelfth century B.C.E. would probably have said that everything was against the success of the Israelite experiment" (Albright, *BP* 17). The broken terrain of the land promoted separatism among both the invading Israelites and the many different tribes already dwelling in Canaan. The walled cities of Bronze and Iron Age Canaan were not only amazingly small (cf. De Vaux, *AI* 66) but also largely independent of one another; they are often classified as city-states, each with its king (cf. the list in Jos 12:9–24) and separate interests. (For the study of one such city-state, cf. A. Alt, *KlSchr* 3, 258–302; *KlSchr* 2, 1–2.) Temporary and often loose federations were formed where provocation demanded such a step, as in the case of the "Amorite" coalition formed to punish the Gibeonites for their surrender to Israel (Jos 10:1–2). It is likely, too, that some such relationships were formed among the Canaanite cities because of various central shrines (thus giving rise to a number of amphictyonies). Nevertheless, we should not forget that when Joshua brought the Israelites across the Jordan he was faced with nothing resembling a unified opposition, but rather with almost innumerable small city-states, most of which had to be taken one at a time, as is described with regard to Jericho and Ai, using ruse or surprise attack because the Israelite army was not well equipped. The more powerful walled cities had simply to be reserved for a later time.

The city was something quite foreign to the Israelites arriving from the desert. "When they encountered it, they usually found it to be their enemy. In fact, at the time of the Conquest, it appeared as the very embodiment of hostility and resistance; the cities of Canaan were so many hateful obstacles, to be overrun and destroyed if possible" (R. A. F. MacKenzie, *CBQ* 25 [1963] 61). When we meet Canaanite tribal listings (e.g., Ex 13:5; Jos 3:10), we should not be deflected from the realization that city-states predominated in Canaan; these city-states have much to do with Israel's history, especially those whose cultural influence was greatest and who were able to resist absorption or conquest by the Israelites for longer periods of time.

In our period, Israel had important contacts with many neighbors, even if some of these neighbors were proportionately small and the contacts were of short duration. The subject is complicated. Biblical data is at times discordant on details; in addition, considerable information from outside the Bible is available, some of which is reliable and some not. To work all these data into a chronological and accurate account is difficult, even if the margin for error is decreasing as the evidence is increased and weighed. The method we follow here, i.e., considering one neighbor at a time, has both advantages and disadvantages. It is less confusing to both writer and reader, but it necessitates a certain amount of repetition. Leaving the smallest groups aside for treatment toward the close of this study, we take up Israel's larger and more persistent neighbors during the period from the Conquest to the Captivity: Assyria; Babylonia; the Arameans; Ugarit (for its religious influence); Phoenicians; Ammon; Edom; Moab; Philistines; and Egypt.

4 **(I) Assyrians.** The history of the Assyrian Empire between the Conquest and the Exile must be split, as far as the historian is concerned, at about 883, for, before this date, the sources are scattered and of doubtful value. We enter Assyrian history just after the Middle Assyrian Kingdom (15th–13th cent.), a period of power and influence. At the time when the Israelite Conquest was getting under way, Assyria and the Hittites had worn one another down through a long series of battles. By this time, Mitanni had ceased to be a buffer state. Under Ashurreshishi I (*ca.* 1150–15) and Tiglath-pileser I (*ca.* 1114–1076), Assyria grew somewhat stronger. Extant are several inscriptions of the latter ruler (cf. *ANET* 274–75), whose name in Akkadian was *Tukulti-apil-esharra*, i.e. "My reliance is the son of Esharra." The "son of Esharra" is none other than the god Asshur, whose temple in the city of Asshur was called (in Sumerian) *e-šar-ra*, i.e., "house of the universe" (cf. *EDB* 2432). This monarch attempted to gain control of both Syria and Lebanon and actually received tribute from Byblos, Sidon, and Arvad; he held Babylonia in check, but did not violate the temple of Marduk in any way. He did much for agricultural advancement and took a lively, patronal interest in Babylonian literature, but his kingdom was being undermined for the Arameans were infiltrating these regions slowly and steadily. He transferred the capital from Asshur to Nineveh. His name does not occur in the Bible.

Under Ashurdan II (*ca.* 932–911), Assyria's economy and military organization underwent a revamping that was to contribute to a great upsurge in the history of the country. The high point in Assyrian power was achieved during the New Assyrian Empire (*ca.* 912–609). At this time all Mesopotamia and Syria, the eastern regions of Asia Minor, and finally Egypt were brought (for a time) under Assyrian domination. Assyria employed a deportation system against her conquered enemies that involved the transfer and resettlement of vast numbers of people, at times whole nations, with the Assyrians in turn establishing settlements in regions vacated by captives (cf. 2 Kgs 17:24–25). The handling of enemies was generally brutal and heartless. This huge empire was administered through a provincial system, which later empires would imitate partially.

Some of the rulers who especially advanced the Assyrian Empire follow. Adad-nirari II (*ca.* 912–890) conquered Babylonia and some of the Arameans. Tikulti-ninurta II (*ca.* 890–883) acquired some of Armenia for Assyria. Ashurnasirpal II (*ca.* 883–859) left numerous inscriptions telling of his campaigns at Carchemish and in Lebanon (cf. *ANET* 275–76) and of his expedition as far as the Mediterranean ("I cleaned my weapons in the deep sea..."). He expanded his kingdom to the north, northeast, and west and moved the capital from Nineveh to Nimrud (i.e., Calah). Shalmaneser III (*ca.* 858–824), one of the really great conquerors of ancient times, inherited a kingdom on the ascendant and made an expedition toward the west almost every year. He was not a mere plunderer, but a man with a master-plan, and is the first Assyrian monarch known to have come into contact with Israel. During his first and seemingly inconclusive engagement with the Syrian coalition army at Qarqar in 853, Ahab of Israel (*ca.* 869–850) was among his adversaries. (For details on this battle and the possibilities of a coalition victory over Assyria, cf. W. H. Hallo, "From Qarqar to Carchemish: Assyria and Israel in the Light of New Discoveries," *BA* 23 [1960] 40–41.) In 841, when he laid siege to Damascus, then under the rule of Hazael,

Jehu (*Ia-ú-a*, in Assyrian records [*ca.* 842–815]) sent him tribute (cf. *ANET* 276–81), but Damascus was not taken. On the Black Obelisk of Shalmaneser III (found at Nimrud in 1846 and now on display at the British Museum), in the second row of engravings (cf. *ANEP* 351–55), is shown "Jehu, son of Omri," kneeling abjectly before Shalmaneser, along with a list of his valuable tribute-gifts. Nothing of these events is found in the Bible and it is highly probable that Shalmaneser's facts and figures are tailored in such a way as to exalt his glory. His reign ended disastrously, for civil revolts of alarming proportion broke out and practically nullified his western conquests. His son and successor, Shamshi-Adad V (*ca.* 824–810) quelled the revolt in his second year, but had to acknowledge Babylonian overlordship to do it. This same monarch fought the Armenians, where the new kingdom of Urartu (OT Ararat) had been founded. He also threw off the Babylonian yoke, but could not recover the territory in the west. Shamshi-Adad V died prematurely and his wife Sammuramat (i.e., the famed Semiramis of Greek legend) functioned as regent for her son Adad-nirari III.

5 This new monarch (*ca.* 810–783) fought against Syria and "Paleshtu" (the first mention of the Philistine territory in the Assyrian records), and received tribute from, among others, *māt Ḫu-um-ri* (the land of Omri), i.e., Israel (long after Omri's death, *ca.* 869). Assyria at times identified Israel with his name (cf. *ANET* 281). From the death of Adad-nirari III until the rise of Tiglath-pileser III (*ca.* 744–727), Assyrian power declined considerably, and there is evidence that before Adad-nirari died his sovereignty was not so great or as sure as his annals claim (cf. Hallo, *op. cit.*, 43). There was even a rebellion against the priests and nobles who had great power. During at least four fighting seasons the Assyrian army remained home (768, 764, 757, and 756) and there were plagues in 765 and 759 (cf. Hallo, *op. cit.*, 44). This time of weakness in Assyria, as well as among the Arameans and in Urartu, gave both Judah (2 Chr 26:1–15) and Israel (2 Kgs 14:25,28) the opportunity to expand. Yet Amos saw that such a condition was not to last (1–2; 6:14) and the northern kingdom began to fall apart as soon as the powerful Jeroboam II died (*ca.* 753).

With the advent of Tiglath-pileser III, however, who proved to be most vigorous, Assyrian domination and internal order were soon restored to full force. He reorganized and divided the unwieldy provinces. He bolstered the economy and revitalized the army. He undertook numerous military campaigns, reconquering Babylonia and Syria along the way and driving Urartu out of the latter country. It was this great monarch who combined the Assyrian and Babylonian thrones, taking the name Pul as king of Babylon (cf. 2 Kgs 15:19,29; 1 Chr 5:26, where his two names are used with obvious inconsistency, especially in 1 Chr 5:26 where the reader would be led to think of two distinct rulers). He received tribute from Ahaz (*Ia-ú-ḫa-zi*, in cuneiform, [*ca.* 735–715]), king of Judah, and from Menahem (*Me-ni-ḫi-im-me* [*ca.* 745–738 BC]), king of Israel. His texts also mention the overthrow of *Pa-qa-ḫa* (Pekah, king of Israel [*ca.* 737–732]) and his installation of *A-ú-si'* (Hoshea [*ca.* 732–724], the last of the northern kings) on the throne of Israel (cf. *ANET* 284; 2 Kgs 15:29–30). At the probable bidding of Ahaz of Judah (2 Kgs 16:10–11), he took most of Israel's territory away from her (the provinces of Megiddo and Gilead, cf. Alt, *KlSchr* 2, 150–62). It was at this time that Hazor was destroyed (cf. Y. Yadin, *BA* 20 [1957] 34–37). A perusal of Tiglath-pileser III's annals (cf. *ANET* 282–84) shows many biblical contacts, e.g., Ammon, Moab, Ashkelon, Jehoahaz of Judah, Edom, Gaza, *rabshaq* (e.g., 2 Kgs 18:17), Rezin of Damascus, Hiram of Tyre, etc.

6 The son and successor of Tiglath-pileser III was Shalmaneser V (*ca.* 727–722), who took Shechem (cf. L. E. Toombs, *BA* 20 [1957] 99) and laid siege against both Tyre and Samaria (cf. 2 Kgs 17:3–6; 18:9–10). The biblical text attributes the fall of Samaria to Shalmaneser after a siege of two or three years. This is probably correct, although in various Assyrian inscriptions Sargon II (*ca.* 721–705), who set up a new Assyrian Dynasty, claims the honors for himself (cf. *ANET* 284–85); Samaria fell at the beginning of the first year of Sargon's reign, but before the death of Shalmaneser V and before he had really taken over the throne (cf. Hallo, *op. cit.*, 51, for an interesting discussion on this matter).

It was under this Sargon (who built a new capital at Dur-Sharr-ukin, i.e., Khorsabad) and his immediate successors, Sennacherib (*ca.* 704–681), Esarhaddon (*ca.* 680–669), and Ashurbanipal (*ca.* 668–627), that the Assyrian Empire reached its greatest expansion (cf. *ANET* 284–301, for a large array of texts referring to their accomplishments). Sargon was faced with a rebellion in Babylonia led by Merodach-baladan II, who was not put down for about a decade. He fought Humbanigas of Elam and Merodach-baladan II at Der, a battle that is triply documented, each major participant giving an account divergent from the other two (cf. R. Follet, *Bib* 35 [1954] 413–28, referring to the Warka discovery). Sargon had better success in his western battles, at Hamath, Ekron, Gibbethon, Gaza, a victory over Egypt with resulting tribute, and the completion of Tyre's defeat. In *ca.* 712, Sargon made a third campaign in the west, but this time through his *turtanu* (commander-in-chief), in agreement with the information of Is 20:1 (referring to the Assyrian *tartan* at Ashdod).

In Akkadian, Sennacherib is written *Sin-aḫḫe-eriba*, meaning "Sin [the moon-god] has compensated me for [the loss of my] brothers" (cf. *EDB* 2163–64). In *ca.* 689, he destroyed Babylon completely, which was regarded even by the Assyrians as a sacrilegious act. Yet in 24 years of rule, Sennacherib undertook no more than eight military ventures, the third of which was his campaign against Phoenicia, Philistia, and Judah, generally dated, as far as Jerusalem is concerned, at 701, during the reign of Hezekiah (*ca.* 715–687). It is remarkable that in this instance we have accounts both in the OT (2 Kgs 18:13–19:36; 2 Chr 32:1–22; Is 36:1–37:37) and the Assyrian annals (cf. *ANET* 287–88). However, mainly for chronological reasons, many scholars believe that Sennacherib made two different attacks on Jerusalem, the first in 701 (represented in 2 Kgs 18:14–16 and not paralleled in 1 Chr or Is), and another *ca.* 689–688, when Tirhakah, king of Egypt, would have reached sufficient age to lead the Egyptian army against the Assyrians (cf. 2 Kgs 19:9). (For more details cf. D. D. Luckenbill, *The Annals of Sennacherib* [Chicago, 1924]; *EDB* 2164; Bright, *Hist.* 282–87; and W. F. Albright, *BASOR* 130 [1953] 8–11; *BASOR* 141 [1956] 25–26; and *JQR* 24 [1934] 370–71.) The reigns of Sennacherib and his two successors were peaceful when we compare them to those of other Assyrian monarchs. Sennacherib transferred his capital from Khorsabad back to Nineveh because of strained relations with his father, Sargon II. Sennacherib was murdered in 681 by his older son(s) because he had appointed a younger son as his successor (cf. 2 Kgs 19:37; 1 Chr 32:21; Is 37:38; *ANET* 288). Manasseh, who reigned in Judah for 55 years (*ca.* 696–642), did not revolt when Sennacherib died. He was noted for his loyalty to Assyria, a fact which may have much to do with his unusually long reign (→ History of Israel, 75:82–83).

7 Esarhaddon (Akkadian *ashshur-aḫa-iddina*, "Asshur [the god] has given a brother"; *ca.* 681–669) is linked in Ezr 4:2 to a deportation otherwise unknown.

He received tribute from Manasseh, king of Judah (cf. *ANET* 291). He rebuilt Babylon, kept the warlike Cimmerians out of Assyria, and in *ca.* 677 destroyed Sidon. Some three years before he died he proclaimed Ashurbanipal heir to his throne. To give this decree the greatest force and solemnity and to avoid the murderous contention that marked the beginnings of his own reign (2 Kgs 19:36–37), he had several important people swear to and attest his decree. Esarhaddon even summoned nine princes of Media and imposed on them a pact of faithfulness to his chosen successor (for documentation and details of this unusual procedure, cf. E. Vogt, *Bib* [1958] 541–43).

Ashurbanipal, although unmentioned in the Bible, left an immense library of some 22,000 clay tablets at Nineveh—the main source of information on ancient Mesopotamia. One of his last accomplishments was the conquest (*ca.* 639) of Iran (Persia), which had joined with his brother in an uprising against him (*ca.* 652) and had revolted again (*ca.* 641). Amon of Judah (*ca.* 642–640) continued the pro-Assyrian policy of his father (cf. 2 Kgs 21:20–21; 2 Chr 33:22), and his assassination is probably connected with a general unrest and marks an anti-Assyrian move (cf. A. Malamat, *IsrEJ* [1953] 26–29; and, for a differing view, W. F. Albright, *JBL* 61 [1942] 119; and in *The Jews* [ed. L. Finkelstein; N.Y., 1949] 44). Ashurbanipal quickly moved in to crush this revolt in 640. Ezr 4:9–10, with its reference to Elamites brought in by "Osnappar," may refer to this period. In 2 Kgs 21:24 and 2 Chr 33:25 is described the desperation of the "people of the land" as the forces of Ashurbanipal moved in, for they killed those who had conspired against Amon and put Josiah on the throne—a gesture of submission to Assyria.

Evidence of Assyria's decline was already visible when Pharaoh Psammetichus I (*ca.* 663–609) was able to drive Ashurbanipal's army out of Egypt—an event causing some of the unrest that we have seen in the western and Babylonian sectors of the Assyrian Empire. With the death of this great Assyrian monarch, disintegration set in rapidly throughout the kingdom. At this time, Josiah of Judah showed himself quite anti-Assyrian, reclaiming Assyria's provinces of Samaria, Gilead, and Galilee, and extending his reform into these areas (cf. F. Cross and D. Freedman, *JNES* 12 [1953] 56–58; and 2 Chr 34:3–7). The last four Assyrian kings were all too weak to oppose Josiah.

When Nabopolassar, a Chaldean, took Babylon and then joined hands with Cyaxares the Mede, they easily captured Asshur in 614 and Nineveh, Nimrud, and Khorsabad in 612. Ashur-uballit II (*ca.* 612–609), the last Assyrian monarch, ruled over a very small area surrounding Haran, the city serving as his capital. Pharaoh Neco II (*ca.* 609–594) had wished to help Ashur-uballit, but when Nabopolassar defeated the Egyptian army at Carchemish in 605, Assyria was wiped out forever, and all its former domains were taken over by the Neo-Babylonian (Chaldean) Empire.

Assyrian culture is largely associated with Babylonian culture, and most Assyrian monarchs wrote in Babylonian. Ashurbanipal's library consisted predominantly in Babylonian literature, and yet many of these works were apparently composed by Assyrians; however, Assyria made fine cultural contributions, especially from the time of Ashurbanipal, in building and art. In this field she far surpassed Babylonia and the Hittites.

Assyria's fall was a heavy impact to the Near East, reflected in Zeph 2:13–15 (Asshur) and Na 1:11,14; 2:1–3:19. Only Egypt remained loyal to Assyria, and that may have been an interested loyalty. With no source of income (plunder!), and no irrigation director to maintain the vital water systems for fields and cities, Assyria reverted to a primitive stage of civilization such as she had not known for some 2000 years.

(Hallo, *op. cit.*, 34–61; = *BAR* 2, 152–88. Hooke, S. H., *Babylonian and Assyrian Religion* [Norman, Okla., 1963].)

8 **(II) Babylonians.** Babylonia, at times called Shinar in the Bible (cf. Gn 10:10; 11:2; 14:1,9; Dn 1:2; etc.), refers properly to lower Mesopotamia, a rather small area of about 10,000 sq. mi. originally. It was noted for its fertile soil and its many canals. Its population was partly Semitic (Akkadian, in the North), and partly Asian (Sumerian, in the South), and its culture was rich, with many stages of development. The ancient capital, Babel, lies about 60 mi. S of the modern city of Baghdad, and the land included many famous cities: Ur, Uruk (Warka or Erech), Larsa, Nippur, Lagash, Kish, Borsippa, Sippar, Eshnunna, etc. Babylonia included all the area between the Tigris and Euphrates, where the rivers are 50 mi. or less apart, and the Persian Gulf. According to Gadd, (*op. cit.*, 96), this territory was "the focus of all the ancient civilizations that flourished in Western Asia from the beginning of history up to and beyond the intrusion of Greek influence in the 5th cent. BC."

By 1170, the 24th (Kassite) Dynasty had come to an end and there followed a period of confusion. Babylonia and Assyria were closely connected in history at this time. From around 1100, Babylonia was invaded by successive waves of a Semitic people, the Arameans, who gradually gave back to Babylonia something of its old power. However, there was a long period when native leaders (Chaldeans) would seize the throne, normally held by Assyrians. One of these, called Merodach-baladan (II) in the Bible (cf. Is 39:1–2; 2 Kgs 20:12–13; lit. *Marduk-apla-idinna*, "Marduk has given me a son), seized the Babylonian throne in 721 (when Shalmaneser V of Assyria died) and held it until 710 when Sargon II of Assyria forced him to take flight. The same Merodach-baladan II regained the rule of Babylonia for some nine months in *ca.* 704–703 when Sennacherib came to the Assyrian throne (*ca.* 704). It was probably before 701, when Sennacherib besieged Jerusalem, that Merodach-baladan sent an embassy to King Hezekiah ostensibly to interest him in an anti-Assyrian league (cf. 2 Kgs 20:12–13; 2 Chr 32:31; Is 39:1–2) (→ History of Israel, 75:11).

9 The Neo-Babylonian (Chaldean) Empire lasted *ca.* 626–539. Nabopolassar (Akkadian *Nabû-apal-uṣur*, "O Nabu [a god], protect the heir!") was the founder of the 31st Babylonian Dynasty and ruled from *ca.* 626 until 605. He was the first Chaldean king to regain the absolute independence of Babylonia. His action was facilitated by the internal strife of Assyria at that time. Nabopolassar was descended from Merodach-baladan and became a ruler of great power and influence. Not content with the recovery of Babylonian independence, he combined his forces with those of Cyaxares, king of Media, and in 612 took Nineveh. Haran, the last Assyrian outpost, fell in 609. Cyaxares was apparently a much better military leader than Nabopolassar. By the time Carchemish was fought in 605, Nabopolassar had withdrawn from battle and had died in Babylon. It was Nebuchadnezzar II (Akkadian *Nabu-kudur-uṣur*, "O Nabu, protect the stone"; cf. *EDB* 1595 for remarks on the most justifiable Eng spelling of this name), ruler from *ca.* 605–562, who roundly defeated Pharaoh Neco at Carchemish. This most famous king of the Neo-Babylonian Empire continued the extensive building projects that Nabopolassar had begun. The latter is not mentioned in the Bible, but he may have been on good terms with Josiah of Judah (*ca.* 640–609), who lost his life at Megiddo trying to turn Pharaoh Neco from going to the aid of the Assyrians (cf. 2 Kgs 23:29) and perhaps intending at the same time to share in the spoils of the Assyrian kingdom that he knew would fall.

Nebuchadnezzar has become better known in recent years through the imperfectly preserved Babylonian Chronicle (cf. D. J. Wiseman, *Chronicles of Chaldaean Kings, 626–556 B.C.*, [London, 1956]), where details not given either in the Bible or Josephus are provided. Some chronological problems, especially, have been cleared up. Nebuchadnezzar helped Babylonia reach its height of power and material culture. After Carchemish (605), he gained control of all Syria and Palestine; Jer 46:2–6 speaks of this victory over the Egyptians. In the same year, he defeated the Egyptian army even more severely at Hamath, putting all Syria at the same time at his mercy. When Nabopolassar died, September 7, 605, Nebuchadnezzar interrupted his military ventures just long enough to go to Babylon for his coronation; he then continued his victorious march through Syria. This march, interrupted once more in April, 604, for New Year's Day celebrations at Babylon, took him into Palestine where he conquered Ashkelon and parts of Judah. Late in 601 he invaded Egypt where a hard but inconclusive battle was fought. As a result, he took his exhausted army home for most of the year 600, while it was refurbished and made ready for new enterprises. It was at this time that Jehoiakim of Judah (609–598), after three years of servitude to Nebuchadnezzar, imprudently rebelled against the Babylonians, who now had Syria, Moab, and Ammon as their allies and who could use them as tools against Jehoiakim if necessary (cf. 2 Kgs 24:1–2). In the winter of 598–597, after victories in northern Arabia, Nebuchadnezzar personally led his army against Jerusalem. As this siege was beginning, Jehoiakim died (December, 598) and his son Jehoiachin (598–597) succeeded him. In mid-March, 597, the city fell to Nebuchadnezzar. Jehoiachin, the nobles, and other residents were deported to Babylon. These events are recounted in 2 Kgs 24:6–15; 2 Chr 36:9–10; Jehoiachin is spoken of in Jer 22:24–30; 24:1; 27:20; etc. Jehoiachin was given freedom in the thirty-seventh year of his captivity in Babylon (560) by Evil-merodach (cf. 2 Kgs 25:28; Jer 52:31), but he died and was buried in Babylon (cf. W. F. Albright, *BA* 5 [1942] 49–55). (→ History of Israel, 75:86.)

The Babylonians placed on the throne as puppet-king the brother of Jehoiakim, Zedekiah, who became Judah's last king (597–587). He ruled precariously and ineffectually until, against the express wishes of Jeremiah, he yielded to the suggestions of the pro-Egyptian party in Judah and attempted to overthrow the Babylonian domination. In mid-January of 588, Nebuchadnezzar began his second siege of Jerusalem and took it by the end of July, 587 (cf. 2 Kgs 25:1–2; 2 Chr 36:13–14; Jer 39:1–7). He almost completely destroyed the city, deporting most of the upper-class citizens of Judah to Babylonia. Zedekiah attempted flight, but was captured and taken to Riblah in Syria where he first had to witness the slaughter of his sons and then had his eyes put out, was chained, and taken to Babylon (Jer 52:7–11). As our period closes, we leave Babylonia at the apogee of its power and splendor, with the Israelites thoroughly humbled by its might.

For an account of the religious practices of the Assyrians and Babylonians, and their influences on society as well as their points of contact with Hebrew religion, see Hooke (*op. cit.*).

(Plessis, J., "Babylone et la Bible," *VDBS* 1 [1928] 713–852. Vogt, E., "Etymologia Nominis Babel," *Bib* 37 [1956] 130.)

10 **(III) Arameans.** The Arameans were a large, but loosely related group of Aramaic-speaking Semites. They were known already in the 14th cent. BC as the Ahlamu (nomads?). The Chaldeans were but one branch of this group. The Arameans came from the Syro-Arabian desert in waves, sweeping over northern Mesopotamia, the Anatolian foothills, and inner Syria. Albright associates their influx with the domestication of the camel, a postulate that certainly accounts for their surprising mobility. There may be much more to their obscure background, however, for Aramean movements antedate any mention of camels in the Assyrian texts by some three centuries. Consolidation gradually took place with independent states resulting. Am 9:7 speaks of their homeland as Kir, the location of which has never been determined.

As already indicated, the Arameans were never politically united as an empire or even as one state, but they did become geographically concentrated. Assyrian inscriptions from the 12th and 11th cents. refer to their building cities and even founding the state known as Bit-Adini (Am 1:5?) on both sides of the Euphrates, S of Carchemish. Tiglath-pileser I (*ca.* 1114–1076) claims to have fought the Ahlamu peoples and the Arameans 28 times, listing only victories over them (*ANET* 275).

By 1000 BC a number of Aramean states had been set up in northern Mesopotamia and even E of the Tigris; an Aramean usurper, Adad-apal-iddin (*ca.* 1070–49) reigned over Babylon and gave his daughter in marriage to the king of Assyria. As a result of merging with Hittite groups in northern Syria, the Arameans founded such city-states as Arpad and Ya'di (also called Samal), the capital of the latter being Zinjirli. Hamath on the Orontes was also an Aramean state. A cultural break around 1000, clearly indicated by archaeological evidence, points to some phase in Aramean settlement. Aramaic spread rapidly; by the 8th cent., Aram notations began to appear on Babylonian contracts (→ Texts, 69:80).

Aramean states attested to in the OT follow. First is Aram-zobah, the region E of the Antilebanon, N of Damascus, as well as a part of the Beqa' (between the Antilebanon and Lebanon ranges). The king of this state, Hadadezer, was defeated by David (first skirmish is mentioned in 2 Sm 10:6–19 [= 1 Chr 19:6–19], second in 2 Sm 8:3–8 [= 1 Chr 18:3–8]) and forced to pay a large tribute in copper (or bronze). Saul's fight with, and perhaps victory over, Zobah is referred to in 1 Sm 14:47.

Second is Aram-beth-rehob, a region in southern Syria including territory near the source of the Jordan (cf. Jgs 18:28) and probably the southern part of the Biqa' (Nm 13:21). This small state (not to be confused with the Canaanite Rehob in Asher) was allied with Aram-zobah and was defeated together with it by David (2 Sm 10:6–7).

Third is Aram-[beth-]maacah, a region S of Aram-beth-rehob, situated in the upper Jordan Valley and probably including the city of Abel-beth-maacah. This state, belonging to the Aramean federation (insofar as this existed), was conquered by David (2 Sm 10:6–7 [= 1 Chr 19:6–7]).

Fourth is Geshur, a territory E of Maacah, between Bashan and Mt. Hermon (i.e., in the Hauran; cf. Dt 3:14; Jos 12:5); it was inhabited by the Aramean tribe called the Geshurites. The region withstood Joshua (Jos 13:13; although 1 Chr 2:23 seems to represent an entirely different tradition). David made an alliance with Talmai, king of Geshur, marrying his daughter Maacah, who bore him Absalom (2 Sm 3:3). While in exile, Absalom stayed with his grandfather, King Talmai (2 Sm 13:37–38; 15:8). There is another Geshur in southern Philistia (referred to in Jos 13:2; 1 Sm 27:8).

Fifth and last is Aram-Damascus (2 Sm 8:5–6), originally a small region around Damascus but later including most of southern Syria with the exception of the Phoenician coast. David conquered this state (2 Sm 8:5–8), but by the time the reign of Solomon had ended it had regained its independence (cf. 1 Kgs 11:23–24).

Damascus emerged more and more as the head of the Aramean peoples, especially after David had conquered the other Aramean states. During the reigns of Baasha of Israel (*ca.* 911–888) and Asa of Judah (*ca.* 913–873), the Damascus Arameans allied themselves first to Israel and then to Judah (cf. 1 Kgs 15:16–22). In 853 (at Qarqar), 849, 848, and 845, Damascus was able to hold off the Assyrians. When Ben-hadad died and Hazael usurped the throne (2 Kgs 8:7–8), the Assyrians attacked the city (841 and 837) and could not capture it. When they withdrew, Hazael strengthened his position and subjected both Israel and Judah to tribute (cf. 2 Kgs 12:17–18; 13:3; Am 1:4). Between 806 and 803, Adad-nirari III came across the Euphrates, laid siege to Damascus, and removed considerable booty (cf. *DOTT* 50–52). Jehoash of Israel (*ca.* 798–783) shook off the Syrian yoke and Jeroboam II of Israel (*ca.* 783–743) won back the territory that Syria had taken (2 Kgs 13:25; 14:25). Damascus, however, could not withstand the heavy attacks launched by Tiglath-pileser III and completed by Shalmaneser V and Sargon II. Thus, in 732, this great Aramean stronghold fell to the Assyrians after trying to force Judah to become its ally against the Assyrians (cf. Is 7:3–4; 2 Kgs 16:1–2).

(Dupont-Sommer, A., *Les Araméens* [Paris, 1949]; VTSup 1 [1953] 40–49. Jepsen, A., "Israel und Damaskus," *AfO* 14 [1944] 153–72. McNamara, M., "De populi Aramaeorum primordiis," *VD* 35 [1957] 128–42. Noth, M., "Die Aramäer," *BBLAK* 68 [1949] 19–36. O'Callaghan, R. T., *Aram Naharaim* [Rome, 1948].)

11 **(IV) Ugarit.** Although it is unmentioned in the Bible, Ugarit (Ras Shamra) was the most important city on the Phoenician coast from roughly 2000 to 1200 BC, at which time it was completely destroyed by the Philistines. Its vast literature has come to light only since 1929. Hundreds of clay tablets have been uncovered, many of which still await decipherment and publication. They date for the most part from the 15th to the 14th cent. and are written generally in an alphabetical cuneiform proper to Ugarit.

The population of Ugarit was basically Canaanite, yet it was a truly cosmopolitan city, standing at the crossroads of the ancient world. Because its contacts with Israel were only through ideas, principally religious, that had passed into Canaanite culture by the time the Israelites entered Canaan (at about the same time that Ugarit fell before the Philistines), our remarks will be confined to religion.

Ugaritic documents thus far published include several religious-mythological accounts. The Baal Epic is the most extensive of the myths found at Ugarit, but it is so fragmentary that a reliable reordering of the tablets is hard to achieve and it is not always certain that they belong together. The story concerns the conflict of the fertility god Baal, helped by his sister Anat, against the sea-god Yamm and the death-god Mot. Baal conquers Yamm and restricts him to the sea, his proper abode, with the result that Baal is able to build a palace on the mountain of the supreme god El, the father of the gods (not to be regarded, however, as an expression of monotheism). Baal is then slain by Mot, who kills all vegetation. Anat laments over Baal and forces Mot to restore Baal to life for half of each year (cf. *ANET* 129–42).

In the legend of King Keret, another myth, Keret loses his wife and children during some calamity. He then leads his army against King Pabal of Udum (not Edom), forcing Pabal to give up his daughter Harriya in marriage. They have many children for El has blessed the union. As an old man Keret becomes sick, but through the prayers of one of his daughters El restores his health. The fragmentary story ends wth one of his sons rebelling against him on the ground that he has not judged his people justly. The legend may have an historical kernel (cf. *ANET*, 142–49).

The story of Aqhat, son of Danel, is a third myth. As a gift from the gods, Danel and his wife Danatiya receive a son, Aqhat. Later the gods give Danel a bow, which he in turn gives to Aqhat, but the war-goddess Anat wants the bow and gets it by slaying Aqhat. Paghat, Aqhat's sister, learns how her brother was slain. Although the rest of the story is lost (at least so far), it may well terminate in keeping with the Tammuz-Adonis theme, i.e., Aqhat would be restored to life for half of each year (cf. *ANET* 149–55).

12 From the Ugaritic texts the dominant place of El in the Canaanite pantheon is clear. This same name is used in the OT in the sense of "God" (general meaning) and refers to Yahweh (cf. M. H. Pope, *El in the Ugaritic Texts* [Leiden, 1955]). On one stele found at Ras Shamra, El is depicted as seated upon a throne with the Ugaritic king making an offering before him (cf. *ANEP* 168, 493). Here the god is represented as advanced in years, fatherly, and full of majesty. El's consort was Asherah of the Sea, the counselor of the gods. Baal (or Aliyan Baal), their son, was the god of rain, storms, and consequently of the vegetation resulting from the proper moisture. He is depicted on one stela holding a mace aloft with his right hand and a kind of thunderbolt with spear head (pointed downward in his left hand (cf. *ANEP* 168, 490). One of his titles is "Zabul [Prince], Lord of the earth," a reminiscence of which is found in 2 Kgs 1:2 and in the Beelzebul of the NT (e.g., Mk 3:22). The names Baal and Asherah both figure prominently in the OT where Canaanite religious practices are brought up. Just as they are mentioned together in such places as 1 Kgs 18:19 and 2 Kgs 23:4, so their names often occur in the same context in the Ugaritic texts, where Baal often proves a rival for first rank among the gods with El who is "old and more or less retired" (cf. R. Lack, *CBQ* 24 [1962] 48).

The mythological "Leviathan" (cf. Jb 3:8; 41:1; Pss 74:14; 104:26; Is 27:1 [cf. Jb 26:12–13]) is clarified through the Ugaritic *L-t-n* (usually vocalized Lotan), with whom Baal comes into conflict, and who is described in the Baal Epic (cf. *ANET* 138) in terms precisely the same as those found in Is 27:1 ("...the nimble serpent... the sinuous serpent, the mighty one with seven heads"; for the latter phrase, cf. Ps 74:14).

The figure spoken of in Ez 14:14,20; 28:3 is not Daniel, but the same as Dan'el (or Dan'il) of the Ugaritic Aqhat story, a wise judge of widows and orphans (*ANET* 149–55). The author of the canonical Book of Daniel may have known about him through Ezekiel and used him as background for the hero. Is 14:12–13, where the king of Babylon (perhaps originally of Assyria) attempts to scale the heavens and set up his throne on "the Mount of Assembly in the recesses of the North" (cf. Ez 28:14; Ps 48:2), is remarkably paralleled in the Ugaritic texts—even the expressions "morning star" and "son of the dawn" (cf. E. Jacob, *Ras Shamra et l'Ancien Testament* [Neuchâtel, 1960] 104–105). This adaptation is assuredly of the ancient and widespread myth where a lesser deity—here the morning star (*hêlēl*) aspires to make himself the chief god, but is thrown to the earth in the attempt.

The religion of the Phoenicians (at least at Ugarit) was centered around Baal, the main concern being the predisposition of providence as affecting nature. Baal promotes order and wards off chaos by disposing of the waters in orderly fashion. This notion, linked to the kingship of Yahweh and duly adapted in the canonical books, seems to find reminiscences in some psalms, e.g., Ps 93. The Ugaritic texts use sacrificial terminology regarding worship, speaking of sacrificial animals in a way that externally resembles the OT language of worship. Ugarit knew of the feast of the first sheaves of the grain harvest, like that described in Lv 23:10. The unusual prohibition recorded in Ex 23:19; 34:26; Dt 14:21 not to boil a kid in its mother's milk—the basis for numerous rabbinical regulations against eating meat and dairy products at the same meal—is clearly a reaction against a Canaanite rite, as shown in Ugaritic texts. Verbal and ideological contacts between the Bible and the Ugaritic writings are numerous and important, but as far as basic religious belief is concerned, they are more external and do not bridge the great cleft differentiating Israelite monotheism from Canaanite polytheism.

(Barton, G. A., "Danel, A Pre-Israelite Hero of Galilee," *JBL* 60 [1941] 213–25. Dahood, M., "Ugaritic Studies and the Bible," *Greg* 43 [1962] 55–79. Eissfeldt, O., "The Alphabetical Cuneiform Texts from Ras Shamra," *JSemS* 5 [1960] 1–49; *KlSchr* 2, 464–514. Finegan, *op. cit.*, 171–74. Ginsberg, H. L., *ANET* 129–55. Gray, J., "Cultic Affinities Between Israel and Ras Shamra," *ZAW* 61 [1949] 207–208; *DOTT* 118–33; *The Legacy of Canaan* [Leiden, 1957]. Jacob, *op. cit.* O'Callaghan, R. T., "Echoes of Canaanite Literature in the Psalms," *VT* 4 [1954] 164–65. Pope, *op. cit.* Rainey, A. F., "The Kingdom of Ugarit," *BA* 27 [1965] 102–25. Worden, T., "The Literary Influences of the Ugaritic Fertility Myth on the Old Testament," *VT* 3 [1953] 272–98.)

13 **(V) Phoenicians.** The term "Phoenicia" is broader than and includes Ras Shamra both geographically and historically. In our period, the only two harbor cities that had escaped destruction at the hands of the "Peoples of the Sea" were Byblos and Sidon. This latter city became the leading city of southern Phoenicia; in fact, the entire region was referred to as Sidonian (cf. Dt 3:9; Jos 13:4,6; Jgs 3:3; 10:12; 18:7; 1 Kgs 5:6, etc.). These people seem to have penetrated inward from the coast, as Jgs 18:7,28 hints. The increasing number of Gk colonies were taking away their trade, and even the Phoenician colonies were competing with their founding country. The worst blow of all, however, was the Assyrian invasion of Phoenicia *ca.* 700. The Babylonians captured Tyre in 572, after a 13-year siege, thus crippling the maritime and commercial activities of this people. The long prophecies of Ezekiel over Tyre in chs. 27–28 give a good idea of this city's commercial importance. The cultural achievements of the Phoenicians in the crafts, especially ceramics, metal work, and art, were important, even if partly borrowed from others, and then, in turn, borrowed and surpassed by other peoples, especially the Greeks. But the greatest achievement of the Phoenicians was their use and development of the alphabetical script (known among the Canaanites possibly as early as the 18th cent.) that they passed on to the Greeks. Ugarit has alerted us to the great literary importance of Phoenicia, the richness of which has by no means been exhausted to date.

(Albright, W. F., "The Role of the Canaanites in the History of Civilization," *BANE* 438–87.)

14 **(VI) Ammonites.** The "sons of Ammon" were an Aramean tribe that settled in the 12th cent. (cf. N. Glueck, *BASOR* 68 [1937] 11–12) near the upper region of the Jabbok, after they had expelled or exterminated the native population—among them the Rephaim (called Zamzummim by the Ammonites, Dt 2:20). Rabbah (Rabbath-Ammon) was their capital (corresponding to Amman, the present capital of the Hashemite kingdom of Jordan). In a folk-narrative, Gn 19:30–38 speaks of the Ammonites as descending by incest from Lot through Ben-Ammi. The story seems to indicate Aramean ancestry (→ Biblical Geography, 73:47–49).

It was only during the period of the judges that Ammonite-Israelite conflicts began. In Jgs 3:18, Ammon is allied with King Eglon of Moab against Israel. In Jgs 10:6–9; 11:1–12:4, there is a long period of Israelite backsliding and final conflict resulting in Jephthah's decisive victory. At the beginning of Saul's reign (1 Sm 11:1–11), King Nahash of Ammon attacked Jabesh-gilead. Saul defeated his army so badly that, according to one tradition, he was crowned king at Gilgal. During David's reign (2 Sm 10:1–11; 12:26–31), the Israelite ambassadors were publicly humiliated at Ammon during a good-will visit arranged by David and, as a result, David took Rabbah (Rabbath-Ammon). On this occasion, according to the MT, David took Hanun's crown from his head and put it on his own; he then subjected the cities of Ammon to brutal reprisals. It is difficult to know whether a state of subjection to David ensued.

It is possible that during the reign of Jehoshaphat (*ca.* 873–849) the Ammonites invaded Judah (2 Chr 20:1–30 sets forth such an account, but it is lacking in 2 Kgs, unless 3:4–27—a battle against the Moabites—is regarded as somehow parallel). The Ammonites paid tribute to Uzziah (*ca.* 783–742; cf. 2 Chr 26:8) and to Jotham after he defeated them in battle (2 Chr 27:5). According to Assyrian annals, Ammon was often subject to the Assyrians (cf. *ANET* 279, under Shalmaneser III, *ca.* 858–824; *ANET* 282, under Tiglath-pileser III, *ca.* 744–727; *ANET* 294, under Ashurbanipal, *ca.* 668–625). From these texts and from royal seals of this period, even while Ammon was vassal to Assyria, it apparently had its own dynasty.

During the Neo-Babylonian period, bands of Ammonites, ostensibly vassals of Neo-Babylonia, attacked Judah while Jehoiakim was king (cf. 2 Kgs 24:1–2) which is explained by the sacred writer as divinely willed punishment on Manasseh and his descendants. Ammon's later history lies beyond our terminus.

Apart from two royal seals, no Ammonite documents have thus far been discovered. Its language was close to Aramaic, if the Assyrian texts can serve as an indication. Molech (Melek) was the Ammonite deity for whom Solomon built a high-place shrine (1 Kgs 11:7) "east of Jerusalem" (perhaps the so-called "Mount of Scandal"). Prophetic utterances against Ammon were numerous: Am 1:13–15; Zeph 2:8–11; Jer 9:25; 49:1–6; Ez 21:33–37; 25:1–7.

Glueck's archaeological work has thrown considerable light on Ammonite culture and history, especially when his investigations are seen against the perspective of other information on the Ammonites.

(Albright, W. F., "Notes on Ammonite History," *Fest. B. Ubach* [Montserrat, 1954] 131–36. Glueck, N., *AASOR* 18/19 [1939] 151–251; *The Other Side of the Jordan* [New Haven, 1940]. Landes, G. M., "The Material Civilization of the Ammonites," *BAR* 2, 69–88. Noth, M., *BBLAK* 68 [1949] 36–37. O'Ceallaigh, G. C., "And So David Did to All the Cities of Ammon," *VT* 12 [1962] 179–89.)

15 **(VII) Edomites.** Edom (*'dm*, "red") is the land of a Semitic people (Edomites) that settled in the highland region of Seir (Gn 36:8), S of the Wadi Zered, around 1300 BC. Their capital was Sela (identified with Petra by some authorities). Their settlement was part of a large-scale migration of Semitic peoples from the Syrian-Arabian desert into the arable regions principally of

Syria and Palestine. The area taken over by the Edomites, only a short time before the departure of the Hebrews from Egypt and their journey toward Canaan (via Edom), had hitherto been occupied by nomads. Thus, Dt 2:12 speaks of the Edomites having driven out the Horites, perhaps an outlying branch of the Hurrians (a non-Semitic people). (→ Biblical Geography, 73:40–42.)

Gn 36:10–43 traces the Edomites, despite some intermingling of races, to Esau (Edom), brother of Jacob. Accordingly, the Edomites would be related to the Hebrews, although highly reputed scholars have advanced rather cogent reasons for not accepting this tradition in all its details (cf. M. Noth, *RGG* 2, 308–309). For a rather elaborate listing of clans and subclans of the Edomites, cf. Gn 36:1–19. Some of this information is based on conflicting traditions, for a large number of the names listed here turn up in quite different contexts. Edom extended S from the Dead Sea on both sides of the Arabah to the Gulf of Aqabah—a large area—and it was only under the Nabateans (4th cent.) that they lost the territory on the eastern side of the Arabah. Their borders were protected by many fortresses and the Edomites were organized as a non-dynastic monarchy before the Israelites adopted that form of government. Gn 36:31–39 (cf. 1 Chr 1:43–54) lists eight kings (along with their royal cities) "who reigned in the land of Edom before there were Israelite kings" over Edom, i.e., before the time of David.

16 Conflict between Israel and Edom was not slow in coming, for Israel's only route to the ports of Ezion-geber (and Elath) on the Gulf of Aqabah was the main trade route, called the "royal road" (cf. Nm 20:17; 21:22), controlled by Edom (cf. Jer 49:7–8; Ez 25:13), and the rich copper and iron deposits in the Arabah were attractive to Israel. Thus Saul fought against Edom (1 Sm 14:47) and David slew 18,000 Edomites in the Valley of Salt (2 Sm 8:13, where the LXX *'ĕdōm* merits preference over the MT *'ărām*; note Ps 60:2, where this victory is assigned to Joab, David's general). The Edomites were subject to David during the rest of his reign and during the reign of his son, Solomon. A rebellion led by Hadad during Solomon's reign seems to have failed (1 Kgs 11:14–22,25b, with the text in troubled condition). At least Solomon seems to have maintained his smelting works at Ezion-geber, which was a vital place in Edom. Before the time of Solomon, the Edomite tribe called the Kenites (a name derived from the term for "smith") had been engaged in iron and copper operations. During the reign of Rehoboam (*ca.* 922–915), when Pharaoh Shishak of Egypt laid waste southern Judah (1 Kgs 14:25), the Edomites probably regained independence. The text of 1 Kgs 22:48, having provided some obscure information on Edom's "deputy" king, tells of Jehoshaphat's (of Judah, *ca.* 873–849) abortive naval ventures, with a base on the Gulf of Aqabah. One of the kings of Edom was in league with Jehoram of Israel and Jehoshaphat of Judah against Mesha, king of Moab (2 Kgs 3:9). During the reign of Joram of Judah (*ca.* 849–842), Edom revolted against Judah and set up its own king. Despite a reprisal attack by Joram, Edom prevailed and remained free "to this day" (cf. 2 Kgs 8:20–22). Yet the southern kings, Amaziah (*ca.* 799–783), and his son, Azariah (Uzziah, *ca.* 783–742), ruled Edom (cf. 2 Kgs 14:7,22). Although in a disturbed condition (Edom read twice for Aram?), 2 Kgs 16:6–7 indicates some kind of recovery of independence for Edom. Soon the might of Assyria bore down on Edom. Already, from the reign of Adad-nirari III (*ca.* 810–783), Edom is mentioned in Assyrian inscriptions (*ANET* 281). Tribute from Edom was registered by Tiglath-pileser III (*ca.* 744–727; *ANET* 282) and by Sargon II (*ca.* 721–705; *ANET* 287), while Esarhaddon (*ca.* 680–669) summoned King Qaushgabri of Edom for tribute delinquency (*ANET* 291). Edom also bent before Nebuchadnezzar, the Neo-Babylonian king (Jer 27:2–3; 49:7–22; Ez 32:29).

Apart from some 7th-cent. jar markings, no Edomite writing has been found. Yet much points to both an Edomite culture surpassing that of Israel and an impressive wisdom literature in the Edomite language (cf. Ob 8; Jer 49:7; Bar 3:23, for allusions to this pursuit of wisdom). The Edomite language was probably close to Hebrew and Moabite. The general similarity of Edomite pottery to the pottery forms of Palestine would illustrate considerable contact at various times between Edomites and the inhabitants of Palestine.

Evidence, at times only conjectural, shows that the Edomites worshiped several gods (2 Chr 25:14). Various theophoric names bear out the Chronicler's report: e.g., Qosh, perhaps represented in Qosh-Yahu (1 Chr 15:17); and in the Assyrian listings, Qaushmalake (*ANET* 282) and Qaushgabri (*ANET* 291). There may also have been a deity called Malik (cf. the Ammonite Moloch) and another called something like Ai. Clay figurines of *ca.* 9th-8th cent., found near Bosra, represent a vegetation goddess.

The Edomites are charged with excessive glee at the fall of Jerusalem in 587, with counter-imprecations by Ps 137:7; Ob 10–12 (cf. 2 Kgs 25:8–12).

(Galling, K., *Fest. A. Bertholet* [1950] 179–80. Glueck, N., "Explorations in Eastern Palestine, II," *AASOR* 15 [1935]; "The Boundaries of Edom," *HUCA* 2, [1936] 1–58; *The Other Side of the Jordan*, 114–34; "The Civilization of the Edomites," *BA* 10 [1947] 77–84; = *BAR* 2, 89–98. Haller, M., "Edom im Urteil der Propheten," *Vom Alten Testament* [BZAW 41; Giessen, 1925] 109–17. Maag, V., "Jakob-Esau-Edom," *TZ* 13 [1957] 418–29.)

17 **(VIII) Moabites.** The land of Moab proper is the remarkably fertile (cf. 2 Kgs 3:25) plateau E of the Dead Sea and about 4300 ft. above its surface. Its boundaries follow: on the east, the Syrian-Arabian desert; on the south, the Wadi el-Hesa (the valley of the Zered; Nm 21:12; Dt 2:13–14), separating Moab from Edom; and on the north, the Arnon gorge (Wadi el Mojib), although the Moabites frequently extended their territory further N. Archaeological investigation shows that the territory was resettled in the 13th cent. after ancient towns (dating from *ca.* 3000) had been abandoned and the area had been meanwhile taken over by nomadic groups. The resettlement took place only a short time before Israel's entry into Canaan. Dt 2:10 records the tradition that the pre-Moabite inhabitants of the region were called the Emim. The Moabites were a pastoral people of the plain. A biblical tradition set forth in Gn 19:30–38 has them, along with the Ammonites, descending from Lot through incest—a piece of folklore intended to heap opprobrium on a much disliked neighbor of Israel.

Iron Age Moab was defended by a powerful system of fortresses, several of which were located on the southern border where the plateau drops down to the Wadi el Hesa. The King's Highway crossed this wadi about 17 mi. E of its Dead Sea mouth. This pass was of the greatest importance for trade and travel and was guarded by the strongest fortresses. The development in watertight cistern techniques had much to do with Moabite expansion into regions not graded by springs. Dibon (possibly the Qarhoh of the Moabite Stone) was one such city.

Among the better known Moabite cities mentioned in the Bible are Kir-hareseth (the capital of Moab, corresponding to the modern Kerak, site of a huge Crusader fortress castle), Aroer, Dibon, Jahaz, Medeba, and

Heshbon. All of the sites except Kir-hareseth were N of the Arnon! Before the Israelite invasion of Canaan, the Moabites had settled in the region N of the Arnon, but the Amorite king, Sihon of Heshbon, had driven them back below the Arnon. Although the incoming Israelites were forced to skirt the territory of Sihon (cf. Nm 21:21–22) as well as that of Moab (cf. Jgs 11:17–18), they later defeated the king of Moab and took over his land; the tribes of Gad and Reuben settled there (Nm 32:33–34). This section of valuable land N of the Arnon thus became a bone of contention between the Moabites and the Israelites for several centuries, for both peoples had claims to it. Dt 23:4–5 summarizes the profound antipathy of the Israelites for the Moabites: "No Ammonite or Moabite may ever be admitted into the community of the Lord, nor any descendants of theirs even unto the tenth generation." Despite this regulation, marriages between Israelite men and Moabite women in post-exilic Judah were frequent enough to be lamented in Ezr 9:1 and Neh 13:23; the Book of Ruth shows, and may even have intended to countenance, leniency in this matter.

Just before the Israelite entrance into Canaan, Balak, king of Moab, hired the Syrian diviner Balaam to curse the Israelites. As recorded in Nm 22:1–24:25, however, the whole operation turned to the distinct advantage of Israel—Balaam, in the process, making important utterances about the peculiar and divinely guided destiny of the Israelite people. In Jgs 3:12–13 is recalled the 18-year servitude of Jericho ("Israel") to Eglon, king of Moab, until Ehud the Benjaminite delivered Israel by treacherously stabbing the obese Eglon to death.

18 Although Saul fought against Moab (1 Sm 14:47), it was only under David that Moab was made tributary to Israel following upon a humiliating defeat (2 Sm 8:2,12). Benaiah, one of David's outstanding warriors, is credited with having slain two sons of Ariel (?) of Moab (2 Sm 23:20; 1 Chr 11:22).

Solomon had Moabite women among his consorts (1 Kgs 11:1) who influenced him to build a high place for Chemosh, god of Moab, "on the mountain east of Jerusalem" (1 Kgs 11:7,33), perhaps the "Mount of Scandal" where other shrines to foreign deities were erected by Solomon at the request of his non-Yahwist wives. At the time of the schism between north and south, Moab may have rebelled (cf. R. E. Murphy, "Israel and Moab in the Ninth Century, B.C.," *CBQ* 15 [1953] 411–12), only to be resubjugated for a time during Omri's reign. King Mesha of Moab may have begun minor rebellions under Ahaz but the rebellion became complete and open after the death of Ahaz, against his weak successors. This conclusion is legitimate, from both 2 Kgs 1:1; 3:4–5 and the Mesha (or Moabite) Stone, discovered in 1868 and now in the Louvre. Neither Israel nor Judah was successful in resubjugating Moab, although Jehoram of Israel and Jehoshaphat of Judah, in alliance with the king of Edom (on this peculiar and dubious alliance, cf. Murphy, *CBQ* 15, 416), may well have been able to have done so had they not defaulted when the Moabite king horrified them by offering his eldest son in burnt sacrifice in the view of the conquering coalition army (2 Kgs 3:4–27; 2 Chr 20:1–30). Moab also continued to hold the territory assigned to Reuben N of the Arnon despite the efforts of Hazael of Damascus. Both for these and for religious reasons the prophets often uttered dire threats against Moab (cf. Is 15:1–16:14; 25:10; Jer 48:1–47; Am 2:1–3; Zeph 2:8–11). In time, Moab, along with many other kingdoms in that region, suffered much from the Assyrians. The Assyrian annals record tributes paid by Moab to Tiglath-pileser III (*ANET* 282), to Sennacherib (*ANET* 287), to Esarhaddon (*ANET* 291), and to Ashurbanipal (*ANET* 294, 298).

The Moabites had kings before Israel adopted a monarchical government. They were polytheistic, but their chief god was Chemosh, whose name is worked into Moabite personal names. At times, Chemosh was offered human sacrifice (cf. 2 Kgs 3:27 and the Moabite Stone, ll. 15–16 [*ANET* 320]). Baal of Peor was worshiped with sexual rites into which some Israelites were enticed (Nm 25:1–15). The language, at least as it is known from the Moabite Stone, is similar to Hebrew.

(Franken, H. J., *VT* 11 [1961] 100–101 [shows serious reservations regarding Van Zyl's methodology]. Glueck, N., *AASOR* 14 [1934] 1–113; *AASOR* 15, 1–102; *AASOR* 18/19, 1–50; *The Other Side of the Jordan* [New Haven, 1940]. Murphy, *CBQ* 15 [1953] 409–17. Noth, M., *ZAW* 60 [1944] 11–57. Van Zyl, A. H., *The Moabites* [Leiden, 1959].)

19 **(IX) Philistines.** About the same time (*ca.* 1200) that the Israelites entered Canaan from the east, one of the "Peoples of the Sea" made its entry into the same land from the west, by water. The group was non-Semitic, perhaps from Crete (Caphtor, cf. Dt 2:23; Am 9:7; Jer 47:4) in the sense that they had lived there for a time, and originally from more northerly and easterly regions; they destroyed the Minoan Empire in Crete. Hence, according to this construction, the Philistines were not ethnically Cretans—they had only sojourned there for a time, and there is so far no archaeological evidence for their occupation of Crete. Early Iron Age pottery (1200–1000) found in Philistia is bichromatic, similar to that found in Asia Minor, the Aegean coasts, and Greek settlements, thus suggesting a connection of Philistines with these regions.

The Philistines (or at least some of the "Peoples of the Sea") had attempted to enter Egypt but were firmly rejected in 1191 and 1188 by Pharaoh Ramses III (*ca.* 1195–1164) in land and naval battles, the story of which is told on the walls of this Pharaoh's temple at Medinet Habu, on the western side of the Nile Valley, opposite present-day Luxor. One of the peoples is here described as *p-r-s-t*, the Egyptian equivalent of *p-l-š-t-y*, i.e., Philistines. Unable to enter Egypt, this people gained entry into Canaan at points near the present-day Israeli city of Migdal-Ashqelon, settling between Gaza and Dor, and even farther northward. By 1180 they had occupied the entire coastal plain, including the inner lowlands known as the Shephelah. The Philistine pentapolis was comprised of Gaza, Ashkelon, and Ashdod on the coast, Gath in the western Shephelah, and Ekron, some 6 mi. inland on the same latitude as Jerusalem. The whole district, and later (in Roman times) the whole land of Canaan, was called *Pᵉlešet*, i.e., Philistia or Palestine (→ Biblical Geography, 73:72).

Like the Hebrews, the Philistines did not wholly displace the earlier population of Philistia, although they obtained dominion over them. Goliath was probably an aboriginal of the region (cf. 1 Sm 17). Gn 21:34 speaks proleptically in calling the region "the land of the Philistines," and the same may be said of Gn 21:33 ("king of the Philistines"); 26:1,8; Ex 13:17; 15:14; and even Jos 13:2–3. Some have suggested that the Egyptians had placed Philistine mercenaries in their frontier garrisons at an early date (cf. W. F. Albright, *JPOS* [1921] 187–88). Such a condition may be hinted at in the words of Ramses III—the Philistines were "settled in fortresses bound in his name" (*ANET* 262)—although the context is not entirely clear. Inasmuch as the Philistine invasion was not much later than that of the Israelites, conflict between the two groups was inevitable. Thus the tribe of Dan, assigned to a territory that partially coincided with Philistia, was forced to seek new lands in the north near the sources of the Jordan (Jgs 13–16,18), despite the mighty deeds of its "one man army," Samson. It was during the times of Samuel, Saul, and David that large-scale conflicts broke out. The Israelites suffered a serious defeat at Ebenezer and Aphek *ca.* 1050, and the Ark of the Covenant, symbol of Yahweh's presence, was taken by the Philistines (1 Sm 4). The Philistines swarmed into various plains, like Esdraelon, as far as Beth-shan (cf. 1 Sm 31:10–11), and also into the hill country, as archaeological investigations at places like Shiloh reveal (cf. Jer 7:12,14; 26:6,9).

The Philistine monopoly on the recently introduced iron weapons and iron work gave them a decided advantage over the Israelites (1 Sm 13:19–22). Their knowledge of iron manufacture and usage may fit into a large and slightly complex historical picture. Meteoric and earthly iron was already known by *ca.* 1500, but was developed and worked on in the mountains of Armenia. Soon after it was used by the Hittites in making weapons. The "Peoples of the Sea," among them perhaps the Philistines, who served at times as Hittite mercenaries, learned the secrets of iron from their masters, and eventually, perhaps during a fresh invasion by their own people, used it to overcome the Hittites. The use of iron, although kept secret by its smiths, spread rapidly and had great cultural and historical consequences (Gn 4:22 is the first member of a long series of biblical "iron" texts). By using iron, small nations were at times able to escape the monopolies and domination of great powers.

The Philistine threat had much to do with the institution of monarchy among the Israelites. Strong, centralized power was needed to turn the Philistine tide. Thus Saul, as first king, was quite successful in checking the Philistine advances in the hill country. During one of the many crises in his life, he and most of his sons lost their lives in a battle with the Philistines at Gilboa.

20 When David came to the throne (*ca.* 1000) with the immense asset of a first-hand knowledge of Philistine tactics (1 Sm 27) and with his own well-trained men, the Philistines continued to threaten the Israelite hold on Canaan. The real turning point is narrated in 2 Sm 5:17–18. Shortly after David's anointing, the Philistines initiated an attack against him, coming up the Rephaim Valley toward Jerusalem. David defeated them decisively at Baal-perazim. On a second occasion, they were driven back from a similar position as far as Gezer. Other skirmishes during David's reign (2 Sm 8:1; 21:15–16; 23:9–10; 1 Chr 18:1) end in the defeat of the Philistines and their mighty warriors (although the time sequence is highly uncertain in these brief accounts). David seems to have broken the Philistine power, despite their later efforts, and he made vassals of them. Some believe that the Cherethites and Pelethites, who are spoken of as David's bodyguards, were Philistines. According to 2 Sm 15:19–22; 18:2, Gath furnished David with some of his most faithful warriors, such as Ittai the Gittite. Solomon ruled with complete mastery over the Philistines (1 Kgs 4:21), but isolated incidents seem to indicate that after his reign the Philistines functioned in practice as independent states with very little control from either Judah or Israel (cf. 1 Kgs 15:27; 2 Chr 17:11; 21:16; 26:6–7; 28:18). The information provided by the chronicler makes the event of 2 Kgs 18:8 fit into a general pattern, for here Hezekiah of Judah severely defeats the Philistines and drives them back to Gaza. The Chronicler is inclined to admit more trouble from the Philistines after the time of David than is the author of Kgs.

In the Assyrian annals, Adad-nirari III (*ca.* 810–783) speaks of imposing tribute on Philistines, among others (*ANET* 281); Tiglath-pileser III (*ca.* 744–727) speaks of capturing the southern Philistine cities of Ashkelon and Gaza (*ANET* 283); Sargon II (*ca.* 721–705) says that he placed Assyrian governors in Ashdod and Gath (*ANET* 286); and Sennacherib (*ca.* 704–681) claims to have received tribute from several Philistine cities (*ANET* 287–88). When the Assyrian Empire collapsed in 612, Philistia along with Judah served as a buffer state between Egypt and Babylonia.

From what has been said, it is clear that the Philistines remained a force to be reckoned with after the time of David, although he certainly turned the tide against them and they won no important military engagements against Israel during or after his reign. Judging, too, by the Assyrian annals and by the exposed condition of Philistia on the coast, these people were very likely kept too busy defending their own position to have the time and resources to make serious incursions into Hebr territory.

No documents in the Philistine language have been found. On arrival in Canaan, they probably soon took up a local dialect; most of the names associated with them are Semitic (Canaanite). King Adon, who wrote in Aramaic to the Pharaoh in 604 for help against Nebuchadnezzar, was probably a Philistine (cf. J. A. Fitzmyer, *Bib* 46 [1965] 41–55).

The chief trait attached to them by the biblical narratives is their lack of circumcision (Jgs 14:3; 15:18; 1 Sm 17:26; 18:25). Little is known of their religion. All their gods about whom information is available have Semitic names. Thus, there were temples to Dagon in Gaza and Ashdod (Jgs 16:23; 1 Sm 5:1–7), another to Ashtoreth in Ashkelon (cf. Herodotus I, 105), and one to Baalzebub in Ekron (2 Kgs 1:1–16). According to Is 2:6, they were known for soothsaying.

(Albright, *AP* 112–16. Bérard, J., "Philistins et Pré-Hellenes," *Revue Archéologique* 107 [1951] 129–42. Dothan, T., "Archaeological Reflections on the Philistine Problem," *Antiquity and Survival* 2 [1957] 151–64. Macalister, R. A. S., *The Philistines* [London, 1913]. Von Rad, G., "Das Reich Israel und die Philister," *PJB* 29 [1933] 30–42. Wright, G. E., "Fresh Evidence for the Philistine Story," *BA* 29 [1966] 70–86.)

21 **(X) Egyptians.** In the Exodus, the Israelites left behind them an enervated Egypt that had grown increasingly hostile and oppressive toward them (Ex 1:8–9) Merneptah (*ca.* 1234–24) had recorded on an important stele his victory over the Libyans, stating that "Canaan is devastated, Ashkelon is fallen, Gezer is ruined, Yanoam is reduced to nothing, Israel is desolate and her seed is no more, Ḫaru (Syria-Palestine) has become a widow for Egypt: all the countries are unified and pacified" (cf. *ANET* 378, for a slightly different translation). This is the first time that Israel is mentioned in Egyptian annals. The ideal conditions described by Merneptah did not last long, and his five successors were so weak that the country was overrun with foreign invaders. Egypt's dominion over Canaan had been lost, for all practical purposes. As we discussed before, Ramses III (*ca.* 1195–64) was strong enough to turn back the Philistines on two different occasions (1191, invasion by land and sea at the Nile Delta; 1188, with the Libyans at Memphis), but he could not prevent their settling in Canaan. It was the weakened condition of Egypt that enabled the Israelites to make their surprising, although not at all sweeping, conquests in Palestine. The account written by Wen-Amon (*ANET* 25–29), an Egyptian official who was sent early in the 11th cent. to Byblos to negotiate a lumber deal (to be used in building a sacred boat for Amon at Thebes), amply shows Egyptian power on the decline in Phoenicia. Solomon had contacts with a pharaoh (1 Kgs 3:1–2; 9:15–16), perhaps Suennes II (Psousennes, *ca.* 984–950) and married his daughter (horse trading and chariots may well have been a substantial aspect of the relationship). Hadad of Edom fled to Egypt in order to escape the massacre of Joab (1 Kgs 11:14-22); it was an Egyptian pharaoh, too, who captured Gezer, giving the site and remains to his daughter, a wife of Solomon (1 Kgs 9:16). None of these events are set down in the Egyptian records.

The first pharaoh to be expressly named in the Bible is Shishak (Sheshonk I, *ca.* 935-919), a Libyan. Although the Libyans had been soundly defeated by Ramses III on at least two occasions, they had gained entrance into Egyptian affairs by serving as mercenaries in the army, eventually comprising its majority. Shishak founded the 22nd Dynasty and ruled from the Nile Delta at Bubastis. While he outwardly seemed friendly enough to Israel he was in reality awaiting an opportunity to gain control over this territory, which was still much coveted by Egypt and which Egypt had never formally lost. Thus, he welcomed Jeroboam when he took flight from Solomon (1 Kgs 11:40), and, at the instigation of Jeroboam (*ca.* 922-901) he attacked Judah, carrying off large quantities of temple treasure (cf. 1 Kgs 14:25-26; 2 Chr 12:9-10). The Egyptians did not write a regular account of this campaign (at least there is none extant), but fragmentary lists of the conquered towns are engraved on the south wall of the Karnak temple at Luxor (*ANET* 242-43). The plunder brought home from this military venture enabled Shishak and his successors to continue their ambitious building program, but the impression of power that this campaign had created was unrealistic and was to prove catastrophic in the face of the Assyrian forces. To conquer a weakened Jerusalem was one thing; to stand up against mighty Assyria was something very different (for an exhaustive study of Shishak's Jerusalem campaign, cf. J. Simons, *Handbook for the Study of Egyptian Topographical Lists* [Leiden, 1937] 89-102, 178-87).

22 Pharaoh Zerah, spoken of in 2 Chr 14:9-10 as an Ethiopian defeated by Asa, king of Judah (*ca.* 913-817), is hard to identify. The equation with Osorkon I, Shishak's successor, is no more than a conjecture. It is firmly rejected by L. Hartman and A. van den Born (*EDB* 141). It is certain that around 715 the Ethiopians, already in control of Upper Egypt, conquered the lower part too.

The identity of So, king of Egypt (2 Kgs 17:4) has long been a problem, but it now appears that there was no such person. One should read, instead, "to Sais, to the king of Egypt" in this verse. The actual pharaoh was Tefnakhte, who was a potential ally of Hoshea of Israel in his revolt against Assyria (cf. H. Goedicke, *BASOR* 171 [1963] 64-66).

In 2 Kgs 19:9 (cf. Is 37:9), Tirhakah (*ca.* 690-664) is mentioned; he was the third king of the 25th (Ethiopian) Dynasty and resided at Tanis where he could survey events more carefully and possibly stir up revolt among Assyria's vassals at Tyre and Sidon. He was reported to be ready to attack Sennacherib when the latter was besieging Jerusalem, but it was during the following year that Sennacherib defeated the Egyptian forces at Eltekeh in southern Palestine. In the fourteenth year of Hezekiah (2 Kgs 18:13)—i.e., in 701—Tirhakah would have been a mere boy of eight years! Hence, apart from the 701 siege of Jerusalem, another *ca.* 689-686 is postulated, at which time Tirhakah could have led an army, and at which time the Assyrian king moved up to Pelusium on the Egyptian frontier, where his advance was stopped by a plague of some kind (Is 37:36; but cf. Brevard Childs, *Isaiah and the Assyrian Crisis* [London, 1967] 69-103). The Bible's information on Tirhakah is limited to the extreme (for more details, cf. *EDB* 2426; J. Jannsen, *Bib* 34 [1953] 23-43).

In 671, Esarhaddon of Assyria (*ca.* 680-669), having lost all patience with Egypt's continual intrigue, swept down on that country, capturing the delta and Memphis. Tirhakah fled to Thebes, and from there, through intrigue with Esarhaddon's Egyptian governors, he recaptured Memphis for Egypt in 669. Three years passed before Ashurbanipal (*ca.* 668-663) sent another Assyrian army against Egypt, taking Memphis and forcing Tirhakah to flee once more. Two years later he died and his nephew Tanutamon (*ca.* 663-656) was crowned at Napata (in Ethiopia). His efforts to reconquer Egypt provoked once more an Assyrian onslaught; this time Thebes was thoroughly sacked (663), an event that left a profound impression on the whole Near East for a long time (cf. Na 3:8-10, written perhaps some 50 years after the event took place). Thus the 25th (Ethiopian) Dynasty ended (cf. *ANET* 296, for the Assyrian version).

23 Assyria's domination in Egypt was short—not more than ten years, if that long. Psammetichus I (*ca.* 663-609), who had been appointed governor of Athribis, revolted and expelled the Assyrians from Egypt. By 653 Egypt was free. Psammetichus was a native Egyptian and founded the 26th Dynasty (*ca.* 663-525). Under his enterprising guidance, trade with the Phoenicians and Greeks was encouraged, and Herodotus relates that he invaded Canaan and laid siege to Ashdod. A new appreciation of Egypt's past glory took life among the people, with the consequence of heavy archaizing in language, art and religion. Tombs were adorned with scenes and inscriptions found in sepulchers of the Old and Middle Kingdoms. Monuments were examined and restored, or imitated. Classical literature was studied and there was an earnest effort to recapture its form and spirit. Ancient titles were given to Egyptian officials. Before falling into a kind of sterility, this Renaissance movement had invigorating effects on Egypt; in 616 Psammetichus, alarmed at Babylon's sudden rise, joined the Assyrians in an anti-Babylonian alliance.

Neco II (*ca.* 609-594), son and successor of Psammetichus I, followed the same anti-Babylonian policy as his father, maintaining an alliance with the Assyrians—all of which was to profit him little. Neco may have attacked and taken Gaza and Ashkelon (Jer 47:1-2), but it is certain that in 609 he was marching via Megiddo when Josiah (who supported Babylon) tried to cut off his march, the result being both the defeat and death of that great king (2 Kgs 23:29-35; 2 Chr 35:20-21). Despite an ultimately losing cause, Neco did bring a lot of Syrian-Palestinian territory under Egyptian rule, even as far as the Euphrates. He deposed Josiah's son and successor Jehoahaz (609; only a three months' rule), sometimes called Shallum (1 Chr 3:15; Jer 22:11), whose reign is described in 2 Kgs 23:31-34 and 2 Chr 36:1-4, and sent him to Egypt as a prisoner. He then put Jehoiakim (609-598), brother of Jehoahaz, on the throne of Judah and imposed a heavy tribute on him (2 Kgs 23:33-34; Jer 22:10-11; 2 Chr 26:3-4). (→ History of Israel, 75:84-87.)

The Neo-Babylonian power, however, was growing, and Neco was checked by Nabopolassar and Nebuchadnezzar. In 605, they badly defeated him at Carchemish (cf. Jer 46:1-2; 2 Kgs 24:7). Shortly afterward, at Hamath on the Orontes, he was so completely defeated that he withdrew any claim whatsoever to Syrian or Palestinian holdings.

Neco's son and successor was Psammetichus II (*ca.* 594-589), who was followed by his son Hophra (*ca.* 589-570), the last pharaoh mentioned in the Bible (cf. Jer 44:30, regarding his deliverance into the hands of his enemies). Hophra, following the policy of his predecessors, turned against the Babylonians, but neither he nor his father ever attempted an invasion of Palestine.

It was to this pharaoh that many Jews (with Jeremiah) fled after the fall of Jerusalem in 587 (cf. Jer 42–44; 2 Kgs 25:26). Hophra met his death at the hands of his own countrymen when he fell in battle against Amasis, his successor. The Jewish refugees were installed at Daphne on the eastern Delta and given kind treatment. Some of them probably went up the Nile at a later date to found the Jewish colony on the island of Elphantine, or, perhaps, to join their fellow-Jews there (cf. E. Drioton, *A la Rencontre de Dieu* [Fest. A. Gelin; Paris, 1961] 181–91). (→ History of Israel, 75:99.)

(Černý, J., *Ancient Egyptian Religion* [N.Y., 1953]. Drioton, E. and J. Vandier, *L'Égypte* [Paris, 1952]. Frankfort, H., *Ancient Egyptian Religion* [N.Y., 1948]. Lambdin, T. O., "Egypt: Its Language and Literature," *BANE* 279–97. Murray, M. A., *The Splendor That Was Egypt* [rev. ed.; N.Y., 1963]. Wilson, J. A., *The Burden of Egypt* [Chicago, 1951]; *IDB* 2, 298–315.)

SOME LESSER PEOPLES

24 **(I) The Hittites.** In our period the great Hittite kingdom had collapsed (cf. A. Goetze, *BANE* 316–27). The "kings of the Hittites" in 1 Kgs 10:29 probably refers to those petty rulers in Solomon's time in the region between N Mesopotamia and Syria who had once been in some way allied to the Hittites. In this region, Hittite hieroglyphic documents were found, e.g., Karatepe. Other Hittite references—e.g., Uriah (and Bathsheba?) 2 Sm 11:3–4—are to the equivalent of "displaced persons," unless they have been confused with Hurrians.

25 **(II) The Jebusites.** The Jebusites are an interesting example of a Canaanite clan that was able, at least as far as its chief fortress city Jebus (Jerusalem) is concerned, to withstand the Israelite Conquest for as long as 200 years. The toponym, Jebus, may be nothing more than a term derived from the Jebusites, the name Jerusalem (Urusalim) being at least as old as the Amarna age. "Jebus" is found in Jos 18:28; Jgs 19:10–11,14; 1 Chr 11:4–5, but it may be either an artificial or a forged name. Already listed in Gn 10:16 among other putative Canaanite clans, the Jebusites are placed beside the Amorites, Canaanites, and Girgashites in Gn 15:21. Adonizedek, however, is counted as both a Jebusite king and an Amorite in Jos 10:5. The Jebusites could well have been Amorites—a much broader term with an ethnological connotation (cf. Ez 16:3,45), whereas Jebusite may be largely a geographical expression.

Theoretically, Jerusalem, the Jebusite stronghold, belonged to the tribe of Benjamin (cf. Jos 18:28), but the boundary line between Judah and Benjamin paralleled the Valley of Hinnom, just S of the Jebusite "shoulder" (Jos 15:8; 18:16). This lack of precision in Jos makes it hard to construct a good geographical argument regarding Jebus' tribal position, although the site of the primitive city is definitely known. The town remained a foreign enclave until the time of David (cf. Jos 15:63; Jgs 1:21; against the proleptic statement in Jgs 1:8). Although David captured this city and made it his capital, he purchased the threshing floor of Araunah to construct there a suitable housing for the Ark of the Covenant (2 Sm 24:18–25; 1 Chr 21:15,18–28). The Jebusites presumably continued to live, at least in part, in the Jerusalem area and were gradually absorbed by the Israelites.

26 **(III) The Midianites.** The Midianites, although given a rather ancient origin in the Bible, their patriarch and founder being a son of Abraham by his third wife Keturah (Gn 25:2; 1 Chr 1:32), are spoken of mostly in the era between the Conquest and the Captivity. Although clearly associated in Gn 25:6 with the "east" (the southern Syro-Arabian desert, i.e., NW Arabia E of the Gulf of Aqabah), and similarly in Ex 2:15–16; 18:1–2, these people seem to have been nomads; Nm 10:29 sees (some of) them at Sinai. They are also found in Moab (Gn 36:35; 1 Chr 1:46), in Ammonite territory (Jgs 7:25; 8:18–19), in the eastern Jordan Valley (Nm 25:6–7; 31:2–3; Jos 13:21), and in Canaan (Jgs 6:1–6,33; 7:1). The Midianites were a pastoral people, whatever their relationship to the Kenites may have been (cf. W. F. Albright, *CBQ* 25 [1963] 1–11), and they were also well acquainted with desert caravan routes (Ex 18:5; Nm 10:29–31). In addition, they appear in the early 11th cent. as camel nomads (Jgs 6:1–7:25), capable of those sudden and dreaded raids known as the razzia. They seem to have been among the first to use the then recently domesticated camel for this purpose (cf. Albright, *FSAC*, 287, with references). In Jgs 6:1–6, they are as far as Gaza, and they plunder Palestine for a seven-year period, ruining crops and cattle. Gideon succeeded in liberating the Israelites from these much feared intruders; Oreb and Zeeb, two of their princes, were captured and beheaded (Jgs 7:24–25). Gideon's unusual and proverbial (Ps 83:10,12; Is 9:4; 10:26; 60:6; Hab 3:7) victory over them was decisive, and he pursued them to their habitation—Karkor, in the Wadi Sirhan (Jgs 8:10)—where he captured two of their "kings," Zebah and Zalmunna, and dispersed their army. The Midianites were never again a threat to Israelite peace (Jos 8:28).

27 **(IV) The Amorites.** The Amorites (with the connotation of "Westerners," as used in Akkadian sources) are hard to localize; in the Bible, they are frequently given a general meaning of pre-Israelite inhabitants of Canaan (Gn 15:16), even Adonizedek, king of Jerusalem, being included among them (Jos 10:5; note information in Ez 16:3,45). Am 2:9 describes them as tall as cedar trees and strong as oaks. The Amorites were still active in the period during the conquest, but references are few (Jos 2:10; 9:10; 24:8; Jgs 10:8; 11:19–20) and the use of the term varies. Sihon of Heshbon and Og of Bashan are both called Amorites in Jos, by Rahab (2:10) and by the Gibeonites (9:10). In his farewell address, Joshua refers to the land of the Amorites "who lived on the other side of the Jordan" (24:8). Jgs 10:8 identifies Gilead with the "land of the Amorites." In Jgs 11:19–20, Jephthah describes the victory over Sihon and identifies the area between the Arnon and Jabbok as the "territory of the Amorites" (N Moab and Ammon). Thus, variant biblical usages of Amorite are evident, yet the term is important in any study of Israel's neighbors. They have left no historical records in their own language. In Samuel's time they were not allied with the Philistines but lived at peace with the Israelites (1 Sm 7:14). Solomon drafted all Amorites into his corvées (1 Kgs 9:20–21; 2 Chr 8:7). When they are mentioned again it is without any further historical indications.

28 **(V) The Amalekites.** The Amalekites are linked to Amalek, son of Eliphaz, a son of Esau (Gn 36:12; 1 Chr 1:36). Their earliest habitat is Edom (Gn 36:16). A nomadic people, the Amalekites ranged over the desert regions of Sinai, the Negeb, the Arabah, and parts of Arabia. Their wanderings are summarized in 1 Sm 15:7 in connection with Saul's victory over them. These people also penetrated Palestine as far N as Ephraim (Jgs 12:15) and W into the Philistine country and around Ziklag (1 Sm 30:1–2). The Amalekites are only spoken of as Israel's enemies. They had done their best to block any Israelite entrance into Canaan (Jgs 10:12; 1 Sm 15:2). In the time of the judges, the Amalekites are found in Transjordan where they seem to have functioned as mercenaries, connected with the Moabites and Ammonites. Their presence near Pirathon in Ephraim is also recorded (Jgs 12:15). They are associated with Midianites in the camel invasions that devastated the Israelite settlements in Canaan (Jgs 6:3,33; 7:12). Although turned back by Gideon, the Amalekites long remained a menace, even during the monarchy. Thus Saul (1 Sm 15) waged battle against them, advancing on their "city" (1 Sm 15:5), a unique reference to Amalekite sedentarization (if the term has any force beyond the notion of a fortress or camp). Saul spared any Kenites in their midst, inviting them to depart while he defeated Amalek, even if he did not carry out Samuel's *herem* instructions. Thus, Saul was rejected and Amalek continued to be a menace.

David, while living at Gath, under Achish, made regular and merciless raids on the Amalekites (1 Sm 27:8–9), but he was not able to wipe them out. His greatest victory was a retaliation (1 Sm 30:1–17), but even then 400 young fighting men escaped. In one tradition, an Amalekite mercenary figured in the final dispatching of Saul (2 Sm 1:1–10) but received no reward from David when he brought the news (2 Sm 1:14; 4:10).

As king, David had his own conflicts with Amalekites (2 Sm 8:12; 1 Chr 18:11), although their activities under both David and Solomon seem to have been negligible. Under Hezekiah (*ca.* 715–687), there was only a "remnant of the Amalekites," and they were defeated at Mt. Seir (1 Chr 4:43). This appearance is their last in the Bible—in the land of their origin—and they are never treated outside the Bible. Archaeology has thus far shed no light upon them.

29 **(VI) The Kenites.** The Kenites were a nomadic or seminomadic tribe of smiths. Their most normal habitat would seem to have been close to the western slopes of the Arabah, ever rich in minerals (cf. Nm 24:21; Jgs 1:16), but they probably moved about, plying their craft on regular routes in a manner analogous to that of gypsy tinkers. In Gn 15:19, they are placed in Canaan, and Balaam foresees their destruction (Nm 24:22)—the only expressly unfavorable judgment on them in the Bible. According to Jgs 1:16, Moses' (here unnamed) father-in-law is connected with the "sons of Kenite." In Jgs 4:11, Hobab is called Moses' father-in-law and he is presented as the father of (at least some of) the Kenites. Elsewhere, Jethro or Reuel is the name of Moses' father-in-law, and he is described as a Midianite (for Reuel, cf. Ex 2:18; Nm 10:29; for Jethro, cf. Ex 3:1; 4:18; 18:1–2). Albright has freshly probed this problem (*CBQ* 25, 1–11), with Reuel emerging as a clan name, Hobab becoming Moses' son-in-law, and Jethro retaining his place as Moses' father-in-law. "Kenite" was originally an occupational term, quite consistent with Midianite. (On the "Kenite theory"—that Yahweh was formerly a Kenite divinity—see H. H. Rowley, *From Joseph to Joshua* [London, 1950].)

According to Jgs 1:16, the Kenites entered Palestine with the tribe of Judah, a relationship that seems to be confirmed by 1 Sm 15:6 where the Kenites are shown favor by Saul because of the *ḥesed* they had shown to Israel during the Exodus. The association of Kenite and Amalek (1 Sm 15:6; Nm 24:20–22) does not mean that the Kenites belonged to Amalek any more than they belonged to Midian. During the time of the judges, a branch of the Kenites under Heber lived in Galilee (Jgs 4:11; 5:24). David's relationship to the Kenites during his Gath sojourn seems to have been cordial; although he plundered in an area named after them (1 Sm 27:10), he sent spoils of battle to his friends living in Kenite cities (1 Sm 30:26–29). (→ Biblical Geography, 73:88.)

30 **(VII) The Jerahmeelites.** The Jerahmeelites are an interesting Semitic group living in the Negeb, not too far from Ziklag. David came into contact with them during his pillaging excursions while a fugitive from Saul (1 Sm 27:10; 30:29). Later, they seem to have been driven N and were gradually absorbed into the Hebr people. In the post-exilic era they are listed as a Hebr clan of the tribe of Judah (1 Chr 2:9,25–27,33,42). Their history may be something like that of the Calebites (1 Chr 2:9,18).

31 **(VIII) The People of the East.** The People of the East (children, or men, of the East) is a vague term denoting all those nations who lived E of the Israelites. In Gn 29:1, Jacob came to their land in Paddan-aram, In Jgs 6–8, the term refers to desert groups who attacked Israel with the Amalekites and Midianites (cf. also Jer 49:28; Ez 25:4,10). In Is 11:14, the term more likely applies to Edom and Moab; the same may be said of Jb 1:3. According to 1 Kgs 4:30 (or 5:10), the People of the East were known for their wisdom.

32 **(IX) The Medes.** Although the Medes, with their capital at Ecbatana in NW Iran, seem to have been very remote neighbors of Israel, they were closer than appears at first sight. During much of our period, they were recognized by Assyria. Shalmaneser III (*ca.* 858–824) entered their territory, and other monarchs speak of them. From the time of Sargon II (*ca.* 721–705) until *ca.* 650, they were probably subject to the Assyrian kings. Sargon exiled Israelites to certain "cities of the Medes" (2 Kgs 17:6; 18:11). The part of Cyaxares (*ca.* 625–585) in building a minor empire, in repelling the Scythians, and in doing more than his ally Nabopolassar to destroy the Assyrian Empire, was great. The Median attack on Babylon, as hypothetically envisaged by Is 13:17–18 and Jer 51:11,28, never took place.

Under Astyages, who succeeded Cyaxares, Media was taken over by Cyrus the Great and became part of the Persian Empire. The Medes have left no known literature. Darius the Mede (Dn 5:30; 6:1–2; 9:1; 11:1) defies strict historical identification and is based on the assumption that the Medes succeeded the Babylonians (cf. R. E. Brown in *PBPS* [no. 34, *Daniel*], 21–22; A. Van den Born, *EDB* 491).

12

INTRODUCTION TO PROPHETIC LITERATURE

Bruce Vawter, C.M.

BIBLIOGRAPHY

1 Balla, E., *Die Botschaft der Propheten* (ed. G. Fohrer; Tübingen, 1958). Batten, L. W., *The Hebrew Prophet* (London, 1905). Bendokat, B., *Die prophetische Botschaft* (Berlin, 1938). Chaine, J., *Introduction à la lecture des prophètes* (2nd ed.; Paris, 1932); ET: *God's Heralds* (tr. B. McGrath; N.Y., 1955). Cornill, C. H., *Der israelitische Prophetismus* (6th ed.; Strassburg, 1906); ET: *The Prophets of Israel* (Chicago, 1895). Duhm, H., *Der Verkehr Gottes mit den Menschen im Alten Testament* (Tübingen, 1926). Eissfeldt, O., "Das Berufungsbewusstsein der Propheten als theologisches Gegenwartsproblem," *ThStKr* 106 (1934) 124–56 (= *KlSchr* 2, 4–28); "The Prophetic Literature," *The Old Testament and Modern Study* (ed. H. H. Rowley; Oxford, 1951) 115–61. Fohrer, G., "Neuere Literatur zur alttestamentlichen Prophetie," *TRu* 19 (1951) 277–346; *TRu* 20 (1952) 193–271, 295–361; "Zehn Jahre Literatur zur alttestamentlichen Prophetie," *TRu* 28 (1961) 1–75, 235–97, 301–74; "Remarks on Modern Interpretation of the Prophets," *JBL* 80 (1961) 309–19. Gelin, A., "Les livres prophétiques postérieurs," R-F 1, 467–582. Graham, W. C., *The Prophets and Israel's Culture* (Chicago, 1934). Guillet, J., *Thèmes bibliques* (Paris, 1951); ET: *Themes of the Bible* (tr. A. J. LaMothe; Notre Dame, 1960). Gunkel, H., *Die Propheten* (Göttingen, 1917). Heaton, E. W., *The Old Testament Prophets* (Penguin, 1958). Heschel, A. J., *The Prophets* (N.Y., 1962). Hölscher, G., *Die Propheten* (Leipzig, 1914). Johnston, L., "Prophecy and History," *ClR* 44 (1959) 602–15. Kirkpatrick, A. F., *The Doctrine of the Prophets* (3rd ed.; London, 1901). Lindblom, J., *Prophecy in Ancient Israel* (Oxford, 1962). McKenzie, J. L., "The Word of God in the Old Testament," *TS* 21 (1960) 183–206. Moriarty, F. L., "The Prophets: Bearers of the Word," *The Bridge* (Vol. 3; N.Y., 1958) 54–83. Mowinckel, S., *Prophecy and Tradition* (Oslo, 1946). Nötscher, F., *Die Gerechtigkeit Gottes bei den vorexilischen Propheten* (Münster, 1915). Porteous, N. W., "The Prophets and the Problem of Continuity," *Israel's Prophetic Heritage* (Fest. J. Muilenburg; N.Y., 1962) 11–25. Rinaldi, G., *I Profeti Minori* (Turin, 1953). Ringgren, H., "The Prophetical Conception of Holiness" (*UUA* 12; Uppsala, 1948) 1–30. Robinson, T. H., *Prophecy and the Prophets* (London, 1923). Ross, J. F., "The Prophet as Yahweh's Messenger," *Israel's Prophetic Heritage* (N.Y., 1962) 98–107. Sellin, E., *Der alttestamentliche Prophetismus* (Leipzig, 1912). Skinner, J., *Prophecy and Religion* (Cambridge, 1922). Smith, J. M. P., *The Prophets and Their Times* (2nd ed.; rev.; Chicago, 1941). Smith, W. R., *The Prophets of Israel* (London, 1882). Snaith, N. H., *The Distinctive Ideas of the Old Testament* (London, 1944). Vawter, B., *The Conscience of Israel. Pre-exilic Prophets and Prophecy* (N.Y., 1961). Widengren, G., *Literary and Psychological Aspects of the Hebrew Prophets* (*UUA* 10; Uppsala, 1948). Ziegler, J., *Die Liebe Gottes bei den Propheten* (Münster, 1930).

2 OUTLINE

THE NATURE OF PROPHECY

3 Although our concern is with the OT prophets, specifically those whose names are attached to its prophetic books, we shall begin with some consideration of prophecy in general. The LXX did not translate the Hebr word *nābî'*, which it rendered consistently as *prophētēs*; rather, it used an equivalent term with a venerable Gk history that meant something in the non-Jewish world of that time. Obviously, therefore, although the Jewish translators would have been among the first to insist that Israelite prophecy was something special, they recognized, and so must we, that it stood in some kind of relation to the greater human culture of which Israel was but a part.

4 **(I) The Phenomenon of Prophecy.** Most religions, if not all, have produced the phenomenon of prophecy either continuously or at some stage in their development. This observation holds good not only for the so-called primitive religions but also for highly sophisticated ones. By prophecy we understand not specifically or even principally the forecasting of the future—a fairly late conception of what is essential to prophecy—but rather the mediation and interpretation of the divine mind and will. It was in this sense that *prophētēs* (lit., "one who speaks for another" or "interpreter") was used, from about the 5th cent. BC, to designate those who interpreted the divine mind as made known in various ways to themselves or to others. The function of the *prophētēs* was considered to be pre-eminently one of public religion; other terms were used to refer to private soothsayers or diviners. The function was also customarily associated with rational speech and interpretation: the inspired person as such, the recipient of a revelation that might require interpretation, was known as a *mantis*. The *prophētēs* and the *mantis* could, of course, be one and the same person; however, the latter term came to be used especially in connection with revelations of the future (cf. H. Krämer, *ThWNT* 6, 781–95).

The means of prophetic communication were, in general, the same that are presupposed in OT prophecy: dreams, visions, ecstatic or mystical experiences, and various divinatory practices. Our respect for the prophets of Israel does not require us to deny that many non-Israelite prophecies resulted from genuine religious experience. For centuries Christians felt no difficulty in recognizing genuine prophecies among the Sibylline oracles (now acknowledged, however, to be Jewish and Christian interpolations), which have even found their way into the Church's liturgy. Since prophecy is a charism that of itself says nothing about the orthodoxy or moral character of the prophet, there is no reason to restrict the prophetic spirit of God exclusively to the "normative" channels of *Heilsgeschichte*. The oracles of Balaam in Nm 22–24 were regarded as true prophecies from Yahweh, although biblical tradition classified Balaam with the enemies of God and his people (Nm 31:8,16; Jos 13:22; 2 Pt 2:15; Jude 11; Ap 2:14). As Thomas explained, because prophecy is a transient motion rather than a habit, the same person might prophesy both truth and falsehood, depending on whether or not he had been touched by the Spirit of God (*Quodl.* 12, q. 17, a. 26).

True and false prophets abound not only in antiquity, in the OT and NT, within and without the people of God, but also in later times. Although the Church has never officially applied the term "prophet" to anyone not so named in Scripture, it is nevertheless plain that God spoke to his people through such instruments as Francis of Assisi, Vincent Ferrer, Catherine of Siena, Bridget of Sweden, and others, often through experiences like those of the biblical prophets.

5 **(II) Prophecy in the Near East.** The most important analogies to OT prophecy are to be sought, of course, in the ancient Near East, of which Israel was a tiny part. A concomitant consideration that naturally arises here is the degree, if any, to which Israelite prophecy was dependent on the analogous institutions of culturally superior peoples, chiefly of Mesopotamia and Egypt, and also of the aboriginal civilization of Canaan.

From the earliest recorded time, a common pattern of seers and diviners existed throughout the Near East who were employed in ascertaining the mind of the protective divinity. "I lifted up my hand to Be'elshamayn, and Be'elshamayn heard me. Be'elshamayn [spoke] to me through seers and through diviners. Be'elshamayn [said to me]: Do not fear, for I made you king, and I shall stand by you and deliver you..." (*ANET* 501). While Amos was prophesying in Israel, an Aramean king was having these words inscribed on a stone in Syria. The explicit reference to seers and diviners clarifies the statements of Mesha, the king of Moab, made on the 9th-cent. Moabite Stone: "Chemosh said to me, 'Go, take Nebo from Israel!'...Chemosh said to me, 'Go down, fight against Hauronen'..." (*ANET* 320–21). The biblical parallel is in such passages as: "David inquired of Yahweh, 'Shall I go and attack these Philistines?' And Yahweh said to David, 'Go and attack the Philistines and save Keilah'" (1 Sm 23:2). David was accompanied by his prophet Gad (1 Sm 22:5), whose duty it was to make such inquiries of Yahweh. Even more explicitly 1 Sm 23:6–12 exemplifies the pattern: Abiathar, the priest of Nob who had joined David's band, brought with him the *ephod*, a divining instrument, by which David obtained yes-or-no answers to such questions as "Will Saul come down?" and "Will the men of Keilah surrender me to Saul?"

The existence of ecstatic prophecy in 11th-cent. Phoenicia is attested by the experiences of Wen-Amon, an Egyptian emissary at the port of Byblos (*ANET* 25–29). The harried Wen-Amon took the inconveniences caused him by the "possessed" boy fairly laconically: it was a routine occupational hazard to encounter the effects of ecstatic prophecy, just as they continued to be an embarrassment to Paul over a millennium later (Acts 16:16–18). The graphic story told in 1 Kgs 18:19–40 is witness to the character of ecstatic prophecy among the Canaanites in the time of Elijah. With few, if any, modifications, the external manifestations must have been hardly distinguishable from those of the bands of ecstatic Yahwistic prophets mentioned in 1 Sm 10:5–7,10–13; 19:18–24 in the time of Saul, and, certainly with no modifications at all, from those of a much later date spoken of in Zech 13:4–6 (this time with opprobrium).

We are even better informed about the Near Eastern pattern of prophecy from the Babylonian evidence. Prophecy was no exception to the rule of rigid organization in Babylonian society. In the Babylonian temples *bārū* priests delivered a *tērtu*, "message," to their clients chiefly through liver divination (one of the means of divination noted as characteristically Babylonian in Ez 21:26). The word *tērtu* is doubtless cognate with the Hebr *tôrâ*, used to designate prophetic instruction in Is 1:10 and elsewhere. Another type of Babylonian priest-prophet were the *maḫḫū*, "ecstatics"; their oracles were given in the throes of divine "possession," like those of the youth who plagued Wen-Amon. Neither must it be thought that these Babylonian prophets merely pandered to the magical conception of religion that perverted so much of Mesopotamian piety; the *maḫḫū* also served as judges and physicians. Their incantation formulas, although admittedly magical, nevertheless sometimes showed an awareness of that connection between religion and morality that is so much insisted upon by the prophets of Israel.

The Near Eastern pattern, as we may already surmise, makes little or no distinction between prophet and priest. In Israel, the pattern seems to have been broken, for the difference between the two was well defined. The Israelite priesthood was hereditary and hierarchical whereas prophecy was charismatic; prophets like Ezekiel and Jeremiah might also be priests, but there is no indication that such a man as Amos was a priest—indeed, many indications are against it. Still, the deviation is not as absolute as might first appear, at least as regards Israelite prophecy in the whole. It is difficult to separate the priestly from the prophetical functions of Samuel in the story of 1 Sm 9:11–26. Throughout he is called "the seer," and in 1 Sm 19:18–24 we see that he heads a band of ecstatic prophets; yet some of his main duties are to bless the sacrifice on the "high place" and to preside at the sacrificial meal. Prophets are repeatedly encountered at the sanctuaries of Israel, at Shiloh (1 Kgs 14:1–2), at Bethel (2 Kgs 2:3), at Gilgal (2 Kgs 4:38), in the Temple of Jerusalem (Jer 23:11; 35:4), etc. Prophets and priests are frequently mentioned in the same breath and, often enough, they are both associated with the sanctuary (cf. Lam 2:20). The divinatory devices used by priests (cf. 1 Sm 14:3) are also used by prophets (cf. 1 Sm 28:6). Many psalms that evidently had their life situation in the Israelite cult also presuppose the presence of prophets performing some cultic function (e.g., Ps 95:7b–11). Among the Arabs, the inspired man, the prophet, is known as the *kāhin*, a word cognate with the Hebr *kōhēn*, "priest." In this respect, too, therefore, prophecy in Israel continues to have analogies with that of the remainder of the Near East.

It is important to see these similarities if we are to evaluate properly the prophets of Israel. There was, indeed, in the ancient Near East, of which Israel was a small and (politically speaking) insignificant part, a fairly consistent pattern of prophecy—of inspired men, who in various ways spoke the Word of God to their coreligionists, whether of Babylonia, Canaan, or Israel. The recognition of this common pattern does not detract from, but instead enhances, the unique qualities of biblical prophecy.

(Eichrodt, W., *Theology of the Old Testament* [tr. J. A. Baker; Phila., 1961] 1, 296–303, 309–38. Guillaume, A., *Prophecy and Divination* [London, 1938] esp. 107–84, 185–232, 290–333. Haldar, A., *Associations of Cult Prophets Among the Ancient Semites* [Uppsala, 1945]. Jean, C.-F., *Le péché chez les Babyloniens et les Assyriens* [Piacenza, 1925]. Mendelsohn, I., *Religions of the Ancient Near East* [N.Y., 1955] 211–19. Pedersen, J., "The Role Played by Inspired Persons Among the Israelites and the Arabs," *Studies in Old Testament Prophecy* [Fest. T. H. Robinson; Edinburgh, 1950] 126–42.)

6 **(III) Prophecy in Israel.** The very prevalence of the prophetic pattern through the Near East precludes the necessity of seeking the origins of Israelite prophecy outside the religion of Israel itself. To the extent that Israelite religion had traits in common with the religions of the other, mainly Semitic, peoples of the ancient Near East, it expressed itself in kindred institutions, one of which was prophetism. To the extent, however, that Israel's religion was something quite apart in this same Near Eastern world, its prophetism also became something unlike that of any other people.

(A) A History of Israelite Prophecy. What did the Hebrew mean when he spoke of a *nābî'*, the word we translate, through the LXX, as "prophet"? This question, apparently so elementary, probably cannot be answered precisely on the basis of our present knowledge. The prevailing scholarly view, which, however, has not been universally accepted, is that *nābî'* is an Akkadian loanword meaning "one sent" or "one made to speak" (therefore, "spokesman"). The Hebr verbal forms derived from the noun and translated "prophesy" merely mean, of course, "to act the part of a *nābî'*." All that we can do to define the meaning of the term is to examine its use in OT literature as it is found in the history of prophecy. This examination will help to answer other questions, including one that arises from the paradoxical fact that the term seems to have been avoided by some of those who come first to mind when we think of the word "prophet."

7 (a) Early Prophecy. Biblical tradition traces the origins of Israelite prophecy to Moses, and, at least in the sense that this means prophecy began with Israel itself, there is no reason not to accept the tradition. The scene described in Nm 11:24–30 (E) is doubtless modeled on assemblies of ecstatic prophets known from later times, but it is to this same kind of prophet that Am 2:11 refers when ascribing the beginning of the *n^ebî'îm* to the Mosaic age. It was doubtless this kind of prophet that was first meant by the term *nābî'*. Admittedly, in later texts the term has become much broader in its signification, where it is applied to any kind of inspired person or, indeed, simply to anyone who was recognized as under special divine protection (as in the case of Abraham, Gn 20:7 [E]). Thus, Moses is commonly called a *nābî'* in the Pentateuch, as are Aaron (not only in Ex 7:1 [P], but also in Nm 12:2–8 [E], where Moses is related to Aaron and Miriam as a prophet greater than they) and Miriam (also in Ex 15:20 [P]). In the deuteronomic Jgs 4:4 (although not in the older parallel in Jgs 5), Deborah is called a *n^ebî'â*. These texts do not tell us much about the early significance of the word; as 1 Sm 9:9 shows, *nābî'* was by this time no longer restricted to any single category of "holy man."

If there is no reason to question the tradition that traces the *n^ebî'îm* to Moses, we must admit that we do not hear much about them before the late period of the judges and the early monarchy, when they are mentioned in connection with the Philistine wars. This circumstance is not surprising because a major function of these ecstatic prophets, as also of the Nazirites (→ Religious Institutions, 76:123), seems to have been to stimulate patriotic and religious fervor. Usually these men prophesied in groups whose communal experiences are described in such passages as 1 Sm 10:6–8,10–13. Hence, they are often given the generic name "sons of the prophets" (*b^enê hann^{e}bî'îm*), which has been variously interpreted "members of prophetic guilds," "professional prophets," and "prophetic disciples" (cf. 1 Kgs 20:35; 2 Kgs 2:3ff.; 5:22; 6:1, etc.). All of these interpretations may be justified. The ecstatic experience that served as the climate for prophecy was often induced by mutual contagion through dance and music. These prophets, too, are often seen to have served as disciples or apprentices under some noted prophet; however, they could also live apart as private individuals (cf. 2 Kgs 4:1). In either capacity, they can be found attached to the sanctuaries as "cult prophets" (cf. 1 Kgs 14:1ff.; 2 Kgs 22:14–17; Am 7:10ff.) or serving the king as "court prophets" (cf. 2 Sm 7:1ff.; 12:1ff.; 24:11; 1 Kgs 1:8; 22:6ff.; 2 Kgs 3:11ff.; Neh 6:7). They wore a distinctive garb of haircloth

(2 Kgs 1:8; Zech 13:4; cf. Mt 3:4 par.) and often bore other distinguishing marks (cf. 1 Kgs 20:38,41; Zech 13:6), possibly at times a tonsure (cf. 2 Kgs 2:23).

The ecstatic experience transformed the prophet, made him "another man" (1 Sm 10:6). In such a state, his antics could become grotesque, so that he could be called with rough familiarity "a madman" (2 Kgs 9:11), while his profession was regarded as hardly in keeping with responsible, respectable citizenship (1 Sm 10:11). In ancient times little distinction was made among psychic abnormalities, whether they originated in inspiration, frenzy, or insanity. Certainly this condition was the medium of genuine religious experience in which true contact was achieved with God. There is no doubt, too, that it could as easily be a source of delusion and superstition, as the later polemics of the classical prophets against the *nᵉbî'îm* show.

Ecstaticism continued to some degree throughout the entire period of Israelite prophecy. Samuel is represented on one occasion as leading a band in ecstatic prophecy (1 Sm 19:20ff.). Both Elijah and Elisha are habitually associated with the "sons of the prophets" as masters and leaders, and in 2 Kgs 3:15 Elisha makes use of a customary device to induce ecstatic seizure. The extent to which ecstaticism played a part in later prophecy, specifically that of the classical literary prophets, continues to be the subject of considerable debate. In 1 Kgs 22:5–28, the false prophet Zedekiah points to the possession of "the spirit of Yahweh" by himself and his fellow ecstatics as proof against the prophecy of Micaiah, who apparently lacks this "spirit." Micaiah simply contents himself with ascribing his prophecy to his vision, by which he also knows Zedekiah's experience to be that of a "lying spirit." Similarly, Jer 29:26 shows that ecstatic prophecy was common in Jeremiah's time, but Jeremiah himself never appeals to any possession of a prophetic "spirit." On the other hand, however, Micah (3:8) does claim "the spirit of Yahweh" as testifying against the false prophets of his time, and Hosea (9:7) defines the prophet as "the man of the spirit." Ezekiel certainly received many of his prophecies in ecstatic trance and testifies on any number of occasions to his having been seized by "spirit" and by "the hand of Yahweh."

The ancient relation of the "seer" (*rō'eh* or *ḥōzeh*) to the *nābî'* is uncertain. Etymologically, the seer would have been a visionary rather than an ecstatic, but it is not precluded that his visions would have been received as the result of ecstatic experience. Gad, a *nābî'*, is also called David's *ḥōzeh* in 2 Sm 24:11; 1 Chr 21:9 (cf. also 1 Chr 25:5), which doubtless reflects the later identification of terms shown in 1 Sm 9:9 (so also 1 Chr 9:22; 26:28; 29:29). Although it is the seer's role to prophesy (i.e., "act the part of a *nābî*," cf. Am 7:12), still the seer is distinguished from the prophet in 2 Kgs 17:13; Is 29:10; 30:10; Mi 3:6–7, etc. Dt 13:2–6 speaks of "prophets and dreamers of dreams," in which case it is doubtless with the latter that the seer is to be identified. In looking to dreams as a source of divine revelation, ancient Israel continued to share the Near Eastern pattern of inspired men. Divinatory usages may also have played a part in the seer's visions; in general, however, Israelitic religion tended to look on divination as superstition. The term "diviner" is never used in the Bible of an authentic spokesman for God.

With the sophistication of religious language, the words honored by non-Israelite religions ("diviners," "dreamers," etc.) became pejorative in connotation, and every kind of inspiration was subsumed in the concept of *nābî'*. This tendency in turn introduced a certain ambiguity, however, which was felt by Amos, who approved of the *nᵉbî'îm* and included himself in their line (3:7), and who yet had to deny that he was a *nābî'* in the sense intended by Amaziah (7:12–15)—i.e., a cult prophet encroaching on the terrain of the priest of Bethel.

(Johnson, A. R., "The Prophet in Israelite Worship," *ExpT* 47 [1935–36] 312–19; *The Cultic Prophets in Ancient Israel* [2nd ed.; Cardiff, 1962]. Mowinckel, S., "Ecstatic Experience and Rational Elaboration in Old Testament Prophecy," *AcOr* 13 [1935] 264–91; *The Psalms in Israel's Worship* [tr. D. R. Ap-Thomas; N.Y., 1962] 2, 53–73. Sparks, H. F. D., "The Witness of the Prophets to Hebrew Tradition," *JTS* 50 [1949] 129–41.)

8 (b) CLASSICAL PROPHECY. By "classical prophecy" we mean the prophecy of those whom the OT has taught us to regard as exemplifying what is distinctive about Israelite prophets—all that separates them from the Near Eastern pattern. These prophets are those whose teaching has been preserved in the OT and especially those whose names appear at the head of the prophetic books. The OT also called them *nᵉbî'îm*, as part of the standardization of terminology, and, with some reservations, they doubtless would have referred to themselves in the same way. As a matter of fact, it is not impossible that some of the classical prophets were also *nᵉbî'îm* in the sense of which we have been speaking. The professional prophet might also become a prophet through Yahweh's special call, although such was not the normal event.

This consideration introduces a question that we may as well treat now—namely, that of the so-called "false prophets." It is not a biblical term: the Hebr Bible knows only of *nᵉbî'îm* (although they may be qualified as prophets who tell lies or who have a lying spirit), although the LXX translators have in a few places introduced the paraphrase *pseudoprophētēs*. Because of the ambiguity of the word *nābî'*, the paradox arises that some of the most bitter denunciations to be found in the words of the literary prophets are addressed to, or concern, "the prophets." These literally countless passages accuse "the prophets," or, frequently enough, prophets and priests together, of every kind of moral and social crime against Yahweh and his people and of co-operating with the worst elements in Israelite rule and practice to frustrate Yahweh's will.

In the eyes of Israel and of the classical prophets themselves, of course, the false prophets were members of the *nᵉbî'îm* class as much as were the classical prophets. Although among them may have been those who simply simulated prophecy, we must not think that first and foremost they were "false" in the sense that they willfully and knowingly pretended to be what they were not. They were, rather, prophets deluded by their own prophetic devices, erring in judgment, confusing their own hopes and aspirations with the authentic word of Yahweh (cf. Is 28:7; Jer 23:5ff.). It was not precluded that the same prophet might alternately prophesy truth and falsehood, for a true prophetic word was in every case a distinct gift received from God (cf. Dt 13:2–6, restricting the somewhat unsophisticated criterion of true and false prophecy in Dt 18:21–22). In OT eyes, the activity of the false prophets was also willed by Yahweh as a means of testing his faithful followers (Jer 4:10; 1 Kgs 22:19–23, etc.).

The false prophets were often court prophets in whose interest it was to tell the king and his officials what they wanted to hear; just as often they were those who derived monetary benefits from favorable prophecies that assured their clients of divine blessings and troubled no consciences. Mainly, however, it is probably true that they were men caught up in the common tragedy of their people—i.e., those who had become so convinced that "the Israelite way of life" represented all that was godly that it had become second nature to measure Yahweh's will according to Israel's performance rather than the reverse. This oft-repeated tragedy has by no means been confined to ancient Israel. In an age when national pride spoke a religious language, it was inevitable that it should also speak in prophecy (Siegman, E. F., *The False Prophets of the OT* [Washington, 1939]).

It should be obvious that the distinction between false and true prophecy in the days of the classical prophets was not always clear. Possession of the ecstatic prophetical "spirit" was no sure criterion: prophets might be touched by the spirit and still prophesy falsehood, and most of the classical prophets give no certain signs of having been ecstatics. The fulfillment of prophecy, even if it had been always evident to the prophet's contemporaries, was not an infallible sign, as Dt 13:2ff. shows; moreover, true prophecy apparently often went unfulfilled, discouraging even the prophet himself (cf. Jer 20:7ff.). When the prophet Hananiah prophesied his own wishful thinking in predicting the end of the Babylonian exile in two years and the restoration of Jeconiah (Jer 28:1ff.), Jeremiah could offer little in rebuttal except his conviction of the truth of his own contrary prophecy. "Amen! thus may Yahweh do! May he fulfill the things you have prophesied...." Wistfully Jeremiah said this, for he would very much have preferred to prophesy as Hananiah did; however, he knew he could not, for such was not the word of Yahweh.

Jeremiah also justified his own prophecy in a way that at first seems strange to us: "From of old, the prophets who were before you and me prophesied war, woe, and pestilence against many lands and mighty kingdoms. But the prophet who prophesies peace is recognized as truly sent by Yahweh only when his prophetic prediction is fulfilled." Actually, Jeremiah is not saying simply that a prophet of doom is to be believed whereas a prophet who predicts peace is to be rejected. He is taking his stand on the prophetic tradition that had served authentic Yahwistic revelation, using essentially the same argument found in Dt 13:2ff. Anyone who really knows God will recognize his true prophet and discern him from the false, for the prophecy must conform to God's nature as he has revealed it. Jesus similarly argued his case before his generation according to Jn 5:37ff., etc. Anyone who recognizes Israel's situation in respect to the moral will of its God must also know that a prophecy of peace like Hananiah's could, in the circumstances, be no true word of God.

If the classical prophets could offer their contemporaries only the testimony of the prophetic word itself, they did nothing more or less than any true prophet could be expected to do: it is the word itself that must find a response in the heart attuned to the reception of God's grace. Their own conviction of the truth of their prophecy rests on the same foundations; therefore, the narrative of the prophetic call, the experience of the divine presence, plays a prominent role in the records of the literary prophets. This testimony constitutes their credentials, both for themselves and for those to whom they have been sent.

9 Recognition of the unique purpose to which Yahweh had dedicated prophecy in its classical age is already found in the OT in the story of Samuel. Samuel was a *nābî'*, at the head of a band of the *b^enê hann^ebî'îm*, the existence of such bands on a wide scale being presupposed in the biblical chronicle; yet when Samuel is first introduced (1 Sm 3:1), we read that "the word of Yahweh was rare in those days—visions were not frequent." In other words, with Samuel, Israelite prophecy was to achieve a new dimension. What that new dimension was, at least in the eyes of the same biblical author, is made plain in Samuel's *apologia* (1 Sm 12:1–5), an anthology of the language of Amos, Micah, Hosea, and Malachi. The same may be said of the prophetic speech attributed to the *nābî'* Nathan in 2 Sm 12:1ff. The fearless revelation of the moral will of Yahweh, the God of Israel's covenant, that is to be the characteristic of classical prophecy setting it apart from all the other prophecy, both of Israel and its neighbors, has already begun with these representatives of the ancient *nābî'* class.

In like manner, Elijah denounces Ahab's sin in 1 Kgs 21:17–24, in language worthy of an Amos or a Jeremiah. 1 Kgs 19:4ff. describes, as a new call to prophecy and as the beginning of a new prophetic line (cf. v. 14), Elijah's experience of the "gentle breeze," in which he heard the voice of Yahweh as he had not heard it before. Immediately afterward, Elisha was called to be Elijah's disciple and, ultimately, his successor as "father of Israel." While the author of the Elisha narrative has been mainly interested in this prophet as a wonder-worker, he still found time to represent his teaching, too, in terms that would find their echo in the later "social" prophets (cf. 2 Kgs 5:26).

Thus it is not hard to see why Amos, although he knew himself to be something more than a *nābî'* as this traditional institution continued into his days and beyond, did not repudiate the ancient institution but rather acknowledged his descent from it. However, he attributed what was distinctive in his prophecy to his special vocation from Yahweh (Am 7:15), as Elijah would have done and as so many of the other literary prophets do (cf. Hos 1–3; Is 6; Jer 1; Ez 1, etc.). In the same spirit, the classical prophets tend to give themselves names other than *nābî*—names that more clearly define their significance as Yahweh's special designates. They are "messengers of Yahweh" (Is 44:26; Hag 1:13; Mal 3:1), "servants of God" (Is 20:3; Am 3:7; Jer 7:25; 24:4), "shepherds" (Jer 17:16; Zech 11:4), "guardians" (Is 62:6; Heb 2:1), "watchmen" (Am 3:4; Is 56:10; Jer 6:17; Ez 3:17), etc.

10 The classical prophets best known to us are the so-called literary prophets of the 8th, 7th, and 6th cents. BC. In a roughly chronological order, these are Amos, Hosea, Isaiah, Micah, Nahum, Zephaniah, Habakkuk, Jeremiah, and Ezekiel. All, with the exception of Hosea, were apparently Judahites, although Amos is also, for all practical purposes, a prophet who continues the northern Israelite tradition of classical prophecy begun by Samuel and Elijah. Classical prophecy should not be limited to these great names, however; there are other literary prophets whose names we do not know. One of them, indeed one of the greatest, is the exilic prophet whom we call the Second Isaiah; in addition, numerous anonymous prophets are responsible for supplements to other of the prophetic books, for many of the psalms, and for other prophetical writings found elsewhere in the OT. Then, too, there were other prophets in the classical tradition whose actual words we have in small part or not at all. We do not even know the names of some. Jer 7:25; 11:7 simply speaks of a continuous tradition of true prophecy from the time of Israel's origins. Of some we know the names only, such as the Uriah mentioned in Jer 26:20–23, whose prophecy was contemporary with Jeremiah's and in his spirit.

The special vocation of Yahweh that plays such an important part in the thoughts of the classical prophets is more than simply their title to prophecy. In the way it has been incorporated into their prophetic words, it is often the key—the leitmotiv—of their prophecy, for the prophets are highly individualistic thinkers whose separate personalities were as many diverse instruments through which the Word of the Lord was given. While it is true that there is a recognizably common prophetic doctrine on the essentials of Yahwistic religion and on many of its details as well, and that in the past there was a tendency to overemphasize the individual prophetic genius and originality, it is likewise true that no one who is at all familiar with the prophetic literature is in much danger of confusing one prophet with another. Their similarities derive from their devotion to common ideals and from their dependence on common traditions and institutions. Their mediation of the prophetic word, however, is quite personal. They rarely cite one another or even acknowledge one another's existence. The authority with which they spoke came, in other words, from their individual serene confidence of having the mind of Yahweh.

While pre-exilic classical prophecy, with variations, tends to be a prophecy of judgment against Israel and Judah, the prophecy of Nahum is apparently an exception. Nahum's prophecy is a paean of triumph over the dissolution of the Assyrian Empire, the end of which he foresaw as imminent. It does not mean, as some have thought, that Nahum was one of those "prophets of peace," whose nationalistic pride was so repugnant to Jeremiah. The humbling of the nations other than Israel is also part of the message of other classical prophets who are far from being "prophets of peace." Another prophet who does not fall easily into the pre-exilic pattern is Habakkuk, not so much because of the content of his prophecy, the precise significance of which can still be debated, as because of its form. However, it would be a mistake to imagine that the prophets have to conform to a given list of uniform characteristics. Habakkuk was possibly a cult prophet, as presumably the prophetess Huldah was (2 Kgs 22:14). Those responsible for the royal Pss were also doubtless cult or court prophets, yet there is obviously some difference between the mind that produced Ps 2 and that which composed Ps 72. Given the nature of prophecy, by which the Word of God has been voiced through every kind of chosen instrument, this result was only to be expected.

(Causse, A., *Israël et la vision de l'humanité* [Strasbourg, 1924]. Davies, G. H., "The Yahwistic Tradition in the Eighth-Century Prophets," *Studies in Old Testament Prophecy* [Fest. T. H. Robinson; Edinburgh, 1950] 37–51. Dürr, L., *Wollen und Wirken der alttestamentlichen Propheten* [Düsseldorf, 1926]. Michaux, W., "Les cycles d'Élie et d'Élisée," *BibViChr* 2 [1953] 76–99. Newman, M., "The Prophetic Call of Samuel," *Israel's Prophetic Heritage* [Fest. J. Muilenburg; N.Y., 1962] 86–97. Rowley, H. H., "The Nature of Prophecy in the Light of Recent Study," *HarvTR* 38 [1945] 1–38. Seierstad, I. P., *Die Offenbarungserlebnisse der Propheten Amos, Jesaja und Jeremia* [Oslo, 1946]. Steinmann, J., *Le prophétisme biblique des origines à Osée* [LD 23; Paris, 1959].)

11 (c) Post-exilic Prophecy. Through the Exile, Israel was granted a new vision of the divine economy—that of the great exilic prophets, Jeremiah, Ezekiel, and the Second Isaiah. The particulars of this new vision will be treated, of course, in the commentaries on these prophets. Here, we wish only to note their influence on the final stage of Israelite prophetism—the period of Palestinian Judaism following the Exile.

Post-exilic prophecy lacks much of the vigor and spontaneity of pre-exilic prophecy; at all events, it forms a category apart that invites its separation from the age of classical prophecy. "To a great extent the prophets of this period lived on the ideas of the earlier prophets, and in particular those of the exilic prophets. Their special characteristics are seen less in original ideas of their own than in certain marked tendencies and in the ways in which they modified the ideas they borrowed" (Lindblom, *op. cit.*, 404). The prophets who pertain to this category, listed in chronological order, are the prophet or prophets responsible for the final section of Is (the so-called Trito-Isaiah), Haggai, Zechariah (chs. 1–8), Malachi, Obadiah, Joel, and the anonymous prophets who produced Zech 9–11, 12–14, not to mention numerous prophetic hands that have intervened in the final production of various of the older prophetic books, especially, Is, Jer, and Ez.

The post-exilic prophetic corpus is probably a more consistent unity than the pre-exilic. The post-exilic Obadiah more or less corresponds to the pre-exilic Nahum in prophesying peace for Israel in the destruction of a hated enemy. However, the fact that the Book of Consolation of the Second Isaiah has preceded Obadiah's prophecy serves to set him in the post-exilic tradition more firmly than Nahum's prophecy sets him in the pre-exilic tradition. In general, the post-exilic prophets could take a more "optimistic" view of Israel's destiny than could the pre-exilic prophets, for the doom that the latter had foretold had now come and gone, and a new hope could be found in the figure of the Servant of the Lord revealed by the exilic Isaiah. Zechariah and Malachi show a concern for the Temple, the Law, and matters of cult that cannot be discovered in a pre-exilic prophet. This concern, however, is a continuation of Ezekiel's, an authentic prophet of Israelite doom who at the same time had seen the vision of a new covenant that Yahweh would effect on Palestinian soil when changed conditions would require new religious unities and stresses. Trito-Isaiah also has been greatly influenced by Ezekiel and the Second Isaiah. The bold apocalyptic imagery of Zechariah, Joel, and the Isaiah supplements (chs. 24–27, 34–35) was foreshadowed in Ezekiel, whom many regard as the father of apocalyptic (→ Post-exilic Period, 20:9–10).

The diversity of post-exilic prophecy, it seems, is mainly one of styles, which are often frankly derivative and lacking in the freshness of the earlier prophetic oracles. The themes are fairly common, proper to a people now living under Judaism, when Temple and Torah had become the enduring realities that would continue as Israel's unity after the voice of prophecy had been stilled. Prophecy itself helped in the transition to conditions under which the people of God could survive for many generations (although its lack would be continually felt, cf. 1 Mc 4:46; 14:41). It did so by responding to needs that Jeremiah and Ezekiel had already foreseen before the Exile, by insisting on individual responsibility and fidelity to the Law, speaking to an Israel with which God would no longer deal simply as a people good or bad, for better or for worse, but as a religion in which each member must follow the rule of life set before him until the dawn of an even better hope (cf. Ez 3:16–21; 33:1–20). After a brief interest in a Davidic restoration (Zech 6:9–15), it reverted to other soteriological themes, the variety of which had already been enriched in exilic prophecy, and in this way continued the prophetic testimony to Yahweh's universal domination (cf. Mal 1:11; Is 19:9–10, etc.). It finally promised that prophecy would return (cf. Mal 3:22–24) and that, in fact, in some fashion it would become the gift of all God's people (Jl 3:1–5).

The disappearance of prophecy in Israel was as unobtrusive as its beginning; it would be impossible to determine who was the last OT prophet. In the last 200 years BC, the wisdom writers consciously carried on the tradition inherited from prophecy (cf. Sir 24:31; Wis 7:27), without, however, claiming to possess the prophetic spirit.

(Chary, T., *Les prophètes et le culte à partir de l'Exil* [Tournai, 1955]. Lods, A., *Les prophètes et les débuts du Judaïsme* [Paris, 1935].)

12 **(B) Its Distinctive Character.** From what we have already said, it should be easy to generalize about the distinctive character of Israelite prophecy, some of the particulars of which we shall treat in the following sections.

To the extent that Israel possessed cult and court prophets, or prophets whose gifts were at the disposal of the nation or of individual clients in public or private consultation, Israelite prophecy was part of the aforementioned Near Eastern pattern. Even in such cases, the conformity to the pattern was not exact, for the content of this prophecy was distinctively Israelite. It would be easy to find a non-Israelite parallel to the 400 prophets at the call of the king of Israel in 1 Kgs 22, but not to the prophet Micaiah, who was also at his call. It would be impossible to find a non-Israelite court prophet who would speak to his king as Nathan did to David, or even one who would speak of the king as the royal psalmists do. No true parallel to such literature has yet been found outside Israel, for it was the expression of a religion without true parallel in its contemporary world.

There is no non-Israelite parallel for classical prophecy, either in form or in content. There seems to be no valid reason to alter the judgment made over 50 years ago by a man who was never reluctant to minimize what was unique in Israel, that "the results of a search for genuine Babylonian prophecies are disappointing" and who thus ventured "to doubt [that Babylonia and Assyria] had any prophecies at all" (T. K. Cheyne, *The Two Religions of Israel* [London, 1911] 7–8). Neither has such a search proved to be productive elsewhere. The few scraps of "prophetic morality" that can be assembled from the hundreds of years of well-documented literary history of ancient Egypt certainly do not add up to anything remotely comparable to Israelite prophecy, let alone anything that could justify the fantastic theory once proposed by Egyptological enthusiasts—i.e., the prophetic moral teaching of Israel was of Egyptian origin. The Egyptian material—wisdom literature of the Middle Kingdom or of the interregnum succeeding the Old Kingdom (cf. *ANET* 407–10)—is evidence that Egypt occasionally produced moral voices worthy of comparison with those of the OT but not that it ever possessed a prophetic tradition like Israel's. Israelite prophecy broke with the ancient pattern when it began to produce men who not only spoke from the Israelite institutions but who also judged them and became their conscience. We thus have the distinctive literary forms that found no genuine echo in the other literature of antiquity.

PROPHECY AND ISRAEL'S INSTITUTIONS

As we have already mentioned, prophecy, at least in the classical sense of the word, was a charismatic phenomenon. Therefore, if we are to understand its historical significance in Israelite religion, it is relevant to see the relation of this phenomenon to the noncharismatic Israelite institutions.

13 **(I) The Law and the Priesthood.** Despite the fact that some prophets (e.g., Jeremiah, Ezekiel) were certainly priests, there has long been a persuasion in critical circles that the prophetic and the priestly offices were somehow opposed, at least in the pre-exilic period. (It was always fairly obvious that exilic and post-exilic prophecy had a concern for cult and priestly law, but this concern was explained by the emphasis laid on these institutions in post-exilic Judaism.) Is it true to say that the pre-exilic prophetic tradition was a rival to the priestly tradition that became canonized in the written Law of Moses in and after the Exile?

The functions of priest and prophet were always carefully distinguished in Israel; however, these functions coincided in part. Jer 18:18 speaks of the "law" (*tôrâ*) of the priest, the "counsel" (*'ēṣâ*) of the wise man, and the "word" (*dābār*) of the prophet. While these three conveyed their teachings in different ways—the priest by an institutional tradition, the wise man by a professional tradition, the prophet by a charismatic prompting—they doubtlessly felt that they were contributing each in his own way to a common objective. When the prophets condemned the priesthood, as they often did, it was not for what the priests were teaching but rather for what they were not: They had rejected knowledge and had ignored the law (*tôrâ*) of God (Hos 4:6). In the same spirit, the "false" prophets were condemned, not to reject the idea of prophecy but rather a travesty of it.

The opposition between priesthood and prophecy was exaggerated because of several factors. One was the persuasion, now considerably corrected, that law was a relatively late development in Israel, representing the triumph of formal over spiritual religion. Another was the distorted perspective in which the religion of the prophets was viewed in respect to the "official" religion of Israel. It is quite true, of course, that some difference invariably existed between the attitudes and interests of priestly and prophetic religion, but they were attitudes and not different religions. At its best, the priesthood did the same work, or part of the same work, that prophecy did, i.e., it transmitted the revealed moral will of the God of Israel. The priesthood did so by the tradition of religious law preserved in the sanctuaries; prophecy accomplished the task by the communication of the living word. In principle, the latter was not intended to oppose the former.

Supposed citations of the Law by pre-exilic prophets are often doubtful and, in any case, very few, which of course raises the question of the extent to which the Law existed in pre-exilic times in written form, and in what form, a question into which we cannot enter here. These problems also point to the nature of prophecy, as we have discussed it, which is to depend for its authority on its own communication of the word and not on other prior, even prophetical authority. The teaching of prophecy is, in any case, always consistent with the Law, even if it is expressed in its own way and with its own stresses.

Am 3:2 expresses the idea of election with the thought, if not the precise words, of Dt 14:2. Amos' description of the Exodus and desert wandering and their meaning (2:10; 3:1; 4:10; 5:25; 9:7) are of a piece with Ex 20:2, wherein Egypt is designated as "the house of slaves." This expression is also used by the prophets (cf. Mi 6:4; Jer 34:13), none of which proves that Amos depended on Dt or Ex as written texts, any more than his reference to a *tôrâ* in 2:4 is necessarily to a written priestly law. It does prove, however, that Amos taught a tradition contained in the Law, and although allusive and casual, his statements presuppose the account told in the Pentateuch, with which he agrees even in trivial details (cf. Am 2:9; Nm 13:32). Hos 8:1 explicitly connects the law of Yahweh with a covenant, which, of course, is precisely what the law professes to be; although Hosea does not say that the covenant is that of Sinai, he does connect it with the Exodus (8:13; 9:3; 11:5; cf. Dt 28:68). Furthermore, the *tôrâ* that Hosea associates with the covenant in 8:1 is seen in 4:6 as a priestly *tôrâ* entailing social morality; from 8:12, there evidently existed some kind of written *tôrâ* or *tôrôt*. From the context, it appears that in the last instance Hosea was referring to cultic precepts, which is typical because the prophets really made no distinction between the law of Yahweh as it regarded morality and as it regarded ritual.

The OT has been transmitted through various streams of tradition that have often mutually influenced one another without, however, becoming assimilated. The prophetic tradition requires no glorification at the expense of minimizing other traditions that served their own truths in their own way, supplementing without necessarily contradicting the truths of prophecy.

(Birkeland, H., *Zum hebräischen Traditionswesen* [Oslo, 1938]. Dürr, L., "Altorientalisches Recht bei den Propheten Amos und Hosea," *BZ* 23 [1935–36] 150–57. Scott, R. B. Y., "Priesthood, Prophecy, Wisdom, and the Kingdom of God," *JBL* 80 [1961] 1–15. Van der Ploeg, J., "Studies in Hebrew Law," *CBQ* 12 [1950] 248–59, 416–27; *CBQ* 13 [1951] 28–43, 164–71, 296–307. Welch, A. C., *Prophet and Priest in Old Israel* [London, 1952].)

14 **(II) The Cult.** An extension of this problem is the relation of the prophets to the Israelite cult. Again, the problem arises with the pre-exilic prophets: No one will seriously question the deep involvement of an Ezekiel, a Zechariah, or a Malachi in the ritual of the post-exilic community.

It might seem that there is little need to deal with this question today, when there is a tendency to exaggerate in an opposite direction by assimilating even the classical prophets of Israel to the Near Eastern pattern of cult prophet with which we have just dealt. Nevertheless, the opinion is still shared by some biblical critics that the pre-exilic prophets were opposed to the cult religion of Israel on principle.

We have seen that there were cult prophets in Israel. Were the classical prophets also of this type? This question cannot be answered with a conclusive yes or no, simply from lack of evidence, but at least the great majority of them probably were not. There are some grounds to permit us to classify Nahum and Habakkuk of the pre-exilic prophets, and Joel and Zechariah of the post-exilic prophets, as Temple prophets. Not even in these cases is the evidence necessarily peremptory (e.g., Zech 7:1ff.); in most other cases there is simply no probability in favor of the "cultic" hypothesis. Isaiah's call to prophecy almost certainly took place during a cultic celebration, but there is no proof that Isaiah was present in the Temple in any capacity other than as a pious Israelite. If mere interest in the cult would qualify a prophet as cultic, we should certainly have to make a cult prophet of Ezekiel. Yet it is simply impossible, for there was no Temple cult in the Babylonia where Ezekiel prophesied, and he apparently prophesied nowhere else.

If they were not cult prophets, however, the pre-exilic prophets were indeed involved with the cult. They were involved with it as Isaiah was, as those to whom it was the normal means of worshiping God, taken as much for granted by them as the Israelite traditions to which they appealed in identifying Yahweh with the moral God who had revealed himself to them. They took it for granted in this way, and yet, of course, they did not take it for granted at all, just as they took nothing for granted in the light of their prophetic vision. It was one of the institutions of Israel over which they had been appointed as judges, and judge it they did. In doing so, however, they no more excluded it than they excluded the priesthood, the covenant, the doctrine of election, or prophecy itself, all of which they also judged.

There are various assertions of the pre-exilic prophets that have been interpreted as expressing opposition to animal sacrifice in principle, as a less worthy or an unworthy way of worshiping Yahweh, possibly because it was imported from Canaan and certainly because it embodied an inferior conception of religion against the constant prophetic call for the spiritual sacrifice of service and personal integrity. Some of the chief passages involved are Am 5:21–27; Hos 6:6; Jer 7:21–23; Is 1:12–17; these are perhaps the strongest assertions of their kind, and they are typical of the rest.

When these passages are read in context and not as part of a preconceived theory of the origin of Israelite religion or of what the prophetic ideal of religion must have been, they make very good sense and are completely consistent with the rest of prophetic doctrine. The prophets are altogether existentialist in their approach to this aspect of Israelite life as to any other. They were not concerned with the issue of animal sacrifice or other forms of external sacrifice as an ideal or an abstraction. What was at issue were the sacrifices then being carried out in contemporary sanctuaries by men who were perpetrating a sacramentalism devoid of meaning. These sacrifices, say Amos and Jeremiah, Yahweh did not command. Love, not sacrifice, is the will of God, says Hosea; or, as we might rephrase it, there can be no true sacrifice without love. Absolutes of this kind are a commonplace of biblical language, in the NT as well as in the OT (cf. Lk 14:26 [note Mt 14:26]; 1 Cor 1:17 [note vv. 14–16], etc.); ordinarily they cause no trouble, as long as we are attentive to the context at hand. Isaiah's denunciation, perhaps the strongest of the lot, if interpreted out of its existential situation, would lead to the conclusion that Yahweh rejected prayer itself (cf. v. 15) along with sacrifices, incense, festivals, and feast days.

One does well not to avoid an extreme by embracing another. We can frankly admit that, on their own reading, certain of the prophets would have had at best a minimal interest in the Israelite liturgy, which does not necessarily mean that they made a fetish of opposing rites the observance of which had become a fetish for others. Jeremiah frequented the Temple that he denounced, as did Isaiah before him. On the other hand, Ezekiel, who certainly left no doubt that for him the restoration of Jerusalem's Temple was a condition without which Yahweh could not be properly worshiped by the people he had made his own, nevertheless knew full well that Yahweh himself was the true sanctuary who alone could give any meaning to the Temple built with hands (cf. 11:16). The prophetic attitude to the cult was like the prophetic attitude to everything—one in which forms were always secondary to the realities they signified. It was only when forms no longer signified anything that they demanded condemnation.

(Hentschke, R., *Die Stellung der vorexilischen Schriftpropheten zum Kultus* [Berlin, 1957]. Rowley, H. H., "The Unity of the Old Testament," *BJRylL* 29 [1946] 326–58; "The Meaning of Sacrifice in the Old Testament," *BJRylL* 33 [1950] 74–110.)

15 **(III) The Monarchy.** In respect to the monarchy, the prophetic attitude was characterized by a concern for spiritual realities and a lack of interest in forms as such. The relation of prophecy to the monarchy is important for many reasons, not the least of which was the influence that this institution exercised on prophetic messianic doctrine. Temporally, prophecy and the monarchy coincided almost exactly: The age of kingship in Israelite history was also the age of classical prophecy. In a history of salvation, the fact alone suggests even more intimate connections between the two.

The monarchy served partly as a stimulus to prophecy, for with it there entered into Israelite life a new conception of the relation of Israel to Yahweh, one that had to be under constant review by prophecy. That the popular call for a king was, in a sense, a repudiation of the covenant relationship (cf. 1 Sm 8:4ff.) was doubtless the preferred prophetic view in retrospect; but in any case, not only the tradition that reflects this antimonarchical view but also the tradition that saw in Saul the heaven-sent ruler to end Israel's woes (1 Sm 9:15ff.) are in agreement that prophecy presided over the transition to kingship. It was this, in fact, that alone could have made the monarchy acceptable to Israel—it provided the charismatic guarantees the lack of which had made Abimelech's ill-starred kingship such an aberration from Israelite tradition (Jgs 9) and the transfer of which from Saul to David established the kingship with a permanency the like of which it could never have obtained under Saul (1 Sm 15:10–11). Paradoxically, therefore, prophecy was instrumental in establishing an institution for which its enthusiasm was always at best lukewarm and which it probably would have preferred never to have taken place.

Nevertheless, prophecy never headed any movement in Israel to replace the monarchy with another form of government that it might have been thought to prefer. That this is true is also singularly fortunate, for there is no indication that the prophetic tradition ever possessed either the taste or the talent for practical politics. Whenever prophecy intervened in these matters, it was as apt to be ill-advised as to succeed in its high purposes. Nathan's approval of Solomon over Adonijah (1 Kgs 1:8) was perhaps the blessing of legal processes and the indications of Yahweh's will (1 Chr 28:5) in opposition to an arrogant assumption that a man should rule simply because he was his father's son; however, from the standpoint of prophecy it could hardly be said that Solomon proved to be a wise choice. It is surely not by accident that nowhere in the biblical traditions is it recorded that Solomon either sought the advice of prophecy or received a prophetic oracle. The revolt of Jeroboam against the Davidic dynasty was similarly blessed by prophecy (1 Kgs 11:29–39), but Jeroboam later had to be repudiated by the same prophetic voice (1 Kgs 14:7–11). As in the case of the prophetic intervention that ended Omri's dynasty (2 Kgs 9:1ff.) by replacing it with another that became, if anything, something worse (Am 7:9; Hos 1:4–5; 8:4), the prophetic record in political intrigue is one of failures rather than of successes. It is just as well, then, that with certain exceptions the prophetic attitude, translated into terms of practical policy, was to try to make the best use of existing institutions.

Of course, this was as it should have been. The function of prophecy was to form the conscience of a people, not to dictate its politics. It did not necessarily desire the coming of the monarchy, but it assured that its coming would be in accordance with Yahweh's will. Once it had come, it played the role that destiny had now allotted it—to insist on obedience to the old covenant precepts relegated to the status of private law through the institution of the law of the king. It is in this role that Elijah is cast by 1 Kgs 21:17–24, where the prophet must denounce the crime that Ahab had committed against Israelite law and custom by submitting to the guidance of his Phoenician wife who had tried to show him how to be a real king as the non-Israelite Near East understood kingship. In this episode, as in the action of the prophet Shemaiah against Rehoboam (2 Chr 12:5–7), Jehu against Baasha (1 Kgs 16:1–4), Isaiah against Ahaz (Is 7:10ff.) or Hezekiah (2 Kgs 20:12ff.), and Jeremiah against the last kings of Judah (Jer 21:11ff.), the labor of prophecy was to make the kingship of Israel truly Israelite.

The effort was largely a failure. There were limited successes, as the historical books and some of the prophetic records testify. But the judgment of the deuteronomic author of Kgs on the history of the Israelite monarchy would doubtless have found agreement on the part of the majority of the classical prophets. Although based on more specific and somewhat different criteria from that which the prophets would always have used, his verdict is a prophetical one—that with extremely rare exceptions the kings had been failures from the standpoint of the issues that really mattered.

16 The messianic doctrine of the prophets (→ Aspects OT Thought, 77:155) fits consistently into the outline of their attitude to the monarchy. The royal messianism of the pre-exilic prophets rests on the same religious premise held by the authors of the royal Pss—i.e., the prophetic oracle given to the house of David (2 Sm 7:4ff.; Ps 89:20–38). The classical prophets accepted this tradition as a revelation of Yahweh that had essentially conditioned their theology, even as the deuteronomic authors did, contrary to their instinctive dislike for monarchy (cf. G. von Rad, *Studies in Deuteronomy* [London, 1953] 88–91). But whereas the court or temple prophets responsible for the royal Pss have, to a greater or less degree, entered wholeheartedly into the mystique that surrounded kingship in the Near East, adopting the *Hofstil*, by which the kings were accorded divine titles and unending days, we find little or no trace of any such thing in the classical literary prophets. This is not to say that the royal Pss reflect a wholly uncritical acceptance of the Near Eastern kingly ideal; the ideal has been thoroughly Israelitized and made part of the Israelite eschatology of Yahweh's universality and the Davidic oracle (cf. H.-J. Kraus, *Psalmen* [Neukirchen, 1960] 1, 14–16). Nevertheless, the psalmists can display an enthusiasm for kingship itself as represented in the anointed of Yahweh, and this has no counterpart in the oracles of the classical prophets. A more radical Israelitization has taken place in these oracles—a spiritualization that has de-emphasized the king as king and stressed the king as the elect of Yahweh.

Isaiah perhaps is closest to the language of the royal Pss in his prophecies regarding the Davidic kingship (cf. 7:13–17; 9:5–6; 11:1–5), yet only a brief reflection is necessary to show how much his thinking differs from theirs. For example, he never uses the royal title, even though it is beyond question that he is speaking of a Davidic king. Awesome titles are used, but they glorify the charismatic actions of Yahweh rather than their recipient. That we have here no mere circumstance but rather a studied policy seems to be borne out through the comparison of other prophetic passages of the same kind. Mi 5:1–4 (whether the work of Micah himself or of another prophet is not here important), also dependent on the ancient Nathan oracle, shows similar traits. All these prophecies predicate glorious things of the messianic ruler, but their entire stress is on the power of Yahweh acting through him. This prophetic peculiarity reaches some kind of culmination in the prophecy of Ezekiel. Ezekiel denies the title of king to the Davidic prince who will preside over the restored Israel (37:25), and, in view of the sharp restrictions that he places on the activity of this prince, we can hardly discern in his prophecy more than a faint reflection of the traditional royal messianic idea (cf. 44:3; 45:7–8; 46:16–18, etc.).

If it is true that Jeremiah speaks of a Davidic scion who will reign as king with the justice of Yahweh (23:5–6), it is likewise true that it is probably the only reference made to him by the prophet in all the material that has come down to us (30:9; 33:14ff. are apparently later additions). Exilic prophecy in general placed no emphasis on royal messianism: the "messiah" (*māšîaḥ*, "anointed one") of Yahweh, according to the Second Isaiah (cf. 41:2; 44:28; 45:1), is no Davidic king, but Cyrus, the king of the Persians! For this prophet the only redeemer of Israel is Yahweh (41:14). In the post-exilic period, Davidic messianism was again in prophetic vogue for a time. In the days of Zerubbabel, the prophets Haggai and Zechariah returned briefly to the old tradition, but their expectation was short, as the corrected text of Zechariah (cf. Zech 6:9–15) shows. It was doubtless in this same period that other prophetic hands interpolated earlier prophetic works with similar references to a Davidic ruler.

We must emphasize, of course, that the prophets never denied the relevance of Davidic messianism to the divine economy. It is only that it was never one of their overriding ideas; they recognized that it had a proper place in Yahweh's salvific plan to the extent that they had been permitted to see it, but its place remained in the background of their thoughts. Amos and Hosea, who prophesied in northern Israel where there was a different, non-Davidic kingly tradition, characteristically prophesy nothing of royal messianism (although such prophecies were later inserted into their works). By disposition the prophets were not royalists, but they had to acknowledge that God had spoken through ancient prophecy regarding the destiny of the Davidic line. It was to honor this prophecy that they could await a king who would reverse the sad performance of most of the kings of Israel and Judah by being the true son of Yahweh that he was proclaimed to be. In all this the prophets anticipated to a marvelous degree the attitude that Jesus himself adopted toward royal messianism when he came to fulfill the expectations of the OT. For Jesus, too, royal messianism was a detail only in the divine economy of salvation. Without rejecting it as irrelevant to that economy, he nevertheless preferred to identify himself with other figures that more clearly defined the nature of the realization he gave to the hopes of Israel.

(Gray, J., "The Kingship of God in the Prophets and Psalms," *VT* 11 [1961] 1–29. Hammerschaimb, E., "Ezekiel's View of the Monarchy," *Studia Orientalia* [Fest. J. Pedersen; Copenhagen, 1953] 130–40. Lagrange, M. J., "Pascal et les prophéties messianiques," *RB* 3 [1906] 533–60. McKenzie, J. L., "Royal Messianism," *CBQ* 19 [1957] 25–52. O'Doherty, E., "The Organic Development of Messianic Revelation," *CBQ* 19 [1957] 16–24. Welch, A. C., *Kings and Prophets of Israel* [London, 1952].)

17 **(IV) The Religion of Israel.** Our final consideration in regard to prophecy's connections with Israelite institutions will be to sum up a few of the key concerns of prophetic teaching as viewed in the light of the popular religion of the times. From this point of view, we can more readily see both the prophetic originality, which is never to be minimized, and the conformity of the prophets to the traditional faith of their ancestors.

(A) Eschatology. Messianism is one aspect of eschatology; therefore, we have already noted one prophetic emphasis by which the prophets were both connected with, and separated from, other Israelites. By eschatology in this context we mean Israel's conviction that it was a people of election, that it had a part to play in the work of judgment and power exercised by God over the universe. As to whether this work was envisioned as a continuous one, extending into the historical future, or as a definitive one, pertaining to a time beyond history, is a secondary matter into which we need not enter. For all practical purposes, the eschatology of Israel's prophets was, in fact, historical, although the idea of a definitive judgment is proper to a later Judaism. However, this distinction probably could never have meant as much to the people of the OT as it does to us who have seen the passing away of the Israel known to the OT and have received the quite distinctive interpretation of eschatology contributed by NT revelation.

What is important, however, is recognition of the historical nature of prophetical eschatology in another sense—i.e., from the standpoint of the biblical conception of time, which has sometimes been called "linear" and opposed to the "cyclic" conception of time supposedly associated with other ways of thought. Perhaps too much has been made of the distinction, and there has doubtlessly been some exaggeration in the conclusions drawn from it. What seems to be a fact, however, apparent to anyone at all familiar with the Bible, is that with quite rare exceptions the biblical authors never conceived of time in the sense of a deterministic pattern but as a series of moments filled with distinctly willed events. To recognize this fact is to rule out the fanciful interpretations of prophecy that have ascribed to the prophet a photographic vision of a near or distant future that somehow had relevance for the people to whom he had been sent to reveal the word of God. "The prophet does not see history stretched out before him like a map, from which he need only pick out individual future events. Such foresight is not the prophet's gift. Rather he sees in which direction events are flowing. This is the scope of prophecy. The Hebrew conception of time excludes any other explanation of it" (C. Tresmontant, *A Study of Hebrew Thought* [tr. M. F. Gibson; N.Y., 1960] 27).

Whatever the explanation, it is verifiable fact that it is not the nature of biblical prophecy to see the future as a photograph. Prediction was, indeed, often part of the prophetic message, but prediction was permitted to the prophet always in terms of the contingencies that he knew and that would be understood by his hearers. Isaiah's prophecy of Sennacherib's invasion (10:27–34) is a classical instance: The prophecy was fulfilled, but under circumstances not envisioned by the prophet. The same characteristics apply to the prophets' vision of Israel's eschatology (cf. J. van der Ploeg, *StudCath* 28 [1953] 81–93).

18 It might seem pointless to have to insist that the prophets shared Israel's conviction of its divine election. Nevertheless, it has been held at times that this was not so, and Am 3:2, for example, has been called spurious because it contradicts Am 9:7. Probably most everyone would agree that the once easy admission of such "contradictions" was in reality to miss much of the point of prophetic teaching. The prophets did believe in Israel's election; the vast majority of their utterances, as a matter of fact, would cease to make much sense if their life situation were not founded in such a belief. Election was part of the fundamental constitution of Israel, and the prophets were quite prepared, even if their contemporaries were not, to accept all the consequences of Israel's status as the chosen of God (cf. Am 3:9–12).

The prophets spiritualized and moralized this belief. It would perhaps be more accurate to say that they remoralized it, for they did so without any claim to innovation. The very idea of election carries with it some obvious hazards, such as the temptation to complacency over its effects or haziness over its grounds. Many Israelites had fallen to these temptations. Israel had not been chosen for Israel's sake, the prophets had to insist, but for God's; Israel had not been chosen for its virtues, but because being drawn near God, it might find the way of virtue. When Amos agreed that Yahweh had chosen Israel, it was to remind Israel that in this fact lay his right to destroy it for its crimes: "Therefore I will punish you" (3:2).

Israelite tradition had expressed the conception of election in various metaphors and analogies, one of the most important of which was that of covenant. This conception, too, is to be found in the prophets, although again with their own proper reservations. The term never appears in Amos, who perhaps felt it impossible to rehabilitate it from its misuse. Most of the other prophets, however, show no reluctance to employ it, but they use it as Amos used the idea of election itself—for them the covenant was a deed of Yahweh's grace and the foundation of moral obligation. The figure of Yahweh summoning his people before the bar of justice, which is so common in the prophets (cf. the technical term *rîb*, "litigation," in Hos 4:1; Mi 6:2, etc., and other equivalents elsewhere), was, we now recognize, borrowed from primitive covenant terminology. The prophets also usually insist on the tradition of the Mosaic covenant, which was conditioned, rather than on the patriarchal or Davidic covenants, which were unconditioned. In the Mosaic covenant, the moral character of election was most apparent. It is unusual for a pre-exilic prophet to dwell on the patriarchal traditions, although these are mentioned more frequently in exilic and post-exilic prophecy (→ Aspects OT Thought, 77:83–85).

19 An idea that assisted the prophets in spiritualizing the conception of election was that of the "remnant." Associated most characteristically with Isaiah, this idea seems also to have been imbedded in Israel's best traditions older than the literary prophets. If Amos hardly considered it a viable possibility (5:15), and even scoffingly described a remnant that was not a remnant at all (3:12), he still seems to have honored the belief in his own fashion. Amos was far too convinced of Israel's perdition to waste time in speculating on the consequences of repentance, but other prophets were not so pessimistic. In the preaching of Hosea, Isaiah, and Jeremiah, the notion of a saved remnant that would survive Yahweh's judgment and become a restored Israel gave to the doctrine of election a theological depth in which the designs of a beneficent God could be envisioned better and laid the groundwork for post-exilic prophecy.

Judgment itself was an eschatological idea profoundly spiritualized in prophetic teaching. The "day of Yahweh" to which Amos referred as something taken for granted by his contemporaries (5:18–20) is subject to various interpretations; in any case, he plainly had in mind some event that would celebrate Yahweh's triumph over his enemies. The significance of Amos' use of the expression was his identification of the enemies not as the unbelieving Gentiles but as Israel itself. Another pre-exilic prophet would take up this theme, agreeing with the popular notion that this day would mean the end of the peoples opposed to the people of God (cf. Zeph 2:1–15), but also agreeing with Amos that Israel was to be included among these peoples (Zeph 1:1–18). There seems to be no doubt that popular eschatology looked toward a future in which Yahweh would have a settling of accounts with his enemies, from which his people would emerge triumphant. Prophecy accepted the eschatology but made it clear, apart from all nationalistic considerations and in the light of moral law alone, just who this people would be. It would not be the Israel of the flesh, but the Israel of the spirit—the remnant, the truly chosen. This prophetic interpretation continues into the post-exilic prophecy, where it becomes even plainer that Yahweh's judgment lies not between Israel and non-Israel but between the just and the wicked (cf. Mal 3:13–21) (→ Aspects OT Thought, 77:143).

(Beyerlin, W., *Herkunft und Geschichte der ältesten Sinaitraditionen* [Tübingen, 1961]. Galling, K., *Die Erwählungstraditionen Israels* [BZAW 48; Giessen, 1928]. Hesse, F., *Das Verstockungsproblem im Alten Testament* [BZAW 74; Berlin, 1955]. Huffmon, H. B., "The Covenant Lawsuit in the Prophets," *JBL* 78 [1959] 285–95. Mendenhall, G., "Covenant Forms in Israelite Tradition," *BA* 17 [1954] 50–76. Rowley, H. H., *The Biblical Doctrine of Election* [London, 1952]. Staerk, W., "Zum alttestamentlichen Erwählungsglauben," *ZAW* 55 [1937] 1–36. Von Waldow, E., *Der traditionsgeschichtliche Hintergrund der prophetischen Gerichtsreden* [BZAW 85; Berlin, 1963]. Vriezen, T. C., *Die Erwählung Israels nach dem Alten Testament* [Zürich, 1953].)

20 **(B) Prophetic Social and Moral Teaching.** The stress on social morality apparent among the pre-exilic classical prophets has sometimes earned for them the designation "social prophets." From what has already been said, it is evidently not precisely to the prophets' credit that we should single out this one aspect of their teaching as though they had given a disproportionate attention to it. The prophets certainly were not, as they were once called, "radical pamphleteers" (E. Renan, *Histoire du peuple d'Israël* [vol. 2, Paris, 1893] 425) or "insurrectionists" (L. Wallis, *Sociological Study of the Bible* [Chicago, 1912] 168, etc.). The social message was admittedly a major emphasis, but its explanation is to be found in the function of an Israelite prophet—serving as a conscience for his people in precisely those matters where conscience was needed. Against the backdrop of Israelite history, prophetic social doctrine fits into its proper place and is not out of proportion. The prophets themselves could only have been puzzled by the designation "social." They were only insisting on the social virtues inherent in the doctrines of election and covenant, virtues which had been flagrantly violated in an Israel that had largely abandoned its ancient ideals, assimilating itself to Gentile ways. In presuming a social character to the religion of Yahweh, the prophets were proposing nothing new but recalling a known, although much ignored, morality.

From this prophetic emphasis, however, there emerges an OT theme that becomes a major assertion and extends into the NT doctrine of the kingdom of God (cf. Mt 5:3). This theme is that of Yahweh's poor (*ʿanāwîm*)—i.e., of the socially oppressed whose redress could only come from Yahweh, and who, therefore, became virtually synonymous with the just, the faithful remnant with the right to call upon the Lord. In this theme, too, prophetic teaching maintained its accustomed balance. Poverty was never sentimentalized by the prophets of Israel; in keeping with the rest of the OT, they regarded it as an undesirable thing. The poor man was not just because he was poor, but the existential fact could not be ignored that poverty and injustice were frequent companions. It was the evil of other men that had created this situation, and the whole of prophetic effort was directed against the evil.

We do not mean to minimize the contribution made by prophecy when we assert that they inculcated a known morality, or at least one that should have been known. To the ancient traditions of Israel they also added the immediacy of the Word of God in their own time drawn from their own experience of the God of Israel's history. Their preaching of the social and moral imperatives to be found in the events by which Yahweh had constituted Israel has given the OT its most authoritative basis for *Heilsgeschichte*.

21 **(C) Ethical Monotheism.** "Ethical monotheism" was the term once used to denote what was considered the most important of all the prophetic discoveries—i.e., the God of Israel had a moral will, and that only by a moral life could he be worshiped according to that will. We have already pointed out that this discovery of the prophets was not new; it was, however, certainly the burden of their message to Israel. They discovered the principle where it was always available to all Israel—in its sacred traditions.

Theoretical monotheism appears relatively later in Israelite times (→ Deutero-Isaiah, 22:12,22). The monotheism of the pre-exilic prophets has been called, for its part, a "practical" or a "dynamic" monotheism—i.e., it was an existential monotheism, the only form of monotheism to be reasonably expected in its historical context, and nevertheless a monotheism for not being theoretical. This monotheism is the same kind found in Israel's most ancient traditions, deriving even from the patriarchal narratives. In view of what we must conclude about the transmission of the words of the classical prophets, it would be simply incredible that the prophetic teaching could have been as much out of the mainstream of Israelite thinking as some critics once imagined. The transmission of the prophetic writings makes sense only when we recognize the obvious fact that they depended for their continued existence on their acceptance by a people who acknowledged in them the Word of a God who was also the God of their faith, however reluctant they may have been to act on the Word as delivered to them. The writings of the classical prophets are not the productions of a "proscribed sect" (Wallis, *op. cit.*), but a heritage of the religion of Israel, that of Ahab as well as Elijah, of Zedekiah as well as Micaiah, of Hananiah as well as Jeremiah. Any other interpretation makes nonsense of history (→ Aspects OT Thought, 77:17–20).

Admittedly, the prophetic connection of religion with morality is something unique. If they found the basis for this connection in the common tradition they shared with their contemporaries, it is nevertheless true that it was owing to their ministry that the connection was cemented so that it could never again be sundered. This very fact has sometimes been held up to prophecy as a reproach, in that its answer to all social and moral problems was always religious rather than practical. As noted above, the prophets furthered no policy for the replacement of outworn institutions by better ones. If, on the one hand, they never proposed any reactionary reversion to the past like the Rechabites (cf. Jer 35), neither did they ever suggest any plan of action by which existing Israelite life could be harmonized with what they considered to be Israel's ancient ideals. To the harried politicians of Israel and Judah striving to give their tiny country a means of survival in a sea of power politics where neutralism was not tolerated, the prophets might have seemed to offer no hope in their reiterated condemnation of all political alliances as treason to the God of Israel's covenant. If Jeremiah could be misunderstood by the senseless partisans of a defeated land whose instincts were suicidal, he could also be misunderstood by honest patriots whose religion was as sincere, if not as informed, as his own. "Do good...perform justice...avoid evil..." are admirable injunctions, but they do not constitute an outline for state business or even for one's private professional life. Is it not a continuing objection against moralists that they content themselves with aphorisms and refuse to come to grips with the harsh realities of practical life?

It all must be faced, but not to denigrate the role of prophecy. The prophets were not moralists, statesmen, or politicians; they were prophets. Their function was to reveal the mind of God, which they had as others did not. In this function they had their *raison d'être*, and it was the function of others to translate the prophetic word into plans of action whether for personal or public life. The tragedy of Israel was not that it received from prophecy anything less than what prophecy was supposed to give, but that it had priests who would not know God and his Law, rulers who made their laws apart from God, and a people who would not heed the prophetic word.

(Bruppacher, H., *Die Beurteilung der Armut im Alten Testament* [Zurich, 1924]. Bückers, H., *Die biblische Lehre vom Eigentum* [Bonn, 1947]. Buhl, F., *Die sozialen Verhältnisse der Israeliten* [Berlin, 1899]. Causse, A., *Du groupe ethnique à la communauté religieuse: Le problème sociologique de la religion d'Israël* [Paris, 1937]; *Les "pauvres" d'Israël* [Strasbourg, 1922]; "Les prophètes et la crise sociologique de la religion d'Israël," *RHPR* 12 [1932] 97–140. Cross, E. B., *The Hebrew Family. A Study in Historical Sociology* [Chicago, 1927]. Day, E., *The Social Life of the Hebrews* [N.Y., 1901]. De Fraine, J., "Individu et société dans la religion de l'Ancien Testament," *Bib* 33 [1952] 324–55, 455–75. Gelin, A., *The Poor of Yahweh* [Collegeville, Minn., 1965]. Herrmann, J., *Die soziale Predigt der Propheten* [Berlin, 1911]. Jacobson, D., *The Social Background of the OT* [Cincinnati, 1942]. Kleinert, P., *Die Profeten Israels in sozialer Beziehung* [Leipzig, 1905]. Kuschke, A., "Arm und Reich im Alten Testament," *ZAW* 57 [1939] 31–57. North, R., "Prophetismus ut Philosophia Historiae," *VD* 29 [1951] 321–33. Peters, N., *Die soziale Fürsorge im alten Israel* [Paderborn, 1936]. Porteous, N. W., "The Basis of the Ethical Teaching of the Prophets," *Studies in Old Testament Prophecy* [Fest. T. H. Robinson; Edinburgh, 1950] 143–56. Van der Ploeg, J., "Les pauvres d'Israël et leur piété," *OTS* 7 [1950] 236–70. Vawter, B., "De iustitia sociali apud Prophetas praeexilicos," *VD* 36 [1958] 93–97. Walter, F., *Die Propheten in ihrem sozialen Beruf und das Wirtschaftsleben ihrer Zeit* [Freiburg, 1900].)

THE PROPHETIC LITERATURE

22 The preceding is a necessary preliminary to our consideration of the prophetic literature of the OT. Only in its light can we understand what is meant by this literature, who produced it, and to what end. We are concerned, of course, with the prophetic literature as defined—i.e., that produced by the classical literary prophets. The Jewish canon (→ Canonicity, 67:27) is more inclusive in counting as "the early prophets" what we customarily regard as historical books (i.e., the deuteronomic corpus). Neither are we concerned with other kinds of literature, which, for various reasons, have often been grouped with the prophetical, represented by Lam, Bar, Dan, and Jon. The literary categories of these works are considered in their respective commentaries.

(I) Literary and Nonliterary Prophets. In one sense, the distinction between literary and nonliterary prophets is based on a misconception of the history of literary prophecy, and, in any case, is incidental. Amos differs from Elijah, to the extent that we know of the latter at all, in little that is more significant than that we can read Amos' own words while we can only read about Elijah's. The distinction, therefore, says less about the prophets concerned than it does about the subsequent fate of their prophecies. On the other hand, the distinction is not entirely accidental. As seems to be the case, it was the disciples of a great prophet to whom we are usually indebted for his prophetic writings—the same *b^e^nê hann^e^bî'îm* who otherwise play such a mixed role in the history of prophetism. That a prophet attracted to himself such disciples as would guarantee the preservation of his prophecies can, at least sometimes, tell us something about the prophet himself.

The prophetic literature does not consist of books written by literary authors in the same way that the Book of Ruth, say, is by a determined literary author, or even the Gospel of John. The names appearing at the heads of the prophetical books do, with some nuances, identify the substance of the words therein contained with distinct prophetical authors. However, these words are collections of prophecies rather than unified books. To this judgment even such an apparently unified work as that of Ezekiel has had to bow. These collections, in turn, are the result of the editorial joining of smaller collections of prophecies connected by catchwords, similarity of topic, literary forms, or some similar consideration.

Could not these collections have been made by the prophets themselves? It is not impossible, but it is unlikely, as an examination of the individual prophetic "books" tends to show. In many instances, the compilers of the prophecies evidently lacked information that would have been available to the authors. Another consideration is the biographical material in the third person that forms a substantial part of many of the prophetic books. It is, again, not impossible that the prophet wrote of himself in the third person; however, it is far more reasonable to think that this material is from the same sources responsible for the collections—the prophet's disciples. We are told explicitly of the existence of such disciples and of the role they played in preserving and transmitting their masters' words—e.g., Is 8:16–20. Jer 36 is also a precious source of information, describing the first stage in the Jeremian collection when some of Jeremiah's prophecies were first written at his dictation by his disciple Baruch. Many prophecies in other prophetic books likewise show signs of having been dictated. Even for Amos, whom we generally think of as an isolated figure, we have not only third-person material (7:10–17) but also first-person accounts that presuppose the presence of friendly auditors whose duty it was to remember and record (cf. 7:1,4,7; 8:1–2). It would have been in the circles of disciples, too, that originally private material such as the "confessions" of Jeremiah (12:1–6; 15:15–21, etc.) would have been preserved, made known by the master to his followers but not initially intended for the general public.

This possibility raises in some measure the question of the *ipsissima verba* of the prophet. To what extent do the prophecies of Amos, Hosea, Isaiah, and the rest appear precisely as they were originally uttered? The answer to this question is not simple, nor does a single answer suffice in every case.

In general, we probably have good reason to think that in the majority of the poetic texts primary to a given prophetical book we have a substantial transcription of the prophet's original words. It is not unthinkable that in some instances these had been actually written by the prophet himself, on ostraca or other familiar recording media. It was not really necessary, however, inasmuch as the poetic structure itself was of such a nature as to facilitate memory and precise transmission. As a matter of fact, from this poetic material distinct literary styles and constants frequently emerge, so that it is possible to speak of an Amosian or an Isaian characteristic, to separate easily the material of Jeremiah from that of Baruch, etc.

The prose material presents additional difficulties. A prophet could, of course, produce prose as well as poetry, and there is a great deal of prose in various of the prophetic books that surely has an authentic life situation in the ministry of the individual prophets. However, what we know of the ordinary processes of prophecy encourages us to think that its ordinary form was the utterance of relatively short poetic assertions. The prose sections of the prophetic literature generally have the appearance of literary productions rather than of addresses to audiences, even when they record words of prophecy that were so spoken. Thus, they seem to be paraphrases and summaries of prophecies rather than the actual prophecies themselves. These paraphrases could also have been the work of the prophet, just as John of the Cross wrote the prose commentaries on his poetical experiences, but it is more likely that they are recollections of the sense of the prophecies, sometimes preserving snatches of the original words as tradition had transmitted them. This hypothesis appears to be especially confirmed in the case of Jeremiah, many of whose prophecies have evidently been handed down in circles that were strongly influenced by deuteronomic style and vocabulary (→ Jeremiah, 19:6–8).

23 **(II) Prophetic Literary Forms.** The most characteristically prophetic of the material found in the prophetical books is the oracle—i.e., the revelation of Yahweh. As we have already pointed out, the oracle is ordinarily a brief poetic utterance, although in the prophetic literature oracles of a similar kind have often been joined into a larger unity, sometimes by the prophet himself but usually by an editor. To underline the divine origin of the oracle, the prophet has often prefaced concluded, or interlarded it with appropriate reminders: "So says Yahweh"; "Yahweh speaks"; etc. However, the prophet may just as easily speak in his own name as the accredited spokesman for God.

Authors are accustomed to distinguish various types of oracle, depending on the precise nature of the Word of God being communicated. It may be distinguished as a woe or a weal prophecy, the revelation of a coming evil or a coming good. Pre-exilic prophecy is predominantly of the woe variety (cf. Jer 28:8), which does not necessarily mean that all or most of the weal prophecies in the books of the pre-exilic prophets result from subsequent supplementation from post-exilic prophecy; even Amos, the most pessimistic of the pre-exilic prophets, could utter a qualified salvation prophecy (5:15). It is true, however, that salvation prophecy is characteristically post-exilic, just as prophecy of doom is characteristically pre-exilic. Prophecies of doom for the Gentile peoples who oppose the reign of Yahweh are proper to pre- and post-exilic prophecy alike.

Obscurity is frequently the characteristic of prophecy: the ambiguity of the Delphic oracle was proverbial in classical antiquity. To this day, it is difficult to determine the precise significance of some of the elements in the mysterious prophecy of Is 7:13ff., and the same oracular quality is apparent in the language of prophecies like Am 3:3ff.; Mi 5:2; Jer 31:22, etc. Sometimes it is even doubtful whether weal or woe was intended, or which was predominant.

The word of God mediated through prophecy is not exclusively or even pre-eminently predictive. A prophetic oracle of woe may be, and far more frequently is, a divine denunciation of sin (cf. Is 1:2–3; 3:12–15, etc.) or a summons to repentance (cf. Am 5:4–5a; Zeph 2:3), which reductively may mean the same thing. It is in such prophecies as these that we find our chief source of the social and moral doctrine revealed through prophecy. As is evident, the oracle can often be at one and the same time a denunciation, an exhortation, and a prophecy of doom or salvation.

The exact circumstances under which the prophet uttered most of these oracles are not described for us, and we can only hypothesize. In some cases, however, the prophet has recounted his prophetic experience, recasting the oracle as part of the narrative; from such descriptions we gain a better idea of the prophetic process. Thus, Amos describes various visions in which the Word of God was made known to him (7:1–9; 8:1–3; 9:1ff.), as do Jeremiah (13:1–11) and other prophets. In Ezekiel, these descriptions are often quite elaborate (e.g., 8:3ff.; 37:1–14) and, as such, become a model imitated in post-exilic prophecy and apocalyptic, in which the vision itself is the substance rather than merely the occasion of the prophetic word. Some of Ezekiel's visions read like ecstatic experiences; however, the earlier prophetic descriptions seem to be of ordinary occurrences into which the prophet was given a special insight through his contact with God.

The recasting of the prophetic word by the prophet takes on many forms other than the vision narrative. Am 1:3–2:8 makes use of an ancient poetic form also found in some of the sapiential literature (cf. Prv 30:15ff.). Ez 19:2–14; 27:3–9, etc., and many other prophetic passages have been put into the form of a "dirge song" (*qînâ*), while Is 5:1–7 begins as a love song like those sung by minstrels in the city streets. We have already mentioned the "covenant lawsuit," a form borrowed from ancient covenant ritual well known to the people. An extended form of this in Mi 6:1–8 looks very much as though it has been modeled on a temple liturgy of which we have other examples in various Pss. Many other prophetic passages have been ascribed to liturgical influence with varying degrees of plausibility. Another form very common in the prophetical literature is the prophetic sermon (*tôrâ*), either in prose or poetry, an instruction corresponding to the priestly *tôrâ* of the sanctuaries. It is particularly from examples of *tôrâ* as found in the various prophetic books that we can extract typically prophetic doctrine and phraseology, for in time it built up its own literary tradition just as the priestly *tôrâ* did.

What are called the symbolic acts of the prophets may also be classed among the prophetic literary forms, for these acts were also prophecies. The symbolic act is found more frequently in Ezekiel than in any other prophet, but it is by no means confined to him. Hosea's marriage (Hos 1–3), Isaiah's nakedness (20:1–6), the name Shear-jashub that he gave to his son (7:3), Jeremiah's celibacy (16:1–4), and his purchase of Hanameel's field (32:6ff.) were all symbolic acts. We call them symbolic because we think of them as signs of some other reality. To the OT mind, however, they were realities in their own right, the prophetic word made visible. When Ezekiel drew the roads leading out of Babylon (21:23ff.), he was not merely figuring an event to follow; he was in a sense bringing the event into existence. The prophets' lives and deeds could be as filled with prophecy as their words, for the biblical mind made no real distinction between the two.

(Buzy, D., *Les symboles de l'Ancien Testament* [Paris, 1923]. Eissfeldt, *Einl.* 87–93. Gerstenberger, E., "The Woe-Oracles of the Prophets," *JBL* 81 [1962] 249–63. Westermann, C., *Grundformen prophetischer Rede* [Munich, 1960]. Zimmerli, W., "Das Wort des göttlichen Selbsterweises [Erweiswort], eine prophetische Gattung," *Mélanges Bibliques* [Fest. A. Robert; Tournai, 1956] 154–64.)

24 (III) Formation of the Prophetic Books. There is not space, nor is this the place, to enter into the history of composition of the individual prophetic books. This history is quite complicated and differs from book to book; the more important considerations for this or that book will be found in the respective commentaries. Here we shall note only those details of the history that apply to the formation of the prophetical literature in general into the books as we now have them.

The prophets' disciples are doubtless responsible for the initial work of gathering together and also, in large part, writing down their oracles, sermons, and other prose and poetic material, some of which was preserved in the prophets' own words and some of which the disciples remembered and paraphased. To this material the disciples added biographical recollections and sometimes other related material (e.g., the creation hymn that has been used to form doxologies in Am 4:13; 5:8–9; 9:5–6). The whole of the collections thus formed was put into some kind of order, on either topical or chronological considerations, or both. Sometimes original unities were preserved (e.g., probably Am 1:3–2:8), but generally speaking the unities that emerged were the work of the disciples, for the prophetic material had usually been produced in bits and pieces during lengthy prophetic ministries. Thus, the biographical Am 7:10–17 has been placed after Amos' own account of his vision in 7:7–9 because of the reference there to the house of Jeroboam. Similarly, the biographical Hos 1, the oracles of Hos 2, and the autobiographical Hos 3 have been unified because of the identity of subject matter. It is in all likelihood a disciple-editor, too, who has put such a verse as Am 1:2, from whatever period in the prophet's career, at the head of the book where it now serves as an introduction to the prophetic collection.

The editorial work of the prophets' disciples doubtless entailed redactional retouching as well as collecting the prophets' words. Other retouching took place through the subsequent use made of these collections once they had left the disciples' hands. References to Judah in the present Hebr text of Am 6:1; Hos 6:4 are probably, and certainly in the case of Hos 12:3, the result of change from an original "Israel." After the fall of the northern kingdom, the prophecies of Amos and Hosea circulated in the south, and such adaptations were made to show their continued applicability. Retouches of a similar kind have adapted other prophecies to a post-exilic situation.

The present editions of the prophetic collections seem for the most part to have been post-exilic. It was at this time that titles and chronological indications were attached to the beginnings of the books. The chronological indications are invariably Judahite, even for works like those of Am and Hos, which were originally concerned exclusively with Israel. Furthermore, the indications do not always agree with the prophetic content.

The post-exilic editors who had seen the fulfillment of the pre-exilic prophecy of doom, and who also had the continuing experience of exilic and post-exilic prophecy, followed a fairly standard outline in distributing the prophetic collections. They tended to gather the woe oracles at the beginning of the book and the oracles of salvation at the end; in between, they placed the oracles against the Gentiles. The purpose of this arrangement was to express their faith in the restoration of a redeemed Israel through the defeat of the enemies of God and his people. At the same time they took advantage of the opportunity to supplement especially the second and third of these sections with other similar prophetic passages, updating the oracles against the nations (e.g., by the inclusion of the oracles against Babylon now in Is 13:1–14:23) and including such new salvation themes as the reunification of Israel and Judah derived from Jeremiah and Ezekiel. All kinds of supplementary material have gone into this amplification of the prophetic books; whether they can be separated, however, according to "strata" (R. E. Wolfe, *ZAW* 53 [1935] 90–129) that cut across the lines of the individual books, may be another question. Even such a thorough prophecy of doom as that of Amos has received a messianic epilogue (9:8b–15), and there are countless other additions of the same kind (cf. Hos 1:7; 3:5b; Mal 3:24b, etc.). For other reasons, other types of supplementation have been made, such as the extensive historical material that was available concerning important prophets like Isaiah (chs. 36–39; cf. 2 Kgs 18:13–20:19) and Jeremiah (ch. 52; cf. 2 Kgs 24:18–25:30).

It is likely that the text of some of the prophetical literature at least remained fairly fluid until its inclusion in the canon (e.g., Jer). There are, of course, still further additions and alterations, the result of glosses or of deliberate interpolation, which are not scriptural.

THE PROPHETIC WORD

25 Our concern with the prophetic literature is not, it need hardly be said, merely the interest we have in an ancient religious phenomenon. Prophecy not only was, but still is, the Word of God. If all Scripture is, in its own measure, the Word of God, it is pre-eminently true of the prophecy in which God chose to speak directly with his people. It is, furthermore, not an archival record, but the living Word of a living God.

This concept, at least, is the biblical view. We have stated that the symbolic acts of the prophets were not signs only but efficacious works. The same is no less true of the prophetic utterances. Ahab's reproach of Elijah as the "troubler of Israel" (1 Kgs 18:17) and the king of Israel's complaint against Micaiah's failure to prophesy good for him (1 Kgs 22:8) are not the irrational petulance they might appear at first glance. They are, rather, a recognition that the prophetic word is power from God and that the prophet is the instrument through whom this power is transmitted. The prophetic word lives a life of its own once it has emanated from the prophet, and the prophet is very much identified with the word that he has uttered.

If we share this biblical view, we must recognize two things. First, the prophetic word is greater than the prophet, which the prophets themselves would have been the first to acknowledge. We know of this greatness from the NT fulfillment, which, in turn, is not an occurrence of the dead past but a continually living and growing reality. Second, the prophetic word is the word of Isaiah, or Amos, or Jeremiah, or perhaps a man whose name we do not know—a man, in any case, who was personally involved in the word, who lived for it and was prepared to die for it. If we are to take in this message as God has delivered it to us, we must take it in as it has come through the prophets of Israel. Anything less is not the prophetic word.

13

HEBREW POETRY

Aloysius Fitzgerald, F.S.C.

BIBLIOGRAPHY

1 Albright, W. F., "The Old Testament and Canaanite Language and Literature," *CBQ* 7 (1945) 5–31. Alonso Schökel, L., *Estudios de poética hebrea* (Barcelona, 1963). Burke, F., " 'Verse' and 'Versification,' " *Encyclopedia Americana* (N.Y., 1962). Cobb, W. H., *A Criticism of Systems of Hebrew Metre* (Oxford, 1905). Condamin, A., *Le Livre d'Isaïe* (Paris, 1905). Gray, G. B., *The Forms of Hebrew Poetry* (N.Y., 1913). Horst, F., "Die Kennzeichen der hebräischen Poesie," *TRu* 21 (1953) 97–121. Kraft, C. F., *The Strophic Structure of Hebrew Poetry* (Chicago, 1938). Kraus, H.-J., *Psalmen* (vol. 1; Neukirchen, 1960). La Drière, J. C., "Prosody," *Dictionary of World Literature* (ed. J. T. Shipley; N.Y., 1953). Mowinckel, S., "Zum Problem der hebräischen Metrik," *Fest. A. Bertholet* (Tübingen, 1950) 379–94; "Der metrische Aufbau von Jes 62:1–12," *ZAW* 65 (1953) 167–87; "Zur hebräischen Metrik II," *ST* 8 (1953) 54–85. Patton, J. H., *Canaanite Parallels in the Book of Psalms* (Baltimore, 1944). Robinson, T. H., "Basic Principles of Hebrew Poetic Form," *Fest. A. Bertholet* (Tübingen 1950) 438–50; "Some Principles of Hebrew Metrics," *ZAW* 13 (1936) 28–43; *The Poetry of the Old Testament* (London, 1947). Torrey, C. C., *The Second Isaiah* (N.Y., 1928).

OUTLINE

INTRODUCTION

3 The title of this article may be somewhat misleading. When those who write about Hebr literature speak of poetry, they generally mean verse. The assumption made is that the distinction between poetry and prose is one between speech that is highly patterned phonetically and speech that is less highly patterned phonetically. Thus, the distinction between the poetic books and the prose books of the OT is based on the fact that the former are written in verse whereas the latter are not. The assumption that the essence of poetry is verse is, of course, an ancient one. Gorgias, the sophist rhetorician, simply affirms, "I call poetry whatever has meter" (*Helena* 9). But objections to this point of view by other literary theorists are equally ancient. Aristotle, for instance, did not accept it. He writes, "If people publish medical or scientific treatises in meter the custom is to call them poets. But Homer and Empedocles have nothing in common except meter, so that it would be proper to call the one a poet and the other not a poet but a scientist" (*Poetics* 1447b). Horace does not consider his satires poetry although they are written in hexameters: "I will take my own name from the list of such as I would allow to be poets. For you would not call it enough to round off a verse, nor would you count anyone a poet who writes, as I do, lines more akin to prose [*sermo*]" (*Sat.* 1.4, 39–42).

4 Modern literary theorists and students of contemporary literatures, although they will differ on what exactly is the nature of poetry, do agree that poetry and verse are distinct concepts. Meter can be one of the differentiae of poetry but is not in itself a sufficient one; therefore, a precise use of terminology more accurately distinguishes between prose and verse (nonmetrical and metrical speech) and prose and poetry (nonliterary and literary speech). (For a discussion and bibliography on these and related questions see J. C. la Drière, "Classification" and "Poetry and Prose," *Dictionary of World Literature* [ed. J. T. Shipley; N.Y., 1953]). But the study of Hebr literature has been influenced little by specialized studies in literary criticism or theory made by students of modern secular literatures. It is, of course, quite understandable, for there has been so much else to do. But it is unfortunate, for modern studies on the nature of poetry and prose and the problem of meaning do have much to contribute to the study and discussion of Hebr literature.

5 Pius XII in *Divino Afflante Spiritu* makes such studies the concern of the exegete: "The interpreter must...accurately determine what modes of writing, so to speak, the authors of that ancient period would be likely to use, and in fact did use." More simply, literary theory and literary classification are important for the advance of biblical studies. It is impossible to read intelligently any piece of writing without at least an implicit understanding of the type of literature being dealt with and of the manner in which that type of literature communicates. It is in this precise area that past confusion has led to many difficulties that a developed system of literary classification could have done much to obviate. Literary theory and literary classification are also important for literary criticism. It is not necessary to have a developed theory of literature to appreciate poetry; however, to distinguish poetry from prose and to remove from the area of opinion the distinction between good poetry and poor poetry, literary theory is necessary. This problem is not the precise problem under discussion here, although it is related. In the context of the present article, it simply remains to be said that the title "Hebrew Poetry" is understood to mean Hebrew verse, however inadequate the terminology may be.

THE MAIN FEATURES OF HEBREW POETRY

6 **(I) The Views of Antiquity.** As far back as it is possible to trace the history of the question, the Jews themselves and other students of the OT have always regarded the OT as in part composed in verse. Josephus, for example, affirms that the songs of Ex 15 and Dt 32 are written in hexameters (*Ant.* 2.16, 4 § 346; 4.8, 44 § 303). He speaks of psalms written in trimeters and pentameters (*Ant.* 7.12, 30 § 305). Origen speaks of Hebr hexameters, trimeters, and tetrameters (Ps 118; J. B. Pitra, *Analecta Sacra* [1876–91] 2.341). Jerome, undoubtedly reflecting the views of his Jewish teachers, affirms that Jb is written in hexameters, but he does recognize the frequent use of feet other than the dactyls and spondees of the classic hexameter. These substitutions are said to have the same time value as the dactyls or spondees they replace (*Praef. in Lib. Job, PL* 28.1081). This last point would seem to indicate that as far as Jerome is concerned the Hebr verse system is based on the patterning of quantities of sound and closely resembles the metrics of classical Gk and Lat verse. Jerome finds psalms written in trimeters and tetrameters (*Ep.* 30, *PL* 22.442). He asserts that he follows Josephus and Origen in regarding the canticle of Dt 32 as written in hexameters and pentameters (*Interp. Chron. Eusebii Pamphili, PL* 27.36), although elsewhere he says that the same canticle is written in tetrameters (*Ep.* 30, *PL* 22.442). He incorrectly denies there is any meter in the writings of the prophets (*Praef. in Is., PL* 28.771).

More extensive evidence can be assembled but there is already enough to indicate that the first centuries of the Christian era were well aware of a more ancient tradition that parts of the OT were composed in verse. At the same time there is no evidence to indicate that there existed any understanding of the basis of this verse system. It is clear that Jerome, for example, is unable to distinguish adequately between verse and prose. He incorrectly seems to regard Hebr prosody as quantitative rather than accentual, and his descriptions of Hebr meters in terms of classical Gk and Lat verse are quite meaningless.

7 Much the same, perhaps, may be said of the tradition that produced the MT. The Palestinian Masoretes, at least, recognized some distinction between Pss, Jb, and Prv and the other 21 books, which is indicated by the fact that a special set of accents are used by Palestinian Masoretes to fix the cantillation, or musical declamation, of these books in the synagogues. The practice of referring to these accents as poetical accents and to the accents of the other books as prose accents is relatively modern. Rabbinical writers do not make such distinctions but speak rather of the accents of the 3 books and those of the 21 books. It is thus uncertain what the reason for this special system of accents is, but if we can suppose that the Masoretes did not know the metrical system that underlies Hebr verse and at the same time were aware of the tradition that some books of the OT were written in verse, these three books would have suggested themselves by their evident repetition of comparatively short, closed thought units of rather uniform length. Besides, the tradition that these three books are written in meter is an ancient one, as Jerome, probably reflecting the views of his Jewish teachers, indicates (*Praef. in Is., PL* 28.771 and *Praef. in Job, PL* 28. 1081).

The fact that short sections of these books were traditionally copied stichometrically by the Masoretes is further evidence of a certain awareness of the presence of verse, but it is also clear that the Masoretes did not understand the verse system involved. Their much too limited use of this stichometric arrangement within the three books, their failure to use it at all in other books that are completely or in large part metrical (for example, the later prophets), and their failure to use it for pieces of verse that appear in prose books indicate their inability to distinguish adequately between prose and verse. This conclusion is further evidenced by the fact that the accents with which they distinguish verses and indicate divisions within them in both the 3 and the 21 books often obscure rather than mark metrical units that are meant to be distinctly set off by caesuras and end pauses.

8 The MT gives some indication that this awareness of the presence of verse coupled with a lack of understanding of the verse system is more ancient than the period of the Masoretes. The traditional manner of copying the Song of Moses in Dt 32 is in two columns, each containing a hemistich of a verse. The system works well and properly indicates the line divisions as long as the lines are all distichs, but the first tristich, v. 14, completely disrupts the parallelism, which remains disrupted until restored by the second tristich, v. 39. This situation would seem to indicate a certain confusion about the nature of a basic Hebr verse line. It is true that the Masoretes, recognizing the parallelism, indicate with accents the proper division of the lines allowing for tristichs, but they preserve the traditional manner of copying the song.

Qumran evidence (P. W. Skehan, *BASOR* 136 [1954] 12–14; VTSup 4 [1956] 150) indicates that this confused awareness of the presence of verse in Dt 32 is at least as old as *ca.* 100 BC. The manuscript (4Q Dt) divides the canticle into hemistichs and copies them in columns, 11 to the column; however, to make the song end at the bottom of the final column, certain lines are written with two hemistichs to the line, which is done without intent to preserve parallelism. The evidence seems to show that the Qumran copyist did know to some extent that he was dealing with a metrical composition. Some psalms among the QL are also copied stichometrically, but the fact that the vast majority of the Qumran metrical material is not copied this way would indicate that even at this time verse and prose were not adequately distinguished (→ Texts, 69:37–38,42).

9 **(II) Modern Scholarship.** In the 19th cent., when modern biblical studies began to take such rapid strides in all areas of research, the question of the nature of Hebr metrics was much discussed. There had been several unsuccessful attempts to deal with the problem previously, the basic assumption underlying which was that Hebr verse was quantitative after the manner of classical Arabic or Greek or Latin verse. In 1753, Robert Lowth surveyed and evaluated these efforts in his pioneering work on Hebr poetry (*De sacra poesi Hebraeorum*). None had been successful, and none could possibly succeed because the proper pronunciation of Hebr is simply unknown. The MT is not an adequate guide in these matters. Although it can safely be said that Hebr poetry is metrical, the discovery and description of this verse system is a task beyond human ability.

In spite of this very pessimistic prognostication, it was impossible that the question would remain long unanswered. Scholars, especially in Germany, addressed themselves to the problem with remarkable energy and erudition (for a survey of this scholarship, see Cobb, *op. cit.*). They faced extraordinary difficulties, the most significant of which was that the MT with which they had to work represents a vocalization that was finally fixed only in the 10th cent. Hebrew at the time was, of course, long since a dead language. What the MT does faithfully mirror is the traditional manner of pronunciation used in school and synagogue. The text itself gives ample indication that this was not the pronunciation of earlier ages. Besides, the MT regularized the pronunciation of a living language that spanned 1000 years. Such regularization does not reflect the facts.

Moreover, OT literature is the product not only of original authors but also of editors. There seems to be little doubt that the editing and combining of texts has sometimes been at the expense of the metrical regularity of original compositions. Then, too, the transmission of the text over so many centuries by copyists, some of whom even as early as the Qumran period did not completely understand the texts they were copying, introduced many corruptions into the text tradition fixed by the MT, especially in the case of books written in verse. The reason seems to be that the conventional style of writing characteristic of Hebr verse was much less rigid in its use of grammar and word order than Hebr prose. In addition, its vocabulary was more extensive, and it tended to use rare words. Under the circumstances it is not surprising that more than a few of the hypotheses of these early researchers have been abandoned.

It was recognized early that the Hebr metrical system was not a quantitative one like those used in classical Greek, Latin, or Arabic verse. The Hebr system, like that used in Eng verse, is based on the obviously regularized recurrence of sounds of greater and lesser intensity. This recognition was a positive gain of the utmost importance, but it must also be said that much of the 19th-cent. investigation of Hebr metrics was characterized by a tendency to oversystematize the loose rhythms of Hebr verse and to find or invent regularity where there was none. These hypotheses were nonetheless important, for their ultimate rejection set up definite boundaries for future attempts to describe the conventions of Hebr verse.

In rejecting these hypotheses, scholars sometimes understandably went too far and denied that Hebr literature is metrical in any modern understanding of the word, but today scholars are in general agreement that meter does exist. They point to the tradition that has already been described. Aside from this indication, there is further evidence within the texts that points to the presence of meter. What has been regarded as verse is written in discrete sense units akin to verse lines. Compositions of this type deviate from prose usage and are characterized by anomalies of syntax, morphology, and word order. These are phenomena that might be expected in a composition meeting the demands of meter. Furthermore, song sometimes indicates meter, and some of these compositions are songs. These arguments, of course, simply show what might be expected. The only way to demonstrate that there is meter in Hebr literature is to describe the prosodic system and to show that the system does apply on a broad basis.

10 **(III) The Nature of Hebrew Prosody.** There are, of course, differences in detail, but present-day scholars have reached general agreement in their descriptions of the conventions of Hebr verse. The stich is the verse unit. In each stich there is a caesura dividing it into two hemistichs. Such a line with two hemistichs and one caesura is called a distich in contradistinction to a stich with three hemistichs and two caesuras, which is called a tristich. This terminology, etymologically considered, is difficult to comprehend. A distich should be two lines but is a line (stich) with two parts. A tristich should be three lines but is a line with three parts. A tristich can only be viewed as containing three hemistichs (half-lines) if it is considered to be one and one-half lines of verse. However, the terminology is widely used with the denotations presumed here. The first half of Dt 32:39, for example, is a distich.

> Learn then that I, I alone, am God,
> and there is no god besides me.

The second half is a tristich.

> It is I who bring both death and life,
> I who inflict wounds and heal them,
> and from my hand there is no rescue.

Scholars may use different terminologies. Sometimes they use the above terminology and understand the individual terms differently. The hemistich, for example, is frequently referred to as a stich. But the phenomena being described are the same.

A word of explanation is needed to relate these matters to the CCD translation. In this rendering of the OT, distichs, tristichs, and the hemistichs that compose them are always clearly distinguished in the printing. The opening hemistich of each line is capitalized; the second hemistich, in the case of a distich, and the second and third hemistichs, in the case of a tristich, begin with small letters and are indented to show that they continue the line rather than begin a new verse. Unfortunately, some recent editions of this new translation have dispensed with this method of printing and print verse in solid blocks like prose. This practice is regretable for several reasons, not the least of which is that it makes it difficult to distinguish verse when it is present. This is often a significant exegetical consideration. Furthermore, a translator's arrangement of verse into distinct lines, stanzas, and verse divisions is a meaningful part of his interpretation of the original text. Anyone who has tried to use an edition in which the verse is printed like prose recognizes the needless obscurity it adds.

11 The length of each hemistich is controlled principally by a count of stresses or accents and also by the number and distribution of unstressed syllables, although great variety exists in the latter. Hemistichs vary in length from two to four accents. The three-accent hemistich is the most common. Verse accents are determined by word accents but also by sentence accents as in Eng verse. There are several difficulties involved here. The accentuation of individual words of a living language can never be completely described by rules. Even when carefully formed by native speakers or by those who have the opportunity to listen to native speakers, rules can only be relatively adequate. The Masoretes could not work under such ideal conditions, and consequently their rules for accentuation are even more unreliable. Nevertheless, scholars think the Masoretic system is sufficiently accurate to make possible a more or less accurate analysis of Hebr word accentuation. But there is an even greater difficulty in the matter of determining the number and position of verse accents. In analyzing or reading a line of accentual verse, it is more important to determine sentence accents than individual word accents, for ultimately it is these accents that become the verse accents. Some appreciation of this difficulty can be gained by listening to nonnative speakers of English read a piece of verse like the opening lines of G. M. Hopkins' "Pied Beauty."

Glory be to God for dappled things—
For skies of couple-colour as a brinded cow.

ó o o o ó o ó o ó
o ó o o o ó o o o ó o ó

The reason why non-native speakers rarely learn English well enough to read poetry as it is intended to be read is that few acquire the delicate sensitivity to intonation needed to place stresses and semistresses in their proper positions. In the case of a dead language like Hebrew, it is simply impossible to acquire this sensitivity. Therefore, any analysis of Hebr verse can be only more or less adequate, which explains how it is possible for scholars to differ in their descriptions of a line of verse. What may be a 3 + 3 line for one scholar may be a 3 + 2 line for another. There is much room for legitimate differences of opinion.

12 The second factor controlling the length of the hemistich is the number of the unstressed syllables. This factor is sometimes completely ignored, and it is said that Hebr verse considers only accents or stressed syllables. Taken at face value, the statement is not accurate. The rhythm that characterizes any accentual verse depends on the recurrence of stressed and unstressed syllables. Such recurrence is characteristic of all speech, even prose that has a certain rhythm. What differentiates prose from verse is that the recurrence of stressed and unstressed syllables is regularized or patterned so as to become obvious to the ear. This seems to be the only rule governing the number of unstressed syllables permissible in a hemistich. They must be sufficiently few to allow the regularized recurrence of stressed and unstressed syllables to become obvious. This happens naturally enough in verse, since it is enunciated more deliberately than prose, and consequently smaller clusters of unstressed syllables tend to group around accents.

There are in English literature some remarkably close parallels to the type of verse characteristic of Hebr poetry. In fact, the earliest English poetry determined the length of lines by counting accents and allowed great variety in the number of syllables to the line. This convention was revived in the 19th cent. by S. T. Coleridge. The opening stanza of Coleridge's "Christabel" illustrates the possibilities of the loose rhythms of Hebr verse. That each line has four accents is carefully controlled, but the unstressed syllables in each line show considerable variation in number.

'Tis the middle of night by the castle clock,
And the owls have awakened the crowing cock,
Tu—whit! — Tu—Whoo!
And hark again! the crowing cock,
How drowsily it crew.

In one important respect, though, "Christabel" is quite untypical of Hebr verse. Much of the effect of the stanza quoted is the result of the *a-a-b-a-b* end rhyme. Hebrew verse avoids end rhyme, although there is some very limited use of this phenomenon. Assonance, consonance (alliteration), and, to a lesser degree, internal rhyme are accepted stylistic devices.

13 The most common Hebr line is 3 + 3 (3 accents, caesura, 3 accents, end pause). This type of line predominates in Jb, for example (Jb 3:3).

Perish the-day on-which-I-was-born, 3 + 3
the-night when-they-said, "The-child-is-a-boy."

In a translation, of course, it is impossible to indicate where the accents fall in the Hebr text, but the hyphens serve to group together the Eng words that correspond to the clusters of unaccented syllables around the accents in the Hebr line. There are, as can be seen, three clusters and three accents in each hemistich. (This grouping will be used for illustration's sake throughout the rest of the article. It will necessitate at times slight modifications of the CCD text.)

A common variant of the 3 + 3 line is the tristich, 3 + 3 + 3 (Jb 21:17).

The-lamp-of-the-wicked, how-often is-it-put-out? 3 + 3 + 3
Destruction, how-often does-it-come-upon-them,
the-portion he-allots in-his-anger?

Another important line is 3 + 2. It is referred to as *qînâ* (lamentation) meter because it characterizes the first four chapters of Lam, although it is by no means limited to dirges (Lam 2:5).

The-Lord has-become an-enemy, 3 + 2
he-has-consumed Israel.

Each hemistich is terminated by a caesura or, in the case of the concluding hemistich of a line, an end pause. These stops are necessitated by natural sense breaks. It is true that in the case of the caesura the sense stop is at times either not strong or nonexistent. It is possible to read through such a caesura, but it is probably more correct to say that once the rhythm of the verse is established the pause will be made naturally enough even when not absolutely necessary. The end pause is always made, and it is a strong pause; there is no enjambment. Each line of verse is a complete thought unit in itself. The rare occasions when this convention is violated are noteworthy. These pronounced caesuras and end pauses serve an important function; they render obvious the balancing of accent groups and thus establish the pattern of the verse.

14 One peculiarity of Hebr metrics is the combination of different types of line in the same composition. Such variation of meters is sometimes referred to as mixed meter. The following chart gives a line-by-line metrical analysis of some of the shorter psalms and shows clearly how Hebr verse in this matter runs from the very regular to the very irregular.

Ps 111	Ps 82	Ps 54
3 + 3	3 + 3	3 + 3
3 + 3	3 + 3	3 + 3
3 + 3	3 + 3	3 + 3 + 3
3 + 3	3 + 3	3 + 3
3 + 3	3 + 2 + 3	3 + 2
4 + 4	3 + 3	3 + 4
4 + 3	3 + 3	3 + 3
3 + 3	4 + 4	
3 + 3 + 3		
3 + 3 + 3		

Ps 64	Ps 4
4 + 4	4 + 4 + 3
3 + 3	4 + 4
4 + 4	4 + 4
3 + 4	3 + 4
4 + 3 + 3	3 + 2
2 + 3 + 3	4 + 4
3 + 3	3 + 4
3 + 3	4 + 5
4 + 2	
5 + 3	

It is true that part of this metrical irregularity of Hebr verse is not original and is the product of faulty text transmission. Apart from the obvious glosses and corruptions in the MT, a glance at the LXX and the other ancient versions often indicates a reading not in the MT, which will "regularize" the meter. Sometimes anacrusis (the prefixing of an accent to a line of verse) helps to explain metrical anomalies (T. H. Robinson, BZAW 66 [1936] 37–40). But mixed meter is clearly an acceptable convention in the Hebr prosodic system. It is also a convention in the literatures of cognate languages of the period. In the case of Ugaritic verse, for instance, where there has been no problem with text transmission, metrical irregularities are also marked (*UM* 13:98–99). Actually, such irregularity is hardly to be wondered at. Ugaritic and Hebrew verse conventions do not allow enjambment, and they both demand a caesura and an end pause in each verse. Under these circumstances it is readily understandable why Hebr prosody would introduce variations in the rhythm of the verse by using various metric lines within the same composition.

15 **(IV) Semantic Parallelism.** An extremely important stylistic adjunct of Hebr prosody is the phenomenon of parallelism. The use of the word "adjunct" in this regard might be misleading. It does not indicate that for a literary analysis of a Hebr work written in meter, the use of parallelism in the work is less significant than the meter. It indicates only that Hebr verse is being discussed and meter constitutes verse. As a matter of fact, Hebr meter and parallelism are quite closely related; certainly the parallelism has in large part made possible the modern study of Hebr metrics by clearly marking the distinct verse units. But the relationship between parallelism and Hebr meter is even more involved. Hebrew verse rhythms are in part based on the obvious repetition of hemistichs and verses containing the same, or approximately the same, number of accent clusters. These groupings are rendered obvious by caesuras and end pauses; thus the exigencies of meter demand the type of divisions characteristic of Hebr parallelism. At the same time, because the hemistichs that constitute a verse line are balanced semantically and grammatically, they tend to have a similar number of accents, and because the juxtaposed, parallel word groups tend to be comparatively short, the number of accents to each parallel hemistich is limited to two, three, or four.

Recently an attempt has been made on this basis to deny that there is any true meter in Hebr poetry. From this point of view, what has been described as meter is simply an accident resulting from semantic and grammatical parallelism; there is no such thing as a genuine Hebr verse rhythm as distinguished from Hebr prose rhythms (*UM* 13:98 and G. D. Young, *JNES* 9 [1950] 124–33). This thesis, of course, does solve the problem that a variety of meters in the one composition presents. It accounts for the irregularities of Hebr meter, but it does not take into account the even more striking regularities. For this reason, it has been generally rejected (see, e.g., W. F. Albright, *HUCA* 23 [1950–51] 6–7), but the fact that it has been seriously proposed does indicate the close interaction between metrics and parallelism in Hebr verse. In fact, no other prosodic system seems more adaptable to a style of writing that relies heavily on the type of semantic balance characteristic of Hebr verse. At the same time it is difficult to imagine a style of writing that seems more adaptable to the Hebr prosodic system. Each factor influences and complements the other.

Anyone who has had any exposure whatsoever to Hebr literature knows what parallelism is and can readily identify it at sight, but to offer a definition of the phenomenon is a much more vexing problem. The reason for this difficulty, perhaps, is that the term has been used traditionally to describe too many things. To some of these it applies quite well; to others it hardly applies at all. Synonymous parallelism and synthetic parallelism, for example, are really not similar things. Mowinckel's phrase, *Gedankenreim* (thought-rhyme, *ZAW* 68 [1956] 100) is a happy one. It is sufficiently vague to cover all instances, and it is sufficiently precise to give a relatively accurate description of the matter. But if a definition is necessary, parallelism is the juxtaposition of semantically (and frequently grammatically) similar word groups. Generally speaking, these word groups are the hemistichs of a distich or a tristich. But parallelism is also found between two or more distinct verses. The first type is referred to as intralinear (internal) parallelism; the second, as interlinear (external) parallelism.

16 In his classic study of Hebr verse mentioned previously, Lowth distinguished three types of parallelism: synonymous, antithetic, and synthetic. These classifications have been universally accepted, although it has often been pointed out that the third category is not actually parallelism but is rather a catch-all to include everything that does not fit into the other two categories. Synonymous parallelism involves the repetition in the second hemistich of what has already been said in the first hemistich (Ps 51:3).

Have-mercy-on-me, O-God, in-your-goodness; 3 + 3
in-the-greatness-of-your-compassion wipe-out my-offense.

In synonymous parallelism, the situations dealt with in both hemistichs are the same, and each hemistich says the same thing while simply varying the words of the affirmations.

In antithetic parallelism, the situations represented and the statements made about them are opposed, but the affirmations are made in such a way that each hemistich says approximately the same thing, for one implies the other (Prv 3:5).

Trust in-the-Lord with-all-your-heart, 3 + 3
on-your-own-intelligence rely not.

Synthetic parallelism involves the completion in the second hemistich of the line of thought begun in the first (Is 40:1).

Comfort, give-comfort to-my-people, 3 + 2
says your-God.

Other types of parallelism can be distinguished, but often they are refinements of Lowth's classifications. In emblematic parallelism one hemistich reproduces the other by means of a metaphor or simile (Ps 42:2).

As-the-hind longs for-running-waters, 3 + 4
so-my-soul longs for-you, O-God.

Thus far we have discussed principally intralinear parallelism; there are also many instances of interlinear parallelism. The categories already listed are in general adequate to classify the occurrences of this phenomenon. In addition, there are two other classifications that are generally discussed only in terms of interlinear parallelism: "staircase" parallelism and introverted parallelism. Introverted parallelism is always interlinear. In staircase parallelism, a series of successive verse units open with the same or similar phrases, whereas the concluding phrases of the verse units contribute to the progression of thought (Ps 29:1–2).

Give to-the-Lord, you-sons-of-God, 3 + 4
give to-the-Lord glory and-praise,
Give to-the-Lord the-glory-due-his-name; 3 + 3
adore the-Lord in-holy-attire.

The parallelism here is intralinear and interlinear. It is synonymous and staircase. It is chiastic or introverted—*ab* + *ac*, *ac′* + *a′b′*. Introverted parallelism is always interlinear. More generally it involves the arrangement of parallel verses in an *abba* (chiastic) order or in some similar order (Ps 30:9–11).

To-you, O-Lord, I-cried-out; 3 + 2
with-the-Lord I-pleaded:
"What-gain-would-there-be from-my-lifeblood, 2 + 2
from-my-going-down into-the-grave?

Dust, will-it-thank-you 2 + 2
or-proclaim your-faithfulness?
Hear, O-Lord, and-have-pity-on-me; 3 + 3
O-Lord, be-helper to-me."

In a style of writing that relies so heavily on balance for literary effects, it is evident that the avoidance of monotony is a major problem. One method Hebr writers used to introduce variety into their use of this style has just been indicated. They employed various types of parallelism in the same work. A fine example of this sort of thing is the preceding set of verses from Ps 29, where a subtle combination of different types of balance makes the total effect of the whole quite unique. But variety can be introduced in other ways. Sometimes the parallelism is complete; more generally it is incomplete. These terms can be applied to both interlinear and intralinear parallelism, but they have more significance in the second case because interlinear parallelism is rarely complete. Complete parallelism exists when the sequence of sentence parts in one hemistich is completely balanced by the sequence of sentence parts in the parallel hemistich (Jb 18:16).

Below, his-roots dry-up, 3 + 3
and-above, his-branches wither.

The balance here is *abc* + *a′b′c′*. In incomplete parallelism the sequence of parts in the parallel hemistich is partially changed. The second hemistich remains parallel to the first hemistich, but the balance is incomplete. The four lines from Ps 30 show some of the possibilities:

abc + *b′c′*; *ab* + *b′c*; *ab* + *b′c*; *abc* + *b′c′d*.

There is also here in the second, third and fourth lines a graphic illustration of how the psalmist works to meet the exigencies of his meter. The second hemistich of each of these lines omits the initial element of the first hemistich. The lack of this element is supplied for by adding a final ballast element.

17 (V) Larger Verse Units. That Hebr verse groups lines into larger units is sufficiently evident. At very least this grouping occurs on the level of thought units where verses fall together to form stanzas in much the same way as the sentences of a prose composition do to form paragraphs. These thought units constitute stanzas in the broad sense of the term. Whether Hebr verse is written in what are called stanzas in the stricter sense (recurring groups of verses with the same length and structure, as the Spenserian stanza), and whether there are conventional Hebr verse forms (as the sonnet) are questions of very great complexity. It is clear that there is some grouping of lines into regularly structured units, which in larger poems are repeated; but there is much uncertainty about how extensive this process is and about how much this structuring has been obscured by corruptions, glosses, and the work of editors.

It has always been recognized that the alphabet has been the basis for some of these larger units and that acrostics of various types are an established feature of Hebr verse. Some of the ramifications of acrostics are just beginning to be understood (P. W. Skehan, *CBQ* 23 [1961] 125–42). The 22 letters of the alphabet are the basis for the conventional use of 22-, 23-, and 11-line units with and without an alphabetic acrostic. For example, Pss 25 and 34 are alphabetic psalms in which the first word of each verse begins with the successive letters of the alphabet, starting with *aleph* and concluding with *taw* (*waw* is omitted). A final verse beginning with *pe* is added. The convention of adding this final *pe* to the series apparently developed because in this way *lamed* becomes the middle letter of a series of 23 letters (the 22 letters of the alphabet + *pe*), and thus the three consonants of the name of the first letter of the alphabet (*aleph*) are at the beginning, middle, and end of the series. This explanation does not apply directly to Pss 25 and 34 because the omission of the *waw* leaves a series of only 22 letters, but it does seem to explain how the custom of adding *pe* originated. Ps 37 works the acrostic device on each second line and includes the *waw*, but it does not add a 23rd couplet beginning with *pe*. Ps 94 is a 23-line psalm that omits the acrostic device. Ps 145 and Prv 31:10–31 are examples of 22-line poems with the alphabetic acrostic; Lam 5 is a 22-line unit without the acrostic. Pss 111 and 112, which work the acrostic on a half-line basis, form 11-line units. Previously Skehan had shown (*CBQ* 13 [1951] 153–63), that the 69 lines of the Song of Moses in Dt break down into three sense divisions of 23 lines each. Within these larger units there are smaller units made up of groups of two and three lines. It is this study that underlies the CCD arrangement of the song.

These 23-, 22-, and 11-line units are also quite typical of Jb and Sir, but certainly the most striking example of this type of structuring is found in Prv (P. W. Skehan, *CBQ* 9 [1947] 190–98; for Jb, see also *CBQ* 23 [1961] 125–42 and *Bib* 45 [1964] 51–62). The opening line of the concluding chapter of the first section of Prv (9:1) speaks of the house that Wisdom built as supported by seven columns. The house referred to is the literary edifice contained in 1–8 (6:1–19 is intrusive and not part of the edifice). It is made up of an introduction (1), a conclusion (8), and seven 22-line poems. These poems are the seven columns of wisdom, seven columns of verse. Although attention is drawn to these facts in a footnote of the CCD translation, the structure is not made clear in the text itself. A conservative editorial policy would not presume the reordering of the verses of the MT necessary to restore what was, as it seems, the original order. A similar convention existed in Akkadian literature. The Babylonian "Theodicy" is a long acrostic poem, although not an alphabetic acrostic, of 27 stanzas of 11 lines each (W. G. Lambert, *BWL* 63). (For the structure of Prv, cf. P. W. Skehan, "Wisdom's House," *CBQ* 29 [1967] 162–80.)

18 Even at a cursory reading, the Song of Deborah (Jgs 5), one of the earliest extant pieces of Hebr verse, presents very obvious sense divisions, which give the impression of regular stanzaic structure. Considering the great antiquity of the song, the text is remarkably well preserved, but any attempt to describe this structure or translate the song requires some textual emendation. The suggested emendations presented by various scholars are diverse. Some are conservative, others preposterously fanciful. But it is amazing to see how, in spite of wide differences in this area, the various studies are in general agreement about the number and division of the stanzas of the song. The only possible explanation of this fact seems to be that the song requires such divisions. The CCD arrangement of the song is in part based on a study by T. Piatti (*Bib* 27 [1946] 65–106; 161–209) and in general follows his divisions, although many of his textual emendations are rejected. In this CCD arrangement there are 16 stanzas. Eleven are three-line stanzas, perhaps twelve if the final stanza is considered as including v. 31, the conclusion. There are four two-line stanzas, in two of which the final verse is a tristich to compensate for the shortening. The eleventh stanza (21–22) and the twelfth stanza (23) are two-line stanzas without this tristich, but there are reasons apart from any consideration of stanzaic irregularity to think there is something wrong with the text in this area. Piatti combines the two into one stanza, but the material is diverse, and it seems better to divide as the CCD has done. It should be noted that the opening stanzas, at least, seem marked off by the repetition of the word "Israel." The first line ends with the word. Both the first and second stanzas conclude with the phrase, "the Lord, the God of Israel." The third, fourth, and fifth stanzas all conclude with the word "Israel." Actually, they conclude with the same prepositional phrase, although this fact is lost in translation. Piatti's study is much concerned with this type observation. His study was preceded by an interesting study by W. F. Albright from another point of view (*JPOS* 2 [1922] 69–86). He tried to show that the song consists of fifteen four-line stanzas arranged 3 + 3, 2 + 2, 2 + 2, 2 + 2. The arrangement includes some arbitrary emendations, and Albright himself has criticized it as "too uniform" (*Studies in Old Testament Prophecy* [ed. H. H. Rowley; Edinburgh, 1950] 5), but such studies do show possibilities and give reason to wonder.

19 Much the same can be said of studies attempting to show stanzaic structuring in certain psalms. Grouping lines according to sense often distinguishes units equal or approximately equal in the number of verses they contain. Ps 82, for example, quite readily falls into the pattern presumed by the CCD arrangement: introduction (1); a corpus of two three-line groups (2–4 and 5–7); and the concluding exclamation (8). Sometimes there are further indications of stanzaic patterning. The opening psalm of the second book (42–43) divides itself into three rather clear sense groups, each of which closes with the same two-line refrain. The three stanzas are eight, ten, and nine lines in length. Whether this irregularity in stanza length is caused by a displaced line is hard to say. Perhaps the conventions within which the Hebr poet worked required only that the stanzas be of approximately equal length. The latter possibility seems to be the more probable. This process of distinguishing stanzas by the repetition of a verse, a phrase, or even a word at the end (or beginning) of a stanza is called inclusion, although the term is more properly applied to such repetition at the beginning and end of the same stanza. (See especially the work of Condamin, *op. cit.*, where occurrences of the phenomenon are printed in boldface.)

CONCLUSION

20 With regard to the present state of scholarship in all the areas discussed, much is tentative, but at the same time some certainties have been arrived at, and there are areas which show promise. Comparative studies, especially in Akkadian and Ugaritic literature, have proved and will continue to prove quite useful in this matter. There are, of course, limits to the investigation. The original pronunciation can never be recovered. A perfect text can never be produced. But it is in this second area, perhaps, that studies in Hebr prosody can contribute most to biblical studies. Textual criticism cannot be based entirely on metrical considerations but, in conjunction with studies from other points of view, they can help guarantee the integrity of a text and even, at times, correct the MT. Finally, as has already been pointed out, the presence of verse can often be a significant exegetical consideration. In the light of this fact and the further fact that so much biblical literature is verse—not only the books that are traditionally regarded as poetical but also much of the prophetic literature and a significant scattering of verse elements throughout the prose books—it should be emphasized that an understanding of the principles of Hebr prosody is important even for those who do not study the OT in Hebrew. An appreciation of the extent to which the OT contains verse can be readily gained from the CCD translation or from any other modern translation where verse is printed in verse lines.

14

AMOS

Philip J. King

BIBLIOGRAPHY

1 Cripps, R. S., *A Critical and Exegetical Commentary on the Book of Amos* (2nd ed.; N.Y., 1955). Driver, S. R., *The Books of Joel and Amos* (CBSC; Cambridge, 1934). Edgehill, E. A., *The Book of Amos* (London, 1914). Fosbroke, H. E. W., *Amos* (*IB* 6; N.Y., 1956). Gordis, R., "The Composition and Structure of Amos," *HarvTR* 33 (1940) 239–51. Harper, W. R., *Amos and Hosea* (ICC; Edinburgh, 1910). Hyatt, J. P., *Amos* (*PCB;* London, 1962). Maag, V., *Text, Wortschatz und Begriffswelt des Buches Amos* (Leiden, 1951). McCullough, W. S., "Some Suggestions About Amos," *JBL* 72 (1953) 247–54. Morgenstern, J., *Amos Studies* (vol. 1; Cincinnati, 1941). Osty, E., *Amos* (*BJ;* Paris, 1952). Rowley, H. H., "Was Amos a Nabi?" *Fest. O. Eissfeldt* (1947) 191–98. Smith, G. A., *The Book of the Twelve Prophets* (rev. ed.; vol. 1; N.Y., 1940). Snaith, N. H., *The Book of Amos* (part 1; London, 1946). Sutcliffe, T. H., *The Book of Amos* (2nd ed.; London, 1955). Touzard, J., *Le Livre d'Amos* (Paris, 1909). Weiser, A., *Die Profetie des Amos* (Giessen, 1929). Wolfe, R. E., *Meet Amos and Hosea* (N.Y., 1945). Würthwein, E., "Amos Studien," *ZAW* 62 (1950) 10–52.

INTRODUCTION

2 **(I) Historical Background and Message.** Amos is the third among the 12 OT prophets, but his words were the first to have been recorded. We do not possess a biography of this Judean herdsman but the book provides some valuable information about him (7:10–17). It is an anthology of oracles and visions delivered by Amos at Bethel and Samaria, probably over a brief period of time. His authorship of these records has never been seriously contested, although in places the hand of a later editor is in evidence. Either Amos or a secretary could have set down the oracles in writing; inasmuch as Amos certainly was no systematic theologian the order of the various passages is probably the work of an editor. The vivid imagery of the oracles reflects the shepherd's life. His style is stark and vehement, in keeping with the harsh severity of his message and his own rugged character. The oracles are cast in a poetic form that has rarely been achieved by the other prophets.

The writings of Amos imply a period of prosperity and strong national consciousness, which, coupled with the information contained in the superscription, leads us to assume that Amos' prophetic activity took place shortly after the victory of Jeroboam II over the Arameans of Damascus, late in his reign, probably before 750. This date fits the conditions reflected in the book. Jeroboam II was a capable ruler and a strong military figure. Under his leadership the northern kingdom reached the summit of power; the Assyrian usurper Tiglath-pileser III and the ominous events associated with his reign had not yet appeared. Judah also was enjoying prosperity, and the two states of Israel and Judah were at peace with each other.

This book furnishes an accurate picture of contemporary Israelite society. An oppressive social pyramid had been constructed and class inequities were having drastic consequences, the poor being victimized by the predatory rich. Religious decay was one root of these social crimes. Yahwism was no longer maintained in pure form and was in danger of deterioration into paganism. Amos, steeped in the Mosaic tradition, saw these egregious social injustices as the antithesis of the covenant spirit. Israel's original covenant with Yahweh allowed no class distinctions; a covenant faith in one God included the concept of the brotherhood of all Israelites. A nation can have a true covenant relationship with God only when the people of that nation deal justly with one another. Social justice is thus an indispensable part of covenant responsibility.

Amos was mainly concerned with the violation of the social order. He inveighed bitterly against the social evils of the times. Because of his vigorous denunciations of such abuses he is often called the prophet of social justice (→ Prophetic Lit, 12:35). He reminded the Israelites of the obligations incumbent upon them because of their unique relationship to Yahweh. Owing to their gross deficiencies, God was about to destroy his people. Their fulfillment of formal religious obligations was insufficient, for the moral element was most important;

worship without morality has no value in the eyes of God. Like John the Baptist, Amos exhorted the people to repent in the true sense, i.e., to return to God. If the Israelites would obey the Word of God they would be saved; if they did not, the "Day of the Lord" would be a day of judgment and doom, contrary to the popular belief. Amos was preparing Israel for the terrible invasion by the Assyrians, the form that God's judgment would take. The God of Israel is at the same time the God of righteousness, the God of the nations, and the God of history.

3 **(II) Outline.** The following is the outline for the Book of Amos:

(I) Oracles Against the Nations (1:1–2:16)
  (A) Superscription (1:1–2)
  (B) Oracles of Judgment Against Neighboring Nations (1:3–2:3)
    (a) Aram (1:3–5)
    (b) Philistia (1:6–8)
    (c) Tyre (1:9–10)
    (d) Edom (1:11–12)
    (e) Ammon (1:13–15)
    (f) Moab (2:1–3)
  (C) Oracle Against Judah (2:4–5)
  (D) Oracle Against Israel (2:6–16)
(II) Words and Woes for Israel (3:1–6:14)
  (A) First Word (3:1–15)
  (B) Second Word (4:1–13)
  (C) Third Word (5:1–6)
  (D) First Woe (5:7,10–17)
  (E) Second Woe (5:18–27)
  (F) Third Woe (6:1–14)
(III) Symbolic Visions (7:1–9:15)
  (A) Vision of Locusts (7:1–3)
  (B) Vision of Fire (7:4–6)
  (C) Vision of the Plummet (7:7–9)
  (D) Historical Interlude (7:10–17)
  (E) Vision of the Fruit Basket (8:1–3)
  (F) Against Greed (8:4–14)
  (G) Vision of the Altar (9:1–6)
  (H) Messianic Perspective (9:7–15)

COMMENTARY

4 **(I) Oracles Against the Nations (1:1–2:16).** This section is Amos' original composition. The first six oracles announce a judgment of doom against six neighboring peoples; the last two concern Judah and Israel. Amos inveighs first against the neighbors of Israel and then against Israel itself.

(A) Superscription (1:1–2). These verses have been prefixed by an editor to supply background information concerning the Prophet. The superscription serves as a title for the whole book. **1.** In the OT, the name Amos (Hebr "burden") is associated only with the Prophet, of whom we have a vague picture. Although a plain man, Amos was not uncouth, and his style shows that he was intelligent and well versed in international affairs. Judging from his writings, we find Amos a person of profound convictions. *a shepherd from Tekoa:* The Hebrew *nôqēd* is not the usual word for shepherd. In 2 Kgs 3:4 it is used in reference to Mesha, king of Moab, where it is understood to mean "sheepmaster." The difference between *nôqēd* (shepherd) in 1:1 and *bôqēr* (owner of oxen) in 7:14 may have no special significance. The Eng "shepherd" in both instances veils the difference. The imagery of Amos' oracles reflects an outdoor life, and some argue, from the lack of information about his antecedents, that Amos' family was of inconsequential social status. Amos' home was Tekoa in Judah. It is located about 10 mi. S of Jerusalem, 3000 ft. above sea level. Situated in desolate, rough country, it is aptly called the wilderness of Tekoa. Amos' activities as prophet were not performed in his native country but in the northern kingdom of Israel.

5 Uzziah (*ca.* 783–742) is mentioned in the superscription not only because of Amos' Judean origin but also because he speaks of the southern kingdom. According to some scholars, Am must have been compiled in Judah because Uzziah is mentioned first. In this same period, Jeroboam II (*ca.* 786–746) was king of Israel. It was an age of material prosperity for both states. *two years before the earthquake:* To fix the date, Amos refers to an approximately contemporary event that had deeply impressed the people. Zechariah (14:5), writing several centuries later, also mentions this memorable event, the precise date of which is impossible to determine.

2. This verse is the keynote of the message. According to this ancient formula, Yahweh's judgment will be felt by both man and nature. *the Lord will roar:* Elsewhere in the OT (Ps 29), God's voice is compared to the rumbling of thunder. *Zion:* The etymology of the words is still uncertain. It is a pre-Israelite, Canaanite name, used as a synonym for Jerusalem. Zion is Yahweh's dwelling place, and, in a very special sense, it is the place of divine manifestation from which the Word of Yahweh originates. Drought will curb the growth of plant life, causing the shepherd to abandon the pastures. *Carmel:* It is located near modern Haifa. The reference is to the vineyards in the area, known for fertility, orchards, and forests. The withering of Carmel, noted for its verdure, suggests extreme desolation.

6 **(B) Oracles of Judgment Against Neighboring Nations (1:3–2:3).** This section is a series of indictments against Israel's neighbors, climaxed by the castigation of the people of Israel. Geography, more than history, is responsible for the manner in which these oracles of doom are grouped. These prophetic utterances were not all pronounced at the same time, although they are all identically structured. They manifest the art of repetition and suspense. They reveal the universal sovereignty of Yahweh, who can make moral demands upon all the nations and not just upon Israel. All offenders are subject to Yahweh's punishment without exception.

(a) ARAM (1:3–5). This oracle is of unquestioned authenticity. **3.** Each of the oracles against the nations is introduced by the same formula, signifying an indefinite but excessive number. *Damascus:* The capital of the kingdom of Aram or Syria here represents the whole nation. Israel had frequently engaged in war with Damascus (1 Kgs 17–2 Kgs 14). The crimes inveighed against in this section concern cruelty in the time of war. *I will not revoke:* Literally, "I will not make it turn back." Yahweh will neither intervene nor revoke his punishment. Some commentators suppose that the antecedent of "it" is the nation just named, and that the meaning is "I will not cause the nation to turn to me in repentance," or "I will not restore it [to my favor]" (Hyatt, *op. cit.*, 618). *Gilead:* It is a region of Israel in Transjordan near Damascus. This frontier territory was often a battlefield. Gilead had been devastated by the people of Aram (2 Kgs 10:32–33), who ruthlessly dragged sledges over the prostrate bodies of the vanquished.

4. Hazael (*ca.* 842–806) was the founder of the reigning dynasty in Syria; Ben-hadad III was his son. These Aramean kings fought against Israel and in turn suffered devastation at the hands of the Assyrians. The combined forces of Israel under Jehoram and of Judah under Ahaziah were defeated by Hazael in a battle at Ramoth-gilead in 842. Jehu, king of Israel (842–815), could not stop Hazael from annexing all Transjordan. *castles:* The plural of *'armôn* means "fortified dwellings" (1:4,12; 2:2,5 etc.). **5.** *bar of Damascus:* Reference is to the beam used in securing the main gate of the city. *Valley of Aven:* It means "vale of wickedness" and designates probably the fertile valley of On, between Lebanon and Antilebanon mountains. *Beth-eden:* Bit-adini of the Assyrian inscriptions, a city in Syria, meaning "house of pleasure." These names may be understood symbolically as disparagements of Damascus; they also designate the territory of Aram from SW to NW. The reference to Kir is obscure, but the Arameans were exiled when Damascus fell to the Assyrians in 732. The fulfillment of this prophecy is told in 2 Kgs 16:9.

7 (b) PHILISTIA (1:6–8). The Phi
lived along the se
cities are name
Ekron. The im
of Palestine, here
center of slave tr
Near East. Philis
her sin against the
(c) TYR
seaport of Phoenic
commercial city,
Phoenicians are als
brotherhood: King I
Solomon and calle
The northern king
relations with Tyre
attacks of the Aram
Ahab of Israel with J
of Tyre, (1 Kgs 16
example.

8 (d) EDOM (
of Seir (Gn 26:8),
probably so named be
that area. Hostility pr
and Israel (→ Excursus I
not only of receiving sla
in war. **11.** *he pursue*
Jacob were twins (Gn
descended from Esau. *p*
means "womb" (*reḥem*);
should link those born o
A district in northern Ed
Teman and Bozrah were
(e) AMMON (1:
judges, Jephthah defeated
they were later conquere
13. *they ripped open expecta*
savage brutality in time of
are accused. **14.** *Rabbah:* I
It is modern Amman, capita
of Jordan. Every Arab tr
standard. Israel, too, had i
formed part of the ritual of
The battle cry was originally ... to
inspire the ranks and intim... the hostile forces.
stormwind in a time of tempest: Similar to a hurricane, the poetic description is of devastation by war. **15.** There will be no hope of restoration after the destruction.

9 (f) MOAB (2:1–3). Moab is the fertile plateau located E of the Dead Sea and bordering on Edom. Moab and Ammon were "descendants" of Lot by his two daughters, according to a savage Hebr tale related in Gn 19:37–38. Thus, they are closely related to the Israelites according to the biblical tradition. The cruel satire of Gn 19 is an indication of the traditional hatred of the Israelites for their close neighbors. The Moabites are guilty of the reprehensible crime of desecrating tombs, an abomination to the Semites who believed that it caused unhappiness to the individual in the afterlife. Significantly, the victimized king is of Edom, Israel's mortal enemy, yet it is still a matter of concern to Yahweh. It points to the universal sovereignty of Yahweh, who reproaches all nations for their crimes.

2. *Kerioth:* According to the Moabite stone, this chief city of Moab was the residence of Chemosh, the god of the nations. The land of Moab will undergo violent devastation. **3.** The annihilation of the officials will preclude any future restoration of Moab; this is part of the stereotype language of impending doom (cf. 1:15).

10 **(C) Oracle Against Judah (2:4–5).** Most
mmentators question the authenticity of this
le. The internal evidence (language, etc.)
at it reflects a later period; it has a deuter-
or. It may date from the period when the
f Amos were circulating in Judah. Inasmuch
regarded both kingdoms as constituting a
, it is not likely that he would address a
against Judah. Then one would have six
e climax in the seventh, against Judah.
convicted of the crimes of infidelity to
disobedience to his law. *lies:* Canaanite
esignated as "lies" because they were false.
favoritism with Yahweh; Judah will
fate as the other nations.
Oracle Against Israel (2:6–16). In a
eveloped and detailed account, Amos
ith crimes against Yahweh and brother-
ther nations, Israel, too, will be punished.
ains a study in contrasts—the crimes of
odness of God in behalf of the Israelites.
man for silver: The just man is one who
oor. This phrase is subject to different
may mean to sell into slavery; or it
dge who accepts a bribe and condemns
the poor man for a pair of sandals: This
fer to the venality of the judges, or
nay sell a man into slavery because of
apacious rich placed little or no value
legal fiction of some kind underlies
n for a pair of sandals" seems certain.
fer of property was ratified by a
4:7). Transactions were validated
emoving his sandal and giving it to
ignifying the surrender of a right.
the transfer of land the shoe was
strument. The poor man in 2:6
ossessed unjustly, but the exaction
earance of legality; cf. De Vaux,
lt to interpret, but in a somewhat
cribes the attitude of the rich
Their exploitation of the poor is
xpected of the faithful Israelite—
... service to a brother in need (Lv 19:18).
the weak: The poverty stricken. *the lowly:* The *'ănāwîm* find themselves in humble circumstances and practice resignation without complaint. This term later designated those who put their complete confidence in God. *son and father go to the same prostitute:* "Same" is not in the

ORACION
DE SAN FRANCISCO

Señor, hazme un instrumento
de tu paz.
Donde hay odio,
que siembre yo amor;
donde hay injuria,
perdón;
donde hay duda,
fe;
donde hay desesperación,
esperanza;
donde hay tinieblas,
luz;
y donde hay tristeza,
alegría.
Oh Divino Maestro,
concédeme que yó busque
no tanto ser consolado
cuanto consolar,
no tanto ser comprendido
cuanto comprender,
no tanto ser amado
cuanto amar;
pues es dando
que recibimos,
es perdonando
que somos perdonados,
y es muriendo
que nacemos a la vida eterna.

Hebr text, but the context suggests it. The reference may be to harlotry, or more probably, sacred prostitution. *my holy name:* The name of God is a manifestation of himself, and every act contrary to God's Law is a profanation of his name.

8. *garments taken in pledge:* They are given as a pledge of payment. Should a debtor default, a creditor could demand a security. The debtor hands over an object to the creditor as a guarantee for his debt; a garment often served as a substitute for the person. But, according to the Code of the Covenant, the poor man's garment had to be restored to him by dusk, because it was his only covering for the night (Ex 22:25–26, repeated in Dt 24:12–13). This garment was a symbolic instrument; its value was not proportionate to the credit. These garments may have been used (cf. "any altar") in idolatrous worship. *the wine of those who have been fined:* This obscure phrase may denote the wine forfeited to creditors, or wine unjustly extorted in fines. The drinking of wine is here associated with the sacred meals following the sacrifices; they were often the occasion of numerous abuses. *their god:* A god honored by such excesses is not the true God. While the details of this verse are obscure, the general idea is clear: Amos is inveighing against the externals of religious practice that are in reality the vehicles of social injustice.

12 **9–12.** This review of the saving acts of God on behalf of Israel is a fitting prelude to the announcement of doom (13–16). In view of such divine beneficence, the Israelites should have responded with gratitude and obedience, but they did just the opposite. **9.** *Amorites:* Here, as often, it is synonymous with Canaanites. The pronoun "I," referring to the Lord, is in the emphatic position of the Hebr text (also in 10). **10.** The Exodus deliverance, along with the Conquest, is recalled here as a sign of the Lord's love, to which Israel has failed to respond. **11.** Similarly, the prophets (cf. Dt 18:15–22) and the Nazirites (cf. Nm 6) were signs of the Lord's provident care. **12.** But these men of God were rejected by the people. Amos singles out the abstinence from wine to characterize the Israelite attitude to the Nazirites.

13–16. Yahweh's punishment will be relentless, as the vivid imagery testifies. The exact meaning of 13 is not clear, but the idea is that Israel shall collapse under crushing power, from which even the most favored (the "swift," the "strong," etc., of 14–16) have no means of escape.

13 **(II) Words and Woes for Israel (3:1–6:14).** The second section of Am contains a series of sermons i.e., warnings and threats, some of which are introduced by "Hear!" (3:1–5:6) and others by "Woe!" (5:7–6:14).

(A) First Word (3:1–15). God's election of Israel involved responsibility rather than privilege. Because Israel failed to comply with her obligations she is to be punished. **1–8.** The keynote of Amos' prophecy. **1.** *hear this word:* An introductory formula (3:1; 4:1; 5:1). *men of Israel:* The people of the northern kingdom. The second part of this verse may be a later editorial addition (notice the abrupt change of person, from "the Lord" to "I"), adapting the message to all Israelites. The reference to the Exodus immediately recalls God's covenant with the Israelites, and it is in terms of this relationship that Amos addressed the people. It is the foundation of his comments.

2. *favored:* The verb (*yāda'*) is usually translated "to know," a knowledge that is also experience. It expresses an intimate relationship between persons (even marital relations, as in Gn 4:1). This verse (with 9:7) is a perfect summary of Amos' theology of the covenant. God had entered into an intimate relationship with his people by choosing them. In no way had the Israelites merited this election because of any special qualifications on their part (Dt 7:6–11). Their election was for service; it was not merely a guarantee of divine protection. Failure to serve calls for punishment.

3–8. Amos defends his authority to speak; he is speaking out of divine compulsion. The climax comes in v. 8; vv. 3–6 are a series of challenging, rhetorical questions justifying his intervention. These examples are borrowed from everyday life, and they imply a cause-effect relationship. Those who heard Amos would have had to respond in the negative to all the situations he describes for them. Agreement goes before harmony; prey prompts the animal's cry; the trumpet sounds the alarm; God is the cause of evil (as well as good—in the OT perspective). The events to which Amos alludes happen for a reason; there was also a reason for Amos' intervention, i.e., the call of God. **7.** This verse interrupts the sequence of questions and may therefore be an editorial gloss glorifying the prophetic role. The phrase, "his servants, the prophets," is a deuteronomic expression. **8.** A prophet must proclaim, because God has spoken; he is seized by an inner compulsion to speak (cf. Jer 20:11).

14 **9–15.** Samaria and Bethel are doomed. **9.** An invitation is extended to the nations, in mocking fashion, to witness the stark evil that has taken place in Samaria. Ashdod is one of the Philistine cities mentioned in 1:8. The LXX reads "Assyria," which gives a better balance to "Egypt." Samaria was the last and most important capital of the northern kingdom, built on the impressive mountain site chosen by Omri (*ca.* 876–869). *the great disorders:* Social injustice, oppression, unrest, and extortion. **10.** Material prosperity caused them to lose all sense of morality; "know not" signifies "will not." **11.** *enemy:* The reference is to Assyria, which is never named. Israel's punishment will be invasion, destruction, and exile. **12.** The vivid images (12d is unclear) used to describe the destruction of Samaria reflect Amos' shepherd background. When a maurauding animal attacked the sheep, the shepherd would recover what he could to serve as proof to the owner (Gn 31:39; Ex 22:13). The sense of the verse is utter destruction, not the preservation of a remnant (despite A. Benson in *CBQ* 19 [1957] 199–212). **13.** *the God of hosts:* Here probably the ruler of creation (→ Aspects OT Thought, 77:14), who will destroy Bethel (by an earthquake? cf. 14). **14.** *Bethel* was the national sanctuary of the northern kingdom which contained a temple and a statue of a golden calf, presumably the throne of Yahweh. Bethel is the object of Amos' severe censure. *horns of the altar:* These projections at the four corners of the altar, resembling the horns of an ox, furnished asylum in time of trouble (1 Kgs 1:50); however, even the altars are to be destroyed. **15.** *winter house... summer house:* These references to the extravagant living of the wealthy designate either two parts of the same dwelling or two distinct dwellings. Amos condemns the comfort and luxury of contemporary urban life. He also condemns the lavish buildings. *ivory apartments:* Ivory-paneled houses (1 Kgs 22:39)i Excavations at Samaria have revealed such elaborate and costly adornments as ivory carvings and ivory-inlaid furniture (see *ANEP* § 129–30, 566). The wide disparity between the rich and the poor was completely contrary to the spirit of the covenant.

15 **(B) Second Word (4:1–13).** The pampered and indolent Samarian women are indicted and denounced vituperatively by Amos for their luxury and indifference to the needy. These jaded wives are represented as urging their husbands to exploit the poor to satisfy their selfish demands. **1.** *lords:* A wife called her husband *ba'al* or "master"; she also addressed him as *'ādōn*, "lord." These well-fed women are compared to the cows of Bashan, a fertile area on the E side of the Jordan, extending S from Mt. Hermon to the Yarmuk River, famous for its prize cows and rich pastures. **2.** These scenes depict people being led away with hooks in their noses. The reference may be to corpses being dragged away to the refuse pile, after the manner of disposal of animal carcasses. **3.** *the breached walls:* Subsequent to the conquest of Samaria, when the wall will be broken. There is an evident contrast between the desperate situation described here and the luxury of the Israelites.

4–5. Amos condemns the sacrifices at Bethel and Gilgal. The reference apparently is to the sacred feasts observed in the shrines of Israel, of which we have no record. This ironical invitation to the sanctuaries of the northern kingdom is caustic and contemptuous. It was perhaps (cf. 7:10–17) delivered during a religious festival at Bethel in the presence of a large crowd. *Gilgal:* The name means "the circle," i.e., of stones; several places in Palestine are so named. The location is uncertain, but it was an old shrine (Jos 4:19–20; 1 Sm 7:16). The Israelites were rendering religion farcical by making ritual an end in itself, hence the ironic "sin the more." *each morning... every third day:* The cult was carried to excess. *sacrifices:* Offering of animals slaughtered by the priests. Part of the offering was consumed by the worshipers in a ritual feast. **5.** *burn:* The portion of the offering presented to Yahweh was consumed by fire upon the altar. *freewill offerings:* Those not required by the Law or by a vow (Ex 35:29). *you love to do:* Their interests are far more self-centered than God-centered.

16 **6–12.** The divine pedagogy. In the past the Lord had recourse to numerous chastisements in an attempt to teach the people that they should return to the covenant, but all proved futile. Amos describes the natural calamities that Yahweh had employed to chasten Israel. The emphatic "I" underscores the fact that it is God's power at work here. **6.** *clean of food:* Famine was a common occurrence in Palestine. *you returned not:* The Hebr verb *šûb* is often translated "to repent." The meaning here is "to turn to Yahweh." Five strophes end with this same refrain (6, 8, 9, 10, 11). **7–8.** Drought is still common in Palestine. A premature cessation of the winter rains resulted in the failure of the crops, harvested in May. The drought worked other great hardships on the people. Sufficient water was stored in each village to supply the needs of its own inhabitants, so there was not enough to share with outsiders. **9.** *blight and searing wind:* The two scourges are frequently associated in the OT (Dt 28:22; 1 Kgs 8:37). The crops were ruined by the hot wind blowing from the desert. Devastation by locust plagues was common in the Near East. **10.** *pestilence:* Plagues were well known in Egypt (Dt 7:15). *stench of your camps:* By reason of the unburied corpses (Is 34:3). **11.** Because of the reference to Sodom and Gomorrah (Gn 19), Amos is probably describing the destruction wrought by a severe earthquake. *brand plucked from the fire:* It is uncertain to what calamity the Prophet is referring, but it is some form of devastation from which the Israelites were saved at the last moment. **12.** The preaching of Amos is another opportunity being offered to Israel—i.e., if the Israelites choose not to repent, they will be annihilated. Others interpret this verb as a threat of doom. **13.** The verse is a doxology differing in thought and style from the oracles of Amos. It bears close resemblance to Dt-Is and may have been inserted by a later editor. Similar passages are found in 5:8–9 and 9:5–6. This doxology portrays the transcendent glory and majesty of God, revealed by the forces of nature.

17 **(C) Third Word (5:1–6).** A lamentation which speaks of the imminent fall of Israel. **1–2.** This typical lament represents the misfortunes of Israel as an accomplished fact; it is written in Hebrew in lamentation meter, called "qînâ." **2.** *the virgin Israel:* Israel is personified as a virgin woman, as in Hos, Is, and Jer. The nation is compared to a virgin who dies in the prime of her youth before experiencing the joys of married life. **3.** The judgment of Yahweh will take the form of an invasion that will depopulate the nation.

4–15. Exhortations to seek Yahweh alternate with strong denunciations. "Life" is possible only on the condition of sincere repentance. **4.** *seek: Dāraš* is often used in the sense of seeking a divine answer at a sanctuary in response to a specific question (Ex 18:15). It has here a more profound meaning—i.e., seeking God in the sense of longing for the Lord himself. *live:* It does not mean physical survival on earth or life in the next world, but rather living in a proper relationship with God. Seeking Yahweh in the sense of ascertaining and practicing his will is the only means of escaping imminent destruction. For the practice of justice, sacrifice is not enough. **5.** *Bethel...Gilgal:* See 3:14, 4:4. Seeking the religious shrines is contrasted with seeking Yahweh. Beer-sheba is located in the extreme south of Judah, 50 mi. SSW of Jerusalem; it is associated with the names of Abraham (Gn 21:33), Isaac (Gn 26:23), and Jacob (Gn 28:10; 46:1–5). Amos advised the people to refrain from visiting the sanctuaries because they had so deteriorated. *Gilgal shall be led into exile: Haggilgāl gālōh yigleh* is paranomasia, a not unusual device in the Prophets. *Bethel shall become nought:* There is another play on words in the Hebrew, i.e., house of God...(house of) nought. Beth-aven (*bēt-'āwen*, "house of evil" [or "nothingness"], cf. Hos 4:15) is thought to be an intentional distortion of Bethel (lit., "house of God") because of the idolatrous worship conducted at this shrine. **6.** *house of Joseph:* Since Joseph was considered the eponymous ancestor of the tribes of Ephraim and Manasseh, the members of these tribes are frequently referred to as the "sons of Joseph" or the "house of Joseph," or simply "Joseph" (6:6). Verse 7 is better placed after v. 9, as in the CCD.

8–9. These verses form a doxology reminiscent of Jb 38 and Is 40ff. Since it interrupts the sequence of thought, it is probably an interpolation. According to the doxology, the physical universe is directly under the control of the sovereign Lord. *Pleiades:* In Hebrew, *kimāh;* it is connected with the Arabic word, *kūm*, "heap" or "herd" (of camels). It occurs only three times in the OT (here and in Jb 9:9; 38:31). *Orion:* This bright constellation is near the Pleiades.

18 **(D) First Woe (5:7,10–17).** **7.** Amos inveighs against venal judges who abuse civil justice and make the court procedure a bitter experience for the poor and oppressed. *wormwood:* A bitter plant, which symbolizes something completely revolting or extremely unpleasant. **10.** It continues the denunciation of v. 7, where it fits naturally. *at the gate:* Reference is to the public square, just inside the city gate, where public meetings and courts of law were held. Disputes and trials were settled by the elders who sat at the gate of the town. Any member of the council of elders who would defend right conduct was repudiated by the court. **11.** *levies of grain:* The reference is to exploitation of the impoverished. Contrary to the law of Dt 23:19, wealthy landlords exacted an excessive share of the produce from those who farmed their land. *houses of hewn stone:* These palatial residences, constructed of costly and durable materials, contrasted to the houses of the poor made from field stones lying about; however, at the time of Yahweh's impending judgment, even the sturdiest of structures would not be sufficiently secure. **12.** The verse exposes the corruption of the very people responsible for the administration of justice. *accepting bribes:* Bribes for acquitting the guilty were forbidden in Ex 21:30; Nm 35:31. *repelling the needy:* A conspiracy existed between the judges and the rich against the needy. Without money, a man would not be given a hearing. **13.** This aphorism differs in tone from the rest of Am. It is more like the wisdom than the prophetical literature. It may be a marginal gloss inserted into the text, or perhaps Amos intended it as sarcasm or irony. The righteous man refrains from bringing his case to the court of law because he knows he will be treated unfairly. It suggests resignation on the part of the prudent man who knows that a protest against the prevailing evil would be useless. **14.** A partial explanation of v. 6: "Seek the Lord, that you may live." *as you claim:* They mistakenly thought that election by Yahweh gave a guarantee of protection; cf. 3:2; 9:7. **15.** *remnant of Joseph:* See comment on 5:6. There is no great hope ("perhaps") for what will remain of the nation after the impending catastrophic events. **16–17.** Described is a day of great lamentation. In the Near East, grief was expressed in a very public and ostentatious manner. *alas! alas!:* The funeral lamentation was a sharp, repeated cry (*hôy, hôy*). *professional mourners:* Laments were usually composed and sung by professionals, men or women (cf. Jer 9:17–22). **17.** Usually vintage time was a time of joy, but mourning will be experienced even in the vineyards. *when I pass through your midst:* This reference to the Lord is reminiscent of Ex 12:12,30, when he passed through the land of Egypt and caused great lamentation by slaying the first-born.

19 **(E) Second Woe (5:18–27).** **18.** *the day of the Lord:* This is the first mention in Israelite literature of the day of Yahweh. According to the popular belief, this technical expression connoted a time of joy or victory, a day of exaltation when the Lord would be victorious over his enemies. Israel's recollection of Yahweh's intervention in the past eventually prompted a belief in an eschatological day par excellence when Yahweh would intervene definitively and actualize his promises to the patriarchs. (cf. G. von Rad, *JSemS* 4 [1959] 97–108). Amos proclaims that Israel can look forward only to a day of judgment, a day of vindication and destruction, a day of disaster and doom. Hos, Is, Zeph also purport the ominous view in Am, applying it to the coming judgment upon the nation for its evil deeds. **19.** The unexpected and inevitable nature of the judgment of doom is described in picturesque language. The OT frequently refers to lions and bears; and even more frequently to the serpent.

21–27. A condemnation, not of ritual worship but of religious formalism—external rites unrelated to interior morality. Worship was being substituted for social responsibility. God himself is the speaker in this section. In the NT, Christ inveighs against cult that is purely external (Jn 4:21–24). **22.** *cereal offerings: Minḥāh* is the oldest generic term for sacrifice in the OT. In the older documents it designates any gift, whether offered to God or man. In later writings it is used of an offering to God consisting of grain, such as flour, roasted kernels, bread, etc. *peace offerings:* In this type of sacrifice only part of the victim was consumed by fire; part was given to the priests, and the remainder was eaten by the donor and his friends. **23.** Religious ceremonies included song and music (1 Sm 10:5). While sacrifice was being offered, hymns were sung to the accompaniment of instruments. There should be an intrinsic relationship between cult and conduct. "Justice" (*mišpāṭ*) and "goodness" (*ṣᵉdāqāh*), translated differently at times, are frequently associated →(Aspects OT Thought, 77:93–94, 136).

25. Amos, Hosea (2:16), and Jeremiah (2:1–3) regard the wilderness period as the time the Israelites enjoyed an ideal relationship with Yahweh. *sacrifices: Zebāḥ* actually designates a sacred "slaughtering." The Israelites' chief offering to Yahweh was the life of the animals, which also, of course, served as their own food. According to the opinion of some commentators, the Hebrews' sacrificial system was not part of their religious practice of the wilderness period but developed in Canaan. In the desert they would have worshiped God in a sincere but simple way, without elaborate ritual. But the Pentateuch contains ancient traditions about the sacrifices in the desert (e.g., Ex 3:18; 5:3; 10:25). Is Am contradictory? In the context of 5:25, Amos in not repudiating the cult itself, but the externals of worship that were in vogue, uses the sincerity of the desert ideal as a contrast. **26.** *Sakkuth:* An Assyro-Babylonian god. *Kaiwan:* The Akkadian name for the planet Saturn. The references may be to images in human form that the Israelites are here represented as carrying in procession as they go into exile. The mention of "star god" suggests that astral deities are denoted. These pagan idols were powerless to save the Israelites. The text is uncertain, making the verse very difficult to interpret. **27.** *beyond Damascus:* In Assyria. The type of religious perversion that Israel was practicing was characteristic of Assyria. **27b.** This solemn formula was perhaps intended to contrast with the Assyrian deities of the preceding verse.

20 **(F) Third Woe (6:1–14).** **1–7.** The self-centered and luxury-loving rulers of Judah and Israel will be punished by exile. **2.** *Calneh:* This city in northern Syria near Aleppo was incorporated into the Assyrian empire by Tiglath-pileser III. *Hamath:* A famous ancient city of Syria on the Orontes River, it is modern Hama. *Gath:* It is one of the Philistine confederation of five cities, once prosperous but eventually destroyed by the Assyrians; the same fate awaits Israel. However, this difficult verse may be an interpolation, for these cities were apparently devastated by Assyria subsequent to Amos' time (Calneh, 738; Hamath, 720; Gath, 711). **4.** They made use of very elaborate furniture, inlaid with ivory panels, and they ate sumptuous food. The remains of a bed inlaid with ivory have been found at the site of Arslan Tash in northern Syria, E of Carchemish. One of the pieces bore the name of Hazael, king of Damascus in the time of Jehu of Israel (*ca.* 842–815). *calves from the stall:* These subsist on milk only, so their meat is very tender. **5.** Musical entertainment was provided at meals. The reference to David may be ironic. **6.** The picture is one of indolence, luxury, and insensitivity. *Joseph:* The northern kingdom; see comment on 5:6.

8. *the pride of Jacob:* The people are vain and arrogant, trusting in material things and showing only contempt for the law of Yahweh. **9–10.** Description of a plague. Very often pestilence would follow a siege. Such will be the experience of Israel, with little hope of deliverance. **10.** *for no one must mention the name of the Lord:* Perhaps out of superstitious fear, lest Yahweh's wrath be incurred. The text is corrupt. **11.** Perhaps a devastation resulting from a severe earthquake. All the house, regardless of size, will be destroyed. **12.** These rhetorical questions designate what is unreasonable or impossible. The conduct described is contrary to the nature of horses and oxen, but Israel had attempted the unreasonable in terms of what God had every right to expect from his people. Her sins of social injustice were unnatural. In the scandalous conduct of her law courts, justice and righteousness had been rendered bitter and poisonous. **13.** *Lo-debar:* A small town on the border of Gad, probably to be identified with modern Umm ed-Dabar, its name means "no thing," perhaps a pun. *Karnaim:* An ancient town in eastern Bashan, it means, literally, "horns," figuratively, "strength." Both towns had been recaptured from the Aramean kingdom of Damascus. Perhaps the reference is ironical in that these were only minor conquests. **14.** *a nation:* Assyria. *Labo of Hamath:* It is located on the northern boundary of the Israelite territory. By associating the first word of the phrase with the Hebr verb *bô'* (to enter), we have traditionally translated it "the entrance of Hamath." But now the first part of the designation is thought to represent Labo, a town in the Lebanon Valley S of Hamath. It is probably identifiable with modern Lebweh. *Wadi Arabah:* The valley extends from the S end of the Dead Sea to the Gulf of Aqabah and is the southern border of the kingdom. These two places designate the extent of the territory established by the victories of Jeroboam II (2 Kgs 14:25).

21 **(III) Symbolic Visions (7:1–9:15).** Amos recounts these visions in the first person. Some commentators think that these visions constitute Amos' call to his prophetic ministry.

(A) Vision of Locusts (7:1–3). Locust plagues were known in Palestine (cf. Jl); therefore, this vision is doubtless based on Amos' actual experience. **1.** *the late growth:* The second crop; the first mowing went to the king as a tax. **2.** The land of Jacob is comprised of people who are helpless and without resources. In this vision, and in the second, Amos intercedes for Israel and prevails upon God to withold judgment. Yahweh grants his petition. **3.** The God of Israel, the God of love and mercy, refrained from executing his plan of doom.

22 **(B) Vision of Fire (7:4–6).** **4.** The land is devastated by a huge conflagration during the dry season. The consuming fire, the instrument of God's judgment, deprived the people of both food and water. *abyss:* The Hebrew *t^ehôm*, is always used without the article, and is therefore considered a proper noun. It is the subterranean ocean, on which the earth was thought to float and the source of rivers and floods (Gn 7:11). **5.** As in v. 2, Amos alleges Israel's smallness and weakness as a reason for Yahweh to intervene.

23 **(C) Vision of the Plummet (7:7–9).** The purpose of a plummet is for testing. Yahweh tested the wall with the plummet and found it wanting, symbolizing Yahweh's test to ascertain if Israel has violated the standards of the covenant. Israel's infidelity ensures her destruction. This time Amos does not intervene; God's judgment is irrevocable. **9.** Destruction wrought by invasion is described. The plummet test has revealed that Israel is a wall so askew that it will have to be leveled. *high places:* The shrines were generally located on the heights. Perhaps the ancients felt that they were thus able to draw closer to God. In Israel, the high place (Hebr *bāmāh*) was originally a place of sacrifice to Yahweh; therefore, at first the high places were not condemned by Israel's religion. Later, the term came to mean an idolatrous sanctuary in sharp contradiction to the Temple of Jerusalem. The prophets stood in vigorous opposition to the service of the high places because they furnished a strong temptation to the practice of syncretism. *the house of Jeroboam:* The reigning dynasty. This prophecy was interpreted as treason (v. 11). *sword:* It is in the hands of the Assyrians.

24 **(D) Historical Interlude (7:10–17).** This passage shows the tension between prophet and priest, the climactic clash between Amos and Amaziah. This excellent piece of narrative interrupts the series of visions but provides most valuable information concerning the prophetic activity of Amos. The intrusion of this biographical insert is best explained by the fact that the third vision ends with a reference to Jeroboam, who also plays a prominent part in the biographical interruption. The passage speaks of Amos in the third person, indicating the work of an editor. **10–11.** The verses contain the message of Amaziah to King Jeroboam II. Amaziah, the chief priest of the royal sanctuary at Bethel, was a member of the official family who served as the spokesman for the king. By taking Amos' words out of context, Amaziah distorted them and accused Amos of conspiracy against the king's person. **12–13.** Amaziah's excoriating attack on Amos results in the latter's expulsion from Israel for speaking against the royal house. *visionary:* The term is contemptuous and pejorative. The prophetic orders seemed to have countenanced and capitulated to pagan practices at the local shrines. Many were little more than time-serving professionals whose chief interest was in their fees. *the king's sanctuary:* Bethel, the national sanctuary of the northern kingdom, was the official sanctuary of the affluent Jeroboam II.

14. In reply to the savage rebuke of the high priest, Amos lists his credentials. He denounces the professional prophets and disclaims any connection with them. Amos had no interest in being a prophet for the purpose of earning money. *a dresser of sycamores:* This insipid fruit, which grows especially in the lowlands of Palestine, is related to, but smaller than, the fig; it was the food of the poor. At a certain point in its development, the dresser had to puncture the fruit so that it would grow large enough to become edible. The occupation was seasonal. **15.** Amos was a prophet, not by his own choice or study or through inheritance, but through the personal intervention of an imperious God. **16–17.** The verses are addressed to Amaziah. The intrepid Prophet has the last word. He gives a typical description of imminent invasion and exile—rape, slaughter of innocents, and plunder. The "unclean land" is Assyria, so called because of its idolatry.

25 **(E) Vision of the Fruit Basket (8:1–3).** This fourth vision suggests that the time for judgment is ripe; the Lord will not relent. **2.** Like other prophets, Amos makes occasional use of the pun; "a basket of ripe fruit" is *qayiṣ* in Hebrew, and "the time is ripe" is *qêṣ* (lit., "end"). **3.** *that day:* The day of the Lord (see comment on 5:18).

26 **(F) Against Greed (8:4–14).** **5.** The Israelites wait impatiently for the termination of the holy days so that they can engage in lucrative business practice. The plutocratic landlords would cheat and oppress the poor (cf. 2:6). *the new moon:* Nm 28:11–15 prescribes that on the first day of each new lunar month a holocaust should be offered consisting of two bulls, a ram, and seven lambs, as well as other offerings and libations; a goat was also to be offered, as a sacrifice for sin. This celebration of the first day of the new moon is ancient in origin. Like the Sabbath, it was a day of rest when no business was transacted. It continued to be a festive day to the end of OT times and even into the NT period (e.g., Col 2:16). *Sabbath:* Our Eng word is a transcription of the Hebr *šabbāt*, a word used only in religious contexts. Its etymology is uncertain but it is probably related to *šābat*, "to cease working" or "to rest." The origin of the institution of the Sabbath is a matter of dispute, but it was ancient (→ Religious Institutions, 76:128). A parallel is drawn between the Sabbath and the day of the new moon because both are days of rest (cf. Is 1:13; 66:23; Hos 2:13). *ephah:* This dry measure equals slightly more than a bushel. Law forbade Israelite merchants to make use of a dishonest ephah measure (Lv 19:36; Dt 25:14–15). *shekel:* It was a conventionally established unit of weight; stones were ordinarily used as weights.

6. This verse differs from 2:6 in that here it is a question of buying, not selling. *refuse of the wheat:* It probably means that the rapacious merchants are so greedy that they sell what should be discarded; otherwise, they are guilty of mixing good and bad grain. **7.** *pride of Jacob:* This may be a synonym for Yahweh himself (6:8). **8.** Amos is apparently describing an earthquake in terms of the (annual) inundation of Egypt by the Nile. Even nature will experience the effects of the divine judgment. **9.** A total eclipse of the sun took place in Palestine on June 15, 763. Eclipses were regarded as signs preceding God's judgment. **10.** Traditionally, the harvest and vintage feasts were joyous occasions. Sackcloth and shaved heads were signs of lamentation. **11.** The people will search in vain for a prophet to proclaim the Word of God. **12.** *from sea to sea:* From one end of the world to another (Zech 9:10; Ps 72:8), i.e., from the Mediterranean to the Euphrates. **13.** The judgment of doom upon idolators will be felt not only by the elderly, but also by the young, the hope of the future. *thirst:* A physical thirst. **14.** The meaning is obscure, but it is surely a condemnation of syncretism. *Dan...Beer-sheba:* Described are the extreme northern and southern limits of the country; both were scenes of idolatrous worship. With Bethel, Dan was raised by Jeroboam I to a national shrine.

27 **(G) Vision of the Altar (9:1–6).** In this fifth vision, the Lord is standing beside the altar. The setting is probably at Bethel with the Israelites gathered at the sanctuary. **1.** No one will escape God's punishment, which will be devastation by war. **2–6.** There can be no place (nether world, heavens, etc.) of escape from divine wrath. The Lord's dominion extends even to Sheol, the subterranean region to which, it was thought, all the dead descend. **3.** *Carmel:* This mountain range W of the Plain of Esdraelon is 15 mi. long, and its highest point is 1800 ft. above sea level. The thick forests and recessed caves of Carmel would have made ideal hiding places. *serpent:* A mythological sea monster; *nāḥāš* is the general word for all serpents. **4.** The Lord's sovereignty extends even to foreign countries. **5–6.** God's cosmic power is described (cf. Gn 1:6–8). This third doxology (cf. 4:13; 5:8–9) probably came from a later time than that of Amos. Heaven was conceived of as a palace, and the sky as a solid firmament in the shape of an arch, its bases resting on the earth.

28 **(H) Messianic Perspective (9:7–15).** **7.** It deals with God's relationship to all peoples. This is a repudiation of Israel's narrow concept of her status as chosen by God; her election is not for her merit. The concept of Yahweh's universal dominion includes both Israelite and non-Israelite peoples and extends over the whole of human history. Yahweh is the God of Ethiopia as well as of Israel (Ethiopia traditionally was a slave nation on the periphery of civilization). Israel did not merit the predilection of the Lord; the initiative came from him. This divine election was to responsibility and not to privilege. Amos is not rejecting Israel's special relation to God because of the covenant but rather the Israelites' perversion of it in making the covenant relation the foundation of self-righteousness and a false security. The Philistines and Arameans were always regarded as Israel's worst enemies. *Caphtor:* It is the island of Crete from which the Philistines migrated to Palestine. *Kir:* This place name has not yet been found in any extrabiblical source; its location is still unknown.

8–15. Many commentators believe that this section was added by editors who wanted to conclude the Book of Amos on a positive note. Nevertheless, many other scholars have vigorously defended the authenticity of the book's optimistic conclusion. **8b.** Some see an indication of the Isaian idea of remnant in this statement. It seems to be a qualification of Amos' earlier statements (e.g., v. 9) about the inevitability of devastation. **9.** An ambiguous verse, it is difficult to know whether it is a threat or a promise. **11.** The fall of Jerusalem seems presupposed, and the Prophet anticipates the rebuilding of the kingdom of David. Judgment will be followed by salvation. *on that day:* The time of the restoration of Israel is designated. *the fallen hut:* The kingdom and dynasty of David terminated with the fall of Jerusalem in 587. This reference is considered as evidence of the post-exilic origin of this section. **12.** *Edom:* A traditional rivalry existed between Israel and Edom (Gn 27:40). Edom had also taken advantage of the situation at the time of the fall of the southern kingdom. *all the nations:* Those which David had conquered are indicated: Philistia, Moab, Ammon, and the Syrian kingdoms. The Prophet looks forward to the time when all these nations will be reunited, as they were during David's reign. **13.** A picture of the prosperity that accompanies the restoration is given. The soil will be marvelously productive. The land will be so fruitful that the various farming tasks will follow in quick succession. The entire passage expresses the typical features of royal messianism—the restoration of the Davidic dynasty and material prosperity (→ Aspects OT Thought, 77:158–161).

15

HOSEA

Dennis J. McCarthy, S.J.

BIBLIOGRAPHY

1 *Commentaries:* Mauchline, J., "Hosea," *IB* 6 (1956) 551–725. Rinaldi, G., "Osea," *I profeti minori* (LSB 2; Turin, 1960) 14–121. Robinson, T. H., "Hosea," *Die zwölf Kleinen Propheten* (HAT 1, 14; 2nd ed.; Tübingen, 1954) 1–54. Sellin, E., *Das Zwölfprophetenbuch* (KAT 12, 1; Leipzig, 1929) 6–143. Ward, J. M., *Hosea: A Theological Commentary* (N.Y., 1966). Weiser, A., "Hosea," *Das Buch der zwölf Kleinen Propheten* (ATD 24–25; Göttingen, 1956) 1, 11–104. Wolff, H. W., *Dodekapropheton 1, Hosea* (BKAT; Neukirchen, 1961). (The last book contains a full bibliography.)

Other literature: Jacob, E., "L'héritage cananéen dans le Livre du Prophète Osée," *RHPR* 43 (1964) 250–59. Maly, E., "Messianism in Osee," *CBQ* 19 (1957) 213–25. McKenzie, J., "Divine Passion in Osee," *CBQ* 17 (1955) 287–99. Östborn, G., *Yahweh and Baal* (LUA NF 1,51,6; Lund, 1956). Rowley, H. H., "The Marriage of Hosea," *BJRylL* 39 (1957–58) 200–33. Rust, E. C., "The Theology of Hosea," *RevExp* 54 (1957) 510–21. Wolff, H. W., "Guilt and Salvation. A Study in the Prophecy of Hosea," *Interpr* 15 (1961) 274–85.

INTRODUCTION

2 **(I) Historical Background.** We know nothing of Hosea, son of Beeri, except what we can glean from the book that collects his prophetic speeches. If it is a hazardous undertaking to try to reconstruct the personality of the man and the details of his life through inferences from the material contained in that book, we can at least learn something of his milieu, a factor indispensable for an understanding of his words. He spoke his oracles in the last days of the northern of the two kingdoms into which the Hebrews had divided themselves after the days of Solomon, Israel. We learn that his prophetic activity extended from the prosperous reign of Jeroboam II into the disastrous times that followed thereupon and saw the final disappearance of Israel from the political scene. All this is reflected in his oracles, which gives us the date of their origin, from *ca.* 750 until after 732.

Although Hosea was of Israel and not Judah, the compilers of the Book of Hosea significantly ignore the miserable kinglets who followed Jeroboam in their superscription dating the prophet (1:1). They do list their contemporaries in the more stable kingdom of Judah, and well they might; the last days of Israel make a painful tale. The last century of the nation's existence was lived out under the sign of Assyria. After its first serious thrust into the west in the 9th cent. BC, Assyria, confronted by enemies near to home and governed by a succession of weak kings, was quiescent during the first half of the 8th cent. In this breathing space the dynasty of Jehu was able to establish itself firmly in Israel, and under Jeroboam II (786–746) it expanded the kingdom to its greatest territorial extent and raised it to its greatest heights of material prosperity.

However, Jeroboam's death corresponded closely to the accession of a vigorous king in Assyria, Tiglath-pileser III (745–727). The renewed pressure which that monarch soon applied to the states of Syria and Palestine revealed the hollowness of Israel's power. The political life of the nation deteriorated to a succession of palace revolutions, assassinations, and dynastic changes. In the 20 years between Jeroboam's death and the end of the kingdom six kings reigned in Israel. Jeroboam's son and successor, Zechariah, was assassinated within six months. The murderer, Shallum, was himself slain after but a month by Menahem, who managed to survive from 745 to 738. He was the king who had to accept Assyrian overlordship and pay a heavy tribute (2 Kgs 15:19–20). Pekahiah, son of Menahem, survived two years; then Pekah, at the head of an anti-Assyrian party, murdered him and took over. To the folly of opposing the invincible Assyrian Pekah added the impiety of an alliance with Damascus against the brother kingdom of Judah in an effort to overthrow David's dynasty and impose a king ready to join the anti-Assyrian coalition. However, Ahaz of Judah rejected the advice of the prophet Isaiah and paid tribute to Assyria. Tiglath-pileser was happy to have an excuse to intervene in Palestine and he came to the rescue of his vassal (2 Kgs 16:5–9). Of course the

Assyrian conqueror removed Pekah and replaced him by a certain Hoshea, who was to be a loyal vassal to Assyria. The kingdom of Israel itself was shorn of Galilee and Transjordan.

Despite everything, the lesson had not been learned. Eventually Hoshea joined Assyria's enemies after Tiglath-pileser's death. It was the end: He was taken captive, and, after a long siege, the capital, Samaria, was conquered in 722–721. Israel was led into exile and strangers were settled on the land. The northern kingdom was at an end.

3 **(II) Doctrine.** It is little wonder that the Prophet favors the form of a judgment (*rîb*) for his oracles. This violent and ever-changing history is reflected on every page of his book. He condemns the empty pomp of Israel's purely external cult as well as the pride of the people in its wealth and military power. This denial can only reflect Hosea's reaction to the attitudes prevailing during the favored days of Jeroboam II. But he has equally harsh words for the self-seeking and irresponsibility of Israel's kings and leaders, their quarrels and plots, and the never-ending revolutions and changes of government. In fact, he has a fundamental quarrel with the monarchy in Israel, condemning the strong dynasty of Jehu and its weak successors, which many interpret as a rejection of kingship as such. However, the Prophet's quarrel is not with the idea of monarchy among the Hebrews; it is with the monarchy of the northern kingdom which separated the nation from Judah and the legitimate kingship of David, at the same time founding the paganizing sanctuaries of Dan and Bethel.

Hosea alludes to the impious war with Judah (5:8–15). Most of all, he holds up the threat of exile and final destruction, fulfilled to the letter in Israel's last days.

However, the political folly and the anarchy of Israel's last days were not Hosea's chief concern. He knew that they were only symptoms of the fundamental disorder: Israel had forsaken Yahweh, its true king and its salvation, to take up the cult of the fertility gods of Canaan, the Baals, so that it attributed its prosperity to this cult and not to Yahweh. This name "Baal" is actually an appellative meaning "lord" (in our Bible "LORD" is a surrogate for Yahweh that does not mean lord at all); used alone it stands for Hadad, the Canaanite fertility god par excellence, and proclaims the fact that each locality had its own Hadad who was lord of the territory.

The exact character of the Baalism that Hosea reproaches in Israel is complex. There was overt devotion to the pagan Baals—witness the reference to the sin with Baal-peor (9:10–14)—but the more pervasive sin was the contamination of the very cult of Yahweh with Baalism. Yahweh was considered a god of the same kind as the Baals, bound to the land and essentially a purveyor of agricultural plenty. His worship was performed with rites borrowed from the sanctuaries of the Baals—e.g., cultic prostitution—and the thought, the theology, behind it was pure Baalism: The ritual was thought to have the inevitable effect of constraining the divinity in a magical way to give what was desired, i.e., fertility. Such was the religion that Hosea saw around him masquerading as Yahwism, and against this he protested.

He understandably characterized this religion as harlotry (*z^e^nûnîm, z^e^nût*). Israel had forsaken its true lover to give itself to the Baals. The language is not merely figurative. It does, of course, refer to Israel's spiritual apostasy, but the Baalizing cults included the practice of the grossest sexual abuses, which were not forgotten in the characterization of Israel's attitude as harlotry. This statement, however, does not exhaust Hosea's thought in the matter. He was preoccupied with Israel's apostasy so that "lie" and "falsity" become characteristic words for sin in his vocabulary (cf. 7:1,3; 10:2,13; 11:12; 12:2,8,12). He repeatedly returns to the thought of an Israel that through its history has forgotten again and again the God who saved it from Egyptian slavery, devotedly strengthened it, and made it a nation. Even when the nation has seemed to return to Yahweh, Hosea sees it as lip service, insincere repentance filled with a proud confidence in its own deserts (e.g., 5:15–7:2).

Hosea draws a very clear conclusion: The people that has turned away from its true God, Yahweh, must suffer punishment. It is a juridical penalty announced in a judicial sentence, but it is no mere legal sanction, i.e., a chastisement imposed from without. It is the natural, inevitable outgrowth of the sin. This concept is implied in the nature of the punishments Hosea proclaims. Yahweh will forsake the people who forsook him. Selfish political schemes have as counterpart the destruction of the kingdom and exile, the loss of the national identity. The false cult, pompous and sensual, will give way to a deprivation of the cult altogether. The orgiastic rites aimed at producing plenty—rich crops and the material for feasts—and at fostering reproduction—animal and human—will actually produce famine and barrenness so that the people will die out.

However, these condign punishments are not the only nor even the principal reversal with which Hosea surprises us. Most striking of all and most basic is his transposition of the ideas of the fertility cult. Yahweh is the loving husband of Israel, an idea surely influenced by the *hieros gamos* of Baal. The vocabulary, such as the references to wine, wheat and oil, rain, (sacred) trees, seeking the divinity, etc., is often that of the fertility cult. It is Yahweh, not Baal, who brings rain and thus bread, wine, and oil. Taking over the enemy's strength is a bold and an effective procedure (cf. Jacob, *op. cit.*, 253–54).

4 So far we have seen Hosea's doctrine as negative. It rejects Israel's politics and denies and attacks the current popular form of religion. But it is much more. Again and again Hosea appeals to history, to the evidence that Yahweh has indeed been Israel's savior. The vehicle for this is a formula like "I am Yahweh who brought you out of Egypt," borrowed from the true Yahwist liturgy. Hosea is an eager proponent of Yahwism—one who, guided by the divinely given spirit, explains and develops the contents of Yahweh's revelation that was handed on to the people and kept fresh through its proclamation at the sanctuaries where the liturgy and the teachings of the priests, its custodians, still reflected the true traditions of Yahwism. He demanded a response in which the basic element is *ḥesed*, "faithful love," (usually "kindness" in CCD), i.e., fidelity to Yahweh in obedience to his demands. The word belongs to covenant making; it denotes the disposition which should characterize the true party to a contract (→ Aspects OT Thought, 77:95–98). To us it has a legalistic sound, but *ḥesed* is no mere matter of courts and rescripts. It does not mean mere justice, *quid pro quo*. True *ḥesed* is a matter of mind and heart, a true devotion to the covenant partner, an idea brought out by another typically Hosean formula. The true covenant partner has pity (*rḥm*) for the other. Our translation is woefully inadequate and misleading; it does not mean sorrowful compassion with its frequent overtone of condescension; rather it means love, a personal devotion eager to help and protect, for ultimately it derives from the attitude of a mother to her child (*reḥem*, "womb").

The richness of Hosea's idea of the true character of covenanted union is best evident in the image peculiarly his own, i.e., the presentation of Yahweh and Israel as husband and wife (chs. 1–3). His own experience of the marriage union, characterized by a tender, understanding love and an unshakable fidelity despite a tragic mismatch, provides the insight through which he can understand and convey something of Yahweh's union with Israel. He knows beyond any doubt that Yahweh's love is unchanging no matter how the partner breaks faith.

With *ḥesed*, Hosea demands knowledge of Yahweh. We shall see that it has nothing to do with speculation but is an affective and effective relation implying complete readiness to hear and obey God's wish, i.e., attention to Yahweh's commandments (4:2). He is not concerned with cult and politics alone; he calls for a social conscience, right, order, and respect for the other man.

Finally, Hosea holds out hope for the future. Warning and judgment are the heart of his message, but he also promises a future restoration that will finally bring Israel to Yahweh. The use of the word "finally" must not be taken to mean that Hosea presents an explicit and developed eschatology. He promises a restoration without claiming anything like the Messianic kingdom of later eschatology. However, he does have the imagery and ideas which will be developed into the full eschatological system: a retributive reformation followed by paradisiac peace and a new, everlasting union (covenant) with God (cf. Maly, *op. cit.*).

5 **(III) Authenticity.** We know when Hosea spoke and what he said—if we have his own words or ideas. How much of the book is authentic? Around the turn of the century, drastic editing was fashionable, and large sections of the text were denied to the Prophet. Especially the positive part of his teaching, the promises of restoration (chs. 11, 14), could not, it was felt, be Hosea's work for he was said to have preached unrelieved doom. Today, scholars have abandoned such fancies. The style of the Book of Hosea is homogeneous. Moreover, the Prophet's passionate nature permeates the book and the ideas are consistent. Even the much-attacked promises of restoration are now known to be Hosean. Hope was integral to his doctrine, for the promise of a new and better covenant is inseparably united to the most characteristic portion of the book, the analogy between Yahweh's love for Israel and human marriage. There are, of course, glosses in our text, but they are identified easily enough (e.g., several insertions of the name of Judah, the proverb-like conclusion). Aside from these, it is agreed that the substance of Hos comes from the Prophet, which does not minimize the difficult problem of textual corruption; the Book of Hosea has suffered more than almost any other OT book in this regard. However, a difficulty in reading a bit of text is no argument against its authenticity.

6 **(IV) The Book.** The circumstances in which the contents were produced are clear enough. Like almost all of the prophetic books it is a collection of the oracles which the Prophet, speaking for God, delivered orally to warn, teach, and convert the people. The production of the book as a book is another matter. We do not know when and how it was composed. We assume that the process was the same as that for the other prophetic books—the Prophet's audience, especially his close followers and perhaps he himself, noted down his sayings and groups of sayings more or less close upon delivery; the collection of these notes along with memorized sayings of the Prophet into a book was a gradual process. Sayings about a common topic would be gathered into small collections (e.g., chs. 11, 12) that would later be combined with other collections and individual sayings until the book emerged. For Hos, where and how long this process took place are matters for conjecture, although the occasional glosses referring to Judah indicate that part occurred there.

7 **(V) Outline.** The method of producing Hos indicates the problem with its organization. The whole is not a conscious, unified, literary production but is the result of more or less haphazard growth. Hence, we cannot expect an organization in the strict sense with logical subordination and real progression. From this point of view, all we can make is a list of topics, not an outline (cf. E. Osty, "Osée," *BJ* 71–72). The various divisions are based on the more or less frequent occurrence of something—a word, an idea, a literary form—that serves as a criterion for division. The individual sections, therefore, are a matter of convenience more than anything else. Usually they do not contain a single oracle that Hosea spoke as a unit at one time and in one place; they are collections of sayings more or less unified. On the other hand, this does not mean that they are merely arbitrary and that the individual sayings can only be interpreted in isolation. For one thing, passages that reveal the Prophet's thought about a given theme are the best commentary on other passages where the theme occurs. Thus collections of passages about a theme as collections are legitimate sources for Hosea's thought, even though he did not speak all the words together nor make the collection. Second, it is the inspired Word of God that interests us, and it is the word as it appears fixed in a biblical context and not only the word as spoken by the prophet in isolation that is inspired.

(I) Hosea's Marriage (1–3)
- (A) The Prophet's Children (1:2–2:3)
- (B) Indictment of the Faithless Wife (2:4–17)
- (C) Reconciliation (2:18–25)
- (D) The Prophet and His Wife (3:1–5)

(II) Condemnation of Hosea's Contemporaries (4:1–9:9)
- (A) Yahweh's Indictment of Israel (4:1–3)
- (B) Indictment of the Leaders of Israel (4:4–5:7)
- (C) Political Upheavals (5:8–14)
- (D) False Repentance (5:15–7:2)
- (E) Corruption of the Monarchy (7:3–12)
- (F) Lament Over Israel (7:13–16)
- (G) Sins in Politics and Cult (8:1–14)
- (H) Exile Without Worship (9:1–6)
- (I) Rejection of the Prophet (9:7–9)

(III) Sin and History (9:10–14:1)
- (A) Sin and Decline (9:10–17)
- (B) Punishment of Apostasy (10:1–8)
- (C) False Confidence (10:9–15)
- (D) Love Overcomes Ingratitude (11:1–11)
- (E) Israel's Perfidy (12:1–15)
- (F) Death Sentence (13:1–14:1)

(IV) Epilogue: Repentance and Salvation (14:2–9)

COMMENTARY

8 **(I) Hosea's Marriage (1–3).** This central experience of the Prophet is a symbol revealing Yahweh's personal love of his people, faithful even in the face of their gross failings. Less often noted is the marriage symbol's clear introduction of the idea of a contract, a union of wills, into the concept of the covenant with Yahweh. The very importance of the matter, as well as the textual obscurities, make it natural that the effort to define the exact nature of the marriage has raised many problems, some of which must be touched on briefly.

First, is it allegorical fiction? The allegorical view does not seem to do justice to the often brutal realism of the symbolic actions of the prophets (Is 20:2–6; Jer 19; Ez 5), nor to the intensity of Hosea's words. Moreover, we would expect details like the name Gomer and the sexes of the children to have meaning in an allegory, but they do not.

Second, do chs. 1–3 recount a continuous story? If they do we have a tale of marriage and children, divorce, and remarriage. A variant of the continuous-story interpretation of these chapters holds that ch. 3 does not tell of a remarriage with Gomer after divorce but of an entirely new marriage, which adds the complication that the new wife must be called adulteress proleptically. In any case, to get a good sequence we must rearrange the text (cf. CCD); even then the reconstruction is incomplete and problematic. For instance, the divorce in ch. 2 need not refer to the Prophet's marriage at all but simply to Yahweh's relations with Israel. The account of the remarriage in ch. 3 is not integrated with ch. 1 as we would expect in a continuous narrative, for the vocabulary is different; it does not make a real sequel, and it is complete in itself. Furthermore, the MT presents three well-defined literary units—1:2–2:3, 2:4–25, 3—that move from accusation through chastisement to reconciliation. This arrangement of the text must surely be conscious, seeking to emphasize the theological meaning of the marriage symbol and not to tell a story. We can then consider ch. 3 to be parallel to ch. 1, not in telling the same tale but in treating the same experience from a different viewpoint.

Third, what is meant by "harlot wife" (1:2)? If it is adultery, then it is applied proleptically to the bride in 1:2. But why then say harlot and not adulteress? In view of this difficulty it is better to look for another explanation. Gomer might have been a sacred prostitute at a Baal shrine, or at least a devotee of a Baal whose worship involved orgiastic rites. Although such conduct certainly occurred in Israel, we can hardly say it was ordinary (Wolff, *Hosea*, 14) in view of the value put on virginity (Dt 22:13–19). In fact, idolatry itself was called harlotry so that merely joining the worshipers of Baal would be enough to earn the title (cf. J. Coppens, *Fest. F. Nötscher* [Bonn, 1950] 38–45).

9 **(A) The Prophet's Children (1:2–2:3).** This account of Hosea's marriage, with its symbolic meaning, is in the third person. Chapter 1 is a series of parallel units but the parallelism is flexible: The birth of each child is told in the same general fashion but with variation. Note the sequence of thought: Israel's idolatry (1:2b) and a specific sin (1:4) mean the loss of divine favor (1:6) and so the end of covenant (1:9).

2. *harlot wife:* Lit., "wife of harlotries." The plural expresses a quality, "faithless" or the like, and need not refer to an actual harlot. So also "harlot's children" can be children of such a mother, not children born of adultery. The "harlotry" of the land is idolatry (cf. 5:4). **3.** *Gomer, daughter of Diblaim:* Neither name refers to Yahweh, as was usual in Israelite names. This may be a further hint at infidelity, i.e., service of the Baals. *bore him a son:* It is the Prophet's own child, not the result of adultery. Yahweh gives the child a name, an action that always emphasizes the function of the person as a sign of divine intentions (cf. Gn 17:5, Abraham; 32:20, Jacob; esp. Mt 1:21, Jesus); hence the names do not represent Hosea's own attitude toward his children. **4.** *Jezreel:* The plain between Galilee, Samaria, and the Jordan. The bloodshed at Jezreel during the overthrow of the Omrid dynasty is described in 2 Kgs 9–10, where it is commended by a prophet (2 Kgs 9:7). Hebrew thought ignored secondary causes; what was from one point of view a punishment deserved by the idolatrous Omrids was from another selfish murder. The punishment affects more than the house of Jehu; the kingdom—i.e., independence—will be removed. Verse 5 gives a new meaning for Jezreel by bringing in another, later saying of Hosea. *break the bow:* It indicates the destruction of Israelite power, probably in the Assyrian invasion of 733. The phrase itself belongs to the curses appended to ancient covenants and thus may imply the fulfilment of the curses that must follow covenant breaking (see Dt 28).

6. *Lo-ruhama:* "She is not pitied" or "she no longer holds the love of the parent," since the Hebr stem meaning "pity" carries overtones of parental love (→ 4 above; cf. ch. 11). "She" need not refer to the daughter; it may be the land (v. 2), feminine in Hebrew, or perhaps we should translate it impersonally. The name of the first child emphasized Israel's sin; this name, the divine attitude: the long-suffering God will have to punish his people. **7.** a later addition in the interests of Judah, whose fate is contrasted with Israel's. Yahweh himself intervened to save Jerusalem from Sennacherib (2 Kgs 19:35–37); cf. Is 31:1; Ps 20:7–9.

9. *Lo-ammi:* "Not my people" indicates that the covenant between Yahweh and Israel is ended, for the covenant made Israel the people of God (cf. Ex 6:6–7; Lv 26:12, Dt 26:18; Jer 31:33). *your God:* The Hebrew is "I am not Yahweh [lit., "not Ehyeh"] to you." The very name of God specially revealed to his people (Ex 3:14) is lost to Israel.

10 **2:1–3.** These lines, which are printed at the end of ch. 3 in the CCD, are a set of sayings reversing the meaning of the children's names. **1a.** A clear reference to the promissory covenant with the patriarchs (Gn 22:17; 32:13). Thus, these verses open and close (*'ammi*, "my people") with a reference to (a new) covenant; the emphasis is on the restored covenant relationship, not on a return from exile. **1b.** *children of the living God:* As his son (cf. 11:1), Israel owes Yahweh exclusive service (Dt 14:1). Yahweh is a "living God" in contrast to the dead Baals (Dt 32:17–21—"no-gods," "idols," i.e., nothings), or because he gives life (6:2). **2.** *other lands:* The Hebr phrase "the land," by referring to the Exodus (cf. Ex 1:10), places the reunion of God's people, separated since Solomon's time (cf. Is 7:17), in the context of salvation history. The idea of the new dispensation as a new Exodus is developed in Is 40–55 and is important in the NT. The Exodus reference explains the neutral "head" instead of "king," which would be anachronistic in this context. Jezreel is no longer a threat but a promise. There is a play on the name's meaning, "God sows"; in the new dispensation, Yahweh will grant great plenty.

11 **(B) Indictment of the Faithless Wife (2:4–17).** **4.** *protest:* The Hebr *rîb* indicates a formal juridical situation, reflected in the style of the whole section. There is an indictment (4a), warning (4b–6), and then accusation plus judgment repeated three times (7–9; 10–14; 15–17). It is the common object and situation that give unity to this collection of sayings, which, as inconsistencies and repetitions indicate, were originally separate units.

4a. Yahweh speaks in the first person as throughout this section. He summons the children to bear witness against their mother (on the procedure, see C. Gordon, *ZAW* 54 [1942] 277–80). In v. 6, the children are themselves subject to judgment. The mother is faithless Israel; cf. v. 7b referring to the service of the Baals (although they are named only in v. 15), to whom are attributed in hymn tones the gifts of a fertile land. The children, of course, are the men of Israel; in the concrete, judgment of Israel must be judgment of the people, so that the image of the trial of the mother alone cannot be sustained. Behind the double role of the children may be the idea of diverse elements within the people—the faithful who are witnesses and the faithless who are judged. This would be an early adumbration of the doctrines of the remnant and of personal responsibility so important in later prophetic tradition.

4b. *her harlotry, her adultery:* Reference is to various insignia worn by devotees of the Baals. **8.** *therefore:* As in vv. 11 and 16 (CCD "So"), it marks the change from accusation to sentence, which here looks beyond punishment to reformation. Faced by thorns instead of fruit and kept from the Baal rites ("runs after" and "looks for" are cultic terms), Israel will learn where her true good lies. The return of the divorcee must symbolize restoration of the relationship with Yahweh; according to the Law, divorced partners might not actually remarry (Dt 24:1–4). **10.** A new accusation is made. Israel has turned Yahweh's gifts to the service of the Baals. The withdrawal of these gifts will show who is the true God. There is no hint of struggle; the Baals can do nothing to protect Israel from the results of her folly. Verse 13 indicates that Baalism was more than a competing cult; it had contaminated the very worship of Yahweh, even the specifically Israelite Sabbath. Verse 14 sets forth the Baalist doctrine: Proper performance of rites must yield fertility, so that it is exact to speak of a half-magical earning of what Yahwism knew to be a grace (cf. Dt 9:1–6). After the renewed accusation in v. 15, a new judgment appears in v. 16: Israel must return to the desert. The point here, as in vv. 8–9, 11–14, is not that the Prophet refers to some particular event, drought or invasion, but to the need to re-establish contact with Yahweh. The desert is not a place for permanent withdrawal, but an ideal place to seek God (cf. 11:2; J. McKenzie, *The Way* 1 [1961] 27–39). It is a necessary discipline, an opportunity to find Yahweh again; the final promise is a return to the fertile land.

17. *Achor:* On the border of Judah and Benjamin (Jos 15:7). It is a "door of hope" because the valley leads from the Jordan, near Jericho, into the fertile land of central Palestine; therefore, the restoration follows the route of the conquest and is thus connected with the Exodus and placed within the scheme of salvation history.

12 **(C) Reconciliation (2:18–25).** A group of sayings unified by a common general theme and some points of style: Yahweh's speaking in the first person, the repeated "on that day." The section is not juridical like 2:4–17, but it is a fitting development of the idea of a reconciliation following Israel's punishment.

18. *on that day:* The time of salvation when Yahweh saves his people, the expression can also refer to judgment (Am 5:18). It retains both aspects as a technical term in Jewish and NT eschatology. In Hos it is not strictly eschatological but expresses confidence in the future restoration of Israel. However, the ideas of a new covenant and true peace here expressed will be much developed in eschatological thought. **19.** *invoked:* Hebr *zkr* refers to the liturgical invocation of a god; hence, 19b means idolatry will cease. **20.** Yahweh restores by mediating a covenant between Israel and creation (cf. Gn 9:8–10). Even a right natural order depends on his free choice and covenant. Coupled with this order in nature is a promise that war will cease. Both are common objects of hope (Is 11:6–8; 65:25; 4:4; 9:4; Mi 4:3), but they are seldom joined as here (cf. Lv 26:6; Ez 35:25–28). **21.** A continuation of the idea of covenant under the image of a marriage contract. *espouse in:* The preposition designates the bride price, the gift the groom offers. The following words therefore describe Yahweh's dispositions, not his demands. *justice:* Lit., judgment, i.e., the concrete working out of "right." *love:* Hebr *ḥesed*, which means loyal adherence to the covenant partner. **22.** *know the Lord:* Not with speculative knowledge but with a religious recognition that brings devotion to his will (cf. 4:1–2,6, where "knowledge of God" is parallel to keeping his law); in Hos, knowledge of the Lord [Yahweh] is religious knowledge in a comprehensive sense, and knowledge of God is especially knowledge of traditional Hebr morality (cf. J. McKenzie, *JBL* 74 [1955] 22–27). Despite Hosea's emphasis on the fact that God loves (*'hb*) Israel, when he speaks of Israel's response he demands knowledge (*yd'*), although we would expect that love should call for love. However, *yd'* has a strong affective color; the Prophet probably shuns the direct *'hb* to avoid its erotic overtones. With its devotion to the fertility rites, Israel was all too ready to mistake the erotic for the religious (cf. W. Eichrodt, *Interpr* 17 [1963] 264). **23.** God answers the prayers of a drought-wasted land for crops. The abuses of the pagan cults had put nature into a condition contradicting its essence, which is to serve man and bring him to God. Hosea's personification pictures a restored nature fulfilling its true functions; the heavens link God to the earth, the earth gives its fruits, and man is brought to God. **24.** *Jezreel:* Israel. The uncommon usage comes from ch. 1 where it is one of the names of the children who symbolize Israel. **25.** *him:* Jezreel-Israel. If this is correct (MT has "her") the image changes. Israel does not receive the harvest but becomes the crop itself, and the divine promise that Israel will increase (Gn 15:5; 32:13) is fulfilled.

13 **(D) The Prophet and His Wife (3:1–5).** Hosea delivers his own account of his marriage; unlike ch. 1, it centers on the wife, not on the children.

1. *adulteress:* Need not be taken strictly; it can refer to unchastity or infidelity in general as in 2:4. However, actual adultery is a more meaningful symbol of Israel's conduct, for Israel fell away after it was chosen by Yahweh. The purchase price in v. 2 is sometimes said to amount to 30 shekels, the price of a slave (Lv 27:4), but we know too little about the money values of the time to be sure. Hence, it is not clear whether there is here question of purchasing a slave or merely paying the usual bride price. The new wife must live secluded for a time, which may be either punishment or a kind of training but more likely signifies that she is ritually unclean because she had joined in pagan rites. Only after a time of seclusion could a follower of Yahweh associate with her. The story of the marriage ends abruptly in v. 4. Only enough has been given to serve as a symbol of Yahweh's relation with an Israel that must suffer the loss of its civil and religious organization, the latter symbolized by legitimate (sacrifice; ephod) and illegitimate (pillar, i.e., the asherah, a pagan symbol; idols) cult furniture. In the natural course of things it would mean loss of national identity in the circumstances of ancient Near Eastern culture. However, the deprivation is temporary, for Israel will return to Yahweh. The reference to David is usually considered an interpolation, but note that 2:2 shows that a reunion of all Israel under one leader was part of Hosea's vision of restoration. **5.** *come trembling:* With religious awe.

(II) Condemnation of Hosea's Contemporaries (4:1–9:9). These chapters are a collection of diverse sayings of the Prophet directed now at particular classes, now at the whole people. The theme of most of the sayings is the judgment that Yahweh passes on contemporary Israel for its sins, although occasional words of hope do appear.

14 **(A) Yahweh's Indictment of Israel (4:1–3).** The collection begins with a general introduction, a judgment on the whole people. The sons of Israel (CCD "people of Israel"), sons of the promise who have received the land in fulfillment of the promise, have proved faithless. Fidelity (*'emet*) and mercy (*ḥesed*) are the virtues proper to covenant relationships; their concrete working out is "knowledge of God," i.e., action according to his moral will (cf. 2:22). The catalogue of Israel's sins in v. 2 obviously recalls the Decalogue: precepts of the sort which were the condition for the continuance of the covenant have been violated and so the covenant is broken. **3.** *mourns:* The alternate meaning of *'bl*, "dries up," fits better with what follows. When the covenant is broken, the object of the covenant, the land, is turned to desert and Israel reverts to its primitive, uncovenanted, unredeemed condition.

15 **(B) Indictment of the Leaders of Israel (4:4–5:7).** These sayings unite around the themes of the infidelity of the ruling classes and of the abuses in the cult. **4b.** *priests:* The MT has "priest"; perhaps the chief priest is addressed as head of the priestly guild, which itself becomes the center of attention in the following verses that use the plural. Once more (v. 4) Yahweh uses legal language: Let no one take up the defense of the guilty priests. It is useless, the sentence has been passed; the priests shall "stumble," i.e., fall, come to ruin, and with them the prophets. These latter are not men of Hosea's stamp but rather the false prophets who troubled most of the true prophets of Yahweh. Here they are linked to the priests in a context concerned with cult, indicating their official place in cult and sanctuary (cf. A. R. Johnson, *The Cultic Prophet in Israel* [Cardiff, 1944] esp. 61). Priests and prophets are condemned for failing in their duty to teach Yahweh's ways, not for corrupting the cult. *in the day...at night:* Perhaps the priests sought oracles consciously, the prophets in dreams, but this phrase may mean simply "always." **5b.** *I will destroy your mother:* Perhaps a concretely expressed threat to wipe out the priestly house (the priesthood was hereditary in Israel); cf. the threat about the priests' sons in 6b. **7–11a.** This passage was originally separate from the foregoing: instead of "you," "they" designates the priests. The people are not looked upon as victims but as subordinate partners in the priests' guilt; not only do the priests fail to teach as they ought, they foster idolatry. **7.** *glory:* The office of a true Yahwist priest. *shame:* The Baal cults involving sacrifices, called "sin" and "guilt" in v. 8, on which the priests thrived. However, punishment must come, and it follows from the crime: Israel's idolatrous sacrificial meals will bring no divine favor, no plenty, and their fertility rites no fruit. This denial is inevitable, for they have abandoned the source of life, Yahweh. **11a.** *harlotry:* Idolatry, but alluding to the licentiousness that was part of the Baal cults.

11b. A new attack on idolatry begins with a proverb about the madness of the orgiastic fertility rites. "New wine" (*tîrôš*) can mean freshly pressed grape juice, not itself intoxicating but still the occasion for wild harvest festivals. However, *tîrôš* appears as wine at a Canaanite banquet for the gods (*UM* 2 Aqhat, VI:7), so we may reasonably assume that here it is an intoxicating element in the rites themselves. In any case, there is no need to reduce the madness of Israel to mere lust after good things as in 7:14. Another aspect of idolatry appears in v. 12—i.e., seeking oracles elsewhere than from Yahweh. **12.** *piece of wood:* Perhaps the asherah, a wooden pole and symbol of the mother goddess that was part of the furniture of the Baalist sanctuaries, or an oracle tree (cf. Jgs 9:37, "diviners' oak"), while the wand may indicate some sort of divining rod. The "spirit of harlotry" brings on (Hebr "seduces to") these aberrations. The "spirit" is not personified; it is a force, an urge to act that comes upon one as though from outside; we might best say impulse. Harlotry is here explained as infidelity to Yahweh (12b), although the context gives it the overtones of licentiousness. **13–14.** High places and green groves were the typical locales for the Baalist sanctuaries (cf. 1 Kgs 14:23; Jer 2:20) where men sought pleasure and profit, not Yahweh. Because of the fertility cults, licentiousness flourishes among the people; however, the priests have the greater guilt because they lead the people to sin by consorting with hierodules as part of religious functions (14b). To get the full force here we must remember that unchastity was severely punished in women, not in men; Hosea reverses the received idea. **14b.** *a people without understanding:* The people lack instruction (6) and are given over to the frenzied cult (11). The sentence rounds out this unit of Hosea's words and v. 15 begins a new set where, in contrast to the foregoing, the nation as a whole is condemned without distinguishing degrees of guilt within it.

16 **15–19.** The text is very corrupt, and interpretation must often be hypothetical. **15.** *Judah:* Often treated as an interpolation but found in the ancient versions as well as in the MT; it serves as a rhetorical foil pointing up the northern kingdom's infidelity. *Gilgal...Beth-aven:* Famous Israelite sanctuaries that symbolize the infidelity and idolatry of the whole kingdom (cf. Am 5:5). *as the Lord lives:* Or "that the Lord lives," it is a Baalist cult formula affirming the return of the god (cf. *UM* Text 49, III:8; F. Horst, *EvT* 17 [1957] 371), evidence of the syncretism that the Prophet condemns. **17.** *associate:* Covenanted friend of idols rather than of Yahweh. *let him alone:* "There is nothing one can do to change him" rather than "do not join him." **18.** The nation, not only the priests as in v. 7, is given over to shame—i.e., the licentious rites—for the "wind" (19) has captured them. Wind is the same word as spirit (12), the impulse to shameful acts, but "pinions" adds the idea of mighty physical force (cf. Pss 18:11; 104:3): The madness of idolatry is bringing material—i.e., political and economic—ruin on Israel.

5:1. A new charge against the leaders. *house of Israel:* The elders who served as judges in certain civil cases. Thus the three classes who held authority in Israel are named. *it is you who are called to judgment:* It should be taken to mean "you should exercise judgment." Judgment is not merely judicial decision; it means right order, civil, moral, and religious. This the leaders have failed to maintain; they have become a "snare" and a "net" (hunting gear) trapping Israel into sin. Mizpah and Tabor may have been centers of idolatry, although aside from the following context we have little real evidence for it. **2.** *they:* The change to the third person turns the charge against a new group, presumably the people. If the chiefs misled, the people were ready to follow. **3.** *Ephraim:* The largest tribe of the kingdom of Israel, it often represents the whole nation. *defiled:* Ritually unclean, unfit to approach God; but more than this uncleanness, Israel's sin keeps it from God. **4.** *spirit of harlotry:* An impulse toward idolatry (cf. 4:12) and from their lack of knowledge of God, i.e., devotion to his wishes. "Recognize" is the same Hebr root as "knowledge" in 4:1,6. **5.** *arrogance:* Ostentation. Jeroboam II's prosperous kingdom probably attributed its well-being to the splendor of its cult (6), so that this very splendor was a sign of its erroneous spirit. *stumbles in:* "Trips over his guilt," i.e., comes to ruin because of it; this is the sentence after the indictment. **6.** Verse 6 also has to do with punishment. The cult, the nation's pride and hope, is inefficacious. *seek...not find:* It may well come from the cult of the dying and rising fertility god (cf. H. G. May, *AJSL* 48 [1931] 77), an allusion to the syncretism Hosea attacks. In any case, this splendid cult does not conciliate; it alienates Yahweh. **7.** *illegitimate children:* Lit., "strange children," i.e., whose birth is not attributed to Yahweh but to fertility rites foreign to him. Once more, error brings its own punishment, for idolatry, symbolized by the feast of the new moon, in itself legitimate but corrupted in Israel, will destroy Israel rather than bring it the desired plenty.

17 **(C) Political Upheavals (5:8–14).** **8.** *Gibeah...Ramah:* Benjaminite villages near Jerusalem on the frontier between Israel and Judah. Normally they belonged to Judah, but Jehoash may well have annexed them to Israel at the beginning of the 8th cent. (cf. 2 Kgs 14:8–14), so that they would be the first Israelite places to feel an attack from Judah. *look behind you:* In fear. The alarm is caused by an attack that probably came at the end of the Syro-Ephraimite war when Judah could attack Israel as its forces retreated N to face Assyria (cf. 2 Kgs 16; Is 7:1–9). **9.** *day of chastisement:* Hebr *yôm tôkēhâ* is an unusual expression for the day of judgment and may well connote remedial rather than vindictive punishment. Israel's punishment is deserved and inevitable; nevertheless, the instrument, Judah, is also culpable (10). The leaders of Judah have attacked their brother Israel. The implication that this action violated the covenant is carried by the image of the boundary movers, which recalls the deuteronomic law of the covenant (19:14), the violation of which brought the curse appropriate to the crime (Dt 27:17). **11.** *filth:* A common word for idols (but the text is uncertain). **12.** Verse 12 plays on the formulas of the cultic theophany (cf. W. Zimmerli in *Geschichte und Altes Testament* [Fest. A. Alt; Tübingen, 1953] 179–209): Yahweh is present not to save but to destroy. *maggots:* Lit., rottenness, corruption. Their difficulties led the Jews to seek help in political alliances; this was actually another sin because ancient pacts meant acceptance of the overlord's gods. Israel's seeking Assyria is usually referred to the reign of Menahem before the Syro-Ephraimite war (2 Kgs 15:19), but later King Hosea was Assyria's vassal too. In any case, such dealings were useless; natural aids could not help. **14.** The figure of illness changes to that of the raging lion to express the terror and inevitability of Yahweh's judgment.

18 **(D) False Repentance (5:15–7:2).** **15.** *my place:* Seems to attach this section to the preceding since it refers to the image of the lion who attacks and then withdraws to his lair.

6:1. *rend:* Continues the lion imagery. However, the theme begun here, false repentance, would fit after any prophetic warning or condemnation, and the sins alluded to in 6:6 are not those of ch. 5. The OT knows the idea of God's having a special place (cf. 1 Sm 26:19), and the comparison of Yahweh with a lion is not unique (cf. 13:7; Am 3:8; Ps 50:22). It seems more likely that a separate saying on repentance has been attached adroitly to the preceding. **6:1.** Hosea puts insincere or at least insufficient words of repentance in the people's mouth—such expressions as they, in their bad will, might use. They seem to realize that Yahweh has punished them and that he alone can save them. **2.** *revive:* Not "raise from the dead" but "restore to health," after wounds have brought them close to death. *two days...third day:* A short interval, not a precise time. The choice of "on the third day" may allude to the cult of the dying and rising fertility gods; at least in Babylonia the reawakening began on the third day (cf. "Ishtar's Descent," *ANET* 55). *to live in his presence:* Death was thought of as definitive separation from God (cf. Ps 6:6). **3.** Continues to exhort to repentance but in terms reminiscent of fertility rituals (rain, spring rain). **4.** Yahweh responds in oracle form. The rhetorical question reveals the struggle, characteristic of Hosea's thought, between Yahweh's will to save and his justice. Then the oracle exposes Israel's insincerity (4b) and failure to understand Yahweh, although he has disciplined it with chastisement interpreted by the prophets (5a). **5b.** Verse 5b (3b in CCD, "and his judgment" etc.) should read "and my judgment goes forth like the light" (LXX). Yahweh's unshakable judgment, figured by the never-failing light of the sun, is contrasted with Israel's inconstancy likened to the ephemeral dew.

6. An explanation of Yahweh's past actions, telling by implication—else it is inappropriate here—why Israel's repentance fails now; it has not learned its lesson and still counts on external cult without submission to Yahweh's commands. Hosea does not reject sacrifice entirely (cf. 9:4 where deprivation of sacrifice is a punishment, therefore the loss of a good thing). In Hebr fashion, he affirms now one aspect, now another, without troubling about nuances. In v. 7, the tenor is less personal and crimes of violence rather than false cult are condemned. This change could indicate a new beginning, but the list of infidelities fits here by broadening the illustration of Israel's unrepentant state of mind, the obstacle to true reunion with Yahweh. This theme is resumed expressly in 7:1–2, in view of which it seems that the present ordering was consciously constructed. **7.** *land:* Hebr *'ādām*, which can indeed mean "land" or "country" (M. Dahood, *Prv and North West Semitic Philology* [Rome, 1963] 57–58). However, the parallel with the place names in vv. 8–9 suggests the name Adam, a town in Transjordan. What particular covenant—the word refers to any sworn agreement—was violated there is unknown, just as we do not know the details of the crimes listed in vv. 8–9. In the CCD version, the "covenant" could be Israel's special relation with Yahweh, destroyed when Israel joined in the Canaanite rites after the Conquest. **8.** *Gilead:* A place in Transjordan. *tracked with blood:* Full of crimes of violence. **9.** *Shechem:* An ancient sanctuary (Gn 33:20; 35:1–4) and an important pilgrim resort (A. Alt, *KlSchr* 1, 79–88); the route thither was thus a good place for brigands whose crimes were worse because they were degenerate priests. **11.** Apparently a gloss applying Hosea's words about Israel to the sister kingdom of Judah. *harvest:* Judgment (cf. Jer 51:33; Jl 4:13).

7:1. Sums up the ideas of ch. 6: Israel's wickedness impedes its salvation although Yahweh wills it. **2.** *remember:* Hebr *zkr*, "summon to testify" (cf. Is 43:26). The "wickedness" and "crimes" of Israel are personified; they stand as witnesses against the people.

19 **(E) Corruption of the Monarchy (7:3–12).** Two aspects of Israel's political activity are condemned: the internal intrigues and disorders that followed the overthrow of the dynasty of Jehu (7:3–7); the search for foreign alliances as though these and not Yahweh were Israel's salvation (7:8–12). The monarchy as an institution is not condemned; it is rather the abuse of that institution—the bloody changes of dynasty, the intrigues, the luxury—that Hosea has in mind.

3. *princes:* Court functionaries charged with civil and military administration—the class from which Israel's frequent revolutions arose. **4.** *kindled to wrath:* The MT has "adulterers," and this, in the sense of deceivers, is possible in view of the accusation of deceit in v. 3. The whole text of v. 4 is badly corrupted and a number of interpretations are possible—e.g., the passions of the intriguers are like an oven that burns its contents; their mood is uncertain like an oven whose fire burns down and does not bake the bread enough; like a baker who puts yeast in the dough and then banks the fire to keep the dough warm without baking it, they repress their passions until everything is ready and they can deliver the decisive blow. The extension of the oven image in 6–7a would seem to support the last interpretation. **5.** *on the day of our king:* Probably the celebration of the king's enthronement. The court is full of sensual corruption as well as intrigue. The Judahite Isaiah also reproves the drunkenness of Israel (28:1–4,7–8): The breakdown of responsibility in the kingdom must have been obvious to all. *he extends...:* The meaning is obscure; most likely it means the king consciously associates with dissemblers, i.e., becomes one himself. However, "dissemblers" is uncertain; it may mean "mockers" or "boasters." **7.** *none...calls on me:* Expresses the theological ground for the Prophet's condemnation of the disorders. It is not merely that rebellion and assassination violate the law; the revolutions are not done for the sake of, and at the direction of, Yahweh. Traditionally, the Israelite dynasties assumed power with the help of prophets speaking for Yahweh (e.g., 1 Kgs 11:29–34; cf. A. Alt, *KlSchr* 2, 116–34).

20 Verses 8–12, like 5:13, condemn alliances with foreign powers. **8.** *mingles:* The verb *bll* is often used of mixing oil in cooking (e.g., Ex 29:2b); hence, it belongs to the figure continued in the second half of the verse, and the translation "is tossed about by the nations," which would support the idea that these verses refer to war and exile, is to be rejected. "Mingle" might still point to the exile Tiglath-pileser inflicted on Israel after 732. However, exile can hardly be reconciled with Israel's ignorance of its bad position (9) and its arrogance (10). Hence, v. 8 must refer to seeking foreign alliances, conduct at once foolish and arrogant. **8b.** A warning that the policy of alliances is, lit., "half baked," useless. Orientals bake their waferlike bread by placing it on heated stones or oven walls; if unturned, one side remains raw. **9.** *strangers:* The foreigners to whom Israel has turned do not strengthen but weaken the nation. *gray hairs:* Symbols of waning vigor. In its headlong rush to destruction Israel ignores the danger signals. **10.** This prophetic saying was already used in 5:5 with a different application. The Hebr *waw* ("yet") should probably be taken as explicative (GKC, 484, n. 1, b); the arrogance of Israel is its self-sufficiency, its efforts to work out its salvation independently of Yahweh. **11.** A new image is introduced, indicating it was originally a separate saying against alliances. *dove:* Defenseless in the world of great powers. *silly:* Easily led. In its folly and despite its impotence, Israel persists in meddling with the great powers. **12.** The condemnation follows the catalogue of Israel's failings. It continues the image of the dove: Like a hunter Yahweh will capture it. The end of the verse in the MT is very obscure, seeming to say "I will chastise them according to their assemblies." If, with the LXX, we read "wickedness" for "assemblies," it simply affirms that the punishment will be fitting. The CCD makes it explicit that Israel deserted Yahweh to seek the aid of strangers; it will be punished by exile.

21 **(F) Lament Over Israel (7:13–16).** The prophet laments the ruin Israel has brought upon itself not, as we would expect after 7:3–12, by its disloyal politics, but by its use of Baalist cultic practices. The lamentation, a common enough form of discourse in prophetic literature, is rare and hence emphatic in Hosea.

13. *redeem:* Hebr *pdh* is a commercial term, used, e.g., of buying the freedom of slaves; perhaps we can paraphrase "ransom." *lies:* Probably refers to Israel's insincere repentance that frustrated Yahweh's desire to save (cf. 6:1–4). **14.** Verse 14 makes clear how false are Israel's religious dispositions; their very pleas for help are tainted with Baalist features. This, apparently, is not simple idolatry, for they "cry to" Yahweh, but not "from the heart" for they do it "upon their beds," which refers to sleeping in the "high places" of the fertility rites as part of a ritual (cf. Is 57:7), and "they lacerate themselves," a pagan practice expressly forbidden in Israel (Lv 19:28). **15.** Yahweh was the God who led Israel in war and gave it victory, but it has deserted him, seeking help from others, or, if from him, in a manner he rejects. **16.** *become useless:* The MT is unintelligible and the CCD follows the LXX, linking 16a to the following image. Another possible emendation attaches it rather to the foregoing: "They turn, but not to me." *they are like a treacherous bow:* A slack bow that will not shoot when needed (cf. G. R. Driver, *Fest. F. Nötscher* [Bonn, 1950] 53–54). The figure of the bow implies a telling reversal: Israel is or should be God's instrument, but it has adopted the pagan concept in which the divinity was to be used for man's ends, compelled thereto by magical-religious rites. **16b.** The condemnation of the faithless nation. The sentence falls primarily on the leaders and through them on all the people. *insolence:* Hebr *zaʿam* means mocking speech with overtones of malediction and denunciation. Perhaps this reference is to a mocking rejection of the Prophet's warnings by Israel's leaders. Punishment in any case cannot be avoided; eventually even the proverbial enemy, Egypt, will have the laugh on Israel.

22 **(G) Sins in Politics and Cult (8:1–14)** We have a new proclamation of Israel's inevitable punishment. First comes a warning (1–3), then condemnation of the political and religious schism from Judah (4–7), the policy of alliances (8–10), and finally idolatry (11–13). Although these units have been linked (e.g., v. 4 explains v. 3; "swallow" links vv. 7 and 8), they must have had separate origins; note, e.g., the alternation between second and third persons.

1. *you who watch:* The MT and the LXX "like an eagle" can be retained: "A trumpet to your lips! Like an eagle (the enemy [v. 3] falls upon) the house of the Lord!" The trumpet was an alarm signal, not a mark of the violation of the Law; furthermore, the CCD leaves the explanatory clause in v. 1b with nothing to explain; hence, another translation is indicated. In his imagination, Hosea sees the enemy already falling upon a sinful Israel. *covenant...law:* The basic relationship with Yahweh formed at Sinai with its conditions. However, the link here with v. 4 hints at the extension of this Sinai covenant in the covenant with David's line (2 Sm 7). **2.** The Hosean theme of insincerity is evident: Israel rejects the Lord and yet calls on him. Rejecting Yahweh means "throwing away" (the Hebr is very strong: "treat as disgusting") all that is good (v. 3), for all good is from Yahweh. Effectively, this is to choose chastisement at the hand of God's instrument, Israel's enemies. **4–6.** Kingmaking and idolatry are linked, specifically the setting up of the "golden calves," which points to Israel's original break with the Davidic kingdom, for Jeroboam I founded the shrines of the calves when he split with Judah (1 Kgs 12:26–31). The difficulty is that Jeroboam's rebellion, like many later dynastic changes in Israel, came at the behest of a prophet speaking on Yahweh's authority (1 Kgs 11:26–40). Hence, it might seem that Hosea condemns only the willful intrigues following Jeroboam II's death. However, Hosea felt free to condemn what other prophets had approved (cf. 9:4), so that it is perfectly possible that he is condemning the original foundation of the northern kingdom. If Yahweh permitted the selfishness of Jeroboam to run its course as punishment for Solomon's sins, it remained selfishness. Part of this self-will was expressed when official shrines were set up to rival Jerusalem. The original purpose was not idolatrous (cf. 1 Kgs 12:28, clearly based on a good Yahwist formula: Ex 20:2), but in fact the plurality of shrines led to idolatry.

23 **5.** *calf:* Not originally an idol. Calves were thought of as the mount on which Yahweh was invisibly present (cf. Albright, *FSAC* 299), but before Hosea's time they had come to be worshiped for themselves. *Samaria:* Jeroboam's shrines were at Dan and Bethel, but certainly Omri built some sort of shrine when he founded Samaria as his capital. In any case, the calf of Bethel was thought of as Samaria's own (cf. 10:5), so the reference to Samaria need not belong to the time after 732 when Dan had been lost to Assyria and replaced by a shrine at Samaria. **5b.** *how long:* The question and the reference to innocence belong to the lamentation style. **6.** The scorn of idols, mere human products, became a favorite theme in later OT literature (cf. Is 44:6–20). **7.** A proverblike reflection on the results of Israel's idolatry; like the whirlwind destroying ripe grain, the false fertility cult brings only ruin. Again, it is like a barren stalk, useless. The figures teach the favorite Hosean idea that punishment is the natural product of sin, not an arbitrary, external judgment. **8.** A reference to the exile that began in 732, a fitting punishment for Israel's seeking help from foreign alliances instead of from Yahweh. **9.** *bargained for lovers:* It is doubly ironical: It is the prostitute (bargain is the same root as the technical "harlot's hire" of 2:14; 9:1) Israel who pays her lovers, and love is not to be bought anyway. Nevertheless, it as well as tribute was an element in alliances (cf. D. J. McCarthy, *Treaty and Covenant* [Rome, 1963] 196, n. 14). **10.** *an army:* Yahweh will bring an enemy force on Israel (but the translation is conjectural). *burden:* The tribute paid to Assyria. **12.** *many:* It links vv. 11–12. Israel has built many altars without following Yahweh's many directions. Since Hosea does not condemn the altars as such but rather their idolatrous misuse, the opposition, altar or law, is not absolute. The neglected law could well be the prescriptions for proper worship. Hosea's knowledge of a written law is important for the history of Israel's religion. **13.** The lawless sacrifices do not please but offend God. The verse thus concludes with the sentence, the common ending of prophetic accusations. **14.** *his maker:* It is unusual for Hosea to refer to God as creator, and the implied theme of ostentatious building at the expense of the poor reflects Amos (e.g., 3:9–15); hence the verse is probably an addition. It condemns the Hebrews' self-sufficiency, their confidence in their mighty works.

24 **(H) Exile Without Worship (9:1–6).** Here the Prophet contrasts the festive cult gatherings and the gloomy assembly in the Exile, an exile that punished the idolatry that had invaded Israel's cult. Regarding form, Hosea speaks about Yahweh, not in the person of Yahweh.

1. *rejoice not, exult not:* Reverses the customary call to rejoice in the cult. *like the nations:* They were not so subject to condemnation as Israel because they were not specifically chosen by God. Israel's very election made it possible to "be unfaithful" (lit., "play the harlot") by imitating pagan fertility rites in search of rich harvests. **2.** In fact, Israel will be disappointed of the expected benefits, for the harvest will "*fail*" (lit., "deceive" or "betray") them. Inasmuch as this verb is drawn from the description of moral qualities, it may be better to translate the parallel "not nourish" by "hostile," a meaning demanding no change in the consonants of the MT. The switch to the third person results from a vivid style: the Prophet is a prosecutor, now addressing the accused, now speaking of him to the judges (cf. Is 10:3 for a similar change). The penalty here is not a bad harvest but the total loss of the land through exile, as v. 3 shows. **3.** Unlike Assyria, there was no forced exile to Egypt, but it was a place of refuge. The return there reverses salvation history. In Assyria, Israel's food is unclean (ritually impure), because it is not produced by the Lord's land but by an unclean land (cf. Am 7:17). **4.** Unclean food could not be offered to Yahweh; therefore, in exile the cult must cease. **5.** The rhetorical questions are ironic, emphasizing the impossibility of the exile situation. *festival day...Lord's day:* Synonymous general terms. Instead of assembling for Yahweh's feasts, Israel gathers in exile while the homeland is given over to desolation (6). **6b.** The Hebrew is very emphatic: "Precious was their silver—weeds will grow over it!"

25 **(I) Rejection of the Prophet (9:7–9).** This brief section resembles vv. 1–6 in not using the prophetic "I" in the name of Yahweh, but it is marked off sharply because of the emphatic ending in v. 6 and the different tenses used here. However, it is a fitting sequel: For the prophet, to attack the joyous cult was to invite rejection.

7. *they have come:* Probably a "prophetic perfect"; so sure is Israel's punishment that it is spoken of as a fact. *let Israel know it:* Read with 7a. However, the LXX implies a Hebr consonantal text that can be read "Israel shouts: The prophet," etc. In any case, these last words quote Israel's scorn for a prophet. In 1 Sm 10:9–13; Jer 29:26, the prophet was evidently often thought mad. Hosea's words are general: Israel has rejected not one but the whole line of prophets, the natural, hostile response of the guilty to the reprover (7c). **8.** The image continues the last idea. The prophet is a watchman, one placed on a tower to see and warn of approaching danger. Although he is God's appointee, he meets opposition even on consecrated ground. **9b.** The usual concluding condemnation.

26 **(III) Sin and History (9:10–14:1).** This last group of Hosea's sayings is frequently concerned with Israel's sinful past, climaxing in the troubles of the Prophet's own day, whereas up to this point there was only passing reference to historical events. The style is somewhat meditative; passion remains, but there is less direct address and more reflection.

27 **(A) Sin and Decline (9:10–17).** Two crimes from Israel's history are recalled, and it is made clear that their results continue; the nation that was to have been numberless as the sands of the seashore will waste away.

10. *grapes in the desert:* Unexpected and so all the more desirable. Like the "first fruits" of the "prime fig," they would certainly be plucked. Hence, the image implies the divine election of Israel, although strangely the election takes place in the desert, not in Egypt (cf. 11:1 where it occurs in Egypt!). At Baal-peor, a shrine on the Moabite border, Israel first came in contact with the Canaanite fertility gods, and Israel fell as soon as the contact occurred. With dramatic speed the fall follows upon election. **11.** *glory:* This divinely promised fertility of Israel serves as a link to v. 10 by contrasting with "shame." The Baal cult works in reverse: It brings not fertility but sterility. **11b.** Verse 11b in the CCD should be v. 16b as in the MT, for here it disturbs the progression: sterility; then, worse, the loss of grown children; then, worst of all, the inaccessibility of God. **13a.** The text is difficult. With the MT, the CCD contrasts two stages of Ephraim's history: Once its prospects were as pleasant as Tyre's, the proverbially wealthy and strong Phoenician trading city, but the nation will fall and its people be slaughtered. The LXX offers a different reading, producing parallelism between vv. 13a and 13b. **14.** Thus far the Prophet has spoken in the person of Yahweh, the accuser; in v. 14a he intercedes for his people. Then, confronted with Israel's guilt, he realizes punishment must come, so that in 14b he pleads for the lesser evil (cf. David, 2 Sm 24:12–14). **15.** The history of Israel's sins is resumed in Yahweh's own words. Gilgal probably refers to the shrine near Jericho. The sequence Baal-peor, Gilgal would thus recall the tradition of the Conquest, but negatively: Further contact with the promised land brings further corruption. *hatred:* The just will to chastise, explained in the rest of v. 15. **16.** Israel's punishment is explained (depopulation as in 11–14). **17.** The Prophet again speaks for himself. He cannot but agree to the justice of Yahweh's sentence because Israel has not heeded its God.

28 **(B) Punishment of Apostasy (10:1–8).** **1–2.** A prosperous Israel has multiplied its cult places, but its religion is "false," i.e., flattering and two faced (Hebr *ḥlq*). *break down:* Lit., "break the neck of," a contemptuous expression. **3–4.** Two connective particles, lost in translation, link vv. 3–4 to the foregoing as an explanation of Israel's falseness. Unexpectedly, the first concern is with social, not religious, faults, but unfortunately the exact interpretation is difficult. If we follow the emended text (CCD "they"; "them," for MT "we"; "us" in 3b), v. 3 seems to recall 1 Sm 8: The people complain that they lack a king like the nations, but the Prophet reproves their seeking a king in place of Yahweh, and without Yahweh Israel is lost, king or no king. However, the MT can be kept, according to which the Prophet identifies himself with his nation and expresses the hopelessness of the situation. Inasmuch as "fear of the Lord," the basis of all society, is gone, there is in effect no king. He cannot govern a group where all honor and fidelity are lost. Justice (4) and right order have given way to disorder like useful plants to weeds. **5–6.** Added to include Israel's religious failure in the condemnation by mocking the cult Israel preferred to Yahweh's service. Instead of being joyful in the cult, Israel will mourn its idol whose exile proves its worthlessness. **5.** *priests:* Hebr *k^e^mārîm* is a contemptuous term used of pagans only; perhaps we could say priestlings. This oracle must date from a time well after 732 when new Assyrian attacks threatened the remaining fragment of Israel, which included Bethel. **6–8.** The picture of devastation is developed in three stages: People, leaders, and religion will all disappear. Indeed, no one will want to survive; they shall ask the land for burial (8b).

29 **(C) False Confidence (10:9–15).** This section differs from 10:1–8 in being a direct address to the guilty. The theme is the futility of self-confidence in place of trust in God.

9–10. They form a complete "judgment oracle" with accusation and sentence. The text is very corrupt, but the general idea of false confidence is clear. **10.** *two crimes:* The second cannot be identified, but certainly it is something recent—current guilt that continues Israel's history of sin and brings current punishment.

11–12. As often (2:17; 9:10; 11:1), Hosea turns to the fair hopes of Israel's beginnings when Yahweh himself took a docile people and set it on the way to a good reward. *justice:* the Hebr word means more than the Eng word, implying total right order, and hence, in addition to moral order, order in nature with due rain, etc., so as to produce material plenty (cf. S. Mowinckel, *The Psalms in Israel's Worship* [vol. 1; N.Y., 1962] 146). All the agricultural imagery surely implies a claim that Yahweh, not the Baals, governed fecundity. **13.** Israel turned to the wrong way, trusting in its Baalist rites and in its strength. **14–15.** As fitting punishment that strength will be crushed. **15.** *at dawn:* Enigmatic; a slight change in the MT allows "like dawn," i.e., swiftly.

30 **(D) Love Overcomes Ingratitude (11:1–11).** This passage, one of the high points of the OT revelation of God's nature, is also one of the most corrupt of OT texts. Even so, there is a clear enough flow of thought: Yahweh's fatherly love and Israel's ungrateful response (1–4) is punished (5–7), which calls forth God's love (8–9) to produce Israel's redemption (10–11). There is an abrupt change in style and content at v. 8. Yahweh's reflections about Israel's unresponsiveness give way to an impassioned proclamation to Israel of his love. However, 8–11 presuppose some history like that in 1–7 to explain the pitying love they proclaim, the love that ultimately governs all history. The sequence is deliberate and the chapter is to be interpreted as a whole.

1. *my son:* The ancient Near East often gave notables a divine ancestry, but this need not be the background here. A context treating of Yahweh's education of Israel with emphasis on the love with which it was carried out more likely reflects the common usage in which the wise man, the educator, was called the father of his protegés (e.g., Azitawadda, king of the Danunians, *ANET* 500; Prv 2:1; etc.). **2.** *I called:* From the LXX. If the MT "they called" should be correct, it alludes to the attractions of the Baal cult or of Canaan's superior culture. **4b.** *healer:* Savior from Egypt (MT 3b). **6.** Because it has deserted Yahweh, Israel must be punished with exile. **6–7.** Too corrupt to permit any sure exegesis beyond this.

8. *How...? How...?:* Punishment is not Yahweh's last word. A startling anthropomorphism presents a Yahweh so moved that he addresses his people in the emotional terms of the lament. He cannot destroy his beloved people. **9.** As startling is the appeal to his "holiness"; God's total otherness, the *mysterium tremendum,* instead of producing awe and terror, explains his mercy! Unlike human love, God's love does not have that inevitable element of selfishness that renders it changeable and destructive, making the vengeance of disappointed love so terrible. Verse 9 can be made a question: "Shall I not give vent, etc."—i.e., a new threat after the moment of pity in v. 8 (Robinson, *op. cit.*, 44–45). However, it conflicts with the lamentation style introduced by v. 8 and the hope expressed in v. 11; hence, v. 9 must be kept as an expression of pity. **10–11.** There is an evident reversal in Yahweh's attitude (note the difference from chs. 2–3, where it was Israel that reversed itself), and this promise of salvation (vv. 10–11) is expected. However, the use of the third person in v. 10, in contrast to the divine "I" of vv. 8–9 and 11, makes v. 10 appear an insertion interpreting the "trembling" (in awe and respect rather than in mere fear) of v. 11. Verse 10 introduces a return "from the west"; v. 11 has only Egypt and Assyria, corresponding to 11:5.

31 **(E) Israel's Perfidy (12:1–15).** The chapter as a whole scarcely shows a complete logical plan. We are dealing with a collection of sayings about a common theme, Israel's perfidy illustrated in history and in Hosea's contemporaries who but continue the way of the past.

1b. The perfidy theme is introduced by a contrast between Israel's treachery and Judah's fidelity, for v. 1b should probably be translated "but Judah still walks with God and is faithful to the holy one" (the meaning of *rād,* "walks with," is uncertain; the parallel "faithful" in 1b indicates the general sense; cf. Vg). The plural *q^e^dôšîm,* "holy one," is also difficult. The translation presumes it to be a plural of majesty formed on analogy with *'ĕlōhîm* but it must be admitted that the parallel *'el* (v. 1b) and *q^e dôšîm* is strange since the parallel is the singular *'el*, and Hosea uses an *'el-qādôš* (sing.) parallelism in 11:9. The meaning "the holy ones," i.e., faithful followers of Yahweh, perhaps the prophets who were especially near to God, would unify the chapter by linking this verse to 11 and 14 (Wolff, *Hosea*, 272). **2a.** A vivid image for fruitless activity, made specific in the last half of v. 2: Israel's empty striving is its policy of alliances ("carries oil," i.e., makes covenants, for covenant by oil was familiar in the ancient Near East; cf. D. J. McCarthy, *VT* 14 [1954] 215–21). Whether with Assyria or Egypt, alliances are vain. Worse, they are betrayals of Yahweh, Israel's unique support. **3.** *grievance:* Once more the standard introduction for a juridical accusation is developed in the following verses. *Jacob:* The Patriarch and the people, his heirs, up to the Prophet's own contemporaries, face judgment. The people are one with their head, who concentrates in himself all their deceit. **4.** *as a man:* Treacherous as a child (Gn 25:24–26; 27:36), in maturity the Patriarch presumed to contend with God himself (Gn 32:22–33). **5.** *angel:* Stands for God (cf. Gn 32, where Jacob's opponent changes from man [25] to God [29, 31]). In the light of the foregoing, we may see Jacob's prayer ("tears" are a standard means of supplication; cf. P. R. Ackroyd, *VT* 13 [1953] 250–51) as a continuation of his trickery and presumption; i.e., it was insincere, a ruse, so that Jacob's great encounter with God at Bethel (Gn 28:10–22; Hosea reverses the order of the incidents in Gn) is reduced to some kind of trick. However, it is possible that v. 5 presents Jacob's conversion: The tribal father on whom Israel prided itself was a sinner like the rest, needing God's grace, although, unlike the people thus far, he at least accepted grace and was converted. This interpretation gives a good introduction to the call to conversion in v. 7 (probably Hosea's and directed to the people, although it might be Yahweh's answer to Jacob's prayer, a call to him to repent, and through him to the people). One way or the other Hosea reverses the view of the Patriarch expressed in Gn: Rather than a special friend of God, he is the first sinner in Israel, the one in whom the people's history of infidelity begins.

32 **6.** An interpolated doxology. **8.** A return to the present condemning Israel's double-dealing and confidence in material wealth. Israel is the "merchant," in Hebr "Canaanite" (for the Hebr farmers, the old inhabitants of the land were the traders par excellence); thus, the very word implies Israel's religious infidelity too, for it has imitated all the ways of Canaan. **9.** Wealth, even though applied to the cult in rich sacrifices, cannot cover Israel's sin (5:6). In a typical contrast to the wealth acquired in Canaan comes the picture of Israel's beginnings, when Yahweh himself saved the people from Egypt. The picture is made more actual by Yahweh's speaking in the first person, a reminiscence of cultic theophanies. Yahweh tells Israel that it must return to the condition of those old days, not for reasons of asceticism but because it will thus rediscover its intimacy with God, for "appointed time" (perhaps we might translate "time of rendezvous") recalls the great meetings with Yahweh in the desert. **11–12.** The idea of God's nearness is continued in the reference to the prophets (11), for God spoke to his people through the line of prophets from Moses (Dt 18:15) on, but in vain, for Israel put its confidence in a cult contaminated with Baalism, a cult that works only ruin (12). **13.** The verse returns to Jacob. In the light of 3–6, the reference to his activity in Aram (cf. Gn 27:41–31) must be condemnatory, another instance of Israel's failings early as late in its history. Perhaps Jacob's willingness to undergo servitude to win a wife alludes obliquely to Israel's serving the Baals in the interests of fertility, or his going to Aram refers to the policy of foreign alliances. **14–15.** In contrast to Israel's continual infidelity is God's never-failing saving action. The abrupt change to the condemnation in v. 15 points up the inevitability of the end: A just God must visit its sins upon Israel.

33 **(F) Death Sentence (13:1–14:1).** This collection of judgment sayings is made up of several units: typical judgment oracles (13:1–3, 13:4–8); a mocking condemnation of the monarchy (13:9–11); and a composite final sentence on the whole people (13:12–14:1). These are arranged to give mounting emphasis to the central theme, that Israel stands before the ultimate punishment, death, instead of mere defeat and exile.

13:1–3. The first oracle exposes the past sins of Israel's leader, the tribe of Ephraim. Admittedly, the past tense "died" seems to close off v. 1 and separate it from the following. However, we can take the death to be moral decline, or sufferings, which the OT often likens to death, or, perhaps best of all, a "prophetic perfect," i.e., the end is so certain that it is given as fact even though it is still to come. Hence, v. 1 may be legitimately connected with the following: Past sin continues in the present idolatry so contemptuously described. Israel's use of a superstitious cult designed to force the divine by magical rites ends in its degrading itself before mere creatures—kissing and adoring calves. The end can only be ruin (v. 3; cf. 6:4 for the same imagery). **4–8.** In contrast to the ruin that idolatry brings, the familiar liturgical formula "I am Yahweh your God since Egypt" puts Israel's true salvation, Yahweh, before us. However, the sequel shows, in terms that will be favorites of the deuteronomic school (e.g., Dt 8:11–20), how Yahweh's very favors have swollen Israel's pride so that it has deserted him. This can only mean that he changes from a savior to an inexorable judge who is depicted as a ravening beast of prey (cf. 5:14), an image all the more vivid in that the predator is the classic enemy of the shepherd, the figure under which Yahweh has just been presented. **9–11.** This mocking of the kings points up the idea that without Yahweh Israel is helpless no matter to what institutions it turns. **10.** A seeming reference to the demand for Saul to be made king as it is reported in the antimonarchical tradition (1 Sm 8), but v. 11 implies an ineffectual monarchy with frequent dynastic changes. This fits the unstable northern kingdom that broke away from the legitimate Jerusalem monarchy and cult (cf. 8:4–6). **12.** The final unit of this chapter is introduced as a legal document which is "wrapped" and "stored," alluding to the procedure in which a judicial sentence was recorded on papyrus that was folded and tied with string and then covered with a seal (cf. Is 8:16); illustration in *AtBib* 98). **13.** *birth pangs:* A favorite image of the judgment in prophecy (e.g., Jer 6:24) and apocalyptic (Is 26:17; cf. Jn 16:21), but it is used differently here. The focus is on the child's folly, not the mother's suffering; i.e., in casting Yahweh aside, Israel, the child, has cast aside its chance to live. **14.** Rather than save Israel, Yahweh will give the powers of death power over it (the verse, except the last sentence, may be taken as a cry of triumph [cf. 1 Cor 15:35], but the context demands that it be read as threatening questions, as in the CCD). **15.** A new image specifies the impending destruction after the general threat: As the sirocco comes out of the desert to wither the bloom of spring, so will Yahweh destroy Israel, whatever its seeming prosperity. **14:1.** The final sentence, on the other hand, is not figurative; it describes the common, terrible fate of the people of a conquered land, the punishment which Israel will in fact undergo.

34 **(IV) Epilogue: Repentance and Salvation (14:2–9).** Hosea's prophecy closes on a note of hope—hope based on the certainty that Yahweh loves his people. The proclamation of this love has two parts: the Prophet's summons to the people to return to its God (2–4) and God's answering promise of love spoken to the Prophet about the people (5–9). This structure is that of a penitential rite; first the people proclaim their repentance, then they receive God's assurance of forgiveness through a prophet. Hosea used the form in 6:1–3, but there it was ironical, for true repentance was lacking; here it is serious.

2. Israel has already "collapsed," suffered its definitive punishment, so the summons to "return" looks to a final repentance and union with Yahweh, an idea to which v. 9 (in the CCD version) returns. The fact of collapse does not prove that the oracle is later than 722; the Prophet could have foreseen both ruin and restoration (which, in fact, he never experienced) much earlier. **3.** True return means more than mere external cult: Sacrifices must represent true repentance expressed in sincere prayer ("words"). This is the good Yahweh will accept that makes the sacrifices ("bullocks") valuable because they symbolize true dedication. (Verse 3b is obscure: the CCD is one possible emendation of the MT, "that we may render bullocks, our lips." The LXX has "we will repay with [the] fruit of our lips," removing all explicit reference to sacrifice—although the implicit contrast with the empty, pompous sacrificial cult still cannot be overlooked—and making the verse a simple call to prayer and penance.) **4.** A sample of the words and attitude demanded: Rejection of all Israel's fetishes, political schemes (such as the alliance with Assyria), military force (horses), as well as idols in the strict sense.

5. Israel is sick with a hopeless disease, infidelity, which only God can cure; hence, God's love is free, i.e., not earned in any sense. **6–8.** The results of Yahweh's love are described: Israel will flourish in beauty (6–7) and plenty (8). The images taken from the plant world recall that Yahweh, not the Baals, gives increase. Moreover, the language reflects the strength and tenderness of God's love, for expressions like "fragrance of Lebanon," "blossom like the vine," "dwell in the shade," "wine," "lily" are taken from the love songs of Israel, such as are seen in Ct (cf. Wolff, *Hosea*, 302). **9.** Probably a separate saying attached to the foregoing because of the cypress image. *I have humbled...:* As in v. 2, a promise of final salvation after punishment. The translation, however, is uncertain; the verse may mean "I have answered him and watch over him," i.e., a simple promise that Yahweh will hear a repentant Israel. *because of me...:* Possibly, "on me fruit will be found for you." In either case, Yahweh is likened to the tree of life. This symbol was familiar from the fertility cults. Applied to Yahweh, it is one more assertion that he is the true master of life. **10.** An addition, in Wisdom style, of the scribes who compiled the Book of Hosea.

16

ISAIAH 1–39

Frederick L. Moriarty, S.J.

BIBLIOGRAPHY

1 Anderson, B. W., *Understanding the Old Testament* (2nd ed.; Englewood Cliffs, N.J., 1966) 252–87. Anderson, G. W., *A Critical Introduction to the Old Testament* (London, 1959) 106–12. Auvray, P. and J. Steinmann, *Isaïe* (BJ; 2nd ed.; Paris, 1957). Blank, S. H., *Prophetic Faith in Isaiah* (N.Y., 1958). Bright, *Hist.* 251–87. Childs, B. S., *Isaiah and the Assyrian Crisis* (Naperville, 1967). Feuillet, A., "Isaïe (le livre d')," *VDBS* 4 (Paris, 1947) 647–90. Fohrer, G., *Das Buch Jesaja 1. Bd. Kapitel 1–23* (Zurich, 1960). Huesman, J. E., *The Book of Isaia, Part 1* (PPBS; N.Y., 1961). Kissane, E. J., *The Book of Isaiah* (vol. 1; 2nd ed.; Dublin, 1962). Knight, G., *Prophets of Israel (1) Isaiah* (BG 7; Abingdon, 1961). Mauchline, J., *Isaiah 1–39* (London, 1962). Moriarty, F. L., *Introducing the Old Testament* (Milwaukee, 1960) 120–37. Penna, A., *Isaia* (LSB; Torino, 1957). R-F 1, 501–12. Scott, R. B. Y., "Isaiah 1–39, Introduction and Exegesis," *IB* 5 (N.Y., 1956) 150–381. Vawter, B., *The Conscience of Israel* (N.Y., 1961) 162–207. Virgulin, O. S., *La "fede" nella profezia d'Isaia* (*BeO;* Milan, 1961). Weiser, A., *OT* 183–97. Ziegler, J., *Isaias* (Echter-B; Würzburg, 1948).

INTRODUCTION

2 **(I) The Man and His Times.** The little that we know of Isaiah is derived from the Prophet's own testimony in Is 1–39. He was a citizen of Judah and prophesied during the reigns of four kings: Uzziah (783–742), Jotham (742–735), Ahaz (735–715), and Hezekiah (715–687). It is commonly believed, on the basis of 6:1, that Isaiah's prophetic career began in the year of Uzziah's death. But the possibility of activity prior to that overwhelming vision of Yahweh enthroned in the Temple must be left open. Isaiah was married and the father of at least two children, each of whom bore symbolic names. It is likely that all of Isaiah's prophetic activity was exercised in the city of Jerusalem. Although the Prophet moved easily among kings and had ready access to the royal presence, there is no reason to believe that he was a member of the royal household. His titles of nobility rest upon his stature as a man and the high office to which God had called him.

Isaiah's task was to guide Judah through one of the most critical periods of her history. With the death of Uzziah Judah's time of prosperity and national glory had come to an end. The shadow of Assyria, once again set out on the path of conquest, lay menacingly over the land. In his own lifetime Isaiah would see the northern kingdom of Israel swept away in the tide of conquest and his own land invaded by the mighty Assyrian armies. But the spiritual crisis of Judah was even more serious than the threat of physical destruction. The same greed, hypocrisy, and injustice that Amos had excoriated in northern Israel were sapping the spiritual integrity of Judah.

To these should be added the national loss of nerve that led its rulers to seek an accommodation with Assyria and her gods, thus undermining the very foundation of Judah's existence as a covenanted people. Judah's king was the descendant of David to whom an eternal dynasty had been promised (2 Sm 7). With Assyria sweeping all before her, many of the Judeans began to doubt the power of Yahweh to preserve the dynasty of David in accordance with his promises. Others took an opposite but equally unspiritual position. Interpreting the covenant with David as a guarantee of absolute invincibility no matter what crimes were committed against Yahweh, they tried to force the nation into revolts that were nothing short of suicidal. When religion becomes a blank check for national wrongdoing, the end is not far off; no one saw this better than Isaiah.

3 His career may be divided into three periods, within each of which we can locate with confidence a number of the Prophet's oracles. The first period, extending through the reigns of Jotham and Ahaz, is represented by the material in chs. 1–12. The highlight of this phase was Isaiah's clash with the national policy of Ahaz in the crisis of 735–733 when Syria and Israel formed a coalition and attempted to coerce Judah into armed rebellion against Assyria. The second period brings us to the reign of Hezekiah, who was severely pressured by both Egyptians and Philistines to join in revolt against Sargon of Assyria. Few oracles can be assigned with certainty to this earlier part of Hezekiah's reign when all Palestine lived under the threatening shadow of Sargon the Great.

Chapter 20 certainly belongs here and, with the help of the Assyrian annals, can be safely dated to the years 714–711 when Ashdod and other city-states joined in an uprising against the powerful Assyrian. The position taken by Isaiah is clear from ch. 20. Walking about the streets of Jerusalem barefoot and clad only in a loincloth, the Prophet dramatically underlined the folly of trusting in Egypt and her allies. His policy appears to have prevailed on this occasion, for Judah escaped punishment when Sargon crushed the revolt.

The last period coincides with the Palestinian campaigns of Sennacherib, who succeeded Sargon on the throne of Assyria in 705. The prose material in the historical appendix (chs. 36–39) provides important information for these trying days that eventually saw the vindication of Isaiah's prophetic word. The military activity of Sennacherib in Palestine remains an historical problem; the two-campaign theory, which appears to satisfy the historical evidence better than other alternatives, will be taken up in the commentary. To this latter part of Isaiah's career belong the oracles assembled in 28:7–33:24. For at least forty long and testing years Isaiah performed his task as Yahweh's spokesman. A late and unverified tradition reports that he was put to death under the impious King Manasseh, who thoroughly repudiated the reforms of his father, Hezekiah.

4 **(II) The Theology of Isaiah.** The holiness of the one God, Creator and Master of the world, dominates the message. Yahweh is the "Holy One of Israel," a conviction that was brought home to Isaiah with overwhelming force in his inaugural vision. Concomitant with this profound sense of the divine holiness went an intense awareness of his own sinfulness and that of his people. Sin, in any form, could not be tolerated in his holy presence. No one in the OT has spoken out more forthrightly than Isaiah in his denunciation of Judah's pride, self-indulgence, and callous injustice toward the poor. He was convinced that Yahweh was about to strike down the nation in judgment. In fact, it was already close at hand in the form of the Assyrian armies. The cosmic character of the judgment should not be overlooked. Not only would the land of Palestine be laid waste but all nature would be involved; the sin of man affected the whole universe, which would therefore experience the wrath of divine judgment. Yet, Judah was still "his people" and Jerusalem was the holy city whose foundation was sure. Again and again Isaiah returns to the idea that Zion has been chosen by Yahweh, the living God, as the place where he dwells and reveals himself (T. Vriezen, "Essentials of the Theology of Isaiah," *Israel's Prophetic Heritage* [Fest. J. Muilenburg; N.Y., 1962] 129–31). For this reason, Isaiah never believed that the nation would be utterly destroyed and the divine promises canceled out. There would be a remnant, cleansed in the fire of judgment, inheritors of the promises made to David. Isaiah's doctrine of the remnant gives a basic optimism to his work without clouding his vision of the inevitable judgment upon wickedness.

Undergirding the doctrine of the remnant was Isaiah's faith in the divine control of history. Even in her greatest hour of trial, with Sennacherib encamped under her walls, Jerusalem was promised deliverance if only she would place her trust in God. Such an attitude could later be perverted into a crass orthodoxy of Jerusalem's absolute inviolability, but this was only a distortion of Isaiah's faith that coupled salvation with repentance and conversion to Yahweh. From this faith stemmed Isaiah's conviction that Yahweh, faithful to his promises, would raise up a king from David's line whose rule of peace and justice would replace the faithless and vacillating service of the kings who had ruled from David's throne. In this royal Messianic figure, Israel's hope took on a permanent form that our faith tells us was fulfilled many centuries later when God sent his only Son to establish his reign of peace and justice over the entire world.

5 **(III) Composition.** The process by which chs. 1–39 reached their present form was long and complicated. No modern scholar would claim that all the material in these chapters comes from Isaiah himself. Moreover, there is very little agreement among scholars when it comes to determining precisely what parts are the Prophet's work. With our better knowledge of the way in which the prophetic collections came into existence and our greater respect for the Hebr tradition, there is today a much greater reluctance to declare categorically that a given passage is in no sense Isaian. That Isaiah personally wrote down and ordered to be saved some of his oracles is certain (8:16; 30:8), but it is no less certain that some of the oracles now attached to his name originate from a much later period. Thus, we have, in these chapters, an anthology of Isaian material, some from the Prophet himself and some from later, unknown authors who may be said to carry on Isaiah's tradition. The reader must be warned that neither chronological nor logical considerations have determined the ordering of this material. Oracles from different times and treating entirely different subjects may be found side by side. To impose a false unity on the collection would only mislead and ultimately confuse the reader. No detailed analysis of these chapters is universally accepted.

6 **(IV) Outline.** The outline that follows is the one upon which the commentary is based; it is in general agreement with the customary division of the book.

- (I) Threats and Promises to Rebellious Judah (1:1–6:13)
  - (A) The Indictment (1:1–31)
  - (B) Zion, Present and Future (2:1–4:6)
    - (a) In Days to Come (2:2–5)
    - (b) Judgment Upon Idolatry (2:6–22)
    - (c) Disintegration of Judean Society (3:1–15)
    - (d) Doom for the Fine Ladies of Jerusalem (3:16–4:1)
    - (e) Vision of Zion Restored (4:2–6)
  - (C) Song of the Vineyard (5:1–7)
  - (D) The Woes (5:8–30)
  - (E) The Inaugural Vision (6:1–13)
- (II) The Book of Emmanuel (7:1–12:6)
  - (A) National Crisis Under Ahaz (7:1–9:6)
    - (a) Two Signs for the King (7:1–17)
    - (b) Invasion of Judah (7:18–25)
    - (c) Warnings and Withdrawal (8:1–20)
    - (d) The Prince of Peace (8:23–9:6)
  - (B) Fall of North Israel and Divine Vengeance on Assyria (9:7–12:6)
    - (a) The Hand of Yahweh's Wrath (9:7–10:4)
    - (b) The Arrogance of Assyria (10:5–34)
    - (c) The Rule of Emmanuel (11:1–9)
    - (d) The Ingathering of Dispersed Israel (11:10–16)
    - (e) Thanksgiving to the Holy One of Israel (12:1–6)
- (III) Oracles Against the Gentiles (13:1–23:18)
  - (A) Oracles Against the Enemies of Israel (13:1–20:6)
    - (a) Oracles Against Babylon, Assyria, and Philistia (13:1–14:32)
    - (b) Oracle Against Moab (15:1–16:14)
    - (c) Oracles on Damascus and Ephraim (17:1–14)
    - (d) Oracles on Ethiopia and Egypt (18:1–19:25)
    - (e) The Symbol of Egypt's Captivity (20:1–6)
  - (B) Visions of Catastrophe (21:1–23:18)
    - (a) Fall of Babylon (21:1–10)
    - (b) Oracles on Edom and Arabia (21:11–17)
    - (c) Oracle on the Valley of Vision (22:1–14)
    - (d) Oracle Against the Royal Steward (22:15–25)
    - (e) Oracles on Tyre (23:1–18)
- (IV) The Apocalypse of Isaiah (24:1–27:13)
  - (A) The Coming Devastation (24:1–23)

COMMENTARY

(I) Threats and Promises to Rebellious Judah (1:1–6:13).

7 **(A) The Indictment (1:1–31).** The chapter brilliantly summarizes the whole message of Isaiah, ranging from mighty protestation against the renegade people to promise of renewal on condition that Israel repents. In fact, the whole book oscillates between the themes of accusation and assurance of divine mercy. Most of the material in these early chapters comes from the earliest period of Isaiah's ministry, but it is not arranged in any clear chronological order. Judah's basic sin lay in the rejection of a suzerain as well as a loving father. From that evil stemmed all her sins of social injustice, hypocritical formalism in religion, and propensity for silly superstitions.

1. The title is editorial; it was added to the book before the anonymous prophecies of chs. 40–66 had been incorporated into the oracles of Isaiah. The name of his father has nothing to do with the prophet Amos. **2.** *hear, O heavens:* The introductory formula of the "covenant-lawsuit" literary form. Yahweh, the suzerain who has concluded a treaty with Israel, appears as the judge of Israel's covenant violations. He solemnly states the accusation before the witnessing universe and then passes sentence. In this scene, Yahweh acts as both plaintiff and judge. The Mosaic covenant between Yahweh the suzerain and Israel his vassal is the presupposition that makes the lawsuit intelligible.

(Harvey, J., *Bib* 43 [1962] 172–96. Huffmon, H. B., *JBL* 78 [1959] 285–95. Wright, G. E., *Israel's Prophetic Heritage* [Fest. J. Muilenburg; N.Y., 1962] 26–67.)

5. *where would you be struck?:* The image is that of a slave covered with wounds inflicted by an outraged master. The ravaged land of Judah was the price she paid for her folly. The reference is, most likely, to the invasion of Sennacherib in 701 when he boasted of having destroyed 46 walled cities and villages without number (*ANET* 288). The following four verses describe the devastation wrought by the Assyrian king. **8.** The personfication of Jerusalem as a maiden is a favorite Isaian image (10:32; 16:1; 37:22). The lonely and fragile hut of the watchman is still set up in the Near East during the vintage season. The "shed in a melon patch" prolongs the image of loneliness. **9.** *a scanty remnant:* The word used here (Hebr *śārîd*) is not Isaiah's ordinary word for "remnant" (Hebr *šeʼār*). It is doubtful that Isaiah considered the survivors of the catastrophe in 701 as the purified remnant. Nevertheless, that there were survivors was another proof of God's mercy, sparing a people that deserved destruction. **10.** This verse is a new "lawsuit" oracle joined to what precedes by the catchwords "Sodom" and "Gomorrah." It is likely that the oracle was delivered on a feast day before a throng of worshipers. The exact date cannot be determined but it was probably uttered early in Isaiah's career. At the end of the oracle (19–20) the possibility of escaping chastisement is left open.

8 **11.** The idea that sacrifice is worthless without the proper interior dispositions is common to the prophets (Am 5:21–24; Hos 6:6; Jer 7:21–23; etc.). Worship that is merely external is sheer hypocrisy. The prophets condemn the abuse but not the institution of sacrifice. **13.** The word for "offering" (Hebr *minḥâ*) seems to mean, in this passage, any kind of gift. The word is used later to designate nonbloody offerings, such as cereal or meal offerings. **14.** The ritual for the celebration of the new moon is found in Nm 28:11–15. This very ancient feast was, like the Sabbath, a day of rest, and it took place on the first day of the new moon (De Vaux, *AI* 469–70). **15.** The gesture of prayer, with hands extended and the palms open toward heaven, is rejected because the hands are bloodstained with crime. **16.** *wash yourselves clean:* Not the purely exterior ritual washing of the Law, but an interior cleansing of the heart. **18.** The image is again taken from the court of law. Judah is summoned to argue her case before the divine judge. Only by repentance and reform could disaster be averted.

21–23. Verses 21–23 are a lament; the first verse is in the *qînâ* meter, a sobbing rhythm produced by the succession of accented syllables in a 3 + 2 pattern. The tone is similar to that of Lam. Religious apostasy is frequently described in the prophets as adultery. **23.** Instead of administering justice, the princes have connived with the despoilers of the helpless. The orphan and the widow were, from the earliest times, the classic example of those who needed the protection of the guardians of justice. **24.** The solemnity of the judgment is reinforced by the titles given the judge. **25.** "Dross" is ore to be smelted. **27.** The tone changes entirely. The "judgment" (Hebr *mišpāṭ*) and "justice" (Hebr *ṣedāqâ*) are of God and not of man. **29.** The "terebinths" were oaks at which Canaanite fertility cults were practiced. Some commentators regard this passage as late because of the ideas and vocabulary, but inasmuch as the Israelites were guilty of observing the fertility rites from the earliest days of their history, the argument lacks a solid foundation. As the trees lost their vigor and the groves withered under the heat of the sun so would the religious renegades dry up and be consumed in the fire of judgment.

9 **(B) Zion, Present and Future (2:1–4:6).** Chapters 2–4 form a unit and contain sermons from the early stages of Isaiah's career. They give us a good picture of the deplorable moral condition of Judah in the second half of the 8th cent. Verse 1 serves as a title for this small collection; its form suggests that these chapters once existed independently.

(a) IN DAYS TO COME (2:2–5). This vision of the nations gathering on Mt. Zion is found, with few changes, in Mi 4:1–3. It is impossible to say with certainty in which of the two works it is original, or whether both borrowed from a common source. Arguments for a later, post-exilic date for the oracle are not persuasive since the idea of a great, universal victory of Yahweh was already present in the very early Hebr belief in the day of Yahweh. It has recently been suggested that the oracle is not original in either book but comes rather from a liturgical source upon which both drew (J. Gray, *VT* 11 [1961] 15).

2. *the mountain of the Lord's house:* The idea of the mountain of God as the goal of all nations is a very ancient one. H.-J. Kraus suggests that the concept may have been borrowed from the old Jebusite Jerusalem cult (*Psalmen* [BK; Neukirchen, 1958] 342–45). The precise reference here is to the northern part of the eastern hill of Jerusalem. This location was developed extensively during the reign of Solomon. **3.** Jerusalem becomes the center of "instruction" (Hebr *tôrâ*) for all the nations. Torah was the way of life revealed by God to his people. **4.** *he shall judge between the nations:* Settle disputes, arbitrate between contending parties. The prophets conceive of the Messianic age as a time of justice and peace.

10 (b) JUDGMENT UPON IDOLATRY (2:6–22). Prosperity and alliances with foreigners had led to pride, superstition, and unbridled luxury. The period reflected in this oracle seems to be the time when the wealth and power of Uzziah's reign still blinded Judah to the impending judgment. **6.** Divination, in many forms, was practiced throughout the ancient Near East; it was forbidden in Israel (Ex 22:17; Lv 19:31; Dt 18:10–11; 1 Sm 28:8–9) but never entirely stamped out. *they covenant with strangers:* Lit., "they strike hands," the sign of a commercial or political agreement with foreigners. From the days of Solomon the Israelites knew that foreign alliances opened the door to strange gods and idolatrous practices. **7.** Foreign trade and a reinvigorated economic life during the long reign of Uzziah had given Judah an outward magnificence comparable to the days of Solomon. Archaeology confirms this new prosperity. Isaiah's protest here is very similar to that of Amos in northern Israel. **9.** [*do not pardon them*]*:* This phrase is omitted in 1QIs^a and its position here is awkward. **10.** The humiliation of human pride before the irresistible power of God is a favorite Isaian theme. **11.** This verse contains the first of 45 occurrences of the phrase "on that day" (*bayyôm hahû'*) in Is 1–39. Stylistically the phrase usually serves as an emphatic element in the narrative, being placed at the climactic point of the passage, at either the beginning or the end. Its temporal significance must be determined from the context. In any case the phrase points to an extraordinary manifestation of Yahweh's power (A. Lefèvre, *Mélanges Bibliques* [Fest. A. Robert; Paris, 1957] 174–79). **13.** Everything suggesting might and grandeur will be overthrown. The cedars symbolize the ostentatious vainglory of man (Jer 22:14–15). The oaks of Bashan, a land E of the Jordan and renowned for its fertility, are awesome in their strength; mention of them may be an allusion to Israel's practices of idolatry beneath these trees (1:29). **16.** During the prosperous Solomonic era the ships of Tarshish, introduced by the Phoenicians, would leave Ezion-geber on commercial missions. Tarshish means "refinery," a name given to this class of cargo ships that plied between the copper refineries of Spain or Sardinia and the Phoenician homeland (Albright, *ARI* 136). Even as late as the time of Uzziah, attempts were apparently made to restore this trade (2 Kgs 14:22). **19.** *into holes in the earth:* These would be cisterns or storage pits, which men would use as a means of escape. The upheaval of nature accompanying the theophany brings to mind the appearance of Yahweh at Sinai. **22.** Missing in the LXX. The idea appears to be that Judah should put no trust in fragile man whose life-giving spirit is but a breath that the Lord can give or take away (Jb 7:7).

11 (c) DISINTEGRATION OF JUDEAN SOCIETY (3:1–15). The day of judgment will see only anarchy, confusion, and despair in Jerusalem and Judah. History provides many examples of the chaos resulting when the forces of law and order lose control of a situation. But this disintegration was not owing simply to the play of historical factors. The opening verse emphasizes that this was a divine judgment, a good example of the interpretation of history that is characteristic of the OT. The divine dimension is never overlooked (Mauchline, *op. cit.*, 71–72). The passage probably originates from *ca.* 734, shortly after Ahaz came to the throne.

1. *support and prop:* The MT uses the same Hebr word (*maš‛ēn*) in its masculine and feminine forms. The words refer to the supports of the established order; they are described in the following three verses. **2.** Judges were open to bribes (Am 5:7); the professional prophets gave their message for a fee (Mi 3:11); the fortuneteller thrived on popular superstition. The elders were the leading citizens of the city (Ru 4:2). As heads of the families within a clan, they settled town disputes and trials, usually at the city gate where community affairs were handled. **3.** The fighting units were made up of 1000, 100, 50, and 10 men, an organization dated to the desert period. The "captain" was a professional officer in the service of the king (De Vaux, *AI* 226). **4.** *I will make striplings their princes:* This phrase may be a reference (see also v. 12) to the youth of Ahaz when he began to rule. **6.** In the destitute land a man who still had an outer garment (Hebr *simlâ*) is asked to take over leadership, but he declines, pleading that he is just as poor as the next man. It is a striking picture of a broken-down and leaderless community. **10.** This and the following verse are a reflective interlude, reminiscent of Ps 1. **12.** *my people:* The repetition of the phrase adds pathos to the situation and reminds the people of Judah of their favored status as a covenanted nation. *a babe in arms:* Lit., a "suckling" (*m^{e}‛ôlēl*), referring to Ahaz who came to the throne at 20 (2 Kgs 16:2) and probably served as regent during the last years of Jotham. *and women will rule them:* Judeans had unhappy memories of the rule of Athaliah, the queen mother (2 Kgs 11:1–16). **13.** Yahweh does not plead for his people but contends with them; He has a controversy with Judah, particularly with her venal leaders.

12 (d) DOOM FOR THE FINE LADIES OF JERUSALEM (3:16–4:1). Isaiah does not seem to have had a much higher opinion of the fashionable ladies of Jerusalem than Amos had of the ladies in Samaria (Am 4:1). This passage gives the longest catalogue of feminine finery in the OT. Not all the ornaments can be accurately identified. **16.** A description of the haughty demeanor of holding the head high. Their affected gait, wanton glances, and fine ankle bracelets are meant to attract men.

17. See 7:20 for the practice of cutting off the hair as a mark of shame. Their wantonness would prove their own undoing, for they would be violated by their captors. **18.** *sunbursts and crescents:* For examples of feminine jewelry excavated in Palestine, see *VBW* 3, 22. **24.** *and for the coiffure, baldness:* An elegant hairdo was a sign of wealth and nobility. The ladies worked diligently at the art of hairdressing, an art probably imported from a foreign country. The coiffure is described in this verse as "well-set" (*maʿ^{a}śeh miqšeh*). Elaborate hairdos have been found on figurines of the Canaanite goddess Ashtoreth (*VBW* 3, 23). *then, instead of beauty:* 1QIs^a reads: "instead of beauty, shame."

4:1. So desperate is the plight of these once pampered and haughty women that they will throw convention to the winds and beg a man to marry them. They will not even ask for support; they will ask only for the status, which, in society of that time, came either from childbearing or, at least, from taking a husband's name. Childlessness and spinsterhood were considered a great misfortune (see 32:9–14).

13 (e) Vision of Zion Restored (4:2–6). **2.** *on that day:* The time of Yahweh's choosing, when he shall fulfill his purposes for Zion (1:26–27). *the branch of the Lord:* "Branch" (*ṣemaḥ*) may refer either to the Messianic king (Jer 23:5; Zech 3:8) who comes from the line of David or to the remnant (→ Aspects OT Thought, 77:158–159), which will escape the impending judgment. The latter seems more probable in this passage. A third possibility, based on the parallelism characteristic of Hebr poetry, matches "branch" with "fruit of the earth." The phrase would, in this case, refer literally to a renewal in nature that would characterize the ideal Judah of the future. **3.** *everyone marked down for life in Jerusalem:* Their names are listed among the living in God's census book; Dn 12:1 and Mal 3:16 refer to this book of life. **4.** Some scholars believe that this part of the oracle is a post-exilic addition, but J. Bright (*PCB* 493) sees no compelling reason to assign it to the post-exilic period. He notes the similarity of this promise to Is 37:30–32. **5.** Yahweh would again be with his people as he was during the march through the wilderness. The cloud was a symbol of Yahweh's protecting presence. The allusion to Ex 13:21–22 is clear. **6.** God's protection is compared to a sheltering "booth" (*sukkâ*) set up in the vineyards to afford shade for the workers. When the harvest had ripened, the booth also served as a watchman's post to guard the property from thieves (cf. 1:8). At night it offered a refuge from the heavy dew. These huts can still be seen in the vineyards of Palestine. At the end of the harvest, the booth was allowed to wash away gradually during the winter rains (*VBW* 3, 24).

14 **(C) Song of the Vineyard (5:1–7).** Composed during the early years of Isaiah's ministry, this poem takes the form of a popular ballad that one might sing at a vintage festival. It is possible that Isaiah himself sang the song on one of these occasions, most likely the Feast of Tabernacles. Beginning on a happy and pleasant note, the singer reveals the hard truth only at the end. **2.** With stones dug from the field, the vine-grower built a fence and watchtower for the protection of his property. The stones were also used to erect terrace walls along the slope of the hillside, making intensive cultivation possible. The terraces were thus leveled for planting, a common sight in Palestine today (*VBW* 3, 25). Despite all this care, the vineyard yielded only wild grapes, unfit for eating. **6.** After the seemingly normal condemnation of the vine in vv. 3–5, the tone clearly becomes divine ("I will command the clouds"), and the symbol is identified in v. 7. **7.** There is a play on words here that escapes most of our translations. God looked for "judgment" (*mišpāṭ*) and all he found was "bloodshed" (*miśpāḥ*), for "justice" (*ṣ^{e}dāqâ*) and he found an "outcry" (*ṣ^{e}ʿāqâ*). *Mišpaṭ* was basically a judgment, the revealed will of God covering the totality of man's duties, to God, to man, and to himself. *Ṣ^{e}dāqâ* was the correlative of *mišpāṭ* and it meant whatever accorded with this divine demand. It could be applied to some particular duty or to the quality of the man who lived according to *mišpāṭ*. We translate it as "justice," which meant both the doing of one's duty and the state of being resulting from doing that duty.

(De Orbisio, T., "El cántico a la vina del amado (Is 5:1–7)," *EstEc* 34 [1960] 715–31.)

15 **(D) The Woes (5:8–30).** Following the Song of the Vineyard is a series of six "woes" against the corruption of 8th-cent. Judah and its decadent aristocracy. **8.** Building up large holdings by grabbing the property of others was a fairly common abuse. The concentration of property in the hands of a few (latifundism) was contrary to the old Israelite tradition of smallholding. The Naboth incident (1 Kgs 21) was probably still fresh in the minds of the people (E. Gerstenberger, *JBL* 81 [1962] 249–63). **9.** The landgrabbers will get solitude, but it will be that of the wasteland. **10.** It is impossible to give modern equivalents for these weights; cf. De Vaux, *AI* 195–209. **11.** For a similar charge against drunkards, see Is 28:1,7–8. **12.** That God is actively engaged in history and dominates human events is a basic theme in the theology of the prophets. The men of Judah were too sotted with drink to give a thought to God. **13.** *because they do not understand:* They have no "knowledge" (*daʿat*) of God, i.e., no moral integrity or willingness to practice traditional Hebrew morality as a response to God's gift of the covenant (cf. J. L. McKenzie, *JBL* 74 [1955] 22–27). Hosea mentions this knowledge of God in 4:1 and 6:6. **14–16.** These lines may be out of context; it has been suggested that they belong to the oracle in 2:6–22. The "nether world" is pictured as a great monster about to devour men. **18.** A Canaanite text from Ras Shamra (49:2:28–30) permits us to propose the following translation for this obscure couplet:

> Woe to those who drag iniquity with ewe-ropes,
> And sin with a calf-halter.

The idea is that the sinners' attachment to sin is as strong as the rope used to lead a ewe, or the halter with which one drags a calf (cf. M. Dahood, *CBQ* 22 [1960] 74–75). In other words, they are harnessed to their sins. **20.** We have reached the limit of depravity when men make no distinction between moral good and evil. One could hardly find a better way to describe unprincipled men. **25.** *for all this, his wrath is not turned back:* For this refrain, see 9:11,16,20, and 10:4. The wrath of God should not be seen in too human a fashion, as a kind of mighty peevishness. It is really the complement of his love and it gives a depth and mystery to that love. Divine wrath is the inevitable disaster brought upon those who reject God's love. **26.** The Assyrians are the invaders and they are summoned by "signal" to do God's bidding. Note the speed, disciplined energy, and fury of the well-equipped army suggested by the images in vv. 26–29 (the brackets in v. 30 indicate that it is a dittography from 8:22).

16 **(E) The Inaugural Vision (6:1–13).** Normally, we would find this chapter at the beginning of the prophecy; perhaps it was set down in writing only after the threats mentioned in the concluding verses had been fulfilled. It now serves as a majestic prologue to the Book of Emmanuel (7:1–12:6). What Isaiah tells us in this record of his overpowering encounter with the Holy

One is absolutely essential for grasping his whole life and message.

1. The death of Uzziah in 742 after a reign of over 40 years brought to an end a period of great prosperity and security. Man's mortality is perhaps contrasted with the eternal glory of a transcendent God. **2.** *seraphim were stationed above:* The scene was the Temple of Jerusalem, probably on some great feast. The six-winged creatures, partly human in form, are often depicted in the art of the ancient Near East (*VBW* 3, 27). **3.** The holiness of God is a central theme of Isaiah, who often refers to him as the "Holy One of Israel." By the triple repetition, the superlative is expressed; God is the all-holy. Holiness is the essential quality of God; its vast range of meaning indicates his otherness, utter transcendence, complete apartness from anything sinful or merely finite. God's "glory" is the radiation of this holiness upon the world. The meaning of the title "Lord of hosts" (*Yahweh Ṣ^ebā'ôt*) is disputed. "He creates the armies [of Israel]" seems best to satisfy the data at our disposal. In all likelihood, the phrase was a part of the hallowed name given to the Ark that accompanied Israel into battle. God the warrior is an extremely important concept throughout the OT (cf. D. N. Freedman, *JBL* 79 [1960] 156; R. Abba, *JBL* 80 [1961] 320–28). **4.** *and the house was filled with smoke:* A sign of the divine presence, the smoke is the same as the cloud of glory which filled the tabernacle during the sojourn in the wilderness (Ex 40:34). It veiled as well as revealed that presence. **5.** *woe is me, I am doomed:* Could a man see God and live (Ex 33:20)? Isaiah was overwhelmed by a sense of his own unworthiness, especially since he was one with a sinful people. The whole passage derives its force from the unalterable opposition between God and sin.

17 **7.** *he touched my mouth with it:* The symbolic act of purification was the result of God's, not man's initiative. **8.** *whom shall I send? who will go for us?:* Borrowing from the imagery of a heavenly assembly found in the ancient religions, and known especially from Ugaritic literature, the Hebrews conceived of Yahweh enthroned above the firmament and holding court with his heavenly advisors. These latter are no longer gods but angels or "sons of God." In this scene, the seraphim are members of the assembly who are consulted about the decrees concerning the government of the world. However, they do not make the decisions; their function is to adore. Yahweh's decision is final and absolute. The use of this image of a divine assembly is a good example of how the Hebrews could borrow from their neighbors and yet drastically transform the image in accordance with the demands of Israelite monotheism (cf. R.E. Brown, *CBQ* 20 [1958] 418–20). **9.** *listen carefully, but you shall not understand:* Isaiah's words would only harden their stubborn wills. This obduracy is foreseen by Yahweh but not directly willed by him. From this moment Isaiah will, like Paul (1 Cor 2:6–8), confront and confound the defenders of traditional wisdom with the wisdom he has learned from God (R. Martin-Achard, *Maqqel Shaqedh* [Fest. W. Vischer; 1960] 137–44). **10.** The first two verbs of the verse are imperatives, used here idiomatically to express a future certainty. The negative purpose clause following these imperatives expresses the consequence of Isaiah's preaching. **11.** *how long, O Lord?:* The question contains a hint of protest as well as a hope that, perhaps through his prophetic activity, Israel's obduracy would not be final and complete. For a similar note of protest, see Jer 4:14 and Ps 74:10. The answer comes that it will last until the land is left empty and desolate. **13.** *if there still be a tenth part in it:* Even the "tenth," which constitutes a remnant, shall have to face a purging judgment. *as with a terebinth:* The second half of the verse is obscure but, on the basis of 1QIs^a and what is now known about pre-exilic spelling, W. F. Albright renders the latter part of this verse as follows:

> Like the terebinth goddess and the oak of Asherah,
> Cast out with the stelae of the high place.

The commemorative stelae of deceased people and the sacred trees of a goddess were standard items of furnishing at a typical *bāmâ* or funerary shrine located usually on some height. These "high places" (Hebr *bāmôt*) were used for cultic purposes by both Canaanites and Hebrews. The destruction and desecration of such cultic centers must have been of fairly common occurrence in the turbulent days of Isaiah. Relapse and reform followed hard upon one another. Accordingly, such a familiar iconoclastic action would make a good simile for the trials in store for the surviving remnant (cf. W. F. Albright, VTSup 4 [1957] 254–55; S. Iwry, *JBL* 76 [1957] 225–32).

18 **(II) The Book of Emmanuel (7:1–12:6).**

(A) National Crisis Under Ahaz (7:1–9:6). These events took place in 735–733. The situation is concisely described in 2 Kgs 16:5–9, the events of the Syro-Ephraimitic war.

(a) Two Signs for the King (7:1–17). **1.** Rezin was the last king of Damascus. In 732, the Assyrian king Tiglath-pileser III destroyed Rezin's capital and put him to death. **2.** The coalition of Aram and Israel threw Judah into a state of emergency. **3.** *your son Shear-jashub:* The proper name means "A remnant shall return," i.e., to God. It has both a hopeful and threatening connotation; disaster shall come but some will be saved. *the conduit of the upper pool:* Ahaz was taking the practical step of safeguarding Jerusalem's water supply. It was a channel through which water from the Gihon spring in the Kidron Valley was brought to the upper city. It was at this same spot that, many years later, the Assyrian commander would hurl his taunts at Judah (36:2). **6.** The coalition planned to depose Ahaz and replace him by a prince of Bet Tab'el, an Aramean land in northern Transjordan. The name of the country is now known from contemporary inscriptions (W. F. Albright, *BASOR* 140 [1955] 34–35). The pretender to the throne was probably a Judean, the son of either Jotham or Uzziah by a princess of Tab'el. **9.** *but within sixty years and five:* The verse is difficult since Ahaz could take little comfort in something that would take place many years later. Perhaps the line should be emended to read "Yet six, nay five more years..." (Kissane, *op. cit.*, 78–79). *unless your faith is firm:* There is a play on words, both verbs of the couplet coming from the Hebr root *'mn*, meaning "confirm" or "establish" and, in the causative form, "believe." This summons to believe is a pointed reminder of the oracle of Nathan (2 Sm 7:12–16) promising an eternal dynasty to David's line. The saying expresses a basic conviction of Isaiah who saw no hope for his people apart from complete reliance upon Yahweh. **12.** Ahaz rejects the offer of a "sign" (*'ôt*), which, in the OT and NT, is usually some event assuring man of a divine intervention. It is a form of revelation; in this case, the sign is meant to be a confirmation of Yahweh's first message to Ahaz (S. Porubčan, *CBQ* 22 [1960] 145). Ahaz's refusal was undoubtedly motivated by his unwillingness to follow Isaiah's advice. **14.** An immense literature has grown up around this oracle and the debate continues. Several points may be noted. Isaiah does not use the technical word for "virgin" (*b^etûlâ*) but a word (*'almâ*) that signifies a young woman of marriageable age, whether a virgin or not. The solemn oracle is spoken before the royal court, fearful lest the Davidic dynasty be overthrown. Such a catastrophe would mean the cancellation of the great dynastic promise made to David's house (2 Sm 7:12–16). It was on the royal successor to David that Judah pinned her hopes for the welfare of God's people. The child about to be born, therefore, may be the young Hezekiah in whose birth Judah would see the continuing presence of God among his people and another renewal of the promise made to David. Nevertheless, the solemnity of the oracle and the name "Emmanuel" lend credence to the opinion that Isaiah's perspective does not stop at the birth of Hezekiah; it moves ahead to that ideal king of David's line through whose coming God could finally be said to be definitively with his people. This does not mean, of course, that Isaiah foresaw the fulfillment of this prophecy in Christ, but he expressed the hope that Christ perfectly realized. Matthew and the Church have seen in the birth of Christ from the Virgin Mother the perfect fulfillment of this prophecy.

(Auvray and Steinmann, *Isaïe*, 48. Coppens, J., "L'interprétation d'Is. 7,14 à la lumière des études les plus récentes," *Lex Tua Veritas* [Fest. H. Junker; Trier, 1961] 31–45, esp. bibliog. Vawter, *The Conscience of Israel*, 182–84.)

15. The diet may refer to a condition of plenty, for "curds and honey" were a delicacy to the nomad (Gn 18:8; Jgs 5:25) and usually symbolized a state of abundance (Dt 32:13–14; Ex 3:8). On the other hand, the phrase may evoke a time of hardship and want when the stricken population can hope for nothing more than the food of nomads. Whichever interpretation is preferred one conclusion is clear: Isaiah prophesied both deliverance and disaster for Judah. First of all, before the child reached the age of discretion, there would be deliverance from the threatening Israel-Aram coalition (v. 16); then there would be devastation wrought by the invading Assyrians (vv. 17–25).

19 (b) INVASION OF JUDAH (7:18–25). The passage is distinct from what precedes, but it amplifies what is said in v. 17 and comes from the same period, dominated by the threat of Assyria. **18.** Egypt and Assyria are described as insects, perhaps because they will blanket the land like a pestilential scourge. It is possible that the "fly" and the "bee" may have been national symbols of each country. **20.** Ahaz had hired the razor, Assyria, to shave his enemies; now Yahweh would turn and shave Ahaz with the same razor! **22.** *curds and honey:* Possibly a sarcastic allusion to v. 15; or it may mean that there would be so few left after the Assyrian blow that the remnant would have plenty to eat. A third possibility is to interpret the verse as a prediction that those who survive would have only the food of nomads instead of the delicacies to which their luxurious living had accustomed them. **24.** Judah will become a hunting area: many wild beasts have settled in the wasteland. Hunting scenes are among the most popular in ancient Near Eastern art.

20 (c) WARNINGS AND WITHDRAWAL (8:1–20). **1.** For "cylinder-seal" it is perhaps better to read "tablet" or "board." Others believe that a sheet of papyrus is meant and that it was to serve as a kind of placard (D. Jones, *ZAW* 67 [1955] 230–31). *in ordinary letters:* Lit., "with a common stylus." The placard was obviously intended for public reading in a place frequented by the people. That the knowledge of writing was widespread in Isaiah's time is supported by the famous Siloam tunnel inscription. *Maher-shalal-hash-baz:* The symbolic name of another son of Isaiah; it means, "the spoil hastens, the plunder comes quickly." **2.** *I took reliable witnesses:* Isaiah gave legal formality to the act. Probably the document received a seal of attestation. In any case, the document was to be put away until the prediction had been fulfilled. Uriah collaborated with Ahaz in his dalliance with Assyrian religion (2 Kgs 16:10–16) Zechariah was probably the father-in-law of Ahaz (2 Kgs 18:2). **4.** *before the child knows:* Damascus and Samaria would be despoiled before the Prophet's son could utter his first words. **6.** Isaiah contrasts the gently flowing waters of Shiloah with the mighty torrent of Assyria. The former symbolizes divine aid, the latter the naked power of Assyrian arms. Shiloah was the open-air aqueduct bringing the waters from the Gihon spring to the "lower pool" within the city. Later, Hezekiah would build a tunnel, over 1700 ft. long, to bring water from Gihon to his newly built reservoir, known as the "Pool of Siloam" (22:9,11). **7.** *the waters of the river:* The Euphrates, symbol of irresistible Assyrian power. **8.** *it shall spread its wings:* The Assyrians are compared to a huge bird of prey, if we allow the text to stand as it is. But some scholars, seeing in the imagery of outstretched wings a sign of protection, place v. 8b with vv. 9–10 to make up a short liturgical poem whose introduction has been lost. The liturgical piece would be a strong affirmation of faith in Yahweh's power to deliver. **12.** *alliance:* "Plot" would be preferable. Isaiah and his followers are not to become upset over rumors of conspiracy that often break out in a time of crisis. **13.** *with the Lord of hosts make your alliance:* If it is conspiracy to oppose Ahaz then the archconspirator is Yahweh; join him in conspiracy! **14.** The same "stone" that causes stumbling is also the cornerstone that supports the new house of the people of God (28:16). The same theme, with a similar polarization, is taken up in the NT (Lk 2:34; Mt 21:42; Rom 9:32; 1 Pt 2:8). **16.** In 734–733, Isaiah ceased prophesying for the time and set down a "record" of what he had said. The "instruction" (*tôrâ*) was not the Mosaic Law but his own prophetic teaching. In depositing a sealed copy of his oracles with disciples, Isaiah is probably taking the first step toward what would eventually be the whole Isaian collection. This is an important passage for the light it throws on the formation of the Isaian tradition. **18.** Among the "children" are undoubtedly the two sons of Isaiah, but the word probably refers also to his disciples who were entrusted with the task of preserving and witnessing to the revelation granted to Isaiah. Our Lord refers to his disciples in the same fashion at the Last Supper (Jn 13:33,35). On the hypothesis that there was, in succeeding centuries, a group of followers or an Isaian school, devoted to the collection and preservation of the master's revelation, the unity of the Book of Isaiah becomes more readily understandable (J. H. Eaton, "The Origin of the Book of Isaiah," *VT* 9 [1959] 138–57). **19.** *and when they say to you:* It was customary to consult the prophets and their disciples, especially in times of national emergency. The paganizing tendencies in the reign of Ahaz are evident here. Contrary to Israelite law the petitioners asked that the dead be consulted (necromancy). The disciples, on the other hand, were to point to the prophetic teaching and testimony as the authentic revelation of God's will for this people.

21 (d) THE PRINCE OF PEACE (8:23–9:6). **23.** Zebulun and Naphthali were the first provinces of Israel to be overrun by Tiglath-pileser III in 733. Some of the population of these territories was sent into exile (*VBW* 3, 32). *but in the end:* Eventually God would restore the ravaged lands to their former glory. Mt 4:15–16 sees in Jesus' Galilean proclamation of the kingdom of God the fulfillment of this prophecy. The swift change in this verse from a vision of ruin to a promise of restoration prepares the way for the following oracle, one of the most important Messianic passages in the OT. The oracle has been incorporated into the Christian liturgy of Christmas Day.

9:1. Some scholars believe that the entire oracle (1–6) is a liturgical piece excerpted from the ceremony of a royal accession. Every time that a Davidic king came to the throne and was hailed as an adopted son of God there was cause for rejoicing. On this occasion, the promises of an eternal covenant with David were reaffirmed and hopes were raised for that ideal king of the future who would perfectly realize the dynastic ideal. Therefore, the oracle does not concern any historical king, such as Ahaz or Hezekiah, but the ideal king who would introduce the definitive era of peace and justice. Once again, the prophetic perspective is focused not on a king of the present but on the ideal Davidic king, the Emmanuel of 7:14. Perfect tenses are used by Isaiah, but they are "prophetic perfects," expressing the certainty of a future event. **3.** The captive's condition is compared to that of a harnessed farm animal, a fairly common image of enslavement. Usually the yoke was made of wood but sometimes of metal (Jer 28:13). The "pole" was the bar of the yoke that pressed down on the captive's shoulders (*VBW* 3, 33). Isaiah later compares the liberation of Israel from Assyrian captivity to the breaking of a yoke and the lifting of a burden (10:27; 14:25). *as on the day of Midian:* An allusion to Gideon's defeat of the Midianites (Jgs 7:16–25). **5.** *for a child is born to us:* On the day of a king's enthronement he was proclaimed an adopted son of God (Ps 2:7), the theological basis for which is found in the dynastic promise to David's house (2 Sm 7:14). *they name him wonder-counselor...:* These are the titles that go to make up the royal "protocol"; they were given to the king on his accession. To this ideal king are ascribed the wisdom of Solomon, the courage of David, and the religious virtue of the patriarchs and Moses. He is the quintessence of the great virtues of his people. The accent is strong on "wisdom," the virtue by which king and counselor established prosperity for the community (J. Bourke, *CBQ* 22 [1960] 134–36). **6.** *judgment and justice:* This is the work of a counselor who is, at the same time, a royal personage. His eternal rule shall be assured by the Lord of hosts. The picture is that of the ideal king, the last representative of David's line and not the next one to succeed on the throne of Judah. Christian tradition has, with one voice, seen in Christ the fulfillment of this promise. Certainly no historical king of Judah adequately realized this hope attached to the ideal king. *the zeal of the Lord of hosts:* God's "zeal" (*qīn'â*) could punish Israel for her sins (Dt 5:9), especially idolatry, but this same quality would also assure the fulfillment of the promises to his people.

(Coppens, J., "Le roi idéal d'Is. IX, 5–6 et XI, 1–5 est-il une figure messianique?" *À la rencontre de Dieu* [Fest. A. Gelin; Le Puy, 1961] 85–108, esp. bibliog.)

(B) Fall of North Israel and Divine Vengeance on Assyria (9:7–12:6).

22 (a) The Hand of Yahweh's Wrath (9:7–10:4). The section is unified by the refrain that occurs four times in the passage. **7.** The "word" (*dābār*) is laden with power and, once released, it has a mighty effect in history, whether for curse or blessing. **9.** *bricks have fallen...:* A proverb meaning: We have suffered a reverse but we will come back stronger than ever. This false confidence of Ephraim probably reflects the time just after the death of Tiglath-pileser in 728. The death of an Assyrian overlord was ordinarily the sign for revolt among the subject peoples. **13.** *head and tail:* Leaders and subjects. *palm branch and reed:* The same idea is repeated. All classes, high and low, are affected. **17.** Evil is compared to smouldering embers that break out suddenly in a raging fire. For a similar image, see Hos 7:4,6. **18.** Complete anarchy and confusion seize the country. The fratricidal strife probably refers to the civil wars that tore Israel apart between 745 and 737 (2 Kgs 15:8–26). **19.** Voracity is described as vividly as possible. The people stuff themselves but are not sated. **20.** *Manasseh devours Ephraim:* That these tribes were closely related only emphasizes the chaos in the north. They could unite only in their hostility toward Judah.

10:1. This section refers to Judah, which is also under judgment. The decrees were official documents and interpretations that defrauded the defenseless of their rights. **2.** *depriving the needy of judgment:* To "turn away from judgment" has resonances in the legal vocabulary of Dt 16:19; 24:17; 27:19 and Ex 23:2,6. All of these passages refer to the perversion of correct judicial process. **4.** *lest it sink beneath the captive:* The text is difficult; perhaps it means that there will be no place for their riches except among the captives or the slain.

23 (b) The Arrogance of Assyria (10:5–34). The editor has drawn together a number of oracles uttered by Isaiah against the pride of Assyria; punishment is foretold as well as the deliverance of Judah. The historical setting is most likely the reign of Sennacherib (705–682), more specifically the events surrounding his second and last invasion of Judah, *ca.* 688. **5.** Yahweh had used mighty Assyria as an instrument to chastise his people. The Assyrians were commissioned by the Lord of history to plunder Judah and trample her in the mud. **7.** The Assyrian king thinks only of annihilating the foe; he has not the faintest notion that a divine sovereign is using him to attain his purpose. **8.** The proudest title of the Assyrian ruler was "King of Kings"; many of his subordinate officers were vassal heads of conquered territories. **9.** Calno and Carchemish, along with Arpad, were in northern Syria close to the Euphrates; Hamath was on the Orontes in central Syria. All were overrun by the Assyrians, some more than once. **13.** The Assyrian king boasts of his self-sufficiency as though he alone were responsible for his victories. **14.** *no one fluttered a wing:* Usually the mother bird causes a great commotion trying to protect her young. The inhabitants of the plundered cities appear to have been paralyzed by the invaders. **15.** The rhetorical questions mock the presumption of the Assyrians. **16.** *and instead of his glory there will be kindling:* "Glory" (*kbd*) may mean "liver," as known from Ugaritic. If we read the preposition as "under," the picture may be that of a fever consuming the man's liver. The writer seems to say that the once-powerful man shall waste away with the disease. **17.** *the Light of Israel:* The glory of the divine majesty that becomes manifest on the day of the Lord (2:10). **19.** *and the remnant of the trees:* Assyria also is to have her remnant, a pitiable one, which survives the raging forest fire of judgment. **20.** *the remnant:* This is a separate oracle connected with what precedes by the word "remnant." It could come from either the early or later part of Isaiah's ministry, more probably from the latter since it was only under Sennacherib that Judah experienced invasion by the Assyrian army (cf. chs. 36–39). Isaiah looks to the day when Judah will depend neither on Assyria nor any other power; she will lean only upon the God of Israel. **21.** *a remnant shall return:* The phrase is identical with the name of Isaiah's son Shear-jashub, carrying with it the double aspect of promise and threat.

24 **24–27.** These verses resume the thought of vv. 12–19, pronouncing relief from the Assyrian oppressor. The historical background is probably the period of disaster shortly after the invasion of Sennacherib in 701. **26.** The reference is to Gideon's defeat of the Midianites

(Jgs 6–8). **28.** Isaiah draws a brilliant picture of the onrushing Assyrian army, moving with incredible speed to the very outskirts of Jerusalem. All the places named are relatively close to Jerusalem; the description wonderfully portrays both the speed of the invader and the panic of the Judean towns. The reference is to the invasion of Sennacherib (chs. 36–39). According to his own annals, Sennacherib mounted a two-pronged attack against the holy city. One column advanced southward along the coastal plain; a second force came over the mountain range that ran from Samaria to Jerusalem. It is the latter that is described in Isaiah's literary masterpiece (*VBW* 3, 35). A number of the places have been identified. Aiath is probably Ai (Jos 7:8), just SE of Bethel; Michmash (1 Sm 14:5–15) is near the modern village of Mukhmas; Geba (1 Sm 14:5) still bears the name and is about 6 mi. NE of Jerusalem; Ramah (1 Sm 1:19) is modern er-Ram; Gibeah of Saul is today Tell el-Ful, formerly the capital of Saul's kingdom. Gallim, modern Khirbet Kahkul, is only a few miles N of Jerusalem, as are Laishah, Madmenah, and Anathoth, home of Jeremiah. Nob is probably modern Mt. Scopus, a ridge just NE of Jerusalem and within full view of the city. **33.** *lops off the boughs:* Assyria is compared to a forest of majestic trees hewn down by Yahweh's judgment. It is a sharp counterimage to the Assyrian shaking his fist at Jerusalem.

25 (c) The Rule of Emmanuel (11:1–9). This oracle is closely related to 9:1–6, as well as to 7:14; it describes the ideal king from David's line. His charismatic gifts are enumerated in three pairs and his rule is seen as the inauguration of that hoped-for reign of idyllic peace, justice, and worldwide knowledge of Yahweh (Coppens, *À la rencontre de Dieu*, 85–108).

1. Jesse was the father of David, from whom Judean kings descended. The mention of "stump" has suggested to some scholars that the dynasty had already been destroyed; but the inference is hardly justified because the image merely suggests that the dynasty has produced a new branch. There is no solid reason, therefore, to hold that the passage is late and non-Isaian, referring to a return from the Exile or to the re-establishment of the dynasty. **2.** *the spirit of the Lord:* It is the life-giving "breath" (*rûaḥ*) that comes from Yahweh to men and endows them with extraordinary power, insight, wisdom, and other qualities enumerated in this verse. This enumeration of gifts, to which the LXX and Vg add "piety" in place of one "fear of the Lord," has become the traditional seven gifts of the Holy Spirit in mystical theology. **4.** The severe divine judgments are compared to a chastising rod and to a hot, lethal breath. **5.** The "band" or "girdle" was a loincloth worn next to the body. Justice and fidelity were to be as close to the king as these two garments. For a similar image, in which virtues are symbolized by the soldier's clothing, see Eph 6:13–17. **6.** A vision of concord in the animal world; a similar idea is expressed in the old Sumerian paradise myth of Enki and Ninhursag where it is said: "The lion kills not, the wolf snatches not the lamb." The image in this verse suggests that the Messianic era will be a paradise restored (*VBW* 3, 36). **9.** *on all my holy mountain:* All of Yahweh's land and not Jerusalem alone. Discord and war are the result of man's revolt against God. Only the knowledge of God—i.e., the observance of his will—can bring about the long-sought era of peace. The whole world, not merely Israel, will share in the coming salvation.

26 (d) The Ingathering of Dispersed Israel (11:10–16). This is a post-exilic oracle describing the restoration of Judah from the Babylonian Exile and the reunion of Israel and Judah. It has been attached to the Isaian collection at this point because of the mention of the "root of Jesse." **11.** *the Lord shall again take it in hand:* The first deliverance took place at the Exodus; return from the Exile would be a second Exodus. Pathros was in Upper Egypt; Ethiopia or Cush was farther S; Elam was E of Babylon, called Shinar in this verse. Hamath (10:9) was in central Syria on the Orontes. The "isles of the sea" were the Aegean Islands. **14.** The "Kedemites" or "sons of the East" were tribesmen from NW Arabia. They had joined with the camel-riding Midianites in their *razzia* against Palestine at the time of Gideon (Jgs 6–7). **15.** *the tongue of the Sea of Egypt:* Probably the Reed Sea traversed by the Israelites during the Exodus. *and wave his hand over the Euphrates:* The Assyrians will be smitten as well as the Egyptians. **16.** For an image of the second Exodus moving along a highway, see Is 40:3–5. "Remnant" is the technical term for the dispersed who will eventually be gathered in.

27 (e) Thanksgiving to the Holy One of Israel (12:1–6). The short chapter is made up of an enthusiastic hymn, possibly two hymns, of gratitude for salvation. Date and origin are not certain; the verses were seen to be a fitting conclusion to a major division of the prophecy. Israel had lifted up her voice in thanksgiving after the first Exodus (Ex 15:1–18); this outburst of thanksgiving would be appropriate for the announcement of the new Exodus.

1. *on that day:* Refers to the time of the new Exodus. **2.** *my courage is the Lord:* Perhaps better translated as "my protection is the Lord" (W. Moran, *CBQ* 14 [1952] 202). **3–6.** See Jgs 5:11 for the kind of scene suggested in these verses. The well was a favorite place for recounting the deeds of Yahweh; its life-giving waters symbolized his saving power. The style and language of the thanksgiving hymn are closer to Pss than to the prophetic literature.

28 **(III) Oracles Against the Gentiles (13:1–23:18).** The oracles spoken against foreign nations come from different dates and sources. Some are the work of Isaiah himself, others of later prophets who belonged to Isaiah's circle and were influenced by his message. Similar groupings of oracles against foreign nations can be found in Jer 46–51 and Ez 25–32.

(A) Oracles Against the Enemies of Israel (13:1–20:6).

29 (a) Oracles Against Babylon, Assyria, and Philistia (13:1–14:32). The historical background of the oracle pronouncing doom on Babylon is much later than Isaiah, probably between the death of Nebuchadnezzar (561) and the accession of Cyrus the Great *ca.* 550. Some think this oracle, and that of ch. 14, was originally applied to Assyria and only later referred to Babylon. **2.** Yahweh has summoned his own hosts for battle. "Gates of the volunteers" may be the name of an entrance into the city of Babylon. The volunteers or "nobles" (*n*^{e}*dîbîm*) are the commanders of the forces assembled for battle. **3.** *my dedicated soldiers:* They were "sanctified" for battle because they were participating in a holy war. **6.** Popular belief saw the day of the Lord as the day of Yahweh's vengeance on the foes of his people; with the enemies destroyed, Yahweh would reign as king. The day takes on universal proportions in this passage. For another interpretation of the day of Yahweh, see Am 5:18–20. **8.** *their faces aflame:* With feverish apprehension and shame. Some prefer to read "pains" (*ḥ*^{a}*bālîm*) for "flames" (*l*^{e}*hābîm*) and translate: "with agony written on their faces." **10.** The heavenly bodies are involved in the great cataclysm; the darkening of the stars, sun, and moon are a characteristic literary feature of this denouement (Jl 3:3–4; Lk 21:25). **12.** *gold of Ophir:* The town is probably on the Red Sea and a port of call for

Solomon's trading vessels. Wherever its location, the word has become proverbial for something precious. Note the parallelism with "pure gold." **14.** *like a hunted gazelle:* Foreigners who had enjoyed the wealth and prestige of the great city now get out as fast as possible. The figure suggests panicky haste. **17.** Up to this point no city has been specified as the victim of this catastrophic judgment; it is impossible to determine a definite historical situation for the oracle. Now the preceding oracle of judgment is applied specifically to the overthrow of Babylon. The Medes were an Indo-Aryan people from Iran who, at one time, joined forces with the Babylonians to overthrow Assyria. "To think nothing of silver" means that they could not be bribed. **21.** Ostrich and jackal were associated with desolation (43:20). The satyrs were probably demons in the form of goats (34:11). The imagery of this section is conventional and suggests utter abandonment. Actually, Cyrus spared Babylon; the description would be more suitable for the destruction of Nineveh in 612.

30 **14:1–4.** These prose lines provide a transition from the preceding oracle to the famous taunt-song that follows immediately. The nation is often called after the ancestor and patriarch "Jacob." **9.** *the nether world below is all astir:* This mocking dirge over the dead king of Babylon is unsurpassed in the OT for beauty and dramatic power. It would be worth studying exclusively as a literary masterpiece. In this verse, the poet describes the reception awaiting the dead tyrant in Sheol, the abode of the dead. A striking analogy in Ez 32:17–32 describes the descent of the Egyptian Pharaoh into Sheol. *the shades:* They are the dead—weak, unsubstantial "beings" (*r^{e}pā'îm*) who inhabit Sheol in a kind of twilight existence between life and death. **12.** *O morning star, son of the dawn:* The king is identified with a mythological figure from Canaanite religion. From the Ugaritic texts we know of Shahar, the god of "dawn" (*šāḥar*); his son is the "morning star" (*hēlāl*), giving us the mythical Helal ben Shahar. The Vg translates "morning star" as "Lucifer." Some fathers of the Church have applied this verse to the fall of Satan, prince of demons. **13.** The entire verse swarms with Canaanite imagery, now familiar from the Ugaritic literature (*VBW* 3, 39). The writer has used an ancient Canaanite myth about a lesser god's attempt to become head of the pantheon to illustrate the pride of an earthly king. The mount of assembly refers to a sacred mountain on the N Syrian coast; it was called Mt. Caseus and today is known as Jebel Aqra. The mount was in the recesses of the "north" (*Ṣāpôn;* cf. Ps 48:3), and hence the epithet Baal Zaphon for the Canaanite storm-god. **19.** *the pavement of the pit:* Lit., the "stones of the pit"; the meaning is uncertain, but it possibly refers to the hasty burial of uncovered bodies by throwing stones over them. The reference would be to the mass graves of those slain in war. **21.** *for the guilt of their fathers:* The strong corporate sense of the Semites led them to join ancestors and descendants into one person. It does not mean that the sons were personally guilty of sin; they participated in the father's guilt, for they were conceived as a part of him. **22.** A prose conclusion is provided for the poem. It may be from the same hand that wrote the transitional prose of 14:1–4a. The preceding oracle is applied specifically to Babylon. **23.** *a haunt of hoot owls and a marshland:* With the collapse of civic order and especially the breakdown of the all-important irrigation system, Babylon would be turned into a wasteland.

25. *I will break the Assyrian in my land:* The historical background of vv. 24–27 is probably the same as that of 10:5–34. Sennacherib had overreached himself and he would not succeed in taking Jerusalem during this campaign. Hezekiah had decided upon resistance, for which he had the backing of Isaiah. Yahweh would destroy the Assyrian on his own land, thus proving his sovereignty. On the position of 8:21–22, see P. W. Skehan in *CBQ* 22 (1960) 47–55. **26.** *this is the plan proposed for the whole earth:* The universality of God's design is the answer to Assyria's pretensions to world conquest. **28.** Ahaz died in 715, but the exact situation presupposed by the oracle is disputed. It is probable that the oracle is Isaiah's answer to the Philistine ambassadors ("messengers," v. 32) sent to invite Judah to join the revolt against the Assyrian overlord, Sargon II. Ahaz had been a loyal vassal of Assyria; with his death, Philistia saw the possibility of persuading Hezekiah to lend his support. **29.** The serpent's root probably stands for the Assyrian nation, which was very hard pressed in the early stages of Sargon's rule. However, Assyria weathered the storm and soon settled accounts with the rebellious vassals. Philistia would be destroyed, root and remnant. For the "flying saraph," see 30:6. **31.** The Assyrian army is compared to a storm cloud coming from the north (Jer 1:13–15; Ez 38:15–16). **32.** In Zion, the place which Yahweh had chosen, the people of Judah could find protection. This is a typical Isaian profession of faith and the reply given to the messengers.

31 (b) Oracle Against Moab (15:1–16:14). Comparison with Jer 48 suggests the possibility that we are dealing with two recensions of the same oracle. Date and historical occasion are difficult to determine; at least a post-exilic date seems ruled out by the archaic character of this lament, written in the manner of an ancient ballad. W. F. Albright has suggested that both recensions of the oracle refer to an invasion of Moab *ca.* 650 by Arabian tribes; as a result, Moab ceased to exist as an independent state (*JBL* 61 [1942] 119).

1. *Kir of Moab:* Known today as el-Kerak, this strong fortress commanded the main highway from Egypt to Mesopotamia, along the plateau E of the Jordan (*VBW* 3, 40). Because of its strength, Kir Moab was a primary objective in every attack on Moab. The city was later taken over by the Nabateans, the ruins of whose temples can be seen close by the site. **2.** *daughter Dibon:* Modern Diban, about 4 mi. N of the Arnon, where the famous Moabite Stone (→ Biblical Archaeology, 74:75) was found in 1868. Nebo is the traditional site of Moses' death; Medeba is N of Dibon. Further N are the towns mentioned in the rest of the chapter. **7.** *the Gorge of the Poplars:* Sometimes called the Brook of the Willows, it is probably the modern Wadi el-Hesa (the ancient Brook Zered), which formed the boundary between Moab and Edom (→ Biblical Geography, 73:43–46).

16:1. *send them forth, hugging the earth like reptiles:* The text is obscure; others read: "They have sent lambs to the ruler of the land," recalling Moab's tribute to Israel (2 Kgs 3:4). *from Sela:* The refugees send their appeal to Jerusalem from their temporary lodging in Edom; Sela, the "Rock," is Petra. **5.** *a throne shall be set up in mercy:* Probably means that mercy shown to the wretched Moabites would ultimately redound to the glory of David's house. **6.** *we have heard of the pride of Moab:* Because of her arrogance, Moab's plea (1–5) is rejected, The poet makes his own, in the form of a lament (7–12), the grief of the stricken land. **7.** *the raisin cakes of Kir-hareseth:* A delicacy made from pressed grapes and used in religious ceremonies as offerings to the Canaanite goddess Asherah (Hos 3:1). **9.** *therefore I weep with Jazer:* Possible to read: "Therefore I weep, O fountain [*mbk* instead of *b^{e}kî*] of Jazer" (G. Landes, *BASOR* 144 [1956] 30–37). **14.** *in three years, like those of a hireling:* The time prediction is taken from judicial terminology. Hired service lasted for three years (see Dt 15:18 where it is noted that the slave has completed double the service required of a hired man). This same stipulation of a three-year period of service is found in the Code of Hammurabi (*ANET* 170–71, 117).

32 (c) ORACLES ON DAMASCUS AND EPHRAIM (17:1–14). The date is *ca.* 734, a few years before Tiglath-pileser III took Damascus, the capital of Aram. The threats against Aram and Israel should be seen in relation to the coalition that threatened Judah at this time and that provides the background for Is 7:1–8:4. **5.** Israel shall be gleaned in judgment as a field is gleaned by the harvesters. The Valley of Rephaim was just SW of Jerusalem and must have been well known by Isaiah and his audience. **8.** *the sacred poles:* They were the symbols of the fertility goddess Asherah; they were set up at the shrines where cult was offered to this Canaanite goddess. **9.** The Hivites are the Hurrians, a non-Semitic people who were an important component of the pre-Israelite population of Canaan. The Amorites were the seminomadic people who swarmed into the Fertile Crescent during the early centuries of the 2nd millennium. The patriarchs were closely related to this latter group; Abraham's migrations are connected in some way with the extension of Amorite influence into Syria and Palestine. Sometimes the word "Amorite" is used to designate the inhabitants of Palestine at the time of the Hebr invasion under Joshua. **10.** The gardens honored the vegetation god Tammuz (Hellenistic "Adonis"), whose annual dying and rising were celebrated in the cult (Ez 8:14). **12.** Isaiah compares the advance of a hostile army to a mighty torrent sweeping all before it. The figure suggests the flash floods that are frequent in Palestine, especially in the Negeb (*VBW* 3, 42). The enemy here is Assyria, whose army included the soldiers of many vassal peoples. **13.** The enemy is compared to chaff blown away from an elevated threshing floor; the "tumbleweed" breaks off at the stem after its fruit has ripened and it is then driven by the wind across the Negeb or other desert areas. Both figures suggest the speed with which Yahweh's enemies are dispersed. The siege of 701 forms the best context for 12–14.

33 (d) ORACLES ON ETHIOPIA AND EGYPT (18:1–19:25). The occasion was the embassy sent by the 25th (Ethiopian) Dynasty of Egypt to persuade Hezekiah to join the revolt against Assyria. The date is sometime after 715, when the Ethiopians seized power in Egypt. The tone of the oracle suggests that it was given before the Ethiopians were defeated by Assyria.

1. *land of buzzing insects:* An appropriate description of the insect-laden Nile valley. *the rivers of Ethiopia:* "Ethiopia" (*Kuš*) stands for the country extending S of Egypt from modern Aswan to the fourth cataract. The "rivers" may refer to the streams issuing directly from the sources of the Nile (J. Simons, *The Geographical and Topographical Texts of the OT* [Leiden; Brill, 1959] 18–19; D. Dunham, "Notes on the History of Kush: 850 BC–AD 350," *AJA* 50 [1946] 378–88). **2.** *in papyrus boats on the waters:* Ships made from papyrus reeds bonded with pitch. *to a nation tall and bronzed:* The Ethiopians were noted for their height and their glossy skins. Isaiah bids the ambassadors take a message back to this people. **4.** *I will quietly look on:* The emphasis is upon the divine serenity, observing the scene and quietly preparing for the harvest of the nations. *like the glowing heat of sunshine:* A 5th-cent. BC ostracon, found at Arad, shows that the word translated here as "sunshine" (*ṣaḥ*) is actually the name of a month in the Hebr calendar. **5.** *then comes the cutting of branches:* At the time determined by Yahweh, the branches of the vine (Assyria) will be cut down with the pruning hook of divine judgment. When the work of judgment is finished, the Ethiopians will bring tribute to Yahweh, dwelling on Mt. Zion.

19:1–15. The oracle or "burden" (*maśśā'*) of Egypt is considered by some scholars to be post-exilic and therefore non-Isaian. But there is good reason for ascribing it to Isaiah, who often warned his fellow citizens of the folly of trusting Egypt. Moreover, a background for the oracle in Isaiah's lifetime is not difficult to find, although we cannot be absolutely sure of the crisis envisaged. Some of the verses seem to reflect the trouble in Egypt when the Ethiopian Piankhi invaded the land; or the author may have in mind the defeat of Egypt by Sargon II in 711 (Is 20). Another possibility is the conquest of Egypt by Esarhaddon in 671, an event that happened after the death of Isaiah but was foreseen by him. Historical evidence thus supports the Isaian authorship of this chapter.

34 **1.** *the Lord is riding on a swift cloud:* A familiar image of Yahweh (Ps 68:5), and not peculiar to Israel. In the Ugaritic literature, Baal is called the "cloud rider." The image suggests an impending judgment. **2.** *Egypt against Egypt:* Possibly refers to the internal breakdown of order just before the Ethiopian Dynasty took control. **4.** *the power of a cruel master:* Probably an Assyrian king, but it is possible that Isaiah refers to Piankhi, the Ethiopian. **6.** *the canals of Egypt:* The translation of *māṣôr* as "Egypt" is unlikely, especially since Isaiah had already used the ordinary word for Egypt (*miṣraim*) seven times in the first four verses. The reading *y^{e}'ore-m ṣur* (with enclitic *mem*), "cataracts," has been proposed. The reference would be to the cataracts of the upper Nile, paralleling the "main streams" (*n^{e}hārôt*) of the upper Nile. Then 19:6b would read, "the cataracts will dwindle and dry up." See also 37:25b (P. Calderone, *Bib* 42 [1961] 427–30). **8.** *the fishermen shall mourn and lament:* Egypt lived from the Nile, as it does today. Should the waters dry up, Egypt would soon become a desert. Egyptian art has left many pictures of the fishermen described by Isaiah (*VBW* 3, 44). **9.** *the combers and weavers shall turn pale:* The raising and processing of flax was an important part of the Egyptian economy from the earliest times. Many representations of the different stages in the flax industry can be found in Egyptian paintings (*VBW* 3, 45). With the drying up of the Nile, economic life in Egypt is pictured as coming to a standstill. **11.** Zoan (Tanis) was built in the Nile Delta by the Hyksos, who were later expelled from Egypt. During the 19th Dynasty, Zoan served as the capital of Egypt. In the Exodus narrative it is known as Raamses (Ex 1:11). Egyptian wisemen enjoyed a great reputation in antiquity (→ Wisdom Lit, 28:13–23). **14.** *a spirit of dizziness:* Egypt is compared to a drunkard reeling about aimlessly.

16. Five short oracles in prose, each introduced by "On that day," follow in rapid succession. Realizing that disaster has resulted from Yahweh's judgment, the Egyptians will cower in fear. **18.** Only one of the five cities is identified: the "City of the Sun," which is probably Heliopolis. **20.** Although the sacred "pillar" (*maṣṣēbâ*) was ruled out by Dt 16:22, the Jewish exiles in Egypt either ignored this prescription or did not know of it. **23.** *a highway from Egypt to Assyria:* United in the worship of Yahweh, an era of peace between the two would be inaugurated.

35 (e) THE SYMBOL OF EGYPT'S CAPTIVITY (20:1–6). The siege of Ashdod (Azotus) took place in 711; it is recorded in the Assyrian annals of Sargon II (*ANET* 286). It was revealed to Isaiah that he should perform the symbolic act described here to warn Judah not to come to the aid of Ashdod nor to revolt against Assyria. What Isaiah predicted by his dramatic action was fulfilled to the letter. The Judeans appear to have followed his advice for the Assyrians did not ravage Judah on this occasion.

1. "General" (*tartan*) is an Akkadian loanword and signifies the second in command. This is the only mention of Sargon in the OT. **2.** *go and take off the sackcloth:* Isaiah was not completely naked but garbed in a loincloth. Symbolic actions frequently marked the prophetic work of Jeremiah and Ezekiel; this is the only clear example (apart from the names given his sons) of such an action in Isaiah's ministry. **6.** *the inhabitants of this coastland:* Philistia is certainly included and probably Judah also.

(B) Visions of Catastrophe (21:1–23:18).

36 (a) Fall of Babylon (21:1–10). Although the passage is usually taken as post-exilic and referred to the capture of Babylon by Cyrus in 539, the opinion encounters certain difficulties. Would an Israelite seer of the 6th cent. have been filled with anguish over Babylon's fall? Another possibility, with a very different interpretation and historical background, has been suggested by Bright (*PCB* 503–504). Assuming that the attacker is Assyria, he believes that the Elamites and Medes had gone to Babylon's assistance and, in this, they were encouraged by the Judeans. A blow struck against Assyria was always welcome. But the outcome was what the Prophet had foreseen—the defeat of Babylon and the crushing of the revolt against Assyria. If this theory is correct, a plausible background may be found in the events of 691–689 when Babylon rebelled while Sennacherib was campaigning in the west. Elamites and other forces from Iran joined the revolt, but in 689 Sennacherib sacked Babylon and destroyed her gods (cf. 21:9c). Judah was left alone to face the menace of Assyria. Given this historical background, we can speak of Isaian authorship of the oracle, although the claim should not be unduly pressed. The commentary will use this reconstruction as a working hypothesis.

1. *the wastelands by the sea:* Probably southern Babylonia, a domain controlled by Merodach-baladan, who twice revolted against Assyrian overlordship. **2.** *go up, Elam, besiege, O Media:* With this cry, the Judeans urged the coalition to assist Babylon in her hour of peril. **5.** *they set the table:* Probably the Judeans were prematurely celebrating Babylon's victory. *oil the shield:* The Prophet warns that the banqueters must get ready to fight; the bad news would come soon. Oiling preserved the shields, which were made of wood or metal, covered with leather. **6.** *go, station a watchman:* Isaiah is the watchman (vv. 8–9). **10.** *my people who have been threshed:* The note is one of great compassion. Judah has suffered, but more lies in store for her now that Assyria has beaten down Babylon's revolt.

37 (b) Oracles on Edom and Arabia (21:11–17). Connection with the preceding oracle is difficult to prove, especially because the oracle on Edom is so cryptic. The reason for juxtaposing the oracles on Seir (Edom) and Arabia may be the geographical proximity of the two countries. **11.** *watchman, how much longer the night?:* In the OT, suffering is often associated with the night. **12.** *morning has come, and again night:* The answer is equivocal. Perhaps it means that the future holds both trouble and respite. The future is unsure; so Edom is invited to inquire later. **13.** *O caravans of Dedanites:* Dedan was in N Arabia. The inhabitants were apparently forced to abandon their usual highways and watering places, to seek refuge in the arid wastelands. **14.** The people of Tema, also in N Arabia, are asked to bring relief to the Dedanites. The historical situation is uncertain but the period of Assyrian invasions would suit the description of the battle very well. **15.** Caravaneers and tribesmen would be no match for the heavily armed and magnificently trained Assyrian army. **16.** Within a year the strong N Arabian tribe of Kedar (Jer 2:10) would be destroyed.

38 (c) Oracle on the Valley of Vision (22:1–14). Isaiah is exceedingly bitter over the carefree irresponsibility of unrepentant Jerusalem. The most likely historical situation would be just after Sennacherib lifted the siege of Jerusalem in 701. The unrestrained rejoicing over their temporary good fortune blinded the people to the ultimate reckoning that would eventually overtake the city. **2.** *O city full of noise and chaos:* The celebration was loud and frenzied. **3.** *all your leaders fled away together:* The army was a disgrace; Sennacherib reports that some of Hezeḳiah's soldiers deserted. Judah had reason to be ashamed rather than exultant. **6.** All the people mentioned were allies of the Assyrians, who ringed Jerusalem about and prepared the final assault. **8.** *the House of the Forest:* A large armory constructed of cedar by Solomon (1 Kgs 7:2; 10:17). The people are chided for making military preparations while they gave no thought to God, the builder of the city. The making of a reservoir (11) is a reference to the basin built by Hezekiah to receive the waters as they emptied out of the Siloam tunnel. **12–13.** Yahweh's invitation to repentance was met by reckless banqueting and the moral cynicism expressed in their irresponsible summons to eat and drink.

39 (d) Oracle Against the Royal Steward (22:15–25). Occasionally the prophets bitterly denounced individuals who obstructed their work or distorted their message (Am 7:16–17; Jer 20:1–6). Shebna was one of the court officials who had tried to persuade Hezekiah to revolt against Assyria and send for Egyptian support, directly opposing Isaiah's policy of noninvolvement (Is 7:4). **16.** *a sepulcher on a height:* Shebna had cut out for himself a sepulcher on some high place, eschewing the subterranean burial plot customary at that time (*VBW* 3, 48). It is possible that the very tomb seems to have been discovered, at the foot of Mt. Olivet on the eastern side of the Kidron Valley. Inscribed over the entrance were the words: "This is [the sepulcher of...] yahu who is over the house...." The name Shebna may well be an abbreviated form of the theophoric name Shebnayahu. Paleographically, the inscription suits the period of Hezekiah (cf. N. Avigad, *IsrEJ* 3 [1953] 137–52). **18.** *you and the chariots you glory in:* Like Absalom (2 Sm 15:1) and Adonijah (1 Kgs 1:5), the royal steward took to riding in chariots as a sign of his high rank. **20.** *Eliakim, son of Hilkiah:* Is 36:3–22 shows that Eliakim did, in fact, succeed Shebna as the officer "over the house." **22.** *the key of the House of David:* The key, symbol of the majordomo's authority to grant or deny admittance to the royal presence, was worn over the shoulder. The images used here to denote the authority of the steward are very similar to those of Mt 16:19 (J. Emerton, *JTS* 13 [1962] 325–31) and Jn 20:23. **25.** This prose supplement describes the ultimate downfall of Eliakim, brought to disaster by dispensing patronage to members of his own family. Nepotism had loosened the firmly secured peg and the whole family went down in Eliakim's collapse. From Is 36:3,22; 37:2, it would seem that Shebna's downfall was not complete, for he appears in these passages, dating from 701, as a royal secretary. This discrepancy would argue for a demotion rather than a complete expulsion from royal service; of course, it may be that Shebna later suffered total disgrace when the folly of his pro-Egyptian policy became evident.

40 (e) Oracles on Tyre (23:1–18). The first part of the chapter, vv. 1–14, vividly describes the shock caused by the news of Tyre's destruction. The historical background of this catastrophe visited upon the great Phoenician island and fortress is not clearly indicated, but there is no compelling reason to deny that it belongs to the Assyrian period. The oracle would thus be authentically Isaian (W. Rudolph, *ZAW* 72 [1960] 76).

1. *O ships of Tarshish:* See comment on 2:16. As the ships approach port, they learn that the city has been destroyed. They were returning from a commercial mission to Cyprus (*Chettim*, or Kittim). **2.** Instead of "silence," read "mourn," a meaning already attested in the Ugaritic literature (Dahood, *CBQ* 22 [1960] 400–401; N. Lohfink, *VT* 12 [1962] 275–77). *whose messengers crossed the sea:* Instead of reading "messengers," it has been suggested that we substitute "salesmen," noting the parallelism with "merchants of Sidon" (Dahood, *CBQ* 22 [1960] 403–404). **3.** Trade relations between Egypt and Phoenicia existed from the earliest times. **4.** *I have not been in labor, nor given birth:* The Phoenicians, as a great maritime power, were thought of as nurtured by the sea. Here the sea repudiates her children. **7.** Phoenician merchants brought Canaanite culture to such distant lands as Greece, North Africa, Sardinia, and Spain (Ez 27). **8.** *Tyre, the bestower of crowns:* An allusion to the power of Tyre, which could make and unmake kings in its trading colonies of the Mediterranean basin. Merchants formed the aristocracy of Tyre at this time. **9.** In this favorite Isaian theme, human pride crumbles before the power of Yahweh. **13.** The brackets in CCD indicate a gloss interrupting the sequence of the lament; it was probably inserted much later to explain that Tyre's definitive overthrow did not take place until the Chaldean period in the 6th cent. (Ez 26–28).

15. *seventy years:* A conventional expression for a certain period of time; here, there is a hint that the period may be the duration of a dynasty. Verses 15–18 are probably a much later addition to the Isaian collection; the song mockingly alludes to the commercial revival of Tyre, which is compared to a harlot's return to her profession. **18.** *her merchandise and her hire shall be sacred to the Lord:* Tyre's wealth will, at that time, be used for the support of Yahweh's people. The dedication of Phoenician profits to the Lord recalls Is 45:14, and especially 60:4–16.

41 **(IV) The Apocalypse of Isaiah (24:1–27:13).** These chapters look beyond the events of here and now to the final judgment of Yahweh. They make a suitable sequel to the preceding oracles against the Gentiles. The whole section shows how easily prophecy could pass over into apocalyptic with its characteristic themes of universal judgment, the victory of Yahweh celebrated by a banquet on his mountain, the ingathering of Israel, and others. That this transition could be made so easily results from the fact that both the prophets and the writers of apocalyptic shared a common eschatological tradition. The only difference is found in the greater elaboration of the eschatological element in apocalyptic. Some commentators refuse the designation of "apocalypse" to Is 24–27, claiming that many features of apocalyptic writing are absent here. J. Lindblom, for example, calls these chapters the "Isaiah Cantata," and he dates the section in the Persian era. For a study of apocalyptic and its relation to prophecy, see B. Vawter (*CBQ* 22 [1960] 33–46) and for chs. 24-27, see G. Fohrer (*CBQ* 25 [1963] 34–45).

42 **(A) The Coming Devastation (24:1–23).** **2.** See Hos 4:9, but here the horizon is world wide. The rest of the verse pictures a total upheaval of the social order. **3.** God's word had once established order in the world (Gn 1); the picture is that of a return to primeval chaos. **5.** *the ancient covenant:* The covenant with Noah (Gn 9:9), which envisages a pact between God and all mankind. When this covenant is broken, judgment comes as a new flood. **10.** The "chaos" recalls Gn 1:2; it is not clear whether the poet has a particular city in mind or a symbol of evil opposed to the city of God. **14.** *these lift up their voice:* They are the ones who have escaped the judgment. Verses 14–16a, a hymn of thanksgiving by the remnant, sharply contrast with the terrifying picture of judgment. **18.** *the windows on high:* Rain was thought to come through the windows of heaven (Gn 7:11). **19.** Palestine was well acquainted with earthquakes in OT times. The prophets often drew lessons from this awesome convulsion of nature (*VBW* 3, 51). **21.** *the host of the heavens:* The sun, moon, and stars—heavenly bodies that were sometimes worshiped, even by the Israelites (Dt 4:19; 2 Kgs 17:16). **23.** *glorious in the sight of his elders:* The 70 elders beheld the glory of Yahweh at Sinai (Ex 24:9–11); at the end of time, Israel's elders would again behold Yahweh enthroned in royal majesty.

(B) Hymns of Thanksgiving; Prophecies of Salvation (25:1–27:1).

43 (a) Psalms of Thanksgiving and Praise (25:1–12). **1–5.** This thanksgiving psalm celebrates the victory of Yahweh as something that has already taken place. This piece is possibly the adaptation to a wider perspective of an old hymn celebrating the fall of a hostile city. **6.** *on this mountain:* This is the eschatological banquet; the imagery of a celestial banquet as a symbol of eternal happiness can be traced far back in pre-Israelite, Canaanite literature. **8.** *he will destroy death forever:* The sentence of death (Gn 3:19) is cancelled out. For the same view expressed in similar language, see Ap 7:17; 21:4. The words at the Last Supper referring to the Messianic banquet (Mt 26:29; Mk 14:25; Lk 22:18) look ahead to the definitive triumph of Christ's kingdom. **10.** The mention of a specific country, Moab, is surprising; probably it is the reuse of an original oracle against Moab to express, symbolically, the fate of Israel's enemies. There is no need to emend "Moab" to "enemy" (*'ōyēb*).

44 (b) Confidence in Yahweh the Vindicator (26:1–27:1). **1.** *a strong city:* It is Jerusalem, contrasted with the "city of chaos" (24:10). **4.** *rock:* This common OT metaphor expresses the dependability of Yahweh. **8.** *your name:* The name stands for the very being of the one named. **13.** *other lords:* Refers mainly to earthly rulers but there may be a reference to the gods of these alien rulers. **19.** More than a conviction of national revival is expressed; there is an explicit hope in the resurrection of individuals (S. Baron, *A Social and Religious History of the Jews* [vol. 1; 2nd ed.; rev.; N.Y. 1952] 137). The LXX and 1QIs[a] read: "They who dwell in the dust shall awake and sing for joy." *a dew of light:* Either the morning dew, which brings vegetation to life, or the dew of the heavenly regions of light (Ps 103:2). **20.** Judgment is not yet finished and God's people are told to take shelter until it has passed. **21.** Guilt has stained the earth with blood. No crime can be hidden from Yahweh.

27:1. *Leviathan, the fleeing serpent:* The identical phrase occurs in a Canaanite myth from Ugarit where Lotan (Leviathan) is described as the "fleeing serpent" or "primeval serpent" (W. F. Albright, *BASOR* 83 [1941] 39). This and other mythical monsters of ancient Near Eastern literature have become, in the OT, symbols of forces in rebellion against Yahweh.

45 **(C) Yahweh's Vineyard; Miscellaneous Fragments (27:2–13).** **2.** Verses 2–4 remind us of 5:1–7, but there is some development. Eventually Israel will become a luxuriant vine filling the whole earth (for a literary analysis of the poem, see L. Alonso Schökel [*EstEc* 34 (1960) 767–74]). **6.** As in 5:7, the identification of the vineyard is held off until the last line. **7.** The passage is obscure and has little connection with what precedes. In general, we have a reflection on the meaning of Israel's suffering. The Prophet asks if Israel will be chastised as severely as those who oppressed her. The implication is that she will not. **9.** *this, then, shall be the expiation of Jacob's guilt:* Not by suffering but by rooting out idolatrous practices. For the "sacred poles," see 17:8.

10. *the fortified city:* Not Jerusalem, as some commentators hold, but a hostile city whose identity escapes us. Perhaps it is the same city whose destruction was announced in 24:10–13. **12.** The Apocalypse closes with two short oracles announcing the triumphant return of the dispersed Israelites. The "valley of Egypt" is more properly the Brook of Egypt, modern Wadi el-Arish, about 50 mi. SW of Gaza. The divine threshing will separate the faithful Israelites from the chaff. **13.** A great trumpet will sound to gather the elect on the last day (Mt 24:31; 1 Cor 15:52; 1 Thes 4:16). Here the trumpet sounds to summon Israelites outside the holy land to come and worship Yahweh on Zion.

46 **(V) Oracles of Warning and Promise for Israel and Judah (28:1–33:24).** The material in these chapters is substantially Isaian and concerns the spiritual and military crisis of Israel and Judah during the second half of the 8th cent. BC.

(A) Covenant with Death (28:1–29).

(a) Drunken Leaders of Yahweh's People (28:1–13). **1.** This woe oracle was spoken before the fall of Samaria in 721. Samaria was set upon a hill and surrounded by a strong wall; its choice site suggested the image of a faded crown on the head of a besotted reveler. **2.** Assyria, the instrument of divine vengeance, is compared to a hurricane of great destructive force. Assyrian kings occasionally compared their invasions to the terror of a great storm (*ANET* 277b, 284a). **4.** An early ripening fig was considered a great delicacy. Late summer is the normal time for figs to ripen. **5.** The poet takes up the imagery of the preceding verses but there is a sudden shift of thought to deliverance for the remnant. **6.** Justice and peace were the two blessings most ardently sought in the Messianic age (2:4; 9:6; 11:1–9). The ideal king dispensed justice and brought peace by defending his country against enemies. **7.** An indictment of Judah's leaders, including priest and prophet; intoxication has robbed them of all powers of discernment. **9.** The scoffing taunt of Isaiah's drunken enemies: Would he lecture them like children? **10.** *command on command:* Only the Hebrew adequately conveys the topers' mocking imitation of the Prophet: *ṣaw lāṣāw ṣaw lāṣāw qaw lāqāw qaw lāqāw*. They are mimicking a class of young students repeating by rote what the teacher tells them. Note how the mockery is taken up in v. 13 and put on the lips of Judah's captors. The lesson they had failed to learn in Hebrew would be taught to them in Assyrian! W. W. Hallo (*JBL* 77 [1958] 324–38) believes that in vv. 10 and 13 we have recovered in proper order a fragment from the ancient system of west Semitic names for the letters of the alphabet. The verses would be a sarcastic reference to a "spelling lesson" administered by Isaiah. **11.** In the language of the Assyrian conqueror, God will speak to those who mock.

47 (b) A Covenant with Death (28:14–22). The background of the oracle seems to be the negotiations for an alliance with Egypt against Assyria when Sennacherib was threatening all Palestine. In pursuing this course, the rulers of Judah were inviting invasion and destruction. The structure of power politics offered a false security; in contrast to it Yahweh would build his own structure (vv. 16–17) whose cornerstone would be faith and its measuring rods judgment and justice. **15.** *a covenant with death:* There is an allusion here to Mot, the Canaanite god of "death" (Hebr *mwt*) and Sheol (S. Rin, *VT* 9 [1959] 324–25). Since Israel sought security in a covenant with Egypt, the "death" of this verse would be Osiris or Seth, or some Egyptian god associated with death. Instead of covenanting with the living God, they put their trust in lifeless idols to avoid the "overwhelming scourge" of Assyria. **16.** *I am laying a stone in Zion:* See 8:14. The cornerstone is called a "tested" stone. This is an Egyptian word for a hard stone made either of granite or diorite (T. Lambdin, *JAOS* 73 [1953] 148). The stone is the salvation guaranteed to the Davidic dynasty. A cornerstone was usually inscribed; this one probably read: "He who puts his faith in it shall not be shaken." Trust in God is the idea underlying the image of the cornerstone. This unquestioning trust is a common Isaian theme (7:9; 8:17; 26:4; 30:15). **17.** Yahweh, the builder, will use two standards or tests. His line will be "right" and his level or plummet will be "justice." **19.** *terror alone...:* Understanding the message can bring only dismay. **20.** A proverb describing a completely frustrating situation. **21.** Mount Perazim refers to David's victory over the Philistines (2 Sm 5:20). Although Assyria might seem to be the punisher, it would really be the invisible Yahweh, as was the case in David's victory.

48 (c) Parable of the Farmer (28:23–29). God deals with the world as a wise farmer works his land. All actions are suited to the proper time and place. The piece is written in the spirit and style of the wisdom literature. **24.** The "loosening" describes the farmer's chopping up the large clods of earth. Harrowing is the work of smoothing and leveling off the surface of the soil, a very important process on the sloping Judean hillsides where terrace farming was extensively practised (*VBW* 3, 54). **25.** *scatter gith and sow cumin:* These plants are used for spicing food. **27.** The type of herb determines the kind of instrument to be used in threshing. Gith and cumin were relatively tender plants; the threshing sledge would have ruined them; hence, rods or flails were used.

49 **(B) Judgment Upon Jerusalem; Vision of Redemption (29:1–24).** The passage dates from the time just before the siege of Jerusalem in 701. This was the great crisis under Hezekiah. The thought ranges from bitter castigation to bright hope of redemption.

1. *Ariel:* This name for Jerusalem comes from Akkadian *arallu*, meaning both the "underworld" and the "mountain of the gods." Here the word probably suggests the altar of the Temple, built after the style of the Akkadian ziggurat or temple tower that symbolized the mountain of the gods. No matter how often and piously the people observe the festivals, distress is inevitable. **5.** *then suddenly, in an instant:* Yahweh intervenes for the sake of his people, and Jerusalem is preserved (vv. 7–8). **9–10.** The imagery is reminiscent of 6:9–10. The moral lethargy of Judah is compared to a "deep sleep" (Hebr *tardēmâ*). Persistent refusal to listen to conscience inevitably leads to the loss of all moral sense. **11–12.** Papyrus was used for a scroll; it was rolled up and fastened with a wax seal (Ap 5:1) so that its contents could not be read. The man who could read it refuses; the uneducated is unable to read it. The meaning of the vision is sealed in impenetrable mystery; the people are spiritually illiterate. **13–14.** Their formalism and ritualism will be answered by Yahweh's "wondrous" dealing, which will reduce their wisdom to folly.

15. *those who hide their plans:* The pro-Egyptian party (30:1) which sought salvation in alliances rather than in Yahweh. **16.** *as though the potter were taken to be the clay:* In their folly they attempt to reverse the relationship between the Creator and creature. **17.** The tone is completely different, for transformation and redemption are promised. Some commentators believe that these lines are from a later hand, but Isaiah's steadfast hope for his people should caution us against accepting this opinion too readily. The verse is probably a proverb, the exact sense of which is now lost. It probably means that God's plan for redemption will be as great a reversal as the one described in the proverb. **20.** The "tyrant" is the proud and selfish ruler who is responsible for the social misery that Isaiah saw around him. The removal of the ruthless oppressors is one of the signs of the Messianic era. **21.** *those whose mere word condemns a man:* By perjured testimony.

(C) Judgment Upon Egypt and Assyria (30:1–31:9).

50 (a) FUTILITY OF AN ALLIANCE WITH EGYPT (30:1–7). **1–3.** An embassy was already on the way to enlist Egyptian support for Judah's rebellion against Assyria on the occasion of Sargon's death in 705. This action was directly opposed to God's plan as announced by Isaiah. **4.** Zoan (Tanis) was close to the NE frontier of Egypt; Hanes (Heracleopolis Magna of the Romans) was S of Memphis near the Fayyum. The Pharaoh in question was most likely Shabaka of the 25th (Ethiopian) Dynasty. **6.** *of the viper and flying saraph:* Desert pests that made transit through the Negeb especially troublesome (Nm 21:4–9). The embassy was laden with gifts for the Pharaoh (*VBW* 3, 56). **7.** Rahab was a mythological monster of chaos; here, as elsewhere, the name is applied to Egypt (Ps 86:4).

51 (b) TESTAMENT OF ISAIAH (30:8–17). Summarizes the prophetic complaint against Judah. The time is the critical period between 705 and 701. Isaiah orders his reproach to be put on the record. **8.** The "tablet" was made of wood; the "record" was a papyrus or leather scroll. **10.** *conjure up illusions:* They do not ask to be deceived but to hear "smooth things" (Am 2:12; 1 Kgs 22:13). **15.** Isaiah counsels political inactivity and the avoidance of foreign alliances that could only harm Judah. Only by politically "sitting still" ("waiting" in CCD), could Judah be saved from the Assyrian threat (M. Dahood, *CBQ* 20 [1958] 41–43).

52 (c) PATIENCE AND MERCY OF GOD (30:18–26). This oracle is ordinarily taken as an expansion of Isaiah's thought; all except the first verse is written in prose and the prose section is simply an elaborate commentary on the introductory line of poetry. **20.** The meaning is not that they will see him face to face (Ex 33:20; Is 6:5) but that they will again see his marvelous works. **24.** *will eat silage tossed to them:* A sign of great prosperity for the silage was usually reserved for cattle who were being fattened for slaughter; work animals were given a coarser diet (*VBW* 3, 57). **25.** *the day of the great slaughter:* A surprising thought in this picture of restored prosperity; possibly it refers to Yahweh's judgment on the enemies of Israel, but the fragment may be displaced from another section. **26.** Nature becomes transfigured during this era of blessing.

53 (d) YAHWEH JUDGES ASSYRIA (30:27–33). **27.** The name expresses the essence of the one named; it stands for the person himself. **28.** *like a flood in a ravine:* In the springtime, flash floods pour through the wadies and make them raging torrents. **30.** *his glorious voice:* Thunder is the voice of God. **33.** "Pyre" is "topheth," meaning "roaster" or "cooking stove," which was identified with the Valley of Ben-Hinnom, S and W of ancient Jerusalem (2 Kgs 23:10). There is a bitter play on words in the phrase "prepared for the king" (Hebr *melek*), immediately recalling the infamous sacrifices to the god Molech. In other words, Yahweh's "topheth" or "roaster" is ready for another *mlk*—the king of Assyria.

54 (e) TRUST NOT IN EGYPT; YAHWEH DEFENDS JERUSALEM (31:1–9). The oracle concerns the same subject as 30:1–7 and, like it, comes from the period shortly before 701. The theme of trust in Yahweh rather than in weapons continues throughout.

1. Lack of cavalry and chariotry had been a weakness in Israel's army until Solomon remedied the deficiency. But even then, and later, the Israelites, depending chiefly on footsoldiers, could never hope to compete on even terms with the strong cavalry and chariot forces of the great empires. Being concentrated in the central hill country, Israel did not develop this kind of warfare and was at a great disadvantage when battles took place on the plains where chariotry could maneuver. **2.** *yet he too is wise:* This sarcastic remark reminds Judah that Yahweh also knows how to plan a suitable fate for those who have no faith in him. Both Judah and Egypt would experience the effects of divine judgment. **3.** The contrast between "flesh" and "spirit" is one between weakness and strength. **4.** The figure of the lion applies to Assyria, which had devastated Judah and was about to devour Jerusalem as a lion devours his prey. The band of shepherds are the Egyptians, whose noisy presence had not deterred the Assyrians in the least. **5.** Yahweh is compared to birds that hover over the nest, protecting the young. To "spare" (Hebr *pāsōah*) probably contains an allusion to the deliverance at the time of the Exodus; "Passover" is from the same root. **7.** *on that day:* The day of Israel's return. Each move to repentance was accompanied by a rejection of idols; the story of Israel was a history of relapse and return. **8.** *he shall flee before the sword:* 1QIs[a] reads: "He shall flee, but not from the sword [of man]." The idea is that the defeat of the Assyrians is not the result of human weapons; it is the work of an avenging Yahweh. **9.** The first part of the verse is extremely obscure. The general impression is of an army fleeing in headlong panic. The reference to the Lord's fire is in keeping with 29:6; 30:33.

(D) Miscellaneous Oracles (32:1–33:24).

55 (a) A JUST KING RULING AN ORDERED SOCIETY (32:1–8). Judah is pictured in the new age, the ideal future, when a just king would sit upon the throne, and a sense of social responsibility would characterize the relations between men. The oracle could be taken in conjunction with other promises concerning the Messianic ruler (chs. 9 and 11). It dates from the latter part of Isaiah's career.

2. The "rock" offers security from rain, wind, and burning sun. In regions where there are vast tracts of arid wasteland with little or no vegetation man can find shelter and protection only in caves or under the lee of great rocks (*VBW* 3, 59). **5.** *the fool:* Not simply a dolt but an impious and corrupt leader, as is clear from the following verse. *be called noble:* The ideal king of the future would be truly "noble" (Hebr *nādîb*) and his claim to this attribute would be found in his "noble acts" (Hebr *n[e]dîbôt* of v. 8). The corrupt leadership of the present regime offered a sad contrast. Apparently the reforms of Hezekiah had not been able to stamp out the cruel injustice of irresponsible leaders. **6–8.** These verses are written in the style of the wisdom literature and offer an expanded commentary on v. 5. There is no reason to deny these lines to Isaiah. The thought is perfectly in keeping with the prophetic message. Moreover, the wisdom genre existed long before the time of Isaiah. It is significant that Prv 25:1 gives evidence of a renaissance in sapiential writing during the time of Hezekiah.

56 (b) COMPLACENT WOMEN AND THE IDEAL ORDER TO COME (32:9–20). The passage about the overconfident women of Judah resembles 3:16–4:1. **10.** The oracle dates from 702, a year before Sennacherib's invasion of Judah. **11.** *strip yourselves bare:* A sign of mourning. **14.** *the castle will be forsaken:* Probably the royal palace. The "hill" (Hebr *'ōpel*) was the original site of Zion, S of the Temple area; the "tower" was a strongly fortified donjon. **15.** An altogether new oracle, sharply contrasting with what precedes, begins here. The date is uncertain but, as a typical prophetic oracle of the ideal future, its Isaian authorship should not be lightly abandoned. As in other parts of the OT (Ez 39:29; Jl 2:28–29; Zech 12:10), the new era is inaugurated by an outpouring of God's spirit. **17.** Justice and peace are characteristic marks of the Messianic era; with them come prosperity and stability in the social order. **20.** It would be a time of unusual security and plenty when the owner could allow his livestock to pasture without thought of drought, wild animals, or brigands.

57 (c) Judah's Peril and Future Restoration (33:1–24). The historical circumstances in back of this connected series of entreaties, laments, and promises for the future are difficult to determine. They may come from the time when Hezekiah submitted to Sennacherib in 701. Some verses (e.g., vv. 14–16) sound as though they had been used in liturgical ceremonies.

1. If the historical background we have just suggested is correct, the "destroyer" (Hebr *šōdēd*) is Assyria. Otherwise it would be some later enemy (the same word is used of Babylon in 21:2) or it might be a general designation for all the oppressors in Israel's history. **4.** *as caterpillars are gathered up:* Perhaps it should read. "as caterpillars gather" (active), suggesting the stripping of vegetation by these pests. **6.** The first line is difficult but the general meaning is clear: wisdom, etc., guarantee the stability of Judah's times. **7–9.** A description of the general breakdown in public order (Jgs 5:6). Sharon is the beautiful and fertile coastal plain of Palestine between Jaffa and the Mt. Carmel range. In ancient times it was heavily forested. Bashan is almost identical with the modern Hauran, E of the Sea of Galilee and extending N from the Yarmuk River to the vicinity of Damascus. The region was renowned for its fertility. **10.** The answer of Yahweh to the preceding lament now begins. **12.** *the peoples:* Israel's foes who come under divine judgment. **14–16.** These verses reflect a liturgy similar to Pss 15:2–5; 24:3–6; this kind of question and answer was repeated on the occasion of entering the Temple. **17.** *a king in his splendor:* Probably the ideal future king of the Messianic age rather than Yahweh himself (32:1). This concluding part of the section contains a promise for the future. Some scholars consider this bright hope an addition to the text, coming from as late as the Persian period. But there are good reasons for maintaining its authenticity as an Isaian oracle from 701. The great deliverance of Jerusalem at this time would provide a most suitable historical background for this outburst of hope concerning Jerusalem's future. **18.** *who counted the towers:* Officials of the conqueror who determined which strongpoints were to be razed. The three classes mentioned stand for oppressive overlords who are now only a distant memory. They are the tax collectors and the officials in charge of demolition. **20.** *a tent not to be struck:* An allusion to the "Tent of Reunion," which preceded the Temple as the chief Israelite sanctuary (De Vaux, *AI*, 294–97). **21.** Abundant rivers will encircle Zion as a source of blessing and defense (Ez 47). They will not be traversed by merchant ships nor, much less, by the hostile flotillas of Israel's enemies. **23.** Not only would enemy ships be unable to break through the protective streams, but their sailors would be unable to run up the sails (*VBW* 3, 60). **24.** Good health is a sign that their sins are forgiven (Ps 103:3; Mt 9:2).

58 **(VI) The Lord as Avenger of Zion (34:1–35:10).** The two chapters, striking in their contrasts, belong together as opposite sides of the same coin, i.e., Yahweh's activity in history. Both bear resemblances in style and thought to the material of Is 40–66; some scholars even attribute these chapters to Dt-Is. More probably they come from a circle influenced by the great Prophet of the Exile, and a date in the late 6th or early 5th cent. BC seems likely. The study of Is 34 as a literary composition is very instructive for its information on Hebr standards of poetic style and taste (J. Muilenburg, *JBL* 59 [1940] 339–65).

59 **(A) Judgment Upon Edom (34:1–17).** The enmity between Israel and Edom was bitter and long. It was only exacerbated when Edom, taking advantage of Judah's collapse before the Babylonians in 587, seized part of Judah's territory. The first part of the oracle (1–8) describes the outburst of divine fury; the second part (9–17) describes the utter destruction resulting from Yahweh's vengeance.

1. The world is summoned to a great trial in which Yahweh passes sentence on Edom. **2.** *he has doomed them:* Given them up to "destruction" (Hebr *ḥerem*) as in holy war (Jos 6:17); the idea is repeated in v. 5. **3.** *the mountains shall run with their blood:* The picture is gruesome but these are probably the only images available to the OT poet when he wishes to describe such a devastating judgment. The spirit, however, is not one of blind hatred; Edom, an enemy of God's people, merited judgment. The scene of total destruction should be balanced by the following chapter giving the other side of Yahweh's intervention in history. **4.** The judgment is cosmic, touching all creation (Mk 13:24–25). **6.** Bozrah was the leading city of Edom (Is 63:1), and it is known today as Buseirah.

9. Edom undergoes the fate of Sodom and Gomorrah (Gn 19:24–28). **11.** The "owl," along with the "raven," was a symbol of desolation (*VBW* 3, 61). The picture of once fertile soil turned into the abode of desert fowl is particularly appropriate for Edom, part of whose land was waterless desert. The "empty waste" is a place of "waste" (Hebr *tōhû*) and "void" (Hebr *bōhû*), expressions to denote the primeval chaos (Gn 1:2). *for satyrs to dwell in:* Added by the LXX; for the meaning of these creatures, see comment on 13:21. **14.** The "lilith" is a female demon whose haunt was desert places. The name comes from Sumerian *lil*, meaning "wind" or "spirit." She is known as *lilîtu* in Akkadian, and has appeared in an 8th-century BC Canaanite charm from Arslan Tash. She turns up later in rabbinical lore as the female who deceived Adam. **16.** *the book of the Lord:* The book of life where the destiny of those who were to be saved was recorded (Ps 139:16; Mal 3:16; Dn 12:1). The meaning is that the names of the wild desert animals are recorded in the book as destined to occupy the territory of Edom. This is to be Edom's fate.

60 **(B) Joy of Restoration (35:1–10).** This exultant outburst of joy and confidence is set off sharply from the preceding chapter. The imagery of the passage resembles Dt-Is (40:3–5; 43:19) and evokes the picture of a second exodus. **2.** Cf. comment on 33:9. **3.** The following message of consolation presupposes the Exile. **5.** *eyes of the blind be opened:* The most unfortunate among the exiled will be among the first to share these blessings (see Mt 11:5 for a sign that the Messianic age has arrived). **8.** The "way" is holy because it leads to Zion, the holy city. **9.** The "redeemed" are those who are being brought out of exile. They have been ransomed from bondage as had their forefathers at the time of the Exodus. The NT (Jn 6:48–51; 1 Cor 10:1–4; Heb 12:18–24) understands the coming of Christ in terms of a new and definitive Exodus. Note that the Exodus from Egypt is a type both for the return from Exile (OT) and for salvation through Christ (NT).

61 **(VII) Historical Supplement (36:1–39:8).** These chapters form an historical appendix, bringing to a conclusion the first part of the Book of Isaiah. The material covered here has been excerpted, with some modifications, from 2 Kgs 18–20 (→ 1–2 Kings, 10:68–72). The Psalm of Hezekiah (38:9–20) is missing in Kgs. The reason for the insertion of this prose account in Isaiah is evidently the major part played by the Prophet during this crisis under Hezekiah.

This brilliant and vivid description of the Assyrian threat to Judah permits the reader to relive the excitement and tension of an ancient confrontation between the dreaded might of Assyria and the people of God, represented by the tiny kingdom of Judah. But the chapters have also left us with a problem that has exercised scholars for many years; the evidence is so complex that it is premature to speak of a certain solution. This is a case in which the opinion may seem best suited to explain the historical data even though there is no unanimity with regard to that solution. Are we dealing here with one or two invasions of Sennacherib into Judean territory? The position taken in this commentary will be that the evidence favors the assumption that Sennacherib conducted two campaigns against Judah, one in 701 and the second *ca.* 688. In the latter campaign, Judah was marvelously delivered by a crippling blow inflicted on the Assyrian army. The following commentary on the text will be based on the two-campaign theory that Albright describes as appearing "to have won the field beyond serious challenge."

(Albright, W. F., *BASOR* 130 [1953] 8–11; 141 [1956] 25–26. Bright, *Hist.* 282–87; *PCB* 514–15. De Vaux, R., *RB* 63 [1956] 426. Freedman, D. N., *BANE* [Fest. W. Albright; N.Y., 1961] 211. Hallo, W. W., *BA* 23 [1960] 59. Rowley, H. H., *BJRylL* 44 [1962] 395–431. Noth, *Hist.* 265–69.)

62 **(A) Invasion(s) of Sennacherib (36:1–37:38).** **1.** The date is 701; the reign of Hezekiah is dated 715(?)–687, and that of Sennacherib, 705–681. Corroborative evidence for the campaign is found in Sennacherib's annals, where he states that he took 46 of Judah's cities and laid siege to Jerusalem (*ANET* 288a). On this occasion, Hezekiah, "shut up like a bird in a cage," sued for peace in the hope of saving his ravaged country. At this point we should insert the evidence supplied by 2 Kgs 18:14–16, which describes in detail the capitulation of Hezekiah and the heavy tribute imposed upon him by the victorious Sennacherib (*VBW* 3, 63). **2.** *from Lachish the king of Assyria sent his commander:* According to the theory adopted here, this campaign is Sennacherib's second against Jerusalem (*ca.* 688). What took place between 701 and 688 may be summarized briefly. Sennacherib had put down the revolt of coastal Palestinian cities and had dealt a crushing blow to the Egyptian army coming to the relief of Ekron. He then turned on Judah, which had joined the revolt, and punished her in the manner described in v. 1. All this took place in and around 701, but Sennacherib's troubles were far from over. Within a decade he faced open revolt in Babylon, and, in 691, he was badly beaten by a coalition of Babylonians, Elamites, and other disaffected groups anxious to strike a blow at Assyria. It was only in 689 that Sennacherib was able to put down the revolt in his homeland and devastate rebellious Babylon.

Meanwhile, Assyrian trouble in Mesopotamia encouraged the west (Palestine and Egypt) to try revolt once again. Goaded on by the energetic Tirhakah, an army commander who had become coregent of Egypt in 690–689, the cities of Syria and Palestine were led to join the rebellion. It is on this occasion that we assume that Hezekiah, encouraged by promises of Egyptian aid, defied Assyria by refusing to pay his annual tribute. It would also be on this same occasion that Isaiah backed the royal revolt, assuring Hezekiah that Jerusalem would not fall. If this theory is correct, it means that the historian has telescoped two campaigns of Sennacherib against Jerusalem; the record of the first campaign would be found only in 36:1 (with the valuable supplementary material of 2 Kgs 18:14–16), and the rest of the account would concern only the second campaign of *ca.* 688. The "commander" (Hebr *rabšāqēh*, the "Chief Steward" or "Chief of Staff"), is a title, not a personal name. *the conduit of the upper pool:* See comment on 7:3. **4.** *the great king:* This customary title for Assyrian rulers is affirmed by Assyrian royal inscriptions. **5.** The rebellion is that of *ca.* 689, fomented by the Egyptians. In 701, Hezekiah did not rebel; he surrendered to Sennacherib and agreed to pay tribute (2 Kgs 18:14–16). **7.** This allusion is a contemptuous one, to the religious reform of Hezekiah (2 Kgs 18:3–5); the implication is that Yahweh, angered by the removal of his altars, would give Judah no help. **10.** The insinuation is that, in destroying Judah, they are the instruments of Yahweh (10:5).

63 **11.** *Aramaic . . . Judean:* Aramaic was dialectically different from Hebrew and, by the 8th cent. had become the international language of diplomacy and commerce, as attested in this scene. The Judean leaders were afraid that the common people would despair if they understood the Assyrian terms. **16.** *eat of his own vine and of his own fig tree:* A conventional way of describing normal and prosperous times (e.g., 1 Kgs 4:25). **19.** *the gods of Hamath and Arpad:* For the location see comment on 10:9. Sepharvaim appears as *Spryym* in 1QIs[a] in this passage and also in 37:13. The Sibraim of Ez 47:16 is another spelling of the same name; *WHAB* locates the town near Riblah on the Orontes. All three places were in the path of Sennacherib's invading army.

37:4. See Is 7:3; 10:20–21; etc., for the Isaian teaching of the "remnant." **7.** The "spirit" (Hebr *rûaḥ*) is a force that would induce Sennacherib to take action. In this case it was a rumor of trouble on the home front. **8.** Libnah is the modern Tell es-Safi, about 10 mi. N of Lachish. **9.** Tirhakah was an Egyptian army commander who became Pharaoh of Egypt in 685–684. Sennacherib's reverses at home encouraged him to foment rebellion. Once the Assyrian army had settled matters in Mesopotamia, they turned to the west. Our Assyrian sources for the reign of Sennacherib virtually dry up at this point and we do not know how he dealt with the rebellious Tirhakah. **10.** *again he sent envoys:* It is difficult to determine whether this reference is merely a doublet of the first account (36:2–21) or that embassies were sent on two different occasions—but during the same siege. **12.** Gozan (Assyrian Guzana) was a city or district through which the Khabur river flowed. Haran, in modern Turkey, was a very ancient city renowned for its worship of the moon-god Sin. Rezeph was W of Haran in the direction of Palmyra. It had, by this time, been in Assyrian hands for several centuries. The "Edenites" came from Bit-adini, an Aramaic city-state between the Euphrates and Balikh Rivers. Telassar was a site in the territory of Bit-adini. **13.** *king of the cities:* Instead of the "cities," read the proper name La'ir, discovered by G. R. Driver in the Arsames correspondence, Aramaic documents of the 5th cent. BC. It was situated on the border of Elam. Ana, or Hena, was in Syria, but the exact site is unknown; Ava, or Ivvah, is probably modern Tell Kefr Aya, near Riblah. The wars referred to in these verses were waged by Assyria when the kingdom was extending its imperial limits to the shores of the Mediterranean, during the 9th and 8th cents. BC. **17.** Sennacherib had insulted God by the mocking reference to his power to save Judah

(36:14–20). **22–29.** This is a taunt-song in which the ephemeral triumphs of Assyria are contrasted with the hidden but irresistible plan of Yahweh. Assyria had brought ruin on others, but when she had finished the task designed to her in the divine plan, Assyria would be chained like a wild beast. The oracle should be compared with 10:5–16.

64 **25.** The abrupt mention of Egypt is surprising, coming immediately after the description of Lebanon's forests. Moreover, it is not Sennacherib who is being taunted, but Esarhaddon, who invaded Egypt in 671. It has been suggested (see comment on 19:6) that we read *y*[e]*'ōrê-m ṣûr* with the meaning "mountain streams." Then 25b would read, "and I dried up . . . all the mountain streams" (Calderone, *op. cit.*, 424–26). **27.** Ps 129:6 refers to the tender grass that sprouted on the flat roofs of Palestinian houses; lacking normal moisture and directly exposed to sun and wind, it quickly withered. 1QIs[a] has preserved, at the end of the verse, an original reading superior to the MT and LXX. It describes the grass "which is parched by the 'east wind' [Hebr *qādîm*]" (S. Iwry, *BASOR* 147 [1957] 28–29). **30.** The sign for Hezekiah guarantees that a remnant will survive. Note the tone changes suddenly from threatening, addressed to the Assyrian king, to hopeful, addressed to Hezekiah. *you shall eat the aftergrowth:* For the current year and the following one the land shall lie uncultivated. Then, in the third year, customary prosperity shall return. The "aftergrowth" consists of that which has grown from spilled kernels (Lv 25:5,11). The following year the people would have as food only the wild grain that grows without cultivation, after which normal agricultural activity would be resumed. **35.** The reference to David recalls the dynastic oracle of 2 Sm 7:12–16. **36.** An "angel" (Hebr *mal'āk*) often appears as a messenger or agent to carry out a divine order. It is a conventional way of expressing the divine origin of an action. In this case, commentators generally believe that the besieging Assyrian army was decimated by a plague. For a similar incident, expressed in the same literary form, see 2 Sm 24:15–25. Herodotus (*History* 2. 141) refers to the disaster that overtook Sennacherib's army, and hints that it might have resulted from the bubonic plague. **38.** Nisroch is unknown from Mesopotamian sources; the name may result from a corruption made by Hebr scribes. It could stand either for the great Babylonian god Marduk or for the Assyrian fire-god Nusku. The violent death of Sennacherib is mentioned in Eusebius (*Chronicles* 1. 25–29). Ararat is modern Armenia, called Urartu in the Assyrian inscriptions. Esarhaddon was an energetic ruler (681–669) who conquered and held Egypt for a short time.

65 **(B) Hezekiah's Sickness and Recovery (38:1–39:8).** **1.** *in those days:* This vague indication should be understood to refer to a period before 701. **21.** The fig plaster was used to drain boils and ulcers; its therapeutic value was known from very early times. The parallel account in 2 Kgs 20:1–11, in which our vv. 21–22 appear after v. 6, provides a strong argument for the order adopted here in CCD. **8.** The account in 2 Kgs 20:9 is slightly different; two alternative signs are offered, either to accelerate the course of the sun's shadow or to reverse the distance already covered by the sun's advancing shadow. Our verse offers only the latter sign. The text of 1QIs[a] has helped us form a clearer picture of the sign proposed by Isaiah. It is not a question of a sundial but of "steps" constructed by Ahaz in such a way that they could be used to measure time (*VBW* 3, 67). While Isaiah was talking to Hezekiah, the sun's shadow had already moved ten steps; he promised to reverse the forward direction of the shadow and bring it back the distance it had already traveled, which would be completely contrary to nature's laws (Iwry, *BASOR* 147, 30–33). **9.** *the song of Hezekiah:* This liturgical hymn of thanksgiving is missing in 2 Kgs 20. It serves as an appendix to the incident of Hezekiah's sickness and recovery. The song can be divided into two parts: a description of the sufferer's misery (10–15); praise of God for restoring the man to health (16–20). **10.** For "noontime" it has been suggested that we read "sorrow," and then translate, "I said in my sorrow: I have marched my days..." (Dahood, *CBQ* 22 [1960] 401–402). **12.** The "last thread" attaches the web to the loom. The metaphor depicts the suddenness and finality of death. **15.** Questioning and protest are of no use; God himself had brought on this calamity. Nevertheless, the stricken one is determined to go on hoping. The text is very obscure. **18.** The "nether world," or sheol, was a dark and uninviting place where the shades of the dead enjoyed a kind of impersonal half-life and had no contact with God (cf. Ps 6:5).

66 **39:1.** Merodach-baladan was a Babylonian tribal chieftain who led a rebellion against Sargon shortly after the Assyrian had destroyed Samaria in 721. With Elamite help he became king of Babylon and ruled the city until Sargon drove him out of Babylon *ca.* 710. In 703, Merodach-baladan again came to power during Sennacherib's reign. It is probably during this time, and certainly before 701, that he sent the embassy to Hezekiah. The emissaries came to Jerusalem for something more important than to congratulate Hezekiah on his recovery from sickness. The motive was clearly political; the "letters and gifts" were the means by which the Babylonian hoped to win over Hezekiah as an ally in the rebellion against Assyria. **3.** Isaiah correctly suspected that some intrigue was afoot. Hezekiah's action directly contravened the consistent warning of the Prophet against foreign entanglements. Judah's only hope was faith in Yahweh (7:3–9; 30:3–5,15). **6.** The reference to a Babylonian captivity is puzzling, and several possibilities are open to the interpreter. Verses 6–7 may have been added by a later writer shortly before the deportation of Jehoiachin and the royal family to Babylon in 597. The prophecy may, however, refer to the captivity of Hezekiah's son, Manasseh, in Babylon, an incident reported only by the Chronicler (2 Chr 33:11–13). Or, finally, the passage may be an authentically Isaian warning that Judah would be punished by the very country from which she expected support. Isaiah would be expressing the conviction that a Babylon that sought Hezekiah's help today would enslave him tomorrow. **7.** The "servants" mentioned here are eunuchs who were put in charge of the royal harem. **8.** In the word "favorable," two states of mind can be detected: Hezekiah is resigned to the inevitability of divine punishment in some indeterminate future; he also congratulates himself that the blow would not fall in his lifetime. It would be difficult to find a better example of "after me the deluge."

17

MICAH

Philip J. King

BIBLIOGRAPHY

1 Anderson, G., "Study of Micah 6:1–8," *ScotJT* 4 (1951) 191–97. Copass, B. and E. Carlson, *Study of Prophet Micah* (Grand Rapids, 1950). Crook, M., "Promise in Micah 5," *JBL* 70 (1951) 313–20. George, A., "Le Livre de Michée," *VDBS* 5 (1952) 1252–63; *Michée, Sophonie, Nahum* (BJ; Paris, 1952). Hyatt, J., "On the Meaning and Origin of Micah 6:8," *AnglTR* 34 (1952) 232–39. Smith, J., *Critical and Exegetical Commentary on Micah* (ICC; N.Y., 1911). Snaith, N., *Amos, Hosea, and Micah* (London, 1956). Wolfe, R., "Introduction and Exegesis of Micah," *IB* 6 (N.Y., 1956) 897–949.

INTRODUCTION

2 **(I) Micah the Man.** Micah, the last of the four great prophets of the 8th cent. BC, was a fearless champion of the cause of the oppressed and the underprivileged. This deviation is not surprising in view of his humble origin. His father's name is not recorded, giving us good reason to think that he belonged to the peasant class. We have little biographical information about him except that he came from Moresheth, an obscure village of the Shephelah (lowlands) in SW Judah. His frontier home must have been very vulnerable at the time of foreign invasion. According to the superscription of the Book of Micah, his prophetic activity extended during the reign of three southern kings—Jotham (*ca.* 742–735), Ahaz (735–715), and Hezekiah (715–687?).

Not only did Micah live in the vicinity of Amos' home, Tekoa, but he was like Amos in many respects. He was so much influenced by the spirit of Amos that he has been called "Amos *redivivus*." Both rustic prophets attacked in a direct and forceful way the socio-economic abuses of their day. It was a period when the wealthy capitalists were oppressing the peasant landholders. These prophets not only sounded the call for social justice but also inveighed against the deplorable religious conditions of their time. The priests and the prophets were as venal as the merchants and the judges. External worship or ritualism was flourishing and religious ethics were being thoroughly ignored. This nonprofessional prophet, Micah—a man of blunt and unpolished language—could not remain silent while the stench of social sin offended both God and man. He will always be remembered as the prophet of social justice.

3 **(II) Historical Background.** Judah had reached the height of her power during the reign of Uzziah (Azariah), *ca.* 783–742. When he contracted leprosy he was succeeded by his son, Jotham, first as regent and later as king. His reign also was prosperous; it was a period of building operations and military victories. Jotham's son, Ahaz, came to the throne about 735, when the only threat on the horizon was Assyrian imperialism. In 732, Tiglath-pileser III conquered Syria; ten years later Samaria met the same fate. Such conquests were bound to make Judah feel insecure. Ahaz was a weak king and a servile vassal of Assyria. His son and successor, Hezekiah, was an energetic reformer who cut himself free of Assyria and carried out a purification of Judah's worship. According to Jer 26:18ff., this reform was influenced by the preaching of Micah. Micah was probably prophesying during the invasion of Sennacherib (701), but an earlier date surely applies to some prophecies.

4 **(III) Structure.** The book appears to be composite. It admits of various divisions, but, to bring out the balance between oracles of doom and oracles of promise, the following arrangement is suggested: 1:1–3:12, prophecies of misfortune; 4:1–5:14, prophecies of good fortune; 6:1–7:6, prophecies of misfortune; 7:7–7:20, prophecies of good fortune. This arrangement is the work of a compiler who reworked the material.

5 **(IV) Date and Authorship.** The exact date of Micah's prophetic activity cannot be determined for he does not refer to specific historical events. If the superscription (1:1) is accurate, the outside dates of his prophetic ministry would be 742–687. Taking into consideration both Jer 26:18ff. and internal factors, we find that the greater part of his career as a prophet was apparently coextensive with the years 714–701. We can assert nothing more definite.

It is unanimously agreed that the substance of chs. 1–3 pertains to Micah. The tendency in the past had been to terminate his contribution at just this point. Today, there is an inclination to attribute at least parts of the remaining chapters to him, but certainly 7:8–20 is not his work.

6 **(V) Text.** The Hebr text is in a poor state of preservation. Of the prophets, only Hosea is in worse condition. In several places, the sense is unintelligible: textual critics therefore, have had to make many conjectures over the years.

7 **(VI) Message.** The theological dimensions of Mi are somewhat limited, yet the influence of Isaiah, also Hosea and Amos, is evident. Micah repeats the truths they proclaimed, but in his own way. In his denunciation of the social evils of his day, he stresses greatly God's wrath, not, however, to the exclusion of God's mercy. To convey the depth of the latter, he uses the covenant word *ḥesed*, the steadfast love that binds two parties together in covenant. In the OT, *ḥesed* designates God's gratuitous love, which is the origin and basis of the covenant. As far as Micah was concerned, liturgical ritual had meaning only when combined with moral integrity; otherwise it was a sham.

8 **(VII) Outline.** The book may be divided into three main parts. The following outline is suggested:

(I) The Judgment of the Lord Against His People (1:1–3:12)
- (A) Superscription (1:1)
- (B) The Impending Divine Visitation (1:2–16)
  - (a) Judgment on the Kingdoms of the North and the South (1:2–9)
  - (b) Divine Chastisement of the Southern Cities (1:10–16)
- (C) Social Sins (2:1–13)
  - (a) Oppressors of the Poor, Beware (2:1–5)
  - (b) Objection to Micah's Preaching (2:6–11)
  - (c) Restoration After Exile (2:12–13)
- (D) Condemnation of Leaders (3:1–12)
  - (a) Violent Oppression by Secular Leaders (3:1–4)
  - (b) Indictment of False Prophets (3:5–8)
  - (c) Venality of the Leaders (3:9–12)

(II) The Glory of the New Israel (4:1–5:14)
- (A) Restoration of Zion (4:1–5)
- (B) The Lord's Reign from Zion (4:6–8)
- (C) Exile and Return (4:9–10)
- (D) The Enemies of Zion (4:11–14)
- (E) The Promised Messiah (5:1–3)
- (F) Deliverance from Assyria (5:4–5)
- (G) The Remnant Among the Nations (5:6–8)
- (H) The Purification of Israel (5:9–14)

(III) The Case Against Israel (6:1–7:20)
- (A) Yahweh Charges Israel (6:1–16)
  - (a) Yahweh's Controversy (6:1–8)
    - (i) Summons (6:1–2)
    - (ii) Yahweh's lawsuit (6:3–5)
    - (iii) True religion (6:6–8)
  - (b) Sin and Its Punishment (6:9–16)
- (B) Lament and Prayer (7:1–20)
  - (a) Pessimism of the Prophet (7:1–7)
  - (b) Triumph of Faith (7:8–20)
    - (i) Israel confesses her sins (7:8–10)
    - (ii) Return of the exiles (7:11–13)
    - (iii) A prayer to Yahweh (7:14–17)
    - (iv) Israel's prayer for forgiveness (7:18–20)

COMMENTARY

9 **(I) The Judgment of the Lord Against His People (1:1–3:12).** Yahweh, the universal judge, will punish not only Samaria but also Judah. Divine wrath had been enkindled by the crimes of the people, especially their corrupt leaders who failed to act in a responsible way.

(A) Superscription (1:1). This title was probably prefixed by the editor who compiled the collection of prophetic writings (→ 5 above).

(B) The Impending Divine Visitation (1:2–16).

10 (a) JUDGMENT ON THE KINGDOMS OF THE NORTH AND THE SOUTH (1:2–9). This vivid oracle is a denunciation of the two kingdoms in general, but especially their capital cities, Samaria and Jerusalem. Micah's primary interest is in Jerusalem. An invitation is extended to all people to listen while the Lord presents his case against those who have failed to abide by his will (on the "lawsuit," cf. H. Huffmon, *JBL* 78 [1959] 285–95; J. Harvey, *Bib* 43 [1962] 172–96). He comes as an accuser to present evidence against his people. **2.** *his holy temple:* God's dwelling; not an earthly building, but the heavenly temple of God (Is 63:15; Ps 11:4). Verses 2–4 are a classic description of a theophany. This fragment of poetry may be dependent upon Is 40:3–5. The figurative language of v. 4 suggests that the coming of the Lord will bring devastation, for it is described in terms of a volcano and an earthquake.

5–7. These verses deal with the condemnation of Samaria, the capital of the north. The infectious disease in the moral order that Micah describes began in Samaria and was spreading to the southern kingdom, even to its capital city, Jerusalem. **5.** *Jacob:* The personal name of the Patriarch, who was also known as Israel. The Israelites were often called the Sons of Jacob. Here, it refers to the ten northern tribes in contrast to the southern kingdom of Judah. **6.** It is difficult to determine when the oracle contained in v. 6 was uttered. Traditionally, it is thought to have been delivered prior to the fall of Samaria in 722. Others associate it with 714, at the beginning of Micah's prophetic ministry. Samaria's fate is intended to serve as a warning to the inhabitants of Judah, lest the same tragedy befall them. **7.** This verse, which may be an addition from post-exilic times, compares the unfaithful people with a prostitute. The analogy is first found in Hosea, and then often with the other prophets. The reference here is probably to ritual prostitution. *wages of a harlot:* From the money paid to cult prostitutes, the Temple was provided with elaborate furnishings. Such abominations are expressly forbidden in Dt 23:18.

8–9. The Prophet's main concern is with his own people, the inhabitants of Jerusalem and its environs. They will be punished in the same way as their northern brethren. Although the punishment is deserved, Micah cannot help lamenting and sympathizing. He describes himself in terms of a mourner. **8.** *naked:* Mourners donned loincloths of coarse material and removed their shoes. *jackals:* They resemble a small wolf; their howl is terrifying and mournful, and they usually travel in packs at night. *ostriches:* The reference is to their mournful night cry. They are mentioned frequently in the OT. **9.** *she:* Jerusalem. The destruction is likened to a flood pounding at the gates of the city of Jerusalem. The historical allusion may be to Sennacherib's invasion of Judah in 701.

11 (b) DIVINE CHASTISEMENT OF THE SOUTHERN CITIES (1:10–16). This is one of the most complicated sections of the OT because it abounds with plays on words and assonances, in which Micah delighted. His disheartening message is conveyed by means of a series of puns on the names of the towns located in the vicinity of Moresheth, his birthplace. Several of the allusions have been lost in the transmission of the text, and emendation of the MT is required for sense. The historical event behind this lament may have been Sennacherib's raid against Judah in 701, or Sargon II's campaign of 711. The Prophet pictures a hostile army advancing from the Philistine country toward Jerusalem, and he addresses the towns on this route.

Micah begins his dirge with words borrowed from the opening verse of David's elegy on the occasion of the death of Saul and Jonathan (2 Sm 1:20). This Davidic reference, in addition to a later one in v. 15 (Adullam), suggests a parallel between the perilous conditions of Micah's time and the desperate situation in which David had found himself. **10.** *Gath:* Gath (lit., "[wine] press") was one of the five principal cities of the Philistines and is to be identified with modern Araq el-Menshiyeh. This city was conquered by Sargon of Assyria in 711. Wine presses were common in ancient Palestine; therefore, many places are so named. *Beth-le-aphrah:* This name signifies "house of dust," but the city is unidentified. The pun recalls mourners, whose custom it was to roll their bodies in the dust.

11. *Shaphir:* This place has been tentatively identified with Khirbet el-Kom, W of Hebron. In keeping with the pun, the place suggests the Hebr word for "trumpet," *šôfār*. It means properly "ram's horn." This musical instrument, the most frequently named in the Bible, sounded all signals in both peace and war. *Zaanan:* An unidentified town in W Judah. *Beth-ezel:* Usually identified with modern Deir el-Asal, 2 mi. E of Debir. **12.** *Maroth:* It means "bitterness," and perhaps it is to be identified with Maarath (Jos 15:59). **13.** *Lachish:* Identified with modern Tell ed-Duweir. The Assyrians captured it in Sennacherib's campaign against Judah in 701. From this place, located midway between Jerusalem and Gaza, the Assyrians attacked Jerusalem. Lachish may have been regarded as a place of licentious worship; at any rate, Micah rebukes it for its moral turpitude. *daughter Zion:* This synonym for Jerusalem occurs over 20 times in the OT, 9 times in Mi.

12 **14.** *Moresheth-gath:* The name of Micah's home means the "possession of Gath." In view of 1 Kgs 9:16, the "parting gifts" may designate a marriage dowry. Just as a bride is cut off from her family, Moresheth-gath will be lost to Judah when she becomes Assyrian property. *Beth-achzib:* Lit., "house of Achzib." Achzib is connected with the Hebr root *kzb*, "deceitful." The town is in the Shephelah of Judah, and is probably to be identified with modern Tell el-Beida, SW of Adullam. In this verse, "Israel" designates the Hebr people in general, not just the ten northern tribes. **15.** *Mareshah:* This city in the Shephelah is identified with modern Tell Sandahannah. This pun is based on the resemblance in sound between the place name *Mārēšah* and *yōrēš*, the Hebr word for "conqueror." *Adullam:* This Canaanite royal city in the Shephelah is first mentioned in the Bible in Gn 38:1, 12–20. Identified with modern Khirbet esh-Sheikh-Madkur, it was probably one of the 46 cities taken by Sennacherib in 701. The fugitive David took refuge from Saul in this fortress city (1 Sm 22:1–2). *glory of Israel:* The Hebr word for "glory," *kābōd*, comes from the root *kbd*, lit., "to be heavy"; it signifies something weighty or important. In the OT it is usually associated with a manifestation of Yahweh; in the present context it may refer to the wealth and power of Judah or to the leaders of Israel who will be forced to seek refuge in Adullam as David did.

16. Micah brings his lament to a close by advising parents to observe the traditional mourning rites because their children would go into exile as slaves. Shaving the head was a sign of mourning (Is 3:24; Am 8:10). This custom was forbidden by deuteronomic law toward the end of the 7th cent. (Dt 14:1). In ancient times hair had a religious significance—because of its steady growth it was thought to contain life. The anxiety communicated by the Prophet through this dirge could hardly have eluded his compatriots.

(C) Social Sins (2:1–13).

13 (a) OPPRESSORS OF THE POOR, BEWARE (2:1–5). **1.** Micah attacks the capitalists who are guilty of exploitation and corruption. Wealthy landowners have been dispossessing the poor by illegal means; even during the night hours these unprincipled men plot ways to rob the underprivileged. Their plans will be frustrated, however, by the Lord's counterplan. **2.** The specific and unpardonable crimes are recorded. In Micah's time, wealth consisted for the most part in real estate; thus land monopoly was a common vice. Among other reasons, land was seized for failure to pay debts. Elijah had already inveighed against Ahab's attempt to expropriate the vineyard of Naboth (1 Kgs 21:1–4). He vigorously defended Naboth's right of "inheritance," a term with a broader meaning than its Eng equivalent. It designates the taking possession of something by any title whatsoever, except by one's own labor. Inherited property was looked upon as a sacred trust to be transmitted to one's progeny.

3. Employing the metaphor of a yoked ox, Micah proclaims that the divine punishment will take the form of slavery and exile. **4–5.** Micah envisions the occupation of Palestine by the Assyrians; the land will fall under their jurisdiction, and they will allot it. **4.** The meaning is uncertain because the text is faulty. The irony of the situation is that the monopolists who had been dispossessing the weak will now themselves be despoiled by the Assyrian invaders. **5.** *to mark out boundaries by lot:* A reference to the original apportionment of the land of Palestine among the Israelites (Jos 13–21). The meaning here is that the monopolists will enjoy no inheritance in Israel.

14 (b) OBJECTION TO MICAH'S PREACHING (2:6–11). **6.** Naturally the Prophet's audience was not pleased to hear him expose their crimes; they were anxious to silence him because he was causing great unrest among the people. Moreover, they felt certain that God would protect them so long as they were punctilious in their observance of the externals of cult. Micah answered his adversaries by charging them with having already broken the covenant by their rank injustice. God could not let such crimes go unpunished. **7.** *house of Jacob:* Reference here is to all the Hebr people. **8.** Like the other verses of this section, v. 8 is textually difficult. Micah continues his litany of charges against the exploiters. In their looting they are comparable to a hostile army. *you have stripped off the mantle:* As security for a debt, they have torn the clothes off the backs of the impoverished (Ex 22:26–27). **9.** Because of foreclosures by heartless creditors, women were compelled to abandon their homes, one of the few comforts that remained to them. *honor:* They were God's people who enjoyed the dignity of freedom. The children, the hope of the future, were being victimized by ruthless exploiters. **10.** *up! be off:* The imperatives are those of soldiers leading the people into exile. Unprincipled men can no longer expect to find a resting place in Palestine, because by their crimes they have forfeited their right to it. *crippling pledge:* According to law, it was forbidden to demand unreasonable pledges for loans (Ex 22:25–26; Dt 24:6,10–13,17), but the law was honored more in the breach than in the observance.

11. This verse is a fragment. The reference is to professional prophets who were inclined to proclaim whatever the people wanted to hear. Such prophets stood in sharp contrast to Micah, the man of integrity. The people loathed the latter and his unpalatable oracles, and they welcomed the former. A prophet who would declare himself in favor of intoxicants would find special favor.

15 (c) Restoration After Exile (2:12–13). These two verses interrupt 2:11 and 3:1. This fragment is out of context and is presumably a late exilic or post-exilic interpolation. Its date, however, is uncertain. This Messianic promise, which looks to the time of restoration after the Babylonian Exile, sounds very much like Dt-Is. It may have been inserted here in an attempt to soften the acrimony of the preceding oracle. **12.** *Jacob...Israel:* The 12 tribes are represented in this passage by Jacob and Israel. The reunification of the remnant in Palestine is described in terms of a shepherd leading his flock; Yahweh will gather Judah and Israel, his sheep. As in the days of the first kings—Saul, David, and Solomon—the Hebr people will again be one flock. **13.** The leader, the king, and the Lord are the same person. *gate:* Gate of exile through which the remnant would pass in their return to Palestine from Babylon.

16 **(D) Condemnation of Leaders (3:1–12).** This scathing denunciation of the religious and secular leaders was probably delivered before an assembly of the prominent citizens of Jerusalem.

(a) Violent Oppression by Secular Leaders (3:1–4). Micah's first indictment is leveled against the secular leaders of the community. Men in responsible positions are expected to know the law, but their conduct is completely to the contrary. **1.** *right:* In the present verse, "to know what is right" is not the ability to recite perfunctorily the entire code of law; it is the capability of rendering to each his due. In stigmatizing injustice, Micah echoes Amos. **2–3.** In an attempt to convey some notion of the violence of the landowners toward the weak, Micah compares them to butchers readying slaughtered animals for cooking. He also likens them to ravenous beasts who tear the flesh from their victims' bones. The leaders had as little feeling for their victims as a butcher for a carcass; those with the responsibility to protect the people in reality destroyed them. **4.** There will be a day of reckoning, however. When the leaders turn to the Lord in time of need, he will forsake them. God is never accessible to those who sin against social justice.

17 (b) Indictment of False Prophets (3:5–8). The prophets here castigated were members of the prophetic guilds. These unscrupulous men were motivated by venality, and Micah, a man of integrity, stands in contrast. Because of the disreputable behavior of mercenary prophets, interested only in their personal gain, religion was being degraded. **5.** When the pseudo-prophets were well remunerated, they proclaimed "peace" (*šālôm*). Peace is a gift of God based on covenant relationship. In the prophetic writings it often means "salvation." The converse of *šālôm* would be announced, if a venal prophet were not generously reimbursed. **6–7.** Micah is not contesting the inspiration of these prophets; he is impugning their corrupt practices. There was no practical distinction between seers and prophets—their functions were very similar. Divination, or the superstitious means of gaining knowledge about the future, was widely practiced in the ancient East. There were numerous objects from which the diviners derived their omens—e.g., the heavenly bodies, cloud formations, the livers of animals. The OT furnishes ample evidence that the Hebr people engaged in this practice. The prophets inveighed against divination and all other forms of magical activity. **7.** *they shall cover their lips:* A sign of shame or mourning. **8.** This verse is autobiographical. Micah is a true prophet, disinterested in material gain from his oracles. He is aware of his own personal inspiration. *spirit of the Lord:* In Hebrew, *rûaḥ yhwh;* the basic meaning of *rûaḥ* is "breath" or "wind." The ancient Israelites looked upon breath and wind as powerful forces. *Rûaḥ* came to be regarded as the life principle. The spirit of God is not distinct from God; it is the power by which he intervenes in the life of man. If a man gave signs of some special charism, it was attributed to the spirit of Yahweh. It was this spirit that inspired the prophets. Authority (*mišpāṭ*) and might are the credentials of the authentic prophet. Jacob and Israel are synonymous here, designating the Hebr people other than the ten northern tribes that had gone into exile.

18 (c) Venality of the Leaders (3:9–12). This third indictment is directed against both the religious and the political leaders. As punishment for their heinous crimes against social justice, Jerusalem will be destroyed. The magnates, judges, priests, and prophets are so naïve as to think that the Lord has no concern for social justice; they have incurred divine wrath for their venality, fraud, violence, oppression, and bribery. **11.** There were three avenues of recourse open to those who were in trouble: the elders, the priests, and the prophets. Even these had their price, and it was useless to appeal to them without money. The elders constituted the aristocracy of the people and played an important role in Israelite life. They were the local rulers. Authority was based on age; therefore, it resided in the hands of older men. These elders, or "leaders," dispensed justice at the city gate and served as counselors. The priests functioned at the local shrines and gave decisions—i.e., instruction and guidance through the law. The law (*tōrāh*) was the particular responsibility of the priests (cf. Ex 22:8; Jer 18:18). The professional prophet would attempt to elicit an answer from God. The verse ends with two assertions that summarize the mentality of the religious and political leaders—as long as the Temple stood, they felt confident that the Lord was in their midst and no danger could befall them, regardless of their conduct. **12.** *because of you:* Because of the depravity practiced by the leaders of the community, Jerusalem and the Temple would be reduced to a heap of ruins. This oracle is cited in Jer 26:18–19, 100 years after the time of Micah, and it saved Jeremiah's life. He, too, had spoken against the Temple, but his life was spared when some elders appealed to the precedent set by Micah. The fact that Micah's words were remembered one century later is an indication of the impression his preaching must have made on the people.

19 **(II) The Glory of the New Israel (4:1–5:14).** These two chapters contain oracles of Messianic hope. Many commentators are of the opinion that this Messianic section pertains to the post-exilic period and not to Micah. Others think that these chapters are attributable to the Prophet, although they have undergone later revision and supplementation; then they may well date from the time when divine intervention saved Jerusalem from Sennacherib's advancing army.

(A) Restoration of Zion (4:1–5). The spirit of this first pericope is unalloyed optimism. It refers to the future glorious reign of Yahweh from Zion when there will be universal peace. **1–3.** Verses 1–3 are the same as Is 2:2–4. Each is a vision of the glorification of Zion as the religious center of the world. It is thought that this prophecy was inserted here to mollify the menacing tone on which the preceding chapter terminated. **1.** *in days to come:* Refers to the Messianic end-time. **2.** Pagan converts will come to Jerusalem to seek instruction (*tōrāh*). "Instruction" and "word" are synonymous terms. **3.** Micah is describing a theocracy, with the Lord as the sole ruler over the world. In this reign of peace, instruments of war will be superfluous; therefore, they will be converted into agricultural implements. Modern man can learn a lesson in disarmament from this oracle. **4.** In a figure borrowed from the Palestinian countryside, this verse portrays peace, calm, and security. **5.** Verse 5 may be a liturgical addition to an ancient prophecy. Israel will always worship Yahweh, although other nations would have their own gods.

20 **(B) The Lord's Reign from Zion (4:6–8).** Employing the image of a good shepherd, Micah describes the restoration of Judah. **6.** *on that day:* At the termination of the exile. *lame...outcasts...afflicted:* Israel in Exile. The image of the shepherd is dominant in the OT, and it reaches its most complete expression in the NT (Jn 10:11). The resemblance to Ez 34 is striking; there the restoration is portrayed in the image of a shepherd and his flock. Yahweh goes about gathering the lost or crippled sheep. **7.** From the remnant, Yahweh, the king, will reconstruct a powerful nation. **8.** *Migdal-eder:* Lit., "tower of the flock" (cf. Eder in Gn 35:21). In the present context, it is used figuratively of Jerusalem. It continues the shepherd theme; the Lord would tend his flock from this tower. *former dominion:* Reference is to the unified kingdom during the golden age of David and Solomon, when Jerusalem was the capital city of the entire nation.

21 **(C) Exile and Return (4:9–10).** It is impossible to date this oracle with certitude. It seems to reflect the period between 597–587, during the reign of Zedekiah, the last representative of the Davidic dynasty to rule in Judah, a weak and vacillating king. Others assign to this prophecy a post-exilic date when abortive attempts were made to re-establish the kingship under Zerubbabel (ca. 516). **9.** *cry out:* Suggests despair. **10.** *for now...your enemies:* This verse may have been added when the exile was an accomplished fact, for the reference to Babylon indicates that it dates from a later period. The restoration will be achieved by the Lord.

22 **(D) The Enemies of Zion (4:11–14).** Again, the historical circumstances of this oracle dealing with the fate of Zion's foes cannot be determined. It may refer to the Assyrian invasion under Sennacherib in 701, when he failed to conquer Jerusalem. Others associate the prophecy with the post-exilic era (516–445), when the neighboring peoples vigorously opposed Israel's attempt to re-establish the monarchy. The nations that come with the purpose of annihilating the people of Zion will themselves be vanquished by the Israelites. **12–13.** The neighboring nations were oblivious to Yahweh's prominent role in the Israelite drama; he was about to grind the nations themselves into chaff. Israel's conquest and devastation of the enemy is pictured in terms of threshing; like grain, they are to be trampled under the feet of the ox. *horn:* Based on the bull's horn, it is often used as a figure of "strength." Israel is here compared to the bull goring its victim or piercing the sheaves on the threshing floor. *devote:* In the present context, it designates a military measure. It is employed here simply in the sense of "destroy" or "exterminate." To procure divine assistance in warfare, the people consecrated the booty to God—i.e., the vanquished people had to be put to death and the remaining spoils destroyed. *Lord of the whole earth:* A post-exilic phrase (Zech 4:14; 6:5). **14.** Jerusalem is under attack, and her leader is helpless to defend her against the aggressor. The enemy forces are probably under the command of Sennacherib. *Bat-gader:* Lit., "house of the fenced-in place," a symbolic title for Jerusalem. *they strike on the cheek:* A grave insult. In some versions (RSV), this verse is 5:1.

23 **(E) The Promised Messiah (5:1–3).** The Davidic ruler of Israel will rise from the district of Ephrathah. This king is not the present, but a future, monarch. The prophet is not saying that the Messiah will necessarily be born in Ephrathah, but that he will spring from the royal line of David. Jesse and David (1 Sm 17:12) came from Bethlehem. Bethlehem seems to be a gloss in the MT; it is lacking in the Gk text. Originally, the text probably read *bêt 'eprātāh*—i.e., "house of Ephrathah"—and Bethlehem would be an explanatory gloss on Ephrathah. Ephrathah is generally associated with Bethlehem. After the conquest of Canaan, Bethlehem was settled by the Ephrathah clan of the tribe of Judah. Therefore, Bethlehem is also called Ephrathah (Jos 15:59; Ru 4:11). Bethlehem, lit., "house of bread," is located 5 mi. S of Jerusalem. In Mt 2:5–6, the midrashic interpretation of this text, it is shown how it was understood at the time of Jesus' birth. This oracle fits in well with the theology of Micah and his contemporary, Isaiah; thus it is unnecessary to deny it to Micah.

1. This optimistic verse stands in marked contrast to the preceding one. *me:* The speaker is Yahweh. *from ancient times:* From the ancient dynasty of David. **2.** Until the new king re-establishes the monarchy, Israel will be subject to other nations. The Israelites anxiously awaiting deliverance are likened to a woman in labor. There is an allusion to Is 7:14 in this verse—Micah has been influenced by the Emmanuel oracle. **3.** The qualities of the future monarch are delineated.

24 **(F) Deliverance from Assyria (5:4–5).** The people are the speakers in this passage. They are extremely confident of their ability to overcome Assyria. *shepherds...men of royal rank:* The leaders of the community. *seven...eight:* This numerical progression, also in Am, indicates an indefinite number. **5.** Nimrod was a legendary figure in the ancient Near East (cf. Gn 10:10ff.). Assyria is the "land of Nimrod"; the name is of uncertain origin. Its source may be the name of the Sumerian god of war and of the chase, Ninurta.

25 **(G) The Remnant Among the Nations (5:6–8).** This description of the triumph of the remnant may date from post-exilic times. By likening the remnant to "dew" and "raindrops," which have a divine origin, the Prophet intimates that what is taking place is beyond man's power. The fate of the remnant is in the hands of God, and no human effort can intervene. **7.** The remnant is compared to a "lion," and the other nations are the "sheep." The latter are defenseless in the face of Israel's strength; cf. 4:11–13; the Messianic era is described, as often, in terms of Israel's present troubles. There are many references to lions in the OT, common animals in biblical Palestine. Because of their attacks on the flocks, they became the symbol of power, violence, boldness, and ferocity. **8.** Probably an editorial addition preparing for the next oracle.

26 **(H) The Purification of Israel (5:9–14).** The scene shifts from the annihilation of Israel's enemies to the purification of Israel herself. The people are to put their complete confidence in the Lord; anything that would distract from that goal must be removed. **9–10.** In this disarmament program, all implements of war must be eliminated. *horses:* In Micah's day, horses were used only for military purposes. The horse was not employed in peaceful endeavors until post-exilic times. *chariots:* Chariotry was first utilized in the Israelite army in the era of Solomon. The prophets inveighed against war in this manner because it was a manifestation of a lack of confidence in Yahweh (cf. Is 31:1). **10.** *cities:* Fortified cities. **11.** All forms of magic were forbidden by law, but there is ample OT evidence that the Hebrews indulged in this superstition. **12.** *carved images:* The

Hebr word is *pesel*, designating an image carved from stone, metal, or wood. A *pesel* is a sculptured image as contrasted with a molten image that was cast in a mold. The Decalogue forbade the making of these idols (Ex 20:4; Dt 5:8). *sacred pillars:* The Hebr word for this sacred object is *maṣṣēbāh* from the root *nṣb*, "to set up," "to erect." It was a stone monument that functioned as a memorial or as an object of worship. Sacrifices were offered at it. Influenced by Canaanite practice, the Hebrews erected these sacred pillars even though it was forbidden (Lv 26:1; Dt 16:22). **13.** *sacred poles:* The Hebrew is *'ăšērāh;* the English is Asherah. Asherah was a Phoenician vegetation goddess, the wife of Baal. Her symbol was the sacred pole, which also bears her name. In the OT, it is difficult to determine whether "asherah" refers to the goddess or the object of the cult; however, in the present verse the reference is to the cult object. The sacred pole wat made of wood and took various forms: a plain or carved pole; a staff; a tree; a cross; etc. These objects were evident in Palestine from the 10th to the 6th cents. BC. **14.** This verse may be a later addition. The nations failing to respond to the Lord will be destroyed.

(III) The Case Against Israel (6:1–7:20). The major portion of these two chapters very likely came from Micah. Some scholars, however, associate them with the post-exilic prophets. After a review of Israel's infidelity to Yahweh, this section closes on a note of confidence in God's mercy.

(A) Yahweh Charges Israel (6:1–16).

27 (a) YAHWEH'S CONTROVERSY (6:1–8). This classic passage is the epitome of the prophetic message; it is the Magna Charta of prophetic religion. There is no good reason for assigning this pericope to a date later than that of Micah.

(i) *Summons* (6:1–2). The scene is set in a lawcourt of cosmic dimensions. The mountains, hills, and foundations of the earth are to act as witnesses. Yahweh is both prosecutor and judge, while Israel is the defendant.

(ii) *Yahweh's lawsuit* (6:3–5). In presenting his case, the Lord enumerates his mighty saving acts on Israel's behalf, beginning with the Exodus and continuing to the Conquest. In the face of the Lord's indictment, Israel has no defense to offer. **5.** *Balak:* After the Israelites defeated the Amorites, this Moabite king feared for his own domain. He summoned Balaam, the diviner from N Syria, to curse Israel; instead, he could only bless her. Except for this reference, every other biblical allusion to Balaam outside of Nm 22 and 25 is pejorative. Micah regards Balaam's oracles as part of Yahweh's saving acts. Shittim was the last camping place of the Israelites in Moab prior to crossing the Jordan, and Gilgal was the first camping station W of the Jordan. The phrase, "from Shittim to Gilgal," indicates the critical period of entering the promised land—a period marked by the "just deeds," i.e., saving acts of the Lord.

28 (iii) *True religion* (6:6–8). One of the best-known parts of Mi, it is also the high point. It tells what Yahweh requires of man. Israel, the defendant, is speaking. What kind of sacrifices should they offer to appease God? **6.** *holocausts:* They were distinct from other sacrifices inasmuch as they were completely destroyed by fire and nothing was eaten by the priests or donors. *calves a year old:* Yearlings were more valuable than the younger animals. This offering would have been made by the wealthy. **7.** *oil:* Cereal offerings were provided with oil. In the liturgy, oil was utilized for the lamps, for sacred anointings, and for purification ceremonies. *first-born:* The first male child in a family enjoyed a special status; he received a special blessing (Gn 27) and a double share of his father's property (Dt 21:7). The ancient Semites believed that the first-born were to be sacrificed to God because they belonged to him. This barbarous practice of child sacrifice was condemned in the Mosaic Law; nevertheless, it was not unknown in Israel (2 Kgs 16:3; 21:6). **8.** Sacrifice without interior religion is futile. This verse is a perfect summary of the teaching of the great 8th-cent. prophets—Amos on righteousness, Hosea on steadfast love, Isaiah on faith and obedience. It is not an ethic but a way of life. The phrases "to do the right," "to love goodness," and "to walk humbly" are so highly charged that they are difficult to define. *Ḥesed* (goodness) is the response made not out of duty but out of love. "[T]o walk humbly," etc., means to live in union with God and to serve him.

29 (b) SIN AND ITS PUNISHMENT (6:9–16). This somewhat obscure section may have been delivered by the Prophet after Sennacherib's siege. In this tirade, Micah is continuing the accusations made in chs. 2–3 against fraudulent merchants who exploit the public. He also indicts the people as a whole for their deceit. **10–11.** Fraudulent manipulation of weights and measures. *ephah:* This dry measure equals slightly more than a bushel. **13–14.** Punishments are to be inflicted for the sins mentioned. The Assyrian siege of 701 was only the beginning of more serious catastrophes. The people would be perpetually hungry; they would be deprived of their financial savings; their grain, oil, and grapes would be appropriated by the Assyrian invaders. These catastrophes spelled doom. **16.** The conduct of Judah is compared to Omri and his son, Ahab—the epitome of sin in Israel, as far as the Deuteronomist is concerned. Judah had followed the example of the northern kingdom, infamous for its cult of Baal, the luxury of its leaders, and its oppression of the impoverished. Omri was the founder of the fourth and strongest dynasty of the northern kingdom of Israel. It was his son and successor, Ahab, who tolerated pagan religious practices in Israel. It was his determined wife, Jezebel, who introduced into Israel the worship of the gods of Tyre.

(B) Lament and Prayer (7:1–20).

30 (a) PESSIMISM OF THE PROPHET (7:1–7). Although the text of this section is poorly preserved, it is easy to grasp the Prophet's pessimistic spirit. Once again he denounces the covetousness, violence, and venality that he perceives on all sides. He searches the city in vain for an upright man. Thus, he manifests an attitude of general and extreme mistrust of his fellow man. **1.** In his pursuit of a righteous man, Micah likens himself to a man who enters the vineyard or orchard after the harvest in search of some fruit and finds not a fig or a grape. **4.** Judah is on the brink of annihilation; the watchman on the city walls warns of the enemy's approach. **5–6.** There was a general breakdown in family relations, so important in the Israelite society. Note the ascending scale. **7.** This expression of confidence in the Lord may be a scribal addition; otherwise, "I" refers to the Prophet (cf. 3:8; 7:1).

(b) TRIUMPH OF FAITH (7:8–20). This closing section of Mi is probably an editorial appendix dating from the exilic or post-exilic epoch. The mercy of God is a dominant theme.

31 (i) *Israel confesses her sins* (7:8–10). Israel is being punished because of her sins, which she now confesses. But she is soon to be delivered from the hands of her enemy, when it will be the enemy's turn to be oppressed. Depending upon the historical occasion of this oracle, Judah's unnamed foe may be Assyria, Edom, or Babylonia, among others.

(ii) *Return of the exiles* (7:11–13). This oracle speaks of the restoration of the walls of Jerusalem after the exile. The city's defenses were rebuilt in the time of Nehemiah. The boundaries of Jerusalem will also be greatly extended. **12.** The dispersed Jews will return to their homeland from all directions. The river is the Euphrates. Tyre was an important Phoenician city known for its navigators and traders. *from sea to sea:* Perhaps from the Mediterranean to the Persian Gulf. **13.** *land:* Babylonia, where Israel had been incarcerated, would be reduced to ruins.

32 (iii) *A prayer to Yahweh* (7:14–17). This prayer seems to date from the time after the return from exile when the Jews were trying to rehabilitate themselves. There is a perceptible note of nostalgia and loneliness in this passage. The Lord is addressed as the shepherd of his people; they ask him to bring them out of the forest and into fertile pastures. **14.** *Carmel:* The splendor and fertility of this mountain on the coast of Palestine made a lasting impression on the Israelites. Bashan was a fertile region in Transjordan, famous for its oaks and forests; it was also ideal for growing wheat and raising cattle. Nearby Gilead was also famous for its oaks, pines, and pasture land. **15–17.** The Lord will work signs comparable to those associated with the Exodus. In the face of such wonders, the neighboring nations will be confounded and terrified.

33 (iv) *Israel's prayer for forgiveness* (7:18–20). The closing verses of Mi are addressed to the God of forgiveness. The book ends by recalling the promises of the covenant binding Yahweh and the patriarchs. The Lord had pledged his "faithfulness" (*'emet*) and "grace" (*ḥesed*) to the Israel of old, and he was not about to renege now.

18

ZEPHANIAH NAHUM HABAKKUK

Richard T. A. Murphy, O.P.

ZEPHANIAH

BIBLIOGRAPHY

1 Bullough, S., "Sophonias" (*CCHS;* London, 1952). Chaine, J., *God's Heralds* (N.Y., 1958). De Vaux, R., "Le 'Reste d' Israel'...," *RB* 42 (1933) 526–39. Dheilly, J., *The Prophets* (N.Y., 1960). Driver, S. R., *Zephania* (CBSC; Cambridge, 1906). Fitzpatrick, A. F., *The Doctrine of the Prophets* (Grand Rapids, 1897–1958). Jerome, *In Soph. Proph.* (*PL* 25. 1337–88). Leslie, E. A., *Zephaniah, Book of* (*IDB;* N.Y., 1962). Nötscher, F., "Sephanjah" *Zwölfprophetenbuch* (Echter-B; Würzburg, 1948) 127–37. Pfeiffer, R. H., *Introduction to the Old Testament* (5th ed.; N.Y., 1941). Pilcher, C. V., *Three Hebrew Prophets and the Passing of Empires* (London, 1931). Smith, J. M. P., *Zephaniah* (ICC; N.Y., 1911). Sullivan, K., "The Book of Sophonia," *Worship* 31 (1957) 130–39. Van Hoonacker, A., "Sophonie," *Les douze petits prophètes* (EBib; Paris, 1908) 498–537.

INTRODUCTION

2 **(I) Background.** Zephaniah (lit., "Yahweh protects") is the only prophet for whom we have a genealogy from the fourth generation. He prophesied during the reign of Josiah (640–609; however, J. P. Hyatt argues for Jehoiachin, *JNES* 7 [1948] 25–29). The Prophet was probably from Jerusalem inasmuch as he knew so much about what happened in the city and in the court. His bold attacks on foreign ways (1:8) and idolatry (1:4–6), as well as his silence regarding the king, indicate that he prophesied *ca.* 640–630, before Josiah was able to implement his religious reform and perhaps even before Jeremiah began his ministry (625). The Hezekiah mentioned in his pedigree (1:1) may have been the king of Judah (721–693), but because he is not given that title, it is not certain that Zephaniah was of royal descent.

The age was a turbulent one. Hezekiah had but recently (701) lost 46 cities to Sennacherib (cf. 2 Kgs 18:13ff.), and Judah, in the reigns of Manasseh (687–642) and Amon (642–640), had fallen continually under Assyrian influence; the religious life of the people had suffered accordingly (2 Kgs 21:1–26). But Assyria, so recently the victor over Egypt and Babylon, began to decline soon after the death of Ashurbanipal (621), and hopes for a national restoration and religious reform quickly revived.

3 **(II) Content and Style.** The first of the writing prophets since Isaiah and Micah, Zephaniah announces the coming of the day of the Lord (cf. Am 5:18), a dread day of catastrophe for all (note the eschatological overtones). Judgment Day for the nations ought to be a warning to the chosen people and it should lead them back to the repentance, obedience and humility that they so sadly lack and only by which can they survive the divine visitation. A "remnant," however, will be left to enjoy the fruits of salvation (3:12–20).

Zephaniah lacks the universal sweep of later revelations as well as the depths of NT spirituality. Despite his fierce nationalism and political rancor, his ignorance of other peoples and of the next life, his insight into the meaning of sin (pride, revolt, lying, lack of faith and love) is original and timeless. His limited messianic outlook explains why he is only once quoted in the NT (Mt 13:41), but his prophecy contains the seeds of universalism and true spirituality: The ʿAnawim and the remnant and the day and the sword of the Lord are his contributions to religious thought. Moreover, he suggests that the oncoming doom (the invasion of the Scythians, if one follows Herodotus 1.105; 4.2) can be the occasion of purification and renewal.

4 **(III) Outline.** The prophecy of Zephaniah treats of the following: (I) the day of the Lord in Judah (1:1–2:3); (II) prophecies against the nations (2:4–15); (III) prophecies against Jerusalem (3:1–8); (IV) promises (3:9–20). The authenticity of various passages has been inconclusively contested, but some of the prophecies (e.g., 2:11, concerning the conversion of pagans; cf. 3:9) seem rather badly fitted in and may have been borrowed from Is 40–55. The final verses (3:18b–20) appear to reflect the period of the Exile. Because of the brevity of the prophecy, such conclusions must remain tentative. The following outline has been suggested for the Book of Zephaniah:

(I) The Day of the Lord in Judah (1:1–2:3)
- (A) Cosmic Extent (1:2–3)
- (B) Strange Gods (1:4–7)
- (C) Court Behavior (1:8–9)
- (D) The Merchants (1:10–11)
- (E) Unbelievers (1:12–13)
- (F) The Day of the Lord (1:14–18)
- (G) Call to Conversion (2:1–3)

(II) Prophecies Against the Nations (2:4–15)
- (A) Philistines (2:4–7)
- (B) Moab and Ammon (2:8–11)
- (C) Ethiopia (2:12)
- (D) Assyria (2:13–15)

(III) Prophecies Against Jerusalem (3:1–8)
- (A) The Leaders (3:1–5)
- (B) The Lesson of Other Nations (3:6–8)

(IV) Promises (3:9–20)
- (A) Conversion of the Gentiles (3:9–10)
- (B) The Remnant of Israel (3:11–13)
- (C) A Joyful Psalm of Zion (3:14–18a)
- (D) Return of the Exiles (3:18b–20)

COMMENTARY

5 **(I) The Day of the Lord in Judah (1:1–2:3).** **1.** Zephaniah abruptly and solemnly announces an all-inclusive oracle of the Lord.

(A) Cosmic Extent (1:2–3). **3.** Inasmuch as the divine displeasure can only be aroused by the sins of man (of which fish and birds, e.g., are incapable), the language is to be understood as poetical and hyperbolical; man is the chief target. Using a play on the words, mankind and earth, (*'ădām* and *'ădāmāh;* cf. Gn 2:7; 3:17,19), the Prophet foretells that God shall cut off sinners from the land they have defiled by their sins.

6 **(B) Strange Gods (1:4–7).** **4.** The Lord is about to punish Judah and the people of Jerusalem for their practical atheism—the cult and worship of Baal, of the stars (the hosts of heaven), and of Milcom, an Ammonite god (cf. 2 Kgs 23; Jer 49:1,3; 2 Sm 12:30). This syncretism, always a temptation for Israel, was in reality a falling away from the Lord (v. 6). **7.** *silence:* Requisite for sacrificial ritual, it is now demanded because the Lord is near. Zephaniah thus introduces his central theme: the dread day of the Lord. Judah will serve as the victim; those who shall partake of the feast must be readied—i.e., sanctified and thus clean (cf. 1 Kgs 18:19–40; Jer 46:10; Ez 39:17)—so that they may serve as God's instruments.

(C) Court Behavior (1:8–9). **8.** First to feel the divine wrath will be the court officials, whose bad example led others astray. *foreign apparel:* The wealthy who abandoned their national garb for that of the conqueror. **9.** *all who leap over the threshold:* In the MT, threshold is *miptān,* used to designate the platform upon which Dagon's image rested, or the threshold upon which his broken idol had fallen (1 Sm 5:4–5), or possibly the stepped platform upon which the royal throne rested. The reference is to a superstitious, or perhaps idolatrous, practice.

7 **(D) The Merchants (1:10–11).** The Prophet pictures himself in the midst of coming ruin and desolation, where he hears sounds of grief. **10.** *the Fish Gate... New Quarter... Mortar:* The first two places were on the N side of Jerusalem; the Mortar cannot be located with certainty; the Tyropoeon Valley is suggested. The merchants shall be punished for injustices in commerce, along with the money-changers, those "who weigh out silver"; it would be several centuries yet before money came into common use.

8 **(E) Unbelievers (1:12–13).** **12.** *I will explore Jerusalem with lamps:* The thoroughness of the Lord's search for the wicked will preclude any chance for escape (in iconography, Zephaniah is identified by the lantern he carries). *men who thicken on their lees:* A metaphor for overconfidence and laziness. The preparation of wine demands great care; unless the liquid is thoroughly stirred and separated from the sedimentation after fermentation, the wine thickens and loses its strength and flavor. *neither good nor evil can the Lord do:* Material prosperity has caused Zephaniah's contemporaries to look upon their present prosperous condition as their own doing, which implies that God has nothing to offer man. **13.** Not to be able to drink of the wine from one's own vineyard is a tragic image commonly used in connection with the divine punishment of injustice (Am 5:11; Mi 6:15; Dt 28:30; etc.).

9 **(F) The Day of the Lord (1:14–18).** In intensely energetic language, which has served as a basis for Jl 2:1–11 and the first strophe of the *Dies Irae* (by the Franciscan Thomas of Celano, *ca.* 1260), Zephaniah begins his ominous picture of the great day of the Lord. The concept of a day of universal judgment is important for the evolution of religious thought. As in Na 2–3, the Lord's intervention in the affairs of man is described in terms so graphic as to have almost an audio-visual impact upon the reader. **14.** Many think that Zephaniah is alluding to the warlike approach of the Scythians, whom the Lord has made the instrument of his wrath; the speed of their approach is terrifying to the onlooker. *hark, the day of the Lord!:* Does one listen to a day? The text is difficult to translate. We might render it as "The hideous noise of the day," followed by "there the warrior cries out," although "there" does not here refer to any particular place and is not easily understood as referring to a time of day (BJ has "now"; CCD, "then"). *bitter... the warrior's cry:* Ordinarily bitterness is associated with weeping or disappointment. Here, the idea is perhaps the shouts uttered by soldiers (either in fierceness or desperation) making personal contact with the enemy. In ancient days, warlike cries and speeches were preliminary to the actual combat (1 Sm 17:8–47). *the warrior:* Might even be identified with the Lord (cf. Is 42:13). **15.** The picture is grim. Clouds, as frequently in the OT, indicate God's presence; the thick darkness suggests the menacing tone of that presence. **16.** *trumpet blasts:* The horrors of war are added to the terror of divine judgment. Behind their high battlements, the defenders shall be struck with fear at the noise of the advancing enemy. **17.** *blind:* The inhabitants of besieged Jerusalem shall, in their futile attempts to escape, resemble the blind, who grope along with unsteady steps. *blood... like dust:* The metaphor is mixed, but the idea is that on the dread day of the Lord a man's blood (i.e., his life) will be considered as dust—i.e., something quite inconsequential. *their brains...:* *Leḥem* is generally translated "bread," or any kind of food (e.g., flesh). One obtains the CCD reading "brains" by supposing *mōḥām* for *leḥem;* the single parallel that occurs in Jb 21:24, however, has the meaning "marrow."

10 **(G) Call to Conversion (2:1–3).** 1. *gather yourselves together:* The meaning is obscure (BJ omits the first line but gives four suggested corrections in a footnote). *nation without shame:* Precisely why Judah is thus reproached is not stated, but there is still time for repentance. 2. *before you are driven away like chaff:* Chaff is a graphic image for everything unstable and worthless. *the blazing anger of the Lord:* This favorite expression of the OT (it is used 33 times) may be a gloss here. There is still time for penance before Yahweh's anger blazes up. 3. *you humble of the earth:* The word *ʿănāwîm* does not refer to poverty so much as to the humble folk who were entirely abandoned to the divine will. They serve and obey the Lord, living in humility. Isaiah declared (61:1) that the Messiah would be sent to the "lowly"—the "meek" who despite adversity would hold fast to justice and humility and would withstand the temptation to adopt as their own the religion and gods of their oppressors. *perhaps you may be sheltered...:* The day of the Lord is likened to a storm or an invasion, and the Prophet does not promise definite deliverance even to the *ʿănāwîm.*

(II) Prophecies Against the Nations (2:4–15). Zephaniah enlarges the scope of his vision; there is to be a day for Israel's neighbors.

11 **(A) Philistines (2:4–7).** The Prophet's gaze turns first to the west and south. 4. *Gaza...Ashkelon...Ashdod...Ekron:* The four Philistine cities lay along the coastal plain; a fifth, Gath, had already been destroyed by Sargon in 711. As hereditary enemies of Israel, the Philistines were often the target of prophecies of doom (Am 1:6–8; Is 14:24–32; Jer 47; Ez 25:17–22). *at midday:* Unprepared for the attack, the city of Ashdod would be easily taken in half a day (e.g., Moabite Stone, lines 15–16). 5. *Cretan folk:* They are the Philistines from Caphtor (Crete; cf. Am 9:7; Dt 2:23). King David had taken the Cherethites and the Pelethites (2 Sm 8:18) as his bodyguard. The *krt* mentioned in the Ras Shamra tablets has nothing to do with the Cherethites (R. de Vaux, *RB* [1937] 445). *I will humble you...:* By reading *ʾaknīʿēk* for *knaʿan,* we have the expected prediction of ruin, instead of a comparison of Philistia with Canaan. 6. *the coastland:* Where cities once flourished there shall be nothing but pasture land, in which shepherds will lead their flocks and use the ruins of houses at night for shelter and fold. 7. This reference to the restored remnant suggests a later addition, but see also v. 9.

12 **(B) Moab and Ammon (2:8–11).** Zephaniah next turns his gaze eastward. 8. Moab and Ammon, along the E shore of the Dead Sea, were Israel's traditional enemies (cf. Gn 19:30–38 for a derisive account of their origin). Their insolence toward Israel was often sharply criticized (Is 16–6; Jer 48:29ff.; Ez 25:6). 9. The curse is impressive, for Sodom and Gomorrah stand as types of wickedness and of total destruction (Gn 19:17–29). In ancient times, victors would sometimes sow the fields of vanquished enemies with salt (Jgs 9:45)—a gesture symbolizing an unproductive area. 11. The mention of the universal worship of Yahweh at this early date is considered suspect and a borrowing from Is 41:1,5; 42:4,10,12; 49:1; 51:5).

13 **(C) Ethiopia (2:12).** Egypt had been ruled by a Cushite or Ethiopian dynasty (the XXVth) from 715 to 663. The oracle is very short and is apparently incomplete. Egypt deserves more than this, having frequently interfered in Israel's politics and religion (cf. Is 18–20; Jer 46; Ez 29–32), and King Josiah was slain at Megiddo in a futile attempt to prevent Neco II from re-establishing Egypt's power northward (2 Kgs 23:29).

14 **(D) Assyria (2:13–15).** For more than 100 years, Israel's enemy par excellence, Assyria, had known nothing but success, and Nineveh, the capital city on the Tigris, had become exceedingly wealthy. 13–14. Nineveh was, in fact, so utterly destroyed in 612 that Xenophon (*Anab.* 3.3,6–12) found no traces of it. The traditional image of an area inhabited only by wild life is presented. *screech owl...desert owl...raven:* The exact identification can only be guessed at. The tremendous palace at Nineveh was artistically decorated; the reference to her columns (by synecdoche) may possibly be to the imposing bas-reliefs discovered in the ruins at Nineveh (cf. A. Parrot, *Nineveh and the Old Testament* [N.Y., 1955] 19). 15. With savage sarcasm the Prophet puts into words the thoughts of future visitors to the ruined city. Self-sufficient Nineveh had supposedly said: "I am and there is no other than I"; Babylon will utter a similar phrase (cf. Is 47:8,10). The Lord shall humble them both. *whoever passes her by hisses:* Not the slightest compassion is felt for the fallen colossus. The hisses and fist-shaking reflect the viewers' attitude toward the proud one that has fallen and express their satisfaction with what they see (cf. Jer 19:8; 49:17; Mi 6:16).

(III) Prophecies Against Jerusalem (3:1–8). Zephaniah turns his attention to Jerusalem and its crimes.

15 **(A) The Leaders (3:1–5).** 1. The city is Jerusalem, where tyranny ruled and in which, owing to social injustice, a religious outlook had practically disappeared. It was not so much a question of weakness as of malice, harshness, and avarice (cf. 1:9; Ez 22:29). 2. *she hears no voice:* The time-honored formula for true piety was to "hear the Lord" (Jer 7:28) and to trust in him (Hos 6:5); Jerusalem has done neither. 3. The administrators of justice (princes, judges) are compared to wild animals on the prowl for food; treachery and violence are attributed to the representatives of religion (prophets and priests). Zephaniah paints a stark picture. The leaders were exploiting the people shamelessly (Ez 22:25–28), and in the face of this bad example the people had, of course, also deteriorated (Hos 4:6). Greed, even among the clergy of that time, was rampant, and since the religious laws governing the religion and life of the people were viewed with such broad toleration by the priests and prophets, there was once again a dallying with syncretism (cf. 1:8–9; Ez 44:23ff.). 5. In contrast, the Lord is just, and his medicinal judgment is manifest in vv. 6–7.

16 **(B) The Lesson of Other Nations (3:6–8).** 6–7. The Assyrian kings had imposed heavy yokes upon many peoples, exacting from them heavy tribute. The Lord speaks as if Assyria had been his instrument; it is he who has destroyed cities. But the religious significance behind the violent century just past was lost upon the people. 8. *therefore, wait for me:* Zephaniah speaks now to those who are faithful to the Lord. In view of what has happened in the past century, those who have remained faithful should await with confidence the intervention and judgment of the Lord. He shall be the accuser, or act as a witness, against the wicked; he shall also be judge and executioner (for the common figure of divine wrath, cf. Hos 5:1; Jer 10:25; etc.).

(IV) Promises (3:9–20).

17 **(A) Conversion of the Gentiles (3:9–10).** Harsh and difficult though the trial has been, its purpose has been conversion, not destruction. 9. *I will...purify the lips:* Those who had called upon false gods shall abandon their idols and turn to the worship of the Lord (cf. Is 6:5). The Prophet pictures an ideal future age in

which the Lord triumphs and salvation is for all. **10.** *the rivers of Ethiopia:* Whether the Nile Delta, the Blue Nile, or the White Nile is meant, the idea is that people from afar (Egypt and Assyria) shall come to pay homage to the Lord.

18 **(B) The Remnant of Israel (3:11–13).** This new oracle which fulfills the promise of 2:3 is one of the chief sources for the understanding of the OT concept of "poor in spirit." The Lord shall help his people to be renewed externally and internally, in their religion, views of morality, and practical social justice. **11.** *on that day:* The Messianic era. *you need not be ashamed:* The Prophet speaks directly to Jerusalem, called Israel in v. 14. **12.** *a people...humble and lowly:* The survivors, without earthly possessions, are but a remnant. The chastisement that comes from the Lord always reflects God's mercy as well. At this date, the remnant of Israel (cf. Mi 2:12) can only mean Judah; Samaria has long since fallen. This remnant shall rely heavily upon God in making its decisions; conversion implies the realization that prosperity and possessions do not constitute morality and right. The Lord alone suffices. **13.** *they shall pasture and couch their flocks:* A poetic description, often used (Is 14:30; 17:2; Ez 34:25, 28; Mi 4:4; 7:14) to depict peace. There shall be no lying or deceit; the virtuous, truthful, sincere remnant shall know peace and prosperity.

19 **(C) A Joyful Psalm of Zion (3:14–18a).** Zephaniah, or a later editor, invites Zion to rejoice because her salvation is at hand. **15.** *the King of Israel, the Lord:* The Lord himself shall stand at the head of Israel's army. With such leadership the nation need fear no enemy, from within or without. **17.** Jerusalem's most important citizen, so to speak, her savior, shall feel toward that city as a bridegroom for his bride (Is 62:5; Jer 2:2; 8:19; Hos 2:21), and in coming to the city he shall be attended by gladness and love, joyous shouts and dancing. The dance played an important role in ancient feasts (Ex 15:20–21; Jgs 21:19–21). The presence of God ("in your midst") is notably emphasized.

20 **(D) Return of the Exiles (3:18b–20).** **18b.** *I will remove disaster ...your disgrace:* This phrase is clearly a promise of restoration, probably dating from the time of the Exile; the Lord shall overthrow those who had treated his people with scorn and derision. **19–20.** The judgment upon the enemies of Israel and the glorification of Zion are themes particularly frequent in Is 40ff.

NAHUM

BIBLIOGRAPHY

21 Burrows, M., *The Dead Sea Scrolls* (New Haven, 1950); *More Light on the Dead Sea Scrolls* (New Haven, 1958). Gadd, C. J., *The Fall of Nineveh* (London, 1923). Gaster, T. H., *The Dead Sea Scriptures* (N.Y., 1956). George, A., *Nahum* (BJ; 2nd ed.; Paris, 1958). Haldar, A., *Studies in the Book of Nahum* (Uppsala, 1947). Jerome, *In Nahum Proph.* (*PL* 25. 1231–72). Laetsch, T., "Nahum," *The Minor Prophets* (St. Louis, 1956) 293–312. Leslie, E. A., *Nahum, Book of* (*IDB;* N.Y., 1962). Maier, W. A., *The Book of Nahum* (St. Louis, 1959). Nötscher, F., "Nahum," *Zwölfprophetenbuch* (Echter-B; Würzburg, 1948) 103–15. Parrot, A., *Nineveh and the Old Testament* (N.Y., 1955). Smith, J. M. P., *Nahum* (ICC; N.Y., 1911). Tournay, R., "Le Psaume de Nahum," *RB* 65 (1958) 328–35. Van Hoonacker, A., "Nahum," *Les douze petits prophètes* (EBib; Paris, 1908) 412–52. Vawter, B., *The Conscience of Israel* (N.Y., 1961). Vermès, G., "À propos des commentaires bibliques découverts à Qumrân," *RHPR* 35 (1955) 95–103.

INTRODUCTION

22 **(I) Background.** Nahum (lit., "Yahweh consoles") lived in the turbulent 7th cent. BC, an era of violence. He prophesied between the spectacular fall of Thebes (663; cf. 3:6) and that of Nineveh (612), probably *ca.* 612. The exultant hopes raised by the fall of proud Nineveh on the Tigris were short lived, for Josiah was soon to be cut down at Megiddo (609), Nebuchadnezzar was to become lord of the west at Carchemish (605), soon after which he would invest and take Jerusalem (587).

Nothing is known of Nahum outside of this prophecy, which reveals him to have been a poet of matchless style and great power. From this book, we learn of the passionate resentment that the Assyrians, who had violated every law and instinct of humanity, had aroused in subject nations. The news of her impending fall brought joy to many hearts. Despite his violent nationalism, however, Nahum has much to offer. He teaches that lasting kingdoms cannot be built on fraud and force, and that God punishes injustice, violence, and idolatry.

23 **(II) Outline.** The prophecy opens with a rather conventionally phrased and incomplete alphabetic psalm (1:2–2:3) describing the wrath of the Lord; its threats and promises, reminiscent of Zeph (1:18; 2:12–15; 3:12–13), form a good introduction to the awesome picture of the fall of Nineveh that follows (2:4–3:19). Nahum's savage lines breathe forth a spirit of vengeance. He gives no indication that the present unhappy situation of slavery might result from Judah's own sins—i.e., that the Lord was using the hated Assyrian as his instrument of punishment.

Toward the end of the Exile, Na 2:1 will be taken up and adapted by Is 52:7, but the NT does not quote Na at all. 1QpNa seeks only to explain the history of the author's own times; its author considers the fiery Prophet as uttering the Word of God and as being a source of truth.

The following outline has been suggested for the Book of Nahum:

- (I) The Wrath of the Lord (1:1–8)
  - (A) Manifestation of Divine Power (1:1–6)
  - (B) Manifestation of Divine Justice (1:7–8)
- (II) Prophecy Concerning Judah and Nineveh (1:9–2:1,3)
- (III) The Fall of Nineveh (2:2,4–19)
  - (A) The Assault (2:2,4–11)
  - (B) Threats to the Lion of Ashur (2:12–14)
  - (C) Warning to Nineveh (3:1–7)
  - (D) The Example of Thebes (3:8–11)
  - (E) Futility of Preparations at Nineveh (3:12–15a)
  - (F) The Swarm of Locusts (3:15b–17)
  - (G) Elegy (3:18–19)

COMMENTARY

24 **(I) The Wrath of the Lord (1:1–8).** The traditional theme of the Lord's anger and longanimity (cf. Ex 15; Is 30:27ff.; Zech 1) is here developed in a striking psalm (probably a later addition because it does not mention Nineveh). Until the letter *kaph*, it is an acrostic psalm; the attempts to reconstruct the entire alphabet are ingenious but not compelling. The metaphors are changing and ever bolder.

(A) Manifestation of Divine Power (1:1–6). **1.** *oracle:* A warning speech or utterance (Jer 23:33–40); a burden not easily handled. Elkosh is an unidentified locality, but surely to be sought in Judah (such a prophecy could never have been voiced in Assyria, although his "tomb" has been venerated at al-Qush near Nineveh). **2.** *jealous...avenging:* Because all law ultimately originates from God, violations of it constitute offenses against him that cannot go unpunished. The Lord is said to be jealous because of his devouring love (Ex 20:5; Dt 4:24). Those who flout his authority will feel the weight of the divine vengeance. Only violent images can express the magnitude of his anger, compared here to a storm. This splendid scene of Yahweh coming to judge (3–6) is more easily pictured than explained. **4.** *he rebukes the sea:* The Lord is absolute master of this chaotic primordial element (cf. Ex 14:16–29; 15:1–19) as evidenced by both the Exodus events and creation itself. Bashan, one of the most fertile of regions E of the Jordan, was noted for its flocks and trees (Am 1:2; 4:1). Carmel near Haifa, was also once heavily wooded. Mt. Lebanon, with its snowy heights, can hardly be pictured as suffering a drought, but the Lord could bring it about and also cause the flowers of Lebanon to fade. **5.** The physical world shall likewise feel the stormy wrath of the Lord when mountains, the very pillars of the earth (Jb 9:5–7) shall tremble and dissolve (note the hyperbole and the vivid metaphor).

(B) Manifestation of Divine Justice (1:7–8). There is another side to the divine judgment; unlike the storm, which when unleashed affects good and evil men alike, it is purposeful and selective. **7.** God knows his own and takes care of his own (Zeph 3:12). **8.** *when the flood rages:* Perhaps an allusion to the flood, for both Noah and Nahum were "consolers." *pursues with darkness:* The plight of those who oppose the Lord is hopeless; his pursuit of them into the night suggests the thoroughness and the tenacity of the avenger. An alternate rendition is possible—i.e., it is the darkness that pursues these enemies. The sense remains the same in either case.

25 **(II) Prophecy Concerning Judah and Nineveh (1:9–2:1,3).** This section is composed of alternating promises of salvation and ruin for Judah and Nineveh, respectively. **9.** *imputing:* The people of Judah are asked what they think of God's plans, but their answer is not recorded. It may be that Nahum asks a rhetorical question, for he continues to say that Yahweh will finish his work—carry out his plan to the end. *the enemy:* Assyria, although not yet named. **10.** *thornbushes...stubble:* The sense is that Yahweh's enemies are like thornbushes cut down and ready for the fire, a common image (Is 33:11–12; 2 Sm 23:6; Mi 7:4; etc.); it underscores the Lord's invincible power. Therefore, let Judah be comforted. **11.** Transpose after v. 13, to avoid too frequent a change in address ("you" in v. 11 refers to Nineveh). **12.** *they:* Judah's enemies are meant; neither their number nor strength shall avail them after they have served Yahweh's purpose—his instrument to humble Judah. From Assyria came forth the unidentified "Belial," "the scoundrel" (v. 11) who has wicked schemes in mind (cf. 1 Sm 1:16). Perhaps it designates Sennacherib, whose thrust upon Jerusalem (701) was still fresh in memory. His punishment is foretold in terms similar to those in Is (14:19–21) and Jer (8:1–2; 22:18–19; 36:30). **14.** *I will abolish the carved and molten image:* Possibly a reference to the "seventy-one halls, lined with stone reliefs...depicting various activities of the king and his armies" (*WHAB* 68). Nineveh was so thoroughly destroyed in 612 that its ruins lay undisturbed for over 2000 years, until rediscovered by Botta in 1843 (Parrot, *op. cit.*, 15–19). *mockery:* Read *qallāsâ;* a prophecy of the future fate of Assyria. Even in death, scorn shall be heaped upon this enslaver of the world. The MT has "for you are worthless." For Judah, there are words of comfort (2:1,3), for the Prophet sees deliverance and freedom at the very doors of the captive city.

2:1. The good news is flashed from one hilltop to the other. *peace:* Nahum sums up the blessings of freedom in one word (Is 52:7 will use these words to describe the coming of the Lord to Zion). No more shall the "scoundrel" (Belial; cf. 1:11) harass and oppress the land. *feasts...vows:* The first such things the Prophet thinks of are the religious duties of the nation—observance of the feast days and fulfillment of vows. **3.** *vine of Jacob...Israel:* A united Israel (both branches) is compared to a "vine," a proud symbol of majesty, restored to a flourishing condition. Israel and Judah (described as a vine in Is 5:1–7; Ps 80:9), had both been devastated by ruthless invaders bent on plunder.

26 **(III) The Fall of Nineveh (2:2,4–19).** This passage is a matchless description of the fall of Nineveh, unsurpassed for sheer vividness (but cf. Is 5:25–30; Jer 46:3–10; 4:5–21).

(A) The Assault (2:2,4–11). **2.** Transposed after v. 3. *the hammer:* Probably refers to the Babylonians and Medes, and perhaps to the Scythians. The Prophet's advice is highly ironical; for all its military defensive precautions, the city cannot be saved (cf. Jer 6:1–5; 46:3–11). **4–5.** A description begins of the tenseness and activity of a siege. *fiery steel are the chariots:* Armored chariots were new; covered with highly polished metal plates, they flashed in the sun as they prepared to attack. *the horses:* The high-spirited war horses, bedecked with tassels and ribbons, quiver with excitement as they sense the fray. In the bright sun the glitter of the chariots would make one think of lightning bolts. **6.** *the mantelet:* The outposts destroyed, the enemy advances eagerly upon the city walls where they set up the mantelet (*sōkēk*), a portable sort of defense designed to protect the attackers from the arrows, stones, or torches hurled from the ramparts (*ANE* 101). **7.** It is not known what part the river gates might play in the city's fall. The river in question is the Tigris, with its affluent the Khoser. Nineveh lay on the E bank of the Tigris (opposite modern Mosul in Iraq), and was protected by a complex of dams, moats, sluices, etc. Its city wall had 15 doors. *the palace shudders:* Probably a description of the panic and terror felt by the inmates. **8.** *its mistress:* Inasmuch as the Assyrian queen was usually unimportant, the reference is probably to the statue of Ishtar, the great goddess of

Nineveh, who was served by sacred prostitutes. *doves:* Because of its plaintive call, the dove is a symbol of mourning (Is 38:14; 59:11).

9. *Nineveh is like a pool:* The difficult text is corrected from the LXX. The defenders do not wait to grapple with the attackers but fly from them, as water drains from a breached dam. No command ("Stop! Stop!") can hold them. **10.** *plunder:* The wealth of Nineveh had become enormous; ancient annals tell of the heavy tribute the Assyrian kings, whose supremacy extended over 125 years, were accustomed to demand and obtain. Statues from Egypt have been found as far away as Nebi Yunus (Parrot, *op. cit.*, 68). **11.** *emptiness, desolation, waste!:* English cannot render the stirring assonance of the MT nouns: *bûqâ, ûmᵉbûqâ, umᵉbullāqâ.* The conquerors reduced the city to a mound and a ruin (*DOTT* 76). *frame:* The loins, the seat of strength, are subjected to intense pain, and the bleak faces of the vanquished reveal their utter defeat.

27 **(B) Threats to the Lion of Ashur (2:12–14).** **12.** *the lion:* The king of Assyria. Excavations have revealed the popularity of the lion motif in Assyrian sculpture; the cruelty of the Assyrian king is thus graphically described (cf. also Hos 5:14; Mi 5:7; Jer 4:7; etc.). *where...den:* This rhetorical question indicates that the den is destroyed. *with no one to disturb them:* Assyria had ruled supreme for 125 years, and Nineveh had become one of the wealthiest cities in the world. Nevertheless, it is the "Lord of Hosts" (v. 14) who achieves the downfall of Nineveh. No more shall tribute be exacted or submission be imposed upon the Prophet's people (cf. 2 Kgs 18:17,19; 19:9,23; Is 33:19; 37:10ff.).

28 **(C) Warning to Nineveh (3:1–7).** A new song, blending warning and derision, describes the judgment to be visited upon Assyria's sins.

1. *bloody city, all lies:* Nineveh is obviously meant. By cunning and unscrupulous statecraft, Assyria had lulled many nations into relaxing their guard, and had then forced them to do her bidding by bloody campaigns that filled her coffers with plunder. Ever rapacious, Assyria richly deserved an unenviable reputation; although she had no monopoly on cruelty, she had great opportunity to exercise it. **2.** An extraordinarily vivid and staccato description conveys the impression of hearing the clatter of horses' hoofs and rumbling of noisy chariots jolting toward the luckless foe. We have no details of the actual siege; the fall is described in a few scant lines (*DOTT* 76). There is, however, little doubt as to the thoroughness of the destruction and looting of the city **4.** *debaucheries...witchcraft:* By her prestige, powerful Assyria had enslaved whole nations, as a harlot seduces men. **5.** *lift up your skirts:* Nineveh is now to receive the humiliating punishment reserved for harlotry—i.e., shameful exposure to the public gaze (Is 20:4; Hos 2:5,12; Ez 16:37; 23:25–30). It is Yahweh who brings such retribution on Nineveh; she shall be pelted with filth (*šiqquṣîm*) and shall be made a spectacle to all, as one subjected to the pillory (a possible derivation from *ra'ah*, "to see"). **7.** The sight of fallen Nineveh will turn people from the scene in horror (cf. Lam 1:2,9). But Nahum's rhetorical question, "Where can one find any to console her?" is grimly exultant. Nineveh will suffer without friends to sympathize and support.

29 **(D) The Example of Thebes (3:8–11).** **8.** *No-Amon...set among the streams:* The "City of the god Amon," or Thebes, lay on the E bank of the Nile in Upper Egypt and was once the great city of the Orient. Her ruins have been described as the "mightiest to be found anywhere in the world." Visitors to Karnak and Luxor will be inclined to agree. Thebes was taken after a long siege by Ashurbanipal in 663, who did not fail to boast of that fact in his *Annals* (for the Egyptian campaigns, cf. *ANET* 294–97). The city can hardly be said to have been "set among the streams," a poetical hyperbole. News of the fall of Thebes shook the entire world; even 50 years later, Nahum uses it as a classical example. **9.** An Ethiopian dynasty ruled over Thebes from 712 to 663, and thus could draw upon all the resources of Nubia. The location of Put is uncertain; a locality to the east near Punt (Somaliland), or to the west in Libya, is probable. **10.** A description of the evils that usually accompany war (cf. Hos 10:14; Ps 137:9). **11.** *you, too, shall drink:* Nineveh shall fall as mighty Thebes once fell. The wicked city must drain the cup of God's anger; defeat and destruction are its ingredients (Is 51:17,21–22; Jer 25:15–27). Assyria found an unlikely ally in Neco II, but his help was ineffectual; after 612 the destruction of Assyrian power was certain.

30 **(E) Futility of Preparations at Nineveh (3:12–15a).** **12.** The ease with which Assyria will be taken is a poetic exaggeration and forms part of the irony of the work (cf. vv. 18–19). **13.** *the troops are women:* So terror stricken are the defenders of the city that their manly courage will desert them (Is 19:16; Jer 49:22). Actually, the siege lasted two years and the defenders acquitted themselves creditably; Nahum writes with no little irony. **14.** *draw water:* Derisively, the Prophet urges the defenders to have a good supply of water. For a Judean, a water supply was a matter of life and death (cf. Is 22:10–11), but it was no problem for Nineveh, situated on the Tigris and Khoser. *tread the clay...brick mold:* A supply of bricks was essential for the defense of the city; they were used to repair walls damaged by missiles or battering rams. Sun-dried brick was the chief building material in Assyria and Babylonia.

31 **(F) The Swarm of Locusts (3:15b–17).** **15b.** *multiply like the grasshoppers:* Nahum ironically urges Nineveh to increase the number of its defenders. **16.** *your couriers...garrisons:* In the wake of mighty Assyria, there had quickly followed hordes of merchants, soldiers, and officials, aptly compared to locust swarms because of their numbers and voracity. **16b.** Transposed after 17a. Whenever resistance and danger arose, these time servers would prudently vanish. They are likened to locusts that light on fence tops in the cool of the day: they remain motionless until, warmed by the sun, they galvanize into destructive action. Their arrival and departure are equally mysterious and dreadful.

32 **(G) Elegy (38:18–19).** The Prophet composes an ironic funeral lament, or dirge, over the fallen city. **18.** *slumber:* A euphemism for death; the rulers have been slain. *O king of Assyria:* Many consider this phrase a gloss because it breaks the rhythm of the dirge originally directed at Ashur, not the king. *your shepherds:* Applies better to the city than to the king, who is himself a shepherd, according to ancient Oriental thought. **19.** *there is no healing for your hurt:* For a similar idea, cf. Jer 8:18–22; 10:19; etc. Nineveh's wound is mortal; she shall now suffer the same fate she had so often inflicted upon others. Her fall arouses only malicious, savage exultation. *clap their hands over you:* Applause is an expression of joy and approval (Is 55:12; Ex 25:6; etc.). Nahum speaks not only for his own nation but also for all those who have suffered at the hands of Assyria.

HABAKKUK

BIBLIOGRAPHY

33 Albright, W. F., "The Psalm of Habakkuk," *Studies in Old Testament Prophecy* (Fest. T. H. Robinson; Edinburgh, 1950–57) 1–18. Barthélemy, D., "Notes en marge...le Midrash d'Habacuc," *RB* 59 (1952) 207–18. Bévenot, H., "Le Cantique de Habacuc," *RB* 42 (1933) 499–525. Brownlee, W. H., "Biblical Interpretation Among the Sectaries of the Dead Sea Scrolls," *BA* 14 (1951) 54–76. Burrows, M., *The Isaiah Manuscript and the Habakkuk Commentary* (New Haven, 1950). Gaster, T., *The Dead Sea Scriptures* (N.Y., 1956). Jerome, *In Hab. Proph.* (*PL* 25. 1273–1338). Leslie, E. A., *Book of Habakkuk* (*IDB;* N.Y., 1962). Moriarty, F., "Habacuc and Recent Controversy," *TS* 13 (1952) 228–33. Nötscher, F., "Habakuk," *Zwölfprophetenbuch* (Echter-B; Würzburg, 1941) 116–26. Roth, C., "The Subject Matter of Qumran Exegesis," *VT* 10 (1960) 51–68. Van Hoonacker, A., "Habacuc," *Les douze petits prophètes* (EBib; Paris, 1908) 453–97. Ward, W. H., "Habakkuk" (ICC; N.Y., 1911). Weiser, A., *Das Buch der Zwölf Kleinen Propheten* (ATD 24/25; 2nd ed.; Göttingen, 1956).

INTRODUCTION

34 **(I) Background.** Very little is known about the prophet Habakkuk. From the liturgies (e.g., 1:2–2:4) some have deduced that he was a member, possibly a leader, of the Temple choir; certainly he was a deep thinker and a man of considerable literary skill, a "wrestler with God" (Jerome). His carefully constructed work opens with a dialogue between the Prophet and God; its novelty consists in its daring but respectful demand that God explain his strange way of governing the world. To be sure, Judah has sinned, but why should God, the holy one whose eyes are too pure to gaze upon evil, have chosen to punish evildoers with those who are more wicked than themselves? Can it be that the Lord is on the side of injustice? Habakkuk is intensely preoccupied with the problem of evil, the perennial stumbling block for all thoughtful men. He is told to write down the divine answer so that all who run may read: in ways paradoxical to us, God is preparing the final victory of justice; the evildoers shall pass away, but the just man shall live, only if he is faithful (2:4). Paul works this "heart of Habakkuk" into his own teaching on faith (Rom 1:17; Gal 3:11; Heb 10:38).

Uncertainty still prevails regarding the circumstances surrounding the prophecy of Habakkuk and whether the oppressor was the Assyrians, the Chaldeans, or King Jehoiakim of Judah (609–598), under whom the deplorable practices of Manasseh's reign had been resumed (cf. Jer 22:13–17). On the whole, the Chaldeans are most probable, being named (1:6) as God's instruments for the chastisement of his people; it is against them that Yahweh will take the field. One might date the prophecy between the defeat of Neco by Nebuchadnezzar at Carchemish (605) and the siege of Jerusalem (597). This chronology places Habakkuk shortly after Nahum, and makes him also a contemporary of Jeremiah.

35 **(II) Outline.** The book falls neatly into three parts: (I) a dialogue between the Prophet and God (1:1–2:4), in which Habakkuk's two complaints are answered; (II) maledictions pronounced over evildoers (here the problem arises: Chaldeans or Judeans themselves?; see, e.g., B. Vawter, *The Conscience of Israel* [N.Y., 1961]) for five different types of crime (2:5–20); (III) the Canticle of Habakkuk (3:1–19), an anguished prayer that the Lord intervene in favor of his people as he had in the past and a description of his coming. The musical indications given for the hymn suggest that it was used in the liturgy. It is interesting to note that 1QpHab deals with chs. 1–2 only; however, this intricate and essentially midrashic commentary simply may not have been finished, and it is no real argument against the authenticity of ch. 3.

The following outline has been suggested for the Book of Habakkuk:

- (I) Dialogue Between Habakkuk and God (1:1–2:4)
  - (A) The Prophet's Complaint: There Is No Justice (1:2–4)
  - (B) The Lord's Reply (1:5–11)
  - (C) Second Complaint: Continued Oppression (1:12–17)
  - (D) The Lord's Reply (2:1–4)
- (II) Curses for Various Crimes (2:5–20)
  - (A) Prelude (2:5–6)
  - (B) The Curses (2:6b–20)
    - (a) Woe Against Oppressive Greed (2:6b–8)
    - (b) Curse Against Unscrupulous Gain (2:9–11)
    - (c) Curse Against Policies of Violence (2:12–14)
    - (d) Curse Against Unwarranted Cruelty (2:15–17)
    - (e) Curse Against the Idolatrous (2:18–20)
- (III) The Canticle of Habakkuk (3:1–19)
  - (A) Title (3:1)
  - (B) Habakkuk's Prayer (3:2)
  - (C) The Vision of the Lord (3:3–7)
  - (D) The Warlike Advance of the Lord (3:8–15)
  - (E) Conclusion: Fear God and Trust Him (3:16–19)

COMMENTARY

(I) Dialogue Between Habakkuk and God (1:1–2:4) **1.** This is the only title in the pre-exilic prophetical writings to name the author as a prophet.

36 **(A) The Prophet's Complaint: There Is No Justice (1:2–4).** **2.** *how long, O Lord?:* The anguish of a downtrodden people finds voice in the plaintive question. Habakkuk finds the Lord's toleration of the wicked very difficult to understand. God's inactivity is intolerable. *ruin...misery...destruction...strife...discord:* The evils here deplored are best identified with oppression by foreigners (cf. vv. 12–17); Nötscher and others, however, think of the reign of King Jehoiakim (Jer 22:13–19). **4.** *the law is benumbed:* If vv. 2–4 refer to foreign expression, the law is not the Torah but everything that has to do with justice; a condition close to anarchy and a general disregard for personal rights seems to prevail (Mi 7:2–3; Is 59:14). If this dialogue was in reality a temple liturgy (A. Weiser), then the Prophet speaks in the name of the community.

37 **(B) The Lord's Reply (1:5–11).** **5.** *a work is being done...:* Yahweh's actions, whether in creating the world or in intervening in history, are often described as a work (e.g., Is 5:12; 28:21; 29:23). Both oppressor and oppressed will be astonished at his choice of the Chaldeans as instruments of his justice. **6.** The Chaldeans lived up to their description in vv. 6–11, being accomplished in violence and savage destruction. Graphic images are now piled up in profusion, characteristic of the warlike invader (cf. Is 5:25–29; 13:16–18; Jer 4:5–7,15–17; Na 3:2–3; Ez 23:22–26; etc.). **7.** *from himself...derive his law and majesty:* Although he is the Lord's instrument, the avenger does not know it and recognizes no law or right other than his own strength and sword. **8.** By his harshly fixed purpose and swift approach, the enemy will inspire terror. Wolves that prey at night are proverbially hungry and fierce. Eagles probably denote vultures, unknown for pity. **9.** *their combined onset...:* All these enemies assemble for violence. The text is unusually difficult; the MT has "the multitude of" or the "ardor [or envy?] of their faces." Thus, either the combined onslaught of cruel enemies, or their greedy look, is compared to a storm wind (*qādîm*) or E wind. The violent and scorching E wind from the desert often serves as a symbol for invasion from the east (Hos 12:2; Jer 18:17; Ez 17:10ff.; 1QpHab 3:9). **10.** The word "he" refers to this savage people already mentioned (vv. 6–8). *princes are his laughing-stock:* The Babylonians compiled an imposing list of vanquished kings. In 612 they had defeated Sinsharishkun at Nineveh, and in 609, his son Ashur-uballit at Haran; at Carchemish, in 605, it was to be the Egyptian, Neco. *heaps up a ramp:* Mounds of earth were sometimes heaped up against the walls of cities so that troops could mount them and set up their engines of war (cf. 2 Sm 20:15), Alexander later joined Tyre to mainland by a mole. The "ramp" may also have been nothing more than breastworks to shield the attackers (Is 29:3; Jer 6:6). **11.** *he veers like the wind:* Like a violent wind, the victor blows suddenly and swiftly and is gone, leaving a trail of havoc. The Assyrian and Babylonian invaders, motivated by greed, left the administration of conquered provinces to local rulers who were to see to the prompt payment of tribute. Habakkuk is indignant over the pride that the conqueror takes in his strength (cf. v. 7; Is 10:13).

38 **(C) Second Complaint: Continued Oppression (1:12–17).** The Lord governs everything that happens to the chosen people; therefore, the Prophet approaches him again. His second complaint concerns the Chaldeans and Nebuchadnezzar, who have already been singled out to do the Lord's purpose. Habakkuk gropes for an answer to so much evil (cf. Jer 12:1–6). **12.** *my holy One...Immortal:* The scribes substituted *namût,* (we shall not die) for *tamût,* to eliminate the blasphemous thought that the Lord might die; this is one of the *tiqqunê sōpᵉrîm* of Jewish tradition. *O Rock!:* The Lord, ever steadfast, is often thus described in the OT cf. Dt 32:4). Surely then he will punish the Chaldean. **13.** *too pure are your eyes:* The Lord is holy and will therefore never inflict undeserved punishment, which only makes it the more perplexing that he should allow the wicked oppressor to maintain his hold on those "more just than himself." That the Lord should say and do nothing is very disturbing. **14.** *man...fish:* In a striking image (found also in Assyro-Babylonian literature), man (God's choicest creation) is compared to the leaderless fish of the sea. **15.** *net:* Only a little less than the angels and totally different from such things as locusts and ants, man is apparently delivered over to an oppressor, to be gathered in as if by nets and hooks. **16.** *sacrifices to his net:* The Babylonians are not known to have sacrificed to their nets (the Scythians, however, are said to have thus honored their swords as symbols of Ares); the meaning is that the victor pays tribute and acknowledges as God only his own strength, which procures for him the good things of life. **17.** *shall he then keep on brandishing his sword:* How long will the Lord tolerate this victorious and merciless Chaldean?

39 **(D) The Lord's Reply (2:1–4).** Acutely unhappy with the events, the Prophet awaits attentively for the answer to his question.

1. *I will stand at my guard post...upon the rampart:* Habakkuk is on the alert in his own home, or in some other place propitious for a revelation. The Lord then tells him what he must do. **2.** *write down the vision clearly:* The Lord's words are not meant for Habakkuk's ears alone; the message was to be written down in letters so big that "he who runs may read" and, at a later date, may check to see if the vision was verified or not (Is 30:8). **3.** *the vision still has its time:* It is as if the vision were pressing on with a sort of inward dynamism to its future realization, which shall take place at the moment determined by God (cf. Is 55:10–11). **4a.** *the rash man has no integrity:* The time-honored theory of retribution finds expression: whereas the wicked man shall come to a bad end, there stretches before the good man the prospect of a long life (Is 3:10). **4b.** *the just man lives by faith:* These famous words summarize the entire vision. The Hebr notion of "faith" (*'ĕmûnāh*) describes the just man, implying not so much faith in our theological sense as faithfulness, loyalty, and steadfastness. The word is used of Moses' uplifted hands ("held steady," Ex 17:12), and of men who could be entrusted with money (2 Kgs 12:16). The "just man" then, if he holds fast to the Law of God, will know vindication and be restored to honor. It is the wicked man (in this context clearly Babylon) who shall founder and come to grief. Paul, following the LXX (Rom 1:17; Gal 3:11; Heb 10:38), says that the just man lives by or is justified by "faith." Faith is compounded of belief and love as well as of trust and confidence amid trials and tribulations.

(II) Curses for Various Crimes (2:5–20).

40 **(A) Prelude (2:5–6).** Suddenly changing the train of his thought, the Prophet refers to the oppressor's thirst for riches. **5.** *wealth too is treacherous:* The reading (*hôn* for *yayin*) appears in 1QpHab 8:3; the "wicked wine" of the MT is difficult to fit into the context. Wealth often makes its owners proud and restless; unable to settle down peacefully with what they already have, they seem never to have enough. **5b.** *he who opens wide his throat...is insatiable:* Like the nether world (Sheol), the rich are never satisfied (cf. Prv 27:20; 30:15–16); in the Ugaritic texts (*UT* 67; *ANE* 112), death is personified as Mot, whose mouth is opened wide to swallow. **5c.** *gather to himself all the nations:* Wholesale deportation of peoples was an ordinary aftermath of ancient wars. **6.** *a taunt...satires and epigrams:* The *māšāl* is basically a comparison. It can be translated in many ways, here best rendered as "taunt-song." Solemnly, five prophetical "epigrams" will be set forth, each beginning with a "Woe"; a curse lurks behind each (cf. Is 14:4; Mi 2:4). The evildoer, never explicitly named, is presumably Babylon.

41 **(B) The Curses (2:6b–20).**

(a) Woe Against Oppressive Greed (2:6b–8). The captive nations shall cry out against their oppressors. The first curse is against those who have enriched themselves at the expense of others. The despoiler, here obviously the Chaldean, will himself be despoiled. **6b.** *debts:* The Hebr *'abṭîṭ*, which the Vg translates *densum lutum* and the Douay (and KJ) as "thick clay," is now known to be something taken from a poor man, such as a "pledge." The idea is that the debtors will seize back their mortgages and pledges. **8.** Measure for measure, injustice and sin will be fittingly punished (cf. Is 33:1).

(b) Curse Against Unscrupulous Gain (2:9–11). **9.** *woe...evil gain...setting his nest on high:* The man who has become rich through injustice and then seeks to escape retribution by flight, i.e., by building his "nest" or house (i.e., dynasty [cf. Jer 22:13–17]) away from the common herd, shall not escape (Is 14:13); misfortune, shame, and death await him (cf. Jer 49:16). **11.** *for the stone in the wall shall cry out:* The very stones and the beams in the ceiling, ill-gotten as they are, cry out in reproach against the master of the house.

(c) Curse Against Policies of Violence (2:12–14). Verses 12–13 may possibly be the reproach mentioned in the previous verse. **12.** Prisoners of war and slaves constituted a cheap labor army that the conqueror literally worked to death (cf. Mi 3:10; Jer 22:13). **13.** *people toil for the flames:* A graphic image of fruitless labor; the city built with blood and wickedness shall end in ashes (Jer 51:58). **14.** *for the earth shall be filled:* The triumph of the Lord is described in this citation of Is 11:9, which implies the disappearance of the oppressor.

(d) Curse Against Unwarranted Cruelty (2:15–17). The Prophet next inveighs against the conqueror who takes pleasure in the shame and degradation inflicted upon his defeated and helpless enemy. **15.** *woe...a flood of your wrath to drink:* To cause another to drink of the cup of wrath is something proper to the Lord (cf. Jer 25:15; 51:7; Is 51:17); because Babylon has usurped this power, she must taste of it in her turn. *till their nakedness is seen:* To be stripped of one's clothing and made a public exhibition is the supreme humiliation (cf. Na 3:4). **15.** *drink, you too, and stagger!:* The wrath of the Lord also inebriates; those who drink of it will know humiliation. In 15c, the MT has a savage thrust: "Show your uncircumcision!"—i.e., "Be despised in your turn because you are completely naked, exposing your uncircumcision." **17.** *the violence done to Lebanon:* A stereotyped idea that expresses the ravaging of the countryside by the invading army (cf. Is 14:8; 37:24). Cities built at the cost of human blood shall not prove stable; retribution shall overtake the Chaldean for his callous use of both men and beasts.

(e) Curse Against the Idolatrous (2:18–20). Verse 19 has been transposed before v. 18 in conformity with the pattern of the previous "Woes." The Israelite prophets have only scorn for idols that can neither help them, nor proffer helpful oracles to their devotees (cf. Is 44:9–20; Jer 10:3–16). **20.** *the Lord is in his holy temple:* Taken with the injunction "Silence before him, all the earth!" (cf. Zeph 1:7; Zech 2:17), this phrase suggests that v. 20 was once part of a liturgical formula.

42 **(III) The Canticle of Habakkuk (3:1–19).** This famous passage describes the Lord's coming in majesty and power to avenge his people.

(A) Title (3:1). Although it is a "prayer," only v. 2 contains a supplication; the rest is a hymn addressed to the Almighty. The pausal indications (*selah*, vv. 3, 9, 19; cf. N. Snaith, "Selah" *VT* 2 [1952] 43–56) are later additions, as is the name Habakkuk.

(B) Habakkuk's Prayer (3:2). **2.** *O Lord, I have heard your renown:* The Prophet has in mind what the Lord did for his people during the time of Moses and the Exodus; the Sinai experience had been a glorious one, and became a prototype for subsequent interpretations of history (Nm 14:15; Dt 2:25; Na 3:19). *I have feared your work:* What is meant is not terror but reverential fear at the manifestation of divine power. *in the course of the years revive it:* The Lord's work continues, but the Prophet urges him to show himself now once again the Lord of old. He had vented his anger at his own people by sending the Chaldean; let him not forget to be merciful as well (Is 26:20; 54:8).

43 **(C) The Vision of the Lord (3:3–7).** Habakkuk in spirit sees the coming of the Lord: theophany (3–7) and an ensuing contest (8–15). Allusions to glorious events of the past arouse confidence in the help of the Lord, for that first deliverance (the Exodus) was the foreshadowing of another for which the Prophet longs. **3.** *God comes from Teman...from Mount Paran:* An archaic form of the word for God (*'ĕlôah*) is used here in Habakkuk's evocation of the past. Teman and Paran represent the district and mountain S and W of Judah. The Lord comes from the direction of Mt. Sinai, and his approach is like that of a violent tempest (cf. Dt 33:2,26; Jgs 5:4,5,20; Ps 68:29; etc.). **4.** *his splendor...rays...power:* The radiance of the Lord is like that of the day; rays of light (lit., "horns"; cf. Ex 34:29–30,35) shoot forth from his hands. The Phoenician storm-god is depicted as holding a thunderbolt in his hands (*ANE* 140). The Lord's power is hidden in brilliance. **5.** *before him...pestilence...the plague follows:* Attending the Lord are two scourges, ready to obey his bidding (cf. 2 Sm 23:1–24:15; Hos 13,14; Ps 91:6); the second of these (*rešep*) is fever (Dt 32:24; Ps 91:6). **6.** A clearer meaning might be obtained by reading *wayyam'ēd*. The Lord halts to look about him and the earth shakes (instead of "to survey the earth"); a glance from him causes the nations to know agitation and fear. The reaction of the earth is described first—the age-old hills upon which the Lord treads are shaken by earthquakes (cf. Mi 1:3; Am 4:13; Ps 77:17–21); the troubles experienced by the nations follow. **7.** Cushan is mentioned only here in the OT; it is probably an archaic name for Midian (Ex 2:15). The route from Sinai is clearly intended. As the Lord advances, all fall before him.

44 **(D) The Warlike Advance of the Lord (3:8–15).** Certain awesome phenomena, similar to those which took place during the Exodus (cf. Jgs 5:4–5; Ps 77:15–21; 114:3–7), accompany the coming of the Lord. **8.** We find echoes of ancient myths of a struggle between divinity and the unruly elements (the abyss, sea, river; see *ANET* 129ff; cf. Ps 89:10–11; Is 51:9; etc.). Steeds, the victorious chariot, and the Lord's weapons convey the idea of a war; God is represented as riding upon the clouds (Is 19:1; Dt 33:26–27). **9.** *bared and ready your bow:* The Lord removes from its case his bow, the symbol of strength and a weapon suited to charioteers (Gn 49:24; Jb 29:20). For arrows he has lightning (v. 4; Pss 29:7; 77:18). *into streams you split the earth:* The torrential rains cut channels into the earth's surface (cf. Ps 77:17–19; Jgs 5:4); these may also be the streams the Lord causes to arise from the earth, dividing it. **10.** Tehom, the primordial ocean or abyss, whose waters join those of the heavens, adds its mighty roar to the tumult. **11.** *the sun and the moon remain in their abode:* The sun does not give its light (LXX); only the Lord's flashing arms (his lightning is compared to arrows and spear) will split the darkness. The brilliance of the Lord puts out the lesser lights. **12.** There is a transition from the symbolic description of a storm to a direct consideration of the triumph of the Lord over the enemies of his people. The Lord in his fury, but in the interests of justice, tramples the nations to separate the good from the bad. **13.** *You come...to save your anointed one:* The context indicates that the anointed is the people (rather than the king). *you crush the heads from the house of the wicked:* A very obscure verse. If the singular (head) is used, as in the MT, the wicked one is the Chaldean (cf. 1:4,13), against whom the Lord has to defend his people. The house of this wicked one must be destroyed. Albright here sees an allusion to the defeat of the impious Mot; Gadd and Tournay refuse to follow his mythological interpretation. **14.** *whose boast would be of devouring the wretched in their lair:* The wicked enemy is compared to beasts of prey that carry their victims to their lairs, where they can devour them at leisure. **15.** *you tread the sea with your steeds...churning...deep waters:* For the image, cf. Ps 77:20; Is 43:16–17; the comparison of storm clouds with horses and chariots occurs frequently (Dt 33:26–27). The reminder of the successful passage of the Red Sea (Ex 14–15) and the defeat of the Egyptian army there is reassuring.

45 **(E) Conclusion: Fear God and Trust Him (3:16–19).** The vision is now at an end, and the Prophet is deeply moved. **16.** So violent has the storm been that he writes, "I hear" (cf. also 3:2; Is 21:3–4; Jer 23:9; Dn 8:18,27; 10:8). *my body trembles...my lips quiver:* Habakkuk's body reacts violently to what he has just seen and heard and he is filled with reverential awe. *decay invades my bones:* Compare Hos 5:12; Prv 12:4; 14:30; Jb 13:28. So frightened is the Prophet that his bones can hardly support him. He steels himself to await calmly the day of distress that will come for the oppressors of his nation. **17.** The picture of agricultural misery that follows may be a gloss (vv. 16 and 18–19 go together), intended to re-enforce the lesson of hope in the Lord. Or, it may also be a description of the damages caused in Judah by the war (cf. Jer 5:17). Van Hoonacker considers the possibility of vv. 17–19 being an addition expressive of the confidence one ought always to have in God, no matter what the circumstances. **18.** Despite hunger and misery, the Prophet and the community that adopted his song lose neither heart nor hope. Habakkuk's trust it rooted in a deep belief in the Lord, upon whom he counts despite all manner of difficulty (cf. Mi 7:7). **19.** Swift movement is proper to the victor, who assumes command of the high places from which he can dominate the area (cf. Ps 18:34; Dt 32:13). The last words refer to the musical rendition of the "song," and are a rubric directed to the choir leader; stringed instruments are to be used. Such directions ordinarily occur at the beginning of psalms.

19

JEREMIAH

Guy P. Couturier, C.S.C.

BIBLIOGRAPHY

1 Bonnard, P., *Le Psautier selon Jérémie* (LD 26; Paris, 1960). Bright, J., *Jeremiah* (AB 21; Garden City, N.Y., 1965). Condamin, A., *Le Livre de Jérémie* (EBib; 3rd ed.; Paris, 1936). Gelin, A., *Jérémie* (BJ; 2nd ed.; Paris, 1959); *Jérémie* (*VDBS* 4; Paris, 1928) 857–89. Muilenburg, J., *Jeremiah the Prophet* (*IDB* 2; Nashville, 1963) 823–35. Nötscher, F., *Das Buch Jeremias* (Bonn, 1934). Paterson, J., *Jeremiah* (*PCB*; London, 1962). Penna, A., *Geremia* (LSB; Rome, 1954). Rudolph, W., *Jeremia* (HAT 12; 2nd ed.; Tübingen, 1958). Skinner, J., *Prophecy and Religion. Studies in the Life of Jeremiah* (Cambridge, 1922). Steinman, J., *Le prophète Jérémie* (LD 9; Paris, 1952). Volz, P., *Der Prophet Jeremia* (KAT 10; 2nd ed.; Leipzig, 1928). Weiser, A., *Der Prophet Jeremia* (ATD 20–21; Göttingen, 1952–55). Welch, A. C., *Jeremiah, His Time and His Work* (Oxford, 1928).

INTRODUCTION

2 **(I) Jeremiah's Time.** Jeremiah lived through one of the most troubled periods of the ancient Near East. He witnessed the fall of a great empire and the rising of one even greater. In the midst of this turmoil, the kingdom of Judah, then in the hands of deplorable kings, came to its downfall by resisting this overwhelming force of history.

(A) The Near East. After the brilliant military campaigns of Ashurnasirpal (884–860) and Shalmaneser III (859–825), Assyria remained the leading power of the Near East for about two centuries. The empire reached its zenith under Esarhaddon (681–670). Ashurbanipal (669–633) could maintain its prestige at the beginning of his reign, but toward the end, signs of the empire's decline were noticeable both within and without. Assyria would rapidly experience her eclipse from history, once Ashurbanipal had died (*ca.* 633).

If Herodotus' sole testimony is correct, at that time Scythian hordes from the Caucasus swept the whole of the Near East, not so much to occupy new regions as to plunder barbarously the already inhabited lands (1.103–106). Meanwhile, Babylon raised its head to see that the time had come for its turn to control the Fertile Crescent. Thus, the crown prince Nabopolassar (626–605) first revolted against Assyria. Once he had gained Babylon's full independence, he launched a series of attacks on Assyria with the help of Cyaxares, king of the Medes. Asshur fell in 614, and Nineveh, the capital, was totally destroyed in 612 (see Na 3). Ashur-uballit II, Assyria's last king, fled to Haran where he resisted Nabopolassar for three years, with the help of Neco, Pharaoh of Egypt. In 609, Nabopolassar took Haran and continued to spread his new empire southward until his death in August, 605. At that time, his son and successor, Nebuchadnezzar, had just defeated the Egyptian armies at Carchemish; this victory yielded to Babylon the prevalence in politics. Nebuchadnezzar (605–561), a warrior by nature, spent most of his life outside Babylon at the head of his armies. Egypt was the only country that resisted his domination. In 601, the two armies met in an indecisive battle at the Egyptian frontier; apparently, the Babylonian king renewed his attempt at conquest only in 568, when he was successful. We now have ample information on this first part of the Neo-Babylonian Empire's history (see D. J. Wiseman, *Chronicles of Chaldaean Kings* [London, 1956]).

3 **(B) Judah.** During Manasseh's long reign (687–642), Judah remained Assyria's vassal; this political dependence brought a resurgence of idolatry in the form of a syncretist fusion of the Mesopotamian astral gods and the Canaanite fertility deities. This political and religious situation persisted during Josiah's (640–609) minority; but in 622–621, when the Book of the Law was discovered in the Temple, Josiah led a thorough reform in Judah, which he extended even to the ancient northern Israel, an Assyrian province since 721. The international political circumstances could permit such a move of independence; within Judah, we presume that a number of people had

remained faithful to the Yahwistic covenant and really supported the king's new policy. In a solemn ceremony, the Mosaic covenant was renewed; there followed total destruction of all the high places where idolatrous practices were performed, leaving Jerusalem as the unique cult center. In 609, this glorious reign came to its tragic end with Josiah's death in Megiddo; the king had tried to stop Neco from joining Ashur-uballit in Haran to rescue him from an imminent downfall. Because Babylon had no control over Syria-Palestine, Neco acted as her suzerain: he deposed Jehoahaz, whom he sent as prisoner to Egypt, and replaced him by Jehoiakim (609–598). Under Jehoiakim the religious syncretism revived in Judah, and politically the country remained under Egyptian influence. Thus, to resist Babylon was the king's first preoccupation, which resulted in Jerusalem's first downfall and in Judah's first deportation in 597. Jehoiakim had died the year before and was succeeded by one of his sons, Jehoiachin. The young king was also exiled to Babylon, never to return, and Nebuchadnezzar replaced him by Zedekiah, his uncle (597–587). The new king did not bear the stamp of a ruler; he was caught between two parties and policies: the one urged submission to Babylon, for it recognized that no power could really oppose its strength; the second urged Zedekiah to join Egypt, and probably also the other minor neighboring states, to overthrow Nebuchadnezzar's domination in the west. This second party finally prevailed. In 587 Jerusalem was sacked and the Judean population experienced a new deportation, Zedekiah was blinded and sent in exile to Babylon; Judah was reduced to a Babylonian province. Then Nebuchadnezzar appointed Gedaliah, a Judean, as governor of the new province with Mizpah as the new adminstrative center. Gedaliah was assassinated two months later, at the instigation of the Ammonite king. Seized by fear, a number of Judeans fled to Egypt to escape Nebuchadnezzar's revenge, taking Jeremiah along with them (for details, see Bright, *Hist.* 288–310; Noth, *Hist.* 269–99; R. de Vaux, "*Israël*" *VDBS* 4, 756–59).

4 **(II) Jeremiah's Mission.** Yahweh called Jeremiah to be a prophet to Judah and to the nations in the midst of these political convulsions. His ministry lasted about 40 years (cf. 1:1–3), and his book testifies that his interventions were numerous. In fact, the last decades of Judah's history required a continual flow of light from Yahweh's messengers; besides Jeremiah, Zephaniah, Habakkuk, Nahum, and Ezekiel delivered the Word of God. In their work of bringing forth the authentic tradition of Yahwism, these prophets were assisted by the pious men responsible for the deuteronomic reform and literature. But of all these inspired men, no one reached the stature of Jeremiah in his great sensitivity to Yahweh's love for his people and in his profound understanding of this very people's duty toward Yahweh through the covenant ties. Thus, Jeremiah's prophetical word is noted for its directness and acuity in stating the true nature of Yahwism and in denouncing the different religious deviations. The two predominant themes of his message are precisely to define true Yahwism and to proclaim the imminent wars as punishments of Judah's aberrations.

The first part of his ministry covers the years from his call (627–626) to the Josian reform (621); most of his early oracles now form chs. 1–6. The religious atmosphere of Judah was very low: Josiah was a young king who could not yet eradicate Manasseh's apostasy. Jeremiah, under the influence of his predecessor, Hosea (see K. Gross, *Die literarische Verwandtschaft Jeremias mit Hosea* [Berlin, 1930]), recalls the covenant as basically a matter of love between Yahweh and Israel—a love symbolized by that which unites a man and a woman in marriage. If the chosen people does not convert itself from idolatry, a disastrous invasion from the north will be Yahweh's revenge against such an adulterous attitude. At this early date, Jeremiah probably had not seen clearly who this invader would be. Finally, with a number of exegetes, we believe that Jeremiah hoped then for the restoration of the northern kingdom (chs. 30–31).

In 621, Josiah led a thorough religious reform of his kingdom on the occasion of the discovery of the Law. Jeremiah certainly approved of the king (11:1–14), which is the reason we hear so little of him until his death in 609. Indeed, we cannot assign any of the Prophet's oracles for this period. We presume that the ideal he had preached was then prevailing.

With Jehoiakim's accession to the throne, a new period opens in Jeremiah's life. The reformation was swiftly eclipsed by a universal return to idolatry; politically, the Egyptian party took power. Jeremiah then resumed his denunciations of idolatry and of the superficiality of the covenantal observances. The threat of war became more urgent. When Babylon defeated Egypt at Carchemish in 605, the Prophet knew too well who the invader would be. That very year, he dictated all his previous oracles to Baruch, who wrote them on a scroll, as a solemn and last warning to both the people and its leaders (ch. 36). The prophetical words of this third period appear mostly in chs. 7–20.

5 Even though Jeremiah's warnings had been explicit, Jehoiakim did not change any of his religious and political designs. We can assume that during the last phase of the king's reign (605–598), the Prophet had to face bold opposition and severe persecution; he then experienced an interior crisis of his faith in his mission and in his God, which he described in lyric poems called his "confessions" (see 11:18ff.). These poems are now scattered in chs. 11–20.

The last period of Jeremiah's life runs from the first downfall of Jerusalem (597) to his death in Egypt soon after the destruction of Judah (587). Zedekiah had been unable to handle the power; in fact, the political parties were the real forces that led Judah to her final ruin. Jeremiah had never been so active in the political field as during this last decade. The king had confidence in him and tried to save him from the hands of the officials who had a completely different policy. Most of his speeches and oracles were preserved by Baruch, who inserted them in narratives recording the circumstances and the effects of his interventions (chs. 27–29, 32–45). Jeremiah then understood that a true conversion to Yahweh was humanly impossible; Yahweh himself had to change the very heart of man, and only then could the New Covenant bind forever the people to its God (31:31–34). This new order of things would unite again Judah and Israel, but only after the Exile had purified their stubbornness in sin.

(III) The Book.

6 **(A) Authenticity.** In 1901, B. Duhm (*Das Buch Jeremia* [Tübingen, 1901]) reduced the authentic passages to one-fifth of the book. This radical position has been progressively put aside, and now the critics hold most of the oracles to be really Jeremiah's, even though some later additions and transformations could still be detected clearly, as in all the prophetical books (see Gelin, *VDBS* 4, 862–64). We must study each passage to decide whether or not it belongs to Jeremiah, but the still highly disputed passages are the so-called deuteronomic discourses.

S. Mowinckel published an important study on the different sources of the book, which is still influential in the present discussion (*Zur Komposition des Buches Jeremia* [Kristiania, 1914]). He distinguishes three literary sources:

the poetical oracles (source A); the biographical narratives (source B); the deuteronomic discourses (source C).

The authenticity of the poetical oracles (chs. 1–25, 30–31, 46–51) is no longer suspect, with the exception of the oracles against the nations (chs. 46–51). Mowinckel, and several others after him, rejected this whole section as a very late addition; however, a closer examination of these poems now proves that some of them are certainly Jeremiah's, and an authentic Jeremian nucleus is at the origin of the remaining ones. The long oracle against Babylon (chs. 50–51) is clearly a late exilic composition.

The biographical narratives consist entirely of prose narratives and are attributed to Baruch (chs. 26–45). Jeremiah's friend and secretary (ch. 36) had great confidence in, and devotion to, his master; he summarized the main lines of Jeremiah's message and set them into their historical context. Moreover, he wrote a detailed history of the Prophet's sufferings during the last siege of Jerusalem (588–587) and the following months when Jeremiah lived at the side of Gedaliah in Mizpah. He was then forced to flee to Egypt, where he died as a witness of his people's deep-rooted idolatrous propensities (chs. 37–44). Again, the authenticity of these chapters is not disputed; in fact, they are of prime value for the reconstruction of Judah's history during these decisive years.

7 The still most disputed section of the whole work is Mowinckel's third source C—i.e., the deuteronomic speeches of the Prophet, which are usually introduced by the formula, "The message that came to Jeremiah from the Lord" (7:1–8:3; 11:1–14; 16:1–13; 17:19–27; 18:1–12; 19:1–20:6; 21:1–10; 22:1–5; 25:1–13b; 32:1–2,6–16,24–44; 34:1–35:19). Duhm had already established a special class for these passages, which he believed to be a post-exilic rewriting of authentic Jeremian oracles in the style and the spirit of Dt. Mowinckel defended the same opinion in his 1914 study; not too long ago, however, he changed some details of this first view: He now would no longer speak of a special "source," but rather of a "circle of traditions" within which certain of Jeremiah's sayings have been transmitted and transformed according to the ideas and the style that prevailed in the deuteronomic circle. In other words, a parallel oral tradition coexisted with that which preserved the poetic pieces, and it was responsible for these deuteronomic passages (*Prophecy and Tradition* [Oslo, 1946] 61–65). This deuteronomic revision or rewriting of Jeremiah's oracles is a view widely held by scholars who differ only in matters of dates and authors assigned to it (Bentzen, *IOT* [5th ed.; Copenhagen, 1959] 119; J. P. Hyatt, *Jeremiah* [N.Y., 1958] 39; Pfeiffer, *Introd.* [rev. ed.; N.Y., 1948] 505; Rudolph, *op. cit.*, xviff.; etc.).

However, such a revision is highly questionable. Why should only Jeremiah's work have undergone this transformation? Also, if true similarities exist between the passages discussed and the deuteronomic literature, there also exist great differences that cannot be overlooked. Bright would even go so far as to affirm that these divergences are sufficient to give to the passages a style of their own that cannot be simply assimilated to the deuteronomic one. Would it not be, as W. O. E. Oesterley and T. H. Robinson first proposed, that we have to deal here with the Judean prose style of the end of the 7th and the beginning of the 6th cents.? Weiser accepts such a view and finds its *Sitz im Leben* in the liturgical exhortations for the edification of the people. Thus, Dt and the deuteronomic discourses of Jer would be two different examples of this prose; even Baruch's memoirs (source B) would be another example, for the same style and language are also recognizable at times (Oesterley-Robinson, *Introd.* 298–304; J. Bright, *JBL* 70 [1951] 15–35; A. Weiser, ATD 20–21,67,482; Eissfeldt, *Einl.* 469ff.; W. L. Holladay, *JBL* 79 [1960] 352; Muilenburg, *IDB* 2, 834; Paterson, *op. cit.*, 541; etc.). Thus, we suspect the existence of this third source, the deuteronomic discourses. We keep these speeches as authentic and we refuse to find in them a distortion of Jeremiah's words in the spirit and style of Dt. In fact, Jeremiah's message in his prose discourses is no different from that in his poetical oracles; the sole difference regards style, and poetry and prose would differ. Nevertheless, it is still possible that the Deuteronomists have left signs of their work; each case must be examined individually.

8 **(B) Composition.** The history of the collection of Jeremiah's work into book form cannot be retraced easily. At first glance, we are struck by the high number of doublets, the loose combination of poetical oracles and biographical and autobiographical narratives, the frequent disorder in the chronological data, etc. Explanations are numerous and varied. In this study most critics begin with ch. 36. We are told how Jeremiah dictated all his oracles in 605, to be re-edited the following year with additions. The attempts to reconstruct this scroll have been in vain. We can only say that the oracles thus written down were those directed against Judah and Jerusalem before 605–604. In general, they are now found in chs. 1–25, but, again, each case must be considered separately.

E. Podechard (*RB* 37 [1928] 181–97) separated three different collections, which have been simply joined to one another. First is the scroll of 605; Podechard thinks that it is now included, for the most part, in chs. 1–17, where the oracles are set in their chronological order, as far as we know. Then chs. 18–20 were joined, being a separate collection of symbolic actions, and still later, chs. 21–23, the booklets on kings and prophets. Finally, the book of the confessions was inserted at different places in this first section.

The second collection, chs. 26–35, is Baruch's redactional work; the theme is the restoration of Yahweh's people. Here also Podechard believes that the compiler used already existing smaller units: chs. 26–29 are a collection of Jeremiah's altercations with the false prophets, thus forming a kind of apology of true prophecy; chs. 30–31 preserve the Prophet's early prophecies on the restoration of Israel; chs. 32–33 unite the similar oracles under Zedekiah; chs. 34–35 are an appendix on diverse matters.

The third and last section, chs. 36–45, is easily recognized as Jeremiah's biography by Baruch. The latter prefaced his work with the story of the scroll of 605, which introduces him as Jeremiah's chief collaborator, and he closed it by the short oracle of hope, which he deserved for his collaboration. Finally, Podechard holds that the collection of oracles against the nations (chs. 46–51) has been set at two different places—after 25:13b and in ch. 45—by very old traditions and that we cannot know exactly the true reasons. The present form of Jer can be dated at the end of the Exile or soon after. Eissfeldt presents a similar explanation, although he would count a greater number of independent small collections, according to literary forms (Eissfeldt, *Einl.*).

9 **(C) The Greek Version.** The LXX, according to K. Graf's calculation (1852), is one-eighth shorter than the MT. Often only words or short sentences are omitted, but sometimes whole passages are missing (see the list in Gelin, *VDBS* 4, 858). Another characteristic of the LXX is the placing of the oracles against the nations after ch. 25; moreover, a different order is given to the nations (→ 109 below). H. Thackeray's study (*JTS* 4 [1902–1903] 245–66) also proved that the translation has been effected in two different stages, the division occurring between chs. 28 and 29. Thus, the textual tradition of the LXX presents problems of its own. We cannot prefer, as a general rule, one textual tradition to another; each case where the MT and the LXX differ has to be examined individually. (For further study of these general questions and several others, we recommend the following introductions: Oesterley-Robinson, *Introd.*; Bentzen, *IOT*; Eissfeldt, *Einl.*; Weiser, *OT*; R-F.)

10 **(IV) Outline.** The following outline has been suggested for the Book of Jeremiah:

(I) Title (1:1–3)
(II) Oracles Against Judah and Jerusalem (1:4–25:13b)
- (A) Call of Jeremiah (1:4–19)
  - (a) The Dialogue (1:4–10,17–19)
  - (b) The Visions (1:11–16)
- (B) Early Oracles Under Josiah (2:1–6:30)
  - (a) A Lawsuit Against Israel (2:1–37)
  - (b) The Return of the Apostate (3:1–4:4)
    - (i) The poem on conversion (3:1–5,19–4:1–4)
    - (ii) Two additions (3:6–18)
  - (c) Evil of Judah and Evil of War (4:5–6:30)
    - (i) The invasion (4:5–31)
    - (ii) The moral corruption (5:1–31)
    - (iii) The correction (6:1–30)
- (C) The Ministry Under Jehoiakim (7:1–20:18)
  - (a) The Mistaken Covenant (7:1–10:25)
    - (i) The Temple discourse (7:1–8:3)
      - (A) The Temple (7:2–15)
      - (B) The Queen of Heaven (7:16–20)
      - (C) Religion and Sacrifice (7:21–28)
      - (D) False Cult and Punishment (7:29–8:3)
    - (ii) Nova et vetera (8:4–10:25)
      - (A) Universal Estrangement (8:4–12)
      - (B) The Sacked Vineyard (8:13–17)
      - (C) The Prophet's Lament (8:18–23)
      - (D) An Attempt at Evasion (9:1–8)
      - (E) Dirge over the Land (9:9–21)
      - (F) True Wisdom (9:22–23)
      - (G) Circumcision is Worthless (9:24–25)
      - (H) A Satire on Idolatry (10:1–16)
      - (I) In Full Flight! (10:17–22)
      - (J) Jeremiah's Prayer (10:23–25)
  - (b) The Broken Covenant (11:1–13:27)
    - (i) Jeremiah and the covenant (11:1–14)
    - (ii) Misplaced logia (11:15–17)
    - (iii) The plot against Jeremiah (11:18–12:6)
    - (iv) Yahweh's complaint (12:7–13)
    - (v) Death or life for Judah's neighbors (12:14–17)
    - (vi) Two parabolic discourses (13:1–14)
      - (A) The Rotten Loincloth (13:1–11)
      - (B) The Broken Wineflasks (93:12–14)
    - (vii) Threatening words (13:15–27)
      - (A) The Dark Night (13:15–17)
      - (B) The Exile (13:18–19)
      - (C) Incurable Sickness (13:20–27)
  - (c) Crime and Punishment (14:1–17:27)
    - (i) The great drought (14:1–15:9)
      - (A) Drought (14:1–16)
      - (B) Lament (14:17–15:4)
      - (C) Tragedy (15:5–9)
    - (ii) The renewal of the call (15:10–21)
    - (iii) Jeremiah's celibacy (16:1–13,16–18)
    - (iv) Disjecta membra (16:14–15,19–17:18)
      - (A) Return from Exile (16:14–15)
      - (B) Conversion of the Heathen (16:19–21)
      - (C) Judah's Guilt (17:1–4)
      - (D) Sapiential Sayings (17:5–11)
      - (E) The Source of Life (17:12–13)
      - (F) A Prayer for Vengeance (17:14–18)
    - (v) Observance of the Sabbath (17:19–27)
  - (d) Symbolic Meaning of the Prophet's Life (18:1–20:18)
    - (i) A visit at the potter's (18:1–12)
    - (ii) Israel forgets Yahweh (18:13–17)
    - (iii) Another prayer for vengeance (18:18–23)
    - (iv) The broken flask and Topheth (19:1–20:6)
      - (A) The Broken Flask (19:1,2bc,10–11a,14–20:6)
      - (B) Topheth (19:2a,3–9,11b–13)
    - (v) Jeremiah's despair (20:7–18)
- (D) The Ministry Under Zedekiah (21:1–24:10)
  - (a) A Consultation from Zedekiah (21:1–10)
  - (b) Booklet on Kings (21:11–23:8)
    - (i) A general address to the royal house (21:11–22:9)
      - (A) Jerusalem (21:13–22:6–7)
      - (B) Duty Toward Justice (22:1–5)
      - (C) Idolatry (22:8–9)
    - (ii) Jehoahaz (22:10–12)
    - (iii) Jehoiakim (22:13–19)
    - (iv) Jehoiachin (22:20–30)
    - (v) The future king (23:1–8)
  - (c) Booklet on the Prophets (23:9–40)
  - (d) The Two Baskets of Figs (24:1–10)
- (E) A Foreword or Epilogue (25:1–13b)
- (F) Judgment on the Nations (25:13c–38)

(III) The Restoration of Israel (26:1–35:19)
- (A) Jeremiah Persecuted (26:1–24)
- (B) Jeremiah's Controversy with the False Prophets (27:1–29:32)
  - (a) A Coalition of the West (27:1–22)
  - (b) Prophecy Against Prophecy (28:1–17)
  - (c) The Letter to the Exiles (29:1–32)
    - (i) The letter (29:1–23)
    - (ii) An exile's reaction (29:24–32)
- (C) The Restoration of Israel (30:1–31:40)
  - (a) Northern Israel will be Restored (30:1–31:22)
    - (i) Introduction (30:1–4)
    - (ii) Jacob's distress at an end (30:5–11)
    - (iii) Healing of Israel's wounds (30:12–17)
    - (iv) The restoration (30:18–24)
    - (v) Good news of return (31:1–6)
    - (vi) The new exodus (31:7–14)
    - (vii) End of Rachel's mourning (31:15–20)
    - (viii) En route (31:21–22)
  - (b) Additional Fragments (31:23–40)
    - (i) The restoration of Judah (31:23–26)
    - (ii) Israel and Judah (31:27–28)
    - (iii) Personal responsibility (31:29–30)
    - (iv) The new covenant (31:31–34)
    - (v) The stability of Israel (31:35–37)
    - (vi) The rebuilding of Jerusalem (31:38–40)
- (D) The Restoration of Judah (32:1–33:26)
  - (a) A Pledge of Restoration (32:1–44)
    - (i) The purchase of a field (32:1–15)
    - (ii) Jeremiah's prayer (32:16–25)
    - (iii) The Lord's answer (32:26–44)
  - (b) More on the Restoration of Jerusalem and Judah (33:1–26)
    - (i) Jerusalem and Judah restored (33:1–13)
    - (ii) An anthology on messianism (33:14–26)
- (E) The Conditions for Salvation (34:1–35:19)
  - (a) Zedekiah's Fate (34:1–7)
  - (b) A Dishonest Deal (34:8–22)
  - (c) The Example of the Rechabites (35:1–19)

(IV) Martyrdom of Jeremiah (36:1–45:5)
- (A) The Scroll of 605–604 (36:1–32)
- (B) Zedekiah and the Prophet (37:1–38:28a)
  - (a) Zedekiah Consults Jeremiah (37:1–10)
  - (b) Jeremiah Is Arrested (37:11–16)
  - (c) A New Consultation (37:17–21)
  - (d) Jeremiah in the Miry Cistern (38:1–13)
  - (e) Zedekiah's Last Interview with Jeremiah (38:14–28a)
- (C) The Fall of Jerusalem (38:28b–39:18)
- (D) A Tragedy in Mizpah (40:1–41:18)
  - (a) Jeremiah at Mizpah (40:1–6)

(b) The Colony at Mizpah (40:7–12)
(c) The Assassination of Gedaliah (40:13–41:3)
(d) The Assassination of Pilgrims (41:4–10)
(e) Flight and Panic (41:11–18)
(E) Sojourn in Egypt (42:1–44:30)
(a) Search for Guidance (42:1–6)
(b) The Divine Answer (42:7–18)
(c) The Refusal to Stay Home (42:19–43:7)
(d) Nebuchadnezzar in Egypt (43:8–13)
(e) Jeremiah's Last Words (44:1–30)
(F) The Consolation of Baruch (45:1–5)
(V) Oracles Against the Nations (46:1–51:64)
(A) Against Egypt (46:1–28) (LXX 26:2–28)
(a) The Battle of Carchemish (46:2–12) (LXX 26:2–12)
(b) The Invasion of Egypt (46:13–28) (LXX 26:13–28)
(B) Against Philistia (47:1–7) (LXX 29:1–32)
(C) Against Moab (48:1–47) (LXX 31:1–40)
(D) Against Ammon (49:1–6) (LXX 30:17–21)
(E) Against Edom (49:7–22) (LXX 30:1–16)
(F) Against Damascus (49:23–27) (LXX 30:29–33)
(G) Against Arabia (49:28–33) (LXX 30:23–28)
(H) Against Elam (49:34–39) (LXX 25:14–20)
(I) Against Babylon (50:1–51:58) (LXX 27:1–28:58)
(J) The Oracle in the Euphrates (51:59–64) (LXX 28:59–64)
(VI) An Historical Appendix (52:1–34)

COMMENTARY

11 **(I) Title (1:1–3).** **1.** *the words:* The Hebr pl. expression *dibrê* also means "actions" or "events," and therefore "history" (preferable here). *Jeremiah:* The prophet's name, *yirm^{e}yāhû*, is relatively frequent in the OT and is attested to in the Lachish letters (1,4). Some exegetes (e.g., Rudolph, Weiser), arguing from the Gk transcription, suppose that the first part of the name is from the verb *rûm* and must be translated "Yahweh has exalted," but we prefer the verb *rāmâ* and translate, "Yahweh has established." *son of Hilkiah, of a priestly family:* This Hilkiah must not be identified with the high priest of Jerusalem at the time of Josiah, who co-operated in the discovery of the Book of the Law in the Temple (2 Kgs 22). Solomon had exiled the priest Abiathar to Anathoth for having supported Adonijah's attempt to kingship; he replaced him by Zadok (1 Kgs 2:26–35). Probably only Hilkiah was a descendant of this Abiathar. Indeed, Jeremiah will recall the destruction of Shiloh (7:14), and Abiathar was related to its priest Eli. *Anathoth:* The present village of Anata, over 3.5 mi. NE of Jerusalem, still preserves the ancient name of the Prophet's native town; however, the precise site is to be situated on a nearby mound called Ras el-Kharrubeh. It was a Levitical town of the northern tribe of Benjamin (Jos 21:18). The name is the pl. form of the goddess Anat, very popular among the Canaanites as Baal's sister (see C. Virolleaud, *RES* [1937] 4ff.). We might assume that a high place was dedicated to her in Anathoth. **2.** *in the days of Josiah . . . in the thirteenth year:* Josiah reigned from 640 to 609, the year he was killed in the battle of Megiddo against Neco II; thus, Jeremiah's ministry began in 627–626. There is no reason to take this date as the year of his birth (J. P. Hyatt, *IB* 5, 779–80). **3.** *Jehoiakim:* Jehoahaz succeeded first to Josiah, his father. After three months, he was deposed by Neco, who put him in chains and sent him to Egypt where he died (2 Kgs 23:31–34). The Pharaoh replaced Jehoahaz by Eliakim, another son of Josiah, changing his name to Jehoiakim as a sign of vassalage. These events all occurred in 609. Jehoiakim died three months before the first downfall of Jerusalem in 597 (2 Kgs 23:30–24:6). *until the downfall . . . :* The LXX omits this expression and the MT reads, "Until the end of the eleventh year of Zedekiah . . . until the exile of Jerusalem in the fifth month." According to 2 Kgs 24:18, Zedekiah did reign 11 years, and according to 2 Kgs 25:2–8, Jerusalem was destroyed the fifth month of the eleventh year of Zedekiah. Therefore, the redactor of the title gave here two synonymous expressions of the same date—i.e., August, 587. Zedekiah became king of Judah in 597 by the will of Nebuchadnezzar, who had also changed his original name, Mattaniah, to Zedekiah as a sign of vassalage (2 Kgs 24:17–25).

This list of kings omits two names—Jehoahaz and Jehoiachin—because their short reigns of three months each were negligible. Thus, Jeremiah preached from 627 to 587, a dating that leaves out chs. 40–44, which narrate his activity after the ruin of Jerusalem.

To clarify the problem, we can retrace the history of the title as follows. Originally, v.2 was the introductory title of Jeremiah's call and must be joined to vv. 4ff. Verse 3 was introduced when a longer collection of oracles was added, mainly chs. 7–39. If vv. 2–3 were from the same redactor, we would expect to find the preposition "*from* the thirteenth . . . ," because the last part of the title mentions "until the exile . . . ." Finally, during the Exile or soon after, Jer took its actual form, including Baruch's biographical notes on his master's ministry; then v. 1 was set at the beginning of the whole work, connected awkwardly to v. 2 by a rel. pronoun. Thus, three redactional stages of the title could be registered.

12 **(II) Oracles Against Judah and Jerusalem (1:4–25:13b).** This collection of Jeremiah's oracles of doom on Judah and Jerusalem covers the Prophet's entire ministry. A certain attempt was made to respect their chronological order, although sometimes the affinity of subjects was regarded first.

(A) Call of Jeremiah (1:4–19). Two sections can be recognized easily in this first narrative: a dialogue between Yahweh and Jeremiah (vv. 4–10, 17–19) and two visions (vv. 11–16). We do not know how these visions were inserted into the dialogue, or when they occurred in Jeremiah's life, although it must have been early. The dialogue bears almost exclusively on the personal effects of this call, for the visions insist rather on the object of the Prophet's mission.

13 (a) The Dialogue (1:4–10,17–19). **5.** *I formed you:* The verb *yāṣar* refers primarily to the modeling of pottery. Inasmuch as the J account of creation imagined God as a potter (Gn 2:7–8), the verb took the technical meaning "to create" (Am 4:13; Jer 51:19; Is 45:18; 49:5; Ps 95:5; see P. Humbert, *Fest. O. Eissfeldt* [Berlin, 1961] 82–88). *in the womb:* After Jeremiah, it became an accepted idea that God himself forms the young child in its mother's womb; the significance is that God knows man and stands as his unique master from the very first moment of his existence (Jb 10:8–12; Pss 22:10–11; 71:6; 139:13ff.). *I knew you:* The verb *yādaʿ* does not refer exclusively to an intellectual knowledge; it involves as well an action of the will and sensibility. *I dedicated you:* The verb *qādaš* can also be translated "to sanctify" or "to consecrate." Its basic meaning refers to the separation of something or someone for a divine service. Jeremiah is set aside by God for his prophetical mission; the text does not permit us to believe that the Prophet was cleansed from Original Sin (on such an opinion, see Penna, *op. cit.*; Condamin, *op. cit.*). *to the nations:* This extension of his mission, repeated in v. 10, is not a later addition. Former prophets were also concerned with the neighboring countries for two main reasons: The history of the chosen people was always closely mingled with the history of the entire Near East; the prophets had a keen sense of the ruling power of Yahweh over the universe—he was the God of all history. **6–9.** Undoubtedly, the word (*dābār*) is characteristic of the Prophet, a witness of God's will for his people. Jeremiah is but a young man (*naʿar*)—i.e., in his early twenties; therefore, he has no authority (Is 3:4). Moses had a similar reaction when Yahweh sent him as his messenger (Ex 4:10–15), but for a different reason: He had a speech defect, which is not the case here. Yahweh's answer (vv. 7–8) shows the nature of both Jeremiah's fear and the prophetical mission quite clearly: Yahweh is the first one responsible for what has to be said; he provides the message and intimately sustains his messenger (see Ez 2:6–7; Dt 18:18; Mt 10:19–20). **9.** *touched my mouth:* This symbolic action realizes the promise just made, which is immediately explained: "I place my words in your mouth." In the prophetical calls of Isaiah (6:7), Ezekiel (2:8–3:3), and Daniel (10:16), a similar ritual is performed on their mouths. In each case, the same conviction of Yahweh delivering his message to the Prophet is sensibly experienced. **10.** *to root up...:* Some exegetes suppress the middle stichos ("to destroy and to demolish"), which gives a verse in chiasmus of opposite verbs; strong arguments for such a restitution have been recently proposed by Holladay (*JBL* 79, 363–64). This antithesis defines the twofold aspect of a prophet's mission: to straighten what is crooked and to deepen the whole religious heritage, including occasionally new revelations.

17. *gird your loins:* This verse and those following are the logical sequence of v. 10. They accentuate the attitude of the Prophet during his ministry. The girding of loins points to the promptness in the accomplishment of an order (1 Kgs 18:46), as well as to the immediate preparation for combat (Jb 38:3; 40:7). **18.** *a fortified city...:* In Ezekiel's call (3:8–9), we find the same steadfast strength expressed in similar imagry. Those who will have to encounter such a firm man of God are the leaders of Judah, both political and religious, and their subjects, even the most humble ones (cf. 4:9; 32:32).

If we compare Jeremiah's call with those of Isaiah (6:1–13) and Ezekiel (2:1–3:15), we are struck by three distinctive notes. The predestination of a prophet to his office is clearly underlined: Yahweh's plan for such a man originated from the first moment of his existence. This early intervention of Yahweh is found also in Samson's story (Jgs 13:5), and will be repeated for the Servant of the Lord (Is 49:1–2), John the Baptist (Lk 1:15), and Paul (Gal 1:15–16). In these last instances, we can easily detect an influence of Jeremiah's call. Second, this dialogue shows how intimate are the relations between Yahweh and his prophet; several other passages will prove that this intimacy never stopped growing. Jeremiah is the sole prophet who revealed to us the inner struggle that such a mission caused him. Finally, the inherent persecution following this mission is strongly stressed: The entire book is crisscrossed with such dark events.

14 (b) THE VISIONS (1:11–16). **11–12.** The first vision presents a pun. The sight of a branch from an almond tree (*šāqēd*) means that Yahweh is watching over (*šōqēd*) the fulfillment of his word. The oracle is comminatory, for in Jeremiah, the verb *šāqad* always foreshadows a calamity (5:6; 31:27–28; 44:27). Recently, W. G. Williams interpreted the vision in the light of Aaron's rod (Nm 17); thus, Jeremiah would recall the original meaning of this priestly symbol (*Fest. W. A. Irwin* [Dallas, 1956] 90–99). This is an overly complex view of a simple experience, as we shall see. **13–16.** The object of the second vision is obscure. The MT reads, "A boiling cauldron whose face is from the North," and the versions do not help clarify its meaning. There are three main interpretations. The object of the vision is not the cauldron itself but its support over the fire, the opening of which is on the northern side. Or, Jeremiah saw a cauldron moving from N to S. Finally, some think that the cauldron was leaning to the north, the most obvious solution (Rudolph, Weiser, Gelin). The meaning of the vision is clarified by another pun, on the verb *nāfaḥ;* "to boil" or "to blow." As a result of the idolatrous practices of Judah, a sweeping invasion from the north will lay waste the entire country. The historical problem of this invasion will be discussed after ch. 6.

Great similarities exist between these visions and those in Am (7:1–9; 8:1–3; 9:1–4): We meet the same interrogations on the object of the vision, followed by the formulations of their meaning in plays on words. It has long been discussed whether these visions were real or mere literary fictions. We are inclined to think that they were ordinary perceptions described in the form of visions; the literary genre served as a means to propose a short and striking oracle. The procedure corresponds naturally to the figurative speech of the Orientals.

15 **(B) Early Oracles Under Josiah (2:1–6:30).** It has long been recognized that chs. 2–6 preserve the central themes of Jeremiah's preaching under Josiah, before the deuteronomic reform, for they give no sign of this renewal of the covenant (627–622). The influence of previous prophets (Amos, Hosea, Isaiah) is apparent, for the prophetic tradition developed in a rather continuous line.

(a) A LAWSUIT AGAINST ISRAEL (2:1–37). The first oracle extends from vv. 2 to 37 (Rudolph, Weiser, Gelin, etc.) and stigmatizes Israel's religious desertion. The main fault is pagan cults, favored especially by heathen alliances; such an aberration would have been avoided if Israel had remained faithful to her covenantal ties with Yahweh. The religious atmosphere reflects the decline of Yahwism during the evil years of Manasseh (687–642) and Amon (642–640; 2 Kgs 21), which probably continued under Josiah's minority. The poem is cast in the "*rîb* (lawsuit) pattern," so characteristic of the prophetical discourse on the breaking of the covenant (see B. Gemser, VTSup 3 [1955] 120–37; H. B. Huffmon, *JBL* 78 [1959] 285–95; and esp. J. Harvey, *Bib* 43 [1962] 172–96). Harvey has shown that the international law of the 2nd millennium BC has given us the literary form of both the covenant and its rupture. Some good parallels are found in Mesopotamia and Anatolia; in the OT, clear examples are Hos 4; Is 1:2–3,10–20; Mi 6:1–8; Dt 32:1–25; Ps 50. The main elements of the pattern are the description of the tribunal calling attention to both the accused and the witnesses, an historical review of the accuser's favors, a list of charges often formulated in an interrogative manner, and, finally, the proposal of an ultimatum or the declaration of war. All these elements figure in this present chapter, although in a complex sequence.

1–7. This first section of the poem is a review of Yahweh's favors toward Israel, whose response has been only ingratitude. The greatest proof of Yahweh's devotion to Israel, constantly repeated in the prophetical preaching, is the Exodus, followed by the conquest of the promised land. **2.** *the devotion of your youth:* The word *ḥesed* defines the relationship between Yahweh and Israel at the time of Exodus; the term refers to their mutual faithful and merciful love, made concrete in the covenant (see N. Glueck, BZAW 47 [1927]; H. J. Stoebe, *VT* 2 [1952] 244–54). This notion of love with the symbolism of marriage in history has been developed by Hosea (1–3; see A. Neher, *RHPR* 34 [1954] 30–49). Jeremiah was certainly influenced by his predecessor; both presented the idyllic desert period as an ideal in the history of Israel. **3.** *first fruits:* They were Yahweh's portion (Ex 22:28; 23:19), and therefore sacred (*qōdeš*), i.e., "separated" or "reserved" to the divine world. Thus an alien was forbidden to partake of them (Lv 22:10–15). Such was Israel by her covenantal bonds; being thus the "first-born" of Yahweh (Ex 4:22), she was therefore "sacred," "untouchable" (*qādôš*; Ex 19:6). Here, the Prophet evokes the period of the judges, when Yahweh repressed severely all attempts of the neighboring peoples to subdue his chosen one. **5.** Idolatry is the central charge against Israel. Yahweh is the only God in Israel (Ex 20:3–5). The heathen gods have no right of existence in her midst; they are therefore "nothingness," "emptiness" (*hebel*); Jeremiah first applied the term to these idols (see Gelin, *VDBS* 4, 184–85). This step was the first taken toward the doctrine of monotheism, which is clearly found in Dt-Is (Is 43:8–12; 44:6–8; 45:5–6,14–15; etc.).

16 **8.** The accusations are now directed to all the leaders. The priests were not only responsible for the sacrifices, but they were also in charge of the divine oracle by the means of *'ēpôd*, *'ûrîm*, and *tummîm*. This mechanical way of consulting the divinity was progressively neglected; the priests then devoted themselves to short instructions (*tôrôt*) on particular matters, especially those related to the sacrificial laws. These instructions even characterized the priesthood (Mi 3:11; Jer 18:18; Ez 7:26; see De Vaux, *AI* 349–57). Now that they are specialists of the law, their "knowledge" of Yahweh, or their entire religion, is reduced to nothing. Earlier, Hosea had addressed the same reproach to them (Hos 4:4–10). The shepherds must refer to all the political leaders. The prophets here concerned are the official ones, the spiritual heirs of the ancient diviners of the Oriental courts. They are already distinct from the "vocational" prophets, whose oracles have been preserved in our biblical books. **9.** For such aberrations, Yahweh puts them all on trial; the technical word *rîb* (lawsuit) is repeated twice. **10.** *coasts of Cyprus:* The MT should be rather translated, "the isles of Kittim," the Hebr name for Cyprus, derived from one of its seaports on the SE coast called Kition; but Jeremiah probably refers here to the islands of the Mediterranean coast, meaning the west. *Kedar:* This nomadic Transjordan tribe (Gn 25:13) represents the east. **11.** *their glory:* This attribute of Yahweh (Nm 14:21; Is 6:3) stands for Yahweh himself. Hosea (4:7) had already spoken of this exchange of glory for idols in the same context of accusations against the priesthood. **12.** *O heavens:* This invocation of "heavens," to which we may add "earth" and "mountains" as found in the previous examples of lawsuits, has been diversely interpreted: they are pure poetical auditors, or symbols of mankind and celestial powers, or simply the divine assembly. In the vassal treaties of the ancient Near East, these very elements appear with the rivers and lakes, and the gods of both parties, as witnesses of the mutual bonds just accepted (see *ANET* 201ff.). In the OT we meet them in the same context of covenantal ceremonies in Dt 4:26; 30:19; 31:29. Thus it is quite natural that these elements must be mentioned in lawsuits following the rupture of such alliances. Therefore, the *rîb* pattern requires such an invocation, so well attested in the extrabiblical parallels (see Harvey, *Bib* 43, 182ff.). **13.** *cisterns:* The scarcity of water in Palestine prompted the device of digging underground cisterns to collect the winter rains. Jeremiah uses the beautiful image of "broken cisterns" to define the futility of foreign alliances, as it appears from v. 18, the natural sequence of v. 13. Forsaking thus Yahweh's covenant, Israel could expect only drought—i.e., severe punishment.

17 **14–17.** This section is an interruption of the poem and alludes to an Egyptian invasion of Judah. It could have happened only after the battle of Megiddo in 609, when Egypt controlled Judah. Even though they are Jeremian in thought and vocabulary, these verses were probably added to the original poem. **16.** *Memphis:* Noph is the Hebr form of the name (*mn-nfr*). Located about 13 mi. S of Cairo on the W bank of the Nile, Memphis was the chief city of Lower Egypt. *Tahpanhes:* A city on the E frontier of the delta, it was called Daphne in the classical period and is now identified with the actual Tell Defneh.

20. *on every high hill...:* The expression, traceable to Hosea (4:13), became a classical designation of the high places or sanctuaries of the Canaanites. The core of the cult there practiced was fertility rites, sacred prostitution being the most common. Hence, prostitution was often synonymous with idolatry in the Prophets. **21.** *a choice vine:* Jeremiah recalls Isaiah's famous allegory of the vine as a description of Israel's religious history (Is 5:1–7; cf. Hos 10:1; Ps 80:9). **23.** *valley:* The reference is to the child sacrifice in the Hinnom Valley, S of Jerusalem (cf. 7:31). **27.** *wood...stone:* Jeremiah points clearly to the *'ăšērâ* (erected wooden post) and the *maṣṣēbâ* (erected stone), both cultic objects of the high places. In the Canaanite fertility cult, the first symbolizes the female principle, and the second, the male. He deliberately interchanges their symbolic significance to cover them with greater derision. **29–30.** These verses correspond to the last part of the *rîb* pattern: The accused is unable to refute the charge. In fact, he rejected all warnings and even went so far as to kill his suzerain's messengers, the prophets (probably an allusion to Manasseh's persecution; cf. 2 Kgs 21:16; Neh 9:26). In the Oriental parallels of the pattern, such conduct calls for a declaration of war on the part of the suzerain, bringing complete destruction to the vassal. This sentence is pronounced in v. 35, after the recall of the slaughtering of the messenger (v. 34; Rudolph agrees, although most exegetes see here an allusion to the child sacrifice). **31–33.** Jeremiah ends his poem with the opening view (inclusion) of the desert period, represented as the first steps in married life. **36–37.** Rudolph holds that these verses were added later, under Jehoiakim; the situation is the same as in vv. 14–17.

It has been maintained for some time that the prophets had little concern with the covenant. We now know that they had a most profound understanding of its religious meaning. Jeremiah seems to have been just as much concerned with the religious apostasy of his people, the rupture of the first stipulation of this covenant, as the former prophets were with the breaking of the other bonds, i.e., social justice and moral laws. We must recall that the covenant was not a purely material obligation but the care of Yahweh's plan of salvation. Therefore, Israel's history can only be a sacred one.

18 (b) The Return of the Apostate (3:1–4:4). Jeremiah's mission was twofold: "to root up and to tear down, to build and to plant" (1:10). The poem in 2:2–37 realized the first part of this task; the present poem is the second panel of the diptych. The gist of the whole section is the working out of the conditions required to bring about the reconciliation between Israel and Yahweh.

The pericope underwent at least three stages of redaction. With Rudolph and Gelin, we isolate an early poem on conversion (3:1–5,19–25; 4:1–4), which was later interrupted by two insertions (3:6–13 and 3:14–18). However, a profound unity of the entire composition was maintained through the constant use of the key word *šûb*. Basically, the root means "to return from one place to another." Transposed on the religious plan, the expression designates both an aversion from, and a conversion to, the right. Here, Jeremiah plays on all these connotations (see W. L. Holladay, *The Root Šûbh in the Old Testament* [Leiden, 1958] esp. 1–2, 129–39, 152–53).

19 (i) *The poem on conversion* (3:1–5,19–25; 4:1–4). **1–5.** The first part of the poem shows that this conversion is impossible, according to the human viewpoint, through an analogous situation taken from the law. **1.** According to Dt 24:14, if a man has legally divorced his wife and she has entered the house of another man thereafter, her first husband cannot remarry her. Such is Israel's case, for she pursued other gods. **2.** *heights:* The Hebr word *šᵉpāyîm* means, lit., "bare heights," and is properly Jeremian. The Prophet certainly took the image of the barren hills of Judah, so clearly seen from Anathoth, to designate the high places of idolatry, still called "harlotry." **3.** *showers were withheld:* The spring rains are of prime importance for the crops; the fertility cult aimed at their safe outcome. God certifies that these rites are vain for he is the one who regulates the rains. If he retains them, the reason is precisely this grave religious error. **4.** *my father:* In 2:27, such an invocation was addressed to a Canaanite symbol in the fertility cult. Baal and Astarte were believed to cause the fertility of the fields, cattle, and even humanity; they were thus called "father" and "mother." The idea has been demythologized and applied to Yahweh by Hosea (11:1ff.), to serve, along with marriage, as a second covenant image. Jeremiah, here and in v. 19, blends fatherly love and marital love as tangible expressions of this same covenant.

3:19–25; 4:1–4. Conversion is juridically impossible, but through sincere human repentance and by Yahweh's mercy, a new spirit will be created in the people. That these verses are the logical continuation of vv. 1–5 is clear from vv. 19–20, developing the idea of v. 4. The literary form of the section seems to have been borrowed from the penitential liturgies; Hosea himself was influenced by such liturgies when he called his people to penance (6:1–6; 14:2–9). Once again, Jeremiah might have depended on his predecessor, for both the literary form and the central thought of the passage reflect the Hosean preaching. **21.** *heights:* Jeremiah uses the same word as in v. 2, but with a different connotation; they are now the scene of lamentations for the evil suffered as the salary of the idolatry once practised there. **22.** *return...:* Yahweh is speaking; it is he who will achieve the return, if only Israel consents by penance and confession of her basic creed—Yahweh is her only God (Ex 20:2–6; Dt 5:6–10; 6:4). This acknowledgment meant a renewal of the broken covenant.

4:2. These expressions—*'ĕmet* (truth), *mišpāṭ* (judgment), and *ṣᵉdāqâ* (justice)—to which we must add *ḥesed* (piety, love), define true religion in Israel and are frequently used in the entire prophetical tradition. Such an accumulation of almost synonymous words intends to stress the absolutism of this true religion, which is not only the observance of external rules but also the dedication of the whole of man's internal values. *nations...in blessing:* Israel, authentic to her faith, will bring forth Yahweh's promises to the Patriarchs (Gn 12:3; 18:18; 22:18; 26:4). The nations, at the sight of such a glory given by Yahweh to his people, will desire to serve him also. Thus, this loyal conversion will cause universal repercussions. **4:4.** The circumcision of the heart is proper to Jeremiah (9:25) and Dt (10:16; 30:6); the Prophet seems to depend on this legal tradition (see H. Cazelles, *RSR* 38 [1951] 13). The rite of circumcision was given to Abraham as a covenant sign (Gn 17:10ff.). However, its observance, as for the rest of the prescription of the law, could not realize the purpose of this covenant as long as the heart remained foreign to it. Here, therefore, a new step is taken in the religion of Israel by this proclamation of the primacy of the interior dispositions over the exterior ones, for the heart is the seat of intelligence and will. Thus, Rudolph could call this *logion* an "eternal word, the gospel" of the OT (cf. 31:31–34). The conversion that Jeremiah is asking of Israel in the name of Yahweh is then much more than the restoration of neglected practices. Indeed, Israel first must forsake the idols, a prerequisite to true conversion. Its real essence rests entirely in Yahweh's mercy, creating a new Israel. Therefore, we should speak much more of a revolution than of a reparation of some damage (see M. F. Lacan, *LumVi* 47 [1960] 5–24). Jeremiah follows in the whole tradition of deuteronomic circles that insisted much on this necessity of conversion as one of their leading themes in their history of Israel, from the Exodus to the end of the monarchy (Dt–2 Kgs; see Welch, *op. cit.*, 57–75; H. W. Wolff, *ZAW*, 73 [1961] 171–86).

20 (ii) *Two additions* (3:6–18). These verses were inserted in the poem on conversion. They consist, in fact, in two different short oracles; if they were introduced here, the reason is that both are built on the same key word, *šûb*, with its triple meaning. **6–13.** This first oracle is unanimously believed to be Jeremian, but its composition date is controverted. Although several critics would propose a date after the Josian reform in 622 (Skinner, Rudolph, Weiser, Gelin, etc.), and others would even find here a condemnation of this very reform (Welch, *op. cit.*, 78; B. Vawter, *The Conscience of Israel* [N.Y., 1961] 247), we still hold that it must be dated between 627 and 622. Indeed, Jeremiah reproaches Judah with idolatry, and in the very same terms as in 2:27 (cf. v. 9). There is no allusion to this reform in our passage, and we have no proof that idolatry regained its popularity after Josiah had destroyed the high places. Jeremiah proposes an allegory of the divided kingdoms, figured as two sisters; Ezekiel will give ample proportions to the parable (Ez 16, 23). Israel, the northern kingdom, had been swept away by the Assyrians a century before for having fallen into idolatry without repentance, even though the prophets had heralded its necessity for salvation. Such a lesson should have profited Judah, but her "return" did not last longer than the "morning clouds or the dew" (Hos 6:4). Thus, her guilt is greater and does not deserve the forgiveness offered to her sister (vv. 12–13). This hope of the restoration of northern Israel is intelligible, and even moving, from a prophet whose native country it is (30:1–31:22).

14–18. The present section is much later than the rest of the chapter. In fact, Jerusalem is already destroyed and the Ark of the Covenant has disappeared, not to be replaced (v. 16); hence, a date after 587 is required. The function of the Ark, Yahweh's throne, will be played by Jerusalem itself, as the final word of Ezekiel's *Tôrâ* proclaims (Ez 48:35). Jerusalem, by its new splendor, will become the center where all nations gather (cf. Is 2:2–3 = Mi 4:1–3; Is 56:6–8; 60:11–14).

Finally, another significant theme of the passage is the reunion of the divided kingdoms, already foretold by the 8th-cent. prophets (Hos 2:2; Mi 2:12). But here this reunion is seen as possible only after both Judah and Israel have undergone exile (Ez 37:15–28; Is 11:10–16, which is post-exilic). For all these reasons, critics would consider this oracle to be a post-exilic work by a disciple of Jeremiah. However, both the vocabulary and the thought are Jeremian (cf. 23:1–8). In his early ministry Jeremiah hoped that with the end of her exile Israel would be restored to her ancient glory. The decline of the Assyrian power and the extension of Josiah's reform to Israel certainly increased this hope. The events did not permit its realization, but it continued to live in the Prophet's mind, and when Judah suffered the same fate as Israel, he included her in this faith. Thus, the actual state of the oracle is quite understandable in the months following the destruction of Jerusalem in 587.

21 (c) Evil of Judah and Evil of War (4:5–6:30). This long section must be considered a single poem, for it deals with one subject matter: Judah must be punished for her sins, to be realized by a swift invasion. Thus, the descriptions of the war—with its effects on both the land and the minds of the people and the Prophet—and the denunciations of moral depravity and exhortations to penance intermingle in vivid colors and pathetic accents throughout the entire poem. This unity is even noticeable on the literary level, especially in chs. 4 and 6: Their exordia are extremely close and they both end with the anguish of a mother in childbirth as a symbol of great suffering (4:31; 6:24–26). For the convenience of the analysis, the poem has been divided into three sections according to the predominant theme.

(i) *The invasion* (4:5–31). **5–8.** Like a clap of thunder in a blue sky, a sudden alarm is heard all over the land: The invaders draw near. **5.** *proclaim it...:* A similar outcry is repeated in 6:1; it echoes the same alarm of Hosea a century earlier on the occasion of the Syro-Ephraimite war (735–734; cf. 2 Kgs 16:5ff.; Hos 5:8). Later, another prophet will proclaim the coming of the eschatological day of the Lord in analogous terms (Jl 2:1). Such an alarm is required, for in wartime all countrymen would flee behind the walls of fortified cities. **6.** *standard:* The Hebr word *nēs* also means "signal," i.e., a fire lighted on a height for the transmission of news (cf. Is 13:2; 18:3; Lachish letters 4, 10–13). *evil from the north:* The same expression figures in the Prophet's second vision (1:14), referring to the same event, which will be discussed at the end of the poem. **8.** *sackcloth:* This rough linen is frequently mentioned as a garment of mourning (6:26; 49:3; Is 15:3; 22:12; etc.). **9–12.** Now Yahweh himself describes the profound consternation of the Judean leaders, both political and religious, before he announces his final judgment. **10.** *peace shall be yours:* This promise of welfare is said to be Yahweh's, and the present event shows that he lied; however, this allusion is clearly to the preaching of the false prophets (6:14; 14:13; 23:16–17). **11.** *daughter of my people:* Jerusalem is thus designated (cf. v. 17). **13–18.** The impetuous march of the invader is compared to a swift disastrous storm from the desert (cf. Hos 13:15). **14.** *cleanse your heart:* The judgment was already given as final. Now it seems that true conversion would save the city; nevertheless, such a "return" is unthinkable. **15.** *Dan:* The town was situated at the sources of the Jordan, on the northern border of the promised land, now identified with Tell el-Qadi. Inasmuch as the invasion was coming from the north, it would be the first town to suffer. *Mount Ephraim:* This name is given to the mountainous region from Shechem to Bethel (see Abel, *GP* 1, 359; 2, 302). **19–22.** If the disaster were "bitter to Yahweh's heart" (v. 18b), it could not leave the Prophet insensible. He portrays here his inner emotions; such a confession will be repeated often. By vocation he had to announce destruction and punishment, but by nature he was a man most devoted to his beloved people. His whole life will be spent in this painful paradox. **22.** This verse is now Yahweh's own lament. The knowledge of God is not an intellectual grasp of a sum of truths, but a conduct inspired by these truths. **23–28.** The Prophet gives a new description of the invasion, which takes on the aspect of a cosmic conflagration. Such a contrast of tone induces some critics to reject the passage as unauthentic (Volz, Skinner, Hyatt); however, we find expressions that are attested to only in Jer, thus supporting its authenticity (see W. L. Holladay, *JBL* 81 [1962] 48). **23.** *waste and void:* The description of the primordial chaos (*tōhû wābōhû*; Gn 1:2) is used to give the impression of a perfect confusion. The entire universe is struck with horror at such a sight. This description is found, almost identical, in Jl in the same invasion context (Jl 2:1–11). Amos (8:9–10), Zephaniah (1:2–3, 14–18), and Nahum (1:2–8) produced the same effects in their proclamations of the day of the Lord, also on the occasion of wars. Finally, the scene will be purely apocalyptical in Is (ch. 24), foreshadowing the eschatological discourse of the Syn. **27.** The CCD correctly brackets "not"; the MT *lō'* (not) is certainly a later attenuation of *lāh* (it). **29–31.** The end is irrevocable, as Yahweh has just assured (v. 28). Jerusalem is personified as a woman attiring herself to seduce the nearing enemy. Jeremiah might recall here the example of Jezebel (2 Kgs 9:30ff.) or of the women of Jerusalem at the time of Isaiah (Is 3:18–24). This first section of the poem closes with the shrieks and the contortions of a woman in travail, symbolizing an extreme anguish (13:21; 22:23, etc.).

22 (ii) *The moral corruption* (5:1–31). In ch. 4, the certainty of the invasion had been so great that no chance of salvation could be expected. The Prophet now gives the reason for such a disaster—the evil of the people. In ch. 2, this evil was exclusively religious, i.e., idolatry. Now the stress is on morals, both social and personal.

1–6. This first part is a dialogue between Yahweh and his prophet. **1.** Yahweh asks Jeremiah to search the city for one just man, for he would spare it as he would have spared Sodom (Gn 18:22–32). *uprightly...faithful: Mišpāṭ* and *'ĕmûnâ* are covenantal realities ruling relations between men as well as between men and God. In the prophetical literature, they occur constantly with *ḥesed* (love) and *ṣᵉdāqâ* (justice). **2.** With Rudolph and Gelin we would transpose this verse after the first stichos of v. 3. False oaths are denounced. **4–5.** The sinful state is universal; the low class could be excused for its ignorance, but not the leading one—i.e., kings, priests, and prophets (cf. 4:9)—for it is at the service of the Word of God. **6.** These wild animals are none other than the invaders (cf. 2:15; 4:7; Hos 13:7–8; Zeph 3:3; Hab 1:8). **7–11.** The Prophet now gives the catalogue of sins prevailing in Judah, particularly adultery, expressed in crude terms. **10.** The outcome of this corruption is the devastation of the land, compared to a vineyard (cf. 2:1). But the original text has been attenuated (see 4:27). **12–17.** Yahweh himself had formulated the previous reproaches (vv. 7–11); Jeremiah now addresses the wicked people. **12.** *not he:* A theoretical atheism did not exist in the ancient Near East, but a practical one did: God was believed to be uninterested in human affairs; therefore, he could not intervene (cf. Am 9:10; Zeph 1:12). **13.** The rejection of the true prophets follows naturally the rejection of God. They were the men of the *rûaḥ* (spirit); they are now called the "men of wind," a play on the double meaning of *rûaḥ*. **14–17.** The results follow once more the accusations; Jeremiah will see the fulfillment of his mission (1:9–10), and the invasion will be a proof of its authenticity.

18–25. It is commonly accepted that this pericope consists of two additions to the original poem. **18–19.** This first addition is certainly unauthentic; it weakens the preceding threats, a device noticed twice already (4:27; 5:10). Both literary form and thought recall the speeches of Dt (e.g., 4:27–28; 29:23–27). The exilic period would be a good date for its composition. **20–25.** With Rudolph and Gelin, we hold this second oracle authentic; however, the general theme is no longer the "God of history" but the "God of creation." On the occasion of a drought, Jeremiah warns the people that this calamity must be a divine punishment for their stubborn apostasy, for Yahweh rules the universe.

26–31. The catalogue of sins continues. The stress now shifts to the social injustices and the oppression of the weak, an accusation common in the 8th-cent. prophets. The climax is reached with the denunciation of the religious leaders: The prophets consult Baal and the priests themselves decide the law. The whole section closes with a dreadful question mark (on this moral evaluation of Judah, see Skinner, *op. cit.*, 138–64).

23 (iii) *The correction* (6:1–30). The general theme of ch. 4 is resumed, but now the enemy is already devastating the country and besieging the fortified cities. However, conversion is still lacking. **1.** *Tekoa:* This Judean town was Amos' native country, about 5 mi. S of Bethlehem. *Beth-haccherem:* Recent excavations suggest Ramat Rachel, on the road from Jerusalem to Bethlehem, as the site (see Y. Aharoni, *BA* 24 [1961] 98–118). The signal, probably by fire, seems to indicate the route of the flight toward the south. **4.** *prepare for war:* The verb *qadd^{e}šû* means, lit., "sanctify" for war; ritual purifications and sacrifices were performed before a battle because it was considered a religious act (see G. von Rad, *Der Heilige Krieg* [Göttingen, 1958]). **9–11.** As in 5:1, Jeremiah is asked to discover one just man; he cannot. No one listens, and his wrath breaks forth; the first part of his mission—"to root up and to tear down"—must be executed.

12–15. The same accusations are repeated—social injustices and teaching of the false prophets. The evil is so anchored in everyone's heart that an absolute impenitence keeps them all impassive. **16–21.** M.-L. Dumeste (*VieSp* 55 [1938] 163) and Skinner (*op. cit.*, 115ff.) hold that we have here Jeremiah's first doubts on the efficacity of the deuteronomic reform. However, these lines are hardly anything other than an appeal to the study of tradition so as to know the conduct pleasing to Yahweh, a theme well known from former prophets. It shows moreover that the prophets were not innovators but men solidly attached to tradition, which they kept alive by their new understanding of its old truths and by their addition of new truths through personal religious experiences and revelations. **20.** *incense:* Jeremiah alludes to incense offerings, a luxury imported from South Arabia. This verse, and many others (Am 5:21–25; Hos 6:6; 8:11–13; Is 1:10–15; Mi 6:6–8; etc.), constitute the so-called "prophetic indictment" against exterior cult. For a long while exegetes believed that the prophets rejected all exterior practices of religion to support only interior ones. Now a more balanced view prevails; the prophets teach that sacrifices and feasts are worth nothing if they are not accompanied with real interior dispositions. Indeed, a religion without a cult is unthinkable in the ancient Orient. **22–26.** The end of the poem is very similar to 4:29–31 (see comment on 4:29–31).

27–30. These last verses of the chapter do not belong to the original poem on the invasion; they are rather a kind of summary of Jeremiah's first ministry (chs. 1–6). The result is rather deceiving! A number of obscurities makes the text difficult to understand; the Prophet's work is compared to the work of a metallurgist (see G. R. Driver, *JTS* 6 [1955] 84–87; J. A. Soggin, *VT* 9 [1959] 95–98; A. Guillaume, *PEQ* 94 [1962] 129–32). **29.** *wicked:* A better translation for the word *rāʿîm* would be "slag" or "dross." As silver could not be extracted from the slag, so is the new Israel through Jeremiah's efforts; therefore, she will be rejected.

24 The problem of the identification of the invader is a most disputed question. This enemy is said to come from the north, from afar (5:15), from the "ends of the earth" (6:22); they are horsemen, they also ride war chariots, they use the bow, and they know how to besiege a city by earthworks (4:7,13,19; 5:17; 6:4,6). Their origin is from "old" and their language is unintelligible to the Judeans (5:15). These are the only characteristics given.

A theory that had great influence identified this foe with the Scythians, who invaded Asia and the Palestinian coasts between 630 and 625 BC, according to the testimony of Herodotus (103–106). First proposed by Eichhorn (1819), the hypothesis received great attention by Duhm (1901), who called these chapters *Skythenlieder*, "The Scythian Songs" (Duhm, *op. cit.*). He has been followed by a great number of critics (Pfeiffer, *Introd.* 495ff.; B. W. Anderson, *The Living World* [London, 1957] 303; H. H. Rowley, *BJRylL* 45 [1962–63] 217–20; etc.; both Pfeiffer and Rowley think that the original poem was rewritten during the Babylonian wars). Because this Scythian invasion is questionable historically, others prefer the Assyrians (Penna, *op. cit.*, 35, 85; P. Dhorme, *BPl* 1, li). This solution seems difficult, for Ashurbanipal died *ca.* 663 and his empire was already declining. A third possible identification is the Babylonians, and the songs would therefore be dated after 605 under Jehoiakim (Condamin, *op. cit.*, 66–67; J. P. Hyatt, *JBL* 59 [1940] 499–513; *IB* 5, 779ff.; Bentzen, *IOT* 2, 122). The difficulty with this last interpretation is explaining why these chapters were antedated under Josiah!

All these identifications being so problematical, other exegetes have searched for a solution in a totally different direction. We have to deal here with a pure mythological question. In the Canaanite myths, the north is not only the residence of Baal but also the source of evil; Jeremiah then simply used these references in his proclamation of a correction to come (O. Eissfeldt, *Baal Zaphon* [Halle, 1932] 22ff.; W. Staerk, *ZAW* 51 [1933] 1ff.; A. Haldar *Association of Cult Prophets* [Uppsala, 1945]). However, except for a short passage (4:23ff.), this enemy is not mythological but is clearly presented as a human agent. Thus, a group of exegetes finally reject all these explanations and hold rather that Jeremiah had no particular people in mind when he first wrote his poem; it was only later that he identified the invader with the Babylonians, after the year 605 (Volz, *op. cit.*, 58ff.; Rudolph, *op. cit.*, 43–45; B. S. Childs, *JBL* 78 [1959] 194; Weiser, *ATD* 16,44; Gelin, BJ 10,43; Gelin suggests that the Scythian hordes might have inspired the Prophet in his description of this still unknown foe).

This last opinion is apparently the most satisfying. Indeed, apart from the alleged Scythian wars, no particular people was threatening Judah *ca.* 626. However, in the whole history of the chosen people, the rupture of the covenant through idolatry and injustice has never remained unpunished. Wars in the time of the judges, the Aramean wars of the 9th cent., and more recently the fall of Samaria (721 BC) under the Assyrians, were too well known not to confirm this prophetical faith in Yahweh's justice. Jeremiah had that same faith; at the sight of Judah's perversity, he was sure that a new war would cleanse her sins. Who would lead this war? He did not know and thus described the foe in very general terms. The northern origin was plausible because only Egypt could come from the south, and for centuries she had been no danger. Undoubtedly, Jeremiah saw the fulfillment of his early prophecies in the rise of Babylon, but we have no proof that he rewrote his early work to make this identification clear. (See Rowley, *BJRylL* 45, 198–234, for an excellent review of the exegetical problems in this first part of Jer.)

(C) The Ministry Under Jehoiakim (7:1–20:18). This section is commonly dated under the reign of Jehoiakim (609–598), only partly accurate because some units are of a later date.

25 (a) THE MISTAKEN COVENANT (7:1–10:25). Another common assumption is that chs. 7–10 form a collection of oracular fragments and short discourses; the identical titles at the beginning of chs. 7 and 11 support this view. On the whole, they reflect the religious and moral state of Judah during the first years of Jehoiakim's rule, which is very similar to that described in chs. 1–6. Josiah's reform seemed to have been dependent on his own personal action and not to have penetrated the people's spirit; in general, it was a failure.

(i) *The Temple discourse* (7:1–8:3). This first pericope is also a cluster of different sayings on related matters—the Temple and the cult.

(A) The Temple (7:2–15). This passage is the Temple discourse proper. Chapter 26 is a parallel narrative, where the message is reduced to its essentials, but the circumstances and the shock produced by this sharp criticism are fully covered. The Prophet's intervention occurred in 609–608, shortly after Josiah's death at Megiddo. **4.** *temple of the Lord:* The triple repetition illustrates the superstitious and magic significance attached to the Temple in the popular mind. As the shelter of the Ark of the Covenant, Yahweh's throne, it was sacred and could not fall to the enemy; for the same reason, the whole country would be preserved. **6–7.** This expected protection is conditional; the moral prescriptions of the covenant, which Jeremiah explicitly recalls (Ex 22:17–24 and par.), should be observed. **9.** *steal and murder...:* The sins listed here are offenses against the Decalogue (Ex 20:1–17 and par.; Hos 4:2), the first stipulations of the covenant. **11.** *den of thieves:* Jesus stigmatized the sacrificial transactions in its midst (Mt 21:13), but Jeremiah meant that the Temple is now nothing but a hiding place for evildoers, for Yahweh has withdrawn his protection. **12–14.** Located at Khirbet Seilun, 14 mi. S of Shechem, Shiloh had been the amphictyonic center of the tribes during the last period of the judges (1 Sm 1–4). The city and the sanctuary of the Ark were destroyed during the Philistine wars; its priesthood is later found at Nob (1 Sm 21:1; 22). Only Jeremiah recalls this destruction of Shiloh (see also Ps 78:60). He was from Anathoth where the descendants of the Shiloh priesthood were exiled; understandably, the event was remembered there. The allusion would be even more plausible if Jeremiah himself were related to these priests (cf. 1:1). In his reform, Josiah gave great importance to the Temple of Jerusalem, the only legitimate temple; however, this materialistic idea of the Temple's sanctity does not correspond to the king's intentions. In other words, Jeremiah does not condemn the Josian reform but recalls the very meaning of the covenant, so well formulated in the blessings and curses as a necessary conclusion of all covenantal ceremonies in the ancient Near East. We can even see here the source of his inspiration for this criticism (cf. Lv 26; Dt 28; etc.).

26 (B) The Queen of Heaven (7:16–20). This short speech is the first of a series on cultic matters. It deals with idolatry, especially the fertility cult of Astarte, a Mesopotamian goddess much honored in Canaan; she was very popular in Judah under Manasseh, with many other Mesopotamian gods (2 Kgs 21; 23:4–14). In Mesopotamia she was also called the "Queen of Heaven" (*šarrat šamē, belit šamē*), a name still attested in the Aram papyri of the 5th cent. BC in Egypt. Inasmuch as she was an astral divinity, her cult took place in the open on terraces (19:13; 32:29; 2 Kgs 23:12; Zeph 1:5); it consisted in cake offerings (*kawwānîm*, a loanword from the Akkadian *kamānu, kawānu*), probably in the shape of a nude woman. Such a cult is another sign of the reform's brevity.

27 (C) Religion and Sacrifice (7:21–28). The present oracle pertains to the "prophetic indictment" of the sacrificial institutions (cf. 6:20). **22.** *no command:* This verse and a similar one in Amos (5:25) seem to deny the divine origin of the sacrifices. What Yahweh expects as essential to religion is obedience of the heart to moral laws, without need of sacrifices. However, these sacrifices in fact exist and are regulated in detail in the P tradition, under divine authority (Lv 1–7). Moreover, it is impossible to admit that their origin is exilic for they were offered long before in Israel, even before the Mosaic times, although we recognize that they take only limited importance in the Code of the Covenant (Ex 20–23) and in Dt (12:1ff.). It appears then, from these legislative texts, that moral dispositions had greater importance. To bring his listeners to this true evaluation of their religious duties, Jeremiah went so far as to deny the divine origin of the sacrificial cult, although he knew its remote past. Later, in his definition of the New Covenant (33:11), sacrifices will still be included (see De Vaux, *AI* 454–56; Rudolph, *op. cit.*, 52–53). **24.** *hardness:* The word *šᵉrîrût*, always used with the word "heart," is properly Jeremian (9:13; 11:8; 13:10; 16:12 etc.; Dt 29:18 and Ps 81:13). Thus, Jeremiah, the prophet most sensitive to the problem of sin, goes so far as to speak of a kind of "sinful state" of man, whereas the other prophets speak only of sinful actions; however, this stubborness of heart is not yet the notion of Original Sin. **26.** *stiffened their necks:* This expression is another frequent one found in Jer and Dt. It is synonymous with "hardness of the heart." In a word, we meet here with one of the most valuable truths of the prophetical tradition: External practices and sacrifices have no value unless they are informed by a sincere devotion of the heart.

28 (D) False Cult and Punishment (7:29–8:3). This last section of the discourse is a collection of different sayings of Jeremiah: v. 29 is a poetic exhortation to mourning; v. 30 is taken from another sermon (cf. 32:34), as are also vv. 31–33 (cf. 19:5ff.); v. 34 is also borrowed from other oracles (cf. 16:9; 25:10). **8:1–3.** This saying on violation of tombs and exposure of the dead bodies was added here probably because question of privation of sepulture exists in 7:33. Such a treatment of the deceased is a terrible curse; they are exposed to the heavenly bodies because they worshiped them. (On this sermon, see A. Vaccari, *VD* 19 [1939] 138–46, 193–200; G. Fohrer, *TZ* 5 [1949] 401–17).

(ii) *Nova et vetera* (8:4–10:25). The following section is a compilation of several fragmentary sayings on different subjects, old and new, that can be generally dated to the early reign of Jehoiakim, *ca.* 605.

29 (A) Universal Estrangement (8:4–12). **4–7.** Jeremiah deplores the obstinate heart of his people, who refuse conversion, through the same word play on the different meanings of the verb *šûb*. The comparison used in v. 7 has its parallel in Is (1:3); in the very nature of these animals there exists an instinct that brings them back to their original place or to their masters; thus should Israel turn toward her covenantal God! Sin therefore is seen as a violence to nature (Weiser, Rudolph). **8–9.** The passage has occasioned a long discussion that still continues. Since K. Marti (1889), several authors have believed that the verses are a clear condemnation of the deuteronomic reform. The scribes would be the priests who created and fraudulently imposed the deuteronomic law (J. Wellhausen, C. Cornill, A. C. Welch, J. Leclercq, etc.), but the origin of Dt as a pious fraud is now rejected and there is no sign here of any opposition to a particular code of law. Therefore, an increasing number of exegetes refuse the idea of a Jeremian condemnation of Dt itself and propose a condemnation rather of the spirit of the reform following its discovery (Skinner) or of the priests' false interpretations of the Law (Vawter, Cazelles, Steinmann, Penna). Rudolph and Weiser, both refusing such a condemnation, would see here a subtle distinction between the "Law of the Lord" (v. 8) and the "Word of the Lord" (v. 9), representing, respectively, the legalistic religion of the priests and the teaching of the prophets; in other words, the opposition is between the "letter" and the "spirit." This last interpretation corresponds well to Jeremiah's attitude toward the priests and the false prophets and to his great insistence on the primacy of the spirit in all religious matters. **10–12.** This pericope, omitted in the LXX, is a doublet of 6:12–15, which is in a better context. This repetition can be explained by the catch word *hōbîšū* (they are odious) in vv. 9 and 12.

30 (B) The Sacked Vineyard (8:13–17). The theme of this comminatory oracle reminds us of chs. 4–6, the northern invasion. **13.** The image of the vine reappears, it is now fruitless. The CCD translation omits the last stichos of the verse, missing in the LXX and obscure in the MT. We prefer Rudolph's emendations and translation: "For I have given them plunderers who have plundered them." Hence, the vine is in such a desolate state. **15.** The verse interrupts the oracle and has been taken from 14:19b where it was in better context. **16.** *from Dan:* The invasion, as before (cf. 4:15), comes from the north; its description recalls these poems on the "Foe from the North." **17.** *poisonous snakes:* Possibly the Prophet here alludes to the serpent episode of the desert (Nm 21:6ff.). The foe is still undetermined; the text provides no clear identifications.

31 (C) The Prophet's Lament (8:18–23). **19.** *her king:* Because of the synonymous parallelism of the verse, the king is Yahweh. Such interrogations are well known in this type of poetry (cf. Pss 43:24ff.; 73:22; etc.). *why do they provoke...:* Usually this last part of the verse is rejected as a gloss; with Holladay, we believe it to be original. Yahweh interrupts ironically the lament to explain his departure from Jerusalem (Holladay, *JBL* 81, 48–49; *VT* 12 [1962] 494–98). This mourning of the Prophet over the sufferings of his people shows his sympathy and love for them, even though his message had to foretell doom constantly. The paradox will create a painful interior conflict that his "confessions" will bring to light.

32 (D) An Attempt at Evasion (9:1–8). Jeremiah, disgusted, is tempted to flee to the desert. The short poem is also in the style of the lamentations, and probably influenced the Psalmist, who experienced the same type of persecution and temptation (cf. Ps 54). Rudolph would date the passage under Jehoiakim, when the Prophet was rejected by his fellow countrymen, family (11:19; 12:6), and friends (20:10).

1. *in the desert:* We are reminded of Elijah's escape to the desert to avoid Jezebel's wrath, but Jeremiah's motive is somewhat different—i.e., his people's treachery by false speech or calumny. **2.** *drawn bow:* The image of the bow, or the sword (Ps 64:4), suggests the lethal results of falsehood (v. 7). Lying is not only an offense against men but also against God, for such an attitude is practically a negation of his existence (cf. Ps 11). **3.** *Jacob, the supplanter:* With Hosea (12:3–4), Jeremiah evokes Jacob's cunning actions against his brother (Gn 25:26; 27:35–36). In all these texts, there is a word play on the different meanings of the root of Jacob's name: *ʿāqab*, "to beguile" or "to supplant," and *ʿāqēb*, "heel." **4–5.** Sin is so general and so deeply rooted in man's heart that no conversion is possible. Faults against a man, especially a member of the chosen people, is also a breaking of the covenant and therefore a rupture with Yahweh. **8.** The verse is found literally in 5:9,29. Jeremiah's assurance of the coming punishment is expressed in the terms of the earlier poems, with the same image of the smelting pot (v. 6; cf. 6:27–30).

33 (E) Dirge over the Land (9:9–21). The original work was disrupted by a later prose insertion (vv. 11–15), in the form of question and answer, as an explanation of vv. 9–10. The process has been already noticed in 5:18–19, and can be the mark of the deuteronomists during the Exile (cf. v. 15). It is also possible that such additions originated in the liturgical reading of Jeremiah's oracles. The poem supposes clearly that the land has been sorely struck. According to the Babylonian Chronicles (Wiseman, *Chronicles*, 73), Nebuchadnezzar's first sweeping campaign in Judah occurred in 597 (cf. 2 Kgs 23:10ff.), which would be the suitable historical context of the present dirge. **9–10.** This description of the country's desolation is extremely frequent in Jer (2:15; 4:25; 34:22; 44:2–6). **16–19.** In the Near East, even now, on the occasion of deaths or calamities, mourning is carried on by professionals, women uttering hoarse shrieks (see *EDB* 1571). **20–21.** This passage is at the origin of the classical imagery of "Death the Reaper." Following U. Cassuto, A. Pohl holds that the idea comes from the Ugaritic Baal myth. The god refuses to have windows cut in the walls of his newly built palace for fear that his enemy, the nether world god Mot, could come through them and take away his daughters, Dew and Rain (cf. *ANET* 134; A. Pohl, *Bib* 22 [1941] 36–37; see also G. R. Driver, *Canaanite Myths* [Edinburgh, 1956] 99). The explanation remains questionable; perhaps Jeremiah has simply personified death (cf. Hos 13:14; Is 28:15–18; Hab 2:5; Ps 49:15; Jb 28:22; etc.).

34 (F) True Wisdom (9:22–23). This beautiful *logion* on true wisdom is in the purest sapiential tradition; it later retained Paul's attention (1 Cor 1:31; 2 Cor 10:17). However, we cannot deny its Jeremian authenticity, for the theme of the true knowledge of God is often found on the Prophet's lips (2:8; 4:22; 9:2,5; 22:16; 24:7; 31:34). This heritage is probably Hosean (Hos 4:1,6; 5:4; 6:4; 8:2). Both prophets believed strongly that true religion—i.e., an existential recognition of God—consists in merciful love (*ḥesed*), right (*mišpāṭ*), and justice (*ṣᵉdāqâ*), all gifts of God himself. The passage can be considered as a climax in the religion of Israel.

35 (G) Circumcision is Worthless (9:24–25). After his criticism of the sacrifices and Temple, Jeremiah turns to the circumcision. The general idea is the same; this external rite has no value if the heart does not inspire it. The list of people given here as practicing circumcision, the "shaved temples" being the Arabs (Herodotus, *History* 2.8), is basically correct (see M. J. Lagrange

Études sur les religions [2nd ed.; Paris, 1905] 242–46). As an historical background of the oracle, Rudolph proposes one of the coalitions of these nations against Babylon under the last three kings of Judah. The hypothesis is interesting: thus, the league is not one of the "circumcised in the flesh" but one of the "uncircumcised in heart," and therefore a checkmate.

36 (H) A Satire on Idolatry (10:1–16). The present satire is rejected by most scholars as unauthentic; however, Weiser, and recently P. R. Ackroyd (*JTS* 14 [1963] 385–90), think that its actual form is a reworking of a Jeremian attack on the idols. For several reasons, we still hold that the pericope is an exilic, or even a post-exilic, addition. First, the order of the verses in the LXX is different, and some of them are missing (vv. 6–8,10); the fact that v. 11 is in Aramaic proves only that we have to deal with a simple gloss, probably a liturgical addition. Most significant is the very theme of the poem; both the ideas and the literary expressions are extremely similar to certain sections of Dt-Is (cf. Is 40:19–22; 41:7–29; 44:9–20; 46:5–7) and to some psalms (115:9–16; 135:15–18; see also Bar 6 and Wis 13–15). A post-Jeremian date is therefore required. These compositions are not intended to correct a deviation of the Israelites, but to prevent them from falling into such a deviation, inasmuch as they are now living among the pagans. Moreover, in these satires the gods are identified with their statues, clearly a negation of their existence (see Gelin, *VDBS* 4, 169–87). This strict monotheism is clearly attested for the first time in Dt-Is. Finally, the theme is interwoven with that of the universality of Yahweh through his act of creation and his power over the elements. **12–16.** Repeated in 51:15–19, the passage is a development on the God of nature, in the style of wisdom literature (cf. Ps 104; Jb 38; Prv 8:27–31; etc.).

37 (I) In Full Flight! (10:17–22). The panic described here is in the dreadful atmosphere of 9:9–21; there is certainly a close connection between the two poems, for the same verb *'āsap* (to gather, to pick up) is used in 9:21 and 10:17. It seems that although the invasion has not yet occurred, the danger is imminent; we are probably close to the year 597. The form of the poem is a kind of dialogue between the Prophet (vv. 17–18,21–22) and Judah (vv. 19–20). **17.** *lift your bundle:* The command is an allusion to exile; Assyrian bas-reliefs represent caravans of captives holding bundles on their backs. **21.** The image of the "stupid shepherds" and the "scattered flock" refers to the kings and Judah, as Ezekiel's long allegory shows (Ez 34). The kings, through their sacred anointing, were Yahweh's representatives for his people. Yahweh adopted them as his sons to continue the work of Moses and the charismatic judges, all of which is implied by the verb *dāraš* (to search), used here. They are now found to be little concerned with this will of their God; they are much more interested in playing a role in the political arena. The rejection of this sacred function is especially true of Manasseh and Jehoiakim, the actual king at the time of the oracle (on kingship, see De Vaux, *AI* 100–114; S. Mowinckel, *He that Cometh* [Oxford, 1956] 21–95). **22.** The "Foe from the North" is Babylon; even if Jeremiah still uses this indefinite expression, the identification is now clear to all auditors. The desolated land is also called a "haunt of jackals" in the other related poem (9:10).

38 (J) Jeremiah's Prayer (10:23–25). Because of its overtones of wisdom literature, this prayer is sometimes eliminated as a late addition. This reason is insufficient, for a class of wise men existed in Jeremiah's time (cf. 18:18) that influenced the prophets both ideologically and literarily (see J. Lindblom, VTSup 3 [1955] 192–204). **23.** *way...step:* These two key words (*derek* and *ṣaʿad*) are common and technical in the wisdom literature; some of its passages are even very close to the present one (cf. Prv 16:9; 20:24; Ps 37:23). For the wise man, the "way" is nothing other than the sum of rules leading to a happy and successful life, which is entirely in God's hands. He has a mastering power over all his creation of which man is a part. **24.** God's educational punishment (*yāṣar*) is another current theme of the wise men (cf. Ps 6:2; 38:2; etc.). The Prophet opposes here two types of justice: one punishes evil according to its objective gravity; the other proportions the correction according to man's weakness. This latter is the justice for which Jeremiah prays to the Lord. **25.** The verse is found literally in Ps 79:6–7. This call of vengeance on the nations for having destroyed Israel is out of context here and reflects the exilic period. It was probably added to attenuate the severity of the preceding prayer.

(b) The Broken Covenant (11:1–13:27). Chapters 11–13 can be considered to form a small unity; a new title is set at the beginning of ch. 14. Principal stress is placed on the rupture of the covenant.

39 (i) *Jeremiah and the covenant* (11:1–14). This prophetic speech on the "words of the Covenant" presents a very complex and much-discussed problem: What relation exists between Jer, Dt, and the Josian reform (622)? A definitive solution is still wanted, although a good number of its elements seem accepted. **3.** *cursed:* All covenantal ceremonies were concluded by blessings if the stipulations had been respected and by curses if they had not. *terms of this covenant:* The same expression reappears in vv. 6 and 8. It is frequently used in Dt, in an identical or analogical form, for the Sinai covenant. Thus, it would be rash to hold that Jeremiah must evoke here exclusively the Deuteronomic Code. Moreover, the context itself recalls Sinai, as does the rest of the prophetical tradition, and Josiah's covenant is basically nothing more than the renovation of the primitive one. **5.** The verse corresponds to the "blessings" of the covenantal treaties. *milk and honey:* This expression is not only found in Jer and Dt (6:3; 11:8) but also in the Pentateuch (Ex 3:8; 13:5; etc.; Nm 13:27; 14:8; Lv 21:24; etc.). Its origin is probably Canaanite (see R. Dussaud, *Les découvertes de Ras Shamra* [Paris, 1937] 79–80), where it meant a kind of paradisiac fertility of the land. The particular blessing mentioned here is the one promised to the patriarchs—i.e., the gift of Canaan (Gn 12:7; 13:15; etc.)—and renewed with Moses (Ex 3:8ff.; 23:27ff.) and Joshua (Jos 24). **7–8.** Although these verses are missing in the LXX, there are good reasons to affirm their authenticity—e.g., the "hardness of the heart" is properly Jeremian (cf. 7:24). However, because the passage is very similar to 7:24–26, some scholars believe that we have to deal here with an interpolation. The end of the speech brings forth the main accusation against the covenantal people, which is still idolatry. The Prophet directs an inquiring eye over the whole history of Israel and notices that this way of breaking the covenant even dates to the "forefathers," the very ones who first contracted it. The incidents at the foot of Mt. Sinai (Ex 32) and on the plains of Moab (Nm 25) are probably in Jeremiah's mind, as they were in Hosea's (9:10). Judgment is inevitable; a disaster will sweep away the chosen people, for its false gods are unable to save anyone (cf. 2:28), and the Prophet is forbidden even to intercede in its favor (cf. 7:16; 14:11).

We now turn to the problem already mentioned: What was Jeremiah's attitude toward Josiah's reform? For a time, the common opinion held that Jeremiah was sternly opposed to this deuteronomic renovation of the covenant (K. Marti, B. Duhm, C. Cornill, G. Hölscher, A. C. Welch, and more recently, J. P. Hyatt, *JNES* 1 [1942] 156–73). The main argument asserted in proof of such an opposition is that Huldah, not Jeremiah, was the one consulted at the time of the discovery of the Book of the Law (2 Kgs 22:14). Also, we remember how severely the Prophet criticized the central religious institutions of Israel, the sacrifices, and the Temple. The real sign of this opposition is found in 8:8, for the present speech (11:1–14) is nothing more than the work of a deuteronomist who wanted to neutralize this negative attitude by representing Jeremiah as a fervent propagandist of the reform (11:6). But if the prophet was not consulted on this discovery of the Law, we must remember that he was still young at that time and certainly not the only true prophet of Yahweh. Regarding his attitude toward the cult, we saw that it does not consist in its simple rejection, but in a severe criticism of its external practices without correspondence to interior dispositions. Finally, this passage cannot be discarded as an interpolation because it falls in the line of the prose discourse of Jeremiah, which must be held as authentic (→ 6–7 above).

40 Most exegetes believe that Jeremiah did approve Josiah's action, although they would differ in more than one detail, which it is not our purpose to discuss; it will suffice to indicate only the clearest signs of this positive attitude. Two main figures are connected with the discovery of the Law and its new application: the priest Hilkiah and the scribe Shaphan (2 Kgs 22). In the difficult hours of the Prophet's life, the families of these two supported him (26:22; 29:3; 39:14; 40:5). Also, if Jeremiah had condemned the reform, we could hardly understand his eulogy of Josiah (22:15–16). Moreover, Jeremiah refers directly to the Deuteronomic Code in some of his incriminations against transgressions (e.g., 3:1; cf. Dt 24:1–4; 34:8ff.; Dt 15:12–18), and his constant attack on idolatry, especially worship of the astral gods, corresponds quite evidently to both the letter of Dt and the spirit of the reform; the centralization of the cult had no other purpose. Finally, the interiorization of religion, so strongly stressed in Jer, was already at work in Dt (6:4ff.; 10:12; 11:13; etc.; see Von Rad, *OT Theology* 1, 223–31). Several other remarks of the same nature could be added, all showing that Jeremiah certainly approved Josiah's religious policy. Now some critics would push their inquiry further and hold that Jeremiah withdrew his first approval when he saw that the reform had not really reached its goal, especially with the revival of idolatry and superstitious cult under Jehoiakim. The hypothesis is plausible, but we should remember that the reproval did not concern the reform and its basis, Dt, but rather the distortions given to this law and the reform (Skinner, *op. cit.*, 96ff.; Pfeiffer, *Introd.* 493–95; H. H. Rowley, *Fest. T. H. Robinson* [Edinburgh, 1946] 157–74; A. Robert, *RSR* 31–32 [1943–44] 5–16; H. Cazelles, *RSR* 38 [1951] 5–36; Weiser, ATD 20–21, 100ff.; Gelin, BJ 76; Rudolph, *op. cit.*, 71ff.).

This last opinion certainly corresponds to what we know of Jeremiah's entire message. It would be most surprising to see him impeding a royal initiative intended precisely to bring forth a renewal. We will probably never know what part he did play in this reform; to see him as its busy missionary is more the work of our imagination. His approval might also explain why we have practically no oracles that can be dated between this reform and Josiah's death (622–609). However, when the new engagement faded away, he spoke out again: The Temple discourse and the present speech could hardly have a better historical context.

41 (ii) *Misplaced logia* (11:15–17). **15.** The verse, obscure in the MT, is better preserved in the LXX (see Rudolph, *op. cit.*); a superficial cult has no salvific value. **16.** In this oracle of doom, Judah is seen as a magnificent olive tree (cf. Hos 14:7) that will be burnt down. **17.** This prosaic verse is a later commentary on v. 16.

42 (iii) *The plot against Jeremiah* (11:18–12:6). A plot against Jeremiah's life, instigated by his immediate family and acquaintances, is discovered by the Prophet through some divine intervention. He then experienced a shock that urged him to reflect on his mission and on the meaning of human existence. The text has suffered a certain violence that has been corrected in different ways; the transposition of 12:1–6 after 11:18 seems sufficient to give a logical sequence to the entire narrative. **19.** *lamb led to slaughter:* This figure of complete innocence and simple confidence inspired the author of the songs on the Servant of the Lord (Is 53:7). The end of the verse tells clearly enough that the plot is one of murder. **20.** *searcher of mind and heart:* A more literal translation would be "of loins and heart." The expression occurs again in similar contexts (17:10; 20:12); elsewhere, it is found only in Pss 7:10; 26:2, which we assume to be Jeremian. The "loins" (k^e*lāyōt*) were understood to be the seat of inner reflections and affections (Pss 16:7; 73:21; 139:13; Prv 23:16; Jb 16:13; etc.). What Jeremiah asks then is the death of these men, according to the law of retaliation. There is no need to insist that we are still far from Christian forgiveness of offenses, demanded by a perfect charity; therefore, this desire of a strict justice on earth is not surprising (see Pss 69, 109).

12:1–5. These last verses consist in a pathetic question on a most difficult problem: Why does a just man suffer persecution? This question appears here probably for the first time in the OT; later, some psalmists will still discuss it (Pss 49 and 73), and we know that it stands at the center of the Book of Job. If it is possible that these last compositions were influenced by Jeremiah, we should not forget that the problem had disturbed others long before him. In fact, the Sumerian original of the Babylonian "Just Sufferer" (*ANET* 434–37) was discovered recently (see S. N. Kramer, VTSup 3 [1955] 170–82); in the 3rd millennium BC, man's mind was already taken by this mystery of evil. **4a–b.** With Rudolph, we would omit this first part of the verse; it refers to a drought and could come from ch. 14. **5.** God's answer to Jeremiah's question could be compared to the one given to Job (38:40ff.); in fact, God refuses to give a solution. Jeremiah has to keep faith and courage in his actual sufferings, for they are negligible compared to the ones to come.

These reflections of Jeremiah on his life and mission are the first of a series, known since Skinner as his "confessions" (15:10–21; 17:14–18; 18:18–23; 20:7–18). They have no parallel in the whole prophetical literature; Jeremiah alone gave insights of his interior life, in the midst of struggles with his faith in God and with the inherent difficulties of his mission. The actual incidents that provoked such pathetic utterances are not always easy to determine; we would be inclined to think that his constant message of doom has been the main cause of repeated plots against him.

(Behler, W., *Les confessions de Jérémie* [Maredsous, 1959]. Gerstenberger, E., *JBL* 82 [1963] 393–408; he believes that these passages are exilic, but his arguments are too one sided. Leclercq, J., *Etudes sur les Prophètes* [Paris, 1954] 111–45. Rowley, H. H., *AJSL* 42 [1926] 217–27. Skinner, *op. cit.*, 201–30.)

43 (iv) *Yahweh's complaint* (12:7–13). This poem set on Yahweh's lips, is in the *qînâ* (lamentation) form

Apart from v. 9, quite obscure in the MT (see Rudolph, *op. cit.*), the subject matter is clear and simple: The Lord's house, Judah (cf. Hos 8:1; 9:15), has been ruined by a recent war. The event is told with a host of Jeremian symbols and images. **13.** The verse is sometimes held as being out of context; however, it can be explained by the fact that the invasion prevented the Judeans from looking after their crops, permitting the weeds to choke out the grain. Or, more simply, the foreign armies ruined them, often considered divine punishment (Lv 26:16; Dt 28:38; Hos 8:7; Mi 6:15; etc.). We notice that the invader is no longer the "Foe from the North," but "vultures," "beasts of the field," and "shepherds." Thus, most exegetes suggest that this invasion is the work of a coalition of several nations; therefore, the raids of Chaldean hordes, Arameans, Moabites, and Ammonites would be the historical background of this lament (2 Kgs 24:2–4). In the new Babylonian Chronicles, Nebuchadnezzar failed to invade Egypt in 601; this loss obliged him to return to Babylon and reorganize his army the following year (Wiseman, *Chronicles*, 71). The setback probably incited Jehoiakim to revolt once more (2 Kgs 24:1); Nebuchadnezzar would have commissioned these neighboring nations to check the rebellion until he could come to settle it himself (598–597).

44 (v) *Death or life for Judah's neighbors* (12:14–17). In this most disputed passage, Judah's neighbors are condemned to exile and extermination for their evildoing to Yahweh's heritage; however, if they convert to Yahwism they will be saved. The pericope has therefore the clear colors of the universalism and proselytism of several other OT passages (Is 2:1–4 = Mi 4:1–3; 19:16–25; 56:6–8; 60:11–14; etc.). Because these texts are exilic, or even post-exilic, the present one would fall into the same period. Inasmuch as some expressions, however, are Jeremian in style (*naḥălâ*, "Yahweh's heritage"; *nātaš*, "to pluck"; *bānâ*, "to build"), an authentic oracle might have been thoroughly reworked (Rudolph, *op. cit.*).

45 (vi) *Two parabolic discourses* (13:1–14). These two discourses were bound by the key word *šāḥat*, "to destroy" (vv. 7–8,14).

(A) The Rotten Loincloth (13:1–11). The narrative has often been explained as a symbolic action, so frequent among the prophets. These actions were dramatizations of a message so as to strike the attention of the hearers; also, the idea of a word's efficacious value might be a source of their inspiration. If they have an analogy with magic, it is only from their exterior aspect, for the realization of their meaning is entirely in Yahweh's power; moreover, this realization is often already under way or at least already decided by Yahweh even before these actions were performed (see G. Fohrer, *Die symbolischen Handlungen* [Zurich, 1953]; J. Lindblom, *Prophecy in Ancient Israel* [Oxford, 1962] 165–73). The main difficulty of this explanation stands in the identification of the river *Perāt*. In the OT, it is the name of the Euphrates, and it was thus understood in the LXX. Jeremiah had to walk twice to the Euphrates, some 600 mi. from Palestine, which seems unlikely. Therefore, this is probably why Aquila translated it as Pharan, referring to a Benjaminite locality called Parah (Jos 18:23), identified with the present Wadi Fara, about 4 mi. NE of Anathoth. Many exegetes accept such an interpretation (Cazelles, *RSR* 38, 31; *BPl* 1, 281; etc.). Because the Euphrates plays an important role for the full meaning of the passage, we cannot accept this hypothesis. To avoid the difficulty, others proposed a vision, real or symbolic (A. Penna, W. Rudolph, H. Weiser, R. Tournay, *RB* 60 [1953] 592; E. Baumann, *ZAW* 65 [1953] 77–81). To this we object that nothing in the narrative has the characteristics of a vision. It seems much simpler to hold that the symbolic action is purely a literary device; therefore, the discourse is to be interpreted as a parable.

However, the meaning of the story is clear enough (vv. 9–11). The loincloth represents the people of God; the prophet is Yahweh himself. Previously, Jeremiah had denounced the alliances with Mesopotamia as a betrayal of the covenant (2:18). Such alliances were necessarily the occasion of religious corruptions by the recognition of foreign gods, exactly the object of the Prophet's reproaches here (v. 10), symbolized by the deteriorating effect of the Euphrates' waters.

(B) The Broken Wineflasks (13:12–14). This simple comparison of the whole people of Judah to broken wine jars presents no problem. A forthcoming destructive war will level the entire land.

46 (vii) *Threatening words* (13:15–27). Three oracles of doom, of different periods, conclude this section of the book.

(A) The Dark Night (13:15–17). Jeremiah gives a last warning to his people before the final blow: A sincere service of Yahweh might withhold the calamity—i.e., light will still be shining over the land. Otherwise, this very land will be cast into darkness, which seems to have a double significance, symbolizing both the invasion and the flight it will occasion (Is 5:20; 8:21–23; Am 8:9).

(B) The Exile (13:18–19). **18.** *queen mother:* The Hebr word *gᵉbîrâ* means, lit., "the high lady," and refers clearly to the queen mother. Apparently, she had an official role to play at the court (cf. 1 Kgs 2:19; 15:13), corroborated by the fact that her name is almost always mentioned in the introductions to new reigns in Kgs. According to 2 Kgs 24:12, Jehoiachin was exiled in Babylon with the queen mother Nehushta in 597, and Jeremiah specified the fact twice (22:26; 29:2). The present oracle certainly has to be understood in the light of this first deportation (cf. 2 Kgs 24:10–17).

(C) Incurable Sickness (13:20–27). Jerusalem is doomed once again! The Babylonian victory at Carchemish in 605 could have been an excellent occasion for the Prophet to give this last warning. **20–21.** Most of the expressions used here occur in the early oracles (chs. 2–6). Even if the "Foe from the North" is not called by his name, everyone knew whom it could be. **22.** *you are violated:* Lit., "Your heels suffer violence"; the word "heels" is an euphemism. The meaning of this threat is clear from the end of the pericope: Judah is assimilated to a prostitute because of her idolatrous practices (vv. 25–27); as a punishment, she will be exposed in the nude (cf. Hos 2:5; Is 47:2–3). Inasmuch as prostitution is a symbol for idolatry, such must be also the stripping of a woman for God's vengeance against this evil. There is no need to interpret the verse as an allusion to sexual violence done to women by the foreign soldiers or to bruises contracted by the long walk to the land of exile. **23.** To this well-known interrogation, a negative answer must be given. The sinful state of Judah has now taken a "natural" character, so to speak; through her repeated downfalls into idolatry, she has set herself in a permanent state of rupture with Yahweh. However, this extremely pessimistic view will be mildly corrected at the end of v. 27, where a slight hope for conversion is still expected.

(c) CRIME AND PUNISHMENT (14:1–17:27). Chapters 14–17 can also be considered as a unit, for ch. 18 opens with a new title. The general theme remains the sins of the people and the vengeance of Yahweh.

47 (i) *The great drought* (14:1–15:9). This long pericope is a kind of lament on the calamities of a drought and a war. Although several poems can be distinguished, they are related through a unity of style—i.e., their life setting is the penitential liturgies; such liturgies were performed on the occasion of a catastrophe brought on by natural or political disturbances (see Jl 1–2; Pss 74, 79). Droughts are frequent in Palestine (cf. 5:20–25; 8:18–23); we do not know when the present one occurred.

(A) Drought (14:1–16). These verses form the first lamentation; the plague is dreadful and strikes both people and wild animals (vv. 2–6). **2.** *her people:* Not in the MT; with Holladay (*JBL* 81, 51), we hold that the subject of the verb "sink down" is still "gates." Thus, we keep the chiasmic structure of the verse: Judah-gates/gates-Jerusalem. However, these gates represent the people, for often the judicial and political gatherings took place at the city gates. **7–9.** This collective lament borrowed its literary form from the penitential hymns. Their main characteristic is the abundance of interrogations of Yahweh, seen especially as the only source of hope. Another frequent theme of these hymns is the honor of God: If he abandons his people to their annihilation, the foreign nations and their gods will be convinced that Yahweh is but a vain God; therefore, he must forget his people's sins! Even though such a theology presents a commercial aspect, it expresses a sound faith in Yahweh's salvific powers. **9.** *your name we bear: Qārā' šēm 'al* means, lit., "to invoke the name upon." The name stands for Yahweh himself and the very same expression is applied to the Temple (7:30), to the Prophet (15:16), and to the people (14:9; cf. Dt 28:10). What is intended here is not that these realities be simply Yahweh's property, but that Yahweh protects them by his salvific presence (see A. M. Besnard, *Le mystère du nom* [Paris, 1962]), this is precisely what the last words of the prayer ask for—i.e., "Do not forsake us!" **10–12.** This passage, and the one following, are written in prose. Here we have Yahweh's answer. First he addresses the people (v. 10): Their iniquities are unforgettable and must be punished (cf. Hos 8:13; 9:9). This evil is called a restless wandering, probably an allusion to the multiple idolatrous sanctuaries or to the frequent attempts to enter foreign alliances. Then Yahweh turns to the Prophet (vv. 11–12). As we have already stated, his intercession will be in vain (7:16; 11:14) and the people's sacrifices are void (6:20; 7:21ff.; 11:15). Therefore, the three classical plagues—war, famine, and pestilence (cf. 2 Sm 24:13)—are inevitable. **13–16.** Jeremiah still pleads for his people. They have an excuse for their evildoings because they were misled by the false prophets who continually promised peace and prosperity, even though the covenantal relationship had been broken (cf. 4:10; 5:12; 6:14; 8:11; 27:11; esp. 23:9ff.). This excuse is rejected for lack of foundation: Yahweh did not send these prophets, so their message can be nothing else but a product of their own imagination. The difference between the false prophets and the "vocational" ones has never been so clear (cf. 23:9ff.).

48 (B) Lament (14:17–15:4). Following Weiser, we take this pericope as a new poem, built on the plan of the previous one—a description of the plague, a collective lament, and Yahweh's answer. **17–18.** Now a war is shattering Judah, personified as a young woman mortally wounded (cf. 8:21; 10:19). **19–22.** This collective lament presents again all the characteristics of its kind (cf. vv. 7–9). **21.** *throne of your glory:* The name given to the Temple (17:12) is here applied to Jerusalem (19a; cf. 3:17). **22.** This verse presupposes a context of drought, and might have been taken from the first poem. The Canaanite Baal cult included rites for the assurance of rains necessary for the fertility of the fields; these rites were adopted by the Israelites in their idolatrous practices. The actual drought is now a proof of their inanity and at the same time an appeal to attribute their power to Yahweh (cf. 5:24; Hos 2:7ff.; see P. Reymond, VTSup 6 [1956] 41–53, 222–28).

15:1–4. This new divine answer parallels the preceding one (cf. 14:10–12). **1.** Moses and Samuel have always been considered great intercessors for their people (Ex 32:11–14; Nm 14:11–25; 1 Sm 7:5–9; 12:19–23; Ps 99:6). The refusal to hear their prayers any longer indicates how irrevocable Yahweh's decision can be. **2.** A fourth plague, captivity, is added to the three classical ones. We have no reason to suppress it, and we are inclined to give to this poem a date close to the first downfall of Jerusalem (597). **3.** The verse is a new development on the war. The dogs might be a reminiscence of Jezebel's story (2 Kgs 9:10,37). Vultures and wild animals feeding on the corpses of the slain figure also as a curse in the vassal treaties of Esarhaddon (cf. Wiseman, *Vassal-treaties of Esarhaddon*, 11. 425–27). **4.** Most critics consider this verse as a gloss. Only Manasseh, the most syncretistic of all the Davidic kings, could be the cause of such a great massacre (2 Kgs 21).

49 (C) Tragedy (15:5–9). This gloomy oracle addressed to Jerusalem is similar to the preceding poem. Nebuchadnezzar's invasion of Judah and Jerusalem in 597 might be the historical context of these pathetic verses. **9.** *mother of seven:* Even such a great blessing (1 Sm 2:5; Ru 4:15) is changed to as great a curse, for the lives of these sons ("her sun") are taken away in their full strength ("full day").

50 (ii) *The renewal of the call* (15:10–21). This fragment of the "confessions" (cf. 11:18ff.) was probably inserted here because it opens with a lament on the Prophet's mother, recalling the end of the preceding passage (15:9). This complaint is cast in extremely severe terms. Jeremiah describes an inner crisis. There are clear references to the narrative of his call (1:4ff.); thus, the present one can be considered a renewal of this vocation, once the crisis has been overcome. The crisis probably occurred during the difficult years under Jehoiakim, as most exegetes believe. However, Rowley would date the complaint at the beginning of the Prophet's ministry; when the people realized that his Scythian threats were unfulfilled, he then became the object of their raillery (*BJRylL* 45, 222–24). But we have already indicated how problematical the Scythian question is in these early poems (chs. 4–6). **10.** This curse will take on greater proportions later (cf. 20:14–18). It also brings to mind a similar one in Jb 3:3. We remember that his call dated from his mother's womb; cursing the day of his birth would then mean nothing else but a rejection of his very mission. *a man of strife:* It is what Yahweh intended him to be (1:10). What brings persecution to him is not his just conduct toward everyone, but precisely his message. **11.** Jeremiah's love for his people has no better proof than his constant intercession for them (7:16; 11:14; 14:11). **12.** The verse is untranslatable and must be a corruption of 17:1; this view is supported by the fact that vv. 13–14 are a doublet of 17:2–3 and out of place here. **15.** The desire of vengeance against persecutors figures in all the fragments of the "confessions" (11:20; 17:18; 20:11–12) and is most frequent in the imprecatory psalms. Such a desire has to be understood in the perspective of earthly retribution (cf. comment on 11:20). **16.** *your words...:* The day of his call, Yahweh had touched his mouth, thus placing his own words on the Prophet's lips (1:9). *I bore your name:* The expression reveals a protective presence of God on his messenger (cf. 14:9). **17.** *I do not sit:* This isolation from the evildoers later inspired two psalmists (Pss 1:1–2; 26:4–5). **18.** *treacherous brook:* During the summer, most Palestinian brooks dry up. Here and in Jb 6:16–21 they symbolize a profound deception; similarly, "broken cisterns" were given as a symbol of vain alliances (2:13). Thus, Jeremiah boldly accuses Yahweh of having forsaken him (cf. 20:7)—the climax of the present crisis. **19–21.** Yahweh now renews and confirms the Prophet's mission, in the very terms of the first call (1:18–19), but this time it is not a gratuitous gift; it will only be conferred once Jeremiah has converted himself—i.e., when he has regained confidence in that very mission by rejecting these rebellious thoughts.

51 (iii) *Jeremiah's celibacy* (16:1–13,16–18). The prophetical word is delivered not only through symbolic actions, but also sometimes through events of the prophet's own lives: Hosea's unfortunate marriage (Hos 1–3), Isaiah's family (Is 7–8), the death of Ezekiel's wife (Ez 24:15–27), and here, Jeremiah's celibacy. In the ancient Near East, and thus in Israel, a large family was a divine blessing (Gn 22:17; Ps 127:3–4; etc.); sterility, on the contrary, was a terrible curse (Gn 30:1; 1 Sm 1:6–8; etc.), and virginity was even a cause for mourning (Jgs 11:37). Celibacy was even cursed in an old Sumerian proverb (see W. G. Lambert, *BASOR* 169 [1963] 63–64). For all these reasons, besides his sensitivity to love and joy, Jeremiah's celibacy could not have been his personal choice, but an order received from his Lord. **3–4.** The prophetical meaning of this single state is here given. Inasmuch as Jeremiah has no family, the existing ones will disappear, and violently. The privation of sepulture, a typical Oriental curse, is reaffirmed in the same terms as before (cf. 7:33; 8:2; 9:21; 14:12; 15:3). **5–7.** His solitary attitude forbids him even to join mourning gatherings for the deceased, because Yahweh has withdrawn the covenantal blessings—peace, love and piety, so often symbolized by the married life itself—and Jeremiah does not experience these joys. **6.** *gash...shave:* Incisions, shaved heads, and beards were signs of mourning (41:5; 47:5; 48:37; Is 15:2ff.; 22:12; Mi 1:16; Ez 7:18; etc.). Because these customs have been condemned at one time (Dt 14:1; Lv 19:27–28; 21:5), we suspect that they were of a pagan origin and had some superstitious meaning (see Lagrange, *op. cit.*, 320ff.). **7.** *break bread...cup of consolation:* These funeral meals have been diversely explained: either they were taken at the occasion of a death or they were offered to the dead person (cf. Hos 9:4; Ez 24:17,22; Dt 26:14). Tobit speaks clearly of food offered to the deceased (Tb 4:17), and the excavations of tombs prove that such offerings were really made; therefore, the belief was that life continued after death in a form similar to the present one (see De Vaux, *AI* 56–61). **8–9.** Even the joyful gatherings have to be avoided. "The voice of the bridegroom and the voice of the bride" must allude to nuptial songs at the occasion of marriages (cf. 7:34; 25:10; 33:11). The Canticle of Canticles might be a collection of such songs. **10–13.** Now we know why the Prophet had to take such an attitude: God's people is idolatrous. **13.** *serve strange gods:* A condemnation to exile. Before the idea of strict monotheism was acquired, Yahweh was believed to exist only in Palestine (cf. 1 Kgs 5:17); therefore, if his worshipers leave this land, they are bound to serve other gods—those of the new land in which they find themselves (1 Sm 26:19). Jeremiah still shared this belief. **16–18.** The means of the punishment will be an invasion, figured by hunters and fishermen. *profaning my land... heritage:* If our exegesis of v. 13 is correct, only Yahweh could be worshiped in Palestine; therefore, he called it his land, his heritage.

52 (iv) *Disjecta membra* (16:14–15,19–21;17:1–18). A number of short oracles or simply fragments of longer ones have been placed in this part of the book, without any clear reasons.

(A) Return from Exile (16:14–15). The passage reproduces 23:7–8, with minor differences. It is probably inserted here to attenuate the threatenings of the preceding oracle.

(B) Conversion of the Heathen (16:19–21). The pericope recalls the poem on the vanity of idolatry (10:1–16) and the oracle on the salvation of the foreign nations (12:14–17), which we dismissed as later additions to the book. In fact, the present passage is similar in thought and is close to certain parts of Dt-Is (cf. 40:20; 42:8; 45:14–25; etc.). We meet with the same negation of the existence of the gods and the conversion of the nations. The opening address to Yahweh (strength, fortress, refuge) might have been borrowed from a thanksgiving psalm (cf. 2 Sm 22:2–3 = Ps 18:2–3; Pss 28:1,7–8; 59:10,17–18; etc.).

(C) Judah's Guilt (17:1–4). This short oracle is similar to 16:16–18, on idolatry. The passage is lacking in the LXX and vv. 3–4 are repeated out of context in 15:13–14. **1.** *an iron stylus:* The expression is attested to in Jb 19:24, indicating the indelible character of an inscription. *tablets of their hearts:* This image, borrowed from the writing techniques (see R. J. Williams, *IDB* 4, 915–21), reappears in Prv 3:3; 7:3, and once again in Jer with a variant (31:33). Sin and virtue are much more than mere external rejection or conformity to rules; they are the expressions of the very heart of man. Through this new image, Jeremiah stigmatizes this profound and permanent reality of sin, elsewhere compared to the leopard's spots and the Ethiopian's skin (13:23). **2b–3a.** This prosaic addition specifies which "altars" the prophet was discussing—i.e., the entire cultic material of the high places. The oracle concludes with a new threat of exile, and must date therefore before 597.

53 (D) Sapiential Sayings (17:5–11). The authenticity of this small collection of wisdom is still highly disputed; in fact, no definitive arguments can be given for or against it. **5–8.** This first saying on "true justice" uses the antithetical synonymity and the literary form of the blessings and curses. The idea of the just man being like a green tree because his strength is in God is well known in the wisdom literature (Ps 52:10; Prv 3:18; 11:13; Sir 24:13ff.), as is also the opposition between the trust in God and the trust in man (Pss 39:5; 117:8–9; 145:3ff.). But the closest parallel is Ps 1, where this opposition is expressed with the very same comparisons, also attested to in the wisdom of the Egyptian Sage, Amen-em-Ope (6:1–12; cf. *ANET* 422). Most exegetes agree that Ps 1 is dependent on Jer, for the trust in the Law is characteristic of later Judaism. The saying intends to put across the real heart of true religion: God is man's sole refuge. We see no evidence to hold, with R. Davidson, that what Jeremiah expresses here is a rejection of Josiah's nationalistic reform after the latter's death at Megiddo in 609, proving that the human policies are futile (*VT* 9 [1959] 204–205). **9–10.** This new saying concerns the root of evil, the human heart. If the secret plots of the heart are hidden to men, they are transparent to God (cf. Ps 138). The expression "probe the heart and test the loins" is properly Jeremian (cf. 11:20; 20:12; Pss 7:10; 64:7), and shows how constantly the Prophet repeated the primacy of the interior sentiments in religious life. **11.** The last saying on riches unjustly acquired uses a comparison that probably originates from a popular proverb and remains quite obscure. The retribution is still situated in this present life—a premature death (cf. Ps 55:24).

54 (E) The Source of Life (17:12–13). **12.** The verse has been rejected by many as contradictory to the Temple discourse (7:1ff.), but it is nothing more than the simple affirmation of Israel's belief from old. **13.** *the rebels in the land...:* The MT is corrupted, and we prefer Rudolph's emendations, showing a greater respect for the text—"Those who turn from you shall be written on the dust"—which gives a beautiful image of the fragile existence of the sinners. Finally, the title, "source of living waters," is already known (2:13); the idea probably stems from the belief in the divine regulation of the rains (cf. 14:21).

55 (F) A Prayer for Vengeance (17:14–18). This is a third fragment of the "confessions" (cf. 11:18ff.; 15:10ff.). **14.** *heal me:* Such a demand figures in the "psalms of the sick" (Pss 6:3; 41:5). However, as v. 15 indicates, the Prophet's sickness is the evil wished on him by his adversaries. **15.** *let it come to pass:* That his prophecies of wars and exile are late in coming is the reason why he is now an object of scorn. He must be a dreamer. This "confession" probably dates before 597. **16.** Jeremiah's message is not his but Yahweh's, for the misfortunes predicted are painful to his love for his own land (4:19; 8:21–23; 13:17; 14:17). The prayer closes on the same desire of vengeance common to the imprecatory psalms.

56 (v) *Observance of the Sabbath* (17:19–27). The present passage is usually listed in the "deuteronomic" speeches of Jer, and its authenticity is most disputed. The institution of the Sabbath is extremely old in Israel, for it figures in all four Pentateuch traditions (Ex 32:12; 34:21; 31:12–17; 20:8–10 = Dt 5:12–14), and is also mentioned in the 8th cent. prophets (Am 8:5; Is 1:13; see J. Morgenstern, *IDB* 4, 135–41; De Vaux, *AI* 475–83). Therefore, it is certainly possible that Jeremiah could have corrected deviations in its observance. However, few exegetes would accept the pericope as it now stands to be entirely from Jeremiah's lips; an authentic oracle has been amplified at a later date (Weiser, Rudolph, Penna; Bright, *JBL* 70, 23–24; etc.). Others, on the contrary, reject it entirely as a post-exilic addition (Volz, Gelin, Steinmann, De Vaux, etc.). In general, it is an accepted opinion that the sabbatical rest assumed great importance after the Exile, and Nehemiah took all the measures necessary to have its observance strictly kept; he went so far as to close the gates of Jerusalem (Neh 13:15–22). With this last text in mind, we understand much better why there is such an insistence on the prohibition of carrying burdens, which does not figure in the former traditions, and why the admonishment is proclaimed at all the city gates. Moreover, it is not in Jeremiah's mentality to defend a law without giving its religious meaning and motives. For all these reasons, the speech would seem to have been composed at the time of Nehemiah. Nevertheless, we still hold that an authentic oracle stands at its origin, as the following remark indicates. **19.** *gate of Benjamin:* This phrase is a correction, for the MT reads, "the gate of the sons of my people." Because the kings are passing through it, it must be a gate between the royal palace and the Temple courts; we see no need to correct the text. The mention of the "kings" is rather difficult to explain if the whole passage is post-exilic; but if an original sermon of Jeremiah had been reworked at that time, the difficulty vanishes. **21.** *as you love your lives:* The statement is attested in Dt 4:15 and Jos 23:11 to introduce a solemn and important admonishment. **26.** *land of Benjamin:* This territory is N of Jerusalem. *foothills:* The Hebr word *š^{e}pēlâ* refers to the plain on the Mediterranean coast of Palestine. *hill country:* It designates Ephraim (cf. 4:15). *Negeb:* It corresponds to the desert region S of Hebron. Thus, sacrifices will be brought from all over the land.

(d) Symbolic Meaning of the Prophet's Life (18:1–20:18). The new title at the beginning of ch. 18 is a sign that the present section of the book forms another small unit; its main subject matter consists in the prophetical meaning of some experiences in the Prophet's life with the insertion of two new fragments of his "confessions."

57 (i) *A visit at the potter's* (18:1–12). The narrative is considered another "deuteronomic" passage. The inspiration of the sermon comes from an ordinary experience of Jeremiah later interpreted as the Lord's command; we have already seen how such simple events were, at times, also interpreted by the prophets as divine visions (cf. 1:11ff.). These are illustrations of the modes of God's inspiration. **3.** *wheel:* The potter's wheel is mentioned nowhere else in the OT; the Hebr word *'obnāyim* means lit., "two stones." Its structure was simple: two stone disks were united by a vertical axis; the lower disk was activated by the feet, while the clay, resting on the upper one, was fashioned by the hands as the disk kept turning (cf. Sir 38:29–30). **4.** This verse states the essential point of comparison in the prophetical oracle. **6.** The symbolism emerging from this workmanship is now specified. First, Yahweh is the potter; the anthropomorphism is old in Israel (cf. Gn 2:7) and is well attested to in Mesopotamia and Egypt, which explains why the verb *yāṣar* ("to shape" or "to fashion") could also mean "to create." Moreover, this symbolic image has been used three times in Is (29:16; 45:9; 64:7) to express the absolute dependence of man on God in the order of creation (cf. Rom 9:20–24, where Paul applies it to the notion of predestination). Second, the clay represents man; the idea that man is made of clay is also a very common idea in the Near East, and its origin correlates to that of the potter. **7–10.** Jeremiah proposes the prophetical meaning of the image, which is not set on the level of creation but on that of God's decrees: As a bad vase can be reshaped into a new one, so a decree of God can be changed to a new one, provided that conversion has been achieved. **7–8.** A decree of doom, expressed in the terms of 1:10, can be suspended by conversion; therefore, God does not act arbitrarily but takes the human will into consideration—a proof of the effective value of penance (cf. 7:3ff.; 26:3; 36:3; Ez 18:21–27; Jon 3). **9–10.** The opposite is also true. A blessing, expressed again in the terms of 1:10, can be changed to a curse if man lapses into sin. In other words, Jeremiah teaches clearly that the free will has an important role to play in both salvation and damnation, even though he does not enter into the complexity of the relation between divine necessity and human freedom. **11–12.** This general principle is finally applied to Judah, but the Prophet has no hope for her salvation, because her evil heart (*š^{e}rîrût*; cf. comment on 7:24) obstructs the way of conversion.

(ii) *Israel forgets Yahweh* (18:13–17). The present oracle of doom has been connected artificially (v. 13a) to the preceding sermon. Undoubtedly, there exists a relationship between this passage and ch. 2; both deal with a flagrant apostasy of the people and use the literary form of the lawsuit (*rîb*). However, there are no clear reasons to set the poem under Josiah, as a manifestation of Jeremiah's deception at the king's reform (Skinner, *op. cit.*, 133ff.). **13.** Such an inquiry among the nations introduces also the long tirade against Judah in 2:10. **14–15.** The Prophet borrows from nature some examples of constant faithfulness, in contrast to Judah's constant unfaithfulness through idolatry. He used the same device elsewhere with a similar complaint: "they have forgotten me," "they did not know me" (cf. 2:32; 8:7). The purpose of these images is to show how unnatural is idolatry for God's people. *paths of old:* The expression was met before (6:16) as a reference to tradition. The prophets not only did not reject it but also urged the people to examine it to stay on the right paths. **16.** *shake their heads:* This action, often joined to the one of "hissing," is a sign of derision and mockery

(19:8; 48:27; 2 Kgs 19:21 = Is 37:23; Pss 22:8; 44:15; 64:9; Lam 2:15). Rudolph's opinion that it bore an "apotropaic" value cannot be proved. **17.** *show my back:* By its apostasy, the people was said to have turned its back to Yahweh (2:27); therefore, Yahweh has rejected his people. Such a harsh threat must have been proclaimed under Jehoiakim, at the resurgence of idolatry.

58 (iii) *Another prayer for vengeance* (18:18–23). **18.** The motive of this new plot against Jeremiah is the same as the one given on a similar occasion, i.e., his message (11:19ff.). The priests and the prophets are often mentioned together (2:8; 4:9; 6:13; 23:11ff.; etc.); only here do we meet a third group, the wise men, although they are well known to the Prophet (9:22ff.). These three classes of the spiritual leaders were characterized by the technical term attached to each function: the priestly instruction (*tôrâ*, "law"; cf. 2:18), the prophetical word (*dābār*), and the sapiental counsel (*'ēṣâ;* see W. Zimmerli, *ZAW* 51 [1933] 177–201). The full activity of all these functions will not be suspended by the suppression of Jeremiah. **19–23.** A new fragment of the "confessions" follows, presenting all the characteristics of these compositions (cf. 15:10–21). **19.** *heed me:* Several other prayers of the "just sufferer" include such a call to God's attention (Pss 17:1; 55:3; etc.). **20.** *good repaid by evil:* The theme will be used by other psalmists in similar circumstances (Pss 34:12; 37:21). **23.** We have already explained how such a desire of vengeance must be understood in the light of earthly retribution (11:18ff.). Jesus, bringing the fullness of its revelation, will pray in a manner opposite to this prayer (Lk 23:34).

59 (iv) *The broken flask and Topheth* (19:1–20:6). This section of Jer lacks unity, as most scholars recognize today. The accepted opinion is that a narrative from Baruch's memoirs has been disrupted by interpolations of an oracle or oracles on Topheth. We follow here Rudolph's division of the test.

(A) The Broken Flask (19:1,2bc,10–11a,14–20:6). We deal here with another symbolic action that shows the dynamic aspect of the prophetical word (cf. comment on 13:1–14). The story is enacted in the presence of a small group of elders and priests at the entrance of the Potsherd Gate. This gate is mentioned only here; it must be located at the S end of the city, for a contemporary tradition specifies that it opens on the Valley of Ben-Hinnom. The hapaxlegomenon word *ḥarsît* could simply mean "pottery"; the gate might have been so called because a potter's shop was installed close to it (see L. H. Vincent, *Jérusalem antique* [vol 1; Paris, 1912] 129, n. 3). But if the word really means "sherd," then we might identify the gate with the Dung Gate in Nehemiah's time (Neh 2:13; 3:13–14); this appellation can be explained by the simple fact that the city dump was close by and could only be toward the south, in the Ben-Hinnom Valley. **10–11a.** The symbolic action proper consists in the smashing of a juglet, which recalls some magic rites often attested in the ancient Near East. In Egypt, one rite dating to the old kingdom consisted in writing the names of enemy people and cities on jars and figurines that would then be smashed to pieces; such an action was supposed to bring about the destruction of those whose names were written down on these objects (see J. A. Wilson, *The Culture of Ancient Egypt* [Chicago, 1951] 156–58). Analogous imprecatory rites were also practiced among the Assyrians, the Hittites, and the Arameans, to cast off a sickness or to set a curse on traitors to covenants. The dismemberment of an animal or the destruction of an object signified that the evil would vanish or that the traitor would be annihilated (see texts in *ANET* 346–51, 353–54; Wiseman, *Vassal-treaties*, II. 608–11; Jer 34:18). However, the magical value of such actions is out of place here. Yahweh alone will realize the curse, for the smashing of the juglet is but a dramatic illustration: "I smash this people. . .as one smashes a clay pot" (v. 11a). **14.** *returned from Topheth:* The oracle first proclaimed at the gate is now repeated in the court of the Temple, thus provoking the anger of the Temple's chief officer. The word "Topheth" is probably not original; it replaced a similar one like "entrance" (*petaḥ*) or "entrance of the gate" (v. 2b), when the oracle on Topheth was later inserted (Rudolph, Nötscher, Volz, Gelin, etc.).

20:1. *Pashhur:* He must be different from the other Pashhur mentioned in 21:1 and 38:1ff. The prediction of his exile (v. 6) probably occurred in 597, for in 594 another priest was holding his office, consisting mainly in the organization of the police guard to watch over the activities going on in the Temple courts (cf. 29:25–26). **2.** *stocks:* The rare word *mahpeket* is usually thus translated. However, because the punishment takes place at a gate and both the LXX and Tg. have translated it as "prison," a "cramped room" at the gate serving for short detentions would appear more suitable to the context (see M. Greenberg, *IDB* 4, 443). *upper Gate of Benjamin in the house of the Lord:* This Temple gate has to be identified seemingly with the "upper gate in the house of the Lord" built by Jotham (2 Kgs 15:35); it can be located between the old court and the new one mentioned for the first time under Jehoshaphat (2 Chr 20:5). The designation "of Benjamin" would be a gloss from a later redactor who wanted to identify this gate with the Gate of Benjamin in the city walls where a second arrest will occur later (37:13; see L. H. Vincent, *Jérusalem de l'Ancien Testament* [vols. 2–3; Paris, 1956] 603–604). **3.** *terror on every side: Māgôr missābîb* is the *omen* of Pashhur's *nomen*. The expression certainly hides a pun that is still obscure, for the very meaning of Passhur is itself uncertain. We conjecture that there must be an opposition between the two names; thus, Jeremiah would have thought that *Pašḥûr* comes from combining two verb roots: *pāšaḥ*, "to be quiet"; *sāḥar*, "go about" or "go around." "Terror on every side" is another Jeremian creation (6:25; 20:3.10; 46:5; 49:29), later used in Lam 2:22 and Ps 32:14. **4–6.** Jeremiah now renders more explicit the prophetical meaning of this new name: Judah and Pashhur's household will be exiled and Jerusalem will be plundered. For the first time, he calls the invader by name—Babylon. The incident, which certainly happened before 597, recalls a similar one in Amos' life (7:10–17).

60 (B) Topheth (19:2a,3–9,11b–13). This discourse interrupts the story of the broken flask. Weiser and Rudolph believe that it pertained, originally, to the short oracle on the same subject in 7:31–33. Although most of these verses are repeated here, there are too many new utterances to be a simple doublet. Jeremiah certainly attacked more than once this dreadful idolatrous cult; if he did not, we believe that the present discourse is the original, and some of its parts have been repeated in the small collection of sayings in 7:29ff. **2a.** *Valley of Ben-Hinnom:* At times just called Valley of Hinnom (*gê' hinnōm*, our "gehenna"), the valley is identified with the actual Wadi er-Rababi, running at first southward on the W side of Jerusalem and then turning sharply to the east on the S side (see Vincent, *Jérusalem antique*, I 124–34). **3.** *kings of Judah and citizens of Jerusalem:* This vast audience in full contrast to the small one mentioned in v. 1, is a sign that two different events have been amalgamated. *ears tingle:* The expression is found elsewhere only in 1 Sm 3:11 and 2 Kgs 21:12, as the sign of a catastrophe unheard of before. **4.** *blood of the innocent:* This is a clear reference to child sacrifice (cf. v. 5; 7:31). Human sacrifices existed in the ancient Near East, especially in Phoenicia and Canaan. In Israel, such a practice was condemned quite early, if the substitution of a ram for Isaac meant precisely its abolition (Gn 22:1–19); but these sacrifices revived under Ahaz (2 Kgs 16:3; cf. Mi 6:7) and Manasseh (2 Kgs 21:6). The sanctuary of the Hinnom Valley was then destroyed by Josiah, at the time of the reform (2 Kgs 23:10); the present text proves that Jehoiakim had reopened it (see De Vaux, *AI* 441–46; A. Bea, *Bib* 18 [1937] 95–107). **6.** *Topheth:* The name derives probably from a root *tāfā'* meaning originally "hearth" or "fireplace." According to the texts and extrabiblical sources, the victims were actually burnt. *Valley of Slaughter:* Here, again, a new name is given as a sign of doom. We suppose that the word "slaughter" is opposed to "Hinnom"; although the meaning of Hinnom is unknown, it could well be that Jeremiah connected it to the assonant adverb *ḥinnām*, "gratuitously," "favorably." **9.** To the other evils often mentioned, Jeremiah adds a new one: The siege will be so long and so strict that the people will be forced to eat the flesh of their own children. This threat (Dt 28:53; Lv 26:29; Ez 5:10) became real in Samaria during the Aramean wars (2 Kgs 6:26ff.) and also in Jerusalem during its last siege (Lam 2:20; 4:10). Josephus relates the same fact when Titus besieged Jerusalem in 70 AD (*JW* 6. 3–4). Outside of Israel, Esarhaddon invokes that very curse on whomever breaks his treaty (Wiseman, *Vassal-treaties*, 11. 448ff., 547–50, 570–72). **11b–13.** Topheth and the whole city will become impure by the contact with dead bodies (cf. Lv 21:1ff.; Nm 5:2; 19:11–22). Josiah profaned heathen high places and altars by the same device (2 Kgs 23:14–20). *host of heaven:* The Mesopotamian astral divinities are thus designated (cf. 7:16–20).

61 (v) *Jeremiah's despair* (20:7–18). The redactor who inserted this last fragment of Jeremiah's "confessions" right after the Prophet's altercation with Pashhur, intended probably to give the event as the occasion of Jeremiah's most dramatic interior crisis. Owing to such utterances, we see that a prophet's mission and inspiration were not purely magical or simply human experiences, but real interventions of God in a man's life that could contradict most dramatically his aspirations and cause serious crises. **7.** *you duped me:* The verb *pātā* means, lit., "to seduce," and is used in the case of a virgin being seduced by a man (Ex 22:15). Quite often, it simply means "to deceive," and is applied to false prophets being duped by Yahweh (1 Kgs 22:19–23; Ez 14:9; etc.). We see how daring Jeremiah's address to God could be! *you were too strong...:* A more literal translation yields "you seized me and you prevailed." The verb *ḥāzaq* (to seize) figures also in the context of sexual seduction (Dt 22:25; 2 Sm 13:11,14; Prv 7:13); we believe that the imagery of the first part of the verse is maintained here. Jeremiah had already called his God "a treacherous brook" (15:18), but here the reproach is much bolder: Yahweh tricked his messenger! **8.** Jeremiah has been sent "to root up and to tear down, to build and to plant" (1:10); until now, his message corresponded only with the first part of the program. Therefore, he had to face constant persecutions. He had been deceived, for if he could have built and planted, the situation would have been different. **9.** The verse is important for the study of the prophetical inspiration; its urge is irresistible. Amos had already expressed the same idea through a series of images (Am 3:3–8). Yahweh is said to be a "consuming fire" (Ex 24:17; Dt 4:24; 9:3; Is 33:14); only Jeremiah applied it directly to his word (cf. 5:14; 23:29).

10–13. This authentic passage is often believed to be out of context, for its deep tone of confidence is a break in the Prophet's depression. Rudolph's remark might be true: In a psychological and spiritual crisis like Jeremiah's, what we should expect is not logic but a real conflict of sentiments. **10.** *terror on every side:* This Jeremian outcry (cf. 20:3) is now turned against the Prophet in derision and mockery. **11.** This confidence has its foundation in Yahweh's promise (1:8,19) which the Prophet often recalled (15:20). In the midst of strong contradictions he keeps his faith in Yahweh's loyalty. **12.** The verse is a literal repetition of 11:20; this fundamental belief in earthly retribution could have been expressed more than once. **13.** The verse is often rejected as a late doxology; but Holladay has shown that the expression "from the hand [power] of the wicked" is found only in Jer (15:21; 21:12; 23:14; see *JBL* 81, 52–53). *the poor:* The Hebr word *'ebyôn* had already exceeded its sociological meaning to take a religious tone; it refers to the pious man, the "client of Yahweh" (see P. Humbert, *RHPR* 32 [1952] 1–6; A. Gelin, *The Poor of Yahweh* [Collegeville, 1953]). Again, in several psalms of the "just sufferer," probably under Jeremiah's influence, we have the same combination of themes: an appeal to glorify the Lord for he has taken care of the poor (cf. Pss 22:23ff.; 35:9–10,27–28; 109:30–31; 140:13–14).

14–18. Jeremiah now gives full expression to cursing the day of his birth (cf. 15:10—influence on Jb 3?). The crisis has reached its peak. **16.** *man:* With most scholars, we change "man" to "day," because the whole passage is centered on the day of his birth; moreover, it would be difficult to explain how "man" could have prevented his birth (v. 17). *cities:* Jeremiah may allude here to the destruction of Sodom and Gomorrah (Gn 19); he did explicitly mention the incident once (23:14).

62 **(D) The Ministry Under Zedekiah (21:1–24:10).** The forthcoming chapters have to be considered as a unit, dealing with two subjects: the kings and the prophets. Most of these oracles can be dated under Zedekiah (597–587); they were probably collected toward the end of his reign to reveal the main authors of the imminent final catastrophe. A small oracle on the first exiles in 597 (ch. 24) sheds a dim light of future hope.

(a) A Consultation from Zedekiah (21:1–10). It is generally accepted that this consultation took place during the siege of Jerusalem by Nebuchadnezzar, probably at its very beginning in 588. Similar consultations will be repeated (cf. chs. 37–38). **1.** *Pashhur, son of Malchiah:* This Pashhur is different from the Pashhur in 20:1ff., as their fathers' names show; not too long after this consultation, Pashhur will be violently opposed to the Prophet (38:1ff.). *Zephaniah:* The man will still be a member of another delegation by Zedekiah (37:3); at the downfall of Jerusalem, he will be made prisoner (2 Kgs 25:18). **2.** For all practical purposes, Zedekiah expects Yahweh to repeat now what he did in 701, when Sennacherib besieged Jerusalem (2 Kgs 19:35–36 = Is 37:36–37); the situations were too much alike not to ask for the same outcome, but Yahweh's answer ruins such hope. **5.** *outstretched hand and mighty arm:* The image of the arm alone is attested in Ex 6:6, and, with the one of the hand, it is frequently used in Dt (4:34; 5:15; 7:19; 26:8; etc., but with the inversion of the adjectives) as well as in another Jer passage (32:21). The idea must go back to the times when Yahweh was said to lead the armies in holy wars (see De Vaux, *AI* 258–65). **7.** Zedekiah, with his household and the rest of the population, will fall to the Chaldeans; it is expressed only in the general and classical terms found in Jer. A reading of 2 Kgs 25 suggests that the prediction is certainly antecedent. **8–10.** This answer to the whole people is repeated almost word for word in 38:2–3, not necessarily a doublet. *life and death:* This choice does not figure in the text just mentioned. The MT reads, "the way of life and the way of death," an expression frequently used in the wisdom literature but with a moral intent. Such a proposal of surrender to the Chaldeans has occasioned all kinds of speculation on Jeremiah's political theory. We believe that his first principle is quite simple; Yahweh has abandoned his people because of their infidelities and Jerusalem's downfall is now inevitable. Slaughter can be avoided only by nonresistance and peaceful surrender. Such an attitude can hardly be called collaboration with the enemy.

63 (b) BOOKLET ON KINGS (21:11–23:8). The present section, as well as the following one on the prophets, probably existed in a separate form, as the titles seem to indicate (21:11a and 23:9a), before their insertion in Jer. We find references to all five kings under whom Jeremiah fulfilled his mission.

(i) *A general address to the royal house* (21:11–22:9). We note the double meaning of the Hebr word *bayit*, "dynasty" and "palace"; indeed, both realities are concerned in the following oracles, united as a general introduction to those on the individual kings. **12.** The collection opens with a general recommendation to the king as guardian of justice, one of the main duties attached to the sacral kingship in the Near East. In Israel, this obligation was never lost; Solomon made it one of the elements of his prayer to Yahweh (1 Kgs 3:9; 8:32) and the royal psalms gave it a great importance (45:4–8; 72:1–4,12–14; etc.). The prophetic criticism of the social injustices certainly did concern the kings as well (Am 5:11ff.; Is 1:17; Mi 3:9ff.; etc.). Whenever the deuteronomists wanted to give a definition of the authentic kingship, they did not hesitate to emphasize faithfulness to the covenant (Dt 17:14–20).

64 (A) Jerusalem (21:13–14; 22:6–7). These lines, joined to the preceding through the word "fire" (21:12–14; 22:7), deal with both Jerusalem and its palace. **13.** *valley-site:* The word *'ēmeq* is probably an additional explanation of the word *mîšōr* (plain), for Jerusalem is surrounded only by deep valleys that could hardly be called "plains." On every side, except on the north, the city was naturally well defended. **14.** *I will punish... deserve:* This prosaic sentence is lacking in the LXX and is foreign to the oracle. *Forest:* Because there is no forest in Jerusalem, it must designate the royal palace. Indeed, Solomon built the "Hall of the Forest of Lebanon" (1 Kgs 7:2–4), so called because its walls were made of cedars from that country (cf. Is 22:9). If the "forest" is the palace, its "surroundings" is the city itself. **22:6.** *for thus says...:* This title was added once the oracle had been separated by another. *Gilead, Lebanon:* These two regions were noted for their forests (2 Sm 18:6–9); the comparison is then natural. **7.** For the same reason, we understand why the Babylonians are called "woodcutters." The passage has certainly inspired a later psalmist (Ps 74:5–7).

65 (B) Duty Toward Justice (22:1–5). This further development, in deuteronomic prose, is of the king's duty toward justice (21:12). As in the texts already quoted, the welfare and continuity of the dynasty depend on its fidelity to this duty (vv. 4–5). What Jeremiah asks of the kings he has already asked of the people in his Temple discourse (cf. 7:1ff.). **3.** The protection that these three classes of the weak deserve is a firm covenant stipulation (Ex 22:20–26; 23:9; Lv 19:33–34; Dt 10:18–19; 24:17). If the king himself ought to fulfill it, it shows that the Mosaic and the Davidic covenants were essentially the same. *innocent blood:* A clear allusion to child sacrifice at Topheth (cf. 19:2aff.). **4–5.** A post-exilic addition; cf. 17:25.

66 (C) Idolatry (22:8–9). This short pericope is to be rejected as an exilic addition (cf. 5:19) in the style of two deuteronomic passages (Dt 29:23–25; 1 Kgs 9:8–9). Idolatry is finally understood as being the basic rupture of the covenant (Ex 20:3; Dt 6:4).

67 (ii) *Jehoahaz* (22:10–12). According to 1 Chr 3:15, Jehoahaz was Josiah's fourth son, and is also called Shallum. He was put on the throne by "the people of the land" (see J. A. Soggin, *VT* 13 [1963] 187–95) after his father's death at Megiddo in 609 (2 Kgs 23:30). Most historians hold that "Jehoahaz" is his coronation name, and that his popular election manifested the will of the followers of Josiah's reform, i.e., the anti-Egyptian party. The prophet transfers the mourning from the "dead" Josiah to Jehoahaz who is "going away." In fact, his reign lasted only three months for he was deposed by Neco (2 Kgs 23:31ff.). In the Babylonian Chronicles, we are told how the Egyptian king hurried in vain to the rescue of Ashur-uballit, king of Assyria, in Haran (Wiseman, *Chronicles*, 63). He then acted as if he were master of Syria-Palestine, establishing his headquarters at Riblah, the modern Rable, some 47 mi. S of Hama. He called Jehoahaz there to depose him and afterward sent him into Egypt in chains; thus, Neco declared his suzerainty over Judah (see Bright, *Hist.* 303; Noth, *Hist.* 279). **11–12.** The same oracle is now repeated in prose, probably from a parallel tradition. The prophetical word must be contemporaneous with the events in 609.

68 (iii) *Jehoiakim* (22:13–19). Jeremiah's philippic against Jehoiakim is one of his sternest oracles. Jehoiakim was a typical Oriental despot (Rudolph) who rejected his father's reform. Because he was chosen by Neco to succeed his brother (2 Kgs 23:34), he must have been a partisan of the Egyptian party. Jeremiah contrasts him with Josiah to show how far he is from fulfilling the idea of true kingship. **13–14.** The first attack is directed at the king's luxurious buildings, constructed at the expense of the people; in fact, since the king was obliged to pay regularly a heavy tribute to his Egyptian suzerain, his royal treasure usually must have been empty (2 Kgs 23:35). It has always been thought that this building activity took place in Jerusalem itself, but recent excavations at nearby Ramat Rachel have brought to light an imposing structure dating from about 600 (see Y. Aharoni, *BA* 24 [1961] 118; *BASOR* 170 [1963] 67; *RB* 70 [1963] 574). This new find would be an excellent illustration of the present oracle. The retention of salary was a direct offense against the Law (Lv 19:13; Dt 24:14–15); the king, by office, had to secure its observance, and he himself is found guilty of its violation. **15–16.** In full contrast to Jehoiakim, Josiah is given as the perfect model of the true covenantal king. The kingly justice already discussed (cf. comment on 21:12; 23:3) found its perfect realization in the pious king; such an eulogy of Josiah is an evident sign that Jeremiah could not have opposed his reform. **17.** Jehoiakim was attached to his "own gain" through his buildings; he favored idolatry by reactivating the sanctuary of Topheth (2 Kgs 24:3–4), and he committed "violence," as is illustrated later in his dealings with the true prophets (cf. 26:20ff.; 36). **18–19.** The divine judgment is pronounced over the impious king. In v. 18 we are given formulas of lamentation (cf. 1 Kgs 13:30; see M. J. Dahood, *CBQ* 23 [1961] 462–64, for a possible translation of the last formula, "Alas, Father! Alas, Mother!"—which would be in a better harmony with the preceding). The burial of an ass (v. 19; cf. 36:30) has always troubled scholars, for Jehoiakim seems to have had a normal burial (2 Kgs 24:6). According to the Babylonian Chronicles (Wiseman, *Chronicles*, 73), Nebuchadnezzar marched on Jerusalem in December, 598, at which time Jehoiakim was already dead (2 Kgs 24:10). The suggestion has been made that at the approach of Nebuchadnezzar's army, the king was assassinated in a palace revolt by partisans of the pro-Babylonian party (W. F. Albright, *BA* 4 [1942] 49; Bright, *Hist.* 306; J. P. Hyatt, *JBL* 75 [1956] 279). If this is correct, then the notice in Kgs would be nothing more than the stereotyped formula used at the end of reigns. The hypothesis is more plausible than the supposed profanation of Jehoiakim's tomb after the first capture of Jerusalem in 597.

69 (iv) *Jehoiachin* (22:20–30). Jehoiakim's 18-year-old son succeeded him on the throne for a short reign of three months (2 Kgs 24:6–8). He was exiled to Babylon, with the queen mother and the Judean noblemen, when Nebuchadnezzar first took Jerusalem in March, 597 (2 Kgs 24:10–16; Wiseman, *Chronicles*, 73). The oracle is a little complex and can be divided into three parts: 20–23; 24–27; 28–30.

20–23. Grammatically (verbs and suffixes are in the feminine) and ideologically, these verses refer to Jerusalem itself. If we remember that the siege and capture of the city covered Jehoiachin's entire reign, such an introduction has its place here. **20.** Jerusalem considers its ruin from all the surrounding heights: Lebanon, N; Bashan, NE of Transjordan; and on the wedge of N Moab overlooking the Jordan Valley, the mounts of Abarim, whose main peak is Mt. Nebo (Nm 27:12; Dt 32:49). *lovers:* The term usually designates the idols or the foreign nations; here, it refers to Judah's own leaders (cf. v. 22). **21.** The cause of the ruin is the people's refusal to obey ever since its origin (cf. 2:31; 3:24; 7:24ff.; 11:7ff.). **23.** Jerusalem is compared to a high cedar of Lebanon; Ezekiel applied the comparison to the whole Davidic dynasty (Ez 17). Jeremiah might also allude to the royal palace (cf. 21:13–14).

24–27. This first address to Jehoiachin, in prose, must have been uttered at the time of the events in 597, for what we read in Kgs is practically predicted in detail. **24.** *Coniah:* The abbreviated form of the king's name is attested only here and in 37:1. *signet ring:* Rings bearing seals of important men were cautiously kept, for they were used to stamp official documents (cf. Hag 2:24); thus, Yahweh abandons the king to his own fate. **26.** *mother:* See comment on 13:18. *there you shall die:* Although Jehoiachin was released under Evil-merodach (see Albright, *BA* 4, 49–55; A. Bea, *Bib* 23 [1942] 78–82), he had to stay in Babylon where he did die (2 Kgs 25:27–30 = Jer 52:31–34).

28–30. This second oracle addresses the king as though he were already in exile. **28.** *vessel despised:* The image recalls the story of the "broken flask" (cf. 19:1ff.); Jeremiah will apply it later to Moab (48:38), as Hosea applied it to Israel (Hos 8:8). **29.** *land:* It is solemnly called to attention, probably as a witness of the final judgment pronounced on Jehoiachin (see ch. 2, the "*rîb*" pattern). **30.** *childless:* Contradicted by 1 Chr 3:17–18. However, Jeremiah specifies the meaning he attached to the adjective: None of Jehoiachin's descendants will ascend the throne. Zerubbabel, his grandson (1 Chr 3:19), returned to Jerusalem after the Exile as high commissioner, not as king. Jeremiah knew well that the exiled king's history was over, not from speculations on political combinations but from insight into a different plan—i.e., Yahweh's plan (Rudolph). Undoubtedly, behind these words concerning Jehoiachin, there must be some kind of popular hope that he will restore the Davidic dynasty (at least, among those who stayed faithful to him and disregarded Zedekiah; see M. Noth, *RHPR* 33 [1953] 81–102; *GesSt* 346–71). Thus, Jeremiah would have cut short such a hope by an absolute rejection of both the king and his descendants.

70 (v) *The future king* (23:1–8). The oracles on the individual kings have followed a chronological order. Therefore, we would expect to read now an oracle on Zedekiah, but the Prophet changes the perspective; the last king of Judah provides only his own name, transformed (v. 6), in the proclamation of a new, Messianic era. The present state of this description of the future also results from the combination of various short oracles.

1–4. This first oracle, in prose, concerns both the "shepherds" and the "flock." **1–2.** The authenticity of these verses is sure; the bad shepherds—i.e., the kings—are still active; however, Yahweh is already at work to bring upon them his judgment. Indeed, all the last kings of Judah met tragic ends. **3–4.** Now Jeremiah turns to the people, in terms similar to the ones of another passage (cf. 3:14–18). Their perspective is that of the restoration of the people after the exile, with the full realization of the covenant's purposes.

5–6. The poetic oracle on the "Shoot of David" is certainly authentic; some have even thought that it is Jeremiah's sole utterance on a personal Messiah (see Skinner, *op. cit.*, 311ff.). **5.** *days are coming:* We should not stress too much the question of time behind this expression; it seems more likely to be simply a way of calling attention to a very solemn proclamation (cf. 7:32). *righteous shoot:* The word *ṣemaḥ*, along with a synonymous expression in Is 11:1, became a classic term for the Messiah (Zech 3:8; 6:12). **6.** Both Israel and Judah will share this messianic salvation; Jeremiah never forgot his own homeland (cf. chs. 30–31). *Lord our justice:* The future king's name is a word play on Zedekiah's own name; *Yhwh ṣidqēnû* (Yahweh is our justice), compared to *ṣidqî-yāhû* (my justice is Yahweh), presents only a change of the pronominal suffixes and of the position of Yahweh's name. The word "justice" here must be given its full meaning, which includes God's salvific presence and action; Isaiah had already given a similar name to this future king—i.e., *'immānû 'ēl*, "God is with us" (Is 7:14). The solemnity of the oracle certainly points to a new era. But just what is that era? The answer depends much on one's notion of messianism proper and of its relation to eschatology (→ Aspects OT Thought, 77:23–24). We believe that Jeremiah spoke of a royal messianism that is closely bound to history. The forthcoming bliss is not fixed at the end of time but at the end of a particular time that has turned bad. Moreover, the messianism here proposed is nothing more than the absolute fulfillment of sacred kingship as the means chosen by Yahweh to realize the blessings of the covenant—the peace and the justice of his people in the promised land. This ideal kingship has been defined in Nathan's prophecy (2 Sm 7) and repeated in the royal psalms (Pss 2, 45, 72, 89, 110). Prophets, in dark periods when the kings were unfaithful, recalled this very ideal and promised its realization in the future, using terms found in our present passage (see Is 9:5–6; 11:1–9; Mi 5:1–5; Am 9:11; Hos 3:5; etc.). Therefore, like his predecessors, Jeremiah predicts the restoration of David's dynasty, not so much on political grounds, but on the level of the religious and moral obligations of the covenant. Knowing the full course of history and being witnesses of the end of revelation, we now see that Jesus alone has accomplished this hope, and on a much higher level. (For further study, see Mowinckel, *He That Cometh*, 155–86; J. L. McKenzie, *CBQ* 19 [1957] 25–52; J. Bourke, *Scr* 11 [1959] 97–110).

7–8. These lines are also read in 16:14–15, where they are out of context. They predict a return from exile of northern Israel in terms of a new Exodus. We have no reason to suspect their authenticity, for Jeremiah had such a hope (cf. chs. 30–31, esp. 31:7–14). However, their connection with the preceding oracle is rather loose; the fact that the LXX located them after 23:40 is a sign of a fluctuation in the tradition.

71 (c) Booklet on the Prophets (23:9–40). A second collection of oracles is relative to a class of leaders in Israel, the prophets, who have also done wrong; Jeremiah never stopped denouncing them (2:8; 4:9;

5:31; 6:13–15; 14:13–16; etc.). **9–12.** These introductory verses do not address the false prophets directly; they are Jeremiah's complaint, recalling his early preaching, on the universal corruption of Judah (cf. 5:1ff.; 9:1ff.). At such a sight, Jeremiah is taken with pain; these accents were heard once before (4:19) and later influenced psalmists (Pss 6:3–4; 31:11; cf. Hab 3:16). The adulterous state of the land has been caused by both idolatry and moral deprivation (cf. 5:7–8); the priests and prophets also have a share in these evildoings. The punishment to come is symbolized by a walk through the night on a slippery road (see Is 18:21–23; Ps 35:6). **10bc.** This gloss is inspired by 4:28; 9:11; 12:4. **13–15.** The first characteristic of the false prophets is their moral conduct. Jeremiah establishes a comparison between those in Samaria and those in Jerusalem; both groups are found guilty. Ezekiel will also compare both cities to assimilate them, as here, to Sodom and Gomorrah (Ez 16). **16–22.** A second way to recognize false prophets is to look at the object of their message. They are but flatterers of the popular passions, always foretelling peace even if evil prevails; thus, they are liars, victims of their own imagination (cf. 6:14; 8:11; Mi 3:5). **18.** A gloss has been introduced to explain the scarcity of true prophets. **19–20.** The verses are also read in 30:23–24, and are out of context in both places. They are usually rejected as inauthentic for their strong apocalyptical trend. **21.** The verse is the logical sequence of v. 17. These prophets have not been sent; therefore, the divine mission is another sign of true prophecy (cf. 14:14; 27:15; 29:9). **22.** Another sign of true prophecy is sitting in Yahweh's council—i.e., in the assembly of angels (cf. 1 Kgs 22:19ff.; Jb 1:6; 2:1). However, Jeremiah does not insist on this new sign, but repeats that the moral and religious character of their words is decisive if one is to know that they are commissioned (see Dt 13:1–6). **23–32.** A final criterion is the form of communication: in itself, the dream has nothing in common with the Word of God. **23–24.** These obscure verses could be explained as Jeremiah's own view on these dreams. Their very nature supposes that God is so near that he can be reached as one desires. Therefore, it is an offense to God's transcendence. **25–32.** Dreams served in the ancient Near East to know the will of the gods, but they were not very frequent in Israel (Nm 12:6; 1 Sm 28:6; Jl 3:1; Jb 33:15–16). Because of the magical and imaginative character of their interpretation, they probably never had much weight, and they were formally rejected as means of revelation (27:9; Dt 13:1ff.; Zech 10:2; regarding this question, see I. Mendelsohn, *IDB* 1, 868–69; especially A. M. Esnoul (ed.), *Les songes et leur interprétation* [Paris, 1959]). **33–40.** The end of the booklet is a development on one word. **33.** A technical term for "oracle" is *maśśā'*, derived from the verb *nāśā'* "to lift up" (see P. A. H. de Boer, *OTS* 5 [1948] 197–214; G. Lambert, *NRT* 77 [1955] 963–69), but the same word also means "burden." The question was, *mâ-maśśā'* (what is the oracle); and, following P. Wernberg-Møller's emendations (*VT* 6 [1956] 315–16), the answer given is, *'attēmâ maśśā'* (you are the burden). **34–40.** A very complicated justification of the avoidance of the term *maśśā'*: Yahweh himself has forbidden its use, but we are not told why. Rudolph sees here a talmudic addition that really says nothing. It must be a very late addition indeed, for the word was still current in the post-exilic period (Zech 9:1; 12:1; Mal 1:1).

72 (d) The Two Baskets of Figs (24:1–10). The closing chapter of this section brings us back to the opening one (21:1–10), with the same condemnation of Zedekiah and of those who survived the siege of 597. Chapter 24 narrates a prophet's vision similar to those in 1:11ff., and especially to Amos' vision of the "basket of ripe fruit" (Am 8:1–3). In all these instances we meet with the same literary structure: the vision itself; a question from Yahweh; the prophetical meaning of the vision. We still hold here that we have to deal with the Prophet's concrete experience expressed in this literary form. **1.** *placed before the Temple:* These words suggest that the figs were first-fruit offerings (Dt 26:2–11); but how is it possible to offer bad ones? Penna's hypothesis that the Temple has a simple symbolic meaning is enlightening; because the Temple is not inviolable (cf. 7:1ff.), it is therefore certain that those who will survive the downfall of 597 will be definitively rejected. *this was after...:* This chronological datum is a short summary of 2 Kgs 24:14–16; the oracle occurred in 597, or soon after. **5–7.** The explanation of the vision begins. The good figs represent the exiles of 597. Surprisingly enough, they are now the choice portion of the people who will constitute the new Israel. **6.** *build...plant:* Jeremiah is now called to fulfill the second part of his mission (1:10). **7.** The new Israel will be faithful to the covenant because the Lord will change her heart. It is only when Israel will "know" Yahweh, or observe his Law wholeheartedly, that the covenant really will be concluded. This change of heart will be at the center of the new covenant (cf. 31:33). **8–10.** The bad figs are all those who stayed in Palestine after 597, including the king and the noblemen. They considered themselves to be the choice portion of Yahweh for they had escaped exile, whereas those who had been exiled were justly punished for their evil deeds. Jeremiah overturns such a belief, as Ezekiel does in a similar speech (Ez 11:14–21). **8.** *settled in the land of Egypt:* The colony might have originated in 609 when Jehoahaz had been taken there (2 Kgs 23:34); it is also possible that partisans of the pro-Egyptian party had fled at the arrival of Nebuchadnezzar's armies in 598. **9–10.** The sentence pronounced on the "bad figs" uses a host of Jeremian expressions for doom (15:4; 21:7; 29:18; 34:17; see also Dt 28:37; Ps 44:14–15).

73 **(E) A Foreword or Epilogue? (25:1–13b).** Commentators agree in taking the present pericope as a summary of Jeremiah's ministry until the year 605–604, for it is dated exactly in the 4th year of Jehoiakim (v. 1). Besides, a reference to a written book is given (v. 13), and we know that in the same year Jeremiah dictated all his oracles to Baruch (ch. 36). There must be a relation between this passage and that book; we are inclined to take it as either its superscription or its epilogue. The many differences between the MT and the LXX are a sign of editorial amplifications. In general, the critics agree to drop the following: all the references to Nebuchadnezzar and the Chaldeans, for in 605 the invader was still left in the shadow; the ending of vv. 3–4, a gloss taken from 7:25–26; v. 6, which interrupts the sequence of vv. 5 and 7a; 7b, which is lacking in the LXX; "and against all these neighboring nations" in v. 9, because the scroll contained only the oracles against Judah (cf. v. 1); v. 12, because the oracle against Babylon was also excluded. The text thus relieved of these glosses gives a logical and clear summary of Jeremiah's preaching. **5.** Jeremiah sums up his message in the necessity of conversion, for it is the basic condition for the fulfillment of the promises of the covenant (cf. 3:1–4:4). If it is not realized, punishment will follow (still expressed in the general terms of an invasion from the north; cf. v. 8; 1:15; 4:6; 6:1ff.; etc.). **10.** There will be no more joy (7:34; 16:9). The halting of the millstone and the blowing out of the lamp are signs of the cessation of life (cf. Eccl 12:3–6, for similar examples as symbols of approaching death). **11.** *seventy years:* This prediction (cf. 29:10), which is certainly at the origin of 2 Chr 36:21 and Dn 9:2, has been the subject of ample and frequent discussions. Today, a few still take this number strictly (Penna, *op. cit.;* C. F. Whitley, *VT* 4 [1954] 60–72; *VT* 7 [1957] 416–18; A. Orr, *VT* 6 [1956] 304–306). But if we remember that 70 is often a symbol of "many" (cf. Jgs 1:7; 8:14; 1 Sm 6:19; 2 Sm 24:15; Ps 90:10; etc.), then we would think that Jeremiah only intended a long period without any specification of time. The hypothesis has an extrabiblical confirmation, for an Assyrian text uses the same number to indicate simply an indefinite period (see E. Vogt, *Bib* 38 [1957] 236; O. Plöger, *Fest. F. Baumgärtel* [Erlangen, 1959] 124–30).

74 **(F) Judgment on the Nations (25:13c–38).** In this new section, Jeremiah acts as "a prophet to the nations" (1:5). The LXX presents these prophecies immediately (25:14–31:44), and sets the opening oracle at their end (32:13–38). On the contrary, the MT reads all these oracles at the end of the book and keeps here only the opening one. We shall discuss this problem later (→ 109 below).

Whatever be the original position of the oracles now placed in chs. 46–51, the present discourse served as either a prologue or an epilogue to the whole collection. Considering its position in the LXX and the parallel problem of 25:1–13b in its relation to the first part of the book, we take it to be a closing summary of the Prophet's new activity. **15–17, 27–29.** The symbol of a cup of judgment has its probable origin in the ordeal procedures (cf. Nm 5:11–31). Besides, drunkenness is also a symbol for a sinful state calling for punishment (13:12–14; 51:17; Is 19:14; 28:7–13). Even more often, the cup of wine symbolizes simply the avenging wrath of the Lord (49:12; Hab 2:15–16; Ez 23:32–34; Is 51:17–23; Lam 4:21; Pss 60:5; 75:9). **18–26.** The list of nations breaks the logical sequence of the preceding passage; it was added once the oracles were put at the end of the book. The following four geographical names are missing in the LXX: Uz, a territory to be looked for probably in the Syrian desert; Zimri, unknown, unless it should be read "Zimki," which would give an *atbash* writing (substitution of Hebr letters in inverse order) for Elam; Sheshach, another *atbash* writing for Babel; and Arabia. These cryptograms are sure signs of late additions (as for the identification of the other names, → 111–17 below). The listing of Jerusalem, Judah, and their people is out of place here and must be crossed out (v. 18). **30–38.** This poem on the universal judgment of Yahweh, presented again as a lawsuit (*rîb*, v. 31), is a kind of second summary of the oracles against the nations. **30.** *the Lord roars:* The anthropomorphism is inspired by the old theophanies is the midst of thunder (Ex 19:16). The present theophany also takes place in a storm (v. 32; cf. 23:19; Am 1:2; Jl 4:16), unless it is the roaring of a lion, to which Yahweh is also compared (Am 3:8; Hos 10:11). **33.** The verse interrupts the development of the poem; it is a gloss inspired by 16:4. **38.** *lion:* Some commentators would reject the entire verse because this lion could only be Nebuchadnezzar (cf. 4:7). This identification cannot be proved; the lion symbolizes also Yahweh, and so the sword, his wrath (Ez 22:1–22). The entire pericope shows well enough that Yahweh's action is not restricted only to Israel, but extends to all known nations.

75 **(III) The Restoration of Israel (26:1–35:19).** As in the other prophetical books, a section on the restoration of Israel (chs. 30–33) follows the "oracles against the nations" (→ 74 above; 80 below). A small collection of narratives concerning Jeremiah and the false prophets has been added (chs. 27–29), for these prophets were also promising such a restoration, but on false grounds. Finally, Jeremiah's open fight with the leaders of the people prefaces the whole section (ch. 26).

(A) Jeremiah Persecuted (26:1–24). The common opinion is that this chapter is Baruch's narrative on the circumstances and results of Jeremiah's Temple discourse (7:1–15). This lively story offers no difficulty and requires an eyewitness. **1.** *in the beginning of the reign:* If this chronological data (*bᵉrēʾšît mamlᵉkût*) corresponds to the similar Akkadian expression (*rēš šarrūtim*), the incident occurred in 609, before the first regnal year in 608. **2–6.** The verses are a résumé of the Temple discourse: Yahweh will suspend his judgment if the people repent and observe the Law. However, a new thought has been added: Yahweh reveals himself only through the ministry of the true prophets (cf. 7:25; 25:4)—a sort of introduction to the following chapters. The Prophet's words provoked a general scandal and brought a charge against him (vv. 7–9). **10–19.** The lawsuit is now described and should be compared to the parallel NT examples (Mk 14:55ff. and par.; Acts 6:11–14; 21:27–31). **10.** *princes of Judah:* Although the word *śārîm* could mean "princes," it often also refers to the high officials, closely associated to the "elders" (*zᵉqēnîm*, v. 17), who were the influential element of the people (see De Vaux, *AI* 69, 138). *New Gate:* It will be mentioned again in 36:10; Vincent identifies it with the "upper gate of the house of the Lord," built by Jotham (cf. comment on 20:2). Court sessions were customarily held at the gates (cf. Gn 23:10–20; Ru 4:1; Prv 31:23; etc.). **11.** *deserves death:* Jeremiah's sermon was interpreted as blasphemous, thus requiring a death penalty (Lv 24:10–16; 1 Kgs 21:13). **12–15.** Jeremiah presents his own defense: the words are not his but Yahweh's for he has been "sent"; this is a sign of true prophecy (cf. 23:21). **16–19.** The civil leaders, struck by the defense, stand against the religious authorities. They argue from a parallel case of a century before (Mi 3:12), thus proving that the oracles of the prophets were preserved and well known. The reaction to Micah's word was altogether different from the present case. Hezekiah did lead a religious reform (2 Kgs 18:4) and the evil avoided, alluded to here, might be Sennacherib's withdrawal in 701 (2 Kgs 19:35–36). **20–23.** Baruch now tells the story of the murder of a prophet, Uriah, who had preached in similar terms, but we do not know when it happened. The biographer's purpose is certainly to show the danger from which Jeremiah escaped. Kiriath-jearim is usually situated at Abu Ghosh, about 8 mi. NW of Jerusalem. Elnathan will be present again in the scroll incident in 605–604 (36:12); he might be Jehoiakim's father-in-law (2 Kgs 24:8). The extradition of political refugees is a frequent clause of the treaties of the 2nd millennium BC (see *ANET* 200–201, 203). We remember that Jehoiakim was set on the throne by Neco in 609 and was obliged to pay him a heavy tribute (2 Kgs 23:34–35); since he was thus a vassal of Egypt, the conjecture that an extradition clause existed in the vassal treaty has solid foundation. It is also possible that extradition had simply entered in the international law. **24.** The verse would be better situated after v. 19. *Ahikam son of Shaphan:* This Shaphan is the royal scribe who participated in the Josian reform (2 Kgs 22:3ff.). If his son, Ahikam, protects the Prophet, Jeremiah must have had good relations with this family. Such is confirmed by the fact that another son of Shaphan, Gemariah (36:10), will sympathize with him (36:25), and Ahikam's son, Gedaliah, will be greatly devoted to him (39:14; 40:5ff.). Such friendly relations between Jeremiah and this influential family in the reform are a clear sign of the positive attitude he must have had for Josiah's policy.

76 **(B) Jeremiah's Controversy with the False Prophets (27:1–29:32).** The following three chapters once formed a separate collection, as proved by both their style and subject. Here the Babylonian king's name is written "Nebuchadnezzar" instead of "Nebuchadrezzar" as elsewhere, and Jeremiah's name is *Yirmᵉyāh* instead of *Yirmᵉyāhû*. We are told of Jeremiah's attempt, during the first years of Zedekiah, to bring the Judeans, both in Palestine and in exile, to complete submission under Nebuchadnezzar, instead of revolting against him as the false prophets urged. The MT is much longer than the LXX; the latter most likely presents the primitive text.

(a) A COALITION OF THE WEST (27:1–22). The date given for the event is the beginning of Jehoiakim's reign; however, in the whole story, there is question of Zedekiah only. According to 28:1, the date is his fourth year (594–593). In fact, this first verse, lacking in the LXX, is but a repetition of 26:1; thus we should also read here "Zedekiah," already attested in the Pesh. This chapter is the only source we have on the coalition of the small western states (v. 3), but its historical context is somewhat illuminated by the Babylonian Chronicles published by Wiseman. In 596–595, Nebuchadnezzar was attacked at home by an unknown enemy (Elam?), and the following year (595–594), he had to muster a revolt within his own frontiers. In 594–593, he led a military campaign into Syria; the Chronicles stop there, leaving a gap from 594–593 to 557 (Wiseman, *Chronicles*, 73–75). The Babylonian king being thus so busy in the east, these small states tried to join forces and overthrow his yoke, but in vain. According to Jer 51:59, Zedekiah sent a delegation to Babylon that same year; historians think its purpose was precisely to justify the king's conduct.

2. The message is first delivered in a prophetical action (cf. 13:1–11). **3–11.** The Prophet first addresses the ambassadors from the Transjordan states and the two city-states of Phoenicia. No doubt their intention was to win Zedekiah to their cause. Yahweh is the Lord not only of creation but also of history; he commissioned Nebuchadnezzar, his servant (v. 6; Ez 30:25), to bring the people under his submission, symbolized by Jeremiah's yoke. Therefore, it is foolhardy to believe in the liberation predicted by their own prophets and diviners. Again, Jeremiah does not judge the situation politically, but according to his faith in Yahweh's direction of world affairs. To resist Nebuchadnezzar is to resist Yahweh, which can only result in one's own destruction (see Welch, *op. cit.*, 195–212). **7.** This verse is missing in the LXX, and is an evident exilic gloss on the downfall of the Neo-Babylonian Empire.

12–15. The same message is now delivered to Zedekiah. **13.** The verse, lacking in the LXX, is a repetition of v. 12, in a different form. **16–22.** Finally, Jeremiah warns the priests and the people of the same false hope of these prophets. Their preaching is a provocation to rebellion, for they are confident that the end of the Exile is near. But this rebellion is against Yahweh, and therefore cannot be of his own inspiration. The text of this last section has undergone several amplifications, as the LXX shows: v. 17 is completely lacking and breaks the logical sequence of vv. 16 and 18; the enumeration of the Temple accessories is also missing in v. 19, and we can hardly see how they could have been brought to Babylon. **21–22.** The LXX has, merely, "To Babylon they shall be brought"—a perfect conclusion for vv. 19–20. The prediction of their return is out of place in this oracle of doom.

77 (b) PROPHECY AGAINST PROPHECY (28:1–17). The narrative is biographical and must go back to Baruch; the pers. pronoun "me" (v. 1) is usually corrected to "Jeremiah." The date of the event is given in a complicated text (v. 1): if, with the LXX, we simply erase "in the beginning" (a probable harmonization with 27:1), then the incident happened in 594–593, about the time that Jeremiah delivered his message to the ambassadors, for he still performs the symbolic action of the yoke.

1. *fifth month:* The precision is important (see v. 17). Gibeon is a town of Benjamin, identified with modern el-Jib, a few miles NW of Jerusalem. **2–4.** Hananiah proclaims his oracle in the style of the true prophets. The core of his message is absolutely contrary to that of Jeremiah (ch. 27): Babylon's yoke will soon be broken and Jehoiachin will return to Jerusalem. This last affirmation inclines historians to think that a part of the population regarded the young king as the only legitimate monarch, and refused to accept Zedekiah. The hypothesis is supported by the discovery of stamps bearing the inscription, "to Eliakim, steward of Yaukin"; these stamps, found at Beth-shemesh, Beit Mirsim, and recently at Ramat Rachel (Aharoni, *BASOR* 170, 67), are dated after the king's exile in 597. **5–9.** Jeremiah's answer is another attempt at establishing a clear distinction between the true and the false prophets. The constant message of the latter is one of peace (cf. 6:14; 23:17); thus, they are opposed to the true prophets who so often proclaimed oracles of doom. Jeremiah sets up another condition for authenticity: A prophecy has to be fulfilled (cf. Dt 18:21–22). **10–11.** Hananiah, with great confidence, performs his own prophetical action to bring about salvation. We need not question the sincerity of such a man; however, his faith depended mainly on political situations; the coalition in its process of formation gave him his great assurance. Such a sudden reaction left Jeremiah completely dumbfounded and without an answer. **12–17.** It is only after a certain length of time that the answer came; the true prophets were not dreamers or victims of autosuggestion, but depended entirely on Yahweh's inspiration. **13.** We prefer the LXX: "You broke wooden yokes, now I will replace them with iron ones." Hananiah was calling for a revolt that would eventually lead to complete subjection to Nebuchadnezzar. **15–16.** Hananiah now gets his own sentence, formulated in a play on the word *šālaḥ*, "to send." He was not "sent" by Yahweh to be a prophet, but he will be "dispatched." He deserves death, for he spoke without mandate (Dt 18:20). The final remark, "Because you have preached..." is not in the LXX and may be a gloss taken from Dt 13:6. **17.** Two months later (cf. v. 1), Hananiah died. This fulfillment of Jeremiah's prediction is seen as an authentication of his mission (cf. vv. 5–9).

78 (c) THE LETTER TO THE EXILES (29:1–32). The imminent and happy end of the Babylonian domination was announced not only in Palestine (ch. 28), but also in Babylon by the same type of prophets. The text, from Baruch's memoirs, has undergone some changes: A number of scholars read vv. 8–9 after v. 15 because they break the sequence of vv. 7 and 10; again, vv. 16–20 (lacking in the LXX) are a severe attack on Zedekiah, which is strange in a letter to the exiles in Babylon—they appear to be inspired by 24:8–10.

(i) *The letter* (29:1–23). **2–3.** This letter is dated after the first captivity in 597, and it was sent through Zedekiah's delegation to Babylon. Even though some scholars think that its purpose was to pay the annual tribute, we hold that it was rather to justify Zedekiah (cf. comment on 51:59) after his attempt to join the coalition of the western states (ch. 27) in the year 594–593. *Elasah:* Son of Shaphan and most probably Ahikam's brother (cf. 26:24). *Gemariah:* Son of Hilkiah and must be also from the priestly family that played an important role in the Josian reform. The two men must have agreed with Jeremiah's "pacifism"; they were an excellent choice to restore Zedekiah's relations with the Babylonian court. **4–7.** The exiles have to settle in this foreign land and to collaborate for its welfare. This last recommendation might permit the hypothesis that the exiles, misled by the prophets, had already caused troubles in Babylon; have they not participated in the revolt of 595–594 (see comment on 27:1–22)? **10–15.** Jeremiah gives the reason for settling down in Babylon: The Exile is going to last for an indefinite period (cf. 25:11; 28:3) and they must promote their new land's welfare (v. 7). No doubt the recommendation was shocking. Yahweh could be worshiped in Babylon, for he protects his people even outside Palestine; Yahwism has finally burst through the enclosure of the holy land (cf. Ez 10:18–22; 11:22–25). **14.** *and I will change your lot...:* The remaining part of the verse is not in the LXX and must be an exilic addition. **21–23.** The letter closes with the severe condemnation of two of these false prophets. They are to be turned over to Nebuchadnezzar to be burnt. This punishment, which is to become a common curse among the exiles, is well known in Babylonia (cf. Code of Hammurabi, 25. 110, 157; Dn 3:6).

79 (ii) *An exile's reaction* (29:24–32). The letter caused great anger in Babylonia and one of the prophets sent a letter to Jerusalem to have Jeremiah arrested. **24.** *Nehelamite:* A locality called "Nahlam" is unknown, unless this adjective derives from the verb *ḥālam* and means simply "the dreamer" (see L. Yaure, *JBL* 79 [1960] 307–309). **25.** *Zephaniah:* He consulted Jeremiah twice in Zedekiah's name (21:1; 37:3); he is now at the head of the Temple police (cf. 20:1). **26.** *stocks:* Again we prefer to translate the Hebr word *mahpeket* by "prison" (cf. 20:2). *or the pillory:* The MT reads, "and into the pillory"; the conjunction is correct if the first word is "prison." **31–32.** Jeremiah's answer to Shemaiah is similar to the one he gave to Hananiah (28:15ff.)—he has no mandate from Yahweh and deserves punishment; he will die in Babylon.

80 **(C) The Restoration of Israel (30:1–31:40).** All agree that this passage is the climax of Jeremiah's message, and some would even say the apogee of all prophecy (31:31–34). The work, even though it existed in a separate form before its incorporation into the entire book, is not one solid composition but a collection of poems on one theme. The question of the date and the addressee of these poems has not yet been satisfactorily answered. For a better understanding of the problem, we separate immediately two main blocks: 30:1–31:22 and 31:23–40.

Many critics believe that the first group of poems was written at Mizpah, after the destruction of Jerusalem in 587, for the consolation of southern Israel—i.e., Judah (Skinner, Penna, Nötscher, Steinmann, etc.). However, there are good reasons to hold that it must date from Jeremiah's early ministry, and concerns northern Israel. In fact, "Judah" (30:3–4) and "Zion" (30:17) appear to be later additions. The accumulation of geographical and personal names such as Samaria, Jacob, Ephraim, Ramah, etc., are better understood if Jeremiah had in mind the northern kingdom (see A. Gelin, *Fest. J. Chaine* [Lyon, 1950] 161–68). Besides, both the expressions and the themes figuring in the present section are very similar to those of the early poem on conversion (3:1–4:4): The "lovers" who prevent Israel from "turning" to her God; the laments on heights; the healing of wounds; the perversity since youth; etc. Moreover, the strong Hosean influence in that poem is also felt here. Thus, the present oracles must date from an early period of the Prophet's life and must be intended for the consolation of northern Israel, suffering exile since 721 (Eissfeldt, Rudolph, Weiser, Gelin). We know that Josiah, once freed from the Assyrian yoke, had instituted a thorough reform in Judah that he extended even to the northern country (2 Kgs 23:15–20). Then Jeremiah thought that her purification was complete and that she would soon return to her homeland, but history has its mysteries. The return could not take place, and a new, overwhelming power dominated Palestine—Babylonia. However, the Prophet's hope did not vanish; he went so far as to extend this hope to Judah as well (31:23–40), and it may very well be that he added the name "Judah" to his first oracles.

81 (a) NORTHERN ISRAEL WILL BE RESTORED (30:1–31:22). The following divisions are an attempt to separate the different poems of this first collection.

(i) *Introduction* (30:1–4). These verses serve as a title to the whole collection, written under Yahweh's command (cf. 36:1–2). The leading message is stated clearly: Yahweh will bring back Israel to her land.

(ii) *Jacob's distress at an end* (30:5–11). The prophet describes in vivid colors the sufferings of over 100 years of exile (vv. 5–7). The pains of childbirth symbolize great distress (4:31; 6:24; 22:23); now men are experiencing them (cf. 50:43). The lament closes on the simple announcement of salvation (v. 7). **8–9.** These prose lines are an addition, although they may be authentic. They deal with the whole people in the messianic times. Before, the new ideal king was said to be a descendant of David (23:5); here he is called simply David, as in Hos 3:5 (exilic) and Ez 34:23–24; 37:24–25. A suitable date for the oracle would be after the destruction of Judah and her monarchy. **10–11.** The passage, not in the LXX, is reproduced almost literally in 46:27–28; in both instances, it is out of context. For the first time, Jacob is called the "Servant of the Lord" and the whole passage is similar to certain parts of Dt-Is, where the same title is used with the exclamation "Fear not" (Is 41:8–10; 43:1–6; 44:2–5; etc.). Hence, these verses have the appearance of an exilic addition, overflowing with confidence in Yahweh's realization of the return of Jacob, i.e., the whole people. However, it might well be that Dt-Is has been inspired by Jeremiah, for such similarities are frequent in the following oracles of undisputed authenticity.

(iii) *Healing of Israel's wounds* (30:12–17). This new poem is similar to the preceding one; Israel's miseries (wounds) are described and her restoration promised (17a is to be read after 17b [Rudolph]). The imagery of wounds and healing has been used more than once by Jeremiah (8:22; 10:19; 14:17), probably under Hosea's influence (cf. Hos 5:13; 6:1; 7:1; 11:7). Here, the "lovers" are no longer the idols, as before, but the foreign nations who have chastised them, to be themselves chastised in return. **17.** *the outcast:* This name of Israel brings to mind the poem on conversion (3:1ff.) and the names given to Israel also by Hosea (chs. 1–3). *with no avenger:* This translation is an attempt to restore a difficult text. The MT reads, "Zion, that nobody takes care of," but in the LXX we find, "Our spoil that nobody takes care of." Thus, we should put *ṣêdēnû* in place of *ṣiyyôn*; because the two words are so close graphically, the change is understandable.

82 (iv) *The restoration* (30:18–24). The restoration just announced (vv. 7 and 17), is now fully described. The material civilization will be recovered; the political community (*'ēdâ*; cf. 1 Kgs 12:20) will be reinstated with a king of its own (v. 21). This new ruler will be the perfect intermediary between Yahweh and his people. Does Jeremiah here think in terms of the divided monarchy? The vagueness of the text does not allow a clear answer. It is true that later he did not hesitate to affirm that the entire people would be united under one Davidic king (see vv. 8–9; 3:14–18; 23:1–6), but at this earlier date he might have held a different view. However, he now considers Jerusalem as the real center of worship for the northern kingdom; the Davidic king then would be also another bond of unity (Rudolph). In other words, Jeremiah seems to expect the return of the glorious era of David with its free and joyous life in the promised land. The spread of Josiah's reform into ancient Israel certainly encouraged Jeremiah to have such a hope and to believe in its near realization. **22.** This covenantal formula is omitted in the LXX and is out of place here (cf. 31:33). **23–24.** This apocalyptical passage is read word for word in 23:19–20, and is also omitted in the LXX. In both places, it is out of context and is to be rejected as unauthentic.

83 (v) *Good news of return* (31:1–6). The following four poems have as their central theme the exuberant joy of the return. They are introduced by a new title (v. 1, absent in the LXX) in which "Israel" refers to the entire people; it must have been added at a later date. Throughout this section, we meet with parallel utterances of Dt-Is, which we can explain by the similarity of subject—the return from exile seen as a new exodus. However, Jeremiah might have influenced this anonymous prophet (cf. comment on 30:5–11). **2.** *favor in the desert:* Jer and Dt-Is (Is 41:17–20; 43:16–21; 48:20–22; etc.) described the return as a new exodus, but in a much more glorious form: they are related as type and antitype (see J. Harvey, *ScEccl* 15 [1963] 383–405). **3.** The covenantal love is said to be "age-old" or "eternal," for it originates from the desert period and it will never cease (cf. Dt 7:8; 10:15; Hos 2:21; 11:1–4; Is 43:4; 54:8; etc.; see W. F. Lofthouse, *ZAW* 51 [1933] 29–35; Eichrodt, *Theology* 232–39). A better translation of the last stichos of the verse would be, "This is why I have drawn you with mercy" (see A. Feuillet, *VT* 12 [1962] 122–24).

84 (vi) *The new exodus* (31:7–14). The triumphal march through the desert is the cause of great joy to both the repatriates and the foreign nations. **7.** The hymn opens with a solemn call to joy, for Yahweh has bestowed salvation on his people (see Is 12:6; 40:9–10; 44:23; 55:11; Pss 47:2,9–10; 68:33–36; 95–99). These people are called the "remnant," i.e., the small number of those who have escaped the calamity of 721, and who have been purified through the exile to constitute the new Israel, faithful to her God (see R. de Vaux, *RB* 42 [1933] 526–39). **8.** *ends of the world:* This expression is synonymous with the "north"—i.e., Assyria, where they have been kept captive; again, Dt-Is speaks in similar terms (Is 43:5–6). The caravan is one composed of weak people, a sign of the miraculous nature of the event (see also Is 35:5ff.; 42:16). **9.** *departed in tears...:* The same opposition between sorrow and joy is the central theme of another hymn on the return from exile (Ps 126). *brooks of water:* We see here an allusion to the "rock" incidents of the first Exodus (Ex 17:1–7; Nm 20:1–13); now it is not an occasional spring but constantly flowing brooks. *level road:* Jeremiah again wants to accentuate the facility of the march, quite different from the one of the first Exodus (cf. Is 40:4). *father to Israel:* The fatherhood of Yahweh toward Israel, his first-born, is sporadic in the OT. The notion first served to define their covenantal relationship (Ex 4:22; Dt 32:6), and Hosea used fatherly love as a symbol of Yahweh's favors for Israel during the exodic period (Hos 11:1–6). Jeremiah's word must be explained in this context: Israel is the first-born not because she is superior to Judah, but because Yahweh will renew this same fatherly love for her. **10.** Nations and distant islands are invited to be witnesses of the marvelous event, as in Dt-Is (Is 42:10; 49:1; see Jer 2:10ff.). The symbolism of the shepherd and his flock for Yahweh's salvific action is also a Jeremian theme (23:1ff.), at the origin of later developments (Ez 34; Jn 10:1ff.). **11.** It is through Yahweh's help that Israel overcomes stronger enemies, as in the first Exodus (Ex 15; Is 49:24–25). **14.** *choice portions:* The Hebr word *dešen* means "fat." Jeremiah does not promise the priests an abundance of sacrificial portions, for the fat was reserved for the divinity. "Fat" is also the symbol of life and prosperity (Pss 36:9; 63:6; Is 55:2; etc.); thus, the priests will share the same prosperity as the rest of the people, which is described in the enumeration of the Palestinian goods (v. 12).

85 (vii) *End of Rachel's mourning* (31:15–20). The Prophet now breaks into a profound lyricism on the afflictions of the northern kingdom, personified by Rachel, mother of Joseph (Manasseh and Ephraim) and Benjamin (Gn 30:24; 35:16ff.). **15.** Ramah, in Benjamin (Jos 18:25; Jgs 4:5), is located at er-Ram, about 5 mi. N of Jerusalem. The oldest tradition placed Rachel's tomb in the vicinity of Benjamin's territory, before a later one brought it close to Bethlehem (Gn 35:19; 48:7; 1 Sm 10:2–3; this was followed by Mt 2:18). **18.** *untamed calf:* The image, is most likely another Hosean influence (Hos 4:16; 10:11). *if you allow me:* The MT reads, "Bring on my return, and I will return." The verb *šûb* has two main meanings: "to return from exile" and "to convert oneself" (see 3:1ff.). In the context (v. 16), the return from exile is fundamental, but the Prophet certainly superimposed the idea of conversion as well (v. 19). **19.** *breast:* *Yārēk* means "thigh"! To strike one's thigh is a gesture of pain and lament (Ez 21:17), attested to also in Mesopotamia (see "Descent of Ishtar" in *ANET* 108) and in Greece (*Iliad* 15.397–98; 16.125; *Odyssey* 13.198–99). *disgrace of my youth:* The sin of the chosen people stems from its very origins; the prophets often recalled this early ingratitude toward Yahweh's faithful love (see 3:25; 22:21; 32:30; Ez 16; 23; Is 48:8; 54:4; etc.).

86 (viii) *En route* (31:21–22). The collection of poems closes on a solemn command to start home. The only difficulty in the passage lies in the last sentence of v. 22: "the woman must encompass the man with devotion." The MT reads *n*ᵉ*qēbâ t*ᵉ*sôbēb gāber*, "woman will surround man"; the LXX has an entirely different text, i.e., "men will walk in salvation." A host of explanations have been proposed, ranging from Jerome's theory of a pure mariological and christological prophecy (PL 28.255; 24.880–81) to Paterson's hypothesis of a simple grammatical annotation, "the feminine replaces the masculine" (*op. cit.*, 556). We shall indicate only three explanations. The verb *sābab* would mean "to protect," as in Dt 32:10 and Ps 32:7,10; thus, woman protecting man is a sign of the great security to be experienced during the return and the new settlement in Palestine (Penna, Rudolph). But this seems to be foreign to the immediate context. C. Schedl would vocalize the first word *niqbâ*, with the meaning it has in the Siloam inscription, "a passage," "a path." Once this meaning has been forgotten, the word "man" was added. Therefore, the original text was "a path is achieved"; this emendation is supported by a similar text in Is 43:19 (C. Schedl, *ZKT* 83 [1961] 431–42). We still believe that this explanation is out of context; hence, we prefer the following one: we deal here with a symbolic language, where "woman" personifies Israel and "man" personifies Yahweh (Gelin; *BPl* 1). Indeed, Jeremiah still talks of Israel as an adulterous wife (Hos 1–3; Jer 2:20ff.) who had to be divorced by Yahweh, her husband (3:1). If she now adheres to her husband, certainly this is something new—something unheard of in her entire history (cf. v. 19).

87 (b) ADDITIONAL FRAGMENTS (31:23–40). To this book of the consolation of Israel, a number of disconnected oracles on a similar subject, in which Judah is included, have been added.

(i) *The restoration of Judah* (31:23–26). This oracle and the one following are often denied to be Jeremian because they suppose the historical context of the Exile. On the literary level, such a rejection is unfounded; we believe that Jeremiah extended to Judah, at her downfall in 587, the hope he had for Israel. **23.** *may the Lord bless you...abode of justice:* This liturgical blessing is on the assembly (cf. Nm 6:24–26; Pss 128; 134:3). *holy mountain:* As in Is (11:9), the whole of Judah is thus designated. **26.** The enigmatic saying seems to be a gloss by someone reflecting on the prophecy.

(ii) *Israel and Judah* (31:27–28). **28.** *watched:* The whole verse is a clear reference to 1:10–11. Yahweh's watchful (*šāqad*) eye was upon the Prophet's first mission; now the time has come for the second one—the creation of a new people.

88 (iii) *Personal responsibility* (31:29–30). In Israel, as in the ancient Near East and many primitive cultures, collective responsibility largely prevailed in the realm of morals and justice (Ex 20:5 = Dt 5:9; Nm 14:18). Both Jeremiah and Ezekiel (Ez 18), who probably depends on Jeremiah, quote the proverb (31:29) of the sons' miseries caused by the fathers' sins. They take the occasion of its rejection to propose a new truth, i.e., personal responsibility. In an excellent study, Harvey has shown how this new truth came to light without overshadowing completely the old belief that remained alive up to the NT times (Jn 9:2; J. Harvey, *ScEccl* 10 [1958] 167–202). Originally, the covenant was concluded with the whole people, for the individuals—Abraham, Moses, the kings—were only its representatives. Through the prophetic influence, religion (and thus the covenant) penetrated the heart of man (31:31–34). Hence, the relations between Yahweh and men became more personal, and, concomitantly, the problem of responsibility and retribution reached the same personal level (see also Dt 7:9–11; 24:16). However, the old and new beliefs needed more time to be synthesized.

89 (iv) *The new covenant* (31:31–34). The short oracle can be justly called Jeremiah's "spiritual testament"; his entire message has been condensed in these few words on the new covenant. **31.** The only time "new covenant" is used in the OT. It is now attested to at Qumran, but it designates nothing more than the Mosaic covenant, with strong legalistic tendencies. We have to wait for the NT—meaning precisely new covenant—to see how these Jeremian words are to be understood and fulfilled (Lk 22:20; 1 Cor 11:25; esp. Heb 8:8–12, the longest OT quotation in the NT; see J. van der Ploeg, *RB* 54 [1947] 217–20). The nature and form of the covenant have been recently the focus of scriptural studies that have proved this religious institution to be as old as Yahwism itself (for a summary article on this, see D. J. McCarthy, *CBQ* 27 [1965] 217–40). *house of Judah:* This later addition, if we compare it with v. 33, makes clear that the new covenant extends to the entire people. Rudolph would link the present pericope to the whole section 30:1–31:22; thus in Jeremiah's mind, Israel originally referred only to the northern kingdom. But, as we have seen, the end of ch. 31 (vv. 23–40) is a cluster of disconnected oracles to be considered separately; also, this new covenant is explicitly compared to the old one, in which all the tribes have been bound. Hence, in the present passage, Israel always referred to the whole people. **33.** *after those days:* Rudolph (*op. cit.*) and J. Coppens (*CBQ* 25 [1963] 15) take the "days" here to be different from those in v. 31; therefore, there exists the idea of an intermediate period—i.e., the Exile or the time between the proclamation of the new covenant and its accomplishment. It is unnecessary; the expression is frequently used by Jeremiah (7:32; 9:24; 16:14; etc.) with an eschatological tone, for it indicates a kind of rupture in the course of Israel's history through a wonderful intervention of Yahweh. *write it upon their hearts:* The old covenant was written on stone tablets (Ex 31:18; 34:28ff.; Dt 4:13; 5:22) or in a book (Ex 24:7). The heart as writing material is a Jeremian creation (cf. 17:1), even though it has a close parallel in Dt (6:6; 11:18; 30:14). *I will be their God...:* This covenantal clause is widespread in Jer and later writings (7:23; 11:4; 24:7; 30:22; 31:1; 32:38; Ez 11:20; 36:28; etc.; Zech 8:8; Lv 26:12; etc.). **34.** *teach:* In this new era, intermediaries such as Moses, priests, and prophets will be useless, for Yahweh will intervene directly (cf. Is 54:13). *to know:* Such a knowledge is the practical recognition of God in every action and situation, a life attitude. *least to greatest:* Men of all ages will enter this new covenant (cf. 5:4).

What is the exact nature of this covenant and what relations does it have with the former one? Although some scholars would see a complete rupture between the two, they are fundamentally the same: Yahweh concluded both on his own initiative; both are God-centered; the people are the same and in both instances; the response is manifested in the same obedience to the Law, which did not change. There is no question of the promulgation of a new Law. Therefore, this newness is not found in the essentials of the covenant, but in the realm of its realization and of its means. It will not be broken, as the old one was repeatedly (v. 33), for everyone will be faithful (v. 34). The reason for such a drastic change is that the covenant has now entered the heart of every member of the community. Thus, the real newness announced here is the new means used to assure faithfulness to it—the thorough "interiorization" of the commitment. Jeremiah could attain this insight through a profound understanding of his message and his personal religious experience. For him, God is one who knows the interior of man, a "searcher of mind and heart" (11:20; 12:3; 17:10; 20:12), and asks for its purification; the heart must be circumcised (4:4; 9:25). In a word, the primacy of interior values, such as obedience, love, knowledge of God, is the condition required for a true practice of religion (cf. ch. 7). We also remember that Jeremiah, like Hosea, conceived the covenant as being basically a reality of love and mercy, symbolized by marriage, which asks for such an interior and sincere relationship. The events through which Jeremiah had to live contributed to his grasp of this newness. He has witnessed an attempt to renew the Sinai covenant, later revealed to be a vain effort; what the Josian reform tried to do by human means could only be realized by a divine gift. Finally, his "confessions" prove that he lived this interior and personal religion; now, the entire people will reach that same level.

This extraordinary prophecy had a great influence and found a certain fulfillment at the hands of Ez and Dt-Is (see S. Porúbčan, *Il Patto Nuovo* [Rome, 1958]). They did not speak of a new covenant but of an eternal covenant, one that could not be broken (Ez 16:60; 34:25; 37:26; Is 55:3; 61:8). It is possible because a "new heart" is created in the people, a "new spirit" is given to them (Ez 11:20; 18:31; 36:26; Is 59:21; see P. van Imschoot, *ETL* 13 [1936] 201–20).

90 (v) *The stability of Israel* (31:35–37). This new oracle evokes the stability of the laws of nature to prove the same stability of God's purposes in the history of Israel (cf. Gn 8:22; Ps 89:35–38). The reasoning proceeds thus from an *argumentum per absurdum*. **35.** *sun...stars...:* We find the same purpose in the P tradition (Gn 1:14–18) and in a later psalm (Ps 136:7–9).

(vi) *The rebuilding of Jerusalem* (31:38–40). In this description of the new Jerusalem, the starting point is the Tower of Hananel, situated NE of the city (Neh 3:1; 12:39; Zech 14:10). The Corner Gate is NW (2 Kgs 14:13; 2 Chr 26:9; Zech 14:10); hence, the measurements are taken counterclockwise. The hill of Gareb is mentioned only here, but the context asks for a western location; Vincent identified it with the long esplanade along the W wall of the city. Goah is also unknown; inasmuch as the following indication is at the south, the Valley of Ben-Hinnom, Goah must be at the southwest corner. The Horse Gate is E, in the vicinity of the royal palace (2 Kgs 11:16; Neh 3:28). The "newness" comes from the purification of the Ben-Hinnom Valley, with the abolition of the child sacrifice (cf. 19:1ff.). This brief description of Jerusalem is not apocalyptic but corresponds to the actual size of the city, destroyed by the Chaldeans and rebuilt by Nehemiah (see Vincent, *Jérusalem de l'Ancien Testament*, 650–54). Even if Jeremiah could have spoken these words, it is preferable to see here a post-exilic addition from the period of Nehemiah.

(D) The Restoration of Judah (32:1–33:26). To the preceding collection of poems dealing mainly with the restoration of northern Israel, a similar collection of events and sayings regarding Judah's future has been added.

91 (a) A Pledge of Restoration (32:1–44). This narrative, probably taken from Baruch's memoirs, underwent amplifications, especially in the last two sections.

(i) *The purchase of a field* (32:1–15). **1.** According to 39:1 and 52:4 (= 2 Kgs 25:1), the siege of the city began in January, 588, to be interrupted during the summer because the Egyptian armies were marching against those of Babylon. Thus, Jeremiah's action took place after this interruption, in 587. **2–5.** A later redactor undoubtedly summarized the events recorded in chs. 34, 37–38 to show more fully the historical context of the fact. **7.** Sometime before, during the interruption of the siege, Jeremiah was already preoccupied with this affair (37:12). *first right of purchase:* Hanamel's transaction conforms with the law (cf. Lv 25:25; Ru 4:1ff.). To keep the patrimony within the family, a brother must buy his brother's property; if there is no brother, the nearest relative is bound to do so. **9.** *shekels:* At the time, the shekel's weight averaged about 11.4 g. **10–12.** The contract is concluded in due form with the obligatory witnesses. The "sealed" and "open" copies are well known; in Mesopotamia, the contract was written on a tablet to be enclosed in a clay envelope bearing the same text for current consultations. A closer parallel is attested in the Jewish community at Elephantine. The papyrus bearing the contract was folded several times and then tied and sealed; attached to it was a second copy, left open for easy consultation (see R. de Vaux, *RB* 45 [1936] 96–97). **14–15.** Jeremiah now explains his action; if he bought a field in an occupied section of the country, one day, even in the distant future, he would be able to use its benefits, and others would also perform similar transactions. In a word, Judah would recover her freedom.

92 (ii) *Jeremiah's prayer* (32:16–25). Only v. 17a ("Ah, Lord God") and vv. 24–25 reproduce the original prayer, for it is the only part connected with the present event. The remaining verses are but a redundant complex of Jeremian and deuteronomic phrases and expressions (see Rudolph, *op. cit.*, for the references). The same anthological style was used in a similar prayer in Neh 9:1ff.; they are post-exilic compositions.

(iii) *The Lord's answer* (32:26–44) This answer has also been greatly expanded: only vv. 27–29a and 42–44 are related to Jeremiah's prayer. Yahweh confirms the future restoration of Judah, geographically expressed in the terms of 17:26 (see comment on 17:26) and prophetically symbolized by the Prophet's purchase of a field in Anathoth. The long addition (vv. 29b–41) is another free composition inspired mainly by a number of Jeremiah's prophecies. The sole differences are that the new covenant is called here "eternal" (v. 40), and instead of the "knowledge of the Lord" there is question of the "fear of the Lord" (vv. 39–40); both expressions are foreign to Jeremiah's vocabulary.

93 (b) More on the Restoration of Jerusalem and Judah (33:1–26). The date of the present oracles is 587, as in 32:1. At the beginning of this century, critics rejected the entire chapter as unauthentic; we argue for an original nucleus behind its two sections.

(i) *Jerusalem and Judah restored* (33:1–13). The style of this hopeful passage is extremely repetitious and gives signs of the apocalyptic style (Rudolph; cf. v. 3: "revelation of mysteries"); if most of the ideas are Jeremiah's, their form is hardly his. Hence, we see here a disciple's reflections on the master's message. **6–9.** The historical context is the period of the rebuilding of Jerusalem after the exile. **10.** A quotation from 32:43. **11.** *the cry of joy...:* This enumeration of joyful manifestations is properly Jeremian (7:34; 16:9; 25:10). *give thanks to the Lord...:* This praise comes from the liturgical thanksgiving hymns (Pss 100:5; 106:1; 107:1; its last part is the refrain of Ps 136). **13.** This geography of the restoration comes from 17:26 (see also 32:44).

94 (ii) *An anthology on messianism* (33:14–26). This new section, missing in the LXX, is a small collection of Jeremiah's messianic oracles, mostly transformed. It is now accepted as being the work of a later redactor. **15–16.** The redactor reuses the Prophet's oracle on the future king (cf. 23:5–6); Jerusalem replaces Israel and is called by this king's new name. **17–22.** The present prophecy is a solemn affirmation of the perennial permanence of the Davidic monarchy and the Levitical priesthood, which are closely connected; the phenomenon corresponds well to the post-exilic institutional atmosphere (Zech 4:14; 6:13; etc.). This is the only place in Jer where the revival of the priesthood is an object of concern. **17.** The permanence of the dynasty is based on Nathan's prophecy (2 Sm 7:11–16; Ps 89:35ff.). **18.** *priests of Levi:* The Hebr expression says "priests-levites," which is deuteronomic (see De Vaux, *AI* 362–64, for its full meaning and historical implications). **20–21.** We meet with another *argumentum per absurdum* to prove the persistence of Yahweh's promises (cf. 31:35–37). **22.** The promise of an innumerable posterity to the patriarchs is now applied to David and the priests (Gn 13:16; 15:5; 22:17; etc.). **23–26.** The atmosphere of these closing verses is one of disillusionment. The restoration was not realized exactly as foretold, and a kind of pessimism was trying the people's faith; the messianic hope had to be stirred up, which is what we find in Is 56–66, Hag and Mal. The same apologetic intention is also present in this passage; the post-exilic period of hardships under Zerubbabel or Nehemiah would be the right historical context (see Bright, *Hist.* 346–55, 362ff.; Albright, *BP* 87ff.).

(E) The Conditions for Salvation (34:1–35:19). Three incidents taken from Baruch's memoirs serve as a conclusion to the "book of the restoration." On the occasion of a gloomy situation in Judah, Jeremiah proclaims the conditions required for the salvation of the country with its people and king. The connection between these incidents are rather loose and should not be stressed.

95 (a) Zedekiah's Fate (34:1–7). The first incident happened at a precise moment of the second siege of Jerusalem by Nebuchadnezzar (588–587). Besides

Jerusalem, only Lachish and Azekah are still resisting the enemy (v. 7). This phase of the war has been illustrated by the *ostraca* found at Tell ed-Duweir, identified with Lachish. On ostracon 4 we read: "Let [my Lord] know that we are watching for the signs of Lachish,... for we cannot see Azekah" (*ANET* 322); either Azekah had already fallen to the invader or an obstacle was hiding the city. Whatever the solution, this letter and the present text probably refer to the situation of the first phase of the war, sometime after January, 588 (see Bright, *Hist.* 308–309; Noth, *Hist.* 284–85). **4–5.** The final condemnation of the city and Zedekiah is only conditional: a peaceful surrender will save both, as Jeremiah has constantly repeated (cf. chs. 37–38). **7.** Azekah is commonly located at Tell ez-Zekariyeh, about 19 mi. SW of Jerusalem.

96 (b) A Dishonest Deal (34:8–22). The second event is also dated from v. 22—"I will bring them back to this city"—which supposes that the siege has been interrupted. The Pharaoh—i.e., Hophra (cf. 44:30)—marched into Palestine, surely to rescue Zedekiah; the Babylonians had to leave Jerusalem to stop this Egyptian advance (cf. 37:5). Ostracon 3 from Lachish (*ANET* 322) mentions a journey to Egypt of an army commander, Coniah son of Elnathan; its purpose must have been to seek such help from the Pharaoh (Bright, *Hist.* 309; Noth. *Hist.* 285). The second event must therefore be during this interruption of the siege, sometime in the summer of 588. **9–11.** Under the king's initiative, a general manumission of slaves, both male and female, has been achieved in a religious ceremony before Yahweh (v. 15). The reason for such a decision must come from the hardships of the siege; either the masters could no longer provide for their slaves, or the number of fighting men had to be increased. The slaves are called *'ibrîm*, usually translated "Hebrews." The word is attested to in cuneiform and Canaanite texts to designate a social class from which slaves and mercenaries are often taken (see R. de Vaux, *RB* 55 [1948] 337–47; H. Cazelles, *Syria* 35 [1958] 198–217; Bright, *Hist.* 84–86). Once freed, here and in the law texts, these slaves are called *ḥōfšîm*, a word also attested to in cuneiform texts to designate a low class of the free society (see Cazelles, *Syria* 35, 200–201; De Vaux, *AI* 88). **14.** The law on the manumission of slaves is found in Ex 21:2 and Dt 15:12. Because Jeremiah does not make any distinction between male and female slaves, he must refer to the deuteronomic tradition (cf. Cazelles, *RSR* 38, 23–24; M. David, *OTS* 5 [1948] 63–79). The actual observance of the prescription had a transitory motive; as soon as the danger disappeared, its obligation was again rejected. **18.** *the calf...they passed:* This rite of covenant making is attested to in the OT only here and in Gn 15:9ff. Its meaning could only be an imprecation: The animal's fate will fall on the covenant makers if they break the agreement. The rite has its parallel in the covenantal ceremonies of the ancient Near East, in which a ram or a piglet is cut into pieces as a substitute for the vassal to serve as symbol of the fate that will befall him in the case of unfaithfulness (see E. Vogt, *Bib* 36 [1955] 566; H. Cazelles, *RB* 69 [1962] 345). In the Mari texts, to "conclude a covenant" is expressed *hayaram qatālum*, "to kill an ass," and this must refer to the same practices (see Noth, *GesSt* 142–54). The rite also explains the etymology of the Hebr expression, *kārat berît*, "to cut a covenant," with its exact correspondent in two tablets from Qatna: *TAR bi-ri-ti* (see W. F. Albright, *BASOR* 121 [1951] 21–22); it also corresponds to the Gk *orkia temnein*, "to cut oaths," and the Latin *foedus ferire*. Finally, the rite must also explain the original meaning of the word *berît*, "covenant," which corresponds to the Akkadian *bîrîtu*, the "in between." If we now return to Jeremiah, we see that he really understood the rite as being imprecatory: "I will make [them] like the calf" (v. 18)—i.e., they will find death in the hands of the Babylonians (vv. 20–21). Thus, Jeremiah's message in all these circumstances is inflexible.

97 (c) The Example of the Rechabites (35:1–19). The third incident occurred under Jehoiakim, when Chaldean and Aramean troops were marching against Judah (v. 11). Our information from 2 Kgs 24:2–4 and the Babylonian Chronicles would indicate the year 601–600 for the invasion, the purpose of which was to crush Jehoiakim's revolt (cf. 12:7–13). **2.** *Rechabites:* The present story is the most extensive information we have on this group of men. According to 1 Chr 2:55, their origin was Kenite, a nomad tribe from the south. They co-operated with Jehu's radical extirpation of baalism in Samaria, showing themselves to be fervent Yahwists (2 Kgs 10:15–17). *one of the rooms:* Around the Temple courts numerous rooms served for the priests' residence and storage (1 Kgs 6:5; 1 Chr 28:12; 2 Chr 31:11). **4.** *Maaseiah:* Of the individuals mentioned, only he seems to be known; he must be the father of Zephaniah, who was sent twice by Zedekiah to consult Jeremiah (21:1; 37:3). *keeper of the doorway:* The title of a high Temple official (cf. 52:24). **6–10.** From this description, the Rechabites appear to be reactionaries; their Yahwism is frozen in its nomadic phase, rejecting absolutely all sedentary culture. When the Israelites settled in Palestine, they encountered the Canaanite religion, which was essentially bound to the agricultural society: its chief god, Baal, was mainly a fertility god. They were constantly tempted to adopt this very religion. Although a form of civilization may be a danger to religion, no religion can be identified with a civilization; for the Rechabites, Yahweh was a nomadic god and Baal a sedentary one. If the prophets often recalled the period of the wanderings in the desert as being the ideal one, this was for noncultural reasons (see De Vaux, *AI* 13–15). **13–17.** What we have just said is now clear from the lesson given by these idealists; Jeremiah does not admire their nomadic reaction, but their sheer obedience to their forefathers' word; the Israelites should be as loyal to their own faith. The example of the Rechabites is entirely religious and not at all cultural. This message (vv. 15ff.) is then proclaimed in the same style and thought of several previous ones (cf. 7:24ff.; 11:1ff.; 13:10; 25:4ff.; 26:2ff.; 29:17ff.; etc.).

98 **(IV) Martyrdom of Jeremiah (36:1–45:5).** The present section forms an homogeneous block, both in spirit and style. The faithful Baruch is held to be the author of this chronological history of the persecutions against Jeremiah.

99 **(A) The Scroll of 605–604 (36:1–32).** This chapter is outstanding in Hebr narrative art; the number of vivid observations permits almost a photographic view of the scene. It has often been studied in order to clarify the history of the composition of the whole book; its importance for this problem must neither be neglected nor exaggerated, but it leaves several questions unanswered (see E. Nielsen, *Oral Tradition* [London, 1954] 64–79).

1–4. In 605, Nebuchadnezzar defeated the Egyptians in Carchemish and became king of Babylon. The "Foe from the North" could now only be this leading power of the Near East; a policy of submission was the sole means of survival. **2.** *scroll:* This was a long strip of papyri sheets or skins sewn together; the text was written in transverse columns. This was to contain all Jeremiah's oracles against Jerusalem (the LXX excepts Israel), Judah, and the nations since his call in 627–626.

Attempts to reconstruct this scroll have reached no definitive results; we can say that these oracles were those of doom proclaimed before 605. They are collected mostly in chs. 1–25 and 46–51; each case must be studied individually before we can decide if it was a part of this first collection. Because three readings were given in a single day, the scroll could not have been too long. **3.** The ultimate purpose of the book is to provoke repentance and conversion. The spoken word passes away; perhaps the written word will remain a permanent plea! **4.** *Baruch:* Baruch's first appearance. If he was Seraiah's brother (cf. 51:59), his family was influential and respected the Prophet. **5–10.** The first reading of the scroll takes place in the Temple in presence of the people. For the clarity of the narrative, v. 9 must be transposed before v. 5. **9.** *fifth year...:* A year passed before the scroll could be read; the precise time is December, 604, for the weather is already cold (v. 22). *fast:* It has to be a special fast on the occasion of some evil; would it not be to avert Nebuchadnezzar's armies? According to his Chronicles, that very month he conquered Ashkelon (see Wiseman, *Chronicles*, 69). **5.** *I am prevented:* The obvious reason is the Temple sermon (7:1ff.) and the speech on Topheth (19:1–20:6), which aroused the Temple officials' anger. Jeremiah has to continue his mission through a secretary, keeping the oracles in a book as credential letters. **10.** Gemariah would certainly have supported both the Prophet and the Josian reform (26:24). *New Gate:* For its location between the Temple courts, see comment on 26:10. Baruch was therefore in a position overlooking the people gathered in the courtyards, where he could be seen and heard by everyone. **11–19.** A second reading of the scroll is given to the heads of the administration, during a session for the state affairs. **12.** The scene takes place in the office of the secretary of state (see De Vaux, *AI* 131). Besides Gemariah, only Elnathan is known: he led the group sent by Jehoiakim to Egypt for Uriah's extradition (26:22). **19.** The attempt to protect the Prophet and his secretary suggests that most of these dignitaries must represent Josiah's old administration. They knew what the king's reaction would be; Uriah's tragedy could not have been that long ago! **20–26.** The last, dramatic reading of the scroll in the king's presence. **22.** *winter house:* Certain rooms of rich houses were built for the cold season (cf. Am 3:15). **23.** The scene of the king cutting the columns of writing to burn them in the brazier is in full contrast, by its cynicism, to the one of his father at the reading of the Book of the Law; this contrast is even suggested in the following verse (see 2 Kgs 22:11–20). Jehoiakim perhaps thought he would neutralize the dynamism of these prophecies by destroying them in a kind of execrative action. Being an Egyptian appointee, he probably still hoped that his former suzerain would be able to upset the political balance of the Near East, despite Jeremiah's oracles. **27–32.** Baruch writes a new edition of the scroll at Jeremiah's dictation, the occasion of a new oracle of doom against the king. **30.** The prophecy was only partly fulfilled, for Jehoiachin, his son, became king. However, his reign lasted only a short time, for he was deposed and died in exile (2 Kgs 24:8ff.). *his corpse:* This dishonorable death has been already announced: he will receive the "burial of an ass" (cf. 22:19). **32.** The second scroll was not just a copy of the first one but a new edition; it is impossible to distinguish the additions. A summary of Jeremiah's preaching had been written that same year and probably served as a conclusion to the entire work (cf. 25:1–13b).

100 **(B) Zedekiah and the Prophet (37:1–38:28a).** The encounters between Zedekiah and Jeremiah recorded here happened during the siege of Jerusalem (588–587). In the following remarkable paragraph, Duhm summarized the situation:

> This scene is just as moving as it is historically interesting: on the one hand is the prophet, disfigured by mistreatment, the prison atmosphere and privations, but firm in his predictions, without any invective against his persecutors, without defiance, exaggeration or fanaticism, simple, physically mild and humble; on the other hand is the king, who obviously against his own will had been led by his officials into the war venture, anxiously watching the lips of the martyr for a favorable word for himself, whispering secretly with the man whom his officials imprisoned for treason, weak, a poor creature but not evil, a king but much more bound than the prisoner who stands before him (*Das Buch Jeremia* [Tübingen, 1901] 301; trans. J. P. Hyatt, *Jeremiah* [N.Y., 1958] 73–74).

(a) Zedekiah Consults Jeremiah (37:1–10). The consultation occurred during the interruption of the siege, in the summer of 588 (v. 5), which occasioned the dishonest deal with the slaves (cf. 34:8ff.). **1–2.** To introduce these chapters, the redactor condensed the account of 2 Kgs 24:17–20 on Zedekiah. **3.** Zephaniah was a member of a similar delegation at the beginning of the siege (21:1–10). Jehucal replaced Pashhur; therefore, we have to deal with two different events. *pray to the Lord:* The object of the prayer must have been that Yahweh should renew the miracle of 701 (cf. 22:2). Zedekiah hoped beyond all hope: Jeremiah had already foretold his fate and that of the city at the beginning of the siege (cf. 34:1–7). **7–10.** The Prophet's answer is as clear and stern as ever. His assurance about the outcome is even greater: even though Nebuchadnezzar was left only with wounded soldiers, he would still win a sweeping victory!

(b) Jeremiah Is Arrested (37:11–16). The arrest took place during the same interruption of the siege (v. 11), when there was a certain freedom of movement. **12.** The purpose of this trip to Anathoth is to be connected with the purchase of the field in ch. 3. **13.** *Gate of Benjamin:* The gate was at the NE section of the city walls (cf. Vincent, *Jérusalem de l'Ancien Testament*, 603). The accusation of desertion had a foundation; some Judeans had already joined the enemy, probably more from fear than simply treason (38:19).

(c) A New Consultation (37:17–21). Still later, Zedekiah consults Jeremiah directly and secretly, thus showing his full character. Even if he is sure of the Prophet's policy of submission, his fear of the officials prevents him from taking a personal decision. **19.** The secret interview ends on a fine gesture of the king, a sign of his love for the Prophet.

101 (d) Jeremiah in the Miry Cistern (38:1–13). Jehucal and Pashhur had consulted Jeremiah on Zedekiah's orders (21:1; 37:3). Gedaliah (not the future governor) may be the son of either this Pashhur or the Prophet's persecutor (20:1–3). **2–3.** This message is exactly that delivered to the people at the beginning of the siege (cf. 21:8–10). Jeremiah's word never changed: Jerusalem's fate is irrevocable. **4.** *he demoralizes:* The full expression is "For he weakens the hands of the warriors"—a phrase attested in the Lachish letters (6.6; cf *ANET* 322). In this letter, the author of the demoralization is doubtful because the text is broken; but inasmuch as in letter 3 there is question of a "prophet" saying "beware," some critics believe that Jeremiah is referred to in both texts. However, the hypothesis has no foundation and is now generally rejected (see R. de Vaux, *RB* 48 [1939] 199–206; D. W. Thomas, *Fest. O. Eissfeldt* [Berlin, 1958] 244–49). Nevertheless, these Lachish texts have their historical importance; defeatism did not exist only in Jerusalem. **5.** The king states his own criticism! The true power is in the officials' hands. **6.** Their final intention was to bring about Jeremiah's death without bloodshed (cf. Gn 37:18ff.). **7–13.** Jeremiah is saved by the sympathy of an Ethiopian courtier (see De Vaux, *AI* 120–23). **9.** *of famine, for there is no more food in the city:* Jeremiah's death would have been caused for an obviously different reason; these words are a gloss taken from 37:21.

102 (e) ZEDEKIAH'S LAST INTERVIEW WITH JEREMIAH (38:14–28a). This last encounter takes place at a vague spot in the Temple area. The king, eager as ever to hear a good word from Yahweh's messenger, appears in extreme anxiety, but he receives the same answer (vv. 17–18; cf. 21:8–10; 38:2–3). The die was cast! **19.** Possible vengeance from those who had already chosen "the way of life" kept the king in his habitual indecision. **22.** *they betrayed you...:* This quotation is probably from an ironic popular song. Jeremiah puts these words in their mouths, for it alludes to mud (in which he himself sank, 38:6). **24–28a.** Zedekiah's recommendation cannot find a better commentary than 38:5! With most exegetes, we prefer to read these verses after 37:21, where Zedekiah did fulfill Jeremiah's plea to be withdrawn from Jonathan's house. Once the passage had been displaced, the remark "thus Jeremiah remained in the quarters of the guard," from the end of 37:21, was added.

(C) The Fall of Jerusalem (38:28b–39:18). This pericope is a fine example of textual imbroglio. Many attempts have been made to restore the text to its primitive form; we will present here only the evident emendations (for further discussion, see Rudolph, *op. cit.*, 225–27). **38b.** *when Jerusalem was taken:* This protasis has been separated from its apodosis in 39:3 by the insertion of 39:1–2, a résumé of 2 Kgs 25:1–4a (= Jer 52:4–7a). The siege started *ca.* January, 588, and Jerusalem fell in July, 587 (see Bright, *Hist.* 308–309).

39:3. *middle gate:* This gate is mentioned here only in the OT; it seems to refer to an opening in a separating wall between two quarters of the city. **4–13.** The passage, missing in the LXX, comes from 2 Kgs 25:4b–12 (= Jer 52:7b–16). It was later introduced here, for the logical sequence of v. 3 is in v. 14, but the role played by Nebuzaradan happened one month after Jerusalem's fall (cf. 2 Kgs 25:8 = Jer 52:12) so he could not have had the mission to free Jeremiah (vv. 11–12). **14.** *Gedaliah:* The future governor's appearance here is also out of place, and contradicts the story of the next chapter; his name should be dropped. With Rudolph we restore the verb *wᵉlābîʾô* (to enter) instead of the noun *ʾel-habbāyit* (home) and translate, "they gave him to go out and to go in"—i.e., Jeremiah is free to move among the people. In a word, a short account of Jeremiah's fate at the downfall of Jerusalem (38:28b; 39:3,14) has been heavily interpolated with information borrowed from Kgs. **15–18.** This passage would be in a better context after 38:7–13. Although we are not told, Ebed-melech probably survived the catastrophe of 587; the redactor inserted the oracle here to show once more the fulfillment of Jeremiah's prophecies.

103 **(D) A Tragedy in Mizpah (40:1–41:18).** The introductory verse of ch. 40 is, in fact, a title covering chs. 40–44—the history of Jeremiah after the fall of Jerusalem; but it is somewhat faulty, for there are very few oracles. Some scholars would reject 40:7–41:18, since the prophet is not mentioned; but this section is the necessary historical background to Jeremiah's flight to Egypt. These chapters present many details concerning the period after the destruction of Jerusalem and throw much light on the short account of the same events in Kgs. An eyewitness is required for this precise record and Baruch must be the author.

(a) JEREMIAH AT MIZPAH (40:1–6). Nebuzaradan came to Jerusalem one month after its fall (2 Kgs 25:8); his mission was to burn down the city and organize the caravans for exile. Moreover, he had Nebuchadnezzar's orders to treat the Prophet humanely and to leave to him the choice of his fate (39:11–12). The Babylonian king must have been informed of the Prophet's policy of submission. Released after the capitulation of Jerusalem, it must have been by mistake that he was taken in the group of captives. **2–3.** Baruch puts this résumé of Jeremiah's preaching on the lips of the Babylonian captain. **5.** *Gedaliah:* This noble figure came from a family that strongly supported both the Josian reform and the Prophet's mission (cf. 26:24). He must have been known by the Chaldeans to have opposed Zedekiah's policy. A seal impression found in Lachish, dating from the beginning of the 6th cent., bears the inscription "To Gedaliah, over the house," i.e., chief minister or intendant. If this seal is his, he had a high post in Zedekiah's cabinet (see R. de Vaux, *RB* 45, 96–102). **6.** Mizpah is usually located at Tell en-Nasbeh, some 8 mi. N of Jerusalem. At the time of the judges and Samuel, the town was a political and religious center (Jgs 20:1–3; 1 Sm 7:5–14; 10:17). If it is now chosen as the new capital or the administrative center, it is because Jerusalem was badly damaged, as were most of the important Judean towns (see Albright, *FSAC* 322–23; see also *BibArch* 179). There are no signs of destruction at Mizpah for this particular period (see K. Kenyon, *Archaeology in the Holy Land* [London, 1960] 290).

(b) THE COLONY AT MIZPAH (40:7–12). Gedaliah tried to organize the small colony of survivors; the future depended on a true submission to the Babylonians. Even if Judah were now simply a Babylonian province, she could keep her identity; no foreigners ever colonized her territory and she had a governor of her own, unlike northern Israel in 721 (2 Kgs 17:24ff.). **7–9.** The notice on the new political organization is identical to that in 2 Kgs 25:22–24. **10–12.** Life resumes its normal course. The invaders had respected the crops, for they were especially good; in fact, it was to their advantage. A wind of hope blows gently over the crushed country.

104 (c) THE ASSASSINATION OF GEDALIAH (40:13–41:3). **13–16.** Our only source of information on the plot; Baalis, the Ammonite king, is given as its chief instigator. In 594–593, the Transjordan kings had tried to move Zedekiah into a coalition of the western states in order to overthrow the Babylonian domination (cf. ch. 27). Thus, Baalis must have disliked Gedaliah's leadership. Gedaliah's refusal to believe that a plot was being fomented against him is another sign of his noble character.

41:1–3. The assassination itself is recorded in much shorter form in 2 Kgs 25:25. Ishmael, of royal origin, may have been shocked to see that the Davidic dynasty had been supplanted, or he may have supported the anti-Babylonian party. Whatever his motives, Baalis saw in him an excellent tool. The brutal massacre produced deep consternation in the minds of the Judeans; they commemorated it by a fast, already attested to at the end of the Exile on the third of Tishri—i.e., the end of September (Zech 7:5; 8:19).

(d) THE ASSASSINATION OF PILGRIMS (41:4–10). Two days later, Ishmael shed more blood, for some unknown reason. The pilgrims, in mourning attire (cf. 16:6; 48:37), were from the three cultic centers of northern Israel. Their pilgrimage to the ruined Temple, to present offerings, indicates that Jerusalem remained the main religious center for honoring Yahweh. Mourning rites continued during the whole exilic period in the ruins of the city and its Temple (Lam; Pss 74, 79; Is 63:7–64:12). **9.** Asa did lead some building operations in Mizpah (1 Kgs 15:22); the excavators of Tell en-Nasbeh may have discovered the cistern (see F. X. Abel, *Géographie* II [Paris, 1938] 389).

(e) FLIGHT AND PANIC (41:11–18). It took some time before Johanan learned of the crime; Ishmael probably waited for his absence, for he must have known of Johanan's suspicion. **12.** *great waters of Gibeon:* This landmark has to be connected to the "Great Pool" in 2 Sm 2:12ff. Gibeon is located at the actual el-Jib; recent excavations there have brought to light an immense pool hewn in the rock (see J. B. Pritchard, *BA* 19 [1956] 68–70; VTSup 7 [1960] 9). Once Ishmael had escaped to Ammon, Johanan and the troop that the assassin had gathered by force took to flight. The crime could only be interpreted as a new revolt against Babylon; retaliation was to be expected (see 52:30). Egypt was the only neighboring country free from the Babylonian domination (cf. 2 Kgs 25:26). **17.** *lodging place of Chimham:* Chimham is only known as a personal name (2 Sm 19:38–41); the Hebr word *gērût* ("lodging place") corresponds to the Oriental *khan*. Alt suggested that the word should be translated "state," "right of a resident alien," or, simply, "fief"; the landmark would be then a reference to a fief concession granted by David to an Aramean foreigner (see A. Alt, *JTS* 11 [1960] 364–65).

105 **(E) Sojourn in Egypt (42:1–44:30).** These chapters present the last act of Jeremiah's martyrdom. The Prophet closed his eyes, forever, on his mortally wounded country and on the undying idolatry of his people. His life had been a tragedy to the end.

(a) SEARCH FOR GUIDANCE (42:1–6). The group of fugitives, still in the lodging place near Bethlehem, hesitate regarding what should be done; an oracle from the Lord would cut short their perplexity. But Jeremiah's precaution to make sure that his answer would be accepted makes us suspect that the decision to go down to Egypt was already definitive.

(b) THE DIVINE ANSWER (42:7–18). The answer came to Jeremiah only ten days later; the delay certainly aggravated the situation, for the fear of the Babylonians could only have increased. Also this delay proves well enough that true prophetical inspiration does not depend upon human insight. **10.** The verse is a clear reminiscence of Jeremiah's call, which has been decisive for his entire life (1:10; 24:6; 31:4,28; etc.). The Prophet affirms that they should not fear Nebuchadnezzar (vv. 11ff.); in fact, we have no proof that the king avenged his governor's assassination (see 52:30). **16.** Jeremiah predicts an invasion of Egypt by Nebuchadnezzar; we shall discuss this historical problem later (cf. 43:8–13).

106 (c) THE REFUSAL TO STAY HOME (42:19–43:7). With a number of critics, we transpose 43:1–3 before 42:19–22 for a more logical sequence of the narrative. Azariah is afraid to attack Yahweh and his messenger directly, so he turns against a third party, the less dangerous Baruch. **43:5.** *whole remnant:* Certainly not all the Judeans left in Palestine after 587 went down to Egypt, but only this small company now stationed near Bethlehem, among whom were some who had taken refuge in Transjordan and had recently returned to Judah (40:11–12). **7.** *Tahpanhes:* A frontier city of the eastern delta (cf. 2:16).

(d) NEBUCHADNEZZAR IN EGYPT (43:8–13). Once in Tahpanhes, Jeremiah reiterates his prediction of Nebuchadnezzar's invasion of Egypt, in a prophetical action (cf. 42:16). **9.** *brickyard:* The Hebr word *malbēn*, "brickmould," is hard to explain in this sentence. The LXX omitted the word, and in a fragment from Qumran, it seems that there is no room for it (cf. DJD 3, 63–64). A dittography of the first three consonants of the preceding word (*bammelet*) might be at the origin of its addition. Thus, we simply read, "and sink them in mortar at the entrance...." *royal building:* Lit., "the house of Pharaoh." Inasmuch as the king had no residence here, it must have been an administrative building, or the governor's palace. **10.** *my servant:* Jeremiah always believed that Nebuchadnezzar had been commissioned by Yahweh to rule over the entire Near East (cf. 25:9; 27:6; 42:7ff.). **11.** A part of the oracle is a repetition of 15:2. **13.** *in the land of Egypt:* Better, read with LXX, "That are in On." On is the Hebr form of the Egyptian name for Heliopolis, situated about 5 mi. NE of Cairo. The city was well known for its temple of Re (sun), whose entrance was preceded by two rows of obelisks, one of which still stands. According to a fragmentary tablet in the British Museum, Nebuchadnezzar did invade Egypt during Amasis' reign (570–526), in his 37th year (568–567), which corresponds roughly to the date given by Ezekiel for the same event (Ez 29:17–20; cf. *ANET* 308; E. Drioton and J. Vandier, *L'Egypte* [2nd ed.; Paris, 1952] 597–98).

107 (e) JEREMIAH'S LAST WORDS (44:1–30). The chapter presents the religious situation of the exiles in Egypt, soon after the fall of Jerusalem in 587. Jeremiah had to fight constantly against the recurring idolatry of his people, which, for him, had been the true cause of the kingdom's downfall; the punishment turned out to be meaningless for these Judeans. The narrative is somewhat verbose; it has been largely reworked in the deuteronomic style.

1. *Migdol:* The name means simply "tower" or "fortress." Several places have this name; the present Migdol, as well as that in Ez 29:10, can be located at Tell el-Her, midway between Pelusium and Sele (see T. O. Lambdin, *IDB* 3, 377). For Noph and Tahpanhes, see 2:16. *Pathros:* This is the Hebr transcription of the Egyptian *p'-t'-rsy*, "Southern Land"—i.e., Upper Egypt. Jeremiah probably addressed only the refugees who had taken him down to Egypt, and who are now in the north. This title must come from a later redactor who extended the sermon to all Jewish colonies in Egypt. Among these colonies, the most well known is that established in Elephantine, opposite Assuan. We now have a number of its 5th-cent. writings in Aramaic, which indicates that the settlement must certainly date at least from the 6th cent. Besides this present occasion of a Jewish immigration into Egypt, there was another, when Neco sent Jehoahaz there as a prisoner (2 Kgs 23:34) in 609. The Judean king was probably accompanied by a number of his people. The Elephantine papyri give clear signs of the syncretist religion of the colony: these Jews already revered a goddess called "Anath-Yahu," Anath of Yahweh! (see E. G. Kraeling, *IDB* 2, 83–85; A. Vincent, *La religion des Judéo-Araméens* [Paris, 1937]). **2–14.** Jeremiah gives his explanation of the present miseries; idolatrous practices have broken the covenant. The original oracle is probably limited to vv. 2 and 7–8 (Rudolph); the remaining part of the speech uses abundantly the former sermons of the Prophet on related subjects (e.g., ch. 7). **15–19.** The people interpret the same history in an absolutely opposite way: These calamities have been caused precisely because idolatry has been eradicated by the Josian reform (cf. D. N. Freedman, *Interpr* 21 [1967] 32–49). When the "queen of heaven" (cf. 7:16–20) had her worshipers in Israel, great prosperity existed; thus, the future could be assured only by a return to that cult. **19.** The women practiced such a worship with their husbands' consent. The Law required this consent in the case of vows made by wives, and here these rites are called precisely "vows" (v. 25; cf. Nm 30:7–16). **20–30.** To this bold speech, Jeremiah answers by a last oracle of doom. **27.** *I am watching:* The threat is pronounced by the key word of the call narrative *šāqad*, "to watch" (cf. comment on 1:11–12; 31:28). **28.** The repatriation of these few exiles in Egypt is historically obscure; we have no source of information on their future return to Palestine. **30.** *Hophra:* Some time before Jeremiah had predicted Nebuchadnezzar's invasion of Egypt (cf. 43:8–13); its only historical attestation is dated 568–567, under Amasis. The Prophet might have expected the event sooner; however, the present text does not specify that Hophra (588–568) will fall into Nebuchadnezzar's hands; it merely compares the fate of Zedekiah and Hophra. From Herodotus (*History* 2.161–63, 169; 4.159) we learn that in 570, on the occasion of a war in Lybia, a revolt broke out in the Egyptian army. The general, Amasis, was sent by Hophra to settle the question, but instead he proclaimed himself king and marched against Hophra, who was killed by the people. It is only after this troubled political situation that Nebuchadnezzar appeared in Egypt. The actual state of Jeremiah's prophecy might be a later adaptation to this historical situation. We hear no more of Jeremiah nor does Baruch tell us how he died. A tradition, known only through Christian writings, reports that he had been stoned in Tahpanhes (see Penna, *op. cit.*, 9–10).

108 **(F) The Consolation of Baruch (45:1–5).** This word of consolation is dated 605, the year of the writing of the scroll (ch. 36). **3.** Baruch uttered his own "confessions" (cf. 20:7–18). One of these sufferings must have been the obligation to hide, with his master, to escape Jehoiakim's persecution (36:26). He certainly grieved over his own people's condemnation. **4.** This new judgment over Judah is expressed again in the terms of Jeremiah's call (1:10). **5.** *great things:* There is much speculation about what these "things" were. From the Lord's answer, he apparently asked Yahweh to suspend his sentence on Jerusalem and Judah. Such a prayer is hopeless; however, Baruch's life will be saved. This short oracle was probably included in the second edition of the scroll after ch. 36; in the final redaction of the book, it found its present place so that the narrative of Jeremiah's tragic life would be uninterrupted (see A. Weiser, *Glaube und Geschichte* [Göttingen, 1961] 321–29).

109 **(V) Oracles Against the Nations (46:1–51:64).** In the LXX, these oracles are found immediately after the title in 25:13c and are concluded by the vision of the cup of judgment (25:15–38); in general, critics agree that the LXX represents the primitive order of the book. In other prophetical books (Is, Ez), the oracles against the nations are inserted between those against Israel and those promising the restoration of the chosen people. Would the synagogal reading of Jer be responsible for the present order of the MT? If so, then we ought to explain why the same transpositions have not been made for the other books. Thus, a definitive answer is still lacking. Within this section, the order of the nations is also different in both recensions. The MT followed a geographical pattern, moving from W to E, and the LXX adopted a logical pattern, the nations' political importance. Finally, the authenticity of this section has been the subject of long discussions. For a while, most exegetes rejected it totally as a later addition (Duhm, Smend, Stade, Schwally, Volz, etc.). Now, such a radical position is no longer accepted and an authentic nucleus is acknowledged; in fact, each oracle has to be considered separately. Again, it would be strange if Jeremiah, like the other prophets, had not addressed the foreign nations! However, we recognize that these oracles underwent frequent expansions, much more so than in any other section of Jer.

110 **(A) Against Egypt (46:1–28)(LXX 26:2–28).** Two different poems are directed against Egypt. The opening verse serves as title to the whole section (chs. 46–51), which had to be repeated (cf. 25:13c) once these oracles had been displaced.

(a) The Battle of Carchemish (46:2–12) (LXX 26:2–12). The first poem is dated the year Babylon and Egypt encountered at Carchemish in 605. The present text was our only source of information on this battle until Wiseman published the Babylonian Chronicles in 1956. We learn once more that Nebuchadnezzar, then the general of the army, did defeat Neco at Carchemish in 605. Soon after, in August, his father, Nabopolassar, died; Nebuchadnezzar returned quickly to Babylon to be proclaimed king, leaving his victory limited to northern Syria. However, the event had been important enough to make Babylon the leading power of the Near East (see Wiseman, *Chronicles*, 67–69). The poem is certainly authentic (compare v. 5 and 6:25; 20:3,10; 49:29). The description, high in color and vivid in style, brings to mind a similar poem in Nahum (3:1ff.). **2.** *Carchemish:* The site of the ancient city is at the actual Jerablus, on the upper course of the Euphrates. **9.** Cush is the ancient name for Ethiopia. The identification of Put is disputed; most likely, it designates a part of Lybia (see Lambdin, *IDB* 3, 971). *Lud:* Although the Bible mentions Lydians as a population related to Egypt and living in Africa (Gn 10:13), we prefer to see here the Lydians of Asia Minor, for they are referred to in Is 66:19 along with Javan (Greece) and the coastal islands. Here and in Ez 30:5 they are part of the Egyptian army. We know that Psammetichus I (663–609) was granted help from Gyges, king of Lydia in Asia Minor, to overthrow Ashurbanipal's domination; since that time, the Greeks' influence in Egypt grew continually in army and commerce (see Drioton and Vandier, *op. cit.*, 575–84). **11.** Gilead figures once more as an ideal place to search for balm (8:22; 51:8). Egypt's sole reaction is to cure her wounds; Herodotus noticed that medicine was a widespread preoccupation there (*History* 2.84).

(b) The Invasion of Egypt (46:13–28)(LXX 26:13–28). We have seen that Jeremiah, soon after 587, had a similar prediction, which was realized only in 568–567, according to our present information (see 43:8–13). Some critics would still date the poem *ca.* 601–600, when Nebuchadnezzar and Neco met at the Egyptian frontier; the battle remained indecisive and Nebuchadnezzar was forced to return to Babylon and reorganize his army (cf. Wiseman, *Chronicles*, 71). However, the terms of the poem are too general to permit such precision. We prefer to situate the oracle toward the end of Jeremiah's career, close to the oracle just mentioned. **14.** For the identification of the geographical names, see comment on 44:1. **15.** *Apis:* The sacred bull of the god Ptah, the protector of Memphis. **16.** *Up! let us return...:* The reflection is from the mercenaries in the Egyptian army, mentioned in vv. 9 and 21, who were quite numerous (Herodotus, *History* 2.152–54). **17.** *the noise...go by:* Most exegetes find here a word play on Hophra's name—*w'ḥ-ib-r'*, and the Hebr verb, *he'ĕbîr*, "go by"—as a sarcastic remark on the futility of the help Zedekiah expected from the Egyptian king during the final siege of Jerusalem (cf. 37:5–6). If this symbolic name is correctly explained, the date proposed for the composition of the poem would be thus supported. **25–26.** These verses, in prose and recalling the oracle against Hophra (44:30), extend the invasion to Upper Egypt, Thebes being her capital and Amon her main god; they are considered to be a later addition. The promise of restoration will be repeated for other nations (48:47; 49:6,39). **27–28.** The restoration of Israel, out of context, is also a later addition, probably to attenuate the preceding promise made to Egypt. We read the same text elsewhere with minor differences (cf. 30:10–11).

111 **(B) Against Philistia (47:1–7)(LXX 29:1–32).** **1.** The original title was only "Against the Philistines," as in the LXX. The date given, "Before Pharaoh attacked Gaza," is therefore irrelevant to the rest of the poem. That event may have occurred *ca.* 609, when Neco had been victorious at Megiddo (see Herodotus, *History* 2.159). The invasion "from the north," i.e., from Babylonia, is described in pure Jeremian style. The prophecy was fulfilled in 604–603; Nebuchadnezzar then appeared on the coastal plain and took Ashkelon after an arduous siege (see Wiseman, *Chronicles*, 69); recent excavations at a nearby mound, Ashdod, have revealed signs of destruction at the end of the 7th cent. (see D. N. Freedman, *BA* 26 [1963] 139). An Aram letter from the king of Ashkelon to the Pharaoh, asking for help, probably dates from this period (see H. L. Ginsberg, *BASOR* 111 [1948] 24–27; J. Bright, *BA* 12 [1949] 46–52). **4.** *Tyre and Sidon:* These two important Phoenician seaports are presented as allies of Philistia, which they no doubt were. *Caphtor:* Generally identified with Crete, where the Philistines originated. However, the term might be generic, to designate the islands of the Aegean Sea, for the Philistines were not exclusively from Crete. They were part of the invasion of "peoples of the sea," originating from the eastern Mediterranean area. They were stopped at the Egyptian frontier by Ramses III (*ca.* 1188 BC) at which time some of these "peoples of the sea" settled down on the coastal plain of Palestine. **5.** *Gaza...Ashkelon...Ashdod:* Added from 25:20, they were the main Philistine cities along the coast. *their strength:* We should read instead, with the LXX, the "Anaqim," a people of high stature who terrified the Israelites on their arrival in Palestine (Nm 13:22ff.; Dt 1:28). Joshua exterminated them, except precisely those living in this Philistine region (Jos 11:22). These cities are now left to their mourning (cf. 16:6).

112 **(C) Against Moab (48:1–47)(LXX 31:1–40).** The long oracle against Moab, the central state of Transjordan, has undergone numerous additions by later hands. For the identification of the large number of geographical names, we refer to Rudolph's commentary (*op. cit.*, 263–65). Moab had been opposed to Israel from the time of the Exodus (Nm 22–24); in the 9th cent., her strong King Mesha succeeded in freeing himself from the Israelite domination, which he celebrated in his famous inscription (*ANET* 320–21). In 601–600, Moabite groups were sent by Nebuchadnezzar to uproot Jehoiakim's revolt (cf. 2 Kgs 24:2; Jer 12:7–13), which may be the occasion of the present oracle. The prophecy was fulfilled in 582–581, when Nebuchadnezzar invaded Moab and Ammon, according to Josephus' testimony (*Ant.* 10.181).

1–10. The first poem describes the total destruction of Moab, personified as a woman; the invasion moves from N to S, obliging the Moabites to seek refuge in the desert (v. 6). **5.** The verse is taken literally from Is 15:5; the traditional Assyro-Babylonian policy of deportations will be applied also to Moab. **7.** *Chemosh:* This chief god of the Moabites is mentioned often in Mesha's inscription. **10.** The bloodthirsty curse is unanimously recognized as a gloss.

11–28. The following verses must be considered as a new poem, for Moab is addressed as masculine. The Prophet proclaims the downfall of the whole land (vv. 11–17) and applies then the same fate to the individual cities (vv. 18–28). **11.** The Moabite wine, the central theme of Isaiah's oracle on Moab (Is 16:6ff.), was reputed for its quality (cf. *RB* 57 [1950] 149, n. 1). Here it symbolizes the land's tranquillity; indeed, Moab was outside the normal route of invasions and was only rarely disturbed. **12–13.** A glossator's reflection on undecanted wine. Inasmuch as Bethel is set in parallelism with Chemosh, it must refer to the god of the same name, worshiped by the Jews of the Elephantine colony (see R. de Vaux, *Ang* 20 [1943] 86; O. Eissfeldt, *KlSchr* [Tübingen, 1962] 206–33). **21–24.** The list of cities interrupts the poem; we reject it as a later addition. **26–27.** These two prose verses are another late insertion; the image of the "cup of judgment" is in the background (25:15ff.).

29–39. The present section is an awkward combination of texts borrowed from Isaiah's oracles against Moab (Is 15–16). The interpolator's purpose is to give the reason for such a punishment—Moab's pride and loftiness of heart against Israel and her God; the same reason figures also in Zeph 2:8–11; Ez 25:8–11.

40–47. This last part of the poem is another mosaic of biblical texts. Rudolph keeps only vv. 40–42 as original. **40.** The image of the eagle is borrowed from 49:22, and has been omitted in the LXX. **41.** *on that day...:* This last part of the verse is also taken from 49:22 and is omitted in the LXX. **43–44.** The verses are a quotation of Is 24:17–18; doom is inevitable. **45–47.** The entire passage is missing in the LXX; in fact, vv. 45–46 are merely a free citation of an old song on Heshbon (Nm 21:28–29), and v. 47 is another latter word of consolation (cf. 46:26).

113 **(D) Against Ammon (49:1–6)(LXX 30:17–21).** This authentic oracle against Ammon can also be dated *ca.* 601–600 (cf. 48; 2 Kgs 24:2). Ammon was situated N of Moab, but her territorial limits were never clearly defined; her capital was Rabbah, modern Amman. The Ammonites rejoiced at the fall of Jerusalem (Ez 25:1–7), and their king, Baalis, was the principal author of Gedaliah's murder (cf. 40:11ff.). For the fulfillment of the oracle, see the oracle against Moab. **1.** *Milcom:* The Ammonites' chief god. *disinherited Gad:* At the time of the conquest, Gad had received as his lot a part of the Ammonite territory (Nm 32:33–37; Jos 13:24–28). But after Tiglath-pileser III had conquered this region in 734 (2 Kgs 15:29), the Ammonites probably kept it under their political influence, for they were themselves vassals of Assyria. In fact, at that time, Amos had already reproached them in the same manner (Am 1:13). **3.** *Heshbon:* The city is located at modern Hesban, in the northern part of Moab; Heshbon had probably been an Ammonite possession in its early history (Jgs 11:26). Now it lies down in mourning (cf. 47:5), and the Ammonite god and people are exiled, as happened to Moab (48:7; Am 1:15). **6.** For this promise of restoration, missing in the LXX, see 46:26 and 48:47.

114 **(E) Against Edom (49:7–22)(LXX 30:1–16).** Edom was the S Transjordan state, extending from the Wadi Zered to the Gulf of Aqabah. Her capital, Bozrah, is now situated at Buseirah, some 22 mi. SE of the Dead Sea. Although the Edomites had some relationship with the Israelites (Gn 25:19ff.; 36:1), their antagonism was ancestral. They rejoiced at Jerusalem's downfall and, apparently, they plundered the south (cf. Ez 35:1–15; Ob 10–17; Lam 4:21; Ps 137:7). We have no record of a Babylonian invasion of Edom; she must have submitted as did her neighbors. The present state of the oracle shows a clear influence of Obadiah; we should probably keep as original only vv. 7–8, 10b–11, and 22. **7.** Edom was reputed for her wisdom traditions (Ob 8–9; Bar 3:22–23; Jb 2:11; etc.). Teman is often identified with Tawilan, just below Jebel Heidan. In the present passage, Teman represents the whole of Edom. **8.** *Dedan:* Ordinarily, it refers to a district in NW Arabia; there is a possibility that a clan of Dedanites had settled in Edom. **9–10a.** The verse is found, with minor changes, in Ob 5–6, where it has a better context. **12–13.** This prose passage is also an interpolation; it alludes clearly to the "cup of judgment" (25:15ff.; see 48:26–27) and reuses frequent Jeremian expressions of doom (cf. 18:16; 22:5; 44:12; etc.). **14–16.** These verses are also borrowed almost literally from Ob 1–4. Edom was, in fact, remarkable for her fortresses perched on high rocks, the best known being Petra (2 Kgs 14:7). The doom on Jerusalem now falls on Edom (cf. 19:8). **18–21.** The same verses will be read later (50:40,44–46), with the simple change of the geographical names where they are in a better context. **22.** This last verse is certainly original (cf. 48:40). The eagle is the image of Nebuchadnezzar; Ezekiel develops the same image into a long allegory (Ez 17:3ff.).

115 **(F) Against Damascus (49:23–27)(LXX 30:29–33).** The true title should be, "Against the Syrian Cities." These cities are not listed in the vision of the "cup of judgment" (25:15ff.). Inasmuch as all the Aramean city-states fell under Tiglath-pileser III in the 8th cent., the present oracle would have a more suitable context in that period. However, Jeremiah could have pronounced these words *ca.* 605, when Nebuchadnezzar crushed the Egyptians at Carchemish, or even more likely *ca.* 601–600, when Aramean groups were commissioned by the Babylonian king to settle Jehoiakim's revolt (2 Kgs 24:2–4; Jer 12:7–13). **23.** *Hamath:* The city is located at the present Hama on the Orontes, 110 mi. N of Damascus. *Arpad:* It is identified with Tell Erfad, about 12 mi. N of Aleppo. **26.** The same oracle is repeated against Babylon (50:30). **27.** The verse is a clear reminiscence of Am 1:4. Damascus had at least three kings by the name Ben-Hadad, from the 9th to the 8th cents.

116 **(G) Against Arabia (49:28–33)(LXX 30:23–28).** Jeremiah now turns to the Bedouin tribes of the Syrian desert, E of Transjordan, i.e., Kedar. In his chronicles, Nebuchadnezzar recorded the raid he led against these tribes in 599–598 (cf. Wiseman, *Chronicles*, 71). **28.** No city named Hazor is known in the region, but we are told that Kedar used to live in *ḥāṣēr*—i.e., an "unfortified settlement" (Gn 25:16; Is 42:11). The Prophet must be referring to these settlements, as v. 31 shows (cf. Ez 38:11). *easterners:* Another appellation of he Arabs (Jb 1:3). **32.** *shave their temples:* For this custom, see comment on 9:25.

117 **(H) Against Elam (49:34–39)(LXX 25:14–20).** Finally, Jeremiah condemns Elam, NE of the Persian Gulf. The country fell under the Assyrian power when Ashurbanipal destroyed the capital, Susa, in 640. Thereafter, Elam came progressively under the control of the Medes; in 612, Cyaxares, the Median king, assisted Nabopolassar of Babylon in his final assault on Nineveh. For the following years, our information on Elam is scanty. If the restitution of a broken text in the Babylonian Chronicles is correct, in 596–595 Nebuchadnezzar had to stop along the Euphrates the advance of the Elamite king, who most likely intended to invade southern Babylonia (Wiseman, *Chronicles*, 73). Thus, the date given for the oracle would be almost correct, 597. We recall that soon after this date, Jeremiah had to write to the exiles in Babylon to convince them that their captivity would be long; they might have hoped that Elam would put an end to the Babylonian Empire, which would permit them to return to Judah (cf. ch. 29). The present oracle cuts short any such hope: Elam will also be submitted to a foreign power, which is Yahweh's will. **35.** *bow of Elam:* The Elamites were recognized as excellent archers (Is 22:6). **36.** *four winds:* Probably Ezekiel's expression for "all directions" (Ez 37:9). **39.** On this late promise of restoration, see 46:26 (cf. also 48:47; 49:6).

118 **(I) Against Babylon (50:1–51:58)(LXX 27:1–28:58).** Very few exegetes would still attribute this long poem or series of poems against Babylon to Jeremiah; we rather have to deal with the work of a disciple who wrote not long before 538, the year Babylon fell to the Persians. In fact, Jeremiah strongly believed that Babylon was Yahweh's instrument for vengeance; one should pray for her and contribute to her welfare for the exile in her midst would be long (27:6ff.; 29; etc.). The present atmosphere is entirely different: Babylon is on the verge of downfall and the exiles will soon return home, the two constant themes of these chapters. Thus, we are in the context of the Exile, and the poems are to be compared to Is 13–14 (*ca.* 550) and Dt-Is (see Rudolph, *op. cit.*, 274–75).

50:1–7. This first section presents the two leading themes: the fall of Babylon (vv. 2–3) and the return from exile (vv. 4–7). **1.** The title shows signs of post-exilic composition: the expression *bᵉyad*, "through" or "by the means of," applied to prophecy, is attested only in Hag 1:1; 2:1; Mal 1:1; etc. The LXX says, simply, "The word that the Lord spoke against Babylon." **2.** *Bel...Merodach:* Bel was the main god of Nippur, whose Sumerian name was *EN-LIL*, "the lord of wind." He was later identified with the main god of Babylon, Marduk (Merodach), who became the head of the Babylonian pantheon. Thus, the poet refers here to this one god. **3.** *a people from the north:* Jeremiah's common expression to designate the future invader in his early poems (cf. chs. 2–6). The author does not use it properly here, for the Persians came from the east. **4–5.** The return from exile coincides with this last event; it is also the occasion to renew the covenant (cf. 31:31–34). **6–7.** The wandering of the sheep must be an allusion to Judah's idolatrous cult on high places (cf. 2:20; 3:2; 23:1ff.; Ez 34; Is 53:6).

8–20. The same themes are given further development. The catastrophe is so imminent that the foreigners—i.e., the exiled people—are asked to flee quickly. **16.** The verse is clearly dependent on Is 13:14. **17b–18.** The passage breaks the sequence of vv. 17a and 19. Assyria had conquered northern Israel in 721 (2 Kgs 17:3ff.) and had been punished; the same fate is now befalling Babylon.

21–28. The destruction of the glorious city is proclaimed in Jerusalem. **21.** *Merathaim:* The dual form of the word *mārâ*, "twice bitter"; the author proposes a word play on the name of the region N of the Persian Gulf where the Tigris and the Euphrates meet, called *nār marrūti*. *Pekod:* It means "visit" or "punishment," another wordplay on *Puqūdu*, a region E of Babylon (Ez 23:23). **23.** *the hammer:* It symbolizes Babylon as the instrument of God's vengeance (51:20–23). **27.** *oxen:* The warriors of Babylon are meant (cf. Is 34:6–7).

29–32. Babylon is destroyed for her insolence! Most of the expressions used here are already found in vv. 14–16, 21, 26–27. **29.** *holy one of Israel:* This name of Yahweh is characteristic of Is; it is found here only in chs. 50–51.

33–40. The second main theme, the restoration of Israel, is now evolved. Yahweh is called the redeemer of Israel (*gōʾēl;* cf. Lv 25:47ff.), a characteristic of Dt-Is (e.g., Is 41:14; 43:1,14; 44:6,22–24; etc.). **33.** The oppression in Babylonia recalled the one in Egypt (Ex 7:14; 9:2; etc.). **35–38.** The word "sword" is repeated emphatically in this frenetic judgment on both the people and the material civilization of Babylon; the enumeration has a close parallel in Dt-Is (Is 44:25,27; 45:3). **39–40.** These verses are certainly dependent upon Is 13:19–22, except that the parallelism with Sodom and Gomorrah has been inverted.

119 **41–46.** The present section is purely a collection of previous texts. **41–43.** The poem on the "foe from the north" is quoted, with the change of "Zion" for "Babylon" (cf. 6:22–24). **44–46.** The oracle against Edom is quoted, with the same required changes (cf. 49:19–21).

51:1–19. The combined themes of the destruction of Babylon and of the return of the exiles reappear. **1.** *Chaldea:* Instead of *kaśdîm* (Chaldeans), the MT has its cryptogram, in *atbash* (cf. 25:25–26), *lēb qāmāy* (the heart of my adversaries). **5.** The author uses two expressions of Dt-Is: Israel is a widow (Is 54:4ff.); Yahweh is the holy one of Israel (cf. 50:29). **7.** *golden cup:* We deal once more with an allusion to the "cup of judgment" (25:15ff.); it is now said to be of gold, for Babylon was fabulously rich. **11–14.** This assault against Babylon recalls the one against Egypt (46:3ff.). *Media's kings:* Previously the author used Jeremiah's expression, "the foe from the north" (50:3,9,41; 51:48); hence, this may be a gloss. Until the middle of the 6th cent., the Medes were the leading power of Iran; they then fell to Cyrus, the Persian king, who incorporated them into his empire. Because the Persians took Babylon in 538, it may well be that the Medes represent them, as in Is 13:17. **15–19.** This passage is a doublet of 10:12–16.

20–26. The image of Babylon as the hammer of God's vengeance (50:23) is now developed in a frenzied war song (cf. 50:35–38). Now that its work is over, the hammer will be shattered, although its might is comparable to a lofty mountain.

27–33. Babylon is under the assault, being reduced to a threshing floor. **27.** *Ararat, Minni, Ashkenaz:* These three geographical names are well known in the cuneiform texts (Urartu, Mannay, Ašguzaya). They are all regions of the actual Armenia, in the neighborhood of Lake Van and Lake Urmia. They were successively conquered by the Medes and the Persians, and some of their contingents were part of the Persian army that conquered Babylon in 538.

34–40. The people of Zion call on Babylon the very fate it inflicted on them. The author reuses his former imagery (v. 37; cf. 50:39; v. 40; cf. 50:27); once more he alludes to the "cup of judgment" (25:15ff.).

41–43. The short passage is an ironical elegy on the fallen city; it is not very original in style (e.g., v. 41a; cf. 50:23; v. 42; cf. 46:7–8; 47:2; Is 8:7ff.; 17:2ff.).

44–48. The present section is a severe attack on Babylon's main god, Bel-Marduk (cf. 50:2), which is the occasion of a general joy for the remaining part of the universe. **46.** The verse is an interpolation that later inspired a section of eschatological discourse in Mt (Mt 24:6ff.).

49–57. The reasons for Babylon's downfall are now enumerated. The law of retaliation has to be applied; the heathens have profaned the Temple by their presence within its enclosure (cf. Lam 1:10).

58. A final verse proclaims the leveling of Babylon's mighty fortifications. The city walls were indeed extremely robust (see A. Parrot, *Babylone et l'Ancien Testament* [Neuchatel, 1956] 14ff.). But Cyrus did not destroy the city in 538, for it surrendered without a fight. It is only in 482 that it was totally laid waste by Xerxes I on the occasion of a revolt. **58b.** *the toil. . . :* The end of the verse is a quotation of Hab 2:13.

120 **(J) The Oracle in the Euphrates (51:59–64) (LXX 28:59–64).** It has been customary to consider this short narrative as fictitious to justify the presence of the long oracle against Babylon. Only a few would still doubt the historicity of this event, which occurred in 594–593, under Zedekiah. The ambassadors of the neighboring kings met in Jerusalem to form a coalition of the western states for overthrowing the Babylonian domination (cf. ch. 27). Zedekiah certainly had to justify his conduct, which would have been the purpose of the present delegation. **59.** *Seraiah:* According to his genealogy, he was Baruch's brother (32:12). *quartermaster:* Lit., "the master of the resting [place]" (Nm 10:33). His function in a royal expedition was to provide the king with a suitable lodging place; thus, Seraiah was a kind of chamberlain, a minor officer in the delegation. Through Baruch, he must have been friendly with Jeremiah. **60.** *all these words. . . :* The end of the verse seems to be an addition referring to the preceding poem on Babylon. The "misfortune" must have been in a much shorter form. **61.** Seraiah has to read the content of the book; we presume that the reading has been done privately, for the divulgation of the oracle in Babylonia would have been quite imprudent. After all, Jeremiah has just assured the exiles that such a downfall of Babylon would be long coming, so that they would have to settle in their new land (cf. ch. 29). **62.** Probably another addition borrowed from the preceding poem (50:3; 51:26). We will never know what was written in the book, and the redactor of the present narrative did not know either. **63–64.** This action is prophetical (cf. comment on 13:1–14), dramatizing the word of doom on Babylon by the sinking of the book in the Euphrates. *weary themselves:* The last word of v. 58 is *weyā'ēpû*, and the redactional note ("Thus far the history [or words; cf. comment on 1:1] of Jeremiah") probably followed it immediately. When the present pericope (vv. 59–64) was introduced here, the note, wrongly separated from its primitive contest, was put after it.

121 **(VI) An Historical Appendix (52:1–34).** This last chapter, a later addition as 51:64 testifies, reproduces 2 Kgs 24:18–25:30, with the exception of 25:22–26, which is Gedaliah's story, recorded in greater detail in Jer 40–41. In the present exposition, we shall limit ourselves to the main differences between the two texts; we refer to the commentary on Kgs (→ 10:77–78) for the remaining parts. **20.** *twelve oxen of bronze:* They are not mentioned in 2 Kgs 25:16, and with reason, for Ahaz gave them as a tribute to Tiglath-pileser III (2 Kgs 16:17–18). **28–30.** The verses are missing in both 2 Kgs and the LXX. A special source, following the Babylonian chronology, has been used; nothing can disprove its historical value. *seventh year:* According to the Babylonian practice of postdating, the accessional year is not counted; thus, Nebuchadnezzar's first regnal year was 604; the first deportation occurred, then, in 597. But the Heb computation takes the accessional year as the first regnal; hence, 2 Kgs 24:12 dated it in the king's eighth year. *eighteenth year:* Both 2 Kgs 25:8 and Jer 52:12 have "nineteenth" for the same reason. *twenty-third year:* This third deportation, in the year 582–581, is known only from the present source. Some historians explain it as a reprisal against Gedaliah's murder, while others would rather believe that in the same year Judah joined in the Ammonite-Moabite revolt, which Nebuchadnezzar mastered (Josephus, *Ant.* 10. 181–82). A final solution has not yet been reached. Moreover, there is a great difference in the number of the deported people. The Book of Kings gives only the number of the first deportation (2 Kgs 24:14,16): 10,000 and 8000! These figures are certainly round numbers and much too high. Those given here, being so precise, must come from official lists of deportees; although we cannot suspect their authenticity, they still could represent only special categories of people and would not constitute the exact number.

This section of Kgs has been reproduced here probably to show how Jeremiah's prophecies were fulfilled. As he so constantly repeated, Jerusalem was to be destroyed and Judah sent into exile. With the liberation of Jehoiachin, his hope in the future was given a first sign of realization.

20

POST-EXILIC PERIOD: SPIRIT, APOCALYPTIC

Carroll Stuhlmueller, C.P.

BIBLIOGRAPHY

Bloch, J., *On the Apocalyptic in Judaism* (*JQR* 2; Phila., 1952). Bonsirven, J., *Le Judaïsme Palestinien* (2 vols.; Paris, 1934). Bousset, W. and H. Gressmann, *Die Religion des Judentums im späthellenistischen Zeitalter* (3rd ed.; Tübingen, 1926). Burkitt, F. C., *Jewish-Christian Apocalypses* (Schweich Lectures; London, 1914). Buttenweiser, M., "Apocalyptic Literature," *JE* 1, 675–85. Černý, L., *The Day of Yahweh and Some Relevant Problems* (Prague, 1948). Charles, R. H., *A Critical History of the Doctrine of a Future Life* (London, 1899); *Religious Development Between the Old and the New Testaments* (N.Y., 1914); *APOT*. Charles, R. H., and W. O. E. Oesterley, "Apocalyptic Literature," *Encycl Brit* 2 (19th ed.; Chicago, 1951) 102–105. Frey, F.-B., *VDBS* 1, 326–54. Frost, S. B., *Old Testament Apocalyptic* (London, 1952). Gunkel, H., *Schöpfung und Chaos* (2nd ed.; Göttingen, 1921). Jansen, E., *Juda in der Exilszeit* (Göttingen, 1956). Ladd, G. E., *JBL* 76 (1957) 192–200. Lagrange, M.-J., *Le Judaïsme avant Jésus-Christ* (3rd ed.; Paris, 1931). Moore, G. F., *Judaism in the First Centuries of the Christian Era* (3 vols.; Cambridge, Mass., 1927–30). Oepke, A., "(apo)kalyptō," *ThWNT* 3, 567–97. Plöger, O., *Theokratie und Eschatologie* (2nd ed.; Neukirchen, 1962). Rist, M., *IDB* 1, 157–61. Rowley, H. H., *Jewish Apocalyptic and the Dead Sea Scrolls* (London, 1957); *PCB* 484–88; *The Relevance of Apocalyptic* (2nd ed.; London, 1947). Russell, D. S., *Between the Testaments* (London, 1960); Torrey, C. C., "Apocalypse," *JE* 1, 669–75. Vawter, B., "Apocalyptic: Its Relation to Prophecy," *CBQ* 22 (1960) 33–46.

2 OUTLINE

THE HISTORICAL DEVELOPMENT FROM PROPHECY TO APOCALYPTIC

When the Babylonian army destroyed Israelite independence and marched the people into exile in 587, they struck at the very heart of biblical life. They demolished what had seemed essential to religion and therefore indestructible—i.e., the Jerusalem Temple and its ritual, the possession of the promised land, and the privileges of the Davidic royalty. The "Israelite" was henceforth to be called the "Jew." Thought patterns dissolved and reshaped in new ways; styles of speaking and writing underwent profound modification. Among the important literary developments was the evolution of "prophetic preaching" into "apocalyptic writing." This article seeks to retrace the steps of this transformation, and, from this historical study, to define the dominant features of apocalyptic.

Apocalyptic derives from the Gk *apokaluptein*, "to unveil" or "to reveal." In the OT, this Gk word generally translates the Hebr *gālâ* (cf. E. Hatch and H. Redpath, *A Concordance to the Septuagint* [vol. 1, Graz, 1897] 131–32). Because a vision is usually unveiled before the eyes of the apocalyptist, we might add that the Hebr word best corresponding to this idea is *ḥāzôn* (vision).

3 Three major periods of Israelite history deserve attention: the last days of the royalty, when the dynamic thrust of David and the golden hopes of Solomon crashed into ruin; the fiery crucible of the exile, when the most sacred traditions were re-evaluated and revitalized through the efforts of Ezekiel and Deutero-Isaiah; the post-exilic age, when theocratic Judaism emerged. Our purpose, however, is not primarily historical, but neither will we feel obliged to present a full account of the religious movements within Israel. We concentrate on a form of speech—one as important to the Bible as prophecy—to observe how religious and political factors recast it into apocalyptic.

4 **(I) The Late Pre-exilic Age (640–587).** This span of years is unforgettable because of two, very significant events: the prophetic revival, inspired by Jeremiah; the deuteronomic reform, championed by Josiah. This period will end in the destruction of Jerusalem by the forces of Nebuchadnezzar. The tragic moment becomes one of the "continental divides" of biblical history, separating and profoundly affecting everything that happened before and after it.

5 **(A) The Prophetic Revival.** We have a ready explanation for Josiah's reversal of the anti-Yahwist policy of the previous kings and inauguration of a religious reform. The reason was not simply the king's courage and piety, both of which he undoubtedly possessed. In the seventh year of his reign, the Assyrian monarch Ashurbanipal was dead (668–633), and at his funeral Assyrian power was solemnly and irrevocably laid to rest. His successor could not hold back the tide of destruction, sweeping in from every side, from the Scythians in the north, the Medes in the southeast, the Babylonians in the southwest. Just one year after the funeral, the Chronicler informs us, this king "... began to seek the God of David his father; and in the twelfth year [the same year that Nineveh, the capital city of Assyria, collapsed before the combined forces of the Medes and Persians, Josiah proceeded] to cleanse Judah and Jerusalem" of Assyrian gods (2 Chr 34:3). This action amounted to a declaration of independence from Assyria. Cries for independence had been suppressed for centuries; now they erupted from every side of the empire.

This tumultuous rise and fall of world empires resounded profoundly in the prophetic preaching of Jeremiah, Zephaniah, and Nahum. They reintroduced the day of the Lord motif, first heard over a century earlier. Amos had announced it as a day of "darkness and not light" (Am 5:18) and Isaiah of Jerusalem as "that day" when men will "hide in the dust from the terror of the Lord" (Is 2:10–11). The phrase rang out the devastating news that God must hurl a whirlwind of destruction through the sinful world (Zeph 1:2–3). Nahum the optimist, turned the phrase into "the bearer of good news, announcing peace" to Judah; but Judah's enemy, he announced, "is completely destroyed" (Na 2:1). Therefore, even before the Exile the prophets had already declared that God would destroy totally all opposition to his hopes and promises, whether among his own people or in the world at large. The apocalyptists will take up this note of prophetic preaching and sound the day of the Lord with even more strenuous determination.

6 Not only in Jerusalem were thunderous outcries and weird premonitions being heard; the whole civilized world was reeling under the shuddering impact of mighty Assyria, sending ruthless armies through the world, scaling heights of power, and then suddenly collapsing in fire and smoke, leaving behind only charred ruins soon to be totally forgotten under desert sands. An eerie fear of the uncontrollable gods reveals itself in the official documents of this time (cf. Albright, *FSAC* 316; Bright, *Hist.* 298). Nebuchadnezzar (from 605–604 to 562) ordered some royal inscriptions to be composed in the long-discontinued script and language of early Babylon; Nabonidus' antiquarian interest (556–539) induced him to dig up some of the ancient sites of Babylon and later to retire to the desert sanctuary of Tema to restore the primitive cult and ritual. Earlier, an Assyrian king of Babylon had employed the long-dead Sumerian tongue. In Egypt, the kings of the 26th Dynasty, who reigned between 660 and 525, made every effort to recapture the glory of the Pyramid Age (2800–2400). Certain characteristics of the apocalyptists may be traceable, at least in part, to these influences—i.e., their interest in ancient personages and events, and their expectation of cosmic wars, leading to Yahweh's universal kingdom.

7 As we seek to trace the prophetic influence upon the apocalyptists, we must devote attention to one of the greatest of the pre-exilic prophets—the timid, highly emotional, extremely sensitive man from "Anathoth in the land of Benjamin," Jeremiah (Jer 1:1). In many ways his character is the complete reversal of the apocalyptists' attitude. He could never submerge the very subjective "I" beneath the texture of his discourse. Personal references, even of a very delicate nature, were continually coming to the surface. The apocalyptists, on the contrary, will assume fictitious names and speak in such a stereotyped style that they become almost faceless. Jeremiah dealt with individual persons and particular situations; the apocalyptists will sweep across the world in grandiose fashion and watch "thousands upon thousands... ministering to... the Ancient One [enthroned amidst] flames of fire, [while innumerable]... holy ones of the Most High... receive the kingship" (Dn 7:9–10,18). But prophetic preaching prepared for apocalyptic writing when it insisted upon the cosmic effects of Judah's sins: "Be amazed at this, O heavens, and shudder with sheer horror" (Jer 2:12). Jeremiah used the rare word *tōhû* (cf. Gn 1:2), which leveled "chaos" across the land of Judah and made its "cities lie waste and empty" (4:7). We can cite other texts to demonstrate the close bond between the cosmos and Israel (Jer 4:23–36; 5:22–23; 9:9; 10:10–13; 27:5–6). Jeremiah is important here, not because he contributed anything new to the message of Zephaniah and Nahum, but because his popularity, after his death, secured an important place in later literature for this cosmic dimension of human behavior.

Although the personalism of Jeremiah was different from the collectivism of the apocalyptists, one feature of his preaching may have indirectly but profoundly influenced the latter. His recognition of the individual's worth and responsibility clearly announced that it was not enough merely to be an Israelite; implicit in this belief is the recognition that Gentiles can be absorbed into the final kingdom of Yahweh. They can fulfill the individual requirements of a right spirit. The apocalyptists, as we shall see, will approach the problem of universality in a much different way, but they did insist that the whole world is to be involved in the new creation kingdom. In the same chapter where Jeremiah stated most emphatically his thesis on individualism (31:29–30), he also proclaimed the new creation (31:22) and the new covenant (31:31–34). The two ideas of individualism and universality will also appear together in Ez (Ez 18:2; 36:26; 37:26). We can trace a chain of influence from the pre-exilic prophets through Jeremiah and Ezekiel to the apocalyptists.

Finally, in any discussion of prophetic influence upon the apocalyptists, we must mention the impact upon them of unfulfilled prophecies (or predictions or promises; cf. R. E. Murphy, *CBQ* 26 [1964] 349–59). The "seventy years" (Jer 25:12; 29:10) turns up repeatedly in the apocalyptic works (Zech 1:12; 7:2; Dn 9:2; *Enoch* 85–90) and is a source of quandary and speculation. When fulfillment was delayed, the apocalyptists sought to look more deeply into the book of divine secrets (cf. Charles and Oesterley, *op. cit.*).

8 (B) The Deuteronomic Reform of Josiah. This religious movement left its mark upon the apocalyptists. Direct relationship is difficult to establish, but we detect both a close sequence of time and a convergence of dominant features. Three characteristics of the deuteronomic movement—very evident in Jos, Jgs, Sm, Kgs—will reappear among the apocalyptists: a theology of history; an actualization of the past; an hostility to the Jerusalem Zadokite priests. There is, first of all, the deuteronomic theology of history, clearly enunciated in Jgs 2:6–3:6. It is summed up in the inevitable succession of sin—sorrow—compunction—salvation. Sin always weakens Israel, exposing her to devastation and suffering; in the helplessness of her sorrow, Israel cries out to God with compunction. "The Lord [then] took pity on their distressful cries of affliction" (Jgs 2:18). The D preachers discovered this theme repeating itself in Israelite history (cf. 2 Kgs 17), and summarized it very forcibly in its series of curses and blessings (Dt 27–28). Moreover, a similar pattern will be discernible in apocalyptic literature: A sinful universe erupts into fearful battle, but out of these eschatological woes there suddenly dawns the new age. The apocalyptic style of curses and blessings will dominate the eschatological discourse of Jesus (cf. Mt 23–25; W. G. Kümmel, *Promise and Fulfillment* [Naperville, Ill., 1957] esp. ch. 2; for bibliography, see 9–14, 156–57; in general, see R. Schnackenburg, *God's Rule and Kingdom* [N.Y., 1963]).

Another controlling feature of deuteronomic preaching is its penchant to view the present as an actualization of the past (cf. Von Rad, *OT Theology I* 69, 72; G. von Rad, *Studies in Deuteronomy* [Naperville, Ill., 1953] 74–91). The Deuteronomist explains the mysterious working of salvation within each generation as a repetition of the Mosaic covenant on Mt. Horeb (Dt 5:1–5). Dt views the past not as a series of inflexible laws, but as many sustaining helps for security and happiness (Dt 1:21,31; 4:1–8; 8:1–5). God is awesome and inscrutable (4:32–36; 5:22–24; 10:14,21), but nothing is so mysterious about God as his goodness and love (Dt 4:31,37; 6:4–12; 7:6–9; 10:15). The apocalyptic writers will lack much of the tenderness of Dt, for they insist upon the wondrous and awesome presence of God, renewing the great, salvific acts of former ages, and thus transforming the world into the promised paradise. They will, however, present their account almost completely in the nomenclature of ancient days.

A third influential factor of Dt, possibly contributing to apocalyptic style and spirit, is its independent and even antagonistic attitude toward the Jerusalem priesthood. In an effort to renew the religious life of Judah, Josiah employed the legislation, traditions, and personnel of the former, northern kingdom of Israel. Ezekiel, Zechariah, and other early representatives of the apocalyptic movement will be staunch members of the priestly circle of Jerusalem, and to that extent opposed to the liberal tendencies of Dt. Dt wanted to open the priesthood to all Levites (Dt 18:1–8), but without success (Ez 44:10ff.; cf. 2 Kgs 23:9). After 250, however, the apocalyptic movement no longer found its leadership among the Jerusalem priests, who were becoming more and more conservative and restrictive. Groups like the Pharisees and the Qumran covenanters, who reacted against the established Sadducean priesthood, continued the apocalyptic belief in angels, cosmic war, and world transformation. It is difficult to establish any direct connection between the deuteronomic movement in history and this very late form of the apocalyptic movement, but the similarities are too great to be overlooked. Dt, it must be remembered, is one of the most copied books among the DSS, is quoted at least 83 times in the NT, and provides an important clue to the eschatological community of the early Acts of the Apostles.

(Cross, F. M., Jr., *The Ancient Library of Qumran* [Garden City, N.Y., 1958] 34. Milik, J. T., *Ten Years of Discovery in the Wilderness of Judaea* [Naperville, Ill., 1959] 23. MacKenzie, R. A. F., *CBQ* 19 [1957] 299–305. Schmitt, J., *RScRel* 27 [1953] 209–218. Stanley, D. M., *CBQ* 18 [1956] 243–44.)

9 (II) The Exilic Age (587–539). Exiled in Babylon and Egypt, with nothing left but the word of the Torah and the threats of the persecuted prophets, the people meditated long upon that word and those threats. This meditation was genuine, realistic, and heroic, and it expressed itself in the writings of Ezekiel and Deutero-Isaiah.

10 (A) Ezekiel. In this man, particularly, the formative elements of the apocalyptic style combined and produced the standard "model" for several centuries to come. Both in the first part of his book, where his prophetic office predominates (1–24, 33–37), and in the last part, where the priestly concern is more manifest (40–48), he acts, speaks, and writes as an apocalyptist. Chapters 25–32, 38–39, which present the oracles against the nations and Gog, require separate treatment. We are baffled by many features of Ezekiel's style: the enigmatic vagueness of his approach; the weird signs and symbols heaped one upon another; the necessity of angelic mediators to explain the visions; the great reversals from total destruction to complete renewal. In these details we can identify the essential elements of apocalyptic style. Even if a later editor, as we readily admit, rearranged the Prophet's message, Ezekiel remains an outstanding example of prophet-become-apocalyptist.

Unlike the preceding "writing prophets," Ezekiel not only spoke but also acted symbolically, enigmatically. In his actions he was "a sign for the house of Israel" (12:6,11; cf. 4:3; 24:24,27). He cut his hair and then proceeded to burn one-third of it, place another third within the city and strike it with a sword, and let another third be scattered by the wind (ch. 5). Curious "apocalyptic" actions such as these, performed in weird silence, became all the more terrifying when explained: "This is Jerusalem!" (5:5).

Many causes were at work, influencing this apocalyptic style of action that flowed over into an intense apocalyptic style of writing. Some of the impulse came from the earlier prophets, who were at times commissioned during supernatural visions (Am 9:1–9; Is 6). Ezekiel's own ecstatic experiences, no doubt, contributed most decisively to his apocalyptic mannerisms (cf. A. Gelin, R–F 1, 539; P. Auvray, *RB* 67 [1960] 481–502). His visions, as described in chs. 1–3, 8–11, and 37 (vv. 1–14), were so overwhelmingly spectacular that they burst the confines of words and grammar.

Ezekiel's apocalyptic style appeared not only in the fact that he was a man of signs but also in the fact that he was a man of the book. He persistently clothed his ideas in the imagery of very ancient, sacred traditions: cherubim (Ez 1; Gn 3:24; Ex 37:7; P. Dhorme and L. Vincent, *RB* 35 [1926] 328–58, 481–95; *BibLex* 353–56); Noah, Daniel, and Job (Ez 14:14; 28:3; Gn 6:9ff.); the dependency of Ez 21:32 upon Gn 49:10 (cf. W. L. Moran, *Bib* 39 [1958] 405–25); the creation story in Ez 28:11–19 (cf. Gn 2:4b–3:24); and the prophecies against Gog of Magog (Gn 10:2 and 1 Chr 1:5 place Magog among the descendants of Japheth; in Nm 24:7 [LXX; Sam], we hear of Gog instead of Agag; and in Am 7:1 [LXX], Gog is the leader of the swarm of locusts; rabbinical literature made frequent references to Gog and Magog; cf. J. Bonsirven, *Textes rabbiniques* [Rome, 1955] n. 231, 473, 1903, 1979). This practice of describing the contemporary scene with stage effects from the very distant past will be more evident in later apocalyptists, e.g., Daniel.

Another, and perhaps the most important aspect of his character, is his position as priest. It is Ezekiel the priest who will dominate the future history of Judaism, eventually transforming it into a priestly controlled theocracy (cf. T. Chary, *Les prophètes et le culte à partir de l'Exil* [Paris, 1955]). Ezekiel's priestly office will have its impact upon post-exilic literature, especially that of the apocalyptic genre. A noticeable feature of both the ancient liturgy and the late, apocalyptic writing is the war, fought between Yahweh and his world-wide enemies. In the liturgical hymns and ceremonies, led by the priests, Yahweh is on the point of achieving a final victory over all other nations and gods (Pss 7:7–9; 9:5–9; 18; 82; 93; 95; etc.). The apocalyptic literature envisaged an eschatological struggle between good and evil, conducted almost as though it were a liturgical ceremony, with the final victory centered in Jerusalem (Zech 2:5–27; 3:1–10; 4:1–3,11–14; 8; 9:8,9–10; 12–14; Jl; Jdt; 1QSa; 1QM). These struggles not only involved the gods of other peoples, but the apocalyptists frequently described this hostility in mythological terms. Ezekiel the priest has the best claims for the honor of channeling this liturgical pattern into post-exilic thought and literature; but other influences were also at work, inducing this penchant for mythological language (cf. J. Barr, *VT* 9 [1949] 1–10). We have already mentioned the mythological references in Ez: the cherubim in chs. 1–3; the paradise motif in 28:11–19; the giants of the primeval age in chs. 38–39. Only through the overwhelming influence of a prophet-priest like Ezekiel, however, could these pagan religious stories and references have survived among the narrow-minded, chauvinistic Jews after the Exile (cf. Hag 2:10–14; Ezr 4:1–5; 9–10; Jl 4).

One final detail deserves mention; Ezekiel certainly occupies an important place in the continuity of the P tradition of the Pentateuch. Although he was to absorb the spirit and vocabulary of the Holiness Code (Lv 17–25), he also left his own imprint upon its closing chapter (26; cf. H. Cazelles, *Le Lévitique* [BJ; Paris, 1951] 16). This fact is important because of the apocalyptists' abundant use of the Pentateuch. Their favorite stories were creation, the flood narrative, the mysterious names of the pre- and post-diluvian patriarchs, the disappearance of Enoch, and the tables of nations. Another aspect of the P tradition to have an impact upon the apocalyptists is P's concept of a divine covenant with all mankind (Gn 1:26; 9:1–17), which will be realized through Israel (Gn 12:1–3; cf. Plöger, *op. cit.*, 42–44).

11 **(B) Deutero-Isaiah.** The other great prophet of the Exile is the unknown author of chs. 40–55 in the Isaian scroll, whom we call, for want of a better name, Deutero-Isaiah. His influence upon post-exilic thought does not seem to have been very great, perhaps because the people were too greatly disappointed when his golden dreams never came true, or because his demands were too taxing upon their spirit of faith (→ Deutero-Isaiah, 22:2–6). We mention Deutero-Isaiah here because an historical study of biblical doctrine is incomplete without a reference to this prophet, one of the most gifted in spiritual perception and literary expression. It is also true that many of the controlling features of apocalyptic literature appeared already in Dt-Is, several of which we shall mention.

According to Dt-Is, the secrets of the eschatological age are first spoken in the divine assembly of Yahweh and his angels; they then echo upon earth, to be heard by the prophet (cf. comment on Is 40:1). Yahweh appears supreme in his majesty, unsearchable in his wisdom (Is 40:10,12–24; 41:13–14,29; 42:8). He not only possesses the fullness of life and knows the secrets of every earthly event, but he is also responsible for the chaos of the Exile and the glory of the new creation (Is 41:4–5, 21ff.; 42:9; 43:9–13; 51:9–11). The Prophet even tells of the new creation in mythological language of a struggle between Yahweh and the evil "gods." But for Deutero-Isaiah, the struggle is past and the gods are reduced to helplessness (44:9–20; 46:1–2). The devastating defeat of these gods may have been the compelling reason why he insisted so repeatedly upon Yahweh's creative power (40:28; 41:20; 42:5; 45:6–7).

These factors can be summarized as follows: the day of the Lord motif, with its terror and hopes, involving Gentiles as well as Jews; the vision of a new covenant that will fulfill, and even surpass, the Mosaic covenant; the actualization of history, found in the deuteronomic tradition; the deuteronomic revolt against the exclusive demands of the Jerusalem priests and their Torah; Deutero-Isaiah's vision of battle among the gods, with Yahweh supreme in his new creation, accomplished through the omnipotent word falling upon earth from the secret, heavenly council; and, finally, the overwhelming influence of Ezekiel, priest and prophet—the man of signs, who stylized his words in the form of visions and symbols, and the man of the book, who became responsible for the dominant liturgical spirit of Judaism and its intense loyalty to the P tradition. Apocalyptic is partly explained as the combination of all these elements, which were present in one way or another in the earlier prophetic movement. It was not so much the parts as their unique combination, under the catalytic force of the Exile, that produced something new. Post-exilic thinking will further strengthen that combination by giving special attention to such features as weird symbolism, cosmic, almost unearthly complications, antiquity renewed, and the eschatological age at hand.

12 **(III) Post-exilic Judaism (539 onward).** With the fall of Babylon before the Persian forces of Cyrus II (the Great) in 539, a new, but obscure, chapter in Israelite history begins. A new community is formed, which looks to the past in an effort to understand itself, but also looks to the future.

13 **(A) The Persian Age (539–332).** The apocalyptic movement will now feel the impact of an anti-Gentile spirit, the demise of prophetism, and the eschatological psalms. (See J. Touzard, *RB* 13 [1916] 302–26; *RB* 14 [1917] 451–88; *RB* 15 [1918] 336–402; *RB* 16 [1919] 5–88.)

14 (a) An Anti-Gentile Spirit. The post-exilic community tended to isolate itself from its neighbors (mixed marriages in Ezr 10, Neh 13; cf. also Ezr 4), an attitude that slowly crystallized into intolerance. There always lived, of course, devout Jews with a large, universal interest, who recognized the goodness of the foreigners. The beautiful pastoral story of Ruth serves to mollify the cruel, adamant stand against mixed marriages by showing that David's ancestor was a devout Moabite woman. The author of Jonah, in a story that bitterly attacked the narrow-mindedness of his coreligionists, showed that there were many good pagans who were included in God's mercy. But these authors were outdone by the larger number who despised foreigners, and among the latter, more popular group we must include the apocalyptist.

The causes of this attitude extended beyond the fact of a narrow, confined way of life in Judah. A fear of pagan, religious infiltration was understandable; it was the Canaanite fertility rites, and their superstitious concern over ritual, as well as the foreign alliances of the royal party in pre-exilic Jerusalem, that drove the Israelites headlong into the debacle of the Exile. They must not repeat past errors; they must keep themselves uncontaminated of Gentile impurity (Hag 2:10–14; Zech 5:5–11; revision of the Holiness Code in Lv 17–26). Therefore, they rejected any offer of help from the local, non-Jewish inhabitants in the rebuilding of the Temple (Ezr 4:1–5); this decision of Zerubbabel and Joshua clearly placed a no man's land of hatred between Jew and Samaritan. Other causes also existed for this growing antagonism against the foreigners; e.g., Israel never forgot how the Edomites attacked them as they fled before the Babylonians and then looted their defenseless country (cf. Is 34:5–17; 63:1–6; Ob 1:2–3).

Although Persian policy was apparently paternalistic, there were certainly high-handed minor officials; there were also periods of general revolt when the monarchs felt obliged to tighten controls and suppress initiative. Darius I Hystaspis (521–486) had to fight his way to the throne and extinguish the revolts that had flared up throughout the empire (→ Haggai, 23:2; Zechariah, 23:12–15). According to some historians, Artaxerxes II Mnemon (404–359) placed a heavy fine on the Jews for some unknown reason (W. Oesterley and T. H. Robinson, *History* II, 139–40). Later, *ca.* 351, the Jews seemed to have been involved in a rather general revolt against Persia. Artaxerxes III Ochus (358–338) put down this insurrection with great severity; Bagoses, his general, led the attack against the rebels (Josephus, *Ant.* 11. vii, 1; cf. Jdt). During these periods of violent upheavals and crushed hopes, we can possibly locate the composition of such energetic, anti-Gentile outbursts as the apocalyptic works of Ezekiel (38–39; if not to be attributed to the man himself), Isaiah (chs. 24–27), Deutero-Isaiah (63:1–6), Obadiah, Zechariah (chs. 9–12), and Joel. The apocalyptists, as Rowley has pointed out, gradually moved into a position of sanctioning revolt. In this attitude they differed from the pre-exilic prophets, who seldom if ever favored the wars that the pro-Egyptian party in Jerusalem stirred up against the Assyrian, and later the Babylonian, masters (Is 8:12; 10:5ff.; 19–20; 39; Jer 26–29; Ez 17). The apocalyptists, however, were not so much in favor of revolt as they counseled fortitude under persecution (Rowley, *The Relevance of Apocalyptic*, 17–20). This feature will become very prominent during the succeeding Hellenistic age.

15 (b) The Demise of Prophetism. Prophetism is now silent. A last gasp is heard *ca.* 460 in the preaching of Malachi, but even in his case the prophet is being judged by the Torah, his position is thoroughly subservient to the Levitical priest, and his hopes center around the Temple. Almost the same evaluation applies to Haggai and Zechariah, whose ministry occurred some 80 years before Malachi. Although Zechariah, at least, condemned social abuses (1:4; 7:9–10), he relied upon the priesthood to gain a hearing (chs. 3–5). In the post-exilic age, preaching no longer strove primarily to instill personal goodness and social justice; its goal was the careful functioning of the liturgy. Formerly, the prophets braved the wrath of priests to hurl judgment upon the nation; now, prophecy is subjected to the Torah and is judged by the priests (cf. Charles, *Religious Development*, 41). If for no other reason than this subservience of prophecy to clerical control, the name "prophecy" no longer fits the new phenomenon. Biblical commentators apply the term "apocalyptic" to what has become a distinctly new religious movement.

Part of the prophetic mantle fell upon the wise man, who became the mentor of the Jewish conscience. The decline of prophetism helps to explain the vigorous upsurge of the sapiental movement; it rushed in to fill the gap. When a new edition of Prv appeared, the editor seems very conscious that the wise man was not only continuing the prophetic office but even correcting its present abuses and excesses. In a long introduction to Prv, the editor inserted many prophetic phrases (Prv 1–9; cf. A. Robert, *RB* 43 [1934] 42–68, 172–204, 374–84; *RB* 44 [1935] 344–65, 502–25). If we are correct in judging the editor's mind, he was cleverly indicating that although the prophets have degenerated into apocalyptic dreamers, the true prophetic role is now performed by the wise man. Apparently little sympathy exists between these two movements.

16 What has happened to prophecy is clearly evident in Jl, composed *ca.* 400 as a temple sermon (cf. M. Delcor, *RB* 59 [1952] 396–99; Chary, *op. cit.*, 194). The preacher quotes frequently from the earlier prophets: Jl 2:27 from Is 45:5,18,22; 46:9; Jl 3:5 from Ob 17; Jl 4:9 from Jer 6:4 and Mi 3:5; Jl 4:18 from Ez 37:1ff. and Zech 13:1. Although Joel certainly expected sincerity (2:13), he did not implement this demand, as the earlier prophets had done, by a summons to social justice, marriage fidelity, and plain living. Joel is concerned, rather, with fasting, sackcloth, sacrifices, oblations, and prayers. The setting of his proclamation is a temple ceremony; the leaders are not prophets but elders and priests (1:2,13). He unifies his sermon around the great and awesome day of the Lord, when "the earth trembles [and] the heavens shake," when "my people shall nevermore be put to shame" and "I will pour out my spirit upon all mankind" (Jl 2:10,27; 3:1; cf. J. Bourke, *RB* 66 [1959] 5–31, 191–212). In a final, panoramic sweep, Joel pictures a divinely triumphant day, when all barriers—geographical, social, and nationalistic—will be eliminated. The great powers, the Persians and the Greeks, are not destroyed but only judged "on behalf of my people and my inheritance, Israel" (4:2). For that matter, Joel is a complete optimist. He seldom finds fault with anyone, except the Philistines, Assyrians, and Babylonians, who have long ago disappeared (Jl 4:1–8). In Jl, temple liturgy and cosmic eschatology have triumphed over reform and compunction.

Another example, typical of what has happened to prophecy, is the work of the Chronicler, most probably composed around this same period (400). Both Joel and the Chronicler speak to Judah and Jerusalem; both use the term "Israel" as applying to the one people of God. Whereas Jl provides a good point of comparison with pre-exilic prophecy, 1–2 Chr show what has become of pre-exilic history writing. The Chronicler has two major concerns: the Temple and the Davidic royalty. He records accurately many historical details and quotes carefully from his sources, but he sometimes expands his themes on an eschatological scale. "The three thousand talents of gold...and seven thousand talents of refined silver," which David is said to have amassed for the projected Temple, far exceeded the resources of Palestine (1 Chr 29:4). Furthermore, David is a man without fault—except that he had battled too fiercely for the kingdom of God (28:3)—and he received, like another Moses, the form of the Temple's structure from the spirit (28:19). These important details help us to recognize the real interest of the Chronicler—i.e., not the David who has died but the new David (17:11) who will appear in the great day of the Lord. The Chronicler's work is prophetic history, with heavy midrashic and apocalyptic tendencies.

This study has deliberately avoided any preoccupation with midrash, although this literary genre also emerged from pre-exilic prophecy and shares some elements with apocalyptic: i.e., use of ancient terminology; species of symbolism (or story form); and a sense of fulfillment. Apocalyptic, however, stresses certain features that are usually absent from midrashic works: a mortal struggle involving the entire universe; the final age of the world; pseudonymity; mythological details.

17 (c) THE ESCHATOLOGICAL PSALMS. Finally, to appreciate the eschatological, even "mythical" trends of this age, we must look at the prophetical psalms. "Mythical" is here used in the general sense of unearthly or transcosmic imagery that breaks the boundaries of known reality in its attempt to communicate a sense of divine mystery. We are thinking of psalms such as Pss 95–98. Most probably composed under the influence of both Deutero-Isaiah and the priestly liturgy, these psalms ignore the Davidic pretensions to royalty and see the final moment exploding with wonder and power in the victory of Yahweh: "The Lord is king" (cf. H.-J. Kraus, *Psalmen* 2 [BKAT 15; Neukirchen, 1960] 664–85; 342–45 discuss eschatology and God's world rule).

We will conclude the Persian period, so far as apocalypticism is concerned, by admitting that its writers have not outgrown the norms nor surpassed the style of Ezekiel. The transition, however, from prophecy to apocalyptic is now irreversible. Prophecy is dead, as the author of 1 Mc was to admit poignantly (1 Mc 4:46; 9:27; 14:41; Ez 7:26; Lam 2:9; *Seder Olam* 30; 1QS 9:11). The mark of a Jew is recognized in such external signs as circumcision, Sabbath observance, dietary laws, fasting (Lv 17–26; Is 56:2; 58:1–7; Zech 7:1–6; 8:18–23; Ezr 10). They believed that as a result (or reward?) of this faithful observance of the Law, God will break through the narrow boundaries of post-exilic Judaism and make Jerusalem the world capital; through a mighty outpouring of the spirit, he will shake the earth and darken the sun, and thus fulfill all the ancient promises. Extravagant symbolism is ordinarily employed, especially in Zech 1–6, but not always (Jl). We must await the Hellenistic period before this latter feature of "surrealism" will be firmly set within the apocalyptic genre.

18 **(B) The Hellenistic Age (332–63).** The smashing victories of Alexander the Great revamped world thought and politics but left the tiny, mountain conclave of Judah unchanged in her hopes and practices. Some unhappiness, no doubt, was felt when Alexander permitted the Samaritans to maintain their own temple at Mount Gerizim (cf. A. Alt, *KlSchr* 2 [1953] 359), and from this time onward, the break between Gerizim and Jerusalem was bitter and beyond repair.

Judaism itself, however, gradually separated into two principal groups, which viewed each other with increasing distrust, jealousy, and hatred—the Jerusalem priesthood, later to be called the Sadducees, and a fervent lay sect, later to be called the Pharisees. Zechariah (11:4–17) condemned the priestly leadership; although the language is very symbolic and therefore very vague for us, it must have been blunt and unmistakable to the original audience. The priests maintained a conservative, slavishly literal attachment to the Torah, unwilling to tolerate any new practice or tradition; the Pharisees gave equal attention and reverence to the "oral Torah" with its new applications and modifications of the written law. An example of priestly caution is Jesus Ben Sira (*ca.* 190). The primary or original Hebr text of his work avoided any reference to retribution after death and consistently praised the priesthood and the Law (e.g., Sir 7:17 [cf. Douay secondary text with the primary CCD text]; 24:8–12,22ff.; 44:19–23; 50).

The other position, open to new religious ideas, such as the resurrection of the body and retribution after death, found expression in apocalyptic and midrashic writings (2 Mc 7; Dn 12:1–3; Charles, *Religious Development*, 33–35). If we may judge from one of the earliest, apocalyptic works of the Hellenistic period, Deutero-Zechariah (→ Zechariah, 23:38), the Jewish attitude toward foreigners was serene and even quite generous. Zech 9:7 admits even the neighboring Philistines among "the remnant for our God." The meteoric conquest of Alexander fired the writer with renewed enthusiasm for Yahweh's quick eschatological fulfillment. In a later revision of Deutero-Zechariah, perhaps at the time when the book was put together or still later when Mal was separated from it (→ Zechariah, 23:18), antagonism toward Gentiles, exploding at times into hatred, worked its way into the text (Zech 9:13; 11:1–3; 14:12). The early Jewish benevolence toward Persia, we will recall, had also given way to distrust and then bitterness.

19 History must move forward almost 150 years before the apocalyptic genre burst the confines established for it by Ezekiel and established itself in a transcendent extravaganza of symbolism. Only an occasion of violence could explain such a violent thrust forward in imagery and expression as we find in Dn 7–12 (→ Daniel, 26: 4–5; 26).

The apocalyptic style of Dn manifests, in a most intense way, the spirit and features of this literary genre: imagery that breaks the bonds of earthly existence; explanation of the heavenly secrets by angelic powers; battle between superhuman forces of goodness and evil; expectation of a sudden and glorious breakthrough; appearance of the divine kingdom; attribution to an author who lived before Ezra (in this case, Daniel of the Babylonian Exile). Special attention should be paid to this last feature, because of later apocalyptic literature. A pseudonym may have been employed by the author of Dn, because he was circulating "resistance literature" against hostile authorities (cf. Vawter, *op. cit.*, 41); Dn set a pattern of pseudonymity to which later writers will feel obliged.

There may have been another reason for this use of fictitious names. The Jerusalem priesthood accepted only the Torah, or Pentateuch, as revised by Ezra (cf. 2 *Esdras* 14). There arose a tendency to attribute the apocalyptic works to great personages of the Pentateuch or to prominent heroes in early salvation history. Only thus would the writer get a hearing (cf. Charles, *Religious Development*, 35–46). One final reason for pseudonymity is in the conviction of post-exilic Judaism that true prophecy was vindicated through its fulfillment; this fact becomes evident from the importance of Dt 18:9–22 in later Jewish writing. The authors wrote about the present situation, but they employed the literary form of an ancient prophecy or early vision. This style is similar to the deuteronomic approach: seeking an understanding of salvation within contemporary events by viewing the present through the lenses of sacred history.

20 Very soon after the appearance of Dn, the (Ethiopic) *Book of Enoch* was written; not long after the Maccabean revolt came the *Book of Jubilees*, which divided history, similarly to Lv 25:8ff., into jubilee periods of 49 years each. This book was followed by the earliest edition of the *Testaments of the Twelve Patriarchs*, and then, *ca.* 50 BC, the *Psalms of Solomon*. Apocalyptic had arrived at its full maturity and we can now draw some conclusions and attempt a definition. (→ Apocrypha, 68:9, 16, 25, 45.)

A DESCRIPTION OF APOCALYPTIC

21 Because apocalyptic grew out of prophecy, we can best understand apocalyptic by determining which features of prophecy it stressed or further developed, which details it tended to minimize or forget, and what type of combination it formed to arrive at its own identity (cf. Lagrange, *op. cit.*, 72–90).

The prophets were men of action, rising to the needs of their time by spontaneous, eloquent preaching; the apocalyptists were men of the written word, communicating their message with deliberate, studied effect. The prophets were personally involved in Palestinian politics; the apocalyptists reached out to a cosmic mission. The prophets presented their message as a judgment upon individual events, while the apocalyptists, especially the author of Dn, developed a religious explanation of universal history. The prophets, for the most part, crusaded for the rule of Yahweh over his people, Israel, and championed the cause of the Davidic royal family; the apocalyptists envisaged a world-wide domain for Yahweh and gave less and less and finally no attention to Davidic messianism. Of the essence of the apocalyptic view of history is the conviction that only the direct action of God can transform the world into the new order (Ladd, *op. cit.*, 197). The prophets spoke bluntly about religious abuses and were seldom misunderstood. The apocalyptists wrote symbolically about "visions" that they did not fully understand and that their audience found still more baffling. Angels usually had to be on hand to explain the symbolic vision.

22 Symbolism, in fact, is one of the most characteristic traits of apocalyptic. Almost everything of this earth was used symbolically. The parts of the human body had their value: eyes symbolized knowledge; hands, power; legs, stability; white hair, antiquity or majesty; mouth, divine oracle. Animals counted also for symbolism: the lion for royalty; the ox, strength; the eagle, swiftness; the dragon or sea monster, evil; the lamb, sacrifice; the horns of an animal, power; the wings of a bird, agility. Clothing took on new meaning: a long robe indicated the priesthood; a crown or ring, kingly status. Colors possessed a symbolic status: white radiated joy or victory; blood red, martyrdom; scarlet, luxury and magnificence. Numbers were often enough utilized for what they said beyond their numerical value: 4, the corners of the created world; 7 or 40, perfection; 12, the new Israel or people of God; 1000, a multitude.

Continuing the parallel study of prophet and apocalyptist, we notice that the prophets insisted upon a day of the Lord, sweeping darkness upon the wicked, bringing victory to the elect. The apocalyptists saw the darkness still deeper and the light still more blinding; goodness and evil were interlocked in mortal struggle. For the prophets, this struggle was mostly between the good and the wicked within Israel, but for the apocalyptists it was a world convulsion. The prophets saw the present, sorrowful moment leading to future victory; the apocalyptists watched the heavens open and the future crash into the present.

23 The two key figures in the onward evolution of prophecy into apocalyptic are Ezekiel and the author of Daniel. As a prophet, Ezekiel acquired a place of leadership within this movement, but as a priest, Ezekiel managed to divert this movement in a different direction! He tended to suppress the moralizing role of the prophets and to emphasize the liturgical renewal. God appeared more and more majestic and transcendent; his worship was surrounded with symbolism, angelic ministers, and eschatological fufilllment. All these features of worship began to dominate the literary genre of prophecy, helping to transform it into apocalyptic.

The author of Daniel signaled the liberation of apocalyptic from the priestly group. The Temple and its liturgy remained the center of attention and hopes. By this time (167–164), however, the Jerusalem priests had become rigidly conservative; they rejected many if not all of the new ideas then in the air, especially belief in angels and the bodily resurrection of the elect. After the time of Daniel, apocalyptic literature flourished among the nonpriestly groups, or at least among the non-Jerusalem priests (i.e., at Qumran). Symbolism tended to become more and more exuberant and fantastic. Pseudonyms were used, drawn from the most ancient times, both to give a sense of fulfillment of prophecies and to avoid retaliation from either the civil or the priestly powers.

24 Apocalyptic, then, can be briefly characterized as an exilic and post-exilic development of prophetic style, in which heavenly secrets about a cosmic struggle and eschatological victory are revealed in symbolic form and explained by angels to a seer who writes down his message under the pseudonym of some ancient personage.

In conclusion, we recognize that apocalyptic found its home within the nascent Christian community of the 1st cent. AD (cf. Burkitt, *op. cit.*, 15). Extreme apocalyptic contributed to the great Jewish revolts of AD 60–66 and 132–135. These led to dreadful defeat and near despair. Judaism thereafter abandoned the hope of an imminent breakthrough of Yahweh's world kingdom and based her religion upon the minute practice of the law. Christianity considered herself to be the eschatological triumph of God in Christ Jesus, transforming the world into a new kingdom of the spirit and thereby fulfilling the ancient prophecies. The NT concludes with the Book of the Apocalypse, and its final words cry out for the great, everlasting triumph: "Marana tha"—"Come, Lord Jesus" (Ap 22:20).

21

EZEKIEL

Arnold J. Tkacik, O.S.B.

BIBLIOGRAPHY

1 *Commentaries:* Auvray, P., *Ézéchiel* (BJ; Paris, 1949). Bertholet, A., *Hesekiel* (HAT; Tübingen, 1936). Bewer, J., *The Book of Ezekiel* (N.Y., 1954). Cooke, G., *The Book of Ezekiel* (ICC; N.Y., 1937). Fohrer, G., *Ezechiel* (HAT; Tübingen, 1955). Matthews, J. G., *Ezekiel*, (Phila., 1939). May, H. G., *Ezekiel* (*IB* 6; N.Y., 1956). Muilenburg, J., "Ezekiel," *PCB* (N.Y., 1963) 568–90. Steinmann, J., *Le prophète Ézéchiel* (Paris, 1953). Zimmerli, W., *Ezechiel* (BKAT; Neukirchen, Kreis Moers, 1959).

Other Works: Fohrer, G., *Die Hauptprobleme des Buches Ezechiel* (Berlin, 1952). Harford, J. B., *Studies in the Book of Ezekiel* (Cambridge, 1935). Herntrich, V., *Ezechielprobleme* (Giessen, 1932). Irwin, W., *The Problem of Ezekiel* (Chicago, 1943). Kaufmann, Y., *The Religion of Israel* (tr. M. Greenberg; Chicago, 1960) 426–46. Klausner, J., *The Messianic Idea in Israel* (N.Y., 1955) 108–34. Reventlow, G., *Wächter über Israel, Ezechiel und seine Tradition* (Berlin, 1962). Robinson, H. W., *Two Hebrew Prophets* (London, 1948). Rowley, H. H., "The Book of Ezekiel in Modern Study," *BJRylL* 36 (1953) 146–90. Torrey, C. C., *Pseudo-Ezekiel and the Original Prophecy* (New Haven, 1930).

INTRODUCTION

For each age is an age that is dying
Or one that is coming to birth.
A. W. O'Shaughnessy

2 Perhaps of no age in human history is this quotation more true than of the era represented by the Book of Ezekiel. It would be even more correct to say that in Ezekiel's age, both processes take place in the life span of one man. It is this Prophet who pronounces the death sentence—and in the prophetic perspective it is the beginning of its execution—upon the kingdom with its entire political and religious structure of king, priest, and prophet. His contribution to the birth of the new order is so pregnant that he has been called, rightly or wrongly, the father of Judaism. Despite the distinctive role assigned to the Prophet, however, more conflicting opinions are vigorously advanced by scholars concerning the date and the place, and even the historical existence, of Ezekiel and his ministry, as they appear in the book bearing his name, than for any other OT prophet. This situation, perhaps, is only natural, for in the evolution of any living reality, the disintegrating and emerging forms have a relationship with, and bear a resemblance to, those that have already disappeared and those that are yet to come.

A lively controversy is waged over three basic problems in Ez. What kind of a man was the Prophet? Who was his audience, and where was the scene of his activity? Is there unity of authorship in the book, and if so, was it composed by the 6th-cent. Prophet whose name it bears? (For the historical background of the Prophet, a contemporary of Jeremiah, → Jeremiah, 19:2–3.)

3 **(I) The Man.** Aside from a few scholars who hold the position that Ez is a pseudepigraphon or the equally few who see it almost as an absolute unity from Ezekiel's hand, the vast majority admit that some passages are not the Prophet's work.

The extent of these passages varies, as we shall see, but, regardless of how much material is considered authentic, there arises from the book the figure of the main protagonist, the Prophet called Ezekiel, at first sight one of the strangest persons in the OT. The ordinary problem of the psychological form of God's communication with his prophets is intensified because of Ezekiel's allegedly unusual personality and actions. No other OT writer has received such varied, even diametrically opposed, interpretations of his person and writings. No other prophet has been treated so unjustly by commentators because of personal prejudices. He has been psychoanalyzed and found to be a victim of "catatonic schizophrenia...unconscious sexual regression, schizophrenic withdrawal, delusions of persecution and grandeur" (E. C. Broome, *JBL* 64 [1946] 277–92). According to

R. H. Pfeiffer, "Ezekiel is the first fanatic in the Bible," who shows traces of a "black and savage atrocity of mind" and whose motto was "for the greater glory of God" (Pfeiffer, *Introd.* 543). He has been described as "une âme raide et dure" by J. Steinmann and as betraying "no inward struggle" by G. Cooke. It is difficult to see how such statements could be made in view of passages such as 9:8, 11:13, and, especially, 33:30–32.

In the introduction to his work, Irwin states with keen penetration, "the critical reader of my study will be more concerned with my psychology than with Ezekiel's" (*op. cit.*, x). Ezekiel has been the touchstone of his commentator's bias, whether it was psychological, cultural, or religious. W. F. Albright has called Ezekiel "one of the greatest spiritual figures of all time, in spite of his tendency to abnormality.... The genius of Hebrew prophets is in the fact that they were not normal" (Albright, *FSAC* 248–49). Perhaps we should characterize Ezekiel and all the prophets as unusual rather than abnormal, for even modern psychology is unsure what constitutes a normal personality.

4 What is the view to be taken of Ezekiel's strange actions and visions in which he was transported to distant places? As Cooke points out (*op. cit.*, xxvii), and most commentators agree, some of the symbolic actions "seem incapable of being literally performed." It is the conviction of the present writer that most of the symbolic actions were never acted out. The prophets are primarily preachers; as such, their specialties are parables and allegories. Ezekiel is specifically called "the maker of allegories" (21:5; cf. 17:2). At most, the symbolic actions, with the exception of one or the other—e.g., the two sticks, the absence of any sign of mourning at the death of his wife—were merely dramatic narratives in his sermons.

His visions were probably not ecstasies in the strict sense. Ezekiel has been described as a mystic; indeed, all prophets are mystics, just as all mystics are poets. Thus, his visions are nothing but the keenly experienced reality of God's world by one whose horizon is bounded by God's transcendence and whose world is filled by God's imminent reality. They are very rationally constructed symbolisms inspired by the hold that the all-absorbing reality of God exerts on his imagination and intellect. Ezekiel was not clairvoyant, for he was physically present (see comment on chs. 8–11). He was a normal, but not mediocre, man, as our age tends to define normality. In Ezekiel, we find blended the priest and the prophet, the poet and the theologian, and an organizer of religion as an institution and a preacher of a religion of morality and even mysticism, with the sense of a deep consciousness of the presence and transcendence of God. Most of his commentators are lost when confronted with a role of such breadth and a personality of such depth; therefore, they resort to either the abnormal or the miraculous. Yet in the disintegration of the nation, the future of the Jewish religion "depended upon the preservation of purified institutions" (C. Howie, *Date and Composition of Ezekiel* [Phila., 1950] 84). For such a task, Jeremiah's emotive power was not enough; Ezekiel's harnessed and disciplined emotions were needed.

5 **(II) The Audience.** The problem on which there is the sharpest disagreement even today is the locale of Ezekiel's ministry and the identity of his audience. Traditionally, Ezekiel was thought to have been deported to Babylon in 597, where he received his call and worked all his life among the exiles. Such, at first sight, is the picture that springs immediately from the text (1:1). The first to question the Babylonian setting of the Prophet's activity was C. C. Torrey, who in 1930 maintained that Ezekiel was created by a 3rd-cent. writer who originally set his ministry in the northern kingdom during Manasseh's reign; such idolatry as Ezekiel condemned fits that age and is not to be found after Josiah's reform. A later editor, writing from the chronicler's theological bias, set the ministry of the Prophet in Babylon; he changed a few dates and revised the text to make it appear that the restored people found its origin in the remnant of the captivity and in the authority of a prophet who also made provisions for a new Temple in Jerusalem, thus nullifying the claims of the Samaritans for their own community and sanctuary. In 1931, J. Smith also maintained that northern Israel was the scene of the Prophet's activity, admitting that he was an historical person taken into captivity in 734 who returned to prophesy in Palestine. In 1932, V. Herntrich (*op. cit.*) stated the thesis that others have maintained with little variation—i.e., Ezekiel prophesied in Palestine and a disciple edited the work in the Exile, adding not a little to it (esp. chs. 40–48). Other studies followed maintaining the Prophet's activity in Palestine, before either the deportation of 597, or that of 587; in either case, his prophesying continued in Babylon, and a double ministry is postulated. Scholars are divided almost equally among an exclusively Babylonian ministry, an exclusively Palestinian ministry, and a double ministry. Of the recent commentaries on Ezekiel, G. Fohrer and W. Zimmerli hold a Babylonian ministry and H. G. May, P. Auvray, and J. Steinmann hold a double ministry.

The present work adopts the double-ministry theory, the major portion of which was carried out in Palestine until the destruction of Jerusalem in 587. Our reasons follow. We cannot say that the Babylonian view is traditional, for there is a rabbinic tradition that Ezekiel began his mission in Palestine (S. Spiegel, *JBL* 54 [1935] 169–70; May, *IB* 6, 51). The structure of the prophecy shows the following: two great visions with different locales—the Jerusalem Temple (ch. 8) and the Chebar River (ch. 1); two themes of proclamation—threats (chs. 4–24) and promise (chs. 33–37); two calls—herald of doom (2:3–10) and pastoral office (3:16); commission to bear a message to two different audiences—nation of rebels (2:3–4) and exiles (3:2); corresponding actions in two locales—Jerusalem and the place of Exile. This view is founded in the text, as Fohrer admits—i.e., 2:3; 3:4,15; 8:1–4; 12:3; the present writer would add 14:7,12; 24:5–26. In the last passage, the death of Ezekiel's wife is to be a sign to his hearers that so also they will lose the "delight of their eyes," the Temple (this to exiles already 1000 mi. from it!). Also, a fugitive is to bring news of the destruction of the city on the "very day" that the Temple is destroyed (24:26), which makes sense only if Ezekiel is living as an exile in a village N of Jerusalem. Finally, and most cogently, is it psychologically possible for a man to hurl condemnations and vituperations at an audience 1000 mi. away while he faces an audience of suffering exiles?

6 **(III) The Book.** The difficulties connected with the Book of Ezekiel are proverbial. The rabbis at the time of the closing of the canon found it difficult to reconcile its prescriptions with the Torah. Had it not been for Rabbi Hananiah Ben Hezekiah, who closed himself in a room with food and 300 jars of oil for light to work, according to the Talmud (Mishnah, *Shabbath* 13b; *Menahoth* 45a), until he had explained all the discrepancies, the book would have been suppressed. But even with the work of Hananiah, the difficulties were not solved, for the Talmud (Mishnah, *Menahoth* 45a) states, regarding passages such as Ez 44:31; 45:18, that the problems will be solved only by Elijah when he makes known all truth in preparation for the Messianic age.

Difficulties of another kind are evidenced by Jerome, who notes in his preface to Ez the rabbinical tradition that no one was permitted to read the beginning and the end of the book (also, the beginning of Gn and all Ct) until he reached the age at which priests began their ministry—i.e., 30—because "full maturity of human nature is necessary for perfect knowledge and mystical understanding," such as are called for by the material in these passages (Jerome, *PL* 25. 17).

Modern scholars face different problems: unity, authenticity, date of composition, and the related problem of chronology within the book. Even these subjects, however, have antique beginnings, for Josephus (*Ant.* 10. 6) states that Ezekiel left behind two books and the Talmud notes that "the men of the Great Assembly wrote Ezekiel, the Twelve Minor prophets, Daniel, and the Scroll of Esther" (Mishnah, *Baba Bathra* 15a). Of modern scholars, L. Zunz (1832) was the first to question the authenticity of Ez, and F. Hitzig (1847) was the first to question its unity. Despite this contention, a consensus obtained among modern scholars well into this century, so that A. B. Davidson could say: "The book of Ezekiel is simpler and more perspicuous in its arrangement than any other of the great prophetical books. It was probably committed to writing late in the prophet's life, and unlike the prophecies of Isaiah which were given out piecemeal, was issued in its complete form at once" (*Ezekiel* [Cambridge, 1906] ix). Since then, the situation has changed completely, so that over 25 years ago C. C. Torrey could compare it to a bomb exploding and scattering the pieces in all directions: "One scholar gathers them up and arranges them in one way, another makes a different combination" (*JBL* 58 [1938] 78).

7 The unity of the book has been questioned on several counts. The first involves a series of doublets (e.g., 3:16–21 and 33:1–9; 18:21–25 and 33:10–20), in which R. Kraetzschmar (1900) saw a double recension, one in the first person (1:1) and one in the third person (1:3). G. Hölscher (1924) tried to reduce the original parts of the book to the poetic passages, claiming the poet could not have written the dull prose parts; he thus managed to retain about 170 of the more than 1200 verses as Ezekiel's. Using poetry as a criterion of authenticity, A. Irwin (1943) saved about 250 verses as authentic, seeing in the rest an attempted explanation of the poetry. G. Fohrer (1955) uses the same criterion, but his canons of poetry are more flexible and less rigidly applied. The latest attempt has been made by A. Bruno (1959), whose canons of poetry are a metric strait jacket that evoked the following comment from P. Tournay: "It is difficult to imagine the prophet of Tel Abib indulging in such arithmetically constraining and perfectly useless calculations" (*RB* 68 [1961] 436). H. G. May (1956) draws up a list of over 40 expressions—e.g., "idols" (*gillûlîm*) and the frequent "Then they will know that I am the Lord," which he attributes to an editor without saying why—and declares as secondary any passage in which they are contained; therefore, about 40 per cent is attributed to a 5th-cent. editor.

Today, the presence of redactional material of varied extent is admitted by all. Particular evidence is the oracles of restoration interspersed among the oracles of doom, softening the latter's harshness. It is generally believed that Ezekiel had some hand in the writing of his prophecies, for, in the judgment of many, the book shows more "literary" aspects than that of any other prophet. Of contemporary scholars, most are hesitant about excising sizable portions of the text; in the words of Albright, "Most of the recent critical dissection of Ezekiel is unnecessary" (Albright, *FSAC* 249).

8 The position taken here is that the editor has joined the work of two prophets—Ezekiel, who prophesied both in Palestine and in Babylon, and another prophet, from whom come the visions of the throne-chariot and also chs. 40–48—with minor redactional material present in both sections, which it is practically impossible to separate from the original oracles of the two prophets. The reason for this two-prophets theory is that the visions of the throne-chariot and allied passages lack the directness of the rest of the book; they are too complicated and undisciplined to have come from the same person.

The evolution of Ez may be considered somewhat as follows. Ezekiel preached in Palestine, first in Jerusalem but after a while in some village N of Jerusalem, to which he may have been banished (for which there is some evidence in the text; cf. 3:25–27; 24:25–27). Here he first preached some of his prophecies to a small circle and wrote others with distinct literary character. These prophecies were taken to Babylon, where Ezekiel continued his activity.

9 Dating of Ez is based upon its internal chronological indications. The earliest date is 593 (1:2) and the latest 571 (29:1); all references to dates follow in chronological order, with the exception of 26:1, 29:17, and 33:21. These dates, however, refer to the passages that follow directly. The "thirtieth year" (see comment on 1:1) still remains a puzzle.

The dependence of Ez upon Jer is acknowledged by all. Some go so far as to maintain that Ezekiel must have heard Jeremiah preach; but the similarity can also be extended to other books—e.g., Ez 12:2 can be found in Jer 5:21; Dt 29:4; Is 6:9. Zimmerli has shown that the formula, "they shall know that I am the Lord" has a long prehistory (1 Kgs 20:13,18; Ex 7:17; 9:14; Nm 16:28; Dt 4:35; Jer 24:7; Is 41:17; 45:3; 49:23). The relationship to Lv, especially to the Holiness Code (chs. 17–26), is discussed in the commentary; scholars are generally agreed that Ez shows a dependence on the Holiness Code, but that it is prior to the P tradition (cf. P. Tournay, *RB* 64 [1957] 128).

(Burrows, M., *The Literary Relations of Ezekiel* [New Haven, 1925]. Miller, J., *Das Verhältnis Jeremias und Hesekiels sprachlich und theologisch untersucht* [Assen, 1955].)

10 **(IV) The Message.** Harford writes, "No other book gives us a more sublime vision of the majesty of God" (*op. cit.*, 1), a judgment echoed by A. Weiser (*OT* 230) as "the towering height of his conception of God." However, M. Buttenwieser insists on Ezekiel's inferior spiritual viewpoint, because he was not able to grasp "the real essence of the religious view of the prophets" inasmuch as "the Temple with its cult continued to have for him the mystic, sacramental significance attributed to them by primitive religion" (*HUCA* 7 [1930] 17–18).

The idea of God is the key to Ezekiel's theological and spiritual ideas, for the recognition and acknowledgment of God's holiness is the Prophet's supreme value and the ultimate criterion of God's activity with men. In the constant appeal to Yahweh's holy name and its vindication among the Gentiles, some have seen a rigid and fanatical doctrinal preoccupation that ignores a concern for man's social and ethical welfare. Yet the concepts of the "glory of the Lord," his "holiness," the "sanctification of the divine name," and "the profanation of the divine name" are religious realities, "the depth of whose meaning the modern scholars have not plumbed to this day" (Klausner, *op. cit.*, 117–18). Although holiness may be the essential note of God, it is also the quality that makes him most human, enabling a relationship to be established between him and the people so that his "holy name" will be called upon them and will be the source of life and dignity to them. Because his "holy name" is upon them, there exists the jealousy of an exclusive possession, which, when scorned, is turned to wrath and fury (5:12; 16:42). Because of the "holiness of his name," Yahweh cannot abandon his people to derision (36:5,23), and the sensitive reader can recognize how deeply Ezekiel feels the scorn in which the people are held among the nations. Because they are called by his name, Yahweh is their next of kin, the *gō'ēl* or one who is bound to vindicate their rights and has the first rights of redemption. Yahweh's personal involvement is affirmed by such formulas as "they shall know that I am Yahweh," which expresses an experience of his personal presence to save them (34:11–30).

Inasmuch as Yahweh acts as a *gō'ēl* in redeeming Israel, the messianic prophecies of Ezekiel have a special characteristic—i.e., that the restoration does not come as the result of repentance. The chain as presented in Jgs—sin–punishment–repentance–redemption—is broken and the links change places—sin–punishment–redemption–repentance. Yahweh redeems his people not because they repented, but because of his holy name, which caused him to enter a covenant with them and which will now cause him to restore them. Then they will "know him," be ashamed of their past unresponsiveness, and turn to him (36:31–32; 16:60,62).

11 **(V) The Text.** The MT is corrupt in many passages, necessitating recourse to emendations and conjectural readings. Among others Fohrer (*Ezechiel*, vii) considers it inferior to the LXX, which is more sober and is strongly supported by other versions, and which he considers to be based on an older Hebr exemplar. However, Tournay is not agreed that the Gk text is to be preferred because it is more concise. He considers the prolixity of the Hebr text to be the Prophet's work, whereas the LXX gives an abridged text because the translator left out what he considered useless repetitions (P. Tournay, *RB* 60 [1953] 417). It is generally agreed that the LXX is from the hand of two translators, chs. 1–27 and 40–48 from one, and 28–39 from another; some regard chs. 40–48 as from a third hand.

12 **(VI) Outline.** The book may be divided into two equal parts: chs. 1–24, the oracles of doom; chs. 25–48, the book of restoration. The oracles against the nations are included with the restoration because the judgment against the nations is considered to be an aspect of Israel's salvation. However, chs. 25–32 probably circulated separately at one time, because they interrupt the narrative left off in 24:27 that is then continued in 33:21. Of the rest of ch. 33, vv. 1–9 parallel 3:17–19 and vv. 10–20 parallel 18:21–32; therefore, they are probably not in their original places. This pattern of composition—i.e., doom–salvation—is common in the prophets (Fohrer, *Ezechiel*, xii). In Is, chs. 1–12 are judgments against Judah and Israel, chs. 13–27 against foreign nations, and chs. 28–66, the prophecy of restoration. In Mi, a double pattern is found: doom, 1:1–3:12; restoration, 4:1–5:8; doom, 5:9–7:7; restoration, 7:8–20. The Book of Ezekiel may be outlined as follows:

- (I) Call to Prophesy (1:1–3:27)
  - (A) Superscription (1:1–3)
  - (B) Vision of the Throne-Chariot (1:4–28b)
  - (C) Call and Commissions (1:28b–3:27)
    - (a) First Commission: Mission to Rebels (2:1–7)
    - (b) The Divine Communication (2:8–3:3)
    - (c) Second Commission (3:4–8)
    - (d) Third Commission (3:9–15)
    - (e) Fourth Commission: The Prophet as Watchman (3:16–21)
    - (f) Fifth Commission: The Prophet Under Restraint (3:22–27)
- (II) Prophecies of Judgment and Doom (4:1–24:27)
  - (A) Actions Symbolic of Judgment (4:1–5:17)
    - (a) Symbols of Siege and Exile (4:1–17)
    - (b) The Wrath of Jealousy (5:1–17)
  - (B) Oracles Pronouncing Judgment (6:1–7:27)
    - (a) Against the Mountains of Israel (6:1–14)
    - (b) Against the Land: Near Is the Day of Yahweh (7:1–27)
  - (C) Idolatry in the Temple and Abandonment by Yahweh (8:1–11:25)
    - (a) Foreign Cult in the Temple (8:1–18)
    - (b) Purge of Jerusalem's Idolaters (9:1–11)
    - (c) The Glory of the Lord Abandons Jerusalem (10:1–22)
    - (d) Security and Redemption Only in Yahweh (11:1–25)
      - (i) False security (11:1–13)
      - (ii) Redemption from the Lord (11:14–25)
  - (D) Further Prophecies Against the Land and Jerusalem, Its Rulers, Priests, and Prophets (12:1–24:27)
    - (a) More Symbols of Siege and Exile (12:1–20)
    - (b) Reality of the Word of God (12:21–28)
    - (c) Devastation Wrought by False Prophets (13:1–23)
    - (d) Hypocrisy of Idolaters and Personal Responsibility (14:1–23)
      - (i) Faithless elders and prophets (14:1–11)
      - (ii) Everyone bears his own burden (14:12–20)
      - (iii) Vindication of Yahweh (14:21–23)
    - (e) The Parable of the Wood of the Vine (15:1–8)
    - (f) The Marriage Allegory on Jerusalem (16:1–63)
    - (g) Allegory of the Cedar and the Eagles (17:1–24)
    - (h) The Lord's Way Is Just (18:1–32)
    - (i) Two Elegies on the Royal House (19:1–14)
    - (j) An Historical Survey in Theological Perspective (20:1–44)
    - (k) With Fire and Sword (21:1–37)
      - (i) The parable of fire in the forest (21:1–12)
      - (ii) Song of the sword (21:13–22)
      - (iii) The road is to Jerusalem (21:23–32)
      - (iv) Sword drawn on Ammon (21:33–37)
    - (l) The Docket of Crime Against the Nation (22:1–31)
      - (i) The indictment of Jerusalem and its sentence (22:1–16)
      - (ii) The melting process (22:17–22)
      - (iii) The abuses of civil, social, and religious responsibility (22:23–31)
    - (m) The Story of Two Faithless Sisters (23:1–49)
      - (i) Maidenhood in Egypt and marriage (23:1–4)
      - (ii) The affairs of Oholah (23:5–10)
      - (iii) The affairs of Oholibah (23:11–35)
      - (iv) Judgment of the two sisters (23:36–49)
    - (n) Ezekiel Shall Be a Sign (24:1–27)
      - (i) The allegory of the pot (24:1–14)
      - (ii) Grief too great for mourning (24:15–27)
- (III) Judgment on the Nations (25:1–32:32)
  - (A) Judgment on Israel's Neighbors (25:1–17)
    - (a) Against Ammon (25:1–7)
    - (b) Against Moab (25:8–11)
    - (c) Against Edom (25:12–14)
    - (d) Against the Philistines (25:15–17)
  - (B) Tyre Will Perish from the Seas (26:1–28:26)
    - (a) The Tidal Wave Against Tyre (26:1–21)
    - (b) Lament on the Wreck of the Ship Tyre (27:1–36)
    - (c) Tyre, the Wise and Resplendent, Brought to the Dust (28:1–19)
      - (i) Tyre—A fool's use of wisdom (28:1–10)
      - (ii) Tyre, God's chosen, is cast off (28:11–19)
    - (d) Sidon, the Thorn, Will Pierce No Longer (28:20–24)

(e) Israel Shall Dwell Secure (28:25–26)
(C) Egypt Will Be Turned Into a Desert (29:1–32:32)
(a) Doom of Egypt, the Monster and Reed of the Nile (29:1–9)
(b) Egypt a Wasteland 40 Years (29:10–16)
(c) Nebuchadnezzar's Wages (29:17–20)
(d) Hope for Israel (29:21)
(e) Day of the Lord for Egypt (30:1–19)
(f) Pharaoh's Broken Arms (30:20–26)
(g) Egypt, the Felled Cedar of Lebanon (31:1–18)
(h) Egypt, the River Monster, Will Be Slain (32:1–32)
(IV) Conditions and Process of Restoration (33:1–37:28)
(A) Responsibility of Man—The Prophetic Charge (33:1–33)
(a) Prophet as Watchman (33:1–20)
(b) Fugitive from Jerusalem (33:21–22)
(c) Claims of the Survivors in Judah (33:23–29)
(d) A Prophet of Fashion (33:30–33)
(B) The Shepherd of Israel and His Flock (34:1–31)
(C) Edom To Be Eternally Desolate (35:1–15)
(D) Increase and Be Fruitful, Israel (36:1–38)
(a) Blessing Upon the Mountains of Israel (36:1–15)
(b) Blessing Upon the People of Israel (36:16–38)
(E) O My People, Rise from Your Graves (37:1–14)
(F) One Nation and David, Its Prince Forever (37:15–28)
(V) Triumph of Israel Over All Forces of Hostility (38:1–39:29)
(A) The Prophecy Against Gog (38:1–39:8)
(B) Evil Turned Into a Benefit (39:9–20)
(C) The House of Israel Will Know the Lord, Its God (39:21–29)
(VI) The Vision of the Restored Community (40:1–48:35)
(A) The Vision of the New Temple (40:1–43:27)
(a) The Area Around the Temple (40:1–47)
(b) The Temple Buildings (40:48–41:26)
(c) Other Structures (42:1–20)
(d) The Restoration of the Temple (43:1–27)
(B) The New Cult (44:1–46:24)
(a) The Official Personnel of the Temple (44:1–31)
(b) The Accessories of the Cult: Land and Offerings (45:1–17)
(c) Feasts and Ritual (45:18–46:24)
(C) The New City and the New Land (47:1–48:35)
(a) The Stream of Life-Giving Water (47:1–12)
(b) The Boundaries and Apportionment of the Land (47:13–48:29)
(c) "The Lord Is Here" (48:30–35)

COMMENTARY

13 **(I) Call to Prophesy (1:1–3:27).** We could say that this passage contains the entire Book of Ezekiel, its characteristics and its problems—i.e., the unity, the location of the Prophet's ministry, and the system of dates. After a cursory reading, we are left with an impression of distinct unity. In a recent literary analysis of the passage, however, P. Auvray has shown convincingly the presence of a double introduction and two different prophetic experiences in two different places at two different times with a marked duality of content in the two visions (*RB* 67 [1960] 481–503 = *TD* 12 [1964] 159–65). He has been able to isolate 1:1,4–28a; 3:13–15 as a distinct literary unit, in which visual data are present almost exclusively on a grandiose scale, with a distinctive vocabulary, e.g., *d*^{e}*mût*, "likeness," and *mar'eh*, "appearance" or "resemblance." He points out that these characteristics are concentrated in chs. 1, 8–10, and 40–48. Then, everything changes abruptly with 1:28b. The vision is predominantly auditory and intellectual in the following passage: 1:2–3,28b; 2:1–3:12,22–23. It has its characteristic expressions in "rebellion" and "rebellious house." A hand appears but it is not the "likeness" or "appearance" of a hand. This hand is in no way associated or connected with the vision in ch. 1, and the voice that is heard is also a new factor. There is no greater contrast between two allegedly unitary passages in all of prophetic literature. Zimmerli's labored analysis (*op. cit.*, 35) is unsuccessful; he tries to demonstrate that both auditory and visual elements are present in the tradition of prophetic calls and that just as we cannot separate the two in Is 6, so we cannot separate them in Ez 1–3. But in Is, there exists an essential connection between the theophany and the call and commission of the Prophet; the reappearance of the throne-chariot in Ez 3:13 only accentuates its absence from the previous section.

Furthermore, Auvray concludes that the throne-chariot vision is out of place here. In 43:3 a sequence of the visions of the "glory of the God of Israel" is given: "when he came to destroy the city," i.e., chs. 8–11; "which I had seen by the river Chebar," i.e., 1:4–28a; 3:13–15; the vision of the return to Jerusalem, i.e., 43:2. If this order is correct, it further confirms that the vision is not a part of the Prophet's original call, for it should follow ch. 11. Some scholars holding the double-ministry theory for Ez place this vision at the beginning of the Prophet's Babylon ministry as a renewal of his call. Its displacement to the beginning of Ez would be considered a fitting introduction to the entire book because of its majestic picture of God.

14 **(A) Superscription (1:1–3).** If the two dates in the introduction have the same point of reference, Jehoiachin's captivity (and there is nothing to indicate that they do not), they are the two extreme dates in the book, 593 and 568. There are those who interpret them as two extreme events in Ezekiel's prophetic career—his commission and the collection and publication of his prophecies as a unit; but this idea seems too modern and therefore anachronistic. Possibly "thirtieth" is a corruption for "thirteenth," in which case it suits well as the inaugural vision in Babylon, for those holding the double-ministry hypothesis. Others choose a different point of reference—e.g., the beginning of the previous jubilee year, the birth of the Prophet, the accession of Nebuchadnezzar to the throne, etc.—to arrive at a date harmonious with the "fifth" year of v. 2. If the vision described in this chapter is from another prophet, as we have suggested, then this date probably refers to his inaugural vision and call.

The location given is the river Chebar (Babylonian records: *nâru kabâri*), an irrigation canal that left the Euphrates above Babylon and flowed SE through Nippur to rejoin the Euphrates. At the latter site, excavations have unearthed Jewish names on contracts and other documents (*DOTT* 95–96). In the second date, the time is reckoned from the captivity of Jehoiachin, who seems to have been considered still the rightful king both in Palestine and by the authorities in Babylon (W. F. Albright, *JBL* 51 [1932] 84ff.). Ezekiel (Hebr *y*^{e}*ḥezqēʾl*, "God strengthens") is introduced as a priest, a fact that is amply demonstrated by the doctrinal content and style of his writing. The introduction in the third person is consistent with the introductions to the other prophets, and the switch from the first person indicates the composite nature of the passage. Note the repetition of place, and also of the formula of revelation in v. 3. **3.** *hand of the Lord:* The phrase invariably conveys a clearly perceived supernatural experience that involves Ezekiel in some action by which God intervenes in the life of the nation (as in 3:22; 8:1; 33:22; 37:1; 40:1). As 20:33 makes clear, it is the hand of the Lord that moves individuals to accomplish his purpose in history just as it is the "strong hand" that directs the destinies of nations, even though superficially it may seem to be an interplay of blind forces (cf. 20:22).

15 **(B) Vision of the Throne-Chariot (1:4–28b).** Inasmuch as the glory of the Lord does not leave Jerusalem until ch. 11, this vision, localized in Babylon, is chronologically misplaced, but the themes of its imagery show a Babylonian influence. As a manifestation of God's transcendent majesty with its imponderable qualities of movement and power totally beyond human comprehension, it sets the tone for the rest of the book, in which God's transcendent holiness and power constantly predominate. The theophany has two distinct phases. The first, 1:4–14, is centered in a storm, which has close similarities with 2 Sm 22:11 and Ps 18:11. The second, 1:15–28, shows some relationship to Dn 7:9. Zimmerli considers 1:15–21 a secondary expansion, and, indeed, these passages on the "wheel-work" seem adventitious here and in 10:9–17.

The CCD rearranges the verses rather extensively in an attempt to obtain a more logical sequence, for which there is no justification in the manuscript tradition. Furthermore, it omits v. 14 with the LXX, v. 21 with some Gk and Hebr manuscripts, and v. 25, which is in the MT through dittography.

5. *living creatures:* They are identified in 10:20 as cherubim, and they are guardians of the throne that they carried. **6–7.** Similar composite forms are to be found in Babylonian and Assyrian sculptures (*ANEP* 644ff.). **10.** *right side...left side:* Each of the four had the face of a lion on the right, of an ox on the left, and of an eagle. **12.** *the spirit:* It is the spirit in the living creatures, but from God, that is the purposeful power of God directing the activities of the universe and man (cf. 1:20; 2:2; 3:12,24; 11:24).

16 **13.** *torches moving:* The image given in the Talmud is an apt one: "Like the flame that goes forth from the mouth of a furnace" (*Hagigah* 13b). **15.** *wheels:* A symbol of cosmic mobility (vv. 16–17). In the Talmud, the "Wheels" (Hebr *'ôpannîm*) are classed with the "Serafim" and the "Holy Living Creatures" and so considered as a class of ("wheel-like"?) angels (*Hagigah* 12b). **18.** *rims...full of eyes:* God's all-seeing presence; hence, intelligent direction is in the most insensitive and the most changing and swift elements in the universe. The wheels move under the same impulse that moves the living creatures and that also moves the Prophet to hear and answer Yahweh's call (1:20; 2:2; 3:14). **22.** *firmament:* In Gn 1:6–8 and Ps 19:2, the firmament is the solid vault of heaven on which are hung the heavenly bodies and above which God is enthroned as Lord of the universe. **24.** *mighty waters:* There is no need here to appeal to any mythological struggles of pagan gods with the deep. As in Ps 29, in which an actual storm taking its origin over the Mediterranean ("mighty waters" or "vast waters") is a symbol of God's power and majesty, so here his presence is made manifest by his creatures. **26–28a.** *upon it:* Strictly speaking, this is the theophany, but it is not central to the call of Ezekiel as is true in Is 6:6–7. Yahweh appears not as a man but as "the appearance of a man." This vision is not of the "glory of the Lord," but of "the likeness of the glory of the Lord." **28b.** *glory of the Lord:* Aside from the fact that the glory of the Lord is out of place in Babylon before it leaves Jerusalem in ch. 10, its appearance here is totally unprepared for. Auvray points out that whenever Yahweh is presented under human form in the Bible the glory of the Lord is never present (Ex 15:2; Is 6:1ff.; Dn 7:9), for the glory is usually represented by a cloud of smoke, or fire surrounded by smoke, in the Temple. The cloud in v. 28a merely contrasts with the rainbow, which is compared to the glory of the Lord. The attempt to relate the two is a clear case of harmonization—to unite the preceding with the following vision of the call, where the vision of the glory is more in place. (See comment on 3:13–15.)

17 **(C) Call and Commissions (2:1–3:27).** This passage contains the essentials of the Prophet's call, and presents some discrepancies with ch. 1 (→ 5 above). In 1:1, Ezekiel is "among the exiles" when the vision occurs, but in 3:15 it is after the vision that he comes to them. The Prophet is set on his feet three different times: 1:2; 3:12; 3:24. In 3:22–27, we find all the earmarks of another prophetic call: vision and commission. The redactor has gathered together several visions and commissions in ch. 3. These seem to be four distinct prophetic calls: 1:28b–3:9; 3:10–11; 3:17–21; 3:22–27.

Five different commissions are generally recognized as being given to Ezekiel in his prophetic call, corresponding to these four prophetic calls, except that the first is divided into two: 1:28b–2:8a; 3:4–3:9. Perhaps the best biblical description of the prophetic experience and the prophetic office is given here. A prophet receives his mission in full consciousness and fully recognizes its difficulties.

18 (a) FIRST COMMISSION: MISSION TO REBELS (2:1–7). **1.** *son of man:* The term is used over 90 times and has no messianic connotation here. Man, essentially mortal flesh, is contrasted with God, essentially immortal spirit, "different in substance though alike in form" (H. W. Robinson, *ZAW* 41 [1923] 1–15). Man's transitory nature stands against God's unchangeable nature, man's weakness against God's might (cf. Ps 8:4; Nm 23:9; Jb 16:21; Is 51:12). **2.** *spirit entered:* To bridge the gap between God and man, God's spirit enters into the Prophet, strengthening him to be attentive to the message of God—"stand up." Ezekiel's consciousness of being moved by the spirit (*rûaḥ*) in his prophetic task will be constantly reiterated (3:12,14,24; 8:3; 11:1,5,24; 37:1; 43:5). The influence of the spirit on the heroes and prophets of Israel before the exile was to fill them with a physical energy beyond their normal portion so that their physical actions seemed ecstatic and out of control (cf. Jgs 6:34; 11:29; 14:6; 1 Sm 10:10; Mi 3:8; etc.). With Ezekiel, the spirit's influence is most commonly exercised upon his psychic powers and often simply in the sense of making him attentive to the Lord's presence and the meaning of his words (cf. Robinson, *ZAW* 41, 3). **5.** *they shall know:* The people may ignore the Prophet's words even though they originate from God, but Ezekiel's presence speaks harsh realities that cannot be ignored (cf. R. E. Clements, *Prophecy and Covenant* [London, 1965]).

19 (b) THE DIVINE COMMUNICATION (2:8–3:3) The eating of the scroll is a graphic representation of an inner religious experience by which the Prophet received an insight into the covenant relationship between God and the people. A recognition of his role in it followed, bringing a sense of harmony and joy (cf. Jer 15:16; Pss 19:9–10; 119:103; Ap 10:9ff.). **9.** *written scroll:* It is possible that the scroll suggests a more extensive use of the written word in Ezekiel's prophecy than in the case of former prophets. **10.** *lamentation:* Only "wailing and woe" appear on the scroll. This lamentation is the totality of the Prophet's message, for a prophet who preaches peace is suspect (cf. 13:10ff.; Jer 28:8; Mi 3:5; Zech 5:1–4). **3:1.** *eat this scroll:* By the eating is signified Ezekiel's total assimilation of God's message, so that his whole being is permeated by it and it torments him until it is expressed (Am 3:8; Jer 20:9).

20 (c) SECOND COMMISSION (3:4–8). Largely a repetition of the first (2:3–8), it is less harsh in its indictment. This reason, and the reference to "barbarous language" suggest that the commission is probably given in Babylon and possibly represents Ezekiel's call to prophesy to the exiles there. Israel's sensitivity to Yahweh's Word is so blunted that the pagans who never heard the Word before could recognize it more easily (cf. Jon; Mt 11:21). **8.** *your face as hard:* The Prophet is hardened by those in whose midst he works, and he consciously steels himself for the task. Because it is provoked by God's commission, it is attributed to God.

21 (d) THIRD COMMISSION (3:9–15). **10–12.** Most commentators consider these verses redactional. We believe they are either part of the second call and commission given Ezekiel in Babylon, as distinct from his call in Palestine, or a commission given another prophet, included here by the editor.

13–15. Characterized by the absence of any intellectual communication and by the "wings...wheels alongside," these verses belong immediately after 1:28a. **14.** *spirit... lifted:* The meaning is "driven" or "impelled" by the spirit of Yahweh that had entered him, as in 1 Kgs 18:12; Acts 8:9. *spiritually stirred:* The CCD is somewhat anemic for the lit. translation, "bitter in the fury of my spirit." **15.** *Tel-abib:* This name of the Jewish settlement is the Hebr form of the Akkadian *til abûbi*, by which are meant low mounds reputedly from the predeluge era (*abûbu*, "deluge"). (Today, Tel Aviv is the largest city in Palestine.) Abib is the pre-exilic Canaanite name taken over by the Hebrews for the first month of the year (later called by the Babylonian name, Nisan), meaning "month of the ears of barley" (Ex 13:14; Dt 16:1). The Prophet has undergone a supernatural experience and is filled with the feeling of exaltation, but also with the inadequacy and dissatisfaction experienced by the mystics.

22 (e) FOURTH COMMISSION: THE PROPHET AS WATCHMAN (3:16–21). The CCD omits the first part of v. 16 as redactional and joins the second part to v. 17. Most commentators agree that they are out of place, put here to complement the call and introduce Ezekiel's prophetic activity. Detached from the parable that they presuppose in 33:1–6, they form a partial parallel to that passage: 3:18–19 = 33:8–9. In vv. 20–21, Auvray sees a development that may spring from changed conditions—i.e., the Prophet is not addressing the rebellious of Palestine as in 33:8–9 but the captives whom he is trying to keep faithful to Yahweh, beset as they are by the temptations of an affluent paganism. According to Jeremiah (24:1ff.), the good element was taken into captivity (P. Auvray, *RB* 71 [1964] 198). The prophet as a watchman has a long tradition in Israel (Hos 9:8; Is 21:6ff.; 56:10, 58:7; Jer 6:17). In Ez, it embodies the principle of personal responsibility applied to the prophetic office.

23 (f) FIFTH COMMISSION: THE PROPHET UNDER RESTRAINT (3:22–27). As we have noted, these verses should be transferred and joined to 2:1–2 (Auvray), or, as seems more likely, it is a renewal of the prophetic call under trying and discouraging circumstances. **25.** These "cords" have been interpreted as an actual persecution of the Prophet, or even, interpreted in conjunction with 4:4–8, as an actual imprisonment in his own house. It is possible, for in the prophetic view, even enforced actions have significant value. But more likely it is the people's bitter resistance that makes the Prophet a prisoner of discouragement, from which he is freed only by a special communication from God. That the words "make your tongue stick to your palate" do not denote a catalyptic state but rather a silence flowing from an overwhelming emotion may be gathered from similar expressions elsewhere (Jb 29:10; Pss 22:16; 137:6). Nor does the condition have any permanency: "When I speak...you shall say." **23.** *like the glory:* These words make evident that it is not the same vision as in 1:28b—it is "like" and therefore not the same glory.

(II) Prophecies of Judgment and Doom (4:1–24:27).

24 **(A) Actions Symbolic of Judgment (4:1–5:17).** These prophecies in action were probably not actually carried out; some seem impossible to fulfill, e.g., 4:4–8. Rather we should think of dramatic preaching and word pictures, for the characterization of the Prophet as one who is "forever spinning parables" (21:5) and proposing riddles (17:2) cannot be stressed enough.

(a) SYMBOLS OF SIEGE AND EXILE (4:1–17). Many see in this passage a conflict between the siege symbolism and the exile symbolism, originally apart, one being spoken in Palestine before the fall and the other in Babylon: 1–3, siege; 4–6, exile; 7–9, attempted blend; 10–11, siege; 12–15, exile; 16–17, siege. There is no reason why both siege and exile cannot be held up as threats, in which case the alternation could be a very effective literary device.

1. *clay tablet:* Clay is found in Palestine, and such tablets are common throughout the Near East. To insist upon a Babylonian locale for this symbol is to go beyond the evidence. **3.** *house of Israel:* Throughout his book, Ezekiel looks to the reunion of Israel and Judah; both are meant by this term. When the "house of Judah" is used, the reference is to the southern kingdom. **4.** There is no consensus as to the symbolism of these numbers. It has been pointed out that the numerical value of the Hebr letters in the phrase "the days of your siege" is 390, leaving 40 unaccounted for. The suggestion here is that 390 is approximately the number of years from the beginning of the monarchy to the great reform of Josiah (climaxed by the destruction of the altar at Bethel). From that point to the destruction of the Temple is another generation, or 40 years, when the second Exodus will take place from which a new people will be formed. Thus, the monarchy is compared to the servitude in Egypt, which also lasted 430 years (cf. Ex 12:4; Gal 3:17). The Exile is a new Exodus: "I will lead you to the desert of the peoples" (20:35). **9.** *single vessel:* The odd mixture of grains suggests the scraping of the bottom of flour barrels, the last action before starvation. **10.** *twenty shekels:* About 8 oz. **11.** *sixth of a hin:* About two-thirds of a quart, the minimum amount of water considered necessary per day per person. **13.** By the dietary laws, Babylon would be an "unclean" land making cultic life impossible. **14.** *made unclean:* Dt 23:13 provides the regulation for uncleanness of human excrement, and Lv 17:10–15 for eating "carrion flesh." Such refuse is commonly used as fuel today. **16.** *breaking the staff of bread:* Very likely refers to the staff on which reserves of bread baked with a hole in the center (still common today) were hung to discourage mice. In other words, all reserves of bread will be destroyed, which seems to be the sense in Ps 105:16; Is 3:1.

25 (b) THE WRATH OF JEALOUSY (5:1–17). Chapter 5 is also an anthology of oracles containing at least two distinct units: vv. 1–4 and 12–17; and vv. 5–11, which have no connection with what precedes or follows, in content or language. Many commentators assign vv.

13–17 to an editorial reworking on the basis of certain recurring phrases, for which we could desire more objective criteria.

1. *sharp sword...razor:* The hair was a sign of dignity (2 Sm 10:4–5), and because it grows more noticeably than any other part of the body, it was viewed as a special manifestation of God's life-giving power (cf. Nm 6:1ff.). The action with the sword as a razor symbolizes destruction of life in the city. **3.** *small number:* These are to be salvaged from the wind as a small remnant will be salvaged from the dispersal of the captivity. **13.** *in my jealousy:* God is presented very anthropomorphically as having a jealous love, which, when scorned, turns to wrath and fury (7:8; 8:18; 20:8, etc.).

26 **(B) Oracles Pronouncing Judgment (6:1–7:27).** These chapters are characterized by spoken oracles announcing punishment in words rather than in symbolic actions.

(a) Against the Mountains of Israel (6:1–14). Some authors (May) find the whole chapter secondary, mainly on the grounds that vv. 3–6 parallel Lv 26:30–31, but if the Holiness Code is older than Ez, as has been claimed, these verses need not be considered later than 587. Verses 8–10 are from the exile after 587, possibly from Ezekiel himself, and vv. 11–12 are an independent oracle with vv. 13–14 taking up the oracle of v. 7. However, vv. 11–14 may very well be one unit. Tournay sees in this chapter possible anti-Samaritan polemic, namely against Mt. Gerizim, especially since the first part of v. 5, speaking of "dead bodies of the people of Israel," is found only in the MT (P. Tournay, *RB* 71 [1964] 526). In v. 6, "your works wiped out" is missing from the LXX. But "mountains of Israel" refers to all of Palestine, not only to the northern part with its Samaritan population. **3.** *high places:* These were cultic places usually associated with mountaintops where an illicit worship was carried on. Despite the centralization of the cult in the Temple under Hezekiah (2 Kgs 18:4) and Josiah (2 Kgs 23), the high places continued. Although they were not necessarily idolatrous, they tended to assimilate local fertility rites practiced by the Canaanites living among the Jews, especially inasmuch as some of these shrines had been Canaanite sanctuaries before the Hebrews took over. *ravines and valleys:* Apparently there were high places in the valleys, which must have been artificially constructed mounds, described by R. de Vaux as 6 ft. high with a diameter of 8 to 25 yd., ranging in date from early Canaanite to the captivity (De Vaux, *AI* 284–85). **4.** *idols:* Probably these took the form of a stone pillar representing a male deity and a piece of wood or a stake representing the female deity, the consort of Baal (Ex 34:11–16). *incense stands:* Appurtenances belonging to the shrines (see De Vaux, *AI* 286). **5.** *their bones:* Contact with a corpse defiled a person and prevented his participation in ritual worship. Here, the very place of worship is defiled and made an object of horror. **9.** *I have broken:* The MT has "have been broken," which several ancient and most modern versions emend; in Ezekiel's perspective it is God who initiates the conversion of Israel, and in vv. 8–10, the restoration is already considered,—"those who have escaped will remember me." The adulterous heart is broken in preparation for a new heart (36:26). Perspectives of restoration are introduced here to soften the harsh language of the preceding condemnations. **11.** *sword, famine, pestilence:* Three traditional scourges by which God punishes his people (Jer 14:12; 27:8,13; 28:8). **13.** *every...mountaintop:* Not found in the LXX, it is considered by some as an anti-Samaritan polemic. *leafy oak:* Certain trees and groves were especially associated with female deities in fertility rites (Dt 16:21; Mi 5:13). **14.** *desert to Riblah:* The boundaries of Israelite territory at its greatest extent, from the desert bordering Sinai and Egypt in the south to northern Syria (1 Kgs 8:65).

27 (b) Against the Land: Near Is the Day of Yahweh (7:1–27). Tightly woven and homogenous from a literary aspect, and possessing a poetic vigor and imagery, this chapter contains some of Ezekiel's best poetry. The MT is sometimes corrupt and the LXX shows sizable variation by omission and transposition. Verses 3–4 are a close parallel to vv. 8–9. In the LXX vv. 3–5 are placed after vv. 8–9; it is possible that one is not necessarily an expansion or a later recension of the other, but a literary device. The LXX presents a shortened text also at vv. 5–6 and 11. The day of the Lord, when all things human will be weighed by God and will receive their judgment, is near (8–9). Under this judgment, all human security will disintegrate: society (10–11); economics (12–19); religion (20–26); and politics (27). Then they will know Yahweh. **10.** *day of the Lord:* The context envisages immediate misfortunes and the direct punishment of present evil, not eschatological perspectives. **12.** *let not the buyer rejoice:* The seller and buyer alike will be engulfed in a greater catastrophe that will nullify any immediate loss or gain in their lifetime. **16b.** *put them all to death:* Because the context, both before and after, speaks of survivors, the MT, "all of them moaning, everyone in his iniquity," should be kept. **22.** *treasure shall be profaned:* Probably a reference to the Temple. **24.** *sanctuaries:* Cf. comment on 6:3–6. *worst of the nations:* This description of the Babylonians painted by Hab 1:6 and Jer 6:22–23 could hardly have been used if the Prophet were in Babylon. **28.** *prophetic vision...instruction to priest...counsel to the elders:* These three sources of guidance were those available to the Israelite for conducting his life in the community. Through the "vision of the prophet" (which need not mean an ecstatic experience but simply an inspired "observation"), God manifested his will to the community in concrete actions. The instruction, or "torah," of the priest concerned the right relationship of man to God in worship and moral life (cf. A. R. Johnson, *The Cultic Prophet* [Cardiff, 1944]). The elders represented the people in giving judgments in local administration. **27.** *the common people:* Lit., "people of the land," in contradistinction to various official bodies, without the pejorative sense the term would later acquire.

28 **(C) Idolatry in the Temple and Abandonment by Yahweh (8:1–11:25).** These three chapters are of a composite character, even though presented as a continuous narrative. It is difficult, therefore, to try to reorder them logically as the CCD attempts to do, for the editor who united the parts undoubtedly thought he was acting logically. The main line of division seems to be a long vision from the same prophet responsible for the throne-chariot vision of ch. 1. It was inserted between 8:1 and 11:1 because the setting in the Temple and the activity of the spirit upon the Prophet were suitable links for its incorporation. In 8:1 and 11:1, we are not dealing with a vision but with the presence of the Prophet in person in Palestine. The "visions" (1:1; 8:4; 40:2) are the trademark of a Babylonian prophet active later in the captivity whose object was to vindicate the justice of God's action in allowing the Exile. Ezekiel, the prophet of Palestine, is moved by the "spirit" (2:2; 3:24; 37:1) to speak and act so as to bring about repentance. He never uses the term "vision."

29 (a) Foreign Cult in the Temple (8:1–18). Such pagan rites in the Temple are attested to elsewhere (2 Kgs 21:7; 23:6; Dt 16:21–22; Hos 10:1–2). Some (e.g., Torrey and Kaufmann) deny that it was possible in the time of Ezekiel. However, with the subjection of

Judah to Pharaoh Neco in 609 and to Nebuchadnezzar in 597, many undoubtedly lost faith in Yahweh and turned to the deities of the victorious nations; the activities of those accompanying Jeremiah in his flight amply demonstrate this tendency (Jer 44:17ff.). With religious syncretism being the prevailing spirit of the time, we should not be too startled to find the cults of the victors' deities in the Temple itself. Various reconstructions of the rites so graphically described have been attempted.

(Albright, *ARI* 164–68. Gaster, T., "Ezekiel and the Mysteries," *JBL* 60 [1941] 289–310. May, H. G., "Some Aspects of Star Worship in Jerusalem," *ZAW* 55 [1937] 269–81.)

1. *sixth year:* September 17, 592. *elders...before me:* Coming to seek an oracle from the Lord, the elders are before him also in 14:1; 20:1; 33:31 (De Vaux, *AI* 138). There is no indication whatever that Ezekiel is in Babylon. **2.** *like a man:* Exactly like the description in 1:27, it is therefore part of that complex of visions. *hand seized me:* It seems impossible to harmonize this action with "spirit lifted me up" (v. 3), into one unit—therefore, there is a conflation of two prophetic experiences. *statue of jealousy:* The LXX has an abbreviated text here, followed by the CCD; "seat" (Hebr *môšāb*, probably here "niche") has been omitted, perhaps to avoid giving the impression that such an image had a permanent place in the Temple. Instead of "statue," the Hebrew (*semel*) means rather a carved or painted slab, probably with mythological scenes of Syro-Assyrian cultic origin (Albright, *ARI* 165–66). **4.** *like the vision:* This editorial phrase joins the two visions—i.e., 8:1 and 1:1. **8.** *saw a door:* It is strange that Ezekiel had to dig into a wall to come to a door; perhaps the operation is a literary symbolism for the clandestine nature of the cult, which, according to Albright, is of Egyptian origin with pronounced magical elements centered on Osiris (Albright, *ARI* 165–66). Wall paintings are reminiscent of illustrations in the mss of the Egyptian Book of the Dead. **14.** *weeping for Tammuz:* Especially appropriate at this time of the year, for the descent of Tammuz, the Babylonian god of fertility, into the underworld brought death to all vegetation and was mourned especially by women. **16.** *twenty-five men:* This last idolatry is the worst according to Ezekiel's observation; the 25 men (MT) represent, according to some authors, the 24 courses of priests with the high priest at their head. Those who prefer the LXX reading (20 men) point out that this number is associated with Shamash, the Babylonian sun-god. **17.** *branch to my nose:* The MT has "their nose" which is acknowledged to be one of the 18 emendations of the text made by the scribes out of reverence for God, enumerated in several places in the Talmud (e.g., Mishnah, *Mechilta* on Ex 17:7). All attempts at identifying the rite have failed, especially since, in the progressive gradation, it should be the worst. The most common interpretation is that it is merely an ordinary gesture signifying provocation (the sense in the Talmud—Mishnah, *Yoma* 77a), or that it is a veiled reference to an obscene rite.

30 (b) PURGE OF JERUSALEM'S IDOLATERS (9:1–11). Inasmuch as the description of the idolatry continues with the wicked council (11:1–13) in the Temple, 11:1–13 should precede the present chapter, in which the evildoers of the whole city are executed. So that the Temple will not be used again for idolatrous worship, it will be defiled with corpses and thus be made unfit for any cult; Yahweh is about to abandon the city.

2. Linen, a ritually clean fabric, was used by priests in temple service (Lv 16:3–4) and by those who serve God in heaven (Dn 10:5). **3.** There seems to be no justification for omitting the reference to the "glory of God," which the CCD transposes to 10:2, for here it is not to be identified with the throne-chariot, but with the presence of Yahweh, "sitting upon the cherubim" (1 Sm 4:4 etc.), similar to the theophany in Is 6:1–2. **4.** *mark an X:* Those to be spared receive the mark of *tau*, the last letter of the Hebr alphabet (which resembles an X) upon their foreheads (cf. Gn 4:15, where Cain is marked that he might be spared, and also Ap 7:3–4). **9.** *bloodshed:* The crimes are enumerated in 22:6ff.

The CCD places 11:24–25 after 9:10. It seems unjustifiable, for we would think that the vision of the glory of the Lord leaving Jerusalem (11:23) would be a very important part of "everything the Lord had shown me," which the Prophet "told the exiles" (11:25).

31 (c) THE GLORY OF THE LORD ABANDONS JERUSALEM (10:1–22). Chapter 10 seems to be a conflation of two visions; one presents the traditional view of the "glory of the Lord" (hidden in a cloud; Ex 16:10; Nm 10:34), and the other is the throne-chariot of ch. 1 with its wheels and shining metals. A key to the whole chapter is in vv. 15 and 20, where the living creatures of the vision by the river Chebar are identified as being the cherubim in the vision in the Temple; this would hardly be necessary if originally they were integral parts of the same vision. **2.** *scatter them over the city:* Thus, the wicked city is given over to fire proceeding from Yahweh's very throne. It has come under the "ban" (*ḥerem*) of Yahweh, and so doomed to complete destruction (cf. Ap 8:5). With the land thus purified, a completely new city, holy to Yahweh, will rise on the spot (40:2).

32 (d) SECURITY AND REDEMPTION ONLY IN YAHWEH (11:1–25). Cast in three distinct units, ch. 11 seems to continue the inspection of the Temple begun in ch. 8, but its style and content are totally different, for instead of visions on a grandiose scale we have oracles, and instead of idolatry described in detail, the wicked council of princes with their arrogant optimism about the security of the inhabitants of Jerusalem.

33 (i) *False security* (11:1–13). **1.** *Spirit...brought me:* The words "in divine visions" (8:3) are not present. The Prophet is brought in person into the Temple. Therefore, it takes place in Palestine, and 11:1 should follow upon 8:1, where Ezekiel is sitting with the "elders of Judah" when "the hand of the Lord fell upon him" and the spirit brought him to the Temple. All that is between 8:1 and 11:1 is a vision (or several visions) of prophets in Babylon either before or after 587. Jaazaniah is not the same person as in 8:11. This name appears on a seal found at Tell en-Nasbeh, dated *ca.* 600 BC and containing the inscription: "to Jaazaniah servant of the king" (*DOTT* 222). **2.** *giving wicked counsel:* From Jer 38:4 we know that the largely pro-Egyptian princes were the moving power in the revolt against Babylon. **3.** *building houses soon:* This phrase seems to be an expression of confidence in the restoration of a prosperity and a peacetime economy that will allow resources of men and money to be turned to building, giving the lie to Ezekiel's warning in 7:12–13. *city is the kettle:* An interpretation of this allegory is to be found in 24:3–7,9–13—i.e., good meat boiling in a good pot is a picture of harmony and well-being, giving hopes of a satisfying meal and contentment, something, perhaps, like our expression "they go together like hand in glove." But the Prophet now tells them the allegory has a meaning they never suspected. **7.** *your slain...are the meat:* The cauldron is rusted with the bloody flesh of the oppressed and slain, still clinging to it, making it unclean ritually as well as unfit for profane use. *you I will take out of it:* Out of the rusty cauldron the meat will be taken piece by piece and inspected for edibility (24:6); the broth will be emptied out, the bones will be burnt, and the cauldron put back on the fire to burn out the rust. **10.** *at the borders of Israel:* Just as the meat is taken out of a rusty pot and inspected, thus will the inhabitants undergo scrutiny in the captivity, away from the protective forms of city and kingdom. The phrase, therefore, has no reference to the historical situation of Nebuchadnezzar judging Zedekiah at Riblah and is not a prophecy ex post facto. **13.** The death of Pelatiah has been a source of embarrassment for those who hold the theory of an exclusively Babylonian ministry. To explain it, recourse is had to parapsychic phenomena, to the unwarranted claim (see comment on v. 1) that this is only a vision and not a prophecy; therefore, Pelatiah could not really die as a result of prophesying (Zimmerli, *op. cit.*, 246), but a mere coincidence occurred. Finally, and unbelievably, the verse on Pelatiah's death was supposedly inserted by Ezekiel in the thirtieth year when the book was edited, after he had received news of Pelatiah's death! It is not stated whether Ezekiel's exclamation was also made in the thirtieth year! *what remains of Israel:* Ezekiel has hopes that, despite his prophecy of absolute destruction, God will spare a remnant of those in Palestine (cf. Am 7:2,4). His love for his people is deep and tender.

34 (ii) *Redemption from the Lord* (11:14–25). Perhaps the next section comes in answer to Ezekiel's anguished cry. We should recall that, on the position taken here, Ezekiel has been living outside Jerusalem, possibly in banishment with some disciples, kinsmen, and friends. **15.** *whole house of Israel:* Throughout the book, Ezekiel is keenly conscious of the split between Israel and Judah, and restoration will involve a union of the two. Now, inasmuch as the northern kingdom had been destroyed and its people scattered for over a century, the inhabitants of Jerusalem were claiming the land of the northern tribes as next of kin. **16.** *removed them among the nations:* The reference is to the captivity of the northern tribes. **17.** *I will gather you:* Yahweh himself speaks for the northern kinsmen of Ezekiel; he will be their redeemer, their *gōʾēl*, against the inhabitants of Jerusalem; he will restore the land to them, from which they will remove all vestiges of idolatry. **19.** *new heart:* Read, with the MT, "one heart"—i.e., a heart of undivided loyalty (36:26; Jer 24:7), as opposed to "hearts devoted to abominations" (v. 21). **22.** *the glory...rose from the city:* The presence of Yahweh departs from the city to go to the exiles, symbolizing at once the coming doom of the city and showing that the land of Israel is not an essential element in the covenant.

(D) Further Prophecies Against the Land and Jerusalem, Its Rulers, Priests, and Prophets (12:1–24:27).

35 (a) More Symbols of Siege and Exile (12:1–20). This section has three parts: exile acted out by Ezekiel (1–7); exile explained (8–16); conditions during siege (17–20). Bertholet's theory is that at this point Ezekiel leaves Jerusalem to live in a neighboring town, but it would seem he had already left Jerusalem.

5. *dig a hole:* The scene is probably outside Jerusalem. A Babylonian locale is not necessarily implied, for mud brick walls were common enough. **6.** *cover your face:* Sign of shame, grief, and despair (2 Kgs 15:30; Jer 14:4), with perhaps the added idea of avoiding the jeers and taunts of onlookers. But this becomes applicable to Zedekiah (cf. v. 12). **11.** *sign:* A sign (*môpēt*) to his viewers. **12.** *the prince:* Inasmuch as the dramatic action was already applied to "them," the "house of Israel" (vv. 10–11), its reapplication in a changed sense (not exile but an attempted escape), to fit a specific historically detailed moment in the life of the king and his bodyguard (2 Kgs 25:4–5), is probably a later addition, perhaps by Ezekiel himself, along with the verses that follow (vv. 12–16). **13.** *there he shall die:* The writer's perspective is from Palestine, not from Babylon. **17.** *the people of the land:* From 7:27 and 2 Kgs 25:3, these are people who have no official position in the government, military, or religious structures in the city of Jerusalem. Because this is not a vision and Ezekiel is to address them directly, Babylon cannot be the locale.

36 (b) Reality of the Word of God (12:21–28). There are at least two oracles here reflecting the ridicule to which the Prophet is subjected, and also his own keen sensitivity and hurt. **23.** *the fulfillment of every vision:* Lit., "the word (or "reality") of every vision." The vision need not be a trance but an observation made by the Prophet in the light of his inspired religious, either reasoned or intuitive, insights.

37 (c) Devastation Wrought by False Prophets (13:1–23). If the previous passage showed the tragedy of true prophecy scorned, no less tragic is the perennial attractiveness of false prophecy to ordinary people who cannot distinguish between the two in the absence of immediate objective criteria (Jer 28:1–15; 14:13–16; Is 9:14; Mi 3:5; 1 Kgs 22). The false prophets claim to speak the word of Yahweh and to fulfill his purpose, but their words are products of their own wishful thinking (2), spawned by their own avaricious desires, "their own spirit" (3). The CCD makes extensive transpositions in an attempt to obtain logical sequence. Outside of vv. 6–10a, a later oracle looking toward restoration from Babylon, possibly from Ezekiel himself, the rest of the chapter stands well as it is. **4.** *foxes:* The vineyard (cf. Ct 2:15) of Yahweh is in a state of disrepair because of the broken covenant. Instead of stepping into the breach in the walls and building it up, the prophets have exploited the damage for their own gain. **6.** *their visions are false:* Verses 6–10a break the analogy of the wall and are an oracle inserted by the editor as an elaboration of the preceding verses. Further evidence is the presence of an unusual number of Aramaisms and words belonging to late Hebrew (cf. Cooke, *op. cit.*, 143). **7.** *divination lying:* In divination, the commission does not come from Yahweh or at his initiative, but man on his own seeks to penetrate the counsels of God. Not only do they lack the commission of Yahweh, but their natural divinations and observations are deliberately falsified. **9.** *register of the house of Israel:* The Book of Life (Ex 32:32; Pss 69:28; 87:6; Lk 10:20; Ap 3:5; 13:8). *nor enter the land of Israel:* Further proof that the perspective is late, and looking toward a restoration. **10.** *cover it with whitewash:* Mud walls must be given a hard, water-resistant coat that will fill in the cracks and cause its faults to show. Whitewash presents a nice appearance and covers the faults, but it will not protect the walls against the downpour of the rainy season. **11.** *whitewash...has fallen:* Probably a play on words: *tāpēl... yippōl.* **17.** *daughters of your people who prophesy:* The reference is probably to magical divination and sorcery outside of the cult of Yahweh, which provided no official scope for women. The whole passage (vv. 17–23) is a unit that again has the perspective of the exile and looks to a consolation and restoration: "you have disheartened the righteous...I will deliver my people" (22–23). **18.** *bands...veils:* Magical practices of unknown nature; possibly used here figuratively for tying the hands from good deeds and blinding the mind to truth with their lying divination. **19.** *handfuls of barley:* Possibly referring to the technique of divination, but also perhaps to the small barter that they took from the poor (Mi 3:5ff.).

38 (d) Hypocrisy of Idolaters and Personal Responsibility (14:1–23). Three distinct oracles are contained in the chapter: faithless elders and prophets (1–11); each one bears his own burden (12–20); Yahweh's vindication in the Exile (21–23). The first two seem to be spoken in Palestine before 597, the third is from the perspective of the captivity in Babylon after 597, and from another prophet. Again, Ezekiel is confronted by the elders, this time of Israel and not of Judah. The sense of vv. 1–11 is not very clear, but it seems to be that one cannot have both the satisfaction of idol worship and the communication of a word from the Lord, and the prophet who tries to accommodate idol worshipers, either out of human respect or out of hopes that seem to be founded upon Yahweh, is deceiving himself and is also guilty.

39 (i) *Faithless elders and prophets* (14:1–11). **4.** *his answer in person:* Even though the Prophet may not be aware of the duplicity, Yahweh is, and he will answer him by deeds of unmistakable significance. **7.** *alien resident in Israel:* Except for this phrase, v. 7 almost exactly parallels v. 4. Because it is not a vision but a direct confrontation with the Prophet, location in Babylon is impossible. **9.** *I shall have beguiled that prophet:* In Hebr thought, all events are directly in the hands of God, the First Cause. Hence, it can be said that he "deceives"—without denying man's freedom and responsibility.

40 (ii) *Everyone bears his own burden* (14:12–20). A man is definitely cut off from solidarity in the guilt or virtue of a people, regardless of how renowned for justice, or how wicked, were the rest of the men who lived in it. **14.** Inasmuch as Daniel (Hebr consonants *d-n-'-l*, Danel, as in Ugaritic) is placed beside Noah and Job, he is probably a figure from antiquity known through popular tradition and not to be identified with the biblical Daniel. Probably, although not necessarily, the reference is to Danel of ancient Ugarit, known for the effectiveness of his intercession with the gods, for attention to their desires, and as a righteous judge (*ANET* 150). Whether God judges a land by famine, a scourge of wild beasts, or the sword of war or pestilence, the intercession of even these three just men could save no one but themselves.

41 (iii) *Vindication of Yahweh* (14:21–23). Those who escape these four executioners will give evidence by their conduct that Yahweh acted justly in sparing them and their children, which will strengthen the exiles' faith in Yahweh.

42 (e) The Parable of the Wood of the Vine (15:1–8). The theme of Israel as a vineyard cultivated by Yahweh is familiar in the prophets (Is 5:1–4; Jer 2:21), but here Ezekiel uses the figure in a unique way, comparing the usefulness of the "wood" of the vine with Israel. The recent translation of v. 2 proposed by G. R. Driver (*Bib* 35 [1954] 151) makes the figure strikingly clearer: "Son of man, how is the wood of the vine better than any wood, [even] the vine-branch growing amongst the trees of the forest?" Israel, the cultivated vine, when compared with the trees of the forest—i.e., the mighty nations of material power (cf. Jgs 9:8–15!)—is as useless for material products as the uncultivated vine, unsuited even to make a peg on which to hang useful things. The implication is that its only value comes from being cultivated by God to bear fruit (cf. Jn 15:1–11). Without fruit, it cannot compete with the trees of the forest for other tasks. When its ends (Israel and Judah) are burnt, it becomes even more useless. Only the scorched center remains—the inhabitants of Jerusalem—destined for the fire as an unproductive vine, having "broken faith" (v. 8) with Yahweh.

43 (f) The Marriage Allegory on Jerusalem (16:1–63). The history is given as an allegory of a marriage between Yahweh and Jerusalem told in luxurious imagery and in distinct stages. **1–7.** Other cities usually had in their epic history a legend of being founded by a god or a hero with a divine commission. Jerusalem came to notice as a city of the Canaanites, without any such legend. Yahweh passed by her the first time and allowed her to live; she was not destroyed or even taken in the conquest under Joshua. **8–14.** With the capture by David and the bringing of the Ark of the Covenant into Jerusalem, Yahweh took her for his own and made her renowned for beauty and wealth under Solomon. **15–19.** But her head was turned by these gifts, and she attempted to catch the eye of other nations, engaging in purely material activities, in the course of which she was drawn into their religious practices. She committed a double harlotry, being unfaithful to Yahweh and adopting the neighboring fertility cult that involved ritualistic prostitution (Hos 4:13–14; 2 Kgs 21:1–18). **20–22.** Even human sacrifice was introduced under Judah's wicked kings (2 Kgs 16:3; 17:17; Jer 7:31). **23–34.** Jerusalem squandered the gifts of her husband, Yahweh, to attract partners in illicit love affairs, thus more shameless than a prostitute, who engages in such conduct for pay. **35–43.** First, she is rejected by her husband, who loses interest in her and jealousy for her (v. 42); ultimately, in contemptuous and cruel treatment, her paramours will exploit her and stone her as an adulteress. **44–52.** Sodom has been the model of the sinful city and God's judgment upon her the model of righteous judgment. Samaria has been scorned by Jerusalem for her illicit worship, but in comparison with Jerusalem, who has received God's favors, both cities appear just. **53–63.** Cast out by her lover and despised and despoiled, resembling the original state in which Yahweh found her, she will be sought out and espoused again by him. Now appreciative of such love, she will be ashamed of her own previous ungrateful conduct and will turn to him in complete fidelity. Most commentators consider vv. 44–63 a later expansion. In vv. 44–58 there is such a homogeneity in style (excepting the glosses on Jerusalem's restoration in vv. 53 and 55, and possibly the reference to Edom in v. 57) that separation from the rest of the chapter is unjustifiable (cf. P. Tournay, *RB* 61 [1954] 430). Furthermore, its pro-Samaritan tone could hardly be understood after the destruction of Jerusalem. Amos already compares Samaria with Sodom (4:11). However, vv. 59–63 are a later addition, possibly by Ezekiel, for they speak of the prior restoration of Jerusalem, with Samaria and Sodom being given to her as daughters.

44 (g) Allegory of the Cedar and the Eagles (17:1–24). Two distinct divisions are evident: events of contemporary history (1–21); messianic restoration (22–24). Inasmuch as an allegory is an extended metaphor in which one series of events and persons represents another in a more or less detailed way, we can make the following identifications. **3.** *great eagle:* Nebuchadnezzar (Jer 48:40; 49:22; Dt 28:49). *Lebanon:* City of Jerusalem (Is 10:34; Zech 11:1–3). **4.** *crest of the cedar:* House of David (Jer 22:5–6,23). *topmost branch:* Jehoiachin. *land of tradesmen:* Babylonia. *city of merchants:* Babylons **5.** *seed of the land:* Zedekiah, Jehoiachin's uncle (2 Kg. 24:17). *planted it:* Made him king. **6.** *vine:* That is, cultivated for its fruit (Hebr *gepen* instead of *z^e^môrāh*, "the vine of the forest"). **7.** *low lying:* Not exalted in material resources. Zedekiah's power was very limited, even over his princes (Jer 38:5). **7.** *another eagle:* Psammetichus II of Egypt (594–588). Thus, we have the drama of Zedekiah, the weak king, caught between the pressures of the king of Babylon and the king of Egypt. **10.** *east wind:* It will come from the desert and dry up vegetation; it is a symbol of Nebuchadnezzar. **19.** *my covenant which he broke:* Both Ezekiel and Jeremiah (27:6–8) consider Zedekiah's breach of his fealty oath to Nebuchadnezzar as a repudiation of God's ordering of history. **22.** *take from the crest:* The allegory continues along messianic lines. Although most commentators see vv. 22–24 as a later addition because of the promise of restoration, it is not spoken from the perspective of the captivity but of the long-range fulfillment of God's plan, similar to 2 Sm 7:13; it is so homogeneous in style and context that it forms a unit with the rest of the chapter. Ezekiel views the restoration as a messianic event of the Davidic dynasty under a descendant of Jehoiachin.

45 (h) THE LORD'S WAY IS JUST (18:1–32). Although the principle of individual responsibility does not originate with Ezekiel (2 Kgs 14:6; Jer 31:29ff.; Dt 24:16), he gives it the most limpid formulations and extensive scrutiny. It has been pointed out by K. Koch that oracles of this nature may be an evolution from the liturgy of access to the Temple in the same genre as Pss 15 and 24 and Is 33:14–16; Mi 6:6–8 (which are also embryonic formulations of individual responsibility), and that it was upon this examination of conscience that the prophets based their message. The cultic, doctrinal, and pastoral overtones of the Prophet's message make it very amenable to such an interpretation. On the other hand, Ezekiel is aware of the influence of corporate wickedness of parents upon children (20:18), as well as of the power of an evil habit in an individual life (6:9; 36:26ff.). Nevertheless, the theory of individual responsibility was contrary to some traditional formulation of doctrine, as in Ex 20:5; Lv 26:39–40; Dt 5:9. The influence of the Deuteronomic Code is visible; parallels with the Holiness Code are particularly striking, indicating that the latter and Ez both depend upon the same collection of laws, perhaps the liturgy of access just mentioned.

(Eichrodt, *Theology* 376. Koch, K., "Liturgie d'accès au Temple et Décalogues," *Studien zur Theologie der alttestamentlichen Überlieferungen* [Fest. G. von Rad; Neukirchen, 1961].)

2. *this proverb:* Apparently a current and somewhat cynical formulation of Ex 20:5; 34:7 (cf. Jer 31:29). *if he does not eat...:* Ritual observance seems to be placed on the same level as moral law; however, for Ezekiel, the moral law finds its foundation in the holiness of Yahweh with which man is in contact by ritual and cult. **9.** *he shall surely live:* Just as surely death awaits everyone. Ezekiel's confident repetition of the phrase envisages something more than the immediate condition of life or death; it has eschatological perspectives, for which a new heart and new spirit (v. 31) are a condition and the "return and live" (v. 32) a beginning.

46 (i) TWO ELEGIES ON THE ROYAL HOUSE (19:1–14). In mournful "qînâ" meter, Ezekiel composed a lament over the tragic end of the last kings of Judah. The figures in the allegory are easily identified. **2.** *lioness:* Judah (Gn 49:9; 1 Kgs 10:19; cf. seal of Shema from Megiddo, *DOTT* 220). **3.** *one whelp:* Jehoahaz, taken captive by Neco in 609 after a three-month reign (2 Kgs 23:30–34). **4.** *with hooks:* A usual technique for leading prisoners (cf. the stele from Zinjirli, showing Esarhaddon leading two prisoners with rings in their jaws, *ANEP* 447). **5.** *another of her whelps:* According to modern commentators, it is to be identified with Jehoiachin, taken to Babylon by Nebuchadnezzar after a three-month reign in 597. Yet the picture in vv. 6–8 fits the description of Jehoiakim and his reign in 2 Kgs 24 too closely to be chance or poetic license (cf. 2 Kgs 24:2; Ez 19:8). The notice in 2 Chr 36:6 that Jehoiakim was a prisoner in Babylon should not be dismissed too lightly. The latter identification is preferred here. **10.** *vine:* Judah (Is 5:1–7; Jer 2:21). **11.** *strongest stem:* Modern commentators identify it with Zedekiah. According to 17:6, however, Zedekiah was a "low-spreading vine," and never "towered aloft" (v. 11); therefore, it can be identified with Jehoiachin. **12.** *its fruit was stripped off:* This should not be interpreted as the execution of Zedekiah's sons. It is the fruit of the vine that is stripped off—i.e., the nobility—that is taken into captivity. **14.** *no scepter:* Ez recognizes Jehoiachin as legitimate king; Zedekiah is merely a pathetic transplant (17:5; cf. Jgs 9:12).

47 (j) AN HISTORICAL SURVEY IN THEOLOGICAL PERSPECTIVE (20:1–44). This sweeping panorama of Israel's history ends with the "whole house of Israel without exception" worshiping Yahweh on the "holy mountain...height of Israel," as the culmination of an unremitting sequence of rebellion, punishment, and deliverance. Israel is accused of practicing idolatry in Egypt (v. 9)—for which the punishment was slavery—and of continuing it in the desert (v. 13). The new generation not only continued the rebellious idolatry of their parents but also adopted new forms in the very land Yahweh had given them (v. 28), finally formally repudiating the covenant with Yahweh (v. 32). But Yahweh will not permit it; he will save them against their will for the sake of his holy name (v. 44), as he had always dealt with them out of his holiness (vv. 9, 14, 22, 40–41, 44) and not out of their evil (v. 44). The covenant theme seems to be absent, but it is present in the insistence on the Sabbath that is presented as a sign of the covenant between Yahweh and the people (vv. 12–13, 20, 24; cf. De Vaux, *AI* 476). The view that "concern for His name and His reputation among the nations is thus the sole *raison d'être* for His grace" (C. Kuhl, *The Prophets of Israel* [Edinburgh, 1960] 129) does less than justice to the prophetic thought; God's holiness consists precisely in taking the initiative on behalf of the people and of bringing it to a successful conclusion, regardless of the people's own evil resistance (Kuhl, *op. cit.*; E. Jacob, *Theology of the Old Testament* [N.Y., 1958] 82–88).

The chapter shows signs of being an anthology of several prophecies from different prophets: 20:1–6,27–31 speak only of Yahweh's frank and generous dealings with Israel in the past and of the present hypocrisy and idolatry of the elders in Palestine. It is a homogeneous unit. There is no mention of Sabbaths and ordinances, and instead of "rebelled," the characteristic attitude is "blasphemed." Another prophecy is vv. 8–26 (a "sermon"), which takes its inspiration from v. 7. It has its own characteristic style and content; because of insistence on Sabbath, it is from Babylon (and late exilic), where the Sabbath observance distinguished the Jew and kept him close to the covenant with Yahweh. Verses 32–38 are written from the perspective of the exile but are very similar in style and vocabulary with vv. 1–6 and 27–31, so that they are probably from Ezekiel. Verses 39–44 are also exilic.

1. *seventh year:* August 14, 591 BC. **9.** *the nations... presence:* Cf. Ex 12:38. *my name's sake:* The name and the person are interchangeable realities in Israelite thought. Yahweh's activity is in keeping with his holiness, which is the source of holiness for the people (vv. 11–12). God's total transcendence stands out in dealing with his people in history (cf. also vv. 22, 39, 44). **26.** *immolation of every first-born:* Some see in vv. 23–26 an apology by Ezekiel for human sacrifices allegedly commanded by the Law and in force (e.g., Ex 22:29b; 34:19)—i.e., that the Law was a punishment from God. However, 16:20 and 20:31 condemn the sacrifices of infants, which would be absurd if Ezekiel considered the practice a divine command. De Vaux (*AI* 444) points out that although Ex

22:29 states categorically "You shall give me the first-born," texts that are just as ancient, Ex 13:11–15; 34:19–20, stipulate that first-born of men be ransomed. In 20:26, we find a Semite's view of the positive, all-pervasive causality of God, which enters the actions of men and directs them to an ultimate good (cf. Ex 4:21; Is 6:9–10). **29.** *high place do you betake yourselves:* There is a play on words here (Hebr *habbāmāh*: "high place"; *habbā'îm*: "to frequent"), suggesting contemptuous derivation of the name for place of worship. **35.** *desert of the peoples:* The coming redemption is patterned after the Exodus. **41.** *pleasing odor:* In the restoration, God will accept the sacrifices of Israel only because Israel itself has been accepted as a pleasing sacrifice. The LXX and Vg 20:45–49 are 21:1–5 in the MT.

48 (k) WITH FIRE AND SWORD (21:1–37). Chapter 21 contains four distinct oracles of doom, three against Israel (vv. 1–12, 13–22, 23–32) and one against Ammon (vv. 33–37), the latter included here and not with the oracles against the nations because of its association in the rebellion of Judah against Babylon. Another reason is to make clear that although Nebuchadnezzar turned away from Ammon for the moment, it would ultimately suffer the same doom because of the indications of the divination. All the oracles are composed with the imagery of the sword as the central element.

(i) *The parable of fire in the forest* (21:1–12). The Prophet states that he is accused of "forever spinning parables." He is commissioned to give an interpretation of the parable, in which v. 2 corresponds to v. 7, v. 3 matches vv. 8–9, and v. 4 parallels v. 10. **2.** *look southward:* Ezekiel could not look southward and face Jerusalem (v. 7) if he were in Babylon. **6.** *parables:* For another prophet whose audience was nonplused by his parables, see Mt 13:10ff. and Jn 16:29. **8.** *my sword:* One of the four traditional instruments of God's judgment (cf. 14:21; Is 34:5; Ap 6:8), it is presented here with dramatic imagery, as in the other prophets (Is 34:5; Jer 47:6; 50:35ff.). **12.** *spirit shall be daunted:* Here, it is the human spirit, the decisive power in man to carry out his conscious purposes.

(ii) *Song of the sword* (21:13–22). **15.** *rod:* Here and in v. 18 the text is corrupt and the CCD reading is a conjecture.

49 (iii) *The road is to Jerusalem* (21:23–32). **26.** *at the fork:* In this lively scene, Nebuchadnezzar is represented as resorting to three forms of divination: headless arrows inscribed with the alternatives of action are shaken in a quiver and then drawn; teraphim, figurines mentioned in various connections in the OT and sometimes associated with oracles or necromancy, are apparently marked with alternatives and picked at random (cf. Jgs 18:14; Hos 3:4; 2 Kgs 23:24; Johnson, *op. cit.*, 32–33); livers of sacrificial victims are examined and the markings interpreted in relation to the alternatives. (Many clay model livers have been found in excavations; cf. *ANEP* 594 for a liver inscribed with omens.) **28.** *mark their guilt:* The decision of the king of Babylon will end in the destruction of Jerusalem, which can only be a punishment from God and therefore evidence of the city's guilt. **30.** *wicked prince:* Zedekiah. **31–32.** *nothing shall be as it was:* This wild reversal seems to extend to Gn 49:10, a text usually taken as referring to David and the *pax Davidica*. Ezekiel reinterprets "to whom it belongs" and applies it to Nebuchadnezzar, "who has the claim against the city" (see W. L. Moran *Bib* 39 [1958] 405–25).

50 (iv) *Sword drawn on Ammon* (21:33–37). **37.** *you shall not be remembered:* The Ammonites have disappeared from history, leaving only a vestige in the modern name Amman, the capital of Jordan.

51 (l) THE DOCKET OF CRIME AGAINST THE NATION (22:1–31). Three distinct oracles are discernible, each consisting in an indictment, in legal form, of crimes: 1–12; 17–18; 23–30. Corresponding sentences follow: 13–16; 19–22; 31. Chapter 22 resembles ch. 18, and seems to be an application and a vindication of the principle of personal responsibility expressed in 18:30: "Therefore I will judge you... each one according to his ways." In vv. 1–13, the principle is applied to Jerusalem as a whole; in vv. 17–22, the application is to those outside the city; in vv. 23–31, it is to all the classes of citizens. All are found guilty. There are points of contact with Dt (10:18; 16:19), the Holiness Code (Lv 17–26), and "liturgy of access" to the Temple (Pss 15 and 24).

52 (i) *The indictment of Jerusalem and its sentence* (22:1–16). In this catalogue, ethical and social transgressions far outnumber the ritual ones. **3.** *sheds blood:* The reference is to acts of violence by which blood is shed, or by which crimes punishable by death are committed (such as the sexual sins enumerated in vv. 10–11 and in Lv 21:11–16). **10.** *who uncover the nakedness of their fathers:* Those who have relations with their father's wife (Lv 18:6). **12.** Lending money at interest to a fellow Israelite was forbidden (Ex 22:24; Dt 23:20–21). Two ways of exacting interest seemed to have been distinguished: taking a cut at the beginning of the loan (Hebr *nešek*, "a bite") or demanding more than was lent at the payment (Hebr *tarbêt*, "increase"); cf. De Vaux, *AI* 170. **12.** *brushing one hand:* A gesture conveying the idea of disgust and rejection of responsibility (21:22; Nm 24:10; Jb 34:37).

53 (ii) *The melting process* (22:17–22). Jerusalem is like a huge smelter, and because the inhabitants are apparently all dross, they must be melted so that gold and silver may appear (Is 1:22,25; Jer 6:28–30). **19.** *gather you within Jerusalem:* Possibly a reference to the people from the countryside who will take refuge in the city with the advance of the hostile army.

54 (iii) *The abuses of civic, social, and religious responsibility* (22:23–31). Each of the official groups has failed in its essential task. There are some indications (e.g., v. 31) that this section may be a later addition, perhaps by Ezekiel himself. **26.** *distinguish between sacred and profane:* "Sacred" (Hebr *qōdeš*) is that which belongs in a positive way to God and partakes of his holiness. "Profane" (Hebr *ḥōl*) is the opposite of sacred, because of its association with man; it is "common," i.e., at man's disposal. Sometimes God and man are both involved in certain affairs. To put at man's disposal for furthering his affairs that which pertains to God is to profane it (cf. N. Snaith, *Distinctive Ideas of the Old Testament* [London, 1944] 21–34). **30.** *I found no one...:* This phrase seems to indicate intercessory power and solidarity in righteousness that is opposed to ch. 14 (cf. Gn 18:22ff.). The claim that such a statement cannot be truly made if Jeremiah is also prophesying at this time is a strong element in C. C. Torrey's argument against the traditional dating of the book (*JBL* 53 [1934] 311; see reply by Spiegel, *JBL* 54 [1935] 151–52).

55 (m) THE STORY OF TWO FAITHLESS SISTERS (23:1–49). This allegory is similar to that of ch. 16, where the infidelity, however, is mainly in the realm of worship. The language may seem offensive to our puritan sensibilities, but it would not be to the realism of the Near East. There is no need to appeal to El and his two wives in Ugaritic mythology nor even to any imagined folk tale of two wanton sisters as the origin of this allegory. The metaphors spring easily enough from Israel's history.

(i) *Maidenhood in Egypt and marriage* (23:1–4). **1.** *harlotry in Egypt:* Israel's sinfulness is so deeply rooted that it is represented as originating in Egypt (cf. 20:5–9).

The reference to the apostasy in Egypt, far from being an editor's interpolation (May, *IB* 6, 188), is the very foundation of the story that will repeat itself. **4.** Oholah means "she who has a tent [her own tent]." Oholibah means "My tent [is] in her." Oholah (Samaria) had her own—schismatic—tent, or place of worship, as opposed to the legitimate cult of Jerusalem, where originally the Ark of the Covenant was under a tent (2 Sm 7:2). But it may also allude to some fact or situation of which we are unaware—e.g., a scornful reference to some aspect of the fertility cults, as in 16:16, has been suggested.

(ii) *The affairs of Oholah* (23:5–10). **5.** *her lovers, the Assyrians:* The prophets before Ezekiel already condemned political alliances as showing a lack of faith in God and as placing a greater value on profane power and wealth (Hos 5:13; 7:11; 8:9–10; Is 7:1–9 with 2 Kgs 16:7–8; Jer 4:30, which uses the same word for "lovers" as Ezekiel). **9.** *I handed her over:* Samaria was destroyed by the Assyrians in 721.

(iii) *The affairs of Oholibah* (23:11–35). **12.** The interchange between Judah and Assyria is seen in the case of Ahaz (735–715) calling for help (2 Kgs 16:7–9; Is 7:1–8:22) and the oppression that later resulted for Hezekiah (2 Kgs 18:1–36). **14.** *images of Chaldeans:* See the reliefs of Merodach-baladan of Babylon and the governor of Mari (*ANEP* 454,533). [This material culture must have been very attractive to the Hebrews. Nothing like it has come to us from ancient Israel.] **16.** *she sent messengers:* Isaiah condemns King Hezekiah roundly for being too familiar with messengers of Merodach-baladan (Is 39:1–8). **18.** *became disgusted with them:* Judah's policy toward Babylon changed several times (cf. Jer 29:3 for one reversal). **32.** *the cup of your sister:* The figure of drinking a cup of grief and suffering to the dregs is a popular symbol in the OT (Jer 25:15–29; Is 51:17–23; Ps 11:6; Mt 20:22; Jn 18:11; Ap 14:10).

(iv) *Judgment of the two sisters* (23:36–49). This section is composite, which the alternation between second person singular and third person plural shows. Verse 29 should be followed by vv. 40–44a (the LXX omits "they sent"). **36–37a, 45.** The final judgment passed on the two sisters. **30, 37b–39.** Editorial verses, explaining harlotry as consorting with idols. **46–49.** Has the character of another prophecy, containing the final judgment of destruction on the two sisters together (Samaria's punishment is considered also in the future) and on Judah in particular. References to contemporary political events seem to be contained in vv. 40–44.

56 (n) Ezekiel Shall Be a Sign (24:1–27). The first time the Prophet's name is mentioned since 1:3, it appears as a signature authenticating the oracles of doom comprising the first part of the book. Two actions symbolic of the city's coming destruction are given, with an accompanying interpretation.

(i) *The allegory of the pot* (24:1–14). This section is an elaboration and interpretation of 11:3–13, with echoes of Mi 3:3. **1.** *ninth year:* January 18, 588 (cf. 2 Kgs 25:1; Jer 52:4; 39:1). **2.** *write down:* In the face of the disbelief of his hearers (21:28), the fulfillment of the Prophet's oracles has begun; the day is worthy of record. **3–4.** *all good pieces:* With the coming of the enemy, all the nobility take refuge in the city, thus ironically fulfilling their optimistic proverb of 11:3 in a tragic sense. **6.** *take out its pieces:* See comment on 11:11. *on the bare rock:* The meaning seems to be the impunity and defiance with which sins of blood were committed in the city. Even the blood of animals was to be covered as something sacred because it contained life (Lv 7:13; 17:11ff.). Flagrant and unexpiated sins are indicated in v. 8: "to excite my [the Lord's] vengeance" (24:8; Gn 4:10; Jb 16:18).

57 (ii) *Grief too great for mourning* (24:15–27). In the Near East, where external manifestations of grief are expected (Mt 9:23), this symbolic action was all the more significant. **17.** *groan in silence...:* All are popular mourning customs (cf. A. Heschel, *The Prophets* [N.Y., 1962] 400). There is a depth of character and personality and genuine human warmth manifested here that cannot be matched by any of Jeremiah's emotive outbursts, to which commentators like to compare Ezekiel's work, to the latter's disadvantage. The ability to turn his grief into a creative pattern harmonious with the mission given him by God reveals a man of unusual psychological balance and disciplined self-control—anything but the pathological personality many of his critics would make of him. **21.** *you left behind:* This phrase is deleted as an interpolation by those who hold the Palestinian ministry theory, for it seems to locate the Prophet and his hearers in Babylon (Herntrich, *op. cit.*). There is no justification for this (P. Tournay, *RB* 69 [1962] 137). However, if Ezekiel had left Jerusalem, others had done so with him, and the phrase would be true of them, especially inasmuch as all young people would have been kept there for the military effort. On the other hand, it is impossible to see how the Temple can be the "delight of their eyes" if they are captives in Babylon. **26.** *that day the fugitive:* On the same day, a fugitive will come to the town where Ezekiel is staying. A fugitive from Jerusalem to Babylon, the land of enemies, is absurd! The tampering with the fugitive's date of the arrival in 33:21 and the unlikely length of the journey in any version is all the more evidence for our interpretation (→ 5 above).

58 **(III) Judgment on the Nations (25:1–32:32).** From the earliest times the great prophets have concerned themselves with the nations whose history interlocked with that of Israel (Am 1–2; Is 13–23; Jer 47–51). The nations are scored for two things especially: their hybris and their attitude toward Israel. Hybris is an arrogance that exalts itself above God and takes credit for its own greatness—e.g., the case with the great nations like Assyria, Egypt, Babylon, and Tyre. This arrogance will be brought to dust to the consternation of those who put their trust in it. The small nations exalted themselves at the expense of God's people by preying upon them and oppressing them, seeking to devour them for their own profit. They will receive the same treatment at the hands of others. Ezekiel prophesies against seven nations: Ammon, Moab, Edom, Philistia, Tyre, Sidon, and Egypt (→ Excursus Israel, 11:9–13).

59 **(A) Judgment on Israel's Neighbors (25:1–17).** War was frequent between Judah and her proximate neighbors. The restoration of Israel and its peaceful existence is seen as demanding these nations' political extermination, especially as a recompense for their malicious treatment of Judah in her days of grief. The oracles seem to be written after the destruction of Jerusalem, probably by Ezekiel. They are all cast in the form of indictment and sentence: "because...therefore."

(a) Against Ammon (25:1–7). The Ammonites were situated on the E side of the Jordan slightly N of Jericho, around Rabbah, the capital city. **1.** This introductory formula is patterned after the biographical narratives. **4.** *easterners:* Nomadic Arab tribes to the east of Ammon (Is 11:14; Jer 49:28).

(b) Against Moab (25:8–11). Situated S of Ammon and E of the Dead Sea. **9.** *shoulder of Moab:* The steep but rounded bluff rising from the eastern shore of the Dead Sea, toward the edge of which most of the Moabite cities were located.

(c) Against Edom (25:12–14). Edom, in particular, profited at the expense of Judah in her tragedy, occupying it as far N as Beth-zur. But the long-standing hostility between the two peoples is reflected in previous prophets (Am 1:11–12; Is 34; Jer 49:7–22). **13.** *Teman to Dedan:* The former is the northern province of Edom (Am 1:12), in popular tradition named after Esau's grandson (Gn 36:11); the latter is the southernmost boundary.

(d) Against the Philistines (25:15–17). Although no longer the formidable foe of former times, bands of Philistine plunderers descended on prostrate Judah, renewing the memory of an "undying enmity" (v. 15). **16.** *Cherethites:* Of the same stock as the Philistines, originally from Crete (Jer 47:4), they lived around Gerar (1 Sm 30:14).

60 **(B) Tyre Will Perish from the Seas (26:1–28:26).** In these chapters, we have the most vivid picture of an ancient civilization painted by an historian of antiquity (A. Parrot, *Babylon and the Old Testament* [N.Y., 1958] 129). In fact, it is with a wistful glance of understandable and excusable human envy that the Prophet describes the glories of Tyre in ch. 27—which most modern commentators deny to Ezekiel, at least in part—while pronouncing doom upon them. In the 6th cent., Tyre was a mighty commercial power whose ships dominated the Mediterranean and not the least of whose exports was our alphabet, taken over and adapted by the Greeks (Steinmann, *op. cit.*, 269–70). The city was involved in anti-Babylonian intrigue along with Judah before 587.

(a) The Tidal Wave Against Tyre (26:1–21). Some authors (e.g., Holscher and Torrey) maintain that the poem describes the capture of Tyre by Alexander in 332, because it speaks of a complete destruction of the city (vv. 3–6, 14). But as Steinmann points out (*op. cit.*, 132), the method of attack (vv. 8–9) is not that employed by Alexander but is similar to that of attackers previous to Nebuchadnezzar (e.g., Esarhaddon in 673).

1. *eleventh year:* 586. The LXX has twelfth year, tenth month. **2.** *gateway:* Caravans from Mesopotamia to Tyre passed through Israelite territory and were subject to duty (cf. 1 Kgs 10:28–29). **3.** *as the sea...its waves:* Tyre was built on an island of rock rising out of the sea about .5 mi. from the mainland. The attacking armies will be like the waves of the sea that wash over it in a storm. **4.** *bare rock:* A play on words, the Hebr word for Tyre and rock being the same (*ṣōr*). After a siege of 13 years, Tyre agreed to pay tribute, but it was not taken. **8.** *his shields:* A weapon of attack, possibly like the Roman *testudo* (Driver, *op. cit.*, 156). This verse is a detailed word picture of a siege, such as is seen on sculptures (*ANEP* 368, 372–73). **11.** *mighty pillars:* Standing before the temple of Melqart (cf. 1 Kgs 7:15ff.). **14.** *never... rebuilt:* Mostly true after destruction by Alexander in 332. **16.** *princes of the sea:* The rulers of the islands and cities on the sea that traded with Tyre. **20.** *the pit...Sheol:* Where the dead continue their diminished existence.

Authors differ on the extent of ch. 26 to be attributed to Ezekiel. With the exception of vv. 19–21, the rest should be assigned to him.

61 (b) Lament on the Wreck of the Ship Tyre (27:1–36). Under the imagery of a proud luxury ship, manned by a crack crew carrying a complement of soldiers and rich traders as passengers and laden with rare cargo, Tyre is pictured as sinking in the sea, wrecked by a storm wind from the east. The chapter is acknowledged to be one of the most striking in Ez. The passage, vv. 10–25a, is judged to be a later interpolation, for it drops the image of a ship and takes up that of a fortified commercial city. **6.** The high plateau of Bashan, to the east of the Sea of Galilee, is mentioned for its oaks also in Is 2:13; Zech 11:2. **9.** *every ship:* The verse switches from the figure of a ship to that of a city served by many ships; it prepares for vv. 10–25a. All the countries with which Tyre traded are enumerated (for an identification of the place names, see May, *IB* 6, 211ff.; Auvray, *Ézéchiel*, 98ff.). Some see in this list a close relation to the table of nations in Gn 10, where the P editor gives a list of nations reflecting the historical situation before the fall of Nineveh in 612. **13.** *exchanging slaves:* The law allowed Israel to buy slaves from foreign nations or from resident aliens (Lv 25:44–45; 22:11; Ex 12:44). **26.** *east wind:* Destructive alike on land and on sea (Ps 48:8; Hos 13:15; Jer 18:17). It is possible that here, as in 17:10, it symbolizes Nebuchadnezzar. **31.** *shave their heads:* Sign of mourning for the dead; forbidden to Israel (Dt 14:1).

62 (c) Tyre, the Wise and Resplendent, Brought to the Dust (28:1–19). There are two distinct but related oracles in this passage. In each, Tyre is personified as an arrogant king who will be brought down to the dust. In the first, Tyre is cast down because, although a man, he exalts himself above human measure; in the second, he is cast down because, having been truly exalted by God, he spurns the honor, to seek one according to his own liking.

(i) *Tyre—A fool's use of wisdom* (28:1–10). Speaking with tongue in cheek and with a sarcastic inflection of the word "wisdom," the Prophet reproaches Tyre for having devoted its great wisdom to the acquisition of riches and splendor.

63 (ii) *Tyre, God's chosen, is cast off* (28:11–19). Almost all commentators agree that a myth of the same kind as Gn 2–3 is contained here. However, no one has been able either to identify the myth or to discern whether it is predominantly of Canaanite or Babylonian origin. It cannot merely be an imaginative handling of Gn 2–3, as J. L. McKenzie has shown (*MR* 154–55; 175–81). He maintains that it is a variant form of Gn 2–3, both accounts being forms of native Hebr tradition with possible foreign mythological coloring. The differences between the two passages, however, are so great (e.g., a garden, as opposed to a locale with precious and fiery stones), that we may well question this claim.

The passage is rather an allegory on the historical relationship between Tyre and Israel. Of all Israel's neighbors, only Tyre is not presented by Ezekiel as positing any hostile action; in all Israel's history, we do not read of any hostility from Tyre (two vague references in Ps 83:8 and Jl 4:4 show nothing concrete). There do exist vestiges of great friendliness, especially in the early days of the monarchy (1 Kgs 5:1,7), and even of a covenant (1 Kgs 9:13–14; Am 1:9; Ps 45:13). The role of Tyre in the building of the Temple was essential (1 Kgs 5–7). In Hos 9:13, Ephraim is compared to Tyre. According to Is 23:18, Tyre will be restored and "her merchandise shall be sacred to the Lord...from her merchandise those that dwell before the Lord shall have their fill." Tyre had this position at one time (vv. 15–16), but sinful trade made her fall away by heaping up her riches (Is 23:18; Ez 28:5). The mountain of God is Jerusalem (Is 2:2; Mi 4:2; Zeph 3:11). The garden of Eden is the land of Israel (Is 51:3; Lam 2:6; Jl 2:3). A baraitha in the Talmud states that the garden is one of seven things created before the world (Mishnah, *Pesahim* 54a). The covering of precious stones could refer to the breastpiece of precious stones on which the names of the tribes were inscribed as seals (Ex 39:10). The pact of brotherhood gave Tyre a place among them by association. But it is also possible that the precious stones refer to the Torah, which is often evaluated and preferred to them. Stones of fire might even refer to the stones of the altar or to the whole Temple area (2 Chr 7:1–3; 3:6). "The anointed cherub drove you out" refers to the high priest Jehoiada, who cast out Athaliah, the daughter of Jezebel (2 Kgs 11:13–16), from the Temple, which ended the long and friendly association between Judah and Tyre. Whatever may be said about this identification, it seems more reasonable than the "Urmensch" myth or some other myth as yet unidentified.

We offer the interpretation that Tyre, after its long and friendly association with Israel, became rich by its trade and haughty as a result. Tyre spurned this relationship with lowly Israel because its concern was to "heap up riches." It became corrupt in its trade until finally, in the person of one of its royal members, it was cast out of the Temple and out of the land. With this action, its destiny was cut off from God's people and its doom was sealed.

(May, H. G., "The King in the Garden of Eden: A Study in Ezekiel 28:12–19," *Israel's Prophetic Heritage* [Fest. J. Muilenburg; N.Y., 1962] 167. McKane, W., *Prophets and Wise Men* [*SBT*; London, 1965] 73–77.)

(d) SIDON, THE THORN, WILL PIERCE NO LONGER (28:20–24). Sidon, another Phoenician city to the north of Tyre, will be punished for its scorn of Israel. It participated in the intrigue against Babylon (Jer 27:3).

(e) ISRAEL SHALL DWELL SECURE (28:25–26). Israel, dwelling in security and depending upon God, will be a sign of God's holiness.

64 **(C) Egypt Will Be Turned Into a Desert (29:1–32:32).** The remains that we have from ancient Egypt give evidence of a powerful and resplendent civilization. From earliest times, Egypt was involved in the history of Israel, either as a master exploiting it or as an opportunist friend, alluring it into a false dependence and a consequent false sense of security. For these two evils especially, it will be punished.

(a) DOOM OF EGYPT, THE MONSTER AND REED OF THE NILE (29:1–9). The oracle is dated January 7, 587, when the siege of Jerusalem had been in progress for one year and after the attempt of Pharaoh Hophra (Gk, "Apries") to lift the siege had failed (Jer 37:1–10). **2.** *Niles:* The reference is to the many mouths of the Nile as it flows through the delta into the sea. **3.** *monster:* Undoubtedly the crocodile is meant (Hebr *tannîn;* cf. Is 27:1; Jb 41); the clinging fish are the dependent nations. **7.** *shoulder out of joint:* This is probably a reference to Hophra's failure to drive the Chaldeans from Jerusalem (Jer 37:1–10).

65 (b) EGYPT A WASTELAND FORTY YEARS (29:10–16). This oracle is another with eschatological perspectives, hence from a later time, placed here as a concrete application of the preceding passages. **10.** *Migdol to Syene:* The northern and southern limits of Egypt; the former is a fortress of uncertain location; the latter is modern Aswan, at the first Nile cataract. **12.** *forty years:* The symbolic number signifies "prescribed or allotted measure" for the fullness or completion of things. **14.** Pathros is located in Upper (i.e., southern) Egypt (cf. Jer 44:1).

66 (c) NEBUCHADNEZZAR'S WAGES (29:17–20). This oracle is Ezekiel's last and is dated April 26, 571, the latest date in the book. Thus, his ministry lasted over 20 years at least. Nebuchadnezzar's invasion of Egypt began in 568 (*ANET* 308). Because it is not the last dated oracle in the book, its presence here is to be explained by the fact that the oracle existed separately and was placed here because of the topic. **20.** *who did it for me:* Conquerors of the nations are often pictured as carrying out God's will (30:10,24; Jer 43:10; 44:30). According to general opinion, Tyre was not taken and therefore not handed over to the soldiers for pillage and booty, even though it apparently agreed to pay tribute.

(d) HOPE FOR ISRAEL (29:21). An independent oracle of Israel's restoration. *horn:* Symbol of power, sometimes in royal and messianic perspectives, as in Ps 132:17, and sometimes merely in the sense of moral or political development. Most likely the latter is intended here.

67 (e) DAY OF THE LORD FOR EGYPT (30:1–19). This prophecy seems to be an oracle inspired by 29:1–6, and probably pronounced by a later prophet of the Ezekiel school. Many points of contact with other oracles have been noted. **3.** *day of the Lord:* In the prophetic writings, "the day" or "the day of the Lord" is a time of God's decisive judgment. It comes to be associated with the messianic age when Israel will be established in security and harmony with God (Jl 2:27–32).

68 (f) PHARAOH'S BROKEN ARMS (30:20–26). The oracle is dated April 29, 587, during the siege of Jerusalem. Pharaoh's arm was "broken" when he was forced to withdraw from attempting to drive the Chaldeans away from Jerusalem (29:6–7). **22.** *his strong arm:* The MT adds, "and that which was broken." This prophecy is of a later defeat that will destroy the military forces of Egypt.

69 (g) EGYPT, THE FELLED CEDAR OF LEBANON (31:1–18). Consisting in a poetic oracle (vv. 2–9) and two oracles in prose (vv. 9–14; 15–18), ch. 31 is an allegory prophesying Egypt's ruin in the symbol of a mighty cedar felled to the ground and abandoned by those who had taken refuge in its shade. Although the allegory has some incidental mythological coloring, its origin is to be sought in fable rather than myth (Ez 17; Jgs 9:8). Commentators are not agreed on how much of the chapter, besides the generally acknowledged poetry (vv. 2–9), should be assigned to Ezekiel. Without the interpretation in vv. 10–14 that continues the symbolism and embodies the prophetic message harmoniously, the poetic verses are meaningless. This is not true of vv. 15–18, which lack a clear prophetic message; the symbolism changes to descent to the underworld, and the text speaks of a total destruction already achieved. Thus, it is to be considered another oracle from the Ezekiel school, with v. 14b a transition prepared by the editor. The date is June 21, 587. **2.** *behold a cypress* [*cedar*]: The CCD is an emendation of the text that changes the MT "Assyria" to "cypress," because "Assyria" seems out of place here and makes the text difficult (but not impossible, however, for Assyria could be held up to Egypt as an example of its own doom). **8.** *garden of God:* Commentators see in this a reference to terrestrial paradise; however, this identification is difficult, for in no text are trees of paradise admired for their stateliness and height. It can be interpreted as a symbol of Mt. Zion (cf. Is 51:3; Lam 2:6; Jl 2:3). The sense would be that Egypt was more blessed with material resources than was Israel (cf. exegesis of Ez 15). **12.** *its foliage:* The far-reaching rule of Egypt (Assyria?) was ended. **15.** *drooped on his account:* Just as in the allegory of the ship Tyre—i.e., all the mariners were troubled on her behalf (27:29–30)—so here the trees of Lebanon pine for Egypt, for they were fed by the same streams of water. **18.** *those slain by the sword:* The reference is to those who were executed, murdered, or came to a sudden, unexpected, violent death (cf. O. Eissfeldt, "Schwerterschlagene bei Hesekiel," *Studies in Old Testament Prophecy* [Fest. T. H. Robinson; Edinburgh, 1950] 73–81).

70 (h) EGYPT, THE RIVER MONSTER, WILL BE SLAIN (32:1–32). There are two dated oracles in this final prophecy against Egypt. The first takes up the allegory of the monster (ch. 29), which is very evidently a crocodile, a fitting symbol for Pharaoh. It is difficult to see any connection between this passage and the battle between Marduk and Tiamat of the Akkadian creation myth, for in the myth, Tiamat's blood is taken by the north wind "to places undisclosed," whereas here, the monster's blood drenches the earth it once ruled. The body of Tiamat is used to make "artful works" (*ANET* 67), but the flesh of the monster is given to "glut all the beasts of the earth," manifestly a spoliation by the subject nations. The first oracle, dated March 3, 585, has two parts: vv. 1–8 (which we may attribute to Ezekiel) and vv. 9–16 (which expand the symbolism, e.g., "all of her [Egypt's] animals perish," and not the monster). The second oracle is dated April 27, 586 (in autumnal dating, April 16, 585; cf. May, *IB* 6, 59, 238). Perhaps vv. 17–19, 31b–32 belong to Ezekiel; the rest lacks a clear prophetic message and may be an adaptation of another oracle from the circle of his followers. **2.** *monster in the sea:* Under different imagery, the same ideas are conveyed in vv. 2–8 as in 31:12–16. **5.** *flesh on the mountains:* The corpses of Egyptian soldiers will be left unburied. This was the worst of all curses (1 Kgs 4:11; Jer 16:4) in the ancient world; the "shade" (Is 14:9; Jb 26:5), was considered to feel in some way what was done to the body (De Vaux, *AI* 56). **16.** *this is a dirge:* Professional mourners from the nations will be called to lament over Egypt. **30.** *princes of the north:* Babylon is not included here because the Chaldeans are considered to be carrying out Yahweh's orders.

Ezekiel's view of life after death in these verses seems at first to be the traditional one. But the following points should make us pause before making a hasty judgment: the faithful Israelite is not mentioned in this multitude, even though there seem to be two degrees of existence—an honorable one and a dishonorable one; all are uncircumcised; all are slain by the sword; their consignment is stated as a punishment—"since he spread his terror" (v. 32). However, we should also recognize that vv. 17–32 are an imaginative description of sheol.

71 **(IV) Conditions and Process of Restoration (33:1–37:28).** With the fall of Jerusalem, Ezekiel turns to the task of assuring the exiles that God's purpose with Israel continues. Israel shall rise from the dead (ch. 37).

(A) Responsibility of Man—The Prophetic Charge (33:1–33). It has been pointed out that ch. 33 is composed of parallels found in the first part of the book (33:1–6 = 3:16b–21 = 33:7–9; 33:10–20 = 18:1–32; 33:23–29 = 11:14–21). However, they should not be seen as exact doublets but rather prophetic variants that the editor used to bind the contents of the book. Quite appropriately, Howie (*op. cit.*, 98) has called the chapter a "literary binder" with which the editor joined the two sections of Ez.

72 (a) Prophet as Watchman (33:1–20). The oracle was doubtless suggested by Nebuchadnezzar's invasion, when warning of the hostile army's advance may have meant the difference between life and death. On the hills of Palestine, such watchmen had always been important (1 Sm 14:16; 2 Kgs 9:17; Is 21:16; cf. Lachish ostracon 4, *ANET* 322). According to Auvray, we have here Ezekiel's definition of the prophetic role, in his case unique (*RB* 71, 191–206). **2.** *to be their watchman:* Verses 1–6 are a parable defining the role of watchman without any allegorical interpretation (except, perhaps, "because of his own sin," v. 6; cf. Auvray, *RB* 71, 191–206). **5c.** *had he taken warning:* This phrase should be taken to refer to the watchman, i.e., the watchman saves his own life by being alert to the dangers of others. **7–9.** The parable is applied to the Prophet. By acquitting himself of his charge, he will save his life. Ezekiel conceives of his mission as being for individuals, because Israel as a body seems doomed. This development presupposes that he is in Palestine. **10.** *our sins:* A rigid and somewhat fatalistic application of the principle of personal retribution—i.e., doom is inevitable because of past sins. The reply in vv. 11ff. contains much the same thought as 18:21–30. **11.** *as I live:* God answers the fatalism of the sinners with a solemn oath, a double affirmation in favor of the sinner: "no pleasure in death...rather...conversion." Coming from God, this affirmation is already a saving power. *turn, turn:* Recalled is the triple "return" of Jer 3:12,14,22. This message is basic to true prophecy. **15.** *that bring life:* Life is the goal of God's Law (Dt 30:15–20; Lv 18:5; see also "wisdom" and "life" in Prv 1–9). **17–20.** *way of the Lord:* Some consider these verses a later addition because they are no longer a commentary on the parable, hardly a sufficient reason.

73 (b) Fugitive from Jerusalem (33:21–22). The date given for the arrival of the fugitive is January 8, 585, fully 17 months after the fall of the city. Even if the year is changed to "eleventh" (v. 21), it is still too long, for Ezra's trip with a whole caravan required only four months (Ezr 7:9; 9:31). The date shows signs of tampering, probably by a scribe who conjectured how long a fugitive would take for such a journey. **22.** *my mouth was opened:* This phrase should be interpreted in the light of 3:27. Ezekiel was never mute! When he spoke, it was only to pronounce Yahweh's judgment of doom, and he refused to involve himself in personal argumentation, "to rebuke them" for specific actions or policies. Now this commission was finished; the doom had overtaken the city and he could give his counsel to individuals.

74 (c) Claims of the Survivors in Judah (33:23–29). It is hard to imagine that this oracle was spoken after the destruction of Jerusalem, for it speaks of making "the land a desolate waste so that its proud strength" will come to an end! This claim must have been made by those who remained after the first deportation; Ezekiel lived among them in a country ravaged by an invasion. **24.** *Abraham:* Yahweh had given the land to Abraham, but it is Yahweh who repudiates their claim because they fail to live up to the conditions for keeping the land.

(d) A Prophet of Fashion (33:30–33). To come and hear Ezekiel seems to have become fashionable, the result apparently of a religiosity that usually follows upon national catastrophe. **32.** *ballad singer:* The CCD is a conjecture for a difficult reading in the MT, which seems to mean: "you are for them like a love song of one with a beautiful voice playing [an instrument] skillfully." His preaching satisfies a sentimental religious sense and leaves them in self-complacency.

75 **(B) The Shepherd of Israel and His Flock (34:1–31).** After a bitter indictment of the wicked shepherds (vv. 1–10), the Lord proclaims that he will be the shepherd of the people. He will judge between the sheep and inaugurate an age of peace (cf. Jer 23:1ff.; Is 40:11). Christ built upon this passage to express the nature of his person and mission (Jn 10:1–18; Mt 18:12–14; Lk 15:4–7). Inasmuch as the meaning of vv. 25–30 fluctuates between the allegory and its interpretation—i.e., between sheep and people—it is probably another prophecy, a "sermon" on the previous passage, inserted by the editor. **6.** *and high hills:* Probably a reference to the worship on the high places that most of the kings encouraged or tolerated. **8.** *wild beasts:* Attacks of foreign peoples. **10.** *pasture themselves:* There is a play on words here: "I will stop them from feeding the flock so that they may no longer feed themselves upon it." **11.** *I myself:* This and the following verses suggest a return to a theocracy (1 Sm 8:7; Pss 73:1; 94:7; Hos 8:4). **17.** *between sheep and sheep:* This theme is not present in any of the other prophets and perhaps may be considered a concrete application of the principle of individual responsibility (Mt 25:32ff.). **18–19.** *your feet had trampled:* Abuse of power and exploitation of the weak. **20–24.** *one shepherd:* The profiteering ways of the previous shepherds are contrasted with the shepherding of Yahweh and the messianic shepherd, David, who is considered the beginning of a renewed dynasty. This ruler is called not "king," but "prince," to refer to the conditions of the tribes coming out of the desert (A. Gelin, *VDBS* 5, 1185–86). In contrast to Jer 33:14–33, there is no explicit association of the covenant concept with messianism (as in v. 25); therefore, this passage can be considered to be earlier. It can be related to 17:22–24; 37:24. **25–31.** *covenant of peace:* Cf. comment on 37:26. The description of the material prosperity promised here is restrained.

76 **(C) Edom To Be Eternally Desolate (35:1–15).** Although this oracle belongs logically with the prophecies against the nations, its purpose here is to prepare for the prophecy on the restoration of the mountains of Israel (ch. 36), which the Edomites occupied partially after the catastrophe of 587. The plaintiff and the defendant, mountains of Israel (36:4) and Mt. Seir (35:2), respectively, stand before Yahweh, the judge. There is an arraignment that, in Oriental fashion, anticipates the sentence (vv. 3–4). The indictment is on two counts, each with its sentence: "because [v. 5]...therefore [vv. 6–9]"; "because [v. 10]...therefore [vv. 11–15]." **5.** *Mount Seir:* The mountainous plateau extending SE from the Dead Sea to the Gulf of Aqaba, the traditional home of the Edomites; it is often used as a synonym for Edom (Gn 32:4; Jgs 15:4; Nm 24:18). **5.** *whom you delivered over:* Indictment on the first count (cf. Ob 10ff.). **6.** *guilty of blood:* The verdict was followed by the sentence, "Blood shall pursue you"—the personification of the unrelenting avenger of blood, the nearest relative of a murdered person; this method was the accepted way of carrying out justice (Nm 35:16–22; Dt 19:6–12; Jos 20:3–4). **10–15.** *lands have become mine:* For the second count of indictment, the verdict was guilty of envy and malicious spoliation, carrying the sentence, "So will I treat you"—the execution of the law of the talion.

77 **(D) Increase and Be Fruitful, Israel (36:1–38).** The two parts of this chapter (vv. 1–15; 16–38) are a reversal of the oracles of doom the Prophet had pronounced upon the mountains and the people of Israel in chs. 6–7. A new creation will result and the blessings of Gn 1:28; 9:7; etc., will be surpassed.

(a) Blessing Upon the Mountains of Israel (36:1–15). As in ch. 6, the mountains are personified (cf. Mi 6:1–3) and presented as plaintiffs in the judgment on Edom; the verdict in their favor is the Lord's "hot jealousy" (v. 5) and their indemnity, "grow branches [v. 8]...settle crowds of men upon you [v. 10]."

8. *soon return:* This striking optimism in the midst of ruin and discouragement finds foundation and vindication in such acts as Jeremiah buying a field during the siege (Jer 32:1ff.) and his words to those left by the Chaldeans on the land (Jer 42:10–12). **13.** *rob...people...of children:* The reference could be to: poverty of soil causing famine; offering of children as sacrifice in past idolatrous worship; inability to defend from foreign oppression. Because of the fertility theme in vv. 13–15 and 37–38, many commentators assign these passages to the time after the return from exile, when the returnees were discouraged by the difficulties of making a new beginning.

(b) Blessing Upon the People of Israel (36:16–38). The motif of the Lord's "holy name" (ch. 20) is introduced as a reason for the restoration, which is described in terms of the inner change in the human heart and spirit (a resumption of 11:19, 18:31). **25.** *to cleanse you:* God must cleanse man—man cannot cleanse himself. Although ablution rites were prescribed in the Law (Ex 30:17–21; Lv 14:52; Nm 5:17; 19:7,9), this cleansing will go beyond them. **27.** *put my spirit within you:* This promise of the spirit will be taken up by Joel (3:1ff.) and extended to all mankind; as such, it will be quoted by Peter at Pentecost (Acts 2:16ff.). The activity of the spirit does not produce a transitory change as in the judges or ecstatic prophets (e.g., Jgs 6:34; 1 Sm 10:6ff.; etc.), but it will give an inner abiding power to "live by my statutes," and thus a new level of life will begin. Creation is taken another step forward by the creative activity of the spirit. How this will be accomplished the Prophet does not say; nevertheless, we have here a truly elevated conception of the Law and the relation of the life of the spirit to it. This is one of the key eschatological passages of the OT. **28.** *you shall be my people:* The covenant by which Israel becomes Yahweh's people is also based upon the gift of the spirit; by it, they become true subjects of Yahweh. **29.** *will order the grain:* The covenant will have repercussions on cosmic harmonies, but they are not the extraordinary manifestations of later apocalyptic. **31.** *you shall remember:* Israel's conversion will result from a humble realization of its relationship to God and to its past history. **37–38.** *multiply them:* Cf. Is 54:1–3; Zech 2:4.

78 **(E) O My People, Rise from Your Graves (37:1–14).** The episode takes place in Babylon, and Ezekiel is led out by the spirit into a plain (on which may have remained unburied the bones of those who had fallen in battle). This mystical experience symbolizes his mission to the exiles; through his prophesying, they will receive a new spirit that will enable them to rise from their lost hope (v. 11) and to lead a new life in the land of Israel (v. 12). **1.** *bones:* The bones are often associated with the stamina a man needs to stand up to difficulties (Jb 4:14; Pss 6:3; 101:4; Is 38:13). **2.** *how dry:* These bones have long been lifeless. **9.** *come, O spirit:* The one Hebr word, *rûaḥ*, means: "wind," "breath," and "spirit"—thus the remarkable play on words in this passage. **10.** One of the most imaginative and unusual scenes in all literature. **11.** The explanation of the vision is given: "these bones are the whole house of Israel." The discouragement of the people ("our bones are dried up") is to be met by the powerful word of God who alone knows (v. 3) that they can live. **12.** The metaphor shifts from "bones" to "graves." **14.** The aim of the prophecy is to give the captives new spirit to rise from their captivity (cf. Hos 6:2). There is no reference here to the resurrection of individuals (cf. Is 26:19; Dn 12:2), but the passage shows that this concept is not far removed. The question, "Can these bones live?" as Jacob points out (Jacob, *op. cit.*, 301), is understood with difficulty if only the nation is meant, inasmuch as this was never questioned. The answer, "you alone know," places resurrection in the hands of the living God. Ezekiel's emphasis on individual responsibility as a key to life with the God whose ways are fair (18:25ff.) provides a motive; the Lord can do it—he should do it. As Jacob observes (Jacob, *op. cit.*, 301), there is a development from Hos 6:1–2.

79 **(F) One Nation and David, Its Prince Forever (37:15–28).** **16.** *Israelites:* Ordinarily in Ez, this term means both the northern and southern tribes, but here the reference is to Judah alone. *Joseph:* The northern kingdom—sometimes equated with Ephraim, the leading tribe—was taken into captivity by the Assyrians in 721. **22.** *never again...divided:* The unity of the future messianic kingdom will be a return to the conditions under David. The union of all tribes is a frequent element in messianic prophecy (Jer 3:18; 31:1; Zech 11:7–14; etc.). The manner of its fulfillment is problematical; for a discussion of prophetic language relative to messianism, see *CBQ* 19 (1957) 11–15, 21–24, 306–11.

26. *everlasting covenant:* God will unite the nation in a new covenant in which there are five essential elements: Yahweh, its God (v. 23); Israel, his people (v. 23); life "on the land where their fathers lived" (v. 25); "my sanctuary among them," as a sign of the presence of the Lord and the Law; David, as one shepherd over them. The description of the new Temple and the new land follows logically upon this chapter.

80 **(V) Triumph of Israel Over All Forces of Hostility (38:1–39:29).** A forerunner of the later apocalypses, the passage on Gog depicts the final and definitive establishment of Israel on the land. As such, it is meant as a continuation of the preceding prophecies on the restoration of Israel. The passage in 39:21–29 is a summary of the preceding chapters on the history of salvation. The final editor inserted chs. 38–39 as a fitting explanation of the messianic community described in chs. 40–48, inasmuch as the restoration depicted in chs. 34–37 seemed too modest to prepare for it in view of the forces of evil and hostility that continued to exist in the world.

These forces of evil are set in motion by the malice of one individual, Gog, who has the traits of all of Israel's persecutors. He is mentioned in *Sib Or* 3 and in the Talmudic literature, where the final war also comes after the messianic era has begun. He leads his hordes out of the "north," whence so many evils of Israel have come, particularly invading armies (Jer 4:6; 6:1; Jdt 16:5). His army is composed of elements from the four corners of the world: Gomer, N; Cush and Ethiopia, S; Sheba and Dedan, E; Tarshish, W. This enemy is all the enemies of whom God "spoke in ancient times through my servants, the prophets of Israel" (v. 17; cf. Jer 1:13–15).

Chapters 38–39 have some traits in common with the apocalypses (Is 24–27; Dn 7–12; Zech 9–14; Ap 20:7–10), but they lack some essential elements, e.g., contemporary history presented as prophecy, the occurrence of marvelous phenomena in nature, etc. Steinmann (*op. cit.*, 302) sees in these chapters midrashim on the prophets, especially Is 34, 37 and Ez 32:1–8, with minor motifs from Is 9; 2:6–21. This identification may fix their character more sharply than is warranted. They are oracles, hortatory compositions, inspired by the themes of Ez, but they reflect the conditions of the community after its return, already modestly secure on the land.

81 **(A) The Prophecy Against Gog (38:1–39:8).** **2.** *Gog:* As the brackets in the CCD indicate, he is glossed as from the "land of Magog"; neither he nor this land can be identified with certainty. Many point to Gyges, king of Lydia (*gûgû* in cuneiform records of Ashurbanipal). Identification is perhaps unimportant, because Gog seems to symbolize the powers of evil threatening Israel. **3.** The territories associated with Gog (cf. also v. 6) are all in the Fertile Crescent and its outer reaches (cf. Gn 10:2–3). The mythological coloring of these invaders appears in v. 6, "the recesses of the North" (cf. Is 14:13). Gog is commissioned to come up against a "land of open villages," yet his mission is doomed because the Lord is using him for his own purposes (vv. 17–23). **14–16.** This second prophecy against Gog is set aside for the sake of clarity in the CCD. **39:1–8.** The third prophecy against Gog proclaims his fall on the "mountains of Israel" (cf. chs. 6, 36), and the divine purpose (vv. 6–7) is once more affirmed.

82 **(B) Evil Turned Into a Benefit (39:9–20).** Gog is slain and the weapons he had intended to use against Israel will be burned. **10.** An indication that the talion law will work in reverse. **11.** *valley of Abarim:* There is a play on words between Abarim and *ʿōbᵉrîm*, "travelers." The hilly country S and W of Heshbon is meant, and it abounds in valleys. **12.** *Hamon-gog:* Lit., "horde of Gog." **14.** *unburied:* Such corpses defile the land (Nm 19:16; 31:19; 35:33). **16.** *Hamonah:* A city shall be named as a perpetual reminder of the event. **17–20.** This passage, apparently a separate unit, speaks of a feast provided by God at the slaughter of an army, different from that of Gog, which has already been buried (cf. Is 34:6; 56:9; Jer 46:10; 12:8–9).

(C) The House of Israel Will Know the Lord, Its God (39:21–29). There is no connection between this passage, which dates from the Exile, and the preceding passages on Gog. The whole purpose of the exile experience is seen as a vindication of the holiness of the Lord before the nations. Israel was punished "because of its sins" (v. 23), but the restoration has now become necessary to prove the Lord's "holiness."

83 **(VI) The Vision of the Restored Community (40:1–48:35).** This final section opens with a vision that continues over eight chapters. On first perusal, the reader is overwhelmed by the wealth of detailed building specifications, the ritualistic prescriptions, and the legalistic proposals for the reconstruction of a society. Ironically enough, these plans were never implemented, but paradoxically they had a tremendous influence upon the community that took up life in Jerusalem after the exile. It may even be said that perhaps the Temple as specified was never meant to be built, just as the high mountain of the vision is not a reality and the city on it only "seemed to be built." These plans for temple, cult, and social structure had only one purpose—to bring home graphically the nature of the post-exilic community and its relationship to Yahweh. It was an attempt to visualize in stone, in ritual act, and in socio-political institutions that city and community of which it could be said, "The Lord is here" (48:35). Chapters 1–24 proclaimed the corruption and the coming destruction of the social, political, and religious fabric of the Israelite community. Nothing was to be kept of the old order on which to build, save Yahweh himself and his holiness. He is to return, to become the nerve center from which life, nourishing (47:1–12) and normative (*passim*), will flow to the community.

The composite nature of this section is generally recognized, but there is no agreement on either the amount or the identity of the material to be assigned to Ezekiel. Generally, 40:1–42:20 are attributed to him or his school. There are those who deny that Ezekiel composed any of these chapters (Hölscher and Herntrich), the view of the present writer. This vision is very clearly related to the vision of chs. 1 and 8–11, chapters that are totally different in character and in content from the rest of the prophecies. Only there does the Prophet act in "visions of God." Elsewhere, he pronounces his oracles or dramatizes them under the impulse of the spirit, without any visions. Even ch. 37 is not a vision, strictly speaking, and the term is not used in it. These chapters belong to a prophet or prophets in the tradition or school of Ezekiel, and their value is not diminished thereby.

(Gese, H., *Der Verfassungsentwurf des Ezechiel, Kap 40–48* [Tübingen, 1957].)

84 **(A) The Vision of the New Temple (40:1–43:27).** It has been remarked (Bertholet, *op. cit.*, xx) that the composer of this section knew the Temple before it was destroyed and also in its destroyed condition. In fact, he may have had plans of it before him, for the specifications given here form a complete model (see the plans in Cooke, *op. cit.*, appendix charts; Auvray, *Ézéchiel*, 177ff.) It is in "divine visions," however, that it is revealed, and he is told to watch intently and report from memory to the house of Israel, just as he told his fellow exiles about the idolatry that he saw in the Temple (11:25).

(a) The Area Around the Temple (40:1–47). **1.** *beginning the twenty-fifth year:* The Hebr *rō'š haššānāh* is meant. In later and in modern Judaism, this phrase indicates the Feast of the New Year, celebrated on the first day of the month of Tishri in the fall, which begins the civil year. The present date would then be September-October 573. De Vaux maintains this identification is unlikely. Ezekiel uses the religious calendar, beginning with Nisan in the spring, for other dates, and the new year would hardly begin on the tenth of the month (De Vaux, *AI* 192, 502). Hence the correct date is April 28, 573. **5.** *measuring rod:* A reed about 10 ft. 4 in. long. There is a slight difference between the large and ordinary cubit: the former is about 20.4 in., and the latter about 17.5 in. On his comments on this section, Jerome expresses his frustration thus: "I hope these things don't seem frivolous to the reader, for I myself am dissatisfied in saying them, feeling myself knocking on a locked door" (*PL* 25. 380). **6.** *climbed its steps:* The Temple seems to have stood on successive elevations of 7, 8, and 10 steps each (cf. vv. 22, 26, 31, 34, 39), the last being for the Temple itself. *east gate:* The other gates have the same measurements. **16.** *palms:* A decoration also in Solomon's Temple (1 Kgs 6:29ff.) and common in the Near East. **25.** *windows on both sides:* The object of these gates seems to be to enable guards to keep out any one who might profane the sanctuary, just as today there are guards at the entrance of mosques in the Near East. **38.** *a chamber:* A "sacristy" for the facilities for preparing the sacrifices. **39.** *sin offerings and guilt offerings:* Beside the two main types of pre-exilic sacrifice, the "peace-offering" and "burnt-offering," there now appear the "sin-offering" (Hebr *ḥaṭṭa't*) and the "guilt-offering" (Hebr *'āšām*), which become so prominent in post-exilic Judaism (also in 43:13; 44:29). They are expiatory sacrifices, but it is difficult to say what distinguishes them, although their use here presupposes that the terms are understood. De Vaux thinks that they simply received greater emphasis when the national calamity had given the people a livelier sense of their culpability and when a finer sense of Yahweh's claims and the gravity of sin had developed (De Vaux, *AI* 420–21).

45–46. *priests:* Two ranks in the Temple's clergy are in evidence: the Levites, "who have charge of the temple"; and the sons of Zadok, "who have charge of the altar" (also 43:19; 44:11–15; 45:4–5; 46:20–24). This is in contrast to Dt, where priests and Levites are identified. The Levites, who are to take the place of foreign temple slaves, are relegated to an inferior position that must have been brought about by the reform of Josiah before the Exile (44:7–14). As a result, the Levites do not return from the Exile in great numbers (Ezr 2:40; 8:18; Neh 7:43).

85 (b) The Temple Buildings (40:48–41:26). The Temple's structure, like the Temple of Solomon and other temples of the ancient Near East, had three distinctly divided areas: the vestibule (Hebr *'ulām*), 40:48–49; the nave or the Holy Place (Hebr *hêkāl*), 41:1–2; the inner sanctuary or the Holy of Holies (Hebr *d^ebîr*), 41:3–4. (See *ANEP* 738–40.) **49.** *columns:* These are probably like the pillars that stood before Solomon's Temple, whose names were Jachin and Boaz (1 Kgs 7:21,41). They are passed over with a mere mention here. **41:3–4.** *went in beyond:* Into the "holy of holies," where the Prophet does not follow him. **6.** *chambers...in three stories:* These are probably for storage of Temple equipment (1 Kgs 6:5–10; 14:26; 2 Kgs 14:1ff.). Possibly they also served to make the building untouchable from the outside and thus free from profanation (Steinmann, *op. cit.*, 209). **12.** *the building:* A free-standing structure of unknown purpose, apparently without a roof. There seems to have been a stable for horses dedicated to the sun near the pre-exilic Temple (2 Kgs 23:11). This building might be intended as a shelter for animals before they were sacrificed. **22.** *table...before the Lord:* Either the altar of incense or the table of the Presence (1 Kgs 6:20–22; 1 Chr 28:16,18), on which were the 12 cakes of pure wheat flour that were a pledge of the covenant between Yahweh and the 12 tribes.

86 (c) Other Structures (42:1–20). The shape and arrangement of the structures given here are not too clear. They were places for storing vestments and the supplies necessary for sacrifices, and also dining halls, where the priests ate meat offered in sacrifice. **20.** The area in which the Temple is situated, 500 square cubits, is holy, surrounded by a wall to separate the sacred from the profane.

87 (d) The Restoration of the Temple (43:1–27). The return of the glory of the Lord is the central point of chs. 40–48. The vision thus far has led up to it as a preparation; the remaining chapters will flow from it as a consequence. **2.** *from the east:* It is in that direction that the Lord departed in chs. 10–11. **3.** Actually, the vision is very different from that seen by the river Chebar (chs. 1, 8–11): There are no living creatures, no wheels, no throne, and no appearance of a man; there is only a voice of "someone speaking...from the temple." But probably the vision "when he came to destroy the city" (cf. ch. 9) was like the one in this chapter. Its pervasive Babylonian coloring places it much later in the exile, by a prophet who grew up in those surroundings—hence, the thirtieth year in 1:1. Notice the order of the vision as given here: at destruction of city; by river Chebar; the return. **7.** The old Jerusalem had started as a Canaanite city; the Lord had entered it as a sojourner, and it rebelled. The Temple in the new city will be his permanent dwelling. Built by him, it will remain his and will have a sacramental significance. The combination of "harlotries...corpses...and high places" in vv. 7–10 seems incongruous, but it is united by the fact that the "high places" were places of funeral services and some of the pillars found there were in memory of the dead (cf. De Vaux, *AI* 287).

8. *their threshold:* Because the pre-exilic Temple was one of a complex of royal buildings, it created the impression of being one of them, a dependency of the king (1 Kgs 7:1–12; cf. Am 7:13; 2 Kgs 23:4–8). It will be so no longer (45:7; 46:21). **13–17.** *measurements of the altar:* This passage is probably out of its original context after 40:47. It is placed at this point as a conclusion of, and as a witness to, the promise that the Lord had just made: "I will dwell in their midst forever"; previous covenants were ratified in this way, in connection with theophanies (Gn 8:20; 12:7; Ex 17:14–16; 24:4–6; Jos 8:30–34). **14–17.** The altar was built in the form of a Babylonian ziggurat, and the terms used for its parts betray a Babylonian background (cf. De Vaux, *AI* 412). The altar is built in three tiers of 16, 14, and 12 square cubits, ending in the altar hearth, "the mountain of God." This latter was reached by steps, the total height being 12 cubits or about 21 ft. The significance of the horns on the corners of the altar is not clear, despite many interpretations (cf. De Vaux, *AI* 414; H. Obbink, *JBL* 56 [1937] 43–49). **18–26.** The ritual for the consecration of the altar is set forth along the lines prescribed in Ex 29:36–37; 40:1–38; Lv 8:14–15. **26.** *dedicated:* Lit., "they will fill its hands," terminology originally applied to the consecration of priests. **27.** *I will accept you:* The acceptance of the sacrifices is the acceptance of those who offer them.

88 **(B) The New Cult (44:1–46:24).** In view of the Lord's return to take possession of the new city and

Temple, provisions are made for a new cult that will be free from any taint of the profanation that often affected pre-exilic worship.

(a) The Official Personnel of the Temple (44:1–31). **1.** *facing the east:* This was the gate by which the glory of the Lord had departed (10:19; 11:23) and had returned (43:4). **3.** *only the princes:* The Hebr construction, an emphatic particle (Hebr *'et*) before "prince," which is repeated and followed by the pers. pronoun "he," should probably be translated, "only the prince, qua prince," i.e., not in any priestly capacity as former kings exercised (Driver, *op. cit.*, 309). **4–8.** *to be excluded...foreigners:* In several places, the Bible mentions foreigners being taken into temple service—Jos 9:23,27; Nm 31:30,47. Other references are more to the point: Ezr 2:43,48, where descendants of Solomon's slaves are associated with Temple servants; Ezr 8:20, where David is said to have given them to the Levites as helpers; Neh 7:46; 11:3,21, where their quarters are located on Ophel and thus near the Temple area (cf. De Vaux, *AI* 89–90, for the origin of the practice). These "uncircumcised both in heart and flesh" could never be the objects of the new covenant, for circumcision of the flesh was a preparation for, and a sign of, the circumcision of the heart, the covenant of the new heart and the new spirit that Ezekiel had stressed (Dt 30:6; Lv 26:41; Jer 4:4; cf. also Dt 29:10). **10–14.** *Levites...temple servants:* In the new Temple and cult, the distinction between the Levites and priests will be that Levites shall attend on the people "to minister for them" (v. 11) and "the priests, the sons of Zadok, shall come near to me, to minister to me" (i.e., Yahweh) (v. 15). This demotion is a punishment for having served the people "before their idols," most probably at the "high places." Josiah's reform closed these sanctuaries and gave every priest the right to serve at the Temple in Jerusalem (Dt 18:1ff.), but the Temple clergy refused to receive them and so "they ate unleavened bread with their brethren in the country" (2 Kgs 23:8–9; Dt 12:12). According to H. H. Rowley (B. Anderson and W. Harrelson, *Israel's Prophetic Heritage* [Fest. J. Muilenburg; N.Y., 1962] 214), the arrangement here is a compromise of the conflict, but also a rationalization, in view of what the Prophet had said about the idolatrous temple cult in 8:3. In Dt (18:1ff.), all the Levites are priests. In the P tradition, they are assistants to the priests (Nm 3:5–10; 18:2). The Book of Ezekiel seems to be the transition point. **15.** The reference is to the descendants of Zadok, who was made high priest by Solomon after Abiathar's banishment (1 Kgs 2:26–27,35), and whom 1 Chr (6:50–53) traces to Eleazar, the son of Aaron (but see De Vaux, *AI* 372–74). **16.** *minister to me:* For the performance of services connected with worship.

23. *they shall teach:* The reference is to the chief function of the priests—to present the "torah," the teaching containing the standard of Israelite worship and conduct. The primary object was to teach the people "to know the Lord," as he revealed himself in his dealings with Israel. From this source flowed norms of worship and conduct (Jer 2:8; Hos 4:1–9; Lv 10:11; Dt 33:9–10). The priests had failed in this objective in the past (7:26; 22:26). **24.** *stand as judges:* It reflects Babylonian custom in which judges are described as standing; in Hebr custom, judges are said to sit (Driver, *op. cit.*, 310). As keeper of tradition and precedent, the priest has become a legal authority (Dt 17:8–12). **29–30.** *under the ban:* The term is a technical one (Hebr *ḥērem*), applied to anything that is to be strictly devoted to Yahweh and therefore taken out of profane use and reserved for sacred use, or, if it had been devoted to the service of a pagan cult, to be completely destroyed (cf. Snaith, *op. cit.*, 33–34; De Vaux, *AI* 260). The conditions described here reflect closely the practices before the Exile.

89 (b) The Accessories of the Cult: Land and Offerings (45:1–17). The apportionment of the land, which begins here (cf. ch. 48) with the allotment to the Temple and its personnel, was never meant to be carried out, but was intended as a means of setting forth ideals. It completely disregards geography and history. The city, the Temple area, the property of the priests, Levites, and the prince are outside the tribal portions; the property of the prince is greater than that of the other four combined, almost equal to that of a tribe. **4.** *ministers of the sanctuary:* The inspiration for this phrase seems to come from the desert tradition, in which the sons of Aaron were camped in front of the Meeting Tent (Nm 3:38). **7–8.** *The prince:* This title for the king seems to indicate the modest role played by royalty in the idealistic description of these chapters. **11–12.** *same size:* The measurements given here seem to vary from the accepted contemporary norms, and it is impossible to say whether the attempt is to revalue them in terms of past norms or in terms of a projected reform never put into effect (for identifications, see De Vaux, *AI* 201–204). Because these norms are given as a prelude to the cult, the implication is that the norms of economic life are to find their validity in the cultic life. **13–17.** *duty of the prince:* The tax imposed here is to be given to the prince (that in 44:30, to the priests), out of which he will make provision for all public sacrifices and offerings. This duty is the only one allowed him, in contrast to past kings (e.g., 2 Kgs 16:11–18) who meddled in the cult.

90 (c) Feasts and Ritual (45:18–46:24). It is in the prescriptions for the various sacrifices that the greatest discrepancy with the Pentateuch occurs. The rabbis were divided in explaining this; some held that the sacrifices are to be understood as dedicatory offerings for the consecration of the new Temple, along with those in 43:19ff., while others understood them as permanent ritual in the new Temple, to be explained by Elijah in the messianic era (S. Fisch, *Ezekiel* [London, 1950] 316). **18.** *to purify the sanctuary:* This provision seems to be unaware of the rite of expiation given in Lv 16:1–34. **21.** *Passover:* The earliest instance of the Passover being joined with the Feast of Unleavened Bread (cf. De Vaux, *AI* 486). **25.** *the feast day:* Apparently the Feast of Booths (Hebr *sukkôt*; Lv 23:33–36). The Feast of Weeks is omitted, the only one for which the Mishnah significantly gives no detailed treatise (cf. De Vaux, *AI* 495). **46:2.** *the prince...shall worship:* The prince may enter the E gate of the inner court all the way to the threshold, from where he can look directly at the great altar in front of the Temple, where the priests offer the sacrifices he has provided. Unlike the E gate of the outer court, the inner gate on the E side is opened on Sabbaths and new moons, and when the prince makes a free-will offering (v. 12). **10.** *the prince...in their midst:* Another provision that leaves the prince in no doubt regarding his restricted role in the cult. **13–15.** This daily morning sacrifice was offered into NT times until the last days of the siege in AD 70 (Josephus, *JW* 6. 2, 1). **16.** Apparently the office of the prince was meant to be hereditary. **17.** *year of release:* Most probably the jubilee year, occurring every 50 years when all lands are to revert to the original patrimony (Lv 25:23–55). The prince's inheritance is mentioned here because it concerns the resources out of which he has to provide the sacrifices and oblations treated in the preceding passage. **20.** These chambers were described in 42:1–9 and are repeated here because cooking is a part of ritual.

(C) The New City and the New Land (47:1–48:35). Although the sanctuary will be strictly isolated from the rest of the land, it will not be without influence, for power and life will radiate from the Temple to the tribes.

91 (a) The Stream of Life-Giving Water (47:1–12). This figure, with more or less the same symbolism, is found in other books (Am 9:13; Jl 3:18; Zech 14:8; Ps 36:8–9; Ap 22:1). **1.** *water flowing:* Probably an allusion to the legend in which the stream of water coming out of Eden (Gn 2:10–14) that had been stopped up by Adam's sin reappeared again during the Exodus in the desert; the water flowed from the rock in 12 streams and finally reappeared in eschatological Jerusalem as one stream (cf. R. Tournay, *RB* 70 [1963] 43–51). **3.** *walked off to the east:* The valley of Kedron, ordinarily a dry wash, contrasts with the stream that increases steadily. **8–9.** The Arabah is the deep geological rift that forms the Dead Sea and continues southward. The life-giving effect of the waters is apparent from the freshening of the salt waters and the abundance of fish. **10.** En-gedi and En-eglaim are two oases on the western shore of the Dead Sea, into which the Kedron Valley leads. The latter is probably the modern Ain Feshkhah, about 2 mi. S of Qumran. *Great Sea:* Mediterranean. **12.** *every month:* The striking fertility is assured by the ever-flowing water. The meaning is clear—the presence of Yahweh is a blessing, revealing itself as a life-giving, creative power.

92 (b) The Boundaries and Apportionment of the Land (47:13–48:29). This section is generally denied to Ezekiel, even by commentators who admit his authorship for the rest of chs. 40–48. Among other reasons, it is not the Prophet who is addressed here but the Israelites. The boundaries (vv. 13–20) seem to be those of the greatest extent of the kingdom under David. However, no territory is assigned in Transjordan, probably for the sake of unity because the tribes who settled there tended to be isolated (cf. Jos 22:10–29).

48:1–7. In the new arrangement, Judah, the leading tribe of the south, is placed among the northern tribes to eliminate the old hostilities and divisions that led to the disintegration of David's kingdom. Reuben, Gad, and the half-tribe of Manasseh are brought from Transjordan for the same reason. The children of the wives of Jacob (Reuben, Simeon, Levi and Judah of Leah, and Joseph [Ephraim and Manasseh] and Benjamin of Rachel) are placed closest to the sanctuary, in contrast to the children of the concubines. **8–15.** Cf. 45:1–7. The profane land of v. 15 simply means land put to ordinary use, as distinct from land used exclusively for worship of Yahweh. The whole land is sacred because it is Yahweh's land, and he is in its midst; at the same time, it is totally separated from the sanctuary by the land of the priests. **16.** *dimensions of the city:* The area is 5000 square cubits, or about 1.6 sq. mi., much larger than Jerusalem at any point in history. The *city* is a federal district (v. 19), and on its gates are written the names of all the tribes (v. 30). **23–29.** Benjamin, Issachar, and Zebulun, originally from the north, are now located in the south.

93 (c) "The Lord Is Here" (48:30–35). Such is to be the name of the new city. The Hebr form is *Yahweh šāmmāh*, perhaps an intended contrast by assonance with *y*ᵉ*rûšālayim*. A change of name for Jerusalem as a symbol of its transformation is found in other prophets (Is 1:26; 60:14; 62:2; Jer 3:17; Zech 8:3). The projected city of *Yahweh šāmmāh* combines God's absolute transcendence with his eternal dwelling among his people.

22

DEUTERO-ISAIAH

Carroll Stuhlmueller, C.P.

BIBLIOGRAPHY

1 Auvray, P. and J. Steinmann, *Isaïe* (BJ; 2nd ed.; Paris, 1957). Cheyne, T. K., *The Prophecies of Isaiah* (2 vols.; London, 1880–81). De Boer, P. A. H., *Second-Isaiah's Message* (*OTS* 11; Leiden, 1956). Dhorme, E., *BPl* 2 (1959). Duhm, B., *Das Buch Jesaja übersetzt und erklärt* (4th ed.; Göttingen, 1922). Feuillet, A., "Isaïe (le livre d')," *VDBS* 4 (1949) 690–729. Frey, H., *Das Buch der Weltpolitik Gottes* (Die Botschaft des Alten Testaments, vol. 18; Stuttgart, 1958). Kessler, W., *Gott geht es um das Ganze* (Die Botschaft des Alten Testaments, vol. 19; Stuttgart, 1960). Kissane, E. J., *The Book of Isaiah* (vol. 2; Dublin, 1943). Muilenburg, J., "The Book of Isaiah, Ch. 40–66, Introduction and Exegesis," *IB* 5 (Nashville, 1956) 381–773. North, C. R., *Isaiah 40–55* (TBC; London, 1952); *The Second Isaiah* (Oxford, 1964). Penna, A., *Isaia* (LSB; Roma, 1958). Rignell, L. G., *A Study of Isaiah Ch. 40–55* (*LUA*; Lund, 1956). Smith, G. A., *The Book of Isaiah* 2 (N.Y., n.d.). Steinmann, J., *Le Livre de la Consolation d'Israël et les prophètes du retour de l'Exile* (Paris, 1960). Thexton, S. C., *Isaiah 40–66* (Epworth's Preacher's Commentaries; London, 1959). Torrey, C. C., *The Second Isaiah* (N.Y., 1928). Volz, P., *Jesaja II* (KAT; Leipzig, 1932). Westermann, C., *Isaiah 40–66* (Phila., 1969).

INTRODUCTION

2 **(I) Authenticity.** Until the 18th cent., it was presumed that Isaiah of Jerusalem wrote all 66 chapters of his book. The tradition was questioned by Ibn Ezra (*ca.* 1167), but the vigorous attack came from J. C. Döderlein (1775) and J. G. Eichhorn (1780–83). These scholars maintained that chs. 40–66 were written by a different author, living some 150 years later during the Babylonian Exile. They named him Deutero-Isaiah (or Second Isaiah). In 1892, B. Duhm argued for a separate author of chs. 56–66, whom he called Trito-Isaiah (or Third Isaiah). (In this article, both the prophets' names and their works are abbreviated as Dt-Is and Tr-Is.) Protestant scholars were generally convinced by the soundness of the new arguments, and Catholics, although with some hesitation, tended to agree (i.e., A. Condamin, *Le Livre d'Isaïe* [Paris, 1905]; A. van Hoonacker, *Les douze petits prophètes* [Paris, 1901] 154; M. J. Lagrange, *RB* 2 [1905] 282). A negative response of the Pontifical Biblical Commission, June 28, 1908, precipitated by the modernist attacks upon biblical inspiration and prophecy, made Catholic scholars revert to an ultraconservative viewpoint (*EB* 294; *Rome and the Study of Scripture* [6th ed.; St. Meinrad, Ind., 1958] 119). Once the theological problems were solved, Catholics began to argue again for the split authorship of Is; the opening came with the commentaries of F. Feldmann (Münster, 1926), J. Fischer (Bonn, 1939), and especially E. J. Kissane (*op. cit.*). Most Catholic scholars now work with the Dt-Is thesis. (On the binding force of the Biblical Commission decrees, see E. F. Siegman, *CBQ* 18 [1956] 23–29; → Church Pronouncements, 72:25.)

The reasons for separate authorship of chs. 40–55 are first of all historical. The addressees are no longer inhabitants of Jerusalem but exiles in Babylon (43:14; 48:20). Jerusalem, in fact, has been captured and destroyed and now awaits reconstruction (44:26–28; 49:14–23). Babylon is no longer a friendly ally (2 Kgs 20:12–13), for she has destroyed Jerusalem and deported the Israelites. The former prophecies about Jerusalem's destruction have been carried out (Is 1:21–31; Jer 7:1–15; Ez 22, 24), and Israel now awaits a new and glorious future (40:1–11,43). Contrary to Isaiah, Dt-Is rarely mentions the Davidic dynasty, and even then he transfers its privileges to the entire nation (55:3–5).

The literary arguments are just as impressive. The tone has changed from threat and condemnation to consolation and hope. The style of Dt-Is is expansive, redundant, solemn, and lyrical; Isaiah of Jerusalem had been brief, cryptic, and imperious. The difference is the same as that between Jn and the Syn. Isaiah is filled with biographical material; Dt-Is does not even reveal his name.

The doctrinal themes of Dt-Is likewise manifest a shift in emphasis. Before the Exile, Israel was relatively prosperous, overly self-confident, and very material minded; Dt-Is saw a people discouraged, dazed, and destitute. They must be consoled, not punished; their faith must be sustained, not further tried. Because their situation seemed humanly hopeless, Dt-Is realized that God must intervene as king and creator of a new world commonwealth. Isaiah of Jerusalem looked upon foreign nations as tempters to apostasy (20:5) or scourges of divine anger (10:5); Dt-Is considers them not only as instruments for saving Israel (ch. 45) but also as recipients sharing Israel's salvation.

3 **(II) The Prophet.** The songs of Dt-Is reveal a man pensive, earnest, sincere, and sympathetic. So sturdy was his faith in the God of history that everything had meaning for the redemption of Israel. He thought prayerfully and profoundly about everything—about a child counting the stars (40:26) or about young men frustrated by hopeless existence (40:30).

The Prophet was devoted to the best traditions of his people. Abraham is a rock of life for all ages (51:1–2); the Exodus out of Egypt is an ever-continuous act of salvation (43:14–21). David and Jerusalem possess a new significance for the people of Israel (49:14–21; 55:3–5). He shies away from the formalistic "liturgism" of the past (his terminology is strictly nonliturgical), but the spirit of the liturgy breaks forth into new life through his hymns, laments, and proclamation of the Word. He seems well acquainted with the P tradition of Gn (40:28; 51:9; 54:9–10), and he may have composed his songs for the Sabbath ceremonies conducted in the homes of the exiles.

Dt-Is probably belonged to an Isaian school of religious thought (8:16), for we hear some echoes of the earlier prophet's thoughts: the people are in sin and afflicted with sorrow; God is moved to assist and save his poor people; God alone saves, and therefore salvation will be wondrously achieved (10:15–20 and 42:19–25; 7:14–25 and 54:1–3). Dt-Is may have been principally responsible for the preservation and arrangement of his master's "book," keeping it alive by adapting its message to the needs of the Exile.

Cyrus is already on the march (41:1; 45), so we must place Dt-Is during the latter part of the exilic period. It is not impossible—but we can never be sure—that Dt-Is returned with the first repatriates and was moved by the oppressive trials of the new commonwealth to write the Suffering Servant Songs. For the character, style, and environment of Tr-Is, see comments on ch. 56.

4 **(III) Religious Message.** Dt-Is is the herald of messianic glory, which all mankind is about to witness (40:5,9). The kingdom of God is at hand (40:9), and the poor and lowly, rather than the Davidic family, will have the most prominent places in it (42:6–7; 43:1–8; 55:3–5). Every divine promise is on the point of fulfillment; thus, he extols the justice of God (41:2,16; 42:6). From his opening statements (40:5,8) to his final summation (55:10–11), Dt-Is dwells more than any other prophet upon the power of the divine Word. This Word is so fraught with invincible power that God's previous words or promises are considered not so much phrases in a book as deeds typifying what God will now do in a most wondrous way. The new redemptive act will be so startling that Dt-Is is led to develop a theology of creation. He uses the proper term for creation (*bārā'*) 16 times, but almost always in a context of God's speaking. Creation is thus a personal act revealing the deepest thoughts of the divine heart. Just as creation is world-wide, so also is Israel's missionary apostolate.

5 **(IV) The Songs of the Suffering Servant.** Duhm first isolated four songs, written more in the style of Jeremiah's soliloquies or confessions than in the exalted lyrics of Dt-Is. Although many phrases link these songs to the rest of Dt-Is (i.e., my servant; my chosen one; pour out my spirit; formed from the womb), there are notable differences (i.e., the Servant is no longer deaf and blind but rather listens and illumines; salvation is not so much achieved through a glorious exodus but rather though the expiatory suffering of the innocent). In *The Suffering Servant in Deutero-Isaiah* (2nd ed.; London, 1956), C. R. North clearly lines up the various opinions regarding author, purpose, provenance, etc., of the songs. The commentary adopts the opinion that they reflect Dt-Is' great disappointment over Cyrus' failure to recognize Yahweh as world king, as well as the Prophet's new insight into the meaning of Israel's suffering for the present and for the messianic future.

The songs portray the ideal Servant of God, the perfect Israelite, whose consecration to the divine will, even in the midst of overwhelming suffering, "takes away the sins of many" (53:12). The Servant is Israel, alive in all of her great leaders and intercessors: Abraham (49:6); Moses (42:6); Jeremiah (49:1); wise men (50:4ff.); David (53:1); and the suffering exiles (52:13–53:12). But the collective interpretation leads to an individual Servant of supreme holiness, greater than any single Israelite of the past. In *Jesaja 53 in Hexapla Targum und Peschita* (Gütersloh, 1954), H. Hegermann has shown that pre-Christian Judaism gave a messianic interpretation to the Servant Songs, but it was Jesus himself who clearly identified himself as the Servant. Paul, however, continues the collective interpretation, for he regards himself as the Servant (Acts 13:47; Gal 1:15; Rom 15:21). As established by the studies of J. Pedersen (*Israel I–II*) and C. R. North (*The Suffering Servant*), the Servant is both a collective personality and an individual messiah (cf. 42:1; 43:27–28).

6 **(V) Style.** Whereas Isaiah of Jerusalem employed a style quick and abrupt, hitting home with force, Dt-Is' manner was more contemplative, repeating, exclaiming, balancing, questioning, and answering, with all the modulated cadence of written literature. Perhaps no other Hebr writer can match his extraordinary ability to bolster ideas with the sound of words.

7 **(VI) Text and Translations.** The MT is very well preserved, and is generally supported by 1QIs. The LXX is quite inferior and of little use in restoring any damaged readings of the MT. The Vg tends to sharpen the messianic interpretations (cf. 45:8).

8 **(VII) Outline.** An outline of Dt-Is follows:

(I) The Book of Consolation (40:1–55:13)
- (A) Prologue (40:1–11)
- (B) Hymns to the Lord Redeemer (40:12–48:22)
  - (a) The Splendid Majesty of God the Creator (40:12–31)
  - (b) Cyrus, Champion of Justice (41:1–29)
  - (c) First Song of the Suffering Servant (42:1–4)
  - (d) Victory of Justice (42:5–9)
  - (e) New Song of Redemption (42:10–17)
  - (f) Another Poem (42:18–25)
  - (g) Redemption and Restoration (43:1–44:23)
  - (h) Cyrus, Anointed of the Lord (44:24–45:25)
  - (i) The Burdensome Gods of Babylon (46:1–13)
  - (j) Taunt-Song Over the Fall of Babylon (47:1–15)
  - (k) Recapitulation (48:1–22)
- (C) Hymns to the New Jerusalem (49:1–55:13)
  - (a) The Liberation of Israel (49:1–26)
  - (b) Israel in Darkness (50:1–11)
  - (c) Strength for the Fainthearted (51:1–16)
  - (d) The Cup of the Lord's Wrath (51:17–23)

COMMENTARY

9 **(I) The Book of Consolation (40:1–55:13).** These chapters, constituting the major work of Dt-Is, are divided into three sections: a prologue (40:1–11); hymns to the Lord Redeemer (40:12–48:22); and hymns to the new Jerusalem (49:1–55:13).

(A) Prologue (40:1–11). God commissions Dt-Is as a prophet during a solemn convocation of the heavenly council. God addresses an assembly of angels with the command, "comfort, give comfort...speak tenderly." Some scholars, however, visualize a group of prophets in whose ranks stands Dt-Is (cf. Am 3:7). Dhorme (*op. cit.*, xl) considers the words addressed to Jerusalem. All the ancient versions have the pl. form of the verbs, but the LXX adds, "O ye priests," and the Tg, "O ye prophets, prophesy consolations." A steady biblical tradition, however, refers to heavenly beings who hear and approve the divine decisions. Earth thus reflects heavenly decisions (1 Kgs 22:19–23; Pss 6; 82:1; Jb 1–2; Dn 7:9ff.; Ap 4:1–11; see G. E. Wright, *The Old Testament Against Its Background* [Chicago, 1950] 30–41).

1. *comfort, give comfort:* This double imperative is the first of many (51:9,17; 52:1; 57:14). A tone of mercy joined to a majestic style sets the pace for this entire ensemble of poems. **2.** *speak tenderly:* Lit., "speak to the heart"; the words are deeply felt and earnestly spoken, like the words with which a lover woos his beloved (cf. Gn 34:3; 50:21; Ru 2:13), one of many delicate expressions of divine love appearing in the Dt-Is poems. Jerusalem at this time is actually in shambles (49:17; 51:17ff.), hardly able to be the recipient of God's words. God is speaking to a different Jerusalem—an ideal kingdom of people bound to him not geographically but personally (cf. Pss 45, 47, 75, 86). To have "received... double for all her sins" does not so much imply an excess of divine anger as it proclaims the fulfillment and the end of purifying sorrow. A new era is dawning, inaugurated by God's Word. Dt-Is has little or nothing to say about temple sacrifice and deliberately avoids all ritual phrases (cf. T. Chary, *Les prophètes et le culte* [Tournai, 1955] 71–117). It is simply the "word of God" that begins and climaxes his poems. This feature strengthens the personal aspects of religion, for a word is formed deep within the mind and heart of God and achieves its effects only when received just as personally within man.

10 The first strophe (3–5) combines the ancient biblical tradition of the Exodus out of Egypt with contemporary scenes of Babylon. The grandiose religious processions of the Babylonian masters, moving solemnly through the colorful city gate of Ishtar, past the wondrous hanging gardens of the royal palace, up to the temple courtyard, with music and song accompanying the glittering statues of the gods and with the expectation of sensuous satisfaction at the Temple—all this pomp tended to attract the Jews away from Yahweh (*AtBib* 94). Dt-Is frequently argues against the temptation, as he does now with the announcement of a new exodus. **3.** *a voice cries out:* Someone speaks up from the celestial assembly—a participle in Hebrew, "crying out" continuously—that the Lord himself is about to lead a new exodus, out of Babylon through the desert back to Palestine. Again, the terms are more theological than geographical: the Mosaic days of covenant, protection, and triumph are being actualized in the contemporary moment; purifying sorrow is preparing a wondrous divine victory. *in the desert prepare the way:* Contrary to the Hebrew, the LXX, Vg, and NT (Mk 1:3; par.) divide the phrases differently, so as to read, "a voice cries out in the desert." At this moment, Dt-Is introduces one of the richest expressions of the Bible. The "Way" is a manner of life, for men (Gn 6:12; Is 55:7) and for God (Dt 32:4; Ez 18:25); there can be two ways of good and evil (Ps 1:6; Jer 21:8; Mt 7:13–14). John the Baptist is to announce "the way of the Lord" (Mk 1:3) and Jesus declares that he himself is that Way (Jn 14:6; Heb 10:20). Christianity, therefore, is called simply "the way" (Acts 9:2; 19:9,23; cf. *BibLex* 2566–67; *ThWNT* 7, 70–101). The DSS saw a fulfillment of Is 40:3 in the community's retreat into the wilderness and in their "studying the Torah which He commanded through Moses" (1QS 8:14–15). **5.** *the glory of the Lord:* The phrase indicates a wondrous manifestation of God's redeeming presence (Ex 14:4,18; 16:7; Is 58:8). The Bible uses the phrase particularly of the divine presence in the Temple (Ex 40:34–35; 1 Kgs 8:10–12). Ezekiel (43:1–2) sees this glory return to a new messianic Temple, but Dt-Is magnifies it into a world-wide theophany (cf. Pss 96:3,7–8; 97:6; *BibLex* 867–71. "All mankind" (Hebr, "all flesh") denotes the helplessness of man who nonetheless is enthralled by the wonder of such an undeserved gift.

6. For the first and, perhaps, only time, the Prophet speaks in the first person. We sense a certain despondency in this second strophe (6–8); its repetitious style lets the burden of human weakness fall all the more heavily upon the reader. The contrast with the preceding passage on divine glory is typical of Dt-Is. He delights in counterbalance; as in the present instance, it gives him an occasion to heighten the respectful, all-powerful care of God by bravely enunciating the helplessness of the people.

The final strophe (9–10) in the prologue moves with mounting crescendo: go up; cry out; fear not to cry out. Glorious Jerusalem is no longer emasculated with sensuousness and hypocrisy, as in the pre-exilic days (2 Kgs 21; Jer 22; Ez 24), but is hailed as the home of God on earth and the center of world redemption (Lk 1–2; Ap 21–22). *the herald of glad tidings:* The Gk form, *euaggelizomenos*, is the NT word for the "gospel" proclamation. Dt-Is deliberately overlooks the Davidic pretenders to the throne and sees only one king, Yahweh. **11.** The transition from "king" to "shepherd" is easily made in the Scriptures; the two words can be synonymous (2 Sm 5:2; Jer 3:15). The Prophet reveals God as a shepherd-king, attracting and even carrying his people (cf. Jer 31:10; Ez 34:11ff.; Ps 23).

11 **(B) Hymns to the Lord Redeemer (40:12–48:22).** These chapters, dating before 539 and the fall of Babylon to the Persians, sing of a new exodus initiated by the "Lord's anointed," Cyrus II (the Great), and of a new creation, performed only by God.

(a) THE SPLENDID MAJESTY OF GOD THE CREATOR (40:12–31). God's voice thunders upon earth in a series of questions. Dt-Is, like Job (38:1–42:6), adopts the style of irony for the divine speech. This "is a delicate, even risky, technique, especially when prolonged.... It may so easily become feeble, or else slip over into sarcasm" (R. A. F. MacKenzie, *Bib* 40 [1959] 441). Dt-Is and Job succeed much better than Amos (3:3–8; 5:20; 6:2). Style in Dt-Is is matched with a majestic theology of the Creator's careful planning, unlimited power, and fatherly concern.

12. The questions of God are not confined to the distant past but demand an answer for what is happening at this moment. The Babylonians believed that the worship of the gods Bel and Marduk, Tiamat and Apsu, kept the process of creation from collapsing into primeval chaos. **13.** Unlike other deities, Yahweh depends on no one else for knowledge. Angels approve and carry out the divine decisions but they never form or challenge them. For Dt-Is, the redemption of Israel amounted to a recreation of the national identity and traditional homeland. In quoting this text, Paul associates salvation with a new creation in Christ Jesus (1 Cor 2:16; Rom 11:34; Col 1:15–16). *spirit of the Lord:* The active, life-giving power of God (cf. Gn 1:2; Ps 104:20). **14.** *the path of judgment...the way of understanding:* Creation follows them (cf. 40:3). *judgment:* This word (*mišpāṭ*) introduces another of Dt-Is' favorite themes; throughout the Bible, it indicates the authoritative declaration of what is just and the effective achievement of it. There are several other words for "justice," of different origin but practically synonymous in Dt-Is. Applying the words to God, Dt-Is confesses God's constant fidelity to act in a way consonant with his own goodness and with the covenant between himself and Israel.

(Descamps, A., *VDBS* 4, 1448–60, esp. 1445–57. Eichrodt, *Theology* 239–49. Guillet, J., *Themes of the Bible* [Notre Dame, Ind., 1960] 24–40.)

12 **15–17.** Not even the mightiest nation can stand in God's "way," neither the distant Gk colonies (along the coast of modern Turkey—Ps 72:10; Is 11:11; Jer 2:10) nor the neighboring giant powers (symbolized by the majestic cedars of Lebanon, just N of Palestine—cf. 1 Kgs 5:6; Is 10:34; Ps 29:6). They can no more oppose God than the "void" of precreation could block his will (Gn 1:2; Is 41:24–29).

18–20 (+ 41:6–7). Dt-Is never tires of ridiculing the pompous pseudodeities of other nations (41:23; 44:9–20; Jer 10:1–9). The CCD and others place 41:6–7 here because of the awkward position of the verses in the next chapter.

21–24. The poem returns to the masterly style of Dt-Is, with rapid questions and answers. Participles sustain the same moment of time, and assonance, the same sound of words. What is eternally enduring is accomplished in a moment! **22.** *are like grasshoppers:* Men (cf. Nm 13:34); the phrase is not demeaning but endearing. **23.** The Prophet comments upon the frequent succession of revolutions in the Near East, dynasties toppling and empires cracking up, even when these appear at the zenith of opulence and power (Is 10:15–19; 13–14).

25–27. *Holy One:* Isaiah popularized this proper name for God while developing his doctrine on faith. God, he saw, was infinitely separated from the weakness of everything earthly. His actions revealed this holiness and therefore were designated "the glory of the Lord" (Is 6:3; 1:4; 5:19,13; cf. R. Otto, *The Idea of the Holy* [2nd ed.; London, 1950]; Eichrodt, *Theology* 270–82). The stars, prominent deities in Babylonian mythology, were created effortlessly by Yahweh, simply by calling out their name. The technical term for creating (*bārā'*) occurs the first of 16 times. Seldom, if ever, used before Dt-Is, it now assumes the special meaning of a mighty act of Yahweh, far exceeding the strength of men and gods, that transforms chaos into a well-ordered universe. God creates for the sake of man's happiness and finds glory when men recognize the source of that joy. Creation of the material universe is not just the first of many creative-redemptive acts; it is a continuing quality of each divine act. As the Exile comes to an end with the conquest of Babylon and the discrediting of the astral gods, Yahweh is proclaimed creator even of the stars (cf. C. Stuhlmueller, *CBQ* 21 [1959] 429–67; E. Beaucamp, *The Bible and the Universe* [London, 1963]). **27.** The question is answered in 49:4–5.

28–31. After stating that Yahweh is eternal—his care reaches back farther than man can ever imagine (cf. Mi 5:1; 7:20; Is 51:9)—Dt-Is extends his creative power to the contemporary moment. He sees God right now "creating the ends of the earth" and "giving strength to the fainting" (ptc. constructions). **31.** The Prophet gives the "classical formulation of the OT hope of faith" (A. Weiser, "Faith," BKW 3, 29). Waiting upon God widens man's sense of his own helplessness and deepens his appreciation of God's redeeming power (cf. Is 8:16–18; Hab 2:3–4; Pss 25:3,22; 27:14).

13 (b) CYRUS, CHAMPION OF JUSTICE (41:1–29). With the sudden rise of Cyrus II (the Great), the Semitic era of world history collapsed for all time. Until then, the great powers controlling the civilized world were usually Semites, originally of the Arabian peninsula and later known as Akkadians, Babylonians, and Assyrians (cf. S. Moscati, *The Semites in Ancient History* [Cardiff, 1959]). Cyrus was a Persian, of Indo-European stock, descended from a people who had migrated out of Europe to settle finally in the high plateau area SE of Babylon. In 559, Cyrus became king in Anshan, a vassal within the larger domain of the Medes, but in 10 years he had already captured Ecbatana, the Median capital. In the winter of 546, he led his army over the frozen mountains of Lydia for a surprise attack upon the "golden" capital of Croesus, and in 539 he was master of Babylon. Yahweh was achieving his eternal plan, and to express this doctrine dramatically, Dt-Is portrays Yahweh, summoning the world to his court of justice (cf. Is 1:2–3; Mi 6:1–2). The Prophet draws upon the legislative procedure of the ancient Near East (cf. De Vaux, *AI* 150–58), using the Hebr technical terms for plaintiff, defendant, witness, accusation, and verdict.

1. *silence before me, Coastlands!:* God's opening words peremptorily demand an echo of what is heard elsewhere (Zeph 1:7; Hab 2:20; Ap 8:1). **2–4b.** According to some scholars (C. C. Torrey, E. J. Kissane, D. R. Jones, and most Jewish writers), God is calling the nations to bear witness to what he accomplished in Abraham, whom he brought from the east and settled in the promised land. There is, perhaps, some allusion to Abraham, but Cyrus is the dominant figure here, coming from the east and championing God's justice (cf. 40:14) by fulfilling the divine plans of redemption. Cyrus may not be conscious of the fact, but God had "called" him from the beginning (emphasis is again on the Word of God—cf. 40:3).

14 **4c–5.** God's verdict enunciates a "theology of history." God is at the beginning of every event, no matter how cosmic and colossal (40:12–13), how familiar and insignificant (40:27–28); he is also at the conclusion, ensuring a perfect fulfillment of his designs (Ap 1:8,17; 21:6; 22:13). In Hebrew, "beginning" (4b) and "first" (4c) are almost identical words. Dt-Is twice emphasizes the divine "I," and frequently throughout his prophecy we are reminded of the sacred name Yahweh, revealed to Moses at Mt. Sinai (Ex 3:14–15). The Prophet recognizes the impact of Israel's God upon every moment of time and upon every point of space; he sees everything converge upon God's covenantal promises to his chosen people. This insight into world history strengthens the interpretation of the divine name that understands it to mean, "I am he who is always there [with you]" (cf. Eichrodt, *Theology* 187–92; A. Gelin, *VDBS* 5, 1202; Von Rad, *OT Theology I* 180–81). **6–7.** The CCD transfers these verses after 40:20.

8–10. To reassure Israel of its strong bond with God, Dt-Is utilizes the Hebr grammar with masterly touch. Each Hebr verb makes a compact unit of action-subject-object: choose-I-you...grasp-I-you...call-I-you. What Martin Buber termed the "I-Thou" relationship of God and Israel shows up very clearly. God reveals the mystery of his love by showing that his solicitude for the great forefathers of Israel converges upon this moment of Israel's history. For the first time God calls the exiles "my servant" (cf. 42:1,19; 43:10). "Servant" is used in the Bible of prophets and kings (Jer 30:10; Ez 28:25), and of Abraham (Gn 26:24). Israel shares another divine title with Abraham: "my friend" (lit. "my beloved"; cf. 2 Chr 20:7; Jas 2:23, and the Arabic name for Abraham, *Khalil Allah*, "Friend of God"). But if Israel receives such love as this from God, it is precisely that she may mediate it to others. Words like "chosen," "taken" (in Hebr, "grasped"), "summoned," "strengthen," "uphold" underline God's decisive intervention in and through Israel to achieve his "justice." For this tense and solemn moment, Dt-Is employs words characteristic of a theophany: "Fear not, I am with you" (Gn 15:1; Dt 20:1; Jos 8:1).

15 **11–12.** These lines retard the rhythm to the sorrowful *qînâ* or lamentation meter of a 3–2 beat (cf. Lam). There is tolled the death of every power opposing God's plans of salvation. **13–16.** The judgment upon the nations continues, addressed by God to his beloved Israel. Like a father fondling his infant child, God whispers words of endearment to his people: "worm Jacob," "maggot Israel." **14.** *says the Lord:* In Hebrew, "the oracle of the Lord," solemnly entoning for the first of 14 times in Dt-Is the title "your redeemer" (43:14; 44:6; etc.). The Hebr word *go'el* always includes two ideas: a close bond, usually of blood; an obligation to come to the other's assistance. Sometimes *go'el* can be translated "nearest of kin" (Lv 25:25). A *go'el* saved his kinsman by raising up a son (Dt 25:5–10), by buying him back from slavery (Lv 25:47–54), or by lifting the outrage of murder (Nm 35:12ff.; see *BibLex* 1994–2003; S. Lyonnet, *Theologia Biblica Novi Testamenti de Peccato et Redemptione* [Rome, 1960]; L. Moraldi, *Espiazione Sacrificale* [Rome, 1956]). God first showed himself a *go'el* by the great redemptive act of the Exodus (Ex 6:6–8; 15:13); he now repeats that same wonder.

17–20. A song of exquisite beauty interrupts the trial scene; God sings of his hopes and plans for Israel. The two key phrases are "I will answer them" and "the Holy One has created it." By his answering "word," God recreates a new paradise for "the afflicted and the needy." In the final day of glory, God promises not to save man's soul but to transform his whole self, body and soul. The biblical theology of redemption presumes a correct grasp of ancient Near Eastern psychology, which eschewed Gk philosophical distinctions of body and soul and viewed the physical and the spiritual, the natural and the supernatural, under the aspect of one, real totality. Man's soul can never be fully "saved" unless his body shares the joy. Dt-Is' doctrine of redemption is not materialistic but real and total.

(Bowman, T., *Hebrew Thought Compared with the Greek* [London, 1960]. Pedersen, J., *Israel I–II* [London, 1926] 99–181. Tresmontant, C., *A Study of Hebrew Thought* [N.Y., 1960].)

21–29. The trial scene continues. Earlier prophets crusaded against the worship of other gods and battled furiously against foreign religious influences contaminating Israelite religion (Hos 2:10–15; Is 1:4; 2:6–18; Jer 2:4ff.). Dt-Is, perhaps for the first time in biblical history, denies absolutely the existence of all gods except Yahweh. Other peoples would dictate what they wanted their gods to announce (1 Kgs 22:6ff.), but Yahweh announced the destruction of his own people as a way leading to their resurgence.

16 (c) First Song of the Suffering Servant (42:1–4). Verses 1–4 are composed in the style of the Servant Songs: quiet, even melancholy; terse and concentrated; different from the other hymns, which are much more expansive, lyrical, and exultant. Verses 5–7 combine both styles, and scholars debate whether they belong to the first song. The Suffering Servant of all four songs represents the finest qualities of Israel and her great leaders. In this first song, he is a "chosen one" like Moses (Ps 106:23), David (Ps 89:4), and all Israel (1 Chr 16:13; Is 41:8); as the Servant, he fulfills the role of Davidic king (2 Sm 3:18), messianic king (Ez 34:23–24), and prophet (Am 3:7). But his kingly prerogative is especially emphasized here. Not only is he set in contrast with the military tactics of Cyrus, but he is commissioned to "bring forth justice" (*mišpāṭ;* cf. 40:14), a legal decision ratifying and executing the divine will. The Bible, except in rare cases (Jgs 4:5; 1 Sm 7:6; 3:20), reserved that power to kings, priests, and local magistrates. Prophetic preaching is called judgment (*mišpaṭ*) only in Mi 3:8. The Servant, however, absorbs still other qualities, for he imparts teaching (*tôrâ*), a task never done by kings but only by prophets (Is 8:16; Zech 7:12) and priests (Jer 2:8; Ez 7:26; see North, *The Suffering Servant*, 139–42).

1. As God speaks, perhaps to the heavenly court (cf. 40:1ff.), his words sweep out to include foreign nations (*gôyīm*), the entire earth as far as the distant isles. *my spirit:* This endowment, necessary for any extraordinary redemptive work, was promised the messianic king (Is 11:1) and will later be predicted of the entire messianic community (Jl 3). While the LXX added the words "Jacob" and "Israel," the NT applied the words to Jesus at his baptism (Mk 1:11) and transfiguration (Mt 17:5). Luke subtly alludes to the LXX form of "whom I uphold" when he writes of Jesus' being "taken up" to Jerusalem (Lk 9:51; cf. NTRG 3 on this verse).

2–3. The Servant accomplishes his mission modestly and quietly, not whipping people into conformity but transforming them interiorly. The CCD omits the last part of v. 3, "he will introduce justice effectively" and the first part of v. 4, "he will never fail nor be discouraged." *the coastlands will wait:* The verb "wait" (*yḥl*) means energetic striving for life (*ThWNT* 6, 194; Jb 6:11; 13:15). *the coastlands:* Like Israel, now in exile, they shall undergo a painful expectancy before new life begins.

(Hegermann, *op. cit.* Kaiser, O., *Der königliche Knecht* [Göttingen, 1962]. Lindblom, L., *The Servant Songs in Deutero-Isaiah* [Lund, 1951]. North, *The Suffering Servant* [most complete study of the Servant Songs]. Rowley, H. H., *The Servant of the Lord and Other Essays* [London, 1952]. Van der Ploeg, J. S., *Les Chants du Serviteur de Jahvé* [Paris, 1936].)

17 (d) Victory of Justice (42:5–9). With the lyrical style of a hymn of praise, Dt-Is again insists upon the power of God's Word in recreating the universe (cf. 40:25–27). After the emphatic declaration "Thus says the [one] God, Yahweh," a series of participles reveal the effects of God's Word. What happened in the beginning continues at this moment, as Israel emerges from darkness to light. Israel is the first to benefit from this creative-redemptive power of God. *breath to its people...covenant of the people:* "People" (*'ām*) ordinarily refers to Israel. (See S. Porůbčan, *Il Patto nuovo in Is 40–66* [Rome, 1958].) **6.** *for the victory of justice:* Cf. 41:8–10. The phrase is a single word in Hebrew, defying adequate translation. L. Dennefeld prefers "conformable to my plan of salvation" (*PSB* 7, 157). *I have formed you:* Evokes the image of the creation of the first man (Gn 2:7), for the verb in each instance tells of a potter carefully modeling clay. The last line of v. 6 probably belongs later in 49:6. **7.** According to God's words, man must recognize his blindness and imprisonment before he can be cured and freed. These lines may help to explain Is 6:9–10. The earlier prophetic preaching at times left the people all the more stubbornly entrenched in sin, but such a condition prepared for the moment when they would desperately admit their need of God. **9.** It is difficult to explain "the earlier things" (perhaps the saving event of the Exodus; lit., "the first things"—cf. 41:4) and "the new things." The latter term probably surrounds with messianic glory the victorious march of Cyrus and his edict of freedom granted to the Jews (see C. R. North, "'The Former Things' and the 'New Things' in Deutero-Isaiah," *Studies in Old Testament Prophecy* [Edinburgh, 1957] 111–26.) Dt-Is could not distinguish any time lag between the return from the Exile and the final day of salvation. He combines prediction with mystery. God reveals the future, yet never in any mathematical way, rendering faith unnecessary; fulfillment will "spring into being," taking people by surprise.

18 (e) New Song of Redemption (42:10–17). After God's announcement of "new things" (9), the Prophet entones a "new song" of "praise" to Yahweh, Israel's redeemer. Each new redemptive act added a new reason why Yahweh was king, and it seems quite likely that Israel celebrated the anniversary-renewal of the great deeds of God by proclaiming him king once more. Even though there is no evidence of a separate feast of the Lord's enthronement (against the thesis of S. Mowinckel, *The Psalms in Israel's Worship* 1 [Oxford, 1962] 106ff.), some of the court ritual passed over into the divine worship: Pss 47, 93, 96–97 (cf. A. Weiser, *The Psalms* [Phila., 1962] 62). God's kingdom will extend to Kedar in the Arabian peninsula (Is 21:16; Jer 2:10) and Sela, S of the Dead Sea and capital of Edom (Is 16:1; Ob). **13.** *like a hero...warrior:* God manifests his zeal for world salvation; Dt-Is' language is reminiscent of Babylonian myths of primeval struggle (cf. 51:9–10), because the titanic struggle between good and evil is raging climactically. *as a woman in labor:* God is in the midst of world sorrow (Is 13:8), vitalizing it in such a way that a new messianic life will be born out of it (Dt 32:18; Ps 2:7).

19 (f) Israel, Blind Servant (42:18–25). Dt-Is here assumes the mantle of the earlier prophets, threatening and condemning. The Lord's "servant" is deaf and blind, no longer "a light to the nations" (49:6) or the obedient disciple and well-trained teacher (50:4). These differences or variations may easily exemplify the Prophet's penchant for contrast. This portrait of a deaf and blind servant may seem to contradict the picture drawn in the Suffering Servant Songs, but is not the latter portrayal composed of features drawn freely from a vast Israelite history (42:1)? That history certainly included, but also superceded, the blind infidelity that now occupies Dt-Is' attention. The style of the opening verse is quick and precise like the step of marching soldiers: "Deaf man, hear! Blind man, look and see!" These orders are just the opposite of those in Is 6:9–10; both times and authors have changed! The CCD omits the second part of v. 19: "Who is blind but my covenanted one, or blind as the servant of the Lord?" (see Kissane, *op. cit.*, 48). Dt-Is deplores blindness in much the same way that Amos fought social injustice, Hosea was outraged at Israel's infidelity, and Jeremiah wept over apostasy (cf. Muilenburg, *op. cit.*, 476). Faith imparted the vision to see beneath surface events and recognize God, purifying, redeeming, and recreating.

20 (g) Redemption and Restoration (43:1–44:23). Emphatically and competently, Dt-Is introduces what many regard as his finest poem and richest presentation. The opening verse begins with "now" and closes with "you," two Hebr words almost identical in sound. The power of God's Word is extended through a series of participles, drawing out the full effects of the phrase: "thus says Yahweh," creating you and forming you (42:5). The melodic sound of this line leads to the majestic tone of the next, where theophanic words are pronounced: "fear not" (41:10). **2.** *water...fire:* They symbolize danger and destruction; demonic monsters haunted thunderstorms and large bodies of water, such as the Great (Mediterranean) Sea and the Reed (or Red) Sea (Ps 89:10–11; Is 51:10; Gn 6–9 [deluge]; Ex 14:21–31; 15:8–13 [Exodus]). **3.** Israel is preferred to all other countries, represented by Egypt, Seba (southern Egypt), and Ethiopia (modern Sudan), but only to be God's mediator for sharing his love with them. "Ransom" is not to be taken literally; in saving his people, God never pays a price to the evil one. **5–6.** The great ingathering is announced (Jer 31:1–22; Ez 37:15–28), but the fulfillment will exceed these words as the world becomes one family in Christ Jesus (Gal 3:26–29; Eph 2:13–16). God speaks of "my sons" and "my daughters" (Ex 4:22–23; Hos 11:1–11; Is 1:2), for he is continually imparting life—a life of love, decision, and devotedness; but not until Jesus sends his spirit into men's hearts will man respond with "Abba, dear Father" (Lk 11:2; Rom 8:14–17). **7.** So thoroughly do God's children share his life that they can be addressed by his name. This experience of divine life, recognized and enjoyed, constitutes God's glory (cf. 40:3).

9–13. These lines return to the trial scene (41:1) but also add a new element—the summons to the Israelites to be witnesses. **9.** Yahweh allows the nations one more chance to demonstrate that they or their gods "foretold... the earlier things" (cf. 40:4; 42:9). Because knowledge, for the ancient Near Eastern, meant a total, experiential involvement, prediction implied a steady control of the flow of events. Questions like this will be repeated (Is 53:1; Jn 12:38; 1 Cor 2:7; 10–16). **10.** Israel, by her extraordinary survival and by her still more wondrous resurgence, witnesses to the world that Yahweh alone is God and savior; in a similar way, the apostles, in NT times, became "witnesses...to the very ends of the earth" (Acts 1:8) that "God has raised up this Jesus" (Acts 2:32). Three strong verbs, "know," "believe," and "understand" lead to the divine declaration "I am he." Unique among the Oriental religions, the Bible never recounts the origin nor the decline of Yahweh. He exists, forever in full possession of life and creativity. **11-13.** Of the 29 words in the MT, 12 are in the first person and the first person pronoun occurs five times. The first line repeats "I, I, Yahweh," but this monotheism does not constitute any strict theory nor proud self-esteem. It is the full, exclusive power of divinity at the service of Israel and the world—foretelling, saving, creating, and making known (44:6-8).

21 **14-21.** The Prophet continues a favorite theme, the new exodus. Yahweh is to be known as the one at work "redeeming you" (the Hebrew uses the ptc. form) and as such is "the Holy One" (cf. 40:25). In other words, nothing is so mysterious and "beyond" about God—as the word "holy" connotes—as the extent of his redeeming love. **15-17.** A series of participles answers the question: Who is Yahweh?—He is the one: "creating Israel...opening a way...leading out chariots." The words portray the Exodus out of Egypt, ending in the final scene where the Egyptians are "lying prostrate, never to be rising" (impf. verb connotes continuous act), "snuffed out and quenched" (pf. form connotes completed action). **18.** No one was more devoted to the redemptive acts of the past than Dt-Is; however, here he warns against a glorying in the past that has no time for application in the present. What is to be remembered as a continuous redemptive act is the new exodus; that great deed will constitute the *anamnēsis* of the eschatological age (cf. Lk 22:19; 1 Cor 11:24-26). **19.** This verse seems to remonstrate: Must you be so blind? **21.** *the people whom I formed:* The LXX reads, "people whom I purchased"; that phrase recurs in Acts 20:28; 1 Pt 2:9.

22-28. Human ingratitude and divine mercy meet; God's invectives, delivered in courtroom style, are followed by forgiveness. The build-up in the Hebr text is massive; each section in vv. 22-24 begins with a negative: "not...not...not...not...not...but nevertheless!" These lines are difficult to understand, precisely because the Prophet shifts from pre-exilic days, when sacrifices were offered as though they were the essence of religion (Is 1:11-15), into the exilic period, when sacrifice was impossible. The proud spirit of the past, glorying in an elaborate ritual, continues into the present, burdening God with its weighty offense. Israel's oppressive feeling of despair over deprivation of temple sacrifice and of all "human" means of expiation is not God's responsibility. Israel is wearying God with her complaints, lit., making God a servant—one of the most daring phrases in the entire OT, but especially so in Dt-Is against the background of Servant theology (42:1ff.; 52:13-53:12). The key word is "weary." Both Israel and God are weary, but for different reasons. **27-28.** The strong "corporate personality" of Israel is here manifest. This trait stems from the desert origin where the individual depended so thoroughly upon the group and where great devotion was paid the ancient patriarch and the first-born son who continued the line. The future is seen to exist already in the forebears; ancient blessings and curses explain the present situation. *our first father:* Jacob (Gn 27; Hos 12:2-7; Jer 9:3). *your spokesmen:* The unworthy prophets and priests of old (Mi 3:5-12; Is 28:7).

(Le Frois, B. J., *CBQ* 17 [1955] 315-23. Pedersen, *op. cit.*, 99-131. Robinson, W., *BZAW* 66 [1936] 49-62.)

22 **44:1-5.** This song is composed of a series of short lines, each beginning with a strong declaration: "hear now"; "thus says the Lord" (formula of an oracle); "fear not" (formula of theophanies). The second half of each line introduces a theme of mercy: "servant...chosen...making you...forming you... chosen." **1.** God speaks the word of divine election, and his people are formed in the womb of sacred history. **2.** God calls this child "darling" (*yᵉšurûn*), a term of endearment, a diminutive probably from *yâšâr* (to be upright) and here rhyming with Israel in v. 1 (cf. Dt 32:15; 33:5,26). **3.** As Israel receives the spirit, extending new life through her offspring, the land will be transformed into the new paradise. As we would expect in a desertlike area, water symbolism frequently accompanies the spirit of God (Ez 36:25; Zech 12:10; 13:1; Jn 3:5; 7:37-38). **5.** The Prophet sees that Gentiles shall confess Yahweh as the only Savior and shall even tattoo the name Yahweh on their hands (cf. Ex 13:9; Ez 9:4; Ap 7:3). Membership in the chosen people will not depend upon blood descent but open faith imparted by the spirit of God (Rom 4:16-17; 8:14-17).

6-8. Yahweh alone is Israel's king; a ptc. construction gives the reason: He is now "redeeming" his people. **6.** *Lord of hosts:* A title common with Isaiah of Jerusalem (Is 6:3,5; 3:1; 5:14) and quite frequent with Dt-Is (45:13; 47:4); "hosts" portrays the entire nation of Israel as an army battling for God and the establishment of his kingdom (Ex 6:26; 15:3). In the present setting, however, Yahweh is discrediting the hosts of sun, moon, and stars worshiped by the Babylonians, and thereby claiming for himself a cosmic sweep of power (see *BibLex* 1031-32). God's redeeming power extends from the beginning to the end of human life (41:4). **7-8.** By his Word, God not only foretells but also accomplishes, and as his will is executed its glorious effects in Israel will make that country his "witness" (43:10). Dt-Is speaks of prophecy and revelation, not at all as words whispered by God in the souls of ecstatic seers but rather as his mighty presence in time and on earth, so directing human history that a man of faith can detect the omnipotent, personal will of God.

23 **9-20.** Whereas other prophets fought the foreign gods as powers hostile to Yahweh and Israel, Dt-Is triumphantly acclaims the total victory of Yahweh (Is 40:18; 41:21). These gods and their manufacturers "amount to nothing" (Hebr *tōhû;* the same word applied to the universe before creation in Gn 1:2; cf. Is 34:11; Jer 4:23). Even though the style of this section is prosaic and far below the strength or vividness of the other poems, still most scholars see no sufficient reason to assign it to another writer. Some, like Torrey, Kissane, and Fischer, recast the lines in poetic form, and Muilenburg recognizes traces of a rhythmic meter in vv. 12-13 and 15-17. Jer 10:1-16 is similar and Wis 13:11-13 was composed under the influence of this passage.

21-23. God carefully formed the character of his people, like a potter forming a vase (42:6), and yet in the face of such love he must still answer their complaint (40:27), assuring them: "by me you shall never be forgotten." 1QIsᵃ expresses this divine promise in a slightly different way: "you shall not disappoint me." **22.** The verbs here are in the pf. tense, denoting the completed action of God's redeeming love. **23.** The final hymn entones "a glad cry" taken up from every part of the earth. With Israel redeemed, the world is transformed (Rom 8:18-22). Dt-Is frequently breaks forth in songs such as this (42:5,10-12; 45:6; 49:13). Was it perhaps to provide choral response during the synagogal service of the exiles?

24 (h) CYRUS, ANOINTED OF THE LORD (44:24-45:25). Dt-Is acclaims the brilliant military genius who reversed the Semitic policy of rapine, cruelty, and deportation (see comments on 41:1–29). Cyrus, the benevolent despot, asked only for power to unite all peoples; for the rest, he allowed captive exiles to return to their homelands, precisely that they might worship their gods and pray for him (Ezr 1:1–4). Dt-Is excitedly looks forward to the moment when Cyrus himself will worship Yahweh; already he is the Lord's instrument, signaling the great messianic day. With alliteration, repetition, rhyme, and assonance, with the full orchestration of all his major themes of redemption, creation, eschatological recreation, Word of God, and prophecy, he announces Cyrus, the Lord's anointed.

24–28. In this introduction to his song, the Prophet utilizes a series of participles; everything is happening at this precise moment: "Thus says the Lord, redeeming you and forming you from the womb of history." To fulfill his plan of salvation, Yahweh, the covenantal God of Israel, is "making all things, stretching out the heavens unaided, spreading out the earth unassisted." The Sinai covenant is remaking the entire world. **26.** *confirms the word of his servant:* The MT has the singular, "servant," with the idea that God confirms the word (work or vocation) of his Servant, Israel (41:8). The plural "servants" in the CCD parallels the second line, "messengers," so that both words would refer to the earlier prophets, who announced the destruction of Jerusalem precisely that God might purify his people and build a new Jerusalem. The moment of fulfillment has arrived. **27.** Dt-Is calls upon the mythological language of Babylon; watery depths symbolized monstrous evil powers, lashing destruction upon the peaceful land (43:2; 51:9–10). **28.** For the first time, the Prophet pronounces the name Cyrus; on God's own word, he is "my shepherd" (or king—40:10–11), for he "fulfills my every wish." The last two lines of this verse are probably added; the introduction is clumsy and the word *hêkāl* (temple) is never again used by a prophet unsympathetic to organized temple sacrifice.

25 **45:1–8.** We now listen to the divine decree announcing the royal enthronement of Cyrus. Only here in the OT is a foreigner called the Lord's "anointed" (*māšîaḥ*, or "messiah"; *christos*, hence "Christ"). The OT never uses *māšîaḥ* as a title for the promised one of the messianic age (*BibLex* 1510–11; E. O'Doherty, *CBQ* 19 [1957] 19; S. Mowinckel, *He That Cometh* [Oxford, 1956] 3–9); the title is reserved principally for kings (1 Sm 16:6; 2 Sm 19:22) but shared also with prophets (Ps 105:15) and priests (Lv 4:3; Dn 9:25–26). **1.** *whose right hand I grasped:* At their coronation, Babylonian kings grasped the hand of the patron god, Bel-Marduk. Dt-Is envisions Yahweh grasping Cyrus as legitimate king over messianic Israel. How disappointed will the Prophet be when later Cyrus grasps the hand of Bel-Marduk and in the name of this god allows the Jews to return to their homeland (see *ANE* 316). **2.** The divine "I" is spoken emphatically here, closely linking the Cyrus conquests with the divine revelation of Sinai (Ex 3:14–15). *level the mountains:* The phrase turns the march of Cyrus' army into another exodus (40:3–4). The "treasures" of such legendary figures as Croesus will fall into Cyrus' hands. **4.** This verse has startling theological implications. Without violating the free will of Cyrus, God was directing his steps "though you knew me not." Here is a practical expression of "God the first" (44:6). The Lord was making sure that world history converged upon his designs for a tiny captured group of people, Israel! Historians like Herodotus and Xenophon would scorn such Jewish braggadocio; Dt-Is knew it was true by faith (see Smith, *op. cit.*, 185–86). **6–7.** Yahweh is "forming light" and "making well-being" (*šālôm;* cf. 44:28), but without attempting to explain the inexplicable, the Prophet declares that Yahweh is also "creating darkness" and "woe" (all participles in Hebrew). Evil is no giant staggering through the world at his own whim; somehow, it accomplishes God's will for purifying and disciplining his chosen ones (Am 3:6; Is 10:5–20; Jgs 2:6–3:6). **8.** A prayer follows, begging God—urgently, in the imper. mood—to bring salvation out of all these earthly events (cf. Is 11:1; 55:10–11). The "justice" (40:14) and "salvation" of the MT were translated by Jerome as proper names—the "just one" and the "savior." His Lat translation is well known in the Advent hymn "Rorate caeli desuper."

9–13. Only here does Dt-Is imitate the invective style of other prophets (Am 5:7,18; Is 1:4,24). Possibly referring to the creation account of man (Gn 2:7; 3:19; Jer 18:2–10; Rom 9:20–22), the Prophet cries out: "Woe! will the potsherd strive with the potter? Will the land strive with the ploughman?" (cf. C. F. Whitney, *VT* 11 [1961] 457–61). He allows no one to question God's wisdom. It was humiliating for a Jew to accept a foreigner as the promised savior. God's demand of absolute obedience is not based, however, on blind subservience to fate or on the passive acceptance of brutal power, but rather on his delicate concern implied in the image of a potter, on his paternal love expressed in the phrase "my children," and on his personal attention, emphasized by the repetition of the first person. Quickly scanning the entire history of creation, Dt-Is sees a plan entirely dedicated to Cyrus' release of the exiles. **13.** *without price or ransom:* Cyrus will ask only that Jews pray for him to Yahweh (Ezr 6:10).

26 **14–25.** The world-wide sweep of Cyrus' conquering army leads Dt-Is to the universal domain of the messianic kingdom. Centuries of preparation are ended and the new, eschatological age is breaking through. Because of one world kingdom, the Prophet thinks only of one true God, and this confession leads up to only one true religion. **14.** The wealth of all nations, symbolized by the gifts of Egypt, Ethiopia, and Seba (cf. 43:3), will flow into Israel (Is 2:2–5; Pss 68:32ff.; 72:10). Nations will willingly sacrifice everything to participate in the faith of Israel, for through this faith their entire earth will be recreated. The rewards of faith, once promised Abraham (Gn 15:5–6; 22:15–18), belong to all men of faith. Paul will develop this doctrine fully (Rom 4). **15.** The Gentile confession climaxes in "God of Israel, Savior." Without an article in the MT, "Savior" is almost a proper name for God. People will say to this savior, "Truly you are a hidden God" (the CCD revocalizes the MT); his redemptive acts are concealed beneath every human means, even beneath the person of the pagan Cyrus. Man recognizes the divine presence only by faith (A. Gelin, *BiViChr* 23 [1958] 3–12). **17.** Despite Israel's repeated infidelities, the humble Israelite will never be shamed before the world. God's words combine judgment and salvation, the two principal characteristics of the eschatological moment. **18.** Solemnly, Dt-Is introduces another hymn. The Hebr style is dynamic, as resounding participles are interrupted with abrupt statements: "he is God...he is the one establishing it," which suddenly reverses to "I, Yahweh, and there is no other" (41:8–10), the refrain echoing the words of 44:6. If God is at times present within chaos, it is only to overcome it and transform it. **19.** God's word is heard, not by a few devotees acquainted with magical formulas but by everyone, including Gentiles who have faith.

27 **20–25.** The style switches to that for a courtroom scene (41:1). **21.** The remnant of the Gentiles are summoned to confess that Yahweh was preparing for this moment of salvation "from the beginning." When

Yahweh foretold the future through his prophets, he was setting in motion the means of its fulfillment. The "remnant" doctrine is implied: "fugitives from among the gentiles" (Am 3:12; 5:3; Is 10:21–22). It is a difficult doctrine to define, for it is not to be limited to a number of people nor does it seem to intend simply an interior state of lowliness. Its answer involves the age-old question: "Lord, are only a few to be saved?" (Lk 13:23). **22.** This call to salvation makes only one requirement: to "return" to God in humble, devoted faith. **23.** Dt-Is ends the court scene with words that an early Christian hymn will direct to Jesus Christ (Phil 2:5–11). The rejection of those who had "vent their anger against him" was necessary so that no unhappiness might mar the glory of the eschatological kingdom. The Prophet concludes the poem with the mention of "Israel," for all the world will then belong to this chosen people of God.

28 (i) The Burdensome Gods of Babylon (46:1–13). Dt-Is has already reflected upon the gods' powerlessness; now he fully presents this theme, extending it into ch. 48.

1–2. The poem begins with the humiliation of the gods. At first it is difficult to know if the Prophet thinks of the statues of the gods as being carried in solemn religious procession or as being carted hastily out of the city for protection against Cyrus' advancing army (see *ANEP* 537–38). In either case, men labor to make the existence of the gods less burdensome. The short, staccato phrases of the Hebr text insist upon the deities' quick downfall. We also suspect a play on words. The word for "idol," *ʿăṣabbêhem*, by a simple change of vowels, becomes "toilsome work." *Bel:* God of heaven and father of gods, patron of the Sumerian city of Nippur, merged with Marduk, the great god of Babylon (Jer 50:2; Bar 6:40; Dn 14:2–21). The elevation of Bel-Marduk was celebrated lavishly in the Babylonian ritual. As the great creation myth, "Enuma Elish," was re-enacted, the forces of chaos were thought to be withstood for another year (*ANET* 60–72; *DOTT* 3–16). *Nebo:* Son of Marduk and "secretary-god" possessed of the tablets of destiny. His popularity can be judged from the many Babylonian names referring to him: Nabopolassar; Nebuchadnezzar; Nabonidus. **2.** When Dt-Is writes of the gods going into captivity, he is certainly composing the poem before the fall of Babylon. Here is no *vaticinium ex eventu.* Cyrus reversed the policy of conquerors; not only did he leave the statues in their own temples, but he also returned those that the Babylonians had stolen.

29 **3.** *the remnant of Israel:* Yahweh calls it his burden and care (cf. 45:20; Dt 1:31; Hos 11:3; Ps 21:10). The word *sābal* (to carry) has a rich meaning. It conveys the legal idea of adoption, a ceremony enacted by placing the child upon one's lap (cf. Gn 30:3; Ru 4:16). The foster parents care for the child during its life, and the child, in turn, cares for the memory of the foster parents after their death (see *Bib* 36 [1955] 266). **4.** Israel always remains a child in need of Yahweh's care. The last part of this verse is powerfully constructed, not only by the repetition of the divine "I" but also by the reversal of tenses; a literal translation would read: "And I have done [this] and I will do [this]; and I will bear [you] and I have saved [you]." God is forever the same in love (Ps 7:9,18). **8–11.** A series of four imperatives turns Israel's attention to the past: "remember the former things" (41:4). Yahweh's great redemptive acts of the past sustain faith in the present. **10.** Yahweh acts according to a personal plan of salvation, and the word predicting the future accomplishes exactly what it says. **11.** *the bird of prey from the east:* This plan reaches its climax in Cyrus. Again, a deft reversal of tenses enforces the thought of how surely and quickly God accomplishes his proclamations.

12–13. *listen to me, fainthearted ones:* The Hebrew reads, "you stubborn ones," those slow to acknowledge God's saving power. Every divine promise is on the verge of fulfillment; there is no time to tarry.

30 (j) Taunt-Song Over the Fall of Babylon (47:1–15). Dt-Is sings a dirge over Babylon in the 3–2 beat of Lam. The sorrow is in mockery because the city before him is still wealthy, carefree, and independent, but the Prophet detects its corrupt interior, its death sentence already formulated in the plans of Cyrus. God is soon to requite of Babylon the savage destruction of Jerusalem and the ruthless deportation of her people. What the Prophet condemns most of all is the city's pride. The humble sinner is ready for conversion; the proud sinner must first be broken. Lest this taunt-song seem cruel it must be balanced against the universal call to salvation in Dt-Is (sorrow is intended to purify and thus save) and against the fact that no Gentile nation suffered more than Israel (Is 5; 8:6–10; Jer 13–14). This poem is one of the finest in the Dt-Is collection. The Prophet's virtuosity is displayed in a rich vocabulary; almost 40 words occur, not found elsewhere in his writings (ch. 40, however, contains 50 to 60 such words, 8 in v. 12 alone). The poem possesses a compact strength through the interlocking of its various lines: 1a, 5a; 5d, 7b; 8d, 10f; 9d, 11a, 11e; etc. There is repetition not only of phrases but also of sound; frequent imperatives (fem. sing.) sustain the same sound throughout. The Hebr text reveals striking onomatopoeia; v. 2a reverberates with the crackling sound of a millstone grinding wheat: *q^{e}ḥî rēḥayim w^{e}ṭaḥănî qāmaḥ gallî sammātēk.* The sarcasm is sharpened by grandiose words of address: "virgin daughter...dainty and delicate...sovereign mistress...voluptuous one."

1. Babylon would like to consider herself a virgin, unravished and unconquered by any nation, but she is so only in her sterility (Am 5:2). She is called Chaldean, for she descended from a Semitic people who migrated *ca.* 1000 BC from an area to the southeast. Chaldea later became famous for soothsayers (Dn 1:5; 2:2). **2–3.** Babylon shall exchange her pampered harem existence for the slave drudgery of grinding wheat and corn (Ex 11:5; Jgs 16:21). She will be deprived of the veil worn by noble ladies to hide their faces from sensuous gazes (Ct 4:3); she will bare her legs, either to work more easily or to be treated more freely like a captive woman (Is 20:4; Na 3:5). **4.** This verse may be a liturgical addition, a congregational refrain, reminding us that sorrow as humiliating as that just described is redemptive.

5–7. The "silence" of Babylon is dark and despairing; the country is left incapable of honest reassessment, of humble contrition, of vigorous adaptation. Babylon had defied the laws of humanity, heaping sorrow upon her captives. **8–11.** Babylon is again seated like a goddess accepting divine honors (cf. Zeph 2:15), even the acclamation reserved for Yahweh: "I and no one else!" (45:5,18, 21; 46:9). What she fears "shall come"; Dt-Is repeats the word five times in two verses! **12.** *keep up your spells:* To this opening phrase the Hebrew adds the polite request, stinging with its satire, "I pray you!" (Am 4:4–5). The last two lines of v. 12 could be marginal sarcasm; 1QIs^{a} omits them, simply adding, "even until this day!" **15.** *your magicians:* An emendation of the MT, which reads "your merchants"—i.e., those who have "trafficked" with you (RSV) for their own gain. Each of them "wanders," or staggers to his quarter (Cheyne, *op. cit.*, 297). The last line contains hope; Babylon is ready to recognize that only Yahweh can save!

31 (k) Recapitulation (48:1–22). With full orchestration, Dt-Is concludes the first part of his prophecy;

every major theme is sounded, some of which—such as Cyrus, idols, and, with a slight exception, Babylon—will never be heard again. He touches upon the familiar themes: things past and things to come; history, prophecy, and creation; the power of the Word; the new exodus. The familiar imperatives reappear: hear; call; name. Other characteristic style features show up in this chapter: participles; questions; repetitions.

1–11. This first section reverts to the ancient prophetic style of threat and condemnation (cf. 49:9). As he ends the first half of his ministry, how disappointing it is to realize so much enthusiastic preaching should evoke so very little response. **1.** The first two verses touch continually upon the idea of name. God's chosen people bear the name *Israel* ("God is strong," Gn 32:22–29; Hos 12:5; See R. de Vaux, *VDBS* 4, 730; R. Kugelman, *The Bridge* [N.Y., 1955] 204–24). **2.** *named after the holy city:* Lit., "city of the Holy [One]" (cf. Neh 11:1; Dn 9:24; Mt 4:5; Moslems still call Jerusalem *el-Quds*, "The Holy"). Dt-Is will develop the full significance of "Jerusalem" in succeeding chapters; this city symbolized the presence of God and the fulfillment of all the convenantal promises. For this reason, Isaiah of Jerusalem gave it the symbolic name "city of justice, faithful city" (Is 1:26; Jer 3:17; Ez 48:35). Israel, however, glories in a city of justice "without" seeking her "justice" (i.e., her salvation) in Yahweh. **3.** *former things:* They included the idolatry of pre-exilic days (v. 5), and the danger of it during exile (41:4,22–23; 44:6). The Babylonians attributed the conquest of Jerusalem to Bel-Marduk; the Israelites might be tempted to believe them, for would Yahweh, if he were divine, inflict sorrow such as that upon his people? Dt-Is answers: Yahweh even predicted it through the persecuted prophets! The Word always appealed to faith, a strong confidence in God who exceeded human thought. **4.** Israel, however, was "stubborn," with "iron sinew" and "bronze forehead" (Is 6; 30:9; Jer 5:3; Ex 32:9; Dt 9:6).

32 **7.** *brought into being:* Dt-Is sings of new things (41:4), such as the salvation of the exiles and the inauguration of the messianic age. The MT reads, "are now being created," and it continues, "lest you say: behold! I knew it" as though you created it yourself. **8.** *treacherous... rebel:* One reason why the Book of Consolation (chs. 40–55) could not have been composed by Isaiah of Jerusalem is this denial that Israel (Dt 32:4; Is 1:2) knew beforehand of the wonders of the present moment. **9.** This verse makes it abundantly clear that salvation depends on God's and not Israel's "justice" (40:14). **10.** This difficult verse is translated in various ways, but the general idea is clear enough: The Exile is another Egypt, which earlier tradition called a "furnace of affliction" (Dt 4:20; 1 Kgs 8:51; Jer 11:4), purifying and strengthening Israel's devoted love for Yahweh. **11.** *for my sake:* God declares that this redemptive work is done for him, so that whoever beholds the redemption of Israel will recognize his divine presence.

12–22. The second part of this recapitulation sings of the new redemption. **12.** The opening verse reverses the apostasy of former times when Israel's "name" was "the lord of hosts," but "without sincerity or justice" (vv. 1–2). But as God now calls out the name Israel, the people are immediately "strong" in their faith and devotedness. Israel's strength relies upon Yahweh who is "the first," at the beginning of every act, and "the last," at its fulfillment. Three times Dt-Is repeats the sacred "I" of Yahweh, emphasizing the strong personal love of God. **13.** This verse moves from the covenant with Israel to the creation of the world. The covenant, however, is but the continuing act of creation, assuring the fulfillment of God's plan in creating. This connection is stressed, not only by the fact that "*name*" and "*call*" are the same word in Hebrew, but also because Dt-Is speaks of creation with the ptc. or impf. form of the verb (40:28; 42:5). Creation thus becomes more and more a historical act of salvation, continuing through the ages and leading to the final age of the covenant. **14–16.** The redemption is achieved through Cyrus. As in earlier court scenes (41:1), God challenges all other gods: Have they foretold and by their word accomplished "these things?" "The first and the last" (v. 12) converge in Cyrus. He is Abraham; he too is "the Lord's friend" (41:8), coming from the east to bring salvation to the nations. **16.** *never from the beginning have I spoken in secret:* Even though no one could have imagined this extraordinary way of salvation (vv. 3, 6–8; 40:3), still, what God accomplished in Abraham should have prepared men to accept the call of Cyrus. The last part of v. 16 is a *crux interpretum.* BJ attributes it to Cyrus; Dhorme explains it as an isolated saying by which the Prophet defends himself against critics (*op. cit.*, 171), but in that case, only here and in 40:6 does the Prophet speak in his own name. By a clever emendation of the text, Kissane arrives at: "And now I Yahweh have sent deliverance" (*op. cit.*, 116–17).

33 **17–19.** This stanza opens in the solemn style of an oracle; participles keep the word of God continually resounding, laying out "the way" of the Lord (40:3). The Word of God has always been the major factor in biblical religion, beginning with Abraham (Gn 12:1–3), continuing with Moses (Ex 19:3–8), and re-envigorated with the prophets.

(Jones, A., *God's Living Word* [N.Y., 1961]. McKenzie, J. L., *TS* 21 [1960] 183–206. Moriarty, F. L., *The Bridge* 3 [N.Y., 1958–59] 54–83.)

18. The Mosaic Commandments, if obeyed, will produce "prosperity" (*šālôm*; cf. 44:28) and "vindication" (*sᵉdāqâ;* cf. 40:14). **19.** From Moses, Dt-Is moves back to Abraham, to whom was promised "offspring" equal to "the sand" of the seashore (Gn 22:17) and a name never to be blotted out, so that all nations will bless themselves by it (Gn 12:2–3; Jer 4:2). **20.** With short, abrupt phrases—each has two beats in place of the usual three—Dt-Is signals the start of the new exodus. He does so "with shouts of joy" (Is 12:6; 44:23; Zeph 3:14—all eschatological references). People "to the end of the earth" will be attracted to believe in Yahweh as they witness his redeeming power in "his servant Jacob" (Is 47:7; Ps 126:2). **21.** This description of the new exodus influenced the *Tg. Onkelos* in explaining Nm 21:17, so that the rock of Moses was thought to follow the Jews through the desert as a ready source of water. Here is the source of Paul's application to Christ in 1 Cor 10:4 (see E. E. Ellis, *JBL* 76 [1957] 53–56). **22.** This verse belongs in 57:21.

34 **(C) Hymns to the New Jerusalem (49:1–55:13).** The familiar themes of Cyrus, the Lord's beloved (41:8; 48:14), and of the foolishness of idols (40:18; 41:23) are no longer heard. Songs of creation and of the new exodus continue to be heard, but less enthusiastically. The deep tones of suffering beat with a heavy rhythm, but they are balanced by loud trumpet calls, summoning Jerusalem to new greatness. Chapters 49 and 40 have much in common, especially their style of introducing a new formal section: the time of servitude has ended (40:2) and the time of grace has come (49:8); a way in the desert is prepared (40:3) and the return along that way is described (49:10). In each section we meet the shepherd image (40:11; 49:9), the leveling of mountains (40:3–4; 49:11), and consolation (40:1; 49:13). Scholars explain the relation of chs. 40–48 to chs. 49–55 differently: each is by a different author (W. Staerk; T. K. Cheyne).

Chapters 49–55 were written by Dt-Is after his return to repatriated Jerusalem (R. Kittel), or in Babylon after the fall of the city (P. Volz). (See Feuillet, *VDBS* 4, 699–701 or Pfeiffer, *Introd.* 453–55, for a fuller presentation of this problem.) Here, we adopt the position that Dt-Is writes from Babylon after Cyrus signed the edict allowing the Jews to return home (Ezr 1:1–4). Their new state is barely large enough to support the Jerusalem sanctuary, and in this poor tract of land, 20 by 25 mi., the people quickly succumb to discouragement, avarice, and cruelty (Hag; Neh 5; Ezr 9–10). Not till 515, upon the insistence of Haggai and Zechariah, did they complete the Jerusalem Temple, the foundation of which had been laid in 536 (Ezr 3:7–4:5; 5:1). Some of this melancholy and sorrow echo in these new poems. Yet, the Prophet's faith pierces the surface of events and sees that this Jerusalem will eventually experience the full glory of the messianic era. Even if Cyrus did not profess faith in Yahweh but instead grasped the hand of Bel-Marduk, the God of Israel will lead the world into one kingdom where all men will be united to him in a covenant of peace.

35 (a) THE LIBERATION OF ISRAEL (49:1–26). This chapter opens with the second of the Suffering Servant Songs (→ 5 above; see comment on 42:1). We face again the literary problem of the song's length. The first six verses, like the other Servant Songs, move in the style of Jeremiah's confessions (Jer 11:18–12:6; 15:10–21; 17:14–18; 18:18–23; 20:7–18)—the personal soliloquy of a sorrowing man of faith; with v. 7, we are again back in the prophetic style of oracle, solemnly pronounced by Yahweh. This song presumes that the Servant has already been at work and is now discouraged by the fruitlessness of his ministry. God responds by widening even further the Servant's apostolate: Go to the Gentiles.

1–6. The second Servant Song, addressed to the Gentile nations, presents the Servant as another Jeremiah: he is called from his mother's womb (Jer 1:5); he has a vocation to the Gentiles (Jer 1:10; 25:15ff.); he brings a message of both doom and happiness (Jer 16:19–21), of both suffering and purification (11:18–12:6); he reacts at times with heavy discouragement (Jer 14:17; 20:7). **1.** *called from birth:* Here we see in action the doctrine of God, first and last (41:4); God sets his chosen ones on the way of their vocation even before their birth: John the Baptist (Lk 1:15), Jesus (Lk 1:31), and the apostle Paul (Gal 1:15). **2.** *he made of me:* Lit., "he made my mouth" sharp in uttering the Word of God (Eph 6:17; Heb 4:12; Ap 1:16). It is not clear, however, why God concealed the Servant—to protect him or to let him feel the depressive insignificance of Judah (51:16; 59:21).

3. The explicit mention of "*Israel*" creates a difficulty for those who interpret the Servant as an individual, for here he is referred to as the collective group of Israel. Even for the collective interpretation, however, the presence of the word "Israel" is embarrassing, for how can the Servant Israel have a mission to Israel (v. 5)? There are also problems of Hebr grammar. North concludes that it is retained only with "justifiable hesitation" (*The Suffering Servant*, 119). The solution, perhaps, is in the mysterious fact that the Servant is the gathering of all Israelites, but especially of the saintly members of the people; such a person certainly has a mission to each sinful member of Israel (cf. Rignell, *op. cit.*, 161). **4.** This verse opens in strong contrast with the preceding one: "he [Yahweh] said to me" (3); "and I myself said [to him]" (4). The Servant honestly expresses his dejection over what seems to him a wasted ministry, "for nothing" (*tōhû;* cf. Gn 1:2; Jer 4:23; Is 41:29). The Servant learns to seek his only "reward" (*mišpāṭ;* cf. 40:14) "with Yahweh," not that he loses all apostolic zeal but rather that he will trust God to reveal the fruit of it in his own time. This lesson is necessary, lest the Servant gauge the effectiveness of his work by human appearance (cf. 1 Cor 4:1–5) or seek the glory for himself (Phil 2:8–11; Jn 17:5). The question of 40:27 is now answered. **5.** The Hebr text is damaged and its thought confusing. The verse is sometimes split apart and placed elsewhere or even deleted entirely. **6.** God encourages the Servant by extending his mission "to the ends of the earth" (Gn 12:3; Lk 2:32; Acts 13:47; on the composition of 49:1–6, see C. H. Giblin, *CBQ* 21 [1959] 207–12).

36 **7–13.** Dt-Is now proclaims the wondrous reversal of Israel's fortunes (cf. North, *Isaiah 40–55*, 110). **7.** Opening solemnly with an oracle, the Prophet sees that through "the one despised" God is redeeming (ptc.) the nations. **8.** *in a time of favor:* This phrase became a common inheritance of Jewish apocalyptic writing (Muilenburg, *op. cit.*, 571); both Jesus and Paul see the fulfillment of this hope in their own age (Lk 2:14; 2 Cor 6:2). *favor:* Salvation comes through God's pleasure. *land:* Always important in messianic promises; how else can the full salvation of man, body and soul, be realized (Mt 5:4)? **9.** God is a shepherd leading his sheep along a new exodus (40:11; 42:7). **10–11.** Dt-Is continues to describe the exodus, giving special attention to the messianic theme of water (cf. Jn 4:10ff. and Ap 7:16). **12.** All nations converge and unite in the great in-gathering, and certainly to be included is the remnant of the former northern kingdom (1 Kgs 12; 2 Kgs 17). The language moves with excited pace: "behold some... behold others...and still others." **13.** This melodic interlude (41:17; 42:5) reminds us of the hymn sung by Moses and the Israelites after being rescued from Egypt (Ex 15; cf. Rignell, *op. cit.*, 64).

14–23. Beautiful lines of consolation are sung to Zion-Jerusalem. **14.** The opening lines form an effective contrast with the preceding hymn. **15.** Here, perhaps, is the most touching expression of divine love in the entire Bible; John will transfer the idea to the fatherhood of God (3:16). Together, they furnish us with an image of divine love so far beyond human love as to constitute the greatest mystery of faith (1 Jn 4:16). **16.** *your walls:* God is speaking to Jerusalem, the entire people of God. **18.** In a majestic oracle, God professes to love Israel not only as his child but even as his "bride." Dt-Is is indebted to the earlier prophets for the Yahweh-as-spouse tradition (Hos 1–3; Jer 2:1–3; Ez 16). **19–21.** Israel was "bereft and barren," and yet the wondrous power of God fills her home with healthy, happy children. This verse, with 54:1–3, may provide a clue for interpreting the difficult 7:14. Life is multiplied in the messianic age, far beyond human power and hope. **22.** *my signal:* In Is, God spoke these words to summon the invaders against Judah (5:26); God now calls upon all nations to work together in the messianic family. **26.** Exaggeration emphasizes what is common both to OT and NT (Ap 16:5–7; 18:5–8). God will not countenance the least sorrow or sin in messianic Jerusalem. "The Mighty One of Jacob" (Gn 49:24) has fulfilled his covenant promises with the world.

37 (b) ISRAEL IN DARKNESS (50:1–11). While the earlier chapters frequently spoke of suffering, the words moved in a strong spirit of hope that very soon prison doors would open and darkness would become light (40:2; 42:7). Dt-Is now speaks with a spirit of resignation, even with a tone of reproach. In ch. 50, there occurs the third song of the Suffering Servant, and, in comparison with the first two, the darkness is heavier, the persecution more violent. Most scholars limit the poem to vv. 4–9. Because of the compact unity of this chapter, we must admit that the song has been carefully knit into the fabric of the whole chapter. The first part of the chapter follows the style of two questions and a statement

(1b, 1d, 1f; 2c, 2e); the same device continues within the song (8b, 8d, 8f). **1–3.** The exile certainly revealed a separation between Yahweh and his spouse, Israel. God addresses himself to both his spouse and the Israelites, who consider Israel or Zion their mother. According to Dt 24:1–4, a divorced woman who has remarried can never be reconciled with her former husband. Because God is anxious to bring back Israel as his beloved spouse, he must never have divorced her (54:6–8; 61:4–5). Dt-Is again manifests a dependence upon earlier prophets; Jer 3:8 tells of God's rejecting the northern Israelites, and Ez 16 relates God's decision to expose Judah to shameful treatment. Dt-Is, however, mildly tempers their words. **2.** God, by his Word, was always coming to assist Israel. From the thought of redemption and the struggle against sin, the Prophet turns to God's might in drying up the sea and destroying its monstrous symbols of sin (Pss 89:10–11; 104:7; Is 51:9–10). We also hear echoes of the plague stories of Ex (Ex 7:18–21). **3.** These lines either reveal the shadow of sin and suffering or introduce a great theophany (Ex 19:16–19; 2 Sm 22:9; Na 1:3–6).

38 **4–6.** The third Servant Song opens with the statement that God's word is the source of salvation. **4.** The Servant must first be a disciple, prayerfully receiving God's word, before he can presume to teach others. Cazelles emends the difficult text: "My Lord Yahweh has given me a disciple's tongue, the trial of stammering. It is a tired man whom a divine Word awakens in the morning. He awakens my ear in the morning to hear as disciples do..." (H. Cazelles, *RSR* 43 [1955] 53–54). Like the prophets before him, the Servant, too, is ignored and even maltreated (Am 7:10–17; Mi 2:6–10; Jer 20:7–18). If the Servant is the collectivity of Israel, then the suffering people are deaf to the saving Word of God that is being spoken (or fulfilled) through their suffering. Within the Israelite community, however, there are saintly men like Dt-Is who obediently listen to God's Word and yearn to speak it to others. **6.** It is not easy to determine whether the Prophet himself was persecuted. His willingness to open the messianic kingdom to Gentiles may have been thoroughly unacceptable to the Israelite community. The first repatriates in Palestine rejected any help from foreign groups, like the Samaritan in rebuilding the Temple (Ezr 4:1–5; Mal 1:2–5), and they were not disposed to countenance a missionary apostolate to Gentiles (cf. Jon). At times Mt 5 depends upon these lines (cf. D. M. Stanley, *CBQ* 16 [1954] 398–99).

7–9. The Prophet reverts to courtroom terminology (ch. 41); this style enables him to present a direct confrontation of good and evil, God and Israel; he can employ the powerful moods of question, answer, charge, and declaration. **7.** *I am not disgraced:* This word is from the same root as "buffet" in the preceding verse and provides strong contrast. *face like flint:* The phrase is frequent in prophetic preaching (Jer 1:8,18; Ez 3:8–9; Lk 9–51). **9.** The second half of v. 9 meshes with v. 3; this fact, according to Cazelles, helps us to piece together the original form of ch. 50 before the Servant Song was inserted into it (Cazelles, *op. cit.*, 16–17). It is also a fitting conclusion to the song. Because clothing is frequently a substitute or metaphor for the person (Jb 13:28; Mk 5:28), the Servant's enemies will disappear like moth-eaten cloth.

10–11. All faithful Israelites must walk in darkness—they have no other choice—and like the Servant, they must still believe. **11.** If they rely on the light of their own ingenuity, they will collapse on a painful bed of their own making.

39 (c) STRENGTH FOR THE FAINTHEARTED (51:1–16). In two skillfully wrought poems (vv. 1–8 and 9–16), Dt-Is manifests a keen appreciation of Israel's epic literature on creation and the first patriarchs (J tradition). He sees history, creation, and eschatology combine in the present moment of salvation. Israel, however, appears languid, almost despairing, and must be shaken to attention.

1–3. To "pursue justice" effectively (cf. Mt 5:6; 6:33), Israel must seek the Lord, who alone can fulfill the promises of the past and the hopes of mankind; he not only obliged himself to those promises (Gn 12:1–3; Ex 19:4–6; 24:8) but he also breathed his own spirit into man, making it impossible for men to rest with merely human ambition (Gn 2:7; Ez 37:9–14). God is the rock, the one source of life for the entire community of Israel (Dt 32:4, 18; Ps 18:3; Is 44:8). **2.** God transmitted his life through Abraham and Sarah. Although their marriage was sterile, they believed that God would bless them with the promised son. Faith opened their hearts to the vitalizing Word of God. God "called" Abraham, as the MT reads, "in order to bless him and make him many." **3.** Jerusalem is now lonely and sterile, only a remnant of her former nation, but she is comforted by the divine Word; the promised paradise will come (Ap 21:10ff.]. The Prophet's faith is so secure that he puts the verbs in the completed (proph. pf.) tense.

4–6. Although this stanza repeats earlier ideas, it is not a mere anthology. **4.** The opening words demand attention, not only from "my people" Israel but also from "my folk" among the Gentiles. No longer is the Law proposed at Zion (Is 2:3) nor given by the Servant (42:4); "law" and "judgment"—God's plan leading effectively to full redemption—are received from Yahweh himself. **5.** The line about the arm of the Lord is sometimes rejected (CCD), but it brings the message to a climax. The arm of the Lord, leading the Israelites out of Egypt (Ex 6:6; 15:16) and creating the world (Jer 27:5) "shall judge the peoples" of the world (Is 40:10; Lk 1:51). **6.** *raise your eyes to the heavens:* Know that the sun and stars and moon, great deities in ancient religions, grow dark and thin like smoke (cf. Hos 13:3; Ps 68:3; Mt 5:18; 24:35).

40 **9–16.** In this poem, as well as in the following two sections (51:17–23; 52:1–12), the meter is the 3–2 beat of Lam, but the words boom with a strong, daring demand. Time has elapsed since Dt-Is chanted chs. 40–48; there are many echoes of other prophets—Micah, Nahum, Jeremiah, Ezekiel, and even the author of Lam. **9.** The opening words do not reveal irreverence toward God but rather a desperate spirit, plunged in darkness and yet firmly convinced of God's goodness and strength (cf. Ps 10:12). God is implored to repeat the mighty, redemptive acts of "the days of old," the days of Abraham, Moses, and David, an echo of Mi 5:1. In the present black moment, the struggle of creation is fought; God is warring against sea monsters as destructive as Rahab or the dragon worshiped at Ugarit and in Egypt (Ps 89:11; Is 30:7; Jb 9:13; cf. C. H. Gordon, *Ugaritic Literature* [Rome, 1949] 11–14, for Texts 129 and 137 in Eng trans.; O. Kaiser, *Die mythologische Bedeutung des Meeres* [Berlin, 1959]). **10.** Dt-Is has the opportunity not only to acclaim Yahweh's conquest of the sea monsters but also to move imperceptibly into his favorite exodus theme. God will again make "a way" (40:3) through "the depths of the [Red] sea." **11.** Cf. Is 35:10. **12–16.** Dt-Is again appeals to God's power to create so as to sustain faith in his power to redeem. Kittel's edition of the MT prints vv. 13b–16 in prose lines, and most commentators feel that the genuine Deutero-Isaian thoughts here have been heavily overladen by another hand; v. 15b quotes Jer 31:35.

41 (d) THE CUP OF THE LORD'S WRATH (51:17–23). In this and the next poem, many themes of Dt-Is converge, each strengthening the other and all enriched with the help of other prophetic writing. The first part is addressed to Jerusalem, an abject widow, haunted by the memory of sons whom she saw swooning at every street corner (Lam 2:19). The regular 3–2 beat continues, showing that the agony is deep but controlled (cf. N. K. Gottwald, *Studies in the Book of Lamentations* [Chicago, 1954] 31). *awake, awake!:* The words (Hithpael in the Hebr vb. form) are much more intense than in 51:9. The "cup of wrath" contains the woes preached by many prophets (Jer 25:15–31; Hab 2:16; Ez 23:31–33; Lam 4:21); it was "drained to the dregs" when the Babylonians breached the walls of Jerusalem in July 587, terrorized the city for an entire month, and, in August (9th of Ab), began the demolition of the city and the extinction of a nation (Jer 39, 52). Verse 19a reflects Na 3:7; v. 19b says, lit., "Who is there to shake their head to and fro in grief?"; in the MT, v. 19d reads "Who? I will comfort you."

21–23. Stunned at so much grief, Jerusalem must be addressed repeatedly by God: "But now, hear this, I pray you, O afflicted one...See." Sorrow was the true result of her sins but it has engendered a poor and lowly spirit, anxiously looking to God for life, peace, and joy. The spiritual movement of the "Anawim," inaugurated by Zephaniah (2:3; 3:12) and developed by Jeremiah (15:10–21), reaches maturity. The psalms will keep this spirit vital and energetic in post-exilic Israel (Pss 9:13; 22:25), and the covenanters of the DSS will make it a way of life (1QS 8:1–9).

(Best, E., *NTS* 7 [1960–61] 225–28. Gelin, A., *The Poor of Yahweh* [Collegeville, 1965]. Schildenberger, J., "Moses als Idealgestalt eines Armen," *A là rencontre de Dieu* [Fest. A. Gelin; LePuy, 1961] 71–84. Van der Ploeg, J. S., *OTS* 7 [1950] 236–70.)

42 (e) Awake and Rejoice, Jerusalem (52:1–12). Dt-Is solemnly intones an enthronement hymn in honor of Jerusalem (→ Psalms, 35:6,9). **1–2.** A series of imperatives strikes attention. Jerusalem, the throne room of Yahweh (52:7), will never again be invaded by any sinful uncleanness (35:8; 48:2). **3–6.** These lines come from a later author, reflecting upon the words of Dt-Is and the history of Israel (Dhorme, *op. cit.*, 184). The meter is very defective, so that the MT and many modern writers print the section in blocked prose. *Egypt and Assyria:* Their oppressive measures continue with the Babylonians; Israel is not their private property. Yahweh owes ransom money to no one (45:3; 50:1). Israel, too, contributed nothing except a strong, humble obedience to God's will in history; thus she was "justified freely" (Rom 3:24). **5–6.** Enemies scornfully mourn over Israel's dead body (cf. Pss 42:11; 79:10; De Boer, *op. cit.*, 77), but God's answer rings out: "Here I am!" at work saving you through this suffering. **7.** *peace...salvation...your God is King!:* The messenger shouts this as he runs on the mountain ridges (40:9–10; Rom 10–15). **8.** This shout is now repeated by the watchmen who guard the ruined walls of Jerusalem. As the Word of God is absorbed into people and land, they see "directly before their eyes, the Lord restoring Zion" (62:6–7). **9–10.** This thanksgiving hymn will resound in other OT texts (Zeph 3:13–18; Jl 2:21) and echo in the NT (Lk 1:26–33; cf. R. Laurentin, *Luc I–II* [Paris, 1957] 64ff.).

11–12. The strong, repeated imperatives are transmitted from one caller to another across the land until all Israel is assembled for the great homecoming. *touch nothing unclean:* The Prophet wants more than a transfer from one geographical place to another; rather, Israel must move out of her spiritual, unclean state into a state of holiness (cf. Hag 2:10–14). **12.** In contrast with the fearful haste of the first Exodus (Ex 12:11; Dt 16:3), the army of God's new people moves peacefully, serenely (Ex 13:21; Is 4:4–6; 58:8).

43 (f) Fourth Song of the Suffering Servant (52:13–53:12). The finest thoughts and the most heroic acts of God's people have been flowing into the composition of the Suffering Servant Songs; in the fourth song, the Servant remains one with all people in sorrow and yet distinct from each of them in innocence of life and total service of God. The doctrine of expiatory suffering finds supreme expression in these lines. Style matches thought, for seldom does the Bible reach such extraordinary power of sound, balance, and contrast. Some 46 words occur, otherwise absent from Dt-Is. (North [*The Suffering Servant*, 168] concludes that this occurrence of rare words does not point to a different author; ch. 40 included about 50 such words.) The style is "broken, sobbing and recurrent" (Smith, *op. cit.*, 351) with the constant intoning of the *-û* and *-ô* sounds of a dirge. The author cannot turn away and yet cannot face all at once the mammoth sorrow of the Servant; he repeatedly returns his gaze and often repeats similar phrases.

The question of the Servant's identity becomes acute. Early, pre-Christian tradition among the Jews interpreted this song messianically (see Hegermann, *op. cit.*). The DSS seldom if ever make use of this song (J. Carmignac, *RQ* 2 [1960] 383–95; J. S. Croatto, *VD* 35 [1957] 356), and the Targums turned the one who suffers into an enemy of God (J. F. Stenning, *The Targum of Isaiah* [Oxford, 1949] 178–81; Mowinckel, *He That Cometh*, 330–33). Expiatory suffering, therefore, does not seem to have been a part of official Judaism's messianic doctrine (O. Cullmann, *The Christology of the New Testament* [Phila., 1959] 52–60). It was Jesus' unique contribution to have combined the Suffering Servant theme with the messianic concept of the Son of Man (Stanley, *op. cit.* 385–425; J. Giblet, *LumVi* 7 [1958] 5–34). The NT identifies Jesus as the Suffering Servant at his baptism (Mk 1:11; Jn 1:34), in his miracles (Mt 8:17), and in his humility (Mt 12:18ff.). John sums up Jesus' public ministry in the words of the Servant (Jn 12:37–43). This attribution of the Servant theme to Jesus occurs in Acts (3:13,26; 4:27,30; 8:32) and in the hymns of the early Church (Phil 2:7; 1 Pt 2:21–15). Paul, however, adapts it to himself (Acts 13:47; Gal 1:15; Rom 15:21). Although the first song was spoken by Yahweh, and the Servant was the speaker in the second and third songs, a strong case can be advanced that converted Gentiles proclaim this most sublime revelation of the OT from 53:1 onward.

44 **13–15.** God speaks the opening lines of the lament, announcing the triumph of the Servant. A dirge usually speaks of past glory and present or future sorrow; here, the opposite occurs. **13.** *prosper:* The word bears an idea of prudence of insight, as though the Servant's victory is a result of obedience to God's wise plan of salvation (cf. Vg "intelligent"; Dn 12:3; Is 50:4). **14.** *many:* A key word in the song (52:15; 53:11–12). *amazed:* The Hebr word is often used of vast desolate wastes (Gn 47:19; Is 49:8,19); Dhorme translates it "horrified." *at him:* The MT, LXX, and 1QIs[a] read "at you," as though Yahweh turns for a moment toward "you," the Servant, but immediately afterwards resumes his words to the nations. North (*The Suffering Servant*, 123–24), transfers the long and awkward parenthetical remark of v. 14bc to the end of 53:2, where it provides a good example of inversion (chiasm). 1QIs[a] has an interesting reading for v. 14c: "I so anointed [his appearance] beyond everyone else"; v. 15 is very uncertain (see textual notes, CCD).

53:1–3. This strophe is attached so carefully to the one preceding that we hardly notice the abrupt change in speakers. Gentiles utter their startled question. They believe in the redemptive presence of God, in "the arm of the Lord" at work saving Israel (51:5). **2.** *like a sapling...shoot:* These words recall the messianic promises made to the Davidic family: even though this family tree has been cut down and the descendants have slipped away into oblivion, God will raise up a shoot from the hidden root (Is 11:1; Jer 23:5; Ez 17:6,22; Zech 3:8; Mt 2:23). The shoot is weak and inconspicuous; so is the Servant. **3.** The Servant now tastes one of the most unendurable types of affliction: rejection by his own. The collective interpretation that considers the Servant to be "Israel" sharpens this bitter sense of loneliness. The Servant relives the role of Jeremiah (15:17) and Job (19:13–19), who were also ridiculed and disowned by their own brethren. *avoided:* The Hebr word *hădal* can mean "fat" or "gross," and, in this Isaian context, "obtuse" and "foolish" (cf. P. J. Calderone, *CBQ* 24 [1962] 416–19). Verse 3cd reminds us of an outcast leper.

45 **4–6.** The Gentiles confess their guilt, admitting that they are responsible for Israel's sorrow. The Servant is no substitute for the Gentiles. Both are closely united, so that the sorrows of one are also endured by the other and the heroic obedience of the Servant infuses a full life into the Gentiles. **4.** *stricken:* A leper (Lv 13:22,32; 2 Kgs 15:5) is used metaphorically here for the sinner's outcast condition. **5.** Both ideas—sinner and outcast—reoccur. *pierced:* In 43:28, the same Hebr word was translated "repudiated," whereas "offenses" denotes a rebellion against God's personal concern (cf. N. N. Snaith, "The Servant of the Lord," *Studies in Old Testament Prophecy* [Edinburgh, 1957] 188). *chastisement:* This word recalls the disciplinary or educative power of suffering. God teaches repentance through the calamity evoked by sin (Jer 2:19,30; Ez 5:15; also, Is 3:2,7; see J. A. Sanders, *Suffering as Divine Discipline* [Rochester, 1955]). **6.** *sheep...way:* These expressions bring other biblical themes into the song (Is 40:3,11; Jer 50:6; Ez 34:5; Jn 10:1–21; 1 Pt 2:25). *laid upon him:* It becomes a technical term frequently used in the Christian kerygma to designate God's handing over his Son to death (Mt 17:22; Jn 8:30,35; Acts 3:13; 1 Cor 11:23).

7–9. The Servant's silence is most unusual, for men of sorrow usually cry out their woes (Hab 1:2; Jer 8:18; Pss 16; 21; 68). *harshly treated:* Recalls the Egyptian oppression; Ex 3:7 uses the same word. *like a lamb:* Brings to mind the humble demeanor of Jesus (Jn 1:29,36; Acts 8:32; 1 Pt 1:19; Ap 5:5–6). **8.** This verse, one of the most difficult *crux interpretum* of the Bible, is variously emended and translated. The general idea sees the Servant's loneliness extending almost to the point of despair. *taken away:* Here is the origin of Mk 2:20. *destiny:* The Vg insinuated the eternal birth of the Servant: "who shall declare his generation?" The MT is best explained through the Akkadian or Arabic forms, meaning a "state" or "change of fortune," in this case, from life to death. Cazelles concludes to a "state" or "place" inaccessible and mysterious (*op. cit.*, 40). **9.** *the sin of his people:* The MT reads "my people," thus strengthening the opinion that Gentiles speak these lines as they recognize by faith a message of salvation in the many Israelites who, although innocent, suffer with their own sinful people and thus can share their own heroic goodness with the wicked.

46 **10–12.** Victory—although never enjoyed by the Servant during his lifetime—is again proclaimed (52:13–15). **10.** Although the verse is corrupt and often rejected, the word "pleased"—a strong, determined love—is a key word in Dt-Is (44:28; 46:10; 48:14) and occurs again in the Hebr text of v. 10e: "the will of the Lord." *offering for sin:* In Hebrew, *'āšām* advances the Mosaic liturgy from sacrifice for sins of inadvertence (Lv 4–5) to sacrifice for willful sins. Through Dt-Is, the heavy sin-consciousness of Israel influences the cult, so that from the Exile onward, penitential liturgies commonly occur (Zech 7–8, Jl, Ps 50; cf. C. Stuhlmueller, *ProcCTSA* 18 [1963]). The LXX *lutron* occurs in Mk 10:45. **11.** Clearly God is again the speaker, announcing the resurrection of the nation; in view of the Gentiles' faith (53:1–9), a world-wide renewal is proclaimed. Bodily resurrection of the individual will not be revealed until later (Dn 12:1–3; 2 Mc 7:11–29). *through his suffering:* The MT reads "by his knowledge" (Dhorme, *op. cit.*, 191), i.e., by a full experiential union with his suffering, sinful people. *shall justify many:* He will share his own goodness with them and thus fulfill all divine promises (cf. 40:14; Rom 3:26). **12.** *among the great... mighty:* The MT reads, "among the many...numerous," which is to be preferred as a key phrase (cf. 52:14). In Prv 7:26, the same two words occur with a similar meaning. The song ends, glorifying the Servant for so closely identifying himself with his sorrowful fellow men. His divine gifts thus become their means of salvation. Although the Servant's innocence separates him from the rest of his brethren, he is always slipping back into the collectivity (→ Aspects NT Thought, 78:11, 22–23, 45).

47 (g) The New Zion (54:1–17). Dt-Is, like his master, Isaiah of Jerusalem, quickly reverses the dominant tone of sorrow lest the effect be exhausting or melodramatic; at the same time, such skillful strokes of contrast intensify the mood of each section.

1–3. The Prophet displays his masterly style; strong imperatives and melodious paronomasia are sustained throughout. He joins the Yahweh-spouse image (44:14; 50:1) with the familiar biblical situation of a sterile wife: Sarah (Gn 15:2; 16:1), Rachel (Gn 29:31), Manoah's wife (Jgs 13:2), and Anna (1 Sm 1:2). All bore children through God's special power. Barren Jerusalem will also be peopled with children if she shares the faith of these earlier saints. Here, perhaps, is an authentic interpretation of Is 7:14 to be continued by later Jewish writers (*2 Esdras* 10:44) and finally fulfilled through Jesus Christ (Gal 4:27). Faith not only enables Jerusalem to "enlarge" her tent to house many new children but to include "the nations" in her family. **2.** *tent:* Recalls the existence and hopes of wandering Abraham (Gn 18:1; Dt 26:5).

4–5. *fear not:* After this solemn introduction of a divine oracle (41:10,13–14; 43:1,5), Israel is assured that she can forget "the shame of" her "youth"—i.e. the oppression of Egypt or her pre-exilic apostasy (cf. 50:1). There follows a series of beautiful addresses to God: "your husband," whose love seeks to surround you with protection and joy, "is your maker"; God's creative power always exists for the sake of his redemptive love.

6–8. We meet the mysterious theology of Gn 6:6; 8:21–22, where God repented of what he had done, or of Hos 2:19–25; 11:1–12 where God could not cast off his beloved despite her repeated adulteries, or of Mal 2:14–15, where God inveighs so energetically against divorce. The last line resounds with the everlasting *ḥesed* of Jer 31:3.

9–10. Dt-Is again calls upon the P tradition. This time he compares the Exile to the flood; both were catastrophes of disobedience to the divine Word. Such a horrendous destruction cannot happen again (Gn 9:11–17) because God's love is stronger than "the mountains." We are reminded of the patriarchal name for God—*'ēl šadday*, "God the mountainous One" (Gn 17:1; 28:3; Ex 6:3; Ez 10:5). **10.** *covenant of peace:* This covenant (Nm 26:12; Ez 34:25; Mal 2:5) will firmly unite the entire universe in harmony and happiness (44:28).

11. *storm-battered:* God seeks to console the flood victims with a vision of the heavenly Jerusalem. Like

Ezekiel (28:13,20), Dt-Is draws color and ideas from a mythological paradise; again like Ezekiel (43:1–9), he explains such luminous glory by the presence of Yahweh (and thus basically differs from all mythologies). The Prophet differs from Ezekiel by carefully avoiding any mention of the Temple. **12.** It is difficult to identify all the precious metal adorning the new Jerusalem, but the vision is that of a wondrous city whose foundations reflect the green and deep blue of the sky and whose golden doors are ablaze reflecting the fire of the sun (Frey, *op. cit.*, 279); cf. Zech 2:6–9; Ap 21:18–21). **13.** All this splendor emanates from the presence of the Lord, where the Word of God is taught. Dt-Is does not eliminate all teachers—although such will be the case in the final age—but contrasts the new holy city with the former, disobedient Jerusalem (Jer 31:34; Jn 6:45). **14.** *justice:* Dt-Is recapitulates such glory in this one word (40:14). **15.** We hear the last great shout of hate against God and his people, but it is powerless (Frey, *op. cit.*, 286). **16.** *created the destroyer to work havoc:* If God does so, he thereby forces a clear issue between good and evil. **17.** *the servants of the Lord:* They will receive full "vindication," the same Hebr word as "justice" in v. 14.

48 (b) CONCLUSION: A NEW INVITATION (55:1–13). With a long series of imperatives and with the full orchestration of his major themes, Dt-Is invites the people to the banquet of divine joy.

1–2. All are invited to this eschatological banquet; the only condition is a "thirst" for God. The theology of the "Anawim" (51:21) resounds in the call. The Bible often evokes the banquet symbol to describe God's love. The Passover out of Egypt is celebrated with a banquet (Ex 12), as well as the Sinai covenant (Ex 24:5,11); the abundance of the eschatological age is often laid out as a banquet (Is 25:6; 65:11–15; Ps 22:5); Prv 9:1–1 draws upon these Isaian passages to portray the wondrous banquet of divine wisdom; Ct 5:1 sings of a nuptial banquet for God and Israel. Dt-Is writes, therefore, from a rich biblical tradition that will flow over into the NT: nuptial banquet (Mt 9:15; Ap 19:9); paschal banquet (Lk 22:16–18); and eschatological banquet (Mt 5:6; Lk 22:29).

(See Danielou, J., *La Maison-Dieu* 18 [1949] 7–33; *The Bible and the Liturgy* [South Bend, 1956] 153–60; Galopin, P. M., *BiViChr* 26 [1959] 53–59.)

49 **3–5.** The Hebr text opens with "bend your ears and come to me, listen," because the source of life is to be found in God's Word. God assures Israel that she will receive the full "benefits" of the "everlasting covenant" made long ago with David. "Everlasting" does not mean a covenant beginning now and lasting forever, but one bringing the promises of the distant past to present fulfillment (cf. Mi 5:1; 7:20; Is 61:8). David had conquered nations but his successors could not maintain his kingdom; the Davidic hopes are now secured as all nations beholding God's redemptive power within Israel hurry to join her ranks. Dt-Is again demotes the Davidic dynasty; David is honored merely as leader and commander, whereas God is declared king (40:9) and Cyrus the anointed one (45:1; see O. Eissfeldt, "The Promises of Grace to David," *Israel's Prophetic Heritage* [N.Y., 1962] 196–207).

6–9. With many imperatives, Dt-Is insists that Israel must "seek the Lord"; here, as elsewhere in the Bible (Am 5:4; Hos 20:12; Ps 9:11), the phrase presumes a humble turning to God with urgent prayer and desperate need. Man must seek God, and yet God's ways are far beyond comprehension. These lines combine those mysterious opposites of divine grace: God is transcendent, yet near enough to help; man is helpless, yet required to act energetically; the ways of God are exalted, yet required of man (Hos 14:10; Jb 42:1–6; Sir 43:28–35; Acts 13:10).

10–11. The Word comes from God, but it can be heard only when it is soaked up in human life and spoken with human accents. Dt-Is explains world history, particularly the sacred history of Israel, through the deep, omnipotent presence of the Word (cf. Wis 8:1; 2 Cor 9:10). M.-E. Boismard attributes to this text the immediate origin of the Johannine theology of the Word (*St. John's Prologue* [Westminster, 1957] 100). We hear its echo in John's doctrine of the Eucharist—the Word come down from heaven and received as bread (Jn 6:32,35).

12–13. This last strophe recalls the constant exodus theme in Dt-Is. All the world breaks into song at the wonder of God's saving power within Israel. The curse of sin is removed forever (Gn 3:18; Is 7:23). The reestablishment of God's people constitutes an everlasting sign of divine love. All the world thus recognizes his "renown," or, in Hebrew, his "name." Dt-Is does not sign his own name at the end of his Book of Consolation—that is forgotten—but the name of Israel's savior.

50 **(II) Exhortation and Warning (56:1–66:24).** This final section of Is, frequently called Trito-Isaiah or Third Isaiah (Tr-Is), evinces a change in tone, vocabulary, and outlook. The golden optimism of the earlier section is now overshadowed with a more sombre atmosphere of guilt and even frustration. A new emphasis upon Temple, worship, Sabbath, fasting, and Law reflects a different spirituality from that with which we had grown accustomed. We meet a phenomenon more or less unknown in biblical traditions—quotations from earlier inspired works. Dt-Is no longer speaks; he is quoted. We also hear echoes of his doctrine: the universalism and the proximity of salvation; the necessity of purification; the fulfillment of hopes for the sterile. Because of this similarity and dissimilarity with Dt-Is, the composition of chs. 56–66 is explained in almost every variety of way; by Dt-Is himself during the Exile (C. C. Torrey, E. König, E. J. Kissane); by a single author after the first return (B. Duhm, K. Elliger, E. Sellin); by a group in post-exilic Judah (T. K. Cheyne, K. Budde, P. Volz). "The extreme divergence of positions...shows that any unilateral solution risks being partially false" (Chary, *op. cit.*, 94). Each section must be studied separately. In this commentary, we will hold for a group of inspired spokesmen—a Deutero-Isaian school, perhaps—who integrated the message of their master with the changed situation of post-exilic Israel. The Temple is probably rebuilt (therefore, after 515 BC), but the energetic reformers—Malachi, Nehemiah, and Ezra—have not yet strengthened the weak spirits and still weaker morals of the Jewish inhabitants. This is the gloomy "day of small beginnings" (Zech 4:10), reflected in the prophecies of Haggai and Zechariah, in the Books of Ezra and Nehemiah (see Bright, *Hist.* 344–50; Feuillet, *VDBS* 4, 715).

51 **(A) Post-exilic Torah (56:1–8).** This poem opens with the familiar themes of Dt-Is—salvation and justice—but the spirit of Dt-Is is almost reversed as it insists on man's enterprise rather than on the power of God's creative Word (40:14; 41:14; 45:8). The same ideas, however, but with more of Dt-Is' spirit, converge at the beginning of Mk: "time is fulfilled...kingdom of God is at hand...repent and believe" (1:15; cf. Kessler, *op. cit.*, 21). **2.** This verse recalls Ps 1:1; it is interesting to compare it with Jer 17:7 and Mt 5:3–11, or with Ps 8:5; Jb 7:17; 1QS 11:20–22; Heb 2:6–9, where the accent on man's work is far less. The terms "man" and "son of man" here imply a lowly, discouraged condition: Dt-Is finds relief in the faithful observance of the Sabbath, a very ancient law but rigidly set during or after the Exile (see *BibLex* 2070–76; R. North, *Bib* 36 [1955] 182–201; H. G. Reventlow, *Gebot und Predigt im Dekalog* [Gütersloh, 1962] 45–60; cf. Jer 17:21–27; Ez 20:16; Neh 13:15–22).

3–5. Foreigners living within Palestine (*gērîm*) were granted certain rights and obligations (Ex 22:20; Dt 10:19), but Tr-Is extends full privileges even to the *nēkār*, those living outside the boundaries of the promised land (Dt 15:3; 23:4–9,21). The disciples of Dt-Is are taking sides with the more universal tendencies (Ru, Jon), reacting against the more chauvinistic stand of Ezr 4:3; Ob; Mal 1:3. *exclude:* This word, especially in the LXX translation, refers to objects set apart for ceremonial uses (Lv 20:26; Nm 8:11); here, as in Gal 1:15, it means to be set apart for the messianic kingdom (A. M. Denis, *RTh* 57 [1957] 405–28). *eunuchs:* They were refused admission "into the community of the Lord" (Dt 23:2), not because voluntary castration was common in the ancient Near East—actually it was practiced only upon foreigners working in the royal palace—but because it seemed improper for a person, deprived of the power of transmitting life, to associate with the God of life (*BibLex* 702–703; *ThWNT* 2, 763–64). Certain Israelites were probably forced to submit to castration by their Babylonian masters. They are now readmitted to full membership among God's people, provided they determinedly seek God's will and communicate spiritual vitality to others (cf. Wis 3:14). Their contribution to Israel's vibrant religious life will be their name and monument within the Temple. Many ancient interpreters—such as Jerome and Cyril of Alexandria—recognized here the OT preparation for the NT teaching on consecrated virginity (Is 54:1–3; Mt 19:11–12; 1 Cor 7:7,25–35).

6–8. The Temple receives its "highest title" (Cheyne, *op. cit.*, 62), one that is frequently inscribed over synagogues today: "house of prayer." Jesus quoted these words when he drove the money-changers from the Temple (Mk 11:17; Mt 21:13), but John (2:13–22) developed the full significance of the event by pointing out that the greatest struggle against sin took place in the Temple of Jesus' own body.

52 **(B) Pre-exilic Discourse Against Idolatry (56:9–57:13).** This poem, somewhat rugged in style and blunt in speech, revives the early prophetic form of invective (Am 2:6–16; 4:1; Is 1:12–17). Many commentators (K. Elliger, O. Procksch, B. Duhm, K. Marti, T. Chary, A. Penna, J. Muilenburg) consider this section an attack either upon the apostate Samaritan cult or even upon the religious excesses at Jerusalem. Other scholars (P. Volz, E. Dhorme, P. Auvray, J. Steinmann) look upon these lines as a pre-exilic composition because of the mention of the offensive fertility cult, the royalty, the injustice to the devout, and the hopelessness of the wicked.

9. *wild beasts of the field:* God summons these foreign nations to devour his sinful flock (Am 3:12; Jer 12:9). **10.** *dumb dogs:* Israel's watchmen are contemptuously so called (1 Sm 17:43), "dreaming" or, as the Hebrew may imply, "uttering incoherent sounds" (LXX; Aquila; Symmachus). **11.** *relentless:* Lit., "strong of life" with a voracious gullet (Dhorme, *op. cit.*, 198), living off their sacred charge (Mi 3:1–5). **12.** Some verses of a drinking song are quoted (Is 22:13; 28:7–10).

57:1–2. The opening words present a seeming contradiction; how is it that "the just man," in whom the divine promises reach fulfillment (40:14; 42:1), "perishes?" Only by faith (40:31) can we know that he "enters into peace" (44:28). The writer does not think of a happy immortality; that doctrine comes only much later in the 2nd cent. BC (Dn 12:1–3).

3–8. The language is bitter and the imagery is strong, but how can the evil be cured unless it is laid bare in all its shamefulness? **3.** *sons of a sorceress:* Children manifest what their parents put into them. *adulterous...race:* Not just because of the fertility rites at the sanctuaries but principally because of the violation of God's personal love (Hos 2:4–25; Is 49:14; 50:1). **5.** *you who are in heat:* The same phrase is used in Canaanite mythology for the divine amours; it refers to the sensuous rites of the high places (Dt 12:2; 2 Kgs 17:10; Jer 2:23–27; 3:2). **6a.** *smooth...wady...portion:* In Hebrew these words sound very much alike; their quick succession is like a burst of pent-up anger. **8.** *indecent symbol:* The Hebr word has the same consonants as "male." The second "symbol" translates the Hebr word *yād* (hand), the phallic symbol in Canaanite literature (*UM* 271; cf. 1QS 7:13).

9. *king:* It is best to leave the word untranslated: Melek, Molech, or Milcom, the god of the underworld to whom first-born male children were sacrificed (v. 5; cf. *BibLex* 1546–47). **10.** *new strength:* In Hebr, "life of your hand" (cf. v. 8; Penna, *op. cit.*, 561). **12.** If God loves his children, then he must "expose" their false "justice," their impossible way of seeking what their whole nature yearns for.

53 **(C) Post-exilic Poems (57:14–59:21).** Three compositions reflect the kindly spirit of Dt-Is during the discouraging post-exilic days: 57:14–21, comfort for the afflicted; 58:1–14, true fasting; 59:1–21, a penitential liturgy.

14–21. We hear "another of those mysterious voices which fill the air round about the prophet" (Cheyne, *op. cit.*, 73). The opening lines seem to quote 40:3–4, but the LXX emphasizes the way of faith and morals. It changes "build up" to "cleanse [the way] before him." **15.** The psalm's rich theology of God is illustrated here, mysteriously combining the concept of an "exalted, eternal Holy One" with God's dwelling among the "crushed" and "dejected." The word *šākan* (to dwell) comes from the desert days of Moses, when it indicated the rough, Bedouin tent dwellings (Nm 16:27; 24:5). God lived with the people then and shared their hardships (Ex 25:8–9; Dt 10:14–15). In later literature, *šākan* was used exclusively of God's dwelling with his people in the Temple, but it usually, as here, evoked a memory of his leading the people through the desert (see F. M. Cross, *BA* 10 [1947] 66–68). **17.** Nothing comes closer to eternal damnation than the terrible silence of God, leaving the rebellious satisfied with himself (54:8; Pss 22:2–3; 27:9). **18.** *I will give full comfort:* Lit., "I will give peace," a promise fulfilled in the next verse (Eph 2:17). **20–21.** These lines, anticlimactic after the preceding promise, may have been added by the influential wise men of post-exilic Israel (Ps 1; Jas 1:6; cf. Steinmann, *op. cit.*, 296); v. 21 belongs here rather than in 48:22.

54 **58:1–14.** The second in this series of post-exilic poems answers questions about fasting. The practice reaches far back into Israelite history; it was invoked for times of bereavement (2 Sm 1:12; 3:35) and national sorrow (Jos 7:6; Jgs 20:26). Fasting days naturally multiplied as sorrow abounded. Fasting commemorated the beginning of the siege of Jerusalem, the breach in the walls, the destruction of the city, and the assassination of Gedaliah (Zech 7:1–5; 8:18–19). Ezekiel (45:20) and Nehemiah (9:1) witness to the effort of concentrating on one great day of fasting, which was eventually placed on the tenth day of the seventh month (Lv 16). (See De Vaux, *AI* 507–10.) Priests continued to call extraordinary fasts (Jl).

1–3b. *full-throated:* The dry climate of the ancient Near East has imparted a heavy, guttural sound to all Semitic languages. Deep tones prevent the expression of surprise, scorn, or anger from being mistaken for spite or exhaustion. The long, meditative spirit of the desert enables the prophet-preacher to draw upon earlier prophetic traditions: Is 18:3; Mi 3:8; Ez 33:1–20. The people feel so proud of their piety that they challenge the Prophet to point out what they are doing incorrectly!

3c–7. The Hebr words for "fast" (*ṣôm*) and "day" (*yôm*) sound almost alike. Tr-Is lampoons the idea that man's activity in fasting could turn this day into one of divine salvation (49:6; 61:2; Lk 41:18). Fasting should unite rich and poor, so that all taste the dust out of which each was made (Gn 3:19). Only the wealthy can fast; they alone have something of which to deprive themselves. In fasting, they share the lot of the poor who are always hungry. To fast and yet neglect the poor is a perverted form of conceit. **7.** *sharing your bread:* Lit., "breaking your bread" (cf. Acts 2:46; Mk 6:41; 14:22). Matthew (25:31–46) makes the eschatological judgment depend upon the kindly acts of charity mentioned here.

55 **8–12.** The Prophet's thoughts expand to include the eschatological day. When lowliness unites all men, then will God fill this need of the whole world with his glorious presence. The final age will then have come. **8.** *your vindication:* Cf. 40:14; 54:14,17. **10.** *if you bestow your bread:* This translation is a slight emendation of the Hebrew—from *napšekā* ("your soul" or "your life") to *laḥmekā* (your bread). The former word will occur again in v. 10b ("the afflicted" soul) and twice in v. 11 (simply "you"; the "satisfy" of v. 10 also appears in v. 11 as "give you plenty." When fasting makes the wealthy poor and when the poor impart their spirit of humble waiting upon God to the wealthy, then the world will confess before God "the parched land" of their whole being and God will answer with "glory" (40:5; Jn 1:14), "light" (Jn 8:12), and "spring of water" (41:17–18; 44:3; Jn 7:37–38). **12.** The poem was clearly composed before the reconstruction of the city walls in 445 (Neh 6:15), and possibly before the rebuilding of the Temple in 515 (Ezr 6:16); for other symbolical names given Jerusalem, see Is 1:26; 60:14; Ez 48:35).

13–14. These closing lines repeat many thoughts of the opening verse, so that the entire poem becomes a strong compact unity. One of the key phrases is "your own pursuits" (or "interests"); the identical Hebr word has been translated "desire," "pleased," and "pursuits" (vv. 2–3). Selfish material-mindedness separates man from God and from all God's children, whereas the "honorable" observance of "the Lord's day" unites everyone in a common vocation (56:2). The final words repeat 40:5.

56 **59:1–21.** This penitential liturgy is one of the most obscure passages in Tr-Is. Some scholars, following Duhm, reject large sections (5–8 and 21); BJ splits it into independent sections: a psalm (1–14); an apocalypse (15–20); a divine oracle (21). We prefer to follow Muilenburg's division, which respects the unity of the chapter. Smith wrote: "The whole of this chapter is simply the expansion and re-enforcement of the first two verses, that keep clanging like the clangour of a great, high bell" (*op. cit.*, 456). After the prophetic preaching of repentance (1–8), there follows a confession of guilt (9–15b) and divine pardon (15c–20).

1–8. Inasmuch as the Prophet must defend Dt-Is' preaching (50:2), we suspect that the golden oratory of Dt-Is had aroused false hopes. **3.** All the human faculties employed in prayer are stained with guilt; the image is one of total depravity (Is 1:5–6; Mt 23:13–36; 3:10–18). **5.** "They brood over purposes as pernicious as the eggs of basilisks...[cf. Jb 20:12–16] and as unprofitable to others as spiders' webs" (Cheyne, *op. cit.*, 81). As clothing, this web reveals the evil dispositions of the person (Jb 29:14; Ps 131:9,16). **7–8.** Running in the way of sin reveals the absence of any qualm of conscience (Prv 1:16).

9–15b. A community confession of guilt admits that sin had put God's "right" and "justice" (40:14) far from them. To "look for" a sudden, marvelous flash of "light" insulted God; God would entrust his people with external wonders only when they were interiorly prepared to receive these gifts as from a father. They growl like hunted bears refusing to give up; they moan like helpless doves (Is 38:14; Na 2:8). **12.** Sorrow always teaches the sinfulness of human misdemeanor; God is the Lord of joy. **13.** *apostasy:* The Prophet is condemning a practical abandonment and denial of God by the violation of charity, justice, and honesty.

15c–20. Although similar to Is 24–27, these lines do not thunder with full apocalyptic vigor. Once man recognizes the full extent of his destitution, he is ready to accept the full power of God's arm of redemption (40:10; 51:5,9). **17.** The symbolic use of armor has widely influenced later biblical writing (Wis 5:17–23; 1 Thes 5:8; Eph 6:14–16). *zeal:* In Hebrew, *qānā'* means "to love dearly." It is often translated "jealous," for in God's case love is very often rejected by Israel (Dt 4:24; 5:9; F. Zorell, *Lexicon Hebraicum et Aramaicum Veteris Testamenti* [Rome, 1951] 737; *ThWNT* 2, 880–82). **19.** *glory:* God's glory is identical with his redemptive presence (40:3). The enemies seem to be world-wide, and the Israelites themselves may be included. They, too, needed purification. The poem ends with the acclamation of God as "redeemer," a word very dear to Dt-Is (41:14; 43:1; 44:22).

21. This verse is usually considered to be a much later addition. The words are ambiguous. "You" can apply to the entire community who receive the spirit (Ez 37:1–14; Zech 12:10; Jl 3:1) or to a series of prophets (Dt 18:15; Is 42:1).

57 **(D) Songs of the First Return (60:1–62:12).** These songs are so close in spirit and vocabulary to Dt-Is that the strongest argument is found here for the Deutero-Isaian authorship of chs. 56–66. The author of ch. 60 is obviously familiar with chs. 47, 49, 52, 54–55; 61:1–3 is sometimes considered to be one of the Suffering Servant Songs. These chapters, especially ch. 60 according to Dhorme (*op. cit.*, xlvii), are a lyrical description of the new Jerusalem. What ch. 54 hails from afar, however, ch. 60 sees in the process of being accomplished. Therefore, we consider these chapters to be the composition of Tr-Is immediately after his return to devastated Jerusalem.

58 (a) Glory of the New Jerusalem (60:1–22). **1.** Typical of Dt-Is, the song opens with a double imperative: "Arise! Be refulgent!" *the glory of the Lord shines:* This phrase always signals an extraordinary illumination, as though God were not wrapping splendor around Jerusalem but rather, by his presence within the city, radiating a dazzling light (Dt 33:2; Mal 3:19). In these lines, A. Feuillet (*RB* 66 [1959] 55–96) sees the source of Ap 12; Ct 6:10 also depends upon this passage. Compare the Mosaic Tabernacle (Ex 40:34); the Solomonic Temple (1 Kgs 8:11); sinful and messianic Jerusalem (Ez 10:2–8,18–19; 11:22–23; 43:1–9).

4–9. This strophe opens by quoting almost verbatim 49:18,22. Verse 4d reads, lit., "your daughters are carried on the hips of their nurses" (49:22). **5.** The Gentiles evidently had a definite contribution to make, enriching the people of God; those whom Jerusalem ostracizes can never help her! **6.** *Midian...Ephah...Sheba:* Descendants of Abraham (Gn 25:1–4), they receive their ancient patrimony. **7.** *Kedar...Nebaioth:* Associated in ancient inscriptions (*ANET* 298–300), they were tribes of northern Arabia, also descendants of Abraham (Gn 25:13). With the help of Is 60, perhaps we can recognize that the main interest of Gn 25 was not biological but theological. One day all nations would become his children through faith

(Rom 4:17). Matthew (2:1–12) weaves these and other themes into the Infancy Narrative, for a similar theological purpose. **9ab.** The CCD and others correct the MT; Dhorme (*op. cit.*, 211), prefers the Hebr text, so as to maintain the quotation of 51:5: "In me the coastlands hope." *Tarshish:* A Phoenician colony in southern Spain (Jon 1:3; cf. S. Bartina, *VD* 34 [1956] 342–48). Muilenburg (*op. cit.*, 697) notes how each major section in this poem concludes triumphantly.

10–16. This strophe sings of peace and reconciliation (Ap 21:24–27). Different from Ezr 4:1–3, the poet possesses the more kindly spirit of 1 Chr 22:2. **12.** This verse is probably a gloss from Zech 14:16–19 (Kissane, *op. cit.*, 268), for it disturbs both the poetical style and the serene thought of these lines. **15.** The charges of 49:14–15 or 54:6–7 are forgotten. **16ab.** Jerusalem receives life's sustenance from the nations (v. 5); v. 16cd quotes 49:26.

19. The sun and moon will always remain in place, but all light will radiate the splendor of the Lord's presence (Ap 21:23; 22:5). **21cd.** In *Bib* 41 ([1960] 175–87) I. F. M. Brayley proposes this emendation: "The guardian of his plantation is Yahweh; the work of his hands, that he may be glorified."

59 (b) Glad Tidings to the Lowly (61:1–11). With words from this poem, Jesus announced that the messianic era had come (Lk 4:18–19), but it is extremely difficult to decide when and by whom the song was composed. It is certainly in the tradition of Dt-Is (cf. 40:1–11; 54; 55:3), especially the Songs of the Suffering Servant. An impressive assembly of scholars classify vv. 1–3 as the fifth Servant Song, but they usually work on the basis of the Deutero-Isaian authorship of chs. 56–66 (see the names cited in North, *The Suffering Servant*, 137–38, and in Van der Ploeg, *Les Chants du Serviteur de Jahvé*, 201–205). Chapter 61, however, is too close to the spirit and style of chs. 60–62 to be disassociated from this section: the rebuilding of the city; the change from darkness to light; the stirring call to salvation. This poem might have been the inaugural vocation of one of the leaders of the early post-exilic Isaian school; the Targum, in fact, introduces this monologue with: "Thus says the prophet."

1–3. Each phrase is rich in biblical tradition. "Spirit" (42:1; 44:3) always signals a stupendous work of God (Jgs 3:10; 11:19; 1 Sm 10:5–13). The pre-exilic "writing" prophets ordinarily avoided the term, stressing as they did the interior rather than the exterior marvels of God (yet cf. Hos 9:7; Mi 3:8; Is 4:4). The spirit had been promised the messianic king (Is 11:1–2) and later was assured all the messianic people (Jl 3; Zech 12:10). In Gn 1:2, the spirit creates God's new paradise (see E. Schweizer, "Spirit of God," *BKW* 3; Eichrodt, *Theology* 24–39.) *anointed:* As used here and also in 2 Cor 1:21; 1 Jn 2:20,27; and especially in Lk 4:18 and Acts 10:38 the Word is linked with the preaching and the hearing of the Word of faith; it designates an interior enlightening to know God's Word and a strengthening to follow it (see I. de la Potterie, *Bib* 40 [1959] 12–69). *to bring glad tidings:* Cf. 40:9; 41:27. *lowly:* Cf. 51:21. *release to the prisoners:* The first word can also be translated "light" (KB, 775; Zorell, *op. cit.*, 664; Dhorme, *op. cit.*, 213) as also in Lk 4:18. The meaning in both cases is the same: Prisoners are led out of dark dungeons to full daylight. Here, as throughout the poem, metaphors are abundant, but the basic idea looks to the total salvation of God's people—bodily, spiritually, individually, and socially (cf. Mt 11:4–6). **2.** *year of favor:* Cf. 49:8. The messianic jubilee has arrived (Lv 25:10; cf. R. North, *Sociology of the Biblical Jubilee* [Rom, 1954]). *day of vindication:* This word, *nāqām*, with but few exceptions, is always used of God, with the thought of his repairing the injured force of messianic salvation (34:8; 59:17). Some texts—e.g., *Oxford Annotated Bible* (N.Y., 1962)—follow a Ugaritic root meaning "to rescue," which also explains the LXX and NT translation (Lk 4:19). *to comfort:* The opening word of Dt-Is is repeated (40:1). **3.** *oaks of justice:* Cf. 40:14.

60 **4–6.** As the new promised land rises from the ruins of 587 BC, "strangers" from all nations will contribute their time and wealth (60:4); Israel will intercede with God for them and teach them the word of salvation. *priests of the Lord:* This text does not abolish a separate order of priests, just as the existence of the priesthood never implied that the rest of the people were profane (Ex 19:6; 1 Pt 2:9; Is 66:21).

7–9. The MT is damaged in 7ab; the CCD translation clashes with the mild spirit of these encouraging lines (40:2; Zech 9:12). **8.** Again occurs the covenantal acclamation of "I, the Lord" (41:4). *a lasting covenant:* The word *'ôlām* is frequently translated "eternal" (54:10; 55:3; 59:21). The promises to Abraham are finally fulfilled (Gn 12:2).

10–11. The Targum correctly interprets the thought of these lines when it introduces them with "Thus says Jerusalem." Jerusalem celebrates the fulfillment of love between herself and Yahweh (54:5–8; Jer 33:10–11; Ap 19:7,9; Jn 2:1–11). Messianic glory springs from the earth—i.e., with and through human beings—but "the Lord God" remains the source of all life (45:8; 53:2).

61 (c) Jerusalem, God's Delight (62:1–12). It is difficult to determine who sings this song. The opening line pulses nervously, and the tense mood of excitement continues throughout. Is God breaking the silence of many years (42:14)? It was particularly during the long, frustrating days after the first return that Israel complained of the divine silence (57:11; 64:12; 65:6). Most commentators, however (Muilenburg, Kissane, Penna, Cheyne), consider the entire poem to have been spoken by the Prophet. While others were becoming small minded, jealous, and miserable (Hag and Neh 5), a disciple of Dt-Is breaks into song over the messianic Jerusalem that will dawn the moment that God's people become fully obedient and trustful.

1–5. So long as God was silent, Zion was desolate; but now that God is about to speak, "her vindication" (41:14; 54:14,17) "shines" with the suddenness of the desert "dawn" (60:1). Never did this hope seem closer to fulfillment than on the Feast of Tabernacles, when lights were kindled "at the place of the water-drawing" so bright that "there was not a courtyard in Jerusalem that was not illumined by the light of the place." These words of the Mishnah were commented on by the rabbis: "He who has not witnessed the rejoicing at the place of the Water-Drawing has never seen rejoicing in his life. He who has not seen Jerusalem in her splendour, has never seen a desirable city in his life" (Mishnah, *Sukkah* 51a–b). It was as the same Feast of Tabernacles that Jesus spoke (Jn 7:37–38; 8:12). **3.** Muilenburg (*op. cit.*, 718) refers to the ancient practice of a god's wearing a crown patterned after the city walls. Yahweh holds such a crown in his hands. Jerusalem is not so much a crown of glory to Yahweh as Yahweh is Zion's glory and protection. **4.** Names like "Forsaken" (*'ăzûbâ*) and "My Delight in her" (*ḥepṣî-bâ*) are known in Israelite history (1 Kgs 22:42; 2 Kgs 21:1). **5.** The Yahweh-as-spouse theme is not just repeated here (49:14; 50:1), but sinful, adulterous Israel is restored to that joyful age of long ago when she was the virgin spouse of God.

6–9. These lines voice the demands of apostolic zeal. Watchmen on the walls of Jerusalem are familiar prophetic figures (Is 21:11–12; Ez 33), but their role is no longer to sound the alarm at the approach of invaders but "to remind the Lord" of his merciful promises. The watchmen must be men of prayer and zeal standing between the people and God, fully conscious of both. **8.** *mighty arm:* Cf. Ex 6:6; Dt 4:34; Is 51:5,9. The curses for disobedience will be removed (Dt 18:15–68) and perpetual peace will be ensured. **9.** *you who harvest the grain:* They will celebrate a perpetual Feast of Tabernacles (Dt 16:13–15).

10–12. These lines have caught the spirit of Tabernacles and especially the joy of the glorious procession "of the first festival day of Tabernacles.... Men of piety and good deeds used to dance before them with lighted torches in their hands, and sing songs and praises. And Levites without number with...musical instruments... proceeded, sounding their trumpets..." (Mishnah, *Sukkah* 51a). Themes not only of chs. 60–62 but also of all Dt-Is echo here: double imperative heralding the way of the Lord; call to all nations; sorrow giving way to salvation; glorious renown of Jerusalem.

62 **(E) The Divine, Solitary Conqueror (63:1–6).** We now meet one of the strongest, most impressive poems in the entire Book of Isaiah. The question "Who is this" and the answer "It is I" evokes memories of Dt-Is and the Servant Songs, but the satisfying delight with which the conqueror tramples the enemy and scatters their blood is totally unlike them. We notice some similarity with 59:15c–20, which confirms some suspicion that chs. 60–62 are a later insertion into chs. 56–66, although not necessarily written later. Unlike ch. 59, this poem identifies the enemy of God as Edom, a mountainous country directly S of the Dead Sea. The Nabateans began early to push the Edomites from their craggy fortress land, and this fact may explain why the Edomites took advantage of the fall of Jerusalem in 587 to raid and loot Judah and to occupy the Negeb district (Ez 25:12–14.) Judah's attitude then turned from hostility to intense hatred, boiling over into lines like these or those in Ob or Mal (1:2–5). It is difficult to date this belligerent poem, for divine judgment lay upon Edom from the 6th to the 4th cent. By 320 BC, the Nabateans had totally wrestled the land away from the Edomites. The poet's primary purpose, however, is theological: Edom represents every enemy of God's people, and God eventually destroys evil, after using it to purify and strengthen the elect. The Fathers often applied these lines to Jesus in his bloody death on the cross, but the poet speaks here of the wicked man's blood on the garments of the divine conqueror.

1. A watchman or prophet (62:6) sees someone approaching from Bozrah, a major city of Edom (Am 1:12; Jer 49:13). As the traveler comes closer, he manifests the majestic bearing of a victorious conqueror (cf. Ap 19:13). In answer, the divine "I" rings out—God, announcing (in Hebr, "speaking"; notice the power of the word) "vindication" (54:14,17). **2.** *red:* Red and Edom have the same consonants in Hebrew. **3.** The apocalyptic vista appears; in the supreme cosmic struggle with evil surpassing human endurance, God is the source of all power. The victory marks the total defeat of God's enemies. **4.** The poet contrasts the theme of the terrifying day of the Lord (Am 5:18; Zeph 1:15–18; Is 2:12–17) with the happy scene of the jubilee year (49:8; 61:2; Lv 25:10). God's people can never enjoy undisturbed peace unless the enemy is completely broken and removed. The Hebr word for "vengeance," *nāqām*, also occurs in Nm 35:19 and Dt 19:6 for "avenger of blood" (cf. 61:2). **6b.** The MT reads: "I made them drunk in my wrath," recalling Jer 25:15–29; Zech 12:2 (Dhorme, *op. cit.*, 219).

63 **(F) A Psalm of Entreaty (63:7–64:11).** In the first days of the return, Haggai spoke his prosaic prophecy, Zechariah, his apocalyptic vision, and this psalmist, his agonizing prayer, which is one of the jewels of the Bible. It comes from that time when Jerusalem lay in ruins, and the people's only hope rested in God. God, however, seemed far away and his great redemptive acts buried in the past. The psalmist here identifies himself with the sinful people and pleads their cause before God.

7–10. The opening verse begins and concludes with the Hebr word *ḥesed*, which defies translation but is explainable as a dutiful love springing from a blood bond (see Guillet, *op. cit.*, 20–46; Eichrodt, *Theology* 232–49). Moved by an urgently demanding love, God has performed many redemptive acts, which the psalmist now recalls. In a context of prayer, *zākar* (to remember) always means to invoke a continuous renewal of the redemptive act (cf. Is 64:4; Jer 51:50; Ez 6:9; B. S. Childs, *Memory and Tradition in Israel* [Naperville, Ill., 1963]). The recall of divine favors mounts in strong crescendo; Israel is called (8), protected (9a), exalted (9b), delivered (11–12), and safely led (13–14). Many covenant texts are alluded to: Ex 4:22–23; 14:9; Ez 16; Hos 11:1. Verses 8b–9 in the LXX clearly refer to Ex 33:14 (cf. R. C. Dentan, *VT* 13 [1963] 34–51. **10a.** *and grieved his holy spirit:* God is affected by man's resistance to the prophets and evangelists (Acts 7:51; 2 Cor 3:17). "Holy spirit" occurs only here and in Ps 51:13 and Wis 1:5; 9:17.

11–14. Participles cast this section in the style of a joyful hymn (40:28; 42:5), but that fact only sharpens the sense of near frustration. "Where is he," now at this agonizing moment? That question is not being asked and repeated through ridicule, as when spoken by foreigners (Pss 42:4; 79:10; Jl 2:17); it lays bare an honest, strong, and humble soul like Jeremiah's (Jer 2:8). **11.** Hab 13:20 applies this text to Christ's resurrection, the only completely satisfying answer to the question of sorrow and death. **12.** Cf. 51:5,9.

64 **63:15–64:4b.** The *qînâ* (3–2) meter of Lam stops; the psalmist no longer mourns the dead condition of Israel but, instead, cries out like a man on the edge of despair. Such trials convince man that God alone saves (2 Cor 1:8–11; Phil 3:7–11); even the sacred humanity of Jesus learned by experiencing this agonizing abandonment (Mk 15:34–35; Heb 5:7–9). **16.** *you are our father:* Occurring three times (63:16; 64:7), the phrase must have been common at prayer. As elsewhere (Ex 4:22; Hos 11:1; Dt 32:5–6; Mal 1:6), God became Israel's father not by creating the people but by redeeming them. Redemption imparted a life that shared God's love and hopes, a life far more precious than any physical life. **19.** The psalmist implores God's personal intervention; he pleads for a theophany more wondrous than Sinai (Ex 19; Dt 4:32–36; 5:23–27; Hab 3:3–15). Mark (1:10) sees the answer to this prayer when the heavens were rent at the baptism of Jesus and the messianic era began (A. Feuillet, *CBQ* 21 [1959] 470–90). **64:1.** *fire:* Symbolizes the wondrous power of God's presence. **3.** Cf. 1 Cor 1:9.

4c–6. In this confession of guilt, the psalmist admits that God has not heaped oppressive sorrow upon the sinner but simply abandoned him to his guilt. **5.** *polluted rags:* The guilty man feels this disgusting (Lv 15:19–24).

7–11. This closing appeal, piercing in its pathetic desperation, is born of a stubborn faith that God is still a father able to help (Pss 22:5–6; 44:2–9). **8c.** The MT reads: "Behold! Look! We pray you! your people, all of us!"

65 **(G) The Final Judgment (65:1–66:24).** The eschatological moment, with its panic and darkness, with its ecstasy and glory, disrupts the order and clarity of these lines. The meter is often uncertain (BJ puts 65:1–10,15–25 in prose lines); the text is damaged. Offensive practises of idolatry are bluntly laid bare, a fact that would make the composition pre-exilic; post-exilic Israel is never condemned for such crimes, neither in the historical books of Ezr and Neh nor in the prophetical books of Hag, Zech, Mal, Ob, and Jl. Chary (*op. cit.*, 99–109) and Kessler (*op. cit.*, 87), considered these lines to be a post-exilic castigation of the idolatrous people whom the returning exiles found in Palestine. There are still other opinions for these difficult verses: the apocalyptic style draws images from the deep past so as to make the post-exilic crisis a build-up of centuries, involving all men of all times. We consider the section an apocalyptic composition from the early post-exilic age, in which the line of judgment does not divide Jew from Gentile but rather the true Servant from the false. Toward the end of ch. 66, the distinction of Jew and Gentile disappears; God sees only the saved and the damned.

66 (a) SALVATION OF THE REMNANT (65:1–25). The opening lines mesh well with the preceding; this fact may explain why chs. 65–66 were inserted here. **1–7.** The Hebr grammar expresses the thought very delicately. The Niphal conjugation is used here "to express emotions which react upon the mind...[or] actions which the subject allows to happen to himself or to have an effect upon himself" (GKC 51c). Paul abandons the literal sense to apply the first part of the passages to the conversion of Gentiles (Rom 10:20). **1.** *nation:* In the MT, *gôy* is used often enough of the Hebr nation (Jos 3:17; Is 1:4; 26:15; 58:2). **2.** *spread out my hands:* God stands in a gesture not of supplication but of welcome. This final appeal immediately evokes a terrible scene of judgment. **3.** *sacrifices in the groves:* The phrase recalls the Canaanite nature cults that contaminated pre-exilic Israel (Am 2:7–8; Hos 2:4ff.; Jer 2:8–3:5). Every sin can be counted an act of adultery against God because of God's excessive love (57:3). *burning incense:* Cf. Jer 1:16; 7:9. **4.** *eating swine's flesh:* Condemned by Dt 14:8, this practice featured in Canaanite worship at Ugarit (R. de Vaux, *Vom Ugarit nach Qumran* [Berlin, 1958] 260–65; Von Rad, *OT Theology I* 27). **5.** The people wanted to be left alone in their practices. **6–7.** God cannot remain "quiet," lest mercy be confused with weakness and the definitive triumph of good be delayed forever.

8–10. The Prophet returns to the remnant theme (45:20). A few will survive the sad ordeal of being crushed like grapes. The full extent of the promised land will revert back to God's people, from the Valley of Achor (Jos 7:24; Hos 2:17) in the SE corner where Joshua began his conquest, to the Plain of Sharon on the NW coast beneath Mt. Carmel (Is 35:2).

67 **11–16.** Very emphatically, the Prophet points to "You!" who have committed all these crimes and who worship "Fortune" and "Destiny." Perhaps it is best to leave these words as proper names. "Gad," "Fortune" in the CCD and *daimonion* in the LXX, was the name of a Syrian god (Jos 11:17), venerated in Phoenicia, Dura Europos, and Greece; "Meni," "Destiny" in the CCD, was the name of an Egyptian goddess of spring and fertility (*ANET* 250; H. Gressmann, *Altorientalische Bilder zum Alten Testament* [2nd ed.; Berlin, 1927] 272). **12c.** God replies to the charge of his remaining silent (cf. 49:14; 64:6). **13–14.** Each line begins with "Behold, my servant," who receives the gifts of the beatitudes (cf. Lk 6:20–26); **15.** The apostate becomes a curse symbol (Jer 29:22). **16.** The last line of v. 15 and the beginning of v. 16 are very damaged in the MT; 1QIs^a leaves a blank! Kessler (*op. cit.*, 84, 89) emends the text to read: "My servants will call out a new name...God is the Amen." In Hebrew, "amen" means to be strong, secure, reliable, and truthful (2 Cor 1:20; Ap 3:14).

17–25. A panorama of joy, with the whole universe sharing man's redemption, now extends before us. Three times *bārā'* (to create) occurs; very plainly the achievement is God's, and he and Israel are united in common joy. The world will not be destroyed but transformed into "new heavens and a new earth," a phrase familiar in apocryphal literature (*2 Esdras* 6:16; 7:30ff.; *2 Baruch* 32:16; *1 Enoch* 91:16; 2 Cor 5:17; 2 Pt 3:10–13; Ap 21:1). **20.** This verse interrupts the light, lyrical movement of the passage and is usually considered a late gloss (Torrey, Marti, Kissane, Muilenburg, Penna). **21.** We glimpse a picture of idyllic peace; but it is not to be accredited to human ingenuity nor proportioned to human merit. **22.** The LXX and the Targum read: "according to the days of the tree of life," clearly referring to paradise (Gn 2:9; Ap 22:2,14). **24.** God's anticipation of every wish, even before man speaks, shows that such happiness is his creation. **25.** Cf. Is 11:6–9. Unlike ch. 11, however, the Davidic messiah is passed over in silence.

68 (b) JERUSALEM, PURIFIED AND JOYFUL (66:1–16). The mood and even the vocabulary of the preceding poem continue in this new section. The same eschatological war is being fought, but now it becomes clearer that the sides do not divide between Jew and Gentile but between the good and the evil, the elect and the damned. The Church of apostolic days, living in the final age of the world and inaugurated by Christ's death and resurrection, frequently quoted this chapter to settle internal quarrels with Judaizing groups and to argue against those Jews who rejected Christianity (J. Dupont, *Les Actes des Apôtres* [BJ 2nd ed.; Paris, 1958] 82, n. *e*).

1–2. The prophetic crusade against formalism in worship is taken up again (Am 5:21–25; Hos 6:6; Mi 6:6–8). The Prophet is not rejecting the Temple—a conclusion reached by Stephen (Acts 7:48–50)—for it is God's footstool (cf. Mt 5:34; 23:16–22).

3–6. Four pairs of participles open this section, and most translators turn them into a series of comparisons: CCD; LXX; Vg; RSV; AV. As such, this verse shouts the fiercest condemnation of temple worship in the entire Bible. Scholars like Muilenburg, Dhorme, and Kessler remain closer to the MT: "he who slaughters an ox also kills a man." God condemns the formalistic attitude that temple liturgy (slaughtering an ox) can blind him to moral faults (killing a man). The language is symbolic, drawing as it does upon pre-exilic conditions (→ 65 above). **6.** *a sound:* In Hebrew, *qôl* means "voice." God proclaims the messianic era (Ps 28; Is 40:3; Jl 4:16).

69 **7–9.** These lines, announcing the wondrous birth of the messianic people, continues a long biblical tradition (Mi 4:8–10; 5:1–2; Zeph 3:14–20; Is 7:14; 54:1; 62:4) and, in turn, will influence future writers (*2 Esdras* 9–10; *T. Joseph* 19:8–11; 1QH 3:9–10). In this tradition are to be included Lk 1–2 and Ap 12:3–5 (see Laurentin, *op. cit.*, 155–59). God is always the source of life, most especially in the messianic age.

10–14. This stanza sings with the ecstatic joy of Dt-Is; the poet is continually crying out "rejoice!" to messianic Jerusalem. All children of God nurse at the breast of Jerusalem—an image that beautifully portrays universal peace, contentment, and love. Imperceptibly, the image changes and God takes the place of Jerusalem—fondling, comforting, and nursing his children (cf. 1 Pt 2:2 and the early baptismal liturgy). **12.** *prosperity:* In Hebrew, *šālôm* (44:28).

15–16. The poem ends with booming thunder and

crackling fire, constant biblical symbols of divine victory, with many parallels in other ancient Near Eastern literature: Is 10:17–18; Ps 97:1–5; Ex 19–18; chariots and clouds in Ps 18:10; Hab 3:8; 2 Kgs 2:11; "slain by the Lord" in Zeph 2:12; Jer 25:33. The symbols continue into the NT: Thes 1:8; Ap 18:21–24; 19:17–21.

70 (c) FINALE TO THE PROPHECY OF ISAIAH (66:17–24). The opening verses (17–21) are snagged with many textual problems. Many scholars transfer v. 17 to vv. 3–6. Devotees follow a priest or priestess into a sacred grove for some kind of secret idolatrous rite involving forbidden food (Lv 11:29). Writing under the influence of Ez, the author of this prose section (18–21) sees the glory of the Lord appearing before all nations (Ez 3:23; 11:22–23; 43:1–9). The "sign" may be the Jewish Diaspora, spread through the world and always protected by God. We glimpse a triumphal procession converging upon Jerusalem from all directions: Tarshish in southern Spain (Ez 27:12; Gn 19:4; Is 60:9); Put and Lud in Africa (Ez 27:10; Gn 10:6,13); "Mosoch" (?); Tubal near the Black Sea; and Javan, in the Ionian Islands (Ez 27:13,19) frequently signifies Greece. **21.** Scholars line up on both sides, arguing whether or not Tr-Is foresees Gentiles functioning as priests (60:10; 61:5).

22–24. *the new heavens and the new earth:* The joy (2 Pt 3:13; Ap 21:1) will be accepted by God as a perpetual act of worship (Gn 2:1–3; 2 Cor 5:1–10). The final verse is terrifying. "They" ("all mankind," v. 23) "shall go out" of Jerusalem to the surrounding Hinnom Valley (Gehenna), where human sacrifice was once practiced (Jer 7:31) and which eventually became the city's refuse heap. This proximity of the greatest sorrow and the greatest horror is typical of the eschatological battle, even as announced by Christ at the end of his ministry (Mt 25:31–46). Many texts are inspired by these lines (Jdt 16:17; Dn 12:2; Mk 9:48; see J. Chaine, *VDBS* 3, 572–73; Feuillet, *VDBS* 4, 719). The rabbis directed that when this chapter was read in the synagogue, part of v. 23 would be repeated after v. 24 (cf. Mal 3:24). To hear the stern warning in good time is the best preparation for the great glory promised in the Book of Isaiah.

23

HAGGAI ZECHARIAH MALACHI

Carroll Stuhlmueller, C.P.

HAGGAI

BIBLIOGRAPHY

1 Ackroyd, P. R., "Haggai," *PCB* 562–63; *JJS* 2 (1951) 163–76; *JJS* 3 (1952) 1–13, 151–56. Bullough, S., *CCHS* 543–44. Chary, T., *Les prophètes et le culte à partir de l'Exil* (Paris, 1955) 118–38. Dhorme, E., *BPl* 2, cvii–cviii, 829–35. Elliger, K., *Das Buch der zwölf kleinen Propheten* (3rd ed.; ATD; Göttingen, 1956). Frey, H., *Das Buch der Kirche in der Weltwende* (4th ed.; Stuttgart, 1957). Gelin, A., *Aggée Zacharie, Malachie* (BJ; 2nd ed.; Paris, 1960); R-F 1, 561–63. Horst, F., *Die zwölf kleinen Propheten* 2 (2nd ed.; HAT; Tübingen, 1954). Jones, D. R., *Haggai, Zechariah and Malachi* (TBC; London, 1962). Junker, H., *Die zwölf kleinen Propheten* 2 (BB; Bonn, 1938). Mitchell, H. G., *Haggai and Zechariah* (ICC; N.Y., 1912). Schumpp, M., HBk 10 (2nd ed.; Freiburg, 1950). Sellin, E., *Das Zwölfprophetenbuch* (KAT; 3rd ed.; Leipzig, 1930). Siebeneck, R. T., *CBQ* 19 (1957) 312–28. Smith, G. A., *The Book of the Twelve Prophets* 2 (Expositors' Bible; N.Y., 1898). Thomas, D. W., *IB* 6, 1035–49. Van Hoonacker, A., *Les douze petits prophètes* (EBib; Paris, 1908).

INTRODUCTION

2 **(I) The Time.** The first prophet of post-exilic Israel, Haggai, was truly a "minor Prophet," with a meagerness of words and crabbed style. His four oracles are dated very clearly between August-September and November-December, 520, the second year of the reign of Darius I Hystaspis (521–486). Darius had seized the throne amidst confusion, intrigue, and revolt. His predecessor, Cambyses, had commited suicide when, returning from an Egyptian campaign, he learned that an upstart named Gaumata had declared himself king. Darius, of the royal family, fought for two years, not only to remove Gaumata but also to suppress uprisings across the sprawling empire. The Jews may have been maltreated by their Persian masters at this time of panic and fear. The prophecy echoes this rumble of world events (2:6–7,21–22).

The "Promised Land" of post-exilic Israel had shriveled to tiny proportions, about 20 sq. mi., and it belonged to the administrative district of Samaria and the 5th Persian satrapy situated E of the Euphrates. Not only Jerusalem but also the other towns and villages were in ruins, the fields were overrun with weeds. Farming enterprises were blighted with crop failures (1:9–11; 2:15–17), and, driven by poverty, fellow Jews took advantage of one another and sold debtors into slavery (Neh 5; Mal 3:5). Jealousy, then hatred, developed against those Jews who had stayed behind and had never gone into exile; the Samaritans to the north were repulsed when they offered a friendly hand (Hag 2:10–14); the Edomites to the south were violently despised (Mal 1:3; Ob).

3 **(II) The Book.** The two short chapters abandon the ordinary poetic style of the prophets; attempts to recast the book in rhythmic lines remain hypothetical. Because Haggai is often referred to in the third person, what has been preserved may be a rather free report of the Prophet's work and preaching (cf. Thomas, *op. cit.*, 1037). The Hebr text has suffered a little damage in transmission; the LXX is often helpful for reconstructing the text, but it is also marked by a tendency to expand (1:13; 2:5,18).

4 **(III) Outline.** The outline for the Book of Haggai follows:

(I) The Superscription (1:1)
(II) Haggai's Ministry (1:2–2:23)
 (A) The First Discourse (1:2–15a)
 (B) The Second Discourse (1:15b–2:9
 (C) The Third Discourse (2:10–19)
 (D) The Fourth Discourse (2:20–23)

COMMENTARY

5 **(I) The Superscription (1:1).** The name Haggai (Aggeus in Douay vs.; Haggai in Jewish and Protestant vss.) occurs only this one time in the OT, although there are similar forms (Gn 46:16; 2 Sm 3:4; 1 Chr 6:30). In Hebrew *ḥag* is "feast"; perhaps Haggai means "festal." Christian tradition considers him a priest, for he reveals a great interest and deep understanding of the Temple, but Van Hoonacker (*op. cit.*, 546) concludes from 2:11 that he could not have been a priest. He may have been a "cultic prophet," officially connected with sanctuary worship (Jones, *op. cit.*, 37; for cult prophet, → Prophetic Lit., 12:25). Although influenced by Ezekiel in many ways (Chary, *op. cit.*, 127–38), he shared neither Ezekiel's proneness for vision (Ez 1:4) and symbolic action (Ez 4–5) nor his poetic gifts (Ez 17, 19, 27–28) and adept handling of doctrinal themes (Ez 14, 16). Haggai was a man of action, wholly intent on having the Temple rebuilt; his style was blunt, awkward, and laborious.

The governor of Judah, Zerubbabel (lit., "offspring of Babylon"), was of the royal Davidic line, a natural (1 Chr 3:19) and legal son of Shealtiel (Ezr 3:2; Mt 1:12) through the levirate marriage (Dt 25:5–10). He was governor, but without all the power of Nehemiah (Neh 5:14); he was a high commissioner with a special, temporary mandate. He was probably middle aged at this time. Joshua, son of Jehozadak (cf. 1 Chr 6:15) is the high priest (cf. Zech 3:1–10).

(II) Haggai's Ministry (1:2–2:23). It is recorded in four, possibly five, discourses delivered within a span of approximately four months.

6 **(A) The First Discourse (1:2–15a).** It describes his efforts to secure the rebuilding of the Temple. The foundations had been laid in April-May 536 (Ezr 3:7–13), but nothing further had been done (Ezr 4). The first discourse (2–11) has textual difficulties. After the opening phrase—"Thus says the Lord of hosts"—we expect the words of God or of the Prophet, but, instead there occurs another introduction. Because of these and other difficulties, Eissfeldt (Eissfeldt, *OTI* 427–28) divides the first discourse into the Prophet's memoirs (1–6, 8) and some recollections added to the collection later (7, 9–11). **2.** *not now has the time come:* The CCD represents a correction of the unintelligible MT. The people may be claiming that Jeremiah's prophecy of 70 years has not yet ended (Thomas, *op. cit.*, 1041), but it is extremely doubtful that the Jews ever interpreted Jeremiah's prophecy that literally (Jer 25:12 was pronounced in 605; Jer 29:10–11, in 593). **5–6.** The people feel that they are too poor for the undertaking; Haggai rejects this reason and accuses them of sloth in building God's house. **6.** *bag with holes:* Possibly the first biblical reference to coins. Coinage, first practiced in Asia Minor in the 7th cent., spread through the Near East by Persian influence (De Vaux, *AI* 207). **7–8.** No mention is made of cutting stones for the Temple; the city was probably filled with the stone remains of pre-exilic Jerusalem. Evidently the hills were then covered with trees (cf. Neh 2:8; 8:15). The style is brisk: "Up to the hills! Fetch lumber! Build the house!"

12–15. The people now respond. **12.** *the remnant of the people:* A prophetic phrase, very similar to that found in other prophetic books (Is 10:20–21; Mi 4:7; Zech 8:6,11–12). **13.** *the messenger of the Lord:* Haggai is so called, a phrase that the Bible sometimes translates "angel of the Lord" (see *BibLex* 87–90). **14.** *they set to work:* Twenty-three days later. Haggai seems to be the only prophet immediately successful in what he set out to accomplish! He did not demand any great interior moral reform, but merely the rebuilding of a place of worship whose miniature size made some of the bystanders weep (Ezr 3:12; Hag 2:3). Some interpreters (Thomas, Gelin, Sellin, Horst, and Chary) transfer 2:15–19 immediately after 1:15a, to conform with the practice of placing the date at the beginning of a new discourse. In that case, there are five oracles instead of four.

7 **(B) The Second Discourse (1:15b–2:9).** It is the seventh month (Aram Tishri, our September-October), during the Feast of Tabernacles, which extended from the fifteenth to the twenty-second day (Lv 23:34; Dt 16:13). This feast was closely associated with the Temple and with messianic fulfillment (1 Kgs 8:2; Jn 7:2,37–39; 8:12–59; cf. J. van Goudoever, *Biblical Calendars* [Leiden, 1959] 32ff.; G. MacRae, *CBQ* 22 [1960] 251–76). **2:4.** These words of encouragement are very similar to those once addressed to Joshua (Jos 1:6–7,9, 18). *people of the land:* This term (*ʿam hāʾāreṣ*) earlier designated the country gentry with full citizenship rights, men who were always loyal to the Davidic family (2 Kgs 11:18; 21:14). Later, as here, it means either the common people, as opposed to the civil and religious leaders (Jones, *op. cit.*, 46), or those Jews whose parents had not gone into exile but had intermarried with foreign elements in Palestine (*BibLex* 1795). In NT times it was a term of contempt for illiterate peasants (Jn 7:49). Verse 5ab is a gloss, missing in the LXX, probably inspired by Ex 19:5; 33:14. It breaks the parallelism of the passage.

6–9. In this messianic section, Haggai sees nature and history united through a world center for God's redemptive plans (Is 2:2–5 = Mi 4:1–5; Is 60). The Temple may "seem like nothing in your eyes" (v. 3), but its construction signals the fulfillment of ageless hopes, a privilege never granted Solomon's Temple, for it had been destroyed. **7.** *the treasures of the nations will come in:* Not so much because Palestine is too poor to raise a sumptuous temple, but because God wants his messianic kingdom to include the spiritual riches of all men—their faith, zeal, and kindness. The nations not only receive the saving knowledge of God from the Jews but they also contribute to the full growth of this salvation. Haggai summarizes every blessing with the word, "peace" (see comment on Is 44:28).

8 This passage raises two questions. The first centers on the Vg translation of v. 7b as a reference to a personal messiah: Et veniet desideratus cunctis gentibus—i.e., "and the Desired of all nations shall come." Both the MT and LXX read the phrase in the plural: "the treasures of all the nations will come in"; they are preferred to the Vg. In support of Jerome's translation, we can adduce the NT doctrine—that the Temple-tradition was realized not "in houses made by hands" (Acts 7:48; Mk 14:58) but in Christ's glorified body (Jn 2:19–21), a body that includes all his members—Jews and Gentiles (Eph 2:20–22; 1 Pt 2:5–6; see Siebeneck, *op. cit.*, 316; A. Dubarle, *RB* 48 [1936] 36–39; A. Škrinjar, *VD* 15 [1935] 355–62).

The second question is more difficult: Is Haggai referring to the present moment of Temple reconstruction as the day of messianic fulfillment, or does he consider the present as a type or pledge of what God will one day gloriously achieve for his people? The Hebr text is not as clear as the CCD translation in referring to the future. Verse 6, as it reads in the MT, "is evidently corrupt" (Mitchell, *op. cit.*, 65), and is differently translated by the LXX. The LXX definitely looks to yet one more messianic act of God, which Heb 12:26 recognized in Jesus' resurrection (see J. van der Ploeg, *RB* 54 [1947] 226). Commentators will often reject either "one moment yet" or "a little while," especially the former. It is safe to hold that Haggai definitely looked beyond the immediate moment, but just how far is problematical. Perhaps, as in Dt-Is, "tomorrow" and the distant future merged in a haze of glory. The theological emphasis, however, remains the unique presence of God in the messianic age; blessings shared by all the world; the liturgical character of the new community; "fulfillment" of the Mosaic priesthood.

9 **(C) The Third Discourse (2:10–19).** *the ninth month:* It is Chislev (our November-December) when Haggai speaks with ancient prophetic insistence upon interior holiness (Am 4:4–5; Hos 6:1–6; Is 1:11–17). But unlike the earlier prophets, he defers to the priesthood for a "decision" (*tôrâ*, an authoritative judgment given orally; cf. Zech 7:2–3; Mal 2:7). The priests' answer probably refers to the rules of Lv 6:20–21 (= 6:27–28 in Douay). **14.** *so is this people, and so is this nation:* Undoubtedly, Haggai wants to insist that evil exerts a much greater influence than goodness, but this vague statement leaves us confused about the identity of the evil or unclean group. It is usually held that Haggai is rejecting Samaritan help. These were descendants of foreigners, brought into Palestine by the Assyrians (2 Kgs 17), who worshiped Yahweh with strange practices and false ideas. Here lies the beginning of a hateful rivalry so evident in the Gospels (Lk 9:52–54; Jn 4:9) and attested to by later history (see J. W. Rothstein, *Juden und Samaritaner* [BWANT 3; Stuttgart, 1909]; J. Jeremias, *Jerusalem zur Zeit Jesu* 2 [2nd ed.; Göttingen, 1958] 224–31). Others like Gelin (BJ 7–17) feel that the verse was later reinterpreted to refer to the Samaritans (Ezr 4:1–5). Haggai was condemning the Jews for their half-hearted effort in keeping the Law.

15–19. (See 1:15, where some commentators transfer these verses.) Prophetic themes again color the words of Haggai. When Israel separates herself from God, she cuts herself off from the source of every blessing (Dt 28:22). **17.** *return to me, says the Lord:* Poverty and disappointment, although a punishment for sin, should move Israel to do so (this translation is an adaptation of a damaged Hebr text, with the help of Am 4:9). **18.** The MT reads, "ninth month," and harmonizes with 2:10; the CCD suggests "sixth month" and associates this verse with 1:15a. The entire verse is usually considered a later gloss. **19.** The text is in very poor condition.

10 **(D) The Fourth Discourse (2:20–23).** Haggai speaks a second time, on the twenty-fourth day of the ninth month (cf. 2:10). **23.** God will save his people through the Davidic dynasty, here represented by Zerubbabel (cf. 1:1). Zerubbabel is addressed with a series of messianic titles: "my servant" (see comment on Is 42:1); "signet ring," used for impressing the royal seal on official documents (3 Kgs 21:8), worn either hanging from the neck (Gn 38:18) or placed on the right hand (Jer 22:24). There is a deliberate reference to Jer 22:24; the words concerning the Davidic dynasty, in the person of Jehoiachin, shall be reversed. It is questionable whether or not Haggai expected the full realization in the lifetime of Zerubbabel. Perhaps, like Deutero-Isaiah, he hoped for this proximate fulfillment but was not sure.

ZECHARIAH

BIBLIOGRAPHY

11 Ackroyd, P. R., *PCB* 564–72. Bullough, S., *CCHS* 545–54. Chary, T., *Les prophètes et le culte à partir de l'Exil* (Paris, 1955) 118–27, 138–59. Dentan, R. C., *IB* 6, 1089–1114. Dhorme, E., *BPl* 2, cviii–cxiv, 836–74. Gelin, A., R-F 1, 564–66, 580–82. Jansma, T., "An inquiry into the Hebrew Text and the Ancient Versions of Zech. IX–XIV," *OTS* 7 (1950) 1–141. Lamarche, P., *Zacharie IX–XIV, structure littéraire et messianisme* (Paris, 1961). May, H. G., "The Key to the Interpretation of Zechariah's Visions," *JBL* 57 (1938) 173–84. Rignell, L. G., *Die Nachtgesichte des Sacharja* (Lund, 1950). Thomas, D. W., *IB* 6, 1053–88. (See also titles listed under Haggai.)

INTRODUCTION

The book is to be divided into two major sections: chs. 1–8, 9–14. That the first part was written by the prophet Zechariah has always been admitted, but there is now an almost universal agreement among scholars that the second part is to be traced to a different and later source.

(I) Chapters 1–8.

12 **(A) The Prophet Zechariah.** (See comment on 1:1.) This man was probably born in a priestly family (Neh 12:4,16), and, like the prophet-priest Ezekiel, he allowed his priestly status to dominate his personality and work. In fact he completed a process initiated by Ezekiel, whereby prophetic leadership succumbed to an almost completely priestly dominated theocracy. Zechariah lived, therefore, at a critical period, when the whole direction of Israel's later religious life, extending even into NT times, was being firmly set. His ministry extended at least from October-November, 520 (1:1) until November, 518 (7:1). These dates coincide with the early years after the return from the Babylonian Exile. He was a contemporary of Haggai, and for a month each re-enforced the word of the other that the Temple must be rebuilt (Ezr 5.1f.).

Not only did his ministry extend over a much longer period than that of Haggai, but he also seems to have been a man of greater versatility in mind and language, with a keener sense of the practical. He possessed the rare combination of grand hopes and plain speech. His was just the approach necessary in this "day of small beginnings" (4:10). A discouraged people needed to be reassured that God would definitely fulfill their messianic dreams. Zechariah therefore, spoke his dreams for the future in the finest apocalyptic style (1:7–6:8). But the people must not conjure up romantic fancies on the distant horizon and leave undone the work immediately at hand (1:1–6). Nor must they argue theoretically about fasting when the widow and the orphan were homeless and hungry (7:1–14). He spoke eloquently in two distinct styles: He was both an apocalyptic artist and a reforming prophet. What is even more extraordinary, he was able to combine both styles in a single speech; many of his visions insist upon moral integrity for the worshiper of God: purification of the high priest (ch. 3); the flying scroll and bushel removing the people's sins (ch. 5).

We suspect, however, that Zechariah never quite achieved the full independence of speech characteristic of the pre-exilic prophets. As G. A. Smith pointed out, he seems over-anxious about his reception as a prophet (*The Book of the Twelve Prophets* [vol. 2; N.Y., n.d.] 266–67) and too insistent that "the Lord of hosts has sent me" (2:13,15; 4:9; 6:15). For the historical background → 2 above.

13 **(B) The Message.** Zechariah's first interest centered around the rebuilding of the Temple and its worthy liturgical worship. Like Haggai, he realized that Judaism could not survive without the Temple, for this building was the symbol of God's presence among his people, the assurance that the great redemptive acts of the past would be repeated in each succeeding age, until the messianic age. The Lord, he tells the people, "will be... an encircling wall of fire" for Jerusalem and "will be the glory in her midst" (2:9; cf. 2:14,16–17; 8:3).

This presence of Yahweh demands perfect purity. Zechariah therefore, sees the flying scroll and the flying bushel (5:1–11) as agents removing from Jerusalem her sins and wickedness. He condemns more than ritual mistakes (Lv 4:1–2); he uses terms designating "sin" and "malice": *ʿāwōn* (3:9; 5:6); *rišʿâ* (5:8). The transformation of Jerusalem must reach to the heart of the people. Even the high priest Joshua must be thoroughly cleansed (3:1–10). The moralism, therefore, is much more pronounced than in Haggai.

The people cannot postpone their reformation to some distant messianic age; what they do right now has a profound effect upon the fulfillment of the promises. "A measuring line" of divine mercy is even now "stretched over Jerusalem" and God is proclaiming: "My cities shall again overflow with prosperity" (1:17).

His concern for the Temple, however, tended to elevate the priesthood above the prophet's role. True, in Zechariah the prophet remains superior. When a delegation asked about fasting, it was he who answered them (7:3). Nevertheless, he is among the last of the authentic prophets whose coherent and extensive work remains (cf. Chary, *Les prophètes*, 159).

14 Zechariah not only advances the cause of the priest over the prophet, but he also witnesses the complete eclipse of the Davidic family. There was a temporary restoration of the royal family in the person of Zerubbabel. Before the Exile, the king controlled the Temple and the priesthood (1 Kgs 1–2; 8); after the Exile, the Davidic heir shared equal power with the high priest. Zechariah sees this governor standing beside the high priest; together, both men act as two olive trees who supply oil for warmth and light (4:1–3), or as two anointed ones who share the ruling power (4:11–14). Zechariah will even perform the coronation of Zerubbabel (6:9ff.). But Zerubbabel slips away from history and thereafter we hear no more of the Davidic family. The Prophet's greater attention toward the Temple assured the succession of the priesthood to complete power.

There is a great advance in angelology through the preaching of Zechariah. Angels exercise a more prominent place in his visons than they do even in the later writing of Dn (cf. H. G. Mitchell, *Haggai and Zechariah* [ICC; N.Y., 1912] 103). The delineation of an evil power (*śāṭān*) appears explicit in 3:1 (→ 26 below). This theological development of angels and demons means that God himself has become more and more transcendent; to maintain the personal concern of the Lord for his people, angels and demons act as mediators.

Zechariah also reaches beyond the limited scope of Haggai's preaching, through a more pronounced universalism. At a time when memories were still haunted with the sorrows and agonies of the Exile, the Prophet is not afraid to declare that "many nations shall join themselves to the Lord" (2:15). They shall even "come to seek the Lord of hosts in Jerusalem and...implore the favor of the Lord" (8:21–22). It is possible, however, that he aligned himself with Haggai in the anti-Samaritan movement (see comments on 7:2–3; Hag 2:10–19).

The reader will discover many phrases usually associated with the NT or with some other, better-known prophet—e.g., Isaiah. Not only the first part of Zech but especially the second part draw heavily from previous sacred traditions. It seems to have been one of the favorite books of NT writers: the four horsemen (1:7ff.; Ap 6:1–8); the measuring of the holy city (1:16; Ap 11:1–2); the two olive trees and lampstands (4:1–3,11–14; Ap 11:4–10); the king meek and riding on an ass (9:9; Mt 21:9); the good shepherd priced at 30 pieces of silver (11:12; Mt 26:15; 27:9–10); the transpierced one (12:10ff.; Jn 19:37; Ap 1:7); the scattering of the sheep (13:7ff.; Mt 26:31); etc.

15 **(C) Style.** According to Gelin (R-F 1, 564), Zechariah originally prepared a diary or journal of his visions; to this autobiographical section, other remembrances were added by the editor of the book. The apocalyptic style is not as fully developed as we find in Dn, but it is far beyond the earlier stage, as evidenced by Is 24–27. An apocalypse is always, as the name implies ("to unveil"), a revelation of a secret, known only to God, and communicated most often through an angel. The author of apocalypse is above all a seer; he sees very deeply beneath the surface of reality and presents his knowledge in the form of a vision. Vision, it must be noted, is a literary feature, not necessarily an actual reality. Because the knowledge is so sublime, the seer feels obliged to use an abundance of images. Each symbol has its own value and meaning, and everything can be a symbol: colors; numbers; clothing; parts of the body; animals; etc. These symbols are heaped one upon another—to an extent that seems weird and baffling to the modern reader but that may be congenial to the modern artist—for the apocalyptic writer is not at all concerned about the total effect. Each symbol must be appreciated independently of the others. The prophet has succeeded, in fact, if he has stunned the reader with the sense of the numinous (→ Post-exilic Period, 20: 12–14; 21–27).

(Boismard, M.-E., *L'Apocalypse* [BJ; 2nd ed.; Paris, 1953] 7–9. Frost, S. B., *Old Testament Apocalyptic* [London, 1952]. Rowley, H. H., *The Relevance of Apocalytptic* [2nd ed.; London, 1947]. Vawter, B., *CBQ* 22 [1960] 33–46.)

16 **(D) Text.** The Hebr for Zech is in very poor condition. The book is strewn with corruptions that must be emended (see comments on 2:10,12–13; 3:7; 6:10–15; 7:2; 8:12; 9:1; 11:5; 14:4–5). It also seems certain that later hands rather freely added explanatory notes or glosses (see comments on 1:1; 2:2,4; 3:8–10; 4:6b–10a; 6:3; 7:1,8; 8:13; 11:17; 12:2–3; 14:7). A severely damaged text, as well as the apocalyptic style of writing, justify Jerome's remark that Zech is the most obscure book in the Bible.

(II) Chapters 9–14.

17 (A) The Prophecy of Deutero-Zechariah. The differences in style between First and Second Zechariah are so great that one must either posit two or more authors or else admit that the single author possessed a weird, split personality. Chapters 1–8 and 9–14 manifest many of the same variations usually noted between Is 1–35 and 40–66. We can summarize the differences as follows:

1–8	*9–14*
clear historical allusions	obscure or no historical allusions
precise dates	no dates
concern over the Temple's reconstruction, Joshua, and Zerubbabel	no mention of rebuilding the Temple, Joshua, or Zerubbabel
prosaic, redundant, involved	poetical, direct, simple
indirectly influenced by the thought of Ezekiel	quotes from, or direct allusions to, Hos, Is, Dt, Jer, Ez, Jl, Jb
messianism centers in Jerusalem and the revival of the Davidic house	messianism centers in Judah, with only secondary references to Jerusalem and Davidic family

Chapters 9–14 are further subdivided into two major sections (9–11, 12–14), each of which is introduced by the succinct formula, *maśśā'*, "a burden." The original portion of the first section included 9:1–8,11–17; 10:3b–12; 11:4–16; the other verses comprising chs. 9–11 would have been added at the same time that chs. 12–14 were joined and the entire ensemble of chs. 1–14 put together. The first *maśśā'* is usually dated very soon after the invasion of Alexander the Great (332); its general attitude is favorable toward the foreigner. In the second, a violent antagonism has built up toward non-Jewish culture. A dependency upon Jl places it after that book. The latest date for this second section would be 200, because Jesus ben Sira, author of the Book of Sirach, explicitly mentions "the twelve minor prophets," as though this part of the sacred Scriptures were complete (Sir 49:10). Scholars are rejecting the opinion of K. Marti, W. Nowack, and B. Duhm that chs. 9–14 originated during the Maccabean period (167–134).

18 (B) The Message. The meteoric conquests of Alexander the Great reminded the Prophet of what God can and will do when the messianic day approaches. Similar to Deutero-Isaiah's attitude toward Cyrus (Is 45), Deutero-Zechariah may have felt that Alexander was the Lord's anointed to establish the universal kingdom of the elect. He speaks of even the once hated Philistine as "a remnant for our God...like a family in Judah" (9:7). The same universalism extends also into the second *maśśā'*, where it is written that "all" shall "come to sacrifice" at Jerusalem (14:21). However, chs. 12 and 14 first foresee a mighty war fought almost ferociously against the foreigners. The Prophet, therefore, is preoccupied with the theocratic war of the final great day.

The original words of both parts centered attention upon Judah rather than upon the royal city of Jerusalem. A later redactor, perhaps the one who joined chs. 9–11 and 12–14, and who possibly formed the present book, inserted tributes to the Davidic royalty and to Jerusalem (9:9–10; 12:7–8).

The victory will be achieved only at the cost of great suffering; God's people must be completely purified before they will be ready to enjoy his kingdom. The sorrows of all people will be experienced by the good shepherd of 11:4–16 and 13:7–9 or by the transpierced one of 12:10–14; through their bond with these great leaders, the people will participate in the former's victory and holiness. Priests have an equal status with the royal family in the day of mourning. From its lowly position, the Davidic family will be thoroughly one with the poor; to these God will grant his kingdom. Therefore, "your king shall come to you...meek"; in him it shall be evident that salvation is from God according to his just promises—"a just savior" is the messiah (9:9).

For the most part, however, the Davidic family is overlooked. The author(s) of the major parts of chs. 9–14 looked to Yahweh as their king and leader (9:16; 14:16). From the sacred liturgy, divine blessings will spread through the land; the messianic reign will be a perpetual Feast of Tabernacles, a constant thanksgiving for a bountiful harvest (14:8,16).

19 (C) The Style. The apocalyptic style of chs. 1–8 continues into this second section; in fact, ch. 14 is written according to the most intense apocalyptic form of the Bible. The poetical meter is much more evident here than in the first part. The language, however, is predominantly much more direct, with less of the weird, staggering scenes of chs. 1–8. Although the words are simple, the details are too fragmentary, or the text is too damaged, for us to reconstruct the historical situation. First Zechariah has given more precise data but at the same time has masked it beneath his strange visions.

Deutero-Zechariah is much less original; or we should say that he draws much more freely upon the ancient, sacred traditions. In an elaborate study, M. Delcor has shown the numerous cases of allusion to and borrowing or quoting of chs. 9–14 from Ez, Is 40–66, Jer, Jl, Jb, and even Mal (*RB* 59 [1952] 384–411).

20 (III) Outline. The Book of Zechariah may be outlined as follows:

- (I) The Prophetic Mission (1:1–8:23)
  - (A) Introduction: A Call to Conversion (1:1–6)
  - (B) Visions (1:7–6:8)
    - (a) First Vision of the Four Horsemen (1:7–17)
    - (b) Second Vision of the Four Horns and the Four Blacksmiths (2:1–4) (LXX and Vg 1:18–21)
    - (c) Third Vision of the New Jerusalem and Amplifications (2:5–17) (LXX and Vg 2:1–13)
    - (d) Fourth Vision of Joshua, the High Priest (3:1–10; 4:4–10)
    - (e) Fifth Vision of the Lampstand and the Two Olive Trees (4:1–3,11–14)
    - (f) Sixth Vision of the Flying Scroll (5:1–4)
    - (g) Seventh Vision of the Flying Bushel (5:5–11)
    - (h) Eighth Vision of the Four Chariots (6:1–8)
  - (C) The Coronation (6:9–15)
  - (D) Questions About Fasting (7:1–14)
  - (E) Messianic Days (8:1–23)
- (II) Messianic Panorama of Deutero-Zechariah (9:1–14:21)
  - (A) The First Burden (9:1–11:17)
    - (a) Invasion by the Lord (9:1–8)
    - (b) The Messianic King (9:9–10)
    - (c) The Restoration (9:11–17)
    - (d) The New Order (10:1–11:3)
    - (e) The Allegory of the Shepherds (11:4–17)
  - (B) The Second Burden (12:1–14:21)
    - (a) Jerusalem, God's Instrument (12:1–9)
    - (b) The Great Lamentation (12:10–14)
    - (c) The End of Falsehood (13:1–6)
    - (d) The Song of the Sword (13:7–9)
    - (e) The Battle for Jerusalem (14:1–21)

COMMENTARY

(I) The Prophetic Mission (1:1–8:23). An unknown editor made an anthology of the prophet Zechariah's preaching and reform measures; his collection constitutes chs. 1–8.

21 **(A) Introduction: A Call to Conversion (1:1–6).** The hand of the editor is evident here: i.e., the rugged style; the abrupt change of thought (v. 2; the indefinite "them" in v. 3); the elaborate notation of year, month, and day. Zechariah began his ministry, according to the editor, in October-November, 520, two months after Haggai's first recorded discourse. **1.** Neh 12:4,16 mentions a Zechariah, son of Iddo, who is not called a prophet but a priest; the two roles, however, are not conflicting. The identification "son of Berechiah," is to be rejected; it is not found in Ezr 5:1; 6:14 or Neh 12:16; the phrase probably came from Is 8:2, and the confusion continues in Mt 23:35. **2.** *the Lord was indeed angry:* An allusion to the Babylonian Exile. We notice the editor's interference in the transition from discourse about Zechariah in v. 1 to a message addressed to him in v. 2. **3.** He preaches a moral, interior conversion. *return:* The Hebr word *šûbû* lies behind the NT doctrine of *metanoia* ("repentance" or "change of heart") in the preaching of John the Baptist (Mt 3:2,8), Jesus (Mt 4:16; Lk 5:32), and the apostles (Acts 2:38; 3:26). Although the word enforces the prophetic message of reform, OT usage also associates it with some kind of liturgical act of repentance and confession (Hos 6:1; Jer 3:12,22; Ps 51:15; Lam 5:21; Jl 2:12–28; see *ThWNT* 4, 976–85). As in Lk 7:36–50, conversion is explained from a twofold point of view: on man's side, faith and love precede God's forgiveness; on God's side, love and revelation must initiate man's good acts. **4.** *former prophets:* The phrase here refers to pre-exilic preachers; later, it is applied to Jos, Jgs, Sm, and Kgs, which were considered a prophetic judgment on salvation history. *be not like your fathers:* A warning that God can again destroy Jerusalem as he did in 587 (Jer 18:11–12; 25:5–11; Ez 24).

22 **(B) Visions (1:7–6:8).** In the apocalyptic style, a prophet is often enough called a "seer" (2 Chr 12:15), for he presents his inner perception under the literary medium of "visions" and the elaborate use of images.

23 (a) First Vision of the Four Horsemen (1:7–17). The first "vision" occurred in January–February, 519 (see Hag 1:1). **9.** Angels are frequently present in apocalyptic genre to explain the mysterious "vision." **10.** After patrolling the earth, the horsemen report that the revolts that erupted when Darius I seized the throne are quieted (→ 2 above). The revolts may have raised Jewish hopes for the messianic breakthrough. **12.** Hence, frustration and anguish gripped the people's morale. *seventy years:* The 70 years of Jer 25:11 and 29:10, a symbolic term signifying a long captivity, seem interminable (see P. R. Ackroyd, *JNES* 17 [1958] 23–27; E. Vogt, *Bib* 38 [1957] 236). Some Jews cried for divine intervention; others began to doubt (Is 59:1,9,11). **15–16.** Even though he does not act at once, God assures his people that the messianic promises will most certainly be fulfilled. Like Ez 40–48 or Hag in the OT, and Lk or Ap in the NT, Zechariah centers all promises around Jerusalem.

24 (b) Second Vision of the Four Horns and the Four Blacksmiths (2:1–4) (LXX and Vg 1:18–21). The second "vision" of the four horns and the four blacksmiths indicates that God will subdue all powers hostile to his messianic kingdom. **2.** *Israel:* The word was probably added to the original text; its presence indicates a continuing belief that all 12 tribes would be reunited in the new kingdom (cf. Ez 37:15–28). **3.** *blacksmiths:* Agents of divine destruction (Ez 21:36).

25 (c) Third Vision of the New Jerusalem and Amplifications (2:5–17) (LXX and Vg 2:1–13). The third vision requires angels to measure the great expanse of the new Jerusalem (Ez 40:3; 41:13; Ap 11:1; 21:15). **8.** Walls will not be necessary, for the days of conflict and fear are past (Is 49:21; 54:1–3). **9.** The messianic Jerusalem will bring back the golden days of Moses, when God was pictured leading his people by columns of clouds and fire (Ex 13:21–22; Nm 9:15ff.; Ez 43:1–5).

The second and third visions are amplified in 2:10–17 (LXX and Vg 2:6–13). These lines are an assortment of divine oracles, continually interrupted by reflections of the Prophet or the editor. The CCD frequently follows the LXX, which has smoothed out some of the quick transitions; vv. 10–13 comment upon the second vision; vv. 14–17 comment upon the third.

10. *up, up!:* Lit., "Woe, Woe!" Announces divine judgment—doom upon God's enemies and joy for the elect. God calls to his people in "the land of the north," i.e., Babylon. **12–13.** These lines, as they stand in the MT, are hopelessly confusing; various changes and explanations are offered. The general idea seems to be that all nations will witness the redemptive power and love of God; they will no longer be scattered and divided but united and blessed. **14.** Earlier prophecies harmonize here (Is 2:2–5; Mi 4:1–2; Zeph 2:14; Is 45:22). This universalism breaks through the narrower vision of Haggai (2:10–14). **16.** *the holy land:* The first use of the term in the Bible; it will occur again in Wis 12:3; 2 Mc 1:7. **17.** *silence!:* (Cf. Hab 2:20; Zeph 1:7; Is 41:1; Ap 8:1.) God comes forth from his Tabernacle (the holy city) to pronounce his powerful saving word.

26 (d) Fourth Vision of Joshua, the High Priest (3:1–10; 4:4–10). The fourth vision presents Joshua, the high priest, before the heavenly court. Almost all interpreters, except Dhorme (*op. cit.*, cix–cx), rearrange the verses in chs. 3–4. F. Horst (HAT 14, 226–34) and many others consider 3:8–10 and 4:6b–10a to be explanatory interpolations. **1.** Joshua, the high priest, is "standing" in the heavenly court "before the angel of the Lord," while being accused by Satan. Although "angel of the Lord" is a circumlocution for God (Gn 31:11–13; Ex 3:2), the mention of Satan marks a definite advance in angelology and demonology. Before the Exile, evil was considered God's providential way of punishing sin; after the Exile, demons were believed to act as mediators in punishing man (cf. 2 Sm 24:1; 1 Chr 21:1). Satan, however, is hostile to man but not to God, for here, as in Jb 1:6, he is in God's throne room. Only much later, in Wis 2:24, is he an enemy of both God and man.

(Foerster, W., *ThWNT* 2, 10–16. Gruenthaner, M. J., *CBQ* 6 [1944] 6–27. Von Rad, G. and R. Kittel, *ThWNT* 1, 75–87; *ThDNT* 1, 76–87.)

2. *brand snatched from the fire:* Seems to be an ancient proverb (cf. Am 4:11), here referring to the remnant of the Israelite nation, recently rescued from exile. **3.** The high priest carries the guilt of priests and people upon himself. We can only conjecture what sins were responsible for the "filthy garments": slackness in rebuilding the Temple; contamination from living in exile; sinful condition of pre-exilic priesthood (Mi 3:11; Is 1:11ff.; 28:7–15). **5.** *guilt:* The word implies moral offenses rather than simply some ceremonial mistake. **6–7.** The priests are granted free access to, and complete control of, the Temple; priests, in fact, will fulfill the function of angels, bringing the people into the divine presence. In this intimacy with God, the priest will be another Moses (K. Elliger, ATD 25, 122). **8.** Joshua and his associates (angelic court? fellow priests?) are "men of good omen," signs of future messianic realities (cf. Is 8:18). The thought turns momentarily to the other messianic figure, the Davidic representative, Zerubbabel. He is "my servant" (see Hag 2:23), or "the Shoot" (Is 11:1; Jer 23:5; Ez 17:22). The latter title is *anatolē* in the LXX and *oriens* in the Vg; it became a messianic liturgical title for the "Orient" (Lk 1:78), or the star whose rise out of the heavens (i.e., from God) will inaugurate the messianic age (Mt 2:2,9; Str-B 2, 113). **9.** *stone:* Many scholars identify it with the gem worn in the high priest's turban (Ex 28:36–38), but such a stone is not placed before him but upon him. The opinion favored here identifies the stone with the Temple (H. Schmidt, *ZAW* 13 [1936] 48–60; H. Junker, *Die zwölf kleinen Propheten* [BB; Bonn, 1938]; Chary, *Les prophètes;* E. Siegman, *CBQ* 18 [1956] 373). The inspiration could easily be Is 28:16, not in the sense that Isaiah considers the precious stone as a symbol of the Temple but in the way that he makes the stone a foundation of the messianic edifice of faith. *seven facets:* Represents God's presence, seeing and directing all activity from the messianic Temple.

27 **4:4–10.** The Prophet enhances Zerubbabel's position as of the Davidic family; see Hag 1:1; 2:23. **6.** Zerubbabel must depend more directly upon divine intervention—a teaching very close to the instruction in Is 7:14; 11:1–9; 42:1–4. **7.** The CCD makes as good sense out of the hopelessly damaged MT as is possible. The Prophet, in his enthusiasm for the building of the Temple, sees the mountains around Jerusalem leveled to a plain as workers quarry rock from these hills; Jerusalem alone remains uplifted (Zech 14:10). **10.** A "day of small beginnings" accurately describes this discouraging period of Jewish history. "The select stone" refers to the "capstone" of v. 7, which completes the Temple reconstruction.

28 (e) Fifth Vision of the Lampstand and the Two Olive Trees (4:1–3,11–14). The fifth vision of the lampstand and the two olive trees is variously explained. The "lampstand" (*mᵉnôrâ*) symbolizes God (T. Chary), hidden providence (Cornelius a Lapide), the Jewish people (H. Junker), the Temple (S. Bullough), and total world power vested in the supreme God (F. Horst, relying upon Sumerian and Akkadian mythology). The Prophet may have left the symbolism deliberately obscure, so as to hint at many interconnected ideas. The stem of the lampstand leads up to a bowl, from which seven pipes carry oil to the seven lamps. **3.** Two trees supply oil and thereby act as divine instruments in the exercise of power; v. 14 indicates that they are symbols of Joshua and Zerubbabel.

29 (f) Sixth Vision of the Flying Scroll (5:1–4). The sixth vision is of an enormous flying scroll, 30 by 15 ft. (length and breadth of the portico to Solomon's Temple, 1 Kgs 6:3). The symbol is not new in biblical literature (Ez 2:9–10; 3:1–3; Jer 36:2ff.). The scroll contains a curse of the kind customarily added to solemn, public oaths (Lv 5:1; Dt 29:18). Because it comes from the Temple, we suspect that it symbolizes the curses attached to the covenant, especially in Dt 28:15ff. These curses declare divine judgment upon social abuses, the wrongs of man against man in every part of the world (Neh 5).

30 (g) Seventh Vision of the Flying Bushel (5:5–11). If God inhabits the Jerusalem Temple, then sin and impurity must be removed. Sin and sorrow are brought to Shinar (Babylon; Gn 11:2; Ap 14:8).

31 (h) Eighth Vision of the Four Chariots (6:1–8). The eighth vision, the four chariots, seems to overlap the first (1:7–17). **5.** *four winds:* Hebrew has one word (*rûaḥ*) for both wind and spirit (cf. v. 8, "my spirit"). It can also mean "anger" (Jgs 8:3). It becomes clear that the chariots or winds that sweep through the universe, but especially through the land of the north (Babylon) and the land of the south (Egypt), bring the presence of God to all men—to punish and purify, to defeat and destroy, and to save and revitalize.

32 **(C) The Coronation (6:9–15).** This section is another that leaves many open questions. Was it a symbolic or a real coronation? If real, was the ceremony public or private? Was Joshua, Zerubbabel, or both crowned? Is it an amplification of the preceding visions (chs. 3–4) or an independent section? The Hebr text is too damaged to allow any certainty. Some have thought that Judah joined the revolts that convulsed the Persian Empire at the accession of Darius I Hystaspis. If so, Persia exacted but little revenge, for work on the Temple continued and permission to rebuild the city walls was later granted. Zerubbabel, however, suddenly disappears from history and nothing more is heard of the Davidic attempt to regain power.

10. The names are difficult to identify; they are not only spelled differently in v. 14, but they are not to be found again in the Bible and are considered appellatives by the LXX. **11.** The MT describes a coronation of High Priest Joshua, but scholars generally substitute the name of Zerubbabel, for he is the one who is hailed as "the Shoot" (cf. 3:8), and he is distinct from the priest (v. 14). **12b–14.** The Prophet's words are cast in poetic lines; the oracle seems to apply exclusively to Zerubbabel. **15b.** The section ends abruptly with an incomplete, conditional sentence. Ackroyd and Thomas see a reference to the blessings of obedience recorded in Dt 28:1.

33 **(D) Questions About Fasting (7:1–14).** Now that the Temple was being rebuilt, the people questioned why they must fast over its sacrilegious destruction. Zechariah directs his questioners to what is more necessary than fasting—the spirit of mercy and fidelity (cf. Is 58).

The introduction and the question in vv. 1–3 are badly preserved in the MT. The clumsy grammar corroborates the opinion that the elaborate style of dating was added by a redactor (cf. 1:1). The mention of Chislev, the Aram name for the ninth month, slipped in still later. The redactor is placing this message in November, 518, when the reconstruction of the Temple was only half completed. The text becomes still more suspect from the fact that the men are ignoring the fast of the next month (the tenth) and inquiring about a fast four months distant (cf. 8:19). **2.** The MT is grammatically impossible and must be corrected. The CCD reads "Bethel-Sharezer" as a proper name; relying upon the Syr text and upon Jer 39:3,13, Ackroyd (*PCB* 568a) explains Regemmelech as an honorary title—"chief officer of the king." Dhorme (*op. cit.*, 849) translates the MT the most literally of all: "[the city of] Bethel sent Sarasar and Rogammelech, and each with their men." In this case, a delegation arrives from northern Palestine, asking for religious co-operation (Hag 2:10–14), but Zechariah, along with Haggai, rejects the offer. **3.** *in the fifth month:* The fast marked the day in July-August when the Temple was destroyed (2 Kgs 25:8–9; Jer 52:12ff.).

The Prophet is commanded to give an answer (4–14) to the question of v. 3. He now refers to the fast "in the seventh month" mourning the assassination of Gedaliah in September-August, 587 (2 Kgs 25:25; Jer 41:1–3). Two other days of national mourning are mentioned in 8:19: the fourth month (June-July), when the Babylonians breached the walls of Jerusalem in 587 (2 Kgs 25:3–11; Jer 39:2ff.); the tenth month (December-January), when the siege of Jerusalem began in 588 (2 Kgs 25:1; Jer 39:1). It is quite likely that these separate days were eliminated and the one great day of Yom Kippur took their place (Lv 16). (Cf. J. van Goudoever, *Biblical Calendars* [Leiden, 1959] 45–48.) **5.** God says clearly that it was not "for me that you fasted"; it was its own failure and sinfulness that catapulted the nation into disaster. **8–14.** These final words echo many biblical texts. We hear again the prophetic preaching of Jeremiah (7:5–6; 22:3), Hosea (2:21), Micah (6:8), Isaiah (1:17,23).

34 **(E) Messianic Days (8:1–23).** A series of ten, separate oracles occurs. In compiling this chapter, the secretary-redactor exercised a rather free hand. He simplified and abbreviated, and as a result disturbed the original, rhythmic form of the oracles. He may have edited out any mention of Zerubbabel; this chapter centers all attention upon the priestly domain of the Temple.

1–2. God is "intensely jealous" (cf. 1:14) to fulfill messianic promises through the glorification of the Jerusalem Temple. **3.** In the second oracle, the Lord announces that he "will dwell within Jerusalem": the verb is the archaic *šākan,* commonly used in the ancient, seminomadic days of Moses for the family tent-dwelling and for God's initial dwelling among his people. In later ages, especially in the P tradition of the Pentateuch, which was redacted at this time, *šākan* designated exclusively God's presence in the Temple, but always with an allusion to what was now considered the idyllic, golden age of Israel's beginning (see F. M. Cross, Jr., *BA* 10 [1947] 45–68, esp. 66–67). It is a familiar, biblical custom to endow Jerusalem with messianic titles: Is 1:26; 62:12; Jer 3:17; Ez 48:35. **4–5.** Healthy children and serene old age image all God's blessings that can come between these extremities of human life (Ex 20:12; Is 65:20; Ps 127). **6.** The fourth oracle of this series issues a warning to "the remnant," those divinely chosen to participate in messianic joy (Hag 1:12).

35 **9–13.** The sixth oracle follows the more expansive style of a synagogal homily, just as a later writer will combine this passage with Jer 31:16 to form another sermon (2 Chr 15:1–7). It echoes ideas from Hag 1:2,6–11; 2:15–19. The contrast between the dismal, present scene with its social inequality and its threat of invasion, and the messianic hope with its expectation of universal peace and undisturbed prosperity, accurately mirrors the early post-exilic state (Ezr 4:1–4; Neh 5; Mal 2:10ff.). **10.** We suspect that Zechariah's original words reflected the people's anxiety over a possible Samaritan invasion. **13.** *and house of Israel:* Because of Israel's hostility after Judah had rejected her offer of co-operation, the phrase is likely a later addition to the text; the redactor is thinking not only of a universe sharing in the blessings of God's people (cf. Gn 12:2–3; 22:18) but also of a strongly united theocracy.

14–17. This seventh oracle recaptures the spirit of the pre-exilic preaching of the prophets and Dt, emphasizing the everyday virtues of honesty and consideration and laying down threats and promises (Mi 6:8; Is 1:17; Dt 5:32–33; 6:16–19; Jos 23:14–16). **15.** Again, an exclusive concern with the south.

18–19. The earlier answer to the question of fasting (ch. 7) directed attention to the more important virtues of charity and social justice; the thought now turns to the glorious, messianic moment, when mourning will cease and all men will realize that God was leading every activity to the fulfillment of his promises. *fast days of the fourth, the fifth, the seventh and the tenth months:* Cf. comment on 7:3–4.

20–23. The last two oracles (20–22,23) portray all peoples seeking Yahweh, for they recognize salvation and peace in him alone. "Salvation is" clearly "from the Jews" (Jn 4:22), for Yahweh revealed himself through these chosen people. The emphatic repetition of going up to the Lord at the Jerusalem Temple implies that God is always ready and anxious to receive his people (cf. Is 2:2–4; 54:6–8).

36 **(II) Messianic Panorama of Deutero-Zechariah (9:1–14:21).** (→ 18 above.) A tentative or working conclusion places the compilation of chs. 9–14 between 300 and 180, sometime after the prophecy of Joel but before the composition of Sirach. It is impossible, at the present moment, to be more exact about a section where historical allusions are very obscure and the language is highly apocalyptic. Another undecided question is whether chs. 9–14 were compiled from the writings of one or many authors. Two major sections can be detected, each introduced by *maśśā',* "a burden."

37 **(A) The First Burden (9:1–11:17).** Dated at the beginning of the Hellenistic age, not long after the amazing, triumphal march of Alexander the Great through Asia Minor. To this initial section belong 9:1–8,11–17; 10:3b–12; 11:4–16. Even though the other verses may have been added later, when chs. 9–14 were assembled, they fit naturally into the context.

38 (a) INVASION BY THE LORD (9:1–8). Elliger (*ZAW* 62 [1949–50] 63–115) dates this oracle 332. After the battle of Issus, in which Alexander had routed the Persian forces, the young Gk conqueror headed S through Syria, taking Aleppo, Hadrach, Hamath, and Damascus; he then turned W to capture Tyre by filling in a causeway to this former island fortress. He continued S along the Mediterranean coast, overrunning the Philistine Pentapolis. Although no record exists of his taking possession of Jerusalem, it was certainly absorbed into Alexander's spreading empire. Just as the suicide of the Persian Cambyses and the revolts rocking the empire during the early years of Darius I's reign (→ 2 above) seem to have occasioned the messianic interest (Hag, Zech), so too the disintegration of the colossal Persian Empire before Alexander's army probably evoked a renewed messianic interest in Deutero-Zechariah. He may have considered Alexander a divine instrument for establishing God's kingdom (cf. Is 45:1). Furthermore, what Alexander was achieving could just as easily be done by Yahweh in his great day.

1. *Hadrach:* According to a 9th-cent. stele, it had formed a league with Damascus to the south. The city was destroyed by the Assyrians in 720 (for this reason Horst [*op. cit.,* 247] feels that this passage should depend upon the Assyrian invasion under Sennacherib), but the name Hatarikka was applied to the larger province by the Assyrians and could have continued to have been used under the Persians.

(Noth, M., *PJB* 38 [1937] 36–51. Simons, J., *The Geographical and Topographical Texts of the Old Testament* [Leiden, 1959] n. 142, n. 1566.)

3. Tyre, one of the strongest and wealthiest commercial cities, was a biblical symbol of pride and arrogance (Ez 27–28; esp. 28:11–19). **5–6**. As in other texts (Zeph 2:4; Jer 25:20), Gath, the fifth city of the Philistine Pentapolis (Jos 13:2–3; Simons, *op. cit.*, n. 1633), is unmentioned. **6–7a.** Eating "bloody meat" and various kinds of "abominations" or unclean food was forbidden by Mosaic Law (Gn 9:4; Lv 3:17; 11; Dt 14). Here, as in Is 65:4 and 66:17, the reference may be symbolic of all non-Jews. **7b.** Just as the Jebusites, the original inhabitants of Jerusalem, were absorbed into the Israelite nation (2 Sm 5:6–9), so also will other Gentiles, even the despised and uncircumcised Philistines, be allowed to participate in the privileges of God's elect and to be a part of the sacred "remnant" (cf. 8:6).

39 (b) THE MESSIANIC KING (9:9–10). Cf. Mt 21:5. **9.** *a just savior:* The MT has the pass. form: "just and saved is he." A similar pass. sense of "being saved" occurs in Is 45:17; 45:22; Jer 17:14; 23:6; 33:16. The CCD follows the LXX in recognizing the act. form of the king's saving others; this commentary prefers the pass. form, in which God's saving power reaches the nation as it is united into the one, corporate personality of the king (→ Deutero-Isaiah, 22:5). *meek:* Without the majestic pomp of royalty (see J. L. McKenzie, *CBQ* 19 [1957] 46). We are witnessing a phenomenon, typical of post-exilic Israel, of various messianic movements overlapping, here the "Anawim" tradition and the royal, Davidic messianism. *riding on an ass:* This phrase in no way indicates humility but rather the peaceful intent of the monarch. The horse was the mount in time of war (Ex 14:9; Zech 1:7–11; *BibLex* 1029–30; De Vaux, *AI* 222–25); the ass was put to use for friendly and solemn entry (Gn 49:11; 1 Kgs 1:33; *BibLex* 154–55). **10.** This verse echoes Pss 2:8; 72:8; Mi 5:4. God's kingdom will be completely universal, reuniting not only the northern and southern kingdoms of Palestine, but also the entire civilized world, from the Mediterrean Sea to the Persian Gulf. Verses 9–10 are sometimes considered an addition to the original form of chs. 9–11, for they contain the single reference to the Davidic royalty.

40 (c) THE RESTORATION (9:11–17). The Lord will fulfill the promises of the Mosaic covenant (Ex 24:8; Jer 31:31; Mk 14:24). **13–15.** These verses, with one military phrase after another, move with the marching tramp of an army; God's people will overcome the last outpost of opposition. How else can eternal peace ensue? *against your sons, O Javan:* An addition to the text from the Maccabean era, resulting from the Hellenistic persecution of the Jews (i.e., after 167). In the Bible, Javan refers to the Greeks (Is 66:19; Jl 4:6; Dn 9:21). **14–15.** The eschatological language of many biblical hymns is repeated in these verses (Jgs 5, 2 Sm 22, Ps 18, Hab 3). The final battle between God and his demonic enemy, between God's people and their gigantic opponents, is at hand. Such hymns can always be sung because every battle participates in the finality of the last mortal struggle (cf. Mt 24; 2 Thes 2:1–12; frequently in Ap). *thunder:* Symbolizes the power of God's Word (Ex 19:16–19; Na 1:3). Especially in the second part of v. 15, the cosmic battle is viewed as a solemn sacrificial act. The enemies' blood upon the Israelite warriors reminds the Prophet of animal blood sprinkled upon the altar (Ex 24:6; Lv 1:5; 16:14–15; 17:11; Heb 9:22). **16–17.** The moment of victory and salvation dawns suddenly, majestically. The earth produces an abundance through the power of God's presence. Many scholars (A. van Hoonacker, *Les douze petits prophètes* [EBib; Paris, 1908] 669; Dhorme, *op. cit.*, cxii; Ackroyd, *PCB* 570g) join v. 17 with 10:1–2.

41 (d) THE NEW ORDER (10:1–11:3). The text and the interpretation of this passage must remain hypothetical. There is no mistaking, however, the general theme of a colossal, divine victory. **1.** Liturgical prayers for rain, possibly a quotation from Dt 11:14, seem to be heard in these lines. **2.** This reference to household gods seems out of place in post-exilic Israel. Some scholars accept idolatrous conditions even after the return from exile because of texts like this one (besides Mal 3:5; Is 65:3–5; 66:17). Because these texts are few in number and poetic in style, and also because idolatry is not mentioned in the historical Books of Ezra or Nehemiah, we hold that the few texts are relics of pre-exilic days, or else they are intended symbolically.

42 The battle for messianic glory now becomes tense and bitter (10:3–11:3). References to shepherds, leaders, chiefs, officers, and warriors cast the passage in a setting of a charismatic war. At times God speaks (6–12); at other times the Prophet speaks (3b–5). But the effect is always terrifying. The transition from the drab post-exilic period to the glorious future is pictured as a new exodus out of Egypt; the Prophet utilizes the rich Exodus tradition of Dt 28, Hos 11, Is 43. **3.** The prophets consistently blamed the leaders for Israel's apostasy and destruction (Hos 4:4–9; Mi 3; Jer 2:26); despite all unworthy "shepherds and...leaders" (lit. "he-goats"), God will achieve his goal. **6.** The framework of the Exodus supports the Prophet's words in this passage; it enables him to recall the days of Moses when the north ("the house of Joseph") and the south ("the house of Judah") were united. **7.** *cheered as by wine:* The phrase probably comes from Ps 103:15. *rejoice in the Lord:* From Is 29:19 or Hab 3:18. Deutero-Zechariah continues to draw heavily upon the now archaic language of the pre-exilic period; his references combine the Exodus out of Egypt with freedom from Assyrian oppression. **8.** God had once whistled or signaled for the Assyrians to invade Palestine because of the people's infidelity (Is 5:26; 7:18); now he is reversing the movement of history and whistling for a numerous people his very own, to be redeemed. **10.** *I will bring them back:* The gem of OT teaching on divine mercy—Hos 11—gleams beneath the words. While Lebanon constituted the northern frontier of the promised land (Dt 1:7; 3:25), the area of Gilead in Transjordan brings to mind its first conquest by Moses. *but these shall not suffice them:* Cf. Jos 17:16–17. The messianic age will not seek to recall the former glory of the golden age of Moses; it will surpass it. This line balances the thought of the remnant theology (cf. 9:7).

43 **11:1–3.** This triumphal hymn concludes with a taunt-song against the mighty enemies of Israel, typified by the stately cedars of Lebanon (Is 10:33–34; Ez 31). The scene is terrifying in its contrast. God's innumerous people march exultantly from every part of the world back to the promised land and the enemy is trapped in a roaring forest fire and crashes down the sides of the mountainous ravine.

44 (e) THE ALLEGORY OF THE SHEPHERDS (11:4–17). This section is unquestionably one of the most obscure passages in the OT. The identification of the shepherds (8) and of the roles of the two shepherds (7, 15) is still moot. The general idea seems to be that of judgment upon the people. The Prophet (?) is told to be the shepherd of the flock to be slaughtered (4, 7); he does away with the three shepherds quickly (8), but his own service is not appreciated (9, 12). The judgment is indicated in the breaking of the staffs, "Favor" (10), and "Bonds" (14). The role of the foolish shepherd (15) is to indicate the punishment in store for an unworthy ruler.

5–6. There is an inexplicable shift from the singular to the plural to the singular in the MT of v. 5, and v. 6 seems parenthetical, if it is not a gloss (T. Chary, *BiVChr*

52 [1963] 14). **8.** The identification of the three shepherds escapes us, despite many proposals; they could possibly represent bad rulers, civil and religious (Dhorme, *op. cit.*, 861). **10–13.** The good shepherd (God, the Messiah, the Prophet, or someone else?) does not labor for a wage, but if the people consider him to be as venal as they are, then let them pay him the wages. *thirty pieces:* The price of a slave (Ex 21:32; Mt 26:15). **15–18.** It is not clear how the "foolish shepherd" episode is to be related to the preceding. He is an instrument of God for punishment but will not himself escape punishment.

45 **(B) The Second Burden (12:1–14:21).** Woe is proclaimed against the foreigner (the Gk conqueror?). We suspect that these final chapters can be traced to the years after the appearance of the prophet Joel but before the lifetime of Sirach. We also have the impression from the following passage that the Jews became bitter in their disappointment over Alexander as a possible messianic figure; they transfer this frustration to the Greeks in the form of a violent antagonism. As in the time of Deutero-Isaiah, Israel's moments of great sorrow and dejection occasion the bravest expressions of hope. Jerusalem will be purified by the sorrow of this moment and thus prepared for the day of the Lord. This hope for Jerusalem, however, had to be tempered: perhaps the unworthiness of the Jerusalem leaders forced a reconsideration of the prophecy (cf. Mi 4:14–5:3). Additions were then inserted, which looked beyond Jerusalem to less important people of the countryside—i.e., 12:2b,3b,4b,6a,7f (see Elliger, ATD 168; Horst, *op. cit.*, 255). These last three chapters, therefore, were prepared over an extended period of years. Finally, they were joined to the first "burden" (chs. 9–11), which in the process was also slightly retouched, e.g., with the addition of 9:13b.

46 (a) JERUSALEM, GOD'S INSTRUMENT (12:1–9). **1.** *the word of the Lord concerning Israel:* Possibly a superscription for this last section, added by one of the last editors; Israel is not mentioned again in these chapters. As in Chr, "Israel" is used of the united people of God (1 Chr 21:1; 2 Chr 29:24). *thus says the Lord:* A new introduction, revealing the patched-up condition of this chapter. The rest of v. 1 contains a hymn to God the Creator, seemingly influenced by Is 40:22; 42:5, but also showing some relation with other texts, e.g., Gn 2:7; Ps 24:4; Jb 10:12; 27:3. The hymnic style is very evident in the MT through the use of participles: "spreading out," "laying," and "forming." The messianic renewal will accomplish the recreation of the universe for the sake of the elect. Both Horst and Dhorme detect an original rhythmic meter beneath most of this section.

2. The Prophet employs a common figure—a bowl containing God's wrath, for poisoning or dazing his enemies (Jer 25:15ff.; Ez 23:31ff.; Is 51:17ff.; Ps 75:9). *all peoples round about:* One of the verbal similarities with Jl (Jl 4:11–12), it helps to build a case of literary dependence upon the latter prophecy. **3.** Jerusalem is like a weighty stone that will cut or lacerate anyone who attempts to dislodge it; the idea comes from Is 8:14; 28:16 (cf. Zech 3:9). **4–5.** The theme of Jerusalem's liberation and triumph appears. *with fright and...with madness:* Introduces the thought of Dt 28:28. **6.** The first half of this verse adopts a different viewpoint from v. 5. *the princes of Judah:* They now take a much more active part in the messianic battle, for they share with Jerusalem a prominent place in setting up the kingdom of God. **7–8.** Until now, God has been announcing his messianic triumph; now the Prophet acts as divine herald. **9.** The prophecy reverts to the first person; God speaks in his own name.

47 (b) THE GREAT LAMENTATION (12:10–14). It is difficult to explain the abrupt change to mourning. If we choose to associate this passage with the section on the evil and good shepherds (11:4–17), we might conclude that the people are now mourning over the rejection and death of the good shepherd. The Syr version actually identifies this good shepherd as Josiah, slain at Megiddo in 609. Lagrange and many other scholars "recognize the analogy of this conception [in Zech 12:10] with that of the Suffering Servant in Is 53" (M.-J. Lagrange, *RB* 3 [1906] 76; Dentan, *op. cit.*, 1108).

10. *I will pour out:* The phrase is frequently found in eschatological passages, such as Ez 39:29; Jl 3:1; Acts 2:17,33; here, it helps to maintain the setting of the final day of the Lord. *a spirit of grace and petition:* Grace indicates an attitude of pleasing God (or anyone else) so as to obtain a favor (cf. Gn 6:8; 33:8; 34:11); petition supposes a request for mercy (2 Sm 12:22; Is 27:11). *they shall look on him whom they have thrust through:* This verse is involved in textual difficulties. The MT reads "on me," and is followed by almost all the ancient versions: LXX, VL, Vg, Tg., Aq, Sym, and the Syr version. But OT theology would never permit the daring anthropomorphism that God was "thrust through," in place of which the LXX reads "insulted" or, more lit., "dance in triumph over." In support of the LXX, M. Delcor understands the Hebr word to mean "profane," as in Lam 4:9 (*RB* 58 [1951] 194); the ordinary meaning of the Hebr *dqr*, however, is "to pierce with a sword" (1 Sm 31:4) or "to pierce with a lance" (Nm 25:8). Dhorme (*op. cit.*, 865–66) and Jones (*op. cit.*, 161) understand the Hebr particle *'ēt* to be the prep. "concerning," rather than the particle indicating a definite object: "They shall look on me [i.e., Yahweh], concerning the one[s] whom they have pierced." The CCD translation, "look on him," is supported by 45 Hebr manuscripts, most of the early Fathers, and such NT texts as Jn 19:37; Ap 1:7. The identification of the transpierced or insulted one remains an open question with many possible solutions. Besides those already mentioned (good shepherd of ch. 11 and possibly of 13:7–9; Suffering Servant; Josiah), the other martyrs of Jewish history are presented—e.g., Onias III, high priest (2 Mc 4–5). Delcor (*RB* 58 [1951] 189–99) offers an interesting solution. He understands God to say, "they shall turn towards me [in repentance], because they once insulted and profaned my name." Jerusalem, in the midst of messianic victory, does not forget her former idolatry and laments it in a penitential spirit. Delcor rests his case upon a strong dependence of Zech 12 upon Ez 36:16–28. The NT certainly recognizes a messianic significance; echoes of this prophecy occur not only in Jn 19:37 and Ap 1:7, but also in the "only son' passages of Jn 1:18; 3:13–19; Col 1:15. These lines of Zechariah, like those in Hos 11 or Is 43:24, seek to enunciate the mystery of the divine "passion," God's reaction toward the redemptive sufferings of his chosen people and especially his only Son.

11. Hadadrimmon can be either the storm-god Hadad, or the chief deity of Damascus, Rimmon (2 Kgs 5:18), whose death was mourned each year at the return of the dry season; Jerome identified the term as a city very near Megiddo, later called Maximianopolis, and today Tell Mutesellim. Because it controlled the trade routes between the countries N and S of Palestine, Megiddo has been the site of great battles throughout sacred and profane history (*BibLex* 1414–16; G. A. Wright, *BA* 13 [1950] 28–46; H. Belloc, *The Battleground* [Phila., 1936]), a tradition reflected in Jgs 5; Jdt; 2 Kgs 23:29–30; cf. Armageddon of Ap 16:16. **12–14.** Men and women mourn separately. Nathan represents the house of David (2 Sm 5:14; 1 Chr 3:5) and is the one through whom Luke traces Jesus' genealogy (Lk 3:31), rather than through Solomon as does Matthew (Mt 1:6). Shimei, descendant of Gershom and a son of Levi (Ex 6:17; Nm 3:18,21) represents the priesthood, which here has equal status with the royalty.

48 (c) THE END OF FALSEHOOD (13:1–6). The messianic kingdom must be cleansed of wickedness and especially of any "professionalism" in sacred offices. The image of a fountain of water, purifying or spreading life across the land, is frequently met in the Scriptures. Whereas Is 12:3; Pss 35:8; 45:4–5 are more general references, in Ez 47:1–12 the water flows from the Temple, in Jl 4:18 it flows from Judah, and in Zech 14:8 it flows from Jerusalem. The idea extends into NT imagery (Jn 4:10ff.; 7:37–39; Ap 7:17). The priesthood and the Temple have completely eclipsed the royalty; also, prophetism (13:2–6) has become decadent. This decline was already in progress during the pre-exilic days, at least in regard to the charismatic prophets who banded together (Mi 3:5–7; Jer 23:9ff.; Ez 13), but the disappearance of the prophets resulted not only from their loss of fervor (Neh 6:12–14) but also from Ezekiel's strong emphasis upon the priesthood. Post-exilic sins are described here in terms of pre-exilic idolatry. **3.** Parents will be so loyal to their God as to reject their own children; "thrust through" is the same Hebr word as in 12:10. **4.** *hairy mantle:* The standard garment of a prophet (2 Kgs 1:8; Mt 3:4; Ap 11:3) becomes a symbol of disgrace. **6.** *wounds:* Probably self-inflicted during prophetic frenzy (1 Kgs 18:28–29) and are not to be considered an allusion to fertility cult practices (Ackroyd, *PCB* 571 n.). The prophets seek to conceal their identity by attributing the cuts to family antagonisms (cf. v. 3).

49 (d) THE SONG OF THE SWORD (13:7–9). It is not clear if this song continues the thought of 11:4–17, and, if so, whether the shepherd here is to be associated with the good or evil shepherd in ch. 11. Even if chs. 9–14 are an anthology with abrupt transitions, it is still an extreme measure to change the biblical order of verses or chapters. In its present condition, this song can envisage a situation very similar to 12:10–14; the leaders will share the guilt and the punishment of the people. Accepted contritely, this sorrow leads to messianic glory (13:9). We can trace this song to the influence of passages such as Ez 21:13–22,33–37; Jer 50:35ff., but especially Ez 5 (Horst, *op. cit.*, 251–54). Messianic perspectives cannot be denied: i.e., the title "my shepherd" or "my associate"; remnant; purification; return to God. **7.** The selfish, disorganized condition of the flock brings sorrow, possibly death (?), upon the shepherd; without a leader, the people's lives fall into chaos. United with the shepherd, the people are purified and thus saved by this sorrow. Matthew (26:31) adapts the words to Jesus Christ. **8.** Remnant theology reoccurs (cf. 8:6; 9:7). **9.** *my people...my God:* Cf. Hos 2:25.

50 (e) THE BATTLE FOR JERUSALEM (14:1–21). Like the final chapter of Zech (ch. 8), this last chapter of Dt-Zech is a collection of many disparate prophecies. E. Sellin has recognized a series of doublets: vv. 1–5 = 6–11; v. 12 = 13–14; vv. 15–18 = 20–21. The theme seems to be clear enough, i.e., the mortal agony that convulses the universe before the day of the Lord. Jerusalem, the center of the world empire, must suffer the worst anguish and thereby be purified the most thoroughly. The apocalyptic style is the most pronounced in the whole book. Like the rest of apocalyptic and midrashic compositions of post-exilic Israel, this one draws heavily upon earlier sacred traditions. The overall influence seems to come from Sennacherib's siege (Is 36–37; 2 Kgs 18–19).

1–5. The first scene reveals the cataclysmic upheavals of the last day. **1.** *spoils...divided:* It informs us that Jerusalem has been victorious (v. 1), but the price of victory has been very dear (v. 2). **3.** *the Lord shall go forth and fight against those nations:* For the mighty contest (cf. Jb 38:22–23). There is good reason for translating the last phrase, "fight with those nations [against Jerusalem]." Hostile forces, therefore, are acting completely within the Lord's providential plan for Jerusalem's redemption. **4.** Within the words of this theophany there can be heard the trembling of mountains and the shattering of eternal hills, told by other biblical passages (Jgs 5:4–5; 1 Sm 7:10; Na 1:5; Hab 3:6; esp. Ez 38:19,21–22). **5.** *the earthquake in the days of King Uzziah:* Cf. Am 1:1. It was attributed by Josephus to Uzziah's usurpation of priestly functions (2 Chr 26:16ff.; Josephus, *Ant.* 9.10, 4). *the Lord...shall come:* The Davidic king is not mentioned; Jerusalem is no longer associated with the royal family but with the Temple.

6–7. This second vignette of the messianic age, again in a highly imaginative apocalyptic style, is hampered by a very damaged Hebr text; different, even contradictory translations are offered. The author wants to emphasize the unbroken peace, the security against natural upheavals. The thought can be best understood if studied from such texts as Is 60:19–20 (cf. Ap 21:23; 22:5).

51 8–9. Jerusalem is the source of life in great abundance for all nations; living water flows E and W. What is expressed symbolically in v. 8 becomes a clear, credal confession in v. 9. There might be some dependence of v. 9 upon the Shema prayer of Dt 6:4–9. The imagery is too different from 13:1 to hypothesize a single author, but the influencing factors were probably the same ancient texts (see comment on 13:1).

10–11. The glory of Jerusalem is again presented symbolically. The entire promised land sinks to the depth of "the plain" or the Arabah; Jerusalem alone stands exalted (cf. 4:7). Strangely enough, the Prophet uses the rather narrow limits of late, pre-exilic Judah. Geba was 6 mi. N of Jerusalem; Rimmon was 35 mi. SW of Jerusalem (cf. Jos 15:32; 18:24; 19:7; see comment on 10:10). We recognize a dependence upon earlier texts, such as Jer 31:38–40; Is 2:2–5; thus, the author gives a sense of all hopes reaching their fulfillment. Because of the corrupt condition of the text, there is difficulty in identifying the various Jerusalem sites and their correct names (cf. Simons, *op. cit.*, n. 1583–84; H. Vincent, *Jérusalem de l'Ancien Testament* [Paris, 1956] 603). The E-W limits of the city extended in the north from the "Gate of Benjamin"—a monumental entrance leading into the temple area from the tribal portion of Benjamin (Jer 37:13)—to the "First Gate" or "Corner Gate" at the NW angle. *the Tower of Hananel:* In the NE area of the Gate of Benjamin. *the king's wine presses:* In the extreme SE district of the city, at the confluence of the Kedron and Hinnom Valleys, where the Pool of Siloam overflowed into the king's garden (Is 22:9; Neh 3:15).

12. The grim, even shocking, language of this verse follows the exaggerated style of apocalyptic writing (cf. Ez 38:21–22; 39:17–20; Ap 16:6; 19:17–18); the author may be calling upon the haunting memories of Sennacherib's invasion. The emphasis here is common biblical teaching: the definitive victory of God in the messianic age; the inevitable punishment that the sinner inflicts upon himself by the nature of his sin (Jer 2:5,19; Wis 11:16).

13–15. Dhorme (*op. cit.*, 872) and Horst (*op. cit.*, 260) prefer to place v. 15 immediately after v. 12. As translated in the CCD, vv. 13–14 cannot possibly harmonize with the rest of ch. 14 and must therefore be from another author. The senseless panic of the Gentile nations, the obvious result of mammoth rebellion against God, will also blind the inhabitants of Jerusalem and Judah. At times in their history, the Israelites sinned and destroyed themselves. It seems preferable to translate the one phrase thus: "Judah shall fight in [or, with] Jerusalem."

52 **16–19.** Originally, the Feast of Tabernacles commemorated God's care for the wandering Israelites in Sinai (Lv 23:43); it gradually absorbed other great acts of divine protection: final harvesting (Dt 16:13–15); consecration of the Temple (1 Kgs 8; Hag 1:15b–2:9); conquest of the land (Neh 8:13–18); even the birth of Isaac (*Jub* 16:21; cf. G. MacRae, *CBQ* 22 [1960] 251–76, esp. 268–70). Through all these blessings, God exercised his kingly rule over his people. But it would be going too far, when no important evidence can be located elsewhere in the Bible, to establish from this text a special feast in honor of Yahweh's ascension to the throne of Israel. The Feast of Tabernacles was celebrated in the month of Tishri, from the fifteenth to the twenty-second day, just before the autumnal rains; hence, the special mention of rain in v. 17, and the Talmud speaks of the pouring of water at this feast (Mishnah, *Sukkah* 4:9). **18.** Because Egypt does not depend upon rain but upon the annual flooding of the Nile, a different punishment, the plagues, are the threat—a bit pedantic, according to Horst (*op. cit.*, 259).

20–21. All military power and former profane practices are placed beneath the religious authority: horses, an instrument of war, are consecrated to the Lord (cf. Ex 28:36); bells, once employed for superstitious purposes, are given a sacred use. Again we note the universalism of worship (cf. v. 16; Is 66:18–21). The exclusion of "merchants" most probably is an attempt to control the commercial practices of the priests at the Temple.

The book closes abruptly, without a conclusion! But the redactor wanted the message to continue into the prophecy of Malachi, which he may have considered as Part 3 of chs. 9–14. Malachi begins with the same phrase that Deutero-Zechariah uses in 9:1 and 12:1: "a burden."

MALACHI

BIBLIOGRAPHY

53 Brockington, L. H., *PCB* 573–75. Chary, T., *Les prophètes et le culte à partir de l'Exil* (Paris, 1955) 160–89. Dentan, R. C., *IB* 6, 1117–44. Dhorme, E., *BPl* cxiv–cxv, 875–87. Gelin, A., R-F 1, 572–74. Lattey, C., *The Book of Malachy* (WV; London, 1934). Neil, W., *IDB* 3, 228–32. Pautrel, R., *VDBS* 5, 739–46. Smith, J. M. P., *Malachi* (ICC; N.Y., 1912). Sutcliffe, E. F., *CCHS* 555–58. Torrey, C. C., *JBL* 17 (1898) 1–17. Von Bulmerincq, A., *Der Prophet Maleachi* (vols. 1–2; Dorpat, 1926, II, 1932). (See also titles listed under Haggai.)

INTRODUCTION

54 This work contains no dates and it apparently even leaves the name of the Prophet anonymous (→ 61 below). It is usually agreed, however, that it represents the preaching of a prophet who spoke sometime before the reforms of Ezra and Nehemiah, i.e., around 460, for he condemned what these two leaders were to correct.

(I) The Prophet. The name Malachi ("my messenger"; 3:1) is probably an abbreviation of *Mal'ăkiyyâ* ("messenger of Yahweh"; cf. Dhorme, *op. cit.*, cxiv). This unknown Prophet shows himself to be a patriotic Jew unable to tolerate mixed marriages lest the land become "unclean" from the "abominable" and sensuous types of worship common among the pagans (Ezr 9:11). Staunchly loyal to his religion, he could not remain silent at the sight of a priesthood that was ignorant, indulgent, and grasping. He was a man very well acquainted with earlier traditions (Dt, Ez). Malachi does not impress us with his education, for his vocabulary is limited and his style is colorless; his book makes little demand upon the imagination.

55 **(II) The Style.** Malachi is well known for his "catechetical style." Almost every new section leads off with a statement, by either God or the Prophet, which is then challenged by a question from the people. This question may have been a literary device, for it conveniently provides the Prophet with an opportunity to develop his thought very bluntly.

56 **(III) The Times.** Inasmuch as the Temple has been rebuilt, it is definitely after 515 (Mal 1:10; 3:1,10; Ezr 6:15). The religious abuses that Malachi excoriated are exactly the same crimes that Nehemiah and Ezra energetically combatted and successfully stamped out. Therefore, it is somewhere before 445, or at least 428–427. Jewish men were divorcing "the wives of their youth" (Mal 2:14) and marrying pretty girls of foreign extraction (Ezr 9–10). The wealthy were cheating the poor (Mal 3:5), even selling them into slavery (Neh 5), and the scandalous cry was heard that irreligious people get along better than devout people (Mal 3:14–15). The leaders, and particularly the priests, bore the greatest responsibility for the general collapse of sincere fervor (Mal 2:1–3,8–9; Ezr 10:15–16,18–24; Neh 13:4–13,22,28–31). Temple worship could not even claim to be correct externally; it was as sick as the animals offered in sacrifice (Mal 1:7–8,13; Neh 13:15–22). All this indifference, unrest, and injustice was contained within the small territory of post-exilic Judah, 20 by 25 mi. square, among a population numbering about 20,000.

57 **(IV) Sources.** The Prophet whose preaching was summarized and edited in Mal stands halfway between the prophet-priest Ezekiel and the final redaction of the P tradition of the Pentateuch. Malachi's center of religious life is the Temple, an orientation quite different from the pre-exilic prophets (Is 1; Jer 7); he also reveals a literary dependence upon Ez (cf. Mal 1:7,12 with Ez 44:16; Mal 1:11 with Ez 36:23; Mal 2:3 with Ez 5:10; 6:5; 12:15; 30:36; and Mal 3:2 with Ez 44:27). The P code (Lv) was not yet fully developed and enforced; this fact is deduced from Malachi's frequent contact with the rival law code of Dt. This code may have continued to dominate Palestinian religious life during the Exile and was finally replaced by the P law only through the strong efforts of Ezra (cf. P. Grelot, R-F 1, 816–18, 828–30; Chary, *op. cit.*, 173–76). The Prophet alludes extensively to Dt (cf. Mal 1:9 with Dt 10:17; Mal 1:12 with Dt 7:8; Mal 2:1,4; 3:3 with Dt 18:1; Mal 2:6 with Dt 33:10; Mal 3:22 with Dt 4:10).

58 **(V) Doctrine.** Malachi seeks to restore the holiness of marriage, restricting Dt's permission of divorce (Dt 24:1–4) and calling attention to God's first design at the creation of man and woman (Mal 2:10,15). He roundly condemns mixed marriages and has God declare, "I hate divorce" (2:16). Messianism centers around the Jerusalem Temple, where an acceptable, liturgical sacrifice will be offered by all men (1:11) with the Lord gloriously present in their midst (3:1–2) destroying evil forever (3:5,19) and, like "the sun of justice, "granting a healthy life and the fulfillment of the Mosaic promises to the elect (3:20). A worthy, sincere priesthood will lead the people of God (2:4–7). A later redactor—or perhaps he who collected the Prophet's preaching?—added a footnote that Elijah shall reappear upon earth to inaugurate "the great and terrible day" (3:23).

59 **(VI) History of the Text.** The preaching of the Prophet was edited before Ezra's reform, which made the P code the law of the land; the anonymous Prophet himself may have been responsible for this first redaction of his preaching, but it seems better to hold that the work was done by the one who added the first appendix (3:22). At first, the collection was part of a series of "burdens" or "oracles" attached to the prophecy of Zechariah (→ 36–37 above; → 61 below). When Mal was separated (perhaps to form a 12-book unit within the scroll of the minor prophets), the introductory verse was enlarged, attributing the prophecy to "the messenger of the Lord" (1:1; 3:1). It may have happened at the same time that 3:23–24 was added and attempts were being made to identify the precursors of the messianic movement. It was not until much later, certainly after the translation of Mal into Greek, that the anonymous "messenger of the Lord" was called "Malachi" and the prophecy had reached its final stage of development. Despite this rugged history, the Hebr text has been well preserved and offers no major problems (Eissfeldt, *OTI* 441–42).

60 **(VII) Outline.** The Book of Malachi may be outlined as follows:

(I) The Superscription (1:1)
(II) The Oracles or Burdens (1:2–3:21)
  (A) The First Oracle: God's Special Love for Israel (1:2–5)
  (B) The Second Oracle: The Sins of the Priests (1:6–2:9)
  (C) The Third Oracle: Against Divorce and Mixed Marriages (2:10–16)
  (D) The Fourth Oracle: Yahweh, God of Justice (2:17–3:5)
  (E) The Fifth Oracle: Ritual Offenses (3:6–12)
  (F) The Sixth Oracle: Triumph of the Just (3:13–21) (LXX 3:13–4:3)
(III) Two Appendices (3:22–24) (LXX and Vg 4:4–6)

COMMENTARY

61 **(I) The Superscription (1:1).** It was added at the time of the final editing of the prophecy. *the word of the Lord...through Malachi:* This second part was probably introduced when these chapters became a separate book and the redactors recognized the need of finding a name for the author. The word "Malachi" was then borrowed from 3:1 where it is not transliterated as a proper name but is translated as the common noun, "my messenger." Only here in the entire OT is Malachi used as the name of a Jewish man. The name is suspect for still another reason; the LXX translated the word "through the hand of his angel" (or "his messenger," for the Gk word *aggelos* has both meanings). We are not questioning that the author was inspired but are merely discussing his name, not necessarily such an important matter in ancient Israel as it is today (cf. Is 40:1; Zech 9:1). Sir 50:47 is the only instance in the OT of an author's signing his name to his work.

62 **(II) The Oracles or Burdens (1:2–3:21).** These follow a general pattern: a statement or reproach from God; a challenge hurled against God's remark; an answer developing God's initial remark.

(A) The First Oracle: God's Special Love for Israel (1:2–5). God's love for Israel is different from that for all other peoples, specifically Edom. **3.** *was not Esau Jacob's brother?:* Blood descent from Abraham and Isaac is insufficient. *I loved Jacob, but hated Esau:* Bluntly states the problem of predestination. Malachi certainly does not cover every angle of this complex question; it would not be legitimate to conclude, therefore, that some men are doomed, despite their most earnest entreaties to God for assistance. We can deduce, however, that although God loves all men more than they deserve, he still loves some more than others (H. H. Rowley, *The Biblical Doctrine of Election* [London, 1950] 44–68; S. Lyonnet, *VD* 34–35 [1956] 193–201, 257–71). *I made his mountains a waste:* The Edomites, Esau's descendants, who lived in the dry, craggy, mountainous region S of the Dead Sea, began to be dislodged by the Nabateans as early as 560. **4.** *land of guilt:* Edom and Israel were age-old enemies (Gn 25:22–26; 27; 32:4–21; 33; Nm 20:14–21; 1 Kgs 11:14–22), but Israel's anger and hatred exploded when the Edomites gloated over the fall of Jerusalem in 587, killed the refugees, and poached upon the stricken land (Ob 10–14; Lam 1:21; 4:21–22).

63 **(B) The Second Oracle: The Sins of the Priests (1:6–2:9).** Judah is indicted, especially the priests, for slovenly ritual. **6.** Cf. Is 1:2–3; the Lord challenges the sacrifices that are being offered. **7–8.** From the questions and answers it is clear that defective animals (forbidden in Lv 22:17–25; etc.) were being offered. Hence, sacrifice will be of no avail (9–10). **11.** This famous verse is obscure and variously translated (cf. Chary, *op. cit.*, 179; M. Rehm, "Das Opfer der Völker nach Malachias 1, 11," *Lex Tua Veritas* [Fest. H. Junker; Trier, 1961] 193–94). In contrast to the polluted Israelite sacrifice stands a "pure offering" (Hebr *minḥâ* indicates a grain offering but also used in a more general sense), a "sacrifice" (Hebr *muqṭār* is associated with incense but also has a wider use). This worship will be universal ("from the rising of the sun..."), and a question arises: Does Malachi have in mind Jews in the Diaspora or the sacrifices of the Gentiles? Innumerable interpretations have been given. K. Elliger (ATD 198–99) finds here a different hand; L. H. Brockington (*op. cit.*, 574d) and H. Frey (*Das Buch der Kirche in der Weltwende*, 4th ed. [Stuttgart, 1957] 148) see an implicit recognition of Yahweh by the pagans. Others look to the Zoroastrian worship of the Persians as the object of the Prophet's praise. Still others find a solution in the unorthodox Jewish worship in Samaria (F. Horst, *Die zwölf kleinen Propheten* 2 [2nd ed.; HAT; Tübingen, 1954] 267; A. Alt, *KlSchr* 2, 316–37) or in the heretical Jewish temple at Elephantine in Egypt (Smith, *op. cit.*), etc. In view of the words of the Council of Trent (DB 1742), A. Gelin (*BJ* 65) regards as "official" the interpretation that Malachi refers here to the perfect sacrifice of the messianic era. We hold that the text looks forward to a ritual sacrifice of the messianic age, a fulfillment and perfection of the Mosaic rite, which will be offered by all men and accepted by God. **12–14.** The contrast with the unworthy sacrifices of the Jews continues. A "gelding" is explicitly forbidden in Lv 22:24.

64 In the final section of this second oracle (2:1–9), Malachi not only lays a curse upon the priesthood but uncovers their serious guilt by showing the high estate from which they have fallen (cf. U. Devescovi, *BeO* 4 [1962] 205–18). **4.** *covenant with Levi:* This phrase is important. It underscores the special privilege of the Levites (mediating and therefore summing up in themselves the covenant of God with all the people), and it also forms an important link in determining the history of the P tradition of the Pentateuch. Mal is dependent upon Dt 18:1–8; 33:8–11, where no distinction is evident between priest and Levite. The distinction belonged to the southern kingdom of Judah, where the Jerusalem clergy had gradually assumed a special role and relegated all other clergymen to the minor rank of "Levite" (cf. Ez 43:10–44:31). Ezekiel insisted upon the rights of the Jerusalem priests, but his "priestly law" did not become completely effective until the reform of Ezra. Nm 25:10–13, of the P tradition, reflects this later development when it interrupts a narrative to insist upon "a covenant of everlasting priesthood" with Aaron and his sons (Aaronic priesthood; cf. Chary, *op. cit.*, 167–70). **5.** The Levitical priest was to transmit life, peace, and reverential love, and would himself possess the fullness of what he was to transmit to others. **6.** *true doctrine:* The full oral instruction handed down by the priest, i.e., his commentary on the Law and application of it (cf. Dt 31:9–13). **7.** Malachi here presents his portraits of the ideal priest. Although many prophetic themes are heard in Mal, still, texts like this one show that the priests, despite their apparent faults, were in complete control of the new commonwealth.

65 **(C) The Third Oracle: Against Divorce and Mixed Marriages (2:10–16).** This protest against divorce and mixed marriage is strong. **10.** The opening statement, spoken by the sinful people, is made to sound as from the depths of despair, so great does their offense appear to Malachi. Yahweh is the father of all Jews; because there is only one God, a person must belong to the people of God in order to be a part of his family circle (Dt 6:4–9; 32:18; Hos 11:1). To marry outside this circle is to break the bond of a divine family and to desecrate the home or "temple" of God. Malachi refers to creation and by this allusion shows that the unique wonder of marriage, set up by God himself, must not be torn apart by man! Creation also reminds us of the moment when God made woman from man and established marriage in such a way that each were "bone of bone, flesh of flesh" (cf. Gn 2:21–25; Mt 19:3–9). **11.** "The temple" that "Judah has profaned" and "which the Lord loves" is none other than the divorced wife. *an idolatrous woman:* Lit., in the MT, "the daughter of a strange god." Malachi applies implacable logic: To marry a pagan woman is to be bound to her gods as well. **12.** *may the Lord cut off:* This phrase pronounces excommunication, civil as well as religious, against the man who divorces his wife.

13–14. Ritual and life go together; liturgy should be like a mirror, honestly reflecting before God one's character and daily activity. With Malachi, prophetism has swung away from its older style of ignoring or condemning liturgical abuses and has thoroughly integrated moral reform with temple worship. **14.** *the Lord is witness:* To every marriage. *wife of your youth:* The phrase has already been used in Is 54:6 and Prv 5:18. **15.** This verse is entangled in great textual problems and various translations are advanced. As God is the one Spirit of all life, so man and wife are united in one spirit and one flesh. Just as God cannot be divided, neither should man and wife be separated. **16.** *covering one's garment with injustice:* The text is obscure; perhaps the garments symbolize the person.

66 **(D) The Fourth Oracle: Yahweh, God of Justice (2:17–3:5).** Yahweh is truly the God of justice, for he will certainly intervene (3:5) to punish the wicked. **13–15.** The problem of retribution is frequent in the OT (Hab 1–2, Jb, Pss 37, 73). **3:1.** The fulfillment of the divine promise is announced. It is difficult to know if Malachi is here thinking of one or many messianic precursors in the titles "my messenger" (*mal'ākî*), "the Lord," and "messenger of the covenant" (*mal'ak habbᵉrît*). Horst (*op. cit.*, 271), Elliger (*op. cit.*, 206), and Chary (*op. cit.*, 117–18) consider these terms to be various symbols for God himself. The fact that the author of the prophecy could later be named *mal'ākî* implies that no precise future messianic person is intended by the title. The name "messenger of the covenant" has already been given to the Jerusalem clergy in Mal 2:4,7 Furthermore, Malachi completely ignores the messianic pretensions of the Davidic family, nor does he otherwise speak of any messianic figures. In 3:1, therefore, he seems to be presenting the eschatological moment in the language of God's great interventions in sacred history: God's speaking to the Patriarchs (Gn 16:7ff.; 22:11) and to Moses (Ex 3:2); God's leading the way through the Red Sea (Ex 23:20) and giving the covenant (Jgs 2:1–5; Acts 7:53; Gal 3:19; cf. Frey, op. cit., 164). These various, wondrous ways in which God had manifested himself will later be applied to messianic precursors (see 3:23). The Tg., Jerome (*PL* 25. 1541–42) and Von Bulmerincq have identified the messenger as the priest-scribe Ezra. Jesus adapted the words to John the Baptist (Mt 11:10).

2. Verses 2–4 speak of God in the third person, and thus differ from vv. 1 and 5. The Prophet seems to be commenting on the scope and meaning ("purification," vv. 2–4) of the divine, eschatological presence. **3.** *refining like gold:* Cf. 1 Pt 1:7; 1QS 8:4. **4.** This verse must be kept in mind when we attempt to interpret 1:11; Mal did not reject the Jerusalem sacrifice altogether but awaited its transformation, just as he expected the priestly messengers of the covenant (2:4,7) to be perfected and transcended by the Lord (3:1). **5.** In the concluding line, God again speaks in his own name; the message is typically prophetic in character: social abuses are roundly condemned.

67 **(E) The Fifth Oracle: Ritual Offenses (3:6–12).** Ritual offenses are condemned. **8.** The

Israelites "rob God" by keeping back the stipulated offerings. Such a statement is novel in prophetic preaching; usually God insisted that he did not need the people's gifts (cf. Is 43:23; Ps 50:7–15). **10–12.** If Israel obeys, blessings will follow.

68 (F) The Sixth Oracle: Triumph of the Just (3:13–21) (LXX 3:13–4:3). Malachi again faces (2:17) the problem of evil: just men suffer; unjust men prosper! **16–18.** The answer is that God cares for those who "fear" him; they are inscribed in his "record book" (Ex 32:32; Is 4:3; etc). **19.** (4:1 in the LXX and Vg.) A day will surely dawn when the least shadow of evil will be totally swept away. **20.** *the sun of justice with its healing rays:* The phrase draws upon a very common symbol in the ancient Near East. The sun, always one of the principal gods, was thought to provide warmth and life, light and law (*ANET* 387–89; *ANEP* 349; J. Finegan, *Light from the Ancient Past* [2nd ed.; Princeton, 1959] 96–97). The Bible uses the same symbolism but identifies the deity as the one God, Yahweh (Ps 19:4–11).

69 (III) Two Appendices (3:22–24) (LXX and Vg 4:4–6). These appendices conclude both the prophecy of Malachi and the scroll of the 12 prophets. These lines reflect a later attempt to sustain loyalty to the Mosaic Law (22) as well as an endeavor to identify the precursor of the great messianic day (23–24).

22. In the first appendix, the language is heavily deuteronomic: Horeb instead of Sinai (Dt 1:6; 4:10,15); the phrase "statutes and ordinances" (Dt 4:1,5,8; 5:1); servant of Yahweh (Dt 3:24; 9:27); the verb "remember" (Dt 9:2,27; 24:9; 25:17). **23–24.** A later prophet seeks to identify the messenger of Yahweh (3:1) with the return of Elijah. The latter's sudden departure (2 Kgs 2:11) gave rise to stories about his reappearance upon earth (Sir 48:10–12; *1 Enoch* 90:31; Mishnah, *Eduyoth* 8:7; etc.). The tradition remains fluid, even in NT writing, for whereas Mt and the Infancy Narrative of Lk recognize fulfillment in John the Baptist, the actual precursor of Jesus (Mt 11:14; 17:10–13; Lk 1:17), Luke prefers to present Jesus himself in the image of Elijah (Lk 3:16; 4:23–27). (See also Ap 11:4–15.) The new Elijah's role is to be concerned with peace (v. 23ef). *the great and terrible day:* It will certainly "strike...doom" upon the wicked. The rabbis, however, did not want the scroll of Malachi and the 12 prophets to conclude on this note, so they directed that v. 23 be repeated in public recitation. The concluding lines, therefore, printed in the CCD, are not the conclusion to the book.

24

THE CHRONICLER: 1–2 CHRONICLES, EZRA, NEHEMIAH

Robert North, S.J.

1–2 CHRONICLES

BIBLIOGRAPHY

1 *Commentaries:* Bowman, R., "I and II Chronicles," *IB* 3, 339–548. Cazelles, H., *Les livres des Chroniques* (BJ; Paris, 1961). Curtis, E. and A. Madsen, *A Critical and Exegetical Commentary on the Books of Chronicles* (ICC; N.Y., 1910). Elmslie, W., *The Books of Chronicles* (CBSC; Cambridge, 1916). Galling, K., *Die Bücher der Chronik, Esra, Nehemia* (ATD; Göttingen, 1954). Goettsberger, J., *Die Bücher der Chronik oder Paralipomenon* (BB; Bonn, 1939). Herbert, A., "I and II Chronicles," *PCB* 357–69. Michaeli, F., *Les livres des Chroniques, d'Esdras et de Néhémie* (Neuchâtel, 1967). Myers, J., *I Chronicles. II Chronicles* (AB; N.Y., 1965). Noordtzij, A., *De Boeken der Kronieken* (2nd ed.; Kampen, 1967). Randellini, L., *Il libro delle Cronache* (Rome, 1966). Rehm, M., *Die Bücher der Chronik* (Echter-B; Würzburg, 1934). Rothstein, J. and J. Hänel, *Kommentar zum ersten Buch der Chronik* (KAT; Leipzig, 1927). Rudolph, W., *Chronikbücher* (HAT; Tübingen, 1955). Van den Born, A., *Kronieken* (Roermond, 1960). Van Selms, A., *I–II Kronieken* (Groningen, 1947). Von Hummelauer, F., *In Paralipomenon* (CSS; Paris, 1905).

Studies: Bewer, J., *Der Text des Buches Ezra* (Göttingen, 1922). Kapelrud, A., *The Question of Authorship in the Ezra-narrative* (Oslo, 1944). Noth, *US* 110–80. Pfeiffer, R., "Chronicles, I and II," *IDB* 1, 572–80. Schaeder, H., *Esra der Schreiber* (Tübingen, 1930). Vannutelli, P., *Libri synoptici Veteris Testamenti* (Rome, 1931). Von Rad, G., *Geschichtsbild des chronistischen Werkes* (Stuttgart, 1930). Welch, A. C., *The Work of the Chronicler* (London, 1939). (→ 81 below.)

INTRODUCTION

2 **(I) Name.** The last books of the Hebr Bible bear the name "Annals," or "events year by year," (*dibrê hayyāmîm*). In *dābār* we recognize the famous Semitic "Word and Event interchangeable," as Augustine put it, and the plural of *yôm* "day" means also period or year. "Chronicle [of the whole divine history]" is the designation proposed by Jerome himself and retrieved by Luther; the Lat Church meanwhile contented itself with Jerome's transcription of the unappetizing Gk name, "Of Leftovers" (not "Traditions" as recently claimed), *paraleipomenōn*.

Hebrew has no word meaning "history," a Gk term for "buttonholing people to ask them questions." *Tôlᵉdôt*, as in modern Hebr dictionaries, really means "acts of generating" and reflects a premodern view that Gn (in which that term occurs, 5:1; etc.) gives us history par excellence. More properly, the Pentateuch is regarded as the Torah, the Law. The books from Jos through Kgs, which to us seem even more "historical," are "Earlier Prophets" in Hebr tradition—fittingly enough when, with Augustine, we understand prophecy as declaring the will of God in present affairs.

A modern insight sees in Dt-Kgs a single complete history, compiled *ca.* 600, the first to be published in the form we possess today (→ 1–2 Kings, 10:79). Much older elements of historiography had already been set down by the "Yahwist" of Judah in Solomon's time, and somewhat later in variant form by an "Elohist" in Ephraim. But these were actually published in a coherent continuous torah only after the Exile, traditionally by Ezra. Why, then, should a third great history of Israel, from Adam to the Chronicler's own day, have been undertaken so quickly after Ezra's *geste*? Partly it was to incorporate the post-exilic events, including Ezra's own, but mostly it was to protect the learner from that pentateuchal glorification of Moses and his Sinai covenant, which risked diminishing the importance of Davidic ritual and dynastic authority.

3 **(II) Structure.** The principal and most characteristic block of Chr sets forth the achievement of David, chiefly the regulation of the Temple cult, narrated in 323 verses (as against only 77 in Sm and 73 in Chr on David's military or civil activities—1 Chr 10–29). Both David's rise to power in displacing Saul and the melancholy saga of succession to David's throne are omitted. In exchange, the emergence of David is introduced chiefly by lengthy genealogies: his own Judah tribe in 100 verses (1 Chr 2–4); the Chronicler's Levite clan in

80 verses (1 Chr 6); a skeletal history of the human race from Adam to Saul (1 Chr 1–9).

The history of David's successors differs in important points from the Deuteronomist record in Kgs. The rulers of dissident Samaria are wholly omitted, and thereby also all basis for checking Judah's chronology. Allusions in which vice seems to be rewarded are expunged, and edifying episodes are either heightened or inserted from elsewhere, or even, as a kind of theological reasoning, "created." From the 822 verses in 2 Chr, 480 deal with 4 pious kings and 342 with the 17 others; including Asa's lengthy flirtation with virtue.

The Ezra books narrate Zerubbabel's building of the Temple *ca.* 520 (Ezr 1–6), the construction of Nehemiah's wall in 445 (Neh 1–6), and the promulgation of Ezra's torah in passages the sequence of which will pose recurrent dilemmas (Ezr 7–10, Neh 7–13).

4 **(III) Genre.** Surprisingly valid is this 1899 summary of the Chronicler's historical aim by T. Soares (*AJT* 3, 261). (1) "Dominated by the notion of the complete observance of the full Mosaic ritual from the earliest times, the Chronicler has presented an ideal, rather than a real picture of the ecclesiastical arrangements of the first temple." (2) "Under the influence of the splendor of the Persian empire, the Chronicler has often presented an exaggerated picture of the condition of the Hebrew monarchy." (3) "Living in different circumstances, and far removed from the events which he narrates, the Chronicler occasionally, like other biblical historians... fails to interpret properly the history." Yet, after due allowance has been made, the Chronicler's historical contribution is essentially accurate and complete.

The case is put more trenchantly by a Jesuit seminarian in the [Woodstock] *Theologian* 13 (1957) 12: "...certainly not history in the modern sense. Numerous improbabilities are to be found, to say nothing of clear divergences from what has been proved by archeology, or even what is stated in other books of the Bible."

Excavation has doubtless done much for exegesis since 1899, yet this confidence in "clear" divergence from "what has been proved by archeology" might be nuanced by tracing the steps through which any excavated reality is shaped by human thinking and fallacious literary data before it attains the stage of "proof." More relevant and new is the emphasis on literary genre for determining the inerrant truth expressed by the Bible, rather than defending it, as done with heavy hand by F. Kugler in *SZ* 109 (1925) 367–82 and more recently by H. Richardson in *JBR* 26 (1958) 9–12. Here the view of the late A. Robert goes about as far as one might wish: "As the final term of its development, [the OT 'prophetic history'] genre takes on the form of edifying narrative or juridico-theological theses, which obviously take liberties with the facts, to the dismay of our occidental outlooks.... Chr has no scruple about reworking its scriptural sources; but it does this palpably without the slightest intention or hope of deceiving anybody, in pursuit of the conventions of a recognized genre" (*VDBS* 5 [1957] 418).

Truly it is no more illicit for the Chronicler to ascribe to David, than for P to ascribe to Moses on Sinai, details of cult formulated centuries later than either Moses or David, but expressing in the spirit of these men the basic historic truth that the sacred writer ultimately aims to convey (cf. H. Lusseau, R-F 1, 728). Just as in the form criticism of the Gospels, we cannot admit a complete disjunction between the David of history and the David of the Chronicler's "faith." On the extent to which these two must coalesce, J. Soggin, *TZ* 17 (1961) 385–98, is preferable to Eissfeldt, *OTI* 539, or W. Stinespring, *JBL* 80 (1961) 209–19. Ultimately, no history is conceived or valued as an expression of the "cold" facts rather than as a record of ideological convictions of the writer.

Despite the assumed dullness of the Chronicler's style, G. von Rad (*GesSt* 248–61) notes six cases of impassioned pleading in 2 Chr and a seventh in 1 Chr. He concludes that the Chronicler's aim was "to sell his ideas." Furthermore, Von Rad's *Geschichtsbild* identifies the Chronicler as largely influenced by Dt; N. Snaith concurs in *OTMS* 109, against the efforts of P. Asmussen, *ThStKr* 79 (1906) 165–79, who would make P the only part of the Pentateuch known to the Chronicler.

More audacious is the hypothesis of A. Noordtzij in *RB* 49 (1940) 168: By portraying how all the forces within Israel, the clergy no less than the royal house, have been blocking establishment of the theocracy, the Chronicler aims to point to Christ as the one shepherd. In antithesis to this is the Chronicler's "total lack of eschatological perspective," accepted by Rudolph from H. Hertzberg, *Werdende Kirche* (1950) 14, and T. Vriezen, *Outline* 350. A middle way, suggested by R. de Vaux (*RB* 64 [1957] 280), is what we will favor: The Chronicler fosters a genuinely messianic hope, but in its pre-exilic dynastic form rather than with the eschatological stress it had come to take on in his own time—as an affirmation of the divinely willed definitiveness of the Davidic line, rather than as a remedy for its current deficiencies.

5 **(IV) Sources.** One of the firmest proofs that the Chronicler did use traceable and reliable sources other than biblical parallels was formulated by Cardinal Bea (*Bib* 22 [1941] 46–58). Eissfeldt (*OTI* 532–34) concludes that a single work entitled "Midrash on Kings" underlies five separate similar titles of 2 Chr (16:11; 20:34; 24:27; 27:7; 33:18) and probably eleven different "prophet" citations as well, such as Iddo in 9:29. However, this Iddo corresponds to an unnamed prophet in 1 Kgs 13:1, where eight others are described under the same name as in Chr. Van den Born concludes that this "Midrash" was known to the Chronicler only via Kgs, which also cites it.

These source materials were largely routine office records. Aptly, D. McCarthy (*TS* 24 [1963] 560) asks "Were these inspired? One wonders just how inspiration affected a dusty chancery clerk"; but he goes on to admit that such records must have been seen to enshrine a truly theological value that today escapes us. On Paul's disdain for genealogies in 1 Tm 1:4; 4:7; Ti 3:9, G. Kittel (*ZNW* 20 [1921] 54, following L. Freund, *Fest. A. Schwarz* [1917] 163–92) holds that the genealogies of Chr were highly valued by Judaism, but could readily be misused to spin myths. If we "strive to flesh out the naked skeleton by subtle insights into lively historical implications" (Hummelauer), "the kaleidoscopic popular and historical growing-process lurking behind these countless names, flashes at times upon the attentive reader like a lightning-peal out of the dry grammatical attributes" (Goettsberger, *op. cit.*).

Brunet's explicit study of the Chronicler's use of biblical and other sources (A. Brunet, *RB* 60 [1953] 481–508; *RB* 61 [1954] 349–86) concludes that to attain his own objective, he by preference omits, suppresses, and slants, although on occasion he also adds. There is no whisper about Solomon's faults at their proper place in his narrative, although he copies out what is stated bluntly in Neh 13:25ff. There is a unity of method between the Chronicler and Sir (44–50) and Wis (10–19), both of which also respect the biblical data but reinterpret and enrich them. An indispensable tool for comparison of Chr with its parallels is Vannutelli (*op. cit.*), who gives Hebrew and Greek in adjacent columns, plus relevant Vg and Josephus. (For a new approach to the analysis of priestly and prophetic content in the Chronicler's source material, see A. Jepsen, *Quellen des Königsbuches* [2nd ed.; Halle, 1956] 106.)

Schematic arrangement of 16 1 Chr variants from Sm-Kgs is given by G. Botterweck (*TQ* 136 [1950] 402–35). Again, these are mostly the Chronicler's omissions, but the accretions seem to form a recognizable block, yet excluding the hypothesis of a third document from which the Deuteronomist and the Chronicler drew the parts they do not share, as maintained especially by H. van den Bussche (*ETL* 24 [1948] 354–94).

6 **(V) Authorship and Date.** The unity of Ezr with Chr as the architectonic concept of a single author is today upheld by as unanimous a consensus as can be found anywhere in exegesis. Actually there is little in either style or content of Ezr and Neh that can "prove" unitary authorship against a dissent like D. Freedman (*CBQ* 23 [1961] 441) or Van den Bussche (*Het Probleem van Kronieken* [Louvain, 1950] 26). Ezr and Neh are a patchwork of separate memoirs and archive scraps, but it seems likely that one would set out to redo the deuteronomic history if he had a few centuries to add. This continuity of thought is advertised by the (posthumous) repetition of 2 Chr 36:22–23 in Ezr 1:1ff. (On the unity of aim, see W. Rudolph, *VT* 4 [1954] 404.)

Freedman dates Chr (apart from Ezr) in 515; it cannot be dated earlier than the deuteronomic history on which it draws, and which itself extends to 587. Ezr brings us near 400, and W. F. Albright maintains that Ezra himself wrote Chr shortly after that time. It is intriguing and seldom remarked that he puts forward this deliberate overturning of the admitted immemorial tradition linking Ezra with P rather than with the Chronicler (*JBL* 40 [1921] 123), dating Ezr to 398, a position he later abandoned (*BA* 9 [1946]). But A. Brunet (*VDBS* 6 [1960] 1228) amasses Jewish and other traditions equating Ezra with the Chronicler, although he refrains from taking issue. A date near 400 is accepted also by Rudolph, who rejects however, the identification with Ezra (also, varyingly, Rothstein, Van Selms, Eissfeldt).

An indication of the latest date at which the entire complex could have been written is its momentous silence about the Hellenizing of Judaism after Alexander. Hence, many commentators reasonably assert a date near 300: De Vaux, Van den Born, Galling, Kittel, Curtis, Robert. Gelin and Kuhl favor 325. Bowman and Bentzen prefer 360. This dating horizon allows time for the process of alteration and accretion that is clearly evidenced within our text. But for the eight generations after Zerubbabel recorded in 1 Chr 3:19–24, the time before 300 is too short. A date after 160 is admitted by Lods, Bousset, and Kennett, if we take in stride that the Chronicler should have kept silence about the Maccabean revolution going on about him. Much more tenable is the position of those who believe he could have been silent about Hellenism only before 200: Pfeiffer, Torrey, Goettsberger, Noordtzij, Noth, Cazelles, Bückers, Arnaldich.

Two dates are thus favored: *ca.* 400 and *ca.* 200. But when we examine them in detail, we find these extremes to be based on strangely identical reasoning. The solid core of Chr-Ezr, whether we call it source material or First Chronicler, exhibits a maximum conservatism and unawareness of Seleucid era developments. But to this core everyone admits noteworthy additions. Some exercise their ingenuity in isolating a complete block or actually a book which they call the Second Chronicler, consisting of the whole genealogical vestibule of 1 Chr 1–9 plus long cognate passages from throughout the work (Hänel, Welch). Their ingenuity helps more moderate scholars to recognize the fact of extensive accretion, even though common sense appraisal of the text disinclines them to postulate a single block of interpolated material, or even a single interpolator or time. What we can call the Second Chronicler must really represent a continuing series of recombinations and adaptations from 400 to 170, or even later. Browne's emphasis on the silence about Alexandrinism does not prevent him from postulating minor redactional insertions, which could just as well have been made after Daniel (160), whom he regards as a predecessor of the Chronicler.

There is fairly general agreement that the Chronicler was a Levite cantor (Rehm). Levites are mentioned 100 times in Chr, plus 60 times in Ezr and Neh, as against once in Kgs and twice in Sm! The Chronicler's mention of the priesthood is by contrast uniformly belittling; he plainly takes as something personal the fact that cultic functionaries, who do so little, should be rewarded in every way more than the Levites and choir, who do so much.

7 **(VI) Canon.** Chr was the last book to be received in the Hebr canon, as is dramatized by its place in the MT. Ezr is placed earlier, recognizably because it had been noticed to deal with important centuries of salvation-history not otherwise represented in the Bible (see T. Denter, *Stellung Esdras im Kanon* [Marienstatt, 1964]; Pfeiffer, *IDB*, 498; P. Katz, *ZNW* 47 [1956] 204). Since the LXX preserves the natural order of Chr before Ezr (although with the embarrassing intrusion of apocryphal Esdras A), we may suppose that the Chronicler's history had been accepted as a whole into the Alexandrian canon, perhaps even before Jerusalem accepted a part of it (see A. Sundberg, "The Old Testament of the Early Church," *HTR* 51 [1958] 205–26). (→ Apocrypha, 68:38–41.)

Doubtless in coherence with the Alexandrian situation, the Christian Church never showed the slightest hesitation about the canonicity of Chr-Ezr, even favoring apocryphal Ezra literature (→ Apocrypha, 68:38). The Chronicler is never cited formally in the NT, but 2 Chr 24:21 or 36:16 may account for Mt 23:35 on the death of Zechariah. Other echoes alleged by Cazelles are far from obvious, and countered by alternatives for every case by Van den Born. The genealogies of Jesus, and especially their theological rather than merely biological perspective, echo the Chronicler's viewpoint.

Paradoxically, this dull and forgotten book, on which no Church Father ever commented (except Theodoret), contributed more than its share to the Christian liturgy. Cathedral dedication enshrines 2 Chr 7:1–16 and 1 Chr 29:17ff. Monday Lauds give the Song of David from 1 Chr 29:10–13. From Chr are adapted antiphons of Christmas, Trinity, Angels, the third Sunday after Easter, and the third and sixth Sundays after Pentecost. Passages from Neh occur on September Ember Wednesday and as Philip's introit; Ezr is not used.

8 **(VII) Theology.** We have defended (R. North, *JBL* 82 [1963] 378) the view that the Chronicler wrote entirely to vindicate the superior definitiveness of David's covenant over that of Sinai. Thus, his major theme is a heightening of the royal messianism already dominant in the Deuteronomist (Sm-Kgs) and in Ps, as analyzed by J. L. McKenzie (*TS* 8 [1947] 187–218; *CBQ* 19 [1957] 46–50). The Chronicler truly awaits a future (eschatological) fulfillment of the Davidic promise, although we have noted above that he exhibits an almost terminal complacency about the existing Davidic leaders, in order to preclude abandonment of the dynastic hope because of their shortcomings (cf. R. North, *CBQ* 28 [1966] 519).

The Chronicler's teaching about God is neither anthropomorphic like the Yahwist's, nor abstract like the Thomist's. Rather it is ethically based upon known existing duties and the reasons discerned behind them. Community genealogies must be carefully kept because by them human activities are channeled and perpetuated according to God's will. From the Deuteronomist, the Chronicler adopted the notion of short-range rewards and punishments for the fulfillment of man's part of the bargain with God. The more closely some men are associated with God in theocratic rule, the more their experience must exhibit that crime does not pay.

Ritual, as practiced currently and as enshrined in the sacred scrolls of the past, is the object of the Chronicler's most tender concern and perhaps also his most alive message for our century. He seems to be a Levite chorister vindicating and promoting a *status quo* from which he derives returns in both prestige and standard of living. To this extent, his recorded efforts can serve as a Kierkegaardian examination of conscience for the clergy of today. But behind his naïve self-seeking can be detected basic values that he sincerely strove to perpetuate: the need human nature feels for a cult that is aesthetic, vocal, and conservative; the ideal of social justice, that workers even in the sanctuary should be remunerated in accord with their realistic output. An eloquent Cazelles (*op. cit.*) shows how the Chronicler's rubricalism is not sterile but enriched by appreciation for every zone of God's revealed Word—wisdom and prophets as well as torah and psalms: "Ultimately it is because certain people have a highly developed feel for what concerns God that they receive the functions of Levites (2 Chr 30:22)... who penetrate into the divine decisions...will live forever and lead others to justice (Dn 12:3)."

9 **(VIII) Outline.** The outline for 1–2 Chr follows:

(I) Threshold Genealogies (1 Chr 1:1–9:44)
- (A) The Semites in the Family of Nations (1:1–27)
- (B) Israel's Affinities via Abraham (1:28–54)
- (C) The Twelve Tribes (2:1–7:40)
  - (a) Judah's Line (2:1–4:23)
    - (i) Judah to Jesse (2:3–13)
    - (ii) Household of Jesse (2:13–17)
    - (iii) First alternative Caleb saga (2:18–24)
    - (iv) Origins of Elishama from Jerahmeel and Egypt (2:25–41)
    - (v) Two variant Caleb sagas (2:42–55)
    - (vi) David's own line (3:1–24)
    - (vii) Three more Caleb sagas (4:1–23)
  - (b) Remainder of the South(east) Amphictyony (4:24–5:26)
    - (i) Simeon (4:24–43)
    - (ii) Reuben (5:1–10)
    - (iii) Gad (5:11–22)
    - (iv) East Manasseh (5:23–26)
  - (c) The Levites (6:1–81) (MT 5:27–6:66)
    - (i) The Moses and Samuel problems (6:1–30) (MT 5:27–41)
    - (ii) Lineage of the Levite choir (6:31–48)
    - (iii) Zadokite legitimacy (6:49–53)
    - (iv) The Levite settlements (6:54–81)
  - (d) Davidic Contingents from the Northern Tribes (7:1–40)
- (D) Proximate Setting for David's Rise (8:1–9:44)
  - (a) The Benjaminite Background of Saul (8:1–40)
  - (b) Ethnic Status of Jerusalem (9:1–44)

(II) The Empire of David (1 Chr 10:1–29:30)
- (A) Legitimacy of the Succession (10:1–11:9)
- (B) David's Militia (11:10–12:40)
- (C) Theocratic Consolidation (13:1–17:27)
  - (a) Recovery of the Ark (13:1–14)
  - (b) Building Up the House of David (14:1–17)
  - (c) Inauguration of the Davidic Tabernacle (15:1–16:43)
  - (d) The Temple Project Deferred (17:1–27)
- (D) Militaristic Empire Building (18:1–21:7)
  - (a) East Jordan Campaigns (18:2–20:2)
  - (b) Philistine Episodes (20:3–8)
  - (c) The Fateful Census (21:1–7)
- (E) David's Temple Project Under Way (21:8–29:30)
  - (a) Religious Import of the Census (21:8–22:1)
  - (b) David's Blueprints (22:2–19)
  - (c) Personnel Lineup (23:1–27:34)
  - (d) David's Entailed Abdication (28:1–29:30)

(III) Solomon's Reign (2 Chr 1:1–9:31)
- (A) The Inauguration at Gibeon (1:1–17)
- (B) The Temple (2:1–7:22)
  - (a) Letting the Contracts (2:1–18)
  - (b) The Building and Its Measurements (3:1–17)
  - (c) Minor Furnishings (4:1–22)
  - (d) Enthronement of the Ark (5:1–10)
  - (e) The Dedication Ceremony (5:11–7:7)
- (C) Solomon's Civil Rule (8:1–9:31)
  - (a) Commerce and Urban Renewal (8:1–10)
  - (b) Domestic Moral Issues (8:11–16)
  - (c) The Fleet and Its Fringe Benefits (8:17–9:31)

(IV) The Kings of Judah-Without-Israel (2 Chr 10:1–36:23)
- (A) The First Israelite Dynasty (10:1–16:14)
  - (a) Rehoboam Causes Trouble (10:1–12:16)
  - (b) The End of Jeroboam (13:1–22)
  - (c) Asa Outlives the Jeroboam Dynasty (14:1–16:14)
- (B) The Century of Social Unrest (17:1–25:28)
  - (a) Jehoshaphat (873–849) (17:1–20:37)
  - (b) Athaliah (849–837) (21:1–23:21)
  - (c) Joash (837–800) and Amaziah (800–783) (24:1–25:28)
- (C) The Rise of Book Prophecy (26:1–32:33)
  - (a) Uzziah's Building Activities and Leprosy (26:1–23)
  - (b) Isaiah's Royal Antagonists (27:1–28:27)
  - (c) Hezekiah's Ecumenical Movement (29:1–32:33)
- (D) Judah's Disillusionment (33:1–36:23)
  - (a) Not-So-Wicked Manasseh (33:1–25)
  - (b) Josiah (34:1–35:27)
  - (c) The Babylonian Puppets (36:1–23)

COMMENTARY ON 1 CHRONICLES

10 **(I) Threshold Genealogies (1 Chr 1:1–9:44).** The Christian will value these chapters as a basis and foreshadowing of those genealogies of Jesus, Son of David, that figure so prominently in Mt and Lk. The Chronicler's title for these pages is really (from 9:1) "genealogical records of all Israel from the Book of the Kings of Israel." Monotony and inconsistencies of this literary form must not blind a modern reader to its indispensable role, replaced nowadays by parish and civil record offices, in vindicating legitimacy of both family and function (North, *JBL* 82 [1963] 70).

The Chronicler also attains indirectly a more cherished objective. By eliminating all narrative from the history of mankind since Adam, he imposes the impression that it was all a rather unimportant preliminary to David. The covenants of Noah, Abraham, Shechem, and especially Sinai, are played down. What is disapproved is not these theophanies themselves, but a popular absorption in them out of proportion to the now pre-eminent ascendancy of the Davidic line. To this extent those covenants are presumed by the Chronicler. To regard the whole of chs. 1–9 as a later addition would be to misconceive his aim.

11 **(A) The Semites in the Family of Nations (1:1–27).** **5.** This classification, borrowed by the Chronicler from some compilation older than the P document of Gn (5:1), is based on purely experiential appearances, as when we say "the sun rises." The norm is not really geographical adjacence. Sidon is made a descendant of Egypt, with which it was linked commercially by sea. Canaan, too, is identified with Egypt, doubtless because of the hegemony Egypt had had there. The assertion of such relationships via a common father will not surprise us when we reflect that a town can be named as father of an individual or of another town (2:50; see J. Simons, *OTS* 10 [1954] 155).

12 **(B) Israel's Affinities via Abraham (1:28–54).** **32.** In so brief a "world-history," the Chronicler allots considerable space to the off line of Abraham. His intention seems to be to clarify for 3rd-cent. readers the bonds of proximity and enmity "uniting" Arabs, Nabateans, Edom-Seir, Midian, and Cain (see comment on 2:3,55; Gn 25:4,13; 36:9; W. F. Albright, *Fest. A. Alt* [Tübingen, 1953] 1–12).

(C) The Twelve Tribes (2:1–7:40).

13 (a) Judah's Line (2:1–4:23). **1.** The Chronicler throughout calls Jacob by his community name, Israel, perhaps to avoid recalling the lusty pranks of Gn 25:26,33; 27:24; 29:25; 30:37. Jacob's sons are given as in Gn 35:23ff., but without the intricacies of their four mothers amplified in Gn 29–30. Dan should be with Naphtali; but 17 different sequences of the 12 sons are found in the Bible, or 20 when we include *Jub* and Philo.

(i) *Judah to Jesse* (2:3–13). **3.** Among the twelve, Judah is not singled out, but he is closely associated with Levi (Temple and priesthood). Their descendants are given at greater length than for the other 11 (two replacing Joseph): Judah, 102 verses; Levi, 81; the rest, 126. Within Judah, a chaotic sequence and repetition result from preservation of every datum regarding the presence of non-Israelite tribes, such as Jerahmeel and even Cain among David's progenitors (see 2:53). The name Caleb occurs in seven separate circumstances, so interwoven that it is impossible to reduce them to even three distinct individuals: sons of Hezron, Jephunneh, and Hur. **4.** Perez is here father of Hezron; the other four sons of Judah are Er, Onan (Gn 38:8!), Shelah, and Zerah. In 4:21, the five sons of Judah are Perez, Hezron, Hur, Shobal, and Carmi (Caleb). The Chronicler thus preserves not only the real genealogy, but also a variant in which some disedifying ancestors are skipped, with the result that a brother may appear as an uncle or even a father. **5.** Hamul, also in Nm 26:21, may be a variant for Mahol of 1 Kgs 4:31, linked via Heman (1 Chr 15:17) with the origins of both wisdom and psalmody. **8.** *Chelubai:* Variant form of Caleb. "Ram as a clan parallel with the great clans of Caleb and Jerahmeel is strange, for it is not known otherwise in the Old Testament.... It may be supposed that Ram owes his position here simply to the Chronicler's desire to incorporate Ruth 4:19, where also this pedigree of David is given. Note also that in verse 25 a Ram is mentioned as a son of Jerahmeel and grandson of Hezron" (Elmslie, CBSC). *Salma:* So in Ru 4:20, but cf. Ru 4:21, Salmon.

(ii) *Household of Jesse* (2:13–17). **15.** *David the seventh:* In 1 Sm 17:12, Jesse has eight sons; David is the youngest. Since only the three oldest are there named, perhaps the Chronicler omits a fifth son who had no descendants, possibly Elihu of 1 Chr 27:18, unless this is a variant to Eliab. **17.** *Jether the Ishmaelite:* Appears in 2 Sm 17:25 as Ithra, where "Israelite" (MT) is a copyist error; Jethro is a Midianite clan name for the father-in-law of Moses (Ex 3:1; cf. W. F. Albright, *CBQ* 25 [1963] 9).

14 (iii) *First alternative Caleb saga* (2:18–24). **18.** *Azubah:* The name of this first wife means "desert waste" in Is 6:12. Caleb's second wife is Jerioth, which means "tents." If his third wife's name, Ephrath, stands for the town of Bethlehem, we may have here the record of a progressive sedentarization (Wellhausen). **19.** On Hur, see Ex 31:1. Caleb's taking his father's wife is a way of indicating the legitimate inheritance of his possessions (2 Sm 16:22; cf. C. Gordon, *RA* 50 [1956] 130). **21.** *Machir:* In Jos 14:31, it is the connecting link between the Joseph tribe Manasseh and the previous occupant of this NE Jordan area, Gilead. Linking of Caleb with Midian via Kenaz in Jos 14:6; Gn 36:15; 1 Chr 1:36; 4:13 (Jgs 3:9) is confirmed by Caleb's late-in-life "espousal" or colonization of Gilead, the refuge of Midian in Jgs 6ff. **22.** *Jair's cities:* Here, 23; in Jgs 10:3, 30 are counted, but 60 appear in Jos 13:30; 1 Chr 2:23. Geshur and Aram stand for Arabia (see comment on Neh 2:19) and Syria. **24.** Ashhur, also in 4:5, undoubtedly represents the Hur of 2:19. (Cf. R. North, "Caleb," *BeO* 8 [1966] 167.)

(iv) *Origins of Elishama from Jerahmeel and Egypt* (2:25–41). **25.** *Jerahmeel:* Here father of Ram, not his brother as in v. 9. **31.** Sheshan has a son Ahlai, but the assumption that he had no sons occasions in vv. 34–41 the pedigree of Elishama, member of a known Egyptian border family, possibly the priest of 2 Chr 17:8, whose educational and reforming activities were so congenial to the Chronicler.

15 (v) *Two variant Caleb sagas* (2:42–55). **42.** *Mareshah:* The first time the MT reads Mesha, the name of the Moabite king whose monument found at Dibon furnishes a background to his mention in 2 Kgs 3:5. The second reading is better; it is the name of the town that in Greco-Roman times supplanted Beth-gubrin near Lachish. **45.** *Beth-zur:* North of Hebron, its chief importance was the fortress of 1 Mc 6:26 (*BASOR* 150 [1958] 8). **50.** The text doubtless means "Grandsons of Caleb: first, the sons of Hur." With this we pass farther N to the region of Bethlehem. Some take this to imply pressure by tribes invading from the south, but the Chronicler's concern is simply to explain how David of Judah is so intimately linked with the non-Israelite clans around Hebron (2 Sm 2:1; 5:5). **52.** Kiriath-jearim is 12 mi. W of Jerusalem and is doubtless Baalah (see 1 Sm 7:1; *Bib* 37 [1956] 215). On the lowest slope descending W are Zorah and Eshtaol (Jgs 13:25). **53.** These may be either personal names otherwise unattested, or descriptive terms, possibly connected with music and thus with David's cult reforms (cf. 1 Chr 15–16; 25; 2 Chr 29; R. North, *JBL* 83 [1964] 377. **55.** *scribes:* "Inhabitants of scribe-city," Kiriath-sepher or Debir (Jos 15:15; 15:49; also "copper city"), equated by Albright with the Mirsim mound excavated by him (*AASOR* [1931]), but sought elsewhere by German consensus (*ZDPV* 70 [1954] 135; *ZDPV* 80 [1964] 46; → Biblical Archaeology, 74:15). *Rechab:* Cf. Jer 35:7.

(vi) *David's own line* (3:1–24). **1.** *sons of David:* Fits after 2:15. *Hebron:* The Chronicler here admits what he cautiously suppresses after ch. 10: David's seven-year wait for the northern crown (2 Sm 5:5). But the birth of Amnon, Absalom, and Adonijah at Hebron diminishes their claim to the succession, as rivals to Jerusalem-born Solomon. Bathshua (Gn 28:2) here for Bathsheba, without mention of her sin (2 Sm 11:4). **15.** Johanan did not reign. Zedekiah is given both as son (by blood) of Josiah and as legal son (successor) of his own nephew, Jeconiah. **18.** *Shenazzar:* See Ezr 1:8. **21.** The RSV prefers the LXX to the MT, making 11 instead of only 6 generations between Hananiah and Shecaniah. **22.** *six:* Thus in the MT and LXX, although both name only five.

16 (vii) *Three more Caleb sagas* (4:1–23). **1.** Continues 2:55, or rather adds further variants. Carmi, as probably also Chelub of v. 11, is to be equated with Caleb of 2:18,19. **3.** The sporty maiden name Hazzelelponi borrows its *poni* from the following name (Penuel) by dittography. **8.** *Koz:* A contemporary of Ezra (2:61). **10.** A pun, by metathesis, *'bṣ/'ṣb:* "his mother called him 'Hurts,' but God made of it 'No-Hurts' " (cf. Hos 2:8–9). **12.** *Recah:* For Rechab of 2:55, as the LXX has. **17.** *Miriam:* A strange addition to our knowledge of the heroine of Ex 15:20, with no hint that she is Moses' sister (see comment on 6:3). For this corrupt text (17–19), Van den Born reads "[Jether] fathered Miriam, Shammai, Ishbah. [Mered had two wives: one from Egypt and one from Judah.] His [Egyptian] wife bore him Jered... Jekuthiel. [17] These were the sons of Bithiah, the daughter of Pharaoh espoused by Mered. His other wife was [Hodiah, i.e., 'she of Judah'] the sister of Nacham; and her sons were fathers of [the towns] Keilah and Eshtemoa." **23.** Jerome's tendency to translate proper names may be accurate because it suggests various guilds rather than localities: e.g., potters, gardeners, smelters.

(b) Remainder of the South(east) Amphictyony (4:24–5:26).

17 (i) *Simeon* (4:24–43). **24.** The Chronicler, with Nm 26:12, overlooks the Canaanite mother of Shaul (Gn 46:10); Mibsam is an Ishmaelite in 1 Chr 1:29–30. **33.** Simeon's prominence results from his adoption into Judah (Jos 15:26; Dt 33:6 omits), hinted by recording without a genealogical connection the cities they "occupied," from Jos 19:2, "they kept their own genealogies." **41.** *Meunim:* See comment on 2 Chr 20:1. We would expect Simeon's displacement to be southwestward (Ham, Gedor, Amalekites), but Seir points us toward Ma'on near Petra in Edom.

(ii) *Reuben* (5:1–10). **2.** The Chronicler's apology for not putting the first-born first is limited to the parenthesis that from Judah came the divine leader. With a proper contempt for the schismatic north, he does not make the transfer of birthright to Joseph's sons (Gn 49:3; 48:5) the occasion for inserting their lineage among the first children. **3.** *Hezron...Carmi:* These suggest transferring to here 2:21 about Gilead, but it would constitute as many problems. **8.** *Aroer...Nebo:* The Reubenite homeland in Jos 13:16.

(iii) *Gad* (5:11–22). **11.** Breaks the pattern of taking the sons' names from Gn 46:16 or Nm 26:15. In both, the key figure is a Joel not sufficiently identified. **14.** Gilead is the tribe owning much of the territory taken over by Gad, euphemistically expressed as a marriage with Gad's daughter(s). **16.** *Bashan:* Merely a NE horizon for Gad, really occupied by E Manasseh, although all the E Jordan clan names fit further S in some variants than in others (Jos 13:30; Nm 21:13; 32:38). *Sharon:* For Mishor, the Moabite tableland, not the Jaffa Plain (cf. *Bib* 41 [1960] 50). **17.** On the compilation of this passage, here attributed to 740 BC, see H. Hänsler, *Bib* 10 [1929] 384. **18.** An expanded notice of a holy war (Von Rad, *Old Testament Theology* 1, 17), common to the three E Jordan tribes, against some descendants of Hagar, i.e., Ishmael (Jetur, Naphish, 1:31). The 44,760 is a number symbolic of Yahweh's unstayable power.

(iv) *East Manasseh* (5:23–26). **23.** Inasmuch as E Jordan possesses a natural unity, it is completed here by a nod to the only tribe not in the southern (Judean) latitude. To fill out this fragmentary list, lacking even the pivotal Machir (7:17; Jos 13:31), the Chronicler applies a moralizing summary of what befell N Israel in 2 Kgs 18:11–12. Senir is Mt. Hermon (Dt 3:9), together with the rest of Antilebanon.

(c) The Levites (6:1–81) (MT 5:27–6:66).

18 (i) *The Moses and Samuel problems* (6:1–30) (MT 5:27–41). The disparity of the MT reflects the fact that vv. 16–30 are a doublet of vv. 1–15 that either add nonpriestly branches or take up in detail a preliminary affirmation of post-exilic Jehozadak's legitimacy (see comment on Ezr 2:62). The Chronicler places his own tribe immediately after the Davidic line and its appendages.

The Levites were not segregated for priestly functions because of any peaceable unworldliness. On the contrary, Gn 49:7 sees in their "violent fury and cruel rage" the reason for their disbanding, "dispersed throughout Israel." They seem to have had liturgy thrust upon them because once their murderousness emerged when it was needed to stop the Golden-Calf abuse (Ex 32:27). There is a modern flavor, indeed, in consigning to this roughest tribe the dice or oracular devices of Jgs 18:20; Dt 33:9 (see comment on Ezr 2:63). Another factor prominent in the Levites' rise to theocratic functions seems to have been their willingness to roam from tribe to tribe (Jgs 17:9), which only a reputation for ferocity could have made safe in those days.

3. The children of Amram (from Ex 6:18; Nm 3:19) are not enumerated in 6:22, where a different Kohath genealogy is supposed. Because Miriam is called Aaron's sister while celebrating Moses' exploit (Ex 15:21), we may wonder whether this genealogy is juridical rather than biological for Moses just as for Zadok in v. 53 (L. Waterman, *JBL* 59 [1940] 397). At any rate, by suppressing any importance or exploits at all with the name of Moses or even of Aaron, the Chronicler attains negatively the main goal of his whole opus—to diminish the value of any vehicle of divine influence other than the Davidic covenant.

8. From Aaron to the Temple is exactly 12 generations, of exactly 40 years each or 480 years (as 1 Kgs 6:1). Another 12 generations of just 480 years carry us to the Second Temple (Jeshua, son of Jozadak, Ezr 3:2). This stylized symmetry is obtained by omitting Jehoiada and Uriah (2 Chr 22:11 [see 26:20 on Azariah]; 2 Kgs 16:11).

28. Samuel and his father, Elkanah *the fourth*, were not from Levi but from Ephraim (1 Sm 1:1), which can scarcely be a geographic rather than an ethnic term. Had Samuel been born a Levite, there would have been no point in his mother's conspicuous surrender of him to the sanctuary (cf. W. Baudissin, *DictB* 4, 70). This Elkanah's connection with the others in vv. 13, 25, 35 is likewise disturbing. Samuel's sons are confused and unimportant (1 Sm 8:2–3). The Chronicler seems to hold that by a revelation God has transferred the "sonship" of the high priest Eli to the non-Levite Samuel.

19 (ii) *Lineage of the Levite choir* (6:31–48). **31.** The Chronicler's own family. The three pioneers are Heman, Asaph (Pss 73–83), and Ethan, second son descendants of Levi's three sons, Kohath, Gershom, and Merari. Despite the punishment Korah underwent for defying his uncle, Aaron (Nm 16:16), he merits in v. 37 independent status as founder of the school that compiled Pss 42–49 and 84–88. The 20 generations between Heman and Izhar are really too numerous to span the 250 years from Moses to David. But to equal them, five names for Gershom and eight for Merari were here supplied beyond those in vv. 16–21. These 13 names are commonly alleged to be of post-exilic type; possibly the Chronicler merely picked out names from his own generation such as presumably had been in use in his clan in those early days, of which no records survive. Ethan is Jeduthun of 16:41 and 25:1; see 2:5.

20 (iii) *Zadokite legitimacy* (6:49–53). **53.** The NT name Sadducees means "sons of Zadok" (*CBQ* 17 [1955] 172), and already in the Chronicler's time the whole legitimacy of the incumbent priests depended upon their descent from Aaron via Zadok. The two sons of Aaron surviving the purge of Lv 10:6 were Ithamar (from whose line came Eli and Abiathar, 1 Chr 24:3,6) and Eleazar. Ahitub is given here and in v. 8 as a descendant of Eleazar-Phinehas (Nm 26:11) and as Zadok's father (also in 1 Chr 18:16; grandfather in 9:11). But the Ahitub of 2 Sm 8:17 should be rather father of Ahimelech (1 Sm 22:9), who is father of Abiathar, the Elid priest supplanted by Zadok. If this (Wellhausen) emendation is admitted, Zadok is left without genealogy. In fact, an imposing convergence of modern experts sees in Zadok some pre-Israelite priest. E. Auerbach (*ZAW* 49 [1931] 327) thinks he lived at Gibeon, which can be identified with Nob; Kiriath-jearim is suggested by K. Budde (*ZAW* 52 [1934] 42). The most plausible is H. H. Rowley's defense of Jebus (*JBL* 58 [1939] 113; *Fest. A. Bertholet* [Tübingen, 1950] 461; so also J. Morgenstern, *AJSL* 55 [1938] 11, qualified by H. Judge, *JTS* 7 [1956] 74, and by C. Hauer, *JBL* 82 [1963] 89). "King (or *melek-*) Zadok" would be like his predecessor Melchizedek, priest-king of (Jeru-) Salem, without genealogy (Heb 7:3), and worshiper of "God Most High" acknowledged by Abraham (Gn 14:18). The enigmatic features of David's seizure of the Jebus crag (2 Sm 5:8) are best understood on the basis of a secret deal made with Zadok assuring to his descendants the high priesthood, second rank in the theocracy after the king. Thus, the lineage arranged for Zadok via Eleazar is a legal adoption.

21 (iv) *The Levite settlements* (6:54–81). **54.** No landed estate was assigned to the Levites in the distribution under Moses (Nm 26:62); it was understood that they were to be supported by whatever population they were sanctifying. But the Levites' functions came to be viewed as having some natural relation to the cities of refuge, which were an earlier usage, a sort of habeas corpus to mitigate the severity of vendetta justice. The cities granted to the Levites by Jos 21 include all the "sanctuary" cities, plus, in fact, practically every metropolis in the whole of Israel except Jerusalem! Yet in none of these cities does the Bible ever show them wielding any political or economic administration. Therefore, it would seem that we have to do here with a purely prestige allotment, as when the churches of Rome are assigned to foreign cardinals, or the provinces of France to various archangels.

55. The case of Hebron was particularly unconvincing, inasmuch as this coveted city had been the occasion for the complex insertion of Caleb into the lineage of Judah. The Chronicler is aware of this inconsistency. He tries to rationalize it by giving the city itself to the priests, but to the civilians all the villages which were subject to the city (L. Delekat, *VT* 14 [1964] 19), much as in Italy's 1929 concordat with the Vatican.

22 (d) Davidic Contingents from the Northern Tribes (7:1–40). Chapter 7 no longer pursues the strictly genealogical links among David's relatives. Because the northern tribes had rebelled, the only good thing to be said about them is that they contributed to the success of David's dynasty (21:1 = 2 Sm 24:1).

1. Issachar's four sons appear as in Gn 46:13; Nm 26:23, yet, perhaps by confusion, for in Jgs 10:1, "Tola son of Puah dwelt [*yāšûb*] in Shamir"; no grandsons are indicated elsewhere. Tola's 22,600 armed descendants must obviously include those of his son Uzzi. The 36,000 then credited to Uzzi must represent a later census; even so, the figures do not total 87,000; Nm 2:6; 26:27 give different figures still.

6. "Sons of Benjamin" should be "sons of Zebulun," as in one Gk manuscript (cf. Brunet, *RB* 60, 485). Zebulun would otherwise be the only unrepresented tribe, whereas Benjamin occupies ch. 8. The names there do not correspond to these or to those in Nm 26:38 or Gn 42:21, except for a few striking cases doubtless inserted by copyists after the corrupt "Benjamin" had become part of this text. The custom of giving "biblical" names, such as those of the younger Benjaminites, originated only after 500 BC (cf. Noth, *Die israelitischen Personennamen...* [Stuttgart, 1928] 60). In Hebr writing, the first three names resemble Sered, Elon, and Jahleel. **10.** Tarshish, an epithet of boats (see 2 Chr 9:21), suggests a coastal tribe, as in Gn 49:13. Even those recent commentators who are reluctant to admit that a real Zebulun genealogy can be produced along the lines of some emendations of our actual text (Curtis and Madsen, *op. cit.*) grant that the passage that should be here has somehow been replaced.

12. "The sons of Dan: Hushim," as in Gn 46:23, must have been in place of the impossible readings Ir, Hushim, and Aher. Huppim from Nm 26:39 may be the Akkadian *hipi*, "so-and-so" (indicating a name that the scribe cannot read), especially inasmuch as Gn 46:21 has Muppim (Böhl). **13.** The sons of Naphtali (from Gn 46:24) are curtailed as badly as those of Dan. **14.** The sons of Manasseh form a geographical allegory (Van den Born). The secondary wife is Aramean, because Gilead is E, toward Aram. We thus detect that the Manasseh or Machir tribe historically advanced from Galilee eastward rather than in the reverse direction suggested by Jos 17:1. On Zelophehad's daughters, see Nm 36:2. **27.** Ephraim's most memorable descendant is Joshua. The Chronicler is determined to insert his genealogy. It has ten generations, whereas Moses is only three removes from Ephraim's peer, Kohath, in 6:3 (= Ex 6:20). Several disparities thus arise.

30. Asher, as farthest from Jerusalem, is the most nebulously portrayed of all the 12 tribes; at the same time it is the most firmly attested in occupancy of pre-exilic Canaan (Heber is perhaps an echo of the Ḫabiru). No place name is indicated; those of Jos 19:25 are without exception unidentified, for Tyre and Sidon are certainly not in Israelite territory, and Acco of Jgs 1:31 is a variant for Umma. Noth (*Das Buch Josua* [2nd ed.; Tübingen, 1953]) rightly insists that the sites could be S of Carmel as well as anywhere else. The personal names are borrowed from Gn 46:17, including the dittography of the Ishvah, not in Nm 26:44.

(D) Proximate Setting for David's Rise (8:1–9:44).

23 (a) The Benjaminite Background of Saul (8:1–40). Just as all David's connections are insistently put first, so Saul's are relegated to the last, where a curt notice of Saul's disgrace can also serve as a bridge to the narrative about David's greatness. **33.** The brother of Kish should be not Ner but Abner, Saul's uncle in 1 Sm 14:50. In 1 Sm 9:1, Ner is bypassed between Kish and Abiel, here called Abdon. **34.** Meribbaal and Ishbaal were names no longer offensive when the Chronicler wrote. During the struggle against Canaanite syncretism, the writers of 2 Sm 2:8; 4:4 changed *baal*, "Lord," to *bosheth*, "abomination."

24 (b) Ethnic Status of Jerusalem (9:1–44). **1.** The "book" is not our canonical Kgs; rather it is a title for the eight preceding chapters. "Israel" is here applied twice, chiefly to Judah. **3.** The Chronicler had carefully located Benjamin and Saul's lineage at the point most suited to leading into the narrative of David's heroism, but an editorial rereading forced an interruption at this point to correct a false impression left by 8:29. We must not imagine that the holy city was properly Benjamin's inheritance. Those of his tribe who lived there really belonged to Gibeon (v. 35). Of the tribe of Levi, the priest-choir-doorkeeper guilds loomed large in Jerusalem's population at the time of Neh 11, from which our list is largely borrowed. Of the tribe of Judah, several clans are enumerated, halfway merged with some from Ephraim and Manasseh not in Neh. But the cardinal fact, well known to the Chronicler and his readers, is that the Jebusite crag of Zion never fell within the distribution to the 12 tribes; it was first occupied by David (2 Sm 5:6–7) as an extraterritorial family fief to serve as impartial center for governing the north and south (A. Alt, *KlSchr* 2, 66–75; *KlSchr* 3, 243–57 = *TLZ* 75 [1950] 213; *ZDMG* 49 [1925] 1).

11. On Meraioth between Zadok and Ahitub, see 6:53. He is too early to be that major Zadok, and may be the 6th-cent. Amariah of 6:11. **13.** Three subtotals in Neh 11:12ff. total only 1192, here 1760—a common fate of numbers in textual transmission. **15.** Bakbakkar, Bakbukiah of Neh 11:17, is cantor, not "building supervisor." **16.** Since Jeduthun is the Ethan of 6:44; 15:17, double parts fall to Merari, whereas the Kohath-Heman line is eliminated. **22.** *Samuel:* He is put here to represent pre-Temple days, when as a child he "opened the doors of Yahweh's house" (1 Sm 3:15). **35.** Saul's line is repeated from 8:33, not only to stress its link with Gibeon, only 5 mi. from Gibeah within Benjamin, but also to cue the account of Saul's doom.

The skeleton of chs. 1–9 is the Chronicler's work, and the insertions are from varied hands, as Rudolph admits, although with Noth he adjudges to the Chronicler less of the total than seems required by the undoubted structural importance of these chapters to the plan.

(II) The Empire of David (1 Chr 10:1–29:30).

25 (A) Legitimacy of the Succession (10:1–11:9). **2.** *Saul:* Only his crimes are mentioned, especially the fact that Yahweh personally slew him (v. 14). Verse 4 clarifies that God's judgment was executed by Saul's own hand (so 1 Sm 31:5; but otherwise 2 Sm 1:10). **13.** Only by the word "unfaithfulness" is it implied that Saul indeed had a divine mission and was the foundation stone of Israelite royalty that David usurped. To show David's innocence is the burden of ch. 10. Saul sealed his own doom by consulting a witch despite his own prohibitions (1 Sm 28:9); cf. F. Vattioni, *Augustinianum* 3 (1963) 461–81. He also defied Samuel, as told ambiguously in 1 Sm 13:13; 15:10. Verse 7 insists that all Saul's line died with him, despite the seven-year resistance of Ishbosheth and the threat of Mephibosheth (2 Sm 2–3; 9:7; 16:3). The Chronicler omits the dishonoring of Saul's headless trunk by his enemies and cremation by his friends (1 Sm 31:10ff.). From this passage, the Chronicler takes over the name of a god, Dagon, but not Astarte, because she was a sex symbol. Some maintain this temple of Dagon was not in the Beth-shan enclave but near Gaza (G. Hedley, *AJA* 33 [1929] 34). J. Howlett (*Dublin Review* 126 [1900] 391) defends ch. 10 polemically against Wellhausen.

11:1–2. Repeated from 2 Sm 5:1ff., but in such a way as to imply an immediate gladsome acclaim by the elders of N Israel, instead of a humiliating capitulation after seven years. Even so, here and in 12:23,38 the Chronicler cannot fail to stress Hebron, which fits nothing in David's Bethlehem background (see comments on 2:3,50). **3.** The manner in which David was brought in line for the succession to Saul involves Samuel here and in 1 Sm 16:1, but emphatically not in the variants 1 Sm 16:18; 17:55. **5.** On Jebus as David's extraterritorial fief taken without a struggle, see 9:1; 6:53; 12:28. **6.** David's rash oath is stressed to explain how various defiances of Joab would be so long unpunished: 2 Sm 3:27–28; 14:19; 1 Kgs 1:7. **8.** Not in Sm; the MT reads, "Joab left alive the rest of the city."

26 (B) David's Militia (11:10–12:40). Here is officiously inserted what 2 Sm 23:8–39 tucks in among the "last words of David." **15.** *Adullam:* This adventure presumes the real facts about David's rise to power, from 1 Sm 22:1, curially ignored by the Chronicler. **19.** The Chronicler alters 2 Sm 23:17, "Is the blood of the men who went 'along with' their lives" to "Will I drink the blood of these men along with their lives?"; he thus recalls Gn 9:4; Lv 17:14, "life is blood." **22.** "Ariels" of RSV are lions or perhaps heroes 'of God,' a common superlative not thought blasphemous (thus in 12:22; cf. J. Smith, *AJSL* 45 [1929] 212; R. de Vaux, *Bib* 40 [1959] 499). Precisely in Palestine could a lion prowl from his jungle-heat up hillsides high enough for sudden snows. **26.** *Asahel:* His slaying will cause the Abner-Joab feud, momentous for David's rise in 2 Sm 2:32–33. On Elhanan, see 20:5. **41b.** The Chronicler here adds 16 names not found in Sm, perhaps to soften the tragic irony of Bathsheba's Uriah as "last of David's heroes" (see G. Gray, *Hebrew Proper Names* 230; K. Elliger, *PJB* 30 [1935] 29–75). C. C. Torrey (*AJSL* 25 [1909] 157–88) claims these names are of E Jordan origin (denied by B. Mazar, *VT* 13 [1963] 310).

12:1. *Ziklag:* Again presupposes anti-party line data from 1 Sm 27:5, where, however, there is no parallel to the Chronicler's lists here. They are partly a soberly historical register of David's actual bodyguard in his self-defense against Saul. Into this roster have been inserted also those feudal dignitaries who decided "soon enough" to make no last-ditch resistance to David's takeover. There is no cogent motive for assuming that this was a post-exilic Jerusalem census. **24.** The fact that there are so few from Judah cannot be ascribed to the Chronicler's here inconsistent reckoning with a prior inauguration of David as king of Judah alone, a *de facto* situation in which this whole census just does not fit. **29.** Zadok's 22 minions may reflect those of Neh 12:1. **32.** The times cultivated by Issachar were likely astrological in origin, but are here explained in relation to opportunist politics. **39.** This description may provide the suitable symbol of an eschatological banquet in the Messiah's kingdom; but for that very reason it is a common sense portrayal of what feasting would actually have surrounded David's takeover after seven years of struggle.

(C) Theocratic Consolidation (13:1–17:27).

27 (a) Recovery of the Ark (13:1–14). **1.** The Chronicler shows two major differences from 2 Sm 6. First, this exploit of piety is put ahead of every civil and military episode in David's administration. Second, there is dramatized a sort of democratic assembly (*qāhāl* occurs 37 times in original passages), at which David adroitly proposes retrieving the Ark, although 1 Sm 14:18 had already shown Saul deploying it. For David, the Ark becomes the symbol and impetus for a new style of political union for the 12 tribes (see comment on 9:3). **5.** This presumes from 2 Sm 8 the imperialistic conquests of David stretching far beyond the tribal terrain, as far NE as the Syrian desert and as far SW as the "River of Egypt." *Shihor:* The "stream of Horus" is really the Nile, but here understood rather of Wadi Arish. **6.** *Baalah:* Kiriath-jearim (see 2:53 and M. Gichon, *PEQ* 95 [1963] 113). **8.** *before God:* The Chronicler changes *yhwh* of 2 Sm 6:5 to *hā'ĕlōhîm*, as he does frequently but capriciously (Rudolph, *op. cit.*, xviii; F. Baumgärtel, *Elohim* [1914] 68). Further divergences from the vocabulary of Sm are stylistic, and do not warrant ascribing to the Chronicler theological or ideological aims. **14.** Fetching the Ark results in disaster, as in 2 Sm 6:7; but the experience of Beth-shemesh in 1 Sm 6:19 is so similar as perhaps to suggest that this is a literary convention. The disaster is made the occasion for interrupting David's theocratic maneuvers for several months. The Chronicler utilizes this interval to insert what he had skipped from 2 Sm 5:11–25.

28 (b) Building Up the House of David (14:1–17). Foreign affairs and maneuvers of diplomacy are the real issues in these apparently domestic scenes. **1.** Hiram's embassy is portrayed as an unsolicited prestige gesture, as in 2 Sm 5:11, but it undoubtedly represents David's concern to cement the benevolent neutrality of his more unbeatable neighbors by extending them commercial opportunities. **2.** Again, the multiplying of wives is not merely tolerated by the Chronicler in view of the solidity it gave to the house of David as a dynasty; the Hebron brood is skipped, and disproportionate attention is paid to Solomon (see comment on 3:5) with no hint that his inclusion results from the least tolerable member of the harem. Really important in these matrimonial alliances is their diplomatic bind. Taking the king's wife from among daughters of neighboring chiefs meant simultaneously a compliment to entice their cooperation and a hostage to prevent their opposition. **8.** With the peaceful building of his new Jerusalem fief, David had to take warlike measures against his former allies. As in 2 Sm 5:19, this activity is portrayed as a crusade, almost as a ritual. **10.** The first *yhwh* of 2 Sm 5:19 is changed to *'ĕlōhîm*, as in vv. 11 and 14ff.; but the second is left unchanged, as in v. 2. **17.** The Chronicler also adds an independent reflection, softening by anticipation the bloody deeds in 18:5; 22:8.

29 (c) Inauguration of the Davidic Tabernacle (15:1–16:43). The Chronicler suppresses the suggestion of 2 Sm 6:12 that David set about securing the Ark because it brought blessings to its possessor. In its place, he introduces an entirely original emphasis on the tent, set up by David in imitation and continuance of the desert situation (Nm 1:50). The Mosaic ritual has not been hitherto acknowledged by the Chronicler as preferred by Yahweh; cf. 2:16. **11.** *Abiathar:* Reference to the two priests is inopportune here and in v. 14, and may be a gloss. **13.** The MT does not make so explicit that the Chronicler feels disaster befell the moving of the Ark because the bearers were not Levites.

16. On the importance of this passage and 25:1 for the history of Second Temple cult singers, see H. Gese, *Fest. O. Michel* (Leiden, 1963) 226–34. **20–21.** Alamoth, "girls," may mean soprano, and Sheminith, "octave" or "bass"; there are similar choir directions in the titles of the psalms.

25. From here to 16:3 the account of 2 Sm 6:12–19 is interpolated almost verbatim (J. McKenzie, *Bib* 40 [1959] 522), but the dramatizing of Michal's contempt in 2 Sm 6:20ff. (and David's nakedness—A. van Selms, *Hervormde Teologiese Studies* 4 [1948] 135) is replaced by the lengthy Levitical thanksgiving of 1 Chr 16. It is made up of Pss 96:1–13; 105:1–15; 106:1,47–48. However, references to the Temple and Diaspora are suppressed in 1 Chr 16:27ff.,35. In 16:13,16, Isaac and Jacob are mentioned and Abraham occurs twice, but the name Moses does not appear.

16:3. On "meat" as date cake, see L. Koehler, *TZ* 4 (1948) 397. **37.** The Ark, attended by Obed-edom (now promoted to Levite status, as in 15:24) and Asaph, is left within the tent that David prepared for it in v. 1. This tent is thus distinguished from the one at Gibeon in v. 29, founded by Moses (21:29), and henceforth attended by Zadok, Heman, and Jeduthun. **41.** It will still serve royal cult after David's death. Intensive recent research aims to show that the Ark and the tent were originally autonomous cult objects, unconnected until harmonized by P (cf. Noth, *US* 137, 170; see comment on 2 Chr 5:10).

30 (d) The Temple Project Deferred (17:1–27). For the Chronicler, David is author of the Temple and of all its ritual. Hence, a high point of his art and skill consists in inserting into his framework the momentous oracle that simultaneously predicts the stability of the messianic line and prohibits the Temple project to David. Searching comparison with the parallels in Ps 89 as well as 2 Sm 7 reveals that the Chronicler may preserve the primitive form of the oracle (Van den Bussche, *ETL* 24 [1948] 354–94; McKenzie, *CBQ* 19 [1957] 46–50; *TS* 8 [1947] 187–218; M. Tsevat, *HUCA* 34 [1963] 71–82). In v. 1 occurs the covenant name *yhwh* instead of Sm *'ĕlōhîm*; in v. 13, the promise to David is unconditioned.

1. David's proposal follows immediately his installation of the Ark in its provisional pavilion; the Chronicler omits "Yahweh had given him rest from all his enemies round about," which nevertheless is implicit in v. 8 and in chs. 18–20. **4b.** *you shall not build the house:* Implies that the essentials of the project are approved (Sm has "a house"). In 21:1 the initiative for the census comes not from David but from Satan (Yahweh's agent in Jb 1:1), and direct from Yahweh is the command that David should build an altar on the Temple site (21:18). **17.** This may mean that God has shown David generations to come; S. Marenof (*AJSL* 53 [1936] 47) reads *ktwr* as *k^{e}rā'ôt*, you have looked upon me as a man looks [upon his friend]." **23.** The humility of David's prayer, exactly as in Sm, now fits perfectly the acceptance of God's "minor" revisions for the Temple project.

(D) Militaristic Empire Building (18:1–21:7).

31 (a) East Jordan Campaigns (18:2–20:2). **2.** The Chronicler omits from 2 Sm 8:2 the savage and humiliating reprisals of David against Moab, his loyal ally in 1 Sm 22:3. **5.** The number of slain Syrians—22,000—may be a hyperbole, but its retention by the Chronicler (if, indeed, he recognizes the ferocity it implies) may vouch for its reliability. **9.** Because Hamath remains outside David's jurisdiction, the northern limit of his empire probably was near Emesa (modern Homs), which could be said vaguely to include as far E as the Euphrates, because everything between was desert except Palmyra (see comment on 2 Chr 8:4). **12.** The death of 18,000 Edomites is charged to David only indirectly in v. 13. It is credited to Joab instead of Abishai in Ps 60:1. **14–15.** This follows 2 Sm 8:15, not its doublet, 20:23. But the Chronicler does not provide that base in the context which is afforded by 2 Sm 9:1. **16.** On Zadok's parentage and the Abimelech of the MT, see comment on 6:53. **17.** David's sons also were priests in 2 Sm 8:18, but the LXX there and the Chronicler here change it to officials. *Cherethites:* These are from Crete, an Aegean people closely associated, but not identical, with Philistines (= Pelethites?). The Egyptian name for Crete was Keftiu (biblical Caphtor) until the Amarna age, 1370 BC, after which time the name was applied to Cilicia (cf. J. Prignaud, *RB* 71 [1964] 215–29). Cherethite and Pelethite had meanwhile become (like Janissary) generalized terms for bodyguard. The Chronicler skips entirely the information about Meribbaal (Mephibosheth) in 2 Sm 9:7, for although it emphasizes David's kindness, it also stresses that there were survivors of Saul with more legitimate claim to the throne (see comment on 10:6;

see 2 Sm 16:3). The Chronicler also suppresses the dramatic story of Rizpah's nonviolent resistance to the bloodthirsty revenge that David allowed the Gibeonites, as well as the weakness of the aging David that induced his staff never to let him take the field again (2 Sm 21:1–17). Ps 18, which is inserted in 2 Sm 22, and a similar psalm in 2 Sm 23:1–7, are not taken over by the Chronicler because they are full of allusions to David resisting Saul. The rest of 2 Sm 23 was already in 1 Chr 11:10.

19:1. Ammon is the modern Amman, capital of Jordan. The most conspicuous feature of its siege in ch. 19 is the omission of everything about Bathsheba, unquestionably a whitewashing of the David who was great in God's plan with his faults, although W. Stinespring (OAB) interprets rather "the new David in the new age would certainly not be guilty of such conduct, nor would a prophet have occasion to rebuke him." **2.** David's protestation of loyalty to Nahash belies his concern for Saul's posthumous honor in 2 Sm 1:17, because the rescuers of Saul's body in 1 Sm 31:11 are the same Jabesh-gileadites who in 1 Sm 11:1,11 were defended by Saul against Nahash and Ammon. **6.** *Mesopotamia:* In the MT, "Aram-naharaim," but in 2 Sm 10:6, "Aram-rehob" (see A. Malamat, *BA* 21 [1959] 96–102). **7.** *Medeba:* Perhaps for "waters of (*mê-*) Rabbah," a name for the capital of Ammon. **16.** This verse leads us to suspect that David's dealings with Ammon were a real provocation, for their suppression was essential to the completeness of his Syrian campaign. **18.** David kills 50,000 more Syrians helping Ammon.

20:2. *their king:* This name should rather be Milcom, the Ammonite god in 1 Kgs 11:5. The Chronicler can rejoice that David's bloodshed at least diverted treasures from pagan to Israelite cult.

32 (b) Philistine Episodes (20:3–8). **3.** The peculiar remarks of 20:3 (from 2 Sm 12:30–31) are followed by a leap to the subject matter of 2 Sm 21:18. The intervening epic of the Amnon-Absalom threat to Solomon's succession is relentlessly suppressed, perhaps because the real guilt is seen there to lie with David's senile indecisiveness. **5.** The exploit of the Bethlehemite Elhanan, son of Jair, was the slaying of the giant Goliath of Gath, according to 2 Sm 21:19. This undoubtedly genuine historical kernel is amplified and credited to the Bethlehemite David in 1 Sm 17. In almost all histories, even today, a literary convention ascribes to the reigning monarch politically important decisions or achievements of subjects. That this really happened here is best proved by the uniform disquiet of text transmitters at the real facts thus leaking out: the LXX substitutes "Godoliah the Hittite" for Goliath of Gath; the Vg follows the Targum in translating Elhanan and Jair as epithets of David, "God's [merciful] gift; son of 'the forest' [or, as the Targum alternatively renders *yā'îr* 'waking up in the middle of the night']." But most audaciously of all, the Chronicler here makes (Beth-)Lehemi(te) the object of Elhanan's slaying and then calls him the brother of Goliath, whom David slew. His inerrant assertion would thus seem to be, "Let there be no doubt that it is legitimate to credit Goliath's slaying to the ruler David."

33 (c) The Fateful Census (21:1–7). Coming immediately after various military exploits and statistics, this event at least begins as an apparent cog in the Chronicler's brief acknowledgment of David's secular activities. In 2 Sm 24, it is set off as an isolated cultic episode between the long digression of 2 Sm 23 and David's end. **1.** *Satan:* In Chr, the instrument of what 2 Sm 24:1 calls Yahweh's own vexed incitement of David to a census. We may agree that for the D editor of Sm, God is unquestionably angry and incites man to sin; this is merely a graphic description of the fact that God respects man's free will and co-operates in implementing it even when it is against his own interests and those of the man. Thus, in a sense, God "hands him over to the power of evil." But the alteration introduced by the Chronicler is in itself no more than an application of Jb 2:6. What God (or any ruler) is popularly said to do directly, may more accurately be attributed to the subordinate officials who normally serve that purpose.

In Jb and Zech 3:1, Satan is the name of an official of Yahweh's court, charged with testing the virtue of the just. The name means "adversary," and the function corresponds remarkably to what is now called "devil's advocate." In Nm 22:22, Satan is called a messenger (*mal'āk*, "angel"). Only with Ap 12:9; 20:2 is the name given to "the slanderer" (*diabolos*, "devil"), who is then further identified with the serpent (Gn 3:15; Wis 2:24; Jn 8:44), and with the chief angel defeated in a battle (cf. Lk 10:18) against Michael, according to apocryphal literature. The name Lucifer in 2 Pt 1:19 means something else.

(Brock-Utne, A., *Klio* 28 [1935] 219. Kaupel, H., *Dämonen im Alten Testament* [Augsburg, 1930] 122. Kelly, H., *CBQ* 26 [1964] 190–220; *Thought* 40 [1965] 165–94. Randellini, L., *BeO* 5 [1963] 127–32.)

Any census project, even that commanded by God in Ex 30:12, seems in the Bible to be considered immoral or irritating to Yahweh. Perhaps it represented a shift in war techniques from reliance on the war-god to taking efficient inventory of human resources; perhaps it was untrustfully intended to discover if God had been keeping his promise to multiply Abraham's seed. Or, perhaps "the watched pot never boils"—i.e., counting one's blessings arrests them—or David intended an aggressive war (Hummelauer) even against the northern tribes (so, implausibly, J. Schäfers, *Katholik* 88 [1908] 128). **2.** The Chronicler significantly suppresses the phrase of 2 Sm 24:1 "and Judah." Yet, he also inverts "from Beer-sheba to Dan," on the assumption that Joab would begin nearest to Jerusalem, including Judah. **3.** Joab incriminates David far more outspokenly than in 2 Sm 24:3. **6.** In the Chronicler's view, Levi is not numbered (until 23:24!), but if Judah were, then why not Benjamin? Perhaps it is because of Gibeon in v. 29, but surely it is neither out of respect for Saul nor on the assumption that the Jebusite Zion enclave belonged to Benjamin any more than to Judah. The total of 1,300,000 draftees for Israel plus Judah (2 Sm 24:9) is cut (by an arbitrary 100,000 each for Levi and Benjamin) to 1,100,000 here; however, by oversight, the Chronicler adds to this the Sm figure for Judah (inexplicably curtailed by 30,000). In either case, we must regard the numbers as symbolical, for the total population, including the nonmobilized, would have had to be an improbable 6 million, apart from the Canaanite "hewers" (22:2; Jos 9:27).

(E) David's Temple Project Under Way (21:8–29:30).

34 (a) Religious Import of the Census (21:8–22:1). Nothing in Sm or Kgs links organically the hybris of David's census with the reopening and definitive localization of his Temple project. The Chronicler narrates the stages of David's punishment in terms so identical with 2 Sm 24 that we hardly notice the radical alteration of perspective that his six emendations effect. With a kind of unconscious art, the Chronicler has begun by seeming to heighten David's mad guilt with the intrusion of Satan and Joab's outburst. But we will gradually be made to feel that David was the unresisting pawn of forces pushing him toward God's goal.

12. This verse anticipates and subsequently dramatizes the "angel," appearing in only one passage of 2 Sm

(24:16–17). This angel is not a "mode of divine presence" as that in Gn 32:31 and elsewhere, but is in dialogue with Yahweh; he hovers "in the air" (v. 16; cf. T. Rosmarin, *JBL* 51 [1932] 71), is furnished with a drawn sword, and is seen by the Jebusite of v. 20 as well as by David. The Gk *angelos* was chosen to render the Hebr *mal'āk*, defined as "messenger" but implying rather "tool" or "executor of a task," as a sort of "demiurge." It is preferred by E to Yahweh's direct anthropomorphic action in J, but it is avoided by D and P; only with Dn 8:16; 12:6 is it called a "heavenly" being, under Persian influence.

15. *Ornan:* It is *K^{e}tîb* in 2 Sm 24:15 for consonantal Araunah, a Hurrian name, but not of the god Varuna as B. Mazar (*BIES* 13 [1947] 112) and M. Goldman (*AusBR* 1 [1951] 138) hold, and not a Jebusite king, as S. Yeivin thinks (*VT* 3 [1953] 149). See comment on 2 Chr 3:2. **22.** David's negotiation is glamorized by borrowings from Gn 23:9. The 50 silver shekel price of 2 Sm 24:24, for what had become by this time one of the world's major real estate parcels, is interpreted as gold and 50 per tribe—a way of saying "priceless"! **26.** The sacrifice ratified by fire from heaven as in 1 Kgs 18:37 is an addition to 2 Sm 24:25, shrewdly calculated to leave as a major total impression that God is well pleased with David.

22:1. This verse is an intentional echo of Gn 28:17 "not at Bethel [house of El] or anywhere in Samaria but here shall be the House of Yahweh." House of God is the only Hebr word used for the Jerusalem Temple; its reference here is unmistakable. By launching immediately into an account of the Temple contracts, the Chronicler introduces a noticeably different interpretation from 2 Sm 24:30, where the aversion of the plague is followed by David's senility and peaceful death.

35 (b) David's Blueprints (22:2–19). For the Chronicler, David made all the decisions regarding the building of the Temple; the initialing of its documents by the little prince was a mere technicality. **2.** In 1 Kgs 5:1, these negotiations are handled by Solomon only after David's abdication, and 1 Kgs 5:31ff. specifies that although the stone quarrying was done by Canaanites (*gēr*, "resident minority," rather than "alien"), a levy of Israelite forced labor was needed to keep the timber moving from the northern borders. **5.** Solomon's age at his accession is unattested; Rashi guessed 12 and Josephus suggested 14 (*Ant.* 8.7, 8 § 211). E. Nestle hypothesized 20 (*ZAW* 2 [1882] 312) and recent experts believe the figure is nearer 40. **7.** David's deathbed bequest to Solomon in 1 Kgs 2:3, expurgated of the vicious vendettas by which it is accompanied, is expanded by elements from 2 Sm 7:13ff. into a *status quo* for authorship of the Temple. Here David dwells with a certain complacency on all the blood he shed for the Lord, incurring thereby a purely technical irregularity as in the pious burial of one's own father (Nm 19:11; Lv 21:11); at worst, David is no less responsible for the Temple than is Moses for the takeover of the promised land; in each case, the final step is left to a successor. **9.** By a double pun on the name Solomon—*š^{e}lōm-ô*, "his peace" and (Jeru-)Šalem—David reduces to mere nominalism the fitness of his son to take responsibility for the building. We do know that Solomon waged one war, paradoxically attested only in 2 Chr 8:17. **14.** "With great pains" is no word for it! The world's total annual production of gold in 1965 amounted to only one-sixth of the 5000 tons here stipulated (see R. North, "Weights" in the second edition of *CCHS*). In 1 Chr 29:4, only 3 per cent of this amount is envisioned, and in Ezr 2:69; 8:26, only 1 per cent. The Chronicler's assertion here, as in 21:25, is simply, "that the Temple is an art treasure the value of which is beyond any figure you could bid." **17.** The help that David orders his officials to give to the nominal builder of the Temple amounts to that which executors are expected to give to the wayward heir of an entailed estate: Protect him from himself if he tries to use my money for anything I wouldn't want it used for!

36 (c) Personnel Lineup (23:1–27:34). De Vaux's chapter on "The Levites in the Work of the Chronicler" (1 Chr 1–9, 23–27) opens with these important observations:

> What makes it difficult is that the author ascribes to ancient times situations and ideas which were unheard of until much later. Indeed, he includes ideas from his own day, and ascribes them to ancient times; to make it worse, the annotators of his work have added ideas and customs from their day too, and backdated them as well.... The theory of the original Chronicler (15:2) was that the Levites were primarily meant for the service of the Ark.... This idea does not originate from the Priestly tradition, for in this the Levites are connected with the Tent (Nm 1:50; 3:8); its source is Deuteronomy (10:8), to which 1 Chr 15:2 certainly refers.... Once the Ark had been laid to rest... the Levites had no more work to do as porters. David set some of them apart for choral service.... Indeed, one of the dominant features of the Chronicler is this interest in sacred music.... The later additions to the book are meant to show the legitimacy of the institution of singers, and to give a more exact definition of their rights.... Only a relatively small proportion of them were musicians.... Their work touches on the domain reserved to the priests, and there must have been conflicts, though they are not mentioned explicitly in Chronicles.... The Levites were also teachers (2 Chr 17:8; 35:3; Neh 8:7ff.).... They continued their intrigues to the end [*Jub; T. Levi*]; some years before the ruin of the Temple, the singers persuaded Agrippa II to let them wear linen vestments, as the priests did, and the other Levites who served in the Temple were all promoted to the rank of singers (Josephus, *Ant.* 20.9, 6) (De Vaux, *AI* 390–94).

De Vaux regards chs. 23–27, as well as chs. 1–9, as later additions. Many recent experts would concur with this judgment, and all would admit that at least considerable portions of these chapters are subsequent insertions. However, the position of some top exegetes today is rather that a certain skeleton of these chapters is essential to the Chronicler's outlook; only with some diffidence can we date specific verses or paragraphs to later interpolators, themselves of various strata. The attribution of sacred chant to David may be no invention, but a reflection of the distressing fact that he descended from Cain's tribe, in which the Bible insistently portrays the development of music (see North, *JBL* 83 [1964] 373).

3. *thirty:* It is the age of service, as in Nm 4:3, but it is reduced to 20 in v. 27, as in Nm 8:24, and it is only 20 in 2 Chr 31:17 (Ezr 3:8) as for the non-Levites in Nm 1:3. Plainly a growing need, or rather a decrease in unemployment, dictated progressively lowering the age, so that even within this chapter we do not have the latest insertions. (For a further intriguing vagary in assigning age to liturgical assignments, see R. North, *Bib* 39 [1958] 90, regarding Y. Yadin's edition of 1QM 2:4ff. and 7:1.) **4.** *officials:* "dates from when the Levites were still priests, Ex 22:9" (Van den Born, *op. cit.;* on the term, see J. van der Ploeg, *OTS* 10 [1954] 185–96). **5.** David's fashioning of musical instruments (cf. 2 Chr 7:6; 29:26; Neh 12:36; Josephus, *Ant.* 7.12, 3 § 305–306) is not protocanonically attested outside Chr, because in Am 6:5, *kol* "all [kinds]" fits the context better than *k^{e}lê*, "instruments" of song. **7.** *Ladan:* Represents Libni of 6:17 (also in 26:21), although Libni's sons resemble those of Shimei here. **10.** Quite possibly the exilic bearers of these patronyms are meant. Inasmuch as some of these names sound like "foreigners in the sanctuary," Van den Born suspects a relevance to Ez 44:7.

14. *Moses:* Although proclaimed sonorously "the man of God" (Dt 33:1), he is effectively eclipsed beside Aaron; his sons are nonpriestly Levites (despite Jgs 18:30; cf. C. Hauret, *Bib* 40 [1959] 509–21; and cf. 1 Sm 2:27), to enhance not their father's glory but that of the Levites, whom the Chronicler prefers to priests as he prefers David to Moses.

37 **24:3.** The Chronicler always avoids the embarrassing mention of Abiathar (see comments on 15:11; 27:34), because it was Zadok who replaced him (see comment on 6:53). In his place, amiably paired with Zadok, is an Ahimelech who should be the father of Abiathar (1 Sm 23:6), but, following 2 Sm 8:17 (MT, not Pesh), he is made his son, called Abimelech in 1 Chr 18:16. Van den Born writes, "Here a historic power-struggle is captioned under slogans of 'God's designation.' "

4. Apart from the allusion in Lk 1:5, the 24 "turns" are recorded in five separate places. To make clear their interrelations, we will call this one X. Furthermore, V will be Ezr 2:36 (= Neh 7:38); W, Neh 12:1; Y, Neh 12:12; and Z, Neh 10:3. Of these lists, X has seven names in common with Y and Z, of which only one appears also in V and W! Only four of the other names in X appear in either V or W. The rest are probably post-exilic party bosses.

25:1–31. Here we have systematized a similar 24-turn calendar for the musicians, the Chronicler's own colleagues, who have been copiously publicized already in 15:16 and 16:4,37. The extra names found here may not only represent actual post-exilic people but also be creative symbols (cf. J. Boehmer, *BZ* 22 [1934] 93–100). **4.** "The most curious feature in it is that the names of Heman's nine last sons (v. 4) when put together, form a little poem, a fragment of a psalm" (De Vaux, *AI* 392); the verse can be translated, "Have mercy, Yahweh, have mercy on me; my God art thou; (who sayest [Is 1:2]) 'I have reared and raised'; helper of him who dwells in hardship, increase my eloquence (and) visions."

38 The goal of ch. 26 is to stress that the "gatekeepers," who in post-exilic Judah enjoyed supreme social and political influence bearing no relation to their functional epithet, should not be too proud, for they are merely relatives of the singers' real aristocracy. **8.** Obededom's descendants rely on their name (cf. 13:14); after they are adopted into the clan of singers, they maneuver to make their gatekeeper branch paramount. **12.** "Here the Chronicler forgets entirely his historical pose and describes the Temple as it is in his time, mentioning the four sides on the *east, north, south,* and *west;* also the gates (v. 13), even giving the name of one (v. 16)" (Stinespring, OAB). **24.** It is remarkable how prominent the Hebronites are here, without their customary Calebite disguise (see comments on 2:3; 2:50; 4:1). **25.** On the Moses treasure, see Nm 31:54. **29.** Outside Jerusalem, not, as Herbert takes it, "outside the cultic sphere." *officers:* See comment on 23:4. *judges:* See Dt 17:8; 33:10. These are actually branches of the teachers' function (2 Chr 17:8; 35:3; Neh 8:7ff.) among unschooled tribes.

Chapter 27 concludes with a list of officials whose status was secular but who are here organized for the services they can render to the hierarchy, or rather render directly to King David for the building of the Temple (28:1–2). The organizational scheme is idealized: "In prosaic terms, 'The king's state was magnificent and secure' " (Herbert, *op. cit.*). The names follow 11:10–25 closer than 2 Sm 23. **1.** Perhaps the Chronicler's intention was to show that David really inaugurated the division into the 12 tax districts of vv. 25–31, ascribed to Solomon by 1 Kgs 4. **4.** *Dodai:* Rather, Dodo's son Eleazar, as in 2 Sm 23:9. **7.** *Asahel:* In 2 Sm 2:23 he had fallen in the Joab-Abner feud (C. Kuhl, *Old Testament Origins* [Edinburgh, 1961] 291).

17. Zadok merits an extra place "for Aaron," but subordinate to the other Levites. **18.** *Elihu:* Unnamed among David's six brothers in 2:15; 1 Sm 17:12 supposes seven brothers. **23–24.** These lines somehow hint that the flaw of David's census consisted only in numbering minors. **33.** The Chronicler pays off some political debts left outstanding by his omission of 2 Sm 15:31–32. **34.** This Abiathar is not mentioned as a priest, even if he is the one whose name (from 2 Sm 8:17) is suppressed in 6:50 and 24:3.

39 (d) David's Entailed Abdication (28:1–29:30). The Chronicler's undoubtedly authoritarian intention, drawn from rereading the sad lessons of history, is that the successful administrator—whether of a company, a family, or a nation—should not depend on his sons to follow in his footsteps but should rather hamstring their personal initiative by as many mandated elders as possible. **3.** The most favorable possible impression of David's over-all plan is created by putting into his own mouth a frank admission of how he effected it. **5.** David's shocking inability to cope with the intrigues of his four principal heirs, which fills eight chapters from 2 Sm 13 to 1 Kgs 2, is here shrugged off by rationalizing that after all, there were many sons, but it was God who made the decision (*min Allah* [and not only among Arabs] today often means "I prefer not to occupy myself with bettering the situation as you request"). **8–10.** Powerful oratory in deuteronomic style. **11.** The blueprint (or possibly scale model) is solemnly and publicly handed over. How could Solomon ever dare to change it! **14.** Not only the building, but also the most meticulous details of its furnishings are inexorably regulated by David, not by Moses as in Ex 25:9,30. Indeed, we have here the inventory of materials already in hand, no longer mere contract specifications. **18.** *golden chariot:* A precious proof that the cherubim on the gold smearing-lid of the Ark enthrone Yahweh's presence, Shekinah (Heb 9:5; Ex 25:20), not statically but dynamically, as in Ez 1:26 and Ps 18:11. **19.** *the hand of the Lord:* The Chronicler has David claim the divine inspiration ascribed to his rival Moses by the harmonizing of Ex 31:18 with Ex 24:4; cf. also 40:2; 43:11. **20.** Taken from Dt 31:18.

40 **29:1.** At no point does David admonish Solomon to bear responsibility with a firm hand. **5.** The counterpart-funds principle is here impressively inaugurated—a noteworthy advance in public relations over the Moses of Ex 25:1; 35:4. **4.** Ophir gold, like Tarshish ships (2 Chr 9:10,21), is just a stock epithet like India ink; the quantities are symbolic. **7.** *darics:* One of the strongest proofs for the composition of Chr after Darius (400 BC). So flagrantly Persian a term could not have been otherwise plausibly inserted, even by an annotator. The invention of minted coins does not much antedate Croesus (550 BC). **9.** A sly ex post facto allusion to Solomon's backslidings in 1 Kgs 11:4, which the Chronicler otherwise ignores. **11.** This exquisite theologizing contains no reference to a future life, but neither does it reduce hope to earthly posterity, as 1 Kgs 8:25. **22.** Solomon is anointed as *nāgîd*, "charismatic leader," a role portrayed as coming to Saul from God, whereas he became *melek*, "king," by popular acclaim (1 Sm 9:16; 10:1; 11:25; Alt, *KlSchr* 2, 23; De Vaux, *AI* 94). As in the P tradition of Lv, the Chronicler extends the anointing rite to the high priest, a custom only after the Exile, when he held civil power (cf. De Vaux, *AI* 347, 399; *RB* 71 [1964] 277). **26.** Mention of the seven-year Hebron reign is so casual as to imply no delay in usurping the northern crown (see comment on 11:1). **27.** The Chronicler hurries frowningly past the doubtful events of 1 Kgs

1:4 (2:22!). **29.** For the Chronicler's sources, see E. Podechard, *RB* 25 (1915) 236–47 (→ 5 above).

Now we may summarize the Chronicler's portrayal of David, as in Rudolph and Goettsberger. The sources, especially canonical Sm, are conscientiously followed in what is taken over from them; however, everything tending to diminish David's greatness is systematically omitted. Even the narrative details are deftly heightened in David's favor, often by the insertion of plausible concretizations. The narration of David's strictly civil activities, omitting what concerns the succession to his crown, occupies roughly the same bulk in Chr (73 verses) as in Sm (45 verses, or 103 with the Bathsheba episode). But in what concerns liturgical piety, the Deuteronomist (Sm) gives only 77 verses for David, as against the Chronicler's colossal 323. Like all empire building, David's cost heavily in blood, but the achievement was unique and stellar within the triangle of great powers surrounding him—the Jewish nation's finest hour, as political history goes. Yet the Chronicler makes all this seem a trivial side issue in comparison with his massive dedication to the organization of liturgy. David so far outshines Moses that no Sinaitic or other covenant is any longer worth fostering as a vital force in the religious life of the people. The Temple was truly David's achievement, from cornerstone to parapet, although even the details of its execution will suffice to dominate and galvanize the ensuing reign.

COMMENTARY ON 2 CHRONICLES

III Solomon's Reign (2 Chr 1:1–9:31).

41 **(A) The Inauguration at Gibeon (1:1–17).** **1.** Although the awaited Temple did not yet exist, Solomon's inaugural ceremony would plainly take place at some suitably impressive religious center. The Chronicler eschews all mention of the Gihon spring (1 Kgs 1:45) either because it conjured up spectres of Moloch or of the rival anointing at En-rogel (1 Kgs 1:9), or because both springs were at the bottom of a gorge, a far less impressive spot than the spacious heights of Gibeon. **3.** There could be no denying the notorious historical tradition that Solomon had in fact gone to solemn ceremonies at Gibeon's high place, for it is impassively recorded in 1 Kgs 3:3–4 as his habitual and reprehensible practice. For the Chronicler, it is transformed into making a virtue of necessity on this single occasion. **5.** At the Ark there was only chant, but David had expressly fostered continuing the sacrifices at Gibeon in veneration not of any high place but of the desert Tabernacle (1 Chr 16:37ff.) and its altar of Bezalel's making (Ex 38:1).

7. The Chronicler expurgates the emphasis on the divinatory dream in 1 Kgs 3:5,15; the name *yhwh* in that narrative is replaced by *'ĕlōhîm*, somewhat more consistently than usual. The Chronicler also omits the confirmatory episode, which crystallizes for posterity the wisdom of Solomon. He considers it repugnant that Solomon should have been sympathetic to the pleas of harlots (cf. Mt 21:31–32), or should have even tentatively advocated child slaughter.

14. Solomon's gradual transformation of David's militaristic domain into an economic empire by skillful commerce is telescoped here as an echo of the divine promise of riches. It is not really said that any of this happened at the Gibeon inaugural or was even planned there.

(B) The Temple (2:1–7:22).

42 (a) LETTING THE CONTRACTS (2:1–18). **1.** The verse (MT, 1:18) reduces to a fleeting phrase all the data of 1 Kgs 7:1–12 on the 13 years given to the building of Solomon's personal residence. **3.** *Huram:* Hiram of 1 Kgs 5:2. The Chronicler seems to imply that the Phoenician timber ordered and actually delivered during David's lifetime was for his private home rather than for the Temple, as in 1 Chr 22:4. We may perhaps read between the lines that the canny businessman Huram felt it would be more diplomatic to make new bids to Solomon, whose free acceptance would lay a basis for more harmonious collaboration.

4. The verse explains to Huram that the new structure will be a place for sacrificing to the deity, not a "dwelling" for some embodied form. **5.** *our God is greater than all gods:* Written to a pagan from the paragon of wisdom among Israel's leaders, it is one of the neglected theological pronouncements of the Bible (see the essay by F. Kortleitner, *De diis gentilium* [Innsbruck, 1912] 68). The name *'ĕlōhîm* is equivalently a plural of El, implying that Israel's one God is as much as the total of whatever is meant by that name among her neighbors. But the existential status of every other El was not so easy to formulate, especially in treating diplomatically Great Powers who worshiped their own El (note the uncommitted tact of Huram's reply in v. 12). Basically, the devout Israelite felt that every other El had been degraded to the status of Yahweh's footstool (Ps 95:7); however, inasmuch as they were—if anything—supraearthly or heavenly beings, their status was thus imperceptibly merged with that of the angels, as the Greek often renders *'ĕlōhîm* (Ps 8:6). The OT rarely or never (even in Pss 96:5; 135:6,15; 115:4) maintains that idols are not gods at all, that only Yahweh is God. Perhaps we will attain a more Christian and ecumenical formulation of monotheism today by re-evaluating the OT caution about denying all reality or divinity to the content of the concept of God among primitive or non-Christian peoples.

10. The Chronicler grafts onto 1 Kgs 5:11 (MT, 5:25) a growing awareness that good fences make good neighbors; a businesslike advance understanding builds better friendships than capricious munificence, which is a more sympathetic way of saying, "Solomon does not let Tyre dictate the price, as in Kgs" (Van den Born, *op. cit.*). In v. 15, Huram outdoes Solomon by stipulating payment in advance. **14.** Very important for successful international deals is the ability to speak the local language, with all the sympathetic insight into local outlooks that it implies. This theory is here concretely expounded in the fact that the liaison is the son of one Phoenician parent and one Israelite parent. The tribes of Dan, as here (perhaps to suggest Oholiab of Ex 31:6), and Naphtali, as in 1 Kgs 7:14, shared rather vaguely the hinterland of Israel, farther N even than coastal Tyre.

16. On the log transfer at Joppa, see comment on 8:17. **18.** For the "ethnic minority work force," the figures are identical with those given in v. 2 for the local work force, as 1 Kgs 5:13 (MT, 5:27). *Gēr*, "alien," does not mean "resident subject of a foreign land" but rather "non-Israelite dwelling permanently within Israel." Thus, v. 2 involves no essential discrepancy with either this verse or 2 Chr 8:8–9. However, the same numbers, repeated in slightly misleading terms, increase the difficulty of reconciling this work force with that of 1 Chr 22:2 (cf. also comment on 1 Kgs 5:13).

43 (b) The Building and Its Measurements (3:1–17). **1.** Moriah (elsewhere only in Gn 22:2) is equated with Jerusalem by both rabbinical tradition and L.-H. Vincent (*RB* 58 [1951] 360–71), but rejected by N. Glueck (*Rivers in the Desert* [N.Y., 1959] 63); Rudolph (*op. cit.*,) plausibly proposes to read, with Pesh, "the Amorite hill" (see also M. Noth, *OTS* 8 [1951] 28–46). *Ornan:* See 1 Chr 21:15. By stressing this link with Abraham, the Chronicler leads to the suppression of Moses (Van den Born). **2.** *fourth year:* This important date is bereft of any link with local or world chronology in 2 Chr 1:1 or in 1 Chr 29:27. It is contrary to all we know of the Chronicler's workmanship, but consistent with his soft pedaling of whatever relates to Moses and Exodus, that he suppresses here a number both concrete and mystical, the 480 years of 1 Kgs 6:1.

3. De Vaux writes that the description, shortened from 1 Kgs 6–7, with no notable insertion, "is very hard to interpret. The editor did not have the interests of an architect or an archaeologist, and he omitted details which would be essential for a reconstruction (e.g., the thickness of the walls, the layout of the facade, the way in which it was roofed). Moreover, the text is full of technical terms, and has been disfigured by scribes who understood it no better than we do; and it has been loaded with glosses meant to enhance the splendour of the building.... It is not surprising that the reconstructions which have been attempted differ considerably from each other" (De Vaux, *AI* 313; → 1–2 Kings, 10:17–18; L.-H. Vincent, *Jérusalem de l'Ancien Testament* [vol. 2; Paris, 1956] 377–590).

However, we will suppose as most reliable the recent Howland model documented by P. Garber (*BA* 14 [1951] 2–24; cf. G. Wright, *BA* 18 [1955] 41–44; *JBL* 77 [1958] 116–29). *measurements:* As in Pesh, they need not be preferred to the MT "foundations" or "ground plan." The old standard is presumed vaguely tantamount to a "royal cubit," some 10 per cent larger than the standard 18 in. attested for Egypt and Mesopotamia (De Vaux, *AI* 197; R. North, *CCHS*, 2nd ed.). **4.** *a hundred and twenty cubits:* Or 180 ft., as against 30 cubits (45 ft.) in 1 Kgs 6:2. S. Yeivin, in "Was There a High Portal in the First Temple?" (*VT* 14 [1964] 331–43), maintains that different stages of the building are being described. Kgs assigns no special height to the porch as distinct from the Temple; otherwise the Chronicler's figure results in a monstrosity, even for the porch. But this is not so if we think rather of an entrance *pylon* as at Edfu, on whose proportions the reconstructions of Solomon's Temple are most warrantably based. **6.** *Parvaim:* Possibly an alternative spelling for Ophir as a gold source (see comment on 8:17).

8. *six hundred talents:* At eighty pounds of 12 oz. each, at 35 dollars per ounce, this amounts to 20 million dollars, only a fraction of the 5 billion in 1 Chr 22:14. **9.** The LXX and Herbert understand this as: Each nail weighing one shekel supported 50 shekels of gold.

10. Wood, as in the LXX, for the MT "embossing," is perhaps borrowed from 1 Kgs 6:23. In that context, the description takes the cherubim for free-standing statues, a suggestion consciously pursued in 2 Chr 5:7. But in 1 Sm 4:4, when the Ark is brought into battle, it includes the cherubim upon which Yahweh is enthroned. Hence, it is hard to agree with De Vaux (*MUSJ* 37 [1961] 94), who dates the Chronicler's free-standing cherubim earlier than the Ark lid relief portrayal in Ex 25:17; De Vaux finds that the cherubs' function was to guard the tree of life and serve as Yahweh's throne (De Vaux, *MUSJ* 37, 122). Even in the texts regarding the cherubim as free-standing statues, the 10-cubit height (1 Kgs 6:23 suppressed by the Chronicler) and the wings reaching to the side walls of the Inner Sanctum may be the same kind of pious exaggeration that we have in the gold reckoning. J. Trinquet (*VDBS* 5, 179) admits that at least in the normative period described by Ex 25:17, the cherubim were a relief ornament on the Ark lid itself. This lid is named *kappôret*, "smearing," a reference to the ritual of Lv 16:14. But by a more spiritual insight into the significance of that ritual, *kappôret* has come to be translated as "propitiatory" or "mercy seat." It is regarded as the throne of Yahweh's "Shekinah" no less than are the cherubim. Astride the Ark lid and the cherubim as a single palladium, the Lord of Hosts gallops into the fray in 2 Sm 22:11; Ez 1:20; 10:12; Pss 17:11; 48:9. **14.** The veil (Ex 36:35; Mt 27:51) is replaced by wood-carving decor in 1 Kgs 6:29. **15.** Free-standing pillars, such as like Jachin and Boaz, are strangely lacking in Herod's reconstruction, but they stood also in front of the Hazor temple, as attested by the plinths unearthed there in 1958; the position of the great bird statue(s) before the Middle Sanctum of Edfu is similar (see also S. Yeivin, *PEQ* 91 [1959] 6–22; Ex 37:10–38:31).

44 (c) Minor Furnishings (4:1–22). This is taken with little variation from 1 Kgs 7:23–26,38–51. **1.** The bronze altar is not in 1 Kgs 7:23 but is presupposed in 8:22,64. **3.** The bronze sea is supported upon a cast base the ornament of which is called gourds in 1 Kgs 7:24, but here probably correctly equated with oxen. **5.** *baths:* Unfortunately seems to be in English a quantification of the remark in v. 6 that the sea was for the priests to wash in. The bath is a measure of capacity, perhaps 10 gal. or perhaps only half that. De Vaux focuses the hopelessness of determining it exactly in the fact that our clearest indication is here 10-cubit diameter by 5-cubit depth, or 590 cu. ft., but the parallel (1 Kgs 23:26) to the same dimensions allots only 2000 baths (De Vaux, *AI* 202). C. Wylie (*BA* 12 [1949] 89) convincingly accounts for this difference by the fact that in Chr the receptacle is cylindrical and in Kgs it is hemispherical. **17.** Succoth is Deir Alla, excavated by H. Franken, (*VT* 12 [1962] 378; *VT* 14 [1964] 417). For *Ṣ*ᵉ*rēdâ*, we have *Ṣārtān* in 1 Kgs 7:46, which may well be the conspicuous peak Sartabeh, although H. Guthe (BZAW 41 [1925] 96–108) and N. Glueck (*AASOR* 25 [1951] 342) claim it is Sa'idiyeh, and new data are pending from J. Pritchard's recent excavation.

45 (d) Enthronement of the Ark (5:1–10). **3.** As in 3:2, the Chronicler replaces the colorful month names of 1 Kgs 6:1; 8:2 with austere numerals, like the medieval *feria quinta* instead of Thor's Day. **4.** The Ark is carried not by priests, as in 1 Kgs 8:3, but by the Levites, as in 1 Chr 15:2. **5.** The priests are inserted as if by oversight, either with the Levites as in the LXX, or, as in the MT, by use of the enigmatic tag, Levitical priests (cf. Dt 17:9). **6.** Our occidental taste finds this literary convention of hyperbole, "too many to be counted," more acceptable than the Chronicler's customary use of a concrete number, which, although exaggerated, actually exaggerates less than this sweeping generalization. **7.** The author may be envisioning unrealistically cherubim wings, which were part of the Ark lid (see comment on 3:10), just as in v. 9 he says the ark poles are there "unto this day" (they scarcely were in his own period, 400–200). **10.** What was in the Ark? Heb 9:4 presumes it (always?) contained a specimen of the manna (Ex 16:32) and the flowering rod of Aaron (Nm 17:25) beside the stone tablets of the Law (Dt 10:2). L. Dürr's opinion, adopted in *EDB* 135, perhaps goes too far in denying any perceptiveness to research hypotheses that the stones in the Ark were originally the oracular Urim and Thummim (Dt 33:8; Nm 27:21; 1 Sm 14:18,41; E. Robertson, *VT* 14 [1964] 73), or even that the Ark itself was the priests' incrusted and eventually free-standing breastplate (W. Arnold, *Ephod and Ark* [Harvard, 1917]). More sober and inescapable is the tracing of the Semitic palladium into the recent Arabic palanquin, called *qubba*, *'uṭfa*, or *maḥmal* by H. Lammens—a view accepted by F. Cross (*BA* 10 [1947] 63) and J. Morgenstern (*HUCA* 18 [1944] 39; E. Nielsen, VTSup 7 [Leiden, 1960] 61–74). Perhaps it was by its very emptiness that the Ark as a throne "contained" the Shekinah or "glory of Yahweh" (B. Stein, *Der Begriff Kebod Jahwe* [Emsdetten, 1939]; G. Henton-Davies, *IDB* 1, 222–26; S. Saba, *L'arca* [Rome, 1948]). Strangely, it is claimed that the Chronicler takes up this older Ark tradition—specifically, the outbursts of joy caused by the empty Ark-throne's arrival—as distinct from the deuteronomic "expurgation," making the Ark a mere container inasmuch as Yahweh is enthroned in heaven (Von Rad, *OT Theology* 1, 237–38, 350; "Zelt und Lade," *GesSt* 109ff.). Doubtless, R. de Vaux (*AI* 300; *À la rencontre de Dieu* [Fest. A. Gelin; LePuy, 1961] 55–70) and T. Worden (*Scr* 5 [1952] 82–90) rightly conclude that the Ark's interior might have served as a container while its exposed surface functioned as an empty seat for the invisible deity (see comment on 1 Chr 16:41).

46 (e) The Dedication Ceremony (5:11–7:7). **14.** As soon as a hymn had been intoned to the newly housed Ark, the Temple was filled with a blinding cloud, doubtless from the censers (1 Chr 28:17 = Ex 37:16; cf. M. Haran, *VT* 10 [1960] 113–29). It gave occasion for Solomon to improvise a lengthy speech, beginning "Yahweh promised that he would dwell on a cloud" and continuing throughout ch. 6 (1 Kgs 8:12–50, almost word for word) in a vein of unusually rich theological and moral content. Goettsberger (*op. cit.*) claims that the cloud was smoke caused by the "sacrificial fire from heaven," which our present text therefore misplaces in 7:1. But 1 Kgs 8:54 ignores this "fire from heaven," which Vannutelli plausibly claims was suggested to the Chronicler by the Elijah episode of 1 Kgs 18:38. The "glory of the Lord filling the house" in 2 Chr 7:1, reminiscent of the inaugural vision of Is 6:4, is rendered outright as Shekinah in Pesh. More imaginatively, astronomical or mythical phenomena have been invoked by A. von Gall (BZAW 34 [1920] 52–60) and R. Eisler ("Jahves Hochzeit mit der Sonne," *MVÄG* 22 [1918] 39–46).

6:11. The Chronicler cannot resist substituting "covenant with the sons of Israel" for the irritating reference in Kgs to Moses' "covenant with the fathers he led out of Egypt" (Van den Born). **13.** The only interruption in Solomon's long prayer is seized as an occasion for the author to correct any misapprehension that the king is usurping priestly functions in the sanctuary. The platform or balcony attributed to him is reminiscent of the special loge erected for the emperor in basilicas like Saint Sophia of Constantinople. This long verse ends with the same conspicuous phrase as the preceding v. 12—not unreasonable grounds for suggesting that we have here not an interpolation but an omission, caused by homoioteleuton in 1 Kgs 8:23. **18.** According to B. Alfrink (*Fest. E. Tisserant* [Vatican, 1964] 5), heaven is the firmament, highest heaven the water reservoirs beyond it, and third heaven God's abode beyond that. **41.** Part of Ps 131:8–11, replacing the 1 Kgs 8:53 reference to Moses' leadership in Egypt, which the Chronicler always finds so distasteful. Strangely, we have here three times the pairing of Yahweh with Elohim, a trait shared almost exclusively by the Chronicler and Gn 2–3.

7:1. *fire...from heaven:* See comment on 5:14. **3.** *glory:* Shekinah; see comment on 5:10. **5.** The sacrificial animals (as in Kgs) are worth one million dollars, a restrained symbol by comparison with 3:8 and 1 Chr 22:14. **6.** This addition to 1 Kgs 8:63 is hardly strong enough to counter the impression that Solomon has simply usurped the priestly functions. **8.** It would seem that the solemn octave of the Temple dedication ended on the very day on which the Feast of Tabernacles began with its octave (Lv 23:36). The dedication service itself, although it has furnished one of the most impressive among the rare OT borrowings in Christian liturgy, does not seem to have become an annual commemoration until the "reconsecration" of 2 Mc 10:5; Jn 10:22, which is perpetuated as the modern Jewish Hanukkah counterpart to our secularized yuletide. **11–22.** The text is taken largely from 1 Kgs 9:1–9.

(C) Solomon's Civil Rule (8:1–9:31).

47 (a) Commerce and Urban Renewal (8:1–10). **2.** One of the most mysterious among all the discrepancies from the Chronicler's sources is this acceptance from Huram of cities that can only be those 20, in Galilee, declared by 1 Kgs 9:11 as ceded to Hiram in payment of Solomon's debt. Actually the enigma is even greater within Kgs, where Hiram, after spurning the cities as "worthless" (*kᵉ-bûl?*), sends Solomon the cost of his own buildings. A safe conclusion may be that to prime the pump of Solomon's trade, Hiram bought the Galilean cities for 120 talents, but returned them when he was dissatisfied, as the Chronicler more coherently reports and Josephus (*Ant.* 8.5, 3 § 141–143) interprets.

3. *Hamath-zobah:* In 1 Chr 18:3ff., in an area loosely bounded by Hamath and the Euphrates, David overcomes an expeditionary force of Arameans from Zobah, Damascus, and (2 Sm 10:6) Rehob. Without unknown Zobah and Rehob, the other points suffice to determine a Syrian desert triangle of which Palmyra is the center. Doubtless however, as today, the polities were concentrated along the western fringe of the desert.

4. The name Tamar in parallel 1 Kgs 9:18 really means what was expressed by the later Lat Palm(yra), but the name was common for desert oases. Palmyra itself was named Tadmor, which the Chronicler or a copyist is thought to have been led by the preceding context to substitute here. Tamar in Judah is allegedly nearer the Baalah beside Beth-horon (and Gezer or perhaps Gerar of 1 Kgs 9:17). But Baalah, "(our) lady," is a widely diffused name, such as "St. Mary's" today (and of similar origin!). Strangely, however, there is one Baalah at or near the recently destroyed Arabic peak Soba indicated by Jos 15:9 (cf. *Bib* 37 [1956] 215; Noth, *op. cit.*, 89–90). We cannot altogether exclude some prior phase of the romantic ruins of Palmyra from the commercial, if not military, conquests of David or Solomon.

6. *chariots...horsemen:* More graphic in 1:14 (= 9:25; cf. also 1 Kgs 9:19; 4:26; 10:26). Certain structures that P. Guy excavated at Megiddo are imaginatively called "Solomon's stables," although identical structures at Hazor are called mere storehouses and dated after Solomon by Aharoni's recent excavation there. Both cities are strangely omitted from the parallel 1 Kgs 9:15. **7.** *Hivites:* Perhaps by this name (or even by Hittites) is meant the Horites (Hurrians) of Gn 36:21, whose Egyptian name Kharu was applied to the whole population of Canaan. **8.** Discrepancies in the *corvée* are explained under 2:18 and 1 Kgs 5:13.

48 (b) Domestic Moral Issues (8:11–16). **11.** *Pharaoh's daughter:* As implied in 1 Kgs 3:1; 7:8; 9:16, she plainly deserved a residence more palatial than those of Solomon's harem conquests of lesser geopolitical importance. The sanctimonious motivation ascribed to him here is made even more incredible by commentators' claims that she would defile the house of David, not because she was a pagan but because all women were ritually less clean than men (Lv 15:19; 12:1). The Chronicler retains this verse only from the long description of the residence that Solomon built for himself in 1 Kgs 7:1–12 (cf. G. Richter, *ZDPV* 40 [1917] 171–225). **13.** *new moons:* They had really no official status in the liturgical calendar, despite 1 Chr 23:31; Neh 10:34. But it is hard to see how De Vaux can so rigidly exclude the influence of the moon on Sabbath origins (De Vaux, *AI* 477; see *NCE* "Sabbath" and *Bib* 36 [1955] 193). This liturgical preoccupation of Solomon through v. 16 is an expansion of 1 Kgs 9:25, where, moreover, Solomon is not kept outside the chancel (see comment on 6:13).

49 (c) THE FLEET AND ITS FRINGE BENEFITS (8:17–9:31). **17.** Eloth is Eilat, the present-day Aqabah on the NE coast of the Gulf of Aqabah. Ezion-geber is a variant name. (On Kheleifeh as the site, see N. Glueck, *BA* 28 [1965] 69, and *AASOR* 15 [1935] 42.) This port must have been Solomon's, opening toward the Indian Ocean and Ophir. "Ophir gold for Beth-horon" is the remarkable content of a 589 BC ostracon (*IDB* 3, 606) discovered at the Jaffa excavations; cf. B. Mazar (*IsrEJ* 1 [1950] 209), who maintains that his excavation is the very site where Solomon's government offices supervised the transshipment of logs (2 Chr 2:16; Ezr 3:7). Ophir may be identical with Supara in India (LXX, 3 Kgs 8:28; Josephus, *Ant.* 8.6, 4 § 164). More probably, Ophir was situated along the S coast of Arabia, so near to Africa's apes and peacocks that its name can be extended to both shores of the gulf, like Sheba, or Cush for Midian (Nm 12:1!). Gold-bearing Parvaim of 3:6 could be simply a variant form of the word Ophir, rather than "Hyperborea" or "Hesperia," debated between P. Grelot and H. del Médico (*VT* 11 [1961] 30–38; *VT* 13 [1963] 158–86; *VT* 14 [1964] 155–63; see R. North, *Fourth Congress Jewish Studies* [Jerusalem, 1965]).

9:1. *Sheba:* As in the Epiphany liturgy (Ps 72:10; Is 60:6). This is the S Arabian port nearest Ethiopia [Josephus, *Ant.* 2.10, 2 § 249]. Hence, Abyssinian royalty traces it origin to a romance between Solomon and this queen, who is called Belqis (E. Ullendorff, *BJRylL* 45 [1963] 486–504; E. Wallis Budge, *The Queen of Sheba* [London, 1932]). More prosaically, the queen's visit was a punitive expedition. She wanted to put a stop to upstart Solomon's interference with her lucrative India-to-Canaan spice monopoly. His "wisdom," which she so much admired (v. 6), doubtless consisted in a canny merger guaranteeing increased profits to them both (v. 12)! The Chronicler omits the mysterious comparison of Solomon's wisdom with Edomite-Egyptian prototypes in 1 Kgs 4:33 (cf. Alt, *KlSchr* 2, 90). **7.** *wives:* The reading of 1 Kgs 10:8, where the Chronicler has "men," in a narrative otherwise meticulously taken over. **10.** Algum is a Phoenician export in 2:8, perhaps better spelled almug, as in 1 Kgs 10:11. It is an unknown tree, probably sandal wood, used in the making of lutes and harps. **13.** The gold glut is an old folk tale: the 666, as in 1 Kgs 10:14, is 660 in the LXX. **16.** *three hundred shekels:* The number is the Chronicler's equivalent of Kgs' "three talents" (*me'ôt* for *mānîm*). The palace is called a "forest" merely because it utilizes so much cedarwood.

21. *ships of Tarshish:* Now agreed to be the name of a special kind of ship suited to commerce between Lebanon and the Tartessus port in Spain (Jer 10:9; Ez 27:12)—probably "far sailing" (L. de Las Muñecas, *Estudis Franciscans* 43 [1931] 135); there is no implication of "refinery." Solomon did not have a second fleet plying the Mediterranean jointly with Hiram. This presentation is just the Chronicler's inept recasting of Tarshish in the first half of 9:21. It seems improbable that Darius' anticipation of a Suez Canal (Herodotus, 2.158) had made the Mediterranean available to the Gulf of Aqabah even in the Chronicler's time, as Van den Born claims. **25.** Notable divergence from 1 Kgs 10:26ff. On the horse mart, see comment on 8:6.

29. At this point, 1 Kgs 11 is recklessly omitted. It passes a savage judgment on Solomon's sexual and cultic morality. Worse, it describes his failures and setbacks, signs of divine disapproval. Moreover, it suggests that the coming split of his realm resulted from his own ineptness. Instead of this condemnation, the Chronicler's farewell for Solomon (as for David in 1 Chr 29:29) emphasizes his good standing with the prophets; on the various names the Chronicler gives to his sources (called Solomon's chronicle by 1 Kgs 11:41), → 5 above.

(IV) The Kings of Judah-Without-Israel (2 Chr 10:1–36:23).

(A) The First Israelite Dynasty (10:1–16:14).

50 (a) REHOBOAM CAUSES TROUBLE (10:1–12:16). The Chronicler discounts interplay of human motivation and weaknesses in the working out of God's salvation plan, saying, in effect, that inasmuch as the divinely established David had united the north and south into one administrative unit, it would remain that way. Any departure from that norm was a sin, and its effecters played no positive role in God's plan. We can discern even more of David's personal merit and of God's guiding hand if we can recapture what the Chronicler left out, i.e., that the division was a declaration of independence by the northern kingdom, restoring the more basic situation of the people of God.

The Deuteronomist compiler also tailored the materials in 1 Kgs 12 to fit his message, but he was more concerned to show God's hand in history by the fulfillment of predictions and similar prophetic feats, especially of Elijah and Elisha. Since these men worked mostly in the north, they fall wholly outside the Chronicler's focus of interest. Unlike the Chronicler, the author of Kgs shows his disapproval of the northern kings by recurrently evaluating them, not by merely ignoring them.

1. Rehoboam went to Shechem after he had begun to reign. He had been at once solemnly inaugurated in Jerusalem as head of the southern group to which his father and grandfather had belonged. The northerners had no objection to holding a similar ceremony. They were on the whole satisfied with the unification arrangement, but they did demand (as is evident in the Chronicler's own expression borrowed from 1 Kgs 12:1) that a separate inauguration ceremony should display their autonomy in principle. **2.** Jeroboam's involvement, as telescoped concisely in the single verse of 1 Kgs 11:28, is a magnificent epic of social justice—as a laborer he was skillful and loyal; when he became a boss, he turned against management. Solomon's decision to kill the young agitator is interpreted by a lengthy prophecy of 1 Kgs 12:29–39, safeguarding the divine initiative and Davidic pre-eminence; in short, when Jeroboam was sent back to his native northland to recruit forced labor for the Jerusalem *corvée*, Solomon's confidence in him turned to hatred. Similarly, Jeroboam's return from Egypt is plainly presented in v. 3 as the will of the northern elders. This presentation may have been borrowed for our present text from 1 Kgs 12:3. The northern civic leaders found Jeroboam a suitable mouthpiece to present Rehoboam with a Magna Charta to sign before they would endorse his leadership. Cf. J. Soggin, *Königtum in Israel* (BZAW 104; Berlin, 1967).

5. The popular demand is received by Rehoboam with a moderation that may have been sincere. He asks for three days to think, and even first seeks advice from the elder statesmen, on whom his father had relied for shaping policy. However, he then turns to his 40 or so peers (2 Chr 12:13), chiefly the numerous descendants of

Solomon, according to A. Malamat (*JNES* 22 [1963] 247–53). Their hot-headed counsel prevails. Bright dates the separation of Israel from Judah to 922, defended also by the article of Freedman and Campbell on chronology (*BANE* 265–99). However, this date is the latest of all those proposed by more recent competent authorities; Ricciotti's *History of Israel* centers on a date ten years earlier; De Vaux endorses 930, and Noth, 926. The divergences are intensified by efforts to synchronize the later kings; the chief research, by E. Thiele, *Mysterious Numbers of the Hebrew Kings* (Chicago, 1951), has not won general acceptance (see his defense in *Andrews Univ. Seminary Studies* 1 [1963] 121; 2 [1964] 120; also A. Jepsen, *BZAW* 88 [1964]; V. Pavlovský and E. Vogt, *Bib* 45 [1964] 321–54).

19. The Chronicler tendentiously and scornfully overlooks Jeroboam's claims to legitimacy, where 1 Kgs 12:20 adds, "There was none that followed the house of David but the tribe of Judah only." Bright defends this passage, but Noth emends it to "Benjamin only"; at any rate, 1 Kgs 12:21 (= 2 Chr 11:1) shows that it was meant as a hyperbole and did not exclude Benjamin. In 11:3, the Chronicler adds "Israel" to the citation of 1 Kgs 12:23. This defiant claim that only Judah is the true Israel is reflected in the phrase, "Israel in the cities of Judah" (2 Chr 10:17, copied from 1 Kgs 12:17). Although this snatch of archaic verse is from the mouths of hostile Ephraimites, it may well have been a taunt in which Judah and the house of David are told to go home: "To your tents, O Israel." It does not seem plausible that at this tense moment Jeroboam would have demobilized! There is insufficient proof in 2 Sm 2:9 that the restriction of the name "Israel" to the north is archaic; there it may be a convenient anachronism, or it may refer to the still pending unity with Hebron effected under Saul.

51 11:1–4. Exactly as in 1 Kgs 12:21–24. The implication is that Judah could easily have crushed the Samaria uprising, but preferred to obey God's prophetic Word. **5.** Only the Chronicler preserves this archival detail, but utterly without chronological link. Rehoboam's defense posts have been imaginatively set forth as a sort of Maginot Line intrenchment, studied exhaustively by G. Beyer (*ZDPV* 54 [1931] 113–34). But we really have here every big village (at least of the strategic Shephelah foothills); therefore, the military measures of Rehoboam were more probably on the order of our civilian defense. Alt notes that Rehoboam's forts include two and only two names in common with the "surrounding belt" of Levite cities of 1 Chr 6:39–66 (= Jos 21:8–42): Aijalon and Hebron. He concludes that the "Rehoboam list" is really a certain number of the previously privileged cities that Josiah fortified in 620, after their Levites had been evacuated to Jerusalem by his new cultic centralization (Dt 12:11; Alt, *KlSchr* 2, 306–15). However, most experts, with Beyer, date the forts to the period to which the Chronicler ascribes them. The author ignores any temporary transfer of Jeroboam's capital to Penuel (cf. 1 Kgs 12:25).

13. The Levites flock to Judah, not because Jeroboam impiously opposed the legitimate worship of Yahweh (as the Chronicler strongly expects to be taken from his words), but simply because he replaced quislings with loyalists! **15.** *the calves:* A scornful summary of 1 Kgs 12:26–33. The winged bullocks, called cherubim, were the legitimate symbol of the divine presence (see comment on 3:11). Jeroboam may have incurred some guilt by duplicating this essential of the Ark cultus. The commentary on 1 Kgs 12:26 sees the evil rather in deceptive resemblance of these bullocks to symbols of Baal worship (→ 1–2 Kings, 10:30). At any rate, Jeroboam's efforts to retain within his own nation both his people's religious loyalties and the economic benefits attendant upon pilgrimages cannot be taken as idolatry or dissent from Yahweh worship, which continued to be as strong in Israel as in Judah. The real abuse was sex-crazed Baal syncretism; Elijah had to fight it in Israel, but it had been ravaging Judah ever since Solomon's time (1 Kgs 11:5; 16:32). The whole of 1 Kgs 13, against northern flouting of a prophet, is of no concern to the Chronicler.

18. *Mahalath:* The Chronicler evidently felt that he was reinforcing dynastic legitimacy by showing how (unknown to 1 Kgs) the blood of Rehoboam's wife was nearly as Davidic as his own. They not only shared one Davidic grandfather, but Mahalath's other grandfather was David's brother! **20.** *Maacah:* Rehoboam's second wife, known to 1 Kgs 15:2, was his first cousin (Van den Born), unless, as Rudolph maintains (after Jerome, *PL* 23.1457), her father was "a different Absalom." His 76 other espousals fall far short of Solomon's (1 Kgs 11:3); it is hard to imagine that the Chronicler records this detail to account for Rehoboam's downfall in 12:1, for the following verses praise him, although he had already been depicted as a vicious character. **22.** *Abijah:* He is Maacah's son also in 1 Kgs 15:2; perhaps by textual corruption in 2 Chr 13:2 (MT, not LXX or Pesh), he is traced to Micaiah bath Uriel of Gibeah. The experts prefer to retain this latter reading because it is not the kind of "plausible" change a copyist would have made.

52 **12:1.** The Chronicler omits Yahweh's crushing rejection of the northern dynasty in 1 Kgs 14:1–20, and also the gruesome details of the moral collapse of Rehoboam and Judah, here called "Israel." But in v. 2 he embellishes with a few further details the devastation of Jerusalem by Pharaoh Shishak. Only he tells us that the Egyptian force included Libyans, Ethiopians, and "Sukkiim." These are called "cave-men" by the ancient translators but are claimed to be "mercenaries" in Egyptian documents known to W. F. Albright (cf. *OTMS* 18).

5. The Chronicler makes Shishak's invasion the occasion for an emphatic prophetic intervention. There is no need to raise the question of whether it is historical, because it is certainly a theological interpretation of the invasion, whether composed as such by Shemaiah, the Chronicler's source, or by the Chronicler himself. The Karnak wall record of Shishak's invasion reveals that Israel was damaged as much as Judah (see B. Mazar, VTSup 4 [1957] 57–66). This fact is not only passed over in Kgs as well as in Chr, but it also makes us wonder how Jeroboam would have been harbored by Shishak in 1 Kgs 11:40. **10.** Rehoboam's replacement of the stolen Temple plaques earns him a softening of the disdain in which he is held. **14.** Harshness returns to dominate his epitaph.

53 (b) The End of Jeroboam (13:1–22). **1.** The heir to the throne of Judah was given the same name as the son of Jeroboam—Abijah (1 Kgs 14:1). When he becomes king, however, he is called Abijam in most Hebr manuscripts of 1 Kgs 14:31; 15:1. This giving of an identical name to contemporary royalty in Israel and Judah is a constant source of confusion in later reigns. Perhaps the similar names were given deliberately to cause this confusion, at least insofar as they represent ideological counterclaims, such as naming the states of eastern Europe democratic republics. **2.** On Micaiah as the mother of Abijam, see 11:22. Abijah's three-year reign is passed over in 1 Kgs 15:1–7, where there are three verses about David and one about Rehoboam. The Chronicler expands the note on war between Abijah and Jeroboam into a tissue of descriptive clichés drawn from famous biblical battles (Jgs 9:7; 20:29; 8:2; Nm 10:9). **3.** Symbolic numbers compounded of 40 are used to show that Yahweh's mighty army in Judah met a bully twice its size (= 2 Sm 24:9). **4.** Abijah's long speech is a reform program recalling Nathan of 1 Chr 17:14 and David's taunt to Goliath in 1 Sm 17:8. Thus, the Chronicler must excuse Abijah from the tag of impiety that in 1 Kgs 15:3 he shares with most rulers. **5.** *covenant of salt:* As in Nm 18:19, it is one sealed by sharing a meal (Ex 24:11). **6.** We have here simultaneously a theology of history and a history of theology (Ex 29:1,38; 30:7; 25:30–31). Fabrication of a speech to express the genuine concrete situation is a device legitimate even in some strictest historiographical traditions. (On the fomenting of anti-Samaritanism, see M. Delcor, *ZAW* 74 [1962] 281–91.) **17.** This slaughter can only be regarded as the Chronicler's theological conclusion; there must have been something stupendous to show that Yahweh favored Judah, or rather true worship as against "sons of Belial," apostates in all times (Stinespring, OAB). **19.** Bethel, although only 10 mi. N of Jerusalem, is not, in fact, a city of Judah a few years later (2 Chr 16:1; Am 7:10); however, the border fluctuated greatly, and Abijam may well have gained control of Bethel, Ephron 4 mi. to the NE, and Jeshanah near (Mt.?) Zemaraim. **20.** The Chronicler is careful to make it appear that part of Jeroboam's punishment was sudden death whereas Abijah continued to reign. The synchronism of 1 Kgs 14:20; 15:9 puts the death of Abijah two years before that of Jeroboam, but by reading 7 instead of 17 years for Rehoboam's reign, J. Bright arrives at the following framework: Abijah, 915–913; Jeroboam, 922–901 (thus also W. F. Albright, *BASOR* 100 [1945] 20).

54 (c) Asa Outlives the Jeroboam Dynasty (14:1–16:14). The reign of Asa in Judah (913–873, Bright) is presented with theological reserves complicating the few known historical facts. We should expect to find the greatest significance attached to Baasha's overthrow of the hated Israel dynasty after its second incumbent had reigned only two years (1 Kgs 15:25). Yet the Chronicler is indifferent and senses no impropriety in the lifelong conflict of Asa against Baasha. Without doubt, he is embarrassed by the fact that Israel's change of regime left it as hostile to Judah as before.

Inconsistencies in the Chronicler's appraisal of Asa pass almost unnoticed in commentaries such as those of Driver or Goettsberger. A problem is seen, but pointedly dispatched, by Herbert: "The argument is that for the first 35 years of his reign Asa was loyal to Yahweh and enjoyed success, but then he began to rely on human help and became weak" (*PCB*). To this, Van den Born (*op. cit.*) adds, with equal brevity, "Dragged-out wars and ill health imply falling away from Yahweh, yet reform measures and long life betoken his favor."

But we cannot overlook the intricate network of incoherences from which Rudolph (also in *VT* 2 [1952] 367–71) strives to draw an over-all convincing motivation for the Chronicler's mode of procedure in these three chapters: Asa was a religious reformer whose lifetime of war with Baasha culminated in a painful sickness, all of which can be adequately reconciled by supposing the sin of mistreating a prophet near the end of an otherwise virtuous life. Because virtue merits peace and prosperity instead of war, the notice of 1 Kgs 15:16 about Asa's lifelong war with Baasha must then be dismissed as an inaccuracy or an exaggeration. Moreover, the Chronicler's own description of the Cushite war (during Asa's virtuous days) has to be regarded as a very transitory episode, although it seems to last from Asa's eleventh to fifteenth regnal year (13:23; 15:10). The conflict with Baasha has to be dated by the Chronicler so late in Asa's reign that Baasha was already dead ten years (1 Kgs 16:8). Furthermore, the clearing away of idols in 15:8 is a doublet of 14:3, and the success attributed to this enterprise by 14:2 seems to be negated by 15:17 (if "Israel" there means Judah, as the context and 15:3 suggest; see comment on 2:3). The claim that characterizing Azariah's speech in 15:3–4 (LXX; Vg; cf. 15:1 in MT) as prophecy, when in reality it is philosophy of history, is an incoherence will not hold if we relieve prophecy of unwarranted implications regarding prediction of the future (*VD* 29 [1951] 321–33; B. Vawter, *Conscience of Israel* [N.Y., 1961] 25; *MR* 232–50).

55 **14:1.** The ten years of peace is contrary to 1 Kgs 15:16—"war with Baasha all their days." **2.** The approval of Asa is equally emphatic in 1 Kgs 15:14, but v. 11 adds "like David," which the Chronicler suppresses. **3.** *hewed down the Asherim:* The phrase "seems hardly to accord with the Chronicler's portrayal of the previous reign" (Herbert). The Chronicler postpones to 15:16 Asa's Spartan measures against the offenses of his own (grand)mother, Maacah (1 Kgs 15:13). **5.** The Chronicler here negates 15:17 (= 1 Kgs 15:14), which states that the high places were not taken away (out of Israel). **6.** *fortified cities:* Such an incessant and emphatic armament program is really a kind of cold war with Baasha. **8.** The standing army was stronger than the wartime force of 13:3.

9. Ethiopian (Hebr Cushite) applies not only to Nubia but also to the adjacent Arabian peninsula, including Sinai (Nm 12:1). Inasmuch as the Sinai Midianites roamed as far as Gilead (Jgs 6:3), we may well have here a raid of Negeb Bedouin encamped at Gerar (v. 14) not far from Mareshah in the SW foothills of Judah. Zerah is a Hebr name, and there is no basis for applying it to the Ethiopian Pharaoh Osorkon or the Euphrates desert monarch Cushan-rishathaim, although in Jgs 3:18, Cushan's undoing is ascribed to Mareshah's neighbors (see A. Malamat, *JNES* 13 [1954] 231–42). Zerah's army is again just neatly double Judah's resistance. **14.** *fear:* Like the nameless chaos-causing dread, which has come to be called "panic" because it was supposedly sent by the god Pan.

56 **15:3.** The "prophecy" of Azariah is a masterpiece of historical theology. Truly in the Judges period (17:6; 21:25), "God alone rules us" meant unbridled selfishness. **8.** Asa's acceptance of the challenge forms a doublet the details of which are inconsistent with 14:5. **9.** In Hebrew, *gērîm* (sojourners) refers to local ethnic minorities. Simeon was part of Judah anyway; the Ephraimite refugees are probably (as in v. 8) the type of border merchants who keep their neighbors' flags handy. **10–11.** The only "spoils" compatible with the Chronicler's narrative are those from the campaign against Zerah, which seems to have dragged on four years (14:1). **13.** This saber rattling is brutal if understood as a serious juridical punishment, but it was not applied in practice. **16.** Maacah, his grandmother, as in 11:21.

57 **16:1–6.** Asa was 36 ten years after the death of Baasha, recorded in 1 Kgs 16:8. The Chronicler's accuracy, or historical intent, can be salvaged only by supposing (without other warrant) that he is here counting from the split of the kingdom (see Thiele, *Mysterious Numbers*, 59; Albright, *BASOR* 100, 20). It is just as respectful of the sacred text to say that the Chronicler, knowing how aging Asa suffered an illness in apparent connection with his mishandling of such men as Hanani (v. 7), has taken from the record (1 Kgs 15:16–22, word for word) this specimen of Asa's reliance on human alliances rather than on Yahweh. **7.** This moral is pointed by the hindsight of Hanani, which naturally enrages Asa. **12.** The Chronicler abominates even the most innocent pursuits that fit the definition of what he excoriates—i.e., seeking help from men rather than from Yahweh. Physicians is exactly the sense of the Hebrew for "healers," even if the Chronicler intends it to mean medicine men or witch doctors.

58 **(B) The Century of Social Unrest (17:1–25:28).** This pivotal era in the history of Yahwism is characterized in Israel by the prophet Elisha's engineering the overthrow of Omri's profiteering dynasty. Judah's painful link with these disorders via its own murderous usurping queen Athaliah, Omri's granddaughter, could not be overlooked in the Chronicler's account. But the origin of all these woes in Judean Jehoshaphat's alliance with the northern king Ahab is transfigured into a lengthy "mystery play" incorporating an obscure prophet. The Chronicler is blindly uninterested in Israel's more momentous earlier prophets or mantic guilds affiliated to Elijah and destined to be transformed into the writing prophets of Judah after 750.

59 (a) JEHOSHAPHAT (873–849) (17:1–20:37). **17:1.** Jehoshaphat means "Yahweh judged," and it has been plausibly maintained that the Chronicler's entire presentation here is a cadenza on this theme. *strengthened himself against Israel:* Lit., "grew strong over Israel"; it may well mean "consolidated his power within Judah" (see comment on 10:16). Verse 2 makes it clear that it indeed involved defense measures against the nearest enemy. Such preparedness is not inconsistent with the jockeying and intrigues of diplomatic matrimonial alliance with Israel (18:1; 20:35). What is meant here is ultimately an unpleasant kind of hostage, under cover of which each side might have been readying an attack.

3–6. There is nothing here that could not be the Chronicler's own legitimate inference from the fact that no strife troubling his coregency (16:12) is recorded. On the other hand, the concrete example of kingly good behavior in vv. 7–9 is inserted from a Levite instructional mission after 500, names and all (Zechariah, Tobijah, Elishama; Zech 6:10; Neh 2:10; 7:62; see comment on 1 Chr 3:24). **11.** Exchange of gifts between neighboring heads of state is minimal protocol; by omitting mention of Judah's return gifts, the Chronicler makes the king of Judah to be a sort of suzerain. **13.** The storage cities of Judah have been searchingly examined by Y. Yadin (*BASOR* 163 [1961] 6–12). **14.** The names of the colonels within Jerusalem are from some doubtless ancient list; the numbers presumably represent the total population on which each could draw, but even so a hyperbole is involved. **19.** The Chronicler's narrative here leaps over 1 Kgs 17–22, which describes the rise of Elijah, and specifically the hoarding of national resources fostered by Ahab's queen Jezebel.

60 **18:1.** The marriage alliance of Ahab's daughter Athaliah with Jehoshaphat's son Jehoram would seem to have been more interwoven with the ensuing diplomatic parleys than the Chronicler cares to indicate. **2.** It is by no means evident why the king of Judah should be paying a courtesy call to the ruler of his people's enemy. That Ahab has summoned Jehoshaphat is a fairly natural implication of 1 Kgs 22:1ff., even apart from the overtones of Ahab's servants around the conference table. Why should the Chronicler, who made out Judah's king to be a terror to his Philistine and Arab neighbors, now have him answer meekly that his army is theirs to command instead of asking himself, "What advantages can I gain for my people by agreeing to cooperate with you on a partnership basis?" **4.** *inquire first:* But this is not the first time; Jehoshaphat has already committed himself to the enterprise before he piously proposes to have recourse to the Lord. **5.** This lengthy and fascinating chapter repeats 1 Kgs 22:4–35 word for word. The implication for both is clearly that the northern kingdom's cultus is very bad. More rationally and theologically, we should infer that Yahweh inexorably makes clear his will to Samaria by the weak and contemptible means he chooses (cf. 1 Cor 1:27). **22.** Even the full responsibility of Yahweh for the lying spirit of the false prophets is taken over by the Chronicler without demur (see comment on 1 Chr 21:1). **31.** Only by the insertion "God helped him" does the Chronicler transform Jehoshaphat's cry of terror and identification of himself into a serene and noble prayer.

61 **19:2.** To the flagrant disloyalty of getting involved with Israel at all is added the stupidity of backing a loser, for all of which the writer merely slaps Jehoshaphat on the wrist because he enhanced the prestige and economic status of the Levites upon his return to Jerusalem (v. 8; see W. F. Albright, "The Reform of Jehoshaphat," *Fest. A. Marx* [N.Y., 1950] 1, 61–82). There is no need to suppose that it is a doublet or that it is connected with 17:7 in any way other than by the Chronicler's overriding sympathy for whatever favors the Levites. It would seem that the civil or priestly judges, appointed by a man whose name means "Yahweh judges" (= Jehoshaphat) within the framework of an older spoils system, were arousing ominous dissatisfaction by their bribery and favoritism. To regain a good public image (e.g., that commended in Dt 16:18; 17:9), these political adventurers are replaced by plodding civil servants, Levitical scribes who will know the law or be able to look it up, and who will apply it with unimaginative and unemotional objectivity. **11.** Moreover, for the execution of their writs and verdicts, they are provided with a corps of Levite bailiffs. *Šoṭēr* ("writer" in Akkadian) is the policeman of the modern Israel state (for its ancient implications, see Van der Ploeg, *op. cit.*, 185–96; De Vaux, *AI* 155).

62 Chapter 20 is entirely unparalleled in the Bible (see M. Noth, *ZDPV* 67 [1945] 45–71). **20:1.** *Meunites:* The Hebrew is here unmistakably a repetition of Ammonites. The chief LXX manuscripts read Minaeans (a S Arabian tribe), which is their rendering in 26:7 and 1 Chr 4:41 for *meʿûnîm*. There is one Maʿon S of Hebron and another near Petra, but both form part of the roaming area of the tribe loosely called (or linked as) Edomites and Nabateans (Seir of v. 10). The fact that the invaders' place of origin will be further designated as Moab-Ammon is perfectly plausible even today. Students or pilgrims centered in Jerusalem looking eastward beyond Jordan see the cliffs of Moab about the capital Amman and tend naturally to give this name to the remoter E Jordan districts. **2.** Even Syria forms a part of the Nabatean area, but "Aram" replacing "Edom" in most Hebr manuscripts is a perennial common error. The compiler of this verse probably did not know any better than we do where Hazazon-tamar was exactly located, but, like us, he felt sure that it was S of Hebron in the region the best known landmark of which was En-gedi. **3.** To "seek the Lord" normally implies the use of some oracular devices (the contrary in 1 Chr 10:14). Here, only prayer and fasting are explicit. **5.** There is no reason to assume that this posturing of the king implies that no military operations are being begun; on the contrary, his prayer is typical of those that send armies into the field (cf. 14:11; 1 Sm 17:45). **14.** Yahweh's choice of a Levite cantor (the writer's favorite; see comments on 1 Chr 25:1; 15:17) rather than a priest or prophet for making known his will is significant (cf. A. Johnson, *The Cultic Prophet in Ancient Israel* [Cardiff, 1944] 61). **17.** Victory was assured. **23.** It may well have been that Judah's immunity hinged upon a failure of recognition among the clans allied against it. **26.** An example of etiology follows: "There is a place called *b^{e}rākâ* (blessing) because at one time a momentous blessing took place there." **36.** Ahaziah's short reign in Israel (850–849; Bright) brings the commercialism of Ahab's dynasty near its end. Thus, toward the close of his reign Jehoshaphat shares responsibility for the troubles precipitating a social justice revolution (see comment on 22:7). On the Tarshish ships, see comment on 9:21. The insertion of this episode here is an unskillful anticlimax.

63 (b) ATHALIAH (849–837) (21:1–23:21). Racine's French classic *Athalie* focused the dramatic nadir of separated Judah's fortunes. The very presence of this evil woman in Jerusalem was a symbol of Samaria's sin from which she was born. She secured power by a trail of massacres equaled only by medieval Marozia's enslavement of the papacy. Athaliah's crisis was reached in the very year in which her mother Jezebel was similarly dominating Israel (842), after pushing it into finance-monopoly. Jehu's uprising effected change, but not before the sister kingdoms had provided an astonishing example of Goldsmith's "Deserted Village":

> Ill fares the land, to hast'ning ills a prey
> Where wealth accumulates, and Men decay.

21:1. Jehoram (849–842), father of Ahaziah (842), reigned in Judah, while the same names in reverse order appear in the Samaria king list: Ahaziah (850–849) and Jehoram (849–842, dates identical with those of Judah's Jehoram, in the Bright chronology). **4.** Jehoram's massacre of his own brothers seems clearly the doing of his wife Athaliah, not only from the explicitness of v. 6, but also because she escaped punishment herself. Verse 6 is taken from 2 Kgs 8:18, where the Chronicler rejoins the deuteronomic narrative after skipping seven entire chapters about Elisha. There is no mention of the massacre in Kgs, but its historicity is unquestionable. Experts are hesitant about Noth's eruditely documented claim that names like Michael or Jehiel could not have been used so early. *princes of Israel:* Judah is, of course, meant; see comment on 10:16. **5.** When Jehoram was 32, his youngest son and successor, Ahaziah, was already three years older, unless we correct age 42 to 22, as in 2 Kgs 8:26. **7.** It was the nation of David rather than his dynasty that Yahweh's fidelity bound him not to destroy in 2 Kgs 8:19. **8.** *Edom:* Because the portion of E Jordan opposite Judah was held by Omri, the only part left for Judah was S of the Dead Sea. Actually the close ethnic and commercial relations between Petra and Hebron were inevitable, and eventually resulted in Judah's submission to Edom in the person of Herod the Great. **10.** Libnah is prominent in Jos (10:29; 21:13). Its site W of Lachish is contested (Safi mound, says F. M. Abel; W. F. Albright prefers Borna, 5 mi. S). The Edom-Libnah troubles are taken from 2 Kgs 8:20ff., with the Chronicler's predictable homespun piety.

12. This sudden burst of Elijah into the Chronicler's narrative, after sedulous suppression of his very name and of a dozen chapters dominated by him, is surprising. However, as far back as 2 Kgs 1:17 we see that Judah's Jehoram became king while Elijah was still functioning. It seems likely that Elijah, while roaming about Samaria, Gilead, Phoenicia, and Sinai (1 Kgs 19:8!), knew what was going on in Judah and expressed himself about it. Whether these views were taken down by a disciple and sent during or after Elijah's lifetime, or were composed by the Chronicler for the occasion, creates no problem for the type of historicity the writer intends. **16.** The Ethiopians (Hebr Cushites, as in 14:9) are the ever-raiding Midianite-Arab tribes of Sinai who shared a boundary with Judah and Philistia. **17.** *Jehoahaz:* The youngest son is called Ahaziah in 22:1 and 2 Kgs 8:24–25. **19.** Funeral bonfires are attested only for Asa (16:14). **20.** They buried him in the city (as 1 Kgs 15:8), a blow to archaeological and exegetical assumptions regarding devout Jews' refusal to live in a city containing tombs, like Tiberias (this assumption continues to be shared by *EDB* 2452 with *IDB* 1, 475, despite such data as in J. Simons, *Jerusalem of the Old Testament* [Leiden, 1952] 274, 309; S. Yeivin, *JNES* 6 [1948] 30–45; S. Krauss, *PEQ* 79 [1947] 102–11).

64 **22:2.** Inasmuch as the Chronicler mentions Athaliah's name now for the first time, her influence doubtless became even more dominant over her son Ahaziah—another reason for supposing he was only 22 when he inherited the crown (see comment on 21:5). **5.** For Ahaziah to share in Samaria's anti-Syrian campaign, narrated in 2 Kgs 8:28–29, meant merely supporting the policy of his grandfather. But for once the Chronicler sees and exploits the dramatic possibilities. The pious editorializing, which elsewhere often renders his text colorless, now (v. 7) blossoms into a profound grasp of the significant politico-social movements of the time: In God's salvation plan, the quick eclipse of Ahaziah was interwoven with Samaria's momentous overthrow of the Omri dynasty.

8. The name of Athaliah's mother (or close kinswoman), Jezebel, is not mentioned in the Chronicler's account of the two kings' demise at Jezreel, but she dominates the scene in 2 Kgs 9:30. **10.** The savagery there shown to Jezebel, even more than the relatively routine execution of Ahaziah, accounts for the pathological cunning of Athaliah's reaction. **11.** The dramatic touch is again supplied by the Deuteronomist (2 Kgs 11:2). **12.** For a six-year reign of terror, Athaliah held all power in Judah. (Cf. H. Donner, *OrAnt* 2 [1963] 229; M. Tsevat, *JSS* 3 [1958] 237.)

65 **23:1.** These "centurions" are *śārê m^{e}ʾôt*, as in 2 Kgs 11:4, but provided by the Chronicler with good Jewish names in place of the ethnic "Carians" (Cretans, 2 Sm 8:18). Jehoiada is left strangely without an introduction. He would appear to be the chief of police, but turns out to be a high priest in v. 8 (= 2 Kgs 11:9). **2.** The Chronicler cannot endure that a king of Judah is brought to power by foreigners invading the sanctuary; therefore, he has them enlist Levite co-operation. He also rather unrealistically has "all the houses of Israel" send delegates to the plot. **4.** The *rāṣîm* ("runners" or "footmen," rather than guards) are systematically eliminated from the Kgs account. **7.** Rudolph goes too far in seeing these orders as intended to protect the sanctuary rather than the royal figurehead. **13.** *people of the land:* They rejoice, as in 2 Kgs 11:14 (W. Rudolph, *Fest. A. Bertholet* [Tübingen, 1950] 477); the term is a disputed technical one (De Vaux, *AI* 70, 524; see comment on Ezr 4:4). *the singers with their musical instruments:* The Chronicler inserts the Levites, even risking the loss of dramatic tension.

66 (c) JOASH (837–800) AND AMAZIAH (800–783) (24:1–25:28). **2.** The seven-year-old monarch does a fine job as long as (correcting 2 Kgs 12:2, "because") he lets the priest make the decisions. **3.** After ten years, even a wife is chosen for the king by Jehoiada, and then another (the Chronicler's additions). **5.** The adolescent king's initiative in putting religious worship on a sound financial basis is somewhat coy, especially when it involves reproaching the priests for not collecting the money fast enough. *from all Israel:* In 2 Kgs 12:5, the priests are expected rather to get the repairs paid for by their own contacts, but the "contact" (*makkār*, "acquaintance") seems rather to be the reason why the money is not going into Temple repairs in 2 Kgs 12:1; and 12:4 contains several obscure technicalities about the source of funds. **6.** The author suppresses the fact that Joash allowed some ten years to pass before taking drastic action. **8.** The king gets credit for the collection box. In 2 Kgs 12:9, Jehoiada also gets the idea. **14.** A correction of 2 Kgs 12:13; it is curious how the Chronicler suppresses 2 Kgs 12:15—the priests kept no audit of the funds that they passed to their paymasters, with whom they had an understanding—as well as v. 16—meanwhile the Temple repairs did not eat into the priests' stipends.

18. The Chronicler found inexplicable the notice of 2 Kgs 12:17–18; after a life of virtue and helping the priesthood, why should Joash be punished by a Syrian invasion? How could he buy off the invaders with consecrated funds? To account for this, the author need only rationalize that after Jehoiada's death, Joash fell from a good life into the sinful idolatry so typical of Judah's kings. **20.** This Zechariah is doubtless that of Lk 11:51, called son of Barachiah in Mt 23:35 by assimilation to Is 8:2. **23.** Even though Joash has now been sufficiently blackened, it galls the Chronicler too much to record that a king of Judah voluntarily opened the Temple treasury to pagan invaders; therefore, all responsibility falls to the Syrians. Their king Hazael is not named. **24.** Joash, instead of going free for his simony, is made out to have died from it. **25.** The conspiracy that 2 Kgs 12:20 laconically condemns here appears as an act of righteous moral retribution (whose punishing is blamed in 25:2–3).

67 **25:1.** Amaziah is a variant of *'Amoṣ*, "Yahweh has made strong." **4.** The singular prominence accorded this maxim (as in 2 Kgs 14:6) doubtless results from the fact that with Jer (31:30 [= Ez 18:20]) and Dt (24:16), the new norm of individual responsibility had gained wide popular support as a reaction against primitive Mosaic morality (cf. Ex 20:5; 34:7). J. Scharbert (*Bib* 38 [1957] 149) holds that it was always implicit in the Mosaic legislation. **5.** The Chronicler expands to 12 verses a brief etiological notice of 2 Kgs 14:7, suppressing its point of departure (Joktheel = Sela). Inasmuch as Sela is doubtless Petra, it is a pity that Hebr lexicography sheds no light on why Amaziah selected this new name. Neither Kgs nor Chr hints that this campaign is in any way defensive or punitive, nor are they disturbed in presenting it as an unbridled aggression. **9.** Amaziah doubtless decided that it is better to lose your investment than be strangled by it, a wise policy that the author calls divinely inspired; but the divine promise is hardly borne out by v. 13. **14.** It was common in the ancient Near East, after successful aggressive wars of conquest, to foster the subjected people's religion, even by adding the statues of their gods to the conquerors' pantheon. Some gesture of this kind may well have been made by victorious Amaziah.

17. In the Chronicler's mind, this action is a manufactured link for the chain of theological argumentation needed to furnish the conclusion that Yahweh's Judah will be humiliated by godless Israel (= 2 Kgs 14:8–14). **24.** The author inserts a good word for his special friend Obed-edom (see comments on 1 Chr 13:14; 25:8). **25.** Strangely, Amaziah is granted 15 years of apparently prosperous reign after surviving his foe. **27.** The Chronicler adds to Kgs only a hint that all this time a plot was simmering against Amaziah; but he seems to have retained official good will, for after his fatal flight to Lachish he is restored to burial in Jerusalem.

(C) The Rise of Book Prophecy (26:1–32:33).

68 (a) Uzziah's Building Activities and Leprosy (26:1–23). Four details betoken the Chronicler's special interest in this king. First, he provides him with a priestly mentor, Zechariah, like Jehoiada in 24:2. Relevance to Is 8:2 being quite remote, this figure corresponds disconcertingly to Jehoiada's son of 24:20, perhaps by a dramatic license. Second, Chr alone furnishes information about Uzziah's military pursuits, both aggressive and defensive. One tower and cistern in the desert (v. 10) have been recognized in the Qumran building nucleus dated by 8th-cent. pottery, and called "salt city," as in Jos 15:62 (M. Noth, *ZDPV* 71 [1955] 111–23). On the inroads into Philistine territory, see D. Freedman on the Ashdod excavation (*BA* 26 [1963] 134–39). Jabneh, matrix of post-Jerusalem Judaism, is mentioned only here in the Bible (= Jabneel? [Jos 15:11]). Another exploit of Uzziah supposedly verified by excavation is his reconquest of the Red Sea port of Eilat (cf. N. Glueck, *BASOR* 72 [1938] 8; G. E. Wright, *BibArch* 161), but it is peculiar how this event is recorded in 2 Kgs 14:22 not as part of Uzziah's reign but that of his father. This anomaly is somewhat rectified in 2 Chr 26:2, which perhaps assumes it is after the king (of Edom! not Amaziah) had died (B. Alfrink, *OTS* 2 [1943] 112). Third, the Chronicler predictably expands the notice of 2 Kgs 14:22 regarding this king's leprosy, making it a punishment dramatically inflicted at the very moment of his intrusion in the cult; it is even more dramatic, with earthquake and lightning, in Josephus (*Ant.* 9.10, 4 § 225; J. Morgenstern, *HUCA* 12 [1938] 3). Fourth, the name the Chronicler gives Uzziah seems to be correct—that by which he is known to the prophets and modern scholars. The same name is used for recording the past in 2 Kgs 15:13,30ff. Strangely, this name is replaced by Azariah to describe both his accession and his entire reign in 2 Kgs 14:21–22; 15:1–8 (also 1 Chr 3:12).

Azariah is the otherwise unattested name of the high priest whose lese majesty caused the king's leprosy (vv. 17–20). This priest thus seems to stand in the same relation of theocratic authority over Uzziah ascribed confusingly to the aforementioned Zechariah. Hence, perhaps grounds exist for the claim that the only Azariah was a priest regent who issued the official documents during a period between Uzziah's incapacitation by leprosy and the effective transfer of full powers to the boy Jotham (cf. R. North, *BCCT* 112, n. 27). The same basic factors lead H. MacLean (*IDB* 4,742) to conclude rather that Azariah (differing only by one letter in spelling, and not at all in meaning, from Uzziah in Hebrew) was the private name resumed after the abdication; see comment on 2 Kgs 14:21; on regnal names see A. Honeyman (*JBL* 67 [1948] 13–25).

23. Uzziah was buried in the royal cemetery "although" (not "because" as in RSV) he died of leprosy. Top experts like Simons accept, perhaps too wishfully, Sukenik's attributing to these remains a gravestone of 800 years later with the Aram inscription, "Hither were brought the bones of Uzziah, king of Judah. Do not open" (→ History of Israel, 75:76).

Neither Chr nor Kgs notice that during Uzziah's reign there came to a head and burst that ferment of charismatic outspokenness which we call book prophecy—Isaiah's inaugural vision (6:1), slightly preceded by the emergence of Am 1:1. J. Milgrom (*VT* 14 [1964] 164–82) ascribes the whole of Is 1:10–6:13 to Uzziah's term.

69 (b) Isaiah's Royal Antagonists (27:1–28:27). The reign of Jotham is in 2 Kgs 15:33ff. a bare transition, mildly approved. The Chronicler expands it into the short ch. 27. Why should he have wished to turn it into a glowing encomium by the rewording of adverse elements as in v. 2? Perhaps it was because of his inclination to see everything in black and white—i.e., whoever is on the right side of the thin line of minimal submission to God is a hero, the rest are criminals. **3.** Jotham's Jerusalem wall, according to J. Simons (*OTS* 7 [1950] 192; *Jerusalem of the Old Testament*, 330), may have been a trial run for the expansion of the city from SE to SW. For some reason the Chronicler also suppresses, or perhaps rather transforms into his data on the successful war against Ammon, the indication of 2 Kgs 15:37 that the Rezin-Pekah threat prominent in Is 7:1–17 was taking shape already in Jotham's time.

70 Against this virtuous foil, the evil of Ahaz is greatly intensified by the author's rewriting in ch. 28. Intriguingly there is no mention either here or in the parallel 1 Kgs 16:7 of the lengthy history supplied in Is 7:1–6. The Chronicler's description of the effects of the Assyrian alliance on the Temple altar is unaccountably euphemistic, if, as seems probable, what is meant is either a diplomatic cultus of Assyria's god installed as partner to Yahweh, or at least a use of Temple funds for political entanglements. In vv. 8–13, the Chronicler describes a remarkable boycott of the Samaria population in favor of Judah. This action betrays in many traits the oversimplified piety of the compiler; yet, in essence, it is so alien to his monolithic condemnation both of Samaria and of Ahaz that it cannot be a fabrication. Apart from these two episodes, we cannot readily summarize the Chr alterations from Kgs-Is under a few heads but must notice some special slanting in almost every verse.

28:3. *burned his sons:* The plural, instead of the singular in 2 Kgs 16:3, is here mere rhetoric; the Chronicler will acknowledge (vv. 7, 27) the survival of other sons; however, there is no real proof that the odious rite reprobated here and in 2 Kgs 23:10 meant "burning to death" instead of an ordeal or branding. **5.** The Chronicler, strikingly and apparently copying from some objective record, depicts the Aramean invasion of Judah as a thing independent of collusion with Samaria, and less gruesome. **6.** *Pekah:* Cf. H. Cook (*VT* 14 [1964] 121–35).

9. The antimilitarist flare-up in Samaria under the prophet Oded is remarkable for two reasons: it is a revolt against the authority of the military commanders and not of any king or civil ruler; it contains no indication that the military maneuver being boycotted was itself under Samaritan leadership. From these undeniably salient facts, Van den Born audaciously concludes that the Chronicler may have inserted here the record of an event in which the Samaritan populace genuinely withstood the successful withdrawal of some invaders of Judah, who had come, however, from Moab or Ammon ("kinsfolk," v. 11) rather than from N Israel. **15.** Not only does the army release its spoils, both human and material, but the "good Samaritans," very much as in Lk 10:34, give clothes to the ragged and food and drink to all. Moreover, they anoint them with oil and bring on their donkeys those who need transportation. Jericho is the frontier where the captives are handed over to their Judean kinfolk.

71 **16.** The appeal of Ahaz to Assyria for help is undoubtedly the result of the Syro-Ephraimite attack from the north in v. 5 (as in 2 Kgs 16:7), although the connection is broken by the Chronicler's insertion of a vivid side issue, as well as by his stress on invasions from the southeast and west, Edom and Philistia, in vv. 17–18. **20.** *Tilgath-pilneser:* As in 1 Chr 5:6, it is an unexplained variant of Tiglath-pileser (or Pul!) of 2 Kgs 15:19,29. Strangely, there is no mention of the emphatic intervention here of Isaiah (7:14!), although he is known to the Chronicler in 32:20. In 29:1, the author seems to accept the synchronisms of 2 Kgs 16:2, making Ahaz only 11 years old (and not yet king!) at the birth of Hezekiah, a factor to be explained by the numerous experts who would consider Hezekiah to be Emmanuel. J. McHugh (*VT* 14 [1964] 452) puts Hezekiah's birth ten years later, during Ahaz's lifetime. We cannot determine from the Is narrative whether Ahaz persisted in his plan of inviting Pul or whether the arrival of the Assyrian army did more harm than good to Judah. This does not seem to be the case in 2 Kgs 15:29; 16:9. The contrary indications of 2 Chr 28:21 ought perhaps to be regarded no less than v. 23 as a theological inference rather than an item recorded in archives. By contrast, v. 24 records details about the altar that are even more damaging in 2 Kgs 16:10–17, although 2 Chr 28:24 may well have exaggerated and inferred Ahaz's motivation. **27.** Burial of Ahaz outside the royal cemetery (or even outside the Davidic part of Jerusalem, as in the MT corrected by the LXX) does not exactly contradict 2 Kgs 16:20, but rather clarifies its thoughtless stock phrase by a warranted theological warning—i.e., such a wicked king could not have received honorable burial.

72 (c) Hezekiah's Ecumenical Movement (29:1–32:33). Hezekiah appears chiefly as a weakling and antagonist in Is 37:6; 38:1) and in 2 Kgs 20:19. But for the Chronicler, Hezekiah was one of the most noble reforming leaders. The ecumenical and national defense energies attributed to him, although not attested elsewhere, are altogether plausible and contribute indispensably toward our understanding of the deuteronomic and Josian reforms. **1.** *twenty-five years old:* Only 15 according to McHugh (*op. cit.*, 452). In fact, a boy king is more apt to be a reformer, docile to the influence of his priests and elders (see 24:1 on Joash and 34:1 on Josiah; but in 20:31, the admired Jehoshaphat begins his reign at 35).

3. Hezekiah's first concern, although in the postdated first month (Nisan or March; → History of Israel, 75:62) of his first complete year, was to restore the cultus within Jerusalem. It is expressed by acts and formulas that set him in direct repudiation of the policies of Ahaz in 28:24. **4.** Nominally, priests are convoked for the task as well as Levites. **5.** The address is to the Levites, perhaps a tacit reproach for the priests' easy compliance with Ahaz in 2 Kgs 16:11. Priests were present where needed, to enter the restricted precincts as in v. 16; however, they were too few, and the Levites more zealous (v. 34; 30:3). **6.** This public confession is a favorite genre of the anguished reappraisal during the Babylonian situation. **12.** The nomenclature of the Levites, with special prominence of the choir directors, echoes 1 Chr 6:18,33; 15:5,17; 16:41; 25:1; it "has nothing to do with Hezekiah's time" (Rudolph). **17.** It is important to keep reminding ourselves that what is really meant by a term such as "holy" or "make holy" is far from easy to define. Here what is chiefly meant is "to sweep out" or "to clean up"; but inasmuch as it is the holy place that is being cleaned and repaired, the rendition "restore to its former and due state of holiness" is appropriate, but leaves holiness indefined. **20.** In "officials," J. Hänel (*ZAW* 55 [1937] 46) sees transfer of the right of sacrificial slaughter from priests to Levites. **23.** This ritual gesture is prescribed in Lv 4:24, 28—male goat for the ruler; female goat for civilians; for the priests and the religious group, bullocks are required, with a similar laying on of hands (Lv 4:4,15). The common assumption is that the hand gesture here and in the context of Heb 10:28 signifies the passing of (unconscious) sin from the offerer to the victim. This notion of substitution would seem to derive from a misreading of Lv 16:21, where only one of the two goats is loaded with the people's sins, then sent away alive into the desert; the other goat is sacrificed, but without any hand ritual or other suggestion of expiatory substitution. **24.** The verb for atone, *kipper*, means really "to smear" (the blood); it is a gesture of obscuring rather than of removing the guilt. **25.** The musical background and its Davidic origins are given with a complacency reinforcing the hypothesis that the Chronicler himself belonged to the choir guild. **34.** Very subtly it is implied here that the alleged intrusion of (post-exilic) Levites into dignities above their station was no fault of their own at all, but of the priests' deficiencies noted as far back as Hezekiah's time. **36.** *suddenly:* Rather, "expeditiously"; there was joy that such a big job had been completed in only two weeks.

73 **30:1.** Hezekiah's ecumenical Passover is not hinted in the (perhaps) relevant Nehushtan episode of 2 Kgs 18:4. Some experts maintain we have here the literary vesture for prophetic hope of the return of the northern tribes to their Davidic loyalty, as in Ez 37:19. Others regard it as the Chronicler's way of saying that Hezekiah could not have fallen short of Josiah (35:18) in the splendor of his Passover. Doubtless the recorded facts of the case were relatively pedestrian. Somehow a small number of worshipers from various tribes of the northern kingdom were persuaded to come for a Passover in Jerusalem. The Chronicler exploits and blows up this fact into the expression of a grandiose plan; however, we cannot imagine that the facts themselves were made up. They show Israel in a light more favorable than the Chronicler would like, and, unlike such allegories as the prodigal son and Jonah, the theological lesson is dependent upon the historicity of the kernel of fact. Hezekiah's wielding of influence in Samaria gains in plausibility if his inauguration (or this Passover) took place after Assyria's annexation of Samaria in 721, as Rudolph and other experts hold. Bright dates Hezekiah's accession to 715. **2.** It is almost incredible that for so momentous a display of faith and unity, the Passover would be postponed a month. Admittedly there is precedent in Nm 9:6 for an individual in a state of ritual impurity to defer his Passover by one month, but it is more plausible to interpret this date (also in v. 13) as "the second Passover month" of Hezekiah's reign. **5.** Rudolph finds disproof of historicity in the fact that no prescription of united Passover celebration in Jerusalem existed before Josiah. This leaves unduly out of account the extent to which Josiah's reform itself may have been the expression of a religious conviction of the north, growing to a climax within Hezekiah's time, as many experts maintain. **7.** It may well be that this eloquent appeal to the separated brethren to return to Davidic unity was formulated in view of the estranged Samaritans of the Chronicler's time. At any rate, it is less smug than the similar allocution of Abijah in 13:5.

74 **14.** The altars were chiefly those tokens of Assyrian divinities, set beside the cult objects of Judah—the price Ahaz had had to pay for Pul's protection (2 Kgs 16:10), according to Middle Eastern traditions for signifying alliance between two nations. Thus, it turns out that Hezekiah's gesture of piety was also an effective step toward repudiating the political commitments of his predecessor, beginning from their impiety. When a crowd of excited pilgrims flood a town, they are easy to rouse to violence against counterirritants that the local population is too cautious to uproot. It may well be that the worshipers' indignation was vented also on purely Israelite superstitions and Canaanite syncretisms, the Nehushtan and Asherah of 2 Kgs 18:4, echoed in 2 Chr 31:1. **18.** We have here an extraordinary trait of the ecumenical Passover: Human values prevail over ritual technicalities (Lv 15:31), and this by decree of the king under pressure of political interests, yet neither the Levites who were there nor the Levite Chronicler see anything insuperably reprehensible in this. **23.** According to J. Segal (*The Hebrew Passover* [London, 1963] 19, 226), ch. 30 was written after ch. 35, so as to outdo its Passover by adding seven days of festival, as a misunderstood application of 1 Kgs 8:66. But Segal's whole thesis, rendering the lamb sacrifice as well as the unleavened bread a sedentary Canaanite ritual, is rejected by De Vaux and is contrary to most expert opinion (→ Exodus, 3:26).

31:1–21. Hezekiah's Passover had economic consequences that he foresaw or at least recognized as important for strengthening Judah's defenses and thereby its autonomy. First, the resumption of traffic to Jerusalem from the northern kingdom meant that free-spending tourists would be in the city, perhaps making excursions to points of interest farther S. **3.** The king contributes from his treasury, but expects the populace to be no less generous; with these details are concluded the 88 verses by which the Chronicler expands the single verse of 1 Kgs (18:4) about the cult. **10.** The superabundance of offerings left a surplus even after the clergy had been abundantly taken care of. As at Delphi, the votive offerings to the shrine were both a symbol and a resource for national defense. Although our text does not say so, the crisis of Sennacherib's approach doubtless warranted defending the people of God out of funds that were surplus after all.

75 **32:1.** The fiercest scourge ever to befall Judah was Sennacherib's invasion in 701. Whether our Bible records two separate invasions of Sennacherib is controverted (→ 1–2 Kings, 10:69–71, and the excursus in Bright, *Hist.* 282–87). The reliability of any Herodotus or Diodorus data is contested by T. Africa (*JNES* 22 [1963] 257). The Chronicler differs from the author of Kgs chiefly by his greater compression; he omits all mention of the towns seized outside Jerusalem, and of Hezekiah's anxiety and capitulation (2 Kgs 18:14; 19:1,6). In place of any such defeatism, he regards the whole episode as a glorious reward for Hezekiah's cultic virtues. Truthfully, we must acknowledge that the survival of Judah's autonomy, even at heavy cost, brought immense and deserved prestige to Hezekiah in comparison with the ignominious obliteration of rival Israel and the disappearance of its royal line.

3. Only the Chronicler records for us the event most explicitly attested to by archaeology in the whole of salvation history. Hezekiah's grandiose engineering project to keep the waters of Jerusalem's Gihon spring away from a besieging enemy was, in fact, a tunnel (32:30). Near its issue into Siloam pool, Hezekiah had carved into the stone a Hebr inscription (*ANET* 321), which was found by chance in 1880 and transferred to the Museum of Istanbul. The tunnel functions perfectly today, and biblical visitors may walk from Gihon to Siloam; the water seldom rises above the knee, generally only to the ankle, and the tunnel is nearly 6 ft. high throughout. The Chronicler's statement (as distinct from 2 Kgs 20:20, referring to the "Book of the Chronicles," not this text) shows that the project was not intended to bring the water into Jerusalem, but only to put it beyond the besiegers' reach. In fact, we cannot even say that Siloam was inside Jerusalem, for we are unsure whether 2 Chr 32:5 means that it was Hezekiah who extended the S wall of Jerusalem to include the whole W (modern Zion) hill. Such is indeed plausibly maintained in the recent mammoth researches of both Simons and Vincent, but other experts put the event as late as Herod the Great (Albright, Germer-Durand) or Nehemiah (Galling, Avi-Yonah), or as early as the Jebusites (Dalman)—an archaeological uncertainty spanning 1000 years!

76 **18.** The Chronicler omits the emphasis of 2 Kgs 19:26 on the consternation of Hezekiah's curia at the fact that Assyria's envoy to Jerusalem talks the local language to the populace. **19.** The author summarizes the speech as indicating to the people of Jerusalem that a test case is imminent to prove whether the god of Israel would be as effective in battle as the god of Assyria.

This situation is fair enough, but what the Chronicler suppresses altogether is the clear indication of 2 Kgs 18:33ff. and earlier biblical passages (most notably Mi 4:5) that it is precisely such a test of strength in which the God of Israel glories!

20. The Chronicler's only mention of Isaiah, who, in fact, had disapproved the lack of faith shown by Hezekiah's defense measures (Is 22:11). The piteous comportment of Hezekiah is quickly passed over to stress the miraculous angel (2 Kgs 19:3,35). Why the author should omit the 185,000 slain in a single night is not clear. **24.** It is also perplexing why the Chronicler should not expatiate complacently on the sign (Isaiah's sundial shadow going backwards, 2 Kgs 20:11), and not mention Isaiah at all in connection with Hezekiah's danger of death. **25.** In fact, the Chronicler makes much more explicit than 2 Kgs 20:1 (or really 20:17; see v. 27) that this threatening death was a punishment for Hezekiah's pride and the sufferings it brought upon Judah. This alteration is alien in spirit to all the others made by the Chronicler in copying the Kgs text; it can be accounted for only as dramatic heightening, in view of the splendid repentance of Hezekiah that quickly follows. **27–29.** These words are largely those which 2 Kgs 20:13 used to describe Hezekiah's friendliness toward the overtures of Babylon, bitterly reproved by Isaiah in 20:17–18 as unconditioned cause of the coming exile. But the Chronicler embodies this inventory of Hezekiah's wealth into his epilogue as proof of the monarch's virtue. **32.** All Judah honored him at his death.

(D) Judah's Disillusionment (33:1–36:23).

77 (a) Not-So-Wicked Manasseh (33:1–25). **6.** The list of Manasseh's iniquities (in 2 Kgs 21:6) so reflects Jer 7:31 that he apparently violated every law in the book. Manasseh's long reign (687–642, Bright) is unmitigated evil to 2 Kgs 21:11. For the Chronicler, a contradiction is involved: long life and power is a reward and blessing of God; it is not compatible with immorality. The author solves this dilemma by finding in the records overlooked by Kgs, but published in Esarhaddon's Prism (*ANET* 291; cf. 294), evidence that Manasseh had been forced to go to Mesopotamia to show his subjection. **11.** The Chronicler regards this humiliating episode as a kind of captivity. **12.** The author's theological inference of a consequent humility and prayer of the captive king is commonly held to have suggested the apocryphal *Prayer of Manasseh*, an official appendix to the Vg (→ Apocrypha, 68:37). More plausibly, Cazelles (BJ) suspects that the apocryphon already existed when the Chronicler wrote, and was taken by him as a historical evidence for the present narration, hinted also in some manuscripts of Tob 14:10. **15.** It would be hard to exclude the possibility that some of the architectural and liturgical activities of an aging monarch would be such as the clergy might approve (regarding the Gihon wall, see Simons, *OTS* 7, 191; *JOT* 328). Neither the events themselves nor their proof of short-range retribution, but simply the principle that good will somehow be rewarded and evil punished is the object of the Chronicler's assertion.

23. Amon's reign is brief enough to be written off as a total loss. **25.** His assassination, despite clearing the path for Josiah, is not condoned. But the anarchist violence by which so-called justice was done seems to have terrified the surviving officers of the curia into guiding the child ruler's steps along more God-fearing paths.

78 (b) Josiah (34:1–35:27). **3.** If eight-year-old Josiah came to power in 640, he would have been nearing manhood in 633. Perhaps his "beginning" then to seek God may refer to the fact that with Ashurbanipal's death in that year it was felt safe to evict Assyria's gods from Jerusalem, as was done by Hezekiah in 30:14. Some commentators, however, emphasize that only Canaanite idolatries are mentioned by either Chr or 2 Kgs 23:13, from which they conclude that the Chronicler correctly asserted that Assyrian syncretism had already been outlawed by Manasseh. **6.** Gradually, as Ashurbanipal's successor turned out to be weak and short lived, the chancery of Judah began taking over the administration of N Israel while the king was still in his late teens. **8.** By the time Josiah was 26, Assyria's weakness was irreparable, and he embarked upon the celebrated reform that dominates 2 Chr 34–35 (= 2 Kgs 22–23), as well as Dt (12:11).

10. The finding of this Book of the Law, the pivotal event of Josiah's reform, occurred not during the actual repairs on the Temple but in a preliminary audit of its finances. Thus, the Chronicler agrees with 2 Kgs 22:3, but differs in seeing Josiah's religious reform already well under way when this event occurred. Even the king's moral and ritual life up to that time is a kind of reform of the Manasseh-Amon tradition, and Van den Born exaggerates when he calls the Chronicler's presentation here a "theological postulate which cannot be historical." **12.** The author gives a detailed account of choir Levite supervisors to replace the curious insistence of 2 Kgs 22:7 (= 12:15; see comment on 24:14) that the less known about financial transactions between curia and contractors the better. Rudolph cites excavated examples from Assyria and Egypt to show (against Von Rad) that there is nothing implausible in having liturgical musicians set the tempo by a beat for masons at work. **19.** The young king's horrified dismay at hearing what the book contained (as in 2 Kgs 22:11) is difficult to reconcile with the Chronicler's assumption that the reform is already in progress. Today, it is generally agreed that the content of Dt was fairly familiar from the preaching of Jeremiah, and probably stems from an origin in the northern kingdom during Hezekiah's reform. Essentially, it was an updating of the Mosaic Torah. The king's violent reaction may indeed have been intended as a dramatic gesture to shake the resistance. **30.** The king reads aloud to the solemn assembly the Book of the Covenant, not Ex 21–23 as is generally understood by that title, but Dt, as is implied by the style of v. 31. **33.** Except for what was anticipated in vv. 5ff. above, the Chronicler strangely omits the picturesque and varied account of Josiah's implementation of his reform, especially at Bethel (2 Kgs 23:4–20).

79 **35:3.** The Chronicler's presentation of the famed Passover celebrated by Josiah in the very year of his finding the book, is greatly expanded from 2 Kgs 23:21ff., chiefly to show that certain post-exilic functions of the Levites were not a modernistic usurpation. This Passover forms the point of departure for the apocryphal *1 Esdras*. **3.** It would be too inconsistent for the author to envision the Levites standing before Josiah with the Ark on their shoulders, despite the fact that David (in 1 Chr 16:37; 23:4) had already replaced this duty with others more suited to the Ark's fixed abode. Rather, we can paraphrase thus: Inasmuch as your clan was by David's activities released from the carrying of the Ark, and the other burdens he imposed on you, do not exhaust your unflagging zeal, you may as well lend a hand with the other sacristy jobs, which the priests are neglecting. **5.** Laymen are prominent here, and the actual slaughter is not done by priests. This verse does not really say that the right of sacrificing belonged more primitively to the lay head of the family (which is true), but it does at least hint such as a basis for transferring the pre-exilic prerogative from priests to Levites. **18.** Samuel emerges in this perspective with an altogether singular emphasis. The Chronicler's unexpected admission that not even peerless David had ever performed the Passover so fully in the primitive spirit, is taken by experts as a way of saying, "What's so unusual about giving the primary role in sacrifice to others than priests when that is the way it was done in earliest times, and in fact even then the priests were recognized to be deficient?" (cf. 1 Sm 2:12). **20.** Josiah's opposition to the Pharaoh was not mere meddling, nor was it a firm stand regarding the administration of Galilee, which he had so recently and cautiously taken over. Instead, it was the necessary groundwork to defend himself against eventual fierce reprisals if the Egyptians should lose the impending battle. The Chronicler omits the statement of 2 Kgs 23:29 that Neco was marching "against [rather than 'to (help)'] the King of Assyria"; it is from Nabopolassar's [Gadd] Chronicle (*ANET* 305) that we know Egypt was really helping Assyria to resist the insurgence of Babylon (see E. Vogt, VTSup 4 [1957] 67–96). **21.** There is insufficient warrant for correcting "house (*bêt*) of my war" to "Babylon (*bābēl*) of my war." **22.** A crux of exegetes is this reproach of the Chronicler against Josiah for having refused to listen to the word of God from the mouth of Neco. A largely Catholic controversy has flared over precisely what god Neco thought he was quoting—surely not Yahweh. B. Alfrink maintained (*Bib* 15 [1934] 173–84) that the king of Assyria was meant, honorifically called a "god" as when the Amarna Pharaoh is addressed by Palestine kings as "all my gods." True, Egypt is no vassal of Assyria, but neither is "my god" as humble as "all my gods," and, in fact, Egypt is helping Assyria. Nevertheless B. Couroyer (*RB* 55 [1948] 388–96), following H. Bückers, insists that it is some Egyptian god, probably that represented on the army standards. According to R. Davidson (*VT* 9 [1959] 205), following *1 Esdras,* we have here Yahweh's reproach to Josiah, echoed in Jer 17:5. Much more plausible is the view of simple theological postulate. For the Chronicler, Josiah could not have been cut off so early unless some sin had been involved, the only semblance of which is that he had done what "God" commanded him not to. **24.** The Chronicler seems to have preserved more accurately than 2 Kgs 23:29 the detail that Josiah did not actually expire until his royal person had been conveyed back to Jerusalem.

80 (c) THE BABYLONIAN PUPPETS (36:1–23). The Chronicler allots only a dozen verses to sum up the last 58 verses of Kgs; then he adds 12 more verses of his own. **1.** As in Kgs, it is the '*am hā'āreṣ*, "the people of the land" as a sociological or perhaps religious technical term (see comment on Ezr 4:4), who promote Jehoahaz. The four monarchs of this chapter confuse us by their multiple and similar sounding names. **3.** By the battle of Carchemish and simultaneous death of Nabopolassar, Nebuchadnezzar becomes warlord of Asia and finally reduces Judah to the province status that had been threatening since the same fate befell Samaria a century earlier. **4.** When Jehoahaz seeks asylum in Egypt, his brother Eliakim becomes king under the name of Jehoiakim. Only now is Jeremiah's prophetic mission begun, according to C. Whitley (*VT* 14 [1964] 467–83). **5.** His son Jehoiachin succeeds him and after three years is called to Babylon; honorably installed there, he survives Nebuchadnezzar! (See E. Janssen, *Juda in der Exilszeit* [Göttingen, 1956].) **10.** The last king of Judah was a younger son of Josiah, called Zedekiah or Mattaniah. The Chronicler calls him Jehoiachin's "brother," a common Semitic term for "relative." **20.** The author's reflection on the evil of not listening to God's prophets culminates in a claim that the Exile would last 70 years in fulfillment of Jer 25:12; moreover, it would be a homeopathic punishment for neglecting the Sabbath year law of Lv 25:4; Ex 23:10. **22–23.** These verses really belong to Ezr (cf. Ezr 1:1–3), but were repeated here when this portion of Chr was inserted into the canon after Ezr. Thus, the narrative is rounded off, and the ending of the Hebr Bible is optimistic.

EZRA AND NEHEMIAH

BIBLIOGRAPHY

81 Batten, L., *A Critical and Exegetical Commentary on the Books of Ezra and Nehemiah* (ICC; N.Y., 1913). Bowman, R., "Ezra and Nehemiah," *IB*. Browne, L., "Ezra and Nehemiah," *PCB* 370–80. De Fraine, J., *Esdras en Nehemias* (Roermond, 1961). Galling, K., *Die Bücher der Chronik, Esra, Nehemia* (ATD; Göttingen, 1954). Gelin, A., *Le Livre d' Esdras et Néhémie* (BJ; 2nd ed.; Paris, 1960). Noordtzij, A., *Esra-Nehemiah* (Kampen, 1961). Rehm, M., *Esra-Nehemias* (Echter-B; Würzburg, 1956). Rudolph, W., *Esra und Nehemia* (HAT; Tübingen, 1949). Ryle, H., *The Books of Ezra and Nehemiah* (CBSC; Cambridge, 1911). Schneider, H., *Die Bücher Esra und Nehemia* (BB; Bonn, 1959). Torrey, C. C., *Ezra Studies* (Chicago, 1910). Welch, A. C., *Post-exilic Judaism* (London, 1935). (→ 1 above.)

INTRODUCTION

82 **(I) Ezr-Neh Chronology and Esdras A.** The first statement Ezra makes about himself in the book which bears his name is that he and some other latecomers finally leave Babylon in the seventh regnal year of King Artaxerxes (Ezr 7:8). That would be 458 BC, if Artaxerxes I was meant—a thing that the biblical text neither affirms nor denies.

Nehemiah's narrative follows Ezra's, except for Neh 8–10, in which a few explicit but perplexing verses make them contemporary. With respect for Torrey, we can say that no one maintains Nehemiah's Artaxerxes to be Artaxerxes II; hence his dates are secure—445 and 432 (Neh 1:1; 13:6). A 20-century unanimity of tradition, in accord with the surface tenor of our text, has dated Ezra's return under Artaxerxes I before Nehemiah in 458.

In his lectures at Louvain from 1880, and especially in a series of publications since 1890 (*RB* 33 [1924] 33–64), A. van Hoonacker dropped a bombshell into the staid fixity of exegetical preconceptions by claiming that Ezra first appeared under Artaxerxes II in 398. His arguments are reduced to eight points: 1) The wall for which Nehemiah is chiefly renowned already exists when Ezra reaches Jerusalem (9:9; *gādēr*). (2) Ezra (10:1) finds Jerusalem already repopulated (by Nehemiah, 11:1). (3) Nehemiah is put before Ezra in Neh 12:26; 8:1. (4) Eliashib, contemporary of Nehemiah (13:4), is (grand-?)father of Jehohanan, Ezra's contemporary (Ezr 10:6 = Neh 12:23?). (5) The silence of Nehemiah's memoirs about Ezra's allegedly earlier Torah promulgation is inexplicable. (6) Nehemiah (11:3) enumerates repatriates led by Sheshbazzar and/or Zerubbabel, but not those led by Ezra (8:2). (7) Ezra (8:33) makes use of a committee of four resembling that instituted by Nehemiah (13:13). (8) Nehemiah's handling of mixed marriages, delayed until his second tour of duty (13:23), could not suppose Ezra (9:14) to have preceded.

A majority of modern exegetes have rallied to this insight rightly credited to Van Hoonacker. Emergence of similar views in M. Vernès (*Précis d'histoire juive* [1889] 582n.), claiming Ezra never existed, and F. de Saulcy (*Études chronologiques...Esdras* [1868] 27), dating *both* after 398, made no comparable dent on scholarship. Not all of Van Hoonacker's specific proofs, especially regarding Eliashib, have resisted criticism (on *gādēr*, see H. Kaupel and others in *Bib* 16 [1935] 82, 213, 443; *BZ* 22 [1934] 89). Among supporters of the 398 date are M.-J. Lagrange, S. Mowinckel, J. Touzard, Schneider, O. Eissfeldt, H. Cazelles, and, with best documentation in English, N. Snaith (*ZAW* 63 [1951] 53–66) and H. H. Rowley (*Servant of the Lord and other Essays* [London, 1952] 131–59).

The traditional dating (458 BC) is upheld by J. Morgenstern (*JSS* 7 [1962] 1; *HUCA* 31 [1960] 1) and by an impressive lineup of Catholic scholars—A. Fernández, A. Miller, J. de Fraine, H. Bückers, R. de Vaux.

Neither dating really comes to grips with the problem of Nehemiah and Ezra working together in Neh 8:9; 10:1. Hence, W. F. Albright (*BA* 9 [1946] 13, renouncing his view set forth in *JBL* 40 [1921] 121) gained solid following for the correction of seventh (Ezr 7:8) to 37th year (J. Wellhausen and O. Procksch, less helpfully, 27th). This dating of Ezra's ministry in 428 is followed by Rudolph's master commentary (also by A. Lefèvre, *VDBS* 5 [1958] 393; V. Pavlovský, *Bib* 38 [1957] 275, 428; J. Bright, *Fest. Y. Kaufmann* [Jerusalem, 1960] 70–87). Concretely, this middle-of-the-road dating involves substituting one textual emendation for another. It is no less lawful to expunge Nehemiah's name from Neh 8:9; numbers are notoriously corruptible, but important names just as notoriously glossable! Browne seems unduly confident of the "impossibility" that Ezra would have tolerated Tobiah's intrusion in Neh 13:7. What is perhaps the most disturbing feature of this 428 compromise is its doubly harmonistic striving.

Resolute suspension of judgment among the three equally tenable alternatives would seem to be the most warranted scholarly posture. Only with the practical scope of dislodging hoary presuppositions, we will accept here as concrete framework the 398 dating. This date will incidentally facilitate our support of another and more momentous insight of Cazelles regarding Ezra's conciliation of the Samaritans, which, however, in principle, leaves open the question of dating.

83 Our canonical Ezr-Neh are combined by the LXX into a single book to which it gives the title Esdras B. Preceding it is Esdras A (= *1 Esdras;* → Apocrypha, 68:39) in which narratives about Josiah and Ezra flank a colorful Susanna-style wisdom riddle attached loosely to the person of Zerubbabel (see chart below).

Torrey attaches great weight to *1 Esdras*, although correcting it momentously. Rudolph's commentary includes it under the Ezr–Neh passages to which it is relevant; then he adds at the end a translation with brief textual criticism of the riddle. We may summarize it here (cf. F. Zimmermann, *JQR* 54 [1964] 179–200). "What is the best of all things?" is the challenge, in typically Hellenistic sophist style. Three unoriginal answers are given: wine, the king, woman. But when it is finished, the contestant who had already spoken third is declared to be Zerubbabel, and it is he who continues with a fourth and victorious answer, "Great is truth, and it does prevail" (4:41; not "will prevail" as often misquoted via the Vg). As Zerubbabel's reward, Darius agrees to allow (Nehemiah?) the rebuilding of Jerusalem. The story concludes with a thanksgiving of the victor's clan.

Schneider dates the *1 Esdras* booklet (→ Apocrypha, 68:38–41) in dependence upon Daniel after 150 BC, and concludes that the canonical Ezr on which it drew existed already in its definitive form, that the compiler's technique gives us a good idea of how the Chronicler's procedures were continued, and that the translation is a confirmation of the original Hebr-Aram wording independent of the LXX Esdras B (see E. Hammershaimb, *Tredje Esdrasbog* [Copenhagen, 1963]; E. Johannesen, *Studier* [Copenhagen, 1946]).

The confident reassembling of all the verses of Ezr–Neh in the original order in which the Chronicler had written them, attempted by Torrey on the basis of Ezr's dating and the *1 Esdras* evidence, although called brilliant and definitive by Browne (*PCB*), will seem to most users far too assured. We will here indicate the chronological sequence that seems to fit best, but no reasonable reading or theological use of our Bible can proceed on the assumption that any Ezr reconstruction

LXX	*MT*	*Content*
A1:1–20	= 2 Chr 35:1–19	Josiah's Passover
1:21–22	unparalleled: cf. 1 Kgs 13:2,32; 2 Kgs 23:14	Records of kings' deserts
1:23–55	= 2 Chr 35:20–36:21	Doomed Josiah-Zedekiah
2:1–3	= 2 Chr 36:22–23 = Ezr 1:1ff.	Resurgence under Cyrus
2:3–14	= Ezr 1:3–11	Temple vessels restored
2:15–26	= Ezr 4:7–24	Samaritan opposition
3:11–5:6	unparalleled	The riddle
5:7–71	= Ezr 2:1–4:5	Repatriate listing
6:1–9:36	= Ezr 5:1–10:44	Temple; marriage reform
9:37–55	= Neh 7:73 (MT 72–8:13)	Reading of Ezra's law

but one is categorically excluded. We hold with the virtual unanimity of modern experts that Chr-Ezr are one book (despite Fernández) by one author (despite Freedman). We also hold, with even more deference to the impressive array of Albright's followers, that the author, the so-called Chronicler, was not Ezra himself, who may indeed have been the author of the Ezr memoir passages in the first person (denied by Rudolph following A. Kapelrud, *Question of Authorship* [Oslo, 1944] 95). With Von Rad and Robert, we consider Ezra to be the redactor of the Pentateuch, from whose Sinai orientation the work of the Chronicler was written as an emphatic dissent. D. Bonhoeffer (in *Junge Kirche* 4 [1936] 653–61) discloses his deep insights into these books.

84 **(II) Outline.** The Books of Ezra and Nehemiah can be outlined as follows:

(I) The Second Temple (Ezr 1:1–6:22)
- (A) Cyrus and the Return (1:1–11)
- (B) Zerubbabel and the List (2:1–70)
- (C) Laying the Cornerstone (3:1–13)
- (D) Interruption: The Samaritans (4:1–24)
- (E) Prophetic Nudge to Completion (5:1–6:22)

(II) Ezra's Return Convoy and Torah (Ezr 7:1–10:44; Neh 8–9)
- (A) Ezra's Priestly Scribal Activity (7:1–28)
- (B) Rounding Up the Convoy (8:1–31)
- (C) The Situation in Jerusalem (8:32–10:44)

(III) The Rearmament of Jerusalem (Neh 1:1–7:5)
- (A) The Susa Report and Sequal (1:1–2:11)
  - (a) The Jerusalem Disaster (1:1–10)
  - (b) The King's Caprice (2:1–8)
  - (c) Nehemiah's Status in Judah (2:9–11)
- (B) Program of Reconstruction (2:12–3:32)
  - (a) Wall Inspection by Night (2:12–15)
  - (b) Public Support Assured (2:16–20)
  - (c) The Local Chapter Masons (3:1–32)
- (C) Triumphalism (4:1–7:5)
  - (a) Embattled Persistence (4:1–23) (MT 3:33–38; 4:1–17)
  - (b) Social Justice Reform (5:1–19)
  - (c) Dramatic Completion of the Mission (6:1–7:72)

(IV) Promulgation of Ezra's Torah (Neh 8:1–9:38)

(V) Nehemiah's Final Ministry (Neh 10:1–13:30)
- (A) The Pledge (10:1–39)
- (B) Forcing People to Live in Jerusalem (11:1–12:26)
- (C) Solemn Dedication of the Wall (12:27–13:14)
- (D) Nehemiah as Defender of the Faith (13:15–30)

COMMENTARY ON EZRA

85 **(I) The Second Temple (Ezr 1:1–6:22).** Today's Jewish people rather tenderly favor the expression "Second Temple." It is a chronological term for an important period of their ethnic existence. That era after the return from Exile to the Diaspora is in a certain sense continuing today. But it focuses chiefly the single century that fostered the three most controversial phenomena of all Jewish history: the baptizing sectaries of Qumran and elsewhere; Hillel and Shammai; Jesus and Paul.

Actually it was precisely Herod's Temple that during that century became a wonder of the world to replace the modest efforts of the returned exiles. Yet Jewish tradition never speaks of Herod's as a "Third Temple," doggedly regarding it as a mere repair job on the Temple of Zerubbabel.

(A) Cyrus and the Return (1:1–11). **1.** Repetition of 2 Chr 36:22f. here is sometimes invoked as a proof that the same author wrote both works. The contrary could also be inferred. Probably once 2 Chr 36:23 continued directly into what is now Ezr 1:4. When the Ezr scroll was detached and put into the Jewish canon before there was felt to be any need for Chr, those two verses were borrowed to stand at the head. Unreasonably literal is E. Janssen's claim (*Juda in der Exilszeit* [Göttingen, 1956] 119, following Wellhausen) that Chr wrongly holds Judah to have been left a desert waste while Ezr admits it continued to be populated (see F. Dijkema, *Nieuw Theologisch Tijdschrift* 29 [1940] 136–50).

The first year of Cyrus' rule in Babylon began actually in October 539, but officially on the (March) New Year's Day of 538. This leaves us a "round" 70 years of exile as meant by Jer 25:11, without supposing that Judah's fall is to be dated from the outset of Jehoiakim's reign in 609 as in 2 Kgs 24:1 (P. Ackroyd, *JNES* 17 [1958] 23; A. Orr, *VT* 6 [1956] 304) or 586–516, as held by C. Whitley (*VT* 4 [1954] 60; see K. Galling in *Fest. W. Rudolph* [Tübingen, 1961] 67–96). (On this decree of Cyrus, see E. Bickerman, *JBL* 65 [1946] 249–75; R. de Vaux, *RB* 46 [1937] 29–57; L. Rost, *Fest. W. Rudolph* [Tübingen, 1961] 301–7.)

2. We cannot exclude that the Chronicler here incorporates a few explanatory notes into his otherwise faithful citation of the decree. **3.** A basic Persian viewpoint is preserved in "Yahweh, the God of Israel, is the God who is in Jerusalem." The fact that this unknown and foreign deity is acknowledged by Cyrus as his superior means merely that the king hereby gives to a cultus of his subjects the stamp of his official approval. It need not imply that Cyrus had taken the step of identifying Judah's Yahweh with Ahura-Mazda, whom his decree undoubtedly regards as "the god of heaven." Even as cited by the Chronicler, the words do not indicate that Cyrus had been converted to the Yahwist religion, in awareness of Is 45:3; 41:25 according to Josephus (*Ant.* 11.1,2). Any conqueror must count on securing the benevolence of the subject population by tolerating and even positively promoting their tenacious usages that do not interfere with his power. Indigenous religion especially, for a nonproselytizing power, is a vehicle of peace, order, and civil obedience, which the Persians are known to have exploited in Egypt (cf. A. Olmstead, *AJSL* 51 [1935] 247; S. Eddy, *The King Is Dead* [Lincoln, 1961] 48). Cyrus boasts of having restored gods to their sees (*ANET* 316).

4. Cyrus has a special motive to favor the Jews as a minority oppressed and hated by his own Babylonian enemies. This does not mean that he took any initiative in suggesting or commanding that the Temple be rebuilt, or that he undertook to pay for the project (despite 6:4,8), even by taxing non-Jewish neighbors. **6.** The return is seen as a re-enactment of the Exodus (11:2). It is also taken by modern Jewry and ecumenism as a prototype of (peaceful) Zionism (A. Gelin, *LumVi* 7 [1952] 95–105; G. Lambert, *Cahiers Sioniens* 1 [1947] 314–37). **7.** Restitution of the sacred vessels confiscated by Nebuchadnezzar was undoubtedly a generous act, and because of it, the name of Cyrus deservedly heads the list of contributors to the rebuilding. It really did not cost him anything, for even the Babylonians had not seen fit to put the liturgical ware to any practical use.

8. Sheshbazzar (Senabassar in *1 Esdras* 3:15), as prince of Judah and civil leader of the returning community, is for the Chronicler merely a Persian surname for Zerubbabel (2:2). In 1 Chr 3:18, Zerubbabel is the son of a Pedaiah to whose name is added Shenazzar, generally taken to be Pedaiah's brother, Zerubbabel's uncle, identical with Sheshbazzar; but even if identical, it could be a kind of honorific surname applicable to Pedaiah and to Zerubbabel also. **9.** This inventory is studied by K. Galling in *ZDPV* 60 (1937) 177; see now his *Studien... im persischen Zeitalter* (Tübingen, 1964).

11. No details of the return journey are given (cf. J. Bewer, *AJSL* 36 [1919] 18). It probably took about 100 days, by the Fertile Crescent route, in the spring of 538. C. C. Torrey (*AJSL* 37 [1920] 91) supplies details from apocryphal *1 Esdras*, on the assumption that by Darius in 5:1 is meant Cyrus (refuted by N. Baynes, *JTS* 25 [1924] 154). The number of repatriates in this first convoy may well have been only a few hundred. The Jews in Babylon had already prospered because of their facility in the Aram chancery language. When Persia conquered Babylon, their usefulness as fifth column in the chanceries was doubled. Moreover, private concerns like Murashu & Co. are shown by cuneiform records to have been tycoons of business (edited by A. Clay in English in 1912, by G. Cardascia in French in 1951). If even Ezra's biblical institute (7:6) was loth to move, we may be sure that no eager torrent accepted the king's invitation to exchange comfort and security for the fulfillment of a religious urge.

86 **(B) Zerubbabel and the List (2:1–70).** Chapter 2 is repeated word for word in Neh 7:6–73. The numbers amount to some 50,000. There is no cogent ground for presuming that the figure excludes women and children, some quarter million in all, but even so, the number better fits the Neh situation, allowing the repatriates a century for growth and expansion. Of the 29 out of 153 numbers that differ in Neh 7, only a few can be explained by word alteration, but many can be clarified by cipher notation (cf. H. Allrik, *BASOR* 136 [1954] 21). The group here enumerated seems to have a flourishing cultus, as if the Temple had already been standing in its midst. On the other hand, Neh 7:5 asserts that the list as there given is old, and the stress on cultus is natural if the homesteaders' primary aim is to build the Temple. The archival and juridical parts of our Bible are now known to have been kept up-to-date by a process of continuous accretion. We may well conclude that the names stem mostly from the first return. But the numbers were progressively increased, and doubtless some important names were added as further caravans returned from Babylon and the population grew by natural increase within Judah. Rudolph finds confirmation in the alternation between clans and locality groups, but there is no reason for his limiting the accretion to the time before 515, even though Ezr 8:1 gives a separate list for his own convoy after 458. K. Galling (*JBL* 70 [1951] 199) holds that the list was a brief drawn up for the Persian court in 519, refuting the views of G. Hölscher, that it was a tax roll, and of A. Alt, that it is a register of land deeds. We may hold that a list as utilized under Nehemiah after 445 was later copied into Ezr 2 because an authoritative scribe found it to be a warranted expansion of the previous data.

2. Zerubbabel, as civil leader of the repatriates with responsibility for the rebuilding of the Temple, is equated with Sheshbazzar by the Chronicler in Ezr 1:8,11, and ambiguously in 5:14,16. The title *peḥâ* is given to both (5:14; Hag 1:1). The equation is tolerable, even though arguments of earlier Catholics in its favor based on frequency of double names among Diaspora Jews are to be discounted. Both names are Babylonian; we would expect one to be Hebrew or at least Persian. No success has attended the attempt of P. Riessler (*BZ* 1 [1903] 232; *TQ* 90 [1910] 1) to prove that *zēr-babîlî*, "born in Babylon," is rather *zᵉrûb bā-'ēbel*, "oppressed by grief," as a synonym of *Naḥam-yâ*, "God has consoled." In this verse, Nehemiah is doubtless not the same as in either Neh 1:1 or 3:16. Zerubbabel represents the dynasty of David through Shealtiel in Mt 1:13, but (perhaps by levirate, Dt 25:5) through Pedaiah and Shenazzar in 1 Chr 3:18 (see comment on 1:8). At the side of Zerubbabel stands Joshua, son of Jozadak, the highest ranking priest (3:2). He is messianically paired with Zerubbabel in Hag 1:12; 2:23 (S. Cook, *Studies in Old Testament Prophecy* [N.Y., 1950] 19–36). Joshua appears doubtfully as a Qumran-style second, or even third, priestly messiah in Zech 6:12; 4:11; 3:8 (but cf. B. Vawter, *BCCT* 86). Bigvai, a Persian name, appears also at Elephantine. Other names in this verse are spelled differently in Neh 7.

87 **20.** A shift from clan groups to localities, all close to Jerusalem, which is unmentioned. The geography is pre-exilic and thus somewhat idyllic. **31.** This intrusion of clan groups is followed by post-exilic Sharon settlements in v. 33. **36–55.** A list of priests, and Levites, including "Oblates" (*nᵉtînîm*, 43) and Canaanites (53) with a minority status regularized under Solomon. **62.** Genealogy, "juridical rather than biological, but extremely important" (De Fraine). **63.** "Governor," *tiršātā'*, is here doubtless an appellation like "his honor"; Sheshbazzar is called "prince" (*nāśî'*) in 1:8. *Urim:* It is remarkable that this rather primitive divinatory use should survive unexpurgated in so recent and priestly a document (cf. Dt 33:8; 1 Sm 14:41; → Religious Institutions, 76:7–8). Galling (*Fest. W. Rudolph*, 91) holds the device to be unmistakably oracular here, and also equated with the jewels of the breastplate (Ex 28:30) as in a Qumran comment on Is 54:11–12 (J. Allegro, *JBL* 77 [1958] 221). E. Robertson (*VT* 14 [1964] 64–74) holds *urim* and *thummim* to mean A and T standing for the whole alphabet—i.e., academic instruction. They are taken as abstractions by the LXX, as "lightgiving and accomplishment" here in Ezr, but as "revelation and truth (or holiness)" in earlier books.

64. Census total is 49,897. Identical figures are given in Neh 7:66–67, except for 45 additional singers. In the preceding subtotals, Neh has only 652 for 775 of v. 5, 845 for 945 of v. 8, and frequent smaller variants. The free citizens total only 29,818 in Ezr, ch. 2 (30,142 in *1 Esdras*), and 31,089 in Neh, as against the total given as 42,360. The other 11,000 would make an unconvincingly scarce number of wives, not to speak of children; rather, some subtotals were just skipped.

68. Daric, as in Hebrew, is an anachronism for the time preceding Darius I; moreover, Neh 7:70ff. has only 41,000, audited according to donor groups. If the Attic coin then current in Persia is meant, some 150,000 dollars in gold may be involved and a roughly equal amount of silver (4200 [Neh 7:71–72] or 5000 *mna*, valued at about 30 dollars each).

88 **(C) Laying the Cornerstone (3:1–13).** **1.** *seventh month:* September just one year after Cyrus took power would have allowed six months for the red tape in Babylon, plus three months after the arrival in Jerusalem—ample time for getting down to work, and corroborated by v. 8. But the very reasonableness of this schedule, plus the choice of a month that was, in fact, crammed with liturgy, makes it legitimate to suspect that the Chronicler is here reasoning rather than drawing on any recorded data. Only by a highly speculative theorizing can we claim that the year 520 is here meant, 18 years after Sheshbazzar's earlier group had begun the Temple building.

2. *built the altar:* Experts differ as to whether this implies that those who had never been in exile had allowed the ruined altar to fall into disuse, despite Jer 41:5, or whether the returning exiles disdained to use the cult paraphernalia of the inhabitants. **3.** *Fear . . . peoples of the lands:* See comments on 4:4; 9:2. Although bracketed as a gloss by Vaccari and Noth, the reference here is doubtless to those Judeans who had not been kept pure in the crucible of persecution and had become absorbed in the province of Samaria.

4–5. *daily . . . continual:* The two types of offerings. *'Ôlâ* is the holocaust (Lv 1:13) for the morning; for the evening, another holocaust is prescribed in Nm 28:4 and at Warka (*ANET* 342). But in Ezr 9:4, the evening offering is called *minḥâ*, identified as *tāmîd* in Nm 4:16 and as grain plus libation in Lv 2:1 (see T. Gaster, *IDB* 4, 150). **6.** That so holy a work should not get under way without meticulous daily fulfillment of the very rites for which the Temple is being built seems reasonable: Probably the Chronicler's reasoning rather than recorded facts.

7. *money:* This stress on an obvious prerequisite is perhaps meant to indicate that religion keeps pace with technology, inasmuch as minted coinage was a recent invention. *Joppa:* More "reasoning," based on Solomon's recorded steps in 2 Chr 2:16; it is not the same as "falsification or fiction," straw men that De Fraine knocks down. **8.** *twenty years old:* The age limits were reduced because of the need (see comment on 1 Chr 23:3).

9. Joshua is paired with Kadmiel as in 2:40; because his father's name is not given, it is hard to be sure the Chronicler regarded him as a Levite distinct from the (high) priest just mentioned. The rather pagan name of Henadad (lit., "grace of Phoenician Apollo") is perhaps tidied up as Hodaviah ("praise Yahweh") in 2:40. **11.** Cf. Ps 106:1.

12. The old men wept chiefly because it was a moment of deep emotion. There may also have been anguish in recalling that the earlier Temple had been destroyed by enemies, for a Babylon cornerstone reads: "I started the work weeping, finished it rejoicing." The weeping may also have betrayed misgivings, aroused by the already perceptible ground plan, that the Temple would be inferior (Hag 2:3) at its completion, but we cannot agree that the finishing of the Temple rather than its founding is envisioned here, although such is maintained by experts (L. Batten [based on *1 Esdras*]; J. Touzard, *RB* 24 [1915] 59; J. Bewer, *AJT* 19 [1915] 108).

89 **(D) Interruption: The Samaritans (4:1–24).** **1.** The adversaries of Judah and Benjamin are doubtless the Samaritans, and chiefly the bureaucrats (even if of Judean origin and part of the remnant) functioning in the Persian province of Samaria to which Judah was humiliatingly made subordinate. **2.** At whatever point in history the Samaritan break became irretrievable, the party line in Judah gradually became what it clearly was to the Chronicler—i.e., owing to the replacement of genuine Ephraimite Israelites by relocated Persians under Esarhaddon (676, not recorded in the Bible but doubtless a continuation of Sargon's policy, 2 Kgs 17:24), the racial purity indispensable to his religion had been lost (see J. Jeremias, *ThWNT* 7 [1960] 88–94; J. Macdonald, *Theology of the Samaritans* [London, 1964]). **3.** Zerubbabel does not deny or question that these Samaritans and their Judah-born collaborators had really been worshiping Yahweh. Rather, he gives free rein to stubbornness and racial prejudice in ascribing to their mixed blood what were doubtless imperfections in their observance of details of Israelite law (Hag 2:12; Zech 3:9; Jn 8:48!). His unacknowledged motivation was doubtless the reasonable one that a powerful entrenched group, offering to help as a unitary block instead of individual volunteers, would foreseeably snatch control of the enterprise right out of the returnees' hands.

4. *people of the land:* Not "foreign-born landowners" (Alt's view is refuted by H. Grosheide, *Gereformeerd Theologisch Tijdschrift* 54 [1954] 67) nor the former poor Judeans, enemies of the Deuteronomist movement, whom the Babylonians favored by furnishing with land (as Janssen, *Juda in der Exilszeit*, 49, 121), but the people of Judah, who were employees or collaborators of the Samaria-based regime (as D. Rothstein, *Juden und Samaritaner* [Leipzig, 1908] 28, 41). Whatever their syncretistic guilt, it can hardly be regarded as worse than that which the earlier prophets of both Israel and Judah had constantly excoriated (cf. G. Ahlström, *Aspects of Syncretism in Israelite Religion* [Lund, 1963]). The uncooperativeness of the repatriates, like every ghetto mentality, is the expression of a legitimate concern to preserve religious truth uncontaminated by contact with the imperfect. But it is not the only attitude religion requires toward outsiders, and a certain tension or apparent contradiction vis-à-vis dawning universalism and proselytizing tendencies must be taken in stride as part of the revealed datum and of God's salvation plan (see W. Braude, *Jewish Proselyting* [*sic*] [Providence, 1940]).

90 **6.** Ahasuerus is Xerxes I (485–465), who scourged the sea during his war with the Greeks in 481. There are three principal hypotheses to account for this insertion from 50 years later. It could be, although denied by A. Thomson (*AJSL* 48 [1932] 129), that to a foreigner all Persian names sound alike, and that this correspondence perfectly fits the reign of Cambyses, between Cyrus (530) and Darius I (521), as v. 24 and Josephus (*Ant.* 11.2, 1 § 21) suppose (also the opinion of Ryle and Kuenen). Or, certain later episodes demonstrating the underhand maneuvers of the Samaritans at the Persian curia are here introduced as a sample of the sort of thing that caused friction in 525. Or, the passage is simply misplaced, and because of v. 12 (about building the wall) it belongs with Neh 4:8.

91 **7.** *Artaxerxes:* (Artaxerxes I, 465–424, in Bright's chronology.) If this is a scientifically inerrant rendition of the Persian name (rather than a foreigner's way of speaking), we have to deal with an episode distinct from, and slightly later than, v. 6. Moreover, the presence of the Aramean named Tab'el as one of the signers has given great popularity to Schaeder's hypothesis that this is no accusation sent to Artaxerxes, but a collation of existing accusations with the aim of defending the Judeans. *Aramaic:* At this point, and with this introduction, the language of MT abruptly changes; we are told that a translation was made, not that it is given herewith—only that what comes after v. 7 is (also) in Aramaic.

92 **8.** Here begins really a third document. Its signatories are non-Israelites, who emphasize their trans-Euphrates origin and citizenship. Bishlam, rather than a personal name, or "with the approval of" (Klostermann), means "in Jerusalem('s regard)." *commander:* Rather "chancellor," according to G. Driver (*Aramaic Documents* [Oxford, 1954] 4–10). But Rehum, too, is expunged from the text by K. Galling (*ZAW* 63 [1951] 70); he makes the subject of the sentence "the chancery-officials of Tripoli (Lebanon, Tarablus!), Warka, and Susa, who judged on the matter."

10. All Syria belonged to the one Persian province Abarnahara, at first along with Babili; Darius I cut off Babylon, and Alexander separated it from Mesopotamia (cf. O. Leuze, *Satrapieneinteilung* [Halle, 1935] 25, 318). Osnappar may be intended as a rendition of Ashurbanipal

(669–633), but might also be referred to Esarhaddon. **11.** There is no cogent reason for supposing either that the Chronicler identifies the three documents, the incipits of which he has already given, or that he distinguishes them. He merely records archival fragments available to him and pertaining in a general way to the situation he is describing.

14. *salt of the palace:* This expression for payroll is oddly paralleled in Lat *sal-arium*, "salt allotment," our "salary." **15.** These warnings sound sincere and well founded; they say nothing of any temple or religious movement, even to disguise subversive intrigue. If truly addressed to Artaxerxes, this is a loyal and salutary warning against letting his affection for Nehemiah overrule his common sense (Neh 2:2). **18.** The answer accords ill with what the Chronicler narrates of Artaxerxes (further, Galling, *ZAW* 63, 66), and would better fit the situation under Cambyses.

24. *and ceased...Darius:* An insertion made in Hebrew, although what follows concerning the reign of Darius is in Aramaic. The claim that this whole Aram sequence forms a unit taken over by the Chronicler integrally (Noth) is convincing. However, there is no real coherence of style between the preceding letter and the repatriates' (prophetic) activities; the "wall" of 5:3 is now plainly that of the Temple ("this 'house,'" the normal term); the events of 4:6–23 tie in no better after 6:18. We will conclude that with 5:1 we are fully in the time sequence of 3:13; we must leave as an insoluble enigma the date of ch. 4.

93 (E) Prophetic Nudge to Completion (5:1–6:22). **1.** Whether or not because of complaints like Rehum's, progress on the Temple seems, in fact, to have been suspended during Cambyses' reign. Without denying the "law of the land" represented by Cyrus' decree, local authorities abetted by the new curia could hold up progress indefinitely. The Judeans themselves, however, were also dragging their feet because of poverty and misfortunes, until there arose among them an articulate leader. Haggai (1:4ff.,10) fearlessly blasts Zerubbabel and his coterie (not sparing Joshua) for their self-indulgent inertia. **2.** The accession of a third monarch in 522 (W. Hinz, *ZDMG* 92 [1938] 136; K. Galling, *ZDPV* 70 [1954] 40) seemed an appropriate occasion to cut through barriers of bureaucratic red tape and confront the Persepolis regime with a *fait accompli*.

3. From Samaria comes the top man to size up the stature of those who defiantly build without a permit. Plainly it is no mere misdemeanor but a political hot potato—a test case engineered to establish the strength of the word of the Persian king. **5.** Tattenai cautiously notes the facts but tolerates no police intervention until he has sent Darius I a report of admirable objectivity. **9.** *structure:* The Aram word means "masonry"; like Italian *muratore*, it derives from "wall" but with no implication of Nehemiah's rampart (cf. C. Tuland, *JNES* 17 [1958] 272). **12.** Both the Jews and the Samaritan governor sedulously avoid any mention of the blame attached to both sides for the unsatisfactory progress of the work since Cyrus.

16. The letter does not say that Sheshbazzar is present or in command of the work. This is doubtless the implication of v. 10, but perhaps the Judeans hoped to avoid more red tape by keeping the operations in the name of the original permit holder, even if he were no longer present. Undoubtedly it is strange that if Zerubbabel was meant, the Chronicler essays no harmonizing with v. 2. The real enigma is that Zerubbabel flits so vaguely across these last pages in the record of the building of "his" Temple!

94 **6:1.** *Babylonia:* The generic name for the whole empire was retained even after the Persians took it over. **2.** Although the official capital of the Achemenids was in Persepolis, the empire outside Persia could be best administered from the more central chancery, which contained also the records of the previous empire. Between the two lay Susa and Ecbatana, where in winter and summer, respectively, a large part of the Persian curia's work was done (cf. R. North, *Guide to Biblical Iran* [Rome, 1956] 31).

4. Vertical rather than horizontal construction units are meant (cf. P. Joüon, *Bib* 22 [1941] 39). *royal treasury:* A mere grandiloquent gesture. Cyrus may have made a cash donation, but even the restoring of gold vessels from Babylon's storehouses sufficed to present the whole enterprise as "financed from public funds." No more than this is reaffirmed by Darius in v. 8. If any actual drawing account had been budgeted, either from the Persian treasury or from taxes in Samaria, the retards owing to both poverty and lack of interest would have been unthinkable. We are told plainly in 2:68 that the Jewish worshipers had to finance their project.

6. The sense is "have no further anxiety"; there was no reason why this decree of Darius should pillory his loyal subordinates, *'aparskāyē*, "inspectors" (cf. F. Rundgren, *ZAW* 70 [1958] 209). **9.** Delivery of sacrificial animals means exemption from bureaucratic meat rationing, rather than tax-supported cultus. **12.** Unmistakable echo of Dt 12:5. Plainly also the measurements and doxologies were taken over *verbatim* from some memorandum solicited from Jews in the chancery.

14. Haggai seems to have been aged (perhaps knowing the earlier Temple, 2:9), and to have ended his career within three months of its dynamic start. His work was continued by First Zechariah (chs. 1–8; Vawter, as in 2:2, doubts the authenticity of precisely the three messianic Temple oracles). Artaxerxes is mentioned here only to take cognizance of 4:23, where we saw that no alternative among the explanations imposes itself.

15. The Second Temple was completed within five years. It was solemnly dedicated on a Sabbath, March 12, 515. Or, to avoid the excitement on Sabbath, we may prefer the date given in *1 Esdras* 7:5 and Josephus (*Ant.* 11.4, 7 § 107), April 1, a Friday, according to Kugler. **16.** The joy was tempered by recognition that this hasty pioneering structure was a far cry from Solomon's. Yet it was destined to be honored by a longer life, even before the rebuilding by Herod.

19. Although the dedication was unexpectedly described in the Aramaic of the chancery documents, the Passover in the following month is told of in Hebrew, continuing into ch. 7. **20.** The lamb is killed "for their brothers the priests"—apparently implying that the Levites and not the priests did the immolating, as in 2 Chr 35:6 (nor lay heads of families as in Ex 12:6). **22.** The Lord "turned the heart" of the king (of Assyria, perhaps for Syria, or to avoid saying "the Great [i.e., Persian] King"); this phraseology "sounds like a mild correction of the way divine and human causalities were set on an equal plane in verse 14" (Rudolph).

95 (II) Ezra's Return Convoy and Torah (Ezr 7:1–10:44) (Neh 8–9). Insertion of this passage suggests strongly that Ezra's ministry occurred between the Temple dedication of 515 and Nehemiah's arrival in 445. This impression is reinforced by the apparent continuity between "Artaxerxes...sixth year" of 6:14–15 and "Artaxerxes' seventh year" of 7:7. Actually, however, neither text gives the slightest indication that Artaxerxes I is meant.

The earliest traditions of Judaism recorded in the *Pirqê 'Ābôt* (sayings of the fathers) regard Ezra as "builder of the wall of the Torah" (Ezr 9:9!), and thus predecessor of Nehemiah in the marriage reform and other isolating structures of the post-exilic community. But Ezra's traditional editorship of the Torah must be seen in the light of its acceptance by the Samaritans. We are representing here the position that Ezra's mission was after Nehemiah and in 398, that the segregationist trends were owing rather to Nehemiah, and that Ezra is not the Chronicler.

(A) Ezra's Priestly Scribal Activity (7:1–28). **1.** *Artaxerxes:* Artaxerxes II, according to most since Van Hoonacker; I, according to De Fraine and those who emend v. 7. **5.** Ezra means "(God's) help." The genealogy accentuates his priestly standing and importance, but it touches less than a third of his progenitors, and strangely omits Zadok (see comment on 1 Chr 6:53). In 1 Chr 6:14 (= MT 5:41), Seraiah is father of the exiled priest Jehozadak; it is suggested that his son, Joshua of Ezr 3:8, before leaving Babylon, fathered another Seraiah who became Ezra's father.

6. Scribe (*sōpēr*) can undoubtedly represent the highly technical term for "official" in Babylon (*šâpirum*), Egypt (Anastasi I papyrus), and Gk Persia (Herodotus, 3.128); but in Ezra's case, we believe its earlier implications of "writing" as authorship or scholarship predominate (see comment on 7:14). *skilled in the law of Moses:* Hence the view deeply rooted long before Wellhausen or Astruc, that Ezra was the definitive "redactor" of the Pentateuch. Jerome wrote, in refuting Helvidius (*ML* 23.190), that we can call Moses the author or Ezra the editor, it's all the same, and Bellarmine wrote in *Controversies* (Milan, 1721) 1, 166: "It was Ezra who after the captivity collected and edited [dispersed annals and papers] into a single corpus, adding to Deuteronomy the last chapter concerning the life of Moses, and various other transitional remarks." (See A. van Hoonacker, *De compositione... hexateuchi* (Brussels, 1949); J. Coppens, *The Old Testament and Critics* [Paterson, 1942]; R. North, *AER* 126 [1952] 249–54.) We should add that this early Christian view was doubtless influenced by the colorful implausibilities of *2 Esdras* 14:22, a book so long considered canonical that it was prescribed for inclusion even in the Clementine Vg as an appendix.

In the perspectives of modern research, we would say that the priests exiled to Babylonia found in the intensified study of their scattered "sacred oracles" a compensation for their inability to perform any longer the concrete ritual and other obligations linked with the soil of Palestine. Hence the "new Temple" of Ez 40ff. and the similarity of his style to the Holiness Code, Lv 17–23. The school of priestly scribes in Neharda had doubtless just embarked upon the mammoth project of publishing a critical edition of the Torah when Cyrus officially ended the Exile. Although their whole life had been dedicated to convincing themselves and others that they must get back to Jerusalem as soon as possible, there were still obvious difficulties in abandoning or relocating such a project. Hence, it was agreed to defer the return to Jerusalem until the work was finished. The years dragged on to decades and almost a century. Meanwhile, Ezra became head of the school (v. 10), and, with the resoluteness his memoirs betray, brought both projects to a head (Rudolph, on Neh 9:37, refutes the view that Ezra's Torah was only D [as now Browne in *PCB* 377] or only P; so also A. Robert, *RB* 46 [1937] 199).

It was altogether in accord with Persian policy to foster the compiling of local legislation, especially ritual and moral codes likely to set public order and civil obedience into a loftier religious framework. Ezra was readily granted an exit visa (v. 11) rather than "concordat," as urged by K. Fruhstorfer (*Studia Anselmiana* 28 [1951] 178) for the convoy he set about to organize. It amounted to transfer of the major departments of the Neharda school to Jerusalem.

96 **7.** *seventh year:* If Artaxerxes II, 398 BC; if Artaxerxes I, 458 BC, but if corrected with Albright to 37th year, then 428 BC. **8.** The hike to Jerusalem was to last 100 days; the end of the journey is awkwardly anticipated here, for much is still to be told until 8:32, before Ezra's convoy ever leaves Babylonia.

14. "Fact-finding mission" describes well the official relation of Ezra to the Persian chancery, although all too often bureaucrats who are sent to make inquiries wield an influence tantamount to punitive or even legislative authority. Hence, in v. 25, Ezra is regarded as "appointing magistrates"; but this is only "to judge those who acknowledge the law of Yahweh" and "according to the wisdom of his God which is in his hand." It is important to insist with Kapelrud (*op. cit.*, 27), despite H. Schneider, that Ezra's scholarly religious pursuits exclude his having been that "Under-Secretary for Jewish Affairs" which seems in fact to have been a Persian chancery post (H. Schaeder). **22.** One cor = 10 bath = 58 gal. (see W. Dubberstein, *AJSL* 56 [1939] 20).

24. Clergy exemption from taxation was a plausible grant, as under Darius to the Apollo clergy of Magnesia; v. 19 extends this explicitly to exemption from "hidden" sales or inheritance tax, but v. 15 had expressly emphasized that any funds given in cash for the project by the king or finance minister were (despite the customary flourish of v. 20) purely personal donations, such as those of Jewish or Gentile contributors.

27. Abrupt transit to the first person indicates that the Chronicler is here incorporating a document rightly called Ezra's Memoirs, not a fiction of the Chronicler as held by Noth and Torrey. This single, unitary, unabridged, artistic source furnished all the passages dealing with Ezra except Ezr 7:1–26; 8:1–14, according to F. Ahlemann (*ZAW* 59 [1943] 98). A later redactor inserted all the Aramaic and all about Nehemiah, according to S. Granild (*Ezrabogens Literaere Genesis* [Copenhagen, 1949]; *ZAW* 63 [1951] 65). (See now S. Mowinckel, *Studien/Ezra: Nachchronistische Redaktion* [Oslo, 1964].) It still remains unexplained why there is no transition from the second person Ezra-Artaxerxes document or from the third person Ezra of vv. 10–11. S. Mowinckel (*Fest. W. Rudolph* [Tübingen, 1961] 233) holds this to be merely a stylistic flourish, consciously borrowed from Neh, suggesting that Ezra can outdo Nehemiah.

97 **(B) Rounding Up the Convoy (8:1–31).** **1.** Ezra counts here (mostly in round numbers, and only 15 by name) 1511 men, plus doubtless as many dependents. The 12 families hint rather than represent the 12 tribes; 11 are families already named in the lengthier genealogy of Ezr 2. **2.** Ezra's own family stands first, thus reversing the order of 2:36, which relegates the priestly families last. Moreover, against Ez 43:19, the Ithamar branch is put equal to the Zadokite, represented only by Phinehas (see comments on 7:5 and 1 Chr 6:53).

15. *Ahava:* Confluence of some unknown canal with the Euphrates. *no sons of Levi:* In the minimal or technical sense. Actually all the priests were sons of Levi, but something more—sons of Aaron. It is remarkable that the Chronicler tolerates this implication that the Levites were missing when needed; a meager 74 had been present in 2:40. Still, the author may well have been gratified at how indispensably important Levites are. **17.** On Iddo's Levite center at Casiphia ("silver town," not easy to identify with Ctesiphon), A. Causse (*Dispersés d'Israël* [Paris, 1929] 77) is often cited, but he knows no more about it than anyone can read in this text.

21. Fasting and prayer, as a suitable replacement of normal "secondary causality," comes from a misapprehension regarding "faith in providence," to which the Chronicler was particularly prone. **22.** It would be more defensible to assume that Ezra, having ascertained in a discreetly roundabout way that he would be unable to get a military escort, made a morale-building virtue of necessity. **24.** Ezra's human resourcefulness in guaranteeing the safe arrival of the funds leaves nothing to be desired. **28.** Holiness has its place, not as a mere tool to an economic end, but as a pertinent factor of the existential situation. **30.** The value of the treasury deposits may be reckoned at some 5 million dollars. It would not contradict the practice of biblical writers or copyists to have added a few zeros to the recorded amounts, thus bringing home more vividly to a remote generation the essential theological truth of the mutual generosity between God and his people.

98 **(C) The Situation in Jerusalem (8:32–10:44).** **32.** Allowance is made for three days of rest and orientation after the 100-day trek. **22.** Ezra's doctrinal prestige, as well as his financial backing, must have engendered a certain obsequiousness in even the highest local hierarchs, but the formalities had to be punctiliously respected. **34.** Witnesses were in attendance, and a receipt was drawn up.

35. The transition to the third person marks the Chronicler's drawing on other, less-formulated sources here, according to some (but see Ahlemann on 7:27). Anyway, we must reckon with the possibility that Neh 8 is to be inserted at this point. It does, in fact, narrate Ezra's activities, in the sequence that best fits here; and inasmuch as it speaks of him in the third person, a transition would be needed. However, it is equally possible that the whole of Ezra's ministry was preceded by the work of Nehemiah, including his mixed marriage reform in Neh 13. In fact, one of the motives of Van Hoonacker's dating Ezr after Neh is that Ezr 9 seems to take for granted the earlier clarification of a juridical situation that Neh 13 copes with as a new urgency. In that case, there is some possibility that Ezra deferred the promulgation of his newly edited Torah until he had taken a firm position on scandalous violations of the Mosaic Law as already expounded.

9:1. The first person merely introduces an extended citation, and could have been an adjustment made after Neh 8–9 was dropped from this point. *Canaanites... Perizzites:* This choice of "disapproved races" is not a concrete historical record of conditions in the 5th cent., but a citation from Dt 7:1. Nevertheless, very significant is the fact that Samaritans are not added alongside Ammon and Moab in Ezra's interracial efforts, not even as obliquely as in Neh 13:12. The major clash with Samaritans recorded in these books is concerned with the rampart building in Neh 4:1–2, especially if Ezr 4 is taken as relevant to that episode. Even the Tattenai inquisition, during the building of the Temple a century before Ezra, ended with the Samaritan bureaucrats showing the Judeans exactly that measure of co-operation that was desired. Moreover, the ethnic segregation demanded in Ezr 10:5 is restricted to the priests, not as in Neh 13:24, where the marriages of the Judean populace are in question.

From these facts, H. Cazelles (*VT* 4 [1954] 122–30) has drawn perceptive conclusions with which we are in substantial agreement. The reforms of Neh are based simply on Dt, not on the Law that Ezra was meanwhile editing in Babylon. When Ezra finally arrived, he was opposed neither by the higher Judean clergy nor by the Samaritans. Both classes were invited to the public mass meeting at which he promulgated his new Torah (Neh 8–9 to be inserted during the five months noted as elapsing between Ezr 7:9 and 10:7). The key contention of Cazelles is that Ezra was completely successful in bringing around the Samaritans, no less than the Judeans, to a wholehearted acceptance of his Pentateuch. This view accounts for the enigma that our Torah is identical with that idolized by the Samaritans despite (or even as a symbol of) their hostility to Judah, generally presumed to have reached its culmination before Ezra's editorship.

Nevertheless, Cazelles continues, Ezra was not successful in establishing a durable unity between Judeans and Samaritans. In fact, his efforts to do so backfired against him. The strongly anti-Samaritan party that inherited Nehemiah's ideology came to prevail in Jerusalem. Its dominance during the 3rd cent. dictates the animus against Samaria in Chr and in Sir 50:26 and 2 Mc 2:13 (cf. A. Bentzen, *ST* 3 [1949] 159). Ezra is even blackballed from inclusion beside Zerubbabel and Nehemiah in Sir 49:11. (Singularly opposite conclusions are drawn by Rudolph [*op. cit.*, 168] with five leading experts: Sirach found it inopportune to praise this flail of mixed marriages in a day when they had become frequent!)

99 **9:2.** Peoples of the lands, although always with both plurals here as in 3:3, is doubtless identical with the "ordinary people," as defended in 4:4. **3.** Ezra's reaction to the denunciation has been called histrionic, or defended on the ground that distinction between genuine and theatrical emotion is an Occidental category. More fairly, it shows that a flair for the dramatic is not out of place in liturgy. **6.** Notably effective is his blaming of himself rather than others for what is after all a corporate guilt (cf. J. de Fraine, *Adam* [Paris, 1959] 237). The biblical theologian will not overlook here a certain isolating protective religiosity. It soft pedals that personal responsibility that appears in Jer 31:30 and Ez 18:20 as a link to the universalism of Is 60:3 and Mal 1:11.

8. *remnant:* Here and in v. 13, *p^{e}lîṭâ* means "escapees," but in v. 14 it is coupled with *š^{e}'ērît*, a technical term for the portion of Judah not exiled (Jer 8:3; 41:10). The remnant so stressed in Is is rather *š^{e}'ār* (10:19,21–22), and is rather an envisioned eschatological penitence group. Similarly, eschatological overtones are attributed by Köhler's dictionary to the remnant in Ezr 9; BDB takes it with a slightly different nuance as "the spiritual elite," which surely seems to be the implication of the context. But if we accept Cazelles' imputation of a more ecumenical outlook to Ezr, it is tempting to see a humble and conciliating compliment to the "Samaritan *'am hā-āreṣ*" in his insistence on God's goodness in sparing a remnant while the elite Judeans were exiled. **11–12.** The only thing wrong with this splendidly apt quotation is that it is not in the Bible, although its spirit doubtless is (see comment on Neh 13:23).

10:3. Natural law obligations of justice and decency toward spouses in good faith and utterly innocent children seem never to have entered into the heads of these reformers, excited by a kind of mob psychosis for which Ezra cannot escape blame, especially if Shecaniah's spontaneity is rigged, as seems to be the case, for in v. 26 he is not one of those involved in a mixed marriage. The dangerous and casual claim that "God's rights outweigh all human considerations" can only be called fanaticism. Still less does "maximum convenience of enforceableness for existing religious authorities" take precedence over profoundly human obligations of commutative justice. On the other hand, the need of safeguarding religious truth and duty is also a natural law obligation, but the fact that the conduct of those influenced by Ezra is presented in the Bible as praiseworthy and normative does not mean that it is impeccable or inerrant. **6.** Ezra's own demeanor is more moderate throughout the episode; he takes his religiosity out on himself rather than on others.

9. The assembly is graphically portrayed as "trembling because of the sin and the rain"; sin is here *dābār*, "matter," not to be corrected, with P. Joüon (*Bib* 12 [1931] 85), to "hail." **11.** Ultimately, Ezra too requires that the guilty (priests only, as 10:5?) should punish the innocent by renouncing their children as well as the wives who were either foreign or *'am hā'āreṣ* (nonexiled Judeans unwilling to conform to the full rigor of separatist Judaism). **29.** These verses are rich in corruptions according to J. Bewer (*Text des Buches Esra* [FRLANT 31; Göttingen, 1922] 91). But Sheal is perhaps Yiš'al, as in the Oriental Hebr *k^etîb*, and on a seal found in the 1963 Ophel excavation (J. Prignaud, *RB* 71 [1964] 378), which adds evidence that before Dt, mixed marriages were not prohibited.

We must conclude that religion of its very nature is both centrifugal and centripetal—simultaneously universalist, to bring all men to the benefits its votaries enjoy, and separatist, to protect them from the contamination and loss of their "treasure of great price." The proportions in which these two antithetical obligations are to be combined will call for human prudential judgments, which even among the maximally sincere and zealous will not always be objectively right.

COMMENTARY ON NEHEMIAH

100 The author of this memoir is one of the most genial personalities portrayed anywhere in the Bible. A volcanically emotional temperament (1:4; 5:12; 13:8,25), a bit of vanity creeping into his designs (2:10,18; 5:15; 6:11), are the side views of a noble and leaderly character. *People* are important for him; he values contacts and spends himself for them (5:16). His eloquence is brief, and succeeds always in gaining the hearer's reaction (2:17; 5:7; 13:25). His optimism refuses to notice pockets of reserve or resistance in public opinion. He reckons with workableness. His attitude toward mixed marriages is more realistic than Ezra's; he has enough assurance to pass the first round and save his bet for the next (10:31; cf. 13:25ff.). He takes time out for reflection, as is indicated by the painstaking preparations at Susa for his mission, his inspection of the walls of Jerusalem all by himself, the cautious preliminaries to joining up communities, his waiting-game in unmasking the blackmail of his foes. His recourse to prayer is based on the conviction that God directs events (2:8,10,20; 4:9; 5:13; 6:16) and that he prompts leaders (2:12; 7:5). This prayer is vibrant (3:36–37; 5:19; 6:14; 13:14, 22,31,39) and is akin in spirit to Jer 3:36–37 (Gelin, *Esdras* [BJ; 1960] 23–24).

The memoir itself as composed by its protagonist was long taken to be a kind of ruler's self-glorification, but G. von Rad claims it is a cult text deposited in a shrine (*ZAW* 76 [1964] 176–87).

(III) The Rearmament of Jerusalem (1:1–7:5).

101 **(A) The Susa Report and Sequel (1:1–2:11).** Nehemiah was a bright young man at the Persian court. His official position as cup bearer (v. 11) implies the ultimate both in confidence and in favor felt toward him by Artaxerxes I. The holder of this position was normally a eunuch, as is verified by traces in the youth's demeanor, according to Albright (*BA* 9, 11); the best LXX manuscripts have *euno-echos* for *oino-choos*. But the eunuch hypothesis accords ill with Nehemiah's unusual energy and authoritativeness, or with the requirements of Dt 23:2 for leadership in the community. Even if the title were "eunuch," it need imply no more than our "chamberlain," as in Acts 8:27.

1:1. Both Hacaliah (MT) and Halakiah (supposed by LXX) defy known Hebr name patterns. The MT reading is defended by H. Gotthard (*Text des Buches Nehemia* [Wiesbaden, 1958] 1, 19) along with the eunuch hypothesis. H. Ginsberg (*BASOR* 80 [1940] 12) doubts that *Hakal-yâ* is the correct reading of Lachish Letter 20.1. *twentieth year:* Of Artaxerxes I, 445; Chislev is the month of December. *Susa:* See comment on Ezr 6:2. **2.** *Hanani:* As in Neh 7:2.

102 (a) The Jerusalem Disaster (1:1–10). **3.** The sad news from Zion was that its rampart had been breached and its gates or courthouse destroyed in flames. Such a report is perplexing. The walls of Jerusalem had been destroyed by Nebuchadnezzar 150 years earlier. Surely Nehemiah knew all about that. Can it be that enough of the wall had been standing to be reutilized for a timber structure that caught fire? J. Morgenstern (*HUCA* 27 [1956] 173; *HUCA* 31 [1960] 16) draws sweeping conclusions from his claim that such a disaster occurred exactly in 485, some 20 years before Nehemiah's birth! Gelin more plausibly prefers the year 448, in which an Egyptian revolt was put down. For Pavlovský (*op. cit.*, 446), a group of Babylonian Jews including Hanani came to Jerusalem and tried to rebuild its wall between 448 and 445; it is their failure that is recorded in Ezr 4:21, as well as in Neh 1:3.

(b) The King's Caprice (2:1–8). **1.** The page, with prayerful shrewdness (like Dn 9:4; Ezr 9:5), waited four months before he showed the king signs of his distress. He was doubtless spying out the moment when weariness and wine would have put the monarch into a maximally sympathetic mood. **5.** Artaxerxes is confronted with a pampered youth's virtual plea to be made ruler and rebuilder of a historic and turbulent metropolis. The city wall was a true fortification (*bîrâ*, 7:2; 1 Mc 13:52; name of NT Antonia; cf. *Ant.* 13.11,2), and the authorization of its rebuilding is a genuine "rearmament." The king asks only how soon he would return. **8.** Politically, the King's concession is a dangerous caprice (see comment on Ezr 4:7). But even if that episode refers to Artaxerxes, there is no obligation to date it in the beginning of his reign, as is said in the preceding verse, but concerning Xerxes. More plausibly the letter of Rehum is a reaction to Nehemiah's coming.

(c) Nehemiah's Status in Judah (2:9–11). **9.** The governors are doubtless Sanballat and Tobiah, although Nehemiah is contemptuous of them. Horonite is for the tiny village of Beth-horon on the NW slopes near Jerusalem, and Ammonite means foreigner from across the eastern border (Dt 23:4!; but cf. A. Alt, *KlSchr* 1, 341). The Elephantine papyrus (30:29; *ANET* 492) records a Sanballat as *peḥâ* or governor in Samaria, but this was 37 years later, in 408 (cf. H. H. Rowley, *BJRylL* 38 [1956] 190). Later still, the Tobiads of Ammon became paramount in Judean affairs (see L. Vincent, *RB* 29 [1920] 189; *JPOS* 3 [1923] 55; A. Spiro and S. Zeitlin, *PAAJR* 20 [1951] 303; *PAAJR* 4 [1933] 172; O. Plöger, *ZDPV* 71 [1955] 70; on the excavated Araq al-Amir fortress, see P. Lapp, *BASOR* 171 [1963] 8–39).

(B) Program of Reconstruction (2:12–3:32).

103 (a) Wall Inspection by Night (2:12–15). **13.** Nehemiah was not afraid of the yokels but did not want to bother with them. Apart from the supposition that there must have been a full moon, what this prowl leaves most in the dark is the burning question of whether at this date the SW wall of Jerusalem included also the W hill where a later Judeo-Christian tradition would locate the "Zion" (and tomb) of David (see comment on 2 Chr 32:5), or only the E hill, Jebusite crag or true Zion of David (now inaccurately called Ophel), as maintained by Galling (see V. Gronkowski, *Collectanea theologica varsoviensia* 15 [1934] 208; M. Avi-Yonah, *IsrEJ* 4 [1954] 239). Even if the maximum area were included, the number of gates so disproportionate to defense notions of that background remains more enigmatic than their localization at various points along today's wall, which owes its entire southern line to a rebuilding by Eudoxia in AD 400, several hundred yards farther N. "Valley" and "fountain" as mentioned here afford not the slightest ground for affirming even in which direction Nehemiah was riding (with all due respect for M. Burrows, *BASOR* 64 [1936] 11–21; *AASOR* 14 [1934] 115–40; A. Alt, *KlSchr* 3, 326; J. Simons, *JOT* 441, 237; L. Vincent, *Jérusalem I* [Paris, 1954] 235–58). "Dung" as a name of a gate is equated implausibly with "potsherds" (as Jer 19:2); *'ašpôt* is claimed to have been euphemized into *š^epôt*, "cheese" (so in 3:13 but not in 3:14!), thus tying it down to the cheesemakers' or Tyropoeon valley (see 3:1,13).

(b) PUBLIC SUPPORT ASSURED (2:16–20). **16.** Whatever the details of his ride, it so encouraged Nehemiah that he summoned a meeting and stirred public interest. "Doers of the work" is claimed by H. Kaupel (*Bib* 21 [1940] 40) to mean "the administration" rather than the doers of the work. **19.** Another wetback now joins the local opposition: Geshem is doubtless one of the Arabs who had gradually been filtering northward as far as Nabatean Petra (cf. *Ant.* 4.17, 2; F. Cross, *BA* 18 [1955] 47; W. F. Albright, *Fest. A. Alt* [Tübingen, 1953] 1; *BASOR* 119 [1950] 15; R. North, *PEQ* 87 [1955] 340). With unexplained brusqueness Rudolph rejects W. Graham's reasonable view (*AJSL* 42 [1926] 276) that Geshem represents an Arab tribe around Petra (rather than Hebron, as C. Kent), which by defeating the Edomites kept open trade routes benefiting Jerusalem. **20.** Through this righteous reply glimmers a spiteful hint that Sanballat and colleagues were genuine Palestinians and worshipers of Yahweh, and that their major guilt was to have really wanted to help in the project and thus share in Nehemiah's glory.

104 (c) THE LOCAL CHAPTER MASONS (3:1–32). The rebuilding of the wall was not an organically or hierarchically structured use of manpower. Complete autonomy was left to rival groups working on separate sections. It is hard to see how this policy could have been considered either more efficient or more expressive of that religious ethnic solidarity by which alone the work could have been begun. More plausible than Van Selms' proposal that Nehemiah was consciously imitating the historic wall building of Themistocles (Thucydides, 1.89) is Simon's suggestion that the team rivalry may be a purely literary artifice.

The separatist groups are not all ethnic. Five only represent clans from the list of Ezr 2. Five others are locality based, as indicated there. Five more are earlier districts as in Jos 15 (Jerusalem, Beth-kerem, Beth-zur, Keilah, and Mizpah). Important nearby towns like Bethlehem and Bethel are not mentioned, which we may read as merely a better organized boycott than Tekoa's (v. 5, perhaps out of sympathy with their Arab neighbors). Furthermore, doubtless in extension of the fact that the Zadok and Levi clans are functional priestly groups, we have also some guilds represented, probably more than the goldsmiths, perfumers (undertakers), and merchants, explicitly named in vv. 8 and 32. Incompleteness of the listing is inferred from several mentions of a "second half" to which no first half corresponds (vv. 11, 16, 19–20). The work was shared by no single fellow traveler of Ezra (8:1–24)—one of the proofs that he came after Nehemiah.

3:1. A prestige name heads the list: Eliashib is Joshua's grandson of 12:10. His connections with disdained Tobiah (13:4–5,28; 2:10) must have made him a cool supporter of what De Fraine thought-provokingly calls Nehemiah's apartheid policy. A sheep market even today is installed periodically inside the NE corner of Jerusalem's wall, where (without proof, neither the priests' nearness to the Temple, nor the "probatica" of Jn 5:2) commentators agree to initiate this allegedly counterclockwise circuit of the wall sections. *built:* Claimed to imply that this corner was more utterly razed than the later sections said to be "repaired," but perhaps merely a style variant as in vv. 13ff. *consecrated:* no need to emend to "renovated" (*ḥdš* for *qdš*, Rudolph) or "roofed"; what is more natural than that in their section, the priests should have given vent to a little extra rite?

6. The "Old" or "Corner" Gate is conjecturally set in the NW corner. **7.** *jurisdiction:* Rather, throne, or capitol as localization. **12.** *daughters:* Perhaps suburbs. **13.** The Valley Gate is located farther S, in either Tyropoeon or Gehinnom, depending on whether one includes the SW hill (2:13), which the "thousand cubits" would seem to require, no matter how near Gihon the Dung Gate is placed. **15.** The fountain *par excellence* would be Gihon, but it must be Rogel if we assume that the Shela-Siloam pool stood between it and the climb to the Jebusite-Davidic citadel. **21.** Thus, we are brought to the priests' residences, appropriately located along the half-mile where the E wall of the city coincides with the retaining wall of the Temple esplanade above the Kedron-Jehoshaphat valley.

(C) Triumphalism (4:1–7:5).

105 (a) EMBATTLED PERSISTENCE (4:1–23) (MT 3:33–38; 4:1–17). **1.** (MT 3:33.) The opposition's lively wit is recorded with surprisingly sympathetic flair. To say here with Rudolph and De Fraine that Jews have always been especially sensitive to ridicule—if it implies out of proportion to their maltreatment and their perceptiveness—is just to perpetuate another of many divisive myths. **2.** (MT 3:34.) Army (*ḥayil*) means "strength," whether military or economic, a sociological term controverted like the *'am hā-āreṣ* (Ezr 4:4; 9:2), to which it is antithesis rather than synonym. LXX takes it as part of the taunt, "So this is Samaria's strength, that the Judeans build a city!" What follows is put in very curtailed form as part of Tobiah's remarks. **7.** (MT 4:1.) *Ashdod:* (See comment on 13:23.) With these Philistines to the west, the circle of the compass is complete: Samaria, N; Ammon, E; Arabs, S (2:9,19). Israel is completely surrounded by its enemies.

10. (MT 4:4.) This snatch of verse, with its epic introduction "Judah said," puts colorfully before us the Semite toiler's habit of singing lustily when the work is hardest, as in Arab excavations still—a monotonous refrain, howled by all, alternates with clever improvisations in the same rhythm. **11.** The opposition's reaction, although not in verse, is a kind of proverb put here artistically as an antiphon.

16. "Half of them worked, half held weapons, and [the third half!] supervised" is plainly an exaggeration for vv. 17–18, "those [few] who carried weapons also worked like the others." **18.** Nehemiah slyly admits that his own skin was the major defense objective, as indeed it was doubtless the enemy's prime target. Van Selms rightly notes it was not so sharp of him to want everybody (including the enemy) to know exactly where he was! **23.** "They slept in their clothes, their weapons 'in hand' " is a conjectural correction of *hammāyim*, "the water" (MT, 4:17).

106 (b) Social Justice Reform (5:1–19). **1.** Another major hurdle confronts the masons. Now that the opposition has been neutralized, the workers find that their own fellow Judeans are causing them miseries. It is the wives who protest, for the household economy and children's welfare are involved. **2.** It does not seem that "concentration on the walls had led to economic crisis" (OAB), nor that the embargo on nightly return to outlying towns had cut off the continuing stream of fresh vegetables (De Fraine). A realistic rereading shows that 4:22–23 is an afterthought not chronologically prior to 4:15; all in all, it must have been a very brief crisis, sufficient to convince the opposition their efforts were useless. The whole enterprise, building and defense alike, was completed in only 52 days (6:15)—not long enough to raise any problem of such annual harvests as would already be stored within the city. Moreover it cannot rationally be thought that Nehemiah had expected Judah's poor simply to starve while donating their services to a project financed (at least nominally, 2:8) by the imperial treasury, or even by the nobility that stood to gain most by the retrieval of Jerusalem's onetime metropolitan status. Therefore, we must see these builders as being economically profited by some small but steady salary above their normal expectations. It is exactly a situation that lenders exploit, very much like the payday of excavation workers whose creditors are lurking at the fringe to grab most of what the workers have imprudently spent in advance.

3. This social evil can scarcely have resulted from a 20 to 40 day pinch of the work project. **4.** The king's tax also is a normal annual burden. The mortgaging must have occurred some time previously, if only now the foreclosure is taking place, or even if the interest payments are becoming intolerable. **5.** *our flesh is as the flesh of our brethren:* The real outcry results from the debtors' view of themselves toiling and endangered side by side with (and for the benefit of) wealthier citizens who are presently going to turn on them, as in Mt 18:28. This temporary crisis merely dramatizes a situation that has lasted, and will last, as long as human nature itself: A free economy will result in debt, bankruptcy, and enslavement for the less energetic, talented, or sly. We shall therefore always have to seek new and better social justice legislation or enforcement. This passage was invoked (North, *Sociology of the Biblical Jubilee* [Rome, 1954] 205) as partial proof that the basic Hebr principle was inalienable distribution of private property among small family holders, although as a genuine benefit to debtors it could be allowed to entail their property or their (sons') persons for a period not to exceed 7, or maximally 49, years (Dt 24:6,14; Lv 25:4).

7. The grandiloquent oratory is suited to the patriotic crisis, but must not be pressed to unrealistic conclusions. First, to grant loans on interest even to victims of misfortune is not harmful to a sound economy. Nor is it even a less desirable situation for the debtors themselves, than simply to become beggars asking for a handout. Nehemiah does not regret that he has been granting such loans at interest (v. 11). Second, what he proposes is simply to take cognizance of the reconstruction crisis by a grand act tempering justice with mercy (Prv 14:31). To write off all the loans as gifts is a tacit invocation of the *š^{e}miṭṭâ* law of Dt 15:1,9. In a crisis this is fine, but it would be impractical and ultimately less charitable if the law required in advance, and as normal, that every loan would simply be transformed into an outright gift after seven years, i.e., by return of the mortgaged property or serf without any benefit having been derived in the meantime.

11. *hundredth:* Rather 100, *m^e'â*, which nowhere else means "1 per cent" (per month, it is generally assumed); hence Geiger reasonably emends to *maššā'* "interest(rate)" (cf. E. Neufeld, *JQR* 44 [1953] 199). **12.** *priests...from them:* Not from the priests (we may hope), but using the priestly office as a sort of law enforcement detail. Such a verse could have given rise to the judgment that in post-exilic Judah "all powers without any exception belonged to the clergy," in J. Pirenne's superficial and undocumented work (*RIDA* 1 [3rd series; 1954] 208).

14. Governor from 20th to 32nd year. Although Nehemiah was doing all the work of a permanent office holder, he had no complaint at receiving none of the perquisites (see R. North, *Fest. E. Volterra* [Florence, 1968], where against virtually universal consensus we deny that Nehemiah held any true "governorship"). **15.** Even the commentators who insist he had a true civil function within the Persian bureaucracy admit here that he puts himself in a series in which he had no predecessor, the only possibilities being his Samaritan rivals. But Nehemiah is plainly thinking rather of the prestige leaders of the Jewish theocratic community who truly preceded him, such as Sheshbazzar (and?) Zerubbabel. **18.** Hardly to be called meager by comparison with Solomon, 1 Kgs 5:2. The generosity of Nehemiah as of wealthy Bedouin sheikhs is felt to consist in the fact that they let any number of poor relations come to dinner.

107 (c) Dramatic Completion of the Mission (6:1–7:72). There is no doubt that Nehemiah is here describing what he firmly holds to have been deep dark plots against his life. But 6:17ff. shows that many prudent and loyal Judeans felt that his judgment in the matter was warped. If Sanballat truly possessed some authority, either superior or at least equal to Nehemiah's within the Persian framework, what else could he do except try to come to an understanding that would avert complete breakdown in co-operation and subsequent cracking together of heads from above?

6:2. Ono is held to be near Lydda; Alt (*KlSchr* 1, 344) claims proof from Sennacherib, and *ANET* indicates only Tutmoses III. The Lydda "plain" begins in any case at Latrun, suspiciously near Sanballat's Beth-horon. **3.** A noble reply to give to associates who try to break off one's idealistic plans and enterprises. **6.** Nehemiah's Gaullist grandeur and separatist assurance lend great plausibility to Sanballat's fear.

10. *shut up:* *'āṣûr* (for Shemaiah's confinement) implies in Jer 36:5 "a state of ritual uncleanness," which, being of foreseen duration, need not have hindered Shemaiah from making plans to enter the Temple that evening. But experts prefer the sense of "performing a symbolic act of prophecy" or "seized by a prophetic spirit," as in 1 Kgs 22:11 (similarly, Is 8:11 but without *'ṣr*). The word really means "imprisoned," and its detective-story overtones are doubtless intentional in this setting, even if in actual fact Nehemiah were merely visiting someone "confined" to his room with a cold. The Prophet's statement is an oracle, whose strong hieratic rhythm is perceptible even in English.

12. "Hired" has the same connotation we would use today for someone who, whatever his motive, has espoused a course of action we disapprove. The plot seems flimsy at best—threats of assassination to induce a political figure to put himself in a position he himself calls ridiculous rather than compromising, with no allusion to any death penalty (Nm 18:7 against 1 Mc 10:43?). **14.** Nehemiah takes a dim view of all prophets, as indeed seems to be the outlook even of several whom we call by that name (Am 7:14; Jer 2:26). **18.** Tobiah's marriage connections within Jerusalem are an afterthought and an unworthily personal motivation of opposition to the city's best interests. More objectively, we must say that there would be two ways of looking at Nehemiah's undoubtedly sincere but also self-glorifying whirlwind activity.

7:1. Mention of the Levite choir so casually in the passive suggests that Nehemiah, in fact, took no interest in the matter, but the Chronicler felt that something had to be said about it. **2.** "Governor" (*śar*) of the "fortress" (*bîrâ*, 2:5) is an even nobler term (= "prince") than Nehemiah claims for himself (*peḥâ*, 5:15). The only authority he really possessed to hand over was that conferred upon him by his personal prestige and favor with the king, and that he leaves to his brother to exercise (not too successfully, 13:7). **5.** At this point is to be inserted Nehemiah's fulfillment of his promise (1:6) to return as soon as possible to his royal patron's side (13:6). The "assembly of the nobles" may in fact refer to Nehemiah's "second ministry" in ch. 10, whether or not it is regarded as contemporaneous with Ezra. For convenience, we here pass over the list, the motives for insertion of which at this point are treated under Ezr 2 (→ 86 above).

108 **(IV) Promulgation of Ezra's Torah (Neh 8:1–9:38).** Ezra's assembly (a continuation from Ezr 8:35? or 10:44?) is here inserted as if his first ministry had been abruptly broken off and then his second begun after Nehemiah's first. Even in this assumption, there is no reason to think that he returned to Babylon because Nehemiah did. A. Fernández (*Bib* 2 [1961] 431) leaves unexplained why Ezra is not mentioned, although he accompanied Nehemiah back from Babylon. In any case, the apparent continuity assured in such hypotheses is troubled by so many loose ends that most experts think Neh 8:1 is a continuation of Ezr 10:44, and that it is equally compatible with a first arrival after Nehemiah, even 40 years later. But if we once admit that Neh 8–9 is notoriously displaced, there is no reason why its original situation must have been after Ezr 10:44 (as in *1 Esdras* 9:37). Thus we consider it to fit better after Ezr 8:35, as there explained (maintained also by Torrey, *Ezra Studies*, 253; Ahlemann, *ZAW* 59, 85). Not indeed impossible, but less plausible, is the supposition that when confronted with abuses, Ezra would have adopted *ad hoc* measures while pocketing his sweeping new codification of Mosaic Law. Doubtless the abuses were attacked after his law was promulgated, and possibly long after the violent measures of Neh 13:23 to cope with similar abuses.

Many experts regard 7:73 or its last half, as the preface of 8:1. There is just as good reason for regarding the whole of ch. 7 as a parenthesis between the "assembly of the few Jerusalemites in their towns" of vv. 4–5, and the summoning of "all the children of Israel in their towns" in vv. 73–74. But the "seventh month" is in a sequence totally unknown to us; it is certainly not envisioned as the next after Elul of 6:15, which was, in fact, a sixth month by the Nisan-based calendar, but twelfth on the basis of the New Year beginning in the seventh month, Tishri (October). There is a similar Jerusalem assembly in a "seventh month" immediately after the identical list of Ezra 2:70; therefore, we must conclude that it is a colophon to the list. Doubtless, the rearrangement of the text resulted in part from overhasty identification among various seventh-month assemblies.

109 **8:9.** The pairing of the two otherwise unrelated leaders affords the chief ground for Albright to date Ezra's ministry in 428 by altering the text of Ezr 7:7. But without such alteration, the present verse too can be upheld on the supposition that Nehemiah, in his twenties in 445, had become during Ezra's ministry in 398 an elder statesman in his seventies. "Governor" is here *tiršātā'*, not *peḥâ* as in Nehemiah's own memoirs; we hold both to be prestige titles of popular acclaim, outlasting the occasion on which they were originally conferred.

10. The clergy make a rather heavy-handed effort to cheer up a mob dismayed by the severity of Ezra's Pentateuch. **14.** (= Lv 23:42.) **15.** The general sense of Lv 23:40 is quoted loosely here. **16.** Galling's claim that we have here one of the Chronicler's famed "theological conclusion" insertions is no less plausible than the view that Hezekiah's passover is an imitation of Josiah's in 2 Chr 30:13; 35:1. This Feast of Booths (Feast of Tabernacles, really; Jn 7:2) has the reading of the Law as one of its characteristics, properly for the seventh year as prescribed in Dt 7:10, but suitably in any year after long desuetude. This Ezra activity of Neh 8–10 is, in fact, dated to the Sabbath year 430 by F. Mezzacasa (*Revista Bíblica* 23 [1961] 94).

110 **9:1.** The Yom Kippur rite of Lv 16:29, or at least a ceremony in its spirit, may well be seen here as transferred from the 10th to the 24th day of the seventh month, because in Neh 8:9 either there had not yet been time to promulgate the Torah, or excessive melancholy had endangered its acceptance. Thus, there is no reason for insertion of Ezr 9–10 here between Neh 8 and 9 (Torrey; Rudolph). Also unlikely is the linking of Neh 9 with Nehemiah's own reforms by Sellin, and M. Rehm (*BZ* 1 [1957] 59). **2.** It is not really separatist to exclude others from our acknowledgment of faults whose guilt we do not wish to imply extends to them. Ahlemann (*ZAW* 59, 88) puts Neh 9:1–5 after Ezr 10:15 "upon this 'fast.'"

6. Ezra's long rhythmic prayer is intensely deuteronomic, as the Chronicler generally is, according to Von Rad (*Das Geschichtsbild des chronistischen Werkes* (Stuttgart, 1930). This does not exclude that the prayer originated as a litany composed for a day of fasting and prayer during the subsistence of the northern kingdom, as set forth by A. Welch (*ZAW* 47 [1929] 136). It is also like Pss 78, 105, and 106 and may be taken as a summary of the Torah in the minds of the listeners to whom it had been read aloud during these days. The summary shows a typical preacher's unconcern for adapting sacrosanct formulas to current situations: the menace and slavery of Assyria (v. 32) and Egypt seem to be more present realities than the freedom and revival fostered by the Persian regime. This prayer, although not preserved as such in the post-Ezra synagogue, influenced strongly the structure of its liturgy (cf. L. Liebreich, *HUCA* 32 [1961] 228; *HUCA* 20 [1947] 21n.). **17.** *in their stubbornness:* The MT reads *b^e^miryām*, but the LXX has *b^e^miṣrayim*, "in Egypt."

111 **(V) Nehemiah's Final Ministry (Neh 10:1–13:30).**

(A) The Pledge (10:1–39). This is a bloodless archive fragment that could fit equally loosely any of the several Ezran assemblies or reforms. Verse 1 undoubtedly dovetails with 9:38, numbered 10:1 in the MT. But this leaves open whether 9:38 was a part of the present archive record, or whether 10:1 (10:2) was inserted or modified to connect Neh 9 with a list originally unrelated to it. A. Jepsen (*ZAW* 66 [1954] 87), with Winckler, joins the passage to Ezr 10:44. The explicit mention of Nehemiah is indeed the likeliest thing for a glossator to have inserted, but it also furnishes the likeliest motive for leaving the chapter just where it is (seconding Neh 8:9, as A. Ibáñez, *EstBib* 10 [1951] 379, but favoring pre-Neh Ezr). It is true that vv. 30–31 strongly echo Neh 13:23,21 (but also 5:11 with an apt but purely theoretical addition from Dt 15:1; R. North, *Bib* 34 [1953] 513), whence the content of 10:30–39 is linked by Schaeder with Neh 13, and also by De Fraine, although he emphasizes that the name Nehemiah is an interpolation. If such an interpolator existed, he might well have added vv. 30–31, whose individuality distinguishes them from the routine prescriptions that follow (cf. Nm 18:12–32). **32.** (Mt 10:33). The devaluation of the half-shekel (Ex 30:13; Mt 17:24) is ingeniously linked with the observation that a Persian shekel weighed 21 g. and a Phoenician shekel 14 g. But H. Montefiore (*NTS* 11 [1964] 61) asserts an original third was raised to half. **34.** (MT 10:35.) The wood offering is indeed unusual, but sufficiently virtual in Lv 6:12 (Josephus, *JW* 2. 17, 6 § 425; J. Epstein, *MGWJ* 78 [1934] 97, 255). On the lottery, see 1 Chr 25:8.

112 **(B) Forcing People to Live in Jerusalem (11:1–12:26).** Chapter 11 really fits after Neh 7:7a rather than the repetition of (Nehemiah era) Ezr 2 inserted there. "The holy (city)" (11:1) has become the name of Jerusalem in Arabic, *al-Quds*. **3.** Another of the genealogies in which the Chronicler delights; in fact, vv. 3–19 are perhaps the original from which 1 Chr 9:2–17 was copied. **23.** Especially heart warming to the author is whatever promotes the economic well being of the Levite choir, of which he was a member (→ 6 above).

Neh 12:1–26 is a further genealogical appendix to 7:39. It could fit equally well with what precedes or what follows. **7.** Chiefs of the priests cannot mean technically here high priests, for they are too numerous; but the term began to be used about this time, and in v. 10 (also 13:28) we seem to have a sequence of high priests continuing 1 Chr 5:41. Hence, in v. 23 it is not our canonical Book of Chronicles from which they were copied. **26.** Nehemiah (445) was not contemporary with Joshua (520); even if the verse is a gloss, the presence of Ezra after Nehemiah may be a chronological clue and not merely hierarchical subordination.

113 **(C) Solemn Dedication of the Wall (12:27–13:14).** The abrupt return to first person between vv. 31 and 39 might be equally applicable to Ezra or to Nehemiah of v. 26. The reading of the Law in 13:1 suggests Ezra, but the continuation in v. 6 is surely Nehemiah. It is his wall that is being inaugurated, and in view of all the other quirks of chronological sequence, we might well attach 12:27 to 7:1 where it normally would belong. Singers are stressed there too, as in 12:27–30, 44–47, but these are additions (3rd pers.) of the Chronicler flanking the relevant Nehemiah memoir. Apparently no peremptory reason exists for not treating as continuous Neh 11–13, dealing with the hero's maneuvers after his return to and from the Persian capital.

27. Dedication (*ḥănukkâ*, "inauguration") is also the name of modern Jewry's yuletide festival commemorating 1 Mc 4:60, the cleansing rite after Seleucid desecration (see Jn 10:22). Its date also comes coincidentally close to the 25 Kisleu (December) assigned by 2 Mc 1:18 for Neh 12:31; but this date cannot be inserted in any provable sequence with 25 Elul (September) assigned by Neh 6:15. **37.** Emending *lim'ôl*, "opposite," of both Hebr and Gk to *liśmôl* is favored by those who find here grounds for locating the Water Gate just S, and the Sheep "Probatica" just N, of the Temple esplanade where the procession would presumably end, as explained by M. Burrows (*JBL* 54 [1935] 29–40) on Neh 12, as distinct from the night ride of 3:1.

13:1. "On that day" shows that the Chronicler considered at least some earlier verses of ch. 13 to belong to the dedication of the wall, which he thus sees as pertaining to Nehemiah's second ministry. Although v. 1 unmistakably echoes Ezr (and Dt 23:4–5; K. Galling, *Fest. A. Bertholet* [Tübingen, 1950] 176), actually everything before v. 14 is sufficiently relevant to a ceremony culminating in the Temple. The wall itself, in the course of the quarter of a mile where it serves to bound the Temple area, would have contained chambers for both storage and lodging, according to usages attested by excavation. Even if the penthouse of Nehemiah's political enemies were none of these, the convergence of the processions on the Temple area gave him occasion for ostentatiously "exorcising" or reconsecrating the sacristies usurped by the "foreigner" (vv. 3, 28), rooms in part identical with the "stations" assigned within the Temple as lodging for the Levites.

7. "Batten is quite clear that the Eliashib who let Tobiah occupy the tithe-room was the high-priest. Rudolph and Galling are equally certain he was not" (PCB); Browne himself concludes that the octogenarian priest can hardly have noticed what tenants were receiving his nominal approval, but that 100 years later, the Chronicler tried to cloak the fact.

114 **(D) Nehemiah as Defender of the Faith (13:15–30).** Glowing with the success of those religious purges occasioned by his architectural and political interests, Nehemiah now frankly busies himself with cult. Like many amateurs, he seems unaware of the profound values of human freedom enshrined in the harshly formulated principle *odiosa sunt restringenda.* Loopholes in good laws will always be misused by evil men, but the effort to close them results progressively in an iron juridicalism (v. 24).

23. Massive silence about the enthusiastic public measures taken under Ezra (10:10) to cope with mixed marriages is taken by defenders of the traditional 458 (or 428) dating of Ezra as a sign that his efforts had been a colossal fiasco. For this there is no evidence, and, at any rate, it is more natural to suppose that the reform of Ezra had simply not yet happened. The argument cuts both ways; in Ezra's reform too there is no mention of that of Nehemiah. But Ezra as a priest and scribe possessed the competent authority in this matter that Nehemiah did not. As we noted before (see comment on Ezr 9:2), it is not clear that Ezra extended the ban beyond priests' marriages. The passages in Ex 34:16; Dt 7:3 do seem to prohibit any mixed marriages. The setting and motivation might encourage casuists to conclude that only those marriages are excluded which would involve anti-Yahwist political entanglements. But there is just as much reason for maintaining that the evils there foreseen are inherent in any wide diffusion of marriage outside the community of one's own faith. On the other hand, Dt 21:13 explicitly approves marriage with enemy foreigners, at least in conditions where the partner is a captive totally without influence or guarantee of religious rights. Advertence to the foreign wives of Joseph, Moses, David, and even Solomon and Ahab is such as to make it appear that only excess or "proximate occasion of sin" is categorically rejected (Gn 41:45; Ex 2:21; Nm 12:1; 2 Sm 3:3; 1 Chr 11:1; 1 Kgs 16:31; cf. G. Kittel, *Konnubium mit Nichtjuden* [1937] 30). We may again conclude that the self-protecting or centripetal character of any religious covenant is as such hostile to seeking a marriage partner in the out-group. Although the centrifugal or diffusive character of religious conviction finds in marriage alliances a most potent vehicle, in a given situation the existing authority may and must decide to what extent ghetto restrictions are called for. **24.** Ashdodite in Zech 9:6 may be a synonym of half-breed, really "bastard" (*mamzēr;* Dt 23:3; cf. S. Feigin, *AJSL* 43 [1926] 59). **25.** Nehemiah's mere guarded threat of physical violence in v. 21 proved so effective that he resorts to the real thing. **28.** One may wonder whether his zeal, and especially the picturesque extroversion of his manhandling, result chiefly from his purely political resentment against Tobiah's extensive support within what is, at any rate, a real hero's undying achievement—the wall of Jerusalem.

25

JOEL
OBADIAH

Geoffrey E. Wood

JOEL

BIBLIOGRAPHY

1 Bewer, J. A., *Obadiah and Joel* (ICC; Edinburgh, 1911). Bič, M., *Das Buch Joël* (Berlin, 1960). Bourke, J., "Le jour de Yahvé dans Joël," *RB* 66 (1959) 5–31, 191–212. Chary, T., *Les prophètes et le culte* (Paris, 1955) 190–216. Dennefeld, L., *Les problèmes du livre de Joël* (Paris, 1926). Kapelrud, A. S., *Joel Studies* (Uppsala, 1948). Morris, P. J., "Joël," *CCHS* 522a–23l. Nötscher, F., *Zwölfprophetenbuch* (Echter-B 4; Würzburg, 1954). Pautrel, R., "Joël," *VDBS* 4, 1098–104. Robinson, T. H., *Die zwölf kleinen Propheten* (HAT 14; 2nd ed.; Tübingen, 1954). Schumpp, M., *Das Buch der zwölf Propheten* (HBk 10/2; Freiburg i. Br., 1950). Steinmann, J., *Études sur les prophètes d'Israël* (Paris, 1954) 147–73. Trinquet, J., *Habaquq, Abdias, Joël* (BJ; Paris, 1953). Weiser, A., *Das Buch der zwölf kleinen Propheten* I (ATD 24; 2nd ed.; Göttingen, 1956). Wolff, H. W., *Dodekapropheton Joel* (BKAT 14/5; Neukirchen, 1963).

INTRODUCTION

2 **(I) Author.** Except for his oracles, little else is known of Joel ben Pethuel. He may have been attached to the Temple as spokesman for Yahweh (1:2–18; 2:1–16,19–27; 3–4) and the community (1:19–20; 2:17), for he manifests great familiarity with the Jewish liturgy (1:13–14; 2:15–17) and devotion to the sanctuary (1:8–9; 2:27; 4:16–17). (See A. R. Johnson, *The Cultic Prophet* [2nd ed.; Cardiff, 1962] 74–75; J. Lindblom, *Prophecy in Ancient Israel* [Oxford, 1962] 277; T. Chary, *op. cit.*, 211 n. 4; 216, although R. de Vaux denies the existence of a cultic prophet—De Vaux, *AI* 384–85.) Some conclude that Joel was, in fact, a priest.

3 **(II) Division, Authenticity, and Integrity.** Jl has two main sections. Chapters 1–2 graphically describe a locust plague and the community's reaction to it; chs. 3–4 are an enthusiastic description of that day when Israel's oppressors will be judged and Israel will itself emerge in every way supreme. Did one man author both sections? B. Duhm (*ZAW* 31 [1911] 1–43, 184–88) has argued that Joel was responsible only for 1–2, which deal with an actual locust invasion (see J. A. Thompson, *JNES* 14 [1955] 52–55). Someone else, recognizing the plague's eschatological possibilities, attempted to convert the work into an apocalypse by inserting 1:15; 2:1a–2b, 10–11 and adding chs. 3–4. Several other reputable scholars have supported this duality of authorship (Bewer, *op. cit.*, 56; Oesterley-Robinson, *Introd.* 357–62; Trinquet, *op. cit.*, 68) and some see a third hand in 4:4–8 (e.g., Weiser, *OT* 239–40). However, there is no need to assign the substance of chs. 3–4 to a different author or to view 1:15; 2:1a–2b, 10–11 as interpolations emanating from chs. 3–4. Joel, reflecting on the insects' attack, could have easily considered it a foreshadowing of the last day when the defiant nations at Yahweh's beckoning would march on him and his people only to meet judgment and destruction. The change from the graphic description, excited imperatives, and supplication of chs. 1–2 to the serene predictions and apocalyptic stereotypes of chs. 3–4 would have occurred normally as the Prophet's interest passed from the present calamity to its eschatological significance. One man would have been capable of such a transition; indeed, the change actually begins with 1:15 and gains momentum in 2:1–11 (see Bentzen, *IOT* 2, 135; Pfeiffer, *Introd.* 575; Nötscher, *op. cit.*, 40; etc.).

4 **(III) Date.** There is no mention of a reigning king or dynasty where one might expect it, e.g., 2:16–17. Elders and priests hold prominence in the community (1:2,13; 2:16–17), which is small enough to live within trumpet-call of the Temple (1:14; 2:1,15–16). Judah can be called Israel (2:27; 4:2,16), which suggests that the northern tribes have disappeared. The fall of Jerusalem (587–586), the Exile, and the annexation of Jewish territory are all memories (4:1–3,17). The book is therefore post-exilic. Further precision is possible. The Temple must be that of Ezr 6:13–18, completed *ca.* 515. Joel seems influenced by two mid-5th-cent. prophets, among others—Malachi (cf. Jl 2:11 with Mal 3:2;

Jl 3:4 with Mal 3:23) and Obadiah (cf. Jl 3:5 with Ob 17; Jl 4:2–3 with Ob 11; Jl 4:19 with Ob 10). Greeks merit only passing notice (4:6), indicating that the Battle of Issus (333) and Alexander's entrance into Palestine still lie ahead. Weighing all this, we may date Jl between 400–350. The particularism, the antipathy toward Gentiles, the liturgical preoccupation that Jl manifests characterized this period. Note the allusion to the *tāmîd* in 1:9,13; 2:14, the daily sacrifice stressed by late Judaism (see Dn 8:11; 11:31; 12:11; Josephus, *JW* 6.2,1).

Noting contacts between Ras Shamra literature and Jl, Kapelrud dates the activity of the Prophet *ca.* 600; he agrees, however, that his oracles were not fixed in writing until the 4th or 3rd cent. He has not received wide support (although see Steinmann, *op. cit.*). Bič, sharing Kapelrud's approach, has recently attempted to revive the traditional dating, relating the book to the reform of Jehoash (837–800).

5 **(IV) Occasion and Purpose.** The vigorous 5th-cent. reform of Nehemiah and Ezra restored harrassed Judah's sense of dignity and destiny. The remnant of Yahweh, rallied around the Temple and the Law, insulated itself from pagan and heterodox contagion and awaited the day of the Lord. Struck by a locust plague, the community, at Joel's insistence, turned from initial panic to intense prayer, for to Joel the plague was more than a passing incident. He soon saw, and he encouraged the community to see, it as a harbinger of the day of Yahweh, a preview or trial run of that final onslaught of God's enemies upon Judah and its God. The locusts are described as an invading army in 2:1–10; cf. 4:9–14. The heaven-sent plague (2:11) must stimulate a holy fear of Yahweh and his power—tighter identification with him in view of the judgment it forecasts. This effect achieved—the people do turn to penance and prayer—Joel delivers a consoling oracle: The locust scourge will be diverted, and Judah will flourish again (2:19–27). Even this immediate deliverance has eschatological application, for just as the locusts shall be dispersed, so shall the charging nations they typify be destroyed on that day when Yahweh intervenes decisively on Judah's behalf. Joel takes up the subject in chs. 3–4.

J. Bourke believes that the locust plague must be understood as more than a herald or preview of the day described in chs. 3–4. To him, it is a distinct day of the Lord itself. The prophets had warned of a day that would purge Israel (Am 5:18; Is 2:6–22; etc.), and the locust plague fulfills that prophecy (see 2:4–14). They also spoke of a day that would strike the nations (Ez 30:3; Is 13:6–9; etc.), and Joel turns to that in chs. 3–4. According to Bourke, the symmetry of chs. 1–2 and 3–4 and the use of apocalyptic clichés in both sections (e.g., 2:1–2 and 3:3–4; 2:10–11 and 4:14–16; etc.) argue for the equal appreciation as moments of judgment. It seems unlikely, however, that Joel, mindful of the national disaster of 587–586, would expect Judah to undergo another day of judgment. Living after the Exile, he, like his contemporaries, expected only one judgment—that of enemies with consequent Jewish emancipation.

6 **(V) Outline.** The Book of Joel may be outlined as follows:

- (I) The Locust Plague (1:1–2:27)
  - (A) Description and Reaction (1:1–20)
    - (a) Effects of the Plague (1:1–12)
    - (b) Summons to Prayer and Penance (1:13–14)
    - (c) The Prayer (1:15–20)
  - (B) Second Description—Eschatological Significance (2:1–17b)
    - (a) Invasion Simile (2:1–11)
    - (b) Second Summons to Prayer and Penance (2:12–17a)
    - (c) The Prayer (2:17b)
  - (C) The Divine Reply (2:18–27)
- (II) Eschatological Expansion of Chs. 1–2 (3:1–4:21)
  - (A) Jerusalem's Final Salvation (3:1–5)
  - (B) Trial and Defeat of the Nations (4:1–16a)
  - (C) Peaceful Aftermath (4:16b–18)
  - (D) Abridgment of B and C (4:19–21)

COMMENTARY

7 **(I) The Locust Plague (1:1–2:27).** The content of chs. 1–2 fits well into a liturgical setting. Joel first dwells upon the seriousness of the plague, then exhorts the people to religious renewal, prompting a solemn prayer to God. This sequence is repeated in ch. 2, where Joel underlines the eschatological lessons of the plague. The build-up finds its release in the comforting oracles of 2:19–27.

(A) Description and Reaction (1:1–20).

8 (a) Effects of the Plague (1:1–12). **1.** The LXX, V, and Pesh read Bethuel, a proper name found in Gn 22:23; 24:15,47, and more probably the correct reading (see Bewer, *op. cit.*, 75). **2–3.** The locusts have already inundated the countryside. There follows quick communal recourse to God at the Temple. The Prophet calls for attention, and throughout vv. 2–12, emphasizes the seriousness of the situation. *hear this: Šimᵉʿû* struck a formal note much as "hear ye" in English (see Dt 6:4; Is 1:2,10; Hos 5:1). *elders:* "Bearded ones"; they were members of the municipal council. Primitively the term referred to the heads of clans within a tribe. During the monarchy, the elders managed affairs on the local level (1 Sm 30:26–31; 2 Kgs 23:1; Ez 8:1). For some of their judicial duties, see Dt 19:12; 21:1–9,18–21; 22:13–21; 25:5–10. They continued to function among the exiles (Ez 14:1; 20:1–3) and more prominently in the restored community (Ezr 5:9; 6:7; 10:8,14). **4.** The "cutter" (*gāzām*), the "locust" (*'arbeh*), the "grasshopper (*yeleq*), and the "devourer" (*ḥāsîl*) have left absolutely nothing. Occurring 24 times in the OT, *'arbeh* is the most common biblical term for the mature insect (see Ex 10:13–19). *Gāzām*, *yeleq*, and *ḥāsîl* seem to refer to particularly noticeable stages in the insect's growth (O. R. Sellers, *AJSL* 52 [1936] 81–85; Thompson, *op. cit.*). See 2:25 for the correct sequence. The *yeleq* is the larval or hopping stage; the *ḥāsîl*, the nymphal stage; the *gāzām*, the final or winged stage. Locust plagues generally come out of the Sudan. Their eggs need moist soil, and, when rain conditions are ideal, vast quantities can be deposited and develop. Seized by a wanderlust, hordes begin to move straight across the land, eating and evolving as they progress. Reaching the winged stage, they rise and extend their quest for food. Under this gregarious and wandering spell they have been known to travel over 1000 mi. For other references to locust plagues, see Am 4:9; 7:1; Dt 28:38; Mal 3:1; Ps 105:34–35. For metaphorical use of the locust, see Jgs 6:5; Is 33:4; Na 3:15–17; Ap 9:3–7. Jerusalem's last locust plague took place in 1915; J. D.

Whiting (*NatGeog* 38 [1915] 511–50) provides a description and photographs.

9 5. The Prophet goes into detail. *wake up, you drunkards, and weep:* The agricultural loss is stressed (1:10–12), suggesting that the plague struck just prior to harvest time and the Feast of Tents, a time of revelry and heavy wine drinking (see De Vaux, *AI* 496; also Dt 16:13; Jgs 9:27; 21:19–21). Those who look forward to these festivities had better weep; there will be no wine! Kapelrud remarks that the neighboring Canaanites considered the god of vegetation, Baal, dead or imprisoned during dry seasons, drought, etc., and by means of wine-induced ecstasies (Hos 4:11–13; Am 2:7b–8) and cultic lamentation (Hos 7:14; 10:5; Ez 8:14), they tried to revive him. He believes that Joel here addresses these devotees of Baal, lax Judeans among them, and says, in effect, "Stimulate yourselves, go through your weeping ritual; it will avail you nothing; this plague is not the result of the imagined death of nonexistent Baal; Yahweh has sent it (2:11) and only conversion to him will bring relief." This might be acceptable if, as Kapelrud believes, Joel preached in pre-exilic times when the cult of Baal had made great inroads among God's people; however, as noted, a post-exilic date seems more likely. **6.** *a people:* Prv 30:25–27 applies this same metaphor to ants and rock badgers. Joel develops the invasion metaphor in 2:2–11. **8.** *lament like a virgin...for the spouse of her youth:* Joel addresses the whole community (Jer 6:26; Lam 1:15). Judah, its harvest nipped, resembles a betrothed virgin "widowed" on the eve of her wedding. Canaanite poetry portrayed the goddess Anath mourning over the body of Baal, god of fertility (see J. Gray, *Legacy of Canaan* [Leiden, 1957] 53–54; *ANET* 139); the image may influence Joel's poetry here. **9.** Only the gravest calamity could force the interruption of sacrifice. (Neh 10:33; Dn 8:11; 11:31; 12:11.) Its cessation now, owing to the consumption of all vegetation, points up the exceptional nature of the present disaster; the vital sacrificial line of communion with God has been cut. **10–12.** By his repetition in Hebrew of hollow "o" and "u" (18 times), the steady tolling of short clauses (*šuddad śādeh*, etc.), and finally the fourfold use of *hôbîš*, Joel effectively conveys his mournful mood.

10 (b) Summons to Prayer and Penance (1:13–14). The defenseless community must turn to God. The Prophet calls priests, Temple personnel, the elders, and the whole population to penance and formal prayer—the traditional reaction to disaster (Jgs 20:26; 1 Sm 7:5–9; Jer 36:5–9). In post-exilic times, the efficacy of fasting and other penances was rated highly (see Est 4:1–3,16; 14:2; Tb 3:10–11; 12:8; Jdt 4:8–10; 8:6; 9:1. **13.** Sackcloth was a penitential garment of camel or goat's hair worn about the waist (2 Kgs 6:30). Ordinarily, one might suspend penances at evening, but especially depressing situations prompted sustained self-affliction (2 Sm 12:16; 1 Kgs 21:27).

11 (c) The Prayer (1:15–20). The Prophet leads the assembly in a plea to Yahweh. The standard motifs of lament are present: a reproachful question, v. 16 (see Pss 22:1; 44:24); a provocative description, vv. 17–18; an outcry and invocation of God's powerful name, v. 19. **15.** See Is 13:6; Ez 30:2–3; Zeph 1:17. Joel begins to reveal the deeper significance of the plague. The day of Yahweh is coming, a day of final conflict and the unleashing of God's terrible might. Post-exilic Judah eagerly desired that day because it meant Judah's exaltation, but its hope was not untainted by anxiety. The thought of the day's full impact, its ingredients of divine wrath, struggle, and cosmic upheaval, causes Joel to pale before it. The locusts have been sent to illustrate as well as herald its imminent terrors. *ruin from the Almighty:* A play on words—*ûkᵉšōd miššadday*. El Shaddai, the mountain ("almighty") god, is an ancient name for Yahweh found frequently in the P tradition (Gn 28:3; 35:11; 43:14; 48:3; Ex 6:3). **16–20.** Before the locusts struck, Judah looked forward to the harvest festival with its songs of thanksgiving; instead, a lamentation rises. Compare these verses closely with festival Ps 65:10–14.

12 **(B) Second Description—Eschatological Significance (2:1–17b).** The sequence is similar to A. The plague is again described (2:1–11), motivating a new summons to penance (2:12–17a), and there follows a lamentation (2:17b). There is no need to consider it the content of a distinct liturgy at the Temple. It can be simply a second stage of the solemnity begun in ch. 1. Joel already senses that the locusts herald and illustrate the final onslaught of the nations upon Judah and its God. To help his audience appreciate this sign, he describes them now as an invading army. Thus shall the final day be; let Judah learn from this present attack the necessity of rallying closely about Yahweh and his Temple.

13 (a) Invasion Simile (2:1–11). See Is 13 for similar language. **1.** *blow the trumpet:* Echoes Hos 5:8; Zeph 1:16; Jer 4:5; Ez 33:1–6. **2a.** *it is near:* Cf. Zeph 1:14–15. **2b.** *like dawn:* Inasmuch as the plague introduces the day of Yahweh, it may be called its dawning. The winged locusts, their rising yellow cloud pierced by the rays of the sun, might actually have created a dawn effect. Even on the ground, their masses, moving over the hills, might be comparable to shifting early morning shadows. **4–9.** The military metaphor of charging horses and men is sustained throughout these verses; Ap 9:7–9 draws upon this passage. The poetry picks up the charge's momentum. Verse 9 has a staccato sound in Hebrew. The frequent use of archaic verb forms adds a somber note. **10.** *the heavens shake:* Joel again underscores his lesson that the locust assault introduces, and he exemplifies the coming final day by applying to it the trappings of cosmic turmoil ordinarily reserved for descriptions of that day (see Am 8:8–9; Is 13:10; 24:23; Ez 32:7). **11.** Yahweh has sent this army to stir Judah to serious religious preparation for his definitive coming.

14 (b) Second Summons to Prayer and Penance (2:12–17a). Having impressed his audience with the eschatological significance of the plague, Joel now intensifies his appeal for penance. **13.** *rend your hearts:* In the true prophetic tradition, Joel calls for more than external or cultic return to Yahweh; their whole conduct must change (cf. Hos 6:1–6; Jer 4:4; Dt 10:16). The imperative *šubû*, "return," summarizes a great theme of prophetic preaching (Hos 2:9; 3:5; 14:2; Jer 3:12,14; 4:1; etc.). **14.** Judah's conversion may be matched by Yahweh's pity. Still, one must not be presumptuous; man cannot demand anything. With Yahweh one must always allow a perhaps (see Am 5:15; Zeph 2:3; Jon 3:9). Yet there are solid grounds for confidence. In v. 13, Joel quotes verbatim Yahweh's own proclamation of his attributes (see Ex 34:6) where the emphasis is on his parental compassion and his benevolence; Yahweh is *rab-ḥesed*—i.e., voluntarily and perpetually committed to Israel's welfare by contract (see Jon 4:2; cf. J. Guillet, *Themes of the Bible* [Notre Dame, 1960] 47–95). *a blessing:* Joel hopes for renewed agricultural and pastoral prosperity (Dt 7:13–14; Hag 2:15–19) and with it the means to a revival of sacrifice. **15–17a.** The trial calls for all-out effort; even the young and aged must be brought before Yahweh. The newlywed, ordinarily dispensed from certain obligations (Dt 24:5; *Berakoth* 2:5), must share this penitential burden. The Temple personnel lead the prayers between the outdoor altar of holocaust and the Temple porch (see 1 Mc 7:36–37).

15 (c) The Prayer (2:17b). Dt 9:26–29 seems to stand behind this appeal. The same approach appears in Ex 32:12 and Nm 14:13–16: Yahweh is reminded of possible scandal; the Gentiles will doubt his protective power. God owes it to himself to deliver his people and his heritage, his piece of property in this world. Judah's prostration makes it the butt of ridicule. The Gentiles can taunt: Where is this superior God of whom Judah boasts? (Cf. Pss 44:10–27; 79.)

16 **(C) The Divine Reply (2:18–27).** The communal fast and appeal win a response. God promises deliverance from the locust plague and its attendant drought. Then, throughout chs. 3–4, he promises a more far-reaching deliverance. Jl 2:18–27 is pivotal; after it, the Prophet's perspective becomes wholly eschatological. **18–19a.** *the Lord was stirred:* The oracle's introduction may be an editorial insert. Utilizing the verb *qānā'*, "to be jealous" or "to be emotionally involved," the writer shows that Joel's approach struck home. Yahweh cannot permit his ability to protect Israel to be questioned. His sensitivity to it is betrayed in the quick response that follows (see also Ez 36:21–30; Zech 1:14–17; 8:1–3). **20.** *the northerner:* Palestine experienced many invasions by its northern approaches. Therefore, the north came to mean trouble and "northerner" became synonymous for troublemaker. As such, the term is applicable to the locusts regardless of the direction of their approach. Another possible explanation is that the Canaanite Olympus, Mt. Casius, modern Jebel Aqra in Syria, was called Saphon or "north mountain." It was the abode of Baal. The Jews considered Mt. Zion to be the "Saphon" of Yahweh (Ps 48:2–3; see also Is 14:13–14). Inasmuch as the term "north" can designate Yahweh's dwelling, a punitive agent sent by him might be termed "the northerner" (Ez 38:6; 39:2). (See De Vaux, *AI* 279–81; Kapelrud, *op. cit.*, 93–108.) *the eastern sea...western sea:* The Dead Sea and the Mediterranean. **21.** *fear not, O land:* The oracle fluctuates between the first (2:19–20, 25,27) and third (2:21–24,26) persons. **23.** *teacher of justice:* In Hebrew, *hammôreh liṣ*ᵉ*dāqāh*. *Môreh* means "teacher" or "diviner" (Gn 12:6; Jos 30:20) and is read as such in Tg. Sym, Theodotion, and Vg (*doctorem*). The passage is very similar to Is 30:19–20, where *môreh* as "teacher" occurs twice. The LXX has *brōmata*, "nourishment," possibly reading *hammāzôn* for *hammôreh*. Some suggest that *môreh* be read *yôreh*, the "early (or autumn) rain" (Trinquet, *op. cit.*). The phrase might then be translated, "He will surely give you autumn rain in just measure." However, if *môreh* is kept and translated "teacher," a compromise might still be made: "The teacher of justice whom God will send is the rain." It will witness to God's fidelity to Judah and teach Judah that its corresponding fidelity is the sure key to prosperity. Some think the reference is to a person, not necessarily the Messiah, but a great spiritual leader to come (see Schumpp, *op. cit.*, 86). The 2nd-cent. BC founder of the Qumran sect was called "teacher of justice" (CD 1:5–12; 1QpHab). His title may have been drawn from this passage but more probably from Dt 18:15–18; 33:9–10 (see T. H. Gaster, *The Dead Sea Scriptures* [N.Y., 1956] 5). **23b.** Because of its link to *malqôš*, the "late (or spring) rain," the second *môreh* in this verse should be read *yôreh*, the "early rain," as in the CCD. The context calls for a future reading of the verbs in this verse (see Joüon, *Grammaire* 118s). **27.** All doubts of Yahweh's power and fidelity will be eliminated.

17 **(II) Eschatological Expansion of Chs. 1–2 (3:1–4:21).** Deliverance from the locusts and attendant problems only illustrates and guarantees final deliverance from all oppression. Joel now focuses upon this belief.

(A) Jerusalem's Final Salvation (3:1–5). **1.** *my spirit:* By his spirit, God creates, vivifies (Gn 1:2; 2:7; Jb 33:4; Ps 104:29–30), communicates creativity (Ex 31:3), propels men to leadership (Jgs 3:10; 6:39; 1 Sm 16:13; Is 61:1), and stimulates religious enthusiasm (Nm 11:25; 1 Sm 10:10; Acts 2:4–13; 10:44). It is no wonder that Moses desired all Israelites to be filled with this breath of Yahweh (Nm 11:29), and Joel here predicts the fulfillment of Moses' desire. A universal and manifold outpouring of the spirit is foretold in Is 32:15; 44:3–5; Ez 11:19; 36:26–27; Zech 12:10. No longer will Israel lean upon an occasional hero or prophet. The whole nation will possess their charisms, and Judah will emerge an ideal community. *mankind:* "Flesh." Frequently, when the Scripture wishes to describe man as weak, perishable, or perverse, it describes him as flesh (Gn 6:3; Ps 78:39; Sir 14:17–18; Mk 14:38; Rom 7:18). The spirit of God will revivify and invigorate dormant, prostrate Israel. God promises a second and greater creation. Compare Ez 37:5, where the spirit of God revives the dried bones of Israel (see Van Imschoot, *Théologie* 2, 11–16,28–35; Schumpp, *op. cit.*, 88). **3.** *I will work wonders:* The Exodus, climaxed at Sinai, was marked by wonders (Ex 7–17), blood (Ex 24:4–8), and fire and smoke (Ex 13:21–22; 19:16–18). Judah's coming delivery will be a new Exodus. **4.** God's intervention will shake the cosmos. The sun and moon were worshiped as deities throughout the Gentile world. God's appearance will cast such "gods" into everlasting shadow. Another possible meaning is that the regular transit of sun and moon will abruptly cease with the commencement of God's eternal day (Zech 14:7). **5.** *everyone shall be rescued...a remnant...survivors whom the Lord shall call:* These expressions refer to Judah and possibly to the Israelites of the Diaspora. Paul did not interpret this verse in so narrow a sense. In Rom 10:12–13, he quotes v. 5a and gives it universal scope: The day of the Lord brings salvation to Jew and Gentile. Acts 2:17–31 interprets the whole chapter in the same way and points to Pentecost as its fulfillment.

18 **(B) Trial and Defeat of the Nations (4:1–16a).** Before the day of Yahweh reaches its high noon of Jewish prosperity, the hostile nations must be dispersed even as the locusts. **1.** *in those days and at that time:* See this formula in Jer 33:15; 50:4,20. Judah's restoration coincides with Gentile decline. Joel manifests the exclusiveness of the post-exilic era. Only Judah would benefit hereafter. The bitter memory of 587–586, the long decades of oppression by its neighbors, left Judah little sympathy for aliens. The Book of Jonah was a refreshing reaction to such particularism. **2.** On the general judgment of the nations, see Zeph 3:8; Jer 25:31; Is 66:16. There was a tendency to locate this place in some valley of ominous name (Is 22:6; Ez 39:1; Jer 19:1–13, although this last refers to Israel). Joel's valley is fittingly called "Jahweh shall judge." Some identify it with Hinnom or the Kidron ravine (see Simons, *JOT* 10); however, *'ēmeq* suggests a broad valley. In the reign of Jehoshaphat, Yahweh single-handedly destroyed Judah's enemies in the Valley of Beracah (2 Chr 20:13–30). Joel may allude to it: There will be another Valley of Jehoshaphat (see Schumpp, *op. cit.*, 92)! But Joel probably had no precise geographical location in mind. *I will enter into judgment:* At the nations' trial Yahweh will be judge and prosecutor. Note how intimately Yahweh identifies himself with Israel; outrages committed against his people are taken personally. The crimes remembered here go back to the disasters of 721 and 587. **3.** *they have cast lots:* See Ob 11. Enslavement of his people was bad enough, but here Yahweh expresses indignation over their low evaluation. They bartered a Jewish boy for a moment's sensual satisfaction; they exchanged a Jewish girl for a quick cup of wine.

19 **4-8.** These lines, apparently an addition, expand upon vv. 2-3. Someone, perhaps Joel himself, wished to draw specific attention to the crimes of Phoenicia and Philistia. Whereas vv. 1-3 and 9-16 are poetry, this is in prose. **4.** *what are you to me:* Yahweh asks why these nations oppressed his people. What pretext did they have for vengeance? If there is any avenging to be done, Yahweh will do it. Again note how he identifies himself with his people. **6.** See Am 1:6-10; 2 Chr 21:16; Homer, *Odyssey* 14-15, on Phoenicia's slave-trading habits. *the Greeks:* The Ionians (*yᵉwānîm*), the Greeks of the Aegean Islands and western Asia Minor. **8.** Yahweh invokes the *lex talionis*. Inasmuch as Phoenicians sold enslaved Israelites to distant lands to the northwest, Israel will sell Phoenicians to a people living in exactly the opposite direction, far to the southeast. The Sabeans were a commercial people conveniently located at the southern tip of Arabia (Jer 6:20; Jb 6:19).

9-16a. The poetic style and more general judgment theme of vv. 1-3 are resumed here; however, the trial setting yields to one of combat. **9.** Yahweh ironically urges the nations to declare a holy war of no quarter upon him and Israel—a conflict which by nature would pit their massed gods against the power of Yahweh. **10.** *beat your plowshares into swords:* Yahweh vehemently expresses his commitment to war by this reversal of the classic description of peace found in Is 2:4 and Mi 4:3. *let the weak man say...:* It may mean to draft every available man, but probably the irony persists; let the nations, in fact so feeble, foolishly play the warrior. **11.** *bring down...:* Apparently a later addition—an appeal that Yahweh draw upon his angelic host. The LXX and Vg offer variant readings (see Zech 14:5). **13.** *apply the sickle...the wine press is full:* Cf. Is 63:1-6; Ap 14:14-20. **14.** The nations answer the summons to battle and judgment; they surge upon Israel much as the locusts of ch. 2. The setting is the Valley of Jehoshaphat, here called the "valley of *ḥārûṣ*," which may mean "of the threshing device," in which case the metaphor of v. 13 is continued, or "of sharp, final decision." the preferred meaning. **15.** See comment on 3:3-4. **16a.** *the Lord roars:* Yahweh simultaneously pronounces and executes judgment upon the Gentiles from Zion. He utters not words but earthquaking thunder (Ex 19:19; Ps 18:14; 29:3-9). Here, as elsewhere, Joel borrows his language from an older prophet (see Am 1:2).

20 **(C) Peaceful Aftermath (4:16b-18). 17.** Israel's complete deliverance will prove God's special attachment. Israelites will know from this experience the power of God's presence in their midst (Ez 38:23; 39:6). *Jerusalem shall be holy:* The particularism and Temple orientation of the period are again manifest. The ideal Jerusalem will be inviolable. Israelites will form a closed, untainted community, the "kingdom of priests" of Ex 19:6 (see Ez 44:9 for a similar outlook). This narrower view of the eschaton contrasts with the broader vision of Mi 4:1-3 and Is 2:2-4. **18.** Water was scarce in Judah; a picture of the future in terms of water would be particularly beneficent. The Prophet emphasizes the sure fecundity of the era to come. An image of an unceasing stream flowing from the Temple is found in greater detail in Ez 47:1-12 (see also Ps 46:5). Rivers and luxuriant vegetation were characteristics of Eden (Gn 2). According to Bewer (*op. cit.*, 141-42), the "valley of Shittim" may be the Wadi es-Sant, which cuts W from Bethlehem to the coast. Ezekiel's stream flows in the opposite direction—E into the Dead Sea. In Zech 14:8, it flows in both directions. The town mentioned in Nm 25:1 and Jos 2:1 is located across the Jordan Valley, NE of the Dead Sea; it could hardly be meant here. As with the Valley of Jehoshaphat, no precise location is intended. Shittim means "acacia trees." Because so many furnishings of the Temple were made of acacia wood (the Ark, the table of showbread, etc.; see Ez 25:10,23), Joel may mean that, along with material prosperity, the Temple or cultic life will also flourish.

21 **(D) Abridgment of B and C (4:19-21).** These verses are a condensation of the themes of Gentile judgment and Judean emancipation, already treated throughout 4:1-18, and may be an appendix to the text. **19.** *Egypt...Edom:* These two nations were especially offensive to Judah for past wrongs; on Israelite feeling toward Edom in Joel's time, see Ob 8-14. **21.** *the Lord dwells in Zion:* Without Yahweh, Judah would have no hope or destiny. It is his commitment to Judah, his presence at Zion, that will sustain and should encourage the nation. The dispersal and destruction of the locusts will flow from, and witness to, his powerful presence amid his people (2:27), as will also the final defeat of oppressor nations (4:17). Joel's immediate objective is to strengthen the population's faith in that presence, their appreciation of all that it means to them. It is not surprising, therefore, that his oracles close with one more vigorous declaration of the point: The Lord dwells and will ever dwell in Zion.

OBADIAH

BIBLIOGRAPHY

22 Bewer, J. A., *Obadiah and Joel* (ICC; Edinburgh, 1911). Bič, M., "Zur Problematik des Buches Obadajah," VTSup 1 (Leiden, 1953) 11-25. Bullough, S., "Abdias," (*CCHS;* London, 1953) 666-68. Cannon, W. W., "Israel and Edom. The Oracle of Obadiah," *Theology* 15 (1927) 129-40, 191-200. Nötscher, F., "Obadja," (Echter-B 4; Würzburg, 1954) 78-81. Robinson, T. H., "The Structure of the Book of Obadiah," *JTS* 17 (1916) 402-8. Rudolph, W., "Obadja," *ZAW* 49 (1931) 222-31. Weiser, A., "Obadja," (ATD 24; Göttingen, 1956) 206-13.

INTRODUCTION

23 **(I) Division, Occasion, and Date.** Verses 1-14 and 15b are addressed to Edom. On the relationship of the Edomites and Israelites, see the Jacob and Esau narratives of Gn 25:19-36:43. Despite kinship, both maintained a perennial feud. David subjugated Edom (2 Sm 8:13-14) but the nation gave his heirs constant trouble (2 Kgs 8:20; 14:7,22; 16:6). Jewish antipathy was especially aggravated in 587–586 when the Edomites assisted the Babylonian armies besieging Jerusalem (Lam 4:21–22; Ps 137:7). Biblical oracles against Edom are frequent and intense (see Am 1:11–12; Is 34:5–17; 63:1–6; Jer 49:7–22; Ez 25:12–17; 35; Mal 1:2–4).

But Edom had other enemies. Arabian pressure increased during the 6th cent.; *ca.* 500–450, Edom was dislodged from its seemingly impregnable highlands S of the Dead Sea (Mal 1:3; Bright, *Hist.* 361). Diodorus Siculus (19.94–98) informs us that the Nabateans were living in Petra, the former Edomite capital, in 312 (F. M. Abel, *RB* 46 [1937] 373–91). This situation probably prompted Obadiah to revive a pre-exilic oracle against Edom (vv. 1–9) and blend into it references to the present debacle. Note how Jer absorbs the same oracle (cf. Ob 1b,2,3a,4,5a,5b,6,8 with Jer 49:14,15,16a, 16b,9b,9a,10,7, respectively). Therefore we may date vv. 1–14 and 15b *ca.* 475–450, although the borrowed base oracle paraphrased through vv. 1–9 would have originated before 600 (see Bewer, *op. cit.*, 7; Bentzen, *IOT* 2, 143; Pfeiffer, *Introd.* 586). Because of the quality of vv. 10–14, other authorities prefer a date closer to 586 (Eissfeldt, *OTI* 402–3, 492; Weiser, *OT* 248).

Verses 15a and 16–21 reflect a later date and occasion. Here the Jews are addressed. The imminent judgment not only of Edom but also of all the Gentiles is announced; the final victory of Yahweh and his people is proclaimed. Obviously Edom had not been entirely destroyed by the pressures that occasioned vv. 1–14 and 15b. Its expulsion from the highlands only pushed its people closer to Jerusalem. Another oracle of broader scope was therefore pronounced. Joel (*ca.* 400) echoes elements from it (cf. Ob 15 with Jl 1:15; 4:4,7,14; Ob 17 with Jl 3:5; 4:17). We may date verses 15a and 16–21 *ca.* 425–400. Both oracles were given in Judah.

24 **(II) Outline.** The Book of Obadiah may be outlined as follows:

(I) Oracle Against Edom (1–14, 15b)
- (A) Edom's Fall (1–9)
- (B) Reason for Edom's Fall (10–14, 15b)

(II) Oracle of Final Victory (15a, 16–21)

COMMENTARY

25 **(I) Oracle Against Edom (1–14, 15b).** Obadiah was witnessing the collapse of Edom *ca.* 500–450, caused by some decisive breakthrough of an Arabian coalition. His satisfaction could not be contained.

(A) Edom's Fall (1–9). **1.** *the vision:* The Hebr word *ḥāzôn* can refer to a strictly visual experience but often, when used in the title of a prophetical book, it has the broader sense of "observation" or "word" (see A. R. Johnson, *op. cit.*, 12–15, 36–37). **3.** *the pride of your heart:* For the Semite, the heart was the seat of intelligence (see J. B. Bauer, *VD* 40 [1962] 27–32). Edom's pride is emphasized; the highland nation's habitual sense of security was its undoing—cf. v. 3b. It had lessened its vigilance—cf. v. 7. The "rock," *sela'*, may mean the whole Mt. Seir region, whose plateaus and purple mountains average about 4800 ft. above sea level and extend 45 mi. S and E of the Dead Sea. But Sela was also the name of the Edomite capital (Jgs 1:36; 2 Kgs 14:7; Is 16:1), probably the Petra of Nabatean times. The normal approach to Sela-Petra is through a mile-long gorge whose walls rise 320 ft. (see Albright, *AP* 160–61; N. Glueck, *The Other Side of the Jordan* [New Haven, 1940] 114–200; M. Rostovtzeff, *Caravan Cities* [Oxford, 1932] 37–53). **4.** *though... your nest be set among the stars:* See Am 9:2. In Is 14:13–14, the metaphor describes pride and ambition. This sense may be included here, considering v. 3. **5.** *if thieves came to you:* Thieves take only what they consider valuable; vintagers were obliged to leave something on the vine for the poor (Lv 19:10; Dt 24:21). Edom would be stripped. *how you are ravaged:* This interjection is absent in Jeremiah's version of the oracle (cf. Jer 49:9). It reveals that the prophecy and its fulfillment are almost concurrent. **6.** *Esau:* Edom is here personified under its ancestor's name. *seek out his hiding places:* The mountain walls around Sela are honeycombed with tombs. The soft sandstone lent itself to easy excavation and ornamental facing. Perhaps Obadiah envisions here the soldiery probing these and other caverns where Edomite treasure lay hidden. **7.** *to the border they drive you:* Obadiah again departs from the borrowed oracle. The Edomites had begun to occupy the neighboring Negeb in the 6th cent. (Ez 35:11). Now they were forced to shift westward across the Arabah in such numbers that the Negeb became known as Idumea (see 1 Mc 4:15,61; 5:3). *those who eat your bread:* This phrase, not found in the Hebrew, is suggested by Ps 41:10. Some carefully nurtured treachery achieved what no frontal attack could. **8.** *says the Lord:* Obadiah returns to his paraphrase of the older oracle. *the wise men:* Edom and Arabia were noted for their sages (see 1 Kgs 5:10–16; 10:1–3; Jb 1:1; 2:11; Prv 30:1; 31:1). **9.** *Teman:* An Edomite city, it here represents the whole country.

26 **(B) Reason for Edom's Fall (10–14, 15b).** During the Babylonian siege of Jerusalem in 587–586, the Judeans expected at least neutrality of Edom. But these kinsmen not only assisted the enemy, they annexed Judean territory. Edom now suffered for those crimes. **12.** *gaze not... exult not:* Wincing at the memory of Jerusalem's fall, the Prophet forgets the present and speaks directly to the Edomites of 586. The rhythmic series of imperatives through vv. 12–14, and the excited repetition of *b^e yôm*, "on the day," betray his agitation. **15b.** *as you have done:* This half-verse fits better immediately after v. 14.

27 **(II) Oracle of Final Victory (15a, 16–21).** Edom survived in the Negeb, occupying even Hebron, David's first capital, only 15 mi. S of Jerusalem. Hence, the same Obadiah (see R-F 1, 579), or another prophet living *ca.* 425–400, pronounced a new oracle. Final retribution for Edom and all the nations would yet come; the day was near. **15a.** *the day of the Lord:* On the lips of the pre-exilic prophets the "day of the Lord" had an ominous ring; it was to be a day of doom for unfaithful Israel, and the nations roundabout were to be Yahweh's agents (see Am 5:18–20; Is 2:10–12; Zeph 1:15; Jer 30:5–7). But to chastened exilic and post-exilic Israel, the coming day meant Israelite triumph and the chastisement of Gentile oppressors (see Jer 50:25–27; Is 63:4; Jl 3:4–4:1). **17.** *a portion shall be saved:* For the remnant theme, see Is 4:2–3; Zeph 2:7–9; etc. The post-exilic community may have seemed but the debris of a once proud state, but to the prophets it was the seed of a new Israel. God's fidelity to his ancient promises and choice insured Israel's permanence and salvation (see, e.g., Hos 11). **18.** *house of Jacob:* Here, specifically

Judah. *house of Joseph:* The northern kingdom (see Gn 48). **19.** Jewish territory hardly extended beyond a 10-mi. radius of Jerusalem in the 5th cent. On the day of the Lord, Jerusalem would reclaim all the territories once held by David: S, the Negeb; W, the Philistine hills and coastlands; N, the tribal lands of Ephraim; E, Transjordan. Perhaps Benjamin should read *b^{e}nê ʿammôn*, the "sons of Ammon" (Pfeiffer, *Introd.* 585).

20. Phoenician territory would be annexed; Zarephath was a coastal town situated between Tyre and Sidon (1 Kgs 17:10). *Sepharad:* Possibly a site in Babylonia, because Judean exiles are mentioned. The *Tg. Jon* and Pesh favor Spain; however, the most accepted identification is Sardis in Asia Minor or Asia Minor itself. J. Gray sees Hesperides in the word and suggests NE Libya (*ZAW* 65 [1953] 53–59).

26

DANIEL

Louis F. Hartman, C.SS.R.

BIBLIOGRAPHY

1 *Commentaries:* Bentzen, A., *Daniel* (2nd ed.; Tübingen, 1952). Brown, R. E., *The Book of Daniel* (PPBS; N.Y., 1962). Charles, R. H., *The Book of Daniel* (Oxford, 1929). De Menasce, P. J., *Daniel* (BJ; 2nd ed.; Paris, 1958). Dennefeld, L., *Daniel* (Paris, 1947). Goettsberger, J., *Das Buch Daniel* (Bonn, 1928). Heaton, E. W., *The Book of Daniel* (London, 1956). Jeffery, A., "Daniel," *IB* (N.Y., 1956). Lattey, C., *The Book of Daniel* (Dublin, 1948). Linder, J., *In Librum Daniel* (Paris, 1939). Montgomery, J. A., *Daniel* (ICC; N.Y., 1927). Nötscher, F., *Daniel* (2nd ed.; Würzburg, 1958). Rinaldi, G., *Daniele* (Torino, 1948). Slotki, J., *Daniel* (London, 1951). Steinman, J., *Daniel* (Paris, 1950). Young, E. J., *The Prophecy of Daniel* (Grand Rapids, 1949).

Studies: Baumgartner, W., *Das Buch Daniel* (Giessen, 1926); "Das Aramäische im Buche Daniel," *ZAW* 45 (1927) 81–133; "Ein Vierteljahrhundert Danielforschung," *TR* 11 (1939) 59–83, 125–44, 201–28. Beek, M., *Das Danielbuch* (Leiden, 1935). Driver, G. R., "The Aramaic of the Book of Daniel," *JBL* 45 (1926) 110–19, 323–25. Ginsberg, H. L., *Studies in Daniel* (N.Y., 1948); "The Composition of the Book of Daniel," *VT* 4 (1954) 246–75. Junker, H., *Untersuchungen über literarische und exegetische Probleme des Buches Daniel* (Freiburg i. Br., 1932). Rowley, H. H., "The Unity of the Book of Daniel," *HUCA* 23/I (1950–51) 233–73; "The Composition of the Book of Daniel," *VT* 5 (1955) 272–76.

INTRODUCTION

2 **(I) Title.** This book is named, not after its author, but after its protagonist, who is presented here as living in Babylonia during the reign of the last kings of the Neo-Babylonian Empire and their first successors, the early kings of the Medes and the Persians—i.e., during most of the 6th cent. BC. The name Daniel, "my judge is God" in Hebrew, was also borne, according to the Chronicler, by one of David's sons (1 Chr 3:1 = Chileab of 2 Sm 3:3) and by one of the Jews who returned from the Babylonian Exile at the time of Ezra and Nehemiah (Ezr 8:2; Neh 10:7) in the second half of the 5th cent. Obviously neither can be identified with the Daniel of this book. The prophet Ezekiel speaks of a certain Daniel (or, more exactly, Dan'el, according to the Hebr consonantal text) who was renowned for his piety (Ez 14:14,20) and wisdom (28:3). Inasmuch as this Daniel, however, is presented as living long before Ezekiel at the time of Noah and Job (14:14,20), he could scarcely have been regarded as living in the 6th cent., either by the author of Dn or by his first readers, who knew their Bible too well to make such a mistake. The Daniel of Ezekiel should probably be connected in some way with the *dn'l* (God judges) who plays an important role in the Ugaritic Tale of Aqhat, which dates from about the middle of the 14th cent. (see *ANET* 149–55). Possibly a distant echo of this wise and pious Daniel of the Ugaritic epic, who "judged the cause of the widow and decided the case of the fatherless" (Aqhat 5.7–8), is found in the wise young judge of the Susanna story (Dn 13).

(II) Contents. As preserved in the Hebr Bible, Dn lends itself to a natural division of two roughly equal parts. The first part (chs. 1–6) contains six edifying stories about Daniel and his three companions at the royal court in Babylonia; the second part (chs. 7–12) is made up of four visions in which Daniel beholds, under symbolic images, the succession of the four "kingdoms" that God's people, the Jews, occupied from the time of the Babylonian conquest of Judea until God's establishment of his own kingdom for them. As the book has come down to us in its Gk version, it also contains the three stories of Daniel's exploits with Susanna, the priests of Bel, and the dragon (chs. 13–14).

3 **(III) Historical Background.** To understand the literary nature of this book, we must have some idea of the pertinent historical circumstances. In the 8th cent. BC, the Assyrians had turned the kingdom of Israel into a province of their vast empire and reduced the southern kingdom to a vassal state. Toward the end of

the 7th cent., Cyaxares, king of the Medes, with the assistance of the Babylonians, captured Nineveh and utterly destroyed the Assyrian Empire. Although Nebuchadnezzar of Babylon soon took over most of the former realm of the Assyrians and even extended it by his conquest of Judah in 587, his successors allowed the Babylonian power to deteriorate until the Persian king, Cyrus the Great, who had already conquered Media and made himself master of both the Medes and the Persians, captured Babylon in 539 from its last king, Nabonidus, and his son, Belshazzar. Thereafter the ancient Near East was ruled by the Persian successors of Cyrus the Great, among whom the only outstanding king was Darius I the Great, until Alexander the Great placed it under Gk dominion in 331. In the 3rd cent., Palestine was governed by the Gk dynasty of the Ptolemies, whose capital was at Alexandria in Egypt. In the 2nd cent., it was under the dominion of the Gk dynasty of the Seleucids, whose capital was at Antioch in Syria.

Useful for an understanding of Dn is a conspectus (see below) of the rulers of these dynasties that controlled the Near East from the 6th to the 2nd cent. BC. (→ History of Israel, 75:86–105.)

Most of the Jews who survived Nebuchadnezzar's conquest of Judah were deported to Babylonia between 598 and 582. But after 539, when Cyrus permitted the exiled Jews to return to their homeland, there was a slow but steady growth in the number of Jews living in Palestine. Under their Persian and Ptolemaic rulers they enjoyed limited political autonomy and complete religious liberty. But the Seleucid ruler, Antiochus IV Epiphanes, in his endeavor, both for political and for cultural reasons, to Hellenize the Jews of Palestine, tried to force them to abandon their ancient religion and to practice the common pagan worship of his realm. The ultimate outcome of this bloody persecution was armed revolt among the Jews, as told in 1–2 Mc. This conflict between the religion of the Jews and the paganism of their foreign rulers is also the basic theme of Dn. However, in Dn it is regarded from God's viewpoint as long foreseen and tolerated by him, both to show the vast superiority of Israel's wisdom over all pagan philosophy and to demonstrate the truth that the God of Israel is the master of history, who "makes kings and unmakes them" (2:21), until he ultimately establishes his universal kingdom on earth.

4 **(IV) Literary Genre.** In developing such a thesis the author makes use of two literary genres that may seem strange to many modern readers: the haggadic genre and the apocalyptic genre. The latter, employed in the second half, consists in a certain mysterious "revelation," received in fantastic visions or transmitted by angels, both about past and present history and about the eschatological establishment of God's messianic kingdom. Inasmuch as this literary device makes use of some famous character of the distant past as the recipient of this revelation, events that are past history to the writer are presented as prophecies of future happenings. In a broad sense, however, this form of writing can rightly be regarded as a kind of prophecy, because it gives an interpretation of history in God's name, as seen by him (→ Post-exilic Period, 20:23–27).

The haggadic genre, used in chs. 1–6 and 13–14, gets its name from the mishnaic Hebr word, *haggādāh*, lit., a "setting forth," a "narrative," but often used in the sense of a "story" having little or no basis in actual history but told for the sake of inculcating a moral lesson. If such a story is a free elaboration of some true event of actual history, it is more exactly called an "haggadic midrash." But the story may also be a pure "haggadah," i.e., a free

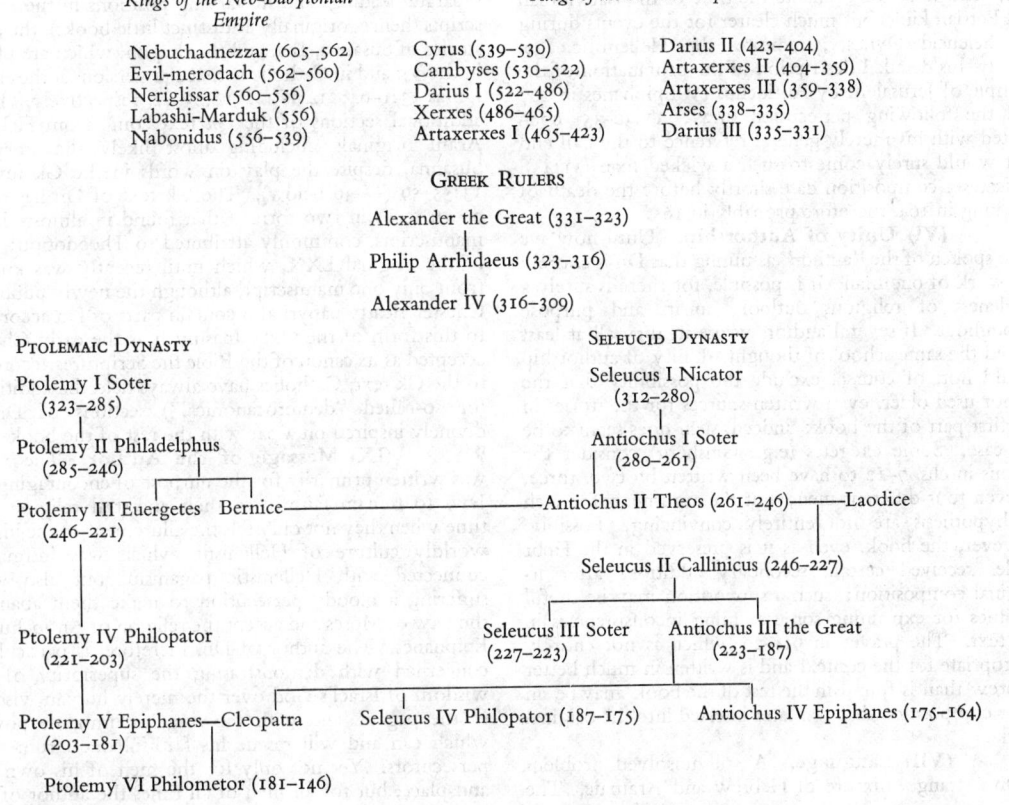

Kings of the Neo-Babylonian Empire	*Kings of the Persian Empire*	
Nebuchadnezzar (605–562)	Cyrus (539–530)	Darius II (423–404)
Evil-merodach (562–560)	Cambyses (530–522)	Artaxerxes II (404–359)
Neriglissar (560–556)	Darius I (522–486)	Artaxerxes III (359–338)
Labashi-Marduk (556)	Xerxes (486–465)	Arses (338–335)
Nabonidus (556–539)	Artaxerxes I (465–423)	Darius III (335–331)

GREEK RULERS

Alexander the Great (331–323)

Philip Arrhidaeus (323–316)

Alexander IV (316–309)

PTOLEMAIC DYNASTY

Ptolemy I Soter (323–285)

Ptolemy II Philadelphus (285–246)

Ptolemy III Euergetes (246–221) — Bernice — Antiochus II Theos (261–246) — Laodice

Ptolemy IV Philopator (221–203)

Ptolemy V Epiphanes—Cleopatra (203–181)

Ptolemy VI Philometor (181–146)

SELEUCID DYNASTY

Seleucus I Nicator (312–280)

Antiochus I Soter (280–261)

Antiochus II Theos (261–246)

Seleucus II Callinicus (246–227)

Seleucus III Soter (227–223) | Antiochus III the Great (223–187)

Seleucus IV Philopator (187–175) | Antiochus IV Epiphanes (175–164)

composition throughout with no historical basis at all. Often it is impossible to say how far, if at all, an haggadic story is based on actual history.

Stories about Daniel are clearly haggadic; in their entirety, they cannot be taken as strict history. Inasmuch as their author does not intend them as historical, he cannot be accused of error if he makes inaccurate statements, from an historical viewpoint. We have no way of knowing whether the Daniel of these stories was really an historical character, about whom popular legends gradually clustered, or whether he was simply a creation of Jewish folklore. A similar case is that of Ahikar of the Aram Ahikar Legend, who, as a wise counselor of the Assyrian kings (see *ANET* 427–30), is not too different from Daniel. For the inspired author of our book this question was unimportant. He stressed the spiritual message that he wished to convey by these haggadic stories. (→ Apocrypha, 68:119.)

5 **(V) Date and Authorship.** Having lost sight of these ancient modes of writing, until relatively recent years Jews and Christians considered Dn to be true history, containing genuine prophecy. Inasmuch as chs. 7–12 are written in the first person, it was natural to assume that the Daniel in chs. 1–6 was a truly historical character and that he was the author of the whole book. There would be few modern biblical scholars, however, who would now seriously defend such an opinion. The arguments for a date shortly before the death of Antiochus IV Epiphanes in 164 are overwhelming. An author living in the 6th cent. could hardly have written the late Hebrew used in Dn, and its Aramaic is certainly later than the Aramaic of the Elephantine papyri, which date from the end of the 5th cent. The theological outlook of the author, with his interest in angelology, his apocalyptic rather than prophetic vision, and especially his belief in the resurrection of the dead, points unescapably to a period long after the Babylonian Exile. His historical perspective, often hazy for events in the time of the Babylonian and Persian kings but much clearer for the events during the Seleucid Dynasty, indicates the Hellenistic age. Finally, his detailed description of the profanation of the Temple of Jerusalem by Antiochus IV Epiphanes in 167 and the following persecution (9:27; 11:30–35) contrasted with his merely general reference to the evil end that would surely come to such a wicked man (11:45), indicates a composition date shortly before the death of this king in 164, therefore probably in 165.

6 **(VI) Unity of Authorship.** Until now we have spoken of the "author" assuming that Dn is entirely the work of one man. It is possible, for there is surely a singleness of religious outlook, spirit, and purpose throughout. If several authors wrote it, they all at least shared the same school of thought. Unity of authorship would not, of course, exclude the possibility that the author used older, even written sources for the stories in the first part of the book; indeed, such does seem to be the case. Some exegetes (e.g., Ginsberg) consider the visions in chs. 7–12 to have been written by two, three, or even four different men; but the arguments for such an hypothesis are not entirely convincing. Possibly, however, the book, even as it is preserved in the Hebr Bible, received certain secondary additions after its original composition; such a supposition may be useful at times for explaining some seeming inconsistencies in the text. The prayer in 9:4–20, which is not entirely appropriate for the context and is written in much better Hebrew than is found in the rest of the book, may be an older composition that was later inserted into the original work.

7 **(VII) Language.** A still unsolved problem is Dn's strange mixture of Hebrew and Aramaic. The difference in language corresponds only partially to the division of the book into its haggadic and apocalyptic sections. The latter is written in Hebrew, except the first vision (ch. 7), which is in Aramaic; the former is in Aramaic, except 1:1–2:4a, which is in Hebrew. Possibly the whole book (except the Hebr prayer of 9:4–20) was originally composed in Aramaic, and later on (to ensure it a place in the Jewish canon of Scripture, or for nationalistic reasons?) its beginning and end were translated into Hebrew, a theory that explains certain difficult Hebr passages as representing faulty translations. Or, perhaps the author of the Hebr visions of chs. 8–12 prefixed to his work an older Aram collection of four stories (chs. 2–6) and one vision (ch. 7), then rounded out the whole by composing or translating in Hebrew the introductory story of ch. 1 and, for a smoother nexus, the opening verses of the second story (2:1–4a).

8 **(VIII) Canonicity and the Deuterocanonical Sections.** There has never been any difficulty regarding the inspired character of Dn as such, although whereas the MT places it in the Hagiographa, the third part of its canon (after Est and before Ezr), the LXX and the Vg put it with the prophets (after Ez). The difficulty is that the canonical Dn as given in the LXX and the Vg is considerably longer than the canonical Dn of the MT. Actually, there is some reason to think that this book circulated at first in more than two forms. We now know from the manuscripts found at Qumran that there were at that time more stories about Daniel in circulation than are contained in any modern Bible (→ 20 below). In any case, the Gk version is much longer than the Aram text of the MT in ch. 3, where the Greek gives, over and above the Aramaic, the Prayer of Azariah (3:24–45) and the Hymn of the Three Young Men (3:46–90). These sections were not deleted from the MT; they never formed part of the edition represented by the MT. Moreover, the Gk version contains, under separate headings and in varying positions in the manuscripts (hence, originally as distinct little books), the three stories of Susanna, Bel, and the dragon, which are placed in the Vg and in Catholic vernacular versions at the end of Dn as 13:1–64; 14:1–22; 14:23–42, respectively. These additional sections of the Gk text come from Hebr or Aram originals, including most likely the story of Susanna, despite the play on words in the Gk text of 13:55–59 (→ 36 below). The Gk text of Dn has come down to us in two forms: that found in almost all the manuscripts, commonly attributed to Theodotion; that of the original LXX, which until recently was known from only one manuscript, although the newly published Chester Beatty papyri also contain parts of Dn according to this form of the text. Inasmuch as the early Church accepted as its canon of the Bible the Scriptures according to the Gk text, Catholics have always held the additional (or so-called "deuterocanonical") sections of Dn as divinely inspired on a par with the rest of the book.

9 **(IX) Message of the Author.** The work was written primarily for the purpose of encouraging the Jews to remain faithful to their ancestral religion at a time when they not only felt the allurement of the higher worldly culture of Hellenism, which was intimately connected with Hellenistic paganism, but also were suffering a bloody persecution to make them abandon the Law of Moses and accept the religion of Antiochus IV Epiphanes. The author of Dn, therefore, is particularly concerned with demonstrating the superiority of the wisdom of Israel's God over the merely human wisdom of the pagans, and with showing his immense power, which can and will rescue his faithful ones from their persecutors. Yet not only for the men of his own age and place, but for all men of all times the author of Dn has a message of enduring worth: God is the master of history, who uses the rise and fall of nations as preparatory steps in the establishment of his universal reign over all men.

(X) Theological Significance. In several respects, the ideas expressed in Dn are of prime importance in the history of religious thought. Even in its literary form, this work presents in its second section the first clear example that we have of the apocalyptic style of writing in its fullest development, a literary genre destined to have tremendous influence during the next few centuries. Then too, in the significant role that Dn gives to the angels as the ministers of God, who reveals through them his will to men, this book goes considerably further than previous books and points the way to the highly developed angelology of the rabbinical and early Christian literature. Likewise, a theological contribution of immense significance is the clear teaching on the resurrection of the body (12:2), which is something unique in the Hebr OT and is much more meaningful to the Semitic mentality than the doctrine of the immortality of the soul. Finally, the messianism of Dn brings Israel's hope of salvation to the final stage before its full realization in the NT. Although the "son of man coming on the clouds of heaven" does not refer directly to an individual messiah (→ 26 below), before long this term was destined to acquire such a connotation and to become the favorite expression by which Jesus of Nazareth would refer to himself.

10 **(XI) Outline.** The Book of Daniel can easily be divided into the following main divisions:

(I) Exploits of Daniel and His Companions at the Babylonian Court (1:1–6:29)
- (A) The Food Test (1:1–21)
- (B) Nebuchadnezzar's Dream of the Composite Statue (2:1–49)
- (C) Daniel's Companions in the Fiery Furnace (3:1–97)
- (D) Nebuchadnezzar's Dream of the Great Tree (3:98 [31]–4:34)
- (E) The Writing on the Wall at Belshazzar's Feast (5:1–6:1)
- (F) Daniel in the Lions' Den (6:2–29)

(II) Daniel's Apocalyptic Visions (7:1–12:13)
- (A) The Four Beasts (7:1–28)
- (B) The Ram and the He-Goat (8:1–27)
- (C) The Interpretation of the 70 Weeks (9:1–27)
- (D) The Revelation of the Hellenistic Wars (10:1–12:13)

(III) Other Exploits of Daniel (13:1–14:42)
- (A) Daniel's Rescue of the Chaste Susanna (13:1–64)
- (B) Daniel and the Priests of Bel (14:1–22)
- (C) Daniel's Destruction of the Dragon (14:23–42)

COMMENTARY

11 **(I) Exploits of Daniel and His Companions at the Babylonian Court (1:1–6:29).** The six stories in this collection are loosely strung together, and most of them probably circulated originally as independent tales. They reveal a fairly good knowledge of the customs in Mesopotamia at the time of the Persian Empire, indicating that these stories go back, at least in part, to this period. However, the many Persian loanwords in the Hebrew and Aramaic in which they are told show that in their present form these stories cannot antedate the Persian period. The Gk names of the musical instruments in 3:4,7,10,15 suggest that at least the story in ch. 3, as we now have it, cannot have been written before the Hellenistic age, even though a considerable amount of Gk culture had invaded the Near East before Alexander the Great. Certain allusions to historical events of the Hellenistic period allow a more precise dating within this period. When the author prefixed these stories to the account of his visions, he may have edited them to some extent. But since they already illustrated sufficiently well the lessons that he wished to inculcate—Israel's religion is superior to pagan wisdom and Israel's God is able to rescue his faithful ones from mortal danger—the compiler left the tales substantially as he found them. He did not even try to make Nebuchadnezzar into a prefigure of Antiochus IV Epiphanes.

12 **(A) The Food Test (1:1–21).** This story, told in Hebrew and not in Aramaic like the other stories, was probably composed by the author to serve as an introduction to the whole collection, even though he may have used older material in its composition. Here he sets the stage and introduces the heroes for the following scenes. The three companions are clearly secondary in the rest of the book. Only the story of the fiery furnace (ch. 3), in which Daniel himself does not appear, is truly concerned with them. In ch. 2 they play a merely minor role, and in the rest of the book they are not even mentioned. In ch. 1, however, because they must be introduced, they are put practically on a par with Daniel. The lesson of this story must have been clear to the Jews, whom Antiochus IV Epiphanes tried to force to eat pork (1 Mc 1:62–63; 2 Mc 6:18; 17:1)—i.e., their God, who did not allow the young men of the Babylonian Exile to suffer harm when they refused to partake of the pagans' food and drink, would also in the present persecution come to the aid of those who refused to violate the Mosaic Law.

1. *the third year:* This year would be 606, but Nebuchadnezzar became king only in 605, and his first siege of Jerusalem was in 597, shortly after Jehoiakim's death (cf. 2 Kgs 24:8–12). The author of Dn, who perhaps combined 2 Kgs 24:1 (Jehoiakim's three-year vassalage to Nebuchadnezzar) with 2 Chr 36:5–7 (Jehoiakim's imprisonment in Babylon), was not concerned with such historical details that meant nothing for his spiritual message; thus, this inaccuracy is not contrary to the inerrancy of inspired Scripture. **2.** The ancient Hebr name for Babylonia (Gn 10:10; 11:2) is Shinar—used here as an intentional archaism. *his god:* Marduk, also called Bel (lit., "lord"; see comment on 1:7).

3. Ashpenaz (MT *'ašpᵉnaz*) is apparently a Persian, rather than Akkadian, name, although its etymology is uncertain. *nobility:* In the MT, *partᵉmîm*, derived from a Persian term. Daniel and his companions, who belonged to this group (v. 6), are thus presented as members of the Jewish aristocracy. **4.** *the language and literature of the Chaldeans:* Not the cuneiform writing of the Babylonians as such, but the well-known omen literature of ancient Mesopotamia. The term Chaldeans designated originally the Aramaic-speaking people who invaded Babylonia in the early centuries of the 1st millennium and to whom the kings of the Neo-Babylonian Empire belonged; it is used in this sense in 5:30. But at a later period, this term was applied to the professional astrologers and fortune-tellers who were skilled in Babylonian omen literature; such is the common meaning of the word in Dn. **5.** *three years' training:* According to the common Persian practice, as prescribed in the Avesta (*Sacred Books of the East* 4,

311ff.). *food:* The MT reads *patbag,* from the old Persian word, *patibaga*; perhaps the author uses this foreign word for alluding to the exotic nature of the food. **6.** The Hebr names are *ḥănanyāh,* "Yahweh is gracious," *mîšā'ēl,* "Who belongs to God?," and *'ăzaryāh,* "Yahweh has helped."

13 **7.** Daniel's name in the MT, *bēlṭ^{e}ša'ṣṣar,* is a word that the author apparently thought contained the name of the Babylonian god, Bel (cf. 4:5); actually, it represents the shortened Babylonian name *balāṭšu-uṣur,* "Guard his life!," the full form of which would begin with the name of one of the Babylonian gods—e.g., Marduk, Nabu, or Bel. The words *šadraḥ...mêsak* are of uncertain derivation; the MT reads *'ăbēd-n^{e}gô* for *'ebed-n^{e}bô,* "servant of [the god] Nabu."

8. *resolved not to defile himself with the king's food or wine:* The author presupposes that this food and drink would be forbidden by Mosaic Law, but the only pertinent legislation would be Lv 11:1–47, part of the Priestly Code, which was probably not promulgated till the end of the 5th cent. The older dietary laws in the Book of the Covenant (Ex 21–23), in Dt, and in the Holiness Code (Lv 17–26), known to the Jews of the 6th cent., were much more liberal. The author of 2 Kgs 25:29–30 saw nothing wrong in the fact that the exiled Jehoiachin "received a regular allotment of food from the king" of Babylon—a passage that served as a literary source for the present passage in Dn. But here the viewpoint is that of a Jew of the 2nd cent., when abstinence from any "Gentile" food became the touchstone of orthodox Judaism. **12.** A spiritual trial of ten days duration is a common motif in the apocalyptic literature (cf. Ap 2:10; *Jub* 19:8; *Test. T. Joseph* 2:7; *Pirqe 'Aboth* 5:4). **15.** *they looked healthier:* Lit., "their appearance seemed better"; also, according to the roughly contemporaneous Jdt 8:6–7, fasting improved a person's looks.

17. *God gave knowledge:* Although the author may have been influenced by the widespread idea of his time that fasting was a necessary preliminary for receiving heavenly revelations, he regards the extraordinary wisdom of the young men, not as the automatic result of their ascetic life but as a gift of God. **19–20.** This general statement regarding the superior wisdom of the young men serves as an introduction to the following stories that give examples of Daniel's superior ability to interpret dreams and ominous signs. **21.** *the first year of King Cyrus:* It is 539–538. The author is concerned with neither Daniel's age—he would then have been almost 90 if he were a young man of 20 in 606 (v. 1)—nor the inconsistency with the date of the third year of Cyrus in 10:1, which may be from another source. The purpose of the present date is probably to imply that Daniel was released from service at the royal court in the year when Cyrus issued his edict in favor of the Jews (Ezr 1:1–4).

14 **(B) Nebuchadnezzar's Dream of the Composite Statue (2:1–49).** This tale is, in a certain sense, a story within a story. The purpose of the main story is to demonstrate the superiority of Israel's God-given wisdom over the highly vaunted worldly wisdom of the pagans, as exemplified by Daniel's ability, with God's help, to divine and interpret Nebuchadnezzar's dream when the pagan soothsayers were unable to do so. The lesson that the author wished his contemporaries, in their conflict with Hellenistic paganism, to learn from this story is stated in v. 47: Israel's God "is the God of gods and Lord of kings and a revealer of mysteries."

Yet this story is really only of secondary importance here. It serves primarily as a frame in which is set the king's strange vision of the multimetal statue. This vision of the four different metals, representing the four pagan kingdoms that successively ruled the then known world but would eventually be supplanted by the kingdom of God's chosen people, is essentially the same in meaning as the apocalyptic vision of the four beasts in ch. 7—a fact that points to the essential bond binding the first and the last of the Aram sections of the book into a distinct literary unit. The purpose of these two visions, as also of the other apocalyptic visions in chs. 8–12, is to strengthen the faith of the author's contemporaries in the ultimate establishment of God's eschatological kingdom.

Although the story of ch. 2, with its vision of the composite statue, may have received its present form only in the reign of Antiochus IV Epiphanes, it is apparently based on older materials—literary accounts as well as oral traditions of a folkloristic nature. It would be hard to say how far our author found them already combined into a single narrative, or to what extent he himself fused them, but their presence is unmistakably revealed in the inconsistencies and unevenness of the narrative.

1. The date is inconsistent with 1:1,5,18, according to which Nebuchadnezzar was king for at least three years before he met Daniel for the first time. The author does not try to bring the older source that he uses here into harmony with his introductory story (ch. 1). **2.** *Chaldeans:* Here, as almost always in Dn, "astrologers," "soothsayers" (see comment on 1:4). This term and the preceding ones have the same general sense in Dn (cf. 1:20; 2:10,27; 4:4; 5:7,11,15). **4.** *Aramaic:* A gloss telling the reader that what follows from here to 7:28 is in Aramaic and not in Hebrew (→ 7 above). *live forever!:* A greeting, derived from the Akkadian, which was used until the Moslem period in addressing the kings of Persia; for similar greetings, see 1 Kgs 1:31; Neh 2:3. **5.** *this is what I have decided:* Lit., "The thing is decreed [Persian *'azdā'*] by me"; therefore, this decree of the king is "immutable and irrevocable under Mede and Persian law" (6:9). The wise men must not only interpret his dream, they must tell him the dream itself! Nebuchadnezzar had not forgotten the dream, as Josephus thought (*Ant.* 10.10, 3 § 195); he was rather using this device to see how reliable the soothsayers' interpretation would be (v. 9).

15 **14–23.** This section is apparently a later insertion into an earlier form of the story. Verse 24 would flow smoothly immediately after v. 13; on the other hand, vv. 25–26 (the king's lack of acquaintance with Daniel) are inconsistent with v. 16 (Daniel's bold entry into the royal court and the obtaining of his request from the king). Verse 16 presupposes 1:18–20 and thus seems to come from the author of the book, who wrote ch. 1 as an introduction to the older stories of chs. 2–6. **14.** *Daniel prudently took counsel:* He acts like the wise scribe of Sir 39:1–11. **17–18.** Daniel's three companions are not mentioned elsewhere in ch. 2, another indication that vv. 14–23 were inserted into the older story by the author of ch. 1. **19.** *the mystery:* In Aramaic, *rāzâ,* derived from the Persian word, *rāz,* "secret"; on the pre-Christian Semitic concept of "mystery," see R. E. Brown (*CBQ* 20 [1958] 417–43).

20–23. In this hymn of praise, Daniel thanks God for having revealed to him the king's dream. The keynote of the whole book is struck in the statement that Israel's God "causes the changes of the times and seasons"—i.e., that he is the master of human history, "who makes kings and unmakes them"; therefore, he can and will lead human history to its climax, the establishment of his universal eschatological reign on earth. The same idea is essentially the theme of the Ap.

28. *in days to come:* Lit., "at the end of days," i.e., in the final period of history when God establishes his kingdom on earth. *this was the dream...in bed:* We would expect the account of the dream to follow immediately.

Besides, v. 29 seems to be merely a variant form of v. 28. Perhaps the author inserted vv. 29–30 from another source to record the statement of v. 30 that this revelation of God's plan in human history is really made by God, with Daniel simply acting as his agent.

31. The image that the king saw in his dream was like the well-known colossal statues of antiquity, except more terrifying. **32.** The ancient concept of world history as divided into four decreasingly happy ages characterized by the four metals of decreasing value—gold, silver, bronze, and iron—was made famous by Hesiod (*Works and Days* 106–80). The Persian variety of this four-age concept—the ages of gold, silver, steel, and iron mixed with clay—is also reflected here. **33.** *its feet partly of iron and partly of tile:* It is not clear how this combination of iron and terra cotta is conceived: perhaps it is either an iron framework filled in with baked clay or a core of baked clay with an iron coating, similar to the clay and bronze statue of Bel in 14:7.

16 **36–45.** Formerly the four kingdoms of Dn were commonly understood as being the Babylonian, the Medo-Persian, the Greco-Seleucid, and the Roman empires. Although this theory, defended by Jerome, was once regarded as the "traditional" Catholic interpretation (in connection with the attempt to explain the "seventy weeks of years" in 9:24–27 as culminating in the death of Jesus Christ), it would now find few modern Catholic exegetes to support it. Daniel's interpretation of the dream and the description and interpretation of the vision of the four beasts representing the same four kingdoms, as given in ch. 7, make it unmistakably clear that the kingdoms are those of the Babylonians, the Medes, the Persians, and the Greeks. The inscriptions of the old Persian Empire speak of three successive empires: the Assyrians, the Medes, and the Persians. After the time of Alexander the Great, the Gk historians added a fourth empire to this traditional series—the Greek Empire. The Jews of the Hellenistic age, taking all the Assyro-Babylonian dynasties as a single unit, substituted Babylonia, with which they were more familiar, for Assyria in their reckoning of the four world empires. Besides, because Cyrus, the conqueror of Babylon, and his successors called themselves "the kings of the Medes and the Persians," it was natural for the Jews to place the Medes chronologically between the Babylonians and the Persians. Although this situation resulted in the historical inaccuracy of having Babylon captured by the Medes (see 6:1), whereas it was really captured by the Persians, who had previously conquered the Medes, our author followed this popular Jewish idea of world history. **38.** *you are the head of gold:* Nebuchadnezzar, with his Neo-Babylonian Empire, is thus identified with the first of the four kingdoms. **39.** *another kingdom...inferior to yours:* The kingdom of the Medes was hardly known to the Jews; therefore, it was inferior to the Babylonian Empire. *a third kingdom...shall rule over the whole earth:* At the height of its power, the Persian Empire was master of almost the whole civilized world. **40.** *the fourth kingdom...subdues all these others:* The empire of the world-conquering Alexander. **41–45.** *toes:* Not mentioned in the dream and therefore perhaps the author's insertion into the older story. *a divided kingdom:* The Greek Empire after Alexander's death was divided among his generals, particularly (as far as the Jews in Palestine were concerned) into the Ptolemaic kingdom of Egypt and the Seleucid kingdom of Syria. *they shall seal their alliances by intermarriage, but they shall not stay united:* The reference is probably to the marriage of Antiochus II to Bernice, the daughter of Ptolemy II Philadelphus, in 252, which ended not in peace but in war between the two kingdoms (see comment on 11:6). *in the lifetime of those kings:* Ginsberg renders this as, "In the days of those kingdoms" (reading *molkayyā'* for *malkayyā'*), and understands this to mean, "while the first three kingdoms are still in existence" (the fourth, Gk kingdom being smashed by the "stone"). He concludes that for the Hellenistic period, such would be true only in 292–261, when there existed a nominal kingdom of Babylon and residual kingdoms of the Medes (Atropatene) and of the Persians (Persis). The original form of this chapter would therefore have been written at this time. Ginsberg regards 2:41b–43 as a somewhat later addition, written between 246 and 220. *the stone...hewn from the mountain without a hand being put to it:* Daniel interprets it as the kingdom that the God of heaven will establish; it will end all of these pagan kingdoms and will itself last forever. The symbolism of the "stone" as representing the holy people of God occurs elsewhere in the OT (Ps 118:22; Is 51:1; cf. also Is 18:14; 28:16). In the NT (Mk 12:10–11; Mt 21:42; Lk 20:17–18; Rom 9:32–33; 1 Pt 2:6–8), the sense of these passages is transferred from the theocratic kingdom to the King, Jesus Christ.

(Gruenthaner, M. J., "The Four Empires of Daniel," *CBQ* 8 [1946] 72–82, 201–12. Siegman, E. F., "The Stone Hewn from the Mountain," *CBQ* 18 [1956] 364–79.)

46–49. Just as Joseph was raised to a high position in the government by Pharaoh as a reward for interpreting his dream (Gn 41), so Daniel is similarly made a sort of prime minister by Nebuchadnezzar, while his three companions (again appearing as secondary elements in the story) are appointed local governors. It is rather surprising that Daniel apparently accepts without demur the sacrifice and worship offered to him as a god (cf. Acts 14:11–17). Probably the author regarded this divine honor as paid, not so much to Daniel as to Daniel's God (thus Jerome). This older story, which portrays the pagan king as practically converted to Judaism, was not changed here by the author of the book to make Nebuchadnezzar a type of Antiochus IV Epiphanes.

17 **(C) Daniel's Companions in the Fiery Furnace (3:1–97).** From a literary viewpoint, this haggadic story is only loosely connected with the other tales in the book; in fact, Daniel is not even mentioned here. On the contrary, this account is concerned with the three Jewish men who, in its original form, are identified only by their "Babylonian" names. The purpose is to show that the God of Israel protects his people from harm so long as they remain faithful to him (see v. 95). Although the story as such probably antedated the 3rd cent., its lesson was pertinent for the Jews in Palestine at the time of Antiochus IV Epiphanes, who set up a pagan idol in the Temple of Jerusalem and ordered the Jews, under pain of death, to take part in pagan worship (1 Mc 1:43–62; 2 Mc 6:1–11), even as Nebuchadnezzar ordered the three companions to worship his pagan idol. Yet the compiler who incorporated this story into the Dn cycle that he edited at the time of the Maccabees did not rewrite it in an attempt to make Nebuchadnezzar into a type of Epiphanes. On the contrary, he let the old story end as it had previously ended, with the pagan king passing a law in defense of the Jewish religion—an ideal situation that would have contented most Jews.

A peculiar literary device in this story is the frequent repetition of certain groups of words, such as the names of musical instruments (vv. 5, 7, 10, 15), the titles of government officials (vv. 2–3, 94), and "nations and peoples of all languages" (lit., "all nations and peoples and tongues" [vv. 4, 7, 96]; but the same phrase is also in 3:98; 5:19; 6:26; 7:14). Likewise, certain set phrases occur over and over again—e.g., "the statue which King

Nebuchadnezzar had set up" (vv. 3, 5, 7; cf. 12, 14, 18).

1. *a golden statue:* Not of the king himself, but of his pagan god; to worship the statue was to serve the god it represented (vv. 12, 14, 18, etc.). *sixty cubits high and six cubits wide:* About 90 ft. high and 9 ft. wide. The great height is seemingly out of all proportion to the narrow width, the monument resembling more an obelisk than a statue, but the use here of the Babylonian sexagesimal system of numerals should be noted. *Dura:* Many place names in ancient Mesopotamia began with this word, meaning "fortress" in Akkadian; perhaps no actual place in particular is intended in the story. **2.** *satraps... magistrates:* The exact meaning of some of these terms in the original is uncertain, but there seems to be a correct order in their descending importance. Of these seven terms, two (*signayyā'*, "prefects"; *paḥăwātā'*, "governors") are of Akkadian origin and the other five are of Persian origin, which would seem to indicate that the original story told in this chapter arose during the Persian period. **5.** *trumpet...bagpipe:* (Verse 4 of CCD.) Of these six musical instruments, three have Gk names: *kîtārôs* (so the *k^{e}tîb*), "lyre"; *p^{e}santērîn*, "psaltery," a sort of harp; and *sumponyâ* (for the Gk word from which the word "symphony" is derived), "bagpipe" (?). These terms could hardly have been introduced into the story before the Hellenistic period. **6.** The execution of criminals by fire, although rare in ancient times, was not unknown either in Israel (Gn 38:24; Lv 20:14; 21:9) or in Babylonia (Code of Hammurabi, paragraphs 110 and 157; Jer 29:22). Jewish martyrs in the persecution under Antiochus IV Epiphanes were sometimes burned to death (2 Mc 6:11; 7:5). The white-hot furnace seems to be pictured here (cf. vv. 20–23) in the form of a limekiln, although there may also be an echo here of the Canaanite-Phoenician custom of throwing human victims into a burning furnace in honor of Molech; therefore, the furnace might be thought of here as a sort of altar of holocaust in front of the statue (thus Steinmann).

18 **8–12.** This story, like that in ch. 6, also contains the motif of professional jealousy among court officials, as in the Ahikar and the Mordecai (Est 3) stories; the three Jews had been "made administrators of the province of Babylon," and they were accused, apparently out of jealousy, by the Chaldeans (i.e., the professional soothsayers), who, as courtiers, had free access to the king. **17–18.** The exact translation of these two verses is somewhat disputed, but their general sense is clear enough: the three Jews do not question God's ability to save them; rather, they affirm it, but at the same time they assert that even if God decides not to rescue them they will still refuse to worship an idol. **21.** *coats, hats, shoes:* The meaning of these terms in the original is uncertain; all three words refer to Persian articles of dress, and when compared with similar Persian words, should perhaps be rendered as "trousers," "shirts," and "hats." The items of clothing are mentioned for the sake of stressing the remarkable nature of the miracle—i.e., the fire consumed the bonds of the three Jews, but not their clothing (vv. 92, 94).

24–90. This part of the chapter, embracing the Prayer of Azariah (26–45) and the Hymn of the Three Men (52–90a), with the prose introduction (24–25), interlude (46–51), and conclusion (90b), is preserved only in the Gk version and the ancient translations made from it. The original was in either Hebrew or Aramaic. Although not present in the MT, this so-called "deuterocanonical fragment" has always been regarded as part of the canonical, inspired Scriptures. However, it is not part of the original story, but rather an addition made by an inspired author who took existing liturgical prayers, adapted them slightly, and inserted them here, with a few sentences of his own to make a smoother nexus.

26–45. The prayer that is here put in the mouth of Azariah is a "supplication of the community," including a confession of national guilt, similar to the older prayer in 9:4–19 and the prayers in Ezr 9:6–15 and Bar 1:15–3:8. **32.** *an unjust king, the worst in all the world:* Antiochus IV Epiphanes is surely meant. **39–40.** These verses are used in part as a prayer in the Offertory of the Roman Mass. **46–51.** Some exegetes regard this prose interlude as part of the original story, because it prepares the reader for the king's surprise at seeing an angel with the three men in the furnace (vv. 91–92). Yet, the secondary nature of this insertion is evident from the inconsistency between v. 46 ("The king's men who had thrown them in continued to stoke the furnace") and v. 22 ("So huge a fire...that the flames devoured the men who threw Shadrach, Meshach, and Abednego into it"), and the dramatic effect is better without this previous explanation of the angel's presence. **52–90.** This hymn of praise, apart from the addition at the end (88–90), consists of two litanies, similar to the litany of Ps 136, in which each half-verse, sung by a soloist or a choir, is followed by the repetition of the same refrain, sung by the people. The first litany (52–56) is a doxology. The second (57–87) is an invitation to all of God's creatures to praise him, similar to, but longer than, the call to praise in Ps 148 (cf. also the litany in the Hebr text of Sir 51:12). **88–90.** These verses were added to the older hymn when it was inserted into the story of Dn 3. The writer overlooked the fact that the three men (here called by their Hebr names!) were themselves pictured as singing this hymn, and so should not be inviting themselves here to sing it. However, in answer to the invitation they respond with the next four lines, "He has delivered us... from the fire." which words are here meant to be understood literally, although originally such expressions were mere figures of speech for deliverance from any mortal danger (cf., e.g., the hymn in Sir 51:1–12, which is itself a cento of older Ps passages).

(Zorell, F., "Canticum trium iuvenum [Dn 3:52–90]," *VD* 1 [1921] 296–99.)

91–97. (Verses 24–30 in the MT.) The king acknowledges the miracle. **92.** *a son of God:* A supernatural being, an "angel" (95) (the same term, but in the pl., appears in Jb 1:6; 2:1; 38:7; Pss 29:1; 89:7). **93.** *the most high God:* Although used by the Israelites, especially in Pss, in speaking of Yahweh, this term, which had a long history in NW Semitic religion, is considered by the OT writers as the name by which their God was known to non-Israelites—e.g., Melchizedek (Gn 14:18), Balaam (Nm 24:15), and the king of Babylon (Is 14:14). **95–96.** The king is not presented as a convert to Judaism, but as passing a law making it a legitimate religion of his realm, protected by the civil authority. He is, therefore, the antithesis of Antiochus IV Epiphanes, who proscribed the practice of Judaism. **97.** The conclusion of the story goes back to the motif of the jealous courtiers; the good men are triumphant in the end and are rewarded with political promotion.

(Kuhl, C., *Die drei Männer im Feuer* [Giessen, 1930].)

19 **(D) Nebuchadnezzar's Dream of the Great Tree (3:98[31]–4:34).** This story is written in the form of an encyclical letter or proclamation published by Nebuchadnezzar in the first person, in which he tells of a strange vision that he had and of his subsequent madness. In the middle of the story, however, the narrative speaks of the king in the third person (vv. 16–30, or at least 25–30), although there is a return to the first-person narrative at the end. If the writer made this shift intentionally, perhaps his purpose was to imply that the king himself could not give a rational account of what happened to him during the period of his insanity.

In general, this story is similar to the one in ch. 2; in both stories, Nebuchadnezzar has a dream that no one but Daniel can interpret. However, this dream concerns not the distant future as in ch. 2, but the king's own fate: he will become insane and live for seven years like a beast, exiled from human society. It happens, but after this period, he is restored to sanity and returns to his throne, where he thanks God for his cure. The moral of the story is pointed out in its concluding words: God humbles the proud, and to him alone belongs all glory (v. 34). On the possibility of an historical basis for the king's insanity, see comment on 4:25–34.

4. *I related the dream:* The king does not make his soothsayers guess what the dream itself was, or threaten them with punishment for their failure, as in ch. 2. **5.** See comment on 1:7. **6.** *the holy God:* In Aramaic, this term (*'ĕlāhîn qaddîšîn*) is plural and is, therefore, sometimes translated "holy gods" (Vg); Nebuchadnezzar would thus be speaking as a polytheist (thus Jerome). More likely, the term is to be understood, like the corresponding Hebr word *'ĕlōhîm*, as singular; the full Hebr equivalent, *'ĕlōhîm qᵉdōšîm*, is, in fact, used of Yahweh in Jos 24:19.

7–14. This account of the symbolic tree that is cut down seems to be borrowed from Ez 31, where the great tree of Lebanon, symbolizing the king of Egypt, is also "cut down" (31:12), "because it became lofty in stature, raising its crest among the clouds, and because it became proud in heart at its height" (31:10). **8.** *its top touching the heavens:* Cf. the tower of Babel "with its top in the heavens" (Gn 11:4) and the king of Babylon in Is 14:14 who boasts that he "will scale the heavens"; in all these cases, the biblical writers had in mind the insolent pride that would raise man above God. **9.** As in Ez 31:8–9, here also there is an echo of the paradise theme; Nebuchadnezzar would take God's place in sustaining man's life. On the great fruit tree with birds of all kind in its branches, see also Ez 17:22–24. **10.** *a holy sentinel:* Lit., "a vigilant and holy one" (*'îr wᵉqaddîš;* cf. v. 14). This chapter is the only place in the OT where the word *'îr*, "watchman," is used in reference to an angel, although it is commonly used in this sense in the Jewish Apocrypha and the QL. Although the concept of the angels as "watchmen" may have been influenced by pagan (especially Persian) notions, it is not foreign even to older books of the OT (e.g., Zech 4:10; Is 62:6). **12.** *its stump and roots:* Cf. Is 11:1; 6:13. *let him...his lot:* The shift from the symbol to the one who is symbolized by it also occurs in Ez 31:14–18. **14.** For the concept of the angels as forming God's council, cf. 1 Kgs 22:19–23; Jb 1:6–12; 2:1–6; Ps 89:7–8. *the Most High rules over the kingdom of men:* This theme is basic in Dn; the kingdom of God will ultimately triumph over the kingdoms of this world (cf. Ap 11:15). **20.** *fettered with iron and bronze:* Hardly to be understood in the sense of a metal band around the trunk of a tree to keep it from splitting, more probably it refers to the chains by which a madman was held in check (Jerome). **22.** The king is afflicted with lycanthropy (a form of insanity whereby a man imagines himself a werewolf); the victim acts like an animal, in the present case like an ox. **24.** These words clearly indicate the efficacy of good deeds, especially acts of charity, in obtaining divine forgiveness of sin (see also Tb 12:9; 14:11).

20 **25.** *all this happened to King Nebuchadnezzar:* There is no historical evidence that this famous king of Babylon was ever afflicted with any form of insanity. However, it seems probable that there were folk tales about the last king of Babylon, Nabu-na'id (better known as Nabonidus), being crazy. Although this king was actually a capable ruler, many of his subjects may have thought that his mind was somewhat unbalanced; he acted strangely by staying for long periods in his desert retreat at the oasis of Tema in Arabia. The Babylonian priests, whom he had alienated by his favoring of the worship of the moon-god, Sin, of Harran, certainly spread calumnies about him after his dethronement, The story of Nebuchadnezzar's madness in Dn 4 was therefore, probably told originally of this later king of Babylon. This supposition has now been made all the more plausible by the discovery at Qumran of a fragment of a "Prayer of Nabonidus" (J. T. Milik, *RB* 63 [1956] 407–11; see also D. N. Freedman, *BASOR* 145 [1957] 31–32). In this prayer, Nabonidus writes, in the first person, that he was once afflicted by God with a bad skin disease, which forced him to live away from other men for seven years, until God sent him a Jewish soothsayer who taught him to confess his sins and give honor and glory to the true God and not trust in idols of silver and gold, bronze and iron, wood, or stone and clay. Some common source probably exists for both this prayer and the story of Nebuchadnezzar's seven-year madness as told in Dn 4. In any case, this and other smaller fragments found at Qumran show that there was a sort of "Daniel cycle" of popular tales in circulation among the Jews in the last few pre-Christian centuries, several of which were used by the inspired author of Dn.

(Hartman, L. F., "The Great Tree and Nabuchodonosor's Madness," *BCCT* 75–82.)

21 **(E) The Writing on the Wall at Belshazzar's Feast (5:1–6:1).** Although the framework of this story—a puzzle that only Daniel can solve and his reward for doing so—is essentially the same as that of the stories in chs. 2 and 4, its substance is quite different. Here the riddle to be solved is not a vision given by God in a dream, but the writing by God of mysterious words on the wall of the royal palace. The king in this story is not the same either in person or in character as the king of the preceding stories. This king does not repent and his doom is absolute. Finally, the moral here is different: God punishes those who, instead of glorifying him in whose hands lies the fate of their lives, worship idols and profane his sacred things at a sacrilegious feast. Yet this story is closely connected, from a literary viewpoint, with the preceding one. Its king is not only presented as the son of the king of the tale that was just told, but he also hears the account of what happened to his father related in almost the same words as in the former story.

The absence of any allusion to the king's persecution of the Jews shows that this story must antedate the time of Antiochus IV Epiphanes; in fact, its conundrum—the meaning of the cryptic words Mene, Tekel, Peres—had perhaps even an older, independent history. But its moral was very pertinent for the time of Antiochus IV Epiphanes. Like Belshazzar, this Syrian king had also desecrated the Lord's sacred vessels (2 Mc 5:16; 1 Mc 4:49). Therefore, the persecuted Jews could receive hope from this story that a fate like that of Belshazzar would also befall Antiochus IV Epiphanes.

1. Belshazzar's name is given as *bēlšaʾṣṣar* in the MT. In the LXX, Vg, and Douay his name appears with the same spelling as that of Daniel's Babylonian name, "Baltas(s)ar." What is unquestionably meant is the Akkadian name, *Bēl-šar-uṣur*, "O Bel, protect the king!" and the Belshazzar of Dn (also mentioned in 7:1; 8:1) is undoubtedly meant to be the *Bēl-šar-uṣur* of history. Although the latter was the son of the last Chaldean king of Babylon, Nabonidus, and as crown prince assisted him in the government of the country, he himself did not bear the title "king," nor did he hold the New Year's festival at Babylon, which was the right of the king alone, in the years when Nabonidus was absent from the capital at the time of this feast (see R. P. Dougherty, *Nabonidus and Belshazzar* [New Haven, 1929]). **2.** Also in Bar 1:11 is Belshazzar called Nebuchadnezzar's son. Although it is possible to argue that Belshazzar's mother may have been the daughter of Nebuchadnezzar, who could thus be called his "father" in the sense of "grandfather" (thus M. J. Gruenthaner, *CBQ* 11 [1949] 421–27), it seems much more reasonable to suppose that Jewish tradition abridged the history of the Neo-Babylonian Empire by confusing Nabonidus with Nebuchadnezzar, as was evidently also done in Dn 4. Neither the author of Bar 1 nor the author of Dn intended to teach history. *entertainers:* The Aram word is feminine, *l*^{e}*ḥēnāt*, and the sense here is rather "harem women." Compared with the "wives" (Aram *šēlgāt*, "queenly consorts"; cf. Ps 45:10; Neh 2:6), they were the women of lower rank in the royal harem (on the two classes of women in the royal harem, cf. 1 Kgs 11:3; Ct 6:8). There is no need to understand the term in an indecent sense, as if the author wished to add a note of lewdness to the sacrilege of Belshazzar's banquet. **4.** *they praised their gods:* The reference is probably to hymns of thanksgiving sung at the banquet; there may have been libations of wine to the gods, but Steinmann goes too far in seeing in this "a sacrificial banquet, a religious rite."

22 **5.** *lampstand:* Probably mentioned merely for the sake of stressing that the writing appeared on a well-illuminated part of the wall; the author possibly meant that the seven-branched lampstand of Solomon's Temple (cf. Jer 52:19) was included in "the gold and silver vessels taken from the house of God in Jerusalem" (v. 3) and was now used at this profane banquet. *the wrist and the hand:* Lit., "the wrist of the hand" (*pas y*^{e}*dâ*); the king saw not only the fingers but the whole hand as far as the wrist. **7.** *collar:* The Aram word used here, **hamyanka'* (for the *k*^{e}*tîb*, *hmwnk'*) is really a Persian word designating a typically Persian ornament of rank, a golden "torque." While there is a clear echo here of the honor that Pharaoh bestowed on Joseph when "he dressed him in linen robes and put a chain of gold around his neck" (Gn 41:42), the royal "purple" and the gold "torque" that Belshazzar offers are more in keeping with later customs. *third in the government:* The Aram term *taltā'* (here "third") is a loanword from Akkadian *šalšu*, originally meaning "triumvir" but later used as the title of various kinds of high officials; hence, there is no need to speculate on who the "second" in the kingdom was. **10.** *the queen:* Not the wife, but the mother of Belshazzar is meant; as the wife of Nebuchadnezzar, she is able to recount the story of her royal husband's madness. *she entered the banquet hall:* Like Queen Vashti of Est 1, she would ordinarily not be present at the king's banquets.

25–28. Daniel must first say what words were written on the wall; evidently no one else could even decipher the script. His interpretation involves a play on words that is possible only in a purely consonantal script, such as Hebrew or Aramaic. The three words that were written in the consonantal script would be *mn'*, *tql*, and *prs*, which could be read, as Daniel apparently first read them, *m*^{e}*nē'*, *t*^{e}*qal*, and *p*^{e}*res*—i.e., as three monetary values, the mina (equivalent at different times to 50 or 60 shekels, and mentioned in Lk 19:12–25), the shekel (the basic unit of weight), and the half-mina. Daniel, however, "interpreted" the writing by reading the three words as verbs, *m*^{e}*nā*, "he counted," *t*^{e}*qal*, "he weighed," and *p*^{e}*ras*, "he divided," with God understood as the subject and Belshazzar or his kingdom understood as the object. Thus, God has "numbered" the days of Belshazzar's reign. (Things that can be counted are few in number.) God has "weighed" the king in the balance of justice and found him lacking in moral goodness. (The idea of the "scales" of justice, which goes back to an old Egyptian concept, is met with elsewhere in the OT: Jb 31:6; Ps 62:10; Prv 16:11; etc.) God has "divided" Belshazzar's kingdom among the Medes and the Persians. For good measure, there is an additional pun on the last of the three words, *prs*, which is also read as *pāras*, "Persia," "Persians." An older form of the conundrum may also have connected the word *māday*, "Media," "Medes," with the root *mdd*, "measure." The conundrum seems to have existed in an older form, independently of its present context. The statement that Belshazzar's "kingdom has been divided and given to the Medes and Persians" does not fit well with the statement at the end of the story, according to which Belshazzar's whole kingdom was handed over to the Medes, with no mention of the Persians. Ginsberg even opines that the conundrum was originally applied to the only three Babylonian kings who were known to the Jews of the Hellenistic period: the mina would stand for the great Nebuchadnezzar, the shekel for the insignificant Evil-merodach, and the half-mina for Belshazzar.

23 **6:1.** *Darius the Mede:* On the idea common among the Jews of the Hellenistic age that the Medes conquered Babylon, see comment on 2:34–35. The "Darius the Mede" of Dn is not an historical character. His name is borrowed from the Persian king, Darius I the Great, who recaptured Babylon in 521 after it had fallen into the hands of the rebel, Nebuchadnezzar IV. According to history, Belshazzar was not slain in Babylon, but he fell on the field of battle N of the city while resisting the Persian army; Babylon was treacherously handed over to the Persians without a struggle, and Nabonidus was taken prisoner as he sought to return from Tema to his capital.

(Alfrink, B., "Der letzte König von Babylon," *Bib* 4 [1928] 187–205. Alt, A., "Zur Menetekel-Inschrift," *VT* 4 [1954] 303–5. Kraeling, E. G., "The Handwriting on the Wall," *JBL* 63 [1944] 11–18. Rowley, H. H., *Darius the Mede and the Four World Empires in the Book of Daniel* [London, 1935].)

24 **(F) Daniel in the Lions' Den (6:2–29).** This last of the haggadic stories in Dn is very similar to the story in ch. 2. The essence of both lies in the readiness of the faithful Jew to suffer martyrdom, if need be, rather than give up the practice of his religion. In both stories, God comes to the rescue of his faithful servants and saves them miraculously from certain death, which instead is inflicted on those who would harm them. Both stories end with the pagan king acknowledging the power of Israel's God; however, in the present case, the pagan king is much more favorably inclined to his loyal Jewish official than is the monarch in Dn 2. Here, the motif of the "jealous courtiers" is much clearer than elsewhere in Dn.

Although nothing suggests a date of composition after the late-Persian or early-Hellenistic period, the Jews at the time of Antiochus IV Epiphanes could find in ch. 6 solace and encouragement in their own religious trials: God would protect them even by miraculous means, as he had protected Daniel in the lions' den. Like Daniel, they too felt the effects of a pagan king's edict that made the public worship of their God a crime punishable by death. Like him, they too would give the age-old answer of the martyrs: God, rather than men, must be obeyed. If it is his will, he will rescue them from death, for "He is a deliverer and savior, working signs and wonders in heaven and on earth" (v. 28).

1. *one hundred and twenty satraps:* The Persian king, Darius I, did indeed institute a good reorganization of his vast empire, but the number of satrapies (large provinces) that he established was never higher than 30. The writer is using the term "satrap" in a broad sense to include various lesser officials who governed the subdivisions of the satrapies (cf. Est 1:1; 8:9). **3.** *three supervisors:* Nothing is known from history of any such "supersatraps." Perhaps the author has in mind Daniel's appointment as one of the triumvirate (see comment on 5:7). **4.** The king planned to make Daniel a sort of grand vizier, such as Pharaoh made Joseph in Egypt (Gn 41:39–41). **5–6.** The hostility of Daniel's colleagues is not primarily a matter of religious bigotry; they merely use his religion as a means of satisfying their political jealousy. **8.** *no one is to address any petition to god or man for thirty days, except to you, O king:* Such a prohibition would be entirely foreign to the religious toleration of the Persian kings, but it would be quite in keeping with the attitude of the Hellenistic monarchs, who regarded themselves as divine and who, on special occasions, suspended the public cult of other gods for a month while all official worship was paid solely to themselves. **9.** *immutable and irrevocable under the Mede and Persian law:* That the Persian kings could not change a law that they had made may have been true for the last kings of the Achaemenian Dynasty (cf. Est 1:19; 8:8), but not for Darius I, who was a strong-minded ruler and was not at all subservient to his courtiers like the Darius of Dn 6.

25 **11.** *to kneel in prayer:* Although the Jews ordinarily stood at public prayer, in the post-exilic period they began the custom of kneeling during private prayer (cf. 2 Chr 6:13; Ezr 9:5; Lk 22:41; Acts 9:40; 20:36). *in the upper chamber:* Either in an upper-story room in a two-story house, or on the roof of any house; such a place of quiet retirement (cf. 1 Kgs 17:19; 2 Kgs 1:2; 4:10–11) was regarded as very suitable for prayer (Acts 1:13; 10:9; 20:8). *with the windows open toward Jerusalem:* Daniel prayed in that part of the house where, through openings that were left in the wall for light and ventilation, he could face Jerusalem (cf. Tb 3:11). In speaking to God in prayer, a Jew naturally faced God's house, the Jerusalem Temple (1 Kgs 8:35; Ps 28:2). *three times a day:* "In the evening, and at dawn, and at noon" (Ps 55:18; see also Dn 9:21). The early Church continued the Jewish custom of praying three times a day (*Didache* 8). **17.** *the lions' den:* Both in Assyria (as known from the inscriptions and the sculpture) and in Babylonia (cf. Ez 19:2,8–10), lions were kept in captivity to be released for a royal hunting party. Their den is pictured here as a deep pit with an opening that could be closed by a large stone (v. 18).

19. *entertainers:* The Aram word used here, *daḥăwān,* is of uncertain meaning and is probably corrupt; the CCD (without textual note) apparently corrects the text to read *l^{e}ḥēnān,* the word that is used in 5:2 (see comment on 5:2). **23–24.** Daniel's rescue by God's angel who "closed the lion's mouths" is referred to in 1 Mc 2:60 and probably also in Heb 11:33. In the early Church, the representation of Daniel standing unharmed among the lions was frequently used as a symbol of the resurrection of the body; in the prayers for the dying, the Latin Church still prays: Libera, Domine, animam ejus, sicut liberasti Danielem de lacu leonum. **25.** *the men... along with their wives and children:* The punishment of a whole family for the crime of one of its members was based on the ancient concept of group solidarity and collective responsibility (cf. Nm 16:25–33; Jos 7:24; 2 Sm 21:6,9; Est 9:13–14). **29.** That "the reign of Darius" ("the Mede") is followed here by "the reign of Cyrus the Persian" is in keeping with the chronology of the whole book, in which the kingdom of the Medes is succeeded by the kingdom of the Persians.

26 **(II) Daniel's Apocalyptic Visions (7:1–12:13).** The second half of the protocanonical Book of Daniel consists of four apocalypses (→ Post-exilic Period, 20:23–27): chs. 7, 8, 9, and 10–12. Although one apocalypse is usually connected in some way to another one in the collection, each one forms a distinct unit. All four were written between 168 and 164, but all were not necessarily written at the same time or even by the same man. In fact, there is some reason to believe that each was written at a slightly different time, although not necessarily in their present sequence in Dn. Moreover, it seems probable that the earlier apocalypses received certain minor additions when the later ones were joined to the collection.

From a literary viewpoint, the Aram apocalypse of ch. 7 is superior to the three following Hebr ones. Strictly speaking, only the first two of the four consist primarily of symbolic visions, which are explained to the seer by an angel. The other two are, rather, direct revelations made to the writer by an angel without the intermediary means of symbolic visions. All four apocalypses use the same device of presenting past events as if these were still to happen. Thus, they instill confidence in the genuine prediction that the pagan kingdom now so hostile to Israel shall soon be overthrown as its pagan predecessors had been overthrown in the past, and that the eschatological reign of God and his holy people shall soon be established.

(A) The Four Beasts (7:1–28). All exegetes now agree that the four beasts of this apocalyptic vision stand for the four successive pagan empires of the Babylonians, the Medes, the Persians, and the Greeks, as the same four empires are represented by the four different metals of the colossal statue in ch. 2. But to understand more fully the symbolism and its application in this chapter, it seems necessary to distinguish, with Ginsberg (*Studies in Daniel*), between a primary stratum—the original vision and its interpretation in this chapter—and a secondary stratum—later additions. The key to the primary stratum of the vision lies in its use of symbolic numbers to distinguish the four beasts. Concerning the fourth beast, which all agree represents the Gk kingdom, it is expressly stated in v. 24 that its ten horns represent ten kings. Two suppositions follow: each of the three preceding beasts have symbolic numbers representing respectively the number of kings in each of these dynasties, although it is somewhat obscured in the present state of the text; inasmuch as the tenth horn of the fourth beast in the primary vision stands for Antiochus IV Epiphanes, the sections concerning the "little horn" springing up among the ten other horns, which also represents Antiochus IV Epiphanes, must be later insertions. The message of the whole chapter, however, is perfectly clear: When the last horn of the fourth beast is broken—i.e., when the reign of the persecutor, Antiochus IV Epiphanes, comes to an end—"then the kingship and dominion and majesty of all the kingdoms under the heavens shall be given to the holy people of the Most High, whose kingdom shall be everlasting" (v. 27).

27 **1.** *the first year:* This date may have been added by a later editor who prefixed successive dates to each of the four apocalypses; in any case, it goes back beyond the last date in the haggadic stories (6:29). *the account began:* More likely a rendering of the Aramaic *rē'š millîn 'ămar* than "he gave a summary of the matters"; cf. v. 28: "The report concluded." **2.** *the four winds:* The four cardinal points of the compass, to show the universality of the cosmic tempest. *the great sea:* The primeval abyss of Gn 1:2, which, according to ancient concepts, was the abode of horrendous monsters hostile to God (Jb 7:12; 26:11–12; Ps 74:13–14; Is 27:1; 51:9–10). **4–7.** Although some of the elements in the description of the beasts may ultimately derive from the widespread mythological images in the ancient Near East, the author drew most of his imagery from the older books of the Bible, particularly from the prophets. In Ap 13:1–2, where the imagery of Dn 7 is applied to the pagan Roman Empire as hostile to God's people of the new covenant, a composite beast is made from the chief characteristics of the four beasts of Dn 7. The bear's feet and the lion's mouth are stressed. It would seem, therefore, that John had a text of Dn 7:4–5 differing from the current MT in that certain words now in the middle of v. 4 were transposed with words now at the end of v. 5. Restoring, therefore, these words to what seems to have been their original position, we may translate vv. 4–5 literally as follows: (4a) The first was like a lion, but with eagle's wings, (5b) and among the teeth in its mouth there were three fangs. It was given the order: "Up, devour much flesh!" (4b) While I watched its wings were plucked, and it was lifted up from the earth. (5a) And behold, there was another beast, a second one, resembling a bear; it raised up one side, (4c) and it was made to stand on its feet like a man, and it was given a man's heart.

In this restored text, each beast has its own symbolic number representing all the kings of each dynasty that were known from the Bible to the Jews of the Hellenistic period. The first beast, the lion, representing the Babylonian Empire, has in its mouth three tusks or fangs (lit., "ribs," but see R. Frank, *CBQ* 21 [1959] 505–7) to symbolize the only three Babylonian kings known from the Bible—Nebuchadnezzar, Evil-merodach (2 Kgs 25:27 = Jer 53:31), and Belshazzar. Its wings were plucked and it was taken from the earth when "Darius the Mede" captured Babylon (Dn 5:30–6:1). The second beast, the bear that takes the natural upright stance of a bear, representing the kingdom of the Medes, lifts up one side (one paw?) to symbolize the only king of the Medes known from the Bible, "Darius the Mede" (Dn 6:1). Its "human heart" points to its humane character in benefiting the Jews by destroying the hated Babylonian Empire. The third beast, the leopard, representing the Persian Empire, has four heads (and also four wings, if this is part of the original text) to symbolize the only four kings of Persia (cf. 11:2) known from the Bible—Cyrus, Ahasuerus (or Xerxes), Artaxerxes, and "Darius the Persian" (Neh 12:22). The fourth beast, representing the kingdom of the Greeks, which is too horrible to be likened to any animal of the earth but differs from the first three beasts (Oriental dynasties) in its Western origin, has ten horns (explicitly stated at the end of v. 7, but omitted in CCD), symbolizing the ten rulers of this dynasty up to the time of the writer. According to Berossus, Seleucus I Nicator was reckoned as the third Gk ruler in the Near East (Alexander the Great being the first, and either Alexander Aegus or Philip Arrhidaeus being the second), so that the tenth horn (ruler) must be Antiochus IV Epiphanes. **8.** This whole verse belongs to the secondary stratum. *a little horn:* This new symbolism for Antiochus IV Epiphanes is taken from 8:9. *three of the previous horns were torn away to make room for it:* This translation is based on the interpretation supposing that three of Antiochus IV Epiphanes' predecessors died violent deaths so that he could succeed to the throne. Even if true, he was responsible for none of these deaths. But in v. 20, also part of the secondary stratum, it is stated that "three of the horns fell before him"—i.e., were defeated by him in battle. Therefore, for the writer of the insertions, the ten horns do not represent ten successive Gk kings, but ten kings of various countries contemporaneous with Antiochus IV Epiphanes—the "little horn" that "sprang up among them" (*silqat bênêhen*, v. 8). Actually, as Porphyry first noted (quoted by Jerome, *PL* 25.531), Antiochus IV Epiphanes "laid low three kings" (*ûtelātâ malkîn yehašpil*, v. 24) in defeating Ptolemy VI Philometor in 170, Ptolemy VII Euergetes II in 168, and King Artaxias of Armenia in 165. *this horn had eyes like a man and a mouth that spoke arrogantly:* The word "man" is here used in a derogatory sense to contrast with God; the whole sentence is based on Is 37:23, which is addressed to the king of Babylon.

28 **9–14.** The description of the celestial court scene at which the fourth beast is condemned and destroyed is all from the primary stratum, except 11a. **12.** *the other beasts:* The second and the third; the first had already been taken from the earth (v. 4). Although they lost their "dominion," i.e., empires, Media and Persia still remained petty kingdoms. *they were granted prolongation of life for a time and a season:* They were allowed to linger on for a short indeterminate period. **14.** *one like a son of man:* An image appeared in the vision resembling a human being, just as the first four images resembled different beasts. These came from the great abyss below, i.e., from the powers of evil; he comes from above, "on the clouds of heaven," i.e., from God. Just as the beasts are figures of the pagan kingdoms, so also the son of man is a figure of the kingdom of "the holy ones of the Most High" (v. 18). In the context, therefore, the son of man is not a real individual but a figure of speech. However, because in Dn the thought of "kingdom" often shifts imperceptibly into that of "king," the concept of the "son of man" eventually shifted from a figure of speech for the theocratic kingdom into a term for the messianic king himself. This change appears in *Enoch*, written a century or two before the time of Christ (on Jesus' application of this term to himself, → Aspects NT Thought, 78:28–30; → Apocrypha, 68:15).

15–27. The explanation of the vision is all from the primary stratum, except v. 20 (apart from the first few words) and vv. 24b–25. Verses 21–22 were probably added still later, combining as they do words from both strata. **16.** *one of those present:* One of the angels attending the divine court. **25.** *thinking to change the feast days and the law:* On Antiochus IV Epiphanes' efforts to do away with the Jewish feasts, the Sabbath, and the whole Mosaic Law, see 1 Mc 1:41–64. *a year, two years, and a half year:* Three and one-half years, i.e., half the perfect number, seven, and thus symbolizing a period of evil (cf. 8:14; 9:27; 12:7). **28.** *I kept the matter to myself:* Daniel understands the meaning of the vision, but he keeps the revelation a secret (so also in 8:26; 12:4,9; but cf. with 8:27). The primary stratum in Dn 7 was written in the reign of Antiochus IV Epiphanes, but before he began his active persecution of the Jews toward the end of 167; the secondary stratum was added after his victory over Artaxias in the second half of 165, but before the end of his persecution in December, 164.

(Feuillet, A., "Le Fils de l'homme de Daniel et la tradition biblique," *RB* 60 [1953] 170–202, 321–46. Manson, T. W., "The Son of Man in Daniel, Henoch, and the Gospels," *BJRylL* 32 [1949] 171–93.)

29 **(B) The Ram and the He-Goat (8:1–27).** There is no difficulty at all in interpreting the symbolism of ch. 8, for it is clearly explained to Daniel by his angelic interpreter. It was probably written by a different author from the one who wrote ch. 7, apparently composed soon after the desecration of the Temple. It is written in Hebrew, although Aramaic may have been its original language. Like ch. 7, it also seems to have suffered some later insertions.

1–2. *Susa in the province of Elam:* Daniel would hardly have been at this capital of the Persian Empire during the reign of Belshazzar (see comment on 7:1). *the river Ulai:* Susa was indeed on this river, but it is not certain that the Hebr word *'ûbal* should be translated "river";

perhaps it should be read as *'ābûl* and translated "city gate" (from Akkadian *abullu*, "city gate"). Daniel would then have had his vision near the Ulai Gate at Susa. **3–4.** Interpreted in v. 20 as representing the kingdom of the Medes and Persians (here regarded as a single kingdom!). **5.** *the he-goat:* The kingdom of the Greeks (v. 21). *a prominent horn:* Alexander the Great (v. 21). **8.** *four others:* The Gk kingdoms into which Alexander's empire was divided after his death: W, Macedonia, under Cassander; N, Thrace and Asia Minor, under Lysimachus; E, Syria, Mesopotamia, and Persia, under Seleucus; S, Egypt, under Ptolemy. **9.** *a little horn:* Antiochus IV Epiphanes of the Seleucid Dynasty; he began his reign as a "little horn" because he inherited a weakened realm, but he soon strengthened his kingdom and extended its sway. *the glorious country:* Palestine. **10.** *the host of heaven...the stars:* God's holy people. *the prince of the host:* Israel's God.

13–14. Probably an insertion, added by the author of ch. 9, to whom vv. 16, 26a, and 27b are attributed; this writer was especially interested in calculating the length of the persecution. *a holy one:* Here an angel, although "the holy ones" are the Jews in v. 24. *the desolating sin:* In Hebrew, *pešaʿ šomēm*, like *šiqquṣ šōmēm* (the horrible abomination of 11:31; 12:11, is an intentional deformation of the Phoenician name *Baʿal šāmēm*, "the Lord of Heaven," for the Gk God Zeus Olympios, whose statue Antiochus IV Epiphanes erected in the Temple of Jerusalem (1 Mc 1:54; cf. Mt 24:15). **14.** The number is equivalent to 1150 days, or three and one-half years (see comment on 7:25). **16.** This verse seems to introduce Gabriel unnecessarily from ch. 9 into this chapter. Originally, this vision was probably explained to Daniel by the unnamed "manlike figure" (angel) of v. 15. **23–25.** A description of Antiochus IV Epiphanes and his persecution. **27b.** *the vision, which I could not understand:* Inconsistent with the words of the angel in v. 17—"Understand...the vision"—and therefore this whole sentence apparently belongs to the later insertions.

30 **(C) The Interpretation of the 70 Weeks (9:1–27).** This chapter consists, not of a symbolic vision, as in chs. 7–8, but of a revelation made directly by an angel. In answer to Daniel's prayer for a solution to the problem of why Jeremiah's prophecy of a restoration of Israel after 70 years has not been fulfilled, the angel Gabriel explains to him that the prophecy means 70 weeks of years—i.e., 7 times 70 years. Moreover, Gabriel divides these 490 years into three very unequal periods of 49, 434, and 7 years, respectively. Because the writer's calculations are only approximate and his historical references not always clear, there is still some difference of opinion in interpreting certain details in Gabriel's explanation. But practically all exegetes now agree that the 490 years terminate in the end of Antiochus IV Epiphanes' persecution; the once common opinion that saw in vv. 26–27 a reference to the death of Jesus Christ is now abandoned by almost all exegetes. If, as claimed by some, there are later insertions from the author of this chapter in chs. 7–8 and 10–12, this was the last chapter of the book to be written (shortly before the end of this persecution), and its author was probably the editor of the whole book. The Hebrew, although often obscure and of poor quality, is probably original and not a translation from Aramaic.

1. The date has no chronological value (see comment on 7:1). Among the Persian kings, Darius I was the father, not the son, of Xerxes. But "Darius the Mede" is the imaginary character (6:1), and any imaginary name can be given to his father. **2.** On two different occasions, Jeremiah spoke of a 70-year period before the restoration of Zion (25:11–12; 29:10). In both cases, the Prophet used the round number 70 to signify a full lifetime (cf. Ps 90:10). His prediction found fairly accurate fulfillment in the return of the first Jewish exiles to Jerusalem soon after Cyrus' conquest of Babylon in 539. But the author of Dn 9 is not satisfied with this fulfillment, which appears to him too incomplete a restoration of Zion. **3.** Therefore, he prays for further enlightenment.

4–20. This whole section is a later addition to the chapter, which originally read: (v. 3) "I turned to the Lord God, pleading in earnest prayer, with fasting, sackcloth, and ashes; (v. 21) and while I was still occupied in prayer, Gabriel, in human form, whom I had seen before in vision, came to me," etc. This mention of Daniel praying, although no prayer is given, suggested to a later scribe the possibility of inserting a prayer here. The older, inspired prayer that he inserted is written in much better Hebrew than that of the rest of the book. It is not a prayer of an individual but of the community, and it is not a plea for enlightenment on the meaning of Jeremiah's prophecy, as the context would demand, but an acknowledgment of public guilt and a supplication for the restoration of Zion. To the later scribe are also attributed the connecting links of vv. 4a and 20. **13.** *as it is written:* The earliest biblical occurrence of this formula for citing Scripture. The sanctions referred to in v. 11 are from Lv 26:14–39; Dt 28:15–68.

31 **24.** *seventy weeks:* Or "seventy Sabbatical periods." The change from the 70 years of Jeremiah to 7 times 70 years is based not only on the fact that Israel's lack of complete repentance merited this sevenfold punishment (Lv 26:18), but also on 2 Chr 36:21, where Jeremiah's prophecy is connected with the Sabbatical years spoken of in Lv 26:34–35. **24.** A brief summary of the whole period of the 490 years. If reckoned at its longest, from the time that Jeremiah first spoke his prophecy (605) to the end of Antiochus IV Epiphanes' persecution (164), this period would be only 441 years. But the writer, who no doubt knew little of the chronology of the early post-exilic period, would not be disturbed by this discrepancy between his symbolic numbers and the historical facts. *a most holy will be anointed:* Almost certainly refers to the consecration by Judas Maccabeus of the restored Holy of Holies in the Jerusalem Temple, but the Church Fathers often applied it to Jesus, "the Anointed One."

25–27. The three main periods of the 490 years. **25.** *one who is anointed and a leader:* Probably Cyrus the Great (cf. Is 45:1); less likely Zerubbabel or the high priest Joshua. Only if one reckons from the second utterance of Jeremiah's prophecy (*ca.* 595) to the anointing of Cyrus as king of Persia (558—a date the writer of Dn 9 would hardly know!) could the required 49 years be approximately obtained. But the following words imply that the first period extends to the beginning of the rebuilding of Jerusalem, which would embrace much more than seven weeks of years. *sixty-two weeks:* The 62 weeks of years, or 434 years, allowed for the rebuilding of Jerusalem are too many by far; from 538 to 171 (the next date) is only 367 years. **26.** *an anointed shall be cut down:* The reference is certainly to the murder of the deposed high priest, Onias III, in 171, in Antioch; hence, "when he does not possess the city of Jerusalem" (cf. 2 Mc 4:5,33–36). *the people of a leader:* The Syrian army of Antiochus IV Epiphanes, which plundered the Jerusalem Temple in 169 and 167. **27.** *for one week:* If counted from the murder of Onias in 171, this period would last from 170 to 163. The writer's hopes that the persecution would not last beyond 163 were fully realized. He probably wrote a few months before the persecution ended in December, 164. *a firm pact with the many:* An alliance made by Antiochus IV Epiphanes with the renegade Jews who favored the Hellenization of their culture (cf. 1 Mc 1:11–14). *half the week:* The second half of the seven-year period beginning in 170. (On the symbolic value of three and one-half years, see comment on 7:25.) The desecration of the Temple actually lasted only three years—from December, 167, to December, 164 (1 Mc 1:54; 4:52).

32 **(D) The Revelation of the Hellenistic Wars (10:1–12:13).** This last apocalypse in the book is also the longest and the most elaborate. After a lengthy introduction that gives the setting of the revelation (10:1–11:2a), an unnamed angel offers Daniel a brief account of the history of the Persian Empire and of Alexander the Great (11:2a–4), and then a very long account of the history of the Seleucid Dynasty, which becomes more and more detailed as the writer approaches his own times, the reign of Antiochus IV Epiphanes (11:5–45). The apocalypse ends with poetic solemnity (12:1–3) and the customary warning to keep the revelation a secret (12:4). What follows (12:5–13) are later additions.

This apocalypse has the usual purpose of guaranteeing the truth of the prediction of ultimate salvation by recounting in the form of prophecies what are actually past events. The author's style is considerably different from the style in the other apocalypses in Dn, which would seem to indicate a distinct author for this section. The Hebrew of this apocalypse is quite poor, and there are some grounds for thinking that it is based on an Aram original. The author must have composed his apocalypse before the campaign of Antiochus IV Epiphanes in the east in the summer of 165, for instead of predicting this, he foretold a successful campaign of the Syrian king in Egypt for this year—a campaign that actually never took place.

1. *a great war:* If this rendering is correct, the reference would be to the Hellenistic wars (11:5–45) rather than to the struggles of individual angels (10:13,20–21). But the translation and purport of the Hebr expression *ṣābā' gādôl*, is very uncertain; it would ordinarily be translated as "a great army" or "a great service," but the sense of such phrases in the context would be obscure. **3.** Daniel's fasting is not in penance for sin, but a preparation for mystical knowledge (v. 12). **4–9.** In the description of his angelic visitor, the author borrows heavily from Ez (especially from chs. 1, 9, and 11), while his description in turn serves as a model for the NT Ap (particularly Ap 1–2). **12–13.** The angel explains why Daniel had to wait three weeks (vv. 2–3) for the revelation: The angelic messenger was prevented for this length of time by the "prince of the kingdom of Persia" from delivering to Daniel this revelation that is partly concerned with announcing the destruction of the Persian Empire. He was finally free to deliver the message only when Michael, Israel's "prince" (v. 21), came to his aid. The idea was common in Judaism that every nation had its guardian angel, but this concept was very old in Israel (cf. Dt 32:8 [corrected according to the LXX]). Inasmuch as Michael is Israel's guardian angel, he is "one of the chief princes" or archangels.

10:20–11:2a. The text seems to be confused. The CCD omits the first half of 11:1. However, by assuming that the order of the clauses has been disturbed in the MT, it can be preserved (with a few slight corrections) to read as follows: (20a) "Do you know," he asked, "why I have come to you? (21a) I will tell you what is written in the Book of Truth. (20b) Soon I must fight with the prince of Persia again; when he [!] leaves, the prince of Greece will come. (21b) No one supports me against all these except Michael, your prince, (11:1) and since the first year of Darius the Mede he has been standing as a reinforcement and bulwark for me." The confusion in the text was probably caused by the author of Dn 9, who inserted here the mention of Darius the Mede (11:1) to identify this unnamed angel with Gabriel, for it was Gabriel who brought Daniel the revelation in the first year of Darius the Mede (9:1).

33 **11:2–4.** Only four kings of Persia were known to the 2nd-cent. Jews (see comment on 7:6). These rich Persian kings (that the last of them was the richest is purely imaginary) are to be conquered by "a powerful king," Alexander the Great, whose empire shall be divided among four of his generals (see comment on 8:8).

5. *the king of the south:* The first ruler of Egypt after the division of Alexander's empire—i.e., Ptolemy I Soter (323–285). *one of his princes:* Seleucus I Nicator (312–280), who at first was a petty vassal of Ptolemy I Soter, but later won a vast kingdom for himself, making Antioch on the Orontes its capital. **6.** In 252, Ptolemy II Philadelphus (285–246) gave his daughter Bernice in marriage to Antiochus II Theos (261–246). But the latter's divorced wife, Laodice, eventually had not only Antiochus II Theos, but also Bernice and her infant son, with their Egyptian entourage, put to death. **7–8.** In revenge for these crimes, Bernice's brother, Ptolemy III Euergetes (246–221) invaded Syria, defeated Laodice's son—Seleucus II Callinicus (246–227)—devasted the land, and carried off enormous booty to Egypt. **9.** In 240, Seleucus II undertook a counteroffensive against Egypt.

10. *his sons:* Seleucus III Soter (227–223) and Antiochus III the Great (223–187) were the sons of Seleucus II Callinicus. The figure of the surging flood is from Is 8:8. **11–12.** The victory of Ptolemy IV Philopator (221–203) over Antiochus III in the battle of Raphia (S of Gaza) in 217. **13–16.** The victories of Antiochus III the Great over Ptolemy V Epiphanes (203–181) in Palestine (202–199), including his successful siege of Gaza. **17.** The marriage of Cleopatra, daughter of Antiochus III, to Ptolemy V at Raphia in 194. **18.** The invasion of Antiochus III into western Asia Minor ("the coastland"), which was checked at Magnesia in 190 by "a leader," the Roman consul, L. Cornelius Scipio. **19–20.** After the death of Antiochus III in 187, while he was plundering a temple in Elam, he was succeeded by his older son, Seleucus IV Philopator (187–175), who sent his minister of finance ("tax collector") to seize the treasury of the Jerusalem Temple, and who was later murdered at the instigation of Helodorus.

21–24. *a despicable person:* Antiochus IV Epiphanes (175–164), who usurped the throne, supplanting Demetrius, the young son of Seleucus IV Philopator. *the prince of the covenant:* The Jewish high priest, Onias III, who was murdered at the court of Antiochus in 171 (cf. 2 Mc 4:33–35). **25–27.** The first campaign of Antiochus against Egypt. Ptolemy VI Philometor, betrayed by his friends and defeated by Antiochus IV Epiphanes in 170, pretended to become a vassal of the king of Syria. **28–30a.** The second campaign of Antiochus IV Epiphanes against Egypt. In 168 he defeated Ptolemy VII Euergetes II, but was forced by Roman legate G. Popilius Laenas to leave Egypt. The Hebr term *kittîm* originally designated the inhabitants of Cyprus; it was later used for other peoples of the eastern Mediterranean, here for the Romans. **30b–31.** On his return from Egypt, Antiochus IV Epiphanes plundered the Temple and began his active persecution of the Jews. *the horrible abomination:* See comment on 8:13–14. **37.** *the one in whom women delight:* The god Tammuz-Adonis (cf. Ez 8:14). **38.** *the god of strongholds:* Probably the Roman god Jupiter Capitolinus, equated with the Greek god Zeus Olympios. **40–45.** Prediction of a successful campaign of Antiochus IV Epiphanes in Egypt, which actually did not take place. **45.** *between the sea and* *the glorious mountain:* Between the Mediterranean and Jerusalem. Although the author is inexact regarding the place of Antiochus IV Epiphanes' death (who actually died in 163 in Persia), he is essentially correct, for the death would be miserable.

34 **12:1–3.** Magnificent poetic conclusion of the revelation given in chs. 10–11. Despite the terrible sufferings in the eschatological crisis, the elect of God, whose names are "found written in the book" of life (cf. Ex 32:32–33; Ps 69:29), will be saved. *sleep:* A euphemism for "are dead" (cf. Jn 11:11–13; Acts 7:60; 1 Thes 4:13). *shall awake:* Shall come back to life. This passage is remarkable as the earliest clear enunciation of belief in the resurrection of the dead (see B. Alfrink, "L'idée de resurrection d'après Dan 12,1f," *Bib* 40 [1959] 355–71). *some shall live forever:* Lit., "some unto life everlasting" (*lᵉḥayyê ʿôlām*)—the first occurrence of this term in the Bible. **4.** Prose ending of this revelation and the original ending of this section. *keep the message secret and seal the book:* Essentially the same expression in 8:26b. By a literary device, common to several apocalyptic writers, an ancient seer is pictured as receiving a revelation that is not to be made public until the proper time, which is, of course, the time of the apocalyptic writer. **5–10.** Evidently an addition to the apocalypse of 10:1–12:4, it is probably by the same writer who composed the apocalypse of the 70 weeks of years (9:1–3,21–27) and who inserted 8:13–14,16,26a,27b into the apocalypse of the ram and the he-goat. Daniel overhears a conversation of two heavenly beings as in 8:13–14. *Gabriel:* As in ch. 9. *a year, two years, a half-year:* Three and one-half years (see 7:25; 8:14). *I did not understand:* Apparently inconsistent with v. 4, where Daniel is told to keep the revelation concealed from others, but not from himself; 8:27b seems inconsistent with 8:26b. **11–12.** Two, distinct, later additions. The time of distress was to last three and one-half years (7:25; 12:7) or 1150 days (8:14). In v. 11, however, a glossator who saw that the period of persecution had not yet ended after so many days increased the number to 1290, and for the same reason a still later glossator lengthened the time to 1335 days. **13.** Perhaps from the same hand that wrote 12:5–10, although it expresses the same belief in the resurrection of the dead as does v. 2.

35 **(III) Other Exploits of Daniel (13:1–14:42).** At the end of Jerome's Lat translation of the Hebr-Aram Book of Daniel, the Vg has three other stories about Daniel that have been translated into Latin from the Gk text that is commonly attributed to Theodotion. The type of Greek used in these stories shows that their original language was Semitic, either Hebrew or Aramaic. The Gk translation, however, was made with considerable liberty, as can be seen in its frequent use of participial constructions. Besides its Theodotion form, the Greek has also come down to us in another form, commonly called the LXX, which is quite different in many places.

All these stories are haggadic folk tales, like the stories in the first half of the protocanonical Book of Daniel. Fragments of a "Daniel Cycle" found at Qumran indicate that all these stories are but a small part of numerous folk tales about a legendary Daniel that circulated among the Jews of the last pre-Christian centuries.

36 **(A) Daniel's Rescue of the Chaste Susanna (13:1–64).** The Theodotion form of this story, on which the CCD is based, is told in a more dramatic form than in the shorter LXX version. Although the latter seems to be, in general, an abridged recension, it has perhaps preserved a few passages that seem closer to the original than the corresponding passages in the other form. One of these is Daniel's question to the false witnesses, which, according to the LXX, reads: "Under what tree and in what part of the garden did you see them together?" It seems to imply that the original Semitic story involved a question, not about trees, but about the locality, in some other sense, of the supposed crime. The Gk pun on the names of the trees (see comments on vv. 55, 59) could then be considered a new element added in the Gk form of the story and thus no argument against the presumed Semitic language of the original.

Superficially, at least, the primary purpose of the story is to show that virtue (here in the form of conjugal chastity) triumphs, with God's help, over vice (here in the form of lust and deceit). Inasmuch as this story belongs to the "Daniel Cycle," it also offers another example of this hero's God-given wisdom. Exegetes, however, have sought deeper meanings in the tale. For some exegetes it is a sort of parable. The two wicked elders ("offspring of Canaan," i.e., idolators) would symbolize the pagans and the apostate Jews, especially at the time of Antiochus IV Epiphanes, who tried to make the Jews, here symbolized by Susanna, fall into the sin of apostasy from Yahweh—the sin that the prophets often called fornication and adultery. The "daughters of Israel"—i.e., the Samaritans—might indeed be seduced by the alluring pagan Hellenism, but not the "daughter of Judah" (v. 57)—i.e., the good Jews. Susanna's heroic statement, "It is better for me to fall into your power without guilt than to sin before the Lord" (v. 23), would then be a fine expression of the sentiments of the Maccabean martyrs when offered the choice between apostasy and death. Still other exegetes would see in this story an indictment by some writer of the Pharisees against the worldly minded Sadducees who acted as "elders" or leaders of the people. In this case the story would be a midrash on the pseudo-biblical quotation of v. 5 (cf. R. A. F. MacKenzie, "The Meaning of the Susanna Story," *CanJT* 3 [1957] 211–18).

2. *Susanna:* The corresponding Hebr word *šûšannâ* is the name of a flower that is traditionally translated as "lily." **5.** *two elders:* An ancient Jewish opinion, witnessed to by Jerome, identifies them with the two false prophets spoken of in Jer 29:21–23; the author of this story may indeed have borrowed the picture of his two wicked elders from that passage. *the Lord said:* Although introduced like a quotation from Scripture, the words attributed here to the Lord are not found in any biblical or apocryphal book. **7–14.** The story as told in the LXX is somewhat different. After seeing Susanna and becoming enamored of her as she walked one afternoon in her garden, each of the elders secretly decided to return there alone early the next day. Scarcely had one of them come there on the following day when the other also arrived and said, "Why did you come here so early and not wait for me?" Thereupon they admitted to each other their common passion. **15–24.** For these ten verses of Theodotion's version the LXX has only three verses; omitting the bathing scene and the running to and fro, it simply relates the elders' resolve to violate Susanna and her refusal (22b–23). Strangely, she is here called "the Jewish." **30.** According to the LXX, Susanna is accompanied by not only her father and mother but also "her 500 male and female servants and her four children." **34.** *laid their hands on her head:* As prescribed in the Law for witnesses (Lv 24:14; cf. Dt 13:9–10; 17:5,7). **45.** *God stirred up...a young boy named Daniel:* In the LXX it is "the angel of the Lord" who acts. Inasmuch as Daniel is presented here as "a young boy" (Theodotion, *paidarion neōteron*) or "a youth" (LXX *neōteros*), in most Gk manuscripts this story is put at the very beginning of Dn. **50.** No doubt the elders say this in sarcasm. **52–59.** By divine inspiration Daniel was sure of the elders' guilt; therefore, there is no need to quibble that the inconsistency of their testimony on a relatively minor circumstance would not necessarily, at least in a modern court of law, prove that their main contention was false. The Gk play on words cannot be adequately reproduced in English: "Under a mastic tree (*hypo schinon*).... The angel shall...split (*schisei*) you in two.... Under an oak (*hypo prinon*).... The angel shall cut (*prisai*) you in two." **56.** The LXX reads "Why have you corrupted your offspring like a Sidonian, not like a Jew?" although "offspring" (Gk *sperma*) should probably be taken here as "seed." **61.** *according to the Law of Moses:* As prescribed in Dt 19:18–19.

37 (B) Daniel and the Priests of Bel (14:1–22). This little "detective story" is another folk tale of the "Daniel Cycle." It is a Jewish satire on the crudities of idolatry, although actually it is a caricature of pagan worship. The offering of food and drink in sacrifice to pagan gods did not differ substantially from similar offerings made to Yahweh in the Temple. In both cases, a certain amount of the sacrificial offerings went quite legitimately to the priests and their families. However, the Jews of the last pre-Christian centuries were so convinced of the folly of idolatry (cf. Wis 13:1–15:17) that this unfair ridicule of pagan worship is understandable.

1. This story is correct in these facts of secular history; Astyages, the last king of the Medes, was in fact defeated and succeeded by Cyrus the Persian in 555. **2.** The LXX, which in general does not differ much in this story from Theodotion, is different here: "A certain priest, whose name was Daniel, son of Abal, was the companion of the king of Babylon." **3.** *Bel:* The Babylonian title (meaning "lord") of the god Marduk (Merodach; cf. Is 46:1; Jer 50:2; 51:44; see also comment on Dn 1:7). **21.** *they showed him the secret door:* According to the LXX, Daniel showed it to the king.

38 (C) Daniel's Destruction of the Dragon (14:23–42). Another short story of the "Daniel Cycle," it is basically a variant of the story told in Dn 6 (Daniel in the lions' den). Here is included another satire on pagan worship—Daniel's blowing up of the Babylonians' divine serpent. Although once an independent story, in its present form it is edited to follow the preceding tale (cf. v. 28); in all the Gk manuscripts, the two stories are together, and the LXX even prefixes to the former the note, "From the prophecy of Habbakkuk, son of Jesus, of the tribe of Levi." **33.** The canonical prophet, Habakkuk (of *ca.* 600), is no doubt meant, although most implausibly at the time of Cyrus. **38.** *O God, you have not forsaken those who love you:* This moral is valid for all time.

27

1–2 MACCABEES

Neil J. McEleney, C.S.P.

BIBLIOGRAPHY

1 Abel, F. M., *Histoire de la Palestine* (Vols I–II; Paris, 1952); *Les Livres des Maccabées* (EBib; 2nd ed.; Paris, 1949). Abel, F. M., and J. Starcky, *Les Livres des Maccabées* (BJ; 3rd ed.; Paris, 1961). Bickermann, E., *Der Gott der Makkabäer* (Berlin, 1937). Dancy, J. C., *1 Maccabees: A Commentary* (Oxford, 1954). Ettleson, H. W., *The Integrity of 1 Maccabees* (New Haven, 1925). Fairweather, W., and J. S. Black, *The First Book of Maccabees* (Cambridge, Eng., 1936). Farmer, W. R., *Maccabees, Zealots, and Josephus* (N.Y., 1956). Grandclaudon, M., *Les Livres des Maccabées* (*PSB;* Paris, 1951). Lefevre, A., "Maccabées, les Livres des," *VDBS* 5, 597–612. Moffatt, J., "2 Maccabees," *APOT* 1, 125–54. Oesterley, W. O. E., "1 Maccabees," *APOT* 1, 59–124. Penna, A., *Libri dei Maccabei* (Roma, 1953). Schaumberger, J., "Die Neue Seleukiden-Liste BM 35603," *Bib* 36 (1955) 423–35. Schotz, D., *Erstes und Zweites Buch der Makkabäer* (Wurzburg, 1948). Tedesche, S. and S. Zeitlin, *The First Book of Maccabees* (N.Y., 1950); *The Second Book of Maccabees* (N.Y., 1954).

INTRODUCTION

2 **(I) Title.** There are four books known by the title "Maccabees." All four owe their name to Judas Maccabeus, the third son of the priest Mattathias who began the Jewish revolt against the Seleucids in 167 BC. The name *Makkabaios*, Judas' surname (1 Mc 2:4), probably derives from a Hebr form, *maqqabyāhū*, meaning "designated by God," although some interpreters have understood it to mean "the hammer" (striking the enemy) or "hammer-headed" (with reference to a physical defect). Each interpretation has defenders, but most likely the first is correct, for Judas' position of leadership (1 Mc 2:66) and honor among the people (1 Mc 5:63–64) calls for divine endorsement (see Is 62:2) rather than for warlike or physical appellations.

The earliest designation for 1 Mc, which originated in Hebrew, seems to be that preserved by Origen's commentary on Ps 1 (cited in Eusebius, *Hist.* 6.25,2) in the textually corrupt phrase *sarbēthsabanaiel.* When this Hebr phrase is corrected, it yields the title *sēper bêt śar bᵉnê 'ēl*, "the book of the house of the leader of the sons of God." There is a corresponding title in the description of Simon (1 Mc 14:27) as "leader of the people of God."

Early Jewish literature, ignoring this title, uses instead the designation "Hasmonean," when referring to Judas and his family. Most scholars take this name to be ancestral. Thus, Josephus, its earliest witness, speaks of *Asamônaios* who is the father (*JW* 1.1,3 § 36), grandfather (*Ant.* 12.6,1 § 265), or even great-grandfather (not reading *Asamônaiou* in apposition with *Symeônos*) of Mattathias, the father of Judas and his brothers (1 Mc 2:1–5). Tedesche and Zeitlin, however, think the term "Hasmonean" is not a personal name but an honorific title equivalent to "prince" (*First Maccabees*, 248).

The earliest explicit Christian reference to these books—in Clement of Alexandria, near the beginning of the 3rd cent. AD (*Stromateis* 1.21,123)—cites *to (biblion) tōn Makkabaikōn*, "the (book) of things Maccabean." This early title, *ta makkabaika*, was perhaps affixed to the beginning of 2 Mc by the Epitomist when he abridged the work of Jason of Cyrene (2 Mc 2:19–32). From there, it passed into use as a title for the first book of things "maccabean," when that came to be translated into Greek. After Clement's time, both Gk and Lat authors shifted the term slightly to speak of the books "of the Maccabees."

3 **(II) Canonicity.** Disillusionment with the politics of the later Hasmoneans explains, in part, why the Qumran community and the Pharisees, both successors to the Hasideans (1 Mc 2:42), had so little regard for these Books of the Maccabees. As yet, no copy of either book has been found at Qumran, nor, as we might have expected, has the rabbinical tradition, which stems from Pharisaic Judaism, preserved the Hebr text of 1 Mc. Josephus, himself a Pharisee, reflects the prevailing view of contemporary and subsequent Judaism when he omits these books from those he holds sacred (*AgAp* 1.8 § 38–41).

Within the Christian community, however, 1–2 Mc have had a better fate. The Roman Church places these works in her canon of the Scriptures, pointing to an ancient tradition as she does so. First to cite them in antiquity is Clement of Alexandria. He is followed by Hippolytus, Tertullian, Origen, Cyprian, Eusebius, Aphraates, Jerome, Augustine, and Theodoret. The provincial councils of Hippo (393) and Carthage (397 and 419) recognized the sacred character of 1–2 Mc, and the general councils of Florence (1441), Trent (1546), and Vatican I (1870) declared them to be inspired by God.

Protestant Christianity, however, does not consider 1–2 Mc to be canonical literature, although it accords these works a special place and esteem among the Apocrypha (→ Apocrypha, 68:5; → Canonicity, 67:21).

4 **(III) Text and Ancient Versions.** The prime witnesses to the text are the Gk uncials and the OL versions. The Hebr original of 1 Mc has been lost. The canonical Gk text is to be found in the uncial codices S (Sinaiticus, 4th cent.), A (Alexandrinus, 5th cent.), and V (Venetus, 8th cent.). The last two also contain the text of 2 Mc.

The OL is represented by three 9th-cent. codices—L (Lyon), X (Madrid), and G (Sangermanensis, which lacks 1 Mc 14ff. and 2 Mc)—and by two 11–12th-cent. codices—B (Bologna) and M (Milan, for 2 Mc). The Vg derives from the OL and the Lucianic recension of the Greek. It can be found in several manuscripts and in two codices—P (Milan, 9–10th cents.) and M (Milan, 11–12th cents., for 1 Mc).

5 **(IV) Sources.** The author of 1 Mc relied, at least in part, on the personal recollections of eyewitnesses for his account of Judas' exploits. To what extent this and the earlier part of his work also contained written sources is not at all clear. The ambiguous text of 1 Mc 9:22 (see 1 Kgs 11:41) has been variously interpreted as pointing to a larger chronicle of Judas, to written notes, or to no written sources at all. Whatever his sources for the deeds of Judas (and of his father), the author of 1 Mc certainly had the Temple treasury at his disposal for his narrative of Jonathan and Simon. In the Temple archives (1 Mc 14:49), which were probably begun by Nehemiah (see 2 Mc 2:13), he could draw upon the annals of the high priesthood (1 Mc 16:24; 10:21; 14:41) and upon the following official documents (dates in parentheses):

(a)	Letter of the Roman Senate to Judas	(161)—1 Mc 8:23–32
(b)	Letter of Demetrius I to Jonathan	(152)—1 Mc 10:3–6
(c)	Letter of Alexander Balas to Jonathan	(152)—1 Mc 10:18–20
(d)	Letter of Demetrius I to Jonathan	(152)—1 Mc 10:25–45
(e)	Letter of Demetrius II to Jonathan	(145)—1 Mc 11:30–37
(f)	Letter of Antiochus VI to Jonathan	(145)—1 Mc 11:57
(g)	Letter of Jonathan to the Spartans	(144)—1 Mc 12:6–18
(h)	Letter of Arius to Onias	(*ca.* 300)—1 Mc 12:20–23
(i)	Letter of Demetrius II to Simon	(142)—1 Mc 13:36–40
(j)	Letter of the Spartans to Simon	(142)—1 Mc 14:20–23
(k)	Decree of the Jews honoring Simon	(140)—1 Mc 14:27–45
(l)	Letter of Antiochus VII to Simon	(139)—1 Mc 15:2–9
(m)	Letter of Consul Lucius to Ptolemy VIII	(142)—1 Mc 15:16–21

Other letters are mentioned in 1 Mc 1:41–51 and 5:10–13.

In addition to these documents and other sources from which he drew his material, the author made particular use of a Seleucid source, which, in detailing the history of that empire, gave him chronological check points for his own narrative.

2 Mc is the work of an Epitomist, who abbreviated the five-volume work of Jason of Cyrene (2 Mc 2:23). It begins, however, with two letters that the Epitomist translated into Greek and prefixed to his own work. Both are addressed to the Egyptian Jews by their Palestinian brethren, and both urge the observance of the feast celebrating the Temple's rededication (in 164).

The first letter, 2 Mc 1:1–9, dated to 124, contains reference to another (vv. 7–8) written in 143. The second letter, 2 Mc 1:10–2:18, which is undated, is considered substantially authentic and a literary unity by Abel and Starcky (*op. cit.*, 27–30), who assign it to a contemporary of Judas writing in 164. Other authors (W. Brownlee, *IDB* 3, 208; Dancy, *op. cit.*, 15–16; Eissfeldt, *OTI* 580–81) consider it spurious, and even a composite, because 2 Mc 1:19–2:15, a later addition, seems to interrupt the flow of the letter.

The major source of 2 Mc, however, is the work of Jason of Cyrene, whose five volumes were abbreviated by the Epitomist for his own theological purposes. Jason's sources are similar to those of 1 Mc—i.e., a Judas tradition, a Seleucid chronicle, and the Temple archives for the following documents:

(a)	Letter of Antiochus IV to the Jews	(164)—2 Mc 9:19–27
(b)	Letter of Lysias to the Jews	(164)—2 Mc 11:16–21
(c)	Letter of Antiochus V to Lysias	(163)—2 Mc 11:22–26
(d)	Letter of Antiochus IV to the Jews	(164)—2 Mc 11:27–33
(e)	Letter of the Roman embassy to the Jews	(164)—2 Mc 11:34–38

6 **(V) Unity and Authenticity.** The authenticity of the final chapters of 1 Mc has been questioned by J. von Destinon (*Die Quellen des Flavius Josephus* [Kiel, 1882]) on the grounds that Josephus discontinued use of 1 Mc as his historical source after the selection of Simon as high priest (Josephus, *Ant.* 13.6,7 § 214; 1 Mc 13:42). But this discontinuity can be explained by Josephus' adherence to his own earlier work, *JW*, in which he leaned heavily upon Nicholas of Damascus, the court historian of Herod the Great, and was apparently unaware of 1 Mc. Another, simpler, explanation is that Josephus' copy of 1 Mc lacked its final roll. In another matter, Oesterley (*op. cit.*, 61–62) has questioned the authenticity of some documents cited in 1 Mc.

These theories, although taken up again by some (Tedesche and Zeitlin, 29–32; see also 38–48), have lost ground since Ettleson's study (*op. cit.*). Dancy's judgment expresses the more recent view: "Stylistically and dramatically the book is a unity, and on those grounds alone it is no longer credible that the work as we have it contains considerable later interpolations, neither documents...nor the whole of the last three and a half chapters..." (*op. cit.*, 6).

Against the unity of 2 Mc, some authors have alleged the later insertion of the prefatory letters and the disarrangement of the text's sequence, when compared with 1 Mc. But the arrangement of 2 Mc has adequate explanation in the Epitomist's use of Jason's work and in his own activity of prefixing the prefatory letters to what he had composed.

7 **(VI) Literary Genre and Characteristics.** A work of history, 1 Mc attempts little at literary artifice, as is evident from the way the sentences are strung together by the Hebr conjunction *waw* (Gk *kai*).

Although translators generally minimize this repetitious "and," it is occasionally obvious (see 1:41–43). Nevertheless, direct and simple as his style is, the author was capable of vivid description (6:39) and even enthusiasm (2:48; 4:24; 5:63). At times, his intense feeling poured out in poetry (1:26–28,36–40; 2:7–13; 3:3–9,45; 14:6–15), but, for the most part, his narrative reflects the sober historian of the events described.

Written in the genre of pathetic or rhetorical history, 2 Mc is characterized by exaggerated numbers (as is 1 Mc also), the invention of dialogue, and the introduction of miracles. Jason's work thus represents the best of this genre, and it can rank well with the similar works of earlier writers in the school of pathetic history: Theopompus of Chios, Clitarchus, and Phylarchus of Naucratis. In this genre, truth alone is not the writer's aim but also the emotional reaction of the reader. Nevertheless, once allowance is made for the literary genre in which he writes, Jason's work has considerable historical value and merit.

Edification is also the Epitomist's aim. He tells the reader that he is not concerned with exact detail (2:28), leaving that to Jason (2:30); instead, he tries to please (2:25), which he does by simplifying Jason's work, excerpting some sections and abbreviating others. Throughout his work there breathes the spirit of piety, in the Pharisaic strain.

8 (VII) Authorship and Date. What little is known about the author of 1 Mc must be gathered from the book itself. He is a Jew, an ardent nationalist, and apparently an enthusiastic supporter of the Hasmoneans (5:61–62). Both his intimate knowledge of Palestinian topography—which marks him as resident, probably in Jerusalem—and the vivid detail with which he writes show that he had access to the participants in the struggle for liberation.

These characteristics also help us date his work. No nationalist author, for example, could have praised the Romans in the manner of 1 Mc 8 once Pompey had captured Jerusalem; therefore, 63 BC is the latest possible date of composition. The earliest chronological limit of 1 Mc lies in the author's reference to the Hasmonean family monument, built at Modin in 143, which remained standing "to this day" (13:27–30). This funerary reference places the book near the end of the 2nd cent. BC, and the note on John Hyrcanus (134–104) in 16:23–24 specifies this date further, because it presupposes that a considerable part, or all, of John's reign had passed. For these reasons, scholars generally agree that 1 Mc was composed in Hebrew about the turn of the 1st cent. BC. At what time it was translated into Greek, its canonical language, is not known.

2 Mc is earlier and was written in Egypt. Its primary source and first author was Jason of Cyrene, a man steeped in orthodox Judaism and skilled in the Hellenistic art of rhetorical narration. He appears more clearly in his work than the canonical author, the unnamed abbreviator. The Epitomist appears to have been a man of Pharisaic tendencies, although these are sometimes ascribed to Jason, and sometimes to both.

The bulk of Jason's report spans 180–160. He must have written shortly thereafter, because the Epitomist, who reduced Jason's five volumes to one, seemingly completed the task in 124, at least if we are to judge by the date found in the first of the festal letters (1:9). Inasmuch as these letters are authentic and were translated into Greek by the Epitomist, there is no need to postulate another author, a later revisor (as Eissfeldt and Dancy hold).

9 (VIII) Purpose and Addressees. Although 1 Mc is an historical work, it is meant to convey a lesson. It is probably intended as a sequel to the work of the Chronicler, to show God at work in Jewish history in the Seleucid Empire as he was in the Persian Empire. The lesson of Mattathias and his sons is there for every true Israelite to learn: fidelity to the Law and faith in God can achieve more than can the size of one's army or the strength of one's arm (2:61–64). Through Judas and his brothers, the agents of a merciful providence, relief from pagan oppression came to Judaism (2:48; 4:24–25; 9:21,73; 14:26,29). Their efforts won independence and a kingdom and prepared the way for God's future intervention (4:46; 14:41). All Israel should look to their example.

Similarly, 2 Mc is intended to instruct and to edify. It is perhaps less political than 1 Mc and places more emphasis upon the importance of the Temple and religious themes. It, too, shows the success of Palestinian Jews against their pagan masters and seeks to strengthen the faith of Jews everywhere by the heroic example of their persecuted brethren (6:31). The book tends also to propagate the doctrines dear to the Pharisaic heart—e.g., the resurrection of the just (7:9; 14:46); how consciously the author pursues this aim it is difficult to say.

10 (IX) Historical Value. Several complaints have been lodged against the historical reliability of 1 Mc. Its author's nationalism and the exaggerated importance he gives Judean events (1:41–43; 3:27–31; 6:5–13) are said to make his objectivity suspect. He is anti-Seleucid (1:9–10), and, moreover, he shows ignorance of the history, geography, and political organization of foreign peoples. His Jewish nationalism leads him to inflate the numbers of the enemy so as to make more striking the divine intervention on behalf of the Hasmoneans. And he has erred in placing the death of Antiochus IV after the dedication of the Temple. These and other historical shortcomings are thought to disqualify him as an accurate reporter of the period.

Nevertheless, we cannot dismiss him so easily. Within the context of his culture and the canons of historiography then in force, he is a trustworthy witness of men and events. His care, for example, in matters of topography (7:19; 9:2,4,33) and Jewish chronology (1:54; 4:52; etc.) illustrate his genuine concern to report matters accurately within the limits of his capabilities and aims. His placing of Antiochus' death is wrong, but his description of it corresponds to that of an independent witness, the secular historian Polybius of Megalopolis (*Histories* 31.9). Despite his limitations, then, 1 Mc's author has, as Dancy notes, "such large stretches of honest and sober narrative that 1 Mc deserves to be regarded as equal if not superior in historical worth, not only to any book of the Old Testament but also to most surviving Hellenistic history" (Dancy, *op. cit.*, 8).

Greater allowance must be made for the rhetorical nature of the "pathetic" historiography of 2 Mc. Yet, without the author, we would not be nearly so well informed about the struggles for the high priesthood involving Onias III, his brother Jason, and the impious Menelaus, or about the other events preceding the accession of Antiochus IV (chs. 3–4). At times, 2 Mc is supported by the secular historian even in details—e.g., the dedication to Zeus of the temple on Mt. Garizim (2 Mc 6:2; Josephus, *Ant.* 12.5,5 § 261). In short, he has historical competence, although this judgment must not be magnified into one of his absolute historicity. His unusual stories and his redistribution of events are to be evaluated in the light of his theological aims.

11 (X) Relationships Between 1 and 2 Mc. It is in the area of relating these two books to each other that the most serious historical difficulties occur. A full description of the problems involved lies outside the scope of this work (see Abel and Starcky, *op. cit.*, 35–49), but the establishment of the correct sequence of Lysias' first campaign and the letters that followed, the death of Antiochus IV Epiphanes, the purification and dedication of the Temple, and Judas' wars with neighboring peoples, is a matter of sufficient importance to merit mention here.

The principal block of material that stands out of historical sequence is 2 Mc 11, describing Lysias' first campaign against Judas while Antiochus IV Epiphanes was still in Persia. Three letters note the outcome—the Jews were to be given their religious freedom. Chapter 11 should properly be moved to follow ch. 8. As it now stands, it errs in attributing this campaign of Lysias to the reign of the next king, Antiochus V Eupator (who succeeds Epiphanes in 2 Mc 10:10–11). The mistake occurred because the Epitomist associated Lysias' campaign and the three letters from Epiphanes' reign (vv. 16–21, 27–33, and 34–38) with the letter of his son Eupator (vv. 22–26). Assigning all the material to Eupator, the Epitomist made this first campaign of Lysias follow the death of Antiochus IV Epiphanes, whereas it actually had preceded it.

In the Maccabean period, Judaism followed a calendar basically similar to that of the Seleucid monarchy. The Seleucid year had an oddity, however: its inception was sometimes counted from spring (from 1 Nisan—our March and April—in Babylon and in Jewish liturgical reckoning) and sometimes from autumn (from 1 Dios—corresponding to the Hebrew Tishri, our September and October—in the official Seleucid reckoning).

Earlier exegetes thought that 1 Mc counted the inception of years in its chronology from the spring, and that 2 Mc (except for 2 Mc 1:1–2:18) counted the year's beginning from autumn. But the discovery of British Museum Tablet 35603 (A. Sachs and J. Wiseman, *Iraq* 16 [1954] 202–12, plate 52) led to the re-evaluation of the chronology of both books by Schaumberger (*op. cit.*, 423–35), whose study has contributed much to the clarification of the Maccabean chronology. In actual fact, 1 Mc follows an autumn computation for the beginning of the year (except where the Temple is concerned), and 2 Mc begins its years counting from the spring, according to the more ancient, Babylonian reckoning.

This reformed chronology demands a revised sequence of the events in 1–2 Mc. The latter is correct in placing the death of Antiochus IV Epiphanes before the Temple dedication (2 Mc 9:1–29; 10:1–9), and 1 Mc has the wrong order (1 Mc 4:36–61; 6:1–17). Antiochus died toward October of 164 (in the Seleucid year 148, if one begins the year in the spring, as Tablet 35603 does; in the Seleucid year 149, if one counts from autumn as 1 Mc 6:16 does), and the Temple was dedicated on December 14, 164 (1 Mc 4:52; 25 Kislev, year 148 of the Seleucids, counted this time as beginning in the spring). The correct placement of Antiochus' death in 1 Mc requires the moving of 1 Mc 6:1–17 to precede 4:36–61.

This change then gives an accurate historical perspective to the battles of Judas narrated in 1 Mc 5, which occurred after Epiphanes had died, as 2 Mc 10 and 12, the parallels to 1 Mc 5, suppose.

These events are properly aligned in the following synopsis:

1 Mc		*2 Mc*
4:1–27	The battle at Emmaus (165)	8:8–29,34–36
4:28–35	Lysias' first campaign and its sequel (164)	11:1–21,27–12:1
6:1–16	The death of Antiochus IV Epiphanes (164)	9:1–29
6:17	The accession of Antiochus V Eupator (164)	10:10–11
4:36–61	The Temple's recovery and dedication (164)	10:1–8
5:1–68	Judas' battles with neighboring peoples (163)	10:14–38; 12:2–45

12 (XI) Theological Teaching. Reflective of a period in Jewish history about which little is yet known, 1–2 Mc have special significance in the development of revelation. Their absolute monotheism is unquestionable. 1 Mc even carries its respect for the transcendent Deity to the point of not mentioning his name at all. So ineffable is God that the author of 1 Mc can do no more than allude to him by the appellation "Heaven" (3:18,50; 4:10; etc.)—scaled down from the earlier "God of Heaven" of the Persian period (Ezr 1:2; Neh 1:4)—or even by the mere personal pronoun "Him" (2:61) or "You" (7:37,41). Distant as he is from his creation, however, God can be found in prayer (3:50–53; 4:30–33) and in the Law (3:48), where his voice is heard now as clearly as it was in the words of the prophets (Jer 1:9), who have disappeared for the time being (4:46; 14:41). The Law continues the covenant of the Fathers (2:20–21,50), the holy covenant (1:15), and observance of the Law brings honor (2:49,64; 3:3; 9:10) and the realization of the ancient promises (Jer 31:31; see Bar 2:35). Infidelity to the Law results in death and punishment (3:21–22; 3:49). Judas and his brethren have acted as savior (9:21; 14:29) and judge (9:72), delivering Israel and restoring its ancient inheritance (15:33–34). Zealous for the Law, the bond between God and his people, they do battle with the pagan oppressors and their allies, the renegade Jews (2:44–48).

Developed as the theology of 1 Mc is, that of 2 Mc is even richer. In Semitic fashion, Jonathan describes the majesty of God by detailing his attributes in 1:24–25. God alone is king and kind, provident, just, and omnipotent. He alone is eternal. So great is his power that his creatures were not made from things that existed (7:28) but *ex nihilo*. He has been provident in choosing his people and watching over them (1:25). He dwells among them in his Temple (13:35–36), the greatest, holiest, and most famous Temple on earth (2:19,22; 5:15; 14:31; 15:41).

The Jews have God's Law, and if they observe it, particularly the Sabbath (8:27; 15:1–4), he will be merciful to them (8:27). But toward the ungodly he is a righteous judge (12:6), and when calamities occur, Israel has only itself to blame (4:10–17; 6:12–16; 7:18; 10:4; 12:40–41). Penance, however, can restore the bond of friendship and harmony with the divine (7:32–33,37–38; 8:5; 12:42–45).

God does not leave his just ones without his aid. He is their defender (7:6; 8:36; 12:11), whose help can be sought in prayer and sacrifice (3:22). He even sends his heavenly hosts to fight for his people (3:23–30; 10:29–31; 11:6–10). Whoever falls in righteous battle (12:45) or in persecution as martyrs (chs. 6–7) can hope to be raised up (7:9,23; 14:46) to full health (7:11; 14:46), whereas the impious will be punished and remain in torment (5:9–10; 7:13–14,17,19,35; 9:18; 13:7–8). Intercessory prayer increases the commerce between heaven and earth, for not only the angels (as formerly, Jb 5:1; 33:23) but also the saints of the past implore God for Israel (15:12–16). There is intercessory prayer on earth, too, by means of which men can help their departed brethren with prayer and sacrifices (12:44–45).

In its doctrinal positions, 2 Mc belongs to the Pharisaic school, while the thought of 1 Mc, less advanced theologically, is closer to that of the Sadducees.

13 **(XII) Outline.** The Books of 1–2 Maccabees may be outlined as follows:

1 MACCABEES

- (I) Preamble (1:1–64)
  - (A) Alexander and the Diadochi (1:1–10)
  - (B) Hellenizers (1:11–15)
  - (C) Antiochus' First Campaign in Egypt (1:16–19)
  - (D) Antiochus Despoils the Temple (1:20–24a)
  - (E) Dirge (1:24b–28)
  - (F) Apollonius Attacks Jerusalem (1:29–35)
  - (G) Dirge (1:36–40)
  - (H) Antiochus Proscribes Judaism and Imposes Pagan Practices (1:41–51a)
  - (I) The Execution of Antiochus' Edict (1:51b–64)
- (II) Mattathias Begins Active Resistance (2:1–70)
  - (A) Mattathias' Lament (2:1–14)
  - (B) Resistance Flares (2:15–28)
  - (C) The Slaughter on the Sabbath and Its Sequel (2:29–41)
  - (D) The Hasideans (2:42–48)
  - (E) Mattathias' Testament (2:49–70)
- (III) Judas Maccabeus Takes Command of the Struggle (3:1–9:22)
  - (A) Praise of Judas (3:1–9)
  - (B) Judas Defeats Apollonius and Seron (3:10–26)
  - (C) Antiochus Goes East (3:27–37)
  - (D) Judas Defeats Gorgias and Nicanor (3:38–4:27)
  - (E) Judas Defeats Lysias at Beth-zur (4:28–35)
  - (F) The Purification and Dedication of the Temple (4:36–61)
  - (G) Judas Battles with Neighboring Peoples (5:1–68)
    - (a) Idumea (5:3–5; 2 Mc 10:14–23)
    - (b) Ammon (5:6–8; 2 Mc 8:30–33?)
    - (c) Gilead (5:9–13,24–54; 2 Mc 12:10–31)
    - (d) Galilee (5:14–23)
    - (e) The Land of the Philistines (5:55–68; 2 Mc 12:3–9,32–45)
  - (H) The Death of Antiochus IV Epiphanes (6:1–17)
  - (I) Siege of the Citadel (6:18–27)
  - (J) Lysias' Second Campaign in Judah (6:28–63; 2 Mc 13:1–26)
  - (K) The Expedition of Bacchides and Alcimus (7:1–25)
  - (L) The Defeat of Nicanor (7:26–50)
  - (M) Judas' Treaty with the Romans (8:1–32)
  - (N) The Defeat and Death of Judas (9:1–22)
- (IV) Jonathan Continues the Struggle (9:23–12:54)
  - (A) Jonathan Succeeds Judas as Leader (9:23–34)
  - (B) Jonathan Avenges His Brother John (9:35–42)
  - (C) Bacchides Ambushes Jonathan (9:43–49)
  - (D) Bacchides Fortifies Judea; Alcimus Dies (9:50–57)
  - (E) Jonathan Escapes and Frustrates Bacchides (9:58–73)
  - (F) Alexander Balas (150–145) Claims Demetrius' Throne (10:1–14)
  - (G) Jonathan Supports Alexander Balas and Becomes High Priest (10:15–50)
  - (H) At Alexander's Marriage, Jonathan Is Promoted (10:51–66)
  - (I) Jonathan Defeats Apollonius, the General of Demetrius II (10:67–89)
  - (J) The Alliance Between Demetrius II and Ptolemy (11:1–13)
  - (K) The Deaths of Alexander and Ptolemy (11:14–19)
  - (L) Jonathan's Pact with Demetrius (11:20–37)
  - (M) Trypho's Intrigue Against Demetrius (11:38–40)
  - (N) Jonathan Aids Demetrius (11:41–53)
  - (O) Jonathan's Alliance with Trypho (11:54–62)
  - (P) War Between Jonathan and Demetrius (11:63–74)
  - (Q) Treaties of Friendship with the Romans and Spartans (12:1–23)
  - (R) Military Activities of Jonathan and Simon (12:24–38)
  - (S) The Capture of Jonathan (12:39–54)
- (V) Simon as Leader of the Jews (13:1–16:24)
  - (A) Simon Becomes Leader of the Jews (13:1–11)
  - (B) Simon Blocks Trypho (13:12–24)
  - (C) Simon Constructs a Family Monument at Modin (13:25–30)
  - (D) Simon Joins Demetrius II (13:31–42)
  - (E) The Capture of Gazara and the Citadel (13:43–53)
  - (F) Demetrius II Is Captured by the Parthians (14:1–3)
  - (G) The Glory of Simon (14:4–15)
  - (H) Renewal of the Alliances with Rome and Sparta (14:16–24)
  - (I) Decree of the Jews Honoring Simon (14:25–49)
  - (J) Antiochus VII Grants Privileges to Simon and Besieges Trypho (15:1–14)
  - (K) The Return of the Embassy Sent to Rome (15:15–24)
  - (L) Antiochus Breaks His Alliance with Simon (15:25–36)
  - (M) John Hyrcanus and Judas Defeat Cendebaeus (15:37–16:10)
  - (N) The Murder of Simon and His Two Sons (16:11–22)
  - (O) Conclusion to 1 Mc (16:23–24)

2 MACCABEES

- (I) Letters to the Jews of Egypt (1:1–2:18)
  - (A) The First Letter (1:1–9)
  - (B) The Second Letter (1:10–2:18)
- (II) The Epitomist's Preface (2:19–32)
- (III) The Decline of the High Priesthood (3:1–4:50)
  - (A) The Episode of Heliodorus (3:1–40)
  - (B) Simon's Plot Against Onias (4:1–6)
  - (C) Jason, the High Priest, Introduces Hellenism (4:7–20)
  - (D) Antiochus Is Received by Jason in Jerusalem (4:21–22)
  - (E) Menelaus as High Priest (4:23–50)
- (IV) Antiochus Epiphanes and the Imposition of Hellenism (5:1–7:42)
  - (A) Antiochus Ravages Jerusalem (5:1–14)
  - (B) Antiochus Despoils the Temple (5:15–23a)
  - (C) Apollonius Attacks Jerusalem (5:23b–26)
  - (D) Judas Maccabeus in the Desert (5:27)
  - (E) Antiochus Imposes Hellenism (6:1–11)
  - (F) The Epitomist's Evaluation (6:12–17)
  - (G) The Martyrdom of Eleazar (6:18–31)
  - (H) The Martyrdom of the Mother and Her Seven Sons (7:1–42)
- (V) The Triumph of Judaism Under Judas Maccabeus (8:1–10:9)
  - (A) Judas Organizes Resistance to the Persecution (8:1–7)
  - (B) Judas Defeats Nicanor and Gorgias (8:8–29,34–36)
  - (C) Judas' Other Victories (8:30–33)
  - (D) The Death of the Persecutor (9:1–29)
  - (E) Judas Purifies the Temple (10:1–9)
- (VI) The Subsequent Struggles of Judas (10:10–15:39)
  - (A) The Suicide of Ptolemy Macron (10:10–13)
  - (B) Judas Fights in Idumea (10:14–23)
  - (C) Judas Defeats Timothy (10:24–38)
  - (D) Victory Over Lysias at Beth-zur (11:1–15; 12:1)
  - (E) The Letters (11:16–38)
  - (F) The Battles with Neighboring Peoples (12:2–45)
  - (G) Lysias' Second Campaign in Judah (13:1–26)
  - (H) The Accession of Demetrius I Soter (161–150) (14:1–2)
  - (I) The Hostility of Alcimus (14:3–11)
  - (J) Judas and Nicanor (14:12–36)
  - (K) The Death of Razis (14:37–46)
  - (L) The Defeat of Nicanor (15:1–37a)
  - (M) Epilogue of the Epitomist (15:37b–39)

COMMENTARY ON 1 MACCABEES

14 **(I) Preamble (1:1–64).** This preamble sets the stage for the Maccabean struggles. Antiochus IV Epiphanes appears and begins his forcible repression of Judaism, thus inducing the resistance of Jews faithful to the Law.

(A) Alexander and the Diadochi (1:1–10). Alexander the Great (356–323) began his victorious march from Kittim (Cyprus in Gn 10:4; 1 Chr 1:7; here and in 8:5, Macedonia) in 334. After defeating Darius III Codomannus (336–331) at the Granicus River (334), at Issus (333), and Gaugamela (331), he pushed on to "the ends of the earth," actually in the east to the Hyphasis (modern Beas) River in the Punjab. The rise of his kingdom is noted in the visions of Dn 2:33,40 (statue's iron feet), 7:23 (fourth beast), 8:5–8,21 (he-goat), and 11:3 (mighty king). **3.** *he was exalted:* Alexander accepted divine honors (see, similarly, Ez 28:2,5).

The author repeats the erroneous story of Alexander's deathbed division of his kingdom among "his servants," his officers who had been educated with him. Josephus (*Ant.* 11.8,7 § 346) contradicts this story, and the slow break-up of the empire—Seleucus occupied Babylon in 311, and he and four others became "kings" in 306—confirms his statement. Eventually, Alexander's successors (Diadochi), especially the Ptolemies and Seleucids, claimed direct inheritance from the Macedonian. Alexander died at Babylon in June 323 at the age of 32, having ruled several months longer than the round number of "twelve years" (v. 7). (For a list of the Seleucids and Ptolemies, → Daniel, 23:3.)

10. *Antiochus Epiphanes:* 1 Mc skips to September 175, when Antiochus IV Epiphanes (175–164) succeeded his brother Seleucus IV (187–175) on the Seleucid throne (see 2 Mc 4:7). Antiochus III, their father, had been defeated by the Romans at Magnesia in 190, and under the treaty of Apamea (188), the younger Antiochus was taken to Rome as hostage. He returned after his brother's murder to assume joint regency with his nephew (another Antiochus, who ruled with Epiphanes until he died in 168), whom he finally later deposed. About 169, the new king took as his title "theos epiphanes," meaning "God manifest," but his subjects soon nicknamed him "epimanes," (madman). (2 Mc 3:1–4:6 can be read here; it narrates events in the reign of Seleucus IV that provide background for Antiochus' robbery of the Temple.)

15 **(B) Hellenizers (1:11–15).** This section is expanded in 2 Mc 4:7–20. Chief among the Hellenizers is Jason (actually, Joshua), the brother of the high priest Onias (III). Jason bought the high priesthood and introduced Gk ways. He gave up the religious concessions won for the Jews from Antiochus III (Josephus, *Ant.* 12.3,3 § 129–53; 2 Mc 4:11) to adopt the "practices of the Gentiles." This Grecian way of life included the establishment of a *gymnasion* (a place of exercise, philosophical lectures, and even worship) and an *ephebeion* (an organization for training youth in cultural, physical, and pre-military affairs; 2 Mc 4:9–10). Inasmuch as the mark of circumcision (1 Mc 1:15)—the sign of the covenant with Yahweh (Gn 17:10–14)—was all too evident in the nudity of the gymnasium, Hellenizing Jews attempted to disguise it by an operation.

Some authors (e.g., Abel and Starcky, *op. cit.*, 54–56) say the most drastic innovation at this time was the change in the city's status. At Jason's request, Jerusalem became a Gk *polis*, and as such was called in time to participate in the feasts and sacrifices of the gods (2 Mc 4:9,18–20). Such a change in the city's constitution amounted to apostasy from Yahwism. Other authors (Bickermann, *op. cit.*, 59–65) hold that at this time Jason established only a *politeuma*, a corporation of Hellenized Jews with certain rights and privileges. It was not until the fortress Akra was built in Jerusalem in 167, these authors say, that the city's status changed.

In all this process of Hellenization, Jews themselves provided the initiative. Abandoning the covenant with Yahweh for a covenant with pagans (v. 15), "they sold themselves to do evil" (see 1 Kgs 21:20,25; 2 Kgs 17:17; Sir 47:24). (The events of 2 Mc 4:21–50 belong here.)

(C) Antiochus' First Campaign in Egypt (1:16–19). Although forbidden by the treaty of Apamea to attack Rome's friends, Antiochus invaded Egypt on a pretext, to establish his control there. This campaign (169) resulted in victory for his forces, although Alexandria was not taken. Tiring of the war, Antiochus left its conduct to his unwilling puppet, his nephew Ptolemy VI Philometor (180–145), who continued to beseige Ptolemy VIII Euergetes II (145–116) in Alexandria.

(D) Antiochus Despoils the Temple (1:20–24a). Although 2 Mc 5:15–21 places this event after Antiochus' second campaign in Egypt, Dn 11:25–30 (esp. 28) shows it to belong after the first. **23.** *hidden treasures:* 2 Mc 5:21 says 1800 talents. Antiochus was supported in this theft by the impious high priest Menelaus who had supplanted Jason (2 Mc 4:23–26; 5:15). **20.** The 143rd year of the Seleucid era would be autumn, 169.

16 **(E) Dirge (1:24b–28).** This lament portrays the universal sorrow in Israel over the sacrilege; even the land is depicted as trembling. **24b.** *deeds of murder:* The allusion is obscure. Starcky (*BJ*) thinks that it recalls the events of 2 Mc 5:12–14 (Abel and Starcky, *op. cit.*). These events are not otherwise noted in 1 Mc. *arrogance:* Antiochus' pretensions to divinity—he identified himself with Zeus Olympios officially—were well known (see Dn 11:36). (Here, 2 Mc 5:1–14 fills in. Antiochus invaded Egypt in 168 for the second time, having himself crowned king at Memphis. Forced by Rome to retire, he turned his wrath on Judah, which he thought to be in revolt.)

(F) Apollonius Attacks Jerusalem (1:29–35). It has a parallel in 2 Mc 5:23b–26. **29.** *two years later:* Than his first Egyptian campaign, hence in 167. *chief tribute-collector:* The text's *archonta phorologias*, "chief tribute collector" is the translator's misreading of *śar hammissim*, "master of levies" (in Ex 1:11, "master of workers") for *śar hammusim*, "chief of the Mysians," as Apollonius is designated in 2 Mc 5:24. This is most likely the Apollonius of 3:10. **30.** *suddenly fell:* The ruse is in 2 Mc 5:25–26. **31.** *tore down...walls:* A typical punishment for a city in revolt (see 2 Kgs 25:8–10). **33.** *fortified the City of David:* In 2 Sm 5:7,9, this is the southern part of the hill between the Tyropoeon and Kedron vallies, the easternmost of Jerusalem's two principal hills. Here J. Simons locates the new citadel (Simons, *JOT* 144ff.). By Maccabean times, however, the city built on the westernmost hill was known by David's name. Consequently, Abel (*Histoire*, 1, 122) locates the fortress here. On this spot, the "sinful people, lawless men," i.e., the Seleucid troops and their Jewish allies (v. 34), built and provisioned the citadel (*akra*) that overlooked the Temple. **35.** *great snare:* A source of danger to the city and Temple. Whether this fortress now became Jerusalem the Gk city, with unwalled Jerusalem regarded as a surrounding village, is uncertain (see 1 Mc 15:28). Seleucid troops occupied the fortress until 141, when Simon drove them out (1 Mc 13:49–50).

(G) Dirge (1:36–40). In a style reminiscent of Ps 79, the author deplores the actions of the Acra's inhabitants and their effect upon Jerusalem, especially upon its religious life.

17 (H) Antiochus Proscribes Judaism and Imposes Pagan Practices (1:41–51a). To unite a kingdom so diverse in ethnic and linguistic groupings, so politically unstable and geographically diffuse, Antiochus thought it necessary to foster the process of cultural and religious syncretism that had received such impetus under Alexander. The cult of a supreme, syncretistic deity—known officially as Zeus Olympios (2 Mc 6:2), but also as Baal or Hadad—was introduced. Judah was especially troublesome, however, because there religion and the surge toward national independence were inseparable and to the same end; the Law cried out for autonomy and theocracy. Antiochus felt that the assimilation of this province into the common social order demanded first the suppression of the local religion. He initiated repressive measures in 167, as soon as the Acra in Jerusalem was sufficiently strong.

The decree of vv. 41–42 is not found elsewhere in ancient historians, and some modern authors question its existence, although conceding that it may echo Antiochus' general policy. As v. 43 notes, many welcomed the change and gladly adopted the king's religion.

The letters sent to Judah (vv. 44–50) were specific and severe, calling for the proscription of Judaism and the imposition of pagan worship under pain of death. They abolished the last of the religious concessions granted by Antiochus III (Josephus, *Ant.* 12.3,3–4 § 129–53). **46.** *the holy ones:* Obscure. The better interpretation extends it to all the faithful (see Dn 7:17–21; RSV reads "priests"). **47.** *shrines for idols:* Niches holding statues and incense altars.

(I) The Execution of Antiochus' Edict (1:51b–64). 2 Mc 6–7 vividly exemplifies the manner of executing the king's edict. **51.** *overseers: Episkopoi.* The chief overseer, the *geronta* of 2 Mc 6:1, has been variously identified as "Geron" (BJ), "senator" (RSV), "an old man" (Abel, EBib 361; Dancy, *op. cit.*, 76). He is an Athenian, probably from Athens itself, and not, as Dancy suggests, from a certain section of Antioch's citizens. **52.** *many:* The "reforms" were accepted gladly by some (v. 43), but only under compulsion by others (2 Mc 6:6–7). **53.** *hiding:* Some were discovered and died (2 Mc 6:11).

On December 7, 167—15 Kislev in the 145th year of the Seleucid era—Antiochus reached the zenith of his evil in the eyes of the faithful; he erected an altar to Zeus in the Temple of Yahweh. **54.** *desolating abomination:* The phrase *bdelygma erēmōseōs* is taken from Dn 11:31. It translates the Hebr *šiqquṣ m^{e}šōmēm*, which conveys the idea of a detestable idol, a horrendous sight to the pious beholder. The *šiqquṣ*, "abomination," substitutes for *baʿal*, the Semitic deity, and *m^{e}šomem* (or simply *šomem* in Dn 12:11) plays upon *baʿal šāmēm* (earlier *šāmayim*), "lord of heaven," by this time a title for the Syrian divinity, which was identified with Zeus Olympios. The way in which this deity was "established" in the Temple was by the erection of an altar upon the altar of holocausts (see v. 59). It then replaced the Holy of Holies as the center of worship in the Temple. Altars were erected in the marketplace of Jerusalem (2 Mc 10:2) and built in the "surrounding cities of Judah." **55.** *burned incense...doors:* Apparently the Jews adopted Grecian shrines in their streets and in the porches of their houses. **56.** *books of the law:* The Pentateuch. **58.** *month after month:* Some Jews did not join in the monthly celebration of the divinized king's birthday (2 Mc 6:7). **59.** *twenty-fifth day of the month:* December 17, 167—25 Kislev. Most likely this was Antiochus' birthday, and it was celebrated monthly throughout Judah (v. 54). **60.** *women:* Cf. 2 Mc 6:10.

As well as the Jews who accepted the king's new ordinances gladly and those who obeyed under duress, there were those faithful Jews who resisted to the death. Eleazar and the seven brothers are examples cited in 2 Mc 6:18–7:42.

18 (II) Mattathias Begins Active Resistance (2:1–70). Mattathias and his followers concentrated on removing the sacrilegious altars, forcing observance of the Law, and striking down apostates from the Jewish religion. But as the religious aspect merged with the political, their struggle soon assumed the proportions of an independence movement.

(A) Mattathias' Lament (2:1–14). **1.** *Mattathias:* In Hebrew, *mattityāhû*, "gift of God." Josephus makes him the "son" (*JW* 1.1,3 § 36)—i.e., the "grandson" (*Ant.* 12.6,1 § 265)—of Asamonaios, from whom the designation "Hasmonean," which is applied to the Maccabean dynasty, is traced. *Joarib:* This is the Jehoiarib of 1 Chr 24:7, who heads the first of the 24 classes of the priesthood. *Modin:* Modern el-Midyah, 7 mi. E of Lod (Lydda). **2.** The surnames of Mattathias' sons are said to mean, respectively, "fortunate," "burning," "designated by Yahweh" (or "the hammerer" or "hammerheaded" as well), "awake," and "favorite" (see Abel, EBib). All died violently.

Mattathias' lament over the Temple is constructed in earlier OT phraseology (cf. v. 9 and Lam 2:11,21), with allusions to current evils (cf. v. 9 and 1:23,61; 2 Mc 5:24). **8.** *without honor:* The sense requires it, although the negative must be supplied. **10.** *what nation...?:* Judah is so weak anyone could despoil her. This is Semitic hyperbole. **14.** *rent their clothes:* Traditional gesture of lament (2 Sm 1:11; Jer 6:26).

(B) Resistance Flares (2:15–28). The enforced sacrifice recalls the monthly celebration honoring the king's birthday (2 Mc 6:7). Mattathias had moved from Jerusalem (2:1), perhaps to avoid such sacrifices, for "those left in Jerusalem" complied (2:18). It was not likely that he would now sacrifice. **18.** *friends of the king:* The lowest of the four ranks in the order of "friends of the king" (friends, honored friends, first friends, and first and preferred friends). There is mention of first friends in 10:65; 11:27; 2 Mc 8:9. **24.** *righteous anger:* Mattathias acted according to the Law (see Dt 13:7–10; Ex 34:13). **25.** *king's man:* Josephus calls him Bacchides (*JW* 1.1,3 § 36), and Apelles (*Ant.* 12.6,2 § 270). **26.** Phinehas' action in Nu 25:6–15 is also recalled in Ps 106:28–31; Sir 45:23.

Mattathias led a group of disaffected into the wild hill country, probably the area E of Modin. 2 Mc 5:27 notes the group's escape.

19 (C) The Slaughter on the Sabbath and Its Sequel (2:29–41). Refusal to worship according to the king's edict meant death or flight. 1 Mc now narrates the fate of some faithful dissenters. **29.** *righteousness and justice:* According to the Law (see Is 56:1; Ps 106:3). *wilderness:* The traditional home of the political outcast (see 1:53; 1 Sm 23:14). **31.** Philip and his men ordered these Jews out of the caves (2 Mc 6:11) on the Sabbath (v. 32) to fulfill the king's edict. **38.** *they died:* By suffocation caused by burning brush heaped against the caves' entrances (Josephus, *Ant.* 12.6,2 § 274–75). The rigors of their piety prevented them from defensive measures, for such action would violate the Sabbath rest. Mattathias and his men made the more practical decision to fight in a similar situation.

(D) The Hasideans (2:42–48). The *asidaioi* are the *ḥăsîdîm*, the "pious" or "faithful." The name fits them well, for their principal interest was the Law and its observance. They now appear as a group for the first time in history. Although 2 Mc 14:6 identifies them with all the followers of Judas, it is an oversimplification (2:42). Later, some of the Hasideans sued for peace (7:13), beginning the drift away from the Hasmoneans. The Hasideans are the forerunners of the Pharisees ("the separated") and the Essenes ("the pure"), two of the three Jewish "philosophical" schools described by Josephus (*JW* 2.8,2–14 § 119–66), the third being the Sadducees ("sons of Zadok"). **43.** *joined them:* 2 Mc 8:1 speaks of the force now actively recruited as though it were led by Judas (as later it was) and not by Mattathias. It numbered 6000. **44.** *organized an army:* What was done with this army is told in vv. 45ff., and in 2 Mc 8:5–7. *sinners... lawless men:* The pagans (1:34; 2:48,62) and the lawless men, apostate Jews (1:11). **47.** *arrogant men:* The Seleucid agents (see 1:21). **48.** *rescued the Law:* By their militant action, they prevented the submersion of Judaism in a syncretistic cult and thus did not permit the "horn" (power) of the "sinner" (Antiochus? cf. v. 62) to abolish their Mosaic Law and Yahweh's covenant.

(E) Mattathias' Testament (2:49–70). The deathbed scene recalls Jacob's farewell admonitions (Gn 49) and Moses' departure (Dt 33). The content of the passage, however, is closer to Sir 44–50, the "Praise of the Fathers." Mattathias recalls the faith of Abraham (Gn 22), Joseph (Gn 39), Phinehas "our father" (v. 26; Nm 25), Joshua (Jos 1), Caleb (Nu 13), David (2 Sm 7), Elijah (1 Kgs 18; 2 Kgs 2), Hananiah, Azariah, Mishael (Dn 1:6), and Daniel (Dn 6). These heroes are to be emulated. The author of 1 Mc shows his acquaintance with the material and aims of the stories preserved in Dn. **49.** *furious anger:* The Lord's anger against his sinful people (see 2 Mc 6:12–16). **51.** *great honor:* As heroes of the people, which, by the time 1 Mc was written, they were. **62.** *corruption and worms:* An illusion to the death of Antiochus, which is described in detail in 2 Mc 9. **65.** *Simon:* Although older than Judas and Jonathan, Simon succeeded to leadership in the family only after their demise. **70.** The 146th Seleucid year places this event in the spring of 166. *Modin:* See comment on 13:25–30.

20 **(III) Judas Maccabeus Takes Command of the Struggle (3:1–9:22).**

(A) Praise of Judas (3:1–9). The author praises Judas' accomplishments in a poetic passage (3–9). **5.** *burned:* See 5:5,35,44; 2 Mc 8:33. **7.** *kings:* Antiochus IV Epiphanes (3:27), Antiochus V Eupator (6:28), Demetrius I Soter (8:31; 9:1). **8.** *wrath:* God's punishment of his sinful people ended (see 2 Mc 6:12–16). **9.** *ends of the earth:* At least to Rome (8:20; see also 3:26).

(B) Judas Defeats Apollonius and Seron (3:10–26). This section has no parallel in 2 Mc. Because 1 Mc only summarizes the first victory—i.e., over the hated Apollonius (1:29–35; 2 Mc 5:23b–26)—it is all the more striking that he should recount the detail that Judas took Apollonius' sword (see, similarly, 1 Sm 21:9). **10.** *Samaria:* Josephus says Apollonius was *stratēgos*, "military commander," and *meridarchēs*, "governor," of Samaria (*Ant.* 12.5,5 § 261, 264; 12.7,1 § 287). He could, then, have recruited much of his force locally.

Next to suffer defeat was Seron, the Syrian commander (3:13–26). Josephus calls him *stratēgos* of Coele-Syria, but it is not likely that he was such an important officer. **15.** *ungodly men:* Renegade Jews, whom Judas had antagonized (see 2:44). **16.** *the ascent of Beth-horon:* There were two towns named Beth-horon, about 3 mi. apart—Upper Beth-horon and Lower Beth-horon. They were situated at the beginning and end of the pass connecting the coastal plains with the highlands N of Jerusalem. Catching his foe in the narrow and steep ascent, Judas could, even with a small contingent weak from fasting (v. 17), defeat Seron's much larger force. Routed, Seron's men tumbled down to the plain and out toward the sea coast, anachronistically called the land of the "Philistines." **18–19.** *heaven:* A circumlocution for God; the author of 1 Mc never uses the names "God" or "Lord." Judas' victories win him renown, bringing him to the king's attention (see 2 Mc 8:7).

(C) Antiochus Goes East (3:27–37). Although 1 Mc seems to make Judas' success the reason for the gathering of Antiochus' forces, other considerations were perhaps more important, such as the necessity to subjugate the Armenian satrap Artaxias, who had declared himself independent after the death of Antiochus III, and the need to recover other eastern provinces while protecting those threatened by growing Parthian power. **28.** *year's pay:* See 1 Mc 10:36. Seleucid kings paid their mercenaries in advance, and probably their own troops as well. **31.** *Persia:* In 1–2 Mc, this term means all the area E of the Tigris (see 2 Mc 1:19).

32. Lysias, the king's "kinsman,"—i.e., one belonging to the highest court order of the realm (1 Mc 10:89; 2 Mc 11:1)—is left in charge of the west (v. 32) and of the younger Antiochus (V Eupator, 164–162), who was then only seven. **34.** *half of his troops:* Josephus says "part" of his force, which seems more likely; Judas was not that serious a threat to Antiochus or he would not have begun other campaigns.

Other monarchs had deported Israelites (2 Kgs 17:6) and colonized their territory (Ezr 4:2,10; 2 Kgs 17:24), but Antiochus went further in his plan to eradicate the Jews. **37.** *hundred and forty-seventh year:* It is 165. By Hellenistic times, the "upper provinces" included the valleys of the Tigris and Euphrates; in the Persian period, only the provinces on the Iranian plateau were meant.

21 **(D) Judas Defeats Gorgias and Nicanor (3:38–4:27).** The parallel account in 2 Mc 8:8–29 gives the preponderant role to Nicanor, one of the "first friends" of the king, associating Gorgias with him as an experienced general or *stratēgos*. But 1 Mc features Gorgias, the commander of the separate contingent in the battle. **38.** *Ptolemy:* In 2 Mc 8:8, he is governor (*stratēgos*) of Coele-Syria and Phoenicia (Coele-Syria designated in Hellenistic times first the region between the Lebanon and the Antilebanon mountains and then also Palestine generally; see 2 Mc 4:45). *Nicanor:* See 1 Mc 7:26ff.; 2 Mc 8:9; 14; 15. *Gorgias:* See 1 Mc 5:58; 2 Mc 8:9; 10:14; 12:32ff. *friends:* See comment on 2:18. **39.** *infantry...cavalry:* The numbers conflict with the 20,000 of 2 Mc 8:9, which is another "round number." For a possible source of the figures involved, see 1 Chr 18:4; 19:18. The comparison of Judas and David is subtle but intentional. **40.** *Emmaus:* In the Shephelah, the foothills of Judah, about 20 mi. NW of Jerusalem. **41.** *traders:* They were invited by Nicanor (2 Mc 8:10–11) to make up a sum of 2000 talents, owed to the Romans as tribute (the indemnity mentioned in the treaty of Apamea?). The price—90 slaves per talent—was half the current price for slaves in Greece.

Unable to go to Jerusalem because the enemy had garrisoned the Acra, Judas assembled his followers at Mizpah, the ancient sanctuary 8 mi. N of Jerusalem, which was associated with the judges (Jgs 20), Samuel (1 Sm

7:5; 10:17), and with Jeremiah and the remnant of the people (Jer 40:6). There, they made ready for battle and prayed for help. The dirge of v. 45 explains why they chose Mizpah for assembly and prayer: No true Israelite remained in Jerusalem; its sanctuary was unclean.

48. After the Exile, the priesthood did not possess the Urim and Thummim (Ezr 2:63; Neh 7:65); therefore, Judas and his band consulted the Book of the Law to discover a sign of the future. The watchword "God's help" (2 Mc 8:23) could be inspired by such passages as Gn 49:25; Ex 18:4. It was customary in classical times to inscribe standards with such slogans (see 2 Mc 13:15; 1QM 4:13; etc.). **56.** The groups sent home are those weeded out of the army by Dt 20:5–8; 2 Mc 8:13 speaks simply of cowardice and lack of faith. As the divisional commanders of Judas' forces, 2 Mc 8:22 gives his brothers Simon and Jonathan, and also Joseph, son of Zechariah (1 Mc 5:18,56). The organization of the army units is that given in Ex 18:21, and it is found, at least in part, in Seleucid and Essene (Qumran) military organization.

22 **4:1–9.** Jewish renegades (Josephus, *Ant.* 12.7,4 § 305) or men from the citadel (v. 2) guided Gorgias to Judas' camp. Judas appeared on the plain S of Emmaus with half his force (v. 6; 2 Mc 8:16,23) and delivered an exhortation (vv. 8–11) that is paralleled in 2 Mc 8:16–20, although the incidents mentioned are different. Here, the reference is to Ex 14. **10.** *heaven:* God (see comment on 3:18–19). **15.** The survivors of Nicanor's army fled to refuge in Gazara (Gezer), Azotus (Ashdod), and Jamnia (Jabneh), three cities in Philistine territory. The "plains of Idumea" (v. 15) apparently stretched farther N at this time, at least N of Beth-zur (4:29). **18.** Judas returned to frighten off Gorgias' detachment, which had searched vainly for him in the hills. In 2 Mc 8:25–26 it is indicated that the imminence of the Sabbath forbade further pursuit. **23.** *great riches:* Including the money that the slave traders could not now use (2 Mc 8:25). **24.** Judas' army gave thanks in the manner of Ps 136. After the Sabbath, they gave some of the spoils to the needy (2 Mc 8:28–30). The survivors of Nicanor's forces (v. 26) and Nicanor himself (2 Mc 8:34–36) reported the results of the fight to Lysias.

23 **(E) Judas Defeats Lysias at Beth-zur (4:28–35).** There is a parallel account of this battle and its sequel in 2 Mc 11:1–15. Lysias was unable to defeat Judas at Beth-zur, retired to Antioch, and negotiated peace with the Jews. **28.** *the following year:* The Seleucid year 148 (3:37; 2 Mc 11:21) or 164 BC. Lysias came with 60,000 infantry and 5000 cavalry to invade Judea. In a fish-hook maneuver, he descended the coastal plain to come up again on Beth-zur (Khirbet et-Tubeiqah), about 20 mi. S of Jerusalem. The stronghold was garrisoned by Jews who were then besieged by Lysias. Judas rushed to arms to relieve the siege, hastily gathering a force of 10,000 men to meet Lysias (4:29; 2 Mc 11:5–7). Seeing the tremendous odds against him (which 2 Mc 11:2,4 inflates further), Judas prayed for divine assistance before joining battle. His prayer (30–33) recalled the exploits of David (1 Sm 17) and Jonathan (1 Sm 14), who also faced superior might and were victorious with divine help. (1QM 11:1–3 contains a similar allusion to David and the Philistines in the prayer of the high priest before battle.) Judas was heard; the heavenly horseman of 2 Mc 11:8 appeared to signify that the battle was the Lord's (1 Sm 17:47). Lysias' ranks, weakened by Judas' imprecatory prayer, began to give way before Judas (35), and Lysias broke off hostilities and retired to Antioch, with every intention of returning later (as he does in 6:31). A more impressive recital of Judas' victory appears in 2 Mc 11:11–15 which also notes that Lysias sued for peace after the battle. (Although 1 Mc narrates the Temple's dedication following the early victories of Judas, the death of Antiochus IV Epiphanes (6:1–16) and the accession of Antiochus V Eupator (6:17) preceded this event. 2 Mc retains the right sequence; → 12 above.)

24 **(F) The Purification and Dedication of the Temple (4:36–61).** (The parallel account is in 2 Mc 10:1–8.) Judas proposed to cleanse (36–51) and dedicate (52–61) the sanctuary, thus providing the name for the annual celebration commemorating this event. Over the years, the feast has had many titles: Feast of Dedication (*enkainismos*, 1 Mc 4:59; 2 Mc 2:9,19; *enkainia* in Jn 10:22); Feast of Purification (*katharismos*, 2 Mc 2:16,18; 10:3,5); Feast of Tabernacles (*skenopegia*) in Kislev (2 Mc 1:9,18), because it was celebrated for eight days in imitation of the Feast of Tabernacles (Lv 23:33–36); Feast of Lights (*phota*, Josephus, *Ant.* 12.7,7 § 325; Mishnah, *Baba Kamma* 6:6); it is more commonly known by its Jewish title, Hanukkah ("dedication" in Hebrew).

Judas and his army ascended Mt. Zion (now inclusive of the Temple area; Is 18:7; Ps 75:2). **41.** *Judas appointed men:* To harass the inhabitants of the Acra while the Temple was under repair. The citadel overlooked the Temple area (1:33–35), a source of constant annoyance until Simon took it in 141. **42.** The priests now began the work of cleansing the Temple, as Hilkiah and his priests had done before them (2 Kgs 23; 2 Chr 29). **43.** The "stones of the impurity" (the altar to Zeus Olympios; 1:54,59) were taken to "an unclean place" (the Kedron Valley? see 2 Kgs 23:4,6,12). **44.** *the altar of holocausts which had been desecrated:* Because of the altar to Zeus built on it, it was itself something of a problem. Fearful lest the use of any profaned object in divine cult incur retribution (see Mal 1:6–14), Judas was reluctant to use the altar. He longed for a prophet, inasmuch as prophets had been associated with the rebuilding of the Temple (Haggai and Zechariah), and were the sources from which to draw God's Word (Jer 1:9). But prophets had disappeared (4:46; 9:27; 14:41), so Judas set the stones carefully aside "until a prophet should come" who could settle the matter (the Qumran sectaries also expected a prophet; 1QS 9:10–11; 4QTest). The altars mentioned in 2 Mc 10:2 were also destroyed at this time.

The new altar was built of "uncut stones" according to the Law (Ex 20:25; Dt 27:5–6), the Temple was repaired in various places, and the furnishing were placed in it. **50.** It was the practice of lighting homes during this feast that earned it the name Feast of Lights, and not the fact that the lights were symbolic of religious liberty, as Josephus reasoned (*Ant.* 12.7,7 § 325).

52. Finally, the repair work was done. Judas and his men dedicated the restored Temple on 25 Kislev, 148, of the Seleucid era (December 14, 164; cf. 2 Mc 1:10; Josephus, *Ant.* 12.7,6 § 319). **53–54.** According to the Law (e.g., Ex 29:38–41; Nm 7:10–88), they offered sacrifices in their renewed liturgy "on the anniversary of the day" on which the Gentiles had defiled the Temple.

This day, 25 Kislev, 145 (December 17, 167) was exactly three years prior to the dedication (1:54,59). The date is confirmed by Josephus, *Ant.* 12.7,6 § 319, and is checked there by cross reference to the Greek Olympiads. The two years of 2 Mc 10:3 are a mistake, based on the author's incorrect dating of the death of Antiochus IV, which he knew preceded the dedication, in 165.

56. The people celebrated the feast for "eight days," like the Feast of Tabernacles (Lv 13:33–36) and the reconsecration of the Temple under Hezekiah (2 Chr 29:17). **60.** To prevent further trouble from those in the citadel, Judas fortified the Temple area itself, and at the same time strengthened the fortifications of Beth-zur to the south, which guarded the approaches from Idumea.

25 **(G) Judas Battles with Neighboring Peoples (5:1–68).** (The parallels are found in 2 Mc 8:30–33; 10:14–23; 12:2–45). The shaky peace established after Lysias' first campaign (4:28–35; 2 Mc 11) was not to last beyond the death of Antiochus IV (6:1–16). According to its provisions, the Jews were to remain subject to the king, but they would be left free to follow their own "food and laws," i.e., to have their own religious freedom (2 Mc 11:27–33). In effect, the king's edict (1:41–50) was revoked insofar as it applied to the Jews. Gorgias, however, smarting under his earlier humiliation (4:1,19–22; 2 Mc 8:9), could not leave the Jews alone (2 Mc 10:14). Other governors shared his hostility (2 Mc 12:2), and soon a wave of anti-Jewish incidents broke out (5:1–3,9,15), so that the Jews were persecuted even unto death (2 Mc 12:3–9). The Jews under Judas fought back, taking up arms against the "Gentiles round about"—the circle of Idumea (5:3–5; 2 Mc 10:14–23), Ammon (5:6–8; 2 Mc 8:30–33),? Gilead (5:9–13,24–54; 2 Mc 12:10–31), Galilee (5:14–23), and the "land of the Philistines" (5:55–68; 2 Mc 12:3–9, 32–45). For the moment, these punitive and defensive measures were not attempts to throw off the Seleucid yoke, but the battles soon escalated the struggle into a war for full independence.

In the description of these battles, archaic titles appear. "The sons of Jacob" (5:2), "Israel" (5:3), contend with the "sons of Esau" (5:3,65), with "Ammon" (5:6), and in the "land of the Philistines" (5:68). The biblical author wants his readers to know that Judas and his brothers are really engaged in a conquest similar to that of David (see 2 Sm 5–8), to establish their rights to an ancient heritage (15:33).

Another cause of anti-Jewish hostility at this time was the Temple's reconstruction and fortification (4:36–61), which the surrounding governors and peoples took badly. For them it was the monument to Jewish nonconformity and contrariness, in which the Jews flaunted their opposition to the stated policies of the empire. Added to their smoldering hatred for Judaism (2 Mc 10:14; 12:2), it led them to persecute the Jewish minorities among them.

It is possible neither to establish a perfect sequence of the battles in 1 Mc 5 and its parallels nor to construct a harmony between 1–2 Mc, because the conflicts obviously were incompletely chronicled (5:7,14; 2 Mc 10:19) and transposition of the material by the biblical authors has occurred (→ 11 above). The events, however, may be assigned to the year 163.

An immediate effect of these battles was the securing of the safety of those Jews who could not be protected adequately at a distance by removing them to Judea (5:23,45). Another sequel, brought on by the siege of the citadel (6:18–27), was the second campaign of Lysias, this time acting for Antiochus V Eupator (6:28–54).

26 (a) Idumea (5:3–5; 2 Mc 10:14–23). After fortifying Beth-zur, Judas began defensive measures further S, by moving against the sons of Esau "in Idumea" (the better reading; A has "in Judea") at Akrabattene (5:3). Presumably he is intent upon pacifying the trade routes harassed by brigands, inasmuch as the Idumeans were waiting to ambush (not "blockade") Israel (5:3) on the highways (5:4), retiring to their strongholds when pressed (2 Mc 10:14–23). The precise location of Akrabattene is uncertain, but it is probably the "ascent of scorpions" (*'aqrabbîm;* Nm 34:4; Jos 15:3; Jgs 1:36) along which lay the trade route from the Gulf of Aqabah to Beer-sheba. **4.** *sons of Baean:* Difficult to identify. They were probably nomads, the mercenaries of 2 Mc 10:14. Abel locates them W of the Jordan near the "stone of Bohan," hence astride the trade route from Jerusalem to Jericho (Jos 15:6; 18:17; Lk 10:30). More likely, however, they lay further S in Idumean territory, again across a trade route. Judas invoked the *ḥerem* upon them, and he accomplished their total destruction (cf. Jos 6:17).

(b) Ammon (5:6–8; 2 Mc 8:30–33?). Triumphant over those who infested the trade routes, Judas then crossed the Jordan to encounter and defeat Timothy and his forces. The particular reasons for this expedition are not given. **8.** *Jazer:* Probably the town in Nm 21:32, modern Khirbet Jazzer near es-Salt. The displaced fragment in 2 Mc 8:30–33 may describe the same series of conflicts.

(c) Gilead (5:9–13,24–54; 2 Mc 12:10–31). The Jews in Gilead (in Hellenistic times Gilead included the district N of the Yarmuk River) were forced to flee for their lives into the stronghold of Dathema, whose location is unknown beyond the fact that it lay within a night's march of Bozrah (5:29). Appeal was made to Judas; if he does not intervene, there will be another massacre like that of the Jews in the land of Tob (in reprisal for Timothy's defeats in Ammon?), because Timothy is preparing to take Dathema. Judas set out to relieve the siege, taking his brother Jonathan with him. As Dancy suggests (*op. cit.*, 105), Judas probably accompanied Simon (5:21) as far N as Beth-shan before crossing the Jordan (5:52) to enter the desert for a three days' journey of about 50 mi. (5:24).

Although the sequence of Judas' campaign in Gilead is not at all clear, the next few paragraphs will attempt to correlate the events narrated in 1 Mc 5:24–54 and 2 Mc 12:10–31.

Judas and his followers met a Nabatean caravan and told them of their plans to attack and wipe out the citizens of Gilead (5:25–27). This situation may have induced the Arab attack mentioned in 2 Mc 12:10–12, in which Judas is the victor. Inasmuch as he was pressed for time, Judas made terms with these preliminary adversaries quickly. After his victory, he took Bozrah and then turned back toward Dathema (OT Edrei, Nm 21:33?) by night. Arriving there at dawn, his three columns lifted the siege, putting Timothy to flight (5:34). Judas then went on to take Alema (5:35), Chaspho (Caspin in 2 Mc 12:13–16; modern el-Mezeirib), Maked, Bosor, and the other "cities" of Gilead (5:36).

Judas' main opponent, however, evaded him. Timothy assembled another force, hired Arab mercenaries, and encamped near a tributary of the Yarmuk, opposite Raphon. Judas meanwhile searched the area for Timothy, and, not finding him (and the captives of 5:13?) at the fortress (*charax*) where he thought him to be (was this modern Kerak?), moved on after detailing some men to besiege the place (cf. 2 Mc 12:18). As Judas approached, Timothy sent women, children, and baggage (of 1 Mc 5:13?) into the stronghold of Carnaim. He then waited to see if Judas were too tired from his pursuit, or too fearful, to enter battle immediately (5:40). Timothy's orders to his officers also smack of the superstitious hope that a divine sign will be given. He had his answer in the orders of Judas to his officers ("scribes," see Dt 20:5–9). Again Judas was victorious in battle; Timothy's army fled to refuge at the sanctuary of the *Atergateion*, the temple of the horned Astarte at Carnaim. Timothy himself fell into the hands of Dositheus and Sosipater, Tobiad Jews, who had been left behind to besiege the fortress of 2 Mc 12:19 and who were then coming to Judas. Timothy persuaded them to let him go, for he had their relatives in his power (2 Mc 12:24–26).

Meanwhile, Judas attacked Timothy's men in Carnaim and took and destroyed the town and its temple (5:44; 2 Mc 12:26).

Finally, Judas removed the Jews of Gilead to Judea. On the way home, he encountered opposition at Ephron (et-Taiyibeh) and crushed it; the people of Beth-shan (Scythopolis of 2 Mc 12:29) were more friendly. Judas arrived in Jerusalem in time to celebrate the Feast of Pentecost (2 Mc 12:31). (For another view of this campaign, see J. Simons, *Geographical and Topographical Texts of the Old Testament* [Leiden, 1959] 422–25.)

27 (d) GALILEE (5:14–23). At the same time that appeal was made to Jerusalem from Gilead, the Jews of Galilee made a similar plea. The same assembly that sent Judas to Gilead commissioned Simon to relieve the distress of the Galilean Jews. **15.** *Galilee of the foreigners:* The "land of the foreigners" in 1 Mc is ancient Philistia (4:22; 5:66,68); therefore, the Galilee spoken of here is along the seacoast. The names of the cities mentioned confirm this hypothesis. The region is distinct from the Galilee of the Gentiles, which is further inland (cf. Is 8:23). Simon also was victorious, crushing the enemy. He returned the Jews of Galilee and Arbatta to Judea. Arbatta is the toparchy of Narbattene, near what was later Caesarea Maritima on the seacoast; it was probably then in Samaria (cf. Josephus, *JW* 2.14,5 § 291–92; 2.18,10 § 509).

(e) THE LAND OF THE PHILISTINES (5:55–68; 2 Mc 12:3–9,32–45). The punitive raids of 2 Mc 12:3–9 apparently occurred before Judas' campaign in Gilead, but it is not certain. The treacherous citizens of Joppa invited the Jews on an outing—at public expense (12:3)—and then drowned them. In reprisal, Judas burned the city's port. When he learned of similar plans in Jamnia, he gave it the same treatment.

The accounts of 1 Mc 5:55–68 and 2 Mc 12:32–45 are interrelated. While Judas was returning from Gilead (Simon was nearly finished with his campaign; cf. 5:22,55), the two commanders he had left in Jerusalem (5:18) disobeyed orders and engaged Gorgias near Jamnia in hope of glory. Joseph (see 2 Mc 8:23) and Azariah (also Eleazar in 2 Mc 8:23 and Esdris in 2 Mc 12:36) were defeated and sent flying homeward, with Gorgias in pursuit. Possibly they were besieged in Beth-zur (4:61), where they had found refuge. If so, it explains the locale of the subsequent battles.

Judas rested his men briefly during Pentecost (2 Mc 12:32), taking to the field later in support of the besieged Azariah (Esdris, 2 Mc 12:36). He met Gorgias, who came out to him (2 Mc 12:32–35), and defeated him near Hebron, which he destroyed (1 Mc 5:65; this destruction need not have been completed at once). Gorgias escaped to Marisa (Mareshah of Jos 15:44). Judas fell upon those besieging Esdris and routed them (2 Mc 12:36–37). Then he bypassed Marisa (5:66; correct "Samaria" of S, A with the OL and Josephus, *Ant.* 12.8,6 § 353) and regrouped at Adullam, where he spent the Sabbath (2 Mc 12:38). Judas then collected the decaying bodies of those who had fallen before Gorgias at Jamnia and returned them to Jerusalem for burial, sending along money for sacrifices for them (2 Mc 12:39–45). Possibly 1 Mc 5:67 is another reference to the defeat of Joseph and Azariah, because the collecting of bodies came at this point. Next, Judas struck at Azotus (OT Ashdod) and unnamed cities; he then returned to Judea with his men (1 Mc 5:68).

28 **(H) The Death of Antiochus IV Epiphanes (6:1–17).** There is a parallel in 2 Mc 9:1–29; 10:9, and possibly in 2 Mc 1:13, which does speak of Antiochus but with a story that differs from the present accounts. The author of 1 Mc assumes that Antiochus died late in the Seleucid year 149 (which 1 Mc 6:16 counts as beginning in autumn) and so after the dedication of the Temple and the campaigns of 1 Mc 5. In fact, Antiochus died early in that year (accepting 1 Mc 6:16 reckoning); thus, the order of 2 Mc is better (→ 12 above).

1. *Elymais:* Ancient Elam (Gn 10:22). There is no city by this name, which designates rather the country around Susa, particularly N and E. The city and temples that Antiochus tried to pillage are in Persia (1 Mc 6:1), but the city was not Persepolis (2 Mc 9:2), about which the king would not need to be told. The city is mislocated in both 1–2 Mc. Otherwise, their accounts match fairly well. Polybius (*Histories* 31.9) narrates Antiochus' death in much the same way. **2.** *temple:* If 2 Mc 1:13 is to be trusted here, this was the temple of the Sumerian goddess Nanaea or Anaitis, worshiped by the Elamites and in Hellenistic times identified with Artemis. *first king of the Greeks:* Alexander (1:1). **4.** Antiochus planned to reach Babylon, but only went as far as Ecbatana (2 Mc 9:3) in Persia (1 Mc 6:5) when he learned of Judas' activities. Ecbatana is often identified with Aspadana (Isfahan), because Polybius says that Antiochus died at Tabae (corrected to Gai or Gagai), S of Isfahan. **7.** The Jews "pulled down the abomination" (cf. 1:54 and 4:43). According to the peace terms of 2 Mc 11:15, which resulted from Lysias' first campaign and which Antiochus had approved, the Jews had gained religious liberty. Consequently, they purified the Temple and fortified Mt. Zion and Beth-zur. The dedication of the Temple, however, came after Antiochus' death, so his anger would have to be posthumous. 1 Mc has simply added to the mention of Lysias' defeat (6:5–6) a summary of the contents of 1 Mc 3–5. **8.** *ill with grief:* Antiochus now fits the nickname some of his subjects have given him—*epimanēs*, "madman." **10.** *friends:* See comment on 2:18. **12–13.** The biblical author sees the king's death as punishment for his crimes against Judah and not for any faults committed in a "strange land." **14.** As he lay dying, the king committed to Philip the tutelage of his son. Earlier this job was given to Lysias (3:33), who was faithful to the charge, declaring Antiochus V Eupator to be the new king (6:17). Apparently Philip later became ambitious (6:55–56,63; 2 Mc 13:23), was defeated, and fled (2 Mc 9:29). Josephus says Antiochus captured and killed him (*Ant.* 12.9,7 § 386). **16.** The 149th Seleucid year is counted here as beginning in the autumn. Antiochus IV died about October, 164. **17.** *Eupator:* The new king's nickname means "of a good father."

29 **(I) Siege of the Citadel (6:18–27).** This passage has no parallel in 2 Mc. Because the citadel, garrisoned by Gentiles and renegade Jews (1:33–34) proved continuously troublesome, Judas besieged it. By this time, the fighting that began with defensive measures and punitive raids had assumed its true appearance of a war for liberation from Seleucid power. Unfortunately for Judas, a few of the besieged escaped and reported to Eupator what had happened, Menelaus among them (2 Mc 13:3). **20.** In the official Seleucid calculation, the 150th year began October 11, 163, and ended September 29, 162. Judas besieged the citadel near the beginning of this year, after the expedition that carried him through Idumea to the "land of the Philistines" in the summer of 163 (5:55–68).

30 **(J) Lysias' Second Campaign in Judah (6:28–63; 2 Mc 13:1–26).** Judas' revolt now assumed great importance in the empire, and the king determined to crush it. He, or rather Lysias, almost did so, but the threat of Philip taking over the whole empire drew the Seleucid army out of Judah. Again Lysias made peace with the Jews.

Upon hearing Menelaus' report, the king conferred with his officers. Actually, because the king was so young, it was Lysias who made the decisions (6:57; 2 Mc 13:2). The importance of the struggle is evident in the force Lysias gathered, which was supplemented by mercenaries, elephants, and chariots (6:29; 2 Mc 13:2), and in the presence of the king himself. The numbers, however, are exaggerated. At the earlier and more important battle of Magnesia (190) and in the parade at Daphne (166), the Seleucid army totaled only 52,200 and 50,500 men, respectively.

Because of the elephants and chariotry, Lysias kept to the coastal plains until he was ready to come up again through Idumea to besiege Beth-zur. The Jewish garrison defended the stronghold with courage (6:31; 2 Mc 13:18–19). Meanwhile, Judas struck at the king's forces near Modin in a nightly foray (2 Mc 13:14–17), then made the mistake of taking his troops to Beth-zechariah to save Judah and "the city" (Jerusalem? Beth-zur?; cf. 2 Mc 13:13). The king turned to meet this challenge with the main body of his forces. Both sides prepared for battle; the king's men intoxicated the elephants with the "juice of grapes and mulberries" (6:33–39). Once on lower ground, Judas and his army were no match for the superior armament and the professionalism of the king's soldiers. Despite heroic courage—notably Judas' brother Eleazar Avaran—Judas was beaten back to Jerusalem (6:40–48).

Beth-zur capitulated for lack of food (6:49; 2 Mc 13:22) because it was a sabbatical year in which the land had to lie fallow (6:49; Ex 23:11; Lv 25:3–7). Lack of supplies also kept the fortress on Mt. Zion undermanned (6:53–54). All seemed desperate, until Lysias received the news that Philip was attempting to seize control of the government (2 Mc 13:23). Lysias made peace with the Jews (6:57–59; 2 Mc 13:23) and went home, permitting them religious, but not civil, liberty. Menelaus was executed, a victim of political expediency (2 Mc 13:4–8). Before he left to defeat Philip (6:63), the king razed the Jewish fortifications on Mt. Zion (6:62). News of the peace treaty nearly provoked a riot at Ptolemais (2 Mc 13:25–26; see 1 Mc 5:22). 2 Mc sees the whole campaign as a series of Jewish victories in the light of its final outcome. The letter of 2 Mc 11:22–26 belongs here; it describes the terms of the peace. The Jews are to be left with the Temple and their religious liberty (the year is 163).

31 **(K) The Expedition of Bacchides and Alcimus (7:1–25).** Demetrius I Soter (161–150), the oldest surviving son of Seleucus IV (187–175), had been frustrated earlier by the Roman Senate in his bid to succeed Epiphanes (175–164), whom he considered a usurper. The Romans had recognized Antiochus V Eupator (164–161) instead, feeling that they could better serve their own purposes with a youth on the Seleucid throne. With the connivance of his friend, the historian Polybius, Demetrius finally escaped from Rome and went to Tripolis, where he set himself up as rightful king (Polybius, *Histories* 31.2, 11–15). The populace and army at Antioch came over to him, and he finally went there to take possession of the "royal palace of his ancestors" in 161. Eupator and his minister Lysias were quickly executed (7:2–4), which opened the way for a new policy toward the Jews—repression. Most of 7:1–25 has no parallel in 2 Mc (see 2 Mc 14:1–11, however). In 7:1, the Seleucid year is counted as beginning in the autumn. When correlated with 2 Mc 14:1,4, it dates the visit of Alcimus to the spring of 161. The "city by the sea" is Tripolis (2 Mc 14:1).

5. With Alcimus, a new priestly line appears. Onias III, who belonged to the traditional family of high priests—who were descended from Zadok (2 Sm 8:17) by way of Joshua (1 Chr 6:8–15; Hag 1:1; Neh 12:10–11) and Jaddua (Ezr 2:36)—had been replaced by his brother Jason (2 Mc 4:7), then by Menelaus (2 Mc 4:23–26). Menelaus was a priest, but of the family of Bilgah (2 Mc 3:4). Josephus (*Ant.* 12.5,1 § 237) makes him the "brother" of Onias, which is incorrect if blood brother is meant. Now, in Alcimus, still another priestly family appears (1 Mc 7:14), perhaps that of Jakim (1 Chr 24:12). It seems that under the peace terms of 163, Alcimus became the high priest when Menelaus was deposed and executed (2 Mc 13:4–8; Josephus, *Ant* 12.9,7 § 385). Alcimus, whose Gk name (meaning "brave") shows his disposition toward Hellenization, is known also by some manuscripts and Josephus (*Ant.* 12.9,7 § 385) as Jakeimos. His full name in Hebrew may have been Eliakim or Jehoiakim (Joakim).

Alcimus' earlier defilement (2 Mc 14:3) is not specified, but the time of "separation" (*ameixias*) from the Gentiles (2 Mc 14:3,38) seems to be that of the persecution under Epiphanes, when even priests defiled the Temple (2 Mc 4:14; 6:3–6), and when those Jews who refused to be defiled died (2 Mc 6:25). If Alcimus were so defiled, Judas would definitely not have wanted him in the high priesthood, even though circumstances in 163 might have forced him to accept Alcimus for a while, until he could prevent him from exercising the high priesthood (2 Mc 14:3) and drive him out (7:6).

The events that follow are best understood if Judas is in possession of Jerusalem. Perhaps the change of regime in Antioch was the signal for Judas to take Jerusalem and drive out Alcimus, who then went to Demetrius to complain. Inasmuch as Alcimus was obviously hostile to Judas and in sympathy with Seleucid interests, the king listened willingly to his complaint (7:5–7; cf. 2 Mc 14:6–10) and then decided to act ruthlessly in establishing Alcimus at Jerusalem. Bacchides' commission was to take vengeance on Judas' followers and to put down any opposition to the high priest.

8. Bacchides was "one of the king's friends" (7:8; see comment on 2:18) and "governor of the provinces beyond the river," i.e., the area between the Euphrates (the "river") and Egypt. His task was to subdue Judah while Demetrius went E—as Epiphanes did (3:27–37)—to meet the challenge to the empire there from Timarchus, the satrap of Media, who had proclaimed himself independent. Eventually, Demetrius defeated and killed Timarchus. **13.** Although Judas was wary of Bacchides' peace feelers, some of his followers from the *ḥăsîdîm* (see comment on 2:42) believed Bacchides' promises and relied too much on the fact that Alcimus was a priest (7:14). Their confidence cost them their lives. No reason is given why they should have now deserted Judas and sued for peace. At any rate, Bacchides soon broke his oath; 1 Mc 7:16–17 applies Ps 79:2–3 to the situation.

Bacchides withdrew from Jerusalem to Beth-zaith. Again he slaughtered without compunction those who had deserted to him from Judas, thus fulfilling his commission (7:9). Then, leaving a force with Alcimus, whom he placed in charge of the province, Bacchides returned to the king at Antioch (7:20). His mission had not been completely successful; Judas was still free and too strong to take by force with the men at hand. **21.** Alcimus strove for the high priesthood, taking his animosity out on the countryside (7:23). Judas realized that he must go forth to prevent further damage to his supporters; thus, he made raids against Alcimus' men and those who had gone over to him. So successful were Judas' reprisals that Alcimus and his partisans could not travel freely in the countryside. Realizing that time was favoring Judas, Alcimus returned to the king to beg a larger force.

32 **(L) The Defeat of Nicanor (7:26–50).** The parallel passage is 2 Mc 14:1–15:36. Demetrius sent Nicanor, who had ample reason (3:38–4:25; 2 Mc 8:8–29) to be "an enemy of Israel" (7:26). Nicanor had escaped Rome with Demetrius (Josephus, *Ant.* 12.10,4 § 402) and was, at the time of his appointment as governor (*stratēgos*) of Judea, in charge of the elephants of Demetrius' army. Those pagans whom Judas had terrorized joined Nicanor (2 Mc 14:14). Judas (the "leader" of 2 Mc 14:16) sent out a party from Jerusalem to reconnoiter. Led by Simon (14:17), they skirmished with Nicanor at Dessau (location unknown), but cautiously, alarmed by the sudden appearance of Nicanor's men (14:16–17).

Nicanor decided on diplomacy and offered acceptable terms, partly that Judas would succeed Alcimus in the high priesthood (14:18–22,26). For a time life continued normally (14:25); then Alcimus, fearful of the growing friendship of Nicanor and Judas, complained to the king, which resulted in the king's orders to send Judas to Antioch as a prisoner (14:26–27). Nicanor then waited to catch Judas by a ruse (presumably because Judas was well defended at all times) because he did not want to stir up trouble, but Judas sensed a change in Nicanor's attitude, assessed it correctly, and fled with his forces, leaving Nicanor in possession of Jerusalem (14:28–30). All these 2 Mc events are capsulized in 1 Mc 7:27–30.

Nicanor suspected the priests of complicity in Judas' escape and blasphemed the Temple, promising to raze it and build a temple to Dionysus if Judas were not handed over to him (2 Mc 14:31–33). Nicanor then left Jerusalem to fight Judas at nearby Capharsalama (location uncertain), where he was beaten (1 Mc 7:31–32). The episode of Razis (2 Mc 14:37–46) may narrate the taking of one of Judas' strongholds nearby.

Returning to Jerusalem, Nicanor regrouped, threatened the Temple again (7:33–35), and went out once more to meet Judas. The priests, in tears, prayed for divine aid to save the Temple (7:36–38; 2 Mc 15:19). Their prayer ironically commented on Is 56:6–8. Nicanor encamped at Beth-horon, there joined by Syrian reinforcements. Meanwhile, Judas is 7 mi. SE at Adasa, encouraging his men before battle (7:40; 2 Mc 15:7–19). Nicanor's plan was to attack Judas on the Sabbath; however, it drew opposition from the Jews with him, and the expedition ended in frustration (2 Mc 15:1–5). In contrast, Judas relied on God to help him and his men and to punish the blasphemer as once he had punished Sennacherib's army (2 Kgs 19:35; 2 Mc 15:20–24).

On 13 Adar (March, 160), Judas was victorious in battle. Nicanor was struck down; his forces fled toward Gazara (OT Gezer) but were cut off by partisans of Judas, driven back toward their pursuers, and destroyed (7:43–46; 2 Mc 15:25–27). Nicanor's head and arm, with which he had blasphemed the Temple, were brought to Jerusalem. There, Judas displayed them before the pagans, hanging them from the Jewish citadel on Mt. Zion (7:47; 2 Mc 15:31,35). The feast of Nicanor on 13 Adar was stricken from the Jewish calendar after the destruction of the Temple in AD 70 (7:49; 2 Mc 15:36; Josephus, *Ant.* 12.10,5 § 412).

33 **(M) Judas' Treaty with the Romans (8:1–32).** By the middle of the 2nd cent. BC, Rome had extended her power throughout the Mediterranean world. 1 Mc now recounts a series of Roman victories to explain her presence and power in the Near East. **2.** *the Gauls:* Most likely the Cisalpine Gauls, whose conquest was complete in the first decade of the 2nd cent. BC. **3–4.** *in the land of Spain:* The Romans came to power after winning the country from the Carthaginians at the end of the 3rd cent. They then exploited Spain's mining interests. *the kings:* Unspecified, unless this is a reference to what follows in vv. 5–8. **5.** Philip V of Macedon was defeated by Titus Quinctius Flamininus at Cynoscephalae (in Thessaly) in 197. Philip's son, Perseus, lost to the Roman general Aemilius Paulus at Pydna (in Macedon) in 168.

6–8. Antiochus III, "the great king of Asia"—i.e., of the lands bordering the eastern end of the Mediterranean—lost at Magnesia to Lucius Scipio, despite having the superior force. The 120 elephants really numbered 54, according to Polybius and Livy. Nor was Antiochus "taken alive"; he escaped. Under the treaty of Apamea (188), he was forced to pay the costs of the war—some 15,000 Euboic talents, a "heavy tribute"—and to give hostages (notably the future Antiochus IV Epiphanes). Antiochus was also forced to retire from Asia Minor, but hardly from India, which he never occupied, nor from Media, which he did. Perhaps India, Media, and Lydia (v. 8) should be read as Ionia, Mysia, and Lydia, territories in Asia Minor given to Eumenes II, the king of Pergamum, who had been Rome's ally at Magnesia.

9–10. 1 Mc notes the defeat of the Achaean League in 146 by the Roman consul Lucius Mummius, who devastated Corinth once he had taken it. The reference to 146 is anachronistic at this point. **10.** *even to this day:* See the similar phrase in 13:30. **13.** *became kings:* The Romans liked to make kings; some they helped were Masinissa of Numidia, Eumenes I and Eumenes II of Pergamum, Prusias and Nicomedes II of Bithynia, Alexander Balas of Syria (10:1), Ariarathes V of Cappadocia, and all the later Egyptian kings. **15.** *every day:* The Roman Senate did not meet daily; it met on the calends, nones, and ides of the month, and on festivals. Nor were there 320 senators; there were 300. **16.** *one man every year:* The consul—one of two—with whom the Jews came in contact (see 15:16). The whole description of Rome in this chapter fits the adage, "too good to be true."

To keep Demetrius off balance politically and to scare him, Judas concluded a treaty with the Romans. The exact moment when the envoys were sent can only be conjectured, but perhaps it was as soon as Demetrius appeared in the east and Judas had driven Alcimus from the high priesthood, for then Demetrius was *persona non grata* at Rome. This estimate is borne out by the letter cited in Josephus (*Ant.* 14.10,15 § 233), in which the consul Fannius Strabo (consul, 161) asks for safe passage through Cos for a Jewish embassy.

17. Judas sent Eupolemus—whose father John had won concessions for the Jews from Antiochus III (2 Mc 4:11), and who was from the priestly line of Hakkoz (1 Chr 24:10; Ezr 2:61)—and with him Jason, son of Eleazar. They were to establish a treaty of amity (*philia, amicitia*) and alliance (*symmachia, societas*) with the Romans, which in effect was often the first step toward Roman domination of a country. **18.** The Gk yoke had not yet been broken to the extent of defeating Nicanor. **22.** The bronze tablets recording the treaty remained in Rome's capitol (Josephus, *Ant.* 12.10,6 § 416); a copy was sent in a letter to Judas.

The treaty (8:23–30) is similar in form to other Roman treaties. In v. 26, the phrase translated as "without receiving anything" was, in the original Latin, exactly the same phrase as in v. 28: "without deception." The original *sine dolo* (*ou meta dolou* of v. 28) was misread as *sine dote* (and so *outhen labontes* in v. 26). **31–32.** The Senate sends a threatening letter to Demetrius at the same time. Its contents are summarized here from the point of view of 1 Mc's author.

34 **(N) The Defeat and Death of Judas (9:1–22).** Demetrius avenges the death of Nicanor (7:43) by sending a larger force to meet and overcome Judas, who is slain in battle.

An enemy force—from the Jewish standpoint, the "right wing" of the descending Seleucid army (9:1)—entered Galilee (the Gk text mistakenly reads *Galgala*; Hebr *gilgal*) and encamped along the highways (Gk *maisaloth* transcribes the Hebr *m^e^sillôt*, "highways") at Arbela, taking and killing many there. **3.** The main body of the Syrian army moved against Jerusalem (again in Jewish hands); the date is May, 160. Not finding Judas there, the Seleucid generals moved the army to Berea, 10 mi. N of Jerusalem, opposite Judas' camp at Elasa.

At the sight of so strong an opponent, the Jewish army dwindled through desertion to 800 men. Discouraged, Judas was still determined to do battle, going against the sound advice of his loyal followers, because he was reluctant to stain his glory (2:51,64; 3:3; etc.).

In battle, the pincers of the Seleucid army surrounded Judas' small band, forcing him to concentrate on only one jaw of the closing trap. He chose to fight against the stronger wing, where Bacchides was, and savagely beat it back toward Mt. Hazor (reading *azôrou orous*; the *azôtou orous* [Mt. Azotus] of v. 15, and also the *azaorous* of Josephus, *Ant.* 12.11,2 § 429 are results of scribal errors). Hazor is mentioned in 2 Sm 13:23; Neh 11:33; 1QapGn 21:8).

The left wing of Bacchides' army swung behind Judas, and before the day was done, Judas was dead. The remnants of his followers fled. Josephus says (*Ant.* 12.11,2 § 432) that Judas' brothers obtained his body under a truce; perhaps they did, for with Judas gone and the Jews defeated, Bacchides could afford to be more lenient. On the family memorial at Modin, see 13:25–30. **21.** This cry combines the plaint over Saul (2 Sm 1:19) with the notion that Judas was a "savior" or "judge" (Jgs 3:9; 2 Kgs 13:5). **22.** *but the rest:* It echoes the stock phrase used of the kings (1 Kgs 11:41; etc.).

35 **(IV) Jonathan Continues the Struggle (9:23–12:54).** With Judas gone, the revolt collapsed for a while, but soon Jonathan took command, and, although he was pursued for a while, he was eventually victorious over Bacchides. Then, aided by Seleucid intrigue for power, Jonathan achieved positions of importance—high priest, governor—under Alexander Balas and succeeding kings. In time, however, he fell victim to the treachery of the ambitious Trypho.

(A) Jonathan Succeeds Judas as Leader (9:23–34). After Judas' death, the "transgressors of the Law" came to power again. Famine sped the collapse of resistance in the countryside; whatever stores were on hand were government controlled. Bacchides and Alcimus used their power to follow up their advantage, rooting out and destroying those sympathetic to Judas. **27.** *a prophet no longer appeared:* Judea's anguish was similar to that experienced in the disappearance of prophecy after the Exile. Josephus (*Ant.* 13.1,1 § 5) and 1 Mc 4:46; 9:54 associate this disappearance rather with Haggai and Zechariah than with Malachi.

The reprisals stirred up Jewish antipathy again. Passing over Simon, the elder brother, for a reason unknown to us, the resistance elected Jonathan as its leader. He accepted, leading his newly assembled followers into hiding at Asphar (i.e., asphalt), a pool now thought to be near Tekoa. **34.** Possibly a misplaced doublet for v. 43.

36 **(B) Jonathan Avenges His Brother John (9:35–42).** For mobility, Jonathan decided to store much of his equipment with the Nabateans across the Jordan, a move made necessary by Bacchides' search for him (9:32–34). **35.** His brother John (Gaddi, 2:2) was detached as "leader of the people," or, rather, the officer in charge of bringing the baggage train (and some families?) to the Nabatean place of safety. Along the way, John was ambushed by "the sons of Jambri," who had their center of operations at Medeba, near the NE tip of the Dead Sea. John's company was killed (9:42) and the spoil taken away.

In revenge, Jonathan and Simon turned the wedding of a Canaanite (or "trader"; the Nabateans were skillful merchants) nobleman's daughter into a massacre. **37.** *Nadabath:* To be read with Josephus (*Ant.* 13.1,4 § 18) as *Nabatha*, the Aram form of Nebo (Nm 32:3). **41.** An allusion to Am 8:10.

(C) Bacchides Ambushes Jonathan (9:43–49). News of Jonathan's attack on the wedding party was brought to Bacchides, who crossed the Jordan (9:34,43) to ambush the Jews returning on the Sabbath (does 1 Mc subtly attribute Jonathan's falling into ambush to this action?). The Jordan marshes (9:42) mentioned here refer to the thickly wooded area at the Jordan's bed, particularly large and swampy in its southernmost extremity near the entrance to the Dead Sea.

45. Before Jonathan reached a ford, perhaps in a loop of the river, the trap was sprung. *before us and behind us:* Bacchides blocked the path to the Jordan; the Nabateans were in pursuit. **46.** *heaven:* The reference is to God. Jonathan fought his way through to the Jordan and crossed it. Bacchides neglected to pursue, perhaps to pick up the spoils of the wedding party (9:40) that Jonathan had to abandon. **49.** Bacchides' losses seem exaggerated.

(D) Bacchides Fortifies Judea; Alcimus Dies (9:50–57). Bacchides strengthened his grip on the land by establishing strongholds and fortifying cities throughout Judea. Fortresses were built at Jericho, Emmaus, Beth-horon (see comment on 3:15), Bethel, Timnath-serah (cf. Jos 19:50), Pirathon (cf. Jgs 12:13,15), and Tappuah (cf. Jos 12:17). The last three are in Samaria, thus outside of Judea (9:50). Bacchides added to the defenses of Beth-zur, Gazara, and the citadel at Jerusalem, also holding hostages in the latter.

54. In the second month (Iyyar) of the 153rd Seleucid year (about May, 159), Alcimus began to renovate the Temple. He ordered the removal of the wall separating "the inner court of the sanctuary," to which the Israelites had access, from the outer court, where Gentiles had access. Thus, "the work of the prophets," Haggai and Zechariah, who brought about the reconstruction of the Temple, was destroyed. The author views Alcimus' stroke as punishment for this nefarious act. **57.** Bacchides' work effectively curbed the resistance movement for two years.

(E) Jonathan Escapes and Frustrates Bacchides (9:58–73). Two years later (157), Jonathan's enemies plotted his capture, but the plot failed and he, in turn, avenged himself on its ringleaders. Then Jonathan withdrew to Bethbasi (S of Bethlehem), which he fortified. Bacchides followed him and besieged Bethbasi, but Jonathan slipped out and created a diversionary nighttime attack upon "Odomera and his kinsmen and the sons of Phasiron," presumably allies of Bacchides; while the latter was distracted, Simon burned his siege machines.

68. Frustrated, Bacchides decided to go home. He vented his anger on Jonathan's enemies—whom he accused of treachery (Josephus. *Ant.* 13.1,5 § 31)—made a pact with Jonathan, and departed. Bacchides did not, however, release the hostages in the citadel (9:53; 10:6). What military necessity or other reason drew him elsewhere, leaving Jonathan still unpunished, is not known, but his departure left Jonathan in peace at Michmash for five years, during which time he pursued his policy of punishing the ungodly whenever possible. He is compared (v. 73) to the judges of old, a warrior fighting the battles of the king of heaven.

37 **(F) Alexander Balas (150–145) Claims Demetrius' Throne (10:1–14).** In the 160th Seleucid year (152), a rival for the Seleucid throne appeared and occupied Ptolemais—Josephus says by treason (*Ant.* 13.2,1 § 35). Alexander, surnamed Balas (for *ba'al*) and also Epiphanes (supposedly after his father), claimed to be the son of Antiochus IV. In this claim he had the support of the kings of Cappadocia, Pergamum, and Egypt; he also won the friendship of Rome. Ancient historians, notably Polybius, the friend of Demetrius, rejected his claim, and called him an imposter from Smyrna. But the chief factor in antiquity for the acceptance or rejection of the new king as legitimate seems to have been the ancients' attitude toward Demetrius. Josephus and 1 Mc accept Alexander at face value for they oppose the reigning monarch. **2.** Other sources say Demetrius lost this first battle to Alexander.

Demetrius put in the first bid for Jonathan's loyalty, allowing him to recruit and equip troops and ordering that the hostages in the citadel (10:6; 9:53) be released to him (vv. 3–6). Jonathan immediately began restoration of the city defenses and of the fortress on Mt. Zion, which Apollonius and Eupator had pulled down earlier (1:31; 4:60; 7:62). Inasmuch as Jonathan was once again in a position of power, the Gentiles fled the strongholds built by Bacchides (9:50); presumably some went to the aid of Demetrius in the battle against Alexander. Only the renegade Jews remained, safe in the defenses of Beth-zur (and, Josephus adds, in the citadel at Jerusalem—*Ant.* 13.2,1 § 42). It seems they retained Gazara as well (11:41; 13:43).

38 **(G) Jonathan Supports Alexander Balas and Becomes High Priest (10:15–50).** Alexander also appealed to his "brother" Jonathan for support. In return, he offered the high priesthood and a position as the king's "friend" (see comment on 2:18). **20.** *a purple robe and a crown of gold:* The first is symbolic of the rank of king's friend; both symbolize the high priesthood. Although the legitimate heir to the high priesthood was Onias IV, who had fled to Egypt when Alcimus was appointed high priest (Josephus, *Ant.* 12.9,7 § 387), neither 1 Mc nor Josephus seems to question the validity of Jonathan's appointment. For them, if Alexander were king, then by long-established Oriental custom he had the right to appoint his choice as high priest. Jonathan was, in fact, a member of a priestly family (2:1).

Abel and Starcky (*op. cit.*, 57–58) give this moment as that in which the *ḥăsîdîm*, later to be known as the Essenes, withdrew their support from the Maccabees. The bulk of the Hasideans continued to favor the Hasmoneans until the time of John Hyrcanus (134–104). The Essenes' disappointment lay in Jonathan's assumption of the high priesthood and its implicit displacement of Onias IV—son of Onias III (2 Mc 3:1ff.)—who was in exile in Egypt. Consequently, the sectaries followed their teacher of righteousness into the desert in protest. (The date of the teacher of righteousness, however, is much disputed. Many authors place him later.) Perhaps, say Abel and Starcky, this is the moment when Onias IV chose to build the rival temple at Leontopolis, near Cairo.

Jonathan put on the "sacred vestments" (10:21; see Ex 28) to begin functioning as high priest at the Feast of Tabernacles, celebrated from the 15th to the 23rd day of the seventh month (Lv 23:33–36) in the Seleucid year 160 (October, 152).

22–25. Demetrius, not to be outdone by Alexander, appealed once more to Jerusalem, not only to Jonathan, but also to the Jews as a whole. **26.** Either he did not know, or pretended not to know, that Jonathan had gone over to Alexander. The prizes he offered included the following: exemption from tribute, i.e., various taxes (10:29), including that on salt (taken from the Dead Sea?); remission of monies paid to the crown (10:29); release of Demetrius' share of the grain and fruit (10:30; see Lv 27:30, where tithes from the land are paid to God); tax exemption for Jerusalem and environs, which, as "holy," have now to pay their former taxes to God (10:31); cession of the citadel to the "high priest" (10:32; here, Demetrius implicitly recognizes Jonathan's new status, which was granted him by Alexander!); the return of captives (10:33; and the restoration of their cattle without payment of back taxes?); freedom for Jews throughout the empire from performance of civic duties on holy days (10:34–35); service in the king's army (10:36–37; at the king's expense, not Judea's, as was customary; with this concession would go positions of status and trust in the military service, and also religious freedom [presumably not to fight on the Sabbath; see 2 Mc 15:1–5]); annexation of three "nomes" (i.e., three toparchies, 11:28, or districts) from Samaria and Galilee (10:30; an administrative division otherwise unknown; the districts are in Samaria [10:38]—Aphairema [Ephraim], Lydda, and Rathamin [Arimathea] in 11:34); the gift (10:39) of Ptolemais and environs (which Alexander now controlled!) with their revenue to be used for support of the Temple; further revenue for the Temple, to be gathered from taxes elsewhere (10:40), unpaid official contributions (10:41), and release of funds formerly appropriated by royal officials (10:42); remission of debt and return of property for those who fled to sanctuary in the Temple (10:43); reconstruction of the Temple at the king's expense (10:44); and defensive construction at the king's expense (10:45). Dancy (*op. cit.*, 146–47) seems unduly hesitant on the authenticity of this letter's contents.

Jonathan (slighted in the letter) and the people rejected Demetrius' offer, preferring Alexander. **47.** *first to address them:* Actually Demetrius was first (10:3–4). The idea here is that Alexander's friendship was preferable. **48–50.** Fortunately for Jonathan, he chose the right side. Demetrius died bravely in battle against Alexander (Josephus, *Ant.* 13.2,4 § 60), and possession of the monarchy was settled (the year was 150).

39 **(H) At Alexander's Marriage, Jonathan Is Promoted (10:51–66).** In the Seleucid year 162 (150 BC), Alexander arranged for his marriage with Cleopatra Thea, daughter of the same Ptolemy VI Philometor for whose sake ostensibly Antiochus IV Epiphanes had invaded Egypt in 169 (1:18). Jonathan was called to the wedding where he met the two kings at Ptolemais. There he was honored by Alexander, who refused to hear complaints against Jonathan and instead promoted him to the rank of "first friend" (see comment on 2:18), making him also a general (*stratēgos*) and provincial governor (*meridarch*), presumably of the enlarged Judea (10:30).

(I) Jonathan Defeats Apollonius, the General of Demetrius II (10:67–89). Three years later, a new claimant to the throne appeared, Demetrius II (145–138, 129–125), son of the slain Demetrius I. Setting out from Crete with mercenaries led by Lasthenes (11:31), Demetrius landed in Cilicia and soon proved a serious threat to Alexander, who hurried home to secure Antioch (Josephus, *Ant.* 13.4,3 § 87). Demetrius appointed Apollonius over Coele-Syria (see comment on 3:38)—the same Apollonius who had helped Demetrius I escape from Rome (Polybius, *Histories* 31.11–15). Apollonius descended on Jamnia, besieging it. His challenge to Jonathan (10:70–73) brought the angry response of battle. **72.** *your fathers:* Probably alludes to Judas' two defeats (6:47; 9:18). **73.** *in the plain:* Wherever superior armament—cavalry, chariots, elephants—could be brought to bear, i.e., on the lower lands along the coast, the Israelites throughout history were generally no match for their technologically more advanced adversaries (note the slow conquest of the Philistines). **74–83.** Jonathan got behind Apollonius, taking Joppa and cutting off his line of communications. Apollonius countered by pretending to withdraw toward Azotus, meanwhile edging further into the plain. He left a large detachment of cavalry behind to swing in behind the pursuing Jonathan. Jonathan fell into the trap, but then stood his ground; when the enemy cavalry was tired, Simon's men (held in a sort of reserve?) moved up to attack the weary enemy phalanx. This counterattack succeeded, and the enemy was routed. **84–86.** Jonathan chased them to Azotus, burned that city and its surrounding towns, and then destroyed those who had taken refuge in the temple of Dagon (a stronghold of sorts?). Ashkelon capitulated without a fight.

87–89. Jonathan returned to Jerusalem with his plunder. The overjoyed Alexander rewarded him by giving him Ekron and its territories, and making him a "kinsman (*syngenēs*) of the king." The insignia of this highest court order in the empire was a golden buckle fastening the purple cloak at the recipient's shoulder.

40 **(J) The Alliance Between Demetrius II and Ptolemy (11:1–13).** Ptolemy VI Philometor tried to add part of Alexander's domains to his own. Josephus says that he was alienated from Alexander by an assassination attempt at Ptolemais, but 1 Mc calls it camouflage (11:11; *Ant.* 13.4,6 § 106). If Ptolemy were still friendly to Alexander, why would he leave his own garrisons in the cities he passed? And why would he listen, even silently, to complaints against Jonathan in Azotus? Apparently he fooled Jonathan, for the latter accompanied him to the Eleutherus River (Nahr el-Kebir, 19 mi. N of Tripolis). Ptolemy certainly made his intentions clear when he reached Antioch; "he put on the crown of Asia" (v. 13). Meanwhile, he took control of the coast northward to "Seleucia-by-the-sea" (slightly N of the Orontes). He also gave his daughter, Alexander's wife, to Demetrius. Diodorus says (*Historical Library* 32.9) that Ptolemy was not ambitious for the whole of Asia but only for Coele-Syria, being content to leave the rest of the Seleucid Empire to Demetrius, partly, at least, because he feared the Romans. Josephus (*Ant.* 13.4,7 § 114–15) supports this theory in part.

(K) The Deaths of Alexander and Ptolemy (11:14–19). To the north, Alexander was busy with revolt in Cilicia, but he returned to do battle with Ptolemy at the Oenoparas River near Antioch (Strabo, *Geography* 751). Defeated, he fled for refuge to the Arab Zabdiel (called Diocles by Diodorus, *Historical Library* 32.9), who murdered him immediately, cutting off his head. Ptolemy also died, of wounds inflicted in battle, but not before he saw the head of Alexander that Zabdiel had sent him. Demetrius now had a clear path to the throne of the whole Seleucid Empire, which, Josephus says (incorrectly), Ptolemy had in mind for him anyway (*Ant.* 13.4,7 § 114–15). With Ptolemy dead, the coastal cities in his power rose against their Egyptian garrisons to kill them. The rest of the Ptolemaic army returned to Egypt. It is at this point that Demetrius became *de facto* ruler of the empire, in the 167th Seleucid year (145). He had begun his bid for power two years earlier. Now, also, he began to call himself Nicator, "conqueror," because of his double victory over Alexander and Ptolemy.

41 **(L) Jonathan's Pact with Demetrius (11:20–37).** Jonathan felt that it was time to rid the citadel in Jerusalem of its pagans and renegade Jews. When report was made to Demetrius of Jonathan's siege, the king summoned him to Ptolemais. Jonathan went at the risk of his life, but he also disregarded the king's command and left orders that the siege was to continue. Once at Ptolemais, Jonathan won Demetrius over, as earlier he had Alexander (10:59–66). Many of the privileges granted by Demetrius I (10:25–45) were confirmed by his son. What reasons, other than Jonathan's personality, impelled the king to generosity with a former adversary (10:67–85) are a matter for conjecture. Perhaps he needed allies, for he was becoming increasingly unpopular at home. **30.** *his brother:* Jonathan was "kinsman" to Demetrius, as he was to Alexander (10:89). *Lasthenes:* Chief minister to Demetrius (Diodorus, *Historical Library* 33.4), and hence he received the original letter for his files. **34.** *all those who offer sacrifice:* They could now pay certain royal taxes to the Temple instead. **37.** The royal rescript granting these privileges was to be publicly posted on Mt. Zion.

(M) Trypho's Intrigue Against Demetrius (11:38–40). Once in undisputed possession of the throne, Demetrius' next objective was to make his reign secure. On the advice of Lasthenes, presumably, who dominated the 16-year-old king, Demetrius dismissed the bulk of his army and did not pay them peacetime wages, as previous kings had done to assure their loyalty in times of stress. He retained only the mercenaries from Crete and the islands (Josephus, *Ant.* 13.4,9 § 129). Naturally, the king became more unpopular, and Trypho, one of Alexander's generals, took advantage of it. This man, Diodotus Trypho (he adopted his surname meaning "self-indulgent" after his victory over Demetrius II), was a native of Apamea and had served in the army of Demetrius I. He had gone over to Alexander, then to Ptolemy. Now he went to Imalkue and promised to set up Alexander's son Antiochus (VI) as king.

(N) Jonathan Aids Demetrius (11:41–53). While Trypho was with Imalkue, Jonathan helped Demetrius put down a revolt in Antioch. **41.** The king offered his troubles with his army as his excuse for not removing the troops from the citadel in Jerusalem and from the fortresses (Beth-zur and Gazara; 10:14; 13:43). He appealed to Jonathan for help and got it. 1 Mc says that the Jews, and Diodorus says (*Historical Library* 33.4) that the Cretan mercenaries, put down the uprising of the populace at Antioch. No doubt both were responsible (as Josephus implies; *Ant.* 13.5,3 § 137), the Jews turning the tide of battle for the mercenaries loyal to Demetrius. Their victory did not help the Jews, however, except for the booty gained, because Demetrius reneged on his word and rewarded Jonathan with "great trouble," which Josephus says was the threat of invasion to collect tribute (*Ant.* 13.5,3 § 143).

42 **(O) Jonathan's Alliance with Trypho (11:54–62).** As Diodorus noted (*Historical Library* 33.4), their subjects were beginning to find the descendants of Antiochus IV Epiphanes a more pleasant lot of masters than the offspring of his brother Seleucus IV. Consequently, when Trypho proclaimed Antiochus VI the new king at Chalcis (SW of Aleppo), he soon had the backing of the dismissed troops of Demetrius, the city of Apamea (NW of Hamath), and the elephants captured from Ptolemy. The young king began his reign in the Seleucid year 167 (145) with Trypho as the real power directing affairs. Disappointment with Demetrius now put Jonathan in Trypho's camp, and he began to serve the new Antiochus VI Epiphanes Dionysius as faithfully as he had served his father Alexander (10:47).

57. When Antiochus gained control of Antioch, he confirmed Jonathan in the high priesthood and in his former ranks of "friend" and "kinsman" (the gifts signify the latter; 10:89). He also reappointed him as governor (*meridarch*; 10:65) "over the four districts" or nomes. Three of these are probably those in 10:34,38; 11:34—Aphairema (Ophrah), Lydda, and Rathamin

(Arimathea of Mt 27:57). The fourth is uncertain, but it is possibly Akrabattene rather than Ekron of 10:89. **59.** At the same time, Simon was made general (*stratēgos*) for the area along the *paralia* or seacoast, from the Ladder of Tyre (N of Ptolemais; Josephus, *JW* 2.10,2 § 188) to the frontier of Egypt at Rhinocolura or Raphia.

Jonathan traveled throughout the country "beyond the River," i.e., W of the Euphrates, gathering troops for the coming struggle on behalf of Trypho; he encountered only temporary resistance at Gaza.

(P) War Between Jonathan and Demetrius (11:63–74). After the battle in which he was defeated by Antiochus' army (11:55), Demetrius established himself at Seleucia-by-the-sea, where he retained control of Cilicia, Mesopotamia, and the coastal cities of Tyre, Sidon, and Gaza (until Jonathan's visit in 11:61–62). In the summer of 144, he sent a force against Jonathan to Kadesh in Galilee with the intention of destroying Jonathan's power. Jonathan went northward to meet this army, leaving Simon to recapture and garrison Beth-zur (11:65–66). Jonathan encamped near the waters of Gennesaret (the plain on the NW shore of the Sea of Galilee, which is also called in the NT the Sea of Tiberias; Jn 6:1). Then he moved to battle in the Plain of Hazor.

Demetrius' generals, Sarpedon and Palamedes (Diodorus, *Historical Library* 33.28) had apparently set another ambush for Jonathan, who had a penchant for falling into them. His soldiers panicked, and Jonathan made the traditional signs of distress (11:71) and prayed. However, Mattathias, Absalom's son (cf. 2 Mc 11:17), and Judas, Chalphi's son, stood firm. Josephus says that about 50 men also stood their ground (*Ant.* 13.5,7 § 161). Once again, as in 10:79–82, determination turned defeat into victory.

43 **(Q) Treaties of Friendship with the Romans and Spartans (12:1–23).** After the defeat of the Achaean League by Lucius Mummius in 146, Sparta, which had not associated with the League, attained new prominence in Hellas. Jonathan now (144) decided that it was time to make a new friend for his people and to renew friendship with the Romans. His envoys were received favorably in Rome, where the official policy was still to foment division as a means of conquering the Syrian Empire. In Sparta, equal acceptance was given the Jewish ambassadors Numenius and Antipater (is his father the Jason of 8:17?). **5.** *senate:* The technical term (*gerousia*) for what was later to be the Sanhedrin. Here, it is equivalent to the "elders" of 7:33; 13:36; 14:20,28.

7. Arius' letter to Onias cited by Jonathan in his letter to the Spartans is accepted by Josephus at face value in *Ant.* 13.5,8 § 167; he cites it in *Ant.* 12.4,10 § 225–27, where he identifies the letter's Onias with Onias III (died 170). Inasmuch as it would be too late for the Spartan King Arius I (309–265) and it could hardly be Arius II, who died as a child of eight in 255, Josephus must be wrong. The proper correlation of sender and recipient exists if they are Arius I and Onias I (high priest *ca.* 300). "Arius" is a correction for "Darius," based on Josephus and 1 Mc 12:20.

The letter itself is thought by modern scholars (e.g., Dancy, *op. cit.*, 167–68) to be fictitious. The practice of constructing a common ancestry for originally distinct peoples or tribes was not unknown in the OT (Gn 10; 35:22–26). It extended into the Hellenistic world too; there is inscription evidence from 126 for a similar diplomatic fiction of a common origin for the Tyrians and the inhabitants of Delphi. Whether a nation honored such common origin depended upon its foreign policy at the moment. The Spartans saw no reason to deny Jonathan's allegation (see 14:20).

In vv. 9 and 14–15, Jonathan somewhat undiplomatically reminded the Spartans that the Jews made no demands on them, for Jewish reliance is on "heaven" (God) and the "holy books" (the Scriptures); the latter are not specified further.

44 **(R) Military Activities of Jonathan and Simon (12:24–38).** Demetrius' generals, anxious to avenge themselves (11:63–74), met Jonathan with a larger army. Again, Jonathan went to confront them, this time warily (12:26; see 11:68). He found them in the "country of Hamath." It cannot be the region immediately adjacent to ancient Hamath, which is too far N. More likely it is the area at the "entrance to Hamath," the great plain between the Lebanon and Antilebanon mountains. Once Jonathan's adversaries were aware that he could not be taken by surprise—apparently he had superior strength—they slipped away by night and retired beyond the Eleutherus, apparently the northernmost limit of Jonathan's military command (11:7,60). Jonathan then continued his march to establish his military power throughout his area. He suppressed the Zabadeans, Arab nomads who had presumably opposed him. Meanwhile, Simon established himself along the coast in his own military district (11:59). He received news of a projected coup in Joppa, and thus placed a more trustworthy garrison there.

35. Jonathan, no doubt in the winter of 144, called together the Jewish elders to plan further defensive structures in Judea. He was particularly concerned with strengthening Jerusalem's defenses, which had been torn down by Antiochus IV (1:31) and Antiochus V (6:62) and were now only partially rebuilt (10:10). He also planned to starve out the men in the citadel (12:36). **37.** Work was begun and completed on Chaphenatha, whose location, although uncertain, is thought to be that of the "second quarter" in NW Jerusalem (2 Kgs 22:14). Simon built a headquarters (13:13) and fortress at Adida in the Shephelah, the foothills or low country between the hill country of Judah and the coastal plain.

45 **(S) The Capture of Jonathan (12:39–54).** Trypho's ambition aroused him to plot against Antiochus VI. For his intended coup to be effective, however, he realized that he must curb the growing power of the Jewish leaders. He decided to neutralize Jewish resistance to his plan by seizing their leader. Jonathan, unsuspecting, met Trypho at Beth-shan and was persuaded to dismiss the army he had brought with him. Trypho lured him to Ptolemais, killed his followers, and made him prisoner there. **49–52.** Jonathan's forces remaining in "Galilee and the great plain" (of Esdraelon) made a strategic retreat to Judea. **52.** *they mourned:* Because they naturally assumed that Jonathan had been killed along with his men (13:23 shows it was not yet true). **53.** News of Jonathan's capture signalled an upsurge of anti-Jewish feeling.

46 **(V) Simon as Leader of the Jews (13:1–16:24).** The last of Mattathias' sons (2:1), Simon did not become the leader of his people until after the deaths of his younger brothers Judas and Jonathan. As leader, however, he was apparently more successful against the deteriorating Seleucid Empire. He fortified Jerusalem and Judea, held off Trypho, allied himself successfully with Demetrius II and for a while with Antiochus VII, built a family tomb at Modin, renewed friendship with Rome and Sparta, and in general showed constructive leadership of the Jews until he, too, was murdered, a victim of the treachery of Ptolemy, son of Abubus.

(A) Simon Becomes Leader of the Jews (13:1–11). With Trypho about to attack Judah, Simon acted quickly to assure leadership for the Jewish defense. He reminded the Jerusalem assembly (presumably the leaders or elders of 12:6; 13:46; etc.) that the house of Mattathias had acted out of zeal for the Law and the Temple to the extent that Judas (9:18), Jonathan (see comment on 12:52), Eleazar (6:46), and John (9:36,42) had all perished in the struggle. Only Simon was left to fight for his people, and he was willing to assume leadership and give himself for their cause. His speech rekindled their enthusiasm, and they elected him their leader (vv. 1–9).

Simon's first defensive measures (vv. 10–11) were to speed construction of Jerusalem's walls and to strengthen the garrison at Joppa (12:33–34), driving out the native populace there because he feared that they would attempt to hand over the city to Trypho (Josephus, *Ant.* 13.6,4 § 202).

(B) Simon Blocks Trypho (13:12–24). 12–19. On the pretext that Jonathan owed the government money, Trypho bargained with Simon for ransom and hostages. Simon, at Adida (see 12:38), knew that Trypho was lying, but he had to meet the demand lest he be thought to allow the death of Jonathan through ambition. Trypho, of course, broke his word.

20–24. With Simon's fortress at Adida blocking the direct route to Jerusalem from the coast, Trypho tried the same fishhook maneuver that Lysias attempted earlier (4:29; 6:31), so as to come up upon Jerusalem from the south. Again Simon was in the way, blocking Trypho at Adora (about 4 mi. SW of Hebron), always staying between Trypho and his objectives. **21.** The men in the citadel begged Trypho to relieve the siege that Jonathan began (12:36) and to try another approach "by way of the desert." This desert is not identified. Possibly Trypho tried to approach Jerusalem from the Transjordan; v. 22 places him in Gilead later, and Abel locates Baskama (13:23) NE of the Sea of Galilee. More recently, however, some authors have identified Baskama with the Sycaminum of Strabo's *Geography* (16.2,27; Tell es-Samak, W of Haifa). In that case, Gilead must be changed to Galilee in 13:22. Trypho then went home the way he came, after killing Jonathan near Baskama.

(C) Simon Constructs a Family Monument at Modin (13:25–30). Amid great lamentation, Simon brought the remains of Jonathan home to Modin, where the last of the Maccabean brothers began construction of a family monument. The memorial tomb now built was covered with polished white marble (Josephus, *Ant.* 13.6,6 § 211–12) and topped by seven pyramids, one each for Simon's parents, his four brothers, and, presumably, himself. In the base of the monument supporting the pyramidal superstructure, columns were set in half-relief, and at the top of the base a decorative frieze of panoplies and ships alternatively encircled the structure. The tomb, which could be seen by sailors, was extant, at least in part, as late as the 4th cent. AD, according to Eusebius (*Onomasticon*, "Modeim").

47 **(D) Simon Joins Demetrius II (13:31–42). 31.** At this point in the Maccabean history, there is some confusion over the order of events. 1 Mc 13:31–32 tells of the murder of Antiochus VI by Trypho, who succeeded the young king in 170 (142 BC). This account is followed in 1 Mc 14:1–2 by the Median expedition of Demetrius II in 172 (140 BC) and the subsequent capture of Demetrius by the Parthians (in 173). Diodorus (*Historical Library* 33.28), Livy (*Periochae* 55), and Josephus (*Ant.* 13.7,1 § 218) say, however, that Trypho killed Antiochus VI (at the age of 10, and thus in 173 or 139 BC—Livy, *Periochae* 55) only after Demetrius had been captured by the Parthians.

The probably correct sequence follows: the deposition of Antiochus VI in 142, the Median expedition of Demetrius (140) and his capture (139), and the murder of Antiochus VI (139), with the subsequent proclamation of Trypho as king, although he had been reigning effectively for four years. Quite possibly, 1 Mc anticipates the young king's murder at the time that it speaks of Trypho's open seizure of power. Josephus and Livy tell the mode of Antiochus' death: Trypho bribed the king's doctors to operate on their young patient for a bladder stone and to kill him in the process.

32. Trypho now "put on the crown of Asia," i.e., of the Seleucid Empire (1 Mc 8:6). **33.** Meanwhile, Simon took defensive measures in preparation for a change in allegiance. Because Trypho's taxes amounted to pillage of Judea, and because he was the murderer of Jonathan, Simon went over to Demetrius. The first step was to send an embassy to the king.

35. The hard-pressed Demetrius was glad to welcome Simon as an ally and to grant him whatever favors would assure his friendship, although Demetrius may not have intended to keep his word (see 11:53). The king's letter repeats many of the concessions of 1 Mc 11:33–36 (see 10:25–45), but of special importance is the remission of the annual tribute from Jerusalem. **36.** The title "friend of kings" was probably added by the author on the basis of 14:39. **37.** *gold crown...palm branch:* Peace offerings, not the crown of annual tribute (v. 39), which was now remitted. **38.** All the tax remissions of 145 BC (11:33–36) remained in effect, and Simon was left in peaceful possession of the fortresses he had built (e.g., Adida, 12:38). **39.** The "oversights and shortcomings," i.e., Jewish support of Trypho, were forgiven, and Jewish troops, of fierce memory (11:41–51), were invited to join Demetrius' soldiery.

41. The remission of the crown tax effected the removal of "the yoke of the Gentiles" from Israel, and a new era began—that of Simon, the great high priest. This new period did not replace the Seleucid era; it simply coincided with the first year of Simon's authority. Simon is also called *stratēgos* (governor) and *hegoumenos* (leader) of the Jews, titles presumably conferred upon him by the king, which show that Jewish independence was not yet complete and that the Jews remained within the framework of the Seleucid Empire. The 170th year is 142 BC. (Here Josephus ends his paraphrase of 1 Mc as the main source of *Ant.;* see *Ant.* 13.6,7 § 217.)

48 **(E) The Capture of Gazara and the Citadel (13:43–53).** Simon evidently decided that while Demetrius and Tryphon were occupied with each other's ambitions and could not afford to invade Judea, the time had come for purging unwanted elements from the midst of Israel. Bacchides had fortified various places in and about Judea (9:50–52), but most of these had since come into Jewish hands (10:12–14; 11:65–66). Only Gazara and the citadel at Jerusalem remained to be taken, and this Simon now proposed to do. **43.** Gazara is taken by storm, with the aid of a siege machine (despite ms. evidence to the contrary, Gazara and not Gaza is to be read as the city here, see 14:7,34; 15:28,35; Josephus, *Ant.* 13.6,7 § 215; *JW* 1.2,2 § 50). **47–48.** The renegade Jews and pagans who garrisoned Gazara, and who had provided refuge for Judas' enemies (4:15; 7:45), were expelled, replaced by "men who observed the Law."

Siege (lasting for three years?; see 13:36; 13:21) reduced the Jerusalem citadel to submission. Again Simon purified his conquest of its "impurities" (Gk *miasmata*; see comment on 4:43), particularly of the idols of the pagan garrison. **51.** The date given corresponds to June 4, 141. **52.** This day is made a festival (for similar decrees, see 4:59; 7:49). The citadel had been a nuisance since Antiochus IV Epiphanes had it constructed in 167.

53. Simon's son, John Hyrcanus, was appointed military commander of the resident forces in Gazara.

49 (F) Demetrius II Is Captured by the Parthians (14:1–3). For the correct order of events see comment on 13:31–42. The Parthian king Mithridates I (also known by the dynastic name of Arsaces VI, 171–138 BC) had extended his rule over the whole of the Iranian plateau; in July, 141, he had defeated Dionysius, Demetrius' satrap, and had also usurped Babylonia. Demetrius began his campaign to dislodge Mithridates from the Tigris-Euphrates Valley, and ultimately from the Iranian plateau, in the 172nd year, or 140. **2.** Initially successful, Demetrius was taken prisoner by the Parthians, who violated an armistice to capture him. Arsaces, "the king of Persia and Media"—i.e., the Parthian conqueror of these territories that Demetrius was trying to win back—treated his captive kindly, and he was freed in 129. For a time he recovered his throne, but he was assassinated in 125 BC.

50 (G) The Glory of Simon (14:4–15). The praise of Simon covers his activities in 1 Mc. **4.** *the land was at peace:* Because no Seleucid army invaded it during Simon's rule. **6.** *he enlarged the boundaries of his nation:* By capturing Joppa, Gazara, and Beth-zur; Josephus adds Jamnia (*Ant.* 13.6,7 § 215). **7.** *he recovered...captives:* In Galilee (see 5:23). For the captured Seleucid strongholds, see 13:43–48; 11:65–66; 13:49–52. **8.** The benefits promised for observance of the Law in Lv 26:3–4 are now realized. **9.** Cf. Zech 8:4. **10.** Cf. 1 Mc 12:34; 12:38; 13:33; 14:33. **12.** Cf. Mi 4:4; Zech 3:10. **14.** The "lowly" are the true keepers of the Law, in contrast to the "lawbreaker and wicked man." It was for the Law that the whole struggle had begun (13:3; 14:29).

51 (H) Renewal of the Alliances with Rome and Sparta (14:16–24). It was customary in Hellenistic diplomacy to renew treaties of friendship whenever one of the governments party to the treaty changed hands. Upon Simon's accession to the high priesthood and leadership of the Jews (in 142; 13:41), he would have sent an embassy to Rome and Sparta to renew the pledges given by Judas (to Rome in 161; 8:1–32) and Jonathan (to Rome and Sparta in 144; 12:1–23). The present position of the materials in 14:16–24 and 15:15–24 gives the impression that the treaty renewals took place after the capture of Demetrius II in 139 (14:1–3). But 14:40 and 15:22 presuppose that Demetrius had not as yet fallen into the power of the Parthians. A more precise dating for the treaty renewal is derived from the Roman reply in 15:16—Lucius Caecilius Metullus Calvus was consul in 142. Thus, the embassy from Simon visited Sparta and Rome in 142 and returned in the same year.

Verses 17–19 refer only to the Romans because Judas did not make a treaty with Sparta; he is referred to in v. 18. The Roman letter is not preserved; only a summary of its contents is found here. An accompanying letter, to surrounding kings and countries, is quoted in 15:15–24. **18.** *they wrote:* In reply to Simon's embassy (14:21–22,24). *bronze tablets:* These are at Rome. See comment on 8:22. **22.** Numenius and Antipater were also the envoys of Jonathan (12:16). Josephus (*Ant.* 14.8,5 § 146) mentions this embassy, but places it much later, in the reign of Hyrcanus II (63–41). He also adds Alexander, son of Dorotheus, to the envoys (see 1 Mc 15:15, "companions"). **24.** *after this:* Although the results of the more important mission to Rome have already been given in 14:17–19, in the order of accomplishment the trip to Rome must have been subsequent to, and a continuation of, the trip to Sparta. The gold shield Numenius brought with him was "worth" (not "weighed") 1000 (silver) minas. Its weight was thus about 100 lbs., comparable in size to decorative shields found at Pompei.

52 (I) Decree of the Jews Honoring Simon (14:25–49). The decree now recorded on Mt. Zion is similar in form to that found praising public benefactors in many Gk cities of the period. It details the merits of the recipient and the honors decreed to him. **26.** *bronze tablets:* For similar important documents so inscribed, see 8:22; 14:18. The tablets were presumably affixed to pillars of the porticoes surrounding the Temple. **27.** This date, 18 Elul (sixth month of the vernal year), 172 of the Seleucid era, the third year of Simon's rule, is approximately September 14, 140. *in Asaramel:* The translator of 1 Mc apparently took it to be a place name, reading an original *beth* before the phrase as the Hebr preposition "in." Following him, several authors (among them Simons and Starcky) reconstruct *Asaramel* in Hebrew as *ḥăṣar ʿam ʾēl*, "the court of the people of God." But the *beth* should rather be read as introducing a description, the *beth essentiae*, and the phrase reconstructed as *śar ʿam ʾēl*. Thus, the translation would read, "...the third year of Simon the high priest as ruler (lit., prince) of the people of God." The title is then the equivalent of the Gk title "ethnarch."

In the body of the decree, the deeds of Simon are largely those mentioned in 1 Mc 13; even the language is similar. **29.** *Joarib:* See comment on 2:1; vv. 29–30 summarize the bulk of 1 Mc and lead to Simon's accomplishments, particularly as noted in 1 Mc 13. **31.** *enemies desired to invade:* Trypho (13:1). **32.** *spent his own money:* An allusion to 13:15–19? Simon also outfitted the army at his own expense, a fact that not only shows him as benefactor of his nation but as an independent prince as well. Earlier, Jewish soldiers were paid out of the royal treasury. **33.** *fortified:* See 13:33. *Beth-zur:* Cf. 11:65–66. **34.** *Joppa:* Cf. 13:11. *Gazara on the borders of Azotus:* See comment on 5:68. The borders of the province of Ashdod now reached to within 5 mi. of Gazara (Gezer). **35.** Cf. 13:7–8; 13:42. **36–37.** See 13:49–52.

Not so much because he wanted to, but because he had to recognize Simon's achievements, Demetrius made Simon the high priest and "friend" (13:36). The king also made him *stratēgos* (governor); see 13:41. **41–43.** The honors are decreed for Simon by the Jews. The Gk cities began the recital of honors by saying, "it seems good to the people...." It is paralleled here in v. 41, "and the Jews...were pleased to make Simon...." Simon (and his family—note the "forever") was established as Jewish high priest and leader until the coming of a "true prophet." The Jews of this time believed that prophecy had ceased (see 4:46; 9:27). When a prophet worthy of belief should arise, he would decide—i.e., God would tell him—whether it was legitimate for Simon's descendants to hold the high priesthood. Apparently some contested the right of the sons of Joarib to the office of high priest (see comment on 10:20). **43.** *contracts...dated by his name:* See comment on 13:41–42. The purple robe and golden buckle (see v. 44) are the insignia of the high priesthood (cf. 10:20). **47.** Simon accepted the roles of high priest, *stratēgos*, and ethnarch (see v. 28). **49.** Inasmuch as these offices were to be hereditary, Simon and his sons were entitled to copies of the decree.

53 (J) Antiochus VII Grants Privileges to Simon and Besieges Trypho (15:1–14). Antiochus VII (138–129) was the son of the slain Demetrius I (see 10:50) and the brother of Demetrius II. Sent by his father to a place of safety, Antiochus VII had grown up at Side in Pamphylia. Hence he was popularly known as Sidetes. His official surname was Euergetes ("benefactor"). Josephus (*Ant.* 13.7,1 § 222; 13.8,2 § 244) gives additional surnames: Soter ("savior") and Eusebes ("pious"). Hearing of his brother's capture by the Parthians, he accepted the invitation of Demetrius' wife, Cleopatra, to come to Seleucia and marry her (for her earlier marriages, see 10:57–58; 11:12), thus establishing a claim to the Seleucid Empire.

1. *from the islands:* Antiochus was at Rhodes at the time. **3.** *wretches:* Notably Trypho. **4.** Antiochus proposed to land his army, probably at Seleucia, where Cleopatra waited. **5–6.** Antiochus, adding to the previous tax exemptions (see 10:28ff.; 13:37ff.), granted Simon and the Jews the right to mint coinage. Actually, no coins have been found that can safely be attributed to Simon's rule; the privilege was soon revoked by Antiochus anyway (15:27). **7.** Jerusalem and the Temple area are declared free (see 10:31; 10:43), but, in fact, all of Judea was effectively in Jewish hands and beyond Antiochus' control (see 15:25–36).

10. The 174th Seleucid year is 139. Trypho's soldiers first went over to Cleopatra (Josephus, *Ant.* 13.7,1 § 221); she, in turn, put them under Antiochus' command. Antiochus then defeated Trypho in battle (Josephus, *Ant.* 13.7,2 § 223) and pursued him to Dor, S of Mt. Carmel. There, Trypho was tightly besieged.

54 **(K) The Return of the Embassy Sent to Rome (15:15–24).** See comment on 14:16–24. This letter of Lucius (Caecilius Metullus Calvus) was addressed to Egypt, to Ptolemy VIII Euergetes II (Physcon, 145–116), who was asked to hand over any rebels to Simon. **22–24.** A copy was sent to Simon. The letter was circulated to five kings in all: Ptolemy, Demetrius II (see comment on 14:2), Attalus II of Pergamum (159–138), Ariarathes V of Cappadocia (162–131), and Arsaces of Parthia (i.e., Mithridates I, 171–138; see comment on 8:13). The letter was also sent to various free states, particularly the cities in Greece, the Gk islands, and various places and leagues in Asia Minor.

55 **(L) Antiochus Breaks His Alliance with Simon (15:25–36).** Antiochus finally succeeded in shutting Trypho up in Dor (15:10–14). In support of this undertaking, Simon sent Antiochus a considerable amount of men and materiel, which Josephus (*Ant.* 13.7,2 § 224) says that Antiochus accepted, although 1 Mc notes the contrary. Instead, the king sent Athenobius to demand the return of places seized by Simon, or at least indemnification for them. **30.** *places...outside the territory of Judea:* Most likely the four districts of 11:57.

Simon's reply to Athenobius justified possession of these territories named on the grounds that they were Israelite lands unjustly taken from his people by their enemies. Despite the practical exigencies of Seleucid politics, the Maccabees, as all true Yahwists, had never conceded ownership of the holy land to a foreign people. Simon was willing, however, to pay an indemnity for Joppa and Gazara. The king became furious when his envoy returned with this message.

56 **(M) John Hyrcanus and Judas Defeat Cendebaeus (15:37–16:10).** Once Trypho has successfully escaped to Orthosia, Antiochus must pursue. Eventually he captured Trypho at Apamea and had him killed (Josephus, *Ant.* 13.7,2 § 224). Meanwhile, he appoints Cendebaeus as *epistratēgos*, "govenor general," placing him over the seacoast (*paralia*; see 11:59) and giving him special powers to deal with the Jews. From Jamnia, the capital of the *paralia*, Cendebaeus built up a forward base of operations at Kedron (about 3 mi. SE of Jamnia) from which he harassed Judea.

When John Hyrcanus, whose Gazara fortress (13:53) was nearest Cendebaeus' activity, reported to his father what was happening, Simon, now about 60, sent John and Judas, another son, to remove the threat. **4.** *cavalry:* First mention of Maccabean cavalry. **6.** John's crossing without fear is reminiscent of the action of Judas in 5:40–43. **7.** Judas' tactic was to place his cavalry so that the infantry protected their flanks; in this way he could offset the numerical superiority of the Seleucid cavalry. **8–10.** Defeated in battle, Cendebaeus and his forces fell back to Kedron and strongholds near Azotus.

57 **(N) The Murder of Simon and His Two Sons (16:11–22).** Ptolemy, Simon's son-in-law, was now driven by ambition to plot against his in-laws. As governor of the fertile region just N of the Dead Sea, he invited Simon and his sons Judas and Mattathias to a banquet at Dok, where he slew Simon. **14.** The 177th Seleucid year is 134; the month Shebat roughly corresponded to February in that year, with the year beginning in the spring. **15.** *Dok:* A hill fortress, 5 mi. NW of Jericho.

Ptolemy wrote to Antiochus VII and to the Jewish troop commanders (*chiliarchs*) to seek support. Meanwhile, he sent other men to Gazara to kill John, who, warned in advance, turned the tables on his would-be assassins and killed them.

(O) Conclusion to 1 Mc (16:23–24). With the escape of John from Ptolemy's assassins, 1 Mc ends his story of the Hasmoneans. The formula of 16:23–24 is similar in style to the summations of 1–2 Kgs (1 Kgs 14:19,29; etc.). The walls alluded to in v. 23 are presumably those built by John after the death of Antiochus VII, who had destroyed the walls of Jerusalem (Josephus, *Ant.* 13.8,3 § 247).

COMMENTARY ON 2 MACCABEES

Since much of 2 Mc traverses the same ground as 1 Mc, it should not be necessary to repeat much of the commentary on events treated in both books. The reader will find amplification of remarks pertinent to 2 Mc in the earlier part of this commentary.

58 **(I) Letters to the Jews of Egypt (1:1–2:18).** For the authenticity and date of these letters, → 5 above.

(A) The First Letter (1:1–9). This letter, urging the observance of the "feast of Tabernacles in the [ninth] month of Kislev," i.e., Hanukkah, was written in the Seleucid year 188 (124 BC). It contains another letter (vv. 7–8), which was probably written to inform the Jews in Egypt of the loss of Jonathan (1 Mc 12:48; 13:23). This earlier letter, dated to 169 (143 BC), contained an account of the apostasy of Jason and its aftermath until the dedication of the Temple (174–164), and presumably urged the Jews in Egypt to observe this feast commemorating the cause for which Judas and Jonathan had struggled. The present letter is a continued reminder to observe the feast. Its incorporation and date (124 BC) probably mark the completion of the Epitomist's work.

1. *greetings:* A Hellenistic salutation (inserted by the translator of the letter). *peace:* The Palestinian, Hebr greeting (original to the letter). **2.** *may he remember his covenant:* See Lv 26:40–46; God will not forsake his faithful in strange lands. **4.** *may he open your heart to his law:* To keep you from the false worship of Onias IV's temple at Leontopolis? **7.** *the critical distress:* The loss of

Jonathan and its sequel. *Jason:* See 2 Mc 4:7–5:10. *holy land:* See Zech 2:12; Wis 12:3. **8.** *we offered:* See 1 Mc 4:36–51.

(B) The Second Letter (1:10–2:18). This letter, written in 164 BC (→ 5 above), asks the Jews of Egypt to join with their Judean brethren in celebrating the new feast of the Temple's purification (1 Mc 4:36–59; 2 Mc 10:1–8). It is to be celebrated in the manner of the Feast of Tabernacles, which coincided with Solomon's dedication of his Temple (1 Kgs 8:2,65) and Joshua and Zerubbabel's establishment of their new altar (Ezr 3:3–4). The added reference in this new feast to "fire"—since commemorated in the special lighting of Hanukkah—recalls 2 Chr 7:1 and is explained in the letter by appeal to the memoirs of Nehemiah (1:19–2:13). For a description of the feasts of Tabernacles and Hanukkah and of the relationship between them, see De Vaux, *AI* 495–502, 510–14.

10. *Aristobulus:* A Jewish "philosopher" of Alexandria, who "taught" Ptolemy VI Philometor (180–145) by dedicating a book to him purported to show that the Greeks derived their wisdom and philosophy from the Law and the prophets (Clement of Alexandria, *Stromateis* 1.22). **11.** The "king" is Antiochus IV Epiphanes (175–164). **12.** *drove out:* Eventually; see 10:1. **13–17.** See comment on 1 Mc 6:1–17. **14.** *intending to marry her:* Antiochus hoped by such "marriages" to appropriate temple treasuries and thus to pay the cost of his wars and indemnities (9:2; 1 Mc 6:1–4). **16.** *leader:* The Gk text leaves the impression that (only) Antiochus was trapped and slain in this way. Actually he was driven off and died later (9 2–3,28–29; 1 Mc 6:4ff.). The information available to the writer of this letter may have confused the death of an officer, the "leader" of a group detailed to rob a temple, with that of the king, the "leader" of the whole army.

59 The section 1:19–2:13 derives from the (lost) memoirs of Nehemiah, including the "records" mentioned in 2:1,4. For the day of the feast to be held, 25 Kislev, see 1 Mc 1:59; 2 Mc 6:7; 10:5. The "fire" (v. 18) probably alludes to the fire from heaven of 2 Mc 2:9–10. Nehemiah did not rebuild the Temple or its altar (Ezr 3:2; 6:14); Ezr 2:2, however, associates him with the first returnees from the Exile. **19.** *Persia:* At that time, Babylonia. The pious priests were given the sacred fire by Jeremiah, according to 2:1. **20.** *thick liquid:* A pool of petroleum (see 1:34). This liquid's "fire" was thought to have fallen from heaven. Thus, the flame that consumed Nehemiah's sacrifices (1:22–23) was successor to that of Moses (Lv 9:24) and Solomon (2 Chr 7:1), although its miraculous element is muted by the appeal to natural elements, such as heat and the sun (see also Jgs 6:21; 1 Kgs 18:38; 9 Chr 21:26). **23.** *Jonathan:* Of the high priestly line (Neh 12:11; 12:22, Johanan). He need not have been high priest at this time. **24–29.** This prayer stresses Israel's monotheism and its special place as God's chosen people. **29.** See Ex 15:17; Dt 30:5. **31–32.** The fire-containing properties of the liquid are now seen clearly in the fact that it flares up when poured out upon presumably heated stones. **34.** The Persians, as Zoroastrians, considered fire holy. **35.** The verse should be translated to say that the king gave the newly founded Temple many gifts. **36.** The Persian word for this petroleum substance is *neft.* "Nephtar" involves a play upon the Hebr root *ṭhr*, "purify"; Nehemiah and his associates call the liquid "nephthar."

60 **2:1–3.** When Jeremiah entrusted the sacred fire to the priests (1:19), he also exhorted them to keep the Law and to avoid idolatry (see Bar 6:3).

4–12. Jeremiah's hiding of the Ark of the Covenant on Mt. Nebo is taken up again by the 1st-cent. apocryphal book, "Lives of the Prophets." Here he also hid the Tabernacle and the altar of incense. The whole story is improbable in the light of Jer 3:16. **4.** *mountain:* Nebo (Dt 32:49). **8.** God, says Jeremiah, will manifest himself so as to disclose the hiding place of the Ark. The manifestation will be like that which took place at the Exodus (Ex 16:10; 40:35) and at the dedication of the Temple (1 Kgs 8:10–11). The mention of the Temple's dedication recalls the fire from heaven upon the sacrifices of Moses (Lv 9:24) and Solomon (2 Chr 7:1), the latter at the Temple's dedication. Verse 11 is obscure (see Lv 10:16–19). **12.** See 1 Kgs 8:65–66; 2 Chr 7:9.

13–15. Nehemiah's memoirs also record his gathering of books considered important to the community. **13.** The "letters of kings concerning votive offerings" are the documents of Persian kings; their inclusion shows that Nehemiah's collection is not a canon of inspired books. Judas similarly makes a collection of "scattered" books, which were then available to the Egyptian Jews. The remaining vv. 16–18 urge the Egyptian community to participate in the new feast of the Temple's purification. **17.** An allusion to Ex 19:3–6 (see 1 Pt 2:9). **18.** See Dt 30:1–5.

61 **(II) The Epitomist's Preface (2:19–32).** Jason of Cyrene's five-volume work will be abbreviated to one, says the Epitomist, but Jason must take responsibility for the accuracy of details in the story (2:28–31). The Epitomist will concern himself with the arduous task of abbreviating so as to produce a result that is readable, memorable, pleasurable, and profitable (2:25). **21.** The miraculous element is characteristic of the genre of Jason's work—"pathetic" or rhetorical history. *Judaism:* The earliest known occurrence of this term (see also 8:1; 14:38; Gal 1:14) to describe the way of life in contrast to Hellenism (4:13). The epithet "barbarian" is not only an allusion to savagery (4:25; 5:22), but also a studied insult to the civilized status that Seleucid Hellenism arrogated to itself. **23.** Jason of Cyrene is otherwise unknown. Culturally, Cyrene was one with Egypt, and from the point of view of religion, the Jews there were dependent upon their Alexandrian brethren. As Jason's book proved, the influence was mutual.

62 **(III) The Decline of the High Priesthood (3:1–4:50).** The author now traces the rapid decline of the office of high priest. Perfect observance of the Law marked the term of Onias III (3:1); a corrosive Hellenization, that of the usurper Jason (4:13); theft and murder, that of Menelaus (4:25,32–34).

(A) The Episode of Heliodorus (3:1–40). After the treaty of Apamea (188), the Seleucid monarchs were badly in need of money for indemnities. Thus, when Simon alleged that the Temple treasury was full of money (with the implication of irregularities?), Seleucus was delighted and immediately moved to confiscate the treasure. God, however, protected these deposits from the king's agent, Heliodorus. (In 4 Mc 4:1–14 the episode happens to Apollonius, not Heliodorus.)

1. *Onias:* Onias III, son of Simon II (cf. Sir 50:1–21) and grandson of another Onias (Josephus, *Ant.* 12.4,10 § 225), whose Gk name appears (from the Hebr text of Sir) to be a contraction based on the Hebr *Yoḥanan*, "God is gracious." The family of Onias were descendants, through Jaddua (Ezr 2:36; 1 Chr 24:7; Josephus, *Ant.* 11.8,7 § 347), of Joshua, the high priest of the post-exilic community (Neh 12:10–11). **2.** *place:* Throughout 2 Mc, the Temple is often referred to in this way. **3.** *Seleucus:* Seleucus IV Philopator (187–175). *king of Asia:* See comment on 1 Mc 8:6. **4.** Simon is of the priestly class of Bilgah (1 Chr 24:14) according to the Lat codices L, B, and P, although the Gk text reads "Benjamin." Simon's office as administrator (*prostatēs*) of the Temple led him into conflict with Onias, who presumably overruled him in some matter relating to administration of the city market. Simon's next step was to go over the high priest's head to the governor of Coele-Syria and Phoenicia with a story calculated to bring about Onias' embarrassment, if not his dismissal, on charges of corruption. **5.** *Apollonius of Tarsus:* The son of Menestheus (4:4,21); therefore, he is identified here as being "of Tarsus" (the Cilician city) and not as "son of Tharseus," as the Gk text might otherwise be read. Apollonius later left office when Antiochus IV Epiphanes became king, going to Miletus (Polybius, *Histories* 31.13). For Coele-Syria and Phoenicia, see comment on 1 Mc 3:38. **7.** *Heliodorus:* Son of Aeschylus and a native of Antioch. Later, he killed Seleucus in an unsuccessful attempt to seize the throne. His present expedition is mentioned in Dn 11:20. **11.** Hyrcanus is properly the grandson of Tobias. The Tobiad family was sympathetic to Ptolemaic interests, and later, when Hyrcanus committed suicide for fear of Epiphanes, his property was confiscated by the Seleucid crown (Josephus, *Ant.* 12.4,11 § 236). **12.** Onias pleaded a form of "sanctuary" for the funds, but to no avail. The amount of the deposits seems exaggerated—their value today would be several million dollars.

22–30. God answered the populace's prayers. Some authors (e.g., Tedesche and Zeitlin, *Second Maccabees,* 128) suggest that Heliodorus made some arrangement with Onias, inasmuch as Heliodorus was shortly to assassinate the king. But 4:1 leaves the impression that some physical evil had befallen Heliodorus. The dressed-up story supplied by Jason of Cyrene (2:21), for whom the Temple's deposits were saved by a miraculous intervention, is typical of the literary form in which Jason writes. In the epiphany, Heliodorus is incapacitated (see a similar story in *3 Mc* 2:21–23). **31–34.** Not wishing to be charged with the murder of Heliodorus, the Jews prayed for his recovery, and once again the divine element was introduced. Verse 33b recalls Jb 42:7–8. **35–40.** Heliodorus acknowledged the supreme might of Israel's God and the protection he affords his sanctuary.

63 **(B) Simon's Plot Against Onias (4:1–6).** Frustrated, Simon continued to plot Onias's removal. **1.** Onias' fear (3:32) was justified. **2.** *laws:* Of the Seleucid kingdom, not the Torah (see B. Renaud, *RB* 68 [1961] 39–67, esp. 64). **5–6.** Onias reached the king too late; Heliodorus had already assassinated Seleucus. After some difficulty, Antiochus IV Epiphanes, the dead king's brother, succeeded him.

64 **(C) Jason, the High Priest, Introduces Hellenism (4:7–20).** For the important changes now taking place in Judaism, see comment on 1 Mc 1:11–15. **8.** Jason promised an increased tribute. The usual amount seems to have been 300 talents (1 Mc 11:28). **11.** *Eupolemus:* See comment on 1 Mc 8:17. *law:* Here, the Law of Moses. **12.** *the Greek hat:* The *petasos* was a wide brimmed hat worn by Hermes, the god of gymnastic skill. To "wear the *petasos*" was to take part in gymnastic exercises. **13.** *no high priest:* Josephus (*Ant.* 12.5,1 § 237) says that Antiochus gave Jason the high priesthood when Onias III died, because the latter's son, Onias IV, was still an infant. But 2 Mc intimates that Jason was no high priest because he obtained the office by bribery. **14.** The priests neglected their own ministry to take part in the "liturgy" (*chorēgia*; the author is being sarcastic) of the wrestling school as soon as the gong summoned them.

18. Games were held at Tyre as early as Alexander's time. **19–20.** *Antiocheans of Jerusalem:* For the importance of this designation, see comment on 1 Mc 1:11–15. *Heracles:* The Tyrian god Melqart was, in Hellenistic fashion, assimilated to Heracles (the Roman Hercules). Even the envoys saw the impropriety of Jewish money appropriated for pagan sacrifices; therefore, they applied it to a less compromising purpose—ship construction.

65 **(D) Antiochus Is Received by Jason in Jerusalem (4:21–22).** Earlier, Epiphanes had recalled Apollonius from Miletus (see comment on 3:5) and had sent him to Rome. Now, in 172, he sent him to Egypt to attend the coronation of Ptolemy VI Philometor (180–145). Ptolemy's mother, Cleopatra I (the sister of Antiochus IV Epiphanes), had governed Egypt for her son in his minority, until her death in 176. Subsequently, the king's ministers Eulaeus and Lenaeus made plans to regain Coele-Syria for Egypt (Diodorus, *Historical Library* 30.16). Antiochus wisely sent an experienced diplomat to assess Egyptian intentions, and Apollonius learned that the newly enthroned king, who had now come of age, was hostile to his Seleucid uncle. Antiochus then prepared for the impending invasion by stationing troops in Joppa and other Phoenician ports. At this time, too, Antiochus visited Jerusalem, where Jason welcomed him warmly with torches and acclamations.

66 **(E) Menelaus as High Priest (4:23–50).** The low state to which the high priesthood had sunk is evident in Menelaus' theft of the Temple's vessels to advance his own career. More successful than his brother Simon, he succeeded in having Onias murdered.

23. *three years:* These are counted from the beginning of Jason's pontificate in 174; thus, the year is 171. **24–26.** By the usual route of bribery (the sum seems excessive; 4:27 bears this out), to which he added flattery, Menelaus won the office of high priest for himself (on his ancestry, see comment on 3:4). Ousted, Jason fled to Ammon, probably to the southern part of Transjordan, held by the Nabateans (5:8). **27–38.** Menelaus and Sostratus, the latter the king's agent and commander of the Cypriot mercenaries at Jerusalem, were summoned to Antioch to explain their delay in forwarding the king's revenue. Coincidentally, Antiochus was called away to suppress a revolt by the Cilician cities Tarsus and Mallus (the latter on the Pyramus River near the Gulf of Issus), whose citizens objected to the transfer of their revenue to the king's concubine Antiochis. Menelaus then bribed Andronicus, the king's deputy in the matter, using vessels stolen from the Temple to obtain a favorable verdict. Onias denounced Menelaus for these thefts, first fleeing to sanctuary in the temple of Apollo at Daphne, about 5 mi. from Antioch. Andronicus' murder of Onias, at Menelaus' urging, shocked even the Greeks, for it violated a solemn pledge and showed contempt for the right of sanctuary. Antiochus promptly executed Andronicus in reprisal, first degrading him (see 1 Mc 10:64–65,89).

39–42. Apparently Lysimachus, Menelaus' brother and deputy (v. 29), had also been his agent in the theft of the Temple's vessels. When the crowds at Jerusalem grew riotous over this, Lysimachus sent a force against them that was beaten back. **43–50.** The Jewish elders (*gerousia*; see 1 Mc 12:6,35) brought charges against Menelaus, but when all seemed lost, bribery again brought Menelaus success. Later, as *stratēgos* of Coele-Syria and Phoenicia, Ptolemy opposed the Maccabean revolt (8:8; 1 Mc 3:38). The Scythians lived N of the Black Sea, in what is now the Soviet Union; they were proverbially cruel.

67 **(IV) Antiochus Epiphanes and the Imposition of Hellenism (5:1–7:42).** The author now turns to the troubles unleashed by the "Greeks," whom the Jews emulated (4:16). Antiochus despoiled the Temple, ravaged the city, and proscribed Judaism, with dire results for those who remained faithful to the Law.

(A) Antiochus Ravages Jerusalem (5:1–14). Antiochus' second campaign in Egypt, during which he was crowned king of Egypt at Memphis but then forced to retire by the Romans, led to the events that culminated in his slaughter of Jerusalem's citizenry. Looking back, Jason of Cyrene describes an ominous foreboding of these events by painting the scene of celestial cavalry in combat over Jerusalem. Josephus describes a similar omen presaging the Temple's destruction in 70 AD (*JW* 6.5,3 § 300–309).

5–7. Jason, hearing the news of Antiochus' check by the Romans in Egypt, was led to believe that the king was dead. With the support of Jerusalem's populace, he unsuccessfully attempted to capture Jerusalem and drive out Menelaus, who was backed by the pro-Seleucid Tobiad faction (Josephus, *Ant.* 12.5,1 § 239). **8–10.** Driven from his place of refuge with Aretas (Harith I, king of Nabateans), Jason set out to seek refuge with the Lacedaemonians (Spartans; see comment on 1 Mc 12:1–23). But he got no farther than Egypt, where he now lies in an unhonored and forgotten grave. **11–14.** Antiochus, frustrated by events in Egypt, interpreted Jason's attack as a Jewish revolt and ruthlessly vented his anger upon his Jewish subjects. In keeping with the rhetorical nature of Jason's account, the number of those killed or sold is exaggerated.

(B) Antiochus Despoils the Temple (5:15–23a). See comment on 1 Mc 1:20–24a. Theological reasons now explain the Temple's spoliation. Had not the people sinned by following Gk ways, Antiochus would have been beaten back, as Heliodorus earlier (3:1–40). Puffed up by his own pretensions, which reached even to divinity, so that he thought himself in control of nature (v. 21), Antiochus could not perceive that it was the power of a God temporarily angry, and not his own, that has allowed the sacrilege. **16.** *other kings:* Seleucus IV, for example (3:3). **21.** *a thousand and eight hundred talents:* Another inflated number. **22.** *administrators: Epistatai;* see 1 Mc 1:51. Philip appears again in 6:11; 8:8. He is not the Philip of 9:29 and 1 Mc 6:14,55. **23.** Andronicus is not the murderer of 4:31,34,38.

68 **(C) Apollonius Attacks Jerusalem (5:23b–26).** See comment on 1 Mc 1:29–35. Josephus (*Ant.* 12.5,5 § 261) notes that Apollonius is *meridarchēs* (governor) of Samaria. Later, Judas defeats and kills him (1 Mc 3:10–12).

69 **(D) Judas Maccabeus in the Desert (5:27).** Mention of Apollonius leads the Epitomist to introduce Judas, Apollonius' nemesis, thus skipping the story of Mattathias in his sources (see 1 Mc 2). But because it does not suffice to explain his own narrative, the Epitomist immediately breaks off to introduce Antiochus' forced Hellenization of Judea, adding stories that elaborate 1 Mc 1:62–63. This done, he returns to Judas in 8:1ff.

70 **(E) Antiochus Imposes Hellenism (6:1–11).** See comment on 1 Mc 1:41–64. To unify his kingdom (1 Mc 1:41), the king commands the adoption of Hellenism and the establishment at Jerusalem's Temple of the syncretistic cult of Zeus Olympios. What had been voluntary (4:7–20) now becomes obligatory. The year is 167.

1. *Geron:* See comment on 1 Mc 1:51. **2.** *Olympian Zeus:* See comment on 1 Mc 1:54. *Gerizim:* The rival Samaritan temple was built on Mt. Gerizim. *Zeus the Hospitable: Dios Xenios,* "protector of strangers." Josephus (*Ant.* 12.5,5 § 261) says that the Samaritans petitioned Antiochus to name their temple *Dios Hellenios,* dissociating themselves from the Jews, whom they knew to be under the king's wrath. **5–9.** Inasmuch as illicit sacrifices (6:18,21; Lv 11:7; 1 Mc 1:47) were offered, a man could not follow Jewish religious law. Instead, thanks to Ptolemy (4:45; 8:8), Jews throughout Coele-Syria and Phoenicia were forced to partake of swine on the king's birthday (1 Mc 1:58) and to join in the popular cult of Dionysus, god of wine and the grape harvest (a Hellenistic Feast of Booths!). **10.** See 1 Mc 1:60–61. **11.** See comment on 1 Mc 2:29–41.

71 **(F) The Epitomist's Evaluation (6:12–17).** See comment on 5:15–20. The Epitomist reminds his readers that the Jewish affliction is medicinal (7:33). God punishes his people now lest they become more wayward through lack of discipline and suffer the effects of a greater divine wrath in a later visitation. This paternal discipline is also found in Prv 13:24; 20:30; 23:13–14; Tb 13:5. With regard to the Gentiles, however, he waits until the measure of their sins is full before he punishes them (see Dn 8:23; 9:24). A complementary biblical view holds that God withholds punishment from men in view of their salvation. He allows them time for a change of heart, thus delaying the day of reckoning (Wis 11:23; 12:20; Rom 2:4–5); this is also why he delays the parousia (2 Pt 3:9).

72 **(G) The Martyrdom of Eleazar (6:18–31).** The story of Eleazar is elaborated in *4 Mc* 5–7 (see also *3 Mc* 6:1ff.; Heb 11:35b). By refusing the unclean food (Lv 11:7–8), Eleazar spurned the unlawful sacrifice and remained faithful to the Law, becoming a witness (martyr) to its importance and to its claims upon Jewish obedience. His refusal of the deception urged by his pagan(ized?) friends shows a conscience alert to the possibility of scandal. **23.** *Hades:* Abode of the dead. **26.** Eleazar seems aware of punishment after death for the sinner, a development over earlier OT ideas (see also Dn 12:2; *Enoch* 22:10–11). **29.** *madness:* See Wis 3:2; 4:16–5:8.

73 **(H) The Martyrdom of the Mother and Her Seven Sons (7:1–42).** Eleazar's example to the young (6:28) is not wasted. The author now shows that women and children are also willing to die for the Law. In this narrative, the author's artifice is more apparent (for a fuller development of the story, see *4 Mc* 8–18).

There is an evident progression in the words the brothers address to the king before dying: the just die rather than sin (7:2); God will vindicate them (7:6; Dt 32:36); God will raise them up (7:9); they will rise with bodies fully restored (7:11); but for the wicked, there will be no resurrection to life (7:14); instead, God will punish them (7:17); the just suffer because of their sins, as will the wicked (7:18–19); the death of the saints has impetratory, and even expiatory, value (7:37–38). Thus does 2 Mc state the theology of martyrdom and the resurrection of the just (see Dn 12:2).

1. *the king:* Inasmuch as the story is contrived, the chief persecutor himself is addressed. **6.** *Moses... canticle:* See Dt 32:36. **8.** *language of his fathers:* Hebrew (see vv. 21 and 27; 12:37; 15:29). **17.** *descendants:* Cf. 2 Mc 9 (Epiphanes); 2 Mc 14:2; 1 Mc 7:2–4 (Eupator); 1 Mc 11:17 (Alexander Balas); 1 Mc 13:31 (Antiochus VI). **22–23.** Cf. Ps 139:13–16; Wis 7:1–2; Eccl 11:5. **28.** The first biblical mention of creation *ex nihilo.* See also Heb 11:3. **29.** *I may get you back:* He will be restored to life with his family in the resurrection of the just, if he perseveres. **33.** See 5:17. **37.** See 9:12. **38.** See also the vicarious suffering in Is 52:13–53:12.

74 **(V) The Triumph of Judaism Under Judas Maccabeus (8:1–10:9).** In this section, the Epitomist follows Jewish resistance to Antiochus' edicts up to the point where the wicked persecutor dies and the victorious Judas purifies and rededicates the Temple.

(A) Judas Organizes Resistance to the Persecution (8:1–7). See comment on 1 Mc 2:42–48. The Epitomist now continues the narrative he had interrupted in 5:27. **2–3.** The guerilla band prays, then fights. Similar descriptions of the woes faced appear in 1 Mc 1:24–28,36–40; 2:7–12; 3:45,50–53. Destruction either visits or threatens the city in 1 Mc 1:31 (see 2 Mc 5:23b–26); 1 Mc 3:35; 2 Mc 9:4,14. (For the historical order of events at this point, → 11 above.)

(B) Judas Defeats Nicanor and Gorgias (8:8–29,34–36). See comment on 1 Mc 3:38–4:27. **8.** *Philip:* See comment on 5:22. *Ptolemy:* See 4:45; see comment on 1 Mc 3:38. **9.** *Nicanor:* He looms larger as the adversary in 2 Mc than in 1 Mc. **14.** *sold their property:* Lest it fall to Nicanor anyway. These men apparently joined Judas. Note the continual emphasis on prayer. **18.** See Ps 20:7–8. **19.** *Sennacherib:* See 2 Kgs 19:35. **20.** *the battle with the Galatians:* This incident of Jewish mercenaries in support of Macedonian troops is otherwise unknown. **23.** *Eleazar:* BJ suggests "Esdris," as in 12:36; see also 1 Mc 5:18,56, where he is called Azariah (which basically has the same meaning, "God—'El or Yāh—has helped"). This Eleazar is not Judas' brother (1 Mc 2:5; 6:43). **36.** Here 2 Mc gives the theological reason for victory: God defends and makes invincible those who keep his Law.

(C) Judas' Other Victories (8:30–33). See comment on 1 Mc 5:6–8,9–13,24–54. The parts of this fragmentary passage are difficult to locate. See 9:3; 10:24–38; 12:10–31. **30.** *Bacchides:* See comment on 1 Mc 7:1–25. **33.** *Callisthenes:* Otherwise unknown. For the gate-burning, see 1 Mc 1:31. (The events of 2 Mc 11 should be placed here, → 11 above.)

75 **(D) The Death of the Persecutor (9:1–29).** See comment on 1 Mc 6:1–17. Antiochus had agreed to peace terms after the defeat of Lysias at Beth-zur (1 Mc 4:28–35; 2 Mc 11 [except vv. 22–26]), but it still did not dispose him kindly toward the Jews. Frustrated in his Temple-robbing expedition, he now resolves to wreak vengeance on the Jews. Perhaps the immediate cause of his death was injury resulting from the fall mentioned in 9:7. What caused this fall, however, is not clear (heart trouble? v. 5). **8.** See 5:21; 9:12. The false god, Epiphanes "(Zeus) manifest," falls by the manifest power of the true God. The vivid account in 9:9–12 of the king's last moments seems more theological than descriptive of events. It echoes Is 66:24; 14:11; Sir 7:17; 19:3; Jgs 16:17. For similar description in the deaths of God's enemies, see Josephus, *Ant.* 17.6,5 § 168–79 (on Herod the Great) and Acts 12:23 (on Herod Agrippa). Antiochus' vow (vv. 13–18) is equally unlikely, or at least it is the measure of a desperate man and not a true change of heart (v. 17; see the fall and conversion of Nebuchadnezzar in Dn 4). 2 Mc does not allow God to hear Epiphanes' prayer (see comment on 6:12–17).

The letter in 9:19–27, if addressed to the Antiocheans and to the Hellenized Jews, is credible. Placed here, it seems to have other recipients—the Jews faithful to the Law, to whom the converted king commends his son. But remembrance of the king's "service" (v. 26) would not likely endear his son to these subjects. **23.** Antiochus III had appointed Seleucus IV his successor. **29.** *Philip:* See comment on 1 Mc 6:14.

76 **(E) Judas Purifies the Temple (10:1–9).** See comment on 1 Mc 4:36–61. Unable to celebrate the Feast of Booths earlier (6:6; 5:27), Judas and his men now celebrate the purification of the Temple in the manner of the Feast of Booths (10:6). **3.** *flint:* Starting a new fire (see 1:19–2:1). **4.** Again the note of prayer and penitence.

77 **(VI) The Subsequent Struggles of Judas (10:10–15:39).** The remaining chapters of 2 Mc detail Judas' various struggles against neighboring peoples and lead up to his victory over Nicanor and the subsequent establishment of a feast commemorating the event.

(A) The Suicide of Ptolemy Macron (10:10–13). Again 2 Mc introduces a fragment somewhat cryptically. The Epitomist notes the accession of Antiochus V Eupator (164–161) and his appointment of Lysias as chief governor over Coele-Syria and Phoenicia (previously, Lysias was Epiphanes' regent in the west; 1 Mc 3:32–33). Then, by contrast to the death of Epiphanes, he narrates the death of an official friendly to the Jews. Ptolemy Macron (the nickname means "long headed") governed Cyprus for the Egyptian king Ptolemy VI Philometor (180–145). When Epiphanes' fleet approached Cyprus for an invasion, he switched to the Seleucids rather than fight. Branded as a traitor even by his new allies, who despised his moderate Jewish policies, he was accused before the king (for another change of allegiance, to Jewish interests?), and, unable to bear another disgrace, he killed himself.

78 **(B) Judas Fights in Idumea (10:14–23).** See comment on 1 Mc 5:3–5. Gorgias is governor (*stratēgos*) of Idumea (12:32) and the "land of the Philistines," the maritime zone (1 Mc 5:68; see 1 Mc 11:59). **16.** Prayer again precedes battle; the author never loses sight of the source of victory. **17.** *twenty thousand:* Like the 9000 of v. 18 and the 70,000 of v. 20, the number seems inflated. **19.** Judas left his brother Simon and Joseph, the son of Zechariah (1 Mc 5:18), to besiege the towers.

79 **(C) Judas Defeats Timothy (10:24–38).** This passage, for which there is no parallel in 1 Mc, belongs chronologically some time after 1 Mc 5:9–13,24–54; 2 Mc 12:10–31. After earlier defeats (8:30ff.), Timothy mounted a more powerful expedition against the Jews. Again penitential prayer (10:25–26) preceded Judas' army into battle (10:27–28), and again divine aid—graphically represented by Judas' angelic bodyguard—assured a Jewish victory (10:29–30). Timothy was defeated, pursued, besieged, and killed (10:32–37). The victors gave God thanks (10:38). **26.** See Ex 23:22. **32.** *Gazara:* Because it was Simon and not Judas who took Gazara (1 Mc 13:43), it is better to correct the text to read Jazer, as in 1 Mc 5:8.

80 **(D) Victory Over Lysias at Beth-zur (11:1–15; 12:1).** See comment on 1 Mc 4:28–35. This narrative chronologically precedes the death of Antiochus IV Epiphanes. Lysias (see comment on 1 Mc 3:32ff.) was angry over the defeat of Nicanor and Gorgias, and set out to accomplish the king's directives (1 Mc 3:34–36); however, he was beaten at Beth-zur.

1. *king's guardian:* Eupator, not Epiphanes (1 Mc 3:33; 2 Mc 10:10). **3.** *high priesthood for sale:* See 4:7–8.24. It was to be the high priesthood of a Hellenized community, once the troublesome Jews had been eliminated (1 Mc 3:34–36). **5.** *five leagues:* Beth-zur was about 20 mi. S of Jerusalem. **6–12.** Again we have the familiar pattern of penitential prayer, angelic assistance, victory, and flight of the opponent. **6.** *good angel:* See 15:23; Tb 5:21. **11.** For different numbers, see 1 Mc 4:34. **13–15.** The sequel to the battle is an agreed-upon peace, in which the Jews are given their religious liberty. See the letters following. The later invasion under Eupator (1 Mc 6:28–63) is anticipated in 1 Mc 4:35.

81 **(E) The Letters (11:16–38).** The three letters in vv. 16–21, 27–33, and 34–38 belong to the peace negotiations following Lysias' campaign. The letter in vv. 22–26 belongs to Eupator's reign.

16–21. Lysias addresses the people, not their leader Judas. The letter alludes to the agreements of v. 15, although Lysias still notes some reservations (11:18). **17.** John may be Mattathias' son (1 Mc 2:2). Absalom's son is also active in the struggle (see 1 Mc 11:70; 13:11). **24.** The 24th of Dioscorinthius (the month is equivalent to the month Xanthicus; see vv. 30,33,38) of the 148th Seleucid year would occur in March, 164.

27–33. The letter of Antiochus Epiphanes to the "senate" (i.e., elders) of the Jews offers an amnesty and religious freedom. **29.** Menelaus was probably sent by Lysias to the king in Persia. Antiochus sent him back with the idea of restoring everything to the *status quo* preceding the imposition of Hellenism (4:50). Apparently Judas had already rejected Menelaus (see the reservations in Lysias' letter when he forwarded the king's decision; note also the disposal of Menelaus in 13:3–8 and Judas' further reluctance to accept Alcimus as high priest, 1 Mc 7). Eventually, the Hasmoneans themselves (Jonathan being the first) assumed the high priesthood (1 Mc 10:21). **33.** The 15th of Xanthicus, in the 148th Seleucid year, would be sometime in late March, 164. (For the problems connected with this impossible dating [and the dates of vv. 21,30,38], see Abel and Starcky, *op. cit.*, 39–43.)

34–38. The letter of the Roman legates confirms Lysias' arrangements and asks that they be informed about the Jewish reaction to the king's disposition of the still unsettled matters (v. 36). **34.** Abel and Starcky (*op. cit.*) correct the text to give three legates: Quintus Memmius, about whom nothing else is known; Titus Manilius (Torquatus), who was the Roman consul in 165 BC and on a diplomatic mission in the east in 164; Manius Sergius, also a well-known diplomat, who had been sent to Antiochus IV Epiphanes in 164.

22–26. This letter, belonging to Antiochus V Eupator, and thus to the peace negotiations after Lysias' second campaign (1 Mc 6:28–63; 2 Mc 13:1–26), reconfirms the religious freedom of the Jews and restores the Temple to them (which they possessed anyway; 1 Mc 4:36–61; 2 Mc 10:1–8). These terms were forced on Antiochus and Lysias by necessity.

82 (F) The Battles with Neighboring Peoples (12:2–45). See comment on 1 Mc 5:1–68. Because of harassment by surrounding peoples, whose governors provoked hostility, the Jews took up arms in a series of punitive raids and defensive measures. **2.** *Timothy:* Cf. 8:30–33; 10:24–38; 12:10–31; 1 Mc 5:24–54. *Apollonius:* Not the mysarch of 5:24–26; 1 Mc 1:29–35; nor the Apollonius of 2 Mc 4:21. *Nicanor:* Not the son of Patroclus in 8:9. This Nicanor commanded Cypriot mercenaries.

3–9. For the atrocity at Joppa, see comment on 1 Mc 5:55–68. **9.** *two hundred and forty stadia:* Approximately 30 mi.; the distance seems excessive. **10–31.** See comments on 1 Mc 5:9–13,24–54. **15.** Cf. Jos 6:1–21. **27.** *Lysias:* Not the governor of 10:11.

32–45. See comment on 1 Mc 5:55–68. **35.** *Dositheus:* See 12:19,24. **40.** The hidden objects were apparently amulets, etc., taken from the enemy dead in the attack on Jamnia (1 Mc 5:58). In Dt 7:25–26, these materials were ordered to be burned, but cupidity had led the soldiers to conceal them. The author makes this theft the cause of the soldiers' deaths, but 1 Mc 5:19,61–62 and Josephus (*Ant.* 12.8,6 § 352) attribute the casualties to disobeyed orders. **42–45.** These verses contain clear reference to belief in the resurrection of the just (see 7:11; 14:46), a belief which the author attributes to Judas (v. 43), although Judas may have wanted simply to ward off punishment from the living, lest they be found guilty by association with the fallen sinners (see Jos 7). The author believes that those who die piously will rise again (v. 45; 7:9), and who can die more piously than in a battle for God's Law (see 14:46)? Thus, he says, Judas prayed that these men might be delivered from their sin, for which God was angry with them for a while (7:32–33). The author, then, does not share the view expressed in *Enoch* 22:12–13 that sinned-against sinners are kept in a division of Sheol from which they do not rise, although they are free of the suffering inflicted on other sinners. Instead, he sees Judas' action as evidence that those who die piously can be delivered from unexpiated sins that impede their attainment of a joyful resurrection. This doctrine, thus vaguely formulated, contains the essence of what would become (with further precisions) the Christian theologian's teaching on purgatory.

83 (G) Lysias' Second Campaign in Judah (13:1–26). See comment on 1 Mc 6:28–63. **1.** The 149th Seleucid year is 163. **2.** The figures differ from those in 1 Mc 6:30; both sets seem inflated. **3–9.** This execution fits more logically after Lysias' frustration in Judea (see v. 4 and Josephus, *Ant.* 12.9,7 § 385). But perhaps another cause led to Menelaus' execution (see 4:27, 43–47). The method of execution was Persian. **4.** *king of kings:* See Ezr 7:7 (Artaxerxes). *Beroea:* The name given to Aleppo by Seleucus I Nicator (305–281). **5.** *fifty cubits:* About 75 ft.

The battles in ch. 13 appear to have been a series of victories for the Jews, but 1 Mc gives a better perspective. The Jews were on the point of complete disaster until news arrived of Philip's coup in Antioch (v. 23). Then the king made peace with the Jews so as to be free to face the greater threat at home. The letter of 2 Mc 11:22–26 belongs here chronologically. It confirms Jewish religious freedom and possession of the Temple (as in v. 23). **24.** *Gerar:* It is S of Gaza, on the seacoast near Pelusium. The administrative district now formed, the *paralia*, seems later not to have extended so far (see comment on 1 Mc 11:59).

84 (H) The Accession of Demetrius I Soter (161–150) (14:1–2). See comment on 1 Mc 7:1–4 and the paragraphs preceding it. **1.** *Tripolis:* So-called because the merchants of Sidon, Tyre, and Aradus once possessed separate walled city quarters (Diodorus, *Historical Library* 16.41).

85 (I) The Hostility of Alcimus (14:3–11). See comment on 1 Mc 7:1–25; 2 Mc omits Bacchides' expedition (1 Mc 7:8–25). The charges subsequently brought against Judas, mentioned in 1 Mc 7:25, are detailed here (see also 1 Mc 7:5–7). **4.** The year is 161 BC. **6.** *Hasideans:* See comment on 1 Mc 2:42–48; 7:12–18.

86 (J) Judas and Nicanor (14:12–36). See comment on 1 Mc 7:26–38. 1 Mc 7:27–30 speaks of Nicanor's "treachery," because it capsulizes 2 Mc 14:18–30 and presents the result. But 2 Mc speaks of friendship between the two for a time. Eventually, however, Alcimus succeeds in restoring the old enmity.

87 (K) The Death of Razis (14:37–46). This story, unparalleled in 1 Mc, resembles the martyrdoms of 6:18–7:42. Perhaps, also, it is related to the defeat of Nicanor at Capharsalama, narrated in 1 Mc 7:31–32. **46.** Razis, too, believes in the resurrection of those who die piously; cf. 1 Sm 31:4.

88 (L) The Defeat of Nicanor (15:1–37a). See comment on 1 Mc 7:33–50. The impending struggle is seen by the author as one between rival majesties—Yahweh (v. 4) and Nicanor (v. 5)—for possession of the holy city and its Temple. Nicanor's reliance on himself and his army (15:5–6) contrasts with Judas' reliance on God (15:7–8). Again, 2 Mc gives assurance of God's help through presentation of a heavenly vision, this time of Onias and Jeremiah.

1–5. Nicanor seemingly did not know, nor did the Jews with him, that Judas' followers had determined to fight on the Sabbath when necessary (1 Mc 2:41). **6–11.** The confident Nicanor, relying on his army's strength, was already contemplating the postbattle memorial of his triumph (v. 6), while Judas, who relied on God, encouraged his men for battle. **11.** *perfidy:* In violating pledges given to the *ḥăsîdîm* (1 Mc 7:12–18). Judas told his soldiers what they could expect if they surrendered (see also 4:34; 5:25; 12:3; 1 Mc 6:62). **12–16.** The vision of Onias III and Jeremiah, representing the Law (embodied in the priesthood of the Temple) and the prophets (v. 9), is a manner of portraying divine support for Judas and the gift (symbolized in the golden sword) of victory. The vision also illustrates the author's belief in the saints' intercessory power. **12.** *Onias:* The description recalls 3:1,31–34; 4:2,37; see 6:18–31. *Jeremiah:* See 2:1–8. **17–27.** The Jews decided to carry the battle to Nicanor (v. 17). **21.** *savagery of the elephants:* See comment on 1 Mc 6:34. **22.** Judas prayed for a victory such as that over Sennacherib (Is 37:36; 2 Kgs 19:35) and was heard. **28–37.** Instead of having a "trophy" or monument to his enemy's defeat (15:6), Nicanor became one (15:35). **36.** *Adar:* This month is the Seleucid Xanthicus (11:30,33,38). **37a.** *Mordecai's day:* Cf. Est 3:7; 9:20–23; 10:3. *the city:* Jerusalem.

89 **(M) Epilogue of the Epitomist (15:37b–39).** The Epitomist has attempted to please his readers (2:25). Picking up the imagery of the tempered wine at a banquet (see 2:27), he says that he has mixed the recitation of history with a pleasing style of narration. He commends his best efforts to his readers.

28

INTRODUCTION TO WISDOM LITERATURE

Roland E. Murphy, O.Carm.

BIBLIOGRAPHY

1 Dubarle, A.-M., *Les sages d'Israël* (Paris, 1946). Duesberg, H., and I. Fransen, *Les scribes inspirés* (Maredsous, 1966). Fichtner, J., *Die altorientalische Weisheit in ihrer israelitisch-jüdischen Ausprägung* (BZAW 62; Giessen, 1933). Gese, H., *Lehre und Wirklichkeit in der alten Weisheit* (Tübingen, 1958). Murphy, R. E., *Seven Books of Wisdom* (Milwaukee, 1960); *Introduction to the Wisdom Literature of the Old Testament* (OTRG 22; Collegeville, 1965). Noth, M. and D. W. Thomas (eds.), *Wisdom in Israel and in the Ancient Near East* (VTSup 3; Leiden, 1955). Schmid, H. H., *Wesen und Geschichte der Weisheit* (BZAW 101; Berlin, 1966). Von Rad, *OT Theology* 1, 408–59.

Specific studies: Castellino, G., *Sapienza Babilonese* (Torino, 1962). Leclant, J. *et al.*, *Les sagesses du Proche-Orient Ancien* (Paris, 1963). Van Dijk, J., *La sagesse suméro-accadienne* (Leiden, 1953). Würthwein, E., *Die Weisheit Aegyptens und das Alte Testament* (Marburg, 1960).

Periodical literature: Murphy, R. E., "Assumptions and Problems in Old Testament Wisdom Research," *CBQ* 29 (1967) 407–18. Robert, A., "Les attaches littéraires bibliques de Prov. I–IX," *RB* 43 (1934) 42–68, 172–204, 374–84; *RB* 44 (1935) 345–65, 502–25.

Encyclopedia articles: Fohrer, G., "*Sophia*," *ThWNT* 7, 476–96. Gese, H., "Weisheit," *RGG* 6, 1574–77. Hamp, V., "Weisheit," *LTK* 10, 999–1001.

2 OUTLINE

CONCEPT AND ORIGINS

3 The Christian Church has customarily applied the name "Wisdom Book" to Jb, Pss, Prv, Eccl, Ct, Wis, and Sir. Only in a very broad sense can Pss be rightfully included here; most psalms owe nothing specific to the wisdom movement in Israel (for the classification "wisdom psalms" → Psalms, 35:16). Canticles is a collection of love songs, and it may owe its preservation and present form to Jewish sages who recognized its contribution to the "good life." Outside of these books, the counsels in Tb 4:3–21; 12:6–13, and the poem on wisdom in Bar 3:9–4:4 deserve particular mention.

4 The concept of wisdom literature is elusive. The idea has been borrowed from OT studies and applied broadly to various extrabiblical works, and scholars vary widely in their use of the phrase. It seems best to define it according to the oldest examples, the *Sebayit*, or teachings of Egyptian monarchs and ministers. These are instructions concerning life and conduct, transmitted from teacher to student (often in the form of father to son). Observation and experience have molded the framing of these teachings. Their purpose is to train a worthy ruler or courtier, and the life setting is clearly the royal court.

Because of the similarity between the Egyptian sayings and the oldest Israelite wisdom (Prv 10ff.), the same life setting of the court and courtly interests is assumed for Israel. This assumption is reasonable because, as we shall see, the OT itself recognizes that wisdom is the property of Israel's neighbors; in fact, it measures Solomon's wisdom by the wisdom of Egypt and Arabia. Such a comparison with foreign models is never made for any other aspect of Israel's thought. Moreover, within the OT itself one can point to the famous parallels between the teaching of the Egyptian Amen-em-ope, and Prv 22:17–24:22, and to the non-Jewish characters, Lemuel and Agur, whose wisdom is recounted in Prv 30–31. The international character of this literature is further confirmed by the very sparse reference to anything specifically Israelite, such as cult, covenant, or salvation history. Courtly education, then, would seem to be the original purpose and life setting of this literature.

5 However, these origins have relatively little importance for the understanding of the OT wisdom books. They are very important for understanding the growth and direction of this literature but not for understanding the religious message. For one thing, the sayings themselves are not limited to courtly occupations. And all these books in their present form date from the post-exilic period when there was no longer king or court and the concept of wisdom was completely religious (cf. Prv 1–9). Hence, one must balance against the courtly origins of the wisdom movement the indisputable fact of the strongly religious and Yahwistic stamp of the post-exilic wisdom literature. Moreover, we shall see that the concept of wisdom in these writings has many facets.

6 The role of Solomon in the development of the wisdom literature was so emphasized in Jewish and Christian traditions that most of these books were attributed to him. Although Prv is entitled *mišlê s^elomoh* (despite the attribution of some chapters to Lemuel, Agur, etc.), only the material contained in chs. 10–22 and 25–29 can be dated to the pre-exilic period, and one cannot be sure how much belongs to Solomon's age. Canticles is entitled "The Song of Songs by Solomon." The author of Eccl presented himself as "David's son, king in Jerusalem" (1:1). The author of the Book of Wisdom likewise speaks in the person of Solomon (Wis 6:22–23). Evidently, pseudonymity was the practice in the world of the sages; it was one way of securing attention to one's message and of emphasizing the value of one's work. Solomon served as the prototype of the wise men, and the attribution to him came naturally (cf. J. Sint, *Pseudonymität im Altertum* [Innsbruck, 1960] 135–40). The very concept of author in the ancient world differs from the modern notion. As R. A. F. MacKenzie has remarked, "In Israelite tradition, in order to express the belief that books were holy and composed under the impulse of the spirit of God, they were connected with great names of the past, prophets and wise men, who were famous as having been instruments through which the spirit worked. For the Jews, this was their instinctive way of expressing a profound truth. They were unwilling to leave a sacred writing entirely anonymous for then there was no affirmation of its origin through a divinely inspired man" (*CBQ* 20 [1958] 4). Thus the Jews felt no difficulty in attributing the Pentateuch to Moses or the wisdom literature to Solomon.

7 In 1 Kgs 4:29–34 (MT 5:9–11) is provided the basis for the traditional association of Solomon and wisdom: God "gave" him wisdom that surpassed that of "all the people of the East and all the wisdom of Egypt." This statement takes it for granted that wisdom is an international affair. Israel knew that she was a latecomer to the wisdom movement and that its origins were to be found among the eastern Arabs and the Egyptians. W. F. Albright is of the opinion that Ethan and the other wise men mentioned in the context were Canaanites and members of orchestral guilds who exerted great influence on Hebr poetry (Albright, *ARI* 127). The mention of trees and animals (4:33) suggests fables of the type still represented in the Bible itself: Jotham in Jgs 9; Jehoash in 2 Kgs 14:9. But we know nothing about what is attributed to Solomon concerning "trees"—from the Lebanon cedar to the hyssop—or concerning "beasts, birds, and reptiles"; it is not clear whether these are wisdom sayings or a kind of wisdom literature (cf. A. Alt, *KlSchr* 2, 90–99); Albright has pointed to an ant proverb in the Amarna letters as a rough parallel to Prv 6:6; 30:25 (*BASOR* 89 [1943] 29–32). Generally, Israelite wisdom literature concentrated on humans, although interest in animals is evidenced in Jb 38–41 and Prv 30. Perhaps onomastica such as that of Amen-em-ope (about 1100 BC) can shed light on this Hebr interest in nature and natural phenomena (→ 21 below).

8 We have already noted that the Egyptian "teachings" had the very practical purpose of regulating the conduct of a courtier. High officials in the state should be excellent in all things: knowledge, reliability, diligence, and morality. They are urged, as by a father, to take to heart the sayings that enshrine these truths because they represent the way to success. One should not identify this attitude with modern pragmatism. It is not just that "honesty is the best policy"; there is a more fundamental philosophy at work for the Egyptian (as well as for the Hebrew): One must integrate oneself into the existing order of things (the Egyptian *Maat*) in an harmonious manner; the opposite is chaos, which is intolerable (H. Frankfort, *Ancient Egyptian Religion* [N.Y., 1961] 59–87; Frankfort's view is urged also by H. Gese and E. Würthwein).

9 Israel seems to have imitated Egypt in cultivating this type of literature, just as she had imitated Egypt in adopting the government of kingship. In 1 Sm 8:5,20, we are explicitly informed that Israel had recourse to kingship in imitation of the surrounding nations. The implications of this move were tremendous; we can see in the pages of the OT the increasing complexity of court life. With the kingship came the bureaucracy and the world of officialdom that royalty entails. Egypt would have been the most imposing model for Israel to follow (we think of Solomon's marriage to an Egyptian princess, 1 Kgs 3:1). The OT provides concrete evidence of the type of court official that functioned in Jerusalem: The list of officials in Solomon's reign (1 Kgs 4:1–6) mentions priests, scribes or secretaries, heralds (the *mazkîr* or "recorder"), and the major-domo of the palace. Training was necessary for all these dignitaries and for the little world of lesser ministers that functioned in the highly organized (1 Kgs 4:1–21) kingdom of Solomon. What more natural than that the training was at least in part patterned after the courtly ideals expressed in the ancient and imposing literature of Egypt? It is precisely in Prv that we find the Israelite instructions for the court officials; cf. W. McKane, *Prophets and Wise Men* (SBT 44; London, 1965).

10 It is not until the Isaian age that we find explicit references to the wise men, or *ḥăkāmîn*, and in the writings of this prophet the references are somewhat harsh: The strange work (of destruction), which the Lord will accomplish, will be exemplified in the case of the wise men—their wisdom shall perish (29:14). It is at least likely that Isaiah had in mind here the educated courtiers who were advisers to the king, as Ahithophel was to David (2 Sm 15:12; cf. R. Martin-Achard in *Maqqel Shaqedh* [Fest. W. Vischer; Montpellier, 1960] 137–44). He castigates Egyptian sages as well (19:11–12). Jeremiah also refers to the sages, describing them as opposed to the word of the Lord preached by the prophets (8:8–9; cf. 18:18; 9:22). He was also aware of wisdom in foreign parts: Teman (49:7) and Babylon (50:35; 51:57). Ezekiel describes the king of Tyre as "wiser than Danel," the almost legendary monarch who plays a role in the Ugaritic myth of Aqhat, son of Danel.

Although most of the sayings in Prv are applicable to the training of a courtier, several treat explicitly of courtier and king, especially in chs. 16 and 25. We learn of the exalted and sacred person of the king (16:10,12), in whose presence the courtier is to be humble (25:6–7).

11 However, it is by no means necessary to conclude that the wisdom sayings are all directly the product of a definite, educated class. It was among the sages, before and after the Exile, that the ideas were formulated and given expression. But we should also notice a popular wisdom that flourished among the peasants, the sturdy backbone of the nation. These roughhewn pearls of human experience are easily discernible in sayings like that quoted by David to Saul, "Out of the wicked comes wickedness" (1 Sm 24:14), or in the reply of the king of Israel to emissaries from Damascus, "Let not him who is girding on his weapons boast as he who is ungirding" (1 Kgs 20:11). The doctrine of collective responsibility was formulated thus: "The fathers have eaten green grapes, and the children's teeth are set on edge" (Jer 31:29; Ez 18:2). More than one of these popular sayings made their way into the prophetical books (e.g., Is 10:15). The riddle has ever been a favorite pastime of the people, and we may surmise that the popular numerical saying derives from the riddle. Thus, the question, "What are the things that never say "enough"?" finds an answer in Prv 30:16: the nether world, the barren womb, the earth, and fire. These examples suggest that popular influence upon the formal wisdom literature is not to be minimized. More stylized form and more specific application were worked out by the sages but folk wisdom also contributed to the sapiential movement.

12 Some scholars have asked whether or not the origins, or the original life setting of the wisdom literature, should not be pushed back beyond the court into the family (cf. J. P. Audet, *25th International Congress of Orientalists* [Moscow, 1960] 1, 352–57). Was the writing in the court schools entirely creative, or did it find a structured and precise heritage given to it by oral tradition, which it then adapted and transmitted in written form? The latter supposition is plausible. The most natural and primary milieu for wisdom in Israel—long before Solomon—would have been the family. Wisdom, then, is the legacy about life and living that a father transmits to his children; the elder Tobit is a good example (Tb 4:1ff.). The advice of the sages is admittedly the advice of father to son, and the "my son" phraseology so frequent in Prv points to the original and proper life setting of the wisdom movement, the home. The point is well taken: The home must have served as a focal point of education of youth. On the other hand, the formative influence of the educated classes and specifically of the Jerusalem court on the Israelite wisdom heritage is not to be disregarded. One should recognize both family and court as tributaries to the wisdom movement; cf. E. Gerstenberger, *Wesen und Herkunft des "apodiktischen Rechts"* (WMzANT 20; Neukirchen-Vluyn, 1966); W. Richter, *Recht und Ethos* (*StANT* 15; Munich, 1966).

EXTRABIBLICAL "WISDOM" LITERATURE

13 All would admit that the total concept of wisdom literature in Israel is not identifiable with the wisdom literature of any of its neighbors; Israel developed its own style, even though it owed much to others. Here we will stress the similarities.

14 **(I) Egypt.** The Egyptian *Sebayit* or "teaching" presents remarkable similarities with Prv. The extant royal teachings extend over a period of about 3000 years, from the instructions of Hor-dedef, Kagemni, Ptah-hotep, Meri-ka-re, Amen-em-het, Kheti (or "Instruction of Duauf"), Ani, Amen-em-ope, to the Insinger papyrus, which dates from the Ptolemaic period (several of these are translated in *ANET* 405ff.). The pattern of the teaching is fairly regular—a teacher transmits to a student certain instructions on conduct: "the beginning of the instruction which X made for his son [or student] Y." A prose introduction sometimes offers details about the circumstances, e.g., the various data in the preface to the work of Amen-em-ope concerning the author and student. The central concept of the Egyptian wisdom literature is *Maat*, the divine order or "truth" established and preserved by God. Man's conduct must agree with this *Maat*—justice or truth—which is also to be identified with God's will. The teachings of the ancients, tested by experience, are designed to put men in harmonious agreement with *Maat*, but, in contrast to the biblical manner, we do not find that things are explicitly commanded by God. There is a certain built-in pragmatism in the Egyptian *Maat* but it is not crass; it is that justice is the one true order, and any infraction of it brings its own revenge—it is the "abomination of God," as the Egyptian phrase has it, although with a nuance different from the biblical "abomination to the Lord."

15 The advice handed down to the student or "son" was designed to preserve him in justice; it would infallibly do so if he memorized and observed these rules. He was not expected merely to have a theoretical knowledge of them; he was also expected to know how to apply the proper rule in a given situation. One of the famous ideals in this literature is that of the "just, silent" man—the man who is master of the situation, in full control of his tongue and emotions—in contrast to the impetuous, rash person. But this ideal did not exclude clever speech, a talent that is particularly recommended by Ptah-hotep and the *Instruction for King Meri-ka-re:*

> If thou speakest, thou shouldst know how thou can explain [difficulties]. It is a [real] craftsman who can speak in counsel, [for] speaking is more difficult than any labor (Ptah-hotep, *ANET* 414a).

> Be a craftsman in speech [so that] thou mayest be strong, [for] the tongue is a sword to [a man], and speech is more valorous than any fighting (Meri-ka-re, *ANET* 405a).

Although the Egyptian wisdom literature developed certain emphases with the change of times and conditions, we will merely summarize here some of the common ideas so the reader may understand the general similarity with the biblical literature.

16 The *Instruction of Ptah-hotep* (vizier *ca.* 2450 BC) illustrates the broad characteristics of the wisdom literature. He counsels against pride and urges taking counsel with the ignorant as well as with the wise: "Good speech is more hidden than the emerald but it may be found with maidservants at the grindstones" (*ANET* 412b; cf. Prv 2:4). Conduct at the table of an important host is to be most circumspect (Prv 23:1ff.; Sir 8:1ff.; 31:12ff.). Absolute reliability is required in the young man who serves as a messenger (Prv 25:13). Friends are to be tested (Sir 6:7ff., and often). Evil women are to be avoided (Prv 6:24ff.; Sir 9:1ff.).

17 The father of Meri-ka-re (probably Wah-ka-re, who lived toward the end of the 22nd cent. BC) admonishes his son about wise rule and tells of some of his problems. But he also delivers himself of some typical sayings: "More acceptable is the character of one upright of heart than the ox of the evildoer" (*ANET* 417; cf. 1 Sm 15:22; Eccl 4:17).

18 The *Instruction of Amen-em-het* (died *ca.* 1960 BC) is directed to his son and successor. He warns him of the bitter disappointment given him by people whom he had favored and protected.

19 The *Instruction of Ani* portrays the virtues of the "just, silent" man, but his son (Chon-su-hotep) objects to his father's teaching as too ideal. Like many another student, he sees no profit in memorizing lessons. But he is told to listen. Many of the traditional exhortations appear: "Do not talk a lot. Be silent and thou wilt be happy.... Thou shouldst not express thy [whole] heart to the stranger, to let him discover thy speech against thee" (*ANET* 420a).

20 Best known to biblical students is the *Instruction of Amen-em-ope*. When E. W. Budge first published it in 1923, he pointed out its similarity to Prv, which was confirmed by German Egyptologist A. Erman in his detailed study of Prv 22:17–24:22 (→ Proverbs, 29:38–39).

21 Thus far the parallels from Egyptian literature have been truly akin to the OT wisdom literature. The common life setting is the reason. One can point also to other loose parallels: the onomastica, the "skeptical" literature, and the love literature.

Alt has called attention to the "nature wisdom" found in the Egyptian literature, which may give the key to the sayings concerning trees, cattle, birds, and fish attributed to Solomon (1 Kgs 4:23). The most outstanding example is the *Onomasticon of Amen-em-ope* (*ca.* 1100 BC), which testifies to an Egyptian interest in nature and natural phenomena. This type of work is a sort of encyclopedia of all knowledge, as the superscription informs us. It is concerned with all that Ptah has created—heaven and all that belongs to it, earth and all that is in it, what is spewed forth by the mountains and the flood waters, everything that Re shines on, all that grows on the earth. There follows a list: creatures in heaven, water, and earth; divine and royal persons, courtiers and officials, classes of work, kings of men (foreign as well as Egyptian); cities and buildings; and vegetables and foods. Some 600 things are listed in systematic fashion, and the work is left unfinished. It is worth noting that this work is also called *Sebayit*, the title used for the famous examples of Egyptian wisdom literature.

Alt points out the possibility that the "nature wisdom" derives from earlier Sumerian and Akkadian lists that have come to light. The most famous series is the so-called Akkadian *Ḫarra-Ḫubullu*, 24 tablets of hundreds of names of things, which progress beyond the earlier efforts of the Sumerians.

22 G. von Rad (*GesSt* 262–71) has pointed to the even greater pertinence these lists have to such biblical texts as Jb 38–39, Sir 43, Ps 148, and Dn 3:52ff., where the phenomena of nature are discussed, one after another. In particular, the Anastasi papyrus offers some similarity to Yahweh's speeches in Jb. Both run through a list of phenomena (primarily geographical in the Egyptian piece), and both resemble a "catechesis" addressed to a learner who has presumed to rebel against the teacher. The Egyptian text is filled with questions that remind us of the manner in which Yahweh smothers Job, "where were you when...?" (cf. *ANET* 475–79).

23 The prime example of skeptical or *Weltschmerz* (world-weariness) literature is the "Dispute over Suicide," or, as it is also called, "The Man Who Was Tired of Life." It presents some similarity with the theme of the suffering of the righteous man that is found in Mesopotamia and also in the OT (Jb, Eccl). But no real problem is posed or solved; the emphasis is simply on suffering and suicide, as the following selection illustrates:

> To whom can I speak today?
> [One's] fellows are evil;
> The friends of today do not love....
> To whom can I speak today?
> Hearts are rapacious;
> Every man seizes his fellow's goods....
> Death is in my sight today
> [Like] the recovery of a sick man,
> Like going out into the open after a confinement.
> Death is in my sight today
> Like the odor of myrrh
> Like sitting under an awning on a breezy day.
> (*ANET* 406b, 407a)

The Egyptian piece does not pose the problem as acutely as do the Mesopotamian and Hebrew counterparts. There is no real conflict, simply a resignation to death, which involves suicide, as the work concludes. For the Egyptian idea of the afterlife, → Aspects OT Thought, 77:168.

24 Another remarkable work is the "Protest of the Eloquent Peasant," which sets forth the theme of the right of the poor man to insist upon his rights. Once again individual lines remind the reader of the OT outlook: "Now justice lasts unto eternity; it goes down into the necropolis with him who does it. When he is buried and interred, his name is not wiped out upon earth [but] he is remembered for his goodness" (*ANET* 410a). This principle of the good name being an eternal memorial for a man after he dies is frequent in the OT (e.g., Wis 8:13, where the author speaks of leaving "to those after me an everlasting memory"). But pseudo-Solomon has also arrived at a deeper and fuller concept of immortality with God, which is expressed in a manner that is verbally similar to the Egyptian phrase, "for justice is immortal" (Wis 1:15); this phrase is much more pregnant with meaning than the aforementioned Egyptian words, "justice lasts unto eternity."

25 **(II) Mesopotamia.** Sumerian wisdom is an area about which we are as yet not very accurately informed, despite the efforts of J. van Dijk and the studies of E. Gordon (*BO* 17 [1960] 122–52). The difficulty lies in the present uncertainty of translation; the Sumerian language and its complex literary expression are not yet adequately understood. The center of this literature, of which the earliest remains date to 2400 BC, was the *e-dubba* (house of tablets), or academy, where the scribes copied the various works and taught others the methods of the academician. Van Dijk and Gordon, operating with a concept of wisdom that is too broad for biblical comparison, have delineated various literary types, such as proverbs, fables, satirical dialogues, precepts, etc. Here we shall illustrate only some of the more obvious points that Israelite and Sumerian wisdom literature have in common.

26 The *Instructions of Šuruppak* (to be dated about 2000 BC) have not yet been completely published (*BWL*

92ff.; S. N. Kramer, *JCS* 1 [1947] 33, n. 208). They contain the advice of a king to his son Ziusudra, the hero of the flood in the Sumerian version. The customary association between wisdom and royalty is found in Sumer also. The following lines are the most pertinent in the fragments thus far preserved and published:

O my [son], instruction I offer thee, take my instruction,
O Ziusudra, a word I would speak to thee, give ear to my word,
My instruction do not neglect,
My spoken word do not transgress.
(*BWL* 93)

Kramer has published a Sumerian text, which he claims is the first written record of human suffering and submission, but the similarity to Jb is questionable (for text, cf. VTSup 3 [1955] 170ff.). The Sumerians were rich in proverb literature, as the several collections being published by Gordon prove, but there are no striking similarities to which we can point here.

27 In his important publication *Babylonian Wisdom Literature*, Lambert supplemented the Babylonian texts in *ANET*. He rightly raises the question: What does wisdom in Assyro-Babylonian literature mean? He points out that "wisdom" is strictly a misnomer as applied to these works and that the classification is derived from the OT where "wisdom" is properly "religion." But in Mesopotamia wisdom had to do with skill in cult and magic lore. However, several texts are similar to the OT.

The *Counsels of Wisdom* is a collection of moral exhortations that may well be the admonitions of a vizier to his son (this address, "my son," is actually used) and is thus reminiscent of the style of the Egyptian and Hebrew sages. The advice is typical of Hebrew Prv and Egyptian *Sebayit:* avoidance of bad companions, careless and improper speech, kindness to the needy, harmony with one's neighbor, marriage prospects, honesty toward the king—all in about 150 lines. The collection is difficult to date, perhaps composed about the 14th or 13th cent. BC. The following example can be compared with Prv 13:3:

Let your mouth be controlled and your speech guarded:
Therein is a man's wealth—let your lips be very precious.
Let insolence and blasphemy be your abomination;
Speak nothing profane nor any untrue report.
A talebearer is accursed.
(*BWL* 101; *ANET* 426)

28 The story of Ahikar is one of the most phenomenal in the ancient world in that it has become part of many different literatures and has been preserved in several different languages: Syriac, Arabic, Armenian, Greek, Slavonic, and Old Turkish. The most ancient recension is the Aramaic, found among the famous 5th-cent. BC papyri that were discovered at the beginning of the 20th cent. on Elephantine Island in the Nile. The story worked its way into the Arabian nights and the Koran; it influenced Aesop, the Church Fathers as well as Greek philosophers, and the OT itself. Ahikar is mentioned by name in the Gk recension of Tb (→ Tobit, 38:5). His story serves as a framework for the advice that he gives his nephew concerning the necessity of disciplining children for their own good, guarding the tongue, being circumspect in dealing with the king, respecting secrets, etc. "Do not spare the rod on your son; otherwise, you cannot preserve him from evil" (cf. Prv 23:13–14). "If I strike you, my son, you will not die, but if I leave you to your own desires [you will not live]" (*ANET* 427–30). His praise of wisdom reminds one of the biblical attitude, "Wisdom [comes from?] the gods; to the gods also she is precious. For [ever?] kingship is hers; in heaven she is established, for the lord of holiness [or holy ones?] has exalted her." The divine character of OT wisdom is to be found in Prv 8:15ff. and Sir 24:4ff., and the association of wisdom with royalty is another OT theme.

29 The problem of the "righteous sufferer"—the theme of Jb—is well represented in ancient Mesopotamia. There are two religious texts from about the 17th cent. that seem to deal with this phenomenon; one is unpublished, and the other, in the Louvre Museum, is somewhat ambiguous. However, there can be no question about the poem *Ludlul bel nemeqi* (a name taken from the first line, "I will praise the lord of wisdom"), which has been termed "the Babylonian Job" or perhaps better (with Lambert), "The Babylonian Pilgrim's Progress." In style this work resembles the hymn or song of praise found in the Psalter. A noble named Shubshi-meshre-shakkan, describes the long list of calamities that befell him; he then relates three dreams, which promise him deliverance; finally, he tells of the intervention of Marduk (who is, of course, the "lord of wisdom"). This poem was written in praise of his lord, in the second half of the 2nd millennium BC. The similarity to Jb is best seen in the following quotations:

I look about me: evil upon evil!
My affliction increases, right I cannot find.
I implored the god, but he did not turn his countenance;
I prayed to my goddess, but she did not raise her head.
(ll. 2–5; *ANET* 434b)

Yet, his suffering is undeserved; like Job he knows that there is nothing in his past that merits this treatment. His present state makes a mockery of his virtuous life:

Like one who did not offer a libation to a god,
and at meal-time did not invoke a goddess,...
Nay, worse than one who became proud and forgot his
divine lord,
Who swore frivolously in the name of his honorable deity
—like such a one have I become.
(ll. 11–12, 21–22; *ANET* 434–35)

His recall of his past life is reminiscent of Job's review of his own life in Jb 29 and the description of Job's activities in Jb 1:

Supplication was my concern, sacrifice my rule;
The day of the worship of the gods was my delight,
The day of my goddess' procession was my profit and wealth.
(ll. 24–26; *ANET* 435a)

So now he can only question the futility of it all—the gods are arbitrary, identifying good with evil as they please:

O that I only knew that these things are well pleasing to a god!
What is good in one's sight is evil for a god.
What is bad in one's own mind is good for his god.
Who can understand the counsel of the gods in the midst of
heaven?
The plan of a god is deep waters, who can comprehend it?
(ll. 32–36; *ANET* 435a)

However, as we have already indicated, the poignancy of the problem is not really explored in the Babylonian poem. The question is "answered" by a convenient divine intervention that brings about the cure. In Jb one should not think that the restoration in ch. 42 is the solution, just as there is a final cure in the Babylonian work. Rather, Job's confrontation with God, his acceptance of God, and his resignation to an inscrutable supreme will—this is the existential answer presented in the Hebr writing.

30 Another poem, dating from about 1000 BC, is called the "Dialogue about Human Misery," or the

"Babylonian Theodicy," and it has often been compared with Eccl. The work is an acrostic poem of 27 stanzas of 11 lines each. Like Jb, it is a dialogue between the one who is suffering and a sympathetic friend. The former develops the point that suffering and evil conflict with the justice of the gods, and he illustrates this principally from the point of view of social evils. Thus, he complains that he was born to his parents when they were advanced in age and that he was soon left an orphan. Why do not the gods defend such helpless creatures? His friend reminds him that all must die—even one's parents—and that prosperity is the result of piety, etc. The dialogue passes on to several other items: Why should the first-born be favored ahead of later children? Why does crime pay? The friend answers him sympathetically—never, like the "friends" of Job, accusing him of sin and saying that he deserved his suffering. But the consolation is not very great; he continues to mouth the old belief that piety will be rewarded, until finally he makes the astounding admission that the gods have made man the evil person that he is: "They [the gods] bestowed upon humanity ingenious speech: Falsehood and untruth they conferred upon them forever" (279–80; *ANET* 440b). As Lambert has remarked, this conclusion undoes the premises of the debate between the two. When one admits that the gods are responsible for human proclivities to evil, one's argument is finished—and no real conclusion is reached. For the Mesopotamian idea of the absence of a real afterlife, → Aspects OT Thought, 77:169.

31 More deserving of comparison with Eccl is the *Dialogue of Pessimism*. It is a conversation between a master and his slave about various topics, including women, piety, and charity. The master states his intention of following a particular course of action, and the slave agrees, giving a reason for this manner of acting. Thereupon the master proclaims he will pursue the opposite plan, and the slave reverses his stand without hesitation, enumerating the profits from such an action and the disadvantages of the plan he had formerly seconded: "'Servant, obey me.' Yes, my lord, yes. 'A woman will I love.' Yes, love, my lord, love. The man who loves a woman forgets pain and trouble. 'No, servant, a woman I shall not love.' Do not love, my lord, do not love. Woman is a well, woman is an iron dagger—a sharp one!—which cuts a man's neck" (*ANET* 438).

The result of this is relativism, pure and simple; nothing is absolute. The climax of the dialogue comes with a statement that nothing is worth doing; death is the only answer: "'Servant, obey me.' Yes, my lord, yes. 'Now, what is good? To break my neck, your neck, throw both into the river—that is good.' Who is tall enough to ascend to heaven? Who is broad enough to embrace the earth? 'No, servant, I shall kill you and send you ahead of me.' Then would my lord wish to live even three days after me?" (*ANET* 438b).

Is this a farce or a serious piece? Scholars have debated: E. Speiser takes it as a farce and has compared the servant to a Dickensian Sam Weller; W. G. Lambert takes it seriously but thinks that the writer was in a disturbed emotional state. In this case, the point of the last lines would be that if the servant were killed first, the master would soon follow, so attractive would death be. It is not easy to absolve the writer of any serious purpose, and in this the work resembles Eccl. Ecclesiastes was quite serious, yet he took extreme positions, somewhat in the fashion of both master and servant in the *Dialogue*. Such readiness to search out contradictions, to portray two sides to a question, and to seek out every possible disadvantage is characteristic of both writings. The servant points to the "ancient ruins" where men are buried and asks, "Which is the malefactor, and which is the benefactor?" In much the same way, Qoheleth lamented that death was the great leveler, in which the distinctions between wise man and fool, between man and beast, disappear, and "there is no remembrance of the men of old, nor of those to come will there be any remembrance among those who come after them" (Eccl 1:11).

32 The great difference between the Hebrew and the Mesopotamian work lies in the basic faith of Qoheleth. He felt himself committed to certain traditional data about Yahweh, even if he could not understand their relationship to the hard facts he observed; and the thought of suicide was utterly foreign to him, as it was generally to the men of the OT. Moreover, Qoheleth recognized a certain value to the joys of life, and he was unwilling to deny these (9:7–10). Several times (2:24–25; 3:12–13; etc.) he returns to the theme of enjoying the pleasures that God gives in this life. Here, he is echoing the kind of advice that had long before been given to Gilgamesh by the barmaid Siduri in the famous Epic of Gilgamesh:

> Gilgamesh, whither rovest thou?
> The life thou pursuest thou shalt not find.
> When the gods created mankind,
> Death for mankind they set aside,
> Life in their own hands retaining.
> Thou, Gilgamesh, let full be thy belly.
> Make thou merry by day and by night.
> Of each day make thou a feast of rejoicing,
> Day and night dance thou and play!
> Let thy garments be sparkling fresh,
> Thy head be washed; bathe thou in water.
> Pay heed to the little one that holds on to thy hand,
> Let thy spouse delight in thy bosom!
> For this is the task of mankind!
>
> (*ANET* 90a)

CONCEPT OF OLD TESTAMENT WISDOM

33 The concept of wisdom is elusive because it is exceedingly complex. Wisdom can stand for the skill of a craftsman, such as that possessed by those who made Aaron's vestments (Ex 28:3) or by the carpenters who constructed the Mosaic Tabernacle (Ex 31:3–5; 36:1). It denotes the ability of a professional mourner (Jer 9:17) or a sailor (Ps 107:27). The sage is an adviser to kings (Jer 50:35; Prv 31:1) but is also an astute old woman (2 Sm 20:16). It also has an intensely religious aspect—fear of the Lord (Prv 1:7; Sir 1:9–10). Wisdom is somehow divine (Prv 8; Sir 24). These many faces of wisdom cannot be captured in any logical schema. Here we can only give some indications of the variety of its uses and implications within the wisdom literature itself (cf. Fichtner, *op. cit.;* Von Rad, *OT Theology 1;* also W. Zimmerli, "The Place and Limit of Wisdom..." *ScotJT* 17 [1964] 146–58).

34 **(I) Wisdom and Experience.** It is in the area of experience and observation that a certain insight came to be recognized as wisdom. Von Rad has called it "experiential wisdom." It results from man's exposure to reality on various levels. His response to environment becomes an attempt to understand and control it. This understanding is an insight that makes reality less confusing and that may come to have the validity of a "general law." Pride goes before a fall (Prv 16:18; 18:12)—has it not been borne out many times in practice? Every one knows that men are susceptible to bribery (Prv 18:16). But sometimes only a paradox is evident: the lavish man grows richer, but the miser grows poorer (Prv 11:24). Often a certain parallel could be drawn between nature's actions and human conduct. What about the man who boasts but never gives? He is like "clouds and wind when no rain follows" (Prv 25:14). Although Israel never really developed a scientific attitude toward nature, the observable phenomena became a handy frame of reference for comparisons with human conduct. Of course, there were no "natural laws"—hence any insight that detected a certain regularity in nature was to be prized.

35 **(II) Wisdom, Moral Conduct, and Retribution.** The connection between wisdom and virtue is clearly and frequently stated; one need only read Prv 10ff. for the many contrasts between the just and the wicked. There is no reason to deny that this religious association would have been made early in the wisdom literature. A courtly training could not very well prescind from ethical values. The wisdom of the Egyptian Amen-em-ope also correlates certain actions with the will of God, but the evidence of post-exilic wisdom literature shows that wisdom takes on an ever more emphatically moral or ethical character.

Perhaps the best example of this development is the introduction to Prv, written after the Exile. Wisdom has become "fear of the Lord." The sage urges the youth to "understand rectitude and justice, honesty, every good path" (2:9), to "trust in the Lord with all your heart" (3:5). The success of the wise man is not merely a happy issue from some venture but "favor and good esteem before God and man" (3:4). Most of all, wisdom means life (8:35). This same point of view occurs among the deuteronomic preachers. Obedience means life; disobedience spells death (Dt 30:15–20). In Dt 5:33, long life is promised to those who are faithful to the commandments and the decrees. These commandments are, of course, the Torah—the liturgical and ethical ideals of Yahwism. But the wisdom teachers realized that there was an area of life not explicitly recognized in the Torah—the area of what might be called moral awakening and training. How is one to be brought into strict observance? Are there not certain preliminary lessons to be learned from human experience? It was in such a connection that the sages recognized the value of the experiential sayings and observations. These covered a large field, a gray area, as it were, in which moral decision was not directly concerned. But the practical details of daily life were the raw material of morality, and they rendered a decision eventually inescapable. Thus, what should be one's evaluation of bad companions? What does jealousy do to a person? To what end does pride lead? How is one to look upon harlots? (cf. Prv 13:20; 14:30; 29:33; 23:26–28). Besides, would it not be expected that experience would bear out the moral order? Kindness benefits; unkindness is destructive of self (Prv 11:17); check a quarrel at once (17:12). Many specifically immoral actions are singled out for condemnation: unjust gain (Prv 10:2); false witness (25:18; cf. Ez 20:16); bribery (24:23–24); lying and flattery (26:28). Conversely, certain moral ideals are inculcated: kindness to the poor (14:31); fear of the Lord (Prv 19:23, and often); trust in the Lord (28:25).

36 The success and prosperity of the wise young man were seen by the sages as identical with the blessings promised by the deuteronomic preachers. Hence, the author of Prv 1–9 adopts the hortatory style of Dt. Here, too, life is promised—the same good life offered for observance of the Torah. The good life is the common denominator between observance of the Law and the pursuit of wisdom. It comes as no surprise to read praise of the sage who studies the Law (Sir 39:1–11). The association between wisdom and virtue has become complete; the Torah is wisdom, as explicitly affirmed in Sir 24:22 and Bar 4:1.

The eudaemonism or "profit motive" in Israelite wisdom teaching, and in Egyptian teaching as well, has been subjected to new evaluation in recent times (H. Gese, against W. Zimmerli in *ZAW* 51 [1953] 177–204). The pragmatism that the wisdom sayings seem at first sight to betray is not the same as our modern concept of pragmatism, nor is usefulness properly the motive of action. The new insight is the recognition that the wise man sees a divine order established in things, according to which he forms his sayings—e.g., the diligent man stores up riches, the lazy man becomes poor (Prv 10:4). That this order is not universal is recognized by many other proverbs that are aware of the problems involved—the poor man is not always blameworthy (Prv 14:21). Hence, the order is not transparently obvious; it is a hidden thing beyond man's control, just as Yahweh himself escapes man. Nonetheless, the wise man urges his audience to conform to this real order insofar as he has discovered it. In other words, the accent is not on personal security: What must I do to preserve happiness or to keep myself from death? Rather, the sage urges his students to form their conduct after a definite understanding of the order that he finds in reality.

37 The rewards promised to those who acquire wisdom are expressed in the concept of life: "A path to life is his who heeds admonition" (Prv 12:28). The attainment of wisdom and virtue is associated with the "tree of life" (Prv 11:30; 13:12; 15:4), "path of life" (Prv 6:23; 15:24), and "fountain of life" (Prv 10:11; 16:22). Under this broad concept were subsumed many values: mere length of days (Prv 10:27; Sir 1:18), but also the goods of this life, such as riches, a large family, success, and prestige. It is not likely that any notion of personal immortality after death is involved in this notion (despite M. Dahood in *Bib* 41 [1960] 176–82, apropos of Prv 12:28). However, the very concept of life is one that is capable of development.

The development of the doctrine of immortality is associated with the wisdom literature in a special way. The books of Jb and Eccl show the impasse reached by the OT sages. Sheol, or the nether world, meant almost nonexistence (Eccl 9:10), and God's justice and mercy had to be experienced in this life according to the classical doctrine worked out by the sages. But this optimism was not borne out by the hard facts of life, as documented by both Job and Qoheleth; no satisfying answer was to be found. Yet their defeat led to the development of the doctrine of immortality. Israel came to realize that Sheol lay open before the Lord (Prv 16:11), that he was not a God who would abandon his faithful (Pss 49, 73). When the triumphant affirmation of immortality finally comes, it is expressed in a typically Israelite way. Immortality is not a conclusion from man's nature (immortal soul), but "justice is immortal" (Wis 1:15). The union with the Lord, which is secured in this life, simply perdures.

38 **(III) Wisdom and God.** Noth has pointed out that it is only in the later books that wisdom is predicated of God (VTSup, 3 [1955] 225–37). In early thought it belongs to the human, not to the divine, level. Yahweh "makes wise" or "gives wisdom," much as he "makes riches" or "gives riches." Wisdom does not really belong to Yahweh. We are unable to ascertain the reason, but it would appear that wisdom had some undesirable connotation that disappeared only later.

Eventually wisdom is predicated of God (Jb 12:13; Dn 2:20), and it is a characteristic of his creative activity (Ps 104:24; Jb 38:37; Prv 3:19). What has been called the "theologizing of wisdom" began. There is no ready explanation of this development, but within the data provided by the OT, the inaccessibility or transcendence of wisdom may be taken as a starting point. This characteristic is itself unusual in view of the stance wisdom takes in Prv 1–9, inviting men to pursue her, not to mention the invitation of the sages to acquire wisdom. The inaccessibility is indicated frequently. According to Jb 28, wisdom cannot be found anywhere in creation; only God, not the wise man, knows the way to it—he knows it "through and through." The sole indication given to man is that "fear of the Lord is wisdom" (28:28). Similarly in Bar 3: God alone knows wisdom. This mysterious transcendence of wisdom is affirmed also in Sir 1:5–7 at the end of the OT period.

Of course, the reason for wisdom's remoteness is that she is divine, "poured forth" (Prv 8:23) "from the mouth of the Most High" (Sir 24:3), "a pure effusion of the glory of the Almighty" (Wis 7:25). Wisdom is represented not only as originating from God but as being active as "craftsman" in creation (Prv 8:30; 3:19; Wis 9:9). These descriptions have given rise to the problem of wisdom as a person. She seems to be no more than a personification, just as other aspects of God are personified in the OT (his Word, Is 55:10–11; his spirit, Is 63:10–11).

The identification of wisdom with the spirit of God is particularly clear in the Book of Wisdom. She is called "the holy spirit of discipline" (1:5), which flees deceit. In 9:17–18, wisdom is in parallelism with the divine "holy spirit from on high," which reveals God's counsels to men and thus saves them. The salvific aspect of wisdom is another favorite theme of pseudo-Solomon. He traces the history of man from Adam to the Exodus, and he describes wisdom at work, saving Noah, the patriarchs, and finally Israel (Wis 9:18–10:18). This application of wisdom to the historical area flows readily enough from the role of safeguard (Prv 4:6), which wisdom exercises on behalf of those who cultivate her.

39 **(IV) Wisdom and Law.** Sirach describes wisdom's divine origin, but he also explicitly identifies her with the Law of Moses (Sir 24:22; Bar 4:1). Thus, wisdom has come a long way from its international courtly origins. Why was this identification made? The answer lies in the all-embracing role the Law came to have in the post-exilic community. It was the axis around which all Jewish life revolved. The identification, however, was not univocal; the Law did not exhaust the teaching of the sages. Sirach is a good example, for most of his sayings have a relatively loose connection with the straight teaching of the Torah. Another reason for the identification may have been the desire and need to concretize the divine wisdom theme of Prv 8. If wisdom has a divine origin, it is some kind of communication. And where is this communication now? Dt 4:6 reflects the easy confidence of a people that has found its wisdom—in the Law.

40 The theme of wisdom as a divine communication is an important theological development. It is a more fruitful insight than is the mere personification of wisdom. Some theologians have seized upon the personification (with a convenient neglect of the personification of the antithesis, Folly, in Prv 9:13–17) as pointing to the Christian mystery of the Persons in God. Such a view is anachronistic, to say the least. Rather, the wisdom literature witnesses that God does communicate himself, which is significant. It leaves open the possibility of a supreme communication in Jesus Christ, whom Paul calls the "wisdom of God" (1 Cor 1:24); cf. A. Feuillet, *Le Christ, Sagesse de Dieu* (Paris, 1966).

29

PROVERBS

J. Terence Forestell, C.S.B.

BIBLIOGRAPHY

1 Brunet, A., "Proverbes (22, 17–24, 22) et la possibilité d'une source égyptienne," *ScEccl* 1 (1948) 19–40. Cohen, A., *Proverbs* (SBB 2; Hindhead, England, 1945). Drioton, E., "Sur la sagesse d'Aménémopé," *Mélanges Bibliques A. Robert* (Paris, 1957) 254–80. Dubarle, A., *Les sages d'Israël* (Paris, 1946) 25–63. Duesberg, H., *Les scribes inspirés* (vol. 1; Paris, 1938). Hamp, V., *Das Buch der Sprüche* (Echter-B; Würzburg, 1949). McGlinchey, J. M., *The Teaching of Amen-em-ope and the Book of Proverbs* (Washington, 1939). Murphy, R. E., *Seven Books of Wisdom* (Milwaukee, 1960) 8–27. Oesterley, W. O., *The Book of Proverbs* (WC; London, 1929). Robert, A., "Les attaches littéraires bibliques de Prov. I–IX," *RB* 43 (1934) 42–68, 172–204, 374–84; *RB* 44 (1935) 344–65, 502–25. R-F 1, 624–41. R-T 1, 365–68. Skehan, P. W., "The Seven Columns of Wisdom's House in Proverbs 1–9," *CBQ* 9 (1947) 190–98; "A Single Editor for the Whole Book of Proverbs," *CBQ* 10 (1948) 115–30; "Wisdom's House," *CBQ* 29 (1967) 468–86. Toy, C. H., *Proverbs* (ICC; N.Y., 1908). Weber, J. J., *Le Livre des Proverbes* (Paris, 1949). Whybray, R. N., *Wisdom in Proverbs* (SBT 44; London, 1965). Wiesmann, H., *Das Buch der Sprüche* (BB 6; Bonn, 1923).

Among the more recent commentaries the following are particularly noteworthy: Barucq, A., *Le Livre des Proverbes* (Paris, 1964). Gemser, B., *Sprüche Salomos* (HAT 16; 2nd ed.; Tübingen, 1963). Ringgren, H., *Sprüche* (ATD; Göttingen, 1962). Scott, R. B. Y., *Proverbs* (AB; N.Y., 1965). Van der Ploeg, J., *Spreuken* (Roermond, 1952).

INTRODUCTION

2 **(I) Nature and Origin.** Proverbs is the earliest of those OT books that are classified as wisdom literature (→ Wisdom Lit, 28:8–10). The book is an anthology of earlier collections. The prologue (chs. 1–9) and the editorial work evaluate this heritage of the past as well as provide it with a new unity and orientation.

3 The origins of Hebr wisdom literature must be traced to the court of Solomon (→ Wisdom Lit, 28:11), although the short maxim or *māšāl*, the predominant literary form of the book, may well have its origin in earlier, popular forms of satire and clever observation (cf. J. Pirot, *RSR* 37 [1950] 565–80). For wherever men are governed, there is bound to grow up a body of astute observations, based on experience, which will serve subsequent generations of administrators in the difficult art of dealing with men and affairs. The Egyptians had already achieved considerable success in this form of instruction for public life when Solomon organized his kingdom along Egyptian lines and with the help of Egyptian scribes (1 Kgs 4:3). Solomon, however, surpassed his neighbors by reason of his personal reputation as a wise man (see 1 Kgs 3:9–12; 5:9–14 [4:29–34]; 10:1–9; A. Alt, *TLZ* 76 [1951] 139–43; also in *KlSchr* 2, 90–99). In this way, he became the patron and founder of a wisdom tradition in Israel.

Although the entire book is attributed to Solomon (1:1), only two collections—10:1–22:16 and 25:1–29:27—are put in direct literary dependence upon him. The latter collection is explicitly ascribed to the men of Hezekiah's court in the 8th cent. In both collections, the simplest form of the *māšāl* predominates, but repetitions, variations, refinements, and additions suggest a constant work of revision by a traditional school of learned scribes. There is no reason to suspect the pre-exilic origin of most of the proverbs in these two collections. The other collections are all dated later. The final editor was responsible for the prologue and the Sayings of the Wise (22:17–24:34); his hand is also evident in the ordering of the two Solomonic collections (cf. Skehan, *CBQ* 10, 115–30). The book most likely attained its present form toward the end of the 5th cent. BC. The peculiar religious needs of post-exilic Judaism prompted the preparation of this anthology.

4 **(II) Purpose.** The priest, the prophet, and the wise man were the traditional teachers in Israel (cf. Jer 18:18). The wise men were associated with the king and political affairs. There were no doubt many faithful Yahwists among the royal scribes who sought to respect Yahweh and the Law in the conduct of public affairs. Nevertheless, political expediency must have prompted many to counsel the foreign alliances, which the prophets consistently denounced (cf. Is 30:1–5; Jer 8:8–9). Events demonstrated the weakness of a too-human wisdom. The fall of Jerusalem (587) and the subsequent exile in Babylon (587–539) occasioned much theological soul-searching among the learned men of Israel. The message of the prophets had been shown to be true; fidelity to the Law of Yahweh is the only hope of salvation. The priests proceeded to the codification of ancient tradition and law. The wise men seem to have profited most from the experience, for they had learned that all human wisdom is futile without the fear of God (Prv 1:7; 9:10; cf. H. Cazelles, *VTSup* 3 [1955] 31–32). It was providential that they learned their lesson well, for they were to become the principal teachers in post-exilic Judaism, where the voice of the prophet was no longer heard and the careful organization of cult and the codification of laws exposed the religion of Yahweh to formalism and to literalism.

The restored community was no new nation. Apathy best describes the attitude of the majority toward the messianic idealism of the past. Individualism and immorality were rampant. Self-aggrandizement led to the exploitation of the poor by the rich. The wise men stepped into the breach and offered immediate happiness to those who would listen to their instructions. The ideal they proposed was the pursuit of wisdom. Such an ideal had both international and individual appeal; it was part of a long and cosmopolitan tradition (→ Wisdom Lit, 28:12–31). Proverbs never explicitly mentions the characteristic Israelite themes of promise, election, covenant, and law; there is no national messianic hope in the book. Yet the author of the prologue has profited from the teaching of the prophets and the priests, especially from Dt, Is, and Jer. His personification makes Wisdom transcendent, divine, and equal to Yahweh. She has by nature the attributes of the messiah and is interested "here and now" in ruling and guiding men, offering them salvation and happiness. The author of Prv sought to adapt the religion of the past to a changed condition in the life of the people. He did so through this notion of personified Wisdom. Unwittingly, under divine inspiration, he prepared for the appearance of one who was greater than Solomon (Mt 12:42). The eternal Word made flesh is divine Wisdom, according to 1 Cor 1:30.

5 **(III) Doctrine.** The Christian reader of Prv is struck by the apparently secular character of much of the counsel offered, especially in the two Solomonic collections. He may even be scandalized by the boldness with which self-interest and personal success appear as adequate motivation for ethical conduct, even for charity to the poor (cf. 28:27; 30:10). Finally, the confidence with which the wise men expect God's justice to be exercised in this life, granting prosperity to the just and destroying the wicked, is at least naïve, if not utterly false. Under what conditions may such literature be inspired by God?

The wise men of the ancient world were primarily interested in guiding the individual to happiness and success in the conduct of his earthly life. Consequently, no phase of human activity was unworthy of their attention, but it is inaccurate to assert that their counsels are secular in character. Religion was inextricably bound up with every phase of man's activity throughout the ancient world (cf. Skehan, *CBQ* 10, 127–28). In all things, man was subject to the divine will. In incorporating this foreign wisdom into the religion of Yahweh, the Israelite wise men transformed it in the light of their unique understanding of God and his relationship to man, so that Israelite wisdom, although comparable with the wisdom of Israel's neighbors, far surpasses theirs (cf. T. Meek, *JRel* 7 [1927] 262). The religious orientation of the prologue and the Yahwistic proverbs of the other collections must be considered to bathe the entire work in their transcendent light (cf. A. Robert, in *Mémorial Lagrange* [Paris, 1940] 163–82; A. Drubbel, *Bib* 17 [1936] 45–70, 407–28).

The Israelite wise men, at this time, had no knowledge of life after death (→ Aspects OT Thought, 77:168). They nevertheless had great faith and confidence in the justice of God. The earliest wise men, therefore, optimistically applied to the individual the retribution theology of Dt; the nation would prosper materially if the people were faithful to the Law of God. The justice of God must be manifested, and to their knowledge it could only be manifested in this life. Experience eventually challenged this faith, as can be seen in Jb and Eccl; the revelation of life after death resolved the tension (→ Wisdom Lit, 28:36). In the meantime, the wise men were forced to exploit every possibility of happiness in this life.

In the light of this limited perspective, the search for personal success and the protection of self-interest is comparable to the Christian's concern for his eternal salvation. Happiness for the Israelite sage consisted in riches, honor, and a long life; these blessings accompanied humility and the fear of the Lord (22:4). This OT perspective needed the NT revelation for perfect balance. In the light of Christian revelation, man's happiness consists ultimately in eternal life in the kingdom of God. He is instructed to store up treasures in heaven (Mt 6:20). The honor of the Christian lies in the readiness with which he sacrifices his life in this world for the kingdom of God (Lk 17:33). Nevertheless, the Christian has also to appreciate and to love the goods created by God. The religious humanism of Prv, for all its shortcomings, will teach the Christian not to despise natural and human values merely because he has a supernatural destiny. (Cf. R. E. Murphy, "The Kerygma of the Book of Proverbs," *Interpr* 20 [1966] 3–14.)

6 **(IV) Outline.** The knowledge of Prv's plan is indispensable for an understanding of its nature and origin (cf. Murphy, *Seven Books*, 8). The Book of Proverbs may be outlined as follows:

(I) Prologue (1:1–9:18)
- (A) Introduction (1:1–33)
  - (a) Title and Purpose (1:1–6)
  - (b) The Principle of Wisdom (1:7)
  - (c) Initial Exhortation (1:8–19)
  - (d) First Discourse of Personified Wisdom (1:20–33)
- (B) The Blessings of Wisdom (2:1–7:27)
  - (a) Attitude Toward the Lord (3:1–12)
  - (b) The Value of Wisdom (3:13–4:9)
  - (c) The Good and the Evil Way (4:10–27)
  - (d) Warning Against Adultery (5:1–7:27)
- (C) Second Discourse of Personified Wisdom (8:1–36)
- (D) The Banquets of Wisdom and Folly (9:1–18)
  - (a) The Invitation of Wisdom (9:1–6)
  - (b) Six Independent Proverbs (9:7–12)
  - (c) The Invitation of Folly (9:13–18)

(II) First Collection of the Proverbs of Solomon (10:1–22:16)

(III) Sayings of the Wise (22:17–24:22)

(IV) Other Sayings of the Wise (24:23–34)

(V) Second Collection of the Proverbs of Solomon (25:1–29:27)

(VI) The Words of Agur (30:1–14)

(VII) Numerical Proverbs (30:15–33)

(VIII) The Words of Lemuel (31:1–9)

(IX) The Ideal Wife (31:10–31)

COMMENTARY

7 **(I) Prologue (1:1–9:18).** The final editor's introduction to the book is a unified composition, broken only by 6:1–19 and 9:7–12. Chapter 1 explains the purpose of the book (vv. 1–6) and enunciates the guiding principle (v. 7); after an initial exhortation (vv. 8–19) it concludes with the first discourse of personified Wisdom (vv. 20–33). Chapter 2 outlines the blessings of wisdom, which are then developed in chs. 3–7. The second discourse of personified Wisdom follows in ch. 8. The prologue closes in the form of a diptych—contrasting sketches of personified Wisdom (9:1–6) and Folly (9:13–18). Chapters 2–7 may have originally consisted of seven poems of 22 couplets each, thus constituting the seven columns of Wisdom's house (9:1; Skehan, *CBQ* 9, 190–98; 29, 468–86).

8 **(A) Introduction (1:1–33).**

(a) Title and Purpose (1:1–6). **1.** *the proverbs of Solomon:* Refers to the entire content of the book but primarily to the two Solomonic collections that form its heart (10:1–22:16; 25:1–29:27). The Hebr word *māšāl* (proverb) designates the predominant literary form—i.e., the short, pithy saying or aphorism, often based on a comparison. A stimulant to thought and reflection, the didactic qualities of such a form are obvious. *the son of David, king of Israel:* The fuller title is absent from 10:1 and 25:1; the numerical value of the three proper names (375 + 14 + 541) may serve to determine the limits of the editor's work (cf. Skehan, *CBQ* 10, 129–30).

Verses 2–6 form one sentence and express the purpose of the work. **2.** *wisdom: Ḥokmâ* sums up the ideal that the teacher desires for his pupil. Its meaning will become clearer through the explanations and maxims that follow. Basically it is an extraordinary ability in any phase of human activity; later Hebr literature saw wisdom as a prerogative of Yahweh in the creation of the world and in his providence over Israel. Consequently, he alone imparts wisdom to men (→ Wisdom Lit, 28:38). *discipline: Mûsar,* "self-mastery," which is the fruit of disciplined learning, correction, and self-control. *intelligence: Bînâ,* the ability to distinguish sound from spurious teaching as well as right from wrong (cf. 1 Kgs 3:9). **3.** The wise man must be circumspect in his "conduct" (*haśkēl*), conversant with the demands of right living (*ṣedeq*), the just decision in each case (*mišpāṭ*), with what is, in short, proper and honest (*mēšārîm*). **4.** *the simple: P^etā'yim;* education in wisdom is offered primarily to the ingenuous youth, who is open to all manner of influence and in great danger of being led astray. *resourcefulness: 'Ormâ* almost always means shrewdness, outside Prv; the young man must learn to choose his way with care and ability. **5.** The wise man himself will profit from this teaching and add to his store of learning (cf. 9:9). **6.** The enumeration may well refer to the various parts of the present collection. *parable: M^elîṣâ,* an obscure metaphorical discourse or allegory. *riddles: Ḥîdôt,* enigmatic utterances, such as the numerical proverbs of 30:15–33 or the riddle of Samson (Jgs 14:12–19).

The author shows the same concern for the well-being of his disciple as do the Egyptian teachers of wisdom. Compare the introduction to the *Instruction of Amen-em-ope:* "The beginning of the teaching of life, the testimony for prosperity, all precepts for intercourse with elders, the rules for courtiers, to know how to return an answer to him who said it, and to direct a report to one who has sent him, in order to direct him to the ways of life, to make him prosper upon earth, let his heart go down into its shrine, steer him away from evil, and to rescue him from the mouth of the rabble" (*ANET* 421b).

9 (b) The Principle of Wisdom (1:7). An independent couplet stands as a leitmotiv to the entire collection and canonizes the quasi-secular character of much of the instruction offered. *fear of the Lord:* The sum of religion and piety toward God; a reverential fear that manifests itself in loving obedience to his will. *beginning: Rē'šît* not so much the beginning (9:10), but the most excellent form of wisdom; this meaning of *rē'šît* appears in the Mari Texts (cf. O. Loretz, *BeO* 2 [1960] 210–11). *fools:* Throughout the book, the wise man is contrasted with the "fool"; the emphasis is not on a lack of intelligence but on the absence of any sense of God or awareness of his Law. The fool is an irreligious man (Ps 14:1), indifferent to all correction and instruction.

10 (c) Initial Exhortation (1:8–19). **8.** *hear:* Docility is a fundamental condition for the acquisition of wisdom. Compare the commendation of the Egyptian sage, Ptah-hotep: "To hear is better than anything that is, and thus comes the goodly love of a man. How good it is when a son accepts what his father says!" (ANET 414a). *my son:* The expression is figurative, referring to the relationship of teacher and pupil. Parental discipline and guidance are the first sources of wisdom. For the role of the mother in education, cf. Prv 6:20; 10:1; 15:20; Sir 3:2–6. **9.** Docility and obedience make a man attractive. **10–19.** A warning against the allurements of evil companions (cf. 4:10–27). **12.** *the nether world, the pit:* Synonyms for Sheol, the common dwelling place of the dead, beneath the earth. A premature death was considered fit punishment for sinners. Verse 16 is a gloss from Is 59:7, suggested by the words "foot" and "path" in v. 15. **17.** The fowling image more probably introduces v. 18; the bandits are the birds whom it is futile to warn. **19.** The principle of retribution permeates the wisdom literature (cf. 15:27; 28:16). Crime does not pay!

11 (d) First Discourse of Personified Wisdom (1:20–33). Twice in the prologue (see 8:1–9:6) wisdom is presented as a woman who goes about the city seeking disciples. The feminine plural form (*ḥokmôt*), used here and in 9:1, designates either an abstraction or the fullness and abundance of wisdom; the verbs are singular, and many contend it is an archaic (Canaanite) sing. form. In such literary personifications, personal activity is predicated of an abstraction. However, the portrayal of Wisdom in Prv 1 and 8, Sir 1 and 24, and Wis 6–9 suggests a deeper insight into the mystery of God. Wisdom appears with prophetic, divine, and messianic traits but stands apart from God himself. In the light of NT revelation (Lk 11:31; Jn 1:1–18; Col 1:15–20), it is not difficult for the Christian to see here a foreshadowing of the revelation of the Second Person of the Trinity and the coming of the divine Logos among men. Without affirming a second hypostasis in God, the authors of Prv, Sir, and Wis suggest the rich, personal life of the divinity (see comments on 8:22–36).

20–21. Wisdom's message is public, like that of the prophets (Jer 17:19). Her message reaches the common people in the "crowded" streets and the rulers at the "city gates," where public business was transacted in Oriental cities. **22–23.** As the CCD stands (MT is uncertain), Wisdom invites the "simple ones" to repent of their indocility and profit from her gifts. *spirit... words:* May be synonymous for teaching; in the prophets, however, the gift of the spirit was Yahweh's prerogative (Is 44:3; Ez 36:27; Jl 3:1); according to Jn 7:37–39, the gift of the Spirit is the proper mission of Christ.

24–32. Wisdom assumes a threatening tone, charging the young with stubbornness in a manner that recalls Yahweh's threats to hardhearted Israel (Is 65:2,12; 66:4). **26–27.** Wisdom will have the last laugh, for disaster will most certainly come upon them with the suddenness of a Palestinian storm. Such unconstrained delight in the downfall of the sinner seems foreign to the Christian conscience, but we must keep in mind the exhortatory character of the text and remember that we are dealing with the just punishment that befalls the obstinate sinner in this life. **28–32.** Like the rich man in the Gospel parable (Lk 16:19–31), they will seek help when it is too late. The evasion of punishment is excluded, but not the possibility of repentance (cf. Ez 33:11). **31–32.** The sinner is punished by that in which he sins (Ps 57:7; Wis 11:16; Gal 6:7). **33.** The harangue ends on a gentle note. The happiness Wisdom promises her disciples echoes the theology of Dt 28:1–14.

12 **(B) The Blessings of Wisdom (2:1–7:27).** Chapter 2 is an independent poem of six strophes (4,4,3; 4,4,3). **1–4.** The first strophe exposes the conditions for the attainment of wisdom—docility, reflection, desire, and industry. **1.** The wise man speaks in his own name, not in the name of the Lord, as did the prophets. **2.** *heart:* The seat of intellectual and moral life in Semitic thought.

5–19. In four strophes, clearly evident in the MT, the advantages of wisdom are enumerated. **5–8.** Intimacy with God and his protection. **6.** God alone gives wisdom to men. **7–8.** Guidance and protection are the consequences of intimate friendship with God (this theme is developed in 3:1–12,25–34). **9–11.** In the possession of wisdom are moral virtue and practical prudence. **10.** The indwelling of wisdom reminds the Christian of the promise of Christ (Jn 14:23); 3:13–24 and 4:1–9 pursue the theme. **12–15.** Wisdom gives protection from the allurements of evil companions (cf. 1:10–19). **13.** There is a natural association of darkness with evil and light with good (cf. 4:19; Jn 3:19–21); 4:10–27 returns to the same topic. **16–19.** The fourth advantage of wisdom is deliverance from the adulterous woman. **16.** *the wife of another, the adulteress:* Lit., "the strange woman" (*zārâ*) and "the foreign woman" (*nokriyyâ;* cf. 1 Kgs 11:1,8). It is clear from v. 17 that the adulteress is meant (cf. P. Humbert, *RES* 6 [1937] 49–64). The theme of the strange woman is frequent in Oriental wisdom literature (cf. Ptah-hotep, *ANET* 413b; Ani, *ANET* 420a). **17.** We are far removed from the polygamous practices of David and Solomon. This high ideal of marital fidelity is a direct consequence of Israel's covenant with Yahweh on Mt. Sinai (Ex 20:14,17; cf. Mal 2:14). **18.** *her path:* Thus in the CCD, preserving the parallelism; the MT has "her house," which can be taken as the entrance to Sheol (cf. 7:27). **19.** *life:* The goal of the wise man. The ideal proposed is a long and happy life on this earth, enjoying an abundance of this world's goods, a good reputation with one's fellow men, and peace with God through worship and fidelity to his Law (B. Couroyer, *RB* 56 [1949] 412–32). This concept will eventually develop into that of eternal life (→ Wisdom Lit, 28:36). Chapters 5–7 develop the warning of vv. 16–19.

20–22. General conclusion. Peace and security in the promised land were the ideal offered by Dt and temporarily achieved in the reigns of David and Solomon (1 Kgs 4:25). The national note is absent here. The ideal will gradually be spiritualized in preparation for the Gospel (Mt 5:5).

13 (a) ATTITUDE TOWARD THE LORD (3:1–12). Particular recommendations based on 2:5–8. The thought falls into strophes of two couplets each. **1–2.** The reward of docility (cf. Ex 20:12). **3–4.** *kindness... fidelity: Ḥesed* and *'ĕmet* are the qualities that characterize the God of the Sinai covenant in his relationship with Israel (Ex 34:6; Hos 4:1); they should characterize man's relationship to God and to his neighbor (Hos 4:1). **5–8.** Self-conceit was a favorite theme of the prophets (Is 5:21; Jer 9:22–23; cf. Rom 11:25; 12:16). Bodily "health" as a reward for virtue may be understood literally or figuratively; sickness was generally considered a punishment for sin. **8b.** Lit., "water for your bones." Dryness of the bone was a common image for distress and desolation (Prv 17:22; Ps 22:15–16; Jb 30:30). *flesh... bones:* Used for the whole person. **9–10.** This is the only act of cult formally counseled in Prv (cf. Lv 27:30; Ex 34:26; Dt 26:1–2). The initial consecration of the harvest assured its abundant completion. **11–12.** Suffering for the wise man is an education, not a punishment. The theme of 3:1–12 is continued in 3:25.

14 (b) THE VALUE OF WISDOM (3:13–4:9). Two strophes of six couplets each deal with the excellence of wisdom (cf. 2:9–11). The first strophe is in the form of a beatitude (vv. 13, 18). **18.** *a tree of life:* A commonplace of Oriental mythologies; it could be found in Assyrian temples. The usage in Prv (11:30; 13:12; 15:4) is sufficient to indicate that immortality is not meant, nor is there any reference to Gn 2:9; 3:22; it is simply an image for happiness, an image that is nonetheless open to the eschatological considerations of Ez 47:12 and Ap 22:2. Wisdom is personified in this passage. **19–20.** These verses anticipate 8:27–31. The most compelling reason for the excellence of wisdom is its role in God's creation and government of the universe. The cosmogony is that of Gn 1 and of the Bible in general. **20.** The Oriental naïvely considered that the dew came down from heaven like the rain. **22.** *your soul:* The Hebr word *nepeš* is used for the self or the person; the primitive meaning "throat" may not be absent, in view of the parallelism. **23–24.** Cf. Pss 91:1–13; 3:6.

15 **25–26.** The wise man, who trusts in the Lord, need not be disturbed when he sees sudden calamity fall upon the wicked. The *Instruction of Amen-em-ope* reads: "Be sincere in the presence of the common people, for one is safe in the hand of the god" (*ANET* 423a). **27–30.** These verses concern a man's relationship with his fellow man; it should reflect his relationship to God. **27.** The poor and helpless have a special claim upon the charity of the well-to-do (11:24–26; 14:21,31; 21:13). **28.** He gives twice who gives quickly. **31–32.** The apparent prosperity of the wicked is a serious temptation to the good man (cf. Ps 37). *abomination: Tô'ēbâ* effectively expresses the mutual separation of God and the sinner (cf. Ani, *ANET* 420a; Amen-em-ope, *ANET* 423b). *friendship: Sôd,* on the contrary, means, lit., "secret," suggesting intimacy. **34.** Cf. Jas 4:6; 1 Pt 5:5. *the humble:* The *'ănāwîm* of the psalms and the prophets; the poor in spirit of Mt 5:3. **35.** This verse may better be read after 4:19–18 (Skehan, *CBQ* 9, 190–98). Honor and shame refer to the reputation one enjoys before others.

16 **4:1–9.** Read with 3:13–24; an exhortation to the pursuit of wisdom, fortified by the teacher's own experience. The traditional character of wisdom is well illustrated here; it is handed down from father to son by oral instruction. **3–5.** In Dt 6:7 the obligation of instructing his son in the Law of Yahweh is imposed upon the father. **7–9.** Unless wisdom is highly valued, the necessary sacrifices will not be made. Wisdom is to be sought and cherished as a bride (cf. Sir 14:20–27; 51:13–22; Wis 8:2); note the gentle solicitation of these verses.

17 (c) THE GOOD AND THE EVIL WAY (4:10–27). Two poems (10–18, 20–27) develop the third blessing of wisdom (2:12–15). Wisdom is a sure guide in the conduct of one's life. **10–13.** The teacher of wisdom is speaking. A long and happy life is the reward of docility to his instruction. **13.** In Dt 30:20, the Law is the life of the Israelite; here, it is the instruction of the wise man. Verses 14–18 sketch the conduct of the wicked. **16.** The wise man's judgment of evil men is without nuance. **17.** Evil is as normal for such men as eating and drinking (cf. Jb 15:16; Jn 4:34). **19.** In contrast, the just man progresses toward ever greater happiness as the sun rises to its zenith at noon (Ps 97:11; Is 2:5; Jb 22:28).

20–27. A new appeal to the student's attention. **20–21.** Ears, eyes, and heart must all be fixed on the master's teaching. **22.** In 8:35, Wisdom herself is life to those who find her. **23.** Compare Mt 12:34; 15:19; 16:23. Custody of the heart is recommended in the Aram story of Ahikar: "More than all watchfulness watch thy mouth, and over what thou hearest harden thy heart. For a word is a bird; once released no man can recapture it" (*ANET* 428b). **25.** The eyes reflect sincerity. **26.** Cf. Heb 12:13. **27.** The Greeks speak of virtue's golden mean.

18 (d) WARNING AGAINST ADULTERY (5:1–7:27). The longest and most artistic section of the prologue is devoted to warning the young man of the wiles of seductive women, a universal danger for the man who is making his way in the world. The counsels are not merely utilitarian but reflect a high concept of marital fidelity. Without suggesting that the present exhortation is an allegory, the author may intend to contrast the attractiveness of Wisdom with that of the adulterous woman.

5:3. Flattery. **4–5.** The forbidden pleasure, once tasted, is bitter (cf. 2 Sm 13:15). *wormwood:* A species of *Artemisia*, better known as absinthe. **6.** The CCD, following the MT, interprets as a warning to the young man. The ancient versions, reading *bal* or *lō'* (not) for *pen* (lest), understand the verse of the woman: She does not prepare a road to life; her paths ramble she knows not where. The latter better fits the context. **8.** Avoid the occasion of sin. **9–10.** Synonymous parallelism; the reference is to the loss of fortune and well-being, which is consequent upon a life of lust. *a merciless one:* The injured husband. **11.** *flesh...body:* Signify the whole person. **12–14.** When it is too late, the young man repents of his indocility.

15–20. Find your pleasure in your own wife. The context restricts the author's consideration to sensual pleasure, although woman is not thought to be merely a means of satisfaction for a man's passion (cf. 2:17; 11:16; 12:4; 31:10–31). The language is figurative. **15.** *cistern:* Because of the scarcity of water in the Near East, any water supply was highly valued, protected, and cherished; hence, the image is apt for one's wife (cf. Ct 4:15). **16–17.** Your wife will become a woman of the streets if you do not lavish your love and affection upon her alone. The interpretation of Hamp and Cohen, that v. 16 refers to children, is erroneous. **18–19.** Real joy and pleasure are to be sought in the physical embraces of one's beautiful wife. Other ends of marriage are not excluded, but are simply not pertinent here. The "hind" and "doe," by reason of their graceful form and gait, are traditional images of feminine beauty in the Orient (cf. Ct 2:7). **19b.** *her love:* The vocalization of the MT would demand "her breasts." **19c.** Read *tiśgeh;* the water of her love will irrigate you as a well-watered plant. In the LXX, the presence of 6:22 is suggested at this point. Inserted here, it complements the purely sensual character of the passage; a man's wife is also his companion and associate. The entire passage rightly affirms the joys of married life. **21–23.** A final consideration is the all-seeing eye of God.

19 **6:1–19.** The mention of "folly" in 5:23 may have occasioned the insertion of these four poems illustrating folly (vv. 1–5, 6–11, 12–15, 16–19). The subject matter and the literary form suggest that they belong among the Sayings of the Wise in 22:17–24:34, or among the numerical proverbs of 30:15–31. **1–5.** Against imprudent liberality. The situation is that of a commercial transaction in which one man pledges himself or his property to cover the losses that another may incur in a business venture. The advice, a commonplace in Prv (11:15; 17:18; 20:16; 22:26–27), is realistic and based on self-interest; do not do it—there is too much to lose. If you have been foolish enough to do so, leave no stone unturned to be free of the obligation. The advice of Sir (29:20) is more nuanced. **6–11.** The ant offers the lazy man an exhortation to industry in a little fable (cf. 30:25). Ancient moralists drew lessons from the simple observation of plant and animal life (as in the Amarna letters, *ANET* 486a). A similar sketch occurs in 24:30–34. The LXX adds the example of the busy bee after 6:8. **12–15.** Against the schemer and the good for nothing. **13.** The judgment is based upon external signs of duplicity and craftiness. **16–19.** The numerical proverb is common to the Bible (Dt 32:30; Am 1:3; Mi 5:4; Ps 62:12; Jb 5:19; 40:5; Sir 25:7; 26:5,19) and to ancient Near Eastern literature. A series of such proverbs appears in Prv 30:15–31; these may be the riddles of 1:6. As a poetic device in synonymous or synthetic parallelism, the numbers indicate a definite enumeration to follow (cf. W. Roth, *VT* 12 [1962] 300–11).

20 **6:20–35.** The theme of the adulterous woman is resumed (cf. 5:23). **26.** Proverbs says little about common prostitution. The prostitute seeks only her livelihood; with her, a man's losses are only monetary. The price of adultery is one's entire well-being, if not life itself (32–35). **30–35.** The lot of the adulterer is contrasted with that of a thief. **30–31.** There is some pity for a man who is forced to steal out of hunger, even though he must pay the penalty of the law. *sevenfold:* No known law of Israel provides for sevenfold restitution; it probably means "abundantly." **33.** *a degrading beating:* The penalty of stoning for adultery (Dt 22:22) seems already to have been replaced by flogging; this was certainly true in the 1st cent. AD (Oesterley, *op. cit.*).

21 **7:1–27.** A clever and artistic sketch of the tactics of an adulteress. Verses 1–5 introduce a small novel (6–23); the conclusion (24–27) makes the lesson explicit. **2.** *the apple of your eye:* The image may be based on the belief that the center of the eye was a window into a man's soul; hence, the expression is synonymous with life. Verse 3a recalls the custom of wearing phylacteries, small scrolls of the Law, upon the head and hands at the time of prayer (cf. Dt 6:8). **4.** The titles "sister" and "friend" suggest that Wisdom is to be loved, not the adulteress. **6.** The author portrays himself watching the scene below through the wooden lattice of an upper room, a common feature of Oriental architecture. **7–9.** Sir 9:7 warns against such aimless strolls at night. **14–20.** A religious occasion offers an excuse for introducing the young man into her house. In thanksgiving sacrifices, part of the victim remained to be eaten in a sacrificial banquet. **18.** The Hebrew *'āhab*, as "love" in English, expresses all forms of love from physical to spiritual. **19–20.** Her husband is away for about a month. All possible objections have been astutely forestalled. **21–23.** The climax of the story, but the author points the lesson in vv. 24–27.

22 **(C) Second Discourse of Personified Wisdom (8:1–36).** The climax of the prologue. Wisdom again speaks in person and enumerates her claims to attention—her sincerity (6–11), her intellectual gifts (12–16), the favors she bestows (17–21), her origin (22–26), and her role in creation (27–31). The poem, in hymn form, falls roughly into seven strophes of five couplets each. **1–5.** For the biblical reader, the proclamation of Wisdom recalls the prophet's annunciation of the coming of Yahweh and of his salvation (Is 40:9). Wisdom seeks to communicate with men; the universality of her mission is indicated not only by the absence of all national language but by the *bᵉnê-'ādām* of v. 4b. **6.** *noble things:* Oesterley, Toy, and BJ correct *nᵉgîdîm* to *nᵉkōḥîm* (plain things); sincerity is the general theme of the strophe. **7.** *truth:* The Hebrew *'ĕmet* indicates the reliability of Wisdom's words; its opposite is "wickedness." **8.** *sincere:* Lit., "injustice" (*bᵉṣedeq*)—i.e., in perfect conformity with reality; notice the parallelism. **10.** The superiority of Wisdom to all material goods (cf. 3:14–15). **11.** A gloss attracted from 3:15.

12–16. Wisdom possesses in her own right all the gifts that a young man requires for success in guiding his own life and for ruling others. Indeed, it is through Wisdom communicated to men that the world is governed. The attributes of Wisdom are the same as those of the messianic king in Is 11:2 and of Yahweh himself in Jb 12:13,16. Verse 13a is certainly a gloss, 13bc belonging rather to the previous strophe or before v. 17. **16b.** Weber, Toy, and BJ, with the LXX, restore the parallelism thus: "and nobles rule the earth." **17.** The love and desire of Wisdom (Wis 7:10; 8:2) are necessary for obtaining her gifts (Jn 5:40). **18.** Material prosperity is the gift of Yahweh to those who fear him in Ps 112:3. **19–21.** Wealth is among the rewards of Wisdom, but she has other superior gifts. The wise men give full recognition to the value of material goods, but place them in order within a higher synthesis (Mt 6:33).

23 **22–31.** The divine origin of Wisdom and her role in creation are developed in the next two strophes. Wisdom is from God and absolutely prior to the visible universe. This priority implies superiority to all created things. The verbs in vv. 22–25, which describe the origin of Wisdom, may all be associated with generation and birth. In all these expressions, the author is trying to assert, in the best way he can, the absolute priority of Wisdom and her origin from God before all creation (cf. Sir 1:4,8; 24:9). Much of the imagery reflects Canaanite mythology (cf. W. F. Albright, VTSup 3 [1955] 1–16), but there is no trace of dependence regarding content.

22. *the Lord begot me:* The verb *qānâ* generally means "to acquire"; here the connotation is acquisition by way of birth (cf. Gn 4:1; Dt 32:6; Ps 139:13). The rendering, "The Lord created me" (also Tg. and Syr), occasioned serious difficulty with the Arians, who used this text to support the created nature of the Logos. Jerome's "The Lord possessed me" reflects Philo, Aq, Sym, and Theodotion. C. F. Burney ("Christ as the *ARXH* of Creation," *JTS* 27 [1926] 172) recalls the acute comment of Basil (*Contra Eunomium* 2. 20; *PG* 29.616–17): "We must not ignore the fact that other interpreters, who have reached the meaning of the Hebrew more aptly, render *ektēsato me* instead of *ektisen*. This will offer them [the Arians] the greatest obstacle against the blasphemy of their creaturely interpretation. For he who said, 'I have begotten a man through God,' manifestly used the expression not as the creator of Cain, but as his generator." (See C. Hauret, *RScRel* 32 [1958] 360–62; W. Irwin, *JBL* 80 [1961] 133–42.) *the first-born of his ways: Rē'šît* may express excellence as well as temporal priority (see comment on 1:7; J. Bauer, *VD* 35 [1957] 222–27). Paul (Col 1:15, *prōtotokos pasēs ktiseōs*) understands the expression of Christ. **23.** *from of old: Mē'ôlām;* Hebrew has no word for eternity, but *'ôlām* signifies an indefinite period of time. *I was poured forth:* The LXX (*ethemeliōsen*) and the MT (*nissaktî*) suggest Ps 2:6, the enthronement of the messianic king. A slight change in pointing produces *nᵉsakkōtî*, as in Ps 139:13: "Truly you have formed [*qānîtā*] my inmost being; you knit me [*tᵉsukkēnî*] in my mother's womb." The translation in the CCD may apply either to the consecration of a king by the pouring of oil or to the conception of a child (cf. Jb 10:10), in parallelism with 8:22. **24–26.** The pre-existence of Wisdom is developed according to the plan of biblical cosmogony.

27–31. Wisdom has a role to play in creation. Proverbs is content to assert her presence at creation with only a vague suggestion of an active role. The author's successors in Sir 24:1–21 and Wis 7:22–8:1 will be more explicit in this regard. The CCD version corrects v. 28b with the superfluous words in v. 29, thus restoring the rhythm. **30.** *his craftsman:* Skehan (*CBQ* 9, 198) and Albright (*op. cit.*, 8) defend the CCD reading *'ommān*. Wisdom is God's architect in creation (cf. Ct 7:2; Wis 7:21—*pantōn technitis...sophia*). In the MT, *'amôn* only appears in an uncertain text of Jer (52:15). Aquila's *tethēnoumenē* (nursling) supposes Hebr *'āmûn* (Wiesmann, Gemser, Hamp); this interpretation is better adapted to the context—Wisdom is God's child (22), playing before him and the object of his delight (30bc); Jn 1:18 may reflect this interpretation—the Word in the bosom of the Father (cf. R. Scott, *VT* 10 [1960] 213–23). **30b.** The CCD translation follows the LXX, confirmed by Wis 9:9; Wisdom always pleases God (Jn 8:29). Weber and Toy consider that Wisdom finds her delight in God and his creation. Verse 31b overburdens the rhythmical structure but provides a transition to Wisdom's salvific work among men in the final strophe.

32–36. A final exhortation. The CCD rearrangement of stichs in vv. 32–34 (32a, 33, 34a, 32b, 34bc) improves the logical sequence of thought without changing the sense. **34.** This verse suggests the clients of a king and Wisdom's house (9:1; but cf. Dt 6:9). **36a.** The Vg "those who sin against me" goes beyond the MT meaning.

(Burney, *JTS* 27, 160–77. Cazelles, H., "L'enfantement de la Sagesse en Prov., VIII," *SP* 1 [Paris, 1959] 511–15. C. Kayatz, *Studien zu Proverbien 1–9* [WMzANT 22; Neukirchen, 1966]. Robert, *RB* 43. Stecher, R., "Die persönliche Weisheit in den Proverbien Kap. 8," *ZKT* 75 [1953] 411–51.)

24 **(D) The Banquets of Wisdom and Folly (9:1–18).** The prologue concludes with a diptych in which Wisdom and Folly each invite young men to a banquet. Wisdom's banquet is the collection of proverbs that follow; the prologue is the entrance hall to this "house of instruction" (cf. Sir 51:23).

(a) The Invitation of Wisdom (9:1–6). The personification of Wisdom resembles rather that of 1:20–33 than the more exalted figure of ch. 8; yet a connection is suggested by 8:34. **1.** *seven columns:* The number seven is symbolic of perfection; there is no archaeological evidence to support the suggestion that seven columns surrounded the inner court of Palestinian houses at this time. Skehan (*CBQ* 9, 190–98) suggests that the "seven columns" are seven poems of equal length in chs. 2–7; this structure is no longer apparent in the present state of the text. **2.** Spices were mixed with wine to increase the flavor (cf. Ct 8:2; Ps 75:9). Meat and wine are festive foods; compare the bread and water of Folly's table (17). **4.** She invites the "simple," those for whom Prv is intended (1:4). Folly addresses them in the same words (16). **6.** The text would suggest to the

Israelite the eschatological banquet promised by Yahweh (Is 25:6; 55:1–5); the Christian thinks spontaneously of the parable of the wedding feast (Mt 22:1–14) and of the Messianic banquet at which Christ himself serves (Lk 12:37; cf. Mt 8:11). The Eucharistic banquet is itself an anticipation of the heavenly banquet (Mk 14:25). In Jn 2 and 6, Christ not only gives the wine of wisdom and the bread of teaching, but also his sacrificial flesh and blood (cf. R. Dillon, *CBQ* 24 [1962] 268–96; A. Feuillet, *NRT* 82 [1960] 803–22, 918–39, 1040–62).

(b) Six Independent Proverbs (9:7–12). These sayings are inserted between the sketches of Wisdom and Folly. **7–9.** Correction is wasted on the arrogant (cf. Mt 7:6). The wise man profits from all instruction (cf. Ps 141:5). **10.** *the beginning of wisdom:* The Hebrew differs from 1:7 (*t^{e}ḥillâ* in place of *rē'šît*); the fear of the Lord is the first step on the road to wisdom. Verse 11 belongs in a discourse of personified Wisdom; v. 12 expresses the principle of individual responsibility (Ez 18:4) and the optimistic law of retribution.

(c) The Invitation of Folly (9:13–18). **13.** If the text is correct, Folly is explicitly called a woman; the personification of Wisdom is merely implied. Folly is described like the adulteress of 7:11. **17.** She offers only the pleasure of the clandestine (cf. 5:15). **18.** She has hidden from him the fact that her fruit is not life (6), but death. Folly's parody of Wisdom serves to enhance the latter's attractiveness. This diptych directly prepares the first Solomonic collection, which to a large extent contrasts the conduct of the wise man and the fool.

25 **(II) First Collection of the Proverbs of Solomon (10:1–22:16).** The heart of the book—375 short independent maxims of two members each. From chs. 10–15, the parallelism is predominantly antithetic, the second member in contrast to the first. From 16:1–22:16, it is synthetic, the second member developing the thought of the first. The aphorisms in the first section are, for the most part, mere observations, and their religious relevance is less obvious. In the second part, the tone is more religious and the proverbs exhortatory. Inasmuch as each proverb is completely independent, the order is quite haphazard. Sometimes proverbs are grouped by subject matter (e.g., 10:18–21 concerning speech); again, a catchword may serve to connect one proverb with the next, even though the thought is completely different—e.g., 10:16 and 10:17 are connected by the expression "to life" (*l^{e}ḥayyîm*); vocal similarity is also another principle of connection. These are mnemonic devices for mastering an extensive and disparate body of knowledge. The erudition of the wise men is evident in the literary finesse with which similar proverbs are varied. It has been plausibly suggested that the extent of the first Solomonic collection—375 proverbs—is conditioned by the numerical value of the Hebrew for Solomon. This may explain the doublets; the editor must attain the number 375 in this collection (Skehan, *CBQ* 10, 115–30). Many of the sayings are self-explanatory; they manifest keen observation of human foibles, sometimes pointing an accusing finger; real pleasure is found in all natural goods within due order, but the wise men are above all sensitive to the real joy that goodness radiates (10:23,32; 11:25; 13:9; 15:15; etc.). All these proverbs presuppose that justice and wisdom are synonymous, as well as wickedness and folly (10:21,31; 11:2,9; 13:19; 14:16; etc.). The duty of parents in the education of their children is frequently emphasized (10:1; 13:24; 15:20; 20:7; etc.).

26 **10:2.** The good man should live long (11:4). **3.** The principle of earthly retribution. The Israelite character of the collection is evident from the use of the divine name, Yahweh. **5.** An agrarian culture is presupposed. **6b.** In the CCD, v. 13b reads as the proper parallel to v. 6a; the MT reads, "The mouth of the wicked conceals violence" (11b, 13b). Great confidence is placed in bodily chastisement (13:24; 19:18; 22:15; but cf. 17:10). **7.** The wise man's notion of happiness includes a good reputation after death. **8.** *a wise man:* Lit., "the wise of heart." The contrast is between the quiet, reflective person and the talkative man who rarely reflects. **9.** *securely:* Confidence is a goal of education and the fruit of virtue. **10b.** Here the CCD follows the LXX. **11.** Cf. Mt 12:37. **12.** See 1 Pt 4:8. Love is active in undoing wrong (cf. 1 Cor 13:7; Jas 5:20). **13.** The MT version is not clear; the CCD hesitatingly places v. 6b here. **15.** The construction is chiastic; wealth protects the rich, whereas the poor are defenseless. **18.** The parallelism is synthetic; to spread slander is more serious than to disguise hatred. **19.** See Jas 1:19; 3:2–12. **20.** *tongue:* Reveals the heart. **21.** The just man is of profit to many, the fool not even to himself (cf. Dn 12:3). **24.** Cf. Jb 3:25. **25.** Cf. Mt 7:24–27. **26.** Cf. Ptahhotep: "If thou art a man of intimacy, whom one great man sends to another, be thoroughly reliable when he sends thee. Carry out the errand for him as he has spoken" (*ANET* 413a). **30.** Cf. 2:21–22. **31.** More is suggested by the antithesis than is actually said: The just man not only produces wisdom, but he shall also prosper; the tongue of the wicked man causes his ruin.

27 **11:1.** See Dt 25:13–16; justice in the market place was a common concern of the Law (Lv 19:35–36), of the prophets (Am 8:5–6; Hos 12:8; Mi 6:10–11), of the wise men (Prv 16:11; 20:10), of Amen-em-ope (*ANET* 423b), and also of the Lord. **4.** *day of wrath:* Natural calamity or death. **7.** The MT is unclear; the LXX reads: "When a just man dies, hope does not perish; but the boast of the wicked perishes" (10:28). **9b.** Knowledge of men and affairs plus personal integrity. **12–13.** Egyptian wisdom literature also exalts the man who observes a prudent silence (Ani, *ANET* 420; Amen-em-ope, *ANET* 422a). **16.** The CCD version follows the LXX, creating two antithetical proverbs. **20.** Religious proverbs are not absent from this collection (10:3,22; 11:1; 12:2; 15:3,8,33; 16:1–7,9; etc.). **22.** The Hebrew juxtaposes two incongruities; nose rings were worn by women as ornaments and charms. **24.** A paradox, which is based upon observation. **25.** The law of retribution. **26.** The proverb presupposes a small, agrarian society (cf. Joseph in Egypt). **28.** The just man trusts in the Lord (Ps 52:9–11). **29.** Negligence in managing one's own affairs will lead to slavery for debt. **31.** Cf. 2 Thes 1:6.

28 **12:4.** The "worthy wife" (*'ēšet-ḥayil*) is described at length in 31:10–31. *a disgraceful one:* A wife who acts shamefully. *rot in his bones:* See comment on 3:8 (Sir 26:1). **5–8.** These verses contain indirect counsel. **10.** Cf. Dt 25:4. **11.** The story of Naboth's vineyard (1 Kgs 21) illustrates how the Israelite prized independence on his own parcel of land. **12.** *the root of the just:* The image connotes the stability of a tree (Ps 1:3). The self-confidence of the wicked is poor protection. **16.** Sumerian proverb: "To converse with a blazing face, to become downcast, to concentrate one's attention on oneself—that is not human nature" (*BWL* 269). **20.** *deceit:* Self-deception and consequent misery. **22.** The social virtue of truthfulness (12:17) is also of concern to the Lord. **23.** Cf. 11:12–13; 21:23; the *Instruction of Amen-em-ope* reads: "Better is a man whose talk remains in his belly than he who speaks it out injuriously" (*ANET* 424a). **26a.** The MT is uncertain; the CCD may mean that a just man is an example to his neighbor. **27.** If correct, the MT is more colorful: "The slothful man does not roast his game."

29 13:4. *soul:* Used here in the sense of appetite or desire. **5.** The antithesis implies that one's attitude to truthfulness either preserves from, or leads to, shame and disgrace. **6.** *virtue:* *Ṣᵉdāqâ*, an all-embracing conformity to what is right. **7.** Social hypocrisy. **8.** The poor man has nothing to offer; therefore he is not threatened. **10.** *stupid man:* The MT reads *raq*, which may be the origin of *raka* in Mt 5:22; the pride of the stupid man rejects advice. **11.** The value of industry (20:21). **13–14.** "Word" and "commandment" more likely refer to the "teaching" (*tôrâ*) of the wise man than to the Torah of Moses (cf. Dt 30:11–14). **17.** For royal or public servants, see comment on 10:26. **19.** In the MT: "Desire fulfilled is sweet to the soul" (cf. 13:12b). The CCD translation reads *tarʿîb nāpeš* for *teʿĕrab lᵉnāpeš* and establishes a connection between a and b; either something is missing, or we have two independent proverbs. **22a.** Cf. 2 Cor 12:14. **22b.** Cf. 28:8; Jb 27:16–17; Eccl 6:2. **23.** The CCD, by very minor changes in pointing (*rib ʾōkēl* for *rab ʾōkel*), obtains a completely original but intelligible proverb. **24.** The Syr Ahikar reads: "My son, subdue thy son while he is yet a boy, before he wax stronger than thee and rebel against thee, and thou be ashamed in all his corrupt doing" (*APOT* 2, 732). **25.** Cf. 10:3.

30 **14:1.** Wisdom (*ḥokmôt* as in 1:20 and 9:1) is constructive; Folly is destructive (cf. 9:1). **2.** The connection between religion and moral conduct. **3.** *a rod for his back:* The MT "a sprout of pride" is to be preferred to an uncertain correction (CCD). **4.** Animals are necessary for a farmer's success. **7.** The text is corrupt; Toy's emendation offers the least difficulty: "Go from the presence of a fool, for his lips do not utter knowledge" (*op. cit.*). **10.** There is an area of everyone's personal life that is incommunicable to others. **12.** Human fallibility. **17.** *quick-tempered:* Lit., "short of face." **18.** The MT reads: "Simpletons inherit folly." The emendation of the CCD creates a more explicit parallelism. **20.** Money makes a difference; cf. Sir 13:20–22. (On 14:26–16:15, cf. Skehan, *CBQ* 10, 118–20). **27.** A variation on 13:14. **29.** *the patient man:* Lit., "long of face." **31.** Cf. Mt 25:40,45.

31 **15:1–2.** Cf. *Instruction of Ani:* "Thou shouldst not express thy whole heart to the stranger, to let him discover thy speech against thee. If a passing remark issuing from thy mouth is hasty and it is repeated, thou wilt make enemies. A man may fall to ruin because of his tongue.... The belly of a man is wider than a storehouse, and it is full of every kind of response. Thou shouldst choose the good and say them, while the bad are shut up in thy belly" (*ANET* 420b). **5.** On correction, cf. vv. 10, 12, 31, 32. **8.** The importance of interior sincerity and purity in cult (cf. 1 Sm 15:22; Ps 50:8–15; Is 1:11–17); cf. *Instruction for King Meri-ka-re:* "More acceptable is the character of one upright of heart than the ox of the evildoer" (*ANET* 417b). **11.** The world of the dead was a deep mystery to the Israelite; man's existence there was but a shadow (Pss 6:6; 88:11–13; 30:10; Is 38:18); but even in Sheol man cannot escape the hand of God (Jb 26:6; Ps 139:7–12). **13.** A man's countenance generally reveals his interior state (but cf. 14:13). **15.** An observation of fact or a veiled counsel to set one's heart in order, that one may be happy. **16–17.** Riches are among the rewards of the just, but they are not to be sought at the expense of piety and true love (cf. 16:8); cf. *Instruction of Amen-em-ope:* "Better is poverty in the hand of the god than riches in a storehouse; better is bread, when the heart is happy, than riches with sorrow" (*ANET* 422b). **19.** Negligence creates obstacles (cf. 24:30–34). **21.** The fool is completely oblivious to the consequences of the things in which he delights. **22.** Cf. 11:14. **24.** *upward, below:* Missing in the LXX. Robert (*Mémorial Lagrange*, 167) considers the MT to be original, dependent on Dt 28:13–14; the reference is to the prosperity of the wise man and not to heavenly bliss (F. Montagnini, *VD* 25 [1947] 157–58). **25.** Property limits were marked by piles of stone, which could easily be moved. The proud are, by definition, in revolt against God (Ps 94:2; Is 2:12); the Lord's concern for the helpless widow is a constant theme of the prophets (Is 1:17; 10:2; Jer 7:6; Zech 7:10; Mal 3:5). **27.** The reference is to unjust judges (Am 2:6; Is 1:23; Mi 3:9–11). **33.** True humility is founded on a proper relationship to God (1:7; 18:12). Proverbs 15:33–16:7 all mention Yahweh; this editorial arrangement joins the two parts of this collection (Skehan, *CBQ* 10, 119).

32 **16:1.** Man proposes, God disposes (cf. 16:9). **3.** *entrust:* The proverb is in the form of a precept. **4.** *the evil day:* Natural calamity or death (cf. 11:4). **8.** Cf. 15:16; the *Instruction of Amen-em-ope* reads: "Better is praise as one who loves men than riches in a storehouse" (*ANET* 423b). **9.** Cf. *Instruction of Amen-em-ope:* "One thing are the words which men say, another is that which the god does" (*ANET* 423b). Five proverbs (vv. 10, 12–15) concern kingship; they may easily belong to the pre-exilic period. The perfection that they confidently expect in the king is also the perfection of the messianic king (cf. Is 9:5–6; 11:3–5). **10.** *oracle:* Originally the pronouncement of a diviner, here the word merely connotes the divine authority of the king's decree. **11.** Cf. *Instruction of Amen-em-ope:* "Make not for thyself weights which are deficient; they abound in grief through the will of god" (*ANET* 423b). **15.** A late rain in spring fills out the ears of grain before they ripen; the monarch was responsible for the material prosperity of his people. **29.** Cf. the bad companions of 1:10–14. **30.** Cf. 6:13–14. **31.** *gray hair:* Old age is a reward of virtue and a sign of wisdom (20:29). **33.** *lap:* The fold of the outer garment at the breast, in which the lots were placed. Lots were commonly used in earlier times to determine the will of God in crucial circumstances (Ex 28:15–30; Nm 27:21; Jgs 1:1–2; 1 Sm 14:41; Is 34:17; Acts 1:24–26); they were used less frequently after the institution of the monarchy. This proverb reflects the Hebr belief in the all-pervading divine causality.

33 **17:2.** Many proverbs in this chapter (vv. 1, 2, 5, 6, 9, 14) concern domestic and social relations. Intelligence can supplant the rights of blood (cf. Eccl 10:7). **3.** The comparison suggests the stern character of the Lord's examination (16:2). **5.** Cf. 14:31. **7.** An argument a fortiori. **8.** A realistic observation; for a moral judgment, cf. 15:27. **11.** *a merciless messenger:* The agent of civil authority or the angel of divine retribution. **15.** Cf. Is 5:23. **18.** See comment on 6:1–5. **19.** *guilt:* The word includes the notion of punishment. *builds his gate high:* Probably a figure of speech for haughty talk; *petaḥ* could mean the opening of the mouth. **22.** See Sir 30:22. **24.** The wise man disciplines his interests, but the fool is easily distracted. **26.** The argument is a fortiori. **27.** *chary of speech:* Lit., "cold of spirit," an Egyptian expression (L. Grollenberg, *RB* 59 [1952] 42–43).

34 **18:1.** The MT is doubtful; the CCD follows the LXX. The solitary man tends to be quarrelsome. **3.** The social consequences of evil. **4.** *deep waters:* Difficult to fathom (cf. 20:5). *a flowing brook:* Clear, fresh, and easily accessible. An antithesis is implied. **8.** Like choice food, gossip is avidly devoured and becomes part of one's person. **10.** *the name of the Lord:* The name stands for the person in Semitic thought.

11. A neutral observation (10:15) acquires moral overtones in association with 18:10. **16.** The power of the well-placed gift. **17.** Hear both sides of the story. **18.** When a decision is referred to the Lord, human prestige has no weight. **21.** *those who make it a friend:* Those who cultivate the proper use of the tongue. **23.** Wealth is a protection (10:15; 18:11). **24.** Hebrew distinguishes the simple neighbor (*rēʿîm*) from the man who truly loves (*ʾōhēb*).

35 **19:1.** Cf. v. 22; the CCD follows the Syr, Tg., and 28:6. **2.** Cf. Rom 10:2. **3.** Every man is slow to accept the responsibility for his own misery. **5.** Cf. v. 9. **6.** *curry favor with:* Lit., "entreat the face of," used also of prayer to God (1 Sm 13:12). **7.** The *Instruction of Amen-em-het* reads: "No man has adherents on the day of distress" (*ANET* 418b). **10.** Two incongruities constitute an a fortiori argument (cf. Eccl 10:7). **13.** Domestic happiness. **14.** The parallelism implies a comparison (cf. 18:22). **16.** *precept, word:* The instruction of the wise man rather than the Mosaic Law. **17.** Cf. 14:31; 17:5; 22:9; Mt 10:42. **18.** Cf. 13:24. **19.** Translation uncertain. **22.** The MT is doubtful; Wiesmann, Gemser, and Weber follow the LXX: "A man's advantage is his kindness." **24.** Hyperbolic and humorous, with reference to the Oriental custom of eating from a common bowl.

36 **20:3.** Cf. the Babylonian *Counsels of Wisdom:* "When you see a quarrel, go away without noticing it" (*ANET* 426b). **6.** *virtue:* Lit., "kindness" (*ḥesed*). The proof of true virtue lies in its "constancy" (*ʾĕmûnîm*). **8.** The justice of the king is presupposed; in Egypt, the Pharaoh rules in accordance with *maat* (justice). **9.** The consciousness of sinfulness is not incompatible with a life of integrity and justice (v. 7); the proverb must not be pressed to the denial of all goodness in man's actions. **10.** Cf. 11:1. **11.** The child is father to the man. **12.** The use of the senses falls under the surveillance of God, who made them. **14.** Bargaining customs of the Near East; to drive a bargain, the buyer depreciates the goods offered for sale. **16.** The man who foolishly pledges himself for another deserves to lose his security (cf. 27:13). The garment was usually given as security (Dt 24:10–13). **17.** *gravel:* A vivid image for the pangs of remorse. **19.** Gossips are treacherous; cf. *Instruction of Amen-em-ope:* "Spread not thy words to the common people, nor associate to thyself one too outgoing of heart" (*ANET* 424a). **20.** *his lamp will go out:* Dire misfortune will destroy his prosperity. The Aram Ahikar story reads: "Whosoever takes no pride in the names of his father and mother, may the sun not shine upon him; for he is a wicked man" (*ANET* 429b). **21.** *possessions:* Lit., "an inheritance." Hasty acquisition in this case presupposes fraud or injustice (cf. 13:11). **22.** Prohibitions of revenge are found in the OT (Prv 24:29; Sir 28:1), in the NT (Mt 5:39; Rom 12:17,19; 1 Pt 3:9), in Egypt, and in Babylon. The *Instruction of Amen-em-ope* reads: "Do not say: 'I have found a strong superior, for a man in thy city has injured me.' Do not say: 'I have found a patron, for one who hates me has injured me.' For surely thou knowest not the plans of god, lest thou be ashamed on the morrow" (*ANET* 424a). The Babylonian *Counsels of Wisdom* read: "Unto your opponent do no evil; your evildoer recompense with good; unto your enemy let justice be done" (*ANET* 426b). In v. 22 it is implied that it is the Lord who will avenge. **23.** Cf. 20:10. **24.** God's providence in our lives is mysterious. **25.** Dt 23:22–24. **27.** *breath:* N^{e}*šāmâ* seems to be used here in the sense of spirit (cf. Jb 32:8; 26:4); self-awareness is a share in God's intelligence. **30.** The exact translation is uncertain, but the meaning is clear: Chastisement is a deterrent from evil.

37 **21:1.** Free will is not at variance with God's universal causality and providence. *stream:* An irrigation canal that is directed according to the good pleasure of the farmer. **2.** Cf. 16:2. **3.** Cf. 15:8; Mt 9:13. **4.** Perhaps fragments of two different proverbs. **7.** *oppression:* That which the wicked plans to execute. **9.** The CCD reads *rāḥāb*, "roomy house," for *ḥāber*, "the house of a companion"; the comparison is between exiguous and spacious quarters. Albright has suggested "public house" (*op. cit.*, 10–12). Cf. 21:19; 25:24; 27:15. **12.** *the just man:* The MT may also be rendered "the Just One," i.e., Yahweh; a real parallelism is thus restored. **16.** Premature death is primarily meant. The verse may be applied to the eternal punishment of the wicked only in the light of subsequent revelation. Verse 18 presupposes that even the just sometimes suffer, but they will be delivered. **19.** Solitude is better than wrangling. **20.** *precious treasure:* Wisdom that is always at the wise man's disposal; however, the proverb may simply refer to prodigality. **28.** The false witness is contrasted with the cautious and truthful witness (cf. G. Driver, *ZAW* 50 [1932] 144–45).

38 **22:1.** *a good name:* Through his reputation, a man lives after death. **2.** Cf. 29:13; this common bond is the foundation of all obligations to the poor. **3.** *evil:* Lit., "an evil woman"; cf. ch. 7. **4.** The clearest and classic statement of the wise man's concept of happiness. **6.** As the twig is bent, so grows the tree. **7.** Cf. Dt 15:2–4. **8.** Cf. Gal 6:7; the Hebrew is uncertain. **11.** *pure of heart:* Sinless. There is no intrinsic connection between the two lines. See Vg: "Qui diligit cordis munditiam, propter gratiam labiorum suorum habebit amicum regis"; spiritual writers have applied this rendering to virgins, the friends of Christ. **12.** *the eyes of the Lord:* Divine omniscience; God provides for those who possess true wisdom. **13.** The lazy man takes refuge in the slightest excuse and exaggerates all difficulty. **14.** *the mouth of the adulteress:* Flattery. **16.** The MT is uncertain; the CCD implies the ultimate punishment of unjust oppression. The couplet may be simply a social vignette: The man who oppresses the poor does so to enrich himself; the man who gives to the rich is only impoverishing himself.

39 **(III) Sayings of the Wise (22:17–24:22).** A new title indicates a new collection. Instead of isolated couplets and impersonal observations, the instruction is given in strophes of four to eight lines each. The address is direct and personal; the paternal tone of the prologue returns—"my son." The similarity of this collection with the Egyptian *Instruction of Amen-em-ope* (*ANET* 421–24) is most apparent in the structure (introduction and 30 chapters; see Prv 22:20) and in at least 17 parallels. The author has not simply copied the Egyptian text but has rethought and reworked his instructions in the light of his own tradition.

17–18. Cf. *Instruction of Amen-em-ope:* "Give thy ears, hear what is said, give thy heart to understand them. To put them in thy heart is worth while, but it is damaging to him who neglects them. Let them rest in the casket of thy belly, that they may be a key in thy heart. At a time when there is a whirlwind of words, they shall be a mooring-stake for thy tongue. If thou spendest thy time while this is in thy heart, thou wilt find it a success; thou wilt find my words a treasury of life, and thy body will prosper upon the earth" (*ANET* 421–22). **19.** The purpose of the collection, "trust in the Lord," betrays the Israelite character of the instruction (16.3). *the words of Amen-em-ope:* Conjecture; the Hebrew is uncertain; the LXX reads, "your way." **20–21.** Cf. the *Instruction of Amen-em-ope:* "See thou these thirty chapters: They entertain, they instruct; they are the foremost of all books; they make the ignorant to know" (*ANET* 424b). With this introduction (vv. 17–21), compare the introduction to the *Instruction of Amen-em-ope* (*ANET* 421b; see comment on 1:6). **22–23.** The prophetic background of these verses (e.g., Is 5:8–9; 33:1; Jer 22:13–19; Mi 2:1–5; Hab 2:6–17) is more striking than the Egyptian parallel; the *Instruction of Amen-em-ope* reads: "Guard thyself against robbing the oppressed and against overbearing the disabled" (*ANET* 422a). **24–25.** Cf. the *Instruction of Amen-em-ope:* "Do not associate to thyself the heated man, nor visit him for conversation.... Do not leap to hold such a one, lest a terror carry thee off" (*ANET* 423a). **26–27.** No parallel in the *Instruction of Amen-em-ope*, but cf. 6:1; 11:15; 17:18; 20:16. **28.** Cf. 23:10. **29.** Cf. *Instruction of Amen-em-ope:* "As for the scribe who is experienced in his office, he will find himself worthy to be a courtier" (*ANET* 424b).

40 **23:1–2.** Good manners; cf. *Instruction of Amen-em-ope:* "Do not eat bread before a noble, nor lay on thy mouth at first.... Look at the cup which is before thee, and let it serve thy needs" (*ANET* 424a); cf. also *Instruction of Ptah-hotep* (*ANET* 412b). **3.** The CCD omits 3a as dittography (6b) and reads 3b as 7b; conjecture. **4–5.** Cf. the *Instruction of Amen-em-ope:* "Cast not thy heart in pursuit of riches, for there is no ignoring Fate and Fortune" (*ANET* 422b); the rest of the chapter deals with stolen goods, which fly away like geese. **6–7.** The suggested parallel in the *Instruction of Amen-em-ope* (*ANET* 423a) concerns a poor man's bread. *a grudging man:* Lit., "evil of eye" (28:22). **9.** Cf. *Instruction of Amen-em-ope:* "Empty not thy belly to everybody, nor damage thus the regard for thee" (*ANET* 424a). **10–11.** The parallel in *Instruction of Amen-em-ope* (*ANET* 422b) is part of a recommendation to personal diligence in earning an honest livelihood; Prv depends here upon Israelite Law and the prophets. **12.** The thought of 22:17–20 is repeated, perhaps as an inclusion; the formal parallels with the *Instruction of Amen-em-ope* cease here. **13–14.** Cf. 13:24; 19:18; the Aram Ahikar reads: "Withhold not thy son from the rod, else thou wilt not be able to save him from wickedness. If I smite thee, my son, thou wilt not die, but if I leave thee to thy own heart thou wilt not live" (*ANET* 428b). **15–28.** These verses recall the instructions of the prologue; v. 23 is out of place in this context. **29–35.** A colorful description of the effects of excess in drinking. Sirach uses a similar essay form in presenting his instructions.

41 **24:1–2.** Cf. 3:31; 23:17. **3–7.** Wisdom is the architect of prosperity; these verses may be part of an earlier alphabetic poem (cf. Skehan, *CBQ* 10, 122); the 30 instructions of the collection are constructed from a common store, and repetitions (e.g., 24:1,19 and 23:17; 24:14 and 23:18) are required to attain the proposed limit. **7.** Read *dᵉmôt* (to be silent) for *rā'môt* (precious coral). *wisdom: Ḥokmôt*, as in 1:20; 9:1; 14:1. **10.** Uncertain in the MT; apparently an exhortation to courage "in time of adversity." **11–12.** The wise man may not regard the unjust oppression of the innocent with indifference. **15–16.** It is futile to plot the ruin of a just man, for God always restores him. The familiar form of v. 16a, "The just man falls seven times a day," appears only in a few Vg manuscripts. **17–18.** The punishment of evildoing belongs to the Lord (20:22). **19–20.** Cf. 23:17–18 and 24:13–14. **21–22.** The authority of the king is comparable to that of God.

42 **(IV) Other Sayings of the Wise (24:23–34).** The title indicates an appendix to the 30 chapters of the third collection. The LXX inserts 30:1–14 before this section. The miscellaneous character of these sayings is an indication that they derive from various sources and are added without any attempt at an orderly arrangement. **26.** *a kiss on the lips:* A unique expression in OT; doubtless a sign of friendship. **27.** Be sure of your livelihood before undertaking to establish a family. **28.** Cf. 30:10. **29.** See comment on 20:22. **30–34.** Cf. 6:6–11; thorns and thistles result from man's negligence and sin (Gn 3:18).

43 **(V) Second Collection of the Proverbs of Solomon (25:1–29:27).** **25:1.** The royal scribes of Hezekiah's court are credited with assembling this collection. Literary activity during his reign (716–687) is highly probable, owing both to the prosperity of Judah and to the religious reform of this pious king (cf. 2 Kgs 18–20; 2 Chr 29–32). The 126 proverbs (CCD) approximate the numerical value of Hezekiah's name (130) (cf. Skehan, *CBQ* 10, 125–27). Literary form varies considerably. In the first half (chs. 25–27), there are several proverbs of four to six lines (25:6–7,8–10,21–22; 26:18–19; 27:10,15–16) and one of ten lines (27:23–27); the parallelism is predominantly synthetic, and comparisons are numerous. In the second half (chs. 28–29), the proverbs all exhibit the two-line form proper to the first collection of Solomonic proverbs; the parallelism is more often antithetic, and religious and ethical counsels are more frequent. **2–3.** Superior knowledge is expected in a king, whereas the knowledge of God surpasses that of all men. **6–7.** Cf. Lk 14:7–11. **8–10.** Cf. Mt 5:25; 18:15. **13c.** An explanatory gloss. **15b.** Cf. the Aram Ahikar story: "Soft is the tongue of a king, but it breaks a dragon's ribs" (*ANET* 429a). **19.** *dependence on:* An explanatory gloss. **20.** The MT version is corrupt; the CCD adapts the LXX. **21–22.** Cf. 20:22; 24:29; Rom 12:20–21: "Be not overcome by evil, but overcome evil with good." *live coals:* Perhaps remorse or embarrassment, but on this difficult passage see W. Klassen (*NTS* 9 [1962–63] 337–50). **24.** Cf. 21:9. **26.** *Corruptio optimi pessima.* **27b.** The MT is uncertain.

44 **26:2.** The effective power of the spoken word is presupposed. **3–12.** All these verses concern fools. **4–5.** The contradiction is only apparent; beware of imitating or encouraging a fool. **7–9.** The fool is unable to put a wise saying to good use. **10.** Translation is conjectural; both fail in their aim. **11.** Cf. 2 Pt 2:22. **13–15.** On laziness (cf. 22:13; 19:24). **17–22.** On minding one's own business. **22.** Cf. 18:8. **23–26.** The flatterer. **27.** Cf. Sir 27:25–27.

27:1. Cf. Jas 4:13–16. **3.** Cf. Sir 22:15 and the Aram Ahikar story: "I have lifted sand, and I have carried salt; but there is naught which is heavier than rage" (*ANET* 429a). **6.** *prays against:* The Hebrew is uncertain. **7.** Cf. the Aram Ahikar story: "Hunger makes bitterness sweet, and thirst sourness" (*ANET* 430). **8.** The wise men were also travelers (cf. Sir 39:5). **10b.** Apparently out of place; Gemser deletes. **12.** Cf. 22:3. **13.** Cf. 20:16. **14.** Hypocrisy. *in the early morning:* Delete for rhythmical reasons. **16.** Uncertain in the MT; a quarrelsome woman cannot be restrained. **17.** The importance of good companions. **19.** The CCD follows the LXX; the MT reads: "Like water is one face to another, so the heart of man to man." **20.** The insatiability of human desire (30:16; Eccl 4:8). **22b.** A superfluous line. **23–27.** A sketch, similar to 24:30–34, concludes the first half of the collection. **27b.** A superfluous line.

45 **28:2.** The history of the northern kingdom may have prompted this proverb. **3.** *a rich man:* Correction; the LXX has "a wicked man"; the MT has "a poor man." **4.** *the law: Tôrâ*, the instructions of the wise men or possibly the Mosaic Law (cf. vv. 7, 9); if the latter is the case, the proverbs are probably later additions. **8.** Unjust advantage of a neighbor in distress

(Lv 25:35–38; Dt 23:20–21); divine providence will right such wrongs. **10c.** Seems to belong to a proverb whose first member is lost. **13.** Cf. Ps 32:3–5; some form of public confession was practiced in Israel, especially in post-exilic times. **16.** Cf. 15:27. **17.** The murderer deserves no pity (cf. Nm 35:31). **18.** Cf. 28:10. **19.** Cf. *Instruction of Amen-em-ope:* "Plow in the fields, that thou mayest find thy needs, that thou mayest receive bread of thy own threshing floor" (*ANET* 422b). **25.** *the greedy man:* Lit., "wide of desire." **26.** True wisdom includes distrust of self and confidence in God (v. 25). **28.** Cf. 28:12; 29:2.

29:1. Cf. 12:1; 15:10. **4.** The MT is uncertain. **9.** Such disputes are futile. **13.** *light to the eyes:* A figure for life (cf. Ps 13:4; Jb 33:30). **16.** The traditional teaching on retribution; cf. 28:12,28. **18.** *prophecy:* Lit., "vision" (*ḥāzôn*), the word used for the revelations of the prophets (cf. Is 1:1; Ob 1; Na 1:1). *law: Tôrâ;* more likely the instructions of the wise men, as elsewhere in the book (e.g., 1:8; 6:20; 13:14). It remains possible, however, that we have here a reference to the canonical Law and the Prophets upon which the wise men base their teaching (cf. Ez 7:26; Lam 2:9; Jer 18:18). **19.** A rod is necessary (cf. Sir 33:25–29). **20.** Cf. Jas 1:19. **24.** The solemn and judicial adjuration will be effective if the witness refuses to answer (cf. Lv 5:1). **25.** Human respect.

46 (VI) The Words of Agur (30:1–14). Four appendices follow the second Solomonic collection: the personal reflections of Agur upon the inaccessible wisdom of God (1–6); the modest prayer of a pious man (7–9); an independent proverb (10); and an enumeration of the wicked (11–14). Only the first poem need be attributed to Agur, although the modest detachment of the other two suggest the same author.

1. Agur is otherwise unknown; Bar 3:23 speaks of the sons of Hagar, likely Edomite sages, in search of knowledge. *the Massaite:* Correction (cf. 31:1); the MT reads: "the oracle." Massa was an Ishmaelite tribe of northern Arabia (Gn 25:14). *I am not God...prevail:* Conjecture; BJ reads: "for Iteel, for Iteel and for Ukal." Weber and Wiesmann translate, "I have wearied myself, O God, I have wearied myself, and been victorious." **2–4.** The wise man has come to realize the superiority and inaccessibility of divine wisdom (cf. Pss 73:22; 135:7; Jb 26:8; 38:5,18). **4.** Cf. Jb 38–39; Sir 1:2–3; Is 40:12–26. Christ offers such knowledge to man because he had this experience (Jn 3:12–13). *his son's name:* The LXX reads: "his sons' names"—the heavenly court or family of God. **5.** Cf. Ps 18:31; the author is dependent upon biblical literature, which he considers to be divine revelation. **6.** See Dt 4:2; 13:1; Ap 22:18–19.

7–9. The only formal prayer in the book; it is based on the earlier teaching of the wise men. **10.** Independent saying, to be associated with 24:28. **11–14.** A simple enumeration of four classes of wicked men. Both vv. 7–9 and vv. 11–14 are similar in form to the following numerical proverbs.

47 (VII) Numerical Proverbs (30:15–33). Skehan suggests that the *ḥîdôt* (1:6) of the final editor also included 6:12–19; 30:7–9,11–14 (*CBQ* 10, 115–16). For the form, see comment on 6:16–19; heterogeneous elements have been added by association (15a, 17, 20, 32–33). Wise counsel is drawn from the mysteries of nature and the customs of animals. **15–16.** Insatiability. **15a.** The MT is obscure. **16.** *the nether world:* Cf. 27:20. *the barren womb:* Cf. Gn 30:1. *the earth:* In the hill country of Palestine, the earth is shallow and the rain flows away quickly. **17.** Read with 23:22; there will be no burial for the ungrateful son. **18–19.** *the way of a man...:* Four things that excite wonderment (the flight of an eagle, etc.) especially the mystery of sex; cf. Eccl 11:5. **20.** Perhaps a gloss; equally incomprehensible (v. 18) is the nonchalance of the adulteress; cf. 9:17 (cf. D. Buzy, *RB* 42 [1953] 5–13; E. Sutcliffe, *IrTQ* 27 [1960] 124–31). **22.** Cf. 19:10. **23.** Cf. Gn 29:31ff.; 16:4ff.; Dt 21:15–17; 24:1–4. **24–28.** Solomon's knowledge of plant and animal life is praised in 1 Kgs 5:13 (4:33). *rock-badgers: Hyrax syriacus,* a small herbivorous mammal (cf. Ps 104:18). **29–31.** Four examples of imposing figures; the text of v. 31 contains several rare words and is probably corrupt. **32–33.** This quatrain was perhaps suggested by the previous numerical proverb.

48 (VIII) The Words of Lemuel (31:1–9). An example of the maternal instruction frequently mentioned in Prv (e.g., 1:8; 6:20; 15:20). Lemuel, an unknown king of Massa, an Ishmaelite tribe, records the instructions his mother gave him for the exercise of his office. The wisdom literature of Babylon and Egypt is frequently concerned with the education of kings' sons for their future office, e.g., the *Instruction for King Meri-ka-re* (22nd cent. BC). The counsels concern the enervating dangers of lust (3), the stunning effects of wine (4–7), and the protection of the destitute (8–9). **6–7.** These lines occasioned the pious service Jerusalem women used to offer the condemned (cf. Mt 27:34). **8–9.** The *Instruction for King Meri-ka-re* reads: "Do justice whilst thou endurest upon earth. Quiet the weeper; do not oppress the widow; supplant no man in the property of his father; and impair no officials at their posts" (*ANET* 415b).

49 (IX) The Ideal Wife (31:10–31). A noble ideal of womanhood is offered for the imitation of the Israelite wife and mother (cf. M. Crook, *JNES* 13 [1954] 137–40). On the advantages of a good wife, cf. Prv 5:15–19; 11:16; 12:4; 18:22; 19:14; Sir 7:19; 26:1–4,13–18. For an Egyptian praise of women, cf. the *Instruction of Ani* (*ANET* 421b).

Each of the 22 verses begins with a different letter of the Hebr alphabet. Other such acrostic poems may be found in the Bible, e.g., Pss 9; 25; 34; 111–12; 119; 145; Lam 1–4; Na 1:2–8; Sir 51:13–30 (cf. P. Piatti, *Bib* 31 [1950] 281–315). **10.** Lit., "Who will find a woman of strength?" This reflection is not pessimistic, as Eccl 7:28, but an exclamation of praise. **13.** She is herself industrious. **14.** Probably a poetic figure; care in buying is meant. **15.** The Oriental housewife rose early to grind corn and bake bread. **16.** Her economy expands the family holdings. **18.** *her lamp:* A metaphor for prosperity, based on an Oriental custom of keeping a lamp lit during the night (cf. Jb 18:6). **22.** *fine linen and purple:* Signs of wealth and nobility. **23.** It is suggested that her good management reflects on the public status of her husband; great wealth and abundant leisure are marks of prominence in the Orient. **25.** No fears for the future. **30.** The only explicitly religious element in the entire poem; the text, however, is uncertain; the LXX reads: "For a wise woman will be blessed; let her praise the fear of the Lord." As indicated earlier (9:10; 1:7), the fear of the Lord is the beginning of wisdom.

30

CANTICLE OF CANTICLES

Roland E. Murphy, O.Carm.

BIBLIOGRAPHY

1 *Recent bibliographical surveys:* Murphy, R. E., *CBQ* 16 (1954) 1ff. Rowley, H. H., *The Servant of the Lord and Other Essays* (London, 1952) 187–234. Würthwein, E., "Zum Verständnis des Hohenliedes," *TRu* 32 (1967) 177–212. A relatively complete bibliography is to be found in the commentaries of A. Robert *et al.*, G. Gerleman, and W. Rudolph.

Commentaries: Bea, A., *Canticum canticorum* (Rome, 1953). Buzy, D., *Le Cantique des Cantiques* (Paris, 1949). Feuillet, A., *Le Cantique des Cantiques* (Paris, 1953). Gerleman, G., *Das Hohe Lied* (BK; Neukirchen, 1963). Gordis, R., *The Song of Songs* (N.Y., 1954). Haller, M., *Die fünf Megillot* (HAT; Tübingen, 1940). Joüon, P., *Le Cantique des Cantiques* (Paris, 1909). Krinetzki, L., *Das Hohe Lied* (Düsseldorf, 1964). Loretz, O., *Gotteswort und menschliche Erfahrung* (Freiburg, 1963) 76–112, Meek, T., *The Song of Songs* (*IB;* N.Y., 1956). Miller, A., *Das Hohe Lied* (BB; Bonn, 1927). Pouget, W. and J. Guitton, *The Canticle of Canticles* (N.Y., 1946). Ringgren, H., *Das Hohe Lied* (ATD; Göttingen, 1958). Robert, A., A. Feuillet and R. Tournay, *Le Cantique des Cantiques* (*EB;* Paris, 1963). Rudolph, W., *Das Hohe Lied* (KAT; Gütersloh, 1962). Van den Oudenrijn, M., *Het Hooglied* (Roermond, 1962).

The most complete treatment of extrabiblical parallels is the excursus by R. Tournay in the commentary of A. Robert *et al.*, pp. 349–426. See also *ANET* and Schott, S., *Les chants d'amour de l'Égypte ancienne* (Paris, n.d.).

INTRODUCTION

2 **(I) Title and Classification.** The title in 1:1 is the Hebr idiom for the superlative (cf. King of Kings), "the greatest song." And a song it is, or, rather, a group of songs that have been loosely united around the theme of love. Hebrew tradition ascribed the work to Solomon, doubtless motivated by the occurrence of his name in 3:7ff. and 8:11ff. Perhaps also Solomon's prestige in wisdom is another reason, particularly if one admits that post-exilic sages are responsible for the preservation and orientation of the work (J. P. Audet, *RB* 62 [1955] 216; *TD* 5 [1957] 88–92). This point of view would support the traditional Christian grouping among the sapiential books. The late form of the language indicates the probability of a post-exilic date for the book, even if some pieces may be earlier (e.g., the mention of Tirzah, capital of the northern kingdom, in 6:4). The Jews grouped Ct in the five "Megilloth" or scrolls, and it was chosen for public reading at the Passover. Before the so-called council of Jamnia in the 1st cent. AD, there was some opposition to the inclusion of Ct in the canon (W. Rudolph, *ZAW* 18 [1942–43] 189–99). Christian tradition is virtually unanimous in accepting the work; the alleged opinion of Theodore of Mopsuestia seems to deny the inspired character of the book. Such, at least (and not simply because Theodore interpreted the work as referring to human love), is the basis for the condemnation by the Fifth Council of Chalcedon in 553 (R. E. Murphy, *CBQ* 15 [1953] 502–3; A.-M. Dubarle, *RB* 61 [1954] 68–69).

3 **(II) Literary Structure and Content.** There is hardly any evidence of deliberate division by the editors, despite some refrains (e.g., 2:7; 3:5; 8:4). Commentators differ widely in enumerating the poetic units (D. Buzy and A. Bea, 7; V. Zapletal, 37; the subheadings in the CCD introduce 24). In any view, the real unity is created by love and love situations; it is probable that Ct is, in fact, a collection of love poems.

Both Catholic and non-Catholic scholars have recognized Ct as drama. F. Delitzsch accepted two main characters: Solomon and a Shulammite shepherd girl, engaged in a love duet. H. Ewald added a third: the girl's rustic lover; the drama then centered around her fidelity to her lover, despite King Solomon's blandishments. In one form or another, the dramatic interpretation has been advocated by E. Renan, W. Pouget and J. Guitton, L. Waterman, and many others. However, there is no example of true dramatic form in any Semitic literature. Moreover, the stage instructions and explanations that have to be added (and about which hardly any two commentators agree) are too subjective. Finally, the conflict that is characteristic of drama does not seem to be present; the mutual love of the man and woman seems to be at the same high level throughout Ct.

But Ct is dramatic in the sense that it is conceived as dialogue. The ancient Gk codex *Sinaiticus* identifies the speakers in marginal notations, as does also the CCD (B = bride; G = groom; D = daughters of Jerusalem). The gender differences are clearly indicated in the Hebrew, and in most of the cases we may be certain about the marginal identifications.

The content of Ct is best described as love lyrics that reflect the moods of lovers in various situations, whether they are united or separated. Thus, the poems contain expressions of mutual love, protestations of fidelity, reminiscences, and descriptions of each lover's charm and beauty.

4 **(III) Interpretation.** Apart from the literary problem of dramatic or dialogue structure, what is the meaning of Ct? The oldest interpretation, in both Christian and Jewish tradition, is religious; Ct describes the love between God and his people in terms of human love, thus continuing a theme common in the prophets (cf. Hos 1–3; see also Is 62:5; Jer 3:1–10; Ez 16; 23).

Some scholars urge this interpretation from the point of view of strict allegory; each detail of the book has a transferred meaning. P. Joüon provided the most scholarly basis for this approach, and it has been continued through the means of "anthological composition" (*style anthologique*, i.e., the meaning of Ct is determined through the supposed allusions to earlier biblical books) recognized by A. Robert, A. Feuillet, and R. Tournay (cf. Murphy, *CBQ* 16, 1ff.; P. Grelot, *RB* 71 [1964] 42–56). This methodology has not proved successful for Ct.

Other scholars (Buzy) have urged that Ct is a parable—i.e., the work as a whole illustrates the covenant relationship by use of the marriage theme. Although it is true that Ct can be fitted into this tradition, there is no indication that such is the author's intention. The marriage symbolism, which is never referred to as Yahweh and Israel in Ct, is always explained when it is used by the prophets, and the Ct would be a difficult exception.

Many recent writers (T. Meek, M. Haller, H. Ringgren) have been impressed by contacts between Ct and the Tammuz-Ishtar myth. Thus, we would have cult songs from this pagan liturgy, perhaps celebrated in the Temple during Manasseh's reign, which later entered the Passover liturgy. There is simply no evidence for such a radical view, and we cannot easily grant that such unhappy origins would have been glossed over by the Israelites. Perhaps a distinction is necessary: We may readily appreciate that these pagan liturgies could have consciously or unconsciously influenced the love poetry and the wedding imagery of the Hebrews and thus indirectly could have influenced Ct. (For details, see H. Schmökel, *Heilige Hochzeit und Hoheslied* [Wiesbaden, 1956].)

The literal sense of Ct seems to be a celebration of the fidelity and love between man and woman (Audet, *op. cit.*, Dubarle, *op. cit.*, 67–86; and M. van den Oudenrijn, *DThomP* 31 [1953] 257–80). Such seems to be the obvious meaning of Ct, from which we should not depart without a compelling reason.

The love lyrics of ancient Egypt provide an atmosphere in which this work can be understood (cf. *ANET* 467–69). We do not mean that there is any direct dependence of the OT songs upon the Egyptian lyrics, but there is a similar approach with a common topic—love between the sexes. In Ct, "the song of the dove is heard in our land," and spring is the time for love (Ct 2:12–13); similarly, in the Egyptian poems the voice of a swallow invites the Egyptian girl to contemplate the beauty of the countryside. It is a commonplace that true love brooks no obstacles: "Deep waters cannot quench love, nor floods sweep it away" (8:7). Neither can the Egyptian lover be put off—even by crocodiles in the stream that separates them—from his beloved (*ANET* 468). The Egyptian poetry uses the same term, "sister," to designate the beloved as does Ct (4:9–10; 4:12; 5:1–2). In short, this is the language of love, no matter what culture is in question.

The literal interpretation should not be rejected as "naturalistic," as though such a subject would be unworthy of divine inspiration. The Bible itself reminds us: "Male and female he created them" (Gn 1:27; cf. J. P. Audet in *Scr* 10 [1958] 65–83), and other passages of the Bible are related to this theme (Prv 5, 6). Hence, the question is not, "How can profane poetry have entered the canon?" Rather, we should ask: "What does the Bible tell us about sexual attraction?" A great part of the answer lies in Ct. However, it appears that a higher meaning, fuller or typical (→ Hermeneutics, 71:56–79) should also be envisioned with Van den Oudenrijn and Dubarle. Human love in itself is an echo of the divine love to which it is inherently directed. Paul immortalized the relationship between the sexes in the framework of Christ and the Church (Eph 5:23ff.).

Canticles has been the favorite work of such Christian mystics as Bernard and John of the Cross, and they have developed penetrating insights into human and divine love. (For a history of interpretation, see P. Vuilliaud, *Le Cantique des Cantiques d'après la tradition juive* [Paris, 1925]; F. Ohly, *Hohelied-Studien* [Wiesbaden, 1958]; D. Lerch, *ZThK* 54 [1957] 257–77.)

5 Canticles presents some unique characteristics. The course of events does not appear to be leading anywhere; the lover and beloved are simply enjoying each other's presence and affection. Feelings are expressed in extreme imagery that yet has the air of folk poetry, not of studied, learned composition (against G. Gerleman). The atmosphere is that of the fields: vineyards and wine, gazelles and hinds, doves and foxes. The geography cannot be unraveled easily: Kedar, En-gedi, Lebanon, Gilead, Heshbon, and other, often unidentified, place-names. Even with a commentary, Ct does not give up its secrets easily. There are many uncertainties in any translation, also in the CCD, which is to be expected in any short piece that has so many unique terms (about 50 that occur nowhere else in the OT). The commentary will explain the CCD as it stands, with some indications of other possible translations and meanings.

6 **(IV) Outline.** From what has been said it is clear that Ct cannot be broken down into any meaningful outline. Instead, the commentary will utilize headings that attempt to present the leading or characteristic theme of each poetic unit.

COMMENTARY

7 **(I) Title (1:1).** (→ 2 above.)

(II) Love's Desires (1:2–4). It begins, typically, with dialogue between the girl and the daughters of Jerusalem. The latter, who seem at times to be part of a bridal party, serve as a foil in developing the love theme throughout Ct (cf. 5:9; 6:1). The girl addresses her lover as though he were present and speaks of the intoxicating effects of his love (as do Egyptian love songs; cf. Schott, *op. cit.*, 81, 85). The vitality of the name in OT thought appears in v. 3. The exchange of address between the daughters and the girl in v. 4 manifests the tension that exists between them and makes the reader marvel at the attractiveness of the absent lover.

8 **(III) Love's Boast (1:5–6).** The swarthiness of the girl's complexion is aptly illustrated by metaphors of the (black, goat-hair) "tents" of Kedar in the Syrian desert (Ps 120:5; Gn 25:13); "Salma" (rather than "Solomon" of MT) is presumably near Kedar. The motif of the vineyard (1:5) is sounded for the first time (cf. 6:11; 7:13; 8:11–12). Although her brothers made her endure the sun's heat as she worked in the vineyard, she has given the real vineyard, herself, to her lover.

9 **(IV) Love's Inquiry (1:7–8).** "Where is the beloved?" the girl asks. The CCD indicates that he replies in v. 8, but many commentators attribute this line to the daughters. The presence or absence of the lover is a constant motif in any love poem (cf. 4:8; 6:1; etc.; the "search" motif in 3:1–5; 5:2–8). The lines evoke the idyllic imagery of flocks, and they imply that the young man is a shepherd, although in 1:4 he is a king. This fluctuation may result from the fact that disparate poems have been joined, but more likely the language of love makes him appear in several "roles." In modern Syrian wedding ceremonies, the bridal couple are celebrated as king and queen.

(V) Love's Vision (1:9–11). Assuming the role of king, the man compares the jewels that set off her beauty to the rich adornment of Pharaoh's chariotry.

10 **(VI) Love's Union (1:12–2:7).** Evokes the reaction the beloved feels in the contact with her lover; "nard," "myrrh," and "henna" are all precious scents that aptly express the delights of love, and they sustain this highly imaginative language. En-gedi, "the well of the kid," is located on the W shore of the Dead Sea. An exchange of compliments begins in 1:15 and continues into ch. 2. The eyes of "doves" (15; cf. 4:1) suggest innocence and fidelity. The duet (which takes place in a shepherd's hut of branches, 16–17) begins with the girl comparing herself to flowers: the narcissus that grows in the Plain of Sharon between Carmel and Joppa on the Mediterranean coast and the "lily" (lotus?) that grows in the valleys. He neatly turns her comparison into a compliment in 2:2 and she replies in kind; he is the choice "apple tree" whose "shadow" and "fruit" she enjoys. The meaning of the "banquet hall" and "emblem" is not clear, but the effect is lovesickness (a common motif in the ancient and modern world), as they embrace (6). The adjuration in v. 7 (repeated in 8:4) has been interpreted as the lover's wish to let the beloved sleep undisturbed. But the CCD takes it as the girl's advice that their love is not something artificial, which is to be reached by human calculation—it has "its own time." *gazelles and hinds of the field:* Seem to be merely part of the pastoral scene, but there is possibly a reference to the deity (gazelles = ṣ^{e}bā'ôt = [Lord of] hosts?), as Gordis (*op. cit.*, 27–28) suggests.

11 **(VII) A Tryst in the Spring (2:8–17).** The girl recreates a scene in which she is visited by her lover who comes speedily to her. His command (10–13) seizes upon the awakening of nature as an invitation to a love tryst. It is not clear why she is addressed in v. 14 as a dove out of sight and reach, unless this verse is from a different context. Her words about "the little foxes" are a reply to his desire to hear her speak, but what does this mean? It may be a snatch of popular song, directed against any hostile power that would destroy their love (the theme of the vineyard again, as in 1:6; etc.). The lines in vv. 16–17, which are attributed to the girl, are repeated almost exactly in separated contexts (6:3; 4:16; cf. A. Feuillet, *RB* 68 [1961] 1–38). Verse 16 expresses the union between the lovers, the delights he finds in her person ("the lilies"); v. 17 continues the same thought, if the girl is symbolized by the mountains of "Bether," which are otherwise unknown, and it also adds the limit of time: until evening.

12 **(VIII) Loss and Discovery (3:1–5).** The search motif (1:7–8; 5:2–8) reappears. Her restless desire moves her to seek him in the city, unsuccessfully. After her appeal to the "watchmen" (3), she suddenly discovers him and resolves not to let him go (cf. Schott, *op. cit.*, 74) until she brings him "home" (4). The adjuration in v. 5 is to be interpreted as in 2:7.

13 **(IX) Regal State of the Bridegroom (3:6–11).** Even if this poem is completely disparate, its position here invites the reader to view the lover as a king, a Solomon, escorted by 60 armed men (David had his "Thirty," 2 Sm 23:13), and coming in royal splendor on his wedding day. *column of smoke:* Suggests the dust of the "desert" raised by the cortege; the myrrh and other perfumes seem destined for the beloved. The "carriage" (the Hebr *'appiryôn* seems to be derived from the Gk *phoreion*, an indication of late date) is made of the same precious material used for the Temple. The CCD indicates that vv. 6–11 are spoken by the daughters; hence, in v. 11 they must be exhorting themselves.

14 **(X) The Charms of the Beloved (4:1–11).** All literatures describe the beauty of the beloved. In the present-day love songs of Palestine, such songs are termed a *waṣf* (from the Arabic word "describe"; concerning this genre in the ancient world, see W. Herrmann, *ZAW* 73 [1963] 176–97). In vv. 1–7, the man singles out the various parts of the body that call for praise. The comparisons are not to be judged by Western aesthetic taste; they evoke a picture rather than give an actual description. Her black "hair" suggests the goats in Gilead, in the northern Transjordan plain. Her teeth are white and full. The pomegranate resembles an orange, deep red in color. The translation of v. 4 is doubtful, but the total effect is to compare the ornaments on her neck to the trophies (?) on the city walls (see the comparison in 1:9–11). Perhaps vv. 5–6 are to be taken together so that the "mountain" and "hill" symbolize her "breasts" (cf. 2:17); they certainly indicate the delights her person offers. Paul may well have had v. 7 in mind in Eph 5:27.

The summons to depart from Lebanon is a sudden change, typical of Ct and suggesting a collection of disparate poems (some, as here, perhaps originating in the northern kingdom). Mt. Hermon, in the Antilebanon range N of Palestine, is also called by the Amorite name, Senir (Dt 3:9); perhaps the translation should be: Senir, i.e., Hermon (for this use of explicative *waw*, see GKC 154a, n. 1[b]). *Amana:* The mountain range (Jebel Zebedani?) where the rivers of Damascus, Abana, and Pharpar (2 Kgs 5:12) originate. The beloved is called "my sister" (4:9,12), as in the Egyptian songs. The *waṣf* ends, as in 4:10 the lover returns the compliment she had paid him in 1:2. The "honey," etc., of v. 11 stands for her words that return his love; the "fragrance" of the beloved's clothing is still a normal feature of sexual attraction (cf. Ps 45:9 and on ancient Egypt, Schott, *op. cit.*, 86).

15 **(XI) The Lover and His Garden (4:12–5:1).** The symbolism of the "fountain," found also in Prv 5:15–19, is clear: It is the beloved, and she is "sealed," "an enclosed garden," reserved for her lover alone. "Park" is a Persian word—*pardēs* (paradise)—possibly another indication of a post-exilic date. The lover acclaims the attractiveness of the girl's person ("all choice fruits") in the symbols of sweet-scented plants, "nard," etc. The invitation to the winds in v. 16 to spread the sweet scent of the beloved is a cue for the invitation that she extends to her lover: rather than the winds, let the lover himself "come to his garden." In the triumphant, joyful cry of 5:1 he announces his possession of her. Although the last lines of the verse are attributed to the daughters in the CCD, they are what one would also expect from friends at a wedding party, such as the wedding guests of Mk 2:19–20.

16 **(XII) A Fruitless Search (5:2–8).** This charming scene is another instance (cf. 3:1–5) of the search motif, and it is matched in spirit by an Egyptian love poem (Schott, *op. cit.*, 83–84). Unable to sleep, the girl hears her lover "knocking." His description of himself as "wet with the dew" fits the imaginative, rustic flavor of the piece. Her reaction in v. 3 cannot be taken seriously; dressing again and soiling her feet are not really obstacles. This action is best understood as teasing between lovers inasmuch as she obviously desires his company, and she arises immediately to let him in. The myrrh (5) symbolizes his presence (cf. 5:13), the place that has been blessed by his presence; myrrh is continually mentioned in Ct (1:13; 3:6; 4:6,14; 5:1,5,13). But the lover is no longer there, and the search begins again. It is difficult to appreciate the significance of the beating she receives from the watchmen (as though she were a harlot, they take her "mantle"), in sharp contrast to 3:3. Now there is no quick discovery and an appeal is made to the daughters to join in the search (5:8).

17 **(XIII) The Charms of the Lost Lover (5:9–16).** If the daughters are to look for him, they must first know how to identify him. It is obvious that their question is merely a cue for the *waṣf*, which the beloved now gives. This description is reminiscent of the Jerusalem Temple (especially 14–15—as the allegorists point out) or of a statue. The enumeration of his physical attributes proceeds from head to toe. The head of "pure gold" is precious; the "palm fronds" symbolize his thick hair. The comparison of the cheeks to "spice" would indicate the usual perfuming of the beard. The beloved continues with the rest of the body and returns to the mouth, "sweetness itself," because of the compliments and kisses she has received.

18 **(XIV) Discovery (6:1–3).** This heading indicates that the lover has now been found, in the sense that he has never been really lost but has always belonged to the beloved alone. Just as the question of the daughters in 5:9 was a cue for the *waṣf*, so now their question in 6:1, which indicates their desire to find such a lover, is a cue for the girl to say that he is hers alone: "my lover has come down to his garden" (cf. 4:12; 5:1). This interpretation at least resolves the problem of the supposed disappearance of the lover. Van den Oudenrijn interprets v. 3b—"he browses among the lilies"—as the reply of the daughters, who intimate that the lover has gone to visit other loves. But this is hardly likely, in view of the parallelism (and cf. 2:16; 7:11) and the spirit of mutual fidelity that the whole work echoes.

19 **(XV) The Charms of the Beloved (6:4–10).** As if to confirm the "discovery" of 6:1–3, the lost lover appears without any introduction, and he delivers another description of the girl's charms. Tirzah is probably Tell el Farʿah, NE of modern Nablus; it was once the capital of the northern kingdom (1 Kgs 16:23), but it could have been chosen here because the word is derived from a root meaning "pleasant." "As awe-inspiring as bannered troops" is a traditional *crux interpretum* (cf. 6:10), but it is no more surprising a comparison than the "goats" that appear in vv. 5–7 (= 4:1–3). The beloved is said to be incomparable in vv. 8–9; the royal harem that would be compared to her is forced to acknowledge her superiority. If v. 10 follows the riddle form (so Van den Oudenrijn; cf. Jgs 14:12ff.), the obvious answer to the question is the beloved; the entire verse seems to illustrate the praises of the harem.

20 **(XVI) Love's Meeting (6:11–12).** These few lines seem to be an isolated poem in the style of the invitation she issued to her lover in 7:13, or of his invitation to her in 2:10ff. She seems to describe her (first?) meeting with him in "the nut garden." We cannot be sure what happened, for v. 12 is completely obscure (R. Tournay, *VT* 9 [1959] 288–309). The CCD is a conjectural rendering but more satisfactory than the chariots of "my princely people" or of "Aminadab," which the Hebr and the ancient versions have. In this view, the girl describes how quickly and definitively she fell in love and became "the blessed one of my kinswomen."

21 **(XVII) The Beauty of the Bride (7:1–6).** The Shulammite has not been identified, despite many conjectures: A girl from Shulam (Shunem? cf. 1 Kgs 1:3) in the Plain of Esdraelon; or it may be an artificial name using the same term—(*šālôm*, "peace")—that occurs in the name of Solomon. W. F. Albright thinks that it echoes the name of the Mesopotamian goddess of war, Shulmanitu (in D. W. Thomas and W. D. McHardy, eds., *Hebrew and Semitic Studies* [Fest. G. R. Driver; Oxford, 1963] 5). The invitation to "turn" (in dancing) affords opportunity for another description of the beauty of the beloved, probably uttered by the daughters. In 7:1c the girl replies to their invitation by a question, as though she were a spectacle like the "dance of the two companies" (in which the dancers faced each other?). This particular allusion is not clear, but it has provided the basis for some commentators to find the so-called sword-dance here, understanding "companies" as the (military) camps. This interpretation is associated with the name of J. G. Wetzstein, who published his observations of Syrian wedding customs (*Zeitschrift für Ethnologie* 5 [1873] 207–302). Scholars like K. Budde and C. Siegfried took up this idea and elaborated a system of interpretation. The wedding festivities, it was noted, last seven days, while the bride and groom are acclaimed as king and queen; they are further characterized by the *waṣf*, and, finally, by the bride's sword dance. These parallels are interesting, but they are not enough to establish a real connection between Ct and the Syrian customs.

The description of the girl's beauty is more sensuous than any previous *waṣf*, although some of the references are obscure. The "feet in sandals" and "rounded thighs" are praise of her agility and beauty in the dance. The "navel" is probably a euphemistic reference to her role as wife and mother—and this mood continues in the figure of "wheat" and "lilies," signs of fertility. Verse 7:4 is a repetition of 4:5, but the "ivory tower" (for the white "neck"; cf. 4:4) is otherwise unknown. Heshbon is the old Amorite capital in Transjordan; the "pools" suggest sparkling eyes. *gate of Bath-rabbim:* Unknown; perhaps one of the gates to Heshbon. Nor can "the tower on Lebanon" be identified. The Carmel promontory is a natural comparison for a proud, stately carriage. The lover is again referred to as a "king."

22 **(XVIII) Love's Desires (7:7–10).** In one of the most passionate songs of Ct, the lover expresses his desire for physical possession of the beloved, who is symbolized by the "palm tree."

(XIX) Love's Union (7:10–8:4). Perhaps more than one poem is included here. At least two alternatives are mentioned; love in the vineyards (7:13); love at home (8:2–4). The construction of 7:10 is artful. The lover begins with a compliment concerning her "mouth," which she interrupts, only to turn it into an expression of her tender love and surrender to him. Their mutual feeling and possession are expressed in familiar words (10; cf. 2:16; 6:3); there is also a reference in v. 11 to the sexual longing (*t^e^šûqâ*, translated in CCD as "yearns") of Gn 3:16. The invitation of vv. 12–14 echoes the thought of 6:11 and is another expression of their trysting. The theme of spring and the blossoming of flowers and plants is a recurring motif to indicate their love. The fragrant mandrakes were regarded as aphrodisiacs in the ancient world (Gn 30:14).

In 8:1–3 there is another typical fluctuation, in which the lover is addressed in both the second and third persons. It would appear that signs of affection in public between brother and sister were more easily accepted than those between lovers—"none would taunt me." The lessons she would learn from him are lessons in love, symbolized by the "wine" and the "juice." The familiar refrain of 2:6–7 and 3:5 ends the poem; this refrain seems to occur when they find themselves in a trysting place: the banquet hall (2:4) or at home (3:4; 8:2).

23 **(XX) Homecoming (8:5).** In this fragmentary scene, the couple are described by the daughters as coming to the girl's home (a desire she expressed in 8:1), but the symbolism of the "desert" escapes us. The lover speaks of a previous tryst, apparently their first, which took place under an "apple tree" near the home where she was born. This passage presupposes a change in the vowels of the MT; as the Massoretes understood the text, these lines would have been spoken by the girl, but nowhere else is the young man's mother ever mentioned.

24 **(XXI) True Love (8:6–7).** The most touching and beautiful lines of Ct are spoken here by the beloved; she asks for constant union and possession, and she describes the nature of love. The "seal" was worn on the hand (cf. Gn 41:42; Jer 22:24) and also on a chain around the neck—hence, on the "heart." Because it was used for signatures and identification, it was a valued treasure that a man would keep about his person. The qualities of "love" (*qin'â*—the same word that is usually rendered by jealousy, zeal, passion) are the qualities of Sheol, the nether world. For the Hebrew, death and the nether world are often personified as the unrelenting powers experienced by man; no one can escape them—in the end they must triumph. True love shares in that same mysterious power, for just as certainly it will prevail. The "flames" of love are compared to "a blazing fire," but in the MT (the CCD is different), the flames are also characterized as "flames of Yah" (*šalhebetyâ*), which some (e.g., Gordis, *op. cit.*, 26) would interpret as a Hebr superlative: a Yahweh flame, one of high-burning intensity. The use of the "deep waters" to symbolize the ocean or sea (Ps 107:23; Ez 27:26) and even a hostile power (Ps 32:6) is well known in the Bible (cf. O. Kaiser, *Die mythische Bedeutung des Meeres* [Berlin, 1959]); no matter what the obstacles, love will triumph. The emphasis of v. 7cd is on the genuine, unartificial character of true love, which is beyond any price.

25 **(XXII) Chastity and Its Welcome (8:8–10).** Many commentators agree with A. Robert (*RB* 55 [1948] 161–83) that the ending of Ct is made up of appendices having little relation to the rest of the poem. But it is better to try to explain the text as it stands. Accordingly, vv. 8–10 can be taken as the final word of the girl to her brothers, who were mentioned in an unfavorable light in 1:6. Here, they are preoccupied with her eventual marriage (8). If she is a virtuous, chaste maiden, they will adorn her ("silver parapet," 9b). But if she misbehaves (yielding, as a "door," 9c) they will curtail her freedom. To this cautious program, which does not evidence great confidence in her, the girl replies by affirming her chastity, which has received a "welcome" (lit., "peace") from her lover. Loretz detects a sly humor in vv. 9–10. When she has matured ("wall"), they will beautify her; when she is marriageable (door"), they will supervise her. But she laughs at them—she is already ripe for marriage and already mature ("towers").

26 **(XXIII) The Bride and Her Dowry (8:11–12).** These enigmatic verses have been variously interpreted. *Baal-hamon:* An unknown place name; but there may be a play on its meaning, "master of wealth." This is the site of a precious vineyard owned by Solomon (the lover, as in 3:7?) and valued at 1000 silver pieces (exceedingly valuable; cf. Is 7:23). The vineyard and its price may be taken as referring to the girl and her dowry. Then she affirms in v. 12 that the important gift is the gift of herself to her lover, although it also brings him a dowry and a smaller settlement (200 pieces) for her brothers ("the caretakers").

27 **(XXIV) Life Together (8:13–14).** As in 2:14–15, the lover asks for a word or a song, and she replies with an invitation similar to that found in 2:17. Van den Oudenrijn makes the interesting suggestion that the life setting here is a game of hide-and-seek at the marriage festivities, where all seek the maiden, who has hidden herself, but only the lover is actually permitted to find her.

31

JOB

R. A. F. MacKenzie, S.J.

BIBLIOGRAPHY

1 *Commentaries:* Older, still important, commentaries: Dhorme, P., in EBib (1926); Eng. *A Commentary on the Book of Job* (London, 1967). Driver, S. R. and G. B. Gray, in ICC (1921; repr. 1950). Peters, N., in EHAT (Münster, 1928).

More recent commentaries: Fohrer, G., KAT (1963). Hölscher, G., HAT (2nd ed., 1952). Gordis, R., *The Book of God and Man* (Chicago, 1965). Horst, F., BK (1962–). Pope, M. H., AB (1965). Steinmann, J., *Le Livre de Job* (LD; 1955); *Job* (Témoins de Dieu; Paris, 1946). Terrien, S., *Job, Poet of Existence* (Indianapolis, 1957); *Job,* (CAT; 1963). Weber, J. J., *Le Livre de Job* (Tournai, 1947). Weiser, A., *Hiob* (ATD; 2nd ed.; 1956).

Translations with introductions and notes: Larcher, C., BJ (2nd ed.; 1957). O'Neill, G., *The World's Classic, Job* (Milwaukee, 1938). Vaccari, A., LSB (Florence, 1949).

Monographs: Crook, M. B., *The Cruel God* (Boston, 1959). Fohrer, G., *Studien zum Buche Hiob* (Tübingen, 1963). Gese, H., *Lehre und Wirklichkeit in der alten Weisheit* (Tübingen, 1958). Lindblom, J., *La composition du livre de Job* (Lund, 1945). Richter, H., *Studien zu Hiob* (Berlin, 1959). Robinson, H. W., *The Cross in the Old Testament* (London, 1955) 9–54. Stamm, J. J., *Das Leiden des Unschuldigen in Babylon und Israel* (Zürich, 1946). Westermann, C., *Der Aufbau des Buches Hiob* (Tübingen, 1956).

Articles: Baab, O., "The Book of Job," *Interpr* 5 (1951) 329–43. Baker, J., "Commentaries on Job," *Theology* (vol. 66; 1963) 179–85. Fine, H., "The Tradition of a Patient Job," *JBL* 74 (1955) 28–32. Hempel, J., "Das theologische Problem des Hiob," *ZSystTh* 6 (1929) 621–89 (also BZAW 81 [1961] 114–73). Kuhl, C., "Neuere Literarkritik des Buches Hiob," *TRu* 21 (1953) 163–205, 257–317; "Vom Hiobbuche und seinen Problemen," *TRu* 22 (1954) 261–316. Murphy, R. E., "*Job* in the New Confraternity Version," *AER* 133 (1955) 16–29. Paulus, J., "Le thème du Juste Souffrant dans la pensée grecque et hébraique," *RHR* 121 (1940) 18–66. Ponthot, J., "Le scandale de la souffrance du juste selon le Livre de Job," *RevD Tour* 13 (1958) 271–75. Rowley, H. H., "The Book of Job and Its Meaning," *BJRylL* 41 (1958) 167–207. Sekine, M., "Schöpfung und Erlösung im Buche Hiob," BZAW 77 (*Fest. O. Eissfeldt;* 1958) 213–23. Skehan, P. W., "Strophic Patterns in the Book of Job," *CBQ* 23 (1961) 125–142; "Job's Final Plea (Job 29–31) and the Lord's Reply (Job 38–41)," *Bib* 45 (1964) 51–62. Tournay, R., *et al.*, "Job, la mort et l'espérance," *VieSp* 95 (1956) 339–406. Ulanov, B., "Job and His Comforters," *The Bridge* 3 (1958) 234–68.

INTRODUCTION

2 **(I) Preliminary Remarks.** This book belongs to the third division of the Hebr Bible, the Writings (*kᵉtûbîm*), of which the first three books are Jb, Pss, and Prv (their relative order varies in different traditions). It is a poetic dialogue in a prose-narrative setting, dealing with the profound theological problem of the meaning and function of suffering in the life of a just man and with the consequences of it for a man's attitude to God. The book has its forerunners in both Egyptian and Babylonian literature, notably in some dialogues dealing with problems of human life and the justice of the gods (→ Wisdom Lit, 28:12–31). The Israelite author may have been familiar with some of these. If so, he surpassed them, both by his theology (monotheism and the transcendence of the God of Israel) and by his literary genius. Any influence on him from Gk sources (e.g., Aeschylus) is very improbable. Within the literary tradition of Israel, Jb's closest connections are not with the wisdom books but with certain psalms, notably 49, 73, and 139. It is definitely influenced by Jer, particularly by the so-called "confessions" (→ Jeremiah, 19:42), but as a whole, the book is a unique composition, not to be classified with any others.

The greater part of Jb is in poetic form; in fact, it is the longest ancient Hebr poem that has survived (perhaps that was ever composed). The core is the second part, the dialogue, making up almost two-thirds of the work, and the originality or otherwise of other parts is judged by reference to it. Thus, the third—i.e., the Elihu speeches—is probably not original but a contribution from a different writer. The unity of the remaining parts is not beyond question and has been denied by many critics; but the modern tendency is to defend it. Allowing for some lesser additions, we may regard the prologue, dialogue, Yahweh speeches, and epilogue as the composition of one author; he was unquestionably a learned man, a very great poet, and a religious thinker of genius.

3 **(II) Date.** Indications of date are rather tenuous. Verses 3:2ff. probably indicate that the author had read Jer 20:14–18. The presentation of "the Satan" (1:6–2:7) resembles that of Zech 3:1–2 and is less developed than in 1 Chr 21:1–8. As probable outside limits, we may indicate 600–300 BC, and we may add that the first half of that period is more likely than the second; 600–450 was the time of the Babylonian Exile and the return, when the preaching of Jeremiah and Ezekiel caused a crisis in the collectivistic ethics of the people of Israel.

4 **(III) Justice in Jb.** That Yahweh was just and the source of justice had always been an axiom. But this justice could be conceived in two very different ways. From the viewpoint of the helpless and oppressed, justice is liberation, salvation; the "judges" of Jgs are heroes and champions, deliverers of Yahweh's people from oppression. In the experience of the Exodus from Egypt, Yahweh's was a saving justice; his intervention produced justice, the state in which men have what they ought to have. His covenant partners, naturally, ought to have security and well-being (→ Aspects OT Thought, 77:93, 136).

But if these covenant partners were disloyal and became his enemies, then they ought to experience the other side of justice, which is destruction. And that, according to the prophets, is what befell Judah in the Exile. Hence, in the post-exilic period, there was increasing insistence on loyalty to Yahweh, which found concrete expression in the ritual and social observance of a detailed external Law.

At the same time, the wisdom teachers stressed the efficacy of righteous living. In their effort to understand human existence, they aimed at reducing the arbitrary and unpredicted elements in life. They held that there are moral laws that govern life, of which God is the custodian and the guarantor. These can be known, and, by prudent choice and blameless behavior, a man can live in harmony with them and assure himself happiness and success.

Ezekiel's extreme individualism (e.g., Ez 18) was a pastoral necessity in his effort to deliver the remnant of Judah from the dead hand of the past. But it heightened the difficulty of squaring real-life experience with "what ought to be." The emphasis of the authors of Prv on their infallible equation—wisdom = virtuous living = "success"—no doubt helped people to form virtuous habits. But for the thinker it aggravated the problem of "justice" in human life (→ Wisdom Lit, 28:34–36).

5 **(IV) Author's Purpose.** The author of Jb undertook to show, in the light of a more adequate concept of the relationship of man to his loving creator (and drawing, very likely, on his own religious experience), that the problem was wrongly posed: i.e., God may have other purposes than merely the exercise of retributive justice. As his medium he chose an old story that was no doubt familiar to his contemporaries. Ez 14:14,20 (early 6th cent. BC) refers to three legendary figures of the past, Noah, Daniel, and Job, as proverbial for their righteousness. The story of Ezekiel's Job would be roughly that which is represented in this book by 1:1–22; 42:11–17. Our author retold it in a careful imitation of the antique style, even increasing the severity of the trial by adding 2:1–10. Then he introduced the three wise friends and began his discussion.

He did not intend to make fun of Eliphaz, Bildad, and Zophar. He is fair to them, and he makes them eloquent defenders of the "traditional" case. Insofar as their doctrine is positive, it is sound and helpful (cf. Ps 37, simple to the point of naïveté yet beautiful and consoling). It contains much moral and religious truth, but they spoil it by exaggeration. They are not willing to leave a margin of uncertainty, to admit limits to their understanding, to write after each of their theses, "If God so wills." All the workings of divine providence must be clear to them, explicit, mathematical. They have fallen victims to the occupational hazard of the theologian, which is to forget that he is dealing with mystery. They have "studied" God as a subject to be analyzed, predicted, and understood. And in forcing facts to agree with their understanding, they become willfully dishonest (Jb 13:6–11).

As the author has carefully constructed it, Job's is the extreme case; here, consequently, they are extremely wrong. But their simplified retribution doctrine has had a long life. In Jn 9:1–3, Jesus' disciples take it for granted; they are intrigued by the man's blindness, only because he was born so. They do not ask: "Is this because of sins?" (of course it is!). Their problem is: "Were they his own sins in a previous existence or those of his parents before his birth?" Our Lord corrects them very explicitly, and what he says would apply equally to Job: He suffers, not because of any sins but "that the works of God may be shown forth in him."

6 The correction of the friends' distortion is comparatively simple and can be accomplished by Job himself. His own error is more subtle, and his correction must come from God. In the prologue, he makes no connection between his suffering and divine justice. But that loyal simplicity is not sufficient to refute the friends' accusations, and in maintaining his innocence as though God were denying it, he overvalues it. It is not a bargaining counter; it is not a token he can hold up to God, saying, "For this, you owe me happiness." He is in the right, against the friends; he is not in the right, against God. He can make no claim on him. Christ was to warn us in that profound text, Lk 17:10, "When you have done all things that you have been commanded, say, 'We are unprofitable servants; we have done what we were obliged to do.' "

The book is full of paradoxes, for it attempts to approach divine truth, incomprehensible to man, from various viewpoints. It is essential to the lesson that Job should be a lover of God, a saint. Otherwise, his affliction would inevitably contain some proportion of just punishment. Furthermore, only such a man could support the test. This observation should temper the scandal some readers feel at what they call the callousness of God in chs. 1–2. We are meant to understand that God trusts his servant to serve him and that this is Job's opportunity. We may compare this concept with the Christian theology of martyrdom. The martyrs, beginning with Stephen (Acts 7) and Ignatius of Antioch, have not accused God of injustice or cruelty in requiring of them the extreme sacrifice; they willingly offer him this ultimate testimony of love (Jn 15:13). But for the encouragement of less eager martyrs, there is the example of the prayer in Gethsemane, in which even God's own Son uttered his lament and prayed to be spared his trial.

7 **(V) God in Jb.** The variety of divine names in Jb is worth noting. In the prologue and epilogue, the narrator refers in normal Israelite fashion to "Yahweh" (the Lord), the one true God and supreme Lord. But the speakers in the prologue, including Yahweh himself (1:8b; 2:3a), employ the generic word *'elōhîm* (God). The one exception is in 1:21b, where Job three times uses

"Yahweh"; but here, the second stich is a quotation. In the dialogue, on the other hand, "Yahweh" is named only once (12:9b), and that again is in a quotation. "Elohim" also is used once (5:8b). Otherwise, three archaic poetic names are consistently adopted: *'ēl*, *'ĕlôah*, and *šadday* (the Almighty). Of these, the first and second never parallel each other, but each may parallel *šadday*. This elaborate convention establishes monotheism—the five names all apply to the one and only God; and it maintains the non-Israelite situation—Job and his friends are "true believers," but they are outside the ambit of the covenant with Israel. They speak for mankind in general, in face of a God known indeed by his revelation to Israel, but to whom these men are related only by the fundamental fact that they are his creatures. They expect no salvation from him other than individual well-being in this life. Only Job is groping for a more intimate and permanent relationship, based, not on the mere exchange of gifts or services, but on a communion of love.

8 **(VI) Style.** (On Hebr metrics and parallelism, → Hebr Poetry, 13:10–19). In the following pages, "stich" is used to denote a phrase in parallelism with another phrase; a "line" includes two parallel stichs (a "distich"—rhymes with "mystic"), or occasionally three (a "tristich"; e.g., 3:9 is one line, a tristich). In citing poetic passages, "a," "b," etc., added to a verse number indicate the successive stichs in that verse. Grouping of lines into stanzas or "strophes" is regular throughout the poem (see the convincing demonstration by P. W. Skehan, in *CBQ* 23 [1961] 125–42). The strophic analysis adopted in chs. 3–23 mainly follows that of Skehan, with occasional variations, as in chs. 16–17, 19, 21, 22.

9 **(VII) Outline.** The Book of Job may be outlined as follows:

(I) The Prologue (1:1–2:13)
- (A) Job's Character and Prosperity (1:1–5)
- (B) The First Scene in Heaven (1:6–12)
- (C) The Loss of Job's Possessions (1:13–22)
- (D) The Second Scene in Heaven (2:1–7a)
- (E) The Affliction of Job's Person (2:7b–10)
- (F) The Coming of Job's Friends (2:11–13)

(II) The Dialogue (3:1–31:40)
- (A) Job's First Soliloquy (3:2–26)
  - (a) The Curse of Job's Anniversary Day and Night (3:3–10)
  - (b) Better an Early Death (3:11–12,16)
  - (c) Reasons for the Curse (3:13–15,17–19)
  - (d) Renewed Lament (3:20–26)
- (B) Eliphaz' First Speech (4:1–5:27)
  - (a) The Doctrine of Retribution (4:2–11)
  - (b) Eliphaz' Revelation (4:12–5:2)
  - (c) Recommendation (5:3–16)
  - (d) Encouragement (5:17–27)
- (C) Job's First Response (6:1–7:21)
  - (a) Job's Misery (6:2–10)
  - (b) A Transition Strophe (6:11–14)
  - (c) Job's Disillusionment with the Friends (6:15–27)
  - (d) Transition Strophe (6:28–30)
  - (e) Soliloquy (7:1–10)
  - (f) Complaint to God (7:11–21)
- (D) Bildad's First Speech (8:1–22)
  - (a) Introduction (8:2–7)
  - (b) Doctrine (8:8–19)
  - (c) Conclusion (8:20–22)
- (E) Job's Second Response (9:1–10:22)
  - (a) God Is Irresistible in Power, Therefore in Judgment (9:2–12)
  - (b) God Is Arbitrary (9:13–24)
  - (c) Job's Helplessness (9:25–10:1a)
  - (d) Speculation and Appeal (10:1b–12)
  - (e) The Mournful Contrast (10:13–22)
- (F) Zophar's First Speech (11:1–20)
  - (a) Job's Foolishness (11:2–12)
  - (b) Counsel and Encouragement (11:13–20)
- (G) Job's Third Response (12:1–14:22)
  - (a) Job's Wisdom Matches Theirs (12:2–25)
  - (b) Summary and Warning Against "Defending" God Dishonestly (13:1–11)
  - (c) Job Reasons with God (13:12–27)
  - (d) Lament over Human Life (13:28–14:12)
  - (e) A Dream and Reality (14:13–22)
- (H) Eliphaz' Second Speech (15:1–35)
  - (a) Job Has Spoken Impiously and Presumptuously (15:2–16)
  - (b) Punishment for the Impious and Presumptuous (15:17–35)
- (I) Job's Fourth Response (16:1–17:16)
  - (a) Afflicted by Men and by God (16:2–17)
  - (b) The Witness in Heaven (16:18–21)
  - (c) Complaint Continued (16:22–17:16)
- (J) Bildad's Second Speech (18:1–21)
  - (a) Rebuke to Job (18:2–4)
  - (b) Fate of the Wicked (18:5–21)
- (K) Job's Fifth Response (19:1–29)
  - (a) God's Doing, Not Man's (19:2–12)
  - (b) Isolation and Loneliness (19:13–22)
  - (c) Hope of the Vision of God (19:23–27)
  - (d) Warning to the Friends (19:28–29)
- (L) Zophar's Second Speech (20:1–29)
  - (a) The Triumph of the Wicked Is Brief (20:2–9)
  - (b) He Must Give Up Ill-Gotten Gains (20:10–29)
- (M) Job's Sixth Response (21:1–34)
  - (a) Introduction (21:2–6)
  - (b) The Happiness of Men Without God (21:7–18)
  - (c) No Evident Connection Between Virtue and Happiness (21:19–21,23–26)
  - (d) Peaceful Death and Posthumous Fame of the Godless (21:27–34)
- (N) Eliphaz' Third Speech (22:1–30)
  - (a) Exordium (22:2–5)
  - (b) Job's Sins (22:6–11)
  - (c) Rebuttal of Job's Argument (21:22; 22:12–20)
  - (d) Recommendation To Be Reconciled with God (22:21–30)
- (O) Job's Seventh Response (23:1–24:25)
  - (a) Yearning for the Encounter with God (23:2–7)
  - (b) God Is Inaccessible and Unpredictable (23:8–17)
  - (c) Misery of the Oppressed Poor (24:1–12)
  - (d) Enemies of the Light (24:13–17)
  - (e) Obscure Section (24:18–24)
  - (f) The Conclusion of Job's Speech (24:25)
- (P) Obscure Chapters 25–27 (25:1–27:23)
  - (a) Third Speech of Zophar, Part 1 (25:2–6)
  - (b) Job's Eighth Response, Part 1 (26:1–4)
  - (c) Third Speech of Zophar, Part 2 (26:5–14)
  - (d) Job's Eighth Response, Part 3 (27:2–6)
  - (e) Third Speech of Bildad (27:7–10,13–23)
  - (f) Job's Eighth Response, Part 2 (27:11–12)
- (Q) Interlude: The Search for Wisdom (28:1–28)
  - (a) No Mine for Wisdom (28:1–6,9–11)
  - (b) No Guidance from Creatures (28:7–8,12–14, 21–22)
  - (c) Man's Wealth Cannot Buy It (28:15–19)
  - (d) It Belongs to God Alone (28:20,23–27)
  - (e) Annotation (28:28)
- (R) Job's Final Soliloquy (29:1–31:40)
  - (a) Past Happiness (29:1–25)
    - (i) The loving presence of God (29:2–7)
    - (ii) Public honor (29:8–11,21–25)
    - (iii) Good reasons for this honor (29:12–17)
    - (iv) Job's hope (29:18–20)
  - (b) Present Misery (30:1–31)
    - (i) Public contempt (30:1–15)
    - (ii) The hostile presence of God (30:16–22)
    - (iii) Reasons against this abuse (30:23–26)
    - (iv) Job's misery (30:27–31)

- (c) Oath of Exculpation (31:1–40)
  - (i) No deceit or injustice (31:1–12,38–40ab)
  - (ii) No failure in equity or charity (31:13–23)
  - (iii) No false worship (31:24–28)
  - (iv) No vindictiveness or hypocrisy (31:29–34)
  - (v) Summary (31:35–37,40c)

(III) The Elihu Speeches (32:1–37:24)
- (A) Introductory Narrative (32:1–5)
- (B) Introductory Address (32:6–22)
  - (a) Rebuke to the Friends (32:6–14)
  - (b) Soliloquy (32:15–22)
- (C) Elihu's First Discourse (33:1–30)
  - (a) Summons to Job (33:1–7)
  - (b) Quotations (33:8–11)
  - (c) Correction and First Thesis (33:12–18)
  - (d) Second Thesis (33:19–24)
  - (e) Conclusion (33:25–30)
- (D) Elihu's Second Discourse (34:1–37)
  - (a) Summons to the Friends and Quotation (34:2–6)
  - (b) Quotation and Correction (34:7–11)
  - (c) First Thesis (34:12–15)
  - (d) Second Thesis (34:16–30)
  - (e) Conclusion (34:31–37)
- (E) Elihu's Third Discourse (33:31–33; 35:2–36:25)
  - (a) Summons to Job (33:31–33)
  - (b) Quotations (35:2–4)
  - (c) Correction and First Thesis (35:5–16)
  - (d) Second Thesis (36:2–15)
  - (e) Conclusion (36:16–25)
- (F) Hymn (36:26–37:13)
- (G) Concluding Address (37:14–24)

(IV) God's Speech and Job's Answer (38:1–42:6)
- (A) Yahweh Speaks (38:1)
- (B) Does Job Understand Yahweh's "Counsel"? (38:2–38)
  - (a) "Who Is This?" (38:2–3)
  - (b) Was Job Present at Creation? (38:4–15)
  - (c) Does Job Know His Way About the Cosmos? (38:16–24)
  - (d) Would Job Know How to Operate It? (38:25–33)
  - (e) Has Job the Needed Authority and Power? (38:34–38)
- (C) Is Job Capable of Providing for the Animals and Birds? (38:39–39:30)
  - (a) Can Job Feed the Little Ones? (38:39–41; 39:26–30)
  - (b) Are the Wildest Animals Under His Control? (39:1–12)
  - (c) The Ostrich (39:13–18)
  - (d) Is Job Responsible for the Fiery Nature of the Horse? (39:19–25)
- (D) Summary and Job's First Response (40:1–5)
  - (a) Challenge (40:2)
  - (b) Job's Response (40:3–5)
- (E) Yahweh Speaks Again (40:6–41:26)
  - (a) Can Job Administer Divine Justice? (40:6–14)
  - (b) Look at Behemoth! (40:15–24)
  - (c) Look at Leviathan! (40:25–41:26)
    - (i) Can you make a pet of him? (40:25–32)
    - (ii) Can anything overcome him? (41:1–26)
- (F) Job's Final Response (42:1–6)

(V) The Epilogue (42:7–17)
- (A) Expiation for Job's Three Friends (42:7–10a)
- (B) God's Blessing of Job Restored and Increased (42:10b–17)

COMMENTARY

10 **(I) The Prologue (1:1–2:13).** This prose narrative is divided into six scenes that sketch vividly the course of the events giving occasion for the dialogue. The style is deliberately archaizing, reminiscent of the patriarchal narratives in Gn—i.e., dramatic, picturesque, schematized, rhythmically constructed, with set phrases and much verbal repetition. The characters are few and sharply defined; their psychology is realized with a minimum of words. Each dialogue is between two persons only, and the speeches are as economical and pointed as possible.

(Fohrer, G., "Zur Vorgeschichte und Komposition des Buches Hiob," *VT* 6 [1956] 249–67; "Überlieferung und Wandlung der Hioblegende," *Fest. F. Baumgärtel* [Erlangen, 1959] 41–62. Rongy, H., "Le prologue du livre de Job," *RELiège* 25 [1934] 168–71. Sarna, N. M., "Epic Substratum in the Prose of Job," *JBL* 76 [1957] 13–25.)

11 **(A) Job's Character and Prosperity (1:1–5).** "Once upon a time..." gives the flavor of this opening. The period is that of the seminomadic patriarchs; the area is the land of Uz, part of the territory of Edom (Gn 36:28; Lam 4:21), S and E of Palestine (but cf. Fohrer, KAT 72–73, for arguments in favor of NE Transjordan). Job is pictured as a great potentate (not an old man, but comparatively young; cf. 15:10), outstanding for his goodness, and blessed with great possessions. His virtue is analyzed in four expressions. "Blameless" (*tām*) is like the Lat *integer* (perfect), a whole man with no defect or inconsistency in his character. *Yāšār* ("upright" or "righteous") means that his life and actions were right, in accordance with a standard. "Fearing" God means realizing one's relationship to him by showing him reverence and obedience. "Avoiding evil" affirms a good conscience deliberately and constantly choosing the good. **5b.** *blasphemed God:* The MT and versions have "blessed" (so also in 1:11; 2:5,9), but it is presumably a euphemism.

12 **(B) The First Scene in Heaven (1:6–12).** Cf. 1 Kgs 22:19ff. (H. W. Robinson, *JTS* 45 [1944] 151–57). Yahweh is anthropomorphically represented as an Oriental monarch seated on his throne receiving the reports of his servants and issuing his commands. These servants, the agents through whom he governs, are the "sons of Elohim," originally conceived as lesser divinities but in Israelite theology reduced to the rank of Yahweh's ministers. Among them is the Adversary ("the Satan"; not to be treated as a proper name), the prosecutor who spies on men's wrongdoing and reports it to his master (cf. Zech 3:1ff.). He is not yet the "devil" of later Judaist and Christian theology; to identify him as such distorts the understanding of the book (A. Lods, *Fest. R. Dussaud* [vol. 2; Paris, 1939] 649–60). Still, he is an unpleasant figure, and his cynical attitude toward human possibilities of good contradicts the optimistic estimate of Yahweh himself. When the latter, with evident pleasure and even a kind of pride, draws his attention to "my servant Job" (a title of high honor) as an example of perfect human loyalty to himself, the Satan skeptically interprets Job's virtue as mere self-interest. **9.** This penetrating question is one of the fundamental themes of the book. *Ḥinnām* (for nothing) means gratis, without looking to payment or reward—therefore, out of love. Does Job serve God thus? And we might ask, does any man? Can he? And should he? The Adversary does not think so and neither do Job's three friends. **12.** Yahweh accepts the challenge and permits the test to be made. The withholding of his gifts from Job will demonstrate whether Job's affections center on them or on the giver.

13 **(C) The Loss of Job's Possessions (1:13–22).** In four rapid stages these are all destroyed in a single day. The items of vv. 2–3 are all accounted for, and in four "moments" Job finds he has passed from wealth to utter destitution. **20–21.** The first effect naturally is that he "goes into mourning" according to the customs of the time. The second is that he proves the Adversary wrong: He blesses Yahweh instead of cursing him. To sharpen the contrast, the narrator has him pronounce, three times, the name Yahweh, which otherwise he avoids; the last phrase in v. 21 is a standard liturgical formula (cf. Ps 113:2); therefore it is natural to use the same name in the preceding stich.

14 **(D) The Second Scene in Heaven (2:1–7a).** Verses 1–3a repeat 1:6–8 almost word for word. In v. 3b, "without cause" is the same adverb as in 1:9, "for nothing"; but with almost grim humor the meaning is inverted: Not Job's loyalty goes for nothing, but the Adversary's cynicism. However, he does not admit defeat. There is a new stress on individualism (as against the older idea of solidarity of the individual with family and tribe) in his answer: Goods and even children are not a man's self. Let Job be stripped of honor and health—of all but bare existence. When he has absolutely nothing left to thank God for, will he still "fear him"?

15 **(E) The Affliction of Job's Person (2:7b–10).** Job is smitten with some unnamed and disfiguring disease, which causes continual pain and sleeplessness and makes him a disgusting sight (its symptoms are frequently alluded to in his later speeches). **8.** *among the ashes:* Seems to imply his exclusion from human society; his place of refuge is a community dump such as may be seen today outside an Eastern village. **9.** Not Job but his wife reacts as the Adversary had expected. She interprets the situation somewhat as the friends will do; but she takes her husband's side. God has now shown himself to be Job's enemy; the latter should express that fact before he dies. **10.** Job's second speech is a parallel to 1:21. His rebuke is kindly but firm (and the plural shows that he is sensitive to his wife's distress; she has, after all, suffered the losses with him). It excludes any obligation on God's part toward his creatures. Man can never say to him, "You ought not to treat me thus." Thus, Job is now very literally fearing God "for nothing." Yahweh's trust in his servant is vindicated, and the Adversary's skepticism is disproved (he is not mentioned again in the book).

The original story probably went on from this point (or even from 1:22) to tell of Job's consolation and restoration, as in 42:11ff. (A. Alt, *ZAW* 55 [1937] 265–68). But the inspired author chose this point to insert his long and profound analysis of what a man like Job might experience, while this desperate situation lasted.

16 **(F) The Coming of Job's Friends (2:11–13).** This passage prepares for the following dialogue. A certain interval of weeks or even months is supposed to have elapsed before the friends' arrival, so that Job has time to meditate on his condition and to experience its full effects. The three are professional wise men from different localities, but all are connected with Edom, the proverbial home of sages (cf. Ob 8; Jer 49:7; R. H. Pfeiffer, *ZAW* 44 [1926] 13–25). Their friendship is genuine, and their intention is truly charitable. Their sympathy with him in his deplorable state—evidently even worse than they had expected—is expressed in the ritual gestures of mourning for the dead and in a week-long silence. (Cf. N. Lohfink, *VT* 12 [1962] 260–77.) They wait for Job to speak before venturing to try to comfort him.

17 **(II) The Dialogue (3:1–31:40).** Apart from brief introductory rubrics (e.g., 3:1–2), this section is entirely in poetic form. Between Job's initial (ch. 3) and concluding (chs. 29–31) soliloquies, we find a series of alternate speeches by the friends, in succession, and by Job. Because of the textual disorder of chs. 25–27, we cannot be sure of the last few speeches, but inasmuch as Eliphaz speaks first (chs. 4–5), after ch. 3, Zophar presumably speaks last, before chs. 29–31. Thus, there are nine addresses by the friends alternating with eight responses from Job. (The conventional grouping of the speeches into three "cycles" obscures this point; it also imposes a modern category of style, which was not the author's, and is better avoided.) In its form, the whole structure is a lament—i.e., a prayer of petition in which a sufferer appeals to God for a hearing, describes his affliction (which may include physical pain, mental anguish, destitution, dishonor, and attacks by enemies), and beseeches God to put an end to it and save him (cf. Westermann, *op. cit.*). The function of the friends is to console, by joining in the lamentation and the petition. But, because of their doctrine on retribution, they come prepared to take part in a psalm of penitence, whereas Job is uttering a psalm of innocence. This clash of views means that to Job they become enemies, unjustly oppressing him and increasing his suffering. Hence, two subordinate themes become prominent in Job's lament: denunciation of enemies and the oath of exculpation. Worse than that, the friends persist in claiming that they are pronouncing God's judgment, that what they profess is divinely guaranteed wisdom; thus, Job is led to include God among his enemies, i.e., God as presented to him by the friends. This is his real trial: Against human authority and outward appearances, he is fighting to maintain and affirm his faith that God loves him.

(Barthélemy, D., "Dieu méconnu par le vieil homme, Job," *VieSp* 105 [1961] 445–63. Feuillet, A., "L'énigme de la souffrance et la réponse de Dieu," *Dieu vivant* 17 [1950] 77–91. Robinson, T. H., *Job and His Friends* [London, 1954].)

18 **(A) Job's First Soliloquy (3:2–26).** It corresponds to the "complaint" theme of the psalms of lament; i.e., it is mere lamentation, a description and expression of pain. It does not include direct petition for relief, and its invocation of God is implicit only, when the sufferer asks the reason for his affliction. Job begins with the most radical possible declaration of his misery, uttering a rejection of life itself (cf. the parallel in Jer 20:14–18; also 1 Kgs 19:4; Jon 4:3,8; Sir 23:14). By cursing the day of his birth, he implies that the life God has given him is not good, and he would prefer never to have received it. The passage contains a skillfully graded transition from the patient Job of the prologue to the impatient Job of the dialogue. The complaint of vv. 3–10 can well be uttered by the speaker of 1:21; 2:10, turning his attention from God to himself; but a crucial development comes with the query "Why?" in vv. 11–12, and again in v. 20. (For the question element in the lament, compare Pss 13:2–4; 22:2; 42:10; 44:24–25; 74:1,10–11; 77:8–10; 88:15.) In the prologue, Job had not asked why. The first two questions are still rhetorical, but they lead to the third in v. 20, which expresses a real inquiry; it formulates a problem concerning God's treatment of men. There is as yet no reference to divine justice (the friends will introduce that theme), but there is bewilderment about God's goodness; how is it shown in a gift that is no gift—i.e., a miserable life? Job is beginning to wonder about the meaning of his experience, which is just what the friends are ready to explain to him. This repeated "Why?" launches the following debate, much as the Adversary's question in 1:9 had initiated the experience.

The speech contains seven strophes, of 4, 4; 3, 3, 3; 4, 3, lines. Verse 16 should follow v. 11 (or possibly 12).

19 (a) THE CURSE OF JOB'S ANNIVERSARY DAY AND NIGHT (3:3–6, 7–10). Job never does curse God, but these imprecations (like Jeremiah's) are directed against something God has created. Verse 3 joins day of birth with night of conception; then vv. 4–6 (reading *yôm*, "day," in 6a) treats of the former, vv. 7–10 of the latter. They are personified as sentient beings not only conscious of, but responsible for, the events they witnessed (cf. Ps 19:3–4); Job wishes God may blot them out of the calendar, may "uncreate" them (4a is, lit., "That day—let there be darkness!" reversing the "Let there be light!" of Gn 1:3). **7–10.** The night, time of conception and fertility—therefore of joy—is to be barren and mournful. **8.** The reference is to magicians who claimed to be able to control the abyss and the monsters that inhabited it. *Leviathan:* "A personification of the evil forces of the primeval chaos which Yahweh overcame when He created the world" (*EDB* 1330; cf. H. Wallace, *BA* 11 [1948] 61–68; J. L. McKenzie, *TS* 11 [1950] 275–82; G. R. Driver, *Fest. Levi della Vida* [Rome, 1956] 234–49). **9.** Not eyes or eyelids but "the eyelashes of the dawn," i.e., the rays fanning out from the still-hidden sun.

20 (b) BETTER AN EARLY DEATH (3:11,16,12). **11.** *at birth:* Read, "[while still] in the womb" (M. Dahood, *Bib* 44 [1963] 205). **12.** *the knees:* Rather than to mother or nurse, this may refer to the father acknowledging his child; if such acknowledgment were refused, the child might be cast out to die.

21 (c) REASONS FOR THE CURSE (3:13–15,17–19). Consigned to the underworld at birth, Job would at least have "enjoyed" an untroubled nonexistence, preferable to his present anguish. He would be in the company of the ghosts of the great ones of the earth (14–15) but also (18–19) of the ghosts of the wretched, whose release from suffering he would share. **17.** *troubling:* The word means distress caused to others; equivalently, "there one is no longer oppressed by cruel tyrants." Notable is the poet's sensitive feeling for the hopeless misery of prisoners and slaves (cf. 7:1; 31:13–15); Job's feelings are similar—and hence, implicitly, slave driver and harsh master are images, in his present experience, of God (supporting the MT reading in v. 20: "Why does He give light...?").

22 (d) RENEWED LAMENT (3:20–23,24–26). Why make a gift that is a painful burden to the recipient? **22a.** "They would rejoice on [arriving at] the tomb," reading *gal*, "tumulus." **23b.** Cf. Lam 3:7. Verse 26 makes an inclusion with v. 13, repeating "ease" (same word as "tranquil") and "rest"; it also echoes the "trouble" and "rest" of v. 17.

23 **(B) Eliphaz' First Speech (4:1–5:27).** Eliphaz is presumably the oldest of the three and therefore the wisest; he is certainly the most courteous and the most eloquent. He has a genuine esteem for Job and is deeply sorry for him. He knows the advice to give him, the wisdom that lays down what he must do to receive relief from his sufferings. But Eliphaz has been mildly shocked by Job's lament, in which he had merely wished for death and had uttered no prayer for recovery of prosperity and happiness. He had even implied unbecoming criticism of God and seemed to consider his misfortune as an unaccountable mystery. For Eliphaz there is no mystery; he has diagnosed Job's case at a glance. Obviously, these calamities have been sent to punish Job for some transgression or culpable negligence, perhaps unnoticed. Eliphaz intends to help him examine his conscience, to repent of his sins, and so to regain God's favor. (K. Fullerton, *JBL* 49 [1930] 320–74.) Psalm 32 would fit Job's case exactly, especially vv. 3–5.

The structure of the speech is elaborate, consisting mainly in eight five-line strophes; a two-line conclusion (5:1–2) ends the first section; the second is interrupted by a three-line strophe (5:14–16) and is ended by the one-line conclusion (5:27).

24 (a) THE DOCTRINE OF RETRIBUTION (4:2–6, 7–11). The friends' speeches regularly start with a question and reference to Job's words. Eliphaz first begins with the utmost gentleness, appealing to Job's own good advice to others in the past. Unfortunately, this approach is already beside the point; Job had accepted the standard retribution doctrine (cf. 29:18–20) unthinkingly, but now he is beginning to question it precisely because it does not explain his present situation. Next (v. 6), Eliphaz bids him take confidence from his past faithful service of God; he acknowledges Job's piety and integrity (corresponding to "God-fearing" and "blameless" of 1:1,8). (Later on, he will deny both: 15:4; 22:4–5.) **7–9.** Eliphaz sums up the orthodox teaching and innocently asks Job if he doesn't remember it. He claims to base it first on experience: He has seen divine justice working infallibly in the world (cf. Ps 37:25). A man who makes this claim must have shut his eyes to many facts, as Job will trenchantly point out (9:22–24; 21:7–17); in particular, Eliphaz is not considering the case before him; he has not investigated Job's position. In short, he has a closed mind and is completely satisfied with his tidy comprehensible doctrine, which he applies complacently and rather unfeelingly to Job. **7.** *perishes:* The word recurs in vv. 9a, 11a, and 20b. **8.** As a general principle, this is sound; but Eliphaz makes it so absolute that he can turn it around and say infallibly, "Those who reap trouble must have sowed it by their wickedness." **10–11.** The author's rich vocabulary finds five different terms for lions.

25 (b) ELIPHAZ' REVELATION (4:12–16,17–21; 5:1–2). Besides experience ("seen," 4:8 and 5:3) Eliphaz can bring a proof from a private revelation ("heard," 4:16). He describes—with great evocative power and mystery—a ghostly audition; but the source of the message remains undetermined. It is called (v. 12) *dābār* (a word) and *šemeṣ* (a whisper), which produced preternatural dread. The speaker seems to be hinting at something he cannot affirm; the passage may be a deliberate parody of attempts to claim a quasi-supernatural authority for wisdom teachings, on a par with that claimed by oracle givers and prophets. The aptness of the message to Eliphaz' argument makes it rather suspect. **17.** The meaning may be general—"Can man be [considered] just and pure, in comparison with the transcendent justice and purity of God?"—or specific—"In a given case, can a man, by proving himself to be in the right and innocent, prove God wrong and blameworthy?" In either case, Eliphaz' point is that Job should accept God's clear verdict that he is a sinner, whether he understands his sinfulness or not.

5:1–2 A warning against mere unprofitable lament. None of the "holy ones" (the servants and messengers of 4:18) can save from God's displeasure and just resentment (CCD, "impatience" and "indignation") a sinner who refuses to acknowledge his offense or to ask God's forgiveness.

26 (c) RECOMMENDATION (5:3–7,8–13,14–16). **3–5.** Eliphaz illustrates the point made in 5:2. Verse 4 refers, callously enough, to the fate of Job's children.

Verse 6 refers to 4:8. **7b.** *sparks:* Or "eagles"; lit., "sons of Resep," a god of fire and pestilence, but also connected with birds. **8.** *in your place:* Not expressed in the Hebrew; the MT has "But I, I would seek God." "Seeking God" (*dāraš*) is a favorite theme with the prophets (e.g., Am 5:4,6). It implies that a man (in this case Job) has for a time abandoned God and must now penitently return to him. **9.** Omit v. 9, transferred in error from 9:10. **10–13.** A doxology in hymnal style (*EDB* 589, 1044). Verses 11, 15–16 are echoed in the Magnificat (Lk 1:51–53).

27 (d) Encouragement (5:17–21,22–26,27). Eliphaz ends with a flourish, with two carefully matched strophes in elaborate sapiential style. **17.** The first begins with a beatitude (cf. Ps 94:12). Verse 19 introduces a numerical "proverb" (cf. Prv 6:16–19; 30:15ff.; Sir 25:7–10; A. Bea, *Bib* 21 [1940] 196–98; W. M. W. Roth, *VT* 12 [1962] 300–11). In vv. 20–21, six calamities are mentioned, which God will avert: famine, death, war, sword, calumny, and ruin. Verse 22a continues with "ruin [same word] and hunger" (repeating the sixth and first calamities), and these add up to the seventh, wild beasts. **23–26.** Next are listed seven blessings God will bestow; six of these each occupy a stich (the calamities were mentioned more briefly, 20–21), and the seventh occupies v. 26 with its picturesque simile. **27.** Eliphaz sums up. Experience and revelation ("searched... heard") make his teaching certain. The last phrase ("You, apply it to yourself") expresses his calm assurance that it only remains for Job to put it into practice.

This speech is eloquent, and its content is orthodox; yet in the context it is a parody. The reader knows from the prologue that Eliphaz' analysis of Job's situation is wrong; in fact, with his stress on the "profit motive," his outlook is indistinguishable from the Adversary's. He takes for granted Job will be encouraged by all sorts of rewards held out to him, whereas the latter (in ch. 3) had desired only the quietude of death. When he does call for something more positive, he will not call for renewed prosperity but for an explanation of God's acts (10:2ff.).

28 **(C) Job's First Response (6:1–7:21).** Job does not answer like a debater, point for point, but develops his own analysis of the situation, quite different from that formed by the friends. Here he first complains of Eliphaz' prejudgment of his case. This would-be consoler has not properly considered the monumental scale of Job's disaster, nor the fundamental problem it has raised in Job's mind. He and his companions are bound to Job by a covenant of friendship and should exercise *ḥesed*, "covenant love," toward him. That would mean expressing compassion (which they did, at first, by their silent mourning) and then sympathetically entering into his view of the case. They should take into account his own testimony as to his sinlessness; or, if they disagree, they should testify in turn (6:24). They should not take his wickedness as proved merely by the fact of his suffering. After this vehement protest, Job reaffirms his innocence, describes his pain, and then makes a pathetic appeal to God, mingled with bitter reproaches for this unkind treatment.

The speech contains 16 strophes, of which every fourth has four lines, and the rest have three lines each.

29 (a) Job's Misery (6:2–4,5–7,8–10). Job continues in the vein of his lament in ch. 3, but with more express reference to God. **2a.** *anguish: Kaʿas,* translated "impatience" in 5:2 (and as "displeasure" in 10:17). Not God's "indignation" at the foolish sinner, but Job's, at his undeserved suffering, is the theme to be considered. **2b.** *with it:* Better, "all my calamity be heaped together in the scales." Anguish and calamity correspond in parallelism; either of them would outweigh the sands. **4.** A Homeric image: the divine archer, shooting poisoned arrows at his victim. The title *šadday* (the Almighty) was used by Eliphaz, 5:17; what he referred to as discipline is felt by Job as torture. Verse 5 justifies Job's "roaring" (3:24b; 4:10); he is deprived of the necessities of life—i.e., what is needed for normal human existence. **6–7.** Eliphaz' advice has been no help to him. "White of an egg" is a traditional rendering of an uncertain text; something nauseating is meant. **8–10.** Job is not allured by the happiness Eliphaz had augured for him; his affliction does not result from any act of his and it cannot be removed by any facile "repentance." All he desires (as in ch. 3) is a speedy death. **10.** His one consolation will be that he has not, as his wife had proposed, failed in loyalty, even when so severely treated (cf. 23:12). Job here seems to have an inkling of the aspect of his trial that is presented in the prologue.

30 (b) A Transition Strophe (6:11–14). With great pathos Job bursts into protests against the increase of his suffering by failure of the expected comfort from his friends. **12.** "Stones" and "bronze" imply reference to statues; men of marble or metal feel nothing, but Job is living flesh and blood. **14.** An obscure verse. "Kindness" is *ḥesed,* owed to a friend. Read, possibly, "He who withholds kindness from his friend forsakes...."

31 (c) Job's Disillusionment with the Friends (6:15–17,18–20,21–23,24–27). Without (as yet) going into any arguments, Job expresses his profound disappointment. Instead of bringing him comfort, they are acting as his enemies. His reaction is illustrated by a Homeric simile, the most elaborate in the book. The streams that flow down wadies, in Arabia and Syria, are mostly not perennial; they run furiously in the rainy season but sooner or later dry up completely when the rains cease. (A few may flow all summer one year and run dry the year following.) Desert travelers who counted on finding water in a particular wady might be exposed to death by thirst, if that stream had ceased to flow. Their disappointment and despair are the images of Job's reaction to his friends' attitude, as revealed in the speech of Eliphaz (21a). **22–23.** He has not asked much of his "brothers" (15a)—not to pay out money nor to risk their lives (their covenant of friendship would oblige them even to that); he has only asked them to show him sympathy by adopting his point of view and by helping him, if they can, to make sense of this waking nightmare. **26–27.** In effect, Eliphaz' complacent lecturing is inhumane. He is more interested in the disease than in the patient.

32 (d) Transition Strophe (6:28–30). Job makes a formal challenge, appealing to the bond of friendship and affirming his own truthfulness. **29a–30a.** The same word is used, *ʿawlāh* (translated "falsehood" in 13:7 and 27:4): There is no dishonesty in him; let there be none in them.

33 (e) Soliloquy (7:1–3,4–6,7–10). Presumably the friends show their rejection of the appeal, and Job ceases to address them. He returns to the theme of his lament. He compares human life in general to forced military service, to the work of a day laborer, and to simple slavery—three proverbially wretched states of life. (Cf. M. David, *Revue philosophique* 147 [1957] 341–49.) It is his retort to Eliphaz' easy optimism in 5:17ff. Each man has a life span and work allotted to him; Job's life span and work are full of misery. Verse 4 is a tristich; therefore, vv. 4–6 form a three-line strophe. **7.** *remember:* Eliphaz' word to Job in 4:7; but now, suddenly, Job is addressing God. From "my eye will not again see..." (so, lit., 7b), he passes to "the eye of my beholder" (8a), and then to "your eye" (8b, lit., "your eye upon me—but I am gone"). The tone of this first address to God is revealing. It is not the penitential plea that Eliphaz had recommended (5:8); Job, accustomed to an untroubled relationship with his divine benefactor, appeals implicitly to the love God has for him. His human friends have failed him, but he takes for granted his divine friend will come looking for him—only, it may then be too late. **9–10.** This statement of the finality of death is important and will recur several times (cf. 7:21; 10:21; 14:10,12, 18–22; 17:13–16). The whole problem would be different if Job knew anything of a judgment and possible happiness after death, but he has no evidence or basis for such a belief (cf. 14:13–17; and see comment on 19:25–27).

34 (f) Complaint to God (7:11,20cd,12; 13–15; 16–18; 19–20ab,21). Job's first formal prayer. Eliphaz must be shocked at hearing it. Job has not conceived his relationship to God as one of retributive justice, whereby a man observes certain rules, does certain things and avoids others, and the just judge rewards him in due proportion (Eliphaz' concept, and also that of the Adversary). Job has known God as a person adored and loved, whom he can address intimately; the relationship is a personal one, whose possible categories are friendship and enmity, love and hatred. This dearly loved friend has now turned on Job, maltreating and tormenting him. There is no question of justice or its opposite; the problem is: Why is a friend suddenly acting like a vicious enemy? Verse 20cd, restored to its probable place after v. 11, provides an emphatic beginning, with its *lāmāh,* "Why?" as in 3:11,20: "Why have you set me up as your target?..." (cf. 6:4). **12.** *yām* and *tannîn* are sea and sea monster, mythological symbols of the powers of chaos, vanquished by the creator in a cosmic battle but still requiring surveillance as potential threats to God's power (cf. comment on 3:8). **13–14.** God is persecuting him night and day. **15.** Read, "My soul prefers choking, my bones prefer death" (N. M. Sarna, *JJS* 6 [1955] 109). **16–18.** A somber analysis of the presence of God, when that presence, as with Job now, is not benignant, fatherly, and loving, but hostile and oppressive. **17.** Psalm 8:5 is an exclamation of wonder and gratitude at God's care for insignificant man; with bitter irony Job quotes it and applies it to the sort of surveillance God is now applying to him (J. Hempel, *Forschungen und Fortschritte* [vol. 35; Berlin, 1961] 123). Surely it is unworthy of the Almighty thus to occupy himself in tormenting so unimportant a creature. **19b.** An idiom still used in Arabic, to request a moment's respite. **20b.** Perhaps read (with LXX), "You Inspector of the hearts of men!" **21a.** This verse follows v. 20b immediately: Even if Job has sinned, he cannot have done any harm to God, and the latter's greatness would be better shown by his function of forgiveness. **21cd.** Job ends by making more explicit the idea in v. 8. God cannot really mean to treat him like this; but when he realizes what he is doing, Job will be dead and it will be too late to put things right.

35 **(D) Bildad's First Speech (8:1–22).** Bildad is younger, more narrow minded, and less tactful than Eliphaz. He is scandalized at Job's freedom, or irreverent familiarity, in speaking about (and to) God. These protests and complaints seem to him to undermine a main principle of religion, that God can do no injustice. Like Eliphaz, he considers that strict retributive justice is the only principle underlying God's dealings with men. In fact, he implies that God's functions are automatic: Men have freedom to choose this or that, but no allowance is made for liberty or love in the judgments of God. The latter can only react, according to the actions of men. Hence, Bildad's crude representation: Mankind is divided into two groups, the wicked and the righteous; the former, perhaps after brief prosperity, God utterly destroys; the latter he blesses. Bildad argues, not from personal experience, but from the tradition of former generations, the unquestionable source of wisdom.

The speech consists in seven three-line strophes.

(Irwin, W. A., "The First Speech of Bildad," *ZAW* 51 [1953] 205–16. Löhr, M., "Die drei Bildad-Reden im Buche Hiob," BZAW 34 [Fest. K. Budde; 1920] 107–12.)

36 (a) Introduction (8:2–4,5–7). Beginning as usual with a rhetorical question and with a reference to Job's words, Bildad firmly concentrates on the question of divine justice—which Job had not raised at all. **4.** He does not shrink from the obvious conclusion: Job's sons and daughters must have been very sinful, and they have received what they deserved. (Eliphaz had only hinted at this, 5:4.) **5–7.** Having made that clear, Bildad proceeds, according to his original intention (2:11b), to comfort Job and to encourage him (ineptly) by promising renewed prosperity if he accepts his friends' advice. Verse 5a corrects Job's last words, 7:21d, using the same verb, *šiḥar:* Job should seek God, not expect God to seek him. **5b.** *make supplication:* For forgiveness for his sins. **6.** Omit first stich as gloss.

37 (b) Doctrine (8:8–10, 11–13, 14–16, 17–19). After citing his authorities, Bildad develops his doctrine in similes, which have an Egyptian coloring. **11–13.** Papyrus and reed promptly wither if their marsh bed dries up; thus do the wicked when God withdraws his favor. **14–19.** The text is corrupt and may be disordered; read, perhaps, 14–15, 18, 16–17, 19. Like a garden plant, the wicked can be uprooted and destroyed in a moment.

38 (c) Conclusion (8:20–22). Bildad ends on an optimistic, even complacent, note. He has surely convinced Job and so "consoled" him. **21.** An adaptation of Ps 126:2ab. **22b.** The last word, *'ênennû,* "is no more," echoes Job's last word, 7:21d, *'ênennî,* "am no more"; i.e., if Job talks like that, he is setting himself among the wicked.

In this strophe, the author's irony is very clear; Bildad's promises will be verified, but not as he intends. **20.** Job has already been declared perfect (*tām;* not "upright") by God (1:8; 2:3), and Bildad uses the singular: "...not cast away the perfect man" (= Job). But "the wicked" is plural (= the friends)! Verse 21 is to come true without Job's following Bildad's advice, and v. 22a is spoken by Bildad against himself (cf. 42:7–8).

39 **(E) Job's Second Response (9:1–10:22).** Has the same general structure as chs. 6–7: a section answering the friends (9:2–24); a briefer soliloquy (9:25–10:1a); and a direct address to God (10:1b–22). It is less personal than the previous speech; in fact, the friends are addressed only indirectly. Bildad's speech is mostly ignored, but Job picks up Eliphaz' remark about the justice of man before God (4:17). God's justice is really his power; he can do what he chooses; none can withstand him; and if he declares a man to be guilty, then it is so. No appeal can be made, and no other standard of justice can be invoked. Yet if the man's conscience is clear, what he suffers is not felt as justice but as divine anger; thus it is with Job. The third section is another impassioned argument and appeal to God, which subsides into a mournful plea that God leave him alone (K. Fullerton, "On Job, Chapters 9 and 10" *JBL* 53 [1934] 321–49; "Job, Chapters 9 and 10" *AJSL* 55 [1938] 225–69).

The first section is in seven three-line strophes interrupted by a transition couplet, 9:11–12. The soliloquy has three strophes, of four, three, and four lines. The address to God has a couplet (10:1b–2), followed by four five-line strophes. Verses 9:24,33–34a; 10:3,15,17 are tristichs (cf. Skehan, *CBQ* 23, 132–34).

40 (a) GOD IS IRRESISTIBLE IN POWER, THEREFORE IN JUDGMENT (9:2–4,5–7,8–10,11–12). **2.** Job changes Eliphaz' dictum (4:17) slightly to emphasize the lawsuit imagery. If God is one party in such a suit he must necessarily win it, not because he will not pervert justice but because justice is whatever he decides. **4a.** The MT does not say "God is..."; the line may mean "What man, however wise...." **5.** Job begins a doxology, more magnificent than that of Eliphaz (5:10–16), but significantly limited to works of power, not of justice or salvation. **9.** (Cf. G. R. Driver, *JTS* 7 [1956] 1–11.) **11–12.** The divine cosmic activity is beyond man's understanding or control; it is strictly a mystery. For Job, the same is true of God's interventions in human life. But the friends insist that they can explain the latter, infallibly, as retributive justice.

41 (b) GOD IS ARBITRARY (9:13–15,16–18,19–21, 22–24). Job passes from the general to the particular; it is impossible for him to "sue" God or to establish his innocence if God condemns him. Nevertheless, that does not mean that he must have given cause for this ill-treatment—i.e., have rebelled against God. **13.** *Rahab:* "A mythological sea monster personifying the forces of chaos" (*EDB* 1977; see comment on 3:8). **22.** *innocent: Tām*, "perfect," as in 8:20; Job contradicts Bildad.

42 (c) JOB'S HELPLESSNESS (9:25–28,29–31,32–10:1a). Soliloquy, but with asides to God (vv. 28b, 31). If suffering is an infallible sign of guilt, then Job has already been condemned by God and there is nothing he can do about it. Guilt is conceived as a state of damnation produced by the judge's sentence; it is objective and independent of the man's conscience. **30.** (On handwashing, cf. R. Press, *ZAW* 51 [1933] 246–47.) **32–33.** If only there were a court of appeal, a super-god to hold the scales even between Job and his oppressor! This daring concept illustrates another grave defect of the friends' theology (according to which Job is arguing): Their idea of a sort of commutative justice between God and man destroys God's transcendence and tends in this respect to bring him to man's level. Hence this *reductio ad absurdum* suggested by Job.

43 (d) SPECULATION AND APPEAL (10:1b–2,3–7,8–12). Job addresses himself to the "real" God. The friends' understanding of his case is false; Job must try to find a truer one. Desperately he speculates on possible motives for this persecution, proposing (and rejecting) wild theories, trying to provoke an answer. **3.** Is God sadistic or (4) making a mistake or (5) jealous of men's happiness because his own is limited in time? **8–12.** "Hand" in v. 7 leads to "hands" in v. 8 and to this most interesting strophe, which outlines the embryology of the ancient world (cf. Ps 139:13–15). Job recalls with awe the process of his formation in the womb, by the hands of God, and the gifts then made and continued. **12a.** *grace and favor:* The MT has "life and *ḥesed*," a special love (cf. Ps 63:4a). For all this solicitude, Job could never be sufficiently grateful.

44 (e) THE MOURNFUL CONTRAST (10:13–17,18–22). **13.** But now, that gratitude is poisoned, if all along God was only preparing a victim to be tortured. **15.** Here is the denial of the friends' idea of the strict moral causality of human acts. Whether Job acts rightly or wrongly makes no difference; God has chosen to torment him for reasons of his own. **17b.** *displeasure: Ka'as*, as in 5:2a; God's "impatience" is not reserved for the foolish; it also afflicts the just. **18.** The last strophe returns to the theme of ch. 3 and begins with an emphatic *lāmāh*, "Why?" echoing 3:11,20. Verse 20 repeats the theme of God's unwelcome presence, as in 7:16,19; Job can desire only that God withdraw from him. Verses 20b–21a quote, with slight modification, Ps 39:14.

45 **(F) Zophar's First Speech (11:1–20).** The third, probably the youngest, of Job's wise friends is Zophar of Naamah. He shows himself the least original and the most vehement. He does not appeal (like Eliphaz) to his personal experience nor (like Bildad) to the tradition of the ancients. His authority is wisdom itself, a self-authenticating knowledge possessed by him and identical (at least in its application to human life) with the wisdom of God. This doctrine is not only clear and certain in itself, but its exemplification in Job's case is equally so. In form, the speech is a well-developed parallel to Bildad's first two strophes; 11:2–6 to 8:2; 11:7–12 to 8:3–4; 11:13–19a to 8:5–7. But where Bildad undertook to defend divine justice, Zophar is glorifying divine wisdom, which he feels must equally be vindicated against Job's scandalous and ignorant criticisms. Finally, like the other two speakers, Zophar encourages Job with the prospect of restored happiness. Instead of foolishly claiming to be innocent (his condition is clear proof of the contrary), let him repent of his iniquity and ask God's pardon; thus he will enjoy renewed prosperity.

The speech consists of three six-line strophes and a concluding couplet.

46 (a) JOB'S FOOLISHNESS (11:2–6,7–12). **2.** *be right:* A juridical sense: "Be judged to be right, and acquitted." Job's words are mere words, without substance. **4.** Not an exact quotation, but summing up what Zophar finds objectionable in Job's attitude (cf. 9:21; 10:7,15b). **6a.** Read "And declare to you the secrets of wisdom, which are marvelous to our understanding"; the fifth line of the strophe. **8–9.** A fine poetic statement of God's transcendence with regard to all human understanding. **12.** A proverb cited as conclusion, whose meaning is obscure.

47 (b) COUNSEL AND ENCOURAGEMENT (11:13–19a, 19b–20). Zophar sincerely desires Job's amendment and recovery. He leaves the latter's sins to his own conscience (14) and glowingly (and naïvely) pictures the rewards of repentance. **15.** *surely then:* Emphatic, contradicting what Job had said in 10:15. **19b–20.** The brief concluding strophe is an implicit warning; the last phrase indicates that the death wish, which Job has repeatedly expressed, is itself a mark of the wicked man; cf. a similar "sting in the tail" of Bildad's speech, 8:22b.

48 **(G) Job's Third Response (12:1–14:22).** This speech is Job's longest apart from his final soliloquy. Each of the three friends has spoken now, and, as he realizes their unanimous and blunt refusal to accept the testimony of his own clear conscience, he turns on them all with withering sarcasm. Much of what they have said is true, but it is the merest commonplace; it needs no great wisdom to declare that God governs the world and can do all things. Job underlines this with another doxology, this time describing the divine government of human affairs, and how God, for his own mysterious reasons, brings about the rise or fall of peoples and kingdoms. But of these principles, in which Job is as well grounded as they, they are making a false application to his case. God's ways, in the concrete, are not so easy to interpret and understand; they are extremely mysterious to men. The friends will not admit the mystery. In the teeth of the evidence, they are defending God in human terms and are even telling lies on his behalf. This outrageous perversion is denounced by Job in strong terms. He, on the other hand, holds that reverence for God demands respect for truth in the first place. He will testify to that truth and will proclaim his clear conscience, if need be, before God himself. For a moment, he proposes the friends' conclusion: If he is a guilty man, let God make clear his guilt. But he knows God cannot do that—he is only treating Job as though he were guilty. Is this then a temporary aberration on God's part? Job seizes on this idea: He could endure this estrangement if assured that there would be a future reconciliation; if, for instance, there would be a happy reunion with God after this unhappy life. But this is wishful thinking: Death is the end; no restoration or recovery of happiness is possible. The speech ends on the same mournful note as chs. 7 and 10.

Strophic division is somewhat uncertain because of textual obscurities. Skehan (*CBQ* 23, 134–37) proposes: nine strophes of five and six lines alternately (chs. 12–13); a four-line transition strophe (14:1–3), three of three lines each, two of five lines.

49 (a) Job's Wisdom Matches Theirs (12:2–6, 7–12,13–19,20–25). **2.** The MT reads "you are people" (no "the"), so a word is certainly missing, probably "of discernment" or something similar. In any case, the sarcasm is clear from the parallel stich. **3b.** The CCD translation rightly omits "I am not inferior to you," inserted here from 13:2b. **4–5.** Text is obscure, probably corrupt. Suggested emendations (Terrien, Horst) would give "...neighbors, as one who calls on God, but he oppresses him; For misfortune there is mockery, for weakness contempt, for one staggering, an extra push...." The point is (as Job is going to develop in the following strophes) that calamities, whether of nations or individuals, demonstrate God's supremacy and mystery, but not necessarily wickedness in the sufferers; therefore, the friends are being unjust to him. **7–9.** *you:* Singular pronoun, so one of the friends is being addressed; presumably the last speaker, Zophar, is being ridiculed for his remarks in 11:7–9. In 9b, the MT reads "the hand of Yahweh," the only occurrence of this name within the dialogue. The phrase is a quotation from Is 41:20, which accounts for the anomaly (cf. the quotation in 1:21). **12.** Possibly a sarcastic phrase at Eliphaz' expense. **13–19,20–25.** These two strophes, praising God's "wisdom and might...counsel and understanding...strength and prudence," surpass what Zophar had to say on the subject, 11:7–10; but he had jumped to a conclusion about "iniquity" (11:11), which Job denies.

50 (b) Summary and Warning Against "Defending" God Dishonestly (13:1–5,6–11). **1.** Job opposes his experience to that of Eliphaz (cf. 4:8,12; 5:3,27); he, too, has seen, heard, and understood. **3.** Eliphaz had said (5:8), "But I would seek God..."; Job repeats the first words, "But I would speak...." Job can say this because he has been accustomed to speaking thus. Throughout the dialogue he alone utters prayers to God. The friends praise him, but they do not address him. They have no need of such personal reference. Their God works retribution in strict accord with human deserts, and they need only act correctly. There is nothing they need or wish to say to him, and there is no place for a relationship of love. They do not "reason with God," only about him—and, in part, wrongly. **5.** A pointed rebuke to wisdom teachers!—cf. Prv 17:28. **6–11.** After the emphatic "Hear!" the remaining lines of this strophe begin each with the same letter. This famous passage is a powerful warning against a temptation that may come to all controversialists and apologists, in theological as in other contexts. **7a.** The Vg version is still more forceful: Numquid Deus indiget vestro mendacio? "Does God need your lies?"

51 (c) Job Reasons with God (13:12–16,17–22, 23–27). This protest and plea for explanation are genuinely religious, inspired by Job's past experience of God's love and by his intense concern over his personal standing with him. Yet the imagery adopted is inevitably forensic; i.e., according to the conventions of the psalm of lament, enemies are thought of as opponents in a lawsuit, against whom the sufferer must defend and establish his innocence. The friends have shown themselves to be such enemies, and such an enemy, according to outward appearances and the general estimation of men, is God himself. Thus, Job pictures him as his adversary at law (cf. 9:32ff.), which leads him to conceive an illusory equality between himself and God and thereby to conceive a relation of justice, one to the other. It is for this misrepresentation that Job must repent at the end of the book. But it does not, happily, corrupt his intense faith in God's love.

12b. *Gabbîm* can be interpreted as "answers": "Your answers crumble like clay" (lit., "are answers of clay"). **14–15.** Job is risking his life in thus approaching God, but he no longer cares for it. **15a.** *I will wait for him:* The reading of the MT and versions; but the older consonantal text has "I have no hope," which better fits the context. Thus, "He may (or will) slay me—I hope for nothing else—yet I will defend...." **16.** Paradoxically, Job sees his readiness to face God as the best guarantee of his innocence, of his truthfulness, and therefore of God's admitting he is right ("salvation"). He has complete faith that God, if he speaks, will speak in Job's favor.

17. The strophe begins with another emphatic "Hear!" (pl., addressed to the friends), parallel to 13:6. **18b.** *in the right:* More technically, "I shall be found innocent, acquitted." **19.** Job promises to abide by the judgment of the court. **20–22.** Job begs (sing., addressed to God) that God will meet his arguments and not use his infinite superiority to crush him. He is willing to be either defendant (22a) or plaintiff (22b). **23.** Receiving no answer, Job speaks first. He repeats the challenge he has uttered to the friends: He is confident he has committed no such misdeeds as would be reason for his suffering. **24.** God remains silent. He neither declares Job's guilt nor confirms his innocence. And Job resumes his reproaches. **26b.** *faults of my youth:* These are mentioned as something inconsiderable, for which the grown man should not be held responsible. **28.** Replace after 14:2.

52 (d) Lament over Human Life (14:1–2,13:28, 14:3; 4–6; 7–9; 10–12). Job generalizes his lament, returning in v. 3 to the theme of 7:17. **4.** A quite obscure verse; possibly some words are missing. The CCD version (like most translations) paraphrases. Some Church Fathers, relying on the OL or Vg versions, saw here a reference to original sin, but it is not justified by the Hebrew. Verses 7–9 and 10–12 are parallel strophes, emphasizing human mortality by a striking poetic contrast.

53 (e) A Dream and Reality (14:13–17,18–22). Two parallel five-line strophes. In the first, Job contemplates, with eagerness and even passionate longing, the possibility of a restoration to God's intimacy after death, a reconciliation in which God would show himself again the loving benefactor that he really is. **13a.** *nether world:* *Šeʾôl*, the abode of the dead (cf. 3:17ff.). Job here supposes a remarkable duality in God: He would hide Job—from his own wrath. Verse 15b echoes 10:8 (rather than 10:3, where the Hebr words are different). Similarly, v. 16b refers to 10:6; God would resume the old relationship of gracious kindness. **17.** Another obscure text; in any case, not a confession of guilt (cf. 13:23). **18–20.** In the second strophe, Job returns to sad reality. **21–22.** He rejects even the traditional consolation of leaving a prosperous family. Anyway, Job now has no children to leave.

54 (H) Eliphaz' Second Speech (15:1–35). Eliphaz' tone is notably different here from what it was in chs. 4–5. At first, he had looked on Job as a fundamentally wise and God-fearing man (4:3–6) who had happened to incur God's sudden and just anger by some particular fault. But now he has heard him, in three successive speeches, deny any such guilt, reject the sacrosanct principle that suffering is always, and only, punishment for wrongdoing, and challenge God to give some other explanation of his affliction. Eliphaz is not only offended at Job's blunt rejection of the traditional doctrine of the sages, he is profoundly shocked at such fundamental questioning, by which he feels his own religious security threatened. His faith in God is bound up with his narrow retribution doctrine, which he must defend at all costs. Hence, the vigor and the angry tone of his attack. Instead of the encouraging subject—reward of the righteous—stressed in his first speech, he now develops the negative and menacing one—punishment of the wicked.

The speech contains six five-line strophes, an intermediate three-line strophe (17–19), and one one-line conclusion.

55 (a) Job Has Spoken Impiously and Presumptuously (15:2–6,7–11,12–16). **2.** *wise:* Emphatic—"a truly wise man" (cf. 8b). **4.** Eliphaz had acknowledged Job's piety (cf. 4:6), but now he claims that his attitude is destructive of piety and prayer; his words are "offensive to pious ears." **6.** Eliphaz no doubt has in mind such passages as 9:20,24; 10:3; etc. **7–8.** Here, there is reference to the myth of the *Urmensch*, the first man, who enjoyed equality with the sons of God, and, in particular, had access to divine wisdom. Rather than in Gn, the theme is reflected in Ez 28:11–19 and in Prv 8:22–26, where it is transferred to divine Wisdom personified. Verse 7b here is practically identical with Prv 8:25b. Eliphaz conveniently forgets that he himself had claimed superhuman wisdom, at least, through the audition of 4:12–21; but then, his revelation was soundly orthodox, in fact, conventional. **10.** Presumably, the speaker is referring to himself. **11.** *consolations... speech:* The latter is *dābār*, more properly "word"; both refer to Eliphaz' first speech (the only one to "deal gently" with Job), and both attribute to it an authority belonging to the words of a prophet—another ironic touch by the author, in view of the ending of the story. **14–16.** Eliphaz repeats in substance his "word" of 4:17–21 (also quoting Job's phrase, 14:1), but with harsher expressions in v. 16; in v. 16b, read "a man," not the genus but an individual, whom Eliphaz need not name.

56 (b) Punishment for the Impious and Presumptuous (15:17–19,20–24,25–29a,29b–34,35). **18b.** Read "and what their fathers did not hide from them." **19.** This verse stresses the antiquity and purity—and hence the authority—of the sapiential tradition, which Eliphaz represents. **20–24.** The first of three strophes describing the frightful calamities that are sure to come upon "the abominable, the corrupt" man. First he is shown as tormented by his evil conscience and in constant apprehension of disaster. **25–28.** Two examples are given (25, 27) of his impiety, which provokes the disasters of vv. 26, 28. Verse 25 especially is Eliphaz' interpretation of Job's attitude. In vv. 27–30, the text is corrupted and uncertain in detail. **29b–34.** The third strophe uses botanical comparisons to illustrate the wretch's downfall. **35.** Summary.

57 (I) Job's Fourth Response (16:1–17:16). This passage continues the lamentation form and especially develops the motif of denunciation of enemies. These are, in turn, Eliphaz, the three together, and God himself. But in the middle comes the unexpected appeal to a "witness in heaven," who is taking up, or will take up, Job's defense. The speech ends as before with consideration of Job's approaching death and final descent to the underworld.

Twelve strophes can be distinguished in the speech, of which the fourth, seventh, and twelfth have four lines each; the rest have three lines.

58 (a) Afflicted by Men and by God (16:2–4b, 4c–6,7–9b,9c–11,17,12–13,14–16). Job starts with a statement of weariness: He has heard all this, and it is unprofitable. He knows these words and gestures; they do not deal realistically with his case. **2b.** In 15:11, Eliphaz had offered "divine consolations." Using a cognate word, Job calls the friends "wearisome consolers." **3b.** The verb is singular, addressed to Eliphaz; in vv. 4–5 the pronouns are plural, referring to all three. Similarly v. 8 (sing.) followed by vv. 9c–10 (pl.). **8b.** A corrupt text, it is omitted in the CCD; emended, it may be read "and utters calumnies to my face." **9c–11.** The friends are called impious and wicked according to the conventions of the psalm of lament. Job is affirming his innocence; therefore, the opposing party in the suit must be "guilty." **17.** This verse should probably follow v. 11. Job reiterates what Zophar had quoted in 11:4, using the same word, *zak*, "pure." **12–13.** But behind the friends is God, and it is his actions that have given occasion for their abuse. In drastic terms Job describes how God has attacked him. Verses 12c–13a repeat the St. Sebastian image (cf. 6:4; 7:20c); Job is God's target, shot full of his arrows. **14–16.** This terrible lament concludes by describing the state to which God's onslaught has reduced Job. The last word in v. 16 is *ṣalmāwet*, "darkness."

59 (b) The Witness in Heaven (16:18–21). Abruptly, from the depth of his despair, Job utters a cry of hope. It is first an adjuration to the earth, which will "receive his blood" unjustly shed (cf. Gn 4:10; Is 26:21; Ez 24:8); according to the old idea, innocent blood cries to God for vengeance on the one who shed it (who in this case is God himself!). Let the earth not stifle this cry. **19.** But for the cry to be effective, there must be some one to hear it; Job envisages that someone as his "witness" and defender in heaven, who on hearing of his fate will intervene to vindicate him. Many attempts have been made to identify this witness as a heavenly being, angel or intercessor (cf. 5:1; and Elihu, 33:23–24; S. Mowinckel, BZAW 41 [Fest. K. Marti; 1925] 207–12); but more probably it is God himself. He seems to be Job's adversary at law, but is really on his side (the same duality as in 14:13); cf. the following verses. **20b.** *drop tears:* Read instead, from Akkadian *dalāpu*, "stay awake" (Horst, BK): "My eyes strain sleeplessly toward God."

60 (c) Complaint Continued (16:22–17:2,3–5, 6–8,10–12,13–16). Job seems to envisage his vindication taking place in heaven, rather than on earth where his situation is hopeless. He is resigned to dying but not to being estranged from God. **3.** Inasmuch as the friends will not "witness" for him, Job begs God himself to find a guarantor who will "go bail" for Job in his presence. **5.** This obscure verse (half-omitted in CCD) may be understood as a proverb applicable to the friends: "A man invites his neighbors to share [food], while the eyes of his children are failing [from hunger]"; i.e., the friends are "consoling" the prosperous, while leaving Job in his misery. **6–8.** That misery is described again, with reference to the scandal that it causes. **9.** Omit as gloss (not Job's doctrine). **10.** A sardonic invitation to the friends (vv. 11, 12 should perhaps change places).

12. Job mocks their easy optimism, e.g., Zophar in 11:17. **13–16.** The speech ends with an ironic and decisive rejection of the prospects of happiness they had earlier held out to him, as part of their "consolation." Job does not believe in them, nor does he particularly desire them; he merely wants to know his standing with God. Meanwhile, he would rather face the grim truth, which he describes with unflinching vividness.

61 **(J) Bildad's Second Speech (18:1–21).** Bildad's answer is comparatively restrained and all the more unfeeling. He rebukes Job for his abusive language and his contempt for ancient wisdom, and he insinuates that suffering as punishment for sin is a universal law from which Job cannot claim exemption. The bulk of his speech is a lurid description of the fate awaiting the man "who knows not God." Like Eliphaz, Bildad this time has no word of consolation for Job, only warning and implicit threats.

The speech contains six three-line strophes and a one-line conclusion.

62 (a) Rebuke to Job (18:2–4). **2.** Bildad begins as in 8:2 with, "How long [will you not put an end...]?" The verbs are plural (also the pronoun "your" in 3), which makes a difficulty. Most commentators make them singular, as referring only to Job. **3.** *beasts:* May refer especially to 16:9–10. **4.** Bildad coldly remarks that Job is the cause of his own torment because he will not take the right means to remove it. He would like the laws of the universe changed to suit himself. The last phrase is a quotation of 14:18b.

63 (b) Fate of the Wicked (18:5–7,8–10,11–14, 15–17,18–20,21). **5–7.** This strophe develops the image of the failing light. **8–10.** Here, the image of the snare that entangles the wicked. **11–14.** Text is corrupted; there should be three distichs. After "...at his side" in the CCD, read "Pestilence consumes his skin, the first-born of death consumes his limbs. He is plucked from the security of his tent, he is conducted before the king of terrors." This last striking phrase is a personification of death, as the "first-born" is of disease. **15.** Begin, "In his tent no trace of him remains, over his abode...." **20.** *after...before:* Better understood as points of the compass (reckoned by facing E); translate, "At his fate men of the West are appalled, and men of the East are struck...."

64 **(K) Job's Fifth Response (19:1–29).** In contrast with the friends' rigid adherence to their predetermined positions, Job's successive speeches show a certain development. The friends' criticisms have compelled him to analyze his situation in order to seek an alternative to their unacceptable verdict. In this, his central discourse, he achieves an insight and a profession of faith, which supply at least a provisional solution and enable him to triumph over his worst temptation. Even the style reaches a certain climax of power and pathos. Job here draws together themes touched on in his earlier speeches: the validity of his clear conscience (6:30; 9:29; 10:7; 16:17), which the judge—if only he will hear the case—must certainly ratify (10:2,7; 13:23; 16:21); his intuition that God must yearn for him, even as he does for God (7:8,21; 10:8–9; 14:15); his longing and hope that God will finally remember and vindicate him (14:13–15; 16:19–20).

65 The problem is the apparent change in God's attitude to him: He was Job's friend; he seems now to be his enemy. Job's solution is an affirmation of faith: The change is only apparent; the abandonment is only temporary. The friends are uncharitable and unjust in their conviction that God is declaring him to be a sinner. His sufferings, which must speedily lead to his death, have been decreed by God in spite of his innocence, and for the moment, for some unexplained reason, he will not receive Job's pleas and protests. Nevertheless, he will eventually, in his own good time, remember him and pronounce his vindication. And Job—even though he has died in the meantime—will be present at this, and will see God as he truly is, his friend.

Between introductory and closing two-line strophes, the chapter contains four three-line strophes, one four-line, another three-line, one five-line; i.e., 2; 3, 3, 3; 3, 4, 3; 5; 2.

66 (a) God's Doing, Not Man's (19:2–3,4–6,7–9, 10–12). **2.** Job begins by throwing Bildad's exordium back at him (using the same expressions, "How long...?" and "words," as 18:2). That he has to bear God's mysterious displeasure is bad enough; need they make things worse by their inhumanity? **4.** If Job is wrong, he will only harm himself; why must they be so bitter and so intolerant? (The reason is that he threatens their religious existence; he must not be right, otherwise their whole faith would be undermined. It is their insecurity that makes them cruel.) **4b.** *and that:* Omit; probably an apodosis. **6.** They persist in seeking "the root of the matter" in him, whereas it is really to be looked for in God; and whatever else it is, it is not God's justice. Job here contradicts Bildad, 18:4a; cf. 18:8. Verses 7–9 and 10–12 picture in highly pathetic terms what Job is experiencing. **7.** *if:* Better, "Behold!" an emphatic appeal introducing the description. To "cry 'Injustice!'" is the technical phrase for a public act, by which a man suffering personal injury could demand that the community (and eventually God) take action to vindicate him and put right his wrong (cf. Hab 1:2). Job's sufferings (8–12) are not felt by him as the automatic and impersonal effects of wrongdoing (cf. the images used by Bildad in 18:5–7,8–10); they are inflicted by deliberate and personal acts of God. Note especially v. 11.

67 (b) Isolation and Loneliness (19:13–15,16–19,20–22). The apparent hostility of God produces hostility of men. A certain climax is probably intended in the sequence of relationships; i.e., they proceed, broadly, from less to greater intimacy. **13a.** *my brethren:* Probably refers to his three interlocutors (cf. 6:15). **17b.** *men of my family:* Lit., "sons of my womb," i.e., of his mother: full brothers. **19.** The inner circle of intimates, of whom even greater loyalty was expected than of wife or brothers. *my intimate friends:* Lit., "men of my secret council." *those...have:* The MT has a sing. pronoun (Vg "quem maxime diligebam"), so this may have been singular originally, "he...has." (Illustration from the Gospels: v. 19a would indicate the group of the twelve, v. 19b the "disciple whom Jesus loved.") The network of human relationships that constitute a man's life has been ripped apart. Job is ostracized, isolated, on the verge of nonexistence. **20.** The translation is uncertain, but the meaning is something like, "I am nothing, and have nothing, but my skin and bones." He is reduced to bare survival, physical existence, but nothing more. **21.** At least the three are still present to him; communication is still possible, and Job utters his famous cry to the only audience he has. *hand of God:* This echoes 1:11 and, especially, 2:5 (cf. also 6:9; 12:9; 13:21). God's hand is the instrument of creation and salvation, but it also works destruction (cf. 5:18). **22b.** *insatiably prey:* Lit., "and are not sated with my flesh?"; this idiom means, "and will not stop calumniating me?"

68 (c) Hope of the Vision of God (19:23–27). Even the foregoing appeal has been in vain, as we see by the speeches that follow. At this climax, Job is utterly alone, abandoned by family, friends, men, and apparently God. Yet from this depth (as in 16:18) he achieves a "leap of faith." If God will not speak now, then he must in the future. It is to the future that Job appeals. Because he will soon die, he wants his testimony recorded, against the day when his case will come to judgment. The record must be an inscription, as permanent and indestructible as possible. **23.** *inscribed in a record:* *Sēper* is usually understood as a scroll of leather or papyrus, but it can mean anything written, an inscription; "inscribed" here is lit. "chiseled" or "incised." Thus, vv. 23 and 24 refer to the same process (H. S. Gehman, *JBL* 63 [1944] 303–7). **24.** *lead:* This word can be explained from Persian practice, as in Darius I's Behistun inscription: "The wedges...cut into the rock were themselves filled in with lead" (G. G. Cameron, *NatGeog* 98 [1950] 844; K. Galling, *WO* 2 [1954] 3–6).

25. Despite the "but," this verse is not to be separated from the foregoing; these are the words (23a) to be solemnly recorded. This important testimony has unfortunately suffered textual corruption, especially in v. 26a, and its precise sense is much debated. *vindicator:* The word *gô'ēl* means the next-of-kin whose obligation it was to rescue from poverty, redeem from slavery, or avenge a death (A. R. Johnson, VTSup 1 [1953] 67–77). Presumably, it must be God himself (cf. 16:19). But does Job hope for the act of vindication before or after his death? And if the latter, how does he conceive his own state at the time? The former solution seems very unlikely, given his constant expectation of an unhappy death, also the preceding "inscription" passage. If the latter is correct, then Job apparently expects to have, in (or from) the underworld, a vision of God pronouncing his vindication "on the dust," i.e., on earth (?). This is admittedly strange, yet consistent with what he has said earlier and, on the whole, the most likely interpretation. *lives:* Or "is living." A much discussed Ugaritic religious text has "I know that [he is] living, mighty Ba'al!" (*ANET* 140; cf. E. G. Kraeling, *The Book of the Ways of God* [N.Y., 1939] 89), but the parallel may be fortuitous; anyway, the Ugaritic concept of Ba'al is considerably different from the figure of Yahweh in the Book of Job. More relevant is the belief of Israel; it stressed that Yahweh was "the living God," and this dynamism seems to provide a connection of thought with Job's "survival of consciousness" after death. The divine vitality is such that it will cause Job, even in the underworld, to have at least momentary knowledge, or rather vision, of what occurs on earth. (A similar line of thought is carried much further in Christ's argument for the resurrection of the patriarchs, from the nature of "the God of the living"; Mt 22:32.) But we must not (as did Jerome in the Vg) read into the text any idea of an actual "resurrection of the body," even if limited to Job's unique case. *at last:* A noun in the MT: "the Last"; it is applied to Yahweh in Is 44:6.

Verses 26–27 have five stichs, but only these phrases are fairly sure: "...from my flesh I shall behold God...my eyes shall see—no stranger! My emotions are consumed within me." "Behold" is *ḥāzāh*, the verb used of seeing visions. This sight of God is what Job really craves (cf. 42:5).

(Dhorme, E., "L'idée de l'au-delâ dans la religion hébraïque," *RHR* 123 [1941] 113–42, esp. 140. Irwin, W. A., "Job's Redeemer," *JBL* 81 [1962] 217–29. Larcher, C., *Le livre de Job* [BJ; Paris, 1957] 27–31. Lindblom, J., " 'Ich weiss, dass mein Erlöser lebt,' " *ST* 2 [1940] 65–77. Martin-Achard, R., *De la mort à la résurrection d'après l'Ancien Testament* [Neuchâtel, 1956]. 133–44. Meek, T. J., "Job XIX, 25–27," *VT* 6 [1956] 100–103. Mowinckel, S., "Hiobs gō'ēl und Zeuge im Himmel," BZAW 41 [*Fest. K. Marti*, 1925] 207–12. North, C. R., "The Redeemer God," *Interpr* 2 [1948] 3–16. Tournay, R., "Relectures bibliques concernant la vie future et l'angélologie," *RB* 69 [1962] 481–505, esp. 489ff.)

69 (d) Warning to the Friends (19:28–29). *persecute:* The same word (*rādap*) as "hound" in v. 22. **28b.** This verse puts in a nutshell the error of the friends. They insist that this reversal of fortune must be explicable by Job's acts; to attribute it to a mysterious action of God would invalidate their claim to understand the workings of divine retribution. **29.** The middle stich may be a gloss. The last word, *šaddîn* (or *šaddûn*), is unknown and hard to explain. It is tempting to understand it as a variant of *šadday*, "that [so] you may come to know the Almighty" (L. R. Fisher, *VT* 11 [1961] 342–43).

70 **(L) Zophar's Second Speech (20:1–29).** This speech closely parallels Bildad's speech in ch. 18; both deal with the same subject—the destruction of the wicked. Together, they frame and set off Job's great credo in ch. 19. In contrast to his living and developing faith, they present the unchanging rigidity of the "traditional" retribution doctrine. Zophar's distinguishing marks are greater vehemence and some rather crude images (vv. 7, 15). The probable strophic division is a two-line introduction, four six-line strophes, and a one-line finale. (B. H. Kelly, "Truth in Contradiction: A Study of Job 20 and 21," *Interpr* 15 [1961] 147–56.)

71 (a) The Triumph of the Wicked Is Brief (20:2–3,4–9). **2.** The MT begins with *lākēn*, "therefore," which suggests that a preceding distich is missing. The CCD version interchanges the first stichs of vv. 2 and 3, which is also possible, but we miss the usual rhetorical question and the reference to Job's words. However, for the first and only time, one of the friends admits to being impressed by Job's utterance; his "reproach" (19:21? or 29?) has momentarily shaken Zophar. But the latter recovers and reacts all the more violently to reassure himself. Prompt disaster falling on the wicked: This is, always has been, and always must be, a fact of universal experience. He wants to hear Job acknowledge this principle and confess that it has been verified in his case. **7.** *fuel of his fire:* Means rather, "his excrement."

72 (b) He Must Give Up Ill-Gotten Gains (20:11–16,17–22,23–28,29). The text is obscure and overloaded, but the main image is clear: The riches of the impious are like food that turns to poison in his stomach. He has to vomit them up. **10.** "His sons must make compensation to the poor, his [or their] hands give back his wealth." The line is out of place and may be a gloss. In the CCD, v. 10b is joined to 21a. **23.** *God:* The word does not appear in the Hebrew, but it must be the subject. In general, the friends avoid speaking of God's actions in crudely physical terms. **29.** A conclusion very like Bildad's (18:21) and ending with the same divine name "El."

73 **(M) Job's Sixth Response (21:1–34).** Job has emerged victorious from his personal struggle; he has overcome the temptation presented to him by his friends, as earlier he overcame that of his wife. He has stated his faith that God knows his innocence and will one day (although after Job's death) testify to it. Thereby, though his present misery is not lessened, his belief in God's goodness is preserved and he has a firm basis for his rejection of the friends' accusations. Now he passes from mere defensiveness to the attack. They have condemned him on the ground of a fixed principle. Job undertakes to show that their condemnation is unjustified because the principle is false. In human experience generally, God does not send sure retribution in this life; the wicked and godless are not destroyed in a moment. The gravity of this statement, which to the sages must sound like blasphemy, is brought out in vv. 5–6. Job himself is horrified by it, but it is the truth: not that the impious always prosper, but that they often do (cf. Jer 12:1ff.; Ps 73; Eccl 7:15).

This speech is the only one of Job's orations that is exclusively polemical; it contains no soliloquy or prayer.

For the moment his own case is "solved," and he is dealing simply with the doctrine of the friends.

The strophic division is uncertain. Verse 16 (and perhaps 18) appears to be a gloss; v. 22 belongs to the following speech; vv. 30–33 are obscure. Probably there are eight strophes, of 5; 3, 4, 4 (or 3); 3, 4; 3, and 5 lines.

74 (a) INTRODUCTION (21:2–6). Job warns them that what he has to say will shock them more than anything they have heard so far. **2.** Cf. 13:5; 16:3. **3b.** *you:* Singular; the other second person verbs in the context are plural; therefore, this address may be directed to Eliphaz. If so, he responds with something worse than mockery (ch. 22). **5.** Laying hand on mouth is a gesture of voluntary silence (cf. 29:9; 40:4), here signifying horror and amazement. **6.** The facts were always there; Job had not adverted to them until his calamities (and his friends' arguments) forced him to look anew at human life and to ask himself whether the principle of retribution works universally and infallibly. Honesty compels him to a flat denial. He himself is appalled to realize how experience contradicts a fixed (and exaggerated) religious doctrine.

75 (b) THE HAPPINESS OF MEN WITHOUT GOD (21:7–9,10–13,14–18 [omit 16]). It is evidence of the author's subtlety and insight that he does not propose the trite example of the successful tyrant who breaks the laws of God and man and sows misery and disaster on all sides. It is too easy to argue (cf. Eliphaz, 15:20; Zophar, 20:12–14,18; and Plato's *Republic*) that such a man finds no real happiness and is the worst sufferer from his own vices. Instead, Job describes "the good pagan," the good-living, moral atheist, who by any external tests that men can apply enjoys a naturally happy life, filled with all the blessings that can be granted by God alone. Such a man, possessing the good things of life independently of any religious belief or practice, feels no need of God. On the other hand, since *ex hypothesi* this happiness really is God's gift, is he not, by such indiscriminate bestowal of his bounty, encouraging atheism? (In Mt 5:45, Christ cites this very fact as evidence of the heavenly father's love for men: He "sends rain upon the just and the unjust alike." This is intelligible in terms of love, but not in terms of retributive justice.) Again are shown the limits and insufficiency of the friends' commercial morality. Throughout the dialogue they have advanced no other motive for serving God than fear of punishment and hope of reward. Anything higher—the possibility of serving God "for love" (as Job did)—is utterly beyond them. **7.** Contrary to 20:5, the prosperity of the "wicked," i.e., the irreligious, does sometimes endure and increase. Job does not bother to give instances; he asks: How do you explain it? ("Why" here stands for the Hebr word *maddûaʿ*, which means "from what cause?"; the other word, *lāmāh* [3:20; 7:20; etc.], means "to what purpose?") Verses 8–13 are to be compared with Eliphaz' description in 5:20–26. All that was there pictured as reward of repentance is here enjoyed without reference to God. **10.** The homely detail of animal fertility is significant; this was regarded as a mysterious and important divine blessing. So, likewise, were numerous and healthy children (11). **14–15.** "What does it profit...?" These happy people have no motive of self-interest or necessity to induce them to acknowledge or worship God. The friends could suggest nothing else. Only Job could say they have an "obligation" of gratitude and love. **16.** Omit as gloss. **17.** Job refers scornfully to Bildad's glib claims in 18:5–6 ("lamp...put out"), 18:12 ("destruction"), and 18:10 ("noose," same word as "portion").

76 (c) NO EVIDENT CONNECTION BETWEEN VIRTUE AND HAPPINESS (21:19–21,23–26). **19–21.** A facile answer could be given to the "difficulty" that an irreligious man had apparently prospered all his life. The sages would appeal to the principle of solidarity and insist that his children would suffer the penalty of his impiety. Job objects that in such a case justice would not be satisfied; the guilty party would know nothing and feel nothing of such "punishment." **23–26.** A blunt and factual summary of human life (cf. Eccl 8:14; 9:2,11). The friends simply will not face this truth (cf. 34b).

77 (d) PEACEFUL DEATH AND POSTHUMOUS FAME OF THE GODLESS (21:27–29,30–34). **28.** Not a verbal quotation, but cf. 18:15,21; 20:9. **34a.** *comfort:* Makes an inclusion with "consolation" (a cognate word) in v. 2. **34b.** *perfidy: Maʿal*, meaning usually a sacrilegious offense against God; the friends are "lying on behalf of God" (cf. 13:7).

78 **(N) Eliphaz' Third Speech (22:1–30).** Eliphaz, of sterner stuff than Zophar, is not in the least shaken by Job's argument. He is horrified, although hardly surprised. From the beginning he has found Job obstinately perverse. His denial of the very foundations of morality (as it seems to Eliphaz) in the speech just heard is the last straw. Eliphaz drops all attempt at gentleness and forbearance and speaks his mind. In his first speech (chs. 4–5) he had been all encouragement; in his second (ch. 15) he had spoken severely of Job's present irreverence; now he declares openly that Job must have been, all along, a hypocrite and a secret sinner, and he cites by way of examples some of the crimes he must have committed. The inspired author here gives a chilling but all-too-credible portrayal of the intellectual and moral corruption of a devoutly religious man, who has confused his own simple reasonings with divine revelation. The theistic principle from which Eliphaz starts is true (that God is just), but it is not the whole truth (God is also loving); and by treating it in isolation and drawing conclusions from it as though it were the whole truth he distorts man's whole relationship to God. Moreover, he himself commits grave sins of injustice and uncharity by uttering lies and calumnies against his neighbor.

The speech contains six strophes, but the lengths of the first four are uncertain. Probably vv. 8 and 18 should be omitted as glosses, and 21:22 should be replaced before 22:12. Thus, the strophes consist of 4, 5; 4, 5; 5, 5, lines.

79 (a) EXORDIUM (22:2–5). Eliphaz still cannot imagine serving God "for nothing." Somebody must gain by it; if—according to Job—religion brings no profit to man, then it must bring profit to God! **2–4.** Eliphaz puts a series of rhetorical questions, meant to show the absurdity of Job's position. Here again the irony of the author is at work, for the questions can, in all seriousness, be answered in the affirmative. Job's love and loyalty are, indeed, a "gain" to the Almighty, who in 1:8 and 2:3 expressed his pleasure in his servant's perfection; he seemed almost to be proud of Job. In a sense, it is precisely because of Job's piety that he is being "reproved"; that was what had prompted the Adversary's attack. But to Eliphaz, confined in his narrow doctrine of retributive justice, these are fantasies. The only possible alternative to admitting God to be unjust is declaring Job to be wicked, which he proceeds to do on no better evidence than the logical requirements of his dogmatic system.

80 (b) JOB'S SINS (22:6–11). Eliphaz takes almost at random the standard list of social crimes that could be committed with impunity by the wealthy and powerful in the ancient world. **6.** Cf. Ex 22:25–26; Dt 24:6,12–13,17. **7.** Cf. Ez 18:7; Is 58:7. **9.** Cf. Dt 24:17–22. **10.** *therefore:* An emphatic word, which makes the fallacy the more obvious. Eliphaz' real reasoning has been just the opposite: Because Job is suffering "snares...terror...darkness...deluge," "therefore" he must have done the deeds of vv. 6–9.

81 (c) Rebuttal of Job's Argument (21:22; 22:12–14; 15–20). **12–14.** Eliphaz suggests that Job thinks God is too far away to see him, whereas it is his own sight that is dim; cf. "he cannot see" (14a) with "you cannot see" (11a). The apparent quotation is hard to connect with statements made by Job so far (cf. later, 23:8). **17.** Eliphaz picks up the sayings Job had attributed to the "good pagans" (21:14–15), insinuating (15) that this is Job's own outlook. In fact, he claims (16), it was the "way" of the ancient sinners destroyed by the Flood; i.e., there were people such as Job describes, but, far from living out their lives in peace, they suffered the most dreadful of disasters. Verse 20b may be intended to link the destruction of Sodom, the next great judgment recorded in Gn, with the Flood, considering its citizens as successors of the ante-diluvian sinners (Gn 6:11ff.; 19:24ff.).

82 (d) Recommendation To Be Reconciled with God (22:21–25,26–30). Despite his denunciations, Eliphaz has not given up hope of his friend's conversion. His admonitions are sincere (and beautifully expressed); but to him "conversion" is making a bargain with God (21) that will be profitable to Job (28). **22.** Betrays Eliphaz' arrogant assurance that he is God's mouthpiece and bearer of his words.

83 **(O) Job's Seventh Response (23:1–24:25).** It is not sure if this speech is complete. Chapters 24–27 are in obvious disorder, and in some places the text is so corrupted it makes no sense.

As ch. 21 was entirely polemical, ch. 23 is entirely devoted to Job's personal reflections and his search for God. There is no reference to the friends or their doctrine, except for the indirect rejection of Eliphaz' calumnies in vv. 11–12. Compared with Job's earlier speeches, this lament is notably less passionate, although it is profoundly mournful. His profession of faith (ch. 19) has resolved his doubts but has not lightened his desolation. He now dwells on God's inaccessibility and remoteness, which make it impossible for Job to "get through" to him. In terms of mystical theology, Job here describes a dark night of the soul, in which the real absence of God is the keenest of all torments to the man who loves him and used to experience him (see *VieSp* 95 [1956] 372–91).

In ch. 23 there are five strophes: the fourth has four lines, the others three each.

84 (a) Yearning for the Encounter with God (23:2–4,5–7). **2–3a.** The MT reads, "Still today my complaint is rebellious, my hand is heavy upon my groaning. Oh, that I knew how to reach him. . . ." Apart from "his hand," the CCD's other corrections seem unnecessary. **3b–7.** Job once more evokes the courtroom scene of 9:13–21; 13:14–27, but in a more peaceful vein. He is no longer afraid that God would crush him or refuse to hear him. Rather, he would listen and respond with words of consolation. **7.** An echo of 13:16. *preserve my rights:* "Secure my acquittal, vindication."

85 (b) God Is Inaccessible and Unpredictable (23:8–10,11–14,15–17). **8–9.** Cf. just the opposite in Ps 139:8–10. **11.** A denial of 22:6–9. **12.** A reference to 22:22. Job has always done this; he does not need to receive God's words from Eliphaz. **14b.** Cf. 10:13. **17.** Corrupt and obscure text. Perhaps a statement: "Because from him I am hidden by darkness, and my face is veiled in thick gloom" (imitating Hebr word order). This is Job's spiritual state—the dark night.

86 (c) Misery of the Oppressed Poor (24:1–12). As in ch. 21, Job passes from his particular experience to the general. In moving terms, he describes the oppression practiced by unscrupulous rulers and the misery of the poor and unprotected. The passage is a negative parallel to 21:7–17. There, God did not intervene to punish the impious; here, he does not rescue the oppressed. These, according to all orthodox Israelite theology, were two of his chief functions regarding men. **1.** *times. . .days:* Namely, of judgment. **9.** "They plunder the field of the orphan, they take pledges from the poor." Omit, with the CCD, as a duplicate of v. 3. **12c.** *treat it as unseemly:* Emended, this may be read "hear [their] prayer."

87 (d) Enemies of the Light (24:13–17). A short wisdom essay: Murderers, adulterers, and thieves have this in common, that they hate the light (cf. Jn 3:19–20). The connection with Job's speech is doubtful.

88 (e) Obscure Section (24:18–24). At some early stage in the ms. transmission of the book, this section must have become nearly illegible. The next copyist did his best but could not make much sense of it; the same is true for us. It may not even be in its right place.

89 (f) The Conclusion of Job's Speech (24:25). *this:* May refer especially to 24:2–12.

90 **(P) Obscure Chapters 25–27. (25:1–27:23).** These chapters should contain the third speech of Bildad, the eighth response of Job, and the third speech of Zophar. Whether through mutilation or partial destruction of a manuscript at some early stage of the book's history—or possibly by deliberate editorial rearrangement—the text has become disordered and probably incomplete as well; some of the original may have been lost altogether. Thus, no complete restoration is possible. The following is suggested as the probable original order:

Bildad	27:7–10,13–23
Job	26:1–4; 27:11–12,2–6
Zophar	25:4–6,2–3; 26:5–14

In this way a plausible sequence is obtained; 26:2–4, which must be spoken by Job to one of the friends, supposes as immediately preceding something like 27:7ff., rather than ch. 25 or 26:5ff. Furthermore, 25:4–6 fits neatly as a retort to Job's defiant claim in 27:5–6, maintaining his "justice." However, for convenience of reference, our commentary follows (with two slight variations) the present order of the text.

(Barton, G., "The Composition of Job 24–30" *JBL* 30 [1911] 66–77. Dhorme, P., "Les chapitres XXV–XXVIII du Livre de Job," *RB* 33 [1924] 343–56. Kuhl, C., *TRu* 21, 277–81. Régnier, A., "La disposition des chapitres 25–28 du livre de Job," *RB* 33 [1924] 186–200. Tournay, R., "L'ordre primitif des chapitres XXIV–XXVIII du livre de Job," *RB* 64 [1957] 321–34.)

91 (a) Third Speech of Zophar, Part 1 (25:4–6, 2–3). The transposition of vv. 4–6 before vv. 2–3 seems necessary, unless we suppose a lacuna; 25:2 can hardly be the beginning of a speech, whereas 25:4 is particularly apt. Verses 4–6 restate an argument twice used by Eliphaz (4:17; 15:14), and a doxology can naturally follow (2–3, continued in 26:5ff.). **4b.** *woman's child:* The phrase used by Job in 14:1. **3b.** Render, "Against whom does not his lightning flash?"; i.e., God's dominion knows no limits. "Lightning" is a parallel to "troops."

92 (b) Job's Eighth Response, Part 1 (26:1–4). Because "you" is singular, some critics would attribute these verses to Bildad or Zophar, addressing Job. But Job has not been giving counsel and advice (it would be pointless now to refer to counsel given before his calamity, as in 4:3–4), whereas the friends have. The content and the sarcastic tone (paralleled only in Job's speeches to the friends; cf. 6:25; 12:2; 13:1ff.; 16:2ff.) indicate that this passage is part of the response to Bildad. **4.** *whose breath:* The friends have several times claimed to be speaking in God's name (15:11; 20:2; 22:22).

93 (c) Third Speech of Zophar, Part 2 (26:5–14). This magnificent passage is the finest cosmological section in the dialogue for scope of imagination and force of language. In vv. 5–11, the verbs are participles or in the imperfect (to be translated as present) describing God's continued cosmic action; in vv. 12–13 they are in the perfect, narrating deeds accomplished at the creation (read "stirred...crushed...," etc.). The couplet in vv. 5–6 about the underworld balances 25:2–3 referring to the heavens. **7.** *the north:* The pole star and the constellations that revolve about it. *nothing at all:* This vision of earth supported in empty space by the power of God is remarkable for an ancient poet. **10.** *circle:* The horizon, over which the sun rises and sets. **11.** *pillars:* Mountain ranges on which the vault of the firmament rests. **13a.** In the MT, "By his breath the heavens are [made] beautiful"; the correction in the CCD (read "clove...pierced") gives good parallelism, according to the Babylonian account of the "splitting" of Tiamat, the dragon (*ANET* 67, line 137). **14.** *the outlines of his ways:* Better, "the fringes of his power" (M. Dahood, *TS* 13 [1952] 593–94). *how faint:* Lit., "what a [mere] whisper." The MT adds, "But the thunder of his omnipotence who could comprehend?" regrettably omitted by the CCD. This tremendous finale ends the dialogue and is followed by 29:1ff.

94 (d) Job's Eighth Response, Part 3 (27:2–6). It is possible that this section was originally between chs. 30 and 31, as an introduction to the great "oath of exculpation." However, the direct address in v. 5 rather favors taking it as the conclusion of Job's last speech to the friends. (In chs. 29–31 the real dialogue is over, and—as in ch. 3—he does not address the friends at all.) He swears that he will never admit they are right, because that would mean confessing to hypocrisy and impiety in his earlier life. Such action would be against his conscience and a denial of the truth. He will stake everything on his truthfulness. **2.** *as God lives:* The most solemn oath possible (J. Guillet, *L'homme devant Dieu* [Fest K. Rahner; Paris, 1964] 19–20). *withholds my deserts:* He refuses to give his verdict and declare me innocent. **4.** *falsehood... deceit:* Same words as in 13:7. **5.** *account you right:* Lit., "justify you," i.e., admit you (pl.) have won your case. *renounce:* Same word as "withholds" in v. 2.

95 (e) Third Speech of Bildad (27:7–10,13–23). Some opening lines are perhaps missing. It should be read in place of 25:2–6; thus, it would follow Job's speech in chs. 23–24. It is the final statement, by this time monotonous, of the friends' favorite theme. Without (as Eliphaz did) openly calling Job a wicked man, Bildad makes covert references to his condition (v. 8, cf. 23:13ff.; v. 9, cf. 19:7; vv. 14 and 19, cf. the prologue).

96 (f) Job's Eighth Response, Part 2 (27:11–12). **11.** *you:* Plural; Job now addresses the three together. *manner:* Lit., "about the hand of God" (see comment on 19:21). Some lines may be missing between these two verses; v. 11 suggests the beginning of a development, and v. 12 its conclusion. The section omitted may have been something similar to 9:22–24 or 19:6ff.

97 **(Q) Interlude: The Search for Wisdom (28:1–28).** This beautiful poem is hard to situate in the dialogue or, for that matter, in the book as a whole. It lacks the personal references of the speeches and is only distantly connected with the problems treated by the speakers. It is best taken (somewhat in the manner of a choral ode in Gk drama) as an interlude, dealing with a "background theme." The theme is the transcendence of divine wisdom and its inaccessibility to men. With his own wisdom, God created and now governs the universe. Man explores that universe and searches out, ingeniously and tirelessly, all its hidden treasures. But wisdom, most precious of all, is beyond his reach. He will never find it, nor can other creatures give him clues.

The piece probably existed by itself and was inserted into the book, but it is so similar, in vocabulary and style, to the dialogue that it may quite possibly be the work of the same author. Its text unfortunately is disordered, and the original sequence of verses is uncertain (the CCD rearranges rather drastically). Four main ideas are developed: (a) man explores the interior of the earth but finds no "vein" of wisdom; (b) the most far-sighted or distant creatures cannot tell him where to look for it; (c) man's greatest treasures cannot purchase it; but (d) God alone knows and possesses it. A refrain (vv. 12,20) occurs at the beginnings of (b) and (d), whereas the abruptness of v. 1 suggests that something previous is missing; perhaps the refrain (initial "and" omitted) should be restored before v. 1 and before v. 15. The proposed reconstruction follows:

(a) (12) 1–6,9–11
(b) 12–13,7–8,21–22,14
(c) (20) 15–19
(d) 20,23,25–27

(Hulsbosch, A., "Sagesse créatrice et éducatrice," *Augustinianum* 1 [1961] 217–35.)

98 (a) No Mine for Wisdom (28:1–6,9–11). The initial phrase was probably "Wisdom—where can it be found? and where is the place of understanding?" **1.** *mine:* The word is, lit., "finding-place." The poet plays on the words "find," *māṣā'*, and "place," *māqôm*, meaning source or origin (in v. 6, "source" is *māqôm*). These verses, although tantalizingly obscure, give an interesting glimpse of ancient mining techniques. **3–4.** A tentative rendering: "[Man] sets a boundary to the darkness, and to the furthest limit he searches out the stones of darkness and gloom. He pierces a passage...in untrodden places they dangle, they swing far from men."

99 (b) No Guidance from Creatures (28:12–13, 7–8,21–22,14). This reconstruction supposes that the central part of this strophe was once omitted by a copyist, and an attempt at reinserting it (perhaps by writing it across the foot of two columns) resulted in its being divided, one half (7–8) going before its context, the other (21–22) following. **13.** *knows nothing to equal it:* Read, with the LXX, "knows not the way to it."

100 (c) Man's Wealth Cannot Buy It (28:15–19). Insert probably before v. 15, "But Wisdom—where does it come from? and where is the source of understanding?"

101 (d) It Belongs to God Alone (28:20,23,25–27). **24.** Omit as a gloss. (It gives a false interpretation: This wisdom is not "under the heavens," it is only "with God.") **25–26.** This passage leads to the climax: "When he gave weight to the wind, and measured out the waters, When he made rules...Then...." **27.** With its four verbs, a solemn and emphatic ending.

102 (e) Annotation (28:28). This homiletic addition to the poem gives quite a different meaning to "wisdom." Real wisdom, as described earlier, is transcendent, a divine attribute unattainable by man. Later sages, such as Sirach (Sir 24:22), were to describe the giving of the Torah, an act of revelation, as a communication of God's own wisdom. But this verse rather has recourse to analogy. For men, what corresponds to real wisdom is the piety praised in 1:8, 2:3: fearing God and avoiding evil.

103 **(R) Job's Final Soliloquy (29:1–31:40).** With its 95 verses, this is the longest of Job's speeches. Technically, it is outside the dialogue, to which it furnishes a conclusion (ch. 3 gave the introduction). It is formally soliloquy, although it supposes listeners who can testify to the oath, if need be. Here is summed up all that Job wishes to affirm, before God and men, regarding his situation and the question of his own responsibility for it. This renewal of the psalm of lament develops three themes: past happiness (ch. 29), contrasted with present misery (ch. 30), followed by the oath (ch. 31) that he is an innocent man. The other important elements of such a psalm—denunciation of enemies and direct plea to God for salvation—are merely touched on—the former in 30:9–14, the latter in 30:20–26 and 31:35–37, where it takes the form of complaint that his prayer has not been heard and assurance of acquittal if it were.

104 (a) PAST HAPPINESS (29:1–25). Job describes in terms of the patriarchal way of life the ideal existence of the great sheikh, rich in material goods, in his family, and in universal esteem and honor. The way of life pictured is not properly nomadic (although the livestock would have to be moved from one pasturage to another), for Job had the place of authority in a sedentary community, a city. There he distinguished himself by his wisdom, his beneficence, and his generous protection of the poor and helpless.

The chapter contains eight three-line strophes. The last verses, 21–25, must be replaced between vv. 10 and 11.

(i) *The loving presence of God* (29:2–4,5–7). There is much pathos in Job's definition of his happy time as "when God watched over me," and when "my children were round about me." **4.** *sheltered:* An echo of 1:10. **6.** Poetic expression for idyllic abundance. **7.** *then:* Not in the Hebrew; omit, and end verse with a period. Verses 5–7 make a unit.

(ii) *Public honor* (29:8–10,21–23,24–25–11). As the great man of the district, Job took his place in the city council and gave decisions with the authority not merely of his wealth (a sign of God's blessing) but of his moral superiority. **25.** *chose out their way:* Means "decided questions of policy," matters of debate in the assembly. **11.** A literal translation is more picturesque: "The ear heard, and blessed me; the eye saw, and commended me."

(iii) *Good reasons for this honor* (29:12–14,15–17). Job was universally acknowledged to be a model of charity and beneficence, an exemplar of power functioning to protect the weak. **16b.** *stranger:* Lit., "one whom I did not know." Over and above kinsfolk and neighbors Job went out of his way to help even people with whom he had no covenant at all.

(iv) *Job's hope* (29:18–20). Naturally, according to the orthodoxy he had learned and accepted, Job expected God's blessings, to which he had responded so loyally, to be continued to the end of his long and happy life (cf. 30:26).

105 (b) PRESENT MISERY (30:1–31). This is felt all the more keenly by contrast (stressed by the repeated "But now" in 1,9,16). The description naturally corresponds to that of ch. 29, only reversing the order of 29: 2–7 and 29:8–11,21–25.

The chapter begins with four three-line strophes, continuing those of ch. 29. Textual corruption in 30:12–27 makes further strophic analysis uncertain.

(i) *Public contempt* (30:1–15). Elders, chiefs, and princes had revered Job (29:8–10); now the meanest and most wretched of men despise him. The description of the latter is surprisingly elaborate (3–8), but cf. similar detailed presentations of enemies in psalms of lament (Pss 59, 64, 73, etc.). **10b.** *spit in my face:* Too literal; it means "spit on the ground in front of me," a sufficiently insulting gesture of contempt.

(ii) *The hostile presence of God* (30:16–22). Worse than men's abuse is God's persecution. **16.** "But now, my soul is dissolved within me, days of affliction have seized me." As in v. 9 "But now..." introduces affliction from men, here it introduces affliction by God. The verse should be retained, after v. 15. **20.** Since his fourth response (17:3), Job has not directly addressed a prayer to God. Now, after the third-person reference in vv. 18–19 (cf. 16:12; 9:31), he resumes the style of petition; but is God listening to him? **22.** Cf. 13:25.

(iii) *Reasons against this abuse* (30:23–26). Verses 24–25 present an intensely poignant passage. In 6:13ff., Job had felt most keenly the lack of sympathy from his friends (cf. also 19:21). Now he ventures to recall the sympathy that he, a mere man, had shown to the suffering and sorrowful (29:12–17). Will not God show as much toward him? (Cf. the praise of sympathy as a Christian virtue in Rom 12:15; 1 Pt 3:8.) Verse 26 contrasts with 29:18–20.

(iv) *Job's misery* (30:27–31). Verses 27 and 30 refer to his disease, v. 29 to his loneliness. **30b.** *heat:* Presumably means fever.

106 (c) OATH OF EXCULPATION (31:1–40). In the legal procedures of ancient Israel, the "oath of innocence" denying an accusation was important. It supplemented testimony or could supply for it. In default of clear evidence, it was accepted as settling a case; i.e., it transferred the decision to God himself, who, if the defendant had sworn falsely, would bring down on his head the curses he had expressly invited in the oath. Thus, the swearing was a solemn religious act, submitting the case to a divine verdict. Furthermore, if the question at issue was not a mere conflict of human rights but involved an accusation of impiety or blasphemy, a man's religious "existence" might depend on it, his right to take part in the worship of God and receive his blessing. Cf. Ps 139, which seems to be an oath denying worship of other gods (E. Würthwein, *VT* 7 [1957] 165–82). Job now swears that he is innocent of the crimes imputed to him by the friends—crimes, which, according to them, are also imputed to him by God. He challenges the divine judge to give his verdict, i.e., to acknowledge Job's innocence.

(Blank, S., "The Curse, Blasphemy, the Spell, and the Oath," *HUCA* 23 [1950] 73–95; "An Effective Literary Device in Job XXXI," *JJS* 2 [1951] 105–7. Horst, F., "Der Eid im Alten Testament," *EvT* 17 [1957] 366–84. Pedersen, J., *Der Eid bei den Semiten* [Leipzig, 1914].)

This oath is no mere formality. Job examines his conscience and spells out exactly what crimes he, in his time and situation, might have been tempted to commit. The code of ethics here implied is that proper to the ancient Oriental aristocrat, the head of a patriarchal family who need fear no constraint from government or other power. Only religious motivation, and, to a lesser degree, public opinion, will impel such a man to virtuous action and self-restraint. Job's motive was simply the desire to please God. His moral standards are, in fact, the highest to be found in the OT; cf. a somewhat similar code in Ez 18:5–9. Notable are the sensitive respect shown for the dignity of fellow men (even slaves) and the stress on interior attitudes toward God. Eliphaz' accusations in ch. 22 are incidentally refuted (as already in 23:11; 29:11ff.): 31:16–18, cf. 22:7,9; 31:19–20, cf. 22:6.

The form is the standard one for Hebr oaths: "If I have done so-and-so, may this happen to me!" (e.g., 31:9–10, 21–22). By dropping off the apodosis, the phrase "If I have..." by itself comes to mean "I swear I haven't..." (e.g., 31:5,16). The exact list of Job's disclaimers is hard to determine (some authors find 12, others 14, others 16); the question is complicated by textual uncertainties and possible glosses. For the same reason strophic division is uncertain.

107 (i) *No deceit or injustice* (31:1–12,38–40ab). Verses 1–4 are omitted altogether by the LXX, and in the MT they pose a problem. The CCD transposes and corrects; the MT has no "if" before v. 1 and nothing corresponding to "man's" and "his" in v. 2—which is almost a repetition, in question form, of 20:29 and 27:13. Verse 3 implies the opposite of what Job maintains, and v. 4b conflicts with v. 37a ("account" is, lit., "numbering"). Thus, vv. 2–4 are most probably early annotations to the text. Verse 6 makes a likely beginning (after 30:31), and the CCD is probably right in displacing vv. 1 and 5.

5. The first disclaimer. By parallelism, one crime is here presented: deceit, with all it implies (cf. 27:4). **7.** Second denial; any deviation or corruption. **8.** The self-condemnation completing the oath formula.

38–40ab. Original position is uncertain; its closest similarity is with vv. 13–15. It denies cruel exploitation of peasants or sharecroppers.

1. In the MT, a simple statement (no "if"). The two stichs are not parallel and may belong to different verses. In the CCD, "made an agreement" (lit., "covenant") has to denote a vicious intention, which is questionable. **9–10.** Denial of adultery. The penalty contemplated is according to the law of talion. **11–12.** Probably a gloss.

(ii) *No failure in equity or charity* (31:13–23). A list of specifically social crimes, showing a remarkably evolved conscience. They are arranged in chiastic order: 13–15 parallels 21–22; 16–17 parallels 19–20. **13–15.** Denies unjust treatment of slaves, who in the ancient world generally were not regarded as subjects of justice at all, any more than were animals. But Job bases their claim to it on the common creation of all men by God. **16–20.** Job insists that he has shared his goods with the poor, whose rights are based on the common fatherhood of God (if v. 18 is rightly interpreted). **21–22.** Job has not exploited his standing in the community to win legal but unjust victories over weaker men. *supporters at the gate:* Friends in court; the local community, sitting in judgment, would have been too much in awe of Job ever to give a verdict against him. **23.** An adaptation of 13:11, probably a gloss.

(iii) *No false worship* (31:24–28). Two kinds of idolatry: The first (24–25) is what the NT calls "worshiping Mammon." "Trust" and "rejoiced" are emphatic—in his money, rather than in God. The second (26–28) is the secret infidelity of invoking as divinities the sun and the moon.

(iv) *No vindictiveness or hypocrisy* (31:29–34). **29–30.** This concern is considerably above the level of most of the OT. The only parallel is Sir 28:3–7 (cf. Prv 24:17—and its following verse). **31–32.** Similar to vv. 16–20, these verses affirm Job's constant practice of the virtue of hospitality—sacred and all-important in that society. **33–34.** He denies hypocrisy, any mere pretense of virtue inspired by human respect.

(v) *Summary* (31:35–37,40c). Job has come a long way from the unquestioning acceptance of 1:21; 2:10, and even from the longing for nonexistence in ch. 3. The vindication of his truthfulness and integrity, which in ch. 19 he had looked forward to in faith, he now demands in challenging terms. The scroll of indictment would be a badge of honor; it could contain nothing to his discredit.

35b. "Here is my *taw;* let the Almighty answer me!"; placed by the CCD after v. 37 (*taw* is the last letter of the Hebr alphabet). However, it is possible that v. 35a should read "Oh that God would listen to me!" and v. 35b follow in parallelism. Then vv. 35c–36 will be a tristich: "If my accuser has written out his indictment, I swear I will carry it on my shoulder, I will wear it as a crown!" **37.** *a prince:* A dramatic affirmation of the proud assurance of innocence with which Job defends his conduct before God (cf. 13:14–16).

108 Thus, Job has delivered his final answer to his friends and his challenge to God. For the former, there is nothing more to be said. The oath must prevail (in default of evidence); therefore, Job has won his case against them. But Job has not won any case against God. The image of a judicial hearing, of plea and argument, simply cannot represent the situation of a man before his creator; it only falsifies it. Insofar as Job has fallen in with his friends' analysis of his situation, thinking of God as his adversary in a lawsuit, he has put himself in a false position. His unblemished record gives him no claim in justice upon God; from it and from his suffering he has no right to draw any conclusion about what God ought to do. To think otherwise is to forget the divine transcendence and the infinite difference between creator and creature.

However, Job has here proclaimed his "right" (cf. 9:20; 13:18; 19:7; 23:7; 27:2,6), his truthful unanswerable demonstration that he has been what God pronounced him to be (1:8; 2:3): God-fearing and morally perfect. And inevitably, there is an element of presumption here, of what the Greeks called *hubris*. The just man's precious integrity has become a barrier between him and God, a condition which God must accept. Job has overshot the mark (Weiser, *op. cit.*, 212–16).

109 **(III) The Elihu Speeches (32:1–37:24).** This section is generally (not universally) admitted to be a supplement inserted in the book by another writer (here, for convenience' sake, called the "critic," as distinct from the author of the book). If so, it was not an independent piece (as was perhaps ch. 28), but was composed expressly for this purpose. The critic presumably was dissatisfied with the original conclusion of the book (chs. 38–42) and wished to provide a more explicit corrective to some of Job's outbursts. He also felt that the friends' speeches had not done justice to the traditional wisdom teaching and that a better case could be made for it. His work, then, is an interesting specimen of early doctrinal and literary criticism and is almost contemporary with the original composition. He had the initiative—we might also say the courage—to dramatize his criticism in speech form, to create another character as his spokesman, and to integrate his own contribution, quite skillfully, into the great masterwork he had studied so closely. (Needless to say, the section is to be regarded as an integral part of the canonical book, and its author, whoever he was, as having had the grace of inspiration.)

From the literary point of view, the Elihu speeches are wisdom writing on a high level, comparable with the best parts of Prv. But they are much inferior to the brilliance of the original dialogue; their style is severely didactic, argumentative, and somewhat repetitious. The language is much less picturesque and also shows a higher proportion of Aramaisms. Doctrinally, the critic disapproves Job's self-assertion before God and his insistence on his own integrity and blamelessness. But he also disavows the exclusively retributory function ascribed to suffering by the friends. Affliction, according to him, may be a warning, a paternal admonition from God against man's tendency to *hubris.* If the man promptly humbles himself, God restores him to his favor; if he is obstinate, God will further punish him for that obstinacy, but with the purpose of leading him to repentance. Thus, Elihu disagrees with the friends on the grounds of suffering, stressing its medicinal purpose; but in practice, his advice to Job is the same as theirs. On the other hand, he forcibly reminds Job of God's infinite superiority to man (which Job had seemed in danger of ignoring), and he anticipates the divine speeches of chs. 38ff. by insisting on God's sublimity and the mystery of the divine plans.

The section begins with a prose introduction and continues with a poetic composition of nearly 150 lines (compare the total of roughly 220 lines allotted to all three friends in the dialogue). This is broken into four unequal sections by the rubrics in 34:1; 35:1; 36:1. However, the last of these (worded differently from the others and from 32:6) is probably an erroneous insertion. In reality, 33:1–36:25 constitute only three discourses, composed in an identical pattern. Each begins with a summons to Job (twice) or the friends, to listen. Then some of Job's sayings are quoted and contradicted. Elihu lays down a first thesis and then a second, developed at slightly greater length. A conclusion admonishes Job and praises the divine goodness and mercy. (This structural analysis is taken, with slight modifications, from Fohrer [KAT]. The strophic analysis is independent but often agrees with the divisions indicated in the CCD.) In Elihu's oration as a whole, therefore, we distinguish: an introductory address (32:6–22); the three discourses (33:1–30; 34:1–37; 33:31–33 + 35:2–36:25); a hymn (36:26–37:13); and a concluding address (37:14–24).

(Dennefeld, L., "Les discours d'Elihou," *RB* 48 [1939] 163–80. Fohrer, G., "Die Weisheit des Elihu," *AfO* 19 [1959–60] 83–94. Irwin, W. A., "The Elihu Speeches in the Criticism of the Book of Job," *JRel* 17 [1937] 37–47. Kroeze, J. H., "Die Elihu-Reden im Buche Hiob," *OTS* 2 [1943] 156–70. Staples, W. E., *The Speeches of Elihu* [Toronto, 1924].)

110 (A) Introductory Narrative (32:1–5). If 38:1 followed immediately upon 31:40, no one would ever suspect a lacuna. The critic, wishing to make room for his own contribution, had to indicate an occasion and a reason why a new character hitherto unmentioned should suddenly break into the discussion. This he does plausibly enough by explaining that the friends have ceased to argue (on the reason, see comment on v. 1); thus, the field is clear for another speaker. He is Elihu, son of Barachel (unlike Job, 1:1, and the other three, 2:11, he is given a patronymic). Elihu is the original "angry young man"; both attributes are insisted on (anger, vv. 2a–3,5; youth, 4,6b,9–10). He is also, at least to modern sensibilities, amazingly self-satisfied, pompous, and naïve. He takes 24 verses (32:6–33:7) to say, in effect, "Look out! I'm going to speak," and outdoes Eliphaz (from whom he borrows some of his material) in his self-confidence and complacency. There is such an odd contrast between the ludicrous self-importance of the character and the serious religious value of the doctrine he imparts (after 33:7), that one wonders if the critic was parodying some particular "younger school" of wisdom teachers.

1. *his own eyes:* The LXX and Pesh read "in their eyes," probably correctly. It is not necessarily the intention of the author of the dialogue, but it gives a logical reason for their ceasing to argue, the critic seems to suppose it by making Elihu distribute blame impartially to Job and to the friends, and it fits better with v. 3. **3.** *a good answer:* Therefore the critic feels that Job had the best of the argument—which the author intended, but which he disapproves. *not condemned Job:* No "not," and, in the original text, no "Job." What the critic wrote was "and [thus] had condemned God." It was so shocking that "God" was changed to "Job" by the scribes; the "not" is introduced by the translators.

111 (B) Introductory Address (32:6–22). A remarkably elaborate and verbose exordium. There are four strophes: The third has three lines, the others have five each.

(a) Rebuke to the Friends (32:6–10,11–14). **8.** *it is a spirit:* The phrase is strange; perhaps read according to the parallelism, "the spirit of God," and omit "that." Elihu claims something like prophetic inspiration. **13.** Brings out the critic's idea that the friends have been forced to agree with Job.

(b) Soliloquy (32:15–17,18–22). Dramatically, Elihu describes the discomfiture of the friends and his own compulsion to speak. **21–22.** Cf. Job in 13:8,10. Elihu, in his hyperbolic style, envisages the extreme penalty.

112 (C) Elihu's First Discourse (33:1–30). There are nine strophes, of 3, 4, 4; 3, 4, 4, 3; 4, 2 lines, respectively.

(a) Summons to Job (33:1–3, 5–6,4,7). **4.** Probably to be read after v. 6 (omit initial "for"; not in the MT). Elihu refers (sarcastically?) to Job's complaint that he could not speak freely in God's terrifying presence (9:17,34; etc.).

(b) Quotations (33:8–11). Elihu cites two of Job's claims: that he is innocent (cf. 9:21; 10:7; 16:17; 23:10–12; 27:5; 31) and that God is his enemy (cf. 10:17; 13:24,27; 19:11).

(c) Correction and First Thesis (33:12–14, 15–18). Elihu deals with the second claim (the other comes in the next speech). **12b.** *greater than man:* "Enemy" implies a certain equality; God is too far above man for this to be apt. (Job's keen awareness of God's personality easily leads him to this too human way of thinking of him.) **13b.** *no account of his doings:* Better, "no answer to your words." **14.** Elihu retorts that God was already speaking to Job, who was refusing to listen. The first way was by the terrifying dreams Job had referred to (7:14); they were meant to warn him against pride and were the effect of God's kindness.

(d) Second Thesis (33:19–22,23–24). God's second way of speaking to men is by affliction itself. Job's sufferings therefore had a medicinal purpose; they were meant to keep him humble, but by his rebellious reaction he has revealed his pride. Note that Elihu avoids the crude simplification of the friends' doctrine; he does not claim that Job's calamities are sure evidence of previous sin or that divine rewards are an automatic consequence of human repentance. **23–24.** A beautiful and much-discussed text (F. Stier, *Das Buch Iyyob* [Munich, 1954] 333–34). Elihu does not share Eliphaz' skepticism (5:1). A heavenly messenger may be mediator, lit., "interpreter"; i.e., make the man understand the meaning of his affliction, show him his faults, and intercede for him with God. Thus, men need grace and instruction even to repent as they should.

(e) Conclusion (33:25–28,29–30). Verses 25, 26 should perhaps change places. **27–28.** A typical thanksgiving psalm (cf. Pss 30, 41, 116). Verse 29 makes an inclusion with v. 14, and v. 30 echoes v. 22 (vv. 31–33 introduce 35:2).

113 (D) Elihu's Second Discourse (34:1–37). Eight strophes, of 5, 5; 4, 5, 5, 5(?); 4, 4, lines, respectively.

(a) Summons to the Friends and Quotation (34:2–6). Elihu now returns to deal with the first point he had cited, in 33:9. **3.** Cf. 12:11. **5.** Cf. 27:2.

(b) Quotation and Correction (34:7–11). To Job's statement of innocence, Elihu joins (9) the saying of the "good pagans" that had so shocked Eliphaz (22:15–17). Elihu prefixes it with his own expression of horror (7) and says (8) that Job agrees with these atheists—which is true, on this one point (cf. 9:22). "Fearing God" is not an infallible recipe for temporal prosperity, as Job has discovered. But Elihu understands Job's words as an attack on the justice of God's providence and denies them accordingly.

(c) First Thesis (34:12–15). God is the supreme Lord, subject to none. If he were unjust, the universe simply could not function. **14–15.** Cf. Ps 104:29.

(d) Second Thesis (34:16–20a,20b–24,25–29). Elihu applies the same argument to the divine direction of human life. **17.** If God were unjust, he would not be supreme (there would be a standard of justice higher than he). But, in fact, all other justice derives from him; all creatures are equally subject to him, and partiality in him is unthinkable. In him might and right are one. **23.** Perhaps an answer to 24:1; God needs to hold no inquiries, no "hearings." (If 25 is placed after 22, with the CCD, the strophe ends with 23.) **26.** (Omitted by the CCD) "On account of their wickedness he blasts them, he binds them in the place of the damned" (the MT, emended). **29.** If God's actions cannot be perceived, a man still has no right to say he is not acting. **30.** With the CCD, omit as doublet.

(e) Conclusion (34:31–33,34–37). Elihu produces an *argumentum ad hominem:* Job disapproves of all God's work—therefore he must disapprove of his customary loving forgiveness! If he denies God freedom to act "arbitrarily" for his own good reasons, then he must (like the friends) want him to exercise merely automatic retribution. Undoubtedly, Elihu here scores a point. Job's criticisms, prompted by his own unhappy experience, are subjective. **33c.** *you who must choose:* Whether to admit that God may temper justice with mercy. **36.** Job has experienced God's warning; because he rejects it, he deserves extreme punishment.

114 **(E) Elihu's Third Discourse (33:31–33; 35:2–36:25).** The missing introduction has been misplaced at the end of ch. 33. There are eleven strophes of 3, 3; 4, 4, 4; 3, 3, 5, 3; 5, 5 lines.

(a) Summons to Job (33:31–33). **32.** Not, as one might think, an invitation to disagree and put forward his point of view. Elihu is not arguing with Job, he is teaching him. Here he invites him to express contrition, which will show that he is "justified."

(b) Quotations (35:2–4). **2b.** Job had not said this, but he is very sure about his own justice, while holding God's to be quite mysterious (cf. 13:18; 19:6–7; 27:2–6). **3b.** *what advantage have I more:* Because of the following strophe, we should read with the LXX, "what harm can I do you by sinning?" and keep "profit you" (so MT) in v. 3a.

(c) Correction and First Thesis (35:5–8,9–12,13–16). Cf. 7:20; 22:2–3. Elihu agrees with both: Men's evil actions cannot harm God (so Job), nor can their good ones benefit him (so Eliphaz), although they have real effects on fellow men. **13.** But simply because he is just, God does impose sanctions. **36:1.** Omit, as mistaken editorial insertion.

(d) Second Thesis (36:2–4,5–7,8–12,13–15). But more than the effects on fellow men are the results of a man's behavior on himself. When God does intervene, he treats men according to their deserts—although always first encouraging the wicked to repent (8–10). **13.** They do not accept the warning to repent, implicit in their affliction. This is the second and graver stage of impiety.

(e) Conclusion (36:16–20,21–25). The text of the first strophe is hopelessly corrupted. **21b.** The consonantal text can be read "for this is why you are being tried by affliction." **24.** Instead of criticizing, Job should join in the hymns of praise, which are men's fitting response to God. **25b.** *from afar:* Cf. 26:14.

115 **(F) Hymn (36:26–29,30–33, 37:1–4,5–8,9–13).** Appropriately, Elihu himself intones a hymn in praise of God, who manifests himself in the winter rains. In these storms are experienced both his mighty power and—because they give fertility to the soil—his solicitude for men (cf. Pss 8; 19:2–7; 29; 104; 147). The text is somewhat uncertain, but there seem to be five four-line strophes.

116 **(G) Concluding Address (37:14–18,19–21, 22–24).** Elihu resumes his address to Job. This section seems to be expressly formulated so as to lead up to the speech of Yahweh that is to follow. Elihu describes an increase in darkness but also a splendor coming "from the north," traditional source of the theophany (Is 14:13; Ez 1:4). **15–16.** The questions anticipate the style of the following speech. **17–18.** Perhaps, in sequence to the preceding hymn, this reference is to the dry season following the rainy one. Verses 22–23 are the description of God's advent; both power and justice are emphasized. **24b.** In the MT, "He does not see all the wise of heart." The CCD correction is possible, but the following is perhaps better: "to him reverence is given by all the wise of heart," a conclusion similar to 36:25.

With these words, Elihu disappears from the book as abruptly as he appeared. The critic has had his say and has felt no need to introduce his spokesman also into prologue or epilogue.

117 **(IV) God's Speech and Job's Answer (38:1–42:6).** The key section of the book. Although its originality and connection with the dialogue have often been questioned, the majority of modern commentators accept it in principle as an integral part of the original author's work. Doubts are still commonly expressed on certain passages within the present text. We here take for granted the originality of at least 38:1–39:12; 39:19–40:14; 42:1–6 (but cf. P. W. Skehan, *Bib* 45 [1964] 51–62).

After the naïve story of the prologue in heaven and the sophisticated debate in the dialogue on earth, a word is spoken from heaven to earth by God himself. He is the Yahweh of the prologue, and he addresses the Job of the dialogue, the tormented, devout, rebellious man who has raged against the human situation and demanded that God "justify his ways to men." The author, with the audacity of genius, tackles the problem of putting in God's mouth words that will not be an anticlimax after the tempestuous eloquence of his hero. He brilliantly succeeds. The divine speech sweeps away all the irrelevancies and false problems in which the argument with the friends had entangled Job. It puts Job's problem in a new perspective and opens up a vista in which, although still without an answer, it ceases to require one. Throughout this long speech Yahweh does not (apart from mere description) make a single statement; he only puts to Job, majestically, patiently, ironically, a series of unanswerable questions. A critic should know whereof he speaks; and he who would "correct God" must himself have divine knowledge. Yahweh pretends to believe this of Job and cross-examines him on the divine activity in the universe. If Job is incapable of the simplest answer, how can he and Yahweh hold debate? How can Yahweh even explain to him the deeper mystery of his providence over men and his treatment of those who are dear to him? The questions cover the most familiar phenomena of nature: the stars, the weather, land and sea, a selection of beasts and birds. Everywhere are marvels, everywhere is mystery. (And be it said parenthetically, the mystery is not less for us today. We know far more than did the ancient poet about the mechanics of these things; but their inner secrets remain as elusive as ever.) Two points clearly emerge: One is the loving concern of Yahweh for his innumerable creatures, even, or especially, those most independent and far removed from man; the other is the infinite variety and richness of creation, extending to beings that to men seem grotesque or monstrous. In the divine wisdom they have their place, and God finds pleasure in them. The analogy holds in the moral order, where also his ways are not man's ways.

But the foregoing is only the superficial meaning of this passage. Its content, after all, adds nothing essential to what has been already affirmed by other speakers, in hymnal praises of God (cf. 5:10–16; 9:4–10; 12:13–25; 22:12–14; 26:5–14). More striking still, Job's personal problem is completely ignored: Yahweh says not a word about his guilt or innocence, his suffering or its meaning. In his acknowledgment (42:5), Job does not say "I understand your teaching"; he says "I have seen you." This speech is a revelation of the speaker. It is God's Word, in which God is known. The theophany, the encounter with God, is Job's real experience, and this sublime poetry gives back a pale reflection of it for the reader's benefit.

The orderly catalogue of creatures belongs to a tradition derived from the onomastica, or word lists, of Egyptian wisdom (→ Wisdom Lit, 28:20–21); cf. similar sequences in Sir 43:1–27; Ps 148; Dn 3:57–87. Ironical questioning is a feature of the so-called "disputation style," as exemplified in an Egyptian satirical composition (Anastasi papyrus 1; cf. *ANET* 477–78; *VDBS* 4, 452). G. von Rad has made these two observations.

(Fohrer, G., "Gottes Antwort aus dem Sturmwind, Hi. 38–41," *TZ* 18 [1962] 1–24. Lillie, W., "The Religious Significance of the Theophany in the Book of Job," *ExpT* 68 [1957] 355–58. MacKenzie, R. A. F., "The Purpose of the Yahweh Speeches in the Book of Job," *Bib* 40 [1959] 435–45. Richter, H., "Die Naturweisheit des Alten Testaments im Buche Hiob," *ZAW* 70 [1958] 1–20. Stange, C., "Das Problem Hiobs und seine Lösung," *ZSystTh* 24 [1955] 342–55. Voeltzel, R., "Ironie biblique à l'égard de l'homme," *Foi et vie* [vol. 51; 1953] 214–15. Von Rad, G., "Hiob XXXVIII und die altägyptische Weisheit," VTSup 3 [1955] 293–301.)

118 **(A) Yahweh Speaks (38:1).** From 3:2 to 26:1, and again in 32:6; 34:1; 35:1, an invariable formula has been used to introduce each speech (CCD varies, for no evident reason): "Then X spoke, and said...." Now, with simplicity, but also with dramatic effect, the formula includes the divine name and two extra phrases: "Then Yahweh spoke—to Job—out of the storm—and said...." The first indicates the fulfillment of Job's longing (cf. 13:22; 23:5; 30:20; 31:35b). The second suffices to evoke the traditional setting of the theophany (cf., e.g., Ps 18:8–14).

119 **(B) Does Job Understand Yahweh's "Counsel"? (38:2–38).** This first part of the speech deals with (what we call) "inanimate" nature—lively enough to the poet. The division, roughly, is by past, present, and future, relative to Job. Does he know the history, how it all started? Was he present at creation? Does he now know "where to find everything" (i.e., all the distant corners of the universe and what they contain)? Does he know the procedure? Could he, from now on, run things, give the necessary orders?

The strophic structure is carefully symmetrical: 11 strophes, of 2; 4, 4, 4; 3, 3, 3; 3, 3, 3; 4, lines. There seems no need to rearrange the text; only v. 36 is intrusive.

120 (a) "Who Is This?" (38:2–3). The tremendous interrogatory begins with this pointed reminder. Who and what, after all, is Job? Another God, rival to Yahweh? **2a.** All he has done is to "darken counsel." The last word, *'ēṣāh*, means the sum total of God's plans and works. **3b.** Job had rashly invited this, in 13:22a.

(b) Was Job Present at Creation? (38:4–7,8–11,12–15). The origins of earth, sea, and light are described in succession (cf. the reverse order in Gn 1:3–10). The earth is pictured as a building: An architect planned it (5a), a surveyor mapped out the site (5b), foundations were laid (6a), then the cornerstone (6b), to the accompaniment of songs and shouts of rejoicing (7). Cf. the ceremonies described in Ezr 3:10–13. The sea, on the other hand—that tumultuous and threatening element—is pictured at first as a baby, which needed and received Yahweh's tender care. **13–14.** The imagery is obscure to us. Perhaps v. 14 indicates first the gray outlines of things seen before dawn, then their full color when the sun rises.

(c) Does Job Know His Way About the Cosmos? (38:16–18,19–21,22–24). It is all familiar to Yahweh: the abyss, leading to the underworld (17); the "places" where light and darkness are kept when they are "not in use" (light during the night, darkness during the day!); the treasuries from which he produces snow, hail, and winds.

(d) Would Job Know How To Operate It? (38:25–27,28–30,31–33). For all of this, Yahweh has his own supreme "counsel," and it is not exclusively for men's benefit (26–27). **31–32.** Stars and constellations were regarded as having an effect on the weather, which explains their position here.

(e) Has Job the Needed Authority and Power? (38:34–38). Even if he gave the right orders, would they be carried out? **36a.** *heart: Ṭuḥôt*, of unknown meaning, but by parallelism it should be the name of a bird. The verse is certainly out of place and may be an addition to the text (cf. its position in the CCD before 39:13).

121 **(C) Is Job Capable of Providing for the Animals and Birds? (38:39–39:30).** Eight creatures are described, in increasing detail (two lines to the first, two strophes to the last): lion; raven, hawk, eagle; mountain goat, wild ass, wild ox; war horse. The first seven are free and independent of man, yet all are wonderfully nourished and cared for by their creator. The horse, in a different way, is the most amazing of all.

39:26–30. Should be restored to its place after 38:41; note the common theme of "their young ones" in 38:39, 41; 39:3–4; 39:30. The three birds go together, symmetrically with the three beasts that follow. **39:13–18.** An insertion that breaks the symmetry. There are seven strophes, of 3, 4; 4, 4, 4; 4, 3, lines.

(a) Can Job Feed the Little Ones? (38:39–41; 39:26–30). Even the strongest and fiercest beasts and birds depend on God for food for their offspring. **39:27b–28.** The CCD omits two variants and combines to get two stichs instead of three, probably correctly.

(b) Are the Wildest Animals under His Control? (39:1–4,5–8,9–12). The mountain goats need no human help in giving birth, but Yahweh knows even the dates of their pregnancies. He sees to it that the wild ass finds the pasture it needs. And the wild ox serves him, although it is comic to think of it as serving Job (9–12), like its domesticated cousin. The animal is the *rîmu*, a sort of buffalo (now extinct), powerful and dangerous to man.

(c) The Ostrich (39:13–18). This wisdom essay is a comparatively recent addition to the test (it is not contained in the LXX). It lacks the interrogative introduction common to all the other items (38:39,41; 39:26,27,1,5,9,19); unlike them, it does not make the specific point, essential in this context, of Job's incapacity. It merely stresses the curious contrast between the ostrich's (apparent) callousness (which was proverbial; cf. Lam 4:3) and its remarkable speed. The reference to the horse in v. 18b explains the passage's insertion here.

(d) Is Job Responsible for the Fiery Nature of the Horse? (39:19–22,23–25). This famous passage is the climax. In the ancient East the donkey was the beast of burden, the ox did the ploughing, donkeys or mules were riding animals. The horse was reserved for warfare or hunting, at first (in pairs) to draw a chariot, then, after about the 8th cent. BC, as a cavalry mount. It is the latter, the war horse, that the poet admires and marvels at. The animal's excitement and eagerness for the battle, its reaction to the trumpet call, its disregard of danger, have deeply impressed him.

122 **(D) Summary and Job's First Response (40:1–5).** In chs. 40–41, the chapter divisions (established in the 13th cent. AD) and the verse numeration (16th cent.) are unhappily varied and may cause confusion in references. The three different systems in use can be tabulated as follows:

Hebr printed Bibles, LXX, BJ, CCD		Non-Catholic Eng versions: AV, RSV, etc.		Vg, Douay-Challoner, Knox
40:1	=	40:1	=	39:31
40:6	=	40:6	=	40:1
40:25	=	41:1	=	40:20
41:1	=	41:9	=	40:28
41:2	=	41:10	=	41:1
41:26	=	41:34	=	41:25

Our commentary uses the numeration of the Hebr text, as followed by the CCD. This table will help readers with other texts to make their own adjustments.

The introduction (40:1), which interrupts Yahweh's speech, creates a difficulty. Like similar anomalies in 27:1 (omitted by CCD) and 29:1, and the repetition in 40:6–7, it is a sign of textual disorder. If we admit that 40:15ff. is an addition to the original text, the process may be plausibly explained thus: The author wrote one divine speech, in which 40:8–14 immediately followed 39:25 and 40:2 was the concluding verse. Following was Job's one answer, 40:3–5; 42:2–6. Later, an editor who wished to insert 40:15–41:26 as part of a speech by Yahweh detached the last section of the original speech, 40:8–14 (replacing it by 40:1), and the second half of Job's answer, 42:2–6 (replacing it by the repetition 40:6–7), and put them in their present positions—as introduction and conclusion, respectively, to his own contribution. (Pfeiffer, *Introd.* 675.) On the other hand, this explanation supposes a very abrupt join of 40:8 with 39:25 (or 30), the "conversion" of Job in two stages is psychologically more convincing, and 40:15ff. may well be original.

(a) CHALLENGE (40:2). Note that this conclusion returns to the solemn use of the third person, as in 38:2 (K. Fullerton, *AJSL* 49 [1933] 197–211).

(b) JOB'S RESPONSE (40:3–5). Job had insisted that the explanation of his problem must be sought in God, not in himself (cf. 19:28). Now his attention has been forcibly transferred to God, and his complete incapacity to understand God's ways has been demonstrated. What can he do but acknowledge the mystery, and the vanity of his efforts? But, at least, the presence of God from which he had prayed to escape, a presence manifested only by successive blows of calamity and suffering, has changed to a speaking presence, in which Job knows God as addressing him personally and concerned with him as his servant.

123 **(E) Yahweh Speaks Again (40:6–41:26).** Here we have two very different sections. The speech in 40:8–14 is in the same style as the first speech: ironic questions and invitations addressed to Job, which make evident to the point of absurdity his human inability to "be like God." The subject matter is different, but related: Instead of divine providence at work in the cosmic order and the animal kingdom, it is shown in the moral order and in the world of men. Job's incompetence in this field also is exposed. The section following, 40:15–41:26, differs in style, and its theme is harder to relate to the preceding. Two strange beasts are described, the second in much detail. Only in 40:15,25–32 is the style of address and questioning maintained, but even here (and more so in the rest) the tone is didactic and objective; the urgency and challenge of chs. 38–39 are missing. Therefore, many critics have denied the originality of this second passage. But its defenders (several recent writers) maintain that it is an essential part of the divine proclamation. Behemoth and Leviathan are symbols of chaotic powers, monstrous, menacing, and incomprehensible to man; yet they, too, are of God's creation; in them he takes pleasure; through them aspects of his being are manifested.

124 (a) CAN JOB ADMINISTER DIVINE JUSTICE? (40:6–14). Verses 6–7 are virtually identical with 38:1,3. **8.** Now, at last, Yahweh makes a reference to Job's situation: He retorts on him his accusation of "twisting justice" (9:24; 19:6; 27:2). Is Job so convinced of his righteousness that he is ready to believe, of the two, that God is unjust? The divine guilt would follow from the concept (which Job had accepted) of a law suit, in which one party must be found right, the other wrong. Job is in error because no such relationship can exist between creature and creator. **9–14.** The essence of the situation (anticipated in Elihu's speech, 34:10ff.): Only the omnipotent and all-seeing governor of the world can lay claim to perfect justice. **14.** *save you:* An emphatic word: "bring you justice and salvation."

125 (b) LOOK AT BEHEMOTH! (40:15–24). The word is the plural of "animal," but one creature is certainly meant, and the description suggests the hippopotamus. The hugeness of the beast, its strength, its sexual potency, are specially marvelous. **17.** Read probably "he stiffens his penis like a cedar-beam, the sinews of his testicles are closely knit." **19a.** The same phrase is used of this creature as is applied to Wisdom in Prv 8:22: He is the masterpiece (first and greatest effect) of God's power (not "ways"). Verse 19b is an uncertain text. **24.** "Can one seize him by his eyes [in traps]? Can one pierce his nostrils?" The brackets must be a gloss, and the whole verse is doubtful.

126 (c) LOOK AT LEVIATHAN! (40:25–41:26). The name belongs to a mythological sea monster (cf. 3:8) and might refer to the same creature as "Behemoth." But the description dwells rather on ferocity and invulnerability; probably a mythical dragon is meant, pictured as a giant crocodile.

(i) *Can you make a pet of him?* (40:25–32). The same idea as in 39:9–12, and the same direct address. The idea is merely ridiculous; yet (it is implied) Yahweh can play with Leviathan as he wishes. **25a.** This verse may mean "draw up Leviathan with a hook," i.e., land him with rod and line like an ordinary fish.

(ii) *Can anything overcome him?* (41:1–26). The belligerence of the crocodile is described, and his hide, which is proof against any weapons (4–9; cf. 18–21). His fearsomeness is conveyed in mythological terms, as of a fire-breathing dragon (10–13); even the ocean is in dread of him (17). **25–26.** This terrifying monster, supreme over all beasts, is beyond human control. Yet he too is one of Yahweh's creatures, whom he cares for and with whom he is pleased.

127 **(F) Job's Final Response (42:1–6).** In the MT three phrases are interjected (3a, and 4), two of which are quotations from 38:2,3b; the third is "Listen now, while I speak." The CCD omits these phrases, with most commentators, as marginal annotations.

2–3. Job acknowledges the lesson. Verse 2b echoes the phrase applied by Yahweh to the builders of the tower of Babel (Gn 11:6). **3.** Job renounces the *hubris* into which he had fallen and confesses that God's ways and plans are infinitely beyond his understanding. **5.** The great contrast. Job's model service had been based on faith. That faith had been strong enough to withstand the assault of the friends' argument, but at what a cost in struggle and pain! Far different is the experience of the face-to-face meeting. The words of Yahweh may have been very different from what Job expected, but that is unimportant.

The dark night is over; God has deigned to let himself be found by Job. **6.** And it costs Job nothing, it rejoices him, to disown his presumption and his misguided although sincere speculations and complaints. He even discards his last support, his famous integrity. He cannot buy his justification from God; he must accept it as a gift (L. J. Kuyper, *VT* 9 [1959] 91–94).

128 **(V) The Epilogue (42:7–17).** This prose narrative is obviously connected with the prologue and has the same characteristics of style and content. It has been carefully linked also with the dialogue; vv. 7–9 at least, and a phrase in 10a, have been composed by the poet for this purpose.

129 **(A) Expiation for Job's Three Friends (42:7–10a).** Without further mention of the storm, Yahweh is presented as speaking to Eliphaz, as he did to Job; but (in spite of repetitions) the speech is a brief one. It declares God's anger against the three, to appease which they must offer a holocaust in Job's presence, with Job uttering prayers for them. (The holocaust appears to be the same as Job had formerly offered weekly for his seven sons, 1:5, and the implication may be that the friends' speeches amounted to blasphemy.) They comply, and Job's intercession is effective. This apparently artless narrative has the following important implications:

(1) It establishes—what the speech to Job himself had completely passed over—the truth of Job's vehement affirmations against the friends, during the dialogue: He is the perfect and blameless man, and his prayers are acceptable to God. Their doctrine, the conclusions they drew, and their accusations against him were false; their bigotry and uncharity (by which they thought they were defending God and his justice) were culpable and have provoked God's anger. Job's warning in 13:7ff. is verified.

(2) Yahweh treats them with mercy and indulgence; his forgiveness is easily obtained—but by means of the man whom they had condemned as obstinately wicked. Four times (7b–8) he contrasts them with "my servant Job" (cf. 1:8; 2:3). If the question of justice is still to be raised, they must admit, by their humble request, that Job is more just than they. This gentle, ironical, decisive turning of the tables fits with the author's taste for irony; he prepared for it in the dialogue by letting the friends condemn themselves in advance (e.g., Bildad in 8:20–22).

(3) If the friends must humble themselves, Job also must forgive them. They have added immeasurably to his suffering; nevertheless, he must be reconciled to them and become their "redeemer," acting out what he had claimed in 31:29. Verse 10a carefully stresses this concept: Yahweh restored Job's fortunes "when he interceded for his neighbor" (MT has sing.).

(4) There is here an approach to the idea of vicarious atonement, developed further in the fourth Servant Song (Is 52:13–53:12). If Job is such an effective intercessor, it is partly because of the sufferings he has borne. Even while the friends were abusing him, he was actually being "qualified" to obtain for them the forgiveness they would need.

130 **(B) God's Blessing of Job Restored and Increased (42:10b–17).** Nothing is said of the removal of Job's physical affliction, the effect of the Adversary's second attack; only the remedying of the loss of children and property is described. **11.** This seems a rather awkward insertion; probably it is quoted by the author from a pre-existing form of the Job story, in which, after the deprivations of ch. 1, this consolation from his family was narrated. The author had replaced it by the visit of the three friends, as a setting for the dialogue; but here he chose to preserve this notation from the older version. **12–17.** The careful doubling of Job's possessions is a similar archaism; it is a way of saying "Job was twice as dear to God from then on." Many readers feel a scruple over this crude emphasis on material possessions, as though it contradicted Job's insistence in the dialogue on the separability of virtue and prosperity. But Job never questioned that material goods are a natural effect of God's love for men; what he denied was that they are always, and only, withdrawn from the wicked. Also, this state is "normal" for such a man as Job, as we see at the beginning of the book. No reason, other than God's goodness, is required for his bestowing gifts on men; it is their absence or withdrawal that requires explanation—which may be men's sins, or, as with Job, their virtues.

32

ECCLESIASTES (QOHELETH)

Roland E. Murphy, O.Carm.

BIBLIOGRAPHY

1 Barton, G. A., *The Book of Ecclesiastes* (ICC; Edinburgh, 1908). Bea, A., *Liber Ecclesiastae* (Rome, 1950). Dahood, M. J., "Canaanite-Phoenician Influence in Qoheleth," *Bib* 33 (1952) 30–52, 191–221. Galling, K., *Prediger Salomo* (HAT; Tübingen, 1940). Gordis, R., *Koheleth—The Man and His World* (2nd ed.; N.Y., 1955). Jones, E., *Proverbs and Ecclesiastes* (TBC; N.Y., 1961). Loretz, O., *Qohelet und der Alte Orient* (Freiburg i. Br., 1964) esp. bibliography. Pautrel, R., *L'Ecclésiaste* (BJ; 3rd ed.; Paris, 1958). Podechard, E., *L'Ecclésiaste* (Paris, 1912). Rankin, O. S., *The Book of Ecclesiastes* (*IB* 5; N.Y., 1956). Ryder, E. T., *Ecclesiastes* (*PCB*; London, 1962). Scott, R. B. Y., *Proverbs. Ecclesiastes* (AB; N.Y., 1965). Weber, J. J., *Le Livre de Job et L'Ecclésiaste* (Paris, 1947). Wright, A. G., "The Riddle of the Sphinx: The Structure of the Book of Qoheleth," *CBQ* 30 (1968) 313–34. Zimmerli, W., *Prediger* (ATD; Göttingen, 1962).

INTRODUCTION

2 **(I) Title.** The Hebr form, *Qohelet*, is the fem. sing. participle of the otherwise nonexistent *qal* form of *qāhal*, from which is derived the noun meaning "assembly," "congregation." The term therefore designates one who has some relationship to a congregation, perhaps indicating a particular office (teacher? cf. 12:9). The Eng form "Ecclesiastes" is reflected in the Lat and in the Gk (*ekklēsiastes*, "leader of the *ekklēsia*," or "assembly"); the "Preacher" derives from Luther (*Prediger*), and ultimately from Jerome (*concionator*).

3 **(II) Date.** The *terminus ad quem* is fixed by the discovery of Hebr fragments found at Qumran, which indicate that a copy of the book was in circulation about 150 BC (J. Muilenburg, *BASOR* 135 [1954] 20–28). Although the presence of Aramaisms is an inconclusive argument, the Persian words ("park," 2:15; "sentence," 8:11) suggest the *terminus a quo* at about 500 BC. Most authors prefer the 3rd or 4th cent. The language is late and similar to mishnaic Hebrew. Some scholars (e.g., H. L. Ginsberg) have argued that it is a translation from Aramaic; M. J. Dahood has urged a strong Phoenician influence upon the writer.

4 **(III) Structure and Theme.** There is clearly an epilogue in 12:9–14, where Qoheleth is described in the third person. The superscription in 1:1 is followed by a thematic summary in vv. 2–3. Perhaps vv. 4–11 are also an addition, because the author seems to introduce himself in v. 12. Many scholars, such as C. Siegfried and E. Podechard, have tried to detect the hand of later glossators (a "wise man," and a "pious man," etc.) throughout the book, but the current trend is to explain the work as of one piece. No division of the work has attracted any consensus, despite the efforts of A. Bea and H. L. Ginsberg. K. Galling has gone in the opposite direction, finding 37 separate sayings (*Einzelsentenzen*). The study of O. Loretz (*op. cit.*, 135–217) argues effectively for a more adequate appreciation of the author's peculiarities. The work is structured according to the *topoi*, or various subjects treated (Loretz counts 71, *op. cit.*, 197–208): divine wisdom reflected in nature; the importance of one's name or memory; commonplaces in the wisdom literature; etc. Thus, there is no contrived logical unity; the development becomes more circular as Eccl passes from one thought to another. A notable variety of literary forms is employed in this short work. Verses 7:1ff. and 10:1ff. are collections of typical wise sayings and admonitions. The "better sayings" are also frequent (4:6; 5:4; etc.). The first person presentation is the author's deliberate choice; it is not meant to be an autobiographical note, but it does lend itself to greater dramatic effect, while remaining within the wisdom movement (Prv 7:6–20; 24:30–34).

5 Although Gk influence upon the author has often been alleged, the evidence for this is hardly visible. Rather, he is in the mainstream of the ancient Near Eastern wisdom movement, especially the Mesopotamian literature; cf. the advice to Gilgamesh (*ANET* 90) with 9:7–10 (→ Wisdom Lit, 28:29–31). In Israel and in Mesopotamia, we find the recurrent themes of the problem of God's justice, the role of one's name, etc. "Vanity of

Vanities" sums up the theme of the book, but it does not convey the interesting variety of tests that the author applies to life. He tests everything—pleasure, riches, toil, wisdom itself—and finds them lacking. He repeatedly returns to the uncertainties of life, to the lack of any clear sign of divine sanction, and to the grievous fact of death (2:15–17; 3:14–22; 8:5–15; 9:11–12). For this human condition the only viable conclusion is to accept whatever small joys God "gives" to man (12 times in the book it is God who "gives" something; 3:12–13; 5:17–18; 9:7–10; etc.).

6 Qoheleth is sharply critical of the wisdom movement. The earlier sages, in their attempt to categorize nature and human conduct, had allowed themselves the luxury of fixed and certain positions: Justice leads to life, wickedness, to death. Even if there existed a theoretical recognition that God's ways were unaccountable (Prv 20:24; 21:30), the tendency was to put the Lord into a strait jacket tailored by human insights. In exercising dominion over creation (Gn 1:26–28), the wise men seemed to be endangering the divine prerogatives. The oversimplified and optimistic theory of divine providence and retribution epitomizes this position. It is in this perspective that the truly religious nature of Qoheleth's writing can be appreciated. He strikes a blow for divine sovereignty and independence: God is not to be limited and coerced by human considerations (cf. W. Zimmerli in *ScotJT* 17 [1964] 155–58). It is Qoheleth who gives back the divine freedom to "give."

7 **(IV) Outline.** The Book of Qoheleth can be outlined as follows:

(I)	Vanity of Earthly Things (1:1–11)
(II)	Vanity of Wisdom (1:12–18)
(III)	Vanity of Pleasure (2:1–12)
(IV)	Wisdom and Folly Compared (2:13–17)
(V)	Vanity of Toil (2:18–26)
(VI)	The Unchanging Order of Events (3:1–13)
(VII)	The Uncertainty of the Future (3:14–22)
(VIII)	Social Disorders (4:1–16)
(IX)	Reverence for God (4:17–5:6)
(X)	Perverted Justice (5:7–8)
(XI)	Vanity of Riches (5:9–6:6)
(XII)	Vanity of Desires (6:7–12)
(XIII)	Wisdom and Folly Contrasted (7:1–12)
(XIV)	The World an Enigma (7:13–25)
(XV)	Women (7:26–8:1)
(XVI)	Obedience to Rulers (8:2–4)
(XVII)	Indiscernible Moral Sanction (8:5–15)
(XVIII)	The Same Lot for All (8:16–9:10)
(XIX)	The Uncertainty of Fortune (9:11–17)
(XX)	Sundry Proverbs (9:18–11:6)
(XXI)	Youth (11:7–10)
(XXII)	Old Age (12:1–8)
(XXIII)	Epilogue (12:9–14)

COMMENTARY

8 **(I) Vanity of Earthly Things (1:1–11).** **1.** (On the meaning of Qoheleth, → 2 above.) The further specification, "David's son," is probably intended as a reference to Solomon (cf. Prv; Ct). Qoheleth uses the fiction of a wise and rich king, for wisdom is usually associated with royalty and the riches enable him to conduct his examination of life's realities. **2.** *Hebel*, or "vanity," is a favorite word (used 35 times in the book), and it sounds the leitmotiv of the work. It literally means "breath" or "vapor" and is expressed in the Hebr idiom for the superlative (as in "King of Kings"). It is also used elsewhere (Ps 39:6–7; 94:11; etc.) to indicate something that is transient, worthless, and empty. As in 12:9, the mention of Qoheleth in the third person suggests that it has been added by the editor. **3.** Another important idea of the author is summarized (cf. 2:18ff.). "Under the sun," a favorite phrase (used 28 times), occurs in Semitic inscriptions and hence constitutes no evidence for Greek influence. **4–8.** A "mashal," or proverb saying, concerning nature ("world," "sun," "wind," "sea") is used to symbolize the human condition. The relentless monotony in all four areas, without any achievement, symbolizes man's failure to accomplish anything; like the elements, human beings constantly repeat themselves and "there is nothing man can say" (8). **9–11.** Neither can human deeds forge a name or "remembrance" (a frequent theme; cf. 2:16; 9:5,15); new achievements will not be of any avail—indeed, they are not "new," but merely forgotten. One can compare here the Babylonian proverb, "The life of last night [is the same as] every day" (*BWL* 249).

9 **(II) Vanity of Wisdom (1:12–18).** **12–13.** The first person, characteristic of Qoheleth, begins here, and is perhaps a sign that the previous lines are a thematic summary of his teaching. As Zimmerli remarks, Qoheleth uses "wisdom" as a basis for questioning reality (cf. 2:3,9; 7:23)—a "thankless task." **14.** The metaphor of chasing after the wind (lit., "pasture the wind") indicates futility (cf. Hos 12:2). **15.** Whatever may have been the original application of this proverb, it is applied here to the totality of life; man is helpless, and only God can straighten out what is crooked (7:13). **16.** The references to his predecessors is not really an anachronism but is part of the fiction practiced by the author. **17–18.** It is striking that Qoheleth "debunks" the class of sages to which he belonged (cf. 7:23–24; 8:17). He illustrates the futility of wisdom by a proverb, which, if it was originally used as a pointer to diligence and discipline in the pursuit of wisdom, underlines the labor and disappointment inherent in a hopeless pursuit.

10 **(III) Vanity of Pleasure (2:1–12).** The fiction of the wise and rich king (cf. 1 Kgs 5–10) continues as Qoheleth turns to a new area of life in an attempt to find something of value. His judgment on laughter and mirth (2) must be weighed against 8:15. The test of wine and of folly is carried out with a critical use of wisdom (3). He describes his trial of luxury (4–9) in words that are reminiscent of the riches of Solomon; the claim to riches and to buildings is part of a traditional convention among ancient Near Eastern monarchs. The "luxuries" in v. 8 is probably a reference to sexual pleasure, although the CCD omits as dittography the obscure phrase that the RSV renders as "many concubines." The completeness of his test is indicated in v. 10; realistically, he cannot deny the joy that is his "share" (*ḥēleq*, regularly used in Eccl for the portion allotted to man by God) in this trial. The considered judgment is expressed in v. 11, when he "turned to all the works" and pronounced the same verdict appearing in 1:14,17. This word is final, and no reason is given in the MT. But the CCD adopts a widely accepted (Galling, Zimmerli) shift of v. 12b to follow upon v. 11, inasmuch as it is ill-placed after v. 12a. In this view, Qoheleth is represented as raising a further consideration: He must die, and his successor (an echo of the worthless Rehoboam, 1 Kgs 12?) will continue in the same way. One would have expected here a conclusion similar to 6:9.

11 **(IV) Wisdom and Folly Compared (2:13–17).** This section should also be taken into consideration when we interpret 2:1–12. In the CCD, v. 12a is taken as the introduction to the evaluation of wisdom. **13–14.** The advantage of wisdom over folly is quite theoretical: light over darkness (cf. Prv 4:18–19). Wisdom does see; it is not blind. However, this statement is true only in the abstract world, that of the proverbs, such as in v. 14. What about the concrete, the wise and the fools? **15–17.** In reality there is one grievous lot (*miqreh*, "happening," "encounter") that befalls both wise and foolish. This "lot" is developed at length in 3:19–21; 9:2–3; basically, it is death (v. 16), which eliminates man from any claim on existence. Should one try to urge the preservation of one's name in posterity—a highly regarded theme in the traditional wisdom literature (Prv 10:7; Ps 112:6)? Qoheleth denies this type of "immortality" (cf. 1:11), because no one remembers. Qoheleth's hatred of life (17) is also contrary to the traditional evaluation of the sages, who associated wisdom and life. His hard questions will gradually lead Israel to a deeper meaning of life.

12 **(V) Vanity of Toil (2:18–26).** The question shifts again; in v. 18 there may be an echo to 2:10, where the author stated that he had joy in his toil. Now he finds reason to detest his labor—i.e., because you cannot take it with you, you must leave it to an heir. Whether he be wise man or fool, he has the disposition of all that he inherits. And Qoheleth is driven to despair. This consideration is repeated in a definitely impersonal way in vv. 20–23. The futility is heightened by the concrete description of the sorrows and trials inherent in labor (23). The reader should not object that Qoheleth disregards the aspect of the family and the natural consolation one finds in leaving an inheritance. If he can find one limitation to life's pursuits, that suffices; in this case, the ugly reality of death is basic to his consideration.

13 Qoheleth's conclusion in 2:24–26 is a steady theme throughout his work: 3:12–13; 3:22; 5:17–19; 7:13–14; 8:15; 9:7–10; 11:7–10. Inasmuch as satisfaction is really unattainable, the best thing man can do is to accept from day to day the little joys that turn up. Such an emphasis has led some commentators to find hedonism or Epicureanism in Eccl. But these joys, concretely expressed in food and drink, are obviously viewed as God's gifts to a creature, and they are offered here as a resigned conclusion that offers some consolation in life (see comment on 9:7–10). Some (e.g., Podechard) have argued that v. 26 enunciates a view of temporal retribution that is contrary to the author's philosophy (7:15; 8:10; etc.). Rather, Qoheleth is saying here that God's will is supreme and inscrutable; he gives to whom he pleases, and, paradoxically, even the prosperous sinner must yield his collected goods to whomever God pleases. Other translations (e.g., RSV) give the impression of a contrast between the good man (in the CCD, "to whatever man he sees fit") and the sinner; but the emphasis bears on the divine will, not on the state of the individuals. Again, the author is thinking in the wisdom tradition (cf. Prv 13:22; 28:8; Jb 27:16ff.; Sir 14:4). His final remark about vanity seems to be a reflection on the uncertainties (and the corresponding freedom of God) that he has mentioned.

14 **(VI) The Unchanging Order of Events (3:1–13).** Qoheleth's meditation upon time and (fixed) times is a famous passage. He relates the events that come off in an order decreed by God (1–8; cf. 1:4–11), and he contrasts man's situation; man cannot know God's purposes in the world because of "the timeless" God has put in his heart (9–11). Hence, he should resign himself to enjoying whatever comes to him as a gift of God (12–13). **1.** The importance of the right time is recognized in the wisdom literature (e.g., Prv 15:23; 25:11). The rule of God over time (and over the event that occurs in time) is presupposed here, and the author is going to present 14 antitheses. **2.** Man cannot even dispose of such times as planting, much less of birth and death; the necessary conditions, it is presumed, stand within the power of God alone. **5.** *scatter stones...gather:* Many varying interpretations have been proposed; the parallelism with "embrace" suggests that this verse is a euphemism for marital intercourse. **9.** This question seems to be the conclusion to the litany of "times," which precedes. The broad structure of life and the individual fixed times within it are known in general, but man does not know the particular hour and is never sure of getting results from his actions. **10–11.** The reason for man's plight is that God has put *hāʿōlām* (lit., "indefinite duration"—hence "eternity," "world," etc.) into his heart. There seems to be a deliberate contrast between *ʿēt* (the fixed time) and *ʿōlām* (the timeless); God runs things off at his own time, and man is not geared to this scheme because of the timeless in his heart. Hence, he cannot discover "the work which God has done,"—a limitation that earlier sages failed to fully appreciate. **12–13.** Cf. 2:24–26.

15 **(VII) The Uncertainty of the Future (3:14–22).** **14–15.** The play on the word *ʿōlām* (translated here as "forever") continues; it is in this sphere that God acts (and hence man's failure to understand, although the timeless is in his heart—v. 11). The description of God's activity as immutable (no adding or subtracting) has a long prehistory (see also Sir 18:6; 42:22). In Dt 4:1–2; 13:1, the same thing is affirmed of the Torah, and it seems likely that the thought derives from the usual warning found in treaties and inscriptions (for the alleged dependence of 3:14 on a saying from Ptah-hotep, cf. the discussion in Loretz [*op. cit.*, 66–69]). The reference to the fear of God ("that he may be revered") is to be understood against the background of Qoheleth's thought. Zimmerli's comment (ATD) is acute; fear of the Lord is "not to walk in paths of light which secure for those who walk therein the harvest of life's fruits and honor. Fear of God here means walking under a heaven that is mysteriously closed, walking without the assurance that lightning might not suddenly shoot out and strike you as you go—at every step relying upon the free gift of God, but with every step also summoned to suffer the riddle and oppression that God can inflict." Verse 15 seems to take up again the thought of 1:9–11 (cf. 6:10), but perhaps the idea here is the total subjection of created things to the divine government. The translation and meaning of v. 15b remains unclear (lit., "God seeks out what was pursued").

16 **16.** Qoheleth puts forward the problem of injustice in human affairs; his comment is found in the following verses. **17.** His first consideration seems to be contradictory to his whole point of view (e.g., 7:15; 8:5ff.). Hence, it is taken by some to be a corrective gloss; others (Gordis, Scott) treat it as a quotation from traditional wisdom against which he is arguing. Perhaps it can stand as a valid statement of the author, which merely affirms his faith in divine government (however unclear to man it is). The "time for every affair" recalls 3:1–8; it is the time that man does not understand, and the mystery of the existence of injustice still stands, even if God is the ultimate judge (by the fact of death). **18.** It is difficult to determine the nuance of "God's way of testing"; perhaps he means that the existence of injustice

is used by God to make man aware of his limited understanding and his human condition, a condition that Qoheleth assimilates to that of the beasts (mortality) in the following lines. **19–21.** We must not make the mistake of approaching these lines with Aristotelian categories; man and beast are compared, not regarding their nature but their lot—i.e., inescapable death. The background to this thought is the concept of Sheol ("both go to the same place"; cf. 9:10). The description is based on Gn 2 ("both have the same life breath"—a picture of God breathing upon matter to make it live; cf. Gn 2:7; 3:19; also Ps 104:29–30). The awful fact of death is at the basis of Qoheleth's restless questioning. It appears that in his day some were trying to find a distinction between the life breath of man and beast (v. 21), but he was unable to find any evidence for this (and 12:7 must be interpreted in the light of these verses). **22.** He closes the discussion with the only consoling thought he can offer (2:24–26; 3:12); here, the word for "lot" (*ḥlq*, "portion") differs from the word for "lot" (*mqrh*, "happening") in v. 19. His final question, at the end of v. 22, betrays a constant preoccupation: Man does not know the future (cf. 6:12).

17 **(VIII) Social Disorders (4:1–16).** This title loosely designates the following observations, which also include the topics of labor, solitariness, and an example of the vanity of wisdom. **1–3.** Qoheleth deeply feels the enigma of social violence and oppression, despite the fact that he does not adopt the prophetical stance of either threat or consolation. The ugly reality leads him to an extreme comparison between the living, the dead, and even the unborn. In this respect, he is very much against the current of traditional wisdom, which set great store by "life." And yet in 9:4 he will pronounce a judgment in favor of life! This dialectic is understandable in view of the particular angle of thought that forms the context of each passage—here, freedom from oppression; there, hope. **4–6.** Against the traditional esteem for diligence (Prv 10:4–5; 12:27; etc.), Qoheleth makes a telling point: the "rivalry" that characterizes human effort. His quotation of two contrary proverbs in vv. 5–6 is characteristic of his constantly shifting point of view. Laziness is condemned in v. 5 (cf. Prv 6:10; 24:33) and overexertion in v. 6 (cf. Prv 16:8; 17:1). Gordis and Scott are of the opinion that Qoheleth's own view is expressed in v. 6, but it may well be that he is simply and deliberately pitting two proverbs against each other to strengthen what he has said in v. 4.

18 **7–12.** The vanity of diligence and toil is illustrated in the case of a solitary man; he will not have the pleasure of sharing it (see the opposite supposition in 2:18–19!) and presumably will have only his own "greed" (Hebr *'ênāw*, "eyes") to nourish. That companionship is "better" than solitariness is illustrated by three examples; the supposition for the "good wage" in v. 9 is the help provided by one's partner (10). **13–16.** This obscure story may be an echo to the futility of rivalry (v. 4). The example is taken from courtly life (despite the efforts to identify the situation—e.g., with the Joseph story of Gn—it should be understood as a type, as Zimmerli suggests; see Loretz, *op. cit.*, 69–72 for the alleged Egyptian background of the story). Riches and power mean nothing for a king when one considers the fickleness of the people who support him.

19 **(IX) Reverence for God (4:17–5:6).** The author takes up the topics of sacrifice, prayer, and vows, from the point of view of a wisdom teacher (note that reasons are given for the admonitions). **17.** This evaluation of obedience and sacrifice is a commonplace in the OT (e.g., Prv 21:3; Hos 6:6; 1 Sm 15:22).

5:1–2. An admonition against wordiness; "to make a promise" (CCD) is, lit., "to proffer a word" and need not refer only to the making of vows (discussed in 3–4). The thought is similar to Prv 10:19. **3–4.** The subject of vows receives similar consideration in Prv 20:25; Sir 18:22–23. Many commentators (e.g., Zimmerli) stress the use of the generic term "God" instead of "Lord" (or Yahweh), undoubtedly the author's practice, reflecting the usual stance of a wisdom writer. However, Yahweh, the God of Israel's experience, is meant. **5–6.** Some interpret these remarks in the light of the context of vows, but Zimmerli points out the applicability to Nm 15:22–31, the ritual in atonement for sins of inadvertence. He also points out in reference to the command "fear God" that Qoheleth's reserve and cautiousness in these matters (vv. 1–6) stem not from any smallness on his part, but from a deep realization of his position as a creature of God. The CCD translation omits v. 6a ("in a multitude of nightmares, and vanities, and many words"—a corrupt text) as a dittography of 5:2.

20 **(X) Perverted Justice (5:7–8).** The meaning of these lines is not clear. The reason why one should not be shocked at oppression (cf. 3:16; 4:1) is the structure of the state, in which constant supervision is the predominant feature. But the reference to the king and the land remains obscure.

21 **(XI) Vanity of Riches (5:9–6:6).** This series of sayings considers the trials that can assail the person of means. **9–11.** The vanity of greed and covetousness (9) corresponds to 1:8—man can never be satisfied. In addition, the rich man attracts greedy "friends" (10). The reference to the owner's "eyes" in 10 may have prompted the remark about the sleeplessness of the rich man (11). **12–16.** In yet another way, riches create a disadvantage: When they are lost by some misfortune the rich man is reduced to poverty; should he have an heir, he would have nothing to leave to him. In vv. 15–16, the author generalizes from these cases ("he goes just as he came") and affirms the futility of man's toil. **17–19.** Another recommendation (2:24–26; 3:12–13) is that man enjoy his "lot" ("God gives"—"gift from God"). There is a sardonic emphasis on "limited days" and "shortness of his life," but the sovereign disposition of God is clearly affirmed.

6:1–6. This section begins with the plight of the rich man (cf. 5:9ff.) who suffers the fate of losing his riches to another; it digresses into the somber fact of death. **1–2.** The circumstances that explain why the rich man fails to partake of his riches are not detailed; God simply so disposes. **3–6.** A grim comparison between a prosperous man and a stillborn infant. The exaggerations concerning children and age (reminiscent of the patriarchs) underline the hard fate that a man may still suffer: failure to enjoy his goods, or deprivation of burial (the worst of tragedies in OT thought). In such circumstances, the "child born dead" has a kinder fate because it has experienced "rest" (cf. 4:2). The extreme hyperbole in v. 6 (twice the age of the oldest antediluvian patriarch; cf. the "hundred children" in v. 3) sharpens Qoheleth's complaint about Sheol, the "same place."

22 **(XII) Vanity of Desires (6:7–12).** The basic fact is that man's desires cannot be fulfilled (the thrust of v. 7 is different from a similar saying in Prv 16:26). Hence, the wise man has no advantage over the fool, nor is there a profit for the poor man for his conduct. The saying quoted in v. 9 amounts to our popular proverb, "a bird in hand is worth two in the bush." Apparently, vision ("what the eyes see") is taken as some sort of possession, at least in comparison with desire. Yet, in view of the many uncertainties that already have been rehearsed by the author, the basic vanity of any alleged "possession" is clear. In v. 10 he returns to the thought of 3:14–15; God's sovereign (and, for man, unintelligible and uncontrollable) causality. In contrast to Job (Jb 13:21–22; 31:37) and Jeremiah (Jer 12:1–5), Qoheleth cannot contend with God; "many sayings" (cf. 5:1–6) cannot disguise the fact that man does not know the future, especially his own (cf. 3:22)!

23 **(XIII) Wisdom and Folly Contrasted (7:1–12).** A series of "better" sayings ("proverbs of comparative value"—Scott) follow in vv. 1–3, 5, 8, 11. **1.** The alliteration and play on the word "name" (*šēm;* whereas "oil" is *šemen*) is striking in the Hebrew. In itself, the meaning of v. 1a is comparable to Prv 22:1, but the parallelism in this verse suggests that Qoheleth's emphasis on death (cf. 4:2) gives a new meaning to v. 1a; then the sense is that a good reputation (after death) is better than beginning life (the ointment applied at birth), or, a life that is well spent is better than a life that has just begun. **2.** This saying continues the thought of v. 1, and it illustrates the author's realism (cf. 6:12; 9:5) about death. **3.** *sorrow:* Closer to the truth of life's reality than "laughter" (cf. Prv 14:13). **4.** Cf. 7:2. **5–6.** The Hebr text is marked by alliteration, and the saying is similar to Prv 13:1,18; etc.; however, the context is not in praise of wisdom. **7.** Cf. Ex 23:8; Dt 16:19. **8.** Cf. 1 Kgs 20:11; however, in the context of this chapter, v. 8 recalls v. 1. The second "better" saying warns against pride ("lofty spirit"). **10.** This admonition logically follows from 1:10–11. **11–12.** The comparison between wisdom and wealth is frequent among the sages (e.g., Prv 16:16), and the relative superiority (cf. 2:13–14) of wisdom, because of its association with life, is indicated.

24 **(XIV) The World an Enigma (7:13–25).** **13–14.** The "work of God" is his government, and his supreme causality is acknowledged in a phrase reminiscent of 1:15. The recommendation in v. 14 shares in the kind of resigned conclusion that has been sounded before—accept the good things that God gives (e.g., 5:17–19). But one must also live with the "evil day" (hardship), and recognize that it comes from God. The CCD translation of the final words in v. 14 is based on the recognition of an Aram idiom ("find fault"), and it is similar to Sir 39:25–34; 42:22–25. **15–18.** This enigmatic passage is frequently interpreted in the sense of *ne quid nimis*, or "virtue stands in the middle," but this interpretation hardly agrees with the author's thought. He clearly affirms in v. 15 the uncomfortable fact of injustice in the world; as Zimmerli remarks, he does not put this fact up as a counter dogma to the optimistic theory of the sages that good is rewarded and evil is punished—it is simply an ineluctable experience of life. In v. 16, "just to excess" and "overwise" seem to indicate a philosophy that would control life according to the dogma of the sages. To a person of this temper, Qoheleth addresses the question (in the CCD, "lest..."), "Why be ruined?" Experience has shown that such a viewpoint carries no guarantee against adversity. On the other hand (17), the sinner cannot expect to fare any better. Finally, in his almost mocking way, Qoheleth advises his reader to look carefully at both these sayings, neither one of which gives security, and both of which were probably current opinions. His own considered judgment is that "fear of God" (18; see comment on 3:14–15) is the only viable attitude—an attitude that carries with it all the questions, but also all the resignation, expressed in this book.

19–20. The evaluation of wisdom in v. 19 is also found in Prv 21:22; 24:5 (cf. Eccl 9:16), and Gordis thinks that the "ten" is a reference to the council of ten in the Hellenistic city. The connection of this line with v. 20 is not clear; v. 20 perhaps refers to the excessive justice of v. 16. **21–22.** This concrete example is related to man's sinfulness (20). God tolerates sinful man; should not man, conscious of his uncharitable speech about others, be able to overlook the criticism of his servant? **23–24.** The author admits that the pursuit of wisdom is vain because wisdom is unattainable (cf. 1:13; Jb 28). **25.** It is not certain in Hebrew that he "recognized that wickedness is foolish"; he seems to be asking if such is so, but such a conclusion is consonant with the author's other statements (2:13–14). It is not clear whether this verse belongs with what follows (Zimmerli) or with what precedes (Gordis).

25 **(XV) Women (7:26–8:1).** The verdict is pronounced on mankind in general (cf. 29), although the author begins with the subject of women. **26.** The "woman" who is meant is the adulteress, a stereotype in ancient wisdom literature of Egypt and of the OT (cf. Prv 2:16–19; 5:3–14; 7:1–27). But Qoheleth, like other sages (cf. Prv 18:22; 31:10–31), could also evaluate a woman positively (cf. 9:9). He does not take the trouble to issue a warning, as the sages do, but returns to the divine sovereignty expressed in 2:26—as God sees fit, a man will escape this trap. **27–29.** The structure of the Hebr text is very complicated, and some (Bea, Loretz) translate in such a way as to indicate that the saying about "one in a thousand" is something that Qoheleth has not found to be true. Most commentators would agree with the CCD translation, which takes the saying as a conclusion that he has arrived at after much investigation. However, the conclusion must be correctly understood; "one in a thousand" does not speak in favor of man as opposed to woman. The real thrust is clearly indicated in v. 29—"mankind" is responsible for its evil. **8:1.** This saying is in praise of wisdom and the wise man, in the style of the early sages (and cf. Sir 13:24). Because it does not seem to follow 7:29, many combine it with 8:2–4.

26 **(XVI) Obedience to Rulers (8:2–4).** Conduct before the king is a commonplace in the wisdom writings (cf. Prv 16:12–15; 25:2–7). Obedience is urged because of one's "oath" (perhaps of loyalty to the king) and because of the king's power, which is unquestionable.

27 **(XVII) Indiscernible Moral Sanction (8:5–15).** The subtitle indicates the general idea of this section, although a few verses do not seem to fit the author's viewpoint. Some commentators continue the discussion about the king (2–4) until vv. 8–9. **5–6.** The quotation marks in the CCD indicate that this saying is put forth for consideration. Does the author agree with it or not? The praise of wisdom is reminiscent of the optimism in Prv 19:16, but the reference to "times and judgments" reflects 3:1ff.; these are really beyond man's control (perhaps the truly wise "heart" knows of times and judgments in this sense, that they are mysterious?). But Qoheleth is not one to deny that God judges; he denies that this judgment is clear to man, even if "there is a time" for it. **7.** The complaint echoes 6:12. **8.** Although the CCD understands *rûaḥ* as "breath of life" (parallel to "day of death"), this word can also be rendered as "wind" (cf. Prv 30:4, where it is said that the wind cannot be mastered). If the "struggle" is translated as "war," (*milḥāmāh*), the fourth element that enters into the saying is "wickedness." The point of the verse is to illustrate certain limits in man's experience, which demonstrate that he cannot control the events of life.

9. It seems better to take this verse as an introduction to the topic in the following lines, although the oppression of one's neighbor is only casually mentioned. **10.** In the light of the ancient versions, the CCD corrects the Hebrew slightly, so that the sense suggests the hypocrisy of the "wicked men" and the vanity of the recognition that others give them for their frequenting the "sacred place" (the Temple). The MT reads: "I saw wicked men buried, and they came and departed from the holy place; and those were forgotten in the city who had acted justly." Most commentators agree that the text is faulty. Many retain the "holy place" as referring to the grave, and this phrase has been characterized as an instance of Egyptian influence (see the discussion in Loretz, *op. cit.*, 75–77); the text itself is too uncertain for building any further upon it. **11–13.** There is a clear affirmation of the "scandal" given by the success and prosperity of the wrongdoer: "The sinner does evil a hundred times and survives." But it is immediately followed by another affirmation that seems to deny it and that seems to side with the traditional optimism of the sages that God will judge the wicked. Hence, this section is viewed as an addition by a later hand, or it is interpreted as ironic or as a viewpoint that Qoheleth merely quotes. It seems better to understand it as a statement of fact—God will judge—although Qoheleth knows nothing of how it shall occur (cf. v. 14!). As Loretz remarks, Qoheleth's "knowledge of the error of the wisdom teaching did not mislead him into denying God's sovereign dominion over the life of man" (*op. cit.*, 296). **14.** The unpleasant fact, to which Qoheleth constantly reverts (and in the light of which vv. 12–13 are to be viewed). **15.** As often before (e.g., 2:24–26), the author turns from a "vanity" to his practical recommendation. It is easy to see that his praise of "mirth" has different motivation here than in 2:2, where enjoyment was envisioned as a possible satisfying value in life.

28 **(XVIII) The Same Lot for All (8:16–9:10).** Once more (cf. 2:15–17; 3:18–22) Qoheleth wrestles with the meaning of death. **8:16–17.** In contrast to the RSV and others, the CCD transposes the words about sleeplessness from v. 16 to v. 17. The conclusion is similar to what he has said before about the "work of God" (7:13–14; 1:13–15) that escapes man's understanding, but here he challenges the pretensions of the sages. As Zimmerli (ATD) remarks, "all his efforts are basically an argument with that wisdom which thinks it can understand the complex affairs of the world, and God as well, and then proceed to construct a confident philosophy of life."

9:1. This idea is not to be interpreted in the sense of Wis 3:1; Qoheleth merely reaffirms that God is sovereign and also enigmatic, because there is no way of judging his attitude from events that transpire in this life ("love from hatred"). It is irrelevant to raise the question of the author's attitude to salvation history and Israel's past; he is working with the present and with the interpretation given by the sages, as v. 2 clearly suggests. **3.** The "lot" (*miqreh;* cf. 2:15; 3:19) mentioned in v. 2 is now made explicit in the poignant description of life and its final issue, death. **4–6.** A typical proverb, contrasting the lowest with the highest, is adduced to support the advantages of life over death (cf. 4:2 against the background of a different context). But the advantage is highly theoretical, as the irony of v. 5 indicates—the living at least know this much, that they must die. This alleged advantage only serves to strengthen the emphatic finality of death (6). **7–9.** Cf. the advice given to Gilgamesh (*ANET* 90; → Wisdom Lit, 28:31). The similarity is all the more remarkable in view of the context of man's fateful mortality. **10.** A classical description of Sheol, the nether world; it is in view of this inactivity that the author recommends a zest for life (cf. 11:9) while one has it.

29 **(XIX) The Uncertainty of Fortune (9:11–17).** The author returns to the theme of time (cf. 3:1–17) and adversity (11–12) and illustrates the vanity of wisdom with a story (13–17). **11–12.** The examples show that sheer human accomplishment does not succeed in escaping the "time of calamity" (hendiadys—lit., "time and calamity"). Zimmerli points to Rom 9:16 as taking up this hard truth in the context of a challenge to believe in the God who holds in his hands this "time." **13–15.** This typical wisdom story (cf. Prv 21:22) is used to illustrate the "time of calamity" suffered by the poor wise man who had saved the city. **16.** The author's conclusion is that the hard fate of the wise man renders vain the proverb ("wisdom is better than force") that exalts wisdom. **17.** In itself, this proverb also exalts wisdom, but in the context one can hear Qoheleth asking himself if it is not vanity.

30 **(XX) Sundry Proverbs (9:18–11:6).** Another group (cf. 7:1–12) of proverbs is found here; we need not think that they were composed by the author. They probably represent the current sayings, which he communicated to his students (12:9), with the changes and modifications that he may have contributed (e.g., 11:6?). **9:18–10:1.** The CCD has omitted v. 18a as dittography and combined 10:1a with 18b; then the line concerning folly forms a commentary on a popular saying. The meaning is that one single mistake can spoil a whole operation, and this observation is particularly applicable to the power of wisdom or money. **10:2.** Like 2:14, this proverb recognizes a certain superiority to wisdom; "right" is favorable, in contrast to "left." **3.** It would be a mistake to absolutize this saying, as though it represented the author's total judgment; yet he recognizes a theoretical superiority for wisdom (cf. 2:14). **4.** Similar to sayings in Prv 16:14; 14:30; 15:4. **5–7.** Typical examples (cf. also Prv 19:10) of the uncertainties in life, of which the author has been complaining. **8.** The first line is a commonplace in the OT (cf. Prv 26:27; Pss 7:16; 9:16; 57:7; Sir 27:26), but it is not seen as a "law" for Qoheleth; it may happen—hence, caution is in order. The possibility of being bitten by a serpent (cf. Am 5:19!) was very real in Palestine. **9.** These sayings reflect the caution expressed in v. 8. The implication is, of course, that wisdom and diligence, the tried virtues of the sages, cannot counter with these possibilities. **10–11.** *though at first...:* This clause is usually translated, "and he did not sharpen the edge." The slight change in the MT presupposed by the CCD makes better sense. Both proverbs underline the fact that the wise man may fail to use his own skill or insight. Sir 12:13 is close in content to v. 11. **12–15.** This praise of wise talk as opposed to foolish words is a commonplace in the wisdom literature (Prv 14:3; 18:7; etc.), but in v. 14, Qoheleth adds what is for him a typical consideration (cf. 3:22; 6:12). **16–17.** Two contrasting sayings, extolling the nobility (cf. 10:5–7) and sobriety of kings. **18.** This condemnation of laziness is similar to those in Prv 20:4; 21:5. The roofs of Palestinian houses needed repair after the dryness of a summer heat. **19.** The last line in Hebrew is ambiguous; it could mean "money ensures all this." These sayings are observations, not value judgments. **20.** Cf. 7:21–22; 8:2–4. The basis for controlling one's tongue is that words become known; the association of bird and word (cf. also "a little bird told me"; "walls have ears") occurs already in the wisdom of Ahikar (*ANET* 428).

31 **11:1.** If anyone might doubt whether Qoheleth's many-sided analysis had reduced him to immobility, this and the following proverbs (v. 9) indicate that he chose to act, despite the vanity. This saying is rather well known and has often been interpreted in the sense of charity and almsgiving. But this is hardly the meaning. Rather, it amounts to recommending to another that he take a chance—he may profit from it. Perhaps the basic reference is to commerce on the sea. **2.** This proverb is in contrast to the daring of v. 1. One should realize that there is a real possibility of failing, but one can guard against it by careful planning and division (as Jacob in Gn 32:6–7). **3.** The examples of the "cloud" and the "tree" suggest the iron law of an "appointed time for everything" (3:1). **4.** Overcautiousness leads to inaction. **5.** The "work of God," the mystery of which has often been mentioned by the author (7:13; 8:17), is compared to the origins of life. **6.** Qoheleth recommends an optimistic diligence with this proverb. There is no sense in retiring from life, however puzzling it may be.

32 **(XXI) Youth (11:7–10).** These lines contrast with the topic of old age (12:1–8). **7–8.** This perhaps unexpected approval of life (cf. 4:2; 9:4) indicates that the author himself appreciated it deeply, especially in view of the "days of darkness" that are to come. Such a positive attitude should be recalled in view of the many allegations about his so-called skepticism. **9–10.** The accent on youth and enjoyment (cf. 7:14, and the many recommendations throughout the work) continues, although still under the shadow of their brevity (10). The lines referring to God's judgment are suspect, inasmuch as the same phrase ("bring to judgment") occurs in 12:14, almost certainly the addition of a later hand. If they are interpreted as a final solution, they are probably an addition. However, they can be understood by comparison with 3:17; 8:5–6 (see comments on 3:17; 8:5–6). The "fleeting" aspect of youth serves as an introduction to the allegory on old age in ch. 12.

33 **(XXII) Old Age (12:1–8).** All would agree that these lines describe the approach of death (cf. the description given by Ptah-hotep, *ANET* 412), but commentators differ in interpreting the individual metaphors (anatomical allusions, as indicated in the footnotes provided for the CCD version; storm phenomena; etc.). Some (e.g., Loretz, who emphasizes the structure in the "before" of vv. 1–2, 6) would deny that this section is an allegory, an extended metaphor in which each detail has a transferred meaning. **1.** Without any allegory, the admonition concerning the "evil days" of old age is given. There is no compelling reason to alter the text from "Creator" to cistern or pit (thus Galling, understanding it in the sense of "grave"). **2.** The typical Palestinian winter, cloudy by day and night, is described here and suggests the unpleasant effect of a closing in upon life. **3.** Some interpret this verse to refer to the desuetude into which a "house" has fallen; the allegorical approach finds the equivalents of the "guardians," etc., in arms, legs, teeth, and eyes. **4.** The silence and inactivity of old age is indicated by metaphors that can refer to the body ("door," lips or ears). **5.** The first two lines describe the natural fears of an elderly man who is no longer agile. As for the rest, interpretations again vary, but the "almond tree" can be taken to refer to the white hair of the elderly; the sluggishness of the locust suggests a labored gait, and there is no use for the "caperberry," a stimulant for the appetite. The last lines contain a clear reference to death—the "lasting home" (lit., "house of eternity," as the grave is also called in Egyptian and Phoenician sources). **6.** The description of the human body gives way to a still-life description—a golden bowl (lamp), suspended by a silver cord; an unused well, with its broken water wheel and pieces of a water pitcher beside it—an apt suggestion of death. **7.** Death is described in terms of Gn 2:7; man is effectively dissolved. One should recall that man lives because of the "life breath" (here *rûaḥ*; also *n^e^šāmāh*), which he has received from God; this concept has nothing to do (in this context) with the soul and its return to God. It is quite clear that Qoheleth had no knowledge of a blessed immortality (cf. 3:19–21; 9:10). **8.** The theme of the book (cf. 1:2) is repeated at its end. Qoheleth has mentioned a long list of alleged values: wisdom, pleasure, work, wealth, etc.; none of them offered him the security and satisfaction he was seeking. Even if there are small, God-given pleasures that he can enjoy as his "lot," the great uncertainty of life is not to be avoided.

34 **(XXIII) Epilogue (12:9–14).** **9–11.** This appraisal of Qoheleth, apparently added (cf. the third pers. reference) by one of his students, evaluates him for himself ("besides being wise") and in relation to his fellow man ("taught the people"; cf. Sir 37:24–25). The description of his activity—"weighed, scrutinized and arranged"—refers to the scholastic work of the sage. The sapiential sayings were the product of deliberate, highly cultivated, literary art ("pleasing words"). *collector:* Lit., "shepherd"—a surprising term that betrays a warmth and respect for the master. **12–14.** Even if one does not agree with Zimmerli that these lines stem from a second epilogist, they do seem to go far beyond the tone of vv. 11–12. Now it is the book, not the man—and the book is accompanied by a warning in v. 12, as if it were a reflection on the extreme sayings of the author. The writer of vv. 13–14 has taken some ideas of Eccl (cf. 3:14; 8:12–13) and absolutized them so as to give a "safe" interpretation. In reality, God's "judgment" (14) is much more mysterious for Qoheleth than it is for this writer, who uses it in the traditional manner of the sages.

33

SIRACH

Thomas H. Weber

BIBLIOGRAPHY

1 Baumgartner, W., "Die literarischen Gattungen in der Weisheit des Jesus Sirach," *ZAW* 34 (1914) 161–98. Box, G. H. and W. O. E. Oesterley, The *Book of Sirach* (*APOT;* Oxford, 1913). DiLella, A., *The Hebrew Text of Sirach* (The Hague, 1966). Duesberg, H. and P. Auvray, *Le Livre de L'Ecclésiastique* (BJ; Paris, 1958). Hamp, V., *Sirach* (Echter-B; Würzburg, 1951). Haspecker, J., *Gottesfurcht bei Jesus Sirach* (AnalBib 30; Rome, 1967). Kearns, C. J., *Ecclesiasticus* (*CCHS;* N.Y., 1953). Levy, I., *L'Ecclésiastique* (Paris, 1898–1901). Murphy, R. E., *Seven Books of Wisdom* (Milwaukee, 1960). Oesterley, W. O. E., *Ecclesiasticus* (Cambridge, 1912). Peters, N., *Das Buch Jesus Sirach* (Münster, 1913). Pfeiffer, R. H., *History of New Testament Times* (N.Y., 1949). Schilling, O., *Das Buch Jesus Sirach* (HBk; Freiburg, 1956). Segal, M. S., *Sēper ben Sîrā' Ha-šālēm* (Israel, 1958). Smend, R., *Die Weisheit des Jesus Sirach erklärt* (Berlin, 1906). Spicq, C., *L'Ecclésiastique* (*PSB;* Paris, 1946). Vawter, B., *The Book of Sirach* (PPBS; N.Y., 1962).

INTRODUCTION

2 **(I) Name and Author.** For the modern reader who may be bewildered by the problems of authenticity and unity of the biblical books, the work of Sirach comes as a welcome relief. Except for possibly the last chapter, the book of Sirach or Ecclesiasticus was written by one author who signed his name. Although Hebr, Gk, and Syr ms. traditions have confused the issue, scholars are in general agreement that Jesus, son of Eleazar, son of Sira, is the author. The book has two names: Ecclesiasticus, the Church book, either because of the extensive use made of it by the Church, or because of the historical dispute regarding its canonical authority; the Book of ben Sira, or simply Sirach, after the surname of the author whose grandfather seemed to enjoy more prominence (the "ch" is the work of the Gk translator who added it to indicate either the final aleph or the indeclinable nature of the name).

Born and bred in Jerusalem, Sirach was a highly respected scribe and teacher, a man of culture and means, who traveled much in his life possibly as a diplomatic emissary to foreign courts. In later years he ran a school in Jerusalem, imparting to youth his deep knowledge and love of the Scriptures as well as the practical wisdom he had acquired empirically.

3 **(II) Date of Composition.** Scholars have come to agree that the book was written 195–168 BC and most probably *ca.* 180. In his eulogy of Simon, the high priest (50:1–21), who must be Simon II (*ca.* 220–195), Sirach creates the impression that he had only recently died. Furthermore, although storm clouds are brewing, there is no indication in the book that the Maccabean revolt had begun. Finally, Sirach's grandson, the Gk translator, tells us in his prologue that he arrived in Egypt in the thirty-eighth year of Ptolemy Euergetes, who can only be Ptolemy VII (170–116). Working backward two generations from 132 BC, we arrive at a date *ca.* 180 BC. However, some scholars argue that the Gk text implies that the prologue to Sir was written in 116 BC (when Euergetes died), or slightly afterward.

4 **(III) Occasion, Purpose, and Destination.** Sirach's book is essentially an apology for Judaism. Writing to defend the religious and cultural heritage of Judaism against the challenge of Hellenism, he sought to demonstrate to his fellow Jews in Palestine and the Diaspora, and also to well-meaning pagans, that true wisdom resides in Israel. He accomplishes his purpose by producing a synthesis of revealed religion and empirical wisdom.

5 **(IV) Text.** The history of the text of Sir is complicated. The grandson's Gk translation became traditional in the Church and formed the basis of the OL, which was taken into the Vg. It even influenced the Pesh, which was made from the Hebrew (between the 2nd and 4th cents). The Gk text has been preserved in two different forms: that of certain codices—S, B, etc.—and a much longer form in 248 and other cursives. The Hebr text simply dropped out of sight in the early Christian era, apart from a few quotations in rabbinical literature, until 1896–1900 when Solomon Schechter and others discovered in the Cairo Geniza about two-thirds of the book among four fragmentary manuscripts (A, B, C, D). Since then, J. Marcus discovered a leaf of a fifth manuscript (E), in 1931; in 1958 and 1960, J. Schirmann discovered more portions of B and C ; in 1963 a fragmentary scroll (chs. 39–44) was found at Masada.

It would seem that the Cairo manuscripts can ultimately be traced to copies taken from the Qumran caves *ca.* AD 800 and utilized by the Jewish Karaite sect in Egypt (cf. A. DiLella, *CBQ* 24 [1962] 245–67). A very few fragments of Sir, stichometrically arranged like two of the Cairo manuscripts (B and E), were discovered in cave 2 at Qumran, and these must date before AD 68. Although the authenticity of the medieval copies from the Cairo Geniza cannot be denied, it must also be admitted that they show evidence of retroversion from the Syriac (→ Texts, 69:29,30,43).

6 **(V) Canonicity.** Sir is one of the deuterocanonical books; it did not fit into the theology of the Pharisaic part of Judaism, which was responsible for fixing the Jewish canon. The book was generally well received in Judaism as is evident from its use in Jewish worship and literature. Its rejection from the Jewish canon may have been partly because of its recent date, but the chief reason is that it was associated with Sadducean literature. Sirach was no Sadducee, but the tone of the work with its preoccupation with cult, the lack of any appreciation for the afterlife, and minimal messianism put it in a class with later Sadducean tenets.

The Church, however, has always regarded the book as canonical. Not only is its influence seen in the NT, but its canonicity is more frequently attested by the Church Fathers than many protocanonical books. However, owing to the Jewish rejection, doubts arose. The question was definitively settled by the Council of Trent (DB, 783–84).

7 **(VI) Outline.** It is generally agreed that the many attempts to produce a clear outline of Sir have failed, which is not to deny all order. Numerous topics can be isolated and classified as in the CCD edition, which is the basis of this commentary. Yet Sirach's general plan has escaped us. In looking for an explanation, we should remember that Sirach was a Semite and a teacher. It would not be surprising, then, if in assembling his rewritten lecture notes, he would follow a recurring thematic presentation in which many digressions might appear.

In the work, several passages have an introductory nature about them. It is on this basis, to help the modern reader, that the following outline is presented. By no means is it suggested that this necessarily represents Sirach's intentions.

Therefore, the Book of Sirach may be outlined as follows:

- (I) Foreword or Prologue
- (II) Section 1 (1:1–16:21)
  - (A) Praise of Wisdom (1:1–29)
    - (a) The Divine Origin of Wisdom (1:1–8)
    - (b) Fear of the Lord (1:9–18)
    - (c) How Man Obtains Wisdom (1:19–29)
  - (B) Duties Toward God (2:1–18)
  - (C) Duties Toward Parents (3:1–16)
  - (D) Humility (3:17–28)
  - (E) Alms for the Poor (3:29–4:10)
  - (F) The Rewards of Wisdom (4:11–19)
  - (G) Sincerity and Justice (4:20–31)
  - (H) Against Presumption (5:1–10)
  - (I) Sincerity in Speech (5:11–6:4)
  - (J) True Friendship (6:5–17)
  - (K) Blessings of Wisdom (6:18–37)
  - (L) Conduct in Public Life (7:1–17)
  - (M) Duties of Family Life, Religion, and Charity (7:18–36)
  - (N) Prudence in Dealing with Other Men (8:1–19)
  - (O) Advice Concerning Women (9:1–9)
  - (P) Choice of Friends (9:10–16)
  - (Q) Concerning Rulers (9:17–10:5)
  - (R) The Sin of Pride (10:6–18)
  - (S) True Glory (10:19–11:6)
  - (T) Moderation (11:7–28)
  - (U) Care in Choosing Friends (11:29–12:18)
  - (V) Caution Regarding Associates (13:1–14:2)
  - (W) Use of Wealth (14:3–19)
  - (X) The Search for Wisdom and Its Blessings (14:20–15:10)
  - (Y) Man's Free Will (15:11–20)
  - (Z) God's Punishment of Sinners (16:1–21)
- (III) Section 2 (16:22–23:27)
  - (A) Divine Wisdom Seen in Creation (16:22–17:18)
  - (B) Appeal for a Return to God (17:19–27)
  - (C) The Divine Power and Mercy (18:1–13)
  - (D) The Necessity of Prudence (18:14–29)
  - (E) Self-Control (18:30–19:4)
  - (F) The Proper Use of Speech (19:5–16)
  - (G) How to Recognize True Wisdom (19:17–26)
  - (H) Conduct of the Wise and the Foolish (20:1–30)
  - (I) Sin Must Be Avoided (21:1–10)
  - (J) The Wise and the Foolish Differ (21:11–28)
  - (K) On Laziness and Foolishness (22:1–18)
  - (L) The Preservation of Friendship (22:19–26)
  - (M) Prayer (22:27–23:6)
  - (N) The Proper Use of the Tongue (23:7–15)
  - (O) Sins of the Flesh (23:16–27)
- (IV) Section 3 (24:1–32:13)
  - (A) Praise of Wisdom (24:1–31)
  - (B) Those Who Are Worthy of Praise (25:1–11)
  - (C) Wicked and Virtuous Women (25:12–26:18)
  - (D) Dangers to Integrity and Friendship (26:19–27:21)
  - (E) Malice, Anger, and Vengeance (27:22–28:11)
  - (F) The Evil Tongue (28:12–26)
  - (G) Loans, Alms, and Surety (29:1–20)
  - (H) Frugality and Its Rewards (29:21–28)
  - (I) The Training of Children (30:1–13)
  - (J) Health of Soul and Body (30:14–25)
  - (K) The Proper Attitude Toward Riches (31:1–11)
  - (L) Table Etiquette (31:12–32:13)
- (V) Section 4 (32:14–42:14)
  - (A) The Providence of God (32:14–33:18)
  - (B) Property and Servants (33:19–33)
  - (C) Trust in the Lord and Not in Dreams (34:1–17)
  - (D) True Worship of God (34:18–35:24)
  - (E) A Prayer for God's People (36:1–17)
  - (F) Choice of Associates (36:18–37:15)
  - (G) Wisdom and Temperance (37:16–30)
  - (H) Sickness and Death (38:1–23)
  - (I) Vocations of the Craftsmen and the Scribe (38:24–39:11)
  - (J) Praise of God the Creator (39:12–35)
  - (K) Joys and Miseries of Life (40:1–41:13)
  - (L) True and False Shame (41:14–42:8)
  - (M) A Father's Care for His Daughter (42:9–14)
- (VI) Praise of the Fathers (42:15–50:24)
  - (A) The Works of God in Nature (42:15–43:35)
  - (B) Praise of Israel's Great Ancestors (44:1–15)
  - (C) The Early Patriarchs (44:16–23)
  - (D) Praise of Moses, Aaron, and Phinehas (45:1–26)
  - (E) Joshua, Caleb, and the Judges (46:1–20)
  - (F) Nathan, David, and Solomon (47:1–24a)
  - (G) Elijah and Elisha (47:24b–48:16)
  - (H) Hezekiah and Isaiah (48:17–25)
  - (I) Josiah and the Prophets (49:1–10)
  - (J) The Heroes After the Exile (49:11–13)
  - (K) The Earliest Patriarchs (49:14–16)
  - (L) Simon (50:1–24)
- (VII) Epilogue (50:25–29)
- (VIII) Appendices (51:1–30)

COMMENTARY

8 **(I) Foreword or Prologue.** The foreword, written by Sirach's grandson, supplies us with valuable information about the author and the book as well as about the circumstances of its translation. Therefore, it is customary to include it with the text, although it is non-canonical and omitted in some Gk manuscripts and versions, which often carry in its place a spurious prologue of Pseudo-Athanasius. Verse references are based on the numbering in Rahlf's edition of the LXX.

9 **1–2.** *the Law...authors:* The first explicit mention of the Hebr Bible's threefold division of the Scriptures. In his three references to the division, the translator remains sufficiently vague about the third section, thereby implying that this section had not as yet been delineated and still remained incomplete. It is clear that the official title, *Keṯûḇîm* (Writings) had not been assigned. Yet, there is no doubt about the authority of these "other books," for they are enumerated with the Law and the Prophets. **11–12.** In accordance with Dt 4:6, Israel has demonstrated her "instruction and wisdom" to the world by making the truths handed down both the foundation of her moral life and the means for imparting wisdom. The translator is stirring up his own people to a proper appreciation of their heritage as well as attempting to attract his non-Jewish neighbors. The *thorough familiarity* of Sirach's knowledge of the Hebr Bible is amply borne out by his characteristically biblical turn of phrase. This phenomenon has been called "anthological composition," and it is characteristic of the sages (Prv 1–9; Wis). Sirach is both a scribe and a wisdom teacher who injects practical norms for living into his religious instruction. His wisdom counsels are sublimated to the higher purpose of helping his readers make "greater progress" (v. 14) in observing the Law.

15–26. The grandson humbly acknowledges the trials of a translator and the difficulties inherent in translating. He is especially conscious of the necessary loss of the flavor and force of words that occurs in translation. It is interesting to read his criticism of the Gk translations of the books of Scripture, which he offers as an excuse for the deficiencies of his own work. This is the first time we meet the expression "in Hebrew" (v. 22) in reference to the Hebr language.

29. *reproduction:* The obscure Gk word *aphomoion* is understood by many to be synonymous with *aphomoiōma*, "copy" (perhaps a reference to the LXX). Basically, *aphomoion* can mean "something different" and yet also "something like" or "similar," the correct nuance to be arrived at from the context. Therefore, the translation can be either "I found a great difference in teaching," i.e., between Palestinian and Egyptian Jews, which would not fit the context, or "I found a great similarity in teaching," which fits the context well. The grandson feels himself duty-bound to add his grandfather's work to the existing treasure of wisdom. **32.** *in the interval:* During his stay in Egypt probably until the death of Euergetes in 116 BC. He came to Egypt "in the thirty-eighth year" (v. 27), i.e., in 132.

10 **(II) Section 1 (1:1–16:21).** The book begins with a praise of wisdom, which we may regard as an introduction to the first section of the book or even as an introduction to the whole work.

11 **(A) Praise of Wisdom (1:1–29).** In his description of wisdom, Sirach gives us a key to his concept of the term. Absolutely speaking, all wisdom has its origin in God, who freely communicates it to his creation. Moving to a more restricted religious context, the author then considers wisdom from man's point of view. True wisdom has its foundation in the fear of the Lord. Finally, because man is a free creature, he concludes with a series of general admonitions on preserving God's gift, or, if lost, on regaining it.

12 (a) THE DIVINE ORIGIN OF WISDOM (1:1–8). **1.** In this topic sentence, Sirach immediately invites us to contemplate Yahweh, the source of wisdom. Created wisdom—all knowledge of reality, be it in the speculative, practical, ontological, or moral order—has its origin in him who loses nothing by communicating it and who alone knows it in a complete fashion. **3.** *heaven's height:* The language is that of the Gn cosmogony. **4.** The author personifies Wisdom as an intermediate creature between God and the rest of creation, in accordance with Prv 8:22–31. **5–8.** A restatement and clarification of vv. 1–4. Wisdom has its origin from God but is not identifiable with God. Neither is Wisdom accessible because only God fully knows her; yet, she is poured out "upon all his works."

13 (b) FEAR OF THE LORD (1:9–18). **9.** The allusion to God's revelation in v. 8c suggests the effects of God's bounty on the Jews, as well as another foundation of wisdom. The author inserts three aphorisms to illustrate the former and introduce the latter. The consequence of revelation should be the virtue of religion and filial piety expressed by the term "fear of the Lord," which carries with it the reward of material and spiritual well-being. **10.** *length of days:* A long life. A premature death was regarded as a punishment by God. **11.** Sirach held the traditional doctrine of Sheol (cf. 14:16) and of retribution in this world. His solution was that the wicked would receive dire punishment in their last hours (cf. 11:26–28). On the contrary, if a man practiced virtue, he would enjoy not only a long life but also a peaceful death. **12.** *beginning:* From the Gk *archē*, indicating not only time but also that which is essential. Fear of the Lord is regarded as a gift, yet it can be lost (cf. 1:23–24). **15.** *house:* The store of treasures for those who fear God. **16.** *peace:* From Hebr *šālôm*, general well-being and prosperity. **18.** Wisdom based on the proper relationship with God will bring the choice reward of a long life.

14 (c) HOW MAN OBTAINS WISDOM (1:19–29). The sudden break in thought as well as the uncertainty of the Pesh and OL text may suggest that the Gk translation has lost something. Perhaps vv. 19–22 are out of place and should be transposed elsewhere. **19–22.** These verses point up the rewards of wisdom in a practical case. *paragon of prudence:* From Gk *parabolai epistēmēs*, "wise proverbs." Maxims profit the sinner little, inasmuch as he neglects the necessary foundation of true wisdom. **23.** Wisdom seems to be considered a reward for observing the Law, whereas in 24:22, wisdom is identified with the Law. Wisdom pre-existed before creation and is God's lavish gift to the Jews from the beginning of their existence. Yet rejection and loss of this gift are possible if one neglects the fundamental basis of wisdom—fear of the Lord—of which keeping the Ten Commandments is its expression. **29.** *heart full of guile:* Mere external conformity is not enough. Sirach aims his remark at his contemporaries.

15 **(B) Duties Toward God (2:1–18).** Sirach realized that his ideas concerning the true basis of wisdom ran counter to those of the Hellenistic world. Therefore, he warns of trials that will come for one who accepts his teaching. Yet he insists that these are God's tests and suggests patience and trust in God as the means of emerging victoriously. This patience and confidence in God are not without their reward, nor were their fruits unknown in the past. One who compromises is lost, whereas one who is resolute can expect the loving kindness that God shows to those who love him. **1.** *my son:* A traditional form used by wisdom teachers to address their disciples (cf. Prv 1:15; 2:1; 3:1). **5–6.** Using a traditional figure, the author points out that all affliction is under Yahweh's control and directed by his providence. Adversity is not a punishment for the just man but rather a test (cf. 4:17; 33:1). Sirach does not abandon the traditional theory of retribution but only its mechanical application (→ Wisdom Lit, 28:34–36). **7–9.** With a triple exhortation, the author spells out the rewards, the chief of which is mercy—Gk *eleos,* which in the LXX usually translates Hebr *ḥesed,* i.e., that loving concern on the part of God for man as the result of the covenant relationship. **10.** *study the generations:* Sirach sends his students to the Scriptures to prove his point. **12–14.** If the faithful can expect a reward, those who compromise even only externally can expect condemnation. **15–18.** Love and fear are paralleled, for fear denotes not the passion of fear but the virtue of true piety.

16 **(C) Duties Toward Parents (3:1–16).** Fidelity to Yahweh implies many particular virtues, and among them Sirach gives precedence to duties toward parents. In halakic fashion, he comments on the commandment of Ex 20:12 and goes beyond it by promising (3) atonement for sin. No excuse dispenses from this law; he who violates it is like a blasphemer. **1.** *live:* The traditional reward—a long and prosperous life. **3.** *atones for sins:* Cf. 35:1. **5–6.** The traditional blessings, which seem to flow almost according to the law of talion, are enumerated.

17 **(D) Humility (3:17–28).** The haughty attitude of unworthy children suggests the virtue of humility to the author. We are told of its nature and advantages and are reminded of the sad plight of one who does not possess it. **17.** *with humility:* Consciousness of limitations and true position before God as a creature and sinner, but cf. 10:27. **18.** *greater:* Humility is especially important for those in a higher social stratum. **21.** *what is committed:* The Law. Hellenism had brought philosophical speculation to Palestine, which often proved disastrous for the faith of a Jew. **25.** *loves danger:* Dangerous curiosity (cf. 20) about things beyond man's comprehension. Again Sirach has in mind Hellenistic speculation. **28.** *wise men:* The author includes himself here. Faithful disciples are a joy to the master.

18 **(E) Alms for the Poor (3:29–4:10).** If kindness toward parents constitutes a sin offering, so does kindness toward the poor and afflicted. We have here a short discourse on kindness to the traditional downtrodden of the OT—the poor, the orphan, and the widow (cf. Dt 24:14–18). **4:1.** *rob not:* The rich have an obligation to take care of the poor. **7.** One who practices the Law will be praised by the elders in the community. Some, however, would see here an allusion to the many rich who had lost their fortunes in the political upheavals of the time. The assembly would then be the assembly of the poor, and a ruler, a former rich noble.

19 **(F) The Rewards of Wisdom (4:11–19).** Up to this point the author has analyzed the virtue of fidelity to God in its basic aspects of attitude toward God, parents, self, and the downtrodden. Before taking up miscellaneous wisdom topics, he shows the fruits of wisdom in an effort to entice his reader to accept his principles. **11.** *Wisdom:* Personified as a mother who "instructs her children" in the ways of life. **15.** *nations:* Traditionally wisdom is associated with rulers (Prv 8:15), and here the sage will enjoy the dignity of a judge and prince over nations. But this interpretation does not seem to fit the context. Perhaps read with Hebr *'ĕmet,* "in truth," "correctly." Wisdom enables man to discern correctly between true and false. **17.** *test:* Although the Jew is born into the heritage of revelation and therefore true wisdom (1:12), the free individual must co-operate. A period of testing is necessary before he can enjoy its fruits. He must decide whether he will remain faithful.

20 **(G) Sincerity and Justice (4:20–31).** Hellenism had induced many of Sirach's contemporaries to adopt a double standard. The author warns against duplicity and also human respect, and counsels the correct attitude. **20.** *use your time well:* The Hebrew is *šᵉmōr ʿēt hāmôn,* "watch [this] time of confusion," i.e,, we live in critical times that militate against the practice of the Law. **21.** *shame:* Cf. 41:14–42:8. **28.** *even to the death:* As long as you live.

21 **(H) Against Presumption (5:1–10).** The double aspect of avarice mentioned in 4:31 suggests those rich whose pride and presumption lead them to their own perdition. Sirach does not condemn riches as such. Rather, he points out the inherent dangers of self-reliance, begotten by wealth. **1–4.** In typical sapiential style (see 15:11), Sirach warns against the sense of power that "wealth" begets, and against false security. **5–9.** There is no escape from the Lord's punishment for one who fails to convert. The "day of wrath" (10) is the day of the Lord's punishment, marked by some reversal or even by death itself.

22 **(I) Sincerity in Speech (5:11–6:4).** A general proverb concerning opportunism and instability is specified by two rules of conduct regarding speech. **14.** *knowledge:* Competence in a subject that implies an obligation to answer. **17.** *thief:* One who through detraction and calumny has robbed his neighbor of his good name is indeed a thief. **6:2–4.** These lines warn against the danger of uncontrolled desires—a subject that is not in line with the author's admonitions concerning speech.

23 **(J) True Friendship (6:5–17).** The thought of a man isolated as the result of the abuse of speech suggests the opposite result for one who guards his speech. He will have many friends. In friendship, however, caution is the keynote. Sirach stresses the subject of friendship more than any other biblical author; many years of personal experience are doubtlessly reflected in his words. **7.** The basic criterion for discerning a true friend is the ability of the friend to withstand a test. **8–12.** Types of "fair weather" friends. **16.** *life-saving remedy:* Thus in the Greek; the Hebrew has *ṣᵉrôr ḥayyîm,* "bag of life." God was thought to conserve the life of the faithful in a bag (cf. 1 Sm 25:29). The idea is that one is secure when he has a faithful friend. **17.** True piety is the guarantee of true friendship; true friends will be alike in that they both fear God.

24 **(K) Blessings of Wisdom (6:18–37).** In three repetitive strophes, developed by a series of metaphors, Sirach insists that the fruits of wisdom will be attained by him who has determination, perseverance, and docility. **18.** Discipline will insure that one will continue to grow in wisdom until he has reached old age. **23.** *discipline:* The Hebr *mûsār* from *yāsar,* "to admonish," "to chastise," "to instruct." With a play on words, he indicates that discipline is "inaccessible" or withdrawn (also, *mûsār* in Hebr) from the man who is unwilling to subject himself to it. **25–27.** The symbol is that of a slave carrying a burden on his back (cf. Mt 11:29–30). **28.**

The metaphor is that of the chase. **30–31.** He who seems a slave is in reality a king. **37.** Again, wisdom is associated with the Law and described as a gift (cf. 1:23; 15:1; etc.).

25 **(L) Conduct in Public Life (7:1–17).** Inasmuch as true wisdom has its foundation in the Law, conduct in public life necessarily excludes all sin. Pride is the particular danger to avoid. **3.** *sevenfold:* Recompense will be full and repeated. **4–6.** The search for honors, although not wrong in itself, is fraught with dangers. At the court of the Seleucids where some Jews functioned as secretaries and pedagogues, many a moral danger arose. Often as not, principle was compromised. **7.** Favoritism and accepting bribes are meant by "*evil.*" **11.** *embittered man:* One whose affliction was regarded as the result of divine wrath according to the traditional retribution theory. Sirach points out that the principle could not be applied in mechanical fashion. **15.** *laborious tasks:* Some see here an allusion to the work forced upon deported Jews. *farming:* Perhaps an allusion to an agrarian crisis as the result of the Jews' preference for commerce (but cf. 38:25–26).

26 **(M) Duties of Family Life, Religion, and Charity (7:18–36).** Having treated the rules of conduct in public life, Sirach returns to the basic rules of conduct in private life (cf. 3:1–4:10). **29–31.** References to liturgy are relatively rare in OT wisdom literature. **36.** The thought of God's retribution in the last days (which must be sad and desolate for a sinner) should deter man from sin (cf. 1:11).

27 **(N) Prudence in Dealing with Other Men (8:1–19).** Having considered the basic rules of conduct in public and private life, Sirach introduces a series of miscellaneous situations in which prudence must be observed. **1.** *contend:* In a court of law. **2.** *quarrel:* The rich man is able to offer a large bribe to win his case. Sirach insinuates that bribery was commonplace in the courts of his day. **9.** *tradition:* The precepts of wisdom have descended orally from generation to generation. The author indeed has in mind experiential principles, yet the traditions of the Law with its interpretations and adaptations are also intended (cf. Dt 4:9). **10.** *coals:* The classic imagery for evil passion. **15.** *ruthless:* The Hebr *'akzārî*, "daring," "bold." The reckless man will take unwarranted chances. **16.** *desert:* In an isolated place a man can give free vent to his passions.

28 **(O) Advice Concerning Women (9:1–9).** If prudence is necessary in dealing with men, above all it is necessary with women. Relaxed caution spells moral disaster. **1–2.** Two extremes must be avoided regarding one's wife. A lack of confidence provokes sin; too much confidence leads to one's ruin. **5.** *damages:* As a result of becoming involved with the girl (cf. 9:9).

29 **(P) Choice of Friends (9:10–16).** Cf. 6:5–17. **11–12.** The law of retribution is applied to these two instances. **13.** Sirach is wary of the powerful. **14–16.** The wise man will form a prudent estimate of his neighbor's character and then associate with the godly.

30 **(Q) Concerning Rulers (9:17–10:5).** The wise man is the ideal friend. He also makes the ideal ruler. With two transitional verses, the author introduces his new subject, in which he briefly considers the consequences of a good and bad ruler. All authority, he points out, comes from God. **17–18.** The genius of the skilled artisan is manifested by the use of his hands; the wise ruler's genius is evident in the deftness with which he can use his tongue and lead his people successfully. **10:4–5.** In his providence, God takes care that his designs are carried out by his instruments, the rulers of the earth, be they good or bad from the human standpoint.

31 **(R) The Sin of Pride (10:6–18).** Perhaps the thought of rulers whose pride and arrogance were almost taken for granted in the ancient world prompted Sirach to take up here the subject of pride. Pride is the "reservoir of sin" and leads man to destruction. **8.** Probably an allusion to the transfer of power from the Ptolemies to the Seleucids. **13–14.** The historical examples cannot be determined. Perhaps he is alluding to the plagues of Ex 7–11, or the fate of Nineveh or Babylon.

32 **(S) True Glory (10:19–11:6).** True glory does not come to the proud but to the humble man who is wise because he fears God (this basic virtue is mentioned four times in five verses). **21.** The text is uncertain. The point seems to be that, whatever one's social status may be, true glory comes from the fear of God. **22.** Poverty is clearly an ambiguous sign; it could be owing to laziness, or be a punishment, but in some cases ("wise but poor") it was simply an unexplained reality. Hence, the sages' attitude to the poor is ultimately ambivalent. **27.** This saying of Sirach is not to be forgotten in view of all his other statements on this topic; ultimately humility is truth, and proper self-esteem is part of it. **30.** This observation concerns the differences that wealth creates (cf. 13:3,20–22).

33 **(T) Moderation (11:7–28).** In three transitional verses, which could just as easily form the conclusion of the previous section on humility, Sirach introduces an extended consideration of the traditional theory of retribution, which regarded prosperity as a sign of divine pleasure. The touchstone of success, he states, is not how much wealth one has accumulated, inasmuch as such depends on God, but rather how one conducts himself in this life. If an evil man seems to prosper, it results from God's pleasure. All will be righted, however, before a man dies. **10.** *avid for wealth:* Such a man will neglect the pursuit of wisdom (cf. 38:24). **14.** *evil:* The idea of secondary and permissive causality is foreign to OT mentality. Yahweh is the cause of good and evil. **17.** *gift:* Stable prosperity is the recompense for the just. Yet it may be delayed (22). **19.** The miser's lot is death when he does not expect it. **21.** *light:* A metaphor for God's deliverance. **26–28.** The last circumstances of a man's life manifest the type of man he has been (cf. 1:11; 7:36).

34 **(U) Care in Choosing Friends (11:29–12:18).** True friends can never be found among the wicked (29–34), who are, as such, hateful to God (12:1–7). **12:1–2.** The sage is convinced that goodness must somehow be repaid; the effect of kindness will be to secure some reward (2–4). **3–7.** This harsh attitude toward the evil is motivated by v. 7 (cf. 27:24). **7.** *vengeance:* As an enemy of God, the sinner merits just retribution in this life. In Sirach's view, this attitude should be shared by the just on earth in their relations with sinners. Thus, sin and sinner are not distinguished. **13.** Cf. Eccl 10:11. **16.** Cf. 13:4–13.

35 **(V) Caution Regarding Associates (13:1–14:2).** Not only is friendship with the proud rich to be avoided, but even associations with them must be kept at a minimum. In the two-class society of Sirach's day, the poor man was often made to feel the class distinction. Companionship is best found with equals. **3.** The bitter contrast indicates the difference that wealth makes. The impious rich man abuses his rights and is able to pay his way out of difficulty (cf. 8:2; 10:30), whereas the poor man must humble himself to avoid greater evils. **8.** *presumptuous:* In thinking one can get along with the proud rich, a man shows himself to be the fool. **14–15.** The basis for his principle of associating with equals is rooted in nature itself. **20–22.** These lines express the difference that the possession of riches creates (cf. v. 3). **23.** Both wealth and poverty are indifferent in themselves from the moral point of view. It is man's attitude toward them that introduces the moral problem.

36 **(W) Use of Wealth (14:3–19).** If man's attitude is the cause of difficulty regarding wealth, that attitude must be regulated by sound principles. The wise man will not be miserly with his wealth but will share it with others. **5–6.** Without proper self-love, no love of neighbor will follow. **10.** The miser acts and lives as the indigent. **11.** *enjoy:* Cf. Eccl 3:13. There is no question of hedonism here; the fear of God must always regulate man's acts in Sirach's eyes. **12.** *grave's appointed time:* The Hebr *ḥōq liš*ᵉ*'ôl* is "the law of Sheol," i.e., the decree that fixes the date for each man (cf. Is 28:15). **13.** *be good:* The author has hospitality, not alms in mind. **14–16.** The advice is motivated by the deprivation one experiences in the nether world (16). **18–19.** The lesson is resignation to the fact that man and creatures are ephemeral (cf. Eccl 1:4).

37 **(X) The Search for Wisdom and Its Blessings (14:20–15:10).** The man who possesses the basic virtue of the fear of the Lord arrives at wisdom (the pursuit of which is vividly described in vv. 21–27) with all its consequent joys and benefits. **21–27.** Wisdom is personified (Prv 1–9) and dwells in a house. Note the progression in thought: The man pursuing Wisdom at first has to force himself upon her. After he wins her favor as a neighbor, he is finally able to dwell in her abode. **15:1.** *practiced in the Law:* The Hebr *tôpēś tôrâ* is the "scribe." This class studied and taught the Law; Sirach here offers them as the prime examples of those who will attain wisdom, virtually identified with observance of the Law. **2–4.** Wisdom is personified as a "bride" as in Wis 8:2. **10.** *praise:* Praise of Yahweh. Only the just man can offer to God a fitting psalm of praise (cf. Ps 32:1).

38 **(Y) Man's Free Will (15:11–20).** If the men of this world are divided into two camps—the wise and the sinners—it is not God's work but that of man himself. This affirmation of free will is rarely made so forthrightly in the rest of the OT. At the same time, there is no attempt to reconcile this idea with the concept that God is the primary cause of all activity. The choice in v. 17 is reminiscent of Dt 30:15. **11.** *say not:* The typical form used to answer an objection in the *bēt midrāš*, "school" (51:23). The objection presupposed here is that evil and sin are simply owing to God. Sin is not from God, because God hates sin—Sirach's strongest argument against the fatalistic attitude of the objector. **13.** *befall:* God not only hates sin but also preserves the religious man from falling into it. **14.** *man:* Unlike the author of Gn, who was interested in explaining the origin of sin in the human race, Sirach is interested in each individual. *free choice:* The solution to the problem of the origin of sin is man's free will. The Hebr *yēṣer* is not the *yēṣer hārā'* or evil tendency of later rabbinical writings (but cf. *Bib* 39 [1958] 334–44). **20.** *command:* The general principle is reaffirmed. Sin is not from God. The power and omniscience of God spelled out in vv. 18–19 do not militate against the general principle. *lies:* Actions that are contrary to God's precepts.

39 **(Z) God's Punishment of Sinners (16:1–21).** Man is free to choose good or evil but, as the responsible cause, he must expect the wrath of God if he chooses evil. Not only does this doctrine follow from a consideration of the nature of God, the just rewarder or punisher, but history (Sodom and Gomorrah, etc.) itself bears witness to the fact. The excuse of man's insignificance before God is a futile rationalization, as is also the self-deception that man can act in secret without God's knowledge. Note that Sirach shares Ezekiel's individualism in religion (cf. Ez 33:10–20). **1–3.** For one like Sirach, who believes in Sheol, man's life continues in his progeny, as long as they are not godless. **4.** An example of the value of even "one wise man." **6.** Cf. Nm 16 for Korah and his "band." **7.** Cf. Gn 6:4; Wis 14:6. **8.** The sexual abuses of the Sodomites are not mentioned, but rather "pride." **10.** Cf. Nm 11:20; 14:12ff. **11.** *mercy and anger:* Mercy tempers justice, yet the unrepenting wicked cannot benefit. **15.** *say not:* Cf. 15:11. The foolish thoughts of the sinner are presented in vv. 15–21. *spirits:* The Hebrew is *rûḥôt*, i.e., the world of living men (cf. Gn 2:7).

40 **(III) Section 2 (16:22–23:27).** Because of the solemn tone and the similarity of this passage to 1:1–18, many regard it as the beginning of a new, major part of the book.

41 **(A) Divine Wisdom Seen in Creation (16:22–17:18).** With the usual sapiential opening, Sirach introduces a treatise on divine wisdom in creation. In typical OT wisdom fashion, he interprets creation under the aspect of the economy of salvation by joining to the works of creation the saving acts of God toward Israel. All the while, the point is made clear that man's wisdom is but a reflection of divine wisdom. Man may hold a privileged position in creation, especially true of the Israelite who has received God's special favor, yet he is a debtor to God. He is free to follow or betray the wisdom he has received, but he can expect compensation for his actions. **24.** *assigned their tasks:* Greek *diesteilen meridas autōn.* If the Greek is rendered according to the CCD, Sirach would move immediately to the first works of adornment of Gn 1:14. Many, however, would take *diastellō* in the sense of separation, thus seeing in this verse the works of separation of Gn 1:3–13. **25.** *ordered:* Regardless of which way the Greek is rendered in v. 24, this verse refers to the works of adornment of the fourth day. Sirach has in mind particularly the stars (cf. Gn 1:14–19). **26.** The author stresses the constancy of the stars to emphasize later the contrasting position of man. **28.** *return:* With a melancholy note, more explicit than in Gn, Sirach points out the limits of life on earth.

17:3. The "power" of man is a participation in the dominion of God. **6.** Here, Sirach parts with Gn, which says nothing of "wisdom" being given to man. *good and evil:* In Gn, man knows evil only after the fall. Sirach gives a liberal interpretation of the Gn narrative; he does not consider man before and after the fall but takes him in his present actual situation. **7–8.** *works... deeds:* Both in nature and history, but for Israel it was especially in history that God's works were revealed. **9–10.** *knowledge:* Revelation. Sirach explicitly joins the economy of salvation with creation by introducing the Sinai covenant. **11.** *eyes beheld:* The author alludes to the elements of the Sinai theophany. In Gn, all Adam heard was Yahweh's voice. **14.** This idea is reflected in Dt 4:19–20; 32:8–9; Dn 10:13–21. **18.** *requite:* No indication is given on the time or manner of retribution.

42 **(B) Appeal for a Return to God (17:19–27).** Sirach has explained man's position in the universe and has contrasted that position with the rest of creation. In so doing, he has pointed out two classes of men, the good and the bad. But he also realizes that even an evil man has a chance to change his status. Provided he repents, he may turn from his way of sin to the merciful God who will receive him. The author extends the invitation and bids the sinner to make haste. **19.** *losing hope:* Those who are despairing of God's mercy even though they have decided to repent. **20.** The three conditions of repentance are enumerated. *make your offenses few:* The Greek is *smikrynon proskomma*, "make small a stumbling block," i.e., remove any obstacle to

God's service (cf. 1 Cor 8:9; Rom 9:32). **22–23.** The time of repentance is this life, for both good and bad go to the shadowy existence in Sheol and are incapable of praising God (cf. Pss 6:6; 30:10; etc.). Sirach has often pointed out that God visits the wicked with a premature death as a punishment. **26.** *thoughts of flesh and blood:* The text is uncertain; the CCD indicates man's inability to understand God's designs.

43 **(C) The Divine Power and Mercy (18:1–13).** Not content with the disproportion between God and man as far as their natures are concerned, the author stresses the superiority of God in his works. Although the disproportion is without measure, the sinner must remember that of all God's works, one of the greatest is his tender concern for man, which far surpasses any human mercy. **1–4.** God is truly the incomparable one. **5.** Finite man cannot comprehend the infinite (cf. Ps 139:18). **6.** Man is insignificant (cf. Ps 8). **7.** *hundred years:* Sirach is exaggerating the limits of the life span to emphasize his point (cf. Ps 90:10). **9–10.** The reason for the Lord's mercy. **11.** A vivid contrast between one's neighbor ("fellow man") and the whole realm of creation ("all flesh").

44 **(D) The Necessity of Prudence (18:14–29).** Sirach has spelled out man's place in the universe and has classified the various types of men. The wise man will observe the commandments; the fool will disregard them. With the foundation well laid, he takes up specific points of conduct, all loosely connected. Beginning with the virtue of charity, suggested by the charity of God in the preceding verses, he moves on abruptly to consider prudence and circumspection. **14.** The manner of giving is more important than the gift itself. **15.** *burning wind:* The sirocco, the effects of which are tempered by the "dew." **19.** *visitation:* Of the Lord, when he intervenes to reward man (in this life). **20.** *repentance:* Cf. 17:19. **21.** *distress:* As a visitation of divine wrath for sin. **24.** *day of death:* Sirach, looking for divine retribution in this life, regarded the day of death as the time God would repay man for his deeds, if he had not already done so (cf. 11:26–28).

45 **(E) Self-Control (18:30–19:4).** A particular case in which the prudent man reveals himself is found in his mastery over sensual desires. The fool lacks this control and thereby brings upon himself not only loss of fortune but spiritual and physical ruin. **32.** *pleasures:* Sirach means especially gastronomic pleasures (33). *poverty redoubled:* The double poverty of purse and health. **19:3.** *rottenness and worms:* His punishment will be a premature death. The motivation is enlightened self-interest.

46 **(F) The Proper Use of Speech (19:5–16).** Control of the tongue is a commonplace warning among the sages. A most difficult task for man is silence when the neighbor's reputation is at stake. However, the law of silence is not absolute. The true facts must be ascertained and fraternal correction given if necessary. **9.** *burst:* The image is that of new wine placed in a wineskin (cf. Jb 32:18). **11.** *arrow:* The speedy removal of the arrow is the point of the comparison. **12.** *admonish:* The Greek, *elegchō*, has a twofold sense of questioning and correcting; the proper nuance is arrived at from the context.

47 **(G) How to Recognize True Wisdom (19:17–26).** The mention of the Law in the preceding verse suggests an excursus on true and false wisdom. A man may possess intellectual talent, speculative knowledge, and a shrewdness in using that knowledge. Yet, the true criterion for determining a wise man is not found in these qualifications but in the possession of that basic virtue of fear of the Lord. **17.** *all wisdom:* At first sight, it seems that Sirach makes an explicit identification of the fear of the Lord and wisdom and then extends that identification further by equating the Law and wisdom. Thus, we have expressed the following thesis: wisdom = fear of the Lord = the Law. Many authors hold this opinion. On closer examination, however, the author seems to express no more than he did in his introduction—that the virtue of the fear of the Lord is the basis of true wisdom (cf. 1:12–18). This interpretation is suggested by a consideration of the Gk text of v. 17b. In the Gk *kai en pasē sophia poiēsis nomou* of v. 17b, we must give some consideration to the preposition *en*. Thus, it might be rendered, "and in complete wisdom, there is a fulfillment of the Law." If such is true, and the parallelism with v. 17a is synonymous, then the *pasa sophia phobos Kyriou* of v. 17a could be rendered, "complete wisdom [includes] the fear of the Lord." **19.** *detestable:* Shrewdness in itself is not bad, but if it concentrates on evil and leads to sin, it becomes bad. *simple man:* One lacking in intelligence can be in a better position than a shrewd man who commits sin. **20.** Sirach doubtless has in mind the Hellenists of his day. The young men of his time were contrasting the Hellenistic intelligentsia with those Jews who had nothing to do with Hellenism. He wishes to point out that the simple equations, intelligence = wisdom, stupidity = folly, are not valid because the essential criterion for determining the sage is fear of the Lord. **25.** The sages thought that both folly and wisdom never failed to be revealed in outward deportment (cf. v. 26).

48 **(H) Conduct of the Wise and the Foolish (20:1–30).** In a lengthy series of often paradoxical and loosely connected maxims, which may be unified under the general theme of the use of the tongue, Sirach witnesses to the complexity of human existence and at the same time indicates a practical course of action in the various circumstances of life. The lessons he teaches are brought home to the reader by means of contrast. The fool will always bungle either by failing to size up a situation properly or by displaying his disregard for the moral law. **1.** *admonition:* Sirach returns to the subject of fraternal correction initiated in 19:12. **3.** An admonition given under passion will bring with it external compliance, but it will not remove the internal sinful attitude. **8–10.** Silence is an ambiguous factor; it has to be interpreted (cf. Prv 10:19; 17:27–28). The wise man does not judge from appearances alone. **8–11.** A series of paradoxes. **13.** *equal to seven:* He will expect in return much more than he gives. **14.** *criticizes:* He criticizes because he has not received gifts in return. **16.** *eat his bread:* The fool thinks that he can buy popularity, not realizing that true friendship cannot be discerned in time of prosperity (cf. 12:8). **19.** Cf. Prv 26:7. **20.** *in this tranquility:* The Greek is *en tē anapausei autou ou katanygēsetai*, "in his rest, he will not be troubled." The man whose poverty keeps him from sinning is like the man who appears wise because he is silent (cf. 20:5). Such a one does not necessarily differ from the loquacious fool just because of the appearance of virtue. **21.** *shame:* Silence proceeding from false modesty can lead to ruin. **27–28.** Factual observations, not moral advice. **29–30.** The wise man has an obligation to teach wisdom. If he does not, he is acting less wise than the fool who has at least the wisdom to keep silence.

49 **(I) Sin Must Be Avoided (21:1–10).** Since the truly wise man possesses the virtue of the fear of the Lord, one who desires wisdom must give up sin, return to God, and be careful to avoid sin in the future. **1.** Cf. 17:20. **2.** *souls of men:* The lives of men. **3.** *two-edged sword:* The author instills a vivid horror of sin by referring to the sword used by the Thracian mercenaries of his time. **5.** *is heard:* By God. *justice:* The Gk *krima* is "judgment," God's judgment in his favor. **8.** *funeral mound:* Such a man can expect the punishment of a premature death. **9.** *bundle of tow:* The comparison of criminals with inflammable tow, destined to be destroyed by fire, is an apt figure to express their final disgrace. *flaming fire:* Their corpses will be relegated to the smoldering rubbish dump located in the Hinnom Valley outside Jerusalem's walls. **10.** *smooth stones:* The Gk *'omalismenē ek lithōn* means "made level without stones." Paved roads were unknown in the East in this period. Keeping the roads in repair meant leveling the ridges made by the wheeled vehicles in use as well as removing stones. The "smooth stones" accelerate the sinners' progress to Sheol. These last two verses, taken out of the total context of the book, might seem to imply some idea of penal retribution in Sheol for the wicked. The Christian can understand them as expressing the eternal punishment of the wicked. But Sirach did not share this understanding, for it is inharmonious with his general teaching. Life after death was a shadowy existence in Sheol for both good and bad (cf. 14:16; 17:22–23; 28:21; 41:4; 48:5). Consequently, he treats the whole problem of retribution in terms of this life (cf. 1:11; 7:1–3; 10:13–17; 11:26–28; 16:14; 23:14–26; 27:3; 34:13–17; 41:5–10; 44:10–13).

50 **(J) The Wise and the Foolish Differ (21:11–28).** The fear of the Lord forms the basis for the sharp contrast between the sage and the fool. The sage who has this virtue will welcome and acquire knowledge. As a result, both his words and conduct will command respect. The fool, lacking this virtue, will scorn words of wisdom and reveal himself in his language and actions. **11.** *impulses:* Probably a reference to the *yēṣer hārā'* or "evil instinct" of later rabbinical literature, which almost corresponds to our idea of concupiscence. Many see here an allusion to the reality of original sin. Although Sirach admits the presence of such impulses, he believes that man can control them, thus placing the origin of sin once again in man's free will (cf. 15:14). **13.** *flood:* The Greek is *kataklysmos.* Inasmuch as it implies something catastrophic, some suggest that the Gk translator read Hebr *mabbul,* the technical word for the flood of Gn, instead of *mabbua'*, a spring of water. **18.** *inscrutable words:* As formulas without meaning (cf. 20:19). **20.** This verse is out of place; v. 21 should be read after v. 19 for antithesis. *laughter:* Without restraint. Even in the expression of joy, the fool and sage are distinguished. **22–24.** The wise man observes proper etiquette, also beyond the fool because it demands self-control. **26.** Fools talk without thinking, but the sage does not express all his thoughts; if he does speak, he thinks beforehand.

51 **(K) On Laziness and Foolishness (22:1–18).** Sirach digresses and concentrates on the lot of the fool. In a series of loosely connected maxims he gives various consequences of folly and counsels the proper course of action in dealing with the fool. Finally, he returns to his original theme by contrasting the constancy of the sage with the instability of the fool. **3.** *poverty:* An unruly daughter brings financial loss as well as disgrace; no one will agree to marry her, and she must be supported at home. **4.** *shameless:* The thought is the same as v. 3b. Some, however, render Gk *kataischynousa* as "one bringing shame," i.e., to her husband. This situation results in grief for the girl's father, because it is his fault that she was not raised properly. **6.** *lashes:* The wisdom teachers are strong believers in corporal punishment (cf. Prv 13:24; 19:18; 22:15; 23:13–14). **11.** *seven days:* The traditional time of mourning is contrasted with "lifetime." **14–15.** Cf. 21:16. Any burden or calamity is preferable to association with the fool. **16.** This common method of construction was of practical necessity in such an area as Palestine. **18.** *small stones:* A reference to the Palestinian custom of placing small pebbles on the walls surrounding a vineyard or garden so that any animals attempting to jump the wall would knock them off, thus attracting the custodian's attention.

52 **(L) The Preservation of Friendship (22:19–26).** Constancy in one's resolve suggests constancy in friendship. Such constancy breaks down at times, but it is only a deliberate violation of moral virtue, which irreparably destroys friendship. On the other hand, standing by one's friend in time of adversity brings its reward. **21–22.** Actions that spring from anger in a moment of dispute do not necessarily result in a broken friendship, for in calmer moments the situation can be righted. *insult...attack:* Such acts are premeditated and deliberate. The result is irreparable. **23.** *poor:* Those in poverty or adversity who needed friends were most usually found without them because poverty and adversity were regarded as just punishments from God for sin. But in this situation true friendship is demonstrated (cf. 6:8; 12:1). The man's poverty or adversity is no deterrent because the mechanical application of the theory of retribution is not valid (cf. 2:5). *thus:* The result of such action will have its reward. Sirach does not offer "prosperity" simply as a motive but as a logical outcome. **24.** This verse breaks the thought and would fit better after v. 20.

53 **(M) Prayer (22:27–23:6).** To conclude this section, Sirach considers at length two areas of human conduct—language and sex—wherein man perhaps experiences the most difficulty in observing the basic virtue of fear of the Lord. To introduce these topics, he offers prayer to God asking divine help for himself so that he might avoid the sins connected with them. The text is somewhat uncertain as the variants in the versions show. Many authors resort to rearranging the order of the verses to enable the sequence of thought to flow more smoothly. A common suggestion is to regard 23:1 as a doublet of 23:4 and to eliminate it on that score. Thus, 22:27–23:3 would form the introduction to the prayer and 23:4–6 the prayer proper. This suggestion is hardly necessary. Inasmuch as two subjects follow the prayer, we might look for two prayers. One deals with the tongue, 22:27 serving as the introduction to the prayer in 23:1; the other deals with sex, with 23:23 forming the introduction for the prayer in 23:4–6. **22.** *who will:* A Hebraism to express the wish—would that there were! **23:2.** *to my mind:* The Gk *epi tēs kardias* means "to my heart." In Semitic thought, the heart symbolizes the intellectual aspect of man. **5–6.** Sirach humbly acknowledges his dependence on God to overcome evil. At first reading, he seems to place the source of evil in man's evil tendency. But in 15:14–15, he also places the blame for evil squarely on man's free choice. Nevertheless, Sirach is not oblivious to the fact that man must struggle against his evil impulses (cf. 21:11).

54 **(N) The Proper Use of the Tongue (23:7–15).** The man who lacks control over his tongue soon becomes a slave to it and invites disaster. Sirach warns especially about swearing, blasphemy, coarse talk, and abusive language, all of which betrays a man's character. **11.** *in error:* Falsely, when he knows the opposite is true. *doubly great:* Not only does he break an oath, thereby offending God, but, by not living up to his word, he offends his neighbor. **12.** *words which merit death:* An allusion to blasphemy, a sin so great that Sirach will not mention it explicitly.

55 **(O) Sins of the Flesh (23:16–27).** Using a numerical proverb, Sirach introduces his consideration of three types of sins of the flesh, all indeed grave, but the third, adultery, is the worst. This third type is given a more lengthy treatment. Not only does it bring with it social sanctions, but above all it violates the Law of God and betrays the sinner as one who lacks the foundation of wisdom. **16.** *for burning passion... breaks forth:* The reference seems to be to a man given to solitary sins of impurity. This then would constitute the first term of the numerical proverb. **17.** *all bread:* The fornicator is not hard to please. Women of any social condition, even the harlot, satisfy him. **21.** *punished:* Because death is not mentioned, the sanction of Lv 20:10 may have been mitigated to that of public scourging (cf. Prv 5:11–14; 6:32–33). *apprehended:* Taken by officials, for public punishment. **24–25.** *punishment:* Besides public scourging, the woman suffered divorce, loss of property rights, and expulsion from the house. The illegitimate children accompanied her, thereby sharing in her disgrace and punishment. **27.** *thus:* This verse certainly concluded the previous consideration of sins of the flesh. Some authors see here also a solemn closing for the first part of the book, or at least the section that began in 16:22.

56 **(IV) Section 3 (24:1–32:13).**

(A) Praise of Wisdom (24:1–31). Sirach introduces his next series of practical subjects with a praise of wisdom that surpasses other similar passages because of its doctrine and poetic beauty. Therefore, it has emerged as one of the most celebrated chapters of the book. Personified Wisdom describes herself as God's first creature who played an intermediate role in the creation of all things. Again, it is in Israel that wisdom is found in a special way. This time, however, she is sent by God's express command. Speaking in his own name, Sirach explicitly identifies wisdom with the Law for the first time. He has implied as much previously in insisting on the religion of Israel as the basis for true wisdom. Now, however, wisdom is the Torah, the book that contains the precise mode of action for men. He does not exclude experiential wisdom; nor does he limit wisdom to the moral order alone. He does insist that the Book of the Covenant not only manifests the basis of Wisdom but makes her incarnate. Finally, Sirach the teacher speaks. He compares himself to a stream in which the waters of wisdom course until they overflow; Sirach must communicate his wisdom to others.

3. *from the mouth:* Just as all creation was the result of God's Word, so also wisdom. Many see here an allusion to, and a prefiguring of, the doctrine of the Logos (cf. Jn 1:1–14 and C. Spicq, *Mémorial Lagrange* [Paris, 1940] 183–95). Although Sirach cannot be said to propose that wisdom is a person, his thought did prepare the way for later revelation. *mistlike:* A symbolic reference to wisdom as the *rûaḥ 'ĕlōhîm* (the spirit of God), which totally enveloped the earth. Wisdom pre-existed with God and participated in all the works of creation (cf. Gn 1:2; 2:6). **4.** *pillar of cloud:* Cf. Ex 13:21–22. The pillar in the desert was the manifestation of God's presence. Wisdom's proper abode is thus with God. **5–6.** Wisdom also finds a place in all creation both animate and inanimate (cf. 1:8). **7.** *resting place:* A special abode on earth. **8.** *formed me:* Sirach clearly regards Wisdom as a personification; she came to dwell in Jacob, i.e., Israel. **9.** This summary statement of the preceding verses serves as an introduction to the more complete description of wisdom's role in Israel that follows. **10–12.** Sirach's interest in cult becomes evident (cf. 50:1–21). **13–17.** In the rich poetic imagery of beautiful Palestinian flora, personified Wisdom describes the privileged position of Israel brought about by her active and special presence. **18–21.** The invitation is now given to seek the true wisdom of Israel. Sirach undoubtedly has in mind primarily those Jews who were enticed by Hellenism. It is said that 24:20–21 inspired Bernard's hymn, *Jesu Dulcis Memoria.* **22.** With the discourse by Wisdom completed, the author in his own reflections moves to specify wisdom in Israel by identifying it with the Law. It is by means of the Law that people adhere to wisdom; it is by its knowledge and practice that man becomes truly wise. And it is Israel's prime possession and heritage (cf. Dt 4:6–8). **23–25.** Sirach mentions the four rivers of Gn 2, to which he adds the Jordan and the Nile. Some propose to identify here the Pishon with the Indus and the Gihon with the Nile. However, it seems clear from the parallelism that Sirach has six rivers in mind, which he uses as fertility symbols. The agricultural time indications cover all the stages of growth. Thus, wisdom as manifested in creation and arrived at by sapiential experience is symbolically joined to revealed wisdom, which has spread from Israel to the Diaspora. **26–27.** *first... last:* Hebraism for all the world. Some, however, understand the terms in a temporal sense. These verses are the *locus classicus* quoted by the Church Fathers in support of the abundance of the scriptural sense.

57 **(B) Those Who Are Worthy of Praise (25:1–11).** After his lofty praise of wisdom, the author takes up again practical precepts. For the next several chapters he will consider various aspects of conduct in family life and society. He begins with two modified numerical proverbs in which charity is opposed to vices, which stifle it. After a slight digression on old age, he resumes the numerical device, this time in its classic usage. Nine manifestations of wisdom deserve praise, but the tenth surpasses all. Again, fear of the Lord is the basis of all true wisdom. **3–6.** Old age and wisdom are normally companions, as in Prv 16:31 (but cf. Wis 4:7–9). **7.** *lives to see:* Not to be understood of a man harboring a merely revengeful spirit. We must remember Sirach's view of retribution in this life; the man rejoices because God's justice is manifested (cf. Prv 24:17–18). **8.** *inferior:* Of lower social status. Perhaps, however, it is an allusion to the heathen in Palestine. **10.** *wisdom:* Culture and experiential knowledge of human affairs.

58 **(C) Wicked and Virtuous Women (25:12–26:18).** Sirach is no misogynist, but he writes from the male point of view dominant in Israelite culture. The wicked woman must be either controlled by her husband or divorced. The praise of the virtuous woman dispels any idea of misogynism. He beautifully describes the virtuous woman and her contribution to man's happiness. **13.** *foes:* In context, this general proverb is applied to a wicked woman. **23.** *sin's beginning:* Alluding to Gn 3:1–24, the author recalls the simple sequence of events in Gn, much in the fashion of 1 Tm 2:14. *because of her:* The transmission of original sin and its punishments was owing to Adam as head of the human race (cf. Rom 5:12). In this context, Sirach finds it expedient to emphasize woman's role: Because she played a part in Adam's downfall, she shares in the responsibility for the punishment. **25.** *cut her away:* Divorce her. In Gn 2:24 the two marriage partners become one flesh, but Mosaic Law permitted divorce (cf. Dt 24:1–4).

26:5–6. A numerical proverb in which the last element, "a jealous wife," is the worst of all. **9.** *eyelids:* Either synonymous for eyes or perhaps an allusion to cosmetics (cf. Jer 4:30). **18.** After this verse, some Gk manuscripts give additional, noncanonical verses, as noted in the CCD translation.

59 **(D) Dangers to Integrity and Friendship (26:19–27:21).** Sirach stresses the dangers that threaten man's integrity; commerce poses a particular danger. A man so engaged can be drawn into dishonesty; therefore, rules are necessary. This concept leads to a more general consideration of the use of the tongue. The section ends with the evil of betraying a confidence. **27:2.** *peg:* A tent peg wedged between stones for stability. **4.** *husks:* The Gk *kopria* means "refuse." After the grain has been threshed, it is placed in a sieve. The refuse, including straw and dung, remains behind. **8.** *attain it:* The author recognizes the possibility of honesty and virtue. **12.** *limit the time:* The same expression as 4:20. In this context, however, it refers to time wasted in the company of the godless. **21.** *hopeless:* Once a confidence is betrayed reconciliation is hopeless.

60 **(E) Malice, Anger, and Vengeance (27:22–28:11).** The insincere man brings hatred upon himself, but the wise man avoids vengeance, which belongs to God. He controls his anger, avoids strife, and forgives his enemies for God's sake as well as his own. **22.** *shifty eyes:* Cf. Prv 6:13. **25–27.** Examples of the inexorable law of retribution. **29.** *pain:* Either the evils of this life or a premature death. Sirach holds fast to the traditional idea of retribution (cf. Jb 21:20–21). **28:2.** Verses 3–5 are almost a commentary on the sixth petition of the "Our Father." It represents a definite advance from the law of talion. **3.** *healing:* In the moral sense of forgiveness (cf. Is 6:10; Jer 3:22). **6–7.** Motivation does not go beyond the perspective of this life. **10.** *strength:* Not in the material but in the moral sense, stemming from his social rank.

61 **(F) The Evil Tongue (28:12–26).** Resuming the specific theme of the use of the tongue, Sirach treats at length the curse of an evil tongue, one of his favorite topics (5:12–6:1; 19:5–16; 20:17–25; 23:7–15). **12.** *both:* Man's tongue can be used for good or evil, peace or strife; the alternative is up to him. **14.** *meddlesome:* Lit., "third tongue." It is a technical term in rabbinical writings for the slanderer. It may refer to the third person who goes between friends or to the three victims affected by slander—the slanderer, the one slandered, and the one who believes the slander. **21.** *gain:* Physical death and the shadowy existence in Sheol are preferable to the harm caused by evil tongues.

62 **(G) Loans, Alms, and Surety (29:1–20).** Another problem of living in society is that of loaning money to others. This activity is fraught with dangers and the fear of loss will keep many from practicing it. Yet a generous soul will regard it as a form of alms and act out of obedience to God's Law. He will also post surety for his neighbor. In this affair, however, as in others, caution is Sirach's practical counsel. **29:1.** The Law forbade the taking of interest; thus, it is not mentioned here. Loans were regarded as one form of fraternal charity. **3.** The man who repays his loan can reasonably expect another if a new need arises. **4.** *adds:* Because he does not repay the loan. **8.** *alms:* A loan for which there is no hope of repayment becomes an alms. **19.** The good man who posts surety for another may find himself ruined as a result of man's wickedness. The sinner who posts surety for the sake of profit inevitably comes to ruin. **20.** Sirach's conclusion is that such action, if caution and prudence are observed, is an act of charity. On the contrary, many old proverbs counsel against the practice (cf. Prv 11:15; 17:18; 22:26).

63 **(H) Frugality and Its Rewards (29:21–28).** Sirach has dealt with the obligations of the man of means. He now turns to the poor man. Economic independence and contentment with basic needs have their rewards. The man who sacrifices his independence to live more sumptuously as a parasite on the rich dooms himself to a life of misery. **24–25.** The parasite paid his way by performing menial tasks in the homes of the rich. **27.** *brother:* Understood here in a broad sense.

64 **(I) The Training of Children (30:1–13).** The author returns to practical wisdom in the family circle and treats the important topic of child-rearing. This subject always has practical interest, but it was all the more important for those who expected rewards merely in this life, because only a careful education of children could bring satisfaction in later years. His practical counsel corresponds to the old adage, "Spare the rod and spoil the child." **6.** The "avenger" and the "one to repay" is his son. **7.** *wounds:* The parallelism suggests that these are the wounds of the child. The pampering parent will have no peace.

65 **(J) Health of Soul and Body (30:14–25).** Good health and contentment are personal benefits that outstrip even riches, whereas constant illness is a scourge to which death is preferable. One means to preserve health is to hold fast to a cheerful disposition and to avoid those things that render it impossible. **18.** The custom of placing food on tombs is considered futile. **19.** The common polemic against idols is used in a new context (cf. Dt 4:28). **22–24.** Sirach is motivated by his view of the life in Sheol, but his observations are rooted in experience. **25.** Following a less ancient ms. archetype, in which two pairs of leaves were transposed, all Gk manuscripts place 30:25–33:16a after 33:16b–36:10a. The present order follows Heb, Pesh, and OL; it makes better sense and is undoubtedly the true order.

66 **(K) The Proper Attitude Toward Riches (31:1–11).** Linking his treatment of riches with the previous topic by showing how undue care for wealth destroys health of body and soul, Sirach proceeds to point out the moral dangers involved for the man seeking riches (1–7). The just rich man, rare as he may be, is worthy of special praise (8–11). **5.** Inordinate desire for riches leads to sin. **8.** *gain:* The Hebrew is *māmôn*, a word of Aram origin (cf. Mt 6:24). **9.** *who is he:* Such a man is rarely found.

67 **(L) Table Etiquette (31:12–32:13).** Following the example of his Egyptian predecessors (see *ANET* 412–13), Sirach gives a small code of table etiquette. His guiding principle is that good manners must be predicated on good morals. **13.** This obscure verse seems to moralize on the significance of tears. **21.** Sirach obviously envisions an exceptional case with no hint of evil intent, not the deliberate practice of the Roman pagans. He intends his advice as a medical remedy. **32:1.** *chosen:* An allusion to the Gk custom of choosing a banquet chief whose duties included the invitation list, placement at table, etc. Sirach does not condemn in principle the practice that had been introduced into Palestine, but rather sets down proper rules of conduct regarding it. **3.** The old sage has the right to speak, yet moderation and consideration for others are necessary. **7.** *more than once:* The Hebr *beḥōzeq paʿămayîm wešālôš* means "at the most two or three times." The young man is to join in the conversation seldom and only if asked to do so. His role is to learn wisdom from others. **9.** *insistent:* With questions. **11–12.** At "home" one can relax from the rules of society, but never to the point of sin.

68 **(V) Section 4 (32:14–42:14).** With a quick succession of themes and ideas already developed in earlier chapters, the author seems to introduce a new section of his book.

69 **(A) The Providence of God (32:14–33:18).** Sirach's intention is to bring his reader to share his own convictions that God controls his universe and that all men, although different, contribute to the divine plan. Unlike pagan determinists, however, the author assumes free will on man's part and exhorts his reader to base his life on the Law and to follow the wisdom of the sages. Thus, the polemic against Hellenism continues. The author concludes by asserting his right to speak. **15.** *the hypocrite:* He who studies the Law but does not observe it; hence, it will be his downfall. **33:3.** *oracle:* Hebrew *kā'ûrîm.* A reference to the Urim and Thummim (cf. Ex 28:30). The Law is as infallible a guide as a direct revelation from God. **7–11.** The author intends to show that just as it is God's will that some days are celebrated as feast days and others as ordinary days, so it is his will that differences among men exist. **12.** The groups mentioned are, successively, the Israelites, the priests and Levites, and the Canaanites. Yet Sirach probably also has in mind the pagan nations of his day. **14–15.** The author affirms the existence of contrasts even among men and insists on the divine will as operative also in this case. One cannot validly conclude that he denies here what he has so firmly insisted upon elsewhere (free will, in 15:11–20). In typical OT fashion, he simply avoids the problem of reconciling the divine causality and human freedom.

70 (B) Property and Servants (33:19–33). Sirach once again begins his particular counsels. Although the Law prescribed generosity and mercy, these precepts do not excuse men from using prudence. One must neither allow oneself to become dependent upon others nor allow an unruly slave any quarter. Although Sirach takes slavery for granted, his attitude toward the dignity of the human person who happens to be a slave is remarkable for the time in which he lived. **25–26.** The hard life of a beast of burden and the life of a slave are compared. **31.** *your life's blood:* With your own money. **33.** A runaway slave was lost forever (cf. Dt 23:15–16).

71 (C) Trust in the Lord and Not in Dreams (34:1–17). The author groups together three apparently different themes: the vanity of dreams; wisdom through experience; and confidence in the Lord. His object is to teach prudence: The prudent sage practices no superstition, enriches himself by experience, and relies on God in all undertakings. **34:1.** *dreams:* Sirach demonstrates his hostility to dreams, an attitude that would hardly be shared by the superstitious world in which he lived. In general, he was following the attitude of Israelite legislators and prophets (cf. Dt 13:2–6; Jer 29:8). **3.** *reflection:* In a mirror. Just as a mirror reflects only that which is placed before it, a dream reflects only what the dreamer reflects into it. **6.** Sirach admits only one exception. **8.** *without fail:* The Law suffices. Superstition is unnecessary, and the wise man will avoid it. **11.** *learned more:* Sirach was certainly not sympathetic to pagan nations, yet he cannot be accused of exclusivism. **13.** It is natural that he would conclude with a hymn of thanksgiving after recalling the dangers of his travels. At the same time, he points to a basic quality of the wise man—confidence in God.

72 (D) True Worship of God (34:18–35:24). From confidence in God, the author turns to warnings against the false confidence generated by pure externalism in religion. For him, as for the prophets, religious practices without internal dispositions are mockery. And yet, he is careful to insist on the necessity of external worship. Those who are sincere can count on God's blessings and protection; those who are not can expect God's visitation. This thought leads Sirach to conclude with a few words about God's protection of Israel now under pagan domination. **18.** *mock presents:* Ill-gotten goods offered to God are a mockery. **19.** Cf. Am 5:21–24. **21.** *bread of charity:* He who fails in charity to provide for the poor is in the same class as those who oppress them. **22.** Injustice is a kind of murder (cf. Dt 24:14–15). **23–24.** The curse of the oppressed poor man nullifies the prayer of the rich. It is as though someone would tear down a building as fast as another puts it up. **35:1.** Observance of the Law constitutes a sacrifice itself equal to the four sacrifices enumerated. Some see here an allusion to the lack of respect for the sacrificial system that prevailed among many Jews, especially those of the Diaspora. Sirach is no critic of sacrifice as such (cf. 50:12–17), but rather of the pure externalism of many who offered sacrifice. **7–9.** Cf. Dt 12:6. **11.** Insincere worship is viewed as a bribe. **19–24.** The subject changes from the oppressed poor to the oppressed Israel. Antiochus III of Syria (223–187) was favorable to the Jews. Yet the fact that the Gentiles ruled by right of conquest and represented Hellenistic culture produced a spirit of resentment and rebellion in the orthodox Jew. Here, for the first time, Sirach introduces a messianic perspective.

73 (E) A Prayer for God's People (36:1–17). The faith and confidence that God will vindicate Israel prompt Sirach to address a prayer to God asking that this take place soon. In this beautiful prayer he recalls God's past acts of power and asks for new ones, so that Israel's destiny might be achieved and all nations might recognize him as the true God. These verses are used in the Roman breviary for Saturday Lauds. **3.** *used as:* In the Exile, God's holiness in punishing Israel was manifested to the world. Sirach understood well Ez 20:41. *use them:* Now it is their turn to be punished, for they have oppressed the chosen people. By so doing, God's attributes will be manifested to Israel. **7.** *day...time:* The messianic era, which is rarely mentioned in the wisdom literature. God is free to advance or delay the appointed time. **10.** *gather:* The author is thinking of the Diaspora; the restoration permitted by Persian rulers remained incomplete.

74 (F) Choice of Associates (36:18–37:15). The author returns to practical counsels, which he began in 33:19. He enunciates general proverbs about discernment and applies them to the subjects of women, friends, and counselors. **21.** Oriental custom gave the man the right to choose his wife. The woman had to accept the husband given her. **37:6.** A sage stands by his friend in times of adversity and prosperity. **11.** Some practical examples of counselors who are not disinterested. *rival:* A second wife. Sirach does not condemn polygamy but is careful to point out its limitations. *about business:* About his own merchandise. *about value:* The price he ought to pay. *seasonal laborer:* One hired at the time of planting. After the crops were in, the man was free to leave and cared little about the harvest.

75 (G) Wisdom and Temperance (37:16–30). The author concludes the subject of discernment by pointing out not only the source of good and bad conduct but the various types of men considered to be wise. He then takes up the subject of temperance to introduce the next chapter. **16.** *word:* Hebrew *dābār* may here perhaps be taken in the sense of "reflection" or "reason." **17–18.** The chiastic structure presents man's basic choice (cf. 33:14). The tongue is the immediate and constant means of bringing to light one's intentions. **19.** Some can give wise counsel to others and yet are wholly inept in counseling themselves. In reality, therefore, they lack wisdom. **20.** Teachers whose words are rejected because of their lack of ability to express themselves or for other reasons will be deprived of the means of subsistence that would enable them to enjoy some of the legitimate pleasures of life. They, too, are not wise. **21–25.** In contrast, the true sage helps himself and therefore enjoys material compensation and the acclaim of his contemporaries. He also helps others and wins for himself a type of immortality (25), although the immortality of the community (23) is of a higher order.

76 (H) Sickness and Death (38:1–23). Although one is careful to preserve his health, there are times when sickness does strike, and the services of the doctor are needed. This bit of common sense, self-evident to us, constituted a problem for some of Sirach's contemporaries who looked upon consultation with a doctor as a lack of confidence in God (cf. 2 Chr 16:12). Therefore, the author extols the role of the physician and proceeds to explain the proper procedure in consulting him. He concludes with a few words about the proper attitude toward the dead. **5.** *sweetened by a twig:* An allusion to the event at Marah (Ex 15:25); all cures come from God, who used the doctor and medicines as instruments. **9–12.** Note the order. A man cleanses his soul, offers prayer and sacrifice, and then consults the doctor; confidence in God does not exclude common sense. **14.** The doctor prays for help in plying his skill. There is no question here of faith healing. **16.** Precise rules governed a funeral service (cf. Jer 9:7; Am 5:6; Ez 24:15–24). **18.** *one or two days:* Cf. 22:11, where seven days are mentioned. The author may be thinking of various parts of the rite, some of which could be stopped after one or two days. **23.** Cf. Eccl 12:7.

77 **(I) Vocations of the Craftsmen and the Scribe (38:24–39:11).** (Cf. "The Satire on the Trades," *ANET* 432.) It is hardly surprising that Sirach would extol his profession. Although others before and after him were apt to disparage the trades in their quest to show the superiority of the scribe, the author here maintains his usual balance and moderate attitude. The scribe's vocation is superior. Yet craftsmen have an important and necessary place in society. From this passage we gain information about the types of craft practiced in Jerusalem in Sirach's day as well as a lofty concept of the work and activity of a Jewish scribe. No doubt much of what the author writes about the scribe is autobiographical. **24.** *free from toil:* From manual labor. **33–34.** There exists a social hierarchy. The work of the craftsman is noble, but in the affairs of government, his lot is to be ruled rather than to rule. **39:1.** Cf. Ps 1:2. The scribe's first duty is to study the Scriptures. Note the threefold division—Law, Wisdom, and Prophets. The sapiential books he places second in the list, owing to his particular interest. True wisdom, after all, consists basically in the Law, and the sage's first activity is to meditate and expound it. **2.** The scribe also occupies himself with oral traditions. Sirach is thinking here principally of sapiential, not legal, traditions. **6.** Above all, he recognizes that God is the source of all wisdom. Therefore, after purging himself from sin through a contrite prayer (cf. 51:19), he seeks divine help in his work. *spirit of understanding:* Cf. Is 11:2; Jb 12:13.

78 **(J) Praise of God the Creator (39:12–35).** Sirach now offers us a concrete example of the scribe's labors. Although many commentators treat this section as a hymn concerning creation and divine government in the world, analogous to 42:15–43:33, it seems that the author is giving a concrete solution to the problem of good and evil. He places the whole subject in a theological context: He offers a hymn to God and then asserts the dogmatic fact stated in Gn that all the works of God are good. However, he is aware of the objection that experience shows that both physically and morally the world is not all good. Therefore, whence evil? Experience seems to contradict his belief. He solves the problem by a distinction. Everything is good insofar as it serves God's purpose. Sin is the villain; not only is it the root of evil, it blinds man to the facts. If the physical universe seems evil, it is only because men fail to recognize that God uses nature to punish sin. The author, satisfied with his solution, offers a prayer of thanks to God to conclude his consideration. **16.** The statement of the dogmatic fact. **21–25.** The answer is given to the supposed objection; God blesses or punishes, as the situation demands. **23.** An allusion to the expulsion of the Canaanites and the destruction of Sodom and Gomorrah. Wicked men regard these acts of God's wrath as evil. In reality, they manifest God's justice, something good. **25–27.** Sirach holds to the traditional view of retribution. **32–34.** A summary and reassertion of his optimistic view. **35.** By way of inclusion and to fulfill the prescription on giving thanks, the author concludes in hymnic style.

79 **(K) Joys and Miseries of Life (40:1–41:13).** This long section deals with various topics. It begins with a lamentation on the troubles of humanity, a continuation of the thought of ch. 39. At first it might seem that the author abandons his optimistic solution for the problem of evil. Once again, however, Sirach's thought must be placed in a theological context. Meditating on Gn 3:17, which is alluded to throughout the passage, he recognizes that all creation suffers the effects of sin. Experience attests to man's woes, but it is sin that explains them. Those who by personal sin add to the first sin receive additional punishment. Therefore, the author's original thesis can stand. All creation is good; what is bad comes as a consequence of sin. He then returns to the main theme of practical counsels, from which he has often digressed. Many things contribute to man's happiness; the best of all, however, is fear of the Lord. One must avoid the life of a beggar. Death is inevitable, but it is a scourge only for the wicked.

40:1. *God allotted:* This universal misery is the consequence of Adam's sin, stemming from God's curse. **5.** Note that there are seven evils, the sign of plenitude. **11.** *what is from above:* The allusion is not to the "soul" in the Christian sense but to the life breath (cf. Eccl 12:7; 3:19–22). **17.** This verse begins a series of "better" sayings, which culminates in fear of the Lord (26–27). **18.** *city:* In the author's day, cities were often named after the men who founded them. **41:1–4.** One cannot but admire Sirach's faith and resignation before the fact of death. **5.** *witless:* Not fearing God. The children will take after their parents. **8.** *forsake:* Sirach has especially in mind those who forsake Judaism in behalf of Hellenism. **10.** *void to void:* The godless with no reputation in life are forgotten after death as though they never existed, in contrast to the virtuous (vv. 11–13).

80 **(L) True and False Shame (41:14–42:8).** Using his usual technique of contrast, Sirach first gives concrete examples of shameful action. There follow examples of actions of which the wise man need not be ashamed. The norm of conduct is that of principle, not human respect. **16.** *prince and ruler:* Advice for those Jews who were engaged at the court. **42:2.** *of the law:* An admonition not to compromise the practice of one's faith to please the Hellenistic Gentiles. **5.** *business:* Sirach never condemns business, but he is aware of dangers. **6.** *seal:* Security measures to confine such a woman. **7.** Written records should accompany all property transactions.

81 **(M) A Father's Care for His Daughter (42:9–14).** The last of Sirach's particular counsels deals with a perennial problem, a father's worry over his daughter. Although the passage reflects the social customs of his day, the author's insistence on vigilance is sound. **9.** *repudiated:* Cf. Dt 24:1. **10.** *in her father's home:* While yet unmarried. **11.** *lattice:* Cf. Prv 7:6.

82 **(VI) Praise of the Fathers (42:15–50:24).** Abruptly, but solemnly, Sirach begins the final section of his work. With a *Te Deum* to God's omnipotence and omniscience as manifested in nature, he wishes to prepare the reader for his eulogy of the fathers in which he uses history to demonstrate one of the themes of ch. 24: True wisdom resides in Israel. This blending of the works of God in nature and history is not Sirach's innovation, for many psalms (e.g., 135, 136) follow the same procedure. What is original is that he abandons the practical moral counsels and the gnomic genre and turns to extended lyric poetry to teach wisdom. Whether one regards this section as the "heart of the book" (Vawter) or a type of concluding doxology (Spicq), it is clear that he wishes to move his pupils to appreciate God's works both in nature and history, thus to combat the advance of Hellenism among his people.

83 **(A) The Works of God in Nature (42:15–43:35).** In this introductory section, the author first considers God's omnipotence and omniscience in general terms. He then proceeds to show how these attributes are manifested in the world of nature. His conclusion is that man is not only incapable of fathoming the attributes of God but that he cannot even adequately praise him.

15. *word:* The creative power in God's word has a role in the doctrine of the Logos (cf. Jn 1:3). In wisdom literature, the usual medium of creation is Wisdom herself as God's first creature. **17.** *holy ones:* The members of the heavenly court, or angels (cf. Jb 5:1; 15:15). **18.** The "depths" of the subterranean reservoir and the "heart" of man are generally regarded as inscrutable. **24–25.** Above all, it is the harmony amid so much diversity in creation that manifests divine wisdom. **43:1.** The material heaven is meant. **6.** *moon:* The Jews followed a lunar calendar. **8.** *how wondrous:* For those who do not understand astronomy, it was a great mystery. **28.** *he is all in all:* Creation is explained only by God, and the contemplation of that creation reveals the divine perfections to man.

84 **(B) Praise of Israel's Great Ancestors (44:1–15).** Sirach now turns to history to substantiate his thesis that true wisdom resides in Israel. In the style of haggadic midrash, he reviews and reinterprets the lives of those great men of Israel's history who can serve to demonstrate this point to his Hellenistic contemporaries. Therefore, not only is his over-all purpose primarily apologetic, but the principle on which he chooses his heroes is the apologetic value of their lives. At the same time, however, the whole eulogy fits into a larger dimension in that this wisdom of Israel's heroes glorifies the wisdom of God, its source. Thus, he completes the praise of God's wisdom begun in 41:15. Some authors also find a future perspective in Sirach's development, but he does not go beyond the general messianic hope inherent in Israel's salvation history.

The whole treatment, theocentric in perspective and dominated by the themes of covenant and cult, falls into four sections: the introduction (44:1–15); a chronological survey from Enoch to Nehemiah (44:16–49:13); a short survey from Enoch to Adam (49:14–16); and a eulogy of Simon, the high priest (50:1–24; P. T. Maertens, *L'Éloge des pères* [Bruges, 1956]; R. Siebeneck, *CBQ* 21 [1959] 411–28).

The first section introduces the reader to the various classes of Israel's heroes. In it, the author stresses the fact that, owing to God's special favor, they became truly wise and thus their names remain illustrious to the present day. **44:1.** *godly men:* Men of *ḥesed.* In this period, the sect of the Hasidim arose (cf. 1 Mc 2:42; 7:13). **2–6.** Sirach lists 12 categories of great men of the past. Because the priesthood is not mentioned, some have supposed that he refers to pagan heroes to whom he will then contrast the men of Israel. It is most unlikely, however, that Sirach would call some of these pagan heroes godly men (cf. 44:10). Most prefer to consider this section as a global view of Israel's great men, whom the author will then proceed to specify. **8–10.** Cf. 37:21–25. Only the godly man lives on in his works and good name. **12.** *covenant:* Throughout this section, Sirach gives the term the wide signification of a gracious promise.

85 **(C) The Early Patriarchs (44:16–23).** Turning to particular heroes, Sirach chooses only two from prehistory—Enoch and Noah. He then considers the patriarchs Abraham, Isaac, and Jacob. Sirach draws heavily from the OT for his information and assumes that his reader is familiar with the incidents to which he alludes. The modern reader will find most of the references in the scriptural cross references of the CCD translation. **16.** *walked...taken up!:* Cf. Gn 5:24. This cryptic piece of P tradition was the cause of numerous legends about Enoch that later found their way into apocryphal writings. *succeeding generations might learn:* The addition shows that Sirach wishes the reader to recall not only the data of Gn but also the apocryphal legends. According to one story, Enoch saw past, present, and future generations in paradise (cf. *Jub* 4:16–19). Therefore, Enoch becomes a pious exemplar who possesses knowledge far surpassing any Gk hero. **17.** *renewed the race:* Because of his piety, Noah was saved from destruction and became the holy remnant in whom God would fulfill his promises. Thus, the author encouraged his readers to remain devout amid the pagan surroundings in which they lived. Not only will the pious be spared chastisement, but he will also receive the promises of God. **19.** *kept his glory:* Of the many facets of Abraham's career, Sirach emphasizes only that he was loyal to God's will, even in the face of difficulty, and as a consequence became the recipient of God's promises. In a nation small in population and dispossessed of its land, it was imperative to keep alive the hope that the ancient promises were still operative for the zealous observer of God's will. **22–23.** Isaac and Jacob were the recipients of these same promises, which were partly fulfilled in the establishment of the nation Israel.

86 **(D) Praise of Moses, Aaron, and Phinehas (45:1–26).** Note that Joseph is not mentioned in Sirach's list. Some have conjectured that his name has dropped out of 45:1, but no textual evidence supports this hypothesis, and, as we read it now, it refers to Moses. Moses, of course, enjoyed special powers from God, but Sirach most emphasizes that he alone was privileged to approach the source of wisdom to receive the Commandments. Israel's wisdom, therefore, comes directly from God. Hellenism could not make this boast. Next, Aaron is extolled in a lengthy passage describing the glory of the high priesthood. Especially noteworthy is the insistence on the perpetuity of this divinely established office and the value of the high priest's services. No doubt, the author saw the storm clouds brewing that in a few years would make the priesthood a political tool (cf. 2 Mc 4:13–17). Thus, he adds the example of Phinehas to insist on the right of legitimate succession; he concludes with an ardent prayer that any abuse of the office might be avoided. **6.** The lengthy treatment of Aaron betrays Sirach's special interest in cult and the priesthood, which far surpassed anything the Greeks could offer. **9.** Cf. Ex 28:35. **14.** The principal office of the high priest was to offer daily sacrifice (cf. Lv 6:7–16). **17.** The high priest also functioned as custodian, teacher, and administrator of the Law. **25.** The sense of this difficult text is disputed. Some regard it as a simple comparison. As David's line and power were hereditary, so also were Aaron's. Others see a contrast between the Davidic heritage and the high priest succession in favor of the latter. **26.** *bless the Lord:* These words are addressed to the contemporary high priest and his successors.

87 **(E) Joshua, Caleb, and the Judges (46:1–20).** Joshua and Caleb, and the judges and Samuel are excellent examples for Sirach's contemporaries. Faithful to the Lord, and strengthened by him, Joshua fought the Lord's battles and won an inheritance for Israel. The pagan nations were forced to acknowledge that a higher power resided in Israel. Sirach selects only the war stories of Joshua's career, wishing to serve notice on the foreign conquerors of Israel. Also faithful to the Lord was Caleb.

He and Joshua were the only ones spared from punishment and rewarded, thus standing as examples for those Jews contemplating Hellenism. The same lessons are manifested in the judges and Samuel. It is the faithful judges who are extolled and blessed, and, like Joshua, Samuel was faithful to the Lord and fought his battles against foreign oppression. **9.** *summits of the land:* The fortified places around Hebron. **11.** Only those judges who were faithful to Yahweh are praised. **12.** *bones return to life:* The parallelism indicates that he prays that there may be found in the present age those who imitate the piety of the faithful judges; it is not a wish for bodily resurrection.

88 **(F) Nathan, David, and Solomon (47:1–24a).** After a brief mention of Nathan, the most prominent prophet after Samuel, Sirach turns to David. He extols David not only as a skilled warrior against Israel's enemies but also as one who made vast contributions to the liturgy. Although a sinner, he repented; therefore, God rewarded him. Once again Sirach is thinking of his contemporaries. He would have them turn from sin to the practice of their faith. Solomon becomes a perfect example of Sirach's basic thesis on true wisdom. As long as he fears God, all is well; when he abandons God, he abandons wisdom, despite his vast erudition. Dishonor and the wrath of God follow. His son keeps alive God's promises, but he, too, suffers for his folly and God punishes him by splitting his kingdom. **2.** *choice fat:* The fat surrounding the inner organs of sacrificial victims (cf. Lv 4:8–10). As this fat was separated from the rest of the victim, so David was separated from the rest of Israel by the Lord. **3–8.** David's strength and bravery became legendary, and his piety equalled his courage. **18.** *name:* An allusion to Solomon's early name, Jedidiah, "beloved of Yahweh" (cf. 2 Sm 12:25; Jer 11:15). **20–21.** As the cause of the schism, Sirach mentions only Solomon's violation of the Law regarding foreign marriages. Unlike the author of 1 Kgs 11:1–10, he says nothing explicitly about idolatry.

89 **(G) Elijah and Elisha (47:24b–48:16).** The careers of the two prophets are depicted as grim reminders of the destruction and devastation that await those who forsake God. They stand as God-fearing men of principle in marked contrast to the kings of Israel among whom Sirach finds none to praise. **11.** A difficult text that may also be rendered, "blessed is he who saw you before he died." In this case, the verse would refer to Elisha and serve as a transition.

90 **(H) Hezekiah and Isaiah (48:17–25).** Only two kings of Judah are praised: Hezekiah and Josiah. Hezekiah withstood the powerful Assyrians and received God's help (701 BC). The author's contemporaries, impressed by the armies of the Seleucids, could not miss the point. The presence of armed force was no excuse for turning toward Hellenism. The guiding force behind Hezekiah, of course, was Isaiah, that illustrious prophet whose wisdom came from God himself. **24–25.** These verses implicitly attest to the fact that in Sirach's time the Book of Isaiah comprised the 66 chapters we have today. They also witness the fact that the author regarded the contemporary of Hezekiah as the author of the whole book (but this fact is no guarantee of the authenticity of Is 40–66). In a context of this kind, Sirach had no intention of settling literary or historical problems. Furthermore, it is quite possible that Sirach alludes here not only to the Book of Isaiah but also to legends that grew up around the Prophet and that are reflected in the apocryphal *Ascension of Isaiah.*

91 **(I) Josiah and the Prophets (49:1–10).** Josiah is the only other example of piety in the long list of Judean kings after David. Again, the author stresses the practice of virtue during evil times. Jeremiah, Ezekiel, and the 12 prophets all deserve mention. The author omits Daniel from this list. It is difficult to understand how Sirach would have overlooked this hero whose life would have offered him a great apologetic tool against Hellenism. The inference, at least, is that the Book of Daniel did not as yet exist. **4.** *they all were wicked:* Only qualified approval is given to Asa, Jehoshaphat, and Jehoash in Kgs. **9.** *he referred to Job:* The way in which Job is mentioned (cf. Ez 14:14,20) suggests that Sirach may not have known the canonical book; however, the author may be using this technique to include Job, a non-Jew, in his list of heroes. **10.** *twelve prophets:* The minor prophets constituted a single book in Judaism.

92 **(J) The Heroes After the Exile (49:11–13).** Zeal for the Law characterized Zerubbabel, Joshua, and Nehemiah. Amid almost insurmountable obstacles, official worship was restored after the Exile and protection was given to God's holy city against brigands. The surprising omission of Ezra, the great scribe and reformer, remains an unsolved mystery. **11.** *signet ring:* Cf. Hag 2:23. **13.** *memory:* Cf. Neh 13:14,22,31.

93 **(K) The Earliest Patriarchs (49:14–16).** Another unsolved problem is Sirach's abrupt transition to the patriarchal and prehistorical periods. Some regard these verses as a conclusion. The author quickly recalls men of earlier epochs so that he can end with the head of the human race. Others see an independent section here. Either Sirach forgot these names in his original list or he became weary at his task and therefore did not complete his original plan but merely appended the names. Or perhaps the indication is that the book represents a first draft, never revised by the author. Finally, there are those who consider these verses as an introduction to the next section. Each opinion has its merits and drawbacks. In any case, Enoch is reintroduced, and, because of him, also Joseph, as the parallelism (14–15) regarding the bodies of each indicates. There follow the pious representatives of the ante- and postdiluvian ages, and finally Adam, the progenitor of all. **16.** *splendor of Adam:* Because Adam originated directly from God's hands, he enjoys a glory above that of the others.

94 **(L) Simon (50:1–24).** One need not rely on history alone to show the superiority of the Mosaic worship over Gk cult. Indeed, in the memory of men, there was one Simon II, a high priest, whose zeal for public worship and very presence on the Day of Atonement stirred the hearts of men. Whether one regards this section as an appendix or as the last of Sirach's list of heroes depends on the view one takes of 49:14–16. In any case, Sirach concludes chs. 44–50 with a renewal of praise to God.

50:1. *Simon:* Most probably Simon II, son of Onias II (*ca.* 220–195). *in whose time:* He was dead when Sirach wrote. *renovated:* Antiochus the Great (223–187) was favorable to the Jews and no doubt supplied the necessary funds for this and other undertakings. **5.** *veil:* Cf. Ex 36:35–38. **15.** *sweet-smelling odor:* A technical term for a pleasing sacrifice. **20.** *glory:* The high priest alone was privileged to pronounce the divine name, Yahweh, on this day. **21.** *blessing:* Cf. Nm 6:24–26.

95 **(VII) Epilogue (50:25–29).** Perhaps the vivid picture of sacrifice suggested to the author the liturgical and religious rivalry between the Samaritans and the Jews; hence, we have an explanation for the numerical invective (25–26) that prefaces the subscription. Other authors, however, regard the invective as out of place. **26.** *in Seir:* The Idumeans (Edomites) occupied the region of Hebron. *Philistia:* The Philistine cities were the centers of Hellenism. *degenerate folk in Shechem:* The Samaritans.

96 (VIII) Appendices (51:1–30). Following Sirach's subscription are appendices of certain canonicity but debatable authenticity, which contain a psalm of thanksgiving for deliverance from danger (1–12) and an alphabetical poem on the acquisition of wisdom (13–20). The latter has appeared in the Hebr psalms from Qumran, cave 11 (cf. J. Sanders, DJD 4). **1.** Some give this psalm a collective interpretation, applying it to the nation. The arguments, however, are inconclusive. Most regard it as the prayer of an individual, and a common view is to attribute the words to Sirach. The exact nature of the danger described is unclear. **12.** The Hebr text adds here a second psalm, quite similar to Ps 136 and possibly reflecting the point of view of the Zadokite priests (cf. P. Trinquet, *VT* 1 [1951] 287–92). Although it may date from Sirach's time, it is not considered authentic or canonical. **13.** Some who deny this poem to Sirach explain its presence by saying that the inspired scribe was not satisfied with Sirach's brief subscription. Most of the poem deals with his intense pursuit of wisdom. **23.** *school:* Hebrew *bēt midrāš*, a technical term for the place where students met under a teacher for instruction in the Law. However, the Greek reads *paideia*, "teaching." **28.** Wisdom is as valuable as silver and gold. The school of wisdom offers a great prize and makes one truly rich. **30.** *work:* Seeking after wisdom.

34

WISDOM

Addison G. Wright, S.S.

BIBLIOGRAPHY

1 In addition to the general works mentioned in the introduction to the wisdom literature (→ Wisdom Lit, 28:1), see: Cornely, R. and F. Zorell, *Commentarius in Librum Sapientiae* (CSS; Paris, 1910). Deane, W. J., *The Book of Wisdom* (Oxford, 1881). Drubbel, A., *Wijsheid* (Roermond, 1957). Feldman, F., *Das Buch der Weisheit* (BB; Bonn, 1926). Fichtner, J., *Weisheit Salomos* (HAT; Tübingen, 1938). Fischer, J., *Das Buch der Weisheit* (Echter-B; Würzburg, 1952). Geyer, J., *The Wisdom of Solomon* (TBC; London, 1963). Goodrick, A. T. S., *The Book of Wisdom* (N.Y., 1913). Gregg, J. A. F., *The Wisdom of Solomon* (Cambridge, Eng., 1909). Grimm, C. L., *Das Buch der Weisheit* (Leipzig, 1860). Heinisch, P., *Das Buch der Weisheit* (EHAT; Münster, 1912). Holmes, S., "The Wisdom of Solomon," *APOT* (Oxford, 1913). Kalt, E., *Das Buch der Weisheit* (HBk; Freiburg, 1938). Oesterley, W. O. E., *The Wisdom of Solomon* (London, 1918). Osty, E., *Le Livre de la Sagesse* (BJ; 2nd ed.; Paris, 1957). Reider, J., *The Book of Wisdom* (N.Y., 1957). Weber, J., *Le Livre de la Sagesse* (PSB 6; Paris, 1946). Ziener, G., *Die theologische Begriffssprache im Buche der Weisheit* (BBB; Bonn, 1956). For a survey of the commentaries, see Emerton, J. A., *Theology* 68 (1965) 376–80.

The critical edition of the text is Ziegler, J. (ed.), *Sapientia Salomonis* (Göttingen, 1962).

INTRODUCTION

2 **(I) Title, Language, Date, Origin.** "The Book of Wisdom" is the title of the work in the Vg; LXX manuscripts entitle it "The Wisdom of Solomon," and it is today referred to under either name. The earliest mention of Wis is in the Muratorian Fragment (3rd cent. AD) where it is listed (as part of the NT canon!) as "Wisdom, written by the friends of Solomon in his honor."

The book is not in the Hebr Bible and is known to us only in the Greek; although some have argued for a Hebr original, it is generally held today as certain that Greek was the original language. Among other indications, the Greek is spontaneous and free from the constraint that is inevitable in a translation; it has rhetorical devices, such as alliteration, assonance, and paronomasia, which a translator could hardly have constructed. Moreover, the author obviously knew and utilized the OT in the LXX translation and thought out his work in Greek.

Clearly, then, despite the claim for Solomonic authorship, Wis was written many centuries after the time of Solomon. It was certainly written after the completion of the LXX of the Prophets and the Writings (*ca.* middle of the 2nd cent. BC), and it is earlier than the writings of Philo (20 BC–AD 54) and the NT, for the writer is ignorant of the former and the latter utilizes Wis (cf. Rom 1:18–32; Eph 6:11–17; Jn; Heb 1:2–3; etc.). These two points of contact give us a *terminus a quo* and a *terminus ad quem* for the work, and if we assign to it a date in the first half of the 1st cent. BC we shall not be far wrong. Wis, then, is the last of the OT books.

The place of composition is apparently Egypt, probably Alexandria, the great intellectual and scientific center of the Mediterranean world and one of the largest centers of the Jewish Diaspora. The language of Wis and that of the LXX (the Alexandrian version of the OT) are closely connected, and the thought of Wis closely resembles that of other Jewish-Alexandrian works of the same period. Another indication is the emphasis on Egypt and its relationship to Israel in chs. 11–19.

The author of the book claims to be Solomon. The claim was questioned by Origen, Eusebius, Augustine, and Jerome, and it is clear from the preceding data that the claim is simply a literary device, conventional in OT wisdom literature (cf. Prv, Ct, Eccl). Unfortunately the author of the book remains anonymous. All efforts to identify him (Philo, Zerubbabel, Apollos, Aristobolus) have been futile, and the most we can say is that he was a devout, Gk-speaking Jew, acquainted to some extent with Gk philosophy and culture, and probably from Alexandria.

3 **(II) Unity of the Book.** Many scholars have proposed that Wis is the work of more than one author, and they distinguish two independent sections (1:1–11:1; 11:2–19:22 or 1–5; 6–19); some point out even three or four sections. Arguments in favor of composite authorship follow: the difference in style and tone between the first and last parts of the book; the absence of references in chs. 11–19 to wisdom (save for 14:2,5) and immortality; a number of striking linguistic differences, especially in the use of particles and in the choice of words (see Holmes, *op. cit.*, 522–23). However, the majority of critics since Grimm defends the unity of authorship, finding that the factors mentioned are far outweighed by the homogeneity of vocabulary and of outlook throughout, as well as by the mutual cohesion of the parts. The differences between the sections are accounted for by postulating that some interval of time elapsed between their composition, the artistically and theologically inferior chs. 11–19 perhaps being written in the author's old age (P. W. Skehan, *Traditio* 3 [1945] 5).

4 **(III) Genre.** From the point of view of content, the book belongs to the wisdom literature and might be classified, with J. Fichtner (*ZNW* 36 [1937] 113–32), as an apocalyptic wisdom book. In form, the first part of Wis is not a teacher's instruction to his pupils (Prv, Sir) or a scholar's meditation (Eccl), but a public address, more popular than the one intended for educated readers in *4 Mc* and therefore closer to the Cynic-Stoic diatribe. The second half of Wis is a midrash in homily form. The first part, of course, was never delivered orally in its present form, for the oratorical manner is clearly artificial; the same may be true of the second part. The poetry of the book (well sustained in chs. 1–5 and 9; sporadic elsewhere, although more prevalent in chs. 6–8, 10–12 than in 13–19) is a blend of Hebr parallelism and Gk prosody; at times it is truly impressive.

5 **(IV) Occasion, Purpose, Doctrinal Significance.** From the book itself we can conclude that the author's purpose was to strengthen the faith of his fellow Jews in Alexandria. Living in the midst of pagans, the Jewish community was in frequent contact with all the elements of the new society that was the Hellenistic world. Conquests in science were opening up to men the beauty and mystery of the world around them (7:17–20). A variety of religions and philosophical systems offered wisdom or salvation or a view on the real meaning of life. There existed the new cosmopolitan and individualistic mentality, skepticism, and dissatisfaction with traditional ideas. It was a time of crisis for faith, which some Jews had abandoned (2:12), replacing it with pagan religions, secular philosophies, or their own superficial versions of these (2:1–20); other Jews were in danger of following their example. The problems created for the Jews by the intellectual atmosphere were compounded by an age-old problem that afflictions and anti-Semitism had evoked once again—retribution. How is it that the wicked and godless prosper and the just man suffers? How and where does God mete out his justice?

It was to these issues that our author addressed himself, and for solutions he searched the Scriptures. The 19 chapters of Wis contain not many lines and few connected passages that have not been derived in large part from fruitful meditation on the earlier sacred books. In fact, if we are to seek a principle of unity in Wis, it is this feature that provides it. To say it is a book about wisdom or immortality or providence will not define Wis. Rather, it is the expression of the fullness of all that one man in Egypt, with what must have been years of devoted study, could draw under divine guidance from the entire sacred literature of his people to give hope and consolation to his contemporaries (cf. A. A. DiLella, *CBQ* 28 [1966] 139–54).

6 On the question of retribution, the author gives us the first and only instance in the OT where future life with God is categorically and clearly affirmed as man's real destiny (→ Aspects OT Thought, 77:168–74). According to the traditional view, the lot of all beyond the grave was to be the same, a weak and pale existence in Sheol separated from God; reward and retribution were to be in this world, with long life, a large family, riches, and prestige for the just man, and misfortune for the wicked. This theory was not borne out by the hard facts of experience, and there had been advanced various solutions to the problem in its national (Dt-Is) and individual aspects (Jb, Eccl). Some psalms had expressed a hope of a life with God beyond the grave for the individual (Pss 16:9–11; 49:16; 73:23–24). But it is Wis that synthesizes and develops these and other texts, states the reward of life with God with an emphatic assurance, reassesses the problem of the suffering of the just and the value of children and old age in the light of his teaching, and presents an understanding of God's plan for the individual—surpassing any other that we know from before the time of Christ. (See R. Schütz, *Les idées eschatologiques du Livre de la Sagesse* [Paris, 1935]; H. Bückers, *Die Unsterblichkeitslehre des Weisheitsbuches* [Münster, 1938]; R. Taylor, *ETL* 42 [1966] 72–137).

The author may have been aided in his thinking by the Gk concepts of body and soul (→ 12 below). However, his reasoning process is Jewish, for he does not conclude to immortality from the nature of man but from man's relationship to God (→ 13 below), and his picturing of the reward of the just in terms of a sharing in the angelic life (5:5) could have been formulated within the framework of the developing aspirations of OT piety without an explicit philosophical knowledge of the immaterial nature of the human soul. It seems to have been so formulated at Qumran (cf. 1QS 11:7–8; 1QH 3:21–23). (For a discussion of similarities and differences between Wis and DSS see A. M. Dubarle, *RSPT* 37 [1953] 425–43; M. Philonenko, *TZ* 14 [1948] 81–88.)

There is no mention of a resurrection of the body in Wis (cf. Dn 12:2 and 2 Mc 7). Some critics have maintained that the silence on this point is out of deference to the Greeks (cf. Acts 17:32) and that the doctrine is implied in chs. 3–5 and in 16:13; 19:6–21 (see P. Beauchamp, *Bib* 45 [1964] 491–526, bibliography; Taylor, *op. cit.*, 131–37). The arguments are unconvincing, and it would seem that Wis (like Qumran thus far) does not envision a resurrection of the body (→ 13 below).

7 In the section on wisdom, the author addresses himself to the problem of the allurements of Hellenism and attempts to show the Jews that they are not barbarians, as it has been alleged, and that they have no reason to envy the wisdom of the pagans inasmuch as they possess true wisdom. He does not reject Gk culture but attempts something of a synthesis. He begins with the personification of God's Wisdom in Prv 1; 8–9; Jb 28; Bar 3:9–4:4; Sir 24, and identifies it with the spirit of the Lord (→ 12 below). He states that it is Wisdom who really possesses the qualities of the world soul of the Greeks (7:22–8:1). It is she who is the true initiator into the divine mysteries (8:4) and who teaches the four cardinal virtues of Plato (8:7). He attempts a synthesis between anthropocentric Gk humanism and theocentric Hebr humanism by broadening the purely ethical connotations of wisdom to include the profane learning of Hellenism (7:17–20). However,

in typically Hebr manner he reminds us that wisdom teaches above all the justice that leads to immortality and that wisdom is not a quality acquired by man but a favor to be asked of God, not merely an ideal of human life but the power that enables man to attain it (see T. Finan, *IrTQ* 27 [1960] 30–48).

In addition, by identifying Wisdom with the spirit of the Lord, by transferring the functions of the spirit to Wisdom, the author bestowed upon Wisdom the contemporaneity and nearness of action that were associated with the Spirit. Whereas Prv and Sir identified Wisdom with the Law, Wis imparts a dynamic vitality to her (cf. J. Rylaarsdam, *Revelation in Jewish Wisdom Literature* [Chicago, 1946] 99–118).

8 In the second part of the book, the author recalls God's earlier dealings with the just and the wicked in Egypt at the time of the Exodus. Thus, he strengthens his coreligionists' trust in God in the present and their hope for a similar eschatological intervention. In a digression, he reworks some OT prophetic texts into a polemic on false worship.

9 Besides its contributions to the theology of retribution and wisdom, Wis also introduces into the biblical vocabulary the Gk terms of providence (6:7; 14:3; 17:2), conscience (17:10), and the cardinal virtues (8:7) to describe ideas already current in Judaism. The author does not express a hope for a personal messiah and apparently belongs to that segment of Judaism that looked for God's direct intervention at the end-time to establish his kingdom; he provides us, however, with the only OT occurrence of the important NT phrase "the kingdom of God" (10:10). Also of interest is the author's explanation of miracles in terms of Gk philosophy (19:18–21), his viewing of the Exodus as a new creation (19:6–13), and his discussion of the possibility of a knowledge of God through creation (13:1–9).

10 **(V) Outline.** A wide variety of outlines of the book has been offered in the past by the critics. However, the author of Wis, like the author of Heb, has used various techniques to structure his work, and with the discovery of these it has become possible to provide an outline of the book that can confidently be proposed as being the one the author intended (cf. A. G. Wright, *Bib* 48 [1967] 165–84).

First, the author has marked the limits of each paragraph with inclusions—i.e., the repetition, at the end of a section, of a word or phrase used at its beginning. The inclusions for each section are indicated in the commentary. The manner in which these paragraphs are to be grouped has been indicated by the author in several ways. Some are arranged in a concentric symmetry (chs. 1–6, 7–8, and the digression of 13–15), others in a parallel symmetry (ch. 9); still others have been arranged in a linear fashion and develop an announced theme by repetition (ch. 10 and the homily of chs. 11–19, in which there is not a sevenfold division, as is often stated, but a fivefold one).

In addition, throughout the book the author has counted his verses (not biblical verses, of course, but poetic verses: monostichs, distichs, and tristichs). In the symmetrical sections there is a quantitative symmetry in the number of verses as well as the qualitative symmetry already mentioned. Moreover, in all parts of the book, except in the two digressions in 11:17–12:22 and 13:1–15:17, the number of verses in each smaller section stands to the number of verses in its neighboring larger one in the same ratio as the larger stands to the sum of the two ($m/M = M/m + M$)—i.e., in the neighborhood of 0.618. The major sections (1:1–6:21; 6:22–9:18; 11–19) also stand to each other in that ratio. This ratio is the well-known golden mean or divine proportion, famous in mathematics, art, architecture, and aesthetic theory and utilized by Vergil, Catullus, Lucretius, Horace, Ennius, Lucan, and Aratus in proportioning sections of their literary works (cf. G. E. Duckworth, *Structural Patterns and Proportions in Vergil's Aeneid* [Ann Arbor, 1962]). Finally, with the addition of ch. 10 and the two digressions of 11:17–12:22 and 13:1–15:17, the book consists in two halves (1:1–11:1; 11:2–19:22) of 251 verses each (for the details, see A. G. Wright, *CBQ* 29 [1967] 524–38). As with the inclusions, so also with the numerical patterns the rationale is to be sought in the artistic sense of the author. He had a sense of, and a desire for, completion; therefore, he repeated at the end of a section a key word from the beginning. He also had a sense of proportion and thus constructed his book on the basis of the golden mean.

Discovery of both inclusions and proportions makes it possible for us to propose with confidence the following plan of the Book of Wisdom as the one the author himself had in mind:

(I) The Praises of Wisdom (1:1–11:1)
- (A) Immortality Is the Reward of Wisdom (1:1–6:21)
  - (a) Exhortation to Justice (1:1–15)
  - (b) The Wicked Invite Death (Speech of the Wicked) (1:16–2:24)
  - (c) The Hidden Counsels of God (3:1–4:19)
    - (i) Suffering (3:1–12)
    - (ii) Childlessness (3:13–4:6)
    - (iii) Early death (4:7–19)
  - (b′) The Final Judgment (Speech of the Wicked) (4:20–5:23)
  - (a′) Exhortation to Seek Wisdom (6:1–21)
- (B) The Nature of Wisdom and Solomon's Quest for Her (6:22–11:1)
  - (a) Introduction (6:22–25)
  - (b) Solomon's Speech (7:1–8:21)
    - (i) Solomon is like other men (7:1–6)
    - (ii) Solomon prayed and Wisdom and riches came to him (7:7–12)
    - (iii) Solomon prays for help to speak of Wisdom (7:13–22a)
    - (iv) The nature of Wisdom (7:22b–8:1)
    - (iii′) Solomon sought Wisdom, the source of knowledge (8:2–8)
    - (ii′) Solomon sought Wisdom as his counselor and comfort (8:9–16)
    - (i′) Solomon realizes that Wisdom is a gift of God (8:17–21)
  - (c) Solomon's Prayer for Wisdom (9:1–18)
  - (d) Transitional Section: Wisdom Saves Her Own (10:1–11:1)

(II) God's Fidelity to His People in the Exodus (11:2–19:22)
- (A) Introductory Narrative (11:2–4)
- (B) Theme: Israel Is Benefited by the Very Things That Punish Egypt (11:5)
- (C) Illustration of the Theme in Five Antithetical Diptychs (11:6–19:22)
  - (a) First Diptych: Water from the Rock Instead of the Plague of the Nile (11:6–14)
  - (b) Second Diptych: Quail Instead of the Plague of Little Animals (11:15–16:15)
    - (i) (11:15–16) plus digression on God's power and mercy (11:17–12:22)
    - (ii) (12:23–27) plus digression on false worship (13:1–15:17)
    - (iii) (15:18–16:4) plus digression on the serpents in the desert (16:5–15)
  - (c) Third Diptych: A Rain of Manna Instead of the Plague of Storms (16:16–29)
  - (d) Fourth Diptych: The Pillar of Fire Instead of the Plague of Darkness (17:1–18:4)
  - (e) Fifth Diptych: The Tenth Plague and the Exodus by Which God Punished the Egyptians and Glorified Israel (18:5–19:22)
    - (i) (18:5–19) plus digression on the plague in the desert (18:20–25)
    - (ii) (19:1–5) plus digression on creation (19:6–21)
    - (iii) Conclusion (19:22)

COMMENTARY

11 **(I) The Praises of Wisdom (1:1–11:1).** The first part of the book is divided into two sections. The first section, sometimes called the Book of Eschatology, deals with the problem of retribution for good and evil and with the blessed immortality that Wisdom offers; it concludes with an appeal to the reader to seek Wisdom (1:1–6:21). The second section describes Wisdom and her operations in the world and explains how she is to be found (6:22–11:1).

(A) Immortality Is the Reward of Wisdom (1:1-6:21). The section is divided into five parts arranged concentrically. The central part contains the author's teaching on retribution. The inclusions (abbrev. Incl.) are given according to the revised CCD translation of Wis (1968).

12 (a) EXHORTATION TO JUSTICE (1:1–15). (Incl.: *justice*, 1:1,15.) The author begins with an exhortation, which the rest of the book will reinforce: Live a virtuous life and trust in God because these qualities make possible union with God and with wisdom (1–5; Incl.: *justice/injustice*, 1 and 5; *counsels; rebuke*, 3 and 5). Grumblings against God's providence do not go unnoticed, and God, who is jealous of his honor, punishes such transgressions by not granting immortality (6–11; Incl.: *tongue[s]*, 6 and 11). The author then introduces the theme of this part of the book: Man is made for immortality; death comes from sin and from man's free choice; God is not responsible for it, nor are creatures to blame, nor can the nether world cause man to lose immortality (12–15; Incl.: *destruction/destructive*, 12 and 14; *death/undying*, 12 and 15).

1. *justice:* Righteousness, virtuous thought, and action. *you who judge:* Rulers. Such an address, fairly frequent as a literary device in the prophetic and sapiential literature (Is 1:2; Hos 5:1; Pss 2:10; 49:2–3; etc.), may have been chosen here in keeping with the "Solomonic" authorship, or perhaps some other allusion is intended that now escapes us. In any event, the book is addressed first of all to the author's everyday associates among his own people. *in goodness:* Have good thoughts about the Lord and do not grumble against his providence. **3-11.** The "perverse counsels" and evil speech seem to refer to grumblings among the Jews about God's apparent disregard for the just and his failure to punish the wicked—the problem that gave rise to the discussion here and in chs. 11–19. **4.** *Wisdom:* Wisdom is personified in Prv 1:20–33; 8:1–36; 9:1–6; Jb 28; Bar 3:9–4:4; Sir 24:1-21, as well as by our author. It is not a person separate from Yahweh but a literary personification of one of his attributes. Such personification is common in the OT (e.g., Spirit, Word, and Justice). In the earlier wisdom literature, wisdom was an effect of the spirit of God; in Wis (here and in 7:22–23; 9:17), Wisdom is identified with the spirit of the Lord and becomes an immanent cosmological principle and the internal principle of physical and moral life (see P. van Imschoot, *RB* 47 [1938] 23–49). *soul, body:* The Hebrews did not conceive of man as constituted of a material body and a spiritual soul (→ Aspects OT Thought, 77:61, 64–66). Under the influence of Hellenism, these concepts appear in the OT clearly for the first time in Wis 8:19–20; 9:15; 15:8, and less clearly here where the terms are in parallelism (cf., however, Taylor, *op. cit.*, 84–100). However, Wis has not adopted the Platonic idea that the body is evil, nor the tripartite division of man into body, soul, and spirit. In Wis, soul (8:19, etc.) and spirit (15:16, etc.) are used interchangeably for the vital principle and are put in synonymous parallelism in 15:11 and 16:14. *body under debt of sin:* The phrase is parallel and synonymous with the "soul that plots evil" in v. 4a. The body is not seen as the source of sin in opposition to the soul. **5.** *discipline:* In the wisdom literature, the term means religious instruction, training, and correction. **12–13.** *death:* It becomes clear in 2:24 that the author is not speaking of physical death but of spiritual death, the second death (Ap 2:11; 21:8), definitive separation from God. Our author seems to be indifferent regarding the fate of the body (cf., however, Taylor, *op. cit.*, 102–16). **14.** *nether world:* Sheol, the abode of the dead, here equated with personified Death. **15.** *justice is undying:* It leads to immortality. As ch. 3 makes clear, the term "immortality" for the author is neither fame with posterity, as in the OT, nor the philosophical notion of the native immortality of the soul, but the unending existence with God (blessed immortality).

13 (b) THE WICKED INVITE DEATH (SPEECH OF THE WICKED) (1:16–2:24). (Incl.: *in its [his] possession*, 1:16 and 2:24.) The author next explains that it is the wicked who invite death by their evil deeds, and he sets forth their erroneous philosophy of life in the form of a speech. Some have suggested that the wicked depicted by the author are Epicureans or Sadducees, or even that the section is a polemic against the views set forth in Eccl. Actually, the philosophy of life pictured here differs essentially from the doctrine of all those mentioned. The wicked the author has in mind are apostate Jews, probably seen as a type of the wicked in general.

(Skehan, P. W., *The Literary Relationship Between the Book of Wisdom and the Protocanonical Wisdom Books of the Old Testament* [Washington, 1938]. Weisengoff, J. P., *CBQ* 11 [1949] 40–65.)

In their view of life and death, the wicked espouse a practical atheism and attribute man's origin to chance. Their concept of man is completely this-worldly, and they deny survival after death and therefore the existence of Sheol (1–5; Incl.: *dying*, 1 and 5). Consequently, they resolve to pursue a hedonistic existence and to make might the norm of right (6–11; Incl.: *use/useless*, 6 and 11). They resolve to persecute the just man because his life and words are a reproach to them (12–16; Incl.: *God*, 13 and 16), and they determine to test the claims of the just (17–20; Incl.: *his words*, 17 and 20). The author concludes the section with his judgment on the thoughts of the wicked and announces the subject of the next section (21–24).

16. *friend:* Irony. *covenant:* The terminology is from Is 28:15,18. **2:1.** *dying:* The word "death" on the lips of of the wicked means, of course, physical death. **2.** *haphazard:* The allusion is probably to the Epicurean doctrine that objects were formed by a chance combination of atoms. **2–3.** *smoke, spark, ashes:* An allusion to a Gk theory that the soul is a fiery principle. **4.** *name will be forgotten:* The wicked reject even the OT hope of remembrance by posterity as a reward for the just (Prv 10:7; Is 56:5; etc.) and state that the lot of the just and unjust is the same. Ironically, the statement is true on the lips of the wicked (cf. 4:19). **7–8.** The emphasis on flowers is Greek. **11.** *weakness proves itself useless:* Therefore, it has no right to exist. **12.** Cf. Is 3:10 (LXX). From 2:12 to 5:23, the author draws heavily on Is 52–66. His teaching on retribution is the fruit of meditation on these chapters in their LXX form, and he sets forth that teaching in a series of characters or types taken from Is, presented in their Isaian sequence and embellished with additional details from elsewhere (see P. W. Skehan, *CBQ* 2 [1940] 289–99; *CBQ* 10 [1948] 384–97; M. J. Suggs, *JBL* 76 [1957] 26–33; G. Ziener, *TTZ* 66 [1957] 138–43).

13. The picture of the just here and in 3:1–9 is based on the fourth Servant Song (Is 52:13–53:12), as well as on Is 42:1 and Ps 22:8. **22.** Announces the subject of the next section. **23.** *image:* The author connects the "image of God" of Gn 1:26 with the blessed immortality to which man is destined but which he can lose by sin. Wis never says that man is by nature immortal but rather that he acquires immortality (3:4; 4:1; 8:13; 15:3). *nature: Idiotētos.* Read, with some manuscripts *aïdiotētos*, "eternity." **24.** Here it is clear that "death" in 1:11–14 and in this verse does not mean physical death but rather spiritual death because it is experienced only by the wicked. Likewise, *aphtharsia* (CCD "imperishable"), here and in its other occurrences in Wis (6:18,19), means blessed immortality and not bodily immortality. The author apparently views physical death as the result of man's earthly origins (cf. 7:1), which would explain his disinterest in physical death and the lack of a doctrine of bodily resurrection. *envy of the devil:* The phrase is usually interpreted as an allusion to the fall in Gn 3, in which case the author apparently interprets the threat of death in that account as referring to spiritual death. If the allusion is to Gn 3, it is one of the rare OT texts that refers to the fall (cf. also 10:1 and Sir 25:23) and the first biblical text to equate the serpent with the devil (see later, Jn 8:44; Ap 12:9; 20:2). A few, however, see here an allusion to Gn 4 and the murder of Abel by Cain. On the text see S. Lyonnet, *Bib* 39 (1958) 27–36; A.-M. Dubarle, *Fest. E. Tisserant* (Vatican, 1964) 1, 187–95.

14 (c) The Hidden Counsels of God (3:1–4:19). In this section, the author begins by stating that blessed immortality is the reward of the just. Then, in the light of that belief, he comments on three points of the traditional discussion of the problem of retribution (the suffering of the just, childlessness, early death), and in each paragraph he contrasts the fate of the just and of the wicked.

15 (i) *Suffering* (3:1–12). (Incl.: *foolish*, 2 and 12; *thought*[*s*], 2 and 10; *hope*, 4 and 11.) The just seem to have died, but they are really alive with God. Their sufferings in this life appear to be punishments (a frequent OT assumption), but their sufferings are not punishments at all but a discipline, correction, and testing of fidelity in which God recognizes those worthy of him. The just are full of hope for a blessed immortality, and at the Judgment the just shall enjoy the kingdom of God. The wicked, however, have no hope for the future and their punishments begin even in this life (on the text, see Taylor, *op. cit.*, 119–31).

1. *in the hand of God:* Under his protection (cf. Dt 33:3; Is 62:3). *torment:* After death (cf. 4:19). **2.** *affliction:* Cf. Is 53:4. **3.** *peace:* See Is 57:1–2. The author is (deliberately?) vague on the state of the souls of the just immediately after death. Some suggest that Wis, like *Enoch*, places them in Sheol with the souls of the wicked until the Judgment, when they will be brought out to be with God (e.g., P. Grelot in *A la rencontre de Dieu* [Fest. A. Gelin; Le Puy, 1961] 165–78). However, because Sheol is seen as a dark and disagreeable place (17:14–21), because it is bound so closely with spiritual death (1:14), and because the wicked seem to be in anguish before the final Judgment (4:19), it would seem that Sheol can hardly be the place in which the just now find peace; rather, they must be with God and the angelic court (5:5), and the last Judgment must merely bring further glory (3:7–9; 5:16; see M. Delcor, *NRT* 77 [1955] 614–30). **4.** *hope:* During their earthly life. *immortality:* Again, blessed immortality; the first occurrence of the noun in the OT. **5–6.** *chastised, proved:* The author takes up the lead of Dt 8:2–5; Prv 3:11–12; Sir 2:1–6; 4:17–19. **6.** *sacrificial offerings:* The idea was suggested by Is 53:7–10. **7.** *visitation:* A biblical term (Is 10:3, etc.) meaning a divine intervention, here referring to the definitive intervention of the last Judgment. *shine, sparks:* Images of triumph (Ob 8; Dn 12:3). **8.** *judge:* Synonymous with "rule"; for the allusion, cf. Dn 7:18–27. *nations, peoples:* The author does not identify them. Many Jews hoped for the rule of Israel over the rest of the nations in the messianic age. Perhaps this image is used here to express the triumph of the just over the wicked. **9.** *truth:* Probably the knowledge of God and of heavenly wisdom (cf. 1QS 4:22). **10.** *thoughts:* Cf. 2:1–5. **11a.** Cf. Prv 1:7. **11b–12.** The ideas of offspring, length of days, and fruit seem to be from Is 53:10–11 (cf. Is 65:23) and are applied to the wicked in accordance with the traditional thought (cf. Prv 10–11; Sir 41:5–10; etc.). **12.** *foolish:* Folly is the equivalent of wickedness in the sapiential books (cf. 1:3). *children wicked:* Because of the example of their parents.

16 (ii) *Childlessness* (3:13–4:6). (Incl.: *wicked*[*ness*], 3:14 and 4:6; *fruit*, 3:13 and 4:5.) The traditional view was that children are a sign of God's favor and sterility a curse, especially inasmuch as one's hopes for immortality dwelled above all in the memory of one's children. Our author, taking up Sir 16:1–4, comments on this view in four paragraphs arranged in a chiasma. The childless, if virtuous, are not cursed, for life's true fruit is virtue (3:13–15), whereas the children of the wicked are a fruit that is not lasting (4:3–6). Children of the wicked either live to a dishonorable old age or die young with no hope of immortality (3:16–19); better than this is virtue, for it is honored by men and is rewarded with blessed immortality (4:1–2).

13. A transfer to the individual order of the promises made to Jerusalem in Is 54:1ff. *childless:* Not celibacy but sterility. *transgression:* The adultery theme throughout this passage seems to refer to all sinfulness (as frequently in the OT) and is here inspired by Is 57:3. **14.** The author sees Is 56:2–5 as being fulfilled in the spiritual order at the last Judgment. *more gratifying:* Than sons and daughters (cf. Is 56:5). **15.** *root of understanding:* The root that is understanding (wisdom). **16.** *remain without issue:* (CCD) Better, "will not reach maturity." **18.** *day of scrutiny:* The last Judgment. **4:1.** *immortal:* In two senses—fame with posterity, and, because it is recognized by God, blessed immortality. **3–5.** Cf. Sir 23:25; Is 57:13; 40:24. **6.** The verse is not completely clear. The misfortunes of vv. 3–5 will suggest a parental sin (according to the OT view of things; cf. Sir 41:5–7; Jn 9:2) when the children (and the parents?) are scrutinized by men at the time of the misfortunes (and by God at the Judgment?).

17 (iii) *Early death* (4:7–19). (Incl.: *honorable*/*dishonored*, 4:8,19.) The traditional view of retribution was that the wicked die young and the just are blessed with an honorable old age. The author, for the first time in the OT, throws a clearer light on the problem of the early death of the just and observes that an early death is no evil for the just because the true "old age" that is honorable is really virtue, and, as in the case of Enoch, God may snatch the just man from the world before his time to preserve him from contamination. But the old age and death of the wicked will not be honorable. **7.** The author has moved on to Is 57:1–2

(LXX; cf. also Is 65:20–23). **9.** Cf. Prv 16:31. *understanding:* Wisdom. **10.** There are allusions to Enoch (Gn 5:21–24), young by patriarchal standards. There is no need to seek an allusion here to the Qumran Teacher of Righteousness with M. Philonenko (*op. cit.*, 81–88). **14.** Cf. Is 57:1. *people:* The wicked. **15.** For the omission of v. 15 in the CCD, see Wright, *CBQ* 29, 221. **16.** *condemns:* Will provide a standard of comparison, which will end with the condemnation of the wicked (cf. Mt 12:41ff.). There may be an allusion to 2:20. **19.** The verse describes the fate of the wicked after death and before the last Judgment in imagery from Is 14:16–19; 19:10; 66:24.

18 (b′) The Final Judgment (Speech of the Wicked) (4:20–5:23). (Incl.: *lawless*[*ness*], 4:20 and 5:23; *confront*, 5:1 and 23). At the last Judgment, the wicked will behold the salvation of the just (4:20–5:3a). In a speech that parallels that of ch. 2, they acknowledge the error of their evaluation of the just as well as the error of their way of life, which has left them with nothing, especially with no sign of virtue (5:3b–13; Incl.: *held*, 3 and 13). The author this time concurs with the statements of the wicked and describes the reward of the just in a picture which develops into an apocalyptic description of God's punishing of evil (14–23; Incl.: *tempest*, 14 and 23).

4:20–5:7. The author has moved on to Is 59:6–14. **5:5.** *sons of God, saints:* The angels (cf. 1QS 11:7–8; 1QH 3:19–23). Wis pictures the reward of the just in terms of an association with, or assimilation to, the angels (see P. W. Skehan, *CBQ* 21 [1959] 526–27). **6.** *light of justice:* Cf. Is 59:9. **7.** *we had our fill of the ways:* Probably to be emended to "we became entangled in the thorns" (Ziegler). **15–16.** For the imagery, cf. Is 62:3,11; similarly 1QS 4:6–8. **17–23.** Cf. Is 59:16–19; 60:12; 13:5–9. **23.** It is not clear if the wicked are thought to be annihilated at the Judgment. Such was the view at Qumran (cf. 1QpHab 13:2–4; 1QS 4:14). *thrones:* A transition to the next section.

19 (a′) Exhortation to Seek Wisdom (6:1–21). (Incl.: *kings*, 6:1,21.) The author resumes the direct address of 1:1 and concludes this section of the book with a warning of impending judgment (1–8; Incl.: *power*, 2 and 8; *scrutinize/scrutiny*, 3 and 8), an exhortation to hear his words (9–11; Incl.: *my words*, 9 and 11), a statement on the accessibility of wisdom (12–16; Incl.: *seek*[*ing*], 12 and 16), and a sorites, which shows how the search for wisdom leads to immortality and an eternal reign (17–21; Incl.: *desire*, 17 and 20).

1. *kings:* See comment on 1:1. **4.** *ministers of his kingdom:* In that their dominion is from God. *judged:* Ruled. **5–6.** Cf. Moses (Nm 20:12) and David (2 Sm 24:10–17). **10.** *learned:* Not a mere intellectual knowledge but also a vital inner correspondence. *response:* A defense at the scrutiny. **12.** Cf. Prv 3:15 (LXX); 8:17. *resplendent:* Because of her divine origin (cf. 7:26). *Wisdom:* For the personification of Wisdom, see comment on 1:4. **13–16.** Cf. Prv 1:20–21; 8:1–36. **15.** *prudence: Fronēsis.* Sometimes identical with wisdom (e.g., "understanding" [CCD] in 3:15 and 4:9; "prudence" in 7:7 and 8:21), sometimes taught by wisdom (8:7). Here it is a moral quality whose completion is the attainment of Wisdom. *free from care:* Like Wisdom herself (7:23). **20.** One step in the sorites is to be supplied from 3:7–8 and 5:17: To be close to God is to reign. Here, again, Wis transposes the traditional teaching of the sages. For them, wisdom and justice assured the stability of an earthly throne (Prv 16:12; 20:28; etc.), but the reign of which our author speaks is eschatological.

20 **(B) The Nature of Wisdom and Solomon's Quest for Her (6:22–11:1).** In this section, the author, identifying himself with Solomon, praises the beauty of Wisdom and describes how he sought her out. After a brief introduction (6:22–25), Solomon's speech (7:1–8:21) is presented in seven paragraphs arranged concentrically with the description of Wisdom in the central paragraph (7:22b–8:1). At the end, and standing outside of this structure, are Solomon's prayer (ch. 9) and a transitional section (10:1–11:1), which leads into the second part of the book.

21 (a) Introduction (6:22–25). The author announces the subject matter of chs. 7–10 and his desire to share with others the mysteries of Wisdom. **22.** *how she came to be:* The author probably has in mind 7:25–26 (cf. the similar brief treatment of Wisdom's origin in Prv and Jb), but the bulk of his attention will be on the effects of Wisdom, especially in Solomon's life. *secrets:* The origin of Wisdom (cf. Jb 28:20ff.), the knowledge of which has been given to the heavenly assembly (Sir 24:1ff.); also the teachings and blessings that she imparts. *beginning: Archē geneseōs.* Either the beginning of Wisdom (7:25–26), or of creation (ch. 10), or of Solomon's life (the same two words occur in this sense in 7:5). **23.** *jealousy:* Possibly a jibe at the pagan mystery religions and philosophers that kept their teachings for the select few. **24.** Cf. Prv 11:14; Sir 10:1–3; Wis 10, where Wisdom saves her own.

22 (b) Solomon's Speech (7:1–8:21).

(i) *Solomon is like other men* (7:1–6). (Incl.: *all; same*, 7:1,6.) Solomon was not especially disposed by birth toward wisdom but had the same origin as all other men. **1.** *mortal:* In sharp contrast to the divine origin claimed by rulers. **2.** *ten months:* Lunar months. **3.** *kindred:* Not that Solomon and the earth were related, but rather Solomon and other men.

23 (ii) *Solomon prayed and Wisdom and riches came to him* (7:7–12). (Incl.: *came to me*, 7:7,11; *riches*, 7:8,11.) Solomon preferred Wisdom over power, riches, health, comeliness, and light. He prayed for her and Wisdom came to him with all these good things besides, much to Solomon's joy. **7.** *prayed:* Cf. 1 Kgs 3:6–9; 2 Chr 1:8–10. The author's version of the prayer is given in Wis 9. *prudence:* Understanding; the spirit of wisdom of the following stich (synonymous parallelism). **10.** *never yields to sleep:* Wisdom never ceases to exist. Cf. 7:29–30.

24 (iii) *Solomon prays for help to speak of Wisdom* (7:13–22a). (Incl.: *hide/hidden*, 13 and 21.) Once again, Solomon expresses his desire to share what he has learned about Wisdom for the benefit of men, but, before beginning his description of her, he asks for help from God who gave him his encyclopedic knowledge. **14.** *discipline:* Wisdom is the spirit of discipline (1:5). **17–20.** Embellishing on the Solomonic material in 1 Kgs 4:32–34, the author attributes to Solomon a knowledge of those sciences that were the special pursuit of the Hellenistic world. **17.** *elements:* The four constitutive elements of the world, according to the Greeks, were fire, water, air, and earth. **18.** *beginning, end and midpoint of times:* The line is so indefinite that it is impossible to be sure of its meaning. Perhaps it is a poetic expression for the knowledge requisite for constructing an astronomical calendar. **19.** *cycles of years:* Perhaps an allusion to the 19-year lunar cycle of Meton of Athens. **20.** *natures of animals and tempers of beasts:* Solomon is supposed to have known the ways and habits of animals and to have spoken parables about all sorts of living creatures (cf. 1 Kgs 4:32–34). *thoughts of men:* Not the thoughts of men's hearts, which are known only to God, but the way the human mind works—its reasonings, plottings, and tricks. **22.** *Wisdom taught:* Wisdom is identical with God (v. 17; see comment on 1:4).

25 (iv) *The nature of Wisdom* (7:22b-8:1). This central of the seven paragraphs begins with an enumeration of 21 (7 [perfection] × 3 [the divine number] = 21 [absolute perfection]) characteristics of Wisdom (7:22b-23; Incl.: *spirit, intelligent, subtle,* 7:22,23). The author then singles out two of these characteristics for further comment. Wisdom is mobile because of her purity and divine origin. She is omnipotent in producing holy men because she is fairer than the sun and wickedness cannot prevail over her (7:24–8:1; Incl.: *all,* 7:24 and 8:1; note the use of the stem [*pas*] seven times in these verses). **22–23.** For the personification of Wisdom, see comment on 1:4. Much of the terminology here and in the rest of the paragraph is borrowed from the Gk philosophers, who attributed these qualities to a world soul, the Nous or the Logos. In using this vocabulary, the author wishes to show that it is really the divine Wisdom that possesses these attributes. It is not always easy to define precisely the meaning of each attribute, especially inasmuch as the author has sometimes repeated himself to arrive at the number 21. *there is in her a spirit:* The mode of expression results from the author's personification of Wisdom. The attributes of this "spirit" are the attributes of Wisdom. *holy:* Because of Wisdom's origin (7:25–26), her avoidance of evil (1:5), and the holiness she produces (7:27). *manifold:* In her manifestations and activity, even though she is one (unique). *subtle:* Spiritual, immaterial. *clear:* In utterance (cf. the same word in 10:21). *unstained:* Despite her contact with the beings she pervades. *certain:* As a moral guide. *keen, unhampered:* In penetrating. *firm, secure, tranquil:* Because she is unchanging in her plans, unerring, and unable to be hindered. **24.** *by reason of her purity:* Metaphysical rather than moral purity; there is in her nothing gross or of the earth as the following lines show. **25–26.** The author, enlarging on Prv 8 and Sir 24, seeks the most immaterial images possible to describe the origin and divinity of Wisdom. **27.** *renews:* Apparently one generation after another. Cf. Pss 104:30; 102:26–27. **29.** *fairer:* A moral purity. *she takes precedence:* The text should be emended to, "she is found more brilliant" (Ziegler). **8:1.** *end to end:* Of the universe. *governs well:* Because of her goodness.

26 (iii′) *Solomon sought Wisdom, the source of knowledge* (8:2-8). (Incl.: *understand*[*ing*], 8:4,8.) Solomon returns to the subject of his quest for Wisdom. He sought her as his bride, for she instructs in knowledge. She is God's friend and collaborator; she gives wealth and skill; she teaches the four cardinal virtues of Plato (*Laws* 631) and the Stoics, the knowledge of past and future, the understanding of the utterances of the sages. **3.** *nobility:* Wisdom's nobility of origin. *companionship:* The term (*symbiōsis*) is normally used of marriage; it is found in this sense in vv. 9 and 16 to describe the marriage with Wisdom that Solomon sought. Unless each element of the symbolism is to be taken separately, the term here must refer simply to Wisdom's association with God (cf. 9:9). **4.** *for:* Refers to "sought" in v. 2. *understanding of God:* The knowledge that God possesses. *selector of his works:* The author conceives of God as giving Wisdom a voice in choosing what his works should be. **5.** *produces:* The Gk verb (*ergazesthai*) also means to make money from something; apparently both meanings are intended here (cf. 7:11; 14:2; Prv 8:18). **6.** *prudence:* Practical intelligence. **7.** *justice:* In the first stich, it designates the ensemble of all the virtues; in the fourth, the cardinal virtue. *works:* Labors. **8.** *turns of phrases... solution of riddles:* The wisdom of the ancients found in maxims and stories (cf. Prv 1:6; Sir 39:2-3). *signs and wonders:* Eclipses, storms, and earthquakes. *outcome of times and ages:* The course of history.

27 (ii′) *Solomon sought Wisdom as his counselor and comfort* (8:9–16). (Incl.: *live/living with,* 8:9,16). Through Wisdom's counsel, Solomon would have glory in life and be remembered in death, for he would be wise and would be a noble and brave king; his private life would be serene. **12.** *hands upon their mouths:* A gesture of respectful silence (cf. Jb 29:9). **13.** *immortality:* In the memory of men, as in the previous OT books.

28 (i′) *Solomon realizes that Wisdom is a gift of God* (8:17–21). (Incl.: *my heart,* 8:17,21). In view of all the blessings that come from Wisdom's company, Solomon went about seeking her for his own. He was of noble birth, but he knew that Wisdom came not with nobility but was a gift of God; therefore, he went to the Lord and besought him. **17.** *heart:* The seat of the intellect for the Hebrews. *immortality:* Apparently in the sense of v. 13, for these lines recapitulate 8:2–16. **20.** Some have proposed that the author here espouses the Gk doctrine of the pre-existence of the human soul. Taken in itself, the verse could appear to reflect such an idea, but it should be read in the context of the whole book. According to the Gk doctrine, the pre-existent soul is sullied by its contact with the body and seeks deliverance through death. Our author's remarks on created things (1:14) and on the possibility of an "unsullied body" (7:20) and a "soul that plots evil" (1:4) show how foreign these ideas are to him. Moreover, in the present context the author is not concerned with the pre-existence of the soul but rather with the pre-eminence of the soul (correcting v. 19, which appears to give priority to the body). *unsullied:* Matching his noble nature. The question of original sin lies outside the author's view.

29 (c) SOLOMON'S PRAYER FOR WISDOM (9:1–18). The author presents his version of Solomon's prayer (cf. 1 Kgs 3:6–9; 2 Chr 1:8–10). The prayer, with phrases reminiscent of Ps, is divided into two paragraphs of identical structure (address, petition, motive, and a supplementary general observation). In the first paragraph, God, who has given dominion to all men, is asked to give Solomon Wisdom because Solomon is a man weak and lacking in comprehension (1–5; Incl.: *man,* 2 and 5). Indeed, even if a man be perfect, without Wisdom he is nothing (6). In the second paragraph, God, who has chosen Solomon to be king and to build the Temple, and who has with him Wisdom, is asked to send her to be with Solomon because she knows what is pleasing to God and can guide him (7–12; Incl.: *your people,* 7 and 12). Indeed, no man can arrive at God's counsels without wisdom, for thus have men always learned what is pleasing to God (13–18; Incl.: *counsel,* 13 and 17).

1. *God of my fathers:* An appeal to God's fidelity to the promises that he made to the patriarchs and to David. *word:* The creative Word of God (cf. Gn 1; Ps 33:6). **2.** *to rule:* Cf. Gn 1:26–28. **4.** *attendant at your throne:* Cf. Prv 8:27–30. *reject:* Solomon deprecates a fate that he knows must befall him if he thinks to dispense with Wisdom. The terminology is reminiscent of Ps 89:38. **8.** *copy:* The Chronicler represents David as having received from God a detailed account of the Temple, which he passed on to Solomon (1 Chr 28:11–19). The holy Tabernacle that Solomon was meant to copy is not the Tabernacle of Moses but an ideal archetype, which the writer pictures as existing in heaven (for the same concept, cf. Heb 8:2,5; 9:23). **9.** Cf. Prv 3:19–20; 8:22–30. **11.** *by her glory:* By her power (cf. Rom 6:4). The divine glory is the manifestation of God's power and attributes. **14.** *timid:* Uncertain. **15.** This verse, reminiscent of Plato (*Phaedo* 30.81c), has caused the author to be accused of a dualism, which pronounces matter evil. Such an idea (espoused by Philo) is foreign to the OT, and the author does not go beyond such texts as Ps 103:14; Jb 4:19; Is 38:12; he merely says that the earthbound body is a weight on the heavenward aspirations of the soul (cf. also Gal 5:17; Rom 7:14–25; 2 Cor 4:7). **17.** *holy spirit:* The author identifies Wisdom with the Spirit of the Lord (see comment on 1:4; on the whole chapter, cf. F. Zorell, *VD* 2 [1922] 264–69). N. Peters sees the prayer as the translation of an alphabetic Hebr psalm (*BZ* 14 [1916] 1–14), but the arguments in favor of a Gk original obtain here as elsewhere.

30 (d) TRANSITIONAL SECTION: WISDOM SAVES HER OWN (10:1–11:1). In this transitional section, which leads into the second part of the book (→ 4 above), the author expands on 9:18 and shows how Wisdom has saved men throughout history: all of mankind in Adam and Noah (10:1–4); Abraham (5); Lot (6–9); Jacob (10–12); Joseph (13–14); and the people of Israel (10:15–11:1). The paragraphs are not marked off with inclusions as elsewhere but with the emphatic pronoun *autē* (she) at the beginning of each paragraph (10:1,5,6,10,13,15). Following his usual custom, the author does not name the individuals discussed but merely refers to each as "the just" (10:4,5,6,10,13,20). Throughout this section, as well as in the second part of the book (chs. 11–19), we find the sacred history embellished with imaginative details and with popular traditions, which we find elsewhere in Philo, Josephus, and the Targums.

1. *father:* Adam. *he alone:* A difficult text and variously interpreted. Perhaps it means so long as he was alone without the temptress Eve. (See, however, A. Dupont-Sommer, *RHR* 119 [1939] 182–203.) *raised him up:* By repentance and expiation (an opinion current in Judaism). **3.** *unjust man:* Cain (Gn 4:8–13). *perished:* Incurred spiritual death. **4.** *on his account:* The wickedness that brought the flood is attributed to Cain instead of to the "sons of God" (Gn 6:4–6). The wickedness of Cain's descendants is a Jewish tradition (Josephus, *Ant.* 1.2, 2) not found in the Bible. *just man:* Noah. **5.** *universal wickedness:* The allusion is to the tower of Babel (Gn 11:1–9). *just man:* Abraham. *pity for his child:* When God commanded him to sacrifice Isaac (Gn 22:1–19). **6.** *just man:* Lot (Gn 19). *Pentapolis:* The five cities of the plain: Sodom, Gomorrah, Admah, Zeboiim, and Bela (or Zoar; Gn 14:2). **7.** *smoking desert:* A legendary exaggeration prompted perhaps by mists rising from the Dead Sea basin or smoke from the bituminous soil. *fruit:* Apparently the "apples of Sodom" referred to by Josephus (*JW* 4.34)—a fruit of the area seemingly fit to be eaten, but with a black, powdery interior. *pillar of salt:* Cf. Gn 19:26. **8-9.** These verses divide the poem into two parts: the rare just men in a wicked world (1–7); Jacob, Joseph, and Israel in a new age (10:10–11:1). The plurals here very likely refer to all that has gone before by way of summary (cf. Wright, *Bib* 48, 175–76). **10.** *just man:* Jacob, who fled from his brother Esau (Gn 27:41-28:10). *showed him:* The reference is apparently to Jacob's dream at Bethel (Gn 28:10–17). *kingdom of God:* The only occurrence of this important NT phrase in the OT. Here, it apparently means heaven, although this usage is unusual (cf. R. Schnackenburg, *God's Rule and Kingdom* [N.Y., 1963] 20 n.). It possibly reflects a belief that Jacob was shown future (even eschatological?) events. *holy things:* Perhaps heavenly realities in general; or perhaps the heavenly sanctuary (cf. 9:8), in which case the allusion would be to the tradition recorded in *T. Levi* 9:3 (cf. E. Burrows, *Bib* 20 [1939] 405–7). **11.** *defrauders... enriched:* The allusion is to Jacob's stay with Laban (Gn 29:1–31:21). **12.** *foes:* Perhaps Laban and his brothers (Gn 31:23–29) or Esau (*Jub* 37–38). *struggle:* At the Jabbok (Gn 32:22–32). **13.** *just man:* Joseph (Gn 37–41). **14.** *glory:* Undying fame. **15.** *blameless:* Holy insofar as they were chosen and set apart by God. The author overlooks Israel's infidelities to her vocation. **16.** *Lord's servant:* Moses. *kings:* The plural is puzzling if the reference is to Pharaoh, but cf. Ps 105:30, where the plural is likewise used. However, perhaps the kings outside Egypt are included. **17.** *recompense:* The precious objects of the Egyptians (Ex 3:21–22; 11:2–3; 12:35–36) and liberation from slavery were Israel's recompense for its slave labor. *shelter:* The cloud was thought of not only as a guide but also as a protection from the heat (cf. Ps 105:39; Is 4:5–6). **20.** *despoiled:* The despoiling of dead Egyptians at the Red Sea is not in the Ex account but is a tradition found in Josephus (*Ant.* 2.16, 6; 3.1, 4). *sang:* The allusion is to the Song of Miriam (Ex 15). **21.** *opened the mouths of the dumb...:* Apparently an allusion to a targumic legend that Israel's children, threatened by death in Egypt, were brought up in the wilderness by angels and later joined in the Exodus (P. Grelot, *Bib* 42 [1961] 49–60).

31 **(II) God's Fidelity to His People in the Exodus (11:2-19:22).** The second part of Wis, a homily on the Exodus, is a separate composition, probably written in the author's later life. It has been attracted to the earlier material because of the theme it has in common with chs. 1-6—retribution for the just and wicked. The homily recalls for the Alexandrian Jews that once before the Jews had suffered in Egypt and the Lord came to their rescue; therefore, it sets forth, in addition to the material in chs. 1–6, an historical basis for trust in God. Because of its present juxtaposition to chs. 1–6, the homily quite probably has an eschatological dimension, the Exodus events being recounted as an image of God's final intervention on behalf of the just (thus G. Kuhn, *ZNW* 28 [1929] 334-41, and others). The idea is explicit in 17:21.

The work is perhaps the best single example in the Bible of a midrash—i.e., a composition that explains the Scriptures and seeks to make them understandable and meaningful for a later generation (on the genre midrash, see A. G. Wright, *CBQ* 28 [1966] 105–38, 417–57; *The Literary Genre Midrash* [N.Y., 1967]). Midrash can take the form of a verse-by-verse commentary, a homily, or a rewritten version of a biblical narrative. Wisdom 11–19 is a midrash in homily form (perhaps a Passover sermon). The work takes its departure from a short summary of the biblical narrative of Israel's desert wanderings (11:2–4), after which one is perhaps expected to supply mentally an *et reliqua*. The author next states a pattern that he detects in the Exodus events: The Israelites were benefited by the very things that punished the Egyptians (11:5), and then, in a *synkrisis* or comparison (cf. F. Focke, *Die Entstehung der Weisheit Salomos* [Göttingen, 1913] 12; on this Gk figure, see F. Focke, *Hermes* 58 [1923] 327–68), he illustrates this observation in five antithetical diptychs (11:6–19:22). The homily also contains examples of the "rewritten Bible" type of midrash (cf. esp. the description of the plague of darkness in ch. 17). Two characteristics frequently found in a midrash are evident in the homily. There is, on the one hand, a careful attention to the details of the biblical account and a desire to explain the reasons for happenings (11:8; 16:3–4,6–8) and to draw out applications for the present (e.g., 16:26,28; 19:22); on the other hand, the biblical material is handled creatively: Details are altered to fit the purposes of the author and events are idealized and even embellished upon with legendary and imaginative material to make them more ample, vivid, and edifying (see R. T. Siebeneck, *CBQ* 22 [1960] 176–82).

32 **(A) Introductory Narrative (11:2-4).** The homily begins with a brief account of Israel's desert wanderings, which is partly dependent, as are several features of the homily, on Ps 107, apparently understood by the writer as referring to the Exodus. **2.** *they:* Throughout the composition the author avoids proper names as in the first part of the book. **3.** *enemies:* The biblical account mentions the Amalekites (Ex 17:8–16), Arad, Sihon, and Og (Nm 21), and the Midianites (Nm 31:1–12). **4.** *thirsted:* Cf. Ex 17:1–7; Nm 20:2–13. *they called upon you:* The writer ignores Israel's murmurings and presents an idealized version suggested by Ps 107:6.

(B) Theme: Israel Is Benefited by the Very Things That Punish Egypt (11:5). Apropos of the mention of the water from the rock, the author makes an observation on the Exodus events that will be the theme of the homily: The Israelites were benefited by the very things that punished the Egyptians. The idea is first attested in Wis and appears later in Philo (*De vita contemp.* 102).

(C) Illustration of the Theme in Five Antithetical Diptychs (11:6–19:22). Immediately after the statement of the theme, the author proceeds, not with a continuation of the narrative of 11:2–4, but with the first of his contrasts. The preposition *anti* ("instead of") serves as the "hinge" of the first four diptychs (11:6; 16:2; 16:20; 18:3).

33 (a) First Diptych: Water from the Rock Instead of the Plague of the Nile (11:6–14). (Incl.: *thirst,* 11:8,14.) Water punishes the Egyptians (cf. Ex 7:17–24) and benefits Israel (cf. Ex 17:5–7; Nm 20:8–11) in the desert (6–7). The Israelites thirsted in the desert as did the Egyptians during the plague, but for Israel it was only a test and to show them how their enemies were punished (8–11). For the Egyptians, the news of Israel's good fortune added to their grief (12–14). **6.** *instead of a spring:* The CCD envisions the wells the Egyptians dug to get water when the Nile was turned into blood (Ex 7:24) and contrasts this meager source with the abundance of water granted to Israel. It is also possible to translate "instead of a river's perennial source troubled with impure blood," in which case the contrast is punishment by water vs. blessing by water. **7.** *decree:* According to Ex 7:14–24, the purpose of this plague was to induce Pharaoh to let Israel go; Wis sees the plague as a punishment for Pharaoh's decree of Ex 1:16,22. *gave them:* The Israelites. **8–9.** In Dt 8:2–5, Israel's sufferings in the desert are interpreted as a testing, and so also below in v. 10, but here Wis gives an additional reason for the thirst. *punish, chastise:* A repetition of the theme of 3:4–10 (cf. also 12:22). **9.** *being tormented:* The author envisions some of the plagues in Egypt as continuing during Israel's desert journey (cf. 16:4,22). **11–10.** For the transposition of verses in the CCD, see Skehan (*Traditio* 3, 9–10). **11.** *those afar off and those close by:* From the point of view of Israel in the desert. **12.** *twofold grief:* Perhaps the memory of their suffering is doubled by their recognition that Yahweh had triumphed over the gods of Egypt; or perhaps the twofold grief is the recognition of Yahweh (13) and of the success of Moses (14). **13.** The writer assumes that the Egyptians are being informed of the desert events, as also in 16:8; (cf. Ex 32:12; Nm 14:13; Dt 9:28). **14.** *proved unlike:* The Egyptians had no relief for their thirst (or cf. v. 10).

34 (b) Second Diptych: Quail Instead of the Plague of Little Animals (11:15–16:15). The diptych is presented in three passages (11:15–16; 12:23–27; 15:18–16:4), each of which is followed by a digression (→ 10 above).

(i) (11:15–16) *plus digression on God's power and mercy* (11:17–12:22). The diptych begins by recalling the plagues of little animals, which were sent upon the Egyptians, according to the author, as a punishment for their worship of animals (11:15–16). **15.** *serpents:* The crocodile, serpent, lizard, and frog were worshiped in Egypt. *insects:* Beetles, scarabs. *dumb creatures:* Frogs (Ex 8:1–15), gnats (Ex 8:16–19), flies (Ex 8:20–24), and locusts (Ex 10:3–15). **16.** The idea, familiar from Pss 7:15–16; 57:6; Prv 26:27; and 2 Mc 9:6, is a truth of experience but not an absolute principle.

35 The digression, prompted by the mention of punishment for sin in 11:16, is divided as follows:

(A) God Is Omnipotent (11:17–22)
(B) Because of His Power God Is Merciful (11:23–12:22)
  (a) God Spares Men Because He Loves Them (11:23–12:8)
  (b) God's Might Is the Source of Mercy (12:9–18)
  (c) The Lesson To Be Derived (12:19–22)

36 (A) God Is Omnipotent (11:17–22). (Incl.: *universe,* 11:17,22.) God could have punished the Egyptians with death and in any number of ways because he is all-powerful. **17.** *from formless matter:* An allusion to the primeval chaos of Gn 1:2. **20.** *measure, number and weight:* God will not unnecessarily interfere with the regular course of nature (cf. *2 Esdras* 4:36–37). The phrase may be borrowed from Plato (see E. des Places, *Bib* 40 [1959] 1016–17). **21.** *for:* Refers to vv. 17–20. **22.** *grain from a balance:* A tiny particle used for weighing in scales.

37 (B) Because of His Power God Is Merciful (11:23–12:22). (Incl.: *mercy,* 11:23 and 12:22; *abandon wickedness,* 12:2,20. The word *metanoia* [*repent,* 11:23; *repentance,* 12:10,19], in its only occurrences in the book, marks the beginning of each of the three subsections.)

38 (a) God Spares Men Because He Loves Them (11:23–12:8). (Incl.: *men,* 11:23 and 12:8; *spare/spared,* 11:26 and 12:8.) God, whose power is irresistible (cf. 11:21) and who is therefore free of constraint, loves all the things that his creative power has made, for only love can explain his having created and preserved them. Because of this love, he pardons them and is patient in their regard so that they might repent (11:23–12:2; Incl.: *sins,* 11:23 and 12:2). God even gave the wicked Canaanites a chance to repent because they too were men whom he had created (12:3–8; Incl.: *land,* 12:3,7).

23. This verse announces the topic of the remainder of the digression. God's mercy is a prolongation of his creative power (11:24–12:2) and of his mastery over his own might (12:16–18). **24–26.** Nowhere else in the OT is there so forceful an expression of God's love for all things or a reason given for it. **12:1.** *imperishable spirit:* Either Wisdom as the agent of God's immanence (1:7; 7:24; 8:1), or as the breath of life put in creatures by God (Gn 2:7; Jb 27:3; 33:4; 34:14; Ps 104:30). **4.** *hated:* Manifestly in a different sense than in 11:24; the word here expresses God's antagonism toward sin. **4–5.** *works of witchcraft...:* Cf. Dt 18:9–12. **5.** For a discussion of the rearrangement of stichs in the CCD and the corrupted text, see Skehan (*Traditio* 3, 10–11). **6.** *willed to destroy:* Cf. Nm 33:52. **8.** *wasps:* Cf. Ex 23:28; Dt 7:20; Jos 24:12.

39 (b) God's Might Is the Source of Mercy (12:9–18). (Incl.: *power,* 12:9,18.) God gave the Canaanites a chance to repent, but not because he was unable to find means to punish them or because he feared that anyone would oppose him or accuse him of acting unjustly, for he is their maker who alone is God and whose might cannot be opposed (cf. 11:21) by any king or prince (12:9–14; Incl.: *condemn,* 12:10,13). God's might is not the source of arbitrary action but is the source of his justice (16a). Therefore, he exercises his might not on the innocent (15) but on those who challenge his omnipotence (17).

God's mastery over all is the source of his mercy (16b), for he is thereby master of his might (18), and hence executes his justice and rule with much lenience (12:15–18; Incl.: *master[y]; lenient/lenience*, 12:16,18). **10.** *for repentance:* Ex 23:29 (cf. Dt 7:22) and Jgs 2:22; 3:1–2 offer other opinions for God's gradual condemnation of the Canaanites. **11.** *accursed:* Probably an allusion to Gn 9:25. **16.** *might is the source of justice:* Cf. 2:11, where the wicked say that their might is the norm of justice. Unlike the wicked, whose weakness and insecurity prompt them to use unjustly what strength they have, God, being all-powerful and unchallenged, experiences no disturbed moral equilibrium and is therefore just and even merciful. **17.** *disbelieved:* By pagans. *those who know you:* Israelites who rashly disregard God. **18.** *judge:* Perhaps refers to God's action in v. 17; but it is also perhaps a generic statement, because the "us" seems to refer to all men. *power:* His omnipotence; it includes God's might as well as his ability to control it.

40 (c) The Lesson To Be Derived (12:19–22). (Incl.: *enemies*, 12:20,22.) By his merciful action, God teaches Israel to temper justice with mercy, and he gives her reason to hope for mercy from him. **21.** *exactitude:* Of leniency, not of severity. *fathers:* The patriarchs. **22.** *thousand blows: Muriotēti.* The idea fits the context of mercy poorly; the text should probably be emended to *metriotēti*, "with moderation" (see A. Vanhoye, *RSR* 50 [1962] 530–37).

41 (ii) (12:23–27) *plus digression on false worship* (13:1–15:17). Having concluded the first digression, the author returns to the Egyptian "panel" of the second diptych. **25.** The Egyptians were treated as if they were children. If children worshiped animals, their animals should make sport of them. *mockery:* Not a mock punishment but a real one that made both gods and people ridiculous. **26-27.** The Egyptians took no heed of the plagues of animals (the child's play). They did, however, come to recognize the true God (Ex 10:16), but, continuing to oppose him, they experienced the final condemnation: the death of their first-born and the destruction of their army in the Red Sea.

42 Apropos of the Egyptians' failure and success in recognizing the true God, the author digresses once again, this time on false worship. He divides such worshipers into two groups: those who worship nature and those who worship man-made idols. The digression is structured as follows:

(A) Nature Worship (13:1–9)
(B) Idolatry (13:10–15:17)
- (a) Introduction (13:10)
- (b) The Carpenter and Wooden Images (13:11–14:2)
- (c) Apostrophe (14:3–6) and Transition (14:7–11)
- (d) The Origin and Evils of Idolatry (14:12–31)
- (c′) Apostrophe (15:1–3) and Transition (15:4–6)
- (b′) The Potter and Clay Images (15:7–13)
- (a′) Conclusion (15:14–17)

(On the digression, see H. Eising, *Bib* 40 [1959] 393–408.)

43 (A) Nature Worship (13:1–9). (Incl.: *succeed in knowing*, 13:1,9.) Foolish were all men who failed to know God from studying his works and who considered the works themselves as gods. The works are great and mighty, but he who made them is exceedingly so and he can be known through these works. Such nature worshipers are well intentioned and look in the right direction; therefore, they are less blameworthy than others. But, because of their superficial use of their intelligence, they are not to be excused entirely. The writer is not presenting an argument for the existence of God. As a Hebrew, he does not even conceive of the pure atheist. That God exists is a fact; it is identifying him that poses a problem for men. The section is unique in the OT. Israel's knowledge of God was derived not from rational arguments, but from the experience of God's saving acts on Israel's behalf. The Greeks, on the other hand, strove to know God in a philosophical manner, and here our author acknowledges this approach, too, as a valid way to know the true God of Israel. The idea is taken up again by Paul in Rom 1:19–25. **1.** *by nature:* Either "not illuminated by wisdom," or, as we say, "born foolish." *him who is:* An allusion to the Hebr name of God in Ex 3:14, but perhaps, under Platonic influence, it also expresses here the idea of God as absolute being and pure existence, something not contained in the Ex text. **2.** *governors of the world:* Cf. Gn 1:16. (On this section, cf. C. Larcher, *LumVi* 14 [1954] 197–206.)

44 (B) Idolatry (13:10–15:17). (Incl.: *dead things; hands; made/makes*, 13:10 and 15:17.) Our author next launches into a satire on idols inspired by Is, Dt, Hos, Jer, and Pss. The central section of the digression attacks idolatry as being of human origin and the source of all evil (14:12–31); it is bracketed by a satirical depiction of a carpenter and wooden idols (13:11–14:2) and of a potter and clay idols (15:7–13).

45 (a) Introduction (13:10). (Incl.: *work[s]; hand[s]*.) Much more miserable than nature worshipers are those who put their hope in lifeless, handmade idols. *useless stone, the work of an ancient hand:* Probably a sacred meteorite with some regularity of shape, either accidental or the result of human workmanship (cf. Acts 19:35).

46 (b) The Carpenter and Wooden Images (13:11–14:2). (Incl.: *produce[d]; art/artificer*, 13:11 and 14:2.) A carpenter produces useful things from wood, uses the scraps to cook his food, and from the worthless wood that is left makes an image in his spare time. Then he and others pray to the helpless thing! The description is taken directly from Is 44 and is enlarged upon in language reminiscent of the same Prophet (Is 44:9–20; 40:18–20; 41:6–7). **14.** *red:* Ancient authors speak of images of Jupiter, Priapus, and Dionysus being painted red.

47 (c) Apostrophe (14:3–6) and Transition (14:7–11). The example of the seafarer develops into an hymnic apostrophe to God (Incl.: *guides/guidance*, 14:3,6), who is the real guide of every ship that puts to sea just as he was the guide of Noah in the ark. **3.** *road:* The terminology is reminiscent of the Exodus but here apparently refers simply to ships. **5.** *products...idle:* The existence of ships makes commerce possible; otherwise, the fruits of the earth would be wasted for lack of the means of distribution. **6.** *giants:* An allusion to Gn 6:4.

In 14:7–11 the thought returns to 13:10 (application of "god" to handmade images), and, by way of transition to the next section, the author adds the idea that the idols themselves will undergo judgment because they ensnare men in evil (Incl.: *comes/become*, 7 and 11). **7.** *wood:* The ark. *justice:* Divine justice in saving the just man.

48 (d) The Origin and Evils of Idolatry (14:12–31). (Incl.: *idols*, 14:12–30.) The initial verses introduce the topics of this central section: Idols are of human origin, and they lead to countless evils (12–14; Incl.: *devising/devised*, 12 and 14). The author proposes two examples of how idolatry originated. A father grieving for a child makes an image of the child; soon it is honored as a god with its own rites; in time, its worship is even prescribed by law. Again, an image of a king soon becomes an object of worship (15–20; Incl.: *honored; man*, 15 and 20). Idolatry, evil as it is in itself, also leads to other evils (cf. Rom 1:26ff.) in the immoral rites connected with it (21–27; Incl.: *evil*, 22 and 27). Idolatry also gives rise to false oaths, and those who practice both idolatry and perjury will be punished (28–31; Incl.: *sworn*, 29 and 31).

14. *vanity:* Empty imagining, foolish fancy. **15ff.** The more natural process would be for children to venerate their deceased ancestors (cf. 2 Mc 11:23), but instances of the worship of deceased children in ancient Egypt and elsewhere are known. **20.** The theory that pagan gods were originally deified rulers had been popularized by Euhemerus about 290 BC. **21.** *grief:* As described in vv. 15-16. *tyranny:* Cf. vv. 17–20. *incommunicable Name:* The name "God," which cannot be shared with creatures (cf. Is 42:8). **22.** *war:* Disturbance of passions within and violence without (cf. 14:23ff.) caused by ignorance of the true God. *peace:* For a Jew, spiritual and temporal well-being. **28.** *go mad...prophesy:* Mantic frenzy. **30.** *thought ill of God:* Thought wrongly.

49 (c′) Apostrophe (15:1–3) and Transition (15:4–6). The discussion of the punishment of the wicked develops into an apostrophe to God (Incl.: *know your might*, 15:2,3), who is merciful and who, unlike the idols, has might. Even if we sin with idols we still belong to God, which we know because we have experienced his mighty deeds on our behalf. But if we know that we belong to him, then we will not sin, for true knowledge of God (i.e., total dedication) is complete justice (and justice is immortal; cf. 1:15). Hence, the first step to immortality is to experience God's might. **3.** *might:* May also mean God's death-destroying power. The verse is difficult (for a survey of opinions and a fuller discussion, see R. E. Murphy, *CBQ* 25 [1963] 88–93). Cf. Jn 17:3.

The following verses (15:4–6; Incl.: *form; long[s]*, 5 and 6; *evil*, 4 and 6), with vocabulary reminiscent of 14:9–11 ("senseless"; "make") and 13:10 ("dead"; "hopes"), sum up the thought to this point and provide a transition into the final section. **6.** *hopes:* Futile trust in idols; or the idols themselves.

50 (b′) The Potter and Clay Images (15:7–13). (Incl.: *vessels: earth[en]*, 15:7,13). The potter, like the carpenter, produces useful vessels for our service (cf. 13:12), but out of the same clay from which he himself and his vessels were made he forms an idol. His whole existence is worthless because he did not recognize his creator but saw life as a time to make profit (cf. 13:19; 14:2). Indeed, the potter who makes idols is more guilty than any other because he knows well the brittleness of those images. **7.** Cf. Is 45. **9.** *vies:* Clay idols were glazed and gilded. *counterfeits:* On two counts: because they are imitations of valuable images and because they represent nonexistent gods. **11.** *soul, spirit:* See comment on 1:4. **12.** *evil:* Unlike the carpenter, this idolmaker has no belief in the idols he produces.

51 (a′) Conclusion (15:14–17). The thought returns to the Egyptians (14) and to the dead, handmade idols of 15:5 and 13:10. **15.** Cf. Pss 115:4ff. and 135:15ff. *idols of the nations:* The author projects back upon the past the religious syncretism of the Hellenistic period. **16.** *spirit:* See comment on 1:4. *has been lent:* Cf. 15:8. **17.** *mortal:* Because man is doomed to die he can only make dead things. "Death" in the second half of Wis means simply physical death (12:20; 16:13; 18:12–20; 19:5).

52 (iii) (15:18–16:4) *plus digression on the serpents in the desert* (16:5–15). (Incl.: *tormented*, 16:1, 4; *came/come*, 16:5, 14). The author returns to the Egyptian "panel" of the second diptych. Worse even than the religious syncretism of the Egyptians (cf. 15:15) is their worship of animals and, indeed, animals that have neither intelligence nor beauty to recommend them; therefore, they were punished by the plagues of little animals. But whereas animals plagued the Egyptians, they became a blessing to Israel in the desert, for God gave them quail (Ex 16:2–13; Nm 11:10–32). Loathsome creatures were sent upon the Egyptians so that they might loathe the sight of food and not be able to satisfy their hunger, whereas Israel received quail to satisfy her hunger. For hunger had to come upon Egypt as punishment for its tyranny, but on Israel only to show her once again (cf. 11:8) how her enemies were being afflicted. **15:18.** *compared as to folly:* From the point of view of the animals' lack of intelligence. *rest:* Of the animals. **19.** *escaped:* The line is obscure. Perhaps the curse of the serpent is thought of (Gn 3:14–15) or perhaps a legend that reptiles were exempted from God's blessing and approval in Gn 1. **16:2.** The author again gives us a glorified account and fails to mention Israel's murmuring in the desert (Ex 16:2–8) and the wrath of Yahweh (Nm 11:33–34). **3.** *turned from craving:* The allusion is apparently to the frogs in the ovens and kneading troughs (Ex 8:3). **4.** *being tormented:* The author implies that Israel's hunger was contemporaneous with Egypt's.

53 Again the author digresses. It is true that Israel also endured a plague of serpents (Nm 21:6–9), but it was not a punishment unto death as it was for the Egyptians. It was only a warning to remind them of Sinai and their dependence on God, and God saved the Israelites from death. The incident also served to convince the Egyptians that it is Yahweh who has dominion over life and death and not man, for man can slay but cannot revive. **6.** *they had:* The author seems to suppose that the sign of salvation (the bronze serpent) already existed when the plague of serpents appeared (yet cf. Nm 21:9). **8.** The writer once again (cf. 11:13) assumes that the Egyptians are being informed of the desert events (cf. Ex 32:12; Nm 14:13; Dt 9:28). **9.** *locusts and flies:* A paraphrase of the plague of little animals. *slew:* Somewhat hyperbolic; perhaps it is based on Ex 10:17 or on the legend recorded by Josephus (*Ant.* 2.14, 3). **13.** *lead back:* Means not an eschatological resurrection but that God can restore to life (1 Kgs 17:17–23; etc.). **14.** *spirit, soul:* See comment on 1:4. *confined:* By the "gates of death" (Pss 9:13; 107:18). **15.** The verse goes with the digression and not with the following diptych (cf. Dt 32:39 and Tb 13:2). *escape:* May form an inclusion with "escaped" in 15:19 to bring the second diptych to a close.

54 (c) THIRD DIPTYCH: A RAIN OF MANNA INSTEAD OF THE PLAGUE OF STORMS (16:16–29). (Incl.: *water*, 16:17,29). The diptych proper, the central one of the five, is set forth in 16:16–22 (Incl.: *rains, hail, fire*, 16:16,22) and is followed by a digression on creation (16:23–29), a theme that will be taken up again at the conclusion of the work (19:6–21). Whereas the Egyptians were punished by wondrous downpours of rain and hail and their crops were destroyed by thunderbolts (fire), passing unquenched through the showers and sparing the animals sent to plague the Egyptians (cf. Ex 9:22–26), God rained down manna—food of angels (Ps 78:25), bread from heaven (Ps 105:40)—upon the Israelites in the desert. The manna assumed every conceivable flavor, and, although similar to hoarfrost and ice, fire did not melt it when it was cooked (Ex 16:23; Nm 11:8) so that Israel, seeing this alteration in nature, might know that fire was destroying Egypt's crops even in the midst of rain. **17.** Cf. 5:17. **18.** *beasts:* Despite Ex 8:13,31, the author presumes that the plagues of animals lasted until the plague of rain and hail. **20.** *conforming:* The legend is found in the rabbinical literature also. This verse is applied to the Eucharist in the liturgy of the Blessed Sacrament. **22.** *snow and ice:* The manna was "like hoarfrost" (Ex 16:14) and had "the appearance of ice" (Nm 11:7 in the LXX). Both comparisons are used here under the influence of Ps 148:8.

The author then takes up the idea of v. 17 in a digression on creation (16:23–29). God works through creation when he punishes and blesses, and he thereby teaches moral lessons. For the nourishment of Israel, creation was transformed in many ways to teach Israel that it is not food but God's Word that saves man (23–26; Incl.: *nourish*, 23 and 26). Moreover, the manna, which was not destroyed by fire in the oven, could nevertheless be melted by the sun (Ex 16:21). Therefore, one must thank God before the sunrise, for the melting manna is an image of the hopes of anyone who is ungrateful (27–29; Incl.: *melt*, 27 and 29). **29.** The Shema was to be recited (according to the Mishnah, *Berakot* 1:2) when the sun's rays lighted up the tops of the mountains.

55 (d) Fourth Diptych: The Pillar of Fire Instead of the Plague of Darkness (17:1–18:4). (Incl.: *darkness; confined*, 17:2 and 18:4). Whereas the Egyptians were imprisoned in the total darkness (Ex 10:21–23), haunted by frightening apparitions, terrified by sounds, and seized by a panic induced by their bad conscience, the Israelites, who had enjoyed great light in Egypt (Ex 10:23), were guided in the desert by the pillar of fire (Ex 13:21–22; 14:24; etc.), for they were the future bearers of the light of the Law. The magnificent description of the plague of darkness is a good example of narrative midrash or "rewritten Bible." The biblical account is embellished with legends, speculations, and the author's imagination to make the account more vivid and to highlight the theological significance.

1. For the thought, see Ps 92:6–7; Wis 5:3ff. **2.** *exiles:* The darkness screens them even from God. **3.** *secret sins:* Cf., perhaps, 14:23. The author sees in this plague another instance of the law of talion (11:16); moral darkness is punished by physical darkness. *apparitions:* A legendary embellishment on the biblical account, as are many of the other details. **6.** *fires:* Probably lightning. *these, that sight:* The fires; they were more fearful than the darkness. **7.** A reference to the magicians (Ex 7:11,22; 8:7; 9:11), who were powerless against the plague. **9-10.** During the protracted darkness, when there was nothing really terrible near the magicians, the memory (or continuation) of the previous plagues caused them to people the darkness with terrors to the extent that they feared even the air. **11.** *cowardly, testifies:* The wicked man is fearful as a result of his wrongdoing, and it bears witness to his guilt. Verses 12–13 develop the thought. *conscience:* The first appearance of *syneidēsis* in this meaning in biblical Greek. **12–15.** Perhaps intended to be a digression (Incl.: *fear; surrender; expectation/unexpected*, 17:12,15). **13.** *expectation:* Fear is uncertain expectation. **14.** *powerless:* The night was powerless to hurt; the nether world is the place whose inhabitants have no strength. *sleep:* Rhetorical; to describe the rest imposed by the darkness the author resorts to terms of night. **15.** *surrender:* Of reason (cf. v. 12). *came upon:* Probably to be emended to "was poured upon" as the more difficult reading. **16.** The subject is no longer the magicians but the Egyptians generally. **18–19.** Seven natural sounds, which became terrifying in the darkness. **21.** *next should come:* In the nether world. *burdensome:* Their bad conscience. **18:2.** *thanked:* Not in the biblical account. *for the sake of the difference:* They pleaded with Israel to leave so that the plague that only Egypt suffered might cease. **3.** *mild:* They were sheltered from its heat by the cloud (cf. 10:17).

56 (e) Fifth Diptych: The Tenth Plague and the Exodus by Which God Punished the Egyptians and Glorified Israel (18:5–19:22). (Incl.: *your people*, 18:7 and 19:22; *glorified*, 18:8 and 19:22.) The diptych proper is set forth in 18:5–19 and 19:1–5.

(i) (18:5–19) *plus digression on the plague in the desert* (18:20–25). There are two digressions (18:20–25 and 19:6–21). In return for their determination to slay Israel's infants (Ex 1:22–2:10), the Egyptians were punished through the loss of their first-born sons (Ex 11:4–6; 12:29–32). They thereby came to recognize that Israel was God's son (18:5–19; Incl.: *perish*, 5 and 19.) **5.** *boy:* Moses. *reproof:* Ex does not assign any relation between the killing of Israel's sons and the tenth plague; but for Wis, the events furnish another example of the law of talion (11:16): The Egyptians who had killed the male children of Israel lost their first-born, and those who had used the Nile to drown Israel's children were themselves drowned in the Red Sea. **6.** *fathers:* Either the Israelites at the time of the Exodus (Ex 11:4–7), or, better, the patriarchs (Gn 15:13–14; 46:3–4; etc.), to whom God swore he would deliver their descendants. **8.** *summoned:* Chosen, out of all the peoples of the earth. **9.** *sacrifice:* The Passover, which created a religious unity. *institution:* Refers either to the law commanding the Passover or to the idea expressed in the next line. *praises of the fathers:* The author pictures the Israelites singing the praises of the patriarchs just as later Israel sang the Hallel (Pss 113–118) at the Passover. **10.** *cry:* Cf. Ex 12:30. **12.** *not sufficient:* An embellishment on Nm 33:3–4. **13.** *sorceries:* Cf. Ex 7:11; 8:7. *God's son:* An amplification of Ex 12:31 (cf. also Ex 4:22–23). **14–19.** The description is inspired by Ex 12:23; Jb 4:13–15; 1 Chr 21:15–27. The liturgy uses the passage in an accommodated sense of the incarnation, a use already attested in Ignatius (*Ep. ad Eph.* 19; see A. Cabaniss, *VigChr* 10 [1956] 97–102). **15.** *word:* In the OT, Yahweh's Word was regarded as the executor of divine judgments (Hos 6:5; Jer 23:29; etc.; cf. also *Tg. Jon* on Ex 12:29). **17.** *them:* The first-born. *dreams:* The detail is from Jb 4:13–15, rather than from the Ex account. Not only were the survivors to recognize God's hand but also the victims.

57 *Digression on the plague in the desert* (18:20–25). (Incl.: *trial; anger*, 18:20,25.) It is true that Israel in the desert also experienced a plague of death as did the Egyptians (Nm 16:44–50), but the parallel is only apparent: The plague did not last long because Aaron interceded. **22.** *smiter:* Called an angel in *4 Mc* 7:11. **23.** *cut off the way:* Blocking the smiter. **24.** *whole world:* Aaron's garments were symbolic. Jewish tradition had it that the long blue robe denoted the sky; the girdle, the ocean; the buttons on the shoulders, the sun and moon; etc. (cf. Philo and Josephus). *four rows:* The four rows of precious stones in the high priest's breastplate, upon which were engraved the names of the 12 patriarchs or tribes of Israel (cf. Ex 28:15–21). *grandeur:* On the high priest's miter were engraved the words, "Holy to the Lord" (Ex 28:36). **25.** *destroyer:* The term is introduced from Ex 12:23. *enough:* To warn Israel; they were not like the Egyptians, who needed to drain the cup to the dregs.

58 (ii) (19:1–5) *plus digression on creation* (19:6–21). The Egyptians, however, pursued the Israelites and experienced in the Red Sea the completion of the punishment begun in the tenth plague (Ex 14:5–31). In all these events, on the other hand, Israel experiences a wondrous journey (19:1–5).

1. *he knew:* God (cf. Ex 14:3–4). **4.** *compulsion:* The Egyptians freely chose their sinful deeds (cf. 19:13). When they did not repent at the initial warnings (cf. 12:26), their unrepented sins led to new sins, and pursuing justice finally overtook them (cf. 14:31; Ex 14:4; Rom 9:17–24). *fill out:* Cf. Dn 8:23; 2 Mc 6:14; 1 Thes 2:16. **5.** *wondrous...extraordinary:* Unprecedented and characterized by miracles and wonders. ("Your people" and "glorious" form an intermediate inclusion with "your people" and "glorify" in 18:7–8.)

59 *Digression on creation* (19:6–21); Incl.: *kind*[*s*], 6 and 21.) The author takes up once again a theme already touched on in the digression to the third and central diptych: Creation ministers to God's commandments (cf. 16:24–29). Here, the further observation is made that creation, in co-operating in the Exodus events, was made over anew, for the miracles were like a repetition of the first creation: The cloud covered the camp (Ex 14:19–20), just as the darkness (or spirit) covered the waters (Gn 1:2); dry land appeared out of the Red Sea (Ex 14:21–22) as it had from the primeval waters (Gn 1:9–10), and from the land came vegetation ("grass," v. 7; Gn 1:11–13); the land brought forth gnats (Ex 8:16–19) instead of animals (Gn 1:24); the waters swarmed with frogs (Ex 8:2) instead of fish (Gn 1:20); a new bird appeared from the sea (Ex 16:13; Nm 11:31), as at the first creation birds had appeared (Gn 1:20 in the LXX); and thunder accompanied the Exodus (Ps 77:17–18) as it had the creation, according to Ps 104:7 (6–13a; Incl.: *sea*, 7 and 12). The author digresses in the second paragraph to observe that the Egyptians' punishment was just, because they were more blameworthy in their treatment of strangers than were the evil Sodomites. The author notes further that both Egyptians and Sodomites were stricken with a similar blindness (13b–17; Incl.: *just*[*ly*], 13 and 17). Returning to the subject of the new creation, Wis suggests that it was accomplished by a rearrangement of the basic elements of the universe in the same way that a rearrangement of notes produces a new melody (19:18–21). **6.** *kinds:* Reminiscent of Gn 1:21,24,25. *its natural laws:* Read "your commandments" with many LXX manuscripts and Latin (cf. the deliberate parallel with the beginning of the digression in 16:24). **7.** *grassy:* Another embellishment on the biblical account (cf. *Tg.Jon*). **13b–17.** Perhaps the mention of the thunderbolts led to the thought of the Sodomites, who were overwhelmed with a tempest of fire (Gn 19:24), and provided the author an opportunity to present one final comparison. **13.** *they suffered:* The Egyptians. *guests:* Hospitality was the supreme law of the ancient Near East. *more grievous:* Than the Sodomites. **14.** *those others:* The Sodomites, who were inhospitable to the angels (Gn 19:1–11). *these:* The Egyptians. *beneficent:* Because of the services rendered by Joseph (Gn 39–47). *guests:* Israel had been invited to come into Egypt (Gn 45:17–18). **15.** Refers to the Sodomites. **16.** "These" (the Egyptians) "oppressed those" (the Israelites). *same rights:* The author supposes that the Israelites already possessed the civil privileges enjoyed by the Jews at this time under the Ptolemies. There may well be allusions in these verses to conditions in Egypt contemporaneous with the author. **17.** *they were stricken with blindness:* The Egyptians, with the plague of darkness. *the just:* Lot. **18.** The author is the first to attempt an explanation of the biblical wonders in the light of the Gk idea of the harmony of the cosmos (cf. Philo, *De vita Mos.* 1.17); cf. J. P. M. Sweet, *Miracles* [ed. C. F. D. Moule; London, 1965] 113–26). **19.** *land creatures:* Apparently the reference is to the Israelites and their cattle going through the sea. *those that swam:* The frogs. **20–21.** Cf. 16:17–22. **21.** *ambrosial:* Heavenly. (On the digression, see Beauchamp, *op. cit.*, 491–526.)

60 (iii) *Conclusion* (19:22). The author draws a conclusion from his discussion for the encouragement of his fellow Jews and provides an inclusion with 18:7–8. The abruptness of the ending has been remarked by most of the commentators, and it has been suggested that some verses have been lost. The numerical patterns (→ 10 above), however, indicate that the text is intact; therefore the author must have been satisfied with chs. 11–19 as a rounded literary unit. (Bibliography for chs. 11–19: Kuhn, *op. cit.*, 334–41; E. Stein, *MGWJ* 78 [1934] 558–75; Fichtner, *ZNW* 36, 113–32; G. M. Camps, *Fest. B. Ubach* [Montserrat, 1953] 97–113; Siebeneck, *op. cit.*, 176–82; Wright, *Bib* 48, 176–84.)

35

PSALMS

Roland E. Murphy, O.Carm.

BIBLIOGRAPHY

1 *Bibliographical information and summaries of modern trends:* De Langhe, R. (ed.), *Le Psautier* (Louvain, 1962). Johnson, A. R., in *OTMS* 162–209. Mowinckel, S., "Psalm Criticism between 1900 and 1935," *VT* 5 (1955) 13–33.

General studies: Becker, J., *Israel deutet seine Psalmen* (Stuttgart, 1966). Drijvers, P., *The Psalms* (N.Y., 1965). Gunkel, H. and J. Begrich, *Einleitung in die Psalmen* (HKAT; Göttingen, 1933). Mowinckel, S., *Psalmenstudien I–IV* (Oslo, 1921–24); *The Psalms in Israel's Worship I–II* (N.Y., 1962) with a complete bibliography in vol. 2, 271–89. Ringgren, H., *The Faith of the Psalmists* (London, 1963). Westermann, C., *Das Loben Gottes in den Psalmen* (Göttingen, 1954); ET: *The Praise of God in the Psalms* (Richmond, 1965). Worden, T., *The Psalms Are Christian Prayer* (London, 1962).

Commentaries: Castellino, G., *Libro dei Salmi* (Rome, 1955). Dahood, M., *Psalms I–II* (AB 16–17; N.Y., 1966–68). Gunkel, H., *Die Psalmen* (HKAT; Göttingen, 1926). Kissane, E., *The Book of Psalms I–II* (Dublin, 1953–54). Kraus, H.-J., *Psalmen I–II* (BKAT 15; Neukirchen, 1960). Podechard, E., *Le Psautier I–II* (Lyon, 1949–54). Schmidt, H., *Die Psalmen* (HAT 15; Tübingen, 1934). Weiser, A., *The Psalms* (Phila., 1962).

Special studies: Barth, C., *Die Errettung vom Tode* (Zollikon, 1947); *Introduction to the Psalms* (N.Y., 1966). Falkenstein, A., and W. von Soden, *Sumerische und akkadische Hymnen und Gebete* (Zurich, 1953). Füglister, N., *Das Psalmengebet* (München, 1965).

INTRODUCTION

2 **(I) Text and Versions.** The MT of Pss is corrupt in many places, but in recent times a reaction has set in against the uninhibited emendation that characterized earlier scholars, such as C. Briggs, H. Herkenne, and H. Gunkel. At the present time, scholars recognize that emendations, even conjectural, are necessary, and they rely on the evidence of ancient versions and also upon the new understanding of Hebrew that the ancient Ugaritic language and literature afford (cf. M. Dahood, *Psalms I* [AB 16; N.Y., 1966] xv–xliii). The LXX is the most important of the ancient versions, even if it presents a bewildering variety of textual forms; there is still no critical edition of the Syr Pesh, but W. E. Barnes published an edition of Pss in 1914. The Lat versions are particularly important because of their influence on ecclesiastical literature and liturgy. Almost all were based on the LXX and thus reflected a numbering that is usually one digit lower than the Hebr numbering. What is called the *Psalterium Romanum* and usually attributed to Jerome's editorial revision seems merely to be the OL Pss. At Bethlehem in 386, Jerome produced the *Psalterium Gallicanum*, which became the Psalter of the Vg and hence of Lat Christendom. It was a revision of OL in the light of the Hexapla, but it retained all the LXX weaknesses, especially the confusion in tenses. Jerome's best effort, the *Psalterium juxta Hebraeos* (ed. by the Benedictine Commission, Vatican City, 1954), was an independent translation from the Hebrew, which unfortunately was never accepted into the Vg. In 1945, a new Lat translation was published by order of Pope Pius XII, the so-called *Psalterium Pianum* (cf. A. Bea, *CBQ* 8 [1946] 4–35). It is a soberly critical translation from the Hebrew and has been generally well received despite criticisms of the Latinity. (→ Texts, 69:100–103.)

The CCD is an independent critical translation of the Hebrew, but it has been influenced by the *Psalterium Pianum* of 1945. There are about 50 instances in which it departs from the Hebr text underlying the *Psalterium Pianum*. For the most part, it agrees with the emendations proposed by that Lat version, but it often departs from the understanding of the Hebrew that the Latin proposes.

The discovery of a Ps scroll in cave 11 near Qumran, which contains 33 Pss in whole or in part from 92 through 151, does not add much to the critical understanding of the text. More interesting, from an historical point of view, is the fact that the scroll contains the Hebr original of three of five noncanonical "psalms," which previously had been preserved only in Syriac (for Ps 151, cf. P. W. Skehan, *CBQ* 25 [1963] 407–9; see also DJD 4; → Texts, 69:27).

3 **(II) The Formation of the Psalter.** The book itself gives evidence of a fivefold division, probably in imitation of the Pentateuch; the divisions are indicated by the doxologies at 41:14; 72:19; 89:52; 106:48, and 150:6 (or perhaps the entire Ps). But these groups (indicated here as I–V) are in turn formed from earlier collections. The "Elohist" Psalter (42–83) receives its name from its use of the generic name for God, Elohim, which has been systematically substituted throughout these poems for the proper name, Yahweh. Further subdivision of the groups is justified by the indications in the titles to the Pss, which reflect ancient Jewish tradition. The following schema gives a quick picture of the situation:

I. David Pss: 3–41
II and III. Pss 42–72 and 73–89
 42–49: Korah (44–48 community songs)
 51–71: David (mostly Pss of individual lament)
 73–83: Asaph (74–82 are community songs)
 84–88: Korah (except 86), a sort of appendix to the Elohist Psalter
IV and V. Pss 90–106 and 107–50.
 93–101: Yahweh's kingship (except 94)
 103–07: Pss of praise
 111–18: Alleluia Pss of praise
 120–34: Pss of ascents
 138–45: David (141–44 are individual laments)
 146–50: Alleluia Pss of praise

C. Westermann, upon whose article in *Theologia Viatorum* 8 (1961–62) 278–84 (= *Forschung am Alten Testament* [Munich, 1964] 336–43) this significant grouping of the Pss is based, argues in some detail concerning the inner groupings of the Pss. But even if there are several Pss that cannot be conveniently grouped, the schema suggests the complicated process of the collection of the Pss. Certainly the literary type alone was not the criterion, yet we should note that most of the individual laments are in I and II, and most of the hymns of praise are in III and V (just as the Book of Lamentations forms a group of national laments, and at Qumran the "praises" were put together to form the *Hodayot*).

4 **(III) Titles: Authorship and Technical Terms.** The titles or superscriptions of the Pss are not part of the inspired text. They were added by pre-Christian Jewish tradition, and they attempt to provide data concerning "authorship," the type of Ps (*maśkîl*, etc.), and even the life setting (e.g., Ps 34 is referred to David "when he feigned madness before Abimelech, who forced him to depart").

The most common designation of "authorship" is *l^e^dāwîd*, which may be interpreted to mean "by," "of," "about," or "for" "David." "Of David" in the CCD translation reflects the time-honored acceptance of Davidic authorship, but most Catholic scholars now acknowledge that this term cannot be taken in the proper sense of authorship. The attribution of Pss to David is more in the simplistic style of the authorship of the Pentateuch by Moses or of the wisdom literature by Solomon. The general trend today among all scholars is to recognize the pre-exilic origins of the majority of the Pss (in contrast to the earlier views of J. Wellhausen and T. K. Cheyne). However, it is difficult to date individual poems with any certainty within this period (cf. the summary of R. Tournay's—necessarily tentative—views by J. Coppens in *ETL* 36 [1960] 911–13). The indications as to authorship are convenient for distinguishing the various groupings of Pss that were made before the final collection.

As far as the dating of Pss is concerned, the verdict of O. Eissfeldt (*OTI* 448) is worth quoting: "We shall have to be content with the very general statement that it [the Psalter] contains, in addition to exilic and post-exilic elements, songs and parts of songs which are old and perhaps very old indeed. This indicates that each individual psalm must be examined with reference to its age...." In the commentary below, the approximate dating given to several Pss should be understood in the light of the above statement.

The superscriptions also contain many technical terms, but the meaning of most of these was already lost by the time of the LXX. The interpretation of these terms can be summarized under the following headings (for details, cf. the commentaries):

5 (a) General Descriptions. "Song" (*šîr*). This was generally accompanied by music; it has the further nuance of a cultic song, something carried out in the liturgy.

"Psalm" (*mizmōr*). This word occurs 57 times as a technical term in the superscriptions. Properly, it means a song accompanied with stringed instruments; it is rendered *psalmos* in the LXX.

Miktām (6 times) remains a mystery. Efforts have been made to interpret it as a penitential Ps or as a secret prayer.

Maśkîl (13 times), on the basis of the vb. *śkl*, has been taken to mean a didactic poem, but it is found also with those that are not didactic. Another possibility is "artistic poem," i.e., one executed with art.

"Praise" (*t^e^hillâ*). Indicates a song of praise, a hymn. The plural (masc.!) of this word, *t^e^hillîm*, came to be applied to the collection of the Pss.

"Prayer" (*t^e^pillâ*). Designates a lament and a plea.

"Song of ascents" (*šîr hamma'ălôt*). There are several explanations advanced for this title, which occurs in Pss 120–34: songs of returning exiles, as they "went up" from Babylon; songs uttered by Levites on the 15 steps ascending into the court of the Israelites in the Temple; the "staircase" parallelism (anadiplosis, joining one line to another by a catchword) found in many of these Pss—e.g., 121:3–4,7–8. It is more probable that the phrase indicates pilgrim Pss, used by pilgrims as they "went up" to Jerusalem for the feasts.

(b) Musical Terms and Directions. "For the leader." This phrase, which occurs 55 times, is usually taken to refer to the director of the music, but the meaning is not certain.

"With stringed instruments" is probably a musical annotation indicating the kind of accompaniment (Ps 4:2); similarly, "with wind instruments" (Ps 5:1).

Idithun (*Y^e^dûtûn*) may refer to the name of David's choir leader (1 Chr 9:16).

"Upon the eighth," in 6:1; 12:1, may refer to the eight-stringed instrument.

Šiggāyôn ("plaintive song" in 7:1) may refer to a lament.

(c) Miscellaneous. *Selah*, which occurs 71 times in 39 Pss, is completely unknown, despite desperate efforts to give it a meaning. It might indicate a lifting up of the tone or of the eyes; others think it is a sign for repetition or that it means bowing.

Maḥălat (53:1; 88:1) is unknown. Many other phrases remain unknown to us, as in 56:1 (*Jonat*); 22:1, "the hind of the dawn." "Lilies" occur in various combinations in 45:1; 60:1. "Do not destroy" in 57:1 is likewise unclear; so also *gittith* (8:1); "Virgins" (46:1); *Mut labben* (9:1); etc.

6 **(IV) Literary Types.** The most important single event in the modern study of the Pss has been Gunkel's literary analysis of types (→ Modern OT Criticism, 70:39). He applied form-critical methods to the Pss and clearly established the various classifications:

hymns, laments, etc. He recognized that these songs generally correspond to a given *Sitz im Leben* (life setting), often liturgical, and that they share in a common fund of thoughts, moods, and even vocabulary. Each group has its particular manner of literary expression and, in some instances, of content. In other words, there were set forms, or molds, in which the Pss were cast; they were not sheerly personal outpourings to God; the stereotyped nature of the language used in the poems should have made this evident. They follow certain definite patterns that already existed, and they grow out of the given life setting with which they are connected, as a thanksgiving Ps grows out of the occasion of the thanksgiving sacrifice. The formal characteristics of the types will be outlined, but at times the content combines with the literary traits to form a classification (e.g., royal Pss). Moreover, one often finds mixed compositions (89, 102). In some instances, the classification must remain doubtful. (On Gunkel, see the summary by Johnson, *OTMS* 162–209; Gunkel's *Einleitung* was edited posthumously by J. Begrich and remains a fundamental work.)

S. Mowinckel built upon Gunkel's foundation and carried the literary studies of the Pss completely into the realm of cult. Gunkel had recognized cultic background for many Pss, but he claimed that there were also several "spiritual" poems, composed privately in imitation of the liturgical pieces. Mowinckel argued that there was a basic liturgical orientation to the Pss, and his profound studies on the nature of kingship and cult, and his recognition of the similarity between certain biblical themes and the Babylonian *Akitu* festival (New Year), led him to assume the existence of a New Year enthronement feast of Yahweh. About one-third of the Pss have this feast as their life setting. At times, he seems to go beyond his evidence (e.g., in considering the large number of Pss associated with the feast and in evaluating the Babylonian evidence for the existence of the feast in Israel), but no one has really refuted the basic enthronement idea in Pss 47, 93, etc. It is hardly an answer to say that there is no evidence for an enthronement feast in the OT historical books. Another characteristic of his approach is the so-called democratization, meaning that certain Pss, which were originally uttered by priest, prophet, or king, came to be applied to and to express the religious sentiment of the average Israelite. Hence, his understanding of "I" and "we" references in Pss is complicated; somehow the community speaks in the first person singular through its cultic representative (the king), who identifies with the people (in the title, *l*^{e}*dāwīd* meant originally the king, not David). The authors of the Pss are, for Mowinckel, Temple singers who composed the songs for someone else, a king or cultic leader. The poet entered into the life situation of the worshiper for whom he composed; hence, there would be no artificiality (cf. Mowinckel, *The Psalms*; A. R. Johnson in *Myth, Ritual and Kingship* [ed. S. H. Hooke; Oxford, 1958] 205–35). For the enthronement feast, → Religious Institutions, 76:151–54.

7 Among the opponents of Mowinckel is H.-J. Kraus, who has offered a theory of his own. On the basis of 2 Sm 6 and 1 Kgs 8, he reconstructs a royal Zion festival commemorating the choice of both the Davidic dynasty and Jerusalem as the Lord's dwelling. The worship involved procession with the Ark, but no enthronement (e.g., Ps 132). With the Exile, there came a change; thanks to the emphasis of Dt-Is upon the kingship of Yahweh, there emerged the idea of an entry of Yahweh, leading his people to Jerusalem where he is enthroned. Such is the life setting of the enthronement Pss (47, etc., excluding Ps 95).

Another basic and somewhat monolithic approach to Pss has been proposed by A. Weiser. The proper life setting of the Pss is the annual feast of covenant renewal. In view of the new awareness of the role of the covenant in ancient Israel (cf. K. Baltzer, *Das Bundesformular* [Neukirchen, 1960]), and of the prominence of the covenant theme in the Psalter, Weiser's theory has some plausibility. The center of the cultic act is the theophany, Yahweh's self-revelation to the believer, just as the theophany is the center of the covenant narrative in Ex. It is in this liturgical re-enactment of the covenant and its implications that the psalmist encounters God; hence, there are many references to Yahweh "enthroned on the cherubim," and to his "name" and to his "face." However appealing this hypothesis is—and it does provide a satisfactory explanation of many Pss—it is hardly the key to the entire Psalter. For the Feast of Weeks as the feast commemorating the Sinai covenant, → Religious Institutions, 76:142.

The most recent significant study on literary types has been done by Westermann (cf. R. E. Murphy in *CBQ* 21 [1959] 83–87). He denies that there are any true thanksgiving Pss (the word "thanksgiving" does not exist in Hebr, as he points out); there are only Pss of praise. These are of two kinds: confessional (acknowledging the Lord's intervention—this would replace the traditional classification of thanksgiving); and descriptive (e.g., 117). However, his views have thus far met with only limited acceptance.

8 The literary approach to Pss was considerably aided by the comparative materials in Egyptian and Mesopotamian literatures that were made available in modern times. A pioneer study was made by F. Stummer, and this line of research was pursued by G. Castellino and G. Widengren for the Babylonian laments. The similarities with Egyptian prayers are noted by A. Blackman (in *The Psalmists* [ed. D. C. Simpson; Oxford, 1926]). The parallels with Ugarit are abundant in matters of vocabulary and poetic structure, although there are no Ugaritic Pss (cf. J. Patton, *Canaanite Parallels in the Book of Psalms* [Baltimore, 1948]). As in all questions of comparative literature, one should not be misled by mere similarities. The same words do not always mean the same things, because they are colored by the particular culture or religious milieu in which they are used. The distinctive differences between Israelite, Egyptian, and Mesopotamian religions should not be glossed over because of a common fund of vocabulary and thought patterns. There are bound to be basic similarities in man's encounter with divinity.

The OT Pss follow the general liturgical and poetic structure common to the Fertile Crescent. Widengren has illustrated the structure basic to the Mesopotamian and Israelite laments (G. Widengren, *The Accadian and Hebrew Psalms of Lamentation as Religious Documents* [Uppsala, 1937]): invocation of the divinity; the complaint about various evils (sickness, etc.); the request for deliverance (and forgiveness, inasmuch as a general connection exists between sin and suffering); and a vow to offer sacrifice. There is a noticeable similarity in vocabulary: Sheol; beasts; a face that is turned away; etc. Scholars have pointed out the monotony and repetition that are characteristic of the Akkadian prayers, especially in the litany of names and epithets given to the gods (e.g., *ANET* 385b). The intimacy with God that characterizes many of the Hebr Pss is lacking in the Babylonian prayers: men are the slaves of the gods. As the creation myth indicates, they were made to relieve the gods of daily menial work. The words of A. Falkenstein and W. von Soden (*op. cit.*, 56) are worth quoting: "The Psalms are much freer in form and more varied in structure. There are decisive differences which stem from the excessive ties the Babylonians have with tradition, and from Israel's unconditioned faith in one God.... In summary we can perhaps say that even the most beautiful Babylonian prayers, despite many related ideas, do not come up to the Psalms in any way, because it was not given to their poets to dedicate themselves completely and without any reservation to the God whose will they believed they knew; they could therefore often proclaim important truths, but not the truth."

9 (a) HYMN OF PRAISE. It is essentially a song of praise, with the following structure: introduction; body; and conclusion. The introduction is an invitation to praise Yahweh ("sing," "rejoice," etc.; cf. 35:1–3), which is expressed by the imperative or volitive mood. The audience varies—the just, Israel, Gentiles, or even the psalmist himself. Frequent reference is made to the gestures of prayer or to the instruments used with the vocal praise. The body is introduced by the causal particle (*kî*, "for" or "because," e.g., 117:2) or a relative clause or participle (e.g., 104:2–4). It presents the reason for the praise: Yahweh's attributes; his work in creation or in salvation history; etc. The theology of the Pss is to be found particularly in the hymns. The Lord can be addressed in the second person, or he can be described in the third person. There is no formal conclusion, but often the invitation is repeated from the introduction, or a wish is expressed (104:35).

The life setting of the hymns is generally some cultic situation, which may be indicated in the poem (e.g., 100:4). Among the famous Near Eastern parallels may be mentioned the hymn to Amon-Re, the hymn to the Aton (Sun) by Akhenaton, or the Osiris hymn (cf. *ANET* 365ff.), which present structural and material similarities to the OT Pss. (For Mesopotamian counterparts, cf. Falkenstein and Von Soden, *op. cit.*, with the literary discussion on pp. 20–22, 43–44.) The following Pss may be classified as hymns: 8; 19:1–7; 29; 33; 46–48; 65; 66:1–12; 68(?); 76; 77:14–21; 84; 87; 93; 95–99; 104; 111; 113–14; 117; 122; 129; 134–36; 139; 145–50. Outside the Psalter, cf. the Song of Deborah (Jgs 5) and the Song of Miriam (Ex 15).

It is convenient to group separately under the hymns the so-called songs of Zion (46, 47, 76, 84, 87, 122), which glorify the holy city of Jerusalem and God's designs for it. They present hymnic characteristics, but the term "songs of Zion" is based on content.

Another division of the hymns is the Pss of Yahweh's enthronement, 47, 93, 97, 99, to which might be added 95, 96, 98, 100. The reader is faced by a triple alternative in the interpretation of these hymns: historical (interpreting the poem of a concrete event); eschatological (e.g., Gunkel, understanding the poem of events in the end time); cultic (e.g., Mowinckel, understanding the poem against the background of the enthronement feast). On any interpretation, the following data should be kept in mind in studying these Pss. First, Yahweh is saluted as king. This does not mean that he was not always a king; in fact, the anchoring of his kingship in creation is proof that it is from of old. But now it is actualized and presented again in the cult. Yahweh ascends his throne: *Yahweh mālak*—Yahweh "is king" or "has become king" (either translation is grammatically possible, but see E. Lipinski in *Bib* 44 [1963] 405–60). Second, Yahweh is king because of his creative power. The allusions to creation are in terms of the mythical battle in which chaos is defeated (Pss 93:1–4; 95:5; 98:7–8). He is king also because of the Exodus event in which he saved Israel (95:6–7; 99:4–8; 100:3). Third, Yahweh's kingship (because it is rooted in creation) is not only over Israel but over the whole earth. Hence, all are summoned to praise him who is "above all the gods." Fourth, although not properly eschatological, these Pss are oriented to the future insofar as Yahweh's rule over, and judgment of, the nations await fulfillment in fact.

10 (b) LAMENT. The laments can be personal (individual lament) or collective (a lament of the community). The individual lament predominates (about one-third) in the Psalter: 3; 4(?); 5–7; 10(9B); 14 = 53; 17; 22(?); 25–28; 35–36; 38–39; 40:12–18; 42–43; 51; 52(?); 54–57; 58(?); 59; 61; 63–64; 69–71; 77:2–11; 86; 88; 102; 109; 120; 140; 141–43. The life setting is indicated by the content: The psalmist is in dire straits and he calls out to God for help.

The basic structure will be indicated, followed by a discussion of particular problems. The song begins with an invocation of Yahweh (5:2; 7:1), or "my God," and a cry for help. Very often epithets such as "God of hosts" or "my rock and my redeemer" are added. The introduction may be continued for several verses, frequently with an expression of trust and a plea. The body consists in the description of the distress and the request. The distress can be manifold: bodily sickness (Pss 6, 38, 88, 102), death (69), sin (51), unjust treatment (35), abandonment (22, 88), and especially persecution by enemies The exaggeration in the descriptions is striking, and at times it is not possible to identify exactly the reason for the complaint because of the stereotyped language. The description leads into the request for the Lord's intervention, which is expressed in the imper. mood, or in the 3rd pers. jussive. Various devices are worked in, such as questions, "why?" (10:1) and imprecations against the enemies. Specific motifs are adduced to move the Lord to intervene: the psalmist's trust in Yahweh; the Lord's own attributes, such as his justice or fidelity—the Lord owes it to himself to intervene; or the psalmist's own innocence. The manner in which Yahweh is "humanized" so as to induce him to have pity and intervene is quite striking. The appeal may include a vow to offer a thanksgiving sacrifice in praise of the Lord (61:9). The conclusion is characterized by an expression of certainty that the prayer has been heard. This may be expressed either modestly or with such force that one has the impression that an answer has actually been rendered. This violent change raises a problem that has not yet been adequately solved (→ 12 below).

H. Schmidt recognized a subsidiary class in the Pss of individual lament, which he called "prayers of the falsely accused." The life setting of these Pss is presumably a judicial procedure at the Temple, in which the accusation cannot be clearly settled by law. The accused presents himself before the priest and receives a decision, and the thanksgiving at the end of the poem is a sign that he has been exonerated—a defeat for his enemies who had calumniated him as a wrongdoer. Although not all would agree with Schmidt, who is also a protagonist of the enthronement feast of Mowinckel, his interpretation has some merit. He reckoned about 20 Pss belonging to this class, but O. Eissfeldt would wisely limit the number to four: 7, 35, 57, 69 (Eissfeldt, *OTI* 119).

11 The "Pss of trust" can be included under the laments because they originate from this literary type. The prayer of trust is an instance of taking one motif, which is characteristic of the lament, and developing it into a Ps type. The following are usually classified as Pss of trust: 4(?), 11, 16, 23, 62, 91, 121, 125, 131.

In the individual laments, three topics have been studied at great length in the past and still remain problematical: the "enemies"; the "poor"; and the sudden change of mood—the certainty that God has heard the complaint.

The enemies are hard to identify, despite many attempts. Some interpretations are now simply discarded (e.g., B. Duhm's understanding of them as the Hellenizers of the Maccabean period). Mowinckel has interpreted them as sorcerers (*pō'ălê 'āwen*, "evildoers") who work a magic spell against the psalmist. H. Birkeland regards them as foreign political adversaries (originally the lament was a royal Ps in which the "I" is the king; "democratization" took place later, and the enemies stand for the private foes of the one who is praying). Others have interpreted the enemies in the light of the poor and oppressed, so frequently mentioned in the Pss; they would then be the rich gentry who oppressed the poor. These interpretations are perhaps too specific. We may agree first of all that the enemies are real persons and not merely symbols of hostile powers; after all, their punishment is prayed for. How can they be so richly described as liars, robbers, men of blood, godless, and blasphemous? How can their opposition be expressed in so many different ways (sometimes in the same Ps; e.g., 22 and 35)? They are animals (lion, ox, dog); they set snares and traps; they are an army that surrounds the psalmist. C. Barth (*Introduction*... 43–48) has suggested that the purpose of this wild language is to present a conventional type of maximum godlessness. Hence the extravagance has become somewhat schematic and stereotyped, as befits the sacral language of the liturgy. Good and evil are opposed—not merely in the abstract, but concretely, and with no middle ground. This mentality helps one to understand the extravagant language in which the enemies are described and also to see the so-called cursing Pss (→ 18 below) in correct perspective.

The "poor" ("needy," "oppressed") in the Pss present a similar problem in interpretation. How specific is this term? Long before the fundamental study of A. Rahlfs (1892), the difference between *'ānî* and *'ānāw* was being debated. Rahlfs's study indicated that *'ānî* was one who was oppressed by misery and distress in life; the *'ānāw* was one who humbled himself before the Lord (hence the *'ănāwîm*, the "faithful"). With R. Kittel a still greater spiritualization of terms denoting social distress took place (*'ebyôn*, "poor"), and in recent times many adopt the thesis of A. Gelin that the vocabulary relative to poverty, although originally sociological, came to carry an intense spiritual meaning. The influence of the prophets (as early as Zeph; cf. 3:12) and of the Exile are invoked to explain this development. Mowinckel, on the other hand, refers the terms to those who are hurt by the "evildoers," or sorcerers, who cast a spell upon them. In view of the wide range of opinion, it seems that the term "poor" can have both a sociological and a religious sense, and the dominant idea must be derived from the context. *'Anāwîm* always occurs in the plural (Nm 12:3 is a doubtful singular form), and it may have had a technical spiritual meaning, but one should beware of spiritualizing it without further ado (cf. the discussion by P. van den Berghe in De Langhe, *op. cit.*, 273–95).

12 The discussion of the structure of the individual lament glossed over a point that is fundamental for the life setting of these Pss: the transition to certainty that the prayer has been heard. Often the expression of certainty is mild enough to go along with the requests that are expressed; they are, as it were, expressions of trust (e.g., 10:17–18; 26:12; 40:18; 43:4–5; etc.). On the other hand, many passages seem to go beyond mere trust or assurance. The change in mood is a violent turnabout: Yahweh "has heard" (cf. Pss 6:9–10; 31:22–23; 54:8–9; 56:13–14; etc.; and esp. 22:23–32). This change is particularly indicated by the change in tense (pf. tense, and it cannot be explained as proph. pf.). In some instances, the change is so sustained that it is difficult to escape the impression that one is reading a thanksgiving song; the danger is over and gone.

The explanation of J. Begrich ("Das priesterliche Heilsorakel," *ZAW* 52 [1934] 81–92) is perhaps the most frequently adopted: At this point the one who is praying would have received an answer to his prayer—an oracle delivered by the priest. One may point to 1 Sm 1:17 as perhaps alluding to such an oracle. Begrich's detailed analysis of the poems in Dt-Is argued that the typical priestly oracular style was imitated by the Prophet in 41:11ff. This explanation has been indicated at several points in the commentary on Ps, but it is no more than a reasonable assumption.

Other solutions have also been proposed. E. Podechard questioned the need of an oracle; if one had been given, why would not the psalmist have quoted it? Rather, such Pss are the "acknowledgment of a past deed," delivered in the Temple before the assembly—the whole story is rehearsed, even those lines (plea, description of distress) that could have been written on a "bed of pain." Thus, the psalmist relives his trials and dramatizes them, and the Ps might better be classified as a thanksgiving (e.g., Ps 22). Weiser's position is similar: The violent transition is merely a question of linking a lament with a thanksgiving; the description of the distress, characteristic of the thanksgiving Pss, has been replaced by the actual lament that was uttered during the distress. Westermann has argued that there is no "pure" lament in the Pss. There is never a lament that is not somehow softened by trust or praise—there is no lament for the sake of lament. The change in mood from lament to joy indicates that the Israelite did not separate the lament from the total religious context in which he understood his God. Hence, what seems to us an abrupt division may not have been so in fact.

13 The "lament of the community" is related in spirit and structure to the individual lament; the individual lament is now cast against the background of the community. The OT provides many concrete situations in which we may find the life setting of these songs: a war crisis (Jos 7:6); a famine (1 Kgs 8:33–34); a plague (Jl 1, 2). At such a time, the nation and its leaders united for a major liturgical action. The following Pss are usually classified thus: 44, 74, 79, 80, 83, 89(?), 90, 94, 123, 126, 129, 137. The introduction to the lament consists in the usual invocation, with epithets that are noticeably national, e.g., "Shepherd of Israel" (80:2). The body is taken up with a description of the national crisis, such as profanation of the Temple (74:7–8), slaughter of the Lord's servants (79:2–3). There are many motifs for "humanizing" Yahweh: Those who are suffering are his people, his flock, his vine; he must intervene "for your name's sake" (79:9)—"for the sake of your *ḥesed*" (44:27)—because the people trust in him. The request is often a strong imperative, "awake!" (44:24). The conclusion usually expresses the same optimism noted in the individual lament—the certainty that the prayer is heard. A vow to praise God is often expressed.

In summary, the significant differences between the individual and the collective laments are those caused by the contrast of an individual with a group. Most scholars, following the study of E. Balla, recognize that the "I" in the Pss is generally to be treated as an individual, not the nation, although Mowinckel, as we have already indicated, has maintained that there is a certain representative character to the first person in many Pss.

14 (c) Thanksgiving Psalm. The following Pss may be classified as thanksgiving Pss of an individual: 10:1–11; 22(?); 30–31; 40:2–11; 41; 66:13–20; 73; 92; 103: 107; 116; 138. This type of prayer was presumably uttered on the occasion of a thanksgiving sacrifice (*tōdâ*), which was offered up after some saving experience. The references to the Temple liturgy are clearer than in the hymn or lament (e.g., Pss 66:13ff.;

107:22–23). The characteristic introduction is an exclamation of praise or thanksgiving to Yahweh, expressed in the volitive mood: "I will give thanks to you, O Lord" (138:1; cf. 9:2). The similarity to the hymnic introduction is noteworthy. Indeed, there is no Hebr word for "thanksgiving": *tōdâ* means, properly, "praise." Hence, as has already been indicated, Westermann has claimed that the so-called thanksgiving Pss are really hymns recited in response to God's perfections or to his saving activity. There is certainly a close relation to the hymn style. The body of the prayer contains two important features: the story of the person who gives thanks and the acknowledgment of Yahweh as the rescuer. In describing the trouble from which he has been delivered, the poet uses the themes of the lament (after all, there is a correspondence in both cases—the human distress), but only to emphasize the deliverance that God has wrought. The acknowledgment of Yahweh as the rescuer (Pss 30:2–4; 40:2–3) is essential, and it has often been expanded into an instruction for those who are present (e.g., 31:24–25; 40:5–11; 66:16–19). It is in this acknowledgment that much wisdom teaching is found. In Ps 66:13–16, there is a reference to the actual *tōdâ* offering. Like the ending of the hymn, this type of prayer returns to the beginning: the declaration of praise.

The collective thanksgiving Pss are relatively rare; perhaps most would agree that 67 and 124 are the clearest examples, and these more or less reflect the structure we have already noted for the thanksgiving prayers of an individual.

15 (d) ROYAL PSALM. These songs include 2, 18, 20–21, 45, 72, 101, 110, 132. The classification is based on content, not on literary characteristics. Actually they can be laments or thanksgivings, but all are royal in that they commemorate some event that has its life setting in the king's experiences: accession (or the anniversary) to the throne (2, 72, 110); marriage (45); thanksgiving for victory in war (18, 21); pleas for the safety and victory of the king (20 and perhaps 144:1–11?). Ps 101 is a "mirror of princes" or guide by which the king is to rule. Exaggeration is typical of many of these poems (2, 45, 72, 110): The king is to rule forever; his empire is world-wide; peace and justice mark his reign; etc. This style is not just the "court style" of the Fertile Crescent, even if some phraseology (e.g., 72:8–9) is borrowed from, or at least influenced by, foreign sources. Such extravagance in a small state like Israel, where the kingship had such remarkable limitations, would be hard to explain. Rather, this use of such exalted themes is based on 2 Sm 7, the dynastic oracle of Nathan (→ Aspects OT Thought, 77:155).

By this oracle Yahweh promised an eternal reign for the dynasty of David. Inasmuch as he was the Lord of the world, the glories of worldly kingdoms could be used to suggest the destiny that was planned for the Davidic dynasty; it was thus that the "court style" was justified. Hence, there developed in Israel what is called "royal" messianism. The royal Pss (and also the prophets, such as Is 7–11) record this vision of the reigning king; he reigns, not so much in and for himself, but insofar as he is a member of a fated dynasty, the vehicle of God's plans. There could be no exaggeration of his glory and power for it was guaranteed by Yahweh. Yahweh had made an eternal covenant with the Davidic dynasty to which this king belonged; through him will come the realization of God's kingdom.

Perhaps the most remarkable witness to the vitality of these prayers is the fact that they were preserved at all. After the fall of Jerusalem and the negative judgment on the kingship by the deuteronomic historian in 1–2 Kgs, these royal Pss were still preserved and adapted, one may assume, to the liturgy of the Second Temple—only possible because they were reinterpreted and eschatologized toward a future era. The Davidic dynasty had received too much support from the oracles in Jer and Ez for these Pss to drop into oblivion. It is important to appreciate their role in sustaining the messianic hope—how their usefulness long outlived their historical pertinence. This observation is also applicable, to a certain extent, to the rest of the Psalter. The Pss were sufficiently above time and circumstance and sufficiently oriented to the future to become the prayers of Jews of all later ages—and of Christians as well. Once Israel became the People of the Book, their writings, and especially the Pss of David, took on another frame of reference. No people could rehearse the salvation history, or even the experiences recorded in the Pss of lament, without hearing in them the announcement of better days and inspiring in them hope for the future. This openness to the future colors the understanding of Christians who treasure their OT.

16 (e) WISDOM PSALM. Recently there has been a trend toward recognizing that the later Pss have come from a wisdom milieu; at least, the sages were probably responsible for the collections and formation of the Psalter. Can one go further and specify a class of Pss that embodies the characteristics of the wisdom literature? The demarcation is not easy, and the opinions of those scholars who have studied the question are at variance (cf. R. E. Murphy, "The Classification 'Wisdom Psalms,'" VTSup 9 [1963] 156–67). Because no one structure is typical of wisdom literature, perhaps the best approach to it is to combine considerations of content with literary characteristics. From the point of view of content, one would expect to find mention of the problem of retribution, the contrast between the just and the wicked, practical advice concerning conduct (responsibility, diligence, etc.), fear of the Lord, etc. The stylistic features one would expect are comparisons and admonitions, alphabetic structure (the "acrostic" Pss). numerical sayings, "blessed" sayings or macarisms, "better" sayings, and the address of father to son. On this basis, the following have some right to the classification as wisdom Pss: 1, 32, 34, 37, 49, 111(?), 112, 128, 129(?), 133(?). Although many would include Pss 73 and 119, the former is rather a thanksgiving song, and the latter is a "Law" Ps, which is unique and combines features of all the literary types. Notable wisdom influence can be detected in the rest of the Psalter, e.g., in laments (25:8–14; 31:24–25) or in thanksgiving songs (esp. 40:5–6; 92:7–9), where the acknowledgment of Yahweh has a tendency to become didactic.

17 (f) LITURGY. Gunkel used this term to indicate songs in which different literary types are brought together and expressed in choral style in Temple service. The liturgical act determines the articulation of the Ps. The most striking examples are the so-called entrance or gate liturgies (called "Torah-liturgy" by Gunkel): 15, 24 (cf. Is 33:14–16). A question is asked and a teaching is imparted concerning the character of the person who can enter before the Lord. Another type of liturgy is oracular or prophetic, in that a divine oracle is imparted to the worshiping community: 12, 50, 60, 75, 81. The rest of the liturgical Pss are so classified because they reflect choral recitation in their structure (although the Ps may be more properly considered a hymn or thanksgiving song): 115, 119, 121, 134 (cf. also 107, 118, 136).

(g) HISTORICAL PSALM. Three Pss (which Gunkel called *Legende*) are frequently classified as "historical": 78, 105, 106. This term does not designate a true type, but it is a convenient term for songs in which elements of hymn, thanksgiving, and even wisdom are to be found. The life setting was probably one of the three great annual feasts of Israel.

(h) Torah Psalm. Kraus uses this rubric for Ps 1, which is classified as a wisdom Ps in this commentary, and Pss 19:8–15 and 119. Again, this classification is convenient, based on the dominant theme of the Pss.

18 **(V) The Theology of the Pss.** No true summary of the theology in the Pss is possible. At least these few considerations may help to underline some of the basic theological realities. Inasmuch as the Pss were composed over a period of 700 years, it is to be expected that they would furnish a cross section of OT belief. But one should also recall that they are primarily cultic expressions of doctrine; they describe Yahweh as he was worshiped and experienced in the liturgy—a crucial area, but distinct from the preaching of the prophets and the sages. The new insight into the liturgical character of the Pss enables us to appreciate their dynamism and even to relive, to a certain extent, the Israelite attitude toward the Lord. The liturgical aspect should be particularly evident to a Christian reader whose religious practice has such deep roots in the liturgy. There is constant reference to the Temple and sacrifice, with which OT piety was so closely enmeshed. It was in the Temple that the Lord was present to the Israelite (e.g., Pss 42–43), and there the worshiper made contact by sacrifice and song. He was not without the means of criticizing liturgical cant (Pss 40, 51, 141) that tried to make sacrifice an end in itself. But without his liturgy, he was dead; there was no psalm singing in Sheol: *Leben ist Loben.*

The literary classification of the Pss runs the gamut of basic human feelings and attitudes before God: praise, thanksgiving, lament, etc. Rarely is the psalmist alone involved, even if his prayer has a personal tone. He is either inviting others to praise the Lord or he is generalizing on his experience and preaching a "lesson" to bystanders (especially in the thanksgiving Pss). The community spirit is never really absent.

Two facts about Yahweh are central to these poems. He is both creator and savior. One need only recall the enthronement Pss, which describe the Lord's victory over the waters and the other mythological expressions of creation (74:13–14; 89:10–15). His creative power is now his word (147:15), now his breath (104:29), now both word and breath (33:6). From this power it is a small step to the description of his providential rule of creation (104:10–18; 147:8–9). The recital of the events of the Exodus and conquest honor him as the savior of his people. The recital may be for the sake of sheer praise (136:10–22) or by way of a didactic rehearsal that pinpoints Israel's infidelity (78).

The prolongation of the salvation theme is found in the Pss of lament, of both the individual and the nation. The God who showed himself the savior of early Israel must stay in character for the individual who yearns for forgiveness from sin or who is threatened with death or by the calumnies and machinations of his enemies. There is only one to whom he can turn, and it is with themes of childlike trust and sometimes petulance that he approaches the saving Lord. It is not surprising, then, to find theology emerging from the laments. The meaning of a "merciful and gracious God, slow to anger and rich in kindness and fidelity" (Ex 34:6) is fully expressed. The experiences of the nation were too deeply rooted in its religious consciousness to be forgotten in moments of crisis: "Where are your ancient favors, O Lord?" (Ps 89:50; cf. Pss 74, 79–80).

Perhaps the most serious threat to the man of the OT was death in all its forms ("pit," "nether world," "waters," etc.). In the face of the bleak existence that confronted him in the nether world, he could but love this life with all the blessings he recognized in it as God-given. Indeed, the possession of God was itself the heart of these blessings. But in Sheol all was gone: "For among the dead none remembers you; in the nether world who gives you thanks?" (6:6). And when the divine blessings were absent from life, when sinners triumphed and the just man failed? We hear the sage in Ps 37 warning against envy of the wicked, who will certainly receive their punishment. But there is also the poignant admission of near defeat by the writer of Ps 73, whose faith finally triumphed in the certainty that God, his "portion forever," would receive him "in glory."

A striking intensity of feeling characterizes the psalmist's dealing with his fellow men. He loves them when they are the "just," the "lowly"; he hates them when they are "oppressors" and "liars." This black-and-white attitude is apt to shock the Christian reader, who is only too ready to point to the superiority of the Sermon on the Mount and to the forgiveness preached by Christ. Such a reaction is neither sympathetic nor necessary (cf. Barth, *Introduction*...43–48, 65–75). One must appreciate the OT desire to see God's justice manifested in the world (the only world of which the Israelite knew). There is no need to judge the personal experience and moral evaluation of the psalmist; he simply recognizes the evil man as opposed to God and hence as worthy of punishment. In many instances the wicked seem to be described in a highly stylized and schematic way; they appear as godless types, God's enemies. As such, they are also the psalmist's enemies (139:21–22) and are deserving of the divine justice that is invoked upon them in the liturgy. Hence, we should understand these as declarations of loyalty and liturgical condemnations of God's enemies rather than as statements of personal vengeance. Some expressions are often misunderstood by the modern reader, e.g., smashing the little ones against the rock (Ps 137:9). This act was not the result of a refined cruelty; it was simply the usual accompaniment of warfare. And war is never humane, in any age.

This same black-and-white attitude appears also in the description of the psalmist as a *ṣaddîq* (just) man or as a *ḥāsîd* (faithful) one who protests his innocence and also as a sinner who asks for pardon. Some Christian readers have expressed surprise at the self-righteous tone that they profess to find in certain Pss. At times the protestations of innocence are quite emphatic (Pss 17:4–5; 18:21–25), and, at other times, they seem to be merely themes to induce Yahweh to intervene (41:13; 59:4). Ps 26 speaks insistently of the psalmist's innocence. On the other hand, an acknowledgment of sin appears in the traditional seven penitential Pss (these are not a literary classification), which have been used in the traditional Lat liturgy (6, 32, 38, 51, 102, 130, 143). Elsewhere also the sense of unworthiness and sinfulness is clearly conveyed (25:7; 39:9; etc.). Complications arise when affirmations of innocence and guilt are combined in the one prayer: e.g., 32:5,10–11; 41:5,13; 51:3,15.

Rather than seek a "psychological" explanation, one should accept the Hebr paradox that it is possible to be just and also sinful (although it is hardly the same as the *simul justus et peccator* of the Reformation). The just man is not the one who has nothing on his conscience; he is the one who is allowed to approach Yahweh in the Temple (Ps 15); then he can confess his guilt. However, it is his justice that entitles him to speak to the Lord; his affirmation of innocence is his right to approach God as one on whose side he has aligned himself. These affirmations are therefore less self-righteousness than they are declarations of loyalty. As Barth puts it, they are not "affirmations" of innocence but "confessions" of innocence in a liturgical context. On the other hand, the confession of guilt is what only a just man who fears God will do.

The Psalter has been justly termed the "prayer book of the Church" because of its extensive use in the liturgy. From many points of view, it is not an easy prayer book, because it represents the wide range of Israel's belief and history over some 700 years. But although it makes some demands upon those who use it in prayer—demands that can be met by a study of the OT and by an appreciation of God's gradual revelation of himself to Israel—it also remains open to men of all classes and all times. For in these prayers is expressed the basic reactions of man before God—faith, joy, fear, trust, and praise—language no one can fail to understand.

COMMENTARY

19 **Ps 1.** A post-exilic wisdom Ps, which has been prefixed to the collection as an introduction; in one of the variant readings to Acts 13:33, Ps 2 is called the first Ps. Structure: 1–3, the just man; 4–5, the godless; 6, the two ways. **1.** A congratulatory formula, "Happy..." is typical of the wisdom style; here, the characteristics of the just man are defined negatively: keeping away from bad companions. **2.** Positively, he is constantly and joyfully occupied with study and observance of the Torah, the expression of the divine will. **3.** Positively, his well-being can be compared to a fruitful tree (Jer 17:7–8; Ps 92:13–15), a common comparison in the ancient Orient (Amen-em-ope, *ANET* 422); the bracketed line in 3e is a gloss formed on the pattern of Jos 1:8. **4–5.** In sharp contrast are the wicked—"chaff," the lighter, useless, parts of wheat that are blown free as the wheat is sifted on a breezy mound. What "judgment" is meant? Either one at the end time, or more probably an effective judgment in this world (cf. E. Arbez, *CBQ* 7 [1945] 398–404). In this world, the judgment would be the exclusion of the sinner from the company and fate of the just. **6.** The biblical sense of "way" as manner of life is apparent (cf. F. Nötscher, *Gotteswege und Menschenwege in der Bibel und in Qumran* [Bonn, 1958]); the just will prosper whereas the wicked will be punished. One should avoid an excessively legalistic interpretation of Ps 1; the ideal held out is one of joyful loyalty and dedication.

20 **Ps 2.** A royal (messianic) Ps, composed on the occasion or possibly on the anniversary of the king's accession to the throne in Jerusalem. Structure: 1–3, description of nations in revolt; 4–6, Yahweh's answer; 7–9, the divine oracle proclaiming the king's legitimacy and firm rule; 10–12, admonition to rulers to heed Yahweh's will. This poem was more probably recited by a court poet. **1–3.** The revolt against the holy person of the king ("anointed') is also against Yahweh. Revolutions were frequent with the accession of a new king, and one might see here a borrowing of Oriental court style, as far as Jerusalem is concerned; at most, only minor lands like Edom could be among the revolutionaries. In the post-exilic period, this revolt could be reinterpreted in an eschatological sense. **4–6.** The "folly" of revolt is clear from the description of the God of the world, whose reaction is vividly described. Yahweh has "set up" (i.e., consecrated) his own king on his "holy mountain"—a move neither appreciated nor understood by the nations. **7–9.** The "decree" (*ḥōq*) is now recognized to be, after the analogy of the Egyptian royal ritual, a written document of legitimation or protocol, authenticating the king (cf. G. von Rad, *GesSt* 205–13). It seems to be announced by the king himself. The sonship is adoptive and not mythological, as in Egypt, and not unlike the divine sonship of Mesopotamian kings, except that the Israelite notion is rooted in the divine promise made to David in 2 Sm 7. Firm world dominion is assured this king—another echo of foreign court style, but meaningful in the light of the Israelite belief that Yahweh rules the world and has his own designs for the Davidic dynasty. **10–12.** The ultimatum given to the kings of the earth is in the wisdom style: Give heed!

21 **Ps 3.** An individual lament attributed to David (as are Pss 3–41). Structure: 2–4, the complaint; 5–7, trustful affirmation of help from God; 8–9, appeal and acknowledgment. Some scholars argue that the author must be a king; others modify this theory and think that it is an individual Israelite who uses phrases that may have been originally part of royal laments (the result of the so-called democratization). **2–4.** Addressed directly to God, with the "how," typical of lament. Trust in Yahweh for salvation is the key motif (3, 8–9); hence, the Lord is his protection ("shield") and also the cause of his dignity (*kābôd*, "glory"). **5–7.** The theme of trust is continued; he is certain of a hearing from Yahweh. The metaphor in 7 is that of a soldier surrounded by a hostile army. **8.** The plea for help is followed by the certainty of being heard (esp. if translated, "for you have struck..."). Many scholars postulate an oracle from a priest or a cult prophet at this point to explain the certainty in Pss of lament. **9.** The invocation upon the community suggests that the prayer was originally by the king, their representative.

22 **Ps 4.** An individual lament, which is practically a Ps of trust. Structure: 2, appeal; 3–6, admonition to enemies; 7–9, contrast between impatience and confidence. The life setting cannot be determined in detail, although some (H. Schmidt) regard this Ps as a prayer of someone falsely accused who spends the night in the Temple. **2.** *O my just God:* Lit., "God of my justice," i.e., the one who must, by saving him, declare him just. The psalmist has regularly experienced the saving intervention of Yahweh in the past ("relieve," lit., "created room for me"). **3.** *men of rank:* Probably his enemies (in the MT they are asked, "How long will my glory be dishonored?"). A relatively mild admonition follows: He appeals confidently to Yahweh's treatment of him, from which they should draw a lesson: reverence, sacrifice, and trust. It is not certain if they are persecuting him or if they are deserting Yahweh; "falsehood" in 3 can indicate idols, as well as calumny. **7.** *many:* Those who lack the confidence of the psalmist; their murmuring is quoted. **8–9.** For the third time (2, 4) he refers to his own experience: His "gladness" is greater than the joy of the harvest festival ("grain" and "wine"). This song is similar to Ps 3, but it need not be joined with it, as some urge. The spirit of the poem is reflected in passages like Is 50:8–9 and Rom 8:34.

23 **Ps 5.** An individual lament. Structure: 2–4, the cry for help, uttered in the Temple in the morning; 5–7, Yahweh will not tolerate sinners in the Temple (motif of certainty of being heard); 8–11, by God's favor the psalmist can enter the Temple, and he asks that Yahweh guide him in trials and punish the deceitful enemies; 12–13, confident prayer for the just. The life setting can be that of a man who ministers in the Temple and who begs the Lord for triumph over enemies who are trying to oust him (prayer of one unjustly accused, H. Schmidt). **4c.** Lit., "at dawn I prepare [my sacrifice] for you and I wait"; perhaps an oracle from a priest would be given in answer. **5bc.** The sinful are excluded from the sacral area (cf. the "entrance" torah of Pss 14:2–5; 23:3–6)—such is the basis of the psalmist's hope; he seems to be a Temple minister whom others are trying to get rid of. **8.** A confident statement of the service he hopes to render, as a "kindness" from Yahweh. **9.** A request for such help from God in his service of him, which will defeat the machinations of his enemies. **10.** *throat:* Compared to an "open grave" because words of calumny and corruption come forth from it. **11.** A request for just punishment of his enemies who must also be hateful (6) to God. **12.** *your name:* You, since the name is the person (cf. Pss 69:37; 119:132). **13.** The certainty of having the protection of Yahweh comes through here.

24 **Ps 6.** An individual lament, one of the seven penitential Pss. Structure: 2–4, complaint and cry for help; 5–6, plea and reason for Yahweh to intervene; 7–9, description of grief designed to move God to intervene; 9–11, Yahweh "has heard" his prayer, thus putting his enemies in confusion. **2.** Apparently a stereotyped formula (Ps 38:2; Jer 10:24), in which God's fatherly love is expressed anthropomorphically. **3.** A request that his sickness (in OT thought a sign of sin, or God's punishment for sin) be healed. **4.** *soul:* As often in OT, it is the person. **5–6.** Two reasons why Yahweh should intervene: his *ḥesed* (kindness); the fact that after death man has no contact with him in Sheol ("nether world"; cf. Is 38:18; Pss 88:11–13; 115:16–17; → Aspects OT Thought, 77:170). Hence, Yahweh owes it to himself not to allow the psalmist to die. **8.** The role of the "foes" is never clearly indicated; at the least, they are triumphant over the suffering they think he deserves. **9–11.** Whence comes the astonishing certainty that "the Lord has heard"? Either these words are recited in the Temple after the psalmist recovered or they are a reaction to the deliverance promised in an oracle of a priest. On the "evildoers" (*pō'ălê 'āwen*), → 11 and 18 above.

25 **Ps 7.** An individual lament and a good example of the type called "prayer of one unjustly accused" (H. Schmidt). The life setting seems to be that of a man who, persecuted by enemies, takes refuge in the Temple and proclaims his innocence; he calls upon the Lord, as a just judge, for aid. Structure: 2–3, plea for help and deliverance from pursuers; 4–6, protestation of innocence in the form of a purificatory oath; 7–10, an appeal to Yahweh, the just one (set aside as a separate Ps by Duhm, Podechard, etc.); 11–14, Yahweh is a savior, but he punishes the unjust; 15–18, a description of how the evil man will be entrapped by his own evil. **1.** *plaintive song: Šiggāyôn*, an obscure term. *Cush the Benjaminite:* Unknown. **4–6.** The casuistic style (if, then) is typical of the purificatory oath (cf. Jb 31). *I who spared:* Others translate, "[if] I pillaged." **7–10.** The appeal is to Yahweh, "enthroned" (on the Ark), judge of "nations," to rise and "do justice," i.e., vindicate the psalmist by defeating his enemies. The imperatives in 7 derive from the old battle cry in which the Ark played a role (Nm 10:35–36). As Kraus remarks, the answer expected would be something like Ps 12:6. The atmosphere of world judgment in 8 does not indicate an eschatological reference; it is merely a description of the judge from whom he is seeking justice. The motif of innocence, another aspect of the oath in 4–6, appears in 9; such protestations can be found in ancient Babylonian prayers. **13.** The CCD has, with most of the ancient versions, "God" as subject; some modern critics prefer to understand the wicked man (described also in 15–17) as the subject. **15–17.** These metaphors are familiar in OT (cf. Jb 15:35; Is 59:4; Prv 26:27; Ps 9:16; Ob 15; Ps 28:4): conception that fails to bring forth; falling into the hole one has dug; evil recoiling on one's own head. **18.** An announcement of thanksgiving (sacrifice), which the psalmist will offer.

26 **Ps 8.** A hymn of praise of God as creator (4–5) and of man as the head of creation (6–9). Structure: The two themes are placed in the framework of community praise (2–3, 10; note the refrain). **2.** The MT of 2–3 is uncertain; "name" and "majesty" are synonymous with God himself, who is "exalted" above all that he has made. **3.** *praise:* Lit., "strength"; the general idea of the CCD is that God's power is the more evident because of the modest means (*babes*) he uses. Others take "strength" as a fortress God constructs against his enemies (powers of chaos?). **4.** *I:* A Temple singer, who is astounded by the contrast between God's majesty and his "care" (5) for man, to whom he has subjected all creation (6–9; cf. Gn 1:26–28). **6.** *angels:* Lit., "elohim" beings, the members of the heavenly court. The reflected divine glory is seen in man (Gn 1); Heb 2:5–9 transposes this idea to the new creation in Christ.

27 **Pss 9–10.** A thanksgiving song and a lament, in an imperfect alphabetic pattern of very loose structure. Praise is proclaimed in the Temple (9:15) by one who acknowledges his own deliverance (9:4,14) and who develops the themes of God's judgment and reign over the peoples (9:5–12,18–21; 10:16). But there remains the scandal of the arrogant wicked (10:1–11, where the style of the individual lament is employed). Let God intervene and save the poor from them. The (LXX, Vg) pattern of one Ps is better than the MT. The uncertainty in interpretation comes from the vagueness ("enemies," "judgment," "wicked man"), and from the sequence of thanksgiving, lament. It is hard to escape Mowinckel's contention that Pss such as this "I-Psalm" are really royal songs in which the king is associated with the people (*The Psalms I*, 76–78). **13.** *avenger of blood:* Yahweh. *afflicted:* Hebr *'ănāwîm* (*Qᵉrê*, and cf. 10:17). This term has been variously interpreted in Pss: an Israelite "party" devoted to Yahweh (A. Rahlfs); the spiritually proficient (A. Causse); those who suffer at the hands of conjurers (S. Mowinckel, H. Birkeland). A summary of various views is given by Castellino (*op. cit.*, 254–63; → 11 above). At the least, the term suggests faithful, pious Israelites who are being oppressed. **14.** *gates of death:* The metaphor comes from the conception of Sheol as a (prison) house with gates. **10:4.** The inaction of God amounts to his nonexistence.

28 **Ps 11.** Song (not a prayer) of trust, by one who takes refuge in the Temple with Yahweh (1, 4), and refuses to follow the advice of his friends to flee (1–3). **2.** Perhaps these are metaphors for calumny (cf. 64:4–5). **3.** Flight is the only solution in a chaotic, lawless situation. **4–7.** Yahweh's justice is the reason for the psalmist's trust. *allotted cup:* Of wrath (cf. Jer 51:17; Lam 4:21). *see his face:* Encounter with Yahweh in the Temple worship (cf. 17:15; 27:4; etc.).

29 **Ps 12.** A liturgy of lament, which expresses trust in Yahweh's word (6) for deliverance from the wicked. The psalmist seems to voice the prayer of the community (2–5), which speaks in 7–9. Structure: 2–3, cry for help and description of deceit; 4–5, wish; 6, a divine oracle, which (7–9) inspires a confident response from the community. **3.** *double heart:* Lit., "with a heart and heart," i.e., duplicity (cf. Jas 1:8). **6.** Rather than merely a summary statement of Yahweh's assurance of help, it is probably a cultic oracle pronounced by a priest (cf. Pss 2:7; 32:8; etc.; and Begrich, *op. cit.*, 81–92). **7.** The words of the Lord are "refined," i.e., no trace of falsity. **8.** The community is confident that the prayer is heard.

30 **Ps 13.** An individual lament. Structure: 2–4, complaint and request; 5–6, confident promise of thanksgiving. The psalmist is tortured more by abandonment by God than by any sickness. **2–3.** *how long?:* A question typical of the lament. **4.** *light...:* The strength and will to live (Ps 19:9). **5.** *enemy:* Those who think his misfortune justifies their accusations against God. To induce Yahweh to intervene, he uses the motif of trust in his "kindness," and he holds out the prospect of singing his praises in thanksgiving.

31 **Ps 14 (= Ps 53).** A lament that has been preserved in two slightly different forms. Structure: 1–3, a complaint about "fools"; 4–6, but God is with the just; 7, request. **1.** A practical, not theoretical, atheism is ascribed to the "fool," i.e., the evil man. **4.** The question is a complaint concerning the activities of the "evildoers" (*pô'ălê 'āwen;* see comment on 6:9). **6.** *you:* The evildoers. **7.** *out of Zion:* In contrast to 2, where Yahweh is in "heaven," this may indicate a gloss (but cf. Ps 20:3,7) that requests a renewal (*šûb šebût*, "to restore the well-being," does not necessarily refer to return from exile) perhaps in the post-exilic period.

32 **Ps 15.** A liturgy Ps of entrance (cf. 24:2; Is 33:13–16), pronounced antiphonally on the occasion of (pilgrims') entering the Temple. Structure: 1, a question addressed to Yahweh by one who enters the Temple; 2–5, an answer (the "entrance" torah) given by a cult minister. **1.** *tent:* The Temple, referred to by the old amphictyonic term for the Tabernacle. **2–4.** A description of the deserving man—his total justice and sincerity, which includes his attitude to his neighbor, especially in matters of justice.

33 **Ps 16.** A Ps of trust. Structure: 2–6, a meditation on his relationship to Yahweh and his separation from idolators; 7–11, trust in Yahweh who saves him from death. **1.** *refuge:* Perhaps in the Temple (Ps 61:5). **2.** Yahweh as the supreme "good" is an operative idea in the development of the OT concept of immortality. **3–4.** Text uncertain; the CCD expresses the psalmist's affection for the "holy ones" (elsewhere almost always used of members of the heavenly court) among the people, and his aversion to idolatry. **5–6.** The terms, "portion...inheritance," are reminiscent of the partition of Palestine under Joshua (Jos 14:1ff.), and the inheritance allotted to Levites (Nm 18:20). A Levite might be the author, but the metaphors are "spiritualized" here as Von Rad (*op. cit.*, 241–43) has pointed out. They bespeak a deep sense of presence and communion (8–9) with God, which prevails over death (10). **10.** Does this verse refer to deliverance from impending or sudden death and restoration to the divine companionship in this life, or to deliverance from "corruption" after death, i.e., immortality? Scholars are divided in opinion. The word "corruption" translates Hebr *šaḥat* as the LXX did (*diaphthora*), but it could be rendered simply "pit," a synonym for the nether world. It seems best to respect, with A. Weiser, the author's vagueness, and to understand his words as indicating a conquest of death without any further specification. The NT applies 8–11 in a fuller sense to Christ's resurrection (Acts 2:25–31; 13:34–37). The apostles naturally rallied to the LXX version of *šaḥat*, a meaning that the word seems to have in the Qumran scrolls (cf. R. E. Murphy in *Bib* 39 [1958] 61–68). **11.** *path to life:* Correct moral conduct is the meaning of the phrase in the wisdom literature (cf. Prv 2:19; 15:24; 5:6; 6:23; the Egyptian parallels are discussed by B. Couroyer in *RB* 56 [1949] 412–32). The evaluation of God's "presence" is noteworthy.

34 **Ps 17.** A lament of an individual unjustly accused (10–12). Structure: 1–5, a cry to Yahweh, with affirmation of innocence; 6–9a, request; 9b–12, a description of his accusers; 13–15, prayer for deliverance and vengeance, with certainty of being heard. **2.** *from you:* He expects some form of God's just judgment, such as an oracle. **3.** He probably spends the "night" in the Temple, awaiting the answer upon awakening from sleep (cf. 15 and Ps 5:4). Kraus suggests that what we have here is Temple incubation, as though the thoughts of man in sleep can no longer be hidden. **4.** His very integrity demands this affirmation of innocence. **6–12.** The tenderness of Yahweh's "kindness," in contrast to the "cruel hearts" of his enemies, is one of the themes he employs to gain a reply from God. The metaphors in 8 betray his deep trust in God; the "wings" are an allusion to the wings of the cherubim over the Ark on which Yahweh is enthroned. **11–12.** *lions:* A frequent symbol for enemies in Pss (7:3; 10:9; 22:22; etc.).

35 **Ps 18.** A royal Ps of thanksgiving for victory over enemies; a parallel recension is found in 2 Sm 22. The life setting is perhaps the Temple (7) where the king gives thanks for a battle victory; the prayer might possibly go back to the time of David (cf. F. M. Cross and N. Freedman, *JBL* 72 [1953] 15–34 for critical translation with notes on archaisms and Ugaritic allusions). Structure: 2–4, hymnic introduction; 5–31, the first description, in terms of a theophany, of his desperate plight and Yahweh's intervention to save him because of his loyalty; 32–49, a second description, more concrete, of the marvelous deliverance in battle by the God who trained the king. **3.** *rock:* A natural symbol of safety and strength (although some, e.g., Kraus, see here an allusion to the old Jerusalem tradition about the "holy rock" that came to be applied to Yahweh). *horn:* A frequent symbol of strength in the OT. **5–6.** *breakers... snares:* These metaphors derive from the ancient myths concerning Sheol, the watery abyss that "hunts" man; the psalmist describes himself as in the "nether world," which is more a condition than a place. **7.** A succinct description of distress, prayer, and deliverance (the latter described in the theophany of 8–20). **8–16.** A graphic description, which borrows the usual literary dress of OT theophany (e.g., Ex 19; Hab 3:4ff.); the enumeration of the cataclysmic phenomena (earthquake, storm, lightning) serves to actualize the Sinai theophany. **11.** Yahweh rides on the "cherub" (see comment on Ps 68:5). In 16, the creation myth is again (5–6) the background for Yahweh's control of the sea. **17–20.** The psalmist is delivered from the "deep waters," here explained as his "foes." **21–31.** The question is: Why does God help the psalmist (and all who are "lowly" and "take refuge in him")? The answer is succinctly expressed in 26–27, and the ways of the just man are described in 21–25; hence, every just man, whether he be king or "lowly," can rely upon the protection (28–31) of Yahweh, who is "light" (source of strength) to the psalmist's "lamp." **32–35.** An expression of confidence in God; this passage begins the second part of the poem, which describes the concrete circumstances of battle in which God fights for the king. The fact that his enemies cried out to the Lord seems to indicate that they were Jews, but the "foreigners" of 45 suggest that they are non-Israelites who have been completely subdued; the references are probably to a series of battles. **47–51.** Acknowledgment and praise of Yahweh for his "kindness" (*ḥesed*) to the king, the "anointed" par excellence. *the Lord live!:* The Israelite form of an old cultic formula reflected in Am 8:14, and perhaps in the Ugaritic formula, "Aliyan Baal lives" (*UM* 49:III,8–9; *ANET* 140).

36 **Ps 19.** A hymn of praise, which unites two themes (perhaps originally separate Pss): 2–7, God's glory in the heavens; 8–15, the wonder of his Law. One may conveniently explain the connection in that the Law reveals God's will, while his glory is spoken throughout nature (cf. Pss 1, 8, 119). **2.** The beauty of the "heavens" is itself a hymn in praise of God. **3–5.** A development of how the "heavens declare." The CCD means that the praise is continuous, "day" and "night," and everywhere. But others (RSV, etc.) understand 3 to mean that no sound is audible. Then, paradoxically, the message is heard everywhere (v. 4), even though it is not voiced. **5–7.** The marvel of the "sun," which is merely God's handiwork. It is compared to a "groom" (coming forth from the "chamber" where the sun rests for the night) and to a soldier-giant, in its course. **8–10.** Praise of the Law: Each verse relates a characteristic, followed by a good effect. The Torah, as embodied in the Pentateuch, is the expression of God's will for Israel; the synonyms are "decree," "precepts," etc. **9.** *enlightening the eye:* Giving health and well-being. **12–15.** The conclusion is the author's personal reaction: loyalty to the Law, even if there are "unknown faults" (e.g., Lv 5:2–4; Ps 90:8). The Bible frequently refers to God's role in keeping man from sin (cf. Is 63:17; Jer 10:13; and the NT "Our Father" prayer). **15.** His very Ps is to be accepted as a sacrifice, obtaining God's "favor" (cf. Pss 104:34; 119:108). It is worth emphasizing that the attitude to the Law in this Ps is characterized by joy and appreciation (cf. Pss 1, 119).

37 **Ps 20.** A royal Ps, a liturgical prayer that the king be victorious. Structure: 2–6, request; 7–10, certainty that Yahweh has granted the request, which is repeated in 10. The Ps is part of the Temple liturgy, spoken by several (6, 10) and also by an individual (7). The name of God echoes through this Ps (2, 6, 8). **2.** The "name" is a surrogate for Yahweh himself, whose name, in deuteronomic theology, resides in Jerusalem. Hence, he gives help "from Zion" (3) as well as from "his holy heaven" (7). **4.** *your holocaust:* The sacrifice that was accompanied by this Ps. **6.** A promise is given to celebrate his coming victory. **7.** *I know...:* An oracle assuring victory is perhaps presupposed by this change of mood. **8.** The antithesis between reliance upon human powers and reliance upon God is a frequent OT theme (1 Sm 17:45; Is 31:3).

38 **Ps 21.** A royal Ps that forms part of a liturgy of thanksgiving. Structure: 2–8, thanksgiving to God for the blessings given to the king (probably rendered by a Temple minister); 9–14, the community expresses good wishes to the king for a victory over his enemies—a fitting prayer on the occasion of a royal accession or its anniversary (cf. 4). **2.** *strength:* Cf. 14; God's power has secured the "victory." **3–5.** The only concrete reason given for thanksgiving is the granting of the king's request for "life," which is to be understood in the full sense of prosperity and well-being. **6–8.** Verses like these illustrate the sacral, superhuman, aspect of Israelite kingship. **9–13.** A direct address to the king by a choir (14) that promises to offer thanksgiving when Yahweh shows his "might" and "strength" (cf. also 2).

39 **Ps 22.** An individual lament (2–22) and thanksgiving (23–32). Two literary types are combined in one Ps, pronounced by an individual who has already experienced deliverance and now offers his sacrifice (26–27). The triumphant affirmation of 23–32 is more than the usual "certainty of having been heard." Hence, 2–22 must be the complaint he made in his suffering. The individual is a private worshiper (rather than a king participating in a ritual, as some modern commentators urge), who suffered from physical pain and from enemies; but the descriptions of his plight are highly metaphorical. Structure: 2–22, the complaint, with repeated requests, descriptions of suffering, and expressions of confidence (4–6; 10–11); 23–32, thanksgiving, in which the community is invited to share (23–27) and worldwide worship of Yahweh is proclaimed. **2.** *my God:* An invocation that implies reliance upon Yahweh for help; but its repetition suggests the dire situation of the abandoned one. **4–6.** The basis of his trust is Yahweh's presence in the Temple and his deliverance of Israel in the past salvation history. **8.** *parted lips:* Lips parted in a wide, sneering, manner. **9.** This quotation, typical of his enemies, reflects the disbelief that one who suffers could be other than a sinner. *if he loves him:* Probably, if God loves him. **10–11.** After the complaint, another (cf. 4–6) affirmation of trust. **13.** *Bashan:* East of the Sea of Galilee in Transjordan, noted for its strong bulls (Am 4:1), which symbolize his enemies. **15–16.** Apparently a description of a mortal, feverish malady. **17.** *pierced:* A conjectural meaning, supported partly by some ancient versions, but it remains doubtful, even if it is better than the MT ("like a lion"). The verse is not quoted in the NT. **19.** These actions indicate that his enemies regard his death as certain. **20–23.** The renewed appeal exemplifies the wide range of metaphors that describe his suffering: "sword," "dog," "lion," "bull." **23–27.** A sharp transition to a thanksgiving ceremony with "brethren" (23, 26) in the Temple, where he fulfills his "vows" in gratitude for deliverance. The mood of these verses hardly permits one to think that he is merely "anticipating" deliverance. They describe an actual thanksgiving: acknowledgment of Yahweh as rescuer (24–26); participation in a sacrificial banquet in which the lowly share (27). **28–29.** The universalism is reminiscent of the enthronement Pss (47, 93, etc.), which describe Yahweh as king; it is unexpected here, although not out of place in an acknowledgment. **20.** *all who sleep...who go down...:* Because one does not normally worship Yahweh from Sheol (Pss 6:6; 90:11–13), these phrases probably indicate "mortal men." *to him my soul shall live:* A conjectural translation; the MT is uncertain. He seems to contrast the prolongation of his life with the death others have incurred. **31.** Yahweh's "justice," i.e., the deliverance of the psalmist, is to be told to future generations. This Ps (2, 8, 9, 16, 19) is utilized frequently in the NT passion narratives—and with true insight. It is not a prediction, but a presentation of an exemplary suffering and deliverance (cf. the Suffering Servant of Is 53) that was fulfilled in a transcendent manner in Jesus.

40 **Ps 23.** A Ps of trust, structured in two parts: 1–4, God as shepherd; 5–6, God as host. E. Vogt (*Bib* 34 [1953] 195–211) has argued that the occasion is the thanksgiving meal of one who has been unjustly accused; one may agree that 5–6 at least indicate a thanksgiving ceremony. **1.** Yahweh as a shepherd is a frequent theme, in the OT (Ps 79:13; Is 40:11; Ez 34:15ff.; etc.) and in the NT (Jn 10:11–18). The ancient Orient generally conceived of the king as shepherd, and Shamash is described as shepherding all who live (*ANET* 387). **2–4.** The vivid metaphors derived from shepherding cover all the contingencies of human life—e.g., the "rod" for hostile beings, the "staff" for sure guidance. **5.** This picture of God as table host, probably at a sacrificial meal in the Temple, is all the more impressive because it is "in the sight of my foes." **6.** In contrast to his former enemies, "goodness" and "kindness" now pursue him. It has been inferred that he is perhaps a Levite, dwelling in the Temple, but a sense of God's presence may be all that he intends to convey.

41 **Ps 24.** A processional hymn, with an "entrance" torah (cf. Ps 15). Structure: 1–2, praise of the creator; 3–6, the entrance torah, question and answer; 7–10, the procession (with antiphonal response) of the king of glory into the Temple. Various feasts have been urged as the life setting of this Ps—e.g., the enthronement festival of the New Year (S. Mowinckel)—but there is no sure answer. **1.** *fullness:* All that the earth contains. **2.** The reason for Yahweh's dominion is his creative power, which conquered the "seas" and "rivers"—a motif frequent in the so-called enthronement Pss. The marvel of the created world is its firmness, although it rests on that unruly enemy the Lord tamed in the creative act, the "seas"; the earth was conceived as resting on pillars in the abyss (Ps 75:4). **3.** The question asks for an instruction, or torah. **4.** There are four requisites: freedom from bribery; purity of heart (i.e., a clean conscience, especially as regards neighbors); aversion from idols ("what is vain"); and, finally, one should not have harmed others by lying oaths. **5.** The "reward" is the "blessing" (b^e*rākâ*), a full, prosperous life. **7.** The address to the "gates" is uttered by the pilgrims and the question in 8 comes from within the Temple. The pilgrims identify the "king of glory" in terms traditionally associated with the Ark (cf. 1 Sm 4:3–4); he is "Yahweh" S^e*bā'ôt*, the Lord of hosts (10), the war hero of Israel. The spirit of this Ps matches the description in the inaugural vision of Isaiah (6:1–6).

42 **Ps 25.** An individual lament in acrostic style. The psalmist is a sinner (7) who is hated by enemies; he prays for deliverance and guidance. Structure: 1–7, a series of requests, with themes to induce Yahweh to intervene (3, 6–7); 8–15, a teaching about the "way" (8) and fear of the Lord (12); 16–21, another series of requests for help, followed in 22 by an apparent addition referring to the community. **4.** Although the poem is a complaint, the key idea is "your ways," which the author asks to know and to observe; this concept is taken up again in 8–15, in which a strong wisdom influence can be seen, especially 12–14. **10.** *kindness and constancy: Hesed* w^{e}*'ĕmet* are the characteristics of the covenant relationship (cf. 14). **12.** Lit., "Who is the man who fears the Lord?" This type of question is found in the entrance torah of Pss 15:1; 24:3. **16–21.** There is found here an unusual mixture of request and expressions of trust. **22.** This verse is certainly an addition because it introduces a prayer for Israel and because it is outside the alphabetical sequence that structures the Ps. When a poem goes beyond 22 (the number of letters in the Hebr alphabet), the standard practice is to begin the next (and last) line with *Pe* (as here, and cf. Ps 34:23 and the observations of P. W. Skehan in *CBQ* 23 [1961] 127).

43 **Ps 26.** An individual lament by one who has been unjustly accused. Structure: 1–2, request for justice; 3–8, affirmation of innocence, request for deliverance, and certainty of being heard. The typical life setting for such a prayer is aptly described in 1 Kgs 8:31–32. **2.** This request should be taken seriously; he is asking for a judgment that will be shown before men by the test he is ready to undergo. **3–8.** Following the positive statement of virtue are the denials in 4–5—a sort of purificatory oath (cf. Jb 31), the ritual of which seems to be described in 6–7; the *Lavabo* prayer of the Roman rite Mass uses these verses. The "thanks" (*tôdâ*) is the proclamation of Yahweh's judgments ("wondrous deeds"). **9.** Let him not be destroyed, as "sinners" are. **11.** *redeem:* Save from the death that is the lot of the sinner; perhaps he refers in 10b to the venality of his judges. **12.** Sure of Yahweh's intervention, he promises a thanksgiving sacrifice in the Temple that he loves (8). Affirmations of righteousness (3–8, and frequently in Pss) should be understood as a legitimate denial of guilt, not as an arrogant claim of self-justification (cf. 11b; → 18 above).

44 **Ps 27.** An individual lament. Structure: 1–6, poem of trust in God for protection; 7–14, the complaint, ending with certainty of being heard (13), and oracle of encouragement. Although many scholars (Podechard, Weiser) claim that two Pss have been combined here, a certain unity can be recognized: Trust is a characteristic of the lament, and in both parts there is mention of enemies (2, 12). He could have expressed his confidence and desire for the "shelter of his tent" (5–6) before he succeeded in making his lament in the Temple. **2.** *devour...:* Destroy completely. **3.** The metaphor is taken from military experience; the victorious spirit of confidence is reminiscent of Rom 8:32–39. **4.** This single desire is also expressed in Ps 23:6. **6.** He is confident enough to vow that one day he will offer thanksgiving for his deliverance from his "enemies." **7–10.** The insistent requests for "pity," are still colored by his trust. (10). **8.** The MT is not clear. **12.** The enemies are identified for the first time: "false witnesses." **13.** The CCD correctly expresses the thought, but in the MT the anacoluthon is striking: "If I were not certain that I should see...!" *land of the living:* The present world, as opposed to Sheol (cf. Ps 52:7). **14.** This is best taken as an oracle of deliverance addressed to the psalmist.

45 **Ps 28.** An individual lament. Structure: 1–2, invocation and plea; 3–5, punishment for the wicked; 6–7, certainty that Yahweh has heard; 8–9, acknowledgment of Yahweh and prayer for the king and people. This prayer is uttered in the Temple (2) by one who is perhaps sick and tormented by the wicked. **1–2.** *pit:* A frequent synonym for the nether world (Ps 30:4, etc.); he is close to death as he addresses God at the Holy of Holies. **3–4.** Let Yahweh punish those who are truly guilty. **5.** The wicked do not recognize God's just rule ("deeds...work") on earth. **6–7.** *he has heard:* This sudden change from pleading may best be explained by presupposing (cf. 6:9–10) that he has received in reply a favorable response from the priest; hence, he now praises the Lord. **8.** He generalizes his experience as applicable to the people of God whom Yahweh protects. The reference to the "anointed," or king, is not enough to classify this Ps as a royal Ps.

46 **Ps 29.** A hymn with many Ugaritic echoes (for references, see F. M. Cross, *BASOR* 117 [1950] 19–21) extolling the power of God the king in the storms of nature. Its precise life setting is hard to determine (naturally, it is associated with the enthronement feast by Mowinckel), but the Canaanite flavor is undeniable. The climactic or "staircase" parallelism (abc—a'b'd) is typical of Ugaritic verse, and several expressions can be duplicated from Ugaritic poetry. Hence many scholars think that it is an adaptation of an "ancient Canaanite Baal hymn" (Cross); if so, it has been radically reinterpreted. It is not possible to determine the antiphonal pattern that may have structured this song. **1.** *sons of God:* The members of the heavenly court (cf. Ps 8:6) who serve Yahweh are commanded to give glory (cf. 9b). **2.** *in holy attire:* Perhaps better, "when he appears in holiness" (cf. Ugaritic *hdrt*). **3.** The voice is "thunder," a figurative expression used also in Ugaritic literature (*UM* 51:5, 70; cf. Ps 68:34; Jb 28:26). The "waters" are the same as the "*flood*" in 10—i.e., the waters above the firmament (Gn 1:7) where God dwells. **6.** Lebanon and Sirion (the Phoenician name for Mt. Hermon; cf. Dt 3:9) are in parallelism, as also at Ugarit (*UM* 51:6, 18–19). *leap:* Tremble. **7.** *fiery flames:* Lightning (cf. Ps 18:9).

8. Kadesh, a "wilderness" in the area of Lebanon, seems to be mentioned in the Keret epic (*UM* 125:7, 108), which some understand as a reference to Kadesh-barnea. **9.** Others translate, "makes the hinds calve and hastens the birth of kids"—a description of the fright the storm causes among the animals. **9b–10.** Yahweh is "enthroned" as king in his "temple" (*hēkāl*) above the firmament and is honored because of the "glory" that his power manifests. **11.** The Lord is associated with Israel, "his people."

47 **Ps 30.** A thanksgiving song of an individual. The title associates it with the dedication (*ḥanukkâ*) of the Temple in 164 BC (cf. 1 Mc 4:35–59). Structure: 2, praise of Yahweh for having saved him from death; 3–4, the story of his experience; 5–6, invitation to bystanders to praise the Lord and to learn from this event; 7–12, a more explicit description of his trouble and deliverance, ending with praise of Yahweh. **2.** His "enemies" would "rejoice" in that his misfortune proves he is one stricken by God. **5–6.** The thanksgiving song regularly appeals to bystanders to associate themselves in the praise of God, and it frequently becomes didactic, as in the expressive lesson of 6. **7–11.** The psalmist goes back over his problem to the days of his overconfidence, and relives it, repeating his prayer (9–11). **10.** As in Ps 6:6, there is reflected here the belief that in Sheol there is no contact with Yahweh, no praise is offered to him; hence God should preserve his life. There is perhaps the nuance that in Sheol it would not be the Lord's faithfulness that would be rehearsed! **12.** A graphic picture of his restoration; sacred "dancing" was known in Israel (2 Sm 6:16).

48 **Ps 31.** A thanksgiving song, by one who has been delivered from his afflictions (sickness, persecution), and who praises God in the Temple. Structure: 2–9, a typical complaint, with strong overtones of trust; 10–19, similar to 2–9, although some consider 10–25 a separate Ps; 20–25, the thanksgiving begins as the author acknowledges deliverance and "teaches" (24–25) those present with him. **2–4a.** Cf. Ps 71:1–3. **4.** The metaphors applied to Yahweh are natural enough without necessarily belonging to the ancient cult tradition of Jerusalem; (cf. Ps 18:3). **5.** The "snare" (of the hunter) symbolizes the opposition, perhaps unjust accusations (12,18–19), of his enemies. **6.** *spirit:* Breath of life (Gn 2:7; Ps 104:29–30). Jesus used the first line of this verse as his prayer on Calvary (Lk 23:46). **8.** The aspect of thanksgiving is best brought out by translating "because" instead of "when." **10.** In a second phase (cf. Pss 18, 29, 102), the author returns to his description of his distress in words that suggest mortal sickness. But it also appears that perhaps his enemies would utterly destroy him by false witness (cf. 14 and Jer 20:10). **13.** *the unremembered dead:* An apt metaphor, in view of the limited knowledge of the next life in the OT (cf. 18). **16.** *destiny:* Lit., "times," which has suggested that the Hebr concept of time is "filled time," periods filled with something. **17.** The emphasis on God's "face" (rendered in 21 by "presence") is noteworthy. Weiser's commentary emphasizes this aspect of theophany, or the experience of God, in the Pss. **20.** The thanksgiving begins in hymnic style and is followed by a testimony before fellow men (24–25), which is typical of this type of Ps. **22.** *fortified:* "Besieged" is perhaps better as a metaphor for his situation. But the text is changed by many to "in a time of distress." On the basis of Pss such as 31, P. Bonnard has written *Le Psautier selon Jérémie* (Paris, 1960), but it is not easy to establish the dependence of these Pss upon Jeremiah; this particular Ps, it must be admitted, does seem to echo the "confessions" of the Prophet.

49 **Ps 32.** Although this is usually classified as a thanksgiving Ps, perhaps it is better considered as a wisdom Ps. The wisdom elements (1–2, 8–11) serve as a wrapper for a thanksgiving testimony (3–7) that is directly addressed to God. The testimony exists only for the lesson that the author wants to communicate ("for this shall every man pray to you," v. 6; cf. Murphy in VTSup 9, 162). Structure: 1–2, macarism formula, a reflection on his past experience; 3–7, a description of this experience, with the lesson that flows from it; 8–9, teaching and admonition; 9–10, a contrast between the faithful and the wicked, with a command to rejoice. **1–2.** The *'ašrê* formula is frequent in wisdom literature as a classic form of moral exhortation. These verses are not to be read in the light of the theology of the scholastics and the reformers; they tell us nothing about the intrinsic nature of justification. The phrases "cover" and "impure" are anthropomorphic descriptions of God's forgiveness, and they are frequent in the OT. Verses 1–2 are the conclusion to which the psalmist has come and the lesson that he inculcates. **3–5.** *as long as...:* His suffering finally led him to the realization of his sin, and led him to "speak," acknowledging it (5); thus, his admission of sin brings pardon. **6–7.** *for this:* Refers to his experience, which becomes a lesson for those whom he would instruct. *deep waters:* Symbolic of death (Ps 18:5–6,17). **8–9.** He speaks as a sage (Kraus would make this a divine oracle communicated through the priest). The advice in 9bc is not clear; the CCD can be understood as urging a willing submission to Yahweh lest he be forced to violent treatment. **10.** After indicating the benefits of confession and pardon, he has a word about the wicked, in contrast to "him who trusts." This Ps is the second of the traditional seven penitential Pss.

50 **Ps 33.** A hymn of praise of Yahweh for his creative Word and his control of history. Structure: 1–3, hymnic introduction, inviting the just to repent; 4–9, the Word of God; 10–12, God's plan; 13–19, God's supervision of mankind; 20–22, an expression of confidence and a prayer. The life setting in the liturgy cannot be exactly defined; it should be noted that the poem has 22 lines, but without acrostic sequence. **4–9.** The poet passes from a general consideration of the divine Word and action to the power of the Word in creation (→ Aspects OT Thought, 77:45–46). God's easy dominion is illustrated by 7: The waters above the firmament (Gn 1:7) are gathered as easily as in a "flask." **11.** His "plan" means his control of history. **13–19.** Nothing escapes God's "eyes" and he governs accordingly; he is the only savior for Israel (for 16–17, cf. Ps 20:8).

51 **Ps 34.** A wisdom Ps, although it is widely classified as a Ps of thanksgiving. It is alphabetical (cf. S. Holm-Nielsen in *ST* 14 [1960] 1–53, on acrostic Pss) and is filled with typical maxims in favor of the just against the wicked (13–22). The testimony in 5–7, which suggests a thanksgiving Ps, is really didactic in character. The reference to 1 Sm 21:10–15 in the Ps title as the life setting is unconvincing. Structure: 2–4, hymnic introduction that anticipates the lesson to be announced ("the lowly will hear me..."); 5–11, a brief mention of deliverance (5), which develops into didactic exhortation to trust and to fear the Lord; 12–22, the psalmist appears as a sage, inculcating typical wisdom lessons; 23, the *Pe* verse (it begins with that consonant) is a didactic device to arrive at a 22–23 line acrostic poem spelling out the root *'lp* (meaning "to teach"; see comment on Ps 25:22). **3.** The *'ănāwîm* (humble) are the dedicated, committed Yahwists, who hence have a claim to Yahweh's help (cf. Ps 10); the term does not designate the virtue of humility. **5.** A succinct description of deliverance (to which 7 is parallel) that serves as a springboard into the wisdom teaching. **8.** *angel of the Lord:* The metaphor is one of a divine messenger at the head of an army that surrounds and protects (cf. Ex 14:19; Jos 5:14; etc.). **9–11.** *taste...:* In the context, it does not refer to inner spiritual sweetness but to the concrete goods, which God gives "to those who fear him." *holy ones:* Perhaps the only time (but cf. Ps 16:3) in the OT that *qdš* stands for humans; usually "holy ones" designates the members of the heavenly court. The motive of material retribution in these verses, it should be remembered, is extended to the poor (19–20), and it is not the same as current materialism, for it includes union with God and what might be called, with Cardinal Newman, a sacramental view of the universe. **12–22.** The psalmist has become a wisdom teacher (in the style of Prv 1:7; 5:7; etc.) inculcating "fear of the Lord" and offering "life" (explained by prosperous days); for a literal Egyptian parallel to 13, see B. Couroyer, *RB* 57 ([1950] 174ff.). The rest of the teachings deal with admonitions and statements of retribution. Although the doctrine of retribution follows the optimistic trend of wisdom tradition, there is a recognition that suffering is part of the lot of the just—but Yahweh "watches over." The *Pe* verse (23) takes up an idea ("guilt") from 22.

52 **Ps 35.** An individual lament by one who has been unjustly accused (7, 11, 15, 20–21). Structure: 1–6, invocation of Yahweh for aid and for punishment of enemies; 7–12, description of enemies and renewed appeal; 13–16, ingratitude of his opponents; 17–28, confident request and promise of sacrifice. **3.** *salvation:* The Lord saves him from the injustice he complains of; the line has the ring of an oracle. **4–6.** These wishes express his desire to see God fulfill justice. *angel of the Lord:* See comment on 34:8. **8.** A wish that his enemies be hoisted on their own petard (cf. Ps 7:15–17). **9–10.** These confident assurances alternate with complaints. **11–16.** The "unjust witnesses" have accused the psalmist not only without cause but also despite his genuine charity toward them. The last line of 13 is vague. The CCD makes it parallel to 13b; it may be a wish that the prayer he offered for them be taken back and returned to himself. **18.** A vow to offer thanks, characteristic of laments (cf. 28). **22.** *have seen:* In contrast to the calumnious words of his accusers in 21. **24.** The appeal to God's "justice" is basic for understanding the point of view of the OT man (cf. 4–6,25–27). His enemies and his friends are vividly contrasted.

53 **Ps 36.** An individual lament by one who is dismayed at the persecutions he suffers, but who trusts in the covenant loyalty (*hesed;* 6, 8, 11) of God. Structure: 2–5, the evildoing of the wicked; 6–10, the joy of God's protection; 11–13, a prayer for protection against the wicked. So understood, the Ps can be taken as a unit rather than as a composite. **2.** *sin speaks:* A bold personification of sin as ruling in a man. **3.** He convinces himself that God will not punish him. However, the MT of 2–3 is obscure. **6.** *kindness...faithfulness:* God's covenant loyalty and reliability. **7.** *the mountains of God:* A kind of superlative—the highest mountains in contrast to the "deep." **8–9.** God's covenant loyalty provides "refuge" in the Temple ("your house"). **10.** *your light:* Cf. Pss 4:7; 31:17; 89:16; etc. This is the light of Yahweh's face (encounter with him in the liturgy). When the Lord's face shines it dispenses good and enables men to "see light," i.e., to live (Ps 49:20). **11–13.** The request and certainty of being heard are typical in the conclusion of a lament.

54 **Ps 37.** A wisdom Ps in alphabetical form (in this acrostic, there are two full lines to a letter). There is no clear structure; the poem is made up of warnings (1–2) and admonitions (3–4) supported by promises of happiness, in which the lot of the good and that of the wicked are described. The author passes as an elder sage (25, 35–36), who recognizes the danger that a youth may be enticed from wisdom by what he sees ("Be not vexed..."). His optimism makes him a champion of the traditional view of retribution. God must punish evil and reward goodness—naturally, in this life. Judgment may be slow, but it shall surely come. **2.** *grass:* Symbolic of the short duration of prosperity that the evil may experience. This common metaphor (Is 40:7) is taken from the rapid desiccation in Palestine caused by the sirocco or the sun. **6.** The idea is that by his intervention (blessings), Yahweh will make manifest the integrity of the man who trusts in him. **9.** *possess the land:* A motif throughout the poem (3, 11, 22, 29, 34). The phrase has the overtones of the divine promise fulfilled for Israel (Gn 12:1), and it is given fuller meaning in the Beatitudes of Jesus. **12–15.** A description of the wicked man and his unsuccessful persecution of the just. **16.** This idea is frequent in the wisdom teaching (Prv 15:16; 16:8; cf. Eccl 5:9). **22.** Illustrates the power of cursing and blessing in the ancient world (→ Aspects OT Thought, 77:40–43). **25–26.** A remarkable example of rigid holding to the traditional wisdom doctrine. **27.** *forever:* As elsewhere in the OT, the meaning is "indefinitely," but the idea is capable of expansion into a life that is immortal (Wis) and eternal (Jn). **30–31.** This close association of wisdom and Law is found in Sir 24:22; Bar 4:1; etc. **34.** *you shall look on:* Not as vindictive as it sounds; the point is that the just will witness God's justice at work. **35–36.** The prosperity of the wicked is transitory and unsubstantial. On this Ps, Kraus comments rightly that it is not a statement that justice exists; rather, it bears witness to Yahweh's intervention in human life. The poet does not call for faith in a just order, but for trust in Yahweh.

55 **Ps 38.** An individual lament by one who is sick, sinful, and persecuted; it is the third of the penitential Pss. Structure: 2–5, a plea, with acknowledgment that his sorrow is a punishment for sin; 6–13, a description of sickness and a reaction of neighbors; 14–17, confidence that Yahweh will answer him; 18–23, themes to induce Yahweh to act, and a final plea. **2.** Yahweh's "anger" is inferred from the psalmist's misery (cf. Ps 6:2). **3–13.** The description is similar to that of Job; he is afflicted with "sores" (4, 6, 8); he goes about "in mourning" (7), separated from men (12) who would, of course, regard him as one punished by God for his crimes. **14–17.** His "deaf" and "dumb" attitude proves his trust in Yahweh alone, whose answer he expects—a motif to induce God to intervene. **20.** *undeserved:* Apparently there was a group that went beyond what was just in condemning him, even to obstruct his conversion (21).

56 **Ps 39.** An individual lament, in a highly original form, by one who has been afflicted with sickness and the accompanying disdain of his enemies and whose life is almost spent (5). Structure: 2–4, a lively description of a resolution he had once taken to control his tongue; 5–7, the complaint; 8–9, an appeal for deliverance; 10–14, the request continues, with motifs as to why Yahweh should intervene. **2.** The psalmist made an effort not to complain about Yahweh's harsh treatment (10), particularly when the wicked man might turn the complaint against God; but he could not hold it in. This description of how this complaint was born is unusual. **5–7.** He wants to unravel the mystery of a life that must end with death (when will it come?); in 6–7 he holds up the brevity and vanity of human life as a motif for God's mercy (unless, with Castellino, we regard these verses as the divine answer to the question in 5). This theme is common in the wisdom literature (Jb 7:6ff.; Eccl 2:18ff.; Sir 14:15). *span:* Lit., "palm," the measurement of four fingers (cf. Jer 52:21), the width of the palm. **9.** The implication is that his enemies consider him condemned because of his "sins." **10.** He begins to persuade Yahweh to have pity on him, and he refers to his resolution in 2–3 (unless 10 is to be translated by the pres. tense; then it is a new resolution); he is bold enough to remind Yahweh that it was his "doing." **12.** *like a cobweb:* Lit., "like a moth" (whose destructive power regarding clothes is a symbol of Yahweh's power over man). **13.** The psalmist does not have time to wait, and he applies to his possession of life the metaphors that are used of the patriarchs' possession of the promised land ("wayfarer," or alien; "pilgrim," or tenant). **14.** With his plea, cf. Jb 7:19. It is no small virtue of this Ps that it ends on a dark note, even though he trusts in Yahweh.

57 **Ps 40.** A thanksgiving Ps and an individual lament. More probably it is composed of two separate Pss: 2–11 (or 2–12, with 13 being a transition to 14–18), and 12–18 (or perhaps 14–18, which is also to be found in Ps 70:2–6). For some scholars (e.g., Weiser) 40A (2–11) is a thanksgiving for past deliverance, which is supposed to serve as an introduction to the lament of 40B (12–18); hence, the whole prayer would be a unit. Structure of 40A: 2–4, the story of how Yahweh delivered the psalmist from the pit (power of Sheol); 5–6, a beatitude formula with recommendation to trust, and a testimony to God's deeds before those who are present in the Temple; 7–11, the psalmist's "sacrifice" of thanksgiving and proclamation of the deliverance wrought by the Lord. **2–3.** Yahweh responded to his firm hope by delivering him from the power of death, symbolized by the "pit" and "swamp" that characterize the nether world. **4.** The "new song" is the present Ps of thanksgiving, which has been inspired by Yahweh's saving act; perhaps it is also new in the sense that it replaces the old "cry" of 2. It is to be a testimony before the "many" (cf. "us" in 6). **6.** The deliverance is connected with God's wondrous deeds of salvation history—a further reason for the trust that is urged in 5. **7–11.** Although a Ps such as this accompanies a sacrifice, the psalmist says that God prefers obedience to any type (four kinds are mentioned) of sacrifice. This emphasis should be interpreted like similar prophetic statements on sacrifice (Am 5:21ff.; Is 1:10ff.; etc.); it singles out dedication and commitment as the only adequate responses to God without rejecting the principle of sacrifice (cf. De Vaux, *AI* 454–56). *written scroll:* The Law or the expression of God's will, which is also within his "heart." Hence, he proclaims in a testimony Yahweh's "justice"—his fidelity in delivering his Servant—on the occasion of a feast before a "vast assembly." In Heb 10:5–9, the LXX of 6–8 is applied to the Messiah, as though the lines were addressed by the Son to the Father. As indicated above, 12–13 can be taken with 14–18; these will be discussed in Ps 70, a doublet form, which circulated independently.

58 **Ps 41.** A thanksgiving Ps by one who has recovered from sickness (9). Structure: 2–4, a beatitude formula; 5–11, a flashback on his distress (mortal sickness, enemies) and his prayer at that time; 12–13, acknowledgment of Yahweh's help; 14, doxology. **2–4.** This assurance of blessing for the one who cares for the poor is a didactic element, often found in a thanksgiving song. **6–10.** He recalls vividly the hostile comment and wishes of his enemies, even of an intimate "friend" (lit., "the man of my peace"). **11.** *repay them:* This desire for vengeance is frequent in OT complaints; God's justice is not to remain inactive. **13.** His recognition of his "integrity" does not exclude sinfulness (5; cf. Ps 38:18–20). **14.** The doxology is a later addition, and it closes the Davidic collection (Pss 3–41).

59 **Pss 42–43.** An individual lament; the two Pss were originally a single poem (cf., besides the refrain, 42:10 and 43:2, and note the absence of a title for Ps 43). The psalmist is at the sources of the Jordan near Mt. Hermon (42:7), where he utters this complaint, filled with yearning for Zion. Structure: three strophes, each ending in a refrain. **42:2–3.** *as the hind:* The comparison, known also in Ugaritic (cf. *UM* 67:1, 17), stresses his yearning to be present in the Temple before ("behold the face of") God. *living God:* Yahweh is the source and the fullness of life for him (cf. 9). **4.** His grief, apparently caused by nothing more than absence from Jerusalem, is increased by those (Gentiles? cf. Pss 79:10; 114:10) who ridicule his reliance upon Yahweh. **5.** The memories of his role in the Jerusalem liturgy are both a consolation and a torment to him now. **6.** The refrain (42:12; 43:5) is full of confidence that he will return. **7.** The complaint continues, specifying Mt. *Mizar* ("the small mountain") in the foothills of Mt. Hermon near the Jordan sources as his residence. **8.** The "roar" expresses his despair and it is suggested by the cataracts of the Jordan and the "deep" (t^{e}*hôm*), i.e., the powers of chaos, which threaten him. **9.** Yahweh's continual *ḥesed* toward him is met by "song" and "prayer," which are concretely expressed in the complaint in 10–12—abandonment, ridicule, and pain. **43:1.** An appeal to Yahweh to intervene against his enemies who are now more clearly described as "faithless," "impious." **3.** *light...fidelity:* Personified, as though members of Yahweh's entourage. **4.** The lament usually includes a vow to give "thanks" in the Temple. The Roman rite appropriately uses the second half (43:1ff.) of this Ps, which is so replete with motifs from the songs of Zion, for the opening of the Mass prayers at the foot of the altar. The poem is a pure expression of yearning for God, with no expectation of reward or other benefit.

60 **Ps 44.** A lament of the community. Structure: 2–4, the introduction rehearses God's saving acts in the past; 5–9, trust should be the response of Israel; 10–17, a description of the present distress; 18–23, protestations of fidelity and trust; 24–27, a bold plea. The life setting is some national catastrophe that we can no longer specify; an individual, probably a king, speaks in 5, 7, and 16, representing the people. **2–4.** Oral tradition handed down the victorious "deeds" of past salvation history; these had been performed by Yahweh alone without help from Israel. **5.** *victories:* Lit., "salvations"; it is clear that a military figure (the king) leads the prayer (cf. Ps 18:33–40). **10–17.** *you...you:* Yahweh is the one responsible for their plight, which seems to have involved exile (12) for some, but no precise date can be given to the Ps. **18–23.** In contrast to the theme of 1–2 Kgs, Israel is pictured here as faithful and loyal to the "covenant" (18–20). In a lament we may expect to find such an idealization—what Mowinckel calls "the innocence of motivation" (*The Psalms I*, 206). **20.** *place of misery:* Thus in the LXX; the MT has "place of jackals," i.e., uninhabited wilderness. **23.** *for your sake:* Israel's suffering is a martyrdom, a bearing witness—a motif to move God to intervene. **24.** *awake:* A bold metaphor, and this is the only time God is explicitly said to "sleep." There is no good reason to hold that this is a Maccabean Ps, as some Fathers and modern commentators have thought.

61 **Ps 45.** A royal Ps, composed on the occasion of the marriage of an Israelite king to a foreign princess (11–13)—a unique situation in the Psalter. Any attempt to identify the king and queen (e.g., a Tyrian princess betrothed to a king of the northern kingdom) is very problematical. Neither can the allegorical interpretation (God, or the messiah, and Israel) be sustained (but cf. R. Tournay in VTSup 9 [1963] 168–212). Structure: 2, introduction by court poet; 3–10, praise of the king for his comeliness, virtue, warlike ability; 11–12, allocution to the bride, urging her to wifely devotion; 13–16, a description of her apparel and the procession; 17–18, concluding remarks, addressed to the king. **2.** The tone and style suggest the work of a court poet, a distinguished person who addresses the bride as "daughter." **3–6.** The admirable qualities of the king—beauty," "majesty," "justice,"—remind us of the sacral character of the Israelite monarch; his warlike qualities are also emphasized. **7.** *your throne, O God:* As the CCD stands, "God" (*'ĕlōhîm*) must be addressed to the king. He is called an "elohim," or superhuman being, just as David was compared to a messenger of elohim (2 Sm 14:17ff.), or David's house to elohim (Zech 12:8), and perhaps just as the members of the heavenly court are called the sons of elohim. Elohim would not connote divinity in a metaphysical sense but a realm of being higher than that of an ordinary mortal. Because of the king's anointing and relationship to Yahweh, he is considered a sacral person, something "divine." This appellation is unique in the OT, and various other translations have been proposed, e.g., "Your throne is a divine throne"; for other attempts to rewrite this verse, see the commentaries and the summary in P. King (*A Study of Psalm 45(44)* [Rome, 1959] 73–84). **8.** *God, your God:* Before the Elohistic recension this phrase would have been "Yahweh, your God." **9–10.** A vivid description of the wedding preparations and cortege; the queen is decorated with gold from Ophir (either in S Arabia or E Africa; cf. 1 Kgs 10:11,22). **11–12.** The instructions to the queen suggest that she is of foreign extraction. **13.** *city:* Lit., "daughter," and some would construe the text as indicating that the queen is a Tyrian princess. **14–16.** Her beauty and the retinue that proceeds into the "palace" are described. **17.** Good wishes for the king: May the union be fruitful and prosperous—an allusion to the importance of the continuation of the royal dynasty. **18.** The final flourish is an illustration of typical court style.

62 **Ps 46.** A hymn of praise, or song of Zion, which was the inspiration of Luther's "Ein' feste Burg ist unser Gott" (Englished by T. Carlyle, "A safe stronghold our God is still"). There is a clear structure of three strophes, each ending in a refrain: With God as a refuge, there is nothing to fear (4, 8, 12). The second strophe singles out God's presence in Zion, which preserves it from the nations; in the third strophe, the congregation is invited to consider Yahweh's deeds, and his oracle of supremacy (11) is quoted. The precise life setting in the liturgy (e.g., Yahweh's enthronement, as proposed by Mowinckel) cannot be defined. Even should there be a borrowing of the old Canaanite traditions—a point not easily proved by Kraus—the reason behind the Zion tradition is Yahweh. The eschatological interpretation of Gunkel and others needs more evidence. **3–4.** Neither earthquake nor the unruly power of chaos ("waters") can counterbalance the presence (which is at the same time a defense) of the "Lord of hosts." **5.** The stream, in contrast to the waters, is symbolic of God's presence (cf. "waters of Shiloah" in Is 8:6). **6.** *dawn:* Perhaps a reference to the answer given to prayer after a night in the Temple (cf. Pss 5:4; 17:3,15; 90:14). **9.** *deeds:* These are described specifically in 10. **11.** This verse has the appearance of a salvation oracle uttered by a priest or prophet in Yahweh's name.

63 **Ps 47.** A hymn of praise, one of the Pss (cf. 93, 95–100) associated with the alleged feast of Yahweh's enthronement (→ 6 and 9 above; cf. Mowinckel, *The Psalms I*, 118–30). Scholars are divided as to the interpretation of this type of Ps: historical (Podechard); eschatological (Gunkel); and cultic (Mowinckel). The kingship of Yahweh is clearly the central idea, whatever be the precise life setting. Structure: 2–6, all peoples are invited to praise the Lord, the supreme king who has chosen Israel; 7–10, Yahweh is enthroned and receives the praise of all. **2.** *all peoples:* This universalism follows upon the Lord's prerogative as supreme ruler (cf. 8–9) and creator. **3.** *Most High:* *'Elyôn* is the common ancient Semitic designation of the chief god, which was appropriated by Israel for Yahweh (cf. R. Lack in *CBQ* 24 [1961] 44–64). **4–5.** The proof of Yahweh's dominion is drawn from the salvation history: the conquest of Palestine ("our inheritance") for Israel. **6.** *mounts:* This term (*'ālâ*) strongly suggests a cultic rite in which the Ark would have been carried in procession (cf. Ps 132; 2 Sm 6:15) and installed in the Temple. *trumpet blasts:* Characteristic of royal enthronement (2 Sm 15:10; 2 Kgs 9:13) and also of the Feast of Tabernacles (Ps 81:4; Nm 29:1). **8–10.** Further theological basis for the celebration of Yahweh's kingship is related. *God reigns:* It can also be translated as "Yahweh has become king"—a cry of acclamation similar to that used for Israelite kings (2 Sm 15:10; 1 Kgs 1:11; 2 Kgs 9:13). It need not imply that Yahweh was not considered as king before; rather, his eternal kingship is actualized in the liturgy. *princes:* It is possible that representatives of other nations could have shared in the liturgical celebration. *guardians:* Lit., "shields"; the parallelism in Pss 84:10; 90:19 shows that the term designates kings or nobles. (For a treatment of this Ps, cf. A. R. Johnson, *Sacral Kingship in Ancient Israel* [Cardiff, 1955].)

64 **Ps 48.** A hymn of praise, or song of Zion. Structure: 2–4, glorification of the "city of our God"; 5–8, report of a siege and its failure; 9–12, proclamation of God's justice and praise to the world; 13–15, invitation to admire the city. The life setting, apart from the reference to the Temple in 10, depends on the interpretation of 5–8; the siege of Jerusalem could be real (Sennacherib in 701?) or merely a theme of invincibility. Like other songs of Zion, the hymnic introduction is lacking. **3.** *his holy mountain:* (Ps 2:6.) Because Jerusalem has been chosen by Yahweh as his residence, no claims can be too extravagant. *the recesses of the north:* Originally Mt. Saphon (the later Mt. Casius, today's Jebel Aqra, N of Ras Shamra), the residence of the Canaanite pantheon, comparable to Mt. Olympus of the Greeks. It was appropriated by Israel for the holy mountain of Zion (cf. Is 14:13; W. F. Albright in *Fest. A. Bertholet* [Tübingen, 1950]). *the great king:* Used also of the great Mesopotamian monarchs (*šarru rabû*). The invincibility flows from Yahweh's presence (Ps 46:5,8); this verse leads into the description of the unsuccessful siege in 5–8, in which the enemies are made to quake because they "see" (Yahweh? just as the waters in Ps 77:17 [cf. Ps 114:4] saw God and shuddered?). *the ships of Tarshish:* Large, seagoing ships capable of voyaging to Tarshish (Tartessus in Spain?). *wind from the east:* Suggests the Phoenicians, not the Israelites, whose only port was S at Ezion-geber. **9–10.** Perhaps an antiphonal response to the description in 5–8, which is something the people "have seen," and the "temple" is indicated as the place where they are, meditating on his "kindness" (*ḥesed*). **11.** The "justice" of Yahweh is, as often in the OT, his saving intervention, the judgments (12) against Zion's enemies (Ps 97:8). **13.** Those present are invited to go about the city and admire its strength, which is ultimately Yahweh (15, "such is our God"). The Hebr text ends with *'al mût*, "concerning [or against] death" (read by the LXX as "forever"). The CCD omits it as belonging originally to the title of Ps 49.

65 **Ps 49.** A wisdom Ps, preoccupied with the problem of retribution; it begins in the style of Dame

Wisdom preaching in the streets (Prv 8), and the author proclaims *ḥokmāh* (wisdom). Structure: 2–5, solemn introduction; 6–13, the triumph of the wicked is transitory because their riches are of no avail; 14–21, and also because of their fate (contrasted with the fate of the psalmist in 16). **2–3.** The breadth of this audience suggests that the author has something truly important to say, and he presents it as wisdom teaching in 4–5. As in Prv 1:6, "proverb" and "riddle" are in parallelism; the psalmist assumes the stature of a prophet who sets his inspired message to music (2 Kgs 3:15). **6–7.** The problem: Should one fear the wicked, who "trust in their wealth"? **8–10.** Man cannot bribe death no matter how wealthy he is. **11.** The reference to the "wise men" is to be understood from the viewpoint of the psalmist; even these die, and how much more the "senseless," because "you can't take it with you." Death is the great leveler for all. **12.** The irony is that the rich who would "remain alive always" (10) are forever in "tombs"; in this stupidity they resemble the "beasts" (13). **14–15.** The end of the wicked: Their riches are replaced by the "nether world." The text of 15 is hopelessly corrupt; the general idea is a description of Sheol and *Môt* (death personified). The CCD translation has retained, with the MT, "the upright rule over them," but it is not certain. **16.** A key verse, although Gunkel and others claim it is a gloss. Two interpretations are possible: Yahweh saves the psalmist from (premature or threatening) death (the "power of the nether world"; cf. Barth, *Die Errettung vom Tode* 158ff.); Yahweh delivers him from Sheol by "receiving" him into his own presence—an intimation of immortality. Two factors argue in favor of the second view. The use of *lāqah* (receive) seems a deliberate allusion to the story of Enoch (Gn 5:21) and to Elijah (2 Kgs 2:9–10; see also Ps 73:24). Then too, 16 seems to be in contrast to 8: The rich man could not "redeem himself" or bribe God—that very God who has the power will "redeem" the psalmist. **17–21.** Words of consolation that take up the ideas of 6–12; 19b is the self-satisfied judgment that the wealthy man passes upon himself. There is an implicit contrast between the one who is received (16) and the one "who shall never more see light" (20). The refrain of 13 is picked up in 21, with a deliberate change that suggests the wisdom teaching ("prudence"), which the psalmist consciously proclaims.

66 **Ps 50.** A (prophetic) liturgy. Structure: 1–6, introduction in the style of theophany: Yahweh comes to summon his faithful; 7–15, the first discourse of Yahweh concerning sacrifice; 16–23, a second discourse on true obedience. The cultic life setting is obvious, but not all agree on the precise feast. Mowinckel holds for the enthronement; Weiser and Von Rad suggest a covenant renewal, such as the Feast of Tabernacles, which seems more probable (cf. 5). **1.** *God:* Lit., "God, God" (*'el, 'ĕlōhîm;* cf. Jos 22:22). **2.** Suggests a liturgical appearance ("shines forth") at Zion, with the usual events that accompany a theophany; the "trial" of his covenanted people is witnessed by "heavens" and "earth" as frequently in the OT (Dt 31:23; Is 1:2). **7–15.** Probably a prophet speaks in the name of Yahweh, the covenant God ("your God"), regulating proper liturgical worship. As both Catholic and Protestant exegetes now agree, it is not a total condemnation and rejection of sacrificial worship as such. Rather, the point is that sacrifices can neither control God nor force him into a corner, for his are "all the animals." Let not the people think they are being rebuked for the number of their sacrifices (8). But he has no need of sacrifices; after all, he does not "eat" or "drink." He is independent of all things, for they belong to him. What is commanded? "*Praise as your sacrifice*" (14)—i.e., the personal involvement and commitment in the liturgical sacrifice (*tôdâ*). **16–17.** The second discourse condemns the insincerity of the "wicked man" (although 16 is dropped by Podechard and others). Three of the Commandments are explicitly indicated in 18–19; theft, adultery, and calumny. **21.** *I am like yourself:* So God would be, if he were not to intervene and "correct" evil men. **22–23.** A threat and a reminder that they are to continue the sacrificial system, but in a sincere fashion (cf. 14 with 23); the "right way" leads to "salvation" (cf. Prv 15:8).

67 **Ps 51.** An individual lament, in sorrow for sin. Ps 51 is the fourth and the most famous of the penitential Pss. There is no indication that it was uttered by David after his sin with Bathsheba (cf. title). Perhaps the most striking emphasis is placed on the awfulness of sin itself; the author cannot rest until it is forgiven. (For details, cf. E. Dalglish, *Psalm Fifty-One in the Light of Ancient Near Eastern Patternism* [Leiden, 1962].) Structure: 3–4, appeal for mercy; 5–8, confession of sinfulness; 9–14, request for cleansing, for heart and spirit; 15–19, a vow and assurance of special sacrifice; 20–21, a prayer for Jerusalem. Life setting: The prayer is composed by a sinner, who feels the weight of his sins more than his sickness (10); one may detect in 19 the influence of Jeremiah (spirit) and the prophets (sacrifice of a contrite heart). **3–4.** The entire complaint (9, 12–15) is permeated with the desire to be completely purified of sin (cf. metaphors, "wash," etc.). **6.** The quotation marks in the CCD indicate that this verse is his acknowledgment of his sin as an offence against God (not just against man). He proclaims his wrongdoing as a justification of God's sentence against him. **7.** He goes further and professes his deep-rooted sinfulness (in the sense of Gn 8:21, not in the sense of the doctrine of Original Sin, which is a matter of later revelation). **8.** *sincerity of heart:* Lit., "fidelity in that which is secret"—the depths of his being. **9.** *hyssop:* A metaphor taken from the ritual cleansing effected by sprinkling blood or water by means of the branches of this bush. **10.** *bones...crushed:* Apparently implies bodily sickness. **12.** *create: Bārā'*. The technical term that designates an action proper to God (Gn 1:1); purification is a work that only God and not ritual can achieve. **13.** *holy spirit:* God's action in man, which saves him and keeps him faithful (cf. Is 63:8–14). He is asking for what Jeremiah and Ezekiel said about the new covenant and the new spirit (Jer 24:7; 31:33; Ez 36:25ff.). **15.** *teach:* A vow to proclaim publicly his experience (in the *tôdâ* sacrifice? cf. 17–18) and thus lead sinners back to God. **16.** *blood guilt:* Lit., "bloods," i.e., blood poured out, or murder. Because he is hardly a murderer, it may be that he fears someone will slay him; perhaps the word should be rendered "death." **18–19.** An unusual idea, influenced by prophetic teaching: He himself, contrite, is the victim. **20–21.** Probably a later addition (after 587) and partly a corrective to the bold idea in 19.

68 **Ps 52.** An individual lament(?). The Ps has been classified in divers ways: trust (Podechard); lament (Gunkel); sapiential (Castellino); thanksgiving (Schmidt); or a composite work (Kraus). Structure: 3–6, an indictment, in prophetic style, of the evil man; 7, a threat; 8–11, the reaction of the just man. The application of this Ps to Doeg (who denounced, but did not lie) in the title is contradicted by the mention of the Temple (10). **3–6.** The indictment is leveled against those who are crass enough to boast of their evil-doing. **7.** Such an evil person is a scandal; the law of temporal retribution demands punishment by God. **8–9.** This is a stereotyped picture in the OT, but more often the unjust ridicules the just; now the tables are turned. **10.** In contrast to the lot of the wicked (7), the author shall flourish like a tree (Jer 11:16). **11.** A vow to offer a thanksgiving sacrifice, and with it, to "proclaim" Yahweh before the congregation.

69 **Ps 53.** See comment on Ps 14; this poem is a variant form. The only significant difference is 53:6 (= 14:5,6), but the "besiegers" cannot be identified.

70 **Ps 54.** An individual lament. The structure is typical of the lament: 3–5, a cry for help against godless enemies; 6–9, an expression of trust, a plea, and a vow to offer sacrifice. **3.** *name:* As elsewhere in the OT, it is a surrogate for God himself; it stands here in parallelism to "might." **6.** A motif of trust. **8.** *freely:* Lit., "with a free-will offering"; the n^e*dābâ* was a spontaneous offering over and above what was prescribed.

71 **Ps 55.** An individual lament. Although some (Kraus, Gunkel) argue that this Ps is a composite work, it can be interpreted as a unit (Podechard, Weiser). The life setting is the suffering of persecution by wicked people, among them a very close friend; the psalmist prays to be delivered and to see divine punishment visited upon them. Structure: 2–3, a cry for help; 3–8, a description of distress; 10–12, a request that God may remedy the evil that is abroad; 13–15, his bosom friend has become his worst enemy; 16–24, a confident request that death will be the punishment of the evil whereas the psalmist will be saved by God (16–24). **8.** The "wilderness" would at least provide respite and "shelter" from persecution and anguish. **10–12.** It is not clear how the "evil" in the "city" involves the psalmist (but cf. 19). **14.** The betrayal by his "bosom friend" (whose action may be described in 21–22) is particularly bitter. **16.** Perhaps an allusion to the revolt in the desert by Korah and others (Nm 16:31ff.). **18.** These are the three periods in the day that are specified for prayer (Dn 6:11). **23.** *your care:* Addressed to one person; either the psalmist is addressing himself, or one of the Temple personnel speaks to him (Pss 28:14; 37:5). The poem closes on a note of serene confidence.

72 **Ps 56.** An individual lament. Structure: 2–3, a cry for help against enemies; 4–5, expression of trust; 6–12, complaint, request, and confidence; 13–14, a vow of thanksgiving for deliverance. It is not possible to determine precisely the machinations of the "enemy." **4.** This remarkable "trust" in God is enough to dispel fear. **5.** *flesh:* In the OT, it designates mankind, with the connotation of man's weakness, as opposed to spirit (cf. Is 40:6). **9.** The metaphors "tears," "flask," and "book" express God's intimate and kindly notice of his suffering. **10.** *with me:* Perhaps better read "for me." **13.** A vow to offer thanksgiving is characteristic of the lament. **14.** This Ps illustrates how broad is the sphere of "*death*" in the OT world of thought, and it ends on the customary note of certainty ("you have rescued me"), which seems to grow naturally out of his great confidence (5, 10–12).

73 **Ps 57.** An individual lament. The poem ends in a thanksgiving (8–12) that also appears in Ps 108:2–6; for the transition of lament to thanksgiving, see also Pss 23, 42, 57. Structure: 2, a cry for pity; 3–6, a description of his situation (calumny) ending in refrain (6, 12); 7–12, despite the plots of enemies (7), he gives thanks to God for deliverance. **2.** The "refuge" in God may be not merely spiritual consolation but the right of asylum in the Temple, where he has been unjustly accused by his enemies (5, 7–9), and where he wakes at "dawn" (9) to give thanks (Schmidt). **7.** The CCD translation understands this verse as a general observation (cf. Pss 7:16; 9:15–16); other translations insist on the past tense. In the latter case, there is more here than mere certainty of having been heard; his enemies have been undone, and he has been delivered—a clear motif of a thanksgiving song. **8–12.** See Ps 108:2–6, which differs only slightly; in both cases, these lines may be a borrowing from a third source. **9.** *wake the dawn:* There are many parallels to this idea, from the *evocat auroram* of Ovid (*Metamorph.* 11. 597), to Shakespeare and modern poets. **10.** The reference to the "nations" and "peoples" does not necessarily mean that the author is in the Diaspora; the presence of foreigners or the thought of the Lord's universal dominion could account for this aspect, which is not unusual in statements of praise (Pss 9:12; 119:46). **12.** The refrain (cf. 6) refers to Yahweh's position above the firmament, and, corresponding to his power in the heavens, it is the "glory" due him.

74 **Ps 58.** A lament. Structure: 2–3, an address to the "gods"; 4–6, description of wickedness; 7–10, imprecations; 11–12, conclusion concerning temporal retribution. For the proper understanding of the poem, the role of the "gods"—i.e., the members of the heavenly court—in governing the world is to be assumed (cf. Dt 4:20). They are derelict in their duty; hence they are excoriated. **1.** *gods:* They are not human judges, but the "sons of God" who assist Yahweh in governing the world. It would be better, therefore, to read "O Gods" instead of the "like gods" of the CCD (cf. Ps 82:1). *men of rank:* Lit., "sons of man" (b^e*nê ʾādām*); this line is better translated, "and judge fairly the sons of men?" **3.** The answer to the question is now given; the "gods" are guilty. **4.** *wicked:* The tools used by the gods; they spew "poison" and they fail to heed admonition, like a "stubborn" snake that will not listen to the snake charmer. **7.** It is God who will punish the wicked ("their teeth" does not refer to the gods). **9.** *snail:* The Hebr word is doubtful in meaning. The "melting snail" in the CCD refers to the empty shells of dead snails, which presumably have wasted away, if one judges from the trail they leave after them. **10.** Any translation of this verse is uncertain. **11.** The bloodthirsty touch is deliberate exaggeration (cf. Jb 29:6). **12.** The traditional Israelite view of temporal retribution is reflected here; the "gods" may fail in the realm of justice, but not Yahweh.

75 **Ps 59.** An individual lament. The psalmist has been accused unjustly, and he awaits God's intervention (at dawn? cf. 17 and Pss 17:15; 57:9). Structure: 2–3, a cry for rescue; 4–5, his situation is that "mighty men" attack him without cause; 5–6, a call for action; 7–11, a complaint about the enemy and an expression of trust; 11–14, complaint and request; 15–18, complaint and confident certainty that his prayer will be heard. **3.** *evildoers:* On this term, → 11 and 18 above. **4.** The affirmation of innocence is frequent in laments (Ps 7:4–6; etc.). **5.** A direct appeal to the Lord as *Yhwh Ṣ*^{e}*bāʾôt*, the ruler and judge of all (cf. enthronement Pss); from this point of view, the reference to nations (6, 9, 14) can be understood. On the other hand, Mowinckel sees here a reason to interpret it as a royal Ps, uttered by the king against his enemies (cf. *The Psalms I*, 226). **7.** This refrain is found again in 15, just as 10–11a are almost repeated in 18. **17.** In his confidence he vows to offer the thanksgiving sacrifice.

76 **Ps 60.** A (liturgy) lament of the nation. Despite the title, which connects the Ps with David's wars (2 Sm 8), the precise occasion escapes us. A serious defeat, perhaps in Edom (11), has prompted this lament, and the oracle (8–10) is offered as an encouraging reply in which the divine ownership of Canaan is affirmed. Structure: 3–7, an appeal and description of the distress; 8–10, the oracle of promise; 11–14, a complaint, and confident request. **4.** The "country" is compared to a house shaken by earthquake. **5.** *stupefying wine:* Not the "cup of wrath" but a drink that weakens and causes one to fall (Jer 25:15–16; Is 51:17). **8–10.** In this cultic oracle, given by priest or prophet, Yahweh is presented as a victorious warrior distributing booty. All of Canaan and

Transjordan belong to him, just as they were once divided and distributed under Joshua. It could possibly be an older oracle that is applied to the present defeat; Kraus and Podechard argue that it dates after 721 and is a promise of repossessing the northern kingdom. *valley of Succoth:* The lower stretch of the Jabbok Valley to Tell Deir Alla. *washbowl:* An allusion to the Dead Sea and an indication that Moab is to perform menial tasks. *set my shoe:* In the sense of "throw my shoe"—a symbol of taking possession (cf. Ru 4:7). **11.** An individual (the king?) asks a question, and it does not express much confidence in the oracle (cf. 12). *fortified city:* Perhaps Bozrah, the capital of Edom. **13–14.** The community expresses a confident request. Ps 60:7–14 is repeated in the artificial poem, Ps 108:7–14.

77 **Ps 61.** An individual lament. The classification is difficult; Weiser takes it as a thanksgiving prayer; others consider it to be a royal Ps (cf. 7–8); Podechard argues that the desire to be restored to the Temple (5, 9) indicates that it is the prayer of a Levite. Structure: 2–3, invocation; 3–5, a confident prayer that he may dwell with Yahweh in the Temple; 6–9, he is certain that his prayer has been heard and offers a prayer for the king. **3–5.** *earth's end:* Not a mere metaphor (against Weiser); he is far from Jerusalem—hence his desire for the "shelter" of the Temple ("your wings" in 5, a frequent metaphor, as in Ps 57:2). **6.** This expresses the usual certainty that his prayer has been heard. **7–9.** Why is the prayer for the king mentioned here? Kraus argues that it is not a later addition (Gunkel) but merely part of the plea in a lament, and he points to similar requests on behalf of the king in Akkadian prayers (cf. Falkenstein and Von Soden, *op. cit.*, 237, 239).

78 **Ps 62.** A Ps of trust. Structure: 2–8, an affirmation of trust in God, despite attacks of his enemies; 9–13, a testimony, characteristic of a thanksgiving Ps. The poem emphasizes the Lord as the "only" (notice the repetition) one in whom to trust. **2.** The refrain in 2–3, 6–7 uses metaphors frequent in Pss (18:3; 46:8,12). **4.** Addressed to his (hypocritical, 5) enemies, but the situation is not described. **9–11.** He turns to the assembly present (in the Temple) and urges them to imitate his trust (9); in the style of a wisdom teacher he describes the vanity of man and human power. **12–13.** He seems to paraphrase the oracle that he has received from God and that is the basis of his trust; the oracle is expressed in the numerical style (x; x + 1) that is frequent in the wisdom books (Prv 6:16–17; 30:15ff.). The union of "power" and "kindness" (covenant loyalty) is characteristic of Yahweh, and this fact lies behind his just treatment of man.

79 **Ps 63.** An individual lament. The psalmist is filled with nostalgia and a strong desire to return to the Temple (Pss 42–43). David (cf. the title) never seems to have had for Saul the sentiments expressed in 10–11. Structure: 2–3, a yearning to be with God; 4–9, a description of what service in the Temple means to him; 10–11, imprecations against enemies; 12, a prayer for the king and for the faithful. **2–4.** A delicate and fervent desire expressed for the encounter with God "in the sanctuary" (cf. Pss 27:4; 42:2–3), "a greater good than life." **4–9.** A description of his hopes and his actual experiences in the Temple; the lines express well his sense of intimate union with God. **11.** He envisions his enemies as sentenced to death and left without burial (hence, "the prey of jackals"). **12.** The reference to the "king" need not be an addition, nor does it necessarily indicate a royal Ps (cf. 61:7).

80 **Ps 64.** An individual lament. The psalmist describes the machinations of his enemies and expresses his confidence that God will punish them and will care for the just man. Structure: 2–3, a cry for help; 4–7 the activities of his enemies; 8–9, God's intervention; 10–11, the acknowledgment of Yahweh as refuge. **2–7.** His enemies calumniate him, for which "swords" and "arrows" are common metaphors—e.g., Ps 57:5. **8–10.** Is God's intervention in the past, so that this Ps is really of thanksgiving (so Weiser and Kraus), or in the future, and hence described here as timeless? The CCD translation favors the second alternative. The punishment (8–9, "arrows") is appropriate to the sins of the evildoers (4, "arrows"). **11.** This verse has the appearance of a "lesson" addressed to those who hear this prayer.

81 **Ps 65.** A hymn of praise. God is praised (not thanked) as one who pardons and blesses, as creator, and as the one who bestows rain and fertility on the land. Structure: 2–5, the gifts that Yahweh's presence in Zion secures for his people; 6–9, Yahweh as savior and creator; 10–14, Yahweh, the source of fertility. **2–4.** A vivid, but simple, description of the mercy that the sinner may expect. **5.** *the man you choose:* The phrase suggests that it is a privilege to approach Yahweh in the Temple. **6.** The universalism expressed here and in 9 is noteworthy; it refers to more than the Israelites of the Diaspora, and it derives from the Lord's status as creator (cf. the enthronement Pss). **8.** In the Israelite concept of creation, God keeps chaos at bay (Ps 89:10–11). **10.** *watercourses:* The water above the firmament, the source of rain. **12.** *paths:* Lit., "wagon-wheel tracks," left by Yahweh as he travels, fructifying the earth. **10–14.** Possibly an original harvest song incorporated into this hymn; it is hardly enough to determine the literary type as a harvest thanksgiving song (cf. Ps 67).

82 **Ps 66.** A mixed type: A hymn of praise and thanksgiving for national deliverance (1–12) and a thanksgiving by an individual (13–20). There is no convincing explanation of the relationship between 1–12 and 13–20. It is not clear that 1–12 are a sort of choral prelude to 13–20 (Gunkel) or that the individual in 13–20 is a king who speaks for the "we" of 1–12 (the "king-Ego" style of Mowinckel). And it always remains possible that two separate Pss have been joined. Structure: 2–4, an invitation to praise God; 5–7, the praise is motivated by his works, especially at the Exodus; 8–12, the invitation is renewed and allusion is made to God's testing of Israel; 13–15, a declaration of an individual that he will offer sacrifice; 16–20, a testimony addressed to God-fearing bystanders about God's kind intervention. **6.** The reference is to God's saving action in the crossing of the Red Sea and the Jordan. **7.** God's world-wide rule is the reason why "nations" and "peoples" (8; cf. 2, 4) can be urged to praise him. **9–12.** These lines acknowledge Yahweh's deliverance of Israel from some trial, presumably the Exodus experiences alluded to in 6. **13.** A thanksgiving song of an individual, accompanying a sacrifice (15), begins here. **16.** Preaching to bystanders (the "testimony") is a characteristic part of a thanksgiving Ps.

83 **Ps 67.** A national thanksgiving Ps (?). The classification is not clear; the poem may be taken as a request for blessings (2, 8) or as a national thanksgiving for a good harvest (7). The remarkable thing in the Ps is how God's blessings on Israel are taken to be a sign of his salvation for the nations (3). Hence, the nations (whom he rules, 5) should praise God (2–6); if they are to share in the blessings, they must "fear him" (8). The structure is determined by the refrain (sung by the congregation?) in 4 and 6. **2.** This line is modeled on the priestly blessing of Aaron (cf. Nm 6:24–26). **3.** *your way:* The divine manner of dealing with men—blessings for those who "fear" him. **5.** This verse recalls the theme of Yahweh as just ruler of the world (cf. Pss 96:10; 99:4).

84 **Ps 68.** A hymn of praise(?). This obscure Ps is difficult to classify; it has been called a collection of incipits, or opening lines of various songs (W. F. Albright in *HUCA* 23 [1950–51] 1–39), an "eschatological hymn" (Gunkel), and a song of enthronement (Mowinckel). The hymn betrays no particular structure, and in many places the translation must remain uncertain. It is perhaps best understood as part of a liturgy that commemorates Yahweh's saving deeds of the past, and that accompanies procession and enthronement in the Jerusalem Temple. **2.** A comparison with Nm 10:3 suggests that the Ark is being carried in procession. **5.** *cloud-rider:* An epithet of Baal, frequently found in the Ugaritic texts (e.g., *ANET* 138), that is also applied to Yahweh (Dt 33:26; Pss 18:11; 68:34). **8–11.** Apparently a summary of the salvation history from the Exodus to the Conquest. Rain is associated with Sinai also in Jgs 5:4–5. The bracketed line in the CCD suggests a gloss, although Albright insists on the translation, "the one of Sinai." **12–15.** An Israelite victory over "kings" at Zalmon (in Bashan) is achieved by the "Almighty." The "dove" is perhaps Israel or else is a notable piece of booty taken in battle (the dove was sacred to Ishtar). **16–19.** *mountains of Bashan:* Serve as a contrast to Zion; they are addressed poetically as though they were jealous of Jerusalem. The Lord's advance "to the sanctuary" suggests that this verse is sung as the Ark is carried in procession. It seems as though Yahweh's transferral from Sinai to Jerusalem is being commemorated. Yahweh is portrayed as a conqueror who has "ascended on high"—i.e., entered his Temple and received homage from his captives. **20–24.** The Lord is acclaimed as a "saving God" who "controls" life and death. The oracle in 23–24 indicates that none can escape him (cf. Am 9:3) and that Israel shall conquer (24). **25–28.** A procession "into the sanctuary" is described; it is not known why these specific tribes are mentioned. *Israel's wellspring:* Designates the family or stock of the people (cf. Ps 87:6–7). **29–32.** Gifts are to be brought to Yahweh in Jerusalem from the "nations" (Egypt is the "beast of the reeds"). **33–36.** This hymn urges "kingdoms" to acknowledge Yahweh, enthroned "in his sanctuary."

85 **Ps 69.** An individual lament. Cries for help and descriptions of misery alternate through 2–30, followed by a vow to offer thanksgiving and expressions of confidence. He is sick (27, 30) unto death (2–3) and persecuted by enemies as a thief (4–5) and as one smitten by God (9–10,19–20). With Ps 22, this prayer is most frequently quoted in the NT in relation to Christ's suffering. Like Ps 22, it can be regarded as a description of the exemplary suffering of an innocent man who relies upon God for deliverance—eminently applicable to the Son of Man. **2–3.** *water, swamp, depths:* Synonyms for the nether world (cf. 15–16) where he finds himself (Sheol is a state rather than a place). **6–7.** Despite his sinfulness (6), he regards his situation as unjust and he appeals to God to change it for the sake of "those who seek you," who will otherwise be scandalized at the suffering of a man who is a martyr (10–11). **15–16.** For the imagery, see comment on 2–3. **17.** *in your kindness:* As in 14, he appeals to the Lord's *ḥesed.* **22.** The "food" and "drink" may refer to the practice of giving a meal to unfortunates, but they gave him "gall" and "vinegar." **23–29.** A series of violent imprecations follows—if God is the just judge, let him act! **23.** *table:* Perhaps the reference is to their sacrifices. **28.** *attain to your reward:* Lit., "come into your justice," as though God's justice were a "safe" and blessed area. **29.** The names of the "just" are presumably inscribed in the figurative Book of the Living (cf. Pss 40:8; 139:16; Ex 32:32). **31.** He vows to praise God in "song," which he considers more pleasing than material sacrifices (cf. Ps 40:7). **33–35.** The lesson that the "lowly ones" are to derive from his deliverance. **36–37.** Perhaps an addition, although the author could easily pass from the individual to the group; it presupposes the destruction of the kingdom of Judah (587).

86 **Ps 70.** An individual lament, almost identical with Ps 40:14–18. It may have been an independent poem originally. The description of the psalmist's distress is very vague. He is persecuted by enemies who seek his life (3–4), and he seems to contrast himself ("afflicted," "poor," 6) with those who "seek" God (5). But his trust is in the Lord as his "help" and "deliverer."

87 **Ps 71.** An individual lament. The so-called anthological style characterizes the composition; it is made up of several expressions borrowed from other Pss (cf. Pss 31:2–4; 22:10–11). This is the prayer of a sick, persecuted old man who in the past experienced God's protection; now he overcomes his fear with prayer and hope. Structure: 1–8, a plea to be delivered from enemies, and expressions of trust, concluding with a vow to praise God; 9–16, a complaint about his enemy, concluding with a vow to praise; 17–24, plea and expressions of trust, concluding with a vow to praise God. There is a fairly consistent alternating of request, confidence, and motifs of trust and vow; the Ps ends with the certainty that God has heard him (23–24). **2–3.** Cf. Ps 31:2–4. **5–6.** For this motif, see Ps 22:10–11. **7.** *portent:* One on whom God's anger has been poured out (cf. 11 and also Dt 28:46 for *môfēt* as a portent and object of God's wrath). **9.** As in 18, he alleges his "old age" as a reason for Yahweh to intervene (cf. Is 46:4). **12.** His appeal is in vivid contrast to the words of his enemies in 11. **15.** *their extent:* The many individual acts of God's "justice" and "salvation" (note the parallelism, as in Dt-Is) are meant. Perhaps these embrace all the salvation history, as the *magnalia Dei* ("mighty works," 16) of the next verse suggest.

88 **Ps 72.** A royal Ps, probably composed on the occasion of the coronation of a new king in Jerusalem. The king is undoubtedly a descendant of David (but hardly the "Solomon" of the title), and the dynastic oracle of 2 Sm 7 forms the basis of the high hopes held out for this ruler: justice, peace, life forever, and world-wide rule. The courtly style, which Gunkel, Gressmann, and others stress, is to be found here, but it is not merely an imitation of foreign courts. The justification lies in the divine plans for the Davidic dynasty. The king's reign is described in "messianic" language; the currently reigning king is viewed in the light of the hopes centered in the dynasty (→ 15 above). In the designs of God, Jesus fulfilled the royal ideals in a transcendent manner. Structure (cf. P. W. Skehan in *Bib* 40 [1959] 168–74): There are five strophes with four full lines of (Hebr) verse: 1–4, a prayer that God grant the king justice for his office; 5–8, the king's rule is to be unlimited in time and space; 9–11, the king's dealings with foreign nations; 12–15, his dealings with his own people; 16–17, wishes for the prosperity, long life, and universal blessings for the king. **1.** The parallelism indicates that the "king" is of royal lineage, not a usurper; he is to be given the divine gift of "justice" for his rule. For the ideal of a just king in the ancient world, cf. the prologue and epilogue to the Code of Hammurabi (*ANET* 164, 177–78). **3.** The prosperity attendant upon the king's just rule is described in hyperbole (cf. Is 32:15–20). **4.** The just judgments are concretely described; 4c overloads the line and is probably a dittography of the first word in 5. **6–7.** The beneficent effects of the reign are described here. **8.** Cf. Zech 9:10; the world-wide rule seems to extend from the Mediterranean Sea to the Persian Gulf (or simply the waters that surround the earth?), and from the Euphrates (the "River") to the "ends of the earth," i.e., the islands in the Mediterranean; cf. Adad-nirari's boast, as a parallel to this court style (*ANET* 281). **9.** The phraseology is also in Mi 7:17 and Is 49:23 and in the Amarna tablets. **10.** Rulers from the far west and the far south will give "tribute." **12–15.** Because of his justice to the "poor," the king will be beloved of his subjects. **17.** There seems to be a clear allusion to Gn 12:3 and other passages where Abraham is said to be a source of blessing for all nations. **18–19.** The collection of the Second Book of the Pss (cf. Ps 41:14) ends with this doxology, and 20 probably indicates the close of a collection of Davidic Pss (Pss 51–70).

89 **Ps 73.** A thanksgiving Ps. Many (Podechard, Castellino) classify this Ps as a wisdom Ps on the basis of content, but the form suggests that it is properly a thanksgiving song. The psalmist describes the crisis he has experienced but only after stating his conclusion about God's goodness (1, which is given in detail in 23–27), and he concludes with an avowal of thanksgiving (28cd). This prayer is unquestionably one of the most sublime and beautiful in the OT. Structure: 1–3, the conclusion he finally reached after being scandalized by the prosperity of the wicked; 4–12, the success and the sins of the wicked are described; 13–17, the crisis that he underwent; 18–23, the fate of the wicked; 23–28, the fate of the good. **1.** The comforting conclusion, reached after his crisis, is now proclaimed in praise of God (cf. Ps 106:1). **2.** *almost:* The rest of the Ps relates how close he came to giving up his faith. **9.** Lit., "they set their mouths in heaven," perhaps speaking blasphemously against God or "in place of" God. **10.** The CCD (doubtfully) takes this verse as a blasphemy against God uttered by the wicked. **13.** *washing:* Probably the liturgical act of purification (e.g., Dt 21:6). **17.** *sanctuary:* The Jerusalem Temple, not the "mysteries of God" (Vg). *final destiny:* Lit., "after[wards]," Hebr *'ăḥarît.* This destiny is described in 18–20 as "slippery road," "suddenly desolate"; it is to be understood in the sense of the traditional "end" of sinners, according to the wisdom teachers. **20.** The text is uncertain; the CCD suggests that the injustices perpetrated by sinners will seem like a "dream" after God rises to judge. **23–28.** Present the psalmist's insight into the lot of the just, such as himself, and he finds it in companionship with God (25, 26, 28); it is his "good." Does 24 indicate that this association with God goes beyond death, "in glory"? Many argue that it does, citing the use of the technical term *lqḥ* (so Elijah, 2 Kgs 2:1ff.; and Enoch, Gn 5:24 [cf. Ps 49:16] were "taken") and also the use of the term "glory" (*kābôd*). If the author does not mean life beyond death, the solution to his crisis is not apparent. Others argue that these lines merely indicate his deliverance from evil and impending death (cf. Barth, *Die Errettung vom Tode* 161–63). However, it seems more probable that the author had some insight into a contact with God that is destined to perdure. **28.** *I shall declare:* The characteristic vow of thanksgiving (cf. 1).

90 **Ps 74.** A lament of the community, on the occasion of a destruction of the Temple. The structure follows the typical framework of the communal lament (cf. C. Westermann, *op. cit.; CBQ* 21 [1959] 87): 1–11, a complaint and description of the situation, with motifs to induce Yahweh to intervene; 12–29, a hymn praising God's power in creation (12–17), to which other motifs for intervention and a final plea are added. **1.** *why:* The question is typical in a lament (cf. 10). **2.** Such terms as "your flock," "inheritance" are highly nuanced and are intended to move God to action. **3.** There is no certainty as to the date of this devastation of the "sanctuary"—but that of 587 is more probable than that by Antiochus in 167. **5.** The text is uncertain, but some kind of damage to the Temple is described. **9.** *deeds on our behalf:* Lit. "our signs"; these are not military symbols, but God's, saving actions, such as "prophet." **12.** *saving deeds:* Creation is considered one of these. **13–14.** A typical description of creation in terms of the mythical primordial battle between Yahweh and chaos, personified in "dragons" and "Leviathan" (for Ugaritic and other biblical parallels, cf. J. L. McKenzie, *TS* 11 [1950] 275–82). The double perspective of creation and Exodus (cf. also 2) echoes in these lines. **18.** Here begins a series of motifs to induce Yahweh to act, culminating in the final appeal (22–23).

91 **Ps 75.** A "liturgy"(?). The classification is very uncertain. The poem acknowledges God as the inexorable judge of the wicked on earth. The life setting is also difficult to ascertain. Scholars have suggested various occasions: a prophetic liturgy portraying eschatological judgment (Gunkel); enthronement festival song (Mowinckel). A liturgical background may be presupposed. Structure: 2, hymnic introduction; 3–5, divine oracle; 6–9, admonition; 10–11, praise proclaimed by an individual. **2.** *wondrous deeds:* In this context, they are the Lord's just judgments upon malefactors. **3–4.** The divine oracle announces that the just judge, who holds the earth firm on its "pillars," will judge when he sees fit; the creator is also the judge. **5–6.** On the strength of the oracle, a priest (?) warns the wicked not to rebel against God. **7.** A deliberate anacoluthon occurs here; one must supply "does salvation [or judgement] come." **8–9.** God alone is "judge." The "cup" (of wrath) is a frequent OT metaphor (Is 51:17; Jer 25:15). **10.** A priest (?, cf. 5) announces "praise," and judgment of the "wicked" and "just." **11.** Perhaps the MT "I will break off" should be changed to the third person (God).

92 **Ps 76.** A hymn of praise, or song of Zion (cf. Pss 46, 48). Structure: 2–4, acknowledgment of Yahweh as inhabiting and protecting Zion; 4–10, a description of his victory at Zion; 11–13, praise of Yahweh by Israel and the nations. The interpretation is again problematical: Is the battle (4–10) an historical, eschatological, or cultic event? It seems more probable that the Lord's saving deeds are actualized in the liturgy—not without a certain orientation toward the future (10–13). **3.** *Salem:* Apparently an older name of Jerusalem (Gn 14:18). **4.** This is more a generalization about Zion's inviolability than a reference to a particular battle; the description continues through 10, with the theophany described in 5. **5.** *everlasting mountains:* A correction of the MT in the light of Hab 3:6; the Lord is pictured as coming from his heavenly residence, striding upon the mountains of the earth (Am 4:13). **6.** *sleep:* Not necessarily death but the torpor and daze (cf. "stilled" in 6) with which God renders his enemies impotent, as in Is 29:10. **11.** *Edom... Hamath...:* The MT, preserved by the RSV and others, does not make much sense; the correction in the CCD affects merely the vowels, not the consonants. The two peoples, S and N, are mentioned here as honoring the Lord, just as in 12 all are invited to "make vows" to Yahweh.

93 **Ps 77.** An individual lament (2–11) and a hymn of praise (14–21). Even if the hymn is an addition, in any case it is a supplement to 12–13, which serve as a transition. The psalmist laments over the sad situation of his people, abandoned by God—an unusual subject for an individual lament—and he then derives some consolation from the memory of the salvation history of the past, which he ponders and relates. **2–8.** After a long description of his misery and brooding, he finally reveals the cause: Yahweh has abandoned his people. **3.** *by night:* Not indicative of sleeplessness; he is probably in the Temple overnight, a custom indicated in many Pss, e.g., 17:3. **6–7.** The burden of his thoughts about years "long past" is revealed in 15–21; they heighten the mystery of the apparent rejection of Israel. **11.** The text is uncertain; the change of the "right hand" means that the Lord who once revealed himself as a saving God has now rejected Israel; the salvation history (cf. the use of "right hand" in Ps 78:54) has been reversed. **14–16.** A hymns begins, recalling the Exodus events (16). *your way is holy:* God's dealings are mysterious, different (not holy in the ethical sense; cf. Ex 15:11). *sons of Jacob and Joseph:* The "people" rescued from Egypt (cf. Ps 81:5–6). **17.** A different meter begins here (an older Ps?) and the Red Sea crossing is described in terms of a victory over the primordial "waters" by the God of "thunder" and "lightning" (18–19) who comes through the "sea" (20; cf. Hab 3:15) without leaving a trace. **21.** The more traditional description of the event.

94 **Ps 78.** An historical Ps (cf. Pss 105–6) in hymn style, showing considerable wisdom influence. Structure: 1–8, introduction; 9–31, the disloyalty of God's people, disobedience and the wonders in the desert; 32–39, Israel's continual infidelity; 40–55, the Exodus from Egypt; 56–64, the conquest and troubles from Philistines; 65–72, Yahweh's intervention and choice of Zion and David. Because the psalmist addresses the people directly and is anxious to teach them, a life setting in some liturgical feast at the Temple is plausible (cf. a similar survey of salvation history from Qumran in 1QS 1:18–24). The influence of Dt, stressed by H. Junker (*Bib* 34 [1953] 487–500), is also likely. The fact that the poem ends with David's reign does not, however, prove its date. O. Eissfeldt has argued, by comparison with Dt 32 and the absence of any reference to the divided monarchy, that is was written before 930 (cf. review in *CBQ* 22 [1960] 88–90). **1–4.** The introduction is composed in wisdom style (cf. Prv 3:1; 5:1); history is used as a lesson, as can be seen from a constant refrain (17, 32, 40, 56). **5.** The "law" referred to is in Ex 10:2; Dt 4:9; the handing down of the sacred traditions was a consistent practice (Dt 32:7). **6–8.** The purpose of instructing "sons yet to be born" is also the purpose of this Ps. The somber note of Israel's characteristic infidelity is sounded in 8. **9.** The reference to Ephraim, the most important tribe in the north, interrupts the context and cannot be satisfactorily explained. **12.** *Zoan:* Tanis, in the Nile Delta, the Hyksos capital, which is not mentioned in the Exodus narrative. In 13–16 is a description of the traditional events associated with the crossing of the Red Sea and the traversing of the "desert" (pillar of "cloud," miraculous "water," etc.). In 17, Israel's rebellion is noted and an extended description of the miracles in the desert (quail and manna, without any particular sequence) begins. The "mighty" (25, *'abbîrîm*) are the members of the heavenly court, whence the "heavenly bread" was thought to come (cf. Wis 16:20). The episode of Kibroth-hattaavah (Nm 11:34) is dramatically described in 30–36; 33 refers to the death of the disobedient Israelites during the 40-year sojourn; 34 echoes the sequence of sin-penitence-deliverance in the deuteronomic theology of Jgs 2:10ff. A very free presentation of the plagues is found in 40–55; only seven (44, blood; 45, flies and frogs; 46, locust; 47, hail (and frost!); 50, plague; 51, first-born) are mentioned, and not in the order of Ex. The series culminates in the conquest of the "holy land" (54–56). In 56–64, the reverses of the Philistine wars (capturing of the Ark and the destruction of Shiloh) are explained by Israel's infidelity. There are two bold expressions in 65–66: the awakening of the Lord and his striking the Philistines *in posteriora* (cf. 1 Sm 5:6–12). The choice in 67–70 of Zion and David (over Ephraim in the north) is a theme dear to the Deuteronomist school (1 Kgs 8:15–16). In contrast to other surveys of salvation history (e.g., Pss 105, 136), this Ps includes Zion and David as the culminating events.

95 **Ps 79.** A lament of the community over the destruction of the Temple (587? certainly not Maccabean times). Structure: 1–4, the complaint; 5–10, several pleas with motifs to move God to intervene; 11–13, final plea, and confident vow of thanksgiving. **2–3.** There is a wild, deliberately exaggerated tone in this description, which is taken up in 1 Mc 7:17. The lack of burial was felt to be a terrible plight (Dt 28:26). **5.** *jealousy:* A basic attribute of the "intolerant" Yahweh who is punishing his people. **9–10.** There is no attempt to escape their own guilt, but the "nations" are described so as to move Yahweh to intervene. **12.** *in their bosoms:* The reason for this metaphorical expression is the ample folds of the outer garment, which served as a receptacle for good or for bad (Lk 6:38).

96 **Ps 80.** A lament of the community. The occasion and date cannot be determined, despite the many theories that have been advanced; the indications in 2 have not yet been understood. The refrain (4, 8, 20) is oddly absent in 12 and 16. Structure: 2–4, a cry for help; 5–8, the present evils are contrasted with the past (9–12); 13–16, an appeal; 17–20, a wish and confident protestation of faithfulness. **1.** *shepherd:* Cf. Gn 48:15; 49:24; Ps 77:21. **2.** The mention of the northern tribes (except Benjamin!) suggests perhaps the troubles of 734–721 or the period of Josiah as the occasion of the prayer. Yahweh was conceived as invisibly enthroned "upon the cherubim," the mythical winged figures, half-human and half-animal, associated with the Ark. **4.** *restore:* Does not necessarily presuppose the Exile; for the beneficent effects of the "face" of Yahweh, see Ps 31:17. **9.** *vine:* For the figure, see Hos 10:1; Is 5:1–7; Jer 2:2; Ez 17. The reference here is to the Exodus and Conquest. **11.** *cedars of God:* Giant trees that, like "mountains of God" (36:7) are God's work, not man's. **12.** *sea:* The Mediterranean. *river:* The Euphrates. **13.** The vines were usually protected by "walls" (Is 5:5) as a guard against humans or beasts. **15–16.** This touching plea is calculated to move God; the line bracketed in the CCD seems to be an accidental duplication of 18b. **18.** The prayer is for the king who sits at Yahweh's "right hand" (Ps 110:1) and who here receives the unusual appellative, "son of man" (no relation to Dn 7).

97 **Ps 81.** A prophetic liturgy. Jewish tradition associates this Ps with the Feast of Tabernacles, and Mowinckel points out the similarity to Ps 95, hence including it in the enthronement Pss. Structure: 2–6, hymn (exhortation to rejoice and the reason); 6–17, an oracle delivered by a prophet, calling for obedience. **4–6.** The solemn feast has been identified with both Passover and Tabernacles; at any rate, it is commanded by God since the Exodus. Tabernacles is probably the occasion; cf. Lv 23:24,34, the blowing of the "trumpet" on the "solemn feast." **6.** *I:* A priest or prophet relates the message, speaking in God's name. **7–8.** Yahweh freed Israel from slavery (the "basket" is for carrying clay bricks, as at the time of the Exodus), and he appeared "in thunder" at Sinai. The saving acts are a prelude to the proclamation of the (First) Commandment in 10–11. **12–17.** The lesson to be learned: Israel disobeyed, but if only she "would hear," then she would prosper.

98 **Ps 82.** A "prophetic" Ps(?). The classification is not clear (see also Ps 58). In a courtroom scene, God accuses the *elohim* beings of injustice and lays down the law to them. There is no hope of their conversion; they will die. (On this Ps see G. E. Wright, *The Old Testament Against Its Environment* [London, 1950] 30–41; A. Gonzalez in *VT* 13 [1963] 293–309; and R. T. O'Callaghan in *CBQ* 15 [1953] 311–14 for the Canaanite background.)

Structure: 1, the introduction portrays God in judgment; 2–4, God questions the judges and warns them; 5–7, he judges them unworthy; 8, a plea that God judge the earth. **1.** *in the midst of the gods:* The scene is the heavenly court, as in 1 Kgs 22:19; Jb 1:6ff.; Ps 89:6–8; etc. The concept of the "gods," or superhuman beings, in Yahweh's entourage has a Canaanite counterpart in the "assembly of the gods" in Ugarit (e.g., *UM* 51: III, 14; *ANET* 132) and in Mesopotamia. Israel adapted this world of thought to Yahwism. Here, the *elohim* beings are condemned for their unjust supervision of earthly affairs (2–4). One answer to evil in this world was to lay the responsibility upon these beings. **3–4.** The classes mentioned in these lines were those who were usually oppressed, as noted often in the OT. **5.** The divine beings seem to be incorrigible. The result of injustice is that the very "foundations of the earth are shaken" (for this relationship between justice and foundations, cf. Pss 96:10; 75:3–4; Is 24:1–6). **6–7.** By divine judgment they shall "die," "fall." The motif of the fall of the "gods" (cf. also Ez 28:17; Is 14:15) is borrowed from Canaanite myths (cf. P. Grelot in *RHR* 149 [1956] 18–48). The judgment implies responsibility for the injustices of 2–4; obviously, the "gods" cannot be human judges for their punishment is to die "like men." The use Jesus makes of 6 (Jn 10:34) is conditioned by the contemporary understanding of his audience. **8.** The appeal to Yahweh may be proclaimed by the congregation—a call to activate the condemnation rehearsed in 2–7.

99 **Ps 83.** A lament of the community. Despite the nations mentioned in 7–9, the specific life setting escapes us; it is tempting to consider these references as symbolic of hostile powers arrayed against Israel. Structure: 2–9, a cry for help against enemy nations; 10–19, God is asked to intervene, as he did with his saving acts in the past. **4.** *whom you protect:* A typical motif, designed to move Yahweh to intervene. **5.** *Israel:* The tribal federation or amphictyony, not the northern kingdom. **7–8.** All these peoples are neighbors of Israel; the Hagrites inhabited the southern desert with Ishmaelites; Gebal was in the mountain country S of the Dead Sea near Petra. The entire list is a free poetic composition that allows no historical inferences. However, the absence of Babylon suggests a date before 612. **10–12.** The examples are taken from early salvation history: The Kishon River and En-dor were the scenes of victory (cf. Jgs 4–8). **14.** *leaves in a whirlwind:* Lit., "a wild artichoke plant," that rolls into a ball and is driven by the wind. **15–19.** *fire...flame:* Terms of comparison for the destruction of the enemy; their defeat will make them acknowledge Yahweh as the Most High.

100 **Ps 84.** A hymn in praise of the Temple, a song of Zion. It is best understood as the song of a pilgrim approaching and entering Zion or the Temple on a feast such as Tabernacles. Structure: 2–4, the desire for the sanctuary; 5–8, the "beatitudes" of those who dwell there; 9–13, the prayer for the king, and expression of desire to dwell in the sanctuary. **2.** For this love of the Temple, cf. Pss 42–43; 48:3–4; etc. **4.** The birds nesting, perhaps in the Temple area, become a symbol of the security enjoyed by those who are around the "altars." **7–8.** A description of the pilgrim's journey. The MT is uncertain; the CCD indicates that even the "arid valley" becomes a "spring," owing to the "early rain," i.e., the first rains after the long, dry summer. For the theme of watering the desert, cf. Is 35:6ff.; 41:18ff. *from strength to strength:* Renewing their strength, the people finally arrive at the Temple to "see" God—this bold expression was softened by the Masoretes to mean "to be seen by" or "appear before." **9–10.** The prayer for the king ("anointed") indicates a pre-exilic date; the king is called "our shield," as protector of the people, and the channel of divine power and blessings. **11.** Cf. Ps 27:4. The comparison of the "wicked" is unexpected, but it can underline the fact that only the faithful, and not the wicked, enjoy God's nearness (as indicated in 12)' **12.** Nowhere else in the OT is God explicitly called "sun'. (rendered "battlement" by some); in combination with shield (cf. also 10), it symbolizes God as the bestower of blessings.

101 **Ps 85.** A lament of the community, to which a divine oracle is given in answer. The situation and date cannot be established, although it is clear that the whole nation is suffering, is dead (6). Structure: 2–4, Yahweh's goodness to Israel; 5–8, a prayer for "life" and "salvation" in the present circumstances; 9–14, a prophet proclaims the blessings that Yahweh will impart. **2–4.** These lines can be interpreted of a past event (return from Exile; so Kraus and many others), or of a future, eschatological, deliverance (Gunkel, who understands the verbs as proph. pf.)—not to mention the background of the alleged New Year feast (a prayer for a prosperous New Year in v. 13?), as argued by Mowinckel. The reference to the return from Exile seems more probable (cf. Ps 126). To "restore the well-being" means to bring back one's former prosperity, without necessarily connoting the catastrophe of the Exile (cf. Pss 53:7; 126:2). **5–8.** The complaint presupposes that Israel's present situation is an unhappy one (such as Is 59:9ff.; Hag 1:5ff.?); hence, the request for "life," "kindness," and "salvation." **9–10.** *I will hear:* A prophet (cf. Ps 81:6) speaks and summarizes the divine oracle he has received: "peace," the meaning of which is spelled out by "salvation" and "glory" (cf. Is 60:2). **11–12.** The blessings are personified (Is 58:8; 59:14–15) as in 14, and they are probably to be given an eschatological, messianic reference. **14.** *and salvation:* A conjectural emendation of the MT which reads, "and shall make his footsteps a way"—a reading retained by the RSV. The parallelism with "justice" lends support to the conjecture, and "salvation" seems to be the theme of the entire Ps (cf. *yešaʿ* in 5, 8, 10).

102 **Ps 86.** An individual lament. The psalmist seems to be persecuted (14), perhaps unjustly accused, and he looks for a sign from the Lord that will confound his enemies (17). The structure is loose because of numerous borrowings from other Pss: 1–7, a cry for help; 8–10, a hymn of praise; 11–17, a renewed appeal with motifs of confidence (15) and thanksgiving (12–13), and a return to the request (16–17). **1.** Cf. Pss 102:3; 40:18. **2.** Cf. Ps 25:20. **3.** Cf. Ps 57:2–3. The use of the term Lord (Adonai, not Yahweh) is characteristic of this Ps. **4.** Cf. Pss 51:14 and 25:1. **5.** Cf. Ps 130:4. **8.** This ancient formula (Ex 15:11) came to be understood in a totally monotheistic sense, as in this poem. **11.** *walk in your truth:* Cf. Ps 25:4–5; if he observes the Lord's command, he is protected by the Lord's "truth" or his fidelity to his covenant with man. **12–13.** A vow to offer thanksgiving, with expression of certainty that his prayer has been heard. **14.** It is not clear how the wicked threaten his very life; cf. Ps 54:5. **15.** An old formula is expressed here (cf. Ex 34:6; Ps 103:8). **16.** *son of your handmaid:* A servant born in his master's house belongs to the master (Ex 21:1ff.); hence, this term is one of total devotion designed to move God to pity (cf. Ps 116:16). **17.** The "proof" may be a providential intervention of Yahweh, or a legal judgment in his favor.

103 **Ps 87.** A hymn of praise, or song of Zion, on the occasion of an undetermined feast. The text is uncertain, but the CCD translation is more sober in its treatment of the MT than the hypothetical reconstructions offered by many commentators. **2.** Yahweh's choice of

Zion, a key fact in the OT, becomes the basis for the universalism that appears in this song. **4.** *I tell:* The speaker is more likely a Temple minister who speaks in the name of Yahweh rather than the poet himself. God recognizes Egypt (lit., "Rahab," the name for the ocean monster [Ps 89:11], which came to be applied to Egypt) and Babylon, those two great areas of the Fertile Crescent, among his worshipers. Interpreters vary in understanding this verse of converted Gentiles or of Jews of the Diaspora. Probably the latter is meant, and 4–6 go on to celebrate Zion as the mother of all (Jews), no matter where they are born. *when they are enrolled:* The reference is to an official list of citizens, which Yahweh is assumed to possess. **7.** *in festive dance:* Dancing was part of the Israelite liturgy (cf. Ps 30:12; 149:3). *my home:* Lit., "my sources."

104 **Ps 88.** An individual lament, by one who is mortally sick and has been abandoned by his friends and, it would almost appear, by God. Even though he cannot understand, he still has the faith and courage to appeal to the Lord. The absence of the motifs of trust and certainty of being heard, so typical of the lament, is conspicuous. Structure: 2–3, a cry for help; 4–9, the complaint; 10–13, a renewed plea, with the "argument from Sheol" as a motif; 14–19, the final plea, even in the perspective of being abandoned by all. **1.** *by day...by night:* Continually, as the parallelism indicates. **3.** *nether world:* He is in danger of death (cf. Ps 20:1, etc.), and in Sheol the "shades" (11) are "cut off" (6) from Yahweh,—whence the motif of praising God is used in 11–13—God should keep him alive so as to praise him (cf. Ps 6:6). **7–8.** *abyss... billows:* These metaphors derive from the OT understanding of Sheol (cf. Barth, *Die Errettung vom Tode*, 14–19). No other Ps describes Sheol as frequently as this one ("pit," and in 12, *'ăbaddôn*, rendered in the CCD "those who have perished"). It is remarkable that this prayer ends on the grim note of abandonment ("darkness," 19).

105 **Ps 89.** A lament of the community, as it stands (39–52!). But it is a mixed composition; the lament is preceded by a hymn in praise of God (2–19) and an oracle concerning the Davidic dynasty (20–38). The one who prays seems to be identified with the king ("my life," 48; "anointed," 52; and cf. 2, 19). But the precise life setting is not easy to establish. There is no proof of a cultic "humiliation" of the reigning king, and an historical occasion (Josiah?) is perhaps the best supposition. **2.** *the favors of the Lord:* These are the actions in history by which Yahweh has shown his covenant love (Ps 107:43; Is 63:7), in particular the dynastic oracle to David (3–5). (On this oracle, cf. McKenzie, *op. cit.*, 275–82 and H. van den Bussche in *ETL* 24 [1948] 354–94.) **6.** *the assembly of the holy ones:* See the comment on Ps 82 concerning the heavenly court. **10–11.** For the mythological allusions in this version of creation, see the comment on Ps 74:13–14. Like Leviathan (Ps 73:14; Is 27:1; and cf. also Is 51:9–10), Rahab is a monster personifying the powers of chaos. **13.** If "north" and "south" are really proper names parallel to Tabor and Hermon, we can identify north as Mt. Saphon, the mount of assembly of the Canaanite pantheon (Ps 48:3; Is 14:13), but there is no Mt. Yamin (south) that we know of. **16.** *the joyful shout:* Hebrew *t^{e}ruʿâ* is conspicuously associated with procession (of the Ark, cf. 2 Sm 6:15). **19.** For the parallelism of "shield" and "king," see 84:10. It is not easy to imagine that 2–19 would have been written by the same author or, at least, by one in the same situation as 39–52. **20.** In place of the CCD "of a stripling..." read *nēzer* for *ʿēzer:* "I have placed the diadem upon the champion"; for the ceremony, see De Vaux, *AI* 103. **21–38.** An expanded version of 1 Sm 7; they highlight royal prerogatives: anointing (21), divine protection (22), victory (23–26), adoptive sonship (27–28), personal and dynastic security (23–26). However, 31–38 show that punishment of an unfaithful descendant of David is still within the framework of Yahweh's eternal "covenant" with David, which he will not "violate" (35). **39–46.** The complaint begins here and is developed in detail; Yahweh is accused of having "renounced the covenant" with the descendant of David. **47–52.** The motifs characteristic of the lament, and designed to move the Lord to take pity on the king, appear: "how long?" shortness of life, the ancient favors," the "insults." **53.** A doxology finishes the Third Book of Pss (cf. 41:14; 72:18–19).

106 **Ps 90.** A lament of the community (but pronounced by an individual), for which no specific occasion can be found. The complaints are general (life is short and troubled), and the poem shows the influence of the wisdom movement. Structure: 1–12, the complaint: God's eternity contrasted with the fleeting and troubled life of man; 13–17, a request for God's intervention. **2.** The eternity of God is emphasized to point up the contrast with man's brief span. **3.** The sentence of death is a reversal of the creative act of Gn 2:7. **4.** The point is the brevity of time for God, exemplified by the sensation of "yesterday" and the night "watch." **5.** Although the MT is obscure, the brevity of life is the theme. **7–8.** The reason for the shortness of life is God's anger and man's iniquities. The "biblical" age for man is three score and ten or, at the outside, 80 years, but these years have little to show. **11.** The question finds an answer in 12; the wise man "knows." The prayer is that we may truly appreciate how brief "our days" are and thus obtain "wisdom" (*ḥokmâ*), or fear of the Lord. For the wisdom traits in 8–12, cf. Jb 4:17–21. **13.** The spirit of this request (13–17) is less somber than 1–12. **14.** *at daybreak:* This imagery may result from the sequence, light after darkness (cf. Ps 30:6). **15.** These "years" cannot be specified. **16.** The parallelism of "work" and "glory" suggests a powerful intervention of the Lord in favor of his people. **17.** The bracketed line in 17c is a dittography of 17b.

107 **Ps 91.** A Ps of trust, with markedly didactic intent. Structure: 1–2, an address to one who takes refuge in God, perhaps asylum in the Temple; 3–12, the protection that Yahweh affords; 14–16, a divine oracle, assuring salvation. **2.** The command to "trust" in Yahweh is strengthened by the following examples of the Lord's saving protection (note the metaphors in 4). **5–6.** The hostile powers described here are probably demonic in origin (night demons, sun rays, etc.). The LXX and Vg translation of "plague at noon" gave rise to the "noon-day devil" (cf. J. de Fraine in *Bib* 40 [1959] 238–49, and in De Langhe, *op. cit.*, 89–106, esp. 102–4). The four crises indicated for night, morning, evening ("darkness"), and noon balance against the four animals of 13. Such trials will not affect the man who is protected by God. **7.** The metaphor of pestilence (rather than war) continues in the felling of thousands. **8–10.** An affirmation of the "traditional" theory of retribution. **11.** The work of God's angels is well illustrated by Gn 24:7; Tb; Mt 4:6. The metaphor in 12 (quoted in Mt 4:6) is derived from the rocky roads in Palestine. **14–16.** This divine oracle confirms the teaching proclaimed in the Ps. To acknowledge the "name" of the Lord means probably to invoke him by name for help (cf. 15).

108 **Ps 92.** A song of thanksgiving, although it is preoccupied with moral retribution. The psalmist has experienced Yahweh's fidelity (3), and he has seen the defeat of his enemies (10–12). Structure: 1–5, introduction in hymnic style, praising Yahweh for his deeds; 6–9, praise of God's deeds and thoughts, which his enemies understand not; 10–12, Yahweh's treatment of the psalmist's enemies; 13–16, comparison of the prosperity of the just to a fruitful tree. **1.** According to the Mishnah, this Ps was sung in the Temple with the libation of the morning sacrifice (cf. Ex 29:39–40). **2.** The parallelism between Yahweh and the "name" is noteworthy. **3.** The indications of time refer to the periods of the daily sacrifice. **4.** For details concerning these instruments, see J. Murray in *VD* 32 (1954) 84–89. **5.** The reasons for praising are introduced, and these refer to God's government, the destruction of evildoers, and the victory of the just, as developed in the rest of the Ps. **7.** The fool's lack of understanding is a perennial wisdom theme (Prv 12:1). **8–9.** Typical wisdom teaching follows: The prosperity of sinners is deceptive; they will perish. The "eternal destruction" does not carry the implications of later, Christian, revelation. **10.** This line seems to be an adaptation of a Canaanite praise of Baal, as indicated in Ugaritic: "Behold, your enemies, O Baal; Behold, your enemies you shall smite; Behold, you will vanquish your foes" (*UM* 68:8; *ANET* 131). There is the same "staircase" parallelism and the same ideas. **11.** Yahweh has given him the strength (symbolized by "horn") of a wild bull and cause for joy (symbolized by anointing with "rich oil"). **12.** It is characteristic of the OT law of retribution that the just man will witness the fall of his foes (Pss 37:34; 91:8). **13.** The comparison to a tree is frequently made to indicate the prosperity of the just (Pss 1:3; 37:35; Jer 17:8). The general idea of the Ps is expressed in 16—praise of God's just government of the world.

109 **Ps 93.** A hymn of praise, commemorating Yahweh as king (→ 6 and 9 above); see comment on Ps 47 concerning enthronement Pss. Structure: 1–2, acclamation of Yahweh as eternal king and creator; 3–4, even the waters of chaos bow to his power; 5, the conclusion acknowledges his decrees (the Torah). **1.** *the Lord is king:* The cry of enthronement does not preclude his kingship from being eternal (cf. Ps 47). *world:* The reference to creation is a consistent feature in the enthronement Pss. The firmness of creation accords with Yahweh's eternal and firm "throne" (2). **3–4.** *floods:* The waters of chaos, which could possibly destroy creation, are held in check by divine power (cf. O. Kaiser, *Die mythische Bedeutung des Meeres in Ägypten, Ugarit und Israel* [BZAW 79; Berlin, 1959]). **5.** *decrees:* The Law; this verse at least suggests the Feast of Tabernacles as a possible life setting (cf. Dt 31:10ff.).

110 **Ps 94.** A lament, of both an individual and a community; violence and injustice are threatening the community (1–15; cf. Pss 14 and 53), and an individual makes this fact his cause for complaint (16–23). Hence, one need not distinguish two separate Pss. Structure: 1–7, a complaint about oppression within Israel; 8–11, an admonition to the fools, in the wisdom style; 12–15, a blessing pronounced upon the just and Israel, because God will intervene; 16–23, an individual complaint, with marked emphasis on trust and on certainty that Yahweh will hear him. **1.** *God of vengeance:* The proper nuance is indicated by the parallel in 2. **3–7.** The complaint is characterized by the typical formula, "How long...?" and by the description of the situation. The "evildoers" oppress the defenseless (cf. 16). **8–11.** A reply to the charge of the wicked (7) that Yahweh does not know what is going on. He does "hear" and "see" all, and he will punish. **12–15.** More wisdom teaching, this time concerning the man who keeps the Law; retribution shall surely follow, for Yahweh "will not cast off his people" (Ex 19:5; 1 Sm 12:22). **16–19.** The psalmist makes this cause his own and speaks in his own name, asking for help because his own experience in the past has been marked by Yahweh's sustaining "kindness." **20–23.** He sees clearly that corruption in the human "tribunal" is totally opposed to God, and he is confident that the Lord will intervene to punish.

111 **Ps 95.** A hymn of praise, commemorating Yahweh as king (see comment on Pss 47, 93; → 6 and 9 above). The liturgical character of this hymn, which resembles Ps 81, is very marked; Gunkel classifies it as a prophetic liturgy on the basis of the oracle in 9–10. Structure: 1–5, an exhortation to praise Yahweh as king and creator; 6–7, exhortation to worship the God of Israel; 7–10, a prophetic admonition against obstinacy and disobedience (cf. Hab 3:7–11). **3.** *above all the gods:* This comparison does not imply effective reality for other gods (cf. Ps 96:4). **4–5.** Yahweh's kingship stems from his creative power (cf. 93:3–4). **6–7.** The invitation to "come" (into the court of the Temple for worship) is motivated by the great events of salvation history, the covenant that "made" (cf. Is 43:1) Israel. **8.** *today:* As in Dt (30:11–20), this verse indicates an actualization or re-presentation of some aspect of the old salvation history. *harden not:* Probably spoken by a prophet (cf. Pss 50, 81, 85), who uses the examples of rebellion in the desert (Meribah, Massah; cf. Ex 17:1ff.; Nm 20:1ff.). **11.** *rest:* Originally it was the possession of the promised land; in this context, it has the overtones of peace with God; the precise reason for the admonition in the Ps remains unknown. This Ps is used for the *invitatorium* in Matins of the Roman Breviary

112 **Ps 96.** A hymn of praise, commemorating Yahweh as king (see comment on Pss 47, 93, 95). In 1 Chr 16, this song is inserted in the context of David's bringing the Ark to the Jerusalem Tabernacle. There is a noticeable similarity to Is (40:10; 44:23; 49:13). Structure: 1–6, Israel is invited to sing of God's incomparable majesty and creative power; 7–10, an invitation to the nations to bring tribute and to worship God as king and creator; 11–13, an invitation to creation to rejoice in the Lord's dominion. **1.** *new song:* So-called because it commemorates a new evidence of God's rule; the divine supremacy is to be acknowledged in liturgical worship. Note the Ugaritic abc–a′b′d pattern (and "staircase" parallelism in 7–8). **2.** *his salvation:* The saving deeds of old, which are now being rehearsed. **4.** Cf. Ps 95:3. **5.** *things of naught:* Lit., "zeros" (*'ĕlîlîm*), a favorite term of Isaiah (2:8; 10:10; etc.); the ineffectiveness of the gods is contrasted with Yahweh's creative power. **6.** The personification of divine attributes in the entourage of the deity is found also in Mesopotamian hymns (cf. Falkenstein and Von Soden, *op. cit.*, 222, 320; Ps 89:15). *his sanctuary:* Probably the Temple. **7–9.** Cf. Ps 29:1–2. **10.** Israel is commanded to say, "The Lord is king"—the characteristic cry of the enthronement Pss; the kingship is shown in creation (from of old) and in rule of the world. Some OL and LXX manuscripts added "from the tree," in a reference to the crucifixion of Christ (cf. "regnavit a ligno Deus" of the *Vexilla regis* hymn). **13.** *he comes:* The coming of the Lord is the actualization of his reign in the cult, which represents and celebrates his rule in the world.

113 **Ps 97.** A hymn of praise, commemorating Yahweh as king (cf. Pss 47, 93, 95, 96). Structure: 1, proclamation of Yahweh as king in majesty; 3–6, description of a theophany; 7–9, the effects produced by God's reign; 10–12, application to the faithful. **1.** Cf. Is 49:13; 42:10ff. **2–6.** The typical theophanic traits are exploited here (cf. Jgs 5:4ff.; Dt 33:2ff.; Is 30:27ff.; Hab 3:4ff.; Ps 18:8ff.): "fire," "lightning," "melting" of "mountains." This cataclysm is witnessed by "all peoples." **7–9.** The reaction of idolators and their gods is contrasted with that of Judah; God's "judgments" (i.e., his instruction) bring shame to the former, joy to the latter. *Most High:* See comment on 47:3. **10–12.** An assurance of Yahweh's beneficent protection for the "faithful" and "just."

114 **Ps 98.** A hymn of praise, commemorating Yahweh as king; it shows great similarity to Ps 96 and to Dt-Is. Structure: 1–3, invitation to praise Yahweh on account of salvation; 4–9, invitation to the world and nature to praise the king who is coming to rule. **1.** *new song:* Cf. 96:1; the emphasis here is on the saving "victory" Yahweh has wrought by his "arm" (Is 51:9; 52:10; 59:16). **2.** The parallelism between "salvation" and "justice" is typical of Dt-Is (cf. 45:8,21). **3.** The victory has been achieved because Yahweh "remembered" his covenant with his people (cf. Ps 106:44–46). *all the ends of the earth:* Again, universality is characteristic of this celebration of Yahweh's kingship. When Deutero-Isaiah says almost the same thing in Is 40:5, he is referring to the end of the Exile, which is a pledge of the messianic era. **4–9.** An extended hymnic invitation to lands and to nature to sing, rejoice, and offer praise "before the King" because he "comes" (cf. comment on 96:13).

115 **Ps 99.** A hymn of praise, commemorating Yahweh as king. In contrast to the other enthronement Pss (47, 93, 95–98), there are no similarities to Dt-Is, and more emphasis is put on Yahweh's relation to his own people (not the world). Structure: The "Sanctus" refrain in 3, 5, and 9 divides the poem: 1–3, let the peoples worship Yahweh, enthroned and awesome; 4–5, Yahweh's justice is the motif for worship; 6–9, another motif is God's relationship with his ministers. **1–3.** A description of the "great" and "high" God invisibly enthroned on the Ark between the "cherubim," his half-man and half-animal bodyguard (cf. Ps 80:2). **4–5.** The "justice" and "judgment" of Yahweh refer here to the covenant and Torah. *footstool:* The Ark. **6–9.** It is difficult to say why these three heroes are singled out; perhaps they represent priests and prophets, interceding for the people. **7.** Cf. Ex 19:9; 33:9–10 for the "cloud"; in 1 Sm 7:7–10 God speaks to Samuel from the Ark (with which the "pillar of cloud" seems later to be associated; cf. 1 Kgs 8:10–12). **8.** *to them:* The reference is now to the Israelites.

116 **Ps 100.** A hymn of praise, composed for a procession to the Temple. The note of joy is emphatic and characteristic. **3.** The reason why God is to be praised is the covenant relationship, expressed in the Dt formula, "the Lord is God" (Dt 4:35,39). **4.** The exhortation to enter the Temple is probably spoken by the priests; the purpose of the visit is thanksgiving and praise. This Ps is often associated with the enthronement Pss, although there is no mention of Yahweh's kingship.

117 **Ps 101.** A royal Ps, spoken by the king, concerning the norm of life that he follows in his office. It is plausible that such a declaration (*Fürstenspiegel* or *miroir des rois*) would have been made upon accession to the throne or in some other ritual. Structure: 1–2, introduction; 2–8, the norm of life. **1.** *kindness and judgment:* The *hesed* and *mišpāṭ* of the Lord, demonstrated in giving him the kingship (cf. Ps 72:1). **2.** *when ...?:* Apparently this question is a prayer expressing his desire for God's help (cf. Ex 20:24; 2 Sm 6:9). **3–8.** Present the picture of an ideal king—his sincere and earnest resolve of personal integrity, his refusal to tolerate evil men in his government, his solicitude for "the faithful of the land," his just exercise of judgment ("each morning," the time for such administration; 2 Sm 15:2).

118 **Ps 102.** An individual lament. However, the form is unusual in that hymnic (13–18) and prophetic (14, 19–23) elements are incorporated into an individual complaint. Structure: 2–12, the complaint of an individual; 13–19, a hymn praising Yahweh as the rebuilder of Zion; 19–23, a prophecy that the Lord shall intervene; 24–27, a final plea (24–25); and a song of praise (26–29). The transition to Zion and restoration has caused great variation in the exegesis of this Ps. It is a natural development (cf. Lam 2:11–17) or the result of the incorporation of another Ps? If we take it as a unit, the psalmist describes himself as mortally sick and then turns confidently to God, more concerned with the fate of his people than with his own destiny. This is the fifth of the so-called penitential Pss. **2–3.** These lines are an echo of other Pss (cf. 39:13; 27:9; 69:18; etc.). **4–6.** He seems to suffer from fever and emaciation, and his spirit is afflicted by the proximity of death. **7–8.** The comparison with "owl" and "sparrow" underlines his loneliness and desolation. **9.** *make a curse of me:* His fate is wished on people as a curse. **10.** *ashes:* The conventional sign of mourning in the OT. **12.** *lengthening shadow:* The evening (of life) approaches. He is close to death, although still "in the midst of my days" (25). **13.** In contrast to his ephemeral existence (12) is the eternity of God, which he now acknowledges. God's eternity forms the perspective for the restoration that is his desire. **14–18.** The description of Zion serves as a sort of motif of consolation for the poet. The exilic period is the presupposition of this passage, which is filled with confidence and hope. **19–23.** The psalmist becomes prophet as he wishes his description of Yahweh's successful intervention recorded as proof to the "generation to come." The restoration will be realized with a conversion of "peoples" and "kingdoms" (Is 2:2ff.). **24–25.** The theme of complaint reappears—the proximity of death, although he is still in the prime of life. **26–28.** As in 12–13, there is another contrast between creation and God's timeless permanence. God is eternal, outlasting "earth" and "heavens," which he changes "like clothing" when it is worn out (the CCD "and they are changed" keeps the play on words of the MT; the sense is that they wear out). **29.** The final verse comes back to his hope for Israel; something of God's permanence is attached to his "servants' posterity."

119 **Ps 103.** A thanksgiving Ps of deep, religious sensitivity. However, it could be just as easily termed a hymn of praise; it is a simple and beautiful reaction to God's goodness. Structure: 1–5, a hymnlike acknowledgment of Yahweh's goodness, which has been shown to him in the past; 6–18, a description of the Lord's treatment of Israel (the change to pl. suggests a choir); 19–22, a conclusion in hymn style. **1–2.** The hymnlike exhortation to one's self ("soul") is also found in Ps 104:1. **3–5.** Although he speaks to the community, he doubtless reflects his own personal experiences. The verses are addressed to himself ("your" in sing. in opposition to the pl. in 6ff.). Yahweh is a saving God, who forgives man's sin and blesses him with good things. The "eagle" is a symbol of perennial youthful vigor (Is 40:3). **6–10.** From the concrete acts of "justice" in the salvation history the author goes to the universal attributes of God (8) that are revealed by such history—expressed in the theological formula of Ex 34:6. The paradox in 10 is noteworthy; "God's grace is greater than man's sin" is Weiser's apt comment. **11–18.** The comparisons (cf. Is 55:8–19) come to a climax in the love of a "father" (13), which is rooted in God's creation of man: "he remembers that we are dust." There is a beautiful contrast between man's brevity ("grass," cf. Is 40:7–8) and the enduring "kindness" and "justice" of God toward those who "keep his covenant." It is such lines as these that give the lie to the popular travesty of the OT as a testament of fear. **19–22.** The closing hymn calls upon the heavenly court, all creation, and the poet himself to praise God.

120 **Ps 104.** A hymn of praise of God as creator; one of the most remarkable songs in the Psalter. Structure: 1–4, praise of God in the heavenly palace; 5–9, God as tamer of the ocean; 10–18, the provider of rain and well-being; 19–23, the regulator of light and darkness; 24–26, God's creatures in the sea; 27–30, God the sustainer of life; 31–35, conclusion. The similarity of this beautiful song to Akhenaton's "hymn to the Sun" has often been noted. If any dependence exists (e.g., 19–23; cf. *ANET* 370), it is largely indirect and relatively insignificant in view of the essentially Yahwistic theology embodied in the poem. There are references to the typically Israelite understanding of creation as it came to be expressed in Gn 1. The life setting of the Ps (e.g., the New Year feast of Mowinckel) cannot be determined. **2–3.** The comparison of "light" to a "cloak" is easily understood if light is viewed as a "thing" as in ancient Israel. God was thought to dwell in a "palace" above the firmament (Gn 1:6–8) and to ride on the "clouds" (Ps 68:5). **4.** *flaming fire:* Lightning, and the "winds" are merely to do God's bidding. **5.** The firmness of the earth results from a "foundation" (cf. Jb 38:4–6). **6–9.** Another description of creation is given in traditional mythological terms: *Tehôm* ("ocean") and the "waters" covered earth in chaos, and the Lord brought order out of this chaos by his "thunder" (his voice), and the waters found their "place" in the "valleys" (8 is variously translated). God's continuous creation is implied in 9. **10–18.** The unruly, chaotic waters have now the mission of giving "drink" to creation, and making the earth produce good things for all creatures. A beautiful scene is evoked by beasts, birds, bread, wine, oil, goats, and man. **19–23.** A quaint picture is given here: Night is for "beasts" (note that lions' "roar" is interpreted as a prayer to God for food) to work and prowl, and day is for "man" to do his work. It is worth noting that in the Egyptian hymn the sun god retires at night when evil powers take over (*ANET* 370a), but in the Ps the Lord hears the beasts pray for food. **26.** *Leviathan:* The mythical sea monster (Is 27:1; cf. *BA* 11 [1948] 61–68), a mere plaything. Another translation could be "to make sport in it" (i.e., the sea). **27–30.** Besides feeding them, God keeps creatures alive by his creative "breath" ("spirit," *rûaḥ*); the picture derives from Gn 1–2. God breathes and creatures live; when he stops breathing, they die. This lively creation poem underlines the Hebr concept of the world as a continuing event, a continuous creation (not a Gk cosmos, → Aspects OT Thought, 77:48). **31.** It is characteristic that he speaks of God's joy in his creation; but he is not unmindful of the mysterious and majestic aspect of this God, whose mere glance or touch is cataclysmic! **35.** The imprecation against sinners does not lessen the power of this poem; it must be judged from his deep appreciation of God's justice, which he desires to see manifested in the very world he made.

121 **Ps 105.** An historical Ps (cf. Pss 78, 105) in hymnic style. Structure: 1–6, an invitation to Israel to proclaim God's wondrous deeds; 7–11, the covenant with the patriarchs; 12–15, protection of the patriarchs; 16–22, the story of Joseph; 23–38, the Exodus from Egypt; 39–43, the marvels in the desert; 44–55, conclusion. This rehearsal of the salvation history follows the traditional sequence of the liturgical credo (Dt 26:1–9, although Sinai is mentioned), and it probably has a cultic life setting for its origin, as suggested by its later use in 1 Chr 16:8ff. **1–3.** The introduction is an explicit invitation to worshipers in the Temple (who "seek the Lord") to acknowledge Yahweh's saving deeds. **6.** Both the saving "deeds" and the condemning "judgments" are to be found in the song. **7–11.** *covenant:* It is emphasized rather than the promises to the patriarchs (but note the promise to the patriarchs of the "land" in 11). **12–15.** A brief summary of the "wandering" of the patriarchs; the term "anointed" for the patriarchs (15) is not in the Gn tradition. **16–22.** The divine initiative ("He") in the Joseph story (and throughout the entire poem, in fact) is emphasized. Joseph's "prediction" refers to the interpretation of the dreams in prison. (For the "wisdom" (22) aspects of the Joseph story, cf. Von Rad, *GesSt* 272–80.) **28–38.** The sequence of the ten plagues is different from the Ex account: 9,1,2,4,3,7,8,10, with no mention of the fifth or sixth plague. **42.** The provision in the desert results from the "word" (covenant) to Abraham. **44–45.** The conclusion on the "statutes" and "laws" ties in Sinai with the events of sacred history; obedience to the laws is gratitude for salvation.

122 **Ps 106.** An historical Ps, conceived in terms of a national lament (cf. 105). Structure: 1–5, the summons to praise God and a prayer for Israel's prosperity; 6–46, the confession of sins, present and past, against the background of the Exodus tradition (7–12), greed for quail (13–15), Dathan and Abiram (16–18), the golden calf (19–23), the desert murmuring (24–27), Baal of Peor (28–31), Meribah (32–33), the conquest (34–39), the judges (40–46); 47, the conclusion, a prayer for restoration. In this exilic Ps, history is not used for a recital of praise but as an expression of sorrow (as 6 indicates). The spirit and mood of a lament move through the historical periods as the author emphasizes disobedient and faithless aspects of Israel. Weiser has pointed to the sequence of praise-confession in the Qumran "manual of discipline"; this sequence is seen also here and in Ps 105. **2.** The question is an idiom, which implies that God's "mighty deeds" cannot be adequately praised by man. The "beatitude" of 3 is unexpected; but perhaps it is only the just man who can or should praise God. **4–5.** In a request that is characteristic of the lament, he asks for a repetition in the present of the "saving help," which he is about to rehearse (cf. 47). The confession of sin (5de) begins the recital. **7–12.** Follow Ex 14–15, but somewhat freely, e.g., there is no mention in Ex of rebellion at the Red Sea. **13.** *counsel:* May be derived from Is 5:19; Ps 108:11, etc., rather than from the Ex tradition. **19.** *Horeb:* The deuteronomic name for Sinai; the Ps shows the general influence of Dt. The murmuring in the desert (24–27) is associated with the Exile in 27, and the present Exile is an appropriate punishment for those who "despised" the land (24). **32.** Cf. Dt 32:51; the strange fate of Moses is merely referred to, but in such a way as to be a source of blame for the people. **34.** The failure to "exterminate" the Canaanites is disobedience to the commands in Dt 7:1ff.; 20:16ff. **37.** Child sacrifice was considered to be in honor of "demons" (cf. demons in Dt 32:17). **40–46.** These verses reflect the Deuteronomist theology of Jgs. **47.** Israel is in exile, but the previous recital, ending on the note of God's kindness (45–46), gives reason to hope for salvation. **48.** A doxology, which closes the Fourth Book of Pss.

123 **Ps 107.** A thanksgiving liturgy; 33–43, hymnic in style, are probably a later addition. Structure: 1–3, an invitation to the redeemed to thank God; they form four groups: those who made their way out of a desert where they were lost (4–9); prisoners who have been freed (10–16); sick who have been cured (17–22); sea voyagers who have been rescued (23–32); 33–43, a hymn praising God for the blessings on the (restored) community. The refrain in 6 and 8, 13 and 15, 19 and 21, 28 and 31 is clearly recognizable and points to a thanksgiving sacrifice in the Temple as the life setting. But it is not clear if this action is collective (Gunkel) or an introduction to the individual sacrifices (Kraus). **1.** Standard summons to praise (1 Chr 16:34; Ps 106:1; the lines were probably recited antiphonally; cf. Ps 118:1). **2–3.** *redeemed . . . gathered:* A clear reference to a community restored from exile, although the following groups of redeemed were not necessarily exiles; hence, these verses may be a post-exilic addition, or rereading. **4–9.** The desert wanderers were saved by Yahweh's *ḥesed;* the particular incident is unknown. But this and also the "prisoner" theme that follows could easily be applied to the post-exilic community. **10–16.** We do not know why these prisoners had been jailed "in darkness" and "in chains," but the applicability to the Exile is obvious. **17–22.** The usual connection between sinfulness and sickness is affirmed clearly in 17. **20.** *he sent forth his word:* The word of the oracle (given by the priest?) assuring a cure. **23–32.** A summons to the seafarers, who saw his "wonders in the abyss," i.e., Yahweh's battle with chaos, the sea, which he "hushed"; the theme of continuous creation (cf. Ps 104) underlies the description. **33–43.** This addition is reminiscent of Dt-Is (Is 35:7; 41:18; 50:2), and the whole is designed to portray the blessings bestowed upon the post-exilic community. However, God's actions refer to no specific events. Rather, his timeless actions (39–40) are described and praised. Thus, in 37 no particular "city" is meant; the idea is that Yahweh has made it possible for the people to live together. **43.** A wisdom saying, urging the people to comprehend the many acts of Yahweh's covenant love.

124 **Ps 108.** A composite Ps, made up of 57:8–12 and 60:7–14. Hence, a thanksgiving song (1–6) with a plea for deliverance (7), and a divine oracle (8–10), ending in a plea for help (11–14). See comments on Pss 57 and 60.

125 **Ps 109.** An individual lament. Structure: 1–5, a complaint against calumny of enemies; 6–19, a series of curses; 20–31, a request that God punish his enemies but bless the psalmist, with motifs why God should intervene (23–26), and a vow to offer thanksgiving (30). This so-called cursing Ps (cf. 6–19) has been interpreted as the words of the author against his enemies. Rather, they should be understood as the curses of his enemies against him: The subject is singular (thus refers to the author); the enemies are always described in the plural (1–5, 21–31); the author's curse is given in 29 (see also the comment on 20–21). With this prayer, the persecuted man tries to offset the curses (6–19) directed against him by his enemies. It appears from 16 that he is accused of having persecuted the poor unto death; hence, he turns to the Lord for help. **1–5.** The attack and the injustice of his enemies are clearly described; they repay him "evil for good." **6–7.** *accuser:* (Hebr *śāṭān.*) Apparently delegated to secure the condemnation of the psalmist (7). The curses begin in 8ff., presumably uttered by the enemies. This interpretation implies that 16 is the specific accusation leveled against the psalmist. **18.** The picture of cursing as a "robe" (cf. 29) or like "oil" is not merely metaphor; the state of being totally cursed seems to be the idea—the words of the curse permeate the accursed. **20.** The CCD translation indicates that the psalmist wishes these curses to recoil upon his enemies, who uttered them, but the verse may be merely a summary sentence indicating that the previous curses are the work of those who would harm him. **21.** A change in tone and emphasis is indicated by "but do you . . ."—a contrast with what his enemies intend. A series of motifs to move Yahweh to pity begins (wretchedness, age, ridicule). **29.** *you . . . have done this:* Explain "your hand," but the reference is obscure. What has Yahweh done? Is he the reason why the poor (16) died? Rather, it is Yahweh who has delivered the psalmist. **30.** He expresses a vow to offer thanksgiving for his deliverance.

126 **Ps 110.** A royal Ps. Both the text (especially 3) and the meaning are a moot question. Structure: 1–3, introduction and oracle; 4, introduction and oracle; 5–7, description of the victory of the king(?). The life setting would seem to be the day of coronation, when the prerogatives of the Judean king are enunciated in oracles. (For the messianism, see comments on Pss 2, 72;→ 15 above). **1.** *the* LORD *said to my lord:* "Yahweh said to my master [the king]." A court poet proclaims an oracle given to the king by God. The purpose of Mt 22:41–45, in which the Davidic authorship (taken for granted by Jesus' audience) is simply presupposed, is to suggest the mystery of his person: How superior to David, how transcendent must be the Messiah! *sit. . .:* This command suggests the enthronement of the new king in a place of honor, the very "right hand" of God. Kingship in Israel is a sacral institution established by God. Fittingly, victory over his "enemies" is promised. The image of the footstool is owing to the courtly style derived from ancient Near Eastern practice (cf. Jos 10:24). **2.** Yahweh is described as holding the royal scepter and commanding the king. **3.** The MT is corrupt, and any translation is problematical. The CCD follows the evidence of the ancient versions, which emphasize the (mysterious?) birth of the king; he is the (adopted) son of God. (cf. Ps 2:7). *daystar:* The morning star (Is 14:12). (For a discussion and bibliography, see J. Coppens in *ETL* 32 [1956] 5–23.) **4.** In a second oracle the royal priestly prerogatives are associated with the ancient Jerusalem traditions of Melchizedek (Gn 14:18); the king is, as it were, the successor to Melchizedek in his royal and priestly function. *according to:* "On the model of." (For a summary of interpretation of Melchizedek, see J. Fitzmyer in *CBQ* 25 [1963] 305–21.) **5–7.** The presence of Yahweh at the king's "right hand" insures the victories in which the warlike activities of God are described. The reference in 7 is obscure; perhaps it pictures Yahweh (rather than the king) as a weary warrior refreshing himself after battle.

127 **Ps 111.** A hymn of praise, written in acrostic style; the half-lines begin with successive letters of the Hebr alphabet. There are many echoes of biblical phrases (the so-called anthological composition). So pronounced is the influence of wisdom teaching that many classify it as a wisdom Ps. Indeed, it looks as if Pss 111–12 are a pair, intended to match; if 112 is wisdom, then 111 is the wise man's hymn of praise—teaching by example. Nevertheless, despite the didactic strain, this Ps is a hymn. Structure: 1, hymnic introduction; 2–9, the reason for praising Yahweh—the greatness of his works; 10, a wisdom ending. **1.** *alleluia:* Lit., "praise Yah." A sort of title, as in 112. The hymn is intoned in the worshiping community, and stress is laid upon inner appreciation ("with all my heart"; Dt 6:4, and notice the emphasis on "delights" in 2). **2–3.** *works:* Events of salvation history, the "renown" (i.e., liturgical remembrance) of which is continued in the worshiping community, as in this Ps. **5.** *food:* Refers to the tradition of manna and quail in the desert. **6.** *inheritance:* Palestine. **7–9.** After the mention of the saving acts comes the praise of the Torah, and 9 is a summary statement of salvation and covenant. Verse 10 is a wisdom tag line; "who live by it," lit., "who do them," i.e., the Commandments. It is worth noting that in this Ps, salvation history has been appropriated and inculcated by wisdom teachers.

128 **Ps 112.** A wisdom Ps. Written in acrostic style, as is Ps 111, it portrays the ideal wise man who would utter such hymns as 111; thus, 111–12 belong together. There is no particular structure but merely typical wisdom sayings, which describe the just, God-fearing man, and which reflect Prv and other wisdom books. **1.** *commands:* Those of the Torah (cf. Ps 1); observance is the practical expression of "fearing the Lord." **2–3.** These rewards are typical of those promised by the wisdom writers; with 3, compare 111:3,9. **4.** The subject of "dawns" is the wise man. **7.** *evil report:* Should be understood in the sense of "bad news." **8.** *till he looks down:* He will eventually witness their downfall. **9.** *horn:* A symbol of strength and power in the OT. **10.** The description of the "wicked man" is in contrast to 1–9, and it is characteristic of OT ideas of retribution.

129 **Ps 113.** A hymn of praise. Structure: 1–3, a summons to servants to praise the Lord; 4–6, exaltation of Yahweh; 7–9, a proclamation of the good deeds of God. **1.** *alleluia:* The superscription has led to the designation of Pss 112–17 as the Hallel, or the Egyptian Hallel, to differentiate it from 146–50, also called the Hallel. The Great Hallel designates Pss 120–36 (songs of ascents), or 135–36, or just 136. **2.** *servants of the Lord:* Priests or Levites probably, but it can also mean the congregation. **3.** *from the rising...:* An ancient Near Eastern formula. **7–9.** These lines stand in happy contrast to 4–6, for they portray the exalted Lord acting kindly with the lowly and unfortunate in this world. His majesty does not exclude his mercy. The MT ends with alleluia, which the CCD, following the LXX, places as the superscription of Ps 114.

130 **Ps 114.** A hymn of praise, which is joined to Ps 115 in LXX and Vg. The usual hymnic introduction is lacking. The poem recalls vividly the saving deeds of the Exodus; the association of the two crossings, Red Sea and Jordan, appears already in Jos 4:23–24. **1.** *people of alien tongue:* A stereotyped phrase for a hostile nation (Is 28:11; 33:19; Jer 5:15). **2.** The parallelism between Judah and Israel appears deliberate; Judah is Israel, after the destruction of the northern kingdom. And this later development is read back into the time of the Exodus. **3.** *the sea beheld:* Yahweh, who appeared (cf. the reference to his "face" in 7); then it "fled" without a fight! The background of the bold figure is the myth of the battle between a god and the sea (cf. *ANET* 130–31 and Hab 3:8; Pss 77:17; 104:7). **4.** The "mountains" may be a reference to Sinai. **5–7.** The answer to the questions is the presence of the Lord (7), who worked the desert marvels described in 8 (Ex 17:6; Nm 20:11). But instead of a flat answer in 7, the poet issues a command. Cosmic effects accompany the theophany in the tradition of the Sinai experience.

131 **Ps 115.** A choir song of Temple liturgy, distinct from Ps 114. Structure: 1–3, a motif from a lament; 4–8, a hymnic satire about idols; 9–18, a series of antiphons, affirming trust in, and praise of, God. **1.** The implicit request will be realized by Yahweh alone, who acts "for his name's sake" (Ez 20), not by Israel. It is impossible to determine the situation that called forth these lines. **2.** The ridicule of the "pagans" is answered in 3: Yahweh cannot be forced to prove he is God; he is free to act as he pleases. **4–8.** A satire against dead idols in the style of Jer 10:3ff.; Is 44:9ff.; etc.; also a reply to 2. **9.** The first line should be understood as a summons to trust, whereas the second is the reply. *house of Israel:* The congregation. The same pattern holds for 10, where "house of Aaron" indicates priests, and for 11, where "those who fear the Lord" are probably the proselytes (cf. Ps 118:1–4). **12–15.** Blessings are spoken by the priests. **16–18.** A hymnic conclusion, in which the "three-story" concept—heaven, earth, and nether world—is neatly indicated.

132 **Ps 116.** A thanksgiving Ps, divided into Pss 114–15 in the LXX and Vg. The life setting is in the Temple (19) where one who has been delivered from dire distress ("death," 3) fulfills his "vows" (14,18) with a "sacrifice of thanksgiving" (*tōdâ*), accompanied by this Ps. Structure: 1–2, the psalmist acknowledges that Yahweh "has heard"; 3–4, a description of the prayer uttered during distress; 5–9, a lesson (for the bystanders at the sacrifice) how Yahweh "keeps the little ones," as exemplified by the psalmist; 10–11, he looks back on his reactions before Yahweh saved him; 12–19, he acknowledges Yahweh as rescuer, as he offers the sacrifice that was vowed. **1.** *I love:* Thanksgiving Pss usually begin with an expression of praise. **3.** See comment on Ps 18:5. **4.** To "call upon the name" is to invoke Yahweh's help, but in 13 and 17 it indicates the proclamation of his name in thanksgiving. **5–6.** The didactic tendency of the acknowledgment of Yahweh is exemplified here; the psalmist teaches a lesson to those present. **8.** On such literal statements as this, see Barth, *Die Errettung vom Tode*, 143). There is more than poetry or metaphor here; death is a power that asserts its grip on man by sickness, etc. **9.** The phraseology is capable of fuller meaning: life with God. **10.** In a second phrase he recalls his trust in God alone, when he was afflicted. **13.** *cup of my salvation:* A cup that saves (in contrast to the cup of God's wrath, Is 51:17ff.), and perhaps a libation is implied. This verse is appropriately used in the Mass of the Roman rite before Communion. **14.** *my vows:* He had vowed to perform the sacrifice he is now offering. **15.** The meaning is that Yahweh will not let his "faithful ones" die; they are too "precious" to lose. **16.** *son of your handmaid:* The houseborn slave, who has absolutely no rights (cf. Ps 86:16).

133 **Ps 117.** A hymn of praise. The structure is a model of hymn style: the summons to praise, followed by the reason for it. The appeal to "nations" to praise Yahweh for his "kindness" and "fidelity" (Ex 34:6) toward Israel is striking, but when Gentiles are invited to praise the Lord in the enthronement Pss, the reasons are based on his qualities as creator and also as savior of Israel. There is no need to associate this short prayer with Pss 116 or 118, as some Hebr manuscripts do, nor to regard it as a liturgical prelude to a festival hymn (Weiser).

134 **Ps 118.** A thanksgiving liturgy. This Ps has received many varying interpretations. As a whole, it is a thanksgiving liturgy, which is structured in three main sections: 1–4, a thanksgiving song divided between several choruses (Israel, Aaron, God-fearers); 5–14, a thanksgiving song of an individual, that has affinity to the so-called gate or entrance liturgies (Pss 15, 24) and in which a victory song (15–18) is to be found; 22–29, a proclamation and summons of a processional. It is tempting to understand the "I" as the king, who heads a public thanksgiving and procession to the Temple. Jewish tradition associated the poem with the Feast of Tabernacles. **1–4.** The whole community is addressed in 1, and in 2–4 a summons is issued to each of three groups (also mentioned in that order in 115:9–11). **5.** If the "I" is the king, he is not the one who addressed the groups in 1–4. He begins here a thanksgiving Ps in which he expresses his great trust in the Lord (6–9), who has "set him free" from his "foes." There is a certain sapiential style ("it is better...") to his acknowledgment of Yahweh as the rescuer and in his recommendation of trust in God. **10.** *all the nations:* These are not identified; once more, he begins to describe his distress and the Lord's saving intervention. There seem to be echoes of the royal Pss (18:29–30,36–39; 27:3). **15.** *shout of victory:* Thus begins the victory song, which has been incorporated into the prayer; it associates the psalmist's salvation with that of the community ("tents of the just"). *right hand:* God's instrument of victory (cf. Skehan, *CBQ* 25 [1963] 94–110). **17.** *I shall not die:* Physical death is meant, and a full life on earth is implied. **18.** *chastised:* Reflects a view of suffering that is similar to Prv 3:11f. **19–20.** *gates of justice:* The gates of the Temple, where the justice of the one who enters is questioned (Pss 15:1ff.; 24:3ff.) and through which only "the just shall enter." A similar concept of the Temple gates exists in Mesopotamian literature (cf. Kraus, *op. cit.*). **22.** *the stone:* A symbol of the psalmist, who has just related the story of his distress, and of the restoration by the Lord. These lines must be spoken by those ("our eyes") who accompany him to the Temple to offer thanksgiving. The NT interpretation (Mt 21:42; Acts 4:11) sees a more eminent fulfillment in Christ. **24.** *day the Lord has made:* The day of his saving intervention. **25.** *grant salvation:* The equivalent is "hosanna!" **26–27.** *blessed...:* These lines fit into the gate or entrance liturgy. **27a.** A kind of confession or "credo." **27bc.** A command given to the community to execute a procession "to the horns of the altar." **28.** The psalmist begins again, and in 29 he repeats the opening verse.

135 **Ps 119.** An acrostic poem; each of the eight verses of the first strophe (aleph) begins with the first letter of the Hebr alphabet; each verse of the second strophe (beth) begins with the second letter; and so on for all 22 letters of the alphabet. The classification is not easy (wisdom?), and it seems best to recognize that it is *sui generis.* It is a Torah Ps (Kraus), which is a composite of several types (hymn, lament), and influenced by various movements (deuteronomic school, wisdom writers, anthological composition). The entire work is in praise of the Law, and the joys to be found in keeping it. It is not "legalism" but a love and desire for the word of God in Israel's Law, which is the expression of the Lord's revelation of himself and his will for man. In almost every verse, a synonym for the Torah is to be found: decrees, ways, precepts, statutes, commands, ordinances, promises. There is no logical progression of thought in the Ps. **10–11.** The intensity of Dt appears in many verses, as here and 17, 18, etc. **14.** The note of joy in observance of the Law is mentioned throughout (cf. 24, 35, 47, etc.); the comparison with "riches" is characteristic of the sages' doctrine. **19.** *wayfarer:* The Hebr *gēr* is one who has no claim to possession of territory; the meaning is spiritualized here to indicate one for whom Yahweh alone is the only claim; he asks not for land but to know the Lord's commands (20). **22–23.** Motifs from the individual lament appear often, as here, and in 28,42,61,81–88. **36–37.** His true reward is not the "gain" of this world but the delight that fidelity brings. **40.** The full implications of this idea (cf. 37, 50, etc., for life as a consistent theme in this Ps) will be drawn by a later writer: Justice is immortal (Wis 1:15). **48.** *lift up my hands:* In a gesture of prayer. **49–56.** This strophe is characterized by motifs of a lament; the exile in 54 is metaphorical (cf. 19). **57.** *my part:* See comment on Ps 16:5. **83.** *leathern flask:* Because wine or water "bottles" were frequently leather, they would become brittle in the warmth of a home. **85.** The second line can be translated: "they who do not follow your law." **89.** Cf. Is 40:8 and Ps 89:3. **96.** The thought is obscure; perhaps he recognizes that his "fulfillment" of God's "command" falls far short of what it should be. **120.** The realistic tone of this formula of "fear of the Lord" is unusual. **131.** The psalmist is fed with the "commands" of God. **147–48.** Through the night he awaits God's "words." **150–51.** Note the contrast between "far" and "near." **159.** See v. 40. **162.** The metaphor of rich spoil is to suggest only his rejoicing. **164.** *seven times:* As often in the OT, it indicates an indefinite number.

136 **Ps 120.** An individual lament by one who is beset with calumnious enemies in a hostile area. Structure: 1–2, a call for help; 3–4, an imprecation against the enemy; 5–7, a description of his unhappy situation. **1.** *song of ascents:* (→ 5 above.) It would be better to translate 1b as "to answer me." The CCD translates the MT, which, as vocalized, indicates a thanksgiving Ps. A change of one vowel would yield "to answer me." If it is a thanksgiving song, 2–7 would have to be interpreted as a flash-back. **3.** *with more besides:* Derived from a common formula of cursing: "May the Lord do such and such, and add more" (cf. 1 Sm 3:17; 14:44; 25:22). **4.** *brushwood:* The broom plant, which provides intense heat. **5–7.** *Meshech:* The name of an ancient people of NE Asia Minor. *Kedar:* A N Arabian desert tribe. Inasmuch as these two places are so far apart, it is likely that they are metaphorical for "barbarians." The "*long*" residence among them has been unhappy.

137 **Ps 121.** A Ps of trust. The prayer is too vague to enable us to reconstruct the life setting with any certainty. Kraus inclines to see it as a pilgrim's departure ceremony from the Temple (cf. 7). Gunkel (with emendations in the text) considers it as a question and answer between pilgrim and priest. The note of trust in God for help and protection dominates the poem. Structure: 1–2, a question and answer; 3–8, an address to the psalmist. **1.** Depending upon the interpretation, the "mountains" designate Jerusalem (and as such it anticipates 2) or, possibly, the surrounding hills on which the pagan sanctuaries were located. In the latter case, the proclamation in 2 would be a rejection of these sanctuaries. **2.** This reply seems to be given by the psalmist himself (rather than by a priest). **3–8.** Addressed to the psalmist, presumably by a priest. The possibility of sunstroke in Palestine is real, and many superstitions about the effect of the moon (6) exist. The poem affirms trust in God as creator, ever vigilant guardian, refuge, and guide.

138 **Ps 122.** A song of Zion, on the occasion of a pilgrimage to Jerusalem. Structure: 1–2, reactions at the start and finish of a pilgrimage; 4–5, praise of Zion; 6–9, prayers for Jerusalem. **1–3.** On his arrival (3), he recalls the joy with which he first heard the invitation to make the pilgrimage to the Temple (1). In 3, he expresses his admiration for the holy city. **4–5.** He describes the religious significance of Jerusalem, the place of worship for the "tribes" (once David had transferred the Ark there), and the place of "judgment" (cf. 1 Kgs 7:7). **6–9.** His prayers for Jerusalem are centered upon "peace": her complete prosperity (Hebr *šālôm,* which can be taken as part of the name, Jerusalem; here, *nomen est omen*).

139 **Ps 123.** A lament of the community, which probably reflects an exilic or post-exilic attitude (3–4). **1–2.** These lines are spoken by a representative of the community. The comparison with the "eyes" of servants is especially fine; as one looks to the largesse that comes from the "hands" of a master, so Israel looks to Yahweh for "pity." **3–4.** The complaint voiced by the community is very general; one cannot be sure if the oppressors are foreign or Jewish.

140 **Ps 124.** A thanksgiving song of the community. **1–5.** A vivid, repetitious expression of what would have been, "had not the Lord been with us." The metaphors ("swallow alive," "waters," "snare") are too vague to allow conclusions about the precise dangers. The "torrents" are an echo of the myth of unruly chaos (cf. Ps 130:1). **6–8.** Thanksgiving and acknowledgment of Yahweh's deliverance are offered by the community.

The "fowlers' snare" was a wooden instrument with nets triggered to capture the prey.

141 **Ps 125.** A national Ps of trust. **1–2.** There are two comparisons: "those who trust" are as immovable as "Zion"; Yahweh's protection of his "people" is like that of the "mountains round about Jerusalem." **3.** The basis for the hope is that for the sake of the "just," "wickedness" must disappear. The "scepter" could refer to internal as well as external oppression. **4–5.** A prayer is offered for the "good," and an imprecation is pronounced upon those who side with the "evildoers." The poem, like 128:6, concludes with a prayer for Israel's prosperity (cf. Ps 122:8).

142 **Ps 126.** A lament of the community. Structure: 1–3, an historical survey; 4–6, a prayer for restoration. This liturgical song can be understood as a prayer during the first years of the return from Babylon (cf. Hag, Zech), although the request in 4 remains vague. **1–3.** The reference is to the end of the Exile. The return could hardly be believed ("like men dreaming") at first. And then both the "nations" and Israel acknowledged the *magnalia Dei*. Some scholars (Gunkel) interpret 1–3 as an announcement of future deliverance. **4.** This request indicates that the return was not all that it had been envisioned to be. In the poet's own time, Yahweh's continuing intervention is needed. The comparison to the wadies in the Negeb ("torrents") bears on the transformation undergone by the dry, caked valley, once water courses through it. **5–6.** A consoling, proverblike saying (perhaps uttered by a priest?). The mourning associated with sowing may hark back to the symbolism of the death of the fertility god (Baal, Osiris), although this background has nothing to do with the meaning here.

143 **Ps 127.** A wisdom Ps. Structure: 1–2, without the Lord's help, human activity is futile; 3–5, the good fortune of being father to many sons. Originally these were probably independent poems, but the two sayings are complementary, if "house" is understood of founding a family. **1.** A vivid comparison: Unless Yahweh is builder and guardian, man's toil is "in vain." **2.** Yahweh is the giver of every gift, no matter the effort made by man; this is expressed paradoxically in the contrast between hard work and "sleep." God gives as he pleases. **4.** *arrows:* A symbol of the protection that "sons" provide for a family, as specified in 5; in the judicial processes that take place at the "gate" of the city, the many sons will support their father.

144 **Ps 128.** A wisdom Ps. It is composed of a beatitude formula (which continues in the 2nd pers.) and a blessing (1–4,5–6). **1.** Fear of the Lord is spelled out by the parallelism, "walk in his ways"; this practical service brings the rewards promised in 2–4, where the ideal picture of family life is depicted—prosperity and a large progeny. The description of the rewards is meant to be an exhortation to fear the Lord. **5–6.** Present a blessing from Yahweh (pronounced by a priest?) that points to the basis of Jewish happiness—"the prosperity of Jerusalem"; the solidarity of the individual with the community lies behind this blessing.

145 **Ps 129.** A lament of the community. After referring to Israel's sad history of oppression and deliverance (from Exodus to Exile?), the psalmist asks for punishment of her enemies. **1–2.** The history of Israel's oppression is compared to that of a man who has somehow survived. *let Israel say:* May indicate a liturgical recital by an individual ("me") who represents the community. **3.** Israel was not merely used as a beast of burden (4), but she was herself plowed up. **4.** *cords:* Those belonging to the yoke placed upon Israel. **6–7.** The grass that happened to grow on the roofs of beaten earth has no root and cannot last; it cannot even be harvested. **8.** Blessing, such as that of the harvesters (Ru 2:4), will be absent from the enemies (who have been compared to unharvested grass in 7).

146 **Ps 130.** An individual lament. Structure: 1–2, a cry for forgiveness; 3–4, trust is adduced as a motif for mercy; 5–6, an affirmation of confidence; 6–7, an exhortation to the community. Greatly distressed by his sinfulness, the psalmist humbly and trustfully requests forgiveness for both himself and the community (8). But if one might possibly understand the perfect tense in 1, 5, 6 as past time, it could be a thanksgiving song for deliverance from sin, in which the psalmist associates the bystanders and the people in God's mercy (e.g., Weiser). This Ps is one (the sixth) of the traditional seven penitential Pss. **1.** *depths:* Chaos and the sphere of death and the nether world, away from God. **3.** This poignant question underlines God's "forgiveness," which is his gift to those who fear him ("that you may be revered"). **5.** *word:* Perhaps the oracle of the priest, indicating forgiveness. **6–7.** The comparison to the watch of "sentinels" is expressive. The admonition to Israel is also a confident claim that she will be redeemed.

147 **Ps 131.** A Ps of trust. The writer is one of the "Anawim" (→ 11 above), a just man who offers his loyalty and modest achievement to God, grateful for the security and satisfaction that he finds in him. **2.** This tender comparison to "a weaned child" speaks volumes about his attitude. **3.** As in 130:7, an appeal is made to Israel.

148 **Ps 132.** A royal Ps. The liturgical character of this Ps is clear, even if the precise feast is disputed (New Year for Mowinckel; the choice of Zion for Kraus; a "constituent part of the covenant festival" for Weiser). The key ideas are evident from the structure: 1–5, a prayer for David because of his care for the Lord's dwelling; 6–10, a description of the procession of the Ark; 11–13, the Lord's promise of an eternal dynasty; 14–18; the Lord's eternal choice of Zion. **1–5.** Reflect an imaginative, expanded version of the events in 2 Sm 7; no record exists of David's "vow" or renunciation of sleep. The lines are presumably spoken by a priest or cultic official. Yahweh is the "mighty one of Jacob," the God of the amphictyony. **6.** *we:* Apparently a choir interrupts and recreates the story of the recovery of the Ark by David. Whatever the precise explanation of "Ephrathah," its association with Bethlehem suggests that in David's home town he and his followers heard of the existence of the Ark "in the fields of Jaar," i.e., Kiriath-jearim. The exhortation in 7 indicates a cultic re-enactment of the event in which the liturgical cry of 8–10 (cf. 2 Chr 6:41–42!) fits very well. Yahweh "advances," enthroned on the Ark (footstool), borne by "priests," as the "faithful ones shout merrily," and a direct prayer (10) for the "anointed" descendant of David is voiced. **11–13.** In the second part of the poem, Yahweh's oath corresponds to David's (2–5). The dynastic oracle of 2 Sm 7 has become an oath (as in Ps 89:4): The dynasty shall be eternal, provided the descendants keep the "covenant" (of Sinai, in which the Davidic covenant [Ps 89:4; Is 55:3] is included), and the "decrees" (of legitimization? cf. De Vaux, *AI* 103, on *'ēdût*). **14–18.** A description of the blessings that flow from Yahweh's choice of Zion. The "horn" is David's strength, his descendants, and so also, in parallelism, is the "lamp."

149 **Ps 133.** A wisdom Ps(?). The classification is difficult; it praises brotherly unity, without specifying within a family or a larger group. **2.** The picture is akin to Ps 23:5; the "head" is anointed generously, and the oil runs down the "beard." The allusion seems to be to the anointing of the high priest (Aaron). **3.** The unity is compared to the beneficent Hermon dew. Inasmuch as no geographical possibility links this image with Zion, it must be understood as a metaphorical allusion. *comes down:* The same verb as "runs down" in 2 (*yōrēd*), which characterizes this poem. *life forever:* To be understood in the OT perspective of no real life after death; hence, it designates the full blessings of this life.

150 **Ps 134.** A hymn of praise, exhorting priests ("servants of the Lord") to "bless" the Lord in the "night" worship. Their reply, akin to the priestly blessing of Nm 6:24, is in 3.

151 **Ps 135.** A hymn of praise. The life setting is the Temple (1–2) on the occasion of some feast (covenant renewal?). Structure: 1–4, introduction; 5–7, praise of God as creator; 8–14, God's work in the Exodus and Conquest; 15–18, the vanity of idols; 19–21, conclusion. Many of the verses are repeated from other parts of the Bible in the style of the so-called anthological composition. It is noteworthy that there is no mention of the Sinai covenant (cf. the liturgical confessions of Dt 26:1–9, etc.). **1.** *servants:* Normally priests, as in Ps 134:1, but it can apply to the community (cf. 19). **4.** The reason for the praise is the choice of Israel (cf. Ex 19:5; Dt 7:6). **5–7.** *I know:* More detailed reasons for praise now follow (proclaimed by an individual on behalf of the community): God's freedom and creative activity, with allusion to the conquest of chaos and to his control of the elements. **8–12.** In the list of plagues, the Conquest, and the gift of the land, the Red Sea is curiously absent. **15–18.** Virtually identical with Ps 115:4–8. **19–21.** An invitation to bless the Lord (see comment on Ps 115:9–11).

152 **Ps 136.** A hymn of praise in the form of a litany. Often called the Great Hallel. Structure (cf. Ps 135): 1–3, introduction; 4–9, creation; 10–22, Exodus, wilderness, and Conquest; 23–26, conclusion. The song is designed for antiphonal rendering: The first line is proclaimed by a soloist; the second line is a refrain by the congregation. **4–9.** The cosmological picture is much the same as that of Gn 1. As in the Pentateuch, creation serves as a prelude to the salvation history (cf. Von Rad, *op. cit.*, 136–47). **13–15.** Unlike Ps 135, the events of the Red Sea are commemorated. **17–22.** These lines are almost the same (without refrain) as Ps 135:10–12. **23–24.** These verses could be understood of the period of the judges as much as of the Exile. The conclusion in 26 returns to the introduction (1–3), as often in the hymns.

153 **Ps 137.** A lament of the community. Structure: 1–3, a flash-back to earlier experiences in the Exile; 4–6, an imprecation on one who would forget Jerusalem; 7–9, an imprecation on the destroyers of Jerusalem. **1.** *streams of Babylon:* Countless irrigation canals from the Tigris and Euphrates watered the Babylonian plain. It is hard to escape the impression that these are personal memories that are being recalled; if so, the prayer is to be dated in the Exile. Kraus argues that the poet recalls a liturgical commemoration of the destruction of Jerusalem. **3.** The request of the "captors" here fulfills the same function as the frequent question motif in the lament: "Where is your God?" (e.g., Ps 79:10). The "songs of Zion" has been adopted as a literary classification of Pss 76, 84, etc. **4.** The question implies that the "foreign" land is unclean as well as hostile. **5–6.** While delivering this imprecation, he is at the same time singing a song of Zion! The reference to "hand" and "tongue" is in view of harp and song. *be forgotten:* So MT; a slight change of consonants yields "dry up," a reading preferred by some scholars. **7.** Edom ravaged Judah with the fall of Jerusalem (Lam 4:21; Ob 8, 15). **9.** This brutal practice was an accepted part of ancient warfare (Hos 10:14; 14:1; Na 3:10), and it is merely a bold cliché for the usual horrors of war (→ 18 above).

154 **Ps 138.** A thanksgiving Ps. Structure: 1–3, thanksgiving for deliverance; 4–6, a hymn proclaiming universal recognition of God; 7–8, expression of trust and acknowledgment. **1.** *angels:* Hebr *'ĕlōhîm*, "God" or "gods." It could stand for the members of the heavenly court or "angels," or there may be an allusion to Yahweh as incomparable among the gods (Ps 86:8; Ex 15:11). **2.** *temple:* Here the thanksgiving liturgy takes place. **3.** A summary statement of the saving act. **4–6.** This idealistic and enthusiastic universalism is characteristic also of other Pss (22:28–30; 47:2; and the enthronement Pss).

155 **Ps 139.** The classification is difficult: a hymn, or a sapiential consideration of God's active presence, or the prayer of an accused man (19ff.)? If the correspondence between 1 and 23–24 is granted (Yahweh *has* probed) with Kraus, we can recognize a thanksgiving Ps. He thinks the life setting is the same as that of the cultic doxologies, in which one glorified God for his judgment in intervening to justify the author. Weiser remarks appropriately that "the poet does not shape his thoughts impersonally in abstract theological definitions, but develops them in the sphere of his personal experience of the reality of God." The "I-Thou" character of this Ps makes it one of the most personal and beautiful expressions in the OT.

Structure: 1–6, praise of God for his marvelous knowledge of the poet; 7–12, the impossibility of escaping from Yahweh; 13–18, praise of the Lord as all-knowing creator; 19–24, a plea to see God's justice and to remain faithful. **1.** *probed:* Full of trust and admiration, he approaches Yahweh, the omniscient God, who "knows" his loyalty (cf. 23–24). This intimate knowledge moves him to praise, and he develops the theme of omnipresence in the following lines. **2.** *sit...stand:* The Semitic idiom states opposites to express completeness—hence, "at all times." **4.** The poet communicates his own astonishment at God's involvement with him. **5.** No matter where he turns, the Lord confronts him. **8.** *heavens:* Were the psalmist, like Elijah, to be taken up, or were he to sink to the "nether world" like Korah and Dothan, he could not escape the Lord. **9–10.** *wings:* The speed with which the dawn comes will not suffice to escape the "hand" of God. **8.** With this verse Kraus compares an Amarna letter to the Pharaoh: "Whether we go up to heaven or go down to the underworld, our head is in your hands." **13.** *formed me:* God's creative activity is the basic reason for the omniscience, which has been described. **14.** *soul:* The person. **15.** *in the depths of the earth:* The womb is meant, but the phrase may originally have reflected the story of man being made from the earth (Gn 2:7). **16.** *book:* God is thought to have the name of everyone inscribed in a book (cf. Pss 56:9; 69:29). **17–18.** *with you:* An expressive indication of God's transcendence; were it possible to grasp his thoughts (Is 55:8), there would still be God himself to reckon with. **19–20.** There is an abrupt transition to this personal problem. The "wicked" are those who persecute him (by forcing him to disloyalty to Yahweh?; cf. "your foes"); he wants to see God's justice demonstrated. **21–22.** His "hatred" is directed against them because they hate Yahweh; it is a sort of declaration of loyalty—God's enemies are his enemies. Little apology is needed for this verse; although one may admit that the OT does not have the extended horizon of the Sermon on the Mount, it does not exclude the NT development (where there is more emphasis on conversion and the identity of the Christian with Christ). The fact remains that as sinners, the enemies of God are worthy of his rejection. **23–24.** *probe:* He asks for a decision from Yahweh that will show he is in the right and that his loyalty will remain; should he waver, Yahweh is to "lead" him back.

156 **Ps 140.** An individual lament. The poet is beset by calumnies of wicked men, but the description is entirely too general to permit of specific conclusions (cf. Ps 64). Structure: 2–4, a cry for help against the tongues of evil men; 5–8, a plea, complaint, and expression of trust; 9–11, a plea for God's judgment on the wicked; 12–14. certainty that the prayer has been heard. **4.** For similar metaphors, see Pss 52:4; 58:5; 64:4. **6.** The metaphor is that of a hunter laying a trap, as in Pss 9:16; 64:6 (see comment on 124:7). **10.** The MT is uncertain; the CCD describes the attitude of the wicked in 10a. **11.** *burning coals:* See Prv 25:21–22. For the ramifications of this metaphor, cf. K. Stendhal (*HarvTR* 55 [1962] 343–55). **12–14.** The lament ends, as usual, on a note of confidence: The wicked cannot prevail against the just.

157 **Ps 141.** An individual lament. Structure: 1–2, a cry for help; 3–7, a prayer not to be led astray by the wicked, who will be judged; 8–10, a trustful prayer. **2.** Here, prayer is considered the equivalent of sacrifice. **4–5.** His real fear is to be seduced by the wicked (cf. Ps 84:11); hence, any discipline from the just man can be only beneficial. **6–7.** The MT is uncertain and obscure; the sequence of ideas seems to call for the punishment and judgment of the wicked.

158 **Ps 142.** An individual lament, which is characterized by simplicity, humility, and trust. Structure: 2–4, a trustful appeal to God; 4–5, the complaint; 6–8, a request and vow to give thanks. The psalmist is in prison (8) because of his persecutors, and he looks forward to God's intervention. **5.** In this moment of crisis he is encouraged by the fact that God knows his "path" of life. **6.** In view of 5, the Lord is his sole "refuge," his "portion" (the prerogative of the Levites—for whom Yahweh was the "portion"—is his; cf. Nm 18:21). Verse 8 contains the vow to offer thanksgiving, and it refers to the participation of the "just" (whose trust in God will have presumably been strengthened by the deliverance) on this happy occasion.

159 **Ps 143.** An individual lament; the seventh penitential Ps, which echoes the phraseology of earlier Pss. The author is a man oppressed by enemies, but he nevertheless trusts in God for deliverance. Structure: 1–2, a cry for mercy; 3–6, a description of his affliction; 7–9, repeated appeals; 10–12, confident requests. **1–2.** The appeal is to God's fidelity and saving intervention; he admits his sinfulness and throws himself upon the grace of God. God's "justice" is to be understood here as the divine ability and will to save him. **3.** *the dark:* The ominous realm or sphere of death, which threatens him even though he lives. **5.** A review of God's saving acts in the "days of old" is a consolation and also a motif to move Yahweh to intervene. **8.** *at dawn:* As often in Pss, the time when God answers. **10.** This plea is typical of the sincerity that characterizes the prayer (cf. Ps 51:12–13).

160 **Ps 144.** The classification is difficult. The Ps is an echo of other Pss, especially Ps 18 (a model?), and it has elements of both the lament and the thanksgiving. It may even be called a royal Ps (cf. 10). Structure: 1–2, thanksgiving for victory; 3–7, the motif of man's frailty and a plea for deliverance; 9–11, vow of thanksgiving and refrain; 12–15, a communal prayer for prosperity. A slightly varying refrain occurs in 7–8 and in 11. The prayer (especially 12–15) is best understood in the light of the role the king has in bringing prosperity to his people (cf. Ps 72:2–14). **1–2.** Cf. 18:2,35,47. **3.** Cf. 8:5. **4.** Cf. 39:6; 102:12. **5.** Compare this request for a theophany with Ps 18:10,15,17. **7.** *waters:* As so frequently in Pss (e.g., 18:5), they symbolize the powers of chaos and death. **10.** The royal background of the Ps is clearly indicated (cf. 18:51). **12–15.** These blessings (children, food, cattle and flocks, peace) are to be associated with the king through whom God communicates them (although Gunkel considers these lines to constitute a separate Ps).

161 **Ps 145.** A hymn of praise. The acrostic pattern (aleph, beth, etc.) is perhaps the reason why other Pss are echoed in it—but without injuring the movement and beauty. Structure: 1–4, hymnic introduction (by an individual, throughout); 5–9, commemoration of God's deeds and goodness; 10–20, universal praise of God as king, provider, savior; 21, conclusion. **2.** Cf. Ps 48:2. **3.** Cf. Ps 96:4. **5–6.** *works...deeds:* Refer to creation and salvation history. **8.** Cf. Ex 34:6, and J. Scharbert in *Bib* 38 (1957) 130–50. **13–14.** The poet changes from second to third person. **15–16.** The beneficent providence of God reflected in these lines has made them a popular prayer (especially at meals) in Christian tradition.

162 **Ps 146.** A hymn of praise, or perhaps a thanksgiving. Structure: 1–2, a hymnic introduction (by an individual, throughout); 3–4, admonition on the vanity of trusting in man; 5–10, hymnic development of Yahweh as creator and savior—the reason for trusting in him (5). This poem inaugurates the last group of alleluia Pss (see comment on Ps 113). **1–2.** Cf. Ps 104:1,33. **3–4.** This admonition, characteristic of thanksgiving songs, points up the contrast to 5–10, where Yahweh is praised as one to be trusted in every crisis. The "princes" are probably to be understood as powerful and rich leaders rather than as members of the royal family. **5–10.** This stirring catalogue of divine attributes is typically concrete and exemplifies the manner in which the men of the OT conceived of Yahweh.

163 **Ps 147.** This hymn of praise is divided into three strophes by an invitation to sound the praises of God: 1–6, praise of the Lord as restorer of Israel and as creator; 7–11, God's providential direction of nature; 12–20, God's power over nature and his care for Zion and Israel. For some of the ideas in this Ps, see Pss 33, 104, and Is 40–66. **2.** The reference is probably to the end of the Exile. **3.** Cf. Is 61:1. **4.** Cf. Is 40:26. **5.** References to Yahweh's "wisdom" are relatively late in the OT. **8–11.** The acknowledgment of the Lord's blessings is followed in 10–11 by wisdom considerations (cf. Prv 21:31). **15.** The creative "word" of Yahweh is to be found in Is 55:10–12; Gn 1; Ps 33:6. Here the word is a messenger that does his will and works in nature (the poet betrays real feeling for nature in the following lines). **16–18.** A description of winter and spring in Palestine. **19.** Another aspect of the "word" of Yahweh: His "ordinances" are for Israel alone (cf. Dt 4:7–8).

164 **Ps 148.** A hymn of praise. Structure: 1–6, the heavens are invited to praise the Lord (reason in 5–6); 7–14, the creatures of earth, especially man, are invited to praise God (reason in 13–14). The poem is related to the *Benedicite*, or Song of the Three Children, in Dn 3:52–90 (Gk text). In both, the influence of the catalogues of natural phenomena (*Listenwissenschaft*) as found in the *Onomasticon of Amen-em-ope* can be felt (cf. Von Rad, *GesSt* 262–71); other OT examples are Jb 28; Sir 43. The series—heaven, sun, moon, stars, etc.—is virtually the same in all, owing to the common "scientific" tradition. **4.** The "heavens of heavens" is over the firmament where the "waters above" (Gn 1:6–8) were stored. **7.** In contrast to 4, the chaotic "depths" are now summoned. **8.** *fire:* Lightning. **11–12.** There is even a certain hierarchy in human levels.

165 **Ps 149.** A hymn of praise. Structure: 1–4, an invitation to praise the Lord for his love of Israel;

5–9, a description of the participants in the warlike mood of the hymn. It is not possible to associate this song with a specific historical event. Rather than referring to an eschatological battle, it is best understood as a cultic celebration (cf. 5–6) of victory. **1.** *new song:* Perhaps in imitation of Pss 96:1; 98:1, the enthronement Pss. **4.** The reason for praise: victory for the "lowly," i.e., Israel. **6–9.** Saved by Yahweh, the faithful execute a victory ritual. *written sentence:* The book of Yahweh's decrees (Jb 13:26; Is 65:6), in this case, judgment.

166 **Ps 150.** A hymn of praise, which is almost entirely a hymnic introduction, answering the questions, where (1), why (2), and how (3–5). **1.** The heavenly "sanctuary" is meant, as the parallelism suggests. **3–5.** On these musical instruments, see Murray (*op. cit.*, 84–89) and O. Sellers (*BA* 4 [1941] 33–47).

36

RUTH, LAMENTATIONS

Geoffrey E. Wood

RUTH

BIBLIOGRAPHY

1 Burrows, M., "The Ancient Oriental Background of Hebrew Levirate Marriage," *BASOR* 77 (1940) 2–15; "The Marriage of Boaz and Ruth," *JBL* 59 (1940) 445–54. Crook, M. B., "The Book of Ruth," *JBR* 16 (1948) 155–60. Gerleman, G., *Ruth* (BK XVIII/1; Neukirchen, 1960). Glanzman, G. S., "The Origin and Date of the Book of Ruth," *CBQ* 21 (1959) 201–7. Gunkel, H., *Reden und Aufsätze* (Göttingen, 1953) 65–92. Haller, M., *Die fünf Megilloth* (HAT 1, 18; Tübingen, 1940) 1–20. Hertzberg, H. W., *Die Bücher Josua, Richter, Ruth* (ATD 9; Göttingen, 1953) 255–81. Humbert, P., "Art et leçon de l'histoire de Ruth," *RTP* 26 (1938) 257–86. Joüon, P., *Ruth* (Rome, 1924). Loretz, O., "The Theme of the Ruth Story," *CBQ* 22 (1960) 391–99. Myers, J. M., *Linguistic and Literary Form of the Book of Ruth* (Leiden, 1955). Penna, A., *Guidici e Rut* (LSB; Rome, 1962) 266–87. Robertson, E., "The Plot of the Book of Ruth," *BJRylL* 32 (1950) 207–28. Rowley, H. H., "The Marriage of Ruth," *HarvTR* 40 (1947) 77–99. Rudolph, W., *Ruth-Hoheslied-Klagelieder* (KAT XVII/1–3; Gütersloh, 1962) 23–71. Van Zyl, A. H., *The Moabites* (Leiden, 1960). Vincent, A., *Juges, Ruth* (BJ; Paris, 1952) 149–64. Wolfenson, L. B., "The Character, Contents, and Date of Ruth," *AJSL* 27 (1910–11) 285–300.

INTRODUCTION

2 **(I) Purpose and Date.** During the reign of Solomon (961–922), or shortly thereafter, Judah made a major effort to collect its laws and traditions. This collection, generally called the Yahwist (J) and now diffused throughout the books of Gn, Ex, and Nm (→ Pentateuch, 1:14), contains a relatively large number of stories in which God wonderfully raises up and sustains select heirs, according to the promises made to Abraham and despite every imaginable obstacle. Sterility threatens the line's continuity in the cases of Sarah, Rebekah, and Rachel (Gn 15:3; 16:1; 25:21; 30:1–2). Elder brothers intrude—e.g., Esau, who might rightfully intercept the promise and bear it away to some other people than Israel. Judah's first-born dies without issue and his brother refuses to raise up an heir to him (Gn 38). But God always saves the situation; taken together, the stories portray him irresistibly preserving a line of descent from Abraham to Isaac to Jacob to Judah to Perez, which issues in David and his dynasty. When one realizes that the Yahwist compilers served the royal house of David this emphasis is understandable.

In many of these stories particular stress is laid upon the women involved. Rebekah arranges a clever stratagem whereby Jacob receives Isaac's solemn blessing instead of Esau (Gn 27); Tamar sacrifices all pride and risks her life to beget an heir to her deceased husband. Awareness of Bathsheba's role in Solomon's succession to the throne over his elder brother Adonijah may have prompted the editors to highlight this motif (1 Kgs 1).

Other stories within the J collection show the editors' preoccupation with this theme of providential preservation of a family line: the Noah narrative (Gn 7–8); the account of Lot and his daughters (Gn 19:30–38). And interest in this theme is not confined to the J tradition (see Gn 22:1–19; Ex 1:15–22; 2:1–10; Jgs 13:1–25; 21; 1 Sm 1). The Book of Ruth dwells upon the same kind of crisis—Will the line of Elimelech go on?—and the outcome is the same—the difficulties give way to a happy ending.

3 Interest in such stories seems to have been more prevalent among earlier Hebrew generations; the stories mentioned are generally dated from premonarchical or early monarchical times. It seems then that Ru requires an early dating. Because it deals specifically with the providential preservation of David's ancestral line, it must have been composed sometime after David's rise to prominence, possibly in the reign of Solomon, the very period during which the J editors were by means of similar stories following the selective finger of God down through the many generations from Abraham to David.

This period was one of great literary activity, of Davidic acclaim (see the court history of David, 2 Sm 9–20; 1 Kgs 1–2), an atmosphere most suitable to the production of a work like Ru. Note, too, how evolved Ru appears when compared with its premonarchical literary counterparts, the stories of Lot's daughter, of Judah, and of Tamar. These reflect a primitive, frank age; Ruth's length, its finely cast sentences, and its delicacy reflect a higher level of culture. Although the setting is rustic, the characters are courtly in speech and manner. G. von Rad ("Josephsgeschichte und ältere Chokma," VTSup 1 [1953] 120) has classified the Joseph story in Gn 37–50 as a product of early monarchical times, a narrative shaped to edify and inculcate good manners, etc., a graphic lesson supporting the principles of Prov. If Von Rad's view has value, it is worth noting that several authorities have remarked on the similarity in style and mood of Ru to the Joseph narrative (Gunkel, *op. cit.*, 85; Rudolph, *op. cit.*, 33; Haller, *op. cit.*, 4). On the other hand, Ru is itself a bit primitive, classically pure in comparison to the baroque narratives of post-exilic times, e.g., Tb and Est (Jouon, *op. cit.*, 11; Gunkel, *op. cit.*, 90). The language of Ru supports its pre-exilic dating. Particular items of evidence may seem weak, but their cumulative effect is strong, as can be seen in the studies of W. F. Albright (*JBL* 61 [1942] 124), J. M. Myers, G. S. Glanzman, and others.

4 Suggestive also of the work's early origin is the author's description of certain Israelite social customs in their early stage of development. The Hebrews had a strong sense of family or clan solidarity (see A. Johnson, VTSup 1 [1953] 67–77). A man begot sons, grandsons, a clan. All the individuals of this clan were considered extensions of the original patriarch, members of a growing body, sharing the same bone, flesh, and blood (see Gn 29:14; 37:27; Jgs 9:1–2; 2 Sm 5:1; 19:11–13). The continuity and integrity of the clan must therefore be of serious concern to all. If some member was slain, the blood shed was not his alone—the whole clan bled. Inasmuch as blood was the seat of life (Gn 9:4; Lv 17:11), something of the whole clan's vitality was drawn off. Therefore, the custom existed whereby a member of the clan might pursue and slay the offender, take something of the aggressor clan's life, and thus re-establish social equilibrium (Nm 35:19–21; Dt 19:6–13). The kinsman who carried out this duty was known as the *gō'ēl haddām*, the clan's "blood avenger" or "redeemer."

Because a man's material possessions, his field, house, etc., were in some way extensions of himself, these too were considered appendages of the clan body. Note Naboth's refusal to give up the family vineyard (1 Kgs 21:3). Any loss of these material goods constituted an impairment of the clan itself, jeopardizing its continuity and vitality. Thus, whenever some poorer kinsman was forced to sell or lose his property, some other kinsman had to intervene—i.e., keep the property in the clan by purchasing it himself or redeeming it from the outsider by whom it was taken (Lv 25:25; Jer 32:6–9). Again, the kinsman who carried out this function was called *gō'ēl*, "redeemer," and the function itself, *ge'ullāh*, or "redemption." (See Ru 4.)

Clan continuity and integrity were again threatened by childlessness. In an age when man had no notion of resurrection, he sought immortality, perpetuated his name, through sons and grandsons (see O. Loretz, *CBQ* 22 [1960] 395). If a man died without a son, he died altogether and left the clan itself stunted. A third custom served to resolve this crisis: The man's brother must wed the widow, and the first-born son of this union was adjudged son of the deceased, heir to his property, and sustainer of his name and lineage (Dt 25:5–6). The brother who fulfilled this function was called the *yābām*, meaning "progenitor" or "procreator" (see KB 359; Burrows, *BASOR* 77, 6–7). The Lat term for brother-in-law is *levir*—hence, the term levirate marriage to designate this practice. In early times, when the sense of clan or family solidarity was stronger, the practice seems to have been more strictly binding. See Onan's fate in Gn 38. In Ru 1:11 also it seems understood that if Naomi had other sons, her widowed daughters-in-law could expect them to meet their obligation (see Rudolph, *op. cit.*, 62). Where brothers to the deceased were wanting, clan solidarity would have required a next of kin to serve as *yābām*, although the obligation was probably less binding—i.e., it could have been passed on to some other kinsman without disgrace.

5 Many authorities agree that Dt 25:5–10 reflects a later, narrower concept of the levirate duty, a time when its extension beyond a man's brothers was unnecessary, when the brother himself was preferably one who had been living with the deceased, when even he could refuse the duty with relative impunity, the penalty being simply public censure. Obviously, by this time a sense of family solidarity, although still strong, was no longer overly demanding in this particular matter. The post-exilic Priestly code went further in legislating levirate marriage out of existence. Lv 18:16 actually sets up an impediment of affinity between brother and sister-in-law, and Lv 20:21 brands such unions incestuous (De Vaux, *AI* 31–32). Ru faithfully reflects that strong clan solidarity proper to early times, when even a remote kinsman could be expected to marry a man's widow and raise his heir. The author himself seems quite at ease with this wider usage of the custom, for he supposes his audience's natural acquaintance with it.

Some have argued that the sandal incident in Ru 4:7–9 shows a dependence on Dt 25:9–10 and that Ru must be postdeuteronomic and post-exilic (Pfeiffer, *Introd.* 718; Joüon, *op. cit.*, 13). But closer scrutiny shows that the formality in Ru is conducted quite differently from Dt 25:9–10, concerning only land redemption and not the levirate, as in Dt (see Wolfenson, *op. cit.*, 293–94; R-F 670; Rudolph, *op. cit.*, 27; Eissfeldt, *OTI* 483). It is true that Ru 4:18–22 shows a Priestly style (see Gn 14:27) and repeats the genealogy found in 1 Chr 2:4–15 of the 4th cent. But scholars generally view this as a later expansion upon v. 17 and therefore no criterion of the date of origin (e.g., Bentzen, *IOT* 183; Joüon, *op. cit.*, 96).

The LXX and Vg place Ru after Jgs, thus amid works of greater antiquity. However, it must be admitted that the Hebr Bible locates it among the Writings—the third section of the Scriptures that contains works of late origin. It is difficult to say which represents a more primitive arrangement.

Some have suggested that Ru reacts to the 5th-cent. reform of Nehemiah and Ezra, thus betraying its post-exilic origin. To avoid spiritual contagion, these leaders made Judah a closed community, forbidding, among other things, intermarriage with aliens (Ezr 9–10; Neh 13:1–3,23–28; see also Dt 23:4–7). This action must have stirred up some opposition, e.g., the creation of stories like Ru to check the reform's ghetto tendency. Ru shows that David himself had a Moabite ancestress; therefore, intermarriage could not be absolutely bad (R-F 672; Weiser, *OT* 304). But this reconstruction seems forced. Joüon, even though he favors a post-exilic date, rejects it in telling fashion (*op. cit.*, 46; Gunkel, *op. cit.*, 88–90). H. H. Rowley (see his *Israel's Mission to the World* [London, 1939] 46–48) has pointed out that as an instrument of 5th-cent. polemics, Ruth might just as well have served the reformers, for she was a Moabite who left country and gods to become an exemplary follower of Yahweh.

6 In summary, the purpose of Ru seems similar to that of so many old biblical narratives: It shows dramatically how an elect family escaped extinction. Other points are made. Ruth is an example of tenacious fidelity to her husband and his kin. Boaz radiates prudence, nobility, and generosity. Both are presented to the individual reader for emulation. One need not judge the work as pure fiction, a moralizing tale without any foundation in fact. Yet the author's chief interest is not in the facts themselves but in how they express God's nature and ways, the favored place of David's house in God's plan of history, the fruits of fidelity and generosity, the consequences of weak faith and selfishness, etc. To underscore these points that most concern him, the author may freely embellish the facts. Ru cannot be considered mere record; it is primarily edifying drama.

The date of origin might be placed *ca.* 950–850 BC, somewhat contemporary with the court history of David and the J tradition. Rudolph (*op. cit.*, 29) offers a wider choice—1000–700—but leans, with Albright (*op. cit.*, 124), Haller (*op. cit.*, 3–4), and Hertzberg (*op. cit.*, 257), toward the 8th cent. Humbert connects the work with the deuteronomic reform, dating it in the late 7th cent. (*op. cit.*, 257–86). Crook suggests that Ru came to national circulation about 832, after Athaliah's overthrow (2 Kgs 11). The not too faithful descendants of David had almost been exterminated by this alien widow of Jehoram; the story of Ruth, an alien widow whose faith revived the ancestral line of David, would have provided the populace with a significant contrast to Athaliah (Crook, *op. cit.*, 155–60).

7 **(II) Outline.** The Book of Ruth may be outlined as follows:

(I) The Death of Elimelech's Line (1:1–6)
(II) The Return of the Widows (1:7–22)
(III) The Encounter with Elimelech's Kinsman (2:1–23)
(IV) The Widow's Demand and the Kinsman's Dilemma (3:1–18)
(V) The Dilemma's Solution (4:1–12)
(VI) The Revival of Elimelech's Line (4:13–17)
(VII) Appendix (4:18–22)

COMMENTARY

8 **(I) The Death of Elimelech's Line (1:1–6).** **1.** *in the time of the judges:* The incidents that follow occur within the period of loose tribal union prior to establishment of a monarchy, *ca.* 1020 BC. The author speaks of it as in the distant past, which need not mean he lived several centuries after the period; a man narrating *ca.* 900 might speak with similar vagueness (cf. the modern American who speaks of not-too-distant colonial times or antebellum days). According to 4:21, Ruth was David's great-grandmother, which would place her and the events narrated *ca.* 1100. *famine:* Periods of famine were frequent in Palestine (1 Kgs 17–18; 2 Kgs 8) and occasioned several biblical migrations (see Gn 12:10; 26:1; 42–46). *Bethlehem:* A settlement ancient enough to be mentioned in Egyptian archives *ca.* 1350, Bethlehem lies 5 mi. S of Jerusalem (Jgs 19:10). It is the traditional site of Rachel's tomb (see Gn 35:19; Ru 4:11). The author distinguishes it here from the Bethlehem in Zebulun (Jos 19:15). *to reside:* The Hebr *gûr* means to reside as a *gēr*, an alien, one who remains free, capable of owning property, but without the full civil rights proper to a native. Israelite law protected aliens, appealing to Israel's own experience as *gērîm* in Egypt (Ex 22:20; Dt 24:14–18; etc.). It did not always save aliens from oppression (Jer 7:1–7; Ez 22:6–7; Zech 7:8–11; De Vaux, *AI* 74–75). *the plateau of Moab:* One must not think here of the low, irrigated flats that lie directly E of the Jordan Delta (Nm 22:1; 26:3,63; 31:12; Jos 13:32) but of the plateau along the E coast of the Dead Sea rising gradually from 2000 to more than 4000 ft. (→ Biblical Geography, 73:43–46).

2. *Elimelech:* The name means "my God is king" and occurs with notable frequency in the Amarna letters—as *Ilimilku* or *Milkilu*—and in the Ras Shamra material. Naomi may be the feminine form of Naaman (Gn 46:21; Nm 26:40; 2 Kgs 5:1), a name sometimes applied to the god of fertility in Canaanite literature (see W. E. Staples, *AJSL* 53 [1957] 150). Its root, *n'm*, expresses delight, pleasurableness. Naomi may match the Eng expression "sweetheart." In 1:20, Naomi herself contrasts the name with Mara, meaning "bitter." Many authorities believe the author has taken liberties with the two sons, giving them symbolic names that better signal their unhappy condition and fate. Mahlon may mean "sterility" or "sickness," and Chilion, a "tiny vessel" or "consumption" (Rudolph, *op. cit.*, 38; but see Glanzman, *op. cit.*, 206). *Ephrathites:* Ephratha was the clan that settled around Bethlehem (1 Chr 2:51; 4:4; see also Gn 35:16; 48:7; 1 Sm 17:2). **3.** *Elimelech died:* The narrator plunges his audience at once into a somber mood. Shadows spread and deepen rapidly with mention of famine, exile, the ominous names of Mahlon and Chilion, and now the death of Elimelech. **4.** *married Moabite women:* The author manifests no scandal over this. Patriarchal figures and Moses himself married foreigners (Gn 41:45; Ex 2:21), and David and Solomon included them in their harems (2 Sm 3:3; 1 Kgs 11:1–8). Only later after pagan infiltration had weakened the nation's moral fiber were strict laws promulgated against intermarriage (Dt 7:3–4; Ex 34:15–16; Ezr 9–10; Neh 10:31; 13:23–27). *Orpah...Ruth:* The author probably placed no special stress on the etymology of these names, but later rabbinical interpreters tended to do so; e.g., *'ōrep*, "neck" or "back of the neck," seems to underlie "Orpah." Thus, the name may nicely intimate Orpah's character, for she will "turn away" or "show the back of her neck" when her loyalty is put to the test. It is indicated later that Ruth was Mahlon's wife. **5.** One might have expected the marriage of Naomi's two sons to herald an upswing in her fortune. In reality, it only serves as springboard for a deeper plunge into tragedy. The sons also die and without issue. Naomi is left alone, the pitiable remnant of this cruelly buffeted family. **6.** *the Lord had visited his people:* This section concludes with Naomi preparing to return home. Judah's renewed prosperity meant Yahweh was powerfully present there again. The narrative thus far has been absorbing but deliberately cursory and introductory, for the author's chief interest is not this family's decline but its wonderful deliverance. From this point on his pace becomes more measured; detailed description and dialogue fill out each scene. *had given them bread:* These final words, *lātēt lāhem lāḥem*, provide a good example of Hebr assonance and alliteration. The author passes into poetry often, especially in direct discourse (e.g., 1:16–17,20–21; 2:12–13; 3:9; 4:11–12,14–15; see Myers, *op. cit.*).

9 **(II) The Return of the Widows (1:7–22).** There were reasons other than Judah's renewed prosperity

that drew Naomi home. Elimelech owned a small piece of land there (4:3), and the destitute widow could not ignore its value. There would also be the consolation of familiar surroundings, customs, cult, etc. Her homeland offered her the most she might now expect of life, but it offered little or nothing to Orpah and Ruth, who were young and might have so much more. She allows them to accompany her part of the way back but then appeals to their good sense. **8.** *go back to your mother's house:* Naomi generously takes the initiative, releasing the women of any sense of obligation to her or their deceased husbands. They were still attractive, productive; they must not deny themselves a full life. It was senseless to remain attached to a family already dead. A widow ordinarily returned to her "father's" house (Gn 38:11; Lv 22:13; see also Dt 22:21; Jgs 19:2–3); in fact, the LXX (Alex) prefers *oikon tou patros* here. But mothers did have their own quarters and probably did exercise direct control over the daughters of a family; therefore, Naomi's advice here need not seem strange (Gn 31:33; Jgs 4:17; Ct 3:4; 8:2). *may the Lord be kind...as you were:* Naomi gratefully acknowledges their *ḥesed* or steadfast loyalty to her and her sons and prays that Yahweh will stand by them as constantly in the future. **9.** *grant you repose:* Naomi makes her prayer more specific. She hopes they will soon find *m^{e}nûḥāh*, not mere passing security but something permanent, true fulfillment. The word has a terminal sense. Palestine was considered Israel's *m^{e}nûḥāh*, its predestined abode, the goal of all its wanderings (Dt 12:9; Ps 95:11); similarly, the Temple was described as God's place of *m^{e}nûḥāh*, for there the Ark came to rest at last (Ps 132:8,14). Given this definitive quality, the word also served to describe the messianic era (Is 32:18). **10.** *they said to her, "No...":* It seems the negative *lō'* should be added here (Joüon, *op. cit.*, 38). See the frequent combination of *lō'* and *kî* in Gn 18:15; 19:2; 42:12; Jos 5:14; etc. Naomi's quiet, matter-of-fact manner may have momentarily obscured the full significance of her words, but only momentarily. Surprised and anguished, Orpah and Ruth quickly protest. Obviously Naomi got along better with her alien daughters-in-law than Rebekah did with hers (see Gn 26:35; 27:46).

10 **11.** Naomi appreciates their devotion but demands that they be realistic. She spells out for them the absurdity of their continuing with her. Like every normal woman of the times, they must desire the esteem, satisfaction, and security that accompany marriage and children (Gn 30:1). Are they really willing to sacrifice all to live with an aging widow amid strange people? They cannot count on the levirate (→ 4–5 above), for Naomi has no more sons, and, being old, no hope of begetting more. But suppose she could. Suppose that before tomorrow morning she not only remarried, but by some fantastic acceleration and accommodation of nature gave birth to twin sons. Were Ruth and Orpah going to waste precious years waiting for them to grow up? One wonders why Naomi did not mention another, less far-fetched alternative. At this stage in history, it seems that in the absence of brothers other kinsmen of the deceased had some obligation or at least the right to marry his widow and beget him an heir—which, in fact, happens ultimately in Ruth's case. Did Naomi fail to mention it because she knew of no other kinsmen in Judah? Such is unlikely despite her reaction in 2:20. Probably she ignored the possibility because kinsmen other than brothers were not as strictly bound to fulfill the levirate and Naomi had been out of touch with the clan for many years. She refused to subject Orpah and Ruth to so uncertain a future when they could take advantage of the better prospects to be had in Moab. Note that she places the welfare of her sons' wives before that of her sons. A man's only hope of immortality in the OT lay in sons and grandsons to carry on his name (Gn 48:15–16; 1 Sm 20:14–16; Ps 72:17); somehow he lived on in them. If a man had no natural son, his continuity must be insured by obtaining a fictitious one through adoption, *errebu* marriage, the levirate, etc. (see Burrows, *BASOR* 77, 3–5; *JAOS* 57 [1937] 259–76). In sending Ruth and Orpah after new husbands at home, Naomi removes whatever chance her menfolk had of survival after death. But this point is the very one the author wishes to make. The line leading to David through Elimelech has come to a dead stop and everything seems to militate against its continuing. Similar crises arose in the past and were wonderfully resolved (Gn 19:30–38; 22:1–19; 38:1–30). The anxious question is: Will Providence intervene again and in what way? The author may be especially mindful of Gn 38 here—an account that offers such a striking blend of contrast and correspondence to Ru (see 4:12). In both accounts, men die without natural heirs. In Gn 38, Judah, the father-in-law, has a young, not yet marriageable son, who might one day serve as Tamar's levir. Judah tells Tamar to go home and wait for the boy to grow up. In Ru, Naomi, the mother-in-law, has no such son, but even if she had, she can see no reason why Ruth and Orpah should waste years waiting for them to mature. She tells them to go home and remarry, fashion new lives for themselves. In Gn 38, Judah considers Tamar an ill-fated woman and has no intention of letting his boy wed her; he really sends her home to get rid of her. In Ru, Naomi considers herself ill-fated and sends the widows home to remove them from possible contagion. The author may wish his audience to compare Naomi's thoughtful openness with Judah's callous deceit and be duly impressed.

11 **14.** *Orpah kissed her mother-in-law good-by:* Naomi's words make sense to Orpah. Despite her attachment to the old woman, she decides to return home. Orpah is not condemned here. By human standards her conduct is correct; she offers a praiseworthy example of common sense. But as such, she serves even more effectively to set off Ruth's greater character. For Ruth steps beyond common sense (cf. Lot and Abraham in Gn 13; Esau and Jacob in Gn 25:27–34). She ventures beyond human horizons, a human estimation of what is correct or safe. She manifests the spirit of Abraham who made a similar leap beyond the frontier of perceptible, tangible security and met not disaster, but prosperity and new vitality (Gn 12). Like Abraham, Ruth goes counter to the sterile Adam tendency—self-interest, retreat into one's self—and just as Abraham's courageous faith turned the tragic, plummeting course of human history upward (Gn 1–12), so Ruth's unselfish commitment to Naomi breaks the unmitigated gloom of the tale thus far and introduces a faint glimmer of hope. The audience knows that such selfless, generous persons can be vehicles of immeasurable divine good. **15.** *gone back to her...god:* The Moabites worshiped Chemosh, a fertility god with martial overtones (Nm 21:29; Jgs 11:24; 1 Kgs 11:7,33). His prominence in Moab is evidenced by his frequent mention in the chief Moabite inscription extant, a stele put up by King Mesha (870–840 BC) and discovered at Dhiban in 1868 (see Van Zyl, *op. cit.*, 193–202). *go back:* Note the progression. Naomi urges Orpah and Ruth to depart three times. Both resist her first attempt—v. 8. Orpah yields to her more intense second urging—vv. 11–14. Ruth, however, resists even this third entreaty. This device is not uncommon in biblical literature: see Gn 18:22–33; 1 Sm 3:1–19 and, in closer parallel, the temptation and Gethsemane scenes in the Gospels, Mt 4:1–11; 26:36–46. **16.** Until now only Naomi's voice has been heard. Here Ruth finally speaks out. The author helps solemnize the moment by having her speak in poetic style. *your people...my people:* Her commitment is total. She willingly leaves her familiar homeland, surrenders the rights she has there, and makes Naomi's land and people her own. *your god...my god:* Ruth delivers herself entirely into the hands of the God of Israel. **17.** *wherever you die I will die:* She will not desert Naomi even in death. She plans to share her mother-in-law's grave and thus insure their proximity even in Sheol. Note Jacob's insistence that he be buried with his fathers (Gn 47:30; 49:29). The ancients believed that family ties could somehow be maintained beyond the grave. Ruth manifests the vehemence of her determination to remain with Naomi by calling down a curse upon herself should she depart. *may the Lord:* She has just confessed Yahweh to be her God; she now summons him as witness. The efficacy of a curse was seriously appreciated; imprecations were not lightly made. Naomi is therefore completely disarmed and recoils from any further insistence. Imprecations were not lightly narrated either; Ruth probably specified something dire but the author timidly leaves the matter vague (see this tendency in 1 Sm 14:44; 2 Sm 3:9; 1 Kgs 2:23). Ruth's over-all response constitutes a vow. To appreciate the binding nature of a vow at her period in history, see Jgs 11:35. Although Ruth is of alien birth, the Israelite audience cannot help but welcome her into the fold. Her career parallels so clearly that of its patriarch Abraham, who, with a barren woman at his side, left his home in Haran to follow Yahweh in Canaan. There his faith was rewarded—he fathered a nation. Ruth's faith will be no less fruitful. She will give that nation its line of kings.

12 **19.** *can this be Naomi?:* After this brief revelation of Ruth's radiant character, the story continues its somber course. The women play upon the root meaning of Naomi's name—"sweetness" or "pleasure." To appreciate the effect, consider some Eng examples: Can this sad woman be Joyce or can this vanquished lady be Victoria? **20.** Mara means "bitter." In the East, names were meant to express something of the essence or character of the thing or person. Thus a change of name might be in order should one's state, character, or destiny change (Gn 17:6, 16; 41:45; 2 Kgs 23:34; 24:17; Mt 16:18). Naomi wearily retorts that the bitter circumstances in which she finds herself indeed suggest a change of name in her case. *for the Almighty:* The divine name *šadday* (almighty) sounds very much like *šōd*, "destruction" or "ruin." Isaiah (13:6) and Joel (1:15) appreciate the likeness and play upon it; they speak of judgment day as *šōd miššadday*. **21.** *destitute:* Naomi refers to her material losses but especially to the loss of her menfolk. She now has nothing and no one. Apparently she does not think Ruth much of an asset. Indeed, the shy Moabite may prove simply an additional burden. Note by this time that Naomi is no paragon of faith. She prefers to stay well within the logic of a situation and brood. *the Lord has pronounced against me:* The ancients believed that suffering was God's just sentence upon one's wrongdoing. Naomi feels that God has not only punished her but publicized her sinfulness. **22.** *the barley harvest:* It took place in April and May.

13 **(III) The Encounter with Elimelech's Kinsman (2:1–23).** Naomi and Ruth are in low spirits, but now seemingly fortuitous yet actually providential events intimate their possible deliverance. *Boaz:* There are various opinions on the etymology of Boaz. It derives either from *bô ʿōz*, "in him is strength," or from *baʿal ʿōz*, "Yahweh is strong." The latter is J. A. Montgomery's interpretation of the name *bōʿaz* inscribed upon one of the pillars of Solomon's Temple, a formula found in Ugaritic literature (see "Kings," ICC 170–71; Glanzman, *op. cit.*, 206) or the name may have some affinity to the Arabic *baǵzun*, meaning swiftness (Vincent, *op. cit.*, 153). *a prominent kinsman:* The Hebrew reads *gibbôr ḥayil*, lit., "a strong man of valor." But the warrior ring must not be pressed. Possibly *gibbôr ḥayil* had become a technical term for a citizen fit for military service and wealthy enough to equip and provision himself when summoned. The emphasis here would be upon wealth and independence rather than actual military prowess (Rudolph, *op. cit.*, 48). **2.** *let me go:* Significantly it is Ruth who suggests the first step that will lead to deliverance. *glean the ears of grain:* Custom required that harvesters leave something in their wake for the needy, specifically the alien, orphan, and widow (Dt 24:19–22; Lv 19:9–10; 23:22). *her fortune happened upon the section belonging to Boaz:* (*Wayyiqer miqrehā.*) The author and his audience do not really attribute it to chance but to providence (see 2:19–20). **4.** *the Lord be with you:* Although the author may intend this greeting to reveal something of Boaz' piety, the point must not be overstressed. The greeting was quite normal. Certainly the harvesters' spontaneous response—the Lord bless you—is no gauge of their piety (see 2:9). **5.** *whose girl is this?:* In the Orient, every female belonged to some male as wife, daughter, or slave. Career women were unknown. **7.** *she asked leave:* The author brings out another facet of Ruth's character; she is not presumptuous. Even though she has a right to follow the harvesters—see Dt 24:19; etc.—she humbly asks permission. *with scarcely a moment's rest:* Moreover, she works hard. Verse by verse her excellence is brought out. **8.** This storyteller avoids giving lengthy portraits of his characters. He introduces them and lets their own direct speech reveal their characters. Boaz speaks like a gentleman, protective, respectful, generous. A sprinkling of archaic verbal forms contributes a note of gravity. *with my maidservants:* These were the women who followed the cutters and bound the sheaves. **10.** Ruth's humility is manifest again in her prostration before Boaz. She naturally wonders why she, an alien, should receive such preferential treatment. *you recognize me and I! I am unknown:* (*Lᵉhakkirēnî... nokriyyāh.*) Ruth indulges in a play on words. **11.** Boaz has somehow heard of Ruth's great act of fidelity, which climaxed ch. 1. The language here echoes Gn 12:1.

14 **12.** Boaz indicates Ruth's chief claim to admiration. She not only chose to stay with Naomi and dwell in Israel, she embraced Yahweh with a faith that might very well shame the natural children of Abraham. *may you receive a full reward from Yahweh:* Boaz uses a term (*maśkōret*) that means "wages" elsewhere in the Bible (see Gn 29:15; 31:7,41). There may be a direct allusion here to Gn 15:1: "Fear not Abram...I am your reward [*śᵉkārᵉkā*] exceeding great." Boaz does not realize that he will be Yahweh's reward to Ruth; indeed, he has already begun to function as such. *under whose wings:* A frequent biblical metaphor (see Dt 32:11; Pss 16:8; 56:1; 62:8; 90:4; Mt 23:37). Boaz lived long before the Temple of Solomon was built and furnished. He would, therefore, be incapable of alluding to it here. However, the author, who is, of course, responsible for the dialogue, was familiar with that structure and may have used the "wings" to depict Ruth's conversion in terms of a spiritual entrance into the Holy of Holies where Yahweh dwelt above the Ark, flanked by the great, winged cherubim (Ex 25:20; 1 Kgs 6:27). Rabbis of later times described proselytes as people who took refuge under the wings of the Shekinah. **14.** After an interval of work, Boaz and Ruth meet and again he treats her with unusual favor. She is permitted to sit among the men and share their rations. *sauce:* Bread moistened by this light vinegar proved very refreshing after long work under a hot sun. For reference to its restorative value, see Mk 15:23,36 and parallel passages. *roasted grain:* Puffed wheat, popcorn, etc., are modern examples of *qālî*; Boaz' helpers put barley through the same process. Easily prepared, it was a common food of the period (1 Sm 25:18; 2 Sm 17:28). **15–16.** In harvesting, the reapers came first, cutting barley stalks by the handful. They were followed by others who bound eight to ten of these handfuls into sheaves. Only after the sheaves were carted off were the poor permitted to pass over the field. But Boaz permits Ruth to glean among his harvesters and instructs them not to bind every handful but leave some loose for her. Ruth was thus able to gather a whole ephah of grain, i.e., about two-thirds of a bushel.

19. Naomi perceives immediately that someone has favored Ruth. Her remarks betray her excitement. Delight, female curiosity, an impulse to bless someone—all are expressed in one breath. The name of Boaz heightens Naomi's joy. She intensifies her blessing, going beyond Boaz to praise Yahweh, whom she now sees working positively in her behalf. Note the sky-rocket pattern of vv. 19–20. One bright burst follows another: the sight of the grain stimulates joy and a general blessing; the name Boaz provokes a further blessing, recognition of Yahweh, gratitude, and a vision of greater possibilities to come, for he is a kinsman with possible obligations to Naomi and the deceased Elimelech. **20.** Naomi now renews her faith in God's fidelity after having nearly despaired of it in 1:20. *to the living and the dead:* Public opinion had concluded that Elimelech and his sons were sinners. Their death in Moab and the impoverished state of their widows could only be understood as divine punishment for some wrongdoing (1:21). But Naomi now envisions the possibility of a change in her fortunes and with it public reappraisal of God's attitude toward her family, and renewed respect for deceased Elimelech's name. *one of our next of kin:* (*Gô'ēl.*) Naomi hopes for even more. She sees God's active fidelity stretching beyond mere exoneration of Elimelech's name. She can demand of him fulfillment of certain *g*[e]*'ullâ* obligations: namely, protection of a small piece of land belonging to Elimelech that the impoverished Naomi now held in futile trust (4:1; and see De Vaux, *AI* 54; Nm 27:1–8; 36:1–9; 2 Kgs 8:3–6), and also marriage to Ruth, that an heir might be raised to Elimelech and Mahlon, insuring their "immortality," the continuity of their line. **23.** Ruth continues working among Boaz' servants throughout the barley and wheat harvest, i.e., into June. But Naomi harvests nothing of her great expectations, for the scene ends with Ruth back home. Naomi and the audience now wonder whether her hopes were premature.

15 (IV) The Widow's Demand and the Kinsman's Dilemma (3:1–18). Naomi's faith remains far from perfect. Like Sarah in Gn 16, she becomes impatient and decides to assist providence. **2.** *this evening he will be winnowing:* Farmers separated the barley from its chaff by tossing it into the wind. The heavier grain would fall to the stone floor while the chaff was blown away. Because suitable winds crossed the Judean highland out of the west from about 2 P.M. until sunset, threshing started late in the day and continued until nightfall. The owners and workers spent the night at the threshing floor to prevent theft. **3.** *bathe... yourself; ...go down:* See Ez 16:9. Naomi tells Ruth to utilize all that will enhance her attractiveness and then delay her entrance until Boaz has reached a most content, pliable frame of mind. **4.** *uncover a place at his feet:* Some authors view this whole section as a euphemistic account of downright seduction (cf. Robertson, *op. cit.*; and also H. G. May, *JRAS* [1939] 75–78). Such intentions would, however, clash violently with the over-all character manifested by the women throughout the book (see 2:8–9,22). Although her plan does leave itself open to misunderstanding (3:14), all Naomi asks is that Ruth undertake a symbolic action, go through an impressive, mimed "invitation" to marriage, and nothing more (see e.g., Haller, *op. cit.*, 13–14).

9. *who are you?:* Boaz is naturally startled by this perfumed presence lying near him. Ruth identifies herself and informs him of his obligation to marry her, the childless widow of a deceased kinsman. *the corner of your cloak:* A man's clothing is a very personal item; therefore, it frequently served to symbolize one's self (cf. 2 Kgs 2:13–14; 9:13). Here the act signifies engagement to marry (see Ez 16:8; Dt 23:1). *you are my next of kin:* Ruth indicates the reason why Boaz must marry her. Custom and his responsibility to the clan as nearest kinsman to Elimelech and Mahlon demand that he raise up issue to their line. **10.** *more loyal now than before:* Far from betraying her deceased husband's memory, Ruth acts here calmly and deliberately out of devotion to him. If Ruth had been merely sensually inclined, she might have consorted easily with younger men. In seeking out Boaz, she shows that her primary interest in this whole affair is the "immortality" of her husband and father-in-law. Her fidelity shone forth admirably when she refused to leave Naomi; it now takes on new radiance. **12.** The willingness of Boaz raises hope of an immediate happy conclusion to the story. But someone else—an anonymous and obviously not too attractive kinsman stands closer to Ruth and Naomi than Boaz. The latter cannot infringe upon that man's priority. **13.** Boaz refuses to let Ruth wander home in the dark. He again shows his great concern for her integrity (2:9). The reader can therefore assume that he took no advantage of the woman.

16 (V) The Dilemma's Solution (4:1–12). **1.** Boaz arranges a definitive hearing on the matter at the town gate where all traffic converged and he could soon expect to find the relative mentioned in 3:12. The town gate was the customary place for commerce, public transactions, etc. (see Gn 23:18; Dt 22:15; Am 5:10, 12,15). *by name:* The Hebrew means "so-and-so," "what's-your-name," as though the narrator meant to keep him obscure, less of a distraction to the audience. Boaz alone must hold the spotlight in this scene. **3.** The audience is meant to experience some anxiety at this point. Boaz must delicately maneuver the kinsman ("goel") into yielding his prior rights over Ruth. But the "goel," so teasingly developed into a man of mystery by the narrator, commands the situation. Which way will he decide? Boaz keeps silent about Ruth. He focuses the attention on the piece of land. Possibly squatters were on the land, rendering it useless to Naomi (see 2 Kgs 8:1–6) for a parallel). **4.** *put in your claim for it:* The "goel," Elimelech's closest kinsman, had to buy the land from Naomi before she let it pass to some nonrelative (see Lv 25:23–25; Jer 32:8). Boaz offers to step up as next-in-line to this obligation if the first "goel" wishes to withdraw for any reason. However, the "goel" sees no problem here. Indeed, he perceives an opportunity to blend piety with profit. **5.** *you must also take Ruth:* Boaz cleverly disconcerts his kinsman before the elders. He offers him an opportunity to act solely out of piety, a chance to forego nobly all profit. Inasmuch as he wills to hold on to his rights and obligations, let him also raise up an heir to Elimelech's line. The man may have thought of this possibility earlier, but knowing how old Naomi must be, he considered the necessity of honoring this obligation safely out of the question. Now he hears of Ruth, the still fruitful widow of Elimelech's son and heir. The line can and must go on. He was emphatic about doing his duty when it was a question of land redemption. Will he be as emphatic about this obligation? **6.** *I cannot:* The man is perplexed. If he redeems Elimelech's property and simultaneously raises up an heir to Elimelech and Mahlon who must eventually be given that property as his proper inheritance (Dt 25:6–7), he will emerge with nothing to show for his expenditure but an additional wife, Ruth, and the possibility of more mouths to feed, more heirs of his own, because her subsequent children will be his responsibility. He envisions the disintegration of his present estate. The mystery man's true nature is unveiled. He is another Orpah, not so unselfish that he would risk his own interests when met with a challenge of generosity. His smallness only serves to set off the bigness of Boaz, as Orpah did for Ruth. *put in a claim yourself:* The man yields his *g^e^ullāh* priority to Boaz. **8.** *drew off his sandal:* Only the owner of a piece of property might rightfully place his foot upon it. This fact probably gave rise to the use of a shoe or sandal as a general symbol of one's power over something, one's right of possession (see Pss 59:10; 107:10). In removing his sandal and handing it to Boaz (LXX adds *kai edōken autō*), the "goel" publicly manifests his renunciation of prior rights to Naomi's land and to Ruth. This symbolic act seems to have been commonplace. Shoes serve as token payment in certain transactions described in the Nuzi tablets (see E. R. Lacheman, *JBL* 56 [1937] 53–56; E. A. Speiser, *BASOR* 77 [1940] 15–18). The author and his audience would have understood the meaning of this action; the explanation given in v. 7 was probably inserted by a postexilic hand to satisfy the curiosity of his generation (cf. 1 Sm 9:9; Wolfenson, *op. cit.*, 294; Glanzman, *op. cit.*, 204; Joüon, *op. cit.*, 14). **9–12.** By his adroit maneuvering, Boaz has now obtained clear and first claim to the land and to Ruth. He heartily declares his willingness to do his duty by them. The elders witness his declaration and, admiring his shrewdness and generosity, wish him well. The elders liken Ruth to Rachel and Leah, the nation's matriarchs, and to Tamar, who perpetuated Judah's threatened line. In so doing, they suggest that this union of Ruth and Boaz may figure as importantly in God's plan of history as those alluded to.

17 **(VI) The Revival of Elimelech's Line (4:13–17).** This story, which began somberly with three deaths, ends brightly with as many births. Elimelech's line has revived contrary to all human expectation. Generosity and faith have borne fruit. **14–15.** *the women said to Naomi:* This scene counterbalances the closing scene of tragic ch. 1. There (1:19), the women expressed dismay over Naomi's situation; now they congratulate her. There (1:20), Naomi, left without husband or sons, bemoaned her absolute want; now the women proclaim her fortunate to have had Ruth, a woman worth more than seven sons. *blessed is the Lord who has not failed to provide you with an heir. May his name be proclaimed in Israel:* The women seem to wish the newborn child fame, but Joüon (*op. cit.*, 92–93) and Vincent (*op. cit.*, 163) would change *lāk* to *lammēt*, rendering "The Lord has not failed to provide the deceased [i.e., Elimelech] with an heir." "His name" would then refer to Elimelech, whose name has been rescued from oblivion. **16.** *Naomi took the child to her bosom:* There is no need to see in this action some form of adoption (cf. Nm 11:12). She merely held the child affectionately and regularly pacified him (L. Köhler, *ZAW* [1909] 312–14). **17.** *The neighbor women called* [*or*] *gave him his name:* Thus MT. But it is unlikely that they would do so. Perhaps "his name" should be dropped and the verse translated, "The neighbor women called out, 'A grandson has been born to Naomi.' They called him Obed." *the father of Jesse, the father of David:* The story originally ended here. Succinctly but eloquently the author reveals the vivifying repercussions of a faith like Ruth's. Her total commitment to Yahweh revived the dead stem of Elimelech, which eventually blossomed forth with David and his elect dynasty.

(VII) Appendix (4:18–22). This genealogy is obviously a later addition, possibly drawn from 1 Chr 2:5–15. The story made it clear that Obed was the legal heir of Elimelech and Mahlon, their legal son, a new link in their line of descent. Whoever added this genealogy has ignored that and has connected David, Jesse, and Obed to Boaz' family tree to emphasize more David's connection to that elect, divinely sustained line of Perez, Judah, and Jacob.

LAMENTATIONS

BIBLIOGRAPHY

18 Albrektson, A. B., *Studies in the Text and Theology of Lamentations* (Lund, 1963). Gelin, A., *Les Lamentations* (BJ; Paris, 1951). Gottwald, N. K., *Studies in the Book of Lamentations* (London, 1954). Kraus, H.-J., *Klagelieder* (BKAT; Neukirchen, 1956). Meek, T. J., "The Book of Lamentations" (*IB*; N.Y., 1956). Nötscher, F., *Die Klagelieder* (Echter-B; Würzburg, 1947). Rudolph, W., *Die Klagelieder* (KAT; Gütersloh, 1962). Weiser, A., *Klagelieder* (ADT; Göttingen, 1958). Wiesmann, H., *Die Klagelieder* (Frankfurt, 1954).

INTRODUCTION

19 **(I) Title.** Hebr manuscripts entitle this work *'êkāh*, a mournful expletive, the usual initial word of a Hebr dirge (see 1:1; 2:1; 4:1). The term *qînôt*, a more definitive title meaning "dirges" or "lamentations," is found in the Talmud and rabbinical writings and in 2 Chr 35:25 (LXX *thrēnoi*). The Vg and modern vernacular translations have kept to this designation.

20 **(II) Author, Date, Place.** In 2 Chr 35:25, reference is made to the preservation of dirges composed by Jeremiah on the death of King Josiah in 609. It is not strange that later generations saw in this passage a reference to the canonical Book of Lamentations and thus concluded that Jeremiah was its author. It is highly questionable, however, whether 2 Chr 35:25 has any relation to canonical Lam, for nothing in Lam refers to Josiah's death. Lam dwells entirely on disasters occurring from 597 on. The true author manifests some relationship in style and spirit to Jeremiah; he was certainly his contemporary. W. Rudolph thinks he was a political or military figure who perhaps participated in the flight of Zedekiah (see 4:19).

The five chapters seem to be the work of one man living in one critical period and not a collection of several poets historically distant from each other. It is true that ch. 1 stands somewhat alone, but closer scrutiny shows its closer relationship to other parts of the book: e.g., cf. 1:4a and 2:6b,8c; 1:4c and 2:10c; 1:7d and 2:17c; 1:1a and 3:28; 1:1b and 5:3; 1:7a and 3:19; 1:15a and 4:2b. Some authorities would separate ch. 3 from the rest on the basis of stricter alphabetical style and a more personal expression than the socially oriented dirges of chs. 1–2, but distinction here seems unnecessary. The over-all style, vocabulary, and content of all the chapters support unity of authorship. Variations in stress are to be noted, but they seem to result mostly from the differing time and circumstance of each lamentation. In ch. 1, the author has not yet experienced the disaster of 587; he knows only the recent and preliminary crisis of 597. In chs. 2 and 4, the experience of the 587–586 debacle intensifies his grief and poetry. Chapters 3 and 5 reflect the chaos, exhaustion, and political oppression that followed upon the fall of the city and the second deportation.

The location seems to be Judean Palestine.

21 **(III) Style.** The poems collected here are written in the Hebr dirge or *qînâ* meter, a form consisting of a long line of three measures followed by a short, grief-aborted line of two measures (see K. Budde, *ZAW* 2 [1882] 1–52; Gottwald, *op. cit.*, 23–46). But the *qînāh* measure is flexible enough to allow pairs of 2 and 2, 2 and 3, and 3 and 3 measures; the fifth poem favors the 3 and 3 pattern (→ Hebr Poetry, 13:13–14).

The poet indulges in further formality throughout the first four dirges by lining up his stanzas in alphabetical sequence—i.e., by commencing each stanza with the letters of the alphabet in their proper sequence. Thus, 1:1 begins with a word whose initial letter is *aleph*, 1:2 with a word whose initial letter is *beth*, and so on through the poem, until the last letter, *taw*, initiates the last verse. Each poem contains exactly 22 stanzas. Chapter 3 shows even more concentrated application of the alphabetical, or acrostic, form. There, the poet not only commences each stanza with *aleph*, *beth*, *ghimel*, etc., but within the *aleph* stanza all three lines are faithful to an initial *aleph*; within the *beth* stanza all three lines are faithful to an initial *beth;* etc. Alphabetical poems are found elsewhere in the OT (Na 1:2–8; Pss 9–10; 25; 34; 37; 111–12; 119; 145; Prv 31:10–31). For an example in nonbiblical Near Eastern literature, see *ANET* 438ff. But with Ps 119, Lam is outstanding in this category.

The wedding of genuine grief to extreme formality may seem impossible at first, but the effort is successfully carried through without damage to emotion or realism. Several reasons are possible as to why the author submitted to such taxing formality. If the poems were to be used cultically, the alphabetical form could serve a mnemonic purpose. But beyond that, Gottwald suggests that the acrostic device supplied a note of wholeness to a theme; when a poet has said everything from *aleph* to *taw* (from A to Z), he has said everything that can be said on a topic.

Tragic reversal, a motif common to lamentations in almost any culture, occurs frequently within this book. Nostalgic memories of past joy and glory provide a context and help underscore the jolt of present death and tragedy; for example, see 1:1: "How lonely she is now, the once crowded city."

22 **(IV) Background and Purpose.** Lam contains much historical data on the tragic period 609–586. It supplements the material of 2 Kgs 22–25, Jer, and Ez. Even a cursory reading introduces the reader into some experience of siege, famine, sudden death, disgrace, and a sense of political and religious vacuum. As poetry, it carries even more impact than a simple narrative of Jerusalem's fall. But Lam has heavy theological import as well. It is, like Jb, a poetic reflection on enigmatic disaster. Events from 609 on brought about a severe crisis of faith in Judah. The reform effort of Josiah, reflected in deuteronomic literature, seemed to lay the foundation for a happy, expanding future. Judah seemed to have deserved a fate similar to that of the northern kingdom for all its syncretism and general laxity, but it had survived long Assyrian ascendancy, and now firm religious reformation was undertaken to ensure the future. The Temple was given central attention; local sanctuaries and syncretism were abolished; the Mosaic Law was re-emphasized and applied to the monarchical situation; reform writing flourished. If Yahweh justly punished infidelity, he also justly rewarded fidelity, and the reform movement of Josiah was an extraordinary expression of fidelity that would hopefully bring favor and perpetuation of the dynasty and nation, a revival of the age of David and Solomon.

But hopes based upon this reform were disappointed at Megiddo where Judah lost its king and fell subject to Egypt. The small nation was tossed about by conflicting world powers. A vain attempt to overthrow Neo-Babylonian domination resulted in 597 in the deportation of King Jehoiachin and important elements of the population. After ten more years under Babylon, Jerusalem rebelled again unsuccessfully; the city was besieged and leveled, and new deportations followed. The Josian return to orthodoxy apparently added up to nothing and the nation began to wonder whether Yahweh himself was a cipher, or at least less potent than the powers that overran his people.

The author of Lam transcended this desperate conclusion. It is true, he sings dirges, but in reality there is no corpse. His is not the dirge an Assyrian might sing over the fall of Nineveh and its gods—an absolutely hopeless lamentation. This Judean poet bewails his dead compatriots, the national want, his disgraced king, and the city's fallen structures. But Jerusalem's God still lives, a just and merciful God who was not simply another Jewish victim of superior Babylonian power but the real agent of Jerusalem's fall, the manipulator of the very forces that struck his people. The debacle was not a consequence of his unconcern or impotence but a righteous act of Yahweh, punishing the shallow fidelity and religious myopia of the nation. These dirges are no irrational outpouring of grief but firm acts of faith in Yahweh's continuing power, mercy, and justice. They manifest confidence in Israel's election, despite appearances.

The poet emphasizes Yahweh's part in Jerusalem's destruction. He does not want his audience to misunderstand the true nature of the disaster. See 1:13–15; 2:1–8; 2:22; 3:1–18; 3:43–45, where Yahweh appears among the enemy troops and shares their ferocity.

If Jerusalem's fall is evidence of a mute Yahweh, then Jerusalem can only despair. But if Jerusalem's fall is evidence of Yahweh's wrath, then it is evidence too of his serious, personal interest in Jerusalem's correction and well-being. Wrath here is a metaphor of divine grace;

but like all moments of passion, it will give way to a more benign, constructive grace once Judah's conversion has been effected.

23 **(V) Outline.** The Book of Lamentations may be outlined as follows:

(I) A Lamentation Over the Events of 597 (1:1–22)
  (A) Jerusalem's Disgrace (1:1–11)
  (B) Jerusalem's Appeal (1:12–22)
(II) A Lamentation Over the Events of 587–586 (2:1–22)
  (A) Yahweh, Agent of Disaster (2:1–17)
  (B) Yahweh, the Only Savior (2:18–22)
(III) The Poet's Personal Knowledge of Suffering (3:1–66)
  (A) The Poet's Bitter Experience (3:1–21)
  (B) The Poet's Hope (3:22–42)
  (C) The Poet's Prayer for Himself and the Nation (3:43–66)
(IV) A Second Lamentation Over 587–586 (4:1–22)
  (A) Jerusalem's Inhabitants (4:1–11)
  (B) Jerusalem's Priests and Prophets (4:12–16)
  (C) Jerusalem's King (4:17–20)
  (D) Judah and Edom (4:21–22)
(V) The Aftermath (5:1–22)
  (A) The Plight of Judah's Survivors (5:1–18)
  (B) A Prayer for Restoration (5:19–22)

COMMENTARY

24 **(I) A Lamentation over the Events of 597 (1:1–22).** This dirge was composed soon after the Babylonian defeat of Judah in 597. The poet makes no reference to the worst disaster of 587 when city and Temple were destroyed. The Temple has been pillaged but not leveled (see v. 10b).

(A) Jerusalem's Disgrace (1:1–11). The poet speaks of Zion in the third person. **1.** *widowed is she:* Sharp contrast is drawn between Jerusalem's once populous condition and its present emptiness. Beside the usual casualities of war, King Jehoiachin and several thousand leading citizens had been deported to Babylon by Nebuchadnezzar. Bereft of her chief son and so many other offspring, deserted by Yahweh, Jerusalem appears a destitute, lonely widow. *the princess among the provinces:* Once the hub of the Judean countryside, the focal point of her own tributaries, Jerusalem is now one of the many humbled tributaries within a much wider Babylonian Empire. **2.** *her friends have all betrayed her:* Jerusalem noticed many a familiar face within the ranks of the Babylonian invader. Small Palestinian nations that shared Judah's history and even dwelt in periodic alliance with her supported invincible Babylon when affairs became critical (e.g., see Jer 35:11; Ez 19:8). **3.** *Judah has fled into exile from oppression:* Invasion was nothing new for Judah, although exile added an unusual note to the experience. Judah's history had been one of oppression and international pressure; out of that context she now steps into exile. **4.** *the roads to Zion mourn:* Although the Temple remained intact and the priesthood free, recent events had suspended cultic life. Pilgrimages had ceased; a general silence pervaded the once active Temple area and a city that profited much from the liturgical cycle. Jerusalem resembles a ghost town. See Pss 118, 122 for presentations of happier scenes for which the poet now yearns. *her virgins sigh:* Could refer to the young women who participated formally in cultic festivities (see Ps 68:26; Jer 31:4,13; Jgs 21:19ff.). Once they sang and played their percussion instruments; now they are in no mood for music. **5.** *the Lord has punished her:* The main theological point of the poet is touched upon here. Both victor and vanquished may have thought that Judean defeat revealed the impotence of Judah's God, but the author sees none other than Yahweh behind the victor. Judah's defeat underscores the power of Yahweh, who is a universal God—not a deity confined by nationality, but one that transcends the nations and actually directs international events. He does not rise and fall with Judah. Rather, Judah rises or falls depending on her ethical and theological response to Yahweh. **6.** *all her glory:* A reference to Jerusalem's nobility. The best of the population had been deported to weaken local resistance. **7.** *Jerusalem is mindful of the days:* Thus in the CCD version. "In the days" is preferable because the catastrophe is still current. The author has kept to three-line verses throughout the dirge; one of the four lines here may therefore be a gloss. The CCD eliminates the second Hebr line, "all her pleasant things that she had from days of old." Rudolph thinks the second line is original and the third line, "when her people fell...her," is a gloss explaining the "homelessness" of the initial line. **8.** *Jerusalem has sinned:* The poet emphasizes the true cause of Jerusalem's fall and disgrace. An innocent victim might bear tragedy with some pride, but Jerusalem's tragedy is aggravated by guilt and shame. **9.** *her filth is on her skirt:* The poet describes Jerusalem as a menstruating woman. Menstruation rendered a woman ritually impure (see Lv 15:19ff.) and a source of contagion. *look, O Lord, upon her misery:* Repentance can reverse events. The author, after his quick recognition of national guilt, calls for a change of attitude on God's part. The excesses of Jerusalem's enemies should now be the targets of his wrath. **10.** The poet calls Yahweh's attention to enemy sacrilege (see Dt 23:3ff.). **11.** If enemy excesses are not enough to attract Yahweh's wrath from Jerusalem, certainly his people's extreme hunger will soften him, turn him to mercy.

25 **(B) Jerusalem's Appeal (1:12–22).** The poet yields to the city; Jerusalem itself speaks directly to its God. **12.** *the Lord afflicted me:* The direct causality of God is again emphasized. **13–15.** The city's fall in no way demonstrates Yahweh's inferiority before alien gods. The current catastrophe is a matter between Yahweh and his rebellious people (see Zech 1:7ff.; Is 13:1ff.; Jl 4:13ff., for similar descriptions of Yahweh's agency in war). **17.** *Zion stretched out her hands:* The poet momentarily moves into the third person as in vv. 1–11. **18.** Jerusalem speaks in the first person again with renewed emphasis upon the true cause of the war—the sins of Judah and the corresponding justice of Yahweh. Judah had continual warning that Yahweh was omnipotent and moral; Dt 28:15ff. was clear enough and the prophets developed this point. Neither divine caprice nor divine impotence lay behind the city's plight, rather divine justice and power. Yet this fact is cause for hope, for if divine caprice or impotence were indeed factors in the city's fall, Jerusalem might rightly despair; but divine justice and power guarantee restoration as well as destruction, depending on Judah's own conduct. **19.** *I cried out to my lovers:* May refer to Jerusalem's king and nobility or to neighboring allies. In any case, her "lovers" proved unsound. **20–22.** The city turns from those who pass her by to Yahweh, who can really do something for her. These verses constitute a confession of guilt and an appeal for help based on enemy excesses.

If Yahweh is concerned about sin, let him turn his attention from Judah to her arrogant, plundering enemies.

26 **(II) A Lamentation Over the Events of 587–586 (2:1–22).** The tragedy of 597, which the preceding chapter laments, was not sufficient to quell Judean nationalism. Another declaration of independence followed ten years later, when this time the empire crushed Judah, destroyed its Temple, and deported more citizens. Judah lost all autonomy and became a Babylonian province. Experience of this more severe trial of faith is evident here, but again the poet stresses Yahweh's role. The fall is a consequence of Jerusalem's infidelity to an omnipotent God who is not indifferent to the laxity of his people and who shows his vital interest in anger, an anger incarnate in the Babylonian armies that have struck the city.

(A) Yahweh, Agent of Disaster (2:1–17). **1.** *how the Lord...has detested daughter Zion:* Yahweh is the subject in vv. 1–8 and 9,17,20–22; thus, his causality is stressed. *the glory of Israel:* The holy city, the Temple and Ark, all the trappings of divine election—along with that election—were Israel's glory. Now apparently all of it has been taken away. Israel seems no longer divinely chosen but an outcast. *his footstool:* A reference to the Ark of the Covenant (see Pss 132:7; 99:5). **2.** *the fortresses of daughter Judah:* The Babylonians destroyed fortress towns in the Judean provinces—e.g., Lachish and Azekah—while besieging Jerusalem (see Jer 34:7). *her king and her princes:* Jehoiachin had been deported in 598. His uncle Zedekiah reigned in his stead in Judah until this second war. Captured by the Babylonians, he saw his sons executed before he himself was blinded and exiled to Babylon. In effect, the Davidic dynasty, to which Yahweh had promised perpetuity (2 Sm 7), was submerged. **3.** *he broke off... the horn:* A bull's horns were symbols of power, and Israel has been shorn of its power (see Ps 75:11; Jer 48:25).

6–7. With the destruction of the Temple, cultic life practically ceased. **8–9.** After the Temple's destruction, the poet dwells upon the plight of the city itself. Yahweh directs the destruction of the city's fortifications (see 2 Kgs 25:10). **10–12.** Aspects of the siege are drawn in detail, especially the horrors of famine. **13.** *to what can I liken you:* Jerusalem's experience is incomparable; it has something of the dimension of the sea. **14.** *false and specious visions:* Jerusalem can turn to no one for help. Her official prophets, whose word was supposed to be efficacious, drew pictures of victory, prosperity, and national restoration. They emphasized Judah's election as guarantee of victory and glossed over the important consequences of election—i.e., responsibility, fidelity to Yahweh's total word. (See Jer 23:9ff.; Ez 13:1ff., for background.) **17.** *the Lord has done as he decreed:* Again, Yahweh's causality is stressed.

(B) Yahweh, the Only Savior (2:18–22). The poet now urges the people to approach Yahweh; he has engineered the siege and defeat of Jerusalem, but he is also involved in irrevocable covenant with Israel. **18–19.** *let your tears flow like a torrent...:* Serious disaster follows upon serious guilt. Therefore, serious, genuine manifestations of repentance are necessary. The situation requires radical conversion and vehement exhibition of it. **20–22.** The poet breaks into direct address, and, as a corporate person, prays for the whole nation. He points to some of the most horrible aspects of the siege—the cannibalism and indiscriminate slaughter (see Lam 4:10; 2 Kgs 6:28ff.; Ez 5:10). Behind Yahweh's wrath lies a basic love and concern that may be stimulated to pity by scenes like these.

27 **(III) The Poet's Personal Knowledge of Suffering (3:1–66).** The author of this dirge is no aloof spectator or recorder of Jerusalem's agony. He has experienced personal affliction throughout the communal crisis. Some think the suffering prophet Jeremiah composed this piece (v. 14 repeats Jer 20:7), but the Jeremian cast of the poem was probably applied deliberately by the same poet who authored the preceding lamentations. This work is an acrostic tour de force (→ 21 above), but because of its formal character, it sacrifices something of sense unity.

(A) The Poet's Bitter Experience (3:1–21). **1.** *the rod of his anger:* The pronominal suffix of *'ebrātô* links this poem directly to ch. 2. There the poet saw Yahweh as agent of Jerusalem's fall. He sees that same punitive hand of Yahweh reaching out to him individually. **4–18.** Hunger, poverty, fatigue, imprisonment, mockery, bitter humiliation, mental anguish—the poet utters his litany of pain. **21.** *but I will call this to mind as my reason to have hope:* His despair was not great enough to obscure certain theological bases for hope. Throughout this biographical confession, the author really sets himself up as an authentic model for the city; he has suffered, but he has reason to hope—reasons that the suffering city has every right to share.

28 **(B) The Poet's Hope (3:22–42).** **22.** *the favors of the Lord are not exhausted:* His suffering had been so great that he could only dwell on one attribute of God, his wrath. For the moment, it seemed his only attribute, his final nature, and in that context the poet almost despaired. So might the city. But the poet knows that God's wrath is not final, and it must be seen within the greater and truly final context of God's graciousness. **24.** *my portion is the Lord:* As an Israelite, he has confidence that Yahweh's eternal covenant with Israel applies to him individually (see Pss 16:5; 73:26; 142:6, for similar expression). **29.** *good is the Lord to one who waits for him:* The author begins to generalize (Ps 130:6). His God is the God of every Israelite and his confidence is something every responsible Israelite may experience. **29.** *there may yet be hope:* The crisis calls for a careful confidence that avoids presumption, that recognizes God's transcendence even in matters of grace (see Am 5:15; Zech 2:3; Jl 2:14, where hope is cautious—aware of God's absolute sovereignty). **34–36.** Evildoers do not go unnoticed by the Lord. **37–39.** Nothing happens without some divine involvement. Judah's oppression is not the result of divine unconcern but the just consequence of Yahweh's serious concern over Judah's sins. **40–41.** *let us...examine our ways:* Radical religious reform is the key to Jewish revival. **42.** *you have not forgiven us:* The problem calls for more than superficial confession and appeal.

29 **(C) The Poet's Prayer for Himself and the Nation (3:43–66).** **43–48.** Addressing himself directly to Yahweh, he acknowledges Yahweh's justified and efficacious wrath manifest in the slaughter, isolation, mockery, and grief experienced by his people. **52–54.** Moving from the communal scene, he depicts his own personal affliction. **55–66.** In his desperate situation, the poet called on Yahweh, and affairs apparently took a happier turn for him. Men who were determined to destroy him were exposed. Jeremian allusions accumulate here (cf. Jer 26:38). Rudolph would eliminate fut. and imper. vb. renderings in this section and make the whole a clear thanksgiving for favors already received. The poet's own experience of Yahweh's favorable intervention supplies foundation for hope of similar intervention on the community level.

30 **(IV) A Second Lamentation Over 587–586 (4:1–22).** This dirge is similar to ch. 2; the details of the siege and the plight of the citizens are fresh in the poet's memory, perhaps in some instances still matters of daily witness (cf. 4:17 with Jer 37:5ff.; 4:19–20 with 2 Kgs 25:4–6 and Jer 39:4–5). But the poet makes little theological capital out of the disaster in this poem. Seemingly exhausted by what he has seen, he simply describes the tragedy, reviewing its effect upon various types of citizens. Whereas Yahweh's role and the religious logic of the fall were stressed in ch. 2, here the author only rises occasionally to that theme (see 4:11,13,16,22). What he has seen is too depressing to transcend right now. Note the comparative brevity of this dirge; each stanza contains two lines instead of the three found in the previous chapters.

31 **(A) Jerusalem's Inhabitants (4:1–11).** **1.** *how tarnished is the gold; how the sacred stones lie strewn:* These metaphors are for the sons of Zion (v. 2). Once the proud offspring of an elect people, they are now disgraced, their value ignored by a victorious enemy. **3.** *as cruel as the ostrich:* By bringing down upon herself the forces of Babylon, Jerusalem denied her children a future. Most birds lay their eggs in high, relatively safe nests; the ostrich lays them in the sand where they are more easily accessible to preying animals. Primitive zoology saw in this act proof of the stupidity of this awkward bird and of its unnatural cruelty toward its young (see Jb 39:13–17). **6.** The poet judges the seriousness of sin by the severity of its punishment. Jerusalem's agony seems unending compared to the sudden destruction of Sodom (see Gn 19:23–29; Ez 16:48; Jer 23:14). **7–8.** *brighter than snow...blacker than soot:* A good example of tragic reversal.

32 **(B) Jerusalem's Priests and Prophets (4:12–16).** **12.** Jerusalem's natural position was remarkably strong. The Israelites had to bypass it in the judges' period (Jgs 1:21). David finally captured it, and during the monarchy it enjoyed long security, withstanding even a siege by the powerful Assyrian war machine in 701. In Israelite circles, Jerusalem's invincibility was owing as much to Yahweh's presence as to the natural defense advantages of the city. And yet the city fell. The poet looks for its hidden weakness and uncovers it in Jerusalem's religious leadership. **13.** The prophets mentioned here were professional seers or ecstatics who delivered oracles in Yahweh's name for a fee. They were an approved part of the Israelite religious structure, although they fell into disrepute over the centuries of the monarchy. (See Jer:13ff.; 23; 26; Ez 22:25ff.) **14.** *they stagger...soiled with blood:* The verse describes their present tragic condition. Stunned, soiled, and unemployed, they wander through a city that their religious complacency and myopia helped to undermine. **15.** *away! unclean!:* See Nm 19:1ff., and Lv 21:1ff; contact with the dead rendered a person unclean, unfit for ritual contact with Yahweh. But now contact with corpses can hardly be avoided. The poet ironically describes Jewish citizens running from their corpse-defiled priests and prophets to preserve their own cleanliness.

33 **(C) Jerusalem's King (4:17–20).** This section seems to describe an incident of the siege: Zedekiah's futile effort to escape the city (see 2 Kgs 25:4–6; Jer 39:4–7; 52:7–9). **17.** *our eyes ever wasted away, looking in vain for aid:* Israel and Judah frequently became involved in foreign alliances that brought more disappointment than security. Authentic prophets regarded such ties as apostasy (Hos 7:8–12; 8:8–10; Is 30; Jer 2:18–37). This verse probably refers to that moment of hope when an Egyptian relief column under Hophra required Babylonian attention (Jer 37; 34:21–22). But the Babylonians soon chased the Egyptians and resumed siege operations. **20.** *our breath of life:* A royal title. Yahweh was the source of all life and blessing (Gn 2:7), but the King's proximity to God made him the primary mediator. The title is an Egyptian import (Rudolph, *op. cit.*, 254).

(D) Judah and Edom (4:21–22). On Edomite and Israelite rivalry, → Obadiah, 25. For bitter Jewish remembrance of Edom's part in Jerusalem's fall, see Ez 25:12–14; Ob 10ff.; Ps 137:7–9.

34 **(V) The Aftermath (5:1–22).** This lamentation is not strictly alphabetical, although its limitation to 22 verses shows alphabetical influence. The meter is unusual; the normal 3 and 2 dirge measure expands to 3 and 3 or 4 and 3. The locale is (occupied) Palestine, shortly after 586. Babylon controls the country (5:2,11); the Temple area has been reduced to jackal-infested rubble (5:18); life in general is chaotic (5:9,12).

(A) The Plight of Judah's Survivors (5:1–18). **2.** The present generation has witnessed a complete reversal of Israel's history. The land had been promised them by Yahweh and conquered by Joshua. Now everything is in the hands of foreigners. **4–5.** A conquered people has no rights; the natives must pay for materials once their own; the Jews cannot expect even minimal protection. They seem to exist only to be abused by overbearing aliens. **6.** The reference is to old alliances that involved Judah in international struggles and were symptomatic of her failure to trust in Yahweh (see Hos 7:11; Jer 2:18). **7.** *our fathers, who sinned, are no more; but we bear their guilt:* A primitive notion based on profound awareness of human solidarity. Ezekiel emphasized that his stricken contemporaries were not fated by their ancestors but free to determine their own present and future, no matter what the waywardness of earlier generations. This poet seems less advanced (see Ez 18; Jer 31:29). **9–10.** *at the peril of our lives:* Babylonian occupancy did not eliminate Bedouin raids at harvest time. **11–13.** Neither sex nor rank nor age are guarantees against violence and humiliation. **14–15.** *the old men have abandoned the gate:* A town's gateway was a favorite place of meeting and business. The population has gone indoors or underground (cf. Jer 16:9; 25:10).

(B) A Prayer for Restoration (5:19–22). In Yahweh's stability and eternity, the fallen, dying nation sees some hope for survival, even full restoration. **22.** *in full measure:* What more can Yahweh do? Considering the over-all picture, he must certainly have exhausted his wrath. There seems nothing left for him now but to be merciful.

37

BARUCH

Aloysius Fitzgerald, F.S.C.

BIBLIOGRAPHY

1 Ball, C. J., "Epistle of Jeremy," *APOT* 1 (Oxford, 1913) 569–611. Dhorme, E., *Les religions de Babylonie et d'Assyrie* (Paris, 1945). Gelin, A., "Baruch," *DTC* (Paris, 1953) tables. Lefèvre, A., "Les Livres Deutérocanoniques," R-F 1 (Tournai, 1959) 733–39. Penna, A., *Baruch* (Rome, 1953); *Geremia* (Rome, 1952). Saydon, P. P., "Baruch," *CCHS* (London, 1952) 596–600. Whitehouse, O. C., "Baruch," *APOT* 1 (Oxford, 1913) 569–95; 596–611.

INTRODUCTION

2 **(I) Divisions.** The deuterocanonical book commonly attributed to Baruch, Jeremiah's well-known secretary, is not a single work, but rather a collection of several distinct pieces covering a wide range of literary types. These pieces are grouped together because all are too short to stand alone and because all are set against the background of the events that led up to and followed upon the fall of Jerusalem in 587. In fact, the process that assembled the book has been in part preserved. The LXX manuscripts generally arrange Jer, Bar, and Lam in that order and after Lam include the letter of Jeremiah as an entirely distinct work. The Vg, certainly reflecting another tradition, rearranges the order to Jer, Lam, Bar, and makes the letter of Jeremiah the concluding part of Bar (6:1–72), although the title of the letter (6:1) clearly distinguishes it from the rest of Bar.

3 **(II) Original Language.** Bar is extant today only in Greek. Even Jerome knew no Hebr text (*In Jer. Proph., PL* 24. 706; *Prol. in Jer., PL* 28. 904), but it cannot be doubted that at least in part Bar was originally composed in Hebrew. The evidence is too technical to be discussed here, but is clearly presented in the textual notes of the CCD translation. An example of the type of argumentation will suffice. A precise translation of the Gk text for 6:71 presents the picture of an idol clothed with purple cloth and marble, both of which are in a state of decay. But marble does not rot and is not worn as clothing like purple cloth. The difficulty is immediately obviated by postulating an underlying Hebr text, for the Hebr word *šš* can mean both "marble" and "linen." The LXX translator, working without modern tools, was confused. On the basis of this type of evidence we can safely say that at least all the prose sections of Bar are translations from an original Hebr text (1:1–3:8 and 6:1–72). The wisdom poem of 3:9–4:4 is probably a translation from the Hebrew. In the case of the prophetic discourses (4:5–29 and 4:30–5:9), it is difficult to decide whether the Greek is original.

4 **(III) Date of Composition.** Superficially, the approximate dates of composition of the parts of the book seem simple to determine. The introduction to Baruch's prayer indicated that he composed it five years after the fall of Jerusalem to Nebuchadnezzar—i.e., in 582 (1:2). The introduction to the letter of Jeremiah indicates that it was sent to the exiles being carried off to Babylon in 597 or 587 (6:1). The prophetic discourses assume the conditions of the Exile, and thus date from before 538. In this context, 3:10–11 clearly refer to the Exile; therefore, the wisdom poem also is referred to the same period.

There are, however, good reasons for assigning a much later date to these various parts. First, certain things indicate that the account it presents is not history in the sense that the narratives of Kgs are history. Consequently, the indications of the date of composition in the book itself must be viewed in this light. The historical books know nothing of the return of the sacred vessels (1:8–9), and the source of the accounts seems obvious enough. There is a contradiction between the prayer itself, which presumes that the Temple is in ruins (2:26), and the introduction, which presumes that the Temple is standing and that the normal worship is carried on there (1:14). Belshazzar is not the son of Nebuchadnezzar (1:11–12), who destroyed Jerusalem, but of Nabonidus, the last Chaldean king. This confusion could not have existed at the time when the prayer is said to have been written, although this telescoping of history, also found in Dn 5:1, seems to have been a commonplace in later Jewish tradition. The letter of Jeremiah is clearly post-exilic. The Babylon described in the prayer is not the great city of Nebuchadnezzar (6:14,48–49). The idolatry against which the Jews are warned seems to be that of the Gk period. In any case, if the letter were really written by Jeremiah to the Jews going to Babylon in 587, it would be difficult to explain why it was not included in the definitive edition of Jer that itself dates from the post-exilic period. Perhaps a more precise indication of the date of composition is contained in 6:2, where Jeremiah's prediction of a 70-year exile (Jer 25:12; 29:10) has become a prediction of seven generations of exile. If 40 years or so (Nm 32:13) are assigned to a generation, a writer of the Gk period would be holding out to his fellow Jews, for whom the conditions of the Exile still existed, the promise of speedy assistance from God. Some older exegetes tended to see in Nebuchadnezzar and Belshazzar pseudonyms for Vespasian and Titus, and they regarded the destruction of Jerusalem described in 1:2 as the destruction of AD 70. On this basis, they variously dated Bar sometime after that date. But it is impossible to imagine a pious Israelite urging his fellow Jews to pray for Vespasian and Titus (1:11).

5 **(IV) Authorship.** Any discussion of the question of authorship hinges very much on the matters already discussed. If Bar is a collection of smaller works, then the question of authorship has to be answered for each individual part. If the book is in part a translation and in part written in Greek, unity of authorship becomes much less probable. If the book as a whole or in part dates from well after the Exile, then neither Baruch nor Jeremiah could have authored whatever dates from this later period of OT history. As is evident, the inconclusive character of much of this discussion already indicates that the question of authorship will yield historical probabilities rather than certitudes, and that generalizations will have to be made for the whole book on the basis of evidence drawn from different sections.

The evident late date of the letter of Jeremiah makes authorship by the Prophet quite impossible. There is a question here of obvious pseudepigraphy, a phenomenon common enough in the OT (e.g., Ct, Wis, Eccl) and paralleled in related literature. This view has been held by exegetes from the days of Jerome (*In Jer. Proph., PL* 24. 706). The introduction attributes the prayer of 1:15–3:8 to Baruch, and the introduction itself is certainly of a late date. Whether the author presents an actual prayer composed by Baruch is problematical, although the arguments in favor of a late date and consequent pseudepigraphy here also seem to carry weight. It would otherwise be somewhat difficult to explain why a prayer written by Baruch was ignored by the Palestinian canonical tradition. The practice of using Baruch as an assumed name is paralleled in the Apocrypha.

Whether in 1:1 the intention is to attribute not only the scroll (the prayer) to Baruch, but also the wisdom poem and the two prophetic discourses is not really clear. In any case, the various alternative positions here, as in the rest of the book, seem sufficiently indicated. Thus, the evidence seems to indicate that Bar is the work of a number of unknown authors working well after the period of the Exile.

6 **(V) Significance.** What has been said thus far, of course, impugns in no way the canonicity or inerrancy of Bar. The Council of Trent settled definitively for Catholics the question of canonicity. As a matter of fact, the canonicity of this book has better witness in the history of the early Church than is generally true of deuterocanonical books. The literary device by which an author makes the speaker in his work some important personage from a time long past and attempts to recreate for his readers the historical circumstances of the period during which this person lived, in no way undermines the inerrancy of the book, even if in his reconstruction of the history of the period the author is guilty of what from the point of view of a modern scientific historian are historical errors. The whole point of this edifying history is not to present an account of the past, accurate in its details. The aim of the author of this type of history is to interpret the past for the men of his day, i.e., to edify. Sufficiently numerous examples of this sort of device exist in the OT (e.g., Jdt and Est), although the measure in which a particular work will combine fancy with history will vary from work to work. Viewed in this light, the purpose of Bar becomes clear. It presents vignettes from the history of the Exile and certain reflections upon that history to the Jews of the Diaspora who knew this history well. For these Jews, the conditions of the Exile were still realities. It was very clear to them that the return of 538 was not the restoration God had promised his people. Bar used the history of the Exile to present to this Diaspora the reason for its distress, the source of its salvation, and the certainty of this restoration. The Jerusalem to be restored is not the Jerusalem of the Exile, but the new Jerusalem of the end time, as seems clear from the second prophetic discourse (4:30–5:9). The return of 538 was the foreshadowing and guarantee of the great event to come.

7 **(VI) Outline.** The first and last section of Bar are prose compositions; the remaining three parts are written in verse. The Book of Baruch may be outlined as follows:

- (I) Prayer of Baruch (1:1–3:8)
  - (A) Introduction (1:1–14)
  - (B) The Prayer (1:15–3:8)
- (II) A Wisdom Poem (3:9–4:4)
  - (A) The Importance of Wisdom (3:9–14)
  - (B) No Man Can Find Wisdom (3:15–31)
  - (C) Wisdom Is the Law (3:32–4:4)
- (III) The First Prophetic Discourse (4:5–29)
- (IV) The Second Prophetic Discourse (4:30–5:9)
- (V) The Letter of Jeremiah (6:1–72)

COMMENTARY

8 **(I) Prayer of Baruch (1:1–3:8).** The prayer itself (1:15–3:8) is prefaced by a brief introduction (1:1–14), which presents the circumstances under which it was composed. Precisely in this introduction are found the exegetical problems of the book that have most exercised commentators. As 1:1b–2a stand, they indicate that the prayer was composed "in Babylon, in the fifth year, on the seventh day of the month." The absence of a number before "month" is strange, but it is generally agreed that the fifth month is intended;

thus, the date indicates 7 Ab 582, the fifth anniversary of the fall of Jerusalem in 587, which was the occasion of the writing of the prayer. But this understanding of the passage presents serious difficulties. First, the introduction presumes that the Temple is standing and that services are being carried on in the normal manner; 1:2 itself and what is known from other sources (2 Kgs 25:8–9; Ezr 3:1–13) indicate that such was not the state of affairs in 582. Second, if the occasion that prompted the composition of the prayer was an assembly held on 7 Ab, the whole chronology of the introduction becomes impossible—assembly, 7 Ab (month 5, day 7); Baruch's arrival in Jerusalem with money and vessels, 10 Sivan (month 3, day 10); the reading of the prayer for the Feast of Tabernacles, 15 Tishri (month 7, day 15). It is not necessary to understand the feast of 1:14 as Tabernacles, but if Baruch and his party depart immediately after the assembly of 1:3–4, this is the feast for which they would arrive. Consequently the feast of 1:14 is usually understood to be Tabernacles.

The CCD translation conceives the circumstances of the introduction differently. It regards 1:2b as the work of a glossator. The gloss harmonizes with 2:26, but in its own context it is completely out of place and obscures the date intended. The fifth year referred to is not the fifth year after the destruction of Jerusalem, but the fifth year of the exile of Jeconiah, i.e., the fifth year of Zedekiah. Another fifth year with no month given is found in Ez 1:2. Here clearly 593, the fifth year of Zedekiah is the date indicated. If Jer 28:1–3 and 29:1–2 are the source of the incident recounted in 1:8 about the return of the silver vessels, we have another reason for understanding the date of 1:2 as 593 (Jer 28:1). In any case, such an understanding of the problem presented by 1:2b harmonizes perfectly with the rest of the introduction.

As for 1:8–9, which the CCD has enclosed in square brackets to indicate it is a gloss, it would perhaps be better to regard these verses as a parenthesis rather than as a gloss. That v. 10 follows logically upon v. 7 is clear enough. Besides, the "he" of v. 8 is Baruch, not Jehoiakim, the priest, for only Baruch was in Babylon (1:3) to accept the vessels. If v. 8 were the sequel of v. 7, this change in subjects would have to be indicated in some way other than by the use of the simple pronoun.

On this basis, the chronology of the events described can be reconstructed using 10 Sivan as the known date. The occasion of the assembly of 1:3 is Passover of the fifth year of Zedekiah, Passover 593 (15 Nisan: month 1, day 15). Baruch and his group depart immediately after the feast for Jerusalem with the money and the vessels and arrive there on 10 Sivan (month 3, day 10), which is five days before the Feast of Weeks (month 3, day 15) according to the Zadokite-Qumran calendar, supposedly the one presumed by the author. The time allowed for the journey is just about right. Ezra and his large party take three and one-half months for the journey from Babylonia (Ezr 8:31; 7:8–9), but Nebuchadnezzar, according to a Babylonian chronicle, gathers his troops in the ninth month of 598 (beginning November 29) and captures Jerusalem March 16, 597, after a siege (2 Kgs 24:10–11; and D. N. Freedman, *BA* 19 [1956] 50–60). The least certain part of this reconstruction is the identification of the day of the assembly of 1:3 as Passover. It seems a rather reasonable conjecture, but there is no reason why Baruch could not have started sooner and been on the road at Passover (Ezr 8:31).

9 **(A) Introduction (1:1–14).** **1.** The "scroll" here and in 1:3,14 is the prayer of 1:15–3:8. The editor, who is the speaker here, attributes this prayer to Baruch. Whether it is intended that the rest of the book be attributed to Baruch is not clear. There is no further indication of authorship for the various parts of the book until the letter of Jeremiah (6:1). For the genealogy of Baruch, see Jer 32:12; there is no parallel for the lengthy genealogy given here. **3.** Jeconiah, otherwise referred to as Jehoiachin, was brought to Babylon by Nebuchadnezzar in 597 after a reign of only three months (2 Kgs 24:6–7). At first a pensioner in the King's court, he was jailed sometime after 592 (W. F. Albright, *BA* 5 [1942] 49–55), probably in connection with some insurrection, that of 587 or another prior to that date. He was later released (2 Kgs 25:27–30). **4.** *the kings' sons:* Male members of the royal family not in the direct line of succession. That they are not sons of Jehoiachin is indicated by the use of the plural, "kings," and also by the order of the groups named (see Jer 36:26 where Jerahmeel is spoken of as "the son of the king" [MT], although he is certainly not the son of Jehoiakim). *the river Sud:* One of the Babylonian canals. It has not been identified. **5–6.** For further indications that there were fixed days of mourning and fasting and that these practices were a standard manifestation of piety during and after the Exile, see Zech 7:1–5; Ezr 8:21; Neh 1:4; 9:1; Dn 9:3. **7.** Jehoiakim was a member of the family of the high priest (1 Chr 6:13–15), but otherwise unknown. It is not clear why the vessels and money are sent to him while the high priest Seraiah and presumably his son Jehozadak were still in Jerusalem (2 Kgs 25:18). **8–9.** If these lines are a parenthesis and are not the work of a glossator who had 587 in mind as the date of 1:2, they presume the following chronology of events: siege and surrender of Jerusalem, 598–597; the making of new vessels for the Temple; the handing over of these vessels to Nebuchadnezzar, possibly as part of the regular tribute to be paid; the return of these vessels, 593. The historical books know only of the return of the sacred vessels under Cyrus (Ezr 1:7–11). There is no reason to think that the account presented in these verses is historical. The basis for the story seems to have been Jer 28:1–3; 29:1–2. **11.** Jeremiah had always advocated acquiescence to Babylon. **12.** *light to our eyes:* The force within the eye that enables a person to see (Ps 6:8, 38:11, Jb 3:20).

10 **(B) The Prayer (1:15–3:8).** The prayer bears marked resemblances to the prayers of Ezr 9:6–15; Neh 1:5–11; 9:6–37, but especially to Dn 9:4–19. **15.** The first part of the prayer (1:15–2:10) is strictly speaking not a prayer, for here the exiles address their fellow Jews in Jerusalem and humbly acknowledge the reasons for their present difficulties. The use of the phrase, "Justice is with the Lord," here and in 2:6, marks the beginning and the end of the section (for a more developed use of this device, see Bar 6). **20.** *and the evils and the curse...:* See, e.g., Lv 26:14–15; Dt 28:15–16.

2:2–3. The reference is to the siege of Jerusalem. Cf. Lv 26:29; Dt 28:53; Jer 19:9; Ez 5:10; Lam 2:20; 4:10. This horror was the greatest under heaven. **9.** This figure presenting God as carefully observing the actions of men, looking for a fit time to punish or reward, is common in Jer (1:2; 31:28; 44:27). **11.** With the change in address, the prayer strictly speaking begins. **14–18.** God is asked to save Israel for his own sake (see Pss 25:11; 79:9–10; 114:9–10; Ez 20:44; Dn 9:19), because the prosperity of Israel is regarded as the measure of God's glory in the world. This belief is so for two reasons: if Israel prospers, then all the world will know that the God of Israel is Lord and will show him respect (15); if Israel prospers and does not perish, then Israel will be able to praise God (17; see Ex 32:12; Nm 14:13–14; Dt 9:26–27; Sir 36:1–2). **15.** *you are... our God* *and Israel and his descendants . . . bear your name:* The phrases mean the same thing. To bear the name of someone in contexts similar to the present one means to be possessed and then protected by that person. The Temple, Jerusalem, and the nation are all spoken of as bearing the name of Yahweh. This scheme is not something purely nominal, but in OT thought conferred on them a real quality implicit in the name. For the city and Temple, such is evident—e.g., in Dt 12:5,11,12 and in the Temple sermon of Jer 7:1–15 (for the nation, see Dt 28:10; Is 43:1; 44:5; 48:1–2).

11 **17.** If Israel perishes, then God's nation will not be able to praise him. For the idea that the dead do not praise God, see Pss 6:6; 88:11; 116:6; Is 38:18. What is being reflected here is the typical OT view of the human composite, death and the afterlife. Dust plus the breath of life (Gn 2:7) or flesh plus God's Spirit (Gn 6:3) make man a living *nepeš,* "being," "person." Death occurs when the two are separated. The dust returns to the earth; the life breath returns to God who gave it (Eccl 12:7). This would seem to leave nothing of man, but an undefinable something does remain (Gn 37:35, 1 Kgs 28:11–19). A live man is a living *nepeš*; a dead man is a dead *nepeš* (Nm 6:6; Lv 21:11). This undefinable something sinks to the nether world, Sheol, located in the depths of the earth (Dt 32:22; Is 14:9), where it endures a shadowy and sorrowful existence (Jb 26:5–6; Is 14:9–10; Ez 32:17–32; Eccl 9:4–10). The doctrine of a true afterlife and of reward and punishment after death is a late development in OT history (Wis 3:1–9; 2 Mc 12:38–46). **18.** The subject of this sentence ("He") is Israel, the nation personified. The sense follows: The dead do not praise the Lord (17), but Israel, although struck a mortal blow, declares his glory and justice. It is done in the following verses, where it is shown that the present condition of Israel, far from being a manifestation of the impotence of God, is a just manifestation of his power. Implicit in the verse is a plea for mercy for God's own sake. If God does not save Israel, soon there will be no one to praise him. **21.** The particular refusal to serve the Lord (19–21) was the refusal to heed Jeremiah's pro-Babylonian policy (Jer 27:12–13). **23.** After Jer 7:34. **24–25.** After Jer 8:1–2; 22:19; 26:30. The historical books present no account of such a desecration of the tombs at the hands of Nebuchadnezzar. Honorable burial was an important consideration, because death was not an annihilation (see comment on 2:17). The dead *nepeš* in Sheol still in some way experienced what was done to the body. Hence, for a corpse to be left unburied, the prey of birds and beasts, was a terrible fate (1 Kgs 14:11; Jer 16:4; Ez 29:5; Eccl 6:3).

12 **26.** *the house which bears your name:* A synonymous expression for the house of the Lord, the Temple, which lay in ruins after 587 (see the prophecy of Jer 7:10–15; see comment on 2:15). Whether the author has in mind 587 or 598–597, here, in vv. 19–20, and in other references to a siege and fall of Jerusalem scattered throughout the prayer, is hard to say. The Temple was not destroyed in 598–597, but if there is one author for both the introduction and the prayer, and if it is necessary that he be consistent, it seems best to say that he has this date in mind. Such seems clear enough from the introduction. Besides, vv. 24–25 appear to be based on what Jeremiah had predicted of the end of Jehoiakim in 598–597. There is, then, in this verse, a conflation of the events of the two sieges, an inconsequential historical inaccuracy, granted the purpose of the book. **27.** The nature of the "clemency" and "mercy" that God has shown his people is made clear in vv. 30–35. God's punishment was not for revenge, but for purification. It brings to his people a change of heart, which is the occasion for God to bestow on them even greater blessings. **29–35.** These words, put into the mouth of the Lord, are an expansion of the thought of Dt 31:24–27, which itself makes use of other biblical texts, notably Dt 30:1–10. **31.** From the OT point of view, the heart was the seat of all rational activity, the seat of the intellect and the rational appetite. *hearts, and heedful ears:* Two parallel expressions signifying the capacity to understand the truth and the willingness to act in accord with it.

13 **3:3.** God, the ruler of all that is, has the power to effect Israel's release from present difficulties (see Ps 29:10–11; Lam 5:19–20). For the exact sense of this passage, see Ps 102:12–13, where the verb "abide" translates the same Hebr vb. *yšb* as "enthrone" in the other passages. **6.** God is called upon to remember his might and his reputation—i.e., what he can do to have his name glorified—the equivalent to asking God to save Israel for his own sake. **7.** The punishment of Yahweh is not vindictive, but purifying (see Jer 31:33). **8.** *a reproach, a curse, and a requital:* Israel has become a reproach, for she has been disgraced by God before the nations; thus, it has become an insult to say to someone: You are like Israel. Israel has been cursed and requited by God in such a way as to become the example of curse and requital (see Jer 29:22; 42:18).

14 **(II) A Wisdom Poem (3:9–4:4).** The poem presents wisdom ("prudence," *phronēsin*) as the most prized possession, for it is the source of prosperity for all who possess it. Without it, man experiences only disaster. But man in no way can achieve it by his own efforts; God alone can bestow it on him. He has chosen to bestow it on the Jewish people to whom he has given the Law, which is equated with wisdom. The observance of the Law is held out as the source of deliverance from present difficulties. In this poem, as elsewhere in the OT (Prv 8:1–36; Sir 24:1–31), Wisdom is personified. In the Gk text it is not clear where exactly the personification begins, but it is obviously present in 3:38. The CCD translation has chosen to begin the personification with 3:15. The speaker in the poem is a wisdom teacher who addresses the Jewish nation.

(A) The Importance of Wisdom (3:9–14). **9.** *commandments of life:* Commandments that give life when they are observed (Dt 30:15–20). The life promised is prosperity of every kind (Dt 30:15). The parallelism between "commandments" and "prudence" in this first verse makes the identification between Wisdom and the Law that is the whole point of the poem (4:1). **10.** Israel is "defiled" by her association with the Babylonians, who are all but dead and ready to depart for the nether world because they do not know and observe the Law, which is the source of life (for the idea that contact with a corpse defiles a person, see Lv 21:1–4; 22:4; Nm 19:11–16). **12.** The genitive seems best taken as an objective genitive; then the "fountain of wisdom" is God, who gives wisdom (for parallel expressions, see Jer 2:13; Jn 4:13–14). **14.** *light of the eyes:* See comment on 1:12. Here, the expression parallels "length of days" and "life."

15 **(B) No Man Can Find Wisdom (3:15–31).** **16.** For the idea that the dominion of the king extends even to beasts and birds, see Jdt 11:5; Jer 27:6; Dn 2:37–38. **17.** The Greek indicates that "they who heaped up the silver . . ." are the kings of v. 16 and not a new group. **20.** To come to see the light is to be born; to see the light is to be alive (Jb 3:16; 33:30; Ps 49:20). **22.** Both Canaan (Phoenicia) and Edom, of which Teman is a part, were renowned for human wisdom (see Jer 49:7; Ez 28:13–14; Ob 1:8–9; Zech 9:2). **23.** The sons of Hagar are the Ishmaelites (Gn 16, 21). Ishmael was the traditional ancestor of 12 tribes localized in NE Arabia (Gn 25:12–13). Midian is the region S of Edom and E of the Gulf of Aqabah (for the Midianites as traders, see Gn 37:28). **24.** As the parallelism shows, "the house of God" is the created universe. **26.** On the "giants," see Gn 6:4; Wis 14:6; Sir 16:7. **29–31.** These verses conclude the section that begins with v. 15 and summarize its content: Man is incapable of discovering wisdom.

16 **(C) Wisdom Is the Law (3:32–4:4).** **33.** Sunset and sunrise are presented as the obedience of the sun to God's commands. **34.** *at their posts:* The stars are described as sentries keeping watch in the night. **37.** *the way of understanding:* The objective genitive is suggested by v. 31. Verses 29–30 are clearly concerned with finding the way to wisdom. Thus, the CCD renders a similar Gk genitive in 31a, "the way to her." The Gk genitive in 31b seems best regarded as parallel, and thus "her paths" signifies the paths to her. This understanding of the genitive makes good sense in similar expressions in vv. 20–21, 23, 27. This interpretation seems preferable to "the path where understanding walks" (30). **4:3.** The idea seems to be that if Israel does not observe the Law, God will forsake her and give his Law to others. Israel's "glory" is the Law; her "privileges" are to know and observe it.

17 **(III) The First Prophetic Discourse (4:5–29).** The speaker addresses in prophetic tones the Jewish nation in exile. He presents to them Jerusalem, the mother of the nation, explaining to her neighbors and her exiled children the reason for the Exile and holding out the assurance of an ultimate return. The poem is a fine example (as is that following) of the Hebr method of indicating stanzaic divisions in verse by the repetition of similar phrases. The poem is divided into five stanzas of approximately equal length (6, 6, 7, 5, and 6 lines). Each stanza is introduced by a vocative and imperative (Fear not/people, Hear/neighbors, Come/neighbors, Fear not/children, Bear/children). What seems like an irregularity in v. 14 is a 3rd-pers. Gk imperative. The CCD clearly indicates these divisions. **6.** *you were sold:* The people of Israel belonged to God in view of the covenant relationship. He handed them over to Babylon as slaves. This event is compared to a transaction in which slaves are exchanged for a cash payment. But, as Deutero-Isaiah (52:3) pointed out, the figure is not completely parallel. God received nothing in exchange for Israel. Israel even in captivity is God's people. This is the foundation of the captives' hope. **8–9.** Jerusalem is here personified and presented as the mother of the nation (10; for the same figure, see Is 51:18).

18 Jerusalem now speaks to the neighbors of Zion (9b–13), an uncertain addressee (14–16), and the nation in exile (17–29). The uncertain addressee of vv. 14–16 is probably the same as in vv. 9b–13, i.e. the neighboring nations. **12.** The condition of Jerusalem is like that of a woman who has lost not only her husband but also her children (see Lam 1:1–2). **17.** Here, the question, as frequently in Hebrew, implies a negative response. **20.** *the garment of peace:* The fine clothing that is worn by a noble lady in a prosperous city during a time of peace has been exchanged for the type of mourning clothing worn after a terrible siege and a crushing defeat. (see 5:1). **24.** *with great glory and the splendor of the Eternal God:* Splendor (*lamprotēs*) here seems to be the effect of God's saving presence on Israel. God is Israel's light (savior). The nation basks in his splendor (cf. Is 60:1–3). Glory seems to be parallel to splendor, and the phrase seems to go closely with God's salvation. The sense, then, is that Israel's neighbors will see the glorious and resplendent salvation God will bring Israel (but see comment on 4:37). The verbal form of "splendor" (*zrḥ*) indicates a theophany in Dt 33:2 and Is 60:2, where it is parallel to the glory of Yahweh, as here. In any case, the two suggested meanings are not far apart. **25.** *trample upon their necks:* Mercy toward enemies was not an OT virtue (cf. Is 51:23). **26.** *rough roads:* The roads to Babylon.

19 **(IV) The Second Prophetic Discourse (4:30–5:9).** The stanzaic structuring of this poem is similar to that of the previous poem. There are three stanzas of 6, 6, and 7 lines, each beginning with the combination of an imperative and a vocative (Fear not/Jerusalem, Look/Jerusalem, Up/Jerusalem). The speaker again echoes the prophetic style, as in 4:5–29. He addresses Jerusalem, again personified as the mother of the nation, but the tone of his message has shifted. The return from Babylon is imminent. In this poem, the two levels of meaning that have been suggested as characteristic of the whole of Bar become more evident. Superficially, the author is talking about the return of 538 as imminent. But this return is from both E and W, and the exaggerated language (esp. 5:6–9) shows that the poet had something else in mind. The poet well knew that 538 was nothing like this. Thus, whereas the poem seems to predict the return of 538, actually the nation to be re-established is the new Israel of the end time, when God will once again establish his kingdom. **30.** The name that Yahweh is said to have given the city is not "Jerusalem." Rather, because he has made Jerusalem his own city, it is "the city of Yahweh," which is referred to here (cf. Is 60:14; Ps 46:5; see comment on 2:15). **35.** *fire shall come upon her...for a long time:* Babylon will become a burnt ruin that will smolder for a long time (cf. Is 34:10). *demons shall dwell in her...:* Babylon will remain an uninhabited ruin. Demons were thought to dwell in deserts and desolate places (cf. Tb 8:3; Is 13:21; 34;11,14; Lk 11:24). **36.** Babylon is due E of Jerusalem. *the joy:* Her exiled children returning are Jerusalem's joy. **37.** *the glory of God:* The phrase indicates the divine presence. In the poem, God is pictured as accompanying the exiles from Babylon to Jerusalem. In 5:9, "the light of his glory" is clearly the light of his glorious presence (for the picture of God accompanying the returning exiles, see Is 40:3–11; 58:8–9).

20 **5:1.** In 4:20, Jerusalem had removed "the garment of peace." *the splendor* (*euprepeia*) *of glory:* The gloriously resplendent and wonderful effect of God's saving action upon Israel. **2.** Not only does God restore splendor to Jerusalem, but also "justice." *displays the glory of the eternal name:* The CCD rendering here is based on Ex 28:36–37, but especially on Wis 18:24. The crown that Jerusalem is told to put on has inscribed upon it the sacred name. **3.** For "splendor" (*lamprotēs*), see comment on 4:24. **4.** The conferring of a name in a context such as the present one involves not only the giving of the name, but the bestowal of the attributes indicated. "Peace," the product of justice, will reign in Jerusalem (Is 32:17). She will be an honorable city; her honor will derive from the fact that she worships God (cf. Is 1:26; Jer 33:16; Ez 48:35, for other names of the new Jerusalem). **5.** *Holy One:* God, as in 4:22. **7.** The road to Jerusalem is made level by God to facilitate the return, as in Is 40:3–4. *in the glory of God:* Israel advances in the glorious presence of God. That God returns with the exiles and leads them personally to Jerusalem is most clear in 5:9 (cf. also 4:37). **8.** To make the return journey as comfortable as possible, God will cause shade trees to grow to shield the exiles from the sun. **9.** *by the light of his glory:* By the light of his glorious presence (for God as the light of Israel, see Is 60:1–2; see comments on 4:24, 37). Divine "mercy" and "justice" personified accompany God and the exiles on the journey.

21 **(V) The Letter of Jeremiah (6:1–72).** The

letter is said to have been written by Jeremiah to those who were being led into exile to Babylon (6:1), but it is not clear whether the Exile of 597 or that of 587 is intended. The introduction indicates that Nebuchadnezzar himself led away the captives, which was strictly true only in 597 (2 Kgs 24:14–16), for the general Nebuzaradan was charged with the deportation of 587 (2 Kgs 25:11). The letter seems to be modeled on Jer 29:1–2, which is a letter addressed to the exiles of 597. But, in fact, no definite solution to the problem is possible. The author presents a satirical attack on the idolatry of Babylon during the Gk period. The same sort of technique, the repetition of set phrases or a refrain, that is more commonly used to mark stanzas in verse (see 4:5–29 and 4:30–5:9), is here used to set off paragraphs (6:14,22,28,39,44,50,56,64,71).

22 **2.** That the author of the letter was well acquainted with the writings of Jeremiah is evident. The change, then, from Jeremiah's 70 years of exile (Jer 25:12; 29:10) seems significant. Allowing 40 years to the generation (Nm 32:13), the return is promised during the Gk period. Perhaps the author, writing shortly before the termination of these 280 years, is holding out to his fellow Jews, for whom the circumstances of the Exile were still real, the hope of a speedy return. But "generation" has not such a determined denotation and "seven generations" can well mean simply a long time, another indication of the double level of meaning operative in Bar. Whereas the book seems to be promising the return that took place in 538, it actually promises God's assistance to the dispersed Jews of a much later period.

23 **3.** Because the gods are carried in procession, they are not made of solid gold or silver but of wood covered with these metals. **6.** *my angel:* A heavenly emissary who will assist Israel (cf. Ex 23:20–21; Tb 5:45). The pronoun is in the first person because the author regards his message as God's message. As was the case with the prophets, God's own words are in his mouth. **8.** The satire here is in the parallel between gods and silly young girls. **10.** *harlots:* The cult prostitutes of the Babylonian temples. **12.** *house:* Here and throughout the letter, it is the equivalent of temple. **17.** The comparison indicates the manner in which these gods are locked in their temples, but the fact that they are paralleled to a criminal who has been condemned to death adds to the satire. **19.** *their hearts are eaten away:* By insects. The idols were made of wood covered with gold or silver (3). **24.** No matter what price is paid for one of these idols, it is without life. There is here an implied contrast with the living God. **25.** *their shame:* The shameful powerlessness of these gods is shown by the fact that they cannot even walk (cf. Is 46:7; Ps 115:7). *shame:* Could also be understood as the nakedness of these idols (Jer 13:26; Na 3:5). **26.** Food is as useful to these gods as it is to the dead. Again, the significant part of the comparison is the parallel drawn between the idols and the dead. The practice of making funeral offerings to the dead was not a part of the Hebr funeral rite (see Sir 30:18 and the difficult verses, Dt 26:14; Tb 4:18).

24 **27–31.** The practices described here were all forbidden by Jewish law. The priests and their wives took a share of the sacrificial offerings, but nothing was given to the poor (Dt 14:28–29). Women who had just given birth and menstruating women were regarded as unclean (Lv 12:2–3; 15:19–20). No woman ever held a priestly office in Israel. Priests were forbidden to bare their heads, lacerate their bodies, shave their beards, or rend their garments (Lv 21:5–6,10). These acts were signs of mourning (Jb 1:20; Jer 16:6; 41:5; 48:37; Ez 24:17), and mourning for dead gods was an established part of Babylonian worship (cf. Ez 8:14). **31.** *a funeral banquet:* When a death occurred in a house, the house was unclean and food could not be prepared there. Consequently, relatives and friends brought food to the house and stayed to console the bereaved family (see Jer 16:7; Ez 24:17,22).

25 **33–39.** The God of Israel can do all that these idols cannot. **40.** The Chaldeans do not ask their god to speak to men who can hear. They thereby acknowledge that the god cannot speak. They rather ask the impossible and the ridiculous. The god cannot speak and the "deaf mute" cannot hear. What underlies this practice is not clear. The Egyptian gods, at least, when carried in procession, gave oracles, made decisions, and were supposed somehow to speak.

42–44. There is a question here of cult prostitution. The "chaff" seems to be an aphrodisiac. The unbroken "cord" was a sign that the rite had not been fulfilled. **50.** *God's work:* The ability to do what God can do. **54.** *they are like crows:* These gods have about as much power as a crow. But what makes a flying crow an image of something particularly powerless is hard to see. **59–64.** The sun, moon, stars, lightning, wind, clouds, and fire are presented as obedient to the command of the true God. There is an implicit contrast between them and the idols. These false gods are not even the equal of nature, which serves the true God.

38

TOBIT, JUDITH, ESTHER

Demetrius R. Dumm, O.S.B.

TOBIT

BIBLIOGRAPHY

1 Bentzen, *IOT*. Lefèvre, A., "Tobie," R-F 1, 740–45. Miller, A. and J. Schildenberger, *Die Bücher Tobias, Judith und Esther* (BB; Bonn, 1940). Pautrel, R., *Tobie* (BJ; 2nd ed.; Paris, 1957). Pfeiffer, R. H., *History of New Testament Times* (N.Y., 1949). Simpson, D. C., "*Tobit*," *APOT*.

INTRODUCTION

2 **(I) Text and Canonicity.** The discovery at Qumran of both Hebr and Aram fragments of Tb confirms the conjecture that the original language was Semitic, and, more probably, Aramaic. The best complete texts are in Greek and follow two rather divergent traditions, one represented by the Sinaiticus codex and OL (which seems preferable) and another found in the codices Vaticanus and Alexandrinus. Although Jerome did not consider Tb canonical, Augustine and Ambrose supported it. Hence it was accepted by the council of Hippo (393) and succeeding councils.

(II) Author, Place, and Date of Composition. The author of this work is unknown. Most scholars fix the date of composition *ca.* 200 BC, either in the Mesopotamian Diaspora or, more probably, in Palestine.

(III) Literary Form. Some scholars (notably A. Miller) still maintain the historicity of the kernel of this story. But most moderns (P. Grelot, O. Eissfeldt, A. Bentzen, R. Pautrel) prefer to call it a religious story merely reflecting an historical situation. The commentary will indicate the reasons why it should be considered an edifying tale.

3 **(IV) Doctrine.** The primary aim of the author is to reassert the validity of faith at a time when God has apparently abandoned his people. Various secondary themes are also discernible—e.g., the importance of mutual support in times of oppression (family life, alms, tribal loyalty), the need to maintain religious integrity in pagan society, the role of angels and demons as agents of God and Satan, and an awareness of the role of Israel in mediating salvation for all men.

(V) Outline. The Book of Tobit may be outlined as follows:

(I) Tobit's Virtues and Trials (1:1–3:6)
(II) Sarah's Tribulations (3:7–25)
(III) Journey to Ecbatana (4:1–6:17)
(IV) Marriage of Tobias and Sarah (7:1–10:13)
(V) Homecoming (11:1–12:22)
(VI) Tobit's Prayer (13:1–14:1)
(VII) Epilogue (14:2–15)

COMMENTARY

4 **(I) Tobit's Virtues and Trials (1:1–3:6).** **1.** *Tobit:* In Vg and some modern versions, Tobias' father is also called (incorrectly) Tobias. **2.** *Shalmaneser:* Shalmaneser V (726–722). The deportation of the tribe of Naphtali occurred about 734 under Tiglath-pileser III (745–726). Such inaccuracies betray the author's lack of concern with historical precision. **3.** *charity:* Tobit is a model of the exiled Israelite who expresses his faith by serving the needs of his fellow sufferers. *Nineveh:* Capital of Assyria, situated on the E bank of the Tigris.

4. *Jerusalem:* The schism took place in 931 (1 Kgs 12:16), long before Tobit's time. The point is theological rather than historical; the author follows the Deuteronomist in emphasizing that legitimate sacrifice can be offered only at Jerusalem. **5.** *calf:* Jeroboam had established schismatic sanctuaries at Bethel and Dan (1 Kgs 12:26–32). **6.** *alone:* Tobit's devotion to the Law contrasts with the general apostasy of the northern kingdom. As a matter of fact, the ten northern tribes also worshiped Yahweh; from the strict Deuteronomist viewpoint, however, it was an illegal and unworthy cult. *first fruits:* The Law prescribed that the Israelites contribute the first and best products of their labors to the sanctuary in acknowledgment of their radical dependence on God (Dt 18:3–5; Nm 18:12–13). It was characteristic of post-exilic piety to stress observance of legal prescriptions, frequently at the expense of the larger and more objective covenant context.

7. *second tenth:* The second tithe was to be converted into money and spent for rejoicing, except on the seventh or Sabbath year. **8.** *third tenth:* The third tithe, offered every third year, was for the poor (Dt 14:28–29). This practice represents a strict, indeed idealistic, observance of the Law. **10.** *carried away:* Presumably in 734 (cf. 1:2). *food of the Gentiles:* Tobit strictly observes the Jewish dietary laws (Lv 11; Dt 14), exemplary and exceptional conduct that the author obviously recommends. **13.** *Shalmaneser:* See comment on 1:2. *buyer of provisions:* Many of the exiled Jews engaged in commercial activities, prospered, and reached high positions. **14.** *Media:* Region E of Nineveh. *ten talents:* Equivalent to many thousands of dollars.

5 **15.** *Sennacherib:* The son and successor of Sargon II (721–705), who had seized the throne from Shalmaneser V. **16.** *alms:* The author takes pains to emphasize this practice, so necessary in exile where many Jews were destitute while others prospered. **17.** *I buried:* The Jewish community's abandonment of its dead members dramatizes the degree of its spiritual disintegration. Tobit strives to reverse this disastrous course by risking his life for the decent burial of his compatriots. It is far more a question of the survival of God's harrassed people in a foreign and hostile milieu than of a simple act of virtue. **18.** *from Judea:* Cf. Is 36–37; 2 Kgs 18:13–19:37. *bodies were sought:* Probably to expose them to public ridicule.

20. *nothing was left:* Tobit's virtue does not shield him from misfortune. The paradox of the just man who is afflicted constitutes one of the major themes of this book. The problem of reconciling belief in God's goodness with daily experience, which seemed to contradict that belief, tortured the conscience of post-exilic Judaism. **21.** *killed him:* Cf. 2 Kgs 19:37. *Esarhaddon:* This warrior monarch ruled Persia from 681 to 669. *Ahikar:* This personage was the hero of an extremely popular and widespread story of antiquity, extant in various forms and in several languages (*ANET* 427–30). According to the story, the sage Ahikar was chancellor of the Assyrian kings Sennacherib and Esarhaddon. He adopted his nephew, Nadab, and carefully groomed him to be his successor. But Nadab, once in power, turned traitor and had his benefactor sentenced to death. By a clever ruse, Ahikar was spared and hid in a cave. Sometime later, the Pharaoh asked Esarhaddon to find a wise man to solve some profound riddles. Nadab declined the challenge and the king regretted having lost Ahikar. Then the executioner revealed the ruse, Ahikar was summoned, solved the riddles, and was reinstated. Nadab was flogged, imprisoned, and eventually died in disgrace. The author's references to this story (see also 2:10; 11:18; 14:10) reveal his desire to contrast Ahikar and Tobit, both wise men assailed by outrageous fortune who are eventually vindicated.

6 **2:1.** *feast of Pentecost:* Celebrated 50 days (seven weeks) after Passover, this feast was a joyful thanksgiving for the wheat harvest (Dt 16:9–11). Tobit faithfully observes the Jewish customs even in exile. **4.** *I sprang up:* Tobit's spontaneous reaction to a situation of need, allowing an "unrelated" incident to spoil his feast and seeing in it the fulfillment of a prophecy, demonstrates his belief that charity is a principle of daily life, not merely an occasional diversion. **8.** *laughed at me:* Tobit's "stupid" repetition of the very act for which he had previously been forced to flee is wise and prudent by God's standards. **10.** *fell into my open eyes:* It is futile to wonder about the nature of this injury because the episode is narrated for theological rather than historical (much less medicinal) purposes. One is immediately struck by the "accidental" aspect of this misfortune. Tobit has just demonstrated his personal belief in a God who controls all history. As if in response to this act of faith, God permits him to fall victim to a ridiculously fortuitous and improbable chance! This incident is meant to illustrate the apparently irrational and uncontrolled course of human events in defiance of faith in an omnipotent and benevolent God. *Ahikar:* If Ahikar were really the king's cupbearer (1:22), he could surely have arranged to have Tobit's money returned. For the story, however, it is necessary that the cache of money remain undisturbed. Literary considerations take precedence over historical probability. **14.** *your charities:* Tobit's scrupulosity concerning the kid given to his wife causes her to blurt out an accusation that is essential to the story. Like Job's wife, she points out the stupidity (by worldly standards) of virtue and hope in the face of the overwhelming curse of bad fortune. Unlucky Tobit is pictured as living proof that there is no real relationship between virtue and happiness.

3:1. *prayed in anguish:* Tobit's prayer sums up the attitude of the believing but bewildered Jew of the post-exilic era. He knows that this suffering must somehow be reconcilable with the reality of a just, merciful, and faithful God; yet, it is so much more severe than known sins would seem to require. Hence, a piteous plea for surcease and oblivion (see also Jb 7:15–21).

7 **(II) Sarah's Tribulations (3:7–25).** **7.** *same day:* The coincidence is deliberate; behind the disarray of a life dominated by evil chance, the reader is permitted to see the "logical" and ordered plan of God unfolding. *Ecbatana:* Capital of Media from 700; captured by Cyrus in 550. *reproached:* Sarah's misery is eloquently presented by these few words. She is, in fact, a victim of that cruel sport of heartless women by which, in subtle but most telling fashion, she is reminded of her failure as a wife. It is a variation on the theme of the barren woman in the Scriptures (cf. 1 Sm 1–6; Lk 1:25). **8.** *Asmodeus:* In ancient times, it was customary to attribute particularly virulent or inexplicable maladies to a demon. No doubt this name is derived ultimately from non-Jewish sources (the Persian god Aeshma-daeva has been suggested). Asmodeus, the destroyer, is paired with Raphael, the healer.

10. *hanging herself:* Sarah represents a person who is driven by merciless and incomprehensible fate to the point of madness. She envisions no rational escape and is diverted from the false solution of suicide only by faith. Thus, Tobit and Sarah are both overwhelmed by the blind irrationality of human misfortune: One is struck down by ridiculous chance; the other is worn out by cruel nagging. **11.** *prayed by her window:* Sarah, ever mindful that she is an exiled Jewess, prays like a prisoner with eyes on home and the land of freedom (cf. Dn 6:11).

Faith impels her to cast herself upon God's mercy, and a great faith it is that, after years of frustration, can still call the deity a "God of mercy"!

14. *innocent:* In the midst of tribulations, to claim innocence is almost as difficult as to declare God's goodness. Both statements seem quite irrelevant. Note also the keen sensitivity to the importance of chastity. **15.** *only child:* Throughout the story, the author emphasizes the radical interdependence of all men. The child is saved as a member of the family; the Israelite is saved as a member of God's people. No one is saved alone! Sarah, too, is keenly aware of her duty as heir of the family name and property.

16. *prayer of both was heard:* The reader is permitted to see how the story will end. From now on it will be merely a question of following the suspenseful course by which God works out his purpose. **17.** *Raphael:* The name, meaning "God heals," aptly describes the role of this angel who will be God's agent in vindicating the faith of two worthy clients. *light of God:* The glory of God (3:16), which, judging from the experience of Tobit and Sarah, shines so dimly in the world, will now enlighten the blindness of the one and will rout the dark demon who enslaved the other. *possess her:* In God's plan, Sarah was saved for Tobias. *that very moment:* Another clear indication that objective history is not intended (cf. 3:7).

8 **(III) Journey to Ecbatana (4:1–6:17). 2.** *my son Tobias:* The mysterious threads of divine providence begin now to weave the design that God intends. **3.** *honor her:* In the style of an Israelite sage, Tobit gives advice to his son. The virtues of good family life—piety, fidelity, continence, obedience—are featured in this story. **6.** *your ways will prosper:* An extraordinary promise in the mouth of one whose own experience has contradicted such an act of faith! **7.** *give alms:* This practice, so important in the eyes of those who know the uncertainty of life, is strongly underlined by the author, who presents it as a truly wise and prudent investment (4:9).

12. *sons of the prophets:* The Israelite who marries a foreign woman thereby compromises his prophetic witness, because he allows personal interest to guide his life rather than a sense of vocation as a member of the chosen race. **14.** *watch yourself:* The literary format is characteristic of OT wisdom literature: The father instructs his son about the wisdom of life. Although much of the advice is based on experience and common sense, it is all permeated by an indomitable spirit of faith. **17.** *place your bread:* It need not mean approval of pagan practices; it could signify sharing food with the pious bereaved. **18.** *seek advice:* The post-exilic era is marked by a profound spirit of docility; Israel's collapse has removed all her smugness. **19.** *not to every nation:* It takes strong faith to claim wisdom for the one nation that is now scattered over the face of the earth! **21.** *great wealth:* True wealth is reverence for God, for it alone brings lasting rewards.

5:1. *I will do everything:* Exemplary obedience toward a father who is blind, poor, and generally out of contact with "reality"! **2.** *the way:* The journey to Media is really the way to fulfillment of God's providential designs. The true Israelite will seek guidance and it will be provided, although not necessarily in an expected or obvious manner. **4.** *an angel:* Angels, as distinct persons who carry out divine missions among men, came to the fore in Israel primarily during the post-exilic period when God's transcendence was emphasized. *did not know:* God apparently prefers to hide his hand in the execution of his saving designs. **6.** *familiar with the way:* God's agent knows well his master's map! *two-days journey:* In fact, the distance between Ecbatana and Rages is some 185 miles, and Ecbatana is at a higher elevation than Rages; Raphael knows the journey of life far better than the route to Media!

9 **10.** *like the dead:* The reader is reminded of Tobit's pathetic situation, which is intended also to excuse his rather searching questions. **11.** *of what family:* In exile, loyalty is frequently a matter of blood relationship. God's providence works by preference within the confines of his own people. **13.** *Azarias:* To be scandalized by this "lie" is to miss the point of the story; Azarias means "God helps." "Raphael" has many names; his true name is never known until the victory has been achieved. **15.** *drachma:* Half a shekel, or about a quarter-ounce of silver; no doubt it was a fair wage. **16.** *route is sure:* Only the reader knows the source of this supreme confidence. *his angel:* A delightful note to show how unknowing faith meshes with God's reality. *dog:* Only here does the Bible take notice of the dog as a domestic animal and a friend of man. The sentiment is certainly imported and its purpose is to reinforce the family atmosphere that the author judges so important.

17. *began to weep:* Anna represents the good but sometimes too-human viewpoint of relatives and friends. The reference to money seems to mean (the text is doubtful) that she does not wish her son's welfare to be exposed to risk for mere money. She does not realize that the money is only an excuse; in reality, this situation is Tobias' challenge—the test of his maturity. **20.** *will return safe:* Tobit's faith dismisses all objections.

6:2. *a fish:* No doubt there were large fish in the Tigris and perhaps boys have at times caught fish in this unusual manner, but it is far more likely that the fish is as symbolic as the journey on which it was seen. **4.** *heart, liver and gall:* The boy obediently follows the apparently meaningless (but cf. v. 7!) directions of the angel; faith sometimes counsels such a course of action. The choice of heart, liver, and gall is not entirely arbitrary, for popular belief frequently attached therapeutic value to these organs.

10. *marriage:* Tobias' marriage to Sarah is not based on romantic love; it is plainly arranged by God and approved by the respective parents. The primary consideration is concern for the good of Israel, for apparently Sarah's inheritance will be lost to God's people should she marry a foreigner. One of the chief lessons of this book is that happy marriage is based upon such altruistic considerations rather than upon purely personal interests. **12.** *also beautiful and sensible:* These are important but strictly secondary considerations! *my plan:* Almost no attention is paid to Tobias' personal opinion. He is expected to play a role in a larger design. *law of Moses:* The author persists; he wishes to leave no doubt about what factors are important in such decisions (cf. Nm 36:5–9). **13.** *I have heard:* Finally Tobias is allowed to make an observation! But even here he questions the wisdom of such a marriage, rather out of concern for his parents than because of the disquieting rumors he has heard. **15.** *your father commanded:* The angel turns the argument against Tobias; filial respect and obedience demand this marriage. *do not worry:* Once again Tobias is asked to trust without any human guarantee. **17.** *destined for you:* God's plan cannot be thwarted. The fact that a course of action is part of that plan already guarantees its wisdom and prudence. *fell in love:* Tobias has in reality fallen in love with God's plan; he has not yet seen his destined wife!

10 **(IV) Marriage of Tobias and Sarah (7:1–10:13). 7:1.** *you are welcome:* Hospitality is one of the most prized virtues of the biblical family. Time and again it is an occasion for special divine blessings. **5.** *my* *father:* God's mysterious plan is beginning to bring happy results. **8.** *large servings:* The author delights in dwelling upon the simple and homely virtue of sincere concern for the bodily needs of guests. **10.** Raguel does not want the transaction to be carried on under false pretenses. There is a certain "commercial" flavor about this conversation. **11.** *be merry:* Sanguine Raguel knows that the world will still be here tomorrow! *heaven:* Raguel unwittingly reveals a thread of God's design. The author is concerned lest his reader fail to see that there is a deeper meaning in the story. **13.** *here she is:* One senses that the author is eager to have done with the ceremonies and to get on to the confrontation of Tobias and the demon. Or perhaps he wishes to remind us that this is the eighth time that Raguel has given away his daughter! **14.** *contract:* A written record is required inasmuch as the rights of inheritance belong to Sarah. **16.** *began to weep:* Sarah has good cause for weeping as she remembers the seven previous failures!

8:2. *ashes of incense:* It would not be unusual to have incense burning in the room to sweeten the air. Tobias' action will produce the opposite effect; this stench will prove intolerable to the demon. **3.** *remotest parts:* Demons were believed to inhabit wild and deserted areas. Fleeing to distant Egypt implies total defeat. *bound him:* Raphael, minister of healing, immobilizes the agent of death. This exorcism does not imply belief in magic; it is presented as a symbolic action by which God's power is unleashed in view of the prayer of the petitioner rather than for any intrinsic value of the ritual. **4.** *let us pray:* This invitation makes it clear that the demon represents lust and passion. He cannot harm those who approach the marriage bed with a deep awareness of the sacred nature of their calling. **6.** *Eve his wife:* Tobit recalls the definition of marriage as it was intended by God, implicitly rejecting all the distortions of that original, wholesome image. **7.** *with sincerity:* Sexual relations should be an expression of sacrificing love rather than a means of self-gratification.

11 **9.** *dug a grave:* Raguel does not yet know how different this marriage is from all the others. **13.** *opened the door:* The author fully exploits this suspenseful situation. **15.** *blessed art thou:* Although he does not know how it has happened, Raguel rightly assigns the credit to God, who enables his children to love without lusting. **20.** *fourteen days:* Obviously a feast is meant for feasting! **21.** *your father:* Note again the insistence on the need to extend the saving bonds of communal life to other persons.

9:2. *get the money:* Tobias was sent to fetch his father's money. But God intended the journey for another (and far more rewarding) purpose. The money now becomes a mere afterthought. **4.** *counting the days:* The thoughtfulness of Tobias is repeatedly underlined. **6.** *wedding feast:* The monetary transaction is completed with a minimum of ceremony; the wedding feast is clearly the important event now.

10:3. *greatly distressed:* One last test is given to Tobit. **7.** *all night long:* Anna fears the worst but dares not give up hope. **9.** *send me back:* As a good son, Tobias knows instinctively that there are certain duties that cannot be delegated to servants. **12.** *now your parents:* The wife follows her husband and becomes a member of his family. *a good report:* The wise father knows that his beautiful daughter is not yet perfect; he hopes, therefore, that she will work hard at being a good wife. *do nothing to grieve her:* The mother realizes how easily a sensitive daughter can be hurt by a thoughtless husband. One notes that all are now stronger for having pooled their spiritual resources. The author sees this fact as extremely relevant to the problems of the post-exilic era.

12 **(V) Homecoming (11:1–12:22).** **4.** *the dog:* No fitting homecoming lacks a barking dog! Cf. also 5:16. **5.** *looking intently:* Many would have called such persistence folly. **6.** *your son:* Anna thinks first of the blind Tobit. Thoughtfulness seems to be the chief characteristic of this ideal family. **9.** *ready to die:* Such happiness is impervious even to the corrosion of death. **11.** *gall:* Bitter gall provides a cure; the eyes of faith are opened only through suffering. *be of good cheer:* A fitting keynote of this story. The beleaguered Jews of the post-exilic period are reminded that only unconquerable faith can lift the burden of adversity.

14. *I see you, my son:* A capricious turn of fate, borne with faith and patience, is converted into a joy that would otherwise have been unknown. The soul is opened through suffering to ever new dimensions of joy. **15.** *afflicted me:* Tobit knew that God permitted his misfortune; now he also knows why! It is not difficult to imagine this scene, which is such a tribute to the author's dramatic ability: The words of adventure spill out of the son's mouth; the father interrupts to clarify obscure points while the mother hears nothing although she listens intently! **17.** *my daughter:* The family bonds are drawn ever tighter as the demon of loneliness is banished from this enclave of love. **18.** *Ahikar and Nadab:* The fact that Ahikar is here accompanied by his ungrateful nephew is evidence that the author does not follow the plot of that story but merely uses the names to enhance his own story by suggesting a similarity of theme.

13 **12:2.** *half of what I have:* New proof of Tobit's generosity. **6.** *praise God:* Raphael reminds his friends that these happenings are ultimately owing to God's favor. The author puts in the angel's mouth the practical lesson of the story: Praise God, do good, pray, fast, give alms. The angel has become an Israelite sage (cf. 4:3–19). **11.** *will not conceal:* Raphael now points out the consistent thread of God's providential design in all the seemingly fortuitous events that led to this happy outcome. **14.** *to try your faith:* Adversity and God's goodness are reconciled by this formula. **15.** *one of the seven:* There is no need to see here a reference to seven well-known angels; more probably, it is a symbolic number signifying the totality of those ministers who are entitled to stand before God ready to do his bidding. *prayers of the saints:* The emphasis here should be placed on the assurance that the prayers of God's faithful servants do, in fact, reach his ears (in spite of appearances), rather than upon the manner in which they are presented (see also Zech 1:12 and Ap 8:3).

18. *by the will of our God:* Raphael insists that there be no misunderstanding about the true source of all this good fortune. **19.** *did not eat or drink:* The author feels the need to explain that a spiritual being need not eat or drink, yet to do so would be no more difficult than to speak. **20.** *who sent me:* Raphael is in essence an emissary of God. It is God, not his agent, who is really at work. *write in a book:* The author here justifies his own enterprise and provides the expected "documentary" evidence. **21.** *saw him no more:* With God's purpose accomplished, Raphael vanishes.

14 **(VI) Tobit's Prayer (13:1–14:1).** In 13:1–8, we have a thanksgiving prayer in the hymnic style of many psalms. **1.** *his kingdom:* God's kingdom, embracing all creation, is a favorite subject of Pss (cf. Pss 47, 93, 96–99). **2.** *no one:* The primary theme of Tb is the hidden but effective divine control of history. **3.** *before the nations:* It is Israel's glorious vocation to bear witness to God's hidden design. *has scattered us:* One purpose of the Exile was to sow God's witnesses among many nations. **5.** *will gather us:* All Israel's hopes are concentrated in the ultimate "ingathering" of her scattered children. The messianic triumph, too, will be a homecoming—and no less joyous or surprising than that of Tobias! **8.** *Jerusalem:* The holy city is the rallying point of God's people.

9. *O Jerusalem:* During the troubled post-exilic period, the kingdom of God took on strong eschatological overtones, frequently featuring an idealized messianic Jerusalem (cf. Is 60). Tobit's prayer in 13:9–18 represents a lyrical address to the new Jerusalem. *holy city:* All Jerusalem's privileges are traceable to her consecration as the sanctuary where God is present among his people. **10.** *raised for you again:* The threads of God's hidden designs for a scattered and oppressed Israel converge upon the new Temple with the new beneficent presence of God with his children. **11.** *many nations:* Israel's witness will cause many nations to look to Jerusalem for salvation. *bearing gifts:* Eventually the God of Israel will be acknowledged and acclaimed by the whole world (cf. Is 2:2–4; 60:1ff.).

12. *all who hate you:* Those who refuse to recognize God's sovereignty freely will do so by constraint. **14.** *your peace:* To God's downtrodden and badgered people, this vision of peace—the positive, fulfilled peace of the Bible—was wonderfully attractive. *rejoice:* The lots will be reversed; those who mourn now will then rejoice. **16.** *sapphires and emeralds:* An attempt to suggest the rare beauty of this home for all the exiled (cf. Is 54:11–12; Ap 21:10–21). **18.** The whole city will ring with a great shout of praise for the God who has so wonderfully rescued those who, like Tobit and Sarah, appear to have hoped in vain.

15 **(VII) Epilogue (14:2–15).** **2.** Tobit's happy death at an extremely advanced age (recalling the demise of the patriarchs) is the fitting conclusion to a life of unswerving fidelity. Men of faith find happiness and peace at the end. **4.** *go to Media:* Writing after the destruction of Nineveh, the author anticipates a logical question in his reader's mind: What then happened to Tobias when Nineveh fell? *Nahum:* The reference is to Na 1–3 (other texts read Jonah). This prophecy, already fulfilled, reinforces the author's argument that God does, in fact, control human history. *in due time:* The time of God's visitation is part of his secret counsel; but the fact of his sovereignty is clearly revealed. *burned down:* The Temple was destroyed by the Babylonians in 587. **5.** *rebuild the house of God:* A second Temple was built under the direction of the prophet Haggai and was completed in 515. This undistinguished structure was replaced five centuries later by Herod's magnificent edifice.

6. *all the Gentiles:* A universalist approach reminiscent of Is 18:7; 19:22. **7.** *land of Abraham:* The promised land will eventually become the permanent inheritance of Abraham's descendants. **8.** *serve God:* While awaiting the fulfillment of messianic hopes, Israel, like Tobit, must keep faith with God. **10.** *Ahikar:* See 1:21 and comment. It is clear from this reference that the point of similarity between these two stories is the eventual triumph of justice and the vindication of virtue in human life. **11.** Like the patriarchs, Tobit imparts a solemn charge just before death. It is the wise and authentic Israel that speaks here. **13.** Note again the emphasis laid upon the humble virtues of family life; it is impossible for man to find God alone. **14.** *hundred and twenty-seven:* Patriarchal virtues deserve a patriarchal longevity!

JUDITH

BIBLIOGRAPHY

16 Cazelles, H., "Le personnage d'Achior dans le livre de Judith," *RSR* 39 (1951–52) 125–37. Dubarle, A., *Judith: formes et sens des diverses traditions* (2 vols., Rome, 1966). Haag, E., *Studien zum Buche Judith* (Trier, 1963). Lefèvre, A., "Judith," R-F 1, 746–52. Miller, A. and J. Schildenberger, *Die Bücher Tobias, Judith und Esther* (BB; Bonn, 1940). Skehan, P., "The Hand of Judith," *CBQ* 25 (1963) 94–110. Steinmann, J., *Lecture de Judith* (Paris, 1953). Stummer, F., *Geographie des Buches Judith* (Stuttgart, 1947).

INTRODUCTION

17 **(I) Text and Canonicity.** The Book of Judith is presently extant in Gk and later versions only. Scholars agree, however, that the Gk edition is a translation of an original Semitic (probably Hebr) text. The best of three divergent forms of the Gk version is represented by codices Vaticanus, Alexandrinus, and Sinaiticus. (For details cf. Dubarle, *op. cit.*, and the review by P. Skehan in *CBQ* 28 [1966] 347–49.) Jdt never came into the Hebr canon, but it was adopted for reading for the feast of Hanukkah, and even Jerome admitted that the work was "read" in the Church. Final recognition of its canonicity came with the Council of Trent.

(II) Author, Date, and Place of Composition. An unknown Jewish author composed this work about 150 BC, probably in Palestine. The author's knowledge of Gk customs (3:7; 15:13) and the strong emphasis on legal prescriptions suggest this late date of composition.

(III) Literary Form. Very few authors still attempt to defend the historicity of the work. Most agree that it is a didactic story concerned primarily with God's providence. The many references to Israel's history are valid, not as elements of a reliable and accurate narrative, but as realistic illustrations of a doctrine concerning Israel's role and destiny in human history.

(IV) Doctrine. Although Jdt may not be considered historical, it is nonetheless devoted to the exposition of a doctrine rooted in the eminently historical fact of God's involvement in human history through the Exodus event (cf. Skehan in *CBQ* 25, 94–110). Widely separated elements of Israel's history are artificially telescoped and interpreted in the light of the overriding fact of the Exodus experience. Judith (Israel) cannot fail to overcome the powers of this world, simply because God led her out of Egypt with outstretched arm! In the historical disarray of the post-exilic period, it is essential that Israel pronounce again her act of faith. This opportunity is provided by this work.

(V) Outline. The Book of Judith may be outlined as follows:

(I) Peril of the Jews (1:1–7:32)
(II) Deliverance of the Jews (8:1–14:10)
(III) Victory (14:11–16:25)

COMMENTARY

18 **(I) Peril of the Jews (1:1–7:32).** **1.** Nebuchadnezzar was king of Babylon from 605 to 561. *Assyrians:* The Assyrian Empire came to an end when Nebuchadnezzar's father, Nabopolassar, destroyed Nineveh in 612. The historically impossible combination of Nebuchadnezzar and Nineveh, not to mention the Persian commander-in-chief (2:4), tells us that the author wishes to create a composite figure representing all the traditional oppressors of Israel. It is the world against Israel (Judith). *Arphaxad:* Unknown. *Ecbatana:* Capital of Media, E of modern Hamadan.

2. The "wall" and its gateway are of such fantastic proportions that one may assume the author merely wishes to suggest an image of massive power and permanence. **5.** *Rages:* Perhaps modern Rai, 100 mi. NE of Ecbatana. **6.** *Hydaspes:* River on the eastern boundary of Persia. *Arioch:* Otherwise unknown; the Elamite kingdom disappeared before the time of Nebuchadnezzar. **7.** *Cilicia:* Southern Asia Minor. **9.** *River of Egypt:* Wadi el-Arish, between Egypt and Palestine. *Tahpanhes:* City in the eastern Nile Delta. **10.** *Tanis, Memphis:* Cities in Egypt. These geographical references are intended to highlight the world-wide arena of this theology of history; vv. 7–11 cover the western portion of the Fertile Crescent. **11.** *lone individual:* An erroneous assessment of Nebuchadnezzar's political strength providing an excuse for his military campaign. **12.** *borders of the two seas:* Possibly a reference to the lands between the Mediterranean and the Red Sea, i.e., Upper Egypt. **13.** Nebuchadnezzar's rout of this vague eastern power (Arphaxad) sets the stage for his vengeance on the west and also serves to establish his reputation of invincibility.

2:1. *eighteenth year:* It is 587, or the exact year in which Jerusalem was leveled by Nebuchadnezzar's army. The author judges this date appropriate for the decision of worldly power to eliminate the witness of faith in this world. **4.** *Holofernes:* The name is Persian. See comment on 1:1. **5.** *lord:* Nebuchadnezzar is God's rival in any age. **7.** *have earth and water ready:* A Persian expression meaning the provisioning of an invading army from the local country. **8.** The satellites who foolishly defied the giant must now accept the inevitable recompense. All the elements of this equation are human, and its logic appears irrefutable. **19.** *he and his whole army:* The image intended is that of a perfectly prepared and, by human standards, invincible force setting out on a military cakewalk.

21. *Bectileth:* Unknown. **23.** *Put and Lud:* These names occur in Gn 10, where Put is a son of Ham (v. 6) and the Ludites are associated with the Philistines. In Gn 10:22, however, Lud is listed among the sons of Shem. *Rassisites:* Unknown. **24.** *Abron:* Unknown. **25.** *Japheth:* Unknown. The author is more intent on displaying the power of Holofernes' war machine than on providing reliable geographical information. **28.** *Sur and Ocina:* Perhaps Dor and Acco in western Galilee. *Jamnia:* Town on the shore of the Lake of Galilee. This campaign follows an impossibly erratic course. Just as the personages involved make up a composite of Israel's enemies, so does this campaign sweep over the general arena where Israel's oppressors had displayed their prowess. Thus, the stage is set for Israel's entrance: A mighty army, crushing all before it, will be challenged by a political and military nonentity!

19 **3:2.** *lie prostrate:* This craven attitude serves as a contrasting backdrop for the "hopeless" defiance of the Israelites. **6.** *seacoast:* Even the hardy and indomitable Phoenicians understand that resistance is futile. **7.** *garlands and dancing:* A Gk feature suggesting a period of Hellenist influence. **8.** *invoke him as god:* It is now clear that the author wishes to situate the real contest between Nebuchadnezzar (human pride and power) and the true God of Israel (acting through his humble and insignificant people). In point of fact, the Assyrian and Babylonian rulers never pretended to be gods. The author attributes to Nebuchadnezzar a claim made by the Seleucids (cf. Dn 3:5). **10.** *Scythopolis:* The Hellenist name of Beth-shan, S of the Lake of Galilee.

4:1. *Israelites:* The people of Judea are in great fear, not for their lives, but for the honor of their God and his Temple. These Israelites represent an idealized picture of God's people in human history. They are as God-fearing as Nebuchadnezzar is godless; the issue must be clearly religious. **3.** *exile:* The return from the Babylonian Exile began in 538. This purification must refer to the rededication of the Temple by Judas Maccabeus in 164, after it had been desecrated by Antiochus IV Epiphanes. The author deliberately telescopes Israel's history.

4. *region of Samaria:* The line of resistance is drawn along the northern border of Judea. Of all the towns mentioned, only Beth-horon, Samaria, and Jericho are helpful. The author conveniently ignores the ancient enmity between the Israelites and the Samaritans. *valley of Salem:* An archaic name for Jerusalem (Gn 14:17–18). **6.** *Joiakim:* A high priest of this name is mentioned in Neh 12:10,12,26, but at that time Jerusalem was controlled by a Persian civil governor. No doubt Joiakim represents the priesthood in general, viewed as the ideal rallying point for God's people in defence of their sanctuary. *Bethulia:* No city by this name is known. It is, quite plainly, a fictitious city, situated in the strategic Plain of Esdraelon and thus blocking the path of Israel's traditional enemies on their way to ravage Jerusalem. In a word, it is the "place" where God's people and the powers of this world engage in inevitable and decisive conflict.

8. *senate:* Such a council was sometimes invoked by the king (cf. 1 Kgs 8:1), but a senate of the high priest is found only in Maccabean times (2 Mc 11:27). Once again, the author's overriding concern is to make this enterprise one of all the ages of Israel. **9.** *cried to God:* All Israel's great victories begin with prayer and penance, for divine intervention can come only after Israel has cried out from the "bondage of Egypt." **12.** *altar:* A ritual unmentioned elsewhere in the Bible. Israel displays her misery before God in the spirit of a beggar showing his rags. **13.** *heard their cry:* God cannot remain deaf to the humble petition of his oppressed people: "As their cry for release went up to God, he heard their groaning..." (Ex 2:24).

20 5:2. *summoned all the rulers:* Israel is so insignificant that Holofernes must call in the better known neighbors for information about these "mountaineers." His questions are standard and prudent, but hopelessly irrelevant in the case of God's people. *satraps:* Another reflection of Persian times. 3. *you Canaanites:* This archaic designation indicates the author's desire to associate all Israel's traditional enemies with the oldest of her oppressors. 4. *why have they refused?:* Holofernes asks the leading question: What makes Israel different? It sets the stage for a long disquisition on the reason for Israel's stubborn nonconformity.

5. *Achior:* This "good pagan," posing as a disinterested observer, tells the strange story of a people whose history cannot be explained by the usual interplay of political and military forces. It recalls Balaam's witness regarding Israel (Nm 22–24). *the truth:* Achior's nationality is supposed to lend credibility to his account. 6. *Chaldeans:* A reference to Abraham. 8. *they fled to Mesopotamia:* In this context, Mesopotamia is the region around Haran where Abraham first stopped after leaving Ur (Gn 11:31). The biblical account gives no hint that this migration resulted from religious persecution. 12. *land of Egypt:* This review of Israel's history is intended to explain her unique character by showing how God has involved himself in her destiny. Israel's remembrance of God's past interventions in hopeless situations makes it possible and "reasonable" for her to defy Holofernes. In a word, Israel's actions cannot and should not make sense unless one takes into consideration the premise of her faith in the reality of the Exodus experience.

15. *Amorites:* Ancient inhabitants of Canaan or, as here, of Transjordan. *Heshbon:* The capital of Sihon in Transjordan (Nm 21:21ff.). 17. According to this interpretation, all Israel's misfortunes are direct results of her infidelity. By the same token, she is invincible when faithful. Achior thus pinpoints the exact source of Israel's courage and strength. 18. Israel's vocation is to seek out and to follow the unlikely path traced out for her by God. 19. The return from the Exile is interpreted as the restoration of a chastened and repentant Israel, the kind of Israel that cannot be defeated. 21. Given the premise of Israel's faith, it is God with whom Holofernes will have to contend. 22. Achior's remarks are greeted with predictable anger and derision. His thesis, being an unequivocal statement of faith in the reality of God in human history, could scarcely be expected to find any other reaction from the general staff of a great army.

21 6:2. *who are you, Achior?:* For such as Holofernes there is no reality but earthly power and no man may suggest seriously that there are perhaps other significant factors in human existence. *what god is there?:* The issue is strictly religious; there can be but one supreme deity. 5. *mercenary:* Achior, like all the prophets, is abused and ridiculed for his advice. *people from Egypt:* Israel does not even merit a proper name. 6. By his "stupidity," Achior has won for himself the fate of the Israelites. 9. *my words shall not fail:* It is typical of the great ones of this world that they reject the very possibility of error or misjudgment.

15. *Uzziah:* Neither this person nor his fellow rulers are mentioned elsewhere. 18. *fell prostrate:* Israel, too, sees that the moment of truth is approaching. It is now faith against steel. 19. *lowliness:* Humility and sincere prayer are the arms of those who trust in God. *consecrated:* The covenant sets the Israelites apart from all that Nebuchadnezzar represents. They are reserved for God's service and must rely on his protection. 20. *consoled Achior:* Israel's faith embraces and sustains this good foreigner whose honesty has won him the same fate.

7:3. Balbaim and Cyamon are unknown. 5. *lighted fires:* To prevent a surprise attack. 6. *his cavalry:* The elite force is paraded to break Israel's morale. 7. *sources of water:* For a successful siege all springs must be located and guarded. The noose is tightening. It is odd that this powerful army should follow the strategy suggested by the Edomites and others. 15. *dire punishment:* A siege requires patience and denies the attackers the satisfaction of personal infliction of punishment; but there is compensation in the knowledge that death is slow and gruesome! The strategy is as flawless as it is cruel.

18. *Acraba...Chusi...Wadi Mochmur:* Probably in the area SE of the city of Samaria. 19. *surrounded:* The author insists on the size and strategy of the invading army to impress the reader with the hopeless situation of the cornered Israelites. The prospect must be as bleak as was that of post-exilic Israel. 22. The strategy is mercilessly effective. Everywhere there is proof that prayer cannot match power. 24. Uzziah is another Moses being assailed for having led the people into the desert to die (Nm 14:1–4). At this point in the struggle, the clamor for compromise is deafening. 27. *be made slaves:* An echo of the complaint made against Moses (Ex 14:12). 30. *five days:* Uzziah seeks to restore morale by setting a definite goal. This faith is not perfect (see 8:11–27), but it is an understandable maneuver.

22 **(II) Deliverance of the Jews (8:1–14:10).** 1. *Judith:* The "Jewess"; this rather uncommon name is chosen because Judith represents the Jewish nation. Her long genealogy firmly establishes Judith's membership in the covenanted nation. 2. *her own tribe:* Later identified as the tribe of Simeon (9:2). 3. *sunstroke:* Judith was widowed early and in a particularly sudden and cruel manner. *in the field:* An archaic reference to patriarchal burials. *Balamon:* Probably a variation of Balbaim; cf. 4:4; 7:3. 5. *a tent:* A kind of summer room on the flat roof where there would be more privacy—an austere retreat. There Judith prays and awaits God's call. 6. The vigil of Sabbath and New Moon was a solemnity of later, talmudic times (maybe a gloss). 7. *beautiful of form:* A providential preparation for Judith's negotiations with Holofernes. In view of the early age of marriage in Israel, she could have been as young as 18. 8. *God-fearing:* Like true Israel, Judith's life is centered in God. She might have had another husband or lived sumptuously on her wealth; she preferred to devote her life to prayer and charity.

11. Judith now takes charge of the desperate situation. God has found his agent and it is, as usual, a surprising choice. 14. *discern his mind:* Israel must learn to trust God, not attempting to anticipate his moves, much less to force them. God's mysterious design for his people must remain inviolate until he decides to reveal it. God is fiercely jealous of his freedom of action while Israel is forever tempted to pry into his counsels. 17. *while we wait:* In desperate situations, calm patience and sincere prayer are the ideal reactions of a true Israelite. There will be a time for action but it must await God's initiative. 18. *gods made by hands:* An optimistic observation generally verified in the post-exilic period. The Exile had thoroughly disillusioned the old, idol-loving Israel; now patience and prayer seem the only recourse in a dark and turbulent world. 20. Judith reasserts Achior's thesis: So long as Israel remains loyal to God she is invincible. 22–23. Each Israelite must carry his personal burden of unflinching faith. The author undoubtedly has his own contemporaries in mind. Judith reminds her countrymen of the ironic possibility that lack of faith may bring

disgraceful defeat just when God was prepared to grant glorious victory!

24. *set an example:* The leaders must assume first responsibility for resolute faith. **25.** *should be grateful:* This occasion ought to be interpreted as an opportunity to join the heroes of Israel, all of whom were tried in the fire of apparent failure. All are thus urged to join hands with the true Israel of faith, personified by Judith herself. *test:* Cf. v. 12. **27.** *admonition:* Israel is God's field, to be plowed and harrowed by suffering before it can yield his bountiful harvest. **29.** Judith's wisdom derives from solid piety rather than from learning or social advantage. **31.** *pray for us:* Uzziah acknowledges his own lack of contact with God. **33.** *by my hand:* The hesitant and compromising leaders are bypassed as God chooses his own unlikely instrument and plots the strange course of his salvation. The author is clearly influenced, here again, by the Exodus narrative where it is "by the hand" of Moses that Israel is liberated (cf. Ex 9 and 14 *passim*; cf. Skehan, *CBQ* 25, 94–110). **34.** *will not tell you:* It is essential that God's plan remain secret so as to guarantee the absolute gratuity of his salvation.

23 **9:2.** *Simeon:* This patriarch had not played a glorious role in Israel's history (Gn 49:5–7; 2 Chr 34:6). Perhaps it is another indication of the "unlikely instrument" theme. *put a sword:* Simeon and Levi slaughtered the Shechemites for having violated their sister, Dinah (Gn 34). The author sees that strangers are once again laying violent hands upon the virgin daughter of Jacob! **3.** The seduction of Dinah must be avenged by the seduction of the offender—an anticipation of Judith's tactics with Holofernes. **5.** The central theological theme of the entire book is stated here: God rules history. Israel is, by definition, a witness to this dramatic, if often disconcerting, fact. It was particularly necessary to reassert this conviction after the Exile when the God of the promises appeared to have lost control of history.

7. The Assyrians here represent all those who maintain that military and political power is the decisive force in human history. *crush warfare:* A quotation from the Song of Moses (Ex 15:3 in LXX). The obvious similarity between this canticle and the theme of Judith confirms the impression that the author is composing a theology of Israel's history. Faithful Israel can never be consumed because her God is the God of the Exodus—the God who successfully defied the Pharaoh. **8.** Israel is inviolable because God has set her apart; she is consecrated and God is sworn to defend her against violent profanation. **10.** *the slave:* See Wis 18:11, where the same statement is found in reference to the victory of the Exodus. *hand of a woman:* Perhaps a reference to Jael's dispatching of Sisera (Jgs 4:17–22), but now the hand is that of Judith.

11. *God of the lowly:* A common theme of Pss and characteristic of post-exilic piety. **12.** *Lord of heaven and earth:* The creator, having molded the first moment of time, controls the last also, and therefore all intervening history. **13.** *my guileful speech:* This deceit is an art of warfare, like spying; Judith's guile is no more reprehensible in this view than David's sword.

24 **10:3.** *festive attire:* It is now time to proceed from prayer to action. **4.** *captivate:* Judith is a woman and fights with a woman's weapons! **5.** *provisions:* Violation of dietary prescriptions must be avoided; Judith's piety is almost scrupulous. **6.** *Uzziah:* Even "official" Israel is merely a spectator at the unexpected execution of God's saving design. **13.** *trustworthy report:* The use of artifice as a tactic of warfare was held in highest regard in those ancient times. It would be naïve to be scandalized by such conduct. **17.** *escort:* The Assyrians are easily gulled by this attractive woman. **19.** *beguile the whole world:* As these proud men walk into the trap they confidently note that this would make a very good trap! Man's wisdom is folly before God. **20.** *tent:* The adornment of this field headquarters, no doubt exaggerated, reflects the character of a shrewd but proud and sensual potentate.

11:4. *take courage:* An ironic situation in which the victim encourages his executioner! **5.** The author makes a point of the veracity of Judith; her ambiguous remarks are, in the wider perspective shared by the reader, substantially true. **6.** Holofernes will indeed play his part perfectly. He does not yet know, however, that he has the villain's role. **12.** *forbade them to eat:* The emphasis on dietary laws is typical of later Judaism (Dn 1). **15.** Judith allows Holofernes to draw conclusions that do not necessarily follow. **16.** *such deeds:* To Holofernes, it refers to his victory; in reality, it is the incredible news of his rout. **17.** *remain with you:* What different meanings these words have for Holofernes and Judith! History admits of various interpretations and only at the end is the true meaning fully revealed. *each night:* Judith twits the sensual Holofernes as she plays the pious and naïve damsel, and so dupes him into granting permission for an important factor in her strategy. **19.** Holofernes is invited to become a partner in a secret plot with a beautiful woman—an infallible device to win his collaboration in a project with quite a different outcome. **20.** They admire her discovery of their own wisdom, whereas her true wisdom is to have perceived their folly. **22.** *God has done well:* Truly spoken, and unwittingly! The author proves himself a master of the storyteller's art. **23.** *my God:* Judith's God will indeed be his God (cf. Dn 5:34–37), but not as he understands it. Holofernes is now completely mesmerized and ready for the slaughter. No one is so blind as the proud man.

25 **12:2.** A reflection of typical post-exilic piety with its concern for ritual observance. **4.** *by my hand:* See 8:33 and comment. **7.** *each night:* A pattern of nocturnal excursions is established so as not to arouse suspicion later. **9.** *toward evening:* Apparently Judith fasted during the day. **11.** *Bagoas:* The name is Persian. **12.** *disgrace:* Holofernes represents the sensual worldy potentate for whom pleasure is the highest law. **15.** *festive garments:* One must be fittingly clad for the day of Israel's victory! **16.** *burning with desire:* The proud are betrayed by their passions. **18.** Note the subtle ambiguity in Judith's statement.

13:1. *excluded the attendants:* Holofernes makes careful preparations for pleasure, and death. **4.** *exaltation of Jerusalem:* The ambiguity now ceases. Judith stands beside the great Holofernes as God's unlikely agent for the protection of his sanctuary and the deliverance of his helpless people. **5.** *your heritage:* All this has come about because God freely involved himself in Israel's history through the Exodus event. **6.** *his sword:* The Gk word suggests a Persian scimitar or dagger, not the heavy battle sword. **7.** *strengthen me:* It is the climactic and decisive confrontation of humble faith and proud worldly power. This story is almost certainly influenced by Jael's victory over Sisera (also on the Plain of Esdraelon; Jgs 4:21) and David's beheading of Goliath (1 Sm 17:51).

11. *open the gate:* The seemingly endless waiting of God's people is rewarded with final dramatic victory. *God... is with us:* Israel's persistent belief in the presence of a protecting God is fully vindicated. This belief was most sorely tried in the desolate post-exilic period. **13.** *all the people:* It is the victory of all God's people—of all ages. *fire for light:* Israel's Exodus victory was described as a light in the darkness (Ex 12:29ff.; 14:24). **14.** *by my hand:* See 8:33 and comment. **15.** *hand of a woman:* Israel's strength lies in what this world calls weakness, namely, faith and prayer. **16.** Judith risked her own virtue to save her people, but it is emphasized that she escaped. **18.** *above all women:* Cf. Lk 1:28,42. **20.** *risked your life:* Israel can be saved only by the sacrifice that subordinates personal needs to the common good.

14:1. *on the parapet:* All the world must witness the ultimate triumph of faith. **2.** *at daybreak:* Again it is at daybreak that Israel's victory is consummated (see 13:13 and comment). The sun's "victory" over darkness is symbolic of faith's triumph over the blind chaos of evil. **5.** Achior can prove the identity of the head, and as representative of Israel's foreign friends, he must witness the vindication of his own faith in her vocation. **10.** *believed firmly:* The good foreigner's honesty eventually brings about his total conversion to the true God. *circumcised:* All legal prescriptions must be observed.

26 **(III) Victory (14:11–16:25).** **11.** *at daybreak:* See 13:13, 14:2 and comments. **13.** *slaves:* A contemptuous reference to Israel's former status in Egypt. **18.** *have duped us:* Wisdom has prevailed over power.

15:3. This dramatic "turning of the tables" is characteristic of all apocalyptic scenes. **4.** These towns cannot be identified. **5–7.** The author delights to spell out the details of the rout and slaughter of the enemy. **6.** *acquired great riches:* See Ex 12:35–36. **8.** *Joiakim:* See 4:6 and comment. **9.** *glory of Jerusalem:* Judith is extolled because she is the perfectly pliable instrument of God. The glory of any Israelite is to permit God to work freely through him. Christian liturgical texts apply these words to the Virgin Mary. **10.** *with your own hand:* See 8:33 and comment, and P. W. Skehan, *CBQ* 25, 94–110. **12.** *formed a dance:* As Miriam led the women of Israel in dancing after the victory over Egypt (Ex 15:20). *garlands:* This distinctively Gk feature suggests a date of composition during the Hellenistic period (333–63 BC).

27 **16:2.** The Canticle of Judith is called a "new song" in the style of Pss 96,98. **3.** *crushes warfare:* See 9:7 and comment. *his dwelling:* Israel's victory is owing to God's invisible but efficacious presence in the midst of his people. **4.** *from the north:* Although Assyria lies E of Palestine, the invasion route is from the north. **6.** *by a woman's hand:* See comment on 8:33, 14:10. **10.** *Persians...Medes:* Even such fearless warriors are stunned by the daring of this maid of despised Israel. **12.** *fugitive slaves:* The mighty ones (like Holofernes) ridicule the Israelites fleeing from Egyptian slavery (6:5); now the tables are turned. **14.** *were created:* A theme from Pss—e.g., 33:9; 104:30. **16.** *sacrifice:* An echo of the prophets' campaign against formalism in worship. **17.** *fire and worms:* Classic imagery to describe the final lot of the wicked (cf. Sir 7:19; Is 66:24).

19. *Judith dedicated:* An attitude of detachment that recalls Est 9:10. The booty belongs to God, who gave the victory. **20.** *three months:* See *3 Mc* 6:30–40. *in Jerusalem:* Clearly it is Jerusalem, not Bethulia, that has been delivered. God's sanctuary proves to be inviolable after all. **22.** *marry her:* Marriage is viewed as an obstacle to that total dedication to God desired by Judith. **23.** *advanced age:* A reflection of patriarchal signs of divine favor. **24.** Such final acts of largesse are the expected concluding gestures of heroic biographies. **25.** *for a long time:* An echo of the era of the judges (cf. Jgs 3:11; 3:30, 5:32). This "long time" may also point to Israel's definitive eschatological peace and joy.

ESTHER

BIBLIOGRAPHY

28 Anderson, B., "Esther," *IB*. Barucq, A., *Esther* (BJ; 2nd ed.; Paris, 1959). Eissfeldt, *OTI* 505–12, 591–92. Gunkel, H., *Esther* (Tübingen, 1916). Miller, A. and J. Schildenberger, *Die Bücher Tobias, Judith und Esther* (BB; Bonn, 1940). Paton, L. B., *The Book of Esther* (ICC; N.Y., 1908). Roiron, F. X., "Les parties deutérocanoniques du livre d'Esther," *RSR* 6 (1916) 1–16. Soubrigou, L., *Esther* (*PSB* 4; Paris, 1949).

INTRODUCTION

29 **(I) Text and Canonicity.** Est has been preserved in two substantially different forms: a Hebr text, assumed by most scholars to be original; and a Gk text (also existing in two rather divergent forms—LXX and Lucian), which freely translates the Hebrew and adds to it six large (deuterocanonical) sections. When Jerome translated this book, he lumped the Gk sections together at the end of his work. In this commentary, they are restored to their proper places, where they are designated by capital letters. The Gk numbering (11:2–12:26; 13:1–7; 13:8–14:19; 15:1–16; 16:1–27) is adopted in many translations. The Greek additions to Est are the "deuterocanonical" portions, and they were, as usual, questioned by Jerome. But they were finally recognized as canonical by the Council of Trent.

(II) Author, Place, and Date of Composition. Est was written by an unknown Jew, either in Susa (Persia) or in Palestine, during the period between the late 5th and late 2nd cents. BC. The Gk translation and additions were probably prepared shortly before 114 (cf. F:11 [11:1]).

30 **(III) Literary Form.** On this point, scholarly opinion ranges from pure myth to strict history. Most critics, however, favor a middle course of historical elements with more or less generous literary embellishments (thus J. Schildenberger, H. Gunkel, O. Eissfeldt, A. Barucq). The Gk additions in particular appear to be essentially literary creations. That neither author intended to write strict history seems obvious from the historical inaccuracies, unusual coincidences, and other traits characteristic of folklore (all of which will be pointed out in the commentary). On the other hand, there is no compelling reason for denying the possibility of an undetermined historical nucleus, and the author's generally accurate picture of Persian life tends to support this possibility. Several details of Est suggest a fictitious story.

The very fact of variations between the Hebrew and the deuterocanonical additions shows that the book was freely embellished in the course of its history. Then there are the many difficulties concerning Mordecai's age, and the wife of Xerxes (Amestris). Moreover, the artificial symmetry suggests fiction: Gentiles against Jews; Vashti as opposed to Esther; the hanging of Haman and the appointment of Mordecai as the vizier; the anti-Semitic pogrom and the slaying of the Gentiles. A law of contrasts is obviously at work. On the other hand, one cannot dispute the possibility of Jewish pogroms during the Persian period, and the story of Esther and Mordecai may have some basis in fact. As it stands, it has been developed very freely as the "festal legend" of a Feast of Purim, which is itself otherwise unknown to us.

31 **(IV) Doctrine.** The Hebr author underscores the dramatic deliverance of the Jews from the power of a great empire that found them guilty of nonconformity. He thus emphasizes the inviolability of God's people in history. This thesis is made the theme of the already existing Feast of Purim, which the author wishes to explain and support. His deliberate avoidance of any explicit references to God is the result, some say, of later editors who did not wish God's name to be associated with the decidedly profane Purim festivities. Others attribute the absence of overt religious references to religious persecution. The Gk translator-author extends the theme of divine providence to the cosmic and apocalyptic arena: God's people, misunderstood but loyal, will be rescued from the apparent hopelessness of a human history dominated by secular power.

32 **(V) Outline.** The Book of Esther may be outlined as follows:

(I) Prologue: Mordecai's Dream and His Loyalty (A:1–17[11:2–12:6])
(II) Esther Replaces Queen Vashti (1:1–2:23)
(III) Haman Plots To Destroy the Jews (3:1–15; B:1–7[13:1–7])
(IV) Esther and Mordecai Appeal to God (4:1–16; C:1–30[13:8–14:19])
(V) Divine Deliverance Is Prepared (D:1–16[15:1–16]; 5:1–16)
(VI) The Lots Are Reversed (6:1–8:12; E:1–24[16:1–24]; 8:13–9:19)
(VII) The Feast of Purim (9:20–10:3)
(VIII) Epilogue: Interpretation of Mordecai's Dream (F:1–11[10:4–11:1])

COMMENTARY

33 **(I) Prologue: Mordecai's Dream and His Loyalty (A:1–17[11:2–12:6]).** **1.** *second year:* It is 484 BC. *first day of Nisan:* About March 15. *Mordecai:* The name is Babylonian, after the god Marduk. **2.** *Susa:* Capital of Elam; later, winter residence of Persian kings (for archaeology, see J. Finnegan, *Light from the Ancient Past* [2nd ed.; Princeton, 1959] 21–22, 243). **4.** *one of the captives:* Since this deportation took place in 598, Mordecai would be well over 100 years old! Some critics suggest that he was a descendant of the captives; others maintain that the author was not concerned about the exact date of the deportation. *Jeconiah:* Or Jehoiachin (2 Kgs 24:8,15).

5–11. The imagery is typical of apocalyptic literature. Israel, at the mercy of powerful oppressors and drained of all human hope, looks for a divine intervention that will dramatically turn the tables and establish her in peace and glory. This divine visitation is usually depicted as a convulsion of nature, followed by the sudden repose of total victory. The Gk redactor adapted the story of Esther to illustrate this eventual cosmic victory of God's people over the apparently invincible powers of this world. The dream itself is interpreted in the Epilogue (F:1–11 [10:4–12]). **12–16.** The Hebr text (6:3) takes a different view of Mordecai's successful thwarting of the plot on the king's life, but here it is explicitly stated that he is rewarded.

17. *Haman:* Identified as a "Bougean," apparently the equivalent of Agagite (cf. 3:1). This term associates him with the Amalekite king defeated by Mordecai's fellow tribesman Saul (cf. I Sm 15:7–9). Thus, the struggle between Mordecai and Haman becomes a continuation of the blood feud between Israel and Amalek, and, in apocalyptic perspective, between God's people and the godless forces of this world. *because of the two eunuchs:* The implication is that Haman was involved in this plot and therefore harbored a grudge against Mordecai. The Hebr text (3:5) suggests a more personal reason for the enmity.

34 **(II) Esther Replaces Queen Vashti (1:1–2:23).** **1.** *provinces:* The Persian Empire was divided into administrative districts called satrapies, of which there were about 13 at this time. The 127 provinces were probably subdivisions of these larger districts. The author is intent in vv. 2–9 on displaying the power of Xerxes I (485–464), who is called "Ahasuerus" here and in Ezr 4:9; cf. Dn 9:1. **2.** *Susa:* The winter residence, as opposed to Persepolis, the real capital. **9.** *Queen Vashti:* No other source speaks of a Persian queen of this name. Moreover, Herodotus names Amestris as Xerxes' wife (*History* 9.108–13). **11.** *display her beauty:* Probably a euphemism. The half-drunk king intended to make an indecent display of his wife. **12.** *much enraged:* The defiance of a potentate and his consequent rash actions are a common theme of popular court stories. **13.** *wise men:* One senses a hint of mockery as the ponderous machinery of Persian government is deployed in such an insignificant matter. **18.** *will rebel:* Another sardonic touch; it is difficult to believe that this situation could really have constituted a problem in view of social conditions of those days. The entire description (17–22) seems to be deliberately exaggerated.

2:3. *all beautiful young virgins:* It would be naïve to take this statement literally. Such a universal canvassing of the empire is meant to highlight Esther's beauty by magnifying the competition. **5.** *a certain Jew:* The Hebr text introduces Mordecai here. The Gk translator, perhaps out of respect for his source, chose not to eliminate this repetition. **7.** Hadassah is a Hebr name meaning "myrtle"; the name Esther is almost certainly of Babylonian derivation. Jews in foreign lands frequently bore two names. *daughter:* The relationship between Mordecai and Esther is characterized by extraordinary tenderness and loyalty. He is the wise, cool head of Israel; she is its warm, tender heart. **9.** *the girl pleased him:* Esther emerges as the winsome, natural beauty who joins physical attractiveness with those more subtle and telling personal qualities of tact, thoughtfulness, and sensitivity.

35 **10.** *her nationality:* The king must not know that he is falling in love with one who is of the "enemy" race. Here, again, one recognizes a familiar theme of popular narrative. **11.** *day by day:* Mordecai could not enter the harem but he stayed abreast of happenings by listening to the usual gossip. It is surprising, in view of v. 10, that he associates himself so closely with Esther. **12.** *beauty treatment:* It seems strange that the king, who was reported to be so lonely, should have had to wait a full year for companionship. Again, literary requirements take precedence over historical considerations. **15.** *she did not ask for anything:* A delicate way of underlining her natural comeliness and also the hidden providence of God (cf. Dn 1).

16. *the tenth month:* About December 15 to January 15. *the seventh year:* It is now more than three years since Vashti's deposition! Some suggest that Xerxes may have been absent on the Grecian campaign (his armies destroyed Athens in 480). **18.** *a great feast:* The frequent mention of sumptuous banquets evokes the spirit of the Purim feast—in view of which Est was doubtless composed—which was marked by feasting and giftgiving (9:22).

19. The MT is corrupt; whatever the exact meaning of the passage, it is clear that the author's intention is to recall the reader's attention (after the harem distractions) to those elements of the story important for the next episode—i.e., Mordecai's position; Esther's hidden nationality; Mordecai's service to the king (presumably unrewarded); and the recording of this fact in the king's annals.

36 **(III) Haman Plots to Destroy the Jews (3:1–15; B:1–7[13:1–7]).** **1.** *after these events:* A common biblical phrase used to introduce a situation that the author does not wish to explain. Haman, the "Agagite," is now in a position to do grave harm to Mordecai, the tribal brother of Saul (1 Sm 15:7–9)! **2.** *kneel and bow down:* There is no reason to believe that the act was more than a convention, out of courtesy and respect, but in the story it becomes a religious concern. **4.** *a Jew:* The nub of the issue: Mordecai is persecuted because he is a Jew—one who is "different," one who gives absolute allegiance to God alone. **6.** *all the Jews:* The immediate extension of Haman's hatred to all Jews confirms Mordecai's intuition that this is the fated enemy of his people.

7. *Nisan:* About March 15 to April 15. *the twelfth year:* It is 474. It is now five years since Esther became queen. The sequence of events is abridged to set the proper dramatic pace. "Pur" is a Babylonian word that the author is careful to translate. The ancients commonly resorted to casting lots to discover the hidden counsel of the gods concerning the propitious moment for an important action. The Babylonian term is introduced to explain the Purim feast, which was probably borrowed from the Babylonians (see A. Bea, "De origine vocis pûr," *Bib* 21 [1940] 198–99). *in Haman's presence:* Some authorized person cast the lots (perhaps marked pebbles) so that Haman could see the results for himself.

37 **8.** The Jews are indicted because they are inassimilable and disobedient. **9.** *to destroy them:* Any secular power claiming total authority must logically consider acknowledgment of divine sovereignty treasonous and has no choice but to proceed against it. *ten thousand silver talents:* This fantastic sum (estimated in millions of dollars) introduces the important element of blood money. God's people will be evaluated in terms of money, not as persons made inviolable by his free and loving choice.

10. *the king:* In this struggle between Haman and Mordecai, King Xerxes plays a strangely neutral role. He emerges as a singularly naïve and ingenuous person who, while basically good and beneficent, is alternately manipulated by good and evil forces. The fact that the historical Xerxes did not conform to this image merely provides further evidence that the author's aim was not primarily historical. **11.** The king's cavalier attitude toward Haman's bribe is far from what one would expect from an Eastern potentate. It may be a diplomatic acceptance, or perhaps the author wishes to preserve the innocence of the king so that all the blame can be concentrated on Haman.

12. *royal signet ring:* A ring the inset of which contained the royal seal, which, when affixed to a document, guaranteed its authenticity and authority (cf. v. 10). **13.** Such harsh and merciless measures, so untypical of the Persian rulers of the Achaemenid Dynasty, must be understood in the light of the author's desire to illustrate the absolutely definitive and conclusive nature of the struggle between God's people and the powers of darkness. The Gk text (13:1–7) provides copies of the document.

38 **B:1[13:1].** *the letter:* This pompous letter, composed by the Gk author, expatiates on the alleged faults of the Jews. It is an apt expression of the sentiments of those who are offended by the attitude of a religious people. **3.** *Haman...wisdom:* As the spokesman for merely human wisdom, Haman will find his best intentions misinterpreted by those who live by the superior dictates of divine wisdom. **4.** *one people of bad will:* The Jewish people, committed to the larger scope of divine vision, must inevitably appear to be disloyal and recalcitrant subjects. Their laws, which set them apart from those guided by merely rational dictates, will be judged contentious and divisive. *the unity of the empire:* Israel's prophetic mission among the nations demands that she bear witness to God's way and thereby disturb the harmony of any exclusively human order. **5.** It is easy to imagine the worst things about people who perform unconventional rites and who are guided by unknown principles. **6.** *fourteenth day:* The lot had fallen on the thirteenth day (3:7)! This discrepancy can perhaps be explained as a literary counterpart to the two-day slaughter of the Jews' enemies at Susa (9:18), or perhaps it results from a variation in the date of the Purim feast.

3:14. *A copy of the decree:* The MT resumes here. In its more sober style, it merely notes the promulgation of of the decree. **15.** *in haste:* With 11 months remaining before the fateful day, there does not seem to be any need for haste. Such remarks are occasionally introduced to increase the pace of the narrative. *to feast:* The king and Haman relax and rejoice. One notes the contrast between a frightened populace (which will later rejoice) and the comfortable, unworried rulers (who will be confounded)!

39 **(IV) Esther and Mordecai Appeal to God (4:1–16; C:1–30[13:8–14:19]).** **1.** *sackcloth and ashes:* A rough camel's-hair garment and disheveled hair effectively publicize a greatly tormented spirit. **2.** *royal gate:* Gossip will soon bring to Esther the news of Mordecai's appearance in the garb of tribulation. **4.** *he refused:* This will tell Esther that the situation is desperate. **7.** *exact amount of silver:* Mordecai is well informed, and the reader is reminded of the venal nature of this crime.

8. *on behalf of her people:* Esther is reminded that high station brings heavy responsibility. Whether she likes it or not, the fate of countless countrymen now rests in her hands. An addition in the Gk text of v. 8 stresses that death faces the people. **11.** *without being summoned:* There is no evidence in profane sources of such drastic penalties for disregarding similar prescriptions. The author probably embellished this episode to accentuate the risk that Esther must take for the sake of her people. *I have not been summoned:* Every easy route is blocked; the risk of death cannot be avoided. **13.** *do not imagine:* The lives of God's people are so intertwined that none of them can ever find salvation without seeking it for his brothers also.

14. *from another source:* The Hebr author refuses to mention God's name. Whatever the exact meaning of the "other source" may be (whether God or some human aid), God's providence is certainly involved. Esther is challenged to prove her faith by sacrificing herself for her people, for only faith can tell her that this act will bring her own salvation. **16.** Faith triumphs, as Esther appoints a fast for the Jews and for herself and her servants. *I perish:* The supreme sacrifice is made. It matters little that death did not actually follow. The essence of worship is this unconditional deliverance of one's whole being to God's discretionary disposition.

40 **C:1–30(13:8–14:19).** *he prayed:* The Gk author, true to his theological perspective, introduces two prayers meant to etch clearly the spiritual physiognomy of the two principal actors. **2–5.** The omnipotent Lord has used his power in Israel's favor in the past. The motifs of omnipotence and omniscience are employed to induce the Lord to intervene. The Gk author realizes that Mordecai's act of defiance could conceivably have been prompted by ignoble motives. For his purposes it is important to eliminate this possibility; the issue must be unambiguous. **8–9.** The usual motifs of a national lament appear: "your people," "your inheritance," "your portion which you redeemed." Cf. Pss 74,79. **10.** *to sing praise:* A familiar theme in the lament: God must spare his people so that they may declare his praises (Ps 79:13). **11.** *death staring them in the face:* No slightest doubt must linger concerning the definitive nature of the threat; it is the apocalyptic alternative of life or death.

12(14:1). *mortal anguish:* The supreme nature of Esther's sacrifice is underlined; she fully expects to die. **13.** *dirt:* Probably a euphemism for dung. **14.** The prayer of Esther combines motifs of individual and national lament: she is "alone"; the nation has "sinned" (17); etc. **22.** The Lord is challenged not to allow idols, which are really nonbeings, to prevail. His failure to rescue Israel now would indirectly endorse idolatry! Ultimately, it would mean the triumph of secular power and, by implication, the nonexistence of God. *their counsel:* It is a question of the validity of God's or man's interpretation of history and reality. Haman personifies merely human counsel—he is powerful, resourceful, decisive, and proud. If this wisdom prevails there can be no God! **23.** *give me courage:* God's agent must recognize that she is too weak to accomplish her mission without God's help. **26.** *abhor the bed:* The Gk author's scruples are again manifest. For his purposes, it is essential that Esther be cleared of any suspicion of willing commerce with the unbeliever. **27.** *sign of grandeur:* No doubt a reference to her crown or some other royal ornament that might appear to imply approval of pagan beliefs. **28.** *at the table of Haman:* But later she will invite him to eat with her (5:4)! **30.** *from my fear:* Esther experiences the anguish of every religious person who undergoes the radical test of his faith.

41 **(V) Divine Deliverance Is Prepared (D:1–16[15:1–16]; 5:1–14). D:1–16.** The Gk author turns the very sober Hebr account (5:1–3) into a vivid, dramatic act in which the mortal peril and intrepid courage of Esther are illustrated This procedure serves his over-all purpose by heightening the contrast between the hopelessness of the Jewish lot and their instantaneous and dramatic deliverance—between the apparent folly of religious hope and its final glorious vindication. **5–7.** The pathos and exaggeration in this scene prepare for the climax in v. 8. **8.** *God changed:* At the moment when, by all human estimates, Esther must be sent away to her doom, God intervenes and the tide is turned. The king's savage anger melts into smiling benevolence (cf. 5:1–3). The change is remarkable: A magnificent and impassive potentate becomes a gentle and solicitous husband! **10.** Although the text is obscure, the implication seems to be that the king knows Esther's nationality (cf. 2:10!).

5:3. *half my kingdom:* An obvious exaggeration. **4.** *come today with Haman:* Esther's strange request initiates a strategy that will lead to Haman's downfall. **8.** *come with Haman tomorrow:* This delay contributes to the suspense of the narrative and gives the author an opportunity to bring Haman to the apex of his pride and self-satisfaction. Attention now shifts from Esther to Haman and Mordecai. It is unlikely that the king would have tolerated such procrastination, but the story demands that Haman die on the very day scheduled for Mordecai's execution.

10. *Haman restrained himself:* Buoyant after his great honor, Haman can afford to be momentarily indulgent. **12.** *no one but myself:* The reader is placed in the advantageous position of one possessing secret knowledge that changes the meaning of the episode. Haman, being prepared for disgrace, boasts of his good fortune! **14.** *fifty cubits:* The incredible height of the gallows (approximately 85 ft.) underlines Haman's irrational hatred. Moreover, his perfect self-assurance prompts him to advertise his victory in grand style!

42 **(VI) The Lots Are Reversed (6:1–8:12; E:1–24[16:1–24]; 8:13–9:19). 6:3.** *nothing was done:* This contradicts a previous statement (A:16) and means either that the reward was insignificant or that a divergent source is used. **4.** *Haman had entered:* The timing provides a perfect dramatic climax as the reader watches this misunderstanding develop with all its savor of poetic justice. **7.** *to reward:* The proud and selfish Haman, seeing everything in relation to his own interests, is trapped into providing a throne for the very one for whom he had erected a gibbet! **10.** *the Jew Mordecai:* Haman—ambitious, clever, and powerful—is blinded by pride and plunges into irreparable disgrace; Mordecai, however, humbly trusting in God, is just as suddenly elevated to honor and glory. **12.** *his head covered:* The great Haman now hides his face in grief and shame. **13.** *the Jewish race:* Even Haman's wife sees that the outcome of the mortal feud between the Israelite and the "Agagite" is already decreed. **14.** *hurried Haman off:* Haman is now swept relentlessly to his doom. With what frightful misgivings he must have attended this second banquet!

7:3. *the lives of my people:* Esther's nationality is presumed to be known to the king (cf. 2:10). **4.** Esther indicates that it is the destruction of her people that motivates her; mere slavery, owing to Haman's bribe, would have been acceptable. **5.** *who and where:* Making full use of the very effective thou-art-the-man technique (cf. 2 Sm 12:7), the author sets the stage for the identification of the despicable culprit who would dare sell the heroic Mordecai or the incomparable Queen Esther! In real life, the king's ignorance would be incomprehensible (cf. 3:11–15); in the story, it serves to underline Haman's culpability.

6. *seized with dread:* He who yesterday was the joyous companion of king and queen is today an isolated and shunned man, darkened by the shadow of death. The same dread that Haman had cast upon the Jews now falls heavily upon himself. **7.** *to beg Queen Esther:* Now Haman, too, knows the desperate fear of the condemned. **8.** *violate the queen:* Such was certainly not Haman's intention, but now everything he touches turns to ashes, as the story moves to its climax. *was covered over:* A sign of doom; he is to be prepared for execution. **9.**

hang him on it: The wheel has turned full circle. The biblical warning that he who digs the pit shall himself fall into it (Ps 7:16) is proven valid.

8:1–3. Mordecai replaces Haman. But the people have yet to be saved. **7.** *what you see fit:* The imperial might is now at the disposal of the just; what had threatened to destroy them is now their servant. **8.** *cannot be revoked:* But a new order will neutralize the effect of the previous "irrevocable" decree. **11.** *attack them:* Defiance of the earlier decree is officially encouraged; in other words, anarchy is invited by royal decree!

43 A copy of the decree is found in the deuterocanonical addition, E:1–24(16:1–24). **E:4.** *the all-seeing God:* The Gk author rather implausibly portrays Xerxes as one duped by a malicious schemer seeking to use the royal power for his nefarious purposes but who is fortunately exposed before irreparable harm can be done. Perhaps he wishes to suggest that irreligious men twist a good creation against God's purposes and must also eventually be exposed and condemned. **7.** *ancient stories:* The sense is that, unfortunately, such perfidy is not restricted to uncivilized times. **10.** *Macedonian:* Haman's identification here as a Greek is probably a reflection of an anti-Greek mentality current at the time of the author. Whatever his nationality, he represents the shrewd worldling who plots to thwart the true purpose of creation. **12.** *of kingdom and life:* Haman's persecution of the Jews, whom he misrepresented as disloyal subjects, was a treasonous act contrary to the best interests of the king. **14.** *Macedonians:* The Greeks, commanded by Alexander (a Macedonian), were the eventual conquerors of Persia. **15.** *not evildoers:* The Jews appear to be disloyal because their patriotism is qualified by their faith; in fact, they are the most loyal subjects for the simple reason that the empire itself can survive only under God. **17.** *to ignore:* The "irrevocable" decree is rendered ineffective by the withdrawal of all sanctions. **18.** *entire household:* Just as the Jews benefit from Mordecai's triumph, so must Haman's "people" go to defeat with him. **19.** *their own laws:* Higher principles demand the disavowal of that rigid conformism that denied the Jews their right to be different. **20.** *help them:* This permission (or polite command) may be intended to explain how a Jewish minority could defend itself successfully. **21.** *has turned that day:* There is no day like the day of doom turned to jubilation! **24.** *ruthlessly destroyed:* This exaggerated threat is further evidence that the Gk author saw this confrontation in the apocalyptic perspective of total victory or defeat.

44 **8:15–17.** The MT records the celebrations in Susa and the provinces. **17.** *embraced Judaism:* God's dramatic interventions in history are designed to force a decision upon all men: Join God's people or scatter. **9:1.** *the situation was reversed:* The day of doom sees the imminent victory of God's enemies become the triumph of his people. **2.** *no one could withstand:* At the end, the weapons will fall from the hands of God's enemies. **10.** *plundering:* It is a holy war, implacable but disinterested (cf. vv. 15–16). The folly of Saul is also corrected (cf. 1 Sm 15:9–23). **13.** *again tomorrow:* The two days of vengeance in Susa will account for the delayed celebration of Purim there; this delay is behind the blood-curdling request. **18.** *fifteenth:* The feasting at Susa is delayed by the extra day of slaughter. Some suggest that the real reason for the divergence in observance had been forgotten.

45 **(VII) The Feast of Purim (9:20–10:3).** **20.** *recorded these events:* A reference to the author's sources. **21.** *celebrate every year:* The chief purpose of the Hebr story was to substantiate, encourage, and interpret the traditional Purim feast. **23.** The story of Purim is now summarized (vv. 23–28). **24.** *foe of all the Jews:* Behind Haman one discerns all the enemies of God's people in all ages. (For the "pur," or "lot," see comment on 3:7.) **27.** *inviolable obligation:* This solemn reminder seems to reflect contemporary Jewish indifference toward this feast (cf. v. 28). **29.** *wrote to confirm:* Queen Esther's influence is added to that of Mordecai. *this second letter:* Although there is no clear distinction between Mordecai's letters, v. 23 indicates that he did, in fact, write more than one letter on this matter. **30–31.** The repeated emphasis betrays a preoccupation with the need to substantiate an already existing practice. *fasting and supplication:* A reflection of the later practice of fasting the day before Purim in imitation of the prayers of Esther and the Jews prior to her appeal to the king.

10:1. *laid tribute:* This irrelevant remark may have been intended to give the narrative a semblance of great antiquity and reliability. *islands of the sea:* The Grecian isles. **2.** *in the chronicles:* A formula borrowed almost verbatim from Kgs (e.g., 1 Kgs 16:14,20,27). *herald of peace:* The figure of Mordecai is evoked as a symbol of the triumph of God's people.

46 **(VIII) Epilogue: Interpretation of Mordecai's Dream (F:1–11[10:4–11:1]).** **F:1.** *the work of God:* A summary of the theological message of the Gk author. The unexpected deliverance of a people about to be crushed by the wheels of secular power is proof that God will vindicate religious hope at the end of time. **2.** Mordecai's strange dream (A:5–11[11:5–11]) is now interpreted as a preview of his own experience, and, beyond that, of the climactic end of history. **3.** *the river:* Esther symbolizes the weak and unpromising instrument that God delights to employ for the dramatic accomplishment of his purposes. **5.** Mordecai and Haman, the "dragons," symbolize the two protagonists in the continuous struggle between good and evil. **6.** *signs and great wonders:* The salvation of Israel, from Exodus to Armageddon, is accomplished by striking interventions of God (the *magnalia Dei*). **8.** *were fulfilled:* Even seemingly fortuitous events are obedient to God's timetable. **10.** *celebrate these days:* Renewal of faith in divine providence is the keynote of the Purim feast. **11(11:1).** *fourth year:* Probably 114 BC, although Eissfeldt, *OTI* 590, thinks it is 78–77. *who said he was:* One detects a note of diffidence on the part of the Alexandrian community toward Jerusalem. *letter of Purim:* The Book of Esther itself. The Gk translation and augmentation no doubt immediately preceded the introduction of this feast into the Jewish community in Egypt. *Lysimachus:* Allegedly the man who translated Est into Greek.

39

JONAH

Jean C. McGowan, R.S.C.J.

BIBLIOGRAPHY

1 Alonso, J., "Lección teológica del libro de Jonas," *Misc. A. Pérez Goyena* (Madrid, 1960) 79–93. Biser, E., "Zum frühchristlichen Verständnis des Buches Jonas," *BiKi* 17 (1962) 19–21. Diaz, J. A., "Paralelos entre la narración del libro de Jonas y la parábola del Hijo Pródigo," *Bib* 40 (1959) 632–40. Dubarle, A. M., "Jonas," *RSPT* 46 (1962) 181. Feuillet, A., "Jonas," *VDBS* 4 (1948) 1104–31; "Le Livre de Jonas," *Revue du Clergé Africain* 18 (1963) 509–21; *Le Livre de Jonas* (BJ; Paris, 1951); "Le sens du Livre de Jonas," *RB* 54 (1947) 340–61; "Les sources du Livre de Jonas," *RB* 54 (1947) 161–86. Freedman, D. N., "Jonah 1, 16," *JBL* 77 (1958) 161–63. Goldberg, A. M., "Jonas in der jüdischen Schriftauslegung," *BiKi* 17 (1962) 18–19. Knoch, O., "Das Zeichen des Jonas—Vorbild Christi," *BiKi* 17 (1962) 15–16. Landes, G., "The Kerygma of the Book of Jonah," *Interpr* 21 (1967) 3–31. Lohfink, N., "Jona ging zur Stadt hinaus," *BZ* 5 (1961) 185–203. Loretz, O., *Gotteswort und menschliche Erfahrung* (Freiburg, 1964); "Herkunft und Sinn der Jona-Erzählung," *BZ* 5 (1961) 18–29. Schildenberger, J., "Was bedeutet die literarische Gattung für die Auslegung der biblischen Bücher," *BiKi* 17 (1962) 4–7. Schreiner, J., "Eigenart, Aufbau, Inhalt und Botschaft des Buches Jonas," *BiKi* 17 (1962) 8–14. Scott, R. B. Y., "The Sign of Jonah: An Interpretation," *Interpr* 19 (1965) 16–25. Smart, J. D., "Jonah," *IB* 6, 871–94. Smith, G. A., *The Book of the Twelve Prophets* (London, 1928). Snaith, N. H., *Notes on the Hebrew Text of Jonah* (London, 1945). Stanton, G. B., "The Prophet Jonah and His Message," *BS* 108 (1951) 237–49, 363–76. Steffen, U., *Das Mysterium von Tod und Auferstehung* (Göttingen, 1963). Van Hoonacker, A., *Les douze petits prophètes* (Paris, 1954).

INTRODUCTION

2 **(I) Authorship and Date.** Commentators who have interpreted the book as an historical narrative identify Jonah with the 8th-cent. Prophet mentioned in 2 Kgs 14:25 and consider him to be the author of the book. However, the majority of scholars today deny Jonah's authorship and date the book between 400 and 200 BC. Their arguments can be summarized as follows. The satirical tone in which the author writes about the Prophet in the third person suggests that he was not writing about himself. The lack of significant details, such as the name of the land where the fish left Jonah and the name of the king of Nineveh, suggests that the author was not writing about contemporary events. The language of the book is not that of the 8th-cent. A number of words used are not found elsewhere in the OT but only in later Hebr literature. The use of a number of Aramaisms indicates a date later than the 8th cent. (cf. A. Gelin, R-T 1, 745; Loretz, *BZ* 5, 19–25). The mentality of the author is more like the mentality of the mid-5th cent. Other OT books, such as Ezr, Neh, and Ru, bear witness to the fact that in post-exilic Israel there was a strong current of interest in the question of Israel's relations to the nations, which would form a natural background for the theme of Jon. For these reasons, this book of unknown authorship is dated between 400–200.

3 **(II) Integrity.** The unity of the book as a composition has been denied by some who find in it apparent interpolations and transpositions. But attempts to recompose the story in its "original" form seem rather artificial. Most recent scholars defend the unity of the book as a whole (cf. Feuillet, BJ 9). However, scholars agree that the psalm in the second chapter does not fit well into the whole. The language is different from that of the rest of the book in that it lacks the Aramaisms found elsewhere. More significant, however, is the fact that the sense of the psalm seems to indicate that it is misplaced. It is a song of thanksgiving with, apparently, a *Sitz im Leben* of deliverance from danger. The danger of death is expressed in water symbolism, because for the Israelites as well as for the Babylonians the sea was the kingdom of death. Jonah's psalm is so worded that it might be a song of gratitude sung by any Israelite delivered from any mortal danger. However, it is hardly appropriate for an individual to recite from the belly of a fish. It would be more appropriate for Jonah to pray this psalm after his deliverance when he was safe on dry land.

A. R. Johnson (*Studies in Old Testament Prophecy* [ed. H. H. Rowley; Edinburgh, 1950] 82–83) is of the opinion that the psalm is an independent composition introduced into the narrative either by the author himself or by an interpolator. The purpose of the insertion would be either to supply the prayer mentioned in 2:2, without regard for appropriateness, or to express Jonah's gratitude for deliverance, in which case it is misplaced. The hymn expresses gratitude in the language that is typical of the psalms of thanksgiving for deliverance from danger without specific mention of particular circumstances. But this fact does not necessarily mean that it is not original, for the psalms do not always adapt themselves to concrete situations.

4 **(III) Literary Form.** If the book is studied in relation to its life setting in post-exilic Israel, if it is compared to the legends of the prophets, the narratives of symbolic action, and the OT parables, if it is examined with sources on which it seems to depend, and if it is analyzed in its outer stylistic form, this composition appears to have the characteristics of didactic fiction rather than historical narrative.

The life setting of Jon cannot be determined with the precision that is possible with some other parts of the OT. The book itself gives no hint of the particular circumstances that influenced its composition. We are told nothing of the author and nothing of the audience for which he wrote. But although we have little knowledge of its particular life setting, we have some idea of the book's general cultural background. Against this background we can understand the author's didactic intention. In an age when Israelites were tempted to hope more for the destruction of their enemies than for their salvation, the author conveys a message about the extent of the Lord's mercy.

Among OT narratives that have the activity of the prophets as their subject matter, there are two types to which the Jonah story can be compared: the legends of the prophets, and the narratives of symbolic action (cf. Bentzen, *IOT* 283–93; A. Robert, R-T 489–91). The legends of the prophets are a later development of the historical genre in which the authors take liberties with historical facts to teach a lesson (cf. 1 Kgs 12:33–13:32; 17–19; 2 Kgs 8:7–15; 9:1–12). The narratives of symbolic action are stories in which the activity of the prophet has sign value (cf. 1 Kgs 20:35–43; 22:11; 2 Kgs 13:14–19; Is 20; Jer 27:1–8; Ez 4:1–15). The similarities between the Jonah story and these two kinds of narratives about prophets suggest that the author of Jon has as his chief concern the teaching of a religious message.

R. B. Y. Scott (*op. cit.*) identifies the literary form of the Book of Jonah as a parable with elements of allegory. This interpretation is shared by others (Van Hoonacker, *op. cit.*, 316–18; Smith, *op. cit.*, 499; Bentzen, *IOT* 1, 145; J. D. Smart, *op. cit.*, 272). Some of the characteristics of the OT parables (2 Sm 12:1–14; 14:6–8; 1 Kgs 20:39–41; Is 5:1–6; 28:24–28) are shared by the book: closely knit structure; vividness; brevity; didactic purpose. Jon is less abstract than the parables; it identifies its subject and delineates his character with the appearance of historicity. All the OT parables make their point inescapable by including usually in the last verse an explicit explanation of the meaning of the story. The author of Jon gives us no such explanatory epilogue. Inasmuch as these two characteristics of OT parables are lacking, it would seem preferable to use the broad term "didactic fiction" rather than the more specific term "parable."

5 By a study of parallels in 1 Kgs, Jer, and Ez, Feuillet ("Les sources du livre de Jonas," *RB* 54, 161–86) reaches the conclusion that Jon is neither a mere popular legend nor a simple historical account; rather it is the work of a highly instructed Israelite who had so assimilated the Scriptures as to be able to use them for his particular didactic purpose.

Although scholars differ as to the term that should be used in determining the literary form of Jon, they would agree that the book is not to be classified as history. Their reasons may be summarized as follows. It lacks the significant topographical, historical, and chronological details that would give the narrative the precision of an historical account. The presence of certain grotesque elements, such as the fish and the plant, gives the narrative the atmosphere of legend. The structure of the book—its neat division into two artfully paralleled parts—underscores in an ironic way the paradox of the plot. The similarity between the situation of Jon 4:3 and 1 Kgs 19:4, and yet the striking contrast between the characters of Jonah and Elijah, suggest that the author deliberately paralleled the Elijah story for didactic reasons. The main characters of the narrative are more typical than realistic. The frequent echoing of other OT passages is evidence that the book is a carefully worked out literary composition. The tone of irony, which has been subtly achieved both in the structure of the narrative and in the way previous Scriptures are echoed, suggests that the author intended to write satire rather than history. The crisp brevity and closely knit unity of the book, which gives no details except those that bear directly on its religious message, suggest a didactic rather than historical purpose. The abrupt ending of the narrative once the moral of the story has been pointed suggests that the author was not attempting to give an account of an historical event with an historical outcome but rather that he was making use of a story as an illustration of his religious message. The formulas used to describe God (1:9; 4:2), as well as the affirmation of the universality of the Lord's mercy given in the final verse of the book, suggest that the story of the recalcitrant Prophet served as a carrier for the author's theological views. For these reasons, Jon is to be classified as a didactic narrative, satirical in tone with a profound theological purpose.

6 **(IV) Outline.** Jon is an artfully structured composition with a twofold division significant with regard to its religious message. Jonah benefits from the Lord's mercy in the first part only to begrudge that mercy to others in the second part. The Book of Jonah may be outlined as follows:

(I) First Mission (1:1–2:11)
- (A) Jonah's Vocation (1:1–2)
- (B) Flight to Tarshish (1:3)
- (C) The Storm (1:4–16)
  - (a) Jonah Under Suspicion (1:4–9)
  - (b) Significance of Storm (1:10–12)
  - (c) Jonah Cast Into the Sea (1:13–16)
- (D) The Large Fish (2:1–11)
  - (a) Jonah Swallowed (2:1–2)
  - (b) Hymn of Thanksgiving (2:3–10)
  - (c) Deliverance (2:11)

(II) Second Mission (3:1–4:11)
- (A) Jonah Sent Again (3:1–4)
  - (a) The Lord's Message (3:1–2)
  - (b) Jonah's Preaching (3:3–4)
- (B) Conversion of Nineveh (3:5–10)
  - (a) Repentance (3:5–9)
  - (b) Forgiveness (3:10)
- (C) Jonah's Anger (4:1–4)
  - (a) Jonah's Plea (4:1–3)
  - (b) The Lord's Answer (4:4)
- (D) Jonah Under the Gourd Plant (4:5–11)
  - (a) Jonah's Bitterness (4:5–8)
  - (b) The Lord's Reproof (4:9–11)

COMMENTARY

7 **(I) First Mission (1:1–2:11).** The division of the book into two parts corresponding to the two missions of the Prophet is significant. In the first part, the recalcitrant Prophet is the recipient of God's mercy; in the second part, he begrudges that mercy to others.

8 **(A) Jonah's Vocation (1:1–2).** **1.** *the word of the Lord:* Jonah is placed in the tradition of the prophets called by God and sent to announce his Word (cf. 1 Kgs 17:2–3; Hos 1:1; Jl 1:1; Mi 1:1; Zeph 1:1; Hag 1:1; Zech 1:1). *Jonah, son of Amittai:* "Jonah" means "dove." Hosea calls Israel a silly dove (7:11) and speaks of Ephraim returning as a dove. Jonah, anxious to limit God's mercy, epitomizes post-exilic Israel, narrow-minded toward her neighbors. The son of Amittai is the Jonah of 2 Kgs 14:25. **2.** *set out for the great city of Nineveh:* Jonah's mission is reminiscent of Jeremiah's mission to the nations (Jer 1:5). Nineveh was the capital of the kingdom that destroyed Israel in 721, and the chief sanctuary of the goddess Ishtar, whose sacred bird was the dove. No explanation for this extraordinary mission (What language? What authority?) is offered.

9 **(B) Flight to Tarshish (1:3).** **3.** *Tarshish:* Most likely the Gk city of Tartessos, a Phoenician colony in S Spain. To the Israelite, it meant the farthest boundary of the world (cf. 1 Kgs 10:1; Pss 48:8; 72:10; Ez 38:13). *away from the Lord:* The author has the Prophet maintain a notion common in the ancient Near East: The presence of a god is localized to the territory inhabited by his believers. The phrase is repeated within the same verse. *Joppa:* This port is the modern Jaffa.

10 **(C) The Storm (1:4–16).** The rebellious Jonah's flight is cut short by a storm sent by the Lord of sea and land (cf. Ps 139:7–12), from whom no one can escape.

11 (a) Jonah Under Suspicion (1:4–9). **4.** The primary causality of God is emphasized throughout the narrative (2:1,11; 4:6,8). **5.** *mariners:* This Aram word is never found in classical Hebrew but is common in the Talmud and in midrashic works. *ship:* The Aram word is used here rather than the Hebr word used in 1:4. **6.** *be mindful:* This Aram expression is found in Dn 6:3, but not elsewhere in the OT. It is used frequently in the Targums. The author's intention here is to underscore the ironic contrast between pagan mariners who recognize the need to cry out each to his own god and the Prophet who has not only fled from the true God but sleeps unmindful of the storm sent as punishment. **7.** *on whose account:* This phrase, omitted in the Greek, reveals the common belief that some individual's offence against a god may cause a storm at sea (cf. 1 Sm 14:36–42). *cast lots:* This device was used in Israel, as elsewhere in ancient times, to decide issues (cf. Jos 7:14; 1 Sm 10:20–21; Nm 26:55). The author includes the storm and the casting of lots in his story to bring out the idea that the reluctant Prophet cannot escape the Lord's demands. **9.** *who made the sea and the dry land:* The author intends the irony of this confession of belief in the omnipresence of the Lord. Jonah knows that his God is Lord of the sea and land, and yet he has sought to escape him by taking a ship for the farthest boundaries of the world. This inconsistency parallels the Prophet's deeper inconsistency in recognizing that the Lord is a merciful God (4:2) and yet hoping that he would show no mercy to the Ninevites (4:1).

12 (b) Significance of Storm (1:10–12). **10.** The sailors find it unthinkable that anyone could resist a god known to be the Lord of land and sea. **11.** *quiet down:* This expression occurs only in late passages of the OT (Prv 26:20; Ps 107:30), but it is common in the Talmud and in the midrashic works. **12.** *throw me into the sea:* Jonah is aware that the only way to save the ship and the sailors is for him, the guilty one, to be thrown overboard. Again the author plays with irony: Jonah shows himself as humane in his willingness to sacrifice himself for the lives of the pagan sailors, yet later he shows himself as far from humane in his attitude toward the Ninevites threatened with destruction. Jonah's request does not indicate a real change of heart, for he merely regrets that his flight has been unsuccessful and dangerous for others, without repenting of his disobedience to the Lord.

13 (c) Jonah Cast Into the Sea (1:13–16). **14.** *as you saw fit:* In their prayer to Jonah's God, the pagan sailors remind him that the responsibility for the storm, the outcome of the lots, and Jonah's fate is not theirs. **15.** *cast him forth into the sea:* Ez 26:27 warns that the pagan sailors and all the wealth and power of Tyre will be hurled into the sea, but here it is the Israelite Prophet who is hurled into the sea by the pagan sailors. **16.** *offered sacrifice unto the Lord:* The implication need not be that they are converted to Jonah's God but rather that they are religious men ready to acknowledge the power of the god who commands storms.

14 **(D) The Large Fish (2:1–11).** The marvelous intervention of the Lord, who demonstrates his power over all creatures and events by using them as his instruments, can be compared to divine activity in the Elijah narrative (1 Kgs 17:6); no one can escape him.

15 (a) Jonah Swallowed (2:1–2). **1.** *a great fish:* The author's intention in making use of this detail is best understood if his story is compared to the legends of the prophets in Kgs (1 Kgs 12:33–13:32; 17–19; 2 Kgs 8:7:15; 9:1–2) and to the narratives of symbolic action (1 Kgs 20:35–43; 22:11; 2 Kgs 13:14–19; Is 20; Jer 27:1ff.; Ez 4:1ff.). In such narratives, the authors take liberties with facts to teach a religious lesson (cf. Bentzen, *IOT* 1, 238–39; A. Robert, *VDBS* 5, 418; J. Delorme, R-F 1, 445–55). If the Jonah story is interpreted symbolically, then the Prophet whose name means dove signifies Israel, the great fish signifies Babylon, and the three-day sojourn in the fish's belly signifies the Exile.

1. *three days and three nights:* Jer 51:34 compares the king of Babylon to a great monster who has swallowed Israel, and Is 27:1 also represents Israel's oppressor as a sea monster. However, J. C. Ball (*Proceedings of the Society of Biblical Archaeology* 20 [1898] 9ff.) points out that the cuneiform characters denoting Nineveh are a combination of the symbols for house and fish, and from this fact, W. O. E. Oesterley and T. H. Robinson argue that perhaps Jonah's sojourn in the belly of the great fish haggadically represents his sojourn in Nineveh (Oesterley-Robinson, *Introd.* 378). In this case, it is possible that the author is suggesting a parallel between Jonah's experience in Nineveh and Israel's experience in Babylon.

16 (b) Hymn of Thanksgiving (2:3–10). This psalm of gratitude for deliverance is an interpolation that serves as the prayer said by Jonah within the belly of the fish (→ 3 above). It is possible that the hymn is a tissue of borrowings from, or at least echoes of, Pss. There are

many parallels (Pss 32:6; 42:8; 66:12; 69:2; 88:18) in which water is used as a symbol of mortal danger. But such parallels are not necessarily the result of direct borrowing, for they can have their source in the common background and stereotyped language of this *Gattung*. Water symbolism for the danger of death is found elsewhere in the OT (Is 8:7; 30:28; Jb 22:11; 27:20). In structure, Jonah's hymn can be compared to other hymns of thanksgiving (Pss 18; 30; 31; 40:2–12; 66; 92; 116; 138; etc.), which include an address to the Lord, a description of distress in vague terms, an acknowledgment of Yahweh as rescuer, a religious lesson, and an announcement of a Temple offering. Jonah's hymn is so worded that it might be sung by any Israelite delivered from any danger. Its appropriateness as a song sung from within the belly of a fish is derived from the references in vv. 4, 6–7. **3.** *the nether world:* The Prophet is exiled from the Lord's presence (cf. 2:4). **3.** *the heart of the seas:* This phrase is a figure of extreme distress (cf. Ez 27:25; Mi 7:19). **7.** *roots of the mountains:* This expression probably means the depths of the seas, for the Israelite envisaged the earth as resting on the seas.

17 (c) Deliverance (2:11). The Exile symbolism can be worked out here, for the Prophet is vomited out of the mouth of the great fish just as Israel is vomited out by the monster Babylon (Jer 51:44). But is is more significant to note that the Prophet is back where he started from—thanks to the merciful but firm intervention of the Lord.

18 **(II) Second Mission (3:1–4:11).** Having been rescued by the merciful Lord, whom he had disobeyed, the Prophet goes to Nineveh to preach, but he begrudges the repentant Ninevites the mercy shown them by the Lord.

19 **(A) Jonah Sent Again (3:1–4).** The Lord makes no mention of Jonah's resistance to the first call. Jonah undergoes no change of heart but merely complies because he has found escape impossible.

(a) The Lord's Message (3:1–2). **2.** *message:* This word (*qᵉrî'â*) is not used elsewhere in the OT, but it is used frequently in postbiblical Hebrew.

(b) Jonah's Preaching (3:3–4). **3.** *Nineveh was:* The use of the past tense suggests that this narrative was written after the destruction of Nineveh in 612. *enormously large city:* Lit., "the city great before God." *three days to go through it:* This expression could be hyperbole, but A. Parrot (*Nineveh and the Old Testament* [N.Y., 1952] 85) explains that people who lived far from Assyria might have understood by the word "Nineveh" the area that is known as the Assyrian triangle, which reaches from Khorsabad to Nimrud in an almost unbroken string of settlements about 26 mi. long. **4.** *forty days more and Nineveh will be destroyed:* Unlike the prophetical books that abound in judgment speeches and oracles of admonition, reproach, and doom, Jon contains only this one brief word delivered in the Lord's name. The 40 days recall the 40 days of the flood (Gn 7:17) and the 40 years of the Exodus (Ex 12; cf. 1 Kgs 19:8). The Greek reads "three days more."

20 **(B) Conversion of Nineveh (3:5–10).** The story of the Ninevites' spontaneous repentance seems like an illustration in narrative form of the Lord's words to Ezekiel (Ez 3:4–7). If the Prophet had brought God's message to a foreign people of unknown language, they would have listened, whereas Israel refused to listen to God speaking through Ezekiel. The Ninevites stand in striking contrast to Israel, who remained obstinate despite all the prophetic preaching (e.g., cf. this unnamed king with Jehoiakim in Jer 36).

(a) Repentance (3:5–9). **5.** *believed:* The Hebr expression is the same as that used for Abraham's belief in Gn 15:6. The text does not make clear whether the people of Nineveh did penance immediately on hearing the Lord's warning or only after the king's decree. **6.** *king of Nineveh:* The fact that his name is not mentioned suggests that this narrative is a free composition, not concerned with "history." **7.** *man and beast:* This expression has parallels in Jer 21:6; 31:27; 33:43; 33:12; 36:29. **8.** *every man shall turn:* Jeremiah's message of personal conversion is echoed here (Jer 25:5; 26:3; 36:7; 18:11). **9.** *blazing wrath:* This expression is used for the Lord's anger in Jer 4:8; 4:26; 12:13; 25:37; 30:24; 49:37.

(b) Forgiveness (3:10). **10.** *he repented:* That the Lord's oracles of doom are conditional, that the Lord will repent of the punishment he threatens if the nation will repent of her evil ways, is the explicit teaching of Jeremiah (18:7–8; 26:3). Feuillet ("Le sens du livre de Jonas," *RB* 54, 344–46) considers this concept of the nonfulfillment of divine oracles to be the fundamental lesson of the book. But this speculative question about the accomplishment of oracles seems secondary for the following reasons: fulfillment of oracles was not the only criterion for the authenticity of prophecy; the conditional nature of oracles of doom must have been well known when the book was written; elsewhere in the OT there is little concern with this speculative problem; and in the Jonah story itself, the central issue is not whether Jonah's threat of destruction is fulfilled but whether the Lord's mercy extends even to Ninevites.

21 **(C) Jonah's Anger (4:1–4).** Jonah's words of disappointment reveal his character and his motivation. He had fled from his mission because he foresaw that the Lord would have mercy on the Ninevites if they repented; now he has been proved right. From the Lord's point of view, Jonah's mission is a success, but from Jonah's point of view, it is a bitter disappointment (cf. M. Buber, *The Prophetic Faith* [N.Y., 1951] 104). Jonah is clearly an object of satire.

(a) Jonah's Plea (4:1–3). **2.** *gracious and merciful God, slow to anger:* This description of the Lord's mercy is especially reminiscent of Yahweh's revelation to Moses (Ex 34:6–7). It is found also in Jer 3-12; 31:20; 32:18, and seems to be a stereotyped formula in Jl 2-13; Pss 86:15; 103:8; 145:8; Neh 9:17 (cf. J. Scharbert, *Bib* 38 [1957] 130). **3.** *take my life from me:* The Prophet feels that the Lord has robbed his life of all meaning by showing mercy rather than blazing wrath to the Ninevites. Jonah's plea for death echoes Elijah's (1 Kgs 19:4). The story of Elijah and the story of Jonah are interestingly similar. In both there are marvelous interventions of divine power and the use of the physical world as the instrument of the divine will—e.g., crows to feed the hungry Elijah, a great fish to swallow the drowning Jonah. The picture of Jonah sulking in the shade of his vine (Jon 4:6) is so reminiscent of the picture of Elijah in the shade of his broom tree (1 Kgs 19:4) that it is possible that the similarity was deliberately contrived by the author. But there are several significant differences between the two stories. The marvels of the Jonah story surpass the marvels in Kgs. The characters of the two prophets and their relationship to the Lord are also very different. Elijah remains a hero to be admired even in his moment of despondency under the broom tree. The reason for his low spirits was the infidelity of the king and people to whom he had been sent. He lamented for the Lord's sake, not for his own. The Lord's response to Elijah's plea was an angelic visitation and divine encouragement. In Jon, the situation is very different. Sulking in the shade, Jonah is no hero; his disgruntlement is ridiculous. His misery results from his own narrow-mindedness. The Lord's response to Jonah's plea is a tantalizing question. Detail after detail underscore the contrast between Elijah and Jonah: Jonah flees from the Lord (1:3), whereas Elijah seeks for the Lord in wind, earthquake, fire, and still small voice (1 Kgs 19:8–12; Jonah rebels (1:3), whereas Elijah obeys (1 Kgs 17:1). It is possible that the irony of this contrast between the two prophets is deliberate. Jonah asks for death because his message has been heeded, and he echoes the words of Elijah, who asked for death because his message was not heeded.

(b) THE LORD'S ANSWER (4:4). **4.** *have you reason to be angry?:* The Lord probes to the heart of the matter: Can one who has been the recipient of divine mercy begrudge it to others? This question, in the form of a rebuke, expresses the core of the religious message intended by the author. There is no little literary artistry shown by creating another "death wish" and question-reply in 4:8–9.

22 **(D) Jonah Under the Gourd Plant (4:5–11).** The Prophet waits and watches outside the city. Evidently he has not given up his hope that he will see the destruction of the Ninevites.

(a) JONAH'S BITTERNESS (4:5–8). **6.** *gourd plant:* Like the storm and the fish, this plant is to be the Lord's instrument in educating his Prophet. **7.** *worm...burning east wind:* Jonah is made to experience something of the destruction that he had wished for the Ninevites. **8.** *better off dead:* Again, as in 4:3, Jonah echoes the words of Elijah but with motivation that is ironically different.

(b) THE LORD'S REPROOF (4:9–11). **9.** *have you reason:* The core of the religious message intended by the author is contained in the Lord's challenge to Jonah. The Lord demands that Jonah examine the motive for his anger, and it is evident that the reason for his bitterness in ch. 4 is linked to the reason for his rebellion in ch. 1. **10.** *I have reason:* But Jonah is blinded by his resentment and does not see the parallel between the Lord's concern for men, whether drowning Prophet or repenting Ninevites, and his own concern for a withering plant. *came up in one night and in one night perished:* Lit., the passage reads, "which was the son of a night and perished the son of a night." This expression is not used elsewhere in the OT. Why should Jonah show such concern over something so ephemeral, with which he was never involved? **11.** *should I not be concerned over Nineveh?:* The abrupt ending of the narrative underscores the Lord's concern for people, for the least intelligent of human beings, and dumb beasts. No limits are to be put upon the God of the covenant, whose mercy extends beyond Israel. This message of mercy is the underlying theme in the narrative in which Prophet, sailors, Ninevites, and cattle are all made the objects of divine pity. It is the thought of the Lord's mercy that causes Jonah to flee. It is perhaps the Lord's mercy that saves him from drowning. And it is because the Lord has been merciful that Jonah sulks outside the city of Nineveh. The very structure of the book brings out the irony of a Prophet who benefits from the Lord's mercy only to rebel because his mercy is extended to others. In the person of Jonah, the author satirizes those narrow-minded Israelites who, despite their long experience of the Lord's mercy to themselves, begrudge the extension of his mercy to others. The author writes for those of his own day who yielded to the temptation of a covenanted people to limit God's freedom. The application to our day is obvious.

Volume II

THE NEW TESTAMENT AND TOPICAL ARTICLES

Edited by

JOSEPH A. FITZMYER, S.J.

RAYMOND E. BROWN, S.S.

40

SYNOPTIC PROBLEM

Frederick Gast, O.C.D.

BIBLIOGRAPHY

1 **General.** Bailey, J. A., *The Traditions Common to the Gospels of Luke and John* (*NovTSup* 7; Leiden, 1963). Bultmann, *HST*. Cambier, J., *et al.*, *La formation des Évangiles* (Rech. Bibliques 2; Louvain, 1958). Da Fonseca, A. G., *Quaestio synoptica* (3rd ed.; Rome, 1952). Farmer, W. R., *The Synoptic Problem* (N.Y., 1964). Farrer, A. M., *St. Matthew and St. Mark* (London, 1954). F–B 33–60. Grant, F., *The Earliest Gospel* (N.Y., 1943). Kilpatrick, G. D., *The Origins of the Gospel According to St. Matthew* (Oxford, 1946). Knox, W. L., *The Sources of the Synoptic Gospels* (2 vols.; Cambridge, 1953). Léon-Dufour, X., *Concordance of the Synoptic Gospels* (N.Y., 1957); *Les Évangiles et l'histoire de Jésus* (Paris, 1963); *Études d'Évangile* (Paris, 1965). McCool, F., "Revival of Synoptic Source-Criticism," *TS* 17 (1956) 459–93. R–F, *INT* 250–86. R–T 1, 563–80. Parker, P., *The Gospel Before Mark* (Chicago, 1953). Sanday, W. (ed.), *Studies in the Synoptic Problem* (Oxford, 1911). Streeter, B. F., *The Four Gospels, a Study of Origins* (London, 1924). Taylor, V., *Behind the Third Gospel* (Oxford, 1926); *The Formation of the Gospel Tradition* (2nd ed; London, 1935). Vaganay, L., *Le Problème Synoptique* (Tournai, 1954). Wik, *NTI* 221–53.

2 **Synopses.** In Gk: Aland, K., *Synopsis quattuor evangeliorum* (Stuttgart, 1964). De Solages, B., *A Greek Synopsis of the Gospels* (Leiden, 1959)—in mathematical form. H–L is the most practical student's edition. In Eng: Throckmorton, B. H. (ed.), *Gospel Parallels* (N.Y., 1957)—this is H–L in the RSV trans. (Beare, F. W., *The Earliest Records of Jesus* [Nashville, 1962] constitutes a commentary on *Gospel Parallels*.) Sparks, H. F. D., *A Synopsis of the Gospels* (Oxford, 1964)—has the advantage over *Gospel Parallels* of having all four Gospels, but in the RV trans. In Fr: Benoit, P. and M.-E. Boismard, *Synopse des quatre Évangiles en français* (2 vols.; Paris, 1965).

3 OUTLINE

THE PROBLEM

4 The first three Gospels, because of the extensive agreement of their materials, can be put in parallel columns for the sake of comparison. This type of arrangement is called a synopsis. Consequently, Mt, Mk, and Lk have become known as the Synoptic Gospels; their authors are accordingly known as the Synoptists.

The similarity of material evidenced by this arrangement coupled with notable dissimilarities within the first three Gospels gives rise to the so-called Synoptic Problem. How is this remarkable mixture of similar and dissimilar material within Mt, Mk, and Lk to be explained?

5 **(I) Similarities.**

(A) Content. On the whole the first three Gospels report the same words and deeds of Jesus. The miracles, parables, discussions, and principal events in his life are the same. The passages that are common to the three Syn are called the "threefold tradition." The "twofold tradition" designates passages found in two Syn. "Unique traditions" are those contained in a single witness, Mt, Mk, or Lk. Traditions employed twice in the same Gospel are called "doublets."

The shortest of the three Syn is Mk. Almost the whole of its material occurs also in Mt or in Lk or in both. Only very little material is peculiar to Mk (e.g., 7:33–36; 8:22–26—stories that Matthew and Luke seem to have found embarrassing). For instance, Mt contains the substance of approximately 600 verses of Mk, or about 90 per cent; Lk contains more than half of Mk's material and substitutes for half of what remains by parallel material. On the other hand, the material peculiar to Mt constitutes about 30 per cent of the total Mt; and in Lk the peculiar material constitutes almost half the total Gospel.

There are discrepancies in the figures presented by different scholars because of text-critical disagreements about the genuineness of certain verses in each Gospel. Numerical comparisons are further complicated by the fact that the matter that constitutes one verse in one Gospel may be spread over two verses in another. The table below shows the approximate statistics of the matter.

	Mt	Mk	Lk
Total verses	1070	677	1150
Unique tradition	330 (approx. 1/3)	70 (approx. 1/10)	520 (approx. 1/2)
Twofold tradition	170–180 (Mt and Mk)	170–180 (Mk and Mt)	230 (Lk and Mt)
	230 (Mt and Lk)	50 (Mk and Lk)	50 (Lk and Mk)
Threefold tradition	350–370	350–370	350–370

6 COMPARATIVE OUTLINE OF THE GOSPELS OF MARK AND LUKE

Mark

INTRODUCTION (1:1–14)

1:1 –11 Baptism of Jesus

1:12–13 Temptation

BEGINNING OF GALILEAN MINISTRY (1:14–3:6)

1:14–20 Call of first disciples
1:21–39 Typical day at Capernaum
1:40–45 Transitional leper healing
2:1 –3:6 Controversy with Pharisees

HEIGHT OF GALILEAN MINISTRY (3:7–6:13)

Training of the Twelve (see 3:14)

3:7 –12 Crowds follow Jesus
3:13–19 Call of the Twelve
(Omission of Sermon on the Mount; see 3:13)

3:20–21 Relatives go to seize him
3:22–30 Beelzebul interlude
3:31–35 Relatives arrive
4:1 –34 PARABLES

4:34–ch. 5 MIRACLES (four)
6:1 –6 Rejection at Nazareth
6:17–13 Sending out the Twelve

MINISTRY OUTSIDE GALILEE (6:14–8:26)
6:14–29 INTRODUCTION: Herod and John the Baptist

Luke

INFANCY NARRATIVE (chs. 1–2)

INTRODUCTION (3:1–4:13)

Baptism of Jesus (3:1–22)
John the Baptist's social preaching
Genealogy (rest of ch. 3)
Temptation (4:1–13)

BEGINNING OF GALILEAN MINISTRY (4:14–6:11)

Rejection at Nazareth (4:14–30)
Typical day at Capernaum (4:31–44)
Call of disciples; Catch of Fish (5:1–11)
Transitional leper healing (5:12–16)
Controversy with Pharisees (5:17–6:11)

HEIGHT OF GALILEAN MINISTRY (6:12–9:17)

Call of the Twelve (6:12–16)
Crowds follow Jesus (6:17–19)
Sermon on the Plain (rest of ch. 6)
Centurion's slave
Widow of Nain
Disciples of John the Baptist
Anointing of feet
Galilean followers
(ch. 7–8:3 Events that happened in Galilee)

= 11:14–23)

PARABLES (8:4–18)
Relatives arrive (8:19–21)
MIRACLES (rest of ch. 8)

Sending out the Twelve (9:1–6)

Interlude: Herod and John the Baptist (9:7–9)
Withdrawal; Feeding of 5000 (9:10–17)

6:30–44	Feeding 5000	8:1–9	Feeding 4000
6:45–54	Crossing to Bethsaida	8:10	Crossing to Dalmanutha
	Loaves not understood	8:11–13	Versus Pharisees
6:53–56	Landing; sick come	8:14–21	Loaves not understood
7:1 –23	Versus Pharisees	8:22	Crossing to Bethsaida
7:24–30	To Tyre and Sidon; healing		Sick come
7:31–37	Spittle healing of deaf	8:23–26	Spittle healing of blind
		8:27	To Caesarea Philippi

GREAT LUCAN OMISSION Mk 6:44–8:27

Mk 8:11–13 = Lk 11:26,29
Mk 8:14–15 = Lk 12:1

TO JERUSALEM (8:27–ch. 10)

8:27–30 Peter's Confession
8:31–38 *First Passion* Prediction
9:1 –8 Transfiguration
9:9 –13 Elijah question
9:14–29 Healing of mute boy
9:30–32 *Second Passion* Prediction
9:33–50 Instructions for disciples
10:1 Journey to beyond Jordan
10:2 –12 Pharisees and divorce
10:13–16 The children
10:17–31 Rich young man; possessions
10:32–34 *Third Passion* Prediction
10:35–45 Ambition of Zebedee's sons
10:46–52 Leaving Jericho; blind beggar

THREE DAYS IN JERUSALEM (chs. 11–13)

Day 1 11:1 –11 Entrance

Day 2 11:12–14 Cursing fig tree
11:15–19 Cleansing Temple
Day 3 11:20–25 Fig tree dried up
11:27–33 Authority for Jesus' actions
12:1 –12 Parable: Tenants in Vineyard
12:13–17 Pharisees: Caesar's coin
12:18–27 Sadducees: Marriage in heaven
12:28–34 Which is greatest commandment?
12:35–40 Jesus turns on Pharisees
12:41–44 Widow's mite
13:1 –37 Eschatological Discourse

PASSION AND DEATH (chs. 14–15)

RESURRECTION (16:1–8)

(Marcan Appendix 16:9ff.)

TO JERUSALEM (9:18–19:27)

Peter's Confession (9:18–21)
First Passion Prediction (9:21–27)
Transfiguration (9:28–36)

Healing of mute boy (9:37–43)
Second Passion Prediction (9:44–45)
Instructions for disciples (9:46–50)
JOURNEY TO JERUSALEM—GREAT LUCAN ADDITION (9:51–18:14)
The children (18:15–17)
Rich young man; possessions (18:18–30)
Third Passion Prediction (18:31–34)
(cf. 22:24–27)
Before Jericho; blind beggar (18:35–43)
In Jericho: Zacchaeus (19:1–10)
Double parable: Pounds / Man becoming king (19:11–27)

IN JERUSALEM (19:28 through ch. 21)

Entrance (19:28–40)
Lament over Jerusalem (19:41–44)
(cf. 13:6–9)
Cleansing Temple (19:45–48)

Authority for Jesus' actions (20:1–8)
Parable: Tenants in Vineyard (20:9–19)
Pharisees: Caesar's coin (20:20–26)
Sadducees: Marriage in heaven (20:27–40)

Jesus turns on Pharisees (20:41–47)
Widow's mite (21:1–4)
Eschatological Discourse (rest of ch. 21)

PASSION AND DEATH (chs. 22–23)

Details peculiar to Lk:
No anointing by woman
Influence of Satan on Judas; in garden
Passover ordering of supper account
Supper: disciples dispute priority
Supper: two swords
Morning trial before Sanhedrin
Trial before Herod
Weeping women on Via Crucis
Three words of Jesus on the cross
Preparing spices on Friday for burial

RESURRECTION (ch. 24)

(→ Gospel Lk, 44:175)

7 **(B) Arrangement.** The course of the life of Jesus and his activity are presented in a similar fashion. The Baptist appears; Jesus is baptized by him and enters into the desert of temptation. After this he begins his public life. The greater part of Jesus' activity centers in Galilee and in the regions bordering it (Decapolis; Philip's territory). His journey to Jerusalem and his trial there are told in similar fashion. All three accounts close with his crucifixion and resurrection. The framework below expresses this graphically.

	Mt	Mk	Lk
Preliminaries to the ministry	3:1–4:11	1:1–13	3:1–4:13
Galilean ministry	4:12–18:35	1:14–9:50	4:14–9:50
Journey to Jerusalem	19:1–20:34	10:1–52	9:51–18:43
Passion and resurrection	21–28	11–16	19–24

There is no attempt by the Syn to present a biography of Jesus as such. Nor do they seek to depict his personality. Their desire is rather to report in popular speech the words and works of Jesus and the impression these made upon those surrounding him. These Gospels, therefore, consist of separate units of narrative and discourse that appear to be complete in themselves. These units are often in sequence without any temporal or spatial connection. There are also sections in which similar materials are placed together, e.g., Sabbath stories, parables. The Syn are also marked by the separate, characteristic sayings of Jesus, short discourses and fragments of discourses. A particular penchant for parables is also evident. In much of this they are quite unlike Jn.

8 **(C) Language.** Many passages show a striking agreement in language or wording. Sometimes all three will agree on an OT quote that is different from both the MT and the LXX. The words of Jesus are often reported in identical Greek. Sometimes all three or at least two of the Syn use unusual Gk constructions or the same comparatively rare Gk words. Occasionally whole sentences or groups of sentences correspond practically word for word.

9 **(II) Dissimilarities**

(A) Content. Some events are recounted by only two of the Evangelists, others are proper to only one.

Even then, the two accounts of the same event differ at times. For example, Mt and Lk give the history of Jesus' infancy, whereas Mk does not; yet these two accounts of Mt and Lk differ considerably. This also holds true for the genealogies of Jesus that they present (Mt 1:1–17; Lk 3:23–38). The same three temptations of Jesus are narrated by Mt and Lk, but the order is changed (Mt 4:3–12; Lk 4:3–12). Even the reports of the resurrection present no uniform tradition (→ Aspects NT Thought, 78:153).

10 **(B) Arrangement.** Although in general there is agreement in the arrangement of the Gospel materials, it must be noted that there are some differences. Where one author groups the material together in one place, the other scatters it throughout his work. The parable section is common to all three, but each has a different number of parables. Although Lk and Mt share many of Jesus' sayings not found in Mk, they organize these sayings differently. In Mt the sayings are grouped in five great discourses of Jesus (→ Gospel Mt, 43:2,16), whereas in Lk much of this material appears during Jesus' long journey to Jerusalem (9:51–18:14). There are divergencies even in individual sections. The best examples of this are the number of petitions to be found in the "Our Father" (Mt 6:9–15; Lk 11:2–4) and the number of the Beatitudes (Mt 5:3–11; Lk 6:20b–22).

Luke follows Mk's order much more closely than does Mt. Perhaps the best way of summarizing the similarities and dissimilarities of content and arrangement among the Syn is to give a detailed comparison of Lk and Mk. Careful study of this comparison will help the reader to understand the different method of the two Evangelists and show him the complexity of the interrelationships. (The comparative outline of Mk and Lk [→ 6 above] is the work of R. E. Brown, S.S.)

VARIOUS SOLUTIONS

11 The Syn Problem as we know it did not arise until the middle of the 18th cent. (→ Modern NT Criticism, 41:21). Even then, thorough investigation of the problem did not begin in earnest until the early 19th cent. The early Church Fathers did not treat this question explicitly. Augustine was aware of some of the difficulties. He considered the literary relationships among the different Gospels in his book *De consensu evangelistarum.* This work was not much more than a harmony of the Gospels, tending to reconcile difficulties rather naïvely; yet Augustine's principles concerning differences in Syn order were actually much more liberal than the literal-minded harmonies of a later period, such as that of Osiander in the 16th cent. (H. K. McArthur, *The Quest Through the Centuries* [Phila., 1966] 51, 93.)

12 **(I) Oral Tradition.** According to the proponents of this theory, the remarkable concordance found among the three Evangelists is the result of a primitive oral gospel. In its most extreme form this solution excludes any common literary dependence on a single written Gospel. The primitive preaching became stereotyped at an early date. This preaching was constantly repeated. The similarities in the written texts are thus accounted for; the dissimilarities are explained by the diversification of the same catechesis necessary in various areas. To support the existence of such a primitive catechesis the extraordinary memory of the Oriental is invoked. In 1818, J. Gieseler gave a firm form to this hypothesis.

Evaluation. Doubtless a period of oral tradition did precede our written Gospels. Modern criticism almost universally admits to the primacy and importance of oral tradition in the Gospels. But the supposition of an oral tradition alone cannot account for the complex problem of similarities and dissimilarities in the written texts. There is in many passages an exact verbal agreement, especially in Mk and Lk. Oral tradition can explain the divergencies in the Gospels but not the similarities. These would seem to demand some literary dependence as well. This theory is therefore inadequate as a single answer to the Syn Problem.

13 **(II) Literary Interdependence.** This type of hypothesis is also known as the Mutual-Dependence Theory and the Use or Utilization Theory. According to this hypothesis, each Evangelist (except the first) depended upon his predecessor or predecessors. The first of the Gospels in date was followed by the two others as derivatives. This would explain the points of agreement among the three Gospels. There are several possible orders of dependence, each having had its proponent at one time or another. Only two of these combinations (shown in diagram below) have really been able to hold any ground: Mt–Mk–Lk, and Mk as the source of Mt and Lk.

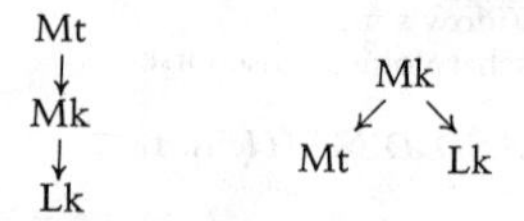

14 **(A) Mt–Mk–Lk Sequence.** This sequence was accepted by Augustine and most Catholic exegetes until relatively recent times. This solution is based on the traditionally accepted order of the Gospels. It is advocated today mostly in a modified form that views Mk as dependent upon a preliminary stage of Mt. This hypothesis is still defended by B. Butler (*CCHS* 760–64; *The Originality of St. Matthew* [Cambridge, 1951]).

Papias, an early bishop of Hierapolis in Phrygia, Asia Minor, stated that Mt put together the *logia* of Jesus in the Hebr language and each person translated them as best he could (Eusebius, *Hist.* 3.39,16; GCS 9/1:292). From this statement it is concluded that there must have been an Aram Gospel of apostolic origin. This Aram Gospel (M) would have been translated into Greek (Mg), and the translation then used by all three Syn in different ways. In addition canonical Mt and Lk used Mk. In this theory canonical Mt would be the best witness to Aram M since Mark abbreviated M and added to it some oral tradition from Peter and his Roman preaching. The diagram below illustrates the theory.

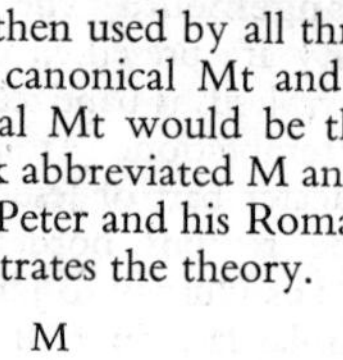

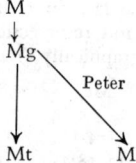

Evaluation. This use of Papias' tradition is an instance of eating one's cake and having it too. If one takes Papias literally, he is not speaking of the canonical Gk Mt that we know today. Any use of Papias to prove the priority of Mt has the hidden assumption that Mt is somehow related to the Aram collection of the *logia* of Jesus of which Papias spoke, and this is simply an unproved assumption. We need not agree with those who say that Papias was mistaken and there never was such an Aram collection made by Matthew, but we must confess the purely speculative nature of any chain M-Mg-Mt. In loyalty to the 1911 and 1912 decrees of the Pontifical Biblical Commission, Catholics have tended to support this solution to the Syn Problem; but now that complete freedom with regard to such decrees has been granted, the limitations of such a solution are being honestly recognized (→ Church Pronouncements, 72:28,25). Recently, W. R. Farmer, a Protestant scholar, has argued strongly for the priority of Mt (*The Synoptic Problem*). For meaning of *logia* see *ETL* 41 (1965) 530–47.

15 **(B) Mk as Source for Mt and Lk.** This alternate sequence is the most generally held theory today, among non-Catholic and Catholic scholars alike. This literary priority of Mk seems almost to be a fixed tenet of the critics.

The Gospel of Mk is certainly independent of Mt and Lk. If Mark abridged Mt as some critics hold, how explain the countless additions? The narratives of Mk are far more lively than those of Mt's stylized form.

16 There is no decisive evidence of any borrowing between Mt and Lk; they are independent of each other. When Mt or Lk do not follow Mk, they disagree with regard to the arrangement of their common materials and the mode of expression. If Matthew had written with Lk before him, how can we explain the omission of so much fine material? There must be another explanation for any agreement that is evidenced. This will be taken up later.

17 The question of whether or not Lk and Mt depend on Mk is greatly discussed. The dependence of Lk on Mk is generally accepted. However, the nature and extent of the dependence is disputed. The problem arises with the doublets found in Lk, i.e., the same episode appears in Lk twice, once in a section where Lk is following Mk, and again in a section where Lk has independent material (e.g., Lk 8:16 and 11:33). Such a phenomenon posits another source somewhat parallel to Mk. Both Mt and Lk omit details that appear in Mk. Vaganay calls these omissions "negative agreements." Thus a simple dependence of Lk on Mk is insufficient as an explanation. This raised a theory, generally abandoned today, of a proto-Mk, i.e., Luke did not have the canonical Mk but a more primitive form. (For another theory, that of proto-Lk, → Inspiration, 66:62.) Vaganay has proposed that Luke had both Mk and a Gk translation of Aram M (not the same as the canonical Mt) and that he simply used Mk without following him slavishly.

That Matthew depended on Mk is widely affirmed but also disputed vehemently. The hypothesis of Mt's priority has never been totally excluded from criticism; the same problem of doublets arises as seen in Lk, e.g., Mt 5:29f. and 18:8f.

18 *Evaluation.* The priority of Mk is generally accepted by scholars today. It seems to answer best the questions raised and is surely a fine working hypothesis. Concerning the dependencies of Mt and Lk on Mk, there has not been a truly satisfactory proposal to solve the problems involved. The dependence of Lk on Mk is to be maintained; that of Mt on Mk is to be maintained, but with more reserve.

(Brown, J. P., "An Early Revision of the Gospel of Mark," *JBL* 78 [1959] 215–27. Taylor, V., *The Gospel According to St. Mark* [London, 1953] 67–77, esp. on proto-Mk. Wood, H. G., "The Priority of Mark," *ExpT* 65 [1953–54] 17–19.)

19 **(III) Documentary Hypotheses.** These form a third type of explanation for the problems encountered from a consideration of the Syn data. The theories of literary interdependence just discussed suppose that two of the Syn depend on the third, in other words on an existing Gospel—even where we spoke of Aram M (→ 14 above), the presumption was that this was substantially the same as canonical Mt. But the three theories we discuss below all suppose dependence on a hypothetical, reconstructed source, no longer extant and not the same as any canonical Gospel. Sometimes these theories are thought to supplant previous explanations of the Syn Problem; at other times they are combined with one of the explanations already given, e.g., with dependence on oral tradition or with dependence on Mk.

20 **(A) Single Document as Basis for Threefold Tradition.** This theory, known as the Primitive-Gospel Solution, first presented by G. E. Lessing in the last quarter of the 18th cent., suggests that the Syn all drew their material from a primitive Aram Gospel that has been lost. In J. Eichhorn's developed form of the theory, the Syn are considered independent of one another. They would all have drawn from a document that contained the entire life of Christ. This document was composed in Aram at an early date and subsequently translated into Greek and revised a number of times. The Syn would have made use of these revisions when composing their Gospels.

Evaluation. The theory, which seemed so simple but which became progressively complex, was unsuccessful and has been abandoned. There would certainly have been much greater uniformity among the Syn in content, arrangement, and language if the theory were fact. There was a positive value to the theory: It paved the way for the recognition that our canonical Gospels represent the culmination of a literary process, and the supposition of a common source for Mt and Lk was the first insight into the proposal of a "sayings" source or document.

21 **(B) Complementary Document as Basis for Twofold Tradition.** This theory attempts to explain the origin of the material common only to Mt and Lk. It is also known as the Two-Source or Two-Document Theory.

(a) Two-Document Theory. This hypothesis holds wide acceptance among Protestants and, in a modified form, among Catholics as well. Despite Mt's and Lk's independence of each other, there are agreements in opposition to Mk that seem to call for a Gk source prior to Mk. This Gk source, whose existence is pure conjecture, consisted almost entirely of words or sayings of Jesus. First mentioned by F. Schleiermacher in 1832, it is referred to as Q (from the Ger *Quelle*, "source"). The two later Syn would have drawn the greater part of their material from this source plus Mk, adapting the material to the different circles they wished to reach. The diagram below approximates the situation as conceived by the proponents.

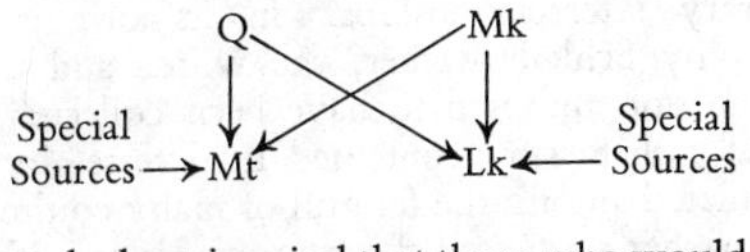

It ought to be kept in mind that those who would identify this Q document with Aram Matthew (M) or its Gk form (Mg), in order to defend the "traditional" sequence giving Mt priority, do so arbitrarily.

Evaluation. The Two-Document Theory has become very complex through numerous modifications. One of its great unsolved problems is that the phenomena positing the existence of Q appear not only in the sayings sections but also in the narrative sections. The Q material has always been considered a Gk collection of sayings, not a true narrative. Moreover, this classical theory does not take into account oral tradition. The Gospels could not have arisen solely as a writing process.

(Barrett, C. K., "Q—a Re-examination," *ExpT* 54 [1942–43] 320–23. Bradby, E. L., "In Defence of Q," *ExpT* 68 [1956–57] 315–18. Bussby, F., "Is Q an Aramaic Document?" *ExpT* 65 [1953–54] 272–75. Farrer, A. M., "On Dispensing with Q," *SGL* 55–88. Petrie, S. "'Q' Is Only What You Make It," *NovT* 3 [1959] 28–33. Rosché, T. R., "The Words of Jesus and the Future of the 'Q' Hypothesis," *JBL* 79 [1960] 210–20. Taylor, V., "The Elusive Q," *ExpT* 46 [1934–35] 68–74; "The Order of Q," *JTS* 4 [1953] 27–31. Throckmorton, B. H., "Did Mark Know Q?" *JBL* 67 [1948] 319–29.)

22 (b) THEORY OF L. VAGANAY. Vaganay introduced a theory taking into account this oral tradition, as a tradition to be found in both Aram and Gk. This was put into writing as small collections of words and/or incidents. In Gospel form these became Aram M, not identical with canonical Mt. Another early collection, consisting of sayings and discourses, he names S (source or supplement); it was also written in Aram. Both of these were translated into Greek. The earliest canonical Gospel, Mk, used as its sources Mg (the Gk translation of Aram M) and the oral tradition of Peter's preaching, but not S. Canonical Mt used as sources Mk, Mg, and Sg (the Gk translation of S), plus elements of Peter's preaching. According to Vaganay, Lk used as sources Mk, Mg, Sg, and elements of oral tradition. The diagram shown here approximates Vaganay's theory.

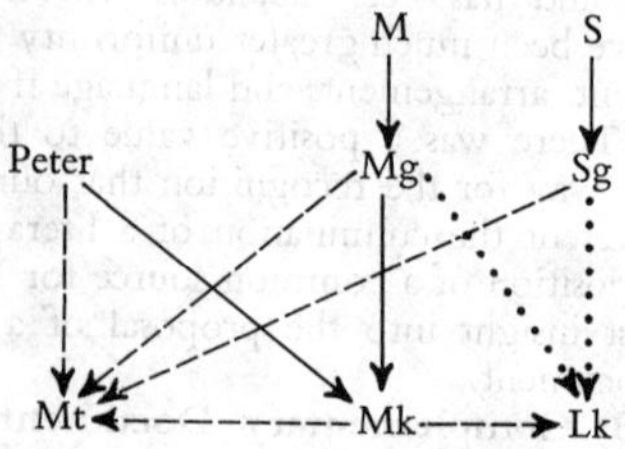

Vaganay introduced S into the solution to the problem because he felt that Aram M translated into Greek was insufficient to explain all the Syn tradition. He claims that this source has nothing in common with Q.

Evaluation. The criticisms leveled at Vaganay's theory have stressed that his system is very complex. In his desire to reject the Two-Document Hypothesis he has reconstructed a similar theory substituting S for Q. There are about 60 passages that scholars commonly allocate to Q; over 40 of them are in S—therefore, is there an actual distinction between S and Q? He presents us with no good reason why Mk should have been written.

23 **(C) Multiple Documentation as the Basis for Whole Gospel Complex.** This theory consists in supposing a rather mixed documentation as the origins of the Syn. It is considered by some as a middle course because it does not insist on the simplistic approach of the Oral-Tradition Theory nor on the rigid approach of the literary interrelationships. In its original form, proposed by Schleiermacher, the words and deeds of Jesus were not supposed to have been collected in one book but rather were contained in diverse documents that circulated among the faithful of many communities. Schleiermacher suggested that the missionary life of the early Christian Church could account for this form, for these various documents would serve as memory aids to preachers and catechists. From these the men involved in this work would draw according to various purposes and the needs of their hearers. These documents would have built up into miniature collections. Later on the Syn gathered these together. (For an important modern study of similar rabbinic, catechetic technique applied to the Gospels, see B. Gerhardsson, *Memory and Manuscript* [ASNU 22; Lund, 1961] and the analysis of this book by J. A. Fitzmyer, *TS* 23 [1962] 442–57.)

The modern interpreters of this theory stress not so much the written sources but rather the fragmentary tradition, whether oral or written, that evolved according to historical exigencies. At this late date it would be impossible to unravel the accretions from the nucleus.

24 The Multiple-Document Theory, with some variations, has found two modern proponents in L. Cerfaux and X. Léon-Dufour. At the origin of the Gospel material there was a standardization of the materials in Aramaic, followed by many partial traditions. All this was put into Greek at an early date. (This would be Aram M or proto-Mt translated into Greek.) Oral tradition would have been a continuing process, and this gospel would be expanded and modified by it. These particular traditions issue in the canonical Gospels. No other documentary source is posited.

Evaluation. The theory combines oral tradition and a single written Gospel flowing from multiple documents. Each of these is insufficient to explain the Syn Problem. The agreements among the Syn seem to require a literary process and not an oral process; the agreements cannot be reduced to a single document. Yet this theory does take into account both oral and written traditions. Perhaps it has not yet been sufficiently worked out. Taking the insights of the other theories and working on more of the minutiae of this theory might produce a closer approximation to the true background of the Syn.

(Cerfaux, L., "En marge de la question synoptique. Les unités littéraires antérieures aux trois premiers Évangiles," *La formation des Évangiles*, 24–33. Léon-Dufour, X., R–F, *INT* 282–86.)

25 **(IV) Summary.** Having considered some of the more plausible solutions to the Syn Problem, we can now summarize the points made throughout the discussion.

(a) Oral tradition must be given a more prominent place in the consideration of any solution to the Syn Problem. Oral tradition alone is not the answer; it cannot explain the similarities in the written texts.

(b) Mk as a source for Mt and Lk is generally accepted by Protestants and Catholics as the sequence of the Gospels. There is a literary dependence of Mt and Lk, therefore, on Mk; and Mk is to be regarded as the oldest of our Gospels in Greek.

(c) The canonical Mt was very probably composed in Greek and is not a *direct* translation of an Aram original.

(d) It should be remembered that sources Q (in Gk) and S (in Aram) are pure conjectures. Moreover, to presume that either Q or S is Aram M or Mg is arbitrary.

(e) Any purely literary solution with no consideration for oral tradition does not present the picture adequately.

(f) Perhaps the nearest approximation to the truth will be found in a multiple-document theory that takes into account a continuing oral tradition and its influence until the final crystallization of our present canonical Gospels. The modern emphasis on *Formgeschichte* and *Redaktionsgeschichte* (which is beyond the scope of this article) is a healthy reaction to an overstress on purely literary-documentary solutions to the Syn Problem (→ Modern NT Criticism, 41:42).

Conclusion. All the time and effort put into the consideration of the Syn Problem over the past century and a half have not been in vain. For each attempt at a solution—though faulty in some area—has contributed some insight. With each new insight we are brought closer to the complete answer. Yet the origins of the Syn, going back as many centuries as they do, are difficult to perceive. We are still a long way from a completely satisfactory answer. Perhaps the problem will never be totally solved. The challenge, however, still remains and will continue to be accepted by dedicated scholars.

41

MODERN NEW TESTAMENT CRITICISM

John S. Kselman, S.S.

BIBLIOGRAPHY

1 Anderson, H., *Jesus and Christian Origins* (Oxford, 1964). Fuller, D., *Easter Faith and History* (Grand Rapids, 1965). Fuller, R., *The New Testament in Current Study* (London, 1963). Howard, W. F., *The Romance of New Testament Scholarship* (London, 1949). Hunter, A. M., *Interpreting the New Testament 1900–1950* (London, 1951). Jülicher, A., *An Introduction to the New Testament* (N.Y., 1904) 8–30. Kümmel, W. G., *Das Neue Testament: Geschichte der Erforschung seiner Probleme* (Munich, 1958). Levie, J., *The Bible, Word of God in Words of Men* (London, 1961). McArthur, H. K., *The Quest Through the Centuries: The Search for the Historical Jesus* (Phila., 1966). Nash, H. S., *The History of the Higher Criticism of the New Testament* (N.Y., 1901). Neill, S., *The Interpretation of the New Testament 1861–1961* (Oxford, 1964). R–F, *INT* 141–54. Schnackenburg, R., *New Testament Theology Today* (N.Y., 1963).

2 OUTLINE

PRE-CRITICISM TO THE NINETEENTH CENTURY

3 **(I) Introduction.** The application to the NT of the principles of literary criticism (a study of the content of the NT) and of historical criticism (a study of the NT as a historical document) has a history that ranges from the 2nd cent. to the present.

(A) Pre-Critical Period. Although criticism of the Bible is a distinctly modern undertaking, there were in the early Church scholars who took the first steps toward scientific study of the NT.

(a) Pioneers in the Early Church. The first of these is Marcion (*ca.* 150), a heretic who repudiated the OT and Judaism and produced a truncated NT canon to conform to his teaching. By so doing, he moved the Church to counter his teaching by producing an orthodox NT canon (→ Canonicity, 67:58,81). Tatian (*ca.* 175), a Syrian convert to Christianity, was another 2nd-cent. pioneer who made an attempt at criticism of the NT. His *Diatesseron* was the first harmony of the four Gospels, presented as a single, continuous narrative.

The greatest ante-Nicene scholar in the Church was Origen (*ca.* 185–254), the head of the famous school of Alexandria. He made two notable contributions to biblical studies. The first was his *Hexapla*, the earliest Christian attempt at textual criticism of the OT (→ Texts, 69:68). The second was his realization of the importance of hermeneutics; although excessive, his allegorical interpretation of the Scriptures was a serious endeavor to make them relevant and meaningful to his contemporaries (→ Hermeneutics, 71:38).

The first Church historian, Eusebius (*ca.* 260–340) gave much valuable early information about the NT in his *Ecclesiastical History* (326). He also divided the Gospels into small numbered sections (still printed in Nestle's Gk NT) and devised a set of tables to show parallels between the various Gospels (H. K. McArthur, *CBQ* 27 [1965] 250–56).

Augustine (354–430), the great theologian of the Western Church, laid down in his *De consensu evangelistarum* (400) the principles that affected the treatment of Syn differences for over a millennium; he was aware that the order of the Gospel narratives sometimes reflects general recollection rather than strict chronological history and that the words of Jesus are often reported with an accuracy that preserves only their sense, rather than being given verbatim.

Although the Middle Ages, especially the great scholastic period, contributed to the better understanding of Scripture (→ Hermeneutics, 71:41–42), the contributions to real NT criticism were not major. (For the critical implications of medieval lives of Jesus, see McArthur, *The Quest Through the Centuries*, 57–84.)

4 (b) The Reformation. In the 16th cent. the Reformation increased the interest in the Bible, especially in the Reformed Churches, though this interest was more dogmatic than critical. One important figure in this period was A. Osiander (1498–1552), an early Lutheran reformer, who published in 1537 a harmony of the Gospels that set the style for Protestant harmonies of the following centuries. His approach was much more rigid than Augustine's, and for him, minor differences in sequence or detail meant different events. (See McArthur, *op. cit.*, 93ff.)

5 **(B) Critical Studies Before the Nineteenth Century.** Against the background of rationalism and the Enlightenment, the 18th cent. saw the rise of the scientific method. When this method was applied to the study of history, and particularly to biblical history, the science of historical criticism of the Bible was born.

(a) R. Simon. A French Oratorian priest, Simon (1638–1712) was the first to apply the critical method to the NT, in the three vols. of his *Histoire critique* of the NT (1689–92; → Modern OT Criticism, 70:6.). J. D. Michaelis (1717–91) built upon Simon's work to produce the first truly historical and critical introduction to the NT (1750). (→ Modern OT Criticism, 70:12.)

(b) H. S. Reimarus. As the German title (*Von Reimarus zu Wrede*) of A. Schweitzer's *The Quest of the Historical Jesus* indicates, Reimarus (1694–1768) is a key figure in the history of NT criticism. In 1778 excerpts from his *Von dem Zweck Jesu und seinen Jünger* (*On the Intention of Jesus and His Disciples*) were published posthumously. In this work Reimarus distinguished between the historical Jesus (a Jewish revolutionary who failed in an attempt to establish an earthly Messianic kingdom) and the Christ found in the Gospels and preached by the Church (a deception created by the disciples who stole the body of Jesus from the tomb and invented the doctrines of the resurrection and parousia). Although prejudiced by rationalism's rejection of the supernatural, Reimarus was the first to try to pierce through the Christological dogma of the Gospels to the real historical Jesus, a concern that has lost none of its urgency in the 20th cent.

6 **(II) Birth of Nineteenth-Century Criticism.** Starting from the work of their predecessors, the scholars of the 19th cent. continued the study of the NT, pursuing two directions: critically, they were concerned with the question of the historical value of the NT; theologically, they were concerned with its meaning. These two directions shaped the subsequent history of NT criticism.

(A) Tübingen School. Few schools have been so influential in NT interpretation as that which took its name from the University of Tübingen. The questions formulated by the leaders of the Tübingen school and the fundamental insights they provided have been determinative for all later NT criticism.

7 (a) D. Strauss. In 1835, Strauss (1808–74), a student of F. C. Baur, published his *Life of Jesus*, a radical reinterpretation of the Gospel accounts of Jesus. Previous lives of Christ had been either orthodox interpretations accepting the intervention of the supernatural into human history, or rationalist explanations of only apparently supernatural happenings. Strauss added a third alternative, the mythical interpretation: the Gospels give us a basis of historical fact transformed and embellished by the faith of the Church. Strauss ended his work by confessing the impossibility of writing a life of Jesus, both because the Gospels refuse to see Jesus simply as a part of history and because the Gospels give us only unconnected fragments, the order being imposed by the Evangelists.

Strauss's work profoundly influenced two other 19th-cent. writers. B. Bauer (1809–82) removed what historical foundation Strauss had allowed and left only myth, concluding that Jesus and Paul were nonhistorical literary fictions. E. Renan (1823–92), in his *Life of Jesus* (1863), equated supernatural with unreal and gave his readers a purely human Jesus.

8 (b) F. C. Baur. One of the most important NT scholars of the 19th cent. and the teacher of Strauss was Baur (1792–1860), undoubtedly the uncontested head of the Tübingen School. Although few of the solutions he proposed are accepted today, the questions he asked are of enduring significance, and he raised NT criticism to a truly scientific level.

According to Baur's Hegelian view, the history of Christianity from *ca.* AD 40 to 160 was one of tension, struggle, and eventual reconciliation. The struggle was between *Pauline libertarianism*, with its message of freedom from the law and the universality of the Church's mission, and narrow *Judaic legalism*, represented by the primitive apostles led by Peter, with its insistence on the supposed prerogatives of Judaism. From this thesis-antithesis came the Catholic Church and the NT canon, which smoothed away differences by putting Peter and Paul on equal footing, a process we can see in Acts. This synthesis came in the 2nd cent. as a result of the gradual cooling of hostilities and the emergent common threat of Gnosticism.

The effect of Baur's hypotheses on the formation and dating of the NT was far-reaching. Before 70 only Paul's "authentic" Epistles existed (Rom, 1–2 Cor, Gal). The Judaism of Mt was an argument for its priority; the Paulinism of Lk vs. the Judaism of Mt produced Mk as synthesis; Acts and Jn were to be dated in the middle of the 2nd cent.

The strict application of Hegelian principles and the overemphasis on the influence of Judaism in early Christianity were obvious defects in Baur's work. But the contributions he made to NT studies were estimable. First and most important, he studied the NT as part of the history of Christianity, showing it to be the product of the history of the early Church and a witness to the spirit of a definite age. Second, this same historical acumen led him to see that the study of the NT must begin with the earliest evidence, the writings of Paul. Third, he gave deserved prominence to Paul and his theology. Finally, he made a clear distinction between the Syn and Jn. (Cf. W. F. Howard, *The Romance of New Testament Scholarship*, 33–44. P. C. Hodgson, *The Formation of Historical Theology* [N.Y., 1966].)

9 **(B) Reaction to Tübingen.** After the critical work of Strauss and Baur there seemed to be only two alternatives: either a naïve sacralization of the Bible and a fundamentalist refusal to subject it to critical study, or an acceptance of German criticism, which seemed to spell the destruction of orthodox Christianity. The task of NT scholarship in the second half of the 19th cent. was to present another alternative: an acceptance of the historicocritical method, but without Baur's presuppositions and conclusions. In England, this task fell to the Cambridge Three; in Germany, to A. von Harnack.

The answer of the three great Cambridge scholars was to attempt a critical commentary on the whole NT, a commentary that was historically and philologically accurate, set against the background of its own era and based on a critically edited Gk NT. Although this proposed commentary was never completed, it would be difficult to overvalue the legacy the Cambridge Three left NT scholarship. (Cf. Howard, *op. cit.*, 55–83; S. Neill, *The Interpretation of the New Testament*, 33–76.)

10 (a) J. B. Lightfoot. Realizing like Baur that a critical study of the NT must begin with Paul, the first task to which Lightfoot (1828–89) set himself was a series of commentaries on the Epistles of Paul, of which he completed his commentaries on Gal (1865), Phil (1868), and Col and Phlm (1875). Lightfoot's work on Paul made him acutely aware of the problem of the dating of the NT. Critical NT scholarship had largely accepted the late dates that Baur had assigned to the books of the NT. But the Tübingen theories would collapse if one could establish an early date for a body of post-NT literature. Lightfoot found such a starting point in the letters of Ignatius of Antioch and the Epistle of Clement of Rome, literature that alludes to most NT books. The results of his labor on Ignatius appeared in 1885, and his edition of Clement was published posthumously in 1890. Because of Lightfoot's careful historical investigation the date of the Epistle of Clement was set at the end of the 1st cent., and the seven authentic letters of Ignatius were assigned to the early 2nd cent. Besides giving a fixed point of time from which we can date the NT, this literature gives us a picture of the life of the Church in the late 1st and early 2nd cent. AD in three great Church centers, Antioch, Ephesus (Ignatius), and Rome (Clement). And rather than giving any indication of prolonged and bitter conflict between a Pauline and a Petrine party, both Ignatius and Clement link the names of the two great Apostles, a practice which, according to Baur, did not occur until the middle of the 2nd cent.

11 (b) B. F. Westcott. The real exegete of the three was Westcott (1825–1901). His commentary on the Gospel of Jn, an outstanding blend of criticism and theology, first published in 1880, was republished as recently as 1958. Also *Epistles of St. John* (repub. 1966).

12 (c) F. J. A. Hort. Of the few works Hort (1828–92) published, two books on the history of the early Church are especially noteworthy: *Judaistic Christianity* (1894) and *The Christian Ecclesia* (1897). To the proposed commentary he added only his work on 1 Pt 1:1–2:17 (1898).

However, it is not on the above works that the fame of Westcott and Hort rests but on the great critical edition of the Gk NT that they prepared (→ Texts, 69:130). Previously, NT study had to rely on the *textus receptus*, substantially the 16th-cent. text of Erasmus, printed in 1516 and based on inadequate ms. evidence (→ Texts

69:123–24). Having formulated a genuinely scientific method of textual criticism, Westcott and Hort published in 1881 the critical text of the NT, with an important introduction on the science of textual criticism.

13 (d) A. VON HARNACK. Perhaps the greatest Protestant theologian of the 19th cent., Harnack (1851–1930) was a universal scholar, proficient in biblical studies, patristics, Church history, and systematic theology. Like Baur, Harnack came to the NT documents as a historian of the early Church. Unlike Baur, he challenged the new orthodoxy of Tübingen with the cry of "Back to tradition!" This was not a call for the abandonment of historicocritical methods nor a naïve acceptance of the NT merely on the authority of earlier ages in the Church. On the contrary, with expert use of the critical method, Harnack examined the evidence and concluded that Baur had rejected overhastily and uncritically the traditional views regarding the origin and growth of the NT.

An illustration of Harnack's method would be his great trilogy on the Lucan writings: *Luke the Physician* (1906), *The Acts of the Apostles* (1908), and *The Date of the Acts and of the Synoptic Gospels* (1911). In these works, Harnack's critical study upheld the traditional view that the author of Lk and Acts was Luke, companion of Paul, a position that had for 60 years been abandoned because of Baur's criticism. (Cf. Howard, *op. cit.*, 44–54.)

Harnack's most famous work is not one of his many critical studies but a series of popular lectures, published as *What Is Christianity?* (1900), the classical exposition of liberal Protestantism. According to Harnack, the essence of Christianity lay in certain ethical truths preached by Jesus: the fatherhood of God, the brotherhood of man, the infinite value of the human soul. It was this position that Schweitzer would attack, with his claim that Jesus preached not a set of timeless principles but the imminent end of his world order. (Cf. *ExpT* 66 [1954–55] 100–103.)

THE TRANSITION TO THE TWENTIETH CENTURY

14 **(I) Studies in Language and Background.** Starting with the insights of Baur and throughout the works of Harnack and the Cambridge Three, the theological question of the religious meaning of the NT loomed ever larger. But before this question could be adequately dealt with the more prosaic study of the language and background of the NT had to progress.

(A) Language of the NT. In a lecture delivered in 1863, Lightfoot stated that if we could recover letters reflecting the way in which ordinary people of the 1st cent. spoke and wrote, our understanding of the language of the NT would be immeasurably increased. Lightfoot's surmise was prophetic—ancient mss. and papyri, discovered in the second half of the 19th cent., have been of immense benefit to NT studies.

15 (a) C. VON TISCHENDORF. In 1859, Tischendorf (1815–74) made one of the most important finds in the history of biblical studies. In a monastery on Mt. Sinai he discovered one of the two oldest biblical mss. we possess, the Codex Sinaiticus, including the complete NT (→ Texts, 69:120,129). Tischendorf's contribution to the study of the text of the NT ranks in importance with that of Westcott and Hort. (Cf. Howard, *op. cit.*, 84–92.)

16 (b) A. DEISSMANN. Starting late in the 19th cent., papyri were found in increasing numbers in Egypt where the dry climate preserved them. These papyri were mostly popular documents—letters, bills, receipts—exactly the sort of material that Lightfoot had spoken of. The documents were written in koine, the common form of the Gk language spoken in NT times. The pioneer in applying to the NT the new knowledge gained from such discoveries was Deissmann (1866–1937). The subtitle of his *Bible Studies* (Ger 1895; Eng 1907) is a good summary of his work: "Contributions Chiefly from Papyri and Inscriptions to the History of the Language, the Literature, and the Religion of Hellenistic Judaism and Primitive Christianity." This book was followed by another with the same aim, *Light from the Ancient East* (1908), still a standard introduction to the field. (Cf. Howard, *op. cit.*, 117–28; → NT Epistles, 47:4.)

17 **(B) Background of the NT.** In addition to progress in linguistic studies, NT study profited in this transitional period from the continuing growth of our knowledge of the world from which the NT came, its history, its geography, its government, its religion, its thought forms and literary forms—in short, all those *varia* we can classify under the rubric of background.

18 (a) E. HATCH. The name of Hatch (1835–89) will forever be linked with that of H. A. Redpath with whom he produced a monumental concordance to the LXX, published in 1897. But our concern here is with a lesser known book published in 1889 (and reissued in 1957), whose importance was immediately recognized by Harnack. In this work, titled *The Influence of Greek Ideas on Christianity*, Hatch examined a subject of continuing interest to NT scholars: the question of the interaction of Christianity and its Hellenistic environment and of the distinction between the Semitic and Hellenistic elements in Christian faith and thought. The relevance of this subject can be seen in the impact it has made on contemporary biblical theology (where the difference between the Semitic and Greek mentalities has become a commonplace) and on the History of Religions School, one of the decisive influences on the thought of R. Bultmann.

19 (b) R. H. CHARLES. Apocalyptic is a literary form alien to the world of the 20th cent., but an understanding of it is absolutely necessary for the interpretation of the NT, which came from a world permeated with Jewish apocalyptic thought forms and literature. Charles (1855–1931) was the great student of apocalyptic literature and of Jewish apocryphal literature in general. He was the editor of and a major contributor to the two vols. of *The Apocrypha and Pseudepigrapha of the Old Testament in English* (1913), still an indispensable tool for research into NT background. Charles put his extensive knowledge of apocalyptic to good use when in 1920 he produced for the ICC his important two-vol. commentary on the Ap. (Cf. Howard, *op. cit.*, 105–10.)

20 (c) W. M. RAMSAY. Archaeologist, historian, and indefatigable explorer of Asia Minor, the early seat of Christianity, Ramsay (1851–1939) is best known for two important books, *St. Paul the Traveller and the Roman Citizen* (1895) and *The Cities of St. Paul* (1907), in which he treats of the historical, political, and geographical background of Acts. Although Ramsay had been skeptical about the historical value of Acts, his historical and archaeological study of Asia Minor as Paul knew and traveled it convinced him of the accuracy and reliability of Luke as a contemporary historian—in the light of archaeological evidence the Lucan writings truly reflect the conditions of the second half of the 1st cent. Ramsay's studies of Paul and the Greco-Roman world in which he moved did much to recreate for us the Apostle as a living man.

Less well known but significant for the study of the Ap is his book *Letters to the Seven Churches in Asia* (1904), which emphasized the importance of the imperial cult as the background for the persecution of the Church in proconsular Asia and the influence of historical geography on the picture of the seven churches of Ap 2–3. (Cf. Howard, *op. cit.*, 138–55.)

21 **(II) Synoptic Gospels: Criticism and Development.** There were two interrelated, crucial problems in NT interpretation that the 19th cent. did not adequately consider: the Syn question and the questions connected with the NT accounts of the life and death of Jesus Christ. Both subjects were to engage the attention of 20th-cent. scholars.

(A) The Priority of Mark and the Two-Source Theory. Mk had long been the least examined of the four Gospels in the history of NT interpretation. Augustine had looked upon it as an abbreviation of Mt. In the 19th cent., in response to Strauss's attack on the historical foundation of Christianity, students of the NT began to turn to Mk in an attempt to preserve Christianity as a historical religion, based on a historical figure, Jesus of Nazareth. The historicocritical method was used as an instrument to discover the sources that underlay the NT accounts of Jesus. Important preparation for this quest was the work of J. J. Griesbach (1745–1812), who recognized the difference between Jn and the first three Gospels. He saw the possibility of arranging Mt, Mk, and Lk in a synopsis, and the impossibility of constructing a harmony, since the Evangelists were in all likelihood not concerned with chronological order.

22 (a) K. Lachmann. A real advance came in 1835, when Lachmann (1793–1851) published a study entitled "De ordine narrationum in evangeliis synopticis," in which he proposed the literary priority of Mk and claimed that Mk was closer to the original tradition than the other Gospels, thereby establishing Mk as a basic source for any attempt to get back to the origins of Christianity.

23 (b) C. H. Weisse. In 1838, Weisse furthered Lachmann's hypothesis by adding another source, a sayings-source common to Mt and Lk (which would eventually be termed the Q source). Thus, by 1838 the main lines of the classic "Two-source Theory" had been discovered (→ Syn Problem, 40:21).

24 **(B) Scientific Source Criticism.** Lachmann and Weisse had proceeded by insight. The next task of NT criticism would be to test their theories scientifically.

(a) H. J. Holtzmann. In 1863, Holtzmann published the results of his painstaking study to verify scientifically the Two-Source Theory, *Die synoptischen Evangelien.* He concluded that Mk was the original apostolic document and that behind Mt and Lk lay another written document, a very early collection of the sayings and teachings of Jesus, including probably some narratives (e.g., the Baptism and Temptation Accounts).

25 (b) B. H. Streeter. We now turn to the 20th cent. and to the scholar who gave source criticism its classic exposition. Streeter (1874–1937) had two advantages in his work: Westcott and Hort's edition of the NT and the work of Holtzmann. Against a background of nearly universal acceptance of the Two-Source Hypothesis, Streeter proposed a refinement of this theory in *The Four Gospels: A Study of Origins* (1924). He theorized thus: if Rome had a cycle of traditions about Jesus enshrined in the Gospel of Mk, written *ca.* 65–70, would it not be likely that the three other great Christian centers of the 1st cent. would also have such local traditions? Working from this hypothesis, Streeter assigned Q (*ca.* 50) to Antioch; the material peculiar to Lk (*ca.* 60) had its origin in Caesarea; and Jerusalem was the home of Mt's special tradition (*ca.* 65). On this basis, Streeter dated Lk in its final form to *ca.* 80, and Mt to *ca.* 85.

Streeter's important contribution was that he proved by careful scientific investigation that four sources, rather than two, underlie the Syn. What is questionable is his concept of four written documents. Scholars today would tend to speak of cycles of oral tradition rather than of written documents. Streeter's work was the final word on source criticism in two senses, for by the time he had published his book, scholars were turning their attention from source criticism to form criticism. (Cf. *ExpT* 72 [1960–61] 295–99.)

26 **(C) Gospel Origins: The Aramaic Question.** The interaction of Semitic and Greek influences in the NT is a subject that has continued to hold the attention of critics. Perhaps the greatest indication of this perennial interest is the NT commentary prepared by H. L. Strack and P. Billerbeck from rabbinic sources, their five-vol. *Kommentar zum Neuen Testament aus Talmud und Midrasch* (1922–55; index 1961); also J. Bonsirven, *Textes rabbiniques des deux premiers siècles chrétiens pour servir à l'intelligence du Nouveau Testament* (Rome, 1955); W. D. Davies, *Paul and Rabbinic Judaism* (2nd ed.; London, 1955).

On the subject of Aram origins in particular, source criticism had noticed in the Gospels much that was of Aram character. In the Q source, for instance, critics had detected an early Aram original, translated into Greek. This is far from surprising; since Aramaic was the language of Jesus and his first disciples, the Aram background of the writers and the ones written of constantly shows through the Greek of the NT.

27 (a) G. Dalman. The trail blazer in this area was Dalman (1855–1941), a great Aram scholar, representative of the conservative or minimal position regarding Aram influence in the NT. His most important book was *The Words of Jesus* (Ger 1898; Eng 1902). Although the hypothesis of an Aram original underlying the Syn tradition was not impossible, Dalman established that Jesus indubitably spoke Aramaic to his disciples; the words of Jesus, as recorded in the Gospels, definitely show Aram influence.

28 (b) C. C. Torrey. The maximal theory of Aram origins found an able defender in Torrey (1863–1956). In two works, *The Four Gospels* (1933) and *Our Translated Gospels* (1936), he argued that the Gospels were translations of primitive Aram writings. His thesis failed to convince the body of NT scholars.

29 (c) C. F. Burney. Burney (1868–1925) focused attention particularly on Jn, supposedly the most Hellenized Gospel, and did NT studies the service of pointing up its Semitic qualities in *The Aramaic Origin of the Fourth Gospel* (1922). A maximalist like Torrey, he held that Jn was a translation of an Aram original.

30 (d) J. Jeremias. A student of Dalman, Jeremias (b. 1900) is a very competent Aram scholar. His interest in this subject is especially evident in *The Parables of Jesus* (Ger 1947; Eng 1954) and *The Eucharistic Words of Jesus* (Ger 1949; Eng 1955). In both works Jeremias attempts to recover the "ipsissima verba Christi" by reconstructing from the Gk accounts given to us by the primitive Church the original Aram spoken by Jesus.

(Cf. *ExpT* 66 [1954–55] 46–49; *ExpT* 74 [1962–63] 115–19.)

31 (e) M. Black. In 1946, Black (b. 1908) published his important survey of the whole Aram question, *An Aramaic Approach to the Gospels and Acts* (3rd ed. rev. 1967). In it he modifies the extremes of Torrey and Burney and takes a mediate position. Since Aramaisms are strongest and most frequent in the words of Jesus, an Aram sayings-source, either written or oral, underlies the Syn tradition.

(Brown, S., "From Burney to Black: The Fourth Gospel and the Aramaic Question," *CBQ* 26 [1964] 323–39. A thorough discussion with extensive bibliography.)

TWENTIETH-CENTURY CRITICISM

32 **(I) New Directions.** Twentieth-cent. NT scholarship presents a variegated picture, influenced as it is by its own heritage of historical and critical studies and by the 20th cent. itself (e.g., consider the impact that modern scientific technology has had on Bultmann's hermeneutic). The dominant issue in 20th-cent. criticism is certainly the series of historical problems arising from the NT account of the life and death of Jesus. The crucial question is this: To what degree has the Church's confession colored or shaped the history? This is obviously a theological as well as a historical question; for the answer, skeptical or otherwise, that we give to the historical question will to a large extent determine the meaning that we assign to that history. Form criticism's search for and investigation of the "Gospel behind the Gospels" is one attempt of NT criticism to give an honest answer to this question.

Theology has come into its own in 20th-cent. biblical studies. In the area of NT interpretation, the great sign of the times is indisputably the *Theologisches Wörterbuch zum Neuen Testament*, begun in 1932 under the editorship of G. Kittel (1888–1948) and not yet completed. Every German NT scholar of importance can be found among its contributors. Although this diversity makes for some unevenness in the quality of the individual articles, this work is still the most valuable source book of NT theology produced in this cent. Happily, its translation into English has finally been undertaken (*ThDNT*).

To understand the present state of NT studies, in particular the alliance of criticism and theology, we must first listen to some of the prophetic voices raised at the beginning of this cent.

33 **(A) Abandonment of the Liberal Quest of the Historical Jesus.** Strauss's attempt to write a life of Jesus was, by his own admission, a failure, as in his opinion any such attempt must be, in view of the nature of the sources. In an analogy later to be elaborated upon by the form-critical school, Strauss believed that the pericopes, the individual stories and sayings of which our Gospels are composed, are, like a necklace of pearls without a string, fragments that had received an artificial order from the Evangelists.

Such skepticism seemed unwarranted later in the 19th cent. First, the discovery and scientific establishment of the Two-Source Theory seemed to make available two sources, Mk and Q, which stood very close to the original apostolic tradition. Second, the Liberal school, under the leadership of Harnack, believed that, with the use of the historicocritical method, one could cut away the Christological dogma that Reimarus had called attention to in the Gospels and get to the historical Jesus behind the Christ of faith proclaimed in the NT.

Consequently, the last half of the 19th cent. saw the production of a spate of lives of Jesus based on the established facts of 19th-cent. criticism: two primitive sources that could be stripped of their dogmatic trappings.

34 (a) W. Wrede. The first serious challenge to this presumed factuality came from Wrede (1859–1906). In his classic, *Das Messiasgeheimnis in den Evangelien* (*The Messianic Secret in the Gospels*) published in 1901, Wrede used the same critical method employed by the Liberals to demonstrate the unscientific character of the picture of Jesus that they had constructed. He contended further that Mk, like the other Gospels, was not a simple biography but a profound theological interpretation of the meaning of Jesus. Literally from the opening words of his Gospel, the Evangelist shows us not a human, but a completely divine Jesus. Wrede's thesis on the Messiahship runs thus: The historical Jesus never made any claim to be the Messiah. Only after the resurrection did the disciples realize that Jesus was the Christ. They then read back Messiahship into the earthly life of Jesus and created the "Messianic Secret" (Jesus' concealment of his Messiahship) to account for the fact that his Messiahship was unknown to them and to the Jews at large before his death. The Messianic secret was therefore a tradition created by the early Christian community and taken over by Mk, who wrote not as an objective historian but from the viewpoint of Christian faith.

Wrede thus dealt the first blow to the Liberals' optimistic quest for the Jesus of history. The *coup de grâce* would be administered a few years later in Schweitzer's famous book. (Cf. *ExpT* 65 [1953–54] 246–50.)

35 (b) A. Schweitzer. In 1901, Schweitzer (1875–1965) too published a study on the Messianic secret entitled *Das Messianitäts- und Leidensgeheimnis* (*The Secret of the Messiahship and the Passion;* tr. into Eng in 1914 and published as *The Mystery of the Kingdom of God*) in which he defended the historicity of the Messianic secret, claiming that it was not a creation of the Church but a conviction of Jesus.

But Schweitzer's most memorable work was *The Quest of the Historical Jesus* (Ger 1906; Eng 1910), an exhaustive survey of the life-of-Jesus research from Reimarus to Wrede. After incisive criticism of the Liberal portrait of Jesus the ethical teacher so attractively presented by Harnack in *What is Christianity?*, Schweitzer reconstructs for us what he considers to be the true picture of the historical Jesus. Following the guidelines that J. Weiss (1863–1914) proposed in *Die Predigt Jesu vom Reich Gottes* (*The Preaching of Jesus on the Kingdom of God;* 1892), Schweitzer stressed the eschatological, apocalyptic element in the life and teaching of Jesus. The Jesus that Schweitzer finds in the Gospel is a heroic figure, a noble but deluded fanatic convinced that he was the Messiah, who preached an apocalyptic message of the imminent end of the world and went to his death to bring it about.

Although few would accept Schweitzer's reconstruction of the historical Jesus, there is general agreement that his work sounded the death knell for the Liberal quest for the Jesus of history and that it pointed up the importance of the apocalyptic background and framework of the teaching of Jesus. (Cf. *ExpT* 65 [1953–54] 206–9.)

36 **(B) Early Catholic Reaction to Critical Study.** Up until the 20th cent. biblical criticism had almost no impact on Catholic studies; the critical tradition that had produced a Strauss and a Baur was looked upon with suspicion. Indifference at best, even overt hostility were the characteristically defensive postures assumed by all but a few pioneers. (Indeed, it was only with Pius XII's encyclical on biblical studies in 1943, *Divino Afflante Spiritu*, that Roman Catholic biblicists could begin to take their place in the vanguard of serious NT study; → Church Pronouncements, 72:20–23.)

37 (a) M.-J. LAGRANGE. The greatest of the pioneers in Catholic biblical studies was the Dominican Lagrange (1855–1938; → Modern OT Criticism, 70:35). He had become aware of German critical study while a student of Oriental languages at the University of Vienna. In 1890, with almost no material or financial support, Lagrange founded in Jerusalem the *École pratique d'études bibliques* (more familiarly known as the École Biblique). The principal aim of the École was to promote study of the Bible not only as the inspired Word of God, but also as a literary work that could be examined with the aid of the historicocritical method developed in the 19th cent. In 1892 Lagrange founded the *Revue biblique*, the first and today the most prominent Catholic journal of biblical studies. In 1902 he launched the *Études bibliques*, a series of biblical commentaries both doctrinal and scientific. In summary, Lagrange's outstanding achievement was that he moved Catholic studies into a field where Protestant scholarship, sometimes rationalistic and skeptical, had dominated, and in so doing he demonstrated that the use of the historicocritical method was not necessarily contrary to faith.

(Ahern, B., "Père Lagrange," *Worship*, 36 [1962] 242–48. Braun, F.-M., *The Work of Père Lagrange* [Milwaukee, 1963]. Murphy, R., "Père Lagrange," *BT* 8 [1963] 478–83.)

38 (b) A. LOISY. Another great scholar, whose career unfortunately ended in Modernism, Loisy (1857–1940) was a gifted philologist and exegete. He was an outstanding teacher of Scripture at the Institut Catholique in Paris from 1884 to 1893. During this time he wrote his doctoral dissertation on the history of the OT canon, which he completed in 1890 and in which the impact of criticism could be felt. Loisy accepted in his work the principles and conclusions of the critical school and soon began to lean toward the hypercritical and skeptical wing of that school. His association with Modernism and consequent clashes with ecclesiastical authority eventually led to his excommunication in 1908. Loisy's work was extremely harmful to Catholic exegesis, casting suspicion even on orthodox scholars and loyal churchmen like Lagrange.

Loisy's most important work was *L'Évangile et L'Église* (1902), his answer to Harnack's *What is Christianity?* In this book Harnack had proposed that, since the essence of Christianity was the interior and individual realization of God in the human soul, Christianity had no need for a Church; indeed, a Church could become an obstacle to and deformation of genuine Christianity. Against this position Loisy defended the Church as an organization that truly mediates God to man, but he denied that the Church was founded by Christ in the form it later assumed. Although the Church developed according to the designs of God, Jesus could never have foreseen what it would become. Loisy developed these ideas further in two later works, *Le Quatrième Évangile* (1903) and *Les Évangiles Synoptiques* (1908), wherein he dissociates the historical Jesus, unconscious of his divinity, and the Christ of faith, and sees the early Christian community as a screen between believer and event.

39 **(C) History of Religions School.** This school (in Ger *Religionsgeschichtliche Schule*) applied the principles of comparative religion to the study of early Christianity and saw Christianity as one religious phenomenon among many in the dying Roman Empire. Parallels like ritual washings, sacred meals, the worship of a dying and rising god, and certainty of eternal life through union with the god suggested a gradual process of syncretism and mutual interpenetration of Christianity and the popular mystery religions from the East. The History of Religions approach marked NT interpretation especially through the influence it exerted on Bultmann and his school. (For a good discussion of *Religionsgeschichte*, cf. Neill, *op. cit.*, 157–90.)

40 (a) R. REITZENSTEIN. One of the key doctrines of *Religionsgeschichte* found an important expositor in Reitzenstein (1861–1931). In *Die hellenistischen Mysterienreligionen* (1910) Reitzenstein traced this supposed Hellenizing process through early Christian history and offered three conclusions affecting NT study: first, that Hellenistic and Eastern religion exercised a profound influence on NT theology, especially on that of Paul; second, that the early Church's proclamation and cult depended on the mystery religions and Gnosticism; third, that early Christianity's idea of redemption by the death and resurrection of Christ was borrowed from a pre-Christian Gnostic redeemer myth.

41 (b) W. BOUSSET. The most influential scholar of the History of Religions school was undoubtedly Bousset (1865–1920). His greatest work is *Kyrios Christos* (1913), a sketch of the development of Christian thought up to Irenaeus. Bousset's primary insight was his recognition of the importance of worship in the early Church. According to Bousset, Paul or his successors transformed primitive Christianity into a mystery cult. Many of the early Christian groups in the Hellenistic world had been mystery fellowships, which now simply worshiped a new god, Jesus, as *Kyrios*, a title commonly given to the god-hero in the cult and ritual of the mysteries.

Because of their continuing currency in NT studies, particularly in the Bultmannian school, we shall summarize here the fundamental theses of the *Religionsgeschichtliche Schule*. First, we have already mentioned the hypothesis of a redeemer myth found in a supposed pre-Christian form of Gnosticism. Second, there is posited a distinctly Gentile form of Christianity (*Heidenchristentum*) independent of the traditions of the Jewish Church and syncretistically influenced by non-Christian religious groups with which they came in contact. Third, even in the NT canon one can find evidence of "Early Catholicism" (*Frühkatholizismus*), the development of an institutional Church as an outward and visible mediator of salvation (*Heilsanstalt*), a process that is viewed as a deformation of genuine Pauline Christianity.

42 **(D) Birth of Form Criticism.** Source criticism was the signal achievement of 19th-cent. NT study. Among its important contributions were the establishment of the priority of Mk, the identification of Q, and the use of these sources in Mt and Lk. Beyond this, however, source criticism could not go, for by definition it was confined to the study of the documents at hand. Twentieth-cent. criticism posed a further question: can we get behind the written documents to the period between the events and the first written records (*ca.* AD 30–60), when the stories of the words and works of Jesus circulated in Aram?

This is the aim of form criticism (or *Formgeschichte* = form history), which attempts to investigate and analyze the origin and history of the preliterary, oral tradition behind our written Gospels. The premise of form criticism is that the Gospels are composed of many smaller pericopes that circulated as separate units in early Christian communities before the Gospels were written. Form criticism is concerned with the forms or patterns of these stories and sayings, and the reasons for their preservation in the Gospels. The original impetus for this study came from the great OT scholar, H. Gunkel, who had developed techniques in OT interpretation by which he tried to establish the underlying oral traditions behind the documents, and the *Sitz im Leben* (life-situation) of these traditions (→ Modern OT Criticism, 70:38). New Testament form criticism developed Gunkel's insight and we may distinguish three levels in the formation and preservation of the Gospel material. First, the *Sitz im Leben Jesu* (the situation in the life of Jesus) is the context and meaning of an individual story or saying in the earthly life of Jesus whenever such a context is recoverable. Second, the *Sitz im Leben der Kirche* (the situation in the life of the Church) is the situation or context of a particular story or saying of Jesus in the life of the early Church. What prompted the early community to preserve this particular reminiscence from the life of Jesus and what meaning did the community give to it? Third, the *Sitz im Evangelium* (the situation in the Gospel) is the context of a saying or story of the Lord in the Gospel itself. What did the Evangelist mean to teach by recording this particular event in this particular setting? This latter question marks a transition from *Formgeschichte* to *Redaktionsgeschichte* (→ Hermeneutics, 71:30).

43 (a) K. L. Schmidt. The form-critical era began in 1919 with the publication by Schmidt (1891–1956) of *Der Rahmen der Geschichte Jesu* (*The Framework of the History of Jesus*). Schmidt's contention was that the Syn were mosaiclike collections of short episodes from the life of Jesus, which had circulated as independent units in the period of oral transmission and few of which had any indication of time or place of origin. (The one important exception was the Passion Narrative, which seemed to have existed very early as a continuous, coherent narrative.) In Mk, the Evangelist supplied a framework of connecting links and "bridge passages" (*Sammelberichte*, generalizing summaries like Mk 1:14–15, 21–22; 2:13, etc.) for these separate, self-contained units. This framework is a product of Mk's theological concerns rather than a picture of the life of Jesus. In form-critical terminology Mk reflects not the *Sitz im Leben Jesu* but the *Sitz im Leben der Kirche*. The early Christian community for which and in which Mark wrote his Gospel preserved and adapted stories relevant for its life, its worship, its pastoral and missionary concerns.

44 (b) M. Dibelius. The year 1919 also saw the publication of *Die Formgeschichte des Evangeliums* (tr. under the title *From Tradition to Gospel;* 1934) by Dibelius (1883–1947). Dibelius's starting point was that the missionary activity and needs of the early Church were instrumental in shaping the early tradition. In his discussion of the tradition, he advanced two principles that were accepted as axiomatic by later form critics: first, that the Syn were not literary works in the strict sense of the word but *Kleinliteratur*, literature designed for popular consumption; second, that the Syn Evangelists were not true authors, but rather compilers of preexisting material. (The most recent trend in form criticism has been a reaction to this second principle called *Redaktionsgeschichte*, the study of the redaction, or editing, done by the Evangelists as creative theologians and not simply as depersonalized compilers. This is the approach adopted by G. Bornkamm in his *Tradition and Interpretation in Matthew* [Ger 1960; Eng 1963] and by H. Conzelmann in *The Theology of St. Luke*; → 68 below.) (For Dibelius's work on Acts, cf. *ExpT* 67 [1955–56] 343–45.)

45 The last figure in the great triumvirate of early form critics is, of course, R. Bultmann, whose form-critical study of the Syn tradition will be discussed below (→ 49). For convenience, however, we shall summarize here the principles on which form criticism generally operates. As was mentioned, the form critics posit a period of oral transmission before the written Gospels, during which time the stories and sayings of the tradition circulated as separate units. These separate units can be discovered in the Gospels and can be classified according to their literary form. The determinative factor in their preservation was to be found in the needs and interests of the Christian community. Such traditions have little historical value. The form critics assumed further that the early Christians were not at all interested in history. Thus the Gospels are not biographies, giving us a consistent historical picture of the life of Jesus, but reflections of the faith and life of the early Church. In fact, history was of so little concern to the early Christian community that they made no great distinction between the earthly history of Jesus and his post-resurrectional history and presence with the Church, to whom he still spoke by the Spirit. Without the strictures of history and with its assurance of Jesus' presence the early Church could freely adapt and even creatively add to the tradition, if the needs of the Church for preaching, apologetics, worship, etc., so required.

Such are the most important conclusions of form criticism's investigation of the Gospels. (For a more extensive treatment and evaluation, the reader is referred to Neill, *op. cit.*, 236–91; Guthrie, *NTI* 3, 178–94; and Taylor, V., *ExpT* 75 [1963–64] 356–58.)

46 **(II) Criticism and Theology: The Work of Rudolf Bultmann.** Certainly Bultmann (b. 1884) is the most influential figure in 20th-cent. NT study, combining immense erudition and scholarship with a profoundly pastoral desire to preach a meaningful and relevant message to his contemporaries in a world where faith is no longer easy. One despairs of attempting to give even an inadequate summary of Bultmann's thought. The University of Marburg, the scene of Bultmann's teaching career, has become a latter-day Tübingen in the influence it has exerted on 20th-cent. Protestant theology. In terms of mere bulk, Bultmann's work extends over a period of almost 50 years and has provoked a library of literature pro and con. The contemporary vitality of his thought is shown in the fact that his followers still dominate the German theological scene. (Cf. *ExpT* 76 [1964–65] 300–306.)

There are a number of dominant influences distinguishable in Bultmann's thought. From Strauss, Bultmann has taken the concept of myth as the key to the interpretation of the NT. He has accepted Wrede's view of the nonmessianic character of Christ's life and the creative genius of the early Christian community. The History of Religions school has contributed its syncretistic view of Christian origins and the assumption of the pervading influence of Gnosticism in the NT world. Form criticism has been one cause of his lack of interest in the historical Jesus. But beneath these diverse elements and bringing them into a basic unity, one can find at the heart of Bultmann's thought and permeating all his work two major influences: a thoroughgoing Lutheranism and the existentialism of M. Heidegger (b. 1889).

47 Lutheranism is a constant in the background and orientation of Bultmann's thought. It can easily be discerned in his strong evangelical emphasis on the preached Word. But Bultmann's Lutheranism goes deeper than this; in fact, Bultmann has understood his own theological enterprise as a logical conclusion of the Reformation doctrine of justification by faith alone. Herein lies the theological reason for Bultmann's lack of interest in the historical Jesus, for to seek a historical basis for faith would be a betrayal of the principle of *sola fide*. So Bultmann's distrust of the search for an objective basis for faith thus underlies his deep skepticism concerning the historicity of the Gospel accounts and his consequent dehistoricizing of the kerygma. In his view, the only history that we find in the kerygma is the *Dass*, the bare fact of the existence and death by crucifixion of the man Jesus of Nazareth. The Word that addresses man in the kerygma is therefore the ground, as well as the object, of faith. Bultmann's definition of faith in terms of personal choice and decision, as an act of the will rather than of the intellect, is as much the legacy of Luther as of Heidegger. Bultmann's attenuated concept of the Church as little more than the arena in which the Word is preached and heard has its roots in Luther's individualism.

48 Heidegger and Bultmann were colleagues at Marburg from 1923 to 1928, and Bultmann readily admits the influence that Heidegger's thought, particularly as formulated in *Being and Time* (Ger 1927; Eng 1962), had on his theology. An analysis of the impact of Heidegger's existentialism on Bultmann is beyond the scope of this discussion. A good treatment of this subject recommended by Bultmann himself is J. Macquarrie, *An Existentialist Theology; A Comparison of Heidegger and Bultmann* (1955). One example, for the sake of illustration, is Bultmann's interpretation of Pauline theology by Heidegger's concept of the transition from inauthentic to authentic existence. Both Heidegger and Bultmann distinguish inauthentic existence, man's life in bondage to the illusory security of a dying world, and authentic existence, which for Heidegger is achieved by personal decision. For Bultmann, authentic existence is a gift of God achieved by abandoning adherence to this world and opening oneself to the word of forgiving grace announced in the kerygma. We might conclude by noting that among Bultmann's disciples Heidegger's philosophy is still a live issue. (For a discussion of this cf. J. M. Robinson and J. Cobb, eds., *The Later Heidegger and Theology*, NFT 1 [1963]; → Hermeneutics, 71:50.)

49 **(A) Bultmann the Form Critic.** Working from the conclusions of Schmidt and Dibelius, Bultmann applied the form-critical method to the Syn in *The History of the Synoptic Tradition* (Ger 1921; Eng 1963). Against the more conservative approach of Dibelius, Bultmann's form-critical investigations are not simply a means of literary classification, but must lead to judgments on the historicity of the stories and the genuineness of the sayings found in the tradition. His skepticism as regards historical reliability is evident in that he assigns most of the material in the tradition to the creative imagination of the early Christian communities. What genuine material there is, he finds chiefly in the sayings of Jesus. But this genuineness does not extend to the contexts of these sayings in the Gospels, the *Sitz im Evangelium*, which is the creation of the later tradition, especially of the Evangelists themselves.

50 **(B) Bultmann the Theologian.** Bultmann's most noteworthy theological contribution has been in the area of hermeneutics. Although many would disagree violently with his proposed solutions, all admit that Bultmann has come to grips with a real problem, namely the difficulty of communicating the Christian message in the 20th cent. As a theologian, Bultmann's major concern is that the NT message should challenge modern man rather than prevent him from making an existential decision by its mythological language. (For Bultmann's *TNT* cf. *ExpT* 66 [1954–55] 15–19.)

51 (a) Demythologizing the NT. Bultmann's manifesto, "The New Testament and Mythology," first appeared in 1941. Since then, this programmatic essay has been the storm center for a continuing debate, often accompanied by misunderstanding. Two initial observations are in order here. First, by myth, Bultmann does not mean an imaginary story or some sort of fairy tale but the use of imagery to express the otherwordly in terms of this world. Second, one should recognize the profoundly pastoral intent of Bultmann's call for demythologizing, i.e., for interpreting the NT in existentialist terms. For Bultmann, demythologizing is not a reduction of the NT but the only way to make its saving message available to modern man.

Bultmann holds that interpretation is necessary because modern man finds the obsolete mythological world view of the NT incredible. Therefore, if man is to be challenged to decision by the kerygma, the NT must be demythologized; the mythological framework of the NT must be interpreted, to expose the understanding of human life contained in it. Bultmann finds in the existentialism of Heidegger a tool suited for such interpretation of the NT.

Further, for Bultmann such interpretation is valid, not only because the very nature of myth demands it, but because we can see this process starting in the NT itself, especially in Paul and Jn. One example of such NT demythologizing is Jn's "realized eschatology," i.e., his emphasis on eternal life here and now, not in some distant future.

Finally, the pastoral aspect of demythologizing becomes clear when one realizes that the elimination of the unnecessary stumbling block of mythology helps Bultmann to expose the real stumbling block, the offense of the Gospel which proclaims that the eschatological act of God "for us and for our salvation" took place in the life and death of Jesus Christ.

Perceptive reaction in disagreement with Bultmann (as distinct from fundamentalist reaction) has not been directed against the basic need to reinterpret, to decode, to "demythologize" some of the mythical imagery of the NT (→ Hermeneutics, 71:49), but against Bultmann's judgment on what constitutes unacceptable imagery or myth. For instance, resurrection from the dead and the miraculous, which for Bultmann are no longer meaningful for modern man, remain very meaningful in the judgment of other scholars.

(An Eng trans. of "Neues Testament und Mythologie" is available in Bartsch, H.-W., ed., *Kerygma and Myth* [rev. ed.; N.Y., 1961] 1–44. See also Fuller, R., *The New Testament in Current Study*, 9–19.)

52 (b) Bultmann on John. Bultmann has been writing on Jn since 1923; his masterpiece is his commentary in the Meyer Kommentar series, *Das Evangelium des Johannes* (1941). Containing the most penetrating critical exegesis of Jn that has yet appeared, this commentary confirms Bultmann as one of the most influential exegetes in the history of biblical studies, even though many disagree with his conclusions.

According to Bultmann, the first step in the formation of Jn is the work of the *evangelist*, quite possibly a Gnostic converted to the Christian faith. He drew his Gospel material from three principal sources independent of one another: (1) a Signs-Source (*Semeia-Quelle*), a collection of miracles, symbolic rather than historical, attributed to Jesus; (2) Revelatory Discourses (*Offenbarungsreden*) a collection of poetic discourses of an Oriental Gnostic origin; and (3) a Passion-Resurrection source, parallel to but independent of the Syn tradition.

After the death of the evangelist comes the work of the *redactor*, or editor, whose work consisted chiefly of organization and harmonization. The organization was necessary because the redactor found the evangelist's work in terrible disorder. He did his best to arrange the material in sequence, but did not totally succeed. Bultmann sees his own attempt to reconstruct the original order of Jn as a continuation of the work of the redactor.

Since the redactor knew the Syn tradition, he attempted to harmonize the evangelist's work with this tradition. More important, he had to harmonize the evangelist's work with standard Church teaching, to make it acceptable to the orthodox Church; he did this by adding, e.g., sacramental references to the antisacramental work of the evangelist, and traditional eschatology to balance and correct the demythologized eschatology of the Gospel. This theological harmonization was necessary because of the Gnostic bent of the evangelist. Bultmann considers the evangelist a convert from Gnosticism who used demythologized Gnostic concepts to interpret the meaning of Christ for his contemporaries. The Gnostic redeemer myth is demythologized by being attached to the historical person, Jesus of Nazareth; Gnostic dualism is demythologized by being transformed from a metaphysical to an ethical dualism.

Bultmann heavily stresses Jesus as the Revealer whose revelation is not the communication of Gnostic secrets about the upper world, but simply the person of Jesus himself. Thus the whole point in Jn is not the salvific action by Jesus but his words: he is truth, he is light, and he has to be accepted. All who *know* him are saved. There is no longer need of salvation history, for Jesus always supplies men here and now with the opportunity for decision.

(Brown, R. E., *The Gospel According to John* [N.Y., 1966] xxix–xxxiii [sources of Jn], lii–lvi [Gnosticism]. Smith, D. M., *The Composition and Order of the Fourth Gospel* [New Haven, 1965], a lucid analysis of Bultmann's approach to Jn. For a resumé of the theology of Jn according to Bultmann, cf. the treatment in his *TNT* 2 [N.Y., 1955] 3–92.)

53 **(III) Reactions to Bultmann.** One measure of Bultmann's influence on NT studies is the extent of the reactions—both favorable and hostile—caused by his work. These reactions stretch across the whole spectrum of Christian thought, from a fundamentalist conservatism that would reject his work totally to the Protestant liberalism represented by F. Buri, who accuses Bultmann of not going far enough in his demythologizing program because he retains the reality of God's act in Christ. In Europe, Catholics like L. Malevez and G. Hasenhüttl have become leading authorities on Bultmann's theology.

54 The Scandinavian traditio-historical school in particular supplies some important correctives to the negativism of Bultmann's form criticism. The traditio-historical approach is well known in OT studies through the work of scholars like S. Mowinckel (→ Modern OT Criticism, 70:45–46); and the Uppsala school of interpretation has begun to apply it to the NT, as in the important study of B. Gerhardsson (b. 1926), *Memory and Manuscript: Oral Tradition and Written Transmission in Rabbinic Judaism and Early Christianity* (1961). Gerhardsson contends that the Gospel narratives are the result not of a creative but of a preservative process, through an institution in the early Church for the delivery of the Gospel tradition, similar to a contemporary rabbinic institution for the controlled transmission of the written and oral torah. Gerhardsson's work is a welcome alternative to the negative judgment on historicity characteristic of much form-critical study (J. A. Fitzmyer, *TS* 23 [1962] 442–57).

The reactions that have stirred up the greatest interest, however, are the debate being carried on in Germany among Bultmann's former students, and the alternatives to Bultmann's radicalism proposed by more conservative German and British theologians.

55 **(A) Reaction of Conservative German Scholarship.** Bultmann's theology has not been without its opponents in Germany, who object to his excessive skepticism and find the hermeneutical key to the NT not in Heideggerian existentialism but in the Bible itself.

56 (a) K. Barth. A systematic theologian rather than a NT scholar, Barth (b. 1886) was an early ally of Bultmann. World War I made him see the inadequacy of liberal theology, and he expressed his disenchantment in his memorable and powerful commentary, *The Epistle to the Romans* (Ger 1918; Eng 1933), which focused on the theological significance of Rom, in its emphasis on the Bible as the Word of God. Scientific historico-critical study was at best only a preliminary to the real task of theological, "pneumatic" exegesis. Whereas Bultmann's studies concerned the human side of the God-man relationship (how man can receive revelation), Barth emphasized the divine side (God as the source of revelation). Bultmann was an early defender of Barth with whom he agreed in principle, if not in methodology. However, Bultmann's demythologizing and existential hermeneutic has not met with agreement from Barth. (For a bibliography of and on Barth cf. his *Faith of the Church* [N.Y., 1958].)

57 (b) O. Cullmann. Cullmann (b. 1902) of the University of Basel is the foremost proponent of salvation history (*Heilsgeschichte*) as the key for understanding the NT. He has proposed this alternative to the Bultmann school in two important books, *Christ and Time* (Ger 1946; Eng 1951, rev. 1962; cf. *ExpT* 65 [1953–54] 369–72) and *Salvation in History* (Ger 1965; Eng 1967). The *heilsgeschichtlich* approach views history as a series of redemptive epochs, with the Christ-event as the midpoint of a time line that includes a previous period of preparation, the present stage of the Church, and the eschatological future. All of biblical history is marked by the permanent tension of promise and fulfillment, the "already" and the "not yet." Against the Bultmannians, Cullmann holds that *Heilsgeschichte* is not a Lucan distortion but is rooted in the teaching of Jesus. Salvation history is thus a characteristic of the whole NT, from Jesus himself to Jn. Cullmann defends the appropriateness of *Heilsgeschichte* as an exegetical tool for arriving at the original meaning of the NT by pointing out that Jesus and the early Church were nurtured on the OT and the view of history it contained.

Mention should also be made of Cullmann's important contribution to biblical theology, *The Christology of the New Testament* (Ger 1957; Eng 1959). In this work Cullmann attempts to define the Christology of the early Church as expressed in the NT, without the developed interpretations of subsequent theology. He examines ten titles applied to Jesus in the NT, referring to Jesus' earthly work, his future eschatological work, his contemporary work in the Church, and his pre-existence. Cullmann emphasizes exclusively the functional aspect of Christology and avoids the static categories of Greco-Roman theology, with its developed notions of person and nature, as beyond the limits of exegesis.

To give an illustration of his method, we can look at the title of Lord (*Kyrios*), which Cullmann discusses under the heading of Christ's contemporary work in the Church. He admits to Bousset's contention that the Church's experience in worship of the presence of Jesus the Lord gave prominence to this title, but against Bousset Cullmann shows that this most advanced Christological title has its roots in Palestinian Christianity and is not the result of the Church's encounter with the Hellenistic mystery cults. (→ Aspects NT Thought, 78:5–7; on Cullmann cf. *ExpT* 77 [1965–66] 4–8.)

58 (c) W. Pannenberg. The most promising challenge to Bultmann's school has come from the contemporary school of Pannenberg (b. 1928), a young theologian from the University of Munich. In *Offenbarung als Geschichte* (*Revelation as History;* 1961) and *Grundzüge der Christologie* (*Principal Features of Christology;* 1964) Pannenberg proposes an alternative to the lack of interest in history characteristic of Barth's theology of the Word and to Bultmann's relocation of revelation in the kerygma rather than in history. According to Pannenberg, God's self-revelation comes to men not immediately (as Barth and Bultmann hold) nor through a special redemptive history (as Cullmann proposes), but mediately and indirectly, mirrored in the events of history. Since history becomes the locus of revelation, revelation is verifiable by the methods of historical scholarship. And if revelatory history is knowable by reason, then faith does not produce, but rather presupposes rational knowledge. Faith does not give us the inner meaning of events of past history, but is trust oriented to the future, to the final end of universal history anticipated in the Christ-event.

(Braaten, C. E., "The Current Controversy on Revelation: Pannenberg and His Critics," *JRel* 45 [1965] 225–37; *History and Hermeneutics* [New Directions in Theology Today 2; Phila., 1966]. Fuller, D., *Easter Faith and History*, 177–87; "A New German Theological Movement," *ScotJT* 19 [1966] 160–75. Robinson, J. M. and J. Cobb, eds., *Theology as History* [NFT 3; N.Y., 1967].)

59 **(B) Reaction of British Scholarship.** Traditionally more conservative than the Germans in theology and exegesis, British scholarship rejected in the main Bultmann's radical skepticism and his existential hermeneutic. Form criticism, however, received a more sympathetic hearing, and British NT scholars were not slow to put the insights of form criticism to good use.

60 (a) E. Hoskyns. The man most responsible for bringing German criticism and theology to a British audience was Sir Edwyn Hoskyns (1884–1937). It was he who translated Barth's commentary on Rom into English. In *The Riddle of the New Testament* (1931) Hoskyns attacked the liberal notion that criticism could arrive at a nontheological picture of Jesus in the earliest tradition. As did the form critics, Hoskyns realized that the crucial problem in the NT, the "riddle," was the relationship between Jesus of Nazareth and the primitive Christian Church. But he had more confidence than they in the ability of scientific criticism to reach the historical Jesus behind the Gospels. His greatest work, however, was his commentary on Jn, edited and published posthumously by F. N. Davey, *The Fourth Gospel* (1940), a commentary in the best British tradition of sound critical study and profoundly theological interpretation.

61 (b) V. Taylor. Another scholar no less aware than Hoskyns of the importance of Continental theology, especially of the influence of Bultmann, is Vincent Taylor (b. 1887). Soon after the appearance of Hoskyn's *Riddle*, Taylor published *The Formation of the Gospel Tradition* (1933), his magistral estimate of the values and excesses of form criticism. Still an excellent introduction to the subject, it is an eminently fair treatment, critical of the extremely negative conclusions but willing to accept the positive contributions of form criticism. Taylor saw that form criticism, far from leading inevitably to skepticism, could supply valuable confirmation of the basic historicity of the Gospel tradition. Fully recognizing the theological nature of the Gospels, Taylor is a vigorous defender of the historical trustworthiness of the Gospels as sources for the authentic words and deeds of Jesus.

This confidence is evident in his trilogy on NT Christology, *The Names of Jesus* (1953), *The Life and Ministry of Jesus* (1954), and *The Person of Christ in New Testament Teaching* (1958). Although Taylor, like Bultmann, sees the importance of the preached Christ, the exalted Lord of Christian faith, he also recognizes the indispensability of the historical Jesus for Christology.

Taylor's most famous work is certainly his commentary, *The Gospel According to St. Mark* (1952), wherein he employs all the tools of biblical science to offer an alternative to Wrede's still current skepticism regarding the historicity of Mk. Revised in 1966, this commentary is a standard work in Syn studies. (Cf. *ExpT* 75 [1963–64] 164–68.)

62 (c) R. H. Lightfoot. Much more sympathetic to German exegesis than his British confreres in NT studies, Lightfoot (1883–1953) was the champion of form criticism in England. The title of a study published in 1935, *History and Interpretation in the Gospels*, indicates the approach he took, viewing the Gospels as theological interpretation rather than as a biography of Jesus of Nazareth. Lightfoot's approach in *The Gospel Message of St. Mark* (1950) was a significant exception to the traditional British acceptance of the historicity of Mk. Finally, he was the author of a moving and beautiful commentary on Jn, *St. John's Gospel*, published posthumously in 1956.

63 (d) C. H. Dodd. The contemporary concern for relevance in communicating the NT message has not been the exclusive preserve of the Bultmann school. As early as the 1930's Dodd (b. 1884) called for an end to the critical atomization of the NT, necessary as such study might have been, and he himself took the first steps toward a synthesis. Although not a member of the form-critical school, Dodd made an invaluable contribution to our knowledge of the Gospel behind the Gospels in *The Apostolic Preaching and Its Developments* (1936), an investigation of the Church's earliest preaching, especially in Acts and Paul. In this primitive apostolic kerygma Dodd found the underlying unity of the NT, and in this he has been followed by many Catholic exegetes.

No less influential was his book, *The Parables of the Kingdom* (1935), an attempt, often successful, to get behind the parables as we find them in the Gospels (the *Sitz im Evangelium*) to the parables as originally spoken by Jesus (the *Sitz im Leben Jesu*). Jeremias, in his study of the parables, freely admitted his debt to Dodd's work. Dodd also formulated in this book his widely discussed theory of "realized eschatology," the fact that the kingdom preached by Jesus in the parables was a present rather than a future reality (→ Aspects NT Thought, 78:69).

Students of Jn have reason to be grateful to Dodd, who has given to Johannine studies two brilliant books. The first of these, *The Interpretation of the Fourth Gospel* (1953), is not a commentary but a study of the background, the leading concepts, and the structure of Jn. One criticism of the book is that Dodd overemphasizes Hellenism as the thought-world that produced Jn, a position that needs serious modification in view of the Qumran discoveries. Ten years later Dodd published *Historical Tradition in the*

Fourth Gospel (1963), a study of the relationship between Jn and the Syn and a defense of the historical reliability of Jn, which Dodd showed to be based on a historical tradition parallel to but independent of the Syn tradition, and deserving of at least as much historical respect. In all his work Dodd shows a high degree of the historical and theological competence that has become a trademark of the best British NT scholarship. (Cf. *ExpT* 75 [1963–64] 100–102.)

64 **(C) Reaction from Bultmann's School: The Post-Bultmannians.** The best-known reaction to Bultmannian orthodoxy is certainly that which has arisen among his own disciples. Despite the individualism of these former students of Bultmann, this reaction is sufficiently well-defined to have introduced a new, post-Bultmannian phase in German exegesis. Two areas in which the post-Bultmannians have built upon Bultmann's work, only to re-examine critically some of his fundamental theses, are the whole question of the historical Jesus and the significance and relevance of Heidegger's later philosophy for exegesis and theology. Because of the complexity of this second question, we shall confine our discussion to the new quest of the historical Jesus and, for the Heideggerian question, refer the reader to the article of Brown and the two vols. of the NFT series cited in the bibliography at the end of this section.

For Bultmann, the kerygmatic nature of the Gospel precludes any attempt to reach the historical Jesus through the early Church's confession of faith in Christ the Risen Lord. According to Bultmann, the early Church had no biographical interest in the historical Jesus of Nazareth but focused its gaze exclusively on the Christ of faith proclaimed in the kerygma. The historical Jesus was therefore irrelevant to Christian faith.

But for all his theoretical skepticism regarding a historical quest that would go behind the kerygma, in *The History of the Synoptic Tradition* and in *Jesus and the Word* (Ger 1926; Eng 1934) Bultmann goes to great lengths to verify the words and deeds of Jesus. It is this direction in Bultmann's own work that the post-Bultmannians claim to be furthering in their new quest of the historical Jesus. M. Kähler (1835–1912) was an early forerunner of this new quest in *The So-Called Historical Jesus and the Historic Biblical Christ* (Ger 1892; Eng 1964), a book that was reissued in 1956, during the initial stages of the post-Bultmannian reaction.

65 (a) E. Käsemann. The new quest was formally launched in 1953 by Käsemann (b. 1906) of Tübingen, in an article entitled "The Problem of the Historical Jesus." Käsemann makes three important points in this article. First, if there is no connection between the glorified Lord of Christian faith and the earthly, historical Jesus, then Christianity becomes a nonhistorical myth. Käsemann strikes here at the danger inherent in Bultmann's dehistoricizing of the kerygma—the danger of a docetic, nonhistorical kerygma. Second, if the early Church was so disinterested in the history of Jesus, why were the four Gospels ever written? The Evangelists surely believed that the Christ they preached was none other than the earthly, historical Jesus. Third, although the Gospels are products of Easter faith and it is therefore difficult to get to the historical Jesus, our faith requires confidence in the identity of the earthly Jesus and the exalted Lord of the kerygma.

Besides this theoretical defense of the necessity of the new quest, Käsemann gives us as well the methodical principles by which the new quest may be carried on. To establish any saying or deed of Jesus as authentic we must eliminate all Gospel material that has a kerygmatic tone. These sayings are not necessarily inauthentic, but since they resemble the Church's proclamation they cannot be proved to be authentic utterances of Jesus. Their *Sitz im Leben* could be a post-Easter situation or faith. Second, we must exclude anything that can be paralleled in contemporary Judaism, e.g., in rabbinic tradition or contemporary Jewish apocalyptic, as not demonstrably authentic. A third confirmatory principle is that an authentic saying of Jesus should reflect Aram features. Käsemann has since modified his position somewhat in that he has replaced Bultmann's Gnosticism with Jewish apocalyptic as the background of primitive Christian theology. After rigorous application of these criteria, Käsemann finds in Jesus' teaching elements that unquestionably stem from Jesus himself. (Käsemann's seminal essay on the historical Jesus and other articles are available in Eng trans. in E. Käsemann, *Essays on New Testament Themes* [SBT 41; London, 1964].) (→ Canonicity, 67:94–96.)

66 (b) E. Fuchs. In 1956 another of the post-Bultmannians, Fuchs (b. 1903) of Marburg published in the *ZThK*, the journal that has become the organ of the post-Bultmannians, an article entitled "The Quest of the Historical Jesus," in which he advanced his canons for the new quest. Fuchs seeks in the behavior or conduct (*Verhalten*) of Jesus something that is historical and relevant for faith. Especially in his gracious table-fellowship with the outcast, his eating and drinking with sinners, Jesus effectively and authoritatively lived out what he preached in the parables: the present redeeming activity of the near God. This declaration of God's love for sinners was authoritative because in receiving sinners Jesus put himself in God's place, identifying his will with God's. Thus in Jesus' conduct we find the key to his self-understanding of who and what he was: God's eschatological representative among men. Fuchs's confidence in the historicity of the Gospel reports of Jesus' activity is grounded in the belief that the Church would be less likely to change the deeds than the words of Jesus. (For an Eng trans. of Fuchs's article cf. E. Fuchs, *Studies of the Historical Jesus* [SBT 42; London, 1964].) (→ Hermeneutics, 71:50.)

67 (c) G. Bornkamm. Thirty years after Bultmann's *Jesus and the Word*, Bornkamm (b. 1905) of Heidelberg published *Jesus of Nazareth* (Ger 1956; Eng 1960), the first post-Bultmannian study of the historical Jesus. Like Käsemann and Fuchs, Bornkamm regards the unmatched authority of Jesus as historically valid and relevant for Christian faith. Käsemann found this authority manifested in the teaching of Jesus; Fuchs, in his conduct. Bornkamm claims that the strongest impression the Gospels make on one is the immediate, unparalleled authority of Jesus, an authority that is absolute and present in both the words and the deeds of Jesus. This authority has its source in the historical Jesus and is not a product of faith. Although faith acknowledged and proclaimed it, faith was not strong enough to create it.

Besides this experience of authority, we can establish the following facts about the historical Jesus. Jesus was a Jew, the son of Joseph the carpenter, from Nazareth in Galilee. He preached in towns along the Lake of Galilee, healing and doing good works, and struggling with opposition from the Pharisees. Ultimately he was crucified in Jerusalem. More important, however, than these bare historical facts concerning the ministry of Jesus was their existential significance—the fact that in the ministry, the crucial, eschatological hour was present, calling men to decision. A historical encounter with Jesus was therefore an eschatological encounter with God. (Cf. *ExpT* 76 [1964–65] 379–83.)

68 (d) H. Conzelmann. Of all the post-Bultmannians Conzelmann (b. 1915) of Göttingen has probably remained the most sympathetic to Bultmann's reaction to the new quest (cf. the article by Bultmann cited in the bibliography at the end of this section). Conzelmann is the author of the long article, "Jesus Christus," in the 3rd ed. (1959) of *RGG* (3, 619–53), which, like Bornkamm's book, is a rather positive synthesis of what he claims we can know of the historical Jesus. For Conzelmann, Jesus is man's confrontation with God; in his ministry Jesus' proclamation of the coming Reign of God already engages men. His word is the definitive Word of God; his deeds make the Kingdom of God present.

For English readers, Conzelmann's *The Theology of Saint Luke* (Ger 1953; Eng 1960) gives an insight into the *Redaktionsgeschichte* practiced by the post-Bultmannians. Conzelmann argues that Luke had a very definite theological point of view, in the light of which he rewrote the history of Jesus and added a supplementary volume dealing with the history of the early Church. According to Conzelmann, the early Christians thought that the coming of Jesus meant absolutely the end of history and that therefore the period between the resurrection-ascension and the parousia would be very brief. With the delay of the parousia, the early Church had to rethink its whole theology. In this task of rethinking, Conzelmann contends, Luke deliberately and radically modified the eschatological perspective of Jesus and the more primitive sources (e.g., Mk) by introducing the perspective of *Heilsgeschichte* into early Christian theology, with Christ's public ministry as an intermediate period between that of Israel and that of the Church. Conzelmann and the post-Bultmannians in general view Luke's concept as secondary and erroneous, in fact as a falsification and distortion of the original Gospel. It is here that Cullmann takes issue with the post-Bultmannians, in maintaining that Luke's view of history is primary and is rooted in the teaching of Jesus, whose eschatological outlook has been seriously overemphasized by Conzelmann.

69 (e) J. M. Robinson. An American representative of the post-Bultmannian school, Robinson (b. 1924) holds that there are two ways of access to the person of Jesus. Besides the kerygma, the existential historiography evolved by the German philosopher W. Dilthey (1833–1911), and by R. G. Collingwood (1889–1943) in his posthumously published *The Idea of History* (1946) offers us the possibility of an encounter with the historical Jesus, who renounced completely the support of this present evil world to live only for God. This existential philosophy of history makes the new quest not only possible but also legitimate. (Cf. J. M. Robinson, *A New Quest of the Historical Jesus* [SBT 25; London, 1959].)

70 (f) G. Ebeling. A Church historian and systematic theologian as well as a biblical scholar, Ebeling (b. 1912) of Tübingen is especially concerned with the problem of faith in its many ramifications: the relevance of the historical Jesus to faith and theology; the problem of the transition from the Jesus of history to faith in Jesus the exalted Lord; and Jesus' teaching about faith.

Ebeling distinguishes the following elements in the teaching of Jesus as historical: the nearness of the Reign of God as the core of his message; the identification of his will with God's, so that he appeals neither to Moses (like the rabbis) nor even to God (like the prophets) but uses the unprecedented words, "Amen *I* say to you"; obedience to the will of God that liberates men from legalism and casuistry; and a call to conversion and discipleship with joy. (Two of his important articles, "Jesus and Faith" and "The Question of the Historical Jesus and the Problem of Christology," are available in Eng in G. Ebeling, *Word and Faith* [London, 1963]. Also cf. *The Nature of Faith* [London, 1961]; *The Problem of Historicity* [Phila., 1967].)

(For Bultmann's reaction to the new quest, cf. Bultmann, R., "The Primitive Christian Kerygma and the Historical Jesus," *The Historical Jesus and the Kerygmatic Christ* [1964], C. E. Braaten and R. A. Harrisville, eds., 15–42. For the philosophical background of the post-Bultmannian school, cf. Robinson, J. M., and J. Cobb, eds., *The Later Heidegger and Theology* [NFT 1; N.Y., 1963] and *The New Hermeneutic* [NFT 2; N.Y., 1964]; also Robinson, J. M., "Basic Shifts in German Theology," *Interpr* 16 [1962] 76–97. For discussion with extensive bibliography, cf. Brown, R. E., "After Bultmann, What?—An Introduction to the Post-Bultmannians," *CBQ* 26 [1964] 1–30; Cahill, J., "Rudolf Bultmann and Post-Bultmann Tendencies," *CBQ* 26 [1964] 153–78; Jeremias, J., "The Present Position in the Controversy concerning the Problem of the Historical Jesus," *ExpT* 69 [1957–58] 333–39. This article was considerably expanded and reprinted by Fortress Press as a pamphlet entitled *The Problem of the Historical Jesus* [Phila., 1964; Harvey, V. A., *The Historian and the Believer* [N.Y., 1967] 164–203. Some new contributions are found in *Theology and Proclamation: Dialogue with Bultmann* [Phila., 1966].)

71 **(IV) Emergence of Catholic Critical Scholarship.** The first 40 years of the 20th cent., from the days of the Modernist crisis and of Lagrange and Loisy (→ 37, 38 above) to the writing of *Divino Afflante Spiritu* in 1943 (→ Church Pronouncements, 72:20) were dark days for Catholic biblical scholarship (→ Church Pronouncements, 72:5–6). Significant criticism of the NT re-emerged only after the papal encyclical. This renewed Catholic critical scholarship, although it has been looked upon as shocking by many within the Church and has only grudgingly received toleration (→ Church Pronouncements, 72:7–8), remains on the whole decidedly right of center, much more in line with the scholarship of Cullmann, Taylor, and Dodd, for instance, than with the Bultmannian or post-Bultmannian schools. (Interestingly enough, however, there are now some very appreciative Catholic writings on Bultmann.)

Over-all, modern Catholic NT scholarship has consisted in a judicious selecting and combining of acceptable elements in Protestant scholarship; it is not yet following its own new paths. It has succeeded in convincing more intelligent Catholics that the ultraconservative biblical positions of the past are no longer tenable; but now it faces the much more difficult task of discussing with scientific objectivity and in detail the sensitive problems of NT exegesis that have vital dogmatic implications, e.g., the limitations of Jesus' knowledge regarding himself, the future, and the Church; the reliability of Acts as a guide to how the Church historically emerged; the extent of creativity exercised in the formation of the Gospel tradition; the historicity of the infancy narratives. One can be certain that such discussion, no matter what results are reached, will provoke heated opposition; for some contend that scientific discussion should not be allowed, since inevitably it will filter into the popular press and disturb the faithful. Nevertheless, the freedom and objectivity of this discussion and the sense of responsibility with which it is conducted will be the real test of the maturity of modern Catholic biblical scholarship in a post-Vatican II Church.

We shall give the briefest survey of some of the more important names in Catholic NT scholarship.

72 **(A) French Scholarship.** That the French writers have been the most productive of all Catholic NT scholars is due to the heritage of Père Lagrange, the Jerusalem École Biblique, and the *RB* (→ Modern OT Criticism, 70:35). In NT the mantle of Lagrange has fallen on P. Benoit and M.-E. Boismard. Benoit, probably the best-known Catholic NT scholar of our time, published a cautious but favorable assessment of form criticism in *RB* 53 (1946) 489–512. He is well known for articles on the *sensus plenior* (→ Hermeneutics, 71:56), inspiration (→ Inspiration, 66:50), the Passion Accounts, the Eucharist, the resurrection and ascension, and the concept of body in Paul; many of these are gathered in *Exégèse et théologie* (3 vols.; Paris, 1961, 1968). Boismard has worked extensively in the Johannine field, e.g., *St. John's Prologue* (London, 1957), *Du baptême à Cana* (Paris, 1956), and *L'Apocalypse* in BJ. (For his important textual contributions → Texts, 69:139,149). The French Jesuits J. Daniélou and H. de Lubac have made important contributions to the history of the spiritual sense of Scripture (→ Hermeneutics, 71:47); and at Rome, S. Lyonnet has written extensively in the Pauline field, especially on Rom. The French Sulpicians have produced a number of notable biblical scholars (A. Robert, A. Gelin, H. Cazelles; → Modern OT Criticism, 70:62); and in NT, A. Feuillet is outstanding for his studies on the parousia (*VDBS* 6, 1331–1419), for *Johannine Studies* (N.Y., 1965), and *The Apocalypse* (N.Y., 1964). C. Spicq, O.P., has done notable commentaries on Heb and the Pastorals in EBib, and a four-vol. investigation of *agapē* in the NT (Paris, 1955–59), which is being translated into English in an abridged form (St. Louis, 1963, 1965, 1966).

73 **(B) Belgian Scholarship.** While most of Catholic scholarship was still under the shadow of fear cast by the stern repression of Modernism, the University of Louvain preserved its proud tradition in the publications of Msgr. L. Cerfaux. His three volumes of collected essays (*Recueil L. Cerfaux* [Louvain, 1954–62]) show a broad range of interest and competency, but he is best known for his trilogy on Pauline theology: *The Church in the Theology of St. Paul* (Fr 1947; Eng 1959), *Christ in the Theology of St. Paul* (Fr 1951; Eng 1959); and *Le Chrétien dans la théologie paulinienne* (1962). His students have carried on the Louvain tradition; perhaps the best known work is *Les Justes et la Justice* (Louvain, 1950) of A. Descamps, now a bishop and the rector of the university. A Belgian Jesuit at the Biblical Institute in Rome, I. de la Potterie, has written extensively on John (cf. his collected essays in *La vie selon l'Esprit* [Paris, 1965]), as has also the Belgian Dominican F.-M. Braun, famous for his many-volumed *Jean le théologien* (Paris, 1959, 1964, 1966). J. Dupont of the Benedictine abbey of St. André at Bruges has contributed to the study of the Beatitudes (*Les béatitudes* [Louvain, 1954]) and of Acts (*The Sources of Acts* [N.Y., 1964; Fr 1960]; *Le discours de Milet* [Paris, 1962]; *Études sur les Actes des Apotres* [Paris, 1967]).

74 **(C) German Scholarship.** The *Regensburger Neues Testament* is, in general, perhaps the best Catholic NT commentary series. It does not have the detailed criticism of EBib, but some of the volumes are more modern and more perceptive. The three volumes on the Syn by J. Schmid are superb. Msgr. A. Wikenhauser contributed important commentaries in this series on Jn and Acts, but is better known for his *New Testament Introduction*, which remains the best Catholic introduction available today. *Facile princeps* in German Catholic biblical circles is R. Schnackenburg, the author of a series of important works: *The Church in the New Testament* (Ger 1961; Eng 1965); *God's Rule and Kingdom* (Ger 1959; Eng 1963); *Baptism in the Thought of St. Paul* (Ger 1950; Eng 1964); *The Moral Teaching of the New Testament* (Ger 2nd ed. 1962; Eng 1965). In 1965 he brought out the first volume of a three-vol. commentary on Jn, *Herders theologischer Kommentar*, a series in which he had already done an important work on the Johannine Epistles; these works also appear in English. More critical in tone than the French Catholic scholars, the Germans are gradually assuming leadership in the Catholic biblical movement.

75 **(D) American Scholarship.** In America, the work has largely been a question of articles and particular studies, often relaying French or German Catholic trends into English. Only very recently have full-scale Catholic NT commentaries begun to appear in English. Although many names might be mentioned (most of them appearing in this volume), the Canadian Jesuit D. Stanley deserves particular commendation for the essays written in the 1950's (collected in *The Apostolic Church in the New Testament* [Westminster, Md., 1965]). These essays introduced the new Catholic trends to English-speaking readers at a time when no one else was writing in such a critical vein in American Catholic circles. Stanley bore the brunt of fundamentalist reaction to new ideas (a reaction which was particularly severe in America in the period 1959–62). Along with him, E. Siegman fought bravely in the struggle to introduce modern NT criticism; as editor of *CBQ* from 1951 to 1958 he put the magazine on a scientific level and published some excellent articles. The subsequent development of the movement in the 1960's in America has been promising.

Other national groups and other scholars might be mentioned, but we shall leave the pleasant task of recording their praises to the specialized bibliographies in this volume. For Protestant American scholarship see R. M. Grant, "American New Testament Study," *JBL* 87 (1968) 42–50.

42

THE GOSPEL ACCORDING TO MARK

Edward J. Mally, S.J.

BIBLIOGRAPHY

1 Burkill, T. A., *Mysterious Revelation* (Ithaca, 1963). Colon, J.-B., "Marc (Évangile selon S.)," *VDBS* 5 (1957) 835–62. Cranfield, C. E. B., *The Gospel According to St. Mark* (CGTC; Cambridge, 1959). Gnilka, J., *Die Verstockung Israels* (Munich, 1961). Gould, E. P., *The Gospel According to St. Mark* (ICC; N.Y., 1907). Grundmann, W., *Das Evangelium nach Markus* (ThHkNT 2; 2nd ed.; Berlin, 1959). Haenchen, E., *Der Weg Jesu* (Berlin, 1966). Huby, J., *L'Évangile selon S. Marc* (BJ; 3rd ed.; Paris, 1961). Johnson, S. E., *A Commentary on the Gospel According to St. Mark* (BNTC; London, 1960). Jones, A., *The Gospel According to St. Mark* (London, 1963) Klostermann, E., *Das Markusevangelium* (HNT 3; 4th ed.; Tübingen, 1950). Lagrange, M.-J., *Évangile selon S. Marc* (EBib; 4th ed.; Paris, 1929). Lightfoot, R. H., *The Gospel Message of St. Mark* (London, 1950). Lohmeyer, E., *Das Evangelium nach Markus* (Meyer 1/2; 16th ed.; Göttingen, 1963). Marxsen, W., *Mark the Evangelist* (Phila., 1969; German ed., 1959). Moule, C. F. D., *The Gospel According to Mark* (CNEB; Cambridge, 1965). Nineham, D. E., *The Gospel of St. Mark* (PGC; Baltimore, 1963). Robinson, J. M., *The Problem of History in Mark* (SBT 21; London, 1957). Schmid, J., *The Gospel According to Mark* (Staten Island, N.Y., 1969). Schweizer, E., *Das Evangelium nach Markus* (NTD 1; Göttingen, 1967). Swete, H. B., *The Gospel According to St. Mark* (London, 1898). Taylor, V., *The Gospel According to St. Mark* (2nd ed.; London, 1966). Trocmé, E., *La formation de l'Évangile selon Marc* (Paris, 1963).

Wik, *NTI* 155–73; R-F, *INT* 191–220; Guthrie, *NTI*, 3, 49–83; F-B 60–72; *IPLCG*, 267–95.

INTRODUCTION

2 **(I) Authorship; Date and Place of Composition.** The tradition of the early Church is unanimous in ascribing the Second Gospel to Mark the disciple of Peter. The earliest statement is from Papias of Hierapolis who, writing in the early 2nd cent., quotes and comments upon a still earlier attestation: "This also the presbyter used to say: 'When Mark became Peter's interpreter, he wrote down accurately, although not in order, all that he remembered of what the Lord had said or done.' For he had not heard or followed the Lord, but later, as I said, [heard and followed] Peter, who used to adapt his teaching to the needs [of the moment], without making any sort of arrangement of the Lord's oracles. Consequently, Mark made no mistake in thus writing down certain things as he remembered them. For he was careful not to omit or falsify anything of what he had heard" (Eusebius, *HE* 3.39; *GCS* 9/1, 290–92). Later testimonies (e.g., the Anti-Marcionite Prologue to Mk; Irenaeus, *Adv. haer.* 3.1,1; Tertullian, *Adv. Marc.* 4.5; Clement of Alexandria, *Hypotyposeis* 6; Origen, *Comm. in Matt.;* Eusebius, *HE* 2.15,1–2; 3.24,5–8) may derive from Papias' statement, but the fact that this Gospel was universally accepted as the work of an otherwise unimportant person in the apostolic Church, may be taken as an index of the soundness of this tradition.

The Evangelist is usually identified with the John Mark of Acts 12:12,25 and the Mark of 1 Pt 5:13. The fact that he had a Jewish name (John) and a Hellenized Lat name (Mark) suggests that he was a Jew from the Gk-speaking world; in fact he belonged to the Hellenists of the Jerusalem community. He was a cousin of Barnabas (Col 4:10) and presumably the same "John who was also called Mark" (Acts 12:12,25; 15:37,39). Paul and Barnabas "had John with them as their assistant" on Mission I (Acts 13:5); but he subsequently left them and returned to Jerusalem (Acts 13:13). Later, at Antioch, Barnabas wished to take him on a missionary tour. But Paul disapproved, and the disagreement between him and Barnabas eventuated in the latter's taking Mark and sailing for Cyprus instead of accompanying Paul (Acts 15:37–39). Writing from house arrest in Rome, Paul mentioned Barnabas' cousin Mark as being with him (Col 4:10); similarly, a Mark is named in Phlm 24 as Paul's fellow prisoner. In 2 Tm 4:11 Paul instructs

Timothy in Ephesus to "get Mark and bring him with you." Finally, the author of 1 Pt sends greetings from Babylon (Rome) from himself "and Mark my son" (1 Pt 5:13). Although the identification is not altogether certain, there is no positive reason why all these texts should not refer to the same person; nothing in the Second Gospel indicates that its author was not a disciple of Peter or a familiar of Paul.

3 According to tradition, Mark wrote his Gospel after Peter's death (AD 64). Mk 13 contains a prediction of the destruction of the Temple; but whereas its parallels in Mt and Lk were written after that event (AD 70) and were to some extent altered to fit the known facts, Mk 13 appears to be a prediction before the event. Accordingly, Mk is commonly dated between AD 65 and 70.

Except for John Chrysostom who assigns the Gospel to Alexandria, tradition connects it with Rome or Italy. On internal evidence it is clear that Mk was written for non-Palestinian Christians of pagan origin: there is little concern to show the connection of the Christian gospel with the OT; conversely, Mark takes care to explain Jewish customs (7:3–4; 14:12; 15:42), to translate Aram words (3:17; 5:41; 7:11,34; 10:46; 14:36; 15:22,34), to give geographical details (1:5,9; 11:1), and to underscore the meaning of the gospel message for pagans (7:27; 8:1–9; 10:12; 11:17; 13:10). Moreover, the references to persecution (8:34–38; 10:38–39; 13:9–13) appear to corroborate the tradition of a Roman provenance (see Wik, *NTI* 166).

4 **(II) Literary Structure and Content.** Until quite recently most commentators endorsed Papias' notice that Mark wrote "accurately, although not in order." "All this amalgam of miracles and instructions is only a collection of remembrances . . . whose sequence is not governed by any rigorous historical or logical principle" (A. Loisy, *L'Évangile selon Marc* [Paris, 1912] 9). More recent commentators have proposed either a geographical or theological structure.

(A) Geographical Structure. C. H. Dodd (*ExpT* 43 [1931–32] 396–400) maintains that the combination of summary passages in 1:14–15,21–22,39; 2:13; 3:7b–9; 6:7,12–13,20, forms a geographical framework, not unlike that preserved in the primitive kerygma (cf. Acts 10:37–39), into which Mark has set the traditional pericopes. Thus V. Taylor (*Mark*, 107–11): The Galilean ministry (1:14–3:6); height of the Galilean ministry (3:7–6:13); ministry beyond Galilee (6:14–8:26); from Caesarea Philippi to Jerusalem (8:27–10:52); ministry in Jerusalem (11:1–13:37); the passion and resurrection (14:1–16:8). Against this view it may be objected that the events of section 6:14–8:26 do not all take place beyond Galilee; both miraculous feedings occur near the Lake of Galilee (6:34,45; 8:10), and Galilee or Galilean towns are mentioned in 7:31; 8:22; 9:30,33.

5 **(B) Theological Structure.** H. Riesenfeld (*SEA* 18–19 [1953–54] 140–60; cf. *IZBG* 3 [1954–55] 386) maintains that the pre-Marcan material was geographically ordered (Galilee, 1–9; journey to Jerusalem, 10; in Jerusalem, 11–13; Passion Narrative, 14–16), but that Mark superimposed a theological structure making 1:1–8:26 a proclamation of Jesus' messiahship in his activity, and 8:27–13:37 an instruction on true discipleship.

The structure proposed here (→ 7 below) confirms Mark's theological purpose, and is based on certain literary indices. After the prologue (1:1–13) Mk falls into two major sections, each having its own distinctive traits:

(a) The Mystery of the Messiah (1:14–8:33). *Structure:* This part is articulated by three summary statements (1:14–15; 3:7–12; 6:6b) each of which is followed by a pericope about the disciples (1:16–20; 3:13–19; 6:7–13,30) and ends with a notice showing how Jesus' true identity was misunderstood by the Pharisees (3:6), by his own relatives and townspeople (6:1–6a), even by his disciples (8:17–21,27–30). *Characteristics:* The emphasis is on the miracles of Jesus; the little teaching that is recorded is mainly directed to the crowds, expressed in parables, and concerned with the coming of God's reign. Jesus strives to conceal his messiahship (the "Messianic Secret," 1:33–34; 3:12; 5:43; 7:36; 8:26), although he rebukes his disciples for their inability to understand who he is (4:13,40; 6:52; 7:18; 8:17–21,33).

(b) The Mystery of the Son of Man (8:27–16:8). *Structure:* This part also falls into three lesser sections: 8:27–10:52; 11:1–13:37; 14:1–16:8. The first of these is articulated by three predictions of the passion (8:31; 9:30–31; 10:33–34) each of which is followed by a mention of the disciples' lack of understanding (8:32–33; 9:32–34; 10:35–37) and by an instruction (8:34–38; 9:35–37; 10:35–45). The second section (11:1–13:37) is concerned with Jesus' self-revelation in Jerusalem, and ends with Jesus passing judgment on Pharisaic Judaism. The Gospel ends with the narrative of Jesus' death and resurrection (14:1–16:8). *Characteristics:* In this section miraculous healings are rare and the emphasis falls more upon Jesus' teaching. This is now directed mostly to the disciples, presupposes their recognition of him as Messiah, and is largely concerned with the nature of his messiahship: His mission is not to be carried out by force or for political ends, but is to entail suffering both for himself (8:31; 9:39; 10:33–34,45) and for his followers (8:34–38; 10:21,35–44). This section, therefore, constitutes a gradual revelation of the Messiah as the suffering Son of Man (8:31; 9:9,12,31; 10:33; 14:21), and finds its culmination in Jesus' answer to the high priest's adjuration, "Are you the Messiah, the son of the Blessed One?" (14:61–62), and in the recognition by the Roman centurion that "truly this man was the Son of God" (15:39).

These two parts overlap in the incident at Caesarea Philippi (8:27–33) when Peter on behalf of the disciples asserts that Jesus is the Messiah, and Jesus undertakes to correct their mistaken notion of his messiahship by predicting for the first time that the Son of Man must suffer and be repudiated. This first glimpse of a recognition of his identity by human beings is the turning point of Mk, and occasions a change in Jesus' tactics: he continues to conceal his messiahship from outsiders who could easily misinterpret it, and concentrates instead on instructing his disciples in its true nature.

(See Delorme, J., "Points de vue nouveaux sur l'Évangile selon S. Marc," *AmiCl* 65 [1955] 193–203. Léon-Dufour, X., R-F, *INT* 199–206. Trocmé, E., *op. cit.*, 56–69. Simonsen, H., "Mk 8:17–10:52 i Markus-evangeliets Komposition," *DanTTs* 27 [1964] 83–99.)

It is presupposed in this commentary that Mk was the earliest written canonical Gospel and served as one of the sources of Mt and Lk. There are certain sections of Mk, however, that appear to reflect a later development over what is found in Mt, and that may derive from a tradition used independently by the two Evangelists. These are, e.g., Mk 2:23–28; 6:7–16,31–34; 9:14–29; 10:11. They do not appear, however, to discredit the basic view of the Two-Source Theory in Syn analysis.

6 **(III) Marcan Theology.** E. Schweizer has pointed out several word groups that Mark has consistently introduced into his redaction of the Gospel tradition and that serve to characterize this Evangelist's theological outlook. Since these notions are discussed in the commentary, it will suffice to state the theological views and to indicate the relevant texts.

The age of salvation prophesied in the OT is the time of the kerygma, or proclamation. This begins with John the Baptist (1:1,4,7), is taken up by Jesus (1:14–15,38,39), continued by the disciples (3:14; 6:12), and eventuates in the Church's universal mission (13:10; 14:9). This kerygma is both a call to repentance and a proclamation of the good news. Significantly, however, Mark reserves to Jesus the proclamation of God's kingdom (1:15; see comment on 6:12).

Closely allied to this is Mark's view that the kingdom that Jesus proclaims is not a body of doctrinal teaching but a mystery or secret that Jesus himself embodies and that he reveals only to his disciples (see comments on 1:1; 4:11).

Jesus' ministry, therefore, is fundamentally a revelation of his own identity or function in God's kingdom and takes place through his "teaching"—a notion that Mark predicates only of Jesus (but see comment on 6:30). Even Jesus' exorcisms and other miracles are almost indistinguishable from what Mark calls his teaching (see comment on 1:21). Moreover, the universality of the gospel message is underscored by Mark's use of the adjectives "all" (1:5; 2:13; 4:1; 6:33,39,41; 13:10) and "whole" (1:28,33,39; 6:55).

A third group of characteristically Marcan expressions brings out the Evangelist's view that even Jesus' closest disciples were incapable of comprehending the mystery of his person, and that Jesus necessarily used an enigmatic form of "teaching." These expressions include *parabolē* (4:2,10–13,33–34; 7:17; 12:1,12; see comment on 4:11), "in private" (see comment on 4:34; cf. 6:31; 7:33; 9:2,28; 13:3), "understand," and "their minds were blinded" (see comments on 6:51; 8:17–21). Only at the first prediction of the passion does Jesus "speak the word plainly" (8:32), showing that the mystery of his messiahship resides especially in his passion and death, a fate that also awaits his disciples (8:34–38; 10:21,35–44).

Not only are these theological preoccupations of Mark reflected in his special vocabulary, they also dictate the structure of his Gospel as a progressive revelation of Jesus' status as Messiah and Son of God (1:1–8:30) and as the suffering Son of Man (8:31–16:9). This status Jesus intentionally concealed during his ministry (1:34,44; 3:12; 5:43; 7:36; 8:20,30; 9:9); it was only imperfectly grasped by his disciples, but came to be recognized at his death by the Roman centurion (→ 5 above).

(Boobyer, G. H., "Galilee and Galileans in St. Mark's Gospel," *BJRylL* 35 [1952–53] 334–48; "The Secrecy Motif in St. Mark's Gospel," *NTS* 6 [1959–60] 225–35. Bratcher, R. G., "Introduction to the Gospel of Mark," *RevExp* 55 [1958] 351–66. Briggs, R. C., "Exposition of the Gospel of Mark," *RevExp* 55 [1958] 367–92. Burkill, T. A., "The Hidden Son of Man in St. Mark's Gospel," *ZNW* 52 [1961] 189–213. De la Potterie, I., "De compositione evangelii Marci," *VD* 44 [1966] 155–69. Denis, A.-M., "Les richesses du Fils de Dieu selon S. Marc [1–6:30]," *VieSp* 41 [1959] 229–39. Faw, C. E., "The Heart of the Gospel of Mark," *JBR* 24 [1956] 77–82. Haenchen, E., "Die Komposition von Mk 8:27–9:1 Par.," *NovT* 6 [1963] 81–109. Hay, L. S., "The Son of God Christology in Mark," *JBR* 32 [1962] 106–14. Hegermann, H., "Bethsaida und Gennesar," *Judentum, Urchristentum, Kirche* [Fest. J. Jeremias; BZNW 26; Berlin, 1960] 130–40. Luz, O., "Das Geheimnismotiv und die markinische Christologie," *ZNW* 56 [1965] 9–30. Peacock, H. F., "The Theology of the Gospel of Mark," *RevExp* 55 [1958] 393–99. Riesenfeld, H., "Tradition und Redaktion im Markusevangelium," *Neutestamentliche Studien* [Fest. R. Bultmann; BZNW 21; Berlin, 1954] 157–64. Schulz, S., "Die Bedeutung des Markus für die Theologiegeschichte des Urchristentums," *SE* 2, 135–45. Schweizer, E., "Anmerkungen zur Theologie des Markus," *Neotestamentica et patristica* [Fest. O. Cullmann; NovTSup 6; Leiden, 1962] 35–46; "Die theologische Leistung des Markus," *EvT* 24 [1964] 337–55; "Zur Frage des Messiasgeheimnisses bei Markus," *ZNW* 56 [1965] 1–8. Strecker, G., "Zur Messiasgeheimnistheorie im Markusevangelium," *SE* 3, 87–104. Tyson, J. B., "The Blindness of the Disciples in Mark," *JBL* 80 [1961] 261–68. Vielhauer, P., "Erwägungen zur Christologie des Markusevangeliums," *Zeit und Geschichte* [Fest. R. Bultmann; Tübingen, 1964] 155–69.)

7 **(IV) Outline.** The Gospel according to Mark is outlined as follows:

(I) Prologue (1:1–13)
  (A) Title (1:1)
  (B) John the Baptist (1:2–8)
  (C) Jesus' Baptism (1:9–11)
  (D) The Temptation (1:12–13)
(II) The Mystery of the Messiah (1:14–8:33)
  (A) Jesus and the Crowds (1:14–3:6)
    (a) Introduction (1:14–20)
      (i) Summary of Jesus' preaching (1:14–15)
      (ii) Call of the first disciples (1:16–20)
    (b) Jesus' Authority (1:21–3:5)
      (i) In teaching and healing (1:21–45)
      (ii) In controversy with the Pharisees (2:1–3:5)
    (c) Conclusion: The Pharisees' Plot (3:6)
  (B) Jesus and His Own (3:7–6:6a)
    (a) Introduction (3:7–19a)
      (i) Summary of Jesus' miracles (3:7–12)
      (ii) Institution of the Twelve (3:13–19a)
    (b) Jesus Retires from the Crowds (3:19b–5:43)
      (i) Jesus' true family (3:19b–35)
      (ii) Preaching in parables (4:1–34)
      (iii) Miracles (4:35–5:43)
    (c) Conclusion: Jesus is Rejected by His Townspeople (6:1–6a)
  (C) Jesus and His Disciples (6:6b–8:33)
    (a) Introduction (6:6b–34)
      (i) Summary statement (6:6b)
      (ii) Mission charge and return of the disciples (6:7–13,30)
      (iii) Interlude: Opinions about Jesus (6:14–16)
      (iv) Interlude: John the Baptist's death (6:17–29)
    (b) The Loaves Section (6:31–8:26)
      (i) Feeding of the 5000 and its sequel (6:31–7:37)
      (ii) Feeding of the 4000 and its sequel (8:1–13)
    (c) Conclusion: The Blindness of the Disciples (8:14–21)
    (d) Appendix: The Blind Man of Bethsaida (8:22–26)
(III) Conclusion of Part II and Transition to Part IV: Peter's Profession and Jesus' Correction (8:27–33; → 51 below)
(IV) The Mystery of the Son of Man (8:31–16:8)
  (A) The Way of the Son of Man (8:31–10:52)
    (a) First Prediction of the Passion and Its Sequel (8:31–9:29)
      (i) The first prediction (8:31–32a)
      (ii) Misunderstanding of the disciples (8:32b–33)
      (iii) Instructions on discipleship (8:34–9:1)
      (iv) Complements (9:2–29)
    (b) Second Prediction of the Passion and Its Sequel (9:30–10:32)
      (i) The second prediction (9:30–31)
      (ii) Misunderstanding of the disciples (9:32–34)
      (iii) Instruction (9:35–37)
      (iv) Catechetical complements (9:38–10:31)
    (c) Third Prediction of the Passion and Its Sequel (10:32–52)
      (i) The third prediction (10:32–34)
      (ii) Misunderstanding of James and John (10:35–40)
      (iii) Instruction on greatness (10:41–45)
    (d) Appendix: Cure of Bartimaeus (10:46–52)
  (B) Jesus in Jerusalem (11:1–13:37)
    (a) Judgment in Action (11:1–26)
    (b) Judgment in Words (11:27–12:37a)
    (c) Conclusion: Jesus' Warning against the Pharisaic Leaders (12:37b–40)

COMMENTARY

8 **(I) Prologue (1:1–13).** After announcing the title of his work Mark establishes in three brief passages that Jesus is the Messiah and Son of God who fulfills OT promises.

(A) Title (1:1). *beginning of the gospel of Jesus Christ, Son of God:* Mark is the only Evangelist who entitles his book *to euaggelion* (the good news, gospel). His use of the word is akin to that in Paul where it can mean either the act of proclaiming the good news or the content of the good news—salvation in Christ. Like Paul, Mark identifies the good news with Christ: in 8:35 and 10:29 to sacrifice or die for the Gospel is to do so for Christ; in 13:9–11 Jesus' call to the disciples to bear witness for him is interpreted as proclaiming the Gospel to all nations, implying that in the very proclamation Christ is made present. Thus in calling his book "the gospel" Mark means that it is not primarily an account about Jesus but a proclamation of the Risen Christ in which he is again made present. What follows is the good news, which re-presents Jesus the Messiah and Son of God in incidents taken from the tradition regarding his earthly ministry through to his resurrection. Some mss. and editions omit "Son of God."

(Hoskyns, E. and F. N. Davey, *Riddle of the NT* [3rd ed.; London, 1947] 85–89. Marxsen, W., *Markus*, 77–101; *Einleitung in das NT* [3rd ed.; Gütersloh, 1964] 123–24.)

9 **(B) John the Baptist (1:2–8).** As in the preaching of the apostles (Acts 1:22; 10:37; 13:24) the Gospel proclamation begins with the ministry of John in the wilderness. Here, however, John's ministry has a place in the Gospel only as the divinely ordained prelude to God's saving act in the coming of Jesus the Messiah. Mark presents this prelude as the fulfillment of OT prophecy. John's proclamation concerns a mightier one still to come. **2.** *as it is written in Isaiah:* The Isaian citation begins in v. 3; v. 2 is an adapted form of Mal 3:1 (cf. Ex 23:20; Mt 11:10; Lk 7:27). *look, I am sending my messenger:* Identified as Elijah in Mal 4:5, he is the one who is to come to purify Israel before the Day of Yahweh (*kyrios*). The text is applicable to John only on the supposition that Jesus is now the *Kyrios;* therefore John was his prophesied forerunner. But elsewhere John disclaims he is Elijah (Jn 1:21) and calls Jesus such (Mt 11:3; 3:10–12). Moreover, Jesus finally makes the startling reversal of roles, stating that "he [John] is Elijah" (Mt 11:14). A solution is that early in his ministry Jesus was taken to be Elijah, Yahweh's forerunner, perhaps on the basis of John's proclamation of the "one to come" (see 1:7); later on Jesus disclaimed the role of the fiery prophet in preference to one of mercy and forgiveness (Mt 11:4–6). Then he transferred the title to John. The citation from Mal is undoubtedly a gloss on the early Marcan text, read back into Gospel tradition from a later stage (see J. A. T. Robinson, *NTS* 4 [1957–58] 263–81). **3.** *the voice of one crying:* Is 40:3 is applied to John in the belief that Jesus is the *Kyrios* whose way is being prepared. Mk thus records a Christian interpretation of the OT. **5.** *were baptized in the river Jordan, confessing their sins:* Both John's baptism and the confession of sins have parallels in the QL (1QS 5:1,13–14; 1:24–25); on the Baptist's possible connection with Qumran, → 43:23. **6.** *clothed in camel's hair with a leather belt around his waist:* Possibly an allusion to Elijah's dress (2 Kgs 1:8). The LXX, however, interprets this to mean that Elijah, like Esau, was hairy; and according to Zech 13:4 a hairy mantle was the customary dress of a prophet. Thus, originally this verse may not have contained an Elijah-Baptist typology (J. A. T. Robinson, *NTS* 4 [1957–58] 263–64). **7.** *one mightier than I:* Elijah (Mal 3:1–3; 4:1–6), in whose role John casts Jesus initially. **8.** *will baptize you with a holy Spirit:* Cf. 1QS 4:18–21: "Then [i.e., in the season of divine visitation] God shall purify with his truth all man's deeds and will refine for himself the body of man, rooting out every spirit of iniquity from the midst of his flesh and cleansing it of all impurity with a holy spirit. Like waters of purification he shall pour over him the spirit of truth." Such a background for this verse would explain why it is immediately followed by the episode of Jesus' own baptism and his temptation by Satan.

(Best, E., "Spirit-Baptism," *NovT* 4 [1960] 236–43. Marxsen, W., *Markus*, 17–32. Robinson, J. A. T., "The Baptism of John and the Qumran Community," *HarvTR* 50 [1957] 157–91. Yates, J. E., "The Form of Mk 1:8b," *NTS* 4 [1957–58] 334–38.)

10 **(C) Jesus' Baptism (1:9–11).** **9.** *baptized by John:* That Jesus submitted to John's baptism of repentance presented a theological problem to the early Church. Only Mk directly affirms it, whereas Mt mentions Jesus' intention to be baptized (3:13) and refers to it as an accomplished fact (Mt 3:16; cf. Lk 3:21); Jn omits it altogether (1:32–34). **10.** *he saw:* Unlike Mt and Lk, Mk recounts the theophany at Jesus' baptism as an apocalyptic vision seen only by Jesus. Four elements of the vision bring out the theological meaning of the event: (1) "The heavens torn open" is an allusion to Is 64:1, part of a prayer that God may inaugurate the *eschaton* as a new exodus. (2) "The spirit coming down" is an allusion to Is 63:11,14 where God's spirit is said to have come down upon the Israelites during the Exodus, just as in Ex 19:11, 18,20 God had come down upon Sinai to form his people. (3) "Like a dove": This was a symbol of Israel in the Bible (Hos 11:11; Pss 68:13; 74:19; 56:1 [LXX]; Ct 1:15; 2:14; 4:1; 5:2,12; 6:9) in rabbinical commentaries (*Midr. Ct* 1:15 [93b]; 2:14 [101a]), and in extrabiblical writings (*2 Esdras* 5:24–27). Jesus is thus designated as the representative of God's new people according to the Spirit. (4) "Out of the heavens came a voice": The allusion is to Is 42:1; it attests that Jesus is the unique Son of God, the Servant of Yahweh, anointed with his prophetic Spirit. By portraying this theophany as a vision seen only by Jesus, Mk keeps Jesus' true identity a secret known only to the reader. It was not shared by those present at the Jordan. **10.** *when he came up out of the water:* A possible allusion to Is 63:11. Thus, this event at the Jordan fulfills the Isaian longing and recalls the passage through the Reed Sea, the Israelites' crossing of the Jordan under Joshua (= Jesus), and the new exodus announced in Is 40:3–4. It has ecclesial significance: Jesus embodies the new people of God, being born in a new exodus.

(Buse, I., "The Markan Account of the Baptism of Jesus and Is 63," *JTS* 7 [1956] 74–75. De la Potterie, I., "L'onction du Christ," *NRT* 80 [1958] 226–39. Feuillet, A., "Le baptême de Jésus d'après l'Évangile selon S. Marc," *CBQ* 21 [1959] 468–90; "Le symbolisme de la colombe dans les récits synoptiques du baptême," *RSR* 46 [1958] 524–44.)

11 **(D) The Temptation (1:12–13).** The account in Mk is so brief compared to those in Mt 4:1–11 and Lk 4:1–13 that certain commentators believe that in Mt and Lk the Marcan story has been expanded with material from Q, or that Mk is an abbreviation of a longer account. There is no evidence, however, that the Q version is an amplification of Mk, or that the Evangelist knew of the Matthaean and Lucan nuances of the temptations. Hence one should resist the inclination to interpret this scene by the fuller accounts in Mt and Lk. The Marcan version, moreover, is complete in itself when seen against the background of the current Jewish belief that in the last days the evil spirit would be conquered in a great contest of strength (1QS 3:13–4:26; cf. T. A. Burkill, *Mysterious Revelation*, 20–23). The temptation is thus a mythologized picture of Jesus' redeeming work: as Son of God and bearer of the Holy Spirit (1:10–12) he overthrows Satan's empire.

12. *the Spirit drove him out:* There is a nuance of compulsion or violence in this word, which is usually used of Jesus' expulsion of demons (1:34,39,43; 3:15,22). *into the desert:* Although Mt and Lk clearly draw an analogy between Jesus' temptations and the 40 years' testing of Israel in the desert (Dt 8:2), this parallelism is all but absent from Mk. Rather, the mention of the desert reflects the belief that the wilderness was the habitat of evil spirits (Str-B 4, 515–16). Similarly, the 40 days simply denote a more or less prolonged period, without any allusion to Dt 8:2. **13.** *tempted by Satan:* The notion of temptation is connected with the view that a state of war existed in the world between good and evil powers, in which the believer was constantly exposed to the devil's attacks. Unlike Mt and Lk, Mk does not indicate the nature of Jesus' temptation, or even that it may have been occasioned by hunger. *he was with the wild beasts:* This may perhaps symbolize the beginning of the Messianic age as paradise regained (Is 11:6–9; 65:25; Hos 2:18). The wild beasts, however, may also symbolize the evil with which Jesus contends (cf. Ps 22:13–22; Is 13:21–22; Ez 34:5,8,25). *and the angels ministered to him:* Namely, in his struggle with Satan. The QL portrays the angels as an army fighting on God's side against the evil spirits (1QM 1:10–11; 12:8,9; 13:10; 17:6). Although Mk does not clearly indicate the outcome of Jesus' struggle, this is clearly stated in 3:27, and the implications of Satan's defeat are spelled out in Jesus' exorcisms.

(Best, E., *The Temptation and the Passion* [Cambridge, 1965] 3–27. Dupont, J., "L'origine du récit des tentations de Jésus au désert," *RB* 73 [1966] 30–76. Feuillet, A., "L'épisode de la tentation d'après l'Évangile de S. Marc," *EstBib* 19 [1960] 49–73. Kuhn, K. G., "New Light on Temptation, Sin, and Flesh in the NT," *The Scrolls and the NT* [ed. K. Stendahl; N.Y., 1957] 94–113. Seitz, O., "Praeparatio evangelica in the Markan Prologue," *JBL* 82 [1963] 201–6.)

12 **(II) The Mystery of the Messiah (1:14–8:33).** Having shown that Jesus is the Messiah and Son of God, Mk now begins the story of how he gradually unfolded the mystery of his identity during his ministry.

(A) Jesus and the Crowds (1:14–3:6).

(a) Introduction (1:14–20).

(i) *Summary of Jesus' preaching* (1:14–15). Mk is punctuated by similar summaries (1:39; 3:7–12; 6:6b), many of which appear to be pre-Marcan units (cf. C. H. Dodd, *ExpT* 43 [1931–32] 396–400), although comparison with Mt shows that the Evangelist edited them in line with his own theological preoccupations. This is especially true of 1:14–15.

14. *after John had been handed over:* A foreshadowing of Jesus' fate (9:31; 10:33; 14:10,11,44). *Galilee:* The Galilean ministry is central in Mk; the Evangelist probably introduced this locale systematically less for informational than for theological reasons: it is not only the scene of Jesus' earthly ministry, but also the meeting-place of the Risen Lord (16:7). Mark may be exhorting the Jerusalem church to turn its sights on this "Galilee," recognizing in the locale of Jesus' earthly ministry the scene of his impending parousia (W. Marxsen, *Markus*, 33–77; F-B 64–65). *proclaiming God's good news:* Possibly Jesus himself called his message "the good news," alluding to Is 61:1–2; 40:9; 52:7. However, the expressions "proclaim the good news" and "God's good news" are Christian terms found in Paul (Gal 2:2; Col 1:23; 1 Thes 2:9). It is thus more likely that this notice is an editorial addition giving a programmatic summary of Jesus' preaching in specifically Christian terms (see 1:1). Similarly "believe in the good news" (1:15b) is a compendium and characterization of the Risen Christ's message. **15.** *God's reign is at hand; repent:* Cf. Mt 4:17, "Repent, for the reign of heaven is at hand." By inverting this order and starting with "the appointed time [of God's saving act] is fulfilled," Mk emphasizes the eschatological nature of Jesus' presence in Galilee (cf. Ez 7:12; Dn 12:4,9; Zeph 1:12; 1QS 4:18–20; Gal 4:4). (On the reign [or kingdom] of God, → Aspects NT Thought, 78:99–101; cf. F. Mussner, *TTZ* 66 [1957] 257–75.)

(ii) *Call of the first disciples* (1:16–20). **16.** *was passing along:* The early Church knew that certain of Jesus' disciples had been with him from the time of John (Acts 1:21–23; 10:37); hence Mk places this episode at the beginning of the Galilean ministry. Although the words suggest an almost casual encounter, the vbs. *paragein* and *parerchesthai* (to pass by), when predicated of Jesus in the Gospels, occur in epiphanic stories (Mt 9:27; 20:30; Lk 18:37; Mk 2:14 [Mt 9:9 par.]; Mk 6:48). In the OT, God (1 Kgs 19:11; 2 Sm 23:4 [LXX]), his goodness (Ex 33:19), or his glory (Ex 33:22) are said "to pass by," i.e., to be shown forth. Here the expression portends an epiphany of Jesus' Messianic power to create disciples (E. Lohmeyer, *NThTij* 23 [1934] 206–24; *Urchristliche Mystik* [Darmstadt, 1958] 59–79). **17.** *come after me:* Jesus makes an imperative claim upon his disciples and gives new direction to their lives. No less important is the immediate effect of his summons. **19.** *he saw James and John:* Mark combines incidents so as to make the three privileged disciples the first to be called (contrast Lk 5:1–11; Jn 1:37,42,43). **20.** *leaving their father Zebedee:* Mark gives the impression that Peter and Andrew answered Jesus' call by leaving behind their livelihood, whereas James and John responded by severing family ties. This may be exaggerated, but Mark's primary purpose is to show that discipleship entails renunciation of possessions (cf. 10:21) and family ties (10:29).

13 (b) Jesus' Authority (1:21–3:5). (i) *In teaching and healing* (1:21–45). Several episodes form "a day's ministry at Capernaum," illustrating Jesus' Messianic authority in word and act. **21.** *Capernaum* (→ Gospel Lk, 44:57). *taught:* Mark records much less of Jesus' doctrine than Matthew or Luke; yet he associates the activity of teaching more closely with Jesus' self-revelation. Except for 6:30 and 7:7 (= Is 29:13), it is always Jesus who teaches (1:21; 4:1; 6:2,6; 11:17; 12:35; 14:49). His teaching is connected with his miraculous power (1:27), and like the latter it causes amazement (1:22,27; 6:2; 7:37; 10:26; 11:18). Those whom Jesus teaches are often specified (the people: 1:22; 2:13; 4:2; 6:34; 10:1; 11:18; 14:49; the disciples: 8:31; 9:31); but what he teaches is specified only in the second half of the Gospel: his passion and resurrection (8:31; 9:31), insoluble marriage (10:1), David's son (12:35), the way of God (12:14), caution against the scribes and Pharisees (12:38). In the first half of Mk, Jesus teaches only "the secret of God's kingdom" (4:10), and in a veiled way through parables (4:10–12, 33,34). Thus the coming section is to be a veiled revelation of Jesus' messiahship. **22.** *as one having authority, not as the scribes:* In the primitive tradition "authority" (Gk *exousia*) probably stood for the Hebr r^{e}*šût*, the "authority" of a rabbi to impose a decision with binding force (cf. 11:28,29). The word "scribe" (*grammateus*) corresponds to the Hebr *sôpēr*, a teacher of lower rank than a rabbi. Thus Jesus would have been contrasted to such lesser teachers who did not possess this r^{e}*šût* (D. Daube, *JTS* 39 [1938] 45–59). In Mk, however, *exousia* implies the Messianic authority that Jesus exercises in act (2:10; 3:15; 6:7; 11:28–33). His teaching constituted an exercise of that same authority by which he overthrew Satan's rule.

(Coutts, J., "The Authority of Jesus and of the Twelve in St. Mark's Gospel," *JTS* 8 [1957] 111–18. Schweizer, E., "Anmerkungen zur Theologie des Markus," *Neotestamentica et patristica* [Fest. O. Cullmann; NovTSup 6; Leiden, 1962] 37–38. Starr, J., "The Meaning of 'Authority' in Mk 1:22," *HarvTR* 23 [1930] 302–5.)

14 (A) Cure of a Demoniac (1:23–28). Jesus' first miracle is, significantly, an exorcism, a sign that in his presence the power of evil is reduced to impotency. God's rule is at hand. **23.** *a man possessed by a foul spirit:* In antiquity sickness was ascribed to evil spirits. Many of Jesus' miracles are recounted in terms of exorcism. *he cried out:* A common feature in miracle stories is to describe the gravity of the sufferer's affliction; this is intimated here by the defiant cries of the demoniac and the details in 1:26. **24.** *why do you meddle with us?:* See Lk 4:34; Jn 2:4. *come to destroy us:* Jesus is in effect recognized as the Messiah, anointed with God's Spirit and possessing power over evil spirits. *I know who you are:* To know one's adversary's name was to give one a magical power over him; the demon names Jesus twice: "Jesus of Nazareth," then "God's Holy One," i.e., a charismatic prophet like Elisha (2 Kgs 4:9). Here as elsewhere in Mk (1:34; 3:11–12; 5:7) Jesus' true identity is a secret kept from the crowds but known to the Christian reader and attested by the demons. **25.** *rebuked him:* The vb. *epitiman* technically also means "exorcise." In the LXX it translates Hebr *gʿr*, meaning "rebuke" (see Zech 3:3; cf. 1QapGn 20:28–29; *CBQ* 22 [1960] 284).

(B) Simon's Mother-in-Law (1:29–31). **29.** *entered the house:* The mention of the private setting and of privileged disciples may be an eyewitness detail; in such settings (4:10,34; 5:37–40; 6:31–32; 7:17,24,33; 9:2,28,33; 10:10; 13:3) and in the presence of three disciples (5:37; 9:2; 13:3; 14:33) Jesus makes important self-disclosures. **31.** *raised her up:* Mark uses the vb. *egeirō*, which is frequently used of Jesus' resurrection (Mk 14:28; 16:6; 1 Cor 15:4; Acts 3:15; 13:37). Possibly the early Church viewed the miracle as a foreshadowing of the eschatological resurrection wrought in mankind through Christ's death and resurrection. *she served them:* The detail suggests the completeness of her cure and service expected of those who have been saved by Christ (10:43–45). (See P. Lamarche, *NRT* 87 [1965] 515–26; X. Léon-Dufour, *Études d'Évangile* [Paris, 1965] 123–48; A. Richardson, *Miracle Stories* [London, 1959] 75–76.)

15 (C) Jesus' Evening Cures and Withdrawal from Capernaum (1:32–39). The first of these two stories (32–34) closes Jesus' Sabbath ministry at Capernaum and shows (1) that his miracles were not restricted to a few, and (2) that they were a manifestation of his messiahship, even if only demons were able to penetrate this secret. **35.** *he prayed:* Jesus' departure was occasioned by the false messianic hopes engendered by his miracles. The other occasions on which Jesus prays (6:46; 14:32–42) are times of stress connected with the true nature of his messiahship. **36.** *Simon and those with him:* This expression usually designates Jesus' disciples (3:14; 4:10; 5:18, 40; cf. 2:25; 16:10). Here Simon is presumably accompanied by Andrew, James, and John; yet Mark avoids calling them "disciples" as if to suggest that their present way of acting puts them rather in opposition to Jesus. **37.** *everyone is looking for you:* In Mk *zētein* always occurs in contexts suggesting an evil intention (8:11,12; 11:18; 12:2; 14:1,11,55) or at least a misguided sort of seeking (3:32; 16:6). Simon implies that Jesus should remain at Capernaum and capitalize on the popularity aroused by his miracles. But Jesus refuses to confine his ministry to one place or to encourage the messianic hopes of the crowds.

(D) Cure of a Leper (1:40–45). **40.** *a leper:* This miracle illustrates Jesus' power to save even those excluded from Israel by the Mosaic Law. **41.** *moved with anger:* Most mss. read *splagchnistheis*, "moved with pity." Jesus' anger was probably directed against the leprous spirit. **43.** *dismissed him:* That is, the demon. The present form of the story is probably a conflation of two earlier accounts, one of which depicted Jesus' pity (1:42) and the other his anger (1:43). Mark may have understood "him" to mean the cured leper, adding the injunction to silence (1:44a) in accord with the Messianic secret. The rest of 1:44 refers to Lv 13–14; by showing Jesus' regard for the Mosaic Law it sets the stage for the controversies in 2:1–3:6. **45.** *he went off:* Theoretically, the subject may be either Jesus or the cured man. It is most likely the latter, and Mark is making a subtle catechetical point: those cleansed by Christ in baptism must "proclaim" and "spread the word"—a technical term for the Gospel coined by the primitive Church (Mk 4:15–20; 16:20; Acts 4:4).

16 (ii) *In controversy with the Pharisees* (2:1–3:5). This section serves to show the growing opposition to Jesus, leading to the Pharisees' plot in 3:6.

(A) Cure of a Paralytic (2:1–12). This pericope may refer to a single incident in Jesus' ministry, or it may have been conflated from a miracle story (3–5,11–12) and a pronouncement story (6–10) by the association of the forgiveness of sins with faith (Acts 10:43; 13:38–39; cf. J. Dupont, *ScEccl* 12 [1960] 156–58; *NRT* 82 [1960] 942). The main difficulty lies in 2:10, which contains an anacoluthon involving a shift in the persons addressed and thus breaks the unity of the passage. It is surprising, moreover, in view of Mark's presentation of the Messianic secret, that Jesus should have disclosed himself so early in his ministry as the Son of Man with authority to forgive sins, the more so since this disclosure is made to hostile scribes (cf. 8:11–13). Possibly, however, 2:10 is not a saying of Jesus, but a parenthetical comment of the Church addressed to the Christian readers of the Gospel and explicating for them the significance of the healing. In that case the passage would form a perfect literary unity in which Jesus establishes the effectiveness of his forgiving word not by a verbal claim but by a miracle whose import is accessible only to those with faith.

4. *roof:* See Lk 5:18–19. The essential point in 2:3–5 is the connection between the actors' faith and Jesus' declaration of forgiveness. Although Jesus' words may simply have meant "God has forgiven your sins (cf. 2 Sm 12:13; *GrBib* § 236), vv. 7 and 10 show that they are reported here in the light of the Church's Easter faith in Christ as the Lord with power to forgive sins personally. **5.** *saw their faith:* Faith, the necessary prerequisite for a miracle (5:34; 5:56 [cf. Mt 13:58]; 7:29 [cf. Mt 16:28]; 9:23; 10:52), and an essential demand of Jesus' preaching (1:15), could not, before the resurrection, have meant an act of belief in Christ as a divine person. The Evangelists, writing as Christian believers, tend to color *pistis* in terms of the specifically Christian faith to which it was leading (see, e.g., comments on 2:10; 1:15). During Jesus' ministry it would have meant a receptivity to God's healing word proclaimed by Jesus, together with a confident self-abandonment to God whose saving power was being exercised in and through Jesus (P. Benoit, *LumVi* 22 [1955] 45–64). **7.** *blasphemy:* A foreshadowing of the condemnation in 14:60–64. **10.** *that you may know:* This verse is a Christian editorial comment on Jesus' miracle; the "you" cannot refer to the scribes. It is addressed to the Christian readers to whom the miracle is being recounted. **11.** *I say to you, rise:* Jesus' cure substantiates his claim to forgive sins and symbolizes the spiritual health of the forgiven sinner. (On the Son of Man, → Aspects NT Thought, 78:28–30.) **12.** *they were astonished:* The amazed people fail to see the miracle as a sign of Jesus' power to forgive sins (contrast Mt 9:8)—another reason for thinking that 2:10 does not represent a saying uttered by Jesus on this occasion.

(Boobyer, G. H., "Mk 2:10a and the Interpretation of the Healing of the Paralytic," *HarvTR* 47 [1954] 115–20. Ceroke, C. P., "Is Mk 2:10 a Saying of Jesus?" *CBQ* 22 [1960] 369–90. Dupont, J., "Le paralytique pardonné," *NRT* 82 [1960] 940–58. Feuillet, A., "L'*exousia* du Fils de l'Homme," *RSR* 42 [1954] 161–92. Mead, R. T., "The Healing of the Paralytic—A Unit?" *JBL* 80 [1961] 348–54.)

17 (B) The Call of Levi (2:13–17). This passage combines a story about Jesus (2:13–14) with a pronouncement story (15–17), both of which deal with Jesus' attitude toward sinners. **13.** *taught:* See comment on 1:21. **14.** *was passing along:* See comment on 1:16. *Levi the son of Alphaeus:* Mk does not suggest, as does Mt 9:19; 10:3, that Levi was the apostle Matthew (→ Aspects NT Thought, 78:166). **15.** *at table in his house:* Before this pronouncement story came to be joined to the call of Levi, it probably meant that Jesus was in his own house. In this context, however, it appears to be Levi's house, thus reinforcing the point that Jesus associated with tax collectors and sinners to the extent of table-fellowship with them. **17.** *need no physician:* The point of the story lies in Jesus' proverbial pronouncement, which Mark understands less as a new principle of moral behavior than as an epiphany of Jesus' Messianic power to forgive sins. He invites sinners to the Messianic banquet rather than letting himself be contaminated by their presence. *not to call the upright, but the sinners:* A Christian interpretation of Jesus' proverb in 2:17a. It is not that those who were upright according to Mosaic Law lay outside the scope of Jesus' invitation, but that in fact those Jews who did accept Christ were, by and large, not from among the scribes and Pharisees, but from among those considered by them as sinners (J. Mousson, *ColMech* 43 [1958] 134–39).

(C) On Fasting (2:18–22). **19.** *can wedding guests fast:* Jesus' answer to the charge of 2:18 takes the form of a parabolic saying based on such OT passages as Hos 2:16–20; Is 54:5–6; 62:45; Jer 2:2; Ez 16, in which God's relation to his covenant people is portrayed as a marriage. *while the bridegroom is with them:* Possibly this means simply "while the wedding is in progress" (J. Jeremias, *Parables of Jesus* [rev. ed.; London, 1963] 52). But Jesus may have intended an allegorical reference to himself as the Messiah-Bridegroom (Str-B 1, 969–70; 2, 393). In either case Jesus' answer means that the *eschaton* is here, and hence there is no reason for his disciples to fast and mourn. *with the bridegroom with them, they cannot fast:* Verses 19b–20 are often thought to be a later addition to Jesus' original saying, for (1) "the bridegroom" is an allegorical trait inconsistent with the Semitic parable form (C. H. Dodd, *Parables of the Kingdom* [rev. ed.; London, 1936] 116–17, n.2); (2) 2:19b–20 are meant to justify the early Christian practice of fasting; (3) they contain a premature prediction of Jesus' death. However, (1) one cannot exclude all allegory from the Semitic parable even as Jesus used it (M. Black, *BJRylL* 42 [1959–60] 273–87; R. E. Brown *NovT* 5 [1962] 36–45); (2) other sayings, such as Mt 6:16, attest an interest in fasting during Jesus' lifetime; (3) the saying may have belonged to a later stage of Jesus' ministry. Thus 2:19b–20 may contain a genuine saying of Jesus. For Mark the pericope shows that Jesus' Messianic authority takes precedence over Mosaic observance; his presence is a source of eschatological joy, and indeed the coming of God's reign is connected with his very person and will entail suffering (O. Cullmann, *Christology of the NT* [2nd ed.; London, 1963] 61–62; K. T. Schäfer, *Synoptische Studien* [Fest. A. Wikenhauser; Munich, 1953] 124–27).

Two parabolic sayings now stress the incompatibility of the new economy with the old Mosaic economy; Jesus' disciples can no longer adhere to the Baptist's manner of life without compromising their new view of things. **21.** *unshrunk cloth on an old garment:* The garment may be a symbol of the universe, which Jesus does not merely patch up but creates anew (cf. Heb 1:10–12; Acts 10:11ff.; 11:5ff.). **22.** *new wine into old wineskins:* Wine may be a symbol of a new era (Gn 9:20; 49:11–12; Nm 13:23–24); Jesus refers to himself as the one who dispenses the new wine at the Messianic banquet (J. Jeremias, *Parables*, 117–18; C. H. Dodd, *Parables*, 117).

18 (D) Plucking Grain on the Sabbath (2:23–28). **25.** *have you never read what David did?:* Jesus answers the Pharisees' charge in rabbinic fashion with a counter-question and an appeal to 1 Sm 21:2–7: even the OT made exceptions to its own regulations (Lv 24:9). Mark makes no comparision between Christ and either David or the Temple, as does Mt 12:5–8. David is excused from the Law as any man would have been, by the circumstances of his extreme hunger. In effect Mark has isolated from the Sabbath controversy a general principle that is considered to supersede the purely positive precept of the Mosaic Law. **27.** *the Sabbath was made for man, not man for the Sabbath:* This conclusion, absent from Mt and Lk, betrays an attitude out of keeping with the Jewish view of the Law, but renders Jesus' argument more convincing to a non-Jewish audience. A similar method of procedure is found in Mk 3:4; 10:11–12; 12:28ff., and hence 2:27 should be attributed rather to the Evangelist than to Jesus. **28.** *the Son of Man is lord even of the Sabbath:* This second conclusion to the episode does not conform to the reasoning found in 2:23–27. Here Jesus justifies the violation of the Sabbath by his authority as Son of Man quite apart from any excusing circumstances.

Probably Mk 2:23–28 is a secondary redaction of the Sabbath controversy as found in Mt and Lk, rather than Mk having been used as their source. For whereas Mt

12:1–8 is a logical unit that recognizes the binding force of the law but argues on an analogy with David that a fortiori Jesus as the Son of Man can presume to exempt himself and his disciples from the law, Mk 2:23–28 by contrast demeans the binding force of the law and invokes the more general (and un-Jewish) principle that man is ultimately the measure of the binding force of God's positive law. This would explain why Mk 2:27 is absent from the parallel in Mt and Lk—it is not that they have omitted it independently of one another, but that Mark has added it to the common tradition with a Gentile church in mind. Likewise the mention of Abiathar in 2:26 is absent from Mt and Lk, not because they have seen the discrepancy with 1 Sm 21:1–2 where Ahimelech is said to be the priest, and omitted it for that reason, but because Mark has added this detail without taking the trouble to verify his faulty memory of the OT story. Nevertheless, since Mt 12:8 existed in the common tradition, Mark retained it; he joined it quite loosely to the inserted v. 27 by the conjunction "consequently."

(Gils, F., " 'Le Sabbat a été fait pour l'homme et non l'homme pour le Sabbat,' " *RB* 69 [1962] 506–23.)

19 (E) Cure of a Withered Hand (3:1–5). The same differences between Mk 2:23–28 and Mt 12:1–8 are found in this next Sabbath dispute. **4.** *is it lawful:* According to Mt 12:11, Jesus answers the Pharisees by citing Jewish practice and using an argument a fortiori: If a sheep falls into a pit on the Sabbath, any observant Jew would rescue it; "of how much more value is a man than a sheep." According to Mk, Jesus invokes a more universal principle: "Is it lawful on the Sabbath to do good or to do harm, to save life or to kill?" This response is less apropos than that in Mt because the man with the withered hand was not a case of life or death. Jesus' words silence his adversaries more by their irony than by their cogency. *they were silent:* A Marcan comment as in 9:34. **5.** Mark's antilegalist strictures are continued in this verse that is also to be attributed to the Evangelist. *he looked around at them:* A formula found only in Mk (3:34; 5:32; 9:8; 10:23; 11:11; and once in Lk 6:10 [Mk 3:5 par.]). *with anger:* Mark is the only evangelist ever to mention Jesus' anger (see 1:41); its mention here reinforces the anti-Pharisaic tone of the passage. *grieved at their hardness of heart:* A typically Marcan theme (6:52; 8:17).

20 (c) CONCLUSION: THE PHARISEES' PLOT (3:6). This verse marks the culmination of the first section of Mk. **6.** *the Pharisees took counsel with the Herodians on how to destroy him:* Ironically the Pharisees have joined forces with the renegade followers of Herod Antipas, but Mark is pursuing an anti-Jewish polemic here, and wishes to say that Jews of all shades of persuasion conspired to kill Jesus. (On Herodians, see H. H. Rowley, *JTS* 41 [1940] 14–29.)

21 **(B) Jesus and His Own (3:7–6:6a).** This section forms a transition from Jesus' ministry among the crowds (1:14–3:6) to that among his close disciples (6:6b–8:33). In the face of growing opposition he restricts his ministry and begins to concentrate increasingly on the formation of his disciples. The structure of this section parallels that of 1:14–3:6.

(a) INTRODUCTION (3:7–19a). (i) *Summary of Jesus' miracles* (3:7–12). This summary, whether freely composed by Mark or elaborated from earlier material, previews the forthcoming section. **7.** *Jesus retired with his disciples:* The mention of the disciples here and in 3:9 looks to such incidents as the choice of the Twelve (3:13–19), the explanation of the parables to them (4:10–20,34), and the miracles performed in their presence (4:35–5:43). *a great crowd from Galilee:* The place names in this verse are like a catalogue of all the regions of Palestine inhabited by Jews. Their gathering around Jesus is the prelude to his creation of a new Israel in the appointment of the Twelve. **8.** *Idumea:* The Gk form of the name Edom, the mountainous area to the S of Judea. *Tyre and Sidon:* Phoenician coastal towns, lying outside Jewish territory, serve to show Jesus' interest in the non-Jewish world, a theme developed in 5:1–20; 6:31–8:10. **9.** *a boat:* This detail looks to a series of incidents on and around the Lake of Galilee (4:1–41; 5:1–21; 6:32–56). **10.** *to touch him:* This foreshadows the two miracles in which Jesus cures by a touch (5:22–43). **11–12.** *you are God's son:* These two Marcan verses again underscore Jesus' identity as the hidden Messiah who binds the "strong man" Satan (3:24–27). (See L. E. Keck, "Mk 3:7–12 and Mark's Christology," *JBL* 84 [1965] 341–58.)

22 (ii) *Institution of the Twelve* (3:13–19a). This passage, together with its correspondent in 6:6b–13, poses a difficult problem in Syn source analysis, for a discussion of which one may consult the bibliography below.

13. *he went up a mountain:* As in Mt 5:1, where this same notice introduces the Sermon on the Mount, the locality sets the scene for a solemn act of Jesus. *summoned those whom he wanted:* Mark emphasizes the authority of Jesus' action. *they came to him:* A verbal reminiscence of 1:20. Their coming is a response to Jesus' summons to be associated with him; in the par. verse in Mt 5:1 the disciples come to hear Jesus teach. **14.** *he appointed:* Lit., "he made," a Semitic phrase used in the LXX of the appointment of priests (1 Kgs 12:31; 13:33; 2 Chr 2:18), of Moses and Aaron (1 Sm 12:6), and in the NT of Jesus as Lord and Messiah (Acts 2:36; Heb 3:2); cf. Mk 1:17. *twelve:* Jesus symbolically claims to found the 12 tribes of the eschatological Israel. *that they might be with him:* This expression comes close to being Mark's definition of the Christian disciple (2:19; 3:7; 4:36; 5:18,40; 8:10; 9:8; 11:11; 14:17,67; 15:41). Its theological significance "is also evident from its frequency in the communion of the last evening (14:14,17,18,20,33), which is shattered by Judas 'with a crowd' [v. 43] and Peter 'with the guards' [v. 54], denying that he had been 'with the Nazarene Jesus' [v. 67]" (J. M. Robinson, *The Problem of History in Mark*, 79–80). **15.** *that he might send them to preach and to have authority to drive out demons:* Mark alone mentions in this context that Jesus was to confer upon the Twelve his own Messianic powers. The shift in subject from "they" to "he," the awkwardness of the syntax, and the fact that the other Syn more logically mention these powers in connection with the mission of the Twelve, all indicate that Mark added these clauses as an anticipation of the mission charge in 6:7 where they rightly belong. **16.** *he appointed the Twelve:* Mark resumes 3:14a after his parenthesis about their powers (→ Aspects NT Thought, 78:162–182). *gave Simon the name Peter:* All the lists place Peter first (Mt 10:2; Lk 6:14; Acts 1:13); Mark alone suggests that his name was changed on this occasion. **17.** *Boanerges, that is, sons of thunder:* The Gk word *boanērges* is not a clear transcription of any recognizable Hebr or Aram phrase that would correspond to Mark's translation. The common explanation is that it reflects *b^e^nê regeš*, which would mean "sons of tumult." Another suggestion is that it represents *b^e^nê r^e^gez*, "sons of wrath," i.e., hot-tempered. No satisfying explanation has been suggested for the vocalic difference at the beginning of the name and so it remains obscure (see G. Bardy, *RSR* 15 [1925] 167–77; *RSR* 18 [1928] 344). *Andrew:* A good Gk name, which is otherwise attested as borne by a Jew. Mark puts him in fourth place after the two privileged brothers who, like Simon, were given descriptive names by Jesus. *Simon the Canaanaean:* "Canaanite" is a mistranslation of the Aram *qan'ānāy*, which Lk 6:15 correctly renders as "the zealot," a member of the chauvinistic and warlike anti-Roman party in Palestine. The rest of the names vary in the lists (→ Aspects NT Thought, 78:162–171). This has led some to think that the choice of the Twelve is a story invented by Christians to substantiate their claim to be the new Israel; the existence of the college, however, is a secure and primitive datum of the NT (Mt 19:28; Lk 22:28–30; 1 Cor 15:5), and there is no reason to think that it did not owe its origin to an appointment by Jesus.

(Burgers, W., "De instelling van de Twaalf in het Evangelie van Marcus," *ETL* 36 [1960] 625–54. Cerfaux, L., "La mission de Galilée dans la tradition synoptique," *ETL* 27 [1951] 369–89; 28 [1952] 629–47. Dupont, J., "Le nom d'apôtres a-t-il été donné aux Douze par Jésus?" *Orient syrien* 1 [1956] 267–90, 425–44. Giblet, J., "Les Douze. Histoire et théologie," *Aux origines de l'Église* [RechBib 7; Louvain, 1965] 51–64. Vaganay, L., "L'absence du Sermon sur la Montagne chez Marc," *RB* 58 [1951] 5–46. Van Bohemen, N., "L'institution des Douze," *La formation des Évangiles* [RechBib 2; Paris, 1957] 116–51.)

23 (b) Jesus Retires from the Crowds (3:19b–5:43). This section recounts a series of events in which Jesus tries, not always successfully, to withdraw from the crowds. In these incidents further charges against Jesus appear.

(i) *Jesus' true family* (3:19b–35). The episode opens with the recording of a reaction toward Jesus on the part of those who knew him well. **19.** *he went home:* Lit., "he goes to a house" (hist. pres.). **20.** *could not even eat:* Lit., "eat bread," which would mean to take food of any kind (see Gn 3:19). **21.** *his people:* Lit., "those around him," which could mean "friends, relatives, household" (Prv 31:21). Verse 31 specifies them as Jesus' kinsfolk. *he is insane:* This is equivalently an accusation of demonic possession (cf. Jn 7:20; 8:48). **22.** *possessed:* Although 3:31–35 may originally have followed 3:21, Mark here recounts the accusation made by religious leaders. The juxtaposition of the two accusations suggests that the personal animosity of Jesus' kin was of a piece with the opposition that eventually led to Jesus' death. *by Beelzebul:* The Vg reads "Beelzebub" ("lord of flies") which in the MT of 2 Kgs 1:2,3,6,16 is the execratory name for the Philistine god of Ekron. This name was corrupted from *ba'al zᵉbûl*, "lord of the dwelling" or "Baal the prince." The Gk NT has preserved the more original name. But it is not elsewhere attested in pre-Christian literature as the name of a demon (see W. Foerster, *ThDNT* 1, 605–6). **23.** *how can Satan cast out Satan?:* Jesus argues that his exorcisms do indeed signal the collapse of Satan's rule, but some power other than that of Beelzebul is needed to explain Jesus' works, since Satan is not so foolish as to destroy his own rule. **27.** *unless he first bind the strong man:* Namely, Beelzebul. Jesus is the "stronger man" (1:14) who has broken into Satan's house and can now proceed to plunder his enemy's household. **28.** *all sins will be forgiven:* Jesus affirms both the universality of God's pardon for all sins and the impossibility of pardon for a blasphemy against the Holy Spirit. **29.** *whoever blasphemes against the Holy Spirit:* This seems to contradict v. 28. The unforgivable sin is that which ascribes Jesus' works to the power of one other than God's Holy Spirit manifest in Jesus' victory over the demons. See comment on Mt 12:31.

(Barrett, C. K., *The Holy Spirit and the Gospel Tradition* [London, 1947] 59–63. Roulin, P., "Le péché contre l'Esprit," *BiViChr* 29 [1959] 38–45. Williams, J. G., "A Note on the 'Unforgivable Sin' Logion," *NTS* 12 [1965–66] 75–77.)

31. *his brothers:* See comments on Gal 1:19; Mt 12:46 (→ Aspects NT Thought, 78:167). **33.** *who are my mother and my brothers?:* The pronouncement, for the sake of which the episode was recalled, is full of disappointment. It is not inconsistent with a tender care for kinsmen. **34.** *looking around at them:* See 3:5. **35.** *whoever does God's will:* Jesus does not deny his natural kinship but radically subordinates it to a higher bond of brotherhood. The reign of God makes demands on the personal commitment of a disciple, which must transcend at times all natural bonds of family or ethnic grouping. However one interprets this passage about the "brothers" of Jesus, it is to be noted that the doctrine of Mary's perpetual virginity is not based on Marcan texts.

24 (ii) *Preaching in parables* (4:1–34). This passage is a redactional unit comprising three parables (3–9, 26–29, 30–32), two sayings (21–23, 24–25), the interpretation of a parable (10, 13–20), a saying about the purpose of parables (11–12), an introduction (1–2), and a conclusion (33–34). Its composite character appears from the following: (1) At the beginning and end (vv. 1, 33–34) Jesus is addressing the crowds from a boat; in v. 10 the scene changes and Jesus is alone with his disciples. (2) The saying in vv. 11–12 separates the sower parable (3–9) from its interpretation (13–20). (3) This interpretation (13–20) as well as the sayings (21–25), although addressed to the same audience, are each introduced by Mark's typical linking formula *kai elegen autois* (13, 21, 24), "and he said to them." (4) The interpretation of the parable of the sower is itself a catechetical rereading of Jesus' original parable (3–9). (5) The question in v. 10 receives two answers with two different introductory formulas: In v. 11 Jesus gives a generalizing explanation of why he speaks in parables; this is introduced by the Marcan formula *kai elegen autois*. In 13–20 he explains only the sower parable; this is introduced by the formula *kai legei autois*, which also occurs in 7:18 to introduce the interpretation of a specific parabolic saying. Since the interpretations of the parables probably did not circulate independently of the parables themselves, and that of vv. 13–20 is clearly not the one primarily intended by Jesus, it is likely that in the pre-Marcan tradition the interpretation (13–20) was immediately joined to the parable (3–9), just as 7:18b–25 was joined to 7:15 (see also comment on 7:14–23).

Several stages in the elaboration of 4:1–34 may be conjectured: (1) The earliest tradition combined the three parables by the pre-Marcan formula *kai elegen* (26, 30). (2) Either because the original point of Jesus' parable of the sower became obscure, or because the early Church wished to draw a new catechetical lesson from it, the allegorical interpretation (13–20) was elaborated and joined to Jesus' parable by means of the question in v. 10 and the formula *kai legei autois* (v. 11). In Mark's source the disciples most likely questioned Jesus not about his parables in general but about the parable of the sower in particular. (3) Into this complex the Evangelist introduced a second and more generalizing answer in vv. 11–12, introduced by his typical formula *kai elegen autois*, and accordingly changed the singular "parable" to "parables" (v. 10). Finally he introduced two other parabolic sayings in vv. 21–23, 24–25. "Moreover he has worked over the framework: *palin, ērxato, synagetai* [hist. pres.], *kai elegen autois, didachē* [vv. 1f.] are linguistic characteristics of Mark; he has expanded the details about the audience in v. 10 by the addition of vv. 11f.; v. 34, too, must come from him, since the phrase *chōris de parabolēs* is a reference to v. 11b [but see comment on vv. 33–34 below]. The three stages of the tradition [Jesus . . . the primitive Church . . . Mark] are recognizable throughout the whole of Mark's Gospel, but nowhere so clearly as in ch. 4" (J. Jeremias, *Parables*, 14, n. 11).

(Boobyer, G. H., "The Redaction of Mk 4:1–34," *NTS* 8 [1961–62] 59–70. Gealy, F. D., "The Composition of Mk 4," *ExpT* 48 [1936–37] 40–43. Marxsen, W., "Redaktionsgeschichtliche Erklärung der sogenannten Parabeltheorie des Markus," *ZThK* 52 [1955] 255–71. Riddle, D. W., "Mk

4:1–34: The Evolution of a Gospel Source," *JBL* 56 [1937] 77–90.)

25 (A) The Sower (4:1–9). **1.** *again he began to teach beside the sea:* This notice resumes the narrative of 3:7–12 after the Marcan interpolation of 3:13–35. **2.** *in parables* (On the nature, purpose, and literary form of the parables, → Aspects NT Thought, 78:131–145). **3.** *a sower went out to sow:* Although the parable begins without an introductory formula, what is meant is that "It is the case with God's kingdom as with a sower who..." (J Dupont, *BeO* 6 [1965] 247–53). **4–8.** *along the path, on rocky ground, among briars, into good soil:* The parable consists essentially in a contrast between the three types of unfruitful soil and the good soil in which the seed grows to maturity. It is on the latter that the accent falls (cf. the Pharisee and the publican, Lk 18:9–14). God's kingdom, like an abundant harvest (cf. Ps 76:17; Hos 6:11; Is 27:6), will surely come despite the various setbacks encountered by the sower. Such a lesson accords with a more advanced stage of Jesus' ministry, when reality seemed to belie the expectations of the people awaiting a great purification before the *eschaton* (cf. Mt 3:10–12 par.). Jesus' parable gives assurance: despite all the disillusionments engendered by the course of his ministry, it is still only the preparatory phase of God's kingdom. "Between his ministry, apparently so modest, and the glorious coming of God's kingdom, Jesus establishes a cause-and-effect relationship, comparable to that between the sowing and the harvest" (J. Dupont, *Assemblées du Seigneur* 23 [1964] 41). **8.** *thirtyfold, sixtyfold, hundredfold:* A 20-to-1 ratio would have been considered an extraordinary harvest. Jesus' strikingly large figures are intended to underscore the prodigious quality of God's glorious kingdom still to come. An implicit warning to be prepared for the coming of God's kingdom by an upright life is the secondary lesson that is taught in the allegorical interpretation of the parable in vv. 13–20. **9.** *whoever has ears to hear, let him hear:* This verse, appended to the parable as an introduction to its interpretation (vv. 10,13–20) implies that not everyone is capable of understanding the parable.

26 (B) The Purpose of Parables (4:10–12). Mark has inserted three verses, or at least vv. 11–12, between the parable and its interpretation. Dodd contends that this saying was created by the early Church to answer the question, "Why did the Church fail to win the Jews to Christ?" However, Schmid, Jeremias, and Cerfaux regard it as an authentic saying of Jesus on the basis of its highly Semitic character. Moreover, the quotation of Is 6:9–10 in Mk 4:10 follows neither the MT nor the LXX, but an Aram translation then in use. The saying may be an authentic logion that has been isolated from its primitive *Sitz im Leben Jesu* and attracted to this context by the catchword *parabolē*.

10. *when he was alone:* See comment on 1:29. *those about him with the Twelve:* A cumbrous phrase to designate "the disciples" (thus Mt 13:10; Lk 8:9; cf. Mk 10:10) or possibly "those about him who belonged to the company of the Twelve" (R. P. Meye, *SE* 2, 211–18). **11.** *"to you...to those outside":* The latter may originally have designated those mentioned in 3:32 (J. Coutts, "'Those Outside,'" *SE* 2, 155–57). Viewed against the rest of Mk, however, the expression presupposes the division between the Jews who by their rejection of Christ have forfeited their privileges, and the new community that replaces the old Israel (cf. Mk 12:9). In the midst of an obdurate Israel, Jesus gathers a new community destined to receive the secret of God's kingdom. *has been given:* "God has given" (theol. pass., see *GrBib* § 236). The communication of this secret takes the form of an *epilysis*, an "explanation" of what they do not understand; see 4:34. *the secret of God's kingdom:* Mt and Lk have the plural *mystēria*, "the secrets," probably more original than Mk's singular (cf. Dn 2:28; 1QM 16:11; 1QpHab 7:4–5,8; 1QH 4:23–4; *Enoch* 46:2; L. Cerfaux, *NTS* 2 [1955–56] 241).

The content of the "secret" may be determined, first, from the parallels in the pseudepigrapha and in QL where the word *rāz* refers to "divine providence and its workings in reference to man's salvation" (R. E. Brown, *Bib* 39 [1958] 430). More specifically the word is used there with the connotation that "evil can impede good in the world...until God's judgment" (e.g., *2 Baruch* 81:4). This connotation is present in Jesus' references to the rocky ground and the briars that impede the fruitfulness of the seed. "Thus it is no novelty to Hebr thought that the varied success of God's kingdom on earth is seen as a divine mystery" (*ibid.*). Within Mk, the content of the "secret" may be further determined by those passages where the disciples show a lack of understanding in the face of what Jesus reveals of himself (4:13–20,36–41; 6:45–52; 7:14–15; 8:14–21; 9:31–2; 10:2–12; 13:3). Thus *to mystērion* is the knowledge that God's kingdom has irrupted with Jesus, the hidden Messiah, along with the reversal of values that his coming effects. *everything is in parables:* Since *parabolē* can mean not only "parable" but also "riddle," "symbol," etc., and since Jesus speaks of "everything" being *en parabolais*, commentators such as Masson (*Les paraboles de Marc IV* [Neuchâtel-Paris, 1945] 28), Lohmeyer (*Markus*, 83–84), Jeremias (*Parables*, 16–18), Schmid (*Markus*, 93–94), Schnackenburg (*God's Rule and Kingdom* [N.Y., 1963] 184–86), and Gnilka (*Die Verstockung Israels*, 24–28) believe that Jesus' saying was not originally concerned with the purpose of parables alone but with the effect of his ministry in general: "To those outside everything becomes a riddle." The Evangelist, however, understood *parabolē* in the more restricted sense of "parable." **12.** *so that:* Since the words following this conjunction are a free quotation of Is 6:9–10, it is reasonable to fill out Mark's thought thus: "in order that [as it is written] they might see...." Thus, Jesus would not have used parables with the intention of withholding the truth from outsiders. (For the purpose or result meaning of the conj. *hina*, see *GrBib* § 412–14, 426.) On the other hand, it is quite possible that Mark is giving an accurate picture of Jesus' pedagogy here, for it was a traditional idea that God withheld his revelation from sinners (Nm 12:8, *2 Baruch* 48:2–3; *2 Esdras* 12:36–7; 1QS 4:6; 9:17,22). Moreover, two-thirds of the Syn parables (41 out of 63) are explained by Jesus, but rarely to nondisciples; those that are explained to them do not deal with the heart of the Gospel message, God's kingdom. Hence it is difficult to ascribe this "parable theory" only to the Evangelist (J. A. Baird, *JBL* 76 [1957] 201–7; → Aspects NT Thought, 78:139). *lest [perhaps] they should turn:* Jeremias (*Parables*, 15) argues that the original Aram *dilᵉmā* would have meant "unless they turn." This would tone down the severity of the statement, but it is questionable whether the Gk *mēpote* can be so understood.

(Burkill, T. A., "The Crypotology of the Parables in St. Mark's Gospel," *NovT* 1 [1956] 246–62. Manson, T. W., "The Purpose of the Parables: A Re-Examination of Mk 4:10–12," *ExpT* 68 [1956–57] 132–35. Siegman, E. F., "Teaching in Parables," *CBQ* 23 [1961] 161–81.)

27 (C) Interpretation of the Parable of the Sower (4:13–20). Both the un-Hebraic style and vocabulary and the allegorical features of this passage suggest that it is an interpretation of the primitive Church rather than of Jesus (J. Jeremias, *Parables*, 77–79). More significantly, it bypasses the main eschatological point of Jesus' parable and, by concentrating on the different types of unfruitful soil, draws a moralistic lesson of perseverance in temptation and persecution. "The word," which appears eight times in these verses, is a Christian term for the Gospel message (Acts 6:7; 12:24; Col 1:6,10; 1 Thes 1:6; 1 Tm 1:8; 1 Pt 2:8; Jas 1:21). **20.** *bear fruit:* The presence of this theme suggests a setting of baptismal instruction as the origin of this passage (cf. Mt 3:7–12; 13:3–8,18–23; Rom 6:21–22; 7:4–6; Gal 5:22–24; Phil 1:11; Eph 5:8–11; Col 1:10–13; R. J. Dillon, *Bib* 47 [1966] 21–33).

(D) Sayings on Concealment and Disclosure (4:21–25). Here Mark arranges a series of disconnected logia into a double parable, 21–23 and 24–25. **21.** *is a lamp brought in to be put under a bushel?:* This saying and its explanation in v. 22 correspond to 4:11–12; parables conceal the truth from outsiders, but the truth will ultimately be disclosed. **24–25.** *the measure you give will be the measure you receive:* Corresponding to 4:13–20, these sayings are a call to an attentive hearing of God's word.

28 (E) Parable of the Seed (4:26–29). **26.** *as when a man scatters seed on the ground:* Like the sower parable, this parable is essentially a contrast between the inactivity of the farmer after sowing, and the harvest (the fulfillment of God's kingdom). The kingdom will surely come because it has already irrupted into the world in Jesus' ministry, and like the seed will inevitably produce a harvest. This point is expressed in v. 29: but when the grain is ripe, he at once puts in the "sickle, because the harvest has come"; cf. Jl 3:13. The details of the seed's growth, however, also appear to be essential to the parable. **27–28.** *the seed sprouts and grows he knows not how:* Jesus thus makes the additional point that God's kingdom does not come abruptly but grows inexorably from hidden beginnings. Jesus' parable may originally have been both an assurance that the coming of God's kingdom was inevitable and an apologia for his not attempting to establish this kingdom by a forceful intervention; to do so would have been to nip the grain prematurely.

(F) The Mustard Seed (4:30–32). **31.** *the smallest of all the seeds:* It is really not, but this is not the point. Jesus contrasts its insignificant beginnings with the unexpected size of the full-grown bush. **32.** *it becomes the greatest of all trees:* The tree as an image of God's rule is found in Jgs 9:15 and in 1QH 6:14b–17; 8:4–9, where, as here, the comparison is based on Dn 4:7–9,11,17–19; Ez 17:23; 31:1–9; cf. F. Mussner, *BZ* 4 (1960) 128–30. *the birds of the air nest in its shade:* An allusion to Dn 4:21 (Theodotion) where God's kingdom is compared to that of Nebuchadnezzar whose empire reached to the ends of the earth, giving shelter to all peoples. Both the contrast between the tiny seed and the full-grown tree, as well as the notion of its growth, are essential elements in the parable. They symbolize the organic continuity between Jesus' ministry, so disappointing to Israel's hopes, and the future Kingdom of God, which would encompass the Gentiles as well as Israel.

29 (G) Conclusion (4:33–34). **33.** *he spoke the word to them as they were able to hear it:* That is, in proportion as they could understand it. This verse presupposes that the people understand the parables to some extent; but this seems to be at variance with v. 34. *he did not speak to them except in parables, but privately to his own disciples he explained everything:* This verse seems to say that the parables were unintelligible unless "solved," and that this solution was reserved only to the disciples. Many commentators think that v. 33 reflects Jesus' intention in using parables—to disclose the truth, and that v. 34 reflects Mark's assumption that they were meant to conceal the truth from outsiders. It is equally possible, however, that both verses are pre-Marcan and reflect the view that the true meaning of a parable is unattainable unless accompanied by an explanation such as that found in 4:13–20. Thus, "he explained everything" would have meant "he unraveled the allegorical meaning of all the parables." The Evangelist's view, however, is different. It is not only that the disciples received a solution to the parables; more significantly, they received the secret of God's kingdom, and that not only in Jesus' explanation of the parables, but in his whole course of instruction to them. Accordingly, the explanation of the parables was only one moment of the process by which Jesus initiated his disciples into the secret of God's kingdom. The discrepancy, therefore, is not between vv. 33 and 34, but between the meaning of the two verses as understood in Mark's source, and their meaning as understood against the background of the whole Marcan Gospel. (See J. Gnilka, *Verstockung*, 62–64, 82–83.)

30 (iii) *Miracles* (4:35–5:43). After the three parables Mk recounts three miracles performed for the benefit of the disciples.

(A) Stilling of the Storm (4:35–41). This pericope is frequently taken to be based on a personal recollection of Peter. Nevertheless the event has been so reworked in its transmission that it is all but impossible to isolate the brute fact from its credal interpretation in the Church. G. Schille (*ZNW* 56 [1965] 30–40) has isolated the basic text consisting of four triadic strophes (4:37,38a,39,41a), which is an early Christian confession of Jesus' power as a wonder-worker. This was then expanded by 4:35–36,38b,40,41b. The mention of the boat in 35, 36, 38b, and 40 introduces an ecclesial nuance. The emphasis on the storm and the need of faith (38b,40) make the incident a lesson in discipleship under stress; and the use of the pres. *hypakouei* (obey, v. 41b) indicates that Jesus' power is still operative in the Church. Excluding the two introductory verses, the pericope may be set out schematically as follows:

Primitive Creed	*Later Accretions*
37 And a great windstorm arose, and the waves beat into the boat, so that the boat was already filling.	
38 And he was in the stern, asleep on the cushion, and they woke him	and said to him, "Teacher, do you not care if we perish?"
39 And awaking he rebuked the wind, and said to the sea, "Silence; be still." And the wind abated, and there was a great calm.	40 And he said to them, "Why are you afraid? Do you not yet have faith?"
41 And they were filled with awe, and said to one another, "Who then is this	that even wind and sea obey him?"

35. *late in the day:* In context this notice may have symbolic meaning. See comment following 5:20. **36.** *just as he was:* This redactional touch of Mark links the miracle more closely with the foregoing context (cf. 4:1). *leaving the crowd:* This and the following miracles are performed for the disciples' benefit. *other boats were with him:* Nevertheless there is an indication that originally this miracle interested a larger audience than just the Twelve (cf. also 5:20 and the repeated mention of the crowds in 5:21–43). **37.** *the boat:* On the boat as an image of the Church, see H. Rahner, "Navicula Petri," *ZKT* 69 (1947) 1–35; E. Hilgert, *The Ship and Related Symbols in the NT* (Assen, 1962); K. Goldammer, "Navis ecclesiae," *ZNW* 40 (1941) 76–86. **38.** *the cushion:* More exactly, the helmsman's seat on the high afterdeck, where Jesus would have been protected from the splash of the waves. *said to him:* What marks this latter part of the verse as an accretion to the early creed is that elsewhere in Mk the vocative "Teacher" always occurs in catechetical passages (9:17,38; 10:17,20,35; 12:14,19,32; 13:1), and that the occurrence of such titles in miracle stories is clearly motivated by catechetical interests (e.g:, see comments on 1:26; 2:10). **39.** *he rebuked the wind:* As if it were a demon; see 1:25. *said to the sea, "Silence. Be still":* Lit., "be muzzled." The religious implication of this miracle is seen in its OT background, where God's work in creation is described as a conquest of the sea or sea dragon (Gn 1:2; Ps 89:10; Job 9:8; 26:12–13) and is paralleled by his deliverance of Israel (Ps 74:12–14; Is 51:9; Ex 15:8; Is 63:12–13). Here Jesus shows the same divine mastery over the sea in his own redemptive ministry. **40.** *"Why are you afraid? Do you not yet have faith?":* Some mss. read, "Why do you not have faith?", which brings out less clearly that it is a question of faith in Jesus. The fact that the disciples are not merely "of little faith" (Mt 8:26), but have no faith, seems inconsistent with a pre-resurrection situation. It looks like the Evangelist's own comment, and may have been prompted by a reminiscence of the disciples' loss of faith at Jesus' death. **41.** *that even wind and sea obey him:* The addition of these words to the disciples' question in v. 41a is tantamount to an answer: he is God (see comment on v. 39 above). This manner of answering one's own question about Jesus is a characteristically catechetical amplification (cf. Mk 1:27; 2:7). The use of the pres. tense "obey" shows that this event was recounted not so much as a past historical incident, but as symbolic of Christ's abiding power to rescue his Church from tribulation (see P. Achtemeier, *Interpr* 16 [1962] 169–76).

31 (B) The Gerasene Maniac (5:1–20). This is one of the most difficult miracle stories to interpret, because (granted the factual value of the swine's stampede into the sea) it is difficult to see its connection with the exorcism of the maniac. To explain the incident as an anecdote about the blindness of the Gentiles who prefer their unclean animals to their own Savior (A. George, *BulComEt* 5 [1961] 396–97) is to bypass this problem. More satisfying, although equally conservative, is the view of A. Richardson for whom "the story teaches that evil is self-destructive; it cannot exist by itself, but only in so far as it can gain a foothold in the good" (*Miracle Stories*, 72–74). Without pronouncing on its factual character, T. A. Burkill thinks that originally the story circulated "in the primitive communities as an account of the way in which Jesus won fame in a foreign land, and it is not impossible that the action of the healed man at the end [5:18] would be seen as a sort of anticipation of the work of apostolic missionaries" (*ST* 11 [1957] 166). H. Sahlin believes that this is a midrash, i.e., a story elaborated on an original factual datum, for the sake of showing Jesus as the Savior of the Gentiles in the light of Is 65:1–5. Without admitting that it is a "midrash," this hypothetical explanation is acceptable, (1) because the theme of Jesus' relations with Gentiles is further developed in Mk 7:24–37; 8:1–10, and (2) because a comparison with other Marcan incidents gives one to suspect that what are customarily considered to be graphic eyewitness details may in reality be a form of religious interpretation. To explain this pericope in this way, therefore, is not to deny its historical basis, but to recognize that certain details may be literary amplifications in the interest of the primary theological point: that Jesus' victorious confrontation with the power of the demons was not without interest to those outside Judaism.

1. *the country of the Gerasenes:* Gerasa (Jerash) is 33 mi. SE of Lake Gennesaret and therefore an unsuitable locale in view of 5:13. Variant readings are "Gadarenes" (of Gadara, 6 mi. SE of the lake) and "Gergesenes" (of Gergesa, an otherwise unidentified place). At all events Jesus is in pagan territory, and his presence there reflects Is 65:1. **2.** *out of the tombs:* This detail is stressed again in vv. 3 and 5; cf. Is 65:4. *no one could bind him any more.* Mk dwells graphically on the impossibility of subduing the maniac, perhaps as an image of the rebellious people described in Is 65:2. **7.** *why do you meddle with me:* See comment on 1:24. *Son of the Most High?:* The adj. *hypsistos* (= Hebr *'elyôn*) is a typically Gentile designation for the God of Israel (Dn 3:26; 4:2). The maniac's desire to keep Jesus at a distance may correspond to Is 65:5a. **9.** *what is your name?:* Jesus is pictured as over-powering his adversary by learning his name; see comment on 1:24. *Legion:* Jeremias suggests that the Aram original read *ligyônā* (soldier); thus, "My name is 'Soldier,' since we [demons] are a great host [and resemble one another as soldiers do]." A translator understood the Aram word for its alternate meaning, "legion," thought that this indicated a plurality of demons, and accordingly added vv. 12–13 (*Jesus' Promise to the Nations* [London, 1958] 30–31). This would explain why, outside of vv. 10, 12, 13, there is no indication that the man was possessed by more than one demon. **11.** *a great herd of swine:* Cf. Is 65:4, where the people are said to sit in tombs, pass the night in caves, and eat the flesh of swine. **13.** *the herd, numbering about 2000, stampeded down the cliff into the sea:* On Sahlin's hypothesis this is an image of the annihilation of the power that held the Gentiles captive (cf. Elijah's slaughter of the prophets of Baal, 1 Kgs 18:40). **15.** *they were afraid:* This looks like the original ending of the miracle story. If so, vv. 16–17 would have been added to supply a motive for Jesus' withdrawal to the other side of the lake (5:21). **18–20.** These verses may have been an integral part of the original story, complementing the reaction of the people mentioned in v. 15: Jesus is shown to be as humane as he was awe-inspiring (Burkill). The present style and vocabulary, however, betray the Evangelist's hand and his interest to interpret this event as an image of the Gentiles seeking to follow Christ. **19.** *he refused:* It is useless to speculate on why Jesus did not allow the man to become a disciple. The important thing is that here Jesus does not enjoin "Messianic secrecy" as he does upon Jews (1:43–4; 3:12; 5:43; 7:36; 8:26), and that the man goes out to "proclaim" how much Jesus had done for him.

(Burkill, T. A., "Concerning Mk 5:7 and 5:18–20," *ST* 11 [1957] 159–66. Sahlin, H., "Die Perikope vom gerasenischen Besessenen und der Plan des Markusevangeliums," *ST* 18 [1964] 159–72.)

32 (C) Jairus' Daughter (5:21–24,35–43) and the Woman with the Hemorrhage (5:25–34). The inter-position of one narrative within another occurs in four other places in Mk: 3:19b–21 (22–30) 31–35; 6:6b–13 (14–29) 30; 11:12–14 (15–19) 20–25; 14:53 (54) 55–65 (66–73). **22.** *one of the synagogue leaders:* Jairus' confident demeanor toward Jesus contrasts with the hostility of the scribes (2:6,16,24; 3:6,22). **23.** *lay your hands on her:* Healing through the imposition of hands is not mentioned in the OT or in rabbinical writings. It does occur, however, in 1QapGn 20:28–29. The verbs used there, *smk* and *g'r*, appear in the LXX as *epitithēmi* (lay upon) and *epitimaō* (rebuke) and recur in NT healings and exorcisms (Mk 6:5; 7:32; 8:23–25; 16:18; Lk 4:40–41; 13:13; Acts 9:12,17–18; 28:8; perhaps also Mk 1:31; 9:27; Mt 9:29 (see J. A. Fitzmyer, *The Genesis Apocryphon of Qumran Cave I* [Rome, 1966] 124–25). *that she may be cured and live:* The verbs are typical of Christian catechesis and, on the deeper level, mean "that she may be saved and have [eternal] life."

25. *a woman with a hemorrhage:* A uterine issue of blood made her ceremonially defiled (Lv 15:19,25). **27.** *reports about Jesus:* The expression *ta peri tou Iēsou* most often refers to the paschal proclamation of Christ (cf. Lk 24:19,27,44; Acts 13:29; 18:25; 23:11; 28:31). **28.** *I will be cured:* See comment on 5:23. The woman's demeanor, as that of Jairus, is presented as a paradigm of access to Christ in faith. **30.** *power:* Jesus is described as possessing an almost magical healing power that operates automatically upon contact with him. Accordingly the following verses correct a possible misunderstanding and show that faith is a necessary disposition, at least in order for the miracle to effect the deeper saving reality it symbolizes. **33.** *in fear and trembling:* Found elsewhere only when used by Paul to describe specifically Christian sentiments (1 Cor 2:3; 2 Cor 7:15; Eph 6:5; Phil 2:12). **34.** *your faith:* See comment on 2:5. *has cured you:* Or "has brought you salvation." *be cured of your disease: Mastix* (disease; cf. 3:10; 5:29; Lk 7:21) means lit. "a scourge" or "whip" and suggests that disease was regarded as a punishment for sin (Ps 38:11; 2 Mc 7:37; cf. Mk 1:30).

35. *your daughter is dead:* This news raises the question of Jairus' faith not only in Jesus' healing power (5:23), but in his power to raise the dead. *why trouble the rabbi any further?:* The messengers' words betray their own lack of faith. **36.** *do not be afraid:* See comment on 6:50. *only believe:* See comment on 2:5. **37.** *Peter, James, and John:* See comment on 1:29. The presence of the close disciples is intentionally stressed by Mk (cf. 5:21); it is largely for their instruction that Jesus performs the miracles of 4:35–5:43. **38.** *commotion, people weeping and wailing:* Jesus pays no heed to such lamentation but proceeds to give a lesson, by word and deed, on the true meaning of death. **39.** *asleep:* It is impossible to decide whether Jesus means this literally or theologically (i.e., her death is only a sleep). The paschal outlook of the Gospel, however, makes it clear that for Mark Jesus' miracles symbolize the passage from death (bondage to sin and the devil) to new life. **40.** *they laughed at him:* The vb. *katagelan* occurs only here and in the par. of Mt and Lk. In Acts 17:32 Paul's mention of the resurrection of the dead meets with similar scorn. **41.** *talitha koum[i]:* As elsewhere (3:17; 7:11,34; 11:9–10; 14:36; 15:22,34) Mark preserves the Hebr or Aram words and translates them for his Gentile readers. *get up:* Lit., "rise"; see comment on 1:31. **42.** *she arose:* The vb. *anistēmi* and its cog. noun *anastasis* are used of Christ's resurrection (Mk 8:31; 9:9,31; 10:34; Acts 1:22; 2:24,31,32; 4:33; 10:41; 13:33,34; 17:3,31; Rom 1:4). *beside themselves with amazement:* The expressions of amazement are unusually strong here; significantly, the same verb and its cog. noun (*existēmi*, *ekstasis*) are used here as in 3:21 where Jesus' relatives accuse him of insanity. Thus the section 3:19b–5:43 is held together by a "inclusion."

33 (c) CONCLUSION: JESUS IS REJECTED BY HIS TOWNSPEOPLE (6:1–6a). **1.** *his native town:* Presumably Nazareth (cf. 1:9). But *patris* can also mean "homeland," and thus Nazareth's rejection of her native son foreshadows the final rejection by his people. **2.** *teach:* See comment on 1:21. There is a certain similarity between this passage and 1:21–27; but whereas Jesus' first appearance in the synagogue met with enthusiasm for his teaching and miracles, here enthusiasm yields first to skepticism (v. 3a), then to opposition (v. 3b), and finally to disbelief (v. 6a). *where did this man get all this?:* Questions like this punctuate Mk (1:27; 2:7; 4:41), in function of an ever-increasing disclosure of Jesus' person and mission. **3.** *the carpenter, the son of Mary?:* Without any explanation, admiration changes to resentment. Mk 6:3 is the only NT text that calls Jesus "the son of Mary." It was Jewish custom to refer to a man as the son of his father (cf. Lk 3:23; 4:22; Jn 1:45; 6:42). Thus "son of Mary" may be intended as an insult (R. H. Lightfoot, *History and Interpretation in the Gospels* [N.Y., 1934] 187–88). Considering Origen's statement (*Contra Celsum* 6.36) that nowhere in the Gospels is Jesus spoken of as a carpenter, and the fact that the Chester Beatty Papyrus (P^{45}) and the minuscule mss. of fam. 13 read "the son of the carpenter," as does Mt 13:55, it may be that "son of Mary" is also a faulty reading. *brother, sisters:* See comment on 3:31. *of James:* Not one of the Twelve; probably the first bishop of Jerusalem (Eusebius, *HE* 2.23,1) who may have been one of the additional "apostles" (→ Letter Gal, 49:15). The other brothers, Joses, Judas, and Simon are unknown. *took offense:* By the time Mk was written *skandalizomai* and its cog. noun *skandalon* (stumbling block) were technical terms to describe the effect of Christ's death on Israel (Rom 9:33; 1 Cor 1:23; Gal 5:11). **4.** *a prophet is not without honor:* This saying, in a form closer to Lk 4:24, is preserved in the Coptic *Gospel according to Thomas*, 31: "No prophet is acceptable in his village; no physician cures those who know him." **5.** *he could do no mighty work there:* A perfect illustration of the latter part of the saying in v. 4. Jesus' miraculous power was rendered ineffective by the disbelief of his countrymen. Mt 13:58 changes "could not" to "did not." Possibly Mark intended this "not as an indication of the impotence of Jesus in face of the disrespect of his compatriots, but as an impressive illustration...[that] those who do not show the respect and honor which are due to the divine prophet, necessarily preclude themselves from receiving the marvelous benefits which he can bestow upon them" (Burkill, *Mysterious Revelation*, 139). *except:* As in 12:41–44, Mark is quick to point out that not all his fellow countrymen rejected Jesus. **6.** *their lack of faith:* Like *skandalon* (v. 3), *apistia* had also come to designate the disbelief of Israel (cf. Rom 3:3; 11:30).

The significance of this episode is obvious: it is a dramatic and tragic end of Jesus' Galilean ministry foreshadowing the greater rejection of Israel; at the same time, it signals a new phase of the ministry in which the Twelve will play a more active role (6:7–13,30) as an anticipation of the mission of the apostolic Church, especially toward those outside Judaism (see comments on 7:1–23,24–30; 8:1–10).

(Burkill, T. A., *Mysterious Revelation*, 137–40. Lightfoot, R. H., *History and Interpretation in the Gospels*, 182–205.)

34 **(C) Jesus and His Disciples (6:6b–8:33).**

(a) INTRODUCTION (6:6b–34).

(i) *Summary statement* (6:6b). *he circulated through the villages:* This summary begins a new phase of

Jesus' ministry; rejected by his own townspeople and relatives, he devotes himself to his disciples, whose mission is being prepared. Mark is fond of pointing out that Jesus preached in the country villages (1:38; 5:14; 6:56); contrast Mt 9:35. *teaching:* See comment on 1:21.

(ii) *Mission charge and return of the disciples* (6:7–13,30). A comparison of this episode with Syn parallel material makes it likely that both Mark and Matthew were drawing on an earlier account, which included as a unit: (1) the institution of the Twelve (Mk 3:13–19; Mt 10:1–4; Lk 6:12–16), (2) the sending out of the disciples (Mk 6:7,12–13; Mt 10:1–4; Lk 9:1–2,6; 10:1), and (3) a discourse of Jesus to the departing missionaries (Mk 6:8–11; Mt 10:5–42; Lk 9:3–5; 10:2–16). Mark has separated (1) from (2) and has drastically abbreviated (3). The effect of these redactional changes in Mk is to present the mission of the disciples less as an account of their preaching than as a preparation for Jesus' self-revelation to them as the Messiah. **7.** *he called to him the Twelve:* Close comparison will show that Mark composed 6:7,12–13 as a parallel of 3:13–19, and indirectly of 1:17–20. His separating the institution of the Twelve from the mission charge is a literary artifice that places the latter after Jesus had begun to preach in parables. Matthew may be closer to the fact in placing it before that point in Jesus' ministry, for Jesus apparently did not begin to use parables until after he had experienced a certain disappointment with the crowds. In fact, his use of this method of teaching represented a certain withdrawal from them. **8.** *he charged them:* This same verb is used in Mt to introduce the mission discourse in 10:5; in Mk, however, there are only the slightest vestiges of a discourse, and even the instructions Jesus gives show differences.

Mt 10:9–10	*Mk 6:8–9*
Take no gold, nor silver,	And he charged them
nor money in your belts,	to take nothing for their
no bag for your journey,	journey
nor two shirts, nor sandals,	*except a staff; no bread,* no bag,
nor a staff;	no money in their belts;
for a laborer deserves his	but to *wear* sandals
food.	and not *put on* two shirts.

Mark has adapted Jesus' instructions by introducing several exceptions that suggest a later stage of missionary activity—that of the Church outside Palestine. For the same reason Mark omits mention of the prohibition to go "among the Gentiles or to any Samaritan town" (Mt 10:5). *no bread:* This mention is emphatic. It prepares for the miracles in 6:35–44 and 8:1–9, where Jesus himself will give bread. **10.** *and he said to them:* Mark's customary linking formula. *wherever you enter a house:* The instruction in this verse is an abbreviation of what Mt reports more fully in 10:11–14. The effect is to highlight the acceptance or nonacceptance of the disciples rather than the eschatological lesson in Mt 10:15. The latter is only suggested in Mk's words, "for a testimony against them," i.e., as proof that they are condemned for rejecting the disciples. **12.** *men should repent:* According to Lk 9:2; 10:9, the disciples proclaim the imminence of God's kingdom; according to Mk, this proclamation is reserved to Jesus, whereas the disciples and the Baptist preach repentance (1:4,15; cf. Mt 3:2) as a preparation for Jesus' proclamation of the kingdom (see comment on 4:10–12). **13.** *drove out many demons:* A prolongation of Jesus' own Messianic activity (1:34,39,43; 3:22–23; 7:26). *anointed many sick people with oil:* The curative powers of the disciples also prolong those of Jesus (1:34; 3:2,10; 6:5). In the anointing with oil the Church sees a prefigurement of the sacramental anointing of the sick. Mark does not explicitly connect this with either Jesus' own practice or with any command to the disciples, although it was apparently a Palestinian custom (Jas 5:14–15; cf. P. Hoyos, *RstaB* 25 [1963] 34–42).

35 (iii) *Interlude: Opinions about Jesus* (6:14–16). In Mk the notice (about Herod's opinion of Jesus) is fuller than that found in Mt 14:1–2; 6:14b–15 (about the opinions of others) is an anticipation of 8:28. The emphasis falls on this addition and sets the theme of the entire section down to 8:30: Who is Jesus? **14.** *King Herod:* Herod Antipas, tetrarch of Galilee and Perea (→ History of Israel, 75:140). *heard:* What he heard is not explained, possibly the disciples' miracles (6:12–13) or the fame of Jesus (6:14a)—or a combination of the two, implying that the disciples' activity resulted in renown for Jesus. *people were saying:* The pl. *elegon* is found in the mss. B, D; VL; an important variant is *elegen,* "he [i.e., Herod] said." Many commentators prefer the former because Mark is concerned here not with Herod's opinion but with that of "the people," "others" (15a), and "still others" (15b). *John the Baptizer has risen from the dead:* This view could only have been shared by those who had never seen Jesus and John together while they were living. This identification attests that Jesus was also thought to be the eschatological prophet (O. Cullmann, *Christology of the NT,* 31–34). *powers are at work in him:* The identification of Jesus with John *redivivus,* made on the basis of their similar behavior, presupposes that John too had performed miracles. The pl. *dynameis* (powers) has a pagan ring that may reflect the thought of inhabitants of Herod's tetrarchy. In the NT Jesus' miracles are often called *dynameis* (Mk 6:2; → Aspects NT Thought, 78:114; cf. W. Grundmann, *ThDNT* 2, 301–3). **15.** *Elijah:* See 1:2; 9:11–13. *a prophet like one of the* [*ancient*] *prophets:* So most mss., but according to ms. D, "he is one of the prophets [returned to life]." In either reading Jesus' presence is seen as a sign of the *eschaton,* but significantly, no one recognizes him as the Messiah. **16.** *John whom I beheaded has risen:* Mark returns to Herod as an introduction to the next passage; the full irony of his opinion becomes apparent in 6:29.

36 (iv) *Interlude: John the Baptist's Death* (6:17–29). Mark presents this as a drama in three scenes.

Scene 1. **17.** *seized John and imprisoned him:* According to Josephus (*Ant.* 18.5,2 § 116–19), Herod imprisoned John in the fortress of Machaerus on the E side of the Dead Sea, where eventually he was put to death. *on account of Herodias, his brother Philip's wife* (For the relationship of Herod and this "Philip," → History of Israel, 75:140). **18.** *it is not right:* The Gospels assign John's rebuke of Herod's adultery as the reason for his death; this does not preclude the further reason mentioned by Josephus—Herod's fear that John's influence might eventually enable him to instigate a rebellion against him. **20.** *Herod stood in awe of John:* Just as the disciples (4:41; 9:32; 10:32), the people (5:15), the healed woman (5:33), even the high priests and scribes (11:18) stood in awe of Jesus. There is in this scene a certain John-Jesus typology. *an upright and holy man:* An early Christian formula applied to Christ (Acts 3:14). *he liked to hear him:* Just as "the mass of the people like to hear" Jesus (12:37).

Scene 2. The attention shifts from the Baptist to Herod who was tricked by Herodias' daughter. Verbal contacts show that the Baptist's death is retold in the light of the story of Esther. **21.** *Herod gave a banquet:* Cf. Est 1:3 (LXX): "[King Xerxes] gave a feast for his friends, and the other nations, and to the notables of the Persians and Medes, and the chief of the satraps." **22.** *Herodias' daughter came in:* Cf. Est 2:15,16. *Herod and his guests were delighted with her:* Cf. Est 2:9. **23.** *up* *to half of my kingdom:* Cf. Est 5:3; 7:2. The frequent references to Herod as "the king" (6:22,25,26,27) recall the same manner of referring to Xerxes in Est.

Scene 3. **27.** *sent a guard with orders:* Cf. Est 1:8; 8:11. **29.** *his disciples came and took his body and laid it in a tomb:* A foreshadowing of Jesus' burial (15:45–46). This closing verse corresponds to the opening verse, 6:16b. Taken together, the two verses anticipate 16:6, and by thus alluding to Jesus' resurrection bring out the irony of Herod's statement in 6:16a.

In summary, Mark has presented the Baptist's death in terms colored by the story of Esther; by developing the parallelism between John and Jesus, he has made it into an anticipation of Jesus' own fate. For other instances of this parallelism, cf. 1:2–14; 9:11–13.

37 The Return of the Apostles (6:30). This verse closes the section begun at 6:7. On the interposition of one narrative within another, see comment on 5:21. This is the only place in Mk where the Twelve are called "apostles," Mark's usual name for them being "disciples." But having just spoken of "his [John's] disciples" in 6:29, he was forced, for clarity's sake, to use another word for the Twelve, and since in 3:14 and 6:7 Jesus "sends them out" (*apostellei*), Mark here calls them *apostoloi*. Here the word means simply "those sent out" rather than "apostles," for the latter term had acquired a technical meaning by the time Mark wrote, which is not fully applicable to the Twelve before Pentecost (→ Aspects NT Thought, 78:172–178). *told him all they had done and taught:* The whole of 6:30 is absent from Mt, where 14:12–13 has a more natural sequence of events. Jesus' retreat to the desert is clearly motivated by Herod's murder of John; in addition, the notice that the disciples had "taught" is at variance with the Syn tradition regarding the nature of their mission, which is to proclaim repentance (Mk 6:12–13) and the coming of God's kingdom (Mt 10:7; Lk 9:2; 10:9). Mk 6:30b represents a postresurrectional viewpoint (cf. Acts 4:2,18; 2:42).

38 (b) THE LOAVES SECTION (6:31–8:26). This section is based upon a presynoptic unit, which L. Cerfaux calls "la section des pains." It is articulated by the two multiplications of bread (6:31–44; 8:1–9) and by a passage recalling both these miracles (8:14–21), giving the following structure:

(1) Feeding of the 5000 (6:31–44)	Feeding of the 4000 (8:1–9)
(2) Crossing the lake (6:45–52)	Crossing the lake (8:10a)
(3) Landing at Gennesaret (6:53–56)	Landing at Dalmanutha (8:10b)
(4) Controversy with Pharisees (7:1–23)	Controversy with Pharisees (8:11–13)
(5) Dialogue with the Syro-Phoenician woman about bread (7:24–30)	Dialogue with the disciples about the bread miracles (8:14–21)
(6) Cure of a deaf-mute (7:31–37)	Cure of a blind man (8:22–26)

39 (i) *The Feeding of the 5000 and its sequel* (6:31–7:37). The series of scenes built about the first story of the multiplication of the loaves is only loosely linked to what precedes.

(A) The Feeding of the 5000 (6:31–44). R. Bultmann would call this account a Miracle Story, whereas V. Taylor (*Mark*, 321) thinks that "it has not yet attained the rounded form of a Miracle-story proper and stands nearer the testimony of eyewitnesses." **31.** *come away by yourselves:* Only Mark emphasizes that Jesus was alone with the Twelve, a detail that presages a revelation of Jesus to them (see 1:29). *rest a little while:* Mt 14:13 suggests that Jesus' withdrawal to the desert was prompted by Herod's murder of John; Mark assigns "rest" after the mission as the motive of Jesus' retreat. The theme of "rest" occurs in the OT to designate the entrance of the Israelites into the promised land after the 40 years in the desert (Dt 3:20; 12:10; 25:19; Jos 1:13,15). It is often connected with the image of God as the shepherd who gives rest to his flock (Is 65:10; Ez 34:15 [both LXX]; Ps 23:2). Thus 6:31 introduces the theme of Jesus as the eschatological shepherd. **34.** *like sheep that have no shepherd:* The motive of Jesus' pity recalls the allegory of the shepherd in Ez 34:5. *he began to teach them:* See comment on 1:21. Jesus' pity moves him to assuage the spiritual hunger of the shepherdless people by bringing God's revelation to them. **35.** *a lonely place:* Lit., "a desert place." The stress on the desert (6:31,33,35), on eating (6:31,36,37,42–44), and on bread (6:37,38,41,44) recalls the miracle of manna (Ex 16:12–35). **39.** *he ordered them all:* The universal significance of this miracle is underscored by the repeated use of "all" (6:33,39,41,42). *sit down:* Lit., "recline" as at table. *in parties:* Lit., "banquet by banquet, eating-party by eating-party." *on the green grass:* This vivid detail, often taken to be an eyewitness recollection that would date the event to early spring around Passover (Jn 6:4), may be only an allusion to Ps 23:2, thus continuing the shepherd and banquet imagery. **40.** *by hundreds and by fifties:* This is possibly an allusion to Moses' apportioning the Israelites into groups of 1000, 100, 50, and 10 (Ex 18:25; Dt 1:15). According to 1QSa 1:14–15; 2:11–12, the same apportionment was to obtain at the Messianic banquet.

41. *took the five loaves:* The original account of Jesus' gestures has been expanded by details from the institution of the Eucharist (14:22). For a detailed analysis see B. van Iersel, *NovT* 7 [1964] 167–94. **42.** *they all ate and were full:* An OT formula recalling the manna (Ps 78:29; 105:40) and the promise of the messianic abundance to come (Is 49:10; cf. 65:10–11; Ps 132:15). **43.** *twelve baskets:* The leftovers, a sign of God's superabundant gifts (Ex 16:19–24; 2 Kgs 4:43–44), are enough to feed the 12 tribes of the new Israel. The customary expressions of wonder are missing at the end of this miracle, corroborating the impression that Mark has presented it less as a miracle than as a Messianic sign intended to disclose to the Twelve the secret of Jesus' person (8:19).

(Boobyer, G. H., "The Eucharistic Interpretation of the Miracle of the Loaves in St. Mark's Gospel," *JTS* 3 [1952] 161–71; "The Miracles of the Loaves and the Gentiles in St. Mark's Gospel," *ScotJT* 6 [1953] 77–87. Cerfaux, L., "La section des pains," *Synoptische Studien* [Fest. A. Wikenhauser; Munich, 1954] 64–77. Clavier, H., "La multiplication des pains dans le ministère de Jésus," *SE* 1, 441–57. Friedrich, G., "Die beiden Erzählungen von der Speisung in Mk 6:31–34; 8:1–9," *TZ* 20 [1964] 10–22. Hebert, A. G., "History in the Feeding of the Five Thousand," *SE* 2, 65–72. Heising, A., "Exegese und Theologie der alt- und neutestamentlichen Speisungswunder," *ZKT* 86 [1964] 80–96. Knackstedt, J., "Die beiden Brotvermehrungen im Evangelium," *NTS* 10 [1963–4] 309–35. Montefiore, H., "Revolt in the Desert?" *NTS* 8 [1961–62] 135–41. Richardson, A., "The Feeding of the 5000," *Interpr* 4 [1965] 144–49. Shaw, A., "The Marcan Feeding Narratives," *ChQR* 162 [1961] 268–78. Ziener, G., "Die Brotwunder im Markusevangelium," *BZ* 4 [1960] 282–85.)

40 (B) Jesus Walks on the Sea (6:45–52). All three accounts (Mk, Mt, Jn) place this miracle after the bread miracle at the height of Jesus' popularity in Galilee. The same atmosphere of rife messianic expectation, mentioned by Jn 6:15, is subtly suggested by Mark and is essential to this episode. **45.** *constrained his disciples to get into the boat:* There is a consistent contrast between Jesus and the Twelve; here it is suggested in their reluctance to leave. *to the other side toward Bethsaida:* A puzzling notice, since Bethsaida was at the NE extremity of Lake

Gennesaret rather than opposite them. The Twelve probably intended to sail the short distance to Bethsaida (8:22; to nearby Capernaum, according to Jn 6:17), but were in fact driven on a SW course to Gennesaret (6:53). **46.** *to pray:* Jesus' retiring from the Twelve to pray (see 1:35) suggests that the messianic fervor engendered by his last miracle constituted a temptation for him. **47.** *the boat was in the middle of the sea:* "25 or 30 furlongs" (Jn 6:19; i.e., 3 or 4 mi.). Mark's expression is from the LXX where it occurs in connection with the passage through the Reed Sea (Ex 14:16,22,23,27,28,29; 15:8; Neh 9:11). **48.** *the wind was against them:* None of the accounts specifically mentions a storm. *around the fourth night watch:* Between 3:00 and 6:00 A.M. *walking on the sea:* Seen against the OT, Jesus' action constitutes a divine epiphany (Ps 77:19; Job 9:8; 38:16; Sir 24:5; Is 43:16). *he intended to pass by them:* See comment on 1:16. There is a striking parallel with Job 9:11 where God is said to "pass by" (i.e., manifest himself), treading on the billows of the sea. **49.** *they thought it was a ghost:* This same motif is found in Jesus' Easter apparitions; cf. Lk 24:37–39. **50.** *they were terrified:* The Gk word denotes fear in face of a preternatural vision or message (Mt 2:3; Lk 1:12,29). *spoke with them:* In the LXX *lalein meta* often refers to God's self-disclosure to men (Gn 35:13,14,15; Nm 11:17; Jgs 6:17; Ex 3:10); this expression further enhances the epiphanic character of this miracle. *take courage:* The word is found in theophanic contexts in Ex 14:13; 20:20; Zeph 3:16; Acts 23:11. *it is I:* Jesus' word comes as an answer to the disciples' question in 4:41. It is a "revelation formula" (lit., "I am"), which in the LXX is attributed only to God (Ex 3:14; Dt 32:39; Is 41:4; 43:10), and which in the redemptive context of Dt-Is emphasizes God's transcendence and fidelity to his promises of salvation. Thus Jesus designates himself as the transcendent agent of God's salvation (J. Brinktrine, *TGl* 47 [1957] 34–36; W. Zimmermann, *BZ* 4 [1960] 54–69). *do not be afraid:* Another expression found in theophany contexts in the LXX (Gn 15:1; Jos 8:1; Dn 10:12,19; Tb 12:17). **52.** *they had not understood about the loaves:* Mark's conclusion is completely different from Mt 14:53; the Evangelist consistently stresses that the disciples were unable to comprehend the secret of Jesus' identity (4:13,40; 7:18; 8:17–21). The vb. *synienai* (understand) is used in the LXX of the God-given understanding of visions and mysteries (Dn 1:17). Had they penetrated the mystery of the miraculous feeding, they would have known who it was who came walking on the sea. *their hearts were hardened:* This NT theme, usually applied to Jews (Mk 3:5; 4:12; 7:14–23; 8:11–13; Jn 12:14) is applied by Mark to the disciples (8:17–21; cf. 4:13; 7:14,18) to describe their inability to perceive the deeper meaning of Jesus' self-revelation in parables and signs.

(Cerfaux, L., "'L'aveuglement d'esprit' dans l'Évangile de S. Marc," *Mus* 59 [1946] 267–79. Dowden, G. F., "The Significance of Mk 6," *ChQR* 158 [1957] 39–48. Lightfoot, R. H., "A Consideration of Three Passages in St. Mark's Gospel," *In Memoriam Ernst Lohmeyer* [Stuttgart, 1951] 110–15. Renié, J., "Une antilogie évangélique [Mk 6:51–52; Mt 14:32–33]," *Bib* 36 [1955] 223–26.)

41 (C) Cures at Gennesaret (6:53–56). **53.** *landed at Gennesaret:* Jesus' presence on the W shore after the miraculous feeding and the crossing of the lake is again mentioned in Mk 8:10,22 and in Jn 6:24–25. But the name of the place varies: Dalmanutha (Mk 8:10), Bethsaida (Mk 8:22), Gennesaret (Mk 6:53), Capernaum (Jn 6:24). The rest of this passage is a synthetic construction of the Evangelist who uses isolated traditional materials more fully recounted elsewhere. *people recognized him:* The enthusiastic Galilean crowds serve as a contrasting introduction to the hostility of the Jerusalem leaders (7:1–23). The subject throughout is "they"; there is no mention that Jesus either taught or preached. **56.** *as many as touched [the fringe of his garment] were made well:* Even the cures are mentioned in the passive, and the impression is that Jesus was still seeking unsuccessfully to evade the crowds.

42 (D) Further Teaching of Jesus (7:1–23). This section contains two pronouncement stories (1–8; 9–13) and a parabolic saying of Jesus (14–23), all of which show his opposition to the code of unwritten law so scrupulously observed by the Pharisees. Together with the previous section (6:31–53) and that following (7:24–8:26) they form a unit continuing the self-revelation of Jesus as the Messiah whose mission extends beyond Judaism and is in opposition to the legalism and particularism of the Pharisaic leaders.

(E) On Hand Washing (7:1–8). **1.** *Pharisees and some scribes from Jerusalem:* As in 3:22, the mention of Jerusalem shows that the scribes represent the official attitude of prominent Jewish leaders toward Jesus. **2.** *ate food with hands defiled:* It is debated whether the washing of one's hands before eating was of obligation for all Jews or only for priests; possibly it was a practice among the pious Jews, Pharisaic or others (see V. Taylor, *Mark*, 338–39). In any case, the custom is expected here of Jesus' disciples, "some" of whom were detected not doing so. The word for food is literally "loaves" (*artous*), a catchword that links this passage with the rest of the Loaves Section. **3.** *unless they have washed their hands:* Unlike Mt 15:1ff., written for Jewish Christians, Mark adds a long explanation of the customs in question for the benefit of his Gentile readers. The Greek contains the additional word *pygmê* ("with the fist"), which may possibly mean "with cupped hand" (S. M. Reynolds, *JBL* 85 [1966] 87–88). **5.** *the tradition of the elders:* A rabbinical term for the body of unwritten laws that the Pharisees considered as equally binding as the written Torah (cf. Gal 1:14; → History of Israel, 75:120). **6.** *about you Isaiah prophesied:* Jesus does not answer the charge directly but cites from Is 29:13 (LXX), which differs from the MT in that it adds "they teach as doctrines the commandments of men" (instead of those of God). Taylor thinks that the MT, even without the added clause, provides a basis for Jesus' charge that the Pharisees' worship of God is largely hypocritical. Other commentators feel that the Hebr text, which Jesus would have presumably used, is irrelevant to the charge, and hence that the quotation was added by Gk-speaking Christians to the original story of Jesus' indictment of the Pharisees. There is an allusion to the same text form of Is 29:13 in Col 2:22; Ti 1:14 (B. Lindars, *NT Apologetics* [London, 1961] 165–66). **8.** *you give up what God has commanded:* Even if Jesus did not cite Is 29:13, this verse fully represents his style and attitude and may well be a pronouncement of Jesus in answer to a question like that of 7:5.

(F) On Qorban (7:9–13). **9.** *he said to them:* This characteristic linking clause joins another isolated pronouncement to the previous passage in order to show concretely how the observance of the unwritten traditions sometimes contradicts God's commandments. **10.** *Moses says:* Jesus quotes the Fourth Commandment (Ex 20:12 = Dt 5:16) and Ex 21:16, showing that he accepts the binding force of the written Mosaic Law. **11.** *anything of mine that might have been of use to you is Qorban (that is, a gift):* In later rabbinical writings *qorbān* was an asseverative or adjuratory formula; in the absence of contemporary parallels, commentators often suggested that Mk 7:11 should more accurately be translated, "I solemnly swear that nothing of mine will be of use to you" (S. Zeitlin, *JQR* 53 [1962] 160–63). However, in 1955 an inscription was found near Jerusalem on an ossuary from the 1st cent. AD in which *qorbān* is used exactly in the sense of the statement in Mk. It is a dedicatory formula, offering the contents of the ossuary to God and removing them from any profane use by its finder (see J. A. Fitzmyer, *JBL* 78 [1959] 60–65; J. T. Milik, *FrancLA* 7 [1956–57] 232–39). Jesus, then, refers to a practice whereby a man would evade the obligation of the written Law to support his parents by dedicating his money to God, declaring it sacral by pronouncing over it *qorbān* (Aram for "gift" offered to God), a legal fiction that still allowed the person to retain possession of the money. **13.** *nullify God's word by your tradition:* Judgment of such traditionally accepted practices is an uncompromising demurral.

43 (G) A Parable on Defilement (7:14–23). There is a close structural similarity between this passage and 4:1–20:

4:1–2	The crowd (*ochlos*)... *and he said to them*
4:3	*"Listen"*
4:3–8	Parable
4:9	*and he said, "Whoever has ears...*
4:10	Alone with disciples, Jesus is asked the meaning of his parables.
4:13	*and he says to them, "Do you not understand...?"*
4:14–20	Jesus explains the parable.

14. *Listen to me, all of you, and understand:* Mark has amplified the "Listen" of 4:2 (1) by the phrase "to me": Jesus directs their attention more explicitly to himself, (2) by the vocative "all of you," an indication of the universality of Jesus' doctrine, (3) by the additional imper. *synete* (cf. 6:51b), implying that what follows is a mysterious revelation. **15.** *nothing that goes into a man from outside can defile him; it is what comes out of a man that defiles him:* The antithetical parallelism of this saying is a feature of Semitic diction and argues for the authenticity of this saying of Jesus. The truth expressed here must have been surprising to Jews, to judge from the fact that no parallels are found in rabbinical literature (Str-B 1, 719). Its implications were only realized when the Church was confronted with the question whether Gentile converts were to observe Jewish dietary regulations (Acts 10:14ff.; 15:28–29; Gal 2:11–17). **16.** This verse is missing in the best Gk mss. **17.** *when he had entered the house and left the crowd:* According to both Mk and Mt 15:15 Jesus is asked to explain his parable; but in Mk this explanation assumes the character of a secret revelation, (1) because it is given privately to the disciples (cf. 4:10–12,32–33); (2) because Jesus rebukes them for their inability to comprehend; (3) because Mark quotes Jesus in a more enigmatic form (compare Mk 7:18b–19 with Mt 15:17–18); and (4) because in Mk the content of the saying is extended beyond the question of eating with unwashed hands (contrast Mt 15:20). By restricting Jesus' instruction to the disciples, Mk continues the theme that Jesus is revealing to them the mystery of God's kingdom—not only its irruption in Jesus' person, but also the reversal of values that he brings. **18.** *are you also without understanding:* The Gk adjective is *asynetoi*, a compound of *synienai;* see comment on 6:52. **19.** *thus he declared all foods clean:* This is an editorial comment of the Evangelist, which draws out the implication of Jesus' words. **20.** *whatever goes out of a man:* Thoughts and words that proceed from his inmost self. **21–22.** Catalogue of vices. Lists of vices were common not only in the Hellenistic world (Aristotle, *Nic. Eth.* 2.7; Wis 14:25–26), but are now known to have been in use in Palestine as well (see 1QS 4:2–6,9–11); see A. Vögtle, *Die Tugend- und Lasterkataloge im NT* (NTAbh 16/4–5; Münster, 1936; S. Wibbing, *Die Tugend- und Lasterkataloge im NT* (BZNW 25; Berlin, 1959). Cf. Gal 5:19–21; Rom 1:29–31; 1 Pt 4:3.

44 (H) The Syro-Phoenician Woman (7:24–30). This pericope continues the universalist theme of the Loaves Section, showing Jesus to be the Savior of the Gentiles as well as of the Jews. A comparison with Mt 15:21–28 shows that in the Gospel tradition the cure of the girl was developed into a pronouncement story on faith, whereas the dialogue between Jesus and the woman remained practically unchanged.

24. *leaving that place:* Mark also uses this formula in 1:35 and 10:1 to signalize a new theatre of Jesus' ministry; here he goes "to the region of Tyre," into the coastal province of Phoenicia, or Gentile territory. *he went into a house:* See comment on 1:29. *yet he could not be hidden:* Mark continues the theme of the Messianic secret, but

7:14	The crowd (*ochlos*)... *and... he said to them "Listen to me"*
7:15	Parable
[7:16	*"If anyone has ears...*]
7:17	Alone with disciples, Jesus is asked the meaning of his parable.
7:18	*and he says to them, "Have not even you any understanding then?"*
7:18b–23	Jesus explains the parable.

intimates that Jesus is soon to be disclosed for what he really is. **25.** *fell down at his feet:* The scene recalls other recognitions of Jesus' known powers in 1:40; 3:11; 5:22–23, even though he is not yet regarded as Messiah. **26.** *a Greek, a Syro-Phoenician:* Thus she stands in contrast to the Jew Jairus who was the "leader of a synagogue" (5:22). Mk is more emphatic than Mt about her being a Gentile both by religion and by birth. The reading "Syro"-Phoenician is not universally attested; P.-L. Couchoud (*JTS* 34 [1933] 120–21) would read *chēra phoinikissa*, "a Phoenician widow," like the widow of Zarephath whose son was revived by Elijah (1 Kgs 17:9ff.). *she asked him to cast the demon out of her daughter:* Such requests are usually reported by Mark in direct discourse; in this story (vv. 26,29–30) the customary graphic touches are absent, and the attention is primarily on the dialogue in vv. 27–28. **27.** *it is not right to take the children's bread and throw it to the pups:* The connection of this pericope with the Loaves Section is maintained by the mention of bread (*ton arton*). It is difficult to account for the connection of this dialogue with the miracle because Jesus' saying is more applicable to teaching than to a cure (cf. Mt 7:6). To say that the two were first combined in the Gospel tradition leaves unsolved the question why Jesus, who first refuses the woman's request, ultimately accedes to it. The "children" are the Jews (Ex 4:22; 14:1; Is 1:2; Hos 1:10; Rom 9:4). Gentiles were vulgarly called dogs (Str-B 1, 724–25; O. Michel, *ThDNT* 3, 1104); but Jesus uses the milder diminutive "pups." His words betray a certain particularism (cf. Jn 4:22), and yet it is significant that he has the children and the pups in the same house and eating from the same table. Lohmeyer sees a Johannine theme in the saying: Jesus is the father who dispenses to his children the bread of life, and although at first he refuses to feed the pups until the children have been fed, the refusal is, as in Jn 2:4; 4:48, followed by a miracle, and Jesus ultimately feeds them too. This thought is quite in keeping with the universalism of the Loaves Section (see comment on 8:1–9). **28.** *even the pups under the table eat the children's* *crumbs:* The woman cleverly retorts that in eating what the children reject, the pups are only taking their due. **29.** *for saying that, be on your way; the demon has left your daughter:* No other miracle is so tersely narrated by Mark; as in Jesus' other cures of Gentiles (Mt 8:5–13 par. Lk 7:1–10; Jn 4:46–54) this one occurs at a distance.

45 (I) Cure of a Deaf-Mute (7:31–37). This miracle story is proper to Mk, whose redactional additions are evident in vv. 31 and 36. Apart from these two verses the story consists of five tripartite sentences arranged in chiastic order: in vv. 32 and 37 the subject is "they" (the crowd); vv. 33 and 35 tell of Jesus and the deaf-mute; the central v. 34 recounts the healing (Lohmeyer). The passage should be seen together with its correspondent in 8:22–26.

31. *Tyre, Sidon, the Sea of Galilee, the district of the Ten Towns:* This geographical route, difficult to accept at face value, serves rather to link this episode with the previous passage and to provide a Gentile setting for the following miracle (8:1–9). **32.** *a man deaf and unable to speak well:* The word *mogilalos* occurs only here and in Is 35:6 where it translates the Hebr word for "dumb." The allusion to Is 35:5–6 in Mk 7:37 would suggest that the man was unable to speak at all, but the fact that his cure enabled him to "speak plainly" (7:35) justifies translating *mogilalos* as "unable to speak well." Mark probably derived the word from Is 35:6; "then, seeing the incident as a fulfillment of the prophecy, and influenced by the literal meaning of the Gk word, he took the miracle to consist in making the man speak 'plainly' (v. 35)" (D. E. Nineham, *Mark*, 202). *to lay his hand on him:* See comment on 5:23. **33.** *taking him aside from the crowd privately:* The privacy of the cure, which echoes 1 Kgs 17:19 and 2 Kgs 4:33 (LXX), is connected with the theme of the Messianic secret (see 7:24; → 6 above). *put his fingers into the man's ears and touched his tongue with saliva:* Jesus' gestures are "sacramental" in that they effect what they symbolize, the opening of the man's ears and the loosening of his tongue. Both gestures and the use of a foreign word (v. 34) were commonplace among contemporary healers, and even suggest a sort of magical ritual. It may be that such details were remembered in the Gospel tradition as a guide to Christian healers in the early Church (M. Dibelius, *From Tradition to Gospel* [London, 1934] 86), but it is also true that these features, together with the absence of any mention of the devil or of faith, accord well with the pagan background of this section in Mk. **34.** *looking up to heaven:* This gesture is less one of prayer than a sign of Jesus' intimacy with God (cf. 6:41; Jn 11:41; 17:1). *he sighed:* A sign either of his deep emotion over the man's pitiful condition, or, as Lohmeyer believes, of Jesus' transcendence, which is constrained by human limits foreign to it. *ephphatha:* Mark retains the Aram word (*'eppeṯaḥ* < *'etpeṯaḥ*), and translates it, " be opened." The vb. *dianoigō*, relatively rare in the NT, occurs 33 times in the LXX, significantly in Ez 24:27: "Your mouth shall be opened, and you shall speak and shall no longer be dumb." **35.** *his ears* [lit., *faculties of hearing*] *were opened:* Mk relates the effects of the miracle in unusually solemn terms; there is possibly an allusion to Is 48:8. *spoke plainly:* Cf. Wis 10:21. **36.** *the more he charged them, the more they proclaimed* [*it*]: The vb. "proclaim" (*kēryssein*), ordinarily reserved by Mark for the preaching of Jesus and of the disciples, is predicated here of the crowd (cf. 5:20). It is a characteristically Christian term, strongly connected with the proclamation of the Gospel (1:14; 13:10; 14:9), and although the object of the man's proclamation is not specified, the implication both of the injunction to silence and of the following verse is that he proclaimed the good news of Jesus as the Messiah. **37.** *they were more than excessively astonished:* Nowhere else does Mk emphasize so strongly the reaction of the crowd—an indication of its unusual significance. *he has done all things well:* Many commentators see here an allusion to Gn 1:31, implying that Jesus has wrought a new creation. *makes the deaf hear and the dumb speak:* This allusion to Is 35:5–6 brings out the theological lesson of the cure: the age of Messianic salvation, announced by Isaiah, has arrived with Jesus.

46 (ii) *The feeding of the 4000 and its sequel* (8:1–13). The relation of this whole section to the feeding of the 5000 and its sequel has previously been discussed (→ 38 above).

(A) The Feeding of the 4000 (8:1–9). This passage (hereafter called B) is most probably a second version of the same miracle recounted in 6:34–44 (hereafter A). Form-critically, it is a miracle story, told again because it foreshadows the Christian Eucharist, this time as food for the Gentiles, whereas A was a sign to the Jews. **1.** *in those days:* Unlike A, B has only the loosest connection with the foregoing narrative; Jesus is still in the pagan district of the Ten Towns (7:31; 8:10). *a great crowd had gathered again:* Cf. 6:34. *they had nothing to eat:* The crowd's physical hunger receives greater stress in B than in A (8:1,2,3,4). *called his disciples:* Cf. 6:35 where the disciples, not Jesus, are the first to notice the crowd's hunger. There is a consistent de-emphasis of the disciples' role in B, and a corresponding heightening of Jesus' role. **2.** *I pity these people:* The same motif of compassion as in 6:34; but whereas there Jesus' pity is theological (they are like sheep without a shepherd), here it is because "they have been staying with me three days now, and have nothing left to eat." In A all takes place within one evening.

3. *if I send them home hungry:* This detail, unparalleled in A, again stresses the crowd's hunger. The rare vocabulary (*prosmenein*, "stay with," and *nēsteis*, "hungry," etc.) and the outlook of this pericope indicate that it arose in a Hellenistic church as an even more noticeably catechetical version of the miracle than A. *they will give out:* The vb. *eklyō* (give out, grow weary) occurs in the NT only here, in the par. Mt 15:32, and in Gal 6:9; Heb 12:3 (Heb 12:5 = Prv 3:11), where it has the connotation of slackening in one's Christian faith. *some of them have come from a distance:* In 6:36 they were close enough to the neighboring villages to buy themselves food. Here the emphasis on the distance is theological. In the OT the Jews in the Diaspora after the Exile are those who are or have come "from afar" (Is 43:6; 49:12; Jer 30:10; 46:27) more significantly, the expression is also used of the Gentiles (Jos 9:6,9; 2 Chr 6:32; Tb 13:11). Mark's phrase in 8:3, therefore, stresses that Jesus' action is especially concerned with the Gentiles in the crowd (F. W. Danker, *JBL* 82 [1963] 215–16). **4.** *where can anyone get bread:* The disciples' question is inexplicable if they had already witnessed a previous multiplication of loaves; but to the reader of Mk it focuses attention on Jesus who alone can satisfy the need for bread. *desert place:* This is the only mention in B of the desert locale; in A it is an essential element and is mentioned three times (see comment on 6:35). *to satisfy these people's hunger:* Again the emphasis is on their physical need, and the vb. "satisfy" anticipates the result of the miracle in 8:8. **5.** *how many loaves have you?:* The disciples' role is emphasized less here than in 6:38. On the difference of numbers between A and B, see comment on 8:9. **6.** *ordered the people to sit down on the ground:* The Messianic and eschatological details of 6:39–40 are suppressed as unmeaningful to non-Jewish Christians. *he took the seven...:* The essentials of this verse occur verbatim in the "Greek" (i.e., non-Palestinian) account of the Eucharistic institution in 1 Cor 11:24, corroborating the hypothesis that B comes from a Gentile church. *they passed them to the people:* An allusion to the early Eucharistic practice in which the deacons distributed the elements received from the presiding bishop (V. Taylor, *Mark*, 359–60). **7.** *a few small fish:* This mention is like an afterthought, the Eucharistic element of bread receiving all the stress. *he blessed them:* The variant in ms. D, "giving thanks," is a harmonization with the previous verse. Among Jews one "blesses" God for his gifts; here Jesus directly blesses the fish, in accord with the practice among Gentile Christians (cf. Lk 9:16). **9.** *seven hampers of surplus fragments:* The word *sp(h)yrides* is found often in Gk papyri meaning a basket for edibles; in 6:43 the word is *kophinoi*, used of food baskets common among Jews. There is a more studied uniformity in B (seven loaves, seven hampers) than in A (five loaves, two fish, twelve baskets). *there were about 4000 people:* Unlike 6:44 it is not specified that only the men were counted. *he sent them forth:* This final notice (*apelysen*) forms an "inclusion" with 8:3 ("if I send them away," *apolysō*); it is like a liturgical "Ite, missa est" at the end of a Eucharistic service.

47 (B) The Sequel: A Sign Refused (8:10–13). **10.** *Dalmanutha:* A site that is as yet unidentifiable. **11.** *a sign from heaven:* Unimpressed by Jesus' many miracles, the Pharisees seek an apocalyptic portent that will substantiate his claims. From their viewpoint the request may have been justified (C. G. Montefiore, *The Synoptic Gospels*, vol. 1 [London, 1909] 186–88), but to 1st-cent. Christians it could only be interpreted as a sign of willful blindness. *to test him:* The classic instance of man's tempting God—the unbelief of the Exodus generation (Ex 17:7; Nm 14:11–12)—is repeated by the present generation's quest for a sign. **12.** *this generation:* Based on texts like Dt 32:5 and Ps 95:10, "this generation" became an execratory term in the NT for all those who distrust Jesus and seek unmistakable signs of his divine mission (Mt 11:16; 12:39,41,42,45; Mk 9:19, etc.). *amen, I say, [may evil befall me] if a sign be given to this generation:* Jesus' answer is more than a refusal to work a sign; it is a tacit claim to the knowledge that God will give no such sign. The expression is Semitic, a strong negation; see *GrBib* § 400. The passive is "theological"; see *GrBib* § 236. **13.** *he left them:* This verse is almost a repetition of 8:10, showing that Mark has artificially placed this pericope in the present context, as a commentary on the Pharisees' reaction to Jesus' miracles. **13.** *the other side:* Opposite Dalmanutha, wherever that may be.

48 (c) Conclusion: The Blindness of the Disciples (8:14–21). In this passage Mark combines a saying about the yeast of the Pharisees and the yeast of Herod with a stern rebuke of the disciples for their lack of comprehension about the multiplication of the loaves. **14.** *they had forgotten to bring bread:* Again the mention of bread (five times in this passage) links this pericope with the foregoing sections. *had but one [loaf of] bread with them in the boat:* This clause appears to have been added by Mark to draw attention to Jesus, the Bread of Life (cf. Jn 6:51). **15.** *be on your guard against the yeast of the Pharisees and the yeast of Herod:* This isolated saying of Jesus is freely associated with the foregoing because of the association of yeast and bread. It breaks the natural sequence of vv. 14 and 16; yeast does not figure in the rest of the passage. It also upsets the otherwise contrasting symmetry of the passage—14 and 16: the complaint of the disciples; 17–21: the response of Jesus. Lk 12:1 has placed the saying in a more logical context of controversy with the Pharisees. Whether or not the saying contributes in any way to the understanding of this passage can only be decided after studying the rest of the section. **16.** *they were arguing among themselves because [or, about the fact that] they had no bread:* Their concern for material food prevented them from seeing that Jesus, who had just fed the multitudes miraculously, is the Messiah capable of feeding them with the bread of life.

Jesus' reaction takes the form of seven questions in which he berates the disciples for failing to understand the meaning of the miraculous feedings, and tries to open their eyes to that meaning. **17.** *why are you arguing:* Jesus picks up verbally the thought of the disciples in 8:16; it is their annoyance over the lack of bread, rather than any failure to comprehend the yeast-saying, which shows that their minds are blinded. *do you not yet perceive or understand?:* An allusion to 6:52. It is to be noticed, however, that what the Evangelist states there (and in 9:32) as a fact is here expressed by Jesus as a question designed to evoke the disciples' understanding (so also 4:13,40; 7:18). *are your hearts hardened?* See 6:52. The allusion to Jer 5:21 and Ez 12:2 is continued in Jesus' next question. **18.** *having eyes do you not see?:* Viewed in the light of 4:11–12, Jesus' questions prove that in Mk the miracles of the loaves were intended to reveal to the disciples "the secret of God's kingdom." *do you not remember?:* In the OT remembering is one of the chief vehicles of God's revelation, and may even be an essential element of the covenant form (see comments on Dt 4:9–15; Jos 24:2–13). Especially in Dt the Israelites are called upon to remember God's past mercies as the basis for their present fidelity to his covenant (Dt 4:32–40; 5:15; 6:20–25; 7:6–11; 8:2–6; 9:1–7; 29:1–8; 32:7). Thus Jesus' question here is a call to such reflection on his two bread miracles as will lead the disciples to see who he is. **19.** *when I broke the five loaves:* Mark resumes the substance of the first miracle (6:41,43–44). **20.** *and the seven for the 4000:* Mark here resumes 8:5–9. In both cases the Eucharistic symbolism of the miracles is emphasized by referring to them as a breaking of bread (cf. Acts 2:42,46; 20:7,11). **21.** *do you still not understand?:* Jesus' final question, resuming his earlier question in 8:17, summarizes the gist of this whole episode: it is intended to evoke from the disciples a recognition of himself as the Messiah because of the two bread miracles. With this in mind we may now proceed to assess the meaning of the yeast-saying in 8:15.

Mt 16:12 interprets the yeast as "the teaching of the Pharisees and Sadducees," and Lk 12:1 as their "hypocrisy." Underlying both interpretations is the Jewish view of yeast as symbolic of a corruptive power (1 Cor 5:6,7,8; Gal 5:9; Str-B 1, 728ff.). Originally the saying must have referred to that hostile attitude of the Pharisees that caused them to be blind to the person and message of Jesus. To suggest that Jesus was warning his disciples not to become infected by that same blindness, while it agrees with Mark's categorical statements in 6:52 and 9:32, is nevertheless at variance with 4:11–12 where Jesus says that the disciples are not among "those outside" whose minds are blinded. Moreover, the obduracy of the disciples springs not from any lack of good will as with the Pharisees, but from lack of insight. By speaking here of the yeast of the Pharisees "and of Herod," Jesus forces us to interpret the yeast as some corruptive force common to both and capable of infecting the disciples too. This can only be their nationalist and political views about the expected Messiah, views that were not foreign to the disciples and that in the present scene prevent them from recognizing the true nature of Jesus' messiahship. In context, therefore, Jesus' yeast-saying is both a strong admonition to the disciples against corrosive messianic hopes, and an invitation to see the real character of his messiahship. Thus the entire passage is a fitting end to the Loaves Section, and leads naturally to the disciples' recognition of Jesus as Messiah in 8:27–30.

(Gnilka, J., *Die Verstockung Israels*, 36–39. Manek, J., "Mk 8:14–21," *NovT* 7 [1964–65] 10–19. Manson, T. W., "Mk 8:14–21," *JTS* 30 [1928–29] 45–47. Smith, D. H., "An Exposition of Mk 8:14–21," *ExpT* 59 [1947–48] 125–26. Ziener, G., "Das Bildwort vom Sauerteig," *TTZ* 67 [1958] 247–48.)

49 (d) APPENDIX: THE BLIND MAN OF BETHSAIDA (8:22–26). This miracle story ends the second cycle of the Loaves Section just as the cure of the deaf-mute (7:31–37) ends the first cycle. Both miracles are recounted only by Mark and show striking similarities of structure and vocabulary (see V. Taylor, *Mark*, 368–69). There are also affinities with the immediately following pericope (8:27–30) and with the cure of the blind man at Jericho (10:46–52).

22. *they came to Bethsaida:* This notice parallels the introduction to the cure of the deaf-mute (7:31). The cure takes place outside Galilee, in the tetrarchy of Philip, just as the cure of the deaf-mute took place in the Transjordanian district of the Ten Towns. The reference to populous Bethsaida as a "village" (8:23) makes it likely that the localization of this cure is Mark's own redactional comment. *they brought him a blind man, and begged him to touch him:* There is a strong parallelism with 7:32 except for an inversion of the vbs. "to touch" and "to lay his hand[s] upon." **23.** *taking the blind man by the hand, he led him outside the village:* There is an evident similarity with 7:33; in this case we have none of Mark's usual expressions to indicate the private setting of the secret revelation of Jesus (→ 6 above). A closer similarity is found in Jesus' removal of the sufferer to a distance, as well as his use of saliva and his laying on of hands; as in 7:31ff., the man's condition is not attributed to demoniacal possession, nor is there any mention of faith. *do you see anything?:* This is the only cure in the Gospels that takes place gradually, in two stages; elsewhere Jesus' word effects an instantaneous healing. This, together with the fact that the ritual gestures were reminiscent of pagan practice, may account for the omission of these two miracles by the other Evangelists. **24.** *looking up:* Cf. 7:34. *I can see people, for I can make out something like trees, only they are walking:* The Greek is complicated here, and the textual tradition varies somewhat, but the idea is clear: the man has begun to recover his sight but cannot yet distinguish objects clearly. *he kept looking and was cured; and he began to see everything clearly:* As in 7:35, Mark recounts the three effects of the cure in three coordinated clauses. **26.** *he sent him home:* The parallelism with 7:36 is evident enough. *do not even go into the village:* A well-attested variant reads: "Do not tell [this] to anyone in the village," which would produce an even more perfect parallelism with the earlier cure (7:36).

Because of the strong formal parallelism with 7:31–36 Bultmann (*HST*, 213) believes that 8:22–26 "is in all probability to be taken as a variant" of the former miracle. Yet, apart from the notable differences between the two stories and the fact that the saying in 8:24 is "a highly distinctive detail which stamps the story as genuine" (V. Taylor, *Mark*, 369), it is also true that "unless Jesus really healed blind persons, it is difficult to see how the whole elaborate interpretation of the meaning of His sight-imparting miracles could have been built up in so short a time" (A. Richardson, *Miracle Stories*, 86). It is most probable that Mark intended the present miracle to complement the previous one in showing that Jesus' ministry is the fulfillment of such OT prophecies as Is 29:18; 35:5–6, which mention both the restoration of sight and of hearing as signs of the Messianic age.

The structural parallelism with 8:27–30 consists principally in the similarity between the gradual restoration of the man's vision and the gradual recognition of Jesus' messiahship by the disciples. In both cases Jesus repeats his gesture or question before the desired effect results. Moreover, the acclamation following the cure of the deaf-mute (7:37) is absent in the parallel cure; but it follows in Peter's confession (8:29). Thus this cure is a prophetic gesture of Jesus symbolizing the opening of the disciples' eyes to his messiahship.

There is also a similarity with the cure of Bartimaeus in 10:46–52 in that (1) both miracles mark the end of sections of teaching about Jesus' messiahship; and (2) the recognition of Jesus as Messiah (8:30), symbolized by the first cure, is paralleled by Bartimaeus' hailing of Jesus as the Son of David.

(Lightfoot, R. H., *History and Interpretation in the Gospels*, 90–91. Nineham, D. E., *Mark*, 216–20. Richardson, A., *Miracle Stories*, 81–90, 98–99.)

50 **(III) Conclusion of Part II and Transition to Part IV: Peter's Profession and Jesus' Correction (8:27–33).** This passage is the turning point of Mk, for it climaxes Jesus' self-revelation with the disciples' first recognition of him as Messiah. It also introduces the theme of the suffering Messiah, which will be developed in the succeeding chapters. Both Peter's confession and the first prediction of the passion form a logical and structural unit in Mk that is not broken, as in Mt 16:17–19, by the interpolation of the Petrine promise. This section really belongs at once to the preceding and the following parts of Mk, for it is the climax of chs. 1–8 and also the transition to the new section; hence the overlapping in the outline.

The episode is classed by form critics as a story about Jesus. The confession of Jesus' messiahship by Simon has indeed been written off as a legend born of Easter faith. But as V. Taylor (*Mark*, 375) notes, "the decisiveness of the confession of Peter and the teaching which followed claim recognition. Joseph Klausner... recognizes their historical character, and goes so far as to say that 'to deny this would make the whole history of Christianity incomprehensible'. The story ought not to be interpreted as if no suspicion that Jesus might be the Messiah had ever dawned on the minds of the disciples before. Without some sense of His greatness and a hope that in Him ancient prophecies might be fulfilled, they are not likely to have forsaken all and followed Him."

27. *Caesarea Philippi:* The ancient town of Paneas (modern Baniyas) was rebuilt by Philip the tetrarch and renamed Caesarea after the Roman emperor. Situated some 25 mi. NNE of the Lake of Galilee, it was called Caesarea Philippi to distinguish it from the coastal city, Caesarea Maritima. *who do men say that I am?:* The sense of *hoi anthrōpoi* (men) must be judged from Mk's other uses of it, where it clearly denotes those outside Jesus' circle (1:17), his enemies (9:31), or "human beings" as contrasted to God (7:7). The last meaning is found in the last verse of this passage (8:33); here it probably has the first meaning. **28.** *John the Baptist; Elijah:* See 1:2–8; 6:14–15; 9:11–13. *one of the prophets:* See 6:15. **29.** *he himself asked them, "Who do you say I am?":* Jesus' second question is emphatically introduced; it becomes clear that the Twelve ("you") are contrasted with the "men" of 8:27. They are "you" to whom has been entrusted the secret of God's kingdom and are contrasted with "those outside" to whom everything becomes a riddle (4:11). *you are the Messiah:* Peter is the first human being to recognize, or at least to acknowledge openly, that Jesus is the expected deliverer. It is, in effect, an act of faith in the messiahship, not yet the divinity of Jesus. (On the notion of Messiah used here, → Aspects NT Thought, 78:8, 24.) **30.** *he warned them not to say this about him to anyone:* Jesus' answer is remarkable on several accounts: (1) for the first time the prohibition to speak openly is explicitly related to his own person (contrast 1:44, 5:43; 7:36; 8:26 [variant]; the only exception is 3:12, but there the injunction is given to the foul spirits); (2) if Peter's confession is a legitimate (and long overdue) recognition of Jesus' identity, why should Jesus enjoin silence? Actually Jesus accepts Peter's Messianic confession, but only with the important qualification made in 8:31—a reaction that is typical of Jesus' attitude toward the popular Messianic titles. Cf. Mk 14:61 par.; Jn 18:37, where Jesus accepts the title used by his questioner, but immediately adds a serious corrective.

51 (IV) The Mystery of the Son of Man (8:31–16:8). Although 8:27–33 is really an indivisible unit, the second half of Mk begins with Jesus' first prediction of his passion (8:31), which forms the end of this unit. A glance at the outline (→ 7 above) will show that the sequence related to the three predictions is the same (prediction, misunderstanding, instruction) so that it is at once impossible to separate 8:27–33 from the first part of the Gospel as it is from the second part. And yet the episode itself functions as the hinge of the two.

52 (A) The Way of the Son of Man (8:31–10:52). This section of Mk comprises those episodes that are articulated by the three predictions of the passion.

(a) First Prediction of the Passion and Its Sequel (8:31–9:29).

(i) *The first prediction* (8:31–32a). This passage must be related to 9:31 and 10:33–34. Its importance in Mk cannot be overstated for its main burden is to correct any possible false notions of the messiahship involved in the confession just made. It is impossible to deny that the formulation of this and the other two predictions has been colored by the events themselves. However, to conclude from this that the whole is a literary device and merely *vaticinium ex eventu* would be illegitimate and exceeding the evidence, such as it is. The major affirmation of these sections is, after all, that Jesus did try to give the disciples some inkling of what lay before him. Undoubtedly, it was only after the event itself that the full import of his hints and the formulation of the story and predictions themselves took shape. **31.** *then he began to teach them:* Jesus' words (quoted indirectly by the Evangelist) now come as a commentary on Peter's admission; they are an instruction on the sense in which he is to be understood as an Anointed One, a Messiah. They follow logically on his prohibition not to tell anyone about him. It is not that others would not understand if the disciples were to tell them that Jesus is the Messiah, but that they themselves have not yet grasped the essential—that the Messiah is the Son of Man who must suffer and die. *it was necessary:* The Gk word *dei* connotes the fulfillment of Scripture (cf. 9:11 referring to Mal 3:23; 4:5, and Ps 118:22 [LXX]). *the Son of Man:* Except for the secondary verses 2:10,28, this is the first occurrence of the title Son of Man (→ Aspects NT Thought, 78:28–30). Hereafter in Mk the title will occur in connection either with the glorious coming of the Son of Man (8:38; 13:26; 14:62) or with Jesus' lowliness of life (10:45) or with his passion and death (9:9,31; 10:33; 12:31; 14:21), i.e., in instructions to his disciples on the nature of his messiahship. Jesus thus transforms the current notion of the Son of Man as the eschatological judge of glory by fusing it with the figure of the suffering Servant of Yahweh (Is 52:13–53:12; → Aspects NT Thought, 78:22). *to undergo much suffering, and be repudiated..., and be killed, and rise again after three days:* As it stands this verse is a prediction of the maltreatment, condemnation, death, and resurrection of Jesus, less obviously a prediction after the event than the detailed statement of 10:33, but showing signs of Christian elaboration nevertheless. In the NT, *paschein* (suffer) is never used to denote the ignominies that Jesus bore before he died; at best it is used of his death itself (e.g., Lk 17:25; 22:15; 24:26,46; Acts 1:3; 3:18; 17:3). Thus, while in the context of Mk 8:31, "to undergo great suffering" refers to the events preceding his condemnation on Good Friday (cf. 10:33), on Jesus' lips the expression would have served to characterize his remaining ministry as that of the suffering Servant of Yahweh. *repudiated:* In context this alludes to the capital sentence passed on Jesus (cf. 10:33, "they will condemn him to death," *katakrinousin...thanatô*). Here, however, the word is *apodokimasthēnai*, a religious rather than judicial term to denote how fools, who rely on human wisdom, repudiate God (Jer 8:9; Wis 20:20) or how God repudiates Israel for its folly or infidelity (Jer 6:30; 7:29; 14:19). As used by Jesus, therefore, the word would have designated his ministry as a "repudiation" by men, a thought akin to Is 53:3. *by the elders, the high priests and the scribes:* The addition of these words, however, transforms the originally theological thought of Jesus into a specific prediction of his condemnation to death, emphasizing the guilt of the Jewish leaders. (On these three groups as constituents of the Council, or Sanhedrin, in Jerusalem, see J. Blinzler, *The Trial of Jesus* [Westminster, 1959] 93–97.) *be killed:* The usual kerygmatic formula is *apethanen*, "he died" (1 Cor 15:3; Ap 1:18; 2:8), whereas the vb. "to kill," referring to Jesus' death, is found in anti-Jewish polemic (Acts 3:15; 1 Thes 2:15; often in Jn, e.g., 5:18; 7:1,19,20,25; 11:53; Mt 23:27). This part of the verse, therefore, is most probably a Christian addition to the original saying of Jesus, and the same polemical motif is recognizable in the addition of the all-inclusive phrase about the elders, high priests, and scribes. *rise again after three days:* Death and resurrection are always combined in the kerygma, and this association easily accounts for the mention of Christ's resurrection after that of his death. Moreover, since in the earliest tradition Christ is proclaimed as "having been raised from the dead by God" (e.g., Rom 4:25; 6:4,9) the use of the act., "to rise again," betokens later Christian usage and the influence of Hos 6:2 (LXX). **32.** *plainly:* This word denotes the openness or public quality of Jesus' revelation (e.g., Jn 7:13,26; 10:24) and in Acts, the outspokenness with which the apostles proclaimed Jesus as Lord (Acts 4:13,29,31; 28:31). It suggests that Jesus now departed from his veiled manner of self-revelation and spoke of his suffering and repudiation in unmistakably clear terms.

53 (ii) *Misunderstanding of the disciples* (8:32b–33). **32b.** *Peter rebuked him:* This is proof that in spite of his calling Jesus a Messiah, Peter still does not grasp that this function entails suffering and death for Jesus. **33.** *turning around and seeing his disciples:* Mk's graphic detail indicates that Jesus' reply, although addressed to Peter, is intended for the others as well. *get behind me, you devil:* Peter plays Satan's role by suggesting that Jesus should be the political liberator of popular expectations. *your views are not those of God but of men:* Implied in Jesus' final word is that he has chosen to follow God's will, whereas Peter and all others who think the thoughts "of men" align themselves against God's salvific plan. The mention of "his disciples" and "men" is a reprise of the same formulas in 8:27 and further unifies the pericope by this "inclusion."

(Cullmann, O., "L'apôtre Pierre instrument du diable et instrument de Dieu," *NT Essays* [Fest. T. W. Manson; Manchester, 1959] 94–105. Dinkler, E., "Petrusbekenntnis und Satanswort," *Zeit und Geschichte* [Fest. R. Bultmann; Tübingen, 1964] 127–53. Hahn, F., *Christologische Hoheitstitel* [Göttingen, 1963] 226–30.)

54 (iii) *Instructions on discipleship* (8:34–9:1). Here Mark topically arranges a series of isolated sayings of Jesus on commitment. **34.** *come after me* [*opisô mou*]: Jesus has just told Peter to "get behind me" (*opisô mou*); this is the catchword bond that links this series to the preceding. His words are now directed to "the crowd with his disciples" and concern true commitment to himself. *let him deny himself:* These words reiterate the original thought of Jesus' saying; it is a question of staking one's whole life for the eschatological good now within reach. *let him take up his cross:* To the Christian reader Christ's cross is a symbol of the redemptive suffering, which all his followers must bear. It is doubtful, however, that here Jesus had his own crucifixion in mind, and outside Christian literature the Roman form of capital punishment was not an image of suffering. The anointing or marking of a person with a cross (+ or ×, the ancient form of the Hebr letter *tau*) was, however, practiced among Jews as a sign of repentance and of "branding" one as God's possession (Ez 9:4–6; *Pss Sol* 15:6–9). It was often connected with penitential and baptismal rites and is at the basis of the NT theme of the baptismal seal (2 Cor 1:21–22; Gal 6:17; Eph 1:13; 4:30; Ap 3:12; 7:2–8; 9:4; 14:1). Jesus' saying may originally have run, "Whoever does not put on [mark himself with] his + [i.e., does not repent and dedicate himself wholly to God] cannot be my disciple" (Lk 14:27).

(Dinkler, E., "Jesu Wort vom Kreuztragen," *Neutestamentliche Studien für R. Bultmann* [BZNW 21; Berlin, 1954] 110–29. Fridrichsen, A., "Sich selbst verleugnen," *ConNeot* 2 [1936] 1–8.)

35. *to save himself:* Lit., "to save his *psychē*," a word that in the LXX translates the Hebr *nepeš* (breath, life principle, hence "living being," "self" [Gn 2:7]). Jesus' words mean that there is an eschatological phase of human existence and that no sacrifice is too great to attain it. *whoever destroys himself for me and the Gospel will save himself:* Mark's expansion of "for me" by "and [for] the Gospel" is tantamount to saying that Christ is somehow present in and identified with the proclamation of the good news (cf. 1:1; 10:29; 13:9–11), and betokens a time when the Church was undergoing persecution for the Gospel. **38.** *in this adulterous and sinful generation:* See comment on 8:12. In the OT, infidelity to God was often called adultery (Jer 3:3; Hos 2:2). *the Son of Man will be ashamed of him:* Jesus demands an allegiance that severs his disciples from "this generation" and is the condition of salvation. The early Church seems to have taken what was originally a saying on eschatological retribution (cf. Lk 12:8; Mt 10:32) and transformed it into a prediction of the parousia by adding "when he comes in the glory of his Father with his holy angels." **9:1.** *there are some who will not taste death:* An analogous eschatological theme—the coming of God's kingdom in power—has attracted this isolated saying to that of 8:38. It is a prediction of the "certain and imminent establishment of God's rule on earth—the Church—by God's power" (J. Huby, *Marc*, 54). It has also been interpreted as an ironic reprimand addressed to those still unwilling to undertake the arduous program of discipleship sketched in 8:34–38: even among my disciples there are those who simply will not take any risk unless they have incontestable evidence that God's kingdom is breaking in upon them (E. Trocmé, *SE* 2, 259–65).

55 (iv) *Complements* (9:2–29). Three complementary episodes follow.

(A) The Transfiguration (9:2–9). It is impossible to reconstruct the original event, yet this story is based on some factual occurrence in which for a fleeting moment the disciples recognized the truth of the revelation at Caesarea Philippi: although Jesus' messiahship involved suffering, he was truly the glorious Son of Man. The account of this experience, however, draws upon motifs from the Sinai theophany (Ex 24:15–18; 34:29–30; 40:34–38)—the overshadowing cloud, the mountain, the awesome majesty, Moses' presence, the tent—; also from the apocalyptic appearances of the Son of Man (Dn 7, 8, 10; *Enoch* 14, 60, 71; cf. *2 Esdras* 10:25–33; Ez 1–2)—the vision, Elijah's presence, the fear, the brilliant clothing, the command to secrecy, the conversation. The transfiguration is one of the central Messianic pericopes and shows similarities with Jesus' baptism (the heavenly voice), and with the Gethsemane story (the three disciples, the mountain, the cry "Abba, Father" corresponding to the heavenly voice, "This is my beloved Son," the prominence of Peter, the incomprehension of the disciples).

2. *six days later:* Although this detail may be symbolic (cf. Ex 24:16), it serves to link the transfiguration with the events of Caesarea Philippi (8:27–9:1) and to corroborate in a dramatic way the Messianic revelation and instruction given there. *a very high mountain:* An allusion to the Moses motif (Ex 24:12–18; 31:18) showing Jesus to be the new Moses radiant in God's presence on the new Sinai. *transfigured:* Metamorphosis—the profound change in the appearance of the just in the world to come—was an apocalyptic theme (*2 Baruch* 51:3–10; Dn 12:3; cf. 1 Cor 15:40–44; 2 Cor 3:18). **3.** *his clothes became dazzling, intensely white:* White clothing is a frequent apocalyptic image of otherworldly glory (*Enoch* 46:1; 71:10; Dn 7:9; Mt 28:3; Mk 16:5; Jn 20:12; Acts 1:10) and of the eschatological glory of the saints (Ap 3:4,5,18; 4:4; 6:11; 7:9,12). **4.** *Elijah with Moses:* Jesus' interlocutors are usually taken as standing for the Prophets and the Law. Both are connected with Sinai (Horeb)—cf. Ex 19:33–34; 1 Kgs 10:9–13—and by their presence on the new Sinai they witness to the fulfillment of the OT in Jesus. **5.** *good to be here:* Their joy is explained by what follows. *three tents:* Or "booths," such as were used at the joyous Feast of Tabernacles. Peter feels that the end time has come when "I will again make you dwell in tents" (Hos 12:9), and wishes to eternalize this experience of God's eschatological presence. **6.** *did not know what to say:* As in Gethsemane (14:40) Peter is lost for words at the mystery of Christ. Mark comments on the naïveté of Peter's statement, for, as it turns out (9:7), Jesus has no need of earthly tents: he is heavenly wisdom embodied (cf. Sir 24:48; Wis 9:7–8) and his glory is that which filled the Tabernacle of the wilderness (Ex 40:35). *a cloud:* An OT image of God's presence (Ex 16:10; 19:9; 24:15–16; 32:9) associates the transfiguration with earlier theophanies (Ex 40: 34–45; 1 Kgs 8:10–12) and anticipates the eschatological appearance of God's glory (2 Mc 2:7–8). *overshadowed them:* An OT image to describe God's dwelling among his people (Ex 40:35). The fact that the disciples too are overshadowed by the cloud shows that, far from being mere spectators, they are deeply involved in the mystery of Christ's glorification as representatives of the new people of God. *my beloved Son:* As at Jesus' baptism (1:11) the heavenly voice alludes to Is 42:1 and designates Jesus as the prophet-Servant of Yahweh. This time, however, the words are addressed to the three disciples, and within the context of the first prediction of the passion they constitute the divine approbation of Jesus' role as the suffering Messiah-Servant. *listen to him:* Jesus is now the prophet like Moses whose teaching must be heeded under penalty of extermination from God's people (cf. Dt 18:15). **8.** *saw no one but Jesus:* Elijah and Moses vanish, ceding their place to Jesus alone. **9.** *as they were coming down:* The descent from the mountain and the command to secrecy are elements of the OT theophany-pattern (Ex 32:15; 34:29; Dn 12:4,9) and form the conclusion of this pericope. *until the Son of Man should rise:* Unlike the other injunctions to Messianic secrecy in Mk, this one explicitly foresees the end of it at Christ's resurrection. **10.** *they kept the matter to themselves:* A continuation of the apocalyptic theme of secrecy (Dn 7:28; *2 Esdras* 14:8; *T. Levi* 6:2).

(Caird, G. B., "The Transfiguration," *ExpT* 67 [1955–56] 291–94. Feuillet, A., "Les perspectives propres à chaque Évangéliste dans les récits de la transfiguration," *Bib* 39 [1958] 281–301. Kenny, A., "The Transfiguration and the Agony in the Garden," *CBQ* 19 [1957] 444–52. Léon-Dufour, X., *Études d'Évangile* [Paris, 1965] 83–122. Müller, H. P., "Die Verklärung Jesu," *ZNW* 51 [1960] 56–65. Sabbe, M., "La rédaction du récit de la transfiguration," *La venue du Messie* [RechBib 6; Bruges, 1962] 65–100.)

56 (B) Elijah's coming (9:10–13). **11.** *first Elijah must come:* That is, before the resurrection from the dead. Elijah's presence at the transfiguration and Jesus' mention of the resurrection of the dead lead the disciples to wonder whether they would see Elijah's coming. **12.** *Elijah does come first and restores everything:* Jesus alludes to Mal 3:2–3; 4:5–6; cf. Sir 48:1–3. Elijah was expected to precede the Day of Yahweh and the general resurrection. As the fiery reformer he would "turn the hearts of fathers to their sons, and the hearts of sons to their fathers." *how is it written?:* Jesus voices an objection based on the supposition that he himself is Elijah (see comment on 1:2): If I am to perform the fiery purification of Israel expected of Elijah, then how can it be that, as Son of Man, I must suffer and die? That supposition is much like the Baptist's own question to Jesus (Mt 11:3), only now it is all the more acute after Jesus' prediction of his passion. Jesus corrects the mistaken supposition in his next statement. **13.** *Elijah has come:* Namely, in the person of John the Baptist. Fittingly enough (since he prepared for the Day of the Lord, i.e., Christ's death and resurrection), "people treated him as they pleased." John's violent death is seen by Jesus as a fitting prelude to his own (see 1:14; 6:17–29).

57 (C) The Epileptic Boy (9:14–29). Although this passage is a composite of several stories, Mark has made of them an artful and unified composition consisting of three scenes, each with narrative and dialogue (14–19c; 19d–24; 25–29), and portraying Jesus as victor over the demon (Léon-Dufour).

14. *saw a great crowd:* Unlike many of the miracles in Part II of Mk that take place privately, the two miracles in Part IV (here and 10:46–52) take place before crowds. They are in the nature of public proclamations of Jesus' Messianic power. *scribes:* Their presence is inconsequential to the story, and they disappear from the scene as soon as Jesus chides his disciples for disputing with them. It may be that Mark saw in Jesus' casual dismissal of them an anticipation of his authoritative expulsion of the demon. **17.** *teacher:* See comment on 4:38. **18.** *they were unable:* The Greek can also mean "they were not strong [enough]." By driving out the demon Jesus will show himself to be the "stronger" one who overpowers Satan (3:27). **19.** *unbelieving generation:* See comment on 8:12. Jesus' exclamation seems out of place in this context, for it is not applicable either to the crowd, to the disciples, or to the boy's father. Originally added in order to enhance Jesus' transcendence in this scene, it shows that without faith in Christ one is doomed to the fate of this unbelieving generation. **20.** *they brought the boy to him:* Because his father had already brought him to Jesus (9:17), this verse probably began an originally independent narrative. *seeing him:* The participle is masculine (*idōn*) and refers to "the epileptic boy"; the same is true of the participles *pesōn*, "falling," and *aphrizōn*, "foaming at the mouth." But the subject suddenly shifts to "the spirit." The possessed boy is obviously secondary in the narrative; the emphasis falls rather on Jesus' confrontation with the demon. **21.** *how long has he been like this?:* Jesus' dialogue with the boy's father is prompted less by a desire for information than by a desire to show the petitioner's extreme distress. **22.** *if you can do anything:* The request betrays an imperfect confidence in Jesus' power, but at Jesus' behest the man is led to make an act of faith. **25.** *he rebuked the unclean spirit:* See comment on 1:25. **26.** *like a corpse:* Mark apparently intends the boy's exorcism as a symbol of resurrection from death. Note the contrasting terminology in vv. 26–27: "like a corpse...he is dead; he raised him up; and he arose"; also the connection of this miracle with the prediction of Jesus' own death and resurrection (8:31,35–37). **29.** *impossible to cast out this sort except by prayer:* Since the demon was deaf and dumb (9:17,25) the disciples could not resort to the usual method of dialogue with the demon in order to expel him. A more profound communion with God is required. Most mss. add "and by fasting," but this phrase is lacking in the best texts (S*, B, P45) and generally rejected by modern editors.

This miracle concludes the section begun with the first prediction of the passion (8:31) and, like Jesus' instructions in 8:34–9:1, is addressed to the crowds. By its content and context it has both Christological and catechetical significance: it is a sign of Jesus' triumph over Beelzebul, a reminder of Jesus' own death and resurrection, and a call to faith in Jesus who alone can deliver one from demonic power.

58 (b) Second Prediction of the Passion and Its Sequel (9:30–10:32).

(i) *The second prediction* (9:30–31). **30.** *leaving that place:* Compare the similar formula of 7:24. **31.** *will be betrayed:* A prediction of Judas' treason, but the word can also mean "be handed over" to death according to God's saving design (Rom 4:25; 8:32). *kill:* See comment on 8:31.

(ii) *Misunderstanding of the disciples* (9:32–34). Mark seems to have compiled 9:33–37 from elements in the Gospel tradition, simply to keep the symmetry with the first and third predictions of the passion.

(iii) *Instruction* (9:35–37). **35.** *if anyone wishes to be first:* This saying is apparently an abbreviation of 10:43–44. **37.** *whoever receives one such child:* Comparison with 9:42, where Jesus refers to his followers as "little ones," suggests that this saying originally meant "Whoever listens to one of my disciples listens to me." Variant versions of this saying occur in Mt 10:40; Lk 10:16; Jn 13:20, where it refers to the reception accorded to Christ's disciples. In 9:37 Mark seems to have adapted the saying into a lesson on how the disciples are to treat others.

59 (iv) *Catechetical Complements* (9:38–10:31). Five complementary episodes follow.

(A) The Exorcist (9:38–41). **38.** *someone casting out devils:* This incident treats a problem that arose in the early Church (Acts 19:13), but that Jesus himself may have faced: what to do when nondisciples cast out demons in his name? **39.** *do not stop him:* The genuineness of Jesus' tolerant solution is sometimes doubted on the score that the apostles were quite intolerant of non-Christians performing miracles in Jesus' name (Acts 8:18–24; 13:6–12; 19:13–20). It may be, however, that the situation in the early Church was complicated by the element of sorcery. It is difficult to think that the early Church would have made up and attributed to Jesus so tolerant a solution without any basis in truth. **41.** *a cup of water:* This saying has been freely appended here by the catchword *en onomati*; the context in Mt 10:42 is more natural.

(B) A Group of Sayings (9:42–50). This pre-Marcan catechetical group of disparate sayings is connected only by catchwords. In Aramaic, vv. 38–45 form a poetic unit with strong assonances (see Black, *AAGA* 127–28). **42.** *whoever causes one of these little ones . . . to stumble:* Whoever shakes their faith in Christ; see comment on 6:3. **43.** *if your foot causes you to stumble:* Verses 43, 45, and 47 contain three parallel warnings against self-ensnarement. The catechetical interest of these sayings must have been especially relevant to the Christians of Rome during Nero's persecution. *Gehenna:* A ravine south of Jerusalem called *Gê-Hinnom* (or *gê'-ben-Hinnom*, "Valley of the Son of Hinnom" [Jos 15:8]), where human sacrifices were once offered to Molech and where in later times rubbish was burnt. Its continually burning fires came to symbolize the place of torment for the wicked (*2 Esdras* 7:36; *Enoch* 27:2; 90:24–26). **48.** *where their worm does not die:* Jesus' words are based on an OT description of Gehenna with its filth and smouldering fires (Is 66:24). **49.** *salted with fire:* Three forms of this saying are attested: (1) mss. S, B, L, W; "For everyone will be salted with fire"; (2) mss. A, C, Θ add: "and every sacrifice will be salted with salt"; (3) ms. D: "For every sacrifice will be salted with salt." Form (2) appears to be a conflation of (1) and (3), and of these (1) is textually better attested, and (3) reflects Lv 2:13. The saying is independent of the previous ones; "fire" scarcely refers to that of Gehenna. Salt and fire suggest the purification the disciples will undergo through persecution and suffering. H. Zimmermann (*TQ* 139 [1959] 28–39) prefers reading (2) and sees this verse as a spiritualization of Lv 2:13: like the OT sacrifices, the self-sacrifices of Christians must be salted—by the fire of the Holy Spirit (cf. Mt 18:3; Mk 8:35; Jn 3:5). **50.** *salt is good:* Like Mt 5:13 this saying is probably addressed to the disciples; they must purify the world and not be contaminated by it or its spirit. *be at peace with one another:* Mark closes with an allusion to the dispute (9:33–34) that occasioned this whole section.

60 (C) Marriage and Divorce (10:1–12). **1.** *he left there:* See comment on 7:24. *taught them:* See comment on 1:21. The use of this verb (contrast Mt 19:2), together with the fact that in vv. 10–12 an explanation is given privately to the disciples (see 1:29), indicate that Mark sees this episode as a further disclosure of Jesus' Messianic authority. **2.** *is it lawful for a man to divorce his wife?:* Mt 19:3 adds "for any reason whatever"—a form of the question that reflects more closely the contemporary rabbinical debate about divorce. Dt 24:1 implied that a man could divorce his wife for *'erwat dābār*, lit., "the exposure of a thing," a euphemism for a wife's immodest exposure to another man (so Rabbi Shammai; cf. Mishnah, *Gittin* 9:10); but the very vagueness of the Hebr expression gave rise to a debate among rabbis as to whether it meant any "reason" (*dābār*) whatever (thus Rabbi Hillel; Mishnah, *Gittin, ibid.*). Mark's omission of the phrase reflects a Gentile church background unfamiliar with the rabbinical dispute and more interested in a universal moral principle (see 2:23–28). **4.** *a certificate of divorce:* Cf. Dt 24:3. **5.** *for your hardness of heart:* Dt 24:1–4 is in reality not a commandment but a permissive rule regulating the relationship between a man and his divorced wife; underlying it is the view that a wife who for any reason whatever had had sexual intercourse with some other man, could not cohabit again with her husband. **6.** *God made them male and female:* Jesus quotes Gn 1:27, and, in the next verse, Gn 2:24, as the reason why marriage is indissoluble. **7.** *for this reason a man shall leave his father and mother:* In Gn 2:24 the reason advanced is not that God created man as male and female, but that woman was taken from man and is "bone of my bones and flesh of my flesh," and this reason explains a man's urge to form a unity with his wife stronger than his affinity to his closest blood relatives. A similar mode of argument, but directed against polygamy, is found in CD 4:20–5:5 (cf. J. A. Fitzmyer, *NTS* 7 [1960–61] 319–20). **9.** *what therefore God has joined together:* Jesus thus claims to voice God's will on the indissolubility of marriage as against even Moses' authority. **11.** *whoever divorces his wife and marries another commits adultery against her;* **12.** *should she divorce her husband and marry another, she commits adultery:* This pronouncement of Jesus is akin to Mt 19:9; 5:32; Lk 16:18, except that (1) Mark does not have the exceptive clause of Mt 19:9, and (2) unlike Mt 19:9 assumes that a women can institute divorce proceedings against her husband. This assumption, however, did not exist among Jews, and reflects rather a non-Jewish church where civil law permitted a woman to divorce her husband. Mk 10:11 is usually regarded as closer to Jesus' own pronouncement on the absolute indissolubility of marriage than Mt 19:9 with its additional exceptive clause. It is at least equally probable, however, that the *porneia* mentioned by Matthew meant "premarital sexual intercourse" on the part of a woman engaged in a Jewish betrothal. Such conduct was envisaged by Jesus himself as grounds for divorce when the marriage had not yet been consummated, because the husband had been deceived into believing that his wife was a virgin. In such a case the husband was obliged by Jewish customary law to sue for an annulment of the marriage contract. If the exceptive clause is regarded as coming from Jesus himself, then Mark's omission of it may simply reflect a non-Jewish milieu where the niceties of Jewish custom were unknown or irrelevant (A. Isaksson, *Marriage and Ministry in the New Temple* [Lund, 1965] 127–41).

Jesus' views on the indissolubility of marriage are a wholly new idea not found in the OT, rabbinical literature, or QL. There is, however, an affinity with the Levitical rule regarding the marriage of priests (Lv 21:7), and especially with the rule of Ez 44:22 regarding the marriage of priests in the new Temple of the Messianic age. Isaksson believes that underlying this ethic of Jesus is both a Messianic pretension and an eschatological view, that "the new Temple has already been established. Jesus Himself is Messiah and the fulfillment of the promise of a new Temple and a new communion with God."

61 (D) Jesus and the Children (10:13–16). **13.** *they were bringing children to him:* A possible reference to the custom of bringing the young to the scribes to be blessed on the eve of the Day of Atonement. *the disciples rebuked them:* Perhaps because they objected to the parents treating Jesus as a mere scribe. **14.** *he was indignant:* Jesus' reaction suggests that some important principle is at stake; perhaps it was that the children's parents "understood his message better than the disciples" (J. Jeremias, *Infant Baptism in the First Four Centuries* [London, 1960] 49). *do not hinder them, for to such belongs the Kingdom of God:* Because only children can "call God 'Abba' with childlike confidence, safe under his protection, and conscious of his boundless love" (J. Jeremias, *Parables*, 191). Jesus' saying is equivalently a word of repentance to his disciples; "only to those whose whole life is a Day of Atonement, a becoming small before God, is entry under God's rule guaranteed" (J. Jeremias, *Infant Baptism*, 49–50).

The vb. *kōlyein* (hinder), found in baptismal texts in Acts 8:36; 10:47; 11:17; Mt 4:13–14; *Gospel of the Ebionites* (see Epiphanius, *Panarion* 30.13,8); *Pseudo-Clementine Homilies* 13.5,1; 13.11,2, may be taken from the ritual where the question was put, "What is to hinder this candidate from being baptized?" Its occurrence in Mk 10:14 suggests to some commentators that Jesus' desire to have the children come to him was an anticipatory approval of infant baptism. **15.** *whoever does not receive the Kingdom of God like a child:* Variants of this saying are found in Mt 18:3; Jn 3:5; Justin, *Apol.* 1.61,4; *Apostolic Constitutions* 6.15,5; the last three instances stress that the new beginning of life occurs in baptism. Originally, however, the saying may have been akin to Mk 9:42.

(Aland, K., *Did the Early Church Baptize Infants?* [London, 1963] 95–99. Cullmann, O., *Baptism in the New Testament* [London, 1950] 71–80. Jeremias, J., "Mk 10:13–16 Parr. und die Übung der Kindertaufe in der Urkirche," *ZNW* 40 [1941] 243–45; *The Origins of Infant Baptism* [London, 1963] 54. Richardson, *ITNT* 360–61. Schilling, F. A., "What Means the Saying About Receiving the Kingdom of God As a Little Child?" *ExpT* 77 [1965] 56–58.)

62 (E) On Riches and Earthly Ties (10:17–31). **18.** *good teacher:* A rarely used epithet for a rabbi, for, as Jesus answers, "No one is good but God alone" (cf. Ps 118:1–4 [LXX]; 1 Chr 16:34; 2 Chr 5:13; Ezr 3:11; Rom 7:18). *eternal life:* Life in the *eschaton*, God's kingdom. **19.** *you know the commandments:* The best commentary on these words is Mt 19:17b. As the sequel shows, Jesus' words are less an answer than a challenge to the salvific power of Mosaic righteousness (Mt 5:20). **21.** *you lack one thing:* Cf. Mk 12:34 where Jesus replies in a similar situation, "You are not far from God's kingdom." *go, sell what you own:* Here Jesus' words are an absolute command; in Mt 19:21 they are conditional: "If you wish to be perfect...."; contrast Mt 19:17: "If you wish to enter life...." Matthew introduces the distinction between what is necessary for salvation and what is a counsel of perfection. Mark's version is closer to Jesus' own thought, for (1) in Mt moral perfection is proposed as an imitation of God's perfection (Mt 5:48—an idea quite foreign to the Jewish mentality (cf. J. Dupont, *SP* 2, 152–54); (2) absolute renunciation as a condition for following him is more in accord with Jesus' eschatological message (Lk 6:20–23; cf. J. Dupont, *Les béatitudes* [2nd ed.; Louvain, 1958] 209–96). **23.** *how hard it will be for those with riches:* The man's refusal to follow Jesus (v. 22) occasions this pronouncement. It seems to displace the accent of the story where the man's wealth is mentioned only parenthetically in v. 22b, and where the point is that the only way to eternal life is to follow Jesus. It may be that Jesus' original pronouncement was not restricted to "those with riches" but applied to any person (cf. 10:24b). **24.** *his disciples were amazed:* Because of the authoritative way in which Jesus reverses the common Jewish thought that wealth is a sign of God's favor.

24b–27. There is a certain unevenness of thought in this passage, suggesting that originally it may not have concerned riches, but God's sovereign freedom to bestow salvation on whomsoever he wills. **25.** *easier for a camel:* The paradox of Jesus' saying is often weakened by accepting the poorly supported variant *kamilon* (cable) instead of *kamēlon* (camel), or by supposing that the "eye of a needle" referred to a particularly narrow gate in Jerusalem. But there is a similar rabbinic proverb mentioning an elephant (J. Jeremias, *Parables* 195). **26.** *who can be saved?:* The disciples' consternation indicates that originally Jesus' camel-saying meant in effect that "many are called but few are chosen" (Mt 22:14). This thought of Jesus is clarified by his saying on the narrow door (Mt 7:13–14; Lk 13:23–24), which may be connected with the camel-saying and originally have been a call of repentance to the obdurate. On this occasion, however, the severity of Jesus' pronouncement is softened by his next saying. **27.** *with God all things are possible:* Jesus' answer renews the disciples' hope of Israel's Messianic salvation. The words are a citation of Gn 18:14 (cf. Lk 1:37), recalling God's omnipotence to fulfill his promise to Abraham. Thus it may be that Paul's vision of Israel's final conversion (Rom 11) was anticipated by Jesus himself (S. Légasse, *NTS* 10 [1963–64] 480–87).

28. *Peter began to say:* Verses 28–31 are an appendix stressing the rewards of those who have sacrificed all for Jesus. **29.** *for my sake and for the Gospel:* See comments on 8:35; 1:1. **30.** *a hundredfold:* Three difficulties complicate these verses: (1) the promise of a recompense "in this time" is unusual; elsewhere all consolations are relegated to the future; (2) the promise of prosperity is contradicted by the phrase "with persecutions"; (3) the distinction between the present age and eternal life seems to reflect the thought of the early Church rather than that of Jesus. It is possible, therefore, that everything after "hundredfold" was added to Jesus' saying. **31.** *many who are first will be last:* An isolated saying (cf. Mt 20:16; Lk 13:30) akin to Mt 23:12; Lk 14:11; 18:14. In its Marcan context it confirms the promise of the preceding verse: the disciples, now among the last, will become the first.

(Goguel, M., "'Avec des persécutions,'" *RHPR* 8 [1928] 264–77. Walter, N., "Zur Analyse von Mc 10:17–31," *ZNW* 53 [1962] 206–18.)

63 (c) Third Prediction of the Passion and Its Sequel (10:32–52).

(i) *The third prediction* (10:32–34). **32.** The prediction begins in the second part of this verse; the long first sentence is an introduction to the whole complex 10:32b–52. *Jesus was walking ahead of them:* Rabbis usually preceded their disciples; but the suggestion here is that Jesus is impatient to "go up to Jerusalem" and fulfill his Messianic destiny. *they were amazed:* Their amazement and fear are best explained by what follows. **33.** *the Son of Man will be handed over:* The detailed prediction of 10:33–34 clearly draws on the Passion Narrative. As in the two previous predictions an anti-Jewish tone is perceptible, and the Gentiles are presented only as the executors of the death sentence passed by the chief priests and scribes.

(ii) *Misunderstanding of James and John* (10:35–40). **37.** *grant that we may sit:* The request recalls Jesus' promise of the 12 thrones (Mt 19:28; Lk 22:28–30); here it is a question of occupying the places of honor (cf. Josephus, *Ant.* 6.11,9 § 235). **38.** *can you drink the cup:* An OT image both of weal (Pss 23:5; 116:13; Jer 16:7) and of woe (Ps 75:9; Is 51:17; Jer 25:15–18; Hab 2:15–16; Lam 4:21). Here it is a figure of Jesus' death (cf. Jn 18:11; Lk 22:20; Heb 9:15) as something that the two brothers must share. **39.** *be baptized:* To be drowned by calamities (Pss 42:7; 69:2; Is 43:2) or to be immersed in the fire of God's judgment (Ps 11:6; cf. G. Delling, *NovT* 2 [1957] 92–115). However, the OT parallels are weak at best, and the formulation of the saying may have been influenced by Mk 14:24,36. **40.** *it is not mine to grant:* Jesus can only point out the way to glory by his own death; only God can bestow that glory, at least until Jesus has received the full measure of his Messianic authority through his resurrection.

64 (iii) *Instruction on greatness* (10:41–45). **43.** *whoever wishes to be great:* The disciples are to reverse the customary practice whereby those in authority rule by force; their new norm of conduct—to be the servant of all—is made possible by Jesus' own mission of service. **45.** *but to serve:* The use of the title "Son of Man," which denotes Jesus' authority, reinforces the paradox of his voluntary lowliness. *to give his life as a ransom for many:* This clause, patterned on Is 53:10–12, specifies the meaning of Jesus' service as an atoning death for all men. The rarity with which Jesus describes his mission in terms of Is 53, and the fact that these texts are found only in the Marcan source, has led Jeremias to suppose that Jesus confided his revelation only to his closest disciples (J. Jeremias, *The Servant of God* [rev. ed.; London, 1965] 99–106). On the other hand, it is not certain that 10:45b, any more than 14:24b, is an authentic dominical saying; possibly it is a Christian expansion of 10:45a in the light of the Eucharistic cup as a share in Christ's sacrificial death. Even if it is, it does not weaken the evidence that Jesus conceived his Messianic role as that of the suffering Servant of God (→ Aspects NT Thought, 78:11, 23).

(Emerton, J. A., "The Aramaic Background of Mk 10:45," *JTS* 11 [1960] 334–35. Jeremias, J., " 'Das Lösegeld für Viele,' " *Jud* 3 [1947–48] 249–64. Lohse, E., *Märtyrer und Gottesknecht* [Göttingen, 1955] 117–22. Tödt, H. E., *The Son of Man in the Synoptic Tradition* [London, 1965] 135–38, 202–11. Urner, H., "Der Dienst Jesu Christi," *ComViat* 2 [1959] 287–90.)

65 (d) APPENDIX: CURE OF BARTIMAEUS (10:46–52). This miracle, together with the cure of the blind man in 8:22–26, frames the didactic section of 8:27–10:45 and preludes Jesus' Messianic entry into Jerusalem (→ 49 above).

46. *Jericho:* A Judean city about 18 mi. NE of Jerusalem in the Jordan valley. The corresponding miracle in 8:22–26 is introduced by an identical geographical notice. *Bartimaeus:* Only Mark names him. **47.** *cry out:* This word occurs in connection with manifestations (6:49) or recognitions of Jesus' transcendence (1:24; 3:11; 5:7; 9:24,26; 11:9); but for the first time this noisy acclamation of Jesus by a Messianic title is made by someone other than a demon. *Son of David:* This title designates Jesus as the heir of the promise made to David through Nathan (2 Sm 7:12–16; 1 Chr 17:11–14; Ps 89:29–38). **48.** *many rebuked him:* In 3:12 and 8:30 Jesus rebukes and commands silence; but here Jesus shows no displeasure over Bartimaeus' acclamation. *cried out all the more:* The repetition not only emphasizes the acclamation, but contrasts it with the gradual restoration of the blind man's vision in 8:22–25, and with Peter's gradual recognition of Jesus as Messiah in 8:27–30. **51.** *what do you want:* Jesus' question is the same as that to James and John (10:36). Their request for seats of honor contrasts with the humble request of Bartimaeus; this shows the blind man has seen better than they the nature of Jesus' kingly authority: it stoops to serve. **52.** *your faith:* See comments on 2:5; 5:34. *followed him along the road:* The Greek can also mean "on the way [of discipleship]." Comparison of the Syn versions of this miracle (→ Gospel Lk, 44:131) shows that in Mk the accent falls on Jesus' commendation of the man's faith rather than on the cure itself; no healing gesture is recounted (contrast Mt 20:24) and the usual expressions of amazement are missing at the end (contrast Lk 18:43).

66 **(B) Jesus in Jerusalem (11:1–13:37).** This section deals with Jesus' ministry in the holy city of David. Together with the Passion Narrative it has all been fitted into a week's time in Mk (see the time indications in 11:11,12,19–20,27; 14:1,12,17; 15:1,25,33); but there are indications that the time was longer (see 14:49: "day after day"). The first part of the section, preceding the Passion Narrative proper, is mostly devoted to teaching and even the narrative incidents have a parabolic character. They are in many cases incidents of a general nature without any specific reference to or consciousness of Jesus' coming fate.

(a) JUDGMENT IN ACTION (11:1–26). The first part of Jesus' ministry in Jerusalem deals with three events surrounding his arrival there; they are fraught with meaning for his revelation of himself, which still remains somewhat guarded.

67 (i) *The Messianic entry into Jerusalem* (11:1–10). In all the Syn accounts the arrival of Jesus in Jerusalem is a point of no little interest; in Lk it has particular significance because of the geographical preoccupation of that Gospel. But the arrival is not without its import in Mk. It is the entry of Jesus as a Messiah—even though some commentators are inclined to deny this aspect of the entry. The association with the Mt. of Olives, the sending for the colt, and the reference to "the kingdom of our father David" give to the entry an implicit Messianic nuance. Mark has not introduced the overtones of OT fulfillment that one finds in Mt, and the question therefore arises whether Zech 9:9 really influenced Mark's composition. There is the further question: Did Jesus intend to convey such an impression himself in entering Jerusalem? It is more than likely that he did. Mark's account is restrained but makes its point: "Unable to deny that He is the promised Messiah, He seeks to show to His disciples and to the crowd the kind of Messiah He is, no man of war, but lowly, and riding upon an ass. The crowd is puzzled, but penetrates His meaning sufficiently to see that he is not to be the Messiah of their hopes" (V. Taylor, *Mark*, 452).

1. *Bethphage:* See comment on Mt 21:1. *Bethany:* The small village on the SE spur of the Mt. of Olives to which Jesus was wont to go (see 8:22; 14:3). Its present-day name is el-Azariyeh because of associations with Lazarus (Jn 11). *at the Mount of Olives:* See comment on 13:3. Its mention is significant here because of the popular belief that seems to have associated it with the coming of an Anointed One; it was the hill of oil, of anointing (see Zech 14:3ff.; Josephus, *JW* 2.13,5 § 262; *Ant.* 20.8,6 § 169; Str-B 1,840–41). *he sent two of his disciples:* More than half this passage recounts the preparations for Jesus' entry into the city; there is a strong similarity with the preparations for the Passover supper (14:13–16), both passages stressing Jesus' foreknowledge of events. Here Jesus' initiative in prearranging his Messianic entry, as well as his cleansing of the Temple (11:15–18) and his parable addressed to his adversaries (12:1–12), appears to reverse his customary cautiousness about Messianic demonstrations. Nevertheless, although Jesus now begins to act more openly, his Messianic self-disclosures continue to have the same parabolic quality as heretofore. **2.** *a colt on which no one has ever sat:* Suggesting that it is to serve a religious purpose (cf. 1 Sm 6:7; 2 Sm 6:2; 2 Kgs 2:20; Nm 19:2; Dt 21:3). Mark does not make any specific allusion to Zech 9:9; cf. Mt 21:2–5. **3.** *the owner has need of it:* It seems more likely that here *kyrios* means "owner" than that it is a self-designation of Jesus as "Lord." **8.** *many spread their garments on the road:* A gesture recalling the royal acclamation given to Jehu (2 Kgs 9:13). *others spread leafy branches:* This allusion to Ps 118:27, describing the festive procession on the Feast of Tabernacles, stresses the religious rather than political nature of the ovation given to Jesus. Matthew explicitly narrates Jesus' entry as a fulfillment of Zech 9:9–10; Mark does not, but he cannot have failed to see the connection of Jesus' act with this prophecy. *hosanna:* Originally a plea for help in distress (2 Sm 14:4; 2 Kgs 6:16) and a prayer for rain (Ps 118:25). Through its connection with the Feast of Tabernacles, Ps 118 came to be an expression of Messianic hope and "hosanna" a liturgical cry of homage to God or to the Messiah as he enters Jerusalem in triumph. See Mt 21:9 for explanation of the word. *blessed is he who comes in the name of the Lord:* Ps 118:26. **10.** *the coming kingdom of our father David:* In context this cry is tantamount to a proclamation of Jesus as Davidic king (cf. 10:47,48). Strictly speaking, however, it is only a prayer that Jesus' coming may signal the proximate restoration of the Davidic kingdom, and does not directly designate Jesus as the Davidic king. It is the later evangelists who shift attention from the "coming kingdom of David" to Jesus "the king" (Lk 13:38), "the king of Israel" (Jn 12:13), "the son of David" (Mt 20:9). As such Mark's version stands closer to the event, suggesting that originally Jesus' action was less a claim concerning himself than a sign of the imminent coming of God's kingdom (see B. Lindars, *New Testament Apologetic* [London, 1961] 112). *hosanna in the highest:* Or, translating the Semitic counterpart, "Hosanna to God" (cf. Ap 7:10; J. Jeremias, *ZNW* 50 [1959] 274). The addition of the phrase "in the highest" to "hosanna" serves to stress the religious nature of this event and to relegate any political motives to the background. **11.** *went into Jerusalem, into the Temple:* The natural sequel to Jesus' triumphal entry would seem to be his cleansing of the Temple (11:15–19) and the challenge of the Jewish authorities (11:27–33). Mark, however, interrupts this sequence, surrounding the story of Jesus' cleansing of the Temple by the cursing of the fig tree, both actions symbolizing God's judgment against Israel.

(Burkill, T. A., "Strain on the Secret: An Examination of Mk 11:1–13:37," *ZNW* 51 [1960] 31–46. Dupont, J., "L'entrée messianique de Jésus à Jérusalem," *Assemblées du Seigneur* 37 [1965] 46–62. Lohse, E., "Hosianna," *NovT* 6 [1963] 113–19. Smith, C. W. F., "Tabernacles in the Fourth Gospel and Mark," *NTS* 9 [1962–63] 130–46. Van Bergen, P., "L'entrée messianique de Jésus à Jérusalem," *Questions liturgiques et paroissiales* 38 [1957] 9–24.)

68 (ii) *The barren fig tree* (11:12–14). **13.** *seeing a fig tree:* Texts like Jer 8:13; Hos 9:10; Jl 1:7; Mk 7:1–6 suggest that the fig tree symbolizes Israel (cf. Lk 13:6–9). **14.** *may no one ever again eat fruit from you:* Jesus' cursing the tree is an acted parable dramatizing God's judgment against barren Israel. Jesus' saying may originally have been a statement that the *eschaton* would occur before the tree could bear fruit; later, the delayed parousia, together with a faulty translation of the Aram imperfect by an optative, may have caused the statement to be reinterpreted as a curse (H.-W. Bartsch, "Die 'Verfluchung' des Feigenbaums," *ZNW* 53 [1962] 256–60).

(iii) *Cleansing of the Temple* (11:15–19). **15.** *he entered the Temple:* It is impossible to determine whether this incident took place at the beginning of Jesus' ministry (Jn 2:13–17) or toward the end (cf. V. Taylor, *Mark*, 461–62; J. A. T. Robinson, *NTS* 4 [1957–58] 272). In any case, it was an eschatological act in the spirit of Mal 3:1–3,8–9, which came to be reinterpreted as the Messianic purification of the Temple (Ez 40–48). *drive out the sellers and buyers:* In the context of Jesus' cursing the fig tree, and in the light of Is 56:8; Ez 40–48; Hos 9:15; Mal 3:1; Zech 14:21, Jesus' action is seen as an exercise of his Messianic authority, symbolizing God's judgment against the abuses of the Temple. **17.** *is it not written:* Jesus cites Is 56:7 and Jer 7:11, the former being a Messianic prophecy that looks to the Gentiles' taking their rightful place in God's Temple. In view of the Gentile orientation of Mk, and of the fact that Jesus' act takes place in the Temple court, which separated the Gentiles from the Jews, it may be significant that Mark alone cites the full verse of Is 56:7 including the phrase "for all the [Gentile] nations" (R. H. Lightfoot, *Gospel Message of St. Mark*, 60–69).

(iv) *The withered fig tree* (11:20–25). This passage is a collection of disparate sayings artificially connected by the catchwords "faith" and "prayer." **21.** *Peter remembered:* See comment on 8:18. *have faith in God:* Jesus proposes his withering curse of the fig tree as the effect of his trust of God, but the connection of this and the following sayings with 11:12–14 is purely editorial. **23.** *whoever says to this mountain:* Variant forms of this proverbial saying of Jesus recur in Mt 17:20; 21:21; Lk 17:6; 1 Cor 13:2. The latter passage shows that Paul understood it of charismatic faith. **25.** *forgive... so that your Father...may forgive you your trespasses:* This verse is closely paralleled by Mt 6:14, and shows that the Lord's Prayer was familiar to Mark's church although he does not cite it in full.

69 (b) Judgment in Words (11:27–12:37). This section comprises five pronouncement stories and a saying portraying Jesus for the most part in controversy with various representatives of contemporary Judaism, and reporting his views on current religious questions. To this complex the Evangelist has added the parable in 12:1–12.

(i) *On authority* (11:27–33). **27.** *the chief priests and scribes and elders:* The chief priests include Caiaphas who was high priest at that time, together with Annas and other former high priests, in general the priestly aristocracy. Mark regards "the chief priests and scribes and elders" as the official leaders of the Jews (8:31; 10:33; 11:18; 11:27; 14:1,43,53; 15:1,31). **28.** *by what authority do you do these things?:* In the context their question refers to Jesus' Messianic entry into Jerusalem and to his cleansing of the Temple; originally it may have challenged his accreditation by the religious authorities to teach (see comment on 1:22) or to baptize (cf. Jn 3:22,26). **30.** *was John's baptism from heaven or from men?:* Jesus' counterquestion confronts his adversaries with a dilemma that is spelled out in vv. 31–32. Unable to voice an authoritative decision about the Baptist, the Jewish authorities prefer to leave Jesus' question unanswered. **32.** *they feared the crowd:* Their fear prevents them from voicing a negative opinion against John, just as in 12:12 the same fear will prevent them from arresting Jesus on the spot. Mark thus insinuates an analogy between Jesus and John (see comment on 6:27). **33.** *neither will I tell you by what authority:* The point of this story lies in this pronouncement of Jesus; it is a tacit claim to possess Messianic authority from God.

70 (ii) *Parable of the vineyard tenants* (12:1–12). This passage is unique among Jesus' parables because it is an allegory of how Israel's rejection of the prophets was climaxed by its murder of Jesus, and how God consequently dispossessed Israel of its birthright. The allusions to Is 5:1–7 make it clear that the vineyard stands for Israel (v. 1) or God's kingdom (vv. 8–9); the owner for God, the tenants for Israel's religious leaders; the servants for the prophets; and the beloved son for Jesus. Since the early Church allegorized many of Jesus' parables in the transmission, exegetes since A. Jülicher (1889) have been concerned to recover the original parables by removing all allegorical traits as secondary accretions (→ Aspects NT Thought, 78:135). Once it is seen, however, that allegory was not altogether foreign to the Semitic parable, there is no reason to think that Jesus could not have spoken this parable substantially as it is recorded by Mark, intending it as an allegory of his own place in the religious history of Israel as God's Son, and as a devastating condemnation of Israel for its impending rejection of him.

1. *in parables* (→ 6 above). *planted a vineyard:* These words have been expanded by a description of the vineyard which follows closely the LXX of Is 5:1–2, indicating that the Gospel tradition understood the vineyard to represent Israel. *let it out to tenants and went off on a journey:* Commentators who do not admit any allegorical features in Jesus' original parables explain the plot of this parable as an accurate reflection of economic conditions in Galilee before AD 66, when large tracts of land were owned by absentee landlords and leased out to local tenant farmers in return for a specified percentage of the produce. This situation stirred up discontent and nationalist feelings against the foreign proprietors and could easily have led to the situation described in the parable. Other commentators feel that the parable does not envision this economic and political situation, and that the repeated missions of the owner's servants and son and their maltreatment by the tenants are so unlikely that they can only be explained as allegorical references intended by Jesus himself. **5.** *and so with many others:* This part of v. 5 appears to be a later addition, both on grammatical grounds (J. Jeremias, *Parables*, 71, n. 83), and because it comes as an anticlimax after the murder of the third servant; it also serves to turn the whole series of mistreated servants into an allegory of the prophets' fate (cf. 2 Kgs 17:13–14). On the other hand, if the mission and maltreatment of the first three servants was intended allegorically by Jesus, v. 5b may be part of the original parable (see comment on v. 1 above). **6.** *one beloved son:* The phraseology recalls 1:11; 9:7 and refers to Jesus. The fact that Matthew's even more allegorized version of this parable mentions only "his son" indicates that Mark's "one beloved son" may be a Christian expansion. In any case, the son is an integral part of the story as a foil for the unrestrained malice of the tenants, and there is reason to think that Jesus intended a reference to himself in the figure of the son. This is all the more likely since this parable shows none of the usual characteristics of the Christian kerygma about Jesus as the Son of God. Christian hymns and creeds explicitly call Jesus "Son of God" (Acts 8:37; 9:20; Rom 1:3–4; Heb 4:14; 1 Jn 4:15), relate this title to such OT sonship texts as Ps 2:7 (Acts 13:33; Heb 1:5; 5:5) and 2 Sm 7:14 (Rom 1:3–4) and connect Jesus' divine sonship with his resurrection (Acts 13:33; Rom 1:4; 1 Thes 1:10). All of these elements are absent from this parable (see comment on 12:10–11), so that Jesus' indirect and enigmatic self-designation as God's son closely resembles such sayings as Mt 11:27 par.; Mk 13:22 par. **7.** *this is the heir; come, let us kill him:* Their plan is to murder the sole surviving heir so that, if his father were to die intestate, the vineyard could be claimed by the occupant tenants. **8.** *they killed him and threw his body outside the vineyard:* Jesus' words are less a prediction of his crucifixion than an expression of his consciousness that he shares the fate of Israel's prophets (cf. Mt 23:39–39; 12:41–42). Matthew and Luke, by representing the son as first being thrown out of the vineyard and then slain, may be allegorizing the story in terms of Jesus' passion and death (cf. Jn 19:17; Heb 13:12). **9.** *what will the owner of the vineyard do?:* As in other parables Jesus poses a question as a challenge to his hearers to see the point of the story (cf. also Is 5:3–4). *come and destroy the tenants and give the vineyard to others:* Answers to Jesus' questions were often written into the Gospel stories by Christian catechists (see comment on 4:41), but Jesus' answer here may be original. An early Christian would have been more prone to speak of the son's return, referring to Christ's parousia (cf. Mt 24:43–44; 25:10–13,21,23), and to specify more clearly who "the others" are. By these Jesus may have meant the poor (cf. Mt 22:1–10 par.; 5:5), although the point of his saying is simply that Israel's birthright is to be taken away. **10.** *that stone which the builders rejected:* Ps 118:22–23 was a favorite proof-text in NT apologetic for explaining how the Messiah, rejected by Israel's leaders for the building up of God's people, became the capstone itself of God's new people (Acts 4:11; Lk 9:22, cf. Rom 9:33; Eph 2:20; 1 Pt 2:7). Jesus probably used this OT image on occasion as part of a devastating answer to his adversaries, but the connection of this Ps text with the present parable is doubtless due either to the Christian tradition or to Mark. Unlike the parable, the Psalm text emphasizes the new importance of the previously rejected stone—alluding to Christ's resurrection—and overlooks the true point of the parable, that the vineyard tenants ("the builders") are themselves rejected. **12.** *the parable:* See 12:1 (→ 6 above).

(Dodd, C. H., *Parables*, 93–98. Jeremias, J., *Parables*, 70–77. Léon-Dufour, X., *Études d'Évangile*, 303–44. Van Iersel, B., *"Der Sohn" in den synoptischen Jesusworten* [Leiden, 1961] 124–25.)

71 (iii) *On the census tax* (12:13–17). A typical pronouncement story in which all the narrative is subordinate to Jesus' saying in v. 17. Although there is no indication of when this incident took place, Mark situates it in a series of controversies at the end of Jesus' ministry.

13. *some of the Pharisees and Herodians:* See comment on 3:6. It may be that Mark sees the Pharisees as representing those who tolerated collaboration with Rome, and the Herodians as representing more nationalistic factions who opposed it. *is it lawful to pay census tax to the emperor?:* Between AD 6 and 70 a census tax was levied on the inhabitants of Judea, Samaria, and Idumea. Aside from being a constant reminder of their subjection to Rome, this tax also raised religious scruples among Jews since it had to be paid in silver coins bearing the emperor's image (cf. Dt 4:16,25; 5:9:10). The question was hotly debated among the Jews, and the attempt to make Jesus voice a decision was calculated to discredit him with adherents of one or the other side. **15.** *bring me a coin:* Since coins were considered as the monarch's personal property, their having the coin of the census was an implicit recognition of the emperor's sovereignty over them. Jesus accordingly retorts that they have an obligation to pay the tax. **17.** *give the emperor what is his due, and God what is his:* In view of the belief that God's kingdom would come imminently and all earthly kingdoms would disappear, Jesus' saying is less a statement of principle about loyalty to Church and state than a pronouncement about the relative insignificance of Rome's political power compared to God's kingdom. By the time Mk was composed, however, expectation of an imminent end of the world had abated among Christians, and Jesus' pronouncement was reinterpreted as sanctioning the principle that a man's loyalty to civil authority need not contradict his obedience to God (cf. Rom 13:1–7). The saying must have been of special pertinence to Roman Christians during the Neronian persecution (AD 64).

(Goppelt, L., "The Freedom to Pay the Imperial Tax," *SE* 2, 183–94.)

72 (iv) *On resurrection* (12:18–27). A third controversy story culminating in Jesus' pronouncement in vv. 24–26.

18. *Sadducees:* These were an aristocratic and priestly segment of contemporary Judaism, religiously more conservative than the Pharisees (→ History of Israel, 75:123). Unlike the latter, the Sadducees rejected the oral Torah of the elders (see comment on 7:3) as well as the more recent beliefs in immortality and resurrection (cf. Acts 23:8). *there is no resurrection:* Resurrection first appears in the OT as a communal experience of God's people (Is 51:17; 69:1; Ez 37:1–14; Hos 6:1–3); belief in individual resurrection only emerges with Dn 12 (*ca.* 165 BC). **19.** *Moses wrote:* The Sadducees cite Dt 25:5–6 (on levirate marriage) and Gn 38:8 and propose a case in which seven brothers, to fulfill this divine precept, successively marry the same woman. **23.** *in the resurrection whose wife will she be?:* The question is evidently unanswerable and was designed to ridicule belief in resurrection as incompatible with the divinely revealed precept of levirate marriage. **25.** *neither marry nor are given in marriage:* The first part of Jesus' answer concerns the manner of life after the resurrection; it is not incompatible with the Scripture cited, once the Sadducees recognize that earthly relationships will not persist after death. *but are like angels:* The idea that men will share in the beatitude of angels is also found in the QL (1QS 11:7–8; 1QH 3:21–23); Paul describes the spiritual state of the risen body in 1 Cor 15:35–50. **26.** *have you not read:* The second part of Jesus' answer establishes the fact of resurrection, by applying to Ex 3:6 a type of rabbinical exegesis. God declared himself to be God of the patriarchs; but, "he is not the God of the dead, but of the living"; therefore, the patriarchs must still be living, and hence resurrection is implicitly taught in the OT. Although Jesus' argument appears illogical, it exploits above all the OT experience of man's communion with a loving and life-giving God. Acts 17:32 attests that belief in resurrection continued to be a stumbling block even for the Gentiles; hence this pronouncement of Jesus may have acquired a new pertinence to Mark's Roman readers in their discussion with pagans.

(Carton, G., "Comme des anges dans le ciel," *BiViChr* 28 [1959] 46–52. Dreyfus, F., "L'argument scripturaire de Jésus en faveur de la résurrection des morts," *RB* 66 [1959] 213–25. Ellis, E. E., "Jesus, the Sadducees and Qumran," *NTS* 10 [1963–64] 274–79.)

73 (v) *On the First Commandment* (12:28–34). This pronouncement story differs somewhat from the others in this series in that it portrays a friendly, rather than a controversial, discussion between Jesus and a scribe.

28. *one of the scribes:* The style of this introductory verse shows that it was composed by Mark to connect this pronouncement story with the previous one. *which commandment is the first of all?:* Teachers of the Torah, such as Hillel (*ca.* 25 BC), argued about the relative importance of the many commandments in the OT, with a view to finding the "parent commandment" from which all others could be deduced. **29.** *hear, O Israel:* Jesus cites Dt 6:5, the opening verse of the *šᵉmaʿ* (hear), which Jews recite daily. **30.** *you are to love the Lord your God:* The command to love Yahweh was considered the fundamental and all-inclusive stipulation of the covenant; since he is one, man's love of him must also be undivided. **31.** *the second is this: love your neighbor as yourself:* Lv 19:18 commanded that the Israelite love his fellow Jew, but even before Jesus the command was extended to include at least resident aliens. Both commandments were central in the religion of Israel, but their combination into a single moral principle appears to be original with Jesus. **32.** *you are right, Rabbi:* The scribe repeats the substance of Jesus' words adding a word about the primacy of love over even ritual sacrifice (cf. 1 Sm 15:22; Hos 6:6). **34.** *you are not far from God's kingdom:* The image is somewhat at variance with the usual concept of God's kingdom as something still to be given to men, and may be a secondary formulation of Jesus' original thought; cf. 10:21 where, in a similar situation, Jesus commends the man, but reminds him that he has not yet reached the goal. *after that no one dared asked him any question:* An editorial comment by which Mark separates the previous stories from the next one in which Jesus takes the initiative.

(Bornkamm, G., *Jesus of Nazareth* [London, 1960], 109–117. Montefiore, H., "Thou Shalt Love Thy Neighbor as Thyself," *NovT* 5 [1962] 157–70.)

74 (vi) *On David's son* (12:35–37a). The Marcan form of this episode records a dominical saying, and lacks any trace of debate such as one detects in Mt; in all the Syn the saying is substantially the same. Jesus questions the contemporary tradition about the Messiah as the Son of David. The background of Jesus' question is the long-standing tradition about the anointed descendant of David, which developed in the last two centuries BC into a full-blown messianism, when an ideal Davidic king was to be expected. This was rooted in such passages as Jer 23:5; Ez 37:23–24; 1 Chr 7:11,14; Dn 9:25–26; see also 1QS 9:11 (Messiah of Israel); 1QSa 2:14,20; CD 20:1; 4Q Patriarchial Blessings 2:4; *Pss Sol* 17:23,26; 18:6,8). **35.** *the Messiah is David's son:* God's Messiah was commonly identified with a descendant of David, and hence as a legitimate pretender to the throne of Israel, according to 2 Sm 7:14 (see R. H. Fuller, *Foundations of NT Christology* [N.Y., 1965] 23–31). Jesus appears to challenge this view in the next verse. **36.** *inspired by the Holy Spirit:* Jesus' argument presupposes the then accepted view that David was the author of the Psalter, and that it was David "in whom the Lord's Spirit has spoken" (2 Sm 23:2). *the Lord said to my lord:* Jesus cites Ps 110:1 in the form of the LXX, which means, "The Lord (*Kyrios* = Yahweh) said to my lord (*kyrios* = the anointed king)." See comment on Mt 22:42 for an explanation of the senses of *kyrios* used here. Although OT commentators debate about the messianic character of Ps 110 and many point out that it is only a royal Ps addressed to the reigning monarch, others consider it as messianic in that it reflects the outlook of David's dynasty (see J. L. McKenzie, *CBQ* 19 [1957] 25–52). There is little doubt that the Evangelist understands it in the latter way. **37.** *David himself calls him "lord"; how then can he be David's son?:* The question Jesus poses is simple in itself, but three different ways have been proposed of understanding it: (1) Jesus in effect is calling in question the Davidic origin of the Messiah. As a Galiliean and "son of Joseph the carpenter" he could not be the Messiah; so he is trying to prove that the Messiah is not really of Davidic lineage. (2) Jesus is in effect insinuating that the Messiah is really something more than a mere son of David, having a more exalted, transcendent origin than David himself. This would be another step in the self-revelation of Jesus. (3) Jesus is supposed to be referring indirectly to the vision of the Son of Man in Dn 7:13; yes, he is the son of David, but something more—the Son of Man in a unique sense. Of these three interpretations only the second one is convincing in the long run (see J. A. Fitzmyer, *Concilium* 20 [1967] 75–87). Jesus' question is not so much a denial that the Messiah is David's son as a statement that he is more than that. While humanly descended from David (Mt 1:1–17; Rom 1:3; 2 Tm 2:8), the Messiah had a character transcending mere blood ties with David; so the latter could rightly refer to him by the name otherwise reserved for Yahweh.

(Gagg, R. P., "Jesus und die Davidssohnsfrage," *TZ* 7 [1951] 18–30. Lövestamm, E., "Die Davidssohnsfrage," *SEA* 27 [1962] 72–82. Michaelis, W., "Die Davidssohnschaft Jesus als historisches und kerygmatisches Problem," *Der historische Jesus und der kerygmatische Christus* [2nd ed.; Berlin, 1961] 317–30.)

75 (c) CONCLUSION: JESUS' WARNING AGAINST THE PHARISAIC LEADERS (12:37b–40). This warning of condemnation against the Scribes climaxes the whole section from 11:1, which shows Jesus' judgment against Pharisaic Judaism. The sayings recorded here may have been abstracted from a larger complex such as that found in Mt 23 and in Lk 11:37–53; their effect is to show the extent of Jesus' antipathy to the Jewish religious authorities.

37. *the mass of the people:* Lit., "the abundant crowd," a strange expression for Mk. **38.** *beware of the scribes who walk about in long robes:* Their use of the *tallîth* (shawl) for other than prayer and religious duties constituted an ostentatious display of piety. *salutations in the marketplaces:* To be greeted with deep ceremonial bows in recognition of their superior position in the community as experts in the Law. **39.** *the first seats in the synagogues:* To sit facing the people on the bench before the Ark containing the biblical scrolls. **40.** *they devour the houses of widows:* To the charge of personal pride Jesus adds those of exaction and hypocrisy. Jesus undoubtedly made some such accusations, yet their formulation here is so sweeping and unqualified as to reflect a later anti-Jewish polemic.

(d) APPENDIX: THE WIDOW'S TWO COINS (12:41–44). This may originally have been a pronouncement story on almsgiving, which Mark has situated here by free association of the widow with v. 40 and of the Temple with Jesus' being in Jerusalem. Other commentators note that close parallels of the story are found in Jewish and other literature and suspect that originally this may have been a parable that was made into an incident of Jesus' ministry. In any case, following upon Jesus' condemnation of the Jewish leaders, it comes as a harbinger of hope in the midst of an otherwise obdurate Israel. It is perhaps noteworthy that Matthew, who portrays Israel as obdurate in its rejection of Christ (Mt 23), omits this story, which Mark and Luke place at the end of Jesus' ministry.

41. *he sat down opposite the treasury:* The temple treasury usually means the cells where the valuables were stored; here it may designate the women's court around whose walls were placed 13 trumpet-shaped chests for offerings. **42.** *two tiny coins:* Mark explains them as equaling in Roman coinage a *kodrantēs* (= Lat *quadrans*, a quarter of an *as*), about one sixty-fourth of a laborer's daily wages. **44.** *she, with less than enough for herself, has given all that she had to live on:* Jesus measures the worth of her offering in terms of the sacrifice or self-offering involved. In this context, his thought preludes the laying down of his own life.

76 (e) THE ESCHATOLOGICAL DISCOURSE (13:1–37). This is the second of the two extended discourses in the Marcan Gospel (see 4:1–34 for the first). Written in apocalyptic style and genre, it seeks to explain what Jesus in his capacity as the Son of Man means for Jerusalem, for the Christian disciples, and for men in general, while exhorting all to vigilance. Even a superficial reading reveals that there is reference to Jesus' own "generation" (13:30) and to "all" men (13:36), with a double perspective. Behind this one must reckon with the composite nature of the discourse. The following sections may be distinguished: (i) The Destruction of the Temple (1–2); (ii) Signs before the End (3–8); (iii) Persecution (9–13); (iv) The Desolating Abomination (14–20); (v) False Messiahs and Prophets (21–23); (vi) The Coming of the Son of Man (24–27); (vii) Sayings and Parables on Watchfulness (28–37). Of these it is easy to single out (iii) and (vii) as clear examples of exhortations, the former of which undoubtedly reflects the stress of the early Church (particularly in a place like Rome), whereas the latter is a collection of sayings drawn from different contexts and applied to the *eschaton*. Sections (ii) and (vi) are the real apocalyptic part of the discourse; many commentators believe that this part existed earlier in an independent composition (representing Jewish-Christian views). Finally, sections (iv) and (v), related to(i), deal with Jerusalem and the destruction of the Temple, revealing a strong Palestinian trait. Aside, then, from the hortatory parts in (iii) and (vii) there is the double perspective: one dealing with Jerusalem, and the other with the coming of the Son of Man (→ Gospel Mt, 43:164). In the mind of the Evangelist (as was true of many in the early Church) the coming was thought to be not far off. But the sayings of Jesus regarding it and regarding the destruction of Jerusalem have been sharpened far more than the modern reader may at first realize, and the effort to say how much of the present discourse represents *ipsissima verba Iesu* is not easy to determine. And yet it is intended in the Syn as Jesus' farewell address to his disciples. There is no indication in Mk that the destruction of Jerusalem had already occurred.

(Beasley-Murray, G. R., *A Commentary on Mark Thirteen* [London, 1957]. Lambrecht, J., "Die Logia-Quellen von Markus 13," *Bib* 47 [1966] 321–60; *Die Redaktion der Markus-Apokalypse* [AnalBib 28; Rome, 1967].)

77 (i) *The destruction of the Temple* (13:1–2). Verses 1–2 form the link of 12:41–44 with the coming discourse. They contain a pronouncement story, the substance of which proves to be the basis of the accusation leveled against Jesus in 14:58 and 15:29; cf. Acts 6:14.

1. *one of his disciples:* The discourse is not addressed to the crowds, but only to disciples. *Teacher:* See comment on 4:38. *what great stones and buildings:* The disciple refers to the Herodian restoration of the Second Temple. The Second Temple was begun under Jeshua and Zerubbabel after the return from the Babylonian Captivity (*ca.* 520 BC) and was only a modest construction (see Ezr 3). Herod the Great finally undertook the reconstruction of it *ca.* 20 BC. The reconstruction of the Temple and its precincts continued long after his death (Jn 2:20) and it was only completed about seven years before its destruction by the Romans (see Josephus, *JW* 5.5,1–6 § 184–226; *Ant.* 15.11,1–3 § 380–402; *Mishnah, Middoth*; A. Parrot, *The Temple of Jerusalem* [SBA 5; London, 1957]; L.-H. Vincent, *RB* 61 [1954] 5–35, 398–418). Its site corresponds roughly to what is known today as the *Ḥaram esh-Sherîf*, or "Dome of the Rock," in the Old City of Jerusalem. Mammoth blocks of Herodian masonry belonging to the Temple precincts can still be seen there (see G. E. Wright, *BiblArch* 223–24). **2.** *not a stone upon a stone:* Hyperbole expresses the utter destruction of the Jerusalem Temple, which Jesus foresees; cf. Mi 3:12; Jer 26:6,18. It was eventually destroyed by fire in AD 70 and then razed along with the rest of the city (→ History of Israel, 75:162). This prediction serves as a springboard for the coming discourse.

(ii) *Signs before the end* (13:3–8). This passage should be read in conjunction with 13:24–27; together they will disclose to the reader the apocalypse proper that deals with a perspective beyond that of Jerusalem and the contemporary generation. Verses 3–4 act as an introduction to the apocalypse linking it with the prediction about Jerusalem (1–2).

3. *Mount of Olives:* See comment on 14:26. An association of this spot with the Day of Yahweh is already found in the apocalyptic part of Zech (14:4). *Peter, James, John, Andrew:* These four disciples were first called (1:16, 19), and so most intimately associated with Jesus. Contrast Mt 24:3, where the discourse is addressed to "the disciples in private" (→ 6 above). **4.** *when will this be and what will be the sign when all this is to be accomplished?:* The two-part question seems to refer immediately to the destruction of the Temple; and yet, as the discourse unfolds, one sees that other expressions refer to a perspective beyond it. Contrast then "this" (*tauta*) and the sign of "all this" (*tauta...panta*); and compare vv. 7, 10, 30, and 37 for similar double references. Cf. Dn 12:7 [LXX]. It is also important to note how Mt (24:3) has sharpened the meaning of the two-part question by an explicit reference to the parousia. **5.** *beware that no one misleads you:* Since apocalyptic is by definition almost a form of persecution literature, it is hortatory and often contains warnings against straying or being misled. The vb. *planaō* (mislead, beguile) is used elsewhere in apocalyptic writing (Ap 2:20; 12:19; 13:14; cf. 2 Thes 2:11). **6.** *in my name:* Cf. 9:37–39. Taylor (*Mark*, 639) and others before him have noted that if this phrase were dropped, the rest of this apocalypse would read like a Jewish-Christian apocalypse, a liturgical poem, or an early Christian sermon. *saying, "I am he":* Or more lit., "I am." The phrase *egō eimi* is not easy to interpret here; cf. 6:50; 14:62. Will they claim to be messiahs, teachers, or *Iesus redivivus?* Mt 24:5 resolves the problem by adding "the Messiah" (*ho christos*). However, before the time of Bar Cochba (→ History of Israel, 75:168) there does not seem to be a clear instance in Jewish history of a messianic pretender previous to him; one can point to Acts 5:36–37 and Josephus, *Ant.* 20.5,1–2 § 97–102, but there is no indication that such men as Theudas and Judas regarded themselves as "messiahs." **7.** *wars and rumors of wars:* Another sign of apocalyptic distress; cf. *2 Esdras* 13:31; *Enoch* 99:4. *this must take place:* An apocalyptic trait, derived from Dn 2:28. This phrase would be read by Christians as a reference to the later Roman war and the siege against Jerusalem. *the end is not yet:* Another reference to the eschatological "end time" (cf. Dn 8:17; 9:25; 11:35,40; 12:4,9,13). As used by the Evangelist, the reference is to a period transcending the impending crisis. Underlying it is the deterministic view of history, which is characteristic of apocalyptic writing; there is the call for calm because the divine purpose is working itself out in all of this. **8.** *kingdom against kingdom:* Cf. Is 19:2; Ez 5:12; 1QM 1:3ff. *beginning of the pangs:* The figure of a woman in travail was often used to describe the prelude to the Day of Yahweh or the Messianic era: Is 13:8; 26:17; Jer 6:24; Hos 13:13; Mi 4:9–10; Str-B, 1, 950; 1QH 3:6–10. The precise reference is unfortunately not explained in Mk.

78 (iii) *Persecution* (13:9–13). An exhortation to fortitude in the face of coming persecution is now addressed to Christians. A catchword (*paradidonai*, "hand over, deliver") joins most of the sayings in the passage together (see vv. 9, 11, 12). The sequence is broken by v. 10, which seems extraneous; it is clearly an addition of the Evangelist that relates the exhortation to his general Gospel theme.

9. *beware:* The same warning occurs in vv. 5 and 23. *they will deliver you to sanhedrins; you will be flogged in synagogues:* The first warning regards persecution from Jewish sources. The Gk word *synedria* (pl.) refers not to the Great Sanhedrin in Jerusalem, but to the local councils of 23 men; cf. 2 Cor 11:24. The division of words used here seems preferable, although some commentators see a different parallelism and translate: "they will deliver you to sanhedrins and synagogues; you will be flogged before [both] governors and kings; you will stand for my sake as testimony to them and to all the nations." This division, however, is forced and inverts *kai epi. will stand before governors and kings:* The second warning regards persecution from Gentile sources. *for my sake:* See 10:29 and recall how there the Evangelist added the phrase "and for the Gospel." It is this same idea that is responsible for the addition of v. 10. The counterpart of this v. 10 in Mt is found in 24:14, not precisely at the corresponding point. It seems then that Mark has explained "for my sake" by adding the whole verse. Mark's addition of it amounts to an interpretation of Jesus' call to bear witness to him, in terms meaningful to the persecuted Church of his own day. "For my sake" is therefore paralleled not so much by preaching about Christ, but by Christ himself as proclaimed and made present to men in the preaching. **11.** This verse finds other contexts in Lk (12:11–12; 21:14–15), and Mt (10:19–20). *the Holy Spirit:* Assurance is thus given to persecuted Christians that they will not be facing this crisis alone, but that the Spirit of the Risen Jesus will be with them. This seems to be the sense of this exhortation in the mind of the Evangelist. The only problem is to try to determine to what extent post-Pentecostal faith has colored the phrasing of the saying. In Lk 12:12 the "Holy Spirit" is mentioned; but in Lk 21:15 (the par.) Jesus says, "I will give you a mouth and wisdom." Given Luke's interest in the Spirit (→ Gospel Lk, 44:11), would he have replaced an original reading of the Spirit with a reference to the influence of the Risen Jesus? Mt 10:20 uses the expression, "the Spirit of your Father," which parallels Lk 12:12, and which may be the more original form of Q for that passage. **12.** *brother will hand over brother:* Mi 7:6 lent itself to the development of the apocalyptic theme of family strife; see *Jub* 23:19; *2 Baruch* 70:3. The role of Elijah (Mal 4:6) was also instrumental in developing this theme: he was expected to put things right in this regard. **13.** *because of my name:* See Acts 4:17–18; 5:40–41; 9:27; 1 Pt 4:14. This was certainly the lot of Christians within a relatively short time: suffering for "the Name" they bore (cf. Tacitus, *Annales*, 15.44,2: "...the populace called Christians, hated for shameful deeds; the author of this name, Christ, was put to death by the procurator, Pontius Pilate."). *endures to the end:* An apocalyptic strain of exhortation; see Ap 2:26; *2 Esdras* 6:25.

(Kilpatrick, G. D., "Mark xiii. 9–10," *JTS* 9 [1958] 81–86.)

79 (iv) *The desolating abomination* (13:14–20). This and the next section should be read in relation to the opening verses of the chapter. These passages present in apocalyptic form Jesus' judgment on Jerusalem uttered in the spirit of such prophets as Mi 3:12; Jer 26:6,18. They envisage some historic destruction of Jerusalem, but a comparison of Mk with Mt or Lk in this matter suggests that Mark formulated this discourse at some time prior to the catastrophe of AD 66–70.

14. *the desolating abomination:* The phrase *to bdelygma tēs erēmōseōs* is taken from the LXX of Dn 12:11 (cf. 9:27; 11:31), a loose translation of Hebr *haššiqqûṣ mᵉšōmēm*, "a desolating abomination." And 1 Mc 1:54, using this Gk phrase, indicates that it refers to the statue of Zeus Olympios erected by the Seleucid ruler, Antiochus IV Epiphanes, "upon the altar of burnt offering" in the Jerusalem Temple in 167 BC; cf. 2 Mc 6:2 (→ History of Israel, 75:107). But to what does the phrase refer in Mk? Some commentators (Bacon, Manson, Torrey) have referred it to Caligula's attempt to have his own statue erected in the Jerusalem Temple *ca.* AD 40 (→ History of Israel, 75:150); but this is scarcely convincing. Because the ptc. *hestēkota* (standing) is masculine and does not agree grammatically with neut. *bdelygma*, it has been considered as an indication that Mark understood the "desolating abomination" as a personal Antichrist; cf. 2 Thes 2:3–10 (Loisy, Klostermann, Streeter). However, the following apocalyptic warning, "Let the reader understand" (cf. Ap 13:18; 2 Thes 2:6–7), would seem to suggest that the literary phrase should be understood as it was in Dn. There it was a cryptic reference to the desecration perpetrated by the foreign occupying government; so too it should be understood here, even though it is no longer Seleucid, and even though it may not yet have (in Mk) the specific reference to the Roman profanation of the Temple in AD 70, which it undoubtedly has in Mt. Writing in the early sixties, although in Rome, Mark could have been aware of the tinderbox situation in Judea; and his formulation needed to be no more specific than it is for the genre he has employed (cf. B. Rigaux, *Bib* 40 [1959] 675–83). *standing where it should not:* That is, desecrating Jerusalem or the Temple. *let those in Judea flee to the mountains:* See Mt 24:15. **15.** *not go down into the house:* The Christian must flee directly from the housetop by way of the outside staircase without going into the house to get anything at all—so desperate and urgent will be the situation. **16.** *to get his coat:* Left on the side of the field as he ploughed, cultivated, or reaped. **17.** *pregnant women and nursing mothers:* The crisis will bring with it all the horrors that war has for such women; cf. *2 Baruch* 10:13–19; *2 Esdras* 5:8; 6:21. **18.** *in winter:* When swollen torrents will impede the flight. **19.** This verse is an allusion to Dn 12:1; cf. 1QM 1:12; Ap 16:18. Other OT phrases describing the great tribulation are also echoed here (Ex 10;14; 11:6; Jer 30:7; 1 Mc 9:27). **20.** *the Lord:* Here *kyrios* refers to Yahweh. *shortened the days:* The great tribulation is thought to have a determined period because God is in provident control (Dn 12:7); indeed, on behalf of those whom he favors he has shortened it (cf. *2 Baruch*, 20:1–2; 83:1; *Enoch* 80:2; 38:2–4 for other references to this motif of shortening).

(Cotter, G., "The Abomination of Desolation," *CanJT* 3 [1957] 159–64. Rigaux, B., "*bdelygma tēs erēmōseōs*," *Bib* 40 [1959] 657–83.)

(v) *False messiahs and prophets* (13:21–23). Taylor (*Mark*, 502–3, 515) thinks that this section is in reality only a doublet of 13:5–8. His reasons for this position are not wholly convincing, even though one must admit a certain similarity in structure and content. The passage is made up of a number of sayings.

21. *here is the Messiah:* The statement is indicative of messianic rumors that apparently circulated in the Palestine of the 1st cent. AD. **22.** *false prophets... signs and wonders:* The composition is most likely influenced by Dt 13:2–4. **23.** *beware:* See comment on 13:9.

80 (vi) *The coming of the Son of Man* (13:24–27). This section is closely related to 13:3–8 (see introductory note there). It is an apocalyptic description of something that transcends the historical dimensions of the destruction of Jerusalem—something that requires Christians to prepare themselves in order to cope with it. This section almost entirely employs OT imagery.

24. *in those days:* A stereotyped expression that lacks any definite association (see 1:9; 8:1). *after that tribulation:* The "great tribulation" of OT and apocalyptic writing; see comment on 13:19. *the sun will be darkened:* OT motifs are incorporated here; see Is 13:10; cf. Is 34:4; Ez 32:7–8; Am 8:9; Jl 2:10. They are images that symbolize divine judgment being passed on those so afflicted. The same motif is also used in extrabiblical writings (*2 Esdras* 5:5; *Assumption of Moses* 10:5; *Enoch* 80:4–7). **26.** *the Son of Man coming on clouds with great power and glory:* This is the crucial affirmation of this section: the vision of the Son of Man. There is little doubt that this verse reflects Dn 7:13; implied is the coming of the Son of Man to inherit his kingdom. Whereas the movement of the Son of Man in Dn is toward the "ancient of days," one may well ask in what direction the "coming" is to be understood here. Verse 27 suggests that it is earthward: "angels" are to gather the elect from the four winds. Again, the "Son of Man" most likely has to be understood in terms of an individual, superhuman person possessing heavenly "power and glory." **27.** *the messengers:* Possibly "the angels"; cf. *Enoch* 61. *from the four winds:* See Ap 7:1. So many of the details in this section are characteristic of apocalyptic writing that it is not easy to assess either the meaning they had for 1st-cent. Christians or the meaning that modern Christians are to draw from them.

81 (vii) *Sayings and parables on watchfulness* (13:28–37). The eschatological discourse, which, as can be readily seen is not wholly concerned with the *eschaton*, ends with a series of hortatory sayings and parables bearing upon vigilance. Their validity is perennial; and in this lies the value of the discourse as a whole. In this section the series comprises a parable of the fig tree (28–29), two sayings on the passing of the present generation and world (30–31), two sayings about the unknown day or hour and the vigilance it calls for (32–33), the parable of the servants of the householder who is abroad (34–36), and the final exhortation to vigilance (37). They are for the most part linked by catchwords.

29. *these things happening:* In the Marcan context it must refer to all that has gone before; if it were restricted to the last section (24–27), the very coming of the Son of Man would be a "sign," and not the end itself. *it is near:* Or, "he is near." It is impossible to say whether the subject of *estin* is masculine ("the son of Man") or neuter ("all these things"). [*even*] *at the gates:* This phrase simply intensifies "is near." **30.** *this generation:* The Evangelist is thinking not merely of a possible destruction of Jerusalem, but of the coming of the Son of Man in power and glory, which is to be witnessed by his generation. This verse is in a sense the answer to 13:4.

32. *of that day or hour no one knows:* This affirmation is essential to the exhortation of vigilance. Underlying the statement is the OT imagery of the Day of Yahweh (Am 5:18–20; Is 2:12; Jer 46:10); that it is known only to God is also an OT conviction (Zech 14:7; cf. *Pss Sol* 17:23). *not even the Son:* The reason is that he is only the Son in Marcan Christology, which is not that of Chalcedon; he is not the Father, who does know. One should not try to explain this away by appealing to the communicative knowledge that Jesus (the Son) has for his mission; this distinction is not grounded in the text itself, but is born of a perspective that is not that of the Evangelist. **33.** The exhortation to Christian vigilance par excellence, which is true for all ages. Its point is brought out by the following parable, which speaks for itself. **35.** *evening, midnight, cockcrow, morning:* Four divisions of the night (into periods of three hours each) were used by the Romans (cf. 6:48); Jewish Palestinian usage divided it rather into three watches (Lk 12:38). **37.** *what I say to you I say to all:* This statement lifts the whole discourse beyond the limits of the narrow perspective of the crisis that the coming destruction of Jerusalem and its Temple would mean to Jews and Jewish Christians.

82 **(C) The Passion and Resurrection (14:1–16:8).** Since the beginning of the modern study of the Gospels the Passion Narrative has customarily been considered as "the first part of the primitive tradition to attain the form of a continuous narrative" (Taylor, *FGT* 44). Hints of such a narrative are found in 1 Cor 11:23; Acts 10:36; 13:27–31. It is not possible simply to identify the Marcan Passion Narrative with this first form. But in any case, the Marcan form comes closest to what it must have been. When the Marcan form is compared with that in Mt or Lk, it is seen to be the most primitive in the stark reality of its description and the smaller amount of what is tendentious editing. It is devoid of peculiar traditions of its own (except for that of the flight of the naked young man, 14:51–52).

The Marcan Passion Narrative is presented as the completion and crowning event in the life of Jesus who is finally recognized as Messiah; it is thus the climax of his *euaggelion*. Mark assumes that the whole career of Jesus was a fulfillment of God's design and is thus anxious to proclaim the shameful climax of Jesus' earthly ministry as an integral part of it. The Passion Narrative in Mk is a description of the dark passage through which the Messiah must proceed before he can appear to the world in glory. The "hour has come" (14:41–42) and he must face it in utter loneliness.

One cannot deny that the Marcan Passion Narrative (like the others) is preoccupied with stressing Jesus' innocence in the face of the decision of the Roman governor who was pressured to make it. Again, there is the stress on the accomplishment of God's will in that death; to this end the OT Scriptures are cited throughout the narrative. This was done apparently to answer the charge of critics who objected that if he were God's Son, God should have saved him. The use of OT citations colors the factual account, giving it a theological character and showing that the Evangelist was not writing sheer history.

(Bertram, G., *Die Leidensgeschichte Jesu* [FRLANT 15; Göttingen, 1922]. Léon-Dufour, X., "Passion [Récits de la]," *VDBS* 6 [1960] 1419–92. Lohse, E., *Die Geschichte des Leidens und Sterbens Jesu Christi* [Gütersloh, 1964]. Schelkle, K. H., *Die Passion Jesu* [Heidelberg, 1949].)

83 (a) THE ANOINTING AT BETHANY (14:1–11). This composite episode consists of a notice about the conspiracy of Judas (14:1–2,10–11) and the inserted story of the anointing (→ 32 above). The latter was once an isolated piece of Gospel tradition; not only does it interrupt the conspiracy account, but it is given a different setting in Jn (12:1–8) and is omitted in Lk in favor of a (different?) story related to the Galilean ministry (7:36–38). This story about Jesus is almost a crystallized pronouncement story, which indicates that it originally had little to do with the Passion Narrative.

1. *the Passover and [the feast of] Unleavened Bread:* The Passover festival (Gk *pascha;* Hebr *pesaḥ*), celebrated in Jerusalem, began at sundown after the slaughter of the lambs in the Temple; the Passover meal marked the beginning of Nisan 15. It was the most important of the three feasts whose observance was incumbent on every male Jew over 12 years of age (Ex 23:14–17). It was followed by *ta azyma* (lit., "the [feast of] unleavened [loaves]"), the seven days from Nisan 15 to 21 (see Lv 23:5–6). The popular linking of these two feasts is inherited from the P tradition of the Pentateuch (see De Vaux, *AI* 485). *two days off:* Lit., "[was] after two days." This ambiguous expression has been understood by some commentators to mean that Passover was still two days off, while others insist that it was the next day (appealing to Mk 8:31 where "after three days" means from Friday to Sunday by counting both ends). *chief priests and scribes:* Two of the three groups mentioned in 14:53; see comment on 8:31. **2.** *not during the feast:* To celebrate the festival (Dt 16:2), huge crowds flocked to Jerusalem. The popularity of Jesus with such pilgrims is implied and suggests a contrast with the hostility of the Jewish leaders.

3. *Bethany:* See comment on 11:1. *ointment of pure nard:* The Gk *nardos*, derived from Persian *nārdīn*, denotes an aromatic oil of a root native to India (Eng [spike]nard). The meaning of Gk *pistikos* is uncertain; if related to *pistis*, "faith," it might mean "unadulterated, genuine, pure." But it might also be the proper name of the nard (see Black, *AAGA* 160–61: "ointment of pistachio"). *his head:* Similarly in Mt 26:7, whereas in Jn 12:3 Jesus' feet are anointed (cf. Lk 7:38). In the OT the head of a king was anointed (2 Kgs 9:1–13; 1 Sm 10:1), and so possibly Jesus' royal dignity is being suggested. However, it may be no more than the anointing of the head of a dinner guest (cf. Ps 23:5). **4.** *some who said:* In Mt 26:8 they become "the disciples," and in Jn 12:4 "Judas." **5.** *300 denarii:* The equivalent of 300 days' wages; see Mt 20:2. **6.** *a fine thing:* Lit., "a beautiful deed," explained by the three remarks that follow. Echoing Dt 15:11 ("The poor will never cease from the land"), Jesus does not dismiss poverty as a fact of life (cf. Mk 10:17–21,28–29). Rather, he contrasts the inevitable continuance of it with his own fleeting presence among men. The woman is praised for her devoted recognition of this in not sparing even so precious a possession. **8.** *anointed my body beforehand for burial:* In her defense Jesus adds an eschatological consideration; see 15:46; 16:1 (Jesus' body was not anointed in the normal way before burial). **9.** *this gospel is preached:* Jesus' third remark about the woman: the symbolic value of the act clothed it with extraordinary value and made it worth remembering. The last verse is probably a comment of early Church provenience, when widespread preaching of the "Gospel" was already in progress.

10–11. Three short sentences, the logical sequel of vv. 1–2, explain how the arrest of Jesus took place "with cunning." Mark offers no psychological explanation of Judas' delivery of Jesus to the Jewish leaders (contrast Jn 12:4–6). Later (v. 21) it will be ascribed to God's will. *Iscariot* (→ Aspects NT Thought, 78:170). *one of the Twelve:* This phrase, often associated with Judas' name in the Gospels (see 14:43), records with horror the recollection of his intimate association with Jesus. It must have often been so used in the early community. *money:* Mark never specifies the amount; contrast Mt 26:15 and Zech 11:12.

(Danker, F. W., "The Literary Unity of Mk 14:1–25," *JBL* 85 [1966] 467–72. Daube, D., "The Anointing at Bethany and Jesus' Burial," *AnglTR* 32 [1950] 186–99. Jeremias, J., "Die Salbungsgeschichte," *ZNW* 35 [1936] 75–82.)

84 (b) THE LAST SUPPER (14:12–25). This section is divided into three parts: (i) Preparation for the Passover (12–16); (ii) The Announcement of the Betrayal (17–21); (iii) The Eucharist (22–25). Together they form the supper cycle, common to the Syn; Lk adds to it a farewell discourse (22:21–38), which parallels after a fashion the Johannine tradition.

(i) *Preparation for the Passover* (14:12–15). In particular, this passage links Jesus' last supper with the Passover, although the essential elements of the meal (lamb, bitter herbs, sauce) never figure in the account. The purpose of the episode: not to announce that Jesus performed the rite of Passover, but to show that he was about to celebrate his own Passover. The structure and wording of the episode are strikingly parallel to that of the entry into Jerusalem (11:1–6); see V. Taylor, *Mark*, 536, for details. The similarity reveals an unstudied and almost stereotyped form of composition.

12. *on the first day [of the feast] of Unleavened Bread:* This date, which should mean Nisan 15, is immediately corrected by the following clause, "when the Passover lamb was slaughtered" (Nisan 14); see 14:1. Mark's loose mode of dating is paralleled in Josephus, *JW* 5.3,1 § 99. *eat the Passover:* Or "eat the Passover lamb." Although Dt 16:7 ordained that Jews "cook and eat it [the lamb] at the sanctuary the Lord your God chooses," and this meant the precincts of the Jerusalem Temple itself (2 Chr 25:1–9; *Jub* 49:16–17), this came to mean all Jerusalem, provided that the lamb was slaughtered in the Temple and the designated parts were given to the priests. **13.** *a man carrying a jug of water:* Jesus' prescient indication singles out the characteristic feature: male water carriers tote it in skins, but women use terra-cotta jugs. Hence, such a man would guide the disciples to the right house. **14.** *the Teacher:* See comment on 4:38. Perhaps the owner of the house was a disciple of Jesus for whom *ho didaskalos* was sufficient identification. *eat the Passover with my disciples:* There had to be a group big enough to consume an unblemished one-year-old male lamb (Ex 12:4). **15.** *a large upstairs room, spread with couches and furnished:* In contrast to the first Passover and early Israelite custom when the lamb was eaten in haste while standing (Ex 12:11ff.), the Passover meal had become in 1st-cent. Palestine a festive dinner at which even the poorest reclined at table (a sign of the liberation of Israel from bondage). The site of the "Upper Room" outside the present S wall of Old Jerusalem and near the Church of the Dormition is based on a 4th-cent. tradition (see C. Kopp, *Holy Places of the Gospels* [N.Y., 1963] 323–34). *prepare for us there:* Did the preparations include the slaughtering of the lamb, the bitter herbs, the *harōset* sauce? No mention is made of these Passover meal elements in the Syn beyond the bread (*maṣṣôt*) and the wine. Hence the character of the Last Supper as a Passover meal is debated. Certainly, no identification of it with a so-called *Qiddûš* meal, or a *Hᵃbûrāh* meal, or an Essene community meal (see 1QSa 2:11–22; 1QS 6:2–6) has been more convincing than the usual Passover identification (see Jeremias, *EWJ* 15–88). (On the problem of the date of this meal, → Gospel Jn, 63:138.) **16.** *found it as he had indicated:* The pericope does not exaggerate the implications of Jesus' foreknowledge.

(Jeremias, J., "Mc 14:9," *ZNW* 44 [1952–53] 103–107. Kilpatrick, G. D., "The Last Supper," *ExpT* 64 [1952–53] 4–8).

85 (ii) *The announcement of the betrayal* (14:17–21). Two different Gospel traditions exist about this announcement. One is reflected here and in Lk 22:21–23; Jn 13:18, which does not identify the traitor; the other in Mt 26:25; Jn 13:21–30 identifies him as Judas. Again, the former is presented at different times: in Mk before the Eucharist; in Lk after it. The position of the announcement in Mk (and Mt, Jn) may be due to an early effort to eliminate the suggestion that Judas had shared in the Eucharist; but see P. Benoit, *Scr* 9 (1956) 101.

17. *when it was evening:* The beginning of Nisan 15; the Passover lamb was to be eaten between sundown and midnight. *the Twelve:* They are not just "the disciples" (see 3:16; 5:10; 6:7; 9:35; 10:32; 11:11). **18.** *one of you will betray me:* Mark adds the words of Ps 41:10, "one who is eating with me," thus suggesting OT fulfillment: the treachery of a table companion. **20.** *who dips into the [same] dish with me:* Either a reference to sharing an ordinary meal or possibly to the sharing of the Passover *harōset* sauce. **21.** This verse is probably the Evangelist's comment. *as it is written of him:* In desperation over finding the OT text that speaks of a "suffering" Son of Man, commentators sometimes point to Dn 7:21—which is scarcely *ad rem*. The verse represents an early Christian conflation of the themes of the suffering Servant of Yahweh and the Son of Man.

(Lüthi, K., "Das Problem des Judas Ischariot—neu untersucht," *EvT* 16 [1956] 98–114. Preisker, H., "Der Verrat des Judas und das Abendmahl," *ZNW* 41 [1942] 151–55.)

86 (iii) *The Eucharist* (14:22–25). The Marcan or earliest Syn account of the institution of the Eucharist represents a liturgical formulation of an incident at the Last Supper. Its vocabulary and style suggest that it comes from a Jerusalem or Palestinian liturgy. Mt (26:26–29) is close to Mk (→ Gospel Mt, 43:184). Mark's concern is not simply to relate what Jesus did and said on that occasion, but to recount it in the interest of Christian faith and worship. Hence the reader is introduced *in medias res*. The probable Passover background gives overtones to many of the verses (see Jeremias, *EWJ* 85–86, for an outline of the Passover meal).

22. *while they were eating:* See 14:18. The meal began with a preliminary course, which is presupposed here. *took bread:* At the beginning of the main course Jesus as the paterfamilias in the group pronounced a grace or blessing over some of the unleavened *maṣṣôt* (before the lamb would have been eaten). For Gk *artos*, meaning "unleavened bread," see Ex 29:2; Mk 2:26; Mt 12:4. *this is my body:* The five words, *touto estin to sōma mou*, are found in all four NT accounts of the Eucharist. Just as the paterfamilias at the Passover explained the meaning of "the bread of affliction" (Dt 16:3), so Jesus interpreted the bread he was about to distribute. It is his body, i.e., himself. Philologically, the vb. *estin* could mean either "is really" or "is figuratively," since both meanings of the vb. *einai* occur in the NT (real sense: Rom 7:18; Lk 1:19; Mt 11:29; 1 Jn 3:1; figurative sense: 2 Cor 6:16; 1 Cor 9:2; Jn 10:7). Thus the text is philologically "open"; Catholic tradition, aided by other NT passages (e.g., 1 Cor 11:24–32), has resolved that openness in terms of identity and real presence. That tradition was crystallized in the Tridentine decree on the Eucharist (DS 1636–37, 1651; DB 874, 883). **23.** *a cup:* This is probably the third cup of the Passover meal, "the cup of benediction" (1 Cor 10:16), which followed the main course and preceded the singing of the Hallel. **24.** *my blood of the covenant:* Inferior mss. add "new," a reflection of Jer 31:31. Jesus interprets the cup of wine in terms of "covenant blood," an allusion to the sacrifice that concluded the Sinai covenant (Ex 24:8; Zech 9:11; cf. Heb 9:15–22). Underlying the identification he makes is the meaning of blood as "the life" of the victim (see Lv 17:11,14). The blessings for Israel implied in the poured out blood of the Sinai covenant are now seen as a type of the blessings to come to all men in the poured out life of Jesus (see B. Cooke, *TS* 21 [1960] 1–44). *poured out for many:* The "many" should be understood in the Semitic sense as designating a great number without restriction. Christ's blood poured out will admit the mass of mankind into a new covenant with God. The Eucharist, therefore, interpreted as bread and wine (food), is clearly the source of new life for men. **25.** *until the day I drink it anew in the kingdom of God:* The eschatological dimension of the Eucharist is implied in its relation to the kingdom in which Jesus and his followers will share at the Messianic banquet. This will be in some "new" and definitive way; and thus the Eucharist takes on a dimension of hope. This dimension is expressed in Lk 22:15–16, before the institution itself; that is perhaps the more original context for this statement, which is more properly related to the first Passover cup.

(Benoit, P., "The Holy Eucharist," *Scr* 8 [1956] 97–108; *Scr* 9 [1957] 1–14; *Cross Currents* 8 [1958] 294–314. Dupont, J., "'Ceci est mon corps, ceci est mon sang,'" *NRT* 80 [1958] 1025–41. Emerton, J. A., "The Aramaic Underlying *to haima mou tēs diathēkēs* in Mk. xiv. 24," *JTS* 6 (1955) 238–40. Turner, N., "The Style of St. Mark's Eucharistic Words," *JTS* 8 [1957] 108–11.)

87 (c) GETHSEMANE (14:26–42). Two subsections may be distinguished here: (i) The way to Gethsemane (26–31); (ii) Christ in Gethsemane (32–42).

(i) *The way to Gethsemane* (14:26–31). This pericope is made up of sayings set in the context of a walk to the Mt. of Olives. In Lk (22:31–34) and Jn (13:36–38) Peter's protest is situated at the supper itself, not afterward as here. It gives another instance of Jesus' foreknowledge and attributes the coming denial to a foreordained divine plan.

26. *having sung a hymn:* In the hypothesis of a Passover meal this would refer to the singing of the second part of the Hallel (Pss 114,115–118). *Mount of Olives:* The hill to the E of Jerusalem beyond the Kidron. Ex 12:22 prescribed that no Israelite was to leave his house after the Passover meal until morning; Josiah's reform, however, applied this to the "sanctuary which the Lord your God chooses" (Dt 16:7), i.e., the Jerusalem Temple precincts. But crowded conditions in Jerusalem elicited in time the interpretation that the environs of the city as far as Bethphage would be included (see Jeremias, *EWJ* 55). **27.** *all of you will stumble:* Jesus predicts the scandalous shock that will come over the Twelve, citing and adapting Zech 13:7; he implies their defection and temporary disbelief in him. **28.** *am raised up:* That is, by the Father (→ Aspects NT Thought, 78:158). *I shall go before you:* The Risen Jesus will be the shepherd, regathering the scattered sheep at the scene of their first calling and of their first realization of him; cf. Mk 16:7. **30.** *before a cock crows twice:* Peter's denial will take place so quickly that a cock will not even have time to crow twice. The hyperbole stands in contrast to the vehemence of Peter's protest. There is no need to refer this saying to a division of the night; cf. Mk 13:35.

(ii) *Christ in Gethsemane* (14:32–42). Peter is often regarded as the Evangelist's source for this vividly described scene, which is so humiliating for him and his companions that it is unlikely to be a complete fabrication. On the other hand, some of the details are undoubtedly an imaginative reconstruction. This section sums up Jesus' confrontation with the climax of his career and attempts to give it a psychological explanation. This story was told over and over again in the early Church for its obvious apologetic and edifying value: Jesus' acknowledgement of his Father's will contrasted with the slumbering disciples, unaware that "the hour had come."

32. *Gethsemane:* See comment on Mt 26:36. *while I pray:* For Jesus' solitary prayers, see Mk 1:35; 6:46. **33.** *Peter, James, and John:* The same three who were present in 5:37; 9:2. What they witnessed on those occasions (raising of the dead, transfiguration) did not predispose them to alertness. Those who had seen his power and glory manifested were now invited to see his distress and his weakness. **34.** *deeply grieved:* Jesus' distress is so great that he reaches the point of wanting to die; death would have been a welcome relief. Ps 42:6 has influenced the formulation here. **35.** *if possible, let this hour pass:* The possibility depends on his Father's will. "The hour" may reflect the eschatological use of *hōra* in the LXX of Dn 11:40,45; it is the hour of destiny for Jesus in his passage to the Father through death and it brings with it only the natural repugnance of mankind. **36.** *Abba, Father:* See comment on Gal 4:6. This verse repeats v. 35 in direct discourse. Even in the horror of Gethsemane Jesus knows God as his Father, expresses full confidence in him, and finally his willingness to face his destiny alone, if this be the Father's will. Note the overtones of the Our Father here. *this cup:* See comment on 10:39 (cf. C. E. B. Cranfield, *ExpT* 59 [1947–48] 137–38). **37.** *Simon:* Since 3:16 he has not been so named in Mk; while asleep, he is not addressed as Peter: "The new character which he owes to association with Jesus is in abeyance" (H. B. Swete, *Mark,* 325). **38.** *temptation:* The sense is that of "the trial" facing all men in the struggle between God and Satan, of which the agony and the passion are the climax. Judas, the agent of Satan, is soon to arrive and the struggle will begin; it will confront the disciples who are now urged to steel themselves for it. **39–40.** The dramatic repetition heightens the poignancy of Jesus' distress and loneliness and the insouciance of the disciples. **41.** *sleep on:* The vb. *katheudete* could be a question, "Still sleeping?" But in conjunction with the following problematical vb. *apechei* (which may mean, "it is enough"), it is better to take it as an imperative. Jesus then utters an ironic command, "Sleep on now and take your rest; it is enough!" (i.e., there's no need to counsel you any more). The ms. D reads *apechei to telos;* if this were the original text, then possibly it would be better understood as a question: "Are you still asleep? Still taking your rest? Is the end [so] far off?—Rather, the hour has come!" (See G. H. Boobyer, *NTS* 2 [1955–56] 44–48.) *the Son of Man is handed over:* Mk presents the end as a betrayal of the "Master" or "Teacher" by one of his own disciples into the hands of "sinners" (*hamartōloi*). The last word could mean either non-Jews or nonobservant Jews (see 2:15,16, 17; 8:38); it may mean merely Jesus' enemies (cf. Ps 71:4; 82:4).

(Cantinat, J., "L'agonie de Jésus," *VieSp* 88 [1953] 272–81. Héring, J., "Simples remarques sur la prière à Gethsémané," *RHPR* 39 [1959] 97–102. Kuhn, K. G., "Jesus in Gethsemane," *EvT* 12 [1952–53] 260–85.)

88 (d) The Arrest of Jesus (14:43–52). At this point the Syn Passion Narrative begins to correspond more closely to details in Jn. Since Judas is introduced here again as "one of the Twelve," it is often concluded that this pericope had an independent, pre-Marcan existence. In fact, Jeremias (*EWJ* 96) regards it as the beginning of the pre-Marcan "short account" of the passion. This episode presents the traitorous act of a follower of Jesus whose complicity in the death of Jesus cannot be minimized. It is linked in Mk to the fulfillment of Scripture (v. 49). In it we also see Jesus as one who makes no apologies for his deeds nor shrinks from the ensuing consequences. He faces them alone from now on.

43. *one of the Twelve:* See comment on 14:10. *chief priests, scribes, elders:* See comment on 8:31. The Sanhedrin dispatched a "crowd" (*ochlos*) along with the high priest's servant (14:47); contrast Lk 22:52; Jn 18:3,12. **44.** *kiss:* Obviously intended as a means to identify Jesus in the dark; but cf. Prv 27:6. **47.** *one who stood by:* Unnamed here, but cf. Jn 18:10. The impulsive act is depicted as revenge for the indignity done to Jesus. **48.** *as if against a robber:* Jesus' ironic remark already identifies the crowd as emanating from the Temple. **49.** *let the Scriptures be fulfilled:* This is an elliptical purpose clause, probably added by the Evangelist who gives no hint to what OT passages he refers. **50.** *all...fled:* That is, the Eleven. **51–52.** This enigmatic detail is found exclusively in Mk. Its purpose is elusive; but it heightens the desertion of Jesus by his own. The young man is not identified; idle conjectures have named various candidates: John the Apostle (Ambrose, Chrysostom, Bede); James, "the brother of the Lord" (Epiphanius); John Mark (many modern commentators).

89 (e) The Trial and Crucifixion of Jesus (14:53–15:41). This section of the Passion Narrative falls into five subsections: (i) Jesus before the Sanhedrin (14:53–65); (ii) Peter's Denials (14:66–72); (iii) Jesus before Pilate (15:1–20); (iv) The Crucifixion (15:21–32); (v) The Death of Jesus (15:33–41).

(i) *Jesus before the Sanhedrin* (14:53–65). This section and the next (Peter's Denials) are the two parts of the Passion Narrative that create the greatest difficulty in interpretation when they are compared with Lk and Jn. The solution used here is basically that of P. Benoit, "Jésus devant le Sanhédrin," *Ang* 20 (1943) 143–65; *Exégèse* 1, 290–311. Briefly, it reckons with a Marcan creation of a literary doublet in the "two trials" of Jesus before the Sanhedrin. He has transferred to the unofficial nighttime interrogation of Jesus by the high priest the details of the morning session before the whole Sanhedrin (as in Lk 22:54–71). The Lucan order of events is here not only more logical, but is supported by elements in the Marcan and Johannine traditions. (On the interposition of narratives here, → 32 above.)

53. *to the high priest:* Mk has preserved an authentic element of historical tradition: Jesus was led by night to "the high priest," who is unnamed both here and in Lk 22:54. Only Mt 26:57 identifies him as Caiaphas; in Jn 18:13 he is Annas. Most likely the latter is correct, for although Annas was not "the high priest of that year," he had once been such and retained the title (→ History of Israel, 75:130). The hasty interrogation by the high priest concerned "his disciples and his teaching" according to Jn 18:19; this is quite different from the inquiry of "the trial" in Mk, the details of which are otherwise more suitable to the morning session. *chief priest, elders, scribes:* See comment on 8:31. This is "the whole Sanhedrin," a detail introduced from the morning trial (see 15:1). **54.** *Peter:* His presence in the courtyard of the high priest is noted in all four accounts; it prepares for the denials to come and is undoubtedly an incident that happened at night. **55.** *the whole Sanhedrin:* The name *Sanhedrīn* is a Hebraized form of the Gk *synedrion*, "sitting-together, session, council." The Hebr name is used in the Mishnah for the body of 71 chief priests, elders, and scribes who met under the ruling high priest to decide religious, legal, and internal Jewish civic matters that did not pertain to the Roman governor. *testimony:* This meeting and the seeking of testimony belong most likely to the morning session of "the whole Sanhedrin." Jewish court procedure knew of no official prosecuting attorney; witnesses were the prosecutors. Witnesses for the defense were heard first, then those for the prosecution. At least two witnesses had to agree in their testimony (Dt 17:6; 19:15). (For other details, see Mishnah, *Sanhedrin* 4:1.) **56.** *testified falsely against him:* As phrased, this is a Christian value judgment of the report of the lack of agreement between the witnesses who were interrogated separately. **58.** See 13:2; 15:29. The destruction of the Temple and the cult for which it stood must have been the object of Jesus' criticism at some time or other; the Gospels refer to it too often for it to be baseless. He and his Church after him were to be the New Temple. However, the witnesses took the critical words literally, as if he were to destroy the Temple with his own hands. **60.** *have you no answer:* The high priest is depicted as intervening because the witnesses did not agree. Jesus' silence may only be the obvious answer to the lack of agreement; but cf. Is 53:7. **61.** *are you the Messiah, the son of the Blessed One?* Undoubtedly, the second part of the high priest's question was intended to mean that only the anointed king of Israel could be called God's son (see Ps 2:7). But from the standpoint of the Christian Evangelist, writing after the fact and with a hindsight born of Easter faith, much more is implied by it. **62.** *I am:* Jesus gives a clear affirmative answer. Contrast Mt 26:64; Lk 22:67,70. Is it to be understood only in the high priest's sense? Or does "I am" (*egō eimi*) connote more, by alluding to the Gk translation of Hebr *'ᵃnî hû'*, the self-identification of Yahweh in Dt 32:39; Is 43:10? (see Mk 6:50). In any case, the rest of Jesus' answer clearly alludes to Dn 7:13 and Ps 110:1, which implies that he will soon be realized to be the enthroned "Son of Man" giving judgment in a perspective of eschatological glory; he belongs to a transcendent sphere. *you will see:* This does not necessarily mean a sensible perception of a visible portent related to the parousia; circumstances and events will bring about the realization. *sitting...coming:* The two present participles cannot be intended literally and simultaneously (especially in the sense of "coming to earth"); these are allusions to OT passages that suggest only the enthronement of Jesus in a suprahuman sphere. (See T. F. Glasson, *NTS* 7 [1960–61] 88–93.) **63.** *rent his robe:* As a sign of formal, judicial horror; see Str-B 1, 1007–8. **64.** *blasphemy:* This is the charge against Jesus, a charge that echoed in the early Church. It was not that Jesus had reviled the name of God (Lv 24:10–23), or pronounced the ineffable name YHWH itself (Mishnah, *Sanhedrin* 7:5), or openly claimed that he was a messiah. Indeed, "blasphemy" seems to have had a much wider meaning in 1st-cent. Palestine (see Mk 2:7; Jn 5:18; 10:33). The blasphemy is undoubtedly to be sought in the implications of the latter part of his answer to the high priest: that he will sit at God's right hand and act as judge in his kingdom (see Ps 110:6 and cf. P. Lamarche, *RSR* 50 [1962] 74–85). *as deserving of death:* The "verdict" is one of condemnation (*katekrinan*, "they condemned him"); according to Lv 24 the penalty should have been stoning. The fact that Jesus did not so die but was executed by the Romans may be partly explained in Jn 18:31–32. Mark certainly knows nothing of the niceties of the legal system of the Mishnah, *Sanhedrin* 4:1, according to which in a capital case "the verdict...must be reached during the day time" and "a verdict of conviction [may] not [be reached] until the following day." But one has to ask whether these mishnaic regulations reflect the period before AD 70 in Palestine and whether the session of "the whole Sanhedrin" in the morning was a "trial" at all. **65.** Cf. Is 50:6; 53:3–5.

(See Blinzler, J., *The Trial of Jesus* [Westminster, 1959]. Kilpatrick, G. D., *The Trial of Jesus* [London, 1953]. Winter, P., *On the Trial of Jesus* [StJud 1; Berlin, 1961].)

90 (ii) *Peter's denials* (14:66–72). The time of Peter's denials and the interval between them differ according to the four Gospel accounts; it is then impossible to reconstruct this incident exactly. This section is really a sequel to 15:54 and probably belongs to the events of the night—possibly coinciding with the interrogation of the high priest. The passage is straightforward and without difficulty. Note the climax in Peter's denials: feigned ignorance, simple denial, finally denial with cursing and swearing.

68. *and the cock crowed:* These words appear in some mss. (A, C, D; the Koine tradition generally) and are read by Merk and Bover. They are omitted by some editors and translators, however, because they are lacking in mss. S and B and seem to have been introduced only to explain "a second time" (14:72). If they were genuine, one would have to suppose that Peter never heard the first crowing. The phrase *ek deuterou* ("a second time," cf. Jn 9:24; Acts 11:9) seems to be an effort to historicize a not very subtle interpretation of Jesus' prediction. **72.** *burst into tears:* The Gk words *epibalōn eklaien* are difficult to translate. They may mean, "having set to, he wept," i.e., he began to weep (Klostermann, Schniewind, Bl-Deb-F § 308); or "having reflected on it, he wept" (Zorell); or (less probably) "having covered his head, he wept" (Theophylact). The ms. D reads a different ptc., *arxamenos*, "having begun." This supports the first interpretation.

91 (iii) *Jesus before Pilate* (15:1–20). The notice at the beginning about the assembly of the Sanhedrin undoubtedly refers to the investigation the details of which Mark has transferred to the interrogation in the high priest's house (14:55–64). The purpose of the investigation was to crystallize the Sanhedrin's "decision"—a sentence of "condemnation" (14:64), which they probably could not carry out (Jn 18:31; → Gospel Jn, 63:161, 169). They, therefore, led Jesus to the Roman governor. Three phases of his appearances before Pilate are recorded in all four Gospels: interrogation, sentence, mockery.

1. *morning:* This is the only time indication in Mk; there was no specific reference to "night" in 14:53–65—which in itself supports the suggestion that Mark transferred the details. *chief priest, elders, scribes:* See comment on 8:31. *the whole Sanhedrin:* See 14:55. *having reached a decision:* This translation is based on the reading of Nestle, *symboulion hetoimasantes* (lit., "having prepared a deliberation"). Another reading has the ptc. *poiēsantes,* "having made, held a consultation." *handed him over:* As far as Mk is concerned, this verse indicates the complicity of the Jerusalem authorities with Pilate in the death of Jesus. See 9:31; 10:33; 14:10,11,18,21,41,42,44 for the use of the significant vb. *paradidonai. Pilate:* The Roman procurator or prefect of Judea (→ History of Israel, 75:143). **2.** *the king of the Jews:* In 14:61–62 Jesus admitted that he was a Messiah; since this was the title par excellence for Israel's king, Pilate's question is understandable—even though it does ring throughout the Gospel accounts with a certain irony, which is exploited by the Christian Evangelists. We do not know the source of Mark's information about this question; it is not impossible that the scene is reconstructed on what was remembered in the Christian community about the inscription on the cross. In any case, the charge of blasphemy is not made here; the overtones of the interrogation are those of political sedition, a cause that would concern the Roman governor. *you say it:* The meaning of this answer is not clear and has often been debated; it probably is a "yes," half consented to, implying that the speaker would put it differently. *accused him of many things:* The account is very vague. Jesus' silence puzzles the cynical Pilate, and it is the innocence of Jesus that the Evangelist implies. **6.** *at the feast:* The custom of a Roman governor releasing a prisoner to the people on a feast day is not attested elsewhere, except in Jn 18:39. Very dubious extrabiblical parallels are occasionally cited, but they prove nothing since there is no indication of the reprieve involved being related to a feast (see A. Deissmann, *LAE* 269). **7.** *Barabbas:* The Aram name means "son of Abba," or more literally, "son of the father." A symbolic interpretation of the latter meaning is probably responsible for the patristic notice and the variant in Mt 27:16 that his name was "Jesus Barabbas" (see H. A. Rigg, Jr., *JBL* 64 [1945] 417–56). The Barabbas incident explains the presence of "the crowd," which would otherwise scarcely have gathered to witness Jesus' trial. This incident is presented as Pilate's attempt to find a way out of an embarrassing situation and obviously shifts complicity in Jesus' death still more in the direction of the "chief priests." **13.** *crucify him:* This mode of capital punishment, apparently Persian in origin, was common practice among the Romans for slaves and non-Jews since the Punic Wars (Josephus, *Life* 75 § 420; *JW* 2.14,9 § 306); even the Hasmonean king Alexander Janneus employed this method (*JW* 1.4,6 § 97). The Evangelist's notice about the crowd's cry clearly implicates them in the execution; but mob psychology must be reckoned with, as well as the part played by the "chief priests" (15:11), before any conclusions are drawn from this notice. **14.** *what evil has he done?:* As in vv. 10 and 12, Pilate is depicted making an effort to defend an innocent person. **15.** *wanting to satisfy the crowd:* Pilate's own complicity is thus clearly stated, even though the involvement of the Romans is played down. Thus Pilate, "naturally inflexible, a blend of self-will and relentlessness" (Philo, *Embassy to Gaius* 8 § 301), yielded to the will of a cynical crowd that did not respect him.

16. *soldiers:* In the context, this can refer only to soldiers in the pay of the Romans. *inside the palace (that is, the praetorium):* The latter word is the official designation of the place where the Roman governor resided when he was in Jerusalem. It is commonly identified with the Fortress Antonia, at the NW corner of the Temple precincts (thus by such archaeologists as L.-H. Vincent, W. F. Albright, G. E. Wright; see M. Aline, *La Forteresse Antonia à Jérusalem et la question du prétoire* [Jerusalem, Jordan, 1956] 119–42). Others, however, insisting more on the literary evidence available, hold that the *praetorium* was at Herod's palace on the W side of the city (see P. Benoit, *RB* 59 [1952] 531–50). The site is not crucial in the interpretation of this passage; but it would call in question the route of the medieval Via Dolorosa (on which see G. Dalman, *Sacred Sites and Ways* [London, 1935] 346–47). *the whole cohort:* The Gk *speira* is the equivalent of either Lat *cohors* or *manipulus;* if either is to be taken strictly here, it would mean 200 to 600 men. But is it to be taken strictly? **17.** *purple:* Unlike Mt 27:28, where reference is explicitly made to a "scarlet cloak" (prob. the military *sagum purpuratum*), the mere mention of "purple" suggests the nuance of imperial robes. *a crown of thorns:* See comment on Mt 27:28. **18.** *hail, King of the Jews!:* The mockery included a parody of imperial acclamation, "Ave, Caesar, victor, imperator." It heightens the destiny of Jesus who draws from ordinary men only a lack of comprehension. To the soldiers he appears only as another prisoner and a means of idling away a weary hour: if you want to be a king, we'll make you one. It also brings out that it was as king of the Jews that Jesus suffered. **19.** *struck, spat:* These verbs remind one of 14:65; some commentators even go so far as to say that Mark has introduced them here from the account of the mistreatment of Jesus by the high priest's servants. *knelt down in homage to him:* The whole incident has often been compared to the contemporary story of the mockery of Herod Agrippa I in a farce acted out in the Alexandria gymnasium in which a lunatic named Karabas was decked out as a king (supposedly Herod Agrippa) and was saluted, consulted, and acclaimed (see Philo, *Flaccus* 6.35–40). There is, however, no evidence that this parallel influenced either the soldiers or the Evangelist.

92 (iv) *The crucifixion* (15:21–32). On the composition of this and the following section, see V. Taylor, *Mark,* 587, 649–51. The impersonal tone of this section, the frequent use of the simple connective "and," the hist. present in some verb forms, and the lack of any overly hortatory cast create the impression that the Evangelist writes not so much an eyewitness account as a compilation of details sifted from many stories about it in the early Church. He attempts to present Gentile Christians with information about the event. On the other hand, his references to the third, sixth, and ninth hours give the account a certain dramatic effect.

21. *they impress:* Pressed into service. This is the first hist. present in the passage, which in the Gk text heightens the vividness of the account; other instances: "lead" (22), "crucify" (24, 27). *Simon of Cyrene:* A colony of Jews had been in Cyrene in N Africa (near Bengasi) ever since the 4th cent. BC (See E. F. F. Bishop, *ExpT* 51 [1939–40] 148–53); possibly, then, Simon was a Diaspora Jew visiting the holy city for the feast of Passover (cf. Acts 2:10; 6:9; 11:20; 13:1). He seems to be a total stranger in the story, although later legend made him a bishop of the church in Bosra (Arabia) and a martyr. *father of Alexander and Rufus:* These are otherwise unknown Christians, but possibly known to the Gentile church for which Mark writes the Gospel (scarcely the Rufus of Rom 16:13; → Letter Rom, 53:10, 143). *coming in from the country:* This does not necessarily mean "from work in the country"; therefore it can scarcely be used as an argument pro or con the dating of the Last Supper as a Passover meal (see Jeremias, *EWJ* 76–77). *carry his* *cross:* The condemned person was normally made to carry at least the *patibulum* (crossbar), and Jn 19:17 suggests that Jesus did. That Simon was pressed into service by the Roman soldiers is likely after the scourging (15:15). **22.** *Golgotha:* A Grecized form of the Aram word for "skull," *gulgultā*. The spot may have been named thus because of a hill shaped like a skull, but the NT does not mention a hill. Later legends (influenced by the Christian Second-Adam motif?) identified the spot as the burial place of Adam's skull. Since about AD 326 the Constantinian basilica of the Holy Sepulcher has stood over an area said to be Golgotha. It still has the best claim for the site because it is now definitely known to have been outside the so-called second N wall of Jerusalem and the gate of Ephraim in the 1st cent. (See G. Dalman, *Sacred Sites and Ways*, 347–81; A. Parrot, *Golgotha and the Church of the Holy Sepulchre* [SBA 6; London, 1957]; J. Jeremias, *Golgotha* [Leipzig, 1926]; [most recently] K. M. Kenyon, *PEQ* 98 [1966] 87. On the merits of the claim of the so-called Gordon's Calvary or Garden Tomb, see J. Simons, *Jerusalem in the Old Testament* [Leiden, 1952] 282–343; L.-H. Vincent, *RB* 34 [1925] 401–31.) It must be recalled that the double destruction of Jerusalem (AD 70 under Titus and AD 135 under Hadrian) razed most of the 1st-cent. city; a pagan temple also occupied the area in question near the agora of Hadrian's Aelia Capitolina. But is it likely that all memory of the area where this event took place would have disappeared from the corporate consciousness of early Christians? The English name "Calvary" comes from Lat *calvariae locus*, "place of the skull" (Vg). **23.** *wine flavored with myrrh:* An anodyne, which probably also reflects Prv 31:6 ("Give...wine to the sorely depressed"). *did not take it:* No reason is given for the refusal. The Christian reader recalls Jesus' words of 14:25 and 10:39. **24.** *they crucify him:* "So, in the simplest possible terms, the dread act is recorded! No attempt is made to describe the harrowing details" (V. Taylor, *Mark*, 589). (For a description of different modes of crucifixion, see *EDB* 462–75.) Through this act, what Cicero once called the "most cruel and repulsive of punishments" (*In Verrem* 5.64) quickly became a symbol of Christian motivation (see Gal 2:20; Rom 6:6; Mk 9:34 par.) and a source of inspiration for centuries. *divided his garments among them:* The Roman custom of permitting the soldiers to take the prisoner's clothes as booty is colored by an allusion to Ps 22:18. The despoiling of Jesus is thus presented as a fulfillment of the OT image of the suffering upright man of the Psalter. Jn 19:24, however, presents a different interpretation of the incident. **25.** *third hour:* About 9:00 A.M., which stands in conflict with Jn 19:14 ("sixth hour," or about noon). The Marcan time framework has an artificial air about it and may reflect a liturgical celebration of the passion in some early Christian community much more than the time sequence of the events. **26.** *the king of the Jews:* Although the wording varies slightly in Mt and Lk, the superscription on the cross is substantially the same in the Syn, which know nothing of the three languages mentioned in Jn 19:27. Roman custom used the superscription to indicate the reason for the penalty ("praecedente titulo qui causam poenae indicaret," Suetonius, *Caligula* 32). It also represents at once Pilate's concession to the political accusation leveled against Jesus as well as his contempt of them. **27.** *two robbers:* The Gk word *lēstēs* may also mean "insurrectionist," for Josephus (*JW* 2.13,3 §254) has used it to describe the chauvinistic "sicarii" who opposed Roman occupation of Palestine (→ History of Israel, 75:155). Mark's account knows nothing of the mishnaic regulation that "two ought not to be judged in the one day" (*Sanhedrin* 6:4). **28.** Missing in the best mss. (S, A, B, C, D), it is most likely a late gloss introducted from Lk 22:37, associating the execution of Jesus with Is 53:12. **29.** *tossing their heads:* See Ps 22:8; but also Lam 2:15; 2 Kgs 19:21–22; Jb 16:4; Sir 13:7. The OT allusions create a certain poignancy in the remarks of the passers-by whose logic is irrefutable but only brings out the folly of the cross (see 1 Cor 1:17ff.). *destroy the temple:* See comment on 14:58. **31.** *the chief priests...scribes:* Not only the passers-by (v. 29) and the fellow crucified (v. 32), but even the chief priests are depicted as taunting Jesus. **32.** *that we may see and believe:* See Wis 2:17–18. The taunts recorded here reflect the charges of the "trial" scene (destruction of the Temple and messiahship) and the charge on the cross itself. But they also sum up the "scandal of the cross," the stumbling block that it presented to contemporary Jews. Mark does not theologize the cross as does Paul, but through the record of these taunts he conveys his message: Faith in the crucified Jesus is not measured by what one sees.

93 (v) *The death of Jesus* (15:33–41). The sober account of Mk continues, as a further attempt is made to supply information and an interpretation of the event. Its singular character is conveyed by the extraordinary phenomena accompanying it.

33. *sixth hour:* Noon; see comment on 15:25. *darkness over the whole earth:* Or possibly, "the whole land" (of Judea). See comment on Mt 27:45 for its significance; cf. Ex 10:22, and the darkness described by OT prophets at a time of Yahweh's visitation (Jl 2:10; 3:4,15; Is 13:10). *ninth hour:* 3:00 P.M. **34.** *Elōi, Elōi, lama sabachthani:* Mark translates the cry immediately. As it stands, it reflects an Aram version of Ps 22:2 ('^{e}lāhī '^{e}lāhī l^{e}mā š^{e}baqtánī [though the Gk *elōi* is closer to the Hebr form with its *ō* instead of *ā*]). The Hebr text of the Ps runs: *'ēlî, 'ēlî, lāmā 'azabtánî*. As a quotation of an OT Ps, it can hardly be taken literally as an expression of real despair or dereliction. Rather, Jesus applies to himself an OT passage that sums up the suffering of the upright individual who turns to his God in the stress of hostile opposition and its ensuing depression. In using the Ps, Jesus does not express the feeling that his life's work has failed and that God has therefore abandoned him; he identifies himself with a biblical precedent, the persecuted upright man who has trusted in Yahweh, and found in him the source of his consolation and ultimate triumph. (See J. Gnilka, *BZ* 3 [1959] 294–97.) **35.** *he is calling for Elijah:* The return of Elijah was expected (see Mk 6:14; 8:28; 9:11; Mal 3:1; 4:5); popular belief considered one of his tasks to be the rescue of the pious from their need (Sir 48:1–11). It is not easy to explain the misinterpretation of *elōi* and *'Elîyāh;* but the form of "my God" in Mt 27:46 (*ēlī*, which may be more original) could more easily have been understood as a shortened form of *'Elîyāh*). **36.** *vinegar...to drink:* See comment on Mt 27:48. In the spirit of Elijah one of the bystanders offered Jesus a soothing drink. But Christian tradition saw it as a fulfillment of Ps 69:22 ("they gave me vinegar to drink for my thirst"). **37.** *Jesus cried aloud and expired:* The loud cry indicates that the end came with violence. Was it a cry of pain? Nothing in Mk or Mt would be against this meaning. Lk 23:46, after having suppressed the cry in Mk 15:34, substitutes an interpretation at this point ("Father, into your hands I commend my spirit"). Likewise, the majestic theologoumenon, "it is finished" of Jn 19:30, stands in contrast to the stark reality of Mk. Patristic writers often regarded the cry as a manifestation of the freedom with which Jesus handed over his life to the Father. **38.** *the curtain of the Temple was rent in two:* Two curtains (both called *katapetasma* [as here] by

Josephus, *JW* 5.5,4–5 § 212, 219, and by the LXX [Ex 26:37 and 26:31]) hung in the Jerusalem Temple: one before the *naos*, and one separating the holy of holies from it. Since *katapetasma* was more frequently used for the curtain before the holy of holies, probably this is meant here. But is a reference being made here to a material Temple veil at all? As the remark stands, it could be a symbolic statement of the Evangelist, commenting on the death of Jesus, which opened the way to God for men in a new way and connoted the end of his inaccessibility for which the inviolable holy of holies stood. It may be Mark's way of expressing what Heb 9:9ff. and 10:19 have formulated more theologically. Access to God is now made through the death of Christ. (Cf. A. Pelletier, *RSR* 46 [1958] 161–80.) **39.** *truly this man was the Son of God:* In a certain sense this verse is the climax of the Marcan Gospel: the full revelation of who Jesus is becomes manifest. The climax is really double, for a very similar manifestation is implied in the question of the Jewish high priest (14:61). Now, by contrast to that incredulity, a Gentile—a centurion of the hated Roman army—makes the admission awaited all through the Marcan Gospel. It is, of course, one thing to ask what the Roman centurion would have understood by the phrase "Son of God" and another to ask what the Christian Evangelist understood by it in recording it. In Lk 23:47 the centurion acknowledges Jesus simply as "upright" (*dikaios*), which may be closer to the original estimate. On the other hand, a man in such service could have used of Jesus an imperial title, saying that he was *divi filius*.

40. *Mary Magdalene:* This resident of the Galilean town of Magdala is probably the same as the woman "out of whom Jesus drove seven devils" (Lk 8:2), who is not, however, the same as the sinner of Lk 7:37, despite the later Western romantic tradition about her. *Mary, mother of James the small and Joses:* James was "little" in stature. If account is taken of Jn 19:25, then she might be the same as "Mary the wife of Clopas." Some would identify this James with James the son of Alphaeus (Mk 3:18; see AG 368); others with James, "the brother of the Lord" (Gal 1:19; → Aspects NT Thought, 78:168). See also comment on Mt 27:55. Their presence is noted here only as a literary anticipation of 16:1ff.

94 (f) The Burial and Anointing of Jesus (15:42–47). The account of Jesus' burial confirms his death; and even though the details are recounted in view of the coming episode of the empty tomb, the story is scarcely a fabrication in which a pious Jew gives Jesus a hasty burial and his own disciples have no part in it (see Bultmann, *HST* 276).

42. *evening had come:* Mk's chronology is confusing for two reasons: (1) The evening mentioned should conclude "the [day of] Preparation" or *prosabbaton* and thus begin the Sabbath itself—when it would be unthinkable for a pious Jew to do what Joseph is depicted doing here. (2) When one compares Mk 14:12, this "[day of] Preparation" just ending must be the Passover itself, or "the first day of Unleavened Bread." On this day it would be equally impossible to do what is described. It should be noted, moreover, that Mk's chronology tends to be closer here to what Jn (18:28; 19:31) suggests—that Passover and Sabbath coincided that year. *Joseph of Arimathea:* See comment on Mt 27:43. Joseph appears here as a pious Jew, a prominent member of the Sanhedrin, who out of sympathy or else respect for the prescriptions of Dt 21:23 sought to bury Jesus. Mt (27:54) makes him a rich Christian disciple; cf. Lk 23:50–51. **45.** *the corpse:* Mark uses the stark Gk word *ptōma*, "cadaver," i.e., that which has fallen. **46.** *linen cloth:* Or burial shroud, which can scarcely be identified with the 14th-cent. Shroud of Turin (see H. Thurston, *Cath. Ency.* 13, 762–63; J. Blinzler, *MTZ* 3 [1952] 403–14; *Das Turiner Grablinnen und die Wissenschaft* [Ettal, 1952]). On the possibility of buying a shroud on the Passover, see Jeremias, *EWJ* 77–78. *in a tomb:* See *EDB* 906–10.

(Braun, F.-M., "La sépulture de Jésus," *RB* 45 [1936] 34–52. Masson, C., "L'ensevelissement de Jésus; Marc xv, 42–47," *RTP* 31 [1943] 193–203.)

95 (g) The Empty Tomb (16:1–8). Commentators do not agree about the ending of the original Passion Narrative; did it include an apparition scene or not? Taylor (*Mark*, 602) thinks that Mk 16:1–8 stands apart from the Passion Narrative proper and stems from a different cycle of traditions. Léon-Dufour (*VDBS* 6, 1472) is, however, inclined to include at least one apparition; in this he is in basic agreement with Jeremias (*EWJ* 96). Cf. 1 Cor 15:3ff. In this regard it is noteworthy that the Syn still agree in general in recording a scene of the discovery of the empty tomb (see Mt 28:1–10; Lk 24:1–12); after this each goes his own way—and Mk may even end at v. 8. In this and the subsequent episodes recorded in the Gospel tradition the emphasis is not so much on what happened as on the Easter message itself: "He has been raised; he is not here. Why seek the living among the dead?" The diversity of apparitions in the Syn reveals merely that there was no need felt in the early Church for one continuous Resurrection Narrative, as was true in the case of the Passion Narrative (see Taylor, *FGT* 59–60). In these verses the resurrection itself is not described—it never is, and never could be—and so the title is usually given as "The Empty Tomb."

1. *when the Sabbath was over:* After sundown, which brought Nisan 15 to a close. *Mary Magdalene...:* See comment on 15:40. *bought spices:* Although the anointing of a corpse was allowed by rabbinical law on the Sabbath (Mishnah, *Shabbath* 23:5), the women respected the Sabbath rest by not purchasing *arōmata* (aromatic oils and salves, used for the burial of the dead). **2.** *very early on the first* [*day*] *of the week:* Lit., "on [day] one of the week." Even though delayed, the action of the women was obviously intended to honor the dead; see also comment on 14:8. **3.** *who will roll back the stone for us?:* Their question is prompted by the heavy weight of the circular flat stones rolled on their edge in a stone track and used in Palestine to cover the entrance to burial crypts. The question, why they did not think about this sooner, or why they wanted to anoint the body if they could not get to it, misses the point of the narrative. **4.** *was rolled back:* Mk does not say how; Mt 28:2 ascribes it to "the angel of the Lord" who descended for the purpose. **5.** *entering the tomb:* Into the chamber or chambers, which were fitted out with *loculi* for the dead bodies. *a young man sitting on the right side robed in white:* The word *neaniskos*, "young man," can be found in 2 Mc 3:26,33 and Josephus, *Ant.* 5.8,2 § 277 as a designation for an angel. This could be meant here by Mark; in Mt 28:5 it is an "angel" who addresses the women; cf. Lk 24:4. For white robes as a symbol of heavenly beings, see comment on 9:3. What Mark is mainly interested in communicating in picturesque fashion is that the women were recipients of a realization of what the empty tomb really meant. **6.** *you seek Jesus of Nazareth, the crucified:* Cf. 1 Cor 1:23; 2:2; Gal 3:1. *he has been raised; he is not here:* Thus Marcan simplicity formulates the fundamental Christian *praeconium paschale;* the Cross has yielded to the Empty Tomb. Although the Gk vb. *ēgerthē* (an aor. pass.) might possibly have a deponent sense, it is most likely intended as a passive at this early stage of the Gospel tradition, given the predominance of the passive in other early NT writings (→ Pauline Theology, 79:72) and other

NT statements using the active (Acts 3:15; 4:10; 10:40; 13:30; → Aspects NT Thought, 78:158). *see the place where they laid him:* This is not a directive to a different tomb in which the body of Jesus lay; such an interpretation would contradict the sense of the whole passage. **7.** *go, tell his disciples and Peter:* Although Peter is singled out, and a reference to the denials (14:68,70,71) is obviously intended, one cannot fail to note that the Easter message is first announced to the faithful, devoted women of the Christian entourage. *going before you to Galilee:* Like Mk 14:28, these words foreshadow the Galilean apparitions. They will see the Risen Jesus, where they witnessed his deeds and miracles; these will be confirmed by his new status. **8.** *fled from the tomb:* This is the effect of the message. *for they were afraid:* Cf. Gn 45:3.

96 **(V) The Endings of the Marcan Gospel (16:9–20).** Mark may have ended his Gospel with v. 8 (→ Aspects NT Thought, 78:156) but the strange ending of that verse with the conj. *gar* and its abruptness indicate that the real ending of the Gospel may be lost to us today. The mss. tradition has preserved three different endings: (1) the long canonical ending (16:9–20), which is missing in mss. S and B and was declared inauthentic by Eusebius (*Quaest. ad Marinum* 1). Even though it is generally regarded today as non-Marcan (on the basis of different style, vocabulary, and subject matter; see Wik, *NTI* 171–72; R–F, *INT* 219–20), it is nevertheless regarded as canonical by Catholics, as a result of the Tridentine decree on the Canon (see DB 784; DS 1504); it was one of the passages explicitly discussed at the Council as an example of a "pars" (see E. Mangenot, *DTC* 2, 1602; *DAFC* 4, 1972–73). (2) the so-called shorter ending, a single verse found in mss. L, Ψ, 099, 0112, 579. It too is non-Marcan in its style and language (see V. Taylor, *Mark*, 614). (3) the Freer Logion, actually a gloss added to 16:14 in the 5th cent. Freer ms. of the Gospels (codex W [Washingtoniensis] is in the Freer Museum of the Smithsonian Institution). This gloss, added by some early scribe to soften the condemnation of the Eleven in v. 14, was known to Jerome (*Contra Pelagianos* 2.15). It too is quite non-Marcan in its style and language, and may have come from a Gnostic circle of the late 2nd or early 3rd cent.

97 **(A) The Canonical Ending (16:9–20).** This ending, which may date from no earlier than the 2nd cent. AD and may be related to other than Marcan traditions in the early Church, is customarily divided into four sections: (a) the Apparition to Mary Magdalene (16:9–11); (b) the Apparition to Two Travelers (16:12–13); (c) the Apparition to the Eleven (16:14–18); (d) the Ascension and Start of the Apostolic Mission (16:19–20).

(a) The Apparition to Mary Magdalene (16:9–11). In style and language these verses are related to either a Lucan or Johannine tradition; see Jn 20:11–18. They are a colorless record of the first apparition of the Risen Jesus to Mary of Magdala (see 16:1), who goes off to report it to the sorrowing, incredulous disciples. **9.** *having risen:* The Gk participle used here is *anastas*, an intr. form, which stands in contrast to the pass. *egerthē* of 16:6. The intr. form represents a later stage in the early Church's Christological awareness when the act of rising was being attributed less to the Father and more to Jesus himself (→ Aspects NT Thought, 78:158). *from whom he had expelled seven demons:* See Lk 8:2; she is not to be facilely identified with the sinful woman who anointed Jesus' feet in Lk 7:37–38. **10.** *mourning and weeping:* The reaction is that of disciples who have lost their Master and are not partaking in the joy of the Jewish festival. **11.** *they would not believe:* Their incredulity is repeatedly stressed in this ending to Mk, see vv. 13 and 14. There is a certain irony in that Jesus appeared first, not to his chosen disciples, but to a woman; Mary Magdalene (and the others, 16:1) became the first herald(s) of the resurrection. But the early Church did not always present it this way; see the fragment of the kerygma in 1 Cor 15:3–8.

98 (b) The Apparition to Two Travelers (16:12–13). These verses remind the reader of the Emmaus incident in Lk 24:13–35; they serve to bring out again the postresurrectional incredulity of the disciples. **12.** *afterward:* The Gk phrase is *meta tauta* (after these things), common in Jn, but not otherwise used in Mk. *in a different guise:* Lit., "in another form," the noun *morphē* indicating his external appearance. This and other Gospel accounts (e.g., Jn 20:14,19) are the basis of the usual conviction that the Risen Jesus presented himself to the early Church in a form that did not in all respects resemble that of his earthly ministry (cf. 1 Cor 15:35–41). *walking out into the country:* See Lk 24:15. **13.** *they went back:* See Lk 24:35.

(c) The Apparition to the Eleven (16:14–18). This section recalls passages in other Gospels such as Lk 24:36–49; Jn 20:19–23; Mt 28:16–20. The apparition forms a climax in this ending, as is seen by the words *prōton* (first) in 16:9, *hetera* (another) in 16:12, and *hysteron* (lastly) in 16:14. It is also brought out by the reproach addressed to the disciples, climaxing the notices that they did not believe. **14.** *he upbraided them:* The vb. *oneidizō* is the same as that used to describe the ranting of the thieves who were crucified with Jesus (15:32). Early commentators (and the Freer Logion) tried to soften this reproach of the disciples. **15.** *go into all the world:* An independent version of Mt 28:18–20. The universalism cannot be missed. *to the whole creation:* Or "to every creature." *proclaim the good news:* See comment on 1:14. **16.** *will be saved:* The conditions are faith and baptism (as in Mt 28:18). The proclamation of the good news will bring either life or death to men, in accordance with their response of belief or unbelief. Men of all ages must take a position toward it. According to V. Taylor (*Mark*, 612), the phrase "he who believes" (being an aor. ptc.), probably refers to a baptismal confession. **17.** *signs:* These are indicated in the following phrases of vv. 17–18; the word *sēmeion* is being used in the usual Syn sense, and differs considerably from its Johannine cognate. They indicate here that the kingdom is established (→ Aspects NT Thought, 78:127–128).

(d) The Ascension and the Start of the Apostolic Mission (16:19–20). Like Lk 24:50–51 this canonical ending of Mk situates the exaltation of Jesus to heavenly glory by what we normally call the ascension on Easter itself. It is the fitting conclusion to the apparitions recorded in this ending. **19.** *after he had spoken to them:* The interval would by all normal understanding of this phrase be a very short one. *was taken up into heaven:* Again the passive is used, and the implication is that this is the "theological passive" (*GrBib* § 236), i.e., "taken up" by God (*theos* = the Father). This interpretation is supported by the fact that the words used here to describe the ascension are taken from 2 Kgs 2:11 (the assumption of Elijah). The same verb (*analambanō*) is used to describe this exaltation in Acts 1:2,11,22; 1 Tm 3:16, whereas the Creeds use *anabainō* or *anerchomai*. (For the relation of the ascension to the resurrection, → Aspects NT Thought, 78:159.) *sat down at God's right hand:* The phrase comes from Ps 110:1, already cited in Mk 12:36. Because he is there, the author of this ending could refer to Christ as "the Lord Jesus," giving him the title *Kyrios* (found elsewhere in Mk only in 11:3). **20.** *they went out and preached* *everywhere:* They set out from Jerusalem and carried the "word of the Lord" forth (see Is 2:3) to all men. *the Lord worked with them:* It is the exalted and Risen Jesus who is said to cooperate with the endeavors of his own disciples and agents in the spread of the kingdom which "the word" was proclaiming. Their "word" is none other than the "gospel" with which the Marcan composition began (*archē*, 1:1). Some inferior mss. add "Amen" to the end of the verse.

99 **(B) The Shorter Ending.** It reads: "But they reported briefly to Peter and his companions all they had been told. Afterwards Jesus himself sent out through them the sacred and incorruptible proclamation of eternal salvation from the east to the west." It is to be read after 16:8.

they: The women of 16:1. *through them:* That is, by Peter and his companions. *from the east to the west:* This has been taken by H. B. Swete (*Mark*, ci) as an indication of composition by a "Roman hand; a Western origin is suggested by the pointed reference to the westward course of the Apostolic preaching." *salvation:* A Lucan word; see Lk 1:69.

100 **(C) The Freer Logion.** It reads: "And they excused themselves, saying, 'This age of lawlessness and disbelief is under Satan, who does not permit the true power of God to prevail over the unclean things of the spirits. Therefore reveal your righteousness now.' Thus they addressed Christ, but Christ said to them in reply, 'The term of the years of Satan's authority has been fulfilled, but other terrible things draw near, even for the sinners for whom I was handed over in death, that they might return to the truth and sin no more, that they might inherit the spiritual and incorruptible glory of righteousness which is in heaven.' "

they: The Eleven of 16:14. *lawlessness:* The juxtaposition of this notion with that of "righteousness" in the logion recalls 2 Cor 6:14. *under Satan:* Cf. Rom 3:9 ("under sin"); see 2 Cor 2:11. *reveal your righteousness:* Rom 1:17 gives a pregnant sense to these words. *Satan's authority:* See Acts 26:18, the commission of the Risen Jesus addressed to Paul: "[the Gentiles] to whom I send you to open their eyes, that they may turn from darkness to light and from the authority of Satan to God." *handed over in death:* See Mk 13:12.

43

THE GOSPEL ACCORDING TO MATTHEW

John L. McKenzie

BIBLIOGRAPHY

1 Allen, W. C., *The Gospel According to St. Matthew* (ICC; N.Y., 1907). Bornkamm, G., G. Barth and H. J. Held, *Tradition and Interpretation in Matthew* (tr. P. Scott; London, 1963). Butler, B. C., *The Originality of St. Matthew* (Cambridge, 1951). Davies, W. D., *The Setting of the Sermon on the Mount* (Cambridge, 1964). Farrer, A. M., *St. Matthew and St. Mark* (London, 1954). Fenton, J. C., *The Gospel of St. Matthew* (Baltimore, 1963). Filson, F. V., *A Commentary on the Gospel According to St. Matthew* (London, 1963). Gaechter, P., *Das Matthäus Evangelium* (Innsbruck, 1963). Hummel, R., *Die Auseinandersetzung zwischen Kirche und Judentum im Matthäusevangelium* (Munich, 1963). Klostermann, E., *Das Matthäusevangelium* (3d ed.; Tübingen, 1938). Lagrange, M.-J., *Évangile selon Saint Matthieu* (EBib; 8th ed.; Paris, 1947). Lohmeyer, E., *Das Evangelium nach Matthäus* (Meyer; Göttingen, 1956). M'Neile, A. H., *The Gospel According to St. Matthew* (London, 1915). Schmid, J., *Das Evangelium nach Matthäus* (RNT; 3d ed.; Regensburg, 1959). Schniewind, J., *Das Evangelium nach Matthäus* (NTD; Göttingen, 1954). Stendahl, K., *The School of St. Matthew* (Uppsala, 1954). Strecker, G., *Der Weg der Gerechtigkeit* (Göttingen, 1962). Trilling, W., *Das wahre Israel* (Munich, 1964).

F–B 72–86. Guthrie, *NTI* 3, 19–48. R–F, *INT* 159–90. Wik, *NTI* 173–99; *IPLCG*, 208–67.

INTRODUCTION

2 **(I) Literary Character of the Gospel.** The outline of Mt (→ 16 below) does not produce well-balanced parts. But the pattern of five books, if it exists, must be intended to suggest the five books of the Law. The outline would then reflect a theme that is clear in the Gospel without the outline: Jesus is the new Moses and the new Israel with a new revelation from God.

Compared to Mk and Lk, Mt is more obviously artificial, even contrived in its arrangement. This does not imply that Mk and Lk are without artificiality in the arrangement; even Mark, who seems to be the most naïve and unstudied of the Evangelists, has arranged his narrative in an order other than the simple order of events. But Matthew apparently wishes to make it clear that his arrangement is his own. He uses a large number of "literary seams," lines intended to connect passages previously unconnected: His most common connecting particle, "at that time," usually has no temporal reference whatever. The discourses are clearly arranged as such, and each of the five major discourses is signified by an individual concluding formula. A synoptic table of the Gospels shows that most of the material in Mt's discourses is found in scattered contexts in Mk and Lk; and possibly the sayings that are peculiar to Mt were assembled by him from scattered contexts also. Each of the discourses revolves around a theme, as the outline indicates (→ 16 below), except for the Sermon on the Mount; and the theme of this discourse is the righteousness of the Gospel as contrasted with the righteousness of the Law.

3 Mt emphasizes the sayings of Jesus both in discourses and in narratives. This interest in his teaching is in sharp contrast to Mk; the same interest appears in Lk, and Jn is almost entirely a report of the discourses of Jesus. The development of interest is obvious here; but Matthew has his own interest in the teaching. In Mt Jesus is contrasted with the scribes, the teacher of Judaism; he is a teacher far superior to them—a new Moses, as we have noted. Mt is as much a presentation of Jesus' teaching as it is a recital of his life; and the primitive form of the Gospel was a proclamation of the life, passion, death, and resurrection of Jesus. K. Stendahl has attributed Mt to a group of Christian scribes, "the school of St. Matthew," who wished to produce a handbook of Christian conduct to be used by teachers. Such a handbook would fill in the Christian community the place that was occupied by scribal teaching in the Jewish community. Thematic grouping of material appears not only in the discourses but also in the narratives; the pieces in 8:1–9:34 focus upon the revelation of Jesus as Messiah and the confession of his messiahship. The numerical groupings may also have a pedagogical purpose, although a symbolism of number is not excluded. There are seven petitions in the Lord's Prayer, seven parables in the parable discourse, seven woes against the Pharisees, and three temptations. Sayings and narratives are sometimes connected by catchwords, a mnemonic device.

Mt is written in good Greek, superior to that of Mk; but a conscious effort to write good Greek is seen more clearly in the narratives than it is in the discourses and sayings, which more frequently reflect an Aram source. But Mt also shows features of Semitic style; he employs synonymous and antithetic parallelism (7:24–27; 16:25), repetition of formulas, and strophic structure (5:3–10; 12:22–32). These cannot all be attributed to an Aram source with equal probability; the Evangelist was sufficiently versed in Semitic style to be able to combine it with Greek.

4 The schematism of the Gospel as a whole is also reflected in details. It can be seen that Mt usually abbreviates the miracle narratives of Mk. A definite pattern can frequently be discerned: introduction of the persons, the request, the reaction of Jesus, command and effect, and the reaction of the spectators. Matthew's writing here loses some of its vitality and results in a dry and monotonous style; this is not because Matthew does not know how to write vividly. By contrast Mark's vividness is in some ways artless. Matthew strives for a hieratic recital in which the miracle becomes a clear epiphany of divine power exercised without effort. When the heavenly reality is manifested, the event is detached from space and time. In Mt the transfiguration of Jesus has begun.

It is no accident that the words of Jesus are quoted more frequently from Mt than from any other Gospel. The Evangelist was deeply interested in Jesus' teaching; he presented the teaching in a compressed economical style that allows the impact of the sayings to be felt with no loss of power. This is not to imply that the sayings of Jesus are feebly recounted in the other Gospels, but simply to give to Matthew the credit for careful composition he so fully deserves. It can be noticed in the commentary that we are not concerned with the question which Gospel reports more accurately "the very words" of Jesus; this question admits to no answer. The form of Mt's sayings often reflects beyond doubt the experience of the primitive Church and its meditation on the person and the words of Jesus. Matthew is an excellent spokesman for this experience and meditation. It is paradoxical that, in spite of the force of his style, he has sometimes recast sayings that in Mk's form were too harsh for his readers.

5 **(II) Relation of Mt to the Other Synoptic Gospels.** The Syn theory adopted in this commentary is the simplest and most widely accepted theory (→ Syn Problem, 40:15). In spite of the difficulties involved, this theory raises fewer problems than any of the more detailed theories that have been proposed. But its adoption here does not imply that it is a final solution; it must be considered subject to revision, and therefore any conclusions that rest upon it should be considered provisional.

The theory can be simply outlined. It supposes that Mk is the earliest of the Syn, and that Mk was used as a source by both Matthew and Luke; and this means Mk in the form in which we now have Mk. It supposes that neither Matthew nor Luke knew each other. The large amount of material that only Mt and Lk have in common is not attributed to any form of interdependence, but to their use of a common source, usually called Q, from the Ger word *Quelle*, "source." If the common parts of Mt and Lk that do not appear in Mk are combined into a single document, this document would not be a gospel; and it is not supposed that Q was a gospel. But one of the difficulties in this Two-Document Hypothesis is the problem of defining what kind of document Q was. A document must be presupposed, in the opinion of the great majority of critics; the resemblances between Mt and Lk are too close verbally to be explained as having derived from a common oral tradition. That there was oral tradition before the Gospels or Q were written is doubted by no one; but the problem of the relationships of the Gospels is a literary one.

Since Q was not a gospel, it is usually assumed that it was a collection of the sayings of Jesus. Such collections appear in the *Pirqe Aboth* and also in Gk literature. However, scrutiny of the Q passages reveals at once that Q was not a collection of isolated aphorisms, like Prv in the OT. The community of Mt and Lk shows that the sayings must have been woven into connected discourse in at least some of the passages. This part of the hypothesis again is not altogether satisfactory, but attempts to multiply this documentary source into several sources have been no more satisfactory.

Besides Mk and Q, Mt has material found in no other Gospel. Since Mk and Q are documentary sources, many critics postulate a third document for Mt's material (often called M). This document cannot be considered a gospel, nor is it a collection of sayings; Mt has narrative passages peculiar to itself. Whether such a written source need be postulated for Mt's own material is not as clear as the postulate of Q; for Q is postulated because of a clear literary relationship. Effectively the symbol M designates nothing except material that is neither Mk nor Q; the character of M or proto-Mt simply cannot be determined. There is no convincing reason why this material may not be stray pieces of oral tradition first put in writing by Matthew.

6 The Evangelist's method of handling his sources can be traced only for Mk. The method can be described in two paradoxical qualities: Mt is dependent on Mk; and Mt is very free in the use of Mk. Where Mt follows Mk, it can be said generally that it betrays the use of no other source. The expansions are few, and almost without exception they admit an explanation that is based on Mt's theological conceptions. It follows the order of Mk closely, but allows some rearrangements that again can be explained by its theological purpose. The general structure—baptism, Galilean ministry, miracles, controversy, confession of Peter, predictions of the passion, journey to Jerusalem, Jerusalem controversies, passion, resurrection—is not substantially altered. At the same time Mt is free in its use of Mk. The exercise of this freedom is most obvious in the abbreviation of narrative passages, usually by the omission of descriptive details. Mt makes little use of the dialogue that occurs in Mk; personal names are generally not retained. Conversely, Mt shows no independence of Mk in its geography; Mt, which has been alleged to be "Palestinian," is much more vague on the geography of Palestine than is Jn, which has so long been attributed to a Hellenistic Christian (or an ex-Palestinian resident of Ephesus).

The sayings of Mt, both its own and those derived from Q, are inserted without dislocating the narrative of Mk. Most of them occur as mass insertions. Where Mk has sayings, Mt by rearrangement of the context sometimes gives them a different turn. This also is an example of freedom; the alterations we find need not be attributed to theological intentions. Some sayings certainly appeared both in Mk and in Q, but in a slightly different form in each. We can easily suppose that other variant forms of the sayings were in circulation, and Matthew felt free to adopt that particular form and context best suited to his purpose.

It is not entirely certain that we can project Matthew's handling of Mk into the handling of his other sources, e.g., Q (→ Syn Problem, 40:17, 21).

Because of Matthew's interest in Jesus' teaching, it may be a poor presumption that he treated the sayings that came to him in the same manner as the narratives of Mk. Certainly he did not regard Mk's sayings as immutable formulas; not infrequently he couched them in a form he considered better. He could have shown the same freedom combined with dependence toward Q that he shows toward Mk, but we have no reason to assert that he treated Q with less freedom than he applied to Mk. For the sayings peculiar to Mt we have no point of reference at all; but if the Evangelist allowed himself liberty in his use of the other sources, it seems improbable that he denied himself liberty here.

7 **(III) The Theological Character of the Gospel.** Matthew, we have noted, has been called a Christian scribe or rabbi. The designation means that he (or the school that he represents) instituted the same kind of study of the Gospel that the scribes of Judaism made of the Law. The parallel should not be pressed too closely; there is a world of difference between Mt and the Talmud. Nevertheless, there are points of contact between Mt and the rabbinical writings that are not found in the other Gospels. These points of contact are more than an interest in the Law and allusions to Jewish institutions. Matthew sometimes moves in the world of rabbinical thought. He not only is familiar with rabbinical dialectic; he uses it. He describes genuine rabbinical discussions. Certainly nothing in this implies undue liberty with the traditions. If Jesus was recognized in any character in the Jewish community, it was as a rabbi. That he engaged in rabbinical arguments and discussions is certain; but the other Gospels are less familiar with this world of thought than Mt, and they report it in less detail. These methods are employed by Matthew because he wishes to make a point that is directed toward Judaism: the thesis that Jesus Messiah is the new Moses and the new Israel, and the fulfillment of the Law and the Prophets. This thesis, which could only be directed to a Jewish audience, is supported by the type of argument accepted in Jewish learning. Mt reflects not only the rabbinical discussions of Jesus himself, but controversies of Jewish Christians with their fellow Jews.

8 Matthew cites the OT 41 times. Of these quotations 21 are common to Mk and Lk, and evidently Mk is the source. But 20, nearly half his total, are not found in Mk and Lk; and 10 of these 20 are found in no other NT book. Here we enter an area where Matthew shows his greatest originality. Of the 41 texts 37 are introduced with a formula; the most common formula is "that it might be fulfilled." Matthew's idea of fulfillment is treated in the commentary on 1:22; it is not the idea of the fulfillment of a prediction, but of the growth of a reality to its destined fullness. There is a certain rough similarity between Matthew's use of OT texts and the type of midrashic interpretation found in QL (see J. A. Fitzmyer, *NTS* 7 [1960–61] 297–333).

The source of these quotations is a matter of interest. Some are quoted according to the LXX, some according to the MT, and some according to neither of the two. That Matthew (or the other authors) used either the MT or the LXX at random or always quoted from memory seems highly improbable. Several scholars have postulated a handbook of OT texts devised for the use of Jewish Christians from which it could be argued that Jesus is the Messiah of the OT (cf. J.-P. Audet, *RB* 70 [1963] 381–405). The existence of such a handbook would explain the lack of consistency in the texts that are quoted in one Gospel or in all the Gospels taken together. Matthew may have supplemented the texts of such a handbook by some he gathered himself; or he may simply have used more of the texts given than Mark did.

9 Mt is called a Jewish Christian Gospel, and in this it differs from Mk and Lk; the allusions to Judaism and the use of the OT are a part of this pattern. The central theological purpose of Mt is to show that Jesus is the Messiah of the OT. The Jews should have recognized him, but they did not; and the messiahship of Jesus emerges against a background of Jewish unbelief and hostility. Jesus is Son of God and Son of David. The humanity of Jesus is transfigured by softening the emotional reactions attributed to Jesus in Mk and by the hieratic style of the miracle stories. In these details Jesus does not appear less human but as a man with a mysterious and superior personality. Matthew retains a number of the texts in which the "Messianic Secret" of Mk appears, but he continues his Gospel after these passages as if they had not occurred. Jesus is transparently the Messiah in Mt, and only willful unbelief can obscure this truth. The obtuseness of the disciples to the messiahship of Jesus, a basic theme in Mk, is softened by Matthew; again he keeps a number of Mk's texts, but continues with his own material in such a way that the disciples appear to have a good understanding of the messiahship, if not a complete one. In this respect Matthew has certainly retrojected the faith of the apostolic Church into the Gospel narrative; but in spite of this it is the faith of the apostolic Church that his Gospel proclaims.

Jesus is Messiah, but not the king Messiah of popular expectation. Mt identifies him as the suffering Son of Man whose saving work is accomplished through his passion and death. He is the lowly Messiah, a friend of the poor because he is one of them. Jesus renounces wealth and power and calls upon his disciples to do the same. He has no political message; only Mt has the verse in which Jesus says that those who take the sword shall perish by the sword. The reign comes with Jesus, but it is not a reign of the king Messiah over a Jewish world empire. The reign is accomplished by free submission to the sovereign will of God.

10 Mt is a Jewish Gospel, but it is also a Gospel of the Church. The reign of God in Mt is clearly identified with the community of the disciples, a community that is identified with Jesus himself. Mt has not the Pauline idea of the body or the Johannine idea of the vine, but Jesus is present where two or three assemble in his name, and he remains with the disciples until the eschatological consummation. Mt's reign is universal. The unbelief of the Jews has opened the Gentile world for the proclamation of the Gospel. The Gentiles are not evangelized simply because of the defect of Jewish faith; Matthew understands that Israel should have proclaimed its Messiah to the world, but has refused to accept him. For the Church is the new Israel, and because the Church alone believes in Jesus Messiah it is the only true Israel. The "fulfillment" of Israel must be realized in the Gentile world without the people of Israel.

But the reign of God is not identified with the Church in such a way that the identification is total. The reign of God is fulfilled only in an eschatological event. Here Mt does not differ from Mk; Mt's contribution is the eschatological thrust of the Christian community. The eschatological event begins with the Church. And indeed the rejection of the Messiah by the Jews initiates the eschatological mystery; this rejection elicits the judgment, which in Mt 24 is merged with the eschatological judgment.

11 Since Jesus is the Messiah of the OT, Matthew finds it necessary to state the position of Jesus toward the Law, the basis of Judaism in NT times. This position is expressed in a classic phrase: Jesus did not come to destroy the Law, but to fulfill it. To fulfill the law means to bring it to the fullness of which it is a developmental phase. The reign—and Jesus himself is identified with the reign—is this full reality. Jesus is lord of the Law; he does not annul it any more than mature manhood annuls childhood, but the "yoke" of the reign removes the yoke of the Law. Jesus reduces all the commandments of the Law to the commandment of love; love is Christian freedom. Love communicates not a lesser righteousness, but a greater; and when the reign has arrived the Law is no longer righteousness.

In this context the controversy between Jesus and the Pharisees is not a controversy between Jesus and the Law. The Pharisees do not represent the true Law; they do not teach and observe the true Law, for they do not recognize that it demands its fulfillment in the Messiah. They have attributed to the Law a sufficiency it does not possess and have maintained its efficacy by adding to it the traditions of men. Jesus flatly rejects the Pharisaic thesis that the Law in its totality included "the traditions of the elders." These traditions have made the Law an intolerable burden. The Pharisees have reduced the union of man with God to a carefully fixed set of routine external observances and have thus reduced righteousness to a man-made product. In effect, they deny man's sinfulness because they do not confess guilt for real sin; they polish the outside of the vessel, but their interpretation of the Law does not touch the heart.

12 In the development of these themes Mt reflects the controversies of Christians and Jews in the apostolic Church; but very possibly it also reflects discussions within the Jewish Christian community. It is clear from Acts and the Pauline epistles that the problem of the Gospel and the Law was the central theological problem of the first generation of the Church. Mt has its place in this discussion; and in spite of the fact that it is called the Jewish Gospel, Mt's thesis on the Law is the same as the thesis of Paul in substance, although it is couched in different terms.

13 **(IV) Authorship, Date, and Place of Composition.** There is no evidence that Mt ever bore any other title or attribution. Nor has there been any doubt that the Matthew meant is the tax collector whose call is related in Mt 9:9–13 and who is enumerated in the lists of the Twelve. There are, however, certain problems here; the name of the tax collector in Mk 2:13–17 and Lk 5:27–32 is Levi, and it must be assumed that Levi (like Simon Peter) had a change of name. Jews did not bear two Semitic names. The Gk *Matthaios* represents the Hebr *Mattai*, abbreviated from *Mattityāhû* or *Mattanyāhû*. The assumption of a change of name is not too difficult; no Levi appears in any of the lists of the Twelve.

The first attribution of literary work to Matthew is the statement of Papias, bishop of Hierapolis in Phrygia *ca.* AD 130, quoted by Eusebius in the 4th cent. (*HE* 3.39,16); the statements of Irenaeus and Origen are probably dependent on Papias (Wik, *NTI* 179–81). Papias does not call the writing of Matthew a gospel, but says that "Matthew collected the sayings [Gk *logia*] in the Hebr language and that each one translated [or interpreted?] them as best he could." The "sayings" are generally understood to mean the sayings of Jesus, and this work would have borne some resemblance to Q. But the *logia* may mean a collection of OT texts, a handbook of texts for apologetic use of the type described above. Irenaeus and Origen speak not of *logia* but of a gospel; and there is no doubt that they meant the Gospel we know.

The text of Papias is open to many questions. Eusebius did not regard him as well informed, and the passages that have survived in quotations indicate that his information—not to say his thinking—was more than slightly confused. There is no evidence that Papias saw the Aram (which he calls Hebr) document to which he refers. There are no citations of the Aram M (→ Syn Problem, 40:14) anywhere in early Church literature. The question of whether Matthew wrote the Gospel that bears his name is thus closely connected with the question of the original language of Mt. If Matthew is not the author of an Aram gospel, it does not follow that he wrote no gospel; but the only ancient literary testimony is that Matthew wrote in Aramaic.

14 That the canonical Gk Mt is not a translation of an Aram original is universally accepted by scholars. It can be retranslated into Aramaic no more easily than Mk or Lk. Its Greek is superior to that of Mk. It contains a number of wordplays (6:16; 21:41; 24:30) possible only in Greek. The 21 OT quotations found in Mt, Mk, and Lk are given according to the LXX; in the quotations peculiar to Mt the Hebr text is followed more closely but with affinities to the LXX, and the indications are that Matthew did not use the MT for these quotations. They may come from a handbook of the type previously mentioned. Matthew's dependence on Mk for his narrative passages is clear beyond doubt; and of special pertinence here is Matthew's dependence on Mk in the story of the call of Matthew—a passage that in the hypothesis of the authorship of Mt must be autobiographical. If an Aram M existed, it would not be the exact original of the present Gk Mt: the Gk Mt would have to be such a substantial and thorough rewriting as to eliminate all traces of the original. If Matthew was the author of the Aram M, he cannot be the author or translator of the Gk Mt.

The case for an Aram M was ably presented by M.-J. Lagrange, and is at present upheld by P. Benoit. Most scholars do not find the arguments for it convincing, for the reasons indicated above; the doubts can be summed up simply in the absence of any trace of the existence of an Aram M except for the quotation of Papias and the use of Papias by writers who depended on him. If the Gk Mt is the original Gospel—and everything suggests that it is—then it cannot be attributed to the tax collector Matthew, one of the Twelve. There is nothing to suggest the personal identity of the author.

15 Irenaeus alone of the early writers suggests a date; he makes the authorship of Mt contemporaneous with the preaching of Peter and Paul in Rome—i.e., before AD 68. This detail cannot be tested. Internal evidence suggests (but does not demonstrate) a date later than the fall of Jerusalem in AD 70. But the familiarity of the author with Palestinian Jewish customs does not allow us to remove the Gospel—in space or in time—too far from Palestinian Judaism before the Jewish rebellion. It is not without interest that Matthew's acquaintance with Jewish customs and practices is not matched by acquaintance with Palestinian geography; his geography lies mostly in Galilee, and Matthew, as a Palestinian Jew, need not have known Galilee. But if the Gospel was written later than AD 70, there are excellent reasons for thinking that it was written outside Palestine. Many scholars suggest Antioch in Syria, a city where Jewish and Gentile Christianity met and mingled, and where the questions of the relations of the Law and the Gospel were very probably acute. The material peculiar to Mt is best explained as drawn from Palestinian traditions directly; and this would have been possible in Syria.

16 **(V) Outline.** To outline Mt or any of the four Gospels might appear to be a simple task; but commentaries on Mt show a surprising diversity in their conceptions of the plan and outline. This diversity is ultimately due to the Evangelist, who in this as in other respects is more subtle than he seems: the plan of the book is a part of his purpose. This commentary is arranged according to the commonly accepted scheme of five books; but not all interpreters think this is the guiding plan, and this approach presents difficulties. That is, the discourse against the Pharisees, which is nearly as long as the missionary discourse, is not treated as a separate discourse; nor is the eschatological discourse counted in the number. But since the discourses are obvious points of division and are easily recognized, this scheme has been adopted here.

(I) Prologue: Genealogy and Infancy Narratives (1:1–2:23)
- (A) The Genealogy of Jesus (1:1–17)
- (B) The Birth of Jesus (1:18–25)
- (C) The Worship of the Magi (2:1–12)
- (D) The Flight into Egypt and the Slaughter of the Innocents (2:13–23)

(II) Book One: The Proclamation of the Reign (3:1–7:29)
- (A) Narrative Section: The Beginning of the Ministry (3:1–4:25)
- (B) Discourse: The Sermon on the Mount (5:1–7:29)

(III) Book Two: Ministry in Galilee (8:1–11:1)
- (A) Narrative Section: Cycle of Ten Miracles (8:1–9:34)
- (B) Discourse: The Missionary Sermon (9:35–11:1)

(IV) Book Three: Controversy and Parables (11:2–13:52)
- (A) Narrative Section: Incredulity and Hostility of the Jews (11:2–12:50)
- (B) Discourse: The Parables of the Reign (13:1–52)

(V) Book Four: The Formation of the Disciples (13:53–18:35)
- (A) Narrative Section: Various Episodes Preceding the Journey to Jerusalem (13:53–17:27)
- (B) Discourse: The Sermon on the Church (18:1–35)

(VI) Book Five: Judea and Jerusalem (19:1–25:46)
- (A) Narrative Section: Journey to Jerusalem and Events There (19:1–23:39)
- (B) Discourse: The Eschatological Sermon (24:1–25:46)

(VII) The Passion Narrative (26:1–27:66)

(VIII) The Resurrection Narrative (28:1–20)

Further subdivisions of the Gospel will be found in the commentary itself.

COMMENTARY

17 **(I) Prologue: Genealogy and Infancy Narratives (1:1–2:23).** Mt and Lk both have accounts of the conception and the birth of Jesus and of some incidents that followed the birth. Neither Mk nor Jn touch upon this period of the life of Jesus. The genealogies of Jesus found in both Mt and Lk are not parallel, nor are there parallels elsewhere in their Gospels. It is difficult to reconcile some of the details in the accounts of Mt and Lk. The absence of the infancy narratives in Mk suggests very strongly that these narratives did not exist in the earliest form of the Christian traditions about Jesus and that various traditions about the infancy were formed later. Mt's version of the traditions is greatly affected by the use of OT texts. Theological imagination and symbolism also play a very large part in the composition of the infancy narratives.

18 **(A) The Genealogy of Jesus (1:1–17).** The purpose of the genealogy is to show that Jesus is the Messiah (1:1,16), the term of the history of salvation that was begun with the promises to Abraham. Mt here takes the view of the E source of the Pentateuch, which also begins with Abraham; Lk, like the J source (Lk 3:23–38), begins with the first man. Jesus is king Messiah, the son of David, and Messiah of Israel, the son of Abraham.

The genealogy is deliberately compiled in 3 sets of 14 names (1:17); 14 is a multiple of 7. It is divided at the two critical points of Israelite history, the foundation of the monarchy of David and the collapse of the monarchy of Judah in the Babylonian conquest of 587 BC. The artificiality of the numbers is maintained by the omission of the names of Ahaziah, Jehoash, and Amaziah between Jehoram and Uzziah; the queen Athaliah was regarded as a usurper, and she would not have figured in the genealogy in any case. Mt follows the line of the kings of Judah; Lk follows a cognate line. Mt's genealogy up to Zerubbabel could be formed by copying from a text of OT books; for the rest of the genealogy, there is no documentary source with which we can compare it.

Four women appear in the genealogy: Tamar, Rahab, Ruth, and Bathsheba. No principle governs their inclusion. Tamar deceived her father-in-law Judah into an incestuous union (Gn 38). Rahab in folklore was the prostitute of Jericho who sheltered the spies and was admitted to the Israelite community (Jos 2). Ruth, the heroine of the Book of Ru, was a Moabite who joined the Israelite community. Bathsheba was the wife of Uriah and the partner of David's adultery. The only common element (probable, but less clear for Bathsheba) is that they were foreigners.

The number 14 in the third group can be maintained only by including Mary or by counting Jesus and Christ as two; it is possible that a name was omitted in the early transmission of the text. One could explain the inclusion of Mary because of the virgin birth, clearly declared in the following passage. If Jesus and Christ are counted as two, the duality could be understood as referring to his nativity in the flesh and to his Second Coming; such an eschatological allusion is common in Mt. **10.** *Amos:* This reading of the critical text stems from an early confusion of the name of King Amon with the name of the prophet Amos.

The reconciliation of the divergent genealogies of Mt and Lk already was a celebrated problem in patristic times. Reconciliation assumes that both genealogies are compiled from reliable records. It is known that genealogies were kept in the post-exilic Jewish community, but this does not prove that genealogies were available to Matthew and Luke. It is much simpler to suppose that each genealogy was compiled artificially where the biblical record failed or where Luke, for reasons of his own, chose not to follow the line of the kings of Judah.

19 **(B) The Birth of Jesus (1:18–25).** In this and the following section some noteworthy differences between the narratives of Mt and Lk appear. Joseph is the central and the active figure in Mt. He is the recipient of revelation, which comes to him through the appearance of an angel in a dream. Mt mentions no residence in Nazareth prior to the birth. It agrees with Lk in the statement of the virgin birth and in the childhood residence of Jesus in Nazareth. **18.** *espoused:* The written contract of marriage had been drawn up between Joseph (or his parents) and the parents of Mary. The Jewish marriage ceremony was accomplished when the groom took the bride into his house; this is meant by "come together" (1:18) and "take" (1:20,24). Premarital unchastity in these circumstances was not adultery in the full sense of the word, nor was the repudiation of a marriage contract "divorce" (1:19) in the full sense of the word. It is very doubtful that the rigorous capital penalty of the Mosaic Law and the talmudic traditions was enforced in NT times. **19.** *righteous:* Joseph is called thus because of his desire to observe the Law. This righteousness was united with an unwillingness to expose his wife; it lay within his power to repudiate the agreement by signing a declaration in the presence of witnesses, but without stating the reasons in public. **20.** *the angel of the Lord:* A messenger figure of the OT (e.g., Gn 16:10; 22:11,15–16; Ex 3:2; Jgs 6:13; 2 Sm 24:16; cf. *EDB* 87–90). The angel of the Lord announces the birth of Samson (Jgs 13:3). Here he announces the name of the child: Jesus. The Gk form *Iēsous* represents the Aram *Yēšuaʿ* and the Hebr *Yehôšûaʿ* (→ Aspects NT Thought 78:3, for the etymology). According to a popular etymology the name means "Yahweh is salvation"; this child will be an agent of salvation but the people will be saved from their sins, not from external enemies or dangers from nature. The greatest to bear this name in the OT was the hero of the Book of Joshua.

22. *might be fulfilled:* Matthew presents the event as the fulfillment of Is 7:14. The formula of "fulfillment" occurs 11 times, more often than in the other 3 Gospels combined. The term does not signify mere prediction and fulfillment; and it is difficult to state in modern terms the kind of thinking involved. The saving event of the Gospel gives the word of the OT, which is a declaration of the power and will of God to save, a new dimension of reality. The text of Is is quoted according to the LXX, except for the reading "they shall call" (LXX: "you shall call"; MT: "she shall call"). **23.** *virgin:* The LXX used *parthenos*, "virgin," to translate the Hebr word in Is 7:14 for "young girl" (*ʿalmāh*). This gives the text of Is a new dimension of reality, and Matthew uses it to affirm the virgin birth. His emphasis, however, seems to be more on the declaration of a savior who shall be called Emmanuel, "God is with us," than on the word *parthenos*. The birth initiates the Messianic age of salvation to which the whole OT looks forward. The age begins with the birth of a child, and this is the force of the allusion to Is. Jesus realizes the presence of God among his people in an entirely new way. **25.** *until she had borne a son:* This verse has caused trouble since the early heresies of the Helvidians and the Jovinians, who concluded from it that Mary and Joseph had marital relations after the birth of Jesus. The implication, easily taken in English, is not present in the Gk particle (*heōs*), and still less if we suppose a Semitic background of the passage. The NT knows nothing of any children of Mary and Joseph. Matthew's interest here is in the affirmation that Joseph is not the natural father of Jesus, and his language is determined by this interest. The agent of the conception of Jesus is "a Holy Spirit" (1:20). This term is used in the OT to designate God's mysterious power; it is not used to designate the agent of human conception.

20 **(C) The Worship of the Magi (2:1–12).** **1.** *in the days of King Herod:* One of the rare chronological pieces of information in Mt places this event in the time of Herod the Great, a satellite king of Judea (37–4 BC). It is impossible to date the year of the birth of Jesus exactly; according to the reckoning of Dionysius Exiguus, Herod the Great died four years before Jesus was born (→ History of Israel, 75:130–34). *Magi:* The visitors are called *magoi* (Lat *magi*, whence the Eng term); it is probably used in a loose sense. Originally the term designated the learned priestly caste of the Persians; later it came to mean any one skilled in occult knowledge and power (much the same as our "magician," which is derived from the same word). It could also mean a mountebank or charlatan. Matthew certainly does not use the word in an abusive sense. The mention of the "star" shows that they are called *magoi* because of their knowledge of astrology. Nothing else is said about them. *from the east:* This suggests Mesopotamia, the home of astrology in the Hellenistic world. The story reflects the popular belief that each person is represented by a star, which appears at his birth. **2.** *his star:* It is impossible to identify a particular heavenly body as the star of Bethlehem; any attempt to do so would be futile. Although the allusion is not explicit, the Jewish reader would recognize the star that rises from Jacob (Nm 24:17)—an allusion to David usually interpreted in a messianic sense.

The story of the Magi, like the genealogy of Jesus, affirms that Jesus is king Messiah. The Magi seek a king, and Herod consults the religious experts of Judaism to find out where they should look. Of this there is no doubt; they should look not in Jerusalem but in Bethlehem. **5.** *in Bethlehem of Judea:* The place of David's birth and the place of origin of the king Messiah of the future. In support of this the text of Mi 5:1–3 is cited. The text is cited neither according to the LXX nor according to the MT; it is conflated with the text of 2 Sm 5:2 (the offer of kingship made to David by the elders of Israel). **7.** *the time of the appearance of the star:* The inquiry about the time looks to the sequel in 2:13–23. No guidance of the star is suggested for the journey prior to the arrival of the Magi in Jerusalem; but now it leads them not only to the town but to the very house. **11.** *gold, frankincense, myrrh:* The gifts that the Magi bring echo Ps 72:10; Is 60:6. The dream motif recurs; the Magi are warned not to return to Herod.

The theme of the story is not only the royal messiahship of Jesus but also the adoration of him by the Gentiles. In contrast to Luke, who places Jewish poor at the scene of the nativity as the first to worship Jesus, Matthew puts the Gentiles first, and the Jews, even when informed of the birth, remain indifferent. This is a theme that is echoed several times throughout the Gospel.

21 **(D) The Flight into Egypt and the Slaughter of the Innocents (2:13–23).** The dream motif recurs again both in the departure to Egypt and in the return. **15.** *out of Egypt:* The quotation of Hos 11:1 (according to the MT) illustrates the freedom with which Matthew employs the OT. The original refers to the "call" of the Exodus. Jesus is presented as re-enacting in his own life the career of Israel; for he is the new Israel. **18.** *a voice heard in Ramah:* Jer 31:14 is quoted with similar freedom; the quotation follows neither the LXX nor the MT exactly. The original text refers to the destruction of the monarchy of N Israel by the Assyrians in 721 BC. The confusion of Ephrath in the territory of Benjamin with Bethlehem is as old as the gloss on Gn 35:19. A Moslem shrine just N of Bethlehem, identified with the tomb of Rachel, reposes on an early tradition.

19. *when Herod had died:* The return from Egypt is dated after the death of Herod (4 BC). Herod's kingdom was divided by Augustus among three of Herod's surviving sons, Archelaus (Judea, Samaria, Idumea), Herod Antipas (Galilee and Perea) and Philip (the territory to the E and N of Galilee). At the petition of the Jews Augustus denied the title of king to Archelaus and gave him the title of ethnarch. His government was so unsatisfactory that he was deposed and exiled to Gaul in AD 6 (→ History of Israel 75:139). The warning given to Joseph in a dream explains why Jesus, although born in Bethlehem, was reared in Galilee and was known as a Galilean. Lk, which agrees with Mt both on Bethlehem and Galilee, explains the relation of the two places in a different way: Joseph and Mary were originally residents of Galilee and were only temporary visitors to Bethlehem when Jesus was born. **20.** *they that sought the child's life:* The influence of the OT appears in this phrase; it is taken almost verbally from Ex 4:19. **23.** *spoken by the prophets:* The text of "the prophets" quoted is found nowhere in the OT. Nazareth is not mentioned in the OT. The most probable explanation of the "quotation" is that it is a wordplay based on the Hebr text of Is 11:1, "A shoot shall rise from Jesse, and a branch (*neṣer*) shall sprout from his roots." There is an assonance between the word *neser* and the town name Nazareth.

22 The tragic episode of the Innocents is mentioned in no other literature, canonical or profane; this raises serious questions about the historical character of the incident. Such a wanton action is in harmony with the character of Herod as Josephus has described it (*Ant.* 15.3,3 § 53–56). Josephus depicts Herod as being pathologically jealous of his power—a number of his family were murdered by him because he suspected them of trying to supplant him. There is no doubt that Josephus meant to paint Herod as black as he could, and it is difficult to explain the absence of the Bethlehem incident in Josephus except on the hypothesis that he knew nothing about it. That he should have omitted it because of its interest for Christians is unlikely; Josephus has demonstrated his ability to write history according to his own ends. Therefore it should be considered that the incidents of ch. 2 possibly represent a symbolic presentation of the royal messiahship of Jesus and the opposition of secular power to this messiahship. The opposition finally achieved its purpose in the passion of Jesus. This type of theological narrative is supported by the use of OT texts.

23 **(II) Book One: The Proclamation of the Reign (3:1–7:29).**

(A) Narrative Section: The Beginning of the Ministry (3:1–4:25).

(a) The Preaching of John the Baptist (3:1–12). The first six verses of this passage follow Mk 1:1–6 closely, adding only the location in the desert of Judea (3:2) and the content of the preaching of John. **1.** *wilderness of Judea:* The desert of Judea is the steep slope that falls from the central ridge of the country to the valley of the Jordan and the Dead Sea. Baptism in the Jordan indicates that John preached near the river, very probably not far from Jericho. This is only a few miles distant from Qumran, and the relations of John to the Qumran sect offer occasion for interesting speculation (see J. A. T. Robinson, *HarvTR* 50 [1957] 175–91). **2.** *repent, for the kingdom of heaven is at hand:* The sentence in which John's preaching is summarized is identical with the summary of the proclamation of Jesus in 4:17. **3.** *this is he:* The mission of John is described in all three Gospels by the text of Is 40:3, quoted according to the LXX, and no doubt originally in Mk. Mt omits Mk's conflation of Mal 3:1. Mt, like Mk, introduces John abruptly; only Lk has the story of John's nativity. John the Baptist was a well-known figure in the early Christian community who needed no introduction; disciples of John appear even at Ephesus (Acts 19:1–5). **4.** *garment of camel's hair:* John's residence in the desert and his garb and diet suggest the prophet Elijah (2 Kgs 1:8); see the question of the return of Elijah in 11:14; 17:10–12. **6.** *were baptized by him:* Mt does not use Mk's phrase, "baptism of repentance for the remission of sins"; possibly by the time of Mt this phrase might have seemed to assimilate the baptism of John to Christian baptism; but see 3:11. Mt alone (3:14–15) expresses the difficulty about the reception by Jesus of a rite that involved repentance and remission.

Mt 3:7–10 (Lk 3:7–9 par.) comes from Q. Mt limits these words to the Pharisees and Sadducees; Lk directs them to the whole crowd. **7.** *brood of vipers:* The epithet occurs also in 12:34; 23:33. This suits Mt's general pattern; the religious leaders of the Jews are responsible for the refusal of the Jews to believe in the Messiah. The words of John are strongly eschatological, reflecting the "coming wrath" of the Day of the Lord (Am 5:18–20; Zeph 1:14–16). **9.** *from these stones:* The threat alludes to the rejection of the Messiah by the Jews and his acceptance by the Gentiles; the Church of Jews and Gentiles is the new Israel and the true people of God. **10.** Cf. 7:19. **11–12.** These verses contain the Messianic preaching of John, expanded by Mt from Mk; 3:12 (Lk 3:17 par.) is from Q. To Mk's baptism with a Holy Spirit Mt and Lk both add "with fire"; this seems to be an allusion not only to fire as the element that symbolizes the presence of the deity, but also to the appearance of the Holy Spirit in tongues of fire in the Pentecost narrative. "The spirit of truth" as purifying water appears in 1QS 4.21 (see J. A. T. Robinson, *HarvTR* 50 [1957] 175–91). The fire in the expansion of Q (3:12) is the destroying fire of Gehenna. It is clear from the importance of John both in Judaism and in primitive Christianity that his messianic witness was of great value. Some apparently were ready to take John as the Messiah; John himself disclaimed this office, and pointed to another. The complete witness of John is given later (11:2–6).

24 (b) The Baptism of Jesus (3:13–17). Matthew depends on Mk, but has added 3:14–15—it was necessary to explain how Jesus could submit to a rite of repentance and confession of sin. **15.** *a fulfillment of all righteousness:* An obscure phrase; it very probably refers to Jesus' identification of himself, as he comes to be baptized, as a devout Jew who observes the Law and the practices associated with good Jewish life. The added dialogue introduces a confession of the dignity of Jesus by John not found in Mk and Lk. **16.** *the spirit of God descending:* In Mt and Mk, Jesus sees this event as the heavens open, but in Lk and Jn 1:32–33 the vision is extended to John (at least). *a dove:* Here only the symbol of the Spirit; in OT imagery the dove represents a symbol of love. **17.** *this is my beloved son:* Love is expressed in the saying formed on Is 42:1 (following Mk). The use of this formula identifies Jesus as the Servant of the Lord. The vision defines the character of the messiahship of Jesus; he is not the royal conquering Messiah but the Servant who proclaims and suffers.

The "voice from heaven" reflects the Jewish belief in the *bat qôl* (daughter of a voice), often mentioned in rabbinical literature as the means of revelation granted after prophecy had ceased (Str-B 1, 125–34).

25 (c) The Temptation of Jesus (4:1–11). Mk's brief notice of the 40 days' fast in the desert and temptation is expanded by Mt (and Lk) into a triple temptation. A common documentary source for Mt and Lk is not obvious; if there is a common source, one of the two Evangelists has handled it freely. The biblical quotations (from the LXX) are identical in the two Gospels. The order of the second and third temptations is inverted in Lk from Mt; the order of Mt seems to have a deliberately arranged climax. The movement of Jesus to the desert occurs under the guidance of the Spirit. **1.** *into the desert:* This area is not specified; probably the desert of Judea (see 3:1) is intended. Jebel Qarantal, named after the 40 days, lies to the W of Jericho and is traditionally associated with the mount of temptation. **2.** *forty days:* This phrase suggests the 40 years of Israel in the desert. The desert sojourn was a time of temptation and failure for Israel; but Jesus, the new Israel, is likewise tempted in the desert. The symbolic character of the narrative is evident; the temptations and Jesus' answers define the true character of his Messianic mission. The answer of Jesus to all three questions is taken from Dt (8:3; 6:16,13). The use of this source shows that the Law itself reveals the true character of messiahship.

The three temptations can be summed up as temptations to power. The first temptation is to use miraculous power to provide for ordinary material needs. **4.** The answer of Jesus (Dt 8:3) does not deny that ordinary needs should be met by ordinary means, but subordinates even basic physical necessities to the revealed word of God. Jesus does not fulfill his mission by providing for basic physical necessities, but by proclaiming the word that is life.

26 **5.** The second temptation also deals with miraculous power; it is the use of this power to produce a "sign" (12:38–42), a spectacular and convincing display that would compel belief. This type of sign Jesus does not give. *the pinnacle of the temple:* It has not been certainly identified. If the ancient structure of Herod's temple had relations to the topography similar to those of the modern Haram esh-Sherif, the SE corner of the esplanade lay well above the level of the slope of the valley of Kidron; this may be the point meant. **6.** Here the tempter supports his proposal with a biblical quotation (Ps 91:11–12). **7.** Jesus responds by quoting Dt 6:16, a warning against rashness. The appeal to the spectacular sign imposes demands upon God that God has not promised to fulfill; it is not the way in which he has chosen to reveal himself. **8.** *a very high mountain:* The mountain of the third temptation does not exist in nature. This is a temptation to secular messianism, the use of political power to accomplish the ends of the Messianic mission. **10.** Jesus' answer to this temptation exceeds his previous answers in severity and is prefaced by a dismissal. The quotation of Dt 6:13 places secular messianism on the level of the worship of false gods.

The temptations of Jesus all touch upon his Messianic mission; even in a theologically symbolic narrative Jesus is not represented as liable to the common temptations of mankind. Nor in the mind of the Evangelist is he really subject to the temptation to abuse his Messianic powers. The temptation comes not to him but to the Church, which carries on his mission. The elaboration of the temptation story by Matthew has an ecclesial purpose. The spiritual dangers that threaten the integrity of the mission of the Church have already been met by Jesus himself; he has shown how the Church must overcome them.

27 (d) The First Proclamation in Galilee (4:12–17). The complete account of the imprisonment of John the Baptist is given in 14:1–12. The three Syn (and Jn in its own way) agree that Jesus did not begin his own proclamation until John had been imprisoned by Herod Antipas (→ History of Israel, 75:144). The associations of Jesus and John are too obscurely known for us to determine what is implied in this situation. The Syn, as we have seen, do not relate any confession of John the Baptist in any way similar to the version we find in the Fourth Gospel. We may conjecture that the preaching of John had aroused a climate of interest into which Jesus could move with his own proclamation. All three Syn also agree that Jesus returned to Galilee, his own country, to proclaim the reign. **13.** *in Capernaum by the sea:* Jesus moved from his own village of Nazareth to the larger city of Capernaum (identified with the ruins Tell Hum near the northern end of the western shore of the Sea of Galilee). In NT times the western shore of the lake was occupied by many busy and prosperous small cities and towns; and we must assume that Jesus wished to reach a wider audience. *in the territory of Zebulun and Naphtali:* Matthew notes that Capernaum lay in the old tribal territory of Zebulun and Naphtali; this enables him to adduce Is 8:23–9:1 (LXX 9:1–2). In the Isaian passage deliverance of 9:2–6 is first announced to the territory of Galilee, which was detached from the kingdom of Israel by Tiglath-pileser III of Assyria in 734 BC and erected into an Assyrian province. The first part of Israel to experience the destroying wrath of Yahweh shall be the first to hear of his salvation. The quotation follows neither the LXX nor the MT.

17. *kingdom of heaven:* Mt compresses Mk's summary of the proclamation of Jesus, using the phrase Mk uses to summarize the preaching of John (3:2) without Mk's allusion to the "time" (*kairos*) and Mk's call to faith. The typical Matthaean phrase, "kingdom of heaven," appears here instead of Mk's "kingdom of God"; the circumlocution of "heavens" for "God" was a common Jewish manner of speech. Jews of this period avoided the use of the divine name or what were regarded as peculiarly divine titles. The word usually translated "kingdom" is more accurately rendered "reign"; this is the word employed in this commentary, except in a few passages. The word does not designate an area in which power is exercised, but the exercise of the power (→ Aspects NT Thought, 78:102–105). What "approaches" (or "is arriving") is the manifestation of the supreme power of God, the assertion of his sovereignty. The first response to this is repentance; for sin is a refusal to accept the reign of God.

28 (e) The Call of the First Disciples (4:18–22). Matthew here depends on Mk, which he has slightly rewritten. Luke, perhaps employing a peculiar source, has rewritten the story more extensively and added the miraculous catch of fish. Jn 1:35–42 has a quite different account: Andrew and another disciple (not named, but presumably John himself) were disciples of John the Baptist, who introduced them to Jesus; and Andrew introduced his brother Simon. The point of the story in Mt and Mk is that the four followed Jesus immediately even though they did not know him; they "dropped" their fishing nets, left their families, and became disciples. There is no implication that they returned to their homes and their livelihood. Three of this first four—Peter, James, and John—formed an inner three who witnessed incidents not seen by the other disciples (17:1; 26:37; Mk 5:37). A similar urgency is expressed in the call of Levi (9:9). The promise to make them "fishers of men" is an intimation of the apostolic office.

29 (f) A Journey in Galilee (4:23–25). This brief passage is compiled by Matthew as an introduction to the first of his major discourses, the Sermon on the Mount. The summary is described in commonplaces: teaching in the synagogues (mentioned several times), proclaiming the good news of the reign, healing diseases, exorcising demons. As a result of these activities Jesus became known "in all Syria" (4:34). The Roman province of Syria was bounded by the Taurus mountains, the Syrian desert, the Nabataean kingdom, and the Mediterranean. Matthew means those parts of the province mentioned in 4:25; Galilee, the Decapolis (N and E of Galilee), Judea and Perea (E of the Jordan). These are regions which Jesus traversed. The region of Tyre and Sidon (Mk 3:8; Lk 6:17) is not mentioned, very probably because Matthew thought that this territory was already included in his enumeration; see 15:21.

30 **(B) Discourse: The Sermon on the Mount (5:1–7:29).** **1.** *the mountain:* Jesus is meant to be the new Moses proclaiming the new revelation on a new Mt. Sinai. Much of the sermon is paralleled in Lk, but the extensive discourse, which contains most of the parallels, is strangely given not on a mountain but in a plain (Lk 6:17). The preceding narrative has gathered the crowds (5:1) that hear the sermon. The discourse is introduced with unusual solemnity; Matthew means this to be the explication of what he has called the proclamation of the reign or the good news of the reign.

(a) The Beatitudes (5:3–12). **3.** *blessed are:* Or "happy is the one who...." This formula is common in Pss and in OT wisdom literature; it also appears elsewhere in other NT books, and in particular in Ap. The beatitudes as such are not attributed to Q; Lk 6:21–24 has four beatitudes and four woes. Lk's beatitudes are parallel to Mt's first, second, fourth, and the expansion of the eighth (see below). The woes of Lk are antitheses of the beatitudes. The beatitudes of Mt are "spiritualized" in comparison to those of Lk, emphasizing the quality of virtue and the activity of virtue; Lk speaks of poverty, hunger, and mourning. *poor in spirit:* The difference between Lk's "poor" and Mt's "poor in spirit" is not substantial; Mt certainly does not mean those who, although they are wealthy, are spiritually detached from their wealth. The phrase very probably echoes Is 61:1 (see Lk 4:18). Both phrases designate the poor class, which constituted the vast majority of the population of the Hellenistic-Roman world. In later OT literature and in the literature of Judaism the name of this class, *'ᵃnāwîm* or *'ᵃniyyîm* (frequently confused because of the similarity of spelling), became almost a technical term for devout and observant Jews. Mt's "poor in spirit" emphasizes less the literal lack of possessions than the lowly condition of the poor; their poverty did not allow them the arrogance and assertiveness of the wealthy but imposed habitual and servile deference. The term is very close to "meek" in the third beatitude. Their reward is "the kingdom of heaven"; in this context "kingdom" rather than "reign" is meant.

4. *those who mourn:* If 5:3 echoes Is 61:1, 5:4 very probably echoes Is 61:2; to console the mourners is one of the functions of the messenger who speaks in this passage of Is. The beatitude at least means those who have no worldly joy, and in this sense would be closely parallel to the first and the third. More probably it means those who mourn the evils of Israel, which are due to its sins. Their consolation will be the experience of the Messianic salvation. **5.** *the meek:* These are the same class as that designated in 5:3, the lowly who are unable to be aggressive. The ideal of meekness is described concretely in 5:39–42. *the land:* The meek shall possess the eschatological land of Israel, restored by the saving deeds of God. The phrase echoes the promises of the land to the OT patriarchs. **6.** *who hunger and thirst for righteousness:* The "righteousness" after which one should hunger and thirst is a word of broad meaning. In Mt it most frequently designates the condition of good relations with God—achieved by submission to his will. In Pharisaic Judaism this condition was thought to be assured by the observance of the Law according to Pharisaic standards. Jesus insists that his disciples must strive for something higher than this (5:20). "Righteousness" can also echo the OT idea of the victory of God over his enemies, his vindication of himself and of Israel. The reward is to obtain what is desired.

31 **7.** *the merciful:* The ideal of mercy or compassion is a frequent theme in all the Gospels. The beatitude is illustrated by the parable of the merciless servant (Mt 18:23–35). The two works of mercy most emphasized in Mt are almsgiving and forgiveness. The reward of compassion is to receive compassion. **8.** *the pure of heart:* Purity of heart is opposed to the external Levitical purity achieved by ritual ablution: this is a frequent object of contention between Jesus and the Pharisees. What is meant by purity of heart is explained in 15:10–20. It is manifested principally by speech, which betrays one's thoughts and desires. The reward of purity of heart is to see God. This does not signify what in theology is called "the beatific vision," but admission to the presence of God (see 18:10). In OT language the members of the royal court are those "who see the face of the king." **9.** *the peacemakers:* This word does not represent the Hebr phrase, "one who produces prosperity," but means those who reconcile quarrels. Reconciliation is a Christian office often recommended in the Gospels; see 5:23–26. The reward is to be called sons of God. This is a title of Israel in the OT; those who reconcile quarrels are genuine Israelites.

32 **10–12.** In spite of the repetition of "blessed" in 5:11, the number of beatitudes is eight, not nine; the beatitude is expanded in 5:11–12. Persecution for righteousness is persecution that is endured in order to maintain good relations with God by obedience to his will (see comment on 5:6). The expansion identifies Jesus with righteousness. He replaces the Law as the one and the sure means by which one maintains good relations with God. This relationship will certainly bring persecution (described in terms of the experience of the primitive Church), but the reward is greater than any reward promised before. The Church is the successor of the prophets, who were persecuted by their own people; the persecution mentioned is most probably the attacks made on the Christian community by the Jews.

It is difficult for us to appreciate the paradoxical character of the beatitudes. They institute a moral revolution that has not yet reached its fullness. They are opposed to all the conventional values of the Jewish and the Hellenistic-Roman world and pronounce blessings on those who do not share in these values. Not only the external values of wealth and status are repudiated but also those goods of the person that are achieved and defended by self-assertion and strife. The general statements of the beatitudes are enlarged by concrete examples in the following passages of the sermon.

33 (b) The Salt of the Earth and the Light of the World (5:13–16). The function of the disciples is illustrated by the homely metaphors of salt as seasoning and the single lamp that was used in the one-room house of the Palestinian peasant. The explanation of the two images (5:16) refers them to the "good works" of the disciples. By living according to the teaching of Jesus, men will manifest the goodness of "their father in heaven" (a common phrase in Mt) and will praise God because of what they see. This is very probably the original force of the images. In Mt's text the image is expanded by the possibility of the loss of savor of salt and the hiding of the light under a measure; he who fails to realize the ideal of the life of the Gospels will be rejected. The related idea of the city on the mountain, which is not explained, appears to be a popular wise saying that is intruded into the context, something like the Eng simile "stands out like a sore thumb." In the context of the sermon these sayings serve as an introduction to the lengthy passage that follows; here the disciples are instructed in the manner in which they can become the salt of the earth and the light of the world, and what the good works are through which God is glorified.

34 (c) The Law and the Gospel (5:17–48). In the initial encounter of the Gospel with Judaism, as well as in those primitive churches that were entirely or largely Jewish in membership, the attitude of Jesus and the Church to the Law was an urgent question. The Law had a sacredness and a saving value in Pharisaic Judaism that do not perfectly reflect the place of the Law in preexilic Israel. The Law was thought to be the summary of all wisdom—human and divine, the revelation of God himself, a complete and a secure guide of conduct and endowed with a sacramental assurance of good relations with God. This value of the Law Jesus did not and could not accept; implicitly for most Jews the Law was the terminal revelation of God.

The attitude of the NT books toward the Law is not homogeneous. This does not mean that it is inconsistent, but simply that it reflects the development of the Christian understanding of the Law and its relation to the Gospel. One can trace the uneasy stages of this development in the epistles of Paul. A certain superficial inconsistency could be found, if one wished to be captious, even in 5:17–20, and much more easily in the entire Sermon on the Mount. To affirm inconsistency ignores the subtlety and the complexity of the problem, as well as the historical conditions in which Jesus proclaimed the gospel. This introductory pericope is Matthew's effort to state Jesus' position toward the Law in general. It must be read with the rest of the Gospel in mind.

17. *not to annul:* It was not the mission of Jesus to annul (break down, as a camp) the Law and the Prophets; these two words are often used to designate the whole collection of the books of the OT, and they are so used here. His mission is to "fulfill" them. *Fulfill:* This word cannot refer to a simple literal observance; the following six examples negate such a facile interpretation. "Fulfill" means to bring the Law to perfection, to give it that finality the Pharisees believed it possessed. Jesus affirms indirectly that the Law is imperfect, unfinished; he will perfect and finish it. In popular messianism the Messiah had a relation to the Law, but it was not a relation of bringing the Law to completeness. Jesus affirms the enduring, even eternal reality of the Law that we find affirmed in the rabbinical writings; but it is the finished and perfect Law that endures, not the Law of Moses with its explanatory oral teachings. **18.** *Amen:* In this affirmation Jesus uses the asseverative *Amen* so common in the Gospels. There is no parallel to this use of the word. It usually expresses agreement with a statement or a wish, particularly a prayer; Jesus uses it as an asseverative particle of his own words. *jot:* The Hebr consonant, *yodh*, the smallest of the 22 consonants in the late or square Hebr script. *tittle:* Lit., "little horn"; it is less certain in meaning, but probably designates the small decorative "horn" added to many Hebr consonants in the square script. *until all things be done:* A deliberately obscure phrase; the Law will not pass until it has been finished and perfected by the Messianic work of Jesus.

19. Jesus accepts the rabbinical distinction between "heavy" and "light" commandments; the rabbis counted 613 distinct precepts in the Pentateuch and classified them according to their seriousness. From the terms "great" and "small" the words of praise and condemnation are derived. This again is not a program of literal Pharisaic observances; in fact, it is most probably the Pharisees who are meant by those who teach and practice nonobservance; see 15:3–6; 23:16–26. The nonobservance by Jesus of the traditional Sabbath ordinances and of the laws of Levitical cleanliness was a frequent source of controversy. Jesus is not recommending here that which he repudiated in teaching and practice. The Law therefore that the disciples are to "do and teach" is again the perfect and complete law. Observance of the Law and the traditions will secure the righteousness of the scribes and Pharisees; this righteousness will not gain admission to the reign. The righteousness of the disciples must exceed the righteousness of the scribes and Pharisees; it is a submission to the will of God that goes beyond the observance of the Law. What this departure from the Law means is illustrated in the following six examples (5:21–48). Paul also speaks of a righteousness of the Law that is not true righteousness and does not save; true righteousness is achieved through faith in Christ Jesus (Rom 3:20; 10:5; Gal 2:16; 3:21; Phil 3:9). For Matthew also, faith is that which saves.

35 (i) *Murder* (5:21–26). In each of the six examples that follow, the statement of the Law (not distinguished from its explanation in tradition) is directly opposed to the pronouncement of Jesus: "I say." The statement of the Law is impersonal; the quotations are not attributed to God himself. This may reflect Jewish delicacy in speaking of the deity, and it also avoids an antithesis between the words of God and the words of Jesus. **21.** *you shall not kill:* The commandment is quoted according to Ex 20:15; Dt 5:18; the added statement concerning the judgment is not a quotation from the OT, but judicial processes for murder are mentioned (see Ex 21:12; Nm 35:16–33). Jesus does not distinguish between willful murder and casual homicide (Ex 21:13; Nm 35:10; Dt 19:4–6), for accidental homicide does not fall under moral consideration. **22.** *anyone who is angry:* What Jesus prohibits is not murder but anger; and the mere feeling of anger is liable to the court's judgment, a procedure that in the Law follows murder. There is an element of hyperbole; anger is not the object of legal action. Jesus rather means that anger, the passion that impels to murder, is as guilty an action as murder itself. The Law is restated. Expressions of anger in speech without violent action are reprobated in even stronger language. There is a climax in the penalties; the words move from the *krisis*, the judgment (which probably designates the local court), to the *synedrion* (council, Sanhedrin), the supreme legal body in Judaism, to the *gehenna* of fire, the final punishment God inflicts. No similar climax can be perceived in *raka* and *mōre*. *Raka* (probably = Aram *rēqā*, found as an abusive term in the Talmud) means "fool," "empty-headed," and can scarcely be distinguished from the Gk *mōros*. Efforts to find a climax in the terms, or to discover some particularly insulting quality in *mōros*, are fallacious; interpreters are deceived by the severity of Jesus, and they cannot believe that he speaks so sternly of simple abusive language. The point is that the two words have no peculiar force beyond that of colloquial abusive terms like "idiot," "blockhead," "numbskull," "stupido," "Dummkopf," and their equivalents in all languages. It is just this type of language as an expression of anger that Jesus totally forbids. He strengthens the prohibition of murder by going to the very roots of mutual dislike.

36 **23.** Should men yield to anger, which is conceived as unavoidable, the sacred duty of reconciliation arises. The directions in 5:23–24 go as far as possible to make clear the urgency of this duty. Worship was to a Jew the most sacred action in which a man could engage. But worship must be postponed for reconciliation. The primacy of fraternal relations over cultic duties is established beyond all doubt; and this again is a restatement of the Law. The case in 5:23–24 is not the case of one who feels anger but of one who has excited anger in another; it is irrelevant to the duty of reconciliation who started the quarrel.

25–26. This saying is found in Lk 12:57–59 in an eschatological context; and it is probably original in this context. *your adversary:* In the context of Lk it is most probably not the brother with whom one has a dispute, but God, whose judgment the sinner is in danger of incurring. By transferring the saying to this context Mt has altered its meaning. He makes of the saying an expansion of the commandment of reconciliation, in which the element of urgency is again expressed. The eschatological threat adds to the severity of the commandment; but it is scarcely possible to overstate the sternness that Jesus everywhere voices toward those who refuse to love.

37 (ii) *Adultery* (5:27–30). **27.** *you shall not commit adultery:* The commandment is quoted according to Ex 20:13; Dt 5:17. Jesus does not attend to the penalties prescribed in the Law for adultery, which was normally a capital crime (Dt 22:22). Neither does he mention illicit sexual relations that are not adulterous, although these are treated of in the Law. **28.** *looks with lust:* As in the discussion of murder, the supreme offense is taken as the point beyond which Jesus advances. The statement is brief; the gaze of lustful desire is as guilty as the adulterous action. The lustful gaze is mentioned very frequently in the rabbinical literature, and it is reprobated with scarcely less vigor than we find in the Gospel passage (Str-B 1, 298–301). The restatement of the Law is directed again at the roots of the impulse. **29–30.** The expansion in these verses is found also in 18:8–9, in a form that shows more clearly the dependence of Mt on Mk 9:43–48. Mt has detached the saying from its original context, in spite of the fact that the hand is less relevant to the topic than the eye. The passage is rewritten for the present context. (On scandal, see comment on 18:6–9.)

38 (iii) *Divorce* (5:31–32). See also 19:9; Mk 10:11–12; Lk 16:18. **31.** *whoever divorces his wife:* The statement of the Law is a very loose paraphrase and compendium of Dt 24:1, omitting the phrases that deal with the occasion of the divorce—the wife does not find favor with her husband because he has found "something shameful" in her. The meaning of this obscure phrase was extensively discussed by the rabbis. Rabbinical tradition tells of two governing views in NT times: the opinion of Shammai, who permitted divorce only for adultery, and the opinion of Hillel, who permitted divorce for the love of another woman or for causes as trivial as inferior cooking (Str-B 1, 312–20). The law of Dt actually deals only indirectly with divorce; its object is the prohibition of the reunion of partners after a divorce. **32.** *everyone who divorces his wife:* The saying was found in Mk and Q, and Matthew used both sources. The clarity of the saying in Mk and Lk is undisputed; there Jesus simply forbids divorce entirely. Mk's formula reflects Roman law, which allowed the wife to institute divorce; Mt and Lk allude to the Jewish practice, in which only the husband could divorce. *except the case of unchastity:* This exceptive clause is universally regarded as an expansion of the original form. Many interpreters and the Greek church understand it as a permission of divorce for adultery. But this is so plainly out of harmony with Mk and Lk that it seems improbable. Mt is the only Gospel that seems to allude to the rabbinical disputes; the allusion is quite clear in 19:3 (see comment). The interpretation of the phrase as an exception to the repudiation of divorce would place Jesus with the school of Shammai. If Matthew meant adultery, he chose a less apt word for it; *porneia* means literally "prostitution," and it designates unchaste conduct generally. *Moicheia* (the cog. word occurs in 5:32) means "adultery." The distinction between the two words is not so rigid as to make it impossible that here *porneia* means adultery. Nevertheless, if the verse is translated "He who dismisses his wife, except for adultery, makes her commit adultery," the saying sounds quaint, to say the least; the divorced wife commits adultery unless she has already committed adultery. J. Bonsirven (*Le divorce dans le Nouveau Testament* [Tournai, 1948]) called attention to a rabbinical use of the Hebr word z^{e}*nūt*, which would be translated by the Gk *porneia*, to designate an unlawful union of concubinage. He proposed that it was this type of union that was designated by the exception. It is easier to understand this interpretation if one recalls that Greek has no distinct noun for "wife." Literally the sentence reads: "Every one who sends away his woman—except in the case of concubinage—makes her commit adultery." This seems to be the most satisfactory interpretation of the passage, and it explains the exceptive clause from the Jewish background that is so often apparent in Mt. (For another explanation of *porneia*, see comment on Mk 10:12.)

(Isaksson, A., *Marriage and Ministry in the New Temple* [ASNU 24; Lund, 1965]. Richards, H. J., "Christ on Divorce," *Scr* 11 [1959] 22–32.)

39 (iv) *Oaths* (5:33–37). **33.** *you must not swear falsely:* The statement of the Law is not a direct quotation, but a paraphrase of such passages as Ex 20:7; Lv 19:12; Nm 30:3; Dt 23:22. The statement in Mt's paraphrase does not distinguish vows and oaths; it prohibits perjury and commands that vows be paid. **34.** *do not swear at all:* In particular Jesus forbids the type of evasion that substitutes for the divine name something less sacred. If a sacred object is mentioned in an oath, it is as if the divine name were being used. The identity of such objects with the deity is shown by quotations from Is 66:1; Ps 47:3 (quoted according to the LXX). **36.** *by your head:* Nor should one swear by one's self. All of the formulas mentioned in this verse, except "by Jerusalem," are attested in biblical or extrabiblical Jewish literature (Str-B 1, 330–36). A simple affirmative or negative is sufficient; more than this is "from evil." **37.** The ambiguity of the Greek permits this last phrase to be rendered either "from evil" or "from the evil one"; see 5:39. In either translation the meaning is the same; the oath is a reflection of the evil condition of man, exhibiting both his mendacity, against which the oath is thought to protect, and his distrust of his fellow man.

The passage is echoed rather closely in Jas 5:12. Like the other antitheses, the statement is paradoxical. The prohibition of perjury is intended to secure truthfulness in situations where a solemn affirmation or denial is demanded. In the new ethics of Jesus truthfulness will be secured not by an oath but by the inner integrity of the person. The oath, because of its implications of men dacity and lack of confidence, can have no place in a society that does not assume evil as a matter of course.

40 (v) *Revenge* (5:38–42). **38.** *an eye for an eye:* The law of retaliation is quoted loosely from Ex 21:24; Lv 24:20; Dt 19:21. The law of revenge was an ancient custom of the Near East that protected individuals by obliging the next of kin to avenge injury or murder or to purchase property to pay the debts of a kinsman. The laws of the Pentateuch are actually restrictions that limit the injury inflicted by the avenger to injury proportionate to the damage done by the aggressor. **39.** *do not resist the evil one:* The customary principle of self-defense is rejected by this saying of Jesus; and the customary principle is not replaced by another principle of self-defense. The saying is probably the most paradoxical of all the sayings of the passage and has certainly been the object of more rationalization than any other. The statement is simply not to resist "evil" or "the evil one"; in the context it seems that the person rather than the neuter is meant, and we almost think of "the evil one" as the aggressor. *if anyone strikes you:* Several concrete examples are given that take the saying out of the mere abstract and general. The first area is the area of physical violence, which is not to be met with physical violence; it is to be suffered. **40.** The second area is that of legal contention; the disciples are told not to meet legal action with legal action, but to yield what is contested and even beyond what is contested. The garments mentioned are the tunic, a long shirt worn next to the body, and the cloak, a heavier outer garment that protected against cold and rain. These were normally the only two garments worn by the Palestinian peasant. In Ex 22:25–26 the creditor who takes the cloak in pledge is directed to return it at sundown so that the debtor may have covering for the night. **41.** The third area is that of forced labor or service, a part of the contribution of the subjects of ancient states to the government. **42.** The fourth area is that of requests for gifts or loans, which are not to be refused. It is difficult to see how the principle of nonresistance and yielding could be more clearly stated. The rationalizations of the words of Jesus do not show that his words are impractical or exaggerated, but simply that the Christian world has never been ready and is not ready now to live according to this ethic. The passage is echoed in Rom 12:17–21; see also 1 Cor 13:5–7.

41 (vi) *Love of one's enemies* (5:43–48). **43.** *love your neighbor:* The precept of the love of one's neighbor is quoted from Lv 19:18; the precept of hating one's enemy is not found in the OT, nor is it a summary of rabbinical teaching as it has been preserved (Str-B 1, 353–68). It no doubt represents the popular understanding of the love of one's neighbor; no one needs to be instructed to hate his enemies (cf. M. Smith, *HarvTR* 45 [1952] 71–73). The saying should not be restricted to personal enemies among one's brotherhood, implying a toleration of hatred of the enemies of one's group; this would not distinguish the Christian from the Gentile or the tax collector (5:46–47). The "neighbor" is the member of one's group or fellowship: one's village or town, one's religion or nation, one's tribe or race. In many languages the same word is used to designate "stranger," "foreigner," or "enemy." The enemy is specified in Mt as the persecutor, probably a reflection of the experience of the early Church; Lk has "those who mistreat you" (6:27). **45.** *be sons of your Father:* The disciples are to show the same indifference to friends and enemies that God shows in his distribution of sunshine and rain; in exhibiting this godlike providence they vindicate their title of sons of God. Love within one's group or fellowship is merely a natural and universal human trait; Mt uses terms that identify two despised classes among the Jews: the Gentiles and the tax farmers. The use of these terms is something of a lapse from the principle Mt is stating; elsewhere the Gospel is friendly to these despised classes; see 9:10; 11:19; 21:31. By this kind of love the disciples will be perfect as the heavenly Father is perfect. **48.** This verse is conflated from Dt 18:13 and Lv 19:2, where the word "holy" is used. "Perfect" represents the Hebr word for "whole" or "integral"; it is the love of one's enemies that assures the integrity of Christian morality and distinguishes it from merely ethical morality. This passage also is echoed in Rom 12:17–21.

42 (d) GENUINE AND SPURIOUS RIGHTEOUSNESS (6:1–18). This passage expands the idea of Christian righteousness as contrasted with the righteousness of the scribes and Pharisees (5:20). Righteousness is illustrated by three basic acts of Jewish piety: almsgiving, prayer, and fasting. In each instance an antithesis is drawn between the spurious piety of display and the genuine piety, which seeks to conceal itself. The ideal of this passage lacks a certain harmony with that of 5:14–16—an inconsistency not so much in the text as in the situation: works of piety should not be done for vain display, but they should have the force of good example. If they stem from the proper motive, they will be seen—a city set on a mountain cannot be hidden.

43 (i) *Almsgiving* (6:1–4). **1.** *righteousness:* In later biblical literature and extrabiblical Jewish writings this becomes the technical term for almsgiving; and the word may have this force here (some mss. indeed read *eleēmosynēn*), although this is not the usual meaning of the word in Mt. The language in which vain display is repudiated is unusually vigorous. **2.** *hypocrites:* This word originally meant "actor," and this meaning may be echoed here; the word "to be seen" used in 6:1 is the Gk verb related to the noun "theater." Genuine righteousness even tries to evade itself. To be hailed as a virtuous man is a sufficient reward for those who seek recognition; they obtain what they seek, and that is all they obtain.

44 (ii) *Prayer* (6:5–15). The saying on prayer follows the pattern of the saying on almsgiving. The prayer in public was prayer that was uttered at set times of the day; the devout Jew stopped wherever he was, unless the place was unclean, and recited the proper prayers in a standing position. Moslems also worship in public at prescribed times, and it is regarded as a sign of great devotion to observe this practice. **6.** *retire to your room:* In a phrase borrowed from Is 26:20, quoted according to the LXX, the saying recommends that one retire to one's private chamber even to recite the scheduled prayer. Prayer said when one is not being observed is surely prompted by the proper motive. The saying does not refer to public common prayer in the temple or the synagogue.

Verses 7 to 15 interrupt the pattern and are placed here under a loose topical arrangement. The Lord's Prayer in Lk 11:2–4 is given in answer to a request from the disciples for instruction in prayer, and this is no doubt the original context of the prayer in Q. The Lord's Prayer is contrasted in 6:7–8 not with Jewish prayer but with pagan prayer, which is dismissed as "babbling." There may be an allusion to the long and tedious magical formulas in which meaningless epithets are piled up (C. K. Barrett, *NTB* 31–35). The saying is not sympathetic to long prayers, however, of which Judaism of NT times presents numerous examples. The lengthy recital of one's needs is discouraged on the ground that God does not need to be informed of them.

The Lord's Prayer in Lk has a shorter invocation and six petitions against Mt's seven, omitting the third petition in Mt. **9.** *Father in heaven:* A common phrase of Mt (5:45; 7:21; 12:50). The first three petitions are really synonymous; they express the desire for the eschatological realization of the reign. *hallowed be your name:* This occurs when it is recognized as holy and confessed to be holy by men. The coming of the reign is the effective actualization of the will of God "on earth as in heaven," where God's supremacy is not questioned. **11.** *daily:* The word *epiousios,* traditionally translated "daily," is of uncertain meaning; it does not appear in any Gk literature before the Gospels, and the etymology is uncertain. "Daily" is a very probable rendering; the word seems to designate the bread of the coming day, and the petition is thus related to the sayings against excessive solicitude (6:31–33). However, K. Stendahl has raised the question whether the petition may not refer to the Messianic banquet (*PCB* 778); see comment on 8:11. This also is in harmony with 6:31–33; for the petition is then not directed even to the simple provision of daily basic needs, but to the ultimate realization of the reign in which basic daily needs cease to exist. In this interpretation the fourth petition belongs with the first three. **12.** *our debts:* The fifth petition is a prayer for the forgiveness of them. Lk has "sins," an easier word for non-Jewish readers. The condition of forgiveness is that one has forgiven. **13.** *lead us not into temptation:* This petition probably does not refer to the daily encounter with evil; Matthew would no doubt agree with Paul that God can give an escape from temptation (1 Cor 10:13). The eschatological tone of the prayer suggests that the temptation meant is the great eschatological test, of which Mt says (24:22) that no one could bear it unless it were abbreviated. *deliver us from evil:* Similarly, the eschatological catastrophe is very probably "the evil" from which the Christian prays to be delivered in the final petition. The ambiguity of "evil" and "the evil one" previously noted (5:37,39) is found here too.

A doxology, "For thine is the kingdom and the power

and the glory forever and ever, Amen" is found in many Gk mss: The presence of a similar doxology in the *Didache* (8:2), a work written before AD 100, suggests that the doxology is a very early expansion. It was normal in Judaism to conclude prayers with a formal doxology, and the early Christian communities often followed the Jewish practice. The doxology, however, is not found in the most reliable mss. It has been used in the Protestant churches; it is sheer accident that it did not appear in the Gk mss that Jerome used in translating the Vg.

Verses 14 and 15 are a commentary on the fifth petition, emphasizing the duty of forgiveness as a condition of receiving forgiveness. The passage is very loosely parallel to Mk 11:25–26. See 5:23–26; 18:35.

45 (iii) *Fasting* (6:16–18). **16.** *when you fast:* In the early books of the OT, fasting appears as a token of mourning or of repentance. No fast is prescribed in the Law except the fast of the Day of Atonement (Lv 16:29; 23:27; Nm 29:7). A fast meant abstinence from food for the entire day from sunrise to sunset. Fasting twice a week was regarded in NT times as a sign of devotion. *they disfigure their faces:* The disfigurement was a part of the ritual of grief or mourning in the ancient world; "sackcloth and ashes" were put on to make the person unsightly. These are rejected as mere external display. The disciple who fasts should wash and anoint himself; washing and anointing were preparations for a banquet, not signs of grief and affliction (see 9:14–15).

46 (e) SAYINGS (6:19–34). This collection of sayings, which are found in scattered contexts in Lk, have as a common theme singleness of purpose. The disciple should attend exclusively to the service of God and should not permit himself to be distracted from this concentration even by what men think are legitimate cares. The paradoxical tone of the sermon is maintained in these sayings.

(i) *True treasure* (6:19–21). The Palestinian archaeologist sometimes finds hoards of coins in the remains of ancient houses. More frequently he finds only traces of such hoards. The ancient peasant or laborer had very little opportunity to use hard money; and when it came into his hands, his instinct was to bury it rather than spend it. He was especially moved to hide his little store of coins at times of political disturbance: and there was always the danger of thieves or robbers (6:19). The saying tells the disciples that no lasting treasure can be stored on earth. The stores of the peasant often included costly garments, which were saved for special occasions. These will be eaten by moths. "Rust" is literally "eating," any type of corrosion. **20.** *dig through and steal:* This could be done by thieves in a house of mud bricks, no longer the prevalent building material in modern Palestine, where stone is now commonly used. There are other references to mud-brick houses; see 7:26–27. *treasure in heaven:* This metaphor is in the same line with the "wages" mentioned in the preceding examples of true righteousness (6:1,4,6). Only righteousness achieves anything of lasting value; and what a man thinks has lasting value determines where his intentions and interests lie.

(ii) *The single eye* (6:22–23). **22.** *the eye is the lamp of the body:* In a naïve physiological conception the eye is the aperture through which light is admitted. The eye should be simple, which means healthy; the Hebr or Aram background is not certain, but this is the most probable meaning of the word. The healthy eye illuminates the whole inner man. The "evil," or wicked, eye is here the diseased eye; if the very principle of light is darkened, then the whole inner man is in total darkness. The force of the metaphor is somewhat obscure both in Mt and in Lk. The "evil eye" is usually envy; and the original saying seems to have been directed against this vice. By inserting it in the present context Mt has turned it to an image of simplicity of intention; this is the clarity of vision by which one seeks true treasure and serves only one master.

47 (iii) *Two masters* (6:24). This saying continues the common theme. The disciple cannot have a divided loyalty. *Mammon:* personified in opposition to God, it is found in the Talmud to designate not only money, but possessions in general. Taken together with 6:19–21 and the following passage, the radical character of the teaching of Jesus on wealth and ownership begins to emerge. Material possessions are a false god that demands exclusive loyalty, as God demands it. The claims of material possessions must be totally repudiated.

(iv) *Solicitude* (6:25–34). The radical teaching of Jesus on possessions is expanded and emphasized. *worry:* "Anxious care" is not to be admitted; it may be worth noting that the word means more than simple thought or planning. Jesus refers to the kind of worry that leads to a divided loyalty and ultimately to an exclusive concentration on possessions. He speaks of the basic needs of food and clothing—the person is more important and deserves more attention than the external goods that sustain him. The example of the birds is proposed as the proper attitude toward food. T. H. Robinson has remarked that this example does not excuse one from earning his food; few men, he says, work as hard for their living as the average sparrow. The audience to which these sayings were addressed was largely composed of peasants and laborers, and Jesus says nothing here or elsewhere that invites them to abandon their life of incessant grinding toil. It is not indolence he recommends (see 2 Thes 3:10). What is recommended is that one's anxiety should not exceed the labor that is required to secure subsistence. It is not the use of the necessities of life that is discouraged, but the accumulation of goods. Accumulation of goods does not prolong the life of the owner as much as a cubit (about 18–20 in.). The spatial and temporal metaphors are mixed in this figure.

25. *what you shall put on:* For the proper attitude toward clothing, Jesus alludes to the wild flowers, which bloom in profusion on Palestinian hills. These hills are a dull brown color most of the year. The example illustrates the observation of nature and the details of daily life that are typical of the Gospels. Yet this display of bright color, which is indeed an impressive sight, lasts only for a few weeks. **29.** *Solomon in all his splendor:* The raiment of Solomon, the proverbial example of wealth in the Bible, did not effectively endure much longer. To make the provision of food and clothing one's major concern, an object of anxiety, is to live like the pagans who know no dedication except to the accumulation of the goods of this world. The disciples have a prior dedication, the reign of God; Mt adds "its righteousness" (see 5:20), not found in Lk. If the disciples seek this, God will provide the necessities of life to those who work for them. **34.** This verse (not found in Lk) emphasizes more clearly the principle that the disciples should not accumulate goods. By a saying paradoxical to modern ears, saving is called anxious care for the morrow; no doubt this is an instance (similar to the legitimation of what was once called usury) of the adaptation of the Gospels to an economics not the same as that in which the Gospels were written. If saving becomes "accumulation," it is still subject to the words of this passage. *sufficient for the day:* The concluding sentence sounds less like a saying of Jesus than a popular proverb used to illustrate the point at issue.

48 (f) COLLECTION OF DETACHED SAYINGS (7:1–27). The remainder of the sermon has no perceptible unity of theme. Obviously Matthew considered the sayings to be basic. Almost all of them are paralleled in Lk; but only one is paralleled in Mk.

(i) *Judging others* (7:1–5). **1.** *judge not:* The meaning of "judge" is not simply to have an opinion—this can scarcely be avoided; the word means to judge harshly, to condemn, and the form in which the saying appears in Lk (6:37–38) makes this explicit. Mt's briefer statement is probably closer to the original. **2.** This saying is found in Mk 4:24 in a different context. It suits Matthew's purpose quite well. Men must judge one another, but they can expect to be called to responsibility for their judgments. By a somewhat popular paradox one who judges others unfairly is apparently threatened with the unfair judgment of God. This is not the intended meaning; harsh judgments will be punished severely, but not unfairly. Lk 6:38 has adapted the saying to a different context; the measure is not the measure of judgment but the measure of generous giving. The name of God is avoided; the threat of judgment is put in the simple passive ("theological" passive, *Gr Bib* § 236). **3.** *the beam:* By a hyperbole the "beam" in one's own eye is contrasted with the "splinter" in another's eye. This may be a popular proverb applied to the Gospel. Acute observance of the faults of others combined with complacency with one's own character is the object to many commonplace proverbs in all languages. This is the attitude of "hypocrites" (see comment on 6:2); the saying is clearly directed against the censoriousness of the scribes and Pharisees.

49 (ii) *Pearls before swine* (7:6). This saying has furnished interpreters difficulty; it is not clear what is concealed by the figure. The saying is chiastic. Its original form may have been: "Give not the holy to dogs/lest they tear you;/nor cast your pearls before swine/lest they trample them." Whatever the original force of the saying was (another popular proverb?), in Mt it most probably refers to the proclamation and teaching of the Gospel. In this hypothesis the dogs and the swine can scarcely be any but those who in Mt are least hospitable to the Gospel: the scribes and Pharisees. The saying is harsh, but more so to us than it would be in its original utterance; the use of popular proverbs in this fashion was a commonplace of ancient Near Eastern wisdom.

(iii) *Prayer and its answer* (7:7–11). **7.** *ask and it will be given:* Prayer to most people means the prayer of petition, and this is the prayer recommended here. The deliberate repetition of the threefold formula, ask–receive, seek–find, knock–be-opened, is intended to assure the disciples that prayer is heard and to encourage them to present their petitions to God. There is no real opposition between this passage and 6:8,32, where Jesus speaks of the prayer of worried anxiety, which reflects the excessive solicitude of those who utter it. It is possible that the type of nervous care discussed in 6:25–34 can reflect itself in the prayer of the worried person. Prayer should be uttered in the spirit of freedom from worry and in the assurance that it is heard and answered. **9.** *if a son asks for bread:* The assurance is illustrated by homely examples from family life; the father will give his children what they ask, and he certainly will not give them something harmful in answer to their requests. The bread is the round loaf that has a strange resemblance to a stone. Mt uses this example instead of the picturesque example of the egg and the scorpion (Lk 11:12); this well-known Palestinian nuisance roughly resembles an egg. **11.** *you who are evil:* Fathers, even though they are "evil," take care of their children; this is merely a statement of the human condition. The Father in heaven is not evil, and can be counted on to act like a father.

50 (iv) *The golden rule* (7:12). This verse has parallels both in Judaism and in other ancient literature (Str-B 1, 459–60). The best known is probably the saying attributed to Rabbi Hillel, given in answer to the challenge of a proselyte to explain the whole Law while the proselyte stood on one foot: "That which displeases you do not do to another. This is the whole Law; the rest is commentary." The saying of Hillel is echoed in the last part of Mt's sentence, not found in Lk; but the saying attributed to Hillel cannot be dated. The addition of Mt does not support the claim that the saying is entirely new in Christianity, as indeed it is not. Not too much, it seems, should be made of the fact that the Gospel saying is couched in the affirmative, whereas the parallels are couched in the negative; this distinction seems to be hairsplitting.

(v) *The narrow gate* (7:13–14). The saying in Lk is given in answer to the question whether few are saved. The question is not found in Mt, but the saying is no less eschatological. The ms. evidence for 7:13b in the form most frequently quoted, "Wide is the gate and spacious the way," is ample; but the critical text reads, "Wide and spacious is the way." Where Lk says there are few who seek the narrow gate, Mt says there are few who find it; Mt's formula is slightly more rigorous. The saying echoes the rather common teaching of the two spirits and the two ways, found in 1QS 3:20–21; *Didache* 1:1–6:2; *Ep. Barnabae* 18:1–21:9.

51 (vi) *Genuine good works* (7:15–20). Lk (6:43–45) does not contain the warning against false prophets; see 24:11. These do not seem to be "false teachers," but those who claim a new revelation; possibly the saying refers to the Zealot prophets who incited to rebellion against Rome during the period preceding the Jewish War AD 66–70. In any case, the addition of Mt seems to reflect the experience of the Church. **16.** *by their fruits:* The true test of prophets or disciples is their life. The comparison of trees and fruits is painfully elaborated. Luke felt the necessity of explaining the comparison (6:45), with the addition of a phrase that makes speech the principal fruit; this is not the real meaning of the original comparison, which refers to deeds. See the recital in Mt 23. **19.** This verse is repeated word for word from the preaching of John the Baptist (3:10), where it has a more suitable context.

(vii) *Self-deception* (7:21–23). **21.** *Lord, Lord:* This address, "Lord, Lord," reflects the experience of the primitive Church. It is most likely that the reference to prophecy, exorcism, and thaumaturgy also refers to the experience of the primitive Church. Devout invocation of Jesus as Lord and the reception of the charismata of the apostolate do not guarantee that one is a genuine disciple. Paul also says that these gifts are vain without love (1 Cor 13:2). In Mt the test is doing the will of the Father (Lk 6:46, "doing what I tell you"). **22.** *on that day:* In the eschatological judgment Jesus will profess that he does not know them. **23.** The formula of reprobation is quoted from Ps 6:9; neither Mt nor Lk quotes the LXX exactly. The form of the saying in Lk 13:26–27 ("We have eaten and drunk with you, and you have taught in our streets") points the saying much more directly to the Jews. In Mt the saying is directed at false disciples within the Christian community.

52 (viii) *Hearers and doers* (7:24–27). The words of Jesus are a call and a challenge to action; they are not mere teaching, and understanding them is an insufficient response. The challenge is serious; failure to meet it is followed by catastrophe—"great is the fall." This again is the eschatological catastrophe. **24.** *upon the rock:* The comparison of the housebuilders presupposes Palestinian conditions; Luke, however, was not familiar with these. He describes the digging of a deep foundation (6:48). It is rather striking that Hellenistic buildings in Palestinian sites were built on deeper foundations than earlier buildings; but this was the practice with large houses or public buildings, not with the ordinary dwelling. The flood Luke envisages is the flood of a river. Matthew knows the Palestinian winter rains that run off in sudden large flows of water. These rains not only fill the stream beds (*wadis*) with rapid torrents but erode the slopes of the hills. The soil is swept from beneath a house that is not founded on the bedrock. The house built of mud brick is particularly vulnerable. It is action, not knowledge or profession of belief, that furnishes the secure foundation for the life of the disciple; and the love without which Paul says charismata are vain is action, not mere profession of belief.

53 (g) CONCLUDING FORMULA (7:28–29). Each of the major discourses of Mt is concluded by a similar formula. The result of his teaching, in a phrase taken from Mk (1:22), is astonishment. The astonishment is not attributed to the content of the teaching, but to the manner in which it was proposed: Jesus teaches with authority unlike that of the scribes. The authority of the scribes was based on tradition: The scribe was careful to repeat the traditional teaching and to show that his own commentary rose from the tradition and was in harmony with it. The first part of the sermon (→ 35–41 above) is a deliberate and explicit departure from tradition. Jesus taught not like a scribe but like a prophet, although the word is not used. The Gk word *exousia* translated "authority" means "authority by commission." Jesus has a commission from the Father to teach—a commission the scribes do not have. He manifests this commission clearly, and the people are astonished.

54 **General Remarks.** The Sermon on the Mount is not "the New Law"; this phrase is nowhere applied to the sermon, and the sermon is not couched either in the form of the Law or in the form of rabbinical teaching. It is very probably a form of Christian teaching (*didachē*), the instruction given to those who had believed in the proclamation (*kerygma*) and received baptism. It was formed by a more or less systematic collection and arrangement of remembered sayings of Jesus, adapted and clarified where necessary for the group that was being instructed.

The sermon is not a complete code of Christian ethics. There are many directions for Christian morality in the NT that are not found in the sermon. Indeed no single passage of the NT contains a complete and systematic code of conduct. The Christian moral revolution consisted in a reorientation of values. This can be expressed in a few simple phrases, most of which can be summed up as directions to love. Other moral directions are applications of the principle of love. The sermon is a statement of those principles "Matthew" or his sources considered basic enough to be collected and placed in the significant position of introducing the account of the words and deeds of Jesus.

(Dupont, J., *Les béatitudes* [new ed.; Bruges, 1958]. Hunter, A. M., "The Meaning of the Sermon on the Mount," *ExpT* 63 [1951–52] 176–79. Jeremias, J., *The Sermon on the Mount* [Facet, Bibl. ser., 2; Phila., 1963]. McArthur, K. H., *Understanding the Sermon on the Mount* [N.Y., 1960]. Schnackenburg, R., *The Moral Teaching of the NT* [N.Y., 1965]. Windisch, H., *The Meaning of the Sermon on the Mount* [Phila., 1951].)

55 **(III) Book Two: Ministry in Galilee (8:1–11:1).**

(A) Narrative Section: Cycle of Ten Miracles (8:1–9:34). This section has as its basic content ten miracles (→ Aspects NT Thought, 78:109–130), most of which are found in Mk. The order of Mk, however, is revised. Mk's "Day in Capernaum" has nearly disappeared as such, and materials that follow the call of the apostles in Mk have been placed before it by Mt. The events are arranged to form an introduction to the discourse on the apostolic mission, which concludes Book Two.

56 (a) THE HEALING OF A LEPER (8:1–4). This passage illustrates how Mt normally abbreviates the narratives of Mk (see 1:40–45) by the omission of picturesque details. In Mt the incident takes place in a location between the "mountain" of the sermon and Capernaum; in Mk and Lk it is placed somewhere in Galilee. Mt, because the incident follows the sermon, makes mention of a crowd with Jesus. **2.** *leper:* Leprosy is loosely used throughout the Bible for unspecified skin diseases (cf. Lv 13), which were as common in the Near East of NT times as they are today. The type of disease is not pertinent to the miraculous character of the cure; eczema seems no easier to heal by a touch than leprosy. **3.** *I will; be made clean:* All three Gospels retain the formula in which the words of Jesus echo the petition of the sick man; faith is not mentioned in the narrative, but the brevity of the petition and the instant echo of the answer illustrate the faith of the sick man and the healing power of Jesus. Both Mt and Lk omit the words that express the emotional reaction of Jesus: "feeling compassion" (Mk 1:41) and "angered" (1:43). Indeed Mk 1:43 must have been as unintelligible to Matthew and Luke as it is to modern readers; the verse surely reflects the constructive work of Mark, and the original form of the story must have represented the leprosy as the work of a demon. It is the demon and not the sufferer who is the object of the anger of Jesus and who is expelled in Mk. The precept of silence is important in Mk; it is a part of that pattern called "the Messianic Secret." Mt and Lk retain the precept, even though the pattern of the secret is not an essential part of their Gospels. Mt consequently omits Mk's notice that the secret was not kept. **4.** *show yourself to the priest:* The appearance of the leper before the priest with an offering to certify his cure is prescribed in Lv 14:2–9.

57 (b) THE SLAVE OF THE CENTURION (8:5–13). In contrast to the preceding incident, this passage illustrates the "saying-story" as opposed to the "miracle story." In the healing of the leper, the miracle itself is the point of the story. In the story of the centurion, the miracle is the occasion by which the faith of the Gentile centurion is manifested; and his faith in turn is the occasion of the saying of Jesus (8:10–12). The story is not found in Mk, and the variations between Mt and Lk are such as to raise some doubt whether the story was found in Q. These doubts do not appear to be well founded; a comparison of Mt and Lk shows that Matthew uses his customary technique of abbreviating narratives.

The scene is Capernaum. **5.** *a centurion:* The petitioner is an officer of the Roman legion whose command was normally 100 men (Lat *centum*, 100); but the number could be more or less. These officers, who corresponded somewhat to our noncommissioned officers, were usually in charge of small local posts and garrisons. It is interesting to note that every one of these officers who appears in the NT is an honest and kindly man. The sick person is called "slave" (*doulos*) by Lk, a "boy" (*pais*) by Mt; but *pais* was a common Gk designation of a young slave. The disease cannot be identified; paralysis means the loss of the use of the limbs, and here it is accompanied with great pain; this detail is not found in Lk. **7.** This verse is understood by many interpreters as a question: "Shall I come and heal him?" Normally a Jew would not enter the house of a Gentile; he would incur ritual uncleanness.

Mt makes the centurion the petitioner; Lk has the centurion send Jews as his emissaries and intercessors, and the centurion does not appear until Jesus is on his way to the house. This is more probably an omission by Mt rather than an expansion of Lk. The omission unfortunately leaves out a pleasing detail of excellent relations between a Gentile and the Jewish community. The omission, however, takes no more credit from one party than from the other; and it is economical rather than tendentious. **8.** The climactic line in both versions is the centurion's belief that Jesus need only speak; a visit and personal contact are unnecessary. **9.** *a man under authority:* He illustrates from his own position. He, a military officer of lower rank, gets instant obedience and execution from men under him; if military discipline can effect things by a word, Jesus is surely no less "under authority." **10.** The answer of Jesus is the first saying in Mt that contrasts the unbelief of the Jews with the faith of the uninstructed Gentile. Actually at this point in Mt's narrative the unbelief of the Jews has not yet appeared; in Mt's version even the request of the Jews that Jesus should come to the house to heal the slave (Lk 5:3) is omitted. In Lk, likewise, the faith of the centurion seems to grow from the initial request to the point where he intercepts Jesus.

11–12. This saying is found in Lk (13:28–30) in a different and entirely eschatological context, which is probably its original situation. "The sons of the kingdom" are simply "you" in Lk. The Gentiles will be admitted with the true Israelites to the Messianic banquet. This theme is based on Is 25:6–8; it conceives the Messianic deliverance as admission to a festive dinner that God prepares. The Messianic banquet is found in apocalyptic literature and in the Qumran writings and is echoed frequently in the NT. It is a part of the idea of the Eucharist (see 26:29). **12b.** An eschatological commonplace in Mt (13:42,50; 22:13; 24:51; 25:30).

The theme of the story is faith—the kind of faith that sets no conditions. The choice of a Gentile to illustrate this faith the first time the idea is raised in the Gospel is certainly deliberate; it sets a tone Mt maintains in the rest of the book: The faith of the Gentiles gives them the title of the true Israel which the Jews have forfeited by unbelief in the Messiah.

No doubt Jn 4:46–52 is a variant of the same story, but it is so profoundly modified that a common source cannot be traced with certainty.

58 (c) Peter's Mother-in-Law (8:14–15). This is another instance of Matthew's economy with Mk's material (Mk 1:29–31). He omits all names except the name of Peter, the intercession of the family, and picturesque details in the cure itself. Commentators believe the change from "she served them" to "she served him" is significant; Jesus is more than one of a group. This episode and 1 Cor 9:5 show that Peter was married.

(d) Healings and Exorcisms (8:16–17). The evening is the evening of Mk's "Day in Capernaum," of which Mt has preserved only this passage and the preceding incident (Mk 1:32–34). The Gospels distinguish between those "possessed by demons" and the "ill"; not every illness was regarded as the work of a demon. It is doubtful that Mark meant to say that they brought all the ill and Jesus cured some; but Matthew in any case alters Mk to say that Jesus healed "all." **16.** *by a word:* A Matthaean addition emphasizing the easy exercise of power. Allusion to the Messianic secret (see comment on 8:4) is omitted, but a fulfillment quotation from Is 53:4 (see comment on 1:24) is added. The text is quoted not according to the LXX but according to the MT; and the meaning is altered by a wordplay. The passage of Is refers to the vicarious suffering of the Servant of the Lord, who takes upon himself the illnesses and the stripes of others. Mt interprets the words "take" and "carry" as take away, which Jesus does by healing.

(e) Discipleship and Renunciation (8:18–22). **18.** This connecting verse is peculiar to Mt, which has its own arrangement. Jesus commands a voyage to the eastern shore of the Sea of Galilee, opposite Capernaum, in order to escape the crowds. Actually the chief reason for the command in Mt is to provide an occasion to insert the stories of the calming of the storm and the demoniacs of Gadara. The two sayings about discipleship are placed in Lk at the beginning of the Journey Narrative; they had no original context in Q. Both the speakers are disciples. Matthew presupposes the formation of a group of intimate associates who accompanied Jesus, although he has not yet described the formation of such a group except in the story of the call (4:18–22). **19.** *a scribe:* The first speaker belongs to a group usually represented as hostile to Jesus, yet there were scribes among the members of the primitive Christian community. His words are not meant to be insincere; they are the occasion for the statement of Jesus that those who follow him must be prepared to have no home, as he has none. There are no other clear references to the fact that Jesus was technically a vagrant, but no home is ever mentioned. The form of expression is possibly based on a popular proverb. **20.** *Son of Man:* This title, used frequently of Jesus, appears for the first time here in Mt (→ Aspects NT Thought, 78:28–30). **21.** *another of his disciples:* The second disciple wishes to bury his father. This does not mean that his father had died (burial normally occurred on the day of death), but that the disciple wished to await his father's death so that he might provide for him. But renunciation of family ties is one of the conditions of discipleship; one cannot wait until all family connections are satisfied, or one would never be able to follow the call. The time is now (see 10:37).

59 (f) The Tempest at Sea (8:23–27). Here Matthew has compressed the narrative less than usual, and his changes are significant. For Mk's "whirlwind" has become a *seismos*, "earthquake," a cosmic disturbance. In Mk (4:35–41) the boat is shipping water, in Mt it is nearly covered by the waves. In Mk the cry of the disciples is not a petition for help—how could they expect to be saved from a storm? In Mt it is a prayer for deliverance addressed to Jesus, the *Kyrios*; and this change is not altogether consistent with the rebuke in which they are called "you of little faith." **24.** *a great storm:* The *seismos* (above). Modern observers have noticed that the Sea of Galilee, a small body of water almost entirely surrounded by hills, is often subject to sudden storms because of currents of air of variant temperatures that roll down the slopes. The storms abate as suddenly as they arise. It seems unlikely that the disciples, who had lived on the Sea of Galilee all their lives, did not know this. The story opens another aspect of the mystery of Jesus: his mastery over nature, which is more awesome than his mastery over disease and demons. The disciples simply ask who he is; the rest of the Gospel is taken up with the revelation of the answer to the question. **27.** *the men:* This word seems to admit others than the disciples as witnesses of the miracle, although he has left no room for others in the preceding narrative; Mk, however, notes that the boat was accompanied by other boats (4:36).

60 (g) The Demoniacs of Gadara (8:28–34). Mt designates the location of the story more correctly than Mk or Lk. The Hellenistic city of Gadara lay nearer to the Sea of Galilee than the Hellenistic city of Gerasa. The variant reading Gergesenes comes from an erudite conjecture of Origen. The story is told in Mk with full and circumstantial details. It has obvious folkloristic traits, is vivid, and moves rapidly. Even Matthew's condensation retains more length than his miracle stories usually have; but he has omitted most of Mk's details. **28.** *two demoniacs:* Instead of Mk's one (5:2–5); Mt omits Mk's description of the ferocity of the demoniac. In the ancient world, Jewish and Gentile, ailments which exhibited some unusually repulsive feature or for which there was no explanation were often attributed to demons. It is rarely possible to define the ailment that is explained in this way; mental illness, of course, was more obviously explained by demonic possession than was physical disease. The important feature of this and other exorcisms performed by Jesus is not whether he accepted the common belief or spoke in terms of the common belief; those who formed the Gospel traditions could not have represented him as speaking in terms other than those familiar to them. The important fact is that the exorcisms show that Jesus liberates men from the fear of demons; demons have no real power and are instantly subdued by a word from him. The power of God overcomes any other power. The significance of exorcism is not that the Christian should or should not believe in demons and their power, but that the Christian should treat demonic power as nonexistent. There is only one power with which men must reckon, and that is the power of God. **29.** *what have you to do with us:* Lit., "what to us and to you?" The phrase expresses dissociation; it denies both community of interest and grounds for hostility and is effectively a dismissal. But the demons recognize Jesus. *Son of God:* The title has rather full implications here. The dark powers of the world of spirits know with whom they have to contend before he is recognized by men (→ Aspects NT Thought, 78:20). *before the time:* The *kairos* is the appointed time for the eschatological consummation, when God will destroy every hostile power (1 Cor 15:24–25). **31.** *the demons begged him:* The request of the demons to be sent into the herd of pigs is not mere mischievousness; the pig, the most unclean of all animals, is the suitable place for a demon. The presence of the herd shows that the episode occurs in Gentile territory. **32.** *rushed... into the sea:* The rush of the pigs into the sea may seem a bit unfair to their owners; but in Jewish thought the unclean pig was good for absolutely nothing at all, and no one could incur a loss when a herd of pigs perished. Does the narrative mean that the demons perished? This seems to be the implication. The demons were driven from men into pigs, but even the pigs reject them; demons have no place in a world in which the saving power of God has entered in Jesus Christ.

Mt also omits most of the details of the recovery of the demoniacs. **34.** *they begged him to leave their neighborhood:* Mk does not exhibit in the story any of the remarkable faith shown by such Gentiles as the centurion. One who has power over demons is a dangerous person and may even himself be a demon of higher power; this is the point of the accusation of the Pharisees (12:24). The story is an instance of the failure of a wonder to inspire faith, and the Gospels make no comment on the reasons. Mt omits the request of the man to follow Jesus, and the commission Jesus gives him to proclaim the wonder (Mk 5:18–19).

61 (h) Healing and Forgiveness of Sins (9:1–8). This passage is a "controversy-story" in which the miracle is the resolution of a controversy. The progress of Mt's arrangement is obvious: from disease to nature to demonic possession to the power to forgive sins, the climactic exhibition of a power that belongs to God alone (Mk 2:7), a phrase Mt strangely omits. **1.** *his own city:* The scene is Capernaum, to which Jesus returns from the eastern shore of the Sea of Galilee. Mt calls Capernaum "his own city" (9:1), which does not indicate that Jesus had a house there (see 8:20); it was the city to which he returned during the Galilean ministry. Matthew abbreviates Mk even in the dialogue, which is the central part of the story; he omits the presence of crowds and the almost bizarre detail of the digging of a hole in the roof in order to get the paralytic into the room. **2.** *their faith:* The appearance of the sick man and his manifest faith elicit not a cure but a declaration of forgiveness of sins, which is not the expected response. Yet it is fully in harmony with the evangelical understanding of miracles (→ Aspects NT Thought, 78:115–128). The miracle is worked in response to the faith of the petitioner; and faith in Jesus is already an implicit confession of sin and of repentance. The afflictions of the human condition are the consequences of sin, and forgiveness of sins removes the root of evil. The miracle is far more than a mere wonder; it is at once a symbol and a token of the saving process, which is initiated in Jesus. This conception of miracle escapes the scribes, who see in the words of Jesus an assertion of divine prerogatives. Jesus does not withdraw from his position but challenges them to an ordeal. **5.** *which is easier:* To say that sins are forgiven, which cannot be tested by observation, or to bid the sick man rise and walk. The effect of the healing power shows that the power that saves from sin is present and active. Unless sin is cured, there is no genuine remedy for human ills. This is the point of Mt's version of the concluding verse; it is the fullness of the saving power—not the mere power of thaumaturgy—that causes men to glorify God.

62 (i) The Call of Matthew (9:9–13). This is a "controversy-story" that ends in a saying; the vocation of Matthew is the occasion of the controversy. The tax collector is named Levi in Mk 2:14; Lk 5:27,29, and only in these passages; the name Matthew appears here and in all the lists of the Twelve (→ Aspects NT Thought, 78:166). The tax collectors are known in the Gospels as a typical class of moral reprobates, sometimes paired with sinners (as in 9:10–11). The Roman taxes were collected by tax farmers, who bid for the right to collect taxes and then extorted them to the limit. They were therefore not only considered oppressors; they were traitors to their own people because they collaborated with the foreign imperial power.

If Matthew is the author of the First Gospel, then this passage would be autobiographical. In this hypothesis, it is strange that this passage shows exactly the same kind of dependence on Mk and the same type of revision found elsewhere. The revisions are actually slight, consisting of a few omissions and the addition of 9:13. Matthew follows the call with the same immediacy that is seen in the call of the fishermen (4:18–22); the promptness of Matthew's response is more remarkable because he is such an unlikely subject. **10.** His second response is a gesture of hospitality; he invites Jesus to a farewell dinner with his friends, "tax collectors and sinners." The "sinners" are nonobservant Jews. **11.** *why does your teacher eat...:* Pharisaic Judaism held strictly to the principle of avoiding contact with Gentiles and Jews who did not observe the Law; these were the social outcasts of the community, and no rabbi could afford to consort with such. The remark may express surprise as much as hostility; but the snobbish attitude that underlies the remark elicits a sharp response from Jesus. **12.** *need no physician:* Jesus' saying is cast in a proverbial form, and in Mt it is strengthened by the quotation of Hos 6:6 (LXX). The quotation places human relations above cultic worship, and of course above mere observance of an external manner of life. The quotation and the saying express the compassion of Jesus for sinners, to whom his mission is directed, but it also strikes at the self-righteousness of the Pharisees. Those who do not recognize their illness will not summon the physician nor receive him; they are beyond healing. No one can approach Jesus unless he confesses that he is a sinner. The position of this story after the story of the healing of the paralytic is extremely apt in the Gospels. The faith that heals demands repentance.

63 (j) FASTING (9:14–17). In Mt the question is asked by the disciples of John; in Mk and Lk the questioners are not identified. Fasting was a recognized Jewish observance (→ 45 above) that was not practiced by Jesus and his disciples. **15.** *can wedding guests mourn:* The question is answered by a saying; possibly the form of the saying is influenced by the fact that fasting was observed in the primitive community. The saying affirms that the sojourn of Jesus with his disciples is considered a time of joy when fasting (or other symbols of grief or mourning) is out of place. Jesus does not reject fasting as such, but asserts the liberty of fasting when it is suitable; he obviously does not regard the Pharisaic customs as obligatory. The comparison of the messianic advent to a wedding festival is found also in 22:1–14; 25:1–13; Ap 19:7–8; these passages, however, are explicitly eschatological. The joy of the eschatological festival is not limited to the end time; it begins with the coming of him who is the bridegroom.

16–17. These sayings have no obvious connection with the preceding, although most commentators seek to establish a relation. The metaphorical language somewhat disguises the radical content of the sayings. The incompatibility of old and new is illustrated with the homely figures of patching with new cloth an old fabric and pouring new wine into used wineskins. The meaning of the figures is that the Gospel is incompatible with the Law. The order Jesus initiates is not a patchwork of elements derived from Judaism and pronouncements of Jesus. It is as new as was the revelation of the Torah through Moses. The statement is as emphatic as anything we read in Paul, although it is in metaphorical language. The novelty of the Gospel should not be overstated, nor is it overstated here; the declaration means that Judaism is not to determine the form the Gospel takes. Whatever value elements of Judaism have in the new order they have from the new order, and not from themselves. Jesus is the supreme interpreter of the Law and the Prophets.

64 (k) THE RULER'S DAUGHTER (9:18–26). The account of Mk is sharply abbreviated in Mt; and here it is easier to trace the theological basis of the abbreviation. The transitional phrase in Mt connects this incident with the sayings; in Mk the miracle follows the return of Jesus from the territory of Gerasa. **18.** *a ruler:* In Mk and Lk the more precise title of synagogue officer appears. In Mt the petition is for a resurrection from the dead; in Mk it is a petition for a cure. The large crowd of Mk does not appear here; this harmonizes with the omission of Mk 5:31–32.

The inserted story of the woman with a hemorrhage (9:20–22) is even more curtailed. The conception of the miraculous power of Jesus is profoundly modified by the omission of Mk 5:29–33. In Mk the power is conceived as a kind of invisible but palpable substance that flows from Jesus by contact, and is effective even when he is touched without his knowledge. But Mt does not conceive power as an emanation; it is operative at the word of Jesus, and the woman is cured not by touching his garment but by his word. Of Mk's narrative Mt preserves the faith that is manifested in her assurance that a touch of Jesus' garment is sufficient to effect a cure. The observant Jew wore a tassel at each of the four corners of his cloak; it was the tassel, not the "fringe," the woman touched.

Mt represents the child as already dead, and the element of suspense becomes superfluous (cf. Mk 5:23,35–36). The musicians and the crowd in the house were professional mourners. **23.** *the girl is not dead:* The sleep from which Jesus awakens is death. The raising itself is reduced by Mt to the bare essentials, and the allusion to "the Messianic Secret" (Mk 5:43) is, like most such allusions in Mk, omitted. The rewriting of the story in Mt heightens the wonder of the incident. Where Mk has a healing story, Mt has a resurrection story. This freedom, which to the modern reader may seem unwarranted, rises from the Gospel conception of the miracles. They are, as we have seen, the response of the power of Jesus to faith; and the release of the power corresponds in intensity to the intensity of the faith. The comparison of Mt with Mk here is a good illustration of the type of development that the stories of the deeds of Jesus experienced in the traditions of the primitive Church.

The structure of this part of Mt also may be related to the theological development of the miracle. The three miracles related in this context touch death, blindness, and the loss of speech and hearing. The intention to present a comprehensive summary of the saving power of Jesus is apparent.

65 (l) TWO BLIND MEN (9:27–31). This episode is a doublet of the healing of two blind men at Jericho (see comment on 20:29–34). **27.** *Son of David:* This title occurs in both accounts; this was a popular Messianic title, for the king Messiah was a descendant of David and a new David (→ Aspects NT Thought, 78:27). This version of the incident is expanded by an explicit demand for faith. **30–31.** An allusion to "the Messianic Secret," rare in Mt. The reason for the duplication of the incident here is no doubt the threefold classification of the miracles (→ 64 above).

(m) A DUMB MAN (9:32–34). In spite of some variations in detail, this passage appears to be an abbreviated doublet of 12:22–24. **34.** *the prince of the demons:* The charge of the Pharisees that Jesus was in league with Beelzebul is the occasion of a long controversy in 12:25–37. The reason for the duplication is the same as that given for the preceding passage.

66 **(B) Discourse: The Missionary Sermon (9:35–11:1).** This discourse addressed to the Twelve closes Book Two. It is, like the Sermon on the Mount, a Matthaean construction. Most of the material comes from Q, and some of it is an expansion of Mk. The missionary discourse itself ends at 10:16; the remainder, which is not separated from the missionary discourse, contains sayings on discipleship that are suitable to the context of missionary endeavor. The first of Mt's great discourses was the proclamation of the reign; the second is the first step in the foundation of the Church. In this discourse Jesus admits others to share both his mission and his powers, and he commissions them to proclaim on a scale wider than he could reach personally.

67 (a) THE SENDING OF THE TWELVE (9:35–10:4). The passage opens with a summary of the itinerant preaching of Jesus in Galilee, which is partly repeated from 4:23; the introduction is thus similar to the introduction of the Sermon on the Mount. The new element is the compassion Jesus feels for the multitudes. **36.** They are "harassed," "bothered"; this somewhat vulgar Gk word is an excellent term to describe the thousand petty persecutions and annoyances to which the poor are subject. *like sheep without a shepherd:* Cf. 1 Kgs 22:17; the quotation is not from the LXX. The line very probably refers to the *'am hā'āreṣ*, "the people of the land," a contemptuous term used by Pharisees to designate the poor and ignorant who did not know the Law well enough to observe it (Jn 7:49), and often could not afford to observe it. The verse is taken from Mk 6:34, where it precedes the multiplication of the loaves. The compassion that Jesus feels for the hungry in Mk is transferred to the spiritually unenlightened in Mt. **37.** *the harvest is plentiful:* This is paralleled in Lk 10:2–3 in the discourse to the 72 disciples. The missionary work of the disciples is also compared to a harvest in Jn 4:35–38 in different terms.

10:1. Mt (with Lk) expands the conferring of power in Mk 6:7 by the addition of the power of healing diseases. This makes explicit what is implicit in Mk; for afflictions are the work of evil spirits, but the attribution to evil spirits is expressed in certain outstanding cases of damage, particularly when the mind is afflicted (see 8:28–34). The designation of the spirits as "unclean" comes from Mk. Although the word usually means immorality associated with sexual experience, this is probably not meant here; the word appears to be synonymous with "evil."

The list of the Twelve has the same names as Mk 3:16–19 with some changes. Peter is singled out as "first" (see comment on 16:13–20). The Twelve are arranged in pairs, with the two sets of brothers mentioned first; this may reflect Mk 6:7, in which the Twelve are sent out in pairs. To the name Matthew is added "the tax collector." The nickname of Boanerges for the sons of Zebedee is omitted. **4.** *Cananaean:* Simon's appellative is not the gentilic name of the pre-Israelite people of Palestine, but a Gk transcription of the Aram *qan'ānā(y)*, "Zealot," a member of the radical anti-Roman revolutionary party. Simon had no doubt abandoned this allegiance. *Iscariot* (→ Aspects NT Thought, 78:170). The Twelve are called "apostles" only here in Mt. No appointment of the Twelve is related by Mt other than this; both Mk and Lk mention the election of the Twelve (→ Aspects NT Thought, 78:162–182).

68 (b) THE DISCOURSE PROPER (10:5–16). Verses 5–8 are peculiar to Mt, except for the commission to proclaim the reign (10:7), where the same words are used that appear in the proclamation of John the Baptist (3:2) and Jesus (4:17). **6.** *to the lost sheep of the house of Israel:* Mt limits the mission of the Twelve to Israel; a similar limitation of the mission of Jesus himself is found in 15:24, also peculiar to Mt. The mission to the Gentiles was as much a fact when Mt was written as it was when Mk and Lk were written, and Mt certainly accepts the mission to the Gentiles. The words are obviously not understood as a precept of Jesus, which the apostolic Church did not follow. They reflect the historical fact, assured in all the Gospels, that the mission of Jesus himself was limited to Jews. More important, they express the principle, not stated so clearly in Mk and Lk, that the Jews had a prior call and a peculiar responsibility. The Jews rejected this call, and the implication is that they lost thereby a peculiar place in the reign. Lk has a similar statement (Acts 13:46–47). These passages suggest that the awareness that there was a mission to the Gentiles developed by stages in the apostolic community; the various NT writings represent different stages. The ideal was that Judaism, transformed by faith in its Messiah, should be the agent of the proclamation to the Gentiles. **8.** *heal the sick:* This is a communication of the powers of healing and exorcism to the Twelve. *freely you have received, freely give:* Jesus' saying is illustrated in vv. 9–12, and it was clearly the understanding of the apostolic Church that the gospel was not sold nor were its apostles paid. Several rabbinical sayings preserved in the Talmud warn the rabbi that he must not accept a fee for instruction in the Law; the scribe should have a trade by which he could support himself (Str-B 1, 561–64). It was a point of honor with Paul that he did not even avail himself of the privilege stated here (10:10b; see 1 Cor 9:12). This passage is a more urgent and practical expansion of the discourse about care in the Sermon on the Mount (6:25–34). The prohibition is rigorous in all three Gospels, but there are some variations in detail. Mk has, "Take nothing," Lk has "Take no money," Mt specifies still further "Neither gold nor silver, nor bronze," the metals from which coins were minted. Even the place where coins were usually carried is mentioned, that is, in the girdle. **10.** *no bag:* The purse or bag was used to hold food; the ancient traveler, if he was poor, traveled with not much more than the Twelve are permitted here. Mk rather practically allows a staff and sandals; the exclusion of these two articles in Mt and Lk is no doubt an ideal heightening of the poverty of the missionary. *nor two tunics:* To carry a change of linen was a luxury in the ancient world. None of these material things will be needed, for the Twelve will have their needs provided by those to whom they proclaim. **11.** *stay with him:* It is not supposed that this provision is the minimum that a hospitable person would offer to any traveler, even to a stranger. This is the food given to the laborer for his labor. Even in the forced labor of the ancient world the laborer received either a small wage or a portion of food for himself and his family for the day. The Twelve are assured this type of support. Paul quotes a saying of Jesus not found in the Gospels (1 Cor 9:14) that makes the proclamation the sole support of the missionaries. It is assumed that they will be unable to support themselves by any other employment. Although Paul did support himself at Corinth, this seems to have been an exception in his own practice. *worthy person:* The adj. "worthy" occurs with unusual frequency in this chapter. "Worth" is shown first by offering hospitality to the missionaries, and secondly by faith in the gospel. **13.** *let your peace come upon it:* The blessing to come upon the worthy house was expressed in the usual greeting, "Peace to you"; Lk makes the greeting explicit by quoting the formula. "Peace" is not an adequate translation; the greeting is a wish that all may be well with the person greeted. It is represented as a dynamic word which is sent out by the speaker, and which returns to him if it is unable to fulfill its meaning. *if it is not worthy:* Those who refuse to give hospitality and to listen to the proclamation are to be left; the symbolic action of shaking the dust from the feet expresses complete dissociation. **15.** The unbelievers are to be left to the judgment of God; the judgment of Sodom and Gomorrah, which in the OT is the proverbial example of the wrath of God (Gn 19:4), is less severe than the judgment for unbelief. This last expression of condemnation comes from Q. **16.** Mt alone has the proverbial saying about the sheep among wolves, the prudence of the serpent, and the simplicity of the dove. Such animal proverbs are found among all peoples, and they appear in the wisdom of the OT. It is a commonplace of wisdom that man combines in himself the paradoxical features of different animals. "Prudent" means that one is thoughtful and perceptive; the serpent always knows where it is going and what it is doing. "Simple" means innocent of malice; the prudence of the missionaries is not the crafty shrewdness of those who are alert to do harm to others. The missionaries are defenseless; this is expanded in the discourse that follows.

69 (c) SAYINGS ON DISCIPLESHIP (10:17–11:1). The rest of this chapter contains a grouping of sayings of Jesus suitable to the missionary endeavor; these sayings have been appended to extend the discourse.

(i) *Persecution of the disciples* (10:17–25). This passage reflects the experience of the primitive Church; it alludes to persecution both by Jews (17) and by Gentiles (18). These verses are a fuller form of Mk 13:9, summarized in 24:9; see Lk 21:12–18. **17.** *councils:* The plural refers both to the great council of Jerusalem of 72 members, which heard the case of Jesus and examined the apostles (Acts 3–5), and to local councils. The Talmud prescribes that in a community that numbers as many as 120 there should be a local council of 23 members. **18.** *governors:* A generic name for Roman provincial officers. *kings:* This refers to such satellite rulers as Herod Antipas and Herod Agrippa. The punishment of flogging was suffered by Paul (2 Cor 11:24); it was limited to 40 stripes, always diminished by one to protect the Law. **20.** The assistance of the Spirit is promised the disciples when they have to bear witness for Jesus (see Mk 13:11; Jn 14:26; Lk 21:14–15; 12:11–12). Such charismatic witness is related in Acts 4:8; 13:9. **21.** The gospel will be a cause of division in families; this seems to refer primarily to Jewish families. The hatred of all men comes from Mk 13:13; Mt uses the line again in 24:9. The line is a strange inversion of the charge of *odium generis humani*, "hatred of the human race," which Roman writers laid against Christians. **22.** *he who endures to the end:* Sustains persecution even to death. *will be saved:* Here "being saved" has not the usual meaning of escaping with one's life, but of assuring one's eschatological salvation. **23.** *flee to the next town:* The disciples are not to sacrifice themselves rashly; the proclamation of the gospel is their primary task, and if they are prevented from proclaiming the gospel in one place they should move on to another. **23b.** *before the Son of Man comes:* This verse is an ancient exegetical puzzle. If it means that the parousia is expected before the disciples even begin the Gentile mission, one can only wonder at the fidelity with which the Church preserved sayings attributed to Jesus that were in such manifest contradiction with the actual course of events. Obviously the saying was not understood in this sense; and it seems most probable that it was understood to refer to the Jewish War of AD 66–70, which elsewhere is associated with the coming of the Son of Man in judgment (→ 164 below).

24. The persecution of the disciples is explained by a cryptic reference to the passion of Jesus. The saying is preserved in nearly identical form in Jn 13:16; 15:20, referring both to the washing of the feet, which is symbolic of the humility recommended to the disciples, and (as here) to the hatred incurred by the disciples (see also Lk 6:40). Matthew anticipates his own arrangement of the Beelzebul controversy in 12:25–37.

This part of the discourse is, as the parallels show, composed largely of material drawn from Mk, some of which is used twice: in the eschatological discourse (where Mk puts it) and detached from its context here. Matthew selects and so arranges the material because it is a suitable continuation of the missionary discourse.

70 (ii) *Confession without fear* (10:26–33). This collection of sayings comes from Q (cf. Lk 12:2–9); two verses are found in Mk also. **26–27.** These verses have a different context from Lk 12:2–3 and quite a different meaning; the saying in Mk 4:22 is closer to the meaning given by Mt. Lk has made the line a warning against the hypocrisy of the Pharisees; it is impossible that "you" should say anything in secret that will not become public; you cannot hide your real mind. Mt refers the saying to the teaching of Jesus. The teaching now reaches only a limited circle, but through the disciples it will be widely published. The saying does not imply that Jesus taught a secret doctrine, but simply that the number who hear his teaching from his own lips is much smaller than the number who will hear it from the disciples.

28. The discourse moves on to a saying in which the prospect of death is stated even more clearly than in the preceding section. The dualism of *sōma* (body) and *psychē* (soul) is unusual in the NT and does not represent the OT conception of the human person. It is remarkable that Luke, presumably a Hellenistic writer, avoids the dualism in his version of the saying; the dualism would be quite germane to several schools of Gk philosophy. *him who can destroy...in Gehenna:* God (see comment on 18:8–9). There is a life after one's earthly life that must be preserved. **29.** God has as much care for the human person as he has for the sparrow, which was one of the cheapest articles sold in the market. God knows when even a small bird dies; he is aware of the death of one of his own, and he will save the life that endures after death. The variant form of the saying in Lk (21:18) is about the hairs of the head. **32.** With this assurance of confidence that God knows and cares what happens, the disciples are urged to confess "in Jesus"; the confession would be the typical confession of the primitive Church that Jesus is Messiah and Lord. The reward of confession or denial is that Jesus will accept or disown according to one's fidelity. A similar saying appears in Mk 8:38 (Lk 9:26 par.); but the formulation is so dissimilar that it is difficult to assume a common source, unless Matthew has rewritten with great freedom. These sayings are also suitable appendages to the missionary discourse.

71 (iii) *Divided families* (10:34–36). The parallel in Lk (12:51–53) exhibits so many variations that some commentators doubt a common source for the saying; in particular, Lk replaces the vigorous metaphor of the sword with an abstraction. **34.** *I have not come to bring peace:* Jesus is of course the messenger of peace in the truest and highest sense of the word; the saying reflects the experience of the primitive Church (see 10:21). The immediate result of the proclamation of the gospel was discord within the Jewish community, which touched even family relations. The same theme is expressed in the words of Simeon (Lk 2:34). The saying is illustrated by the quotation of Mi 7:6 (not according to the LXX, but quite faithful to the MT). The lines lead to the saying in the following verse.

72 (iv) *The renunciation demanded by discipleship* (10:37–39). Cf. Lk 14:26–27 and 17:33; see Mk 8:34–35; Lk 9:23–24. If the gospel introduces a division into families, then the disciple has no choice except to prefer the new community to the community of blood. Mt softens "hate," found in Lk, to "love more"; the language of Lk is closer to the original Aramaic, which had no other way of saying "love less." The example of this renunciation has already been given in the call of the disciples (4:18–22; 9:9–13). **38–39.** Two sayings are joined that Lk has in different contexts; but Lk, like Mt, uses the sayings twice (16:24–25). Here again, as in other parts of the discourse, Matthew has used doublets to compile his material. Mk also has the sayings; and the verses are a rare example of sayings found both in Mk and in Q. The very fact that they are quoted so often shows that the early Church, like the modern Church, recognizes these as sayings that express in a remarkably clear manner a basic principle of the gospel and of Christian life. **38.** *take up his cross:* This is the first time that Mt uses the word "cross." Other allusions (some have appeared already) to the passion will be found before Jesus predicts it openly. Crucifixion, a method of execution of Oriental origin, was used by the Romans for rebels and for slaves. Roman law prohibited its use on Roman citizens. The conventional use of the cross as a

Christian symbol makes it difficult for modern readers to grasp the harshness of this saying as it was originally uttered. Jesus tells the disciples that there is no extreme to which they may think that faith and the proclamation of the gospel will not take them. The personal renunciation implied will go far beyond renunciation of one's own family. **39.** The oxymoron assures the disciples that there is no other way in which they can save themselves. The word *psychē*, "soul," is used here in a sense that reflects the OT use (see comment on 10:28). The word should be rendered "self" rather than "soul" or "life." The preservation of the person is achieved only by yielding the person entirely to Jesus. One who saves his life may lose himself.

73 (v) *Conclusion* (10:40–11:1). The final words of the discourse express praise of those who show the disciples hospitality. The praise is based on the identification of the disciples with Jesus; he is encountered in those who proclaim the gospel. The saying is adapted from Mk 9:37 (see Lk 9:48; Mt 18:5); it is another doublet. **42.** *little ones:* The "child" of Mk's saying becomes the plural and refers here to the disciples; they are told to become as little ones in 18:1–4. A similar saying is found in Lk 10:6. The saying about the cup of cold water (Mk 9:41 par.) is aptly placed here because of its association with hospitality.

The concluding verse narrates that Jesus continued his teaching and proclaiming. The mission of the twelve "disciples" is not mentioned again, nor is their return from the mission; the discourse has a somewhat artificial character and situation.

74 **(IV) Book Three: Controversy and Parables (11:2–13:52).**

(A) Narrative Section: Incredulity and Hostility of the Jews (11:2–12:50).

(a) The Question of John the Baptist (11:2–6). The correspondence between Mt and Lk (7:18–23) in this and the following sections, except for Mt's omissions, is extremely close; these passages are among the best illustrations of Q. The relations between John the Baptist and his followers and between Jesus and his disciples are somewhat uncertain in the traditions (see 3:13–17). There seems to be little reason for thinking that the question of John was other than sincere, or that he sent his disciples in order to elicit an open profession of messiahship either for their sake or for the sake of a wider public. John was quite capable of expressing his own faith to his own disciples. It is more difficult to explain the reasons why John asked the question. With the little information we have about him, we can surmise that the heavy emphasis on the eschatological judgment the Gospels report in John's preaching (see 3:1–10) did not appear in the proclamation of Jesus, and that this caused John wonder. The messianism and eschatologism of John had to be corrected by the proclamation of Jesus. **2.** *John in prison:* Mt postpones the explanation of John's imprisonment until the story of his death (14:3–12). According to Josephus (*Ant.* 18.5, 2 § 119), the prison was in the palace-fortress of Machaerus, built by Herod the Great on the desolate heights of Moab near the E central shore of the Dead Sea (*JW* 7.6, 1–2 § 164–77). *the Coming One:* This title is not attested in Jewish literature for the Messiah, but there could be no doubt of its meaning (see Mal 3:1). **4.** Mt has omitted (or Lk has added) a recital of miracles performed in the presence of the disciples of John; this certainly adds vividness to the quotations in which Jesus answers the questions. **5.** This verse is not actually a quotation either according to the MT or according to the LXX but a cento of allusions from Is 29:18–19; 35:5–6; 61:1. The raising of the dead is added in Q; it replaces the liberation of captives in Is 61:1. The answer of Jesus, although it is not a formal claim of messiahship, alludes to phenomena that in the OT and Judaism were expected in the Messianic era. More important, the quotations establish the type of messiahship that Jesus lets those see who will look. It is not a messiahship of the eschatological judgment of wrath, nor the establishment of a Messianic empire over all the kingdoms of the earth, nor a war of extermination against the enemies of the elect people. The messiahship here suggested is a messiahship of the healing of ills and the conferring of blessing. **6.** *not be scandalized:* The *skandalon* is anything over which one stumbles and falls; the use both of the noun and the verb in the NT is exclusively metaphorical to designate something that makes faith difficult; see 18:6–9. That this type of messiahship was a scandal even to the disciples of Jesus is abundantly clear from the Gospels.

75 (b) The Witness of Jesus to John the Baptist (11:7–19). Except for the insertion of 11:12 (Lk 16:16 par.) from a different context, Mt and Lk still are very close. The witness of Jesus to John is given both to John's manner of life and to his genuine prophetic mission. **9.** *to see a prophet:* In Jewish belief prophecy had ended with the closing of the canon of the prophetic books, and the next prophet to appear would be the prophet "like Moses" (Dt 18:15; → Aspects NT Thought, 78:14). **10.** This is clearly the meaning of the witness that Jesus gives to John; Jesus applies to John the text of Mal 3:1 (quoted according to the MT), one of the texts on which the belief in the "Coming One" was based. This makes John the last and the greatest of the prophets; but Jesus calls him even more: the greatest figure of the dispensation of the Law and the prophets. By implication John is greater even than Moses. *is greater than he:* John lived and worked before the reign. Therefore even the least in the reign, who will have the light of the gospel and the communication of the power of faith, will accomplish greater works than John.

12. This verse is obscure in both Mt and Lk (16:16); and it is hard to say whether Lk has compressed a difficult sentence or Mt has expanded it to explain it. It may mean either "the reign does violence" or "the reign suffers violence." In the first meaning the reign is said to make a violent entrance into the world (see 10:34), and those seize it as a prize who are willing to be as violent as the reign demands—by the kind of renunciation Jesus imposes upon his disciples. Many interpreters find this sense somewhat forced; they prefer to say simply that the reign has always been under the violent attack of its enemies and is now under attack. This interpretation does not fit well with the word "snatch" or "carry off"—a word that is used in Greek of taking plunder. Another possibility relates the verse to the contemporary scene and identifies the violent with the party of the Zealots (see comment on 10:4), who sought to establish the reign by violence. No proposed interpretation is entirely satisfactory. Mt's interpretation of the discourse, because of the occurrence of the name of John in 11:12, is somewhat violent itself. **13.** *prophesied until John:* Mt returns to the topic, reaffirming that John terminates the Law and the prophets. **14.** *he is Elijah:* Cf. Mal 3:1,22; *Elias redivivus*. The messianic prophet was sometimes identified with Elijah returning; Elijah had never died but was carried off in a chariot (2 Kgs 2:11–12). This statement is repeated in 17:10–13 in a longer form. **15.** *let him who has ears hear:* A tag used when a cryptic saying is proposed; it was a sign of the wise man that he could speak in riddles and solve them.

16–19. The first indication in Mt of a wide disbelief in the proclamation of Jesus; it is the sole indication of remarks directed against John the Baptist, respect for whom is attested both in the Gospels and in Josephus (*Ant.* 18.5, 2 § 116–19). Jesus and John followed quite diverse manners of life. John was a hermit who reduced his use of material goods to an absolute minimum. Jesus, although he was poor and preached renunciation, made no similar radical departure from the usual manner of life of the Jews. The austere prophet was called a demoniac; the rabbi who lived much like other rabbis was called a glutton and a drunkard who liked low company. No approach could satisfy the Jews if it suggested a change in their belief and their life. Jesus uses the homely parable of children who always want to play some other game than the one suggested by their companions. **19b.** *wisdom is justified by her deeds:* Another obscure saying. It is probably proverbial and would make good sense in the wisdom tradition, in which wisdom is proved genuine both by the success of the wise man (Prv 3:13–18) and by the wisdom he teaches his children (Prv 10:1). But precisely what Jesus means by wisdom here is not clear. Most obviously it is the divine wisdom, which in one reading proves itself by its works and in the other reading by those who accept it—here, the disciples of Jesus. Some interpreters think that the Church has formed the saying and that Jesus himself is meant by wisdom; he too is proved both by his deeds and by his disciples. Lk 7:35 reads "by her children," a reading that has also contaminated the Matthaean ms. tradition.

76 (c) Doom of the Cities of Galilee (11:20–24). This passage is from Q. Luke makes it a part of the farewell words of Jesus to Galilee; Matthew probably saw an opportunity to contrast the praise of John the Baptist with the reproach delivered against those who had seen much more of Jesus than John had. **21.** *Chorazin, Bethsaida, Capernaum:* Of the three towns mentioned Mt has related no miracles except for Capernaum. Chorazin appears only here and in Lk 11:13. It is identified with Khirbet Kerazeh, about 2 mi. NW of Tell Hum, the site of Capernaum. Bethsaida is the home of Peter, Andrew, and Philip in Jn 1:44, the scene of the healing of a blind man in Mk 8:22, and near the place of the multiplication of the loaves in Mk 6:45; Lk 9:10. The name seems to have belonged to a fishing village on the shore of the Sea of Galilee and to a new city, 2 mi. N of the sea and E of the Jordan, founded by the tetrarch Philip. For Capernaum, see comment on 4:13. *would have repented:* The people of these towns have not done so. In spite of the works of power they had seen, repentance was a part of the proclamation of Jesus (4:17). Plainly the works of power should have moved them to faith. **22.** *Tyre and Sidon:* These towns were not eminent examples of wickedness; they were Gentile cities that were near. **23.** *Capernaum:* The object of a peculiar reproach, for it was the city of Jesus (9:1); Mt has expanded the reproach by repeating vv. 21–22 and by comparing Capernaum not to Tyre and Sidon but to the outstanding proverbial example of wickedness in the OT, Sodom. *exalted to heaven:* The words of Is 14:13,15 are adapted to Capernaum. On the basis of this and similar passages elsewhere it must be concluded that the mission of Jesus in Galilee produced only a few disciples. The mass of the population was interested—all the Gospels refer to crowds attracted by Jesus—but they remained unmoved by the proclamation.

77 (d) Thanksgiving to the Father (11:25–27). This passage also is from Q. The verbal correspondence of Mt and Lk is nearly perfect except for Mt's omission of a phrase in v. 25 and a merely grammatical variation in v. 27. Lk places the saying after the return of the 72 disciples; it is a prayer of thanksgiving for the success of their mission and for the understanding that has been granted to them, "the little ones." The position of the saying in Mt—after the reproach of the Galilean cities—contrasts the little ones, the disciples, with the wise and prudent, who are the Jews, in particular their spiritual leaders, the scribes and Pharisees. **26.** *such was your good pleasure:* The tone of thanksgiving mixed with resignation is, however, apparent in the form of the saying itself; for resignation is expressed in v. 26. Jesus has not reached the wise and prudent; his message has been grasped only by a few disciples who are drawn from the peasant and working classes. But this is the work of the Father. The message of Jesus is not grasped by wisdom and understanding; it is known only by revelation. The saying does not mean that revelation has been denied to the wise and prudent in the Jewish community; Jesus has proclaimed the reign, and this is revelation. But only the simple have accepted the insight the Father grants to those who wish it. There is a sense in which Jewish wisdom and learning, which was the knowledge of the Law, was a genuine obstacle to the understanding of the message of Jesus. The more one knew about the Law, the more difficult it was to see that the messianic revolution would supersede the Law; see 5:17–20.

27. *all things have been given over to me by my father:* This verse is so singular in the Syn that it has been the object of many conjectures; it has been called "a meteor from the Johannine heaven." The intimate relation of Jesus and the Father is mentioned frequently in Jn, rarely in the Syn. But the saying is as well attested in Q as anything in the Gospels; we have noticed that the correspondence of Mt and Lk is unusually close. The saying is formal, even labored, particularly in Mt. Jesus claims that "all" has been handed over by the Father; in the context "all" probably means revelation. *knows the son:* The prerogative of the Father; only by the revelation of the Father can the true identity of the Son be recognized (11:25; and see 16:17). Conversely, only the Son can reveal the Father. In the context this is a direct contradiction of the Jewish claim to have the complete revelation of God in the Law and the Prophets. The saying fills out the implications in the usual way in which Jesus speaks of the Father; he has a relation with the Father that other men do not share. (See A. Feuillet, RB 62 [1955] 161–96; A. Gelin [ed.], *Son and Saviour* [Baltimore, 1962] 77–78.)

78 (e) Invitation to the Weary (11:28–30). This saying is peculiar to Mt. But since the studies of E. Norden in 1913, some commentators have been convinced that the triple strophe which can be seen in 25–30, and which is paralleled elsewhere, is the original form. One can hardly imagine why Lk would have omitted these verses, which are so much in harmony with the themes of his Gospel. If Mt has the original form, the saying must have come to Lk already mutilated. **28.** *the weary and the burdened:* Those who are under the "yoke" of the Law; the metaphor of the yoke is used in rabbinical writings. In this context perhaps this suggestion is intended. But the import of the saying in itself is more general; the weary and the burdened are the poor (see 5:3–5), who have the good news proclaimed to them (11:5). Jesus invites them because he is one of them; the adjectives used in 11:29 are identical in meaning and very close verbally to the adjectives of the first and third beatitudes (5:3,5). **29.** *take my yoke:* The yoke and the burden of Jesus are submission to the reign of God. This imposes no further burden on those who accept it, but rather makes it easier for them to bear the burdens they already have. Jer 6:16 (quoted according to the MT) promises rest to those who follow "the old paths," the traditions of Israel. This saying flows easily from the preceding claim of a unique relation of sonship. The revelation of the Father is not conceived as the revelation of new obligations but as a knowledge of the Father that releases from burdens and weariness and makes it easier to live under his will.

79 (f) SABBATH CONTROVERSY: PLUCKING CORN (12:1–8). Most of the remaining episodes in this book resume the theme of controversy begun in 9:1–8. The order followed is the order of Mk except for the insertion of some material from Q. The first two controversies deal with the Sabbath. The incident of the plucking of ears on the Sabbath illustrates the "saying-story." It appears that the original material consisted only of the sayings in Mk 2:27–28. Of these sayings Mt retains only one. The dialogue is constructed in the framework of a dispute that is resolved by the sayings. **1.** *through the fields:* The journey is presented as a trip to the synagogue on the Sabbath (12:9). The disciples plucked ears of wheat and rubbed the grains in their hands to make a rough meal; Lk found it necessary to make this explicit for his readers. The preparation of food was listed by the rabbis as one of the 39 forms of work that were forbidden on the Sabbath; the inclusion of such an action as that of the disciples illustrates the rigorist school of Pharisaic interpretation. The plucking of stray ears in a field, permitted in Dt 23:26, was prohibited by the rabbis on the Sabbath.

3. The answer of Jesus is twofold; and like a good rabbinical argument it is based on the Scripture. The first example is the story of David (1 Sm 21:2–7); he and his men ate the showbread (Lv 24:5–9) in the Tabernacle because they had no other food. The second example is given only in Mt, which elsewhere in this passage follows Mk more closely than usual. **5.** *how the priests...profane the Sabbath:* The work of the priests in the Temple is "work" in the rabbinical sense, but it is justified by its holy purpose. The application to the disciples is obvious, but much more suggestive than the version of Mk. The disciples of Jesus may work on the Sabbath in his company because this service is greater than the service of the Temple. Mt turns the dispute into a Messianic affirmation. **7.** This verse, also peculiar to Mt, quotes again Hos 6:6 (quoted in 9:13) in support of the humanitarian interpretation of the Law. Rigorism is condemnation of the innocent. Thus the two answers are a plea for a humanitarian interpretation of the Law and a claim that Jesus is greater than the Law. The example of David does support this interpretation, but is does not apply directly to the Sabbath. **8.** The saying is ambiguous, even though the omission of Mk 2:27 makes it less so. Mk 2:27 is a bold statement of the humanitarian view; the Sabbath law is to be interpreted according to human needs and possibilities. *Son of Man:* If this phrase is to be interpreted as "man" (a sense that the Aram equivalent will bear), the saying is synonymous with Mk 2:27. This, however, is probably not the meaning of the sentence. It is not a claim that the Sabbath is under the decision of man, but that it is under the decision of Jesus (→ Aspects NT Thought, 78:28–30). The episode in all three Gospels lies in the same pattern of thought we see in Mt 5:17–48. Jesus is the supreme interpreter of the Law; and he interprets it in humanitarian terms. The Sabbath law does not oblige one to go hungry.

80 (g) SABBATH CONTROVERSY: HEALING (12:9–14). Lk (6:6–11) has not only a parallel to this passage, but two other incidents of healing on the Sabbath (13:10–17; 14:1–6), which illustrate the same principle. The controversy about the Sabbath was sufficiently important to appear in both Mk and Q and perhaps in independent sources. Mt makes the Pharisees inquire of Jesus instead of observe him; and the challenge uttered by Jesus to their unspoken question becomes a challenge uttered by the Pharisees. **11.** This verse (Lk 14:5 par.), missing in Mk, may have had no context in a miracle story in Q. Rabbinical practice as attested in the Talmud did permit one to render assistance to an animal on the Sabbath; but the Talmud also attests a more rigorous view that apparently did not prevail in NT times (Str-B 1, 629–30); but cf. CD 11:13–14. **12.** The argument proceeds from the superiority of man to animals. Rabbinical opinion generally permitted the practice of healing on the Sabbath if there was danger of death, but not if the healing could be postponed until the next day (Str-B 1, 622–29). This practice is so much in agreement with modern medical and hospital practice on Sundays and holidays that it scarcely calls for comment. **13.** Jesus, however, affirms by the miracle that it is permitted to do good on the Sabbath whether the work can be postponed or not. Matthew abbreviates Mk by omitting any reference to the anger and grief of Jesus (Mk 3:5). **14.** He also omits the mention of the Herodians (Mk 3:6) as partners with the Pharisees. If the omission here is due to the fact that the party had long ceased to exist when the Gospel was written, this motive was not operative in the composition of 22:16. The omission is more probably another abbreviation. The movement is climactic; this is the first mention of a plot against the life of Jesus.

The theme of the story is the same humanitarian interpretation of the Sabbath as that of the preceding incident. The first example illustrates self-help on the Sabbath, the second example illustrates assistance rendered to others.

81 (h) JESUS THE SERVANT OF THE LORD (12:15–21). Matthew has sharply reduced the material in this passage where Mk (3:7–12) summarizes the mission of Jesus in Galilee. Matthew has given a similar summary in 4:23–25. The purpose of the summary here is to introduce the quotation from Is 42:1–4, which is introduced by another of Matthew's rare allusions to Mk's "Messianic Secret" (see 8:4). Matthew here takes account of the secret, but he explains it as a "fulfillment" (see comment on 1:18–25) of Is 42:1–4. The passage is quoted not according to the LXX but according to the MT translated very freely. The identification of Jesus with the Servant of the Lord of Dt-Is was a key idea in the Gospels and of the primitive Church (→ Aspects NT Thought, 78:22–23). Matthew has already quoted one Servant passage, which is applied to Jesus in a very broad sense (see 8:17). Here the passage is quoted not with reference to the mission of Jesus to proclaim the reign, but as an explanation of his retirement from proclaiming before a wider public. **15.** *knowing:* The motive for the retirement is given by Mt alone in this one obscure word; the implicit object of the participle is the plot mentioned in v. 14. The quotation from Dt-Is refers clearly to a mission of the Servant to the Gentiles, and Matthew includes this in his quotation. These passages are relevant in the interpretation of such passages as 10:5; 15:24. The quotation in which the Servant passage is applied to Jesus is very probably intended as a striking contrast to the accusation of the Pharisees reported in the following passage.

82 (i) THE ACCUSATION OF THE PHARISEES (12:22–24). The accusation of the Pharisees is the occasion of one of the major controversial statements of Jesus (see the following passage). The accusation is found in Mk (3:20–22) without the miracle story; both Mt and Lk (11:14–16) have the miracle story from Q; and it seems that the accusation also followed the miracle story in Q. The miracle is described in only the bare essentials; the interest is not in the miracle but in the discussion that follows. **22.** *a blind and dumb demoniac:* Mt adds "blind" to the "dumb" of Lk. The description illustrates the current popular demonology (see comment on 8:28–34).

Where Lk has a question expressing wonder, Mt has a question whether Jesus is not the Son of David, a Messianic title. Mt specifies the accusers as Pharisees; Mk has "the scribes," Lk "some." We have noticed that Mt anticipates this incident in 9:32–34. **24.** *Beelzebul:* The name comes from 2 Kgs 1:2–6. The NT has preserved the correct reading of the name; the MT has corrupted it (a not infrequent occurrence when divine names occur in the MT) to *Ba'alzᵉbûb*. The name means "Baal the prince" and is not attested elsewhere in Jewish literature as the name of a demon (cf. W. Foerster, *ThDNT* 1, 605–6). The accusation reduces Jesus to the level of a common magician; it was understood that such feats could be performed with the assistance of demons.

83 (j) Response to the Accusation (12:25–37). A comparison of the three Syn shows that this episode was found both in Mk (3:23–30) and in Q (Lk 11:17–23; 12:10 par.). This indicates the importance this discussion had in the early Church; and it is altogether probable that the composition of the passage reflects the controversies of the primitive Church with the Jews. Verses 25–26 are an abbreviation of Mk 3:23–26, but vv. 27–28 agree with Lk 11:18a–20 with no parallel in Mk. Verse 30 agrees with Lk 11:23, again with no parallel in Mk. Verses 31–32 conflate Mk 3:28–29 and a Q passage that appears in a briefer from in Lk 12:10. Verses 33–36 are an expansion peculiar to Mt (→ 84 below).

25. *a kingdom divided against itself:* The first argument in response is based on the absurdity of the charge of the Pharisees. If Jesus expels demons by Beelzebul, then the kingdom of Satan is doomed by its own internecine strife. This consequence the Pharisees are unwilling to admit. Implicit, no doubt, is the principle that the collapse of the reign of Satan will not occur until the advent of the reign of God. **27.** The second argument, missing in Mk, is drawn from exorcisms worked by Jews. *your sons:* A Semitism for "yourselves," "members of your own group." The genuineness of the exorcisms worked by Jews is not called in question; it is neither affirmed nor denied. There is a subtlety in this argument that eludes the modern reader; our ignorance of the ritual of Jewish exorcisms makes the force of the argument somewhat difficult to see. The exorcisms of Jesus in the Gospels are accomplished by a simple command, sometimes accompanied by a touch. It is highly probable that Jewish exorcists used long and complicated rituals, with perhaps more than a touch of magical formulas. **27.** *they will be your judges:* Jesus challenges the Pharisees to compare the displays of power. Jewish exorcists themselves will be the judges; they can attest the implications of a successful exorcism performed by a simple command. **28.** *God's Spirit:* The power of Jesus shows that the spirit of God is at work; Lk 11:20 has the more picturesque "finger" of God (see Ex 8:15). Lk's phrase is probably more original; Mt's change to "spirit" leads into the saying about blasphemy, which Lk has in a different context (12:10). *the reign of God has overtaken you:* Lit., "has come upon you," i.e., when they were not looking. Such a display of the power of the Spirit clearly shows that the Messianic age is dawning. This Messianic claim is more explicit than Mk's customary style.

29. The parable of the strong man shows that Jesus is completely master of the demons. Satan is a robber lord whose "goods," which means here those who are bound by demonic possession, are kept in his castle. No one can release them unless he has mastered the strong one and his fortress. **30.** Here Q added a saying that is not found in Mk and does not seem to belong to this context. A similar idea is expressed in Mk 9:40; Lk 9:50. The saying affirms that Jesus demands a decision that cannot be evaded. Neutrality toward him is impossible; to be neutral is to reject him.

31. *blasphemy against the Spirit:* The saying about blasphemy against the Spirit has long presented difficulty, particularly in Catholic theology, which affirms the possibility of repentance up to the moment of death. This teaching is solidly founded in the NT, and this saying of Jesus cannot be understood in a way that contradicts his invitations to repentance. Refusal to recognize the Son of Man as Messiah can be forgiven; faith atones for previous denial of faith. This Messianic claim is missing in Mk. Blasphemy against the Holy Spirit, however, attributes the activity of the Spirit to some other power. The present activity of God can be attested only through the actions of the Spirit. If these are not recognized, then there is no means by which God can reach man. The one who will not accept the work of the Spirit has made it impossible for himself to recognize the word and the work of God. Only he can be forgiven who confesses that he has something to be forgiven.

84 **33–37.** These verses are an expansion of Matthew composed from a passage of Q that is at the base both of Lk 6:43–45 and Mt 7:16–20; the passage adapted to the present context to describe the dogmatic unbelief of the Pharisees. **34.** *brood of vipers:* See 3:7; 23:33. The sayings all touch upon the theme of speech as revealing the genuine character of the person. Speech is the fruit that discloses whether the tree is good or bad. The evil person cannot speak good things; for speech is the overflow of the heart. *out of the abundance of the heart:* The heart in the Bible generally is not the organ of sentiment, as it is in our metaphorical language, but rather the mind and the sentiments. Even the hypocrite cannot long conceal his real convictions. Goodness or wickedness will manifest itself in word. **36.** The final saying is peculiar to Mt; its severity is apparent, but the entire context is couched in a severe tone. *idle word:* This does not mean merely the trivial or unnecessary word; it is the word spoken without foundation, the word that serves no purpose. Such a word may be mendacious or calumnious simply because the speaker has not reflected on the content and implications of his speech. The saying echoes the ancient conception of word as an existent and dynamic reality. If the reality the speaker creates is an agent of evil, the speaker must accept full responsibility for the evil. It was in his power to speak with reflection.

85 (k) Signs (12:38–42). The present passage is based on Q (Lk 11:29–32 par.) with a distinctive adaptation of Mt. A similar request for a sign is found in Mk 8:11–12 (cf. 16:1–4; Matthew has again used the same or similar material in two different passages). **38.** *a sign:* The "sign" in the OT was an extraordinary or paradoxical event that manifested the present activity of God (see Is 7:10). Isaiah invites Ahaz to ask a sign as deep as Sheol or as high as heaven; some phenomenon in nature is clearly indicated. When the king refuses the challenge, Isaiah gives him the sign of the birth of a child. The essential feature of the sign is not its marvelous character but its significance; it is an event that admits an obvious interpretation. In the context the request is directed toward a Messianic sign, the type of event that in Jewish belief would precede the coming of the Messiah; see 24:3. The Beelzebul controversy is thus followed by an indirect, but not subtle, demand for a verification of the Messianic claims. **39.** *a wicked and adulterous generation:* "Adulterous," which echoes an OT metaphor for the infidelity of Israel (see Jer 2:1–3,20–25,32–33; 3:1–5; Hos 2:3–22), does not appear in Lk. In Lk there are two parallel signs, the repentance of the Ninevites at the proclamation of Jonah (Jon 3:5) and the journey of the queen of Sheba (in southern Arabia, "the ends of the earth" in ancient geography) to hear the wisdom of Solomon. In these instances the Gentiles exhibited repentance and an eagerness to hear the wisdom that Yahweh gave; the Pharisees show neither of these attitudes. The theme of the faith of the Gentiles in contrast to the unbelief of Israel is repeated. **40.** This addition in Mt alters the significance of the sign of Jonah. The repentance of the Ninevites is a sign that the unbelieving Jews will be judged; the sojourn of Jonah in the belly of the whale for three days and three nights (Jon 2:1) is a foreshadowing of the resurrection of Jesus. This will be the sign the Pharisees seek. Matthew anticipates his own account of the resurrection, which emphasizes the refusal of the Jews to accept this sign. No sign can be given them, for they have blasphemed against the Holy Spirit. (See A. Vögtle, "Der Spruch vom Jonaszeichen," *Synoptische Studien* [Fest. A. Wikenhauser; Munich, 1953] 230–77.)

86 (l) THE RETURN OF THE EVIL SPIRIT (12:43–45). This saying from Q is preserved in a very close verbal parallel in Mt and Lk (11:24–26). The force of the saying is obscure. In Lk it is arranged in closer connection with the Beelzebul controversy. The saying casts some light on exorcisms performed in NT times (see 12:27); the cure was sometimes only temporary, and the patient relapsed into a worse condition. This should certainly cause no surprise when we recall that many pathological conditions were attributed to demons, and any apparent cure could be only the work of suggestion. The saying may have originally been intended to contrast the healings and exorcisms of Jesus with the merely temporary results achieved by other exorcists. **43.** *waterless places:* The expelled demon wanders through the desert, in the Bible the home of evil spirits (see 4:1; Is 32:21; 34:14; Tb 8:3). There he finds seven like himself; when all return to the man whom he previously haunted, they find the dwelling swept and clean—but empty. The demonic power has not been replaced by power for good. **45.** *with this evil generation:* In Mt the figure is explicitly applied to the Jews. The Jews have experienced the coming of the reign that expels the reign of Satan. The power of Satan has been rolled back, but the Jews have not accepted the reign of God. Nothing can happen but another and stronger invasion of the power of Satan.

87 (m) THE BRETHREN OF JESUS (12:46–50). In Mk (3:31–35) this passage is probably a resumption of Mk 3:20–21, a passage so difficult that both Mt and Lk omit it. "His own" (so we may render Mk 3:21) are here specified as his mother and brethren. **46.** *brothers:* This word must be taken as kinsmen, unless one insists that Mary had children who are never mentioned in the NT or in any other source of early tradition (see comments on 1:25; Gal 1:19; → Aspects NT Thought, 78:167). The kinsmen, very probably from Nazareth, seem to have felt that Jesus was acting imprudently. Most commentators have failed to regard the kinsmen as being kind; the allusions in the Gospels to the hostility of the Pharisees are to be taken seriously, and it is more likely that the kinsmen were motivated by a desire to take Jesus out of a situation of growing danger than by envy or fear for his sanity. **47.** This verse is not attested in the most important mss. and is largely a repetition of 12:46. **48.** Matthew has here abbreviated so sharply that he becomes obscure. The response of Jesus seems harsh, but it is not harsher than his words in 8:22 and 10:37, which are here illustrated by his conduct. The new unity Jesus forms about himself is a unity in which other bonds, even the bonds of kinship, are sublimated. Jesus does not reject the bonds of kinship, but raises all who believe in him to an intimacy of kinship. His own kin exclude themselves from this new unity if they do not believe in him. Again in fairness to the kinsmen, the saying does not imply that they do not believe in Jesus.

88 **(B) Discourse: The Parables of the Reign (13:1–52).** The parable in the NT designates a wise saying or fictitious short story used by Jesus to expound his teaching. The roots of these literary forms lie in the OT, particularly in the wisdom literature, and in the rabbinical literature (Str–B 1, 653–55). The fictitious anecdote leads the listener to concede a point that he does not immediately perceive is applicable to himself (see 2 Sm 12:1–14; 14:1–11; 1 Kgs 20:35–40). The story also sharpens the curiosity and attracts attention. The rabbinical parables, of which about 2000 are counted in rabbinical literature, are told in answer to the question of a disciple and show that the scope of the answer is broader than the disciple perceived. These purposes are all apparent in the parables of Jesus.

For most of the parables of the Gospels it is possible to find a situation in the life and teaching of Jesus himself and a situation in the life and teaching of the primitive community. The parables were modified in the teaching of the community; such modifications can be seen by comparing different versions of the same parable in different Gospels. The commentaries on the parables (see 13:18–23,36–43) and most allegorical features are almost universally regarded by modern scholars as expansions made by the primitive Church. Other modifications include the creation of a new setting for the parable and the addition of a saying of Jesus (→ Aspects NT Thought, 78:131–145).

89 (a) THE PARABLE OF THE SOWER (13:1–9). The collection of parables is one of the two extended discourses in Mk, and Mt uses the entire collection except for Mk 4:26–29, adding other parables drawn both from Q and from a private source. Matthew abbreviates Mk less in the discourses than in the narratives; here he follows Mk in placing the teaching in a boat by the seashore; Lk alters the scene.

3. This parable is a simple description of the process of plowing in Palestine, of the type of ground upon which seed is sown, and of the usual results. The "road" is not the highway, but the soil trodden hard in paths through the fields. The wild thorns, the most common weed in the country, are not cleared before plowing but turned under by the plow. The fields are sown throughout, even in the edges and corners where the limestone base lies very near the surface. Verse 9 is a saying that indicates that the preceding utterance has more than a superficial meaning (see comment on 11:15).

Setting aside for the moment the explanation given in the Gospel (13:18–23), one observes that 13:8 is a very apt conclusion. Modern interpreters are at variance on the meaning of the parable, possibly because they try to give the parable a more precise meaning than it was intended to convey. The reign (or the proclamation of the reign) is certainly the central theme of the parable. The reign will arrive in spite of obstacles; it is as infallible as the growth of the harvest, which reaches maturity and even richness in spite of what seem to be nearly insuperable difficulties. One perceives the optimism that should inspire the preachers of the Gospel and is assured that such opponents as the Pharisees in the present context will not prevail; these responses are inferred, not stated. The parable is presented as a theme on which one can reflect and from which one can draw as much meaning as one wishes: on this basis the earliest explanation of the parable (18–23) was composed.

90 (b) The Parables as Revelation (13:10–15). Mt omits Mk's notice (4:10) that this explanation was given when Jesus was alone with the disciples; but the character of the explanation remains the same. The reason for parables as given in Mk seems extremely harsh, and in both Mt and Lk it is softened—in Mt by altering the syntax and expanding the passage, in Lk by reducing the passage so sharply that it becomes nearly incomprehensible. **11.** An implicit difference between the general patterns of Mk and Mt is pertinent here: in Mk the disciples are represented as not understanding the preaching of Jesus until the final moment, whereas in Mt this theme of obtuseness is much less perceptible. That knowledge is "given" to the disciples and withheld from "them" (Mk has "those outside," but the omission seems not to alter the meaning) is not due to a refusal to give, but to a refusal to receive. **12.** *to him who has more will be given:* Mt expands the saying by transferring Mk 4:25 to this point: he who has (= receives) the reign shall receive more; he who has not (= refuses) the reign shall lose what he has (for the Jews, their position as the chosen people who have received the revelation of God). **13.** *because seeing they do not see:* The harshness of Mk 4:12 is due to the use of a Gk particle expressing purpose (*hina*); this reflects an ambiguity implicit in Hebrew and Aramaic, which do not distinguish grammatically between purpose and result (*GrBib* § 351–53). Indeed, biblical writers could scarcely conceive of a divine purpose that did not achieve its result nor of the result of a divine action that was not from a purpose. **14.** The formulation of Mk 4:12 is based on Is 6:9–10; Mt again eases the harshness by quoting the text in full in a "fulfillment" formula; see 1:22. This is the longest explicit quotation in Mt, and it follows the LXX exactly except for one word; some interpreters believe that it is an extremely early expansion of the Gospel. Obscurity cannot be entirely removed here; the basic problem is the problem of obduracy, which ultimately has no perfectly rational explanation. In the biblical conception denial of faith becomes itself the punishment of denial of faith. In Mt the saying fits his general pattern of the growing hostility of the Pharisees to Jesus; in a sense they have already reached the peak of unbelief in the Beelzebul controversy (12:25–37) and have closed their eyes and ears to any communication. The ultimate problem in the passage is not the meaning and the purpose of the parables, but the problem of the refusal of the Jews to accept their Messiah. For this reason most commentators think the saying has its original context in none of the Gospels.

91 (c) The Blessing of Faith (13:16–17). Luke (10:23–24) places this saying from Q immediately after the thanksgiving of Jesus for the Father's revelation to the simple (see 11:25–27); he thus connects it with the revelation. Matthew's use is not an alteration. He uses the catchwords "see" and "hear" from 13:13 to identify the disciples as those who, unlike the unbelieving Jews, perceive the revelation of the reign. **17.** *prophets and righteous:* These terms occur together in 10:41 and in 23:29; strangely both in 23:29 and here Lk does not have the same pair. Lk is probably closer to the source, for it is difficult to see why "righteous" should be altered to "kings."

92 (d) The Interpretation of the Parable of the Sower (13:18–23). This passage is now generally regarded by commentators as the interpretation given the parable by the primitive Christian community. We may thus call it a second level of interpretation; the first level is of a more general character, outlined in 89 above. The second level proceeds by allegorizing. The terms of the allegory reflect the conditions of the primitive Church rather than the proclamation of the reign by Jesus, and this so clearly that there is little room for doubt that the Church is interpreting the parable. This interpretation does not annihilate the first level of interpretation but rather builds upon it. The soil represents various types of members of the Church, those who have heard the Gospel and accepted it with faith. But the faith is not always persevering. **18.** Mt softens Mk 4:13, which includes the disciples among those who do not understand the parables. **19.** *the word of the reign:* This is the seed. *do not understand:* A phrase peculiar to Mt; this does not signify intellectual apprehension, but the full acceptance of the Gospel. *the wicked one* (see comment on 6:13). He easily "snatches" the word. **20.** *hears and receives with joy:* This is synonymous with "understand" in v. 19. This second class are "opportunists" who cannot meet the challenge of suffering and persecution. **22.** *the cares of the world:* The third class also hears and accepts, but is distracted by secular interests. **23.** The fourth class hears, understands, and performs. Each of the classes illustrates the sayings of Jesus in the Gospels about the word of the Gospel; the interpretation is not original but is a synthesis of Gospel material. It is not without interest that the primitive community was able so early to classify its delinquent members. Mt's revision of Mk is quite extensive in this passage, but the revisions are intended for clarity rather than for any alteration of the sense. The abbreviations are few, in contrast to Lk, which abbreviates the passage much more sharply.

93 (e) The Parable of the Darnel (13:24–30). Matthew omits the parable of the seed that grows secretly (Mk 4:26–29) and gives this parable instead, peculiar to himself. **25.** *darnel:* The weed, "tares" or "cockle" in the older Eng versions, is commonly recognized as darnel, a weed that has a resemblance to wheat. This parable is explained in vv. 36–43. The form of the parable does not allow a statement of the first level of interpretation (→ 92 above). The composition of the parable in its present form reflects the experience of the primitive community.

(f) The Parable of the Mustard Seed (13:31–32). The mustard seed must have been proverbially small (see 17:20); but it is not the smallest of seeds, nor is the tree (more properly a shrub, which grows to a height of 10–12 ft.) remarkably tall. The point of the parable is the contrast. **32.** *nest in its branches:* These words are based on Dn 4:21, but on no existing Gk version. No allegorical explanation is given, but it would be quite easy to form one. Without allegory the parable signifies the arrival of the reign from beginnings so small that they are hardly perceptible. The humble beginning of the reign in Jesus was a scandal to Judaism and even to his own disciples.

94 (g) The Parable of the Leaven (13:33). This parable is found in Q (Lk 18:20–21 par.). In its present form it falls into the same pattern with the parables of the sower and the mustard seed, illustrating again the irresistible growth of the reign from small beginnings. *three measures of meal:* The size of the lump of dough is exaggerated to make the point. Leaven, mentioned rarely in the NT, is used only in this passage as a figure of something good (see 16:6; 1 Cor 5:6–8; Gal 5:9). It is possible that the original saying has a force something like that of 1 Cor 5:6, and that it was given a different meaning when it was incorporated into the collection of the parables of the reign.

95 (h) Speaking in Parables (13:34–35). In Mk these lines are the conclusion to the collection of parables; Matthew follows the order of Mk (4:33–34), even though he adds other parables. He omits Mk's allusions to the inability of the crowds to understand and to the explanation given privately to the disciples. This agrees with his treatment of Mk 4:10–12 (see 13:10–15). The parables are a form of revelation, not of concealment. The point is further expanded by a fulfillment quotation (see comment on 1:22). The text quoted is called the words of a prophet, although the source is Ps 78:2; David is called a prophet in Acts 2:30. The text follows neither the MT nor the LXX; it is freely adapted to fit the revelation of Jesus.

96 (i) THE INTERPRETATION OF THE PARABLE OF THE DARNEL (13:36–43). The explanation is entirely allegorical; but even with the explanation the parable and the allegory raise questions. It has been noticed above that the form of the parable is such that it suits the allegorical explanation; and thus it seems likely that the parable is either composed by Matthew or his sources or it is a substantial reworking of a parable of Jesus. **38.** *the field is the world:* The scandals and the workers of lawlessness are collected from "the kingdom of the Son of Man." This must mean the Church. The problem is not the existence of the wicked in the world at large, but the existence of wicked men where the Son of Man has sown good men; the seed is the members of the Church, not the word. **39.** The solution to the problem is purely eschatological. The angels are the ministers of judgment (see 13:49; 24:31). The Church has come to recognize that it is not entirely a community of the elect; it has unfaithful members. God will tolerate such members in the Church as he tolerates them in the world at large; but the judgment will determine the final destiny of righteous and wicked and will purify the kingdom entirely. The lesson is certainly one of patient tolerance of the presence of the wicked even in the community of the reign. **43.** To the explanation is added the phrase, "Let him who has ears hear," which is elsewhere attached to the parable itself. The explanation is not entirely consistent with itself; possibly it shows more than one level of interpretation.

97 (j) THE PARABLES OF THE TREASURE AND THE PEARL (13:44–46). These parables, peculiar to Mt, have a common theme. Where the other parables speak of the reign and of its members as a group, these parables are addressed to the individual person. In both, the man sells all he has (see 19:21). The reign demands total renunciation (6:24; 8:18–22; 10:37–39). Here the emphasis is less on the renunciation than on the supreme value of the reign; renunciation has its reward. Small hoards of coins and jewelry are still found occasionally in Palestine both by chance and by archaeological exploration. In the unsettled ancient world when the danger of foreign invasion or brigandage was almost always present, many a householder buried his little store in the hope of a return, which he never made. The finder of the treasure does not tell the owner of the field; Jesus passes no judgment on the ethics of the finder, but uses his avarice as an example of the zeal with which the believer should pursue the reign at any price. The pearl merchant similarly puts all his possessions in one investment that he knows will repay him handsomely.

98 (k) THE PARABLE OF THE NET (13:47–50). This parable, also peculiar to Mt, is very close to the parable of the darnel (24–30,36–43). The theme of the presence of both good and wicked in the Church is even clearer here, and the eschatological solution is identical. In this parable, however, it is possible to trace an earlier form of the parable beneath the allegorizing second level of interpretation. The introductory verse makes no mention of good or wicked, but states simply "from every kind." The reign is thus described as universal in its scope and excluding no one. The net (Gk *sagēnē*) is the large dragnet. The eschatological line in 50a is repeated from 42a (see 8:12).

99 (l) CONCLUSION (13:51–52). Matthew has already used Mk's concluding formula (13:34–35), but he has placed these verses, peculiar to himself, at the end of his collection. **52.** *every scribe:* The saying of v. 52 need have had no reference to the parables in its original context. The question in v. 51 concerns the "understanding" of the parables; see 13:19, where the same word is added by Matthew. The question may be composed to introduce the saying. There are no references in the NT to Christian scribes; but it has to be assumed that the members of the primitive Christian community included some scribes. Many commentators think that "Matthew" himself was such a Christian scribe. The saying is a restatement in a different form of the principle of the relations of the Law and the Gospel (5:17–20). The scribe who has become a disciple will employ both the old, the Law and the Prophets, and the new, the Gospel. Neither is sufficient without the other; for the Gospel is the fullness of the Law.

100 (V) Book Four: The Formation of the Disciples (13:53–18:35).

(A) Narrative Section: Various Episodes Preceding the Journey to Jerusalem (13:53–17:27).

(a) REJECTION AT NAZARETH (13:53–58). The parable discourse in Mk is followed by 4:35–5:43; Matthew has used this material in 8:23–34 and 9:18–26. In both Mk and Mt the Nazareth episode forms a climax of the Galilean ministry and the rejection of Jesus. Matthew's revisions and omissions are significant. Jesus is called "the son of the carpenter" and not "the carpenter"; Matthew may have wished to raise Jesus above the actual practice of a trade. It is quite strange that in neither Mk nor Mt is the usual patronymic employed, which would be Jesus *bar*-Joseph; indeed, in Mk he is called the son of Mary, a designation that is extremely suggestive. It appears that in Nazareth it was known that Jesus was not the carnal son of Joseph, with all the implications that would be attached to this designation. **55.** The kinsmen of Jesus mentioned in general in 12:46–50 are here named; it is impossible to identify them positively with others in the NT who bear these names, and the mss. are not uniform in the reading of the names. It is clear that they were never persons of importance in the primitive Jerusalem community. **57.** Where Mk says Jesus "could" not work miracles, Mt says he "did" not; the phrase in Mk is harsh, but it is in agreement with the general conception of the Gospels of the miracle as a response to faith. The saying about the prophet who has no honor in his own country is found also in Jn 4:44. Mk's note of the amazement of Jesus at the unbelief of the Nazarenes is reduced in Mt to "because of their unbelief"; this amazement is an emotional response of Jesus of the type that Mt usually omits.

The incident is not only climactic in the Galilean ministry, it also summarizes the rejection of Jesus as a whole. The response of the Nazarenes was, "We know him, and therefore he cannot be anything out of the ordinary." In a proper sense the entire Jewish community could say this. The incident illustrates the saying in 10:34–36.

101 (b) HEROD HEARS OF JESUS (14:1–2). This Herod is Herod Antipas, son of Herod the Great and Malthace. After the death of Herod the Great in 4 BC Antipas received Galilee and Perea as his portion of Herod's kingdom according to Herod's will, ratified by Augustus (→ History of Israel, 75:140). Mt reports only one of the various bits of gossip current about Jesus (Mk 6:15). **2.** *this is John the Baptist:* On the assumption that the words attributed to Herod bear some resemblance to what he said, it seems unlikely that they express a superstitious fear. John had worked no wonders, but one risen from the dead would be full of power. The burden of the remark is, "Here is another John the Baptist"—who may expect the same treatment as the first. Herod no doubt shared the common superstitious belief in miraculous power; but this would not prevent him from executing the wonder-worker if Jesus threatened to be another moral prophet as explicit as John had been (→ 102 below).

102 (c) The Execution of John the Baptist (14:3–12). In both Mk (6:17–29) and Mt this incident is strangely parenthetical, inserted almost as an afterthought to explain the words of Herod. Matthew has abbreviated Mk very sharply. **5.** The desire to kill John has been transferred from Herodias to Herod, and Herod's fear has been transferred from John to the crowd; and there is no mention of Herod's willingness to hear John. These alterations have the result of making Herod look still blacker. **8.** The exchange between the daughter and the mother in Mk 6:24 is omitted, probably to make the narrative run faster. **12.** *they went and told Jesus:* This is a Matthaean addition, which not only establishes a clearer connection between the death of John and the departure of Jesus from Galilee, Herod's territory, but also makes Jesus more explicitly the successor of John.

According to Josephus (*Ant.* 18.5, 2 § 116–19), the scene of the murder was the palace-fortress of Machaerus (see 74 above). He also informs us that the name of the daughter was Salome (for her relation to Herod, → History of Israel, 75:140). According to Josephus, the scandal was less in the degree of kinship than in the open adultery that preceded the divorces. The execution of John was so barbarous and so lawless that a number of historians have questioned the historical character of the details. But the incident is quite in accord with the nature of the house of Herod as it is described by Josephus, our only witness—and, it must be confessed, a deeply prejudiced witness.

103 (d) The Feeding of Five Thousand (14:13–21). Mt connects this incident with the killing of John the Baptist and the withdrawal of Jesus from Galilee. Mk associates it with the return of the Twelve from their mission and a withdrawal into solitude for rest. The scene is not clear in any of the three Syn. **13.** *a desert place:* It is not identified, nor can it be said with certainty that it was on the E shore of the Sea of Galilee. However, it lay near enough to villages to make possible the purchase of food; consequently the locale is not "the desert" in the technical sense of the term. *from the cities:* The names of the cities from which the crowds followed Jesus are not given, but one has to assume that the cities on the shore of the Sea of Galilee are meant. **14.** *healed their sick:* Contrast Mk (6:30) which speaks of teaching. **15.** It is unlikely that very many of the crowd would leave home for a day's journey without carrying some food; the modern Palestinian peasant would not be so improvident. **17.** *only five loaves and two fish:* The amount mentioned would not even suffice for Jesus and the Twelve. **19.** The ceremonial with which Jesus blesses and distributes the food anticipates the Last Supper (26:26). **20.** The Twelve hand out the food and collect the fragments, one basket for each. Mt heightens the number of the people: uncounted women and children besides 5000 men, who were mentioned in Mk 6:44. The number is very probably exaggerated, and it is not the result of a head count in any case; oral tradition tends to raise such figures.

The usual note of wonder that follows miracles is not mentioned here. The incident is related less for the element of the miraculous than as a symbol and an anticipation of the Eucharist and of the Messianic banquet (see 8:11–12). The association with the Eucharist is more explicit in Jn 6, where the multiplication of the loaves is followed by John's Eucharistic discourse. It is a Messianic sign and symbol that will find its fulfillment in the true Messianic banquet, the Eucharist.

Matthew has abbreviated here less sharply than elsewhere; but his abbreviations, achieved by the omission of some details and dialogue, have the effect of heightening the symbolic significance of the incident. The exception to this is his omission of Mk 6:39–40.

104 (e) Jesus Walks on the Water (14:22–33). The geography remains vague; there are no "mountains" in the immediate vicinity of the lake to which Jesus could retire, but the word could be used loosely. **23.** *to pray:* This is one of the few occasions when Jesus retires to pray alone (see 26:36–46). **24.** *many stadia off:* Where Mk says that the boat was in the middle of the sea, Mt particularizes with "many stadia"; the *stadion* was about 600 ft. **25.** *the fourth watch:* The last watch of the night, the period of about three hours before dawn. **26.** *a ghost:* This is the usual meaning of *phantasma.* In Mk the wind stops, and the disciples were astonished; but Mt, as usual, omits Mk's note that the disciples were still without understanding. Mt replaces this by a very explicit confession that not only anticipates 16:16, but comes near to making 16:16–18 meaningless.

The incident is so singular in the Syn narrative that many commentators propose that in its original context it belongs after the resurrection of Jesus. Whether this was the original context or not—and it seems probable that it was—the story, like the preceding story, has a symbolic significance. This chapter begins that portion of Mt that is called the ecclesiastical portion. The disciples in the boat represent, in a not too subtle way, the Church, from which Jesus is never far even when the situation is threatening and he is invisible.

28. *on the water:* Mt alone adds the incident of Peter's attempt to walk on the water. This addition increases the symbolic significance of the story. Peter emerges into prominence in Mt's Book Four. His special position in the Twelve is clearly affirmed; here it is suggested that Peter has responsibilities not shared by the others. If he is to meet these responsibilities, he must have faith. The faith of Peter is also a prominent theme in the story of the confession of Peter (16:13–23).

105 (f) Healings (14:34–36). Matthew has made a summary of Mk (6:53–56); adhering to Mk's order of events, but abbreviating the material by the omission of graphic details. **34.** *Gennesaret:* The plain at the NW shore of the Sea of Galilee, mentioned also by Josephus and regarded as a fertile and salubrious territory. **36.** On healing by the touch of the tassel, see 9:20.

106 (g) Exterior and Interior Cleanliness (15:1–20). This is a controversy-story concluding in a saying and its explanation. Matthew has rewritten Mk, with his expansions outbalancing his abbreviations. He omits Mk 7:2–4, an explanation of Jewish ablutions, and rearranges Mk 7:8–13 so that these lines begin the response of Jesus. **2.** *the tradition of the elders:* The question is about tradition, and not about the Law. In rabbinical interpretation the traditions of the elders ranked only beneath the Law itself as a source of obligation. *wash their hands:* This particular tradition was based on a rigorous interpretation of Lv 15:11. Things that "defiled the hands" need not be articles that were technically unclean; the holy—for example, the text of the Bible—also defiled the hands, which should be washed after handling the text. **3.** *he answered them:* The question is not answered directly, but by a charge: The disciples ignore the traditions, but the scribes and Pharisees nullify the Law (quoted from Ex 20:9; Dt 5:16; Ex 20:12, very nearly according to the LXX). **5.** *an offering to God:* The practice to which Jesus obscurely alludes permitted the son to vow to give to the Temple the resources by which he might support his parents. This gave him the use of the resources, but the vow forbade him to convert the property to profane uses (see J. A. Fitzmyer, *JBL* 78 [1959] 60–65; J. Bligh, *HeythJ* 5 [1964] 192–93). **6.** *for the sake of your tradition:* The force of the example is that in this instance the traditions of the elders nullify the Law; and the implicit conclusion is that the traditions impose no obligation. **7.** *well did Isaiah prophesy of you:* The attitude of the Pharisees is illustrated from Is 29:13, quoted according to the LXX, and not the MT.

10. The saying (pronounced to "the crowd") terminates the controversy; here the question concerning ablutions is answered. But the answer goes beyond the tradition of the elders; as in the Sermon on the Mount, Jesus restates the Law, which clearly enumerates the types of unclean food (Lv 11; 17:10–16). The saying is actually an annulment rather than a restatement. **11.** The controversy about the dietary laws in the primitive Christian community is frequently echoed both in Acts and in the epistles; and it is thought by many commentators that it is also reflected here. The position that is taken in Mt is also taken in the story of the vision of Peter (Acts 10:9–16; 11:1–10). In Acts, however, the principle is extended to apply by an allegorical interpretation to the admission of Gentiles to the Church. The connection is loose; but the controversy shows that the dietary laws could have become a major obstacle to the admission of Gentiles to the Church. The controversy, however, does not begin with a question about unclean foods but about ablutions; the saying is general, covering uncleanness that might be contracted by handling unclean objects and unclean foods. Matthew has abbreviated the saying with no loss of clarity. *profanes:* There is a play on the word "profane" (lit., "to make common"), which is explained in vv. 18–19.

107 **12–14.** Matthew has expanded by the addition of these verses, including the saying in 14, which comes from Q (see Lk 6:39). The expansion is pointed; the question of Pharisaic scandal is briefly handled by the saying in v. 13. Those who take scandal at the teaching of Jesus are not planted by the Father. **15.** The question is proposed by the disciples in Mk, by Peter in Mt (see comment on 14:28–31). The saying is called a "parable," which means a saying with a hidden meaning, not merely a short story. **16.** The disciples cannot understand the saying because it is so explicitly contrary to the prescriptions of the Law. Here Matthew, contrary to his usual practice, retains Mk's words about the failure of the disciples to understand. It may not be fanciful to think that he retains the saying here because the issue involved is the relation of Jesus to the Law, in particular his competence to interpret and even to annul the Law. The Jewish Christian who does not grasp this is indeed obtuse. **17.** *whatever goes into the mouth:* The explanation of the saying is one of the most earthy passages of the Gospels, but the earthiness only adds to the earnestness of the passage. **18.** *profanes:* Here the play on words is explained. Legal "cleanliness" is nothing, for all that man eats ultimately issues in the height of uncleanliness. This is irrelevant to morality. True cleanliness or uncleanness is determined from the heart. Actually not all the things mentioned proceed from the mouth; but in biblical idiom the mouth is the channel through which the heart externalizes itself, and the line between "word" and "deed" is thin. **19.** Here Matthew has altered Mk 7:19 in a peculiar way; with the exception of "wicked plans," he enumerates the vices that are forbidden in the Decalogue. The wicked plans of the heart lie at the root of the crimes men commit. **20.** *these are what profane a man:* The concluding verse returns to the subject with which the controversy began. The discussion has ranged widely to reach this answer; and it is probable that not only Matthew but Mark also has related a construction formed from several sayings.

108 (h) THE CANAANITE WOMAN (15:21–28). Just as the vision of Peter is associated with the Gentile mission in Acts 10–11, so here the controversy over cleanliness and the annulment of the dietary laws is followed by one of the rare encounters of Jesus with Gentiles. The story should be compared with the healing of the centurion's slave (8:5–13). **21.** *to the district of Tyre and Sidon:* That is, in southern Phoenicia. In Mk it is not clear whether Jesus left the territory of Galilee, but the implication is that he did. Mt puts him near Gentile territory but not in it; the woman "comes out." Mt's addition sharpens the point that Jesus never left Jewish territory. **22.** *a Canaanite woman:* The woman is called a Syro-Phoenician in Mk, a Canaanite in Mt; both of these gentilic names occur only here in the NT. The name Canaanite suggests the OT use of the name; there, particularly in the deuteronomic and postdeuteronomic literature, the Canaanites become the sinful race that embodies all that is wicked and godless, the race that is to be exterminated. Matthew's choice of this word reflects the OT background. Contrary to what we usually find, Matthew's account is longer; and the expansions suit his general theme and purpose so well that no special source need be postulated. *Son of David:* In Mt the woman gives Jesus the Messianic title (→ Aspects NT Thought, 78:27); this is highly improbable in the speech of an uninformed Gentile, but it illustrates the readiness of the Gentiles to confess the messiahship the Jews denied. **23.** Mt adds to Mk the intercession of the disciples; "dismiss" here means to dismiss by granting the petition. *to the lost sheep of... Israel:* Mt also adds these words of Jesus; effectively they are an explanation of the proverb in v. 26, which no doubt sounded as harsh to Hellenistic readers of the Gospels as it does to modern commentators, many of whom think that it cannot be an authentic saying of Jesus. The restriction of the mission of Jesus to the Jews is clear in the entire NT, but rarely is it as explicit as here (see comment on 10:6). The affirmation in this context heightens the difference between the believing Gentile, to whom Jesus has no mission and to whom he denies any relationship, and the unbelieving Jews. The proverb is less harsh in a Near Eastern context than it would be to us, but it is not gentle. The dialogue is an instance of the kind of wit that was and is admired in the Near East, the same wit that is called wisdom in the OT; it is the ability to match riddle with riddle, to cap one wise saying with another, to match insult with insult, or—as here—to turn the insult into a commitment. There is nothing unrealistic about the exchange at all; Jesus would not have been a genuine Palestinian if he had not occasionally engaged in a duel of wit. The scene is much more a scene of peasant good humor than it is of solemn theological debate. **28.** Mark appreciates the tone when he has Jesus tell the woman that the favor is granted because of her saying. Matthew introduces the more solemn praise of her faith, the same theme that is illustrated in the healing of the slave of the centurion (8:13).

The story is not really a miracle story, nor can it be called a saying-story; it is the saying of the woman, not the miracle or the saying of Jesus, that is the climax of the episode. In this respect the story is singular. It is no doubt composed in the light of the problems of admission of Gentiles to the Church, but it is not composed entirely for this point. The story does not assert that Jesus did recommend a mission to the Gentiles; it does assert that he did not refuse faith wherever he found it.

109 (i) The Healing of the Sick (15:29–31). Mt omits the geographical details of Mk (7:31–37), which show a remarkable misunderstanding of Palestinian geography. Matthew's geography is usually no more precise, but he probably found Mk unintelligible. The remarkable feature of this passage is that Matthew turns a single cure into a summary statement of several cures. It is possible that he preferred not to relate a cure that was accomplished through the use of touch and spittle; but it was also possible for him to omit these details and describe the cure by the use of a word. It is also remarkable that the praise of Jesus (Mk 7:37) is reduced to the colorless statement that they glorified the God of Israel, although the praise is actually more suitable to Mt's summary than it is to the single incident narrated in Mk. The purpose of the summary in Mt seems to be to create a transition between the story of the Canaanite woman and the feeding of the 4000; this episode explains how the crowd came to be present in a remote and unpopulated area, "the hill country."

110 (j) The Feeding of Four Thousand (15:32–39). Of this passage one can say that if it is not a duplicate of the feeding of the 5000 (14:13–21), then there are no doublets anywhere in the Bible—or indeed in all literature. The variations are neither numerous nor significant: the presence of the crowd for three days; the initiative taken by Jesus; the number of loaves; the number of baskets of fragments; the number of persons (and here, as in the feeding of the 5000, Mt is careful to note that the number counts only the men). The common points are numerous: the motive of Jesus is expressly said to be compassion; the crowd is in a remote uninhabited place; the people recline on the ground; the Eucharistic formula is used; the scene is near the lake, and the miracle is followed by a trip in a boat. The terminus of the trip is Magadan in Mt, Dalmanutha in Mk. Neither name occurs elsewhere and neither can be identified.

The existence of the doublet can be explained only by the assumption that the variations occurred in the sources of Mark, and that they had been so well developed by the time they reached him that the two accounts could be taken as narratives of two different incidents. The presence of doublets is not uncommon in Mt, as we have noticed several times; but doublets are rare in Mk. That this story should have given rise to variant forms so early may indicate that it was very often told; and this in turn suggests that the connection of the story with the Eucharistic rite was present from the beginning.

111 (k) Signs and Times (16:1–4). Matthew here repeats what he has already used in 12:38–39. **1.** *a sign:* See comment on 12:38. **2b–3.** These words are missing in many important mss., and many critics regard them as a secondary gloss. Lk 12:54–55 is not an exact parallel, and this suggests that the substratum in Q was different from both Lk and Mt. It is easier to suppose that weather phenomena, which are peculiar to most regions anyway, would be altered when the Gospel traditions were retold in another climate. The Mediterranean climate is generally uniform throughout the whole basin; but Palestine has its own peculiarities. The redness of the sky comes from atmospheric dust that accumulates during the dry summer months. The sign can only refer to the beginning of the rainy season. The type of cloudiness that indicates the first rain of the winter is such that once observed, it is not likely to be misconstrued. The Arabs say "Rain tomorrow" (predicting a day in advance of the time indicated in 16:3) with an assurance that the foreigner will do well to respect. **3.** *the times:* The Messianic times (Gk *kairoi*). **4.** See comment on 12:38.

112 (l) Leaven (16:5–12). Mt's abbreviations of Mk (8:14–21) are significant. Lk (12:1) gives the saying and the situation in a much more compressed form, but adds an explicit note that the leaven of the Pharisees is hypocrisy. This is not clearly the force of the saying, and it is quite possible that the original context is not preserved. The most obvious meaning of the figure is the teaching of the Pharisees and Sadducees; but Mk has Pharisees and Herod, and Herod cannot be considered a teacher. Mt's change of "Herod" to "Sadducees" may have been made to suggest the idea of teaching. **7.** *we brought no bread:* The disciples failed completely to grasp the figure and thought that it referred to their own forgetfulness; this elicits an extremely sharp rebuke from Jesus, which is considerably softened in Mt by the omission of Mk 8:17b–18. **9–10.** The direction of the story is then turned from the Pharisees and the Sadducees to a lesson of faith; Jesus has proved that he can provide for their needs. This is doubtfully a part of the original saying-story. **12.** *then they understood:* Mt still further softens the rebuke of the disciples by adding that they understood after the rebuke and gives the explanation of the figure as teaching; Mk leaves the rebuke hanging in the air.

The episode is placed on "the opposite side" by Mt, in the boat by Mk. This journey takes Jesus and the disciples to a point from which they can travel to Caesarea Philippi, the scene of the next incident. Mt omits the healing of the blind man of Bethsaida (Mk 8:22–26).

113 (m) The Confession of Peter (16:13–23). The scene of this conversation is the neighborhood of Caesarea Philippi, the modern Baniyas, a little over 20 mi. N of the Sea of Galilee near the sources of the Jordan. The city was founded by Philip the tetrarch, brother of Herod Antipas; it was an entirely Gentile community. The variations of Mt from Mk here are some of the most interesting in the entire Gospel. The question of Jesus concerns the Son of Man where Mk has "me"; Son of Man is usually understood to be a Messianic title, but suggestive rather than explicit. To the answers John the Baptist (see 14:2) and Elijah, or another of the prophets, Mt adds Jeremiah. The belief in the return of Elijah was derived from Mal 3:23–24; see Sir 48:10; Mt 17:3,10–13. The addition of Jeremiah may not be unrelated to the belief expressed in 2 Mc 15:13–16. The question is turned directly to the disciples; and the construction of the passage leaves no doubt that it is a challenge. "Simon Peter" answers for all with a profession that Jesus is the Messiah; Mt alone adds "the son of the living God." This additional title, which goes beyond the confession of messiahship, very probably reflects the more developed faith of the primitive Christian community; Mk has preserved the original saying. By speaking of the more developed faith of the community we do not imply that the community had a full understanding of the sonship of Jesus; but they professed their belief in the entirely unique relationship of Jesus with the Father (see 11:27; T. de Kruijf, *Der Sohn des lebendigen Gottes* [AnalBib 16; Rome, 1962]).

114 Verses 17–20 have no parallel in Mk and Lk; and there can be no explanation of this omission except that Mk and Lk did not have the words. Some writers have suggested that the verses have been removed from their original context, which was postresurrectional, and that they can be compared to Jn 21:15–19, in which Peter is given a peculiar position in a postresurrectional narrative (see R. E. Brown, *CBQ* 23 [1961] 159). The arguments for this hypothesis are not convincing; and in the context of Mt the words are spoken to Simon Peter in response to his faith. **17.** *but my Father who is in heaven:* Simon's confession of messiahship is attributed to divine revelation; it could not come from his own perception or from the instruction of others. This itself is an interesting testimony to the way in which the primitive Church thought that the messiahship of Jesus was recognized. **18.** *you are Peter:* Jesus then gives Simon bar-Jona a new name and a commission, which is set forth in the most vigorously discussed passage of the Gospel. (For a full discussion see O. Cullmann, *Peter* [rev. ed.; London, 1962]; O. Karrer, *Peter and the Church* [QD 8; N.Y., 1963].) Simon gets the name by which he is usually known in the NT; and those who doubt that Jesus spoke these words forget that the NT has no other passage in which the change of name is explained. This does not imply that Mt has preserved "the very words" of Jesus; this can rarely be said of any passage in the Gospels. "Peter" comes from the Gk *petros*, the masculinized form of the fem. noun *petra*, "rock," which represents the Aram *kēphā*. The Aram name occurs once in the Grecized form *Kēphas* in Jn 1:43; 1 Cor 1:12; 3:22; 9:5; 15:5; Gal 1:18; 2:9,11,14; Paul uses *Petros* only in Gal 2:7,8. *upon this rock:* That Peter is the rock upon which the *ekklēsia* is to be built is clear; but in what sense he is the foundation is not. The word *ekklēsia* is used only here and 18:17 in all the Gospels; and it is highly doubtful that Jesus himself used the word, which becomes the common designation of the Christian community in the epistles. Whether Jesus used the word has nothing to do with whether the primitive community understood him correctly when they believed that he intended to form an enduring community.

In the context the reason why Peter is called the rock is the faith that he has just shown in his confession. He has made vocal the faith of the disciples; and it is upon faith in Jesus as the Messiah that the group Jesus has formed will endure. Peter is the speaker and the example of this faith. As long as this faith endures, "the gates of Sheol" will not have power over the group. *gates of hell:* The common translation is misleading; the phrase means not the powers of evil but the power of death; for Sheol is the biblical abode of the dead.

115 **19.** *the keys of the kingdom:* The conferring of the keys is a clear statement of a position of leadership and authority. The phrase echoes Is 22:22, in which Shebna receives the keys of the royal palace. The key was the symbol of the office of master of the palace, the highest of the officers of the Israelite court; and Peter is thus declared master of the palace in the *ekklēsia*. The phrase "kingdom of heaven" is used here not in its usual sense of reign, but of the community established by the reign, practically synonymous with *ekklēsia*. *whatever you bind...you loose:* The meaning of the office conferred is further specified in the conferring of the power to bind and loose. This phrase is obscure; it has no background in biblical language, and in rabbinical Judaism it signifies rabbinical decisions; to bind is to give a decision that imposes an obligation, and to loose is to give a decision that removes an obligation. If this is the sense in which the phrase is used, it does not mean that Peter becomes chief rabbi in the Church; for his decisions are accepted in heaven. The same phrase is used of the Church as a whole in 18:18; there it refers to expulsion from the Church. The phrase certainly signifies the exercise of authority; but the nature and use of the authority are not specified. That Peter had a special position in the early Church is clear from other passages in the NT; see Lk 22:31–32; Jn 21:15–19; Acts 1–12.

116 **20.** By the insertion of vv. 17–19 Matthew has taken some of the point from Mk's arrangement; but he retains what Mk has. In Mk the question leads from a confession of messiahship to an instruction in the suffering of the Messiah. This is a crisis in the Gospel narrative; for the idea was entirely foreign to the Judaism of NT times. *the Christ* [or *the Messiah*]: The confession is followed by a prohibition to reveal the messiahship; Mt makes this explicit by the addition of "the Messiah." If the faith of the disciples is firm, they are ready for this instruction. **21.** Where Mk has "the Son of Man" (9:31) Mt has "him," with "Jesus Messiah" as subject. Mt also adds Jerusalem as the place of the events. The Gospels describe very briefly what must have been one of the great disillusionments in the minds of the disciples; but the early disillusionment had long been forgotten. **22.** *Peter...started to reproach him:* Not forgotten, however, was the response of Peter; Lk spares Peter by omitting the passage. Mk mentions that Jesus saw the disciples present before he answered Peter, which adds to the humiliation of Peter. **23.** *You are a scandal to me:* Mt's additional phrase is no less humiliating. *scandal:* See comment on 11:6. Peter is called an obstacle, an adversary, an enemy; and the occurrence of this verse immediately after the confession and the conferring of the name and the commission is certainly striking. Contrary to his usual practice, Matthew makes the exchange more vivid by quoting Peter's words directly. The revelation of Jesus as Messiah was more easily received than the revelation that the Messiah must suffer, die, and rise.

117 (n) DISCIPLESHIP (16:24–28). This passage contains a collection of sayings brought together by Mk; but Mt does not follow Mk closely. The connection with the prediction of the passion is established by Mk; the word "cross" does not appear in the prediction, but the association is obvious. Mt omits Mk's crowds (8:34); the scene of Caesarea Philippi made this detail unlikely. Matthew has used the sayings of 16:24–25 earlier (see 10:38–39); the form in which they are set here is almost identical with Mk. **24.** *let him deny himself:* The "denial of self" does not mean the renunciation of some optional good, as the phrase is commonly used; it means the affirmation that the self is nothing, that it has no claims and no values. The phrase is echoed in Paul's saying that Jesus emptied himself (Phil 2:7). *take up his cross:* Lk adds "daily," thus giving the phrase a more clearly metaphorical turn; but the original phrase very probably echoes the martyrdoms of the primitive Church. **26.** *self:* See comment on 10:39. This translation does not take away the implicit affirmation of the verse that the true and lasting value of the person transcends the conditions of the present existence. The whole world is not a sufficient recompense for the surrender of the self (*psychē*) to prolong one's earthly life. Matthew omits Mk 8:37–38; he has already used this saying (in a variant form) in 10:33, although there are many other instances where he uses the same saying twice. **27.** *the Son of Man is to come...:* Because of the omission Mk 8:38b had to be recast; and the allusion to the judgment becomes more general in Mt. The judgment is a coming in glory with the angels; see 24:29–31. The function of the angels in the judgment appears in the parables of the reign; see 13:36–50. The judgment is described in terms drawn from Ps 62:13. The allusion to the glory is a catchword by which 16:28 is attached to the preceding passage. **28.** The saying was paradoxical enough even in the primitive Church to be preserved in three forms (Mk, "the Reign of God coming in power"; Mt, "the Son of Man coming in his Reign"; Lk, "the Reign of God"). It has been remarked on 10:23 that such sayings are inexplicable on the hypothesis that they indicate that the parousia is near. Like 10:23b, this saying must have been understood to refer to another display of judgment in power, and this display was most probably the catastrophic destruction of Jerusalem in AD 70.

118 (o) THE TRANSFIGURATION (17:1–8). Matthew has condensed Mk (9:2–8) in some parts of this narrative and expanded it in others. In 17:2 he has added a glow to the countenance of Jesus where Mk speaks of the whiteness of his garments, but he has omitted Mk's allusion to the fuller. In 17:4 he has omitted Mk's reference to Peter's ignorance and the fear of the disciples; but in 17:6–7 he has added a deeper note of fear and reverence and presents Jesus himself as arousing the disciples. The effect of these modifications is to heighten the majesty and the mystery of the experience and to remove, as he often does, suggestions that the disciples did not understand what was happening.

1. *mountain:* Traditionally understood as Mt. Tabor in the plain of Esdraelon; but since Tabor is not notably high, Mt. Hermon north of Caesarea Philippi (over 9000 ft. high) has been suggested. It is far more probable that this mountain, like the mountain of the sermon (5:1) has no geographical location. It is the symbolic mountain on which the events of Sinai are re-enacted in the life of the new Moses. *Peter, James, and John:* The three who accompany Jesus are the same three who are his exclusive companions in other events (26:37; Mk 5:37, not followed by Mt). *after six days:* The interval is thought to echo Ex 24:16, but the parallel is not close; the themes of the episode, however, do echo the Sinai narrative. **2.** *was transfigured:* The luminous clarity with which Jesus is surrounded recalls the brightness of the face of Moses after the Sinai revelation (Ex 34:29–35), which made it necessary for Moses to veil his face; this feature is added in Mt. **3.** *Moses and Elijah:* They are symbolic figures, representing respectively the Law and the Prophets. These two words are used to designate the entire collection of OT books, and thus the fullness of the revelation of God to Israel. Jesus joins the two as the fulfillment of the Law and the Prophets (see 5:17). **4.** *I will make three booths:* The remark of Peter alludes to the Feast of Tabernacles. This feast commemorated the sojourn of the Israelites on Mt. Sinai while they received the revelation of the Law through Moses. But this is not the revelation of another Law; a greater reality is manifested here. The external symbol is again derived from the Sinai narratives. **5.** *a bright cloud:* The luminous cloud is the Shekinah, the symbol of the presence of God. In a cloud God comes to declare the Law to Moses (Ex 19:9; 24:15–16), and he speaks from the cloud as he does here. *my beloved Son:* The words spoken are a revelation of the sonship of Jesus; Mt repeats the formula of the baptism (3:17), with the addition of Mk's phrase, "Hear him." Jesus is the son and the revealer. The formula very probably echoes the Servant passage of Is 42:1 (see 3:17). **7.** The suggestion that the disciples were asleep is much clearer in Lk; this extraordinary experience was more easily conceived as a dream-vision.

119 The transfiguration has no parallel in the Syn except the Baptism Narrative; and for this reason some scholars have suggested that it is a postresurrection narrative transferred to this point. This opinion is not accepted by the vast majority of commentators. The external features of the narrative, we have noticed, are derived from the Exodus narratives rather than from the resurrection narratives. The heavily symbolic character of the story indicates that this story, like the story of Jesus' baptism, is more theological than historical in character. The narrative must rest upon a mystical experience of the disciples, but the experience is described in symbolic imagery in such a way that the experience itself is impossible to reconstruct. The course of events in the Gospels compels us to suppose that the fullness of perception into the reality of Jesus that the transfiguration suggests was not possessed by the disciples until after the resurrection. The position of the narrative here—after the confession of Peter and the prediction of the passion—makes it a reaffirmation of the messiahship of Jesus and of the Messianic glory in which he will be revealed. He is no less Messiah when his Messianic glory is hidden in the incarnation and the passion.

120 (p) THE COMING OF ELIJAH (17:9–13). The precept of Jesus not to reveal "the vision" (this word occurs in Mt but not in Mk) is a part of Mk's Messianic secret, which Matthew has retained. But he has not retained Mk's observation that the disciples did not understand what was meant by the resurrection; as usual, he omits passages that show their lack of insight.

The context of the preceding chapter and of the transfiguration has been Messianic; and the question of the disciples about the coming of Elijah supposes that Elijah would return as a messianic precursor (see 16:14). If Jesus is Messiah, what has happened to this sign of the Messianic age? **12.** *has already come:* The answer of Jesus is that Elijah has come (alluding to Mal 3:23, LXX) but has not been recognized (added by Mt). As "Elijah" was treated by men according to their will, so shall the Son of Man suffer; Mt transfers this allusion to the passion from its position in Mk, and thus secures a parallel between the death of John the Baptist and the death of Jesus. **13.** Mt adds explicitly that "Elijah" was John the Baptist. It seems very probable that this dialogue is constructed in the light of the controversies between Christians and Jews in the primitive Church. Jews would have asked about the traditional Messianic signs, and Jewish Christians were obliged to meet their request.

121 (q) THE HEALING OF AN EPILEPTIC CHILD (17:14–21). This exorcism story, one of the most vivid in Mk (9:14–29) has been condensed in Mt to less than half, including the expansion in 17:20. The healing-story issues in a saying, but Matthew has changed the saying (see comment on 17:20). **14.** *to the crowd:* The presence of the crowd at the foot of the mountain is introduced in Mt without any of Mk's explanation; but the geography, as we have noticed, is more ideal than real, and the conjunction of the incidents seems to be artificial. Nor does Mt retain the dispute between the disciples and the scribes, which in Mk has no object. **15.** *an epileptic:* The nature of the ailment, which in Mk is demonic possession, is called "lunacy" in Mt; in the ancient world attacks of mental disease were attributed to the phases of the moon. But there is no doubt that the symptoms of epilepsy are described. Mt omits the details given in Mk concerning the symptoms, the attack the child suffers when he is brought to Jesus, and the dialogue of Jesus with the father concerning faith; but Mt does retain the theme of faith and places it in the concluding saying. **17.** The apostrophe to the "unbelieving and perverse generation" (possibly in Mt an allusion to Dt 32:5) is difficult to explain; it seems to refer directly not to the father, nor to the crowd, but rather to the disciples who have failed in the use of the power that Jesus communicated to them (see 10:8; 17:19–20). **18.** *rebuked him:* Mk's account of the healing suggests an unusual struggle and resistance; Mt reduces the healing to a bare minimum.

20. Mk's answer to the question of the disciples, "This kind is expelled only by prayer," was too difficult for both Matthew and Luke. Matthew has substituted a saying on faith adapted from Mk 11:22–23, which he uses again in 21:21. The failure of the disciples is due not to lack of prayer but to lack of faith; it is doubtful that any real difference between the two is intended. The saying on faith introduces a theme that is both more familiar and easier to grasp. The saying is cast in a hyperbole that contrasts the smallness of the grain of mustard (see 13:31–32) with the mountain. The explanation removes any idea that the power communicated to the disciples has any essential limitations; it was simply a lapse in that which is the basis of all the power that Jesus communicates. **21.** A number of mss. add this verse based on Mk 9:29 with the addition of "fasting" to "prayer"; but it does not belong to the critical text.

122 (r) The Second Prediction of the Passion (17:22–23). The "gathering" of the disciples is for the journey to Jerusalem (19:1). Mt omits Mk's notice (9:30) that Jesus traveled without wishing to be known, as well as Mk's statement that the prediction of the passion was the object of the teaching of Jesus. This prediction of the passion has fewer details than the other predictions; the slayers are simply "men," and the only detail added is that Jesus will be betrayed. Mk's frank statement that the disciples did not understand the saying is altered by Matthew, according to his practice, to a statement that they were grieved.

123 (s) The Temple Tax (17:24–27). This episode is peculiar to Mt; and it is another in this series of texts that raises Peter to a special position in the company of the disciples (see 16:13–23). But the position of Peter is not the main point of the story. According to Ex 30:13–15 (a late passage), each adult male Jew owed a half-shekel annual tax for the maintenance of the Temple. The payment here is made in Attic coinage; the double drachma was equal to a half-shekel and the stater, four drachmas, was payment for two persons. **24.** *Peter:* Aware of Jesus' habitual observance of the Law joined with affirmation of his independence of the Law, Peter assured the collectors that Jesus paid the tax. This passage gives occasion for a saying. **25.** *their sons:* The "sons" from whom the kings of the earth do not collect taxes are the subjects of the king as opposed to residents who are citizens of other countries. Rome at this period did not tax Roman citizens; the revenues of the government were obtained by taxing allies, provinces, and satellite kingdoms. **26.** Jesus claims the same freedom for himself and for his disciples; by their association with him they share to this extent in his own freedom. **27.** *not to give offense:* The reason for paying the tax is purely to avoid scandal. The stater will be obtained by catching a fish. That foreign objects are often found in fish is not to the point. It is remarkable that there is no statement that the coin was actually found in this manner.

The saying and the construction of the dialogue in which it occurs seem to reflect the position of Jewish Christians in the first generation of the Church toward the Temple tax. They regarded themselves as Jews and observed the Law and the cult. But the idea of freedom was not limited to Paul and Hellenistic Christian communities. If Jewish Christians paid the Temple tax, it was to preserve the decencies and not because they lay under the obligation of the Law to pay the tax. Jesus is greater than the Temple (12:6).

124 **(B) Discourse: The Sermon on the Church (18:1–35).** From 18:1–14 this discourse is almost entirely drawn from Mk with some additions from Q; the rest of the discourse is peculiar to Mt. The theme of the discourse is the relations between the disciples. The word *ekklēsia* occurs here for the second and last time in the Gospels. Mt arranges the sayings to fit the idea of a community with many close relations between the members. The discourse is not "ecclesiastical" in the sense that it speaks of the structure of the Church; no officer of the Church is mentioned, and the single allusion to pre-eminence in the Church is followed by a warning against pride of place. The discourse sets forth the spirit that should be exhibited by the members in their relations with one another. The topics are not treated in a logical and consecutive structure.

125 (a) Greatness in the Reign (18:1–5). The theme of this saying appears elsewhere in the Gospel; see 20:26–27; 23:11–12. Mk (9:33–37) has combined two unrelated sayings in a single unit by the catchword "child." Matthew has rewritten Mk in such a way as to reduce the two sayings to one; but he adds the second saying of Mk in an appendix (18:5). **1.** *who is the greatest:* The saying in Mk arises from a dispute among the disciples, a dispute they recognize as altogether foreign to the mind of Jesus. Mt omits this unflattering detail and has the disciples ask the question about rank directly. *reign:* Here, as in a few other passages, *basileia* is more properly translated "kingdom," referring to the community of the Church. The question is not unrelated to the position among the disciples (see 16:13–23). **2.** *calling a child to him:* The answer is given by bringing the child into the group; even in the modern Near East it is rare that a group of adults gathers without at least one small child standing right behind them. **3.** *unless you become...:* The saying is closely related to Mk 10:15 and nearly identical with Lk 18:17 (Q par.). Becoming like a child is not only a condition for greatness in the reign, it is a condition of admission. **4.** *whoever humbles himself:* Mt adds the precept of lowering oneself to clarify what is meant by becoming like a child. In ancient law the child was not a person in the full legal sense. He was not only under the authority of the parents, he was their property; he had no power of self-assertion and no power of independent action. This "denial of self" (16:24) is the proper posture of those who would be "great"—that is, the bearers of authority—in the reign. **5.** The saying is joined to the preceding by the catchword "child." "Child" here is possibly not meant in its literal sense, although the same idea is stated in 19:10–13; the word may designate the simple who become disciples and who already have that simplicity that Jesus states as the condition of membership. With these "little ones" Jesus identifies himself. Elsewhere those who receive the disciples receive Jesus (10:40).

126 (b) Scandals (18:6–9). By a change from "child" to "little ones" the association is retained, but the little ones become more clearly the simple disciples "who believe." **6.** *scandalizes:* That is, causes to stumble (see comment on 11:6). Presumably the simple are in greater danger of being misled (see 11:6). The words of Jesus are severe. *great millstone:* A millstone drawn by an ass would be notably larger than the hand millstone so frequently found in Palestinian sites and of a type still used; actually the hand millstone is large enough for the purpose, but by hyperbole probably the larger stone is meant. This is a flat circular stone that is revolved over the lower stone, of corresponding shape and size, to make meal. A favorite material is basalt, which has a high specific gravity. **7.** This verse is peculiar to Mt; it is an assertion of the ineradicable malice of man, which brings woe to the world. The inevitability of the scandal, however, does not excuse the individual person who is responsible for it. **8–9.** These sayings already occur in 5:29–30. Here Mt follows the text of Mk more closely, but compresses the first two of Mk's pronouncements into one. The obstacle, the object by which one is tempted to sin, may be in oneself as well as in another person. A woe cannot be pronounced upon the self, but the occasion of offense must be removed. The fact that the saying is couched in a rather intense hyperbole does not entitle interpreters to reduce it to a vague form of spiritual detachment. *eternal fire:* This and "the Gehenna of fire" are derived from Jewish literature; and the image in turn is derived from Is 66:24 (quoted by Mk 9:48, but not by Mt). "Gehenna" (Gk *geenna*) refers to the ravine S of Jerusalem (the modern Wadi er-Rababy), which in ancient times was the place where rubbish was burned. In Is the bodies of the enemies of Israel are thrown here.

The sayings on scandal are addressed to the entire group of disciples; but without any direct reference to the leaders in the Church, it is evident that the words of Jesus about the scribes and Pharisees (see v. 23) show that these words have a special reference to those in the Church who by their position of leadership are both better able and more likely to place obstacles in the way of the simple. The saying is addressed to all members; but the "little ones" are presumably mentioned in contrast to "the greater."

127 (c) The Lost Sheep (18:10–14). This parable comes from Q; but it has different forms and different applications in Mt and in Lk. Lk gives the parable as the answer of Jesus to the charge that he fraternizes with tax collectors and sinners; in Mt it illustrates the saying of 18:10 (peculiar to Mt) addressed to the disciples. **10.** *little ones:* Again the simple disciples are meant, whom the "great" may be tempted to despise. But the simple have powerful friends: "their" angels. The belief that angels guard the righteous appears in the OT and very frequently in the literature of Judaism (Str-B 1, 781–83). *see the face:* A technical term that designates the prerogative of those members of a royal court who immediately attend upon the king; the phrase shows the intercessory power of the angels. **11.** Some mss. add this verse taken actually from Lk 19:10.

12. The precept is reinforced by the parable of the shepherd. The shepherd can with some assurance leave the entire flock alone for a short time even in the mountains (Lk, "in the desert"); sheep are gregarious and do not readily scatter. But the one that has strayed may have fallen and must be sought out. The parable does not suggest that one person is equal in value to one hundred, but that the shepherd must not let one go because it is only one. It is the will of the Father that not even one should perish. Deliberately or not, the passage echoes the words about the watchman in Ez 33:1–9. The responsibility that Jesus takes as his own in Lk becomes the responsibility of the shepherds in the Church in Mt.

128 (d) Fraternal Correction (18:15–20). This passage shows one of the ways in which the members of the Church must seek out the sheep that has wandered. To the saying about correction is added a saying about prayer (19–20). The passage is peculiar to Mt. **15.** *sins against you:* Many Gk mss. (and the Vg) add the prepositional phrase "against you" (*eis se*); but it does not belong to the critical text. The duty of correction is therefore not limited to offenses that are personal. The whole point of the preceding parallel would be annulled by this reservation. Any individual member of the community should try to "gain" the offending brother, the stray sheep; and this is done privately, so that the brother is not humiliated. **16.** But should he be recalcitrant, a few witnesses are to be summoned for another reproval. In the law of Dt 19:15 the evidence of a single witness is not enough for a conviction; the principle is applied here somewhat loosely. The witnesses are to add weight to the reproval, which they can only do by sharing it. **17.** Failure to heed this more solemn warning demands that the process be brought before the *ekklēsia*, here the local church community. A similar procedure was used in the Qumran community (1QS 5:25–6:1; cf. H. Braun, *TRu* 28 [1962] 134–36). *as a Gentile and a tax collector:* If the offender will not accept the verdict of the Church, he must be expelled from membership. Expulsion was used by Paul against an offender at Corinth (1 Cor 5:1–5). The words of excommunication are strangely discordant with the general tone of the Gospels, in which Jesus is called a friend of sinners and tax collectors; and these classes as well as Gentiles are sometimes praised for their faith and repentance. The words are a stock phrase to designate those who were unacceptable within the Jewish community. Together with other features of the passage, they suggest that this saying was formed within the primitive Jewish Christian community. **18.** *bind... loose:* See comment on 16:19. In this context the words clearly have the force of "condemn" or "acquit." The whole assembly of the Church has the power that is given to Peter in 16:19; and it should be noticed that the acts of the Church in Acts are always the acts of the whole Church, not of its officers. The apostolic Church was a true assembly.

19–20. The idea of assembly leads by association to the next saying. *should two of you agree:* This saying affirms the efficacy of the common prayer of the Church, but common prayer does not mean the prayer of the entire Church; even two or three form an assembly where the prayer of the Church is offered. The reason for this efficacy is that Jesus himself is present in any community of Christians, and two or three are as small a number as one can have in a community. The idea of Christian community expressed here seems to reflect a more developed conception of the Church; and the saying, like the saying that precedes it, appears to derive its form from the primitive Church.

129 (e) Forgiveness (18:21–22). The saying is a development by Mt of a saying found in Q (Lk 17:4). Mt makes it an answer to a question asked by Peter. *seven times:* If account is taken of the symbolic value of the number seven, it should signify a definite but not specified number; there should be a point at which forgiveness becomes perfect, and the duty to forgive ceases if the offense continues. By the multiplication of seven by itself and ten Jesus uses another symbolic significance of the number and makes the number indefinite; no definite number makes forgiveness perfect. The phrase surely echoes the saying of Lamech in Gn 4:24, in which a limit is denied to the satisfaction of blood revenge. The Gospel inverts the old dispensation.

130 (f) The Parable of the Unmerciful Servant (18:23–25). This parable, peculiar to Mt, is one of the sternest passages of the Gospels. It reinforces the duty of forgiveness by appealing to another motive: the forgiveness granted by man to man as a condition of forgiveness granted to man by God (see 6:15). **23.** *the reign of God:* Again, that to which the "king" is likened is rather the "kingdom," the community of the Church; the parable describes conditions in the Church. The king is an Oriental despot, and the "slave" with the immense debt is not a domestic; he is a high officer of state, a viceroy, who has the disposal of enormous funds and has defaulted in his payment of revenue. **24.** *ten thousand talents:* The value of the talent cannot be reckoned in terms of modern coinage with any degree of accuracy; the sum of 10,000 talents is intended to represent an incredibly large sum, something like the national debt of the United States falling upon a single citizen. **25.** *to be sold:* The unreal sum is matched with a very realistic and common procedure, the sale of the man and his family into slavery for debt; but the sale would not pay the debt. **26.** *imploring him:* The slave promises payment, and the king not only accepts the promise but forgives the whole debt. This generosity is contrasted with the attitude of the slave, who assaults and imprisons a fellow slave for a debt of 100 denarii, a comprehensible sum;

the denarius was the daily wage of common casual labor (20:2). **34.** *until he would pay all his debt:* The king punishes the slave with torture because he has not forgiven as he was forgiven; torture does not repay the debt, and no end to the torture is possible under these conditions.

The parable illustrates the principle that details should not be allegorized. The conduct of the king is not a model by which we should learn the providence of God. The detail that is most significant is the difference in the debt owed by the merciless servant and the debt that he claims. The model is the forgiveness of God, which knows no limit; and neither should man's forgiveness. If man does not forgive, he cannot expect forgiveness; if he does not renounce his own claims, which are small, he cannot ask God to dismiss the claims against him.

131 **(VI) Book Five: Judea and Jerusalem (19:1–25:46).** The events of this book represent a very brief period; as in the preceding books, there is a narrative section and a discourse (for the treatment of ch. 23, → 16 above).

(A) Narrative Section: Journey to Jerusalem and Events There (19:1–23:39). The journey to Jerusalem is related in chs. 19–20, and the entire remainder of the Gospel covers a period of eight days from the entrance into Jerusalem to the day of the resurrection.

(a) Marriage, Divorce, and Celibacy (19:1–12). The opening verse is Mt's standard concluding formula to the discourses. The geography, vague in Mk (10:1–12), becomes impossible in Mt; there was no "Judea across the Jordan." The phrase somewhat clumsily designates a journey from Galilee to Judea through eastern Palestine; this route would avoid the territory of the Samaritans. For Mk's "taught," Mt has "healed" (19:2).

3. The discussion on marriage and divorce is a fuller treatment of the principle stated in 5:31–32. Mt adds that the Pharisees' question was posed as a "temptation." *for any cause:* The question is rephrased so that it does not deal simply with divorce (Mk 10:2) but with divorce "for any cause"; Jesus is asked to give an opinion on the dispute between the rabbinical schools of Hillel and Shammai (Str-B 1, 303–321). Hillel permitted divorce literally "for any cause," but Shammai permitted it only for adultery. It is rather important in interpreting Mt to notice the question. Mt has transposed Mk 10:4–5 so that these verses follow 19:6. **4.** *have you not read:* Jesus' answer is given in good rabbinical style by quoting the text of the Law; he appeals to Gn 1:27 and 2:24 as arguments for a permanent state of unity created by marriage. The quotations follow the LXX rather closely, but the LXX here is faithful to the MT. **6.** *what God has joined:* Since this union is a work of creation and formally stated in the Law, it is the work of God, with which man may not tamper. This is an appeal to the primitive institution of marriage; Jesus goes behind the Law to creation, an argument that would not please the questioners but one they could hardly contest. **7.** *why then did Moses...:* Their rebuttal (placed in this position by Mt) asks why the Law makes provision for divorce (Dt 24:1). The obscure allusion to "some indecency" in this verse of Dt furnished the occasion for the various interpretations of Hillel and Shammai. **8.** *from the beginning it was not so:* The answer of Jesus is a candid devaluation of the Law (see 5:17–20). The law of divorce is a concession to "hardness of heart," a deviation from the original institution. Jesus then states the law as restored to its original force.

132 **9.** In Mk the statement (10:11) is given to the disciples alone, in Mt to the questioners. Mk's statement is written in the light of Roman law, which permitted either the husband or the wife to institute divorce. Mk's formula is a clear, total prohibition of divorce. Mt has in a briefer form the exception contained in 5:32 (→ 38 above). The preceding context is completely in harmony with the interpretation that Mt's statement does not contain an exception permitting divorce for adultery. The exception would be in open contradiction with the argument on which the statement is based and would place Jesus simply on the side of the school of Shammai. This opinion could have been given without the argument that is employed.

10. *if such is the case:* Only Mt reports the disciples' reaction: They do not understand an exception permitting divorce. Their naïve reaction was that the single state is preferable to an indissoluble marriage. By association this leads to another saying, found only in Mt. Indeed celibacy can be preferable to marriage, but not for many. **12.** Some live without marriage by reason of a natal defect or surgery; the state of celibacy is not always of one's own choice. But it is also possible for one to renounce marriage because of the reign of God. The statement is extremely daring in a Jewish context, and the final phrase, "Let him take who can," shows awareness of the challenge. For what purpose is this renunciation made? Jesus does not specify; but the saying is not unrelated to the sayings that insist on renunciation (see 19:29). If the Christian vocation can divide families, it can also detach one from founding a family. The saying has no antecedent in Judaism. Continence was practiced at Qumran, but it is not clear that it was more than temporary abstinence.

133 (b) The Blessing of the Children (19:13–15). In Mk (10:13–16) this episode is a saying-story; the readiness of Jesus to receive children is the occasion of the saying in Mk 10:15. But Matthew has transferred this saying to 18:3 (→ 125 above). He has made both the request of the parents and the action of Jesus more formal, even ritual, than they are in Mk; but he leaves out the embrace of the children. As usual, he omits Mk's notice that Jesus was irritated at the officiousness of the disciples. Mt's version of the incident has the same meaning as it has in Mk, even with the transfer of Mk 10:15 to another context. The main purpose is not to show the affability of Jesus—for modern readers one of the most precious traits of the Gospels. **13.** *children:* Jesus accepts the children because they are the "little ones," the simple to whom the gospel is proclaimed. The gospel was not literally proclaimed to children: but the dispositions demanded for the reception of the gospel impose upon the disciples the necessity of reducing self-importance. The lesson is the same as the lesson of 18:1–5; and the affability of Jesus toward children suits what is said of him in 11:19.

134 (c) The Rich Young Man (19:16–30). This passage, the source of the evangelical counsels in Catholic tradition, contains a number of sayings of Jesus that revolve about the theme of wealth. The sayings are set within a framework of dialogue. Matthew has made some changes in Mk (10:17–31) without altering the character of the sayings. He omits Mk's vivid description of the approach of the man and changes the form of both question and answer. **16.** *Master, what good deed...:* Matthew omits the adjective "good" modifying "master" (Mk 10:17) and changes the question to "What good shall I do?" This allows him to change the answer of Jesus; that Jesus should reject the title "good," and still more that he should affirm the exclusive goodness of God in such a way that he seemed to deny goodness of himself, was too difficult for Matthew to retain. *to have eternal life:* Jewish moral thinking underlies the man's question; "eternal life" has no reference to the peculiarly Christian idea of life developed in other NT books. **17.** *keep the commandments:* The answer of Jesus is also couched within the scope of Jewish moral thinking; five of the ten commandments are cited, with the addition of the commandment of love of God and neighbor. This last commandment is not found in Mk (10:19); but Mk adds "Do not defraud," omitted in Mt. Curiously Mt represents Jesus as eliciting the enumeration by a Socratic question; in Mk, Jesus himself enumerates the commandments. The way to eternal life in the answer is the way of Jewish morality; there is no call to faith in Jesus nor to any new morality. This is more contrary to the proclamation that Jesus gives elsewhere in the Gospels than most commentators have noticed; and the presentation must be meant to be pedagogical. **20.** *what do I still lack:* Jesus brings the man to the point where he himself asks for something more. The word "lack" is taken from the words of Jesus in Mk 10:21. Mk notes that Jesus looked on him and loved him; Matthew omits this trait, as he usually omits emotional expressions attributed to Jesus. Matthew calls the man "a youth," and this is probably derived from Mk 10:20; but the words of Mk suggest a mature man rather than a youth. **21.** *go, sell what you own:* The call to renunciation of wealth is then clear and unambiguous, echoing both the teaching of Jesus (6:19–21,24–34) and the practice of the primitive Church (Acts 2:44). These allusions must be remembered in interpreting the meaning of Mt's addition of the phrase, "If you would be perfect." "Perfect" here does not designate a special state within the community of the disciples; the man does not become a disciple, and the only invitation Jesus gives him is the call to renounce his wealth. As in 5:48 (Mt's only two uses of the word), "perfect" designates the quality of discipleship. The man is not invited to practice "evangelical counsels," but, as in Mk, to become a disciple of Jesus. **22.** The invitation is refused.

135 **23.** *it will be hard for a rich man:* The dialogue with the youth is followed by a saying of Jesus about riches and the reign; "reign" here suggests the idea of kingdom. Matthew omits the astonishment of the disciples and the repetition of the saying; this reflects the slowness of the disciples to understand, a trait that the Evangelist usually softens. **24.** *easier for a camel:* The figure of the camel and the eye of the needle means exactly what is said; it does not refer to a cable or a small gate of Jerusalem. **25.** *who can be saved:* The response of the disciples shows that they understood the saying clearly enough. Their question shows no great perception of the principles enunciated in such passages as the eight beatitudes. In popular Jewish belief wealth was one of the rewards God conferred upon righteousness; and the saying of Jesus was more paradoxical than modern readers perceive. **26.** The paradox is not softened by the saying that what is impossible with men is possible to God, and this does not mean that it is possible by a miracle for the rich to retain their wealth and still be saved. It means that God makes possible what man finds impossible—the renunciation of riches.

136 **27.** *then Peter said:* The question of Peter at this point seems to fall to a lower level; and Jesus' answer (Mk 10:29–30) makes no effort to raise the level. The reward of renunciation is put in terms that suit the tone of the question; and there may be more irony in the answer than most interpreters suspect. Matthew has tried to spiritualize the answer by compressing Mk's enumeration of the goods to be received a hundredfold and by the insertion of v. 28 (concerning the eschatological thrones). *judging the twelve tribes of Israel:* "Judge" is used here in the OT sense of "rule," not of passing a verdict. The Twelve are the leaders of the Church, and their position will be vindicated in the eschatological judgment. **29.** *manyfold:* The ironical answer concerning the "manyfold" (Mk, "hundredfold") may be couched in terms that reflect the communism of goods of the primitive Church; all will enjoy common possessions equally. The saying then returns to the words "eternal life," with which the passage began, and the question of the man is finally and fully answered. But the final answer is not the answer Jesus gave in 19:17. The dialogue, as we have seen, is constructed in a pedagogical manner. The answer given in terms of Jewish morality leads step by step to the revolution of Christian morality; and only then is it stated clearly that Jewish morality, unless it leads to the fullness of the gospel, does not serve its purpose.

30. This statement, which cryptically alludes to the reversal of social positions in the reign, is also found in 20:16, where it is better suited to the context.

137 (d) THE PARABLE OF THE LABORERS IN THE VINEYARD (20:1–16). This parable appears only in Mt; and it seems that it belongs to the "Jewish" Christians. No parable better illustrates the principle that allegorical interpretation is to be employed with great reserve; the vineyard, the denarius, the hours of the day when the men are hired, and the reverse order of payment have all been exploited for allegorical meaning. But the allegorical interpretations miss the point, and are mostly in contradiction with each other. The parable illustrates the dreadful condition of casual labor in the Hellenistic-Roman world, but that is not the point. **1.** *to hire laborers:* Employers looked in the agora of the city for unemployed men waiting there to be hired. Such men worked for as little as the employer would pay. **2.** *denarius:* A coin representing subsistence wages at the lowest level for a day. As the day goes on and more laborers are needed, more are hired at the same wage. **11.** *they grumbled:* The dissatisfaction might seem reasonable to us; but the capitalist of the ancient world was master of his money, as the employer says (20:15). **14–15.** The laborers are rebuked not for dissatisfaction with what they receive, but for dissatisfaction that others receive as much; and the employer insists on his right to be generous. By giving to one he takes nothing away from another.

138 The most obvious meaning of the parable is that it compares Jews and Gentiles in the reign; the Gentiles are admitted late, but they are admitted on an equal standing with the Jews. We know that the controversy over the admission of Gentiles was the major problem of the apostolic Church, and that it was ultimately resolved in the manner indicated in the parable. The parable must reflect this experience. **16.** The saying does not really suit this situation because it is not a question of a reversal of positions—unless we suppose that from the Jewish-Christian point of view the admission of Gentiles on an equal plane was a degrading of the Jews.

But this parable, like others, may have several levels of meaning. Supposing that the interpretation indicated—the interpretation most widely accepted by the commentators—is the primary and basic interpretation, the position of the parable in the Gospel suggests that it may look in more than one direction. It is preceded by the promise that the Twelve will sit on 12 thrones, and it is followed very shortly by the request of the sons of Zebedee for the first places in the reign. Thus the parable may look not only to Jewish Christians as contrasted with Gentile Christians, but also at early disciples—even the Twelve—and others who became disciples much later. The parable indicates that an early call has no relevance to standing in the reign of God. Whenever one is admitted, one is admitted to full participation; the reign does not become the property of those who first sought admission, even if they are its officers.

139 (e) THE THIRD PREDICTION OF THE PASSION (20:17–19). See the first two predictions: 16:21 and 17:22–23. The predictions are evidently arranged in such a way that they increase in vividness and detail. Mt alone mentions the crucifixion, but all three versions of the predictions reflect the passion narratives. Mt, following Mk (10:32–34), mentions the betrayal, the condemnation by the Jewish council, and the execution of the sentence by the Romans ("the Gentiles"). Mt omits the wonder and fear the disciples exhibit when Jesus begins to lead them to Jerusalem; the emphasis falls upon the fact that Jesus foretold the events of the future.

140 (f) THE SONS OF ZEBEDEE (20:20–28). Lk 22:24–27 contains only the second part of the saying (= Mt 20:24–28) in a different context and in a different form; and this saying very probably was found both in Mk (10:35–45) and in Q. The boldness of the request of the two disciples and the depth of misunderstanding it implies is sufficient explanation for Lk's omission of the request. Matthew has softened the request in his own way by introducing the mother as the petitioner; but she does not appear after 20:21. Though Matthew adds the mention of the mother, he abbreviates the request. The petition reflects popular messianic belief; but allusions to the glory of the Messiah are not missing in the Gospels, and it would be rather bold to say that Jesus never mentioned it. At the same time, the setting of the petition in the context immediately following the third prediction clearly emphasizes the common theme of the Gospels that the disciples did not grasp the reality of the sufferings of the Messiah. **21.** *that my two sons may sit:* The petition asks for the two first places; and the petition is related to the question of precedence in 18:1–5. This does not imply that it is merely a doublet of the earlier question; no doubt more than one saying circulated about this highly important principle. **22.** *are you able to drink the cup:* The answer of Jesus uses the metaphor of cup for suffering but omits Mk's metaphor of baptism, both used elsewhere. This association Jesus promises them. **23.** *prepared by my Father:* By referring the assignment of places to the Father, Jesus says nothing about his personal relations to the Father but simply removes the question from discussion (see 24:36). The saying about the cup is certainly not couched in a form determined by later events. James was executed by Herod Agrippa in AD 42 (Acts 12:2); but the NT knows nothing of any tradition about a martyrdom of John.

24. *when the ten heard it:* The indignation of the disciples is easy to understand; but it arose from the same motives that prompted the petition of the two disciples and is therefore rebuked by Jesus. The position of the leaders in the Church is contrasted with the position of the rulers of the nations; the type of rule described suggests the courts of Hellenistic kings and of satellite kings in the Roman empire such as Herod. **25.** *lord it over...exercise authority:* These words indicate absolute authority. This was the type of rule familiar to most subjects in the ancient world; Jesus is not judging this use of power favorably, nor is he condemning it. He simply describes existing institutions. **26.** But absolute power is not to be used by the leaders in his Church. If the leaders wish to know how they should use their authority, they should consider that in the Church, social positions have been reversed; leaders in the Church are to be slaves. In the ancient world the slave was legally not a human person. This represents the lowest social stage (like the child in 18:2–4), the class of persons who are unable to impose their will on anyone but must suffer the imposition of the will of others. **27.** This is the position that the first among the disciples should consider proper to himself in the Church. **28.** Jesus adds that this is his own position. He has become the servant of all, and the service that is imposed upon him is the supreme sacrifice of life. It should be noticed that the term "ransom" follows the context of service. The ransom, the price paid, means that Jesus describes himself as reduced to the level of a means by which a purpose is achieved for others. The value of his life is determined not by self-assertion or self-aggrandizement even in a legitimate sense, but simply in terms of its value for other persons. This carries out the figure of the slave, who could have no personal ends to achieve.

141 (g) THE HEALING OF TWO BLIND MEN (20:29–34). This is the final miracle story in the account of the public ministry of Jesus; it occurs just before the entrance into Jerusalem. Matthew has abbreviated Mk (10:46–52). by the omission of the name of the blind man and of picturesque details, but he has some interesting variations. As in the story of the demoniac of Gadara (8:28), he has two men instead of one. He adds the kind of detail that he usually omits and that is not given in Mk, the mention of Jesus' compassion and of his touching the eyes (→ 65 above).

The story illustrates the rise of messianic feeling as Jesus approaches Jerusalem. Even blind men know who Jesus is, and they greet him with the Messianic title "Son of David" (see comment on 9:27). The impatience of the crowd with the noise of the beggars has no theological implications; it is simply a normal reaction to their importunity. When the blind men are cured, they follow Jesus—that is, they join the crowd that is gathering to accompany Jesus into Jerusalem. There is no longer any precept of silence nor any effort to restrain enthusiasm; Jesus is ready to enter Jerusalem acclaimed as Messiah because he will shortly demonstrate how the Messiah is to accomplish his saving act.

142 (h) THE ENTRY INTO JERUSALEM (21:1–9). The action in this incident is continuous from the preceding passage; Mt, following Mk, puts all these episodes into a single day, the description of which ends at 21:17. The scene is a Messianic display. **1.** *Bethphage:* The village, where the incident begins, cannot be precisely located; it lay on the slopes of the Mount of Olives. **2.** *go into the village:* Matthew abbreviates the instructions of Jesus to the two disciples (see Mk 11:2–3). *a she-ass and a colt:* This is a striking variation from the colt mentioned in Mk; the alteration is made in view of 21:5. Matthew also omits Mk's account of how events proceeded according to the instructions of Jesus. **3.** *the Lord:* It is not without interest that the Greek of 21:3 can also mean "The owner has need of them [it]." There is no other parallel in the Syn to the use of the title *Kyrios* in the sense in which it is used of Jesus in the Pauline epistles; this title was understood to belong to Jesus after his resurrection. **4.** A fulfillment text is introduced (see comment on 1:22). The text is compiled from Is 62:11, the introductory line, and Zech 9:9, both quoted according to the LXX, but with the omission of a phrase in Zech that alludes to the victory of the king. The text of Zech includes the king among the "lowly" (see comment on 5:3,5) and lacks the usual traits of the royal messianic figure. Although only Mt quotes the verse, the scene appears to be a deliberate re-enactment of the prophetic saying. This was the only type of Messianic claim Jesus would publicly profess—the claim to be the Messiah who was one of the lowly. The mention of the ass and the colt in Zech is nothing but poetic parallelism, the use of two words to indicate a single animal; but Matthew has taken the verse with rigorous literalism; therefore he not only has the disciples take two animals but actually has Jesus riding both of them (21:7).

The ride into Jerusalem then becomes a Messianic procession, with a large crowd taking part in the acclamations. **8.** *spread their cloaks:* The spreading of cloaks in the paths was in imitation of the red-carpet treatment accorded royalty in the ancient world. *others cut branches:* The branches were also intended to soften the road. It is curious that none of the three Syn mentions the palms, which have become traditional in the liturgical commemoration of the procession; these occur in Jn 12:13. **9.** *hosanna:* The acclamations of the crowd are based on Ps 118:25–26. The Hebr word *hôšî'āh-nā'* becomes in Gk *hōsanna* (really = Aram *hôša'-nā'*), lit., "save, we pray"; but in these Gospel passages it has become a shout of acclamation with no regard to its meaning. *he who comes:* A Messianic title (see comment on 11:2); Mt adds "Son of David," a more explicit Messianic title (see comment on 9:2). The shout of *hōsanna* and the use of branches suggest the ritual of the Jewish Feast of Tabernacles.

143 (i) THE PURGING OF THE TEMPLE (21:10–17). Mk (11:15–19) places this episode on the day following Jesus' entry into Jerusalem, but Matthew makes it part of a climactic description of the first day of Jesus in Jerusalem. Mt alone relates that the whole city was stirred at his entry. **10.** *stirred:* Lit., "shaken," the word that would be used to describe an earthquake. This effect on the whole city heightens the import of the Messianic procession. **11.** *the prophet:* It is strange, however, that the Messianic titles do not appear in the words of "the crowds"; Jesus is not described as the king but as the prophet from Nazareth (→ Aspects NT Thought, 78:14).

The purging of the Temple is put at the end of the public ministry by the Syn, at the beginning by Jn (2:13–22); Jn for his own reasons has adopted an artificial chronology (→ Gospel Jn, 63:65). **12.** *the Temple:* The Gk phrase *to hieron* designates the entire temple complex of courts and buildings. The business, however, could only have been transacted in the Court of the Gentiles, the outermost court into which any person could enter. The business was the sale of animals for sacrifice; the doves that were used by the poor as substitutes for the larger animals required of the wealthy are mentioned explicitly. *the money-changers:* Still a regular part of the Near Eastern urban scene, they performed a necessary service in a period when all sorts of coins were in circulation. It is assumed by commentators that these commercial services were a concession of the priests of the Temple; and it is difficult to see how such business could have been conducted without their participation. Jesus therefore attacked the Jerusalem hierocracy directly; this body appears rarely in the Gospels before the arrival in Jerusalem, but it is frequently mentioned thereafter. **13.** *it is written:* Jesus justifies his action by a quotation of the OT combined form Is 56:7 and Jer 7:11 (quoted according to the LXX). Mt (and Lk) omit the phrase found in Mk (11:17), "for all nations." For Mt at least, the omission may be deliberate; the worship of the true God is to be communicated through Jesus the Messiah and not through the Temple of Jerusalem. The action of Jesus is a Messianic action. It corresponds to his assertion of supremacy over the Law (see 5:17–42; 12:1–14; 12:22–37). He asserts also his authority over the Temple, the second great institution of Judaism of the time. This leads to a question about his authority (see 21:23–27). By actions like this Jesus shows that he recognizes none of the existing authorities in Judaism; the implication that he has a greater authority is clear.

144 (j) THE CURSING OF THE FIG TREE (21:18–19). This episode is so difficult that it is omitted in Lk. Mt's abbreviations leave out some of the details, but the most startling alteration is that the fig tree withers instantly at the words of Jesus; in Mk the tree is seen to be withered when the party passes it on the following morning. Mk apparently has transformed a prophetic saying into a slow miracle, whereas Mt has transformed the slow miracle into an instantaneous miracle. The saying of Jesus is symbolic. It was not the season for the fig tree to bear fruit, but it did bear leaves. This is a symbol of Judaism, which has the appearance of religion without the reality. The words are addressed not to the fig tree but to Judaism; Judaism has come to its final crisis, and has rendered itself unproductive.

145 (k) THE INTERPRETATION OF THE FIG TREE (21:20–22). The lesson of the fig tree is the same in Mt as in Mk, in spite of Mt's modifications in the cursing of the fig tree. But in neither Gospel can these sayings be in their original context. The withering of the fig tree becomes the occasion of sayings on faith, and the symbolism of the barren fig tree is left without explanation. Mt has already given these sayings in very nearly the same form (17:20); and Lk has them in a different context (17:6). Their attachment to the story of the fig tree is later than the transformation of the saying-story into a miracle story. This apparently had already happened in the sources of Mk.

146 (l) THE AUTHORITY OF JESUS (21:23–27). Here Mt follows Mk (11:27–33) with no more than a few insignificant omissions. Both in Mt and Mk the question of the chief priests and elders (Mk adds "scribes") belongs properly after the purging of the Temple. Composition from various sources has put it back here, where it now refers to all of the words and works of Jesus. **23.** *by what authority:* A question of a commission can refer only to his extraordinary act in purging the Temple. **24–25.** The answer of Jesus is a counterquestion about the commission of John the Baptist. The Gospels reconstruct the attitude of the religious leaders of the Jews with little credit to the leaders; if they admit John's divine commission they convict themselves of unbelief, and if they deny it they risk inciting mob anger. Actually the evasion would have incited mob anger just as much; it is equivalently a refusal to recognize in John a man sent by God. The refusal of Jesus to answer the question about his own commission is a tacit rejection of the authority of the questioners. If they are religious leaders, teachers of the Law and cultic officers, they should be able to fulfill one of their fundamental responsibilities: to discern true and false prophets. **27.** *we do not know:* They have professed themselves unable to reach a decision about the most prominent figure in their day before Jesus himself. This confession of incompetence releases Jesus from any obligation to submit himself to their judgment.

This is the first of five controversy stories in the days preceding the passion (see 22:15–22).

147 (m) THE PARABLE OF THE TWO SONS (21:28–32). This parable, found only in Mt, stands as the first of three parables that deal with the same basic theme. The contrast between verbal rebellion and ultimate obedience as opposed to verbal obedience and failure to act is clear, and the adversaries themselves are compelled to admit that action is the test of obedience (see 7:21). **31.** *tax collectors and prostitutes:* The application to the Jewish leaders contrasts them with the despised classes of tax collectors and prostitutes, who "push ahead" of them into the reign; the word is vivid. **32.** *in a way of righteousness:* This does not mean that John led a righteous life but that he showed a way by which men could become righteous. The work the Jews profess but do not execute is not the observance of the Law but the work of faith. They have not admitted that the life of the Law leaves room for the repentance proclaimed by John and by Jesus as a condition of entrance into the reign. They have met the supreme demand of Judaism with professions of obedience. In its present form the parable no doubt reflects the faith of the Gentiles as contrasted with the unbelief of the Jews.

148 (n) THE PARABLE OF THE WICKED HUSBANDMEN (21:33–46). Matthew has somewhat expanded this parable in order to make the point entirely clear, although the parable is not obscure in Mk. The description of the vineyard is given in words that closely echo Is 5:2, where the vineyard symbolizes Israel. The parable of Jesus has allegorical features. The owner is an absentee landlord, and in the NT world such disputes between landlords and tenants were not unknown. **34.** *he sent his slaves:* Matthew increases the number of the slaves so that their allegorical significance may be completely clear; the slaves represent the prophets (see 23:29–31). **37.** *he sent his son:* The allegorical significance of the son is not equally clear. No OT figure can be intended; and the death of John the Baptist cannot be attributed to the Jews. If the son is an allegorical figure, he can represent no one but Jesus; and one would expect more to be made of this feature of the parable. **38.** *let us kill him:* As a suggestion that Jesus himself is the son who is killed, this passage is extremely delicate; that it is an ecclesiastical expansion inserted in the primitive Church seems unlikely, because it is a part of the climactic structure of the parable. Some scholars have proposed that the entire parable is of ecclesiastical origin; but most recent commentators do not favor this opinion, in spite of the allegorical elements in the parable.

The plan of the tenants to kill the son is not unrealistic, as J. Jeremias has pointed out (*The Parables of Jesus* [rev. ed.; N.Y., 1963] 76). When a proselyte died intestate, his property became unoccupied land that went to the first claimant; and the tenants had the first opportunity to claim by occupation. **41.** It is not without interest that Mt, for which an Aram original is alleged, is the only one of the three Gospels that has a pure Gk play on words: "Evilly those evil men he will destroy." Mt heightens the tension by the dialogue form, which elicits the words of condemnation from the Jews themselves. The application of the parable is much more explicit in Mt than it is in Mk or Lk. **42.** The quotation of Ps 118:22–23 (LXX) is applied in a broad sense; and as it stands it can refer only to the admission of the Gentiles to the Church. Quite possibly this biblical explanation of the parable is an ecclesiastical expansion. **43.** The same is almost certainly to be said of Mt's addition, where the displacement of the Jews in favor of the Gentiles is suggested beyond all doubt. It was hardly necessary for Matthew to retain Mk's notice that the chief priests and Pharisees recognized that Jesus spoke about them. The high popular esteem in which Jesus was held kept them from action at the moment. This esteem is often attested in the Gospels; how deep it was cannot be said, but it should be remembered when the question of the general popular Jewish attitude toward Jesus arises. The agents of hostility in the passion narratives are the religious leaders of Judaism, not the mass of the people.

149 (o) THE PARABLE OF THE WEDDING FEAST (22:1–14). The dissimilarities in detail between Mt and Lk are so great that there is room for doubt that both Gospels are using the same source (Q); but the evidences of extensive rewriting in Mt are clear. Instead of a dinner Mt has a royal wedding feast; in addition to the excuses presented by the guests in Lk, Mt introduces a violently discordant note in the killing of the messengers and the ensuing war. This feature very probably represents the destruction of Jerusalem by the Romans in AD 70; it is not intruded into an existing form of the parable but is the reason for the change of the main figure of the parable from a host to a king. **8.** *those invited were not worthy:* These guests are intended to signify both the Jewish people and their leaders; in Lk only the Jewish people as a whole are meant. In Lk the parable then proceeds to the call of the Gentiles, signified by the invitation of anyone who happens to be in the neighborhood. **11.** Matthew has altered this part of the parable in such a way that it becomes a second parable. The theme of this modification is set by the introduction of the phrase "good and bad" (22:10). Even after the rejection of the guests first invited, one still appears who is not suitably attired for a wedding feast; a clean white garment was the proper dress for such festivities. This feature should not be forced into an allegorical significance. The point of the second parable is that the reign contains wicked as well as righteous, the same point that is made in the parables of the tares and the net (see 13:36–43,47–50). In these parables the mixed condition of the Church endures until the Judgment. **13.** Matthew by the use of his tag line (see 8:12; 13:42,50) introduces an eschatological note that changes the image of the wedding feast from the Church to the eschatological Messianic banquet. The punishment is instant and severe.

14. Language is used here that later became the language of predestination. No complex theological theory lies behind the verse. The parable represents God as making every effort to bring guests to the eschatological feast; the invitation to all who pass on the highways and byways, even "the good and the bad" (as contrasted with Lk's beggars, destitute, blind, and lame) is clear. All these are called; the chosen are those who accept the call and do not reject the invitation, like the first guests, or who do not accept it fully, like the man who comes to dinner but is too much of a boor to dress in the proper manner. Because the parable does not exhibit Matthew's usually fine literary unity and coherence, there is no reason to postulate a compilation from various sources; rather it is a rare example of substantial rewriting by Matthew; and it shows that he did not rewrite skillfully.

150 (p) THE QUESTION OF TRIBUTE PAID TO CAESAR (22:15–22). This is the second of the five controversy-stories in this section (see 21:23–27). The narrative is taken from Mk (12:13–17) with only slight revisions; Lk (20:20–26) has altered it more extensively. **16.** *the Herodians:* The Pharisees make common cause with the Herodians to "trap" Jesus. The Herodians (see Mk 3:6) were supporters of the dynasty of Herod, represented at the time by Herod Antipas, tetrarch of Galilee. The Herodian fortunes were founded on unswerving loyalty to Rome; Herod the Great had proved this by magnificent political dexterity during the civil wars that followed the assassination of Julius Caesar. **17.** *taxes:* The position of the Herodians on the payment of the poll tax (Gk *kēnsos* = Lat *census*) exacted by the Romans was clear. The party of the Zealots refused to admit the subjection of the people of God to a foreign power; the theoretical position of the Pharisees was identical with the position of the Zealots, but they did not believe in the use of force to achieve independence. The question was bound to alienate one party or the other. The flattering words in which Jesus is addressed suggest that he was expected to take the Zealot position; this, as Lk (20:20) says, would render him liable to arrest. **18.** *Jesus perceived their malice:* In Mk mention is made of the "hypocrisy" of the Pharisees. **19.** *the tax coin:* Jesus calls for the actual coin, the denarius, for his answer. The right to mint coinage is an act of sovereignty, and it was jealously guarded by the Roman government. Satellite kings and free cities were permitted to issue coins, but it was clearly understood that this was done with Roman authorization. The minting of coins without authorization was an act of rebellion. **20.** *whose likeness...:* The coin provides an answer to the question; it belongs to Caesar, and it is within his power to demand it.

Jesus thus rejects the position of the Zealots without accepting the position of the Herodians. Effectively his answer evades the question rather than solves it. He does not appeal to right but simply to the *de facto* existence of Caesar's power, symbolized by Caesar's coinage. Whether Caesar has a right to rule is not touched by the answer. The explanation, "Give Caesar what is his and God what is his," offers no basis for a theory of politics. Jesus certainly did not intend to divide the world into areas belonging to Caesar and God, each with his respective and exclusive jurisdiction. Nor did he answer the question what belongs to Caesar and what belongs to God. This he left to the personal decision of each man, who must solve the problem of the opposing claims of God and Caesar. The saying is valid here that no man can serve two masters (6:24).

151 (q) MARRIAGE AND THE RESURRECTION (22:23–33). This is the third of the controversy-stories in this series. The Sadducees are less well known in biblical and extrabiblical sources than the Pharisees (→ History of Israel, 75:123–24). They were the party of the priestly aristocracy and seem to have represented the wealthy landowning class as well. They were thoroughly conservative. In politics they accepted the Roman rule of Palestine, and in theology they accepted only the Law as the basis of Judaism. They based their denial of the resurrection on the absence of the resurrection in the text of the Law.

Matthew has compressed Mk's account (12:18–27) without any significant change of the sense. The case presented to Jesus is intended by the Sadducees to show the absurdity of belief in the resurrection. **24.** *if a man dies without children:* The very free citation of the law of the levirate is based on Dt 25:5–6 and Gn 38:8, but it is not an exact quotation of either text; and Matthew has abbreviated the citation. The law of the levirate provided for continuity of the family. When a man died without children, his brother was obliged to have a child by the widow; the child would bear the name of the deceased. **29.** *you are wrong:* Jesus answers the case by denying the presupposition that marriage endures in the afterlife. The conception here is related to that expressed by Paul in 1 Cor 15:35–50; the resurrection is affirmed, but a transformation of the body is also affirmed. "Flesh and blood will not possess the reign." **30.** *like angels in heaven:* The example of the angels refers to a life in which sex plays no part; it does not designate the absence of the bodily component in the afterlife, for this would itself be a denial of the resurrection and an affirmation of Platonic immortality.

31–32. These verses are a supplementary argument about the resurrection independent of the question about the seven brothers. The Sadducees denied the resurrection because they could not find it in the Law. **32.** The argument of Jesus, genuinely rabbinical in character, is based on Ex 3:6. The patriarchs had been long dead when God spoke to Moses, yet God *is* the God of Abraham, Isaac, and Jacob. This he could not be if they had ceased to exist; therefore they must live in some way other than the life of the terrestrial body. The answer does indeed raise questions, but the Sadducees were unable to answer them. In their doctrine there was no relation between God and the dead, and they could not explain this text.

152 (r) THE GREATEST COMMANDMENT (22:34–40). This is the fourth of the controversy-stories. The three Syn diverge more than usual in their versions of this incident. Lk (10:25–28) has placed it in a different context and has appended to the discussion the parable of the Good Samaritan, peculiar to itself, the classic exposition of the meaning of the term "neighbor." Lk also makes the "lawyer" (more frequently "scribe," and always "scribe" in Mt except here) state the two commandments in answer to the question of Jesus. Mk, particularly by the addition of 12:32–34 (peculiar to itself), presents the scribe in a favorable light, and Jesus praises his answer. In Mt and Lk, however, the questioner is hostile and asks the question to "tempt" Jesus; in Mt he speaks as the representative of a conspiracy. Mt regularly views the scribes and Pharisees in a less friendly manner than the other Gospels.

36. *which is the greatest commandment:* The question is placed in terms of the rabbinical understanding of the Law. The rabbis counted 613 distinct commandments in the Law, of which 248 were positive precepts and 365 were prohibitions. These commandments were distinguished as "light" and "heavy" according to the seriousness of the subject. This type of question was normal in rabbinical discussion, and it is difficult to see how it could have been conceived as a "trial" of Jesus. On the other hand, he is represented as claiming the power to interpret the Law independently and even to restate it. **37.** *you shall love...:* The answer of Jesus quotes two texts of the Law that form the foundation of the new morality of the gospel. The commandments are quoted from Dt 6:5 and Lv 19:18. The text of Dt 6:5 forms a part of the Shema, the Jewish profession of faith; Mk quotes 6:4, the introductory verse. The novelty of the statement of Jesus does not consist in quoting this commandment; no rabbi could have called this anything but an excellent answer. The novelty consists in placing Lv 19:18 on the same level, making it equally "heavy." To this arrangement of the two commandments so that they become effectively one there is no parallel in Jewish literature. The *T. Issachar* (5:2 [*APOT* 2, 327]), often quoted in this connection, does indeed urge the love of God and of the neighbor; but these are not stated as the two greatest commandments of the Law, nor are they so explicitly given equal weight. **40.** *on these two commandments:* Mt alone adds that on these commandments "hang" the Law and the Prophets—that is, the entire revelation of the OT. Good works have value as acts of the love of God and of the neighbor.

153 (s) THE SON OF DAVID (22:41–46). This is the fifth and last of the controversy-stories. Up to this point Jesus has responded to questions; now he himself puts an exegetical question to the Pharisees, which they cannot answer. Mt makes it much more explicit that he "tests" the Pharisees; in Mk (12:35–37a) he "teaches," and in Lk (20:41–44) he continues his discourse. **42.** *whose son is he:* In Mt the affirmation that the Messiah is the son (descendant) of David is elicited from the Pharisees. The Gk and the Eng versions of Ps 110:1 (quoted from the LXX except for one word) contain an ambiguity not found in the MT. The Jews of this period did not pronounce the divine name Yahweh, but substituted for it the title *'ădōnāy*, "lord" (lit., "my lords," a grammatical form used only of the deity); *'ădōnî*, "my lord," is in the OT the usual form of address to a king. Thus the Greek represents the pronunciation of the verse used at the time: "*'ădōnāy* said to *'ădōnî*," instead of "*Yahweh* said to *'ădōnî*." The question assumes several accepted rabbinical views in terms of which the question is put and within which it would have to be answered: (1) David wrote "in the spirit," under divine inspiration; (2) David is the author of Ps 110; (3) *'ădōnî* designates the Messiah. The modern exegete would solve the problem by rejecting the authorship of David and the assumptions of (3). Within Jewish exegetical tradition this could not be done, and the problem remained insoluble. **45.** The saying is obscure, and modern commentators differ in its interpretation. That

Jesus meant to "teach" anything by proposing a question his adversaries could not solve and he did not solve seems doubtful. The question implies no claim of his own to the title of Messiah and Son of David; such a claim would have to be discussed on the basis of other texts. Nor does the question imply a rejection of the idea of king Messiah and Son of David. Jesus certainly did reject most aspects of the popular understanding of the king Messiah, but he does not do it here. Nor does he imply a deeper and mysterious reality in virtue of which the Messiah is both son of David and David's lord; this again would have to be discussed on the basis of other texts. The point of the story is that the Pharisees could not solve a simple exegetical problem. Jesus thus demonstrates that they are not competent religious teachers; even their vaunted skill of interpretation breaks down. They cannot be judges of the identity of the Messiah if they cannot deal with a messianic text. Whether they accept Jesus as the Messiah or not is meaningless because they do not understand the Scriptures in which the Messiah is revealed (→ Gospel Mk, 42:74).

154 (t) INVECTIVE AGAINST THE SCRIBES AND PHARISEES (23:1–36). Chapter 23 is a construction of Mt like the discourses previously noticed. In its present position it serves both as a conclusion of the controversy-stories and as an introduction to the eschatological discourse that follows (see 23:36). Mk has a much briefer invective against the Pharisees, but Matthew has made little use of Mk (12:37b–40). Some of the sayings come from Q (Lk 20:45–47; 11:39–51 par.), and the rest of the chapter is peculiar to Mt. The discourse frequently reflects the controversies between Jews and Jewish Christians; in its present form it clearly conveys the experiences of the Palestinian church and the fall of Jerusalem in AD 70. The discourse is composed of an introduction, seven woes against the scribes and Pharisees, and a conclusion. Mk speaks only of the scribes; Lk divides the woes between the scribes and the Pharisees. In all three Gospels the discourse is delivered to a crowd; Mt and Lk mention the disciples explicitly.

155 (i) *Introduction* (23:1–12). **1.** *the chair of Moses:* This designation of a teacher's podium is otherwise attested for the 4th cent. AD but not for NT times. The phrase is most probably a metaphor for the authority of the scribes to teach. In rabbinical tradition the interpretation of the Law was carried on in a scribal tradition that theoretically went back through an unbroken chain of scribes to Moses. This view is, of course, entirely unhistorical. Jesus does not discuss the historical character of the tradition, nor does he question the authority of the scribes to teach. The basis of this authority was no more than custom in the post-exilic Jewish community; the scribes grew up with the development of the Law as the basis of Jewish religion and life. **3.** *observe and do what they tell you:* Jesus does not attack the teaching of the scribes; actually there is a lack of consistency between this general statement and some particular interpretations of the Law that are discussed in Mt (see 5:17–42; 12:1–14; 15:1–20; 19:1–12). The position of Jesus toward the Law was variously interpreted in the apostolic Church (see 5:17–20), and for this reason the position of the apostolic Church was not clear and firm from the beginning. It can be said, however, that the Gospels contain no formal and total repudiation of the teaching authority of the scribes. What is principally criticized here is not the teaching of the scribes but their practice; it does not cohere with their teaching. **4–6.** These verses state two complaints: the rigor of scribal interpretation and the vanity and hypocrisy of the scribes and Pharisees (see 6:1–8,16–18). A general statement that scribal teaching is always rigorous would go too far. The text deals with attitudes, not with particulars, and the influence of Pharisaic theory and practice on interpretation led to a severe rather than a humane interpretation of the Law. This is verified not only by the incidents recorded in the Gospels but also by the Talmud. Rabbis themselves were sometimes as critical of rigorism as are the Gospels. The second complaint—vanity and hypocrisy—is expanded in 23:5–6, and it runs through much of the discourse. Jesus echoes the ancient prophetic charge of mere formalism in religion and adds to it the charge of vain display. **5.** *phylacteries:* Small boxes containing parchment on which is written the text of Ex 13:1–16; Dt 6:4–9 and 11:13–21. These were fastened to the left wrist and to the forehead in such a way that they hung in front of the eyes. Thus the injunction to keep the Law as a sign on the hand and as a memorial between the eyes (Ex 13:9; Dt 6:8; 11:18) was literally observed. *tassels:* On the four corners of the cloak tassels were worn in observance of Nm 15:38–39 as reminders of the Law. The size of these was obviously a token of great devotion; one need not look far for parallels in Christian devotional practices. **6.** *the place of honor at feasts:* The desire for such places in synagogues or at dinners is not well supported by the Talmud. These are ordinary marks of human vanity, and the protocol of precedence in modern times is as rigorous as anything found in Pharisaism. **7.** *salutations:* Near Eastern courtesy demanded that the length of the salutation be in proportion to the dignity of the person, and thus the greeting was a status symbol. This should be remembered. *rabbi:* The Aram title, "my master," was used for a teacher of the Law; it is attested for NT times only in the NT; but it appears in postbiblical Judaism and must have been coming into use at this time. The term or the Gk equivalent is often used by those who address Jesus in the Gospels.

8–12. These verses echo the theme of 18:1–5 and 20:23–28 and appear to be a digression originally unconnected with the invective against the scribes and Pharisees. Three honorific scribal titles are rejected: master (Aram *rabbî*), father (Aram *'abbā*), and teacher (Hebr *môrēh*). The title of "father" is not well attested in Jewish literature, but the text does not indicate that it was common. **8.** Honorific titles are rejected because the disciples are all brothers—there is one Father, God; and one teacher, the Messiah. Scarcely any verse in the Gospels is so clearly an ecclesiastical expansion as this one. This text would seem to exclude all honorific titles within the community of the disciples; Christian tradition has taken this verse in an extremely restricted literal sense, and even in this restricted interpretation has found room for the modern clerical title of "Father." Other honorific titles have not been considered excluded by this verse. **11.** A repetition of 20:26. **12.** This verse is used twice by Lk in different contexts (14:11; 18:14). The sense is not that one should await the place that God finally grants.

156 (ii) *The first woe* (23:13). The metaphor of the keys of the reign, used of Peter in 16:19, is applied to the scribes and Pharisees. The reign here means the reign inaugurated by the proclamation of Jesus. The Pharisees refuse to believe in Jesus, and they exclude from the Jewish community those who do believe. This modification of Lk 11:52 again seems to be an ecclesiastical expansion; Lk has a more difficult phrase, "the key of knowledge," which seems to be more original. **14.** This verse (Mk 12:40 par.) does not belong to the critical text of Mt and is omitted by modern editors.

157 (iii) *The second woe* (23:15). There is ample evidence that Jewish proselytism was extremely active in NT times. This missionary activity came to an end with the Jewish War and the destruction of Jerusalem in AD 70. *proselyte:* As contrasted with "the fearer of God," he accepted circumcision and the full observance of the Law. The "fearers of God" professed faith in one God and attended the synagogue but did not become full members of the Jewish community. *twice as much a son of Gehenna:* This is a very forceful expletive, and it is difficult to discern what lay at the base of this severe condemnation of proselytes. The verse must, it seems, reflect the experience of the apostolic Church (and most probably, as elsewhere in this discourse, the Jewish Christian community). It is very possible that proselytes showed greater hostility toward Jewish Christians, whom they regarded as renegades, than native Jews did.

158 (iv) *The third woe* (23:16–22). Here Pharisaic teaching is criticized. On the problem of oaths see 5:33–37. **16.** *blind guides:* See 15:14. The point at issue is the rabbinical teaching on the obligation of oaths. The examples used cannot be paralleled from the Talmud, but the principle that is attacked is easy to identify. The question is whether or not the formula of an oath is to be regarded as obligatory. One who wished to evade the obligation could seek out an interpretation that denied the validity of the formula used. One might illustrate in modern terms by saying that an oath by God would oblige, but an oath by Gosh or by Golly would not. The casuistry of such evasions is what Jesus attacks. If a man intends to swear, he swears. If he intends that another should think he swears, but deliberately uses a formula that he believes is invalid, he swears. This passage, like 5:33–37, is peculiar to Mt; and in these discussions of rabbinical casuistry we have the traditions of the Palestinian Christian community. But the vigor with which these evasions of truthfulness are attacked goes back to the source of the Gospel.

159 (v) *The fourth woe* (23:23–24). This woe again attacks the teaching of the scribes and Pharisees. The question at issue was what forms of produce came under the law of tithing. In the rigorist interpretation every natural growth was subject to the law; a more humane interpretation would limit the obligation to the traditional "grain, wine, and oil." Mint, dill, and cumin are examples of tiny seeds or plants, which it would be ridiculous to tithe. But Jesus does not object to this rigor in itself; he objects to the interest shown in such trivia while the "heavy" commandments (see 22:34–40) are ignored. The heavy commandments are cited as "judgment" (equivalent to "justice"), mercy, and fidelity. An example of the difficulty Gentile Christians had in apprehending such a thoroughly Jewish passage as this can be seen in Lk 11:42, which is put in much more general terms. **24.** *you strain at a gnat:* The final touch of ridicule is the example of straining out the gnat and swallowing the camel. In the ancient world, strainers were commonly attached to the mouths of decanters because any liquid might contain foreign matter. Pharisaic observance used the strainer not only for this purpose but also to strain out any unclean substance that one might inadvertently consume. Casuistry can get so lost in details that it forgets to ask simple questions like Is this fair? Is it decent? The camel was the largest animal known to Palestinians; to judge by the use of the camel in figures like this and in 19:24, such hyperbole was common in popular speech.

160 (vi) *The fifth woe* (23:25–26). In some instances Pharisaic devotion to cleanliness approached the fanatic (see 15:1–20). The dish and the cup here are not, however, meant literally; it is doubtful that Pharisaic practice would be content with washing the outside of the vessel. The vessels are metaphors for the person; and the woe is directed at the care for external correctness in observance without regard for the interior disposition. The vices mentioned are "plunder," not otherwise mentioned in Mt (but see Mk 12:40), and "intemperance," which is so remotely associated with plunder that the mss. have several variations, of which the colorless "injustice" is the favorite. The combination, however, does echo Am 2:6–8.

161 (vii) *The sixth woe* (23:27–28). These lines are similar in structure to the preceding woe. The whitewashing of tombs in present-day Palestine dates back to NT times, when it was common practice. Since contact with death caused Levitical uncleanness, the whitewashing served to identify the tombs and ward off those who might otherwise touch them accidentally. The interior of the tomb was the supreme degree of uncleanness and the figure is strong. **28.** The point is again Pharisaic practice. The vices cited are hypocrisy (the word is a refrain in the discourse) and lawlessness; the observance of the Law, of which the Pharisees boasted, was a cloak for a life that was lived in complete contradiction with the Law.

162 (viii) *The seventh woe* (23:29–36). This is the longest of the seven, and it no doubt reflects the execution of Jesus, the Messiah and the ultimate fulfillment of prophecy, and the attacks of Jewish authorities against the apostles and missionaries of the primitive Christian community. Hostility to the prophets is traced back in an unbroken chain to the origins of the nation—indeed, to the origins of humanity, for the series begins with Abel; and Israel could hardly be blamed for his death. The hostility of Israel to the prophets is somewhat schematized, just as Ezekiel traces the rebellion of Israel to its origins (Ez 16). There are few instances in the OT of prophets who were killed by the Israelites, nor is the number notably increased in the folklore of the apocryphal literature. The argument by which the present generation of Jews is linked with its ancestors in the killing of the prophets is somewhat involved and rabbinical in character.

29. *you build the tombs of the prophets:* By building the tombs of the prophets and disclaiming the actions of the ancestors, the Jews confess that they are sons of prophet-killers; and by the peculiar Hebr conception of sonship the designation, which they themselves accept, shows that they have the dispositions of their fathers. **32.** *fill up the measure of your fathers:* That is, by continuing to kill prophets. **33.** *brood of vipers:* See 3:7; 12:34. *being condemned to Gehenna:* The fate is inevitable. The whole passage is to be read in the light of the catastrophe of AD 70, but condemnation to Gehenna goes beyond God's judgments in history. **34.** *I will send you prophets:* The sending of "prophets, wise men, and scribes" (Lk 11:49, "prophets and apostles," a more candid allusion to Christian missionaries) is conceived in the same terms we find in Is 6:9–10 (see 13:10–15) and Ex 4:21; 7:3; 10:20,27. The benevolent purpose of divine revelation is frustrated by the unbelief of men, and the effect of the revelation is to harden the hearts of those who refuse to receive it. **35.** *from the blood of Abel:* The collective guilt of the murder of all the innocent from Abel to Zechariah is indeed a terrible load to bear; and it is here especially that the passage is to be understood in the light of the great catastrophe of AD 70, in which Jerusalem and the Temple were destroyed and thousands of Jews perished. To those who were accustomed to think biblically this event was a manifest judgment of God; and the horror of the disaster showed that it was a judgment for no ordinary crime but suitable to a vast burden of guilt. Abel (Gn 4:8) is the first victim of murder in the Bible; and the prophet Zechariah (2 Chr 24:20–22), killed in the reign of Joash of Judah, is the last victim of murder in the Hebr Bible, in which the books of Chronicles stand last. This is no doubt the reason why these two names are mentioned. "Zechariah" has been an exegetical problem: In 2 Chr 24:20 he is called the son of Jehoiada. The only

Zechariah the son of Berechiah is the eleventh of the twelve prophets (Zech 1:1); but some uncertainty about his patronymic is excusable inasmuch as he is called the son of Iddo in Ezr 5:1, his grandfather in Zech 1:1. There is no doubt a confusion of the patronymics in the tradition; Zechariah the minor prophet was a much better known figure than the Zechariah of 2 Chr 24. The difficulty, however, has led some interpreters to identify Zechariah with Zechariah the son of Baris, killed in AD 70 shortly before the fall of the Temple (Josephus, *JW* 4.5,4 § 335). All this blood comes upon this generation in the war with the Romans.

163 (ix) *Conclusion* (23:37–39). The apostrophe to Jerusalem, taken from Q, is placed in Lk (13:34–35) in a different context at the departure of Jesus from Galilee. In both Gospels a different phrase appears, which permits the verses to follow easily from what precedes, and there is no reason to think that either Gospel represents the original context or that the saying was preserved with any context. **37.** *killing and stoning:* The allusion again seems to reflect the experience of the early Christian missionaries. **38.** *your house will be left you:* The prediction echoes such prophetic passages as Jer 12:7; 22:5; Ez 10:18–19; 11:22–23, in which Yahweh is said to depart from Jerusalem. **39.** In Lk the final verse could refer to the entrance of Jesus into Jerusalem (see 20:9 par. Lk 19:38); but by placing the prediction here, Matthew has made the eschatological reference clear beyond doubt. The coming to which Jerusalem can look is the parousia of the Son of Man; and thus the discourse leads into the great eschatological discourse that follows. It is probably because of this close connection that Mt omits the story of the widow's mite (Mk 12:41–44 par. Lk 21:1–4).

164 **(B) Discourse: The Eschatological Sermon (24:1–25:46).** The basis of Mt 24 is Mk 13. The eschatological discourse is the only portion of Mk that can properly be called a discourse; this was plainly the most important collection of the sayings of Jesus in the circles in which the Gospel of Mk arose. Matthew has expanded the discourse in ch. 25 by the use of materials from Q and from private sources.

The ambiguous attitude of the apostolic Church toward the parousia of the Son of Man and the end of the world is a celebrated exegetical and theological question that cannot be settled here. But the materials of Mt's discourse must be employed in reaching an understanding of the attitude of the apostolic Church, and they should be explained clearly and objectively. The discourse refers both to the fall of Jerusalem and to the eschatological end; but it is impossible to sort out which verses refer to which event. One must understand that in much biblical thinking, both in the OT and in the NT, history and eschatology are merged in a way that is alien to modern thought. Particular historical events that are seen as judgments of God are described in eschatological terms; the examples are too numerous for citation here, but one may mention the fall of Jerusalem in 587 BC, the fall of the Assyrian and the Babylonian kingdoms, and even minor historical events such as the fall of Edom and the fall of Tyre. A blurring of perspective in the consideration of the fall of Jerusalem, far from being strange to the thought and language of Judaism, is native to it. Jesus did not depart from biblical language; and the precedents for such language in the prophetic literature were numerous enough to preclude that type of misunderstanding that would identify the fall of Jerusalem with the beginning of the end catastrophe.

This sermon must also be read with the awareness that its composition was affected by the fact that the catastrophe of Jerusalem had already occurred; the narratives describe an event that was remembered. This is not to say that Jesus did not predict it; but his exact words were not remembered any more precisely for this than for other sayings, and the historical impact of the event could hardly have been conducive to a more accurate preservation of them.

It is the reality of the eschatological event that is the object of the discourse, not its date. There are clear warnings—not necessarily original—against attempting to calculate the date. The point is that man in history lives under an eschatological judgment, which means a final judgment. In particular events, such as the fall of Jerusalem, the judgment seems to break into history. When it does, it reminds man of his eschatological destiny; and he is warned in terms such as those used in Mt 25 that the judgment is to be awaited with unremitting vigilance. There is a sense in which the eschatological judgment can and must always be conceived as "near"; for there is no one to whom it is irrelevant.

165 (a) THE PREDICTION OF THE DESTRUCTION OF THE TEMPLE (24:1–3). In 21:23 Mt has presented Jesus entering the Temple; in the chapters that follow controversies and invective against the Pharisees occupy the period since that entry. Here in 24:1 Mt depicts Jesus leaving the Temple and arriving at the Mt. of Olives (24:3). The change of locale is rather sudden; the rough transition is due to a compilation in Mk (13:1–4), which in Mt is somewhat smoothed over.

The remarks of the disciples allude to the restoration of the Second Temple initiated by Herod the Great in 19 BC (Josephus, *JW* 1.21, 1 § 401; but cf. *Ant.* 15.11, 1 § 380). The reconstruction was finished by the time of Jesus' public ministry; the 46 years of Jn 2:20 would place the period in AD 26–27. But embellishment of the structure was continued until AD 66; all work was completed only four years before the Temple was destroyed by fire in AD 70. The observations about the size of the stones in Mk are fully justified by the remains of Herodian masonry in Palestine. Jesus' comment on the remarks of the disciples includes a prediction that introduces a sombre note.

The western slope of the Mt. of Olives affords the best panorama of the city of Jerusalem. In NT times the Temple occupied the prominent position in the foreground, roughly where the Dome of the Rock now stands.

Matthew has made two changes in Mk (13:1–4): The discourse is addressed to all the disciples instead of to Peter, Andrew, James, and John; and the question of the disciples is made more clearly eschatological. **3.** The disciples in Mk and Lk ask vaguely when "these things" will happen; in the context the question refers to the prediction of the destruction of the temple. Mt adds to this the question of the sign of the parousia of Jesus and the end of the world. Both these phrases are used only by Mt in the Gospels, and parousia is used only in Mt 24–25. The word *parousia* in Hellenistic Greek designated either the manifestation of a hidden god or the visit of an emperor or potentate to a city. In the NT and later Christian literature it becomes a technical term for the Second Coming of Jesus (→ Aspects NT Thought, 78:80, 87). The question is framed by Mt from the contents of the discourse.

166 (b) THE SIGNS OF THE PAROUSIA (24:4–8). The sermon proper begins with a warning against deception. **4.** *many will come:* This claim to be the Messiah is generally ascribed to a number of Jewish rebels against Rome before the outbreak of the Jewish War. Mt introduces the word "Messiah" into the claim (cf. Mk 13:5). **6.** Widespread wars, earthquakes, and famine are commonplaces in biblical and extrabiblical apocalyptic literature. There can be no allusion to events contemporary with the composition of the Gospel unless we suppose that the author exaggerates the Jewish War into a cosmic catastrophe, which he may very well do according to the principle mentioned (→ 164 above). **8.** *the beginning:* But the disciples are not to take these events as "the end"; they are the beginning of the birth pangs. "The birth pangs of the Messiah" are a designation of convulsions in nature and in history that usher in the Messianic era; the term is used in rabbinical literature.

167 (c) PERSECUTIONS AND DISSENSIONS (24:9–14). Mt deviates from Mk in this section because Matthew has already used Mk's material in the missionary discourse (10:17–21); 24:9b parallels Mk 13:13a, and 24:13 (Mk 13:13b par.) is repeated from 10:22b. The material peculiar to Mt does not refer to persecutions but to dissensions within the Church; scandal, mutual distrust and hatred, betrayal, and deception through false prophets (see 13:36–43,47–50). This is summed up as the growth of lawlessness to the point where love grows cold. Here again no allusion to events contemporary with the writing of the Gospel can be traced; but little is known of the conditions of the Jewish-Christian community in Palestine during the years of the Jewish War. Mt 24:14 parallels Mk 13:10; this line, by virtue of its transfer to this position, leads clearly into the following section and strengthens the eschatological thrust of Mt's form of the discourse. The proclamation of the Gospel to all nations is a gradual development in the Gospels; but only here is the fulfillment of the mission made a sign of the near approach of the end. Thus Mt's reconstruction suggests that what follows is to be referred to the end; this suggestion is not made in the versions of Mk and Lk.

168 (d) THE ABOMINATION OF DESOLATION (24:15–22). In spite of the last verse of the preceding section, these lines are quite clearly referred to the Jewish War. **15.** *the abomination of desolation:* Cf. Dn 9:27; 12:11 [LXX]. In Dn the abomination signifies the erection of the image of Zeus Olympios in the Jerusalem Temple by Antiochus IV Epiphanes in 168 BC. Luke (21:20–24) is quite correct in referring this sign here explicitly to the presence of hostile forces; he omits the Hebr phrase as scarcely intelligible to Gentile readers—or to himself. *let the reader* [of Dn] *understand:* An occult interpretation of Dn is intended. This is a warning to the Palestinian Christian community to escape. A tradition preserved by Eusebius (*HE* 3.5,3) relates that the Palestinian Christians fled to Pella in the northern valley of the Jordan to escape the Jewish War. **16.** Oddly enough this town is not in "the mountains," i.e., the hills of the desert of Judea. The escape must be made with no delay. **17.** *he who is on the roof:* The roof of Palestinian houses was reached by an outside stairway; one who must flee should leave at once without trying to bring anything from the house. **18.** The man who is plowing should not even go back to the edge of the field where he left his cloak. **19.** The note of compassion for pregnant women and nursing mothers is obvious; so is flight in the rainy season, when one is exposed to rain and chilly weather. **20.** *on a Sabbath:* But the allusion to flight on the Sabbath is meaningful only to Jewish Christians who observe the Sabbath, a day on which a journey in excess of 2000 paces was prohibited in rabbinical interpretation. **21.** *such as have not been:* The troubles of the Jewish War are described by hyperbole in a phrase based on Dn 12:1 as the greatest in human history. The "salvation," which no one would attain unless the time of tribulation were shortened, does not mean spiritual salvation but escape from death; unless God mercifully shortened the time (Mt in Jewish style uses the impersonal "theological" passive instead of the divine name [*GrBib* § 236]), no one would have escaped alive from this disaster. The narrative of Josephus does indeed indicate a terrible loss of life in the Palestinian Jewish community. That even a few escape is attributed to God's mercy toward "the chosen," that is, the Christian members of the Palestinian Jewish community.

In calling this "the end," Mt merges the historic and the apocalyptic. To understand his point of view we must remember that to the Palestinian Jewish Christian community, of which Mt is here the spokesman, the total collapse, as it seemed, of Palestinian Judaism was truly the end of their world. A world in which Yahweh was not worshiped by his people in his land in his Temple was not the world of history. No similar act of judgment was related in the OT; for there could be no messianic hope to survive this ruin—the Messiah had come and initiated the reign. This community was aware, perhaps better aware than Gentile Christians, of the magnitude of the historical and theological crisis of the fall of Palestinian Judaism. With the disaster a new phase of the reign began.

169 (e) FALSE MESSIAHS (24:23–25). These lines are a fuller doublet of 24:5, taken from another source. There are echoes in the NT of false prophets in the apostolic Church who cannot be positively identified, nor can the signs and wonders that are attributed to them. The disciples have been forewarned against such pretenders (cf. Mk 13:21–23).

(f) THE DAY OF THE SON OF MAN (24:26–28). These lines are inserted from Q (Lk 17:23–24,37 par.) and do not belong in this context originally. The theme is related to the theme of the preceding lines. **26.** *in the desert:* Christians need not go out into the desert to seek the Messiah, as some went out after Theudas, a messianic leader whose insurrection was suppressed by the procurator C. Cuspius Fadus (AD 44–46; cf. Josephus, *Ant.* 20.5, 1 § 97). Nor should they accept invitations to join secret meetings in inner chambers. **27.** *as the lightning:* The coming of the Messiah will be as easy to see as the flash of lightning across the sky. **28.** A proverb of cryptic meaning is cited; the gathering of vultures shows that there is carrion that attracts them, and the parousia of the Son of Man will be just as easily discerned.

170 (g) THE PAROUSIA OF THE SON OF MAN (24:29–31). **29.** This verse is the sequel to 24:22. Mt has made the junction of history and eschatology even tighter by adding "immediately." He has expanded Mk's description of the parousia in 24:30–31. The parousia is described in terms largely taken from OT apocalyptic passages; for comparisons see Is 13:10, 34:4 (24:29); Zech 12:12–14 (24:30); Is 27:13; Zech 2:10 (24:31). It is influenced by the Son of Man epiphany in Dn 7:13–14. The cosmic disturbances are a conventional part of OT imagery when the approach of God's judgments are described. **30.** *the sign of the Son of Man:* This is not clear. A sign from heaven is asked in 16:1–4, but Jesus denies that it will be given; this answer is not directed toward the eschatological event. The sign of the Son of Man may be identical with his epiphany "in power and great glory." Apocalyptic imagery, of course, should not be taken in a crass literal sense; what is described is a manifest vindication of the Son of Man as one endowed with power and glory and a gathering of his elect, expressed in language that suggests the OT theme of the ingathering of Israel. The eschatological essence of the event is that it is final. The coming of the Son of Man as Mt conceived it could easily be the establishment of the community of the Risen Son of Man as the new Israel after the destruction of the old Israel. This is not identical with the eschatological parousia, but it is an event that anticipates the parousia and moves closer to it.

171 (h) THE PARABLE OF THE FIG TREE (24:32–33). The blossoming of the fig tree occurs at the end of the rainy season and signifies that the dry season of summer is at hand. One may ask more precisely what are "all these things" that are to happen, and what is it that is "near, at the door." Although the saying has an eschatological intent, it does not seem to lie in its original context. In its present position, the coming of the Son of Man is the sign that the Son of Man is coming. The events that are the "beginnings of the pangs" indicate the catastrophe of Jerusalem, which is presented as one event with the parousia. Yet the "signs" of the end event are of such a general character that they can hardly furnish the kind of precise indication suggested here. Furthermore, there is a more than superficial lack of harmony between these lines and 24:34-36, which follow. The apostolic Church was alive with speculations about the parousia of which we have only traces; and these verses reflect some of these speculations, which could, of course, arrive at no certain conclusion (cf. Mk 13:28-29).

172 (i) The Time of the Parousia (24:34-36). The speculations mentioned above are also reflected in these verses. The affirmation that "all these things" will happen in this generation is clear, and there is no reason to alter the meaning of the word "generation" from its usual sense except a fear that the Scriptures may be in error if it is not so altered. The sentence can be understood only in the light of that merging of history and eschatology upon which we have remarked above. **35.** This saying may originally come from another context in which it serves as an asseveration of the statement that these events will come in this generation. **36.** *nor the Son:* Yet what seems to be as clear an indication of time, apart from an exact date, as one could wish is followed by a statement that not even the Son knows the day and the hour. Distinctions between the fall of Jerusalem and the parousia have no basis in the text; and reservations on the ignorance of the Son likewise have no basis in the text. The words mean that Jesus did not know the time, and he did not add "in my human nature" or "with my experiential knowledge." Perhaps it would have made no sense had he added such phrases, but in this case it would have been better to omit a completely unnecessary remark. We are, of course, not dealing with "the very words" of Jesus; but it is hard to understand how the apostolic traditions would have preserved such a difficult saying if it did not rest on the memory of something Jesus had said. The first Christian writer to find this sentence difficult was Luke (21:32-33) and he solved his problem by omitting it. We cannot do this; and perhaps the only remark that can be made is that there is much about the relations of Jesus and the Father that we do not know.

Both Mk (13:33-37) and Lk (21:34-36) conclude the discourse at this point with an exhortation to watchfulness. Matthew has expanded the discourse by the use of the material in 24:37-25:46.

173 (j) Exhortations to Vigilance (24:37-41). These sayings come from Q, but the forms they have in Mt and Lk (17:26-27,34-35) exhibit variations. **37.** *the days of Noah:* The warning about the deluge is significant; it does not say that men were sinning, but that they were engaged in innocent secular occupations. Their sin was to give no thought to impending catastrophe. The disciples are warned against that interest in secular business that makes them forget the parousia. The saying may originally have referred more precisely to the fall of Jerusalem rather than to the parousia. **40.** The parousia will manifest the difference between men—a difference that is not now apparent. Two men plowing or two women grinding meal share the same occupation and look alike externally, but God knows the difference and will make it clear. The precise meaning of "taken" and "left" is not made clear, nor need it be. Those who are "taken" will be taken because they are ready; they have shown the vigilance that is recommended.

174 (k) The Prudent Householder (24:42-44). The parable of vigilance occurs in variant forms (see Mk 13:33-37; Lk 12:39-40). The parable reinforces the uncertainty of the time of the parousia (see 24:34-36). **43.** *the thief in the night:* It will come without warning, as the thief comes in the night; the same image is used in 1 Thes 5:2. *digs through:* The Palestinian house was often built entirely or partly of clay bricks. The parable clearly does not envisage signs by which the near approach of the parousia can be discerned.

(l) The Faithful and Prudent Servant (24:45-51). This parable comes from Q, and Mt and Lk (12:42-46) are unusually close to each other. In Lk the parable is spoken in answer to a question of Peter; and although the parable is certainly eschatological, its primary reference is to those who have authority in the Church and are the stewards of the goods of the Church. **45.** *set over his household:* It is their duty to dispense these goods, which are not their own but have been entrusted to them precisely so that they may be dispensed. **47.** *set him over all his possessions:* The reward of fidelity in this is commitment of a greater trust. **48-49.** Tyrannical treatment of those over whom one has the charge and the use of the goods for self-indulgence is infidelity in the commission. This is more than lack of vigilance; but the excuse for such conduct is the delay of the parousia. Let all know that the Lord will come when he is not expected. **51.** *will punish him* [*or cut him in pieces*]*:* The punishment threatened to the unfaithful servant is dismemberment, a vigorous and to us disagreeable metaphor taken from the practices of the Hellenistic-Oriental world; after this the assignment of his lot with the hypocrites seems anticlimactic. The hypocrites are the same against whom the invective of ch. 23 is directed; the parable recognizes that the faults of Jewish religious leaders can be found also in Christian religious leaders. **51b.** A tag of Mt (8:12; 13:42,50; 22:13).

175 (m) The Parable of the Wise and Foolish Virgins (25:1-13). This parable, peculiar to Mt, has a remarkable combination of a homely scene with a tragic end. The point of the parable is foresight, not vigilance in the strict sense; all the girls sleep, five of them are ready. **1.** *bridegroom:* Some mss. add "and the bride." There is a lack of detailed information about wedding practices in NT Judaism. There was certainly a solemn wedding procession from the home of the bride to the home of the bridegroom; the taking of the bride from her father's house to his own by the bridegroom was the symbolic act of marriage. The critical reading ("bridegroom" only) indicates that the bride's female attendants went to meet the bridegroom and his party and accompanied them to the house of the bride. Whether the wedding feast was held in the house of the bride's father or in the house of the bridegroom is not clear; but it is the wedding feast from which the foolish girls are excluded, and since the groom speaks it appears that his house is meant. The wedding ceremonies were held at night, and the bridal couple was accompanied by torches and lamps. **5.** Obviously there was no set time for the bridegroom to appear, and provisions had to be made for a long delay. **10.** The closing and barring of the house door was not a simple task, and it was not opened again except for a real emergency; guests who could not arrive in time for the feast could not expect to be admitted. The parable restates yet again the uncertainty of the time of the parousia and recommends constant alertness, not the calculation of the signs of the times. The conception of the Messianic era as a wedding festival appears also in 9:15; 22:1-14 (see Jn 3:29).

176 (n) The Parable of the Talents (25:14–30). The parable comes from Q, but there are a number of differences in detail between Mt and Lk (19:12–27). The point of the parable, however, is the same in both, and it seems unnecessary to postulate different sources. The sum in Mt is much larger, but this scarcely touches the point. The slaves who trade with the money double the investment; the timid slave buries the sum in the earth (see 13:44). **19.** *settled accounts:* The point is not the uncertainty of the time of the parousia but the reckoning that will be demanded. It is possible here also to discern that the original form of the parable was directed to the officers of the Church. **21.** *will set you over much:* The reward of fidelity is again the commission of greater responsibility; the admission to the joy of the lord means that the slave is admitted to intimate association with the owner. **24.** This verse, which should not be allegorized, does indicate that the owner is demanding; and this is indeed the point of the whole parable. The slave has lost nothing, but he has gained nothing. He could at least have invested the sum with moneylenders, who gave an excellent rate of interest in NT times. **28.** *give it to him who has ten:* That the one talent is given to the slave who received ten is again not an allegorical feature; it affords room for the saying of v. 29. This paradoxical saying indicates that the powers conferred on the disciples grow with use and wither with disuse. The punishment for this type of infidelity is as severe as the punishment for more positive sins; it is expulsion into outer darkness, to which Mt has added the tag used in 24:51b.

177 (o) The Last Judgment (25:31–46). This chapter in its present form has been produced by ecclesiastical expansions of sayings of Jesus. The usual designation of the passage as "The Last Judgment" is somewhat misleading; it is an imaginative scene in which is set the core of the moral teaching of Jesus. It has no parallel in the other Gospels. **32.** The scene is the parousia, and "all nations" mean all mankind. But the process is addressed to the disciples; the standards on which they will be judged are set forth. That faith is not mentioned should lead to no theological conclusions; it is clear that for Mt as for other NT writers faith in Jesus is the first movement of man toward God. The point of this scene is that faith is not the whole movement; that it should transform the disciple. **32.** *the sheep from the goats:* The separation of the sheep from the goats can be easily observed in modern Palestine when the time comes to transfer the animals to other pastures; sheep and goats feed together, but they are moved separately. **34.** *the King:* Jesus is here given the title of king, unusual in the Gospels, and one of the signs of ecclesiastical expansion. *the kingdom:* This is not the reign that Jesus proclaimed but the eschatological kingdom; this is prepared "from the foundation of the world." In rabbinical theology the kingdom of the Messiah was one of the items created before the world. **35–36.** The source of "the corporal works of mercy." Ministry to the basic needs of one's fellow man is the only canon of judgment mentioned here. One could paraphrase by saying that man is judged entirely on his behavior toward his fellow man. The evasion that this does not include man's duties toward God is met in this passage; Jesus identifies himself with those to whom service is given or refused, and their behavior toward men is their behavior toward God. The works mentioned are not those we usually call necessary works; and perhaps the word necessary is misleading here. The passage says nothing about what we would consider duties; man is judged on those things that he is accustomed not to consider duties. **44.** *and did not minister to you:* The surprise of those who are condemned is easy to understand; they never accepted the fact that they encountered Jesus in other men and that they cannot distinguish between their duties to God and their duties to man. They are ranked with the devils, whose proper element is the fire of Gehenna. Eschatology means man is capable of a final decision that gives his life a permanent character. Both the righteous and the wicked here have made decisions that are irrevocable.

The position of this chapter in Mt at the conclusion of the final discourse of Jesus suggests that it is intended as the last word of Jesus to the disciples. The chapter is weighty theologically. Like the last discourse in Jn, the theme is love based on the identity of Jesus with men. In the last analysis, it is love that determines whether men are good or bad. If their love is active, failure to reach perfect morality in other ways will be rare, and it will be forgiven. But there is no substitute for active love.

178 **(VII) The Passion Narrative (26:1–27:66).** Interpreters generally agree that this part of the Gospel tradition was the first part to acquire a fixed structure. No part of the life of Jesus is related in such detail and with such close agreement in the sources. The amount of space given to the passion in Mk as compared to the rest of his Gospel shows the place this narrative had in the apostolic Church; in Mt, the disproportion, although smaller, is still notable. The earliest proclamation of Jesus centered on the story of the death and the resurrection. This was the great saving act of God, the climax of the saving acts in the history of salvation. Paul said that he preached Christ and him crucified (1 Cor 2:2).

Mt's Passion Narrative shows a few expansions of his own. Some of these are legendary details, others come from a "fulfillment" interpretation of OT texts of a character similar to that observed frequently in the infancy narratives, less frequently elsewhere in the Gospels. It is not an account of the words of Jesus; although Jesus speaks more frequently in Mt than in Mk, he is generally silent. Strangely to us, the Gospels have no theological exposition of the passion, either through the words of Jesus or the words of others. This was left to the apostolic teaching, which we can see illustrated in the epistles of Paul.

The Passion Narrative was of all the portions of the Gospels certainly the first to be included in a liturgical recital as well as in the proclamation, and liturgical influences must have operated in the formation of the narrative. The detailed investigation of these traces is a work still to be done.

179 **(A) The Conspiracy of the Jewish Authorities (26:1–5).** Matthew notably expands Mk (14:1–2) here. He connects this passage immediately with the preceding discourse. The prediction of Jesus, peculiar to Mt, is a solemn introduction to the narrative; the words give purpose and clarity to the sequence of events that were not realized by the disciples until after the resurrection. **2.** *after two days:* This phrase, from Mk 14:1, has been given an entirely different force. The conspiracy also is described in an expanded form. The prediction of Jesus is balanced against the decision of the Jewish authorities; he knows what they are doing and is master of events. **3.** *chief priests and elders:* These are the parties to the conspiracy (Mk, "chief priests and scribes"). "Chief priests" in the plural is not exact; there was only one "high priest," and the chief priests were the heads of the leading priestly families. *Caiaphas:* He is mentioned here only by Mt. Joseph Caiaphas was appointed high priest by the procurator Valerius Gratus in AD 18 and deposed by Vitellius in AD 36. He was the son-in-law of Annas, who controlled the priestly aristocracy for many years. **5.** *not during the feast:* The desire that Jesus should not be killed on the feast leads to the question of the chronology of the crucifixion, which cannot be resolved here; but there seems to be no reason for the introduction of the phrase except to show that the conspiracy was frustrated in this detail. Jesus was certainly crucified during the Passover feast, which is what the conspirators wished to avoid. He is master of events.

180 **(B) The Anointing at Bethany (26:6–13).** The story of the anointing appears in all four Gospels, and it is unlikely that such an incident occurred more than once. Lk places it earlier in the life of Jesus (7:36–50), does not name the host, and identifies the woman as a sinner. Jn places it before the passion (12:1–18), but locates it in the house of Martha and Mary at Bethany, and identifies the woman as Mary. Mt follows Mk; the host is Simon the leper (a difficult epithet, usually thought to identify him as one whom Jesus had healed), and the woman is neither named nor identified as a sinner. Jn also has substantially the same dialogue as Mk and Mt, but he identifies the complainer as Judas Iscariot. **7.** Mt omits Mk's identification of the perfume as nard, but notes that it was expensive. To retain its fragrance, enough perfume for one application was sealed in small alabaster vases; it could be used only by breaking the vessel. It was the custom to anoint the head generously at banquets; in Lk's account the host did not furnish ointment for Jesus. **8.** *why this waste:* It was not the anointing but the costliness of the ointment to which "some"—probably the disciples—objected. **10.** Jesus accepts the gesture in the spirit in which it was intended, although he was no more in favor of luxury than anyone else; and he excuses the extravagance by an allusion to his impending death and burial, which permits him to accept it. The narrative illustrates his graciousness in accepting a service he would never have accepted if he had first been asked, and he reads the disciples a lesson in the interpretation of motives. The gesture was foolish but generous; it is the only action in the Gospels that is promised a perpetual and universal memory. The exchange surely made a profound impression on those who witnessed it.

181 **(C) The Treachery of Judas (26:14–16).** **14.** *then:* The adverb does not indicate any inner connection between the betrayal and the preceding event; Matthew uses such connecting particles throughout his account of the last days of Jesus and thus makes the events follow in rapid sequence. *Judas:* In all the Gospels the initiative comes from Judas. The Gospels do not always refrain from representing the inner thoughts of persons; Mk 14:4 in the preceding incident describes the objection that was thought but not expressed. But no Gospel attempts to probe the motivation of the most astounding act they relate, the betrayal of Jesus by one of the Twelve. Speculations are numerous, but here they seem useless. **15.** *thirty silver coins:* Only Mt specifies the amount (30 [silver shekels]). The number comes not from tradition but from Zech 11:12, and Zech in turn probably alludes to Ex 21:32, in which damages for the life of a slave killed by a goring ox are set at 30 silver shekels. Certainly there were difficulties in apprehending Jesus that the Gospels have not set forth fully; the priests were ready to accept help in doing it clandestinely, but this is not altogether easy to combine with the public display they not only permitted but encouraged. The phrases used both here and in 26:4 suggest assassination rather than a judicial process. There were no doubt varied counsels in the priestly ruling class on how to deal with the matter.

182 **(D) The Preparation for the Passover (26:17–19).** A night elapses between the anointing at Bethany and the preparation of the Passover (on the problem of Passion Week chronology, → Gospel Jn, 63:138). In the Syn the last dinner is a Passover dinner. **17.** *on the first day of matzoth:* The phrase is somewhat imprecise (→ Gospel Mk, 42:83). Matthew's abbreviation of Mk is startling here; he omits all reference to the man carrying the pitcher and the implications of second sight possessed by Jesus and gives a narrative that supposes that arrangements with someone (whose name he does not give) have been previously made for the use of his house for the Passover dinner. Such reserve is not characteristic of Matthew; there can be no reason for his omission except that he saw nothing extraordinary in the incident reported in Mk.

183 **(E) The Traitor (26:20–25).** **20.** *reclined:* Jews of NT times had adopted the Hellenistic practice of reclining around the table on couches. In Mt and Mk it is at the very beginning of the meal that Jesus chose to reveal the treachery of one of the company; Lk postpones the announcement until after the Eucharistic words. Jn also puts it early, but solves the problem by sending Judas out of the room after the announcement. **21.** *one of you will betray me:* That this news cast gloom over the assembly is not surprising; and this is a better argument than most for proposing that the announcement of the betrayal at this point is a later expansion. That each of the disciples should ask seriously whether he was the traitor would exhibit a surprising insecurity, and this also points to a period of reflection when the Church came to realize that each of its members carries potential treachery within him. The answer of Jesus does not identify the traitor. **23.** *dipped in the dish:* The dinner was served in large bowls, set in the succession of courses in the center of the group; each reached into the bowl for a morsel. In Jn (13:26) this custom leads to the identification of Judas by a morsel that Jesus hands to him. To eat together and share the same bowl denotes fellowship; and the contrast of fellowship and treachery is heightened by that act that negates the community of those who eat together. **24.** *had he not been born:* The condemnation of the act of Judas is the most severe in all the Gospels; the death of Jesus is inevitable, "as it is written," but it is not inevitable that one of his disciples should betray him. **25.** *is it I?:* Matthew adds an expansion of his own in which Jesus expressly discloses to Judas alone that he knows who the traitor is; this is a step in the development that is completed in the account in Jn.

184 **(F) The Institution of the Eucharist (26:26–29).** Paul has the earliest of the formulas in which the institution of the Eucharist is preserved (1 Cor 11:23–25). The variations between Paul and Lk (22:15–20) on the one hand, and Mt and Mk (14:22–25) on the other, should not be exaggerated; but the texts do vary. That this passage was a liturgical text is certain, and thus it was assured a relatively fixed form very early. Mt follows Mk closely with only one major expansion (in v. 28). Verse 29 suggests a reference to the last cup of the Passover dinner. **26.** All three Syn mention the blessing, the breaking, and the distribution; Mt adds the unnecessary command to eat. *this is my body:* Here without any modification; but Paul and Lk add, "which is for you." **27.** Mt also adds the command to drink; Mk has the simple indicative ("they drank"). **28.** *this is my blood of the covenant:* Paul and Lk have "This cup is the new covenant in my blood." The formula of Mt and Mk is more explicitly sacramental than that of Paul and Lk. The "blood of the covenant" is an allusion to Ex 24:4–8, where the covenant between Yahweh and Israel is concluded with the offering of sacrifice. The blood of the victims, sprinkled on the altar, which symbolizes Yahweh, and on the elders, who represent the people of Israel, signifies the community of the two parties in the covenant. The blood of Jesus likewise, which means his death, is the effective symbol of the community that he establishes between the Father and men. *is shed for many:* For all without restriction. *for the remission of sins:* Only Mt adds the phrase that expresses more clearly the effect of the reconciling death. Certain Israelite sacrifices atoned for sin and guilt, by which were meant ritual offenses. The atoning death of Jesus liberates man not only from ritual sin and guilt, but from sin simply, for which there was no atonement in the Israelite sacrificial system. **29.** *when I drink it anew with you:* This is the final cup Jesus shares with his disciples; he will not drink with them again until they meet in the Messianic banquet (see 8:11). Mt and Mk do not have the precept to repeat the act, but nothing suggests that they diverged from the practice of the apostolic Church. The Eucharistic meal celebrated in the Church was an anticipation of the Messianic banquet (26:29), and the belief that Jesus was present to share the meal was implicit in the idea of the Messianic banquet. (See P. Benoit, "The Holy Eucharist," *Scr* 8 [1956] 97–108; 9 [1957] 1–14.)

185 **(G) The Prediction of Peter's Denial (26:30–35).** Mt follows Mk (14:26–31) closely with a few expansions of no special significance. **30.** *a hymn:* Sung to conclude the dinner, this would have been Ps 114/5–118, the second part of the Hallel. Considering Jesus has spent the preceding nights in Bethany, there was nothing remarkable in the journey of the group to the Mt. of Olives; because Jesus had traversed this path nightly, it was possible for Judas to tell the priests where he could be apprehended with no disturbance. **31.** But while only one betrays, all the others will be offended by him this very night; he will disappoint their messianic hopes. *for it is written:* The text is an inexact quotation of Zech 13:7, but the point is not lost; the group will be helpless when they lose the leadership of Jesus. **32.** They will not see him again until they go to Galilee after the resurrection. Mt has an apparition in Galilee, but Mk does not.

33. Attention is again drawn to Peter, who speaks now for himself and not for the group; Mt expands the words of Peter's asseveration. But Peter's excessive self-confidence will be followed by a fall more grievous than the fall of the others; the rest will be offended, but Peter will deny Jesus, and that this very night, "before cockcrow," that is, before dawn. **35.** Not only Peter but the others join in affirming their loyalty. Certainly one of the most indelible memories of the group of disciples was their breakdown at the time of the passion, and they told this part of the story without sparing details or persons. It was an expression of their awareness that in the disciple infidelity lies always very close to the surface.

186 **(H) Gethsemane (26:36–46).** Mt still follows Mk (14:32–42) closely with amplifications in small details. This is one of the most remarkable scenes of the Gospels, and it has been pointed out that the witnesses—according to their own testimony—slept through it and that they must therefore have reconstructed the incident. But this is hypercritical. The incident shows that Jesus was under severe emotional strain comparable to nothing else in the Gospels, and that once in his life he sought the help of others. These things could be observed; and the reconstruction of the memory is built upon these observations.

36. *Gethsemane* [*oil press*]*:* An olive grove grew on the western slope of the Mt. of Olives near Jerusalem. It is not certain whether the modern grove that bears the name is the same site, but it lies in the immediate area. **38.** Jesus openly confessed his agitation and asked that the disciples remain awake with him; he does not tell them what they are awaiting. The words are addressed to Peter, James, and John, who also witnessed the transfiguration (17:1–8), and only they could attest anything about the prayer. **39.** The narrative supposes that Jesus spoke distinctly enough to be audible at a short distance. *if it be possible:* The prayer expresses a repugnance for the experience of the passion; the Gospels report only what could be seen and heard and do not attempt to analyze the thoughts and feelings of Jesus, and the modern commentator will do well to follow their example. **40.** The words in which Jesus asks for the companionship of the disciples are loosely adopted from Ps 42:6; this is derived from Mk. In keeping with Matthew's usual treatment of Peter, he is the one being addressed, not the disciples. **41.** Matthew has altered the form of the prayer slightly and has repeated it a second time. *to enter into temptation:* Not merely to experience temptation in our sense of the word but "temptation" as it is meant in the Lord's Prayer (6:13): a difficulty that one does not overcome. "Spirit" and "flesh" are a common biblical antithesis, used frequently in the Pauline epistles. The spirit is not merely the internal psychic principles of man, but the psychic principles strengthened by a divine impulse. Even with the divine impulse, the "flesh," which means man in his concrete existence, is not able to sustain "temptation" in the biblical sense of the word.

45. The disciples were too weary to remain awake; men rose and retired early in the ancient world, and no one here remains awake except Jesus and the arresting party. Most interpreters see a gentle irony in the permission to sleep that Jesus grants; it is now unimportant whether the disciples remain awake or not. **46.** There is a certain incoherence in the permission to sleep followed immediately by the command to arise. This incoherence no doubt reflects the confused memories of the disciples, who doze in a manner that makes them half-aware of what is going on, and who are suddenly aroused to the greatest catastrophe in their experience. Jesus himself saw the approaching party; the Passover falls during the full moon, and the party no doubt carried torches.

187 **(I) The Arrest of Jesus (26:47–56).** Mt still follows Mk (14:43–52) except for some minor abbreviations and two notable expansions. **47.** *Judas:* He is mentioned as if he were the leader of the party, but this is unlikely. Judas knew where Jesus should be sought, at least in what neighborhood. That he should bring the party immediately to the very spot seems astonishing; this detail can probably be attributed to the confused recollections of an exciting and confused evening. **48.** *the one I kiss:* The kiss, a normal form of greeting, was necessary to identify the person whom the party sought in the darkness illuminated only by the full moon and the torches. Jesus was not that well known to the arresting party, and the priests had no desire to apprehend the whole group. **50.** *why are you here:* The first of Mt's expansions is a response of Jesus to the greeting of Judas. Tradition was not satisfied with the silence recorded in Mk; Lk (22:48) has another variation of the response of Jesus, and Jn (18:4–8) makes the signal of Judas entirely unnecessary. Modern interpreters (against most Eng translations) take the words of Jesus as an elliptical imperative, rather than a question: "Friend, for what you have come!" meaning, "Do the business for which you have come." **51.** *cut off his ear:* The disciple who offered resistance is named only in Jn (18:10) as Peter; Jn also names the slave. Matthew's usual interest in Peter suggests that neither he nor Mark had this bit of information. *the slave of the high priest:* He may have been the leader of the party. The arresting group is unsatisfactorily described as "a crowd" by Mk, which Mt makes "a large crowd" (26:47), sent by the priests and elders (Mk adds "the scribes"). This is equivalent to saying that they did not know who the party were. The Temple had its own police, and since the priests were the chief actors in the passion, the Temple police were probably sent on this mission; it is unlikely that it was merely a mob. **52–54.** Mt's second expansion contains the response of Jesus to the attempt to defend him. The response is probably composed of sayings taken in part from other contexts, particularly the proverb of 52a. But the sharp rejection of the use of arms is entirely in accord with the teaching and the practice of Jesus; and no one else is said to intervene in a scene that would certainly have led to massive violence if some one had not stopped it. **52b.** The rejection of the use of arms is general, not a remark adapted to this particular situation; it condemns the use of arms as futile rather than as immoral. **53.** *twelve legions of angels:* If Jesus wished or needed this type of help, it was available in far greater strength than the disciples could furnish. **54.** But if resistance is offered, the Scriptures will not be fulfilled; the reign of God will not be established in that way in which God intends. That there can ever be other situations in which the reign will be advanced by the use of arms is not denied by this saying; but the saying lends little support to such an understanding of the reign.

188 **55.** The words of Jesus to the crowd show that he freely surrenders himself. They need not have sought him out in a lonely place when he was within easy reach in the very Temple precincts. That the Jewish leaders did not desire a public arrest is a constant theme in the Passion Narrative; and this is revealing about public sentiment toward Jesus. For the same reason there is no mention of the invocation of Roman authority at this stage of the passion; the Gospel tradition is clear that the arrest was the act of Jewish religious leaders.

For the rest of the Passion Narrative the disciples were not eyewitnesses, but there was no difficulty in reconstructing events that occurred in the presence of large numbers of people. The disciples were ready to defend Jesus by force; when he himself rejected defense, they did not know what to do.

189 **(J) Jesus Before the Council (26:57–75).** The arresting party led Jesus to the house of the high priest. Here the council (Sanhedrin) was assembled, composed of 72 members drawn from the priests, the scribes, and the elders. That the house of the high priest, however large it was, could seat this assembly seems unlikely. **57.** *Caiaphas:* The name does not appear in Mk (cf. 26:3; but also Jn 18:13). **59.** *false testimony:* Mt condenses Mk's account of the witnesses, but the sources are at one that the witnesses were perjured and even then could not reach a satisfactory agreement on their testimony. The testimony on which two witnesses agreed is reported in a saying in Jn 2:19, the only place in the Gospels where anything remotely resembling the charge is found. Two witnesses were the necessary minimum for a condemnation. As the story proceeds the two witnesses did not support the charge, and the high priest then puts Jesus under an oath to answer a direct question. The charge concerning the Temple was blasphemy against the Temple; see Jer 26:1–19, where Jeremiah was threatened with death for a prediction that the Temple would be destroyed. **62–63.** The question of the high priest is a question concerning the messianic claims of Jesus; but the formula "the Messiah, the son of God" should probably be regarded as a Christian rather than a Jewish formula. This raises a critical problem concerning the charge on which Jesus was convicted. **64.** The answer of Jesus combines two messianic texts, Ps 110:1 and Dn 7:13; by the use of these texts Jesus declares himself the king Messiah and the Son of Man. That this claim should be treated as blasphemy has long been a problem. *you have said it:* This must have been in Matthew's mind equivalent to Mk's "I am" (14:62); the use of the two OT texts is certainly a clear affirmation. But we have nothing in Jewish sources to suggest that a claim of messiahship was regarded as a blasphemy, even if the claim were proved false. **65.** The claim is here immediately taken as a capital crime. The rending of one's garments was an ancient token of grief; in Pharisaic Judaism it was a sign of grief at seeing or hearing of some grievous violation of the Law. **67.** The rough treatment to which Jesus is subjected following the sentence is not attributed to any group in particular. Mt's amplification of the taunt in which Jesus is challenged to prophesy gives point to the taunt; Jesus was among strangers.

190 This trial is one of the most complex problems in Gospel interpretation. See further J. Blinzler, *The Trial of Jesus* (Westminster, 1959); P. Winter, *On the Trial of Jesus* (SPB 1; Berlin, 1961); K. H. Schelkle *Die Passion Jesu* (Heidelberg, 1949); E. Lohse, *Die Geschichte des Leidens und Sterbens Jesu Christi* (Gütersloh, 1964). The problem is not simplified by the fact that Mt 27:1 (like Mk 15:1) follows immediately after 26:56 (Mk 14:51 par.). It has often been noticed that the process deviates in many ways from the standards of legal process set down in the Talmud. The Talmud is a post-Christian collection that is not always valid for the practices of NT times; and in describing the legal process of the council, the Talmud describes an institution that was extinct after AD 70. But it can and does preserve some genuine historical memories. As the trial is described there was no effort whatever to maintain a just process; but until the contrary is clearly proved it should be assumed that the council would adhere to legal forms, and that all the more closely in a case the verdict of which was prearranged.

In addition there is the problem of a certain lack of coherence in the narrative, noted above. It appears that the testimony of blasphemy against the Temple would have been a better charge for the purpose of the council than the charge of blasphemy for messianic claims, and it should not have been too difficult to arrange a harmonious testimony; one has the impression that the competence of the priests has strangely broken down. That the accused should be put under oath to make a statement by which he could be condemned is a strange procedure that has never been satisfactorily explained.

For these reasons, the hypothesis that the night trial scene is a theological recital rather than a historical account should be considered. The purpose of the recital is not to charge the council with perversion of justice; this charge is abundantly clear already. Its purpose is to set forth the real reason why Jesus was condemned to death by the Jewish leaders. The real reason, whatever the alleged reasons, was that he claimed to be and was their king Messiah and the Son of Man. The question of Caiaphas and the answer of Jesus are both couched in terms of the Christian profession of faith. When the Jewish leaders encountered their Messiah and refused to believe in him, they could do nothing else but remove him.

191 **69.** To this recital is attached the story of the denial of Peter, which is independent of it; the denial represented as occurring at the court of the high priest, the open space around which the house was built. Thus far Peter could follow Jesus with some safety. The threefold denial occurs as predicted with some modifications in detail. Mk attributes the first denial to the teasing of a slave girl; Mt introduces a second slave girl and specifies how it was that Peter was recognized as a Galilean. Dialectal differences were numerous in ancient Palestine, as they are in the modern Arabic spoken in Palestine. No explanation of the failure of Peter's courage in such hostile territory is necessary. **75.** Both Mt and Lk add "bitterly" to the statement that Peter wept. The lapse of the Rock of the apostolic group was remembered because it was such a striking demonstration of common human weakness; but it was also remembered because Peter neither concealed nor excused his lapse. For such lapses there is no remedy but repentance.

192 **(K) Jesus Delivered to Pilate (27:1–2).** Matthew has rewritten Mk 15:1a somewhat extensively, but he leaves Mk 15:1b (Mt 27:2 par.) almost unchanged. The purpose of the rewriting in 27:1 is to make more coherent the transition from the night session to the morning session. Hence he adds the explicit purpose "to kill him." Lk has handled the problem more radically by placing the interrogatory process in the morning session. We have noticed that Mt 27:1 and Mk 15:1 can be read immediately after Mt 26:56 and Mk 14:51. **2.** Mt alone adds the title of Pilate, Gk *hēgemōn*, Lat *procurator*. This officer was a subordinate of the provincial governor (Lat *legatus*) in the Roman system of provincial administration (→ History of Israel, 75:142–43). In the provinces the right of passing a capital sentence (Lat *ius gladii*) was reserved to the Roman authority (→ History of Israel, 75:147).

193 **(L) The Death of Judas Iscariot (27:3–10).** This passage is peculiar to Mt. There is another tradition of the death of Judas in Acts 1:18–19 which shows definite variations; Judas there purchases the field himself, and he dies by a fall and not by suicide. Both passages are better understood as legendary material about the death of Judas. **4–5.** The remorse of Judas and his throwing the money into the Temple are vividly and dramatically described. We do not know of any prohibition that disallowed putting such money into the Temple treasury. **8.** *field of Blood:* In Gk *hakeldamach* (Aram *ḥaqel dᵉmā* [Bl-Deb-F § 39, 3]); see Acts 1:19. That there was such a burying ground near Jerusalem must be assumed, and it is very probable that the name was connected by Jewish Christians with the legend of Judas. **9.** The quotation of Zech 11:12–13 under the attribution of Jer is a celebrated problem; it is also one of the most striking examples of "fulfillment" texts in Mt. The text is not quoted exactly from either the MT or the LXX, although had it been, the passage would have been more pointed. The use of the text hinges on an ancient variation. Where the MT twice reads "potter," the LXX reads much more probably "treasury." In this respect the quotation follows the MT rather than the LXX; and it is not impossible that the source of the quotation was aware of the wordplay (treasury, *'ôṣār*; potter, *yôṣēr*). Yet the form of 27:10 suggests the story of Acts 1:18 rather than the story of Mt. In the story of Mt, Judas fulfills the text in both readings. The attribution to Jer is credited by most scholars to Mt's source and possibly to a florilegium of texts, but it seems unlikely that a florilegium would have circulated with this attribution. Some scholars see an allusion to the purchase of a field in Jer 32:6–15 and to Jeremiah's visit to the potter in Jer 18:2–3, from which allusions the entire text is attributed to Jer. This seems unlikely; and it is more probable that the source, which quoted from memory, attributed the passage to Jer by unconscious association of the text with these passages of Jer.

194 **(M) The Hearing Before Pilate (27:11–14).** Mt here follows Mk (15:2–5) closely with only verbal modifications; the addition of the elders to the priests as accusers (27:12) is not significant. **11.** *are you the king of the Jews:* The charge of claiming kingship is introduced abruptly, and it was not a part of the account of the night hearing; again we encounter a certain lack of consistency in the traditions about the trial. This must have been the charge laid by the accusers, but the narratives do not say so explicitly. The answer of Jesus, like his answer in 26:64, is noncommittal; he neither accepts nor denies the charge. Jn, in which the theme of kingship is much more prominent in the Passion Narrative, adds an explanation of the nature of the kingship of Jesus (18:33–37). **13.** *how many things:* What these things were of which the priests and the elders accused him is not stated. It is quite possible that the early Church saw in the silence of Jesus a fulfillment of Is 53:7; but if this awareness were deep when Mt was written, one would expect another fulfillment text. The charge of claiming the kingship of the Jews was a charge of treason against the authority of Rome. Pilate obviously did not take the charge seriously. Jewish messianic insurrections in Palestine were dealt with severely by the Roman authorities.

195 **(N) The Sentence of Death (27:15–26).** Matthew's modifications of Mk (15:6–15) are again merely modal. He omits Mk 15:7b, the details of the crimes of Barabbas, expands Mk 15:11–14 (27:20–23 par.), the dialogue of Pilate and the Jewish leaders, and adds two episodes of his own, the dream of Pilate's wife (27:19) and Pilate's symbolic washing of the hands (27:24–25). **15.** The custom of an amnesty at Passover is not elsewhere attested, but such a practice was not foreign to Roman policy in the provinces, and similar practices are attested for other territories. The narrative supposes that the selection is made by popular petition, and Pilate seeks to direct the petition to Jesus. **16.** *Barabbas:* Described by Mk as a revolutionary, one of the party of the Zealots. The play on his name is evident; *Bar-'abbā* in Aramaic means "son of the father," and he is chosen in preference to Jesus, the true son. The play on the name is not a sufficient reason for calling the Barabbas episode legend or midrash. **19.** The story of the wife of Pilate, on the other hand, must be characterized as legend. The dream motif occurs also in the infancy narratives of Mt (1:20; 2:12,13,19). The Gentile woman learns by revelation that Jesus is a "righteous man"; in the context the word would mean no more than innocent, but the OT echoes of the word are clearly audible. **20.** Mt here as earlier adds the elders to the priests as accusers; their work is now to persuade those who had come to petition for the amnesty to select Barabbas.

196 What follows is not the description of a legal process. There is no further hearing, no interrogation of witnesses. The sentence is implied in 27:26. That there was a process must be assumed, but this was not something tradition described in detail. The important factor was not the process, but the pressure that determined the outcome of the process. The traditions clearly affirm that Pilate knew that there was no genuine charge against Jesus. Matthew's addition of the symbolic washing of the hands emphasizes this. The traditions do not flatter Pilate in this respect; he who condemns an innocent man under pressure is morally not very far above those who put on the pressure. **25.** *all the people answered:* Matthew's addition of the acceptance by the Jewish spokesmen of the guilt is a theological addition, written with the disaster of the Jewish War in mind; this was seen by the early Christians as a terrible judgment on the people who had secured the killing of their Messiah by the perversion of justice (see further J. A. Fitzmyer, *TS* 26 [1965] 667–71). It is scarcely Matthew's thought that the plea of innocence that he puts in the mouth of Pilate (27:24) could be regarded as genuine.

Historians have noticed that no process is described and that the career of Pilate as described by Josephus is not in harmony with this picture of a man who easily yields to popular pressure. On this basis a number of scholars have argued that the Gospel traditions have transferred the responsibility for the death of Jesus from the Romans to the Jews, who in this hypothesis had no part in the process. To remove the Jewish leaders from the narrative of the passion is effectively to deny that we have any history of the passion at all. We do have a history, popular as its character may be, and in this history Jews and the Roman authorities both collaborate in the execution of Jesus. In the simplified Gospel narrative it is very likely that the attitude of Pilate has been softened. Pilate would have been ready to accept the charge that Jesus was a revolutionary; the story of his administration as related by Josephus shows that he was extremely harsh toward revolutionary movements. The Jewish leaders laid the charge against Jesus, and Pilate found little difficulty in accepting the charge. The purpose of the form that the Gospel narrative takes at this point is not to absolve Pilate of guilt but to affirm the legal innocence of Jesus in terms of Roman law as well as in terms of Jewish law.

26. The scourging was regularly inflicted in the Roman process before execution by crucifixion. The Gospels (except Lk) mention it casually, and although a scourging could be a dreadful process, they do not suggest that it was other than routine.

197 **(O) The Mocking of the Soldiers (27:27–31).** The scene of this episode, the *praetorium*, was the official residence of the Roman governor who had the rank of praetor; Pilate did not have this rank, but *praetorium* had come to mean "headquarters." Opinion is divided whether Pilate resided at the Fortress Antonia, at the NW corner of the Temple area, or at the Herodian palace, the site of which was occupied by the police station of recent Jordanian Jerusalem (see P. Benoit, *Exégèse et théologie* [Paris, 1961] 1, 316–39). At full strength the cohort numbered 600 men, but it seems improbable that the entire force was gathered there. **28.** *scarlet cloak:* Matthew has changed the "purple" of Mk to a scarlet cloak. Purple (the celebrated Phoenician dye) was the color of royalty and of the Roman aristocracy; the cloak of the Roman soldier was scarlet, and Matthew's change is no doubt correct. *crown of thorns:* It could not have been woven in a wreath. The long thorns used for fires would have been stored in the courtyard, and they could easily be arranged in a radiate crown of the type worn by Hellenistic kings (and familiar to us from its appearance on the Statue of Liberty). **29.** *hail, King of the Jews:* The crude sport of the soldiers expresses their contempt not only for the alleged king but also for the people whose king this was supposed to be. In the Gospel traditions the scene had a mysterious significance. Jesus is acclaimed as king at the time when he fulfills his kingly duty, which is to save his people by his own death. It is only in the passion narratives and the infancy narratives of Mt and Lk that the theme of kingship appears in the Syn.

198 **(P) The Way of the Cross (27:32).** The sons of Simon must have been members of the Roman church, and Mk mentions their name; but they were not known to Mt, who omits them. The Roman military had the right of impressing anyone for forced labor. What was carried was not the cross but the transverse beam; the upright stake was a permanent fixture at the place of execution. If Golgotha is to be identified with the site of the Church of the Holy Sepulcher, the distance was not long either from Antonia or from the Herodian palace.

199 **(Q) The Crucifixion (27:33–44).** In spite of the innumerable references in Christian literature and art to the hill of Calvary, the site is nowhere described as a hill in the Gospels. It is now sufficiently well established that the site of the Church of the Holy Sepulcher lay outside the 1st-cent. wall of Jerusalem; but this of itself does not authenticate the site. **33.** *Golgotha:* Interpreted in all three Syn as "skull," it comes from an Aram word, *gulgultā*. **34.** *wine:* The drink offered Jesus is changed in Mt from Mk's "wine flavored with myrrh" to "wine mixed with gall," an allusion to Ps 69:22. It was the practice of Jewish women to offer a strong narcotic drink to men condemned to execution; Jesus refused this. **35.** No details are given concerning the crucifixion. This was not a Roman punishment but an Oriental punishment adopted by the Romans. It was prohibited by Roman law to crucify Roman citizens; and normally crucifixion was used only for slaves, bandits, and rebels. The crucifixion of Jesus with two bandits shows the charge on which Jesus was condemned by Pilate. The division of the garments was a privilege of the squad of soldiers who handled the execution; the crucified were stripped entirely nude. Christian tradition saw here a fulfillment of Ps 22:19, quoted in all the Gospels. **37.** *the title:* Affixed to the cross of the criminal was his charge; it indicated that Jesus had attempted to establish himself as king. **39.** The mockery of those executed has been a universal feature wherever public executions have been practiced. The taunts are attributed to those who chanced to pass by and to the priests and scribes; Mt adds the elders, as usual. The taunts reflect the Messianic character of Jesus and the charge that he had threatened to destroy the Temple (26:61). **40.** Mt has added "son of God" and "king of Israel" to the taunts mentioned by Mk. Mt 27:43 is added from Ps 22:9. **42.** *he saved others but cannot save himself:* This taunt is an expression of the faith of the primitive Christians that this was the supreme saving act of Jesus. He is now the Messiah at the moment when he is jeered for failing to show what the Jews believed to be the Messianic qualities.

200 **(R) The Death of Jesus (27:45–56).** Mt and Lk have omitted Mk's note of the third hour (midmorning) as the hour of crucifixion (Mk 15:25), but have retained the sixth hour (noon) and the ninth hour (midafternoon). The darkness that covered the land is a legendary feature in Mk; no explanation is offered, and the word does not mean a heavy overcast. It is a symbol of "the hour of darkness" (Lk 22:53). **46.** *Eli, Eli, ...:* The words of Jesus are quoted from Ps 22:2, the opening line. This Ps, already cited, was used by the early Church as a Ps of the passion; it is as such a prophecy that it is used here, and not as a cry of interior abandonment expressed by Jesus. Mt quotes the psalm partly in Hebrew and partly in Aramaic. **47.** The bystander who recognized the name Elijah can hardly have been one of the soldiers. **48.** The drink offered Jesus was sour wine or wine vinegar, a cheap, thirst-quenching drink used by the poor; it was not unpalatable when mixed with water. Jesus was offered a share of the drink the soldiers no doubt carried with them. The tradition saw here another fulfillment of Ps 69:22. The loud cry uttered by Jesus is inarticulate in Mt and Mk.

51–53. Mt has a number of legendary features peculiar to itself. The veil of the temple divided the Holy Place from the Most Holy Place, accessible only to the high priest; Mk and Mt mean that the Most Holy Place at this moment ceases to be holy. The earthquake in the poetry of the OT is the tread of Yahweh's footsteps. The holy men who were buried in Jerusalem rise at the saving act of the Messiah; they recognize him, but Israel of the flesh does not. Even the centurion and the soldiers profess their belief that Jesus is the Son of God; this is a Christian formula of faith, and it is anticipated in the mouths of these Gentiles. Mt makes the confession a result of the signs; Mk, somewhat more impressively, presents it as the result of their witness of the death of Jesus. **55.** The women who had followed Jesus and served him in Galilee are mentioned in anticipation of the Resurrection Narrative. Mk mentions Mary of Magdala, Mary the mother of James (the Less) and Joses, and Salome. Mt mentions the two Marys (Joses must be the same as Joseph) and the mother of the sons of Zebedee, who need not be the same as Salome. This is the first time these names occur in Mt and Mk; and romantic identifications of them with nameless women mentioned earlier in the Gospels remain romantic. Mk mentions "many others" besides; Mt omits this.

201 **(S) The Burial of Jesus (27:57–61).** Mt has abbreviated Mk (15:42–47) by omitting the detail of Pilate's surprise that Jesus had died; crucifixion was a slow death that sometimes took two or even three days. **43.** *Joseph of Arimathea:* Mt designates him "a rich man" instead of a respected member of the Jewish council; he has also made Joseph a disciple instead of one "who expected the reign of God." But the term in Mk indicates one who looked for the true reign and not for the spurious messianism of the Pharisees, the Sadducees, or the Zealots. Mt may have seen a problem in the discipleship of a member of the council that had voted the death of Jesus. Arimathea is identified with the modern Rentis, about 20 mi. NE of Jerusalem. **60.** *laid it in his own tomb:* The burial took place on the eve of the Sabbath; Mt and Mk describe a simple enveloping of the body in a new linen shroud. The tomb belonged to Joseph; it was a rock-cut tomb of a type very common in the vicinity of Jerusalem. The circular stone that was rolled in front of the entrance was used on some 1st-cent. tombs, which can still be seen. **61.** It was not unimportant that the two Marys took careful note of the location of the tomb. The areas surrounding the walls of Jerusalem had literally hundreds, if not thousands of tombs, and the resurrection apologetic demanded that the spot where Jesus had been buried should be known exactly. For the same purpose it was important that the tomb was new, not previously used.

202 **(T) The Guard at the Tomb of Jesus (27:62–66).** This passage is peculiar to Mt; it seems to be based on a local tradition, which is not without problems for interpreters. The following day here can be only the Sabbath, the day after the death of Jesus. **62.** It is remarkable that the priests and the Pharisees show such an accurate knowledge of the prediction of a resurrection the disciples seem to have forgotten completely. **65.** It is also somewhat remarkable that Pilate so readily granted a guard for a purpose he could only have thought to be absurd. Most remarkable is that this more than trivial detail of the resurrection apologetic is unknown to the other three Gospels. What can be concluded from the story is that the Jews charged the disciples with the theft of the body of Jesus. What can also be concluded is that Jews and disciples both agreed that the body of Jesus was missing from the tomb on the third day.

203 **(VIII) The Resurrection Narrative (28:1–20).** In this concluding narrative of the Gospels it is impossible to speak of a harmony of the Gospels. Each of the four Gospels goes its own way; even the correspondence between Mk 16:1–8, Mt 28:1–10, and Lk 24:1–11 is less close than usual, and Mk possibly ends at 16:8. Thereafter each Gospel has collected separate traditions. Evidently the Resurrection Narrative was not fixed in the way that the Passion Narrative and the Syn tradition of the life of Jesus was fixed. In addition, there is an allusion in 1 Cor 15:6 to an apparition that has no clear parallel in the Syn or in Jn. That the apostolic Church made no effort to harmonize these divergent and even conflicting accounts is of itself extremely significant; the faith in the resurrection did not depend on the fact that everyone had the same story. Nor should too much be made of the divergence; the resurrection is the most unique and shattering of all the events related in the Gospels, and confusion in the details is rather to be expected (→ Aspects NT Thought, 78:146–159). Nor does the admixture of some legendary details have anything to do with the faith in the resurrection.

204 **(A) The Empty Tomb (28:1–10).** Matthew seems to use Mk here, but his rewriting and additions are extensive. Mt says nothing of the women's purpose of anointing the body with spices; in Mk this is the motive for their visit to the tomb. The number of women is reduced from three to two. **1.** The time is dawn on the day after the Sabbath; Mt's opening phrase means "after the Sabbath," not "on the evening of the Sabbath." **2–4.** In Mt it is unnecessary for the women to ask who shall remove the stone; Mt's legendary expansion makes them witnesses of the removal of the stone by an angel. The guards Mt has placed at the tomb are completely overcome by the apparition. Mt calls the being "the angel of the Lord" (see comment on 1:20); Mk and Lk more cautiously speak of "a youth" and "two men," but the description of their white garb and their luminous appearance is the same, and no doubt is left that celestial messengers are meant. The women are called to witness the vital fact that the tomb is empty. **7.** The messenger commissions them to inform the disciples; Mt omits special mention of Peter. Both Mk and Mt, in contrast to Lk and Jn, record apparitions to the disciples located only in Galilee. For obvious reasons Mt changes Mk's note that the women told no one that they went to tell the disciples. Mt does not relate that they made their report; the apparition of Jesus himself completes the Resurrection Narrative. **9–10.** Peculiar to Mt; but there are resemblances between this episode and the apparition of Jesus to Mary Magdalene in Jn 20:14–18. The words of Jesus are very close to the words of the angel in 28:7, and the two verses are very probably variations of the one saying.

205 **(B) The Bribing of the Guard (28:11–15).** This section, peculiar to Mt, completes 27:62–66. It is remarkable that the guards should report to the priests instead of to their commanding officer. The purpose of the narrative is to explain the current story that the disciples stole the body. It is even explained how the guards could give this explanation and escape punishment for dereliction of duty.

206 **(C) The Apostolic Commission (28:16–20).** This passage also is peculiar to Mt. **16.** No mountain has previously been mentioned, and the location of this mountain need not be sought; it lies in the same geographical order as the mountain of temptation (4:8), the mountain of the sermon (5:1), and the mountain of the transfiguration (17:1). The mention of doubt on the part of some is candid (see Jn 20:24–29). Through all the resurrection stories there runs the idea that those who saw Jesus did not recognize him. **19.** The apostolic commission is couched in the terms of the experience of the early Church. Brief as it is, it is an unusually clear presentation of what the apostolic Church understood itself to be. The Church acts in virtue of the commission that Jesus has received—a commission that is without limit. By his authority they may make disciples of all nations; there is no longer any question of the restriction of the mission to Jews. *baptizing them:* Their work is to baptize and to teach. Baptism is a rite of initiation; to baptize "into the name" is to signify that the person baptized belongs to the Trinity of persons whose names are invoked in baptism. It seems unlikely that the Trinitarian formula was the earliest baptismal formula employed, and Mt here reflects a more mature practice. **20.** The object of the teaching is "all that I have commanded you." This phrase echoes Mt's habitual presentation of Jesus as the new Moses of a new Israel. The word "command" does not affirm the establishment of a new Law, but of a new way of life, just as the Law of Moses established a way of life. *I am with you always:* The final word is an assurance of the living presence of Jesus in the Church, a presence that looks to the eschatological fulfillment of the Church. That Jesus lives in the Church is a belief that is elaborated much more in detail in the Pauline epistles, but it is not an exclusively Pauline idea. The resurrection was not a mere restoration of life nor a mere vindication of the Messiah, but the beginning of a new existence in which the life of the Messiah becomes the enduring life of that group which continues his mission. The Church itself is the witness of the resurrection; for its life and activity are a constant testimonial that Jesus lives.

(Bruce, F. F., "The End of the First Gospel," *EvQ* 12 [1940] 203–14. Dodd, C. H., "The Appearances of the Risen Christ," *Studies in the Gospels* [Fest. R. H. Lightfoot; Oxford, 1957] 9–35. Michel, O., "Der Abschluss des Matthäusevangelium," *EvT* 10 [1950] 16–26. Trémel, V., "Remarques sur l'expression de la foi trinitaire dans l'Église primitive," *LumVi* 29 [1956] 41–66.)

44

THE GOSPEL ACCORDING TO LUKE

Carroll Stuhlmueller, C.P.

BIBLIOGRAPHY

1 Arndt, W. F., *The Gospel According to St. Luke* (St. Louis, 1956). Cadbury, H. J., *The Making of Luke-Acts* (2nd ed.; London, 1958). Cerfaux, L. and J. Cambier, "Luc (Évangile selon Saint)," *VDBS* 5 (1953) 545–94. Conzelmann, H., *The Theology of St. Luke* (N.Y., 1960). Creed, J. M., *The Gospel According to St. Luke* (London, 1953). Ellis, E. E., *The Gospel of Luke* (London, 1966). Flender, H., *Heil und Geschichte in der Theologie des Lukas* (Munich, 1965). Geldenhuys, N., *Commentary on the Gospel of Luke* (NICNT; Grand Rapids; 1956). Gilmour, S. M., "Luke," *IB* (Nashville, 1952) 8. Ginns, R., "The Gospel... According to St. Luke," *CCHS* 744–75. Grundmann, W., *Das Evangelium nach Lukas* (ThHkNT 3; 2nd ed.; Berlin, 1961). Hastings, A., *Prophet and Witness in Jerusalem* (Baltimore, 1958). Klostermann, E., *Das Lukasevangelium* (HNT 2/1; 2nd ed.; Tübingen, 1929). Lagrange, M.-J., *Évangile selon Saint Luc* (EBib; 4th ed.; Paris, 1927). Lampe, G. W. H., "Luke," *PCB* 714–34. Leaney, A. R. C., *A Commentary on the Gospel According to St. Luke* (HNTC; N.Y., 1958). Manson, W., *The Gospel of Luke* (MNTC; N.Y., 1930). Osty, É., *L'Évangile selon Saint Luc* (BJ; 2nd ed.; Paris, 1953). Ott, W., *Gebet und Heil: Die Bedeutung der Gebetsparänese in der lukanischen Theologie* (StANT 12; Munich, 1965). Plummer, A., *The Gospel According to St. Luke* (ICC; 10th ed.; N.Y., 1914). Rengstorf, K. H., *Das Evangelium nach Lukas* (NTD 3; Göttingen, 1962). Schmid, J., *Das Evangelium nach Lukas* (RNT 3; Regensburg, 1960). Taylor, V., *Behind the Third Gospel: A Study of the Proto-Luke Hypothesis* (Oxford, 1926). Valensin, A. and J. Huby, *Évangile selon Saint Luc* (VS 3; 41st ed.; Paris, 1952). Wellhausen, J., *Das Evangelium Lucae* (Berlin, 1904).

F–B 86–106. Guthrie, *NTI* 3.84–113. Léon-Dufour, X., R–F, *INT* 221–49. Wik, *NTI* 199–221. *IPLCG*, 295–331.

INTRODUCTION

2 **(I) Author.** Christian tradition has consistently named Luke, Paul's "beloved physician" (Col 4:14), as the author of the Third Gospel. Irenaeus (*Adv. haer.* 3.1,1; 3.14,1 [written *ca.* AD 185, in Gaul]) is probably the earliest witness. In the beginning of the 3rd cent. confirmation comes from Africa (Tertullian, *Adv. Marc.* 4.5), from Egypt (Clement of Alexandria, *Stromateis* 1.21; 5.12), and possibly even earlier from Italy (Muratorian fragment). As J. M. Creed points out, Luke was not a prominent figure in the apostolic church; he was neither an apostle nor an eyewitness of Jesus' earthly life. It is much more difficult, therefore, to explain how Luke's name later became attached to the Gospel than it is to accept the Church's long-standing tradition.

The fullest defense that the author of the Third Gospel was a physician has been made by W. K. Hobart, *The Medical Language of St. Luke* (Dublin, 1882; repr., 1954). Thorough studies by H. J. Cadbury (*The Style and Literary Method of Luke* [HTS 6; Cambridge, 1919]; *JBL* 45 [1926] 190–209) have shown that one cannot prove from the language of the Third Gospel that its author was a physician. Not only is the same vocabulary shared by other ancient Gk writers who were certainly not medical men, but it also seems certain that physicians in those days did not possess a technical language all their own. Nonetheless, Luke makes enough significant changes in his sources, particularly in what he drew from Mk, to make the tradition about "Luke the physician" very plausible: e.g., Lk's reference to a "great" fever in 4:38 (modifying Mk 1:30f.); his statement in 5:12 about the "man covered with leprosy" (expanding Mk 1:40); his omission of a derogatory remark about physicians in 8:43. Finally, in Acts 28:7–10, Paul and his traveling companion, Luke, are highly honored for curing many sick persons on the island of Malta. A number of other texts fit most conveniently with a medical profession: 6:18; 8:42; 13:11,32; Acts 3:7; 9:33.

3 Another tradition, voiced by Eusebius (*HE* 3.4,6) as well as by Julius Africanus and the Monarchian prologue to Lk, identifies Luke's hometown as Antioch on the Orontes (A. Strobel, *ZNW* 49 [1958] 131–34). Granting that Luke is also the author of Acts, we can appreciate his acquaintance with church affairs in Antioch (Acts 11:19ff.; 13:1–3; 15:1–5,22–35; 18:22). The Western Text introduces a "we" clause at 11:28; this is probably not the original reading but it is best explained

by the Antiochian tradition of Luke's origin. That his background was Gentile and pagan is implied in Col 4:10–14.

Luke appears rather suddenly and unobtrusively at Paul's side during Mission II (→ Life of Paul, 46:35); Acts begins to relate events in the first person plural. These "We-Sections" occur in Acts 16:10–17; 20:5–21:18; 27:1–28:16. From these sections it seems that Luke accompanied Paul from Troas (in northern Asia Minor) to the seaport of Philippi in Greece. He remained at Philippi for six or seven years until Paul returned on Mission III. Both men traveled by boat to Miletus and Caesarea; after landing at Caesarea they went to Jerusalem. Luke remained near Paul during his imprisonment at Caesarea; he went with Paul and Aristarchus on the perilous journey to Rome. Paul names Luke as one of his most faithful companions during the Roman house arrest (Col 4:14; Phlm 23f.). During this time at Rome, Luke may have made personal contact with Mark. In 2 Tm Paul is made to say: "Demas has deserted me, loving this world [cf. Col 4:14]... only Luke is with me" (4:9,11). Later Christian tradition continues the life story of Luke, but its historical accuracy cannot be demonstrated. According to the Anti-Marcionite Prologue, Luke was unmarried, labored in Achaia (Greece), and died at the age of 84. The *Acta* of his alleged martyrdom are unreliable. The Emperor Constantius II transferred his relics to Constantinople in AD 357; a later legend tells of a second transfer (1177) to Padua, Italy. In the 14th cent. it was believed that Luke was a gifted painter and the artist of a famous icon of Mary, now preserved in Rome (S. Maria Maggiore); but cf. Augustine, *De Trin.*, 8.5,7; M.-J. Lagrange, *Luc*, xviii–xix. Another, hardly acceptable tradition claims that Luke was one of the 72 disciples and the unnamed disciple of Emmaus (Lk 24:13–35). The Western Church celebrates his feast on Oct. 18.

4 **(II) Literary Style and Characteristics.** Luke ushers the NT into the world of literary excellence. He moves with masterful control and delicate smoothness from the classical style of the Prologue (1:1–4) to the strongly Hebraic tone of the Infancy Narrative (1:5–2:52) to the heavily septuagintal pattern of the rest of his Gospel; in Acts he reverts to the classical style. For instance, his use of the Gk vb. *egeneto* (it happened) is striking: the LXX form (*egeneto* followed by a finite verb without *kai*) occurs 22 times in Lk, but never in Acts; the classical Gk construction (*egeneto* followed by an infinite) is found 5 times in Lk and 15 times in Acts (see *GrBib* § 389).

Luke the physician writes with an observant eye to mannerisms, psychological reactions, hidden motivations. He alone gives the psychological setting in 3:15; 4:14f.; 9:43; 11:1,29; 13:1; 17:20; 18:1,9; 19:11. His pagan origin as well as his extensive traveling is probably responsible for his broadminded openness to all groups of peoples. He shows a favoritism for minorities, segregated groups, and the underprivileged. Samaritans, lepers, publicans, soldiers, public sinners in disgrace, unlettered shepherds, the poor—all these receive special encouragement in his Gospel.

5 Luke writes primarily for Gentiles, and for their sake he makes many changes in the Gospel tradition. He will either omit Semitic words or find a substitute for them. He never uses the following Semitic words that occur in other Gospels: *abba* (Father) in Mk 14:36 (cf. Lk 22:42); *Boanerges* (sons of thunder) in Mk 3:17 (cf. Lk 9:54); *ephphatha* (be opened) in Mk 7:34; *hōsanna* (save, we pray) in Mk 11:9; Jn 12:13; Mt 21:9 (cf. Lk 19:38). Instead of the Hebr title *rabbi*, Luke prefers *didaskale* (teacher), and especially *epistata* (master). He will give the meaning of the word instead of its Aram form; he uses *kranion* (Gk word for "skull") instead of *golgotha*.

Another concession to Gentile readers is his practice of seldom—at least as compared with Mt—quoting the OT. But he has another way of inferring the fulfillment of OT hopes and promises. For Luke, Jesus himself is the prophet; he uses this title for Jesus more often than Mk (Lk 4:24; 7:16,39; 9:19). Jesus appears especially in the role of Elijah, the prophet sent to Gentiles. And yet Luke never presents Jesus preaching to Gentiles. The comparison with Elijah will be appreciated only if we keep one other factor in mind. Luke not only parallels the ministry of Jesus in his Gospel with that of the Church in Acts, but he sees a fulfillment of Jesus' prophetic ministry in the Church. The following parallels can be noted: baptism of the Spirit (Lk 3:21f.; Acts 2:1ff.); preaching about the Spirit (Lk 4:16–19; Acts 2:17); rejected (Lk 4:29; Acts 7:58; 13:50); cure of multitudes (Lk 4:40f.; Acts 2:43; 5:16); glorification (Lk 9:28–36; Acts 1:9–11). Luke, therefore, not only veers away from OT quotations, of less interest to his Gentile readers, but also directs attention to Jesus' prophetic ministry, which finds fulfillment in the Church's ministry among the Gentiles.

6 Another characteristic of Lk appears in the way earlier events or statements anticipate or "prophesy" future events; hopes are thus seen eventually to reach fulfillment in Jesus' passion–glorification. Some statements suspend the reader between the present and the future: 1:24,56,80; 2:33–35,39,49–52; 4:13,43; 5:35. At other times we detect a definite parallel between the present and the future: (1) 4:29; 20:15; 23:18; (2) 3:21f.; 12:49f.; 22:15,42; (3) 2:14; 19:38; (4) 13:35; 19:38; 9:31,51; chs. 22–24. Luke, however, not only has a way of foreshadowing the future but also feels the necessity of imparting a literary symmetry to an episode. He will round out the description of an event by including details of what will happen later: 1:24,56,80; 3:19f.; 4:14–30. He rearranges the sequence of events at Jericho, so that something important happens before, during, and after (19:1–28). He recasts ch. 14 according to an artificially contrived chronological sequence: entering the house (v. 1); taking one's place at table (v. 7); lunch or dinner (v. 12); evening dinner (v. 16).

In a desire for order, Luke ordinarily avoids unnecessary repetitions of similar events: only one anointing of Jesus (7:36–50); one multiplication of loaves and fishes (9:12–17); one account of the barren fig tree (13:6–9); one return of Jesus to the apostles in the garden (22:39–46); one trial scene before Jewish authorities (22:66–71). This arrangement and suppression of details from an artistic point of view did not keep Luke from a double citation of certain sayings, or logia, of Jesus. Luke was a careful historian besides being a sensitive artist; he respected his sources. Some logia, therefore, occur twice; derived once from Mk and perhaps again from Q: 8:16 = 11:33; 8:17 = 12:2; 8:18 = 19:26; 9:24 = 17:33; 9:26 = 12:9; 9:50 = 11:23. Luke thus parallels the first (4:1–9:50) and the second stage (9:51–19:28) of Jesus' ministry.

7 **(III) Doctrinal Characteristics.** More light will be cast upon the literary qualities of Lk as we investigate the author's religious emphasis. Some of Luke's doctrinal attitudes have already been mentioned in the literary study: Jesus as prophet; the parallel between Jesus' activity in the Third Gospel and the Church's ministry in Acts; the concern for the Gentiles, the poor, and the outcasts.

An overarching plan reaches from the Gospel into Acts. Each begins in messianic Jerusalem with the imparting of the Spirit (Lk 1:5–2:52; 3:21f.; Acts 1–2). The Gospel then presents Jesus' Galilean ministry (4:1–9:50) and his journey to Jerusalem (9:51–19:28). Acts subsequently takes up the early ministry of the apostles, confined for the most part within Judaism (Acts 8–15), followed by Paul's journey to the center of the world, Rome. Each ends with a rejection of Jesus by his own people, which leads to a world-wide apostolate. Not only is there this parallel between the Gospel and Acts, but we also find that Acts continues where the Gospel leaves off. In Lk, Jesus never preaches immediately to Gentiles, nor is the kingdom fully established with Jesus. The kingdom must include the Gentiles, but this universal scope is realized only after Jesus' ascension, in the ministry of the Church, as described by Acts. Lk repeatedly reminds its readers that the time of the parousia is quite indefinite; the kingdom did not appear in full glory with the resurrection of Jesus, nor with the fall of Jerusalem; now, within the Church it is gradually but surely being revealed—in anticipation of the final fulfillment of all promises and hopes.

8 Within this larger framework, Luke will develop other, subordinate themes. He writes the "Gospel of Mercy" or the "Gospel of Great Pardons." Lk alone of the Syn includes such episodes or parables as: the sinful woman (7:36–50); the lost sheep, the lost coin, and the prodigal son (ch. 15); Jesus' presence in the house of Zacchaeus (19:1–10); Jesus' executioners (23:34); the good thief (23:39–43). Lk (6:36) records Jesus' words, "Be merciful as your Father is merciful," which Mt (5:48) reads as "Be perfect...." The entire sermon "on the plain" focuses attention upon the social bond of charity (Lk 6:17–49); Mt's catechetical sermon "on the mount" delays over the legal aspects of the subject and the relevance of the Mosaic Law. Luke makes other, notable additions to the text of Mk: at 5:32, he inserts the phrase "to repentance" after the statement that "I have not come to call the just but sinners" (cf. Mk 2:17; Mt 9:13). A similar modification occurs at Lk 8:12 (cf. Mk 4:15; Mt 13:19).

The pardon of Jesus reaches out to all men, so that Luke has composed the "Gospel of Universal Salvation." The genealogical table (3:23–38) does not limit Jesus' ancestry to the royal line of David, as in Mt 1:1–16, but places Jesus within the family tree of the entire human race as a son of Adam who was of God. The faith of Abraham can be shared with all men, thereby making them Abraham's children (Lk 3:8). Immediately preceding this statement was the fuller rendition of an Isaian text; Mk 1:3 and Mt 3:3 omit the words that "all mankind shall see the salvation of God" (Lk 3:6).

9 This same merciful concern reaches to the poor and lowly, so that Lk merits to be called the "Gospel of the Poor." This spirit shines brightly in the Infancy Narrative, where the poor and insignificant are chosen for the greatest privileges: the childless couple, Zechariah and Elizabeth; Mary and Joseph from unknown Nazareth; shepherds from the countryside; an old man and elderly widow at the Temple. Luke preserves the strong regard for actual poverty in his beatitudes; in writing "happy are you poor," he keeps the direct address of the second person and does not add, like Mt, "poor in spirit" (Lk 6:20). He includes the full Isaian text about the poor to whom the gospel is brought (4:18; 7:22). The parable of the rich man and Lazarus is exclusive to Lk (16:19–31). Still other words about poverty, including a parable, are found only in Lk (12:13–21).

10 It is not surprising, therefore, that Luke should write the "Gospel of Absolute Renouncement." Disciples must leave "all things" (Lk 5:11); in a similar statement, Mk and Mt restrict the renouncement to nets and father (Mk 1: 16–20; Mt 4:18–22) to follow Jesus. Yet another statement, only in Lk (9:62), insists upon total dedication to Jesus. Lk alone adds the word "wife" to the list of what some will be asked to renounce for the sake of the kingdom (14:26). Again, where Mt writes "lay up for yourselves treasure in heaven" (6:20), Lk has, "sell what you have and give alms" (12:33). Lk extends the cross-bearing of the single eschatological moment (Mk 8:34; 16:24) to the continuous daily sorrows of life (Lk 9:23). The necessity of renunciation and suffering as the way to glorious fulfillment shows up in repeated assertions that Jesus "must" suffer (9:22; 13:33; 17:25; 22:37; 24:7, 26,44).

11 Such detachment and renunciation are possible because Jesus and his followers are shown continuously dedicated to God in this "Gospel of Prayer and of the Holy Spirit." Lk explicitly portrays Jesus at prayer before every important step of the Messianic ministry: at his baptism (3:21); before the choice of the Twelve (6:12); before Peter's profession of faith (9:18); at the transfiguration (9:28); before teaching the "Our Father" (11:1); in Gethsemane (22:41). Jesus was the master of prayer and frequently insisted that his disciples be men of prayer themselves (6:28; 10:2; 11:1–13; 18:1–8; 21:36).

Lk constantly alludes to the role of the Spirit (1:15,35, 41,67; 2:25–27; 3:16,22; 4:1,14,18; 10:21; 11:13; 12:10,12). Where Mt 7:11 speaks of the good things the heavenly Father gives to those who ask, Lk 11:13 speaks of the Holy Spirit who is the gift par excellence. Once given to the OT judges, this Spirit is now sent to John the Baptist (1:15,80) and his parents (1:41,67). Jesus is conceived through the power of the Spirit (1:35) and is himself filled with the Holy Spirit (4:1). What happened to Jesus must continue to happen to the Church—until the parousia. The Spirit, consequently, occupies the same prominent position in Acts. The implication is clear enough. The Church continues the mission of Jesus; the eschatological age, inaugurated by Jesus, persists until the Spirit brings it to perfection at some future moment.

12 The Spirit, possessed by Jesus, spreads joy and peace among those who listen to him. Luke wrote the "Gospel of Messianic Joy." Various Gk words for joy or exultation occur with notable frequency in Lk: *chairō* (12 times in Lk, 6 times in Mt, twice in Mk); *chara* (8 times in Lk, 6 times in Mt, once in Mk); *agalliasis* (twice in Lk; not at all in Mt and Mk); *agalliaō* (twice in Lk, once in Mt; not in Mk); *skirtaō* (3 times in Lk, but not in Mt or Mk). Even a cursory reading of the various Gospels leaves the impression that Mt has a serious, almost majestic setting and Mk the relaxed candor of a diary; but Lk rebounds with joy after one has had time to ponder the wonder of what has taken place. More than any of the other Evangelists, Luke tells of the admiration of the crowds following Jesus (5:26; 10:17; 13:17; 18:43). Such a spirit among the people fulfills Jesus' promise that his followers will be "happy" and "fortunate" (Gk *makarios*, 1:45; 6:20–22; 7:23; 10:23; 11:27f.; 12:37f.; 14:14f.; 23:29).

13 **(IV) Sources.** Lk 1:1–4 states strenuous efforts were made to acquire firsthand knowledge about Jesus. Various written documents or official traditions, as well as many oral traditions, privately circulating in the Church, were tracked down. At Antioch, where he may have been baptized, Luke came into contact with Manaen, a boyhood companion of Herod Antipas (Acts 13:1); perhaps through him he met Joanna, the wife of Antipas' steward, Chuza (Lk 8:3). These persons could have informed Luke about Herod's dealings with Jesus, which are related only in Lk (13:31–33; 23:7–12). In Asia Minor he must have moved at times among the Johannine disciples; either from the apostle John or his disciples, Luke absorbed some of the themes characteristic of Jn and acquired the Infancy Narrative as well as the substructure of his Passion–Glorification Narrative. Johannine traces in Lk are: the motifs of Jerusalem and the Temple; the importance of Jesus' glorification; exclusive facts about Jesus' ministry at Nazareth (4:22b–30, which John learned from Mary?); Johannine influence on the transfiguration scene (Lk 9:28–36); Jesus' hymn of praise (10:22); the exhortation to trust in God (12:32). (See J. A. Bailey, *The Traditions Common to the Gospels of Luke and John* [NovTSup 7; Leiden, 1963]; P. Parker, *NTS* 9 [1963] 317–36.)

14 Luke had almost two years at his disposal—during Paul's imprisonment at Caesarea (Acts 24:27)—to seek information and interview persons who had known Jesus or heard about him from firsthand witnesses. He met the deacon Philip, the apostle of Samaria (Acts 8; 21:8); from him Luke could have gained knowledge of events described in 9:52–56; 17:11–19. The penitent woman, whose name Luke kept secret, felt confident to relate her conversion to Luke the physician (7:36–50). Although Luke, like Paul, never married for the sake of the Kingdom of God and the apostolate (14:26; 18:29), he recognizes a more important role for women than does any of the other evangelists. The reason for this can be traced to his Hellenistic background, where society permitted women to occupy a more prominent, public place than was true within Judaism (Acts 8:27; 16:13–15; 18:26; 24:24).

15 Another source, more important for Luke's general attitude than for detailed information, lay in his association with the apostle Paul. The commentary will discuss this Pauline influence at 7:9; 10:7f., 39; 11:13; 17:7–10; 18:1,14; 21:19,28,34–36. Paul may have contributed to Luke's strong positions on the universality of salvation; Jesus' will to save; and his cool attitude toward the Law. A detailed study of Lk's contact with Paul is given by A. Plummer (*Luke*, xliv–xlv, liii–lix).

16 Besides these oral sources, Luke employed several documents and, in fact, drew from them rather freely. His most important written source was the Gospel of Mk. Lk incorporates 60 per cent of Mk's 661 verses; Marcan passages make up one-third of Lk's 1149 verses. The main parallels between Lk and Mk occur thus:

Lk 4:31–6:19 follows Mk 1:21–3:12
Lk 8:4–9:50 follows Mk 4:1–9:41
Lk 18:15–21:38 follows Mk 10:13–13:37.

The question is still open whether Lk depends on a text of Mk's Gospel anterior to the one we now possess.

The dependence of Lk on Mt is still more complicated. Narratives sections seem to have come at times from Mt through Mk: Lk 4:1–3 relies immediately upon Mk 1:13, which may have depended on Mt 4:1–3; other similar cases are Lk 5:26; Mk 2:12; Mt 9:8; or again Lk 8:25; Mk 4:41; Mt 8:27; or again Lk 8:44; Mk 5:27; Mt 9:20. There are occasions, especially in the report of Jesus' "sayings," where Lk has a word-for-word agreement with Mt; here Lk and Mt are probably depending upon a common written source, Q (→ Syn Problem, 40:21). Some examples are: Lk 3:7–9 and Mt 3:7–10; Lk 4:3–12 and Mt 4:3–10; Lk 7:19–35 and Mt 11:4–19. Because Lk shows important differences from Mt in particular sayings, we suspect that he is at times using another source, e.g., Lk 6:47–49 (see Mt 7:24–27); Lk 12:54–56 (see Mt 16:2f.); Lk 13:25–27 (see Mt 7:22f.).

The thesis has been advanced by B. H. Streeter (*The Four Gospels: Study of Origins* [London, 1924]) and V. Taylor (*Behind the Third Gospel*) that Luke first composed a document (proto-Lk) from Q material and other information acquired at Caesarea (the latter was called L by Streeter); only later, after his arrival at Rome, did Luke combine proto-Lk with Marcan material. The main objection to this hypothesis is the sturdy position that the Marcan material occupies in Lk; it seems to be the backbone of the Gospel, the framework in which other narratives and sayings were inserted (→ Inspiration, 66:62).

17 The manner in which Luke used his sources further illuminates the style and characteristics of the Third Gospel. Luke handles the material taken from his sources respectfully but never slavishly. He insinuates his own viewpoint with delicate tact. For the sake of a smooth, literary style, he makes many omissions: details that would bore or offend his Gentile readers and incidents that would disrupt his over-all plan (an early ministry in Jerusalem; trips outside Galilee; postresurrection appearances in Galilee). A sense of delicacy keeps Luke from including scenes of violence and disrespect: the murder of John the Baptist (Mk 6:16–29); the gruff remarks of the disciples (compare Lk 8:22–25 with Mk 4:35–41); the outrages committed in the passion (Mk 14:65; 15:15–19). He also suppresses remarks that may seem to limit Jesus' knowledge about the future or about men's thoughts (Mk 4:40; 13:32).

Besides omissions, Luke also retouches and expands his material. The effects of this editorial work have already been noted in pointing out the various doctrinal themes.

18 **(V) Date and Place of Composition.** The position has frequently been taken, particularly by Catholic scholars, that Lk was written before the end of Paul's Roman house arrest (*ca.* AD 63), because Acts stops with Paul still in custody. If Acts was completed before Paul's release, the Gospel must have been written still earlier (Acts 1:1). But the phrase that "for two full years he [Paul] remained in his own rented house" (Acts 28:30), involves a technical term of Roman jurisprudence, designating an uncontested case in which the defendant is allowed to go free. Acts, therefore, sets no definite date for the composition of the Lucan works.

Sometimes a date after the fall of Jerusalem (AD 70) is advocated because of the detailed description of this catastrophe in the discourse beginning with 21:5ff. Most of Lk's descriptive language is indeed drawn from OT texts and it could just as easily be dated before the fall of the city. But a comparison of this section with Mk and Mt does reveal important modifications, best explained by a date after AD 70. Lk deletes the reference to a flight in the winter, eliminates "the abomination of desolation," and speaks instead of an army besieging the city. A still more convincing argument for a date after 70 comes from the general attitude of the entire Gospel. Lk divides the eschatological discourse of Jesus, so that one part speaks only of the parousia and the presence of the kingdom (17:20ff.), whereas the other is almost completely preoccupied with the fall of Jerusalem (21:5ff.). Whereas Mk 13 and Mt 24 combine both momentous acts of God, Lk separates them, as if to say that the fall of Jerusalem did not inaugurate the Second Coming of Jesus. The Church is still expecting the parousia. The Commentary will point out how Luke has edited the words of Jesus or of John the Baptist, as found in Mk or Mt, so that the kingdom is no longer announced as imminent. The full eschatological kingdom is still being prepared for by the ministry of the Church. The Lucan version of the Lord's Prayer adds the simple but important word "daily" in the petition for bread; Mt, for his part, leaves the impression of asking for strength in the single, eschatological moment (Lk 11:3; Mt 6: 11). Lk again adds "daily" to Jesus' demand that his disciples carry their crosses. Lk makes it clear that Christians face a long, continuous testing (9:23). We conclude, therefore, to a date after AD 70; there is no reason to go beyond 80 or 85. A very old tradition supplied by Irenaeus and the Monarchian prologue and accepted by Jerome and Gregory Nazianzen, gives southern Greece as the place of composition.

19 **(VI) Outline.** The Gospel according to Luke is outlined as follows:

(I) Prologue (1:1-4)
(II) The Infancy Narrative (1:5-2:52)
  (A) Diptych of the Annunciation (1:5-56)
    (a) The Annunciation of the Birth of John the Baptist (1:5-25)
    (b) The Annunciation of the Birth of Jesus (1:26-38)
    (c) The Visitation (1:39-56)
  (B) The Diptych of the Births (1:57-2:52)
    (a) The Birth of John the Baptist (1:57-80)
    (b) The Birth of Jesus (2:1-40)
    (c) The Boy Jesus in the Temple (2:41-52)
(III) Preparation for the Public Ministry (3:1-4:13)
  (A) John the Baptist (3:1-20)
  (B) The Baptism of Jesus (3:21-22)
  (C) The Genealogy of Jesus (3:23-38)
  (D) The Temptation (4:1-13)
(IV) The Galilean Ministry (4:14-9:50)
  (A) Two Typical Events: At Nazareth and Capernaum (4:14-44)
  (B) From the Call of Peter to the Naming of the Twelve (5:1-6:16)
  (C) The Full Ministry (6:17-9:9)
  (D) The Climax (9:10-50)
(V) The Journey Narrative (9:51-19:28)
  (A) Section Proper to Lk (9:51-18:14)
  (B) Section Common with Mark's Gospel (18:15-19:28)
(VI) The Jerusalem Ministry (19:29-21:38)
  (A) Events at Jesus' Entry (19:29-48)
  (B) Controversies in Jerusalem (20:1-21:4)
  (C) Discourse on the Fall of Jerusalem (21:5-38)
(VII) The Passion and Glorification of Jesus (22:1-24:53)
  (A) The Paschal Meal (22:1-38)
  (B) The Passion, Death, and Burial (22:39-23:56)
  (C) The Resurrection and Ascension (24:1-53)

Further subdivisions of the Gospel will be found in the Commentary itself.

COMMENTARY

20 **(I) Prologue (1:1-4).** Luke introduces his Gospel in the style of Gk classics; similar introductions are found in Dioscurides, *Concerning Medical Matters* (1.1); Josephus, *AgAp* (1.1, 1 § 1-3) and *JW* (1.1,1 §1-3); and *Aristeas* (1). Luke is thus claiming to write a work of literary importance, and critical judgment will agree that he has admirably succeeded in this goal. The grammar and diction of vv. 1-4 carefully and majestically obey the classical norms; they form one sentence, closely interlocked with subordinate clauses and participial constructions, and bound with a protasis and apodosis. **1.** *inasmuch as many... I also:* Each of these two major parts contains three cola, or sections; these can be lined up in parallel columns with corresponding phrases. Finally, this prologue introduces both of Luke's books, the Gospel and Acts; classical style permitted a second preface (Acts 1:1) at the beginning of the second half of a major work (cf. Josephus, *AgAp* 2.1, 1 § 1; Diodorus Siculus, *History*, 2.1). The stately compound conj. *epei-dē-per*, common enough in classical Greek, occurs nowhere else in the NT (or the LXX); it has the meaning, "with reference to a fact already well-known" (see Bl-Deb-F § 456, 1). *draw up:* The Gk vb. *ana-taxasthai* implies a repetition by which facts have been memorized. *an account:* Luke avoids Mk's introductory word *euaggelion* (gospel or good news). Instead of that more theological term, he prefers one that lays more stress on the historical genre of his composition. Later on in the prologue, he insists that what he is writing about has really happened. *fulfilled among us:* Luke does not pretend in any way to be an eyewitness. The pf. form of the Gk participle indicates that what happened in the life of Jesus was perfectly completed and that its effects are now being felt "among us" in the Church. **2.** *eyewitnesses:* Avoiding the Gk word *martys*, ordinarily reserved for the apostles who lived with Jesus, Luke has in mind a much wider group of witnesses, like the deacon Philip (Acts 8:5; 21:8), Symeon Niger (Acts 13:1); Manaen (Acts 13:1); various women (Lk 8:1-3; → 13 above). *ministers of the word:* "Word" (*logos*), with its biblical background in Hebr *dābār*, refers to events as well as to statements. We find a vague indication here of what form criticism has propounded with scientific learning. Luke is drawing not only upon strictly eyewitness records but also upon the instructions, prayers, and popular stories through which the eyewitness accounts were "ministered" in the Church. **3.** *after following up all things carefully:* The Gk pf. tense of the verb indicates Luke's competence; he has made a thorough investigation. *from the beginning:* The apostolic kerygma ordinarily began with John the Baptist (Mk 1:2-8; Acts 13:24f.); Luke actually goes beyond that and prefixes an Infancy Narrative. *Most Excellent Theophilus:* The title honors a high-ranking government official (Acts 23:26; 24:3; 26:25). H. J. Cadbury claims that Theophilus was probably not a Christian; Luke was writing a defense of Christianity for the Roman government (*Beginnings* 2, 510). It seems unlikely, however, that Luke would compose such a theological gospel as his actually is for an apologetical purpose. *Theophilus:* The name means "beloved by God," very similar to the Hebr *y^edîdāh*, found under various forms in the OT (2 Kgs 22:1; 2 Sm 12:25 [*y^edîdyāh*]). The Gk name has appeared on Jewish inscriptions and papyri from the 3rd cent. BC, and there is good reason to think that Theophilus was a prominent Christian to whom Luke dedicated his work because the former may have defrayed the cost of the parchment or performed other services for the Church. The Gospel, in this case, would actually be intended for the entire Church. *an orderly account:* This need not be chronological; it could be geographical or follow a more theological plan according to the successive stages of salvation history. **4.** *the certainty of the words:* The Greek can also mean "that you may be more solidly and certainly grounded in the mysteries of salvation."

21 **(II) The Infancy Narrative (1:5-2:52).** Mt, Lk, and Jn add some kind of "infancy gospel" to their major undertaking. Jn's can be described as an early Christian hymn, proclaiming Jesus' pre-existence as well as his becoming flesh; Mt's account is cast in the form of an official, catechetical statement; Lk's narrative combines the hymnic, doctrinal, and meditative style. That these "infancy narratives" were not an original part of the apostolic preaching can be established, not only from the fact that Jesus' redemptive ministry began only with his baptism by John but also from the fact that the apostles' ministry depended on what they had seen as eyewitnesses. In preaching, the apostles worked backward from Pentecost to the resurrection to the passion and death to the public ministry and eventually to the "hidden life" of Jesus. The infancy narratives emerged out of the endeavor to impart an ever fuller understanding of the redemptive work and words of Jesus (cf. E. H. Maly, *BT* 1 [1962–63] 172–78).

22 Whereas Mt 1–2 consistently quotes Scripture, Lk 1–2 alludes to Scripture, with the single exception of the scene of Jesus' presentation in the Temple (2:23). Moreover, Mt's scriptural citations, in fact his entire Infancy Narrative, bear the form of an explicit, official statement of the (Jerusalem?) Church; conversely, Lk's scriptural allusions are more intuitive and meditative, more along the style of a popular or private tradition. Each Infancy Narrative has the earmarks of a miniature gospel, but Mt more completely covers the basic areas of the Christian message: genealogy (messianic promises through Israel); role of Joseph (through whom Jesus acquires Davidic or royal prerogatives); conversion of the Gentiles (typified in the Magi); the Exodus motif (in the flight into Egypt); victory through sorrow and death (case of the Innocents, whom the fuller citation of Jer 31 shows to be victorious); full consecration to God (exemplified in the Nazirite vow). Most of these elements can be detected in Lk's Infancy Narrative: the Jewish background of Jesus is abundantly clear; he is said to inherit the throne of his father David (1:32); universality of salvation is seen in the call of the lowest strata of Jewish society, the shepherds; a prophecy is made about contradiction and the sword; full consecration is performed through the presentation in the Temple. Both Lk and Mt, therefore, are not primarily concerned with the actual details of Jesus' infancy but with a gospel of redemption.

A Qumran influence may be uncovered in Lk's Infancy Narrative. A verse in the early chapters of Acts (6:7) hints at a possible, large-scale conversion from the Qumran covenanters (F. M. Braun, *RB* 62 [1955] 34f.). Not only is Lk's Infancy Narrative significantly different from the rest of the Gospel in giving only scant (if any) attention to Gentiles, but its messianism is close to Qumran's in other ways. Both emphasize the messianic role of a prophet-precursor (Lk 1:16f.; 1QS 8:14–16; 9:19f.); the importance of both a priestly messiah and a Davidic messiah within a liturgical setting (Lk 1:32; 2:46; 1QS 9:11, 1QSa).

23 Our tentative conclusion is that Lk's Infancy Narrative originated at Jerusalem within the early, post-Pentecostal days of Jewish Christianity—a conclusion that can be strengthened by a study of stylistic details. An original Hebr text appears at times beneath the surface of the present Gk version. The strong parallelism within most verses indicates an author of Semitic background. The parallelism, however, extends beyond ideas to the sound of words, when the Greek is translated back into Hebrew. Assonance can be detected: in 1:17,76, "before him" (*l*^{e}*pānāw*) and "to prepare" (*l*^{e}*pinnôt*); in 1:56, "she remained" (*wattēšeb*) and "she returned" (*wattāšob*); in 2:11, "messiah" (*māšî*^{a}*ḥ*) and "savior" (*môšî*^{a}*ʿ*). See R. Laurentin, *Structure et théologie de Luc I–II* (EBib; Paris, 1957) 12–13, n. 5; P. Winter, *NTS* 1 [1954–55] 111–21. The major difficulty, however, with this early dating of the first stage of Lk's Infancy Narrative lies in the prominent place which the narrative gives to Mary. Would the Church during those first six years after Pentecost have bestowed such honor upon Mary? The Infancy Narrative seems to demand a longer period of reflection, at a time and place more distant from Mary. This difficulty does not neutralize the Jewish influences within Lk 1–2, but it makes us more cautious in our conclusions.

Many indications point to a second stage in the evolution of the Lucan Infancy Narrative, within a Johannine group. The abundant use of number symbolism in Lk 1–2 reminds us of both Jn and Ap. Lk 1–2 favors: the number twelve (2:42), which was the number of the tribes of Israel and the full number of God's elect (Ap 7:4–8; 21:10–21); the number three (2:46), the length of time between Jesus' death and resurrection (Jn 2:19); 70 weeks of Dn 9:24, which knit together the events of Lk 1–2 (6 months, or 180 days, from the announcement to Zechariah to Mary's annunciation; 9 months, or 270 days, from Mary's annunciation to the birth of Jesus; 40 days from Jesus' birth to his presentation in the Temple—giving the total of 490 days, or 70 weeks of 7 days); Jn's Gospel makes great use of the symbolic number seven: 7 days of Jesus' first ministry (Jn 1:29,35,40,43,47; 2:1); 7 great discourses; 7 principal miracles.

24 The schematization of scenes in Lk 1–2 reminds one of Ap and thus strengthens the dependence upon a Johannine circle of disciples (cf. W. Heidt, NTRG 14, 10–11). An outline of Lk's Infancy Narrative, dependent upon the studies of R. Laurentin, *Structure*, 32–33, shows the drama format within this section.

The Diptych of the Annunciation

(a) The annunciation of John the Baptist (1:5–25)	(b) The annunciation of Jesus (1:26–38)
Presentation of the parents	Presentation of the parents
Apparition of the angel	Entrance of the angel
Anxiety of Zechariah	Anxiety of Mary
"Do not fear"	"Do not fear"
Announcement of the birth	Announcement of the birth
Question: "How shall I know this?"	Question: "How shall this happen?"
Answer: The angel's reprimand	Answer: The angel's revelation
Sign: "Behold, you shall be dumb"	Sign: "Behold, your kinswoman has conceived"
Silence of Zechariah	Response of Mary
Departure of the angel	Departure of the angel
	(c) Complementary episode (1:39–56): The visitation
	Conclusion: Mary's return (1:56)

The Diptych of the Births

(a) The birth of John the Baptist (1:57f.)	(b) The birth of Jesus (2:1–20)
Joy at his birth	Joy at his birth
Indication of a canticle	Canticle of the angels
Circumcision and manifestation of John (1:59–80)	Circumcision and manifestation of Jesus (2:21–35)
First manifestation of a prophet	First manifestation of the Savior at Jerusalem
Canticle: *Benedictus*	Canticle: *Nunc Dimittis*
	Supplementary episode of Anna (2:36–38)
Conclusion: Growth refrain (1:80)	Conclusion: Growth refrain (2:40)
	(c) Complementary episode (2:41–52)
	The finding of the boy
	Conclusion: Growth refrain

25 Other indications of Johannine influence can be seen in the Temple symbolism. Not only does Lk 1–2 begin and end in the Temple and reach its climax in the presentation of the infant Jesus in the Temple, but Mary herself is compared to the Temple or Ark of the covenant (1:35,43,56), and Jesus' first recorded words refer to his Father's house (2:49). The overshadowing of the divine presence (Lk 1:35) brings to mind the reference to the Temple in Jn 1:14.

The question whether John received the Infancy Narrative from Mary is much more difficult to answer. In favor of an affirmative reply is the intuitive or feminine approach toward the mysteries of salvation; but must an intuitive approach be necessarily feminine? The intimacy of details would seem to demand Mary's willingness to share these secrets with the early Church; but need she have given anything more than a few facts? The details and style of the narrative are symbolic and biblical; they communicate the mystery of redemption, not a diary of early events.

26 Lk's Infancy Narrative is a cento of OT-LXX texts. We can cite a few examples: 1:12 (Dn 10:7,12); 1:16f. (Mal 3:1,4f.); 1:19 (Dn 9:20–23); 1:28–32 (Zech 3:14–17); 1:35 (Ex 40:35); 1:40–46,55; (2 Sm 6); 1:42 (Jgs 5:24); 1:64f. (Dn 10:16f.); 1:76 (Mal 3:1).

In conclusion, we admit the difficulty of placing the Lucan Infancy Narrative within any known literary genre. It shares some features of what is called "midrash," but it does not follow the midrashic procedure of scriptural quotation and homiletic application in story form. Neither can Lk 1–2 be classified simply as "haggadah," for this literary genre deals almost completely with fictional stories. Lk not only places his narrative within history (cf. 1:5; 2:1) but also brings many important historicodogmatic facts to the surface: names of people, geographical locations, chronology (as in 1:56, "about" six months), virgin birth, Davidic prerogatives of Jesus. Lk's Infancy Narrative, however, manifests some of the stylistic touches of both midrash and haggadah: comparison with ancient scriptures and great men or events of old; homiletic application to the present; story form to expound doctrinal truths; compenetration of various periods of time.

27 **(A) Diptych of the Annunciation (1:5–56).** See the detailed plan given in 24 above.

(a) The Annunciation of the Birth of John the Baptist (1:5–25). **5.** *Herod:* The Great, son of Antipater II, an Idumean, who was master of the palace for Hyrcanus II, the next to the last Hasmonean king. (→ History of Israel, 75:130). The Roman senate constituted Herod king (in 40 BC), but he had to fight his way to the control of Palestine. Gradually, Rome extended Herod's domain E of the Jordan into Perea and N as far as Paneas at the base of Mt. Hermon. He actually ruled from 37–4 BC. *Judea:* Lk uses the term for all Palestine. *Zechariah:* His name means "Yahweh has remembered." He belonged to the eighth division of priests, those descended from Abijah, one of the 24 grandsons of the first high priest, Aaron (1 Chr 24:10). *Elizabeth:* Her name means "God has sworn [to protect us]." She was a kinswoman of Mary, although the exact relationship is not known (1:36). The couple had had no children. This opening verse is not only very similar to Jgs 13:2 (LXX), but it recalls the many great women of Israel who had remained sterile for a long time: Sarah (Gn 15:3; 16:1); Rebekah (Gn 25:21); Rachel (Gn 29:31); the wife of Manoah (Jgs 31:2); Hannah (1 Sm 1:2). **6.** *both were just:* Unlike the Pharisees (Lk 16:15), they looked to God for the fulfillment of the promises and were always willing to be guided by his will (Acts 3:14; 7:52). *commandments and ordinances:* The phraseology echoes Dt 6:1f.,17,25; 7:11;10:13.

28 **8.** *serving as priest:* It was decided by lot which of the 800 priests of the division of Abijah would have the privilege each day of offering incense in the Holy Place, the first of two rooms constituting the Tabernacle (Ex 30:1–9; Mishnah, *Tamid* 3:1). This moment would have been the culmination of Zechariah's priestly life. **10.** *a large multitude:* This implies the evening, rather than the morning incense offering. **11.** *the angel of the Lord:* The phrase, in the OT, is often a circumlocution for the presence of God (see comment on Mt 1:20). In this case, however, the angel identifies himself as Gabriel (v. 19), the angel who announced the 70 weeks of years (→ 23 above), the final eschatological struggles, and the messianic consecration of the Holy of Holies (Dn 9). Like Zechariah, Daniel was frightened by Gabriel's appearance and was told not to fear (Dn 10:7,12). Again like Zechariah, Daniel was struck dumb, but his speech was restored (Dn 10:15f.). These parallels to apocalyptic literature make it extremely difficult to sift out the historical kernel of Luke's theological document. **13.** *do not be afraid:* These words frequently introduce a great redemptive act of God (Gn 15:1; Jos 1:9; Is 41:14). The angel's words repeat a birth formula very common in the Bible: Gn 16:11; Jgs 13:3; Is 7:14. *John:* His name means "Yahweh has shown favor" (*Yᵉhôḥānān*), a name that symbolizes the role of John in the redemptive plans of God. **14.** *joy and gladness:* Indicative of the Messianic age: Pss 96:11f.; 97:1,8; 126:2,5f.; Is 12:6; 25:9; R. Bultmann, *ThDNT* 1, 9–21 (→ 12 above). **15.** *before the Lord:* The prep. *enōpion* is found 22 times in Lk, 13 times in Acts, and nowhere else in the Gospels (excepting Jn 20:30)—an indication of a Lucan rewriting of the Infancy Narrative. *no wine or strong drink:* The boy will be dedicated as a Nazirite before birth (Nm 6:1–21). An even more important feature of the Nazirite was the provision of not cutting his hair (Jgs 16:17; 1 Sm 1:11; Acts 18:18; 21:23–26), which is not mentioned of John the Baptist. Luke may be adapting the language of an earlier passage in the Samson story (Jgs 13:14); or else the Nazirite vow—rather vague in history—could have taken different forms, like the ascetical life practiced at Qumran. *filled with a holy spirit:* The absence of the definite article shows that the reference is not to the third person in the Trinity but rather to God as exerting extraordinary salvific power. *from his mother's womb:* Like another Jeremiah (Jer 1:5). This figure of speech, similar to another in Lk 7:28, proclaims that every action of the Baptist was initiated and sustained by God; no one, therefore, was better suited to be a forerunner of the final, eschatological fulfillment in Jesus. **16.** *bring back:* The reference may be to the priestly role of reconciliation or else to the Exodus theme of coming back to the promised land (Is 40:3ff.; Mal 2:6; 3:1,24). **17.** *spirit and power of Elijah:* The attributing of Elijah's spirit to the Baptist is distinctly avoided by Luke, except in the Infancy Narrative—another indication of an original, non-Lucan authorship of the latter. Jewish tradition expected the return of Elijah before the "Day of the Lord" (see Mal 3:23). The combination of spirit and power occurs in 1QH 7:6f.; in accord with QL and the Hebr text of Sir 48:10; *Jub* 23:26; *Enoch* 90:6f., the idea seems to be that the people will no longer be proud, independent "fathers," but devoted, obedient "children." The parallel here is between fathers (the disobedient) and sons (the wisdom of the just).

29 **18.** *how shall I know this:* Zechariah's question is similar to Abraham's (Gn 15:3–5). To seek a sign accords thoroughly with biblical practice (Gn 15:8; Jgs 6:36ff.; 2 Kgs 20:8); at times, God himself volunteers a sign (Ex 3:12; Is 7:11). Zechariah's consequent punishment, therefore, is very surprising. The affliction, however, was only temporary and was tempered by the joyful expectation of a son. We sense also something of ecstatic joy, too overwhelming for words: Dn 10:15f.; Lk 24:41. This is the impression left with the people in v. 22. **19.** *Gabriel:* See comment on 1:11. His name means: "El [God] is my man [hero]." *to bring this good news:* The Gk *euaggelizō* alludes to Is 40:9; 52:7; and to the Baptist's role in Messianic salvation. **23.** *departed to his own house:* The conclusion is similar to that in the story of Hannah (1 Sm 1:19f.). Zechariah lived in the tribal portion of Judah (v. 39); an ancient tradition localizes his home at *ʿAin Karim*, some 4 mi. from Jerusalem in a valley leading into the Shephelah. **24.** *hid herself:* Did Elizabeth seclude herself for the same reason that her husband was left speechless, overcome by joy at such an unbelievable event? *five months:* Luke's way of directing attention to the next, even more wondrous event. **25.** *reproach:* Cf. Gn 30:23; 1 Sm 1:5–8,11 (see P. Benoit, *NTS* 3 [1956–57] 169–94).

30 (b) The Annunciation of the Birth of Jesus (1:26–38). The strict parallel in details between this annunciation scene and that of the Baptist, along with the overwhelming textual evidence, disqualifies any attempt to delete verses like 34 and 35, where Mary's virginal conception of Jesus is stated explicitly. To claim that the idea of virginal conception did not come from the Jewish-Christian background of these chapters but rather from pagan, Greco-Roman mythology (cf. J. M. Creed, *Luke*, 13–16) clashes with the reasons already given for the very early Jewish origin of the Lucan Infancy Narrative.

26. *sixth month:* That is, of Elizabeth's pregnancy. *Nazareth:* An insignificant town, never mentioned in the OT, in the Talmud, or by Josephus, despised by the Palestinians of Jesus' own time (Jn 1:46), and inhabited by jealous, material-minded people (Lk 4:23–30). **27.** *virgin:* Lk twice stresses Mary's virginity. In Hebrew her name, *Miryām*, means "exalted one" (see E. Vogt, *VD* 26 [1948] 163–68). Joseph, Mary's betrothed, seems to have been of Judean stock, possibly an inhabitant of Bethlehem. Through Joseph, therefore, as Jesus' legal father, and not through Mary, did Jesus inherit a claim to the Davidic throne.

31 **28.** *hail, full of grace:* The Greek is melodious, *chaire kecharitōmenē.* The word "grace" (*charis*) is associated in Lk with joy (*chara*) and wisdom (*sophia*). Greek verbs, ending in *oō*, as is the case here, do not imply fullness but rather instrumentality. Luke's word puts the emphasis upon the source of goodness rather than upon its effects. In regard to Mary, therefore, he points out that she is the object of God's grace and favor. Because the verb is also a participle, Mary is shown to have been chosen for a long time past; God's full flow of favor has already been concentrating upon her (cf. M. Cambe, *RB* 62 [1963] 193–207). P. Joüon translated the passage: "I salute you, object of [divine] favor" (*NRT* 66 [1939] 797). The Hebr form of the salutation would be *šālôm lāk*, "Peace to you" (cf. 24:36; Jn 20:19,26). Mary, more than any other human being in the Bible, is the recipient of the most impressive salutations: 1:28,30,35,42–49; 2:19f.,34. The Bible, which makes no clear distinction between body and soul, is not referring simply to Mary's physical charm. In her, more than in anyone else, God's messianic fulfillment is achieved. As such, she has received more—from and through God's anticipation of Jesus' redemptive work—than anyone else in the OT or NT. *the Lord is with you:* Although the phrase can be a simple greeting (Ru 2:4), still when it comes from God, it implies a particular office or special prerogative. The Redeemer-God professes to find an eminent fulfillment of his promises in the recipient of the greeting. Because of v. 31, some commentators (S. Lyonnet, Th. Maertens) see a reference to Immanuel of Is 7:14. Some inferior Gk mss. add: " 'Blessed are you among women.' When she had seen him." Lk, therefore, does not speak of any vision but rather of a communication of a message. The Bible speaks of angelic mediators at other great moments of salvation history (Gn 16:10; Ex 3:2; 33:2f.). The problem about the reality of the angel has already been discussed (v. 11). In support of an affirmative position is the widespread popular devotion to angels among the Jews at this time, attested in the apocalyptic or haggadic books of the Bible (Dn, Zech, Tb) and extrabiblical literature (such as QL). **29.** *kept pondering:* The Gk vb. *dielogizeto* implies intense, prolonged reflection, activating a strong spirit of faith.

32 **30.** *do not be afraid:* See 1:13. *you have found grace [favor] with God:* This announcement parallels and partially explains the first greeting of the angel (v. 28). Mary did not need to apologize, as frequently happened before her declaration, "If I have found favor in your eyes..." (Gn 18:3; 19:19; 30:27) (cf. M.-J. Lagrange, *Luc*, 29–30). **31.** The birth formula is repeated again (cf. v. 13). Because of the messianic intensity of the context, a reference to Is 7:14 is quite likely. **32.** Mary's future son is described with language ordinarily reserved for God's redeeming presence among his people. The boy will grow up to be "great" (Tb 12:22; Pss 48:2; 86:10; 96:4); "Son of the Most High" (Gn 14:19ff.; Sir 24:2); "the Holy One" (Is 1:4; 5:24; 41:14); "everlasting King of all the earth" (Pss 24:7,10; 97:1; Gn 21:33; Dn 12:7; cf. H.-J. Kraus, *Psalmen* [BKAT 15/1; Neukirchen, 1960] 197–205).

Did Mary understand the angel to announce that her son would be divine, the second person of the Holy Trinity? The following should be recalled: First of all, Luke is not giving a diary of the day of the annunciation, but a gospel of salvation. Second, Mary, as a Semite, was not accustomed to think in later philosophical terms of person and nature and would have been impressed with the dynamic thrust of divine power and infinite goodness in the words and works of Jesus. Even after Pentecost the apostles thought in this way (Acts 2:33–36; 3:26; Rom 1:4). Third, there are indications that before Pentecost Mary did not fully appreciate the divine mission of her son (2:48–50). Mary, therefore, pondered, ever anew, the words and works of Jesus during his lifetime; through the light granted by the Spirit at Pentecost, she plumbed ever deeper into the realization that nowhere as in her son Jesus was God so dynamically and personally at work saving the world. The Infancy Narrative, composed in the post-Pentecostal age within a Johannine circle, rather obviously insinuates the divinity of Jesus. The Lucan text draws upon Zeph 3:14–17 and Jl 2:21–27, describing the Messianic age and God's presence among his people (S. Lyonnet, *Bib* 20 [1939] 131–41). The OT does not state God's presence in a divine-human person, but Luke does by applying the texts very carefully to Jesus.

33 **34.** *how shall this happen, since I do not know man [as a wife does her husband]:* From the OT, with the possible exception of the controversial passage of Is 7:14 (see C. Stuhlmueller, *Marian Studies* 12 [1961] 165–204; see also J. J. DeVault, "The Concept of Virginity in Judaism," *Marian Studies* 13 [1962] 23–40), we could never conclude to the virginal conception of the Messiah. Mary's previous espousal to Joseph indicates that she looked forward to a normal married life. Yet, her question to the angel raises the objection of virginity. Various answers are given by scholars and commentators. Mary's difficulty and question, according to S. Muñoz-Iglesias (*EstBib* 16 [1957] 329–82) and J. Gewiess (*BZ* 5 [1961] 221–54), are a literary device, modeled on OT parallels (Gn 17:17–19; Ex 3:11ff.; Jgs 6:13ff.), allowing the editor to expand upon a doctrinal involvement, viz., Mary's virginity. As such, Luke's document witnesses to apostolic preaching, upon which our faith rests. By those who accept Mary's question as genuinely historical, various solutions are proposed: (1) Mary, understanding the angel to imply an immediate conception, objected that marriage relations were not allowed till the year of espousal was completed (P. Gächter, *Maria im Erdenleben* [3rd ed.; Innsbruck, 1955] 96–102). (2) A commonly held opinion among Catholic exegetes (still forcefully argued by M.-J. Lagrange, M. Zerwick, and S. Lyonnet) holds that Mary had made a vow of perpetual virginity even before her espousal to Joseph; Joseph accepted marriage under this most unusual condition. (3) Still others maintain that Mary decided upon perpetual virginity at the time of the annunciation, either because of the demands of Is 7:14 (J.-P. Audet, *RB* 63 [1956] 346–74) or because of the impelling necessity of the mystery of the divine maternity (J. Auer, *Geist und Leben* 23 [1950] 411–25; 27 [1954] 331f.).

(Ceroke, C., *CBQ* 19 [1957] 329–42. Dillon, R., *DunR* 1 [1961] 1–37. Flanagan, N., *Marian Studies* 7 [1956] 103–21. Laurentin, R., *Structure*, 176–78. Lyonnet, S., *Le récit de l'annonciation* [Rome, 1954]. Maly, E. H., *Marian Studies* 13 [1962] 41–61. Zerwick, M., *VD* 37 [1959] 212–24, 276–88.)

34 **35.** *will overshadow you:* The Spirit's overshadowing of Mary reminds one of the Jerusalem Temple: Ex 40:35; 1 Kgs 8:10; Hag 2:6–9. Not only the text of Hag, but the descent of God's Holy Spirit (used without the article) and the proclamation of the Son of God give an apocalyptic tone to the verse. Both the Temple theme and the eschatological spirit demand virginity or continence, required by the Bible of the worshiper and the warrior (Lv 15:16–18; 1 Sm 21:4f.; 2 Sm 11:11). Mary's virginity thus points to the apocalyptic struggle of the cross and the liturgical setting of the early Church. **37.** *nothing will be impossible:* Mary's virginity reveals a new depth of meaning, that of complete trust and obedience before God, as Hos depicts Israel in her role of virginal spouse of God (Hos 2:21f.). **38.** *let it be done: Genoito* is the optative of desire, a more subtle, deferential form than *genēthētō* in the "Our Father" (Mt 6:10).

35 (c) The Visitation (1:39–56). Mary visits her kinswoman (the relation is very generally stated) to offer assistance and to seek advice. **39.** *with haste:* The Gk phrase (*meta spoudēs*) can also mean "very thoughtfully" (cf. B. Hospodar, *CBQ* 18 [1956] 14–18). **41.** *the babe leapt:* This action of Elizabeth's unborn child not only reminds us of Rebekah's children (Gn 25:22ff.) and David's dance before the Ark (2 Sm 6:16) but also of the messianic leap of joy among the poor (Is 35:6; Ps 114:6; Mal 3:20). **42.** *loud voice:* Another phrase redolent of messianic fulfillment (1 Chr 16:4–5; Ps 66:1; Is 40:9). *blessed are you...:* Many OT texts are echoed in this declaration of Elizabeth: Deborah's praise of Jael (Jgs 5:24); the people's acclaim of Judith (Jdt 13:18); the abundant blessings of Dt 7:12–14.

36 **46.** *and Mary said:* Mary's song of thanksgiving, often called the "Magnificat" (from the first word of the Vg translation), has been put together from many OT phrases (see the margins in A. Merk or E. Nestle; cf. J. T. Forestell, *Marian Studies* 12 [1961] 205–44). Such a heavy use of scriptural allusions has produced a ponderous piece of poetry with little originality or imagination. Yet it expresses deep emotion and strong conviction. Some mss. of the VL read here, "and Elizabeth said," but the Gk mss. attribute the canticle to Mary. The similarity of the "Magnificat" to the canticle of Hannah (1 Sm 2:1–10) favors the attribution to Elizabeth: both Hannah and Elizabeth have been childless for a long period of their married life; both dedicated their child as a Nazirite; both bear a child who will "anoint" a future king. **47.** *my spirit rejoices:* Lit., "has rejoiced" (an aorist in Greek, to be explained by a Hebr original in which the preceding verb was a participle and this a *wayyiqtol* form continuing the same tense; this would ordinarily be translated by the past tense). **48–50.** The first stanza extols the fruits of faith and of lowly dependence on the merciful God. Luke has already cast Mary in the role of handmaid before God (1:38). So evident will be the transition God has achieved in Mary, of loneliness turned into fruitfulness, that all men will find hope. There is, therefore, a prophetic or eschatological ring to Mary's words, strengthened by OT allusions such as Mal 3:12; Zech 3:17; Ps 111:9. God appears as the Mighty One; yet he exercises his power most of all in caring for the needy. **51–53.** The second stanza insists upon the great reversals of salvation history; one must be in need to be saved, one must be blind to be given light by God—as Dt-Is often sang (Is 40:29–31; 41:8–10,17–20; 42:7; 57:15; 61:1–3). A series of aorists occur here (as also in 1 Sm 2:4f. [LXX] = pf. in the MT); these gnomic aorists point out how God is accustomed to act; he has always done it and will always continue to do it this way. *his arm:* This phrase has the nuance of OT redemption through battle (Ex 6:6; Dt 4:34; Jer 27:5; Is 40:10; 51:9). **54–55.** The conclusion gathers up the ideas of the Magnificat in the Servant theology of the OT and particularly of Dt-Is (Is 42:1–4; 49:1–7; 50:4–9; 52:13–53:12). Jesus applied this theology to himself (3:22; 5:35; 9:22) and the very early Church thought of him in those same terms (Acts 3:13). **56.** Luke stylistically closes the scene; Mary must have remained longer, in order to be of service at the birth of John the Baptist. *about three months:* Possible allusion to the period of time in which the Ark remained in the house of Obed-edom (2 Sm 6:11); if so, the qualifying word "about" adapts the allusion to this new historical situation.

37 **(B) The Diptych of the Births (1:57–2:52).**

(a) The Birth of John the Baptist (1:57–80). **57.** *time was fulfilled:* A Hebraism (cf. Gn 25:24). **58.** *Lord had magnified his mercy:* Cf. v. 46; 1 Sm 12:24; Gn 19:19. In the Bible God's omnipotence is most clearly revealed in the extent of his mercy; "magnified" connotes a revelation of God's redemptive acts. **59.** *to circumcise the child:* Circumcision, especially in post-exilic Israel, became the most important act, initiating a male child into the covenanted people of God. Its necessity for receiving salvation through Christ was emphatically denied in Paul's epistles. But Lk 1–2 make the ceremony of circumcision a climactic moment when God and his people are covenanted in the perfect fulfillment of the promises on God's part and the perfect observance of the Law on Israel's part. **59.** *after his father:* Naming a boy after his father was a very late custom in Israel (Tb 1:1,9; Josephus, *Ant.* 20.9, 1 § 197; Str–B 2, 107–8). **64.** *blessing God:* Cf. Dn 10:16–20; Lk 9:16. The "Benedictus" (vv. 68–79) belongs here. **66.** The people's question prepares the reader for the future—a common stylistic device of Luke. **67.** *prophesied:* By recording the effects of the Spirit's activity within the mind and life of one of God's servants.

38 **68–75.** At least the first part of the "Benedictus" is distinctly Jewish, modeled in many ways on prayers said at the circumcision ceremony (cf. Th. Maertens, *Le Messie est la!* [Bruges, 1954] 94). R. Bultmann and others feel that the verses originated in Jewish circles, were completed with a Christian (or Baptist) addition (vv. 76–79), and were inserted very early into the Infancy Narrative (*HST* 296–97, 441). Like the "Magnificat," this hymn of Zechariah resounds with OT allusions (see the margins in Merk or Nestle; W. Grundmann, *Evangelium*, 72). **68.** *blessed:* An imitation of the style of the hymns of praise in Pss 34:2; 67:2; 103:1; 113:2 and in QL (1QH 5:20; 10:14; 11:27). The verbs that follow, as in the "Magnificat," are in the aor. tense; the hymn blesses Yahweh for what he has achieved of salvation. *visited:* A common biblical word, meaning either favor or punishment; according to the context God cannot be present in any neutral way (Ex 3:16; 4:31; Lv 18:25; Is 10:12; 23:17). **69.** *horn of salvation:* A Semitism, whose meaning is expressed thus in NEB, "Deliverer of victorious power" (cf. 1 Sm 2:1; Ps 18:2; Zech 2:1–4). *David his servant:* Cf. Acts 4:25. **72.** *forefathers:* Lk speaks of them now in the heavenly paradise (13:28; 16:23; Jn 8:56), as they look forward to the complete fulfillment of all hopes and promises. *holy covenant and oath:* Cf. Gn 12:1–3; 15; 17; 22:15–18. **75.** *all our days:* The words reflect a hope in a proximate fulfillment of the messianic promises; liturgical texts, and especially the hymns of praise, spread a spirit of glory now—through the presence of the redeeming God.

39 **76–79.** The second stanza sees the hopes of the (OT) Fathers at the dawn of fulfillment through the intervention of Zechariah's son. **76.** The child will be Elijah, whose coming before the *eschaton* was announced by Mal 3:1,23f. (cf. Is 40:3). So close is this verse to the OT expectation voiced by Mal and Dt-Is that no mention is made of a Messiah; God will wondrously intervene among his people. The Christian people saw a new meaning in both Mal and this canticle, when God intervened to save his people in Jesus (→ Aspects NT Thought, 78:88). **78.** *the orient from on high:* The Messiah, hinted at in a mysterious name, "shoot" or "sprout" in the MT (Str-B 2, 113), or the "rising" [sun or star] in the LXX (Jer 23:5; Zech 3:8; 6:12; Nm 24:17; *ThDNT* 1, 351–53). Like the terms "servant" and "son of man," this Messianic title quickly passed out of use in the Christian community. **79.** *in darkness and in the shadow of death:* A combination of Is 9:1–2 and 42:7 (as found in the LXX). When the darkness of sin and need is blackest, men will understand that God alone is Savior. **80.** Luke stylistically closes the scene; it is possible that as a young boy John was entrusted to the covenanters at Qumran.

40 (b) The Birth of Jesus (2:1–40). **1–2.** These verses are distinctly different in style from the Semitic tone of the rest of chs. 1–2 and are quite Lucan; Luke has thus made his own contribution to the Infancy Narrative. *when Quirinius was governor of Syria:* Luke's reference to the census of Quirinius poses an historical problem that is still unsolved. It rises chiefly from Acts 5:37 and Josephus, *Ant.* 17.13, 5 § 355; 18.1, 1 § 1–2, which refer to a census under Quirinius while Coponius was procurator of Judea (→ History of Israel, 75:136). This would have been *ca.* AD 6–7. For attempts to justify Luke's chronology, see *EDB* 336–38; W. Grundmann, *Evangelium*, 76–79; W. F. Arndt, *Luke*, 76–80. **3.** *each to his own city:* A Roman census could be based on residence in one's native city; an Egyptian papyrus contains an edict of the governor of Egypt in AD 104 ordering a "census by household" and stipulating that all who are out of their districts are to return to their own home (see A. Deissmann, *LAE* 268–69). **4.** *to the city of David:* Emphasis is put here on the royal privileges that come to Jesus through Joseph (1:32–33). *Bethlehem:* The distance between Nazareth and Bethlehem would be about 90 mi. (cf. C. Kopp, *Holy Places of the Gospels* [N.Y., 1963] 1–48; E. Lussier, *BT* 1 [1962–63] 158–62; M. W. Schoenberg, *BT* 1 [1962–63] 152–57). **6.** *days... fulfilled:* Lk uses the word "fulfilled" eight times in chs. 1–2 (cf. Gal 4:4); centuries of longing and prayer, inspired and sustained by divine promises, are about to end. Lk might be making a special allusion to Mi 5:1f., an important text not only because it sees ancient promises reaching fulfillment in the Davidic messianic king, but also because another passage, Mi 4:9f. sees the chosen people experiencing the travail of messianic agony while giving birth to ultimate victory. **7.** *first-born son:* The Gk word, *prōtotokos*, is consistently used throughout the OT (LXX) for the child who will continue the name and receive the double portion of property of the ancestral line (Gn 27; Dt 21:17). In certain cases the name carried strong messianic significance; through the first-born the patriarchal blessings or religious heritage of Israel were transmitted (Gn 27; Ex 4:22; Rom 8:29; Col 1:18). The strong Jewish character of the Infancy Narrative, therefore, explains the use of *prōtotokos* in place of *monogenēs* (only-begotten) of 7:12; the former word in no way demands that Mary had other children by Joseph (see *EDB* 777–79; *ThDNT* 4, 737–41; R. T. Siebeneck, *BT* 1 [1962–63] 194–200). *wrapped him up:* In the long strips of cloth, customary in Palestine, so that the child grows straight and strong. *manger:* A feeding trough for animals. Jesus was born in one of the caves in the hills around Bethlehem. These caves were used at times as homes for families by adding a lean-to at the entrance of the cave; the family's livestock was housed inside the cave. *in the inn:* The word *katalyma* means a room for a guest or for eating (Lk 22:11). Because the outer room attached to the cave was already fully occupied or at least did not afford privacy, Joseph brought Mary inside the cave where the livestock ordinarily rested.

41 **8.** *shepherds:* The poor, as typical of Lk, are first to receive the message of salvation in Jesus' presence among men. A double tradition or reputation surrounds the shepherd. The patriarchs were shepherds, so was David; "to shepherd" was a synonym for ruling (2 Sm 7:7; Jer 2:8). God himself is called the shepherd of Israel (Pss 23:1; 80:2). In both pagan and patristic literature (Vergil, *Eclogues* 4; Origen, *Catechesis* 20) shepherds are the innocent ones to whom divinity reveals itself; but this idea seems outside the scope of biblical thought. Another Israelite tradition, however, held that the shepherds were so destitute as to be always on the point of stealing and therefore completely untrustworthy (Str-B 2, 113–14). **9.** *the angel of the Lord:* See comments on 1:11 and Mt 1:20. *glory of the Lord:* The wondrous presence of God the Redeemer. In the OT this phrase is associated with great redeeming acts of God (Ex 14:4,18; 16:7) and especially with the Ark or Temple (Ex 40:34f.; 1 Kgs 8:11). Whereas Luke prefers to restrict the term "glory" to Jesus' ascension or parousia (9:26,31f.; 19:38; 21:27; 24:26; Acts 7:55), John applies it to the entire life of Jesus (Jn 1:14; 2:11). **10.** A parallel sequence of promise and fulfillment can be traced between the annunciation of Jesus' birth to Mary and this angelic visitation to the shepherds: angel(s) appeared (1:26; 2:10); said to her (them) (1:30; 2:10); do not be afraid (1:30; 2:10); grace or joy, *charin* or *charan* in Greek; you will bring forth, or, there has been born (1:31; 2:11); Jesus, Savior (1:31; 2:11); Son of Most High, or, the Messiah Lord (1:32; 2:11); throne or city of David (1:32; 2:11); sign (1:36; 2:12); angel(s) depart (1:38; 2:15). See R. Laurentin, *Structure*, 126–27, n. 3. *good news:* See 1:19.

42 **11.** The contents of the Gospel are now revealed: the fulfillment of OT promises about a Davidic Messiah, the Lord's Anointed, who is himself Savior and Lord. Note how three significant titles are given to Jesus in this one verse: *sōtēr* (Savior), *christos* (the Anointed), *kyrios* (Lord). For Luke the most significant title is "Savior," for "salvation" is one of the main themes of his Gospel. Among the Syn he alone employs the title and the noun *sōtēria*; he uses the verb *sōzō* (save) 30 times in the Gospel and Acts, more than the combined number of occurrences in Mt and Mk (see W. Grundmann, *Evangelium*, 454–56; W. Foerster, *ThWNT* 7, 990–92). **14.** *men of good will:* That is, of God's good pleasure. The phrase does not refer to the good dispositions of men themselves but to the predilection of God. God is not to be thought of as taking delight in man's goodness but rather as bestowing goodness on man through his divine election and mercy. The phrase has a parallel in QL (1QH 4:32–33; 11:9; see J. A. Fitzmyer, *TS* 19 [1958] 225–27; E. Vogt, "Peace Among Men of God's Good Pleasure, Lk. 2:14," *The Scrolls and the NT* [ed. K. Stendahl; N.Y., 1957] 114–17; C.-H. Hunzinger, *ZNW* 44 [1952–53] 85–90). The song of the angels gives a liturgical setting to the birth of Jesus as well as an eschatological aura (19:38). **15.** *to see this thing:* The Gk word *rēma* could also mean "this word," reflecting the Hebr *dābār*, which can mean both "word" and "event" (see comment on 1:4). **16.** *with haste:* The same root word is used as in 1:39. **19.** *Mary kept in mind:* Cf. Dn 7:28; Gn 37:11; Lk 8:4–21 (see B. F. Meyer, *CBQ* 26 [1964] 31–49).

21. *was circumcised:* The circumcision of Jesus is told in a way reminiscent of that of John (1:59). Jesus is formally stamped as a member of God's chosen people, through whom world salvation was to be achieved. Such hopes were now fulfilled in Jesus, even in his name (1:31). **22.** *their purification:* The pl. "their" is textually preferable to "her" (Syr^{sin}) or "his" (D, VL); Mary is thus seen united with Jesus and possibly with Joseph in the Temple ceremony. Mary's uncleanness was not moral but only ceremonial (Lv 12:2–4); but just as Jesus followed the full Mosaic Law and completely immersed himself in humanity, thereby to transform it, so Mary is presented as one with all womankind in giving birth to her child. Her purification, like Jesus' act of redemption, belongs to everyone of Israel. This interpretation agrees with the earlier presentation of Mary in the symbol of the Jerusalem Temple (1:35). *to present him to the Lord:* That is, to Yahweh. Jesus' presentation in the Temple, in accord with Ex 13:1–16, is a climactic moment in the Infancy Narrative; throughout the Gospel Jerusalem will occupy a principal spot. Lk says nothing about Jesus' being redeemed or bought back (Nm 18:15f.); he was possessed by his Heavenly Father even before this ceremony; this act formalized or externalized what was and would remain always true. **24.** *a pair of turtledoves:* Rather than a year-old lamb, Mary and Joseph give the "offering of the poor"; one bird was for a holocaust of adoration, the other for a "sin" offering (Lv 12:6–8; 5:7–10). **25.** *Simeon, just and devout:* The adjectives denote care in observing the moral obligations of the Law, a care springing from a healthy fear of the Lord (Acts 2:5; 8:2; 22:12). *consolation of Israel:* According to the rabbis, this denoted the final, unrecorded words that passed between Elijah and Elisha (2 Kgs 2:11; cf. Str-B 2, 124–26) and that would be made known when Elijah reappeared (1:17). *Holy Spirit:* God at work in saving his people, particularly in the final eschatological age (Jl 3; Acts 2; 1QS 4:2–8,15–26). **26.** *the Lord's Anointed:* That Jesus should here be called the Anointed or the Messiah is indicative of composition after his baptism. **28.** The rabbis took children into their arms in order to bless them (Str-B 2, 131). The Gk word *edexato* implies that Simeon "received" what was being presented to him. **29.** Simeon, most probably a member or close associate of the Sadducee group, must have waited amidst great suffering, as he witnessed the priestly betrayal of many sacred obligations. *dismiss in peace:* Simeon is the watchman released from duty. *servant:* The Gk *doulos* implies the difficult service of Simeon's days in the Temple. *Lord:* The Gk *despota* is used with *doulos* in only one other NT passage (Acts 4:23–30), which is also highly liturgical (see D. Rimaud, *La Maison-Dieu* 51 [1957] 99–101). **31.** *all peoples:* The universal scope of salvation reflects Is 42:6; 49:6; 52:10. Revelation under the image of light is characteristic of Johannine literature: Jn 8:12; 12:46; 1 Jn 1:5–2:27. When the glory of the Lord descended upon the Ark, Moses could not enter lest he die (Ex 33:18–20; 40:35); having seen the glory, Simeon can die peacefully.

43 **34.** *Simeon blessed them:* He proclaimed the fulfillment of Messianic blessings in them and announced their involvement in the continuation of these blessings among other men. *for the fall and rise of many:* The reference is most probably to an idea found in Is 8:14; 28:16. The goals and goodness, preached and lived by the Messiah, force all men to face up to their great sinfulness (their "fall"). This knowledge can completely destroy, as it will the proud; or it can prompt the humble to turn to the Messiah and through him to rise to new life. The Gk word for "rise" (*anastasis*) is elsewhere used in Lk exclusively for resurrection from the dead (14:14; 20:27,33,35f.). *a sign contradicted:* Cf. Lk 4:23–27; 11:14–28,29–32. **35.** *a sword will pierce...:* Some of the Church Fathers interpreted the sword as one of doubt or hesitation in faith (so Origen, Chrysostom, Basil, Cyril of Alexandria); but this meaning seems unlikely in the context of the Infancy Narrative where Mary is extolled. The sword could be indicative of the sorrow experienced by a humble person before the demands of an exalted vocation, by a delicately thoughtful person before the profound mystery of salvation (1:29; 2:19,50; 11:28), or by a sympathetic person before the revenge inflicted on the innocent. (cf. A. Feuillet, "L'épreuve prédite à Marie," *A la rencontre de Dieu* [Fest. A. Gelin; LePuy, 1961] 243–64; C. Stuhlmueller, *Marian Studies* 16 [1955] 94–120; P. Benoit, *CBQ* 25 [1963] 251–61). *that the thoughts of many hearts:* The introductory particle, *hopōs an*, refers this passage to all that preceded, thereby linking Mary with Jesus' sorrowful redemptive undertaking.

36. *Anna a prophetess:* Rabbinical literature recognized seven (the symbolic number) prophetesses: Sarah; Miriam (Ex 15:20); Deborah (Jgs 4:4); Hannah, mother of Samuel (1 Sm 2:1); Abigail, wife of David (1 Sm 25:32); Huldah (2 Kgs 22:14); and Esther. The Bible also mentions the wife of the prophet Isaiah as a prophetess (Is 8:3). These women witnessed to God's will, at least by holiness of life, sometimes by speaking in his name. It is difficult to decide whether or not the Infancy Narrative wants to insist upon the symbolic meaning of "Phanuel" (face of God) and "Asher" (good luck). **37.** *till she was eighty-four:* Anna would be 104 years old; this age may place her symbolically in the person of another devout widow, Judith, who lived to be 105 years old (Jdt 16:23). Both Jewish and Christian tradition found an honorable place for widows in the service of the community (Str-B 2, 141; 1 Tm 5:9f.). **38.** *awaiting:* The poise of those who receive salvation. *redemption of Jerusalem:* The holy city represents all the elect. **40.** *the child grew:* Very simply the Gospel points out the necessity of Jesus' hidden life at Nazareth, that he might grow strong in the full experience of a human nature; thus he might be able to bring the Spirit of God into immediate contact with every human area. *filled with wisdom:* God's practical, all-embracing plan of salvation (Prv 8:22ff.; Sir 24).

44 (c) The Boy Jesus in the Temple (2:41–52). This sole incident, breaking the Gospel silence of "the hidden years" of Jesus, is narrated in a way sharply different from other, apocryphal gospels. Mary and Joseph presume Jesus to act as any normal boy would act; the apocryphal gospels multiply all kinds of extravagant miracles. The same penchant for the miraculous or the unusual colors the pages of the boyhood accounts of other ancient heroes: Cyrus, Alexander, Apollonius, or Moses. The closest parallel is Josephus' story of his own boyhood (*Life* 2 § 9), describing his reputation for learning among the chief priests and rulers of Jerusalem. Luke's account, by contrast, is reserved and unassuming.

41. *went to Jerusalem every year:* The law prescribed the Jerusalem pilgrimage for three major feasts: Passover, Pentecost, and Tabernacles (Ex 23:14; Dt 16:16); but custom excused those who lived at a distance from all but the Passover. The rabbis were not in agreement whether or not women and children were required to make the pilgrimage (Str-B 2, 141–42). **42.** *twelve years old:* A year before the age at which a boy officially reached manhood; the event is celebrated today with the ceremony of *bar miṣwāh.* **43.** *fulfilled the days:* The feast had an octave (22:1). **44.** *in the company:* Entire villages joined in the pilgrimages. **46.** *three days:* Used here with a possible symbolic reference to the three days of Jesus in the tomb (see Lk 9:22; 13:32; 18:33; 24: 7,21,46; 1 Cor 15:4). *sitting in the midst of the teachers:* In one of the outer halls of the Temple. Jesus is not acting with any braggadocio; he is listening, asking questions, and giving answers to the questions put to him. By implication, however, Jesus is presented as the teacher at the center of a circle. He knows the Torah and its interpretations; in no way is he in opposition to Jewish Law and practice. **49.** *in my Father's house:* The Greek can also be translated "about my Father's business." The latter is favored by the Gk construction in such texts as Mt 16:23; Jn 8:29; 9:4; 14:31. The phrase implies a close personal relationship between Jesus and the Father. The addition of the word "house" accords with the immediate situation and is supported by the interpretation of many of the early Fathers; see also Gn 41:51; Est 7:9. This interpretation also fits in with the main thrust of the Lucan Gospel where the climactic moment is reached in the Jerusalem Temple, not only in the Infancy Narrative (2:22), but also at the end (19:45). By way of foreshadowing, the Infancy Narrative ends where the Gospel will. Mary finds Jesus at his work; he is not simply her son, but the heavenly Father's Son, sent on a mission in which she finds him totally involved; at this she sorrows, for it means separation. The words "my Father" are a sharp reversal; up till now Joseph was called by that title.

50. *they did not understand:* That is, neither Joseph nor Mary. One of a parent's greatest sorrows afflicts Mary—not to understand her own child. This statement makes it highly improbable that Mary appreciated the divine sonship of her son at this time. **51.** *was obedient to them:* This last reference to Joseph in the Gospels is a beautiful tribute to him. Obedient to his guidance, Jesus grew to perfect manhood. **52.** *Jesus advanced in wisdom:* Lk stresses his connatural condition; he grew as any boy would. *in physical stature:* The Gk word could also mean "age," but this idea seems like tautology in this statement of growth. *and in grace:* Lovableness in the sight of God and men, including not only spiritual holiness but also graciousness, tact, charm, and attractiveness. Jesus grew in all ways—physically, intellectually, emotionally, spiritually—for the work that lay ahead of him.

(Burrows, E., *The Gospel of the Infancy* [London, 1940]. Van Iersel, B. M. F., "The Finding of Jesus in the Temple: Some Observations on the Original Form of Luke ii. 41–51a," *NovT* 4 [1960] 161–73. Wilson, R. M., "Some Recent Studies in the Lucan Infancy Narratives," *SE* 1, 235–53.)

45 **(III) Preparation for the Public Ministry (3:1–4:13).** For the information in this section, Luke depended mostly upon Q (→ 16 above). Not only this written memorandum of the sayings of Jesus, but also Mk (1:1–8) and the early kerygmatic discourses in Acts (10:37; 13:24)—all these early sources—inaugurate the Messianic lifework of Jesus with the preaching of John the Baptist. After the section on John the Baptist (3:1–20), Lk presents the baptism of Jesus (3:21f.), the genealogy (3:23–38), and the temptation (4:1–13).

(A) John the Baptist (3:1–20). Lk, composed after Mk and Mt, manifests suspicion against an attempt in early Christianity to make the Baptist a rival or even an open opponent of Jesus. Jn, the last Gospel, will be most explicit in pointing out that the Baptist is not the Messiah (1:8,19–34). Comparing Lk with Mt (both depended upon Q), we find that: (1) Lk omits John the Baptist's announcement that the Kingdom of God is close at hand (Mt 3:2) and reserves this statement for Jesus (Lk 10:9,11); (2) Lk suppresses the description of the Baptist in the role of Elijah (Mt 3:4 par. Mk 1:6) and an account of the Baptist's activity, especially his baptizing (Mt 3:5f.); (3) in the statement, "There is coming one after me, mightier than I" (Mk 1:7; Mt 3:11), Lk removes the words "after me," lest Jesus be considered a disciple of the Baptist or even an intimate friend. Lk considers John the last and greatest prophet of Israel, but clearly distinct from the glorious Messianic moment that begins with Jesus (Lk 16:16; Acts 13:24f. where it is stated that John came "before his [Jesus'] entrance").

46 **1.** Although the practice of introducing a prophet with the names of contemporary rulers has OT parallels (Is 1:1; Jer 1:3; Hos 1:1), still Lk's style is closer to that of classical Gk authors, like Thucydides (2.2) who similarly begins the account of the Peloponnesian War. *fifteenth year of the reign of Tiberius Caesar:* The most precise, chronological reference in all the Gospels for dating the ministry of Jesus. Although coregent from AD 11 to 12, Tiberius succeeded Augustus as sole emperor on Aug. 19, AD 14 and reigned till 37. The fifteenth year of his reign is AD 28–29 according to Roman computation; but Luke possibly used the Syrian method, which counted the interval between Aug. 19 and the beginning of the new year (Oct. 1) as the first regnal year. In that case, the fifteenth year extended from Oct. 1, 27 till Oct. 1, 28. Jesus, therefore, was baptized toward the end of the year 27. *Pontius Pilate:* He was the "procurator" or "prefect" of Judea (not really the "governor" [Lk's terminology is vague]), AD 26–36. *Herod:* This is Herod Antipas, the son of Herod the Great by Malthace; he ruled as tetrarch over Galilee and Perea from 4 BC to AD 39. *Philip:* The son of Herod the Great by Cleopatra of Jerusalem, he was by far the most sincere and upright of Herod's children. At Herod's death he became the ruler of Batanea, Trachonitis, Auranitis, and a certain portion of the domain of Zenodorus (see Josephus, *Ant.* 17.11, 4 § 318; → History of Israel, 75:141). *Lysanias:* His identity is problematical. Josephus (*Ant.* 19.5, 1 § 275; 20.7, 1 § 138) speaks of a king of Abilene by this name, who was, however, killed in 34 BC on the order of Anthony and Cleopatra. Ptolemy, his father, had been executed three years earlier. Several Gk inscriptions (*CIG* 4521, 4523; cf. R. Savignac, *RB* 9 [1912] 533–40) seem to indicate that the name Lysanias was hereditary among the sovereigns of Abilene (see J. de Fraine, *VDBS* 6, 595); possibly Luke is referring to one of the latter rulers of the same name. If Luke is accurately informed in this matter, he must have drawn upon sources of information other than Josephus. **2.** *during the high priesthood of Annas and Caiaphas:* Luke now identifies the religious rulers of Palestine. Annas had held the office of high priest from AD 6 to 15, but his dominant influence insured the appointment to this office of five sons, one son-in-law (Caiaphas, AD 18–36), and one grandson (Matthias, AD 65). All in all, this list of names draws a gloomy picture. Tiberius by this time was in semiretirement on Capri, and the affairs of state were in the grip of the unscrupulous Sejanus until AD 31. Palestine was arbitrarily divided by Rome and the high priesthood was granted to the scheming family of Annas. "It was thus the Lord took pity on their distressful cries of affliction under their oppressors" (Jgs 2:18).

3. *The word of the Lord came to John, son of Zechariah:* The Gk phraseology with the prep. *epi* is rather singular, found only here and in Jer 1:1 (LXX). Although the idea parallels the introduction of many prophetic books (Hos 1:1; Mi 1:1; Hag 1:1), Luke calls special attention to John's continuation of the role of Jeremiah: Consecrated before birth (Jer 1:5; Lk 1:13), he announces eschatological judgment (Jer 1:10; 25; Lk 3:9,16f.), messianic glory (Jer 31; Lk 1:14; 3:15f.), and the new and final covenant available even to the least important of men (Jer 31:31–34; Lk 7:18–23). In the notice "son of Zechariah" we detect a point of contact between the major part of Lk and the Infancy Narrative. *in the desert of Judea:* Another connecting link with the Infancy Narrative (1:80); both references leave the topography rather vague: 1:80 has simply "in desert areas." Here "the desert of Judea" means the semimountainous, bleak wilderness rising between the Dead Sea and the central mountain ridge. The Jordan Valley cannot properly be called a desert, especially that around Jericho, the traditional spot where John is said to have baptized. Jn 3:23 states that John was baptizing in the north. We must agree with H. Conzelmann (*Theology of St. Luke*, 18–22) that Luke is combining geography and theology. The OT contains a tradition of desert spirituality; it signifies the place to which God led Israel and, alone with his people, formed a covenant or marriage bond with them (Jer 2:2f.; Dt 2:7; 32:10; Ez 16). The text of Dt-Is, soon to be quoted by Lk, continues the same desert theme. The Qumran covenanters also went out "into the desert" that they might be thoroughly consecrated to God and be made ready for the final eschatological war. *he went all over the Jordan valley:* Another vague topographical indication. *preaching a baptism of repentance for the remission of sins:* Identical with Mk 1:4; Mt 3:2 has simply: "[he was] saying, Repent!" The word "preaching" (*kēryssō*) envisages an initial proclamation to non-Christians; another word, "teaching" (*didaskō*), imparts a deeper understanding of the mystery of Christ and is reserved for instruction given by Christ in the Gospels and for work done among baptized Christians in Acts and Epistles (D. M. Stanley, *The Apostolic Church in the NT* [Westminster, 1965] 199–213; *CBQ* 17 [1955] 336–48). *baptism:* A ceremonial purification by water that has deep roots in biblical tradition (1 Sm 7:6; Lv *passim*; A. Oepke, *ThDNT*, 1, 529–46). The Qumran covenanters, living near the traditional spot where John baptized, built an elaborate water system in their community house in order to provide for their many lustrations (see J. Delorme, "Baptism in Judaism," *Baptism in the NT* [Baltimore, 1964] 25–60). The Mishnah legislates for baptism along with sacrifice (and for males, circumcision) in the reception of gentile converts. John's baptism differed from Jewish proselyte baptism in that it was administered to Israelites, and it differed from Qumran purification in that it was given once for all time to soldiers, to publicans, and to sinners, who were not usually accepted in full communion with God's people. The prophetic, eschatological aspects of John's baptism can possibly be traced to texts like Is 1:16; Jer 4:14; Ez 36:25; Zech 13:1. *repentance:* In Gk literature *metanoia* denotes "repentance" after some misdemeanor. In the LXX, it almost always translates the Hebr *niḥām* (to be sorry, be moved interiorly with sorrow or pity [Jer 18:8; Am 7:3,6]). Later Gk translators of the OT (Aq, Sym) as well as Hellenistic Jewish literature employed *metanoia* to translate *šûb* (return, e.g., Is 31:6; 53:7; Jer 18:8; Ez 33:12; Sir 48:15). This Jewish background of *metanoia* focuses attention on the deeply interior quality of repentance; for the Syn some kind of interior renewal must accompany the forgiveness of sin.

47 **4–6.** John the Baptist is introduced with the words of Dt-Is (40:3–5)—the identical phrase with which the Dead Sea covenanters explained their way of life. Whereas John prepares for the way of the Lord, whom the Evangelists know to be Jesus, the Dead Sea covenanters explain: "This means studying the Torah which He commanded through Moses" (1QS 8:14). Slightly different from the NT and the LXX, the Hebr text of Is 40:3 connects the phrase "in the desert" with the second member: "A voice cries out: 'In the desert prepare the way of the Lord!' " The NT also changes the final words of the next line to read "make straight his paths" instead of "the paths of our God" (MT), so that the reference is more clearly to Jesus. Dt-Is was describing the return from the Babylonian exile as a new Exodus, leading across another Sinai desert to a new and more glorious promised land (Is 41:17–20; 43:1f.,14–21). John the Baptist is depicted as realizing the dreams of Dt-Is. Lk will point out that the "desert" will be the trials of Jesus' sufferings and death, and that the promised land and the new Jerusalem will be gained through Jesus' resurrection–ascension. **6.** *all mankind shall see God's deliverance:* Lk adds to Mk and Mt this concluding line from Dt-Is, stressing here as throughout his Gospel the universal scope of Jesus' salvation. Luke also omitted a line, "the glory of the Lord shall be revealed," because in Lk the glory of the Lord, though partially anticipated at the transfiguration (9:31), will be fully manifest only at Jesus' ascension (24:26). Luke deliberately omits Mk's statement that the Baptist comes in the role of Elijah (2 Kgs 1:8); the Third Gospel reserves that for Jesus.

48 **7–9.** Lk now presents a summary of the Baptist's preaching on many occasions (cf. v. 18). *the crowds:* Lk often substitutes this more general word where the other Gospels read Pharisees, Sadducees, or scribes; cf. 11:15 (par. Mt 12:24; Mk 3:22); 11:29 (par. Mt 12:38f.); 12:54 (par. Mt 16:1). Lk thereby gives a wider scope to Jesus' words. From the subject matter of John's words (the eschatological theme and especially the question about Abraham), it seems that Mt and Mk more accurately identify the learned, Jewish audience. *brood of vipers:* "A genuine memory of John's words" (A. R. C. Leaney, *Commentary*, 106), one of many desert images in John's preaching, e.g., stones, dried bushes, barren trees. Luke customarily edits such harsh phrases, as he did in the case of Jesus' final words about Judas (Mk 14:21). "Vipers," throughout the Gospels (Mt 12:34; 23:33) and in QL (1QH 3:1–8), is an eschatological term referring to men under diabolical power at the time of the final struggle. *who has shown you how to flee from the coming wrath?:* This question is also packed with eschatological terminology: "shown" (*hypodeiknymi*) is a technical term for revealing something hidden (Sir 48:25; Lk 12:5); "the coming wrath" contains all the fury of such prophetic words as Is 13:9; 30:27; Zeph 2:2; Mal 3:2; *Enoch* 90. John demands sincere, total turning to the Lord at once. **8.** *fruits befitting repentance:* While Mt has the sing., referring to the final preparation before the last day, Lk has the pl., "fruits," denoting good actions in general. *out of these stones...sons to Abraham:* A play on words in the Aram language of John, *banayyā* (sons) and *'abnayyā* (stones). The Baptist, like Paul many years later (Rom 4:13–17), clearly states that no human works, but only God's act of infusing faith produces life within the chosen people and membership in their ranks. **9.** *thrown into the fire:* See v. 16.

49 **10–14.** These verses, which are exclusive to Lk, reveal the Evangelist's interest in the universal aspect of redemption. John the Baptist pronounces his sociological message to publicans and their bodyguards. **12.** *publicans:* These were tax collectors, men who bought from the Romans the right to collect taxes; they were despised by the Jews (Mk 2:15; Mt 11:19 [Lk 7:34 par.]) and also by Gentiles (Herodas, 6. 64). **14.** *soldiers:* These men did not belong to the regular troops of Herod Antipas or the Roman procurator; they rather provided armed support for the tax collectors (so M.-J. Lagrange, A. Plummer, I. de la Potterie). *rob no one:* Lit., "shake no one violently," in order to extort money from them. Luke does not ask of these men a high mysticism but only a practical spirituality.

15–17. Luke now presents the Baptist's Messianic preaching. But first, in a verse exclusive to himself, he gives the psychological setting: "The people were on tiptoe of expectation" (NEB). **16.** *mightier than I:* Jesus is the great liberator in the war against Satan. The word "mighty" is often used in Scripture for the leader of the final struggle with evil: Mk 3:27; Lk 11:20–22; Ap 18:8 (cf. W. Grundmann, *ThDNT* 3, 399–401). In the Gk text the chiasm (a-b b-a arrangement of words) of the next part of v. 16 highlights the sublimity of Jesus' baptism over that of John:

I with water (a) baptize you (b)...
he you (b) will baptize with holy spirit and fire (a)

This style is typical of Lk. *baptize with the Holy Spirit:* The Scriptures frequently attribute messianic achievement to the Spirit (Ez 36:26ff.; Is 44:3; Jl 3:1), but special prominence is given to the Spirit in the Lucan writings (→ 11 above). Throughout the Bible many extraordinary accomplishments reveal the presence of the Spirit (the life-power) of God: creation (Gn 1:2); warriors (Jgs 3:10; 11:29; 1 Sm 11:6); particular offices (Gn 41:38–40; Nm 11:17,25; 27:18); Servant of the Lord (Is 42:1); messianic king (Is 11:1ff.). (See *ThWNT* 6, 330–453; M.-A. Chevallier, *L'Esprit et le Messie dans le bas-Judaïsme et le Nouveau Testament* [Paris, 1958].) *baptize with...fire:* In Scripture, fire very often indicates the presence of the Savior-God. Fire has a prominent place in liturgical services where man meets his savior (Lv 1:7ff.; 6:2,6). Great theophanies surround God with fire (Gn 15:17; Ex 3:1ff.; 13:21f.; Nm 14:14; Is 6; Ez 1:4ff.; Jl 3:3). God comes "in fire" to judge, that is, to fulfill his promises to the elect and remove evil from their midst; and this nuance shows up in the Qumran texts: 1QpHab 10:5; 1QS 2:15; 4:13. The "fiery" arrival of messianic judgment may have its roots in Nm 31:23 and/or Mal 3:3,19 (see G. W. H. Lampe, *The Seal of the Spirit* [London, 1951] 27; F. Lang, *ThWNT* 6, 927–53). In view of this rich biblical background it is difficult to decide whether the Baptist's statement about Jesus identifies fire with the Spirit's purifying and sanctifying action or, instead, adds a new dimension of eschatological judgment. The latter, more convincing opinion is adopted by P. van Imschoot (*ETL* 13 [1936] 653–66); R. Bultmann (*HST* 246, 424); E. Schweizer (*ThWNT* 6, 306).

17. *his winnowing fork:* The image of winnowing wheat is a frequent one in the Bible for separation (purification) and fiery judgment (Is 29:5–6; 41:16; Jer 15:7). With a wooden shovel the Palestinian farmer tossed the crushed stalks of wheat into the air. The heavier grain fell quickly to the ground, while the lighter chaff was blown by the wind to the edge of the threshing area, where it was gathered and later burned. *unquenchable fire:* Ferocious heat (Is 66:24; Mk 9:43f.).

18–20. Lk concludes the Baptist's apostolate, stating that he frequently exhorted the people with this good news; the use of a participle (*parakalōn*, root for the word "paraclete") and the impf. tense of the verb (*euaggelizō*, root for the word "gospel") indicate constant repetition. **19.** *but Herod:* Luke records what actually takes place later, the incarceration of the Baptist by Herod Antipas at Machaerus, a fortress E of the Dead Sea (Mt 14:1–12; Mk 6:14–29). Luke not only rounds out the story of the Baptist with a fine literary conclusion, but he effectively removes John from the Messianic work now entrusted by the Father to Jesus (see C. H. H. Scobie, *John the Baptist* [Philadelphia, 1964]).

50 **(B) The Baptism of Jesus (3:21–22).** **21.** *all the people were baptized:* This stylistic device links a new episode with the preceding one about John the Baptist. Luke might also intend a fulfillment of the mission confided to John before his birth: "to prepare a perfect people for the Lord" (1:17). Men have been led to the final moment of world salvation through the baptism administered by John; they are ready to become the messianic, eschatological people of God (Acts 15:14); see P. M. Dutheil, *FrancLA* 6 (1955–56) 85–124. Luke, however, never mentions John by name in the account of Jesus' baptism. In fact he hurries over the act of Jesus' baptism, assigning it no more than a participial construction, and at once speaks of Jesus at prayer. Jesus' baptism by John was more and more embarrassing for the early Church, and we can watch the notice being gradually edited from the NT: Mk (1:9) clearly states that Jesus was actually baptized by John; Mt (3:13–15) tones it down by saying that Jesus presented himself to be baptized; Lk removes all mention of the Baptist's name and directs attention away from the baptism; Jn gives no account whatsoever of Jesus' baptism; the *Gospel of the Nazareans*, as recorded by Jerome (*Contra Pelagianos* 3. 2; see E. Hennecke, *NT Apocrypha*, 1, 147), has Jesus question why he must be baptized. The theophany rather than the baptism is the focal point for Luke, who alone states that Jesus "remains at prayer" (pres. ptc.). Often in Lk Jesus is portrayed at prayer before an important decision: election of the Twelve (6:12), confession of Peter (9:18), instruction on prayer (11:1), agony before his death (22:41), on the cross (23:46). This present moment is crucial and Messianic. *heaven was opened:* This imagery frequently implies a vision of heavenly secrets in apocalyptic writing (Ez 1:1). The strongest influence upon the present passage comes from Is 63:19. Not only does the pathetic and stirring prayer of Is 63:19 entreat God to open the heavens, but the Gk word of Mt and Lk closely follows the LXX of this passage. Mk, to maintain the violent rending of heaven implied by the MT, uses a different Gk word, *schizō*. This intensifies the eschatological tone of the baptism, for the Isaian prayer begs God to repeat, for one last time, the great redemptive acts toward his people, especially the Exodus out of bondage. Jesus' baptism, therefore, answers that prayer and envisages a whole community advancing to the new and most joyful promised land (see A. Feuillet, *CBQ* 21 [1959] 472–73; M. Traub, *ThWNT* 5, 529–30). Jesus' baptism, however, remains more of a promise to be fulfilled at Pentecost when the heavens will open again and the Spirit will descend upon the community (Acts 2). Jn takes a different viewpoint: the heavens remain open and heavenly beings are continually descending upon Jesus throughout his entire ministry (1:51).

51 **22.** *the Holy Spirit:* The Messianic gift to be bestowed on the Church at Pentecost (see I. de la Potterie, *NRT* 80 [1958] 225–52). *in bodily form:* These words, found only in Lk, move the discussion away from the apocalyptic vision of Mk and Mt, the description of which approximates Ez (1:4–5) and Dn (7:4–5), which speak of "someone or something like the appearance of...." Later writers will further enhance the external phenomena accompanying the baptism: The waters burn with fire (Justin) and the dove sings (*Odes of Solomon* 24). *like a dove:* Representing the new people of Israel, the eschatological community. The oldest traditions make this comparison: Hos 11:11; Ps 68:14 (see E. R. Goodenough, *Jewish Symbols* 8 (New York, 1958) 43) Some explain the dove as a symbol of the Spirit, but this symbolism is not explicitly present in the Bible but is found only in late rabbinic literature (Str-B 1, 123–24). We find again, therefore, the eschatological aspect of the community and a prefigurement of Pentecost in the baptism episode (A. Feuillet, *RSR* 46 [1958] 524–44). Another question can be asked: Was there an actual dove? As already noted, the earliest tradition in Mk implies an apocalyptic style in which visions and symbolism constitute major features of the literary medium. Symbols communicate the hidden qualities of an impelling reality. That reality, in the baptism of Jesus, was the burning conviction that the Father impressed upon his mind—that world salvation was under way and the final age imminent. By the phrase, "dove in bodily form," Luke intends to say that Jesus could almost reach out and touch the new community taking shape around him, especially when Pentecost would achieve the promise of Jesus' baptism. *a voice came from heaven:* A common biblical style, occurring in various modalities, indicates that a message or an action expresses God's hopes and determination (cf. Ex 19:9; 1 Sm 3:4ff.; 7:10; Ps 29). *you are my son, the dearly loved one; in you I am well pleased:* Many scholars accept this reading supported by the major NT mss. (S, A, B, W, etc.); thus A. M. Dibelius, E. Lohmeyer, H. Conzelmann, M.-J. Lagrange, J. M. Creed; and all the critical editions of the NT. But the Western Text changes the verse to read: "you are my son; this day I have begotten you." A large number of scholars prefer it (F. Hauck, W. Grundmann, H. Sahlin, P. Benoit [BJ], W. Manson, A. von Harnack, B. H. Streeter). The former reading, however, is preferred not only because of textual evidence in the mss. but also because Luke otherwise reserves Ps 2 (and its reference to the royal glorification of Jesus) for the moment of his ascension and Pentecost (Acts 2:29–36; 13:33; see J. Dupont, *RSR* 35 [1948] 522–43). According to the preferred reading, the heavenly voice proclaims over Jesus what was once announced to the *'Ebed Yahweh* (Servant of the Lord) in Is 42:1. Because the Servant is both an ideal individual and the representative of the corporate community (cf. C. R. North, *The Suffering Servant* [2nd ed.; London, 1956]), Jesus is declared to be thoroughly incarnate in the eschatological community, even to the point of being baptized as they were; but he also combines in the uniqueness of his person and mission their highest ideals and hopes. Because of his total union with all human weakness, the Servant Jesus must descend into human death, so as to infuse a new life into every area of man's existence. This association of Jesus' baptism with his later death and resurrection comes clearly to the fore in Lk 12:50 (Mk 10:38 par.). The first Servant Song (Is 42:1–4) enables us to understand Jesus' baptism as a solemn investiture in the prophetic role of establishing righteouness (i.e., the fulfillment of divine promises) all over the earth (see Is 42:4). The words "my son" are a deliberate NT substitution for the Hebr *'ebed* (servant) and the LXX *pais* (boy = servant). The expression "my son" complemented by the earlier reference to the Holy Spirit seem in Lk to be a confession of Jesus' divinity (J. Knackstedt, *VD* 38 [1960] 76–91).

(See further Cullmann, O., *Baptism in the NT* [London, 1950]. Daniélou, J., *The Theology of Jewish Christianity* [Chicago, 1964] 224–33. Stanley, D. M., *The Apostolic Church in the NT* [Westminster, 1965] ch. 11. Thompson, G. H. P., *JTS* 11 [1960] 1–12.)

52 **(C) The Genealogy of Jesus (3:23–38).** The genealogies of Jesus in the NT raise many problems when they are compared—a situation recognized as far back as the 3rd cent. in a letter of Julius Africanus to Aristides (Eusebius, *HE* 1.7). Lk proceeds backward from Jesus to Adam, Mt, however, moves forward from Abraham to Jesus. The Lucan procedure is more normal, to start with the contemporary representative of a family and work back (cf. Nm 27:1; 1 Sm 9:1; Zeph 1:1). Like Mt, Lk also makes use of the number seven; there are eleven series of seven names (with some variation in the Syr and Lat mss.). Only Lk provides the names from Abraham to Adam (depending on Gn 5:3–32; 11:10–26 [according to the LXX, which alone has the name Cainan]). Between Abraham and David, Mt and Lk agree, except that Lk adds Arni. Between David and Jesus, Mt and Lk completely disagree, except for the rare names, Zerubbabel and Shealtiel. "It is highly improbable that these are different persons.... That at the same period of Jewish history there should be two fathers bearing the rare name Salathiel or Shealtiel, each with a son bearing the rare name Zerubbabel, and that both of these unusually-named fathers should come in different ways into the genealogy of the Messiah, is scarcely credible...." (A. Plummer, *Luke*, 103). Various explanations for these differences are given, none of them convincing: e.g., that Mt makes use of the levirate marriage and gives legal or royal descent (cf. Dt 25:5–10), whereas Lk adheres to blood descent. Every solution must recognize both the highly artificial literary style of ancient genealogies and the religious purpose of the writer. Genealogies can be a literary device for spanning unknown centuries (Gn 5) or for insinuating the renown of one's ancestors (cf. the ages of the patriarchs in Gn 5 and *ANET* 265). In Mt, the term "to beget" can be a literary way of connecting two names, as happens when the Evangelist omits three names and tells of Joram begetting his great great grandson Uzziah.

23. *when he began his ministry:* The genealogy opens with a problematic ptc. *archomenos.* Perhaps we should translate the verse thus: "When he was about 30 years old, Jesus was beginning [his manifestation]." It is a reference to the "beginning" of the final stage of salvation (see 4:21). *being the son, as was believed:* A further problem is met in the phrase *hōs enomizeto,* "as was supposed, believed," which modifies the statement that Jesus was the son of Joseph. A number of scholars (Grundmann, Sahlin, Creed) claim that the words were added later to support the virginal conception of Jesus; but Lagrange notes that not only do all the mss. contain the words, but that even if the words had not been present, the genealogy of Jesus does not depend on carnal descent but on the spiritual ancestry derived from God himself. **38.** *Adam, who was of God:* This phrase reveals Luke's religious purpose; he stresses the divine origin of the human race, with a universalism that does more than seek to bring salvation to all men. It sees divine sonship already present among them and waiting to be fully realized through Jesus, to whom the Father had just announced for all to hear, "you are my son." Some scholars (Hauck, Grundmann, Lagrange) recognize Pauline influence here in the presentation of Christ as the new Adam (see Rom 5:14; 1 Cor 15:22,45–49).

(See further Jeremias, J., *Jerusalem zur Zeit Jesu* [2nd ed.; Göttingen, 1958] 145–68. Lambertz, M., Fest. F. Dornseiff [Leipzig, 1953] 201–25. Vögtle, A., *LTK* 4, 661–62.)

53 **(D) The Temptation (4:1–13).** In the baptismal scene as well as in the genealogical table, Jesus appears as the son of God, commissioned for the messianic-eschatological work of bringing men to the fullness of divine sonship. The temptation scene now makes it clear that Jesus is fully human too. As man, he undertakes his work in full obedience to the Father (cf. Heb 2:10,18). Mk (1:12–13) has the shortest account of the temptation; in this earliest narrative there is already a strong doctrinal orientation. Jesus relives the Exodus experience of Israel in the desert (see Dt 8:2). By going out into the desert, a desolate land inhabited by demons and ferocious beasts (Lv 16:22; Tb 8:3; Zech 5:11), Jesus subdues the hostile powers and becomes a new Adam living in perfect harmony with the beasts (Is 11:6–9; Gn 3:19–20; see A. Feuillet, *EstBib* 19 [1960] 49–73). Though Lk parallels Mt (4:1–11), there are distinct embellishments so that it is difficult to decide which one stands closer to the original form of Q. Mt develops the two themes of Moses and the kingdom: Jesus, like Moses, is found atop "a very high mountain" (Mt 4:8, cf. Dt 34:1–4); Mt adds "forty nights" to the fast of "forty days," thus more closely associating Jesus' fast with that of Moses (Dt 9:9,18; Ex 34:28); the third and climactic scene in Mt concerns the kingdom, as Jesus rejects that of the devil ("all the kingdoms of the world," 4:8) to mount another mountain in Galilee, there to proclaim the true kingdom. All these differences in Mt from the Lucan version stress the theological viewpoint of the First Gospel. But Luke has his own doctrinal viewpoint too, which will be developed below. (See A. Hastings, *Prophet and Witness* [Baltimore, 1958] 122–23.)

1. *full of the Holy Spirit:* A Lucan phrase (Acts 6:5; 7:55; 11:24). The double mention of the Spirit in this verse explains why Luke is called the Evangelist of the Spirit. *returned:* The Gk word (*hypostrephō*) occurs 35 times in Lucan writings, and only 4 times in the rest of the NT. This is an indication of a strong Lucan redaction of the Temptation Account. *he was led by the Spirit up and down the wilderness:* Luke here employs Gk phrases that show a delicate nuance of meaning, different from Mt. The Spirit accompanied Jesus during 40 days in the desert, and only after this period of prayerful communion with the Father does Jesus engage in battle with the devil. The full force of the godhead confronts the world of diabolical power; it is the eschatological moment. **3.** *if you are the son of God:* The temptation centers on the kind of a Messiah Jesus will be: Will he win the people by granting what they immediately desire, or will he thrust them into suffering by the divine ideals demanded of them? *tell this stone to turn into bread:* Luke uses the singular; Mt refers to stones and many loaves of bread. Mt sees all Israel being tempted in Jesus; Lk portrays a more personal temptation for Jesus alone. **4.** *not by bread alone:* Jesus responds with Dt 8:3 (cf. Ex 16). Jesus' thoughts are expressed in what must have been the favorite OT book of the early apostolic Church (see Lk 10:27; Acts 3:22). **5.** *took him up:* It is usually stated that Lk reverses the sequence of the temptation scenes, for Mt places the episode on the mountain last. Each Evangelist's arrangement fits so well into his own "theology" that it is difficult to decide whose order better corresponds to the original order in Q. *in a single moment:* These words, found only in Lk, remove the idea of any physical translation of Jesus; it happened in a vision. *all the kingdoms of the inhabitable* [*world*]*:* Lk clearly refers to political domains. Verse 6 is a Lucan addition, not found in Mt. We sense here the Johannine idea that the world is under the power of the devil (Jn 12:31; 14:30; 16:11; Lk 22:53; Acts 26:18). A battle of cosmic proportions is being fought to the bitter end (Ap 13:1–8). In rejecting a political messiahship, Jesus again quotes Dt (6:13; 10:20; cf. Ex 23:24).

54 **9.** *to Jerusalem:* Jerusalem constitutes the climax of Luke's Temptation Account, as it will of his entire theology. He presents Jesus' entire ministry as a journey leading to Jerusalem; but the true Jerusalem, perfectly fulfilling every prophetic hope, will be Jesus himself (Lk 9:51; 21:37f.; 24:50–53; Acts 1:12; Ap 21:2). **10.** *his angels charge over you:* Again with Dt 6:16 (cf. Ps 91:11), Jesus rejects the proposal to be the Messiah of the gaudy and the marvelous, even though this is the kind of a Messiah many people want. Salvation is to be attained in the humble and at times sorrowful way of faith. **13.** Luke writes his own conclusion, different from Mt. *finishing every temptation:* The idea seems to be that Jesus has perfected himself through the experience of every temptation (cf. Heb 2:10; 5:9). Jesus as man completes his role as Messiah and so conquers for every man. The full effects of Jesus' victory is now to be seen in his public ministry. *departed from him for a while:* Luke anticipates the passion (22:3,53). He edits all temptations out of his narrative of the public ministry, even omitting the incident of Mt 16:23. Even though the devil returns at the end in the Passion Narrative, Jesus, nonetheless, dies a man of peace and strength; the victory seems already achieved. His entire ministry will show that the way of the cross is a way to victory.

Some scholars deny the historicity of the temptation scene. However, we must reckon with the fact that the other Gospels portray trials and temptations in the later life of Jesus, and we must recognize the strong tradition, favoring the reality of the desert scene. Mt and Lk (or Q) could have expanded an early but brief tradition (Mk) and added details drawn from later events because of a distinctly theological viewpoint. Lk's first temptation reminds us of Jn 6:26–34; the second, of Jn 6:15; the third, of Jn 7:1–4 (cf. R. E. Brown, *CBQ* 23 [1963] 152–55). Other similarities occur in Mt 12:38–42; 16:1–4; 27:42. Just as Matthew and Luke rearranged the sayings and activities of Jesus, disregarding chronological and geographical details, in order to form either the Sermon on the Mount (Mt 5–7) or the Journey Narrative (Lk 9:51ff.), so a similar process could be responsible for the way in which real temptations scattered through the life of Jesus are retold in a new setting in order to focus attention upon theological involvements. Why did the Church do this—for the temptation story already existed in Q when Luke wrote? Perhaps it was to counteract the claims of false Messiahs with their bizarre miracles; or it may have been to re-emphasize the humanity of Jesus against those who considered flesh to be evil.

(See Bultmann, *HST* 254–57, 426–27. Dupont, J., *ScEccl* 14 [1962] 7–29; *NTS* 3 [1956–57] 287–304. Feuillet, A., *Bib* 40 [1959] 613–31. Köppen, K. P., *Die Auslegung der Versuchungsgeschichte unter besonderer Berücksichtigung der alten Kirche* [Tübingen, 1961]. Riesenfeld, H., "Le caractère messianique de la tentation au désert," *La venue du Messie* [Tournai, 1962] 51–63.)

55 **(IV) The Galilean Ministry (4:14–9:50).** The Syn, like the early apostolic preaching, omit any Judean ministry at the beginning of Jesus' public life (cf. Acts 10:37f.), which is so prominent in Jn. If one uses Johannine data, Jesus, before inaugurating an extensive effort in Galilee, would have been in Jerusalem for a Passover (Jn 2:13,23), at which time he swept the Temple clean of money enterprises (Jn 2:13–22) and met secretly with the Pharisee Nicodemus (Jn 3:1ff.). His extraordinary deeds attracted the attention of Galilean visitors (Jn 4:45). Then he traveled N through inhospitable Samaria (Jn 4). While Luke, theologically minded, states that Jesus returned to Galilee "in the power of the Spirit" (4:14), Mt explains that Jesus "withdrew," fleeing before the hostility of the priests and Pharisees (Mt 4:12; Jn 4:1).

Lk presents an orderly account of the public ministry; it does not bring Jesus to Jerusalem till the very end, for the climax of rejection by the Jews and the beginning of a world-wide apostolate to the Gentiles. The universal extent of the kingdom begins with Pentecost (Acts 2). Here is one of the clues for Luke's select use of Mk's Gospel. Although Lk 4:14–9:50 reproduces Mk 1:14–9:39, it deliberately omits Mk 6:45–8:26; it therefore says nothing of Jesus' journey into the Gentile area of Tyre and Sidon. At Lk 9:18 (Mk 8:27; Mt 16:13 par.) nothing is said about Jesus' presence among the villages of Caesarea Philippi. Luke wants an uninterrupted Galilean ministry so that the full force of the Jerusalem rejection can be understood.

56 **(A) Two Typical Events: At Nazareth and Capernaum (4:14–44).** These incidents symbolize the rejection of Jesus by his own people and the appreciation of him by outsiders.

(a) JESUS AT NAZARETH (4:14–30). Lk introduces the incident at Nazareth with a notice of Jesus' return to Galilee (Mt 4:12; Mk 1:14 par.). The two verses (14–15) are loaded with words or phrases particularly favored by Luke. Not only is the role of the Spirit emphasized, but he also delights in noting the crowd's enthusiastic celebration of Jesus' presence in their midst. An almost identical phrase occurs again in 5:25f.; 7:16; 13:13; 17:15; 18:43; 23:47; Acts 4:21; 13:48; 21:20. The psychic reaction of the audience is often noted: 3:15; 9:43; 11:1,29; 13:1; 17:20; 18:1,9; 19:11. While Mk 1:14f. issues a call to repentance because the kingdom is imminent, Luke keynotes the call of the lowly to the Kingdom of the Spirit.

Lk's account of Jesus' rejection by his fellow townsmen combines three or at least two separate visits to the city. The first visit (Lk 4:16–22a) is recorded also by Mt 4:13; that both writers depend upon a common source here seems attested by the unique spelling "Nazara," found nowhere else in the NT. Mt provides the historical context for the visit. Some argue that Lk 4:22b–30 represents two distinct visits to Nazareth, because only vv. 22b–24 find a parallel in Mt 13:54–58 and Mk 6:1–6 (= Jn 4:44; 6:42?). Later, when Lk is relying upon Mk for information (Mk 5:43 = Lk 8:56; Mk 6:7 = Lk 9:1), he passes over the Nazareth incident (Mk 6:1–6). Because vv. 25–30 are distinctly Lucan, not just in content but more especially in doctrinal outlook, Luke may simply be using the occasion to develop his own theology of Jesus' rejection by his own people and the call of the Gentiles (cf. A. George, *BiViChr* 59 [1964] 17–29).

16–22a. Jesus' first visit to Nazareth after the opening of his ministry is now recorded (Mt 4:13 par.). We cannot be certain in reconstructing the Sabbath synagogal services in Jesus' times, but somewhat later it included: (1) two prayers, the Shema (Dt 6:4–9; 11:13–21; Nm 15:37–41; cf. Lk 10:27) and the *Shemoneh 'eśreh* (Eighteen [Blessings]); (2) two readings, one from the Torah and the other from the Prophets (either the earlier prophetic books [Jos-Jgs-Sm-Kgs] or the later prophetic books [Is-Jer-Ez and the twelve Minor Prophets]); (3) an explanation or homily (cf. Acts 13:15); (4) finally, the priestly blessing (Nm 6:22–27); see Str-B 4, 153–88; E. Schürer, *HJPTJC* 2/2, 52–89; A. Edersheim, *The Life and Times of Jesus the Messiah* [8th ed.; N.Y., 1904] 1, 430–50).

17. *he found the place:* Either by accidentally opening the scroll to a passage in Is (H. Preisker, *ThDNT* 2, 769–70) or by deliberately seeking the exact spot (majority of commentators). This is the only clear reference in the Scriptures that Jesus knew how to read. **18–19.** In quoting from Is 61:1–2, Jesus leaves out one of the lines, "to heal the brokenhearted." Luke reserves the Gk word, "to heal" (*iaomai*), for physical cures; a little later (v. 23) Jesus refuses to work any such cures in Nazareth, for his concern here is with preaching and interior renewal. A line, therefore, is added instead from Is 58:6; "to send away free the oppressed." Although the Vg and some late Gk mss. include the line "and the day of vindication" at the end of v. 19, important mss. do not contain the words, which for Luke put too much emphasis upon punishment; he deletes the same words in 7:22 when he once more cites Is. **18.** *the spirit of the Lord is upon me:* In Lk this would refer to Jesus' own baptism (3:22; Acts 10:38). *to bring good news to the poor:* In 7:22 Jesus points to this action as indicative of his Messianic mission. Used without an article in Greek, the word "poor" refers to a quality or state rather than to individual poor persons (cf. *GrBib* § 171). *he has sent me:* The pf. tense of the Gk verb means more than merely to be sent; it declares that the one sent has already arrived and is to be found in the person of Jesus. *to announce the year of grace accorded by the Lord:* All the hopes of the jubilee year (Lv 25:8–55), when debts were wiped out and all possessions returned to their original owner, are fulfilled in the Messianic presence of Jesus. Universalism characterizes the jubilee year, for the celebration rests on the explanation given by God that "[all] land is mine, and you are but aliens" (Lv 25:23). God graciously divides it among all his elect.

21. *in your hearing of my words, Scripture has been fulfilled:* These words are spoken out of the biblical understanding of the power of the word of God (Is 55:10f.). Again, the pf. tense of the verb (*peplērōtai*) indicates that the moment of salvation is already being achieved in the person of Jesus; the effects of his presence, or rather, his continuing presence through the gift of the Spirit in the preaching of prophets and apostles (Eph 2:20), keeps the divine word always being felt (see H. Conzelmann, *Theology of St. Luke*, 36–37). **22a.** *kept wondering:* With the impf. tense of the verbs, Lk indicates the continuing admiration and astonishment of the people at the charm and eloquence of Jesus. Although the phrase "words of grace" is ordinarily understood in an aesthetic sense, still the close connection with the Isaian citation leads some commentators to give it a more spiritual meaning: words proclaiming God's good pleasure.

22b–24. The abrupt change in the attitude of the Nazarenes is best explained by a lapse of time. Luke is now relating a subsequent visit (Mk 6:1–6; Mt 13:54–58 par.). *is not this Joseph's son?:* Luke has already recorded very clearly the virginal conception (1:26–38) of Jesus, and so he can afford to give the normal reaction of the Nazarenes. Mt 13:55 has "son of the carpenter," whereas Mk, which lacks any Infancy Narrative, has the people speak in a way contrary to Jewish custom, "the son of Mary" (6:3). **23.** *you will surely quote at me this proverb:* Luke purposely employs the fut. tense, for in his Gospel Jesus has not yet appeared in Capernaum. After his miracles in this other city of Galilee, the Nazarenes will want to see Jesus (8:19–21), i.e., to see some miracles, though like Herod they lack faith (9:9; 23:8). At this point, Mk (6:5) has "one of the boldest statements in the Gospels" (V. Taylor, *The Gospel According to St. Mark* [London, 1953] 301): "he was not able to perform any miracle there." The implied reason: because of their unbelief. Evidently, Jesus' miracles were intended to deepen faith in Messianic salvation and not to exert external force on a person's freedom. **24.** *Amen I say to you:* Lk usually omits this Semitism; *amen* is a transliterated Hebr word meaning "true, steadfast." It is used as an adverb, and the entire phrase always introduces a solemn declaration uttered only by Jesus in the Gospels (31 times in Mt; 13 times in Mk; 6 times in Lk).

25–27. These verses may introduce us to a third visit of Jesus to Nazareth. But they are not only without parallel in Mt and Mk but their whole theology is distinctly Lucan. Scholars, therefore, will always suspect here an independent Lucan composition summarizing the entire work of Jesus. **25.** *in the days of Elijah:* Jesus compares himself to Elijah and the drought (1 Kgs 17–18) and to Elisha and the cure of Naaman (2 Kgs 5). Like both of these prophets, Jesus too will eventually direct his apostles beyond Judaism to the entire Gentile world. We must accept the comparison as it is intended, for the parallel is not complete. Elijah was not greatly honored at Zarephath, nor was Elisha ever rejected by Israel. Nazareth does not necessarily represent all Israel, nor Capernaum the Gentile country. Clearly implied here is a theology of election. The Gentiles may not be as worthy as the Jews, but God in his mercy has chosen them for his own. *three years and six months:* Although 1 Kgs 17:1 announces a three-year drought, Lk, like Jas 5:17, extends the time to three and one-half years. The latter number echoes the classic figure used in apocalyptic literature for the duration of persecution and distress, even the eschatological struggle (Dn 7:25; 12:7; Ap 11:2; 12:6,14).

28–30. The conclusion of the episode is written in language very similar to the rejection of Stephen (Acts 7:58) and of Paul (Acts 13:50). Luke evidently sees universal Church history already taking place in Jesus, for the spirit of Jesus is responsible for whatever happens in the Church. **29.** *to the brow of the hill:* Nazareth, clinging to a hillside, had several steep slopes from which a man could fall to his death. *passed through their midst and went away:* This does not necessarily imply a miracle. At the decisive moment no Nazarene dared to molest him. Such spasmodic changes of attitude are recorded in many social revolutions (M.-J. Lagrange, *Luc*, 146). Similar incidents are more frequent in Jn (Jn 7:30,45f.; 8:59), with the theological implication that the hour had not yet come. Only in 9:51 will Lk admit that the days were completed for his "being taken up."

57 (b) A Day at Capernaum (4:31–44). Like the preceding account, this one too records a typical day in the ministry of Jesus and as such provides a thumbnail sketch of his entire ministry. The setting is Capernaum, a city that Luke identifies for his Gentile readers as belonging to the larger district of Galilee. An important town on the NW shore of the Lake of Galilee (686 ft. below sea level), Capernaum was a trade and toll station between the seaport city of Ptolemais on the Mediterranean and Damascus further north on the edge of the desert, or between Philip's territory and the cities of the Decapolis SE of the lake (cf. 3:1).

31–32. These introductory verses (Mk 1:21f. par.; cf. Mt 7:28f.) imply that no single day was to be described. *on the Sabbath* [*days*]*:* The plural indicates a typical day in the ministry of Jesus. Luke is now following Mk's Gospel, but always with careful editing. He omits the indelicacy of Mk's phrase that Jesus was not teaching like the scribes. For his part, Matthew transfers the phrase to the conclusion of the Sermon on the Mount. *with authority:* This phrase brings out the impact of Jesus' words upon the conscience of his audience.

(i) *Expulsion of a demon* (4:33–37). See Mk 1:23–28. Jesus enters the synagogue that a Roman officer had built (7:5), distinct from the one erected *ca.* AD 200 whose ruins are still visible at Tell Hum (the modern name for ancient Capernaum). Jesus meets a man possessed by an unclean spirit that made him unfit for worship and godly joy. Because the Bible attributes evil, physical as well as moral, ultimately to a diabolical force (Gn 3), it is not always easy to determine the exact nature of demonic possession in any biblical incident. The Evangelist, however, was certainly convinced that Jesus' presence instigated a vehement confrontation between superhuman forces of goodness and evil. **33.** *he shrieked at the top of his voice:* What he cried is put in idiomatic Greek: the first word (*ea*) is an interjection registering anger and surprise; the second phrase (*ti hēmin kai soi*), lit., "what to us and to you?" always draws a line of division (cf. Jos 22:24; Jgs 11:12; 1 Kgs 17:18; Jn 2:4). **34.** *I know who you are, the Holy one of God:* Here is the cry of a conscience-stricken man, sensing his separation from God's goodness in Jesus, frantically attempting to control the divine by uttering its name. In the Bible to name someone is to have authority over him by thoroughly understanding that person's power and vocation. **35.** *muzzle your mouth:* Jesus' reply to be silent bears all the strength of spontaneous, colloquial language. *threw the man down:* Luke changes Mk's picturesque word for tearing and rending and substitutes a medical term employed by Hippocrates and Galen for convulsions. *without harming him at all:* An important observation by Luke the physician. **37.** *reports:* Luke is ever conscious of the reactions of the crowd (4:20, 22,32,36; 5:26) and the quick spread of news (4:14f.,37; 5:15,17). "What is this word?" Luke takes this question intact from 2 Sm 1:4 (LXX). Even though "word" can denote action and often has that connotation, Luke may be deliberately intending to draw the readers' attention away from excessive preoccupation with a miracle and invite them to concentrate on a fuller appreciation of the good news of salvation.

(ii) *Cure of Peter's mother-in-law* (4:38–39). See Mk 1:29–31; Mt 8:14f. Lk's more majestic account lacks the homey, eyewitness details of Mk's Gospel; no longer is Jesus said to take her by the hand, but instead he stands over her to "rebuke" the fever.

(iii) *Healing of the sick* (4:40–41). See Mk 1:32–34; Mt 8:16f. Now that the Sabbath is over (Jer 17:21f.), the sick can be carried to Jesus. While Lk carefully distinguishes between the sick and the possessed, Mt combines both cases so as to quote from Is 53:4. The possessed cry out in dismay and frustration, but Jesus quiets them, lest he be recognized simply as a wonder-worker and political messiah.

(iv) *Jesus leaves Capernaum* (4:42–44). See Mk 1:35–39; cf. Mt 4:23; 9:35. Lk again portrays the psychological reaction of the crowd, how in Jesus they find their hopes fulfilled and their anxieties overcome. "They did not leave off seeking *until* they reached Him and they *tried* to stay Him from going away from them" (A. Plummer, *Luke*, 140). **43.** *the kingdom of God:* This intimate bond is achieved through announcing the good news of the Kingdom of God—a favorite theme of Paul but never found in the Gospels outside Lk (9:2,11,60; 16:16), except for a citation in Mt 11:5 (→ Aspects NT Thought, 78:93–108). Lk includes the Johannine theme of being "sent" (Jn 4:34; 5:23). **44.** *he was preaching in the synagogues of Judea:* Some mss. read "of Galilee." Jesus is actually in Galilee, and Luke knows it (4:14,31). For him, however, the holy land, chosen by God for the manifestation and completion of world salvation, is Judea and especially Jerusalem. Jesus' Messianic works, though technically occurring in Galilee at this time, can be described theologically as happening in "Judea" (W. Grundmann, *Evangelium*, 126).

58 **(B) From the Call of Peter to the Naming of the Twelve (5:1–6:16).** Although the account of the Galilean ministry (4:14–9:50) rather carefully follows

Mk's master-gospel, Luke does not place the call of Peter before the day at Capernaum (as happens rather abruptly in Mk); instead he composes his own account of Peter's vocation and introduces a more orderly arrangement of events (1:3). A. Plummer (*Luke*, 141) recognized the symmetry: call of leading disciples (5:1–11); two healings that provoke controversy (5:12–16,17–26); call of another disciple (5:27–39); two incidents on the Sabbath that stir new controversy (6:1–11); naming of the Twelve (6:12–16).

(a) The Call of Simon Peter (5:1–11). See Mk 1:16–20; 4:1f.; Mt 4:18–22; cf. Jn 1:35–42; 21:1–11. Luke's account is either a composition that he prepared from various sources (the more probable opinion, for the section is exceptionally heavy with Lucan turns of style) or else the result of oral transmission with details of different stories intermingled. The description of the place (5:1–3) corresponds to Mk 4:1f., but Mk then proceeds with the parable of the sower. The story of the miracle (5:4–10a) contains many points of similarity (and difference!—see A. Plummer, *Luke*, 147) with the postresurrection event in Jn 21:1–11. The call of Simon (5:10b–11) reminds us of Mk 1:17,20. It seems very unlikely that Peter would have forgotten or Mark overlooked the miraculous draught of fishes if such a wonder had occurred at the momentous time of Peter's vocation. Luke probably combines several events, in order to highlight symbolically the fuller meaning of Peter's vocation. Just as the Nazareth incident prefigured the rejection of Jesus by his own and the Capernaum account his enthusiastic reception by outsiders, the vocation of Peter is told in such a way as to symbolize the great number of Gentile converts in the Messianic community.

1. *the lake of Gennesareth:* The other Evangelists speak of the Sea of Galilee, but Luke more properly calls it a lake (for it is a small, pear-shaped body of water, 13 mi. long and 7.5 mi. wide, with fresh, cool water, abounding with fish). *Gennesaret:* The name is derived from that of the plain just NW of the lake. H. Conzelmann recognizes a special theological meaning in the "lake." Just as the "mountain" is the favorite setting for communications with the Father in Lk, so the lake provides a place for manifestations of power. **5.** *Master: Epistata* is a favorite title for Jesus in Lk, replacing the Hebr *rabbi*. Though the men had worked exhaustively through the night, Peter will let down the net "on the strength of your word" (proper meaning of the prep. *epi*; cf. 2:20). **8.** *Lord:* The change from "Master" to "Lord" (Gk *Kyrie*) reflects Peter's religious fear before the awesome presence of the divine (→ Aspects NT Thought, 78:25). **10.** Distinct from Mk 1:17f., where Jesus addresses Andrew as well as Simon and a little later James and John, this section of Lk portrays Jesus, speaking exclusively to Peter: "from this moment forward you [sing.] will be catching men." *this moment:* The phrase is heavily underlined in Greek; it implies a crisis in Peter's life (cf. same phrase in 1:48b). Peter will be catching men in order to save their lives, rather than fish to be consumed at a family dinner; the fut. tense of the verb plus the participle assign Peter to a lifelong vocation. Writing after AD 70, Luke infers that Peter's leadership will never be vacated in favor of anyone else, including James, as some scholars maintain because of Acts 10 (cf. O. Cullmann, *Peter* [N.Y., 1958]). **11.** *brought the boats to land:* The vb. *kat-agō* forms an elegant conclusion to the introductory word in v. 30, *ep-an-agō*, "to put out from the shore" (M.-J. Lagrange, *Luc*, 160). *they left everything:* Luke's addition to the other Gospels, for he writes the "Gospel of Absolute Renouncement" (→ 10 above). Luke makes the call to an apostolic vocation all the more heroic and single-minded on this occasion of an abundant draught of fishes. (See L. Grollenberg, *TT* 5 [1965] 330–36. G. de Raucourt, *RSR* 29 [1939] 610–15.)

59 (b) Two Miracles and a Conflict Story (5:12–26). From 5:12 to 6:11 Luke relies heavily upon Mk and makes only slight modifications in his source. In structural arrangement, the next two episodes evenly match the two incidents after the call of Levi (→ 58 above).

(i) *The healing of a leper* (5:12–16). See Mk 1:40–45; Mt 8:1–4. Lk's opening phrases are not only characteristically biblical in style, in imitation of the LXX, but they link this event with 4:43. Mk 1:39 seems to place the event in the open country where a man in the advanced stages of a highly contagious skin disease (see comment on Mt 8:2) is more likely to be encountered (Lv 13:45f.). Throughout the Gospels Jesus meets lepers only in the central districts of Samaria or Galilee. For the leper to come to Jesus is a manifestation of faith in Jesus' power to cure. Mk states that Jesus "was angry" at meeting him; many mss. read "moved with compassion"; however, not only is "angry" a more difficult reading and therefore less likely to be a scribal correction, but Luke would have taken up the word "compassion" if he had found it in Mk. Here as elsewhere, Luke edits out of his source any expression of Jesus' strong emotion. In the present episode, Luke also removes most of the direct discourse to produce a smoother but less personal account. **12.** *you can make me clean:* The leper did not ask to be cured but rather to be cleansed; this feeling reflects the entire biblical tradition that the most poignant sorrow about leprosy was the lonely despair in being excluded from the community. Only a person ceremonially clean could take part in community services and assemblies. **13.** *stretched out his hand:* The Gk word (*ekteinō*) almost always occurs in the LXX in a hostile sense of God's hand outstretched to punish; but the idea of God's outstretched hand or arm became a cliché for God's redeeming power at the Exodus (Ex 6:6; 14:16; 15:12; Jer 17:5). **14.** *tell no man:* Mk makes a great deal of the "Messianic Secret" and accuses the cured leper of disobedience for not following the order; Lk does not press the point. *show yourself to the priest:* Another instance of Jesus' compliance with the Mosaic Law (cf. Mt 5:17; Lv 14:1–32). **16.** *constantly retiring to lonely places for prayer:* While Mk insinuates that Jesus was forced to flee into deserted areas lest the excitable people riot in a political messianic movement, Luke stresses that Jesus' withdrawal for prayer was spontaneous and continued. Through prayer he gained what people sought from him.

60 (ii) *Cure of the paralytic* (5:17–26). See Mk 2:1–12; Mt 9:1–8; cf. Jn 5:8f.). Luke has completely rewritten the introduction of this account otherwise taken from Mk. Right at the beginning he groups the full galaxy of Jewish leaders, who in opposing Jesus lose all right to their spiritual heritage. **17.** *the power of the Lord was with him:* The Gk construction implies that Jesus was under a divine impulse to act in favor of the sick (Zerwick, *Analysis*, 144). **18.** *on a bed:* The paralytic is being carried to Jesus, lying not on a *krabattos*, a poor man's "mattress" (Mk 2:4), but on a *klinē* or *klinidion*, a "bed" or "small couch." Luke also calls the paralytic by the word more commonly used in the medical profession. **19.** Luke did not understand too well the Palestinian way of building homes (outside stairway, leading up to a flat roof of clay and straw trodden hard upon wooden rafters); he describes how a man would be let down through the tiled roof of Greco-Roman houses. **20.** *man, your sins are forgiven you:* Mk uses a more affectionate form of address, "son." When we expect a physical cure, Jesus forgives sin; Jesus' activity is directed against the kingdom of Satan and its manifestation in sorrow and death. **21.** *who is this...:* Luke again corrects the Gk style of Mk, (accidentally?) putting some of the speech into iambic verse. He has smoothed over the sharp contemptuous words of the adversary: "Why does this [fellow] talk like that? This is blasphemy! Who is able to forgive sins, but the One—God" (Mk 2:7; NEB).

24. This verse bristles with difficulties. There is a disjointed sentence structure. Many scholars, among them E. Klostermann and R. Bultmann, claim that Mark had stitched together two separate stories: a miracle story (Mk 2:1–5a,10b–12 = Lk 5:17–20a,24b–26) and an apothegm or conflict story (Mk 2:5b–10a = Lk 5:20b–24a). These same scholars also feel that the term "Son of Man" was not used by Jesus till much later. Others, such as M. Dibelius, C. H. Turner, and J. M. Creed, argue for the unity of the section, claiming that the anacoluthon is a common enough occurrence in Mk and that "Son of Man" need not necessarily contain all the overtones of the later days of Jesus' ministry. Moreover, it is not at all impossible that the dispute between Jesus and some leaders would have been entirely overlooked by the crowd in their amazement over a miracle. Ordinarily, a miracle story leads to a climax of awe and wonderment; a conflict story ends in a saying of Jesus that answers a problem or need of the early Church (see R. Bultmann, *HST* 14–16, 382–83; C. H. Turner, *JTS* 26 [1925] 145–46; M. Dibelius, *Die Formgeschichte des Evangeliums* [2nd ed.; 1933] 221–22; R. T. Mead, *JBL* 80 [1961] 348–54).

Son of Man: In using this term, Jesus seems to combine or move between two OT traditions. In one of these, "Son of Man" indicates the lowly condition of mortal flesh (Ps 8:5; Job 25:6; Ez 2:1; 1QS 11:20–22); in another association, that stemming from Dn 7:13, "Son of Man" implies the exultation of the lowly, persecuted saints of Israel. Jesus joined the glorious Son of Man, in his eschatological role as judge (Lk 17:22ff.) with that of Suffering Servant (→ Aspects NT Thought, 78:28–30). **25.** Lk alone notes that the man, now able to carry the couch upon which he had been forced to lie so long, was glorifying God (7:16; 13:13; 17:15).

61 (c) The Call of Levi (5:27–39). See Mk 2:13–22; Mt 9:9–17. **27.** Lk omits Mk's references to the Sea of Galilee and to the crowd. At once Jesus turns away from everything else and peers intently (*theaomai*) at Levi, detecting his noble hopes and genuine compunction. *publican:* See comment on 3:12. *Levi:* Usually considered to be the same as the apostle Matthew (Mt 9:9; 10:13); but the name Levi is never included in any list of the Twelve (→ Aspects NT Thought, 78:165–166). **28.** Lk alone states that Levi "left everything" behind to follow Jesus. This addition, along with the word "rising," is expressed by an aor. participle, indicating the continual and ready disposition of discipleship (M. Zerwick, *GrBib* § 363–65). **29.** The income Levi renounced must have been large, if he was able to spread a banquet for the many invited guests. **30.** *the Pharisees and their scribes:* They heard that Jesus did something worse than inviting unclean persons to his own home: He went to their homes, where one could never be sure that the dietary laws were being observed. **32.** *not to call the just:* Thus Jesus refers ironically to the self-righteous. *to repentance:* Luke's addition gives a more religious and conventional form to the saying. While sinners invite Jesus to be their guest at a dinner, Jesus invites them—by repentance—to become his guests at the eschatological banquet. Jesus, by his presence, transforms their banquet into his own (W. Grundmann, *Evangelium,* 133; A. Schlatter, *Das Evangelium des Lukas* [Stuttgart, 1931] 62).

62 **33–35.** In his editing of the Marcan material, Luke closely connects the following series of parables with the preceding episode. To balance the sentence structure he refers to the "disciples of John [the Baptist] and... those of the Pharisees"; actually, the Pharisee as Pharisee had no disciples, even though as a rabbi he might. Mk 2:18, therefore, is by contrast less elegant but more precise. **33.** *supplication:* Formal prayer at specific times (cf. 1 Tm 2:1). Luke was certainly acquainted with the Baptist's style of prayer (cf. 11:1). *fast often:* The Pharisees fasted twice a week (18:12): on Thursday, in honor of Moses' ascent of Mt. Sinai; on Monday, commemorating his descent (A. Plummer, *Luke,* 161). They never fasted, however, on the Sabbath, nor is it likely that they did so at a wedding feast. **34.** *can you make wedding guests fast?:* Jesus reminds them that the Messianic age is a continual wedding banquet. In this regard the NT combines various OT themes of the banquet symbol: the paschal or covenant banquet (Ex 12; 24:11; Lk 22:29f.); the nuptial meal (Ct 5:1; Ap 19:9); the eschatological feast (Is 55:1f.; 65:11–13; Ap 3:20; 19:9; Lk 22:29). **35.** *taken away:* A clear enough reference to Jesus' death, and possibly to the suffering Servant of Dt-Is (Is 53:8,11 [LXX]). By his continual insistence that the disciple must carry his cross after Jesus, Luke places the present age of the Church within this time of mourning. Although full eschatological glory came with Jesus' ascension, it is not yet fully experienced by the Church. The early Church fasted (Acts 13:2f.; 14:22; *Didache* 8).

63 **36–39.** With an editorial addition, Luke connects three independent sayings; their abrupt intrusion is much more evident in Mk and Mt. Typical of the Bible, this whole section (vv. 27–39) is not built up by chronological or logical sequence but rather by association of words and ideas for mnemonic purpose. **36.** *tears a piece from a new garment:* Luke deliberately rewrites the Marcan parable. Mk is truer to the Palestinian practice of not sewing a raw unbleached or unfulled piece of cloth onto an older garment. The new piece would shrink and thereby make a worse tear. Lk's revision has more of an aesthetic touch! **37–38.** *new wine...into old wineskins:* An old skin would stretch and burst with the fermenting juice. Bottles made of animal skins, attested in the Bible (Gn 21:14b; Ps 119:83; Job 32:19), are still in use by Bedouins in the Near East today. **39.** This final saying, found only in Lk, has textual difficulties. The preferred reading is: "no one, after drinking old wine, wants new wine; for he says, 'The old is good.'" In the present setting, Luke is insisting that anyone rigidly and proudly bound up with the past can scarcely sustain the fresh vitality of the new. Studying these sayings in the apocryphal *Gospel According to Thomas* (§ 47), we find a more general context, stating that the old and the new seldom meet peacefully. Grundmann recognizes here an allusion to the problems between Jewish Christians and Gentile Christians in the early Church. The final saying of Lk, however, seems to restrain one from completely rejecting the old; the new, to be palatable, must contain the genuine spirit of the ancient Law (cf. J. Dupont, *CBQ* 25 [1963] 286–304).

64 (d) Sabbath Controversies (6:1–11). See Mk 2:23–3:6; Mt 12:1–14; cf. Jn 5:9). As these conflict stories were repeated, details were gradually sloughed off and attention was directed to a pronouncement, important for the early Church. Even if a miracle occurs, it is subordinated to the controversy and pronouncement.

1–5. The first story opens with a very difficult reading in the Koine and Western Texts: "the second first Sabbath." It is possible that the phrase was inserted into Lk in accord with a solar calendar, used by the Jews before the Exile, later maintained by priestly groups such as the Dead Sea covenanters and by some Christian groups. The reference would be to a Sabbath, the second after Passover but the first after the Feast of Unleavened Bread (cf. 22:1). The dating of the Gospel, in that case, is not exact, because grain would hardly be ripe at the time of Passover (see J. P. Audet, *ScEccl* 10 [1958] 361–83; E. Vogt, *Bib* 40 [1959] 102–5; A. Jaubert, *VT* 3 [1953] 250–64; *The Date of the Last Supper* [tr. I. Rafferty; Staten Island, 1965]). The Law permitted one to pick grapes or grain while walking through a neighbor's field (Dt 23:25), but the rabbis forbade harvesting on the Sabbath (Mishnah, *Shabbath* 7:2). **3–4.** Jesus answered the human objection by citing the divine Scriptures. **5.** Lk omits a crucial saying in Mk (2:27), which may have been Jesus' final reply, "Sabbath was made for man, and not man for the Sabbath." Mk then adds what may have been an independent saying, which Luke makes his conclusion: *the Son of Man is lord of the Sabbath.* If this saying had circulated independently of this episode, then the phrase "Son of Man" could have been meant with all the force of an exalted title (→ Aspects NT Thought, 78:28–30). But if the saying were always part of this story, then "son of man" may be an Aramaism, meaning simply "any man," whose needs are always more important than any legal decision. The ms. D here includes an otherwise unknown saying: "On the same day, seeing someone working on the Sabbath, he said to him, 'Man, if you know what you are doing, blessed are you; but if you do not know, then you are led astray and are a transgressor of the Law.' " M.-J. Lagrange and J. Schmid reject the saying as a Gnostic gloss, but W. Grundmann accepts it as representative of Jesus' thought, provided the man knowingly works on the Sabbath out of mercy and love.

65 **6–11.** The rabbis debated under what conditions a man was allowed to seek and accept medical aid on the Sabbath (Str-B 1, 623–29). Jesus would not quibble over details; he wants a quick, simple answer. **9.** *is it lawful on the Sabbath to do good [as I intend] or to do evil [as you intend against me]?:* Not to do good is to do evil. **10.** Luke edits out of the account how Jesus looked around with anger and sorrow, lest Jesus seem too emotionally affected. **11.** Luke also removes Mk's statement that the Pharisees plotted with the Herodians for Jesus' death. The Evangelist will not dwell upon Jesus' violent death till he makes immediate preparation for the Journey Narrative (9:20–50). Even then he will stress Jesus' free desire in approaching death.

66 (e) THE NAMING OF THE TWELVE (6:12–16). See Mk 3:13–19; Mt 10:1–4; Acts 1:13). Not only does this section fit neatly into the symmetry of 5:27–6:16 (→ 59, 61 above), but it also climaxes the progressive hostility of the Jewish leaders. **12.** *into the hills to pray:* Once again, before a decision crucial to his Messianic mission, Jesus prays (see comment on 3:21); atop a mountain, where Jesus communes with his Father, he chooses 12 disciples. Jesus is conscious of establishing a New Israel, symbolically a people of 12 tribes. **13.** *whom he named apostles:* Mk indicates that Jesus "sent" (*apostellē*) the Twelve to preach, but here in Lk, Jesus is said to have called them *apostoloi.* (For the meaning of this word in the NT, → Aspects NT Thought, 78:162–179, and especially 178 for the discussion of the problem that this verse in particular creates.) Each of the other three Evangelists uses the word "apostle" but once, but it is more common in Lk (9:10; 17:5; 22:14; 24:10). For the most part, Luke follows the list of the Twelve as given in Mk, except that he replaces the name of Thaddaeus with that of "Judas, the son of James" (as in Acts 1:13). The name Levi does not occur, but Matthew does (→ Aspects NT Thought, 78:162–171).

67 **(C) The Full Ministry (6:17–9:9).** Luke's orderly account of the Galilean ministry (4:14–9:50) began with two typical events: one at Nazareth, highlighting the rejection of Jesus by his own townsfolk (4:14–30); the other at Capernaum, symbolizing the enthusiastic reception of him by outsiders (Gentiles) in a town where he had not grown up (4:31–44). Luke then proceeded to add other important details in the story of the establishment of the kingdom (5:1–6:16), especially that of the naming of the Twelve and the controversies with various hostile groups. The stage is now set for a presentation of the full Galilean ministry.

68 (a) THE GREAT DISCOURSE (6:17–49). Although this sermon corresponds in many ways to Mt's Sermon on the Mount (Mt 5–7), there are many important differences. What Jesus originally said in a kerygmatic discourse, promising divine mercy to well-intentioned persons who look to God for salvation, was first of all preserved in an Aram document. Matthew and Luke adapt this material, each to his own purpose, or else each depends upon two different Gk translations of the Aram original. Mt has 107 verses; Lk, 30 or 32. Much of Mt's excess material will reappear in Lk's Journey Narrative (9:51–18:14); Lk 6:38a,39,40,45 are absent from Mt's Sermon on the Mount but show up elsewhere in Mt. As regards the audience, Mt portrays Jesus drawing a select group of disciples up on the mountain, so that he might instruct them to be leaders in the kingdom; Lk pictures Jesus' coming down from the mountain and meeting a large group of disciples, of poor, and of disabled. In Lk, Jesus is always conscious of his audience, "*you* poor," whereas in Mt, he speaks more objectively about "*the* poor." Mt has preserved a catechetical discourse of the early Church, pointing out that law in some way still remains in force for Christians; Lk reflects the eschatological urgency of Jesus' original words. Luke has also rewritten Jesus' words, widening their scope to include Gentiles, underlining the social point of view, and strengthening the sacrificial demands of charity.

17–19. These introductory verses (and 4:41) are found more expansively in Mk 3:7–12 (= Mt 12:15–21; 4:25). When Jesus comes down from the mount (see M. Schoenberg, *BT* 1 [1963] 232–39), he is surrounded by Jews and Gentiles. *power went forth from him and he healed them:* These miracles must be understood in the context of the following beatitudes. The poor and needy who seek Jesus for salvation are the very ones who are brought into the Messianic kingdom (cf. 4:18f.).

69 (i) *The beatitudes* (6:20–23). While Mt has nine beatitudes and no woes, Lk has four of each. Lk, not only rearranges the sequence of the beatitudes from Mt's first, fourth, second, and last; but the woes follow the reverse pattern of the beatitudes. Such stylistic patterns are typical of Lk's Gospel. To the blessedness of the poor, the hungry, the weeping, and the persecuted there corresponds the sadness of the popular, the happy, the full, and the rich. **20.** *lifting up his eyes:* An action recorded of Jesus on especially solemn occasions (16:23; 18:13; Jn 4:35; 6:5; 17:1). *blessed:* "How happy" (J. B. Phillips *The NT in Modern English* [London, 1958] 120); "how blest" (NEB); *makarioi* in the Greek translates Hebr *'ašrê* (lit., "the happiness of...," Pss 1:1; 32:1; Is 56:2). It is a form of congratulation or joyful outburst: "how fortunate is such a man...." It is different from the Hebr *bārûk*, a liturgical expression of blessing, praise, or thanksgiving. *you poor:* The second person is certainly more direct, but the third person of Mt's Gospel is much more common in the OT; it is difficult to decide what grammatical form was used by Jesus in his address. There is a peculiar Semitic flavor in the Gk construction, using the nominative with article in place of the vocative—perhaps, an echo of Jesus' own voice. *poor:* In the LXX *ptōchoi* usually translates the Hebr *'ănāwîm*, the lowly ones who depend desperately upon Yahweh for help (Zech 2:3; 3:12; cf. A. Gelin, *The Poor of Yahweh* [Collegeville, Minn.] 1964). While Mt writes of the "poor in spirit... who hunger for justice," Lk writes more simply of "you poor...who hunger now...weep now." Lk makes great demands and expects strong simplicity in following Jesus. **21.** *hunger now:* The word "now" is Luke's own addition; cf. Am 8:11f. and the famine for the word of God; also Dt 8:3; Lk 4:4. Hunger and thirst are often messianic terms: Is 49:10; 55:1; 65:13; Jn 6:35; Ap 7:16. **22.** In Mt (5:19) the Greek of this saying is somewhat awkward stylistically (even though his version may be more original); Luke has recast the saying to emphasize that every follower of Jesus must share the Son of Man's rejection. Dn 7:13f.,18 understands "Son of Man" in a corporate sense of the persecuted saints in the climactic moment of messianic trial. Jesus used the term "Son of Man" when speaking of himself in the passion prophecies and Luke immediately added the requirements of suffering in the followers of Jesus (9:22–27). **23.** *on that day:* A messianic term, launched in biblical literature by Am (2:16; 5:18) and given a firm place by Is (2:11; 3:18; 4:2; 7:20). *reward in heaven:* The reward that will be enjoyed on this earth already exists with God.

70 (ii) *The woes* (6:24–26). These woes, found only in Lk, cast Jesus in a prophetic role (cf. Am 5:7,18; 6:1; Is 5:8,11,18ff.). The condemnation seems directed to those not present; the immediate disciples of Jesus are again addressed in v. 27. **24.** *you have your comfort:* Lk uses a technical term for someone who has undertaken a debt (Zerwick, *Analysis* 147). Woe or bankruptcy upon each man who does not acknowledge that he owes every comfort to Jesus.

71 (iii) *Love of one's enemies* (6:27–36). Lk has a different arrangement and at times a more expansive presentation than Mt; Lk shows a marked similarity to Rom 12:14; 1 Cor 4:12, and 1 Jn 3:16–18. **27.** *love your enemies:* Followers of Jesus must love others to an heroic degree and so become with Jesus "children of the Most High" (v. 35), manifesting the life of God among mankind. **28.** *who curse you:* The Gk word implies spite, jealousy, and bad will (Zerwick, *Analysis* 147). **29–30.** These two verses have the second person singular, whereas the preceding and following verses have the plural; Luke evidently is combining sources. The Lucan Sermon on the Plain as well as the Matthaean Sermon on the Mount derives from Church documents that combined various statements of Jesus. *strikes you on the cheek:* In Mt it is clearer that Jesus is referring to legal or verbal action rather than to physical rebuffs (cf. S. D. Currie, *HarvTR* 57 [1964] 140–45); Mt, in fact, casts the entire sermon in a much more legal setting. *cloak...tunic:* Lk reverses the order found in Mt. In Palestine, the cloak used for sleeping outdoors is more important than the tunic; it once had a special value as bond (Dt 24:10–13; Ru 3:9). **31.** *so do to them:* The golden rule is found in a negative form in Tob 4:15, Philo, Confucius, and *bShabbath* 31a. Jesus gives the supreme example of it to his followers and expects the same heroic charity from them. **32–33.** Where Mt identifies the wrongdoers as "publicans and Gentiles," Lk more tactfully refers to "sinners." **35.** It is difficult to explain why Luke lacks an equivalent to Mt 5:45, which is so typical of his own Gospel: "Who makes the sun to rise upon the wicked and the good and sends rain on the just and the unjust." If Luke had had the present edition of Mt before him, he certainly would have included the saying. *kind:* In Gk *chrēstos* implies tenderness, liberality, amiability. **36.** *be merciful:* Mt reads "be perfect." In the OT, mercy is attributed to God, rarely to men, while perfection is a goal to be sought by man (T. W. Manson, *The Sayings of Jesus* [London, 1949] 55).

72 (iv) *On judging* (6:37–42). See Mt 7:1–5; 15:14; 10:24f. **38.** *measure:* The word used in Mt is a standard of judgment, but in Lk it is the capacity of one's generosity. *into your lap:* That is, the fold of a garment that hangs over the belt (Is 65:7). **39.** In Mt these words are addressed to "scribes and Pharisees" (15:14); but Lk directs them to disciples who must exercise self-criticism in the example and inspiration of Jesus. **41–42.** *speck... beam:* "Frankly hyperbolical. One utter absurdity is exposed by another" (T. W. Manson, *Sayings of Jesus*, 58). **42.** *hypocrite:* See comment on Mt 6:2. A "hypocrite" deliberately gives a false impression; Jesus refers to men, pitifully deceived about their own condition.

43–46. Mt directs these words against false prophets (7:16–21) and/or Pharisees (12:33–35), but Lk gives a much more universal application.

(v) *The conclusion of the discourse* (6:47–49). See Mt 7:24–27. Luke adapts this parable. Mt reflects the Palestinian setting where the bedrock is close to the surface and deep foundations are unnecessary. The foolish man builds his house on the sandy surface of a wadi, dry in summer but swollen with water during the rainy season.

(Bornkamm, G., *Jesus of Nazareth* [New York, 1960] 221–25. Brown, R. E., *BT* 18 [1965] 1176–80. Davies, W. D., *The Setting of the Sermon on the Mount* [Cambridge, 1964]. Dupont, J., *Les béatitudes* [2nd ed.; Louvain, 1958]. Hunter, A. M., *A Pattern for Life* [Phila., 1953]. Jeremias, J., *The Sermon on the Mount* [Facet Books, Bibl. ser., 2; Phila., 1963].)

73 (b) The Centurion's Servant (7:1–10). See Mt 8:5–13; Jn 4:46–53. This is the only Q section in which the center of interest is an action story rather than a saying of Jesus. Mt and Lk agree only in the dialogue, but not in the details of the action. There are points of similarity with the stories of Jairus' daughter (Lk 8:40ff.), the official's son (Jn 4:46–53), and the Syro-Phoenician woman (Mk 7:24–30); another section (Mt 15:21–28) absent from Lk, inclines us to suspect that in the process of oral transmission details and even the pattern of one story merged into the other. A common feature in all, very attractive to the early Church, is the way in which Jesus, though physically absent, saves a distressed person by the use of his word. This is heightened in Lk; for in Mt, the centurion comes personally to Jesus to plead for his servant, but in Lk he sends two delegations, the one of Jewish leaders, the other of friends. If, as seems likely, Mt more closely represents the original form, then Luke is deliberately adapting his material to the situation of the early Church. Throughout Lk Jesus never preaches immediately to Gentiles; that ministry begins in Acts after Pentecost.

2. *centurion:* See comment on Mt 8:5. The man was a Gentile (vv. 5 and 9), most probably serving under Herod Antipas (3:1). In Mt, the servant is a paralytic; Luke, who is always conscious of human relations, not only says that the servant is near death, but also states that he "was very dear to" the centurion. The word *entimos* (very dear) connotes something that can be obtained only at a great price. **6.** *do not trouble yourself:* The word originally meant to flay or mangle, and then took on the meaning of annoyance or inconvenience. The Gentile did not want Jesus to become legally unclean by entering his house (Jn 18:28; Acts 10:14). **9.** *marveled:* Only as a man, could Jesus experience this surprise and wonderment and so grow in knowledge. *turning to the crowd:* Luke delights in citing this reaction of Jesus (7:44; 9:55; 10:22f.;

14:25; 22:61; 23:28). *I have not found such great faith in Israel:* The first of many examples of faith in Lk (7:50; 8:25,48,50), and as such an element close to Paul's theology. Mt has a longer statement, which Luke puts elsewhere (Mt 8:11f.; Lk 13:28f.). **10.** *in good health:* The word *hygiainonta* is much stronger than Mt's *iathē*; it indicates someone able to take full advantage of a vigorous, physical condition.

74 (c) The Widow's Son at Nain (7:11–17). This incident, only in Lk (cf. 4:25–30; 5:1–11), shows the Evangelist's special delight in portraying Jesus not only overwhelmed with pity at the sight of tragedy but also turning with kindly regard toward women (cf. 7:36–50; 10:38–42). Luke's hand is also evident in the vocabulary, uniquely his own. The episode has literary links with the preceding one: The servant was dear to his master (7:2); this dead youth was his mother's only son. It also prepares for the Baptist's query in 7:20,22. This narrative possesses the charm, color, and pathos of an excellent story: two large crowds meet, approaching from different directions; the silence with which Jesus touches the bier and stops the funeral procession; the thundering message, calmly spoken, bringing the dead back to life. **11.** *Nain:* A village (modern Nein), not mentioned elsewhere in the Bible, two to three hours by foot SE of Nazareth, and about eight to nine hours SW of Capernaum. Rock graves are found just E of the city (F.-M. Abel, *Géographie de la Palestine* [Paris, 1938], 2.394–95). **12.** The large crowd accompanying the widow may have included not only relatives and friends (burying the dead was a very deserving work of mercy—Str-B 4, 578–610), but also hired mourners and musicians. **13.** *the Lord:* The title *ho kyrios* is used here for the first of many times in Lk (e.g., 10:1,41; 11:39; 12:42; 13:15; → Aspects NT Thought, 78:25). It is the Gk translation in the LXX for the divine name, Yahweh. It is very appropriately used on this occasion when "Jesus appears clothed with that exalted power over life and death by which he becomes the object of his Church's faith and worship..." (W. Manson, *Gospel of Luke*, 77). **15.** *sat up:* The Gk word occurs only here and in Acts 9:40 in the NT; its intr. form is very rare in nonbiblical Greek except among medical writers (W. K. Hobart, *Medical Language*, 11–12). *gave him to his mother:* Identical Gk words occur in the Elijah story of 1 Kgs 17:23; another instance of Luke's intent to present Jesus as Elijah and Elisha *redivivi* (1 Kgs 17:17–24; 2 Kgs 4:17–22,32–37). **16.** *great prophet:* One of the figures expected in 1st-cent. Palestinian Judaism (→ Aspects NT Thought, 78:14–15; cf. O. Cullmann, *The Christology of the NT* [Phila., 1959] 13–50).

75 (d) Jesus and the Baptist (7:18–35). See Mt 11:2–19. This collection of sayings about the Baptist from Q is given a different location in Lk than in Mt. Here again we sense the anxiety of the early Church, neither to overestimate nor to undervalue the role of John the Baptist. **18.** Luke omits that Jn is in prison; he has already recorded that fact (3:19f.). *all this:* The ministry of Jesus, including his cures as well as his preaching; Mt writes, "the works of Jesus." Against the position of T. W. Manson (*Sayings*, 66) and others, the contrast is not between the fierce, eschatological preaching of the Baptist (3:7–18) and Jesus' more gentle style of beatitudes (6:17–49). Jesus himself enunciated strong woes or curses against proud, self-sufficient persons. **19.** *you are the one who is to come?:* The emphasis is plainly on the first word, "you." Ever since the time of the early Fathers, this question of the Baptist has puzzled commentators. Was he losing faith in Jesus? Since he was not "a reed shaken by the wind" (v. 24), his attitude toward Jesus did not waver. Like Mary (2:48–50), however, he could be surprised and even doubt; but it is difficult to determine the reason: Jesus' slow accomplishment of Messianic plans (É. Osty, BJ)? Jesus' failure clearly to identify himself? personal discouragement like Jeremiah's (Jer 15:10ff.)? *one who is to come:* This technical term is derived from Mal 3:1,23; it designates a figure expected in Palestinian Judaism who should not be too facilely equated with the Messiah (*pace* J. Schneider, *ThDNT* 2, 670; see J. A. T. Robinson, *NTS* 4 [1957–58] 263–81). **22.** Originally in poetic rhythm (cf. C. F. Burney, *The Poetry of Our Lord* [Oxford, 1925] 117). The citations are from Is 61:1 and 35:5–6 (cf. Lk 4:18f.). *poor have the gospel:* Clearest sign of Jesus' being the Messiah (A. Plummer, *Luke*, 204). It is not as though Jesus heals the wealthy but simply preaches the gospel to the poor. The poor are to be identified with the lame, blind, etc., and the gospel always looks forward to the full alleviation and total redemption of God's people. **23.** *blessed:* Recalls the beatitudes (6:20f.). *is not scandalized:* See comment on Mt 11:6. *in me:* That is, on account of something that one sees in Jesus, different from one's expectation. This is aimed at John.

24. *what did you go out to see?:* A piercing question. Did you look for what you expected to find? Or for what would appeal to you? **27.** This quotation from Mal 3:1 (and Ex 23:20 [LXX]) is adapted from an announcement of God's coming to that of Jesus'. Luke deliberately omits the explicit comparison of the Baptist with Elijah (see Mt 11:14) **28.** *none born of woman is greater...:* We sense a finality in Jesus' words: John may have been the greatest of all prophets and patriarchs, but a new and final epoch has begun with Jesus. How much more fortunate are those who belong to it!

29–35. The first two verses here are a commentary, proper to Lk (cf. Mt 21:31f.). In their baptism of *metanoia* (3:8) sinners expressed their faith that God would redeem them and through the Messiah reunite them to himself. Thus would God's promises or "purpose be justified." **31–35.** Jesus does not want to contrast himself with John, nor his own followers with those of the Baptist; he is pointing out the childish indecisiveness of the people (W. Grundmann, *Evangelium*, 167). A similar poetic line is found in Herodotus 1. 141, and in Aesop's *Fables* 27. Cf. Prv 1:20, "wisdom cries aloud in the street"; 9:2–6, "she has spread her [banquet] table." *wisdom:* God's plan of salvation. Mt identifies wisdom with Jesus, but Luke deliberately associates it with the publicans and sinners in 29f. Note the inclusion between 29f. and 35; the double use of "justified"; the parallel between "purpose" and "wisdom." See A. Feuillet, *RB* 62 [1955] 161–96.

76 (e) The Penitent Woman (7:36–50). See Jn 12:1–8; Mk 14:3–9; Mt 26:6–13. Not only is the Lucan narrative of this episode ensnarled in difficulties, but a comparison of it with a similar story in the other Gospels compounds the problem: (1) In Lk, the story centers around an unnamed, sinful woman; in Mk and Mt, the woman in no way is presumed to be sinful; in Jn her name is Mary; (2) In Lk, the host is Simon the Pharisee; in Mk, Simon; in Mt, Simon the Leper; in Jn, it takes place at a house where Mary served and Lazarus reclined at table; (3) in Lk, it happens up north in Galilee; in the other three Gospels, down south in Bethany; (4) in Lk and Jn, she anoints the feet of Jesus; in Mk and Mt, his head; (5) in Mk, Mt, and Jn, there is a complaint about the waste, and Jesus replies that this is done for his burial; (6) in Lk, it happens in the early part of the ministry; in Mk and Mt, two days before the final Passover; in Jn, six days before. Evidently, during the period of oral transmission, details of one story passed over into another. Each Evangelist, and especially Luke, may have further refashioned the story; Luke could have added the parable (vv. 40–43) where he mentions the name of Simon for the first time. **36.** *one of the Pharisees:* Because of the hostility of the Pharisaic sect to Jesus, it was courageous of this one to invite Jesus to dinner. Not only does Lk frequently present Jesus as a dinner guest (5:29; 10:38; 19:5) but on three occasions his host is a Pharisee (7:36; 11:37; 14:1). Lk has just spoken of the Son of Man eating and drinking; this provides the proper setting for the present incident. **32.** *and behold:* The opening words, *kai idou*, demand attention and register surprise. Lk delicately does not name the woman, simply characterizes her as a sinner (a prostitute, or else a woman married to a man considered an outcast, like a publican). The woman's name is certainly not Mary of Magdala (8:2), nor is there reason to identify her with the sister of Lazarus (Jn 12:3). **38.** *at his feet:* She intended simply to anoint his feet with a fragrant myrrh, but as she leaned over, tears gushed forth, which she ingenuously wiped away with her long hair. Completely overcome, she repeatedly kissed his feet. **39.** *a prophet:* Some mss. read "the" prophet (Dt 18:15,18; Acts 3:22; Jn 1:21), but in any case there seems to be a reference to v. 16. **40.** While Simon silently condemns Jesus for not divining the character of the woman, Jesus proves himself to be a prophet by reading the secret thoughts of Simon. **41.** The story bears similarity to rabbinical anecdotes (Str-B 2, 163). **43.** *I suppose:* We can still feel the insolent frigidity of the speaker. **44–46.** These phrases, almost in poetic rhythm, beautifully portray Oriental etiquette. **47.** *for she has loved much:* This verse has been a classic text for showing that perfect charity has the power of forgiving sins. Zerwick comments: "The context, however, renders the interpretation just referred to almost impossible; for Our Lord goes on at once to add, 'but he to whom less is forgiven, loves less,' with evident reference to the parable whereby He had shown Simon that the greater mercy calls forth the greater love of gratitude. ...The sense demanded by the context...is 'she loves because she is forgiven,' and not 'she is forgiven because she loves.' And this is in fact the sense of the Gk expression, so long as the *hoti* is understood in the special causal sense which gives the reason not why the fact *is* so, but whereby it is *known* to be so" (*GrBib* § 422). For Pauline influence, see J. Winandy, *BiViChr* 47 (1962) 38–46.

77 (f) THE MINISTERING WOMEN (8:1–3). This section, found only in Lk, manifests the Evangelist's hand in several ways: Lucan words or phrases; particular attention bestowed upon woman; exclusive source of information, especially about Herod Antipas. Jesus imparts a new dignity and role to woman in granting her a right not only to learn the "good news of the Kingdom of God," but even to participate in the ministry (cf. 1 Cor 9:5). Some of the rabbis doubted woman's ability even to learn the Torah (W. Grundmann, *Evangelium*, 174; Str-B 1, 1046f.). In the Gospels women bring the first news of the resurrection to the apostles (24:1,10f.; Acts 1:14). **1.** *journeying:* Jesus has already appeared as a wanderer, seeking out men for the kingdom (4:43–44; 5:12), and as a guest (see 7:36ff.), distributing forgiveness and salvation. **2.** *Mary Magdalene:* That is, from Magdala (= modern Mejdel), a city at the halfway mark along the western coast of the Lake of Galilee, never mentioned in the Bible. There is no reason to identify Mary Magdalene with the sinful woman of 7:36ff.; Lk introduces Mary as someone new. *seven devils:* Such possession can indicate only a very serious illness. **3.** *Joanna, wife of Chuza:* Possibly a source of information about Herod Antipas for Luke. If Chuza were the royal official of Jn 4:46–53, then we could understand why he would allow his wife to minister to Jesus. **3.** *many others:* Cf. Mk 15:41.

78 (g) PARABLE OF THE SOWER (8:4–18). See Mk 4:1–9; Mt 13:10–15. (For the nature, purpose, and use of parables, → Aspects NT Thought, 78:131–145.) "Parable" is very difficult to define, not only because there are between 30 and 72 different parables in the Gospels but also because the term is applied to many different kinds of literary pieces: a solemn sentence (Mk 7:17); counsel (Lk 14:7); metaphor (Lk 4:23); two short images (Lk 5:36; 6:39); stories (Lk 13:6), and yet the term is not used of such a typical parable as that of the good samaritan (Lk 10:30–37). Perhaps, it is best to conclude very generally that a parable is a story illustrative of some teaching of Jesus. The parable is more than a "mere analogy," because "an inward affinity [exists] between the natural order and the spiritual order; ...the Kingdom of God is intrinsically *like* the processes of nature and of the daily life of men" (C. H. Dodd, *The Parables of the Kingdom* [3rd ed.; London, 1961] 10). Luke adapts parables as he does other material drawn from his sources: He abbreviates the parable of the sower; he adds clarifying elements (5:36; 11:21f.), doctrinal ideas (8:12), or something similar (11:9–13); he will even reinterpret (20:10–12). Luke, in fact, has the largest number of parables; he introduces parables with a reference to the coming of Christ (18:8b; 19:11–14,27), to the mission to the Gentiles (14:22f.); he adds instructions on prayer (11:9–13), on the responsibility of the apostles (12:41), on renouncement (14:33; 16:9–13), and on humility (17:7–10; 18:14b).

This parable corresponds to Mk 4:1–9, which one should compare; it would be better to call it the "parable of the different sowings," the better to bring out its main meaning. The sower walks over the field, fallow since the harvest, covered with thorns, and crossed by a footpath made by trespassers. Recently softened by the first winter rains, it is ready for seeding. Important to note is that "in Palestine ploughing comes after sowing" (*bShabbath* 73b); this explains why the seed falls where it does. Once sown, it is ploughed under, and all else with it—the thorns and the footpath as well. **4.** Luke suppresses the notice that the crowd made Jesus enter a boat and put out a little from the shore to address them (Mk 4:1). **5.** *a sower went out to sow:* The alliteration (even in the Greek) may be onomatopoeic. *on the path:* The Gk phrase does not necessarily mean "alongside" the path; the seed fell on the trespassers' path, which was to be ploughed under, but before this was done it lay on the hardened surface. **6.** *rocky soil:* Many outcroppings of limestone are found in Palestinian fields. **7.** *thornbushes:* These would have sprung up since the harvest and would not yet have been uprooted; they would be ploughed under. **8.** *a hundredfold:* Luke has simplified the obscure Marcan text. "Hundredfold" is an expression for an abundant crop from good soil (see Gn 26:12). The point: The seed sown on good soil yields an abundant harvest. **9–10.** Luke has softened and shortened these verses from Mk. The Marcan "to those outside" becomes "to the rest." Lk completely omits the clause, "lest they turn and be forgiven." A parable would so present the truth that the ill-disposed would be more puzzled than enlightened (yet, this too would be a grace). The parable kept the kingdom continually before the attention of the sincere Israelites. **10.** *mysteries:* Mk has the sing. *mystērion*, which refers to the single secret of the coming of the kingdom (4:11), but both Lk and Mt use the plural, expressive of the many secrets of the nature of the kingdom (see H. Conzelmann, *Theology of St. Luke*, 103–4). *so that they look and see nothing:* The clause expresses the result of preaching in parables, not its purpose.

79 *An explanation of the parable of the sower* (8:11–15). This is an explanation of the parable Jesus once uttered, an explanation that developed in the early Church; here in Lk it is simply appended to the preceding saying about parables. (For reasons for regarding it as an early Christian interpretation of the parable, see J. Jeremias, *The Parables of Jesus* [rev. ed.; N.Y., 1963], 77–79.) **11.** *the seed is the word of God:* That is, the Gospel or the Christian preaching of salvation proposed to men. **12.** *the devil:* The comparison of the devil with birds that gobble up the seed on the footpath may be inspired by a passage in *Jub* (11:11): "Mastema [another name for Satan] sent ravens and birds to devour the seed which was sown in the Land.... Before they could plough in the seed the ravens picked [it] from the surface of the ground" (*APOT* 2, 30). The reaction to the word of God symbolized here is defection. **13.** *in time of trial:* Weakness in persecution is indicated. **14.** *choked by cares:* Double-mindedness. **15.** *the seed in good soil:* This seed corresponds to those who persevere and adjust to the problems of faith.

(See Dupont, J., "La parabole du semeur dans la version de Luc," *Apophoreta* [Fest. E. Haenchen; Berlin, 1964] 97–108. Laliberté, J., *RUnLav* 4/6 [1950] 475–90.)

16–18. These verses are an additional parable, the parable of the lamp (cf. Mk 4:21–22). Luke envisages a Hellenistic house with an entrance from which the light would shine on those entering it; in Mt the lamp gives light rather to all who are in the house. In either case the application is clear: for Luke, the lamp is to shed its light on the Gentiles who are "entering" the kingdom. **17.** Most likely this verse represents a separate logion, attached to the foregoing parable by free association (cf. the *Gospel According to Thomas* [§ 5, 6]). **18.** *the man who has:* A willing reception to the word of God brings with it a receptivity for still more, and less of a chance of failing to recognize it in the future.

(Harrington, W. J., *A Key to the Parables* [Glen Rock, N.J., 1964] 135–54. Siegmann, E. F., *CBQ* 23 [1961] 161–81.)

80 (h) The True Family of Jesus (8:19–21). See Mk 3:31–35; Mt 12:46–50. In place of the Marcan conclusion to the parable of the sower, Lk uses a story that Mk and Mt place in a context of controversy. Lk omits that very difficult section of Mk 3:20–21, which provides a reason why Jesus' relatives visit him. The sharp separation between Jesus and his natural kin is thus modified. By the final sentence of this episode (Mk has "whoever does the will of God") Luke deliberately links it with the preceding parable of the sower who sows the seed of the Word of God (v. 11). Read against the background of the Infancy Narrative, where Mary ponders the Word (1:29; 2:19,51), these verses might point to Mary as the supreme example of the receptive hearer. Yet because Mary, his brethren, and Herod Antipas all desire "to see" Jesus (cf. Lk 9:9), Conzelmann concludes that the reason is the same in each case: to see a wondrous "epiphany" or miracle. And Jesus proceeds to reject them on this condition (cf. Lk 4:23). We must remember, however, the vastly different character of each in Lk.

81 (i) The Stilling of the Tempest (8:22–25). See Mk 4:35–41; Mt 8:23–27. Luke edits out many colorful details found in Mk; perhaps, we can also say that an eyewitness account (Mk) is becoming a "miracle story" (V. Taylor, *The Formation of the Gospel Tradition* [London, 1935] 119–41). Luke removes Mk's phrase, "they took him just as he was [in the boat]," and writes a new introduction. He effectively cuts any close connection with the preceding parables. It is, consequently, difficult to consider this miracle an example of "the mysteries of the Kingdom of God" (v. 10), which Jesus hides from the crowd but reveals only to his disciples. Luke rephrases some of the details: he states that Jesus fell asleep before the storm swept down upon the lake; he softens the gruff remarks of the disciples ("Is it no concern of yours that we are perishing?") and even the remark of Jesus ("Is it still possible that you are without faith?"). **22.** *the other side of the lake:* The spot is unspecified. The lake, however, again becomes a setting for the manifestation of power (see comment on 5:1). **23.** *he fell asleep:* Luke omits the detail in Mk that "it was evening." There is the further implication that he who will work the miracle is no superman, but one subject to the fatigue of ordinary men. **24.** *Master:* See comment on 5:5. *rebuked the wind and the surging deep:* The vb. *epitimaō* is usually used for the rebuking of demons; the suggestion is that the surging deep and winds were controlled by demons too (cf. Zech 3:2). In the OT the sea was often presented as the abode of such powers (Is 27:1; 51:10; Ps 89:10–11; Jb 9:13). In calming the lake, Jesus appears as the conqueror of the demonic forces of the world of nature; like Yahweh (Pss 65:7; 89:9; 107:23–29) he is the lord of the winds and the waves. **25.** *where is your faith:* Jesus' comment goes to the heart of the matter; a disciple of Jesus, faced even with the worst, should draw consolation from his faith and proximity to the Master. *who can this be:* The question that the whole Gospel tries to answer for its readers.

82 (j) The Gergesene Demoniac (8:26–39). See Mk 5:1–20; Mt 8:28–34. For this one time in Lk, Jesus leaves Jewish territory, but the Evangelist is careful to associate it with his story of the Galilean ministry—he explicitly notes that it is "opposite Galilee" (v. 26). The scene is strange and fraught with tension; in Mk the details are even stronger and the discourse is direct. Of all the miracle stories in the canonical Gospels this one comes closest to the type found in the apocryphal Gospels. **26.** *the country of the Gergesenes:* The mss. have two different readings here: either *Gerasēnōn* ("of the Gerasenes" [probably modern Jerash]) and *Gergesēnōn* ("of the Gergesenes," inhabitants of Gergesa, or modern Kersa, directly opposite Magdala). It is best to follow the latter reading. Note that Mt 8:28 reads *Gadarēnōn* ("of the Gadarenes"); this fluctuation of the name of the locality and other details in the story should caution the reader against trying too hard to reconstruct what really happened. **27.** *a man possessed by demons:* Luke here smooths out the repetitions of Mk's account and adds that the man had roamed the tombs for a long time unclothed. **28.** *what do you want with me:* See comment on 4:33. *Son of the Most High God:* The possessed man—a Lucan addition—recognizes divinity within Jesus. **30.** *what is your name:* Knowledge of one's name presupposed or granted power over that one. *Legion:* A Latinism transcribed into Greek; the name implies the presence of a vast number of demons. **31.** *to the abyss:* This phrase heightens the attack on the demonic forces present; they are to be sent either into the abode of the dead (Rom 10:7; Ps 106:26) or to the final prison of Satan (Ap 20:3). Though aware that this is their destiny, they beg not to be sent there yet. **32.** *many pigs:* See comments on Mt 8:31–32. **33.** *was drowned:* Obviously the problem of the "ensuing loss" of someone's property was of no concern to the Evangelist—and it should not be that of the modern reader of this story. To ask about it is to miss the point. **35.** *sitting at his feet:* In the attitude of a disciple before the Master or the Rabbi (cf. 10:39). **36.** *how he had been saved:* Luke insists that Jesus has accomplished a work of salvation (see 8:12). **39.** Jesus recruits this Gentile as one of his first "evangelists" (see C. H. Cave, *NTS* 11 [1964–65] 93–97).

83 (k) TWO MIRACLES FOR WOMEN (8:40–56). See Mk 5:21–43; Mt 9:1,18–26. Only here in the Gospels are two miracles told in a single account, probably because they happened that way (J. M. Creed, *Luke*, 122). On the other hand, the number 12 (the age of the girl and the number of years of the woman's sickness) may have been the literary link for the separate units. **41.** *Jairus:* A Gk form of the Hebr name which means "he gives light" (Jgs 10:3). As a ruler of the synagogue, he was under no obligation to kneel before Jesus; desperation has pulled him to his knees. According to Lk (4:33–37), Jesus had worked his first miracle in Jairus' synagogue. **42.** *an only child:* Luke's addition (see 7:12; 9:38). **43.** The mss. B and D omit the brusque remarks about physicians. **44.** *tassel of his cloak:* Required on the four corners of men's garments (Nm 15:37–41; Dt 22:12). Jesus obeys the Law, but he also informs the woman that she was cured because of her faith, her confident dependence upon God. Jesus also went beyond the Law in allowing an unclean woman (Lv 15:25–27) to touch him, and later in touching a dead body himself (Nm 19:11). **45.** In Lk, Peter is the spokesman. The words, as recorded here, are much more deferential than the impetuous reply in Mk. **47.** *in the presence of all the people:* Luke alone records this fact; he delights in public acclamations. **49.** *someone comes:* The only time Luke has preserved the historic pres. tense from the Marcan sections in his Gospel (J. M. Creed, *Luke*, 123). **50.** *she shall be saved:* The phrase is only in Lk (cf. 8:12,36). **51–54.** Luke has noticeably shortened Mk's description, so that a careful reconstruction of the episode is difficult from his account. **54.** Lk omits the Gk form of the Aramaic *talitha koum(i)* of Mk's Gospel. **56.** *tell no one:* For the first time, Luke includes the "Messianic Secret" so frequent in Mk; he usually concludes with a public manifestation and praise (5:17ff.; 7:16f.; 8:38f.).

84 (l) THE MISSION OF THE TWELVE (9:1–6). See Mk 6:7–13; Mt 10:1,9–11,14. Luke now omits Mk's account of Jesus' visit to Nazareth (Mk 6:1–6); he has already incorporated the material in an earlier thumbnail sketch of Jesus' entire ministry (4:14–30). Another instruction by Jesus to missionaries will be given in ch. 10 (Q), and a final reference will be made to it in the Last Supper scene (22:35f.). A comparison of these various charges makes us suspect that either the early Church or else the Evangelists adapted Jesus' original instruction. For instance, Lk 9:3 and Mt 10:10 forbid a staff, but Mk 6:8 allows one; Lk 10:4 and Mt 10:10 forbid sandals, but Mk 6:9 allows them. If Mk is closer to Jesus' own words, then Mt and Lk are spiritualizing the charge into an interior ideal of total trust in God. Because of the necessity of shaking off foreign dust before entering the Jerusalem Temple and the prohibition against bringing profane money into the sacred precincts (Jn 2:14), the passage can be interpreted metaphorically: in all your undertakings, act as though you are standing in God's presence; enter the home of each Christian as you would the Temple of God.

1. *called the Twelve:* Different from the instructions to the seventy[-two?] disciples in 10:1–16, the Twelve are not sent out two by two. In the early Church, each of the Twelve was a rule to himself through the special charism of his office. *power and authority:* Said of Jesus in 4:36. **2.** *to preach the kingdom of God and to heal:* Before Pentecost, the Twelve are never commissioned to teach a deeper understanding of the mystery of salvation but simply to preach that the kingdom is at hand (cf. D. M. Stanley, *CBQ* 17 [1955] 336–48). Healing as well as preaching indicates that the kingdom is not simply a spiritual enterprise, but one that looked forward to the full renewal of man in both body and soul. Curing sickness was an assault upon the kingdom of Satan (4:33–37, 40; 5:18–26). **3.** Like the Levites in the OT, the Twelve inherit the right to community support (Nm 18:31; 1 Cor 9:7–18). **5.** *dust from your feet:* See Acts 13:51. **6.** *everywhere:* Lk adds this universal note to Mk's account.

85 (m) PERPLEXITY OF HEROD ANTIPAS (9:7–9). See Mk 6:14–16; Mt 14:1f.) While the Twelve are absent on their missionary journey, the Gospels fill in the gap with an episode that, in Lk especially, prepares for the final moment of the passion (13:31–33; 23:8–12). Herod Antipas thus plays a significant role in each of the three parts of Lk. Luke passes over the brutal details of the Baptist's execution (cf. Mk 6:17–29; Mt 14:3–12). **7.** *the tetrarch:* More exact than Mk's "the king." *perplexed:* Luke's reflection modifies the self-confidence of Antipas in Mk, for throughout the Lucan account Antipas is incredulous: Not Antipas but "some people" claim that the Baptist has risen from the dead. **8.** *Elijah had appeared:* Thus Luke changes Mk's clear statement that "it is Elijah," for he sharply distinguishes Jesus from the Baptist and the "prophets of old." In Mk, Jesus is "like one of the prophets." **9.** Antipas even boasts that it was "I myself [who] beheaded John," and so there is no point in speaking of John's return. So too for Lk, interest does not center in any return to the old, but in the entirely new phenomenon in Jesus. *to see him:* Luke is preparing for the future (23:8).

86 **(D) The Climax (9:10–50).** Lk climaxes the Galilean ministry with acts or statements of Jesus that lay the blueprint of the Kingdom-become-Church: the Eucharist (9:10–17); Peter's profession of faith (9:18–21); announcements of the passion (9:22,44f.); transfiguration–ascension (9:28–36). Luke is consciously pursuing a literary, theological unity in this section: the day began to decline (v. 12); eight days after (v. 28); the following day (v. 37); while all were marveling (v. 44). There is, of course, the well-known break between vv. 17 and 18, where the "Great Omission" occurs. Here Luke, who since 8:4 has been carefully following Mk, skips over Mk 6:45–8:26. Conzelmann (*Theology of St. Luke*, 52–55) lines up various explanations for this omission and with Taylor concludes that Luke is not so much rejecting the content of the Marcan section as the general context or framework (V. Taylor, *Behind the Third Gospel*). Lk keeps the ministry of Jesus ostensibly within the confines of Galilee; journeys among the Gentiles will be the work of the Church apostles.

87 (a) RETURN OF THE TWELVE—FEEDING OF THE FIVE THOUSAND (9:10–17). See Mk 6:30–44; Mt 14:13–21; cf. Jn 6:1–13; Mt 15:32–39; Mk 8:1–10. **10.** *the apostles:* The Twelve (v. 1) are now given this other name (see 6:13). *taking them with him, he withdrew privately to a town called Bethsaida.* There are several textual variants for the three last words in different mss.: "city" (S^a, B, L, X), "town" (D), "desert place of a city" (A, W), or simply "desert place" (S^{*b}; Mk 6:32; Mt 14:13). Bethsaida, originally a village, was embellished by Philip the tetrarch (cf. 3:1) and raised to the status of a city, called Julias, in honor of a daughter of Caesar Augustus. Philip, Andrew, and Peter came originally from Bethsaida (Jn 1:44). It was not really in Galilee, and Luke is silent about its location. **11.** *he welcomed them:* Proper to Lk. **12–17.** This episode is the only miracle story common to all four Gospels; it constitutes a climax of Jesus' Galilean ministry, for after this he concentrates upon the training of his apostles, with his thoughts centering upon his destiny. Eucharistic symbolism is certainly evident in this account, and the manner in which all four Evangelists link the multiplication of the loaves with the announcement of the passion underlines the "sacrificial" feature of the Eucharist. **12.** *began to wear on:* Luke associates the need for food with the late hour of the day. Mk's Gospel must have been further enriched after Luke had drawn from it, for Luke certainly would have included Mk's reason for the miracle: "he had compassion on them because they were like sheep without a shepherd." **13.** Luke softens the apostles' impatient reply to Jesus (Mk 6:37). **16.** *taking...:* In each of the multiplication scenes (Mk and Mt record two such events), in the words of institution of the Eucharist, and at the Emmaus supper (24:30) the same words, in the same sequence, occur: "took...looked up...blessed...broke...gave." Luke further intensifies the Eucharistic resemblance, for he suppresses Mk's double reference to the fish, thus giving more attention to the bread. **17.** *twelve baskets:* Did the 12 apostles collect the fragments (Lagrange), or are we to see a more symbolic significance in the number 12? *fragments:* The Gk word is *klasmata* and is used in the *Didache* (9:3–4) as the technical term for the broken particles of the Eucharist.

88 (b) PETER'S CONFESSION; PASSION-RESURRECTION FORETOLD (9:18–22). See Mk 8:27–33; Mt 16:13–23. The "Great Omission" takes place between vv. 17 and 18 (→ 86 above). This deletion of Mk 6:45–8:26 makes it difficult to identify the audience. From Lk one would never know that this episode took place at the foot of Mt. Hermon, N of Palestine, and in the territory of Philip. **18.** *praying by himself:* A characteristic Lucan addition; see comment on 3:21. *disciples were with him:* This is the meaning of the preferred reading, *synēsan*, but the Gk text of ms. D has *synēntēsan* (met him), which makes better sense, yet is suspect for this very reason. *who do the crowds say I am?:* We sense a feeling of loneliness, almost frustration, in the question. **19.** The same answers as were given to Herod Antipas (9:8); again Lk qualifies the notion of prophet as "old." **20.** The emphasis is upon "you"—"who do you say I am?" It is Peter who answers. *God's Messiah:* The Gk *christos* and the Aram *mešîḥā*, mean "anointed." Peter, therefore, does not confess—or deny—the divinity of Jesus; he recognizes the fulfillment of OT hopes in Jesus. **21.** Jesus at once demands silence, lest the crowds acclaim him according to their false political or national ideas. The "Messianic Secret" of Mk thus becomes in Lk the mystery of a suffering Messiah (W. Grundmann, *Evangelium*, 189). **22.** Lk introduces this section with a participle, depending upon the preceding verse. *Son of Man* (→ Aspects NT Thought, 78:28–30). *must suffer:* All three Syn use the word "must" here; but Lk most frequently connects this pressing necessity with Jesus' passion (4:43; 13:33; 17:25; 22:37; 24:7,26,44). *rejected:* Cf. Ps 118:22; Lk 20:17. Lk omits Peter's blustering remonstrance and Jesus' stern reply (Mk 8:32f.; Mt 16:22f.). See B. Willaert, *ETL* 32 (1956) 24–45.

89 (c) CONDITIONS FOR DISCIPLESHIP (9:23–27). See Mk 8:34–9:1; Mt 16:24–28. Luke not only has removed Peter's contradiction from the text but he now proceeds to apply the message of the Cross to all Christians. In fact, Jesus' approaching death overshadows all his words from now on. **23.** *all:* In Lk's Gospel, the reference would be to those who were fed at the multiplication of loaves (9:12–17), thereby linking the sacrifice of the cross with the Eucharistic symbolism of the miraculous feeding. *come after me:* The phrase fits into the many biblical references to the "way": Is 40:3; Acts 9:2; *EDB* 2566–67; *ThWNT* 5, 475–88. *take up his cross:* Not only was crucifixion a common enough Roman execution, but the Jewish king, Alexander Janneus (103–76 BC), is said to have ordered the crucifixion of 800 Pharisees. This reference to the cross, therefore, need not be a later Church addition to the Gospel message. *daily:* By adding this word to Mk's version, Lk changes the focus of discussion from the unique, eschatological moment of death to the day-by-day struggle of following Jesus (1 Cor 15:31; Gal 2:20). Even in Mk the "cross" had a symbolical meaning, but doubly so in Lk, which reapplies Jesus' words to the new situation of a Church that must patiently wait for a remote parousia. In any case, "the last risk is to be taken" by the follower of Jesus (V. Taylor, *St. Mark*, 381). **24.** "Few sayings of Jesus are so well attested as this" (Taylor, *ibid.*, 382), for it occurs not only in Mk but also in Q (Lk 17:33; Mt 10:39). *for my sake:* Lk omits "and for the gospel" (Mk 8:35), concentrating attention much more personally upon Jesus. **25.** *destroys or injures himself:* Lk strengthens the Marcan statement by adding "destroys." **26.** Compared to Mk and Mt, Lk emphasizes the glory of Jesus as Son of Man by adding that Jesus comes in "his own" glory as well as in that "of the Father and of the holy angels." **27.** Lk removes the reference to Jesus' "coming in power" (Mk 9:1) and thereby avoids any suggestion of a fixed time for the appearance of the kingdom.

90 (d) THE TRANSFIGURATION (9:28–36). See Mk 9:2–8; Mt 17:1–8. Attempts have been made to explain this account as an Easter story read back into the public ministry, but as Taylor has remarked (*ibid.*, 391), Peter's embarrassing words (Mk 9:5f.) always stand in the way of such hypotheses. Later liturgical adaptations may be present: The "eight days" (v. 28) may refer to the Christian celebration of the octave of Tabernacles, just as the "six days" (Mk 9:2) may refer to the six days after which Moses heard God's voice on Mt. Sinai (Ex 24:15f.). Another literary embellishment appears in comparing this account with that of the agony on the Mt. of Olives (A. Kenny, *CBQ* 19 [1957] 444–52).

28. *after these words:* The transfiguration confirms Jesus' previous message that suffering is the way to glory. *the mountain:* In using the article, Luke has a definite mountain in mind (see 6:12 or 22:39). *to pray:* See comment on 3:21. **29.** *was altered:* Lk omits Mk's prosaic description of Jesus' garments (Mk 8:3), "robed in light as with a cloak" (Ps 104:2). **30.** *behold, two men:* The identical Gk phrase appears at the resurrection (24:4) and the ascension (Acts 1:10). *talking with him:* The disciples are asleep, and so the conversation is for Jesus' sake alone. **31.** *his death:* Lit., "his departure." This was the topic of conversation. Just as baptism brought to Jesus an experimental awareness of his awesome ministry, so he now learns the full extent of his suffering. The Gk word for "departure" is *exodos*; Moses and Elijah see the real and perfect Exodus in the passion and resurrection. As the Exodus lasted 40 years, so Jesus will appear in Jerusalem during 40 days before his final leave-taking (his ascension). **32.** Lk gives a less embarrassing explanation of the disciples' sleep than Mk. *his glory:* See comment on 2:9. **33.** *three tents:* A reference to the Feast of Tabernacles (cf. Zech 14:16). **35.** An echo of the baptismal scene (3:21). *hear him:* This is the all-important phrase in this scene; Moses and Elijah have disappeared and Heaven declares that henceforth men must "listen to him," especially in what he will say of his suffering and death, the way to glory and salvation. There is probably also a reference here to the deuteronomic prophet who has been promised (Dt 18:15–18 [see LXX]). **36.** Luke suppresses details about the conversation of Jesus with the disciples during the descent from the mountain; Mk (9:9–13) indicates that it centered on the roles of John the Baptist and Elijah.

(See Baltensweiler, H., *Die Verklärung Jesu* [Zurich, 1959]. Ramsey, A. M., *The Glory of God and the Transfiguration of Christ* [London, 1949]. Sabbe, M., "La rédaction du récit de la transfiguration," *La venue du Messie* [RechBib 6; Bruges, 1962] 65–100.)

91 (e) THE EPILEPTIC BOY (9:37–43a). See Mk 9:14–29; Mt 17:14–18. Lk and Mt abbreviate what is one of the most vivid and moving accounts in Mk and the most popular miracle in the early Church because of its combination of exorcism, faith, and prayer. The extent of agreement between Mt and Lk, though small in detail, brings up the question of the dependence of Lk upon Mt or of both upon a common source. **37.** *a great crowd:* Moses too, on descending from Mt. Sinai, found a crowd, bewildered and unbelieving (Ex 32; Nm 14:27; Dt 32:5,20). **38.** *my only child:* The Lucan addition (cf. 7:12; 8:41). The child is epileptic, as the symptoms show. **41.** It is difficult to determine at whom these words are aimed. Mark and Matthew depict Jesus as being fatigued and depressed from the faithlessness of the immediate crowd, but Luke possibly envisages later generations of Christians. Jesus' words are drawn from Dt 32:5,20; he speaks as though he were no longer a part of this world, somewhat according to the style of Wisdom in Prv 1:22–28. **43.** By abbreviating the account, Luke makes the whole story converge upon the wonder of the people.

92 (f) SECOND PREDICTION OF THE PASSION (9:43b–45). See Mk 9:30–32; Mt 17:22f. **43b.** Lk omits those details of Mk that announce Jesus' return to Galilee; Lk does not consider Jesus ever having left Jewish territory. Instead, Lk surrounds Jesus with a crowd and plays upon their psychological reaction of wonderment (3:15; 4:20). **44.** *lay these words within your ears:* Jesus' remark to the disciples; an obvious Semitism (Ex 17:14) meaning: Think seriously about what you have seen and heard, for my life is moving determinately to a violent death. *handed over:* From Is 53:12 (LXX), the fourth song of the Suffering Servant. **45.** This passage is rather prolix. *hidden from them:* The pf. pass. participle expresses the effects of this concealment, which will be felt for some time to come. *that they might not perceive it:* The Gk participle "that" (*hina*) here implies a consequent result, not purpose (*GrBib* § 351; Bl-Deb-F § 391, 5). Luke delicately attributes the disciples imperceptiveness to a providential design.

93 (g) DISPUTE ABOUT GREATNESS (9:46–48). See Mk 9:33–37; Mt 18:1–5. Luke cuts away from Mk's reasons for the dispute; he uses the incident not only as a conclusion to the Galilean ministry—Jesus must die humbly—but also as a reason for the disciples' obtuseness in understanding the prediction of the passion. **46.** *who was the greatest?:* That is, entitled to the most prominent place in the future kingdom. **47.** Lk states explicitly that Jesus intuits their thoughts. *beside him:* Lk omits the Marcan detail that Jesus gathered the child into his embrace. **48.** Two ideas merge here: (1) The greatest is the one who confesses his greatest need before God, for God will proportionately satisfy his wants. (2) The greatest is the one who loves even the lowliest person.

94 (h) THE EXORCIST, A STRANGER (9:49–50). See Mk 9:38–41. This story no doubt reflects difficulties and controversies within the early Church (Acts 3:6; 16:18; 19:13–16; 1 Cor 12:3), but during Jesus' lifetime unauthorized disciples could have imitated the style of the Twelve (9:1–6). Jesus again allows no neutral ground between good and evil (6:43–45) and banishes exclusivism from his own.

95 **(V) The Journey Narrative (9:51–19:28).** Here Luke constructs his own Christology: the full meaning of Jesus as Savior of mankind. To acquire greater independence of expression, Luke leaves aside his Marcan source (for the largest part of this section: 9:51–18:14) and presents material either from Q or from his own exclusive sources. Mk indicates a journey into Judea (10:1); Lk draws attention to the journey several times (9:51–57; 10:38; 18:31,35; 19:1), and especially to a journey to Jerusalem (9:51–53; 13:22; 17:11; 18:31; 19:11).

The question arises: Did a journey take place? Yes, Jesus passed from Galilee to Judea several times, as Jn attests; however, Luke's interest, we must insist, is not merely geographical but theological. In many ways he is indifferent to actual geographical locale. He does not seem to realize that Perea is across the Jordan and outside Palestine proper; he gives the impression that Jesus traveled S from Galilee, through Samaria, into Judea. There is, moreover, an artificial grouping of details, independent of geography: conflicts (11:14–14:25); logia (12:1–12; 14:25–35; 16:16–18); groups of three, such as three vocation stories (9:57–62), three instructions on prayer (11:1–13), three parables on divine mercy (15:1–32), three sentences on law (16:16–18), and three notices on scandal (17:1–6).

Lk presents a similar sequence of events in the Galilean ministry (4:14–9:50) and in the Journey Narrative (9:51–19:28): concern over the self-awareness of Jesus; common introduction with a rejection of Jesus; the mission of the disciples; a scene involving Herod Antipas; Jesus' close relatives (H. Conzelmann, *Theology of St. Luke*, 64).

The theme in this new section is stated in 13:31–34: The way leads to death in Jerusalem, but through death comes perfect fulfillment. All four gospels present Jesus' constant journeying, but none of them speaks of his goal—so clearly before his eyes—as does the Lucan Journey Narrative. Luke thus demonstrates that Jesus' example and his teaching lead his followers to suffering; but this suffering is the opportunity of full consecration and glorious triumph. Jesus' steps proceed doggedly to Jerusalem, the city of promise (2 Sm 5–7), where devout Israelites entered the Temple of the divine presence (1 Kgs 8; Pss 122, 125, 147). For that city to be established in glory, Jesus must be cast out of the Jerusalem of the scribes, the Pharisees, and the priests; at that moment, the hopes and fulfillment of the holy city left with Jesus, and in him rose the new holy city, which would extend its sway to the ends of the world, when all men would acknowledge Jesus as Savior.

(Benoit, P., *RB* 60 [1953] 446–48. Blinzler, J., "Die literarische Eigenart des sogenannten Reiseberichts im Lukasevangelium," *Synoptische Studien* [Fest. A. Wikenhauser; Munich, 1953] 20–52. Evans, C. F., "The Central Section of St. Luke's Gospel," *Studies in the Gospels* [Fest. R. H. Lightfoot; Oxford, 1955] 37–53. Girard, L., *L'évangile des voyages de Jésus.* [Paris, 1951]. Grundmann, W., *ZNW* 50 [1959] 252–270. Schneider, J., "Zur Analyse des lukanischen Reiseberichtes," *Synoptische Studien* [Fest. A. Wikenhauser; Munich, 1953] 207–29. Simson, P., *Scr* 15 [1963] 65–80.)

96 **(A) Section Proper to Lk (9:51–18:14).** Here Luke depends upon Q, the source he shared with Mt, and upon his own sources.

(a) SAMARITAN REFUSAL (9:51–56). This major section begins, as did the preceding one at Nazareth (4:14–30), with a rejection of Jesus. The incident provides the initial momentum that will ever more forcefully impel Jesus to face rejection and death at the hands of his own people. **51.** *to be taken up:* An almost identical expression, using the same basic word, is used of Elijah's assumption (2 Kgs 2:9–11), of the Suffering Servant's exaltation (Is 42:1), and of Jesus' own ascension to glory (Acts 1:2,11). *set his face:* A Semitism, frequently used in the OT for opposition and hostility (Ez 6:2; 13:17; 14:8; Is 50:7; cf. J. Starcky, *RSR* 39 [1951] 197–202). Jesus' life, therefore, is seen to be an ascension—through hostilities and the agony of death—to consummate glory. **52.** *Samaritans:* A primarily Gentile people, descendants of foreigners who were settled in Israel after the deportation of the Israelites in 721 BC (2 Kgs 17; Ezr 4:1–3;

Neh 4:1–9). **54.** *do you want us to bid fire to come down upon them:* We can now understand why Jesus called James and John "sons of thunder" (Mk 3:17). Some mss. (A, C, D, W, etc.) add "as Elijah did." **55.** Another addition to this verse comes from the same mss., but it is usually rejected from the critical text (cf. 19:10). This incident provides a practical illustration of nonresistance to force (J. M. Creed, *Luke*, 141). **56.** *to another village:* Possibly also a Samaritan village; according to Acts 8:5–25, Samaria was well-disposed toward Christianity. Luke never again mentions Samaria, as he never again speaks of Nazareth, to stress how rejection leads to Jesus' death.

97 (b) DEMANDS OF DISCIPLESHIP (9:57–62). The first two logia, placed in Mt 8:19–22 (Q) at the beginning of the Galilean ministry, teach the disciple how persistently he must follow the way. **58.** *foxes have holes...:* Jesus does not trick anyone into following him; he wants total dedication. When speaking of Jesus' extreme poverty, Luke uses terms of exalted dignity: "Son of Man" and "Lord." **60a.** *let the dead bury their dead:* A play on words: Let the spiritually dead bury the physically dead; mine is a message of life. Filial piety, especially in burying one's parents, is deep within Judaism (Gn 49:28–50:3; Ex 13:19; Tb 4:3; 6:15); Jesus did not intend to be taken literally, but rather he wanted to stir thought. **60b.** *for your part, go and proclaim the Kingdom of God:* This is proper to Lk. **62.** *and looks back:* Jesus demands more than Elisha (1 Kgs 19:19–21); ploughing for the kingdom entails sacrifice; one cannot look back, lest the work suffer (see L. Cerfaux, *Recueil*, 1 [Gembloux, 1954] 498–501).

98 (c) MISSION OF THE SEVENTY-TWO DISCIPLES (10:1–12). See Mt 9:37f.; 10:7–16. Lk presents two missions: one of the Twelve, relying upon Mk (Lk 9:1–6; Mk 6:7–13); and one of the seventy-two, details of which are drawn from Q. The instructions in both chapters are similar, at times even identical. The seventy-two are mentioned only here in the NT, and significantly Jesus applies the words of 10:4 to the Twelve at the Last Supper (23:35–36). What Jesus said in commissioning the Twelve was later applied in the early Church to larger missionary bands; and so Lk records it. **1.** *seventy-two:* This number is read in mss. P^{75}, P^{45}, B, and D; but "seventy" is the number found in other mss., among them S, A, C, and W. The evidence for the two numbers is about equal (see B. M. Metzger, *NTS* 5 [1958–59] 299–306). Commentators often detect a symbolical meaning in either number, seeing connections between the "70 disciples" and the 70 nations in the table of Gn 10, the 70 elders who assisted Moses (Ex 18:21; 24:1; Nm 11:16), or the name by which the common Gk translation of the OT is known, the Septuagint—or again, between the "72 disciples" and the 72 nations of the table of Gn 10 (according to the LXX), the 72 translators of the LXX (according to *Aristeas* 50:307), or the multiple 6 times 12 (the number of the Israelite tribes). But all of this is fanciful (see S. Jellicoe, *NTS* 6 [1959–60] 319–21). **2.** *the harvest is abundant:* See Mt 9:37–38, where the saying occurs just before the call of the Twelve. **3.** *like lambs among wolves:* The image shifts from reapers to animals, and the contrast between the lambs and the wolves suggests the hostility that marks the "journey" to be made by Jesus himself. **4.** *do not carry a purse:* See 9:3. The instruction suggests the urgency of the situation that will face the disciples; not even ordinary greetings should deter them (see 2 Kgs 4:29). **5.** *peace be to this house:* This is the peace that the Lucan Gospel associates with the salvation being brought by Christ (cf. 1:79; 2:14,29; 7:50; 8:48; 12:51; 19:38). See *ThDNT*, 1, 400–17. *son of peace:* What is implied here is that peace has the power of begetting tranquillity in others. **7.** *the laborer deserves his wages:* This saying is quoted in 1 Tm 5:18 as "Scripture" (cf. 1 Cor 9:7,14). **8.** *eat what is set before you:* Dietary laws have no force any more (cf. 1 Cor 10:27; Acts 10:25). **9.** *the Kingdom of God has come near to you:* It was brought near in the coming of Jesus, and now it would be brought even nearer in the mission of the disciples who extend his activity. **11.** *the dust of your town:* See comment on 9:5. **12.** *Sodom:* See Gn 19. Sodom did not have the opportunity for repentance that is being offered to these towns.

99 (d) THE IMPENITENT TOWNS (10:13–16). See Mt 11:21–23; 10:40. **13.** *Chorazin:* A village in the hill country, about 3 mi. NNW of Capernaum; modern Kerazeh. We know nothing of Jesus' own ministry in this village. *Bethsaida:* See comment on 9:10. What Jesus did in these two places would have been regarded as tantamount to a summons to repentance in the wicked towns of Tyre and Sidon, the classic examples of heathenism. **15.** *Capernaum:* The town that is confident in its lofty reputation and character will be brought to the lowest status because it has not responded to the offer extended to it in the mission of Jesus.

100 (e) THE RETURN OF THE SEVENTY-TWO (10:17–20). These verses, modeled on 9:10 (Mk 6:30 par.), give the Evangelist an opportunity to record words of Jesus apropos of the proper attitude of a disciple. **17.** *subject to us in your name:* The Twelve had been promised the power of exorcism (9:1). The report gave indication that Jesus' mission was having an effect in the world of evil (see 9:49–50; Acts 19:13). **18.** *I saw Satan fall like lightning:* Satan ("the adversary") is found at times in the OT in the throne room of Yahweh arguing like a prosecuting attorney against the true welfare of God's people (Jb 2:1ff.; Zech 3:1ff.); cf. Ap 12:9; 20:1–3. The fall of Satan (cf. Is 14:12) is a symbolic way of telling the disciples of the effect of their mission. **19.** *I have given you authority:* The gift has permanent value, for the pf. tense of the verb stresses that Jesus has already conquered Satan in principle; the effects of his victory will be realized in the Church (cf. Ps 91:13; Acts 28:6). **20.** *that your names are written in heaven:* Luke is counteracting the danger in the Church of overemphasizing external wonders (1 Cor 12). On the books of heaven, see Str-B 2, 169–76.

101 (f) JESUS' HYMN OF PRAISE (10:21–22). Except for the introductory words, this section is almost identical with Mt 11:25–27 (→ Gospel Mt, 43:77). The verses may be a hymn of the early Church, so well known as to be quoted verbatim by both Mt and Lk. Luke opens the text in a characteristic way: He alone mentions the rejoicing of Jesus in the Spirit. See A. Feuillet, "Jésus et la sagesse divine d'après les Évangiles synoptiques," *RB* 62 (1955) 161–96.

(g) THE PRIVILEGES OF THE DISCIPLES (10:23–24). See Mt 13:16–17. **23.** *blessed are you:* An isolated beatitude (cf. 6:20). **24.** *prophets and kings:* Such figures of the Old Dispensation lived in hope; but the disciples of Jesus now enjoy a rare privilege of fulfillment witnessed.

102 (h) THE PARABLE OF THE GOOD SAMARITAN (10:25–37). The theme of discipleship continues with a question put by a lawyer who asks of Jesus how salvation is to be achieved. Jesus' answer indicates what should be the conduct of the real disciple; it is the conduct of the wise and the prudent (not just of those learned in the Law) and of the little ones; recall 10:21–22. **25–28.** In the opening scene Luke depends on Mk 12:28–34, because he will omit this story later (at 20:40). The spokesman is a Pharisee in Mt, a scribe in Mk, and a lawyer in Lk. In Mk and Mt he inquires about the great commandment in the Law, but in Lk, where the Gentile-Christian audience is not overly concerned about the Law, he asks about "eternal life." **26.** Because Luke has changed the opening setting Jesus' answer makes little sense; it has to be understood in the background of the Marcan context. **27.** *you shall love the Lord...:* The answer here combines Dt 6:4 and Lv 19:18, as they are combined in the *T. Issachar* (5:2; 7:5). **28.** Jesus' comment is reminiscent of Lv 18:5 (cf. Gal 3:12; Rom 10:5). **29.** *who is my neighbor:* The lawyer would have the "neighbor" of the commandment further defined so that he would be sure of eternal life. Jesus' answer in the parable involves an extreme example: He compares the failure of the ministers of God with the unselfishness of the hated Samaritan, and his hearers would then be able to measure the unlimited nature of the duty of love (so J. Jeremias, *Parables*, 204). **30.** *going down from Jerusalem to Jericho:* The verb is expressive of the great descent involved in the journey; Jerusalem is roughly 2500 ft. above sea level and Jericho is roughly 800 ft. below sea level. *robbers:* The Gk word (*lēstēs*) is the same that is used of Barabbas (Jn 18:40) and of the "bandits" crucified with Jesus (Mk 15:27). **31.** *a priest:* A representative of the religious leaders of the people. **32.** *a Levite:* An assistant in the Temple. Were the two of them afraid to approach the man because they thought he was dead and consequently a source of ritual defilement? **33.** *a Samaritan:* One of those with whom Jews normally did not deal (Jn 4:9). In the course of the parable, he who possesses the secret of eternal life turns out to be this stranger without the lawyer's learning and concern for security and without the dignity and status of the priestly and Levitical condition. *moved with compassion:* His love was spontaneous and did not have to inquire into the Law; it was disinterested, kindly, personal, and effective. **37.** *the one who showed mercy on him:* The definition of a neighbor. The lawyer cannot bring himself to mention the name "Samaritan."

(Cerfaux, L., *Recueil*, 2, 51–59. Daniélou, J., *Mélanges bibliques* [Fest. A. Robert; Paris, 1957] 457–65. Derrett, J. D. M., *NTS* 11 [1964] 22–37. Spicq, C., *Agape in the NT* [St. Louis, 1963] 1, 108–18.)

103 (i) MARTHA AND MARY (10:38–42). A chiastic structure (a-b b-a) connects this episode with the preceding one: (a) the word of God about charity; (b) the story of the Samaritan; (b) the story of Martha's neighborly concern; (a) the logion about the love for God. The parable of the good Samaritan stressed practical, effective helpfulness, and Luke now uses another story to point up the primary necessity of faith in the Christian. **38.** *a woman named Martha:* Her name means "lady," being the fem. form of *mārêh*, "lord." **39.** *a sister called Mary:* Not to be confused with Mary of Magdala. The description of Martha's and Mary's character in Lk harmonizes with that given in Jn (11:1ff.; 12:1–11). *on their way:* The reference to a journey in connection with this episode is entirely stylistic; from Luke's point of view Jesus is nowhere near Bethany, the hometown of the sisters. **40.** *much serving:* Jesus probably brought several guests with him. **42.** *there is need of one thing [only]:* Here the ms. tradition is not sound: (1) "Only a few things are needed, indeed only one" (mss. P^3, S, B); (2) "only a few things are needed" (ancient versions); (3) "there is need of one thing [only]" (mss. P^{75}, A, C, W, Vg, Pesh). The latter reading is usually preferred. Whereas (2) seems to indicate that only a few things on the dinner table are needed, (3) makes it a need of something more spiritual and (1) combines the two interpretations. The doctrine behind the words comes close to other Lucan texts (4:4; 8:21; 11:27–28; see A. Baker, *CBQ* 27 [1965] 127–37).

104 (j) ON PRAYER (11:1–13). See Mt 6:9–13; 7:7–11. This section opens with Luke's rendition of the "Our Father," different enough from Mt's version to indicate that each must stem from a separate liturgical tradition in the early Church. Mt has seven petitions, whereas Lk has only five. K. G. Kuhn translated both forms into Aramaic, and compared each with the Jewish prayer *Shemoneh ʿeśreh* (see *Achtzehngebet und Vaterunser und der Reim* [Tübingen, 1950]). Both prayers were originally composed in rhyme; this type of poetry can be traced to Jewish synagogal prayers of the 1st cent. AD. T. W. Manson (*Sayings*, 167) gives examples of Jewish prayers similar to the "Our Father."

1. *at prayer:* See comment on 3:21. John the Baptist taught his disciples to pray (5:33). **2.** *Father:* The Lucan introduction to the prayer; Mt has added words, "Our Father who art in heaven." Mt is closer to the form of Jewish prayers, Lk to Christian prayers (see Gal 4:5; Rom 8:15), whose expression probably goes back to Jesus himself (Mk 14:36). The fatherhood of God is known by experiencing the mystery of Jesus' sonship. Lk usually imparts an eschatological nuance to the fatherhood of God (6:35; 20:36). *hallowed be thy name:* The same as Mt 6:9. The aor. pass. form of the verb gives a "once-for-all aspect" to the petition, again an eschatological motif (Is 29:23). God manifests his holiness and sanctifies his name in Jesus (Mk 1:23f.; Jn 12:27f.)—especially at the moment of his return to the Father and his sending of the Spirit (Jn 16:14). *thy kingdom come:* Eschatological overtones predominate (4:6; 22:18). In place of this petition, Marcion, followed by Gregory of Nyssa and Maximus, read: "May the Holy Spirit come upon us and cleanse us," an idea thoroughly consistent with Lucan theology. **3.** *give us each day our daily bread:* Mt not only employs the aor. form ("once-for-all" eschatological moment), but he also reads *sēmeron* (this day), whereas Lk has *kath' hēmeran* (day after day) and the pres. tense (expressing continuation). The eschatological interpretation thus yields to the more pressing daily problems. A Eucharistic nuance is also present, for "to give bread" has a Eucharistic meaning throughout the Gospels (cf. Lk 9:17). **4.** *forgive us...:* Lk has "sins" in place of Mt's "debts" and puts both parts in the pres. tense. Here is the only instance in the entire "Our Father" of an action on the Christian's part, and even this act is to be modeled upon God's. *lead us not into trial:* Lk uses *mē* with the aor. subjunctive and therefore refers to a single great future trial, the final onslaught of the demon (1 Thes 1:6,10; 3:2–5; 5:6). By employing the article, Mt has in mind "the" evil one, the devil.

(Brown, R. E., *TS* 22 [1961] 175–208. Jeremias, J., *The Lord's Prayer* [Facet Books, Bibl. ser., 8; Phila., 1964]. Schürmann, H., *Praying with Christ* [N.Y., 1964]. Van den Bussche, H., *Understanding the Lord's Prayer* [N.Y., 1963].)

105 5–8. Only Lk gives this parable, which teaches that the petition of the "Our Father" for daily bread is always heard. **5.** In Greek the opening words expect a ringing "no!" "Can you imagine that any of you...?" (J. Jeremias, *Parables*, 158). From the start, attention is focused upon the housekeeper, who will certainly not refuse the request. *friend:* One does not go to just any neighbor under these circumstances. **7.** *door is shut:* To remove the large wooden or iron bar is tiresome and noisy. *my children and I:* The entire family slept on a mat in the raised part of a single-roomed, peasant house. *I cannot:* I will not! **8.** *shamelessness:* A much better translation than "persistence"; friendship allows such bold requests. The housekeeper cannot say "no," because of the strong bonds of friendship.

A parable about prayer (11:9–13). See Mt 7:7–11. Luke inserts another section on prayer, this one taken from Q. The relationship here is not between friend and friend but between father and son. **9.** *I tell you:* In Greek the opening words imply, "Not only the preceding parable, but I personally tell you." The verbs are pres. imperatives: "keep on asking...seeking...knocking..."; the verbs are also without an object, indicating that Jesus is not teaching what to pray for but how to pray. Nor is he guaranteeing that the object of every prayer will be granted, but inculcating faith in God's continual and effective fatherly concern. **11–12.** Cf. Ps 91:13f. The Palestinian scorpion is black and can never be mistaken for an egg. **13.** *Holy Spirit:* There are textual variants here: Some mss. read either "good Spirit" or (like Mt) "good things." The gift of the Spirit accords with the tone of Lk; attention is directed to the Spirit who enables us to share Jesus' sonship (Rom 8:23; 2 Cor 1:22; 5:5; Eph 1:13f.).

106 (k) TWO STATEMENTS ABOUT A SIGN (11:14–36). The opening verses (14–23) are found, with variations, in Mt 12:22–27; dependence on Mk 3:20–30 is much more difficult to decide. **14.** *a demon that was dumb:* Miracles are an attack upon Satan (4:33–37,40–41); sickness is viewed as the effect of a diabolical hold upon the human race. *the crowds marveled:* Typical of Lk. **15.** Critics do not challenge the reality of the miracle. *Beelzebul:* Cf. 2 Kgs 1:2. *Baʿal-zebūl* ("Lord of the divine abode" or "Baal the Prince") was chief god of the Philistine city of Ekron; the Israelites mockingly changed the name to *Baʿal-zebūb* ("Lord of Flies"). **16.** Jesus has just worked a sign for the poor and needy; his opponents wanted a different kind of sign, one of national splendor or military victory. **18.** Luke's explanation. **19–20.** Almost identical in Mt and Lk. Jewish exorcisms are described by Josephus, *Ant.* 8.2, 5, § 45; see Str-B 4, 533ff. **20.** *finger of God:* The phrase spoken by the magicians of Egypt in admitting their inability to duplicate the miracles of Moses and Aaron (Ex 8:15–19). Jesus' adversaries have less faith than these foreigners. **21–23.** Cf. the incident of David and Goliath (1 Sm 17). The binding of Satan is an eschatological concept (Is 24:22; Tb 8:3; Ap 20:2f.). **24–26.** Mt separates these verses from the preceding by the parable of a fruit-bearing tree and the answer about the sign of Jonah. **24.** *waterless places:* An abode of an evil spirit (Is 13:21; Tb 8:3; Lv 16:10,22). *seeking rest:* As did the evil spirits at Gergesa (Lk 8:32f.). **26.** External cleanliness is not sufficient; it may house a pride far worse than the condition of other "sinful" men. **27–28.** These verses are found only in Lk. Jesus now gives the true sign of holiness. *hear the word of God and keep it:* Not even the greatest of external honors, being Jesus' mother, sufficed; Mary is "blessed" for pondering God's word (1:28–29,42–45; see comment on 8:19–21).

107 *The sign of Jonah* (11:29–32). See Mt 12:38–42; 16:1–4). Lk now describes another sign of hearing the Word of God with compunction. Jesus' opponents think of a sign simply in terms of a miracle; he, however, speaks of a sign as a way of salvation, which eventually, like the cross, leads to an external, wondrous transformation. **29.** *this generation:* In Mt the scribes and the Pharisees are meant; in Lk Jesus refers to all his faithless contemporaries in general. *evil:* Luke suppresses Mt's word, "adulterous"; his Gentile readers would probably not have appreciated its scriptural connotation of Israel, Yahweh's spouse, unfaithful through sin. *sign of Jonah:* Mk 8:11–13 pictures Jesus adamantly refusing a sign. Mt 12:39 and Lk here add a qualifying clause after the refusal; each then proceeds to interpret the sign. As is evident from vv. 30–32, Jonah is intended as a sign: in his coming from distant Palestine to Assyrian Nineveh and in his preaching repentance to the Ninevites, who, even though they were pagans, were converted to God (see Jon 3:2–10). Note that in Mt this is also the "sign" to be given to this generation; but Mt adds a second meaning (a reference to the resurrection), derived from a post-Easter realization of the meaning of the sign. **31.** *queen of the South:* The introduction of this motif really distracts from the "sign of Jonah" as such, but by free association it is introduced because she too came from afar—to seek wisdom from Solomon (1 Kgs 10:1ff.). *something greater than Solomon:* This is Jesus, not as the sign of Jonah, but as Wisdom incarnate. **32.** *at the preaching of Jonah:* The point of the comparison is made explicit. If only "this generation" would repent "at the preaching" of "the Son of Man"! *something greater than Jonah:* Jesus is greater than Jonah in the Lucan version of the story in that with him the preaching of the kingdom takes place. Lk makes no reference to Jonah in the belly of the great fish. (See A. Vögtle, *Synoptische Studien* [Fest. A. Wikenhauser; Munich, 1953] 230–77.)

33–36. To conclude this section on signs, Luke gathers together a number of sayings on light, phrases of which are found elsewhere in his Gospel. **33.** *on a stand:* See 8:16. **34.** *the lamp of your body:* See comment on Mt 6:22. *your body is full of darkness:* When the Light that is Christ does not illumine man's "body," then his whole existence shares only in the opposition to him. The dualism of light and darkness used here echoes that of QL (see 1QS 3:6–7,17ff.; T. W. Manson, *Sayings*, 92). **36.** This verse is proper to Luke. The logion is so dull and so unlike Lk, that early mss. wanted to change it.

108 (l) DENUNCIATION OF THE PHARISEES AND LAWYERS (11:37–54). See Mt 23. Luke has drawn his information from Q and expanded the account with the help of Mk 12:38 and other sources. However, there is another alternative: since Mt also contains additional verses with a strong Jewish coloration, these may have existed in Q but were bypassed by Luke. Lk alone separates the condemnation of the Pharisees from that of the lawyers (scribes), but the new introduction at v. 45 is forced, and the strictures that follow are not specifically directed against lawyers. **37.** *to dine with him:* Jesus is again at table, and once more the guest of a Pharisee (see 7:36). **38.** *began to ponder:* The Pharisee does not seem to have invited Jesus in order to trap him. *did not wash:* The Gk vb. *baptizō* is used in its ordinary sense and not with the meaning of immersion. *before dinner:* An early meal or lunch around noon. **39.** *outside...inside:* Jesus contrasts the outer cleansing of dishes and the inner cleansing of the heart. **41.** A very obscure verse, perhaps meaning that alms effect a true cleansing because they unite the affluent with the poor in one great human need for salvation. **42.** *mint and rue:* Pharisees paid tithes (10 per cent) not just on what the Law required (Lv 27:30), but also on the most insignificant herbs. *justice and love of God:* Mt has "mercy and faith." Justice, in the Scriptures, is God's "just" fulfillment of his promises of salvation; love is that bond of love inciting him to do so. This passage and Mt 24:12 are the only times that the noun *agapē* (love) occurs in the Syn. Mi 6:8 also condemns the people for subjugating justice and charity to external legal holiness. **46.** *load men with burdens:* Nothing gives a man as great a sense of superiority as does the handling of another's conscience! **47.** *you build the tombs of prophets:* Only when dead do prophets receive a respectful hearing; they are persecuted while they live. These words point to the necessity of Jesus' own death. **49.** *wisdom of God:* Mt 23:34 refers the wisdom to Jesus himself. **51.** Abel's murder is recounted in Gn 4:8 and Zechariah's violent death in the final book of the Hebr canon (2 Chr 24:20–22). **53–54.** This passage is textually very difficult. Lk counterbalances two ideas: continuous and fierce verbal assaults; silent, stealthy ambushing. In elegant Greek, Luke writes of this dark tragedy of the mounting opposition to Jesus (see 6:11; 19:48; 20:19–20; 22:2).

109 (m) EXHORTATIONS AND WARNINGS (12:1–13:9). Luke gathers material from Q that in Mt is located variously: in the Sermon on the Mount, the charge to the Twelve, and the final eschatological discourse. He thereby implies that eschatological trials will not be confined to the one great moment of the parousia, but will spread over an indefinite period of time.

1. This opening verse is proper to Lk; it not only provides a link with the preceding section against the Pharisees but pictures Jesus in Luke's favorite style, surrounded by multitudes. *many thousands:* The Gk word *myrias* lit. means 10,000. Even when Jesus addresses his disciples, as here, he does not speak to them privately but within the larger circle of many people. *leaven of the Pharisees:* Mt (16:12) calls it their teaching; Lk their hypocrisy (see 6:42). **2–3.** *shall be proclaimed:* God's word tears off the mask of all pretense and false security. Verses 2–9 have the same sequence here as Mt 10:26–33, the charge to the Twelve. **6.** *five sparrows sold for two pennies:* Jesus does not promise to save his disciples from suffering and death but to vouch for their loyalty on the final day. **8–9.** Heavenly court scene (cf. Jb 1:6ff.; Is 40:1ff.; 41:21ff.; Zech 3). *acknowledge:* The Gk vb. *homologeō* means "to proclaim" what God has accomplished in one. **10.** This verse has another setting in Mk 3:28 and Mt 12:32. Those who rejected the Son of Man, i.e., Jesus during his earthly ministry, will be forgiven and given another chance through the gift of the Spirit at Pentecost; but how can one who rejects the Spirit as he offers forgiveness, repentance, and renewal be forgiven? As v. 11 will make clear, Luke is speaking within a Christian setting and of the danger of apostasy (Heb 6:4–6; 10:29). *speaks a word:* A euphemistic phrase, meaning to curse; to "curse God" (Jb 2:9) is translated in the LXX: "speak a word against the Lord." **11.** *magistrates and authorities:* Jesus' words are applied to Gentiles of non-Palestinian territory during the post-Pentecostal period. **12.** Confessors of the faith, like Jesus, will be Spirit-possessed.

110 **13–21.** The parable of the rich fool is found only in Lk. **13.** The Mishnah has a section on inheritance (Nm 27:1–11; Dt 21:15ff.; *EDB* 1062–64), to guide the rabbis when they are consulted. Jesus eschews family disputes over money. **14.** *man:* A stern salutation. **15.** *not in an abundance:* The Gk text implies that a real and meaningful life cannot be drawn out of an abundance of material possessions (*ek tōn hyparchontōn*). A similar dialogue is recorded in the apocryphal *Gospel of Thomas* (§ 72). **16–21.** The doctrine of the Cross (cf. 9:23–25) is exemplified by the parable, in which the main thrust is not sudden death but the continuing eschatological judgment of the Spirit's presence.

22–34. Sayings from Q on trust in God (see Mt 6:25–33). In vv. 22–28 Jesus points out that human anxiety cannot speed up the growth of plants in the field nor give added luster to the plumage of birds—as if they needed it!—nor can it extend one's life an added cubit or step (cf. Ps 39:6). **32.** After v. 31, Mt continues the theme of anxiety about tomorrow; Lk, on the contrary, has his own words about the kingdom, which he develops in terms of each one's own death. **33.** Mt 6:21 gives this logion in a negative form, "do not lay up treasures on earth"; Lk keeps his ideal more positive and demanding.

111 *Vigilance and loyalty* (12:35–48). Where Mt and especially Mk speak of the fall of Jerusalem and the parousia, Luke refers to the presence of the Spirit of Jesus in the daily life of the disciples, for he writes under a double tension: The eschatological moment does not come for Jesus till his death; but for the disciples who read the Gospel, the Spirit has already been given. **35–38.** Similar ideas occur in the parable of the ten virgins (Mt 25:1–13). *loins be girt:* The long, Oriental robes were drawn up and tucked into the belt at the waist to facilitate movement (Ex 12:11; 1 Pt 1:13). The nuptial banquet is a messianic biblical theme (see comment on Lk 5:34). **38.** *second watch:* Jewish practice divided the night into three watches, but Roman into four. It does not matter how long the delay lasts; Luke thinks only of the indefinite period of the Church's existence. **39–46.** These verses parallel Mt 24:43–51. **39.** *thief:* For the same motif, see 1 Thes 5:2–11; 2 Pt 3:10; Ap 3:3. **41.** *Peter:* The spokesman for the group. Judging from the following section, he is also the administrator of Christ's household. It is difficult to determine the exact point of Peter's question; is the banquet only for the Twelve or for all Christians? Jesus ignores the question, implying that it was out of place. **47–48.** These verses are found only in Lk. The point of this passage concerns the leaders in the Christian community, who bear the greater responsibility. God's own agents, loved more by him, will suffer the more if they fail to correspond to the graces accorded for their role (cf. Am 3:2; Hos 4:4–11; Jer 2:19).

49–56. How to interpret the present (see Mt 10:34–36). These sayings, originally detached, are loosely joined here. Verses 49–50 allow us to glimpse into the depths of Jesus' soul as he utters a statement about his mission. *to cast fire upon the earth:* Fire is usually a figure of judgment (see 3:16–17); here it seems to be the fire that will separate and purify those who are meant for the kingdom. It will work through Jesus' word and his Spirit. See the *Gospel According to Thomas* § 9. **50.** *a baptism with which to be baptized:* Jesus refers to his coming passion, into which he will be "plunged." The image is derived from the OT (see Ps 124:4–5) and indicates the depths of sorrow and suffering that await him in his human condition. See Mk 10:38 (Jesus' martyrdom). *distressed [or constrained]:* The Gk vb. *synechomai* conveys an anxiety of distress, an intolerable force against restraint (see V. Taylor, *Jesus and His Sacrifice* [London, 1937] 164–67; O. Cullmann, *Early Christian Worship* [Chicago, 1953] 19). **51–53.** *not to give peace:* This does not contradict 1:79 or 7:50. Jesus will not tolerate peace at any cost. His utterance is ironical. He will not bring the sobriety of the *status quo*, but the sword that will divide the eager from the contented. **54–59.** Even though the parousia may be delayed—this anxiety was one of the trials of the Church after AD 70—one must keep faith in the presence of the Spirit. **56.** *the present time:* See Mt 16:2–3. The weather manifests itself in advance by its "signs," and men learn to read them. The present (the period of the kingdom) is likewise manifesting itself, but this generation fails to perceive its meaning. Men are not asked to be clever but just to correspond to the proffered aid.

57–59. These verses continue the exhortation to a proper mode of conduct with one who opposes and accuses a disciple (see Mt 5:25–26). The verses contain little more than sound advice; but it is sound advice that men should normally be able to arrive at themselves (just as in the case of reading the "signs" of the present). In a crucial situation, men know how to come to a settlement; a fortiori there is all the more need for one to seize the opportunity for brotherly forgiveness.

112 **13:1–9.** The last exhortation of this section treats of repentance or the consequences of the failure to repent. These verses are found only in Lk. **1.** *Galileans whose blood Pilate had mixed with their sacrifices:* This incident is recorded only here, and is otherwise unknown in secular historians. It fits, however, into the picture of

Pilate that is known to us from Josephus (→ History of Israel, 75:143; see *Ant.* 18.3, 2 § 62; *JW* 2.9, 4 § 175–77). Jesus does not condemn Pilate, but he merely comments on the guilt of those so murdered, or lack thereof. **4.** *the tower in Siloam:* Probably one of the towers that guarded the aqueduct bringing water to the pool of Siloam (cf. Jn 9:3), to the S of the eastern corner of Jerusalem. Jesus does not give his support to Zealot plots or to acts of terror against Rome; he concludes only to the urgency of repentance. **6–9.** The parable of the barren fig tree may compensate for the omission of the equivalent of Mt 21:18–22 and Mk 11:12–14,20–25. **7.** *three years:* Some commentators think that this might refer to the duration of the public ministry. **8.** *let it alone:* God's mercy is symbolized in the digging and manuring of the tree (see Hos 9:10; Is 5:1–7; Jl 1:7). Jesus does not believe that Israel's final answer to him will be a "no."

113 (n) THE UNIVERSAL KINGDOM BEGINS SMALL AND HIDDEN (13:10–21). Here we encounter another of those incidents, exclusive to Lk, in which Jesus' kindly regard for the unfortunate and for women is attested. **10.** *one of their synagogues:* Lk's final mention of Jesus' appearance in this place of worship. **11.** *caused by a spirit:* Cf. 4:33–37. **12.** *saw her:* Jesus always had an eye for the needy. **14.** Although the ruler addresses the crowd, Jesus was the object of his hateful words. **15.** *loose his ox:* In Greek the vb. *apo-lyō* echoes v. 12, "delivered" (*lyō*). The Mishnah gives intricate rules for the Sabbath. Tying and loosing knots are among 39 kinds of forbidden work (Mishnah, *Shabbath* 7:2), whereas *Shabbath* 15:1–2 exempts certain kinds of knots. Another document states that a stubborn animal can be led no more than 2000 yd. and can never be whipped on the Sabbath (CD 11:5–7). **17.** A typical Lucan conclusion. **18–21.** Two parables are joined to the preceding episode by Luke, each showing how the kingdom begins small and hidden, suddenly breaks forth with life, and is not confined to any single group. Mt 13:31–33 contains both parables; Mk 4:30–32 only the first. **18–19.** The fact that this parable is in Q and in Mk makes it "one of the best attested elements in the teaching of Jesus" (V. Taylor, *St. Mark*, 268). *garden:* Luke reveals his city background; this plant does not grow in gardens; it is found wild around the Lake of Galilee. It attains a height of 8 to 12 ft. **19.** *birds of the air:* From Dn 4:11; cf. Ez 17:23; 31:6; emphasis is upon the universal aspect of the kingdom. **20.** *leaven:* Once it is added, leaven inevitably transforms the mixture.

114 (o) THE REMNANT (13:22–35). Lk introduces the problem, how many will be saved (Am 5:3; Is 10:19–22). **22–30.** Parallels to this section are scattered throughout Mt. **23.** The question may be Luke's stylistic device, for he has reconstructed the following section, mostly from Q. **24.** *strive:* In Gk *agōnizomai* denotes strenuous exercise of muscle and power (Jn 18:36; 1 Cor 9:25; 1 Tm 4:10). Jesus is not declaring that many are doomed from the very start, despite their persistent effort to be saved. **25.** This verse is closely linked with the preceding and gives the sense: Many will seek too late, after the Kingdom has come; each one can and must strive now. *I do not know:* Jesus must first recognize and love, and thus impart justifying faith; cf. Is 63:16; Mt 25:12. **26.** No one has a prescriptive right to the kingdom by birth or by any other external criterion. **28–29.** Mt 8:11f. uses these lines to conclude his story of the centurion (Lk 7:9f. omits them in his account). *from the east...west:* Cf. Is 2:2f.; 25:6–8; 49:12; Mi 4:1f. **30.** This verse is applied differently in Mk 10:31 (Mt 19:30) and in Mt 20:16. It was a proverb, able to fit into various contexts.

31–33. Another story about Herod Antipas, only in Lk. **31.** *on that same day:* Luke wants the following episode to be understood in the context of the preceding one. Is Luke referring to a plot to lure Jesus into Judea where the Sanhedrin exerted more power than in Herod Antipas' territory? Or was Herod intending to treat Jesus as he had the Baptist (3:19f.)? **32.** *fox:* Crafty, unprincipled. *today, tomorrow, and the third day:* This phrase, along with an unfinished day in v. 33, may be explained by the biblically symbolic number "three and one-half," which indicates a time of dark persecution that will certainly and gloriously end, but in God's time (thus the number symbolism in Dn 7:25; 8:14; 12:12; Lk 4:25). *I will end:* The same Gk word in Jn 5:36; 17:4; 23; 19:28; Heb 2:10; 5:9—referring to the perfection of Christ's redemptive mission. **33.** *prophet:* Lk 4:25–27; 7:16,39; 24:19. *outside Jerusalem:* "There is...a bitter irony in the words. Herod must not be greedy: for Jerusalem has first claim on the blood of God's messengers" (T. W. Manson, *Sayings*, 277).

34–35. This sad, tender apostrophe to Jerusalem occupies a more appropriate place in Mt (23:37–39) so far as the circumstances of Jesus' life are concerned. Mt places the words after Palm Sunday, so that they clearly refer to the parousia. Spoken here before Palm Sunday in Lk, the words find a fulfillment in that triumphal procession where they are in a sense repeated (19:39–44). Lk has a different meaning. He wants the Church amid persecution to wait perseveringly for the Lord's coming. *blessed is he...:* From Ps 118:26, a psalm connected with the great pilgrim feasts, especially with Tabernacles, which had a particular messianic significance (Zech 14:16; Lk 9:33). *he who comes:* See Lk 7:19.

115 (p) LUCAN SYMPOSIUM (14:1–24). Luke organizes heterogeneous material under an external and internal unity. For internal unity, all the episodes or stories center around a banquet, with a subsequent interdependence of thought. The groups that cannot come to the great supper (vv. 18–20) are the rich neighbors (v. 12). External unity is achieved by maintaining the setting of the same banquet. Luke even binds the parts together by an artificial, chronological progression: they enter to take food (v. 1); choose places at table (v. 7); at a lunch or dinner (v. 12); at dinner (v. 16). In all this, Luke is following the norms of classical Gk style (X. de Meeûs, *ETL* 37 [1961] 847–70).

1–6. Major synoptic problems are met in this symposium. Although this miracle (the cure of the man with dropsy) is proper to Lk, the concluding logion in v. 5 was known to Matthew (12:11), as seen in his rendition of a miracle story from Mk. Mt 12:9–14 expands Mk 3:1–6 and uses the parallel in Lk 6:6–11. Although Lk 6 does not include the logion in question, Luke does repeat it in another form in 13:15–16. **1.** *one of the rulers of the Pharisees:* The Greek can more properly be translated "one of the rulers [who came] from the Pharisees"; the Pharisees were not a sect with rulers or superiors and disciples; for that reason in 5:33 Luke produced an inaccuracy while stylizing Mk's account. **5.** *an ass or an ox:* Better mss. read "son" (*huios*) instead of "ass" (*onos*). M. Black explains "a son and an ox" as a pun in the Aramaic spoken by Jesus: "ox" (*beʿîrā*), "son" (*berā*), "well" (*bērā*).

7–11. These verses are found only in Lk. The concluding logion (v. 11) shows that Jesus is not teaching social etiquette, but from good manners at table he draws conclusions about the kingdom: Attendance depends upon an invitation from God. God invites those who recognize their lowliness and their need of salvation. Because the logion occurs again in Lk 18:14, in Mt 18:4 and 23:12—all in different settings—some scholars feel that Luke exercised great freedom in composing the present parable.

12–14. Found only in Lk. The recompense lies in a growing likeness to God himself who tells the least worthy to go up higher (vv. 7–11). "It is impossible to achieve, even for a moment, a pure unselfish kindness without knowing a blessedness that comes in no other way, a foretaste of something to be made perfect at the resurrection of the just" (T. W. Manson, *Sayings*, 280).

116 *The parable of the great banquet* (14:15–24). See Mt 22:1–10. This is an allegorical parable in which men's reactions to the invitation to a share in the Messianic and salvific banquet prepared by God are described, and also how God will provide for a share in it even for the outcasts of Israel. **15.** *blessed...:* An exclamation of blessedness not only links the new section with the preceding verse, but it also follows the Lucan style (12:13; 13:1,23) of introducing a new section by means of a statement from a bystander. **17.** *he sent his servant:* Jesus is the Servant. A second invitation is required by ancient Near Eastern etiquette (see Est 5); to refuse it is a serious breach of friendship. **18.** *with one accord:* Lit., "from one," which may be an Aramaism (*min ḥ*ᵃ*dā*) and could possibly mean "all at once" (see Bl-Deb-F § 241, 6). **18–20.** Lk expands what is a simple remark in Mt 22:5, "one went off to his farm, another to his business." Only Lk adds the excuse about the wife (cf. Dt 20:7; 24:5). The true reason for the excuses lay in "the riches and pleasures of life" (8:14). **21.** *to the streets and lanes of the city:* The invitations are extended to others than those who were the leaders of the Jewish people. **23.** *to the highways and hedges:* The invitations to share in the banquet go also to the Gentiles (outside the city). **24.** *those men who were invited:* The speaker is no longer the man who gave the banquet but Jesus himself. Certainly nobody will remain outside the kingdom because he was uninvited. Whereas Mt's parable presents the qualifications for entering the kingdom, Lk's preoccupation is with the Jew–Gentile issue (see A. Hastings, *Prophet and Witness*, 131–33; Sr. Jeanne d'Arc, *VieSp* 110 [1964] 718–31).

117 (q) DISCIPLESHIP'S TOTAL DEDICATION (14:25–35). Lk admirably introduces this new section against the background of the preceding parables. People, streaming from all the "streets and lanes, the poor and maimed and blind and lame," now cured (v. 21), form the great crowds, surrounding Jesus as though the eschatological kingdom had already come. Just as the Cross followed Palm Sunday, so Jesus now shifts attention from exultation to the demand for total dedication in his disciples (v. 26f.,33–35). The two intervening parables (vv. 28–32) are artificially stitched into the context by the Gk particles, *gar* (for) and *oun* (therefore, vv. 28, 33), but their theme has a different center of attention: careful, conscious acceptance of a great task.

26. *wife, children, brothers, sisters—yes, even his own life:* Luke adds these words to the form found in Mt 10:37; however, no convincing reason can be found to show that Jesus did not utter them. *hate:* The force of the word is Semitic; in Mt the expression "loves father or mother more" shows that hate must be understood in the sense of "love less." Luke's fuller logion corresponds well with 12:51–53 and is supported by the Qumran messianic interpretation of Dt 33:9 (in 4QTest, see J. M. Allegro, *JBL* 75 [1956] 182–87). The sacrifice of marriage for the sake of the kingdom is supported by Luke's addition in 14:20 and by 18:21–22. Just as the kingdom returns life more fully, it will transform the renunciation of marriage into a new, personal fruitfulness. **27.** *carry his cross...after me:* See Lk 9:23. Lk alone has the Gk word *bastazō* (to carry), which Jn 19:16 uses of Jesus on the way to Calvary; Lk alone in the Passion Narrative (23:26) has the Gk prep. *opisthen* (after), which occurs here and in Mt 10:38. Luke expects a very close—we might even say, literal—following of Jesus in his sufferings and death. **28–33.** "Counting the cost" is an element in every invitation to enter the kingdom and to partake of the Messianic banquet; the disciple of Jesus cannot act on impulse, but only on a carefully considered program of involvement. **34–35.** The involvement demanded of the disciple is that which will season the world as salt does food. Mt 5:13 has a much better context; in Mk 9:50 the connection with the immediate section is merely verbal and the meaning of the saying is not too clear.

118 (r) THE PARABLES OF MERCY (15:1–32). In this chapter Luke presents three parables that have in common the note of divine mercy toward sinners; he thus presents the distilled essence of the good news, the gospel within the Gospel. **1.** *tax collectors and sinners:* See 5:30; 7:34. **2.** *this man receives sinners:* An exclamation quickly gives the setting or the provocation of the parables (see 14:15; cf. W. R. Farmer, *NTS* 8 [1961–62] 301–16). Similar coupling of parables exists in 12:24–28; 13:18–21; 14:28–33.

3–7. The parable of the lost sheep is given first (see also Mt 18:12–14; cf. Jn 10; Ez 34:11–16). Mt includes it among the instructions to the apostles about their obligations as pastors of the Church; Lk, on the other hand, uses the parable to answer why Jesus welcomes sinners. Mt emphasizes seeking; Lk, the joy of finding (J. Dupont, *LumViSup* 34 [1957] 15–23). **5.** This verse is exclusive to Lk. A lost sheep will lie down helplessly and refuse to budge. The shepherd is forced to carry it over a long distance; this can be done only by putting it on his shoulders. He clutches the forelegs and hindlegs with each hand; if he must use his shepherd's staff, he holds all four legs with one hand firmly against his breast. **6.** The invitation to friends and neighbors is given only in Lk. **7.** *just:* Are the words spoken ironically in the sense of the self-justified, with no need of redemption?

8–10. The parable of the lost coin is second and has the same lesson as the first; it has a special appeal to women and is proper to Lk. A woman with only ten small silver coins for her headdress is probably poor. She sweeps the dark room—it has only a single opening at the door—hoping to hear the tinkle of the coin against the floor.

119 **11–32.** The parable of the two brothers (often called the "Prodigal Son") is found only in Lk. Luke knits the chapter together by repeating the concluding refrain (vv. 7, 10, 24, 32). **12.** *my share of the property:* A father can abdicate before his death and divide his wealth (1 Kgs 1–2; Sir 33:19–23). **13.** *loose living:* The Gk word speaks of unrestrained sensuality and spendthrift extravagance. The elder son describes his brother's conduct more precisely in v. 30. **16.** *pods:* The fruit of the carob tree (*ceratonia siliqua*). He was too disgusted to eat with the pigs; no one gave him anything else. He must have stolen his food. **18.** *I will...return:* Cf. Hos 2:9 (Vg 2:7). *against heaven:* Circumlocution for God. The remembrance of his father's goodness revives hope and compunction. The father first seeks the lost son by the memory he has instilled; he is seeking the boy before the lad thinks to return (v. 20b). **22.** Cf. Gn 41:42. **29.** The elder son omits the polite address, "Father," used by the younger son (v. 21). **30.** He contemptuously speaks of "this one" instead of saying "my brother." **31.** *son:* There is an affectionate ring in the Gk *teknon*, lit., "[my] child." This parable not only vindicates Jesus' kingly regard toward "sinners" (v. 2; not just immoral persons, but those too poor or too ignorant to know every legal refinement), but the refrain, "dead but come to life," makes us think of Jesus' passion and resurrection. Jesus, by his union with human nature, becomes the wayward son! (Cf. C. H. Giblin, *CBQ* 24 [1962] 15–31, for a different view.)

120 (s) TWO PARABLES ABOUT RICHES (16:1–31). As in ch. 12, Luke, in presenting two parables, places a series of isolated logia between them.

1–13. The first parable about the dishonest manager consists of Jesus' words (vv. 1–8a) and of some early Christian moralizing upon them (vv. 8b–13). To understand Jesus' parable we must recall the Palestinian economic situation (P. Gaechter, *CBQ* 12 [1950] 121–31; J. D. M. Derrett, *NTS* 7 [1960–61] 198–219). The manager, usually a slave born in the household, possessed great liberty and full responsibility. Like the tax collector, the manager must show a profit for his master, but he could also procure personal benefits perhaps by means of adroit loans and extravagant interest. **2.** The master has learned that his own property has been squandered; the manager is dishonest. **4.** *I know:* Aor. tense in Greek: "I have known all along what I shall do in a case like this." He faces a crisis. **6.** *a hundred jars of oil:* At least 900 gal., the yield of about 146 olive trees. **7.** *a hundred kors of wheat:* At least 1100 bu., the yield ot about 100 acres. We note the Oriental story teller's delight in exaggeration, which Jesus has shown on more than one occasion (cf. J. Jeremias, *Parables*, 27–31). **8a.** *commended the dishonest manager:* In no way is he condemned; as such, he reminds us of the "dishonest judge" in 18:2–8. He was "dishonest" only to the extent of endangering the master's security or wealth. What the manager probably did was to cancel the excessive interest he required for his own personal profit. *he had acted shrewdly:* He took decisive steps in the time of crisis, knowing what to do ahead of time.

8b–9. First moralization of the parable. **8b.** This verse is probably an independent logion of Jesus, which is intensified against the background of the very ingenious manager. *children of this world...of light:* Cf. similar expressions for good and evil people in Essene writings: CD 20:34; 1QS 1:9; 2:16; 3:13,24; 1QM 1:1,3,9. *mammon:* The word's only occurrence in the OT is in Sir 31:8; we find it in QL: 1QS 6:2; CD 14:20. It is probably from the root *'amēn* (be firm); *ma'môn* means "that in which one puts his trust" (cf. vv. 10–12; *ThDNT* 4, 388–90). Verse 9, a difficult one, can be explained thus: Use prudently the wealth that you have, in order to ensure your status within the final age; remember that wealth tends to lead men to dishonesty. When earthly goods fail, you will be welcomed into the everlasting tents of the Kingdom of God. (Some Gk texts and the Vg read, "when you fail.")

10–12. In this second moralization, emphasis shifts from the eschatological age to day-by-day fidelity. The Christian must make a prudent, restrained use of earthly goods. **13.** The third moralization, a saying from Q (Mt 6:24 par.), has nothing to do with the parable. It repeats the total dedication Jesus expects of his followers (Lk 9:23f.; 12:52f.; 14:26). The catchword "faith," related to the Hebr *'amēn*, unites the three short applications and occurs in each moralization in at least some derivation: *mammon*, from *'amēn*, a verb that can also mean "to believe" or "be faithful." (See J. A. Fitzmyer, *TS* 25 [1964] 23–42; a different explanation by D. R. Fletcher, *JBL* 82 [1963] 15–30; for vv. 9–13 see also A. Descamps, *NovT* 1 [1956] 47–53.)

121 **14–18.** Three independent sayings of Jesus (vv. 16–18) are here grouped together under the catchword "law." **14–15.** These introductory verses are connected with the preceding parable and its threefold application by the word "just," also a derivation of the Hebr *'amēn*. The Pharisees could quote from Dt 27–28 that wealth was God's reward to the just. As a rule, the Pharisees lived poor lives; their "wealth" or human security consisted in their meticulous "work" at keeping the Law. **16.** This saying has a completely different setting in Mt 11:12f., where it is part of Jesus' comments on John the Baptist. Luke sees three periods of salvation history: the Law and the Prophets, John the Baptist, and the Kingdom of God in the presence of Jesus. *forces his way in:* The last part of v. 16 is very difficult. The vb., *biazetai*, may be passive as in Mt 11:12, "Kingdom of heaven has been violently assaulted"; or better, it may be the Gk middle voice, "everyone forces his way in" (NEB). R. Schnackenburg suggests that God's eschatological acts in Jesus have unleashed a storm that "is forcing its way in" every area of human existence (*God's Rule and Kingdom* [N.Y., 1963] 129–32). **17.** The second saying (cf. Mt 5:18) states that the Law in its true spirit is completely fulfilled by and in Jesus. *tittle:* A slight brush of the pen to distinguish one Hebr letter from another. **18.** The final saying removes all specious reasons for divorce from the perfect fulfillment of the law of marriage. Lk, as opposed to Mk (10:11), does not record any qualifications (cf. Mt 5:32; 19:9; also see comments).

122 **19–31.** In this story of "The Rich Man and Lazarus," known only through Lk, Jesus is addressing "the Pharisees who were fond of money" (v. 14) and who thought to find justification in their own punctilious observance of the Law (11:37ff.). The rich man is similar in many respects to the "Dishonest Manager" (16:1–8a); both seem successful for a time, both are unaware of evil in mishandling "mammon." Similar stories existed in Egypt and among the rabbis; Jesus could easily have adapted this tradition to his own purpose (cf. references in J. M. Creed, *Luke*, 209–10; W. Grundmann, *Evangelium*, 325–26).

19. *clothed in expensive purple:* Woolen garments dyed with Tyrian purple. *linen:* Fine Egyptian undergarments (Ez 16:13; Ap 18:12). **20.** *Lazarus:* In Hebr, "Eliezer" (Gn 15:2). The only case in a parable where a name is assigned to a character; for this reason it is suspect. Was the name borrowed from Lazarus of Bethany who was at a banquet and whose resurrection from the dead failed to convince the Jewish leaders of Jesus' messiahship? (See Jn 11:1–44; 12:1–11.) Because the poor man is called Lazarus, we find that the rich man also was given a name in some mss. and versions: "Nineveh" (see J. A. Fitzmyer, *CBQ* 24 [1962] 175–77; H. J. Cadbury, *JBL* 81 [1962] 399–402; K. Grobel, *NTS* 10 [1963–64] 373–82). In the oldest text of Lk (P^{75}) it is written *Neuēs*. *a poor man:* Because every Jewish landowner was Yahweh's tenant (Lv 25:23), he owed "taxes" to Yahweh's representatives, the poor, and was thus expected to share the land with them in the form of alms (Mi 2:9; Is 58:7; Neh 5). **21.** *the dogs:* The owner's pets would eat the bread with which the guests wiped the plates or their hands and then tossed under the table; how Lazarus longed to have some of even that food! The rich man's sin consisted in his blind indifference to the agony of the poor. **22.** *Abraham's bosom:* The image is expressive of either the eschatological banquet (5:34) or of an intimate fellowship with Abraham (both known in rabbinical literature; see *ThDNT* 3, 825–26). **23.** *in Hades:* Hell, Sheol, abode of the dead. *Enoch* ch. 22 speaks of adjoining quarters for the evil and the good in this abode of the dead and seems to imply that they remain there till the judgment and general resurrection. This notion corresponds to the rabbinical teaching that after the apocalyptic battles of the messianic age, there would dawn the "age to come" (cf. W. D. Davies, *Torah in the Messianic Age* *and/or the Age to Come* [Phila., 1952]). **31.** This punch line not only emphasizes that knowledge of the Law is insufficient, for the Law must be kept with humble compunction, but also teaches that wondrous events, even resurrection from the dead, do not automatically save men (cf. J. Cantinat, *BiViChr* 48 [1962] 19–26).

123 (t) THREE SAYINGS AND A PARABLE (17:1–10). It is difficult to locate any catchword or motif that unites the three (or four) sayings and the parable of this section, unless it be the common themes stretching throughout Lk's Gospel: God's concern for the lowly, faith in the hidden presence of the kingdom, and man's need for redemption. **1–6.** These three sayings are found in different settings and sequence in Mk (9:42) and Mt (17:20; 18:6–7,15); the intricate interrelation of the Syn here is beyond the scope of this brief commentary. **1–2.** *cast into the sea:* Jesus states that it is better to die a violent death than to lead another into sin. *little ones:* This phrase has the same meaning as "the poor" or "lowly ones" (6:20); in Mt they are adults, for they "believe in me." **3–4.** Some commentators would make v. 3a a conclusion to the preceding logion, but as the beginning of a new logion, the words provide a handy connective: Not only take heed of others (the phrase is found again in Lk 12:1; 21:34; Acts 5:35; 20:28) so that you do not give scandal, but also look to yourself so that you forgive sin and scandal. **4.** *seven times:* Cf. Gn 4:24; 1 Cor 13:4f.,7. **5.** *increase our faith:* To the apostles' request for more faith, Jesus replies that it is the quality rather than the quantity of faith that needs revitalization. The nuance of the Gk verbs indicates that if you "would say...it would have already obeyed you," almost as though fulfillment anticipates faith. **7–10.** Addressed to the apostles (v. 5), this parable (only in Lk) warns Church leaders that they can never stop and rest in the belief that they have worked enough. Lk is the Gospel of total dedication (cf. 1 Cor 9:16). If the story is understood as spoken to the Pharisees of Jesus' lifetime or to Judeo-Christians of the early Church, then it echoes the Pauline doctrine on the insufficiency of human works and justification by faith. In this case, there might be an association with the preceding logion.

124 (u) THE TEN LEPERS (17:11–19). This narrative, only in Lk, is thematically linked with the preceding parable: One waves aside gratitude (v. 9), whereas the other inculcates it (v. 15ff.); the first and certainly the second section conclude with the necessity of faith. A number of scholars, following R. Bultmann, consider the episode of the ten lepers to be a mere parable, a Lucan construction based upon Mk 1:40–45 and 2 Kgs 5. As a parable does, this story ends with a statement rather than with the wonderment of the onlookers as a miracle story does. However, Luke has already recorded the Marcan text in 5:12–16 and is known not to repeat stories. It is possible, however, that in the process of oral transmission details of a parable passed over into a miracle story. This story along with 18:1–8 and 18:9–14 gives the dispositions for prayer: gratitude, perseverance, compunction (W. Grundmann, *Evangelium*, 335). **11.** *through the borderlands of Samaria and Galilee:* Lit., "through the middle of Samaria and Galilee." This phrase (*dia meson*) is very difficult to explain; if correct, this is the only place in the NT where *dia* governs the accusative in a local sense, "through." This is probably the reason why ms. D omits the *dia* (hardly correct); see Bl-Deb-F § 222. If the reading *dia meson* is correct, then it must mean that Jesus passed along the borders of the two provinces to go to the Jordan Valley and down to Jericho (18:35), whence he would make his way to Jerusalem (but see H. Conzelmann, *Theology of St. Luke*, 71–73). This verse is important for his thesis that Luke was poorly informed about Palestinian geography and that therefore his geographical references have a theological purpose. **12.** *stood afar off:* Cf. Lv 13:45–46; Nm 5:2. Misery so loves company that this group consists of both Jews and a Samaritan! See comment on 10:33. **14.** *to the priests:* See comment on 5:14. The Samaritan most probably would have gone to his own priests near Mt. Gerizim. **15.** *turned back:* The foreigner Naaman also returned to Elisha after his cure from leprosy (2 Kgs 5:15). **16.** *giving thanks:* The ptc. *eucharistōn*, in its OT background of *bērak* (bless), means the same as "give glory to God" (v. 18) by proclaiming God's redemptive acts in one's midst (see 22:19).

125 (v) THE KINGDOM OF GOD; THE DAYS OF THE SON OF MAN (17:20–37). Throughout Lk, Jesus has been denying that the Messianic age is realized simply by keeping the Law or following the Prophets, even the greatest of them, John the Baptist. Luke now faces the question. Where and how does one find the kingdom? **20.** *not with signs:* The answer must be considered in connection with 19:11; 21:7; and Acts 1:6. Practically the same reply occurs again in v. 23. Jesus' answer in vv. 20–21 would mean in the context of his own ministry that the kingdom is not entered by the Law nor is it to be identified with portents and wonders. In the period of apostolic preaching, the saying of Jesus was undoubtedly related to questions about the observance of the Mosaic Law by Christians. In the context of Lucan theology there is a further understanding: Because of 19:11 we must conclude that the kingdom, at least in its full external brilliance, will come only in the unpredictable future (→ Aspects NT Thought, 78:88). World history, for Luke, can be divided into: (1) one of preparation, climaxing in John the Baptist (16:16); (2) the presence of Jesus, whose life and words preach what is the kingdom; (3) the reign of the Spirit within the Church at the present time; (4) the future and full manifestation of the kingdom at the parousia. The first three periods manifest something of the kingdom. The same Spirit that led Jesus through the cross to glory is now being sent to the Church by the glorified Lord; the Church experiences the same journey through suffering and persecution to eventual glory. Luke writes, therefore, that in some way, the kingdom has been and always will be "within you." The unusual Gk phrase, *entos hymōn*, has been variously translated: "within you" (*Gospel According to Thomas*, Hippolytus, Origen, Athanasius, Ambrose, Jerome, Bede); "in your midst" (Ephraem, Cyril of Alexandria, Theophylact); or "within your grasp" (Tertullian, Cyprian). The same differences are found among modern interpreters. In any case, the kingdom is not merely the immanent presence of the Spirit; it has an external as well as an internal manifestation; the presence "within" must be determined according to the period of salvation history.

(Conzelmann, H., *Theology of St. Luke*, 113–25. Noack, B., *Das Gottesreich bei Lukas* [*SBU* 10; Copenhagen, 1948]. Schnackenburg, R., *God's Rule and Kingdom*, 134–37. Sneed, R., *CBQ* 24 [1962] 363–82. Strobel, A., *BZ* 7 [1963] 111–13.)

22–37. Lk expands upon the answer just given about the presence of the kingdom. These verses are another form of the eschatological discourse (cf. Mt 24), which Luke uses in the context of his Journey Narrative. Mt 24 and Mk 13 combine the parousia discourse with the account of the fall of Jerusalem, but Lk separates the two events. Luke, therefore, clearly indicates that the final kingdom did not definitively appear at the fall of the holy city; he adds, moreover, that it remains, so far as man is concerned, in the indefinite future. **22.** *one of the days of the Son of Man:* The plur., "days," is important to note. The great eschatological moment can no longer be imagined as one self-contained event. It extended through Jesus' earthly ministry and is still awaited as the Church relives the mysteries of transfiguration, cross, resurrection, and Pentecost. **23.** Statements about exact days for the parousia or about local appearances are not to be trusted (Ap. 6:10). **24.** *as lightning:* Suddenly, unmistakably, gloriously. **26–30.** *choked by the cares and riches and pleasures of life:* See 8:14; the poor will truly find happiness "because of the Son of Man" (6:20–23). Both Lot (Gn 18:16–19:28) and Noah (Gn 6:5–8; 7:6–24) witnessed great catastrophes and sorrow. **31.** Decisive, total dedication will be needed. The flat roof was used in the cool evening; it was reached by an outside stairway. **32.** *remember Lot's wife:* She hesitated and turned around (cf. Gn 19:26). **33.** Cf. 9:24. **34–35.** *one will be taken, the other left:* The day of the Son of Man will indiscriminately touch everyone: husband and wife, master and servant. **37.** Mt (24:28) gives this saying a more natural setting, it is placed after the equivalent of Lk 17:23–24. According to Mt, all will gather with Christ at the parousia. Lk makes it the conclusion, giving a last vague answer to the question of vv. 20–21: Do not seek definite, external signs.

126 (w) Two Parables on Prayer (18:1–14). Just as the preceding section took up the question, When and how will the kingdom come? so Luke continues the same questioning mood of the Church, insisting upon perseverance and humility. Jesus teaches by means of two parables found only in Lk. Luke prefaces each parable with his own introduction.

1–8a. The first parable (the "Dishonest Judge") begins with typical Pauline expressions: "pray always" (1 Thes 5:17; 2 Thes 1:11; Rom 1:10; 12:12; Eph 6:18); "do not lose heart" (2 Thes 3:13; 2 Cor 4:1,16; Gal 6:9; Eph 3:13). **3.** *kept coming:* Cf. Sir 35:10–15. *my adversary:* Probably a rich, influential man. The widow was too poor to bribe either the judge or his assistant; and these officials did not wish to alienate important citizens. **7a.** *hasten to rescue his elect who cry...day and night:* Cf. Ap 6:10. **7b.** *will he delay...:* A difficult clause to translate, much less explain: God delays. Is it out of a merciful patience, giving the wicked time to repent (2 Pt 3:9) and providing the elect with time to complete their renunciation and dedication? **8a.** *quickly:* The final parousia may be long in coming, but it will come surely, speedily, and in a completely unexpected way.

8b. This is an independent saying; no other parable ends with a question. *will he find faith:* The thought of 17:37 is continued in this verse: Can men sustain their confidence in God while they carry their crosses to the darkness of Calvary?

127 **9–14a.** This is the last of Luke's own parables (the "Pharisee and the Publican"). Although it prominently displays Luke's doctrinal emphasis (universal salvation, failure of the Law alone to sanctify, divine mercy), it reveals many idioms of Semitic Palestine (e.g., the omission of conjunctions). See J. Jeremias, *Parables*, 140. **9.** Luke's own introduction. *because they were just:* It is better to translate *hoti* "because" than simply "that." The Pharisees were completely "just" before the Law; that is why they had such confidence in themselves (2 Cor 1:9). **10.** *to pray:* Hours of prayer were 9:00 A.M. and 3:00 P.M. **11.** Because of its Aram background, J. Jeremias (*Parables*, 140) translates the verse thus: "He took up a prominent position and uttered this prayer." **12.** *fast twice a week:* Pharisees abstained even from water every Monday and Thursday. *tithes:* See Lk 11:42. **13.** *the sinner:* The publican identified himself as "the" special sinner (cf. Ps 51:3). **14a.** Conclusion to the parable. *justified:* One of Paul's favorite words, used here in a Semitic way not found in Paul. Paul's doctrine of justification finds its roots in this statement of Jesus. **14b.** This part of the verse is found elsewhere: in 14:11; in Mt 18:4 and 23:12. Each instance in Mt and Lk seems independent of the other.

128 **(B) Section Common with Mark's Gospel (18:15–19:28).** Without any abruptness, Luke returns to his Marcan source, which he had left at 9:50; he will carefully follow Mk until the Passion Narrative at ch. 22. Lk, however, omits a few episodes found in Mk: one that he would find distasteful, the ambition of James and John (Mk 10:35–45; cf. Lk 9:46–48); two others for which he had already given an equivalent, the curse of the fig tree (Mk 11:12–14,20–26; cf. Lk 13:6–9) and the anointing at Bethany (Mk 14:3–9; cf. Lk 7:36ff.).

(a) Children and the Kingdom (18:15–17). See Mk 10:13–16; Mt 19:13–15. The incident flows normally from the preceding section in Mk, which dealt with marriage and divorce (10:1–12). Luke has summarized that matter in 16:18. But we must admit that Luke has neatly stitched his parts together, for the blessing of the children not only follows a passage treating of humility, but it forcefully answers the question put to Jesus at 17:20: "when is the kingdom of God coming?"—when you become like these children! Luke edits from his Marcan source any mention of Jesus' anger and the comment that Jesus gathered the children into his arms—he rarely portrays Jesus showing human emotion.

129 (b) Danger of Riches (18:18–30). See Mk 10:17–31; Mt 19:16–30. To inherit eternal life in the kingdom demands a sloughing off of material possessions. The lesson is brought home in the answer Jesus gives to the ruler's question. **18.** *ruler:* Lk presents the "young man" (Mt 19:22) as a "ruler" (*archōn*); in Mk 10:17 he is designated simply by the Aramaism "one" (*heis*). *good Teacher:* The question in Lk follows that of Mk. **19.** *no one is good but God alone:* Jesus implies that the epithet "good," being proper to God, should not be used indiscriminately and casually. **20.** The three Evangelists differ in the order of the commandments. **22.** Lk omits that "Jesus fixed his eyes on him and loved him" (Mk 10:21). *sell all:* Lk adds "all," for this is the "Gospel of Absolute Renunciation" (→ 10 above). **24.** *how hard it is:* In Mk the man has already departed when Jesus speaks these words; Luke makes sure that they are addressed to the rich man himself. **25.** *camel...eye of needle:* See comment on Mt 19:24. **26.** *who can be saved:* The listeners are shocked at the radical view that Jesus has assumed. And his answer only confirms that view. **28.** *Peter said:* His boast elicits from Jesus a corrective statement. **29.** *or wife:* Added in the Lucan list of renunciations (see 14:26).

130 (c) Third Prediction of the Passion (18:31–34). See Mk 10:32–34; Mt 20:17–19; cf. 9:22,43b–45. **31.** *to Jerusalem:* The goal of his journey is now explicitly linked with his destiny. *written of the Son of Man by the prophets:* Cf. 24:25,27,44; Acts 3:18; 8:32–35; 13:27; 26:23 (for further allusion to prophetic prediction of his passion). But which prophets are meant is not indicated; Luke could not be troubled to specify. **32.** *delivered...mocked...:* The details are formulated from the postresurrectional standpoint, so that the prediction sounds like a *vaticinium ex eventu.* **34.** *they understood none of these things:* Luke's addition. He not only anticipates the desertion of the Twelve but also points to the necessity of the gift of the Spirit.

131 (d) Blind Man at Jericho (18:35–43). See Mk 10:46–52; Mt 20:29–34. Before this incident, Mark included the ambitious request of James and John; Luke can thus compare the spiritual blindness of the Twelve

(v. 34) with the physical blindness of the beggar at Jericho. By the miracle, Jesus shows that he can cure spiritual blindness as well. There are interesting differences in the Syn account of this miracle. Mt and Mk place the miracle after Jesus' departure from Jericho; Lk has it at Jesus' entrance into the city. Luke arranges to give one incident a setting within the city (19:1–10), and places another long account at the conclusion of Jesus' visit. Where Mt, the author of which delights in "twos" speaks of two blind men, Lk has only one. Mk also has only one, who is called Bartimaeus. Lk further rearranges the sequence of Mk and for the convenience of his Gentile readers omits not only the Hebr name of the man but also his exclamation, "Rabboni." Typically, he concludes the episode with the whole group praising God.

132 (e) Zacchaeus the Publican (19:1–10). Another wealthy man, perhaps unethical in some of his business practices, freely detaches himself of his goods; he does not refuse the opportunity from which the wealthy man in 18:18–30 turned away. Again, Zacchaeus exemplifies the practical piety of the publican in the parable of 18:9–14. This story, told only by Luke, shows many signs of Lucan composition: joy (v. 6); detachment (v. 8); universal salvation (v. 10); Jesus, the redeemer and friend of the sinful and the lost (v. 10); Jesus a guest at dinner (v. 5). Bultmann and others claim that Luke is rewriting and expanding one of the brief notices in Mk 2:14–17. What was said at 17:11ff. applies here; Lk has already given his version of the call of Levi (Lk 5:27–32). **1.** *Zacchaeus:* "The pure or innocent one" (cf. Ezr 2:9; Neh 7:14). **2.** This sentence has a strong Semitic flavor. **4.** *sycamore tree:* A short trunk and wide lateral branches make it easy to climb. **8.** Zacchaeus goes beyond the requirements of law in restitution (Ex 21:37; Nm 5:5–7). **9.** Although Jesus has already entered the house, he addresses his words to the crowd. Oriental custom allowed people to enter freely and gather at the edge of a banquet (7:37). Throughout Lk, as Jesus speaks to an individual, we sense a large group of disciples hovering in the background. *to this house:* The entire household shares Zacchaeus' blessing as they had earlier suffered from his unjust practices (Acts 10:2; 11:14; 16:15,31; 18:8). Here is an example of "corporate personality." *son of Abraham:* Thus typifying the Gentile believers (cf. Gal 3:9,29; Rom 4:11f.). **10.** See Ez 34:16 (cf. Lk 15:4–7).

133 (f) Parable of the Pounds (19:11–28). See Mt 25:14–30. A comparison with Mt makes it clear that Luke has combined two parables: one of the pounds (vv. 12–13 and 15b–26); the other of the acquiring of a kingdom, where allegorizing is much more evident (vv. 12, 14–15a, 27). There is overlapping in some verses. If details about the acquiring of a kingdom are lifted from Lk, we get an integral parable, very close to Mt. Luke has not only moved his parable away from the strongly eschatological context of Mt, but by adding the story of the nobleman who goes into a distant country to obtain the title of king, he situates the parable in the interim period of the Church: after the ascension but before the Second Coming. The "kingdom story" is heavily allegorized, reflecting many details about Jesus: departure from his land; rejected by his people; the latter's punishment and loss of privileges; kingdom's administration by disciples; its expansion; his eventual return. Lk, or Jesus, drew the details of the parable of the kingdom from an incident in the life of Archelaus, son of Herod the Great, who at the death of his father went to Rome to procure the title of king along with the domain of his father. A Jewish delegation promptly appeared before Caesar Augustus to protest. Rome refused the title of king and gave him control only over Judea and Samaria, till he was deposed in AD 6 (cf. Josephus, *Ant.* 17.11, 1 § 299–302). **12.** *went:* The Gk verb used here, *eporeuthē*, is often used by Luke (see 22:22) for Jesus' proceeding toward his destiny. **13.** *ten servants:* In Mt there are only three; note that vv. 16–25 refer to only three. *a pound each:* Lit., "a mina," a monetary unit of weight, in value about 30 dollars (1965). The master in Mt is far more generous, dividing his wealth: five talents (in silver over 1600 dollars) to one, two to another, and one to the third. The smaller sums in Lk suggest that the nobleman wants to see if his servants can be trusted with the much greater gifts of the future. **20.** *napkin:* In Lk the servant can hide the small sum in a napkin, but in Mt the unprofiting servant must dig a hole to bury his talent. **21.** *I was afraid of you, because you are a severe man:* This detail of the parable of the pound must not be allegorized; it is simply part of the story. **24.** *give it to him who has ten pounds:* See v. 17; he had earned ten pounds with his entrusted pound, and has been made the lord over ten cities. **26.** Luke has already used this saying in 8:18 (Mk 4:25; Mt 13:12 par.); its original setting has been lost. This parable appears in a modified form in the *Gospel of the Nazareans* (§ 18, as recorded in Eusebius, *Theophania* on Mt 25:14–15; see E. Hennecke, *NT Apocrypha*, 1, 149). Of the three servants one wastes the money on harlots, one increases it by trading, and one hides it and earns nothing; as a result one is accepted with joy, another rebuked, and one cast into prison. **28.** *he went on his way, going up to Jerusalem:* With this verse the Journey Narrative is complete; note how frequently Jerusalem is mentioned in this chapter (vv. 11, 28, 37, 41). See M. Zerwick, *Bib* 40 (1959) 654–74; P. Joüon, *RSR* 29 (1940) 489–94.

134 **(VI) The Jerusalem Ministry (19:29–21:38).** In Lk this section is almost as important as the preceding ones; the ministry even seems to be of long duration (19:47; 22:53). Attention is shifted from the emphasis in Mk and Mt on the final day, or parousia. Here in Lk Jesus is seen taking possession of Jerusalem, especially of the Temple, and cleansing it so that it might be a fitting place for his ministry. The antagonists, for the most part, are no longer the Pharisees, as in the preceding sections, but the scribes and the priests (compare Lk 20:20 with Mk 12:13). Luke is gradually developing the theological notion that the physical city and the material Temple are no longer the sacred places of God's presence: Jesus has taken over that prerogative and honor in himself. Luke relies principally on Mk 11:1–13:37.

135 **(A) Events at Jesus' Entry (19:29–48).** These include his Messianic entry, his lament over Jerusalem, and the cleansing of the Temple.

(a) Messianic Entry (19:29–40). See Mk 11:1–10; Mt 21:1–9; Jn 12:12–16. Mk is closest to the actual occasion; after the triumphal procession in Mk, Jesus silently looks around the Temple and withdraws with the Twelve to Bethany. Mt enhances the event with prophecies fulfilled, miracles worked, and the Temple cleansed. Lk develops the notion of a struggle within Jerusalem and its destruction. Jn stresses the royal prerogatives of Jesus and the Lord's glorification on Easter; the latter event enabled the disciples to understand his glorification on Palm Sunday. **29.** *at the mount:* Lk locates the great moments of Jesus' life on mountains: transfiguration (9:28); the Messianic triumph at this moment; ascension (24:50; Acts 1:12). *Bethany:* A village on the eastern slope of the Mt. of Olives about 2 mi. from Jerusalem. *Bethphage:* Another village situated toward the top of the mountain, 2673 ft. above sea level. **30.** *colt:* Its owner was probably a follower of Jesus. The ass was historically the mount of a prince who entered a town peacefully and joyfully: Gn 49:11 (rule of Judah over the twelve tribes); 1 Kgs 1:38 (Solomon's coronation); Zech 9:9 (the peaceful character of the messianic king). **35–36.** Regal honors (2 Kgs 9:13) are given to him, but Lk omits the cutting of palm branches. **37.** Lk adds the note of rejoicing and praising God. *miracles:* The cures witnessed up to this time in Lk. **38.** The first two lines are from Ps 118:26 (see 7:19 and comment on 13:35). This Ps was part of the Hallel (= Praise [Yahweh], Pss 113–118), sung on major feasts. Attention focuses upon the person of Jesus, as Lk modifies Mk's word "kingdom" to "king." Yet this king remains one of the *'anāwîm*, as in Zech 9:9. Lk thus suppresses the Marcan mention of the "kingdom of David." Lk also removes the Aram word *hosanna* (see comment on Mt 21:9). Gentile readers would not appreciate the foreign language! Lk then adds two lines from the Infancy Narrative (2:14), thereby drawing the angelic chorus into the song. **39–40.** These verses are only in Lk, although a similar passage is found in Mt 21:14–16. *some of the Pharisees:* It is difficult to know if they are friendly (cf. 13:31). Jesus answers them in the form of a prophecy. By silencing the disciples of Jesus, their persecutors will witness a still more resounding judgment that will come upon them in the destruction of the city and Temple. A somewhat similar statement occurs in the Babylonian Talmud, commenting on Hab 2:11, "Perhaps you will say, 'Who witnesses against me?' The stones and boards of a man's house witness against him" (*bHagigah* 16a).

136 (b) LAMENT OVER JERUSALEM (19:41–44). Suddenly the singing stops; Luke frequently writes with heavy contrast—Pharisee and publican [18:9–14]; rich man and Lazarus [16:19–31]; blessedness and woes [6:20–26]. This section is found only in Lk—though it bears resemblance to 13:34–35, which Lk shares with Mt 23:37–39. It need not have been a *vaticinium ex eventu* simply because Luke draws his imagery and language from Jer: vv. 41–46 (Jer 6:13f.); v. 43 (Jer 6:6); v. 44 (Jer 6:21,17); finally, v. 46 is a direct quotation from Jer 7:11 (cf. A. Hastings, *Prophet and Witness*, 116–20). **41.** *wept:* The Gk vb. *klaiō* registers great emotion: at departures (Acts 21:13); with deep, interior agitation (Phil 3:18; 1 Sm 1:7); because of shame and regret (Lk 7:38; Lam 1:16); in mourning for the dead (Mk 5:38f.; Lk 7:13,32); cf. *ThDNT* 3, 722–26. Seldom does Lk reveal such anguished emotion in Jesus. The occasion is Jesus' first glimpse of Jerusalem in Lk since the boyhood episode (2:41ff.). **42.** *that make for your peace:* This exclamation of Jesus stops abruptly—the sentence is incomplete, and the words are disjointed. The peace proclaimed by the disciples (v. 38) is not acceptable; yet peace shall come, but only through the most tragic sorrow and sternest detachment. It is ironic that the second part of the word "Jerusalem" (*šālēm*) means "peaceful" (cf. Heb 7:1f.). **44.** *children:* This word includes all the inhabitants, as in Ps 137:9. *not one stone upon another:* Hag 2:15 employs this expression to describe the building of the Temple; the prophet speaks of this Temple messianically (2:6–9).

137 (c) CLEANSING OF THE TEMPLE (19:45–48). See Mk 11:11,15–19; Mt 21:10–17; Jn 2:13–22. Meditation upon Mal 3:1–2 prepares us for what now follows, "And suddenly the Lord will come to the Temple.... But who will endure the day of his coming?" This OT text is certainly behind Jn 2:13–22 where the cleansing of the Temple is placed at the beginning of Jesus' ministry, right after the announcement of John the Baptist. The Syn place the episode during Holy Week, but each Evangelist does so for his own doctrinal purposes. Chronology is not their main interest: Mt and Lk record the event on Sunday, but in Mk it occurs on Monday. Lk, moreover, does not develop the eschatological significance of the cleansing of the Temple, as do Mk and Mt; Lk reserves that aspect for Acts 7 and the days of the Church. In Lk Jesus prepares the Temple for the place where he can teach (H. Conzelmann, *Theology of St. Luke*, 77–78). Gradually the notion of Temple becomes identified with Jesus himself. Luke again stresses prayer; he suppresses, so far as possible, any mention of acts of violence and villainy in the temple. If he is relying upon Mk, as seems to be the case, then it is difficult to explain why he omits the further quotation from Is 56:7, found in Mk: "house of prayer for all peoples." The final phrase would fit so neatly into Luke's theology of prayer and universal salvation.

138 **(B) Controversies in Jerusalem (20:1–21:4).** In this section Luke carefully follows the sequence and contents of Mk (11:27–12:44). These conflict stories may have happened earlier; they follow the pattern and at times even the style of the introductions (5:1,12; 6:1,6; 8:22) in the account of the early ministry. The connecting links between the sections are vague. By placing the episodes here, Luke intensifies the sense of hostility against Jesus from official Jewry.

(a) AUTHORITY OF JESUS (20:1–8). See Mk 11:27–33; Mt 21:23–27. **2.** *by what authority do you do these things:* In Lk the question refers to more than the fact that Jesus, an unordained rabii (Str-B 2, 647–61), was teaching in the Temple; it challenges his Messianic entry into Jerusalem, the acclamation by his disciples, and the cleansing of the Temple. **4.** Jesus was not attempting to evade the question by asking one himself. *John's baptism was from heaven:* If it were "from God," then one must accept John's recognition of Jesus as the promised One (7:18–30).

139 (b) PARABLE OF THE VINE DRESSERS (20:9–19). See Mk 12:1–12; Mt 21:33–46. In the OT the chosen people are frequently compared to a vineyard that God plants and then gives to the leaders to tend (the main source, Is 5:1–7; cf. Jer 2:21; Ez 15:1–6; 19:10–14). Luke slightly rewrites the story of the various delegations. Only the fourth, consisting of the owner's son, is killed. Lk states, contrary to Mk, that the son is first cast outside the vineyard before being slain (cf. Heb 13:12f.). Applied to Jesus, it means that Jesus' redemptive death is no longer within the narrow limits of Judaism but is meant for the universe. Judaism rejects Jesus, not vice versa. **13.** *What shall I do:* The soliloquy of the Heavenly Father is expanded in Lk; the Evangelist likes to present the interior reaction of people. **17.** *he looked on them:* A psychological detail, proper to Lk. Ps 118:22, cited here, is one of the most quoted OT texts in the NT (Acts 4:11; Rom 9:32f.; 1 Pt 2:6,8). It must have been part of an early Christian collection of *Testimonia*, and in its earliest form went back to Jesus himself. NT usage has also absorbed ideas from similar texts: Dn 2:35 and Is 28:16 (cf. F. F. Bruce, *The Book of Acts* [2nd ed.; London, 1952] 99–100). That which the Jewish leaders were rejecting was soon to become the foundation or keystone of the Church or the new people of God. **18.** *everyone who falls...:* Luke's own addition. Those who reject Jesus will suffer crushing defeat and total rejection; those who follow Jesus must undergo total renunciation and death as the only way to glory.

In the *Gospel According to Thomas* the parable ends with the death of the son. The differences between the various Gospels may very likely be due to endeavors of the early Church to adapt and apply the parable more pointedly to Jesus. In making further adaptations themselves, the Evangelists were simply following the pace already set within the early Church.

140 (c) Tribute to Caesar (20:20–26). See Mk 12:13–17; Mt 22:15–22. Luke is much more careful than Mark or Matthew to point out that Jesus was innocent of any crime against the state. **20.** *so watching for their opportunity:* This refers to the chief priests and scribes, the ones who would accuse Jesus before Pilate (23:1ff.); in Mk the questioners are "Pharisees and some of the Herodians," and in Mt "the Pharisees," but in Lk they are called "spies." They seek only to know what he considers is correct so that they might conform their conduct to it. **21.** *the way of God:* See Acts 18:26 (cf. in QL the same phrase in CD 20:18). **22.** *taxes to Caesar:* See comment on Mt 22:17. **24.** *show me a coin:* Mt 22:19 makes it the "tax coin," which gives more point to the debate. And the irony is that in producing it (i.e., having it in their possession) they themselves acknowledge the propriety of the taxation. **25.** *render to Caesar...:* Without prejudice to what is due to God, they must also render to the emperor what is his due. Jesus' answer has not directly replied to the initial question proposed, but has rather cut to the heart of the problem.

141 (d) Sadducees and the Resurrection (20:27–40). See Mk 12:18–27,34; Mt 22:23–33,46. A controversy now ensues with another group of Palestinian Jews (for the identity of the Sadducees, → Gospel Mt, 43:151). The special Lucan additions to this passage occur in vv. 35–36. **28.** *the brother of a man dies:* The question refers to the so-called levirate marriage (Dt 25:5–10; see comment on Mt 22:24). **34.** *the children of this world marry:* This phrase, when contrasted with "the sons of God" (v. 36) may be an allusion to Gn 6:1–4. **35.** *those worthy of a place in the age to come:* Such Christians will share the heavenly blessedness of freedom from "the cares and pleasures of life" (8:14). Renunciation of marriage for the sake of Jesus (14:26; 18:29) now appears more positively; the vocation contains the fullness of heavenly life, which has nothing more to desire. **36.** *neither shall they die any more:* As "sons of God" and "sons of the resurrection," they will be free; the risen life of Jesus brings them the life that makes them perpetually sons of God. **38.** *for all live to him:* This Lucan addition applies Jesus' ideas of the resurrected life to everyone alive right now within the Church. Christians, therefore, need not be overanxious about the parousia. We sense a kinship of ideas with Paul: cf. 2 Cor 5:1–10; Phil 1:20–23; Gal 2:19. Mk 12:28–34 (and Mt 22:34–40) now treats of the great commandment; in Lk this section served as an introduction to the parable of the good Samaritan (10:25–28).

142 (e) Son of David (20:41–44). See Mk 12:35–37a; Mt 22:41–46. Luke follows Mk verbatim except that he suppresses the mention of the scribes. Strangely enough, in view of his theology of the Spirit, he substitutes the title "Book of Psalms" for Mk's reference to "the Holy Spirit." Luke is probably clarifying a point for his Gentile readers (→ Gospel Mt, 43:153).

(f) Condemnation of the Scribes (20:45–47). See Mk 12:38–40; Mt 23:1–7. Luke has already recorded Jesus' condemnation of the Pharisees and scribes (11:37–54); he took this material from Q (Mt 23 par.). With only slight retouching, he now repeats Mk's condemnation of the scribes.

(g) The Widow's Mite (21:1–4). See Mk 12:41–44. Luke makes no more than his usual stylistic changes or abbreviations in Mk's account. In stating that Jesus looked up, Luke may be thinking of Jesus as seated in a teacher's chair (W. Grundmann, *Evangelium*, 377).

143 **(C) Discourse on the Fall of Jerusalem (21:5–38).** At times Luke copies Mk 13 verbatim and then suddenly drops, modifies, or expands this material, or else substitutes something else. Here is the Syn Problem compounded. At v. 12, Lk's style is very close to Mk's, and yet more bumbling. Some will argue that Luke, the NT stylist, must have had a different text before him than our present Mk. Otherwise, he would have surely incorporated here Mk's smoother style. Possibly, the "Little Apocalypse" of Mk 13 circulated as a separate unit, independently of the Second Gospel. T. W. Manson and V. Taylor attempt to explain Lk's divergences from Mk by reconstructing another source. They thus arrive at a proto-Lk document. H. Conzelmann, it seems convincingly, explains the differences as Luke's editorial work, undertaken for theological reasons. Luke insists that Christians must not expect to be given a proximate and definite date for the parousia. Despite the fall of Jerusalem and the destruction of the Temple in AD 70, even despite contemporary persecutions, they must still wait "until the times of the nations be fulfilled." Luke, therefore, removes almost all eschatological references from this discourse; he has already presented his discourse on the parousia (17:20–37), where he separates what Mt 24 and Mk 13 combine: the fall of Jerusalem and the parousia. The basic doctrinal teaching occurs in each section of Lk: Christians must adjust to a long period of waiting and persecution. In doing so, they are following the sorrowful way of the cross, taken by Jesus to arrive at glory.

144 **5–7.** See Mk 13:1–4; Mt 24:1–3 par. Luke deliberately changes the locale and audience. Mk presents Jesus "sitting on the Mount of Olives," opposite the Temple, "[with] Peter and James and John and Andrew [who] asked him privately," when his words about the destruction of the Temple would be fulfilled. Luke makes the entire discourse public; Jesus is speaking, as usual during this last period of his ministry, in the Temple. **7.** *these things will happen:* Mk's words are much more eschatological, "when the fulfillment of all this is at hand" (NEB).

(i) *The signs* (21:8–11). See Mk 13:5–8; Mt 24:4–8. Luke not only modifies the eschatological language of Mk, but he carefully points out at the beginning of the next section (v. 12) that the tumultuous anarchy among nations and the elemental upheavels in the cosmos lay beyond his own contemporary age. **8a.** We are reminded of 17:20f.,23. *the time is near:* Mk 1:15 speaks of "the [messianic] kingdom"; Lk uses the word *kairos*, a moment, definitely determined by God for salvation history—as was the fall of Jerusalem—but not necessarily the parousia. **9.** *first come to pass:* Lk adds the word "first," thereby indicating a period beyond that of international crises. Similar language occurs in Is 19:2; 2 Chr 15:6. **11.** Standard biblical expressions for great sorrows, to be understood symbolically: i.e., 2 Sam 24:13; Is 8:21; Jer 21:9; Ez 5:12. *pestilences:* This word is absent from Mk; it adds a stylistic flourish to "famines," perceptible only in Greek: *limoi kai loimoi.*

145 (ii) *Beginning of the troubles* (21:12–19). See Mk 13:9–13; Mt 24:9–14. Lk clearly points out that the parousia is still distant; persecution must come first, during which his disciples will be accused of heresy in the synagogues and of disloyalty before civil courts. **14.** *not to meditate beforehand:* Only use of this word in the NT, although a similar idea occurs in 12:11f. The Gk word *pro-meletaō* means to practice gestures or rehearse a dance; Christians are not to be stage actors. **15.** *a mouth and wisdom:* Lk 12:12 ascribes this inspiration to the Holy Spirit; Jn 16:13–15 enlarges on the same thought. **16–17.** An almost verbatim rendition of Mk 13:12. **18.** *will perish:* The future resurrection of the body sustains the martyrs; cf. Lk 12:7 (Mt 10:30 par.). **19.** Not only is this verse an echo of Lk 8:15, but the insistence upon "patience" (*hypomonē*, steadfast endurance amidst tribulation [AG 854]) resembles the Pauline epistles (Rom 2:7; 5:3; 8:25; 15:4f.).

146 (iii) *Jerusalem surrounded* (21:20–24). See Mk 13:14–20; Mt 24:15–22. Although vv. 20a, 21a, and 23a show word-for-word agreement with Mk, the rest is noticeably different. Luke modifies the references to the fall of Jerusalem, so that the event is no longer considered in the context of an eschatological or apocalyptic prophecy. **20.** *Jerusalem surrounded:* This verse begins verbatim with Mk but omits the mention of "the Abomination of Desolation," which Christians, according to Mk, can read about in the prophecy of Daniel (Dn 9:27; 12:11; 1 Mc 1:57). *its desolation:* The profanation of the Temple, in Luke's time, was no longer to be read about in prophecy; it was known to have taken place, without the parousia accompanying it. **23.** Luke drops what is in Mk: "and pray that it be not in the winter." The final siege of Jerusalem took place in the summer, from April to September. Luke also omits Mk's notice about the merciful shortening of the final sorrows, for wrath was "on this people." **24.** *until the times of the nations be fulfilled:* This detail is found only in Lk. Before the siege of Jerusalem, the Christians fled the city for refuge across the Jordan to Pella (Eusebius, *HE* 3.5, 3). This abandonment of their countrymen at such a tragic time forced the final break between Christianity and Judaism. *the times of the nations:* Again Lk uses the Gk word *kairos* (see comment on 21:8a). Luke transferred to ch. 17 the subsequent sections in Mk (13:21–23), strongly eschatological, about false Messiahs and the day of the Son of Man.

147 (iv) *The coming of the Son of Man* (21:25–28). See Mk 13:24–27; Mt 24:29–31. Luke takes up the idea of "signs" and cosmic upheavels from v. 11. By now he has made it clear that these eschatological details are not to be associated with the fall of Jerusalem nor with any contemporary or near future moment; but faith in the eschatological victory offers strong support to suffering, persecuted Christians of every age. The language here is deeply prophetic. **25–26.** Cf. Jer 4:23–26; Am 8:9; Mi 1:3f.; and especially Is 13:9f.; 34:4. **25b–26.** The psychological observations are proper to Lk. **27.** *coming upon a cloud:* Symbolical language from Dn 7:13f. **28b.** *your redemption is near:* The last part of this verse is found only in Lk. Only after the cosmic upheavels will the final achievement of Jesus' mission—world redemption—"be near." The Gk word for redemption, *apolytrōsis*, occurs only here in the Gospels; it is found seven times in Paul (Rom 3:24; 8:23; 1 Cor 1:30; Eph 1:7,14; 4:30; Col 1:14). Although the Gk word literally means "a buying back," it is rooted in the OT idea of redemption, God's powerful acts of liberating his chosen people in need.

148 (v) *The parable of the fig tree* (21:29–33). See Mk 13:28–32; Mt 24:32–35. An inclusion occurs here, uniting vv. 29–31. The conclusion of v. 28 stated that "redemption is near" (*eggizei*); v. 31 ends with another form of the same word, "the kingdom of God is near" (*eggys*). This short parable of the fig tree exemplifies and clarifies the meaning of v. 28. No tree of Palestine seems so dead during winter as the fig tree; but with the annual return of sap through the bare spiky twigs, the tree bursts with new life out of death (see J. Jeremias, *Parables*, 120). The figure fits neatly into Luke's theology. Only after Christianity has weathered the storms of winter and experienced the agony of apparent death (vv. 9–11,25–28) will "the kingdom be near." Jl 2:22 uses the image of the fig tree's blossoming to signify divine blessing. **30.** *you know by yourselves:* No one else needs to tell you that it is here or there (v. 8). **32f.** Luke drops the word "these" in the phrase "till all things have been accomplished," and thereby gives this logion a much more extensive meaning than Mk; it thus refers to the entire process of salvation history. **33.** According to Semitic idiom, Jesus was understood to say: "Even if the sky and earth...still my words."

149 **34–36.** In these verses Luke concludes the discourse with an exhortation to vigilance. They are written in Hellenistic style without parallelism. Bultmann notes that we have here "a quite late Hellenistic formulation with a terminology so characteristic and akin to Paul's that one could hazard a guess that Luke was here using a fragment from some lost epistle written by Paul or one of his disciples" (*HST* 119). For v. 34, see 1 Thes 5:1–3; for v. 34a, see 1 Thes 5:7; for v. 36, see 1 Thes 5:8–10,18. Even the rare Gk word *agrypneō* (be watchful) occurs. **36.** *praying at all times:* A typical Lucan idea. It is clear from this short section that Luke (different from 1 Thes) eliminated the idea of an immediate parousia. Sudden trials will strike everyone, and so there is need of continual vigilance. Everyone, however, will eventually take part in the parousia. How a person lives now, determines how he will "stand before the Son of Man." In these final public words of Jesus we hear some of his first words resounding again: cf. 6:20–23; 8:14; 9:23–27.

37–38. With these verses Luke ends the public ministry of Jesus; he is surrounded by a spirit of prayer, uniting him with his Father, and with a spirit of compassion, attracting all the people to himself. Because of the similarity of v. 38 with Jn 8:1f., it is sometimes thought that the whole section about the adulterous woman (Jn 7:53–8:11) was composed by Luke or is dependent on him. Indeed, it occurs here in the Freer family of minuscule mss.

150 **(VII) The Passion and Glorification of Jesus (22:1–24:53).** The longest single section of any Gospel is the Passion Narrative. This account seems also to have been the first to take definite shape within the early Church (see V. Taylor, *Formation of the Gospel Tradition*, 44–62). The first preaching of the apostles, as recorded in Acts, hurriedly passes over the passion and death of Jesus and even seems to apologize for such an humiliation (Acts 2:23f., 36; 3:13–15,17; 10:39; 13:28). Paul states how the death of Jesus was a stumbling block to both Jew and Gentile (1 Cor 1:17–2:16). Immediately after Jesus' resurrection, however, rumors began to spread, distorting the facts about Jesus' death (Mt 28:11–15). It was necessary to set the record straight; in this we uncover the initial impulse, governing the Passion Narrative of Mk. Gloom and sorrow shroud the verses of Mk's account, as Jesus walks to his death in loneliness. A comparison of Mk's description of the agony in the garden with that of Mt and Lk or with the arrest scene in Jn reveals a vast contrast in style and tone.

Another factor in the development of the Passion Narrative would have been the Eucharistic liturgy in which Christians "proclaimed the death of the Lord till he comes" (1 Cor 11:26). Liturgical services demanded solemnity, a profound sense of adoration, a stylizing of language. This tendency shows up in Mt's account of the passion. In Mt we are in the presence of a divine drama that ends with earthquakes and supernatural apparitions. Mt also reflects the Evangelist's curiosity of wanting to know more and more details about the last hours of Jesus. Biographical details and anecdotes about Judas or about Pilate and his wife are added. Catechetical needs are also met by Matthew, as he frequently matches prophecy and fulfillment.

In Luke's Gospel the reader is not so much invited to adore the person of Jesus who comports himself as the Son of God (Mt and Jn), nor to learn about him (Mt), nor again to look on at a distance in overwhelming sorrow (Mk), rather, the Evangelist invites the reader to be another Simon of Cyrene, taking a position next to Jesus and even carrying his very cross. In the weakness of Peter as well as in the hope of the good thief, the reader sees himself. Other themes and characteristics of the Lucan Passion Narrative will be noted in the commentary below.

The relation of Lk to the other Gospels deserves special attention here. Although Lk is not dependent upon the written form of Mt, some compenetration of Mt and Lk is admissible in the presynoptic stage. Yet there are notable omissions in the passion narratives of Mt and Lk: e.g., the hour-structure of the passion and the names of Simon of Cyrene's sons, Rufus and Alexander, found in Mk. There is also a more positive agreement of Mt and Lk against Mk: The reply of Jesus to Judas after the arrest is introduced by the same phrase, even if the content of the reply is different (Lk 22:47–48; Mt 26:47,50); the words addressed to Jesus by his mockers (Lk 22:64; Mt 26:68); the section on Peter's denials (Lk 22:62; Mt 26:75b). In the Passion Narrative, therefore, Luke moves away from what was his major written source throughout the Gospel.

Among the Syn Lk shows the greatest affinity to Jn's Passion Narrative. This relation, however, does not show up in mere words or phrases, but rather in ideas. If it were the former, we would expect Jn and Lk to agree in the declaration of Jesus' innocence, but such is not the case (Jn 18:38; 19:4; Lk 22:4,14,22). As in the case of Mt's Passion Narrative, Luke relied upon the early stages of the Johannine tradition. Luke, we might conclude, was influenced by a Johannine circle of traditions and doctrines.

The contact between Lk and Jn in the Passion Account can be listed in the following negative ways: no explicit naming of the garden as "Gethsemane" (Lk 22:39; Jn 18:1); no deliberation of the Sanhedrin during the night; no audition of witnesses; no explicit condemnation to death by the Sanhedrin (Lk 22:66–71; Jn 18:19–24); omission of the cry, "My God, why have you forsaken me?"; no rendezvous in Galilee after the resurrection. We can also cite positive accord between Lk and Jn: The attitude of the apostles at the announcement of Judas' betrayal (Lk 22:23; Jn 13:22); a farewell discourse (Lk 22:24–38; Jn 14–17); Jesus' custom of praying in the garden (Lk 22:39; Jn 18:2); the specification of Malchus' "right" ear (Lk 22:50; Jn 18:10); the triple declaration by Pilate of Jesus' innocence (Lk 23:4,14,22; Jn 18:38; 19:4,6).

(Fransen, I., *BiViChr* 25 [1959] 20–38. Léon-Dufour, X., "Passion (récits de la)," *VDBS* 6 [1960] 1419–92. Lohse, E., *Die Geschichte des Leidens und Sterbens Jesu Christi* [Gütersloh, 1964]. Osty, É., *RSR* 39 [1951] 146–54. Ramsey, A. M., *The Narratives of the Passion* [CST 1; London, 1962]. Schelkle, K. H., *Die Passion Jesu in der Verkündigung des Neuen Testaments* [Heidelberg, 1949]. Schniewind, J., *Die Parallelperikopen bei Lukas und Johannes* [2nd ed.; Hildesheim, 1958].)

151 **(A) The Paschal Meal (22:1–38).** It is difficult to decide whether or not Luke places the passion of Jesus in the setting of the Passover. The linking of the passion with the Passover (and the Eucharist) highlights its sacrificial aspect (cf. 9:12ff.). Lk, however, omits the reference to a specific number of days before Passover (found in Mk and Mt) and gives the reader the impression that Jesus stayed for a relatively long time in Jerusalem.

(a) The Conspiracy Against Jesus (22:1–6). See Mk 14:1–2,10–11; Mt 26:1–5,14–16; Jn 11:47–53. Judas, one of Jesus' own disciples, enters into a plot with certain leaders of Jerusalem to do away with Jesus. **1.** *feast of the Unleavened Bread, called Passover:* Mk is more accurate in separating what are really two feasts. The Passover occurred on 14 Nisan, at sunset after the slaughtering of the lambs; the Feast of Unleavened Bread began on 15 Nisan and lasted for a week (see Ex 12:6,15; Lv 23:5–9). Josephus, also writing for non-Jewish readers, identifies the two (see *Ant.* 3.10, 5 § 248). **2.** Lk omits the detail found in Mk and Mt, that the chief priests and scribes feared a tumult among the people. Because Luke delights in noting the allegiance of the people to Jesus, particularly in the Passion Narrative, it seems unlikely that he had Mk's text before him. In Mt and Mk there follows the banquet and anointing at Bethany (cf. Lk 7:36–50); in the Passion Narrative Luke wants to give special attention to an anointing after the death of Jesus, which prepares for his glorification (23:55f.). Jesus is to be comforted and strengthened for the sufferings ahead, not by a woman, but by an angel.

3–6. In narrating the story of the betrayal (Mk 14:10f.; Mt 26:14–16), Luke brings the history of Jesus around full circle. Satan had left Jesus at the beginning of the public ministry (4:13) but only "for a while." Satan now reappears and Luke transforms the Passion Narrative into a struggle against him. *Satan entered into Judas:* These words are very close to Jn 13:2,27; cf. 1 Cor 2:8, where Paul states that the diabolic rulers of this world crucified Jesus. Whereas Mt attributes Judas' action more to cupidity—Judas bargains with the chief priests (26:14)— Luke attributes the action to diabolical possession. The Christian must also carry his cross after Jesus and engage in active battle with Satan; for this reason Jesus leaves him the food of the Eucharist so that he might "continue with me in my trials" (*peirasmoi*, Lk 22:28,40—the same word used in 4:13). *Judas, surnamed Iscariot:* Cf. 6:14–16; Mt and Mk state that he was of the Twelve, but Lk calls him "one of the number of the Twelve," thereby implying that he was not of their spirit. **4.** *and captains:* Recruited from the Levites. The first captain was an important official, consulted on important arrests (Acts 4:1; 5:24). Luke does not tell us exactly how Judas betrayed Jesus. **6.** *without a disturbance:* Judas informed those interested where Jesus could be apprehended quietly at night; the crowd is also adroitly dissociated from the arrest of Jesus.

152 (b) Preparation for the Passover Meal (22:7–13). See Mk 14:12–16; Mt 26:17–19. **7.** *when Passover had to be sacrificed:* Or possibly, "when the Passover lamb had to be slaughtered," for *pascha* is used to designate the feast or the victim (see 1 Cor 5:7; Dt 16:2,6). Luke again points out the necessity of the passion by his use of *dei* (must); cf. 9:22; 13:33; 17:25; 24:7,26,44. He thus describes Jesus in the role of the Passover lamb. **8.** *sent Peter and John:* Only Luke names them. He will continue to draw attention to John (Acts 3:1,3; 4:13,19; 8:14), who seems to have been one of his principal sources for the Passion Narrative. **10.** *a man carrying a pitcher of water:* This task was ordinarily performed by women, who even today in the Near East carry home toward sundown clay jugs of water on their heads. There is a sense of prophecy in Jesus' words, similar to those uttered at his entry into Jerusalem (19:29–30). Conjectures and arbitrary interpretation of Acts 12:12 and Mk 14:50–52 have resulted in the identification of the man with John Mark, father of the evangelist Mark! **12.** *furnished:* With carpets, pillows, couches, and perhaps a low table. **13.** *they prepared:* By obtaining a lamb killed at the Temple and by purchasing herbs, wine, and unleavened bread (see Ex 12:1–27; cf. J. Jeremias, *EWJ* 41–84).

153 (c) The Passover Meal and the Eucharist (22:14–20). See Mk 14:22–25; Mt 26:26–29; 1 Cor

11:23–25. Luke combines here two traditions: one a farewell testament and the other a liturgy of the institution of the Eucharist. The tradition of the "farewell" comes from a Johannine circle that sought to understand the significance of what the Master did at his last supper with the Twelve. Jn 13–17 is the fullest expression of this tradition; Lk 22:14–15,24–30,35–38 comes next; and vestiges of it are still to be found in Mk 14:25; Mt 26:29. This tradition, however, must not be ascribed too quickly and solely to a Johannine church; Jesus probably did utter part of it at least. At the Passover meal it was the custom for the youngest boy to ask the head of the household four times "What does this mean?" about the meal, the lamb, the unleavened bread, and the bitter herbs (see Ex 12:26; 13:8,14). The father would answer in turn with the following texts of Scripture: Dt 26; Ex 13; 12:29; 1:14. John was the youngest at the Last Supper.

The other tradition, more liturgical and connected with the Eucharist, was passed down in two independent accounts (Mk and Mt—1 Cor and Lk).

A serious textual problem ensnarls the interpretation of this passage. The NT mss. tradition divides into a shorter text (represented mainly by D, the Western text, VL), a long text (represented mainly by P^{75}, B, S, A, C, W, Vg), and a mixed text (in the Old Syriac versions). The shorter text stops after the word "my body" in v. 19a and lacks v. 20 entirely. The long text includes vv. 19b and 20 (thereby including the mention of a second cup after the bread). The shorter text has been preferred since Westcott-Hort's edition of the Gk NT (and still is by many, including Fransen, Leaney, the NEB, RSV); however, lately there is a shift of opinion that tends to favor the long text, especially since the discovery of Papyrus Bodmer XIV; it is favored by Jeremias, Schürmann, Benoit, the BJ (see P. Benoit, *Exégèse et théologie* [Paris, 1961] 1, 163–203; J. A. Fitzmyer, *CBQ* 24 [1962] 177). However, arguments in favor of the shorter text can be summarized as follows: (1) Luke usually avoids mentioning the same incident twice; (2) there is no mention of the consecrated cup in the early scenes of Acts (2:46); (3) omission of the cup in the Emmaus scene (Lk 24:30–35); (4) Luke's habit of avoiding what will offend Gentile readers, such as the drinking of Christ's blood. Arguments, on the contrary, in favor of the long text seem stronger: (1) the overwhelming evidence of the mss. tradition; (2) the difficulty of accounting for the long text as a series of corrections or additions to the "genuine" shorter text; (3) the weakness of some of the arguments proposed for the latter: e.g., that Gentile readers would be any more offended than Jewish readers would be by the reference to drinking someone's blood; or that the long text is a liturgical elaboration of 1 Cor 11:24 and Mk 14:24 (an argument that is too hasty and facile for the complexity of the existing differences). However, it should be noted that nothing is lost from Christian doctrine if the shorter text is adopted here. The Christian Eucharist does not depend on a single Gospel text.

154 **14.** *the apostles:* This is the best reading (in mss. S, B, D, P^{75}); inferior mss. read either "the twelve apostles" (as in the Vg) or "the Twelve." **15–16.** These two verses are found only in Lk. *I have greatly desired:* Lit., "with desire have I desired," a Semitism most likely in imitation of septuagintal style, even though the use of the associative dative of a noun cognate to the verb is known in classical Greek too (see Bl-Deb-F § 198, 6). *I shall eat of it no more until:* A similar idea occurs in Mk 14:25 and Mt 26:29 after the words of institution over the bread and wine. Mark and Matthew thereby seem to refer Jesus' words to his Second Coming. But Luke transfers the sentences to a place before the words of institution. Thus each liturgical celebration of the Eucharist becomes a new manifestation of the glorious Lord. Up till now Luke has consistently presented the kingdom of Jesus as "within" (17:20–21), i.e., not yet fully manifested externally. The Lord has not yet returned in all his glory (19:11–28). The eschatological demands of the kingdom, however, are felt already within the Church because Jesus, having ascended to the right hand of the Father, with full regal power pours forth the Spirit within the Church (Acts 2:33–36). This Spirit is even now bringing the Church to glory, as it brought Jesus, through the agonizing struggles of the cross (Lk 9:23–27; 13:24). Luke makes important references to the kingdom, both in the Passion Narrative (22:69; 23:37–38,42) and in the Eucharistic account (22:14–15,29–30). The Eucharist, Luke seems to infer, expresses that moment when Jesus, now enthroned at the table of the heavenly kingdom, makes his presence most vitally experienced within the community; by this presence, with its overwhelming demands of charity and unity, he causes the Church to suffer greatly. The weak and sinful Church can sustain and be transformed by such a presence only through mortal struggle. The Eucharistic meal symbolizes the joy of the eschatological kingdom and thereby brings its realization ever closer, but at the same time it results from and induces even more suffering. Thus it "proclaims the death of the Lord till he comes" (1 Cor 11:26; see C. Stuhlmueller, *ProcCTSA* 18 [1963] 47–76).

155 **17.** *having taken a cup:* A cup will be mentioned again, in v. 20 of the long text, and each time it is given a Eucharistic significance. The words, "took, gave thanks, said, take, share," are reserved to the Eucharist (see 9:12–17). The first cup, followed by the mention of a second, may be due to the passing of three cups of wine at the Jewish Passover meal in the time of Christ. The first ritual cup followed the opening blessing (the *Qiddûš*); the second cup came after the *haggādāh* ("Passover Story") and the singing of the first part of the Hallel (Pss 113–14; see 19:38). Then the head of the household took a piece of unleavened bread in his hands and pronounced the Passover blessing; he broke it and distributed it to each one present. At this solemn moment Jesus must have consecrated the bread (v. 19). After the main course was served, including the Passover lamb, a third cup of wine was drunk, called the "cup of blessing" (1 Cor 10:16). The head of the gathering raised a cup with his right hand and pronounced the Passover thanksgiving. It must have been this cup that Jesus consecrated. Then followed the second part of the Hallel (Pss 115–118).

19. *this is my body:* In Aramaic the copula ("is") would have been omitted: *den biśrî*, "this my body" (see Jeremias, *EWJ* 201). Throughout his Gospel, but particularly here in the Eucharistic account (see 22:14–18), Luke writes simultaneously of the Church-life and the Jesus-life. This fact, along with the close resemblance of his Eucharistic account to the Pauline tradition (1 Cor 11:23–26), makes us see an identification between the Eucharistic body of Jesus and the Church-body. Paul mysteriously identifies the two in the one Lord Jesus (1 Cor 10:17; 11:24–25; 12:12,27). Just as Jesus is truly within the Church, so he must be truly within the Eucharist. Furthermore, what the Eucharist symbolizes of eschatological peace it gradually but effectively achieves. *my body given for you..., my blood shed for you:* In both instances the participles ("given" and "shed") are present; but since use of the fut. participle was on the wane in NT Greek, and the pres. participle often had a future nuance (see *GrBib* § 207–8), it is not impossible that these participles are to be so understood here: "will be given" and "will be shed." The present would have special meaning when the words are repeated in the Church's Eucharistic ceremony; but the future would rather reflect a reference in Jesus' words to his death on the morrow. Finally, if "my body... my blood" include the Church in some way, then the words "for you" indicate the intercessory power of the Church's prayer and suffering as these continue with his body, the Church (Acts 2:42; 4:31; 6:4; 12:12).

156 *do this in remembrance of me:* This instruction is not found in Mk and Mt but is repeated again over the cup in 1 Cor 11:23–25. The words are primarily a rubric, but a subtle theology lies behind them, especially when they are read against the background of other prayers at the Jewish Passover. We are told in the Bible that the Passover was to be celebrated as *l^ezikkārôn*, "as a remembrance" (from the Hebr *zākar*, "to remember" [Ex 12:14; 13:9; Dt 16:3]). In the *Qiddûš* prayer, God is praised as the one who gives his people festal seasons for joy and *l^ezikkārôn*." In Ps 111:4 Israel chanted that God makes "his wonderful works to be remembered." One of its doxologies reads: "Praise to you, O Lord, who remembers the covenant." In all these examples, it is God, not his people, who is said to remember and by doing so to repeat the great acts of redemption. God's remembering makes it possible for the people to experience and thus remember the great moments of the passion-glorification. God's remembering, like his words and symbolic actions, amounts to something much more than mere recollection; he effects what he recalls. **20.** *the new covenant in my blood:* The Passover is associated with the sacrifice of the covenant (see Ex 24:3–8; Heb 9:18–22). The blood was not offered to God in the covenant sacrifice (it never was in the OT), but rather was sprinkled on the twelve pillars (representative of God) and on the people. Because blood is life (Lv 17:11; cf. Gn 9:4) and the flow of blood unites in one life, Jesus' blood symbolizes and effects a forceful union between God and his people.

(Benoit, P., *Exégèse*, 1, 163–261. Betz, J., *Die Eucharistie* [Freiburg, 1955]. Cullmann, O., and F. J. Leenhardt, *Essays on the Lord's Supper* [Richmond, Va., 1958]. Dahl, N. A., *ST* 1 [1947] 69–95. Delorme, J. [ed.], *The Eucharist in the NT* [Baltimore, 1964]. Dupont, J., *NRT* 80 [1958] 1025–41. Kilmartin, E. J., *The Eucharist in the Primitive Church* [Englewood Cliffs, N.J., 1965] 167–70. Lietzmann, H., *Mass and Lord's Supper* [Leiden, 1953]. *Proc. First Precious Blood Study Week* [Rensselaer, Ind., 1959] 33–64; 2 [1962] 11–35. Schürmann, H. *Der Abendmahlsbericht Lucas 22, 7–38 als Gottesdienstordnung, Gemeindeordnung, Lebensordnung* [Paderborn, 1957]. Thurian, M., *The Eucharistic Memorial* [2 parts; London, 1960–61].)

157 (d) The Betrayer (22:21–23). See Mk 14:18–21; Mt 26:21–25; Jn 13:21–30. Mk and Mt place the prediction of the treachery of Judas before the account of the institution of the Eucharist. Luke uses this sorrowful announcement of Jesus not only as a means to continue the farewell discourse (v. 14f.) but also as a subtle warning to the Christian community. The Eucharist is no absolute guarantee against the possibility of a serious betrayal and flagrant violation of trust. Every sin is like Judas', in that in effect it uses the hand that is with Christ on the table to strike against him. Verses 21–22 are closely interlocked by the particle *gar* (because); Judas' betrayal is explained not just by the latter's deliberate wickedness but also by the Father's determination. **22.** *as has been determined:* The word *hōrismenon*, a favorite Lucan term (Acts 2:23; 10:42; 11:29; 17:26,31), is a pf. pass. participle; what has been done (by Judas) remains an abiding effect of what God had determined in the plan of salvation. Lk leaves out the harsh words of Mk: "better for that man if he had not been born." **23.** Cf. Jn 13:22.

158 (e) Dispute over Rank (22:24–30). See Jn 13:1–20; Mk 10:41–45; Mt 19:28; 20:25–28). The first part of this section (vv. 24–27) seems to report Jesus' reply to an argument among the apostles, triggered by a request of the sons of Zebedee, James and John, to sit at Jesus' right and left hand in the kingdom. Luke deliberately struck out any mention of this rivalry where it should have stood, namely between 18:34 and 18:35. However he seldom incorporates such an incident later, once he has rejected it (except Lk 8:19–21, relying upon Mk 31–35). A similar logion of Jesus, that the least is the greatest, occurs at Lk 9:48 (Mk 9:35; Mt 18:4 par.). It seems, therefore, that Luke might be depending upon a separate third tradition (H. Schürmann, *Jesu Abschiedsrede* [Paderborn, 1957] 63–99). **25.** *are called benefactors:* The Gk vb. *kalountai*, if considered as the middle instead of the passive form, can be translated: "allow themselves to be called" *Euergetēs*. The latter term is a Gk transposition of the Lat word "benefactor," a title assumed by several Syrian kings. For Syrian readers there is a sting of irony in these words. **27a.** *who reclines at table:* This phrase probably prompted Luke to place the logion here at the Last Supper; it may also account for the position of the following saying, which could have been spoken on a different occasion. **28–30.** All commentators recognize the very archaic character of this logion, echoing the sound of Jesus' speech quite distinctly. Luke probably introduced v. 28 because of the theme of quarrels "at table." Up till now, Jesus has borne the full brunt of opposition and shielded his disciples from trouble. Because the apostles share in Jesus' mission, which reaches glory only through the cross, and because all Christians are strengthened by Jesus' royal presence in the Eucharist, they must now face trials (see 11:4). **28.** *having continued:* The use of the pf. tense of the Gk vb. *memenēkotes*, informs the apostles that the condition of this moment of trial persists for a long time. **29.** *appointed:* Lit., "disposed," the Gk root being the same as that from which *diathēkē* (covenant) is derived. Jesus implies: We have been covenanted together in a kingdom—the same kingdom with which I am covenanted with the Father. **30.** *judging the twelve tribes:* "Judge" is to be understood in the sense of the OT judges, men chosen by God and endowed with a charism, either to vindicate God's rights, compromised by sin, or to take an active role in proclaiming that God's promises of salvation are fulfilled. "Twelve tribes" symbolizes the new Israel, the Christian community (Ap 7:4–8; 21:12).

159 (f) Peter's Denials Predicted (22:31–34). See Jn 13:36–38; Mk 14:27–31; Mt 26:31–35. Mk and Mt locate this announcement of Jesus after he has left the upper room and is walking with his disciples to Gethsemane. In Lk and Jn, instead, it happens at the supper table. In Lk, the episode continues the theme of trials (v. 28) and has some implications for the Eucharistic celebration. The intimacy of the dinner table casts deeper shadows of shame and guilt about Peter's denials; Jesus' anticipated forgiveness lays down a basic condition how Christians are to approach the table. **31.** *desired:* The Gk vb. *exētēsato* implies "desired of me." According to A. Plummer (*Luke*, 503), the aorist of the compound verb indicates success in the petition; Satan obtained Peter from the Lord. *to sift as wheat:* By violent agitation. God permitted this severe temptation, as he placed Job in the hands of Satan (Jb 1:12; 2:6). **32.** *your faith may not fail:* Faith is to be taken in the biblical sense of loyal attachment to Jesus through trust, love, and confidence. That kind of faith in Jesus never collapsed. *strengthen your brethren:* Matthew has placed this promise to Peter of leadership in the group of the Twelve at an earlier juncture (Mt 16:18–20). Each Evangelist disregards chronology and rearranges events for the sake of theological nuances. Peter, in a sense the greatest among the brethren, becomes the least experientially, so as to know how to lead them by being one with them (v. 26). **34.** *cock will not crow:* The third Roman watch extended from midnight to 3:00 A.M., "cockcrow" can be a semi-official way of referring to 3:00 A.M. Mk states that Peter will deny Jesus thrice before the cock crows "twice." On this unforgettable night in Peter's memory, a cock was heard to crow before this hour.

160 (g) THE HOUR OF COMBAT (22:35–38). It is difficult to trace the origin of these words, found only in Lk. What was stated in v. 28 is given additional force; in that long, indefinite time between Jesus passion-ascension and his parousia, the Church will face much opposition. **35.** This verse seems to be a definite reference to Jesus' instruction to the 72 disciples in 10:4 (see also 9:1–11). **36.** Practically all commentators take the reference to purse, wallet, and sword figuratively. The disciples must be ready for any and every circumstance (see v. 28). Perhaps these words stem from a departure ceremony for missionaries in the early Church (cf. Acts 13:1–30; H. Schürmann, *Der Abendmahlsbericht* [Paderborn, 1957] 60–69). **37.** *was reckoned with the lawless:* Jesus refers to himself as the Suffering (not military) Servant as poignantly portrayed in the Servant Songs (Is 53:12). The quotation is introduced by the Gk particle, *gar*, which links what follows with what preceded, thereby associating Jesus and the disciples in common suffering and trial. **38.** Luke skillfully delineates the contrast between Jesus and the disciples and also sets up a contrast between this verse and the preceding one: "But they said... but he said on the contrary...." *two swords:* The disciples understand Jesus literally and fail to grasp the hidden depth of meaning in Jesus' figurative language about opposition from others and service to them within the long period before the parousia. *enough:* That is, "enough of this!" (a formula of dismissal in Dt 3:26 [LXX]); it seems that Jesus speaks the word with a sigh of sadness, almost of failure.

161 **(B) The Passion, Death, and Burial (22:39–23:56).** Jesus' teaching, especially at the supper table, was to remain wrapped in mystery until the disciples saw that he lived it completely in his death and glorification. But these final acts of Jesus' life surrounded his words with even more mystery until he sent the Spirit to enable them to live through the same mystery.

(a) AGONY IN THE GARDEN (22:39–46). See Mk 14:32–42; Mt 26:36–46; Jn 12:27; 18:1. Luke removes much of the tragic, oppressive gloom found in Mk in order to focus more attention upon the violent opposition the apostles (and the Church) are to face. In Lk Jesus does not come to the apostles three times for comfort, begging them to keep watch with him, nor at the end of the Lucan episode is it said that the apostles abandoned him completely. Lk pictures Jesus on his knees in prayer, not prostrate on the earth. Nor is it said that sorrow alone has reduced Jesus to the point of death. Lk's account is more reflective, with a recommendation that the apostles continue in prayer during their long period of trial; Mk and Mt look upon prayer as Jesus' means of preparing himself to accept the violent eschatological battle immediately at hand. Finally, Jn transfers the entire scene to an earlier moment when Jesus prays for his glorification, i.e., for the wondrous fulfillment of world redemption and thus the glorious revelation of God's love (Jn 12:23–33). A still more theological explanation of the agony in the garden is given in Heb 5:7–9.

162 **39.** *according to his custom:* By these words, found only in Lk, the Evangelist not only implies that Jesus was frequently at prayer (a theme of his Gospel; see comment on 3:21) but also that Jesus did not come to the garden simply to escape his enemies. The owner of the garden must have been a friend of Jesus to allow this frequent access. *Mount of Olives:* Separated from the "mount" of Jerusalem by the Kidron Valley; the garden has been traditionally located at the base of the Mt. of Olives, immediately to the E of the Kidron Valley. Lk omits the Semitic name, Gethsemane ("oil press," from *gat–šᵉmānê*; or "oil valley" from *gê' šᵉmānê* [Jerome]). **40.** *pray, that you may not enter into [succumb to] temptation:* See v. 28. Mk 14:34 reports Jesus' other words, "wait here and watch"—to watch for the return of the Lord is much more eschatological (cf. 1 Thes 5:6). Mk also includes a strong desire on Jesus' part that the disciples watch in his company and so console him. **42.** *Father,... remove this cup:* Lk omits the Aram word, *'abbā* (cf. 11:2). In the OT, "cup" symbolizes the anger of God against those who block or oppose his plans of salvation for his people (Jer 25:15; Is 51:17f.). In Jn 18:11 and Mk 10:38 "cup" seems to take on a more general meaning of a fearsome and most difficult task. Both ideas may be combined here; in the Bible the sorrowful effects of sin, which Jesus is enduring, are the means of purification and redemption. **43–44.** These two verses are missing in the most important mss. (P^{75}, B, S^c, A, W, T) and many patristic writers noted their absence (see J. A. Fitzmyer, *CBQ* 24 [1962] 177–79). It is much easier to explain their omission than their addition. The lines constitute a problem for anyone "defending" the divinity of Jesus. The angel strengthens Jesus, perhaps by reminding him of the full effects of his passion–glorification; and in the agony of what lay ahead (cf. 13:24), Jesus steeped his thoughts and desires in those of the Father and there found acceptance. *sweat like heavy drops of blood:* His sweat, which became noticeable after the ordeal was over, resembled drops of blood. **45.** *for sorrow:* Luke excuses the sleeping of the apostles, for he attributes it to the overwhelming sorrow of this occasion (the use of the Gk article indicates this nuance). He also suppresses the embarrassing fact that Jesus thrice found the apostles asleep.

163 (b) THE ARREST (22:47–53). See Jn 18:3–11; Mk 14:43–52; Mt 26:47–56. Luke never states explicitly that Judas kissed Jesus, an Oriental form of greeting. Furthermore, he has omitted any mention of a pre-arranged sign between Judas and the soldiers with him; one has the impression that Jesus intervened before Judas actually kissed him. **49.** This passage is found only in Lk (see v. 38). **50.** *one of them:* Jn 18:10 identifies the assailant as Peter. **51.** *no more of this:* Jesus' reply, as given here in Greek, can mean (1) "Let events take their course—even to my arrest" (Creed), (2) when the phrases are interrupted "Let everything alone! Enough!, or (3) when these words are connected with the following sentence "Wait! Let me do this—touching the man's ear, he cured him." Only Lk records this miracle of great sympathy. **52–53.** Luke introduces this reply of Jesus with artistic mastery, but in Mt it begins more majestically, "In that hour...." *the chief priests, captains, and elders:* So Luke identifies the crowd; Mk and Mt state that the crowd was sent by them. In Lk's Passion Narrative, the crowd is almost always friendly to Jesus, and the Jewish leaders bear the responsibility of Jesus' sufferings and death. **53.** *daily:* Again Lk lengthens the time of the Jerusalem ministry. *your hour and the power of darkness:* Cf. 22:3; Jn 13:1–3; 1 Cor 2:8. Jn 18:4–11 dramatically brings out the confrontation between light and darkness in the scene of arrest.

164 (c) PETER'S DENIALS (22:54–62). See Jn 18:12–18,25–27; Mk 14:53f.,66–72; Mt 26:57–75). Peter loyally followed Jesus; the other disciples, except John, had vanished. Now Peter was trying to lose himself in a group gathered around a fire in the open courtyard. This courtyard, surrounded by rooms of the house, was accessible from the street by a vestibule. In Lk three different persons accuse Peter, whereas in Mk the maid speaks twice and the bystanders once. Luke politely says nothing about Peter's cursing and swearing and replying with an oath. Only in Lk, however, we find recorded that memorable detail that "the Lord turned and looked at Peter" (cf. Mk 10:21).

165 (d) The Mockery (22:63–65). See Jn 18:22f.; Mk 14:65; Mt 26:67f. Luke passes over the fact that Jesus was mocked by the dignified members of the Sanhedrin lest the indignity to Jesus seem all the worse. He also suppresses the notice that they spat on Jesus and struck his face; all these outrages are grouped together under "many other things."

166 (e) Trial Before the Sanhedrin (22:66–23:1). See Mk 14:53–64?; 15:1; Mt 26:57–66?; 27:1f.; Jn 18:12–14,19–24?,28). We encounter one of the major problems in the history of the passion, the interrelation of the Gospels in the trial scenes (cf. P. Benoit, *Exégèse*, 1, 265–359). Mt places the trial and inquiry at night in the house of Caiaphas; Lk, in the morning before the Sanhedrin. In Lk the morning session is all-important, Mt and Mk dispatch it quickly, and Jn does not speak of it at all. Jn has Jesus brought first to the house of Annas, where an inquiry takes place at night; Jn mentions Jesus being taken to Caiaphas' house (18:28). Lk has no night sessions before Annas or Caiaphas. Luke, according to his habit, groups various scenes. He also omits all reference to witnesses. Not only have the authorities already reached a decision that Jesus must die (22:2), but Jesus' death was also determined by the heavenly Father (22:22). Mt and Mk give more attention to the trial before the Sanhedrin, whereas Lk and Jn emphasize the process before Pilate. Another crucial problem arises here: Did the Sanhedrin possess the *ius gladii*, the power of capital punishment? (See Jn 18:31; J. Blinzler, *The Trial of Jesus* [Westminster, 1949] 157–63; P. Winter, *On the Trial of Jesus* [StJud 1; Berlin, 1961].)

66. *elders, priests, scribes:* These three groups, together with the high priest, constituted the 71 members of the Sanhedrin, which was permitted under the Romans to control religious matters. "Sanhedrin" is an Aramaicized form of the Gk noun *synedrion* ("council" [= syn, "with" and *hedrion*, "little seat"]). *the Christ:* The Messiah (cf. 9:20). This title stresses the fulfillment of OT promises. Mt adds here, "the son of God"; and Mk, "the son of the Blessed One." But Lk reserves this title for the climax of the series (v. 70). **67b–68.** Only in Lk; for Gentile readers the words underline the innocence of Jesus. In his reply Jesus swings the discussion into a different direction. The phrase, "or let me go," found in some inferior mss., is best omitted. **69.** *from now on...:* Luke carefully edits this reply of Jesus, known through tradition. He leaves out the statement that "you will see"; the vision of the Son of Man coming upon the clouds is reserved for the martyrs or confessors of the faith (Acts 7:56). Luke deletes another phrase from Dn 7:13, "coming upon the clouds," which leads the discussion into the eschatological moment of the parousia (21:27). That wondrous event remains in the distant future; Luke confines Jesus' pronouncement to that long, enduring time of the Church when Jesus is "seated at the right hand" (Ps 110:1). This expression is a favorite one of Acts (2:33f.; 7:55); it portrays Jesus in glory, sending the Spirit upon the Church. Jesus has consistently linked his role of Son of Man with the necessity of suffering (Lk 9:22,44; 18:31, 32); such was the way Jesus arrived at glory. **70.** *you are therefore the Son of God?* The conj. "therefore," only in Lk, closely connects the titles given to Jesus—Messiah, Son of Man, Son of God—as though this last one contains all others in a supereminent way. The Sanhedrin meant no more by this title than it signified in the OT—the specially chosen one, particularly the Davidic king, through whom God's promises to the nation would reach fulfillment (2 Sm 7:14; Ps 2:7). In the Sanhedrin's eyes, that Jesus should claim such a privilege insulted God; for this humiliated, rejected man to presume to reveal and mediate the Lord's glory to Israel was a supreme irreverence to God. Lk, however, reflects more than the thinking of the Sanhedrin; the Evangelist is writing for the Church, and so he places in climactic position the assertion that the one being rejected by Jewish leaders is none other than the one whom the Church worships as God's divine Son.

167 (f) Jesus Before Pilate (23:2–7). See Mk 15:2–5; Mt 27:11–14. At this point Mt records what happened to Judas (27:3–10). **2.** This verse is proper to Lk. Coming so close to the charges preferred against Jesus in the Sanhedrin, it underscores the deceit of the Jewish leaders. Their charge of crimes against the state makes Pilate's triple declaration of Jesus' innocence all the more significant before the Gentile world of Luke's time. *claiming to be a Messiah, a king:* The leaders clarify the meaning of Messiah for Pilate; there had been enough of messianic military claimants for Pilate to understand what they meant (Acts 5:35–37). Readers of Lk would remember Jesus' brilliant reply in 20:25. **3.** *you have said so:* Pilate must have understood Jesus' answer (which can possibly be translated, "'King' is your word") as a denial; Jesus was certainly not the kind of messiah or king that Pilate imagined. **4.** *I find no case:* This was a legal sentence of Roman jurisprudence, officially declaring a case ended for want of sufficient evidence. **5.** *but they grew stronger and louder in saying:* Thus we might translate the opening phrase. This entire section, vv. 4–16, is found only in Lk. **7.** Luke not only seems to have had a special source of information about Herod Antipas (Acts 13:1; Lk 8:3), but he also gives Herod a prominent place in each section of his Gospel (3:19; 9:7–9; 13:31–35). *he sent him up to Herod:* The phrase implies that Pilate recognized Herod as a higher court of appeal (Zerwick, *Analysis* 204).

168 (g) Jesus Before Herod (23:8–12). Some, among them M. Dibelius (*ZNW* 16 [1915] 113ff.), have claimed that this section, found only in Lk, was fabricated from such notices as Lk 9:7–9 and Acts 4:27 [with Ps 2:1]. Others, including R. Bultmann, have stated that Luke found the "legend" already in existence (*HST* 273). Luke, however, may have rearranged the chronology and may have disregarded Palestinian geography for the thematic development of his theology; still, he claims to rely upon eye witnesses and reliable sources; he even hints at his source for the Herod material (Acts 13:1; Lk 8:3). **8.** *desiring for a long time to see Jesus:* See 9:7–9. **10.** Lk omits the mockery by the Roman guard and speaks only of the ridicule made of Jesus by the Jews (22:63–65) and by Herod. A glistening white robe was worn by royalty, especially on state occasions. Mk 15:17 describes a purple robe placed on Jesus by the Roman soldiers. *sent him back to Pilate:* As though to Herod's higher court of appeal (cf. v. 7).

169 (h) Jesus Again Before Pilate (23:13–25). See Jn 18:38b–19:15; Mk 15:6–15; Mt 27:15–26. The opening vv. 13–16, only in Lk, line up the entire Jewish nation: **13.** *chief priests, rulers, and people:* It becomes clear that they, not Pilate, wanted the death of Jesus. **14.** Pilate a second time declares Jesus' innocence. **15.** *he sent him back to us:* This is the preferred reading (mss. S, B, Θ); that found in mss. A, D, W, and the Koine tradition, "I sent you to him," is inferior. **16.** *I will chastise him and free him:* Luke deliberately avoids speaking explicitly of scourging, that extremely cruel punishment in which a man was beaten with strips of leather, tipped with knots or bits of metal. He uses a Gk word, very close to that in Is 53:5 (LXX), "the chastisement of our welfare." Mk places the punishment after Jesus' final condemnation—where Roman custom called for it—as the preliminary act to crucifixion. For Luke and John it was an expedient taken by Pilate to appease the mob and hopefully save himself the necessity of condemning Jesus to death. **17.** This verse, missing in mss. P^{75}, A, B, and L, is usually rejected as an explicatory gloss from Mk 15:6. Although there is no historical evidence for such releasing of a prisoner in Palestine, similar instances in the Roman world are recorded by Livy and other ancient writers. **18.** *away with this man:* This is the only time in Lk that the crowd turns against Jesus, and even here Lk does not clearly identify them as such. The Vg is not accurate, for the Greek states, "they" cried out together; the reference is to v. 13. It is understandable, however, that the crowd would be violently angry, because this situation makes a mockery of their acclamations of the preceding Sunday (19:35–40). *Barabbas:* The name is suspect; in Aramaic it means "son of the father." Is it a substitution for his real name, Jesus, dropped out of reverence for Christ (according to some mss. at Mt 27:16)? **20.** *desiring to release Jesus:* The third time that Pilate seeks to release the innocent Jesus. It is clear that Pilate finally acted for the sake of his own reputation and career. **25.** *he handed over to their will:* Not only does the statement record that the Jewish leaders, not the Roman authority, crucified Jesus—notice the absence of Roman soldiers in Lk's entire account—but an allusion to Is 53:6,12 casts Jesus in the role of the Suffering Servant.

170 (i) The Way of the Cross (23:26–32). See Jn 19:16; Mk 15:20b–21; Mt 27:31b–32. Lk omits the crowning with thorns and the taunting by Roman soldiers; he expands a brief notice in the other Gospels into a way of the cross. It is difficult to estimate the distance, perhaps no more than a quarter of a mile. The site of the *praetorium* is not settled (see comment on Mt 27:27). **26.** *laid the cross on him to carry it after Jesus:* Simon of Cyrene is every Christian, fulfilling the injunction of 9:23. Ordinarily, the condemned man carried only the crossbeam; it was slung across his shoulders with his hands attached to it—a hideous sight, especially when the criminal was stripped naked. In Judea the Romans respected the Jewish sense of modesty. **27–28.** Only Lk, the Gospel of women, contains this episode; they alone are presented mourning over the sorrowful condition of Jesus (cf. Zech 12:10–14). They were not Galilean women (8:1–3; 23:49), but inhabitants of Jerusalem. The Talmud speaks of the practice of aristocratic women to prepare a drink to dull the pain of the tortured criminal. **28.** *Daughters of Jerusalem:* Cf. Is 3:16; Ct 1:5. *weep not for me:* A Semitism for "weep not so much for me as for...." As in the garden, Jesus was portrayed by Luke not as one seeking comfort from others, but rather as one bestowing it upon others. **29.** *days are coming:* The same phrase occurs in 19:43, indicating that Jerusalem must endure overwhelming sorrow. So must the Church, till she—like Jerusalem—be cleansed of all impurity. The words, here and in v. 30, are either citations of Hos 10:8 or else echoes of this and other passages such as Hos 9:14; Ap 6:16. **31.** Jesus may be repeating a proverb. The idea seems clear enough: If innocence meets such a fate, what will be in store for the guilty? **32.** Cf. Is 53:12.

171 (j) Jesus on the Cross (23:33–43). See Jn 19:17–27; Mk 15:22–32; Mt 27:33–44. Luke has softened the dark gloom of Mk and Mt and soothed the terrifying agony of Jesus' death. No Evangelist can steel himself to describe at length the actual crucifixion; Mt uses a participle to pass quickly beyond the terrifying remembrance of that ordeal. In Lk, however, the crowd watches silently and in the end returns repentantly to Jerusalem. Jesus is not heard to cry out from the lonely abandonment of his soul (Ps 22:1), and he dies, peacefully commending his soul to his Father. Luke also shows Jesus continually exercising his ministry of pardon.

33. *place called The Skull:* Luke suppresses the Aram name of the hill, Golgotha (*gulgultā*). From the Lat word for skull, *calvaria*, comes the Eng word "Calvary." That it was outside the city depends upon such texts as Heb 13:12f.; Lk 20:15 (see A. Parrot, *Golgotha and the Church of the Holy Sepulchre* [London, 1957]; C. Kopp, *The Holy Places of the Gospels* [N.Y., 1963] 351–94). **34.** *forgive them:* This prayer of Jesus, found only in Lk, is missing in mss. P^{75}, S^{a}, B, D*, and W; it is present in mss. S*, A, C, D^{2}, L, and N. It is easier to explain its deletion in terms of anti-Jewish prejudice than to say why it was added later. Jesus' pardon of enemies and great sinners is typical of Luke's portrait of the Savior. His is the Gospel of the great pardons. The modeling of Acts 7:60 upon the death scene of Jesus also argues in favor of the authenticity of the prayer. Because of the impf. form of the verb (*elegen*, "kept saying"), Jesus is presented repeating the forgiveness over and over again. The motivation is laid to ignorance; Luke frequently returns to this excusing cause in Acts—3:17 and 13:27 in regard to Jews; 17:27,30 in regard to Gentiles (cf. Lk 12:8–10 and see comments). *dividing his garments:* This incidental detail is recorded because it provides a link with Ps 22:19 and an opportunity to see Jesus as the innocent sufferer of the Ps. Luke's sense of order prompts him to place the incident here rather than after the affixing of the title, lest he interrupt his development on the kingship of Jesus. **35a.** Lk clearly distinguishes the people who stood silently looking on from the rulers who kept sneering at Jesus. The Gk particle *de* (but) adds that important nuance. This distinction is all the more significant because Ps 22:7, which is alluded to here, combines "looking" and "sneering" indiscriminately of those ridiculing the sufferer. *sneering:* Lit., "turning up the nose." *let him save himself:* This phrase, along with others in the context, especially as found in Mt, combines Ps 22:7–8 with Wis 2:13,17–20. Rather than give the exact words of those who mocked Jesus, the Gospels portray these men in the poise of the biblical enemies of salvation; as such, they take on a universal bearing (cf. J. Daniélou, *La Maison-Dieu* 4 [1957] 17–34). *the chosen one:* Cf. 9:35. **36.** *common wine:* Not the soporific drink offered Jesus in Mt 27:34, but the common drink of soldiers. Mk 14:35f. links the event with the question about the coming of Elijah; Luke always thinks of Jesus in the role of Elijah.

172 **37–43.** These verses form an inclusion held together by the mention of Jesus' kingdom. Through the cross Jesus will rise to glory and reign as king. But only the martyrs and the confessors at death arrive at this kingdom. Luke definitely does not encourage the Church to wait impatiently for the coming of the kingdom in the parousia; a long period of sorrow must ensue, but a fidelity strong enough to endure martyrdom ushers one into the kingdom. **38.** *an inscription:* The title is put very emphatically in Luke's Greek: "The king of the Jews is this one." See the variant formulas in Mk 15:26; Mt 27:37; Jn 19:19. **42.** The impf. form of the verb (*elegen*) indicates that the good thief spoke his request repeatedly. His words can bear a double translation and even refer to the parousia: (1) "Jesus, remember me when you come into your kingdom"; (2) "...when you come with regal glory." The latter translation accords better with the Lucan preference not to identify the kingdom geographically; for it is within (17:21). **43.** *today in Paradise:* Jesus' reply, his last words to any person on earth, puts the emphasis upon "today"—before the sun sets. *with me:* He tells the thief that he will not be simply in Jesus' retinue (*syn emoi*) but will also be sharing his royalty (*meth' emou*)—A. Plummer, *Luke*, 535. "With Christ" resounds with Pauline theology, sometimes referring to the future life (2 Cor 5:8; Phil 1:23; Rom 8:38f.; 14:8f.) and at other times to the "now" (Gal 2:20; Rom 6:5,8; 8:17,28–32). *paradise:* A word derived from Old Persian, meaning a walled garden or park; it was used occasionally in the LXX for man's homeland before the fall (Gn 2–3; 13:10; Ez 28:13; Is 41:3) and in the NT for the abode of the righteous (Ap 2:7; 2 Cor 12:2–4). The noncanonical *T. Levi* states that the Priestly Messiah will open its gates (NTRG § 3 [2nd ed., 1964] 152; cf. G. W. MacRae, *Worship* 35 [1961] 234–40; B. M. Ahern, *ProcCTSA* [1961] 9–10).

173 (k) The Death of Jesus (23:44–49). See Jn 19:25–37; Mk 15:33–41; Mt 27:45–56. **44.** The powers of darkness are now at their fiercest moment of energy and seeming triumph (22:53). **45b.** *curtain of the temple:* This refers to the one hanging between the Holy Place and the Holy of Holies (Ex 26:31f.). In Heb 9:12 and 10:20 this event is interpreted as the suppression of the Mosaic cult and the admission of all men, Gentiles as well as Jews, into the heavenly sanctuary. Mt connects the episode with earthquakes after the death of Jesus; Luke probably wants to show that Judaism, not Jesus, was vanquished at this moment. **46.** *loud cry:* Jesus dies with full consciousness, earnestly commending himself to the Father. In quoting Ps 31:6, Luke adds the word "Father." **47.** In Mt and Mk the centurion confesses Jesus as a "Son of God"; in Lk, he calls Jesus a "just man," totally innocent of any crime against the state. **48.** *beating their breasts:* Lk shows that the crowd is already converted, at least incipiently. **49.** *stood at a distance:* Lk concludes with Jesus' acquaintances prayerfully looking on.

174 (l) The Burial (23:50–56). See Jn 19:38–42; Mk 15:42–47; Mt 27:57–61. *Joseph of Arimathea:* Though a member of the Sanhedrin, he was good toward his fellow men and just toward God. His justice implied a firm faith that God would fulfill his promises about the kingdom. For the sake of his Gentile readers, Luke identifies Arimathea as "a town of Judea." **52.** *went to Pilate:* Just as Luke eliminated a great deal of Pilate's responsibility in the death of Jesus, so he now cuts through the details about Pilate's verifying the death of Jesus before consigning the body to Joseph. Dt 21:23 forbade corpses to remain exposed overnight. **54.** *the day of Preparation:* For the Sabbath. In Greek *paraskeuē* (from which came the Lat word used in the Western Church for Good Friday till 1955, *Parasceve*) means "preparation." Even though this pre-Sabbath day was also the first day of the Feast of Unleavened Bread (see comment on 22:1), rabbinical law allowed on that day the care of a dead body, but not the digging of a grave. The use of this phrase, Preparation day, by Jn involves our discussion in a most intricate problem of the chronology of the passion (see *EDB* 1910–11; → Gospel Jn, 63:138). In caring for the corpse of Jesus, Joseph became unclean for taking part in sacred ceremonies (cf. Jn 18:28). (For the baptismal symbolism of Jesus' burial, cf. R. Mercurio, *CBQ* 21 [1959] 39–54.)

175 **(C) The Resurrection and Ascension (24:1–53).** Luke had an independent source for the events of Easter and he narrates the material within the space of one day. From his gospel alone, we would not know of any 40-day period between the resurrection and the ascension. This is the first day of a new age—Sunday—which the Church will set apart as its new Sabbath of heavenly rest and joy (→ Aspects NT Thought, 78:147–159).

(a) The Women at the Tomb (24:1–12). See Jn 20:1–10; Mk 16:1–8; Mt 28:1–10. **1.** *they came:* Their names are given in v. 10. **2.** *they found:* Luke records only what the witnesses discovered, though he does so with the insights of faith. All Evangelists write about the Easter events with remarkable simplicity. **4.** *two men:* Mt records an angel; Jn, two angels; Mk, one young man clothed in white. It is best to explain the Lucan details theologically, as a deliberate modeling upon the transfiguration scene (Lk 9:31). In Acts 1:10 and 10:30 angels are called "men." *dazzling raiment:* Lightning frequently expresses some kind of heavenly or unearthly visitation in Luke's writings (Lk 9:29; 10:18; 11:36; 17:24; Acts 9:3; 22:6; W. Grundmann, *Evangelium*, 440). **5.** *among the dead:* That is, in a graveyard. **6.** *while he was still in Galilee:* Like Jn, Lk mentions no postresurrection apparitions in Galilee. (Jn 21 is an appendix to the Gospel.) Each recognizes a highly symbolic value to Jerusalem in the ministry of Jesus. *remember:* Though not as much as Matthew, Luke sees a real importance in prophecy, especially those made by Jesus of his passion, death, and resurrection (9:18–22,43–45; 18:31–33) and those whereby Jesus saw the OT fulfilled in himself, particularly the "Son of Man" and the "Suffering Servant" passages. **7.** *must:* Again Luke insists that the Son of Man "must" suffer (see comment on 9:22). **8–9.** *told all this:* In Lk the women appear much more peaceful and communicative than in Mk 16:8. **10.** Textually, this verse is difficult. An added problem arises in comparing it with Mk 16:1; Lk substitutes Joanna for Salome. Joanna is only known from Lk (see 8:3). **11.** *this tale seemed nonsense:* The Gk word *lēros* applies to the wild talk of a sick person in delirium (A. Plummer, *Luke*, 550). All four Gospels state the doubt and hesitation of the Eleven and other disciples; they did not easily accept the resurrection (Mk 16:10f.,14; Mt 28:10,17; Jn 20:18,25,29). The fact has important apologetical value. **12.** *but Peter...:* This verse seems to summarize Jn 20:3–10. Although it is absent from the Western Text, all the other mss. include it, and v. 24 presumes it. The textual differences between Jn and Lk are too numerous and important for interdependence; each probably drew upon a common source (J. N. Sanders, *NTS* 1 [1954] 29ff.). The verse is rejected by many modern editors (RSV, NEB, Nestle).

176 (b) Emmaus (24:13–35). A number of differences show up upon comparison with the account of Jesus' appearance to the Eleven: (1) The two men are not leaders of the community but represent all followers of Jesus; (2) they are troubled and do not understand why Jesus is absent; (3) at first they do not recognize Jesus; (4) the apostles seem to recognize Jesus but do not believe their senses; (5) after recognition, these men do not hesitate to believe; (6) once recognized, Jesus disappears. We begin to find points of resemblance with several other types or themes within the NT. This simple, charming story in many ways parallels the meeting of deacon Philip with the eunuch on the road to Gaza (Acts 8:26–40): (1) an ignorance of scripture; (2) an explanation that Jesus must suffer, drawn from Scripture; (3) an insistance to stay longer; (4) sudden disappearance. The Emmaus account fits into a series of stories where Christ manifests himself in the person of traveling preachers: the 72 preachers (Lk 10:8,16); Paul (Gal 4:13; 2 Cor 5:20); all the needy (Mt 25:31–46). Finally, before this tradition reached Luke, it had been modified by the Eucharistic liturgy; it follows the sequence of the latter: a reading and explanation of Scripture (vv. 25–27) and the breaking of bread (v. 30).

177 13. *two of them:* Mk 16:12f. refers to this occurrence. *that very day:* Luke gives the impression that all the events of ch. 24 happened on Easter day. *Emmaus:* The site is disputed. The traditional place at 'Amwas, on the Jerusalem–Jaffa road, is 20 mi. from Jerusalem, too far for the "sixty stadia" (7 mi.) mentioned here. The village of el-Qubeibeh has been pointed out as "Emmaus" since the Crusades (AD 1280)—a rather late start for a tradition, but its distance of 8 mi. NW of Jerusalem better suits the biblical account (see C. Kopp, *Holy Places*, 396–402). **18.** *one of them, named Cleopas:* Hegesippus, quoted by Eusebius (*HE* 3.11, 1) identified him as the brother of Joseph, Jesus' foster father, and the father of Symeon; Symeon succeeded James as bishop of Jerusalem and after AD 70 led the Christians back to Jerusalem. The names of the men may not be too important for salvation history, but the tradition brings out that the "brethren of Jesus," his close relatives, did not completely reject him (Lk 4:38f.; Mk 3:21; Acts 1:14). **19.** *a man, a prophet, mighty in word and work:* At most, Jesus had impressed these men as the expected prophet (9:19); the next phrase is said of Moses (Acts 7:22) who is also called a redeemer (Acts 7:35). The presence of the word "man" indicates that these disciples never passed to belief in Jesus' divinity; they remained with his messiahship. **20.** Again Luke declares the guilt of the Jewish leaders. **24.** A reference to Peter and John (v. 12; Jn 20:3–10). **26.** *necessary:* This verse repeats the Lucan theme that "the Messiah must suffer" (see comment on 9:22). *so enter his glory:* The past tense in this expression presumes that the ascension has already taken place. **27.** *Moses...Prophets...Scriptures:* It is still clearer in v. 44 that a reference is being made here to the entire Jewish Bible, which was divided into three sections: the *Tôrāh*, or Law, the *Nebî'îm*, or Prophets, and the *Ketûbîm*, or Writings. The Gk form of "all the prophets" implies that Jesus touched upon each and all the prophets. **29.** *stay with us:* Jesus was not play-acting; he really would have departed. Without him, darkness would have descended; this indication of the time of the day also alludes to a favorite Lucan, Johannine, and Pauline contrast—of darkness and light (Lk 22:53). **30.** *took, blessed, broke, gave:* The terminology is definitely Eucharistic (cf. Lk 9:16). We need not maintain that Jesus consecrated the Eucharist; Eucharistic formulas, however, were absorbed into the story as it was retold at liturgical gatherings. **31.** *eyes were opened:* The verb occurs only eight times in the NT; except for Mk 7:35 and Lk 2:23, it is found either in Lk 24 or in Acts, where it always means a deeper understanding of revelation. *he vanished:* Is this phrase also a liturgical addition to the effect that Jesus' miraculous appearance is hardly necessary when one has his presence in the Eucharist?

(Desreumaux, J., *BiViChr* 56 [1964] 45–56. Dupont, J., *LumVi* 31 [1957] 77–92; *The Eucharist in the NT* [Baltimore, 1964] 105–21. Flanagan, D., *Furrow* 13 [1962] 95–104. Grassi, J. A., *CBQ* 26 [1964] 463–67. Orlett, R., *CBQ* 21 [1959] 212–19.)

178 (c) JESUS' APPEARANCE TO THE DISCIPLES (24:36–49). See Jn 20:19–23. Mk and Mt record an appearance in Galilee; Lk's account bears some similarity to Jn's. Although the literary origin is too complicated to be resolved, it seems that Lk combines both traditions in vv. 36–43. The presence of broiled fish, as M.-J. Lagrange remarks (*Luc*, 613), is a rare occurrence even today in Jerusalem but common in Galilee (v. 42) and may point to Mk and Mt. **36–38.** *afraid, startled, panic-stricken, doubts:* Such a repetitious insistence makes it clear that the acceptance of the resurrection: (1) rests upon faith and cannot be the result of any human proof, including divine apparitions; (2) cannot stem from earlier announcements of Jesus, which remain insufficient. **38.** *doubts:* The Gk word has a wide range of meaning: thoughts (2:35), opinions, reasoning, doubt, dispute (9:46), argument, murmuring (Phil 2:14). **39.** *hands and feet:* In Jn 20:20,25 Jesus shows his hands and side. Ignatius of Antioch comments: "Immediately they touched him and, through this contact with his flesh and spirit, believed" (*Ep. ad Smyr.* 3.2). The Spirit must reveal what the flesh touches. **41.** *for joy:* Lk here shows himself possessed of keen psychological insight; as the Gk text indicates, joy was so great as to leap beyond belief; lit., "they disbelieved for joy." **42.** *and a honeycomb:* This phrase is found only in very late mss. and is not really part of the text. **43.** *ate:* The glorified body of Jesus was no longer in need of food (Tb 12:16–22), but was still able, and willing, to partake of it for the sake of the brethren.

179 **44–49.** These verses, found only in Lk, manifest the origin of apostolic preaching and especially of apostolic tradition. There is an initial insistence upon the fact that Jesus must suffer and rise again. The Passion Narrative was the first to reach formulation in the early Church. This narrative was gradually expanded by reference to the earlier Scriptures for insight and meaning. The preaching of the passion and resurrection stirred compunction over sin (Acts 2:37f.). As the converts wanted to know more about the way of salvation, they appealed to the apostles who had been witnesses of all that Jesus said and did; the other parts of the four Gospels, beyond the Passion Narrative, thus began to take shape. But the apostles spoke not simply as eyewitnesses but also as men possessed of the Spirit, and as such became the foundation of the Church which rests upon the cornerstone, Christ (Eph 2:20; 2 Cor 10:13; 1 Tm 1:18; 4:11).

44. *he said to them:* A stylistic introduction, like v. 36; we have the impression that it is still Easter (cf. v. 13). *while I was with you:* The past tense of the verb shows that Jesus' presence is now different from that before the resurrection. **45.** Luke insists upon the importance of scriptural interpretation either by Jesus or by one of the apostles (Acts 8:31–35). **47.** *in his name:* A frequent theme in Acts (2:38; 3:6; 4:10,30). This phrase expresses faith in the divinity of Jesus; what was formerly said only of Yahweh is now used of Jesus. *to all nations, beginning from Jerusalem:* The theme of Acts of the Apostles (Acts 1:8). For this reason, in his Gospel Luke never pictures Jesus at work among Gentiles; that was to be the undertaking of the Church. **49.** *I send forth:* The pres. tense frequently stands for the proximate future in the NT (*GrBib* § 278). Again, taking ch. 24 as it stands, one gets the impression, given also by Jn 20, that the resurrection, the ascension, and the giving of the Spirit take place on the same day. *wait here:* The command prepares for the events in the Book of Acts.

180 (d) THE ASCENSION (24:50–53). Cf. Acts 1:4–14; Mk 16:19f. Stylistically, this section is interlocked with the preceding, as though it treats of the same Easter day (→ Aspects NT Thought, 78:159). **50.** *toward Bethany:* Cf. 22:39. *he lifted his hands and blessed them:* Jesus acts as the Messianic high priest; Lk's language echoes Sirach's description of the high priest Simon, son of Jochanan (Sir 50:1,20). **51.** *he parted from them and was carried up into heaven:* Only the first clause is contained in S*, D, and VL. It is easier to explain a shortening of the original text than a later lengthening of it; it is likely that efforts would be made to conform Luke's conclusion with the other Gospels, which say nothing of the ascension (except the later addition to Mk); Luke, furthermore, depicts the ascension in Acts, and therefore some would think that the account does not belong in the Gospel.

was carried up into heaven: The Gk word *anephereto* occurs very often in the OT in the liturgical sense of offering or burning a sacrifice (Lv 2:16; 3:5,11,14,16). In Lv *anapherō* most frequently is the LXX translation of the Hebr liturgical word *qāṭar* (burn a sacrifice). In Is 53:11; Heb 7:27; 1 Pt 2:24; and Jas 2:21 *anapherō* is employed in a more extended sense; but a liturgical connotation always remains. **52.** *great joy:* Luke brings one of his favorite themes into the concluding verses. Evidently, the Spirit of Pentecost provides the individual with greater strength and with a stronger, more personal and more appreciative union with Jesus within the community than was experienced ever before. **53.** *continually in the temple:* In the sense that the Church constitutes the new Jerusalem and the new Temple, where all mankind worship God in and through Jesus. *blessing:* In the scriptural sense they proclaimed God's great redemptive acts, which were being re-experienced by the Church.

(Benoit, P., *RB* 56 [1949] 161–203. Schillebeeckx, E., *Worship* 35 [May 1961] 336–63. Van Goudoever, J., *Biblical Calendars* [Leiden, 1959] 195–205. Van Stempvoort, P. A., *NTS* 5 [1958–59] 30–42.)

45

ACTS OF THE APOSTLES

Richard J. Dillon

Joseph A. Fitzmyer, S.J.

BIBLIOGRAPHY

1 Bauernfeind, O., *Die Apostelgeschichte* (ThHkNT 5; Leipzig, 1939). Bruce, F. F., *The Acts of the Apostles* (London, 1951); *Commentary on the Book of Acts* (London, 1954). Cadbury, H. J., *The Making of Luke-Acts* (N.Y., 1927); *The Book of Acts in History* (London, 1955). Conzelmann, H., *Die Apostelgeschichte* (HNT 7; Tübingen, 1963); *The Theology of St. Luke* (N.Y., 1960). Dibelius, M., *Studies in the Acts of the Apostles* (ed. H. Greeven; London, 1956). Dupont, J., *Les Actes des Apôtres* (BJ; Paris, 1954); *The Sources of Acts: The Present Position* (London, 1964); *Études sur les Actes des Apôtres* (LD 45; Paris, 1967). Flender, H., *St Luke: Theologian of Redemptive History* (Phila., 1967). Foakes Jackson, F. J. and K. Lake, *The Beginnings of Christianity: Part I, The Acts of the Apostles* (5 vols.; London, 1920–1933). Haenchen, E., *Die Apostelgeschichte* (Meyer 3; 12th ed.; Göttingen, 1959). Jacquier, E., *Les Actes des Apôtres* (EBib; Paris, 1926). Keck, L. E. and J. L. Martyn (eds.), *Studies in Luke–Acts* (Nashville, 1966). Knox, W. L., *The Acts of the Apostles* (Cambridge, 1948). Lampe, G. W. H., "Acts," *PCB* 882–926. Munck, J., *The Acts of the Apostles* (AB 31; Garden City, 1967). O'Neill, J. C., *The Theology of Acts in Its Historical Setting* (London, 1961). Packer, J. W., *Acts of the Apostles* (CNEB; Cambridge, 1966). Stählin, G., *Die Apostelgeschichte* (NTD 5; 10th ed.; Göttingen, 1962). Trocmé, É., *Le "Livre des Actes" et l'histoire* (Paris, 1957). Wikenhauser, A., *Die Apostelgeschichte* (RNT 5; 3rd ed.; Regensburg, 1956); *Die Apostelgeschichte und ihr Geschichtswert* (Münster, 1921). Williams, C. S. C., *A Commentary on the Acts of the Apostles* (BNTC; London, 1957).

Mattill, Jr., A. J. and M. B. Mattill, *A Classified Bibliography of Literature on the Acts of the Apostles* (NTTS 7; Leiden, 1966).

Cerfaux, L., R–F, *INT* 327–68. F–B, *INT* 106–34. Guthrie, *NTI* 3, 303–48. Wik, *NTI* 320–45.

INTRODUCTION

2 **(I) Author, Date and Place of Composition.** Acts is widely recognized as the continuation of Lk, even though its first five verses present a problem. The dedication of the two books to Theophilus argues in favor of the continuity between them; again, it is impossible stylistically to separate Acts from Lk (→ Gospel Lk, 44:2–6). That the common author of these books is Luke the Antiochene is derived from extra-biblical ecclesiastical tradition. The earliest attribution of both works to Luke may be found in the Anti-Marcionite Prologue to Lk (dated by some scholars *ca.* AD 160–180): "...afterwards the same Luke wrote 'Acts of Apostles'" (see K. Aland, *Synopsis quattuor evangeliorum* [Stuttgart, 1964] 533); cf. the Muratorian Fragment (34–39). The question of the sources of Acts (→ 6 below) is related to that of its authorship; but the evidence from them scarcely offers any proof against the Lucan authorship of Acts (see J. Dupont, *Sources*, 168). That this Luke was the companion of Paul is also widely recognized; it is questioned at times because the "Paulinism" of Acts is not that of the Pauline corpus (see P. Vielhauer, "On the 'Paulinism' of Acts," *Studies in Lk-Acts*, 33–50). Obviously, one must make a clear distinction between Paul's teaching in his letters and the Lucan presentation of his teaching in Acts. But granted this, does the evidence rule out the possibility that the author of Lk-Acts was a companion of Paul for the brief time that the "We-Sections" of Acts (→ 6 below) might seem to call for? To admit this is not to admit that Luke was with Paul during the major part of his apostolic activity or while most of his letters were being written. That the author of Acts was Luke of Antioch, a part-time companion of Paul, is still a plausible hypothesis to explain the authorship of Acts.

If the date of AD 80–85 is reasonable for Lk (→ Gospel Lk, 44:18), the same can be used for Acts (→ Canonicity, 67:58, 66). The ancient tradition that it was written in Greece (Achaia or Boeotia) cannot be proved; but it has nothing against it.

3 **(II) The Literary Purpose and Character of Acts.** The second book addressed to Theophilus continues Luke's story about the origin and growth of

Comments on chs. 1–5 are the work of R. J. Dillon; the introduction and the remaining commentary are by J. A. Fitzmyer.

Christianity under the guidance of the Spirit, who directed the authenticated witnesses to testify to what Jesus had done and taught (1:1). Lk itself told how Jesus fashioned such witnesses during his ministry. Acts now carries the historical account forward, spelling out in detail—and above all through the activity of two prime witnesses, Peter and Paul—how the Word of God spread from Jerusalem to "the end of the earth." Indeed, the purpose of Acts is set forth programmatically in 1:8: "You are to be my witnesses in Jerusalem, throughout Judea and Samaria—yes, even to the end of the earth." Acts thus depicts the emergence of Christianity from its Jewish matrix into a religion of world-wide status. Cf. Lk 24:46–47 (see J. Dupont, *NTS* 6 [1959–60] 139–41). A glance at the outline of Acts (→ 8 below) shows how Luke's geographical perspective dominates his story, as it did in Lk too (→ Gospel Lk, 44:7). Stage by stage Luke will depict the Word of God—either under stress of persecution or commission from Jerusalem—spreading from the mother church to Samaria (8:1,5) and Judea (8:26), to Caesarea (8:40) and Galilee (9:31), to Damascus (9:2), Phoenicia, Cyprus, and Syrian Antioch (11:19), to the Roman provinces of Cilicia, Galatia, Asia, Macedonia, and Achaia, and finally to Rome itself. Symbolically, Rome is "the end of the earth" (as in *Pss Sol* 8:15).

But Luke does not so much write a "history" of the early Church or an early Christian apologetic, as he does a theological essay that describes, somewhat idyllically, the character, growth, and problems of the early Church for the sake of Gentiles or Gentile-Christian readers. History and apologia are present in Acts, but Luke is above all concerned to stress two things: (1) the importance of Jerusalem as the mother church, the seat of the Twelve, and the doctrinal focal point of Christian missionary activity; (2) the work of the Spirit in guiding the spread of the Word, in forming the Christian community, and in bringing men into the fold.

The book was given the title of "Acts" (*Praxeis*) in antiquity, thus relating Luke's composition to a Hellenistic literary form that recounted the deeds of outstanding men (such as Alexander the Great, Hannibal, or Apollonius of Tyana). The careers of Luke's two heroes, Peter and Paul, might seem to justify the use of such a title. But the purpose of the book as described above indicates sufficiently that Luke's work is something more. Though it is scarcely a Pauline apologia, it is a religious or theological essay in which a concern for "assurance" (as Lk 1:4 suggests) is present. In no sense can it be understood as the "Acts" of the Twelve Apostles.

4 **(III) The Composition of Acts.** Only a few words can be devoted here to three features of the literary composition of Acts.

(A) Summaries. Luke has composed three sorts of summary statements in Acts to describe the growth and character of the early Church, or else to generalize after his particular descriptions. These summaries are, as it were, signals to the reader; they remind him of the progress that the spreading Word of God is making despite the author's preoccupation with details. The three sorts of summaries are: (1) *Major:* 2:42–47; 4:32–35; 5:11–16. These give an idyllic view of the growth of the Church in its springtime; they are probably composite or conflated (→ 23 below; cf. P. Benoit, "Remarques sur les 'sommaires' des Actes des Apôtres," *Aux sources de la tradition chrétienne* [Fest. M. Goguel; Paris, 1950] 1–10; *Exégèse*, 2, 181–92; L. Cerfaux, *ETL* 16 [1939] 5–31; J. Jeremias, *ZNW* 36 [1937] 205–21). (2) *Minor:* 1:14; 6:7; 9:31; 12:24; 16:5; 19:20; 28:30–31. These summaries, which are usually of only one verse, have been used by C. H. Turner to divide Acts into six historical "panels" (see J. Hastings, *DictB* [1900] 1, 421; cf. A. H. McNeile, *Introduction to the Study of the NT* [2nd ed.; Oxford, 1953] 97–98). This use, however, is not too convincing; for possibly 5:42 should also be listed here. (3) *Numerical:* 2:41; 4:4; 5:14; 6:1,7; 9:31; 11:21,24; 12:24; 14:1; 19:20. Some of these are identical with those in (1) or (2). They build up the impression of the growth of the Church.

(See Cadbury, H. J., "The Summaries in Acts," *Beginnings* 5, 392–402.)

5 **(B) Discourses.** Roughly a third of Acts is devoted to speeches, and they are obviously an important literary device for Luke. Instead of a prosaic reporting in indirect discourse (as in 17:2–3), Luke more often uses discourses to supply for the lack of psychological analysis or reflection on historical events—a device that ancient historians did not normally employ. Speeches put on the lips of principal characters reveal the meaning of the events with which they are associated.

The discourses in Acts are in the last analysis Lucan compositions; their Lucan style is manifest and found everywhere. Some of the discourses are quite freely composed, without regard of historical detail. Others reflect the missionary preaching of the first apostolic generation. To the latter belong the so-called kerygmatic discourses of Peter (2:14–39; 3:11–26; 4:8–12; 5:29–32; 10:34–43) and of Paul (13:16–41). And yet, even these missionary discourses are far from word-for-word reproductions of what was said by Peter or Paul—they are too short for that. Although they echo the primitive apostolic kerygma, they do not necessarily reflect it in detail; their pattern is stereotyped (→ 18 below), and they are not without an overlay of Lucan theology and terminology in many cases. It is not easy to sort out what can be called primitive, Petrine, Pauline, or even Lucan in these missionary discourses. In the long run, they are best regarded as Lucan compositions, intended for his readers and designed to further his own story. This is also true of the other great discourses of Paul (on the Areopagus, 17:22–31; at Miletus, 20:18–35; in Jerusalem, 22:3–21; before Felix, 24:10–21; before King Agrippa, 26:1–23; to the Jews of Rome, 28:17–20,25–29), and of that of Stephen (7:2–53). The discourses in Acts have often been compared to the speeches composed for principal characters in classical Gk historians and even to the choruses of Gk tragedy; in another sense they are analogous to the great sermons of Jesus in Mt. They mark the decisive stages of the spread of the Word.

(See Bruce, F. F., *The Speeches in the Acts of the Apostles* [London, 1945]. Dibelius, M., *Studies*, 138–85. Dodd, C. H., *The Apostolic Preaching and Its Developments* [London, 1950]. Dupont, J., "Les discours missionnaires des Actes des Apôtres," *RB* 69 [1962] 37–60. Wilckens, U., *Die Missionsreden der Apostelgeschichte* [WMzANT 5; Neukirchen, 1961].)

6 **(C) Sources of Acts.** The reader of Acts soon realizes that Luke was not present for all that he describes or narrates; that he has freely composed parts of his story must be admitted. Furthermore, it is obvious to the careful student of Acts that Luke has often rewritten, telescoped, juxtaposed, and even conflated accounts (e.g., ch. 15 [→ 72 below]) for the sake of his story. Such literary activity and the so-called We-Sections (passages in which the narrative shifts abruptly from the third person singular to the first person plural [16:10–17; 20:5–15; 21:1–18; 27:1–28:16; and 11:28 in ms. D]) have raised the question whether Luke used sources in writing Acts. The "We-Sections" have often been described as extracts from a travel diary, written by a companion of Paul.

Many attempts have been made to isolate other sources; for instance:

A Palestinian (or Jerusalem?) *Source:* 1:6–2:40; 3:1–4:31; 4:36–5:11; 5:17–42; 8:5–40; 9:32–11:18; 12:1–23.

An Antiochene Source: 6:1–6; 6:8–8:4; 11:19–30; 15:3–33.

A Pauline Source: 9:1–30; 13:3–14:28; 15:35–28:31 (except for the We-Sections and Speeches).

Such attempts have not yet commanded the consensus of scholars. If Luke did use them, he must have reworked them in stages and imprinted them with his own vocabulary and style.

(Bultmann, R., "Zur Frage nach den Quellen der Apostelgeschichte," *NT Essays* [Fest. T. W. Manson; Manchester, 1959] 68–80. Cerfaux, L., "La composition de la première partie du Livre des Actes," *ETL* 13 [1936] 667–91. Dupont, J., *Sources* [London, 1964; a fundamental survey]. Haenchen, E., "Tradition und Komposition in der Apostelgeschichte," *ZThK* 52 [1955] 205–25. Kümmel, W. G., F–B, *INT* 123–32. Shepherd, Jr., M. H., "A Venture in the Source Analysis of Acts," *Munera studiosa* [Fest. W. H. P. Hatch; Cambridge, 1946] 91–105.)

7 **(IV) The Gk Text of Acts.** Acts is unique among the books of the NT because of the two forms of the Gk text in which it has been preserved: the "Egyptian" (or Alexandrian) Text, found mainly in the mss. B, S, A, C, P^{45}, P^{74}; and the "Western Text," found mainly in mss. D, E, P^{38}, P^{41}, P^{48}, and in some ancient versions (VL, Syr^{vet}). The latter is also used in some patristic citations (Irenaeus, Cyprian, Augustine, Ephraem). Though it seems to be almost as old as the Egyptian Text, the Western Text is almost a tenth longer than the commonly used Egyptian Text, for it contains many additional phrases, clauses, and even whole verses. Though it is still a matter of scholarly debate, many NT text-critics feel that the Western Text is a conscious revision or adjustment of the Egyptian recension. In many cases the difference in the Western Text is clearly a solution to a textual problem (see comment on 15:34). Significant passages in which the Western Text differs are: 13:27; 15:29; 18:27; 19:1; 28:31. Occasionally the reading in ms. D is judged to be superior to that of the Egyptian recension (e.g., 12:10; 19:9; 20:15; 28:16). A more pronounced anti-Jewish tendency has also been detected in ms. D (see E. J. Epp, *HarvTR* 55 [1962] 51–62).

(Epp, E. J., *The Theological Tendency of Codex Bezae Cantabrigiensis in Acts* [N.Y., 1966]. Klijn, A. F. J., *A Survey of the Researches into the Western Text of the Gospels and Acts* [Utrecht, 1949]; *NovT* 3 [1959] 1–27, 161–74. Metzger, B. M., *The Text of the NT* [N.Y., 1964] 45–51, 162, 213–14. Ropes, J. H., *Beginnings* 3.)

8 **(V) Outline.** The structure of Acts can be seen from the following outline.

(I) The Mission in Palestine (1:1–9:43)
(A) Foundations of the Missionary Era (1:1–2:13)
(a) Preface (1:1–8)
(b) The Ascension (1:9–12)
(c) The Filling of the College of the Twelve (1:13–26)
(d) The Pentecost Event (2:1–13)
(B) The Mission in Jerusalem (2:14–8:3)
(a) The Pentecost Discourse (2:14–41)
(b) First Major Summary (2:42–47)
(c) The First Jewish Persecution (3:1–4:31)
(i) Peter's healing miracle (3:1–11)
(ii) Peter's Temple discourse (3:12–26)
(iii) The apostles before the Sanhedrin (4:1–22)
(iv) The prayer of the apostles (4:23–31)
(d) The Community Ideal of the Apostolic Church (4:32–5:16)
(i) Second major summary (4:32–35)
(ii) Examples (4:36–5:10)
(iii) Third major summary (5:11–16)
(e) The Second Persecution (5:17–42)
(f) Stephen and the Hellenists (6:1–8:1a)
(i) The Hellenists (6:1–6)
(ii) Summary (6:7)
(iii) The account of Stephen (6:8–15; 7:54–8:1a)
(iv) The discourse of Stephen (7:1–53)
(g) The Third Persecution and the Dispersion (8:1b–3)
(C) The Mission in Judea and Samaria (8:4–9:43)
(a) The Story of Philip (8:4–40)
(i) The Samaritan mission (8:4–25)
(ii) The Ethiopian eunuch (8:26–40)
(b) The Vocation of Saul (9:1–19a)
(c) Saul at Damascus (9:19b–22)
(d) Saul's First Jerusalem Journey (9:23–30)
(e) Summary (9:31)
(f) Peter's Mission in Palestine (9:32–43)
(II) The Mission to the End of the Earth (10:1–28:31)
(A) Inauguration of the Gentile Mission (10:1–15:35)
(a) The Cornelius Event and Its Effects (10:1–11:18)
(i) Peter's vision and its consequences (10:1–33)
(ii) Peter's discourse (10:34–43)
(iii) Deliberations on the event (10:44–11:18)
(b) The Mission at Antioch (11:19–30)
(c) Herod's Persecution and Death (12:1–23)
(d) Summary and Lucan Suture (12:24–25)
(e) The First Missionary Journey of Paul (13:1–14:28)
(i) The sending of Barnabas and Saul (13:1–3)
(ii) Cyprus (13:4–12)
(iii) Pisidian Antioch (13:13–52)
(iv) Iconium (14:1–5)
(v) Lystra (14:6–20a)
(vi) Derbe and return (14:20b–28)
(f) The Apostolic "Council" (15:1–35)
(i) Preliminaries (15:1–5)
(ii) The convocation and Peter's address (15:6–12)
(iii) James' discourse (15:13–21)
(iv) Apostolic letter (15:22–29)
(v) Proclamation of the decree (15:30–35)
(B) The Universal Mission of Paul (15:36–28:31)
(a) The Great Missionary Journeys (15:36–21:14)
(i) Paul and Barnabas differ and separate (15:36–39)
(ii) Beginning of Mission II: Departure for Syria and Cilicia (15:40–41)
(iii) Visit to Derbe and Lystra: Timothy becomes Paul's companion (16:1–4)
(iv) Summary (16:5)
(v) Paul crosses Asia Minor (16:6–10)
(vi) The evangelization of Philippi (16:11–40)
(vii) Success and failure at Thessalonica (17:1–9)
(viii) Paul in Beroea (17:10–15)
(ix) Paul in Athens (17:16–21)
(x) Paul's discourse at the Areopagus (17:22–34)
(xi) Paul in Corinth (18:1–17)
(xii) Paul's return to Syrian Antioch (18:18–22)
(xiii) Beginning of Mission III (18:23)
(xiv) Apollos in Ephesus and Achaia (18:24–28)
(xv) Paul in Ephesus: Disciples who had not received the Spirit (19:1–7)
(xvi) Ephesian ministry and encounters (19:8–19)
(xvii) Summary (19:20)

(xviii) The riot of the silversmiths (19:21–40)
(xix) Paul leaves for Greece and returns from there (20:1–6)
(xx) Paul restores Eutychus to life at Troas (20:7–12)
(xxi) Paul's journey to Miletus (20:13–16)
(xxii) Discourse to the Ephesian elders at Miletus (20:17–38)
(xxiii) Paul arrives at Tyre (21:1–6)
(xxiv) Paul arrives at Ptolemais and Caesarea (21:7–14)

(b) Paul in Jerusalem (21:15–23:11)
(i) Paul's arrival, greeting, and purification (21:15–26)
(ii) Paul's arrest (21:27–40)
(iii) Paul's discourse to the Jerusalem crowd (22:1–21)
(iv) Paul imprisoned in the Fortress Antonia (22:22–29)
(v) Paul before the Sanhedrin (22:30–23:11)

(c) Paul in Caesarea (23:12–26:32)
(i) Transfer to Caesarea (23:12–35)
(ii) Paul's trial before the governor Felix (24:1–21)
(iii) Paul's captivity at Caesarea (24:22–27)
(iv) Paul appeals to Caesar (25:1–12)
(v) Festus invites Agrippa to listen to Paul (25:13–27)
(vi) Paul's discourse before King Agrippa (26:1–23)
(vii) Reactions to Paul's discourse (26:24–32)

(d) Paul's Journey to Rome (27:1–28:16)
(i) Departure for Rome (27:1–5)
(ii) Storm and shipwreck (27:6–44)
(iii) Winter in Malta (28:1–10)
(iv) Paul's arrival in Rome (28:11–16)

(e) House Arrest and Unhindered Proclamation of the Message at Rome (28:17–31)
(i) Paul's testimony to the Jews (28:17–28)
(ii) Summary (28:30–31)

COMMENTARY

9 **(I) The Mission in Palestine (1:1–9:43).**

(A) Foundations of the Missionary Era (1:1–2:13).

(a) PREFACE (1:1–8). **1.** *in the first book:* Unmistakable resonances of the polished Gospel prologue (Lk 1:1–4) are in contrast to the truncated structure of the present passage. The initial clause, *ton men prōton logon,* has no corresponding *de*-clause to summarize the volume at hand. Hence the various interpolation-theories: that vv. 3–12 were inserted in place of a successfully completed prologue (cf. W. G. Kümmel, *TRu* 17 [1948–49] 9, n. 1; *TRu* 22 [1954] 196); that the two Lucan volumes were originally one continuous work, joined at Lk 24:49 and Acts 1:6, but were divided when arranged in the present NT canon (P.-H. Menoud, *Neutestamentliche Studien* [Fest. R. Bultmann; Berlin, 1954] 148–56; E. Trocmé, *Le Livre,* 31ff.). Both theories are contradicted by the manifest Lucan quality of the "interpolations." Nor is it necessary to think that this preface is deformed; other "second volumes" in contemporary Gk literature have this kind of secondary prologue, with unnoticed transition from the review of a former volume's content to the material at hand (cf. Josephus, *Ant.* 13.1, 1 § 1; H. J. Cadbury, *The Making,* 198–99). A closer look at vv. 3–8 reveals their programmatic character. Verse 4 announces the disciples' reception of the Spirit; v. 5 has the baptism in the Spirit that they are to confer; and v. 8 programs the movement of the missionary endeavor: Jerusalem, Judea-Samaria, "to the end of the earth." Haenchen (*Apostelgeschichte,* 114) correctly observes that v. 8 accomplishes an outline of the book more effectively than the classical prologue-form would have, for it makes the book's contents globally a fulfillment of the Risen Lord's own words. *began to do and teach:* The vb. "began" (*ērxato*) is intriguing. Is it a mere pleonasm, as in popular Gk and Lat (*coepi*) speech? Or is this Luke's typical interest in the beginning of Jesus' work, to which he insists his account and its source-witnesses reach back (see Lk 1:2,3; 3:23; 23:5; Acts 10:37; cf. the noticeably parallel *arxamenos* in 1:22)? It may not be forcing things to translate: "what Jesus did and taught from the beginning" (*Beginnings* 4, 3). **2.** *apostles... whom he had chosen:* The vb. *exelexato* echoes Lk 6:13, the designation of the Twelve whose membership, excluding Judas, is again spelled out in 1:13. This is Luke's characteristic emphasis on the exclusive apostleship of the Twelve; their unique witness is prepared by both association with Jesus' entire ministry (1:21–22) and the Risen Lord's 40-day instruction (1:3; cf. 13:31 and G. Klein, *Die zwölf Apostel* [FRLANT 77; Göttingen, 1961] 202ff.; → Aspects NT Thought, 78:172–179). *he was taken up:* The slight ms. tradition against *anelēmphthē* has the same origin as the more considerable one against Lk 24:51b (→ Gospel Lk, 44:180), viz., the embarrassment of two apparently conflicting dates of the ascension (see P. Benoit, *Exégèse,* 1, 395). The vb. *analambanō* occurs in the LXX with the meaning of heavenly ascension (2 Kgs 2:9ff.; 1 Mc 2:58; Sir 48:9; 49:14); but some commentators ask if it need signify this here in view of the use of *analēmpsis* in Lk 9:51, where Jesus' "taking up" refers to his death and resurrection, as does *exodos* (departure) in Lk 9:31 (see P. A. van Stempvoort, *NTS* 5 [1958–59] 32–33; E. Lohse, *EvT* 14 [1954] 263). However, the ptc. *enteilamenos* (having commanded), which is subordinate to the vb. *anelēmphthē,* seems to refer to Lk 24:44–49. Hence, the vb. "taken up" probably is a reference to Lk 24:50ff., resuming the sense of that scene.

10 **3.** *after his passion:* *Paschein,* meaning the integral passion-death sequence of Jesus, is peculiarly Lucan (see Lk 22:15; 24:26,46; Acts 3:18; 17:3; 26:23). *during forty days:* As a delimitation of the period of appearances the number is surely symbolic. But of what? Of Moses on Sinai (Str-B 3, 511, 530; Str-B 4, 440), of Jesus' own desert preparation (M. Goguel), or of just a "sacred period" between the "epochs" (H. Conzelmann, *Theology,* 203)? Menoud's suggestion is valuable (*Neotestamentica et patristica* [Fest. O. Cullmann; Leiden, 1962] 151ff.): the intent of the 40 days is not to date the ascension, with which it is not connected as a chronological notice, but to imitate the rabbinic use of 40 as a norm for the disciples' learning and repetition of their masters' teaching. The apostles' teaching is shown to be authentic and authoritative because it was received in normative instruction from the risen One. Tertullian (*Apol.* 21. 23) attests this view rather than the dating of the ascension. Menoud has a point, against Haenchen, that since no Christian author proposes a 40-day dating of the ascension until the 4th cent., Luke was probably not following an early tradition but was using a symbolic figure of his own. One should not rule out the intent to match the periods of Jesus' preparation (Lk 4:1–2) and that of the apostles', since the subject of their instruction (the Kingdom of God) is also that of Jesus' own preaching (Lk 4:43; 8:1; 9:11; 16:16; cf. Acts 19:8; 20:25; 28:23). **4.** The rarity of the vb. *synalizō* probably explains the textual variants. Its meaning is uncertain: "coming together with [them]" or "eating together with [them]." Lk 24:43 and Acts 10:41 (*synephagomen*) would support the latter; and M. Wilcox (*Semitisms of Acts* [Oxford, 1965] 106–9) finds further support for it in the rendering of Ps 141:4 in a hexaplaric fragment. *he charged them not to depart from Jerusalem:* See Lk 24:49. This suits, indeed, the Lucan geographical design. Galilean appearances of the Risen Jesus (Mk 14:28; 16:7; Mt 28:16) are systematically omitted by Luke, and the tradition about them apparently corrected (Lk 24:6; → Aspects NT Thought, 78:153). Jerusalem remains the stable situs of the Twelve (cf. 2:43 l.v.; 5:16; 5:28; 8:14; 16:4), even when persecution has scattered the rest of the first community (8:1). The centrality of Jerusalem in the Lucan history emphasizes the continuity between the era of Israel and that of the Church. The "holy city" is the geographic center of sacred history, and the primitive community is bound to it not just in fact, but of necessity (H. Conzelmann, *Theology*, 213; cf. B. Gerhardsson, *Memory and Manuscript* [Uppsala, 1961] 214–20; J. C. O'Neill, *Theology*, 63–64,67). *the promise of the Father:* A traditional (pre-Lucan) designation of the Spirit is *epaggelia* (Gal 3:14; Eph 1:13); cf. Lk 24:49 and Acts 2:33. The latter probably reflects a traditional derivation of the "promise" from Jl 3. *which you heard:* The transition to direct address is a compositional technique (cf. Lk 5:14; Acts 14:22; 17:3; 23:22; 25:5); it does not point to a difference of sources. The former book's résumé is being expanded into the present book's program. **5.** The promise quoted is really a saying of the Baptist, showing the tradition's tendency to assimilate the two figures, John and Jesus. Luke will refer to this Baptist-tradition in his exposition of apostolic baptism (2:38ff.). Cf. 19:1–6.

11 **6–8.** These verses strike the keynote of Acts. The question asked is of present concern to the author's community, and the answer is that which the Lucan history is intended to give. The basis of this pivotal exchange is the tradition of Jesus' eschatological sayings (cf. 1:7 with Mk 13:32 par.); this has meaning for the study of Lucan compositional techniques. **6.** *now when they had come together* [or *now they who had come together*]: The second rendering means a continuation of the scene of vv. 4–5; it would imply a wider circle than those "whom he had chosen" (1:2), especially if it alludes to Lk 24:33. A wider group is similarly presupposed by 1:21. *will you at this time restore the kingdom to Israel?:* A noticeable contrast is presented to the universal mandate of 1:8. The apocalyptic vision of the final *apokatastasis* ("restoration," see 3:21) is the motive for the question put to Jesus, together (probably) with the idea of proximity that his promise (1:5) aroused in the minds of the disciples. Still, what is being stressed as the disciples' mistaken hope is not a "wordly, nationalistic" messianism so much as a hope of an immediate parousia, to which the proximate outpouring of the Spirit was to lead (see F. Mussner, *Lex tua veritas* [Fest. H. Junker; Trier, 1961] 297). Essentially, it is the preoccupation of an impending parousia that Jesus corrects (1:7–8), not the idea of Israel's restoration (see Jer 33:7; Pss 14:7; 85:2; Hos 6:11; Sir 48:10). **7.** *times or seasons:* The Gk phrase *chronous ē kairous* is also found in 1 Thes 5:1, where the uncertainty of the time of the parousia is likewise the issue. For the authenticity of the logion, see Mk 13:32 par.; cf. W. G. Kümmel, *Promise and Fulfillment* (SBT 23; London, 1957) 42. **8.** *but you will receive power when the Holy Spirit comes:* The Spirit is the substitute for the parousia. This is the force of *alla*, "but," the conjunction that joins the two parts of Jesus' reply. The Spirit is the principle of continued Christian existence in a new era of sacred history, the era of the Church and mission. These realities must take the place of an early parousia as the focal point of Christian awareness. The Spirit in the Church is the Lucan answer to the problem of the delay of the parousia and of the continuance of history (see H. Conzelmann, *Theology*, 136). *Jerusalem, all Judea and Samaria, and to the end of the earth:* The movement of the apostolic mission follows this pattern. It begins from Jerusalem (Lk 24:47), the geographic center of sacred history; from it "the word of God" (Acts 4:31) must spread to the whole earth (see H. Conzelmann, *Theology*, 73ff.; J. C. O'Neill, *Theology*, 63–64). The three geographical stages of the missionary command indicate the structure of Acts, corresponding roughly to chs. 1–7, 8–9, 10–28. In ch. 28 Rome, as the capital of the civilized world, apparently qualifies as "the end of the earth" (see P.-H. Menoud, *NTS* 1 [1954–55] 46–47). This phrase anticipates 13:47 with its citation of Is 49:6 (LXX); hence it reveals that the Savior's command is a fulfillment of OT prophecy (see J. Dupont, *NTS* 6 [1959–60] 139–41). "In this manner the history of the primitive community has become *Heilsgeschichte*" (E. Haenchen, *ZNW* 54 [1963] 161).

12 (b) The Ascension (1:9–12). If one does not agree with Menoud that Luke did not intend to date this event (see comment on 1:3) and hence did not create a conflict with Lk 24:50–53, he may safely agree with Conzelmann that Luke's tradition at least followed the broader consensus (Jn 20:17,19; Lk 24:50) that the resurrection and ascension were not separated in time. This passage in Acts would be the only NT source fixing a distance in time between them; of precisely 40 days there is no other witness before the 4th cent., though certain apocrypha assert similar periods (see P. Benoit, *Exégèse*, 1, 370ff.; for other NT data on Jesus' exaltation, → Aspects NT Thought, 78:159).

9. *was lifted up:* The visible departure, or conclusion of the Risen Jesus' sojourn on earth, was probably the developing tradition's response to the problem of the delay of the parousia. It even appropriated older parousia imagery for the scene (see Mk 13:26 par.; 14:62; 1 Thes 4:17), which may explain the explicit comparison made by the angel interpreters in 1:11. **11.** *why do you stand looking...?:* This was apparently the stance of some in the Lucan generation (see E. Haenchen, *Apostelgeschichte*, 119). **12.** *the mount called Olivet:* See Lk 24:50! Zech 14:4 (LXX) indicates the significance and place of the Mt. of Olives in Jewish eschatological traditions.

(Benoit, P., "L'Ascension," *RB* 56 [1949] 161–203; *Exégèse*, 1, 363–411. Lake, K., "The Preface to Acts and the Composition of Acts," and "The Ascension," *Beginnings* 5, 1–7, 16–22. Lohfink, G., "Der historische Ansatz der Himmelfahrt Christi," *Catholica* 17 [1963] 48–84. Van Stempvoort, P. A., "The Interpretation of the Ascension in Luke and Acts," *NTS* 5 [1958–59] 30–42.)

13 (c) The Filling of the College of the Twelve (1:13–26). Haenchen regards this passage as a "test case" of Lucan compositional method in Acts (*ZNW* 54 [1963] 161); and the radical difference of his analysis (cf. *ZThK* 52 [1955] 206ff.) from that of K. H. Rengstorf (*CINTI* 178–92) is most instructive concerning the basic issues in Acts research. The pericope has two components: the tradition on the death of Judas (vv. 18–20) and the account of the election of his successor, Matthias. The latter event is interpreted for the reader by means of Peter's discourse (vv. 16–22), the first discourse, properly speaking, in Acts. The illustrative role of Peter's discourse, i.e., its editorial origin, becomes clear in the speaker's recounting of the Judas affair with its scriptural proofs and etiological corollary. Nevertheless, most would admit that a pre-Lucan tradition underlies the account, whether its placement between the ascension and Pentecost comes from the tradition (Rengstorf [*ibid.*]; cf. P.-H. Menoud, *RHPR* 37 [1957] 73) or was Luke's design (E. Trocmé, *Le Livre*, 199). We should inquire about the function this pericope has in the editorial plan of Acts. Why did Luke choose to narrate this event? It seems to have little importance for the subsequent history and the chosen Matthias never appears again. The answer is found in the pivotal vv. 21–22, where Peter enunciates a theology of apostleship and of the Church's foundations, which is, in fact, a first principle of Lucan presentation. **13.** The 12 names listed here are the same as in Lk 6:13ff., but the order is different. **14.** This verse is the first example of a frequent Lucan compositorial technique, a minor summary (→ 4 above). **15.** *in those days:* Apparently a conscious placement between the end of the appearances and Pentecost. *stood up:* The ptc. *anastas* is a LXX pleonasm, occurring 18 times in Acts, specifically marking the beginning of a discourse, as in 13:16 and 15:7; cf. *statheis* (2:14; 5:20). *the brothers:* The idea of the new community as a brotherhood and the mutual address of "brother" are frequent (28 times) in Acts (cf. *Beginnings* 5, 378–79). *together:* The phrase *epi to auto* is a LXX idiom, but it has a special nuance in the early Church (M. Wilcox, *Semitisms*, 99). It has become, in Christian usage, a quasi-technical term for "in unity" or "in fellowship" of the believing community (cf. 2:44,47). *one hundred twenty persons:* Not an accidental number. The Mishnah (*Sanhedrin* 1:6) enacts that any community's officers will number one-tenth of its numerical strength; 120 was the minimum number for a small Sanhedrin. **16.** *scripture had to be fulfilled:* The sing. *graphē* indicates that the two verses from Pss 69:26 and 109:8 are taken as one text. Reference to the Scriptures in general would require *hai graphai* (cf. 17:2,11; 18:24,28). Note the singular in 8:32,35. The traditional LXX expression for the necessary fulfillment of God's will is *dei*. Here the necessity arises from the divine will revealed in the Scriptures. The expression was frequent in the Syn tradition; but Lk markedly expanded its use (Lk-Acts has 44 out of 102 NT occurrences, with 10 in the properly Lucan stratum of the Gospel). In Lk *dei* applies to Jesus' passion (Lk 9:22; 17:25; 24:26; cf. Acts 17:3), but also to events of his earthly ministry: his preaching (Lk 2:49; 4:43), his journey (13:33)—in general, to the fulfillment of "all that was written" concerning him (22:37; 24:44). If Jesus' life is thus shown to be a saving event that unfolded in necessary steps planned and willed by God, a similar demonstration is made concerning the history of the early Church by the 25 instances of *dei* in Acts (H. Conzelmann, *Theology*, 153–54). Here the impf. *edei* refers to the traitor's end, already accomplished in accordance with Ps 69:26; a corresponding pres. *dei* (1:21) refers to his replacement among the Twelve (Ps 109:8). The divine will is made known by the Spirit through the Scriptures; hence the noteworthy first association of *dei* with the Spirit in this passage (cf. 20:28; E. Fascher, *Neutestamentliche Studien* [Fest. R. Bultmann; Berlin, 1954] 246).

14 **18–19.** The death of Judas. Comparing this tradition with Mt 27:3–10 and with the report of Papias (*Beginnings* 5, 23f.), one sees how diversely the Christian "popular mind" expressed its deep impressions of the traitor and his terrible deed. **19.** *Akeldama:* The variant etiological stories in Mt and Acts refer to Akeldama, a place known to the Christian community at Jerusalem (cf. M. Dibelius, *Die Formgeschichte des Evangeliums* [2nd ed.; Tübingen, 1933] 113; P. Benoit, *Exégèse*, 1, 341). Each story seeks in its own way to demonstrate that Judas' death agreed with what the Scriptures proposed as the worthy end for nefarious people (*Beginnings* 5, 29f.). The different scriptural passages appealed to in each case (in Acts: Pss 69:26; 109:8; in Mt: Zech 11:12–13) probably account for the different details about the manner of Judas' death and the reason for the name "field of blood." Quite probably his suicide, perhaps by hanging, is the historical core that underlies these stories. Insertion by Luke of the Judas-tradition into a written document of Peter's discourse is improbable, for the two are woven too carefully together. Reading v. 20 after v. 17 would give the impression that no one could fill the place of Judas. *falling headlong:* Jerome's translation "suspensus" (Douai: "being hanged") was an attempt to harmonize the text with Mt 27:5. No rare meaning need be sought here, not even the occasionally suggested "swollen." The rendering of *prēnēs genomenos* is simply: "falling headlong" (i.e., in his ill-gotten field, e.g., by stumbling). *burst asunder:* Perhaps inspired by the death of the wicked who persecute the just (Wis 4:19: *rēxei autous aphōnous prēneis*). Quite similar is the folklore concerning Herod's death in 12:23. *in their own dialect:* Is anything else needed to show that Peter's words are informing Luke's readers rather than Peter's hearers? *Akeldama:* The Gk form (*Hakeldamach*) reflects an Aram name (→ Gospel Mt, 43:193) given to the field because of Judas' terrible death there, and not because the betrayal money was used to purchase it (Mt). The "blood" in question is, in the one case, that of the betrayer; in the other, that of the betrayed.

15 **20.** The Ps text quoted (69:25) presumes the LXX rendering; the MT has the pl. possessive, "their," instead of the sing., "his." This is a situation hard to imagine for Peter or a Semitic source transmitting his words. The Gk word *episkopē* (Ps 109:8) here designates the apostolic office (see 1:25). **21.** The prerequisites of apostolic "service" (*diakonia*) are now given. *must:* The Gk vb. *dei* states the necessity of the new appointment that arises from the Ps. *one of the men who accompanied us all the time:* This condition would gravely undermine the Pauline claims of apostleship (Gal 1:1; 1 Cor 9:1; 15:8). Scholars have correctly asserted that this is a later criterion of apostleship, making the apostles coextensive with the Twelve (e.g., H. von Campenhausen, *ST* 1 [1949] 116; E. Lohse, *TZ* 9 [1953] 269ff.), not one, however, that Luke invented (*pace* G. Klein, *Die zwölf Apostel*, 206), but one that he inherits and presupposes (W. Schmithals, *Das kirchliche Apostelamt* [FRLANT 79; Göttingen, 1961] 233ff.; E. Haenchen, *Apostelgeschichte*, 102, 679–80). A later generation of Christians was anxious to secure its roots in an authentic and carefully traced apostolic witness; the tradition transmitted by the Twelve was thus guaranteed (→ Aspects NT Thought, 78:179–182). What characterizes the apostle above all is his association with the life of Jesus, which is the "beginning" (*archē*) of legitimate tradition and of the continuing Church (Lk 1:2; cf. Acts 10:39; 13:31). Hence, his unique witness to the resurrection rests upon his having also "begun" with Jesus. The apostle's "historical uniqueness" is, for Luke's second-generation Christianity, "the historical foundation for the Church of the present" (H. Conzelmann, *Theology*, 216), guarding it against the anarchy of private revelations and ungoverned charisms. The later Church, seeking a norm of belief and life, looks back to the privileged initial period of her history and sees in the Twelve the unique transmitters of the Word and the Spirit during that period. This accounts for the extended criterion of apostleship encountered here. Of it Paul has no knowledge. **22.** *witness of his resurrection:* This is the traditional apostolic function (1 Cor 9:1; 15:8–9; see K. H. Rengstorf, *ThDNT* 1, 431ff.; *Die Auferstehung Jesu* [Witten, 1960] 117–27, 136–45). The use of the noun *martys* (witness) to embody the concept is Lucan, but even this has roots in the tradition (1 Cor 15:15). The real development here is not in vocabulary but in the extension of the apostle's requisite experience to include the "beginning" of Jesus' ministry. **24–25.** This prayer, like others in Acts (e.g., 4:24ff.), is composed of established formulas. The phrase "knowing the hearts of all" (*kardiognōsta pantōn*) doubtless represents one in use among Gentile Christians (cf. *Apostolic Constitutions* 3.7, 8; cf. *Beginnings* 4, 15). *this ministry and apostolate:* These words resume v. 17 and show that the apostolic office is what the former term designates. **26.** *with the eleven apostles:* Whatever one thinks of the authenticity of the logion in Mt 19:28 (Lk 22:28,30 par.), dismissed by Klein in but a sentence (*Die zwölf Apostel*, 36), the ancient creed of 1 Cor 15:3–5 makes the Twelve an historical reality to be reckoned with. But the equation of the older institution, the Twelve, with the probably later designation *apostolos*, is first encountered in the postapostolic era.

(Benoit, P., "La mort de Judas," *Synoptische Studien* [Fest. A. Wikenhauser; Munich, 1954] 1–19. Cerfaux, L., "Pour l'histoire du titre *apostolos* dans le Nouveau Testament," *RSR* 48 [1960] 76–92. Lohse, E., "Ursprung und Prägung des christlichen Apostolates," *TZ* 9 [1953] 259–76. Menoud, P.-H., "Les additions au groupe des Douze Apôtres d'après le Livre des Actes," *RHPR* 37 [1957] 71–80. Rigaux, B., "Die 'Zwölf' in Geschichte und Kerygma," *Der historische Jesus und der kerygmatische Christus* [eds. H. Ristow and K. Matthiae; Berlin, 1961] 468–86. Von Campenhausen, H., "Der urchristliche Apostelbegriff," *ST* 1 [1948] 96–130.)

16 (d) The Pentecost Event (2:1–13). Luke now describes a formative event in the early Church's existence. **1.** *when the day was fulfilled:* This introduction assures us that we have reached an important date in Luke's history of the Church's formative past; see E. Lohse, *EvT* 13 [1953] 432; *EvT* 14 [1954] 261ff.). The same formula announced the birth of Mary's child (Lk 2:6) and the inauguration of Jesus' exodus-journey (Lk 9:51). It is thus a guidepost for the inauguration of major stages in Luke's sacred history. Here it signals the *terminus a quo* for the new era of the Church, which the gift of the Spirit inaugurates (H. Conzelmann, *Apostelgeschichte*, 25). The "fulfillment" refers to the promise of Lk 24:49 and Acts 1:4–5,7 and again brings out the over-all conception guiding Luke's two-volume composition. *of the Pentecost:* (For the origin and original agrarian character of this feast, → Religious Institutions, 76:142). The Christian adoption of this Jewish festival is surely significant (see 1 Cor 16:8; Acts 20:16; cf. E. Lohse, *ThWNT* 6, 49–50). Pentecost must have been the occasion of a real formative event in the early community's history (see G. Kretschmar, *ZKG* 66 [1954–55] 248; P.-H. Menoud, *RHPR* 42 [1962] 145; but cf. H. J. Cadbury, *The Book*, 101). This "Feast of Weeks" may have acquired more than its original agrarian content as early as the time of Jesus. The character of covenant renewal or Sinai commemoration, which all admit the Jewish feast had acquired by the 2nd cent. AD, may have come only as a gradual result of the Temple's destruction in AD 70. Yet there is earlier evidence for Sinai commemoration in the feast, at least in some refractory circles (cf. *Jub* 6:17–21 [cf. 2 Chr 15:8–15]; QL). Jesus' followers may therefore have been familiar with a fiftieth day feast celebrating Moses' reception of the Law on Mt. Sinai. Besides, Philo and certain rabbinic traditions associated with Sinai such visual theophany elements as the "tongues," fire, and wind. The typology of Moses ascending "to God" (MT: Ex 19:3) and returning with the gift of the Law (*Tg. Ps* 68:19; cf. Eph 4:8) may have inspired an early Palestinian tradition's association of Jesus' ascension with his Pentecostal gift of the Spirit, the "law" of the new covenant (see G. Kretschmar, *ZKG* 66 [1954–55] 216ff.). Given these ancient associations of the fiftieth day after Passover, it may be that we are dealing with a Christian retention analogous to the situation of the Passover itself. The association of the ascension and Pentecost is quite ancient; indeed, in the earliest sources the two events are consigned to the same fiftieth day (*ibid.*, 209–11). Whatever the origins of the Christian Pentecost tradition, the fact remains that the present account originated not with Palestinian Christians, but in a community "which was guided by Judeo-Hellenistic theology" and "in which Sacred Writ was read in the language of the LXX" (W. Grundmann, *SE* 2, 586). **2.** *a mighty wind:* There was even a phonetic relationship in Greek between the words *pnoē* (wind) and *pneuma* (spirit); the latter is not mentioned until v. 4. **3.** *divided tongues as if of fire:* The first occurrence of the thematic word *glōssa* (tongue), which is then used in a quite different sense in vv. 4, 11. The qualifier *hōsei* (as if) reminds us of the apocalyptic comparative that often appears in accounts of visions, emphasizing the disproportion between images and the celestial realities they mean to express. The pedagogy here is similar: to communicate the meaning of an essentially interior spiritual experience of heavenly realities in terms and images familiar to an audience. The mighty wind and fire are familiar from OT theophanies; cf. Is 66:15ff. (LXX), the scene of the final judgment and gathering of nations. *rested upon each of them:* The image brings out that the Spirit (still unmentioned) came to everyone present. **4.** *Holy Spirit:* The great gift of the final age (v. 17) and the fulfillment of the risen One's promise (1:7). The immediate effect is that Jesus' witnesses begin to speak according to the Spirit's dictates. The scene becomes programmatic, for precisely this missionary speaking on a universal scale (vv. 5ff.) is the matter of history in Acts. The Spirit instructs early missioners (8:29; 10:19f.; 11:12; 13:2; 19:1 [in ms. D]; 21:11); it is the decisive and driving force in the proclamation of the message (4:31; cf. 4:8; 2:4; 6:10; 11:23) and in conversion to faith in Christ (2:38; 8:15ff.; 10:44ff.; 11:15; 19:2ff.). It also gives strength to endure persecution (4:29ff.; 9:16–17; 13:52) and remains the guiding force in Paul's missionary efforts (13:4ff.; 20:22–23; 21:4,11; cf. 9:17–18) as it had been in earlier efforts (see 8:39). The Spirit is the principal mover in the decisive event of Acts, the one which opens the Church to the uncircumcised (10:19; 11:12); the apostles' confidence in this is remarkably expressed in the decree of 15:28. As parousia-replacement in Christian consciousness, therefore, the gift of the Spirit inaugurates the era of Church and mission, the new epoch of salvation history (E. Lohse, *EvT* 14 [1954] 263; H. Conzelmann, *Theology*, 213).

17 Luke appears to have complicated the original unit of the paschal experience (resurrection, ascension, outpouring of the Spirit; cf. Jn 20:22; Mt 28:19). It is not that he placed the gift of the Spirit on Pentecost only because he had accepted the 40-day ascension-tradition (E. Haenchen, *Apostelgeschichte*, 137). The Pentecost of Acts and the risen One's first giving of the Spirit are evidently not the same reality. Jn and Mt do not record a mission activity immediately following the Easter experience; Jn in fact suggests an intervening period of inactivity (Jn 20:26; 21:1–3). The historical basis of Luke's Pentecost is probably the first public preaching about the Christ. In this "Luke gives way to his inclination to schematize history, presenting the Spirit uniquely as the divine energy communicated to the witnesses of Christ...in view of the task they are to perform. Neglected here is the aspect that John and Matthew expressed: The believer whom the risen One encounters lives thenceforth by his Spirit" (P.-H. Menoud, *RHPR* 42 [1962] 147). *in other tongues:* It is possible that the earliest version of this story had not recorded a speaking of the apostles "in other tongues" (v. 8 uses the Gk word *dialektos*), but simply their speaking "in tongues" (= glossolalia). The ecstasy or frenzy that accompanied the episode is attested in vv. 7 and 12 (*existanto*). The cynical reaction of some witnesses (v. 13), although hard to explain if the apostles were really speaking in foreign tongues, would be natural if their speech was the ecstatic speaking "in tongues" known to certain early Christian circles (cf. 1 Cor 12:10; 14:2; cf. Acts 10:46; 19:6). The interpretation of the Pentecostal glossolalia in terms of an intelligible apostolic speech "in other tongues" is judged by many to be the innovation of the author of Acts in the interest of his universalist mission theology (cf. É. Trocmé, *Le Livre*, 201–6; E. Lohse, *EvT* 13 [1953] 434–36; G. Kretschmar, *ZKG* 66 [1954–5] 234–37). It is possible that an historically solid oral tradition reported the first public proclamation of the gospel by Jesus' disciples amidst circumstances of frenzied enthusiasm and an emission of the ecstatic speech that persuaded the ancients of the Spirit's operation. Luke's generation, if indeed it retained an accurate notion of glossolalia (Lake and Conzelmann claim that 10:46 and 19:6 show that it did not), had most likely inherited Paul's evaluation of the "tongues." Far from being comprehensible to all ethnic groups, they were understood by no one; consequently, they could not be compared with inspired preaching in service rendered to the Church (cf. 1 Cor 14:1ff.). If Luke shared this view (É. Trocmé, *Le Livre*, 202), it is understandable that he would interpret ecstatic speech as a speaking in "other" tongues, thus causing the first, immediately sensible effects of the Pentecost experience to be clothed with its lasting significance: the inauguration of a mission to all the world, which would overcome every division of mankind.

5. *Jews...from every nation:* The diverse national origins of the Diaspora Jews are enumerated in the catalogue of vv. 9–11. Some confusion in the transmission of this verse makes it difficult to decide whether *katoikountes* (dwelling) and more especially *Ioudaioi* (Jews), are original (cf. *Beginnings* 5, 113f.). But it is quite clear that the Gentiles cannot enter into the Lucan missionary schema until after the Cornelius event (ch. 10). "Jews and proselytes" (2:10) probably constitute an exhaustive division of the audience. Haenchen insists that Luke is not thinking of pilgrims sojourning in Jerusalem for the feast. But v. 14 indicates that *katoikountes* bears a sense not much different from *epidēmountes* (visiting) of v. 10. **6.** *they were confused:* The use of *sygcheō* may be influenced by the use of the same root in the LXX of Gn 11:7,9 ("Tower of Babel"), where *glōssa* is once the verb's object. Thus the Pentecostal Spirit overcomes the ancient division of men's tongues that began at Babel (LXX: *sygchysis*). This allusion is reinforced by the occurrence of the rare vb. *diamerizō* (2:3), which occurs in the reference to Babel in Dt 32:8 (LXX); cf. *Recueil L. Cerfaux* [Gembloux, 1954] 2, 185. Perhaps it is only the inauguration of the healing of Babel's division that the author sees in Pentecost. **7.** *they were beside themselves:* The vb. *existanto* expresses the common ecstatic experience (cf. v. 12). In their ecstasy the polyglot group expresses, quite eloquently and with a catalogue of the nationalities represented (vv. 9–11), Luke's own analysis of the event and its lasting significance. Seen no longer as a momentary and largely incomprehensible religious ecstasy, the apostolic utterance at Pentecost becomes the inauguration of a truly universal preaching that will transcend every boundary of nationality and speech. **9–11.** The 15 nationalities of Diaspora Jews (and proselytes) represent the universality of mankind spread out over the earth and divided by difference of language. Whether the Diaspora was actually so widespread at this time is hardly important; the list is a literary device that proposes the nationalities in a more or less regular geographical sweep from E to W and achieves at least an Oriental's impression of universality (J. A. Brinkman, *CBQ* 25 [1963] 419). Similar catalogues, with possibly similar origins, are found in later Gk literature; one may assume that they were, for contemporary authors, "a stock literary expression for the 'whole world'" (*ibid.*, 425). Jewish authors used this kind of catalogue to describe the extent of the Diaspora (Str-B 2, 606ff.). One must reckon with Luke's adaptation of the prior list. **9.** *Judea:* Probably an interpolation. It neither belongs between Mesopotamia and Cappadocia geographically, nor could it be considered a place where a language other than the apostles' was spoken. **11.** *Jews and proselytes:* These words do not denote additional language-groups, but indicate the entire group's religious status, and so one would normally expect that they conclude the list. However, because "Cretans and Arabians" may be interpolated (in light of Ti 1:5 and Gal 1:17?), the list as Luke prepared it could have ended, as his book does, with Rome. *the mighty works of God:* What these are will be made explicit in Peter's discourse (2:22–36). **12.** The repetition of *existanto* (v. 7) does not indicate a source (*pace* É. Trocmé, *Le Livre*, 202). It is intended to form a transition to the Petrine discourse that follows. Thus the ecstatic observers ask, "What does this mean?" The discourse will not interpret the linguistic miracle. Hence the need for a transition to vv. 7–11. **13.** *others:* Are these in addition to the ecstatic *pantes* (all) of v. 12? Perhaps, in Luke's mind they are Jerusalem Jews who did not know the foreign tongues and could thus judge the apostles to be drunk. One may rather wish to see in this verse an echo of the tradition, which spoke of an ecstatic experience to which the reaction of the "others" would be just what we should expect.

(Cerfaux, L., "Le symbolisme attaché au miracle des langues," *ETL* 13 [1936] 256–59. Grundmann, W., "Der Pfingstbericht der Apostelgeschichte in seinem theologischen Sinn," *SE* 2, 584–94. Kretschmar, G., "Himmelfahrt und Pfingsten," *ZKG* 66 [1954–55] 209–53. Lohse, E., "Die Bedeutung des Pfingstberichtes im Rahmen des lukanischen Geschichtswerkes," *EvT* 13 [1953] 422–36; "*Pentēkostē*," *ThWNT* 6, 44–53. Menoud, P.-H., "La Pentecôte lucanienne et l'histoire," *RHPR* 42 [1962] 141–47.)

18 **(B) The Mission in Jerusalem (2:14–8:3).**

(a) THE PENTECOST DISCOURSE (2:14–41). The first of the "missionary discourses" observes closely the typical outline: (1) an introduction relating the discourse to the narrative framework (2:14–21); (2) the essential facts of the Jesus-kerygma with scriptural demonstrations (2:22–36); (3) a call to penance and conversion in light of the kerygma (2:38–39). A growing consensus today views the discourse as substantially a Lucan composition, but with an inner fabric of prior tradition. Significant in this discourse, and difficult to explain on M. Dibelius's "ancient preaching-*typus*" hypothesis, is the use of Jl 3:1–5 (LXX), not to substantiate the Jesus-kerygma, but as "the carefully placed and aptly chosen link joining narrative-situation and sermon" (U. Wilckens, *Missionsreden*, 34). This may be a hint of compositorial design; but it does not mean that Luke was the first to associate the Joel prophecy with the Christian possession of God's Spirit. Jl 3:5 (= Acts 2:21) can certainly be traced to much earlier preaching (cf. Rom 10:13; C. H. Dodd, *According to the Scriptures* [London, 1952] 47). A possible trace of the prophecy's use concerning the Spirit is the occurrence of Joel's vb., "pour out" (*ek-cheō*), in the formula of Ti 3:6, where God is said to have "poured out [the Holy Spirit] upon us abundantly through [*dia*] Jesus Christ...." Even if the Joel passage were a fixed "testimonium" in Luke's time, it is he who has undoubtedly given it this pivotal position in the literary construction of his two-volume history. Having remained in Jerusalem in accordance with the programmatic instructions of the risen One (Lk 24:49; Acts 1:4), the apostles receive the promised Spirit for bearing universal witness (1:8; 2:1ff.). Peter's argument from prophecy shows that the "promise" (*epaggelia*) of the Father has truly been fulfilled (cf. 2:39). Hence this first Petrine discourse is a careful elaboration of the theme that unifies and links the two-part Lucan history. Moreover, the discourse is carefully anchored in the immediate narrative context of the Pentecost event (vv. 14ff., 33, 39). Any assertion, therefore, that the discourse is a block of tradition taken over as such (e.g., from an Aram source [see C. H. Dodd, *Apostolic Preaching*, 20]) flies in the face of clear and pervasive editorial designs (see U. Wilckens, *Missionsreden*, 59). Still possible, however, is the assertion that a solid tissue of pre-Lucan tradition underlies the Petrine sermon; this we shall attempt to discover in individual instances.

14. *stood up:* The ptc. *statheis* typically denotes the assumption of the speaker's position (5:20; 11:18; 17:22; 25:18; 27:21). *with the eleven:* Cf. the significant parallel in v. 37: "Peter and the other apostles." The equation of "Peter and the Eleven" with "the apostles" is presupposed, and there is a recurring emphasis on their common action in the chapters that follow (cf. E. Haenchen, *ZNW* 54 [1963] 163). *let this be known to you:* It is difficult to ascribe this Semitism (*gnōston einai*) to the influence of the LXX, where it is rare. It occurs thrice elsewhere in Acts (4:10; 13:38; 28:28) and may be a vestige of a late Semitic expository idiom (so M. Wilcox, *Semitisms*, 90–91). **15–16.** The speaker's correction of a misunderstanding of the event by onlookers serves as a bond between the discourse and the narrative. This technique will be used again (3:12; 14:15; cf. 4:9b, 17:22–23) and confirms the role of a single composing hand in the discourses (E. Schweizer, *Studies in Lk-Acts*, 210–12).

19 **17–21.** The LXX text-form of Jl 3:1–5 argues for the composition of the discourse in Greek, for it is quite clear that the discourse as such never existed without the citations (H. Conzelmann, *Apostelgeschichte*, 28). Small interpretative alterations of this passage occur in the Western Text and appear to be improvements of the prophecy's relation to the Pentecost situation (cf. *Beginnings* 3, 16f.). Whether or not Luke originally reproduced the exact LXX wording, he surely preserved the essential structure of the prophecy: (1) the eschatological outpouring of the Spirit, resulting in the gifted people's prophetic activity; (2) cosmic signs of the "day of the Lord" before its dawning; (3) the coming of that day and the salvation of all who call upon the name of *Kyrios*. **17.** *in the last days:* This Western reading (ms. D) is an important departure from the LXX, which simply reads "afterward" (*meta tauta*). Some mss. have the latter, but this is most probably a secondary LXX-assimilation (so L. Cerfaux, *Aux sources de la tradition chrétienne* [Fest. M. Goguel; Paris, 1950] 47; U. Wilckens, *Missionsreden*, 33, n. 2; F. Mussner, *BZ* 5 [1961] 263). Besides, the simple "afterward" would have been unsuitable where the citation was introduced without its context, as here. Yet if we choose the Western reading, is the discourse then a fundamentally Lucan product? The Spirit's outpouring cannot inaugurate the last days for Luke; rather it must initiate the era of the Church, an historical epoch *iure suo*, albeit the final one. Why would he have altered the LXX reading from the first point of view? This question embarrasses the Lucan analysts. It causes Haenchen to opt for the improbable *meta tauta* (*ZThK* 51 [1954] 162; *Apostelgeschichte*, 142); it forces an unwilling Conzelmann to suggest that a tradition is employed that diverges from Luke's own conceptions (*Theology*, 95). The latter approach is more satisfying. For Luke regards these "last days," in an expanded sense—the final epoch of redemptive history (E. Grässer, *Parusieverzögerung*, 209). A "demythologizing" of "the last days" is suggested. The divine Spirit, which inaugurates the new epoch and confers the powers of perseverance and mission, takes the place of the dramatic eschatological "rescue" (Jl) as the "Lord's" act of salvation on his "day." To put forth this new view, Luke has, as elsewhere in Lk-Acts, employed traditional material; in this case, it came to him stamped with the view that the "last days" (in the traditional sense) had arrived with the postresurrection and imminent parousia. *all flesh:* This becomes plural (*pasas sarkas*) in ms. D, and the possessive "your" with "sons and daughters" becomes "their." These touches sharpen the passage's universalism; but they may also violate Lucan economy. For missionary preaching is directed exclusively to the Jews at this point (E. Haenchen, *ZThK* 51 [1954] 162). **18.** *and they will prophesy:* This expansion of the LXX text has been omitted by ms. D (which is doing the LXX-assimilating now). Luke has not equated glossolalia with prophecy (*pace* E. Haenchen, *Apostelgeschichte*, 149; H. Conzelmann, *Apostelgeschichte*, 29), for he did not consider the Pentecost activity of the apostles as a mere ecstatic phenomenon. Prophecy is here understood according to the widespread early Christian usage, as a manner of Spirit-filled preaching (cf. Acts 19:6; 21:9; 1 Cor 14:1). Missionary preaching as the multilingual work of the Spirit rather than a mere ecstasy has aroused derision (v. 13). Prophecy is the missionary function and belongs to all the new "people of God" (H. Kraft, *TZ* 17 [1961] 411). **19–20.** *wonders in the heavens... and signs on the earth:* It is hard to tell whether Luke explains these elements precisely. The repetition of *terata kai sēmeia* (v. 22) may suggest that the miracles of Jesus had taken their place among the premonitory signs of the end time. But then the prophecy's fulfillment has been explicitly located in the situation at hand (v. 16, *touto estin*), making the oblique reference to the ministry unlikely. **21.** *whoever calls upon the name of Kyrios will be saved:* The Pentecost phenomena, as signs of the final age, here become a "mission-motivation"—for belief and penance among the hearers. Peter's subsequent exposition leads up to an identification of the *Kyrios* (v. 36) and a call for penance (v. 38). If the argument from prophecy is proposing the approaching end time as a motive for invoking Jesus as the Lord, as the argument in 3:19–21 certainly will do, is this not a traditional substratum of the discourse traceable to a stage of more proximate parousia-expectation than Luke's own? Luke admittedly does not develop the sign-motivation in the discourse proper, but that may support the view that the confession of Jesus as Lord, when first derived from Jl 3:5 (cf. Rom 10:9,13) was motivated by the perspective of an impending parousia-judgment.

20 **22–24.** The Jesus-kerygma is the central element in the schema of the missionary discourses. It proposes, in short summary, the name, works, death, and resurrection of the proclaimed One. The statement at hand has one main clause ("you killed... this Jesus") and several subordinates, including the usually central statement about the resurrection ("whom God raised up"), which comes in a rel. clause here. The sentence as a whole therefore emphasizes the accusation against the Jewish audience: In contrast to the clear, divine attestation (*apodedeigmenon*) of the miracles, the Jews handed Jesus over to death; therein lies their guilt. To their wickedness is contrasted the mighty action of God in raising up Jesus. The central affirmation of the Jews' guilt, which the grammar brings out, has its counterpart in each of the other missionary sermons (3:13b–15a; 4:10–11; 5:30; 10:39–40; 13:27–30). The contrast of that rejection and the divine saving action in Jesus consistently provides the preacher with the basis of his concluding call for penance and conversion (2:38; cf. 3:19; 5:31; cf. U. Wilckens, *Missionsreden*, 119). The sharp antithesis of the kerygmatic statements and their omission of a formula for Jesus' death, such as "for our sins" (1 Cor 15:3), have led many to propose as characteristically Lucan the tendency to deprive the cross of the saving value given it by Paul and his *paradosis* (e.g., H. J. Cadbury, *The Making*, 280; P. Vielhauer, *Studies in Lk-Acts*, 45; H. Conzelmann, *Theology*, 201). The death of Jesus, though indeed foreseen and provided for in God's plan, was the sinful rejection of their Messiah by God's people; God's action in raising up Jesus thwarted this wickedness and became the unique cause of forgiveness and salvation (cf. 5:30–31; 13:38–39). Yet however one is to explain the different evaluations of Jesus' death in the kerygma of Acts and the *paradosis* of 1 Cor 15, one cannot be content to label the motif in Acts as a Lucan theologoumenon. The same emphasis on the sinful treatment of Jesus and the same lack of a soteriological evaluation of his death are found in the Marcan predictions of the passion (Mk 8:31; 9:31; 10:33–34). There is also in these predictions a climactic and antithetical emphasis on the resurrection. Mk's tradition shares the "third day" notice with Paul's *paradosis* (1 Cor 15:4); and yet it does not include the latter's phrase, "for our sins."

22. *which God did through him:* God is master over salvation history (see 1:7) and Jesus' role is instrumental; he is "anointed," "attested," "raised up," "exalted," by the Father. Conzelmann (*Theology*, 173–76) terms this Lucan "subordinationism." **23.** *according to the definite plan and foreknowledge of God:* This phrase is an example of the Lucan semantics of salvation history (see H. Conzelmann, *Theology*, 151–54; cf. S. Schulz, *ZNW* 54 [1963] 105–6). Especially characteristic is the combination of *boulē* (plan) with *horizō* (determine) or *proorizō* (determine in advance; see 4:28); also the use of words with the prefix *pro-* for God's antecedent disposition of saving events (see 1:16; 3:18,20; 4:28; 10:41; 13:24; 22:14; 26:16). The concept of a powerfully provident God interprets the traditional Scripture fulfillment motif in the light of a more properly Hellenistic theodicy (see S. Schulz, *op. cit.*, 106, 111). *delivered up . . . crucified:* Both words are *hapax legomena* in the NT and in the LXX. The adj. *ekdotos* echoes the traditional *paradidonai* of the Marcan predictions and other passion-traditions (1 Cor 11:23; Rom 4:25; 8:32), whereas *prospēgnynai* (crucify) alludes to Dt 21:22; cf. 5:30 and 10:40 (also Gal 3:13). **24.** *having loosed the pangs of death:* The LXX version of Ps 18:4 was probably a misreading of the MT, *ḥbly* ("bands" or "cords") of death. Contemporary usage gave *ōdines* the meaning of the messianic "woes" (Mk 13:8; Mt 24:8; I Thes 5:3; M. Wilcox, *Semitisms*, 48). A similar uniting of the kerygmatic rel. clause asserting the resurrection with the verse from Ps 18 occurs in Polycarp (*Ep. ad Phil.* 1.2). This formula initiates a new segment of the discourse, consisting of resurrection-kerygma with its scriptural demonstration (vv. 24–32). Scriptural argumentation in support of the resurrection belongs to the earliest NT traditions (1 Cor 15:4) and may be regarded as a natural outgrowth of the biblical necessity (*dei*, "must"), which occurs in the passion-tradition.

25–28. Here and in the first Pauline sermon (13:35) we have the only use of Ps 16:8–11 in the NT. The liberties the Gk translator took with the original Hebrew (*ep' elpidi*, "in hope," for *lbṭḥ*, "securely"; *diaphthora*, "corruption," for *šaḥat*, "pit") are good reasons for thinking that the Ps was not in Christian usage before the stage of Gk language propaganda (J. Dupont, *ETL* 29 [1953] 310–11). Yet the practice of some *targumîm* and some QL (see R. E. Murphy, *Bib* 39 [1958] 61–66) of rendering *šaḥat* with *ḥbl'* (destruction, decay) makes inadequate the usual argument that the pivotal *idein diaphthoran* (to see corruption) proves dependence on the LXX (see B. M. F. van Iersel, *'Der Sohn' in den synoptischen Jesusworten* [Leiden, 1964] 46). Moreover, the contention of U. Wilckens (*Missionsreden*, 141–42) and F. Hahn (*Christologische Hoheitstitel* [FRLANT 83; Göttingen, 1963] 278, n. 2) that Luke was the first to find a resurrection-argument in Ps 16 seems quite improbable, given the peculiarly rabbinic brand of exegesis that Peter employs in vv. 29–31 (see J. W. Doeve, *Jewish Hermeneutics* [Assen, 1954] 168ff.). **29.** The grave of David (1 Kgs 2:10; Josephus, *Ant.* 1.2, 5, § 61; cf. *Ant.* 7.15, 3 § 393–94) is proof that the patriarch was not speaking of himself in the Ps, but was speaking *ep' elpidi* of his descendant. Here, as elsewhere (8:30–35; 2:33–34; 13:35–37), the scriptural argument follows a set schema: (1) Scripture reads thus; (2) the words apply either to the one speaking in the text or to another; (3) but they do not apply to the speaker; (4) hence they apply to another, namely Jesus, whom they fit perfectly (see H. J. Cadbury, *Beginnings* 5, 407–9). Once again, such a fixed schema does not necessarily prove literary creation by Luke himself (contra Cadbury; cf. B. M. F. van Iersel, *'Der Sohn,'* 43–44). **30.** The ideology of Davidic succession is quoted from Ps 132:11–12 to indicate of whom David prophesied in the Ps. The transitive sense of *kathisai* (cause to sit) is confirmed by the fact that God is the subject in v. 36 (*Beginnings* 4, 25). It was God's action that raised Jesus up (vv. 24, 32) and exalted him (vv. 33, 36). **32.** The kerygmatic statement of v. 24 is reaffirmed and the usual formula of apostolic witness is added (cf. 3:15; 5:32; see comment on 1:8). To deny all continuity of this sequence (resurrection-statement and witness-formula) with the Pauline *paradosis* (1 Cor 15:4–5,15) is hypercritical (e.g., U. Wilckens, *Missionsreden*, 148–49). This is not to say that Lk does not employ elsewhere in Acts the concept of "witness" in senses properly his own (cf. 10:39,41–42; 13:31).

21 **33–36.** Exaltation kerygma. **33.** The sentence contains two participles that embody pre-Lucan ideas, and a main verb that probably represents Luke's own innovation. Presupposed is the identity of him whom God raised up (*anestēsen*, v. 32) and him who was "exalted" (*hypsōtheis*); it is such that this participle would seem even to explain the preceding aorist (E. Schweizer, *Lordship and Discipleship* [SBT 28; London, 1960] 38). In support of this is the statement of v. 31, where David, mindful of the promise of heavenly enthronement for his descendant, is said to have spoken of the resurrection of the Christ. On the other hand, Luke's own theology tends to separate the resurrection from the heavenly triumph (e.g., his ascension accounts, Acts 10:41). At least we should expect him to add *analēmphtheis* (having been taken up) before *hypsōtheis*, for he was careful to include the former in the summary of Acts 1:2. Yet the nearly unnoticed transition from *anistanai* (raise up) to *hypsōthēnai* (be exalted) is more in the style of Rom 8:34; Eph 1:20; 1 Pt 1:21, where the risen One's heavenly enthronement is part of a temporally undifferentiated paschal event. It is unlikely that the present statements originate with Luke and that he omitted *analēmphtheis* for "economy of expression" (H. Conzelmann, *Apostelgeschichte*, 30; U. Wilckens, *Missionsreden*, 151). *at the right hand of God:* Familiar citation of Ps 110:1, the *locus classicus* for the early doctrine about Jesus' exaltation. The phrase designates the exalted One's position of sovereignty; it is a dative of place rather than of instrument. Christian exegesis of the Ps helped to form a concept of the already exalted Jesus which could be dissociated from the imminent parousia and the apocalypse of the Son of Man (cf. F. Hahn, *Hoheitstitel*, 113–17, 126–32, and the criticisms of P. Vielhauer, *EvT* 25 [1965] 42–52). *receiving the promise of the Spirit: Epaggelia* is traditional as a designation of the Spirit (see comment on 1:4). But can the same be said of *labein* (receive) as expressing the risen One's being endowed with the Spirit? The NT text does not provide us with a clear affirmative answer. But the similar idea that the Risen Christ became powerful in the Spirit finds expression in the old formulas of Rom 1:4 and 1 Tm 3:16 (cf. 1 Cor 15:45). Luke's usual doctrine is rather that Jesus received the Spirit at the beginning of his public ministry, endowing him for the activities thereof (Lk 3:21–22; 4:18–21; Acts 10:38). In itself, then, this second participial phrase of v. 33 embodies a pre-Lucan view. As Luke uses it, its meaning is that Jesus received the Spirit to "pour out" on his followers only when he was raised up and exalted (cf. E. Haenchen, *Apostelgeschichte*, 146; J. C. O'Neill, *Theology*, 126). *he has poured out that which you see and hear:* The reference to the situation is quite Lucan. Moreover, this is the only instance in either testament where the agent of the Spirit's "outpouring" is other than God (cf. Ti 3:6, where the subject is God "through" Jesus Christ). Thus it is that the two subordinate clauses of v. 33 are traditional kerygmata that Luke has subordinated to his own insight and to the historiographical function of Peter's discourse. The present sovereignty of the Risen Christ involves the very function that inaugurates and maintains the new era of the Church: the outpouring of the Spirit. **34–35.** Only here and in the controversy concerning the Messiah's Davidic sonship (Mk 12:35–37a par.) is Ps 110:1 quoted in full. The controversy and the formula of Rom 1:3–4 belong to the level of a "two-stage Christology" (G. Bornkamm, *Jesus of Nazareth* [London, 1960] 228; F. Hahn, *Hoheitstitel*, 115, 251–62), according to which Jesus' Davidic sonship is an attribute rather of his earthly condition and activity than of his heavenly, exalted state. The distinction between Davidic sonship and full messiahship (*kyriotēs*) probably belongs to the level of the post-Palestinian Jewish mission—as may be the case with the use of Ps 110 itself, with its ambivalent *kyrios*. *until I make your enemies:* Perhaps this second strophe's inclusion reflects Luke's understanding that the era of the Church, i.e., of the exalted Lord's "pouring out" of the Spirit, is to last until the consummation of his kingdom (cf. 1 Cor 15:24–28; Heb 10:12–13). In the meantime, Jesus' heavenly session (cf. 5:31; 7:55–56) is "as the Lord who through his Spirit directs the work of his Church on earth" (C. K. Barrett, *Luke the Historian* [London, 1961] 57). **36.** *God has made him both Lord and Messiah:* This core, at least, of the climactic verse belongs to the traditional kerygma, even if we concede to Wilckens (*Missionsreden*, 171) that the other portions of the sentence are compositional in origin and function. The unusual use of *poiein* (make), not Lucan by any means, clearly refers to the exaltation, which is being proclaimed. The saving name (2:21) henceforth belongs to the exalted Messiah, and the same correlation between resurrection-faith and *kyrios*-confession is asserted as in Rom 10:9–13 (cf. Phil 2:9–11). Luke elsewhere uses the title *kyrios pantōn* (lord of all), which occurs in Rom 10:12.

Verses 33–36 constitute a kerygmatic unit, asserting Jesus' heavenly enthronement as Messiah-king; to the traditional material Luke has only contributed here the specification of Jesus' present heavenly activity (the outpouring of the Spirit). Luke's own tendency is to attribute the titles of v. 36 to the earthly Jesus (e.g., Lk 2:11; 2:26; 4:41; 5:8,12; 7:13,19; 10:1–2; 11:1; 13:23; 19:8;—cf. Acts 10:38); hence the substance of v. 36 cannot be his formulation (E. Haenchen, *Apostelgeschichte*, 150; J. C. O'Neill, *Theology*, 124–27; F. Hahn, *Hoheitstitel*, 116; contra U. Wilckens, *Missionsreden*, 173). We cannot agree with Conzelmann (*Theology*, 174, n. 3) that Luke drew the two titles from Ps 2:7, for *Kyrios* in the Ps is Yahweh, whereas v. 36 places both titles in a clearly "adoptionist" setting: God has made Jesus *kyrios* and *christos* by raising him and exalting him. Such a proclamation has not yet recognized the divine implication of the *kyrios*-title (Hahn, *op. cit.*, 117); that perhaps Luke did when he came to associate the traditional formula with his definition of the exalted One's function (v. 33) is possible (cf. O. Lafferty, *DunR* 6 [1966] 248).

22 **38–39.** Call to penance and conversion. The crowd has interrupted with the required question, according to compositorial technique. The contrast of "God has made" and "you crucified" (2:36) has "pricked" the consciences of the hearers. What Peter proposes in turn is an *ordo salutis* (U. Wilckens, *Missionsreden*, 179): (1) *metanoia* (cf. 3:19; 5:31); (2) baptism in the name of Jesus, which results in (3) the forgiveness of sins (cf. 3:19; 5:31; 10:43; 13:38) and (4) the reception of the Holy Spirit. The two results of penance and baptism cause the baptized to "be added" to the number of the elect—which means that for them the promised "salvation" (Jl 3:5 = Acts 2:21) from the evil age has already taken place (v. 40; cf. 4:12; 13:26). The possibility that Luke has drawn this sequence from Hellenistic Christian missionary preaching is suggested by comparing 1 Thes 1:9–10; Gal 4:8; Heb 5:11–6:2; Acts 14:15–17; 17:22–31. But is there not a more primitive tradition that suggests the same order, viz., the Baptist-tradition (Mk 1:8 [cf. Acts 1:5])? Luke seems to be exploiting for his formulation of the apostolic preaching several elements received from Mk. **38.** *repent:* Man's first initiative in the cycle: He turns away from his besetting sin (the rejection of the Messiah in the case of the Jews, idol-worship in that of the heathen); see Lk 5:32; 15:7; 18:3 and the complementary *epistrephein* in 3:19,26; 14:15. *in the name of Jesus:* As a formula with *baptisthēnai* this is not attested outside of Acts. Luke varies the preposition (*eis*, 8:16; 19:5; *en*, 10:48; *epi*, here), apparently without altering the sense. Other NT baptismal formulas consistently use *eis*, both with the well-known Pauline incorporative sense (Gal 3:27; Rom 6:4; 1 Cor 1:13,15; 10:2; 12:13; → Pauline Theology, 79:136) and with confessional force (Mt 28:19). The unusual use of *epi* in this verse is explained by the final words of Joel, "whoever calls upon (*epikalesētai*) the name of *Kyrios*. . . ." The new baptism is superior to John's not only because of the gift of the Spirit (1:5; 19:2–6), but also by reason of the saving name, which can now be pronounced (H. Kraft, *TZ* 17 [1961] 403, 411). *gift of the Holy Spirit:* Luke regards Christian baptism and the Spirit as inseparable (10:44–48; 11:15; 15:8), and such texts as appear to contradict this (18:15,17–19; 19:2,6) will rather reinforce it. **40.** *be saved:* The aor. inf. *sōthēnai* expresses a present reality for believers, no longer a hope of preservation from an impending judgment (cf. E. Grässer, *Parusieverzögerung*, 211). Here again is Luke's adjusted eschatology.

23 (b) First Major Summary (2:42–47). Luke's information about early apostolic history was rather scant, with considerable gaps among the individual situations and the teaching elements that were his data. Like Mk, he used the "summary" technique to fill in the gaps and to create the impression of a continuous history (cf. Mk 1:39; 3:10–12). Characteristic of the summary is a generalizing function by which single incidents and situations of the adjacent narrative are shown to be usual, typical, and continued (cf. Mk 1:39 with 1:21–27; cf. H. J. Cadbury, *The Making*, 58; M. Dibelius, *Studies*, 9–10; E. Haenchen, *RGG* 1, 505). In the three major summaries (→ 4 above) a certain repetitiveness of phrase and parallelism of structure recall Luke's reworking of the Marcan summaries (e.g., Mk 1:28 = Lk 4:14,37; 7:17). The following parallels are to be observed in the major summaries: 2:42 = 2:46 (cf. 1:14); 2:43a = 5:11 (cf. 5:5b); 2:43b = 5:12a; 2:44–45 = 4:32,34–35; 2:46a = 5:12b (cf. 1:14a); 2:46b = 2:42; 2:47a = 4:33b = 5:13b; 2:47b = 5:14 (see *Beginnings* 5, 397–98). The same summary material seems, in fact, to be reproduced twice in these passages so that the last two summaries (in chs. 4 and 5) practically equal that of ch. 2. Moreover, some of the material in the present summary seems out of place: "Fear" (2:43) is more meaningful after the episode of Ananias and Sapphira (5:11); vv. 44–45 fit better into the summary of ch. 4, which is followed by two illustrative instances of shared possessions (4:36–37; 5:1–10). Here Luke has combined some elements to form the present summary, just as he added some of this summary to the second (4:32a) and the third (5:12b–14), and elements of the third summary to the second (5:12 = 4:33; cf. H. Zimmermann, *BZ* 5 [1961] 75–78). Here in ch. 2, at the beginning of the primitive history, Luke has provided in an enlarged summary a general view of the subsequent narrative (cf. L. Cerfaux, *Recueil*, 2, 74).

Three steps seem to be involved in the formation of these passages: (1) traditional material: exemplary stories (3:1–10; 4:36–37; 5:1–10), venerated prayer-forms (4:24–30), apostolic ideals and practices (*koinōnia*, Temple observances, the community meal); (2) an earlier stage of the book's redaction at which these elements were generalized in summaries directly associated with the corresponding narrative (e.g., 2:42,46–47; 4:32b,34–35; 5:11–12,15); (3) later redactional activity, which enlarged the summaries by combining their elements.

24 **42.** *fellowship:* This unique Lucan occurrence of the Pauline *koinōnia* forbids the view that this verse is Luke's distillation of vv. 46–47 (*pace* L. Cerfaux, *Recueil*, 2, 77–78; H. Zimmermann, *BZ* 5 [1961] 75). The particle *de* in this verse and the following verses binds the summary to the concluding v. 41 of the Pentecost Account, which has the correlative *men*. The apostolic *didachē* (teaching) as source of unity is a generalization of the Petrine discourse just concluded. The traditional term "fellowship," inherited from Pauline circles, means the community of the gospel based on the apostolate (Gal 2:9). *breaking of the bread:* Eucharistic overtones in this community meal are hard to deny (cf. Lk 24:30,35; O. Cullmann, *Essays on the Lord's Supper* [Richmond, Va.; 1958] 8). In fact, Luke seems not to distinguish the Eucharist and the common meal (H. Conzelmann, *Apostelgeschichte*, 31, contra E. Haenchen, *Apostelgeschichte*, 153). The ideal first community enjoyed table-fellowship with those who were privileged table-fellows of the risen One (cf. 1:4; 10:41); Paul's followers will later have the same fellowship with him as a successor to the Twelve (20:7). *the prayers:* Does this element suggest that v. 42 is really a liturgical protocol? See J. Jeremias, *EWJ* 118–21. The summary character of the verse contradicts that hypothesis; the ideal facets of the first community's life, not its liturgical program, are what the summary presents. **43–45.** Much of the material of these verses was apparently not originally adapted to this context (see comments on 4:32–35; 5:11–16). The importation of the elements of "fear," "signs and wonders," and of "shared goods" (*koinōnia*, v. 44) may have been dictated by the transition to the story of 3:1–10 (which includes Peter's disavowal of monetary means [3:6]; cf. H. Zimmermann, *BZ* 5 [1961] 77). **46.** *of one mind:* The adv. *homothymadon* has idealized the apostolic *koinōnia*. *in the temple:* Here is an area of special Lucan interest. The Temple is the principal institution of OT Judaism that continues into the Christian era; having served as Jesus' forum in Jerusalem, it remains a Christian missionary forum (cf. Lk 2:27,49; 19:45; 22:53; 24:53; Acts 3:11; 4:2; 5:20–21,42; H. Conzelmann, *Theology*, 164–65).

(Glombitza, O., "Der Schluss der Petrusrede, Acta [2:]36–40," *ZNW* 52 [1961] 115–16. Kraft, H., "Die Anfänge der christlichen Taufe," *TZ* 17 [1961] 399–412. Lafferty, O. J., "Acts 2:14–36. A Study in Christology," *DunR* 6 [1966] 235–53. Mussner, F., "'In den letzten Tagen' (Apg 2, 17a)," *BZ* 5 [1961] 263–65. Zimmermann, H., "Die Sammelberichte der Apostelgeschichte," *BZ* 5 [1961] 71–82.)

25 (c) The First Jewish Persecution (3:1–4:31). (i) *Peter's healing miracle* (3:1–11). To show that Jesus' healing ministry was continued by his chosen apostles Luke records an event that had been preserved in community tradition. The structure and motifs are familiar from the Syn healing-stories: the setting (vv. 1–2); the doctrinal point (v. 6); the healing by word and gesture (vv. 6–7); success and demonstration (vv. 7–8); the edifying reaction of onlookers (vv. 9–10). The early communities narrated the apostles' miracles as they did the Master's, so that one got the impression that it was the Lord himself who was operative in the deeds done in his name by his witnesses (cf. K. H. Rengstorf, *ThDNT* 1, 433). The continuity between the present narrative and the controversy and persecution in ch. 4 (see 4:7,9,10,14,16,22) suggests source material in which that was the original sequence (so É. Trocmé, *Le Livre*, 194–95), the discourse of 3:12–26 being a subsequent and not completely graceful addition to the context. The miracle and subsequent persecution were probably preserved together by the tradition out of a didactic concern to illustrate the power of the saving confession of Jesus' name and the dauntless determination of those who preached that name.

1. *Peter and John:* John's passive presence in the account is probably not original. Bauernfeind holds that his name may have been interpolated here and in vv. 3–4 so that there might be the required two witnesses of the event before the Sanhedrin (4:19–20). It is Peter who speaks and acts for the Twelve. **2.** *the gate called the Beautiful:* This name occurs in no Jewish source (*Beginnings* 5, 480). Josephus and the Mishnah agree that the eastern front of the Temple was the most beautiful (facing the Mt. of Olives). Whether we should settle on that side for the gate in question and for "Solomon's Porch" (v. 11) is uncertain, as indeed is the whole question of Luke's topographical information (see *Beginnings* 5, 485–86). **6.** *neither silver nor gold:* This climactic saying prepares for the name of Jesus as the powerful source of salvation (cf. 2:21,38–39; 3:16; 4:7–12). The illation from physical restoration to redemption was likewise the didactic intent of the Gospel healing-stories. The judgment that this use of the name of Jesus is Lucan in origin (H. Conzelmann, *Theology*, 177–78) has no conclusive evidence. **11.** *at the porch called Solomon's:* The Western redactor reacted to the difficulty of this location in view of the group's having entered the Temple in v. 8. Verse 10, which contains the last of the typical elements, was probably the end of the old narrative. Verse 11 would then be Luke's suture, providing a transition to the discourse and based on meager topographical information (cf. E. Haenchen, *ZThK* 54 [1957] 53).

26 (ii) *Peter's Temple discourse* (3:12–26). The connection of this sermon to the narrative at either end is tenuous: Only v. 12 and the ill-fitting v. 16 connect it to the miracle story, and it is followed by a rather inept summary of Peter's remarks in 4:2 ("resurrection from the dead" could there refer only to 3:15b). Regardless of these difficulties, however, we are dealing with a Lucan composition, based once again on a substratum of prior tradition. One should therefore not compare the "Christologies" of the discourses of chs. 2 and 3 as if divergent kerygmatic statements in them proved the discourses as such to be documents from pre-Lucan ambients (so J. A. T. Robinson, *Twelve NT Studies* [SBT 34; London, 1962] 140, 148–53; O. Lafferty, *DunR* 6 [1966] 252). It is, of course, useful to compare the traditions of which Luke made use (cf. R. H. Fuller, *Foundations of NT Christology* [N.Y., 1965] 159, 184), but this should not obscure the prevailing role of the author in molding a sermon to fit the plan of his book. The apparent *post factum* attachment of the discourse to the narrative context may result from separate stages of the book's redaction.

12. This verse connects the discourse with the situation and is possibly an adaptation to Jewish circumstances of the situation in 14:11. Peter again begins by correcting a misunderstanding. **13.** The kerygma begins. The continuity of the Church with Israel is brought out by the use of hallowed OT titles of God (Ex 3:6,15). *has glorified his servant Jesus:* Is 52:13 is doubtless alluded to. The vb. *edoxasen* (glorified) cannot refer to the healing miracle, for there is no comparable employment of *doxazesthai* in reference to miracles in the Lucan work. Besides, v. 16 does not suggest that God was the agent of the Petrine miracle, whereas he is always the agent of Jesus' resurrection and exaltation in the discourses. Luke probably inherited a venerable exegesis that applied this statement of the Isaian Servant Song to Jesus. Yet there is not a drawing out of the idea of Jesus' redemptive suffering, as one might expect from the song's influence (see R. H. Fuller, *Foundations*, 168–69). *Pais* (Servant) is a title for the exalted Jesus, probably rooted in early liturgical usage (cf. 4:26–27,30; *Didache* 9:2–3; 10:2–3; *1 Clem.* 59:2–4; see H. Conzelmann *Apostelgeschichte*, 33; J. C. O'Neill, *Theology*, 135–36; E. Schweizer, *Lordship*, 50). Yet since v. 26, like 4:27, appears to apply the title to the earthly Jesus who is a prophet like Moses (vv. 22–26), Luke's *pais*-tradition does not seem to be uniform. **13b–15a.** Passion summary. Ancient messianic titles are employed in this Lucan summary: the Holy (4:27,30; Mk 1:24; Lk 4:34; Jn 6:69) and Righteous One (7:52; Mt 10:41?; *Enoch* 38:2; 53:6; cf. 1 Tm 3:16), the Leader to life (Moses-figure; cf. 5:31; 7:35; Heb 2:10; 12:2). The summary includes elements of a specific scene from the passion narratives, viz., the trial before Pilate; it reflects Luke's editing of Mk in the Gospel. Peter emphasizes the antithesis of the Jews' denial and Pilate's judgment of Jesus' innocence; Luke had made the governor an outspoken witness of Jesus' innocence (Lk 23:4,14,22) compared with the uninterested, compliant attitude he had had in Mk 15:15. *decided to release him:* These words recall the thrice-repeated judgment of Pilate that Jesus was innocent (Lk 23:16,20,22; cf. Mk 15:9,11,15; H. Conzelmann, *Theology*, 87). Luke's emphasis on Pilate's advocacy of Jesus' release may have had a contemporary apologetic objective. **14.** *denied:* The oft-repeated vb. *arneisthai* acquires the same sense as the traditional *paradidonai* (handed over, 3:13). The usage may have been inspired by the ancient Q-logion concerning confession and denial of the Son of Man (Lk 12:8–9; Mt 10:32–33). It probably had a place in the persecution-ideology of Christians in Luke's time (see U. Wilckens, *Missionsreden*, 130). *you asked that a murderer be granted to you:* The "granting" of Barabbas is once again Lucan language (see Lk 23:23–25); cf. Mk 15:7–15. On the textual problem of this verse, cf. M. Wilcox, *Semitisms*, 139–41. **15a.** *leader to life:* Here the Gk word *archēgos* does not mean "author" (contra *Beginnings* 4, 36; 5, 370). The genitive is one of direction, in view of 26:23 and the Moses-typology (cf. 7:35; Heb 12:2; cf. Bl-Deb-F § 166). With Jesus' resurrection, the resurrection of all believers has its beginning (cf. 4:2; 17:31). Here and in 5:31 the title ("Leader and Savior") is based on a tradition of which a variant occurs in *2 Clem.* 20:5 (*sōtēra kai archēgon tēs aphtharsias*). **15b.** A brief and usual resurrection-statement; the more common NT vb. *ēgeiren* replaces the Lucan *anestēsen*. **16.** Peter's argument is interrupted by this stylistically unfortunate reference to the situation of the miracle. Its grammatical disorder is usually dealt with by postulating glosses or Semitic originals (cf. M. Wilcox, *Semitisms*, 144–46). But it may represent the original conclusion of the miracle story, transposed by Luke to this point in the discourse as a connective measure (U. Wilckens, *Missionsreden*, 41). *faith:* This is a typical motif of NT healing-narratives, and Jesus' "name" returns to prominence in the narrative of ch. 4; but elsewhere neither of these motifs enters into this discourse.

27 **17–26.** Call to conversion. **17.** *acted in ignorance:* The *agnoia*-motif was doubtless a traditional missionary theme (cf. 13:27; 17:30); it does not dilute the Jews' guilt but rather explains why God still offers the chance to repent (v. 19). Luke's own interest in this theme may be attested by the logion of Lk 23:34 (textually sound? → Gospel Lk, 44:171). In his schema of sacred history missionary preaching removes the *agnoia* and finalizes the rejection of Jesus. *as did your leaders:* The tendency to distinguish the people from their leaders appears in Lk 7:29–30 (cf. 3:7); 23:35; 24:20; Acts 4:10,21; 13:27; 14:5. The *archontes* (leaders) are prototypes of impenitent Judaism, placing themselves resolutely outside the course of saving events, beginning at John's baptism (Lk 7:29–30) and continuing through the apostolic preaching (Acts 4:4–5,16–17)—this makes their refusal definitive (H. Conzelmann, *Theology*, 146, 164, 186). **18.** The ignorance of the Jews is here given salvation-historical meaning. *his Messiah must suffer:* This expression (*pathein ton Christon*) is not so much a Lucan property (*pace* J. A. T. Robinson, *Twelve NT Studies*, 145–46) as an inherited association of the *Christos*-title and the vb. *pathein* (cf. 1 Pt 2:21; 3:18; Heb 9:24–26; see R. H. Fuller, *Foundations*, 162, 178–79; F. Hahn, *Hoheitstitel*, 215–16, 385). The same title is consistently used in statements of Jesus' saving death in the Pauline literature. Closely related to the present statement is the Marcan prediction (Mk 8:31): *dei ton hyion tou anthrōpou polla pathein*. Luke has exploited the Marcan tradition in this same sense in the Emmaus account (Lk 24:6–7,26,46). Cf. also Acts 17:3; 26:23. **19.** *reform...and turn:* Luke's conversion-semantics involve the fine distinction of *metanoiein* (the negative turning away from an evil course) and *epistrephein* (the positive turning toward God and his *kyrios* [20:21] and a new way of life [26:20]). The association of conversion and parousia (vv. 20–21) is pre-Lucan (cf. 1 Thes 1:9–10; see F. Hahn, *Hoheitstitel*, 184).

20–21. An eschatological motive for conversion. Both Conzelmann (*Apostelgeschichte*, 34–35) and Wilckens (*Missionsreden*, 43) remark that the sequence would be smoother without these verses. The OT citation in vv. 22–23 supports the call for repentance (v. 19) and bears no evident reference to the parousia; nor does "these days" (v. 24) refer to the "times of refreshment," as one might expect from vv. 20–21, but rather to the accomplished prophetic ministry of Jesus (v. 26). Since the train of thought of vv. 24–26 seems to return to that of vv. 17–19, why does the peculiar apocalyptic digression occur in between? Possibly it represents a piece of late-Jewish speculation concerning the return of Elijah as the harbinger of the final event. Primitive Christians would have "baptized" this speculation to make it refer to Jesus' parousia, especially if it had been exploited by followers of John the Baptist. Supporting this view is the fact that the "translated" prophet Elijah was associated with the function of "restoration" in Mal 3:22–23 (LXX), for which he was to be "sent" by God (cf. Mk 9:12). This tradition possibly accounts for the singular use of *apostellein* (send) in Peter's allusion to the parousia, and for the unusual "time for restoration" (*chronoi apokatastaseōs*). Whether one accepts this interpretation (of W. G. Kümmel, *TRu* 14 [1942] 165–66; U. Wilckens, *Missionsreden*, 153–56; F. Hahn, *Hoheitstitel*, 184–86) or rejects it (with E. Haenchen, *Apostelgeschichte* 170–72; P. Vielhauer, *EvT* 25 [1965] 47–48), there remain elements that set the present passage remarkably apart from the mainstream of NT exaltation-statements: (1) The term *dexasthai* seems to indicate that the exalted One's present existence is a hidden (inactive?) one. (2) Until the time of redemption Jesus is "Messiah-designate" (*prokecheirismenos*—see J. A. T. Robinson, *Twelve NT Studies*, 144); this stands in noticeable contrast to the kerygma of 2:36. (3) The penance and conversion the preacher calls for will hasten the exaltation event. (4) The usual reference in exaltation-statements to Ps 110:1 (sitting at the right hand) is lacking. (5) The parousia is nowhere else designated a "mission" of Jesus.

Explaining Luke's designs for this embryonic Christological proposition is a challenge. Should one say that he has used it to endow the delayed parousia with an apocalyptic rationale ("heaven must receive [him]")? Or is the "mission" of the Christ to the repentant in the "times of refreshment" to be understood as a present encounter with the exalted One (in which case that phrase could be equivalent to the puzzling "days [pl.] of the Son of Man" in Lk 17:22,26)? See H. Flender, *St Luke*, 96–98. In any case, we note a triangular relationship between the two Petrine speeches and the programmatic passage 1:5–8: The latter passage had juxtaposed two realities that Jewish tradition associated with the final age, viz., the outpouring of the Spirit and the "restoration" of Israel. Now Peter's two speeches have proposed both of these in turn as fruits of repentance: the Spirit (2:38) and the restoration (3:21). Does Luke understand the restoration to be in some way anticipated in the present, as he understands the outpouring of the Spirit? *all the things which God spoke:* The antecedent of the rel. pronoun is *pantōn* rather than *chronōn*. Otherwise "these days" of v. 24 takes on the future meaning that v. 26 then contradicts. Or we might refer the rel. pronoun to the phrase *apokatastasis pantōn* as a case of attraction of the relative. "Times of restoration" and "times of refreshment" are synonymous apocalyptic terms for the age of salvation, which Luke views in an expanded dimension.

28 **22–26.** Scripture is introduced as a motive for conversion, showing again that OT citation has not a fixed berth in the schema of the discourses. Bauernfeind (*Apostelgeschichte*, 67) asserts that the same Malachi text that underlay the tradition in vv. 20–21 provided a basis for identifying Elijah with the Mosaic prophet of Dt 18:15, as some Jewish speculations did (cf. Mal 3:24 [LXX]; but cf. R. H. Fuller, *Foundations*, 49; F. Hahn, *Hoheitstitel*, 185). The point of the sequence seems to be that the future Messiah, expected to come like Elijah, is the same Jesus whom God has already sent as the prophet like Moses and the Servant to call each faithful Israelite away from his evil deeds (v. 26). **22–23.** Dt 18:15,18 is one of four OT citations in Acts that depart significantly from the LXX. The wording is nearly identical when Moses' words are cited again in 7:37. Common to this and the other citations (Ex 3:6; Dt 21:22; 33:3,4—or Wis 5:5?) is that each occurs twice in Acts, always in discourse material, and with the same odd text-form each time. Wilcox (*Semitisms*, 32–37) suggests that a different Gk version was used at either editorial or source level in these cases. The apparent admixture of Lv 23:29 in the present citation may point to a collection of testimonia (C. H. Dodd, *According to the Scriptures* [London, 1952] 53ff.; cf. H. J. Cadbury, *The Making*, 56–57). The view of Jesus as eschatological Mosaic prophet is a favorite of Luke; but it finds expression in such diversified forms (Lk 24:19; Acts 7:37) that it were better not thought of as a Lucan theologoumenon. Cf. Mk 9:2–8 par. and Jn 1:21,25; 6:14; it may even claim early Palestinian origins (→ Aspects NT Thought, 78:14). **24.** *all the prophets:* The Scriptures' united testimony to salvation in Jesus was an early Christian conviction. *these days:* The present time of the preaching, not the "times" of vv. 20–21 (as v. 26 shows). **25.** *Abraham:* Jesus' prophetic ministry fulfills the blessing promised to Abraham's posterity. In view of the Jewish audience the citation of Gn 22:18 is altered from "all the nations" to "all the families of the earth" (cf. Ps 22:28 [LXX]). As in Gal 3:16, Abraham's "seed" (*sperma*) is taken as a single individual, Jesus Christ. **26.** *first:* This adv. *prōton* refers to the first of the missionary epochs in the schema of Acts (cf. 13:46): first the Jews hear the preaching, then the Gentiles. *raised up:* The establishment of Jesus in his role in salvation history (U. Wilckens, *Missionsreden*, 138, 164). This is the single instance in Acts where *anistanai* refers to Jesus' earthly ministry rather than to his resurrection (see J. A. T. Robinson, *Twelve NT Studies*, 150). This sense of the word is drawn from its use in the Dt citation (v. 22) and is certified by the aor. *apesteilen* (sent). *his servant:* The titles of prophet and *pais* are thus joined. *that each might turn from:* The announcement of salvation is the blessing on Abraham's progeny; its fruit is their conversion.

(Bauernfeind, O., "Tradition und Komposition in dem Apokatastasisspruch, Apg. 3, 20f.," *Abraham unser Vater* [Fest. O. Michel; Leiden, 1963] 13–23. Dupont, J., "Repentir et conversion d'après les Actes des Apôtres," *ScEccl* 12 [1960] 137–73. Mussner, F., "Die Idee der Apokatastasis in der Apostelgeschichte," *Lex tua veritas* [Fest. H. Junker; Trier, 1961] 293–306.)

29 (iii) *The apostles before the Sanhedrin* (4:1–22). The arrest of the preachers at the moment when salvation is being announced to Israel begins the tide of opposition that will culminate in the dispersal of the community (8:1) and in the announcement of the message to the Gentiles (chs. 10ff.). The narrative raises enormous historical difficulties so that one must admit extensive editorial reworking of a basically historical tradition. The limits of the latter cannot now be traced within the text, but it may well have included the miracle account (3:1–10) together with the framework of what follows in ch. 4.

1. *Sadducees:* Because the principal doctrine of this group was a denial of bodily resurrection (23:8), Luke regards them as the archenemies of the Christian movement and places them in the front ranks of its persecutors (cf. 5:17; 23:6–10). On the other hand, the Pharisees, the "most exact" practitioners of Judaism (26:5), appear as defenders of belief in the resurrection and of the Christian preaching (5:34–40; 23:9). The apostolic faith was in continuity with the truest aspirations of Judaism, according to Luke, and was rejected only by those who were no longer faithful Jews. **2.** *the resurrection of the dead in Jesus:* The sense of this is clarified by 26:23. The apostles' preaching proposed Jesus as *archēgos tēs zōēs*, the first to be raised from the dead. Luke therefore regards the resurrection as the central issue in the apostles' arrest; it was this above all that unfaithful Judaism rejected (E. Haenchen, *ZNW* 54 [1963] 157–58). The questions, then, of whether such an issue could have caused an arrest, whether the Sadducees could have arrested anyone, and why the resurrection is not mentioned in the subsequent hearing (vv. 7ff.) are not really to the point. These are motifs of editorial origin (H. Conzelmann, *Apostelgeschichte*, 35; U. Wilckens, *Missionsreden*, 61). **4.** The number of converts amplifies the contrast between persecuting leaders and believing common folk (→ 4 above). **6.** *Annas:* Of these members of the high-priestly family, Annas (AD 6–15) was not high priest at this period, and John and Alexander are unknown (but see A. Wikenhauser, *Apostelgeschichte*, 64–65; É. Trocmé, *Le Livre*, 95–96). **7.** *by what power:* The authorities' question is an editorial device for introducing the discourse.

8–12. Peter's first discourse before the Sanhedrin. A nucleus of this short speech may have been preserved in Luke's tradition. Indication of this is that the redactor's motive for the arrest (v. 2) plays no part in Peter's response or the leader's question. Did the miracle and controversy go together in some "Acts of Peter"? The discourse transfers the healing in Jesus' name from the physical sphere to the spiritual (*sōthēnai*). And this is wrought in that name alone. The absence of the typical call for repentance from this discourse is not explained simply by the narrative situation. The sermon of 5:29–32 occurs in the same situation, yet includes the repentance motif. **10.** *whom you crucified, whom God raised:* Here is perhaps the simplest form of the kerygmatic antithesis. The rel. clauses are inserted into Peter's explanation of the healing in the name of Jesus. **11.** *this is...:* The Gk demonstrative (*houtos estin*) refers awkwardly to the preceding demonstrative *en toutō*, which means Jesus' "name." Ps 118:22 knows two different modes of exegesis in the NT: one makes it express the triumph of the risen One over his enemies (Mk 12:10 [Lk 20:17 par.] and the present passage); the other applies it to the new community founded on the rejected but Risen Christ as the foundation (1 Pt 2:4–5; also Mt 21:42–43). The first of these exegetical traditions was particularly well adapted to the rejection-glorification antithesis of Peter's kerygma. But the rather different wording in this verse from both Mk (= LXX) and 1 Pt suggests again that Luke was using a collection of testimonia (E. Haenchen, *Apostelgeschichte*, 176, n.5). *nor is there any other name:* Possibly a Christianized version of a Jewish formula used of the name of Yahweh (cf. *Hermas*, Vis. 4, 2, 4). **13.** *boldness: Parrēsia* is a traditional attribute of the preaching of God's word, beginning with Jesus' announcement of his passion (Mk 8:32) and continuing in the kerygma of the apostles (Acts 2:29; 4:29,31); it is applied equally to Paul's preaching (9:27–28; 13:46), till it finally marks his teaching at Rome (28:31). *had been with Jesus:* The essential note of apostleship reiterated. **16–20.** The exchange is artfully constructed to bring out the undaunted courage of the apostolic witnesses in the face of callous and unyielding resistance. **21.** *finding nothing:* The reader is assured that no legal fault could be found with the preaching (an apologetic motif?). *the people:* The redeemed *laos* forces the unredeemed *archontes* to release the apostles (see comment on 3:17). *Laos* (people) stands for Israel in 10:2; 21:28; 28:17; for the Christian community in 15:14; 18:10. The continuity between the two is taken for granted (see H. Conzelmann, *Theology*, 164, n.1).

30 (iv) *The prayer of the apostles* (4:23–31). The early liturgical traditions preserved in this passage have been widely discussed (see O. Bauernfeind, *Apostelgeschichte*, 78–79; J. C. O'Neill, *Theology*, 135–38; M. Wilcox, *Semitisms*, 69–72, 74); but the prayer's conclusion (vv. 29–30) shows that it has grown out of the situation narrated and is therefore not a previously independent formulary. It is more likely that Luke, inspired by Hezekiah's prayer in Is 37:16–20 and by an established Christian application of Ps 2:1 to Jesus' passion (vv. 25–28), composed the prayer to fit the situation (E. Haenchen, *Apostelgeschichte*, 186). Contemporary liturgical usage supplied the invocation *despota* (sovereign, Lk 2:29; *1 Clem.* 59–61; *Didache* 10:3), and the title *pais theou* applied to Jesus and David (*Didache* 9:2–3; 10:2,3; *1 Clem.* 59:2–4; *Mart. Pol.* 14:1,3; 22:2). The LXX influence is seen by comparing Ex 20:11; Ez 6:14; Hos 7:1; Is 8:18.

23. *came to their own:* To the group of the Twelve (J. Dupont, *RB* 62 [1955] 45ff.). **25.** The disturbed text of this verse is hard to remedy, except by conjecture. The RSV reads a text that is basically that of ms. B: "who [by] the mouth of our father David, thy servant, didst say by the Holy Spirit." The variant reading of ms. D ("who spoke through the Holy Spirit by the mouth of David thy servant") is probably an attempt to correct the text of ms. B. The Koine tradition offers a text that may be too facile a solution (*Beginnings* 3, 40): "Who said by the mouth of your servant David." In this case "our father" and "Holy Spirit" may have come from scribes who were distracted respectively by a marginal gloss and a stock citation formula (see E. Haenchen, *ZThK* 51 [1954] 157). **25b–28.** A pre-Lucan exegesis applies Ps 2:1–2 (LXX) to the story of the passion (H. Conzelmann, *Apostelgeschichte*, 37). The elements are carefully matched: "kings of the earth" (Herod), "rulers" (Pilate), "Gentiles" and "peoples"—all of them conspire in the death of Jesus. **27.** *Herod and Pilate:* Only Lk's Passion Narrative included the role of Herod and his subsequent friendship with Pilate (Lk 23:6–12). Is Luke therefore composing here with retrospect to his Passion Narrative (U. Wilckens, *Missionsreden*, 133, n.2), or does the present passage contain the tradition that influenced Lk 23:6–12 (so M. Dibelius, *Botschaft und Geschichte* [Tübingen, 1953] 1, 289–92)? Conzelmann (*Theology*, 91) groups this passage with 2:23; 3:13–14; 13:28 as a type of pre-Lucan formula "which traces the death of Jesus back to the combined efforts of Jews and Gentiles, including Herod." Where the Romans (*ethnē*) are presented as sharing the responsibility for Jesus' execution we are probably dealing with pre-Lucan passion material, for his verdict consistently underlines the initiative and guilt of the Jews (cf. Lk 23:25–26 with Mk 15:15; cf. X. Léon-Dufour, "Passion," *VDBS* 6, 1434). In fact, if the passion-tradition had recorded any complicity of Pilate and Herod in Jesus' execution, as Acts 4:27 does, that aspect has been edited out of Lk's Passion Narrative (Lk 23:14–16), and we should therefore regard the passage in Acts as standing closer to the tradition. *your holy servant...whom you [had] anointed:* Servant and Christ (the "anointed") are understood as interchangeable here, and the terminology of the prophet-Christology of ch. 3 is echoed. The aor. *echrisas* is understood as a pluperfect, referring to the prophetic anointing of Jesus at his baptism (Lk 3:22; 4:18; Acts 10:38) with which the tradition had associated Ps 2 (*christos—huios*) and Is 42:1 (*pais*). Luke has used traditional material to create this confluence of his favorite Christological designations; a contrast is immediately visible between the application of *echrisas* to Jesus' baptism and the proclamation concerning the exalted One in 2:36. *Pais theou* was probably an inherited designation of the prophet-messiah (3:26; contra J. Ménard, *CBQ* 19 [1957] 91; → Aspects NT

Thought, 78:11). In the light of Lk 3:22 (Ps 2:7), *pais* might even be rendered "son" here. We are not necessarily in the presence of a primitive Suffering-Servant Christology; there is no hint of the passion's salvific value such as one would expect from reflection on Is 53 (see U. Wilckens, *Missionsreden*, 163–68; J. C. O'Neill, *Theology*, 136–39; but cf. J. Dupont, *RB* 69 [1962] 51–52). **28.** Here the point of the exegesis appears: The foes of God and of his Christ accomplish the divine plan (see comment on 2:23), which the Servant-psalmist had enunciated. **30.** *through [the name of] your [holy] servant Jesus:* Cf. *Didache* 9:2; *1 Clem.* 59:3; *Mart. Pol.* 14:3; 20:2. **31.** A resonance of the Pentecost. Bold, unhampered preaching (*parrēsia*) is the Spirit's basic endowment. *the word of God:* This is a favorite Lucan way of expressing the Christian message (see 6:2,7; 8:14; 11:1; 13:5,7,44,46,48; 16:32; 17:13; 18:11). Variants of it are "the word of the Lord" (8:25; 13:49; 15:35,36; 19:10,20; 20:35) or simply "the word" (4:29; 6:4; 8:4; 10:44; 11:19; 14:25; 16:6). See G. Kittel, *ThDNT* 4, 114–17.

31 (d) The Community Ideal of the Apostolic Church (4:32–5:16).

(i) *Second major summary* (4:32–35). The generalized sharing of possessions (vv. 32, 34–35) in this major summary (→ 4 and 23 above) has been derived from single instances supplied by tradition (4:36–37; 5:1–10). That the universal surrender of goods is a product of later idealizing is confirmed by 5:3–4, which appears to presume that Ananias' donation was voluntary and that his sin lay in the false pretense of total giving (*Beginnings* 5, 148). Besides, popular memory would not have preserved the name of Barnabas (4:36) unless his gesture, like Ananias', was really exceptional (M. Dibelius, *Studies*, 16; E. Haenchen, *Apostelgeschichte*, 190–91). The summary's connection with the two subsequent episodes was therefore brought about by Luke and not before him (É. Trocmé, *Le Livre*, 196). Even within the summary there emerge two distinct ideas: on the one hand, that things were possessed in common in the first community (v. 32); on the other hand, that there were individual possessors who sold what was theirs for distribution (vv. 34–35). The first idea conforms to contemporary Gk ideals of community life (H. Conzelmann, *Apostelgeschichte*, 31; A. Wikenhauser, *Apostelgeschichte*, 69), whereas the second stands closer to the deuteronomic ideal (Dt 15:4, "there shall be no poor among you") and would seem to be the original core of the summary. But then again, v. 32 has the same interpretation of Christian fellowship (*koinōnia*) in terms of a community of goods (*panta koina*) as we encountered in 2:44. The redactor apparently developed this idea on the basis of vv. 34–35, then combined both notions in 2:44–45. Verse 33, which separates the two ideas in this summary, appears to have been condensed from 5:12–13 and to have been occasioned here by vv. 30–31 (H. Zimmermann, *BZ* 5 [1961] 77). Whether influenced by Gk speculation or by actual contemporary ventures (→ Apocrypha, 68:93), Luke's "communistic" ideal is proposed as a characteristic of the ideal first Church rather than a continuing norm for Christian communities.

32 (ii) *Examples* (4:36–5:10). The poverty of the primitive Jerusalem community is recorded elsewhere (Gal 2:10; Rom 15:3; Acts 6:1; 11:29), and a gesture for its relief like that of Joseph-Barnabas would have made a lasting impression on the tradition. The etymology of "Barnabas" is popular and inaccurate.

The chilling tale of Ananias and Sapphira (5:1–10), like most popular narratives, can be presumed to have some foundation in fact (contra H. Conzelmann, *Apostelgeschichte*, 39); but the present sequence and the interpretation of the deaths as a divine punishment unparalleled in the NT are doubtless products of the popular imagination. The well-known view of P.-H. Menoud, that the basic tradition here grew up as an interpretation of the first deaths in the primitive, parousia-oriented community (*Aux sources de la tradition chrétienne* [Fest. M. Goguel; Neuchâtel, 1950] 153–54), is more imaginative than sound. No one doubts, of course, that the story had some edifying purpose, perhaps summed up best by Jerome (*Ep.* 130.14, 7): "... ut poena duorum hominum sit doctrina multorum." But what the point of the story was depends on what the couple's sin was conceived to be. Clearly it was one of deceit, not of refusing to make a mandatory offering. Was there a core of "perfecti" in the community (cf. Mt 19:21) of whom a total surrender of goods was demanded (as at Qumran; cf. 1QS 8:20ff.)? In that case, the sin of the spouses would have been the pretense of total offering while concealing a portion of their goods (1QS 6:24–25; cf. É. Trocmé, *Le Livre*, 198; H. J. Cadbury, *The Book*, 96–97). On the other hand, our story has to do more with a split-second, Spirit-directed apostolic judgment (cf. 1QS 2:4ff.) than with the application of a norm of discipline. It is an instance of the pneumatic scrutiny of the sinner by the believer (cf. 1 Cor 14:24–25), demonstrating in a fearful way the Spirit's presence in the first community (E. Haenchen, *Apostelgeschichte*, 197–98): "Thus you shall exterminate the wicked person from your midst" (Dt 13:5; 17:7). This seems to sum up the instructional or edifying motif that the old story served.

2. *held back:* The rare vb. *nosphizō* occurs only here and in Jos 7:1 (LXX), indicating the possible influence of the account of Achan's sin and punishment on our story. **6–7.** A most improbable sequence. Defenders of Qumranite parallels render *neōteroi* "novices" (É. Trocmé, *Le Livre*, 199). The suggestion of such parallels should be viewed with critical reserve in this matter (see J. A. Fitzmyer, *Studies in Lk-Acts*, 242–44) and in the material of Acts generally (E. Grässer, *TRu* 26 [1960] 159–62).

33 (iii) *Third major summary* (5:11–16). This major summary (→ 4 and 23 above), which has the powerful "signs and wonders" of the apostles as its theme, takes the awesome Ananias event as its point of departure. It is here that the motif of fear (2:43) has its natural place. **11.** *great fear came upon the whole Church:* The word *ekklēsia* makes its first appearance in connection with *phobos* (5:5,11), which may again indicate the influence of the deuteronomic *ekklēsia* (*qāhāl*), especially since reverential fear of God and his works was a precise demand made of the deuteronomic assembly on the "day of the assembly" (*hēmera tēs ekklēsias*, Dt 4:10; cf. Dt 10:12,20; 31:31). **12b–14.** The combining editorial hand is again at work, inserting this material from the first summary (2:46a,47). It is probably the subsequent episode (5:17–21) that occasioned the insertion (H. Zimmermann, *BZ* 5 [1961] 78). *Solomon's portico:* See 3:11; cf. the "Temple" as the area of gathering in 2:46. **15.** Here is a core of community-tradition which, in the pre-editorial summary (see comment on 2:42–47), was generalized on one side by v. 12a, on the other by v. 16. The effect was a demonstration of the fulfillment of the apostolic prayer, 4:30.

(Bihler, J., *Die Stephanusgeschichte im Zusammenhang der Apostelgeschichte* [Munich, 1963] 197–202. Lake, K., "The Communism of Acts," *Beginnings* 5, 140–51. Schmitt, J., "L'église de Jérusalem, ou la 'restoration' d'Israël," *RScRel* 27 [1953] 207–18.)

34 (e) The Second Persecution (5:17–42). Many regard this section as a doublet of the persecution-sequence in ch. 4 (Bauernfeind, Reicke), but J. Jeremias maintains that the second narrative progresses notably beyond the first and complements it (*ZNW* 36 [1937] 208ff.). Mishnaic prescription actually provided for legal admonition after a first violation (4:17), with punishment meted out only in case of recidivism (5:40). Moreover, the legal admonition (*apeilein*, 4:17,21), followed the officials' notice that the apostles were "uneducated, common men" (4:13; cf. J. Dupont, *Sources*, 46). True, the admonition would not have required a Sanhedrin session (4:5–6; cf. É. Trocmé, *Le Livre*, 103), and the Mishnaic trial-protocol is generally recognized to be of later provenance; but Jeremias's reconstruction of the traditional material underlying chs. 4–5 remains a viable hypothesis (W. G. Kümmel, *TRu* 14 [1942] 169; J. Dupont, *Sources*, 49–50).

20. *this life:* Cf. 13:26, "this salvation." Again the Temple is the proper locale of apostolic preaching (see comment on 2:46). **28.** *you have filled Jerusalem with your teaching:* For Luke, the apostles' preaching is bound to Jerusalem according to the divine ordering of sacred history (see comment on 1:4). Hence the apostles' only self-defense is: "We must obey God rather than men."

29–32. Peter's second Sanhedrin discourse. This tiny discourse displays the schema of composition of the missionary discourses in its "pure form" (→ 18 above; U. Wilckens, *Missionsreden*, 45). The abrupt transition from a reference to the situation (v. 29b) to kerygma (vv. 30–32) emphasizes the apostles' necessary and decisive rejection of the command not to teach.

30. *you killed:* Luke's kerygmatic vocabulary is by no means limited; here the rare vb. *diacheirizō* (26:2; cf. 2:23, *dia cheiros*) supplants *anaireō* (2:23), *stauroō* (2:36; 4:10), and *apokteinō* (3:15). *hanging him on a tree:* Dt 21:22 belonged to the early Christian homiletic treasury (cf. 10:40; 2:23; Gal 3:13). Paul took the words from Dt 21:23 because his emphasis was on the curse that lay upon the crucified (*epikataratos*), whereas Luke could quote v. 22 because he was stressing the deed and the perpetrators' guilt. The difference is that in Paul the citation from Dt implements a soteriological evaluation of Jesus' death, whereas in Acts it does not (U. Wilckens, *Missionsreden*, 126). **31.** *Savior:* The first appearance of this Christological title. Like the Mosaic *archēgos* (leader) it is a title of the exalted One, whose function is to save (2:21,40; 4:12). In contrast, *sōtēr* is applied to Jesus in his earthly mission in Lk 2:11; Acts 13:23, which leads one to think that the designation of the exalted Jesus *archēgos kai sōtēr* came to Luke from his tradition (see Heb 2:10; *2 Clem.* 20:5; cf. U. Wilckens, *Missionsreden*, 176–77; J. C. O'Neill, *Theology*, 143). *exalted him:* The juxtaposition of *ēgeiren* and *hypsōsen* is in the traditional equivalent sense, not according to the two "moments" of 1:1–11. Cf. the parallel *anestēsen* (aor.) and *hypsōtheis* (ptc.) in 2:32–33. **32.** The association of the apostles' and the Holy Spirit's witness is not without reference to the preceding narrative: cf. Lk 12:11–12 (modifying Mk 13:11; Mt 10:20); cf. Lk 24:48–49; Acts 2:32–33. **34–39.** *Gamaliel:* The voice of caution is fittingly raised by a Pharisee (see comment on 4:1). That a Pharisee—a student of Gamaliel—later appears as the worst of the persecutors (22:3–4; 26:5,9–11) is a point of tension between Luke and the tradition. **36–37.** Examples of unsuccessful contemporary movements. On the chronological problems here, see M. Dibelius, *Studies*, 186–87; *Beginnings* 4, 60–62). These movements illustrate the argument: If it be not God's initiative, as these movements were not, the new faith will perish of itself. **38–39.** The switch from the subjunctive *ean ē* to the indicative *ei de...estin* indicates the conclusion that Luke's readers cannot avoid. The ms. D paraphrased vv. 38–39, and it shows that some copyists took the cue. Gamaliel is made to articulate the core of the apologetic in Acts: The Christian movement is indeed from God, hence its opponents are *theomachoi*, "fighters with God." **42.** A small concluding summary (→ 4 above).

(Campeau, L., "Theudas le faux prophète et Judas le Galiléen," *ScEccl* 5 [1953] 235–45. Winter, P., "Miszellen zur Apostelgeschichte. I. Acta 5, 36: Theudas," *EvT* 17 [1957] 398–99.)

35 (f) Stephen and the Hellenists (6:1–8:1a). The first indication of dissension in the Jerusalem church is now encountered in Luke's story. Persecutions from outside sources disturbing its tranquillity have already been noted; now an inner crisis disturbs the idyllic unity of the church. In effect, it remotely foreshadows the emancipation of the Church from Palestinian Judaism, for the crisis arises between two groups of Jews converted to Christianity, the "Hebrews" and the "Hellenists."

Thus far the Word has spread to Palestinian Jews, or to Israel; but the leaders of the nation (principally the Sadducees [see comment on 4:1]) have rejected it and persecuted its witnesses. Now Diaspora Jews hear the Word, preached by the Hellenist Stephen.

(i) *The Hellenists* (6:1–6). These six verses are peculiar in Acts in that for the first time Christians are here called "disciples" (*mathētai*), and only here does Luke speak of "the Twelve" (6:2) or of "the Hebrews." Do these six verses come to him from a special source? The strife between the "Hebrews" and the "Hellenists" points up the need of "assistants" (*diakonoi*) in the early community—in effect, a need for a structuring of the community itself. With the appointment of such assistants three classes appear in the Jerusalem mother church: apostles, elders, and assistants. The early hierarchy did not hesitate to restructure itself.

1. *disciples:* This term has not been used for Christians since Lk 22:45; it will reappear in the story of Paul (9:1,10,19, etc.). *Hellenists:* See 9:29. Since the time of John Chrysostom (*In Act. Ap. hom.* 14; *PG* 60.113) *Hellēnistai* has been understood as "Gk-speaking Jews," Diaspora Jews sojourning in Jerusalem. However, H. J. Cadbury (*Beginnings* 5, 59–74) argued that *Hellēnistēs* meant no more than *Hellēn*, "a Greek," because it was a derivative of *hellēnizō*, which means "to live as a Greek," not "to speak Greek." For him "Hellenist" was the title for Gentile members of the Palestinian church. His explanation has not been widely accepted, mainly because there has been no indication so far in Luke's story of anything but a Jewish-Christian Church. Since Paul, a Gk-speaking Diaspora Jew, calls himself "a Hebrew" (Phil 3:5), C. F. D. Moule (*ExpT* 70 [1958–59] 100–102) has plausibly suggested that the "Hellenists" were "Jews who spoke *only* Greek," while "Hebrews" were "Jews, who, while able to speak Greek, knew a Semitic language *also*" (cf. J. A. Fitzmyer, *Studies in Lk-Acts*, 237–38). **2.** *the Twelve:* In Luke's story these are the apostles (see 1:26; 2:14). *neglect the word of God to wait on tables:* Or possibly "to keep accounts" in the dole to the poor (see AG 832). **3.** *seven men:* Though they are not called *diakonoi* ("assistants," and later "deacons"), their task is a *diakonia* (6:1, "service") and they are said to "serve" (*diakonein*). In this basic idea their ministry in the structured church does not differ from the "service of the Word," which is the task of the apostles; both are to "serve." *of good repute, full of the Spirit and of wisdom:* See Nm 27:18. Such qualities may seem superfluous for the function immediately envisaged in their selection; but in Luke's subsequent story they never appear carrying out the relief to the poor. Instead, Stephen and Philip, two of the assistants, are almost immediately depicted in the role of preachers and debaters. The qualities mentioned, then, have this role in view. **4.** *prayer:* See 1:14;

2:42; 4:23–31. *ministry of the word:* The spread of the Word or of the Christian message (see comment on 4:31) is thus depicted as a service (cf. Lk 1:2). **5.** *by all the assembly:* The Jerusalem community is designated as *plēthos*, "multitude," a word that is used in a somewhat similar way as the Essene word *rabbîm* (the many) in QL (see J. A. Fitzmyer, *Studies in Lk-Acts*, 245–46). The seven men chosen all bear Gk names and are intended by Luke to be regarded as Hellenists. (For an attempt to show Stephen to "have been a Samaritan," see W. F. Albright and C. S. Mann, "Stephen's Samaritan Background," in J. Munck, *Acts*, 285–300.) *Stephen:* The description of him anticipates the role he is to play in 6:8ff.; he is known only from this episode. *Philip:* See 8:5–8; 21:8–9. *Prochorus, Nicanor, Timon, Parmenas, Nicolaus of Antioch:* Otherwise unknown; later legends associated the proselyte Nicolaus with the Nicolaitans of Ap 2:6,15 (see A. von Harnack, *JRel* 3 [1923] 413–22). **6.** *imposed hands:* The subject of the verb is not clear; is it "the Twelve" or "the community"? The imposition of hands was an expression of solidarity between the persons so acting and so treated, a self-identification of one person with another in respect of status, office, or quality. It connoted the taking of another into association with oneself in the matter of some spiritual gift, blessing, or function (see comment on 13:3).

(Baumgartner, E., "Zur Siebenzahl der Diakone in der Urkirche zu Jerusalem," *BZ* 7 [1909] 49–53. Cerfaux, L., "La composition de la première partie du Livre des Actes," *ETL* 13 [1936] 667–91, esp. 681–83.)

36 (ii) *Summary* (6:7). A minor Lucan summary marks the further progress of the Word of God. *a great number of priests:* Members of many Jewish priestly families embraced the faith (lit., "were obedient to the faith," a Pauline expression, Rom 1:5; 16:26). Were there Essenes among them? Given the basically priestly nucleus of the Qumran community, it is possible that this Lucan notice would refer to them, but there is no way to prove it. A difference is to be noted between the role of the converted priests in the Christian Church and the clearly defined roles of priests and Levites in the Qumran community (see 1QS 1:18,21; 2:1,11,19; 1QM 7:15; 13:1; 15:4; 1QSa 2:18–19; cf. J. A. Fitzmyer, *Studies in Lk-Acts*, 249–50).

37 (iii) *The account of Stephen* (6:8–15; 7:54–8:1a). These two sections, taken together here, tell the story of Stephen and form the framework of his discourse. The charges leveled against him resemble those leveled against Jesus in the Gospel tradition; it was Luke's intention to make Stephen similar to Jesus. The charges are three: (1) He has uttered blasphemies against Moses and God. (2) He has spoken against "this holy place" (the Jerusalem Temple) and the Law. (3) He has maintained that Jesus of Nazareth will destroy this place and change Mosaic customs. Though the Stephen episode is prima facie a defense, it is actually more a taking of position, a discussion in which Judaism is confronted with Christianity. It depicts the last Jerusalem crisis; the persecution that ensues drives the Word to Samaria, Judea, Galilee, and Syria.

8. *a man filled...:* This description of Stephen echoes the foreshadowing of 6:5. **9.** *synagogue of Roman Freedmen:* Luke's text uses a Gk form of the Lat proper name: *Libertinōn* (= Libertini); it refers probably to the free descendants of those Jewish captives taken to Rome in 63 BC by Pompey for his triumph, who had later been freed (see 2:10). (For an inscription possibly related to this synagogue, see C. K. Barrett, *NTB* § 50.) Luke undoubtedly wants it to be understood that the following groups of Jews are meeting in the synagogue of the Freedmen. **11.** *blasphemies:* The precise nature of the blasphemy against Moses and God is not explained. Even though Stephen does touch on the Temple and Moses in his discourse, he really never answers the charge itself. "Blasphemy" is the one charge that all the Evangelists have recalled in their recollection of the accusations made against Jesus. **12.** *to the Sanhedrin:* See comment on Mk 14:55. **13.** *false witnesses:* See Mk 14:57–58. Luke echoes the Gospel tradition about false witnesses here, even though he omitted mentioning them in his own Passion Narrative. **14.** *the customs which Moses handed down:* Luke does not specify which ones are meant; cf. 15:1,5; 21:21,28; 25:8; 28:17 for similar accusations in the story of Paul. **15.** *like the face of an angel:* The implication is that his face was resplendent; the reason for it is given in the sequel to this verse, which is 7:55–56. The discourse of Stephen interrupts the sequence.

38 **7:54.** This verse is an editorial suture used by Luke to join the continuation of the Stephen story to the end of the discourse (cf. 5:33). **55.** *filled with the Holy Spirit:* See 6:5,8. *Jesus standing at God's right hand:* The vision of Jesus is the confirmation of the truth of the speech (H. Conzelmann, *Apostelgeschichte*, 51). Cf. Lk 22:69. **56.** *the Son of Man:* Aside from Jn 12:34 this is the only occurrence of this expression in the NT, when it is not on the lips of Jesus himself (→ Aspects NT Thought, 78:28). **57.** *they rushed at him:* Even though Stephen was made to appear before the Sanhedrin (6:11,15), there is no indication of a sentence; the crowd's action can only be described as a lynching. The execution of Stephen is scarcely an indication that the Sanhedrin at the time had any right to put a condemned man to death (cf. Jn 18:31). **58.** *began to stone him:* Stoning—carried out outside the city—was a punishment for blasphemy derived from Lv 24:10–16 (cf. Mishnah, *Sanhedrin* 7:4); it was also the fate of the prophet Zechariah (2 Chr 24:21). Cf. Stephen's words in 7:52. *the witnesses:* Probably those of 6:13–14 are meant. *a young man named Saul:* Luke obviously intends to be highly ironic in this mention of Saul, his future hero, who will first be presented as the furious persecutor of the early Church. The clothes are laid at the feet of the future apostle of freedom. Cf. 22:20; 26:10. **59.** *receive my spirit:* Stephen's prayer echoes that of Jesus (Lk 23:46), as does its continuation (Lk 23:34). **60.** *with that he died:* Since the 5th cent. the traditional spot of Stephen's martyrdom has been located a short distance to the N of the Damascus Gate of Old Jerusalem. The Empress Eudocia had a basilica erected there *ca.* AD 420, which was later destroyed by the Persians in 614. On this site the French Dominicans built the Église St-Étienne in 1898 and started the École Biblique in 1890 (→ Modern OT Criticism, 70:61).

39 (iv) *The discourse of Stephen* (7:1–53). This discourse, which is clearly an insert between 6:8–15 and 7:55–60, is the longest speech in Acts. Prima facie it is supposed to be Stephen's defense, but Stephen does not really (i.e., directly) answer the charges leveled against him. In the development of Acts this discourse represents the beginning of the formal break of Christianity with Judaism. Stephen's speech is part of the larger context of the emergence of the Hellenists; as one of these, Stephen addresses and confounds Diaspora Judaism. The result is his death, "and on that day a great persecution started against the church in Jerusalem" (8:1b). The rift is between Jews and Christians. From now on Christianity will continue to emerge from its Jewish matrix, even though Paul in his last speeches will strive to show that Christianity is only the logical conclusion of Pharisaism (23:6; 26:6–8). Hence Stephen's speech heralds the emancipation of Christianity from Judaism.

Stephen's discourse is really a sermon in which the history of Israel from Abraham to Solomon is recast in terms of opposition to Jesus. In this regard it resembles the missionary speech of Paul at Pisidian Antioch (13:17–22), which is the springboard for his proclamation to the Jews of that town (13:23–41). Opposition to Jesus is the climax of the discourse of Stephen (7:51–53); but the implications in the rest of the speech are clear: The history of the Jewish people has always been one of opposition to God's appointed guides and of idolatry. The strictly polemical verses of the discourse are 35, 37, 39–42, and 48–53 (possibly 25 and 27). The edifying historical summary imitates Jos 24 or Ez 20 or Neh 9 after a fashion. One should note the typology in the discourse: Joseph and Moses are types of Jesus, but not David, Solomon, or the Israelites. The basic theme of the discourse can be summed up thus: The holy promise of God has been dishonored by the disobedience of Israel; in rejecting the challenge of the promise, Israel has denied its own history and its inheritance.

40 Six parts of the discourse can be distinguished: 2–7, 8–19, 20–39, 40–43, 44–50, 51–53. Stephen's allusions to the OT are dependent in the discourse on the LXX, not on the MT.

1. This verse is transitional. *the high priest:* The presiding official in the Sanhedrin (cf. 4:5; Mk 14:60). **2–7.** God's promise of "this place" to Abraham. Stephen begins his speech by recalling the historic vocation of Israel's forefather; the seminomadic Abraham is called to settle "in this place." Abraham's obedience to that call was the real beginning of Israel's history. **2.** *my brothers and fathers, listen to me:* Stephen's discourse opens in the manner of Gk rhetoric, but it immediately becomes a tissue of OT texts. *the God of glory:* The chief actor is described with a phrase from Ps 29:3; at his stoning Stephen will behold him (cf. 3:13). *still in Mesopotamia:* According to Gn 11:31; 12:1 the vision took place in Haran; Luke is rather using a form of the Abraham story that was current in later Judaism (see Philo, *De Abrahamo* 62). However, recall that Gn 15:7 passes over the mention of Haran. *Haran:* An ancient city on caravan routes (from Babylonia to Asia Minor and from Persia to Egypt); it was located at modern Sultan-tepe, a mound near the village *Harran* on the Upper Balikh River in Turkey. **3.** *leave your country:* Stephen quotes Gn 12:1. Abraham the wanderer is called to settle in a definite land. **4.** *the land of the Chaldeans:* The town of Ur (Gn 11:31) was not in "the land of the Chaldeans" in the time of Abraham; this is an anachronism confusing about 1000 years (cf. *EDB* 341–42). *after his father died:* See Gn 11:32; 12:1. **5.** This verse echoes Dt 2:5; Gn 12:7; 17:8. **6.** See Gn 15:13. **7.** *I will judge that nation:* An allusion to Ex 3:12, in which a "mountain" appears (referring to Horeb); this is now changed to "this place" (referring to Canaan, or Israel, and in particular to Jerusalem). In all of these verses the important idea is that God's call came to Abraham as a wanderer.

41 **8–19.** In contrast to the obedient Abraham, the patriarchs who were born of him manifested their opposition to God by their jealousy of Joseph; yet despite this opposition God's promise remained and events proceeded to the fulfillment of it. Stephen's indirect accusation of his opponents begins with the story of Joseph, who is the type of Jesus, the rejected one. Through Joseph God brought it about that Jacob, the eponymous ancestor of Israel who died in a foreign country, came to be buried "in this place" (in Israel). **8.** *a covenant of circumcision:* As Luke reads the OT, circumcision is the "sign of the covenant" (Gn 17:11); he is completely unaware that ch. 17 of Gn is derived from the P source (→ Genesis, 2:13) and that the relation of circumcision to the covenant is due to a later addition of P material. *circumcised him on the eighth day:* An allusion to Gn 21:4. **9.** *sold Joseph:* An allusion to Gn 37:28. The motive of the sale is all important for Luke, because it is an indirect description of the opponents of Stephen. **10.** *granted him favor:* An allusion to Gn 39:21. *governor of Egypt:* See Gn 41:43; Ps 105:21. **12.** *there was grain in Egypt:* See Gn 42:2; cf. 1QapGn 19:10. **13.** *Joseph made himself known:* An allusion to Gn 45:1. **14.** *seventy-five persons in all:* The MT of Ex 1:5 reads "seventy persons," but 4QEx^a, with which the LXX agrees, reads "seventy-five persons" (see F. M. Cross, Jr., *RB* 63 [1956] 56; similarly Philo, *De migr. Abrahami* 199). **15.** *Jacob went down to Egypt:* See Gn 46:6; 49:33. **16.** *at Shechem:* Stephen's discourse confuses the land of Jacob's burial, which took place at Mamre near Hebron (Gn 23:17–19; 49:30–31) in ground bought from Ephron the Hittite, with the land bought by Jacob from the sons of Hamor at Shechem (Gn 33:19), where according to tradition Joseph was buried. **17.** *the time of the promise:* The time for the fulfillment of the promise. This refers to the Exodus primarily, but it obviously alludes as well to the time of the fulfillment of God's promise in Christ. *grew more and more numerous:* See Ex 1:7–8. **18.** *who knew nothing of Joseph:* See Ex 1:8. This Pharaoh was possibly Seti I (→ Exodus, 3:8). **19.** *dealt craftily with our people:* See Ex 1:10. Throughout this section Joseph is presented as the type of the innocent one who suffers, but is eventually victorious because God is with him.

42 **20–39.** Then Moses, raised in a foreign land, became Yahweh's instrument; he brings the divine promise to a certain fulfillment, even though Israel rejects him too. He is the type of Jesus, because Jesus is "the prophet like me" (Dt 18:15–18). **20.** *an exceedingly handsome child:* The physical beauty is intended to express God's favor and to be a sign of his exceptional vocation (cf. Heb 11:23; Ex 2:2). **21.** *Pharaoh's daughter adopted him:* See Ex 2:10. **22.** *in all the lore of Egypt:* Stephen makes a point of the foreign birth and the upbringing of Moses; such was the instrument who was to lead God's people to "this place." *powerful in word and deed:* The same description is used of Jesus in Lk 24:19 (cf. Acts 2:22). **23.** *visit his kinsmen:* The implication of Jesus' coming to his own people is obvious (cf. Ex 2:11). **24.** *slaying the Egyptian:* See Ex 2:12. **25.** *using him to bring them deliverance:* The typology is obvious. **27.** *pushed Moses aside:* Cf. 7:39. Again, reference to Jesus is implied. *who appointed you ruler:* See Ex 2:14–15. **30.** *an angel appeared to him:* Ex 3:2 is alluded to here. **32.** A quotation of Ex 3:6 and 3:5. **34.** See Ex 3:7,8,10. **35.** Another allusion to Ex 2:14 (cf. 7:27). **36.** See Ex 7:3 and Nm 14:33. *return to Egypt:* According to Ex 16:3 they longed to have stayed in Egypt. **37.** The climax of the Moses story is reached here, with the quotation of Dt 18:15 (see comment on 3:22–23). One should note Stephen's delicate treatment of Moses and the Law: even the promulgation of it by angels (7:38; cf. Gal 3:19); thus Stephen answers the charge about blaspheming against Moses (6:11).

43 **40–43.** Israel's idolatry in the desert. Having rejected Moses and the oracles of God that he brought to them, the Israelites turned instead to man-made idols. The reference is to the Golden Calf (7:41). This was another open expression of Israel's opposition to God and rebellion against his Spirit in the past. Thus from its inception the chosen nation, wandering in the desert, rejected its God and adored the idols of its heart. **40.** *make us gods:* A quotation from Ex 32:1. **41.** *they fashioned the* *calf:* See Ex 32:4. *a product of their own hands:* Stephen's pejorative description of the Golden Calf paves the way for his criticism of the Jerusalem Temple. **42.** *abandoned them to the worship of the host of heaven:* Idolatrous cult of astral deities, i.e., stars regarded as gods (see 2 Chr 33:3,5; Jer 7:18; 8:2; 19:13). *the book of the prophets:* See comment on 15:15. *did you bring me sacrifices...:* Stephen quotes Am 5:25–27 (LXX), with a change of "Damascus" to "Babylon." Amos' words refer indeed to the cult of astral deities, venerated by Assyrians: Sakkuth and Kaiwan. However, the words of Amos were misunderstood by the LXX translators, just as they were by the Qumran author of CD 7:14–16 (see J. A. Fitzmyer, *NTS* 7 [1960–61] 311–12, 321–22). **43.** *the tent of Moloch:* This is the LXX translation of the words that in Hebrew mean "Sakkuth your king." It involves a confusion with the god Molech of Jer 32:35; 2 Kgs 23:10. *the star of the god Rephan:* Variants in the LXX and in NT mss. read *Rompha, Raiphan, Remphan*, etc., which represent a pre-Christian corruption and misunderstanding of Amos' text that reads *Kaiwan* (possibly = Saturn). *Babylon:* Stephen's quotation changes Amos' "Damascus" to the capital of the country where Israel spent its historic captivity—and thus sees in that captivity the fulfillment of Amos' words.

44 **44–50.** Israel's substitution of a man-made temple for the Tent of Testimony. In this section of his discourse Stephen formulates his main argument against the Jerusalem Temple; it is also a climax to his description of Israel's idolatry in the desert. The Tent of Testimony, constructed according to a heavenly pattern, had moved with Israel and symbolized Yahweh's presence among his people for generations. But Israel's kings replaced it with a man-made building. This misguided act made Yahweh the equivalent of a pagan idol. Stephen's criticism of the Jerusalem Temple must be understood against the background of a growing tendency in Judaism to spiritualize the Temple; elements of such a tendency can be found in 2 Mc 14:35–36; 1QM 2:5; 1QS 9:3ff.; Jn 4:20 (see B. Gärtner, *The Temple and the Community in Qumran and the New Testament* [Cambridge, 1965]). **44.** *had the Tent of Testimony:* See Ex 25:8–9. Note that Stephen has apparently forgotten in this verse what he said in v. 42. The shift of topic calls for a new emphasis. *according to the pattern:* An allusion to Ex 25:40 (cf. Heb 8:5; *2 Baruch* 4:5). **45.** *Joshua:* Ironically enough, the name of this charismatic leader in Luke's Gk text is *Iēsous* (the form used in the LXX indeed). The identity of it with that of Jesus carries unmistakable overtones (see Jos 3:14). **46.** *a dwelling place for the house of Jacob:* This reading of the mss. B, S*, D, H is the preferred reading, because it is the *lectio difficilior*. Another group of mss. (A, C, E, and the Koine tradition) reads, "for the God of Jacob," which agrees with Ps 132:5, to which allusion is being made. But this reading is suspect, because it could be an obvious scribal correction. In the context of criticism of the Jerusalem Temple (as a building made by man) would Luke mention the "dwelling of the God of Jacob"? **47.** *Solomon:* See 1 Kgs 6:2; 8:20–27. **48.** *does not dwell in buildings:* Cf. Acts 17:24; Mk 14:58; Heb 9:11,24. *made by human hands:* In the OT this epithet was used commonly enough for idols (see Is 2:18; 10:11; Lv 26:30); in Is 16:12 (LXX) it occurs even for the Temple. This verse sums up Stephen's attack on the Jerusalem Temple. *the prophet:* Isaiah, whose words (66:1–2) are quoted in vv. 49–50.

45 **51–53.** Stephen's open attack now shifts to Israel's leaders. After rehearsing the history of Israel's opposition to Yahweh and his agents, its reluctance to fulfill its true calling, and its idolatry (both in the desert and in Jerusalem), Stephen ends with a stinging rebuke of Jerusalem's leaders. **51.** *stiff-necked people:* This description is found in Ex 33:3,5. *uncircumcised in heart:* Cf. Jer 9:25; 6:10; Ez 44:7. *opposing the Holy Spirit:* In this section this phrase sums up Stephen's main accusation against his opponents (cf. Nm 27:14; Is 63:10; 2 Chr 30:7–8). **52.** *did not persecute:* For Israel's persecution of the prophets, see 2 Chr 36:14–16; 1 Kgs 19:14; Mt 5:12; 23:31,37. The tradition of the rabbis also tells of the slaying of Isaiah, Uriah (Jer 26:30), Zechariah (2 Chr 24:20–21); cf. Str-B 1, 943. *the Upright One:* This reference to Jesus implicitly equates him with the Servant of Yahweh, who in Is 53:11 is so described (see Acts 3:14; 22:14). **53.** *angels:* See 7:38. The angelic promulgation of the Mosaic Law is not meant here to demean it (as in Gal 3:19); rather it expresses its sacred character, which Stephen accuses his opponents of ignoring (cf. Heb 2:2).

Stephen's speech should not really be regarded as his defense; it has often been noted that most of it is irrelevant to the charges that are made in the story of Stephen's martyrdom (→ 37 above). The didactic character of the speech predominates, and it serves to advance Luke's own story of the spread of the Word from Jerusalem to the end of the earth.

(Barnard, L. W., "Saint Stephen and Early Alexandrian Christianity," *NTS* 7 [1960–61] 31–45. Bihler, J., *Die Stephanusgeschichte im Zusammenhang der Apostelgeschichte* [Munich, 1963]. Charlier, C., "Le manifeste d'Étienne (Actes 7)," *BiViChr* 3 [1953] 83–93. Conzelmann, H., *Apostelgeschichte*, 45–51. Dibelius, M., *Studies*, 167–70. Foakes Jackson, F. J., "Stephen's Speech in Acts," *JBL* 49 [1930] 283–86. Haenchen, E., *Apostelgeschichte*, 227–50. Klijn, A. F. J., "Stephen's Speech—Acts vii. 2–53," *NTS* 4 [1957–58] 25–31. Mundle, W., "Die Stephanusrede Apg. 7: Eine Märtyrerapologie," *ZNW* 20 [1921] 133–47. O'Neill, J. C., *Theology*, ch. 3. Pesch, R., *Die Vision des Stephanus: Apg 7:55–56 im Rahmen der Apostelgeschichte* [SBS 12; Stuttgart, 1966]. Simon, M., *St. Stephen and the Hellenists in the Primitive Church* [London, 1958].)

46 (g) The Third Persecution and the Dispersion (8:1b–3). See 3:1ff.; 5:17–42. These verses represent a redactional suture linking the story of Stephen's martyrdom to the spread of the Word from Jerusalem to Judea and Samaria under the influence of the Hellenists. The death of the Hellenist Stephen leads to a persecution of the Church; and this results in furthering the spread of Christianity. In reality, v. 2 belongs with the preceding episode; vv. 1 and 3 belong together, serving as the introduction to 9:1–19a

1. *except the apostles:* Luke is concerned to depict the Twelve as still the nerve center of Christianity in Jerusalem. **2.** *devout men:* In the context of the persecution Luke possibly intends them to be understood as Jews (see 2:5). **3.** *Saul wrought havoc against the Church:* See 7:58; 8:1a. The "youth" has now become the organizer of the persecution; he has passed from the silent, passive witness to the active destroyer.

47 **(C) The Mission in Judea and Samaria (8:4–9:43).** In this section Luke depicts the spread of the Word and tells the story of the call of the hero whose role will occupy the latter part of Acts.

(a) The Story of Philip (8:4–40). As an example of the spread of the Word from Jerusalem, Luke uses the story of Philip, the evangelist, who is not to be confused with the apostle (1:13); he is the Hellenist elected as one of the seven assistants (6:5; cf. 21:8). The two scenes in which he is here involved concern the evangelization of Samaria (4–25) and the conversion of the Ethiopian eunuch (26–40). These scenes show the spread of the Word from Jerusalem under the stress of persecution (a feature that Luke emphasizes almost as if it were a condition of that spread) and under the influence of the Hellenists (first Stephen, now Philip). The two scenes further depict the acceptance of the Word by persons who were considered outcasts of Israel: Samaritans and eunuchs (who, according to Dt 23:1, were cut off from "the assembly of the Lord" [see Jos 24:1]). The detail of Dt 23:1 no longer has any significance for Christianity, which is rather to be guided by the words of Is 56:1–5.

(i) *The Samaritan mission* (8:4–25). Philip undertakes the evangelization of Samaria on his own; though quite successful, his missionary effort is not regarded by Luke as a fully authorized endeavor. This is why the early institutional Church sends Peter and John, who by the imposition of hands confer the Spirit and incorporate the immature Christian community of Samaria into the fold. Luke makes it clear that the Spirit is given only in conjunction with the authorized college of the Twelve. The incident reveals that Luke, in writing Acts, was aware that there were splinter groups in early Christianity that the mother church sought to incorporate (cf. 18:25–27; 19:2–6; 20:29–30).

5. *a city of Samaria:* This is the more commonly accepted reading today; some mss. (B, A) read "the city of Samaria," which would refer to Sebaste, the Hellenistic capital built by Herod the Great. If Luke meant this town, why did he not name it? Since the episode concerns the evangelization of the Samaritans, the indefinite reference to a city of Samaria may be to some other place like Shechem (= Sychar? [Jn 4:5], or later Flavia Neapolis [cf. *EDB* 2203–4]). *preached to them the Messiah:* The Samaritans, who were regarded as heterodox by the Jews, by this time shared with them a belief in the coming of a messianic figure, the "Returning One" (Aram *Tā'eb*; see Jn 4:25). **7.** *were cured:* Even one of the seven assistants is depicted performing the miracles that Jesus promised his disciples would work (see Mk 16:17). **9.** *Simon:* From this passage he is known in later Christian literature as Simon Magus. Justin Martyr, who came from Flavia Neapolis, associated Simon with the village of Gitta in Samaria (*Apol.* 1. 26, 56; *Dialogue with Trypho* 120.6); see further Irenaeus, *Adv. haer.* 1.23; Hippolytus, *Refutatio* 6.13; 6.17, 1–2; *Ps.-Clementine Homilies* 2.22; 18.12; Epiphanius, *Panarion* 21.2. He is often regarded as the first of the Gnostics, probably because of the title given to him in v. 10 ("the so-called Great Power of God"). In this episode he is not depicted as having anything to do with Samaritan tenets or practices (cf. *Beginnings* 5, 151–63; L. Cerfaux, *RSR* 27 [1937] 615–17). **14.** *Peter and John:* Two of the Twelve are sent from the mother church in Jerusalem to incorporate the Samaritan community into the greater body. *receive the Holy Spirit:* The distinction implied here between the reception of baptism and the reception of the Spirit has always been a problem (cf. 2:38; 10:44; 19:5–6). Undoubtedly the distinction is a Lucan device to insist that the gift of the Spirit comes through the Church, represented by the college of the Twelve in Jerusalem. **17.** *they received the Holy Spirit:* Just as 2:1–4 depicted the Christian Pentecost for the Jews, now Luke depicts the "gift" (v. 20; cf. 2:38; 10:45) of the Spirit to the Samaritans (the Samaritan Pentecost); later he will present the "falling" of the Spirit on the Gentiles in the Cornelius episode (the Gentile Pentecost, 10:44). This reception of the Spirit must be understood in some visible manifestation; whatever it was, it prompted Simon to offer to buy this power (vv. 18–19). **21.** *heart is not steadfast:* An allusion to Ps 78:37. **22.** *repent:* See comment on 2:38. Peter's rebuke recalls OT expressions (Dt 29:17; Is 58:6) and represents an official reaction to an attempt to buy spiritual power. The word "simony" is derived from this story.

48 (ii) *The Ethiopian eunuch* (8:26–40). Another episode involving the activity of the Hellenist evangelist Philip reveals the spread of the Word to a pagan who had not first been fully converted to Judaism.

26. *angel of the Lord:* See comment on Mt 1:20; note that in v. 29 "the Spirit" speaks. *to Gaza:* The desert road led to what was once the old city of Gaza in SW Palestine, near the Egyptian border (→ Biblical Geography, 73:72). Destroyed by Alexander the Great, the new city did not rise on the same site before AD 66 (see *EDB* 843–44). **27.** *Candace:* The title *kntky* appears on Egyptian inscriptions as the name for the ancient Nubian queen; it is not a proper name. The eunuch in charge of her treasury must have been a "God-fearer" (*sebomenos*); the conversion of such a person from a distant land helps to convey Luke's concern to show the spread of the Word (cf. Ps 68:31). **32.** *like a sheep he was led to the slaughter:* Quotation of Is 53:7–8 (LXX). The part of the Servant of Yahweh Song that is quoted emphasizes the death and suffering of the Righteous One (cf. Acts 3:14; 7:52). Strangely, it omits any reference to the vicarious aspect of that death. **37.** This verse is omitted in the best mss.; it probably represents a later formulaic baptismal confession that crept into the Western Text. **39.** *snatched Philip away:* Cf. 2 Kgs 2:16. **40.** *Azotus:* The Gk name of the ancient Philistine town of Ashdod (see *EDB* 181). *Caesarea:* On the site of the ancient Tower of Strato, situated on the coast of Palestine S of Mt. Carmel, Herod the Great built a Hellenistic town and named it in honor of Caesar Augustus. Caesarea Maritima (Gk *Kaisareia Sebaste*) was furnished with a lavish palace, civic halls, and a fine harbor. It later became the seat of the provincial governor of Judea (see Josephus, *JW* 1.21, 5–8 § 408–15; *Ant.* 13.11, 2 § 313; 15.9, 6 § 331–41; cf. L. Haefeli, *Cäsarea am Meer* [NTAbh 10; Münster, 1923]; A. Reifenberg, *IsrEJ* 1 [1950–51] 20–32; A. Calderini, *BTS* 57 [1963] 1–19).

(Lösch, S., "Der Kämmerer der Königin Kandake (Apg. 8:27)," *TQ* 111 [1930] 477–519. Van Wanroy, M., "Eunuchus aethiops a diacono Philippo conversus," *VD* 20 [1940] 287–93. Wilson, R. McL., "Gnostic Origins Again," *VigChr* 11 [1957] 93–110.)

49 (b) THE VOCATION OF SAUL (9:1–19a). Having foreshadowed the spread of the Word to the Gentiles in the episode of the eunuch of the Ethiopian queen, Luke now turns to the person who will be the hero of the latter part of the book. Before the mission to the Gentiles is officially begun, Luke must incorporate his hero into the early Church. The narrative of Saul's conversion is thus introduced at this point. It is not merely a conversion story, because it relates more than Saul's psychological conversion; it is rather the story of his call to be "the instrument chosen to bring my name to the Gentiles" (9:15). This is but the first of three accounts of Saul's vocation in Acts (see 22:1–16; 26:9–18). Though attempts have been made to relate these accounts to different sources Luke had (ch. 9 from the Antiochene church; ch. 22 from the Jerusalem church; ch. 26 from Paul), they have scarcely been convincing. (For comments on the agreements and disagreements in the three Lucan accounts of Saul's conversion, → Life of Paul, 46:17–18.)

The account of Saul's conversion found in Gal 1:11–16 is closest to the Lucan account of ch. 26. The threefold repetition of the story in Acts comes at decisive moments in the story of the spread of the Word from Jerusalem, and the emphasis that Luke gives to it at these moments seems to be deliberate. In ch. 9 the account is related to the spread of the Word to the Gentiles (sandwiched in between the episode of the Ethiopian eunuch and that of the conversion of Cornelius); in ch. 22 it is related as part of the great struggle of Christianity for liberty and independence from its Jewish matrix; in ch. 26 it is recounted at the time when Rome's authority has been invoked to protect Christianity, and under such protection it symbolically makes its way "to the end of the earth."

One can also detect a further difference of the three accounts in the way in which Saul is depicted. Even though Luke is reluctant to give Saul the title of "apostle" (only in 14:4,14), nevertheless his call to evangelize the Gentiles in ch. 9 ascribes to him certain features that had been experienced by the apostles. Compare 9:15–17 with Acts 1:9; 2:4,40: He has seen the *Kyrios*; he has been filled with the Spirit; and he has begun to proclaim Jesus. Luke is implicitly suggesting an equality of Saul with the Twelve, even though he would never put it just that way. In ch. 22 one detects an emphasis on Saul's role as witness; note the number of instances in that account of *martys, martyrein,* etc. (22:5,12,15,18,20) as well as the reference to Stephen (22:20). This accounts for the greater emphasis on the seeing of the light, the *doxa,* and "the Righteous One" (22:14). Finally, in ch. 26 Saul's role is that of a prophet. In vv. 16–18 there are allusions to the inaugural visions of Ez 2:1,6; Jer 1:8, and even more clearly to Is 35:5; 42:7; 61:1. Moses and the prophets support his message about Christ (26:21); he finally asks Agrippa if he believes the prophets (26:27). In all there is the Lucan tendency to present Saul as the one who is continuing the work of Jesus, the *Kyrios*; in the person of Saul he is at work. Saul thus becomes a worthy successor of the Twelve.

(Girlanda, A., "De conversione Pauli in Actibus Apostolorum tripliciter narrata," *VD* 39 [1961] 66–81, 129–40, 173–84. Haenchen, E., "Tradition und Komposition in der Apostelgeschichte," *ZThK* 52 [1955] 205–25, esp. 210–17. Hirsch, E., "Die drei Berichte der Apostelgeschichte über die Bekehrung des Paulus," *ZNW* 28 [1929] 305–12. Lake, K., "The Conversion of Paul and the Events Immediately Following It," *Beginnings* 5, 188–95. Lohfink, G., *Paulus vor Damaskus* [SBS 4; Stuttgart, 1965]. Munck, J., "La vocation de l'apôtre Paul," *ST* 1 [1948] 131–45. Prentice, W., "St. Paul's Journey to Damascus," *ZNW* 46 [1955] 250–55. Stanley, D. M., "Paul's Conversion in Acts: Why the Three Accounts?" *CBQ* 15 [1953] 315–38. Von Dobschütz, E., "Die Berichte über die Bekehrung des Paulus," *ZNW* 29 [1930] 144–47. Wikenhauser, A., "Die Wirkung der Christophanie vor Damaskus auf Paulus und seine Begleiter nach den Berichten der Apostelgeschichte," *Bib* 33 [1952] 313–23. Windisch, H., "Die Christusepiphanie vor Damaskus (Act 9, 22 und 26) und ihre religionsgeschichtlichen Parallelen," *ZNW* 31 [1932] 1–23.)

50 The account of Saul's vocation in 9:1–19a should be regarded as a sequel to Acts 8:3. The vocation should probably be dated about AD 36 (→ Life of Paul, 46:16). Both Luke and Saul in his letters present this event as a great turning point, the significance of which cannot be adequately grasped today (→ Pauline Theology, 79:12–14).

1. *the Lord's disciples:* Cf. Gal 1:13; Phil 3:6 for Saul's own statements about his persecution of the Church. *the high priest:* Though Luke does not name him, he might possibly have been Joseph Caiaphas (→ History of Israel, 75:133); but cf. 4:5. **2.** *letters to the synagogues in Damascus:* The letter in 1 Mc 15:16–21 is usually cited to show that the Roman authorities had granted the Jewish high priest, as leader of the Sanhedrin, the power to pursue fugitives with letters of extradition. Perhaps this is what Luke has in mind here, though one may ask to what extent the high priest in Jerusalem really had such authority over Jews of the Diaspora. Josephus (*JW* 1.24, 2 § 474) suggests that only Herod had enjoyed such privileges of extradition. The number of Jews in Damascus was apparently considerable; Josephus (*JW* 2.20, 2 § 561; 7.8, 7 § 368) mentions both 10,000 and 18,000. Luke's account implies that Christianity had already spread to Damascus, even before the conversion of his missionary hero (see F. A. Schilling, *AnglTR* 16 (1934) 199–205). *Damascus:* An important city of Syria, situated at the foot of Mt. Hermon on the western edge of the Syrian desert and at the crossroads of important caravan routes. It became part of the Roman Empire in 64 BC and eventually one of the cities of the Decapolis. After the death of the Emperor Tiberius (AD 37) it came under the control of the Nabateans; at the time of Saul's conversion it was governed by the Nabatean ethnarch, King Aretas IV (cf. 2 Cor 11:32). See E. F. Bishop, *TTod* 4 (1947) 383ff.; J. Sauvaget, *Les monuments historiques de Damas* (Beirut, 1932). *the Way:* See comments on 16:17; 18:25. **3.** *a light from the sky:* Cf. 22:9; 26:13. **4.** *fell to the ground:* An OT motif is echoed here: cf. Ez 1:28; 43:3; 44:4; Dn 8:17; 10:9; 2 Mc 3:27. *Saul, Saul:* The Hebr form of the name (*Šā'ûl*) is transcribed here; it occurs only in the conversion accounts (→ Life of Paul, 46:3). Cf. 22:7; 26.14. *why do you persecute me?:* The "me" should not be too facilely identified with the concept of "the Church" (→ Pauline Theology, 79:149). Saul has been persecuting here "the Lord's disciples" (9:1), or "the Way" (9:2). **5.** *who are you, sir?:* The vocative *kyrie* may mean, of course, from Luke's standpoint "Lord" (cf. 22:8; 26:15). *I am Jesus:* This is an important affirmation in Luke's story; the Christian community is to be regarded as identified with its Lord, even though it is not yet regarded as "church." In this sense it prayed in 4:24–30. **6.** *get up, go into the city:* Cf. 22:10. In ch. 26 everything takes place between Jesus and Saul on the road, and the latter never makes his way to the city. **7.** *stood there speechless:* Contrast 22:9; in 26:14 "we all fell to the ground." **8.** *got up:* Or possibly "was raised up" (by his companions), if *egerthē* should be understood as passive.

51 **10.** *a disciple named Ananias:* See comment on 22:12. *in a vision:* Or "in a dream" (see A. Wikenhauser, *Bib* 29 [1948] 100–111). **11.** *Straight Street:* A thoroughfare running E-W in Damascus. *Judas:* Undoubtedly a Jewish Christian, who is otherwise unknown. *Saul:* Here the Gk text used the Gk form *Saulos*; contrast the form in 9:4. *Tarsus:* Saul's native town (→ Life of Paul, 46:11). **12.** *imposing his hands on him:* The imposition of hands in order to cure is not really found in the OT, nor in rabbinical literature; however, it does appear in QL (1QapGn 20:28–29; cf. J. A. Fitzmyer, *CBQ* 22 [1960] 284). **13.** *your holy people:* Lit., "your saints" (see 9:32,41; 26:10). The expression designates Christians as persons consecrated to God and Jesus, i.e., the community of the elect. **14.** *call upon your name:* See comment on 2:21; cf. 2:38; 3:6,16; 4:7,10,12,17,18,30; 5:40; 8:12,16; 9:27,29; 10:48; 15:26; 16:18; 19:5,13, 17; 21:13; 22:16; 26:9. **15.** *the instrument I have chosen:* Lit., "the vessel of election." Saul is an agent enjoying divine favor in the mission he is to accomplish. *to bring my name to the Gentiles and their kings, and to the people of Israel:* This verse formulates the three groups before whom Luke will depict Saul appearing in the course of his missionary endeavors. He will appear before Jews (13:5,14; 14:1; 16:13; 17:1–4,10,17; 19:8), before Gentiles (17:22; 18:6–11; 19:10), and before a king (26:1–29). **17.** *filled with the Holy Spirit:* It is this gift of God that incorporates Saul into the early Church; in virtue of it, all else follows. The reception of the Spirit is, therefore, mentioned prior to and, as it were, independently of baptism. This is, however, no more than the Lucan way of emphasizing what for him is the important element, the reception of the Spirit. **18.** *something like scales:* Lit., "as [it were] scales fell from his eyes" (cf. Tb 11:13). *was baptized:* See E. Fascher, *TLZ* 80 (1955) 643–48.

52 (c) SAUL AT DAMASCUS (9:19b–22). The dramatic change in the life of Saul is depicted by Luke in terms of his immediate preaching about Jesus in the town of Damascus.

19b. *the disciples:* Christians in Damascus were apparently more hospitable to Saul than those in Jerusalem; contrast 9:26. **20.** *the Son of God:* Contrast the title used in 9:22 ("the Messiah"; → Aspects NT Thought, 78:8–10; cf. H. Conzelmann, *Theology*, 171). The title "Son of God" occurs again only in 13:33 (a discourse attributed to Paul). **21.** *caused havoc:* Luke uses the same verb (*portheō*) that Saul employs in Gal 1:13,23 to describe the ravaging of the early Church. **22.** *proving:* Luke means that Saul constructed arguments from OT passages to bolster his preaching.

Luke makes no mention of Saul's withdrawal to Arabia (Gal 1:17), which would have to be fitted into the Lucan information about Saul's life at this point (between vv. 22 and 23; → Life of Paul, 46:20). Does Luke omit because he knows nothing about the journey, or because he pursues his plan of depicting Saul preaching first to the Jews and only on rebuff turning to the Gentiles (see 17:2; 28:25–28)?

53 (d) SAUL'S FIRST JERUSALEM JOURNEY (9:23–30). Acts makes mention of six different visits of Saul to Jerusalem after his conversion: 9:26; 11:30; 12:25; 15:2; 18:22 [implied]; 21:17. (On the problem the visits raise in reconstructing Saul's career, → Life of Paul, 46:19–24.) This first visit is clearly the same as that in Gal 1:18.

23. *after a considerable time:* Luke's use of *hēmerai hikanai* (a goodly number of days) indicates that more than "the few days" of v. 19 is intended. Gal 1:17–18 speaks of three years that Saul spent in Damascus after his return from Arabia. *the Jews:* The motive for Saul's departure from Damascus is thus ascribed by Luke to Jewish opposition (as in many other episodes in Acts: 13:50; 14:2; 14:19; 18:12); but in 2 Cor 11:32 Paul notes that the governor under the ethnarch Aretas guarded the city to seize him. Dupont (*Actes*, 94) reconciles the two notices by indicating that Aretas had been in a difficult position with Herod Agrippa and that it was to his advantage to seek the favor of the Jews. **25.** *some of his disciples:* This reading of the verse (*hoi mathētai autou*) is the best attested; it implies that Saul had already made some converts in Damascus. Inferior mss. read *auton* (acc., object of the ptc. "taking") *hoi mathētai*, which would mean simply "the disciples" (cf. 9:19b). *lowering him:* Cf. Jos 2:15. **27.** *Barnabas:* See 4:36–37. He is the mediator between the former persecutor of the Church and the apostolic college. Luke makes no mention whatever of the issue that is discussed in Gal 1:18–20, whether Saul in any way depended on the Jerusalem community for what he preached about Jesus. If anything, Luke depicts Saul acting even in Jerusalem in a very independent fashion. *who spoke to him:* The Lord spoke to Saul. This is the more probable meaning of the clause, which could, however, be understood more naturally, "and he [Saul, the same subject] spoke to him [the Lord]." **29.** *the Hellenists:* The title refers here clearly to Jews; most likely they are those who spoke only Greek (→ 35 above). **30.** *the brothers:* See comment on 1:15. *Caesarea:* See comment on 8:40. *Tarsus:* Gal 1:21 speaks of Saul's departure from Jerusalem for "the regions of Syria and Cilicia." These two notices are not necessarily contradictory (*pace* H. Conzelmann, *Apostelgeschichte*, 60); cf. E. M. B. Green, *ExpT* 71 (1959–60) 52–53.

(Bauernfeind, O., "Die erste Begegnung zwischen Paulus und Kephas Gal. 1:18," *TLZ* 81 [1956] 343–44. Cambier, J., "Le voyage de S. Paul à Jérusalem en Act. IX 26ss. et le schéma missionaire théologique de S. Luc," *NTS* 8 [1961–62] 249–57.)

(e) SUMMARY (9:31). Another minor summary explicitly mentions the spread of the Word (and of the Church) to Judea, Galilee, and Samaria. (For similar summaries, → 4 above.) The mention of "peace" is strange in view of the preceding motif of persecution. The summary provides a transition to Peter's missionary activity.

54 (f) PETER'S MISSION IN PALESTINE (9:32–43). Having incorporated Saul into the Church and related him to the apostolic college in Jerusalem, Luke now begins his picture of the formal mission to the Gentiles. It is not Saul who undertakes it immediately.

32. *was traveling about:* Peter seems to have been making a tour of areas already evangelized. *Lydda:* A town about 28 mi. NW of Jerusalem, about halfway between it and Joppa. **34.** *Jesus Christ cures you:* The cure that the disciple of Jesus effects is done through the invocation of his name (cf. 3:6; 4:10). **35.** *Sharon:* A region in the coastal plain of Palestine in which Lydda was situated (→ Biblical Geography, 73:75–77). **36.** *Joppa:* A coastal town about 12 mi. NW of Lydda, and 30 mi. S of Caesarea Maritima. *Tabitha:* The Aram name is *Ṭabyᵉtā* or *Ṭᵉbītā*, which means "gazelle," as does the Gk *Dorkas*. *acts of charity:* Almsgiving to the poor is often emphasized by Luke (see 10:2,4,31; cf. Lk 3:11; 6:30; 11:41; 12:33; 18:22; 19:8). **37.** *in an upstairs room:* Cf. 1 Kgs 17:19. **38.** *two men:* Cf. 10:7,20. There is a certain similarity between this story and that of Jesus' cure of the daughter of Jairus (Lk 8:40–42,49–56). Cf. Nm 22:16. **40.** *made everyone go outside:* See 2 Kgs 4:33; Lk 8:51. *Tabitha, stand up:* Compare the command in Mk 5:41, *talitha koum*[*i*], "maiden, get up" (Aram *ṭalyᵉtā qūm*[*y*]). **41.** *raised her:* Cf. 3:7. **42.** *believed in the Lord:* Cf. 9:35. **43.** *Simon, a tanner:* The appositive has most likely been added to distinguish this inhabitant of Joppa from Simon Peter himself; but cf. 8:9. Despite Conzelmann's skepticism (*Apostelgeschichte*, 61) the detail may also be intended to emphasize Peter's willingness to lodge with a man whose occupation was normally despised by the rabbis (see Str-B 2, 695). Luke does not even indicate whether this Simon was a Christian.

55 **(II) The Mission to the End of the Earth (10:1–28:31).** The second great section of Acts depicts the spread of the Word from the geographic center of sacred history, Jerusalem, to the third stage of missionary endeavor indicated in Jesus' command (see comment on 1:8).

(A) Inauguration of the Gentile Mission (10:1–15:35). Two important features characterize this part of Luke's account: first, the influential activity of one of the Twelve, Peter; and second, the major problem that faced early Christianity at this point in its development: the break with its Jewish matrix and with Jewish practices. This part of Acts includes the story of Saul's first missionary journey, the latter also serves in its own way to present this major problem too.

(a) THE CORNELIUS EVENT AND ITS EFFECTS (10:1–11:18). This episode symbolizes the universal evangelization of the Gentiles, initiated by Peter, one of the apostles. In it Peter justifies his attitude toward the Gentiles before Jerusalem Christians, and this leads logically to the apostolic "Council" of ch. 15. The Cornelius episode is, however, not just another conversion story, such as the account of the Ethiopian eunuch (8:26–40); rather, Cornelius and his household symbolize the Gentiles, to whom the Word now spreads—and indeed, not just under the aegis of one of the Twelve, but at the direction of God himself. The story of the conversion and of Peter's justification of his actions serves to emphasize the heavenly direction given to this spread. The explicit formulation of this does not come until the

"Council," when Peter insists that "from early days God selected me from your number to be the one from whose lips the Gentiles would hear the message of the gospel and would believe" (15:7). Cf. the words of James in 15:14. Instead of such an explicit formulation Luke presents the idea dramatically, by the recounting of the double vision. These visions do not have as their purpose the glorification of Peter or the enhancement of his role among the Twelve; rather, they make it clear that it is God's will that Gentiles are to become part of the Christian community without having to obey the prescriptions of the Mosaic Law. The emphatic repetition of the double vision serves this purpose: Cornelius' vision is recounted in 10:3–8 and 10:30–33; Peter's vision in 10:9–16 and 11:7–9. The effect of the vision on Peter is brought out immediately by the subsequent narrative, which depicts him inviting Gentiles to stay with him as guests (10:23), entering the house of a Gentile (10:27), and staying with them "for a few days" (10:48).

Dibelius (*Studies*, 109–22) has convincingly shown that the story of the centurion Cornelius was not invented by Luke, but that he did enrich an existing tradition: "A story about the centurion Cornelius, which was current in the community, tells how Cornelius was commanded by an angel to send for Peter from Joppa. Peter, instructed by a voice from heaven, accepts the invitation; he finds Cornelius and his household assembled, and they break forth into an ecstatic 'speaking with tongues' when they hear his words. This he takes as divine confirmation of their belief and does not hesitate to baptize Cornelius and his household. Luke has added the vision of Peter, the mention of it before Cornelius, the speech and Peter's justification, besides, probably, the content of 10.48b and the mention of Peter's Jewish-Christian companions."

56 (i) *Peter's vision and its consequences* (10:1–33). **1.** *Caesarea:* See comment on 8:40. The really important thing for Luke in this geographical notice is that Caesarea is a sort of halfway point between Jerusalem and Antioch. *a man named Cornelius:* He was probably a descendant of one of the freedmen liberated by Cornelius Sulla about 80 BC; many such emancipated slaves took the name Cornelius (see comment on 22:28). *of the Cohort Italica:* This undoubtedly refers to the *Cohors II miliaria italica civium romanorum voluntariorum*, a contingent of auxiliary archers stationed in the province of Syria (for details see T. R. S. Broughton, *Beginnings* 5, 437, 440). *God-fearing:* Luke uses the Gk phrase *phoboumenos ton theon* in a technical sense in the same way that he uses *sebomenos* (revering), to designate Gentiles who had become half-converts to Judaism (see 10:22,35; 13:16,26, 43,50; 16:14; 17:4,17; 18:7). Such persons accepted the ethical monotheism of the Jews, attended their synagogue services, but did not keep the whole Mosaic Law, and usually were not circumcised. In these latter respects they differed from "proselytes" (see 13:43). See K. Lake, *Beginnings* 5, 74–96. **2.** *to the people:* That is, the Jews, as is clear from 10:22 (cf. Lk 7:4–5). **3.** *about three o'clock:* Lit., "about the ninth hour," a moment of prayer for Jews (see 3:1). *the angel of God:* More often called "the angel of the Lord" (5:19; 8:26); cf. 10:7,22, 30. **4.** *before God as a reminder of you:* Cornelius' prayers and generosity are interpreted by the heavenly visitor in terms that recall the "memorial portions" of OT sacrifices (see Lv 2:2,9,16); cf. Tb 12:12 for a similar interpretation of prayer. **5.** *Joppa:* See comment on 9:36. **6.** Cf. 9:43. **9.** *roof terrace:* The isolation it afforded is regarded as particularly conducive to prayer (cf. Jdt 8:5). Thus it is with prayer that an important part of the story is begun. *about noon:* Lit., "about the sixth hour" (cf. 22:6). **10.** *became hungry:* The vision Peter is about to have is thus related to his physical condition. **11.** *the heavens opened:* Cf. 7:56 and Lk 3:21. *an object:* Lit., "a vessel"; the Gk word is *skeuos*, the same that was used figuratively of Saul in 9:15. **12.** *four-legged creatures...:* See 11:6. The various animals recall the usual classes mentioned in the Bible (Gn 1:24; 6:20; Lv 11:46–47; Rom 1:23). **13.** *slaughter and eat:* The heavenly instruction directs Peter not to worry about what animals are clean or unclean. The background for this instruction is Lv 11:2–23; Dt 14:3–20 (see E. Schürer, *HJPTJC* 2/2, 106–11). **14.** *never have I eaten anything unclean:* Peter's reply recalls that of the prophet Ezekiel (5:14). The Gk word translated "unclean" here is actually *koinos* (common), but it was used by Jewish writers to designate what was "profane, accessible, and permissible to all" (see *ThDNT* 3, 790–91), from which it acquired its nuance of uncleanness. **15.** The main point of the vision is stated here. *what God has purified:* The meaning is not that God has brought about this purification through this vision; rather, this has always been so (cf. 1 Tm 4:4). The heavenly proclamation is, however, understood by Luke as the norm for Christians.

17. This verse is transitional to a narrative that eventually explains the meaning of the vision to the Christian reader: the abolition of Jewish dietary regulations for Christians and of a deeper distinction between Jews and non-Jews. **19.** *the Spirit:* See 11:12. *two men:* Luke seems to have already forgotten the "devout soldier" of 10:9, at least if this reading of ms. B is preferred (as it is by most modern editors). Inferior mss. either correct the text to "three men" or leave out the number completely. **22.** *the whole Jewish nation:* See 22:12; cf. 1 Mc 10:25. **23.** Peter's invitation becomes the first effect of the vision; he has no scruples about dining with these men. *some of the brothers from Joppa:* Six of them are mentioned in 11:12. (On the meaning of "brothers," see comment on 1:15.) **25.** *bowed before him:* This gesture was normally regarded as cultic, implying that the person so honored was either divine or angelic (cf. 14:15). Cornelius' reception of Peter in this fashion reveals his esteem of the heavenly authority attached to Peter's mission. **27.** *Peter went in, talking with him all the while:* His entrance into the house of a Gentile is the second effect of the vision that Luke carefully notes. The detail of the conversation, which is omitted in the ms. D, enhances precisely Peter's willingness to accept the Gentiles. **28.** *one should call no man unclean:* The vision concerned clean and unclean animals and was intended to encourage Peter; but this verse gives it a figurative meaning. This is Luke's conclusion, explicitly drawn and formulated, about clean and unclean people; the sequence in 11:9 and 15:9 confirms this conclusion. **29.** *without raising any objection:* Lit., "without contradicting." Luke thus makes Peter obedient to the Spirit's directive (v. 20). **30.** *just three days ago:* The indication of time given here is not easily translated; it seems to say, "from the fourth day until this hour I was praying the ninth[-hour prayer]." It is apparently a combination of two different references to time, an attempt to say, "Three days ago at this very hour I was praying...." *a man in dazzling white robes:* He was called "the angel of God" in v. 3 (see comment). **31.** *your prayer has been heard:* The same formula is used by the heavenly visitor in Lk 1:13. **32.** See v. 5.

(Bishop, E. F. F., "Acts 10:25," *ExpT* 61 [1949–50] 31. Macnicol, J. D. A., "Word and Deed in the New Testament," *ScotJT* 5 [1952] 237–48. Sint, J., "Schlachten und Opfern. Zu Apg 10, 13; 11, 17," *ZKT* 78 [1956] 194–205.)

57 (ii) *Peter's discourse* (10:34–43). The last great discourse of Peter in Acts is the classic proclamation of the gospel to the Gentiles. Though Peter will speak again in 15:7–11—on a topic that is more related to the subject at issue here—the extent of that speech can scarcely compare with the discourse attributed to him here. According to Dibelius (*Studies*, 111), this discourse, which has nothing really to do with the topic of the episode as such, follows the pattern of other speeches of Peter in Acts and of Paul at Antioch in Pisidia. "By developing the same scheme several times Luke wants to show what Christian preaching is and ought to be. It is a literary-theological, not an historical task, which he wants to fulfill here." However, U. Wilckens (*ZNW* 49 [1958] 223–37; *Missionsreden*, 46–50) believes that it is basically a Lucan composition. Three parts of it may be distinguished: 34–35 (introduction), 36–41 (kerygma), 42–43 (conclusion and appeal to the Scriptures).

34–35. These verses serve as the introduction and in a sense seek to relate the discourse to the situation in which Peter finds himself. **34.** *God shows no partiality:* Lit., "God is not one showing favors," an allusion to Dt 10:17, which denies that God respects persons or accepts bribes (cf. Lv 19:15). The adj. *prosōpolēmptēs* (along with its related forms) is found only in the Greek of the LXX and NT. The Gk expression is fashioned from the Hebr *pānîm nāśā'*, "lift up the face" (of a humiliated suppliant or suitor). The expression refers to bribery and corruption; but, Peter asserts, nothing like this is found in God, especially in the matter of salvation available to Jews and Greeks (cf. Rom 2:10–11). **35.** *acts uprightly:* Lit., "practices righteousness." Peter seems to imply that this could be done even if one were not a Jew.

58 **36–41.** The kerygma of Peter. Verses 37–39 give a résumé of Jesus' ministry, which is very close to an outline of the Syn. Is it an outline of Mk? Or is it merely an outline of the Lucan Gospel? See C. H. Dodd, "The Framework of the Gospel Narrative," *New Testament Studies* (Manchester, 1953) 1–11 (or *ExpT* 43 [1931–32] 396–400); D. E. Nineham, "The Order of Events in St. Mark's Gospel," *Studies in the Gospels* (Fest. R. H. Lightfoot; Oxford, 1957) 223–39; U. Wilckens, *Missionsreden*, 63–70; J. Dupont, *RB* 69 (1962) 43–44. If it is assumed that this kerygmatic fragment is simply a résumé of the Lucan Gospel, one would have to explain why Luke has written such miserable syntax at this point (vv. 36–38); the syntactic state of these verses, coupled with the allusions to Is 52:7 and 61:1, points much more to a reflection of the primitive kerygmatic preaching than to a complete Lucan composition.

36. *the word:* The proclamation that was made first to the Jews ("the children of Israel") will eventually be made to the Gentiles (see Ps 107:20). *announcing peace:* These words allude to Is 52:7, which describe the function of the herald of the good news that was to be made known to Jerusalem (cf. Na 1:15). The syntax is confused here, because the ptc. *euaggelizomenos,* which is masc. nominative, seems to agree with "God," the subject of "sent." *he is the Lord of all:* This refers to "Jesus Christ," but the syntax is again not uncomplicated. The pron. *houtos* (here translated "he") should refer to *logos*, "the word." But this is impossible. For a close parallel, see 1QapGn 20:13. **37.** *you know:* These words must be understood as addressed to the Christian reader of Acts, and not to Cornelius; they are obviously Lucan in their formulation. Cf. 10:1–6, which implies that Cornelius, as a God-fearer, might be expected to have known something about the OT; but that he should know the essence of the Christian message now being made known is scarcely credible. *all over Judea:* The phrase is intended to describe the Roman area so designated (cf. Lk 23:5). *starting from Galilee:* Possibly the nom. ptc. *arxamenos* (starting) represents a frozen, pre-Lucan formula, which originally applied to Jesus. In this context, however, it must refer to "the word," i.e., early Christian preaching. *the baptism which John preached:* Cf. 1:22; Lk 3:23. **38.** *how God anointed him:* The baptism of Jesus is here interpreted as an "anointing" of Jesus through the Holy Spirit (see comment on 4:27). This scarcely means Jesus became the Messiah at his baptism, so far as Luke is concerned; Acts 2:36 and 3:12–20 suggest an entirely different understanding of Jesus' messiahship. So does the Lucan Infancy Narrative (1:32–33). But cf. Lk 4:16–19 (= Is 61:1–2); Acts 4:27. For Luke Jesus is the Spirit-filled agent of God's salvific activity. **39.** *in the country of the Jews:* The way from Galilee to Jerusalem. **40.** *hanging him on a tree:* A figurative expression for crucifixion, derived from Dt 21:23; see 2:23; 5:30; and cf. Gal 3:13. (→ Letter Gal, 49:22.) *God raised him:* The resurrection ascribed to the Father (→ Aspects NT Thought, 78:158). *on the third day:* See S. V. McCasland, *JBL* 48 (1929) 124–37, for a discussion of the OT basis of the phrase used in connection with the resurrection of Jesus. Cf. 1 Cor 15:4; Hos 6:2. **41.** *witnesses chosen beforehand by God:* The witnesses to the resurrection were not indiscriminate (cf. 1:8; Lk 24:48). *ate and drank:* Cf. 1:4; Lk 24:41–43. **42–43.** Conclusion. **42.** *commissioned:* See 1:8; Lk 24:47–48. *to the people:* Compare the phrase in 13:31. The expression refers above all to the people of Israel. *judge of the living and the dead:* This role of Jesus is presented again in 17:31. This role will be exercised by the Risen Jesus, precisely as *Kyrios*. **43.** *all the prophets:* Again we would love to know to which OT prophets Luke refers, in making such an assertion (cf. 3:18; see comment on 26:22).

59 (iii) *Deliberations on the event* (10:44–11:18). In this part of the Cornelius episode Luke really makes his point: Peter justifies his activity and converse with the Gentiles by making it clear that all this is the will of God. This is indicated by the "Gentile Pentecost," which is the immediate reaction to Peter's speech.

44. *the Holy Spirit fell upon all who listened:* As in the case of the Jewish Christian Pentecost, 2:4. **45.** *believing Jews:* Lit., "the faithful from the circumcision." They are those who came from Joppa (10:23). *the gift of the Holy Spirit:* Cf. 2:38; 8:20; 11:17. **46.** *speaking in tongues:* See comment on 2:4. *glorifying God:* Cf. 2:11. **47.** *hinder these people:* See 8:36 for the same expression in a baptismal context. The separation of baptism here from the outpouring of the Holy Spirit should not be overstressed; for Luke the all-important thing which incorporates men into the Christian community is the gift of the Spirit, which comes through the representatives of the apostolic college and the early institutional Church. He is aware of the necessity of baptism, but he does not correlate the two elements as closely as they were later understood, or even as Paul understood them. **48.** *baptized in the name of Jesus Christ:* See comment on 2:38. *they asked him to stay with them:* This clearly Lucan notice stresses again the effect of the vision on Peter.

11:1. *the apostles:* The rest of the Twelve. *the brothers:* See comment on 1:15. *Gentiles too had accepted the word of God:* The official report is thus recorded by Luke; in a similar way the spread of the Word to Samaria was recorded (8:14). **3.** *you entered:* As in 10:27. *and ate with them:* This detail is undoubtedly implied in 10:23 and 10:48b, but it has not been explicitly mentioned before; it is a Lucan explication. **5–12.** This is an emphatic repetition of the vision recounted in 10:11–20. **12.** *these six brothers:* See comment on 10:23. *the man's house:* See 10:27. **13.** Repetition of 10:5. **14.** *you and all your household will be saved:* A paraphrase of 10:33b. **15.** *as I began to address them:* This detail is the major discrepancy between the first account and the repetition here (cf. 10:44). This discrepancy is a good reason for maintaining that Peter's kerygmatic speech (10:34–43) was not an integral part of the Cornelius story; it is really intended for Luke's Christian readers. He does not bother to refer to it here. **16.** A clear reference to 1:5. **17.** *the same gift:* The Pentecostal gift of the Spirit, accorded as a result of faith in Christ Jesus. **18.** *God has granted even to the Gentiles life-giving repentance:* The recognition Luke now records is part of his general story of the acquiescence by real Christians in the spread of the Word beyond their own immediate confines. The community itself officially recognizes the evangelization of the Gentiles; and yet, the battle is not wholly won, as the episode of the "Council" will reveal.

(Fenasse, J.-M., "Pierre et Corneille, le centurion," *BTS* 41 [1961] 4–5. Filson, F. V., "The Christian Teacher in the First Century," *JBL* 60 [1941] 317–28.)

60 (b) THE MISSION AT ANTIOCH (11:19–30). This section should really be divided into two parts: 19–26, an account of the mixed community in Antioch; 27–30, Agabus' prediction and the collection for the church in Jerusalem.

19. *the persecution that arose because of Stephen:* Luke refers to what he recorded in 8:1,4. *Antioch:* The largest town in ancient Syria, situated on the Orontes River; it had been the capital of the Seleucid Empire, but was at this time the seat of the Roman governor of Syria. There was a large colony of Jews there, as Josephus attests (*JW* 7.3, 3 § 43; cf. *Ant.* 16.5, 3 § 148; B. M. Metzger, *BA* 11 [1948] 69–88; C. H. Kraeling, *JBL* 51 [1932] 130–60). *to none but Jews:* This notice fits in with the general missionary policy that Luke has adopted; later he will depict Paul following this policy quite consistently. Only after the Jews react against the Word do the Christian missionaries turn to pagans. **20.** *Cypriotes:* Jewish Christians like Barnabas (4:36). *Cyrenians:* Possibly Jewish Christians converted at the first Pentecost (2:10). Both Cypriotes and Cyrenians (like Lucius, 13:1) would be understood as Diaspora Jews, possibly even Hellenists. *even to the Greeks:* The mission to the Gentiles had been launched by Peter; now other unnamed Jewish Christians join in. "Greeks" (*Hellēnas*) is the preferred reading; but some mss. read "Hellenists" (*Hellēnistas*; acc. pl.). The context of this episode, however, demands that these be understood as Gentiles, "Greeks" who have not been circumcised. **21.** *the hand of the Lord:* Luke makes use of an OT expression (2 Sm 3:12 [LXX]) to convey the divine approbation that is given to this less official mission to the Gentiles. **22.** *Barnabas was sent to Antioch:* Again an official representative of the Jerusalem mother church is sent out to incorporate the new Christians into the fold; the Jerusalem church thus officially approves of this work. Compare the sending of Peter and John (8:14). In this case it is not one of the Twelve, even though later Luke will use the title "apostle" of Barnabas (14:4,14). Note the description of him in v. 24. **25.** *Tarsus:* See comment on 9:11. Saul withdrew there after his visit to Jerusalem (9:30); the time lapse between that and this activity of Barnabas is difficult to assess; possibly a number of years is implied (→ Life of Paul, 46:22). **26.** *for a whole year:* This would be roughly AD 45–46. *to be called Christians:* The implication of this verse is that the name *Christianoi* was first applied to them by outsiders. *Christianos* is a Gk form of a Lat word, formed from *Christus* and the ending *-anus*; compare *Hērōdianoi.* It means "follower of Christ," and reveals that *Christos* was already treated as a proper name for Jesus (as indeed it was by Paul). It has been maintained that this title was first used by Roman officials, who sought to distinguish Jesus' followers from Jews; the evidence, however, is not cogent.

(Bickerman, E. J., *HarvTR* 42 [1949] 109–24. Mattingly, H. B., *JTS* 9 [1958] 26–37. Moreau, J., *La nouvelle Clio* 1–2 [1949–50] 190–92. Spicq, C., *ST* 15 [1961] 68–78.)

27. *prophets:* Christian prophets, as in 1 Cor 12:28–29. **28.** *Agabus:* He is mentioned in 21:10, but is otherwise unknown. *a severe famine all over the world while Claudius was emperor:* He reigned AD 41–54; a plausible date for this famine is AD 46 (→ Life of Paul, 46:5). **30.** *sent it off with Barnabas and Saul to the elders:* This is the second reference of a visit of Saul to Jerusalem after his conversion (→ 53 above); it is usually called the Famine Visit. Was it a real visit, distinct from that in 12:25 and 15:2? (→ Life of Paul, 46:24.)

(Benoit, P., "La deuxième visite de Saint Paul à Jérusalem," *Bib* 40 [1959] 778–92. Funk, R. W., "The Enigma of the Famine Visit," *JBL* 75 [1956] 130–36. Giet, S., "Le second voyage de Saint Paul à Jérusalem. Actes 11:27–30; 12:24–25," *RScRel* 25 [1951] 265–69.)

61 (c) HEROD'S PERSECUTION AND DEATH (12:1–23). To the three notices of the persecution of the early community already indicated by Luke, another is now added, and this one from a more official source.

1. *Herod the King:* Herod Agrippa I (→ History of Israel, 75:149). **2.** *James:* The son of Zebedee (→ Aspects NT Thought, 78:164). Herod's actions, as described by Luke, are marked by caprice and serve as a foil to the miraculous preservation of the early community to be depicted, especially of another of the Twelve (Peter). No obligation is felt to replace James, one of the Twelve, as was felt in the case of Judas (1:15–26). **3.** *the feast of Unleavened Bread:* Called Passover in v. 4 (→ Gospel Mk, 42:83). This time-notice plays no real role in the story of Peter's arrest and deliverance. **7.** *the angel of the Lord:* See comment on Mt 1:20; note that in v. 17 Peter ascribes his deliverance to "the Lord." **9.** *it seemed to be just a vision:* That is, a dream of the night. **10.** *the first guard, and then the second:* Possibly the guards are to be thought of as asleep. It is impossible to determine from Luke's account where the prison is located in which Peter was locked up; not even the additional detail in the ms. D ("they went out, descended the seven steps, and walked down a narrow alley") gives any real clue to its location (cf. Ez 40:22,26). **12.** *the house of Mary, the mother of John, who is called Mark:* The house is obviously somewhere in the city of Jerusalem (for its "traditional" location, see C. Kopp, *Holy Places of the Gospels* [N.Y., 1963] 327–28; for the identification of John Mark, → Gospel Mk, 42:2). **15.** *his angel:* This expression preserves a popular belief in guardian angels considered to be the double of the persons whom they guarded (cf. Mt 18:10). **17.** *report this to James:* This is the "brother of the Lord" (Gal 1:19), who is depicted in Acts somewhat like a residential bishop of Jerusalem (see 15:13; 21:18; → Aspects NT Thought, 78:167–168), even though he is not one of the Twelve, nor ever given the title *episkopos.* Peter acknowledges his prominence. *to another place:* The implication is that Peter left Jerusalem for security; there is, however, no evidence that he went to Rome. He becomes a traveling apostle (cf. 1 Cor 9:5; Gal 2:11). **18.** *Caesarea:* Caesarea Maritima, where Herod the Great had built a sumptuous palace. **20.** *Tyre and Sidon:* See comment on 11:19. *food from the king's land:* Cf. Ez 27:17. **21.** *arrayed in royal robes:* Josephus, who recounts the same incident (*Ant.* 19.8, 2 § 343–44), describes Agrippa's robes as "woven completely of silver so that its texture was indeed wondrous...; the silver, illumined by the touch of the first rays of the sun, was wondrously radiant and by its glitter inspired fear and awe in those who gazed intently upon it. Straightway his flatterers raised their voices from various directions—though hardly for his good—addressing him as a god." Herod Agrippa was attending a spectacle in honor of Caesar (the *Vicennalia*) when his death occurred.

23. *the angel of the Lord struck him down:* Josephus (*ibid.*) tells it in this way: Herod "looked up and saw an owl perched on a rope over his head. At once, recognizing this as a harbinger of woes just as it had once been of good tidings, he felt a stab of pain in his heart; he was gripped in his stomach by an ache that he felt everywhere at once.... They hastened to carry him to the palace.... Exhausted after five straight days by the pain in his abdomen, he departed this life in the fifty-fourth year of his life and the seventh of his reign" (= AD 44; → History of Israel, 75:152). *because he did not ascribe honor to God:* In the Lucan context this means that he persecuted the early Church. *eaten with worms:* The Lucan detail recalls the gruesome deaths ascribed by ancient writers to those who condemned God; compare the death of Antiochus IV Epiphanes (2 Mc 9:5–28) or that of Herod the Great (Josephus, *Ant.* 17.6, 5 § 168–79; → 14 above).

62 (d) SUMMARY AND LUCAN SUTURE (12:24–25). Another minor summary (→ 4 above) records the growth of the early community despite the persecution (cf. 6:7; 9:31). *the word of the Lord:* See comment on 4:31 (cf. Is 55:11). **25.** *Barnabas and Saul:* Note the order of the two names in this Lucan suture; Barnabas is still mentioned first, as he is in 11:30; 13:2,7; 15:2,7,12,25. But contrast 13:43,46,51; 14:3; 15:22, where precedence is given to Saul (Paul). Is the difference of order due to different sources that Luke is using? *in completion of their mission:* Lit., "having fulfilled the ministry [*diakonia*]," i.e., the bringing of relief from the Antiochene community to the poor of Jerusalem (11:29–30). The aor. ptc. *plērōsantes* is not easy to interpret because of the uncertainty of the reading of the preposition that follows the main vb. *hypestrepsan* (they returned). *to Jerusalem:* This is the *lectio difficilior* and therefore the reading to be retained in the verse (*eis Ierousalēm*). It should be understood as a second reference to the "Famine Visit" made by Saul to Jerusalem (cf. 11:30). However, the ms. A reads *ex*, "from [Jerusalem]": "Barnabas and Saul returned from Jerusalem, when they had fulfilled their mission." The ms. D reads *apo*, "from" (which amounts to the same easy solution). Retaining the reading "to Jerusalem," it is necessary to understand the ptc. *plērōsantes* in a more generic sense, as is suggested above. *taking with them John:* This would mean that the Jerusalemite John Mark had been in Antioch for some reason or other.

(Dupont, J., "La mission de Paul 'à Jérusalem' (Act 12:25)," *NovT* 1 [1956] 275–303. Giet, S., "Le second voyage de Saint Paul à Jérusalem. Actes 11:27–30; 12:24–25," *RScRel* 25 [1951] 265–69.)

63 (c) THE FIRST MISSIONARY JOURNEY OF PAUL (13:1–14:28). The first part of Luke's description of the evangelization of the Gentiles concerned the activity of Peter (9:32–11:18) and the common efforts of Barnabas and Saul at Antioch (11:19–30). Now Luke begins his story of a topic that will occupy a major part of Acts, the missionary journeys of Paul. The classic number of Paul's missions is three; but it is a real question whether Paul was ever conscious of being on simply three missionary journeys, or even whether Luke so intended them. The transition from Mission II to Mission III in 18:22–23 is very abrupt, and one can ask whether they were meant to be distinguished. At any rate, for the sake of convenience one can continue to speak of Paul's three journeys. These missions are not wholly a Lucan fabrication, for the sequence of Paul's movements from his conversion to his arrival in Rome is confirmed by data in Paul's own letters, as T. H. Campbell (*JBL* 74 [1955] 80–87) has convincingly shown. (For an attempt to relate this sequence and other data in Acts and Paul's letters to what can be called Paul's "life" or "career," → Life of Paul, 46:25–42.) Luke's information about these missions of his hero Paul is not complete; indeed, it is often quite skimpy. Whenever there is question of deciding between Lucan or Pauline data, the preference must be given to the latter. On this entire question, one should consult P. Vielhauer, *Studies in Lk-Acts*, 33–50; P. Borgen, "Von Paulus zu Lukas," *ST* 20 (1966) 140–57.

The starting point for Mission I is Antioch, as it also is in the later missions (15:35–36; 18:23); to this town Saul returns in each case, except at the end of Mission III (see 14:26; 18:22; cf. 21:17). Luke's account of Mission I gives an idyllic view of Saul's missionary activity, first among the Jews, then among the Gentiles. In its own way it sets the scene and develops the problem to be handled at the Jerusalem "Council" (15:3–33).

64 (i) *The sending of Barnabas and Saul* (13:1–3). Up to this point in Acts Luke has depicted the Jerusalem community as the center from which the official evangelization moved. He records duly that "Barnabas was sent to Antioch" (11:22). Progress in the spread of the Word is now shown in the rise of the Antiochene church to a position of importance. It will send out missionaries too, and indeed under the guidance of the Spirit. The charismatic leaders, commissioned by the "prophets and teachers" of the Antiochene community, are Barnabas and Saul.

1. *at Antioch:* In Syria (see comment on 11:19). Even though Antioch is secondary to Jerusalem, which is the doctrinal center from which the Word of the Lord goes forth (Is 2:3), Antioch becomes the historical center for its spread into Gentile territory. *prophets:* Christians who enjoyed gifts of the Spirit (see 11:27; 15:32; 19:6; 21:9–10; cf. 1 Cor 12:28–29). *teachers:* The charisms Paul mentions in 1 Cor 12 were enjoyed by such men too; they were men gifted with a knowledge of the Scriptures and capable of instructing others in Christian faith (see 11:19–20,22,25–26; cf. Eph 4:11). Among the five men who belong to these categories are Barnabas and Saul; they all seem to be officials of the Antiochene church. The list of them recalls that of the Jerusalem apostles (1:13) and of the seven assistants (6:5). *Pace* A. Wikenhauser (*Apostelgeschichte*, 147), they are not all Hellenists; this description would scarcely fit Saul. *Symeon called Niger:* A Lat surname (the Black) has been added to the Semitic name of an otherwise unknown Antiochene church official (see comment on 15:14). *Lucius of Cyrene:* He is not necessarily the same as the Lucius of Rom 16:21; but he could be among those mentioned in Acts 11:20. There is no evidence that this Lucius is Luke the evangelist (*pace* B. Reicke, *The Gospel of Luke* [Richmond, Va., 1964] 10–24); see *Beginnings* 3, 416. *Manaen:* Otherwise unknown. His name is a Grecized form of the Hebr name *Menaḥem* (consoler). *brought up with:* The Gk title *syntrophos* denotes an honor given to this boyhood companion and friend of Herod Antipas (see Lk 3:1; → History of Israel, 75:140). *Saul:* Though a recent arrival in Antioch, he is regarded as one of the "prophets and teachers" of that church. The order of names, Barnabas and Saul, describes the precedence of the former over the latter at this point; it will gradually shift, especially in Lucan formulations. **2.** *engaged in the liturgy of the Lord:* The phrase could also mean more generally, "as they were serving the Lord." Yet is hard to exclude the cultic sense of *leitourgein* (esp. in view of this usage in the LXX: Ex 28:35, 43; 29:30; Nm 18:2). *fasting:* This is not a prelude to revelation (H. Conzelmann, *Apostelgeschichte*, 73), but a simple notice of early Christian cultic conduct (see 13:3; 14:23). *set apart:* Saul's great missions will continually be portrayed by Luke as Spirit-guided, and this guidance is now made explicit (13:4). *the work:* The carrying of the "name" of Jesus and of the "Word" of God to the "people of Israel" and to "the Gentiles and their kings" (9:15; cf. 22:21). **3.** *imposed hands on them:* In a cultic context the Antiochene church commissions Barnabas and Saul for their mission. One might think of this imposition of hands as a sort of "ordination," but the context argues for a missionary mandate and a blessing rather than for a sacramental bestowal of powers; the mission differs little from that of 11:22. The phrase used in 14:26, "commended to the favor of God for the task," supports this interpretation. The mandate stems from a community commissioned itself to preach to the Greeks. The imposition of hands does not necessarily connote even that which is implied in 6:6.

65 (ii) *Cyprus* (13:4–12). Barnabas, the leader of the group, takes Saul to his homeland, the first stage of Mission I.

4. *Seleucia:* This port on the Mediterranean Sea, 16 mi. to the W of Antioch, served the town; it was called Seleucia Pieria to distinguish it from other towns founded by the Seleucids (see *OCD* 822). *Cyprus:* A large colony of Jews dwelled there (see 1 Mc 15:23; Josephus, *Ant.* 13.10, 4 § 284). **5.** *Salamis:* In antiquity, the principal port on the E coast of the island, a short distance from the modern Famagusta. *in Jewish synagogues:* This detail suits Luke's typical presentation of Saul's missionary endeavors in Acts; the principle is formulated in 17:2 (cf. 13:14; 14:1; 16:13; 17:10,17; 18:4,19; 19:8; 28:17,23). *John:* John Mark, the cousin of Barnabas (Col 4:10). *an assistant:* He bears the Gk title *hypēretēs* (cf. Lk 1:2), "a minister" (of the Word). This title has often been related to the Hebr *hazzān* a synagogue official (cf. Lk 4:20; cf. B. T. Holmes, *JBL* 54 [1935] 63–72). **6.** *Paphos:* The town on the SW coast of Cyprus is the goal of the journey through the island. Nothing is said of missionary activity en route. Luke is more interested in joining to his story an account of the meeting of the missionaries with the Cypriote magicians in this town. *a Jewish magician named Bar-Jesus, who posed as a prophet:* Lit., "a false prophet." The name Bar-Jesus differs from the man's name given later, Elymas; this may indicate that two stories have been conflated: one about a Jew, Bar-Jesus, and another about a magician, Elymas (cf. M. Dibelius, *Studies*, 16). **7.** *Sergius Paulus:* The propraetor of Cyprus here enjoys the title of proconsul (*anthypatos*). He was a member of the famous Roman family *Paula*. Inscriptions from Cyprus, Pisidian Antioch, and Rome mention him, but unfortunately his proconsulship cannot be dated precisely (see *EDB* 2172). **8.** *Elymas the magician:* This new name for the magician is strange, and the etymology that Luke offers for it is baffling. The name *Elymas* was used in Libya; it certainly has nothing to do with the fanciful explanations often suggested for it (from Aramaic or Arabic). Its root is possibly Gk *ly-*, "loose." Whatever the meaning of the name, it is clear that Luke seeks to convey a negative and adverse criticism of wizardry. **9.** *Saul, also known as Paul:* The use of a double name was common among Jews; it has nothing to do with a change of the name at the time of Paul's conversion. "Paul" will be used by Luke from now on, except in the conversion accounts (22:7,13; 26:14). Because Luke's notice about the double name occurs in the episode with Sergius Paulus, commentators have often thought that the shift in the Lucan story is due to the name of Paul's "first convert" (see H. Conzelmann, *Apostelgeschichte*, 74). But does Luke consider the proconsul to be Paul's first convert? See 9:25 ("his disciples," in mss. P^{74}, B, S, A, C) and 11:26. Luke certainly knew of Paul's two names (→ Life of Paul, 46:3). *filled with the Holy Spirit:* See 4:8,31. **10.** *exclaimed:* Cf. the Lucan denunciation in 8:20–23. *the straight paths of the Lord:* An allusion to Hos 14:10 (cf. Prv 10:9; Sir 1:30; Gn 32:11). **11.** *for a while:* Cf. Lk 4:13. *groped about:* An allusion to Dt 28:29. *impressed by the teaching:* Luke wants to make sure that the reader does not conclude that the proconsul believed out of fear.

66 (iii) *Pisidian Antioch* (13:13–52). The visit of Barnabas and Paul to this town will give Paul his first real opportunity on Mission I to address a discourse to the Jews.

13. *Paul and his companions:* With this notice one begins to detect the emergence of Paul as the leader in Luke's account. *Perga:* This town lay some 5 mi. N of the port Attalia (14:25) in the center of S Asia Minor; it belonged to the territory of Pamphylia and was the capital of the Roman province of that name. *John left them:* No reason is given for the sudden departure of Paul's (noncommissioned) campanion (see 15:38 for Paul's reaction to this departure). **14.** *Pisidian Antioch:* This town had been built by Seleucus Nikator (300–280 BC) on the frontiers of Pisidia and Phrygia; it actually lay in Phrygia near the Pisidian border. It later became a Roman colony (*Colonia Caesarea*) under Augustus (see Pliny, *Nat. Hist.* 5.94). It served as an administrative center of the southern part of the province of Galatia. A considerable number of Jews lived there, as an inscription bears witness (see H. Conzelmann, *Apostelgeschichte*, 75). **15.** *an exhortation:* Lit., "a word of exhortation, or consolation" (cf. Heb 13:22). The exhortation was to take as its point of departure the reading from the Law and the Prophets, which together with the recitation of the Shema, the "Eighteen Blessings," and the homily formed the bulk of the ancient synagogue service (see Str-B 4, 153–88). The invitation sets the scene for Paul's first great discourse in Acts. It is a model missionary sermon, composed by Luke, conceived as one that would convince a synagogue audience (Jews, proselytes, and God-fearers). In its first part (vv. 17–22) it echoes the discourse of Stephen; but in its totality it is the Jewish counterpart of Paul's discourse to the Gentiles on the Areopagus. Lacking any attempt to render the audience benevolent, it begins *in medias res.* It falls into three parts, clearly marked by the repeated address in vv. 26 and 38: 16–25, 26–37, and 38–41.

67 **16–25.** Salvation history under the guidance of God leads from Israel to the Church. **16.** *rose, motioned for silence:* Luke shows Paul addressing his audience in the stance of the Gk *rhētōr* (cf. 21:40; 26:1); this is in contrast to the posture of the synagogue preacher, who is seated (cf. Lk 4:20). *fellow Israelites:* Paul addresses this audience of Diaspora Jews by their cherished name, fraught with historical and religious connotations. *who reverence our God:* The technical term for the "God-fearers" (see comment on 10:2). **17.** *this people Israel:* An OT expression, echoing Is 1:2; 3:7; 6:9–10. *chose our fathers:* A reference to Ex 6:6; Dt 5:15. **18.** *put up with them in the desert:* An allusion to Dt 1:31 (LXX); cf. Ex 16:35. **19.** *seven nations:* Listed in Dt 7:1 as the Hittites, Girgashites, Amorites, Canaanites, Perizzites, Hivites, and Jebusites (cf. Jos 3:10; 24:11). **20.** *four hundred and fifty years:* The mss. differ in supplying this time-reference; either they associate it with vv. 17–19, or else with the following mention of the judges. In either case it is not clear. If it goes with what precedes, then the figure 450 must equal the 400 years before the Exodus (Gn 15:13), plus 40 years in the desert, plus 10 years for the conquest of Canaan (but cf. Ex 12:40–41, which gives 430 years). If the phrase is read after *kai meta tauta* (and later), then it would mean that the period of the judges lasted for 450 years until Samuel—which is impossible in any mode of reckoning. Whatever the clumsy time reference really means, Luke's main intention seems to be to stress that God in his providence provided for Israel even before he raised up for it the charismatic leaders

(Jgs 2:18) and the prophets, especially Samuel (1 Sm 3:20). See Acts 3:24. **21.** *asked for a king:* See 1 Sm 8:5. *Saul, son of Kish:* See 1 Sm 10:1. *of the tribe of Benjamin:* Like Paul himself (Phil 3:5). *ruled for forty years:* The length of his reign is not given in the OT (see 1 Sm 13:1). However, Josephus (*Ant.* 6.14, 9 § 378) records it as 40 years (18 years during the life of Samuel, and 22 years after it); but elsewhere (*Ant.* 10.8, 4 § 143) he gives it as 20 years. **22.** *God removed him:* See 1 Sm 15:26. *David as their king:* See 1 Sm 16:13; 2 Sm 2:4. *I have found David:* A conflated quotation describes David's obedience in contrast to Saul's disobedience; phrases are taken from Ps 89:21; 1 Sm 13:14; Is 44:28. In this historical introduction of Paul's discourse this is the main point: David is the type of Jesus as well as his ancestor (see 2:30–32). **23.** *brought forth:* The better reading here seems to be *ēgagen*; but some mss. (C, D, 33) read *ēgeiren* "raised up," which has an ambivalent sense: "raised" (in general) or "raised" (from the dead). *a savior for Israel:* This is the main Pauline proclamation to the Jews. For the description of Jesus as Savior, see comment on 5:31. **24.** *John:* The Baptist (see Lk 1:76; 3:15–18; Acts 19:4). **25.** *as John's career was coming to an end:* This clearly Lucan expression refers to the end of the period of Israel that came with John the Baptist; it is the first stage of Luke's view of salvation history (see Lk 16:16). John's "course" (*dromos*) gave way to Jesus' "way" (*hodos;* see 9:2; 16:17). The "One who is coming" was announced by John (Lk 3:16). Since John the Baptist never appears in Paul's letters, it is clear that introducing him here is a mark of Lucan composition.

68 **26–37.** The proclamation, briefly set forth in v. 23, is now explicated by Paul in a structured form (cf. 2:39; 3:25–26; 10:36–41; see U. Wilckens, *Missionsreden*, 50–54, 70–71, 133–36; E. Haenchen, *Apostelgeschichte*, 357–60). **26.** *who reverence our God:* See comment on 10:2. *this message of salvation:* Lit., "the word of this salvation" (see 11:14; 16:30–31; an allusion to Ps 107:20). **27.** *the inhabitants of Jerusalem and their rulers:* Luke's anti-Jewish polemic is manifest here, but it is careful to specify which Jews he has in mind; cf. 2:14, 23,36 (see comment on 3:17). An "ignorance motif" is used to excuse the Jews (→ 27 above); it is, however, presented in a more subdued manner in ms. D (see E. J. Epp, *HarvTR* 55 [1962] 57–59). *fulfilled the words of the prophets:* Luke does not specify which prophets he is thinking of; this is a common Lucan mode of reference to the OT (see 3:18,21,24; 4:28; 10:43). **28.** *begged Pilate:* See 3:13; Lk 23:25. **29.** *laid him in a tomb:* See 1 Cor 15:4. **30.** *God raised him from the dead:* See comment on 10:40. **31.** *many days:* A vague, but significant, allusion to the 40 days of 1:3. *he appeared:* This detail is more important for Luke than that of the resurrection as such. Note that he is careful not to include Paul among such witnesses to the resurrection. His hero depends on the testimony of others; contrast 1 Cor 9:1; 15:8. **32.** *promised to our fathers:* Recall v. 23. **34.** As in Heb 1:5 and 5:5, Luke applies Ps 2:7 to Jesus as of the resurrection (cf. Rom 1:4; see J. Dupont, *RSR* 35 [1948] 522–43; E. Lövestam, *Son and Saviour* [*ConNeot* 18; Lund, 1961] 8–48. *give you the covenant benefits assured to David:* Lit., "the trustworthy holy things of David." This difficult phrase must be understood against its OT background (Is 55:3), "the benefits assured to David." These benefits are part of the "everlasting covenant" mentioned in the first part of the Isaian verse; they are now realized in Jesus, the Risen *Kyrios* (see Lövestam, *op. cit.*, 48–81). **35.** *you will not suffer your faithful one...:* Ps 16:10 is quoted as in 2:27, and the argumentation is the same as in 2:24–31 (see comment on 2:29); see Lövestam, *op. cit.*, 81–83. A free association of *hosia* (holy things) and *hosion* (holy one) has joined the two quotations. **36.** *David... fell asleep:* See 1 Kgs 2:10.

38–41. The conclusion of Paul's discourse stresses that the Risen Jesus is the mediator of salvation and of the forgiveness of sins, which must not be spurned by men. **38.** *forgiveness of sins:* The exhortation in the missionary discourse appeals to a common topic (see 3:19). *is acquitted of every charge of which you could not be acquitted in the Law of Moses:* Luke introduces here a specific Pauline outlook (cf. Gal 2:16; 3:10–14,24; Rom 6:7; 8:3; 10:4). **41.** *look, you cynics:* A quotation from Hab 1:5 (LXX); this form of the text is also found in 1QpHab 2:1. The MT reads, "Look at the nations" (*bgwym*), instead of "cynics" (*bwgdym*). The conclusion of Paul's discourse to the Jews of Antioch foreshadows that which he will address to those of Rome (28:25–28), when he will fling at them the reproach of Is 6:9–10.

69 **42–52.** The reaction to Paul's synagogue discourse is immediately favorable. Paul and Barnabas are invited to speak again; but Luke records no further synagogue discourse (which indicates that vv. 16–37 were intended only as a sample). Instead he reports only further encounters with the Jews. **43.** *proselytes:* Converts to Judaism, won by Jewish missionary efforts, who submitted to circumcision. **44.** *the whole city:* To ask how the whole population would have found places in the Jewish synagogue is to miss the point of Luke's story. Luke's purpose is to contrast the widespread enthusiasm of the populace at large with the jealousy of the Jews (cf. 5:17; 14:2; 17:5). **46.** *first:* The Lucan principle is invoked again (see comment on 17:2). *we now turn to the Gentiles:* This becomes a major theme of Luke's presentation from now on (14:1; 16:13; 17:1,10,17; 18:4,6,19; 19:8; 28:28). **47.** *a light to the nations:* This quotation of Is 49:6 (LXX), a part of a Servant Song, associates Paul as a missionary with the Servant of Yahweh; his preaching of the Word is to be an illumination for the Gentiles (see comment on 1:8). **50.** *persecution:* Once again the reference to the persecution emphasizes the further spread of the Word (→ 46 above). **51.** *shook the dust from their feet:* This gesture of repudiation is also found in Lk 9:5; 10:11 (cf. Acts 18:6). *Iconium:* An important town (modern Konya) in central Asia Minor, about 87 mi. ESE of Antioch; it was part of the Roman province of Galatia and capital of the region of Lycaonia (cf. 14:6; 2 Tm 3:11).

(Dupont, J., "'*Ta hosia David ta pista*' (Ac xiii 34 = Is lv 3)," *RB* 68 [1961] 91–114. Glombitza, O., "Akta XIII. 15–41. Analyse einer lukanischen Predigt vor Juden," *NTS* 5 [1958–59] 306–17.)

70 (iv) *Iconium* (14:1–5). The pattern set up in Pisidian Antioch is repeated in the missionary activity of Paul and Barnabas in Iconium. Luke's account records the founding of a small Christian community here and its subsequent persecution. The sequence of verses in this section is most likely disturbed; v. 2 would more logically follow v. 3.

1. *likewise:* The prepositional phrase *kata to auto* is not easy to translate; it may rather mean "together, in each other's company" (see AG 123). This would then refer to Barnabas and Paul entering the synagogue together. **2.** *unconvinced:* Luke's ptc. *apeithēsantes* may even have a stronger nuance, "being incredulous, refusing to believe." It forms part of his anti-Jewish motif (see 19:9; 28:24). *the brothers:* See comment on 1:15. **3.** This verse is really the sequel to v. 1. *his grace...signs and wonders:* This description is part of a pattern of the Lucan success story (cf. 15:11–12; 19:11–12; 20:24,32; cf. Mk 16:17–20). **4.** *the apostles:* It is surprising to find Luke using the title, which he otherwise reserves for the Twelve in Jerusalem, for Paul and Barnabas; it occurs again in 14:14. It may be that its use represents a pre-Lucan element of the story, derived from a source, which he is simply repeating here.

(v) *Lystra* (14:6–20a). The evangelization of the town of Iconium ended with the same reaction to Paul and Barnabas as that at Pisidian Antioch. The persecution (14:5) drives the Word of the Lord on still further.

6. *Lystra:* About 25 mi. SSW of Iconium, this town also belonged to the region of Lycaonia; under Augustus it became a Roman colony (*Colonia Iulia Felix Gemina Lustra*). *Derbe:* See comment on 14:20b. **8.** *a man lame from birth:* This cure worked by Paul is a literary parallel to that wrought by Peter in 3:2ff. **9.** *faith:* This is mentioned because it is the presupposition of the miracle (see 3:6; cf. Lk 8:48). **10.** *stand up:* Recall Ez 2:1. **11.** *saying in Lycaonian:* The detail enhances the story, because Paul and Barnabas do not understand immediately what is meant. **12.** *Barnabas Zeus, and Paul Hermes:* More prominence is thus given to Barnabas, but the implication is that Paul as Hermes is the spokesman of the gods. With this scene one should compare Ovid (*Metamorph.* 8.611–28) who records the legend of a visit of Zeus and Hermes to Philemon and Baucis in Phrygia. **13.** *the temple of Zeus:* It was outside the walls of the city, dedicated to "Zeus Before the Gates" (see W. M. Calder, *Expositor* 7/10 [1910] 148–55). **14.** *apostles:* See comment on 14:4. *tore their garments:* A gesture of distress and violent protest (cf. Jdt 14:16). **15.** *we are only men:* The refusal of divine honor is found also in 10:26. Paul's protest—actually Luke makes both Barnabas and Paul utter these words—is really a speech condemning idolatry and advocating monotheism. *the living God:* This was the expression par excellence by which Yahweh was distinguished from false gods (see 2 Kgs 19:4,16; Is 37:4). *the one who made heaven and earth:* An allusion to Ps 146:6 and Ex 20:11 (cf. Neh 9:6). **16.** *to go their own way:* This statement contrasts the Jews and the Gentiles; the former were chosen by God and to them he made manifest his way of life. In 17:30–31 Paul's speech on the Areopagus will repeat the idea of God's overlooking the idolatry of the past. **17.** *he has not hidden himself without a clue:* Luke echoes a favorite OT idea (Jer 5:24; Pss 145:15–16; 147:8). **19.** Luke's conclusion to this episode is a return to the theme of persecution. For the treatment of Paul, see 2 Cor 11:25; 2 Tm 3:11.

71 (vi) *Derbe and return* (14:20b–28). The persecution drives the Word on to yet another town in Lycaonia. One verse suffices to record the success Barnabas and Paul had there.

20b. *Derbe:* This town was situated about 60 mi. E of Lystra; its site has been definitely identified through an inscription discovered in 1956 at Kerti Hüyük (see M. Ballance, *Anatolian Studies* 7 [1957] 145–51; P. W. Skehan, *CBQ* 20 [1958] 59; G. Ogg, *NTS* 9 [1962–63] 367–70). **22.** *persevere in the faith:* This Lucan expression is an exhortation to the unflinching practice of Christianity. Luke passes over all mention of the persecution that Barnabas and Paul had experienced in the towns through which they now pass on their return. **23.** *they installed elders:* Paul and Barnabas see that a structure and an institution are set up locally; it apparently resembled that of Jerusalem (see 11:30; 21:18). These elders are significantly not elected by the local communities, but are appointed by the traveling missionaries (cf. 20:17). The ptc. *cheirotonēsantes,* which at times means to "elect by raising the hand" (2 Cor 8:19), here means simply "appoint, install" (AG 889). Some commentators think that Luke has here retroverted a later institutional structure.

24. *Pisidia:* The region near Antioch (see comment on 13:14). *Pamphylia:* See comment on 13:13. **26.** *Antioch:* In Syria (see 13:2–3). **27.** *all that God had accomplished with them:* See 15:4,12; 21:19. *opened the door of faith:* This figure is also used by Paul in 1 Cor 16:9; 2 Cor 2:12. Here it signifies the access that God had given the Gentiles to salvation through the missionaries. **28.** *some time:* Lit., "no little time." The amount of time is hard to specify. Mission I seems to have lasted from AD 46 to 49 (→ Life of Paul, 46:25–26). This notice would indicate some interval between Paul's return to Antioch and the "Council" in Jerusalem.

(Gärtner, B., "Paulus und Barnabas in Lystra. Zu Apg. 14, 8–15," *SEA* 27 [1962] 83–88. Lerle, E., "Die Predigt in Lystra (Acta XIV. 15–18)," *NTS* 7 [1960–61] 46–55. Van Imschoot, P., "S. Paul à Lystres," *Collationes Gandavenses* 16 [1929] 155–61.)

72 (f) THE APOSTOLIC "COUNCIL" (15:1–35). This episode falls designedly in the middle of Acts, for it is the turning point of Luke's story, when the apostolic and presbyteral college of Jerusalem officially recognizes the evangelization of the Gentiles, which has been initiated by Peter, Barnabas, and Paul. Thus the Christian Church officially breaks out of its Jewish matrix. This is the last act that Luke records of Peter or of the apostolic college; the implication is that the Twelve now disperse too, contrary to the indication in 8:1. The mother church of Jerusalem will continue to exert its influence, but under the direction of James. Paul dominates the rest of Luke's story, but in the Diaspora and in the mission to the heathen. Up to this chapter all has been directed by Luke with Jerusalem as the doctrinal focal point of his story; towns and regions in Palestine or Syria that were evangelized were incorporated into the mother church by its emissaries. Even Paul's Mission I foreshadowed the actions of the "Council" and the emergence of the Church from its matrix. There is a last brief reference, in 16:4, to what the apostles did in Jerusalem; after that the Word marches freely and maturely to the "end of the earth."

Though the question of the sources of Acts is still debated, ch. 15 is a prime example of a part of Acts that argues for the theory of sources (→ 6 above). An Antiochene source is possibly represented in 11:19–30, and its sequel is found in 15:3–33. If this cannot be proved, the reader should nevertheless keep it in mind in reading this chapter, because Luke's account of the "Council" reported here most likely depends on some non-Jerusalemite information. Verses 1–2 are undoubtedly a Lucan suture joining the continuation of the Antiochene source with chs. 13–14 (see P. Benoit, *Bib* 40 [1959] 778–92). The conflated character of ch. 15 is widely admitted today; and it is felt that the historical aspect of its report must be carefully distinguished from the Lucan purpose in telescoping his materials (→ Life of Paul, 46:32–33). As Luke presents the event, the "Council" handled two issues: circumcision and the dietary problems. He has done this so that he might stress the break with Judaism without any conditions being laid on Gentile converts by the apostolic and presbyteral college of Jerusalem. Luke presents Peter as the one whose voice prevails in the question of circumcision through an appeal to his experience (the Cornelius episode), James as the influential figure who decides the issue of dietary regulations. Paul's contribution to the "Council" is at most implied and indirect. What is important is that he is not depicted as simply accepting a decision but as having played a part in forming it.

(In addition to the bibliography cited in the Life of Paul [→ 46:34], see Dupont, J., *Études sur les Actes des Apôtres* [LD 45; Paris, 1967] 56–75; *Les problèmes du Livre des Actes* [Louvain, 1950] 51–70. Lietzmann, H., "Der Sinn des Aposteldekretes und seine Textwandlung," *Amicitiae corolla* [Fest. J. Rendel Harris; London, 1933] 203–11. Parker, P., "Once More, Acts and Galatians," *JBL* 86 [1967] 175–82. Reicke, B., "Der geschichtliche Hintergrund des Apostelkonzils und der Antiochia-Episode (Gal. 2:1–14)," *Studia paulina* [Fest. J. de Zwaan; Haarlem, 1953] 172–87.)

73 (i) *Preliminaries* (15:1–5). The first five verses set the Lucan stage for the "Council"; they describe the tension of the Antiochene church—a tension that is repeated in Jerusalem when the emissaries of Antioch arrive there.

1. *some men:* This vague reference reveals the suture-like character of the opening verses; note the more definite "converted Pharisees" of 15:5. *from Judea:* The vague reference points to the Jerusalem church (see 15:24) *unless you are circumcised:* Luke's introduction singles out the main issue at the historic "Council" in Jerusalem (*ca.* AD 49). The dietary regulations are not a concern here. *according to Mosaic practice:* According to the prescriptions of the Mosaic Pentateuch. The practice of circumcision was actually related in Jewish tradition, not to Moses, but to Abraham (see Gn 17:9–14; cf. Rom 4:9–12). **2.** *dissension:* Luke gives this motivation for the sending of Barnabas and Paul to Jerusalem, but in Gal 2:2 Paul speaks of a "revelation" as the reason for the visit to Jerusalem. *Paul and Barnabas:* The order of these names betrays a Lucan formulation (as in 13:43,46,50; 15:22); contrast 14:14; 15:12,25. *to see the apostles and elders in Jerusalem:* The officials of the Jerusalem church are thus clearly specified; they are distinguished from the "whole church" (cf. 15:4,22). The *sedes apostolica* was to be consulted. According to Gal 2:9, Peter and John were among these "apostles"; James, "the brother of the Lord," could also be so counted, if the Gk *apostolos* (Gal 1:19) is understood in a broader sense than the Twelve (→ Letter Gal, 49:15; Aspects NT Thought, 78:168). But does Luke consider James an "apostle" in his sense of the word? Hardly.

3. This verse may really be the sequel to 11:30. *the church:* In Antioch. *Samaria:* See comment on 8:5. On their return journey, Luke has the emissaries go through the districts through which the Word of the Lord gradually spread from Judea to Antioch. **4.** *by that church, and by the apostles and elders:* See comment on 15:2. **5.** *converted Pharisees:* Lit., "some who had come to believe (pf. ptc.) from the sect of the Pharisees." There is no solid reason not to identify these men with the "false brothers" of Gal 2:4. Note that Titus is not a companion of Paul (cf. Gal 2:1–4); nor is there any question of his circumcision here. But then Luke never mentions Titus at all. The converted Pharisees rose in some church meeting, which is not to be too facilely identified with the "Council" itself.

74 (ii) *The convocation and Peter's address* (15:6–12). The debate, which began in Antioch and was carried in effect to Jerusalem, occasions a separate "Council" of the apostolic and presbyteral college in the latter church. In contrast to Paul's account in Gal 2:2,5–10 he and Barnabas play a minor part in Luke's retelling of the "Council."

6. *after considerable discussion:* The conciliar nature of the meeting is thus made clear. Peter's voice is not necessarily meant to carry more weight because of who or what he is. He is, in fact, the only representative of the Jerusalem college who has had the experience to which appeal can be made. The issue was already decided in 11:18, but the official stamp of the corporate body of apostles and elders is now sought—and Peter succeeds in securing it. **7.** *to be the one:* In the Cornelius episode (10:1–11:18). **8.** *reads men's hearts:* See 1:24; Lk 16:15. *granting them the Holy Spirit:* As it was recounted in 10:44–47; 11:15–17. **10.** *put God to the test:* An OT expression (Ex 17:2,7). *a yoke which neither we nor our fathers have been able to bear:* The "yoke" was the symbol expressing the religious obligations of the Jews ("the yoke of the Torah," or "the yoke of the kingdom of heaven"). It denoted the linking of Yahweh and Israel and per se did not connote a burden (see Str-B 1, 608–10). Jesus' reference to his teaching (Mt 11:29–30) with this figure, however, implies the latter nuance, as do Peter's words here. **11.** *by the favor of the Lord Jesus:* Peter's words echo those of Paul in 13:38–39 (cf. Gal 5:6; 6:15; Rom 3:24). *we are saved:* The aor. inf. *sōthēnai* is used; Lake and Cadbury (*Beginnings* 4, 174) admit that it is "timeless' in its meaning, but translate it, "we shall be saved," since the salvation referred to was thought of eschatologically. One may wonder, however, whether it is exclusively so here. **12.** *grew silent:* Peter's words bring the discussion (*zētēsis*, v. 7) to a close. *signs and wonders:* See 2:43; 5:12.

75 (iii) *James' discourse* (15:13–21). This and the following section of ch. 15 undoubtedly had to do with an incident historically independent of the "Council" that decided the issue of circumcision. James' discourse is a Lucan composition that partly links the two incidents; it highlights Luke's description of the Jerusalem mother church in its effort to emancipate Christianity from its Jewish ties and fetters.

13. *when they stopped talking:* A Lucan suture joins the two stories. *James:* See comment on 12:17. **14.** *Symeon:* As this name (a Grecized form of Hebr *Šimᵉʿôn*) stands in Luke's account, it is the apt way for the Jewish-Christian elder James to refer to Peter, who elsewhere in Acts is called either *Petros* or *Simōn Petros* (10:5,18,32; 15:7). However, in the source on which Luke depends it undoubtedly did not refer to Peter, but to another Symeon, possibly Symeon Niger of Antioch (13:1; → Life of Paul, 46:33). *a people from among the Gentiles:* Luke uses a paradoxical expression; the Gentiles become "the people" of God. For the OT roots of the saying, see Dt 14:2; 26:18–19. *to bear his name:* See Jer 13:11 ("be for me... a name"). **15.** *the prophets:* This phrase probably denotes the minor prophets, as in 7:42; 13:40. **16.** James cites Am 9:11–12, but not according to the MT, as one might have expected of him. His argument depends indeed on the variants in the LXX; it could scarcely have been based on the Hebr form of these verses in Amos. Possibly the Gk text has even been influenced by Jer 12:15 and Is 45:21. **17.** *all the rest of mankind may seek out:* The MT reads, "they may possess the remnant of Edom." The text used here reveals that the Gk translator confused *'dm* (Edom) with *'dm* (man, mankind). *that bear my name:* The MT reads, "who are called by my name." This OT expression (see 2 Chr 6:33; 7:14) denotes a consecration to Yahweh; Amos thus spoke of nations that belonged to God. But James applies it rather to the Gentiles who have been called to be a new "people" of God. A similar, but unrelated, extension of the words of Am 9:11–12 is found in QL (CD 7:15–16; 4QFlor 1:12–13 [see J. M. Allegro, *JBL* 77 [1958] 353; J. A. Fitzmyer, *NTS* 7 [1960–61] 311–12, 328–29). **19.** *in my judgment:* James' words establish the principle, as did Peter's at the "Council." James speaks as a presiding elder of the Jerusalem church. The vb. *krinō* can possibly mean, "I decree" (with authority; cf. 3:13; 13:27; 16:4; 20:16; 21:25); and yet, the "decree" seems to emanate from the assembly and "the whole church" (15:22—on the nature of this verse, → 76 below). **20.** *anything contaminated by idols:* Meat sacrificed to idols (see 15:29). *illicit sexual union:* The mention of *porneia* (unchastity) disrupts the sequence of the other three things that concern diet. It also presents the same problem in interpretation as do Mt 5:32 and 19:9 (→ Gospel Mt, 43:38). The things James forbids seem to be four of the things proscribed by Lv 17–18 for the alien (Hebr *gēr*) residing in Israel: meat offered to idols (Lv 17:8–9), the eating of blood (Lv 17:10–12), the eating of strangled animals (Lv 17:15; cf. Ex 22:31), and intercourse with close kin (Lv 18:6–18); see H. J. Richards, *Scr* 11 (1959) 22–32. Against this background *porneia* would refer to sexual union within certain degrees of kinship, a situation often called *z^{e}nût* (lit., "fornication") by the rabbis. James argues that Christians of pagan background, having lived among Jews, must certainly be aware of such Mosaic proscriptions because they have been proclaimed again and again. His argument is thus an appeal for a sympathetic understanding of Jewish-Christian sensitivities (see 1 Cor 8–10; 2 Cor 6:14).

76 (iv) *Apostolic letter* (15:22–29). The decree is sent in the form of a letter, a copy of which may well have been available to Luke in Antioch. In introducing the letter into his story, he has constructed for it a short introduction (vv. 22, 23a) that paraphrases part of the letter itself (v. 25). But did he understand the letter correctly in paraphrasing it? Our historical reconstruction of the events associated with the "Council" and the subsequent Jerusalem decree depends on the supposition that the letter was sent to the Gentile Christians of Antioch, Syria, and Cilicia "along with Barnabas and Paul" (i.e., the latter, believed still to be in Antioch, were intended to be among the recipients of the letter). But Luke's introduction (v. 22) paraphrases v. 25 in such a way as to make it seem that Paul and Barnabas (note the Lucan order of the names) are sent with the letter. To appreciate Luke's paraphrase, one should read the texts in parallel columns:

Letter	*Luke's Introduction*
We have resolved	It was resolved by the apostles and elders
unanimously	in agreement with the whole church
to choose representatives	to choose representatives . . .
and to send them to you	and to send them to Antioch
along with [*syn*] our beloved	along with [*syn*]
Barnabas and Paul.	Paul and Barnabas.

In the letter itself the prepositional phrase "along with..." can modify "you," but in Luke's introduction it must modify the vb. "sent." For other instances of this use of the prep. *syn* (almost the equivalent of "and"), see Acts 16:32; 21:19; 14:5; Lk 20:1; 23:11; cf. AG 789, 4b.

22. *apostles and elders:* The Lucan introduction repeats the two groups mentioned in 15:2,4. *Judas called Barsabbas:* He is otherwise unknown, but may have been related to Joseph Barsabbas (1:23). *Silas:* Paul's future companion (see comment on 15:40). *the brothers:* See comment on 1:14. **23.** *Antioch, Syria, and Cilicia:* The decree sent in the letter is directed to local churches of a specified area; the action taken by James and the Jerusalem assembly scarcely was intended for the universal Church. As Luke combines the two incidents, however, the decision acquires this broader extension. Antioch was actually in Syria (see comment on 11:19); Syria and Cilicia probaby denote here the Roman provinces (cf. Gal 1:21). *some of our number:* In Luke's account this refers to the "some men" of 15:1; but it really may have referred to the "certain men...from James" (Gal 2:12). The implication is that their conduct has been unauthorized. **25.** *to you along with our beloved Barnabas and Paul:* Given the introduction in v. 22, this would mean that Barnabas and Paul were sent with Judas and Silas, who in v. 27 are mentioned alone as the emissaries bearing the letter. In the letter itself Barnabas and Paul seem to be among the intended recipients of the missive. **28.** *the Holy Spirit:* The true guide of the Church as it spreads from Jerusalem directs the work of the authorities making the decision; cf. 5:32. **29.** *to abstain:* See comment on 15:20. *farewell:* The conventional ending of Hellenistic letters (→ NT Epistles, 47:6).

77 (v) *Proclamation of the decree* (15:30–35). The prosaic ending of this dramatic chapter records the delight and the encouragement the news from Jerusalem brought to the Antiochene church.

32. *prophets:* The inspired preachers of the early Church (see comment on 13:1). **33.** *they were sent back:* Silas thus leaves Antioch. Verse 40 records that Paul chose him as a companion as he departed from Antioch on Mission II. It is not clear, however, just when Silas joined Paul on this journey. To solve the problem, later scribes of the Western Text tradition (see mss. D, C), which is followed by the Vg and translations dependent on it, added v. 34 ("But Silas decided to stay there, and only Judas left for Jerusalem"). Yet it is more likely that Luke's original text did not resolve this problem, which is undoubtedly due to the undigested information or sources that Luke used. **35.** *had been spending some time:* Lit., "were spending" (impf.). As Luke's text now stands, Paul and Barnabas (note the Lucan order again) were in Antioch when the emissaries Silas and Judas arrived with the letter. In reality, however, it is more probable that Paul had already set out from Antioch on Mission II, shortly after the "Council" and the "Antioch Incident" (→ Life of Paul, 46:31). He seems to learn about James' decree for the first time in Acts 21:25. Certainly there is no reference to it in either 1 Cor 10, Rom 14, or Gal as something that had been decided at the "Council."

(Kümmel, W. G., "Die älteste Form des Aposteldekrets," *Spiritus et veritas* [Fest. K. Kundzinš; Eutin, 1953] 83ff. Molland, E., "La circoncision, le baptême et l'autorité du décret apostolique (Actes 15:28sq.) dans les milieux judéo-chrétiens des Pseudo-Clémentines," *ST* 9 [1955] 1–39.)

78 (B) The Universal Mission of Paul (15:36–28:31).

(a) The Great Missionary Journeys (15:36–21:14). Luke now begins the description of the peak of Paul's missionary activity. It includes Mission II (to northern Asia Minor, Macedonia, and Achaia) and Mission III (during which Paul is based in Ephesus for several years). He uses Ephesus as a city from which to carry on his evangelization—a city from which he is finally forced to flee. Luke apparently uses a new source of information here, possibly Pauline (see J. Dupont, *Sources* 71).

(i) *Paul and Barnabas differ and separate* (15:36–39). The separation of Paul and Barnabas is the beginning of their distinct apostolates; it is difficult to determine to what extent the difference in Antioch, recounted in Gal 2:13–14, was responsible for it. Luke makes no mention of this, although he implies that there was another reason.

36. *after a certain time:* Lit., "after some days," the number of which is impossible to determine; indeed, the phrase may be merely transitional. It is probably autumn AD 49. *Barnabas:* See 4:36; in the Lucan account he has been involved with Paul in recent events (see 15:2,12,22,25,35). *in each of the towns:* Lit., "in every town (sing.) in which (pl.)...." The construction is pregnant. The reference is to towns in Cyprus and southern Asia Minor visited by Barnabas and Paul on Mission I. Paul's suggestion is not immediately to be understood as a proposal for a new missionary campaign, even though it so eventuates. **37.** *John who was called Mark:* See comment on 12:12. **38.** *deserted them at Pamphylia:* See 13:13. Depending on how strictly one interprets the vb. *ēxiou*, Luke may be suggesting that Paul considered Mark not "worthy" (*axios*) to continue in apostolic work.

on that mission: Lit., "for that work," i.e., of the apostolate on which he might now embark. When last heard of, Mark had returned to Jerusalem (13:13); now, however, he is in Antioch. But Luke has not told us anything of his transfer (see comment on 12:25). **39.** *so sharp a disagreement:* Lit., "there occurred a provocation"; the Gk noun implies actually a bitter quarrel between Barnabas and Paul. This notice is precious because it discloses a tension between two missionaries, both regarded as "apostles" in the early Church (14:14); it shows that the situation was not always idyllic (cf. 1 Cor 9:6). *sailed for Cyprus:* Barnabas' homeland (4:36), to which he and Paul had first gone on Mission I (13:4). When Mark is next heard of in the NT, he seems to be in Rome, reconciled with Paul (Phlm 24; Col 4:10).

79 (ii) *Beginning of Mission II: Departure for Syria and Cilicia* (15:40–41). Paul's itinerary on this mission takes him from Antioch in Syria to Cilicia, Derbe, and Lystra; and from there into Phrygia, (N) Galatia, Mysia, and Troas; after a dream-vision he crosses into Europe: to Neapolis in Macedonia, Philippi, Amphipolis, Apollonia, Thessalonica, and Beroea. Thence he flees into Achaia: to Athens and Corinth. From there he finally leaves by ship from the port of Cenchreae for Ephesus, Caesarea Maritima, Jerusalem (?), and Antioch. The mission lasts roughly from AD 49 to 52. Luke's account implies that Mission II followed close on the heels of the meeting described in Acts 15:3–33; no room is left in his account for anything like the Antioch incident (Gal 2:11–14).

40. *Silas:* See 15:22ff.; he is called Silvanus by Paul (1 Thes 1:1; 2 Thes 1:1; 2 Cor 1:19; cf. 1 Pt 5:12). *Silas* is the Gk form of the Aram name *šᵉʾîlā*, "asked for" (= Hebr *Šāʾûl*; → Life of Paul, 46:3); *Silvanus* is a Latinized equivalent. *commended:* Lit., "handed over" (cf. 14:26). *by the brothers:* By fellow Christians (see comment on 1:15). **41.** *through Syria and Cilicia:* Paul was already in Syrian Antioch. The phrase "Syria and Cilicia" sounds like a redactional summary, possibly influenced by 15:23. However, in the light of 21:25, where Paul seemingly first learns of the apostolic letter about dietary matters, the reassurance given to these churches must have concerned circumcision.

80 (iii) *Visit to Derbe and Lystra: Timothy becomes Paul's companion* (16:1–4). Mission II begins with a revisit of the churches founded by Paul on Mission I. In one of them Paul acquires a new companion, and Silas retires momentarily into the background.

1. *at Derbe and at Lystra:* See 14:6. *there:* Does this adverb refer to Derbe or to Lystra? See 20:4; Origen (*In Romanos* 10.39) calls Timothy "Derbaeus civis" (Rufinus' tr.). *Timothy* (→ Pastoral Letters, 57:3). *his mother:* Eunice (2 Tm 1:5). *a believing Jew:* Despite her Gk name; in 2 Tm she appears as a Christian. *his father was a Greek:* Does the past tense (*hypērchen*, 16:3) indicate that his father was already dead? In any case, Timothy was born of a mixed marriage, forbidden by the Law (Dt 7:3); he was therefore considered illegitimate, and yet a Jew because of his Jewish mother (see Str-B 2, 741; cf. S. Belkin, *JBL* 54 [1935] 46). He had, however, not been circumcised (because of his pagan father?). Luke's picture of Timothy is not easily reconciled with 2 Tm 1:5; 3:15. **2.** *Iconium:* See comment on 13:51. One can only speculate about the reason why Timothy, who was sometimes regarded as a native of Derbe, was so well known to the Christian "brothers" in Lystra and Iconium. **3.** *circumcised him:* Any Israelite could perform the rite (see Str-B 4, 28–29); the text does not necessarily mean that Paul did it himself. Is there a reference to this in Gal 5:11? Paul seems to imply that he once did preach circumcision—even as a Christian. At any rate, this circumcision of Timothy is justified by Luke by appealing to Timothy's background; contrast Gal 2:3, the case of the "Greek" Titus (→ Letter Gal, 49:16). Timothy's circumcision is certainly strange after Acts 15:5–11, especially in view of Paul's attitude in Gal 5:2–3 (which polemical statement he had not yet written at this period). Perhaps Paul's attitude is rather to be judged in the light of 1 Cor 9:20 (cf. Acts 21:26). Luke's mention of it, however, may in reality be part of his presentation of Paul's mission as one first of all directed to the synagogue, and then only when he is rebuffed, to the Gentiles. **4.** *the decisions made by the apostles and elders in Jerusalem:* This notice must have referred originally to the decisions of the Jerusalem "Council" (15:5–11) and not to the letter of James. "Apostles and elders" are in fact mentioned in both contexts (15:4,6,22,23); possibly this is the reason why Luke telescoped the two incidents (→ Life of Paul, 46:28–33). See comment on 15:35.

(iv) *Summary* (16:5). A minor Lucan "summary" (→ 4 above); it emphasizes the steadfastness and the growth of the local churches (cf. Col 2:5; 1 Pt 5:9).

81 (v) *Paul crosses Asia Minor* (16:6–10). Leaving the region of Iconium, Derbe, and Lystra (towns in S Galatia), Paul makes his way first to N Galatia, and from there to W Asia Minor. Luke's data for this account of Paul's itinerary are not entirely satisfying; he writes as one with little firsthand acquaintance of this region. Suddenly in v. 10 he injects himself into the account with the first of the "We-Sections." His interest is really expressed in v. 9, where the evangelization of Europe is itself proposed as the Spirit-guided motive of the journey through western Asia Minor.

6. *Phrygia:* See 2:10. This large area in central Asia Minor had borders that varied from time to time. In 25 BC the eastern region of ancient Phrygia became part of the Roman province of Galatia (which also comprised the old "Galatian country" in northern Asia Minor); the western region belonged to the province of Asia. Some commentators would prefer to understand Gk *Phrygian* as an adjective and translate, "the Phrygian and Galatian country." If correct, it still would not rule out the identification of the latter with N Galatia, the ancient home of the Galatians with their towns of Pessinus, Ancyra, and Tavium (→ Letter Gal, 49:4; see H. Metzger, *St. Paul's Journeys in the Greek Orient* [SBA 4; London, 1955] 30–50). The text itself seems to suggest here that Paul, having been in S. Galatia, went from there into a more distant area (= N Galatia). *prevented by the Holy Spirit:* Although Luke makes it clear that Paul's mission was guided by the Spirit (cf. 13:2,4,9; 19:2,6; see comment on 2:4), the form in which Paul perceives this guidance is not indicated (see 16:9). *the message:* See comment on 4:31. *the province of Asia:* Paul and his companions probably wanted to go to Ephesus via the great Roman post road. **7.** *Mysia:* This territory was in NW Asia Minor, the northern part of the province of Asia (see Strabo, *Geography* 12.564–65, 571). *Bithynia:* Part of the Roman province of "Bithynia and Pontus" in N Asia Minor, established by Pompey (cf. 1 Pt 1:1). The Spirit prevented them from swerving either to the left (Asia) or to the right (Bithynia). *the Spirit of Jesus:* This formula occurs only here in the Lucan writings; it is parallel to the more usual "Holy Spirit" (v. 6); cf. Rom 8:9; Gal 4:6; Phil 1:19; 1 Pt 1:11. **8.** *came down to Troas:* The Roman colony, Alexandrian Troas, was a seacoast town in NW Asia Minor, near the site of ancient Troy; it often served as a port for crossings to Greece (see 20:5–6; 2 Cor 2:12–13). **9.** *a vision one night:* That is, a dream; the context suggests that it was Spirit-instilled. *a Macedonian:* To ask how Paul knew he was such is to miss the point of the story, and of the dream itself. **10.** *we:* The first "We-Section" (16:10–17) begins here (→ 6 above). It reads like an eyewitness account and has commonly been regarded as an indication that the author Luke joined Paul and his other companions at this part of Mission II. Though the inclusion of Luke in the first person plural here is contested (see E. Haenchen, *Apostelgeschichte*, 430), it still remains the best hypothesis (see J. Dupont, *Sources*, 75–165). It may, of course, merely indicate that in this part Luke was using a diary or notes from the journey. Luke accompanies Paul as far as Philippi, where Paul later finds him (20:5).

82 (vi) *The evangelization of Philippi* (16:11–40). Paul's evangelization of Europe begins with the story of his missionary activity in Philippi—a story that is not uncomplicated. This first part merely sets the scene for his imprisonment. Non-Jewish elements in the town are first to show opposition to him.

11. *Samothrace:* An island in the N Aegean Sea, about halfway between Troas and Neapolis. *Neapolis:* This port (modern Kavalla) served ancient Philippi. **12.** *Philippi, a leading city in that district of Macedonia:* The Roman province of Macedonia was divided into four districts; Philippi was a prominent city (but not the capital) of its first district (→ Letter Phil, 50:2). **13.** *the river:* Most commentators identify it as the Gangites, about 1.5 mi. from Philippi. But A.-J. Festugière (*RB* 54 [1947] 133) questions this identification because such a distance would be too far for a Sabbath-day's journey (Acts 1:12; Mishnah, *Erubin* 4:3: 2000 cubits = 880 yd.). He therefore proposes the closer creek Crenides. *a place of prayer:* The noun *proseuchē* can mean a "synagogue," but since Luke otherwise uses *synagōgē* in this sense, and he speaks of women being present, it may be that for want of a "synagogue" in Philippi the Jews used to go to an outdoor place of prayer near a stream for privacy (cf. Dn 8:2; 10:4; Ez 1:1). **14.** *Lydia:* Her name corresponds to the land from which she came, for Thyatira was in Lydia (see Ap 2:18,24). Paul goes first to the Jews (see comment on 17:2). *reverenced God:* She was a half-convert to Judaism (see comment on 10:2). *what Paul had to say:* See 8:6. **15.** *she and her household:* See 11:14; 16:31,34; 18:8; 1 Cor 1:16 for household baptisms (cf. G. Delling, *NovT* 7 [1964–65] 285–311). The baptism follows immediately on the profession of faith. Lydia's persistence wins out over Paul's reluctance to accept her hospitality. **16–24.** Paul is beaten and imprisoned. **16.** *a slave girl with a spirit of clairvoyance:* Lit., "having a *pythōn* spirit." The Gk word *pythōn* originally designated the dragon or serpent that guarded the Delphic oracle and that was slain by Apollo. Later the word came to mean a "spirit of divination," and even a "ventriloquist" (see A.-J. Festugière, *RB* 54 [1947] 133). **17.** *and us:* The last use of the first person plural until 20:5, where a new "We-Section" begins. *servants of the Most High God:* This name for God (derived from OT *'El 'Elyôn* [Gn 14:19; Ps 46:4]) is found elsewhere in NT contexts of demonic possession (Lk 8:28; Mk 1:24). *a way of salvation:* See 2:28; cf. the absolute use of *hodos* (way) as an early designation of Christianity (9:2; 19:9, 23; 22:4; 24:14,22). **18.** *in the name of Jesus Christ:* Acts 4:12 supplies the theological background for the charge given to the demon (see also 3:6; 4:10). **19.** *public square:* The agora was the seat of the local authorities (*archontes*) and of the city jail. **20.** *magistrates:* The *stratēgoi* probably were the *duoviri* of this Roman colony, who were responsible for adjudicating cases. *unlawful for us Romans:* A Roman could not adopt Judaism without liability according to Roman penal code (see Cicero, *De leg.* 2.8, 19; Dio Cassius, *Rom. Hist.*, 67.14). Luke so formulates the charge against Paul in his account that it can readily be repudiated; Paul and Silas are not directly accused of proselytizing. **22.** *flogged:* See 1 Thes 2:2; Phil 1:30; 2 Cor 11:25. **23.** *guard them securely:* This detail is emphasized (as in the case of Peter, 12:6) in order to enhance the deliverance and the climax of the story: the conversion.

25–34. The tone of this section is quite distinct from that of the rest of the Philippi story; it is basically a folkloric insert.

25. *as Paul and Silas prayed:* Their deliverance is ascribed to their pious prayers. **26.** *earthquake:* "It is evident that the author does not intend to speak of a natural phenomenon; it is a question of the manifestation of God's presence and of a testimony which he is making for his servants" (J. Dupont, *Actes* 148). **31.** *put your faith in the Lord Jesus:* This briefly formulates the "way of salvation" (16:17; cf. 2:21; 11:14; Rom 10:9–13). **33.** *was baptized:* Again baptism follows immediately upon the profession of faith in the gospel (see 16:15). **34.** *spread a table for them:* There is no evidence that this meal was in any sense Eucharistic.

35–40. This section is undoubtedly the normal sequel to 16:15–24 because it continues that story without any reference to the miraculous deliverance. The Western Text seeks unabashedly to remedy this lack by reading v. 35 thus: "When it was day, the magistrates gathered at the public square; they recalled with fear the earthquake which had occurred and dispatched officers to say, 'Release those men whom you took into custody yesterday.'" **37.** *though we are Roman citizens:* Luke makes Paul defend himself, not by declaring his innocence in the matter charged, but by appealing to his rights as *civis romanus*. The *Lex Porcia de provocatione* forbade under severe penalty the flogging of a Roman citizen (see Livy, *History* 10.9, 4; Cicero, *Pro Rabirio* 4.12–13; *OCD* 501); cf. Acts 22:25. **38.** *alarmed to hear:* Because of the possible consequences (cf. 22:29). **39.** *escorted them out:* This action of the magistrates is an implicit admission that the preaching of the gospel was not contrary to Roman law.

(Rees, W., "St. Paul's First Visit to Philippi," *Scr* 7 [1955] 99–105. Torrance, T., "St. Paul at Philippi: Three Startling Conversions," *EvQ* 13 [1941] 62–64.)

83 (vii) *Success and failure at Thessalonica* (17:1–9). Ousted from Philippi, Paul moves on to another Macedonian town, where he again approaches the Jews first and manages to found a mixed Christian church.

1. *the road:* The Via Egnatia led from Neapolis to Dyrrachium and Apollonia on the Adriatic. *Amphipolis:* This was the capital of the first district of the province of Macedonia, situated about 33 mi. W of Philippi. *Apollonia:* Another Macedonian town some 30 mi. farther W. *Thessalonica:* This was the capital of the second district of the province of Macedonia, the seat of the Roman governor (→ Letters Thes, 48:2); it lay about 34 mi. W of Apollonia and is the modern Saloniki. **2.** *his usual custom:* See 13:5,14; 14:1; 16:13; 17:10,17; 18:4,19; 19:8; 28:17,23. His custom was based on a theological conviction shared by Paul and Luke, that priority of salvation was a privilege of Israel (see 3:26; 13:46; Rom 1:16; 2:9–10). *three sabbaths:* This notice need not mean that Paul's sojourn in Thessalonica lasted only three weeks or a month; the Letters to the Thessalonians and Phil 4:16 suggest that he had been there a considerable time. *the scriptures:* This phrase is Luke's typical way of referring to the OT (see 3:18; 17:11; 26:23; Lk 24:26,46); cf. H. Conzelmann, *Theology*, 153, n. 3. **3.** *the Messiah had to suffer and rise:* One would love to know what OT passages Luke had in mind as he composed this. **4.** *of Greeks sympathetic to Judaism:* Lit., "of Greek (God-)fearers" (*tōn te sebomenōn*

Hellēnōn), or possibly "of God-fearers and Greeks" (if one reads with mss. A, D: *tōn te sebomenōn kai Hellēnōn*). In the latter case three groups would be distinguished, not counting the women. (On "God-fearers," see comment on 10:2; cf. L. H. Feldman, *TAPA* 81 [1950] 200–208.)

5. *the Jews:* The pejorative sense of the term (see 12:3; 13:45; 14:2; 17:13) is evident; it is enhanced by the motive of jealousy ascribed to them (see 5:17); cf. 1 Thes 2:15–16. *Jason:* Obviously a prominent Christian convert in Thessalonica, not necessarily the same as the Jason of Rom 16:21. *some brothers:* Possibly Aristarchus (Acts 20:4) and Secundus (27:2). **6.** *upsetting the whole world:* See 16:20; 24:5. **7.** *Caesar's decrees:* See comment on 16:21; cf. 25:8. *rather a certain Jesus is king:* The name of Jesus stands in emphatic position (cf. 2:36; 3:20; 4:27; 13:23; 18:5,28). **8.** *the town's magistrates:* Non-Roman magistrates of Macedonian cities were called politarchs, the very term Luke uses here (see E. de Witt Burton, *AJT* 2 [1898] 598–632; *Beginnings* 4, 205).

84 (viii) *Paul in Beroea* (17:10–15). Having fled to Beroea, Paul at first succeeds there in interesting both prominent Jews and Greeks in the gospel; this success draws opposition and persecution from his Thessalonian opponents. As a result he moves on to Athens.

10. *the brothers:* See comment on 1:15. *Beroea:* A town (modern Verria) situated some 50 mi. SW of Thessalonica on a road leading down to central and southern Greece. In the time of Nero it was given the Gk title *mētropolis*, implying some importance. *to the Jewish synagogue:* See comment on 17:2. **11.** *more high-minded:* The Gk adj. *eugenesteroi* really suggests nobility of origin; but in the context it must refer rather to their attitude. **14.** *to the sea:* The text is obscure here; if one reads with the best mss. *heōs epi tēn thalassan*, it could mean that Paul sailed from some point in N Greece to Athens. But if *hōs* is read instead of *heōs* (as in mss. H, L, P), it might mean, "as it were, toward the sea," expressing a subterfuge to mislead Paul's opponents, while he was escorted overland toward Athens. In v. 15 ms. D adds, "he passed through Thessaly, but was prevented from preaching the word to them." Some commentators wonder whether *thalassan* (sea) in v. 14 might not have been originally *Thessalian* (Thessaly); if so, the overland route would be indicated. **15.** *Silas and Timothy:* In 1 Thes 3:1–2 Paul indicates that Timothy had escorted him to Athens and then returned to Thessalonica, which he eventually left again in order to be with Paul in Corinth (cf. Acts 18:5). Luke's information is either abridged or inaccurate.

85 (ix) *Paul in Athens* (17:16–21). This section prepares the scene for the great discourse. Luke brings his hero to the town which, though it had been illustrious in its past history and culture, was in the 1st cent. AD politically insignificant in the Mediterranean world. It was still a center of Gk intellectual life and symbolized Hellenistic learning and piety. It was thus the ideal Lucan stage for a sample discourse of Paul's proclamation to the Gentiles. Christianity is depicted in open confrontation with Gk philosophy.

16. *exasperated at the sight of idols:* It is hard to say whether this is really Paul's reaction or the Christian reaction of Luke. In a sense it would be consonant with Paul's Jewish background. *everywhere in the city:* Lit., "the city to be idol-ridden." Ancient Lat and Gk authors relate the same impression of Athens (see Livy, *History* 45.27; Pausanias, 1.17, 7; Strabo, *Geography* 9.1, 16). **17.** *God-fearers:* See comment on 10:2. In Athens no opposition is recorded from Jews or from those in sympathy with Jewish religion. *public square:* The famous agora of Athens was the heart of the ancient city (see *Beginnings* 5, 209–10) and the meeting-place of members of four prominent schools of Gk philosophy. **18.** *some of the Epicurean and Stoic philosophers:* Only two of the schools of philosophy are mentioned. Epicurean philosophers were followers of Epicurus (342–271 BC), who opened a school in 311 at Mitylene and another at Lampsacus. He came to Athens in 306, bought a house with a garden (*kēpos*), which became the well-known scene of his philosophical school. For Epicurus philosophy was a mode of attaining happiness by discussion and natural reasoning; in ethics he sought thereby to free man from the fear of death and pain, the ensnarement of politics, and the superstition of the gods (cf. *OCD* 324–25). The Stoic philosophers were followers of Zeno of Citium (Cyprus), who founded a school about 320 BC; its name was derived from the *Stoa Poikilē* (the beautiful colonnaded public hall in Athens), where Zeno and his followers taught. The reference here would be to members of the Late Stoa, whose philosophy was completely dominated by ethical questions. To be free, man had to live "according to nature" (*kata physin*). It involved a certain pantheism, and this is probably the reason that Luke mentions them here (cf. *OCD* 861–62). *babbler:* This derogatory Athenian term for Paul implies that he is a "seed-picker" (*spermologos*), i.e., a glib gossip, newsmonger, picking up bits like a bird (see AG 769). *promoter of foreign gods:* The charge echoes that leveled against Socrates (Plato, *Apol.* 24b; Xenophon, *Mem.* 1.1, 1); it foreshadows the discourse that is to come. *"Jesus" and the "Resurrection":* It is not easy to determine the nuance Luke associates with these words. One obvious sense is understood by a Christian reader; but does Luke suggest that the fem. noun *Anastasis* (Resurrection) was understood by the Athenians as the name of a consort to the foreign deity "Jesus"? **19.** *Areopagus:* The name once denoted the hill to the S of the Acropolis (the hill of Ares, Mars' Hill); from it came the name of the supreme Athenian council, which in Paul's time held its sessions rather at the *Stoa Basileios* (Royal Colonnade) or at the Stoa of Zeus Eleutherios (see H. J. Cadbury, *The Book*, 52, 57). However, Luke is probably referring to the hill; by its historic connotation it is the ideal stage for the debate. **20.** *what this is all about:* The interest of the Athenians is polite, but it is not without a serious concern. **21.** A parenthetical observation of the author.

86 (x) *Paul's discourse at the Areopagus* (17:22–34). Luke makes of this Pauline discourse one of the highlights of the Apostle's missionary activity. It is actually a Lucan composition, another example of the inserted discourse. It mirrors the reaction of a Christian missionary confronted with pagan culture, Gk intellectual life and piety, as Paul speaks from the depths of his faith. After the introductory words of vv. 22–23, three parts and a conclusion can be discerned: 24–25, 26–27, 28–29, and 30–31. In contrast to Luke's enthusiastic description here one should recall Paul's own impressions (1 Cor 1:18–25).

22. *scrupulously religious:* The Gk adj. *deisidaimōn* (lit., "demon-fearing") is sometimes translated "superstitious," but it rather means here "reverently devout" (cf. 25:19). At the outset Paul seeks to render his hearers benevolent; but his words bear an irony that the Christian reader readily perceives. **23.** *to a god unknown:* No altar has yet been found at Athens with precisely this dedication. Ancient authors (Pausanias, 1.1, 4; Philostratus, *Vita Apollonii* 6.3, 5) mention Athenian altars to "unknown gods." They apparently mean altars erected without a dedication to some named god. Luke, aware of such literary references, has probably recast the phrase into the singular to make it the starting point of Paul's discourse. Thus Paul begins his address, not with elements of Gk philosophical monotheism, but with popular religious ideas. *I would make known to you:* Paul's message is a proclamation, not a reasoned argument; yet it is not simply the primitive kerygma proclaimed to Israel. He proclaims faith in one God—a God not really unknown to the Greeks. **24–25.** These verses state the relationship of that God to the world: He is its creator and preserver. His nature is described in terms borrowed from both the OT and Hellenistic philosophy. *made the world and all that is in it:* An allusion to Ps 146:6 or to Is 42:5 (see comment on 14:15). *made by human hands:* See 1 Kgs 8:27; cf. 7:48 (Stephen's strictures on the Jerusalem Temple). **25.** *not in need:* Paul echoes a conviction common to both the OT (Ps 50:12; Am 5:21—23; 2 Mc 14:35) and Gk philosophers (e.g., Aristobulus, fr. 4; cf. Eusebius, *Praep. evang.* 13.12, 3). *gives life and breath:* See Is 42:5; 2 Mc 7:23. The God of whom Paul speaks is not just the creator; he needs nothing, least of all shrines (see the similar opinion of the Stoic philosopher Zeno, quoted in Clement of Alexandria, *Stromateis* 5.76, 1). But contrast 2 Mc 14:35. **26–27.** The nearness of this God to man: Proximity. *from one:* The word *henos* is used absolutely and lacks a noun; its interpretation is difficult. Two main translations are given: "from one he made every nation of mankind dwell on the face of the earth," or "from one he made every nation of mankind, to dwell on the face of the earth." In the former interpretation the vb. *epoiēsen* (made) is modal, expressing the causative form of the main idea "to dwell." In this interpretation *ex henos* means something like "from one stock" (the ms. D adds *haimatos* in this sense, "from one blood"). In the latter interpretation *epoiēsen* is the main verb, and the inf. *katoikein* is epexegetical. Then *ex henos* means "from one man [i.e., Adam]." The former is the more likely and more natural interpretation, since the real purpose of the unity of all men is stated further on, "to seek for God" (v. 27). *set the limits of their times and the boundaries of their territories:* This translation understands the words as an historical limitation set by God (cf. Gn 10; Dt 32:8); it is possible, however, that they should be understood more philosophically: "He ordered the seasons and the boundaries of their habitations" (M. Dibelius). Indeed, the last phrase may even refer to God's setting limits to the seas for man. In any case, the aim of the verse is to set forth the destiny of all men: to seek out the God who is near. **28–29.** This God is related to men: Kinship. *we live and move...:* This Gk saying may be modeled on one of Epimenides of Knossos (6th cent. BC [see *Beginnings* 5, 246–51]); cf. Ti 1:12. *one of your own poets:* Paul quotes the 3rd-cent. Cilician poet, Aratus of Soli or Tarsus (*Phaenomena* 5); see also the *Hymn to Zeus* (4) of the Stoic Cleanthes. There is, in fact, a considerable resemblance in Paul's discourse to the beginning of Aratus' poem. The thought-content is also found in Ps 139; in Lk 3:38: Adam is God's son. **29.** *divinity is not like a statue of gold:* Cf. Acts 19:26. Paul is echoing here Jewish stock arguments against idolatry and polytheism (Is 40:18–20; 46:5–6; Wis 13:10). **30–31.** Paul's conclusion; he alludes to Jesus as the risen Judge of individual men. **30.** *overlooked bygone periods:* Contrast Paul's treatment in Rom 1:18–25; 3:25. Here he proclaims to Athenian philosophers the eschatological judgment of all men by God through Jesus. **31.** *judge the world with justice:* An allusion to Pss 9:9; 96:13; or 98:9. *by a man:* The ms. D adds the name of "Jesus" to the dat. *andri*. This is scarcely a reference to the "Son of Man" motif (*pace* K. Lake, *Beginnings* 4, 219). *by raising him from the dead:* Cf. Rom 14:9; 2 Tm 4:1; 1 Pt 4:5 (→ Aspects NT Thought, 78:158).

32–34. The reaction to Paul's discourse. **32.** *the resurrection:* The polite but firm rejection of this idea by the Athenian philosophers should not be confused with their own ideas of "immortality"; for Sadducee and Christian hesitation about the resurrection of the dead, see 23:8; 1 Cor 15:12–18. **34.** *Dionysius:* Not to be confused with either St. Denys of Paris nor with the Syrian writer (Pseudo-Dionysius) of the 5th–6th cent. Eusebius (*HE* 3.4, 10) identifies this Dionysius as one of the early bishops of Corinth. *Damaris:* Otherwise unknown.

The significance of this discourse is seen in that the primitive proclamation of Christians (that Jesus is the Son of God whom God has raised from the dead [cf. Rom 10:9]) has now been cast in a different form due to the needs of preaching to Gentiles. The form of the confession now becomes, "One God, one Lord" (cf. 1 Cor 8:6), who is the author of creation and salvation.

(See Conzelmann, H., "The Address of Paul on the Areopagus," *Studies in Luke-Acts*, 217–30. Dibelius, M., "Paul on the Areopagus," *Studies*, 26–77. Eltester, W., "Gott und die Natur in der Areopagrede," *Neutestamentliche Studien* [Fest. R. Bultmann; Berlin, 1954] 202–27; "Schöpfungsoffenbarung und natürliche Theologie im frühen Christentum," *NTS* 3 [1956–57] 93–114. Gärtner, B., *The Areopagus Speech and Natural Revelation* [ASNU 21; Uppsala, 1955]. Nauck, W., "Die Tradition und Komposition der Areopagrede," *ZThK* 53 [1956] 11–52. Pohlenz, M., "Paulus und die Stoa," *ZNW* 42 [1949] 69–104.)

87 (xi) *Paul in Corinth* (18:1–17). After the disappointment in Athens Paul moves to Corinth (about the beginning of AD 51; → Life of Paul, 46:9, 35). In this politically and commercially important town of Greece, the capital of the Roman province of Achaia, he helps to found a Christian church (→ Letter 1 Cor, 51:2–4).

2. *a Jew named Aquila:* Though he is called a Jew, the context suggests that "Jewish Christian" is meant. He and his wife were scarcely converted by Paul (see 1 Cor 1:14–16; 16:15). Their presence shows that some Christians were already present in Corinth at Paul's arrival—indeed, Christians from Rome. *from Pontus:* His origin was the Roman province in N Asia Minor on the coast of the Black Sea. *Priscilla:* She is called Prisca by Paul (1 Cor 16:19; Rom 16:3; cf. 2 Tm 4:19). *edict of Claudius:* Issued in his 9th year (AD 49; → Life of Paul, 46:6; Letter Rom, 53:142). **3.** *tentmakers:* This activity confirms what Paul insinuates about his own self-supporting, day-to-day existence in 1 Thes 2:9; 2 Thes 3:8; 1 Cor 4:12; 9:1–12 (see P. Kost, *TPQ* 77 [1924] 271–78). Paul's "trade" has usually been identified as the weaving of *cilicium*, a coarse cloth made of Cilician goat hair, because he came from Tarsus in Cilicia (9:11). Objection has been raised to this identification because such cloth is not known to have been used for tents, whereas leather was more common for this purpose. Hence he is sometimes said to have been a "leather-worker"; according to the Pesh he was a "saddler" (see W. Michaelis, *ThWNT* 7, 395–96). **4.** *in the synagogue:* A lintel inscription of a Corinthian synagogue has been found, reading [*syn*]*agogē Hebr*[*aiōn*]; see *LAE* 16, n. 7. Paul's first appeal is again made to the Jews (see comment on 17:2). **5.** *from Macedonia:* See comment on 17:15. *the Messiah was Jesus:* See comments on 17:3,7. **6.** *shake out his garments:* A gesture of repudiation (cf. 13:51). *on your own heads:* This was an OT expression for responsibility (see Jer 28:35 [LXX]; Ez 18:13; Lv 20:9; 2 Sm 1:16; 3:29; H. Reventlow, *VT* 10 [1960] 311–27). *turn to the Gentiles:* See 13:46–47. **7.** *withdrew:* Paul changed his place of teaching from the synagogue, and probably also withdrew from his residence and from work with Priscilla and Aquila. *Titius Justus:* Some mss. (S, E) read "Titus." A Gentile "God-fearer" (see comment on 10:2). **8.** *Crispus:* He is undoubtedly the same as the one mentioned in 1 Cor 1:14. *many...were baptized:* According to 1 Cor 1:14–16 this would mean that their baptism was not conferred by Paul. **9.** *do not be afraid...I am with you:* An allusion to Gn 26:24. The vision emphasizes the importance of the Corinthian church in Luke's account of Paul's missionary activity (see M. Goguel, *RHPR* 12 [1932] 321–33). **10.** *my people:* This term means first of all the Jews; but in this context it must rather be understood in the Pauline sense of "sons of Abraham" (by faith; cf. Gal 3:7–9). **11.** *a year and a half:* Roughly from AD 51 to the middle of 52 (→ Life of Paul, 46:9). **12–17.** Paul is accused before the governor Gallio. This was L. Junius Gallio Annaeus, the elder brother of the philosopher Seneca (cf. *CIG* 7, 1676; → Life of Paul, 46:7, 9). *the Jews:* See comment on 17:5. **13.** *against the law:* Prima facie this equivocal expression would imply that Roman law was being contravened (cf. 16:20; 17:7). But Gallio treats the affair as if it were a matter of Jewish law (18:15), which was, however, normally supported by the Roman administration in accordance with a general policy favoring ethnic groups in the provinces. **15.** *your own law:* Cf. 23:29; 25:18–19. The Roman governors were apparently sensitive to the attempts of minority groups to have provincial authorities decide issues for them. **17.** *Sosthenes:* Possibly the same as the one mentioned in 1 Cor 1:1. No explanation is given by Luke of the conduct of "the Jews" toward a "leader of the synagogue" (for this title, see 13:15; 18:8).

88 (xii) *Paul's return to Syrian Antioch* (18:18–22). This journey back to Antioch marks the end of the so-called Mission II; there is no reason to think that Paul left Corinth immediately after the trial.

18. *quite a while:* Luke uses the indefinite phrase *hemēras hikanas*, which elsewhere (cf. 9:23,43; 27:7) suggests more than a few days; it connotes a considerable amount of time. *the brothers:* Christians (see comment on 1:15) in Corinth, among whom we must suppose that Silas stayed, because he now disappears from the story in Acts (see 1 Pt 5:12). *Syria:* This is the goal of Paul's journey, but he actually lands at Caesarea Maritima (18:22). Are we to suppose that the winds carried the ship to Caesarea instead, or that a ship headed there was the only one on which Paul was eventually able to secure passage? *Priscilla and Aquila:* They settle in Ephesus (Acts 18:19,26; 1 Cor 16:19; → Letter Rom, 53:10, 137). *Cenchreae:* See Rom 16:1 (→ Letter Rom, 53:136). *shaved his head:* The subject is most likely Paul, not Aquila. The reference seems to be to the Nazirite vow, which Paul makes (see Acts 21:23–27; cf. A. Isaksson, *Marriage and Ministry in the New Temple* [Lund, 1965] 189–96). In Nm 6:1–21 the shaving of the head is prescribed as an act to be done in the Temple at the end of the vow-period (usually of 30 days). Hence the mention of Paul's shaving his head here is somewhat enigmatic. **19.** *Ephesus:* The capital of Asia (→ Letter Eph, 56:2). *discussions with the Jews:* See comment on 17:2. **21.** *come back to you again:* Ephesus will be the base of Paul's operations during Mission III (see 19:1). **22.** *Caesarea:* See comment on 8:40. *he went up to greet the church:* The cryptic ptc. *anabas* (having gone up) suggests that Paul paid a visit to the Jerusalem Christians before going to Antioch in Syria. The geographical situation of Jerusalem (over 2500 ft. above sea level) made the expression "go up" a natural one to describe the approach to it (see 8:5; 9:32; 11:2; 15:2). The purpose of the visit is otherwise unknown. *went down to Antioch:* The term of Paul's Mission II is the same as that of Mission I (14:26).

89 (xiii) *Beginning of Mission III* (18:23). The transition from Mission II to Mission III is almost obscured in Luke's account (→ 63 above). Possibly Paul stayed in Antioch from the autumn of AD 52 to the spring of AD 54 (→ Life of Paul, 46:35).

23. *systematically:* The same adverb is used here that appears in Lk 1:3 (*kathexēs*). *the Galatian country and Phrygia:* See 16:6; the form *Phrygian* is clearly a noun here, not an adjective.

(xiv) *Apollos in Ephesus and Achaia* (18:24–28). These five verses are really parenthetical; they interrupt the story of Paul's new mission. Probably they are inserted because of the mention of John's baptism (18:25), which foreshadows 19:4.

24. *Apollos:* The ms. D gives his name as *Apollōnios*, of which Apollos is a shortened form; ms. S* gives *Apellēs* (which reading is probably influenced by Rom 16:10). Apollos was a cultured Alexandrian Jew, learned in the Scriptures, reminiscent of Philo, or even of Stephen (cf. 6:10). Verse 27 suggests that his influence in Achaia was such that Paul's reaction to him in 1 Cor 1:12; 3:4–11,22; 4:6; 16:12 is mixed; although he recognized Apollos' good influence and even his role as that church's "second founder," he was troubled by the factions in the church that developed after his arrival there. Yet this rivalry does not interest Luke. *instructed:* The same word in Lk 1:4 implies only partial knowledge. **25.** *the Way:* See comment on 16:17. *full of spiritual fervor:* Lit., "boiling with the Spirit." This statement is strange because it seems to conflict with Apollos' awareness of "only John's baptism." The latter usually means a mere water-baptism in contrast with the Spirit-baptism of Christianity (see Mk 1:8 par.). The passage in 19:1–7 is related to this notice about Apollos, not only in regard to the deficient awareness of Christian baptism and its meaning, but also in the way Luke uses them both to fill in details of Paul's missionary activity. Apollos is not said to have been baptized by Priscilla and Aquila and it is hard to say that this is presupposed. In this respect the Apollos episode differs from the one that follows; Luke's account, however, implies that the new instruction Apollos receives incorporates him into the official teaching body of the primitive Church. Luke suggests, nevertheless, that Apollos possessed the Spirit in some way even though he only knew of John's baptism. *spoke and taught accurately about Jesus:* Again this is difficult to reconcile with what precedes and follows. This whole episode represents another Lucan effort to assimilate immature forms of early Christianity into the mainstream (cf. 8:14–17; E. Käsemann, *Essays on NT Themes* [SBT 41; Naperville, Ill., 1964] 136–48). **27.** *Achaia:* Apollos' future field of work was Corinth itself (as 1 Cor indicates). *writing:* For ancient letters of recommendation, see Rom 16:1ff.; 2 Cor 3:1–6; Col 4:10. *the Messiah was Jesus:* See comments on 17:3,7. This is a Lucan refrain in Acts.

90 (xv) *Paul in Ephesus: Disciples who had not received the Spirit* (19:1–7). Paul's Ephesian ministry begins with an encounter with 12 isolated, immature Christians who are not much different from Apollos in their awareness of the character and necessity of Christian baptism.

1. *Apollos:* This reference merely forms a suture with the parenthetical note in 18:24–28; Apollos has no other connection with these 12 Christians. *the interior of the country:* The Gk adj. *anōterika* means "upper [parts]" and may refer to the highlands or mountains of Asia Minor or simply to the hinterland of Ephesus through which Paul passed from Galatia and Phrygia (see 18:23). *Ephesus:* See comment on 18:19. *disciples:* The absolute use of *mathētai* elsewhere in Acts (6:1,2,7; 9:1,10,19,25, 26,38; 11:26,29) as a designation for Christians suggests that these disciples are also "Christians." Dibelius would explain the situation by saying that they were disciples of

John who later became Christians; but then why should the question whether they received the Spirit be put to them? Whether one argues that there were disciples of John in Ephesus or that Luke has arbitrarily transferred them here is in a sense irrelevant. For his account seems to suggest that these "disciples" are Christians, and yet immature in their understanding of Christian baptism and its implications. **2.** *when you became believers:* The ptc. *pisteusantes* can only refer to the faith of Christians. Their deficient knowledge of the character of baptism does not relate them necessarily to Apollos. *that there is a Holy Spirit:* This saying makes sense only in that a new outpouring of the Spirit was understood as an essential of the Christian experience, incorporating men into the Church. The Western Text softens the statement: "We have never even heard that some people receive the Spirit." The ignorance refers to the Pentecost episode (see 2:38; 8:16). Note a similar editorial comment to explain the outpouring of the Spirit in Jn 7:39. **3.** *the baptism of John:* See 18:25; Mk 1:8 par. **4.** *baptism of repentance:* Acts 13:24–25 is echoed here. *the one who would come after him:* The coming "after" John is a note found in Mk 1:7; Mt 3:11, but it is strangely absent in the Lucan parallel (3:16). **5.** *in the name of the Lord Jesus:* See comments on 2:38; 8:16. **6.** *imposed hands on them:* Apparently as part of the baptismal rite (see 9:17); and yet the rest of the verse may imply that the imposition of hands had another function—a charismatic office to be exercised in the Church (see comment on 8:17). *speak with tongues:* Glossolalia (see comment on 2:4). *utter prophecies:* Cf. Acts 2:17. **7.** *twelve:* Is this number fortuitous, or does it imply the link of the nucleus of the Ephesian Christian community with the Twelve in Jerusalem?

91 (xvi) *Ephesian ministry and encounters* (19:8–19). Paul's activity in establishing the Ephesian church is similar to that in Corinth (18:1ff.).

8. *the synagogue:* In this case Paul's efforts to convert Jews follow his work among "disciples"; contrast "his usual custom" (17:2). *the kingdom of God:* Cf. 8:12; 20:25; 28:23. The preaching of the kingdom was not substantially different from that in which Paul announced that the Messiah was Jesus (18:5). **9.** *the Way:* See comment on 16:17. *left them:* Paul's influence causes a rift in the Jewish community at Ephesus. *his disciples:* Jewish-Christian converts. *lecture hall of Tyrannus:* A hall possibly used by some otherwise unknown Gk philosopher; however, Tyrannus could have been merely its owner. **10.** *two years:* In 20:31 Luke will indicate that Paul's activity at Ephesus lasted for three years; perhaps these brief time-references are not mutually exclusive (see 19:8,21). *all the inhabitants of Asia:* Hyperbole. "Asia" probably means merely the area about Ephesus and not the entire proconsular Roman province in W Asia Minor. *the word of the Lord:* The Christian message (see comment on 4:31). **11.** *miracles:* Luke describes Paul's wondrous deeds here as "powers" (*dynameis;* → Aspects NT Thought, 78:113); cf. 2:22; 8:13. **12.** *diseases...evil spirits:* The collocation of these two ills should not be overlooked; they express a related belief in demon-sickness. **13–17.** Paul is mentioned only indirectly in the following Ephesian episode—an anecdote used by Luke to fill in details of Paul's Ephesian ministry. **13.** *Jewish exorcists:* See Mt 12:27; Lk 11:19 for other NT references to such persons; in 1QapGn 20:28–29 Abraham is depicted as one (cf. Josephus, *Ant.* 8.2, 5 § 45). *the name of the Lord Jesus:* Cf. Mk 9:38; Lk 9:49–50. **14.** *Sceva, a Jewish high priest:* This person with a Roman name is otherwise unknown as a high priest; certainly he does not figure among those of Palestine (→ History of Israel, 75:133). Moreover, a "Jewish high priest" in an Ephesian context is a good clue to the folkloric character of this legend about Paul and his cures. **16.** The false exorcists are depicted as being at the mercy of the possessing demons. **17.** *this became known to all:* Another clue to the folkloric character of the story (cf. 1:19; 9:42). **18.** *confessed their former practices:* They admitted them to be sinful practices, but did not necessarily disclose the formulas of charms and spells. **19.** *collected their books and burned them in public:* Luke may be referring here to the so-called Ephesian Writings (*Ephesia grammata*), well-known books of spells and charms (*RAC* 5, 515–20; C. C. McCown, *TAPA* 54 [1923] 128–40).

(xvii) *Summary* (19:20). A minor summary (→ 4 above). Not even the demonic and magical arts of the Ephesian capital of Asia can hinder the progress of the Christian mission.

92 (xviii) *The riot of the silversmiths* (19:21–40). The passage begins with a statement about Paul's future travel plans; he intends to leave Ephesus and make his way to Greece, to Jerusalem, and finally to Rome. Thus vv. 21–22 foreshadow the latter part of Acts. Luke passes over the object of Paul's visits to Greece (reconciliation of himself with the Corinthian church; see 1 Cor 16:5–7; 2 Cor 1:15–3:3) and to Jerusalem (the carrying of the collection for the poor of the mother church; see 1 Cor 16:1–3; 2 Cor 8–9; Rom 15:25–29; Gal 2:10). The reason for Paul's hasty departure from Ephesus might rather seem to be the riot of the silversmiths; and yet it is precisely this impression that Luke wants to correct by inserting at the beginning of it the statement about Paul's travel plans; his departure was foreseen, even heaven-inspired.

21. *Macedonia:* See 16:9–12; 18:5. *Achaia:* See 18:12,27. *I must visit Rome too:* The necessity is expressed by the usual Lucan vb. *dei* (see comment on 1:16); the reader learns to understand this as part of Paul's appointed destiny. **22.** *Timothy:* See the comments on 16:1; 17:14–15; 18:5; cf. 1 Cor 4:17; 16:10. *Erastus:* Possibly the same as the one mentioned in Rom 16:23 (→ Letter Rom, 53:145). Luke does not tell of the sending of the peacemaker, Titus (see 2 Cor 2:13). **23.** *the Way:* See comment on 16:17. *Demetrius:* He is otherwise unknown and scarcely to be identified with a person of the same name mentioned in an Ephesian inscription (see H. Conzelmann, *Apostelgeschichte,* 113). The account of the riot Demetrius inspired is hardly a Lucan fabrication (*pace* E. Haenchen, *Apostelgeschichte,* 511–14) or an historicization of the event of which Paul speaks in 1 Cor 15:32; 2 Cor 1:8–10. Luke may have stylized or dramatized certain elements of it, indeed; but the story is not wholly invented. *miniature shrines of Artemis:* This would imply silver models of the shrine of Artemis in her famous Ephesian temple, which was one of the seven wonders of the ancient world (see Strabo *Geography,* 14.1, 20; Achilles Tatius, 8.2ff.). Cadbury (*The Book,* 5) mentions that silver replicas of Artemis' image and terra-cotta models of her temple are known; but to date there is no evidence of silver images of the Ephesian temple. Artemis was venerated at Ephesus in a cult that was syncretistic; there she resembled much more the Asiatic mother goddess and patroness of fertility (the Phrygian Cybele or the Phoenician Astarte) than she did the virgin huntress of classical Greece (see *Beginnings* 5, 251–56; J. Finegan, *Light from the Ancient Past* [Princeton, 1959] 247–48; *RAC* 1, 714–18). **26.** *man-made gods are no gods at all:* Demetrius' charge has shifted from the trade in miniature shrines to the goddess herself; the formulation that he uses recalls 17:24–25 and echoes like a refrain in Acts. **27.** Commentators usually compare this verse with the famous report the governor, Pliny the Younger, sent to the Emperor Trajan (*Letters* 10.96, 10) about the impact of Christianity on pagan religion in Asia Minor. *great goddess:* The formulation here repeats Artemis' famous ritualistic title (see Xenophon of Ephesus, *Ephesiaca* 1.11, 5; Acts 19:28). *she whom all Asia and all the world revere:* Artemis' cult was widespread in the Greco-Roman world as well as in the East (Pausanias 2.2, 6; 4.31, 8). **29.** *Gaius:* According to Acts 20:4 he came from Derbe, a city of Lycaonia in Asia Minor (14:6). *Aristarchus:* A Thessalonian (20:4; 27:2; see comment on 17:5); cf. Col 4:10; Phlm 24. **30.** Cf. 21:40. **31.** *Asiarchs:* The exact function of such an official is disputed; *Mart. Pol.* (12:2) suggests a cultic function; he is therefore usually identified as the priest in charge of the cult of Augustus and Roma at Ephesus. Others would rather identify him as a deputy of the assembly of Asia, which met in Ephesus (see further *Beginnings* 5, 256–62). Luke's comment implies the good relations that existed between his hero and the influential men of the town of Ephesus. **33–34.** The account is not clear at this point. Luke seems to be saying that Jews pushed a spokesman forward to make it clear to the crowd that Christians were not Jews; but even this attempt at clarification failed (recall 16:20). **35.** *the town clerk:* The Gk text has simply *grammateus* (scribe, clerk), which could either be *grammateus tou dēmou*, an authority of the municipality, or *grammateus tēs boulēs*, a clerk of the council (assembly). At any rate, he was a man of authority, who understood the legal implications of the situation. *her image which fell from the sky:* This is the only reference in Gk literature to such a legend about a statue of the Ephesian Artemis; Euripides (*Iphig. Taur.* 87–88, 977, 1384–85) alludes to a similar legend about the Taurian Artemis. Was it made of meteoric stone? **37.** *are not temple robbers:* Paul and his companions are thus exonerated of the charge often brought against Jews (see Rom 2:22; Josephus, *Ant.* 4.8, 10 § 207). *these men:* Gaius and Aristarchus (19:29). Could this also allude to Paul's Ephesian imprisonment? (→ Letter Phil, 50:5–6.) **38.** *proconsuls:* The plural is used in a generic sense, for there was only one proconsul (provincial governor). **40.** *we risk being accused:* The clerk refers to regulations of Roman provincial law.

(Duncan, G. S., *Saint Paul's Ephesian Ministry: A Reconstruction* [London, 1929]. Michaelis, W., "The Trial of St. Paul at Ephesus," *JTS* 29 [1927–28] 368–75. Rowlingson, D. T., "Paul's Ephesian Imprisonment: An Evaluation of the Evidence," *AnglTR* 32 [1950] 1–7.)

93 (xix) *Paul leaves for Greece and returns from there* (20:1–6). Paul probably departed from Ephesus in the summer of AD 57 (→ Life of Paul, 46:36–37). His departure is not presented by Luke as a banishment; it is the consequence of his own plans (19:21–22).

1. *when the disturbance was over:* Luke's editorial note links the coming journey with the riot of the silversmiths. But the rest of the passage is a natural sequel to 19:22. *encouraged them:* Paul's final words to his disciples are a Christian exhortation, as in 14:22; 15:32; 16:40. **2.** *traveled through its regions:* Somewhere in Macedonia, probably Philippi, Paul wrote 2 Cor on this journey, having been met by Titus on his return from Corinth (see 2 Cor 2:13; 7:6). *Greece:* This is the only place in the NT where the classic name of the country (*Hellas*) is used; in popular speech at this time it bore the official Roman designation, Achaia. Paul undoubtedly stayed in Corinth during the three months of the winter AD 57–58, at the end of which he wrote Rom, before his departure for Syria (= Palestine). Thus his intention of 1 Cor 13:5–6 was realized. **3.** *on the point of embarking:* Was Paul about to sail on a ship carrying Jews to Palestine for the Passover? *a plot:* The nature of it is not indicated. *by way of Macedonia:* The overland route would have led through towns such as Beroea, Thessalonica, Apollonia, Amphipolis, and Philippi. Was it on this occasion that he went into Illyricum (see Rom 15:19; → Life of Paul, 46:37), or earlier? Seven named companions go along with Paul from Greece; Luke makes no mention of the collection for the poor—the object of Paul's journey (Rom 15:25–29). **4.** *Sopater:* Probably the same as Sosipater (Rom 16:21). *Aristarchus, Gaius:* See comment on 19:29. *Secundus:* Otherwise unknown. *from Derbe:* Since the ms. D reads *Dubērios* instead of *Derbaios*, some commentaters would change Derbe here to Douberes (a town in Macedonia); this would eliminate the difficulty noted in 19:29; but see 16:1 (comment on Timothy). *Tychicus:* An Ephesian mentioned in Col 4:7; Eph 6:21; Ti 3:12; 2 Tm 4:12. *Trophimus:* Another Ephesian (see 21:29; 2 Tm 4:20). **5.** *waited for us in Troas:* The second "We-Section" begins here (20:5–21:18; → 6 above). Luke apparently rejoins Paul at this point (on Troas, see comment on 16:8). **6.** *Philippi:* Paul spent the Feast of Unleavened Bread with the first European Christian community that he had founded (16:11–40). He then sailed from Neapolis (see 16:11).

94 (xx) *Paul restores Eutychus to life at Troas* (20:7–12). Luke had described Paul as performing "no ordinary miracles" during his stay in Ephesus (19:11) but gave no details other than a generic statement about cures of demon-sickness. Now he presents Paul in the act of bringing about a miraculous resuscitation. As Jesus was a man authenticated by miracles, signs, and wonders (2:22), so his commissioned agent is similarly depicted.

7. *first day of the week:* That is, of the Jewish week (cf. 1 Cor 16:2; Ap 1:10). *for the breaking of bread:* See comment on 2:42. **8.** *many lamps:* There is no symbolic or apologetic meaning in this detail; the author wants merely to explain that Eutychus had fallen asleep because of the hot and smoky atmosphere of the upper room in which Paul prolonged his discourse. **10.** *bent over him:* Lit., "fell upon him," i.e., threw himself upon him. Paul's action recalls that of Elisha in 2 Kgs 4:34 (cf. Mk 5:39). *there is life in him:* The sense is not, "There is still life in him," for the miracle is the whole point of the story. In v. 9 he was recognized as "dead."

(Cabaniss, A., "Early Christian Nighttime Worship," *JBR* 25 [1957] 30–33. Roberts, J. E., "The Story of Eutychus," *Expositor* 8/26 [1923] 376–82.)

95 (xxi) *Paul's journey to Miletus* (20:13–16). The story of Paul's travels resumes.

13. *Assos:* No indication is given why Paul chose to travel overland to this town that was situated around a small cape, slightly to the SE of Troas. Was it to visit some friends? **14.** *Mitylene:* The chief town on the island of Lesbos, almost due S of Assos. **15.** *opposite Chios:* They sailed across the open sea toward the island of Chios in order to round the long promontory that has Smyrna on the N and Ephesus on the S. *Samos:* An island to the SE of Chios. *Miletus:* An important town (modern Balat) on the W coast of Asia Minor, at the mouth of the Maeander River. **16.** *sail past Ephesus:* This town was really off Paul's course and would have demanded a detour; he was in a hurry, but we are not told why he had to be in Jerusalem by Pentecost.

(xxii) *Discourse to the Ephesian elders at Miletus* (20:17–38). Paul's third great discourse in Acts is addressed to Christian pastors; it serves at once as Paul's last will and testament, as an example of Christian hortatory preaching, and as the conscious farewell to his missionary activity. As a testament, it is apologetic and defensive, for in a sense Paul seeks to explain himself to the Ephesian elders and to justify his conduct among them;

as an exhortation, it urges the elders to be aware of their pastoral obligations; and as a farewell, it sums up Paul's motivation in his missionary endeavors. Of all the Pauline speeches in Acts, this one most echoes Pauline phrases; hence the abundant references to Pauline writings (even to the Pastorals) in the following notes. The discourse falls into four parts: (1) 18–21; (2) 22–27; (3) 28–32; (4) 33–35.

17. *the elders of that Church:* The *presbyteroi* are authorities of the Ephesian church. This title, which also occurs in 11:30; 14:23; 15:2,4,6,22,23; 16:4; 21:18, designates officials in local churches founded by wandering apostles. They constitute a group or college in the church, for their title is always plural. Only in 20:28 is the title *episkopoi* applied to them in Acts (implying no distinction in the titles). Authorities in Jewish communities were called "elders" (see 4:5,8,23; 6:12); it was therefore a natural title for Christians to adopt to denote their officials. **18–21.** Paul begins his discourse with a recollection of his Ephesian ministry. **18.** *from the day I first came to Asia:* His first arrival in the Roman province of Asia must have been about four years earlier (→ Life of Paul, 46:36–40). *how I lived among you:* Cf. 1 Thes 1:5. **19.** *served the Lord:* This is a favorite Pauline expression (see Rom 12:11; 14:18; 16:18; Col 3:24; Eph 6:7). *with all humility:* Cf. Phil 2:3. *plots of the Jews:* None have been recorded by Luke, although he does mention Ephesian Jewish opposition to Paul in 19:9 (cf. 21:27). **20.** *for your own good:* Cf. 1 Cor 10:33. **21.** *insisted solemnly* [or *adjured*]*:* Cf. 1 Tm 5:21. Paul's strong language was an appeal for repentance and faith. *faith in our Lord Jesus:* See 17:30–31; 1 Thes 1:9–10; 1 Cor 8:4–6.

96 **22–27.** Paul's premonition of the troubles, and possibly of death, that await him in Jerusalem and his sense of accomplishment. **22.** *to Jerusalem:* The phrase sounds like an echo of the destination of Jesus' journey in Lk 9:51; 13:22; 17:11. *compelled by the Spirit:* Given the emphasis in Acts on the Spirit's guidance of the missionary endeavor (see comments on 2:4; 16:6), this translation is preferable to another that is also possible, "constrained in [my own] spirit." **23.** *from city to city:* Rom 15:30–31 discloses Paul's apprehension about going to Jerusalem, when he was about to leave Corinth; his remarks here foreshadow the premonitions in Tyre and Caesarea (21:4,10–11). **24.** *my life:* Cf. 21:13; Phil 1:21–23; 1 Thes 2:8. *finish my race:* See 2 Tm 4:7; Phil 2:16; cf. Acts 13:25. *gospel:* Luke uses the noun *euaggelion* only here and in 15:7. **25.** *see my face again:* Cf. 20:38. Paul's plans were to take him to Rome and to Spain, if he were to come through the impending troubles in Jerusalem (see Rom 15:24–28). His words can scarcely be used as an indication of the date of Acts. *the kingdom:* See 1:3. Here it refers to God's reign over men as presented in Christ. **26.** *innocent of the blood of all:* See 18:6. Paul implies that he has fulfilled the service assigned to him by Christ; he has unhesitatingly preached the good news of the kingdom and of divine bounty to men. Thus their failure to achieve a new life is not a burden that weighs upon him in the sight of God. This is not a boast, but a frank statement of his sense of accomplishment despite the charges that may have been leveled against him at Ephesus.

28–32. Aware of his imminent separation from the Ephesian church, which he suspects will be definitive, Paul urges the elders to carry out their duties as pastors serving the Church of God. **28.** *keep watch over yourselves:* This is the first duty of all Christian elders (cf. 1 Tm 4:16; 1 Cor 9:26–27; 1 Pt 5:1–3). *the flock of which the Holy Spirit has made you guardians:* The second duty: to be like shepherds guarding and serving a flock. The same image recurs in 1 Pt 5:1–3; Mt 9:36; it depends in part on Ez 34:1–6; Zech 10:2–3. The elders are to be "guardians" (*episkopoi*); the Gk word is the equivalent of the Hebr *m*^{e}*baqqēr* (overseer), the title for certain officials in the Qumran community of Palestinian Essenes. The Gk title, however, is never found in the NT as a designation of authorities in the Palestinian Christian church, despite its obvious Essene background. When it is used, as here, it designates "elders," officials in local churches founded by apostles in the Hellenistic world (1 Tm 3:1–6; Ti 1:5; possibly also in Phil 1:1; cf. J. A. Fitzmyer, *Studies in Lk-Acts*, 247–48). For the combination of "guardian" and "shepherd," cf. 1 Pt 2:25. Note once again the role of the Spirit in the governing of the Church (recall 13:2–4). *the church of God:* The title, often used by Paul for the church in Jerusalem and Judea and extended to that of Corinth (1 Cor 1:1; → Pauline Theology, 79:150), is here used by Luke in a generic sense. The phrase echoes the Hebr *q*^{e}*hal 'El*, the name of the Essene community written on one of its banners (1QM 4:10). *acquired with his own blood:* This obvious meaning of the phrase creates a difficulty with the antecedent "God." For this reason some mss. read "the Lord" (*kyriou*) instead of "God" in the preceding phrase (see R. E. Brown, *TS* 26 [1965] 552–53). For the same reason some commentators suggest the translation, "with the blood of his Own" (i.e., Son [see Rom 8:31]). In any case the sense is: Through the blood of Jesus, the Christian community has become God's own possession, the people of his new covenant. There is an allusion to Ps 74:2; cf. Eph 1:4; 1 Pt 2:9. **29.** *savage wolves:* False teachers (cf. Mt 7:15; Rom 16:17–18). **31.** *three years:* See comment on 19:10. *to warn:* Cf. 1 Cor 4:14–16. *tears:* Cf. 2 Cor 2:4. **32.** *commend you to the Lord:* As in 14:23. *which can build you up:* Cf. Rom 16:25; Eph 1: 14,18; 4:12–16,29. *inheritance:* An allusion to Dt 33:3–4.

97 **33–35.** Paul's distinterestedness and his charity toward the Ephesians. **33.** Cf. 1 Cor 9:12. **34.** *these very hands:* Paul's rhetoric reflects the situation in 18:3 (see comment); cf. 1 Sm 12:3–4. **35.** *words of the Lord:* The discourse attributes to Jesus a saying not preserved in the Gospels, not even in Lk; cf. *1 Clem.* 2:1; Sir 4:31 (see K. H. Rengstorf, *Die Liebhaftigkeit des Wortes* [Fest. A. Köberle; Hamburg, 1958] 23–33).

36–38. The reaction of the elders to Paul's farewell discourse. For the Christian kiss of farewell, see comment on Rom 16:16.

(Dupont, J., *Le discours de Milet: Testament pastoral de Saint Paul* [LD 32; Paris, 1962]. Munck, J., "Discours d'adieu dans le Nouveau Testament," *Aux sources de la tradition chrétienne* [Fest. M. Goguel; Paris, 1950] 155–70. Reicke, B., "A Synopsis of Early Christian Preaching," *The Root of the Vine* [ed. A. Fridrichsen; N.Y., 1953] 128–60.)

98 (xxiii) *Paul arrives at Tyre* (21:1–6). The continuation of his journey leads him to the Phoenician seacoast.

1. *we put out to sea:* The "We-Section" had been interrupted by the discourse of Paul at Miletus, but this narrative resumes it. *Cos:* An island in the Aegean Sea off the SW coast of Asia Minor. *Rhodes:* This may be the name of either the island in the Aegean, S of the western part of Asia Minor, or of its main town. *Patara:* A Lycian town on the S coast of Asia Minor. The mss. D and P^{41} add here "and Myra," a better known Lycian town to the E of Patara; but this name has probably been inserted by conjecture because of 27:5. **2.** *Phoenicia:* See comment on 11:19. **4.** *should not go up to Jerusalem:* See comment on 20:23.

(xxiv) *Paul arrives at Ptolemais and Caesarea* (21:7–14). Suspense is carefully being built up by listing in detail Paul's stops at various towns en route from Tyre to Jerusalem.

7. *Ptolemais:* This seacoast town in Phoenicia, often called Ptolemais Acco, was founded by Ptolemy II in 261 BC (→ Biblical Geography, 73:80). **8.** *Caesarea:* See comment on 8:40. *Philip the evangelist:* See 8:40. *one of the seven:* Not the seven named companions of Paul (20:4), but the seven assistants (6:5). **9.** *daughters gifted with prophecy:* See Acts 2:17 (cf. P. Corssen, *ZNW* 2 [1901] 289–99). **10.** *Agabus:* The same as in 11:28. Like certain OT prophets he acts out his message; cf. Is 20:2; Ez 4:1; Jer 13:1. **12.** *not to go up to Jerusalem:* See comment on 20:23. **13.** *for the name of the Lord Jesus:* See 5:41; 1 Pt 4:14. **14.** *let the Lord's will be done:* An echo of the Gethsemane prayer (Lk 22:42).

99 (b) PAUL IN JERUSALEM (21:15–23:11). The end of Mission III takes place in Jerusalem, which proves to be for Paul just as much of a city of destiny as it was for Jesus.

(i) *Paul's arrival, greeting, and purification* (21:15–26). The main point of this episode is Paul's greeting of James, who seems to be ruling the Jerusalem church in the manner of the later residential bishop (see comments on 12:17; 20:28). Luke has James persuade Paul to go through a Jewish rite in order to make the proper impression on Jewish Christians at Jerusalem.

15. *those days:* Those mentioned in 21:10. **16.** *Mnason, a Cypriote:* This "early disciple" is otherwise unknown; his house, at which Paul and his companions stop, was undoubtedly about halfway between Caesarea and Jerusalem. The next verse suggests this, although the wording of v. 16 is not such as to make this certain. **17.** *the brothers:* Christian disciples (see comment on 1:15). **18.** The second "We-Section" ends here; see further 27:1. **19.** The same sentiment is expressed in 15:12. **20.** *praised God:* James and the Jerusalem elders are quite willing to rejoice over the reports of Gentile converts to Christianity; but they also want Paul to make a good impression on the Jewish Christians of Jerusalem, some of whom seem to have heard pejorative reports about him. *how many thousands of Jews:* Lit., "how many myriads [ten thousands] of Jews." This must be a Lucan rhetorical exaggeration. *staunch defenders of the law:* The Jewish Christians who would adhere rigorously to the observance of the Mosaic Law and would insist on its observance by all who would become members of the New Covenant (Christianity). **21.** *have been informed:* Apparently by Jews of the Diaspora. *to abandon Moses:* One will look in vain in Paul's letters for the position so formulated; cf. Rom 3:31. One should also recall the circumcision of Timothy (Acts 16:3) and the statements in Acts 24:14; 25:8. Yet his attitude toward "Moses" as a legal system would be the basis of the report (see Gal 3:10–25; Rom 3:19–20; 10:4; Eph 2:15). James' statement foreshadows in Luke's account the charge to be made in 24:5; and Luke is at pains to present Paul as one who does have regard for the Mosaic Law. Paul himself was apparently aware of the hostility he would encounter (see Rom 15:31). For "Moses" as a designation of the books or of the law of Moses, see 2 Cor 3:15. *give up circumcision:* See Rom 2:25–29; 4:9–12; 1 Cor 7:17–20. **22.** *they are surely to hear:* Not only the Jewish Christians of Jerusalem, but even the Jews. **23.** *have made a vow:* James urges Paul to join the four men who have temporarily consecrated themselves to Yahweh with a Nazirite vow (see Nm 6:1–21; Philo, *De ebrietate* 1.2; Str-B 2, 80–89). See 18:18; 24:17. **24.** *rite of purification:* Acts 21:27 seems to imply that the period of Paul's vow lasted for seven days only. Has Luke confused the vague "all the days of his separation" (Nm 6:4 [usually understood as 30 days; see Mishnah, *Nazir* 1:3]) with the purification required on the seventh day after an unexpected defilement of the Nazirite (Nm 6:9–12)? *pay the expenses:* See the requirements for the termination of the vow in Nm 6:14–15; they would not have been light. *shave their heads:* In accordance with Nm 6:18–19. **25.** *a letter:* Here in Acts James seems to inform Paul about the letter of 15:23–29 for the first time (see comment on 15:35). *meat sacrificed to idols...:* See 15:29. **26.** *the completion of the days of purification:* See Nm 6:13; 1 Mc 3:49.

100 (ii) *Paul's arrest* (21:27–40). Luke describes this scene of Paul's arrest with great detail and with obvious rhetoric ("the whole city was in turmoil"). Its purpose is to set the stage for the coming discourse of defense, addressed to the people of Jerusalem.

27. *seven days:* See comment on v. 24 above. *Jews from Asia:* Luke is careful to stress that the disturbance did not originate with Jewish Christians of Jerusalem but rather with Diaspora Jews (from Ephesus [see v. 29]) who were apparently present in Jerusalem for the feast of Pentecost. **28.** *against the law and this place:* The charge echoes that brought against Stephen in 6:13 (cf. 18:13–15). *brought Greeks into the temple:* See 24:5–6; 25:8. Lest they defile the sacred precincts, Gentiles were not permitted beyond the Court of the Gentiles, which was marked off by a stone balustrade with inscribed slabs (in Latin and Greek) warning foreigners of the death penalty for trespassing (see *JW* 5.5, 2 § 194; *Ant.* 15.11, 5 § 417). Two copies of these inscriptions have been found (see E. J. Bickermann, *JQR* 37 [1946–47] 387–405; cf. *NTB* § 47, 205). **29.** *Trophimus:* See 20:4; cf. 2 Tm 4:20. **30.** *its gates were closed:* Presumably by the Temple police. **31.** *the commander of the cohort:* When a report was carried to Claudius Lysias (named in 23:26), he intervened on Paul's behalf. He is here called a *chiliarchos,* which suggests that the cohort (*speira*) posted at this time in the Fortress Antonia at the NW corner of the Temple area (→ Gospel Mk, 42:91) was a detachment of 1000 men. One of the purposes of the Roman cohort was precisely to quell riots in the area of the Temple, such as were likely to break out on feasts. **32.** *charged down on them:* Verse 35 suggests that a stairway led down from the barracks to the spot where Paul was being assaulted. **36.** *away with him:* The same cry occurs in the Lucan Passion Narrative (23:18); cf. Jn 19:15. **38.** *that Egyptian:* Josephus tells of an Egyptian who came to Jerusalem, claiming to be a "prophet," and who persuaded a mob of people to march out by a circuitous route "from the desert" to the Mt. of Olives, where they were to watch the walls of Jerusalem fall. The uprising he caused had to be put down by Roman soldiers under the governor Felix (*Ant.* 20.8, 6 § 169–72; *JW* 2.13, 5 § 261–63). Though thousands were killed, the Egyptian escaped; the Roman garrison commander obviously thought he had caught him. *4000 cutthroats:* Lit., "4000 men of the sicarii" (→ History of Israel, 75:155). Josephus (*JW* 2.13, 5 § 261) gives their number as 30,000, which is probably a scribal error for 4000. **39.** *a Jew:* Even though Paul is a Christian missionary, he identifies himself to the Roman commander by his ethnic background, implying that he is not an Egyptian. *Tarsus in Cilicia:* A Roman provincial town with the right of citizenship (→ Life of Paul, 46:11). **40.** *motioned for silence:* The same orator's gesture occurs in 12:17; 13:16; 19:33; cf. 26:1. *in Hebrew:* As in 22:2 and 26:14, this phrase apparently means "in Aramaic," the more commonly used Semitic language in Palestine at this time. Aramaic may even have been Paul's first language (2 Cor 11:22; Phil 3:5). Some commentators try to make a case for Paul's discourse being actually addressed to the crowd in Hebrew (see J. P. Hyatt, *JBL* 76 [1957] 10; J. M. Grintz, *JBL* 79 [1960] 47).

101 (iii) *Paul's discourse to the Jerusalem crowd* (22:1–21). In the form of a discourse of defense Luke presents the second account of Paul's conversion. Many of the details are identical with the narrative in 9:1–19; see the introductory remarks on that passage (→ 49 above) for a comparison.

1. *my brothers and my fathers:* Stephen began his speech with the same formula (7:2). To address a crowd in this way seems a little inappropriate, but it must be related to Luke's presentation of Paul's defense, which is in effect being made to all Israel. **3.** The first part of this verse repeats 21:39. The emphasis lies on Paul's protestation, "I am a Jew," for Paul seeks to explain why despite this background he lives and acts as he does. *brought up in this city:* Paul's early education was at Jerusalem (see W. C. van Unnik, *Tarsus or Jerusalem: The City of Paul's Youth* [London, 1962]; but cf. N. Turner, *Grammatical Insights into the NT* [Edinburgh, 1965] 82–85; → Life of Paul, 46:13). *at the feet of Gamaliel:* Paul was a student of rabbinics under the rabbi mentioned in 5:34 (see M. S. Enslin, *JRel* 7 [1927] 360–75). *the law of our fathers:* What Paul says here is confirmed in Gal 1:14; Phil 3:6. *a staunch defender of God:* Lit., "God's zealot." Luke insists that Paul was a loyal, strict-living Pharisaic Jew whom the *Kyrios* himself (22:10) has won over and commissioned for missionary work. **4.** *I persecuted this Way:* See comment on 16:17. Cf. Gal 1:13; Phil 3:6 ("the church"; → Pauline Theology, 79:149). **5.** *the high priest:* Paul's appeal to the high priest's knowledge is puzzling, because at this time he should be Ananias, son of Nedebaeus (→ History of Israel, 75:133); cf. Acts 23:2; 24:1. He is scarcely the same as the one who might have been involved in Paul's commission to go to Damascus (probably Joseph Caiaphas, the son-in-law of Annas). However, in the "council" (*presbyterion* = Sanhedrin), there should have been elders who remembered the commission of which Paul speaks. **6.** *traveling along:* See 9:3. *about noon:* This detail is lacking in 9:3; it seems to stress that Paul's vision was not a dream of the night. The repetition of details noted in ch. 9 enhances the importance of this event for Paul. **7.** *Saul, Saul:* See comment on 9:4. **8.** *Jesus the Nazorean:* The appositive is lacking in 9:5; for its meaning, see comment on Jn 18:5. **9.** *saw the light, but did not hear the voice:* See 9:7, where these details differ—a strange thing in a composition by the same writer; the difference sheds light on the Syn Problem in the Gospel tradition. **11.** *because of the brilliance of that light:* The reason for Paul's blindness is given here, but not in 9:8. "Brillance" is really *doxa*, a word that often designates for Paul the "glory" of the Risen Jesus (→ Pauline Theology, 79:72–73). **12.** *Ananias:* In 9:10–17 this hesitant agent of God in Paul's conversion appears as a devout "disciple" of the Way; here in ch. 22 he appears as a Jewish Christian, using OT expressions and enjoying good relations with the Jews of Damascus. The overlay of Jewish-Christian detail is explained by the setting of the discourse. **13.** See 9:17. **14.** *the God of our fathers:* Ananias sounds like an OT preacher (Dn 3:26,52; Jos 18:3; Dt 1:11,21; 4:1; Ex 3:13); contrast the title, "the Lord," in 9:17. Paul's conversion is thus attributed to the venerable God of the patriarchs of Israel (see 3:13). *the Just One:* This title for Jesus as the Messiah occurs also in 3:14; 7:52; it is derived from the epithet used of the scion of David in Jer 23:5–6; 33:15 (see *ThDNT* 2, 186–89). **15.** *a witness... to what you have seen and heard:* Paul thus relates his commission to the Risen Jesus; its origin, then, is the same as that of the Twelve (1:8). *before all men:* In 9:15 it was restricted to "the Gentiles"; once again the exigencies of the situation call for a broader view. **16.** *calling upon his name:* See 2:38. **17.** *returned to Jerusalem:* This apparently refers to Paul's first visit to Jerusalem, three years after his conversion, about AD 40 (see Gal 1:18; Acts 9:26). *trance:* The ecstasy is not mentioned in ch. 9, nor is it to be identified with that in 2 Cor 12:1–4. The locale of the trance ("in the court of the Temple") is noteworthy, not only because it discloses that Paul still prayed in the Jerusalem Temple after his conversion (cf. 21:24–28), but because his commission "to the Gentiles" is conferred, according to Luke, in the very heart of Judaism's religious cult. **18.** *leave Jerusalem* Acts 9:29–30 rather ascribes Paul's departure from the city to a plot of the Hellenists. According to Gal 1:21 Paul withdrew after 15 days in Jerusalem to the regions of Syria and Cilicia, which probably included a sojourn of some time in his native Tarsus (see O. Linton, *ST* 3 [1949] 79–95). *they will not accept your testimony about me:* This Lucan refrain runs through the story of Paul's missionary endeavors (see 13:46–48; 18:6; 28:25–28). *I imprisoned those who believed in you:* See 8:3; 9:2; Gal 1:13. Such a reason should have ingratiated Paul with the Jerusalem crowd; but it is not, of course, the whole story. **20.** *your witness Stephen:* See 7:58–60. Stephen here merits the title *martys*, which fits in with the general refrain and purpose of Acts; it does not yet have the later connotation of "martyr", i.e., a witness by blood (see Ap 2:13; 6:9; 17:6). **21.** *far away:* These words echo 2:39 and its allusion to Is 57:19. *to the Gentiles:* Paul's mission to the Gentiles is thus explicitly stated and confirmed; contrast the destination in 22:15 (and cf. 26:18). Paul calls himself "an apostle to the Gentiles" (Rom 11:13), but Luke rarely gives him the title *apostolos* (14:4,14).

(See Badcock, F. J., "St. Paul's Apostolic Commission," *Theology* 8 [1924] 13–20, 79–88. Rigaux, B., *Saint Paul et ses lettres* [Bruges, 1962] 86–90.)

102 (iv) *Paul imprisoned in the Fortress Antonia* (22:22–29). The Jerusalem crowd reacts violently and terminates Paul's address to them; he is arrested and is about to be tortured for information, when, to save himself, he invokes his status as a citizen of the Roman Empire.

22. *away with him:* The cry of 21:36 against Paul is repeated. *not worthy to live:* See 25:24. Paul is regarded as a defilement "of the earth" (*tēs gēs*); or should it be translated "of the land" (= Israel)? **23.** *to fling dirt* [or *dust*]. This was a sign of contempt and loathing for Paul (see H. J. Cadbury, *Beginnings* 5, 269–77). **24.** *examined under the lash:* Claudius Lysias' interrogation of Paul (21:38–39) and the crowd's reaction to his address did not clarify the issue in the mind of the Roman commander. He now proceeds to use the more drastic means of securing information by flogging, which was permitted in the case of aliens and slaves (see T. Mommsen, *Römisches Strafrecht* [Darmstadt, 1955] 983–84). **25.** *legal for you to flog a Roman without a trial:* Paul again invokes the *Lex Porcia* (see comment on 16:37). **28.** *quite a sum of money to get my citizenship:* Dio Cassius (*Rom. Hist.* 60.17, 5–6) attests to the great expense involved (see A. N. Sherwin-White, *The Roman Citizenship* [Oxford, 1939] 181–89; *OCD* 195). The commander's name, Claudius Lysias (23:26), suggests that he had acquired his citizenship in the reign of Claudius, since new citizens customarily added the name of the reigning emperor. *I was born one:* Because he was a child of Palestinian Jewish parents (→ Life of Paul, 46:13) who, as residents of Tarsus, had been granted Roman citizenship by Mark Antony. **29.** Compare the reaction of the Roman officials in 16:38.

103 (v) *Paul before the Sanhedrin* (22:30–23:11). The motivation of the Roman commander at this point is hard to assess. Was he solicitous for Paul's safety? Impressed by Paul's Roman citizenship, he might have been expected to release him immediately. But because he wants to discover why Paul's activity has brought on a riot, he retains him and brings him before the Jerusalem Sanhedrin. Could a mere "commander" summon the Sanhedrin? For Conzelmann (*Apostelgeschichte*, 127), the proceeding is "historically impossible." But "the main difficulty is really psychological, not critical or historical. Paul is represented in this section as defending himself before the Sanhedrin by alleging that he was a good Pharisee, who had got into trouble merely because he preached doctrines which no good Pharisee doubted. That, it is said, was simply not true, and it is inconceivable that Paul would have put forward an untrue defense" (*Beginnings* 4, 286).

30. *the chief priests:* Former high priests (see 4:6). *the whole Sanhedrin:* This would have meant the 70 elders, chief priests, and scribes of Jerusalem who normally met together with the high priest in office (→ Gospel Mk, 42:52). **23:1.** *with a clear conscience:* Cf. 24:16; 1 Cor 4:4; 2 Cor 1:12. As presented here, Paul's conversion to Christianity is only the logical consequence of his Pharisaic past. As Haenchen notes (*Apostelgeschichte*, 565), one should not ask at this point about Paul's part in the stoning of Stephen and the persecution of other Christians. *I have lived my life:* This figurative religious meaning is demanded by the context; the Gk vb. *pepoliteumai* literally means, "I have conducted myself as a citizen" (cf. Phil 1:27). **2.** *the high priest Ananias:* This is Ananias, the son of Nedebaeus, who held office from AD 47 to 59 (Josephus, *Ant.* 20.9, 2 § 205). He was later assassinated by Zealots (?) at the beginning of the First Revolt against Rome (*JW* 2.17, 6 § 426; 2.17, 9 § 441). See comment on 22:5. *to strike Paul:* The motivation of the high priest's order is not clear. Was it a protest against Paul's statement or against his curt mode of address (using only "brothers" before such an august gathering)? See Jn 18:22–23. The effect of the order is to present Ananias (and all that he represents) in the blackest light (see 1 Cor 4:12–13). **3.** *you are the one God will strike:* Is Luke referring Paul's predictive curse to the fate of Ananias, writing with hindsight? *whitewashed wall:* The same figure is used for hypocrisy in Mt 23:27. Despite attempts to explain the figure in terms of Ez 13:10–15, the hypocritical meaning of it seems to fit the situation best here, as the rest of the verse indicates. *yet you violate the Law:* Possibly Paul refers to Lv 19:15 ("You must do no injustice in judging"). His whole answer is ironical; he poses as the exemplar of obedience toward the Law and would not think of insulting the high priest, quoting Ex 22:27 to support his contention. **6.** *some were Sadducees and some Pharisees:* In general, the chief priests would have belonged to the Sadducees and the scribes to the Pharisees; the elders might have been associated with either class. (For a description of these two classes of Jews, → History of Israel, 75:120–24; → 29 above; cf. *Beginnings* 1, 436–38.) *I am a Pharisee:* See Phil 3:5; Acts 26:5. *my hope and the resurrection of the dead:* This is hendiadys: Paul means his hope is the resurrection of the dead. The Pharisaic belief to which Paul refers is based mainly on Dn 12:2. Realizing that it is a point of division between the two classes represented in the Sanhedrin, Paul cleverly relates his belief in the Risen Jesus to the Pharisaic belief in the resurrection of the dead (see Acts 4:2; 13:32–33; 24:15,21; 26:6–8; 28:20). **8.** *no resurrection, no angels, no spirits:* Only the first item of their tenets mentioned here is attested in Jewish sources (see Josephus, *JW* 2.8, 14 § 165). As Haenchen notes (*Apostelgeschichte*, 567), it is not easy to understand how they could deny angels, which appear in the written Torah that they acknowledged. Luke does not make it clear that the Sadducees denied the resurrection because it does not appear in the Pentateuch. **9.** *a spirit or an angel has spoken to him:* The reference would be to the apparition of the Risen Jesus on the road to Damascus, which is understood here by the Pharisees of the Sanhedrin as an angelic communication. This becomes the divisive issue. **10.** *the dispute became worse:* The division of the Sanhedrin is thus achieved, and the implication is that the two chief parties among the Jews cannot agree on their religious tenets. **11.** *the Lord appeared:* This dream of consolation (cf. 18:9; 27:24) marks a stage in Luke's account; his hero must now move on from Jerusalem. The end of his journey in Rome is foreshadowed. Again the important word *dei* (expressing necessity stemming from the divine plan; see comment on 1:16) appears in the account. The next stage of the journey takes Paul to the Roman procurator in Caesarea. Thus this passage ends with the fury of the Jews contrasted with the protection afforded to Paul by the Romans

(Pope, A. M., "Paul's Address before the Council at Jerusalem," *Expositor* 8/25 [1923] 426–46.)

104 (c) PAUL IN CAESAREA (23:12–26:32). The arrest and detention of Paul are ostensibly to protect him from further maltreatment; a contributing factor is, however, the Roman commander's reluctance to release Paul, because he occasioned a riot. Lysias decides, then, to send him to the procurator of Judea, who will keep him in prison in Caesarea for two years.

(i) *Transfer to Caesarea* (23:12–35). News of a plot against Paul's life demands immediate action, and the commander sends Paul under escort to Caesarea.

12. *when it was day:* This phrase forms the transition from the mention of night in which Paul had his dream; equivalently, it means "on the next day." *conspiracy:* The Gk word *systrophē* may mean simply a "meeting," but it often has the connotations of a protest meeting (AG 803: "disorderly, seditious gathering"). *bound themselves by oath:* Lit., "laid themselves under anathema [curse]." **13.** *forty of them:* From v. 15 it would seem that all of these are not necessarily members of the Sanhedrin, who met in 22:30. **16.** *the son of Paul's sister:* Apparently resident with some of Paul's family in Jerusalem. His ability to get access to Paul and the latter's influence with the centurion suggest that the Apostle was not in maximum security. **18.** *the prisoner:* Paul is so regarded by the centurion, despite 22:30, where it is said that the commander "released him" (*elysen auton*). **23.** *to leave for Caesarea:* The seat of the provincial governor of Judea was at Caesarea Maritima. *the third hour of the night:* About 9:00 P.M. *two hundred infantrymen, seventy cavalrymen, two hundred spearmen:* This fantastic number amounts to almost half of the cohort stationed in the Fortress Antonia (see comment on 21:31). The meaning of the Gk word *dexiolabous*, here translated "spearmen," is quite uncertain. **24.** *mounts:* Lit., "animals," which could have been either horses, mules, or donkeys. *the governor Felix:* Antonius Felix, a Roman freedman and brother of Pallas, the intimate and influential friend of the emperors Claudius and Nero, became the procurator of Judea despite his social background (see Suetonius, *Claudii vita* 28; Tacitus, *Histories* 5.9; *Annales* 12.54; Josephus, *Ant.* 20.7, 1 § 137–38; 20.8, 9 § 182; *JW* 2.12, 8 § 247). His procuratorship (roughly AD 52–59 or 60) was marked with cruelty and rapacity (see 24:26). **25.** *to this effect:* How would Luke have gotten access to this letter? Most likely it represents a free composition of his own, setting forth what Lysias must have explained to Felix. It presents the whole affair from a Roman point of view, making no distinction between Jews and Jewish Christians and laying the blame on the Jews. **26.** *his Excellency:* The governor is addressed with the epithet *kratistos* (= *egregius*), the same one used of Theophilus in Lk 1:3. As a freedman, Felix was scarcely of the equestrian order. *greetings:* The Gk form is *chairein*, as in 15:23 (→ NT Epistles, 47:6). **27.** *the Jews:* The commander lays the blame on them. *having learned that he was a Roman [citizen]:* The actions of the commander are telescoped here; this heightens his own account of his chivalrous intervention (see 21:31–33; 22:25–29). **28.** *before the Sanhedrin:* See 22:30–23:11. **29.** *their own law:* The commander's reaction is similar to that of the proconsul Gallio (18:15); cf. 25:18–19. Some mss. of the Western Text read, "the law of Moses and a certain Jesus." *in no way guilty:* Luke stresses Paul's innocence (see also 23:9; 25:18,25; 26:31; 28:18). **30.** *a plot against his life:* See 23:19–22. *I have instructed:* Since Lysias would hardly have done this before Paul was safely out of Jerusalem, this may be either an epistolary past (to be judged from the standpoint of the recipient of the letter), or possibly it is an indication of the free redactional quality of the letter (H. Conzelmann, *Apostelgeschichte*, 131). **31.** *Antipatris:* A town founded by Herod the Great and named in honor of his father, Antipater II; its exact site is contested, but it lay apparently in Samaria, about halfway between Jerusalem and Caesarea Maritima (→ Biblical Geography, 73:76). The area they would traverse from Antipatris was largely Gentile and the heavy escort was no longer necessary. **34.** *Cilicia:* See 21:39; 22:3. Was Felix thinking with this question of remitting Paul to the jurisdiction of the governor of that province? See Lk 23:. **35.** *in Herod's praetorium:* The palace of Herod the Great became the residence (*praitōrion*) of the Roman procurators of Judea (see P. Benoit, *RB* 59 [1952] 532–36; J. Maigret, *BTS* 41 [1961] 3–4; → Gospel Jn, 63:161).

105 (ii) *Paul's trial before the governor Felix* (24:1–21). The two speeches that occur in this section serve to pit Paul and the Pharisaic element of Jerusalem even more sharply against each other. It gives Paul the chance to insist again that his belief and his missionary activity are but the logical conclusion of the cardinal Pharisaic tenet, the resurrection of the dead. In a concrete way this scene presents the words of Jesus reported in Lk 21:12 about disciples being haled before "synagogues" and "governors"; later (26:1ff.) Paul will appear before a "king."

1. *Ananias:* See comments on 23:2; 22:5. *Tertullus:* An otherwise unknown Jerusalem (Jewish?) "advocate" or "pleader" (Gk *rhētōr*) accompanies the delegation of the Jews to present their case before the procurator. **2.** Tertullus begins his accusation by seeking to render Felix benevolent; he recalls the efforts of the procurator to rid the country of the sicarii who were disturbing the peace (see Josephus, *JW* 2.13, 2 § 252); see S. Lösch, *TQ* 112 (1931) 295–319. **3.** *your Excellency:* See 23:36. **5.** *a pest:* Paul is so regarded because his activity was considered seditious and exciting to riot; hence the foregoing allusions to Felix' efforts for peace (see 25:8; cf. 1 Mc 10:61; 15:21). Similar accusations had been leveled against Paul before (16:20; 17:6). *a ringleader of the sect of the Nazoreans:* The word "sect" (*hairesis*) would imply that Christianity was a "school" within Judaism; but when used on the lips of adversaries (as also in 24:14; 28:22), it has a definite pejorative connotation, even though it may not yet have the later meaning of "heresy." *Nazoreans:* See comment on Jn 18:5. The "sect of the Nazoreans" obviously means the Christians, as followers of Jesus of Nazareth. **6.** *to desecrate our temple:* See 21:28. This, not that he was a sectarian, becomes the real charge against Paul. See 24:18. **6b–7.** This verse and a half in the Vg is derived from the Western Text, which adds an improbable invective against Lysias, modeled in part on 23:30. It is not found in the best Gk mss. To add it here (as does J. Dupont [*Actes*, 192]) would be to make the Jews claim jurisdictional competence over Paul. **8.** *him:* With the omission of vv. 6b–7 this pronoun refers to Paul who is to be interrogated by the procurator. If vv. 6b–7 were added, then it would be Lysias who is to be interrogated. He is later summoned to Felix (24:22), and perhaps this is the reason for the addition of the verses in the Western Text. **10.** *Paul replied:* His discourse is a systematic apologia in which he defends himself on the points made against him. The speech has a short introduction (11–13) and three parts (14–16, 17–19, and 20–21). **11–13.** Paul's introduction seeks to render Felix benevolent and rejects the accusations made against him. **11.** *a judge over this nation for many years:* Paul graciously appeals to Felix' experience and competence; he has been a procurator since about AD 52, longer than any other since Pilate (→ History of Israel, 75:155; but cf. H. Conzelmann, *Apostelgeschichte*, 130). *twelve days:* The chronological notices that appear in Luke's account (21:17,18,26,27; 22:30; 23:11–12,32; 24:1) add up to more than 12 days. Luke's figures are often unclear; here it may be that the "twelve" is nothing more than an addition of "seven" (21:27) and "five" (24:1). The implication is that the time has been too short for him to incite a riot. *to worship there:* The goal of Paul's journey is expressed as a pilgrimage such as any pious Jew would make (see 8:27). Again, Luke makes no mention of the collection for the poor (see comment on 20:3; but cf. 24:17). **14–16.** Paul tries to assure Felix that even if he is a member of the sect of the Nazoreans, this is still in line with all that the Pharisees hold most dear. **14.** *the Way:* See comments on 16:17; 18:25. In effect, Paul rejects the pejorative connotation of Christianity as a *hairesis*; he would be dismissing the implication of arbitrary choice the word suggests. He is at pains to show that his allegiance to Christ is not arbitrary, but the logical outcome of Pharisaism. *I worship the God of our fathers:* Lit., "the paternal [ancestral] god"; see comment on 22:14. The God whom he worshiped as a Pharisee is still the same as the one he now worships. *all that is written in the Law and the Prophets:* Christianity is thus presented by Luke as the fulfillment of Judaism (see Lk 24:44–45). Paul in his letters would not express his position just so; see 2 Cor 3:6–18 (cf. P. Vielhauer, *Studies in Lk-Acts*, 33–50). **17–19.** Paul insists that he did not defile the Temple. **17.** *after several years' absence:* Perhaps over five years have elapsed since the visit implied in 18:22 (→ Life of Paul, 46:35, 40). *to bring alms:* Luke finally mentions the goal of Paul's journey, as it is stated elsewhere; see 20:3 and 24:11 by contrast (cf. C. R. Brown, *JBL* 42 [1923] 49–58). Now this matter is introduced to exclude the charge of his inciting riots in the Temple area. *offerings:* These were made in the Temple. *completing the rites of purification:* He alludes to his Nazirite vow (see 21:24). The reference to his "sanctifying" himself in this way stands in pointed contrast to the accusation that he was actually defiling the Temple. **19.** *Jews from Asia:* See 21:27. **20–21.** The conclusion of the discourse recalls that when Paul was brought before the Sanhedrin, no charge could be sustained against him. **21.** *because of the resurrection of the dead:* This phrase rings like a refrain in this part of Acts (see comments on 23:6; 26:6–8). In the immediate context it refers to the Pharisaic belief in "the resurrection of the dead" (*anastasis nekrōn* [pl.]); but the larger implication of the phrase does not escape the Christian reader of Acts ("the resurrection of the Dead [One]").

(Allo, E.-B., "La portée de la collecte pour Jérusalem dans les plans de Saint Paul," *RB* 45 [1936] 529–37. Goguel, M., "La collecte en faveur des saints de Jérusalem," *RHPR* 5 [1925] 301–18. Nickle, K. F., *The Collection* [SBT 48; London, 1966].)

106 (iii) *Paul's captivity at Caesarea* (24:22–27). Paul's words did not win his freedom; he must now be a witness in detention at Caesarea.

22. *the Way:* See comment on 16:17. *Lysias:* See comments on 21:31; 22:28; 24:8. **23.** The conditions of Paul's custody at Caesarea are somewhat similar to those he will be subjected to at Rome; he has fewer privileges than he will have during his Roman house arrest (28:30). **24.** *came:* This verb evokes no little speculation. Was Felix away? Or does it mean that he came to Paul's place of detention (see rest of verse)? *with his Jewish wife Drusilla:* The Roman procurator had married the very beautiful young daughter of Herod Agrippa I, after considerable intrigue to win her away from her husband Azizus, the king of Emesa (in Syria); see the details in Josephus, *Ant.* 20.7, 2 § 141–44. The adulterous marriage is the background for the reaction of Felix to the topics that Paul chose to discourse on (uprightness, self-control, the coming judgment) instead of the topic suggested to him ("faith in Christ Jesus"). **26.** *a bribe:* Lit., "money." This Lucan detail fits into the black picture of Felix painted by Tacitus and Josephus (see comment on 23:24). Felix' hope for the bribe may have been aroused by the mention of the "alms" in v. 17. **27.** *two years passed:* This refers to the duration of Paul's Caesarean imprisonment, but possibly also to the end of Felix's procuratorship. Dupont (*Actes*, 196) understands it as the technical legal term for the maximum duration of such a detention as Paul was experiencing. At its expiration Paul should have regained his liberty (cf. 28:30). *Felix was succeeded by Porcius Festus:* The conscientious new procurator, who held office most likely from AD 60 to 62, is otherwise almost entirely unknown. Josephus (*JW* 2.14, 1 § 271–72; *Ant.* 20.8, 9–10 § 182, 185) remembers him only for his efforts to rid the country of the bands of sicarii; he died in office (*Ant.* 20.9, 1 § 200). *wishing to ingratiate himself with the Jews:* See 25:9.

107 (iv) *Paul appeals to Caesar* (25:1–12). After taking over the procuratorship of Judea, Festus goes to Jerusalem, where the Jewish leaders seek to have him agree to a trial in this city so that they can waylay Paul en route and lynch him. Paul, suspecting the worst, appeals to Caesar in virtue of his right as a Roman citizen.

1. *province:* The Gk word *eparcheia* should perhaps be better translated here as "district," since it could also denote a district ruled over by a prefect (the title the procurator of Judea also held). *Iudaea* was ruled by a procurator and had not yet been made into a Roman *provincia* in the strict sense. **3.** The same procedure for the capture of Paul was to be followed as in the plot of 23:12ff. **6–12.** The trial before Festus. Paul insists that he has committed no crime either against Judaism or against the empire. Luke emphasizes this not so much because of Paul himself as because of Christianity. **6.** *took his seat on the bench:* On the *bēma*, "the gubernatorial tribunal." **8.** *neither against the Law of the Jews:* See 18:13–15; 21:21,28; 24:14. *nor against the temple:* See 21:28. *nor against Caesar:* See comment on 16:21; 17:7. **9.** *to ingratiate himself with the Jews:* See 24:2. *to stand trial before me there:* Festus recognizes that a religious issue is at stake between Paul and his accusers; in order to do them a favor, he is willing to go along with the Sanhedrin's demand for a trial in Jerusalem. But in the long run he does not recognize its authority; eventually he shall conduct the trial himself. **10.** *before Caesar's bench:* Paul will not admit that the Sanhedrin has any competence over him. Since he has been haled before imperial authorities, he will make the most of this situation. He forces the hand of the Roman procurator. Because Paul knows that Festus has already gone too far, he will invoke his right as a Roman citizen. **11.** Paul fully recognizes the legal right of the Roman tribunal to put him to death were he a criminal. Yet he insists that "no one has a right to hand me over to them," making it obvious that he means, "not even the Roman procurator." *I appeal to Caesar:* Paul uses his right as a Roman citizen to claim the privilege of a trial before an imperial tribunal at a higher level. This was the right of *provocatio* or *appellatio* (see *OCD* 742, 72; see *Beginnings* 5, 297–338; J. Dauvillier, *BLitE* 61 [1960] 10–11; A. H. M. Jones, *Studies in Roman Law* [Oxford, 1960] 51–65).

(Holzmeister, U., "Der hl. Paulus vor dem Richterstuhle des Festus (AG 25, 1–12)," *ZKT* 36 [1912] 489–511, 742–83.)

108 (v) *Festus invites Agrippa to listen to Paul* (25:13–27). Paul by his appeal to Caesar does not succeed in being sent immediately to Rome; Festus needs to write a report in accordance with Roman law: "After an appeal has been introduced letters must be sent by the one with whom the appeal is filed to the person who will have to decide about the appeal" (*Digest* 49, 6, 1). This provides Festus with a reason for hearing Paul in the presence of Agrippa. Paul has already appeared before the "synagogue" and the "governor"; now he will appear before a "king" (see Lk 21:12).

13. *King Agrippa:* Marcus Julius Agrippa II whose sister was Bernice (→ History of Israel, 75:153). The reason why Festus brings Paul before them is stated in 25:26–27. *to pay a courtesy call:* Luke uses the aor. ptc. *aspasamenoi* to express purpose here (see W. F. Howard, *JTS* 24 [1922–23] 403–6; A. T. Robertson, *JTS* 25 [1923–24] 286–89). **15.** *demanded his condemnation:* What was not explained in 25:2–3 is now filled in; Luke makes it clear that from the Jewish viewpoint Paul was guilty ("asking for a sentence against him"), but from the Roman point of view his guilt was not established. **16.** See 25:11. The principle of Roman law invoked by Festus is the following: "This is the law we abide by: No one may be condemned in his absence, nor can equity tolerate that anyone be condemned without his case being heard" (*Digest* 48, 17, 1); cf. Appian, *Civ. Wars* 3.54, 222; Justin, *Apol.* 1.3; see J. Dupont, *RSR* 49 (1961) 354–85. **18.** *stood around him:* See 25:7. **19.** *issues in their own religion:* Luke's apologetic intention is obvious here. Festus expresses a Roman reaction to the whole affair that echoes 18:15; 23:29. He uses the noun *deisidaimonia*, which is related to the adjective used by Paul of the Athenians (see comment on 17:22), and which must mean "religion," not "superstition" (RSV). The word is used by Josephus to describe the Jewish desire to die for their beliefs (*JW* 2.9, 2 § 174). The motivation of the Jewish reaction to Paul in their seeking support from the Roman procurator apparently depends on a custom that Julius Caesar had sanctioned in the time of Hyrcanus II in favor of the Jewish high priest: "Whatever high-priestly rights or other privileges exist in accordance with their laws, these he and his children shall possess by my command. And if, during this period, any question shall arise concerning the Jews' manner of life, it is my pleasure that the decision shall rest with them" (Josephus, *Ant.* 14.10, 2 § 195). **20.** *a certain Jesus... whom Paul claimed was alive:* See Acts 17:31; 1 Thes 1:10; 2 Cor 13:4; Rom 4:25. As Festus sees it, the issue is merely whether Jesus is dead or alive. *to Jerusalem:* Implied now in Festus' statement is the thought that Jewish authorities in Jerusalem would be better represented and the issue would be better debated there. A different motive is given in 25:9. **21.** *for an imperial decision in his case:* Lit., "for a decision (*diagnōsis*, the technical legal term) of the Augustus." The Gk *Sebastos* (Lat *Augustus*) is the title that was given to Roman emperors since the principate of Octavian who received it from the Roman senate (16 January 27 BC). The title was intended to be used by his successors, but Tiberius hesitated at first to employ it (see *OCD* 124). **23–27.** Luke's idyllic description of the arrival of Agrippa and Bernice sets the stage for Paul's last defense. **23.** *military commanders:* These were chiliarchs (see comment on 21:31). **24.** *clamoring:* Cf. 21:36; 22:22. **25.** *nothing deserving death:* Again the refrain of Paul's innocence (see comment on 23:29). **26.** *to write about him:* This verse gives the reason for Paul's speech, his last defense in Luke's story. From the account so far it is obvious that Festus already has enough material for the letter he must send to Caesar. *to our sovereign:* Lit., "to the Lord." Luke makes Festus refer to Nero here with the title *ho kyrios* (used absolutely, without the emperor's name). He thus provides the earliest example of the absolute use of *kyrios* for the Roman emperor attested so far (see *LAE* 354; *ThDNT* 3, 1055). Is this an anachronism derived from the period of Luke's writing? **27.** Festus hopes that Paul's appearance before King Agrippa will bring out a further clarification of his position that can be used in the report to be sent to Rome.

109 (vi) *Paul's discourse before King Agrippa* (26:1–23). In Luke's story, this—Paul's last defense—is the culmination of his career. He has been depicted evangelizing the Gentiles and the "children of Israel," and now he brings the name of the Lord before "kings," thus fulfilling what was said of him in 9:15. The speech begins as an apologia but ends as a missionary discourse. It excels in its careful literary construction and style. After a brief introduction (2–3), it has three parts (4–8, 9–18, and 19–23). The whole is dominated once again by a concern to present Paul's belief and ministry as the logical consequence of Pharisaism and the fulfillment of Scripture.

1. *Agrippa said to Paul:* The king now takes over the meeting. *Paul stretched out his hand:* The orator's gesture (see comment on 21:40). **2–3.** Paul's introduction echoes the one addressed to Felix (24:10); he seeks to render his principal listener benevolent. **3.** *expert in all Jewish customs and questions:* Agrippa's experience and competence are acknowledged without any contrast with Festus being implied (on the *de facto* situation of Agrippa's acquaintance or concern with Judaism, see *HJPTJC* 1/2, 197–99).

4–8. The first part of the discourse stresses the connection of Paul's present status with his Pharisaic background and beliefs. **4.** *since my youth:* See 22:3 for a fuller statement. *my own people:* Lit., "in my nation." Paul's past is known to his *ethnos* (= the Jewish people, not the Cilicians). *at Jerusalem:* See 22:3. Since he is well known in Jerusalem, his juridical and religious status should be assured. **5.** *I have lived the life of a Pharisee:* See 23:6; Phil 3:5. *from way back:* The adv. *anōthen* means "from the beginning" just as *ap' archēs* does (see E. Haenchen, *ZThK* 58 [1961] 362–64). Both of these expressions emphasize the phrase "from my youth." **6.** *my hope in the promise made by God to our fathers:* This formulation of the charge made against Paul is more explicit than the earlier ones in terms of the divine "promise" being fulfilled (see 23:6; 24:21). But Luke is vague and does not specify what promise he means. From 26:8 it is obviously the fulfillment of a promise that was begun as of the resurrection of Jesus. This is the basis of the hope that Paul has—a hope he sees as the logical consequence of his Pharisaic belief. Paul implies: The true Pharisee must logically become a Christian. **7.** *worship God:* Paul appeals to the Temple cult and argues that it makes no sense unless it is related to the resurrection. *because of this hope...I stand accused:* No other reasonable charge can be brought forth; Paul thus implies the absurdity of the accusation lodged against him. **8.** *why do you of all people...?:* Paul's argument shifts to the plural, as he in effect addresses the Pharisees. However, this last sentence sounds much more like Luke posing the question to Jews of his own time. We note here the shift in the speech from apologia to missionary proclamation. *raises:* The pres. tense of the Gk verb obviously alludes to the resurrection of Jesus.

9–18. The second part of Paul's discourse repeats the story of his conversion; cf. 9:3–18; 22:6–21. Paul begins by emphasizing that he too reacted negatively to the preaching of the Risen Jesus—just as the Pharisees are now reacting to his own preaching about him. **9.** *the name of Jesus:* See 3:16; 4:17–18; 5:28,40; 8:12; 9:27; 21:13. **10.** Paul's arrest echoes 8:3; 22:4. *many of the saints:* This title for Christians is also found in the Conversion Account of 8:13,32,41. **11.** *compelled them to blaspheme:* To speak out against the name of Christ Jesus, as was done in later persecutions (see Pliny the Younger, *Letters* 10.96, 5; *Mart. Pol.* 9:3). Cf. 1 Cor 12:3; 1 Tm 1:13. *to foreign cities:* For example, Damascus (9:2). **12.** *I was traveling:* See 9:3; 22:6. *with the commission of the chief priests:* See 9:1. **13.** *at midday:* "Noon" is mentioned in 22:6, but not in 9:3. *a light shining from the sky, more brilliant than the sun:* Acts 9:3 mentions only a "light from heaven," and 22:6, "a great light from heaven." Its brilliance is emphasized, for in this third account of the conversion the dramatic effect of the story grows. **14.** *we all fell to the ground:* In 9:4 and in 22:7 it was only Paul who fell. *I heard a voice:* In 9:7 Paul's fellow travelers also heard the voice, but not in 22:9. *in Hebrew:* See comment on 21:40. *Saul, Saul:* See comment on 9:4. *it is hard for you to kick against the goad:* Though Jesus addresses Paul in "Hebrew" (= Aramaic), yet he quotes a proverb which is otherwise not found in Jewish literature. It is, however, very common (in variant forms) in Gk literature (see Euripides, *Bacchae* 795 ["than kick against the goads"]; Aeschylus, *Prometheus* 323; *Agamemnon* 1624; Pindar, *Pythian Odes* 2.94–95; see E. Nestle, *Ph* 59 [1900] 46–57; R. C. Horn, *LCQ* 11 [1938] 281–88). It expresses a useless resistance to divine influence in future conduct; from this moment on Paul is pressed into the service of Jesus. See his own remarks in Phil 3:12 ("seized" by Christ Jesus) and in 1 Cor 9:15–18 (a "necessity, compulsion" [*anagkē*] was laid on him). **15.** *whom you are persecuting:* "Jesus" is here identified with "the saints" (v. 10). **16.** *stand on your feet:* This allusion to Ez 2:1–2 relates Paul's conversion and call to that of the prophet. *I have appeared to you:* In 9:15 Christ addresses the equivalent of these words to Ananias; in 22:14–15 Ananias speaks similarly to Paul. Here, however, the intermediary is eliminated; and Jesus' speech is moreover filled with allusions to OT passages that deal with prophetic mission. The implication is that Paul's own mission is of the same strain. *to designate you as my servant:* Paul is now cast in the role of *hypēretēs* (assistant), but not of *doulos* (slave). That title, joined with "witness" (*martys*), forms a phrase that echoes the functions implied in Lk 1:2. Paul is thus implicitly made the equal of the apostles; cf. 1:8 (witness to the end of the earth); 1:22 (witness to the resurrection); 22:15. **17.** *delivered you:* The allusion to Jer 1:7–8 relates Paul's call to that of another of the OT prophets. **18.** *to open the eyes:* This seems to be an allusion to Is 42:7,16. By references to Ezekiel, Jeremiah, and Dt-Is, Luke relates Paul's mission to an OT mission to the Gentiles; see further 1 Chr 16:35; Is 35:5. But his mission includes the Jews ("this people") as well as "the Gentiles" (= the nations, 26:17). The latter are specifically called from Satan's power to a share in the lot of the saints (= Jewish Christians). *forgiveness of sins:* See 2:38; 5:31; 10:43; 13:38.

110 **19–23.** The third part of Paul's discourse is missionary; it contains a résumé of his preaching and presents Christianity as the fulfillment of Scripture. **19.** *I could not disobey:* That is, as a strict Pharisee, for the Christian mission is of heavenly origin (cf. Gal 1:15–16). **20.** *the people of Damascus:* See 9:20–22,27. *of Jerusalem:* See 9:28–29 for Paul's activity in this area. It is significant that this fits in once again with the general Lucan presentation of Paul's work: first among the Jews, then among the Gentiles (see comment on 17:2). *in all Judea:* We know nothing more than this cryptic reference to such apostolic activity. Is Haenchen (*Apostelgeschichte*, 612) right in writing this all off as "an ancient and false gloss"? Such a judgment is too arbitrary. *even to the Gentiles:* See 22:21. This is not a reference to Paul's Gentile apostolate, which is derived from Rom 15:19—significant though this reference may be for the understanding of this verse. Luke scarcely had access to Rom. *a message of reform and conversion:* A Lucan refrain (see 3:19; 21:27–31; Lk 3:8,21). **22.** *differs from what the prophets and Moses foretold:* Cf. 24:14 ("the law and the prophets"); 3:22–24; 28:23; Lk 24:17,44. The formula used is customary. But once again Luke's reference to the OT is vague; the reader is supposed to believe that in the OT Christianity is in some way foretold. But specific references to OT passages as support for the following summary of Christian belief are strikingly lacking; they reveal Luke's cavalier manner of handling the OT. **23.** *the Messiah must suffer:* Such a formulation is Lucan; it may be derived from the gospel tradition before him; but it cannot be found in OT tradition (see comment on 17:3). Luke joins the OT Messiah-theme with that of the Servant of Yahweh who is said in one place to suffer. Not only does he conflate the two figures (Messiah with Suffering Servant)—a conflation that is still unattested in pre-Christian times—he even asserts that the OT implies the resurrection of this conflated figure; yet no references are given to OT passages. We are thus face to face with a typically Lucan theologoumenon that has profoundly influenced later Christianity. It may well be correct; but it should be recognized for what it is. *the first to rise from the dead:* Through his resurrection Jesus has become the "author of life" (3:15; 5:31). The word *archēgos*, which may mean not "author," but "leader," does not connote a causal connection between the resurrection of Jesus and that of the Christian (H. Conzelmann, *Theology*, 205–6 [quoting Bultmann]). As long as such authors pose the question in terms of causality (with all its Aristotelian connotations), why should not the causality be exemplary? This would scarcely rule out the implications of either Luke or Paul. Yet perhaps these authors err in introducing—even in dependence on older discussions—the very question of "causality" itself. See 1 Cor 15:20; Col 1:18. *light to our people and to the Gentiles:* Jesus' role is seen to be an influence on both Jews and Greeks (see 26:18 and Is 49:6). Paul's discourse to the Jewish king Agrippa II thus ends with a brief summary of the early Christian belief in Christ Jesus. One should note what it affirms and what it omits.

111 (vii) *Reactions to Paul's discourse* (26:24–32). Agrippa's calm is contrasted with the emotional reaction of the Roman Festus, who is struck by Paul's erudition (whatever that would be!), his strange mode of argumentation, and his acquaintance with Jewish Scriptures. But even more operative in the discussion is the talk about the resurrection of the dead; Festus undoubtedly finds this hard to accept.

24. *Festus interrupted:* The discourse of Paul is conveniently ended by an interruption as in 22:22—the audience breaks in. It is a literary device. **26.** *the king is well acquainted:* As a Jew, aware of the Pharisaic belief in the resurrection of the dead and probably also of the death of Jesus of Nazareth, he is one to whom Paul can legitimately appeal. *done in a dark corner:* A Gk proverb (Epictetus, 2.12, 17) serves Paul's purpose at this point. Haenchen (*Apostelgeschichte*, 618) correctly notes: "This phrase actually illustrates the Lucan presentation in Acts from the very beginning on." For the author obviously treats the whole question as if it were perfectly obvious to everyone. Thus, Paul's arguments are based on incontestable facts that invite the observer acquainted with the OT to recognize that the Scriptures have been fulfilled. The death and resurrection of Jesus and the proclamation of these events by the apostles are widely known. **27.** *do you believe the prophets?:* Paul's question to King Agrippa at this juncture is a real challenge, because in effect it asks a Jew to conclude to what Paul considers obvious. **28.** *would you even make a Christian of me?:* The precise nuance of this verse is not easy to grasp. Agrippa seems to be jesting a bit; and yet his jesting answer conceals no little embarrassment. See 1 Kgs 20:7 for a parallel (cf. A. Fridrichsen, *ConNeot* 3 [1939] 13–16). **29.** *might become what I am:* Paul's idyllic hope for all men is that they would become Christians. **31.** The theme of Paul's innocence appears again (see comment on 23:29); it is affirmed both by Roman and by Jew. **32.** *if he had not appealed to Caesar:* Some obscure nicety of Roman law is involved here that escapes us; see *Beginnings* 5, 318.

112 (d) Paul's Journey to Rome (27:1–28:16). In a sense this is the build-up to the finale of Acts. Paul had said in 19:21, "I must visit Rome too." His plans have, however, taken a different turn; his visit to Rome is made under circumstances not precisely envisaged. The composition of ch. 27 by Luke gives a detailed description of the voyage and shipwreck, the nautical correctness of which is due to literary models that the author has certainly consulted. The real question, however, is why Luke has gone to all the trouble to present us with the details. Dibelius (*Studies*, 134) offers a plausible reason:

> We are reminded of another passage in his work which had an obviously literary quality—his characterisation of the Athenians prior to the Areopagus speech; this served to emphasise a symbolically important scene, the encounter of the gospel with the Greek spirit. As he now undertakes this journey, Paul, the real apostle to the nations, is on his way to the metropolis of the Empire. But Luke cannot allow him now, as he did in the scene on the Areopagus, to enter the forum as a speaker, for Paul is making the journey as a prisoner; he does, however, emphasise the significance of the story of the voyage by adding nautical details and so giving prominence to the story as such. Thus he shows at the end of his book that the promise by Jesus in the first chapter has been fulfilled: "You shall be my witnesses in Jerusalem and in the whole of Judaea and Samaria, to the ends of the earth." So we see Luke once more as an historian who expounds the meaning of an event by striking description; we see him also in his capacity as *herald* and *evangelist*, a rôle which he fulfils completely in his first book and wishes ultimately to fulfil also in Acts.

(i) *Departure for Rome* (27:1–5). The third "We-Section" begins here and continues until 28:16, except for a few inserts that are clearly Lucan, but also clearly different from the "We-Section" itself.

1. *we were to set sail for Italy:* The Western Text reads, "And so the procurator decided to send him to Caesar. The next day he summoned a centurion of the cohort Augusta, named Julius, and handed over to him Paul and the other prisoners." In this form of the text Luke would be dissociating himself from the captive status of Paul, which is perhaps implied in the Alexandrian Text quoted. *cohort Augusta:* This was apparently the Cohors Augusta

I, which was stationed in Syria during most of the 1st cent. AD, and which was made up largely of Syrian mercenaries. **2.** *Adramyttium:* The home port of the ship on which they were to sail was a town on the SE coast of Mysia, an area in NW Asia Minor (to the E of Troas). *Aristarchus:* This is undoubtedly the same man as the one mentioned in 19:29 (see comment) and 20:4. *Sidon:* The first port of call is the Phoenician town on the coast N of Tyre. Here Paul enjoys a little freedom. **4.** *sheltered side of Cyprus:* This would mean a course to the N of Cyprus along the coast of Cilicia and Pamphylia. *strong head winds:* These must have come from the NW. The Western Text adds, "for 15 days." **5.** *Myra in Lycia:* On the S coast of Asia Minor (see comment on 21:1).

113 (ii) *Storm and shipwreck* (27:6–44). The account of the storm and the shipwreck is remarkable for its factual detail. It is occasionally interrupted, however, by interventions of Paul (9–11, 21–26, 31–38); the style occasionally shifts to the third person plural; possibly Luke uses a different source here.

6. *an Alexandrian vessel bound for Italy:* This was probably an Egyptian grain ship coming from Alexandria, which is almost due S of Myra (cf. Suetonius, *Claudii vita* 18; Lucian, *Navigium* 7–10; L. Casson, *TAPA* 81 [1950] 43–56; *TAPA* 87 [1956] 239–40; B. S. J. Isserlin, *TAPA* 86 [1955] 319–20). **7.** *Cnidus:* A seacoast town on a southern promontory of W Asia Minor. The difficulty in making port was due either to its position on the promontory, or possibly to the passage N of the island of Rhodes. *Salmone:* A town on the NE tip of Crete, called *Samōnion* by Strabo (*Geography* 10.3, 20; 10.4, 3) and *Samonium* by Pliny (*Nat. Hist.* 4.58, 71). **8.** *Fair Havens:* The modern name Kali Limenes has preserved the ancient one, which is not attested in any ancient author. It was situated on the S coast of Crete. *the town of Lasea:* The nearby town lay somewhat inland. **9–13.** Note the shift to the third pl. verbs in this passage, otherwise regarded as a "We-Section"; it coincides in part with Paul's intervention. **9.** *the fast was already over:* Luke thus refers to the Day of Atonement, the fast kept in accordance with Lv 16:29–31 (see *ThDNT* 4, 925; → Religious Institutions, 76:155–58), about the time of the autumnal equinox, on the 10th of Tishri (late September or early October). It is curious to see a Jewish calendaric reference being used for a navigation problem, which is otherwise determined by Gk or Rom standards. Luke's remark means that it was but a short time before the period (11 November to 10 March; see Vegetius, *De re militari* 4.39) when sea journeys were no longer undertaken because of winter storms. **10.** *Paul warned:* Paul's intervention in this matter is rather strange; does it represent a Lucan effort to extol his hero? According to Conzelmann (*Apostelgeschichte*, 142), Luke is not interested in the decision of the centurion; he only wants to indicate that all the important people on board took a position opposed to Paul's. But in the long run the latter is shown to have been right. **12.** *Phoenix:* Farther to the W on the S coast of Crete (see Strabo, *Geography* 10.4, 3; cf. C. Lattey, *Scr* 4 [1949–51] 144–46; R. M. Ogilvie, *JTS* 9 [1958] 308–14). *exposed to the southwest and the northwest:* Lit., "looking toward Lips and Corus [or Caurus]," the Gk and Lat names (respectively) for winds from the SW and NW. **16.** *Cauda:* The modern island of Gaudos or Gozzo, about 25 mi. S of Phoenix. The ancient name is given as *Clauda* in some mss.; Diodorus Siculus (5.12, 4) gives it as *Gaulos*. *the ship's boat:* There was a chance that the dinghy, used for landing passengers and for other purposes, might be lost. **17.** *they used cables to brace the ship:* Commentators have sought to give various explanations of this phrase; the most that can be said is that the ptc. *hypozōnnyntes* implies some sort of undergirding of the ship's hull. How this would have been done in a storm is a question. Note the shift again to the 3rd plural in this verse. *the reef of Syrtis:* The *Syrtis Maior* was a sandbank or shoal on the N coast of Africa, W of Cyrene (see Pliny, *Nat. Hist.* 5.4, 27). *lowered the kedge anchor:* Lit., "having lowered the instrument [or gear]." In the sense used here, the phrase would mean that the "anchor" (*skeuos*) was to serve as a sort of brake. However, some commentators interpret the phrase to mean rather, "having unfurled the sail" (see J. Renié, *RSR* 35 [1948] 272–74). **18.** *jettisoned some cargo:* In an effort to lighten the ship so that it might ride out the storm better (cf. Jon 1:5). **20.** *neither the sun nor the stars were to be seen.* This left the sailors without aids to navigation; lacking compass and sextant, they normally checked their positions by the sun and stars. A storm made this impossible.

114 **21–26.** Paul's second intervention in the conduct of the voyage. The logical sequel to v. 20 is v. 27. **21.** *had eaten nothing:* Because of the roughness of the voyage (see J. R. Madan, *JTS* 6 [1904–5] 116–21). **23.** *a messenger of the God to whom I belong:* This circumlocution for an angel sent by the God of the Jews is presumably used in the interest of the pagan travel companions (see Jon 1:9). **24.** *destined to appear before Caesar:* The Roman goal of his heaven-guided journey is thus expressed again (see 19:21; 23:11). *God has granted safety to all who sail with you:* Paul is thus the bringer of salvation to men, in a physical sense in the immediate context; but the Christian reader hears the overtones of the words in a larger context. **26.** *shipwreck on some island:* Foreshadowing of 27:42–44.

27. This verse is the sequel to v. 20. *the Adriatic:* The Mediterranean Sea between Crete, Africa, and Sicily is so designated by the ancient geographer Ptolemy; Josephus also, in describing a sea journey between Judea and Rome, uses this name (*Life* 3 § 15). *began to suspect that land was near:* Probably a change in the roar of the waves prompted this conjecture. **29.** *from the stern:* The anchors were to brake the forward progress of the ship toward land—and disaster. **30.** *to abandon the ship:* The action of the sailors is strange and inexplicable. One can only say that they felt their situation to be desperate, that they panicked, and sought their own safety by a means that was scarcely sure to guarantee it. **31.** *Paul alerted the centurion:* Though the third Pauline intervention in the description of the voyage and shipwreck strictly begins in v. 33, it could also be said to start here. **32.** *the soldiers:* Most likely the centurion ordered the soldiers to cut the ropes by which the dinghy had been lowered. **33–38.** Paul's intervention on behalf of the voyagers. **33.** *for fourteen days:* See 27:21,27. **34.** *lose a hair of his head:* An OT expression (1 Sm 14:45; 2 Sm 14:11) echoed also in Lk 12:7; 21:8. **35.** *took some bread, gave thanks..., broke it, and began to eat:* According to common Jewish custom, Paul "said grace" before eating. The expressions used, however, have a Eucharistic ring to them (see Lk 22:19). Yet they cannot be interpreted in this context as if Paul celebrated the Eucharist (cf. B. Reicke, *TZ* 4 [1948] 401–10). **38.** *they lightened the ship:* Cf. 27:18. Note again the shift to the third person plural in vv. 36–44. *the wheat:* Italy derived much of its wheat from Egypt, and this reference is not merely to the provisions for the voyagers, but to the rest of the cargo. **39.** *a bay:* This is known today as St. Paul's Bay, on the NE coast of Malta. **41.** *sandbank:* They did not make it all the way to shore; hence the need to abandon the ship and swim. **44.** *all came safely to land:* Paul's prediction (27:25) is fulfilled.

(Dauvillier, J., "À propos de la venue de Saint Paul à Rome: Notes sur son procès et son voyage maritime," *BLitE* 61 [1960] 3–26. Hermesdorf, B. H. D., "Sint Paulus temidden van zeerechtelijke vraagstukken," *StudCath* 29 [1954] 237–48. Leonard, W., "From Caesarea to Malta. St. Paul's Voyage and Shipwreck," *AusCRec* 37 [1960] 274–84. Ramsay, W. M., "St. Paul's Shipwreck," *Expositor* 5/6 [1897] 170–73. Richard, R., "Navigations de Saint Paul," *Études* 190 [1927] 448–65. Rougé, J., "Actes 27, 1–10," *VigChr* 14 [1960] 193–203. Smith, J., *The Voyage and Shipwreck of St. Paul* [4th ed.; rev. W. E. Smith; London, 1880].)

115 (iii) *Winter in Malta* (28:1–10). The worst is over; the shipwrecked party (Paul and his companions) has found safety and has been welcomed by the inhabitants of Malta, where they spend the winter.

1. *once safely ashore:* Lit., "having been brought safely through" (the wreck of the ship). *Malta:* The main island situated S of Sicily (see Strabo, *Geography* 17.3, 16; Diodorus Siculus, 5.12, 2; cf. A. Brunot, *BTS* 89 [1967] 8–17). **2.** *the natives:* Lit., "the foreigners." Like any Gk writer, Luke calls the Maltese *barbaroi*, "speakers of a foreign language," i.e., people who do not speak Greek (see Rom 1:14; 1 Cor 14:11; cf. H. Windisch, *ThDNT* 1, 546–53). The Maltese were probably speaking a form of Phoenician (a Semitic tongue related to Hebrew and Aramaic) at this time; Punic inscriptions from Malta are known (see *CIS* 1.124). **3–6.** Paul's victory over the viper proves to the credulous natives that he is an extraordinary person; he escapes from divine "justice" (really the pursuing goddess Justice). *viper:* The Gk word *echidna* denotes a nonpoisonous constrictor snake (AG 332). *fastened on him:* This does not necessarily mean "bit him." **5.** *no ill effects:* See Mk 16:18; Lk 10:19. **6.** *he was a god:* Cf. the analogous estimate in 14:11. **7.** *Publius, the headman of the island:* The legate of the praetor of Sicily, who ruled over Rom Malta, was called "Melitensium primus omnium" (*CIL* 10.7495). The Gk word *Poplios* is the equivalent of Lat *Publius*. **8.** *imposed hands on him:* The imposition of hands to cure is found also in Lk 4:38–41 (cure of Peter's mother-in-law); see comment on 9:17. *cured him:* Paul cures the man miraculously; this is the meaning of the short episode. The fact that it is recounted in a "We-Section" is no evidence that Luke, the author, was a physician, or that he exerted his medical skill in this case. **10.** *when we eventually set sail:* After 10 March (see comment on 27:9; cf. Josephus, *JW* 2.10, 5 § 203).

116 (iv) *Paul's arrival in Rome* (28:11–16).

11. *three months later:* This would be roughly late February or early March AD 61 (→ Life of Paul, 46:42). *Heavenly Twins as its figurehead:* The Gk *Dioskouroi* (Lat Castor and Pollux) were carved on the prow of the ship. They were the twin brothers of Helen and the children of Zeus (and Tyndareus?). Sailors cherished them as astral deities and saviors in time of storms (cf. the twin lights of St. Elmo's fire; cf. *OCD* 290). **12.** *Syracuse:* An important town on the E coast of Sicily. *Rhegium:* The town on the "tip of the boot" of Italy (modern Reggio di Calabria). *Puteoli:* An Italian town in Campania (modern Pozzuoli) on the Gulf of Naples to the W of Naples. Even in ancient times it was the chief port of entry to Italy from the islands (see Josephus, *Life* 3 § 16). A Christian community had already been founded there; Paul was greeted by its members. He was still 125 mi. from Rome itself. **14.** *brothers:* See comment on 1:15 (cf. T. Fahy, *IrTQ* 26 [1959] 182–91). *how we finally came to Rome:* The solemn introduction of Paul to his city of destiny. *Appii Forum:* The town of the "Forum of Appius" was situated about 43 mi. from Rome on the Appian Way. *Tres Tabernae:* The town of the "Three Taverns" was about 33 mi. from Rome. We are not told how the Roman community of Christians learned about Paul's approach or how he recognized them when they came toward him on the road. All this is taken for granted by Luke. **16.** *entered Rome:* The geographical goal of the world mission is reached (see 1:8). *with a soldier guarding him:* In Rome Paul is put under house arrest. It is usually thought that Paul would have been led first to the Praetorian camp, which was to the E of Rome, and there put in military custody. Just how this would have been carried out is not easily determined, given the permission to live in his own house. "Chains" are mentioned in 28:20. The last "We-Section" of Acts ends with this verse; but a further passage is added by Luke giving a brief summary of the next two years that Paul spent in Rome.

(See Kinsey, R. S., "Rome in the Time of St. Paul," *LCQ* 18 [1945] 407–11. Mackinnon, A. G., *The Rome of St. Paul* [London, 1931].)

117 (e) House Arrest and Unhindered Proclamation of the Message at Rome (28:17–31). The last part of Acts depicts Paul striving earnestly to present himself in a good light to the Jews at Rome. It gives him once again the opportunity to make a defense of his loyalty to Jewish beliefs, but also (by way of difference from the earlier defenses) to throw a final challenge to the Jews.

(i) *Paul's testimony to the Jews* (28:17–28). Paul's last speech of defense emphasizes that he has committed no crime against the Jewish people. The Jews of Rome prudently invite him to expose his views; and thus once again the Lucan theme appears: Paul addresses his message first to the Jews.

17. *the Jewish community:* The Jews in Rome were organized into a close community (see H. J. Leon, *The Jews of Ancient Rome* [Phila., 1960]; J.-B. Frey, *RSR* 20 [1930] 269–97; *RSR* 21 [1931] 129–68; *Bib* 12 [1931] 129–56; G. La Piana, *HarvTR* 20 [1927] 183–87). *done nothing against our people:* Paul rejects the charge echoed by James (21:21); cf. 25:8; 26:31. *handed over to the Romans:* The phrase echoes the formulation of the Passion Narrative in the Syn Tradition (see Lk 9:22; 24:7; cf. Acts 3:13; 2:23). *from Jerusalem:* The implication is that this was brought about by the Jews; Luke silently passes over any Roman complicity (see 25:9). **18.** This verse formulates specifically Paul's innocence as far as the Romans are concerned (see comment on 23:29). **19.** *I was forced to appeal to Caesar:* See 25:11; 26:32. He was forced to do this, though it conflicts with his affection for his fellow Jews. **20.** *the hope of Israel:* This is not the "messianic hope" of Israel (*pace* G. W. Lampe, *PCB* 925), but rather the hope of the resurrection, as is evident from 23:6 (see comment). *I have requested to see you:* This is the more likely translation of a difficult phrase, which could possibly also mean, "I have requested you to see [me in chains]." *I wear these chains:* See 26:29. Is it possible that Paul uses the term "chains" figuratively of his Roman house arrest? **21.** *with a report:* An official communication from Jerusalem authorities. *or a rumor:* An unofficial hearsay statement. **22.** *this sect is denounced everywhere:* See comments on 24:5,14; cf. 13:45. This would seem to imply that the Roman Jews did not know much about Christianity; yet the reason that is usually given for the expulsion of the Jews from Rome under Claudius is precisely dissension between Jews and Jewish Christians (about AD 49; → Life of Paul, 46:6). Luke cannot be completely unaware of this situation, for he refers to it in 18:2. The real point, therefore, seems to be that Luke is simply making it obvious that it is Paul who brings the news of Christianity to Rome. This is the climax of his whole story. **23.** *the kingdom of God:* See comment on 1:3. At this point in the development of Luke's story it means the gospel message about the reign of God that he would achieve through Jesus (see 8:12;

19:8; 20:25). *about Jesus:* This is a summary expression for all the aspects of the life, ministry, passion, death, and resurrection of Jesus as well as of his meaning for men. The kerygmatic proclamation of 2:22–23,36 is certainly implied in this formulation. *by appealing to the Law of Moses and the Prophets:* See comment on 17:3 and cf. Lk 24:26–27. **24.** *some were convinced:* As in 4:4; 13:48; 14:1; 17:4,12,34; 18:8. *others would not believe:* The theme of divided Judaism has already been presented by Luke (see 23:9–10). The real emphasis here lies not so much on the willingness of some Jews to believe as on the hopeless situation of the Jewish people. So the author of Acts views it. They are Paul's fellow kinsmen by race—yet they will not see what he has seen. **25.** *one final word:* The aggressive part of Paul's speech begins here. Paul makes it clear that the reaction of the Roman Jews to his message has already been foretold in Scripture. **26.** To prove his point Paul cites Is 6:9–10, a text that was often used in early Christian preaching when the refusal of the Jews to accept the gospel message confronted those who were proclaiming it. It is derived from the inaugural vision of the prophet Isaiah, who fears to go to his own people and announce to them Yahweh's message. Its pertinence in the proclamation of the gospel was often sensed—to judge by the frequency with which it is quoted (see Lk 8:10 par.). Here the text is quoted according to the LXX. **28.** *God's salvation has been sent to the Gentiles:* This allusion to Ps 67:2 forms precisely the high point of Luke's whole story; the witness of the Risen Jesus has now been carried even to the Jews of the symbolic capital of the inhabited world; given their reaction to it, Paul can proceed to announce it to the Gentiles there without further ado. The testimony has thus been carried to "the end of the earth" (1:8), symbolized by Rome itself. See Acts 13:26. **29.** This verse does not occur in the best Gk mss.; its appearance in the Western Text may well be influenced by 28:25.

118 (ii) *Summary* (28:30–31). This minor summary is not quite like the earlier ones in Acts; and yet the character of these verses is clearly that of a summation of Paul's activity during his two years of Roman house arrest.

30. *two years:* Roughly AD 61–63 (cf. 24:27). *welcomed all who would come to him:* See 24:23. This verse recalls the programmatic goal of Acts in 1:8. **31.** *the kingdom of God:* See 28:23 and comment on 1:3. *with all assurance:* See 13:46. *taught about the Lord Jesus Christ:* Paul undoubtedly used Scripture to show that Jesus was the Messiah and the Lord (see 2:36). Thus the "Word" has been brought to Rome itself.

119 THE END OF ACTS. Luke's account ends very abruptly; it surprises the modern reader, to say the least. Is it unfinished? Has it been mutilated? Such questions have often been asked to which no certain answer can be given. The following brief survey indicates merely some of the attempts to answer such queries. (1) Luke died before finishing his account. But this often proposed answer encounters the difficulty that vv. 30–31 in ch. 28 are a summary statement that resembles to a degree at least the others that punctuate Luke's account; it seems to be designed as an ending. (2) Paul's journey to Spain (see *Acta Pauli;* the Muratorian Fragment 38–39 [*EB* 4; cf. D. J. Theron, *Evidence of Tradition* (London, 1957) 109]) and his martyrdom followed as the sequel. But there is no evidence of a different ending of Acts in any mss. (see *Beginnings* 5, 326–38). (3) Luke intended to write a third volume, as his own preface indicates (T. Zahn, *NKZ* 28 [1917] 373–95), for Acts 1:1 uses the adj. *prōtos* (first), and not *proteros* (former). But such an implied meaning of "first" cannot be substantiated philologically (see AG 733). (4) Acts was written before Paul's Roman trial in the early sixties. But this view gives a peculiar perspective to Paul's farewell address in 20:18–35 and encounters the objection that Lk-Acts was almost certainly written after AD 70.

The foregoing are simply the most frequently proposed hypotheses to explain the truncated ending of Acts; however, the more modern tendency seeks to reckon with Acts as a book complete in itself, with a distinct literary purpose, achieved by the symbolic meaning of Paul's last defense of himself and his career and his final challenge to the Jews of Rome, the capital of the civilized world of his time.

(See É. Trocmé, *Le Livre*, 34–35, 50–59. Pherigo, L. P., "Paul's Life After the Close of Acts," *JBL* 70 [1951] 277–84.)

46

A LIFE OF PAUL

Joseph A. Fitzmyer, S.J.

BIBLIOGRAPHY

1 Allo, E.-B., *Paul, apôtre de Jésus-Christ* (Paris, 1942). Bornkamm, G., "Paulus," *RGG* 5 (1961) 166-90. Cambier, J., "Paul," *VDBS* 7 (1962) 279–387. Davies, W. D., *Paul and Rabbinic Judaism* (2nd ed.; London, 1955). Deissmann, A., *St. Paul: A Study in Social and Religious History* (London, 1912). Fascher, E., "Paulus," PWSup 8 (1956) 431–66. Feine, P., *Der Apostel Paulus* (Gütersloh, 1927). Foakes Jackson, F. J., *The Life of St. Paul* (N.Y., 1926). Dibelius, M., *Paul* (ed. W. G. Kümmel; London, 1953). Holzner, J., *Paul of Tarsus* (St. Louis, 1944). Hunter, A. M., *Paul and His Predecessors* (rev. ed.; London, 1961). Klausner, J., *From Jesus to Paul* (London, 1944). Knox, J., *Chapters in a Life of Paul* (N.Y., 1950). Knox, W. L., *St. Paul and the Church of Jerusalem* (Cambridge, 1925); *St. Paul and the Church of the Gentiles* (Cambridge, 1939). Lattey, C., *Paul* (Milwaukee, 1939). Maier, F. W., *Paulus als Kirchengründer und kirchlicher Organisator* (Würzburg, 1961). Nock, A. D., *St. Paul* (N.Y., 1938). Penna, A., *San Paolo* (2nd ed.; Alba, 1961). Prat, F., *Saint Paul* (London, 1928). Ogg, G., *The Chronology of the Life of Paul* (London, 1968). Ramsay, W. M., *St. Paul the Traveller and the Roman Citizen* (11th ed.; London, n.d.); *The Cities of St. Paul: Their Influence on His Life and Thought* (N.Y., 1908). Ricciotti, G., *Paul the Apostle* (Milwaukee, 1952). Robinson, B. W., *The Life of Paul* (2nd ed.; Chicago, 1928). Tricot, A., *St. Paul, the Apostle of the Gentiles* (London, 1930). Von Loewenich, W., *Paul: His Life and Work* (London, 1960).

Ellis, E. E., *Paul and His Recent Interpreters* (Grand Rapids, 1961), 11–23. Metzger, B. M. *IPLAP*, 4–24. Rigaux, B., *Saint Paul et ses lettres* (Studia neotestamentica, Subsidia 2; Bruges, 1962), 53–138.

2 OUTLINE

INTRODUCTION

3 **(I) Paul's Name.** In his letters the Apostle calls himself *Paulos*. This name is used also in 2 Pt 3:15 and in Acts from 13:9 on. Prior to Acts 13:9 he is called *Saulos* (7:58; 8:1,3; 9:1, etc.), which is the Gk form of *Saoul*. The latter spelling is found only in the Conversion Accounts (9:4,17; 22:7,13; 26:14) and stands for the Hebr *Šā'ûl*, the name of the first king of ancient Israel (1 Sm 9:2,17; 10:1; etc.; cf. Acts 13:21). It means "asked" (of God *or* of Yahweh). Acts 13:9 marks the transition from "Saul" to "Paul" (except for *Saoul* in the later Conversion Accounts). Here we find *Saulos de kai Paulos*, "Saul, also known as Paul." The name *Paulos* is the Gk form of the well-known Roman cognomen, or family name, *Paulus*, used by the great Aemilian gens.

We can only conjecture how Paul got such a Roman name. Possibly it can be linked to the Roman citizenship (Acts 16:39; 22:27–28; 25:10) his family enjoyed as inhabitants of Tarsus; or perhaps an early ancestor of Paul took the name of his Roman manumitter. It is undoubtedly pure coincidence that Saul begins to be called Paul in the account in Acts when the Roman proconsul Sergius Paulus is converted (13:7–12); it is hardly likely that Paul assumed the name of his illustrious Roman convert from Cyprus (*pace* Jerome, *In Ep. ad Philem.* 1; *PL* 26.640). More likely the Apostle was called *Paulos* from birth, and *Saoul* was the *supernomen* (added name) used in Jewish circles. For like many Jews of the period he had two names, one Semitic (Saul), the other Greek or Roman (Paul); cf. Acts 1:23; 12:25. The names were often chosen for their similarity of sound. There is no evidence that "Saul" was changed to "Paul" at the time of his conversion. Indeed, *Saulos* is used in Acts even after this. The change there is probably due to different sources of Luke's information. Although *paulus* in Latin means "small," "little," it had nothing to do with Paul's stature or modesty.

(Boudou, A., *Actes des Apôtres* [VS 7; Paris, 1933] 275–76. Dessau, H., "Der Name des Apostels Paulus," *Hermes* 45 [1910] 347–68. Harrer, G. A., "Saul Who Also Is Called Paul," *HarvTR* 33 [1940] 19–33.)

4 **(II) Sources and Chronology of Paul's Life.** What little is known about the Apostle comes to us from two sources: (1) from his letters, principally Gal 1:13–23; 2:1–14; Phil 3:5–6; 4:16; 1 Cor 7:7–8; 16:5–8; 2 Cor 2:1,9–13; 11:32–33; 12:2–4,14,21; 13:1,10; Rom 11:1; 15:22–28. Details in the Pastorals can be used only if these letters are authentic Pauline compositions (→ Pastoral Letters, 57:6–11); and (2) from Acts 7:58; 8:1–3; 9:1–30; 11:25–30; 12:25; 13:1–28:31.

Some information from these sources corresponds to events of the known history of NT times, which enables us to establish the chronology of Paul's life with some probability. Certainty is not attainable; but five extra-biblically controlled events help to structure the sketch of Paul's life. These are:

(1) The return of Pontius Pilate, the prefect of Judea, to Rome in AD 36. The legate of Syria, Lucius Vitellius, sent him back to answer before the emperor for his conduct. The removal of Pilate and the arrival of the new prefect Marcellus was the plausible occasion for the trial and death of Stephen (Acts 6:8–7:60) and for the subsequent persecution of the Jerusalem church (Acts 8:1). Paul's conversion was connected with these events (see Josephus, *Ant.* 18.4, 2 § 89).

5 (2) The famine in the reign of the Emperor Claudius (Acts 11:28–30; cf. 12:25), *ca.* AD 46. The date of this widespread famine is not easily established; it apparently affected the eastern Mediterranean area for several years. But some evidence indicates that it occurred in Judea about the beginning of the procuratorship of Tiberius Julius Alexander (AD 46–48; cf. Josephus, *Ant.* 20.5, 2 § 101; → History of Israel, 75:154). If the so-called Famine Visit was an actual visit, distinct from others that Paul made to Jerusalem, then it probably occurred *ca.* AD 46. (Gapp, K. S., *HarvTR* 28 [1935] 258–65; Rigaux, B., *Saint Paul et ses lettres* [Bruges, 1962] 105–7.)

6 (3) The edict of Claudius expelling the Jews from Rome, *ca.* AD 49. According to Suetonius (*Claudii vita* 25), Claudius expelled them because of the constant disturbances between Jews and Jewish Christians over *Chrēstos* (Christ): "Iudaeos impulsore Chresto assidue tumultuantes Roma expulit." Orosius (*Hist. adv. pag.* 7.6; CSEL 5,451) dated this expulsion to the 9th year of Claudius' reign (AD 49). This edict caused Aquila and Priscilla to move from Rome to Corinth not long before Paul's arrival there on Mission II (Acts 18:2).

7 (4) The proconsulate of L. Junius Gallio Annaeus in Achaia, *ca.* AD 52. Paul was haled before him at the end of Mission II in Corinth (Acts 18:12). (→ 9 below.)

8 (5) Porcius Festus succeeded Antonius Felix as the procurator of Judea, *ca.* AD 60. The precise date of this succession is difficult to establish; the one given here is used by E. Schürer, *HJPTJC* 1/2, 182–84; C. Erbes, TU 19 (1899) 16–36; cf. J. Finegan, *Handbook of Biblical Chronology* (Princeton, 1964), 322–24. On the arrival of the new procurator Paul appealed to Caesar for trial in Rome (Acts 24:27; 25:9–10).

9 Of these five events the most important for the determination of the chronology of Paul's life is the proconsulship of Gallio in Achaia. It is mentioned in a Gk inscription originally set up in the temple of Apollo and discovered at Delphi in Greece in 1905. It is a fragmentary copy of a letter from the Emperor Claudius to the Delphians:

> [1]Tiber[ius Claudius C]aes[ar August]us G[ermanicus, Chief High Priest, invested with tribunician po]wer [2][for the 12th time, acclaimed Imperator for t]he 26th time, F[ather of the Fa]ther[land, Consul for the 5th time, Censor, sends greetings to the city of the Delphians]. [3]For a lo[ng time I have been well] dispos[ed toward] the ci[ty of t]he Del[phians, and have been friendly from the [4]beg]inning, [and I] have always observed [th]e cul[t of Pythian] Apo[llo. But for all that] is [5]now being said and [th]ose stri[fes of citizens] such a[s Lucius Ju]nius [6]Gallio, my fr[iend] an[d procon]sul [of Achaia has made known to me. . . .][7] will still have the fo[rm]er [boundary . . . .].

The brackets enclose restorations of the fragmentary text of the inscription; but they are certain restorations, since the epigraphic style of such an inscription is stereotyped and well known. From it we learn that L. Junius Gallio was the proconsul of Achaia in the reign of Claudius, and specifically after the latter's 26th acclamation as "imperator." The emperor was so acclaimed by the Roman army after an important victory. Unlike his tribunician power, with which he was invested each year and which thus marked his regnal years, his acclamation as imperator was sporadic. To date an event by it, therefore, we must know when the specific acclamation took place. From other inscriptions it is known that the 22nd, 23rd, and 24th acclamations took place in Claudius' 11th regnal year, and that the 26th and 27th occurred in his 12th regnal year. The latter began on 25 January AD 52. Since the 27th acclamation took place before 1 August 52, the 26th occurred between 25 January and 1 August 52 (*dēmarchikēs exousias to dōdekaton... autokratora to eikoston kai hekaton;* cf. *CIL* 8.14727; 6.1256). (See J. Finegan, *Biblical Chronology*, 317.)

Achaia was a senatorial province, governed by a proconsul appointed by the Roman senate. Such a provincial governor normally remained in office for one year, and was expected to take his post in early summer (Dio Cassius, *Rom. Hist.* 60.11,6; 17,3: middle of April). At the 26th acclamation of Claudius as imperator, therefore, Gallio could have been near the end of his proconsulate (51–52) or at the beginning of it (52–53). The latter seems to be the preferred date. Many scholars conjecture that Paul's opponents would have used the arrival of the new proconsul on the scene as the occasion to bring him to trial. This, then, could have occurred in the summer of either 51 or 52. The latter fits in well with other data, even though it cannot be regarded as certain (cf. J. Dupont, *RB* 62 [1955] 55–56). Having lived in Corinth for 18 months prior to his arrest, Paul would then have arrived there at the beginning of 51. If we allow about 15 months for the events that preceded his arrival in Corinth, he would have left Antioch on Mission II in the autumn of 49, after the "Council" in Jerusalem. If this reckoning, based on a common interpretation of the Delphi inscription, is not correct, it cannot be wrong by more than a year. In any case, it is the pivotal date in Pauline chronology, enabling us to fit other details into a coherent and satisfactory outline.

(*Beginnings* 5, 460–64. Bourguet, E., *De rebus delphicis* [Montepessulano, 1905] 63–64. Deissmann, A., *St. Paul* [London, 1912], frontispiece and pp. 235–60. Hennequin, L., "Delphes, Inscription de," *VDBS* 2, 355–73. Nikitsky, A. V., *Epigraphical Studies at Delphi I–VI* [Odessa, 1894–95], pl. VII. Ogg, C., "A New Chronology of Saint Paul's Life," *ExpT* 64 [1952–53] 120–23. Roberts, J. E., "Gallio," *Dict. of the Apos. Church*, 1 [1915] 439–40. Spadafora, F., "Gallione," *Enciclopedia catt.* 5 [1951] 1904–5.)

PAUL'S CAREER

10 **(I) Youth and Conversion. (A) Paul's Youth.** The date of Paul's birth is unknown, but it must have occurred in the first decade AD. Since he is said to have been a youth (*neanias*) at the stoning of Stephen (Acts 7:58), i.e., between 24 and 40 (cf. Diogenes Laërtius 8.10; Philo, *Cherubim* 114), and he calls himself an old man (*presbytēs*) in Phlm 9, his birth could not have been later than AD 10.

Paul was born in the Hellenistic town of Tarsus in Cilicia (Acts 22:3). He came from Jewish parents who traced their descent back to the tribe of Benjamin (Rom 11:1; Phil 3:5). According to Acts 23:16 he had a sister. From birth Paul enjoyed the status of a Roman citizen (Acts 22:25–29; 16:37; 23:27). Both the Hellenistic environment of Tarsus and the Jewish heritage of his family left their marks on the young Paul.

11 The origins of Tarsus are obscure. Greek legends ascribe the founding of the town to Perseus, Heracles, or Triptolemus; but it is also said to have been a Phoenician foundation. The first historical attestation of Tarsus is found inscribed on the 9th-cent. BC Black Obelisk of the Assyrian king, Shalmaneser III (1.138; cf. D. D. Luckenbill, *ARAB* 1.207) who took "Tarzi" in the campaigns of his 26th regnal year. In the 4th cent., Xenophon (*Anab.* 1.2,23) called it a "great and prosperous city," and its Gk coins from the 5th and 4th cents. reveal its early Hellenization. During the Seleucid period its name was changed to Antioch on the Cydnus, but later, when it regained its autonomy, the old name was reassumed. The heavy Hellenization of the town is attributed to Antiochus IV Epiphanes (175–164 BC), who is also said to have established a colony of Jews there (*ca.* 171) to foster commerce and industry.

In 66 BC, when Pompey reorganized Asia Minor after his conquests, he set up the *provincia Ciliciae* and made Tarsus its capital. Later on freedom, immunity, and citizenship were granted to the town by Mark Antony; and Augustus confirmed these rights. Paul's status as a *civis Romanus* is undoubtedly related to this free status of the city. Tarsus was known as a center of culture, philosophy, and education. Strabo (*Geography* 14.673) tells of its schools, which surpassed those of Athens and of Alexandria. The students were native Cilicians, not foreigners, as was the case in Athens and Alexandria—an indication of the cultural level of the native populace. The Stoic political philosopher, Athenodorus Cananites, famed as the counselor and teacher of the Emperor Augustus, retired to Tarsus in 15 BC. There he was given the task of revising the city's democratic and civic processes. Other philosophers, too, both Stoic and Epicurean, settled in Tarsus and taught there. Famous Romans visited the town: Cicero, Julius Caesar, Augustus. It was there that Mark Antony accorded a royal reception to Cleopatra as she disembarked. This, then, was the city where Paul was born and where he probably received some of his early education—hence his boast that he was a "citizen of no mean town" (Acts 21:39).

12 Coming from a Hellenized town such as Tarsus, Paul knew Greek (cf. Acts 21:37); his letters reveal that he could write it rather well. There are traces of the rhetoric of Stoic diatribe in his writings (→ Pauline Theology, 79:11), showing that he must have had at least some Gk education. Although he calls himself a "Hebrew" (Phil 3:6), he used the Gk OT (usually the LXX) as a Diaspora Jew would. It is not easy to assess Paul's Hellenistic background, but it cannot be dismissed.

(Böhlig, H., *Die Geisteskultur von Tarsus* [Göttingen, 1913]. Welles, C. Bradford, "Hellenistic Tarsus," *MUSJ* 38 [1962] 41–75. Ruge, W., "Tarsos," PW 2 Series 4/2 [1932] 2413–39.)

13 But Paul boasted of being a "Jew" (Acts 21:39; 22:3), an "Israelite" (2 Cor 11:22; Rom 11:1), a "Hebrew, born of Hebrews..., and as to the Law a Pharisee" (Phil 3:6; cf. Acts 23:6). "I lived as a Pharisee according to the strictest party of our religion" (Acts 26:5; cf. Gal 1:14). Moreover, he was "educated at the feet of Gamaliel" (Acts 22:3). This refers to Rabbi Gamaliel I, the Elder, whose *floruit* in Jerusalem was *ca.* AD 20–50. In calling himself a "Hebrew" (*Hebraios*), Paul probably meant that he was a Gk-speaking Jew who could also speak Aramaic (see C. F. D. Moule, *ExpT* 70 [1958–59] 100–102; cf. Acts 21:40; 26:14). Jerome records the rumor that Paul's family came from Gischala in Judea (*In Ep. ad Philem.* 23–24; *PL* 26.653). Indeed, if one accepts W. C. van Unnik's thesis (*Tarsus or Jerusalem: The City of Paul's Youth* [London, 1962]), then most of Paul's early training took place in Jerusalem itself: "I am a Jew, born in Tarsus of Cilicia, brought up in this city [Jerusalem], and educated at the feet of Gamaliel" (Acts 22:3). This would imply that Paul's native tongue was actually Aramaic, and that his mode of thought was Semitic. There is much to be said for this thesis, but it still does not adequately explain the important Hellenistic mark of Paul's culture and outlook.

14 Paul's training at the feet of Gamaliel suggests that he was preparing to be a rabbi. According to J. Jeremias (*ZNW* 25 [1926] 310–12; *ZNW* 28 [1929] 321–23), Paul was at his conversion not merely a rabbinical disciple (*talmîd ḥākām*) but a recognized teacher with the right to make legal decisions. This status is presupposed in the role he played in going to Damascus (Acts 9:1–2; 22:5; 26:12); such authority would only be given to someone qualified. It seems to be confirmed by the vote that Paul cast against the Christians (Acts 26:10), apparently as a member of the Sanhedrin. From this Jeremias concludes that, since the age of 40 was required for rabbinical ordination, Paul was converted in middle age, and also that Paul was married because marriage was required of rabbis. Consequently, when Paul wrote 1 Cor 7:8, "I say to the unmarried and the widowed, 'It is good for them to remain as I am,'" Paul would be classing himself with the widowed (*chērais*) rather than with the unmarried (*agamois*); cf. 1 Cor 9:5 (Paul would not have remarried). However, the evidence for this interesting view is not such as to be entirely convincing and raises many further questions. (See E. Fascher, *ZNW* 28 [1929] 62–69.)

15 If Paul had much of his early education in Jerusalem and had sat "at the feet of Gamaliel," did he know Jesus? He never gives any indication in his letters that he did. Not even 2 Cor 5:16 necessarily implies that he did: "Even though we once regarded Christ from a human point of view, we no longer regard him in this way." This most likely refers to Paul's attitude toward Jesus when Paul was persecuting the Church; undoubtedly he knew what Jesus stood for and what his disciples were claiming on his behalf. Otherwise it would be difficult to explain his ardent persecution of the new "Way."

(Jungel, E., *Paulus und Jesus* [*HUzT* 2; Tübingen, 1964]. Ridderbos, H., *Paul and Jesus* [Phila., 1958].)

16 **(B) Paul's Conversion.** The date of Paul's conversion is not certain, but it is related to the martyrdom of Stephen, when the witnesses piled their garments at the feet of Saul (Acts 7:58; cf. 22:20) so that he might guard them. This martyrdom and the subsequent persecution of the Church finds a plausible setting in the change of prefects in AD 36. This date fits in well with the 14 years that elapse between Paul's conversion and the "Council" visit to Jerusalem (Gal 2:1; AD 49). However, some commentators would rather date the conversion in AD 33, adding together the 3 years of Gal 1:18 and the 14 years of Gal 2:1 (see J. Finegan, *Biblical Chronology*, 321).

Paul himself and Luke in Acts both describe the experience on the road to Damascus as the turning point in the Apostle's career. It was an encounter with the Risen Lord (*Kyrios*) that made Paul adopt a new way of life; it was the experience that turned Paul the Pharisee into Paul the apostle. For the significance of this event in Paul's understanding of Christ and his gospel → Pauline Theology, 79:12–13.

17 Paul gives an account of the event in Gal 1:13–17 from his own apologetic and polemic standpoint. Three other accounts are given in Acts (9:3–19; 22:6–16; 26:12–18), all of which stress the overwhelming and unexpected character of the experience, which came in the midst of his persecution of the Christians. Although there are variants about certain details in the three accounts (whether the companions stood by speechless or fell to the ground; whether they heard the voice or not—and although Jesus addresses Paul "in the 'Hebrew' language," he quotes a Gk proverb [Acts 26:14]), the essential message conveyed to Paul is the same. All three accounts agree on this: "Saul, Saul, why do you persecute me?"—"Who are you, Lord?"—"I am Jesus (of Nazareth) whom you are persecuting." The variants may be due to the different sources of Luke's information.

18 Paul himself wrote of that experience that God had been pleased to reveal His Son to him so that he might preach the good news of him to the Gentiles (Gal 1:15–16). It was an experience that he never forgot, and to which he always associated his apostolic commission. "Am I not an apostle? Have I not seen Jesus our Lord?" (1 Cor 9:1; cf. 15:8). That revelation of Jesus the Lord on the road to Damascus proved to be the decisive factor dominating the rest of his life. For the sake of Christ he "became all things to all men" (1 Cor 9:22). As a result of it he became "the servant of Christ" (Gal 1:10; Rom 1:1; etc.), like the great servants of Yahweh in the OT (Moses, 2 Kgs 18:12; Joshua, Jgs 2:8; David, Ps 78:70), and possibly even like the Servant of Yahweh himself (Is 49:1; cf. Gal 1:15).

(Darby, J. H., "The Conversion of a Pharisee," *Scr* 6 [1953] 3–8. Lilly, J., "The Conversion of St. Paul: The Validity of His Testimony to the Resurrection of Jesus Christ," *CBQ* 6 [1944] 180–204. Pfaff, E., *Die Bekehrung des hl. Paulus in der Exegese des 20. Jahrhunderts* [Rome, 1942]. Stanley, D. M., "Paul's Conversion in Acts: Why Three Accounts?" *CBQ* 15 [1953] 315–38; "The Theme of the Servant of Yahweh in Primitive Christian Soteriology and Its Transposition by St. Paul," *CBQ* 16 [1954] 385–425. Wikenhauser, A., "Die Wirkung der Christophanie vor Damaskus auf Paulus und seine Begleiter nach den Berichten der Apostelgeschichte," *Bib* 33 [1952] 313–23.)

19 **(II) Paul's Visit(s) to Jerusalem.** After Paul's experience on the road to Damascus, Ananias cured his blindness by imposing hands on him. Paul was baptized and remained in Damascus "for some days" (Acts 9:19).

At this point in the reconstruction of Paul's life we meet with a very difficult problem: the relationship of the events recounted in Gal 1:15–2:14 to the account in Acts. Since the available data are so meager, we can never hope for a fully convincing solution. We adopt the one that has been used often in the past, and modify it slightly. It admits to the identification of Paul's first visit to Jerusalem (Gal 1:18) with Acts 9:26–29, and to the identification of the "Council" visit (Gal 2:1–10) with Acts 15:3–12.

20 Not long after his conversion Paul went to Arabia (Gal 1:17); strangely enough, Luke makes no mention of this in Acts. Most likely *Arabia* means the Nabatean kingdom of Aretas IV Philopatris in Transjordan. The purpose of his withdrawal is unknown. Commentators have speculated about it: for some, Paul withdrew in solitude and meditation to prepare himself for the coming ministry; for others, he journeyed in pilgrimage to Mt. Sinai, to the mountain of the Law, before he would declare it abrogated; for others, he preached Christ in Arabia. Whatever he did, his sojourn was short, and this is probably the reason why Luke omits it. It would best fit into his account between Acts 9:21 and 22.

21 After returning from Arabia (possibly in the spring of AD 37), Paul spent about "three years" in Damascus (Gal 1:18). This period corresponds to the "considerable time" of Acts 9:23. During his stay he confounded the Damascene Jews with proofs that Jesus was the Messiah, and when it drew to a close, he already had acquired disciples of his own. It is not unlikely that at this time Paul came under the influence of Essenes who still dwelt in the Damascene area (see J. Daniélou, *Études* 293 [1957] 221; cf. R. E. Osbourne, *CanJT* 10 [1964] 15–24). Although Paul insists on his Pharisaic background and never mentions any connection with Essenes—nor does Acts, for that matter—the number of significant parallels in his letters to passages in QL (especially in relation to dualism, angels, the "mystery" of God, and the gift of uprightness) suggests that at some point or other in his career he came into contact with Essenes or converted Essenes. (See P. Benoit, *NTS* 7 (1960–61) 288–95; *TD* 11 (1963) 167–72.) Finally Jewish opposition, supported by the ethnarch of King Aretas IV in Damascus (2 Cor 11:32), made Paul leave the city. His flight was arranged by his disciples who lowered him over the city wall in a basket. Making his way to Jerusalem, he visited the town for the first time since his conversion (Acts 9:26; Gal 1:18). This took place *ca.* 40. Barnabas allayed the natural suspicions of the Jerusalem Christians about Paul and saw that he was accepted (Acts 9:27).

22 The purpose of this visit is stated in Gal 1:18 as *historēsai Kēphan*, the meaning of which is debated: "To get information from Cephas," or "to visit Cephas" (→ Letter Gal, 49:15). It is unlikely that he did not compare notes with Peter and James about his preaching. During his visit Paul experienced the ecstasy in the Temple mentioned in Acts 22:17. A Hellenist plot against him eventually made him withdraw from Jerusalem to Tarsus (Acts 9:30), "to the regions of Syria and Cilicia" (Gal 1:21). Paul apparently remained at Tarsus from 40 to 44, but nothing is known of his activities during this period. In this time he probably had the vision to which he refers in 2 Cor 12:2–4 (*ca.* AD 43–44). His stay in Tarsus ended with a visit from Barnabas who took him back to Antioch, where he stayed "a whole year" (Acts 11:25–26), engaged in the evangelization of the town.

23 During this Antiochene apostolate a prophet named Agabus came from Jerusalem, announcing an imminent famine (Acts 11:28). This announcement inspired the Antiochene Christians to take up a collection and send it to the poor of the Jerusalem church. This incident must be related to the widespread famine that affected the eastern Mediterranean in the reign of the Emperor Claudius (Acts 11:28), and Palestine in particular about AD 46 (→ History of Israel, 75:154).

24 Paul's visit to Jerusalem, as he brought the collection, is mentioned in Acts 11:29–30 and 12:25; in the latter case the reference is enigmatic and the text is corrupt (→ Acts, 45:62). Since the "Famine Visit" receives no attention in Gal, the question has been raised whether it was a real visit, distinct from others (e.g., the "Council" visit in Acts 15). Have Luke's sources of information, being multiple and containing references to numerous visits of Paul to Jerusalem, been understood by him as separate and distinct visits, when some of them actually refer to one historical visit (e.g., 11:29–30; 12:25; 15:3)? It is unlikely that a satisfying answer to this question will ever be found; but since the text of Acts is composite, conflated of several sources, we must be careful not to adopt an oversimplified solution (see J. Dupont, *The Sources of Acts* [London, 1964]; P. Benoit, *Bib* 40 [1959] 778–92; → Acts 45:6). At any rate, if the "Famine Visit" is to be regarded as a distinct visit, the best date for it would be *ca.* AD 46; on that occasion, Paul's second visit, he would have stayed in Jerusalem only very briefly before returning to Antioch.

25 **(III) Pauline Missions.** This covers the period AD 46–58, the most active years in Paul's life as he preached the gospel in Asia Minor and Greece.

(A) Mission I (AD 46–49; Acts 13:3–14:26). The account in Acts is obviously abbreviated, being confined only to essentials; a fleeting reference is found in 2 Tm 3:11. Paul's mission was inaugurated by the Spirit who designated him and Barnabas for it. The prophets and teachers of the Antiochene church imposed hands on them (Paul's ordination?) and sent them off, accompanied by John Mark, Barnabas' cousin (Col 4:10). The precedence given to Barnabas' name in the first part of the account suggests that he was the real leader at the start.

26 Departing from Seleucia, the port of Antioch in Syria, they headed for Cyprus and passed through the island from Salamis to Paphos. Here Paul made an illustrious convert in the proconsul Sergius Paulus (Acts 13:7–12). Unfortunately the time of his proconsulate cannot be dated exactly. From Paphos the missionaries sailed to Perga in Pamphylia on the southern coast of central Asia Minor. There John Mark deserted Barnabas and Paul, to the latter's great disappointment, and returned to Jerusalem. Paul and Barnabas made their way inland to the towns of southern Galatia: to Pisidian Antioch, Iconium, Lystra, and Derbe. In Antioch Paul preached first to the Jews in their synagogue, as was his wont, and when he was openly resisted asserted his intention of returning henceforth to the Gentiles (Acts 14:48–50). After evangelizing the area and meeting with opposition in each town, Paul and Barnabas retraced their steps from Derbe through Lystra, Iconium, and Pisidian Antioch to Perga; they sailed from Attalia for Antioch in Syria, where Paul spent some time with the Christians (Acts 14:28).

27 The many conversions Paul had made during the three years of Mission I brought problems to the nascent Church. In particular, the relation of Gentile Christians to the older Jewish converts was a burning issue that had to be settled. Were the Gentile converts to be circumcised? Were they to observe the Mosaic Law? Were they to adhere to Pharisaic prescriptions in dietary matters? This issue was acute in the Antiochene church when Paul returned at the end of Mission I.

(Bérard, J., "Les itinéraires de Saint Paul en Asie Mineure," *RevArch* 5 [1935] 60–70. Campbell, T. H., "Paul's 'Missionary Journeys' as Reflected in His Letters," *JBL* 74 [1955] 80–87. Metzger, H., *Les routes de Saint Paul dans l'Orient grec* [Neuchâtel, 1954].)

28 **(B) "Council" Visit** (AD 49). During Paul's brief sojourn in Antioch at the end of Mission I, Judaizers (most likely converts of Pharisaic background) arrived there and began to teach that circumcision was necessary for salvation. This led to a dispute between them and Paul and Barnabas. The Antiochene church decided to send Paul, Barnabas, and some others (Titus [Gal 2:1]) to Jerusalem to consult the apostles and elders for a decision about the status of the Gentile converts. This visit to Jerusalem is reckoned by Paul in Gal 2:1 as his second since his conversion ("once again in fourteen years"). In Gal he states that it was occasioned by a "revelation," a detail not mentioned in Acts 15:2. This visit resulted in the so-called Council of Jerusalem.

29 The subject matter of this "Council" must be carefully determined. From Gal 2:1–10 one gathers that the sole issue brought up and settled at it was circumcision. The same impression is derived from Acts 15:6–12. It was an issue with important doctrinal implications: Does salvation depend on faith in Christ, or on faith *with* circumcision and observance of the Mosaic Law? The disciplinary question of the observance of dietary prescriptions (Acts 15:13–29) was another issue, which should be carefully distinguished from the problem of circumcision (→ 31 below).

30 Upon arrival in Jerusalem, Paul and Barnabas met with the whole Jerusalem church, including the apostles and elders. Here too, converted Pharisees ("the false brothers" of Gal 2:4) insisted on the circumcision of Gentile Christians and their obligation to observe the Mosaic Law. Paul resisted such a form of Christianity. This open conflict caused the "apostles and elders" (possibly the "men of repute" in Gal 2:2) to convene to look into the matter. After considerable discussion of the problem, Peter's voice prevailed. The assembly acquiesced in his decision against the obligatory circumcision of the Gentile converts and their adherence to the Mosaic Law. The Jerusalem "Council" thus freed the young Church from its Jewish roots and opened it up to the world apostolate then confronting it. Paul's position was vindicated; the "men of repute" added nothing to his Gospel (Gal 2:6).

31 **(C) Antioch Incident** (Autumn AD 49). After the Jerusalem "Council" Paul went to Antioch, and before long Peter followed him. At first both of them ate with Gentile Christians. But soon "some people from

James" (Gal 2:12), undoubtedly Christians with pronounced Pharisaic leanings, arrived and were critical of Peter for eating with the Gentile converts. Peter yielded to their criticism and separated himself from the Gentiles; his action led many other Jewish Christians, even Barnabas, to do the same. Although Paul recognized his position in relation to Peter he felt obliged to protest, and "opposed him to his face" (Gal 2:11). He showed Peter that he was violating his principles and not "walking straight according to the truth of the gospel" (2:13). In Gal, Paul does not directly state that he was successful, but it seems to be implied. And yet the problem of Jewish dietary prescriptions and Gentile converts persisted.

The sequence of events is not certain here; we must assume that Paul departed soon after on Mission II, having separated from Barnabas who eventually went off with John Mark on his own mission. For during his second and third missionary journeys Paul apparently never knew about James' letter on dietary matters. He does not refer to it in Gal, when there would have been occasion for it; apparently he first learned of it on his return to Jerusalem in AD 58: James informed him that he had sent such a letter (Acts 21:25).

32 **(D) Jerusalem Decree on Dietary Matters** (Acts 15:13–29). Paul's opposition to Peter did not solve the problem in the Antiochene church as to how the Gentiles were to conduct themselves with the Jewish Christians. Emissaries were again sent to Jerusalem, presumably in Peter's absence. The decision reached by James who convened with the apostles and elders present was sent in the form of a letter to the local churches of Antioch, Syria, and Cilicia.

33 Chapter 15 of Acts is very problematic. Most likely Luke has telescoped two incidents that are really distinct in subject and in time. This judgment is based on the following details: *First*, the chapter is composite. Verses 1 and 2 are a literary suture joining information from different sources. Verse 34 is absent in the best Gk mss., but added in the Western and Lat textual tradition in an effort to explain where Silas was at the beginning of Mission II. When v. 34 is omitted, as it must be, the location of Silas is a real problem. When does he join Paul on Mission II? *Second*, who is Symeon (Acts 15:14)? Usually he is identified with Simon Peter, who elsewhere in Acts is called either *Petros* (15:7) or *Simōn Petros* (10:5, 18,32), but never *Symeōn*. This name is given to Peter only in 2 Pt 1:1; but even there the ms. tradition is not constant, and P^{72}, the oldest text of 2 Pt, reads *Simōn*. Moreover, John Chrysostom, who reflects the traditions of the Antiochene church, did not identify Symeon with Peter; he mentions that some even identified him with the old man of Lk 2:25 (*In Act. Ap. hom.* 33.1; *PG* 60.239)! The Symeon of 15:14 was probably originally understood as Symeon Niger, one of the prophets or teachers of the Antiochene church (Acts 13:1). He was apparently one of the emissaries sent by it to consult James and the Jerusalem church about the problem of the dietary laws. *Third*, the lack of harmony between Peter's speech (Acts 15:7–11), which deals with circumcision and the Mosaic Law, and the purported summary of it made by James (Acts 15:13–21) in which the subject is mainly the disciplinary problem of the avoidance of certain foods and illicit sexual unions. Such reasons as these suggest that ch. 15 is a conflation of reports about two distinct incidents—the Jerusalem "Council" handling circumcision and the Jerusalem "Decree" (or "Letter") handling the problem of dietary laws in the local churches of Antioch, Syria, and Cilicia.

34 As a result of the consultation of the Jerusalem church a letter was sent by James, recommending that Gentile Christians abstain at least from meat sacrificed to idols, from blood, from the meat of strangled animals, and from illicit sexual unions. James sent it with Judas Barsabbas and Silas to Antioch and to Paul and Barnabas. Acts 15:35 mentions that Paul and Barnabas had been spending some time in Antioch teaching and preaching, but we must suppose that this refers to the time immediately following the "Council." As the Jerusalem letter is sent, it is *presumed* that Paul and Barnabas are still in Antioch; but Paul had apparently left, because he never learned about the Jerusalem letter until later (Acts 21:25). (For further exegetical details regarding the interpretation of James' letter, see Acts 15:22,25; 16:4; → Acts, 45:72–80.)

(Benoit, P., "La deuxième visite du Saint Paul à Jérusalem," *Bib* 40 [1959] 778–92. Dupont, J., "Pierre et Paul à Antioche et à Jérusalem," *RSR* 45 (1957) 42–60. Funk, R. W., "The Enigma of the Famine Visit," *JBL* 75 [1956] 130–36. Giet, S., "Le second voyage de Saint Paul à Jérusalem," *RScRel* 25 [1951] 265–69; "L'assemblée apostolique et le décret de Jérusalem. Qui était Siméon?" *RSR* 39 [1951] 203–20; "Les trois premiers voyages de Saint Paul à Jérusalem," *RSR* 41 [1953] 321–47; "Nouvelles remarques sur les voyages de Saint Paul à Jérusalem," *RScRel* 31 [1957] 329–42. Rigaux, B., *Saint Paul et ses lettres*, 103–23.)

35 **(E) Mission II** (AD 49–52; Acts 15:40–18:22). Paul refused to take John Mark with him on Mission II because of his earlier desertion. Instead Silas (Silvanus) accompanied Paul. Setting out from Antioch, Paul made his way through Syria and Cilicia to the towns of southern Galatia, Derbe and Lystra (where he took Timothy as a companion, Acts 16:1–3). From there he passed through Phrygia to northern Galatia (Pessinus, Ancyra, and Tavium) and founded new churches. Prevented from proceeding to Bithynia, he moved on from Galatia into Mysia and Troas. Here he was joined by Luke—or at least Luke's diary begins at this point (Acts 16:10–17, the "We-Sections"; → Acts, 45:6).

In response to a dream-vision Paul passed over to Neapolis, the port of Philippi, and the latter became the site of his first Christian church in Europe. After imprisonment and flogging at Philippi because he had exorcised a slave girl who had been a source of much gain to her masters, he passed on to Thessalonica (Acts 17:1). His short stay in Thessalonica was occupied with evangelization and controversy with the Jews; it ended with his flight to Beroea (Acts 17:10), and eventually to Athens (17:15). Here Paul tried to interest the Athenians, renowned for their love of novel ideas, in the gospel of the Risen Jesus (Acts 17:22–31). But he failed: "We'll listen to you on this topic some other time" (17:32). After this disappointment Paul moved on to Corinth, at that time one of the most important towns in the Mediterranean world. Here he lived with Aquila and Priscilla (Acts 18:2–3), Jewish Christians recently expelled from Rome by an edict of Claudius (→ 6 above). During his stay in Corinth, which lasted for 18 months, he converted many Jews and Greeks and founded a vigorous, predominantly Gentile church. Toward the beginning of AD 51 Paul wrote his letters to the THESSALONIANS. Near the end of his stay Paul was haled by Jewish opponents before the proconsul L. Junius Gallio who dismissed the case, regarding it as a matter of questions about words (Acts 18:15). After some time Paul withdrew from Corinth, sailing from its port of Cenchreae for Ephesus and Caesarea Maritima. After paying a visit to the Jerusalem church (Acts 18:22), he went to Antioch, where he stayed well over a year (possibly from the autumn of 52 until the spring of 54).

36 **(F) Mission III** (AD 54–57; Acts 18:23–21:17). Leaving Antioch, Paul traveled overland once again through northern Galatia and Phrygia to Ephesus. The capital of Asia became the center of his missionary activity for the next three years (Acts 20:31), and for "two years" he lectured in the hall of Tyrannus (19:10). Shortly after his arrival in Ephesus Paul wrote his letter to the churches of GALATIA (*ca.* 54). To this missionary period also belongs the letter to the PHILIPPIANS, written most likely from an Ephesian imprisonment *ca.* 56 (→ Letter Phil, 50:5–6). During the spring of 57 reports came to Paul about the condition of the Corinthian church. To cope with the situation there—doubts, factions, resentment of Paul himself, scandals—he wrote at least four letters, of which only two survive, and these probably in composite or fragmentary form. One preceded 1 Cor (see 1 Cor 5:9), warning the Corinthians against associating with immoral Christians. Then, to comment on reports and to answer questions sent to him by the CORINTHIANS, Paul wrote 1 Cor shortly before Pentecost of 57. This letter, however, was not well received and his relations with the faction-torn church of Corinth worsened. The situation called forth a hasty visit to Corinth (2 Cor 12:14; 13:1–2; 2:1 ["a painful visit"]; 12:21), which really accomplished nothing. On his return to Ephesus Paul wrote to the Corinthians a third time, a letter composed "with many tears" (2 Cor 2:3–4,9; 7:8,12; 10:1,9). Finally, Paul sent Titus to visit the Corinthians personally in an attempt to smooth out the situation.

37 During Titus' absence the revolt of the Ephesian silversmiths occurred (Acts 19:23–20:1). Paul's preaching of the new Christian "Way" incited Demetrius, a maker of miniature silver shrines of Artemis of Ephesus, to lead a riotous mob into the theater in protest against Paul and the spread of Christianity. This prompted Paul's decision to leave Ephesus and to set out for Macedonia. He met Titus in Macedonia (possibly at Philippi) and learned the consoling news that a reconciliation between him and the Corinthians had been effected. From Macedonia Paul wrote to the CORINTHIAN CHURCH a fourth time, the second canonical letter (autumn 57). It is not possible to say whether he proceeded immediately to Corinth or went from Macedonia into Illyricum first for a brief visit of evangelization (cf. Rom 15:19). At any rate, Paul arrived in Corinth—his third visit there—probably in the winter (December) of 57 and stayed for three months in Achaia (Acts 20:2–3; cf. 1 Cor 16:5–6; 2 Cor 1:16).

38 Paul had by this time been thinking of returning to Jerusalem. Mindful of the injunction of the "Council" that the poor should be remembered, Paul saw to it that his Gentile churches took up a collection for the poor of Jerusalem. This was done in the churches of Galatia, Macedonia, and Achaia (1 Cor 16:1; Rom 15:25–26). He planned to take it to Jerusalem and thus terminate his evangelization of the eastern Mediterranean world. He intended to visit Rome afterward (Rom 15:22–24) and from there to go to Spain and the West. During his three-month stay in Achaia Paul wrote the letter to the ROMANS (probably from Corinth, at the beginning of 58). Then when spring came, he decided to sail from Corinth for Syria. As he was about to embark, a plot was hatched against him by some Jews and he resolved to return overland, by way of Macedonia.

39 Disciples from Beroea, Thessalonica, Derbe, and Ephesus accompanied him. They spent the Passover of 58 in Philippi. After the feast Paul left by ship for Troas and journeyed overland to Assos, where he took ship for Mitylene. Skirting the coast of Asia Minor, he sailed from Chios to Samos, then to Miletus where he addressed the elders of the Ephesian church whom he had summoned there (Acts 20:17–35). He was not deterred by their prediction of his coming imprisonment, but sailed on to Cos, Rhodes, Patara in Lycia, Tyre in Phoenicia, Ptolemais, and Caesarea Maritima. An overland journey brought him to Jerusalem, which he had hoped to reach in time for the feast of Pentecost, 58 (Acts 20:16; 21:17).

40 **(IV) Paul's Imprisonment.** This covers several years after AD 58, a period of trial for Paul as he endured a long captivity and came to the end of his life.

(A) Last Visit to Jerusalem and Arrest (AD 58). Arriving in Jerusalem, Paul and his companions paid their respects to James in the presence of the elders of that church (Acts 21:18). James immediately realized that Paul's presence in Jerusalem would cause a disturbance among the Jewish Christians. He therefore counseled Paul to join four men who were to go through the ceremony of the Nazirite vow and to pay their expenses as a gesture of good will toward Jewish Christians. Paul consented and the seven-day ceremonial period was almost over when he was seen in the Temple precincts by Jews from the province of Asia. They accused him of advocating the violation of the Mosaic Law and of having defiled the sanctity of the Temple by bringing a Greek into it. They set upon him, dragged him from the Temple and tried to kill him. He was saved, however, by the tribune of the Roman cohort stationed in the Fortress Antonia. The tribune eventually put Paul under protective arrest (Acts 22:27) and brought him before the Sanhedrin the next day. But fear of the Jews made the tribune send Paul to the procurator of Judea, Antonius Felix, who resided in Caesarea Maritima (23:23–33). Felix, who expected Paul to bribe him (24:26), kept him in prison for two years, 58–60.

41 **(B) Appeal to Caesar; Journey to Rome** (AD 60). When the new procurator Porcius Festus arrived (probably in 60), Paul "appealed to Caesar," i.e., requested trial in Rome (Acts 25:11), because of his Roman citizenship. Festus had to grant the request. Escorted by a Roman centurion (and by Luke, as the "We-Sections" indicate), he set sail from Caesarea Maritima for Sidon and passed Cyprus to come to Myra in Lycia. In late autumn of 60 they left Myra on an Alexandrian ship, expecting bad weather (Acts 27:9). Their route took them first to Cnidus (on the southern coast of Asia Minor), then southward "under the lee of Crete off Salmone" as far as Fair Havens, near the Cretan town of Lasea (27:7–8). When they tried to reach the harbor of Phoenix, a northeaster blew up and carried them for days across the Adriatic to Malta, where they were finally shipwrecked (28:1).

42 After spending the winter on Malta, Paul and his escort sailed for Syracuse in Sicily, then for Rhegium (modern Reggio di Calabria), and lastly for Puteoli (modern Pozzuoli, near Naples). Their overland journey to Rome took them through Appii Forum and Tres Tabernae (Acts 28:15). Paul arrived in the capital of the empire in the spring of 61, and for two years he was kept in house arrest (61–63) with a soldier to guard him (28:16). This situation, however, did not deter him from summoning Roman Jews to his quarters and evangelizing them (28:17–28). During this house arrest Paul wrote his CAPTIVITY LETTERS (Phlm, Col, and Eph). (See F. F. Bruce, "St. Paul in Rome," *BJRylL* 46 (1963–64) 326–45.)

43 **(C) End of Paul's Life.** Acts ends with the brief account of Paul's house arrest. His arrival in Rome and his unhindered preaching of the gospel there form the climax to the story of the spread of the good news from Jerusalem to the capital of the civilized world of the time—Rome symbolizing "the end of the earth" (Acts 1:8). But this was not the end of Paul's life. The mention of "two whole years" (28:30) does not imply that he died immediately thereafter, no matter what interpretation is given to the enigmatic end of Acts.

If the PASTORAL LETTERS were regarded as genuine Pauline writings (→ Pastoral Letters, 57:6), they would have been composed by Paul after his Roman house arrest. They would suggest that Paul visited the East again, Ephesus, Macedonia, and Greece; and 1 Tm and Ti would have been written from Macedonia (*ca.* 65). Knowing that the end of his life was near, Paul set up Titus as the head of the Cretan church and Timothy as the head of the Ephesian church. The two letters would have been written to these disciples and their churches—2 Tm would be Paul's last will, written as he was about to face death. It suggests that he may have been arrested at Troas (4:13) and brought to Rome again (1:17), where this letter was written in prison (1:8,16–17; 2:9), *ca.* 67.

44 For other details of the end of Paul's life we are dependent on later ecclesiastical tradition, which became heavily embellished with legend. It is difficult to decide in particular whether Paul ever visited Spain or whether this is merely an historicization of his plans expressed in Rom 15:24,28. The tradition tells us that Paul, freed after two years of house arrest, went to Spain. Clement of Rome (*1 Cor.* 5.7) records that Paul "taught the whole world uprightness and traveled to the extreme west (*epi to terma tēs dyseōs elthōn*). And after he had borne witness before the authorities, he was taken from this world and went to the holy place, having proved himself the greatest model of endurance." Clement's testimony (*ca.* 95) suggests the visit to Spain, another trial, and martyrdom. The Muratorian fragment (lines 38–39; *EB* 4; *ca.* 180) implies that the last part of Acts, recounting "the departure of Paul from the City [Rome] as he set out for Spain" (...*profectione Pauli ab Urbe ad Spaniam proficiscentis*), has been lost. Eusebius (*HE* 2.22,2) is the first to mention Paul's second imprisonment in Rome and martyrdom under Nero: "After defending himself, [Paul] was again sent on the ministry of preaching, and coming a second time to the same city suffered martyrdom under Nero. During this imprisonment he wrote the second epistle to Timothy, indicating at the same time that his first defense had taken place and that his martyrdom was at hand." Eusebius further quotes Dionysius of Corinth (*ca.* 170), who had stated that Peter and Paul "were martyred at the same time" (*HE* 2.25,8). Tertullian (*De praescrip.* 36) compares Paul's death to that of John (the Baptist), i.e., by beheading. The Eusebian testimony about Paul's death in the persecution of Nero is generally accepted. This persecution lasted, however, from the summer of 64 to the emperor's death (9 June 68), and it is difficult to pinpoint the year of Paul's martyrdom. The notice of Dionysius of Corinth that Peter and Paul "were martyred at the same time" (*kata ton auton kairon*) has often been understood to mean in the same year. But the preferred year for the death of Paul is 67, toward the end of Nero's persecution, as Eusebius' account seems to suggest. This chronology is not, however, without its difficulties.

45 Paul was buried on the Via Ostiensis, near the site of the modern basilica of San Paolo fuori le Mura. In 258, when Christian tombs in Rome were threatened with desecration in the persecution of Valerian, Paul's remains were transferred for a time to a place called *Ad Catacumbas* on the Appian Way. Later they were returned to their original resting place over which Constantine built his basilica.

47

NEW TESTAMENT EPISTLES

Joseph A. Fitzmyer, S.J.

BIBLIOGRAPHY

1 Champion, L., *Benedictions and Doxologies in the Epistles of Paul* (Oxford, 1935). Deissmann, A., *Bible Studies* (Edinburgh, 1901) 3–59; *Light from the Ancient East* (London, 1910). Eschlimann, J.-A., "La rédaction des épîtres pauliniennes d'après une comparaison avec les lettres profanes de son temps," *RB* 53 (1946) 185–96. Exler, F. X. J., *The Form of the Ancient Greek Letter: A Study in Greek Epistolography* (Washington, 1923). Fascher, E., "Briefliteratur, urchristliche," *RGG* 1 (1957) 1412–15. Finegan, J., "The Original Form of the Pauline Collection," *HarvTR* 49 (1956) 85–103. Lohmeyer, E., "Briefliche Grussüberschriften," *Probleme paulinischer Theologie* (Darmstadt, 1954) 9–29. Lyonnet, S., "De arte litteras exarandi apud antiquos," *VD* 34 (1956) 3–11. Mitton, C. L., *The Formation of the Pauline Corpus of Letters* (London, 1955). Roller, O., *Das Formular der paulinischen Briefe* (BWANT 58; Stuttgart, 1933). Schubert, P., *Form and Function of the Pauline Thanksgivings* (BZNW 20; Berlin, 1939). Stange, E., "Diktierpausen in den Paulusbriefen," *ZNW* 18 (1917) 109–17.

See also F-B 176–77; Guthrie, *NTI* 1, 282–94; Michaelis, 144–49; R-F, *INT* 383–87 (J. Cambier); R-T 1, 542–55 (A. Robert); Wik, *NTI* 346–50.

2 OUTLINE

GENERAL REMARKS

3 **(I) "Epistolē" as a Literary Form.** Of the 27 NT books 21 are called *epistolai*, whereas not one of the OT books is so designated. There are letters in the OT, but the use of this form of writing for a religious purpose, though it owes much to the popularity of the form in the Hellenistic world, becomes particularly prominent with Paul, who was imitated by later Christian writers.

In the OT, summaries of official correspondence in the time of the pre-exilic kings are given (2 Sm 11:14–15; 1 Kgs 21:8–10; 2 Kgs 5:5–6; 10:1–6; etc.). Further summaries are found in the exilic and post-exilic periods, but in the latter period, the summaries tend to preserve more the form of the ancient letter (Ezr 4:11–16,17–22; 7:12–26). In Est 9:20; 12:4 we find mention of a memorandum of Artaxerxes and of a letter about the feast of Purim; and the deuterocanonical parts of the book appropriately present the text of such documents, the result of literary effort in Greek. Similarly, Bar 6 preserves the so-called Epistle of Jeremy or Letter of Jeremiah (cf. Jer 29:1–23). The many letters preserved in Mc (1 Mc 5:10–13; 8:23–32; 10:18–20,25–45; 2 Mc 1:1–2:19; etc.), written by Jews, Roman officials, Seleucid rulers, and Spartans, deal mainly with national or political aspects of the lives of Palestinian Jews. In itself letter writing is an ancient practice, as attested in Egyptian and cuneiform literature antedating the OT (*ANET* 475–90). Although the religious use of the form is found in Jer 29:1–23, such use became prominent in NT times. Some NT letters, however, are no more specifically religious than many in the OT (Acts 15:23–29; 23:26–30).

4 **(II) "Letter" or "Epistle."** Since the comparative studies of A. Deissmann it has become customary to distinguish a "letter" from an "epistle." "A letter is something nonliterary, a means of communication between persons who are separated from each other. Confidential and personal in its nature, it is intended only for the person or persons to whom it is addressed, and not at all for the public or any kind of publicity" (*Light*, 218). Its style, tone, and form are often as free, intimate, and familiar as conversation; but it can also be an official letter intended for a group or several groups. Ancient "letters" exist in thousands of papyri from Egypt (A. S. Hunt and E. E. Edgar, *Select Papyri* [LCL; London, 1952]; cf. D. Brooke, *Private Letters Pagan and Christian* [London, 1929]). Most of the OT examples cited above are "letters."

"An epistle is an artistic literary form, just like the dialogue, the oration, or the drama. It has nothing in common with the letter except its form: apart from that one might venture the paradox that the epistle is the opposite of a real letter. The contents of an epistle are intended for publicity—they aim at interesting 'the public'" (Deissmann, *Light*, 220). The epistle is a careful literary composition, possibly but not necessarily occasioned by a concrete situation, and destined for a wide audience. Developed in Gk philosophical schools of the 4th cent. BC, it resembles a treatise, dialogue, or essay devoted to an instructive or polemical discussion of some theme. Ancient "epistles" are found in Seneca's *Ad Lucilium epistulae morales*, in Epicurus' epistles preserved by Diogenes Laërtius (*Lives of Eminent Philosophers*, bk. 10), and in such Jewish writings as *Aristeas* (in reality, an apologetic narrative; → Apocrypha, 68:32–33), Bar 6:1–73 (a homily), and 2 Mc 1:1–2:18. (See J. Moffatt, *Introduction to the Literature of the NT* [Edinburgh, 1918] 44–50.)

5 The NT *epistolai* constitute a corpus today. But this does not mean that they were originally intended to be "epistles." The private letters of famous litterateurs have become part of a country's literature, and the collection of Paul's letters did not radically change their character as epistles. Philemon is a biblical "book" for us today, but it was written as a letter. Nor does inspiration, by which the letters were destined by the Spirit for the edification of the Christian Church, radically alter the human author's destination of them to one person or group. Hence their literary form must be respected for what it is.

6 **(III) Ancient Letter Form.** Four parts are customarily distinguished in the contemporary Greco-Roman letter form: (1) *Opening Formula.* This is not the "address" (usually written on the outside of the folded papyrus), but the *praescriptio*—an elliptic sentence giving the name of the sender (nom.) and of the addressee (dat.) with a short greeting (usually *chairein* [an inf. with the stereotyped meaning, "Greetings"]). See 1 Mc 10:18,25; 11:30; etc.; in the NT only in Acts 15:23; 23:26; Jas 1:1. (2) *Thanksgiving.* A widespread custom called for an epistolary introduction expressing a religious or nonreligious sentiment of thanks. It often began with either *eucharistō* (I thank) or *charin echō* (I am grateful). (3) *Message.* The body of the letter. (4) *Final Greeting.* Usually *errōsō* (pl. *errōsthe*), "Goodbye" (lit. "be well"; cf. Lat *vale, valete*). (See 2 Mc 16:21,33,38; Acts 15:29 [and 23:30 in some mss].) In official letters the date was often added. The final greeting took the place of the modern signature; in the case of dictated letters it was sometimes written by the sender himself.

7 The form of contemporary Jewish letters, written either in Hebrew or Aramaic and derived from older Assyrian, Babylonian, or Canaanite models, was not very different from the Greco-Roman form. Although a thanksgiving rarely appears, the opening formula was either like the Greco-Roman form with *šālôm* (Peace) instead of *chairein* (see Mur 42,43,44,46), or more frequently a double sentence. The first part named the sender and the addressee ("To our lord Bagoas, the governor of Judah, your servants Yedoniah and his colleagues, the priests..."), and the second part expressed a blessing ("May the God of Heaven seek the welfare of our lord at all times" [see *ANET* 322, 491–92; cf. Dn 4:1; *2 Baruch* 78:2 in *APOT* 2,521; Str-B 1, 154, n. 2]).

NEW TESTAMENT LETTER WRITING

8 **(I) Form of the Pauline Letter.** The form of the Pauline letter shares features of the contemporary Greco-Roman and Jewish letters.

(A) Opening Formula. The *praescriptio* is normally an expansion of the Greco-Roman form, using Semitic elements. Paul (nom.) to X (dat.) with appropriate epithets in Semitic fashion to express the relations between him and the addressees. Co-senders (scribes?) are sometimes mentioned: Timothy (2 Cor 1:1; Phil 1:1; Phlm 1); Silvanus and Timothy (1–2 Thes 1:1); Sosthenes (1 Cor 1:1). Paul never uses simply *chairein*, but expresses a wish involving *charis kai eirēnē* (1 Thes 1:1) usually expanded: "Grace and peace be yours from God our Father and the Lord Jesus Christ" (2 Thes 1:2; Gal 1:3; Phil 1:2; etc.; cf. the modified form in 1 Tm 1:2; Ti 1:4; 2 Tm 1:2). At first sight, *charis kai eirēnē* looks like a Pauline adaptation or combination of the Greco-Roman *chairein* and the Jewish *šālôm*. But there is certainly more to it than this, for it uses the two notions of *charis* (covenant favor) and *eirēnē* (peace) that are rooted in the old priestly blessing of Nm 6:24–26. Again, *charis* has the Pauline connotation of the merciful bounty of God manifested in Christ Jesus (cf. Rom 5:1–11). The two words are Paul's summation of the *bona messianica* of the Christian era. Its solemnity suggests that it may even be a liturgical formula that has been adapted to epistolary introduction. These are the spiritual gifts that Paul normally sends to his readers. His formula occurs also in 2 Jn 3 and Ap 1:4; it is strangely infrequent in later Christian letters.

(B) Thanksgiving. In common with Greco-Roman letters most of Paul's letters have a thanksgiving. Structurally, it is usually a periodic sentence whose function is to "focus the epistolary situation, i.e., to introduce the vital theme of the letter" (Schubert, *Form and Function of the Pauline Thanksgivings*, 180). In Gal Paul replaces the thanksgiving with a rebuking *thaumazō* ("I am amazed..."; 1:6–9), which much more effectively sets the tone of that letter. In 2 Cor he appropriately makes the thanksgiving an extended blessing on the Corinthian church, striking the note of reconciliation with the congregation that caused him so much trouble—a note which is the burden of the letter. In Eph 1:3–14 an extended blessing precedes the thanksgiving (not voiced until 1:15–23). Titus completely lacks a thanksgiving. In this section Paul is usually at prayer, and although it resembles the Greco-Roman letter form, the sentiments uttered in it are often phrased in characteristic Jewish "eucharistic" formulas and sometimes recall the Qumran *Hôdāyôt* (Thanksgiving Psalms; → Apocrypha, 68:74). It is not always easy to decide where the thanksgiving ends and the body of the letter begins (so in 1 Thes, Col). (Among the Catholic Epistles only 1 Pt has a sort of thanksgiving [1:3–12], actually a blessing like 2 Cor and Eph.)

(C) Message. Undoubtedly reflecting early Christian preaching, which often joined an ethical exhortation to its doctrinal exposé, the body of the Pauline letter is usually divided into two sections, one *doctrinal* (discussing truths of the Christian message), the other *hortatory* or *paraenetic* (giving instructions for Christian conduct).

(D) Conclusion and Final Greeting. The final section of a Pauline letter often contains personal news or specific advice for individuals. It is followed by Paul's last greeting—never the ordinary Gk *errōsō*, but a characteristically Pauline blessing, "The grace of our Lord Jesus Christ be with you" (1 Thes 5:28; 2 Thes 3:18; Gal 6:18; Phil 4:23; 1 Cor 16:23; 2 Cor 13:13; Rom 16:20,24; Phlm 25); a shortened form is found in the later letters (Col 4:18; Eph 6:24; Ti 3:15; 1 Tm 6:21; 2 Tm 4:22 [cf. Heb 13:25]).

9 **(II) Paul's "Letters."** Having set up the categories of "letter" and "epistle," Deissmann classed Paul's writings as letters, not literary epistles. Although guilty of a certain oversimplification, he was basically correct, as is generally admitted today. Paul's writings are fundamentally "letters," compositions for an occasion, often produced in haste, and written mostly in complete independence of each other. Philemon is a private letter to an individual; Gal a letter addressed to a group of local churches that is imbued with Paul's personal concern for his converts. Also, 1 Cor, 1–2 Thes, Col, Phil, despite all the great truths they discuss, are basically "letters" handling concrete issues in the churches addressed. Much of the unintelligibility of 2 Cor is due to its genuine letter-like character; it contains many allusions no longer fully understood and yet so expressive of Paul's feeling in his relations with that church. The letters of the Pauline corpus that come closest to being an "epistle" are Rom, written to a church Paul had not yet evangelized, and Eph, an open letter or "encyclical." Both are the literary manifesto of Paul's gospel, his understanding of the message of Christ Jesus—what it meant for all men, Jew and Greek alike. It should be noted that the Pastorals also are less like "letters."

10 Although Deissmann's characterization was basically correct, it must be remembered that Paul rarely wrote the letters as a private individual. He was primarily an apostle, a missionary, a preacher. His letters were written to various communities and individuals to serve his missionary purpose of building up the Church. He used the letter form as a means of spreading his understanding of the Christian message and especially of applying it to the concrete problems that arose in areas he could not visit personally. The problems often served as the springboard for a broader, transcendent treatment of truths fundamental to Christian faith and conduct. He used the letter form to communicate his theological conception of the "mystery of Christ." It was part of his genius to adopt a manageable form of writing for evangelization—a form to be imitated by later Christian writers in conscious literary dependence.

11 Into the letter form Paul the apostle, the theologian, and the orator introduced—often in an unpolished way—scraps of the early kerygma (e.g., Gal 1:3–4; 3:1; Rom 1:3–4; 1 Thes 1:10; 1 Cor 15:1–7; Rom 2:16; 10:8–9); homilies (e.g., Rom 1:18–32); exhortations (Gal 5:19–24 [lists of vices and virtues; see also 2 Cor 12:20; 1 Tm 6:11]; Col 3:18–4:1 [domestic instructions; see also Eph 5:22–6:9; 1 Tm 2:8–3:1; etc.]); hymns (Phil 2:6–11; Rom 8:31–39; 1 Cor 13; etc.); liturgical formulas (1 Cor 11:24–25; 12:3; 16:22); midrashim (Gal 4:21–31; Rom 4:1–25; 2 Cor 3:4–18); "testimonia" (i.e., chains of OT proof-texts, Rom 3:10–18; 15:9–12); and short "diatribes" (Rom 2–3). In many cases the material so introduced was derived from the early Church's nascent tradition (1 Cor 11:23; 15:3; etc.), but reshaped by Paul's preaching and teaching for some time. Many of these sections reveal subordinate literary forms that were not composed for the first time when they were put into a Pauline letter. Consequently, although a Pauline composition is to be considered basically as a "letter," careful scrutiny of its parts often discloses a homiletic or rhetorical formulation of the kerygma and of revealed truths—a formulation that must be respected in interpretation. Paul rarely wrote with the precision of the modern dogmatic theologian, of conciliar definitions, or of canonical legislation. Rarely has he given us in one place a complete exposé of any of his cherished beliefs. His theological language is much more that of a man who speaks than that of one who writes. His formulation is often dependent on the process of dictation (→ 20 below).

12 **(III) The Pauline Corpus.** Although Paul undoubtedly wrote many letters during the course of his missionary career, only 13 are preserved in the NT canon. Thirteen were attributed to him in the Muratorian Canon (ll. 39–63; *EB* 4), but since the time of Cyril of Jerusalem (*Cathechesis* 4.36; *PG* 33.499; *ca.* AD 348), 14 letters (with Heb) have been ascribed to him. Modern scholars, however, both Catholic and Protestant, following the lead of ancient writers like Origen, doubt the Pauline authorship of Heb (→ Epistle Heb, 61:2–3). (For the authenticity of 1 and 2 Tim, Ti, → Pastoral Letters, 57:6–11.)

13 However, several Pauline passages suggest that he wrote other letters beside the 13 preserved. Reference is made in 1 Cor 5:9 to a letter written previously to the Corinthian church; 2 Cor 2:3–4 speaks of a "letter written in tears," composed apparently between 1 Cor and 2 Cor. In Col 4:16 a letter to the Laodiceans is mentioned; a letter so entitled and another addressed to the Alexandrians are rejected in the Muratorian Canon as extracanonical (l. 64; *EB* 5). It is not unlikely that Rom 16 is part of some other Pauline letter; Phil is possibly made up of more than one letter written to that church (as a passage in Polycarp [*Ep. ad Phil.* 3.2] suggests). The integrity of 2 Cor has often been questioned in this regard too. References in Paul's canonical letters to other letters that have not been preserved gave rise to the literary fabrication of apocryphal Pauline letters; 2 Thes 2:2 may even refer to such fabrication (→ Canonicity, 67:59).

14 The collection of Paul's canonical letters was apparently made toward the end of the 1st cent. AD (→ Canonicity, 67:58). Paul himself in 2 Cor 10:10 was aware that his letters were being widely read and causing comments. The reference in 2 Pt 3:15–16 to "all the letters" of "our dear brother Paul" may be an allusion to a Pauline corpus of some sort. The earliest indication of such a corpus comes to us from Marcion who drew up at Rome *ca.* AD 144 a canon into which he admitted ten Pauline letters apparently in the following order: Gal, 1–2 Cor, Rom, 1–2 Thes, Eph (= for him "To the Laodiceans"), Col, Phil, Phlm (cf. Epiphanius, *Panarion* 42.9,4; GCS 31/105).

15 Of the 13 Pauline letters Phil, Phlm, Col, and Eph are usually called "Captivity Letters" because imprisonment is mentioned in them (Phil 1:7,13,14; Phlm 1,9,10,23; Col 4:3,18; Eph 3:1; 4:1; 6:20); 1 Tm, Ti, 2 Tm bear the name "Pastoral Letters" because of their concern for the establishment of hierarchical and ecclesiastical discipline. The title "Great Letters" is often given to Rom, 1 Cor, 2 Cor, Gal, because of their length and the importance of the teaching in them. The order of the Pauline letters in the modern Bible follows that of the Vg and is not chronological. The letters to the seven churches precede those to the four individuals. It has often been suggested that the order is that of dignity; whereas this may account for Rom being first, it is difficult thus to explain the precedence of Gal over Eph and of Phil over 1–2 Thes. The purely material factor of length is most likely the reason for the order within the groups, for the length of the letters decreases from Rom to Phlm. According to some counts, Eph is considered to be slightly longer than Gal (see Roller, *Das Formular*, 38); in the Chester Beatty Papyrus, too, Eph precedes Gal (P^{46} from 3rd cent.; → Texts, 69:142). Note that Heb, despite its length, which is greater than most of the letters, is significantly left outside the Pauline group traditionally so ordered; however, in P^{46} it follows Rom.

(Bahr, G. J., "Paul and Letter Writing in the First Century," *CBQ* 28 [1966] 465–77; "The Subscriptions in the Pauline Letters," *JBL* 87 [1968] 27–41.)

16 **(IV) Hebrews and the Catholic Epistles.** The title "epistle" is better suited to Heb and the remaining seven NT epistles, except for 2 Jn and 3 Jn, which are "letters" (even though the "chosen lady and her children" [2 Jn 1] may refer to a community rather than to an individual). Hebrews is in reality an ancient hortatory sermon, rich in instructive theological discussion and Alexandrian exegesis of the OT; unlike the Pauline letters its exhortations are scattered throughout the composition. There is no evidence that it ever had an opening formula, and the concluding section with its final greeting and request to be remembered to "all your leaders and all the saints" (13:24), which give it a bit of epistolary form, is really secondary to the whole composition. Jas, 1–2 Pt, 1 Jn, and Jude are "epistles" because they are actually homilies in epistolary form; 1 Pt is an outgrowth of a homily for the baptismal liturgy; Jas is written in the traditional style of Hellenistic Jewish exhortations; Jude and 2 Pt are didactic homilies full of admonition and exhortation.

17 The "Catholic Epistles" (Jas, 1–2 Pt, 1–3 Jn, Jude) are distinguished by the name of the writer to whom they are attributed rather than by that of the addressees. Eusebius (*HE* 2.23,25; GCS 9.174) was the first to speak of "the seven called catholic." It is difficult to say to what extent the number seven played a part in the grouping of these letters (and, in fact, of the two times seven Pauline letters in the traditional counting). However, the number seven of these epistles was arrived at only after a long varied history (→ Canonicity, 67:71–80).

The title, *katholikē epistolē*, was apparently first used of 1 Jn by Apollonius, an anti-Montanist (*ca.* AD 197; see Eusebius, *HE* 5.18,5; GCS 9.474; cf. the corrupt text of the Muratorian Canon, 1. 69; *EB* 5). From 1 Jn the title seems to have spread to the group. The Sixto-Clementine Vg, however, uses it only for Jas and Jude. The title's meaning is debated. In the East it apparently meant "addressed to all the churches," whereas in the West the group was often also called *epistulae canonicae*, which suggests that "catholic" there was understood as "canonical" (i.e., recognized in all the churches). If we assume that the title in the Eastern sense is the more applicable, it is somewhat difficult to justify, since 2–3 Jn and 1 Pt are addressed to specific communities.

18 In Eastern lists (see Athanasius, *Ep.* 39.85; *PG* 26.1177,1437; and codices B, S) the Catholic Epistles follow Acts and precede the Pauline corpus; apparently they were considered more important because they were attributed to original apostles or members of the Jerusalem mother church. In Lat lists, however, they follow Paul's letters, which are considered older and more important. Within the group the present order (Jas, 1–2 Pt, 1–3 Jn, Jude) may depend on the order of the names in Gal 2:9. A different order found in the decrees of the councils of Florence and of Trent (*EB* 47, 59; DB 784) reflects an estimate of dignity in use in the West (1–2 Pt, 1–3 Jn, Jas, Jude).

19 **(V) Writing or Dictation.** Four modes of letter writing are known to have been used in antiquity: (1) to write oneself; (2) to dictate word for word (sometimes even syllable for syllable); (3) to dictate the sense, leaving the formulation to a secretary; (4) to have a friend or secretary write in one's name, without indicating the contents. The most commonly used modes were (1) and (3); ancient writers complain often about the wearying mode of dictation (2), especially if the scribe was not skilled.

20 What method did Paul use? Rom 16:22 suggests that he dictated to Tertius (this may refer only to Rom 16 [→ Letter Rom, 53:10]). In 2 Thes 3:17; 1 Cor 16:21; Col 4:18 Paul added the greeting in his own hand—this implies that the rest was dictated to a scribe. This may be the point of the remark in Gal 6:11, when Paul contrasts his handwriting to that of the trained scribe, who wrote the preceding part. But it is impossible to say for sure whether it was dictation of the sort (2) or (3). The individuality of style in his letters would argue for dictation of most of them in mode (2). Eschlimann (*RB* 53 [1946] 192) thinks that Rom and 1 Cor were dictated in mode (3) because of their length—at least certain parts. But Paul, concerned for the correctness of expression in important doctrinal passages, would have composed these himself. Thus Eschlimann would account for the "mixed" style of certain letters. At any rate, dictation of the form (3) would certainly account for the difference in vocabulary and style noted in some of Paul's letters (2 Thes, Eph, Pastorals); this must be kept in mind when their authenticity is discussed and judged on stylistic criteria. In Phlm 19, "I, Paul, have written this with my own hand," may indicate that the whole letter was so written. Anacolutha, inconsistencies of style, and the lack of consistent terminology would also argue for dictation to a scribe. Distractions must have occurred that would be responsible for such stylistic phenomena; it is unlikely that a long letter like Rom or 1 Cor would have been finished in one sitting or in one day.

21 Little can be said about the writing of the other NT epistles. But as 1 Pt 5:12 suggests, it was written by Silvanus as the scribe ("By Silvanus...I have written you this short letter"). Since he is known to have been a disciple of Paul (2 Cor 1:19; 1 Thes 1:1; 2 Thes 1:1), this almost certainly accounts for the marked Pauline flavor of 1 Pt.

22 Did the NT writers dictate to scribes who used shorthand? Shorthand was known in the Roman world; but it is usually thought that it was not practiced by Gk scribes before *ca.* AD 155 (however, cf. the as yet undeciphered stenographic Gk text in Murabbaʿat 164 from a possibly earlier time [DJD 2, 275–79; → Apocrypha, 68:106]).

On the question of epistolary pseudepigraphy see Guthrie, *NTI* 1, 282–94; J. A. Sint, *Pseudonymität im Altertum* (Innsbruck, 1960).

48

THE LETTERS TO THE THESSALONIANS

J. Terence Forestell, C.S.B.

BIBLIOGRAPHY

1 Bicknell, E. J., *The First and Second Epistles to the Thessalonians* (WC; London, 1932). Brinkmann, B., "Die Lehre von der Parusie beim hl. Paulus in ihrem Verhältnis zu den Anschauungen des Buches Henoch," *Bib* 13 (1932) 315–34, 418–34. Dupont, J., *Syn Christō: L'union avec le Christ suivant Saint Paul* (Bruges, 1952) 39–113. Erdman, C. R., *Epistles of Paul to the Thessalonians* (Phila., 1935). Feuillet, A., "Parousie," *VDBS* 6, 1331–1419. Frame, J. E., *The Epistles of St. Paul to the Thessalonians* (ICC; N.Y., 1912). Masson, C., *Les deux Épîtres de S. Paul aux Thessaloniciens* (CNT 11a; Neuchâtel, 1957). Milligan, G., *St. Paul's Epistles to the Thessalonians* (London, 1908). Morris, L., *The First and Second Epistles to the Thessalonians* (NICNT; Grand Rapids, 1959). Neil, W., *The Epistles of Paul to the Thessalonians* (MNTC; N.Y., 1950). Oepke, A., "Die Briefe an die Thessaloniker," NTD 8 (9th ed.; Göttingen, 1962) 155–85. Plummer, A., *A Commentary on St. Paul's Second Epistle to the Thessalonians* (London, 1918). Rigaux, B., *Les Épîtres aux Thessaloniciens* (EBib; Paris, 1956). Staab, K., *Die Thessalonicherbriefe* (RNT 7; 3rd ed.; Regensburg, 1959) 7–63. Vawter, B., *I Thessalonians; II Thessalonians* (NTRG 6; Collegeville, 1960).

Cambier, J., R-F, *INT* 388–99. F-B 181–90. Guthrie, *NTI* 179–97. Metzger, B. M., *IPLAP* 115–19. R-F, *INT* 388–99. Wik, *NTI* 362–72.

INTRODUCTION

2 **(I) The Founding of the Church at Thessalonica.** Thessalonica, an important port city on the Thermaic Gulf in northern Greece, was founded about 316 BC by Cassander, a general under Alexander the Great, and named after the former's wife, a half sister of Alexander. Conquered by the Romans in 168, it became the capital of the Roman province of Macedonia after 146. The city supported Octavius at the battle of Philippi (42 BC) and consequently became a free city, with its own deme, boule, and politarchs (cf. Acts 17:5–6). In the 1st cent. AD, it was a cosmopolitan city with a large Jewish colony and many pagan cults (Rigaux, *Les Épîtres aux Thessaloniciens*, 11–20). Paul, Silvanus, and Timothy arrived in Thessalonica in AD 50, in the course of Mission II. Paul and Silvanus had been arrested and expelled from Philippi (Acts 16:16–40). Passing along the Via Egnatia, through Amphipolis and Apollonia, they came to Thessalonica, about 97 mi. W of Philippi. There they began to preach the gospel in a Jewish synagogue "amid much anxiety" (1 Thes 2:2).

3 As usual, Paul's success with the Jews was minimal. After three Sabbaths in the synagogue, he apparently centered his activity in the house of a certain Jason. A large number of the "God-fearing" Greeks, along with many pagans (Acts 17:4; reading the Gk conj. *kai*, as in the mss. A, D, and the Vg) and important women, were converted. The Jews, however, jealous of Paul's success, stirred up a mob against the missionaries and forced their expulsion from the city (Acts 17:1–9). Acts, being chiefly interested in the spread of the gospel among pagans, gives few details about Paul's stay in Thessalonica. Most commentators feel it must have lasted two or three months, because the two letters reveal a flourishing Christian community, strong in faith, hope, and charity despite constant persecution by their fellow citizens and Jews—a prolongation of that begun while Paul was there. In this short time a strong bond of affection was forged between the Thessalonian Christians and their apostle; within the scope of eight short chapters Paul addresses them as "brothers," the term of Christian endearment, 21 times, a higher proportion than in any other letter.

4 **(II) Occasion and Content of the Letters.** After leaving Thessalonica, Paul met more opposition at Beroea (Acts 17:10–15) and escaped alone to Athens. His preaching to the Athenians failed to produce any results (Acts 17:22–34). When Silvanus and Timothy finally rejoined him at Athens, he was deservedly anxious about

the church at Thessalonica. Unable to return for some unknown reason (1 Thes 2:18), Paul sent Timothy to Thessalonica to inquire about the situation there and to strengthen the new Christians in the faith and in their attachment to the apostles (1 Thes 3:1–2). In the meantime Paul moved on to Corinth. Timothy joined him there (Acts 18:5), bringing news of the Thessalonian church. Shortly after Timothy's return (1 Thes 3:6), Paul wrote in the name of all three apostles (1 Thes 1:1), assuring them of his love and affection, encouraging them, and giving them the instructions and admonitions they needed (1 Thes 3:10). There were no serious abuses to correct at Thessalonica so that the tone of the first letter is entirely gentle and optimistic. The faith is not acquired once for all, but is open to constant growth in understanding; the initial preaching must be reinforced by further clarification and repeated admonition. This is sound pastoral care motivated by disinterested love. The date of 1 Thes is probably AD 51 (→ Life of Paul, 46:35).

5 A few months later 2 Thes was written. News seems to have reached Paul of disturbances in the otherwise fervent community: Persecution was continuing; some enthusiasts were declaring that the parousia was already here (2 Thes 2:2). In the first letter Paul had warned against idleness and meddling (4:11–12; 5:14); in the second, he deals more sternly with these abuses (3:6–15); perhaps the eschatological exaltation of the young community led some to neglect fruitful work and to busy themselves disturbing others; Paul uses his apostolic authority to restore order. These problems are the sole concern of the letter.

6 **(III) Authenticity.** Both letters were readily attributed to the apostle Paul throughout antiquity. Nineteenth-cent. radical critics, led by the Tübingen school under F. C. Baur, questioned their authenticity. The arguments against 1 Thes are based on a priori assumptions of Paul as an anti-Jewish Hellenist; since 1909 (R. Scott) the Pauline character of 1 Thes has been universally recognized.

7 The arguments against the Pauline authorship of 2 Thes are based on elements of vocabulary and style not found in any of Paul's major epistles—the eschatological passages of the two letters appear to be in contradiction: 1 Thes teaching the suddenness of the parousia, and 2 Thes the signs that will precede it; finally, many precise literary similarities between the two letters suggest a forgery. None of these arguments, when carefully weighed, is sufficient to impugn the traditional attribution of 2 Thes to Paul (M. Goguel). Since 1903 (W. Wrede), most critics accept Pauline authenticity of 2 Thes. In fact, over 80 per cent of the vocabulary in 1 and 2 Thes is found in the major epistles; subject matter often dictates a select vocabulary. The eschatological teaching is based on the teaching of Christ and the traditional Jewish apocalyptic schema of the end time; in both cases, there are signs that precede the end but do not point to it in such a way as to determine the exact time. The literary similarity is perhaps the strongest argument of all, but it is not surprising that two letters written within a short space of time on similar subjects should employ similar phraseology. Arguments in favor of reversing the order of 1 and 2 Thes (P. Ewald, J. Weiss, W. Michaelis) are as unconvincing and unnecessary as those in favor of proposing different addressees for the two letters (A. von Harnack, M. Goguel, E. Schweizer).

8 **(IV) Doctrinal Importance.** The letters to the Thessalonians do not have the doctrinal importance of the four Great Letters or the Captivity Letters. Nevertheless, since they are the earliest NT writings, they provide us with a vivid picture of a young and fervent Christian community 20 years after the ascension. The letters presuppose an initial doctrinal formation of considerable clarity and amplitude (1 Thes 1:5; 2:1,2,5,11; 3:3,4; 4:2; 5:2; 2 Thes 2:6; 3:7). Faith, hope, and charity characterize the Christian way of life (1 Thes 1:3). Jesus is Lord and Son of God, who raised him from the dead (1 Thes 1:9–10). God has given the Holy Spirit to those who believe in the gospel of Jesus Christ (1 Thes 4:8; 2 Thes 2:13). Christians must live a life of chastity, justice, order, and charity, working at earthly tasks, in expectation of the coming of Christ as Judge and Savior (1 Thes 1:10; 5:9–10; 2 Thes 1:7–10). Persecution is an integral part of the Christian vocation (1 Thes 1:6; 3:3,4,7; 2 Thes 1:4,6,7). Moreover, Paul manifests a clear consciousness of the nature of the apostolic mission; it is a commission from God (1 Thes 2:4), to be discharged with disinterested love (1 Thes 2:3–12), in constant prayer and thanksgiving (1 Thes 1:2; 2:13; 3:11–13; 5:23–24; 2 Thes 1:3; 2:13,16–17; 3:5,16); the success of his preaching depends not on himself but on the power of God (1 Thes 1:5; 2:13). The same confidence in prayer and the power of God is necessary for growth in the Christian life.

9 The primary doctrinal value of the two letters lies in their eschatological teaching. The thought of the parousia of the Lord pervades both letters and is the source of courage and patience in the face of tribulation (→ Pauline Theology, 79:157). The coming of Christ to judge the living and the dead is an integral part of Christian faith and hope; it is embodied in the later creeds and taught by the IV Lateran Council (DB 429; DS 801); at that time Christians will share with the Risen Christ the glory he already enjoys (1 Thes 3:12; 2 Thes 1:10). Paul had already instructed the Thessalonians in this faith (1 Thes 1:9–10). Since Christ had not revealed the time of his coming (Mt 24:36 par; Acts 1:7; 1 Thes 5:2), it was natural that early Christians would have desired it and expected it to happen soon, even in their own lifetime. Paul writes from such a point of view in 1 Thes 4:15–17 (cf. Bibl. Commission, *Resp.*; *EB* 419–21; → Church Pronouncements, 72:25, 28). These Christians were nonetheless anxious about those who died before the coming of Christ. Paul writes to assure them that those who are living at the time of the parousia will have no advantage over the dead; the dead will rise first and together with the living all will go to meet Christ and be with him forever. This is the positive teaching of 1 Thes. In 2 Thes Paul teaches that before the parousia of Christ takes place, there will be apostasy and the appearance of an Antichrist, an agent of Satan who will attempt to destroy the work of Christ. Satan is already at work, but the Antichrist cannot appear because someone or something is at present preventing it. When he does appear, Christ will come and destroy him.

10 In the eschatological passages of both letters (1 Thes 4:13–18; 2 Thes 1:7–10; 2:1–12) Paul uses the "apocalyptic" form of writing (→ Apocalypse, 64:3), in which concrete symbols are used to convey a more transcendent mystery. In such writing, the correspondence between figure and reality escapes us.

11 **(V) Outline of 1 Thes.**

(I) Paul's Personal Relations with the Thessalonians (1:1–3:13)
- (A) When the Church Was Being Founded (1:2–2:16)
- (B) Since the Foundation of the Church (2:17–3:13)

(II) Instructions and Exhortations (4:1–5:24)
- (A) Holiness and Chastity (4:1–8)
- (B) Charity and Order (4:9–12)
- (C) The Fate of Departed Christians (4:13–18)
- (D) The Date of the Parousia (5:1–11)
- (E) Exhortations for Community Living (5:12–24)

(III) Conclusion (5:25–28)

12 **(VI) Outline of 2 Thes.**

(I) The Persecuted May Expect Deliverance at the Judgment (1:1–12)
(II) The Coming of the Lord (2:1–3:5)
  (A) Signs of the Parousia (2:1–12)
  (B) Thanksgiving, Encouragement, and Prayer (2:13–3:5)
(III) The Admonition of the Disorderly (3:6–15)
(IV) Conclusion (3:16–18)

COMMENTARY ON 1 THES

13 **(I) Paul's Personal Relations with the Thessalonians (1:1–3:13). 1:1.** Address and salutation. Silvanus is to be identified with Silas of Acts 15:22, etc., one of the leading men of the Jerusalem community sent to Antioch after the Council of Jerusalem (cf. 1 Pt 5:12). Timothy, the son of a Jewish mother and Greek father, joined Paul and Silvanus at Lystra (Acts 16:1–3) and remained a most important collaborator of Paul (→ Pastoral Letters, 57:3). Paul does not address individual converts, but "the church of the Thessalonians," i.e., the assembly of Christians gathered at Thessalonica. The relationship of the Church to God and to Christ is expressed by the preposition *en* with the dative (also 2 Thes 1:1); sometimes Paul says "the church of God which is in Christ Jesus" (1 Thes 2:14; 1 Cor 1:2), thereby distinguishing God's initiative in founding the Church as his special possession (1 Pt 2:9; Ti 2:14) from the personal union of believers with the Risen Christ, which actually constitutes the Church (→ Pauline Theology, 79:150–51). The concept of God as father is not original with revealed religion, but the true nature of God's fatherhood is revealed in Christ. *the Lord Jesus Christ:* The full profession of Christian faith is contained in this title; Jesus of Nazareth is the divine, Messianic king (→ Aspects NT Thought, 78:37). By speaking of Christ and God in parallel fashion, Paul implies the divinity of Christ (3:11). *grace and peace: Charis kai eirēnē* is Paul's regular salutation and blessing (2 Thes 1:2; → NT Epistles, 47:8).

14 **(A) When the Church Was Being Founded (1:2–2:16).** This section deals with Paul's relations with the church of Thessalonica at the time of his foundation of it. **2–5.** As in most letters, Paul begins with a thanksgiving addressed to God in prayer. He uses the plural, although he has himself primarily in mind (3:1). It is his public recognition and declaration of benefits received from God (Lk 17:16,18). "Prayer" (*proseuchē*), signifying invocation, is a more general term than *deēsis*, which connotes primarily petition. **3.** The thanksgiving is occasioned by the faith, hope, and charity of the Thessalonians in their service of God (*emprosthen tou theou*). This triad expresses the essence of man's response to the preaching of the gospel. *the achievement of your faith: Ergon* here signifies the total and personal assent the believer gives to God and to his plan of salvation revealed in the gospel (cf. J. A. Kleist, *CBQ* 6 [1944] 61–68). The content of this faith is outlined in 1:9–10. *your active charity:* Lit., "labor of love." *Kopos* connotes hard work (AG 444); Christian faith manifests itself in the labor of fraternal charity (Gal 5:6); this charity or love (*agapē*) is an imitation by man of the love that God revealed in Jesus. *the steadfast character of your hope: Hypomonē*, in its biblical usage, connotes the patient endurance of all suffering in expectation of the salvific work of God; in the NT it is intimately associated with "hope" (*elpis*) in the Lord's parousia, the ultimate object of Christian expectation (1 Thes 1:10; Mt 24:13; Lk 8:15; 21:19). This expectation is the source of strength in present tribulation Rom 5:3–4; cf. C. Spicq, *RSPT* 19 [1930] 95–106; J. de Guibert, *RSR* 6 [1913] 565–69; W. Grossouw, *RB* 61 [1954] 481–532). **4–5.** Acceptance of the faith is the consequence of election (*eklogē*) by God (Rom 8:29–30); this divine initiative was motivated by love, as was the election of Israel (Dt 7:6–8). The divine election was evident in the manner in which the gospel was preached (4–5) and received among them (6–10). *Euaggelion* is the good news of God's salvation (Is 52:7); its content is the mystery of Christ. Yet it is not a mere message or doctrine but a divine activity, *dynamis theou eis sōtērian* (Rom 1:16). Paul emphasizes the point by contrasting the "word" of his preaching with the "power," the "Holy Spirit" and the "great abundance," which accompanied it and was operative among the Thessalonians (2:5–12); the three words are almost synonymous in this context. The Holy Spirit is responsible for all spiritual manifestations (1 Cor 12:3–13).

15 **6.** *imitators:* Cf. 1 Cor 4:16; Paul's example is also the Lord's (1 Cor 11:1). Christianity is an imitation of God after the manner revealed by Jesus (Eph 5:1–2); cf. Gn 1:26; Lv 19:2; Mt 5:48. Paul and Christians effectively offer this example (*typos*, v. 7) to others (cf. 1 Thes 2:14; 2 Thes 3:7–9; D. M. Stanley, *Bib* 40 [1959] 859–77). *the word:* Of the gospel (cf. 2 Cor 11:4; Mt 13:19). Joy in the faith in spite of persecution is the work of the Holy Spirit and the imitation of Christ (cf. 2 Cor 4:10; 1 Pt 2:21; Phil 3:10). *tribulation: Thlipsis* acquired in the NT a peculiarly Christian connotation, based on the Jewish apocalyptic notions of the oppression of the just in the last times: Salvation comes only through suffering (Mt 24:9–25). The passion and death were the *thlipseis* of Christ (Col 1:24); hence *thlipsis* is part of the Christian vocation (1 Thes 3:3–4; Acts 14:22) and the path to glory (Ap 7:14). **8.** *in every place:* A rhetorical exaggeration, or every place to which Paul went in Macedonia and Achaia. **9b–10.** These verses constitute a succinct expression of the apostolic kerygma to the pagans. In rhythmic prose, Paul presents the essence of the faith as a monotheism, a Christology, and an eschatology. As was customary in the Jewish tradition, the kerygma to the pagans began with a polemic against idols (Acts 14:15; 17:22–29). "Idols" (*eidōla*) in the LXX and in the NT are synonymous with false gods; they do not exist (1 Cor 8:4–5) and their worship is related to demons (1 Cor 10:20). "Conversion" involves a departure from the worship of idols for the service of a God who, in contrast to the idols, truly lives and is such as he claims to be (*alēthinos*, not *alēthēs*); both epithets are used of God in the OT (Ps 42:3; 2 Kgs 19:4,16; Ex 34:6). *to serve God:* A traditional biblical expression for cult (Ex 23:33) and the total relationship of man to God (Rom 6:22). To monotheism is added a Christology—Jesus of Nazareth is the Son of God, and God has raised him from the dead. Also an eschatology—this same Jesus will come and rescue us from the definitive manifestation of God's wrath. *his Son:* True divine sonship (cf. Gal 1:16; 4:4,6; Rom 1:3,9; 8:29; 1 Cor 1:9, etc.). *from heaven:* The dwelling place of God, where Jesus is

at his right hand (Acts 2:33; Ps 110:1; Dn 7:13; Mk 14:62). The apostolic kerygma regularly speaks of God raising Jesus (Acts 2:24; 3:15; 4:10; 13:30; → Pauline Theology 79:72). *who rescues us:* The Gk pres. participle is to be preferred to the Vg perfect; in Koine it may refer to the present or the future (*GrBib* 282–83). The salvific activity of Jesus is already operative but will have its supreme manifestation at the parousia. *wrath that is coming:* *Orgē* connotes God's punitive justice toward the unrepentant sinner; it is already operative in history (Rom 1:18), but will have its supreme manifestation at the end of time (5:9; 2 Thes 1:5–10). For the coming day of God's wrath, cf. Am 5:18–20; Is 2:10–22; Zeph 1:15; *Jub* 24:30; *2 Enoch* 44:2.

16 **2:1–12.** These verses develop the thought of 1:5, picking up the word "welcome" (*eisodos*) from 1:9. **1.** *has not been fruitless* (NEB): The pf. tense indicates that the effects of Paul's activity among them still endure (cf. *great abundance* of 1:5). **2.** The human obstacles overcome in the preaching of the gospel indicate the supernatural character of the work. For the physical (*propathontes*) and moral (*hybristhentes*) suffering of the apostles at Philippi, cf. Acts 16:19–40. *we had confidence in our God:* *Parrēsia* usually connotes the freedom of speech proper to a democratic assembly; in the NT it becomes boldness and courage to proclaim the gospel with trust in God (Acts 4:13; Mt 10:20,26). *amid much anxiety:* The interior struggle with which Paul began his mission at Thessalonica, after the persecutions of Philippi. **3.** *our appeal:* *Paraklēsis* and *parakaleō* are characteristic descriptions of early Christian preaching (2 Cor 5:20; Acts 2:40; 13:15; Phil 2:1; cf. Is 40:1); an exhortation with a certain touch of passion that seeks a response to the preached word. Paul is not preaching "error," nor does he act out of "impure motives"; *akatharsia* denotes primarily sexual impurity, which may affect the body and the mind. *with guile:* No trickery was used in the preaching itself (2 Cor 4:2; 2:17; cf. Jn 1:47). These three vices characterized itinerant rhetoricians, philosophers, and charlatans of religious mysteries in those days, whereas their absence characterized the new Israel (cf. A.-M. Denis, *ETL* 33 [1957] 245–318). **4.** Paul is responsible only to God, who has chosen and approved him for this task (1 Cor 4:1–5; 9:16; Gal 1:10,15–16; Acts 5:29). *our hearts:* The plural may be from Jer 11:20, or have reference to Silvanus and Timothy as well. The *heart* connotes the whole interior life of man in Semitic thought. **5–7.** Three more base motives are excluded. **5.** *flattery:* A vice of contemporary rhetoricians; the Thessalonians themselves can testify in this matter. *pretext for self-seeking* (J. Moffatt): *Pleonexia* is more than avarice (*philargyria*, 1 Tm 6:10); in the NT it is constantly associated with sexual impurity, and is called idolatry (Col 3:5; cf. P. Rossano, *VD* 32 [1954] 257–65). It is the base egoism that seeks to turn everything to one's own advantage. Being deeply rooted, only God can detect it in a man, and so Paul calls upon the witness of God (Rom 1:9; 2 Cor 1:23). **6.** Cf. Jn 5:41–44; 12:43. **7.** *we might have made our weight felt* (NEB): More than likely a reference to apostolic dignity and authority than to material support, as in 2 Cor 11:9. (For the notion of apostle, → Aspects NT Thought, 78:174–177). Read *ēpioi* (gentle) in place of *nēpioi* (children); cf. 2 Tm 2:24. *in your midst:* As one of you, in contrast to 7a (Mt 20:25–28 par). *a nursing mother:* Paul wants to express the gift of self, which nursing implies (1 Cor 3:2; Eph 5:29; Gal 4:19). **8.** *our very selves:* *Psychas* has the same connotation as *kardias* in 2:5; the Apostle's love is even more self-sacrificing than that of a nursing mother (Acts 15:26; 20:24). **9.** Added proof of Paul's disinterestedness (2 Thes 3:8; Acts 20:34; 1 Cor 4:12; 9:12,15). Paul was a tentmaker (Acts 18:3). *we preached:* Paul uses the technical vb. *kerysső*, synonymous with *euaggelizomai* (Mk 1:38; Lk 4:43). **10–12.** A third reaffirmation of selfless concern. **10.** *holy:* Interior goodness and fidelity to God (= Hebr *ḥāsîd*). *just:* As in 1 Cor 15:34, "in due order, proper." *blameless:* The quality with which the Christian desires to appear at the parousia (1 Thes 3:13; 5:23). **11.** A new metaphor for the tenderness of Paul's affection; a mother nourishes (2:7); a father instructs. Paul's pastoral concern is for each individual (Acts 20:31; Jn 10:3). **12.** Pastoral care consists in further appeal (*parakalountes*), encouragement (*paramythoumenoi*, almost synonymous; 1 Cor 14:3; Phil 2:1), and even in solemn adjuration (*martyromenoi*). *walk:* See comment on Rom 6:4. *who is calling you:* Pres. participle as in 1:10; God's call is always pressing. *his kingdom and glory:* The goal of the Christian life. In Paul, both kingdom and glory are transcendent goods, proper to God (Rom 1:23; 1 Cor 15:24). Christ has already entered this inheritance (Eph 5:5).

17 **13–14.** The reception of the gospel by the Thessalonians (cf. 1:4–10). **13.** *you received the word of God which you heard from us:* Lit., "the word of the preaching," i.e., that which is heard, *logos akoēs* (Is 53:1; Jn 12:38; Rom 10:16). "To receive" (*paralambanō*) is the technical NT word for the acceptance of traditional teaching (1 Thes 4:1; 1 Cor 11:23; 15:1,3). *you welcomed not a word of men:* The gospel rests in no way on the authority of the preacher, nor is it effective through him (1 Cor 3:5–9). *word of God...made active in you who believe:* The gospel becomes effective through God's power (cf. Jer 23:29; Is 49:2; Rom 1:16; Eph 6:17; Heb 4:12). **14.** Discipleship implies conformity. Jews were the source of persecution at Thessalonica (Acts 17:5,13), as they had been in Palestine (Acts 8:1–3; 9:1–2; 12:1–4).

18 **15–16.** Moved by anger at the thought of the persecution of God's people, Paul very eloquently retails a list of complaints against his fellow Jews (cf. Phil 3:2–3). The death of the Lord Jesus was the culmination of such opposition to God (Mt 5:11–12; 21:34–35; 23:29–32; Acts 2:23; 7:52). A similar theme is found among Jewish writers themselves (1QS 1:21–26; 1QH 4:30; CD 20:29). For Jewish opposition to Paul, see Acts 9:23,29–30; 13:50; 14:2,5,19; 17:5,13; 18:6. *hostile to all men:* Opposed to their salvation; note the scorn of Tacitus (*Histories* 5.5). *they are filling up the measure of their sins:* A Jewish expression (Gn 15:16; Dt 8:23; 2 Mc 6:12–15; Str-B 1, 939) reflecting a theology of history. God has fixed certain moments of history for the punishment of sin and the rewarding of good actions; it is a mark of divine displeasure when this chastisement is postponed (2 Mc 6:13–16). Jews who are hostile to Christ and persecute Christians are left to multiply their sins in view of divine vengeance. *wrath has already come upon them:* God's avenging justice is already manifest in his failure to effect their conversion. The interpretation of the final phrase, *eis telos* is greatly disputed: CCD, "to the utmost"; NEB, "for good and all"; RSV, "at last"; Moffatt, "to the bitter end." Paul's point of view is eschatological; it is already the end time when God's justice will be manifest. A direct literary dependence of 1 Thes 2:16 on Mt 23:31–36 remains uncertain (cf. B. Rigaux, *op. cit.*, 445–46; B. Orchard, *Bib* 19 [1938] 19–42; E. Cothenet, *RSR* 42 [1954] 5–39). Paul does not appear to have a precise historical event in mind, e.g., either the loss of Jewish independence, or a famine (Acts 11:28), or banishment from Rome (Acts 18:2; cf. E. Bammel, *ZThK* 56 [1959] 294–315), or the death of Agrippa I in AD 44, or the insurrection of Theudas (44–46), or even the destruction of Jerusalem. His concern is rather with contemporary persecutors. For another expression of his view on the Jewish question, cf. Rom 9–11.

19 (B) Since the Foundation of the Church (2:17–3:13). Paul now discusses the relations which he has had with the Thessalonian church since his foundation of it. **17.** Physical separation is like the severing of the bond between parent and child. **18.** *I, Paul:* Perhaps Paul intends to distinguish himself from Silvanus and Timothy. Obstacles to apostolic work must be attributed to the devil, the enemy of God and the adversary of man's salvation. *Satan:* A transliteration of Hebr *śāṭān*, "adversary"; in Jb 1 and Zech 3 this figure is simply the prosecutor of man in the heavenly court. In Jewish theology he becomes the leader of the wicked angels; it is in this sense that the term is used in the NT. The nature of the obstacle is unknown. **19.** *who is our hope... who but you?:* His own converts both at Thessalonica and elsewhere (cf. Phil 4:1). *crown of glory:* Lit., " a crown of boasting, or pride," see Ez 16:12. Although the apostle can glory only in what Christ does in and through him (Rom 15:17–18; 1 Cor 15:10), part of his expected reward will be a legitimate pride in his converts and of them in him (2 Cor 1:14).

20 **3:1–5.** The mission of Timothy. **1.** The vocabulary expresses Paul's attachment to his converts. *our brother and cooperator with God:* As Paul's colleague, for all apostles are God's helpers (1 Cor 3:9). Christ is the source and author of the gospel, but also its object (*GrBib* 36–37). "Faith" is used here in the sense of perseverance in and attachment to the Christian way of life. **3a.** This verse repeats 2b in a negative fashion: The Gk verb (*sainesthai*) properly connotes the action of a dog wagging its tail. Metaphorically, it would seem to indicate the interior threat to perseverance, which Christians experience in face of exterior trials (cf. H. Chadwick, *JTS* 1 [1950] 156–58). **3b–4.** *tribulation:* See comment on 1:6. **5.** A repetition and inclusion for the whole passage. The cause of fear is the devil's work to neutralize Paul's efforts and God's will (2 Thes 2:7; Mt 6:13). *our labor:* See comment on 1 Cor 3:8.

21 **3:6–10.** The results of Timothy's report. **6.** *Faith and love* sum up for Paul the Christian life; later he will give some instructions for their hope (4:13–5:11). **7.** *Accordingly* (*dia touto*) recapitulates v. 6. *in all our distress and tribulation:* The apostolic *anagkē* (Lk 21:23; 1 Cor 7:26) and the eschatological *thlipsis* (1:6) are joined. "All" connotes intensity rather than extension. **8.** The knowledge of God's favor is a source of joy in life (Ps 119:40,93; Is 38:16; 2 Cor 6:9). *in the Lord:* In the Risen Christ, an accepted formula for the nature of Christian existence (→ Pauline Theology, 79:138). **9.** The good news and joy occasion thanksgiving to God, the source of all good things; Paul considers such prayer a debt to be repaid. *for all the joy which you have brought us:* The short phrase *di'hymas* expresses the cause of Paul's joy, not merely its occasion. *before our God:* This phrase governs the whole sentence; for thanksgiving and joy characterize Paul's constant relationship to God. **10.** Now a prayer of petition for what is still lacking to his joy. Chapters 4 and 5 will provide the further instruction and clarification desired. *night and day:* The constant disposition of gratitude and dependence on God with which he goes about his work (1:2; 2:13; 5:17; 2 Thes 1:3,11; 2:13; cf. Lk 18:1). *more and more:* Rhetorical emphasis (2 Cor 1:8; Eph 3:8; 1 Cor 4:13; 15:8).

22 **11–13.** An invocation, embodying the petition of v. 10, concludes the first part of the letter. A sing. verb (*kateuthynai*, "may he direct") treats the Father and Jesus as one source of action. In v. 12, Christ alone is the immediate source of growth in love. Three requests are made: (1) the opportunity of returning to Thessalonica; (2) an increase of love for the Thessalonians; (3) the achievement of the goal of the Christian life. **13.** *holiness:* Likeness to God. *with all his saints:* If Paul has Zech 14:5 in mind, the reference is to the angels (Mk 8:38; 13:27; Mt 25:31). The formula, however, is stereotyped, and Paul probably has the whole scene of the parousia in mind, as described in 4:13–18. The reference would then be to all Christians, living and dead, who will be with the Lord on that day (4:17).

(II) Instructions and Exhortations (4:1–5:24). The *hysterēmata*, or "what is lacking in your faith," of 3:10 are now supplied by Paul. Teaching is always an occasion for exhortation in Paul's letters.

23 (A) Holiness and Chastity (4:1–8). **1.** *in the Lord Jesus:* Such instruction is handed down (2:13) from Christ himself through the apostles. Christ is the norm and authority of all Paul's teaching and exhortation. **2.** Paul recalls past instructions and announces the following. **3.** Christian morality is not viewed as natural law, but as the will of God (Mt 6:10). *sanctification:* This connotes a progress toward holiness, a likeness to God (3:13). Such holiness must extend to the body. *porneia:* Lit., "fornication," but it can express all forms of sexual immorality. The pagan society from which the Christians came considered sexual promiscuity and license perfectly normal (cf. Cicero, *Pro Coelio* 20. 48). **4.** *that every one of you learn how to control his own body:* Lit., "to acquire his vessel." Commentators and translators, ancient and modern, are divided on the interpretation of this expression. Insisting on the basic meaning of the verb and on 1 Pt 3:7, as well as certain rabbinic expressions, many understand the phrase to mean, "to take a wife" (RSV, J. Moffatt, E. J. Goodspeed); others (NEB, R. Knox) invoke a more common use of *skeuos* as a metaphor for the "body" in general (2 Cor 4:7; 2 Tm 2:20,21; Rom 9:22,23); see Rigaux, *op. cit.*, 504–6. In the light of the general theme of vv. 3–8, the second interpretation is preferred. *in holiness and honor:* In consideration of the will of God and in giving to one's body (or wife) the respect which is its (or her) due (*timē*, originally, "price"). **5.** The description of the pagans—*who do not know God*—is drawn from the LXX: Jer 10:25; Ps 78:6. In Rom 1:24–32 the connection between idolatry and lust is elaborated upon. **6.** *matter:* "Business dealings" or "adultery" are two meanings that have been suggested here by ancient and modern commentators; *pragma* refers to a lawsuit in 1 Cor 6:1, but to an unspecified abomination in 2 Cor 7:11. According to others, it can mean "business dealings." *Pleonexia* (covetousness) is regularly associated with *porneia* in the NT (cf. R. Beauvery, *VD* 33 [1955] 78–85). **6b–8.** *Triadic* Christian motivation for justice and chastity (1 Cor 6:13b–20): (1) the coming judgment and punishment by the *Lord* Jesus (cf. 2 Thes 1:7–10); (2) *God's* call to holiness; indifference in these matters is a rejection of God and his will (Lk 10:16); (3) the Father has given his "Holy Spirit" to all believers (Ez 36:27; 37:14; 1 Cor 6:19).

24 (B) Charity and Order (4:9–12). **9.** Whereas *philadelphia* means properly love of one's fellow Christians, Christian *agapē* extends beyond the community to all men (cf. 3:12; 2 Pt 1:7; Gal 6:10; Mt 5:43–48). "Taught by God" (*theodidaktoi*) reflects the thought of Is 54:13; Jer 31:33–34. God teaches men his own nature (1 Jn 4:8) by the interior instruction of the Holy Spirit. **11.** *live quietly:* Cf. Thes 3:6–15. Some Christians at Thessalonica, for reasons of false enthusiasm or zeal, had been neglecting their own work to disturb others and live at their expense. Paul realistically calls them back to their duties (cf. 5:12–14).

12. The Christian community must offer an example of propriety and order to non-Christians (1 Cor 14:23–25,40); laziness and begging are unbecoming and scandalous. *be dependent on nobody* (RSV), or *be in need of nothing:* Christian charity demands that those who are able to support themselves be not a burden upon others; the independence proposed here is not Stoic self-sufficiency but Christian liberty and charity (1 Cor 3:21–22; Rom 13:8).

25 **(C) The Fate of Departed Christians (4:13–18).** Their present anxiety concerns not the judgment of the living and the dead (1:10), but the participation of their dead friends in the glorious coming of Christ. **13.** *we would not have you ignorant:* This Pauline formula draws attention to an important point; see comment on Rom 1:13. *concerning those who sleep:* The Christian dead. Death is spoken of as a sleep even in pagan literature, without necessarily presupposing faith in immortality or resurrection. The image is used in the OT (Gn 47:30; Dt 31:16; 3 Kgs 2:10, etc.), but in Christianity it acquires a special sense because of faith in the resurrection of Jesus (Mt 9:24; Acts 7:60; 1 Cor 15:18,20,51, etc.). *lest you should grieve:* Not with a natural sorrow at the loss of dear ones, but with a pagan sorrow that is without Christian hope (Col 1:27; Eph 2:12; 1 Thes 4:5). The object of this hope is specific, viz., the resurrection and a life of glory with Christ. **14.** *if we believe:* A real condition; the certitude of faith is presupposed. The death and resurrection of Christ (cf. 1 Cor 15:3–4; Rom 14:9; Acts 17:3 at Thessalonica itself) bear a causal relationship to the resurrection of Christians (*houtōs kai*). *God will bring into his company those who have fallen asleep through Jesus:* The resurrection of Christians is likewise attributed to God (1:10). Jesus is not the cause of death, but a bond persists between the Christian and Christ in death as in life (Rom 14:7–9; 1 Thes 5:10). Moreover, his death is full of hope because of Jesus; cf. "the dead in Christ" (4:16). The goal of God's activity is the reunion of the believer with the Risen Christ. **15–17.** These verses explain v. 14 in the traditional language of Jewish apocalyptic writing. *word of the Lord:* Paul's teaching appears to be based on the eschatological teaching of Christ (Mt 24–25), or on a special revelation (Acts 16:9–10; 27:23; 2 Cor 12:1; Gal 2:2; cf. 1 Cor 15:51). Perhaps Paul, under inspiration, merely applies the teaching of Christ to this situation. *we who live, who survive:* Not knowing the time of the Lord's coming (5:2; Mt 24:43 par), Paul cherishes the hope of living until the day of the parousia (cf. Dn 12:12–13; *2 Esdras* 5:4; 13:24) and so includes himself and his Christians among the survivors on the last day (1 Cor 15:51; → Pauline Theology, 79:46). *shall not precede:* The living "shall have no advantage over" the dead when Christ comes (cf. A. Wimmer, *Bib* 36 [1955] 273–86). **16–17.** A partial description of the parousia based on current cosmology; heaven, the dwelling place of God and the Risen Christ is above the earth and so the Lord descends; in going out to meet him, Christians must therefore ascend into the air. *command, voice of archangel, trumpet of God:* Probably synonymous, proclaiming the hour of the parousia and the assembly of God's people; the trumpet plays a role in OT theophanies and assemblies of God's people at Sinai (Ex 19:13,16,19), and in the prophets (Zeph 1:16; Is 27:13, etc.; cf. Mt 24:31; 1 Cor 15:52). In Ap 1:10; 4:1 the voice of the angel and the trumpet are one; angels mediate the orders of God in Ap 5:2; 7:2. *caught up:* 2 Cor 12:2,4; Ap 12:5; the passive voice suggests that God himself is the cause of this rapture. *clouds:* The traditional veil and accompaniment of God and of the Risen Christ as the Son of Man (Dn 7:13; Ap 14:14–16; Mk 9:7; 13:26; Acts 1:9; cf. R. B. Y. Scott, *NTS* 5 [1958] 127–32). "Going out to meet the Lord" may reflect either the Hellenistic reception of royal visitors or Ex 19:10–18. The Hellenistic ceremonial probably serves to portray a strictly religious concept, the reunion of Christians with Christ their king. *we shall always be with the Lord:* The climax of Paul's teaching in this pericope (5:10; 1 Cor 1:9; Rom 8:17; → Pauline Theology, 79:137).

26 **(D) The Date of the Parousia (5:1–11).** **1.** *times and seasons:* Synonymous and eschatological: the moments of divine intervention predetermined by God (Dn 2:21; 7:12). Knowledge of these times is a traditional concern of apocalyptic writing (Dn 9:2,24–27; *2 Baruch* 24:4; *2 Esdras* 6:59; *Sib Or* 3:55; Mt 24:3). **2.** *day of the Lord:* The parousia of Jesus now replaces the OT "day of Yahweh" (Am 5:18; Jl 2:1; Zeph 1:7; etc.). *thief in the night:* The image refers only to the suddenness of his coming, not to the time of day (Mt 24:43; 2 Pt 3:10). **3.** The great threat to vigilance is complacency and false prophets of continued prosperity (Jer 6:14; Ez 13:10,16; Mt 24:37–39; Lk 17:26–30). Bammel (*TLZ* 85 [1960] 837–40) sees here a reference to Roman peace (cf. *Pss Sol* 8:18,20). *sudden destruction:* Lk 21:34–36; eternal separation from God (2 Thes 1:9), opposed to salvation (v. 9). *birth pangs:* A prophetic image for sudden pain and eschatological distress (Hos 13:13; Is 13:8; 26:17; etc.). *they will not escape:* Impersonal and vague; the inevitability of divine justice (Jl 2:3).

27 **4–8a.** An exhortation to moral vigilance, playing upon the suggested opposition between day and night, light and darkness. **4–5.** Christians are united to Christ, the light of the world (Jn 8:12; 12:36; Eph 5:8; Col 1:13) and consequently are no longer subject to the assaults of darkness. Light and darkness are associated with the good and wicked in the OT and with the day of the Lord (Am 5:18; Is 5:20; Jl 4:14–16; Dt 28:29; Ps 118:105; Jb 29:3). In Judaism, especially at Qumran, light and darkness become two opposing kingdoms (1QS 1:9–10; 3:18–22; cf. Rigaux, *op. cit.*, 560–61). **8.** Christians exercise vigilance by faith, charity, and hope (1:3). The imagery of a warrior's panoply (cf. Eph 6:14–17) is based on Is 59:17 and Wis 5:17–23, where God arms himself in preparation for the eschatological judgment of his enemies. Here faith, hope, and charity (1 Cor 13:13) become the divine armor of the Christian (cf. Eph 6:11–13) against the satanic powers inimical to his salvation. Paul leaves hope until last, for his thought is directed by the tension toward eschatological salvation. Salvation is the object of Christian hope and preaching (Rom 1:16; Eph 1:13; Acts 4:12; 16:17; cf. S. Lyonnet, *VD* 36 [1958] 3–15). **9–10.** The Christian has not yet attained the full possession of salvation. *wrath:* God's punitive justice is only for his enemies (see comment on 1:10). **10.** *died for us:* The redemptive character of Christ's death is thus expressed. *wake, sleep:* Metaphors for life and death (cf. Rom 14:8–9). While entertaining the hope of living until the parousia, Paul took into account the possibility of dying before that day. **11.** Cf. 4:18. *edify one another:* To be understood in the strong sense of building up the temple of the Holy Spirit (1 Cor 6:19) and of the Church (1 Cor 14:4; cf. 1 Cor 3:9–17; Eph 2:20–23).

28 **(E) Exhortations for Community Living (5:12–24).** **12–13.** Respect for superiors; perhaps the *presbyteroi* whom Paul established in the communities he founded (cf. Acts 14:23). **12.** Their functions: (1) labor on behalf of the entire community; (2) leadership over others; (3) admonition or teaching (cf. Col 1:28; 3:16). *in the Lord:* Such superiors exercise the role of Christ in the community. **13.** *esteem them very highly in love:* Christian *agapē* is required to recognize the need of authority in the community, to ease the burden of its exercise, and to bear the inevitable friction that results. Such esteem and love are motivated by the "work" (*ergon*) that superiors perform for the community. **14–15.** Relations among Christians. Some commentators (John Chrysostom, Thomas Aq., Findlay, Vosté) consider these verses to be addressed to the superiors of 5:12–13; the majority, however, hold the exhortation to be general, even though those in authority are asked to take it most to heart. **14.** *reprove the disorderly:* Those described in 4:11–12 (cf. 2 Thes 3:6–15). *the fainthearted:* Those suffering despondency because of persecution or those concerned for the dead or because of the delay of the parousia (cf. 3:3–4; 4:13–17; 5:1–11). To comfort the fainthearted is a divine work (Is 57:15). *weak:* That is, in the faith (1 Cor 8:9,11; 9:22; Rom 14:1). *be patient toward all men:* The imitation of a divine quality (Ex 34:6; Ps 85:15; Gal 5:22). **15.** *do good to one another:* Cf. Mt 5:43–48; 1 Pt 2:19–21; Rom 12:17–21; a constant concern for the well-being of others is the fruit of charity (Rom 13:10; 1 Cor 13:4–7). **16–18.** The Christian spirit. Paul depicts Christianity not merely as a series of obligations toward God and the neighbor, but as a way of life oriented to God in joy, prayer, and thanksgiving. **18.** *in Christ Jesus:* God's plan for our sanctification and happiness (4:3,7; 5:9) is realized only through Christ. **19–22.** The recognition of charisms (1 Cor 12–14). **19.** True manifestations of God's Spirit must not be suppressed in the Church (Acts 7:51; Is 63:10), although the "distinguishing of spirits" is a necessary charism (1 Cor 12:10; 14:29) to deal with the inevitable risk of false spirits (2 Thes 2:2). **20.** *prophecies:* The inspired words of consolation and admonition spoken by members of the community in special contact with God; it denotes a transitory charism, not a specific class of Christians (1 Cor 14:31). **21–22.** Although Paul would give full scope to the work of the Spirit, he is also conscious of the dangers involved. **21.** *all things:* All extraordinary manifestations of the Spirit. **22.** The context and the use of *eidos* (appearance) suggest that this recommendation concerns the testing of spirits; it is not merely an exhortation to moral excellence, as Jb 1:1,8; 2:3 might suggest.

29 **23–24.** Final invocation (cf. 3:11–13). God is ultimately responsible for all Christian attainment. **23.** *God of peace:* A common formula in Paul (Rom 15:33; 16:20; 1 Cor 14:33; 2 Cor 13:11; Phil 4:9), designating God as the source of full eschatological salvation (Mi 5:4; Na 2:1; Hag 2:9; Zech 9:10; Is 9:5–6; 26:12). Sanctification is not only the will of God (4:3,7), but also his work (Ex 31:13; Lv 21:8; Ez 37:28; Jn 17:19). A sing. predicate, "whole" (*holoklēron*), indicates that the three nouns, "spirit," "soul," and "body," refer to the individual human being. Paul uses the three nouns together only here to describe man; it would therefore be improper to seek Paul's anthropology in the rhetoric of a final prayer. Although some ancient and modern commentators (Jerome, Thomas Aq., Estius, Luther, Allo, Buzy, Amiot, Oepke) think that Paul held for a tripartite division of man, the more common opinion (Eusebius, Theodore of Mopsuestia, Chrysostom, Theodoret, Ambrose, Cornelius a Lapide, Vosté, Milligan, Frame, Prat, Rigaux, *et al.*) holds that Paul does not depart from the current Jewish notion of soul and body as constituting the unity of man. All, however, do not understand the relation of spirit and soul in the same sense. *Pneuma* is used elsewhere by Paul of the spiritual part of man, in opposition to the body (e.g., 1 Cor 2:11; 5:3,4; 7:34; Rom 8:10, etc.), without any relation to the supernatural possession of the Spirit. *Psychē* in the NT often designates the seat of life, the person, even life itself. Paul is no doubt dependent on the OT usage of *rûaḥ* and *nepeš*. The former would designate the divine part of man; the latter the human person himself. But *bāśār* refers to the visible existent; all three can be used singly for man. If a distinction between *pneuma* and *psychē* is justified, it would be the distinction of the higher from the lower powers in man (cf. B. Rigaux, *op. cit.*, 596–600; A.-J. Festugière, *RSR* 20 [1930] 385–415; J. N. Sevenster, *NTS* 1 [1955] 291–96). **24.** God's fidelity to his own promises (2 Thes 3:3; 1 Cor 1:9; 10:13) will assure the effective completion of his election (1:4) and call (2:12; 4:7).

(III) Conclusion (5:25–28). **25.** Cf. 2 Thes 3:1; Rom 15:30; Eph 6:18–19; Col 4:3. Mutual prayer is an expression of love and a means of assistance, uniting distant friends. **26.** *holy kiss:* See comment on Rom 16:16. **27.** The public reading of Paul's letters in Christian assemblies assured their preservation and reception into the canon (cf. Col 4:16). **28.** A Christian blessing terminates all Paul's letters; the supreme mark of affection is to desire the grace of Christ for one's friends.

COMMENTARY ON 2 THES

30 **(I) The Persecuted May Expect Deliverance at the Judgment (1:1–12).** **1–2.** Paul begins the second letter with an address and greeting similar to that of 1 Thes, but with the addition of "from God our Father," etc., the one source of peace and grace. **3.** Cf. 1 Thes 1:2–8; a grateful acknowledgement of their faith, patience, and charity in spite of persecution. Paul offers them encouragement to endure in the thought of the parousia and the judgment of Christ. **4.** *even we take pride in you:* The Apostle cannot help but be gratefully cognizant of the good God has seen fit to achieve through his instrumentality (Rom 15:17–19; 1 Cor 15:10). *your endurance and faith:* Christian hope is manifest in *hypomonē* (steadfastness, 1 Thes 1:3) and *pistis*. The latter, repeated from v. 3, is not merely fidelity (Rom 3:3) nor charismatic faith (1 Cor 12:9; 13:2), but the fundamental Christian commitment considered in its constancy under persecution. **5.** The thought shifts, but the sentence continues. *a sure indication* [*endeigma*]: This noun stands in apposition to "endurance and faith in all your persecutions," etc. To suffer persecution for the faith is a guarantee of a future reward, for God is a just judge (Phil 1:28; Rom 2:5–11; 2 Cor 4:16–18). **5b–7a.** These verses express the twofold character of this judgment. **6.** *just:* The "just judgment" of v. 5 is first of all a retribution, in accordance with the law of talion. *Eiper* expresses a rhetorical but real condition; render (as in CCD) "Indeed it is just." *with affliction those who afflict you:* A verbal development of *thlipsis* in v. 4; there is a deliberate alliteration. **7a.** The reward of the faithful is "rest" (*anesis*) from sufferings (Acts 3:20; 1 Thes 4:17; 5:10). **7b–10.** A description of judgment dependent on the OT and on Jewish apocalyptic writing. Isaiah 2:10 is the primary source, but all is related to man's response to the gospel of our Lord Jesus (v. 8). **7b.** *revelation of the Lord Jesus:* Christ's coming will be an unveiling (*apokalypsis*) of the glory which he has attained with the Father and in which Christians are to share (v. 10). In Jewish apocalyptic literature God comes in judgment with angels who execute the decrees of his power (*2 Enoch* 29:3; *T. Judah* 3:10; *Enoch* 61:10). The NT transfers this imagery to Christ (Mt 13:39,49; 16:27; 24:30–31; 25:31; Mk 8:38; Lk 12:8–9), and the power of God becomes the power of Christ (1 Cor 1:24; 6:14; 2 Cor 13:4). **8.** *in flaming fire:* The glow of his majesty (Ex 3:2; Is 66:15; Acts 26:13; cf. P. Katz, *ZNW* 46 [1955] 133–38). Ignorance of God (1 Thes 4:10) and refusal to accept the gospel preached by Paul (3:14; Rom 10:16) characterize the enemies of Christians. **9.** The *punishment* is *eternal* [*unending*] *destruction*, a deprivation of the presence and glory of Christ, which is the lot of the faithful (1 Thes 4:17; 5:10); their continued existence is presupposed. **10.** *to be glorified in his saints:* Cf. Ps 68:36; 89:8; Is 49:3; 66:5; *en* with the dative connotes both the place and manner of Christ's glorification. The manifestation of the glory of God is the eschatological good (Is 40:5) and takes place at the revelation of Jesus Christ (Ti 2:13; 1 Pt 4:13; 5:10). Christians are to share in the divine glory of Jesus (Col 1:27; 3:4; Rom 8:18; Phil 3:21; 1 Cor 2:7; 15:43). *to be marveled at:* Cf. Wis 8:11; the admiration of the saved in Christ their Savior. *our testimony:* The passage concerns those who have accepted or rejected Paul's preaching. *on that day:* Placed at the end of the sentence, to create a triumphant effect (1 Thes 5:2). **11–12.** The above expectation becomes a prayer, a concise expression of the delicate co-ordination of divine initiative and grace with human effort in the progressive work of man's glorification. *worthy of his call: Klēsis*, the call from paganism to Christianity, is also an orientation to glory (Eph 1:18; Phil 3:14; 2 Tm 1:9–10; Heb 3:1). Perseverance in the vocation must be sought for as a gift (1 Thes 5:23). *bring to fulfillment every desire for good:* God must second all human efforts of progesss. *Eudokia* (good will) refers to a man's own good dispositions (Rom 10:1; Phil 1:15). **12.** *the name:* The very person of Christ. In the ancient East the use of the name called forth the effective power of the person (cf. L. Cerfaux, *Christ*, 478). All depends on the good favor and gift (*charis*) of God and Christ.

31 **(II) The Coming of the Lord (2:1–3:5).** Paul now turns to correct misunderstandings concerning the time of the parousia. The instruction (2:1–12) occasions a thanksgiving (2:13–17) and a prayer (3:1–5).

32 **(A) Signs of the Parousia (2:1–12).** **1.** *concerning the coming:* The Vg *per* is inaccurate. Paul writes about the event that all Christians desire (1 Thes 4:14,17). The final "assembly" (*episynagōgē*) of the people of God is a traditional prophetic and apocalyptic notion (Is 27:13; Sir 36:10; Ps 106:47; Mt 24:31; *T. Naphtali* 8:3; 2 Mc 2:18; *Pss Sol* 17:28,50). **2.** Something has shaken (*saleuthēnai*, aor. inf.) the peace of mind of the Thessalonians so that they are in a perturbed state (*throeisthai*, pres. inf.; cf. Mt 24:6; Gal 1:6–9). **2b.** Three possible causes: (1) a spirit: a charismatic gift, most likely of prophecy (1 Thes 5:19–21); (2) an utterance: a charismatic discourse of wisdom or knowledge (1 Cor 12:8), or a supposed report from Paul; (3) a letter attributed to us: although Paul takes care to authenticate this letter (3:17), it is not clear that such forged letters were actually circulating. *that the day of the Lord is already here:* The Vg *instat* is a facilitating interpretation (cf. Rom 8:38; 1 Cor 3:22). We do not know how they would have understood this false teaching, but it appears to have confirmed some of them in idleness (2 Thes 3:6–12). **3.** The danger of seductive error in the last days is a NT theme (Mt 24:4,11,24; 1 Cor 6:9; 15:33; 2 Tm 3:13). Two signs must precede the coming of Christ: (1) the apostasy; (2) the revelation of the Man of Sin (*hamartias*) or of lawlessness (l.v. *anomias*), a word that connotes all opposition to God (1QS 3:2–3; 5:10–11; 2 Cor 6:14–16). *apostasy:* Defection from the worship of God (Jos 22:22; Jer 2:19; 2 Chr 28:19); under the persecutions of Antiochus IV Epiphanes (175–164 BC) such defection was extensive among the Jews (1 Mc 2:15; Dn 9:4–11). Since that time, apostasy was a recognized phase of the final drama (*Enoch* 91:7; *Jub* 23:14–16; *2 Esdras* 5:1–2; cf. Mt 24:12, the cooling of love in face of *anomia*). The theological content of the apostasy is the final attempt of Satan to destroy God's kingdom through the defections of men. *Man of Sin:* Satan's agent in this work. The Hebr expressions, "man of sin" and "son of perdition" (cf. Jn 17:12), simply connote his intimate association with these realities (cf. Ap 9:11; 19:20; 20:14). The man of sin has commonly been identified with the Antichrist of the Johannine epistles (1 Jn 2:18,22; 4:3; 2 Jn 7); Paul describes him as an individual (2:4,9–10), although 1 Jn sees Antichrists in the heresiarchs of his day (1 Jn 2:18–19). The "Man of Sin" is an apocalyptic symbol for which Paul does not provide an historical identification. Commentators have sought to identify him with both ideologies and individuals throughout history. Following medieval heretics, Reformers saw the Pope as Antichrist; this opinion is abandoned by respectable Protestant exegesis today (cf. Rigaux, *op. cit.*, 259–73 for an history of the exegesis). **4.** He rebels against all forms of religion and cult (*sebasma* means a "cultic object"), and arrogates divine honors to himself. *all that is called God:* A Christian adaptation of Dn 11:36, "the God of gods." The rebellion is described in terms of the rebellion of Antiochus (Dn 11:36–37), and of the self-divinization of the kings of Tyre and Babylon (Ez 28:2,6,9; Is 14:13–14). *he sits in God's temple:* A figurative arrogation of divine honors; Paul considers the Temple of Jerusalem a symbol for God's throne.

33 **5.** Without completing his sentence, Paul concludes in a different manner. **6–10.** These verses develop vv. 3 and 4 by a theological and apocalyptic description of the conflict between Christ and the man of sin, now and at the end of time. **6–7.** The present conflict goes on in secret, for there is someone or something impeding the revelation of the Man of Sin. The "restrainer" (neut. *katechon*, masc. *katechōn*) is a new element in the drama, of which the Thessalonians are already aware; the word appears without an object and both as a neut. and a masc. singular. The meaning is lit.: "And now you know that which restrains, until he is revealed in his own time; for the mystery of lawlessness has already been put to work; (it operates in secret) only until he who is at present restraining gets out of the way." Satan has a secret plan (*mystērion*) and the Man of Sin will have a parousia, just as God has a secret plan (*mystērion*), and Christ will have a parousia. Among the Church Fathers, the civil order of the Roman Empire was a favorite candidate for the "restrainer"; the prayer of the Church or the preaching of the gospel are popular interpretations among the moderns; a divine decree, the Holy Spirit, Michael the Archangel have been other suggestions (cf. B. Rigaux, *op. cit.*, 274–79). But if Paul and the Thessalonians knew, they have not told us. The checking of Satan's power against the Church Triumphant during the present time is spoken of in Ap 20:1–3. **7.** *mystery:* The word *mystērion* is regularly used by Paul of God's plan for the salvation of men (→ Pauline Theology, 79:32–34). Satan has a similar plan for their destruction. The biblical use of *energeō* and *energia* suggests a superhuman activity (cf. Eph 2:1–2). **8.** Biblical language for the ease and irresistible power of Christ's victory over "the lawless one" (the Gk phrase *ho anomos* for *anthrōpos* *anomias*); cf. Is 11:4; Jb 4:9; Wis 11:20; 1 Cor 15:24–26; Ap 19:15,20. *by the manifestation of his coming:* *Epiphaneia* connotes both the manifestation of Hellenistic deities and the joyous arrival of divinized kings. In the LXX it is used of the manifestation of God (2 Sm 7:23; 2 Mc 2:21; 3:24; 15:27). **9–10a.** A parody of the parousia of Christ (Ap 13:11–14); signs and wonders accompany the manifestation of God (Ex 7:3; 11:9), the activity of Christ (Acts 2:22), and that of the apostles (Acts 5:12; 6:8; 14:3; 2 Cor 12:12). Deceit (*pseudos*), wickedness (*adikia*), the lost (*apollymenoi*) are the eschatological characteristics of the enemies of God, in contrast to truth (*alētheia*), justice (*dikaiosynē*), and the saved (*sōzomenoi*). The dualism recalls that of QL (1QS 3:18–4:26); but as 10b–12 show, God is in complete control and man exercises his free will in accepting or rejecting the gospel. **10b.** *love of truth:* Man's free acceptance of the gospel; this love is presented as a gift, which man may reject (1 Thes 1:6; 2:13). **11.** *a power of delusion:* Cf. 3 Kgs 22:23; 2 Thes 2:9; God punishes man's rejection of his gift by handing him over to the deceptions of Satan (Rom 1:25–26; 1 Cor 5:5). **12.** The purpose of God's action; the passage suggests the terrifying responsibility of human freedom. Not to believe the truth is to take pleasure in wickedness (1 Cor 13:6; Rom 1:18).

(Andriessen, P., "Celui qui retient la venue du Seigneur," *Bijdr* 21 [1960] 20–30. Brunec, M., "De 'homine peccati' in 2 Th 2,1–12," *VD* 35 [1957] 3–33. Buzy, D., "L'adversaire et l'obstacle," *RSR* 24 [1934] 402–31. Cothenet, E., "La IIe Épître aux Thessaloniciens et l'Apocalypse synoptique," *RSR* 42 [1954] 5–39. Cullmann, O., "Le caractère eschatologique du devoir missionaire et de la conscience apostolique de Saint Paul. Étude sur le *katechon(ōn)* de II Thess.," *RHPR* 16 [1936] 210–45. Furfey, P. H., "The Mystery of Lawlessness," *CBQ* 8 [1946] 179–91. Orchard, J. B., "Thessalonians and the Synoptic Gospels," *Bib* 19 [1938] 19–42. Rigaux, B., *L'Antéchrist et l'opposition au royaume messianique dans l'Ancien et le Nouveau Testament* [Louvain, 1932]. Schmid, J., "Der Antichrist und die hemmende Macht (2 Thess 2,1–12)," *TQ* 129 [1949] 323–43.)

34 **(B) Thanksgiving, Encouragement, and Prayer (2:13–3:5).** The instruction on the parousia closes with personal reflections and recommendations, as if the letter were drawing to a close. **13–14.** Gratitude to God that the Thessalonians have not refused the gospel; they are loved, chosen, and called by God. *chose you as first fruits for salvation:* So Nestle and Merk, who read *aparchēn;* or *from the beginning for salvation:* so Tischendorf, Westcott-Hort, Souter, Vogels, who read *ap'archēs.* The latter is more consonant with Paul's ordinary mode of expression (1 Cor 2:7; Col 1:26; Eph 1:4); it is hard to see how the Thessalonians would be the first fruits (cf. M. J. Suggs, *NovT* 4 [1960] 60–68). *salvation:* See comment on 1 Thes 5:8. *by the sanctification of the Spirit and faith in the truth:* The work of the Spirit is coordinated with the human response of faith in the gospel message. **14.** *through our gospel:* Preaching is the instrument through which the call of God is made known (Rom 8:30; 10:14–17; → Pauline Theology, 79:125). **15.** *hold to the traditions:* The *paradoseis* include the practical instructions and orders of the Apostle (3:6–15) as well as the general kerygma concerning the mystery of Christ (cf. *Recueil L. Cerfaux,* 2, 253–63, 265–82). **16–17.** Christ precedes God the Father; sing. participles and verbs follow; cf. Rom 15:5. *eternal encouragement and good hope:* The invocation prepares the petition; all is directed to the glory of the parousia. Understand *en chariti* as "graciously," stressing the gratuity of the gift.

35 **3:1–2.** A request for prayers (1 Thes 5:25) and the continuous progress of the gospel (Rom 9:16; 1 Cor 2:6); the reception of the gospel is its glorification (see comments on 2 Thes 1:10,12). **2.** Cf. 2:7,10–11. **3–5.** These verses repeat the thought of vv. 2:16–17. **3.** *the evil one:* Satan (see comments on 1 Thes 2:18; 2 Thes 2:9). **5.** Prayer for an increase in the gift of God's love and in the patient endurance of which Christ is both the example and the donor (Rom 15:5).

36 **(III) The Admonition of the Disorderly (3:6–15).** Cf. 1 Thes 4:11–12; 5:14. Paul exercises his apostolic authority to remedy an abuse that must have worsened since the first letter; there is no indication that it was widespread. **6.** To correct a particular abuse, he invokes the authority of Christ (1 Cor 5:4; 1:10). The community need not support the lazy and the disorderly; the withdrawal suggested here is not as drastic as the excommunication of 1 Cor 5:5,11. The *paradosis* here refers to a particular precept, reinforced by the Apostle's own example. **7–8.** Paul's example presented negatively and positively (1 Thes 2:9; 4:12; 1 Cor 9:12,18). **10.** *if anyone is not willing to work:* The *paradosis* announced in v. 6: the emphasis is on the vb., *ou thelei.* There is no fanatical exaltation in Paul; while ardently awaiting the parousia, the Christian is to engage fully in his earthly tasks. **11.** *for we hear:* Pres. tense, as if the news is quite recent; only *some* are involved. Their disorderly lives consist in the neglect of fruitful work and great activity disturbing others (a play on words: *mēden ergazomenous alla periergazomenous*). **12.** Every Christian must support himself if he is able. **13–15.** A sanction against the obstinate, preserving fraternal charity. **14.** *our word:* The order given in v. 12. Withdrawal of the community from the recalcitrant is intended to shame them into a conversion of life; *synanamignysthai* signifies intimate association, not just ordinary converse. **15.** The undisciplined remain brothers, even while being sternly corrected.

(IV) Conclusion (3:16–18). **16.** Cf. 1 Thes 5:23; "Christ" replaces "God" in 2 Thes. **17.** Although the letter was dictated, Paul writes the closing words himself (cf. 1 Cor 16:21; Col 4:18; → NT Epistles, 47:20). It is also an added precaution for Thessalonica (cf. 2:2). Paul's writing was distinctive (Gal 6:11) and served as an equivalent to the modern signature. **18.** The final blessing; cf. 1 Thes 5:28.

49

THE LETTER TO THE GALATIANS

Joseph A. Fitzmyer, S.J.

BIBLIOGRAPHY

1 Amiot, F., *Saint Paul: Épître aux Galates; Épîtres aux Thessaloniciens* (VS 14; Paris, 1946). Beyer, H. W. and P. Althaus, *Der Galaterbrief* (NTD 8; Göttingen, 1962). Bonnard, P., *L'Épître de Saint Paul aux Galates* (CNT 9; Neuchâtel, 1953). Burton, E. deW., *The Epistle to the Galatians* (ICC; N.Y., 1920). Buzy, D., *L'Épître aux Galates* (*PSB* 11/2; Paris, 1948). Duncan, G. S., *The Epistle of Paul to the Galatians* (MNTC; London, 1934). Grayston, K., *The Epistles to the Galatians and to the Philippians* (Naperville, 1957). Kürzinger, J., *Die Briefe des Apostels Paulus: die Briefe an die Korinther und Galater* (Würzburg, 1954). Kuss, O., *Die Briefe an die Römer, Korinther und Galater* (RNT 6; Regensburg, 1940) 248–84. Lagrange, M.-J., *Saint Paul: Épître aux Galates* (EBib, 2nd ed.; Paris, 1950). Lietzmann, H., *An die Galater* (HNT 10; Tübingen, 1932). Lyonnet, S., *Les Épîtres de Saint Paul aux Galates, aux Romains* (BJ, 2nd ed.; Paris, 1959). Maurer, C., *Der Galaterbrief* (Zürich, 1943). Oepke, A., *Der Brief des Paulus an die Galater* (ThHk 9, 2nd ed.; Berlin, 1957). Ridderbos, H. N., *The Epistle of Paul to the Churches of Galatia* (NICNT; Grand Rapids, 1956). Sanders, J. N., "Galatians," *PCB* 973–79. Schlier, H., *Der Brief an die Galater* (Meyer 7, 12th ed.; Göttingen, 1962). Schmidt, K. L., *Ein Gang durch den Galaterbrief* (2nd ed.; Zollikon-Zürich, 1947). Tenney, M. C., *Galatians, the Charter of Christian Liberty* (Grand Rapids, 1950). Viard, A., "Paul 4. Galates (Épître aux)," *VDBS* 7 (1961) 211–26; *Épître aux Galates* (SB; Paris, 1964). Zahn T., *Der Brief des Paulus an die Galater* (Kommentar z. NT 9; Leipzig, 1905).

Cerfaux, L., R–F, *INT* 400–412; F–B 190–98. Guthrie, *NTI* 1, 72–91; Metzger, B. M., *IPLAP* 82–94. Wik, *NTI* 372–80.

INTRODUCTION

2 **(I) Authenticity.** The Pauline authorship of Gal was doubted by a few 19th-cent. scholars (B. Bauer, G. A. van den Bergh van Eysinga, R. Steck); but no one seriously questions it today, just as it was not contested in antiquity (see F–B 198; R–F, *INT* 400–401).

3 **(II) Destination.** Paul writes to the "churches of Galatia" (1:2). The *Galatai*, originally an Indo-Aryan tribe of Asia, were related to the Celts or Gauls ("qui ipsorum lingua Keltae, nostra Galli appellantur" [J. Caesar, *Bell. gall.* 1.1]). About 279 BC some of them invaded the lower Danube region and Macedonia, descending even into the Gk peninsula. After they were stopped by the Aetolians in 278, the remnant fled across the Hellespont into Asia Minor. There they harassed the country widely until Attalus I, king of Pergamum, defeated them (*ca.* 239 BC) and fixed their territory between the Sangarius and Halys rivers around the three towns Ancyra, Pessinus, and Tavium. But they continued to annoy their neighbors until Manlius Vulso, a Roman consul, subdued them in 189 BC. Rome subsequently used their territory as a buffer state against Pergamum. In the Mithridatic wars they remained loyal to Rome, and as a reward their territory was gradually expanded. About 40 BC some areas of Pisidia, Phrygia, Lycaonia, and Isauria became part of Galatia. When the last king of the Galatians, Amyntas, willed his land to the Romans, it was incorporated into the empire and in 25 BC was made into a province, *Galatia*, by Augustus. As such it took in more than the original "Galatian country" in northern Asia Minor, including a large part of the south and center as well. In the southern region were situated the towns of Pisidian Antioch, Iconium, Lystra, and Derbe. The population of the whole area was quite mixed: Galatians, Greeks, *Gallograeci*, Romans, and Jews (see *EDB* 829–31; *OCD* 376).

4 In what sense did Paul use the name "Galatia"? In antiquity commentators understood the term to refer to N Galatia, the region about Ancyra, Pessinus, and Tavium. In 1748 J. J. Schmidt proposed what has come to be called the "South Galatian theory," which was later espoused by E. Renan and especially by W. M. Ramsay, the famous Anatolian explorer. It still enjoys considerable vogue among NT scholars. According to this theory Paul would have written to the churches of Antioch, Iconium, Lystra, and Derbe, which he had founded on Mission I (Acts 13:14,51; 14:6) and visited again on Mission II (Acts 16:1–2). The reasons for the South Galatian theory are mainly these: (1) Unlike Luke, Paul normally used the official Roman province names for regions of which he spoke rather than names of countries (e.g., Achaia [Rom 15:26], Macedonia [1 Thes 1:7–8], Asia [Rom 16:5], etc.). (2) Neither Acts 16:6 nor 18:23, which mention Paul's passage through Galatia, suggests the foundation of any Christian communities in N Galatia. (3) Paul probably did not even speak the Galatian language, which in Jerome's time was still a form of Celtic. (4) Gal 3:2–3,13–14,23–24; 4:2,5; 5:1 seem to presuppose Jewish-Christian readers, who would only have been found in the Hellenized towns of S Galatia. However, it may be asked whether any of these reasons is really valid. Apropos of (1), Gal 1:21 shows that Paul uses "Syria and Cilicia" as names of countries, not as names of the Roman provinces; in Gal 1:17 he speaks of "Arabia," which did not become a province until AD 106. Moreover, even if one hesitates about "Galatia" in 1:2, there is little room for hesitation about the meaning of *Galatai* (3:1), the name of a barbarian race, which Paul, himself a native of southern Asia Minor, would scarcely apply to inhabitants of the Hellenized cities of Pisidia and Lycaonia. (2) The argument proceeds from the silence in Acts, in which many of Luke's accounts are known to be telescoped résumés. But Acts 18:23, in fact, presupposes communities already established. Further, the natural explanation of Acts 16:6 is that Paul passed from Lystra and Iconium into Phrygia and the "Galatian country"—note the expression, also found in 18:23. (3) If it is true that the Galatians of the N spoke a different language, it probably would not have been the only place where Paul might have had to use an interpreter; cf. Acts 14:11. (4) Finally, none of the verses of Gal cited need be so interpreted as to mean that Jewish Christians apart from the Judaizers were really members of the Galatian communities. In fact, Gal 4:8; 5:2–3; 6:12–13 suggest rather the pagan background of the majority of the readers. In Antioch, Lystra, etc., where Jews are known to have lived, it is not unlikely that the problem of the relation of the Law to Christianity would have been faced even earlier. The infatuation with the Law presupposed by Gal 1:6 seems to be of recent vintage. All of this makes it more likely that Paul wrote the letter to the predominantly Gentile communities in N Galatia.

(F–B 191–93. Guthrie, *NTI* 1, 72–87. R–F, *INT* 401–3. Wik, *NTI* 374–76.)

5 **(III) Date.** The letter is not easily dated—Gal 4:13 suggests that it was written after a second visit to Galatia, probably that of Acts 18:23 on Mission III. Ephesus is the likely place of the letter's origin. At any rate, it seems to belong to the period of Paul's major struggle with the Judaizing influence in the early Church, when he also wrote 1 Cor, 2 Cor, Rom, and probably Phil. Almost certainly Gal preceded Rom (*ca.* AD 58); its relation to 1 Cor and 2 Cor is problematical. A not unlikely date for Gal is *ca.* AD 54–55, not too long after Paul's arrival in Ephesus on Mission III. An earlier date is often given by proponents of the South Galatian theory, but it is difficult to reconcile it with all the data. C. E. Faw (*Biblical Research* 4 [1960] 25–38) argues for a date situating Gal between 2 Cor and Rom.

6 **(IV) Occasion and Purpose.** Shortly after Paul's second visit to Galatia "some agitators" (1:7) there impugned Paul's authority as an apostle (apparently on the grounds that his commission did not come from Christ personally); they claimed that he was not preaching the true gospel (apparently because he neglected the Mosaic Law). They seem to have accused him of opportunism for having permitted circumcision (Gal 5:11; possibly an allusion to Timothy's circumcision "because of the Jews" [Acts 16:3]) and for watering down the requirements of the gospel for the sake of the Gentiles. Paul had learned of the fascination of the Galatians for these new demands of these Judaizers and of the confusion this caused in the Galatian communities. This prompted him to send a strong letter, warning the churches against this "different gospel," defending his position as an apostle, stressing the Christian's new-found freedom vis-à-vis the Law, and insisting that his gospel was the only correct view of Christianity, as recent events had shown. Although he calls the Galatians "senseless" (3:1), he still finds room in his heart for "my children" (4:19) and "brothers" (4:12; 5:11).

7 Who were the Judaizers of the Galatian communities? They seem to have been Christians of some exaggerated or strict Jewish background, which set them apart from the group of moderate Jewish Christians represented by apostles such as Peter, Paul, and even James. They are often thought to have been of Pharisaic background, such as those in Acts 15:5 who insisted on circumcision for all Christians. But there is no certainty that the Judaizers of Asia Minor are the same as those in Acts, or that they had anything to do with "the people from James" (Gal 2:12) who influenced the Antiochene church. It is not unlikely that they were syncretists: Christians of Jewish (perhaps Essene) background, affected by other Anatolian influences. They seem to be related to the false teachers of not-too-distant Colossae, who advocated reverence for the "elemental spirits of the world" (Gal 4:3,9; Col 2:8,20) and observance of special "days, months, seasons, and years" (Gal 4:10; Col 2:16). The Galatian Judaizers apparently were not advocating the observance of the whole Mosaic Law, but the adoption of certain Jewish practices. Paul rejects their claims for circumcision, the celebration of special (Jewish) feasts, and the reverence for angels or spirits. He argues that to submit to circumcision obliges a man "to keep the whole Law" (5:2–3). It is hard to say whether they knew of the decision of the Jerusalem "Council" on circumcision (Acts 15:1–12). But it is to be noted that Paul in effect quotes it to them. Long before the discovery of the Qumran scrolls, J. B. Lightfoot related the "Colossian heresy" to Essenism (*Saint Paul's Epistles to the Colossians and to Philemon* [London, 1892] 81ff.). The data from the Qumran scrolls confirms this relation (cf. Col 1:12–13; 1QS 11:7–8; Col 2:16; 1QS 10:1–8; CD 8:15; etc.); cf. P. Benoit, *NTS* 7 (1960–61) 287. Without stressing the Gnostic element as much as Lightfoot did, we think it likely that the Galatian Judaizers are somehow related to the same general background in Asia Minor.

8 **(V) Relation of Gal to Rom.** Clearly, Gal is not merely an outline or rough draft of Rom, for a difference of perspective marks the two letters. In Rom Paul presents his apostolic and missionary reflections on the historic possibility now offered men through the preaching of the gospel—to be justified and sanctified, and to live a life for God in Christ. It is basically an exposé of uprightness and the love of God, which brings about man's justification and sanctification—the process of Christian life that man must inaugurate by an act of faith. This gospel is the "power of God for the salvation of man" (Rom 1:16). In Gal, however, Paul writes a polemical letter, warning the Galatian churches against a Judaizing error. His emphasis is on the new freedom bestowed in Christ; the rejection of the Law and of circumcision are uppermost in his mind. Justification by faith and life in Christ are somewhat secondary. These rather emerge as the principal themes in Rom. Nothing in Rom corresponds to Gal 1:1–2:14, but the résumé of Paul's gospel in Gal 2:15–21 is almost an outline of Rom 1–8, with the same positive progress of thought.

9 **(VI) Outline.** The Letter to the Galatians is outlined as follows:

(I) Introduction (1:1–9)
 (A) Opening formula (*praescriptio*) (1:1–5)
 (B) Amazement (1:6–7) and Anathema (1:8–9)
(II) Part I (1:10–2:21) Personal and Historical: Paul Defends His Gospel
 (A) Paul's Gospel Is Not of Human Origin, but Divine (1:10–24)
 (B) Paul's Gospel Approved by the Jerusalem Leaders (2:1–10)
 (C) Paul's Gospel Revealed Peter's Inconsistency at Antioch (2:11–14)
 (D) Paul's Résumé of His Gospel (2:15–21)
(III) Part II (3:1–4:31) Scriptural: In God's Plan Faith, Not the Law, Saves Man
 (A) The Reign of Faith (3:1–28)
 (B) The Reign of Christian Freedom (3:29–4:20)
 (C) The Allegory of Sarah and Hagar Illustrates This Freedom (4:21–31)
(IV) Part III (5:1–6:10) Hortatory: Preserve That Freedom in Christ
 (A) Warning Not to Lose Such Freedom in Christ (5:1–12)
 (B) Instructions for the Correct Use of Christian Freedom (5:13–6:10)
(V) Conclusion (6:11–18) Paul's "Signature" and Résumé; Farewell Blessing

COMMENTARY

10 **(I) Introduction (1:1–9).**

(A) Opening Formula (1:1–5). As in Rom, Paul expands the opening formula (1–5) by incorporating into it motifs of the letter: the defense of his apostolate (its independence and divine origin); the divine plan for the justification of man through Christ. **1.** *Paul an apostle:* Paul will argue against the idea that because he was not one of the Twelve, he has no real authority. Here he deliberately assumes the title "apostle" to emphasize his equality with the Twelve. His authoritative commission comes from the Risen Lord. The word *apostolos*, rarely found in extrabiblical Greek, developed a specific Christian nuance under the influence of the contemporary Jewish (rabbinical) usage of *šᵉlîaḥ* (one sent): a representative sent with full powers to perform a definite (legal, prophetic, or missionary) charge (see K. H. Rengstorf, *Apostleship* [*BKW* 6; London, 1952]; *ThDNT* 1, 437–43; → Aspects NT Thought, 78:174–177.) *God the Father who raised...:* Paul's commission to proclaim the gospel is divine, not human; directly received, not delegated by men. Its ultimate origin lies in him who put the final seal of approval on the very mission of Christ himself (see Acts 17:31). Note that the resurrection is attributed to the Father (cf. Rom 4:24; Acts 13:34; → Pauline Theology, 79:72). **3.** *grace and peace:* Paul's greeting invokes a share in the Messianic blessings (→ NT Epistles, 47:8), derived from both the Father and Christ; contrast his anathema (1:8–9). **4.** *who offered himself:* The letter's dominant motif is sounded: salvation through Christ according to the Father's plan. *from the present wicked world* [*age*]*:* Contemporary Jewish theology contrasted "this world [age]" with "the world [age] to come." Paul echoes that contrast here, and sees the former dominated by Satan (see 2 Cor 4:4; Eph 2:2; 6:12). Christ's "giving" of himself has brought about the meeting of the two ages (1 Cor 10:11) and freed man from the influence of "this age" (cf. Eph 2:6).

11 **(B) Amazement (1:6–7) and Anathema (1:8–9).** Instead of his customary thanksgiving (→ NT Epistles, 47:8) Paul voices his surprise and shock at Galatian fickleness. Denouncing any other teaching as a spurious gospel, he affirms that his alone is the real "gospel of Christ." **6.** *so quickly:* Either in the sense of "so soon after your conversion [and my evangelization]" or "so easily." His amazement is really mild, when it is compared with the curse invoked on those who mislead them. *him who called you:* The Father, since Pauline usage usually makes *theos* the subject of "to call" (Gal 1:15; Rom 4:17; 8:30; 9:24; 1 Cor 1:9; etc.); the Father's plan is executed through the grace (benevolence) of Christ. A possible, but less probable interpretation: "turn away from Christ who has called you in grace." **7.** *any other* [*gospel*]*:* Since the gospel is a "force for salvation" (Rom 1:16), emanating from Christ, who is not divided (1 Cor 1:13), there can be only one gospel (Eph 4:5). This Paul has already proclaimed to them. *some people:* The Judaizers (→ 6–7 above). **8.** *an angel from heaven:* Cf. 2 Cor 11:4. In Gal 3:19–20 Paul refers to the Jewish belief that the Mosaic Law was given to men by angels. Even if one of them were to appear again with a modified gospel, he is not to be heard—in fact, Paul curses him. *anathema:* The word originally meant "a votive offering set up in a temple" (Lk 21:5; cf. AG 53), but in time, especially under LXX influence (Nm 21:3; Dt 7:26), it came to mean an "object of a curse." So Paul uses it to utter a solemn curse on the Judaizers (see 1 Cor 12:3; 16:22; Rom 9:3).

12 **(II) Part I (1:10–2:21) Personal and Historical: Paul Defends His Gospel.** The Judaizers had apparently accused Paul of having derived his message not from Christ, but from other preachers, and of having watered it down for Gentiles by eliminating the obligation of circumcision. His reply is to reaffirm the divine origin of his apostolic commission and to explain his relations with the mother church of Jerusalem.

13 **(A) Paul's Gospel Is Not of Human Origin, but Divine (1:10–24).** **10.** A transitional verse. *am I courting the favor of men—or of God?:* Paul rejects the accusation that he was watering down the Gospel to win many converts (see 1 Thes 2:4; 2 Cor 5:11). *still trying to please men:* As formerly, in the time before his conversion, when he persecuted the church of God (1:13). Now service of Christ has delivered him from such motivating vainglory. *a slave of Christ:* His conversion has freed him from the "yoke of slavery," which was the Mosaic Law (5:1), with its emphasis on human achievement. He has become a slave of Christ, prompt to obey him (Rom 6:16–20). There is also a further nuance. In Rom 1:1; Phil 1:1 Paul calls himself a "slave" like certain great OT figures who served Yahweh faithfully (Moses, 4 Kgs 18:12 [LXX]; Joshua, Jgs 2:8; Abraham, Ps 104:42). If he were courting human favor, he would not be true to such a calling. **11.** *I assure you:* The same solemn affirmation introduces the kerygmatic fragment that Paul "received" and "passed on" in 1 Cor 15:1. But his "gospel" is from Christ; as in 1 Thes 2:13 it is even said to be "from God." *the gospel I have preached:* The essence of what Paul likes to call "my gospel" (Rom 2:16; 16:25; 2 Cor 4:3; 1 Thes 1:5; etc.) is that salvation is possible for all men alike through faith in Christ (→ Pauline Theology, 79:27–34). **12.** *through a revelation of Jesus Christ:* The genitive can be either objective (see 1:16) or subjective (in contrast to "from man"). The revelation on the road to Damascus (Acts 9:5) illumined Paul about Christ and his meaning for all men—about the essential dynamic character of the gospel, not necessarily its "form." Verses 11 and 12 do not mean that facts about the life of Christ were communicated miraculously to Paul so that he never had to depend on an early tradition emanating from the Jerusalem church. Fragments of the kerygma in his letters (1 Cor 11:23–25; 15:1–7) reveal a form similar to that found elsewhere in the NT (see B. Gerhardsson, *Memory and Manuscript* [Lund, 1961], 263–73, 288–306; W. Baird, *JBL* 76 [1957] 181–91).

14 **13.** *my former conduct as a Jew:* Paul's former way of life hardly provided the psychological background from which his "gospel" would naturally have developed. As a Pharisee (Phil 3:5–6; Acts 22:3), he resolutely rejected what was opposed to the Mosaic Law and the traditions of the Fathers (Pharisaic interpretations of the written Torah; see Mk 7:1–13). *I persecuted the church of God:* See Acts 8:3; 9:1–2. The phrase, "church of God," reflects the OT *q*^{e}*hal Yahweh* (Nm 16:20; 20:4), the cultic assembly of the People of God in the desert. As used by Paul, it was, above all, a honorific title for the Jewish-Christian churches in Jerusalem and Judea, the Christian counterpart of the old cultic assembly (see 1 Thes 2:14; 2 Thes 1:4; 1 Cor 11:16; 15:9; → Pauline Theology, 79:150). **15.** *from my mother's womb:* Like Jeremiah (Jer 1:5) and even like the Servant of Yahweh (Is 49:1), Paul had been destined for the apostolate by a gratuitous call from the Father, antedating his very existence. Did Paul consider himself another Servant of Yahweh? (see D. M. Stanley, *CBQ* 16 [1954] 385–425). **16.** *to reveal his son to me:* Lit., "in me"; but *en* with the dative can equal the simple dative (Bl–Deb–F § 220,1; see 1:12; 1 Cor 15:10). Paul emphasizes that he has "seen the Lord" (1 Cor 9:1) and is therefore an apostle. Another translation, "through me," is also possible, but seems redundant in view of the following clause. *that I might announce the good news of him among the Gentiles:* Cf. 2:7; Acts 9:15,20; 13:47. Paul connects his apostolic mission to the Gentiles with the revelation of Christ, but his words do not force us to conclude to a simultaneity of these two events (see A.-M. Denis, *RB* 64 [1957] 335–62, 492–515; B. Rigaux, *Saint Paul et ses lettres* [Bruges, 1962] 82–97). *I consulted no human being:* Lit., "flesh and blood" (1 Cor 15:50; Eph 6:12). This emphatic denial of the human origin of his commission is explained by the chronological and geographical details that follow. **17.** *to Jerusalem:* His basic insight into Christ did not come from the traditional center from which the "word of the Lord" went forth to men (Is 2:3; Lk 24:48). *apostles before me:* Although conscious that he is the "least important" of the apostles (1 Cor 15:9), he emphatically denies that he is an apostle of only second rank. *to Arabia:* Most likely the Nabatean kingdom of Aretas IV Philopatris (2 Cor 11:32) in Transjordan, east and south of Damascus, and stretching westward south of Palestine toward Suez. The nature of this withdrawal is not indicated, and his sojourn there is passed over in Acts. Perhaps it fits in chronologically between 9:22–23 (→ Life of Paul, 46:24). How long did he stay? We are not told.

15 **18.** *then after three years:* To be reckoned from his return to Damascus; this detail is probably analogous with "some time" (Acts 9:23). *to get information from Cephas:* The meaning of the Gk inf. *historēsai* is disputed. Basically it means "to inquire about, into [a person, a thing]," "to go and examine" (a thing). Many ancient Gk and Lat interpreters understood it simply as "to see" (Vg *videre*), which has often been said to mean simply "to pay a [social] call on" Cephas. But there is little evidence for such a meaning. Hence, Paul visited Peter for the purpose of inquiry (LS 842), to get from him information about Jesus' teaching and ministry. (See G. D. Kilpatrick, "Galatians 1:18 ΙΣΤΟΡΗΣΑΙ ΚΗΦΑΝ," *NT Essays* [Fest. T. W. Manson; Manchester, 1959] 144–49.) It was probably during the 15 days he spent with Cephas that Paul learned "traditions" of the Jerusalem church (2 Thes 3:6; 1 Cor 11:2,23–25; 15:3–7). Although the identity of Cephas and Peter is sometimes questioned (see C. M. Henze, *DThomP* 61 [1958] 63–67), it is normally and widely accepted (see O. Cullmann, *Peter* [Phila., 1953] 18, n. 7; *ThWNT* 6, 99–112). *Kēphas* (a Gk form of the Aram *kēphā*, "rock, stone") was not a common personal name, but rather a title denoting the quality of the bearer (like Maccabee, "the hammer"). Although Peter is in virtue of this title a "rock" in the Christian eschatological Temple, he is also one of its "pillars" (2:9). **19.** *but only James:* Or possibly, "except James." The conj. *ei mē* can be either adversative ("but," as in Gal 2:16; Mt 12:4), or exceptive (see *GrBib* § 470). If the first meaning is correct (and it seems preferable), then James is distinguished from the apostles. If the second is used, then James is said to be an apostle; but this does not mean that he is to be identified either with James, son of Zebedee, or James, son of Alphaeus. James, the "brother" of the Lord, was the first "bishop" of Jerusalem, but not one of the Twelve (→ Aspects NT Thought, 78:167–68). *the brother of the Lord:* In classical and Hellenistic Greek *adelphos* means "blood brother." In the LXX it translates Hebr *'āḥ*, even when used in the sense of "kinsman" (Gn 13:8; 29:12–15; see AG 15). Greek papyri from Egypt also preserve the wide sense of *adelphos*, "relative" (see J. J. Collins, *TS* 5 [1944] 484–94). In view of the NT teaching on the virginal conception of Jesus (Mt 1:18–25; Lk 1:34) and the Christian tradition about Mary "ever virgin," in the Creeds, *adelphos* is understood as "kinsman, relative." **21.** *Syria and Cilicia:* To Tarsus actually (Acts 9:30), his native town, which became the center of his apostolate for several years, so that he was not "personally" a minister to the "churches in Judea."

16 **(B) Paul's Gospel Approved by the Jerusalem Leaders (2:1–10).** **1.** *once again in fourteen years:* The usual translation, "14 years later," has been questioned by S. Giet (*RSR* 41 [1953] 323–24) on the score that elsewhere in Paul's writings *dia* with the genitive means "during (the course of)." This meaning, plus the use of "again," seems to imply a reckoning of the date from his conversion (*ca.* AD 36). Correlation of this visit to Jerusalem with the data in Acts constitutes one of the most difficult exegetical problems of the NT. Nevertheless, one cannot escape the impression that Gal 2 refers to Acts 15 (vv. 1–12 at least); but many problems remain in this identification (→ Life of Paul, 46:29–34). *Barnabas:* A Cypriote Levite, named Joseph, subsequently called Barnabas by the apostles (Acts 4:36) with the popular etymology, "son of Consolation." He was Paul's companion during Mission I (Acts 13:1–14:28), up to the Jerusalem "Council." *Titus:* A Gentile Christian, who reconciled Paul with the Corinthian church (2 Cor 3:13; 7:6,13–14; 8:6,16,23; 12:18), and was later left in Crete to organize the church there (Tit 1:4). **2.** *because of a revelation:* In Acts 15:2 the reason for the visit is given as a decision of the Antiochene community. If Paul means that he himself had the revelation, then he mentions it at least to show that he was not summoned by the Jerusalem apostles. *privately to those of repute:* He slightly disparages the Jerusalem "pillars" whose authority he nevertheless recognizes. **3.** *not compelled to be circumcised:* It is impossible to say whether Paul means that Titus was in fact not circumcised or that he was not "compelled," but agreed to submit to it. The general tenor of the passage would be in favor of the former. **4.** *false brothers:* More than likely these are the same persons as the Jewish-Christian converts from Pharisaism of Acts 15:5, who pressed for the circumcision of Gentiles and their obligation to observe the Mosaic Law. *the freedom we have in Christ Jesus:* This short phrase sums up the message of Gal: in Christ we have secured freedom from the Law and "the flesh" (5:1, 13; cf. Rom 6:18,20,22; 7:3; 8:2). **5.** *not even for a moment did we yield:* Paul boasts as if he influenced the assembly, but Acts 15:7 gives the credit to Peter. **6.** *the men of repute:* Undoubtedly James, Cephas, and John (2:9). *what kind of people they were:* A difficult, parenthetical statement that seems to mean that Paul was not overawed by the prestige they had gained for having been eyewitnesses of Jesus' mission. Such an experience and such prestige could not outweigh the truth of the God-given gospel. *added nothing to me:* His essential message was not deficient, despite the claims of the Judaizers. **7.** *I was entrusted with the gospel for the uncircumcised, as Peter was for the circumcised:* Paul was thus acknowledged to be the equal of Peter, and the mission-field was divided among them (see Acts 15:4,12; Rom 15:17–19). The division must be understood geographically rather than ethnically, for Paul often began his evangelization of an area with the Jews (Acts 17:1ff.; 18:4; Rom 2:10–11). **9.** *James, Cephas, John:* James, the "bishop" of Jerusalem (1:19), is given precedence over Peter and John, the son of Zebedee. The order suggests that even the head of the Jerusalem church agreed to Paul's gospel and mission. Are these called "pillars" (*styloi*), because together they were ruling the Jerusalem mother church? (See C. K Barrett, in *Studia Paulina* [Fest. J. de Zwaan; Haarlem, 1953] 1–19.) **10.** *remember the poor:* Not a special designation for the Jerusalem community. It may be an imitation of the expression used by the Qumran Essenes of themselves (*'ebyônîm*, 4QpPs 37 2:10; 1QpHab 12:10; see L. E. Keck, *ZNW* 56 [1965] 100–129).

17 **(C) Paul's Gospel Revealed Peter's Inconsistency at Antioch (2:11–14).** Not only did the "pillars" of the Jerusalem church approve Paul's gospel, but in the Antiochene church of Gentiles and Jews it proved to be the only answer. **11.** *opposed him to his face:* Although frank in his assertion, Paul apparently regarded Peter as a person of greater consequence than himself. Presumably both Peter and Paul came to Antioch shortly after the decree on circumcision at the Jerusalem "Council." *because he stood condemned:* By his own actions; explained in 2:12–13. Paul seems to forget here that he allowed Timothy to be circumcised (Acts 16:3); later he will submit himself to the Nazirite vow ritual (Acts 21:20–26). His guiding principle, however, is stated in 1 Cor 9:20 (cf. Rom 14:21). But a greater issue is at stake at Antioch, involving the unity of the Church itself. **12.** *some people came from James:* They are not necessarily the same as the "false brothers" (2:4). The issue now involves Jewish dietary laws, quite distinct from the issue of circumcision settled at Jerusalem (Acts 15:1–12). It had not yet been resolved by the Jersualem church authorities, although the composite and conflated account of Acts 15 might suggest this prima facie (→ Acts, 45:72). *he withdrew:* Peter refused to eat further with the Gentile Christians and gave the impression that only the Jewish Christians, still observing the Levitical dietary laws, were the real Christians. See Est 14:17; Lk 15:2; Tb 1:10–11. **13.** *the other Jews:* Jewish Christians. *played the hypocrite along with him:* Although Peter's influence on a minority of the Antiochene community might be explained in various ways, Paul saw it only as inconsistency and compromise. For this reason he rebuked Peter for it publicly. **14.** *the truth of the gospel:* The "freedom we have in Christ Jesus" (2:4–5), not only from the custom of circumcision but also from Jewish dietary laws. Cf. Acts 10:15,28; 11:3. Paul found fault with Peter because he was not "walking straight toward" this truth (see G. D. Kilpatrick, BZNW 21 [1954] 269–74). *if you, a Jew, live like a Gentile:* See Acts 10:23; Gal 2:12. *why do you force the Gentiles to become Jews?:* Since Peter's example had already misled Barnabas and others, it would tend to compel Gentile Christians in a similar way. Was Paul's rebuke effectual? The passage suggests that it was; he cites his opposition to Peter in order to establish the validity and logic of his own gospel. He made his point with Peter. Whether the issue of dietary laws was settled in the Antiochene church by this incident is another question. Apparently, it arose again after the departure of Peter and Paul, and the Antiochene church sent for instructions from James in Jerusalem (Acts 15:13–33; → Life of Paul, 46:31–34).

18 **(D) Paul's Résumé of His Gospel (2:15–21).** The first part of Gal ends with a summary of Paul's teaching on faith and the Law, and represents a reformulation of Paul's address to Peter at Antioch. Much of the doctrine of Rom and Gal is compressed in the next seven verses with remarkable conciseness.

15. *we:* Primarily Peter and Paul. *Jews by birth:* Lit., "by nature," or natural condition and inheritance (see Rom 2:27; Eph 2:3). Paul thus acknowledges his Jewish background. *not sinners of pagan origin:* Paul ironically contrasts his privilege (echoing the claim of his Judaizing opponents) with the lot of pagans who not only failed to observe the Law, but did not even possess it. Being "law-less" (*anomoi*), they were sinners (see Lk 6:32–34; Mt 18:17). But for Paul, the Jew as well as the Greek was really a sinner (Rom 3:9,19). **16.** *no man is made upright:* The passive of *dikaioō* expresses the status of a man standing before the tribunal of God. It may mean no more than "is pronounced upright," if understood by its LXX usage; but Pauline usage seems to demand more, "is made upright." First, verbs ending in *-oō* are usually causative, producing the quality expressed by the root; second, OT prophets apparently believed that God could change a man internally (his heart: Jer 31:33; Ez 36:26–27); third, Paul believes that the Christian so judged actually lives a new life in vital union with Christ—"Christ lives in me" (Gal 2:20). The verb, therefore, merely expresses a juridical aspect of what divine benevolence actually effects in man as a result of his faith. (See E. J. Goodspeed, *JBL* 73 [1954] 86–91; → Pauline Theology, 79:94–97.) *by deeds of the Law:* The frequency with which Paul uses this succinct expression (Gal 3:2,5,10; Rom 2:15; 3:20,28) suggests that it was a commonly used formula for acts prescribed by the Mosaic Law and/or its Pharisaic interpretation. But the exact expression is unknown in the OT and in rabbinical (Pharisaic) writings (see *ThDNT* 2,646; Str-B 3, 160–62). Strangely enough, it has turned up in QL (*ma'aśê tôrāh*, "deeds of the Law," 4QFlor 1:7 [*JBL* 77 (1958) 352; cf. 1QS 6:18; 1QpHab 7:11]). In using it, Paul refers to the Mosaic Law, which cannot be restricted to ceremonial prescriptions. *through faith in Christ Jesus:* Lit., "through [the] faith of Christ Jesus" (obj. gen.); see Rom 3:20,28. By faith Paul means that attitude of man by which he accepts the divine revelation made known through Christ and responds to it with a complete dedication of his personal life to him (→ Pauline Theology, 79:125–27). *even we believed:* Paul appeals to the conviction shared by him and Peter at the time of their conversion that a Jew fully realizes his inability to achieve uprightness by the "deeds of the Law." *no mortal is made upright:* Ps 143:2 is implicitly quoted: "Before you no living man is just." Paul omits "before you," diminishing the statement's forensic nuance, but adds the decisive phrase, "by [doing] the deeds of the Law." The sense of the Psalm is thus greatly restricted (cf. Rom 3:20).

19 17. *through Christ:* The phrase, *en Christō*, seems at first sight to be the Pauline formula of union with Christ (→ Pauline Theology, 79:138); but here in contrast to "by deeds of the Law," it is more likely instrumental. *we too turn out to be sinners:* That is, like the pagans (2:15), because as "Christians" we are "law-less." *does that make Christ an agent of sin?:* This translation understands the particle *ara* as interrogative. But it could be inferential, introducing an illative statement, "Then Christ is...." Because of the following exclamation the question is preferred. *by no means!:* A strong negative used after rhetorical questions. Paul resolutely rejects the suggestion and turns it back on the imaginary objector: To submit to the Law again would be to sin again. **18.** *if I [try to] rebuild what I tore down:* Paul's first reason to justify the rejection; commentators dispute its precise meaning and hold that: Either Paul would admit that, in restoring the Law as a norm of conduct, he had sinned in abandoning it; or, more probably, he would commit himself, in setting up the Law as a norm again, to a life of certain transgression (Rom 7:21ff.; 4:15; see W. Mundle, *ZNW* 23 [1924] 152–53). In either case it emerges that it is not Christ, but the Judaizer, who is the real "minister of sin." **19.** *because of the Law I died to the Law:* The second reason. The clue to this difficult verse lies in recognizing that Christ is not "an agent of sin," because the Christian has been crucified with him and now lives for God. Living for God is hardly sinful. But this status of the Christian has been made possible for him through his crucifixion with Christ. So crucified, he has died to the Law ("is dead to the Law," Rom 6:11; cf. 2 Cor 5:15). But how has this status resulted "because of the Law"? Its proximate cause is the crucifixion of Christ himself, but its remote cause is the Law, the curse of which was leveled against Christ (3:13). It was the Mosaic Law and the mentality it produced among men that was responsible for the crucifixion—and indirectly for the emancipation of Christians from it. *I have been crucified with Christ:* See Rom 6:8–10; 7:6. Through faith and baptism (Rom 6:3ff.) the Christian has been identified (pf. tense, expressing the state or condition of identification) with the phases of Christ's passion, death, and resurrection. And so he can "live for God" (→ Pauline Theology, 79:137). **20.** *Christ lives in me:* The perfection of Christian life is expressed here, since it is not merely an existence dominated by a new psychological motivation ("living for God," 2:19). Faith in Christ does not substitute a new norm or goal of action; rather it reshapes man anew internally, supplying him with a new principle of activity on the ontological level of his very being. A symbiosis results of man with Christ, the glorified *Kyrios* who has become as of the resurrection a "vivifying Spirit" (1 Cor 15:45), the vital principle of Christian activity. *I live by faith in the Son of God:* Paul's profound insight into the Christian experience: the reshaping of man's very physical life by the transcendent influence of Christ's indwelling. It must eventually penetrate to his psychological awareness, so that he realizes in faith that his real life comes only from the redemptive and vicarious surrender of the Son of God. **21.** *I am not nullifying the grace of God:* Like the Judaizers, who insist on legal obligations and imply thereby the inefficacy of Christ's surrender.

20 **(III) Part II (3:1–4:31). Scriptural: In God's Plan Faith, not the Law, Saves Man.** A scriptural and doctrinal defense is now presented for Paul's gospel. It falls into three sections in which he explains the reign of faith and the reign of Christian freedom, and illustrates them with an allegory on an OT passage.

(A) The Reign of Faith (3:1–28). Two arguments are offered for the replacement of the Law by faith: one from experience (3:1–5), the other from Scripture (3:6–28). The first is proposed in three questions. **1.** *portrayed crucified before your very eyes:* Paul had preached Christ crucified (1 Cor 1:23; 2:2) so eloquently as to "placard" him before the Galatians, perhaps like Moses with the serpent of bronze (Nm 21:9). The position of the participle ("crucified") is emphatic, and its pf. tense expresses Christ's status as initiated on Calvary (see V. Burch, *ExpT* 30 [1918–19] 232–33). **2.** *did you receive the Spirit?:* Paul appeals to the conversion experience of the Galatians, when they received the Spirit by accepting the message of faith (see 4:6; Rom 8:7–17). In this they are like other Christian communities (2 Cor 1:22; Eph 1:13; Acts 10:44–45; 11:16–19). Some commentators restrict the meaning of *pneuma* to charismatic gifts (as in 1 Cor 12:28–29). But Paul does not make the clear distinction of later theology between the created and uncreated gift of the indwelling Spirit; *pneuma* designates rather the outpouring of the Spirit in a pregnant, eschatological sense. Having mentioned *pneuma*, Paul proceeds by rabbinical logic, using catchword bonds, to another meaning of the word, now in contrast to *sarx* (but not in the sense of 5:16–19). Because the "deeds of the Law" can never be on the same level as the Spirit (2 Cor 3:6–8) they must belong to the realm of "flesh"—earthly unregenerate man. But the word "flesh" has still another connotation here, for Paul is scornfully referring to the Judaizers' demand for circumcision. *Pneuma* was the power they began to live by as Christians (5:18; Rom 8:14); they cannot abandon this gift now for any sign in the flesh. **4.** *experienced so much in vain:* A return to "deeds of the Law" now would mean that the Spirit was received to no avail. *if it is really in vain:* A cryptic afterthought, revealing Paul's hope that the Galatians will not yield to the new fascination. Another possible translation: "inasmuch as [AG 152] it would really be in vain." It would then express a Pauline regret. **5.** *when he supplies you with the Spirit and works wonders among you:* The subject is "God" (as in 1 Cor 12:6; 2 Cor 1:22; 1 Thes 4:8; Gal 4:6). Note that the *dynameis* (wonders) are given along with the Spirit; elsewhere (Rom 15:13,19; 1 Cor 12:11) they come from the Spirit. Both are here expressed in a complementary sense, for neither gift came to the Galatians because they performed "deeds of the Law." This is the testimony of their own experience.

21 6. The argument from Scripture. *just as Abraham put faith in God...:* An implicit citation of Gn 15:6. It introduces the first of four midrashic developments (3:6–14; 3:15–18; 3:29–4:7; 4:21–31) of details in the Abraham story in Gn. Paul incorporates into his letter a theological argument, probably developed by him (or others?) in missionary work among Gentiles and Gentile Christians under the pressure of Jewish opposition. In writing now to the Galatians to counteract the Judaizing influence, he adapts that argument to his situation (see W. Koepp, *WZdUR* 2 [1952–53] 181–87). The theme of the first development: Men of faith are the real children of Abraham. The Christian status of the Galatians is like that of Abraham who was upright in God's sight, not because of "deeds" but because of faith. Paul does not imply that Abraham was a sinner before he believed in Yahweh and then was only considered upright by some legal fiction. He merely insists that his upright status was the result of faith (cf. Rom 4:3). Note the inclusion marking this section: *ek pisteōs* (3:7a) and *dia tēs pisteōs* (3:14c). **8.** *scripture foresaw...and proclaimed:* A well-known rabbinical personification of Scripture (Str-B 3,538) emphasizes its divine origin. Paul thus implies that uprightness through faith was part of the divine plan for the salvation of all men. His gospel, now preached alike to Jews and Greeks (Rom 1:16), was first announced to

Abraham. *will be blessed in you:* Allusion to Gn 18:18 (or 12:3). In Gn, Yahweh's promise to Abraham immediately meant a numerous posterity and the possession of Canaan. The meaning of the verb in the Hebr form of blessing in Gn is disputed. It probably meant, "Through you shall all the families of the earth invoke blessings on one another" (will wish to be blessed by God as you were; see Gn 48:20; Jer 29:22). This gives a reflexive meaning to the verb; but it could also be taken passively, and it was so understood in the LXX, Vg, and Pesh. Paul also understands it in this way, reflecting a common Jewish interpretation of the verse of Gn. Gentiles were to share in the blessings promised to Abraham, provided they would worship Yahweh and submit to circumcision. Paul, however, insists that Scripture foresaw their share in the blessings of Abraham, as the children of Abraham through faith in Christ Jesus. **9.** *with Abraham, the believer:* A favorite Jewish epithet for Abraham, *pistos*, which expresses his fidelity (see 2 Mc 1:2; 1 Mc 2:52; Sir 44:20; Philo, *De post. Cain* 173). Paul uses it, however, in his own more nuanced sense. Those who believe like Abraham are his "children" (3:7) and will share in the blessings promised to the patriarch.

22 **10.** *all who insist on deeds of the Law:* Paul's phrase (lit., "those who are of the deeds of the Law") is really a parallel to his expression, "the men of faith" (3:7). *are under a curse:* Explained by Dt 27:26; see also 28:58–59. For Paul the Law could not transmit the blessings of Abraham; rather it imposed a curse, obliging men under such a penalty to the impossible burden (Acts 15:10) of having to observe every word of it. This obligation was laid on man extrinsically, without any help being given him to observe it (see Rom 7). Having cited the OT text that lays a curse on those who do not obey the Law, Paul proceeds to show that the OT itself teaches that life in the real sense comes to men through faith. **11.** *the upright man will have life through faith:* The Scripture argument continues with a quotation of Hab 2:4 (quoted as in Rom 1:17; see comment there). Life for an upright man is derived from faith, not from an observance of the Law. Actually, the MT of Hab reads, "because of his fidelity." But Paul is using the LXX, and understands the Gk *pistis* in his own pregnant sense of Christian faith. Such "faith" will produce in men "life" in the full sense. **12.** *the Law does not depend on faith:* Its principle is rather the universal observance of its prescriptions; cf. Lv 18:5, "The man who carries them out will find life through them." Although the Lv text teaches that life comes to the observer of the Law, and Paul in another context would admit to this (cf. Rom 2:13), here his attention is nevertheless centered on the phrase "through them" (i.e., through the minute prescriptions of the Law, the "deeds of the Law"). These things, Paul insists, have nothing to do with faith. Gentile Christians, then, who believe in Christ and have come to faith in him as *Kyrios* cannot now have recourse to any quest of uprightness through the observance of details of the Mosaic Law, whether few or all. **13.** *Christ has bought us [Jewish Christians especially] from the curse of the Law:* The Law with its manifold prescriptions enslaved man (5:1), and from this enslavement man has been delivered by Christ's "purchase" (1 Cor 6:20; 7:23). Like Yahweh of the OT who through his covenant "acquired" his people (Ex 19:5–6; Is 43:21; Ps 73:2), so Christ by his covenant blood, shed on the cross, "bought" his people. This purchase, however, emancipated the new people of God from the Law and its curse; through faith in Christ Christians have become "free" (5:1). (For the redemptive liberation connoted by the vb. *exagorazō* used here, see F. Büchsel, "*Agorazō*," *ThDNT* 1,126–28; S. Lyonnet, *Bib* 42 [1961] 85–89; → Pauline Theology, 79:90–93.) *becoming a curse for us:* After the fashion of rabbinical logic, Paul passes from one meaning of "curse" to another: from the curse on the man who does not observe all the Law's prescriptions to a specific curse uttered in the Law against a man hung on a tree (Dt 21:23, which Paul then quotes). The latter curse was directed against the corpse of an executed criminal displayed as a deterrent to crime (see Jos 10:26–27; 2 Sm 4:12). It was accursed in God's sight and so defiled the land of Israel; hence it was not to remain suspended beyond sunset. In Roman times, when crucifixion became a frequent punitive measure, the OT verse was apparently applied to it. The early Church considered crucifixion a "hanging" (Acts 10:33). This idea underlies Paul's reference to Christ crucified as a "curse," i.e., something cursed. In citing Dt 21:23, Paul delicately omits "by God," and so clearly excludes the suggestion offered by later commentators that Christ was cursed by the Father. Paul's image is bold, and even though it offers only "a remote and material analogy" (Lyonnet) with a corpse suspended after death, it should not be watered down. The verse must be understood in connection with 2:19: Christ was crucified "through the Law." In dying as one on whom a curse of the Law fell, Paul sees Christ embodying the totality of the Law's curse "for us" (just how he does not say). But he died to the Law, and in his death we died vicariously; he put an end to the Law with its prescriptions (Eph 2:15), and became the "end of the Law" (Rom 10:4). So Mosaic observance and Christian living are henceforth incompatible. **14.** *we might receive the promised Spirit:* Promised not to Abraham but to the people of Israel through the prophets (Ez 36:26; 37:14; 39:29; Jl 2:28).

23 **15.** *no one can annul or alter a man's will:* Only the testator can do so (by cancellation or a codicil), but no one else. A fortiori, God's will, made manifest in his promises and covenant, cannot be altered by the Law, which came later and was administered by angels (3:19). Paul plays on the meaning of *diathēkē*, which in Hellenistic Greek meant a "last will and testament." But the LXX translators used it (instead of *synthēkē*, "treaty") to express the Hebr *b*ᵉ*rît*, "covenant," probably because it characterized more closely the covenant in which God made promises and set stipulations Israel was expected to obey. Paul begins his discussion by using the word *diathēkē* in the Hellenistic sense, but he gradually shifts to the LXX sense (3:17).—The second midrashic development of the Abraham story: 3:15–18. **16.** *to Abraham and his lineage:* Lit., "his seed" (coll. sing.). Cf. Gn 15:18; 12:7; 13:15; 17:7–8; 22:16–18; 24:7. In Hebrew the plural of *zera'* is not used to designate human descendants, but in Greek the plural *spermata* is so used. With rabbinical logic Paul, therefore, interprets the Hebrew singular as a reference to the historical Christ. This verse interrupts the argument begun in 3:15, but it prepares for 3:19b, insinuating that the covenant promises are the real basis of man's relations with God. **17.** *four hundred and thirty years later:* The time given in Ex 12:40–41 (MT) for Israel's sojourn in Egypt. The LXX gives the same time span for Israel's dwelling in both Egypt and Canaan; but cf. Gn 15:13; Acts 7:6. Actually, the calculation may be inaccurate by some 200 years (→ Exodus, 3:31), but this does not really affect Paul's argument. The unilateral disposition (*diathēkē*) made to Abraham was not altered by subsequent obligations imposed in the Mosaic Law. The Judaizers' contention is thus rejected that the covenant promises were subsequently made conditional to the performance of "deeds of the Law." **18.** *if the inheritance [of the promise] depends on the Law:* It would become a bilateral affair, destroying the very notion of a promise. In the LXX *klēronomia* is the term par excellence for the "inheritance" of the land of Canaan; here it denotes rather the blessings promised to Abraham in general. **19.** *added to produce transgressions:* Lit., "for the sake of transgressions," which some ancient commentators try to interpret as "to curtail transgressions;" but the sense is clear from Rom 4:15; 5:13–14,20; 7:7–13. A law is made to stop crimes but not to stop transgressions of the legal prescription, which can only begin with the law. Paul does not employ the later theological distinction of God's positive and permissive will—a distinction unknown to the Jewish world. *until the descendant came:* The Law was a temporary measure adopted by God; see 3:25. *enacted through angels:* An echo of a contemporary Jewish belief that angels, and not Yahweh himself, gave the Law to Moses (cf. Dt 33:2 LXX; Josephus, *Ant.* 15.5,3 § 136; *Jub* 1:27–29; Acts 7:38,53; Heb 2:2). Not only was the Law an interim measure, but its mode of promulgation revealed its inferiority when it is compared with promises made directly by Yahweh. *through an intermediary:* Moses; see the vague allusion in Lv 26:46; Dt 5:4. This is the most likely interpretation of this highly disputed phrase. **20.** *an intermediary is not needed for one party:* As a principle, this is not necessarily true because an individual can use an agent. But Paul thinks of the angel promulgators as a plurality and as dealing with Israel, another plurality. So they needed an intermediary. Thus the Law is inferior to the covenant promises, which Yahweh made directly without an intermediary (see J. Danieli, *VD* 33 [1955] 10–13; J. Bligh, *TS* 23 [1962] 98). **21.** *which could bestow life:* Paul's view of the basic defect of the Law: It tells a man what he must do, but cannot "give life"; see 3:11; Rom 7:10–12. **22.** *scripture:* Especially the Law, and the texts quoted in Rom 3:8–10. *has imprisoned all in sin:* Rom 11:32 would suggest that "all" (*ta panta*, neut.) refers to men. But being neuter, it may refer to the wider effects on all creation of the state in which men existed before Christ (cf. Rom 8:19ff.).

24 **23.** *in view of the coming revelation of faith:* The reign of the Law was divinely ordained to prepare for the reign of Christian freedom (see 4:3). **24.** *our attendant:* Lit., "boy leader," "tutor," a slave charged to lead a boy to and from school and to watch over his conduct while still a minor. The termination of such discipline was Christ, the "end of the Law" (Rom 10:4). Freedom from such discipline came with uprightness through faith in Christ. **26.** *sons of God:* Filial adoption is the relation of Christians to God, achieved "through Christ Jesus," or possibly "in union with" him. The phrase *en Christō* does not depend on *pisteōs;* it does not mean "faith in Christ Jesus." The formula suggests rather the mode of union with Christ the Son as a result of faith and baptism (see A. Grail, *RB* 58 [1951] 506). **27.** *baptized into [union with] Christ:* Baptism is the sacramental complement of faith, the rite whereby man achieves union with Christ and publicly manifests his commitment. For *eis* as the preposition expressing the initial movement of incorporation into Christ (→ Pauline Theology, 79:136). *put on Christ:* As a garment. Either Paul borrows a figure from Gk mystery religions, in which the initiate identified himself with a god by donning his robe (cf. AG 263), or else he uses an OT expression for the adoption of someone's moral dispositions and outlook (Jb 29:14; 2 Chr 6:41). As Paul uses it in Rom 13:14; Col 3:10; Eph 4:24, it seems to have the latter nuance (see V. Dellagiacoma, *RBibIt* 4 [1956] 114–42). **28.** *you are all one:* Secondary differences vanish through the effects of this primary incorporation of Christians into Christ's body through "one Spirit" (1 Cor 12:13). This verse is really the climax of Paul's letter.

25 **(B) The Reign of Christian Freedom (3:29–4:20).** The second section of Paul's scriptural and doctrinal defense of his gospel begins with the third midrashic development of the Abraham story (cf. 3:6,15). To become an heir to the promises made to Abraham, performance of the "deeds of the Law" is not required, but rather faith, which makes one his offspring in the real sense. This is illustrated by Hellenistic and Palestinian legal customs of inheritance.

26 **4:2.** *under guardians and managers:* A comparison of man's status with that of a freeborn, orphaned son explains the interim character of the Law. Paul is not thinking of Roman law, but of Palestinian usage. A father appointed an *epitropos* (guardian) who could handle the son's possessions in his interest (see S. Belkin, *JBL* 54 [1935] 52–55, but cf. J. D. Hester, *Oikonomia* [Fest. O. Cullmann; Hamburg, 1967] 118–25). Outwardly, and for a time, the minor son was not free. **3.** *elemental spirits of the world:* The meaning of *stoicheia tou kosmou* (4:9; Col 2:8,20) is quite disputed: *stoicheia* could mean "elements, rudiments" (of learning, as in Heb 5:12); or "elemental substances" (earth, air, fire, water); or "elemental signs" (of the Zodiac); or "spirit-elements" (celestial beings controlling the physical elements of the world [cf. Ap 16:5]). In the first case it would mean, "slaves to rudimentary ways of thought and conduct." Opinion today seems to be in favor of the fourth interpretation: "slaves to the spirit-elements." They seem to be personal beings parallel to the "guardians and trustees," and are described (4:8) as "by nature not gods." In Col 2:8,20 they are contrasted to Christ and seem to be like the principalities and powers (cf. AG 776). **4.** *fullness of time:* From the "date set" (4:2) Paul widens the application of his comparison to the point in history when God's salvific intervention took place. Man's freedom came with Christ. *God sent forth his son:* The vb. *(ex)apostellō* developed in the early Church a specific religious meaning: to send someone in the service of the kingdom with authority fully grounded in God (see *ThDNT* 1, 406). The "sending" is functional, expressing the mission of the Son in the purpose clause. Here nothing is said explicitly about the Son's pre-existence; it is at most implied (→ Pauline Theology, 79:53). *born of a woman:* The ptc. *genomenon* is aorist, emphasizing the assumption of human condition for the mission. So born, he submitted to the Law by being circumcised, and thus became capable of falling under its curse. But lest the Galatians draw a wrong conclusion, Paul does not mention Christ's circumcision. **6.** *the proof that you are sons:* The conj. *hoti* could mean "because"; then adoptive sonship would be the basis for the gratuitous sending of the Spirit. However, Rom 8:14–17 seems to suggest that the gift of the Spirit is the constitutive element of Christian sonship. Hence many commentators prefer the sense, "the fact that." (Cf. S. Zedda, *L'adozione a Figlio di Dio* [Rome, 1952].) *the Spirit of his Son:* The Spirit is also the object of a personal mission from the Father (*ho theos*); elsewhere he is the gift of the Risen *Kyrios.* (For the pertinence of this phrase to Paul's lack of a clear distinction between Son and Spirit, → Pauline Theology, 79:75–79.) *Abba [my] Father:* The vivifying Spirit of the Risen Son is the dynamic principle of adoptive sonship (see Rom 1:3; 8:15–17). It empowers the Christian's inmost conviction, as he exclaims of God, "Father!" Although the Aram *'abbâ* means "the father," this emphatic form was often used as a vocative and frequently had the meaning, "my Father" (see *ThDNT* 1,5–6). The Christian prays to the Father with the same formula that was used by Christ. When taken up in Gk communities, its literal Gk equivalent *ho patēr* was added, and the combination became a liturgical formula. But without the Spirit a Christian would never be able to utter this cry. **7.** *no longer a slave:* The Christian is free of the Law. *through God:* Inferior mss. read "through Christ" or "an heir of God through Christ."

27 **8.** *in your ignorance of God:* The pagan background of the Galatians is recalled (cf. 5:2–3; 6:12–13). Like the Jews before Christ's coming, the pagans were also enslaved—but to idols (1 Thes 4:5; 1 Cor 12:2; Rom 1:20). From here to v. 20 Paul criticizes the spiritual immaturity of the Galatians. **9.** *known by him:* Cf. 1 Cor 8:3. The Galatians' knowledge of God did not merely spring from within them; it is the result of the divine predilection, of God's gratuitous election (an OT idea, cf. Gn 18:19; Am 3:2; Jer 1:5). *how can you return?:* To adopt Jewish practices is not outright paganism. But regard for such material practices, subjecting the practitioners to the angels of the Law (3:19), would be the equivalent of a reversion to reverence for the elemental spirits. **10.** *you keep [special] days, months, seasons, and years:* Cf. Col 2:16. Days like the Sabbath and *Yôm Kippûrîm* are meant; months like the "New Moon"; seasons like Passover and Pentecost; years like the sabbatical years (Lv 25:5). Such observances would be the material practices of 4:9; Paul can see no reason for a Gentile Christian observing these. **12.** *I have become like you:* Freed from enslavement to the Law, and hence "law-less" (1 Cor 9:21), Paul began to preach to Gentiles. He now appeals to them directly (vv. 12–20), as one who saw fit to abandon it: "Be imitators of me, as I am of Christ" (1 Cor 11:1; 1 Thes 3:6; cf. D. M. Stanley, *Bib* 40 [1959] 859–77). **13.** *physical illness:* This suggests that Paul's first evangelization of the Galatians (Mission II; Acts 16:6) was occasioned by some sickness. *the first time:* The phrase *to proteron* seems to imply that more than one visit to Galatia preceded this letter (cf. Bl-Deb-F § 233,3). **14.** *what might have been a trial for you:* An allusion to some repulsive physical ailment? Paul never explains it further (cf. 2 Cor 12:7). *an angel of God:* Paul uses *aggelos* not in the sense of "messenger," but of "angel" (1:8; 3:19; 1 Cor 4:9; 11:10; 13:1). This expression is surprising in view of his attitude toward angels elsewhere in this letter. **15.** *would have torn out your eyes:* This might seem to suggest that Paul suffered from some affliction of the eyes, but the hyperbole is obvious: they would have given him what was most precious to them. **16.** *telling you the truth:* The Galatians were once overjoyed at his evangelization. Now Paul fears that this letter, in which he warns them of the danger of Judaizing, will alienate them. **17.** *want to shut you out:* Of the Christian community, by preaching to you "another gospel" (1:6). Their aim is that you regard them as authorities and masters. **19.** *I am in labor again until Christ be formed in you:* The reshaping of Christians after the form or model (*morphē*) of Christ is the goal of Paul's missionary endeavors. His concern for his spiritual "children" springs from an almost maternal instinct; cf. 1 Thes 2:7–8; 1 Cor 3:2. (On the metamorphosis of the Christian see 2 Cor 3:18–4:6.)

28 **(C) The Allegory of Sarah and Hagar Illustrates This Freedom (4:21–31).** Perhaps the use of the metaphor of a mother suggested to Paul a fourth midrashic development of the Abraham story, an allegory on Sarah, the mother of the true heir, Isaac. **22.** *Abraham had two sons:* Gn 16:1–16 (Ishmael born to Hagar the Egyptian slave girl); 21:2–5 (Isaac born to his wife Sarah). Paul ignores the children by Keturah (Gn 25:2). **23.** *in the normal course of nature:* Gn 16:4,15. *through the promise:* Not the generic one made to Abraham (Gn 12:2), but the special one in Gn 15:4; 17:16–21 (cf. Gn 21:2,9). God's intervention, consequent on the promise, brought Isaac to life. **24.** *are meant allegorically:* Paul tells his readers that the historic figures of the Gn story have for him a deeper significance (on *allegoreō* see *ThDNT* 1, 260–63). *the women represent two covenants:* Hagar represents the Sinai covenant, and Sarah represents the one made with Abraham. Jews and Judaizers may take pride in the Sinai pact, but for Paul it "enslaved" all the children born of Abraham "according to the flesh"—like Hagar's offspring born into slavery. But Christians can boast of the real covenant made by God with Abraham, for they are sons of Abraham "according to the promise"—like Sarah's offspring "law-less" and free. For from Sinai came the Law that enslaves. *one [covenant coming] from Mount Sinai..., that is Hagar;* **25.** *but Mount Sinai lies in Arabia, yet it corresponds to the present Jerusalem:* This is the reading of the oldest Pauline ms. (P^{46}) and it is supported by several others. Another well-attested reading is: "Now Hagar means Mt. Sinai in Arabia." In either case, wishing to emphasize that the slavery the Law introduced was the condition of the rejected son of Abraham, Paul identifies Hagar with the Sinai pact and the "present Jerusalem." Verse 25a is a geographical detail explaining how Hagar, although connected with a holy place outside of the Promised Land, is yet equated with the "present Jerusalem." Geographically, Hagar represents a place in Arabia, but even so she stands for enslavement and so corresponds to Jerusalem. But why does Paul mention Arabia at all? Possibly because Mt. Sinai is in Arabia, which is Ishmaelite territory: he thus associates the Sinai pact with the eponymous patriarch of Arabian tribes (see Gn 25:12–18; Ps 82:7). He thus suggests that the Law itself stems from a situation extrinsic to the Promised Land and to the real descendants of Abraham. Paul's Jewish colleagues would not have been happy with this allegory. *corresponds to the present Jerusalem:* Since the earthly Jerusalem is for the Jews what Sinai once was, the place whence the "word of the Lord" goes forth (Is 2:3). **26.** *the Jerusalem above:* The "heavenly" Jerusalem (Ap 3:12; 21:2; Ez 40; Zech 2; Hag 2:6–9) is implicitly identified with Sarah and her offspring, the freeborn children of Abraham. **27.** *for Scripture says:* A common introductory formula (see *NTS* 7 [1960–61] 301). Is 54:1 is quoted from the LXX (close to the MT). The prophet's words are addressed to deserted Zion, bidding it rejoice at the return of the exiles. Paul applies his words to the allegorized Sarah, to "Jerusalem above." The Christians of Galatia must rejoice in their freeborn children. **29.** In Gn (21:10) Sarah, seeing Ishmael as the potential rival to Isaac's inheritance, drives him and his mother out. Nothing is said in Gn of Ishmael's persecution of Isaac, but Paul uses a Palestinian haggadic explanation of Gn 21:9 (see Str-B 3, 575–76; cf. Ps 83:6; 1 Chr 5:10). **30.** *"send away the slave girl":* Paul quotes Sarah's words (Gn 21:10) as if they were God's. Accommodating the text, he bids the Galatians rid themselves of the Judaizers—and, ironically enough, obey the Torah itself. **31.** *children of the free woman:* Thus the OT itself supports Paul's thesis that in Christ God's new freedom reigns. To adopt the practices of the Judaizers is to forfeit this Christian freedom.

29 **(IV) Part III (5:1–6:10). Hortatory: Preserve That Freedom in Christ.** From the foregoing doctrinal exposé Paul draws certain practical conclusions. This part has two sections.

(A) Warning Not to Lose Such Freedom in Christ (5:1–12). **1.** *for [real] freedom Christ has set us free:* The emphatic position of the first phrase sums up the doctrinal message of the letter. It is not license, but a freedom from the Law and its material observances, its yoke of slavery (4:5,31). Purpose is expressed by the dative (*eleutheriā*). **2.** *Christ can do nothing for you:* Cf. 2:21. The Galatians must choose one or the other: Christ and freedom, or the Law and slavery. No compromise is possible. **3.** *the whole Law:* The Judaizers in Galatia seem to have insisted on the adoption of certain Jewish customs (circumcision, observance of feasts, respect for angels, etc.). Paul warns: if you accept the "sign" of a Jew, then you oblige yourself to the whole way of life (cf. Jas 2:10). But this is not to walk according to the truth of the gospel (2:10). **5.** *the hope of uprightness:* The full measure of man's uprightness is still a thing of the eschatological future (cf. Rom 5:19; 8:19–25). Here *elpis* is used in the sense of "the thing hoped for," and *dikaiosynēs* is an appositional genitive (*GrBib* 46). **6.** *neither circumcision nor the lack of it matters:* Lit., "neither circumcision nor the foreskin." The Galatians might retort, "Then why oppose circumcision?" But Paul's words have to be understood in the light of 5:2 (cf. 3:28). *only faith active in love:* The principle of uprightness is faith working through love after the fashion of Christ himself (2:20; Rom 5:5–8; cf. 1 Thes 1:3). This phrase shows that Paul's faith is not the mere intellectual assent to monotheism (cf. Jas 2:18–19). In NT Greek *energeō* with an impersonal subject is always used in the middle voice; hence "faith working [expressing itself] through love" (cf. Bl-Deb-F § 316, 1; AG 264–5). **7.** *running well:* Paul often compares Christian effort to that expended by the runner in a Gk race (2:2; Rom 9:16; 1 Cor 9:24–26; Phil 2:16; 3:14). But the Judaizers have been getting in the way; to follow their advice is to ignore God's call, cf. 1:6 note. **9.** *"a little yeast":* A proverb (cf. 1 Cor 5:6; Mt 16:6) brings out the power of that Judaizing influence to spread. **11.** *still advocating circumcision:* The Judaizers apparently claimed that Paul himself admitted to the validity of circumcision, when it suited his purpose. Perhaps they even cited the case of Timothy from Lystra (Acts 16:3), whose mother was Jewish, and whom Paul had had circumcised "because of the Jews." Paul's answer is to stress that if he were still of that mind, he would not be opposed by the Judaizers (see 2:3). *the stumbling block of the cross:* Paul's preaching of the Cross made circumcision unnecessary, and it thus became a stumbling block to the Jews (cf. 1 Cor 1:23, for another reason; Phil 3:18). **12.** *would that they would castrate themselves:* Paul's sarcasm (cf. Phil 3:2) may allude to the ritual emasculation of the priests of Cybele who were undoubtedly known in Galatia.

30 **(B) Instructions for the Correct Use of Christian Freedom (5:13–6:10).** Paul's concrete advice illustrates the love of which he spoke in 5:6. **13.** *an incentive for the flesh:* Supply *poieite*, "Do not make freedom an incentive." If he does away with the Law, Paul wants to stress that the Christian cannot abandon himself to an earthly, material, Godless conduct. His freedom must be one of service, motivated by love, a freedom for others. **14.** *the whole Law:* Cf. Lv 19:18. Is Paul thinking directly of Lv, or of a well-known rabbinical summary (see Str-B 1, 907–8), or of Christ's summary (Mt 7:12; Mk 12:31 par.)? Whatever the answer is, neither here nor in Rom 13:8–10 does he include the love of God. In Lv the "neighbor" meant a fellow Israelite, but for Paul "there is no distinction between Jew and Greek" (Rom 10:12; cf. Gal 6:10). **16.** *live by the Spirit:* Lit., "walk by," in the Semitic sense: "conduct oneself." The Spirit that is the principle of Christian sonship must also be the principle of Christian activity (5:18; Rom 8:14). (On "spirit and flesh," → Pauline Theology, 79:119.) **17.** *you do not do:* The Christian in union with Christ and endowed with the Spirit still struggles with the "flesh," the symbol of all that is man in his opposition to God. See the elaborate description of the struggle of *sarx* with *nous* ("reason," agreeing with the Law) in unregenerate man (Rom 7:15–23; cf. P. Althaus, *TLZ* 76 [1951] 15–18). **18.** *guided by the Spirit:* The Christian under the influence of the indwelling Spirit has an interior principle to counteract the "flesh," and is no longer merely confronted with the extrinsic norm of the Law. **19–21.** The catalogue of vices, which the Christian must avoid if he would share the blessings of the "kingdom of God," i.e., enter into definitive communion with God at the parousia. This catalogue (like that of the virtues) is most likely derived from the primitive didache of the Church (→ Pauline Theology, 79:161). **22–23.** The catalogue of virtues; cf. 2 Cor 6:6; Col 3:12–15; Eph 4:2; 5:9. Note how Paul speaks of the "deeds" (*erga*) of the flesh, but the "fruit" (*karpos*) of the Spirit. "Fruit" can be applied to the flesh, but never "deeds" to the Spirit, cf. Rom 6:21; 7:5. The catalogues, however, show that "good deeds" are not to be excluded from Christian life. *against such there is no Law:* There is no need of a Law to be enacted against such virtuous actions. The Law "was added because of transgressions" (3:19). Paul may be alluding to a statement of Aristotle (*Politics*, 3.8), uttered in a different context. **24.** *have crucified the flesh:* The Christian, crucified with Christ (2:19) through his faith and baptism, has died not only to the Law but also to his *sarx*-self—to himself with all his earthbound, limited, and degrading tendencies. He has also died to the "world" (6:14). Paul speaks, of course, of the ontological, basic reorientation of man and not of his psychological awareness of it. That is why he must continue to "mortify the ways of the body" (cf. Rom 6:6; 8:9,13).

31 **6:1.** *you who are spiritual:* The mature Christians are addressed, those guided by the Spirit (1 Cor 3:1). They are to correct a man "detected in some sin" (cf. Mt 18:15–18; Jas 5:19–20). **2.** *the Law of Christ:* Freed of obligation to the Mosaic Law, the Christian becomes *ennomos Christou*, "under the Law of Christ" (1 Cor 9:21) and a "slave of Christ" (1 Cor 7:22). The "law of Christ" is the "law of the Spirit of life" (Rom 8:2), and in this context it is specified as the law of love, for Christians must bear the burdens of one another in fraternal charity (→ Pauline Theology, 79:160). **3.** *thinks he is somebody:* Either because he thinks he is without sin, or that he is charitable enough to correct an erring brother. **5.** *his own load:* Not to be confused with the "burdens" of 6:2. **6.** *share all good things:* Another practical manifestation of love is to be shown in due support for the catechists of the community; cf. 1 Cor 9:11; Phil 4:15; Rom 15:27. **8.** *will reap eternal life:* This verse sums up 5:16–26. "Eternal life" is the equivalent of the "kingdom of God" (5:21). The former expression is characteristically Johannine, occurring only rarely in Paul (Rom 2:7; 5:21; 6:22–23; 1 Tm 1:16; 6:12; Ti 1:2; 3:7).

32 **(V) Conclusion (6:11–18). Paul's Signature and Résumé.** **11.** *with my own hand:* Thus far the letter has apparently been dictated to a scribe (→ NT Epistles, 47:19). Paul now writes the conclusion himself by way of a "signature." **12.** *not to be persecuted for Christ's cross:* According to Paul, the Judaizers fear that if they preach the real "message of the cross" (see comment on 5:11), they might be persecuted for it by the Jews or other Judaizers. They prefer to make a good showing before men by preaching circumcision instead. **13.** *not even the circumcised:* The pf. ptc. *peritetmēmenoi* seems to be the preferable reading (P^{46}, B, Koine); other mss. read the pres. participle "Those who are being circumcised." The context refers to the Judaizers. *do not observe the Law themselves:* Although they insist on circumcision and a few other legal obligations, the Judaizers do not observe the Law in its entirety. Hence Paul's warning in 5:3; cf. Rom 2:21–25. **14.** *to boast in anything but the cross:* To the vanity (6:12) of the

Judaizers Paul opposes his own boast; it is not one of self-reliance, but of dependence on the grace and favor of God (cf. 1 Cor 3:31; 2:2; 2 Cor 11:16–12:10). "Cross" here means the whole Christ-event. *through which [or whom] the world has been crucified to me and I to the world:* The word *kosmos* denotes all that stands at enmity with God—the sphere of pleasures and ambitions related to the "flesh" in which the Judaizers find their boast. To all this Paul has died (2:19; 5:24), not by some interior psychological or mystical experience, but through the historic event of Calvary, which is the realization of the Father's salvific plan. The pf. tense expresses the condition in which he finds himself through his share in the Christ-event by baptism (Rom 6:3–11). **15.** *circumcision means nothing:* Echo of 5:6; cf. 1 Cor 7:18–19. *but a new creation:* This is the concluding declaration of what is really of prime importance in Christianity: a new ontological reshaping of man's existence, not through a mere extrinsic norm of conduct, but through a life-giving principle that is the Spirit of Christ. This is accomplished through the *doxa* of the Risen Christ (2 Cor 3:18–4:6). Man thus transformed in Christ becomes a new "creature." The word *ktisis* has the active sense of "creation" only in Rom 1:20; elsewhere it is passive, i.e., "creature, created thing." Cf. 1 Cor 7:19; 15:47–49; Rom 6:3ff.; Col 3:10; Eph 2:10; 4:24; Ti 3:5 ("rebirth"). (See E. Sjöberg, *ST* 9 [1956] 131–36.) **16.** *the Israel of God:* The Christian people of God, as the new "offspring of Abraham" (3:29; cf. Phil 3:3; Rom 9:6), in contrast to "Israel according to the flesh" (1 Cor 10:18). In this greeting Paul modifies the last words of Ps 124:5 or 127:6, "Peace be upon Israel." The extension of the blessing beyond those immediately addressed follows the model of contemporary Jewish blessings. Cf. the 3rd cent. Kefr Bir'im Synagogue inscription: "May peace be upon this place and all the places of Israel...." (K. Galling, *Textbuch z. Geschichte Israels* [Tübingen, 1950] 82 § 56.) **17.** *the marks of Jesus:* The Gk word *stigmata* did not mean what this word means in English today. Paul had suffered so much from illness (4:13; 2 Cor 12:7), floggings (Acts 16:22; 2 Cor 11:25), and stoning (Acts 14:19) for the cause of Christ that he could speak of the evidence of these sufferings as "brands" that mark him as the "slave of Christ Jesus" (Rom 1:1; Gal 1:10) forever. In antiquity *stigmata* often designated the branding used to mark a slave or an animal as someone's possession. These "marks" in his flesh Paul gladly bears, boasting of them to those who would try to glory in another mark in the flesh (circumcision). **18.** Cf. Phil 4:23; Phlm 25; 2 Tm 4:22. In calling the Galatians "brothers," Paul finally implies his reconciliation with them.

50

THE LETTER TO THE PHILIPPIANS

Joseph A. Fitzmyer, S.J.

BIBLIOGRAPHY

1 Barth, K., *Erklärung des Philipperbriefes* (5th ed.; Zollikon-Zürich, 1947). Beare, F. W., *A Commentary on the Epistle to the Philippians* (BNTC; London, 1959). Beasley-Murray, G. R., "Philippians," *PCB* 985–89. Benoit, P., *Les Épîtres de Saint Paul aux Philippiens, à Philémon, aux Colossiens, aux Ephésiens* (BJ, 2nd ed.; Paris, 1953) 17–37. Bonnard, P., *L'Épître de Saint Paul aux Philippiens* (CNT 10; Neuchâtel, 1950). Dibelius, M., *An die Thessaloniker I, II. An die Philipper* (HNT 11, 3rd ed.; Tübingen, 1937). Friedrich, G., *Der Brief an die Philipper* (NTD 8, 9th ed.; Göttingen, 1962) 92–129. Huby, J., *Saint Paul: Les Épîtres de la Captivité* (VS 8, Paris, 1947) 261–376. Lohmeyer, E., *Die Briefe an die Philipper, an die Kolosser und an Philemon* (Meyer 9/1, 11th ed.; Göttingen, 1956) 1–193. Martin, R. P., *The Epistle of Paul to the Philippians* (TynNTC; London, 1959). Médebielle, R.-P., "Epître aux Philippiens," *PSB* 12 (Paris, 1938) 75–100. Michael, J. H., *The Epistle of Paul to the Philippians* (MNTC, 5th ed.; N.Y., 1948). Müller, J. J., *The Epistles of Paul to the Philippians and to Philemon* (NICNT; Grand Rapids, 1961) 13–156. Peterson, E., *Apostel und Zeuge Christi* (3rd ed.; Freiburg i. Br., 1952). Segovia, A., "Carta a los Filipenses," *La Sagrada Escritura: Nuevo Testamento II* (BAC 211; Madrid, 1962) 735–98. Staab, K., *An die Philipper* (RNT 7, 3rd ed.; Regensburg, 1959) 167–200. Tillmann, F., *Die Gefangenschaftsbriefe des hl. Paulus* (BB 7, 4th ed.; Bonn, 1931) 121–62. Vincent, M. R., *The Epistles to the Philippians and to Philemon* (ICC; London, 1906).

Cerfaux, L., R-F, *INT* 472–82; F-B 226–37. Guthrie, *NTI* 1, 140–60. Metzger, B. M., *IPLAP* 102–9. Wik, *NTI* 431–37.

INTRODUCTION

2 **(I) The Philippian Church.** In the time of Paul, Philippi (*Philippoi*) was a prominent town of the Roman province of Macedonia (Acts 16:12), situated in the plain E of Mt. Pangaeus on the Roman Via Egnatia (leading from Byzantium to Dyrrhachium and Apollonia on the Adriatic). Although founded in 358–357 BC by Philip II of Macedon on the site of the ancient Thasian town of Crenides (Tiny Spring), it came to be heavily populated by Romans (see Appian, *Civ. Wars* 4.105–31; Dio Cassius, *Rom. Hist.* 47.42–49; Strabo, *Geography* 7. fr. 34,41). In 42 BC, M. Antony defeated Brutus and Cassius in a double battle there. After Antony was defeated at Actium (31 BC), Octavian established a military colony at Philippi (*colonia Iulia Augusta Philippensis*) and gave the *ius italicum* to veterans and Antony's partisans, evicted from Italy. In addition to Romans, there were also many Macedonian Greeks and a small settlement of Jews in the town. Through his preaching (*ca.* AD 50 on Mission II) Paul established his first European Christian community there. Because he exorcised a slave girl whose powers of divination had been the source of income to her masters, he and Silas were arrested, flogged, and thrown into prison (Acts 16:16–24). An earthquake at midnight gave them an opportunity to escape, but Paul appealed to his status as a *civis Romanus* to secure proper redress of the indignity shown to him. During his stay in Philippi he evangelized the Jews at their "prayer-place" near the Crenides stream and converted several Gentiles. To judge from the names of his converts, the Philippian church must have been predominantly Gentile (Lydia, Epaphroditus, Euodia, Syntyche, Syzygus). Like other Gentile Christian churches, Philippi too apparently had visits from Judaizers who followed in Paul's wake.

(Collart, P., *Philippes, ville de Macédoine* [Paris, 1937]. Lemerle, P., *Philippes et la Macédoine orientale à l'époque chrétienne et byzantine* [2 vols.; Paris, 1945]. McDonald, W. A., "Archaeology and St. Paul's Journeys in Greek Lands," *BA* 3 [1940] 18–24. Schmidt, J., "Philippi," PW 1 Series, 19/2 [1938] 2206–44.)

3 **(II) Authenticity.** Although the Pauline authorship of Phil was once contested by the Tübingen School, it is not seriously questioned today.

4 **(III) Occasion and Purpose.** After the foundation of the Philippian church on Mission II, Paul had apparently not visited it again before writing Phil. While he was evangelizing Thessalonica (*ca.* AD 50), the Philippians had sent him money for his needs on two occasions (Phil 4:16). Now during imprisonment

(1:7,13,17), another gift from them has been brought to him by Epaphroditus (2:25; 4:14,18). Imprisoned because of his apostolic activity, Paul knew that the local Christians were continuing his work; his gospel was being preached (1:14–15). He wrote from prison to thank the Philippians for their generosity and told them that he was sending Epaphroditus back, now that the latter had recovered from an illness contracted during his stay with him (2:25–30). Apparently the Philippians were anxious about Epaphroditus and were wondering why he was not returning. Paul had learned too that Judaizers were in the area, and he wrote to warn the Philippians against the influence of such "dogs, these mischiefmakers, with their amputation" (3:2). Phil is a fine example of Paul's care for a fellow worker, of his warm apostolic affection for a cherished community, and of his own serene composure about his lot. He exhorts this church, which seems to have been his "joy and crown" (4:1). Only Euodia and Syntyche are singled out among them for stern admonition (4:2).

5 **(IV) Date and Place of Composition.** Traditionally, Paul's house arrest in Rome (AD 61–63) was regarded as the "prison" from which he wrote Phil. Marcion wrote: "scribens eis a Roma de carcere" (see J. Knox, *Marcion and the NT* [Chicago, 1942] 170). The *praetorium* (1:13) was accordingly understood to refer to the headquarters of the Praetorian Guard in Rome (cf. Acts 28:16); and "those of Caesar's household" (4:22) were converts in the imperial palace at Rome. The imprisonment and proximity of trial, which cause Paul some concern (1:20–26), would easily suit this Roman situation. The Roman origin of Phil is still advocated by some modern commentators (F. W. Beare, L. Cerfaux, C. H. Dodd, D. Guthrie, E. F. Harrison, J. Schmid, *et al.*). But at the end of the 18th cent. some scholars proposed rather the Caesarean origin of Phil (H. E. Paulus, O. Pfleiderer, F. Spitta, E. Lohmeyer). Most of their arguments, however, although not entirely disproving the traditional Roman origin, are better suited to the more recent, plausible hypothesis of the Ephesian origin of Phil. This view was first proposed by H. Lisco in 1900 and has many supporters today (A. Deissmann, P. Feine, W. Michaelis, G. S. Duncan, M. Goguel, P. Benoit, *et al.*). For the understanding of the letter itself the question of origin is of little importance; but for the collocation of Phil in the Pauline corpus and its relation to the rest of Paul's teaching, it makes a difference.

6 The reasons for the Ephesian hypothesis are: (1) Inscriptions from Ephesus make it clear that *praetoriani* were stationed there on the extensive property of Augustus in Asia. (2) Other Ephesian inscriptions reveal that persons belonging to the *familia Caesaris* cared for the imperial bank in Asia (*fiscus asiaticus*). Consequently the *praetorium* (1:13) and "Caesar's household" (4:22) do not necessarily demand a Roman setting. (3) Phil seems to call for at least three, possibly four, journeys back and forth between Paul in prison and Philippi. The journey between Rome and Philippi, reckoned usually at four or five weeks, would thus demand a considerably long time. The situation is more readily intelligible in terms of a six- or seven-day journey between Philippi and Ephesus (see Guthrie, *NTI* 1, 146–47). (4) Although Acts is silent about an Ephesian imprisonment, Paul himself spoke of facing death in Asia (1 Cor 15:30–32; 2 Cor 1:8–10). This confrontation with death in Ephesus could have been the setting for Phil. (5) Topically or doctrinally, Phil is better related to Paul's Great Letters (written during Mission III, AD 54–58) than it is to the Captivity Letters (Col and Eph). These reasons do not provide certainty, but they do make it plausible that Phil was written from an Ephesian imprisonment, *ca.* AD 56–57 (preferably before 2 Cor).

(Bowen, C. R., "Are Paul's Prison Letters from Ephesus?" *AJT* 24 [1920] 112–35, 277–87. Dacquino, P., "Data e provenienza della Lettera ai Filippesi," *RBibIt* 6 [1958] 224–34. Duncan, G.S., *St. Paul's Ephesian Ministry* [London, 1929]. Manson, T. W., "St. Paul in Ephesus. The Date of the Epistle to the Philippians," *BJRylL* 23 [1939] 182–200.)

7 **(V) Unity.** Is Phil one letter or does it represent a conflation of several Pauline letters to the Philippians? Polycarp, writing to the Philippians, mentions that Paul "wrote letters" (*egrapsen epistolas*, 3:2; ACW 6, 77 [though some hold that the pl. is used for the sing., like *litteras*]). An ancient Syr stichometry also mentions two letters to the Philippians (E. Preuschen, *Analecta* [Tübingen, 1910] 68). Moreover, the transitions between certain parts of Phil are so abrupt (2:19; 3:2; 4:10) that modern commentators have often asked whether Phil is a composite work. The reasons for their query are: (1) the abrupt beginning of 3:2 after a farewell; (2) the tone of 3:2–4:3, a section devoted to the Judaizing problem, so different from the rest of Phil; (3) the independent character of 4:10–20, in which Paul's gratitude is expressed after another "farewell" (4:4–9). Why is this relegated to the end of the letter? (4) 4:4 seems to be the natural sequel to 3:1; (5) the letters of Polycarp *To the Philippians* apparently suffered the same compilatory fate (see P. N. Harrison, *Polycarp's Two Epistles to the Philippians* [Cambridge, 1936]; B. Altaner, *Patrology* [N.Y., 1960] 111).

8 Although these reasons are not conclusive, the view that Phil is a conflation of three Pauline letters (or of parts of three letters) helps to understand the disjointed character of the letter. These parts may be isolated as follows: *Letter A*, 1:1–2; 4:10–20 (a note in which Paul thanked the Philippians for their aid). *Letter B*, 1:3–3:1; 4:4–9,21–23 (the letter in which Paul explained his personal situation, gave news of Epaphroditus and Timothy, and sent his instructions to the community). *Letter C*, 3:2–4:3 (a short note to warn the Philippians about the Judaizers).

(Bornkamm, G., "Der Philipperbrief als paulinische Briefsammlung," *Neotestamentica et patristica* [Fest. O. Cullmann; NovTSup 6 (1962)] 192–202. Delling, G., "Philipperbrief," *RGG* 5 [1961] 333–36. Jones, M., "The Integrity of the Epistle to the Philippians," *Expositor* 8/8 [1914] 457–73. Mackay, B. S., "Further Thoughts on Philippians," *NTS* 7 [1960–61] 161–70. Rahtjen, B. D., "The Three Letters of Paul to the Philippians," *NTS* 6 [1959–60] 167–73. Schmithals, W., "Die Irrlehrer des Philipperbriefes," *ZThK* 54 [1957] 297–341.)

9 **(VI) Outline.** The Letter to the Philippians is outlined as follows:

(I) Introduction (1:1–11)
- (A) Opening formula (*praescriptio*) (1:1–2)
- (B) Thanksgiving (1:3–8)
- (C) Prayer (1:9–11)

(II) Part I (1:12–3:1) News and Instructions for the Community
- (A) News of Paul's Personal Condition (1:12–26)
- (B) Instructions for the Community (1:27–2:18)
  - (a) Steadfastness (1:27–30)
  - (b) Harmony (2:1–2)
  - (c) Humility (2:3–11)
  - (d) Obedience and Selflessness (2:12–18)
- (C) News About Timothy and Epaphroditus (2:19–3:1)

(III) Part II (3:2–4:9) Paul's Example To Be Followed in the Path of Christian Salvation
- (A) Beware of the Judaizing Danger (3:2–4:3)
- (B) Counsels of Harmony, Joy, and Peace (4:4–9)

(IV) Part III (4:10–20) Paul's Gratitude for the Aid Sent by the Philippians and for Their Concern toward Him

(V) Conclusion (4:21–23)

COMMENTARY

10 **(I) Introduction (1:1–11).**

(A) Opening Formula (1:1–2). *Paul and Timothy:* Out of courtesy Paul includes Timothy (see comment on 1 Thes 1:1) in the greeting; but actually it is Paul who writes, as evidenced by the first person sing. in 1:3 and by the reference to Timothy in the third person in 2:19–24. *servants of Christ Jesus:* See comment on Rom 1:1. *to all God's holy people in union with Christ Jesus:* Lit., "all the saints in Christ Jesus," all Christians set apart from the profane by their union with Christ (see comment on Rom 1:7). *and the guardians and assistants:* This early mention of *episkopoi* and *diakonoi* in a Pauline church is significant, even if they cannot yet be understood in the modern sense of "bishops" and "deacons." As at Ephesus (cf. Acts 20:17,28) the "elders" of the community acted collectively as its "guardians" (cf. Acts 14:23; 1 Pt 5:2). Although *episkopos* means the same as the Qumran *m^ebaqqēr* (overseer, superintendent, 1QS 6:11,20; CD 14:8–11; 13:7), there is no evidence of such "overseers" in the early Jewish-Christian church in Palestine; *episkopoi* first appear in the Gentile communities of Pauline foundation. Paul's greeting is sent to the Philippian Christians "with" (= and, i.e., including) these community officials, undoubtedly singled out because they saw to the gift that was sent to him. **2.** *grace and peace:* The greeting invokes a share in the Messianic blessings (→ NT Epistles, 47:8) coming from both the Father and from Christ (not through him).

11 **(B) Thanksgiving (1:3–8).** **3.** *I thank my God:* Using a well-known epistolary formula (→ NT Epistles, 47:8), Paul thanks God on behalf of the Philippian Christians. A note of joy is struck, a note that runs through the letter (see 1:18,25; 2:2,17,18,28,29; 3:1; 4:1,4,10). **5.** *for your participation in [spreading] the gospel:* Their share was shown by their contributions to Paul (4:14–16) and by their suffering for the gospel (1:29–30). *from the first day:* Since their conversion (Acts 16:12–40). **6.** *he who has begun the good work in you:* God (= the Father) is the prevenient author of all the good that the Philippians do. *until the day of Jesus Christ:* The parousia, as in 1:10; 2:16 (cf. 2 Thes 2:4; 1 Cor 1:8). Then the "good work" so begun and continued will be rewarded with the glorious destiny of the Christian: to be "with the Lord" (1 Thes 4:17; 5:10). The parousia is often proposed by Paul as a motive of Christian ethical conduct. **7.** *in prison:* Lit., "in my bonds," see 1:13,17. Remembrance of the cherished Philippian community lightens his dismal condition. **8.** *with the very affection of Christ Jesus:* This affectionate yearning for the Philippians has motivated his thanksgiving (3–8) and will motivate his prayer for them (9–11).

(C) Prayer (1:9–11). *your love may grow and grow in deep knowledge and insight:* Their progress and growth in union with Christ is to bring an increased personal knowledge of the Christian reality, marked by a refined and keen awareness of its meaning. **10.** *that you may sense what really matters:* Lit., "may assess the things that differ to your advantage." *for the day of Christ:* See comment on 1:6. **11.** *filled with the fruits of uprightness which come through Jesus Christ:* The term of Christian growth and development is the status of uprightness before God, yet it is not a status that one achieves by oneself; rather it is begun by God (1:6) and has its fullness in that which comes only through union with Christ (see 3:9). *for the glory and praise of God:* As in 2:11 the career of Jesus and his influence on man are ordained only for the glory of the Father (cf. Rom 15:7; 1 Cor 10:31; 2 Cor 4:15). The expression, "for the glory of God," is not found in the LXX, but occurs in QL (1Q*19* 13:1; 1QSb 4:25).

12 **(II) Part I (1:12–3:1) News and Instructions for the Community.**

(A) News of Paul's Personal Condition (1:12–26). Although Paul is imprisoned, he knows that local Christians are boldly preaching the gospel (1:12–18). **12.** *my situation:* Paul's arrest and imprisonment were only of advantage to the gospel. **13.** *the whole praetorian guard:* Because Paul is in the custody of soldiers of the Praetorian Guard, the men know about him: he is imprisoned for the cause of Christ. Even in chains, Paul is a witness to Christ. *Praitōrion* (Lat *praetorium*) originally designated the praetor's tent in a Roman camp; but it came to mean also the governor's official residence in a Roman province (Mk 15:16; Mt 27:27; Lk 18:28; 19:9; Acts 23:35). In the Ephesian hypothesis the Praetorian Guard refers to that serving the provincial governor at Ephesus (cf. J. T. Wood, *Discoveries at Ephesus* [Boston, 1877] app. 7, no. 2). In the Roman hypothesis it would mean the imperial guard camped outside the walls of Rome (cf. *OCD* 727). **15.** *some:* Paul is in prison, and he discloses that some of those who are preaching Christ during this time do so from base motives. To whom does he refer? They are scarcely those who have been made confident by the Lord (1:14); nor do they seem to be Judaizers (whom he normally accuses of preaching "another gospel"; here they would be preaching Christ!). They are probably Christians exploiting Paul's absence for their own purposes; see 2:3. He refuses to be concerned about any personal hostility. *preach Christ:* The object of the early kerygma is Christ himself (as in 1 Cor 4:23; 15:12; 2 Cor 1:19; 11:4; Acts 8:5; 1 Tm 3:16) or his gospel (1 Thes 2:9; Gal 2:2; Col 1:23; → Pauline Theology, 79:27–30). **18.** Paul rejoices at the thriving of Christianity, even though Christ is proclaimed for other than pure motives. Following Paul's example, the Church later refused to make the validity of the Sacraments depend on the minister's worthiness.

13 **19–26.** Paul, however, being imprisoned and realizing that he might be facing death, could not help but reflect on what this would mean. First, the spread of Christianity would have to go on without him; then, he would not live to see the Day of the Lord. He ponders the implications of all this—the alternatives of his living and dying. **19.** *for my deliverance:* Paul alludes to Job 13:16 (in the LXX), as he weighs the beneficial effects of his imprisonment; it will all contribute to his ultimate salvation because of the prayers of the Philippians and the support of the Spirit. **20.** *shall not be ashamed:* Brought to disgrace by frustrated efforts or disappointed hopes. *Christ will be honored in my body:* Faced with the prospect of bodily death, Paul does not simply say "in me," for his physical life is to be spent in toil for the gospel or else surrendered in death. **21.** *To live is Christ:* This does not mean simply a share in the life of Christ (as in Gal 2:20; Rom 6:11), for the culmination of such existence is to be ultimately "with Christ"—and that is why "to die is a gain." For the whole purpose of life in union with Christ (*en Christō*) is to be one day with him in glory. Rather "to live" means to be able to "preach Christ" still more, as 1:22 indicates. **23.** *to depart and to be with Christ:* To "be with the Lord" was the expectation of Paul for the parousia (1 Thes 4:17; 5:10). Now—due to the proximity of death—he realizes that another possibility exists, to enter sooner than the ultimate resurrection into a state of companionship with Christ in glory (cf. 2 Cor 5:2,6–8; Col 3:3). Paul's words indicate that he reckons with an intermediate state in which the deceased Christian is "with Christ" after death and before the resurrection. **24.** *to remain in the flesh:* To continue in earthly life (= "in the body," 2 Cor 5:6). *for your benefit:* Paul thinks not only of the Philippians, but of all the converts he has made or can still make for Christ. **25.** *I know:* There is an awareness that he may come through this present experience alive. This is not really a change of mind from 1:20. Paul is meditating on his situation as he writes; and 2:17 shows that the other possibility, death, is not yet fully excluded. **26.** *my coming to you again:* Subsequent visits of Paul are recorded in Acts 20:1,3,6.

14 **(B) Instructions for the Community (1:27–2:18).** After a description of and a reflection on his own personal situation Paul exhorts the Philippians to steadfastness, harmony, humility, and obedient selflessness. In their witness to Christ they should strive to conform themselves to him.

(a) Steadfastness (1:27–30). **27.** *show yourselves citizens:* Or, conduct yourselves. The Gk verb, which primarily refers to conduct in civil society, is here used figuratively, because the Christian is already a citizen of the Kingdom of Heaven; see 3:20; Eph 2:19. *worthy of the gospel of Christ:* Inasmuch as they have been evangelized and have been brought under the influence of the "power" of the gospel (Rom 1:16), the Philippians should reflect this in their social conduct. *stand firm:* His first exhortation counsels steadfastness; they are to be like soldiers at their posts (cf. 1 Cor 16:13; Gal 5:1; Phil 4:1). *in one spirit:* Because of the parallelism with "one purpose," *pneuma* does not refer to the Holy Spirit; rather it designates an attitude. **29.** *to suffer for him:* Their steadfastness does not refer to personal sufferings, but to apostolic sufferings for the sake of the spread of the gospel of Christ. This is part of the Philippian contribution; see comment on 1:5. **30.** *you saw to be mine:* An allusion to Paul's imprisonment in Philippi itself (Acts 16:22–24; 1 Thes 2:2). *you now hear about:* His present imprisonment, most likely in Ephesus (2 Cor 1:8–10; 7:5).

15 (b) Harmony (2:1–2). **1.** *if there is any encouragement in Christ:* Paul affectionately adjures the Philippians by what they should esteem most. If "union with Christ" (*en Christō*) means anything, then it should be an encouragement, an incentive of life, to which he can appeal for his second recommendation of community harmony (cf. Rom 15:5; see B. Reicke, "Unité chrétienne et diaconie, Phil ii. 1–11," *Neotestamentica et patristica* [Fest. O. Cullmann; NovTSup 6 (1962)] 203–12.)

16 (c) Humility (2:3–11). His third counsel is an exhortation to humility. **3.** *do not act for selfish ends:* For the meaning of the difficult word *eritheia* (self-seeking), see comment on Rom 2:8. Paul is probably referring to the base motives of 1:17; he fears that petty jealousies are at work among them (cf. 4:2); he counsels humility, selflessness, and concern for others as a remedy. **5.** *have for one another the attitude which Christ Jesus had:* Lit., "have this attitude among you which was also in Christ Jesus." The second *en* with the dative is understood as an equivalent of the simple dative (expressing possession; cf. *GrBib* § 120). In this interpretation Paul exhorts the Philippians to an imitation of Christ; his humility and abasement would be the model for the conduct that should be found in the Philippian community. But it is also possible to render the verse, "Have for one another that attitude which you also have in Christ Jesus." In this case the vb. *phroneite* is supplied in the rel. clause. The sense would then be: Let the vital union between you and Christ so come to the fore as to manifest itself in your harmonious and self-effacing conduct with others. The stress is not on the moral imitation of Jesus, but on the vital principle of new Christian communal life.

17 Into this hortatory context Paul inserts a hymn to Christ, possibly of Jewish-Christian liturgical origin, which he has modified slightly by adding the words, "even death upon a cross." The hymn represents an early kerygmatic confession. The hymnic interpretation of this section is based on the rhythmic quality of the sentences, on the use of parallelism (found in OT psalms and poetry), and on the rare, characteristically un-Pauline expressions (*kenoun*, meaning "to empty," *harpagmos, hyperypsoun, morphē, schēma, isa theō einai*). Though there appear to be two periodic sentences, each is composed of nine cola and the whole is conveniently divided into six strophes. Each strophe has a main verb and two subordinate determinations (*thanatou de staurou* is an addition *extra metrum*). In the first three strophes Christ is the subject; in the last three, God. Strophes 3 and 6 begin in Greek with *kai.* The version shown at the bottom of this page follows the arrangement of E. Lohmeyer (*Kyrios Jesous. Eine Untersuchung über Phil. 2.5–11* [= *SHAW* Phil.-Hist. Kl., 1927–28, 4. Abh.; 2nd ed., 1961]; *An die Philipper*, 90).

18 **6.** *who:* Paul proposes to the Philippians the historical Christ who enjoyed according to this hymnic confession of the early Church also a divine pre-existent quality and an exalted celestial reward. *of divine status:* Lit., "originally being in the form of God; having as a

6	Who, though of divine status, did not treat like a miser's booty his right to be like God,	Divine Pre-existence
7	but emptied himself of it, to take up the status of a slave and become like men;	Humiliation of Incarnation
8	having assumed human form, he still further humbled himself with an obedience that meant death— even death upon a cross!	Humiliation of Death
9	That is why God has so greatly exalted him and given him the name which is above all others:	Celestial Exaltation
10	that everyone at Jesus' name should bend his knee in heaven, on earth, and under the earth!	Adoration by the Universe
11	that every tongue should proclaim unto the glory of God the Father that Jesus Christ is LORD!	Jesus' New Title: *Kyrios*

possession the form of God." The "form of God" (*morphē theou*) is not to be understood in an Aristotelian sense, expressing Jesus' internal constitution (*Physics* 1.7 [190b 20]); nor even in the patristic sense, expressing "God's nature" (*physis:* Chrysostom, *PG* 62.219; Theodoret, *PG* 82.569). For the word *morphē* expresses rather the "outward appearance," and is only so used in the LXX (Jgs 8:18; Jb 4:16; Is 44:3; Dn 3:19; 4:3; 5:6,9,10; 7:28). In the Gk world *morphē theou* was used for the external (usually human) form of a god in a theophany. For a Jew, however, to think of God in a human form was out of the question (cf. Josephus, *AgAp* 2.22 § 190). The equivalent of the external form of God in the OT would be his "glory" (Hebr *kābôd;* Gk *doxa*); cf. Ex 16:10; 24:15; Lv 9:6,23; Nm 14:10; etc. If *morphē* is understood in this hymn to refer to Jesus' possession of that quality associated with the external manifestation of Yahweh in the OT, then it can be said that he was of divine status. *did not treat like a miser's booty:* Lit., "considered it not a thing-to-be-clutched[-at]." The word *harpagmos* is rare. Derived from *harpazō* (seize), it has been understood actively as an "act of plundering" (Vg *rapina*). But this meaning is usually rejected today. What would Jesus be plundering? Passively, it could mean either a "prize, booty" to be snatched at (*res rapienda*) or a "prize held fast, snatched to oneself" (*res rapta et retinenda*). Commentators have debated the pros and cons of these two nuances, and even of a third meaning of *harpagmos* (= windfall, godsend, piece of luck). (See P. Henry, *VDBS* 5, 22–27; L. Bouyer, *RSR* 39 [1951] 281–88; H. Kruse, *VD* 27 [1949] 355–60; *VD* 29 [1951] 206–14.) We prefer the sense of *res rapta et retinenda* as the one most in keeping with the context: Jesus did not treat the status of divine glory (i.e., being equal with God) as a privilege or possession to be clutched so tenaciously that it might be exploited in the future; it was not for him a miser's booty. *his right to be like God:* Lit., "to be equal with God." This expresses in another way what his divine status was. Although Jesus possessed divine equality and its consequent privilege to appear like Yahweh in glory, he did not stand on his dignity. Some would see here an implicit comparison with Adam (J. Héring, O. Cullmann, L. Bouyer, P. Bonnard, *et al.*) as the heavenly man. But none of the reasons for this interpretation are really convincing.

19 **7.** *emptied himself:* Jesus, in becoming man, divested himself of the privilege of divine glory; he did not empty himself of divinity, but of the status of glory to which he had a right and which would be restored at his exaltation (cf. Jn 17:5; Mt 17:1–8). His voluntary giving up of *doxa* was the humiliation of the incarnation. *the status of a slave:* The use of *morphē*, "form of a slave," shows that it is not to be understood as expressive of intrinsic constitution. It refers to the condition of a slave. There is a double contrast: (1) with *morphē theou* (2:6); (2) with the title *Kyrios,* which is ultimately to be bestowed on him. He who made himself a "slave" eventually became the "Lord." He who was equal to God did not cease to be such on becoming man and abasing himself (cf. 2 Cor 8:9; Heb 5:8). In the use of *doulos* there may be an allusion to the "Servant of Yahweh" (Is 52:13 [Aquila tr.]); cf. also Is 53:12 (MT: "He poured out his lifeblood to the utmost"); *morphē* also occurs in Is 52:14 (Aquila tr.). *become like men:* Not only did he become a real man, but was like all other men, without exceptional privileges; cf. Gal 4:4; Rom 8:3. *having assumed human form:* Lit., "in outward appearance found as a man." His external shape, as he appeared to men in the days of his flesh (Heb 5:7), was that of a man. **8.** *humbled himself:* An echo of Is 53:8 (LXX). This is the second stage of Jesus' humiliation. This stage sums up his whole life on earth and his devotion to the Father, which comes to a climax in death on the cross. *an obedience that meant death:* As was to be expected of a "servant" (*doulos:* cf. Rom 6:16–18; Col 3:22; Heb 5:8). That obedience was not ordinary, but heroic. *even death upon a cross:* The lowest depth of Jesus' humiliation is set forth in this phrase, added by Paul and expressive of the point farthest removed from his celestial and glorious status. From this nadir the upward movement of the hymn begins. **9.** *has so greatly exalted him:* Lit., "has superexalted him, raised him to the loftiest heights." The hymn refers to the ascension of Christ (cf. Eph 4:10). It is "Johannine" in its immediate passage from the cross to exaltation, and un-Pauline in its passing over the resurrection. The Father has exalted Christ to a status that contrasts superabundantly with his condition of abasement. *the name which is above all others:* Lit., "above every name." The name is *Kyrios,* which appears at the end of the hymn; this LXX equivalent of *'ᵃdōnai* (my Lord) was used as the substitute for the ineffable tetragrammaton *YHWH.* It is the name that surpasses that of all celestial beings (Eph 1:21; Heb 1:4; 1 Pt 3:22; → Pauline Theology, 79:59–67). **10.** *at Jesus' name:* When *Kyrios* is pronounced. *should bend his knee:* In an act of religious devotion. The hymn alludes to Is 45:23 and transfers to the new *Kyrios* the adoration given there to Yahweh. It is a universal and cosmic adoration paid to a sovereign. **11.** *unto the glory of God the Father:* His occupying of the heavenly throne constitutes no rivalry to the Father, to Yahweh himself; rather his voluntary abasement and the acknowledgement paid to him by creation in his rewarded status bring honor to the Father. *Jesus Christ is Lord:* This essential profession of early Christian faith in Jesus forms the climax of the hymn. The same profession is echoed in 1 Cor 12:3; Rom 10:9; cf. Col 2:6. Jesus' lordship involves a cosmic influence over all creation, as it is presented here. "Christ died and lived again that he might be Lord both of the dead and living" (Rom 14:9).

(Cerfaux, L., "L'hymne au Christ-Serviteur de Dieu [Phil. II,6–11 = Is. LII,13–LIII,12]," *Miscellanea historica A. De Meyer* [Louvain, 1946] 1, 117–30; *Receuil L. Cerfaux* [Gembloux, 1954] 2, 425–38. Dupont, J., "Jésus-Christ dans son abaissement et son exaltation d'après Phil. 2,6–11," *RSR* 37 [1950] 500–514. Feuillet, A., "L'hymne christologique," *RB* 72 [1965] 352–80, 481–507. Martin, R. P., *An Early Christian Confession: Philippians II.5–11 in Recent Interpretation* [London, 1960]. Stanley, D. M., "Carmenque Christo quasi Deo dicere...," *CBQ* 20 [1958] 173–91. Talbert, C. H., "The Problem of Pre-existence in Philippians 2:6–11," *JBL* 86 [1967] 141–53.)

20 (d) OBEDIENCE AND SELFLESSNESS (2:12–18). Paul's fourth counsel concerns a further application of the previous one. **12.** *with fear and trembling:* A stereotyped OT expression (Ex 15:16; Is 19:16; Ps 2:11; Jdt 2:28), expressing not a pagan's dread before a capricious diety or inscrutable fate, but a humble reverence and dependence born of faith in God. *work out your salvation:* The eschatological fulfillment of Christian hope, both in its corporate and individual aspects, depends on the moral conduct of the individual. It is not that God may turn against the Christian, but the Christian's activity should not prove to be in vain. **13.** *God is at work in you:* The prevenience of God's aid "energizes" the Christian's desire and effort toward salvation. "In you" does not have merely a corporate connotation. God's dynamism is that which comes through Christ (Rom 1:4; 1 Cor 6:14; Phil 3:10). **14.** *without grumbling:* Cf. Nm 14; 1 Cor 10:9–10. **15.** An adaptation of Dt 32:5 (LXX); in the LXX the "blameworthy children of God" are themselves the "crooked and perverse generation." Paul, however, uses "blameless" of the Christian "children of God," whom he sets "in the midst of" the "crooked and perverse generation." *like lamps in the world:* Paul's vision of the mission of Christians in the world (cf. Mt 5:14–16). **16.** *day of Christ:* See comment on 1:6. *holding fast the word of life:* Others translate, "offering [men] the word..." **17.** *poured out as a libation:* Using a figure from sacrificial offering, Paul considers his death still as a possible end to his present imprisonment. (Cf. A.-M. Denis, *RSR* 45 [1957] 567–70.)

21 **(C) News About Timothy and Epaphroditus (2:19–3:1).** **19.** *Timothy:* See Acts 16:1–3; 17:14–15; 19:22; 1 Cor 4:17; 16:10. Timothy will be sent to Philippi to secure a fresh report for Paul and to care for the Philippians as Paul once did. **23.** *how it will go with me:* What the outcome of his imprisonment will be. Timothy's departure depends on the outcome of the trial. **25.** *Epaphroditus:* The bearer of the gift to Paul in prison (cf. 4:18) will depart shortly. Paul feels obliged to explain his situation, and even to defend him somewhat. The reason for Epaphroditus' proximity to death is not explained; Paul insists that he be received with joy. **3:1.** *goodbye:* So Paul says farewell to the Philippians "in the Lord." He does not hesitate to repeat it; cf. 4:4. Those commentators who strive to preserve the unity of Phil prefer to translate the greeting, "Rejoice in the Lord."

22 **(III) Part II (3:2–4:9). Paul's Example to Be Followed in the Path of Christian Salvation.** The connection between what follows and the preceding is difficult to explain (→ 7 above). There follows a warning against Judaizers who seem to be working in the area of the Philippian church.

23 **(A) Beware of the Judaizing Danger (3:2–4:3).** **2.** *the dogs:* In an otherwise calm and affectionate letter the use of such an epithet is striking. It is a contemporary Jewish term for pagans; Paul turns it about. But would Paul use such a figurative expression of Christians, even though Jewish? Some commentators think that he is referring to Jews as such. *with their mutilation:* A derisive term is used to scoff at circumcision. Is he comparing circumcision to the self-inflicted mutilations of the prophets of Baal (1 Kgs 18:28), or to the slashing of the devotees of Cybele? **3.** *we are the true circumcision:* Christians, who are "the seed of Abraham" (Gal 3:29), the "sons of Abraham" (Gal 3:7) because of faith in Christ Jesus (cf. Jer 4:4; Gal 6:14–15; Col 2:11–13). *who worship God by the Spirit:* The Spirit is considered to be the dynamic source of Christian life; see Gal 4:6; Rom 8:15. Through it the Christian is enabled to pray to the Father. *not relying on the flesh:* Seeking a reason for salvation in the circumcision of the flesh; it is not a guarantee, says Paul. **4.** *I myself:* If there is any reason for confidence in circumcision, Paul as a Christian of Jewish background can claim it as well as the Jews. He recalls his Jewish past (cf. Acts 22:3ff.; 26:4–7; Gal 1:13–14; 2 Cor 11:18–22; Rom 11:1). **5.** *when eight days old:* As the strict regulations of the Law prescribed (Gn 17:12; Lv 12:3). *tribe of Benjamin:* From it had come Israel's first king, Saul (1 Sm 9:1–2). In it the Shekinah dwelt, for Benjamin was the only patriarch born in the Holy Land. It was the elite tribe. *a Hebrew:* A Gk-speaking Jew who also spoke "Hebrew" (= Aramaic; cf. Acts 21:40; → Life of Paul, 46:13). *a Pharisee:* Noted for the strict observance of the Mosaic Law and the tradition of the Fathers. **6.** *persecutor:* See Acts 8:3; 9:1–2; 22:4–5; 26:9–11; 1 Cor 15:9; Gal 1:13. The "church" in Palestine and Syria. *irreproachable:* This significant statement that the Christian Paul makes about his Pharisaic past should deter one from using Rom 7:7–25 or 3:20 as an indication of Paul's psychological background for his conversion (cf. Gal 1:14). **7.** *because of Christ:* Or "for the sake of Christ." Now that the barrier between Jew and Greek has been eliminated (Gal 3:28; Eph 2:14–16), Paul no longer has any reason to boast. **8.** *the knowledge of Christ Jesus:* The knowledge of Christ accorded to the Apostle in the revelation on the road to Damascus inaugurated a relationship between him and Christ that far surpassed all former advantages. This knowledge will be further specified in 3:10. But it reveals the mature reflections of Paul on his former condition, recorded now some 20 years after his conversion (cf. J. T. Forestell, *CBQ* 18 [1956] 123–26). *rubbish [dung]:* A strong expression used for what Paul once regarded so highly. *to gain Christ:* The knowledge of Christ as a mere intellectual acquisition is not sufficient. Paul describes his communion with Christ as a goal to be attained—in a race still to be run (Phil 2:16; 1 Cor 9:24; 2 Tm 4:7). This communion with Christ is an identification ever to be deepened until it reaches its consummation at the parousia. **9.** *be found in him:* At the Last Judgment; cf. 1 Cor 4:2; 15:15; 2 Cor 5:3. *not having my own uprightness, based on the Law:* The goal of his life as a Pharisee was to be found blameless in the sight of God through a perfect observance of the 613 prescriptions of the Mosaic Law. *that which comes through faith in Christ:* His uprightness will be rather that which is freely bestowed by God and dependent only on man's willingness and humility to accept the fact that he must seek his salvation not in himself, but in God through faith (cf. Rom 1:16–17; 3:20–28). *uprightness from God depending on faith:* The very "uprightness of God" (*dikaiosynē ek theou*) is communicated to the Christian so that he can even be said through the Christ-event to "become God's uprightness" (2 Cor 5:21; cf. Rom 5:19; → Pauline Theology, 79:94–97). **10.** *the power of his resurrection:* Having become *Kyrios* and "Son of God in power" (Rom 1:4) as of the resurrection, the Risen Jesus possessed a *dynamis* that is the vital principle of the new Christian life, the New Creation (cf. 1 Cor 1:18; 6:14). This *dynamis* is nothing more than his "glory" (*doxa*), bestowed by the Father (Rom 6:4); it gradually brings about the transformation of the man of faith into an image of Christ himself (2 Cor 3:18; 4:6; Phil 2:21). This influence of Christ enables man to be identified with Jesus in his sufferings, death, and resurrection. **12.** *not that I have already achieved it:* The goal of Paul's striving—and of Christian striving in general—is not yet attained in this life. *since I have been snatched up:* Paul probably refers to the experience on the road to Damascus. But he still is the runner in the race straining for the goal (see comment on 2:8). **14.** *the upward call:* The destiny of the Christian who is called is to share a life with Christ in glory (cf. 1 Thes 4:17; Rom 5:2). **15.** *we then who are mature:* Well formed in Christian life, and no longer just babes or neophytes (cf. 1 Cor 2:6; 14:20; Heb 5:13–14); but not yet consummately perfect (2:12).

24 **17.** *join in imitating me:* Paul does not hesitate to propose himself for imitation (4:9; 1 Thes 1:6; 2 Thes 3:7,9; 1 Cor 4:16), since he himself is an imitator of Christ Jesus (1 Cor 11:1). **18.** *enemies of Christ's cross:* Paul is most probably thinking of the Judaizers; his strong words could apply to tenets of their propaganda. However, some commentators think that he is referring rather to libertine Christians of another sort. *destruction:* Cf. 1 Cor 1:18. *their god is the belly:* Probably a derisive reference to the dietary observances of the Judaizers (cf. Rom 16:18). *their shame:* Probably a reference to the circumcision, which they advocate. *earthly things:* Cf. Gal 4:9. **20.** *our commonwealth is in heaven:* Union with Christ has transferred the Christian in a sense to the "heavenly realm" (Eph 2:6,19). He is there where Christ is (Col 3:1–4). *we await a savior:* See Acts 1:11; 3:21.

21. *will change our lowly body:* Cf. 1 Cor 15:47–55; 2 Cor 3:18; 5:1–5; Rom 8:23 (cf. N. Flanagan, *CBQ* 18 [1956] 8–9). **4:2.** *Euodia and Syntyche:* Women of the Philippian church, otherwise unknown. **3.** *Syzygus:* Otherwise unknown. See comment on 1 Cor 7:8. This may not even be a proper name but a common noun, "yokefellow," an affectionate title with which Paul addresses some individual. *Clement:* Otherwise unknown. Later tradition (Eusebius, *HE* 3.15,1) identified him with Pope Clement of Rome. *the book of life:* An anthropomorphic OT expression (Ex 32:32–33; Ps 69:29; Dn 12:1) for a heavenly record of the names of the Elect (cf. Ap 3:5; 13:8; 17:8).

25 **(B) Counsels of Harmony, Joy, and Peace (4:4–9).** **4.** *goodbye:* See comment on 3:1. Paul says farewell in the Lord in view of his still uncertain destiny. **5.** *the Lord is near:* Paul hopes once again to see the Lord's parousia. He echoes the prayer of the early Church (*maranā tha,* 1 Cor 16:22; Ap 22:20 under a different form). This assurance should be the foundation of the Philippian Christians' forbearance. **7.** *the peace of God:* The peace that God gives is personified; like a sentinel it will stand guard over the hearts and minds of Christians. *surpasses all understanding:* Either because the ordinary mind of man cannot comprehend it, or such a state of serenity surpasses all human efforts to attain it. **8.** *whatever is true...:* Paul recommends as the pursuit of his cherished Philippian community a whole series of distinctively Gk virtues. He is not afraid to recommend to them the ideal of contemporary philosophers. Verse 9 gives them a new setting; he speaks as if all these things represent what has been seen and heard in him. If they pursue such things, then the God of peace (see comment on 1 Thes 5:23) will be with them.

26 **(IV) Part III (4:10–20). Paul's Gratitude for the Aid Sent by the Philippians and for Their Concern Toward Him.** He deeply appreciates the aid sent to him by the Philippians through Epaphroditus. But above all he is cheered by the sentiment that it manifests. **11b–13.** This is a short parenthesis that shows Paul did not depend on such material aid. He accepts what was sent as an expression of the Philippians' concern for him, but he does not seek it. **13.** *I am capable of all things in him who strengthens me:* The word *panta* (all things) refers to the personal experiences just mentioned and has little to do with martyrdom or persecution. Christ gives to his apostle the power to endure all things for the sake of the spread of the gospel (see 1:12). **14.** *my tribulation:* In using the word *thlipsis,* Paul relates his imprisonment to the apostolic struggles of the time that precedes the parousia. This is the sense that *thlipsis* often has (cf. Rom 5:3; 8:35; 1 Cor 7:28). **15.** *in the beginning of [the preaching of] the gospel:* Philippi was the scene of Paul's first evangelization of Europe and to this he undoubtedly refers here. Acts 16:9–10 tells the story of his moving from Asia Minor into Europe and of his first arrival in Philippi (Acts 16:12). From there he moved on to Thessalonica (Acts 17:1) and finally left Macedonia, having set up a Christian community in Thessalonica (Acts 17:2–9) and possibly also in Beroea (Acts 17:10–14). **15.** *entered into partnership with me in giving and receiving:* This does not mean merely the conversion to Christianity that also occurred at Thessalonica. As a rule Paul never accepted pecuniary remuneration (cf. 1 Thes 2:5–9; 2 Thes 3:7–9; 1 Cor 9:4–18; 2 Cor 11:7–10; 12:13–18) even when he could have done so. He seems to have made an exception for the Philippians because of his extraordinarily cordial relations with them. **18.** *I am paid in full:* In these verses Paul uses a number of commercial terms to express the situation in which he finds himself now that Epaphroditus has arrived with the gift of the Philippians. *a fragrant incense:* Allusion to several OT passages (Ex 29:18; Ez 20:41; Gn 8:21; Lv 1:9,13). It expresses the quality of the gift sent and the meaning that it will find with God himself. **19.** *my God will supply your every need:* It is not necessarily a *quid pro quo*; but just as he has seen fit to support Paul with a gift from the Philippians, so he will see fit to aid them and supply their needs. **20.** A solemn doxology that flows from the joy of the whole letter. It is addressed only to "our God and Father" (cf. 1 Thes 1:3; 3:11,13; Eph 5:20). (Cf. F. Cabrol, *RSR* 18 [1928] 9–30).

27 **(V) Conclusion (4:21–23).** The conclusion includes a farewell (4:21–22) and a final blessing (4:23). Paul sends his greetings to all the individuals among the "holy people of God" (= the saints; cf. 1:1 note). **22.** *those of Caesar's household:* This does not refer to the immediate family of the Emperor Nero, nor to high dignitaries in the imperial court, but rather to minor officials whom Paul had converted. Indeed, if the Ephesian origin of Phil is correct, they would belong to the *familia Caesaria* stationed in the province of Asia (cf. *CIL* 3.6082, 6077; *CIL* 6.8645, 8653, 8654; O. Hirschfeld, *Kleine Schriften* (Berlin, 1913) 516–75. **23.** *the grace of the Lord Jesus Christ:* See comment on Gal 6:18.

51

THE FIRST LETTER TO THE CORINTHIANS

Richard Kugelman, C.P.

BIBLIOGRAPHY

1 Allo, E.-B., *Saint Paul: Première Épître aux Corinthiens* (EBib; 2nd ed.; Paris, 1956). Cerfaux, L., *L'Église des Corinthiens* (Paris, 1946). Cornely, R., *Prior epistola ad Corinthios* (Paris, 1890). Dupont, J., *Gnosis: La connaissance religieuse dans les épîtres de Saint Paul* (Louvain Dissertations 2/40; Louvain, 1949). Gutjahr, F. S., *Die zwei Briefe an die Korinther* (2nd ed.; Graz, 1922). Héring, J., *The First Epistle of Saint Paul to the Corinthians* (London, 1962). Huby, J., *Saint Paul: Première Épître aux Corinthiens* (VS 13; Paris, 1946). Hurd, J. C., *The Origin of 1 Corinthians* (N.Y., 1965). Kuss, O., *Die Briefe an die Römer, Korinther und Galater* (RNT 6; Regensburg, 1940). Lietzmann, H., An die Korinther I, II (HNT 9; 4th ed.; Tübingen, 1949). Moffatt, J., *The First Epistle of Paul to the Corinthians* (MNTC; N.Y., 1938). Parry, R. St. J., *The First Epistle of Paul the Apostle to the Corinthians* (CGTSC; Cambridge, 1937). Robertson, A. and A. Plummer, *First Epistle of St. Paul to the Corinthians* (ICC; 2nd ed.; Edinburgh, 1914). Sickenberger, J., *Die beiden Briefe des hl. Paulus an die Korinther und Römer* (BB 6; 4th ed.; Bonn, 1932). Simon, W. G. H., *I Corinthians* (TBC; N.Y., 1960). Spicq, C., "Épîtres aux Corinthiens," *PSB* 11/2 (Paris, 1949) 161–297. Thomas Aquinas, *In omnes S. Pauli apostoli epistolas commentaria*, vol. 1 (Turin, 1924). Thrall, M. E., *I and II Corinthians* (CNEB; Cambridge, 1965). Wendland, H. D., *Die Briefe an die Korinther* (NTD 7; Göttingen, 1963).

Cambier, J., R–F, *INT* 413–33. F–B 198–205. Guthrie, *NTI* 1, 46–71. Metzger, B. M., *IPLAP* 58–75. Wik, *NTI* 381–90.

INTRODUCTION

2 **(I) The City and Church of Corinth.** Situated at the southern end of the narrow isthmus that joins the Peloponnesus to the Gk mainland, Corinth was destined by geography to play a prominent role in the history of Greece and the Mediterranean world. It commanded the land route connecting the Peloponnesus to central Greece, and it had easy access to two seas, the Aegean on the E and the Adriatic on the W. Homer and Pindar speak of "wealthy Corinth." It was primarily an industrial and shipbuilding center, but was also celebrated for its architecture and its cultivation of the arts. Cicero extolled it as "the light of all Greece" (*Pro lege Manil.* 5). The ancient city, which had become a center of Gk resistance to Rome, was destroyed by the Romans in 146 BC and its territory confiscated. The site lay in ruins until in 46 BC Julius Caesar founded a new Corinth under the name *Laus Julii.* Augustus made it the capital of the Roman province of Achaia. With its two ports, Lechaion on the W and Cenchreae on the E, the new Corinth soon regained the commercial importance of the ancient city.

3 In Paul's day Corinth was a bustling city with a cosmopolitan population drawn from all parts of the Roman Empire. It was a center of government and of commerce; its population included Roman officials and military, businessmen, merchants, and sailors from Greece, Italy, Syria, Palestine, Egypt, and other parts of the empire. The city was also a famous sports center. It was the home of the Isthmian games celebrated every second spring. Athletes from all of Greece and the empire flocked to Corinth to compete in these contests. In a pagan world notoriously tolerant of sexual license, Corinth had a reputation for debauchery and licentiousness. In Koine the vb. *korinthiazein*, "to live like a Corinthian," came to mean "to lead a dissolute life," whereas the expression *korē korinthē*, "Corinthian girl," was a euphemism for prostitute. The patron deity of the city, whose cult was popular with the seafaring population, was Aphrodite Pandemos. Her temple dominated Acrocorinthus, the great rock rising abruptly behind the city to a height of 1750 ft.; it is said to have been serviced by a thousand priestesses, who were sacred prostitutes.

4 The patient excavations of the American School of Classical Studies have revealed much of the Corinth known to Paul and have uncovered evidence of the city's wealth. At the rear of a colonnade 100 ft. long and 80 ft. wide, the largest nonreligious structure of ancient Greece, were discovered 33 taverns. The founding of the church in Corinth by Paul in early AD 51 is recorded in Acts. Despite many difficulties and sufferings (cf. Acts 18:12–17) when Paul departed from the city after 18 months of apostolic activity he left behind a flourishing community of Jewish and Gentile converts. The epistles to the Corinthians, especially the first, permit us to gaze intimately on the exuberant life of one of the earliest urban communities. Without these letters our knowledge of the spiritual movements within primitive Christianity and of the problems that tried the Apostle would be vague. They present a vivid and detailed picture of Christian life in a pagan city of the 1st cent. The parallels between this 1st-cent. Corinth and the great cities of the modern world give Paul's letters to the Corinthians an exceptional relevance for modern Christians.

5 **(II) Occasion and Purpose.** This epistle is Paul's response to information about disorders in the Corinthian church communicated to him at Ephesus by messengers from Chloe; he also formulates answers to questions put to him in a letter from the Corinthian community. The messengers had reported the tension created by factions in the community as well as a serious scandal (incest). The letter delivered by the delegates of the community, Stephanus, Achaicus, and Fortunatus, asked for Paul's advice on a variety of problems: marriage and virginity; the licitness of eating the meat of animals sacrificed to idols; the behavior of women in sacred assemblies, and other problems.

6 **(III) Authenticity.** Scholars of all persuasions number 1 Cor among the undisputed Pauline writings. It has been recognized as authentic since Clement of Rome (*ca.* AD 95).

7 **(IV) Date.** This letter was written during Paul's sojourn in Ephesus (AD 54–57), probably in the early spring of 57 (→ Life of Paul, 46:36).

8 **(V) Outline.** The letter is divided into two distinct sections corresponding to the double occasion that prompted the Apostle to write. The first part, chs. 1–6, contains Paul's reaction to the information sent by Chloe; it is a vigorous denunciation of the disorders reported to him. The second part, chs. 7–15, gives his answers to the problems proposed in the letter from the Corinthian church. K. Prümm (*ZKT* 4 [1940] 302–4) contends that the concept of Christian wisdom that Paul uses to combat the disunity of the community runs through the entire letter and unifies it.

(I) Introduction: Greeting and Thanksgiving (1:1–9)
(II) Part I: Condemnation of Disorders in the Corinthian Church (1:10–6:20)
- (A) Factions and Christian Wisdom (1:10–4:21)
  - (a) The Nature of the Dissension (1:10–17)
  - (b) The Message of the Cross (1:18–25)
  - (c) The Membership of the Corinthian Church (1:26–31)
  - (d) Paul's Method of Preaching Illustrates the Axiom of 1:25 (2:1–5)
  - (e) True and False Wisdom (2:6–16)
  - (f) The Spiritual Childishness of the Corinthians (3:1–4)
  - (g) The True Christian Estimate of Preachers of the Gospel (3:5–4:21)
- (B) The Incestuous Man and a Warning Against Sexual Sins (5:1–13)
  - (a) The Incestuous Man (5:1–6a)
  - (b) Do Not Permit Any Moral Irregularities in the Community (5:6b–8)
  - (c) Immoral Christians Should be Excommunicated (5:9–13)
- (C) Litigation Before Pagan Courts (6:1–11)
- (D) The Evil of Sexual Sins (6:12–20)

(III) Part II: Answers to Questions in the Letter of the Community (7:1–15:58)
- (A) Marriage and Celibacy (7:1–40)
  - (a) Marriage and Its Duties (7:1–24)
  - (b) On Virgins (7:25–38)
- (B) Concerning the Eating of Meat That Was Offered to Idols (8:1–11:1)
  - (a) On Knowledge and Charity (8:1–13)
  - (b) Paul an Example of Unselfish Charity (9:1–27)
  - (c) A Scriptural Illustration: The History of Israel Warns Christians About Self-Discipline and Renunciation (10:1–13)
  - (d) Practical Solution of the Problem of Eating Idol-Meat (10:14–11:1)
- (C) Good Order in Christian Assemblies (11:2–14:40)
  - (a) Women Must be Veiled (11:2–16)
  - (b) The Celebration of the Lord's Supper (11:17–34)
  - (c) On Spiritual Gifts (12:1–14:40)
  - (d) On the Resurrection of the Dead (15:1–58)

(IV) Conclusion (16:1–24)
- (A) The Collection for the Poor of Palestine (16:1–4)
- (B) Paul's Itinerary and Some Recommendations (16:5–18)
- (C) Greetings and Concluding Blessing (16:19–24)

COMMENTARY

9 **(I) Introduction: Greeting and Thanksgiving (1:1–9).** 1. *Paul:* An authentic apostle, like the Twelve, by virtue of a divine call. *Sosthenes, the brother:* A Christian well known to the Corinthians. Probably not the Sosthenes of Acts 18:17, since nothing suggests his conversion. The name was quite common. **2.** *the church of God:* This phrase recalls the *ekklēsia* (assembly) of the Lord in the LXX (Dt 23:2–4), the *qᵉhal Yahweh* of the MT (→ Pauline Theology, 79:150–151). *sanctified in Christ Jesus:* Incorporated by baptism into Christ, whom God has made our wisdom and our justice, our holiness and our redemption (1:30; 6:11), Christians are holy, just as Israel was a holy nation by divine election (Ex 19:6). *Klētois hagiois,* usually rendered "called to be saints," probably means "the convoked saints" or "the holy convocation," an allusion to the *klētē hagia* (LXX) and *miqrā' qōdeš* (MT) in Ex 12:16 and Lv 23:2–44. Christians constitute in Christ the Israel of God (Gal 6:16); they form a "sacred assembly," the community of the Lord (see L. Cerfaux, *The Church in the Theology of St. Paul* [N.Y., 1959] 114–20; K. L. Schmidt, "*Ekklesia*," *ThDNT* 3, 501–36). *in Christ Jesus:* An original and favorite Pauline formula to express the Christian's intimate and vital union with the risen Jesus (→ Pauline Theology, 79:138). *all who call upon the name of our Lord Jesus Christ in every place:* The expression, to call upon the name of the Lord, occurs frequently in the OT with the meaning to adore God (e.g., Ps 99:6; Jl 2:32). In the NT it designates the faithful united by their adoration of Jesus as "Lord." The expression clearly indicates Christian faith in the divinity of Christ. *theirs and ours:* That is, Lord. A common adoration of Christ unites all the faithful. Paul is stressing the unity of the faithful in contrast to the divisions of the Corinthian community. *together with all... in every place:* This implies that *ekklēsia* in this verse designates the local community of Corinth, the assembly of God's people in that city, and not the universal Church (→ Pauline Theology, 79:150–151). **3.** *grace and peace:* Paul's customary salutation signifies the gracious goodness of God and the gifts that are the effect of the divine liberality. In the NT *charis* is a soteriological term; it is the favor God shows and the gift he gives to men whom he saves in Christ. "Peace" is the fruit of the salvation God gives in Christ. It includes the forgiveness of sins and reconciliation with God as well as

harmony among men. Perfect peace will be realized only at the parousia, when Christ's redemptive work is completed. These blessings, grace and peace, are desired by Paul for all his correspondents (→ NT Epistles, 47:8). *Kyriou Iēsou Christou:* Grammatically this phrase may modify *theou patros* as does *hēmōn*, i.e., "from God, the father of us and of the Lord Jesus Christ." Grace and peace, the essential blessings of Christianity, come from God. The Corinthians enjoy them because they are brothers of Jesus Christ, children of his father. But it is more probable that "God" and "the Lord Jesus Christ" are coordinated. Grace and peace are given by God the Father *and* the Lord Jesus Christ.

10 **4–9.** A *captatio benevolentiae* that takes the form of a thanksgiving for the gifts conferred by God on the Corinthian community. Paul refers to the many charismatic gifts in the community. The source of the gifts is Christ, in whom the Corinthians have been incorporated. **5.** *with every utterance:* The phrase would cover all the charismatic gifts of speech: discourse of wisdom, discourse of knowledge (12:8), as well as the gift of tongues, of interpretation, of teaching, of making known a revelation, even of singing a psalm (14:26). *with all knowledge:* This is the first appearance of *gnōsis* in the NT, and its exact meaning varies with the context in which it occurs. Here it designates the charismatic gift of "knowledge" about which Paul speaks in chs. 8–10, when treating of meat offered to idols. **6–8.** *the testimony rendered to Christ:* The apostolic kerygma preached by Paul in Corinth, about Christ (obj. gen.). The abundant effusion of charismatic gifts is God's confirmation of Paul's preaching in Corinth and a pledge of his continued grace so that the Corinthians may be found irreproachable on the day of the Lord's parousia. **7.** *while you await the revelation of our Lord:* The parousia, Christ's revelation in glory and power, was a cardinal doctrine of Paul's preaching (1–2 Thes) and the object of Christian hope. **8.** *irreproachable:* An exclusively Pauline term (Col 2:22; Ti 1:6–7; 1 Tm 3:10), meaning "free from blame, not offering any cause for an accusation." **9.** Paul's hope for the blamelessness of the Corinthians on the day of judgment rests on God's fidelity, not on their actual moral state. God's fidelity to his promises is extolled in both the OT and the NT (e.g., Dt 7:9; Is 49:7; 1 Cor 10:13; 2 Cor 1:18; 1 Thes 5:24). Salvation history, the record of this divine fidelity, reaches its climax in the mission of Jesus, the Son, who is the "yes" of the divine promises (2 Cor 1:20). God, who has called the Corinthians to an ultimate and vital union with his son through the gift of faith, will perfect the work he has begun in them. *company:* *Koinōnia* means fellowship, communion, participation. Paul uses the term to designate the vital union of the faithful among themselves that arises from their union with Christ. Reception of the Eucharist is the expression and the cause (nourishment) of this fellowship (1 Cor 10:16–17).

11 **(II) Part I: Condemnation of Disorders (1:10–6:20).**

(A) Factions and Christian Wisdom (1:10–4:21).

(a) The Nature of the Dissension (1:10–17). The perfect harmony that should have reigned among Christians because of their fellowship and unity in Christ had been shattered at Corinth. Chloe's messengers informed Paul of the factions in the community. After he had left Corinth, other missionaries and Jewish Christians representing different movements that were agitating the Church came to the city. Within a short time, rival factions formed within the community. Apollos, an Alexandrian Jew trained in the Philonic school of exegesis and an eloquent orator, had made a strong impression on the better educated minority of the Corinthian Christians. Jewish Christians originally from Palestine or Syria boasted of their attachment to Cephas (Peter) and won a following among their Corinthian colleagues. The majority of the faithful, poor freedmen and slaves, incited by the pretensions of the other factions, boasted of their attachment to Paul, the apostle of Corinth. Was there a fourth faction, a Christ party? Or is the cry "I belong to Christ" Paul's personal protest against the factions in the community? Although Paul never again expressly mentions a Christ party, and Clement of Rome (*ca.* AD 95) in his letter to Corinth omits a Christ party in his enumeration of the factions that disturbed the community in Paul's day (*1 Clem.* 48), the phrase does suggest a group whose members boasted of a special relationship to Christ not shared by other Christians. H. Lietzmann and E.-B. Allo see the Christ party as mystics who rejected all human teachers and pretended to be guided by revelations received directly from Christ through the charismatic gifts. Paul would refer to them again in 2 Cor 10:17. A moral laxity is attributed to them. But J. Huby and others think the Christ party were Judaizers who had known Christ during his earthly life and now challenged Paul's apostolic authority. They would be the adversaries he excoriates in 2 Cor 11:12–29.

12 There were in the Corinthian community Christians with "knowledge" (*gnōsis*), who entertained liberal ideas about the right (*exousia*) given them by Christian liberty. There were others, called "the weak," who were scrupulous about eating meat offered to idols (ch. 8–10). The attitudes of both groups, similar "to the strong" and "the weak" of Rom 14:1–15:13, point to a Jewish rather than to a Hellenistic origin.

13 Observant Jews had a traditional horror of anything connected with idol-worship and considered food offered to idols to be "unclean" (Dn 1:8; Jdt 12:1–2; Acts 15:20,29). Paul's references to "the knowledge" of the strong seem to indicate a special gift or charism that conferred a skill in practical morality and casuistry similar to the special knowledge of the Law and its applications that distinguished the scribe from the ordinary Jew. J. Dupont offers strong evidence for this conclusion. He would identify "the knowledgeable strong" with the Christ party. "If the charismatic phenomena of the Corinthian church show a connection with the spiritual experience of the primitive Jerusalem community, the importance attached to *gnōsis* in the list of the charisms is due to the influence at Corinth of Jewish preachers who would seem to have been at the bottom of the factions in the community, and, to be more precise, would be the promoters of 'the Christ party' " (*Gnosis*, 261). The Gentiles in the community probably ranged themselves with these "pneumatics" and with the Apollos faction (*ibid.*, 257–61, 374–77; cf. S. Lyonnet, *Bib* 35 [1954] 489–97; *Bib* 37 [1956] 17–27).

14 In 1 Cor 16:12 Paul suggests that Apollos and Cephas had no personal responsibility for the formation of the factions that rallied around their names. There is no evidence that Peter had ever visited Corinth before the composition of this epistle.

15 **10.** This solemn appeal for unity is based on the Christian profession of faith in the Lord Jesus. *all say the same thing:* This common Gk expression does not refer to agreement in words only, but means "to be in perfect agreement." *perfectly united:* The word *katartizō*, "to restore, put in order," suggests a mutual adjustment and adaptation, a readiness to give in to one another in the interests of harmony. *purpose:* Christians must be united in their thinking (*nous*) and in the goal and direction (*gnōmē*) of their lives. **11.** *quarrels:* This suggests that the factions had reached the stage of recrimination and sharp language. **12.** *Apollos:* The Alexandrian Jew converted to Christ at Ephesus by Aquila and Priscilla and described as an eloquent speaker, well versed in the Scriptures (Acts 18:24–28). *Cephas:* From Aram *kēphā*, "rock," "which is translated Peter" (Jn 1:42), is the surname given to Simon by Jesus. **13.** Such factions founded on attachment to ministers of Christ involve a dogmatic absurdity. Paul indicates this with biting sarcasm. There is only one Savior, Christ who died on the cross, into whom men are incorporated by baptism, no matter who administers it. **14–16.** Paul has baptized so few persons in Corinth that no one can seriously pretend he was baptized in Paul's name. *Crispus:* The former head of the Corinthian synagogue, his conversion sparked the growth of the church (Acts 18:8). *Gaius:* A wealthy man with a house large enough to accommodate the Christian assembly (Rom 16:23). *Stephanas:* The first Christian convert in Corinth. Paul praises him for his dedicated service to the church. Accompanied by Achaicus and Fortunatus, he delivered to Paul at Ephesus the letter from the Corinthian community that Paul answers in the second part (1 Cor 16:15–18). **17.** No special mission was needed to baptize, and Paul usually left the administration of baptism to others. This does not imply any disdain for it; Rom 6:3–12 and 1 Cor 6:11 indicate Paul's high regard for the sacrament of incorporation into Christ. Yet Paul is an apostle sent by Christ to preach the gospel. *not with wisdom of discourse:* Not with wordy wisdom, employing the technique of the philosopher or the rules of studied eloquence and artificial rhetoric, but by speaking simply and forthrightly in order not to detract from the power of Christ's cross.

16 (b) THE MESSAGE OF THE CROSS (1:18–25). It is foolishness to those who are perishing, but to those who are being saved it is the revelation of God's saving power. **18.** *foolishness:* Thomas Aq. remarks that men are accustomed to regard as foolishness whatever surpasses their understanding. **19.** Paul cites Is 29:14 (LXX) to illustrate his statement. When Sennacherib invaded Judah, the king's counselor advised an alliance with Egypt. But the Prophet told the king to do nothing but trust in the Lord. God himself would save Jerusalem and bring to naught "the wisdom of the wise" and "the cleverness of the clever." **20.** Today, as of old, God confounds human wisdom. The wise men, i.e., the Greek philosopher and the Jewish scribe, count for nothing before God. It is not from among them that he chooses the preachers of the good news of salvation. There is an allusion to Is 33:18 (LXX). **21.** *in the wisdom of God* and *through wisdom:* Several interpretations are possible: (1) In God's wise plan the world (Jew and Greek) failed to know God by "wisdom," i.e., either through the Law, which is wisdom for the Jew, or through philosophy, which is wisdom for the Greek; (2) In the manifestation of God's wisdom in the created universe (Rom 1:20), in history (Acts 17:26–27), and in the Law (Sir 24:22–31) the Jew and Gentile failed to come to know God and his wisdom. Or perhaps better: through the wisdom of this world, which is carnal and under Satan's power (1 Cor 2:6; 2 Cor 4:4). *world:* This word (*kosmos*) in Paul usually has a pejorative meaning as in the Johannine writings, signifying either the material universe still under Satan's power or, as here, unredeemed men, "worldlings." *to know God:* This is not a mere speculative knowledge of his existence and attributes, but a practical knowledge that renders him homage and obeys his will. Failure to know God is not simply ignorance or error, but sin. *those who believe:* To those who surrender themselves to God revealing his wisdom and love in Christ, the preaching of the cross brings salvation. **22.** The gospel message shocks Jewish nationalism and Greek intellectualism. The Jews expected and demanded *signs*, i.e., spectacular miracles that showed divine intervention. They looked for a messiah who would inaugurate their nation's sovereignty over the Gentiles by a display of miraculous power (Mt 12:38; 16:4; Jn 4:48; 6:30–31). The Greeks searched for "wisdom," i.e., philosophies that pretended to give a satisfactory explanation of man and the cosmos. **23.** To the Jew, the Crucified Christ is a *scandal*, i.e., a cause of offense and revulsion and an object of vigorous opposition and anger (see R. A. Knox, *Trials of a Translator* [N.Y., 1949] 66–73; A. Humbert, *Bib* 35 [1954] 1–28). **24.** *to those called:* Paul stresses the primacy of God's action in the genesis of faith; for man believes because God calls him (Rom 9:16). In Christ, crucified and risen, God reveals to the called his wisdom and his saving acts (see J. Dupont, *Gnosis*, 82–83).

17 (c) THE MEMBERSHIP OF THE CORINTHIAN CHURCH (1:26–31). It illustrates the paradox of 1:25.

Few of the educated class in Corinth, few men of authority, few of the aristocracy, have been called to the faith. But God has called the lowly, the poor, the slaves, and—most shocking of all paradoxes—"the nonentities," i.e., the Gentiles (Rom 9:24–26). Thus he might *destroy* (*katargēsē*) the pretensions of all who account themselves as something. Most exegetes would regard *ta mē onta* (the nonentities) simply as a climax, summing up all the preceding phrases. The omission of *kai* (and) in many mss. supports this exegesis. In any case, Paul is alluding to his basic doctrine that the call to faith is due to the merciful goodness of God and not to the works of man, whether naturally good or of the Law (Rom 3:27; Eph 2:9). **30.** God is the efficient cause of *your existence in Christ Jesus*. From being nonentities the Corinthians are by God's call and action transformed into a new creation (2 Cor 5:17). In Christ, the Christian possesses all that the Greek and the Jew yearned for: wisdom, justice, holiness, and redemption. Christ crucified and risen is the wisdom of God (1 Cor 1:18; Col 2:3). "Christ's act of redemption disproves the basic thesis of Greek philosophy, viz. the impossibility of divine intervention in the cosmos. Paul's experience at Athens and at Corinth had taught him the need of presenting 'a crucified Christ' who was risen from the dead as the incarnation of God's Wisdom." (D. M. Stanley, *Christ's Resurrection in Pauline Soteriology* [Rome, 1961] 109). *justice:* Christ, who is "the yes" to all the promises of God, embodies the divine justice, i.e., God's faithfulness to his promises of salvation (Rom 3:21–30). *sanctification:* As the embodiment of God's holiness and the dispenser of the Spirit of holiness imparted at baptism, the Risen Christ has become holiness for us. *redemption:* Christ by his death and resurrection has freed man from slavery to sin, the flesh, the Law, and death. Paul mentions redemption last because it is completed only with the bestowal of the last grace, the glorious resurrection of the body (Rom 8:23). "The Greek difficulty in accepting Christianity was a desire for human wisdom: 'a crucified Christ' was 'folly' to them. The Jews were in search of miracles: the Cross was 'a scandal' (1:22–23). Paul does not isolate the Greek religious problem from that of the Jews, but replies to both simultaneously. Hence, in proposing Christ Jesus to the Greeks as *Wisdom*, he appends an explanation which points out Christ to the Jews as the culmination of the three chief tendencies in the OT search for God. The Mosaic Code and cult strove to impart justice and sanctification. The prophets proclaimed Yahweh's definitive act of redemption. The sapiential literature strove to teach humano-divine wisdom. Thus Paul shows that the striving of pagan religion as of the Jewish faith finds its consummation in Christ Jesus" (D. M. Stanley, *Christ's Resurrection*, 109–10). **31.** The Apostle concludes by citing rather freely Jer 9:23–24.

18 (d) PAUL'S METHOD OF PREACHING ILLUSTRATES THE AXIOM OF 1:25 (2:1–5). This section seems to be directed against the Apollos faction. Paul's failure at Athens, where he attempted to speak as a philosopher (Acts 17), probably prompted him to preach the gospel at Corinth in all its shocking realism without any attempt to play the rhetor. **1.** *the testimony of God:* The apostolic preaching of Christ crucified and risen. The resurrection is the Father's testimony to Christ. Instead of the phrase "the testimony of God" important mss. (P^{46}, S*, A, C) read "the mystery of God." **3.** Paul may be alluding here to the many difficulties he experienced in Corinth (Acts 18:5–17). **4–5.** The conviction Paul's message conveyed and the success that met his preaching at Corinth were due to the Holy Spirit, and not to rhetorical eloquence or philosophic reasoning. Thus the faith of the Corinthians rests on God's power, and not on human wisdom. "In the manifestation of the Spirit and power" is probably a hendiadys: "in the manifestation of the Spirit's power." This refers to the inspired conviction with which Paul preached and to the charisms that were manifested in him and in his converts (see E.-B. Allo, *Première épître*, 26–33; J. Huby, *Première épître*, 74–80).

19 (e) TRUE AND FALSE WISDOM (2:6–16). Both "wisdom" and the "perfect" are emphasized. Christ crucified and risen is the Wisdom of God. In him the divine economy of salvation decreed before creation has been revealed and realized. As a gift bestowed by the Spirit upon the "perfect," wisdom brings a deep understanding of the mystery of Christ. All the baptized have some knowledge of this mystery (1:5), because all have faith. But only the "perfect" are capable of grasping Paul's inspired discourse on the mystery. Two groups are contrasted in this section: (1) *psychikoi* (from *psychē*), "material" men who use only the natural faculties of knowledge and understanding (*nous*), and *pneumatikoi* (from *pneuma*), "spiritual" men in whom the Holy Spirit dwells and acts; (2) *nēpioi*, "infants" in Christ (3:1), beginners in the spiritual life, and *teleioi*, the "perfect," Christians full grown in Christ, the spiritually mature Christians. The *nēpioi* received the Holy Spirit at baptism and he dwells in them (Rom 8:23; 2 Cor 1:22; 5:5), but they cannot be treated as "spiritual" men, because in their thinking and behavior they still walk according to "the flesh" (1 Cor 3:1–13; Gal 5:16); they still behave as "infants" who are enslaved to the elements of the world (Gal 3:3). The *teleios* is the *pneumatikos* in the full sense of the term: perfectly docile to the indwelling Spirit. By this distinction between the "perfect" and the "infants" Paul reproves the Corinthians who were boasting that they were "spiritual" because of the charismatic gifts they had received (see J. Dupont, *Gnosis*, 151–80). **6.** *this world:* This *aiōn* is the world that has not yet been transformed by the redemptive power of Christ and that lies in subjection to Satan and the wicked spirits until the final act of the drama of redemption, the parousia of the Lord. See comment on Gal 1:4. *the rulers of this world:* The wicked spirits who, since Adam's sin, hold this world in slavery (Col 2:15; Eph 6:12; 2 Cor 4:4). *the wisdom of this world:* The philosophy of the pagans who, blinded by sin, failed to recognize and worship God the Creator (Rom 1:19–20), and Jewish interpretations of Scripture, which failed to see in Jesus the promised Messiah. Both Jew and Gentile are enslaved by the elements of the world, the wicked spirits who rule this *aiōn* (Gal 4:3,8–9; Col 2:20). **7.** Since Christ, the Wisdom of God, is a mystery, men can know him only by revelation. The divine wisdom lies hidden in the folly and scandal of the cross. The end of this divine economy of salvation is our glory, our participation in the glorious resurrection of Christ (→ Pauline Theology, 79:129). **8.** Had the wicked spirits known the mystery of Christ, they would never have incited men to crucify him. His death and resurrection are the world's redemption and the destruction of their power and empire. *the Lord of glory:* This implies Christ's messiahship and divinity (Phil 2:10). **9.** A citation confirms the Apostle's statement that the Christian mystery lay hidden. *as it is written:* The formula suggests that a biblical text is being quoted, but the source of the citation is doubtful. There are a few verbal resemblances to Is 64:3 and 65:16; otherwise, the actual Pauline citation is not found in the OT. Possibly the Apostle is using a free paraphrase of the Isaian verses, or perhaps he is quoting (as Origen, Ambrosiaster, and Jerome thought) from the *Apocalypse of Elijah*, an apocryphal writing of which only fragments are extant (cf. J. A. Fitzmyer, *NTS* 7 [1960–61] 304; J.-B. Frey, *VDBS* 1, 456–58).

20 **10.** *to us:* Either Paul and his fellow preachers, or all the baptized. If the former, vv. 10–16 treat of the discourse on wisdom that Paul delivers to the perfect; if the latter, these verses refer to the revelation of the mystery of salvation communicated to all the baptized. The former seems to be indicated by the context. *the depths of God:* The profundity of the mystery of God's love and saving power in Christ (Rom 11:33; Eph 3:18). **11.** *man's own spirit within him:* In our terminology, "his own soul"; *pneuma* in this phrase is almost equivalent to *nous*. Just as no one knows the secrets of a man except himself, so only the Spirit of God can make known the mysteries of God. **12.** *the spirit of the world:* The habitual mental attitude and disposition of those who evaluate everything by natural and temporal standards. Perhaps there is an allusion to the influence of the wicked spirits on the worldling. Christians have not received the spirit of the world, "the spirit of slavery," but rather the Holy Spirit, "the spirit of adoption" (Rom 8:15). *the spirit which is from God:* The Holy Spirit's presence in the baptized and his gifts to the perfect make Christians know and come to an ever deeper understanding of the graces bestowed on them in baptism, especially of "the glory" that awaits them. **13.** This is a description of the *sermo sapientiae* that Paul delivers to the "perfect." It is a charismatic discourse inspired by the Spirit and distinct from the kerygma, "the testimony of God," which is described in 1:17–2:5. The special subject of this charismatic discourse is "the gifts that have been given to us by God," above all the eschatological blessing, the final glory of the blessed. In 2:9 the Apostle declared that the hidden wisdom was destined by God "for our glory," and in 15:51 he introduces his description of the fate of the just who are living at the time of the parousia with the words, "Behold I tell you a mystery" (see J. Dupont, *Gnosis*, 225). *Pneumatikois* may be masculine or neuter. If neuter: "It is of these (gifts given us by God) that we speak, not in words taught by human wisdom, but in words taught by the Spirit; thus we give spiritual truths a spiritual form." If masculine: "...not in words taught by human wisdom, but in words taught by the Spirit; thus we interpret (explain) spiritual truths to the spiritual," i.e., to the perfect. *sygkrinontes:* The basic meaning of this word is "to combine, bring together"; but it can also signify "to compare, explain, or interpret." The LXX uses it of the interpretation of dreams (Gn 40:8,16,22; 41:12,13,15; Dn 5:7); but cf. 2 Cor 10:12 (to compare). **14.** The "material man" (*psychikos*) is one animated only by the *psychē*, the life received from Adam; he has only natural knowledge and understanding and is therefore not responsive to the truths taught by the Spirit. He regards the Christian mystery as sheer nonsense, and he cannot even know it. **15–16.** The Spirit of the Lord dwells and acts in the "spiritual man" (*pneumatikos*) so that he thinks as Christ does and judges all things rightly from a supernatural point of view. These verses recognize the principle that in order to know a truth one must have a cognitive faculty proportioned to it. Sense faculties cannot grasp the object proper to the intellect. So, to know and appreciate the mysteries of faith man's intellect must be elevated. The Christian enlightened and led by the Spirit evaluates correctly all human events and knowledge. The Spirit does not supply information for study, industry, or science, but he does enable the "spiritual man" to judge everything in the universe according to the divine plan for man's destiny. The "spiritual man" himself can never be properly judged by the "material man." **16.** Paul quotes Is 40:13 to confirm the argument. The MT reads *rû^{a}ḥ:* "who has directed *the spirit* of Yahweh?" This would be better adapted to Paul's argument, but he cites the LXX, where *rû^{a}ḥ* is translated by *nous,* "mind." Therefore Paul must conclude: "But we have the mind (*nous*) of Christ." However, his meaning is clearly, "We have the Spirit of Christ." For he addresses a discourse of wisdom to "the spiritual." "The Apostle applies to the *pneumatikos* what the context affirms about the Spirit of God. The *pneuma* alone is capable of searching all things, even the depths of God. Since the *pneumatikos* possesses the *pneuma* and receives his revelations, he also can understand everything. On the other hand, since no one can understand the Spirit of the Lord, it follows that no one can understand the *pneumatikos.* Possessing the Spirit of Christ, he is in some way introduced into the divine inaccessibility" (J. Dupont, *Gnosis,* 324). See R. Scroggs, *NTS* 14 (1967) 33–55.

21 (f) The Spiritual Childishness of the Corinthians (3:1–4). The factions in the Corinthian community are proof of their spiritual immaturity. Consequently, the Apostle cannot treat them as *pneumatikoi* and deliver to them his *sermo sapientiae.* **1.** *men of flesh and blood:* The adj. *sarkinos* means made of flesh, belonging to the realm of the flesh, which is weak, sinful, and transitory. In Rom 7:14 Paul defines *sarkinos* as "sold under sin," and such were the Corinthians in the past. **3.** *worldly:* Lit., "fleshy," i.e., *sarkikos,* "belonging to flesh," to the order of earthly things; it describes the present state of the Corinthians. Their estimate of their preachers is motivated by vanity and prejudices and shows that they are still earthly minded, men behaving as *psychikoi* and not *pneumatikoi.*

22 (g) The True Christian Estimate of Preachers of the Gospel (3:5–4:21). **5.** Apollos and Paul are *diakonoi,* "servants" in the employ of a master, Christ. They are simply the instruments through whom God has called the Corinthians to the faith. Each has a distinct mission, which is not of his own choosing but assigned to him by Christ. **6.** Paul was sent to found the Corinthian church, Apollos to develop it. The success of both ministries is due to God. **8.** *are one:* The ministers are basically equal, because they are sent by the same master and work for the same end. Each will receive "a salary" commensurate to his labor. *laborious toil: Kopos,* "hard work," is the Pauline term designating the apostolic ministry (1 Cor 15:10; 16:16; 1 Thes 3:5; Gal 4:11; Rom 16:12, etc.), but also the constant spiritual and moral effort of Christian life (1 Cor 15:58; 1 Tm 4:10). **9.** *God's fellow laborers:* Not working together in God's interests, but cooperating with a God who acts in and through his apostles. Dropping the agricultural metaphors (planting, watering a field), Paul shifts to one of his favorite metaphors for the Church, God's building (Eph 2:20–21; 1 Tm 3:5), the temple in which God dwells (→ Pauline Theology, 79:156).

23 **10.** Developing the metaphor, Paul describes his ministry and the responsibility of all who follow him, as they build upon the foundation he has laid. **11.** Christ, as the unique foundation, may be an allusion to Is 28:16 or Ps 117:22 (cf. Eph 2:20 and 1 Pt 2:6–8). This Christ, preached by Paul, dwells in the hearts of the faithful (Eph 3:17) and communicates his Spirit to them. Succeeding preachers must take care how they build on this foundation. **13.** *the Day:* The Lord's Day when Christ returns as victorious judge (1 Thes 5:4). *fire:* It is to test the quality of various building materials. Fire is the customary biblical metaphor describing the might and majesty of the divine judgment. *it:* Probably the neut. pron. *auto* refers to *ergon,* "work." The fire tests the work, destroying what is of poor quality and perishable. **14.** A wage will be paid only for good, durable work. **15.** The man whose work will not endure the searching test of judgment will suffer a loss. Like one escaping from a burning house, he will be saved, but his work and his reward will be lost. This metaphor clearly teaches the responsibility of ministers of the gospel, who will be rewarded or punished for the manner in which they have fulfilled their ministry. That the preacher will be saved implies that his sins were not serious and have not ruined the Christian community, because God destroys such a one. Although the doctrine of purgatory is not taught in this passage, it does find support in it. The metaphor suggests an expiatory punishment—which is not damnation—for faults that, although not excluding salvation, merit punishment. When Paul wrote this epistle he was still hoping for the coming of the Lord's Day in his lifetime. Consequently, he locates this expiatory punishment at the final judgment. See J. Gnilka, *Ist 1 Kor 3, 10–15 ein Schriftzeugnis für das Fegfeuer?* (Düsseldorf, 1955); S. Cipriani, *RBibIt* 1 (1959) 24–43. **16–17.** *you:* The Corinthian community is a temple of God, because the divine Spirit dwells in it. Later, in 6:19, the metaphor of the temple will be applied to the body of the individual Christian, because the Spirit dwells in every one of the baptized. This individual application is secondary. The Spirit comes into the community and gives himself to individuals through the community. In 2 Cor 6:16 the metaphor is applied to the Corinthian community as here; but in Eph 2:19 it designates the universal Church (see L. Cerfaux, *Church,* 146–49). Pagans, as well as Jews, regarded desecration of a temple as a heinous crime.

24 **18–20.** In their vain and merely human appraisal of the ministers of the Gospel the Corinthians have shown themselves to be fools, judging by the wisdom of this world. Two biblical texts, Jb 5:12 and Ps 94:11, are cited in confirmation. Paul seems to have used a Gk translation of Jb somewhat different from the LXX. He adapts the verse of the Ps to his argument, substituting "wise" for "men." **21–22.** No Christian should glory in men, calling himself a disciple of any preacher, to the detriment of the unity of the Church. The ministers of the gospel are for the faithful, not the faithful for them. Carried away by his enthusiasm, Paul associates to the preachers all creation and all the happenings of history. God ordains all things for the good of those who love him (Rom 8:28). Belonging to Christ, who in turn belongs to God, the Christian dominates the world and its happenings. He shares already by faith and hope in the triumph of the Lord.

25 **4:1–5.** *servants: Hyperetēs* (from *hypēreteō*) designated the rowers on the lowest bank of the galleys; thence it came to mean "assistant, helper." *managers:* The *oikonomos* was the servant entrusted with the administration of the house. Paul insists on the inferior position of the "manager" who administers his master's property, and not his own. The apostles are Christ's assistants and "managers" of God's mysteries, charged with preaching divine revelation, and not their own doctrines. **2.** *dependable:* The first and indispensable quality demanded of a manager is trustworthiness, a conscientious devotion to his master's interests. **3.** *by a human court:* Lit., "by man's day," an expression that is analogous to the "Lord's Day" and signifies any human judgment or criticism. **4.** The faithful have no right to pass judgment on the Lord's manager. Only the Lord, not even the apostle himself, can judge the faithfulness of his ministry. The Lord will make known his judgment at his parousia.

26 **6.** *I have applied:* Lit., "transformed, disguised"; but the verb is used in a rather unique sense here: "I have applied this by way of example to Apollos and myself." *for your sakes:* In order not to offend any sensitive Corinthians, Paul has used his and Apollos' names in the discussion of apostolic ministry. He hoped thus to make more palatable the lesson they must learn. The next phrase (*to mē hyper ha gegraptai*) is obscure, and many conjectures have been made to explain it. It may be a popular proverb (Allo), e.g., "never go beyond the letter." Or it may be a warning against "hyper-scripturists," Judaizers who found in the OT more than was there, e.g., the obligation of circumcision for Christians (Sickenberger). Or it may be an allusion to the texts cited in 1:19,31; 3:19 (Gutjahr). **7–13.** Paul contrasts, with biting irony, the humiliations and sufferings of the apostles with the smugness of the Corinthians who, in forming factions, make pretense of a spiritual superiority over their fellow Christians. Every supernatural and natural quality by which they may be distinguished is God's gift. The Corinthians have lost the sense of their own indigence and spiritual poverty that is the basic disposition of the true Christian (Mt 5:3). They behave as though they have already reached the summit of perfection and are reigning in the Kingdom of Heaven. The apostles, on the contrary, have been made a spectacle to all the universe, like the basest of men, criminals condemned to die in the games of the arena. **13.** They have become the world's offscourings, the scum of all. *Perikatharmata* means the rinsings of a dirty vessel; *peripsēma* means what is rubbed, washed off, the scum. Since the removal of the "offscourings" is a purification, the word can refer to an expiatory offering or a ransom (Prv 21:18); so perhaps here, "the scapegoats of the world." *Peripsēma* may also mean "scapegoat" (Tb 5:19). The epithet was used by the Greeks for the poor wretch called the *pharmakos*, who was sacrificed in order to free a city from an infection or plague that afflicted it. The *pharmakos* (lit., "sorcerer"), usually a poor beggar or cripple, was supposed to have taken upon himself the city's *miasma*, "infection." If these terms have a cultic meaning in this verse, the passage would suggest an association of apostolic sufferings with the sufferings of Christ "for his body, which is the Church" (Col 1:24–29; cf. 2 Cor 6:4–10). However, in ordinary speech *peripsēma* was used simply as a polite expression of self-depreciation, something like "most humble servant" (see F. Hauck, *ThDNT* 3, 430–31; G. Stählin, *ThWNT* 6, 83–92). **14–16.** From biting sarcasm Paul turns to tender pleading. He has spoken sharply to bring about the amendment of the faction-split community. A father has a duty to correct his children, and Paul has a relationship to the Corinthians not shared by any other preacher. He is their father, having begotten them in Christ; so Christians must follow the example of their apostle. In doing so, they will be following Christ and measuring up to the ideal of the new life they have received (1 Cor 11:1; 1 Thes 1:6; cf. D. M. Stanley, *Bib* 40 [1959] 871–73). **17.** *Timothy:* See comment on 1 Thes 1:1; he appears in 1 Thes 3:2 as Paul's agent again. He was to remind the Corinthians of the rule of faith and conduct that Paul had imparted to them, as to every church that he founded (11:2,16; 14:36). Paul now threatens punishment, if they do not amend. The sovereignty of God is present and manifests itself not in the boasting of the factions but in the power possessed by the apostle, who is the minister of God's severity as well as of his mercy. (Is there an allusion here to Jb 37:13? See C. Spicq, *RB* 60 [1953] 509–12; *TS* 15 [1954] 406.)

27 **(B) The Incestuous Man and a Warning Against Sexual Sins (5:1–13).**

(a) The Incestuous Man (5:1–6a). A Corinthian Christian had entered an incestuous union with his stepmother, and the community took no action against him. Str-B (3, 358) conclude from rabbinical writings that in NT times the rabbis permitted a proselyte to marry his father's widow, because all former family ties were considered to have been destroyed by the Gentile's entrance into the community of Israel. This may have furnished the incestuous man and the Corinthian community a pretext for tolerating the union. Both Roman and Jewish law forbade such marriages and held them to be incest (Lv 18:8; 20:11; Caius, *Inst.* I, 63). A passage of the Athenian orator Andocides, *On The Mysteries* (399 BC), implies that such unions were severely reprobated in ancient Greece, too. **3–5.** The meaning of the passage is clear, but the exact nuance of each phrase depends on the punctuation. Probably: "As for me, though absent in body, I am present in spirit; and as thus present I have already passed sentence on the man who has done this deed. In the name of our Lord Jesus, you and my spirit, united in assembly and empowered by our Lord Jesus, do decree to hand this man over to Satan for the destruction of his flesh, so that his spirit may be saved on the Day of the Lord Jesus." *I have passed sentence:* Paul in Ephesus has already pronounced judgment on the guilty man. With full apostolic authority he now commands his decree of excommunication to be promulgated to the assembled community. The excommunicated man is not only excluded from the community; he is also delivered to Satan to be afflicted physically, even unto death (1 Tm 1:20). "This is a mitigated transposition, in the spirit of the New Covenant, of the law of the *ḥērem*, which included expulsion from the community, exile, and death. The terms Paul uses are those of the Mosaic Code; compare 2, 5, 7, 13 with Dt 17:7; 19:19; 22:24" (C. Spicq, *PSB* 11/2, 204). The punishment is medicinal. While the man's flesh, i.e., his body enslaved by sin, suffers and is even destroyed through this punishment, his *pneuma*, the life that is the effect of God's creative breath and by which man is the image of God (Gn 1:27; 2:7), is saved on Judgment Day.

28 (b) Do Not Permit Any Moral Irregularities in the Community (5:6b–8). **6b.** *a little leaven:* Unlike the gospels, where leaven is a symbol of the inner dynamism of the Kingdom (Mt 13:33; Lk 13:20–21), Paul uses it as a metaphor for the corruptive influence of evil (Gal 5:9). **7.** This is a reference to the Jewish custom of destroying all leaven in preparation for the Paschal festival, during which only unleavened bread was permitted (Ex 12:15–16; 13:7). Incorporated in Christ, who has become for us "holiness and redemption" (1:30), Christians individually are unleavened. Paul exhorts them as a community to rid themselves of the old leaven, i.e., to clean out the wicked. The Church is always engaged in a Paschal celebration, because Christ by his death and resurrection has accomplished the salvation foreshadowed in the Exodus. Paul sees in the lamb sacrificed at Passover and eaten at the festal dinner a type of Christ's redemptive sacrifice. **8.** *let us celebrate the feast:* The Christian life should be joyful because Christ has become "for us redemption" (1 Cor 1:30), and at his parousia the faithful will be glorified with him (Phil 4:4–7). In 5:7 the unleavened bread symbolizes the Christians; in this verse, the virtues that should characterize them. "Sincerity," single-mindedness or purity of intention, as well as "truthfulness" should distinguish the Christian. Perhaps the paschal metaphors of this passage were suggested by the time of year (16:8).

29 (c) IMMORAL CHRISTIANS SHOULD BE EXCOMMUNICATED (5:9–13). **9.** A reference to a lost Pauline letter to the Corinthians. **10–13.** Leaving to God the judgment and punishment of the unbaptized, the Apostle forbids association with immoral Christians. Paul's citation of the frequent refrain of Dt (17:7; 19:19; 22:21,22,24; 24:7) is inspired by his concept of the Church as the Israel of God.

30 **(C) Litigation Before Pagan Courts (6:1–11).** This abuse was probably occasioned, or at least fomented, by the rivalries of the various factions. **1.** *heathen court:* Lit., "the unjust," but not simply in the sense of corrupt or venal men; rather of "unbelievers" as distinct from "the saints," the faithful. **2–3.** The saints share in Christ's royal power and will participate in his judgment of the world. Paul probably has in mind Dn 7:9,22,27; cf. Ap 20:4; 1 Thes 3:11–13. The book of *Enoch* speaks of a judgment pronounced by the Son of Man on angels and men. Associated with the Son of Man (Dn 7:17–18), the elect will also participate in his judgment. **4.** Biting sarcasm! **5.** The Christian community should institute its own courts or at least invite "a prudent brother" (*sophos*) to decide disputes among the brethren. **7–9.** *failure:* The noun *hēttēma* denotes "disaster"; it implies an "utter defeat" for them, that they engage in lawsuits against one another. It may perhaps also have the meaning of "a great loss." The Corinthians not only do not endure injustice patiently as Jesus counseled (Mt 5:38–42), but they inflict injury on their own fellow Christians! **9.** *wrongdoers:* Those guilty of injustice (*adikoi*). Grave sins exclude the guilty from the Kingdom of God. This warning is probably directed against the laxists who stretched Christian liberty from the Law into an antinomianism (6:12) and condoned the vilest depravities. The sexual vices that Paul enumerates were all too frequent in Gk city life. *sensual perverts:* Lit., "the soft, those who lie with males," those addicted to pederasty. **10.** As in Rom 1:28–31; Gal 5:19; Col 3:5; Eph 5:3–5, Paul lists certain vices that were characteristic of the pagans. A comparison of this list with those of the other epistles suggests the greater debauchery and sensuality of Corinth. **11.** Paul does not spare the Corinthians. They were once given to the shameful vices mentioned. *you have been washed:* In baptism with its purifying effect (Acts 22:16; Heb 10:22). *you have been sanctified:* Holiness, which implies a state of consecration to God, has also been conferred at baptism (Eph 5:26). *you have been justified:* Placed in a state of justice, made just. *in the name of the Lord Jesus Christ:* Purification from sin, sanctification, and justification are the consequences of baptismal incorporation into Christ. The "name" here signifies the person. *and in the Spirit of our God:* That is, of the Father. The Spirit is the agent of this spiritual regeneration, of this new creation that is God's gift to us in Christ (Ti 3:4–5). C. Spicq invites us to note "the trinitarian formula used with reference to the effects of baptism (cf. Mt 28:19). Christ is the meritorious cause of justification, the Holy Spirit by appropriation is the efficient cause of it; both operate in the sacramental rites, which create a state of interior and spiritual holiness by the action of the Father" (*PSB* 11/2, 211). This precise theological exposition may be reading into the verse more than Paul actually expresses, but the text emphasizes the real change wrought in the sinner by baptism. Sins are remitted, "washed away," and the justice of Christ is imparted.

31 **(D) The Evil of Sexual Sins (6:12–20).** **12.** Some Corinthians were invoking Christian liberty to justify serious violations of morality. Exegetes usually see in these laxists converts from paganism who had erected into a principle of libertinism the aphorism with which Paul expressed the Christian's liberty from the dietary regulations of Jewish Law. "All things are permitted me" might have been said by Paul with the same meaning as "all things are pure" (Rom 14:14). But J. Dupont has adduced strong arguments against this interpretation. The aphorism does not reflect the usual antilegalistic vocabulary of the controversy over food with the Judaizers. That question is always discussed in terms of "clean" and "unclean" (Rom 14:14,20; Acts 5:14–15; 11:8–9; Ti 1:15). The vb. *exestin,* related etymologically to *exousia,* which figures so prominently in the passages dealing with the eating of meat sacrificed to idols (1 Cor 8:9; 9:4–6,12,18), suggests another interpretation. In profane usage *exousia* signifies a "power" one can use, a right or liberty that a man can exercise at his own pleasure. The vb. *exestin* has a similar connotation. However, the NT uses the verb with a specifically religious meaning: an *exousia,* "a right," can be conferred by a positive law. For the Jew, the Law is the expression of the divine will. Therefore, what the Law permits (*exestin*) is a right, a liberty, conferred by God. The vb. *exestin* with this religious connotation occurs frequently in the Gospels and always in a context of Jewish casuistry (e.g., Mt 12:2,10,12; Mt 14:4, Mk 2:24; Lk 6:2,4,9; Jn 5:10). The Greeks did not use *exousia* in a religious sense. When they wished to express what was religiously permissible they employed the terms *themis, themiton* or *hosion.* Dupont remarks that a Jew would speak as Tobit does (Tb 2:13) in Codex Sinaiticus: "We do not have an *exousia* to eat anything stolen," and a Greek would say with Codex Vaticanus: "It is not *themiton* to eat what has been stolen" (J. Dupont, *Gnosis,* 312f.). The vb. *exestin* and the noun *exousia* in the religious sense in which they are used in 1 Cor are not part of Paul's customary vocabulary. The frequency of *exousia* in the section where Paul refers to those who boast of their "knowledge," supports the conclusion that the aphorism *panta moi exestin* is not Paul's but that of the Christ party, those charismatics who pretended to have received from the Spirit a gnosis that made them the Christian counterparts of the Jewish doctors of the Law, masters of biblical interpretation and of practical morality. They founded their rights and their liberty on a divine permission they pretended to discover in Scripture. In Corinth they adopted the popular philosophical axiom *tou sophou panta einai* and declared *panta moi exestin* (see J. Dupont, *Gnosis,* 282–321). *not all things are profitable:* Thus Paul answers the libertine aphorism. Christian liberty is not license, and the Christian must not allow himself to be enslaved by any self-indulgence.

32 **13.** The libertines argued that sexual gratification is simply the satisfaction of a natural appetite, as permissible as eating and drinking. Paul refutes the fallacy, appealing to the dignity and role of the Christian's body in the divine economy of salvation. The argument indicates the centrality of eschatology in Paul's teaching. Eating and drinking belong to mortal life in this world and will have no place in the life of glory. Hence these functions have no religious value. But the body is destined to be glorified, to become "a spiritual body" (15:42–44). The argument turns on the ideas of use and union. Food, drink, and sex are designed by God for use. This use can be licit or illicit, e.g., gluttony, drunkenness, fornication.

But even the licit use will cease with the resurrection. However, regarding the use of sex, there is a result proper to it; it effects a union between the partners. If the union is illicit, as in the case of fornication, it profanes the union established by faith and baptism, between Christ and the body of the Christian. This Christian union is destined to be perpetual, for "God has raised up the Lord and will raise us up also by his power" (6:14). In baptism the Christian was incorporated into Christ, so that his body is a member of Christ. The Christian is united in a personal, "bodily" relationship to the Lord. The evil of fornication consists in setting up a personal, "bodily" relationship that is opposed to the Christian's relationship to Christ. **14.** The Risen Lord is the model as well as the principle of the glorious destiny of the Christian's body. *by his power:* This phrase probably refers to the Risen Christ, who is the life-giving spirit imparting glorious life to men (15:45). **15.** *don't you know:* Indicates the emphasis Paul places on this doctrine in his teaching. The Christian's body belongs to Christ; incorporated into Christ, his body is a member of Christ. This is the earliest Pauline expression of the doctrine on "the Body of Christ" (→ Pauline Theology 79:140). Because our bodies are members of Christ, the Church is a visible reality in this world. The malice of fornication lies in uniting the members of Christ in an intimate relationship with a harlot. **16.** The fornicator becomes "one body" with a harlot; he enters with her into a relationship so intimate that Scripture (Gn 2:24) can be quoted to characterize it as "one flesh." **17.** *one spirit:* The parallelism of this verse with the preceding would lead us to expect "one body." But Paul is thinking of the power of the Risen Christ, who has become a life-giving spirit (15:45), sending the Spirit to the baptized and incorporating them into his own glorious life. This effects the transformation of their mortal bodies into the "spiritual" bodies of the resurrection. The fornicator degrades himself to the soiled flesh of his partner, whereas the Christian who cleaves to the Lord is no longer "in the flesh, but in the spirit," since the Spirit of God dwells in him (Rom 8:9–11).

33 **18.** Another consideration proving the horrible malice of sinful sexual relations. Although the body serves as the instrument of sin in other vices, e.g., drunkenness and gluttony, it is not intimately united to another person, handed over to the power of another, as it is in fornication. The fornicator sins against his own body, his own person, because he tears it away from the Lord and deprives it of its glorious destiny. **19.** The Christian's body is a temple inhabited by the Holy Spirit, and therefore it belongs to God. The Christian has no right to give it to another. Fornication partakes of the malice of sacrilege. **20.** *you were bought for a price:* Paul's formulation emphasizes that Christians are God's property, his precious possession, his people whom he has united to himself in a new covenant that was effectively sealed by the sacrifice of his son on Calvary (see comment on Gal 3:13; → Pauline Theology, 79:90–93). *glorify God:* This phrase has cultic overtones. "A Christian can be thought of as the priest in the temple of his own body, in which sanctuary he serves God and keeps out whatever might profane it" (L. Cerfaux, *Church*, 148–49). Paul exhorts the Romans "to present your bodies, a living sacrifice, holy, well-pleasing to God, your spiritual service" (Rom 12:1).

34 **(III) Part II: Answers to Questions in the Letter of the Community (7:1–15:58).**

(A) Marriage and Celibacy (7:1–40). To understand Paul's teaching on the value of marriage and virginity one must study it in the eschatological framework in which the Apostle has placed it. Paul considers virginity good because of "the present distress" (7:26); those who marry will have "tribulation for the flesh" (7:28); "time is running out" (7:29). All these expressions have an eschatological connotation. For Paul the *eschaton* is a present reality and is pressing on to its final, definitive stage, which will be ushered in by the parousia of the Lord. Christians are already living in "the last days" (1 Cor 10:11). The *eschaton* became a reality in the glorious resurrection of Jesus. In the Risen Lord who has taken his place at the right hand of the Father, humanity is already redeemed and glorified. Baptism has incorporated the believer into the Risen Lord (Rom 6:3–4; Col 2:12–13). By faith and hope the Christian is already in the future. He passes his life in this world with his eyes fixed on heaven, awaiting patiently the glorious revelation of the Lord at the parousia and in eager expectation of the glorification of his own body (Gal 1:20; Rom 8:9–11,23; Eph 1:19). The Holy Spirit who has been given at baptism dwells in the believer as *arrabōn*, the "first payment" and the guarantee of the full payment of the glorious Christian inheritance (Eph 1:13–14; 2 Cor 1:22; 5:5). Since at the resurrection there will be neither marrying nor giving in marriage (Mk 12:25; Mt 22:30), virginity is a better state of life for the Christian than marriage. The virgin already anticipates the life of the resurrection. Virginity places the baptized existentially in the future. The cares and responsibilities of the married state involve both husband and wife in the affairs of this world, which is passing away, and are a hindrance to undivided devotion to "the things of the Lord." The celibate and the virgin, being free from the cares of family life, realize already in anticipation the perfect consecration to God in body and spirit that will characterize the life of glory (7:32–34).

35 Paul emphasizes throughout this pericope that the call to Christianity involves to a certain extent the state of life in which the Christian was placed at the time of his baptism. God calls to the faith and sanctifies in Christ both slave and free, circumcised and uncircumcised, married and unmarried. Not only the individual but also the state of his existence is brought under the power of Christ's redemption. Provided always that there is no sinful opposition between the situation in which he is living at his baptism and his new relationship to the Lord, the Christian should regard his state of life as the sphere of activity assigned him by God, in which, as the member of Christ, he must glorify God and cooperate in the world's redemption. With particular reference to the subject of this pericope, marriage and celibacy, the Apostle calls both states of life "gifts" from God (7:7). Consequently, the actual life-situation in which the Christian finds himself at the moment of baptism, when he enters into "the last days," should determine the state, free or slave, married or celibate, in which he will carry on the Lord's work in this world, while time presses on to the parousia. "Each one should lead the life the Lord has assigned him, just as he was when the Lord called him" (7:17,21,24,27–31). This principle, as well as the doctrine on virginity as an anticipation of the life of the resurrection, is valid whether the parousia is near or far off. But of course they have greater urgency if, as Paul hoped when he wrote this epistle, the Lord's coming in glory would be soon. In applying these doctrines the Apostle shows himself to be a practical moralist, a realist. He takes into consideration the strength and urgency of the natural appetite, which differs in individuals. Even after baptism, it is better to marry than to be on fire with yearning (7:9).

(Blinzler, J., *ZNW* 28 [1957] 254–70. Maly, E., *Marian Studies* 13 [1962] 41–61. Neuhäusler, E., *BZ* 3 [1959] 43–60.)

36 (a) MARRIAGE AND ITS DUTIES (7:1–24). **1–2.** *it is good for man not to touch a woman:* Paul's reply suggests that the question of the Corinthians concerned not the licitness of marriage but its advisability for Christians. It seems that there were some members of the community who, repelled by the licentiousness of their city and inspired by the Apostle's teaching on the dignity of the Christian's body, thought that the marriage union was evil and contrary to the new life in Christ. They may have thought that married Christians should not make use of their conjugal privileges. Paul answers: Celibacy is good, but marriage is also good, especially in view of the strength of passion. *because of much immorality:* Lit., "because of fornications"; see comment on 1 Thes 4:3. To avoid immorality, men and women, even the baptized, should marry. Paul's reason here for marriage may seem negative and minimal. To obtain a fair and balanced concept of his thoughts about marriage one must also consider his teaching on the sublimity of the marriage union as a symbol of Christ's union with the Church (Eph 5:22–33). **3.** Paul here has in mind those who regarded the conjugal act as something evil. The married have a mutual obligation in justice to engage in marital relations. They incurred a debt (*opheilē*) to each other. **4.** In the marriage contract the spouses hand over their bodies to each other so that each has the right or power over the partner's body, and neither has power over his (her) own. The repeated adv. "likewise" (*homoiōs*) emphasizes the equality of both spouses in the marriage contract. They have equal rights and obligations. **5.** *do not refuse one another:* The refusal of marital relations can be an injustice, unless there is mutual agreement to the abstention. Paul advises that such abstinence be limited in time and for a religious motive. The Jews recognized the value of a temporary abstinence from the pleasures of the marriage bed as a preparation for participation in solemn religious acts (e.g., Ex 19:15; 1 Sm 21:5; Jl 2:16).

37 Since man must prepare and recollect himself before prayer, nighttime is particularly favorable for this holy duty (Lk 6:12). But the night is also the customary time for marital relations. Allo and Spicq insinuate that this may be the reason for the Apostle's recommendation. Allo translates *pros kairon* "at the suitable time." Others understand it: "for a season." At any rate, the Pauline expression, "to devote yourselves" (*hina scholasēte*), seems to be customary to designate interior and external preparation for religious acts (cf. Ps 46:11; Philo, *De spec. leg.* 2. 196); so C. Spicq, *PSB* 11/2, 215. The spouses should renew relations again after a temporary abstinence lest they be tempted to immorality because of lack of self-control. **6.** *concession:* Does this "concession" refer to the verse immediately preceding, i.e., to Paul's advice to spouses not to prolong abstinence from marital relations, or does it refer to his teaching in v. 2 that the Corinthians should marry lest they commit fornication? Verse 7 suggests the latter. The Apostle is not commanding the Corinthians to marry; he would prefer them to be celibates like himself, but he recognizes that not all receive this gift from God. **7.** *as I myself am:* That is, without a wife. In view of v. 8 this can only mean that Paul had never married. *special gift:* Marriage, as well as celibacy, is a gift from God, and like all the *charismata* is for the good of the Church.

38 **8–9.** Applying the principles enunciated in vv. 17, 21, 24, 27, 31, Paul admonishes the unmarried and widows to remain single. *as I am:* The verb to be supplied is *emeina*, "I remained," which implies that Paul had never married. Since Luther, some have tried to conclude from this verse that Paul was a widower. Most of the Fathers held that Paul was never married, although Clement of Alexandria (*Stromateis* 3. 53,1) found a reference to the Apostle's wife in the *gnēsie syzyge* of Phil 4:3, since *syzygos* as a fem. noun means "wife" in classical and Hellenistic Greek (see AG 783 and G. Ricciotti, *Paul the Apostle* [Milwaukee, 1954] 540). The application of Paul's principle "to remain as you are" is conditioned and limited by the moral strength of individuals. Since marriage is a remedy for concupiscence, those single persons who cannot control themselves should marry. "It is better to marry than to be continually on fire" with sexual desire. **10–11.** *to the married:* Paul's advice is now addressed to Christian partners; "the others" of v. 12 are Christians married to unbelievers. The Apostle teaches the indissolubility of Christian marriage in the absolute terms with which Mk 10:9 records our Lord's prohibition of divorce. To that teaching of Christ he appeals, "not I, but the Lord commands." Marriage and cohabitation are not merely temporary expedients to be used only to relieve burning desire. The married are obliged to live together. The wife may not separate from her husband, as pagan laws allowed; nor may the husband divorce his wife, as both Jewish and pagan laws permitted. A separation, whether permitted for serious motives the Apostle does not mention or contrary to the command of Christ, does not dissolve the marriage bond. The separated wife must remain single or be reconciled to her husband.

39 **12–16.** These verses treat of marriages in which only one partner has become a Christian. May the Christian partner continue to live with the unbelieving pagan or Jewish spouse? The Lord himself did not treat of this question, so the Apostle cannot invoke a precept of Christ. He must decide the question by his own apostolic authority. Paul settles this problem, which must have been causing considerable anxiety to many Corinthians, by appealing to his principle: Remain in the state in which you were when called to Christ. Should a Christian, a member of Christ, continue after baptism to cohabit with a pagan or Jewish spouse? Paul attaches a condition to his affirmative answer: The unbelieving partner must consent to cohabit peacefully with the Christian. **12–13.** *he [she] should not divorce her [him]:* Is this a precept or a counsel? Theodoret, Oecumenius, Tertullian, Jerome, Cajetan, and most modern exegetes interpret the phrase as a precept prohibiting the Christian from divorcing the unbelieving partner when that partner consents to continue in the marriage. Cyril of Alexandria, Augustine, Ambrosiaster, Pelagius, and almost all medieval commentators, including Thomas Aq., regarded it as only a counsel, a recommendation to the Christian spouse not to dissolve the union with the unbelieving partner. The Gk phrase itself, *mē* with the imperative (*aphietō*), as well as the conditions expressed in the context (13, 15) are weighty arguments in favor of interpreting the passage as a negative precept, i.e., a prohibition. Paul would then forbid the Christian spouse to divorce the unbelieving partner who consents to cohabit peacefully. **14.** The baptized Christian has been consecrated, has been made holy (6:11); the Christian's body is a member of Christ (6:15). The unbelieving spouse, therefore, who becomes one flesh with the Christian in the marriage union, shares in this consecration. Unlike fornication, the marriage union is not opposed to the Christian's union with the Lord. If it were, then the children of these marriages "would be unclean, but as it is they are holy." "Unclean (*akatharta*) suggests the Jewish distinction between legally "pure" (*katharos*) and "impure" (*akatharos* or *koinos*) and indicates the precise nuance of the holiness referred to. The Christian and unbelieving spouses are united in a legitimate marriage, and the Christian community must regard it as such and the children born of it as legitimate.

Perhaps, as J. Sickenberger thinks, some Jewish Christians of the community were attacking the licitness of such marriages. Perhaps they were permitting the Christian spouse to repudiate the unbelieving partner and abandon the marriage by applying to baptism the rabbinical principle that entrance into Israel freed the proselyte from all former ties. **15.** *has not been bound:* Does not lose freedom of action. *in peace:* The connection of this phrase (*en eirēnē*) with the context is not clear. The sentence, "God has called us (to live) in peace," may express positively what was stated negatively in *ou dedoulōtai*, "has not been bound." If the unbelieving partner abandons the marriage, the Christian should let him (her) go. The Christian is not obliged to oppose the separation and involve himself in a life of marital discord, mutual antagonism, and continual wrangling. By consenting to the unbelieving spouse's departure, he will be assuring for himself that peace which is the proper atmosphere of a Christian life. Verse 16 suggests that the only reason for a Christian to continue to live in a marriage with an unbeliever is his hope of saving the unbeliever. There is little foundation for such a hope when the unbeliever does not want to continue in the marriage.

40 Perhaps, however, the sentence, "God has called us in peace," may be a summary of all the advice given on this matter of mixed marriages. The Christian's conduct should always be governed by his desire to preserve peace. This peace will be preserved by continuing in the marriage after his conversion, if the unbelieving partner is willing to live with him. But if the unbeliever departs, peace will be maintained by not opposing the desertion.

Does v. 15 imply permission to contract another marriage? Do we have here what canonists call the "Pauline Privilege"? Or is the Apostle merely telling the Christian that he is not obliged to resist the departure of the unbelieving spouse? Since the 4th cent. Christian tradition, with some hesitation, has concluded from this passage that the Christian convert is free to contract another marriage if the unbeliever refuses to cohabit peacefully. However, Paul's words grant explicitly only a separation (see P. Dulau, *CBQ* 13 [1951] 146–52). **16.** The interrogatives imply that there is little chance of conversion to the faith (which is a call to salvation) for the unbeliever who refuses to live peacefully with a Christian.

41 **17–24.** Modern exegetes are quite unanimous in taking the difficult introductory conjunction (*ei mē*) of v. 17 as an adversative, equivalent to *alla* or *plēn* (cf. Bl-Deb-F § 376); it means, "aside from that." The separation just granted by Paul is an exception to the principle that each one should continue in the state of life in which he was living when called to the faith. The Jewish Christian should not be ashamed of his origin and "pull over his foreskin," i.e., try to cover his circumcision. This curious surgical operation by which Jews at times sought to escape the annoyances and persecution of pagan anti-Semitism, is mentioned in Jewish literature (see 1 Mc 1:15; Josephus, *Ant.* 12.5,1 § 241; Str-B 4, 33f.). The Gentile should not be circumcised. In Gal (5:1–6) the Apostle vigorously opposed the circumcision of Gentile converts because of the doctrinal implications of such a practice. It implies the inefficacy of Christ's redemptive death and resurrection and denies our freedom from the Law. **21.** The principle, "everyone ought to stay as he was when he was called," is applied even to the poor slave who has become a Christian. Rather than seek emancipation, he should make the most of the opportunities offered him by his servile condition, which is an excellent school of humility and enables him to become more like Christ, "the Suffering Servant" (1 Pt 2:18–25).

42 Some exegetes give this verse an entirely different meaning. They think that Paul urges the slave to seize any opportunity for emancipation that may present itself (see A. Robertson and A. Plummer, *First Epistle*, 147–48). But such an interpretation contradicts the context, which calls for an application of the principle of v. 20. All exegetes agree, however, that Paul is giving a counsel to the slave, not commanding him to refuse emancipation.

43 The Apostle saw the incompatibility of the institution of slavery with the dignity of man created in God's image and elevated to a new life in Christ, in which there is no distinction between slave and free (Gal 3:28; 1 Cor 12:13; Col 3:11). He insisted that master and slave were equals in Christ, who is no respecter of persons (Eph 6:5–9). However, except for a very veiled hint to Philemon that he emancipate Onesimus (Phlm 21), he never urged Christian masters to free their slaves. The economy of the Greco-Roman world was built on slavery; and slave uprisings, of which the Romans had a great fear, were ruthlessly suppressed. The Church, numerically very small in relation to the population of the empire and composed almost entirely of people from the lower classes of society, could not at that time entertain a hope of changing the social and economic structure. Had the Apostle publicly proclaimed the incompatibility of slavery with man's dignity, he would have been prosecuted as a slave agitator; the slaves would not have benefited, and the Church would have been ruthlessly persecuted. Paul was content to preach the Christian doctrine which in the course of centuries led gradually to the abrogation of slavery. Because of the hard conditions of his life, the slave had an opportunity to practice really heroic virtue and share more fully in the sufferings of the Lord. It is to this heroism that Paul invites the Christian slave in this verse.

44 **22–23.** The slave should remember that in baptism he has become a free man in Christ; free from bondage to sin, the Law, and death. The Christian who is free must never forget that he is bound entirely to the service of the Lord (Rom 6:18,22). All Christians, both slave and free, are God's property, acquired at a price. *bought for a price:* See comments on 1 Cor 6:20 and Gal 3:13. The reference to the passage from a servile to a free state shows that the Apostle has in mind the Gk use of *agorazein* in the purchase of slaves and probably in the custom of "sacred manumission." The "price" refers to the blood of Christ, which is the blood of the new covenant (→ Pauline Theology, 79:87). *do not become slaves of men:* Just as the slave should not worry about his bondage and does well if he remains in it, so too the free Christian should not sell himself into slavery in order to practice heroic virtue. Each should remain with God in the state in which he was when called. Slaves and freemen should jealously guard their Christian liberty from sin and dedicate themselves entirely to the service of Christ. They should never enslave themselves to the prejudices, passions, and errors of men.

45 (b) On Virgins (7:25–38). Concerning virgins, men as well as women, the Apostle can cite no precept of the Lord as he could for the married in v. 10. Was he ignorant of the Lord's saying of Mt 19:12? That saying is only a counsel and not a precept (*epitagē*); but we should expect Paul to have alluded to it, had he known it. He gives his opinion on this matter as an apostle who by the Lord's mercy is trustworthy (*pistos*), i.e., worthy of confidence. **26–28.** Because time is pressing on to the parousia, it is good for everyone to remain as he is, whether single or married. *the present distress:* The crisis and sufferings that precede the parousia. V. 29 clearly imposes this exegesis. In Zeph 1:15 the Day of the Lord is "a day of anguish and distress" (LXX *thlipseōs kai anagkēs*); and there will be *anagkē megalē* (great distress) upon the earth (Lk 21:23). Since in Paul's teaching we are already in the last days, all the afflictions of this life belong to the present *anagkē*, which leads up to the parousia (cf. the "travails of the Messiah," to which apocalyptic and rabbinical writings refer; see W. Grundmann, "*anagkē*," *ThDNT* 1, 344–47). Because time is pressing on to the Lord's coming, Christians should remain in the state in which they are: The single should not marry, and the married should not separate. But the virgin who marries does not commit sin. The Apostle's counsel to the virgin to remain unmarried is prompted by a paternal love; he would spare her "the tribulation for the flesh," which is the lot of the married. **28.** *human troubles:* Lit., "anguish for the flesh." The OT associates *thlipsis* (MT *ṣārāh*), "anguish, tribulation," with *anagkē* in its description of the Day of Yahweh (Zeph 1:15). Jewish apocalyptic and rabbinical writings speak of "the travails of the Messiah" as a period of "distress" and "tribulation." The LXX renders the *ʿēt ṣārāh* of Dn 12:1 as *hē hēmera thlipseōs*, "the day of tribulation." The NT uses both terms for the sufferings that precede the Lord's return in glory at the end of time. In Mt 24:8,9,21 *ōdines*, "travail" expresses the natural catastrophes (plague, famine, earthquakes) and *thlipsis* the persecutions that will afflict the faithful. Such sufferings are related to the *thlipsis megalē*, "the great tribulation," which will usher in the great day of judgment and final victory. See H. Schlier, "*thlipsis*," *ThDNT* 3, 139–48. Consequently, the married, who are intimately bound by the cares and duties of their state to the "flesh" (*sarx*) are more susceptible than the celibate to "the tribulation." Jesus' apocalyptic discourse singled out the pregnant woman and the nursing mother as particularly pitiable victims of the tribulation (Mt 24:19). Marriage involves the Christian in the cares of this world (v. 34) and thus implicates him more than the single person in the afflictions that accompany the ever-pressing end of time and the cosmos.

46 **29.** *the time is short:* Lit., "has been drawn together, shortened." With this phrase Paul expresses his conviction that the last period of salvation history is running its course. The parousia of the Lord may come at any moment. The Christian, therefore, must live as the Lord admonished him: in prayer and watchfulness awaiting the return of his Lord (Mt 24:43–44; 25:13; 1 Thes 5:1–2). He must keep himself detached from this world that is passing away. In this sense, even the married must live with detachment, i.e., fulfilling the duties of their state that involve them in the cares of this world, without attaching their hearts to this world. **31.** *shape:* "This world in its present form is passing away" (AG 805). *those who make use of this world without devoting themselves fully to it:* The preposition strengthens the signification of the simple verb, giving it a special coloring: *chrōmenoi . . . katachrōmenoi*. The author of 1 Jn 1:18; 2:15–17 says that we are in "the last hour" and gives a similar counsel of detachment. This apostolic teaching is valid and applicable to Christians of all times, because it is independent of any personal hope Paul entertained for the coming of the Lord in his lifetime. Its basis is the revealed truth that with the Lord's resurrection and Pentecost the last days of salvation history have begun, and time is pressing on to the consummation of redemption.

47 **32–34.** Marriage involves spouses in many worldly cares that make it difficult for them to consecrate themselves perfectly and completely to the Lord's service. The married are tied by flesh and blood in many relationships that subject them to this world and can easily impede their complete dedication to God. The husband must try to please the wife, and the wife the husband. Consequently, they are "divided," i.e., impeded from devoting their attention solely to the Lord. The virgin, being freed from the cares and duties of family life, can devote herself with undivided attention and heart to the Lord. *holy:* In the cultic sense of dedicated to God, consecrated, sacred, i.e., reserved for God and his service. In these verses Paul teaches that virginity is a better state than marriage because it is better adapted to the contemplation of God and to the apostolic life. (On the relation of virginity to the apostolate, see J. Blinzler, *ZNW* 28 [1957] 254–70; E. Maly, *Marian Studies* 13 [1962] 48–52.) **35.** *restraint:* The "halter" (*brochon*) used to restrain animals. In counseling virginity, Paul does not intend to restrict the Christian's liberty to contract marriage, but only to point out what is advantageous for him (her), what is proper, and what enables him to devote himself to the Lord without distraction. *good order:* Virginity is "proper," suited to "these last days," because it puts the Christian existentially in the future virginal life of the resurrection; or perhaps the meaning here is simply, "What is proper," i.e., what is ideal.

48 **36–38.** The Apostle applies the preceding teaching to a particular case. There has been a lively discussion among exegetes concerning the precise relation of the man (*tis*) to his "virgin" in these verses. The general meaning of the passage seems to be clear. In view of the eschatological situation in which baptism has placed the Christian and because it enables the Christian to devote himself entirely to the Lord, virginity is to be preferred to marriage. But marriage also is good, and the Christian is free to contract it.

49 The traditional exegesis considers the case to be that of a father or guardian (*tis*) of a virgin daughter or ward, who fears that he is bringing discredit on himself and behaving dishonorably (*aschēmonein*) toward the girl because she has already passed the customary age for marriage (lit., passed the bloom of youth, *hyperakmos*), and he has not yet fulfilled his parental obligation of providing her with a husband. He does not sin, answers Paul, if he gives her in marriage; but he does better if he keeps her in her virginal state. This interpretation has the advantage of maintaining the usual significance of the words *hyperakmos*, past the *akmē* (full physical maturity, which a girl was considered to have reached at about eighteen), and *gamizō* (v. 38), "give in marriage." It also places the case in the framework of Hellenistic society, where the decision on a girl's marriage rested with her father or guardian. Both ancient and modern exegetes point out how the condition placed by Paul in v. 37 limits the absoluteness of the *patria potestas* and safeguards the girl's freedom. He may decide to keep the girl in her virginal state only if he is "under no necessity" (*mē echōn anagkēn*), i.e., provided the girl does not desire to marry. *Houtōs opheilei ginesthai*, "it must be thus," in this interpretation would be a discreet way of expressing the father's concern because of his fear that the girl might not be able to live in perpetual virginity. In such a case, advises the Apostle, "let them marry" (*gameitōsan*). This pl. imperative would imply that an unmentioned suitor whom the maid accepts has already asked the father or guardian for the girl's hand, and he fears that if he does not consent to the wedding, the girl may yield to the suitor's desire. This traditional exegesis would see the Corinthian father's problem as very similar to that of the parent of Sir 42:9–14. One of the worries that keeps a father sleepless is "lest she pass her prime unmarried" (*parakmasē*), or "lest she be seduced," or "lest she conceive in her father's house." The difficulties of v. 36 in this interpretation are the meanings given to the pl. imperative (*gameitōsan*), the indef. pronoun (*tis*), and the noun (*parthenos*). The Western Text and the Pesh, Armenian, and Vg versions eliminate the first difficulty by employing the sing. *si nubat*, "if she marries." E.-B. Allo notes (*Première épître*,

186): "The elliptical plural *gameitōsan* is no stranger than that of 1 Tm 2:15, *ean meinōsin en pistei*, where the subject *gynē* is singular, but where the husband and children are perhaps connoted." In this verse the plural would include the girl's suitor. The context supplies a plausible reason for calling the daughter or ward "a virgin" (*parthenos*), but the *tis* remains obscure.

50 An interpretation favored by many modern exegetes sees in the man (*tis*) and "his virgin" an engaged couple who have become Christians. What should they do in the light of the Apostle's teaching on virginity? The Apostle answers: If the man's "passions are strong, and if it has to be, let him do what he will, he does not sin; let them marry. But whoever is firmly established in his heart, being under no necessity but having his desire under control, and has determined this in his heart, to keep her as his betrothed, he will do well. So that he who marries his betrothed does well; and he who refrains from marriage will do better" (RSV). The principal difficulties in this and similar interpretations are the unusual meanings attached to *hyperakmos* (understood etymologically), *exousian*, *echei*, and *gamizō*, which is taken as a synonym of *gameō*, "to marry." Some exegetes have even been guilty of the anachronism of attributing to the Corinthian community the origin of the *virgines subintroductae* condemned by the Fathers and Councils of the 3rd and 4th cents.

(Kruse, H., *VD* 26 [1948] 344–50. Kugelman, R., *CBQ* 10 [1958] 63–71. Leal, J., *VD* 35 [1957] 97–102. O'Rourke, J., *CBQ* 20 [1958] 292–98.)

51 **39–40.** Paul applies the teaching of this entire section on marriage and celibacy to the case of a married woman. As long as her husband lives she is obliged to live with him. After his death she is free to marry a Christian ("only in the Lord"); but she will be "happier" (in the religious sense of the word, "more blessed") if she follows the Apostle's advice and remains unmarried. This advice does not contradict 1 Tm 5:14, which treats of young widows of unstable continency.

52 **(B) Concerning the Eating of Meat That Was Offered to Idols (8:1–11:1).** The Corinthians had inquired in their letter whether it was permitted to eat the flesh of animals that had been sacrificed to idols. The problem was a very practical one. A considerable part of the meat sold in the market came from animals sacrificed to idols. Usually, only certain portions of the sacrificial victims were burned; the remainder became the property of the temple priests. Much of this meat was sold to butchers. Moreover, the duties of social life involved joining pagan friends and relatives in common meals celebrating family festivals. At times these meals were held in a temple and were intimately associated with the worship of a pagan deity. Even when the meal was held at home, the meat would frequently be that of a sacrificial victim. With reference to their attitude toward this problem Paul distinguishes two groups among the Christians: those who have an enlightened conscience about Christian liberty because they have knowledge and those with "a weak conscience," who attributed a tangible impurity to sacrificial meats and felt that in eating such food they were entering into a relationship with pagan deities or demons. (A similar problem is discussed in Rom 14:1–15:13, where Paul calls the two groups "the strong" and "the weak.") Exegetes dispute whether the groups at Corinth represent Jewish or pagan tendencies. Allo, Huby, Kuss, and most other exegetes see in the brethren of weak conscience recently converted Gentiles, whose attitude toward idols and idol-meat was still influenced by the beliefs and superstitions of their pagan past. Allo sees in the liberals, whose "knowledge" leads them to participate in temple banquets, Greeks who virtually identified religion with knowledge. According to a few commentators, among them R. Cornely and J. Dupont, the brethren of weak conscience are a little group of Jewish Christians who retain the typical orthodox Jewish repugnance for idol-meat. Their conduct is still inspired by the Jewish laws concerning legal purity and pollution. Dupont also thinks, and argues quite convincingly, that those who have "knowledge" represent another Jewish-Christian mentality. They are Jewish Christians who pretend to possess as a charismatic gift a knowledge of Scripture and its application to practical living that makes them superior to others. They are the Christian counterpart of the scribes or doctors of the law (see J. Dupont, *Gnosis*, 265–377; S. Lyonnet, *Bib* 37 [1956] 17–27; W. Schmithals, *Die Gnosis in Korinth* [Göttingen, 1956]).

53 Two principles govern Paul's solution of this problem of eating idol-meat. They flow from his doctrine on the Christian's incorporation into Christ: (1) freedom from servitude to the Law, the world, and Satan; (2) the primacy of charity in Christian morality.

54 (a) On Knowledge and Charity (8:1–13). **1.** *we all:* Paul and all other Christians, and not only "the liberals" who boast about it, have knowledge. In v. 4 this knowledge possessed by all Christians is defined by reference to monotheistic faith. To have knowledge means to adhere to the one true God and to be freed from servitude to false gods. Christian liberty to eat idol-meat is a practical application of this knowledge. Paul insists on the religious insufficiency of knowledge without charity. *Quicumque habet scientiam, non modum utendi ea, habet scientiam insufficienter* (Thomas Aq.). The knowledge possessed by Christian faith can lead to spiritual snobbishness unless charity, the love of God and the love of neighbor for God, is joined to it. It is charity (*agapē*) that "builds up" (*oikodomei*) the Church (Eph 4:16). *Agapē*, a noun found rarely, if at all, in profane Greek before the Christian era, has become in the NT the technical term for what we call the virtue of charity. It is used to express God's unmotivated love for men exercised in Christ and passed on to believers that they may love one another. The Christian who boasts of his religious knowledge shows that he does not know the basic truth that this knowledge is the gift of a loving and merciful God. **3.** *he is known by God:* We should expect as the antithesis to the preceding verse "he knows God," i.e., he has a true knowledge of God. But Paul casts the phrase in the passive, "is known by God." The Christian knows God only because God has first known him, i.e., only because God in his merciful goodness has loved him and called him and made him his own in Christ. Paul told the Galatians that they, who as idolators were ignorant of God, knew God as Christians because God had known them, i.e., called and chosen them (Gal 4:8–9). In the final analysis, what counts is that God has known us, and that we afterward because of his gracious call know him by faith is only a consequence of his love and graciousness. Man's love for God is thus the effect not of his own knowledge of God, but of God's gracious gift to him. This concept of "knowledge" is a development of the OT teaching on the divine initiative in man's salvation. Paul's concept of our knowledge of God is thus a Jewish, not a Greek concept (see J. Dupont, *Gnosis*, 51–104).

55 **4–6.** All Christians, who have received the faith, know that there is only one true God and that idols are nothing, i.e., the deities represented by them are not really gods. In 10:19–21 the Apostle declares that hidden behind the idols of the Gentiles are demons. The Gentiles speak about many gods and many lords, but the Christian knows that there is really only one God, the Father and Creator of the universe who has made us for himself, and only one Lord, Jesus Christ, through whom all things were made and through whom we are brought to the Father. Christ is called "Lord" because the Father has given him all sovereignty over heaven, earth, and the nether regions (Phil 2:9–11). Jesus is the exalted Messiah and King who reigns until the work of redemption is accomplished at the resurrection of the dead, when he hands his kingdom over to the Father (15:24–28). *through whom are all things:* The role of the Son in creation is thus expressed. Col 1:16 shows that the expression does not imply a subordination of the Son to the Father as his instrument in creation because it designates the Son as the end of creation (Col 1:15–16). *through whom we exist:* This expresses the mediatorial role of Christ. He is the way that leads us to the Father, the ultimate goal of our life. "To him alone belongs the title of Lord in all the fullness of the term, because we derive from him at every moment our existence as creatures and our life as children of God" (J. Huby, *Première épître*, 195–96).

56 7. *knowledge:* In this and in the following verses, knowledge has a slightly different meaning than in the preceding. There, it referred precisely to the knowledge of the one true God and of Christ that distinguishes the Christian from the pagan. Here, it has a practical connotation. It is the knowledge of the practical consequences of Christian liberty for everyday living. *intimacy:* The reading *synētheiā* is better attested than *syneidēsei* (conscience) and suggests that those of "weak conscience" (mentioned later in the verse) are recent converts from paganism. The word expresses their "intimacy" with idols. If this interpretation is correct, then Paul would be referring in "the weak" to Gentile Christians who had not succeeded in ridding themselves completely of superstitions and pagan concepts. In spite of their conversion and their faith in God and Christ, they still felt that in eating meat offered to idols they would be participating in the worship of pagan deities. For E.-B. Allo and others this verse alone is sufficient evidence that "the weak" are not Jewish Christians. But, as J. Dupont points out, this interpretation is correct only if "the intimacy with the idol" means being accustomed to idolatry, i.e., to the worship given to idols. If that is the meaning, then Paul's expression *heōs arti*, which signifies literally "up until now" and not "in former times," is extremely ill chosen and difficult. The "weak" are certainly Christians. How can it be said that "until now" they are addicted to idolatry? *Synētheia heōs arti tou eidōlou* consequently signifies not idolatry, but an attitude toward idols and their cult. In eating idol-meat, the weak "defile" their conscience. This vb. *molynō* is typical primitive Christian vocabulary and is borrowed from Judaism, where it designates the contraction of a legal impurity. "The history of the primitive Church never indicates among converted pagans scruples such as those that would be attributed to the Greek Christians of Corinth; the decision of the Council of Jerusalem, on the contrary, shows us the repugnance that Jewish Christians had for idol-meat" (J. Dupont, *Gnosis*, 285). The attitude of "the weak" at Corinth is what one would expect of Christians accustomed to consider idolatry and everything connected with idols with the horror and repugnance so characteristic of orthodox Judaism (see J. Dupont, *Gnosis*, 283–85; W. Foerster, "*Exousia*," *ThDNT* 2, 570; F. Hauck, "*Molynō*," *ThDNT* 4, 736–37; S. Lyonnet, *Bib* 37 [1956] 1–26). *syneidēsis:* This word meaning "consciousness" was employed in the ethical sense of moral consciousness or conscience by philosophers and was current in the popular moral philosophies of the Hellenistic world. It was unknown to Palestinian Judaism (it occurs only twice in the LXX: Eccl 10:20 and Wis 17:10), and Paul borrows it from his correspondents. C. Spicq indicates the importance of this verse and its originality. Paul, he maintains, was the first to discover what is called the erroneous conscience; i.e., a conscience that judges to be evil what is really good and that, none the less, obliges. **8–9.** Eating is a morally indifferent act; in itself it does not affect a man's relationship to God. But the morality of an indifferent act is determined by, among other factors, the circumstances surrounding it. The "knowledgeable" must therefore take care lest the exercise of their "right" to eat idol-meat lead a brother of "weak conscience" to do what he considers sinful. **10.** This scandal would certainly be given by a Christian so boastful of his "knowledge" that he would dare to take part in a temple banquet. With sarcasm Paul castigates this scandal as an "edification" of the weak to commit sin. The horrible wickedness of scandal is that it destroys spiritually the brother for whom Christ died. It is spiritual murder (Rom 14:15). **12.** This grave sin against fraternal charity is a sin against Christ. **13.** Paul is ready to abstain from meat forever in order to avoid scandalizing his brother.

57 (b) Paul an Example of Unselfish Charity (9:1–27). The Apostle illustrates and enforces his appeal for the renunciation, in the interest of others, of the use of rights by his own practice in regard to some of his apostolic rights. He waives these rights (vv. 1–18) and accommodates himself to all men so that they might share with him in the salvation and graces of Christ (19–23). **1–2.** Paul has just declared himself ready to abstain from meat forever (8:13). This is a renunciation, not an obligation, since he enjoys the same Christian liberty of which "the knowledgeable" Corinthians boast. Moreover, he is an apostle called by the Lord himself in the Damascus vision (Acts 9:3–6,17). The Corinthian church is the fruit and proof, "the seal" of his apostolate. If others may question his apostolic authority, the Corinthians certainly cannot do so.

58 3. *This is my defense to those who are criticizing me:* Apparently, at Corinth, and in other communities, Paul was being criticized for not using the rights of his apostolate. Some were concluding that his nonuse of such rights was proof that he was not really an apostle. **4–6.** Paul lists, besides his freedom in matters of food and drink, two other apostolic rights that he has freely renounced—marriage and support from the churches. *to have a Christian wife:* As it is often interpreted, this would mean to take a Christian woman on his journeys, as a missionary assistant. The Church Fathers interpreted this phrase with reference to the women who accompanied Christ and took care of his material needs on trips during his public ministry (Lk 8:2). Many Catholic exegetes have repeated this interpretation. But *adelphē* means "a sister in Christ," i.e., a Christian woman (7:15), and even in classical Gk usage, *gynaika periagein* means "to have a wife," and not "to take her about with one" (see J. Bauer, *BZ* 3 [1959] 94–102). Peter was a married man when Jesus called him (Mk 1:30); probably all the Twelve were married except John, whom tradition has called "the virgin apostle." Like other apostles, Paul and Barnabas had the right to be freed from the necessity of working to support themselves, so that they might devote themselves exclusively to the ministry. They, too, had the right to be supported by the churches.

59 **7–14.** Paul defends this apostolic right to support from Christians. The OT text he cites in v. 9 is taken from Dt 25:4. Paul's argument proceeds *a fortiori;* perhaps, because of the phrases, "does not the Law itself say this" and "indeed it has been written for our sakes," there is here a typological interpretation of the OT (see

J. Bonsirven, *Exégèse rabbinique et exégèse paulinienne* [Paris, 1939] 308–11. The same text occurs in 1 Tm 5:17–18). Paul and his companions have not made use of this right to support, in order not to cause any hindrance to the gospel. Such a hindrance could come from the complaints of the faithful burdened with the support of missionaries or from unbelievers who murmured that the missionaries were self-seeking in their apostolate. **13.** *those employed in the temple:* Lit., "performing the Temple rites." Paul's strange expression *ergazomenoi ta iera* is probably due to the LXX use of the verb when referring to the work of Levites (Nm 3:7; 8:15). Just as Jewish Levites and priests (pagan priests, too) received their support from the sacrifices and offerings made to the Temple, so Christ commanded that those who preach the gospel should be supported by those to whom they preach.

60 **15.** *I have made no use of this right:* Extremely sensitive on this matter, Paul fears lest the Corinthians think that his defense is a hint that they should begin to contribute to his support. *I would rather die:* The Gk sentence is left unfinished; his readers could readily supply the phrase he omitted for fear of offending them. **16–18.** Paul considers his renunciation of support from the churches a work of supererogation that will receive a special recompense from the Lord. *commission:* The apostolate itself is a "stewardship" (*oikonomia*) entrusted to Paul, which he is obliged to fulfill. **19.** *the more:* He renounces the freedom he enjoys in many things in order to accommodate himself to all men in the hope of winning over to Christ "as many as possible" (*tous pleionas*). Following his Master's example and precept he has made himself the slave of all (Lk 22:25–27; Mk 10:43–45). **21.** *those without the law:* The pagans who do not have the Law of Moses; see comment on Gal 2:15. *under the Law of Christ:* The Gk word *ennomos* means "obedient to law" or "subject to law"; while freed from the Jewish Law in Christ and living among Gentiles, Paul knows only the law of Christ, which is charity (Jn 15:12). **22.** So he respects in his own behavior the erroneous and scrupulous conscience of "the weak." *to save at least some of them:* There is a certain sadness in the last expression, *hina pantōs tinas sōsō;* it suggests the many sacrifices and efforts of the Apostle that had not produced visible results, or his preaching that seemed to fall on deaf ears. **23.** *for the sake of the gospel:* Paul carries on for one reason: to procure for others and for himself a share in the blessings brought by the gospel.

61 **24–27.** Christian zeal and prudence demand sacrifice and self-renunciation. Corinth was famous for the Isthmian games celebrated there every two years. These sporting contests suggested to Paul the examples he now uses. **25.** *a perishable crown:* The prizes for the great Gk games were not money or expensive gifts, but honorific crowns, symbols of victory and supremacy: a laurel wreath for the victors of the Pythian games at Delphi; an olive wreath for the victors in the Olympics at Athens; and at Corinth, a wreath of pine branches for the victors of the Isthmian games. **26.** *not aimlessly:* Paul keeps his eyes fixed on the goal. **27.** *I pommel my body:* The vb. means "I strike under the eye," or in our parlance, "I uppercut." This blow under the eye was considered the knockout blow of the Gk boxer. Paul applies it to himself figuratively. *I treat as a slave:* Perhaps an allusion to the custom of humiliating the vanquished boxer. The winner of a boxing match would throw a rope about his vanquished opponent and drag him about the arena to the cheers and jeers of the crowd. Paul does not specify the practices by which he acquired mastery over his body. In 2 Cor 6:4–10 he speaks of his fasts and vigils along with the persecutions, hardships, and sufferings he experienced in the apostolate.

62 (c) A Scriptural Illustration: The History of Israel Warns Christians About Self-Discipline and Renunciation (10:1–13). In the history of Israel the Exodus prefigured Christianity, the new "Israel of God." Long before Paul, the prophet Hosea had looked back with nostalgia to the *qāhāl* of the desert and seen in it the *type* of restored Israel (Hos 2:16–17). In his fervid discourse before the Sanhedrin, Stephen pointed to Moses as the ancient *type* of Jesus, the "redeemer" (Acts 7:20–40). Paul's contribution to this sort of typology is his discovery of the Christian sacraments of baptism and the Eucharist in the events of the Exodus. The typology is expressed very vividly by the use of Christian sacramental terminology to describe the events of ancient times. **1.** *I do not want you to be ignorant:* This Pauline formula indicates the importance the Apostle attaches to the typology he is going to develop; see comment on Rom 1:13. *our fathers:* Incorporated into Christ, who is the seed of Abraham in whom the promises are fulfilled, all Christians, Gentiles as well as Jews, are children of Abraham (Gal 3:16,29). *under the cloud:* A column of cloud, symbol and manifestation of God's protective presence, led the Jews to the Reed Sea (Ex 13:21). Paul's expression "under" would indicate that he is following the tradition preserved in Ps 105:39, "He spread a cloud to cover them." *all passed through the sea:* According to Ex 14:15–16 the sea split in two and the Israelites marched through on dry land. In employing an expression that suggests passing through water, Paul has his mind fixed on the antitype, Christian baptism. In passing through the sea, the Israelites were delivered from Egyptian bondage under Moses' leadership. So the Apostle, looking to the Christian's deliverance from sin, Satan, and death, which is effected by his incorporation into Christ in baptism, says of the ancient Israelites that they "were baptized into Moses, in the cloud and in the sea." The latter phrases are clearly inspired by Christian baptism in water and in the Holy Spirit. **3–4.** *spiritual food:* Because the manna and the water struck from the rock by Moses' staff typify the Eucharist, Paul calls them "spiritual" food and drink. What is the precise nuance of this adjective? Some exegetes take it to mean, "having a spiritual symbolism." Applied to the food, drink, and rock, it would be merely a synonym for "figurative," "symbolical," or "prophetic." In Ap 11:8 the adv. *pneumatikōs* has a similar meaning. The great city where the martyrs are slain and the Lord was crucified is called "spiritually," i.e., figuratively, Sodom and Egypt. Others think the adj. "spiritual" is used because of the miraculous origin of the manna and of the water from the rock. Ps 78:24 describes the manna as "bread from heaven," and Wis 16:20 calls it "the food of angels." For further details see E.-B. Allo, *Première épître*, 230–31; C. Spicq, *PSB* 11/2, 237.

63 Following a hint of J. Guillet (*Themes of the Bible* [Notre Dame, 1960] 14–15), D. M. Stanley compares the term "spiritual" in this passage with v. 21. There, the Apostle refers to the Eucharist as "the chalice of the Lord" and "the table of the Lord"; and in 11:27 as "the body and blood of the Lord." Since "Lord" is the title of the risen, glorified Christ, who has become in his resurrection a "life-giving spirit" and whose risen body is described as "spiritual" (*sōma pneumatikon*, 15:44,46), Stanley concludes: "The use of this same adjective, *pneumatikos*, in the present passage shows the importance of Christ's resurrection for the Pauline concept of the Eucharist. *They drank from a spiritual rock that followed them; and the rock was the Christ.* This might be called the extreme case of Pauline typology. The cadre of the OT narrative is too narrow to serve as a type of the Eucharist. Accordingly, Paul widens it by introducing a rabbinic legend. He wishes to teach the two main points in his Eucharistic theology: the fellowship of the Christian with the risen Christ (1 Cor 10:16) really present to nourish him upon his own substance (1 Cor 11:23–27). The tale of the rock which rolled after the Israelites during their years in the desert serves Paul's didactic purpose, and he does not hesitate to use it (cf. Allo). What is important is Paul's fidelity to the primitive Christian tradition which had seen a connection between the Eucharist and Christ's resurrection. The present passage is sufficient to contradict the thesis of Lietzmann that the sorrowful Pauline commemoration of the Last Supper and Christ's death superseded the joyous *fractio panis* of the Jerusalem community" (*Christ's Resurrection* 116–17). For the rabbinical legend about the rock from which Moses struck the water following Israel in her wanderings in the desert as an ever-ready source of water, see Str-B 3, 406–8. This rock becomes for Paul a symbol of the Risen Christ who in the Eucharist refreshes the faithful, in this life that is a journey to the land of his peace and glory. See A. T. Hanson, *Jesus Christ in the OT* (London, 1965).

64 The chastisements inflicted on the unfaithful Israelites in the desert are a warning to Christians (5–11). Paul recalls the punishment of the worshipers of the golden calf (Ex 32:6), of the 23,000 (MT: 24,000) who had taken part in the shameful rites of Baal of Peor (Nm 25:1–9), of the grumblers who fell victims to the fiery serpents (Nm 21:4–6) and to "the Destroyer" ("the angel of Yahweh," who is God inflicting punishment; Ex 12:23; Wis 18:25; Heb 11:28). **11.** *as a type:* All this history of Israel of the Exodus is a type. This verse is important for the existence of the typical sense of Scripture. Paul is declaring that God, the master of history and the inspirer of the Scriptures, has willed that OT history should serve for the instruction, admonition, and profit of his Church, of the new people of God who would live in the last days that precede the glorious coming of the Messiah to complete his work. The Christian should read the Scriptures, even OT history, as God's work addressed to him. The chastisement of ancient Israel was recorded for our admonition, as a warning to us to be on our guard. *the ends of the ages:* The Messianic period, the last period of salvation history (see Heb 1:1–2; 9:26; Gal 4:4; Eph 1:10). **13.** The Christian must have a healthy fear of his own weakness, joined to an invincible confidence in God. Our trials are all human, common to mankind. *God is faithful:* He keeps his promises; he never permits us to be tried beyond our strength. He always gives with the trial the means needed to come out of it successfully (*tēn ekbasin*, lit., "the way of escape").

65 (d) Practical Solution of the Problem of Eating Idol-Meat (10:14; 11:1). **14–22.** Participation in a sacrificial meal in an idol's temple is not an indifferent act. The very circumstance of place makes it a participation in the worship of idols, a communion with the demons who are the deities represented by the idols. This is an abomination for Christians, who in the Eucharistic banquet enter into communion with the Lord. **16.** *the cup of blessing:* The third ritual cup of the Passover meal, over which the ritual thanksgiving was pronounced, was called the cup of the blessing ((*kôs šel* b^{e}*rākāh*). *the bread which we break:* The early Christians called the Eucharist "the breaking of the bread" (Acts 2:42; Mk 14:22). *communion: Koinōnia,* "fellowship." Through eating the bread and drinking the cup Christians are united to Christ in an intimate fellowship, because the Eucharist is his body and blood (11:27–31). From this Eucharistic fellowship with Christ follows the real union of all the faithful with one another in one body. Baptism incorporates the Christian into the body of the Risen Lord; the Eucharist in which each communicant receives the body of Christ strengthens and cements this union. The Eucharist is consequently *sacramentum unitatis ecclesiae* (Augustine), and when we receive the Eucharistic bread, Christ assimilates and transforms us, making us his body. **18.** *consider Israel:* The parallelism that Paul draws between Jewish and pagan participation in their sacrifices through eating the meat of the victims and Christian fellowship with Christ through the Eucharist shows that he considers the eating of the Eucharist a sacrificial repast and implies that the Eucharist itself is a sacrifice. *Israel according to the flesh:* The Corinthians know of another Israel, "the Israel of God" (Gal 6:16), which is also Israel according to the promise (Gal 4:21–31). The Jew—and the argument includes the pagan also—considers participation in a sacrificial meal as fellowship with "the altar," i.e., with the deity to whom the altar was consecrated and the victim offered. **19–20.** Paul does not contradict his statement of 8:4 on the nothingness of idols. The idols do not represent divinities, for there is only one God. But behind idolatry stand the evil spirits, so that, as the Law says (Lv 17:17 and Dt 32:17), the Gentiles sacrifice to demons. **21.** *cup of demons:* Participation in a sacrificial meal in a pagan temple is cooperation in idolatry; one enters into fellowship with demons, a relationship absolutely incompatible with union with the Lord. *partake of the table of demons:* To eat the flesh of victims sacrificed to idols is a parallel expression for the Christian sacrificial phrase, "to partake of the table of the Lord." **22.** Paul freely accommodates the text of Dt 32:21 and concludes that the Lord will punish severely the brazen insult perpetrated by those who, while participating at his table, would dare to share in the table of demons. He reminds them that the Lord whom they thus insult is all powerful.

66 **10:23–11:1.** May a Christian eat idol-meat at home or at meals in pagan homes to which he is invited? Yes, answers Paul, except when charity demands that he forego this right (cf. Acts 15:29). **23–24.** See comment on 1 Cor 6:12. Charity is the supreme law that must regulate the Christian's behavior. He must always take into account the spiritual well-being of his brother and be concerned with the building up of the Church. He must be ready to sacrifice himself in the interest of his brother and the community. **25.** Anything sold in the market can be eaten without inquiring if it has been offered to idols. **26.** *the earth and all that is in it is the property of the Lord:* As understood by Paul, Ps 24:1 means that everything belongs to Christ, the Risen Lord to whom the Father has subjected the universe. The sacrificing of an animal to demons does not remove it from the Lord's ownership. **27.** The Christian is free to accept invitations to pagan homes and to eat whatever is offered without inquiries about what is served. **28–30.** *someone:* Presumably "a weak" Christian who might call attention to the character of the food as idol-meat; then "the knowledgeable" Christian should refrain from eating it, not for the sake of his own conscience, which is rightly informed, but for the sake of the erroneous conscience of the other, lest he be scandalized.

67 The concluding questions of vv. 29–30 are the object of much discussion. Are they objections of "the knowledgeable," defending their freedom to use their right? Perhaps, but they could be another expression of the obligation to abstain from the use of one's rights in the interests of fraternal charity. *why am I denounced?* Or "why am I spoken ill of?" J. Dupont explains these difficult interrogatives. The term *syneidēsis* (conscience) was evidently used by "the knowledgeable" of Corinth, from whom Paul borrowed it. They in turn had borrowed it from the popular moral philosophy of the Stoics. A frequent theme of this popular philosophy was that the wise man should regulate his conduct by his own conscience and should not follow the opinion of others. Paul takes up this axiom, perhaps cited by "the knowledgeable" of Corinth in defense of their liberty, and reverses it completely. For the autonomy of the wise man who considers only his own conscience when deciding on an action, Paul substitutes the law of charity, making the Christian consider the effect of his actions on others and regulate his behavior by the duty of edifying his brother (see *Gnosis*, 266–68). **31–33.** The Apostle concludes with an exhortation to live only to give glory to God, taking care to give no offense, i.e., to place no obstacle to the conversion of Jew and Greek (Gentile) and to the growth and edification of the Church. This they will do if they follow his example, because he seeks never his own interest but always that of the rest of men, to bring them to salvation in Christ. C. Spicq (*PSB* 11/2, 244) notes that, in distinguishing the Church of God (which may here designate the universal community of believers? → Pauline Theology, 79:151) from Jew and Gentile, Paul lays the foundation for the theory of the *tertium genus* elaborated by Clement of Alexandria, Tertullian, and others. **11:1.** In imitating the Apostle, the faithful will be imitating Christ, the perfect exemplar of renunciation for the salvation of men.

68 **(C) Good Order in Christian Assemblies (11:2–14:40).**

(a) Women Must Be Veiled (11:2–16). The Corinthians were in general obedient to the instructions Paul had given, but some difficulties were expressed in their letter about the behavior and dress of women in religious assemblies. Some Christian women, influenced perhaps by the liberal atmosphere of cosmopolitan Corinth and emboldened by the attitude of "the knowledgeable" toward their freedom, were attending the assemblies without wearing a veil. Paul reprobates this behavior as unbecoming to a woman, because God has established a hierarchy, in both the natural and the religious spheres, in which the female is subordinated to the male sex. This hierarchical subordination of the woman should be recognized in her behavior and dress. The veil is a symbol of this subordination.

69 **2.** *the traditions:* The concept is Jewish. It suggests a depositum that has been received and handed on integrally in the primitive Christian community, as having come from the Lord or from the first apostles (1 Cor 11:23; 15:3). These traditions embrace customs (14:34) and religious rites like the Eucharist (11:23–24), as well as doctrinal and moral teachings (1 Cor 15:3–4; Rom 6:17; 2 Thes 3:6; 1 Cor 7:10,12,25; 9:14). (See F. Büchsel, "*Paradosis*," *ThDNT* 2, 172–73.) **3.** *head:* God has established a hierarchy. The term "head" imports authority and precedence in the three unions enumerated. Christ is the head of every man (*anēr*, "husband"); the man is the head of the woman (Eph 5:22–23); and the Father (*ho theos*) is the head of Christ. As Son, Christ comes from the Father; as Redeemer, he has been sent by the Father. He receives both his divine nature and his mission from the Father. **4.** *dishonors his head:* Perhaps "head" is ambivalent here. The man praying with covered head dishonors himself by abdicating the dignity God has conferred on the male sex; he also dishonors his hierarchical head, Christ. **5.** *dishonors her head:* The expression may mean "wounds her feminine dignity" and/or shames her husband by publicly repudiating the sign of female subjection. Her shame is that of the woman whose head has been shaved; an allusion perhaps to the shameful chastisement predicted by Is 3:24, as well as to natural repugnance. There is no evidence for the statement of some commentators that prostitutes in Greece shaved their heads. Rather, in the pursuit of trade they took great pains with their coiffure (see *Dict. des Antiquités*, "Mérétrices," 4, 1832B, 1838A,G). **7–9.** An argument from the creation story in Gn 1:27 and 2:22–23. Created by God in his image, man is a reflection (*doxa*) of the divine majesty. Woman, formed from man and created *qua* woman to be man's helper, is his image, reflecting his glory. **10.** This natural hierarchy should be respected "because of the angels" whom the Jews considered the guardians of the natural order. John Chrysostom saw here a reference to angels considered present at Christian liturgical assemblies. This interpretation has received support from the DSS. The Essenes of Qumran thought that angels assisted at their community worship; see J. A. Fitzmyer, *NTS* 4 (1957–58) 48–58; H. J. Cadbury, *HarvTR* 51 (1958) 1–2. *a power:* That is, a veil as symbol of her submission to male authority, i.e., to her husband. Is *exousia* (power) used because of a similarity between the Aram words for veil and power? The context seems to impose the meaning "sign of authority" or "of submission to authority," but the use of *exousia* with such a signification is unknown (See W. Foerster, "*Exousia*," *ThDNT* 2, 573–74; C. Spicq, *RB* 48 [1939] 557–62; S. Lösch, *TQ* 127 [1947] 216–61, would see in the unveiled Corinthian women devotees of the mystery cults). **11–12.** The preceding argument must not be pressed as though man did not need woman. There is a mutual dependence "in the Lord"; both are necessary to and have their proper roles in the Church. As the first woman was formed from the man, so now every man is born of woman. **13–14.** An argument from "nature," i.e., conventional concepts of what is proper. **16.** The matter is finally settled by an appeal to the custom of the primitive communities of Judea, "the churches of God" (1 Thes 2:14; 2 Thes 1:4; → Pauline Theology, 79:151).

70 (b) The Celebration of the Lord's Supper (11:17–34). The Corinthians, like the churches of Palestine, celebrated the Eucharist in the setting of a fraternal meal, which Paul calls the Lord's supper. The factions that divided the Corinthians resulted in serious abuses of charity and even of good manners in its celebration. Christians who were well off, possibly the Apollos faction, brought ample food and drink to the assembly but refused to share these with the other groups. Some also overindulged, even became intoxicated, while others were left hungry. All this was reported to Paul. **19.** *factions:* Not "heresies" in our modern sense; they served at least one good purpose, for they distinguished the virtuous Christians who kept aloof from them from those who were failing in charity. Although gathered in the same place, the Corinthians no longer partook of a common meal expressing their union with one another in the Lord, but each group ate apart.

71 **23–34.** Paul points up the shamefulness of these abuses by reminding them of the doctrine of the Eucharist. **23–25.** He recalls the original Last Supper; it is a teaching that he had learned from the primitive community and had faithfully handed on to the Corinthians (→ Pauline Theology, 79:15–16). This is the earliest extant testimony about the institution of the Eucharist. Written about eight years before Mark's Gospel, the Pauline record of the words of institution is very similar to Lk 22:19–20 and probably represents the form used in the Antiochene liturgy. That of Mk and Mt probably represents rather the Jerusalem liturgical form (see J. Jeremias, *The Eucharistic Words of Jesus* [Oxford, 1958] 118–20; C. Da Cruz, *VD* 37 [1959] 232–36). *the new covenant in my blood:* An allusion to the sealing of the Sinaitic covenant with the blood of the sacrificial victims (Ex 24:8). "New" recalls the promise of Jer 31 (LXX 38): 31–32. **26.** Until the day of the parousia, the Church must proclaim the Lord's redemptive death when celebrating the Eucharist. It is the sacrament of the unseen Presence, recalling the past death and pledging the future triumph. In this pericope the Apostle stresses the sacrificial aspect of the sacrament as memorial and symbol of the Lord's death. Just as the Passover celebration commemorated the deliverance of Israel from Egyptian bondage (Ex 12:14), so the Eucharist commemorates the deliverance brought about by Christ. The Eucharist is the proclamation (*kataggellete*) of the Lord's redemptive death that the Church makes until his coming, when there will no longer be need of his sacramental presence.

72 **27.** *will have to answer for the body and blood of the Lord:* This verse implies the doctrine of the real presence, suggested also by v. 29. **28.** *let one examine himself:* A man should see whether he has the dispositions of faith and fraternal love required for worthy participation in the Lord's Supper. **30–32.** Paul sees in the sicknesses and deaths afflicting the Corinthians a punishment for the abuses in their celebration of the Eucharist. God is calling them to repentance. **33–34.** Does Paul only correct the abuse of the lack of charity in the celebration of the Lord's Supper (Allo, Kuss, and many others)? Or does he abolish the meal with which the Eucharist was celebrated (J. Huby, Coppens, *VDBS*, 2, 1174)?

73 (c) On Spiritual Gifts (12:1–14:40). Their test, value, and exercise. Genuine spiritual gifts are distinguished by their conformity to Christian faith (12:1–3). Diverse as they are in operation and manifestation, all the gifts come from the one divine source and are directed to the one aim of promoting the well-being of the Church (12:4–30). The relative value of the various gifts is to be estimated by their usefulness to the Church. Better, however, than all such gifts is charity (ch. 13). The relative value of the gifts is illustrated by a comparison of prophecy and the gift of tongues. Practical rules are given for regulating the exercise of the gifts (ch. 14). See L. Cerfaux, *L'église des Corinthiens* 81–95.

74 (i) *The test of the gifts* (12:1–3). **1.** *spiritual:* This adjective is probably neuter (14:1), "the spiritual gifts." **2.** A reference to the unbridled religious enthusiasm and emotionalism so highly esteemed by pagans, such as the prophetic trance of the Pythia of Delphi and of the priestesses of Dodona, and the orgiastic frenzies of the devotees of Dionysos (see K. Prümm, *Religionsgeschichtliches Handbuch für den Raum der altchristlichen Umwelt* [Rome, 1954] 230f., 248f.). **3.** Conformity to the faith is the test of a genuine charismatic. No one can confess the divinity and sovereignty of Jesus unless he is enlightened and inspired by the Holy Spirit.

75 (ii) *Many gifts but one giver* (12:4–31). **4.** *gifts:* Paul's use of the term *charismata* is wider than the technical theological use of it today. It embraced for him all graces given primarily for the benefit of the Church: the gifts of administration and of assistance to the neighbor, as well as the extraordinary manifestations of the Spirit in miracles, tongues, etc. **5.** There are many spiritual gifts, but all come from the one divine source, the Spirit, the Lord, and the Father. The terms "gifts," "ministries," and "operations" designate the spiritual gifts according to different aspects that permit their appropriation to the Spirit, Lord, and Father. As *gratiae gratis datae*, the "gifts" are attributed by appropriation to the Holy Spirit, who is himself *the Gift* sent by the Lord Jesus and the Father. As "ministries" or "services," the gifts are attributed to the Lord Jesus, who was sent as the Son in the Incarnation to minister and serve. As "activities" or "operations," the gifts are attributed to God the Father (*ho theos*), the source of all being and activity.

76 **7.** *the common good:* One in source, all the gifts manifesting the Spirit's presence have one purpose, the "common good." The Gk word for this concept is *to sympheron*, which denotes what is advantageous; it connotes the "utility" these gifts have for the building up or "edification" of the Church, as the context shows. Paul now lists nine charisms, which may be arranged in three groups: (1) a discourse of wisdom, a discourse of knowledge, and faith (i.e., the confidence in God that moves mountains); (2) the gift of healing, miraculous powers, and prophecy; (3) the discernment of spirits, the gift of tongues, and the gift of interpreting tongues. All of these are directed to the welfare of the Church, just as the members of the human body exist for the good of the whole.

77 **12.** Christ is one, just as the human body is one, in spite of the diversity and number of its members. **13.** *baptized into one body:* Baptism incorporates the Christian into the risen, glorified body of Christ, so that the Church, the assembly of the baptized, is the manifestation and extension of the Lord's body in this world. The Church is the body of Christ because it is composed of members who share in the life of the Risen Lord.

(See Ahern, B., *CBQ* 23 [1961] 199–209. Benoit, P., *RB* 63 [1956] 5–44. Cerfaux, L., *Christ in the Theology of St. Paul* [N.Y., 1959] 350–56. Robinson, J. A. T., *The Body* [SBT 5; London, 1957].)

27–30. The application of the analogy of the human body, just set forth in vv. 14–26. All the gifts, like the members of the human body, were given for the good of the whole Church. The "higher" gifts are those that contribute more to the Church's welfare. Better than all the gifts is charity.

78 (iii) *A description and praise of charity* (13:1–13). This is one of the most sublime passages of the entire Bible. The loftiness of Paul's thoughts and the enthusiasm of his expression elevate his prose to an almost poetic sublimity. *love:* This is supernatural love, what theology terms the virtue of charity. It is distinguished sharply in v. 3 from philanthropy and humanitarianism. (For the term *agapē* see C. Spicq, *Agape in the NT* [3 vols.; St. Louis, 1963–67].) **1.** *tongues of men and of angels:* All possible tongues; the allusion is to the gift of tongues. The rabbis speculated on the language of the angels (see Str-B 3, 449 for some of the rabbinical ideas; H. Riesenfeld, *ConNeot* 5 [1941] 17–18). **5.** *does not brood over injuries:* That is, is not resentful. Some commentators, however, would translate the phrase as in Zech 8:17 (LXX) where it means "does not plot evil" (see the MT). **6.** *is not happy when others are treated unjustly, but rejoices in the truth: Alētheia* is a synonym here for justice, moral rectitude. **7.** *covers:* That is, "excuses" or "passes over in silence" (*stegei*). **8–11.** Charity is eternal, but the gifts (*charismata*) are transitory and temporal. There will be no need or use for them in heaven, just as a man has no use for the toys of his childhood. **12.** *then face to face:* This expression of the eschatological hope in terms of a knowledge of God is unique in Paul's writings, although it is a common Jewish theme (*4 Ezra* 7:98; Ap 22:3–4; Mt 5:8). In comparing the knowledge we have of God in this world (now) with that hoped for in the world to come (then), Paul employs two metaphors; one borrowed from the OT, "in an enigma" (Nm 12:6), the other from the popular Cynic-Stoic philosophy, "in a mirror." The first contrasts the privileged revelations given to Moses with those given to the prophets. Not even Moses could see God "face to face" in this world (Ex 32:20). The second refers to the indirect vision of an object seen in a mirror; one sees not the object itself, but its reflection. Since the passage occurs in a context devoted to a consideration of the spiritual gifts, the Apostle is comparing with the "face to face" vision of God the knowledge possessed through the charismatic gifts of gnosis and prophecy. *I have been known:* This phrase refers to the prevenient and merciful love of God shown in Paul's election to the faith and apostolate. *then I shall know:* This corresponding phrase implies a relationship between the perfect vision or knowledge of God and the charity by which we love God even in this life. So, of the three virtues that are abiding in this present life (*now*) and that are therefore greater than the transitory spiritual gifts, the greatest is charity (see J. Dupont, *Gnosis*, 105–48; G. Kittel, "*Ainigma*," *ThDNT* 1, 178–80).

The literature on 1 Cor 13 has been well summarized by J. T. Sanders, *Interpr* 20 (1966) 159–87. Many commentators feel that the term "hymn" is not applicable to this chapter, for it is quite unlike the recognized NT hymns in christological content and parallel format. To many scholars it seems to be an afterthought added to the original sequence of the letter, since the first part of 12:31 matches the second part of 14:1 very well. Paul's original thought would then have been that the Corinthians were not to seek after a lowly gift, like speaking in tongues, but rather a higher gift, viz. prophecy. However, on later reflection he thought of the gift that they should really seek after, which would make even prophecy insignificant by comparison, viz. love. It would also negate the tendency of the charismatics to be proud and self-seeking. So Paul added what is now ch. 13, inserting it along with 12:31b and 14:1a. The eschatological aspect of *agapē* has been emphasized by K. Barth, especially in the light of the context of ch. 15. The classic treatment of love in Paul and the NT is that of A. Nygren, *Agape and Eros* (London, 1953). He stresses that unlike the highest form of human love, whereby man seeks self-perfection in what is noble and spiritual, *agapē* comes from God to us in Jesus Christ. It is unmotivated and creative, seeks nothing and is unattracted by goodness. God loved us as sinners in Jesus. We must open ourselves to that love and allow God's love to be active in us in the unmotivated love of others. (See also V. Warnach, *Agape* [Düsseldorf, 1951].)

79 (iv) *The relative value of gifts illustrated by a comparison of prophecy with the glossolaly* (14:1–25). **1.** *that you may prophesy:* Prophecy, which is a divinely inspired message of exhortation, warning, comfort, or correction, is the best of the charisms because it contributes most to "the building up" of the Church. It is better than the gift of tongues so highly esteemed and avidly desired by the Corinthians. **2.** *glossolaly:* The gift of tongues was an extraordinary manifestation of the Spirit's presence and activity (Acts 2:4–6; 10:46; 19:6). The precise nature of this gift remains obscure. Many exegetes think that it consisted in incoherent shouting. Impelled by the Spirit, the charismatic would shout exclamations consisting of words or phrases in his own or in foreign languages but without logical sequence or meaning. The gift of tongues for these exegetes would be a Christian parallel to the emotional excitement and religious enthusiasm of pagan cults like that of Dionysos or Bacchus. Seized by a religious emotionalism under the impulse of the Spirit, a Christian would begin to shout in a fervid improvisation the praises of God. Very soon, carried away by his emotion, he would lose the thread of his discourse; his language would become incoherent, interspersed with words and phrases taken from the liturgy (*Abba! Alleluia! Maranatha!*), or, if he were not a native Greek, from his maternal tongue. The purpose of the gift was to manifest the Spirit's presence in the Christian community and to excite the bystanders to praise and glorify God. The glossolaly would thus have been a divine condescension to the mentality and cultural world of the primitive Christian converts similar to that recorded in the OT descriptions of the "prophets" (see 1 Sm 10:5,10,11; 19:18–24). Acts 2:13 certainly suggests that the glossolaly was an exhibition of great emotional excitement and religious exaltation. Such charismatic, fervid effusions were without meaning and consequently useless to the community, unless some Christian present had the gift of the "interpretation of tongues" (vv. 5, 6, 11, 13, 18, 19). See S. Lyonnet, *VD* 23 (1944) 65–75. **2.** *in spirit he speaks mysteries:* The glossolalist prays in that part of his being that is directly under the impulse of the Holy Spirit (his *pneuma*), and not merely with his understanding (his *nous*). So, he utters things that are obscure (mysteries) by reason of their incoherent expression and consequently unintelligible to others.

80 **6.** If Paul had received only the gift of tongues, he could never have imparted a knowledge of Christian doctrine. The comparison of the glossolaly to sounds produced haphazardly by musical instruments, without melody or rhythm (vv. 7–11), as well as the application of the example in vv. 13–19, supports the interpretation of this charism given above. **20.** The Christian should strive to be like a child in moral innocence, but he should always be mature in his judgment. The Corinthians' attachment to the gift of tongues is childish. **21.** *in the Law:* In the OT, God announced through Isaiah (28:12) that, because the people would not heed the Prophet's message, he would send the foreign-speaking Assyrians to invade their land; but even so, they would not be converted. So, concludes Paul, glossolaly is a sign for those who, like Isaiah's contemporaries, are unbelieving, whereas prophecy is for the faithful. **23–25.** The Corinthians also esteemed the gift of tongues for its apologetic value; it manifested the divine presence in the community. But Paul remarks that prophecy has even a greater apologetic value, whereas an excess of the glossolaly may bring ridicule upon the Church. *uninstructed or unbelievers:* These terms (*idiōtai* and *apistoi*) could be used of Christian visitors who were not accustomed to the excitement and enthusiasm of the Corinthian assemblies with their many glossolalists. But it could also designate non-Christians who had shown an interest in Christianity but were not yet fully instructed. The latter interpretation seems implied by the reference to "the place" of the *idiōtēs* in the Christian assembly (v. 16); see AG 371; H. Schlier, "*Idiōtēs*," *ThDNT* 3, 215–17.

81 (v) *Let the gifts be used for the edification of the Church* (14:26–40). Unlike pagan enthusiasts and ecstatics, Christian glossolalists must control their gift; they should use it only when an interpreter is present. The edification of the community must always regulate and restrict the exercise of the spiritual gifts. **34–36.** The custom of the churches of Palestine (of the saints) prohibiting women to speak publicly in the Christian assembly should be observed also in Corinth. Thus Paul abrogates the Corinthian practice of permitting women "to prophesy" in the assemblies (11:5). As one of many churches that have received the gospel, they should not presume to institute practices contrary to the customs of the primitive Palestinian communities. **37–40.** The true charismatics will be recognized by their docile obedience to the Apostle, the Lord's envoy. Since it is a gift of the Holy Spirit, the glossolaly should not be forbidden, provided reverence and good order regulate its exercise.

82 (d) On the Resurrection of the Dead (15:1–58). It is not clear whether Paul is answering questions about the resurrection asked by the Corinthians in their letter to him or whether he treats of this subject because of reports he has received from Corinth. In any case, he knows that some Corinthians deny the resurrection of the body. This denial, it seems, was due to their concept of the body as a hindrance to the soul's activity,—a characteristic Greek and Platonic concept. Paul answers by declaring that the bodily resurrection of Christ, which lies at the very heart of the apostolic preaching, is a fact duly attested by chosen witnesses (vv. 1–11). If, as some Corinthians assert, the dead do not rise, then it would follow that Christ, who died, did not rise, and there has been no redemption. Faith in Christ would be fruitless; the faithful, who lead self-sacrificing Christian lives, would be the most pitiable of all men, and the apostles would be liars (vv. 12–19). But Christ has risen, and his resurrection guarantees the bodily resurrection of those who are united to him by baptism. The glorious resurrection of the body is a consequence of incorporation into the Risen Christ. This final fruit of redemption will manifest the perfect victory of Christ over mankind's enemies and inaugurate his supreme triumph (vv. 20–28). Faith in the resurrection of the body is confirmed by some arguments *ad hominem* (vv. 29–34). Finally, the Apostle deals with the difficulties attending a materialistic conception of the resurrected body that the Corinthians had probably acquired from Jewish speculation on the subject. The resurrected body will be transformed into a perfect instrument for the new conditions of the life of glory (vv. 35–58).

83 (i) *Christ has risen* (15:1–11). **1–2.** The death, burial, and resurrection of Christ are fundamental doctrines of the *paradosis*, the "tradition" that Paul faithfully transmitted to the churches he founded (→ Pauline Theology, 79:15–17). **3–4.** *according to the Scriptures:* For the passion, death, and burial of Jesus, the primitive kerygma cited Is 53 on the "Suffering Servant of Yahweh" (Lk 20:37; Acts 8:32–35; 1 Pt 2:22–25); for the resurrection, the apostles appealed to Ps 16:8–11 (Acts 2:25–28; 13:34–35). Perhaps Paul also has in mind Jon 2:1 (Mt 12:39–40) and Hos 6:2 (see J. Dupont, *Bib* 40 [1959] 742–61). **5–11.** Paul appeals to the testimony of those who saw the Risen Christ. He omits the apparitions to the holy women, mentioning only those to persons whom Jewish law would accept as responsible witnesses. Peter and the Twelve rank first; they are the chosen, official witnesses. *the twelve:* The consecrated designation of the apostolic college (→ Aspects NT Thought, 78:173). **7.** *to all the apostles:* Is this a synonym for the Twelve? Or does it refer to a larger distinct group of authorized witnesses of the resurrection chosen from among the immediate disciples of Jesus? See L. Cerfaux, *Church*, 202; H. Lietzmann, *HNT* 9, 78; these prefer the second opinion; for the first opinion see R. Cornely, E.-B. Allo, and J. Sickenberger. Apparitions to the Twelve are found in the different traditions recorded in the Gospels; we do not know to which Paul is referring, nor do we know from the Gospels about appearances to James, to all the apostles, or to more than 500 brethren (→ Aspects NT Thought, 78:152–55). The apparition to James is described with legendary trimmings in the apocryphal *Gospel According to the Hebrews* (cf. Jerome, *De Viris Illustr.* 2). Christ's apparition to Paul at his conversion has constituted him an official witness to the resurrection. *one untimely born:* Lit., "an aborted fetus"; when applied to an adult, the Gk *ektroma*, like the Fr *avorton*, has a secondary meaning, "an object of horror and disgust." It is somewhat similar to our Eng expression, "monster." This probably is the sense in which Paul, recalling his persecution of the Church, uses the term, "the monster of the apostolic family" (see G. Björck, *ConNeot* 3 [1939] 3–8).

84 (ii) *If Christ has not risen, the apostolic preaching is a waste of time and Christian faith is fruitless* (15:12–28). Christ's resurrection is the crowning event of salvation history and man's victory over sin, Satan, and death. As Adam brought death, Christ brings resurrection from the dead. The Christian who is incorporated in Christ by baptism shares in his risen life. This final fruit of redemption in Christ will be realized for the Christian at the Lord's parousia when the dead rise in glory. **20.** *first fruits:* This denotes more than first in time. It is a Jewish cultic term. The offering of the *aparchē* (first fruits) was the symbol of the dedication of the entire harvest to God. So, the resurrection of Christ involves the resurrection of all who are in him. **21–22.** This parallelism and contrast between Adam and Christ is a favorite Pauline teaching (Rom 5:12–21; 1 Cor 15:45–49). **24.** *then comes the end:* The consummation of time when Christ, having completed his redemptive mission and brought all the elect to the glory of his resurrection, manifests his total victory over the evil spirits. Then, having completed his work, he hands over to his Father the royal authority that was conferred on him as Savior of the world and Head of the Church. (Concerning the interpretation of H. Lietzmann who sees in *eita to telos* (then the end) an allusion to an interval of messianic wars and a terrestrial millennium, see E.-B. Allo, *RB* 41 [1932] 187–209; J. Leal, *VD* 37 [1959] 225–31). **25–28.** Paul applies to Christ, the new Adam, "the Son of Man," what is predicated of Adam and mankind in general in Ps 8:7. The Father has subjected all created things to his Incarnate Son who was sent to redeem the world and establish divine sovereignty. Since his glorious resurrection, Christ reigns in glory; he is the Lord (Ps 110:1). At his parousia, his royal majesty will be manifested to all. Death is personified as in Rom 7. With the resurrection of the dead at the end of time Christ's victory will be complete: "everything [death included] has been placed under his feet." **27.** This verse is a parenthesis. Paul notes that Scripture does not include in "everything" the Father who has made all things subject to Christ. *it says:* The subject is not expressed; probably we should supply "the Scripture." But God, or even Christ, may be the understood subject. **28.** The submission of the Son to the Father refers to the homage that the Incarnate Son, the Savior of redeemed humanity, will render to his Father together with all redeemed creation. With the completion of Christ's redemptive mission, God the Father will be manifested as the first principle of all life and the final end of all creation and of salvation history.

85 (iii) *Otherwise the full life of Christian sacrifice is foolish* (15:29–34). After the digression of vv. 23–28 Paul returns to his argument about the resurrection of the dead. He appeals to what he and other Christians have been struggling and laboring for; all this would have no sense if there were no resurrection. Again, the Apostle alludes to a practice of the Corinthian community as evidence for Christian faith in the resurrection of the dead. **29–30.** It seems that in Corinth some Christians would undergo baptism in the name of their deceased non-Christian relatives and friends, hoping that this vicarious baptism might assure them a share in the redemption of Christ. Paul sees in this strange practice an implied faith in the resurrection of the dead. The passage is obscure, and many hypotheses have been proposed (see B. M. Foschini, *CBQ* 12 [1950] 260–76, 379–88; 13 [1951] 46–78, 172–98, 276–85; M. Raeder, *ZNW* 46 [1956] 258–60). **32.** *I fought with beasts at Ephesus:* A metaphor for the bitter opposition he had encountered; his life was endangered. Neither Acts nor 2 Cor 11:23–29 mentions a condemnation to beasts in the arena among Paul's sufferings. **32.** *let us eat and drink for tomorrow we die:* Isaiah (22:13) places these words on the lips of the selfish pleasure-seeking people of Jerusalem who gave no heed to the misfortunes of their countrymen. In Wis 2:6 similar words are put in the mouths of the materialists who have no faith or hope in an afterlife.

If there is no resurrection of the dead, concludes Paul, we are fools not to follow this selfish advice. If the dead do not rise, Christ has not risen; there has been no redemption; Christian faith and hope are a chimera. **33.** Paul warns the Corinthians, citing a popular proverb taken from Menander's *Thais* (cf. LCL 356), to guard themselves against those who would corrupt their faith and morals. *shake off your drunken stupor:* This suggests that the deniers of the resurrection were being heeded by some of the community. **34.** *ignorance of God:* This expression characterizes the pagans in Wis 13:1 and 1 Pt 1:13–14. Paul here uses it to stigmatize the deniers of the resurrection. They are no better than pagans!

86 (iv) *The manner of the resurrection* (15:35–53). The Jews engaged in much speculation about the resurrection of the dead. Some entertained hedonistic conceptions of the life of the resurrection similar to the Mohammedan teachings about Paradise (see J. Bonsirven, *Le judaïsme palestinienne* [Paris, 1934], 1, 483–85). Such materialistic conceptions seem to have influenced some Corinthians to deny the doctrine of the resurrection of the dead. The Apostle shows that God wisely provides each being with a "body" adapted to the conditions of its existence. He can provide glorified man with a body suited to his glorious state. **35–36.** Paul employs the Gk mode of argumentation called *diatribē*, imagining an objector whom he refutes with an epithet common to that literary form—"foolish fellow!" (→ Pauline Theology, 79:11). Nature itself shows that the death of a seed is not an obstacle, but the condition for its passage to a higher and richer life. **37.** *naked kernel:* Without leaf or blade, it becomes a plant with a full ear of grain, for God provides each seed with its proper "body." **39–41.** God provides every being with a body adapted to the circumstances of its existence. The earthly bodies of fish, birds, animals, and men have each their proper flesh; each of the heavenly bodies has a glory proper to itself. The sun, moon, and stars all have their own "brightness" (*doxa*), just as earthly bodies have their proper splendor. **42–44.** The analogy is applied to the resurrection of the dead. Four antitheses illustrate the new qualities of the risen body. In this life, man's body is *psychikon*, the instrument of the *psychē*, which is the principle of mortal existence. The risen body will be *pneumatikon*, the perfect instrument of man's *pneuma*, which in the life of glory will be completely possessed by and perfectly docile to the divine Spirit. **45–49.** The model of this "spiritual body" is the risen body of Christ, "the heavenly man." Just as the first Adam is the source and model of natural *psychic* life, so the Risen Christ, the new Adam, is the model and source of "spiritual" life. Gn 2:7 says that God made Adam "a living being" (*psychē* in the LXX). The new head of humanity, Christ, became in his resurrection a life-giving spirit, who sends the Holy Spirit and makes men sharers in his risen, glorified life. **46.** Perhaps Paul has in mind and rejects the Hellenistic Jewish interpretation of the two accounts of man's creation, which saw in Gn 1:27 the creation of "the ideal man" and in Gn 2:7 the creation of the earthly man, Adam, the sinner and father of humanity. According to this Philonic theory the perfect, "the ideal," would be prior to the earthly. Paul insists that the opposite is true. **47.** First came Adam, formed from the earth, and long afterward came the second head of humanity, the glorified Risen Christ. **48–49.** From the first Adam mankind inherited a mortal and corruptible body; from "the heavenly man," the glorified Christ, the baptized inherit his life and glory. Even now they share in the life of the Risen Lord; by the action of the indwelling Spirit whom he has sent to them they are being transformed ever more perfectly into his image (2 Cor 3:18), until at the parousia their bodies will become like his risen body, incorruptible and glorious. **50.** *flesh and blood:* The corruptible body of man must be transformed in order to participate in "the kingdom of God," i.e., in the life of glory. **51.** The Apostle solemnly announces a mystery, a truth of God's revelation. The faithful living at the parousia will not die (will not fall asleep), but they will be transformed. The dead will rise, and the bodies of those still living at the Lord's coming will be transformed instantly into glorified, incorruptible, "spiritual" bodies. Paul alludes to the traditional apocalyptic scenario (the sound of the trumpet) and shows by his use of the first person plural that he still entertained the hope of witnessing the Lord's coming during his own lifetime. The false rendering of the Vg *omnes quidem resurgemus, sed non omnes immutabimur* introduces a contradiction into vv. 51–52. The mystery announced here, that the just who are living at the parousia will not die, is also found in 1 Thes 4:15–17 (see F. Prat, *Theology of St. Paul*, 1, 76–77; 2, 364–69).

87 (v) *Hymn of triumph over death* (15:54–58). Paul ends his discussion of the resurrection of the dead with a hymnic passage. **54.** When the bodies of the elect by resurrection or change become incorruptible and immortal, the last enemy, death, will have been vanquished and Scripture fulfilled. Paul cites Is 25:8 according to a text that differs from the LXX but is similar to the versions of Theodotion and Aquila. **55.** Is this a citation from Hos 13:14, or simply an exclamation of Paul's in phrases borrowed from Scripture? If a citation, it is a very free accommodation of the prophet's words (see J. Bonsirven, *Exégèse rabbinique et exégèse paulinienne*, 327). **56.** *sting:* That is, the sting of a serpent. Sin has been vanquished by Christ the Redeemer. Thus death, like a serpent deprived of its venomous sting, can no longer harm those who are in Christ. Paul suggests this is due to the abrogation of the Law that gave sin its power by giving a knowledge of God's commandments and threatening death to the sinner, without giving the poor man the strength to keep them (Rom 7:7–25). **57–58.** The hard work (*kopos*) of Christian life is not in vain, because the Christian is "in the Lord," who has already won the victory.

88 **(IV) Conclusion (16:1–24).**

(A) The Collection for the Poor of Palestine (16:1–4). Paul orders collections to be taken up for the Christian poor of Palestine in compliance with the request made at the time of the Jerusalem Council (Gal 2:10; cf. 2 Cor chs. 8–9; Rom 15:25–29). **1.** *the saints:* See comment on Rom 1:7. **3.** *I will send those whom you accredit:* The Apostle will not compromise his boast (9:15) by personally handling the money. See K. F. Nickle, *The Collection: A Study in Paul's Strategy* (SBT 48; London, 1966).

(B) Paul's Itinerary and Some Recommendations (16:5–18). Writing from Ephesus during Mission III, Paul plans to come again to Greece. He will pass through the Roman province of Macedonia (see Acts 19:21) to come to Achaia. The riot provoked by the silversmiths of Ephesus forced Paul to leave the capital of Asia, perhaps sooner than he had planned (Acts 20:1). **6.** *wherever I go:* Paul does not say so here, but he may already have had the trip to Rome in mind. His plan to visit Rome is formulated in Rom (1:10; 15:23), in the letter he will write from Achaia. **8–9.** See Acts 18:19; 19:9. **10.** *Timothy:* See comment on 1 Thes 1:1 (→ Pastoral Letters, 57:3). At this time Timothy was very young and timid, yet Paul tried to send him to Corinth to deal with the problems of that disturbed community (cf. 1 Tm 4:12). **12.** *Apollos:* See comment on 1:10; cf. Acts 18:24–26. Apollos seems to have been disturbed over his unwitting role in the factions of Corinth. **13.** Paul's exhortation to the Corinthians ends once again with an appeal for love. **15.** *Stephanas:* See comment on 1:16.

89 **(C) Greetings and Concluding Blessing (16:19–24).** **19.** *the churches of Asia:* The communities founded by Paul in the Roman province of Asia in western Asia Minor, of which the capital was Ephesus. *Aquila and Prisca:* Paul always refers to the wife of Aquila as "Priska" (see comment on Rom 16:3), but Acts uses the diminutive "Priskilla" (18:2,18,26). **20.** *a holy kiss:* See comment on Rom 16:16. **21.** *with my own hand:* Paul pens the final greeting and blessing (→ NT Epistles, 47:20). Was Sosthenes (1:1) his scribe for this letter? **22.** *maranatha:* Paul uses, even in writing to the predominantly Gentile Christian community of Corinth, an Aram liturgical exclamation, probably meaning "Our Lord, come!" (For an explanation of the term, → Pauline Theology, 79:61.) Ap 22:20 plays on the meaning, "Come Lord Jesus!" **23.** Our Lord, who reigns at the right hand of his Father and will come in majesty at the parousia, is to be with all the Corinthians through his bounteous favor, according to this final prayer of Paul. **24.** *my love:* The Apostle concludes this letter in which he has stressed the primacy of love in Christian life by assuring his readers of his love for them in Christ Jesus.

52

THE SECOND LETTER TO THE CORINTHIANS

John J. O'Rourke

BIBLIOGRAPHY

1 Allo, E.-B., *Saint Paul: Seconde Épître aux Corinthiens* (EBib; 2nd ed.; Paris, 1956). Erdman, C., *The Second Epistle of Paul to the Corinthians* (Phila., 1929). Hanson, R. P. C., *II Corinthians* (TBC; London, 1954). Jacono, V., *Le epistole di S. Paolo ai Romani, ai Corinti e ai Galati* (Turin, 1952). Kürzinger, J., *Die Briefe an die Korinther und Galater* (Echter-B; Würzburg 1959). Kuss, O., *Die Briefe an die Römer, Korinther und Galater* (RNT 6; Regensburg, 1940) 197–247. Lietzmann, H., *An die Korinther I-II* (HNT 9; 4th ed.; Tübingen, 1949) 97–162. Lyonnet, S., *Exegesis epistulae secundae ad Corinthios* (Rome, 1955–56). Osty, E., *Les Épîtres de Saint Paul aux Corinthiens* (BJ; 2nd ed.; Paris, 1953) 73–116. Plummer, A., *The Second Epistle of Saint Paul to the Corinthians* (ICC; N.Y., 1915). Rees, W., "2 Corinthians," *CCHS* 1099–1111. Spicq, C., "Deuxième Épître aux Corinthiens," *PSB* 11/2 (Paris, 1951) 299–479. Strachan, R. H., *The Second Epistle of Paul to the Corinthians* (MNTC; London, 1935). Tasker, R., *The Second Epistle of Paul to the Corinthians* (Grand Rapids, 1958). Wendland, H. D., *Die Briefe an die Korinther* (NTD 7; Göttingen, 1963) 143–234. Windisch, H., *Der zweite Korintherbrief* (Meyer 6; 9th ed.; Göttingen, 1924).

Cambier, J., R–F, *INT* 433–46. F–B 205–15. Guthrie, *NTI* 1, 46–71. Metzger, B. M., *IPLAP* 75–82. Wik, *NTI* 390–98.

INTRODUCTION

2 **(I) Authenticity and Unity.** Today the Pauline authorship of 2 Cor taken as a whole is admitted by everyone. However, many consider it a collection of various works or fragments of works by Paul. Especially questioned are 6:14–7:1; chs. 8–9; and chs. 10–13. To consider the first of these sections a fragment of the first lost epistle (cf. 1 Cor 5:9–13) seems a gratuitous hypothesis, even though the passage seems strange to the context. Something more can be said for the opinion that ch. 9 is a doublet of ch. 8, and hence did not belong to the same letter. Nevertheless, these chapters can be reconciled: The past generosity of the Corinthians could have served as an example to the Macedonians, and their present generosity can serve as model to members of the church of Corinth and their fellow Christians of Achaia. (On the relationship between 2:13 and 7:5, see F–B 212.)

3 Chapters 10–13 are considered by many as "the tearful letter" (2 Cor 2:4) or as a subsequent letter to the Corinthian church sent after Titus had arrived in Corinth for the second time. Argument for separating these chapters from the rest of the epistle is found in the apparently brusque change in tone found therein; it is claimed that no author would have spoken in such different ways in the same letter. Connected with this question is the identity of the tearful letter. According to many scholars, Paul made a short visit to Corinth and then sent the tearful letter, during the interval between the composition of the canonical 1 and 2 Cor (→ Life of Paul, 46:36).

4 This reconstruction of one of the most obscure periods in his life does not seem demanded by the facts. Furthermore, 1 Cor 1–5, not to mention ch. 11, is of such a tone as to warrant the Apostle's calling the whole of 1 Cor written "through many tears"; as will be seen, the whole of 2 Cor, save for chs. 7–8, could be called a tearful letter. Paul did not like to be harsh, yet his words are often quite harsh in both 1 Cor and 2 Cor 1–7. It is not impossible that a second visit to Corinth had been made by Paul before he wrote 1 Cor, nor does 2 Cor 12:14 or 13:1–2 necessarily mean that two journeys to that city had preceded the projected trip, although the obvious interpretation of these texts is that he had been there twice before. Certainly "to come again in sorrow" hardly refers to his first sojourn there (Acts 18:1–18); the more natural reading of 2 Cor 2:1–4 demands that a coming in sorrow precede the tearful letter (but cf. 1:15).

5 Whatever may be said of a tearful letter distinct from canonical 1 Cor, such a hypothesis does not require that chs. 10–13 be separated from the rest of 2 Cor. These last chapters cannot be the intermediate letter, because the confrontation of the adversaries mentioned in them is not referred to in chs. 1–9. Moreover, greater vehemence would be expected in the earlier parts of 2 Cor if the last chapters had been written earlier. Most

likely, chs. 10–13 merely restrict the scope of the final part of the letter to that part of the Corinthian church that is giving a hearing to Paul's adversaries or that is indulging in moral laxity. In chs. 1–9 he does defend himself, and expressions of sympathy and reconciliation are not lacking in the final chapters (cf. 10:8; 11:2; 12:14; 13:7). Moreover, the opening words of ch. 10 suggest that Paul is aware that he is about to continue in a somewhat different vein than in the preceding chapters.

All the textual evidence favors the unity of 2 Cor. The Pauline corpus seems certain to have existed by AD 100 (cf. G. Zuntz, *The Text of the Epistles* [London, 1953] 279–83). It is unlikely that an early editor would have joined pieces of various letters into one, especially when it must have been known that at least one letter to the Corinthians was not included in the collection (cf. 1 Cor 5:9).

6 **(II) Time and Place of Composition.** According to 2 Cor (7:5–7; 2:12–13; 8:1–15; 9:2), Paul composed it in Macedonia after leaving Ephesus. This would have been during the journey narrated in Acts 20:1–2. Probably it was in the autumn of AD 57 (→ Life of Paul, 46:37).

7 **(III) Nature.** This epistle is the one most like a letter of all those that are admitted as being genuinely Pauline, just as Rom is the one most like a treatise. As is evident in many places, the author's emotions were close to the surface when he wrote. He is seen as a very affectionate man, hurt to the quick by the misunderstanding and evil-doing of some of his beloved Corinthians, yet he is very happy when he can praise the recipients in any way. What hurts him most is the dogmatic implications of the wrong being done at Corinth. The letter is in great part concerned with combating evils found in the communities of Achaia; apparently universal or general statements should not be interpreted to the letter, for preachers tend to speak in general terms when they know that their words have but particular application. Although deeply personal, the letter contains much Pauline teaching.

In 1914 K. Lake had suggested that the opponents of Paul in 2 Cor were different from those in 1 Cor: if Paul had Judaizers in mind in 1 Cor, he now faced non-Jewish allegorizing pneumatics in 2 Cor. In more recent times many scholars are proposing that Paul's opponents in 1 Cor were Gnostics. Yet many of them feel that those with whom Paul differs in 2 Cor are still different. E. Käsemann has argued that the opponents of Paul in 2 Cor are not Gnostics, since Paul is no longer arguing against libertinism. Recently, D. Georgi took up the question of the peculiarities of Paul's opponents in 2 Cor, basing his opinion on what Paul says in 2:14–7:4 and chs. 10–13 (see *Die Gegner des Paulus im 2. Korintherbrief* [Neukirchen, 1964]). For him the opponents are missionaries from Palestine who have come to Corinth; but they are more than the crude Judaizers who had appeared in Galatia. They regard themselves as supermen, heavenly men, the seed of Abraham, Hebrews par excellence. They think that they have the power to make others supermen like themselves. Much of this is reconstructed from what Paul says of the "superfine apostles" of 2 Cor 11:5ff. They are supposed to have allegorized the OT and to profess a superior wisdom in the gift of the Spirit (see 2 Cor 3:15–16: they remove the veil from the OT). They seem to think of Christ as the supreme example of the heavenly man, despising his humanity. His death made no difference because he was just as "heavenly" before his death as after it. They seem to have no use for suffering or sacrifice, regarding their own success and wealth as a proof of their power as missionaries. Paul attacks these proud men and stresses the importance of the Lord over against them. He emphasizes the death of Jesus and the sufferings of the true Christian missionary.

8 **(IV) Outline.** The purpose of the letter can be seen from the three main divisions of the body of the letter:

(I) Introduction: Greeting and Thanksgiving (1:1–11)
(II) Part I: Paul's Defense Before the Corinthians (1:12–7:16)
- (A) His Sincerity in Deferring the Visit to Corinth (1:12–2:11)
- (B) His Ministry (2:12–7:16)
  - (a) The Recent Journey to Macedonia (2:12–17)
  - (b) Testimonial (3:1–3)
  - (c) Comparison of the Old and New Covenants (3:4–18)
  - (d) His Sufferings and the Motives Thereof (4:1–5:21)
  - (e) Paul Shows His Love and Exhorts the Corinthians to Reciprocate (6:1–7:1)
  - (f) His Delight at the News Given by Titus (7:2–16)

(III) Part II: Collection for the Church in Jerusalem (8:1–9:15)
- (A) Give Generously as Do the Macedonians (8:1–15)
- (B) Recommendation of His Representatives (8:16–9:5)
- (C) The Rewards of Generosity (9:6–15)

(IV) Part III: Paul Confronts His Adversaries and Those Who Receive Them (10:1–13:10)
- (A) Paul Is Not Weak; He Glories in God (10:1–18)
- (B) Paul Praises Himself to Defend His Apostolate (11:1–12:13)
- (C) Announcement of His Coming Visit (12:14–13:10)

(V) Conclusion: Appeals, Salutations, Blessings (13:11–13)

COMMENTARY

9 **(I) Introduction: Greeting and Thanksgiving (1:1–11). 1–2.** In his customary manner, Paul identifies himself and his associate(s) at the beginning of the letter. *Timothy:* See comment on 1 Thes 1:1. He was with Paul at the foundation of the Corinthian church (Acts 18:5). *church of God:* See comment on 1 Cor 1:2 (→ Pauline Theology, 79:150–151). *with all the saints:* The members of the church; by virtue of being members of the Church, they are holy. The Roman province of Achaia was approximately equal to modern Greece; Corinth contained the principal Christian community of that region. *grace and peace* (→ NT Epistles, 47:8). **3.** Reasons are given for praising God; this is typical of the beginning of Paul's letters. *the God and Father of Our Lord Jesus Christ:* The Father of Jesus is Father par excellence (Eph 3:15; cf. Mt 23:9); he can also be called the God of Jesus, for the Son possessed a true human nature by becoming incarnate (cf. Rom 15:6; Col 1:3; Jn 20:17). **4.** *us:* Primarily Paul; he receives consolation not for himself but for others. **5.** *as the sufferings of Christ abound for us:* Paul's sufferings are sufferings of Christ, because they are borne for him, in imitation of him, and above all, borne as a member of Christ (cf. Col 1:24). **6–7.** These verses are confused in Greek, though the general meaning of the variants is the same. Solidarity with Christ means solidarity with one's fellow Christians; thus Paul's sufferings help the Corinthians, and the consolation given to him enables them to bear tribulation. **8.** What the particular affliction in Asia was is not known; it does not seem to have been the affair of the silversmiths at Ephesus

(Acts 19:23–40), in which apparently Paul's life was not menaced. **9.** *sentence of death:* The Gk word *apokrima* designates an official judgment. *who raises the dead:* This refers to God's action in having raised Jesus and in raising all men in the future; the pres. participle expresses durative action. Paul's confidence was based on God, who is the cause of our hope in the resurrection (cf. 1 Cor 15:12–28); this is a reference to one of the questions that had earlier bothered the Corinthians. The resurrection was one of the stumbling blocks to the Greeks (cf. Acts 17:32). **10.** God, who raises the dead, can certainly deliver from lesser evils. **11.** *by many:* As many prayed for the Apostle's safety, so should many give thanks for it. Prayer, both of petition and of thanksgiving, has an important place in Paul's teaching.

10 **(II) Part I: Paul's Defense Before the Corinthians (1:12–7:16).** The Apostle is intent to show that he has no reason to be ashamed of his comportment vis-a-vis the Corinthians.

(A) His Sincerity in Deferring the Visit to Corinth (1:12–2:11). **12.** The "boasting" of the Apostle is based not on worldly motives but on the "sanctity" and "sincerity," mutually complementary, given him by God; these are in open contrast to worldly power and wisdom (cf. 1 Cor 1:18–31). *conscience:* Used here in the rare NT sense of good conscience (see comment on 1 Cor 8:7). **13.** *completely: Heōs telous,* "to the utmost." **14.** *in the day of Our Lord Jesus:* Cf. 1 Cor 1:8; this is the time of the parousia. **15.** *second grace:* Does this indicate that Paul had been to Corinth only once before this projected visit? It would be a grace for them because Paul is an apostle. **17.** *with fickleness:* Paul's adversaries accused him of forever making great plans and fulfilling none of them. **18.** *God is faithful:* Introductory formula for an oath (cf. 1 Cor 1:9; 10:13). *our word was not yes and no:* He did not speak in an inconsistent or in a deceiving manner. **19–20.** *the Son of God... did not become yes and no, but yes came to be in him:* Paul could not be vacillating or uncertain, because Jesus was absolute truth, who in his life and work brought to fulfillment the previous divine promises. *came to be: Gegonen,* pf. tense, denotes an action that has happened and continues in its effect; the divine promises were fulfilled in the person of Jesus Christ, and we are still affected by the results of his life. *amen:* Hebrew for "yes." The goal of God's revelation is divine glory manifested through us; only by his grace are we moved to give God glory. **21.** *giving strength to us with you:* God ever gives his help to those who believe in him. *having anointed us, having marked us with a seal, having given the pledge of the spirit:* Paul retails three effects of our initiation into the Christian life at baptism. The "seal" was the personal mark placed by an owner on his property; the "pledge" (*arrabōn*) was a down payment signifying that the rest of the payment would be made; here the pledge is God's Spirit. The fullest possession of messianic bounty is yet to come (cf. Eph 1:13–14; Rom 8:23). The Spirit dwelling within Paul is a guarantee of the Apostle's sincerity. **23.** *upon my soul:* Another form of an oath: May God take away Paul's "life" if he does not speak the truth. *spare:* Words of anger do not hurt as much when they are not delivered in person. **24.** *not because we are acting as lord:* The only *Kyrios* of the context is Jesus, who alone is to act as Lord (*kyrieuei*). Paul's foes may have charged him with being overly dominant.

11 **2:1–4.** Paul's tearful letter. **3.** *lest I have sorrow:* Paul hoped that his letter would cause the Corinthians to mend their ways; their actions and attitudes should have been such as to bring joy to him. **4.** *that you know the love which I have:* Paul wanted their self-correction to be motivated by his loving care for them. **5.** *if anyone has caused sorrow:* A reference to the one who had acted scandalously among the Corinthians; by using *tis* (anyone), the Apostle shows delicacy in making the reference almost hypothetical. Evidently the sinner has changed his ways and has been received back into the community, whose actions Paul now approves. *not to put it too severely:* Or "not to labour the point" (NEB), or "let's exaggerate nothing" (BJ). The Gk vb. *epibarō* causes difficulty because all other known examples of it are transitive; if it be such here, what is its object? Most modern commentators take it as intransitive (cf. AG 290). *to you all:* Their prior attitude toward the sinner was the cause of the tearful letter; from this it does not follow that the affair of the sinner was the only subject treated in that letter. **6.** *by the many:* The community that acted against the sinner. **7.** *lest he be overwhelmed:* The punishment was to be medicinal, not such as to leave the man without hope (cf. 1 Cor 5:5). **10.** *whom you pardon I also pardon:* Just as he associated himself with the punishment, so does Paul join himself to the Corinthian community in forgiving the sinner (cf. 1 Cor 5:4). *in the presence of Christ:* Christ looking on and approving (cf. 1 Cor 5:3). **11.** *lest we be defrauded by Satan:* To drive the sinner to despair would give Satan a victory. To allow the sinner to remain outside the Church and hence in the power of the devil for a while can be a salutary punishment; to be overly harsh or unforgiving to one who repents would make Satan victorious; this would be in accord with "the designs" (*noēmata*) of the devil. The various elements mentioned here in Paul's approval of the Corinthians' action recall the elements of the excommunication ordered in 1 Cor 5:1–8: the sinner, salutary punishment, action of the community united in spirit to Paul in Christ, and Satan. Not everyone believes that the sinner mentioned here is the incestuous man of 1 Cor 5; the majority of recent commentators see no reference here to 1 Cor 5.

12 **(B) His Ministry (2:12–7:16).** Paul describes his activity first in Troas and then in Macedonia; it culminates in his meeting with Titus for reasons that concern the Corinthians.

(a) THE RECENT JOURNEY TO MACEDONIA (2:12–17). **12.** *door:* A favorite Pauline expression for an opportunity of preaching the gospel (cf. Acts 14:27; 1 Cor 16:9). **13.** *I had found no peace of mind:* Most commentators take the perfect (*eschēka anesin tō pneumati*) as equivalent to an aorist (cf. Bl-Deb-F § 343); yet a pluperfect would be very much in place here, the terminal point of the duration of the effect on Paul being the return of Titus (7:6). **14.** *leads us in triumph in Christ:* As a victorious general heads his triumphal march, so God manifests his power throughout the world through the works of the apostles who are united to Christ, through whom God has brought salvation. This union of the apostles and other Christians to Christ—whose members we are elsewhere said to be (Col 1:24)—is a central theme of Paul's teaching. **15.** *fragrance: Euōdia* is a technical term for the "aroma" of a sacrifice acceptable to God. Those who preach the gospel please God by their work, which is Christ's work. **16.** *odor of death... odor of life:* This implies an advance from bad to worse and from good to better. The preaching of the gospel places those who refuse to accept it on the road to perdition and those who accept it on the way to eternal life (cf. Lk 2:34). *who is sufficient for these things?:* As v. 17 shows, those who speak truly in the name of Christ can undertake such a mission, bringing eternal life or eternal death to others. **17.** *like so many, trading in the word of God:* That is, peddlers; it is to be hoped that this statement is a rhetorical exaggeration. *Kapēleuō* originally meant "to keep an inn," but developed a pejorative connotation and could mean "adulterate" (Vg). It refers to the work of the false teachers at Corinth.

13 (b) TESTIMONIAL (3:1–3). In response to an accusation of his adversaries that he is ever recommending himself, Paul notes that whatever testimonial he needs is written in the very hearts of the Corinthians who by their faith bear witness to his worth. Unlike other teachers, Paul does not seek letters of recommendation; this does not mean that he condemned the practice, for he may have been aware that the church of Ephesus had written such a letter to the Corinthians concerning Apollos (Acts 18:27). **2.** *you are our letter:* Paul does not shrink from praise of the Corinthians; they bear witness to his worth by their conduct. These words must be kept in mind when we read the harsh sections of the epistle; many members of the Corinthian church were good. *by all men:* A literary exaggeration. **3.** *letter from Christ:* Paul changes his metaphor somewhat, for now Christ becomes the author of the testimonial; it is Jesus who produces the good in the Corinthians that testifies to Paul. *by the spirit of the living God:* God effects all good things, using the services of his ministers. This is another expression of the truth that man's sanctification depends ultimately upon God alone. *on tablets which are hearts of flesh:* Durable records were cut into stone tablets. "Flesh" does not have a pejorative sense; rather it indicates men who are tractable and docile. There is possibly an allusion here to Ez 11:19; 36:26. God's grace cannot affect those who will to be obdurate.

14 (c) Comparison of the Old and New Covenants (3:4–18). In this section Paul takes up a theme that he develops more fully and differently in Gal and Rom: the life-giving qualities of the Christian dispensation as opposed to the Mosaic Law, which of itself did not bring men to salvation but only made sins and the effects of sin more manifest (Rom 7:7–12). The polemic against the Judaizers—so evident in Gal and Rom—is not quite as strong here. **4–5.** Continuation of the profession of the belief that God alone moves unto good. Verse 5 was cited by the Second Council of Orange in AD 529 (DB 180; DS 377) against the Semi-Pelagians; this decree was approved in AD 531 by Pope Boniface II. Directly, the verse concerns any thought or any plan for carrying out the apostolic mission; by an *a pari* argument the council deduced the necessity of grace for the initial act of faith. **6.** *the letter kills, but the spirit gives life:* The letter, the OT Law, brings spiritual death because, in proclaiming commands and prohibitions that must be heeded without at the same time giving the inner grace necessary for their observance, it places men in the condition of being bound by what they cannot always observe fully. The Spirit, the graces given in the new economy of salvation, gives power to do what God wants. Paul gives a résumé of his teaching in Gal and Rom. **7.** Here is begun an a fortiori argument based on the description of the giving of the Mosaic Law on Sinai as found in Ex 34:29–35. *glory of his countenance was to pass away:* The transitory glory of Moses' face showed that the splendor of the OT was to give way to the greater glory of the NT—and has now given way to it; this is the glory due to it as an economy of salvation. **10.** *for what was glorified has come to have no glory because of the glory that surpasses it:* The OT's glory was insignificant when compared to the splendor of the New Covenant. **11.** *if indeed that which was transitory was glorious, much more is that which remains in glory:* The Mosaic dispensation had its glory, being a great work of God, but it has given way to the NT, which must be all the more glorious because it is to last. **12.** *having much hope:* Founded on the durability of the New Covenant, which fulfills and perfects the OT covenant, while putting an end to it. *liberty of speech:* Paul speaks openly, in contrast to Moses, and begins to use the OT in a manner similar to that employed by the rabbis. With John Chrysostom we might classify it as allegorical. According to Ex 34:30–34, Moses veiled his face because the Israelites were afraid to come near him when they could see the brightness of his countenance. **13.** Paul uses a daring comparison: The fading away of the splendor of Moses' face was a sign of the transitory nature of the earlier covenant. **14.** *their thoughts were hardened: Noēmata* are the products of the mind, *nous;* the hardening of them, the refusal to see what should be seen—in the present case that the Old Law was merely transitory—is the result of what elsewhere (Mt 19:8) is called *sklērokardia*, a spiritually pathological condition. Because of this, the Jewish nation as a nation refuses to understand; the "veil on the Old Testament," the covering up of its significance, remains for them; in this sense it is not revealed to them that in Christ it is made void. Revelation has been given to them, but they refuse to accept it; they do not uncover themselves so that they may see that Jesus is the Christ, who has put an end to the Mosaic dispensation by perfecting and fulfilling it. **16.** This is an adaptation of Ex 34:34 to the present situation. In the text of Ex, the subject of the statement is Moses; here, the subject of "turn" could be Moses, Israel, any man, or their hearts (v. 15). Grammatically the last is preferable; however, since Paul is using the whole passage of Ex 34 here, it would seem that Moses, not as a person but as a personification of the Jewish nation of which he was the founder, is the subject. If the Jews will turn to God, then the veil of unbelief will be lifted from them just as the face of Moses was uncovered when he turned to God. **17.** A celebrated problem of Pauline exegesis. *Ho Kyrios* elsewhere in Paul refers to Jesus. If such is its meaning here, then Jesus himself is the vivifying spirit, so to speak, of the New Covenant, who is opposed to the letter that kills (3:6). Others hold that Paul follows LXX usage, in which *ho Kyrios* translated the sacred name Yahweh; the God of Israel is spirit, indeed *the* spirit, for God is most perfect. Still others hold that the reference is to the Holy Spirit (cf. P. Grech, *CBQ* 17 [1955] 420–37). Seemingly, 3:6 is the key to the whole section. *liberty is where the spirit of the Lord is:* Those who have embraced the New Covenant are freed from the death brought by the Old Law (cf. 3:6). **18.** *all of us with face uncovered, looking at the glory of the Lord, are transformed into the same image from glory to glory by the spirit of the Lord:* By becoming Christians we are made into the image of Christ by his Spirit that is Jesus himself; we are united to him, gazing here by faith upon him and his meaning, able to advance to greater perfection (*apo doxēs eis doxan*), until we shall see him as he is (cf. 1 Cor 11:7; 13:12; 15:49).

Throughout this section "spirit" refers to the spiritual nature of the New Covenant, which it has from Christ, who is the personification of the New Dispensation, and therefore its spirit.

15 (d) His Sufferings and the Motives Thereof (4:1–5:21). **1.** *we do not lose heart:* The greatness of his ministry prevents Paul from letting weariness or other difficulty overcome him. **2.** *we have renounced the hidden things of shame:* He renounces acting in an occult manner for which one should be ashamed. *does not walk in craftiness:* The word *panourgia* characterized the manner in which Satan beguiled Eve (cf. 11:3). *not deforming the word of God:* He preached the truth even though it was a stumbling block (*skandalon*) to some and foolishness (*mōria*) to others (1 Cor 1:23). *commending ourselves to the awareness of men in the face of God:* For this translation of *syneidēsis*, cf. C. A. Pierce, *Conscience in the NT* (SBT 15; London, 1955) 87. **3–4.** Cf. 3:14, the teaching of which is now applied to the Gentiles. *who are lost:* Those who are on the way to perdition. Obviously Paul does not mean that such men are definitively lost; otherwise there would be no reason for a further ministry in the areas already evangelized. *god of this world:* If the genitive is objective, the god is over this world; he is Satan (Jn 12:3; 14:30; 16:11; cf. Eph 3:3), to whom the nonbelievers have surrendered themselves by their evil dispositions. If the genitive is epexegetic, the god is the world, which they virtually worship by their actions (cf. Phil 3:19). *who is the image of God:* In Jesus, the likeness of God the Father is fully present (cf. Jn 12:41,45; Col 1:15; Heb 1:3). *gospel of the glory of Christ:* The apostolic teaching proclaims Jesus, who was crucified and rose in glory; the death because of its effects was glorious (cf. Phil 2:10–11). **5.** Paul preaches Christ and not himself except as the servant of the Corinthians (cf. 1 Cor 3:5–9). **6.** *that the light shines from darkness:* An allusion to Gn 1:3 (cf. Jn 1:4–5). *on the face of Christ:* If *prosōpon* could have meant "person" when Paul wrote, as C. Spicq thinks, we would have an indication of the mediation of Jesus; however, the word apparently did not then have that meaning (AG); thus it is stated here that the glory of the NT shines forth perennially on the face of Christ, whose members we are, whereas the passing splendor of the OT mirrored on the face of Moses gradually disappeared. God now shines forth in the Apostle's heart—and by deduction in ours—in such a way that the knowledge of the divine glory can produce such knowledge in others. There is here an allusion to Paul's conversion (cf. Gal 1:16).

16 **7.** The Apostle returns to the theme of his own weakness; because of the poor instrument that God uses, his divine power and glory are all the more manifest. *treasure:* The apostolic ministry. **10.** The life of the apostle has a twofold aspect just as did Christ's here on earth: one of continual dying through which it contributes to the realization among men of the redeeming death of Christ; the other of spiritual successes that show the efficacy of the redemption and the consequent diffusion of grace among those who, being justified, await future glory. **11–12.** Death, the danger of physical death either at the hands of enemies or from the labors of the ministry, works in the Apostle because he gives himself over to the ministry to the Corinthians so that the spiritual life gained for them by Jesus may be found among them (cf. 1 Cor 1:4–7). **13.** A citation of Ps 116:10 according to the LXX; the Hebrew has "I believed, even when I said." The causality of faith is announced in both. **14.** We may have here an implicit statement that Paul did not expect to be alive on the last day (cf. 1 Cor 15:51–52 in Gk); however, this is stated secondarily here (cf. 5:1). What is important to him is the announcement of the reason for his hope (cf. 1 Cor 15:12–24). **15.** *all things:* Nothing done or supported by Paul as apostle is excluded from this consideration. These things are intended immediately for the salvation of those who come to faith, but ultimately and principally for the glory of God. **16.** *our outer man is decaying:* Paul's body is being spent (cf. v. 10). *our inner man is renewed day by day:* The inner man here is the durable part of human nature; it is not only the soul but the soul with a right to a glorious body—we are concerned here with one who has grace—at the resurrection. The inner man is renewed daily in that the person who strives continuously to please God grows in the life of Christ, becoming more and more like him. **17.** *the present light thing of our affliction:* Compared to the rewards of eternal life the trials of this life are nil. **18.** *those things which are unseen:* Supernatural realities, or perhaps the good, and hence supernatural, things of the future.

17 **5:1.** *for we know that if our earthly dwelling place, the tent, should be destroyed we have from God a building, an eternal dwelling, not made by hands, in heaven:* "We know" is an expression of the firmness of Christian hope. Our body is "earthly" (*epigeios*) because it is not the glorious body to be had after the resurrection. *Tou skēnous* (the tent) is a genitive of apposition. Profane authors also used the figure of the tent to show the mortal condition of human bodies. Paul did not share the view of some of these authors or other Gk philosophers that the body was a prison of the soul; for him we shall not exist forever as disembodied spirits, but rather at the parousia we shall be given bodies of a different nature from those we now possess; they will be immortal and unable to suffer (cf. 1 Cor 15). The word *oikodomē* (building) was especially used for a temple building (AG); therefore God will provide us with a sacred body, not made by hands because not the result of natural processes. **2.** In the middle of the verse the figure changes somewhat when the Apostle speaks of being clothed with a dwelling; this use of mixed metaphors is found elsewhere in Paul, as in Eph 4:24 where *endysasthai* is also employed. **3.** *if as indeed is the case* [ei ge kai], *having clothed ourselves we shall be found not naked:* The understood object of *endysamenoi* is the glorious body; thus Paul gives another reason that should help the faithful overcome their instinctive fear of death (v. 4). Although the glorious body will not be possessed by each believer until the general resurrection, the right to it is already possessed; moreover, we have as our head one who already has his glorified body, the Lord Jesus. *naked:* In the OT, nakedness connoted guilt and moral wretchedness (cf. Gn 3:10; Is 33:11; Ez 16:7,37–39; E. E. Ellis, *NTS* 6 [1959–60] 219–21). Here the Apostle does not consider the possibility of the believer's losing justification. **5.** Cf. 1:22.

These five verses are an adumbration of the teaching found in Rom 6–8. See K. Prümm, *Diakonia Pneumatos* 2, part 1 (Rome, 1960) 168–75.

18 **6.** *being of good cheer:* While on this earth we are not definitively united to God, but we have hope. **7.** Cf. 1 Cor 13:12. *by faith:* *Dia pisteōs* means during the time of faith. *Dia eidous* causes some difficulty; generally it is taken to mean "during [the time of] seeing"; but that *eidos* can have that meaning is not admitted by all, e.g., F. Zorell, F. Prat (*Theology* [London, 1927] 2, 376, n. 2); and E.-B. Allo. For such commentators the phrase would mean "in the presence of the reality which is seen" (cf. NEB). Usually, *eidos* is distinguished from *opsis*, but seemingly *eidos* can mean "seeing" (cf. AG 220). In either case there is an essential difference between the state of the just in the present life and their state in the next. **8.** Certainly the good Christian can desire death; nevertheless, the average Christian can do so only as he meditates upon the true meaning of death in the new economy of salvation. Even then the horror at separation of body and soul will generally remain. **9.** *thus we aspire:* The word *philotimeisthai* is found elsewhere in the NT only in Rom 15:20 and 1 Thes 4:11. We are led by our zeal and honor to try to do what is right. *to please him:* The end of all activity of men, whether in this life or the next, is to please God. *being at home* [*endēmountes*]...*living apart* [*ekdēmountes*]*:* Directly, these words seem to refer to the definitive possession of the fullness of heavenly glory (with the glorious body) and to our lives on earth respectively. The Apostle prescinds from any consideration of the intermediate state of the blessed in heaven before the general resurrection (cf. C. F. D. Moule, *NTS* 12 [1965–66] 106–23). **10.** The direct reference is to the general judgment.

19 **5:1–10.** This passage has been the object of much discussion. At least eight general classes of interpretation can be found. Among Catholics perhaps the most common one is that which sees here—or at least in 5:6–10—the doctrine of the possession of essential beatitude by the just (prescinding from purgatory) following the particular judgment.

(Cullmann, O., *Immortality of the Soul or Resurrection of the Dead* [N.Y., 1958]. De Langhe R., "Judaïsme ou Hellénisme en rapport avec le Nouveau Testament," *L'attente du Messie*

[Brussels, 1958] 154–83. Dupont, J., *Syn Christō* [Bruges, 1952]. Ellis, E. E., "II Corinthians v. 1–10 in Pauline Eschatology," *NTS* 6 [1959–60] 211–24. Feuillet, A., "La demeure céleste et la destinée des chrétiens," *RSR* 44 [1956] 161–92. Garofalo S., "Sulla 'eschatologia intermedia' in S. Paolo," *Greg* 39 [1958] 334–52.)

20 **11.** *we attempt to persuade men:* The word *peithomen* is a conative present. Paul acts rightly, knowing that God is judge. God knows the Apostle's dispositions that are correct; Paul trusts that they appear as such to the Corinthians. *to your consciousness:* Cf. 4:2. **12.** *that you have it:* That the Corinthians will be able to respond to the insincere critics of the Apostle, those who "glorify themselves" outwardly (*en prosōpō*) without any good reason for doing so (*mē en kardia*). **13.** *if we are out of our mind, it is for God; if we are reasonable, it is for you:* Undoubtedly Paul's adversaries accused him of madness because of his doctrine and zeal, just as the Jews considered insane a doctrine that was difficult to accept (cf. Mk 3:21; Jn 10:20). Paul acted thus for God's sake. At the same time he often acted with great deliberation and circumspection; this, too, evidently caused adverse comment. Paul's irony shows here. **14.** *the love of Christ spurs us on:* The love that Christ had for Paul produced a resultant love for the Lord Jesus. By its nature, love is mutual; there must be a movement from within and without; that is, of each of the lovers toward the other. The love that Christ has for us works on us interiorly by grace. **15.** *for all:* The universality of the redeeming act of Jesus is announced here. *who died and rose for them:* Both the death and the resurrection (→ Pauline Theology, 79:68–74) of Jesus were intended for our salvation; both have their part in our justification. The same thought is expressed in Rom 4:25. *those who now live:* Those who are justified have their reason for being in Jesus the Christ (cf. Rom 14:28), who has made us a new creation (v. 17).

21 **16.** *we know no man from now on according to the flesh; and, if we knew Christ according to the flesh, we by no means know him:* Now we do not know, we do not make judgments, according to merely human standards. Paul had once judged Jesus according to purely outward appearances and had persecuted him in his Church. But now Paul does not consider him in that light, but rather in accordance with the revelation he has received. Although it is possible that Paul saw Jesus when the future apostle lived in Jerusalem, it cannot be deduced from this statement (see J. Cambier, *Littérature et théologie pauliniennes* [Bruges, 1960] 72–92). **17.** *a new creature:* The redemptive activity of Jesus radically changes those who allow themselves to be affected by it (cf. Rom 6:4; 8:10; Gal 6:15; Eph 4:24; Col 3:10). The old things, the Old Covenant, are no more; cf. 3:11. The word *kainē* (new) designates not just something that has recently appeared but rather a new manner of being, differing essentially from what was habitual before (so J. Behm, *ThDNT* 3, 447–50). Thus the crucifixion and resurrection of Jesus are for Paul the dividing line between two periods of the history of human, indeed of all, activity in this world. **18.** *from God:* God alone is the author of the new economy. *through Christ:* Cf. Rom 5:10–12. *ministry of reconciliation:* This refers to the apostolate confided to Paul by God through Jesus (cf. Acts 9:4–6; 22:10; 26:15–18, and for the general idea, Jn 17:18; 20:21). **19.** *that God was reconciling to himself the world:* The word *kosmos* here refers primarily to mankind, but to men as their sins have affected the rest of creation; cf. Col 1:19, where the verb is *apokatallaxai* and its object is "the things on earth" and "the things in heaven." For Paul *kosmos* does not generally have a pejorative connotation. The lack of the article before *theos* is unusual grammatically; for this reason, some consider *theos* as predicate and *katallassōn* as subject of the clause, virtually a noun (cf. C. F. D. Moule, *Idiom-Book of NT Greek* [2nd ed.; Cambridge, 1959] 17, 116); the essential idea would remain the same in this interpretation. The use of the imperfect shows that the process of reconciliation is here considered as taking place throughout the life of Christ on earth, though its high point is reached at the Savior's death (cf. Phil 2:9; Rom 5:9; → Pauline Theology, 79:81–82). *not reckoning their offenses against them:* Through the divine mercy because of the obedience of Jesus (Rom 5:10), guilt has been wiped away; this is what theologians call the objective redemption. God now acts toward the human race as a race as though sin had not been committed (cf. Rom 5:18–21). This new attitude of God's toward mankind reached its high point and continues on that level, at the death of Jesus, but it was already operative during the whole of his life on earth, as the periphrastic impf. (*ēn*) *logizomenos* shows. *placing in us the word of reconciliation:* *Themenos* is aoristic; hence the action is punctiliar: At a given point in time Paul was fully constituted an apostle. He is the herald of the act of divine mercy. **20.** *we function as legate:* A beautiful description of the Apostle's work; as an apostle he is God's instrument (*hōs theou parakalountos*). *Hōs* is used here to show that what is stated is true (cf. Bl-Deb-F § 425). *we beseech you, allow yourselves to be reconciled:* The Apostle makes a practical exhortation. Reconciliation can be lost; those who have accepted the gospel must ever allow it to exercise its effect upon them. In one sense, reconciliation is obtained with the acceptance of the first justifying grace, but in another, it is not achieved until one enters into definitive possession of the eternal reward; the former was emphasized in the earlier parts of the chapter; the latter aspect is mentioned here, in passing as it were, as a prelude to ch. 6. It also seems implied here that sin after baptism can be remitted—which is taught elsewhere in this epistle (cf. 2:5–11; 12:21)—for this letter was not addressed to only the good members of the churches of Achaia. The command would have more immediate application for some than for others. **21.** *who knew not sin:* The word *gnonta* means not theoretical knowledge but personal experience gained by action (cf. Hebr *yāda'*); Jesus was without sin (Rom 7:1). *he made sin for us:* God is the subject. Some commentators hold that Jesus was made a member of our sinful race, though not himself possessing personal sin; others think that *hamartia* means "a sacrifice for sin"; still others contend that Jesus became by juridical fiction the personification of sin. Whatever opinion is right, *hamartia*, each time it is used in this verse, has a different sense; moreover, in the LXX, it sometimes translates the Hebr *ḥaṭṭā'* when it is used to signify "a sacrifice for sin," although the phrase *peri hamartias* is more common when the Hebrew has this meaning. Because here it is a question of the work of reconciliation that was accomplished by the sacrifice of Jesus (cf. 1 Cor 11:24–26; Mt 26:28; Mk 14:24; Lk 22:19–20), *hamartia* most likely means "sin sacrifice." This is supported by the fact that the verse alludes to Is 53:9–11, where in the LXX there is a reference to such a sacrifice; in accordance with the LXX the MT should be interpreted (so L. Sabourin, *ScEccl* 11 [1959] 419–24; *Rédemption sacrificielle* [Bruges, 1961]); cf. Rom 3:22–26. *that we become the justice of God in him:* The purpose of the redemption—and hence its effect—was that we might be identified with a divine attribute, not the justice of God considered in itself, but the salvific justice of God that makes men just (cf. Rom 3:21–22; → Pauline Theology, 79:96–97). "In him" may mean because of our union with Jesus; perhaps *en* here could be translated "by." Both meanings are Pauline, but which is meant here is not certain (→ Pauline Theology, 79:138).

22 (e) Paul Shows His Love and Exhorts the Corinthians to Reciprocate (6:1–7:1). **1.** *cooperating:* That is, with God (cf. 5:20). *lest you receive God's grace for naught:* They would have received God's grace to no avail if they had fallen again into the ways of the pagans or if they had allowed themselves to be seduced by false teachers. **2.** The citation is from Is 49:8 (LXX); it is a portion of one of the Servant poems. In it God answers the Servant, showing by the use of the proph. perfect the certainty of his help. In applying the text to his own situation, Paul made his time "the acceptable time." *in the accepted time: Kairō dektō* translates Hebr b^{e}ʿēt rāṣôn, "in the time of good favor," i.e., of the pouring forth of God's graces. The Corinthians must make use of their present opportunity, the most accepted time (*kairos euprosdektos*) in God's sight, the day of salvation. Here the Apostle views salvation as realized eschatology. The whole verse is a parenthesis; the thought of v. 1 is continued in the following. **3.** *giving:* The ptc. *didontes* refers to the subject of v. 1. Paul has no reason for being ashamed of the manner in which he has conducted himself. **4–7a.** Paul shows himself a true minister of God by his way of life. *in much patience:* His *hypomonē* (endurance) is manifested by three groups of trials, each of which consists of three things that put Paul to the proof. *afflictions: Thlipseis* indicates those trials in which physical or mental pressure was exerted on the Apostle. *necessities: Anagkai* are necessary cares. *distresses: Stenochōria* is almost a synonym for *thlipseis.* The next two groups of trials are more particular; the first is made up of those inflicted on Paul by other men; the second, those to which the Apostle subjected himself for the sake of his apostolate. *wounds:* Cf. Acts 16:23, a beating with rods; cf. Acts 14:19, stoning. *imprisonments:* Cf. Acts 16:22–23. *tumults: Akatastasia* means mob action (cf. Acts 13:30; 14:5,19; 17:5; 18:12; 19:23). *labors:* the tiring work Paul had to do to fill his wants (cf. 1 Thes 2:9; 2 Thes 3:8; Acts 18:3; 1 Cor 4:12). *in vigils:* The loss of sleep caused by his various works (cf. 2 Cor 11:27; 2 Thes 3:8). *periods of fast:* These could indicate works of penance, something certainly not alien to the life of Paul (cf. 1 Cor 9:27); however, most likely this means those times when Paul had little to eat because of his way of life; but cf. 11:27. Next, the Apostle gives a list of positive marks of his ministry. *in purity:* Not in the precise sense of chastity, but in that of integrity, holiness of life. *in knowledge:* That is, of the gospel principles and their application in concrete circumstances (cf. 1 Cor 14:6; Rom 15:14). *in long-suffering: Makrothymia* is the patient acceptance of the shortcomings of others. *in goodness:* That is, toward others; it is a sympathetic attitude toward them (cf. 1 Cor 9:19–22). *in a holy spirit:* The position of this phrase seems to indicate that it denotes a quality of Paul's ministry, viz., a spirit of righteousness. *in unfeigned charity:* The love for others that he shows is real. *in the word of truth:* A quality not possessed by the false teachers; possibly they could pretend to have other qualities, but their teaching was opposed to the true gospel. *in the power of God:* Paul's success comes not from himself but from God (cf. 1 Cor 2:4; 2 Cor 2:17; 4:2). **7b–8a.** Here the nouns are in the genitive governed by *dia,* no longer in the dative after *en;* thus there seems signified some notion of instrumentality. *by means of the arms of justice of the right and of the left:* The qualities by which were promoted the cause of justice, which was the justification of others. Offensive arms were carried in the right hand; defensive ones in the left. One should not try to determine which qualities correspond to the various arms; what the Apostle wanted to say was that his armament was complete (cf. 1 Thes 5:8; Eph 6:13–17). *by means of glory and dishonor:* Caused by the reckoning made by others of Paul's work and personal worth. These estimates of him nevertheless served as a means of Paul's carrying out his divine mandate; thus, for example, the attacks of his adversaries were at least part of the reason for Paul's writing this letter to the Corinthians, just as the claims of the various parties, some of whom were opposed to him, were part of the reason for his writing 1 Cor (cf. 1 Cor 1:11–12). *by means of bad report and good report:* The words of others as they brought dishonor or glory to the Apostle; their causality was the same as that of the estimates of his worth. **8b–10.** *as... and yet:* The words *hōs... kai* (*aei*) create an antithesis: The former introduces the false report; the latter, what is true. *as having nothing and possessing all things:* From a worldly point of view, Paul was an insignificant man; his adversaries at Corinth claimed that he was not much of a teacher; yet in being a Christian apostle Paul had everything. Compared to this, his apparent lack of skill and his poverty were nothing.

23 **11.** *our mouth was open:* The Apostle spoke his innermost thoughts without dissimulation to the Corinthians. *Corinthians:* Rarely in the body of an epistle did Paul address the recipients by name, though he did in Gal 3:1 and Phil 4:15. This shows to how great a degree Paul's emotions were stirred up by his writing the previous section in which he had bared himself to them. *our heart was enlarged:* He showed great love for them in making known his secret self. **12.** *you are not constrained by us:* Paul's love for them knows no bounds. *you are constrained by yourselves:* Lit. "in your bowels"; according to the beliefs of that epoch, these were one of the seats of affection. Any lack of charity is on their side. This was true as far as some were concerned, and Paul was hurt thereby. **13.** As an affectionate father in the faith, Paul beseeches the Corinthians to show reciprocal love for him.

24 **6:14–7:1.** This paragraph is one of the passages in 2 Cor that creates problems about its unity (→ 2 above). Because of the affinities it bears to QL and because it makes sense when removed from the context, it is considered by some commentators to be a non-Pauline interpolation. This view, probably correct, is a basis for considering the letter to be a collection of fragments (see J. A. Fitzmyer, *CBQ* 23 [1961] 271–80; J. Gnilka, *Neutestamentliche Aufsätze* [Fest. J. Schmid; Regensburg, 1963] 86–99; P. Benoit, *NTS* 7 [1960–61] 279, 289–90).

14. *do not be joined together with unbelievers:* A strong expression, for *heterozygountes means* "yoking together different kinds of animals." By his acceptance of the gospel, the Christian is of a different species, so to speak, from the unbeliever; the believer cannot live like the one without faith. Contact with unbelievers is necessary (cf. 1 Cor 5:10), but a sharing of their way of life is impossible. The figurative expression is undoubtedly influenced by Lv 19:19; Dt 22:10. The Apostle is not directly referring to marriage. The following five verses are explicative of this one. **15.** *Beliar:* A designation of the devil in non-rabbinic Jewish literature; e.g., 1QS 1:18,24; 2:5,19. In the mss. tradition there is much fluctuation in the spelling of the name. The alternate form *Belial* preserves the original Hebr spelling b^{e}līyaʿal ("worthlessness"). **16a.** *the temple of the living God:* Cf. 1 Cor 3:16. **16b.** The citation that begins here is a free joining together of several OT verses, starting with Lv 26:12; Ez 37:27. **17.** *wherefore:* An addition made by Paul. The verse is made up of Is 52:11 and Jer 51:45. *do not touch that which is impure:* In Is the reference is to contact with whatever would cause ritual impurity; Paul raises the injunction to the moral plane: If the ancient Jews were forbidden to contract ritual impurity, then Christians must contract no moral stain. The analogy is from the lesser to the greater (for other examples of this type of application, cf. the use of Ps 8:7 in 1 Cor 15:27,

Ps 8:4–6 in Heb 2:6–9). **18.** The citation is made up of 2 Sm 7:14; Jer 31:9; Is 43:6 (or Hos 1:10; Am 4:13 in the LXX; Zeph 3:20 in the LXX). *Almighty: Pantokratōr* is found only here in Paul, and in a citation at that; it is quite common in the LXX and Ap. **7:1.** *these promises:* Those mentioned in 6:16b–18; the NT is the fulfillment of the OT. *let us cleanse ourselves:* An aorist, therefore meaning once and for all. *from every defiling of flesh and spirit:* Sins that soil body and soul. The word *sarx* is not used pejoratively, for sin affects the whole human person. Others take *kai* (and) as adversative here and think that the reference is to external and interior sins. *perfecting our holiness:* In WV and NEB the pres. participle is given the force of an imperative. Although possible (cf. Bl-Deb-F § 468), such an understanding of the grammatical form is not necessary; by cleansing ourselves we begin the work of perfecting ourselves that must endure until the end of our days. *in the fear of God:* Our motive for right action is the knowledge that God will judge us.

25 (f) His Delight at the News Given by Titus (7:2–16). **2.** *make room for us:* That is, in their minds and hearts. *we have not ruined: Ephtheiramen* most likely has reference here to monetary matters. That Paul was charged with financial fraud is seen from 12:17–18. By implication he accuses the false teachers of making demands for their support, something Paul did not do even though he had a right to do so (1 Cor 4:12). Since they were proclaiming falsehood, they had a right to nothing; thus they were trying to ruin the Corinthians spiritually and materially. **3.** *not for condemnation:* Paul does not wish the Corinthians to think that he is making a judgment against them; at least that is not his principal purpose. As he had already said, he loved them. *to die together and to live together:* The logical subject of these infinitives is Paul, though by grammatical position "you," the Corinthians, would be preferable. The meaning, however, seems clear: Paul will always love them; not even death can separate him and them (cf. Ru 1:17 in Hebr). **4.** *frankness toward you:* Paul has addressed them without dissimulation. *boasting about you:* A reference to the effect his tearful letter had upon them; it was such that he could not joyfully point to them as an example to be imitated by the other churches. Paul here begins to prepare them for the appeal that he is going to make for money for the Jerusalem community. **5.** *our flesh had no rest:* In 2:13 Paul's "spirit" had no rest at the time of his arrival in Macedonia; *sarx* now designates the sphere of suffering. Mental stress often has physical repercussions. *struggles without, fears within:* The whole of his apostolic mission was marked by the opposition of those who would not believe; at the same time he was ever concerned that Satan would seduce his converts (cf. 1 Cor 7:5; 2 Cor 11:3). **7.** *your yearning, your lament, your ardor for us:* The repetition of "your," which in each instance is in an emphatic position in Greek, indicates that these attitudes on the part of the Corinthians brought great comfort to Paul: They yearned to see him once more; they lamented at having caused him grief; they acted ardently in righting what was wrong. *I rejoiced the more:* This probably means that not only the reappearance of Titus but also and above all his message gladdened immensely the Apostle's heart. **8.** *even if I caused you sorrow in the letter* (→ 2–4 above). *I do not regret it:* The reaction to the letter on the part of the Corinthians shows that Paul was correct in sending it, even though it caused them unhappiness. *although I did regret it:* This is a nice touch; the Apostle reveals that he did not like having to act sternly. *for I see...:* A parenthesis. **9.** *not that you were saddened, but that you were saddened unto repentance:* Paul is happy not because he caused hurt to them but because whatever grief he effected among them moved them to mend their ways, to have a change of heart (*metanoian*), which was as he desired. To write merely to cause grief would not be in keeping with the apostolate or with the spirit of Christian charity; moreover, sorrow on someone's part without his making an attempt to right the wrong is of no avail. *according to God:* Their becoming sad was in accord with the wishes of God. If they had only taken offense in a human sense, they could have become hardened in their ways; this Paul had feared. *that in nothing: Hina* here seems to introduce a result clause (E.-B. Allo; cf. *GrBib* § 352). By being docile to his teaching, they have bettered and thus not worsened their condition. If they had acted otherwise, their new state would have been worse than their prior condition, and in this sense they would have suffered harm from the letter. **10.** The word *ametamelēton* can modify either *metanoian* or *sotērian;* word order makes the latter preferable; thus "salvation that is not repented." No one should be sorry for having made any sacrifice in order to obtain salvation. *grief according to the world:* Mere sorrow without any attempt to right a situation when such is possible; it "works unto death" because it is a refusal to obey an impulse unto good. **11.** *how great eagerness:* To do what was demanded. *defense: Apologia,* a verbal defense of the Apostle. *indignation:* Against the wrongdoer. *yearning, zeal:* Cf. v. 7. Their desire to see him who had addressed them harshly was certainly a sign of their fundamentally good dispositions, and this perhaps more than anything else brought solace to Paul. *punishment: ekdikēsis* of the one who had done wrong (BJ, RSV, AG). *you showed yourselves to be guiltless in the affair:* Their innocence was shown when their subsequent actions indicated that they had not realized how greatly their previous attitude with regard to the sinner compromised Christian virtue and reputation. **12.** Here Paul is not saying that he did not desire the punishment of the sinner or the vindication of the one who had been wronged, who was apparently the Apostle himself; rather, by employing a Semitic oratorical device, which expresses by contrast what we would express by comparison, namely "not so much this as that," he states that he wrote so that their good dispositions might be made manifest. That it was Paul who was wronged does not prevent one from saying that the sinner was the incestuous man of 1 Cor 5; Paul was father of the Corinthian church and hence hurt by any wrong done by one of his spiritual children (cf. 12:14–15). *among you before God:* That the Corinthians would become aware of their own true regard for and loyalty to Paul, which were sentiments in accord with God's will and of which they should show their regard openly, was one of the reasons for Paul's writing to them.

26 **13.** Here is another nice touch. The joy felt by Titus because he was present when the Corinthians changed their ways made the Apostle rejoice all the more. Not only the knowledge of what the Corinthians had done but also and especially the effect of this upon Titus gladdened Paul's heart, for he had visual proof as it were of the sincerity of their repentance. Furthermore, he is happy because another is made happy (cf. Rom 12:15). **15.** The memory of the docility shown by the Corinthians and of the good reception given him by them makes Titus love them the more. **16.** *I rejoice because I have confidence in you in every respect:* This concludes this section and provides an introduction to the one that follows. The Apostle has been made happy by the Corinthians; he is confident of their good dispositions. It is implicit in this statement that he can make further demands upon them, knowing they will react with generosity. Thus Paul has prepared them for the appeal for material contributions for the mother church in

Jerusalem. In no way does this detract from his sincerity, but it shows that he knew full well that it is better not to scold someone immediately before asking a favor of him; compare the similar procedure in 1 Cor 15:58–16:4 as contrasted to earlier sections of that letter.

27 (III) Part II: Collection for the Church in Jerusalem (8:1–9:15).

(A) Give Generously as Do the Macedonians (8:1–15). 1. *the grace of God given in the churches of Macedonia:* Paul praises the Macedonians in order to rouse the Corinthians to emulate them. The *charis* was the opportunity of contributing to the collection for the Jerusalem community (cf. 1 Cor 16:1–5); it is a grace because it is an opportunity for doing good. The churches of Macedonia were those centered in Thessalonica, Philippi, and Beroea. The generosity of the Philippians is underscored in Phil 4:15. This collection had been recommended to the Galatians by indirection (Gal 2:10). An earlier collection for the Jerusalem church had been made by the faithful of Antioch; Paul himself had been one of those who had taken its proceeds to Jerusalem (Acts 11:27–30). **2.** *in the multiple trial by tribulation:* Reference to the persecutions directed against the Christians of Thessalonica are found in 1 Thes 1:6; 2:14. Paul had been persecuted in Philippi (Acts 16:20) and Thessalonica (Acts 17:5); these were trials for those churches. *the abundance of their joy:* A fruit of the Spirit (cf. Gal 5:22). Christian joy enables one to do anything that is necessary and more besides (v. 3). *depth of their poverty:* To give when one has little is to give the more in God's sight (cf. Mk 12:21–24; Lk 21:1–4). *have abounded unto the riches of their uprightness:* The word *haplotēs* is peculiar in the NT to Paul. In the LXX it translates Hebr *tōm*, which signifies "perfection" or "integrity" (1 Chr 29:17); many commentators render it here (and in Rom 12:8) "generosity." However, the basic meaning gives good sense, and it seems questionable if the other translation can truly be called such. The Macedonians give without any ulterior motives; thus their moral integrity is made the more manifest. **3.** *spontaneously:* In Greek, this is an adjective referring to the Macedonians. Without any prodding on Paul's part, they gave not only what he asked but more besides. **4.** *the grace and the sharing of the ministry:* To give unto others in the person of the Jerusalem community was a grace, a divine favor, because it was an opportunity for doing good and for showing thereby the bonds of love uniting the Macedonians to their fellows in faith; it was a participation in the ministry of service to those in need, a ministry already recommended to the Galatians and requested of the Corinthians (cf. Gal 2:10). This service is a charism (cf. 1 Cor 12:5). *the saints:* The members of the Jerusalem community, who in a sense were "the saints" par excellence inasmuch as they belonged to that community from which the gospel had gone forth to the world, the mother church. "Saints" was a common Pauline appellative for Christians (cf. 1 Cor 1:2; 6:2; 16:1,15; 2 Cor 1:1; 9:1; 13:12; Rom 1:7; Eph 1:1; Phil 1:1; Col 1:2; 1 Thes 3:13). But in 1 Cor 16:1 the collection for the Jerusalem community is said to be simply "for the saints" (cf. L. E. Keck, *ZNW* 56 [1965] 100–129). **5.** *and then to us through the will of God:* The Macedonians gave not only material goods but also of their members; a number of Paul's intimate collaborators came from Macedonia; among them Sopater, Aristarchus, and Secundus (Acts 20:4), Jason (Acts 17:6; Rom 16:21?), and Gaius (Acts 19:29). One associated himself in the active apostolate from a divine impulse. **6.** *that he complete this grace for you as he has begun:* Titus was known to the Corinthians as a man whom Paul trusted. The Apostle had given them instructions for systematic collecting for the mother church (1 Cor 16:1–4); it is evident that Titus, following Paul's directives, had already begun the work of organizing such a collection while he was in Corinth. *charin:* "Gracious work" (cf. vv. 1 and 4). **7.** *you abound... in your love for us:* Cf. 7:8–13; their love was shown in their way of reacting to Paul's earlier letter, which had made them aware of their love. Here the Apostle continues his appeal by mentioning the Corinthians' spiritual resources; the others mentioned here were highly prized in that community (cf. 1 Cor 1:5; 12:8–9). *in this work of charity: Chariti* here refers to the sustained act of giving to others.

28 **8.** *not as a command do I say this:* This softens the imperative of v. 7; Paul feared that he might seem overbearing. *to prove once more by your diligence for others:* The ptc. *dokimazōn* indicates purpose (Spicq, KL, RSV). Some take *heterōn spoudēs* as meaning "by means of others' diligence," referring the phrase to the example of the Macedonians; this does not seem natural. Rather, the solicitude the Corinthians will show for the Jerusalem church will prove their love. **9.** *you know the favor of Our Lord:* The favor (*charis*) is the life of Jesus lived for them on this earth from his birth to his ascension and continued for them now (Heb); the emphasis is on the period of his earthly existence. *although rich, he impoverished himself that you might be enriched:* Paul speaks briefly of the manner and the meaning of the redemption (cf. Phil 2:5–11). As Son, Jesus was rich, being equal to the Father, possessing the fullness of the godhead (Col 2:9); however, he took to himself a human nature—becoming thereby a part of this world of weakness and death—so that the Corinthians and others who believe in him might be made rich with riches that surpass all earthly riches. This verse suggests that in the Church's primitive catechesis the story of the life of Jesus, at least its general outline, was given. Paul appeals to the profound truths of faith in what is a matter of secondary importance, the taking up of a collection. As a manifestation of Christian charity it was not unimportant; its motivation was to make concrete the union existing among Christians. **10.** *I give a counsel in this:* A reference to v. 8. *not only to do but to desire:* The Corinthians had started to take up the collection before the Macedonians did; moreover, they began that work quite willingly. Thus the charity of the Corinthians had first served as example to the Macedonians. Nothing arouses generosity more than to suppose its presence in those whose generosity is desired. **11.** *finish it:* Having softened the previous imperative (v. 7), Paul can now return to this manner of speaking. Whereas the Macedonians are rhetorically said to have impoverished themselves (v. 3), the Apostle asks the Corinthians to be generous in accord with their possibilities. **12.** *if promptness is there:* One is judged only according to his capabilities. **13.** *not that others should have relief, while you have a burden:* In Greek the statement is laconic. Paul does not want the Corinthians alone to shoulder a burden that should be borne by all. *as a matter of equality: Ex isotētos* stands in an ambiguous position. Though most consider it a part of v. 13, placing it with v. 14 seems to give a better meaning, since nothing has to be supplied to complete the sense. **14.** *at the present time your abundance should be for the needs of others:* No one is bound to assist others to such a degree that their condition becomes better than that of the donor; however, equity demands that those who have more help those who have less so that a measure of equality is established, provided that those who have less are in true want. The "abundance" of the Jerusalem community refers to the spiritual gifts they bestow on the rest of the Church; a few commentators would explain it as referring to possible future material goods that would be given in succor to the Corinthians in some future need. This opinion seems impossible grammatically, for the verb of the purpose clause is an aor. subjunctive, hence conceptually at least, a single action; and there is no compelling reason for stating that the reality underlying the concept is broader here. Moreover, is Paul not proposing the highest possible motive in v. 9? He does not seem to have changed his attitude here. **15.** Paul quotes Ex 16:18 (LXX). The OT passage refers to the collecting of manna during the Israelites' journey through the desert. As God did not allow anyone during that phase of the Exodus to have too much or too little, so the Corinthians should not allow a condition of gross inequality to exist. By citing a portion of a passage, Paul intends his readers to remember the context from which it comes; in the present case at least, Ex 16:17 must be understood.

29 **(B) Recommendation of His Representatives (8:16–9:5).** **16.** *thanks be to God:* The good sentiments presently in Titus' heart for the Corinthians come from God, the ultimate author of all good. **17.** *being more eager:* Titus' desire to go to the Corinthians was greater than any care on his part to accept Paul's exhortation. *of his own accord: Authairetos* does not cause any difficulty with regard to Paul's statement that he had exhorted Titus to go; Titus acts in a manner that had made Paul's speech unnecessary. *he went to you:* This seems to indicate that Titus had already departed with his two companions; if so, 2 Cor would probably have reached Corinth after their arrival and would serve to reinforce their presence. But the aorist may be epistolary, meaning Titus and his friends were the bearers of the letter to Corinth (cf. 13:12). **18.** *the brother famous in all the churches:* This man had helped Paul preach the gospel; this he had done well. Who he was is not known. Since Origen, he has been identified as Luke; if so, there is no allusion to his literary work here, for that almost certainly was written at a later date. **19.** *appointed by the churches:* Under what circumstances this appointment was made we do not know. Elsewhere it is patent that the early churches were not organized according to the model of Gk city-states. What is curious is that Paul does not name this man; the same is to be said regarding the other emissary (v. 22). **20.** *lest anyone blame us:* The Apostle is circumspect with regard to handling the collection because he is aware that those who administer funds derived from the alms of others can be suspected of mismanagement or worse. Perhaps this gives a clue to the reason for the appointment of the other men by the churches: to audit the records. Paul wanted the communities to assign their own representatives so that the members of those churches would not suspect him of malfeasance. From 12:16–18 it is evident that his enemies did cast aspersions on Paul's probity and on that of two of these men in monetary matters. **21.** Paul alludes to Prv 3:4 (LXX); cf. Rom 12:17. A moral leader must have a good reputation to be able to work effectively. **22.** *our brother:* His identity is unknown (cf. v. 19). **23.** *apostles of the churches, the glory of Christ:* These men who have been approved and sent forth by their respective churches are Christ's glory, because they bring glory to him by their character and mission. **24.** *give proof before all the churches of your love and our boasting about you to them:* The charity of the Corinthians and Paul's boasting are identified; in Greek the sing. article is used only once (*tēs agapēs... kauchēseōs*). By showing their charity to Titus and his companions, they show it to the churches from which these men came; at the same time they give honor to Paul.

Paul wanted the Corinthians to contribute to the collection, but it is impossible to determine from these verses what the moral obligation incumbent upon the Corinthians was. Did he intend to impose an obligation gently or did he want to give counsel strongly? All that can be deduced from this passage is that it is desirable for Christians to contribute to their brothers who are in need.

30 **9:1.** → 2 above. *for:* The conjunction shows a close connection with what precedes. *superfluous for me to write:* Much of what follows repeats the content of ch. 8: This does not indicate that these chapters were not part of the same letter, for it is a common practice of preachers and petitioners to repeat themselves. Just as the preacher can, so Paul uses many devices in the same context: flattery, exhortation, appeals to honor; a multiple motivation is proposed. **4.** *be put to shame:* A delicate touch. By ostensibly turning the possible insult against himself, the Apostle urges them to be generous, while making it clear that in reality they are the ones who would be disgraced the more. **5.** *as a blessing and not as what is grudgingly granted: Pleonexia* is difficult to translate; lit., it means "greed," but it must be understood here as a "gift grudgingly given" (AG 673). Thus their gift should be large and not small; by being sizable it will be a blessing for the Corinthians, for the largess will bring God's grace on them.

31 **(C) The Rewards of Generosity (9:6–15).** **6.** *this then:* An elliptical expression that must be filled out with something like "is said." The elliptical expression presumes a common understanding of mind and heart between the writer and recipients of the letter (cf. Bl-Deb-F § 481). **7.** *God loves a cheerful giver:* A rather free citation of Prv 22:8 (LXX) that is lacking in the MT; cf. Dt 15:10; Rom 12:8. The idea that one should give willingly was not without support among pagans. **8.** *grace:* Every good thing that comes from God. A person should not fear that his generosity will impoverish him. **9.** Paul quotes Ps 112:9 (LXX). *his justice: Dikaiosynē* (righteousness) can mean "almsgiving"; however, when Hebr *ṣ^{e}dāqāh* is so understood, the LXX generally renders it *eleēmosynē*. Moreover, in Ps 112:3 "justice" means that which comes from moral virtue; such must be the meaning here. **10.** *provides seed...:* The description of God is taken from Is 55:10. *fruits of justice:* The word *genēmata* is found only here in Paul; it is the technical term for the produce of fields, vines, and trees. The Corinthians should have confidence therefore in God (cf. Mt 6:25–34). **11.** *generosity which produces through us thanksgiving to God:* This generosity on their part will increase and cause Paul to thank God, the source of all good, who gives them the power to be charitable and who will reward them. **12.** *the administration of this service:* In Jewish and Christian literature "service" (*leitourgia*) always connotes an action that is public and religious; the Corinthians would worship God by being generous. *is abounding through thanksgiving:* The generosity of the Corinthians will move the Jerusalem church to thank God for the gifts coming to them from Achaia. Again it is brought out that the ultimate source of all good is God. **13.** Obedience and generosity are here identified; their obedience consists precisely in their being generous. This is shown in the Greek, where *epi* appears but once. The Corinthians will thus show their awareness of what the gospel and its service entail: The internal unity existing among Christians must be manifested externally by good works. **14.** *they long for you:* Yearning to be with the other party is a sign of love; here that love is religious, motivated by the manifestation of God's grace among the Corinthians and their correspondence to it. **15.** *unspeakable gift:* The generosity of the Corinthians and the resultant attitude of the Jerusalem community is an outward sign of the unity of the Church; this unity in the Spirit is so great a reality that its meaning cannot be fully explained in human language. Moreover, this unity and all that it implies is a gift from God.

That the collection was successfully made appears from Rom 15:25–27.

32 (IV) Part III: Paul Confronts His Adversaries and Those Who Receive Them (10:1–13:10). The first seven chapters were a defense of Paul's ministry; in chs. 8–9 there were some words of self-defense against possible opponents. Now the Apostle turns against his opponents directly. Although this may seem strange coming immediately after an appeal for funds (see comment on 7:16), it is really not so; for the collection to be a success he must remove all doubts instilled in the minds of the Corinthians concerning its principal promoter, himself, and his agents.

33 (A) Paul Is Not Weak: He Glories in God (10:1–18). **1.** *I myself Paul:* This change from the plural to the first person singular shows that the Apostle is concerned about defending himself against the personal allegations made against him. Contrasted to the plural usage that preceded, it gives added emphasis to what is to be stated, for the author is more personally involved in the verbal counterattack. Except in final greetings, the use of the expression *egō Paulos* is rare in his writings (cf. Gal 5:2; Eph 3:1; Phlm 19). *by the meekness and gentleness of Christ:* Paul wants them to remember these qualities of Jesus. This phrase suggests that Paul had described the moral picture of Jesus to the Corinthians (cf. 8:9). About these qualities the Apostle himself had to be instructed by others; this is another indication of the content of the primitive catechesis. Paul wished to be able to exemplify personally such qualities when he would be once more among the Corinthians. (Cf. R. Leivestad, *NTS* 12 [1965–66] 156–64.) *I who am so humble...:* This is a charge made by Paul's adversaries that he repeats sarcastically. **2.** *us as walking according to the flesh:* That is, according to natural sentiments arising from the weakness of human nature. Paul slips back into the plural of authorship, which was more natural to him when composing. **3–6.** Here we find a skillful and somewhat sarcastic expression of the Apostle's thoughts. Paul may be physically weak, a poor specimen of a man as it were, but his means of combat are not those of a weak man or of weak human nature. **4.** *the arms of our warfare: Hopla tēs strateias hēmōn.* Others prefer the variant *stratias,* "expedition" in a military sense: "arms of our expedition." Paul likes to use metaphors based on soldiering (see comment on 6:7). The preaching of the gospel is a warfare (cf. 1 Tm 1:18). *strongholds:* Anything opposed to God and his ways can be called an opposition "stronghold." *knowledge of God:* That is, a belief in and service of God, in accordance with the Hebr concept of knowing. The things that follow do not exhaust the list of what is opposed to God; to them Paul opposes those that "are powerful for the cause of God" (*dynata tō theō*). **5.** *arguments:* Cf. Rom 2:15; these are the fallacious arguments raised up against the teaching of the Apostle, whether they are expressed publicly or not. *taking captive every mind:* The term *noēma* is also found in 2 Cor 2:11; 3:14; 4:4; 11:3; elsewhere in the NT only in Phil 4:7. Here it means "mind," the seat of thought; it refers to the minds of those who think rightly. They are taken captive because they bow to a higher power, to God. (For what human minds did when they refused to bow to the natural light given to them by God, cf. Rom 1:18–27.) *in obedience to Christ:* Faith requires that we submit our wills to the wishes of Christ. **6.** *hold ourselves in readiness: En hetoimō echontes* is a Latinism, *in promptu habere;* it is found in other Gk authors of the epoch. *to punish all disobedience:* Although a good part of the community practiced obedience (cf. 2:9; 7:15), their practice was still not strong enough to allow the Apostle to act with all vigor against those who attacked him; this is actually a backhanded compliment for the Corinthians, who had not of themselves acted with due energy against them.

34 **7.** *what is before your eyes:* The evidence is there, and the Corinthians should take heed of it. *if anyone believes he is Christ's:* An evident statement of the claim made by some of the false teachers. Does this indicate that "the party of Christ" mentioned in 1 Cor 1:12 was a group of troublemakers? *as he is Christ's, so are we:* Sarcasm. Paul truly belongs to Christ; his opponent should too. **8.** *if I should boast a little too much:* For the sake of argument Paul accepts as possible the claim that he is overly boastful; later he will rightfully boast at some length (11:1–12:13). *which the Lord gave for building you up and not for tearing you down:* The power that Paul had came from Christ; this is a statement of fact. The direct purpose of this power was the salvation of the Corinthians and others; the power will, however, cause damnation for those who do not accept its meaning for them. The same idea is found in 13:10; cf. also 2:15–16. *I shall not be ashamed:* The Apostle knows that he is correct. **9–11.** Here Paul returns to the charge against him mentioned in v. 1. If necessary, he could, even if not the most eloquent preacher (cf. 1 Cor 2:1–4), speak sternly when present among them. Let his adversaries know, therefore, that he will not be as meek as a lamb upon his arrival in Corinth if necessity dictates otherwise. *in word... in act:* Perhaps both refer to words, the former to the written word and the latter to the spoken. Paul, who had faced imprisonment, beatings, stoning, and angry mobs (cf. vv. 23b–27; 6:5), was not going to be afraid of any member of the Corinthian church upon his arrival there. **12.** Heavy sarcasm. His detractors, in their ignorance of the meaning of the gospel, judge themselves according to their own standards, but do not understand (*ou syniasin*). **13.** The standard of comparison Paul uses for justifying whatever boasting he does is the measure that God has made known to him. *to reach you:* This expresses the fact that Paul is one of God's instruments. God made known to Paul the standard by which one could judge if someone truly pertained to Christ; this standard Paul had to make known to the Corinthians (cf. Gal 1:8). **14.** *we were the first to come with the gospel:* Paul has every right to write to the Corinthians, since he was the first to evangelize them. He continues to be sarcastic; for his adversaries, even though living among the Corinthians, overreach themselves, not knowing the meaning of the gospel. **15.** *boast beyond measure in the works of others:* Paul is considering only what he himself has accomplished when he boasts; he does not take credit for the work of others, such as that of Apollos (1 Cor 3:5–9). For Paul's own circumspection in treating with a church in which he had not preached, cf. Rom 1:8–17; 15:20. It seems implicit in this statement that the false teachers were claiming as their own accomplishments things done by others, possibly by Paul himself, and also taking advantage of the vestiges of the factionalism that had existed in the Corinthian church (1 Cor 1:12–17). **15–16.** *and not to boast according to the standards of others for things already done:* Paul's standard of judgment is the realization that he is but an instrument in God's hands. He wishes to be held in esteem among the Corinthians because they will thus show their awareness of the worth of a true teacher. Moreover, their esteem for him will facilitate his work of spreading the gospel, for others will be influenced by the Corinthians whose judgment they respect. The Corinthians will have proper esteem for Paul by accepting the implications of the faith that they received through Paul's labors among them. He does not wish to be considered an equal of any false teacher and thus have a cause for boasting according to such an incorrect standard. Here the Apostle does express a measure of confidence in the Corinthians.

Others translate, and consequently comment upon, this verse in various ways. V. Jacono renders v. 16: "That is to announce the gospel beyond you, to boast not in someone else's field, in [land] already prepared" (brackets his). Similar is E.-B. Allo's interpretation. Yet different translations can be found in the WV, RSV, NEB, KL, and Vg. The principal difficulty is the meaning of *kanōn*, "standard"; almost as difficult is the proper understanding of *hetoimos*, "ready, prepared."

35 **17–18.** Paul freely cites Jer 9:22–23 according to the LXX, which gives it the sense of the MT. Whatever cause one has for boasting, it comes from God. Such a cause can only be present when a man's works are worthy of divine commendation. Once again Paul emphasizes two truths: God alone moves a man to do good; only what is good is worthy of praise. The first of these is the unifying thought found throughout 2 Cor. Implicitly the Apostle states that his adversaries have neither cause for boasting nor approval from God.

36 **(B) Paul Praises Himself to Defend His Apostolate (11:1–12:13).** In this section the Apostle will speak in even greater detail of himself than he did in 6:1–11, so important does he consider his defense of himself for the good of the Corinthian church and the success of the collection. **1.** *foolishness:* He is about to make known what he has accomplished; this apparent commendation of himself he calls *aphrosynē*, "a lack of common sense," because self-commendation is worth nothing. However, he knows not only that he has true cause for boasting, but also that God commends him because his is God's work, as he has just stated (10:17–18). *put up with me:* Another nice touch, which like vv. 16–18, 21 (but only to a slight degree), and 23, softens by anticipation what is going to be extremely sarcastic (cf. Bl-Deb-F § 495). The Corinthians heed the false teachers but will not give Paul a hearing. Paul knows that the Corinthians will listen to his boasting. **2.** *with the jealousy of God:* The Apostle shares the divine sentiments (*zelō*) regarding the Corinthians and all other Christians; he does not want them to be shared by others, that is, by those who are opposed to God. The idea of God's love as a burning ardor demanding an exclusive love in return is a commonplace in the OT (cf. S. Lyonnet, *De Peccato et Redemptione* 1 [Rome, 1957] 46–50). *I betrothed you to one husband to present you as a chaste virgin to Christ:* The one husband and Christ are the same person. The relationship of the Jewish people and Yahweh in the OT is now predicated of the NT faithful and Christ. The love that existed between the Israelites and God is presented under the figure of an engagement or marriage in Hos 2:21; Is 54:5–6; 62:5; Jer 3:1; Ez 16:6–43. Christ is called the bridegroom of the Church in Eph 5:27–32; Ap 21:9; 22:17. His bride, the Church, should be without stain (Eph 5:27). As betrothal to Christ means that the Church's relation to him is exclusive, so should the relation of its members be. That Paul was father of the Corinthian church is seen in his betrothing it to Christ; in that epoch a father arranged the marriage of his daughter. **3.** The Apostle fears that the Corinthians will allow themselves to be led into sin and thus will not be the chaste virgin bride. He recalls the temptation of Eve (Gn 3:1–7), lest they, like her and Adam, lose the simplicity and innocence proper to those who stand in a special relation to God. This passage shows that the early Christians were instructed in the content of the OT even though they were members of a predominantly Gentile community such as Corinth. **4.** *preaches another Jesus:* Not another historic personage, but one who differs doctrinally from him whom Paul preached. *another spirit:* Other than the spirit of Christ (Rom 9:2; Gal 4:6). *another gospel:* An announcement of messianic good news at essential variance with Paul's preaching; such a gospel would not be a gospel (cf. Gal 1:8). *you tolerate him indeed:* Sarcasm. Paul knows full well that someone cannot be in radical disagreement with him and preach truthfully, and he knows that the only true spirit the Corinthians can receive is the Holy Spirit. **5.** *superapostles:* This can refer to true apostles such as Peter and James, not because they were in opposition to Paul but because they were presented as such by the false teachers, or to the false teachers themselves. According to some commentators the reference is to true apostles, because of vv. 22–23 and 12:11; but from v. 15 one might think that the false teachers are meant. The other apostles were apostles before Paul, who was as it were "a miscarriage" (*ektrōma*, 1 Cor 15:8), because he alone of the apostles had persecuted the Church. This consideration makes them superior to Paul. *I am not inferior:* Paul has done as much as, indeed more than, the other apostles to further the work of Christ (cf. 1 Cor 15:9–10). This is a great boast on Paul's part, but a true one. **6.** *inexpert in speech:* A reference to Paul's relative lack of skill as a preacher; actually, he used his own method of preaching by design after the lack of success he had at Athens, where he had employed a more artful delivery. This had taken place immediately before his arrival in Corinth for the first time (see 1 Cor 2:3–5, to be compared with Acts 17:21–32). Nevertheless, Paul did not have the rhetorical skill of some of the true preachers for Christ, as for example, Apollos. *in knowledge:* Paul is not the inferior of anyone in knowing the content of the true gospel. *manifesting it in every way for you:* He had used every means at his command to preach Jesus and his gospel to the Corinthians.

37 **7.** *did I make a mistake:* Here seemingly *hamartia* refers not to a moral fault but to an "error"; Paul resumes his sarcasm, asking if his mistake was in not demanding payment from them for his teaching. Others (e.g., WV, RSV) understand *hamartia* to mean "sin" here; according to this interpretation, the sarcasm is not only present but is even greater. *that you be exalted:* According to his detractors, Paul had shown himself unworthy of any attention or payment, because all true teachers expected recompense for their efforts. Others perhaps blamed him for allowing by his manner of acting that such a charge be made against him; according to these men, Paul had not taken sufficient care of his reputation when he had not demanded payment for his preaching. The Apostle's purpose in so comporting himself was to lift the Corinthians from the mire of sin. **8.** *I pillaged other churches, taking pay:* Here are found two military figures dear to Paul. *Opsōnion* is "a soldier's pay." The strong vb. *esylēsa*, "I plundered," is intended to show the Corinthians that they are indebted to him; from others he had taken much, indeed too much, but from the Corinthians nothing. While humiliating the Corinthians, his statement gives the lie to the charge that he was not a real teacher because he had not accepted any recompense. **9.** *Macedonia supplied my needs:* Cf. Phil 4:10–15; Acts 18:5. *keep myself from being a bother to you:* He continues to humiliate the Corinthians; he allowed the Macedonians to help him, but it is and will be another matter when it comes to the Corinthians. **10.** *by the truth of Christ which is in me: Estin alētheia Christou en emoi* is an introductory formula for an oath. *boasting:* his refusal to accept help from the Corinthians. **11.** No matter what his opponents may say, Paul indeed loves the Corinthians. But he cannot allow his enemies to say that he preached only to receive compensation. His answer echoes another of the charges made by his foes.

38 **12.** Paul will not allow his enemies to claim

that he is like them. The verse is sarcastic. **13.** *false apostles:* These men are perhaps distinct from the superapostles of v. 5, for the teachers of falsehood are in Corinth; they are fraudulent workmen trying to pass themselves off as true apostles of Christ. **14.** *Satan... angel of light:* No OT text describes the devil under this guise, nor has any other explicit parallel of the description yet been found; however, cf. CD 5:18; 1QS 3:20,24. **15.** Paul levels a terrible accusation against those who oppose him: They claim to be ministers of Christ, but in reality they are ministers of the devil. *their end shall be according to their deeds:* They will be condemned by Christ if they persist in their ways; thus they will receive not good but evil (5:10; cf. 1 Cor 3:17).

39 **16.** Returning to the theme of v. 1, his foolishness, Paul begs a hearing from the Corinthians. His boasting in great part will consist in his recalling to them his sufferings for the service of Christ. **17–18.** *I do not speak according to the Lord but as it were in foolishness:* Paul does not relish boasting about himself, but he must do so in order to combat the false teachers; thus he must imitate those who boast "according to the flesh," i.e., "in a worldly manner." **19.** Here Paul is extremely sarcastic: Sensible Corinthians willingly put up with those who are foolish. They have paid heed to false teachers who are truly foolish; let them give some attention to Paul, who now imitates his foolish foes in their boasting (cf. 1 Cor 4:8–10). **20.** The sarcasm continues: They honor those who unlike Paul mistreat and maltreat them. *makes you slaves:* The Judaizers attempt to make everyone observe at least part of the Mosaic Law, though it is apparently not a case here of their imposing circumcision, as it was in Galatia. This accusation must have been especially forceful in a community where some members were freed slaves or descendants of such. *devours:* Probably a reference to the rapacity characteristic of a false teacher. *slaps:* In this way the Corinthians were reduced to silence; they were treated as slaves or young children. This is probably to be understood literally. **21.** *as though we were weak in this regard:* The strong sarcasm is softened by *hōs* (as though), which suggests that what follows is an assertion of his opponents. Paul uses the pf. *ēsthenēkamen*, "we have shown weakness." He did not treat them with harshness and disdain; the results of this continue until the time of writing, for the Apostle is not honored by the Corinthians. If this mode of action was weakness, then let them make the most of it.

40 **21b.** It is made clear that the false teachers are Judaizers, for it is they who make Paul refer to his Judaic background. There seems to be a gradation in the terms, "Hebrews," "Israelites," "seed of Abraham." Paul is a Hebrew, a son of Hebrews (Phil 3:5), because he was born of Jewish parents; he is an Israelite (see comment on Rom 9:4), because he had followed faithfully the precepts of the Jewish religion according to the strict sect of the Pharisees (Acts 22:3; 26:13); he is of the seed of Abraham, because he participated from birth in the divine promises made to the patriarch. If the reference is to the true apostles, Paul is describing them as they were presented by the false teachers and is showing that he does not differ from the other apostles in this regard; if the reference is to his opponents, then he is showing that he is as much a Jew as they, with at least as much right to speak as they. The key to the correct interpretation is to be found in "I speak as one insane." If it goes with the statement, "they are ministers of Christ," Paul is then referring to the false teachers, who are anything but ministers of Christ. They are ministers of Satan (v. 15). If the self-depreciation goes with "I am still more," Paul is contrasting himself to the true apostles, for he is a minister of Christ even more than they, inasmuch as he has done more in the service of the gospel (cf. v. 5). Unfortunately, the position of the clause is such that it can be drawn to either statement. Most likely, the superapostles were other apostles (see comment on 11:13). **23.** *in prison more often:* Up to this point in his life we know with certainty only of his Philippian imprisonment, and that it was of very short duration (Acts 16:22–23); perhaps there is mention of another in 1 Cor 13:32. *forty minus one:* According to Dt 25:1–3, a man could receive no more than 40 blows when whipped; later custom decreed that no more than 39 be given, lest perchance more than 40 be applied. We do not know when these beatings were administered; however, the synagogues in the Diaspora had according to custom the power to punish Jewish troublemakers by whipping. *three times did I pass through the rods:* This was a punishment inflicted by Roman authorities. We know of only one instance of this, at Philippi (Acts 16:23). *once I was stoned:* At Lystra (Acts 14:19). *three times I was shipwrecked:* Of these events we know nothing, though we know that Paul made many sea voyages (cf. Acts 13:4,13; 14:26; 16:11; 18:18–22; 20:2). *I passed a day and a night in the deep:* When this happened we do not know. It is possible that at the time of writing, the memory of this peril still affected Paul deeply (hence his use of the pf. tense; see J. Moulton, *A Grammar of NT Greek* [3rd ed.; Edinburgh, 1908] 144). **26.** Dangers to travelers from highwaymen and other brigands were common in Paul's time. *dangers from my race:* Cf. Acts 11:23; 13:50; 14:2–5,18–20; 17:5; 18:11 (in Corinth); 1 Thes 2:14–15. *dangers in the city:* In addition to dangers that came to Paul from the Jews in various cities, see Acts 16:14–23; 19:23–20:1. *dangers among false brothers:* Cf. Acts 15:1–3; Gal 2:4. By placing this one last, Paul shows how much suffering this type of trial caused him; the efforts of those who taught what was opposed to the true gospel of Christ were intended to make the death of Christ meaningless. This is what he was faced with from the false teachers at Corinth. **27.** *in hunger:* Use of *en limō* here shows that in 6:5 *en nēsteiais* means "in fasting" and refers to penitential acts. **28.** The daily trials of caring for the churches were without end; being truly conscientious, Paul could find no rest from these, as this letter witnesses, being sent to the Corinthians from another church. He had to watch over not only those whom he was temporarily with, but all his churches. **29.** *who is scandalized and I am not indignant:* True Christian charity demands that one be righteously angry at what causes others to fall; cf. Mt 23. *Pyromai* can mean that the Apostle suffers as though being burnt alive when members of the Church are led into sin.

41 **30.** *I will glory:* Paul has boasted not of the great works that he performed but of his sufferings and his affective union with the other members of the Church. If boast he must, he will continue to boast of these aspects of his life. The sarcasm recurs: let his opponents show what proves their care for the Corinthians. **31.** *the God and the Father of the Lord Jesus:* See comment on 1:3. *may he be blessed forever:* This phrase, of Jewish origin, expresses a pious desire (so Spicq, Osty, NEB); compare the indicative formula using with *estin* in Rom 1:15. As Spicq observes, it was psychologically necessary for Paul to proclaim solemnly here that he had told the truth. **32–33.** The episode recalled here is narrated in Acts 9:23–25, where it is stated that the Jews of Damascus were responsible for this action against Paul; obviously there is no contradiction. It is most likely that this event took place in AD 40, for Aretas IV, king of Nabatea, did not assume rule over Damascus until at least 37 (→ Life of Paul, 46:21; cf. Gal 1:17–18; Acts 9:23–26).

42 **12:1.** *one must boast about oneself:* Paul realizes that he must describe some of the divine favors accorded him; he adds, with a fine touch of humor, that this boasting does not bring any particular good to him. **2.** *I know a man in Christ:* Paul cannot refrain from mentioning a special experience once accorded him. However, his humility forces him to speak of it as if it had happened to another Christian. *fourteen years ago:* We do not know where this occurred (→ Life of Paul, 46:22). *whether in the body I do not know, whether out of the body I do not know:* Those who have had mystical experiences often find them difficult to describe; it is said that such is true of any type of ecstasy. There seems to be no reason for attempting to derive from this statement any of the notions Paul may have had about the relationship of the body to the soul. *third heaven:* Identified with Paradise (v. 4). The first heaven was our earth's atmosphere; the second, the region of the stars; the third, the place where God dwells and is seen as he truly is (cf. *T. Levi* 2–3; *APOT* 2, 304–6; *ThWNT* 5, 535). According to another Jewish tradition there were seven heavens (*2 Enoch* 8; *APOT* 2, 433–34). What the Apostle is saying here is that he was made to enter into very close contact with the deity, and this overwhelmed him. **3.** The repetition of his ignorance of the actual state of his soul at the time of the experience emphasizes the extraordinary character of the event. His whole consciousness was enraptured. **4.** *ineffable words which man is not permitted to speak: Arrēta rēmata* was the technical expression in the language of the Gk mystery cults for formularies and teaching that were not to be revealed to the noninitiated. However, Paul rather finds here that his vocabulary fails him; in this sense he cannot speak. For this experience, cf. A. Wikenhauser, *Pauline Mysticism* (N.Y., 1960) 218–20; Thomas Aquinas, *Super Secundam ad Corinthios*, cap. 12, lect. 1–2. **5.** *of this man will I boast:* The vision that Paul had was in no way his own doing; he could boast of the one who experienced it because the event manifested God's power, but he must speak of it as having happened to another, for he did not have even the power of refusing. **6.** *if I wish to boast, I shall not be foolish for I shall speak the truth:* Lest his enemies think that he has no grounds for boasting, he wants them to know that he truly has such; however, he will not mention them lest anyone have too exalted an idea of his own person. There is still at least a hint of sarcasm. **7a.** *by the greatness of the revelation:* This phrase can be attached to "lest it be reckoned to me" of v. 6, or by anacoluthon to "lest I be elated" of v. 7. The latter is harsh if *dio* (therefore) is retained. It is lacking, however, in many mss., including P46, D, E, K, L, P, Vg, and Pesh; it is found in A, B, F, G, and S, and read by Merk, Nestle, Bover, Allo, Spicq, and Plummer. **7b–9.** *thorn in my flesh, an angel of Satan:* This affliction was relatively permanent, as the pres. subjunctive of the verbs suggests. It is possible, however, that when Paul wrote 2 Cor, the affliction was no longer with him. Three general interpretations of the nature of this affliction have been given: persecution, disease, and concupiscence (cf. H. Pope, *IrTQ* 10 [1915] 418–35). The last of these seems necessarily excluded, for concupiscence is something that afflicts everyone to some degree. Moreover, it is difficult to conceive that Paul had not earlier been bothered by such inclinations more or less habitually. As for the general nature of this affliction, modern exegetical opinion generally opts for some physical malady. It is called "an angel of Satan" either because the devil was regarded as responsible for sin (cf. Gn 3:1–4), and to him the cause of physical disease was attributed (cf. Lk 13:16), or because those who are called Satan's sons attempt to pervert others (cf. 2 Cor 11:15; Acts 13:10). **8.** *three times:* That is, either many times or the exact arithmetical number (cf. Mk 14:35 regarding the number of times Jesus prayed in Gethsemane). *I prayed to the Lord:* The prayer was addressed to Jesus; the aorist suggests that Paul was no longer praying for this intention. *he said:* The pf. tense of the verb suggests that the statement still affects Paul's way of acting. *my grace is sufficient for you:* As an answer to his prayer the Apostle obtains not the removal of the affliction but the promise of the continuation of Christ's grace, which is all that is essential for him and all that he truly needs. *power is perfected in infirmity:* The more a man is weak, the more the divine power is made manifest when it works through him (cf. 1 Cor 1:25). **10.** *therefore I am content:* The certainty of God's favor and assistance satisfies Paul. For the various afflictions and trials, cf. 11:23b–29; 6:4–7. These are all borne "for the sake of Christ," that is, for the spread of his Church. *whenever I am weak, then am I strong:* The power of God is more evident when the instrument through which that power is exercised is naturally weak. The conscious instrument, realizing his own debility and seeing results from his efforts, knows that these are accomplished not by himself alone, but by God's power working through him (cf. 1 Cor 1:27; Phil 4:13).

43 **11.** *you compelled me:* The needs of the Corinthians forced the Apostle to write about himself. *commended by you:* Instead of doubting him or allowing themselves to be misled by false teachers, the Corinthians should have taken Paul's part against them; indeed, they should have been lauding him before there was need for such a defense. *the superapostles:* See comments on 11:5,22. *I am nothing:* A favorite theme of Paul's (cf. 1 Cor 3:1–7,12). **12.** *signs of an apostle:* Paul's adversaries seem to have denied that he performed marvelous works. The "signs" were promised to the apostles as a power of their ministry (cf. Jn 14:12; Mk 16:17). *in all steadfastness:* Most scholars translate *en pasē hypomonē* "in all patience," but in the present context this does not seem to make sense. *signs: Semeia* demonstrate the divine revelation. *wonders: Terata* arouse admiration. *powers: Dynameis* show that God is intervening. This brief mention of the works shows that the Apostle had performed some such prodigies in Corinth (cf. K. Gatzweiler, *ETL* 37 [1961] 831–34). **13.** The sarcasm returns and it is biting.

44 **(C) Announcement of His Coming Visit (12:14–13:10).** **14.** *third time* (→ 4 above; → Life of Paul, 46:36). Two visits to Corinth are mentioned by Luke; the first is the one made at the time of the foundation of the Corinthian church (Acts 18:1); the second (Acts 20:2–3) must be identified with the one mentioned here as proximate. This verse of 2 Cor seems to imply that another visit occurred between these two. **14b–15.** As good parents try to obtain good things for their children, so Paul tries to obtain what his spiritual children, the members of the Corinthian church, truly need. For their salvation he would willingly give everything: He who loves them so much should be loved by them. There is poignancy in the Apostle's question, for their answer to it must be "no" if their previous attitude is any indication of their true sentiments. Paul writes here as a preacher; the number of those adversely affected by the false teachers was not necessarily great (cf. 7:4–7). **16.** *but be it so:* Paul has rebutted the arguments of his adversaries up to now; yet there remains still another accusation, namely that Paul, who did not take money from them personally, has obtained it by fraud through his agent, Titus, or someone else. His enemies must have accused him of getting money under the pretext that it was for the Jerusalem community. **18.** *the brother:* Again it seems strange that he is not identified more explicitly. Since only one companion is mentioned with Titus, some commentators wish to cut off chs. 10–13 from the rest of 2 Cor, claiming that they formed part of a separate letter. However, in 8:18 the first companion is called "the brother" as here; the second companion is referred to as "our brother" in 8:22. Moreover, the introduction given in ch. 8 to the two companions and the praise given to Titus have no counterpart here. If, therefore, chs. 10–13 formed part of a separate letter, they would seem to be from a later letter than chs. 1–9. Although a case can be made for this, it would be difficult to find a period in Paul's life when it could have been written unless immediately after chs. 1–9. *did Titus defraud you of anything?:* That is, during his first visit to Corinth as Paul's agent (cf. 7:6–7). *did we not walk in the same spirit?:* Titus followed Paul's example in not taking anything for himself from the Corinthians, even though he set up the organization for the collection (cf. 8:6).

45 **19.** The main purpose of Paul's writing as he does is not to present a defense of himself but to strengthen the Corinthians, the objects of his loving concern. **20–22.** Paul did not wish to appear before them as a severe judge (cf. 1:23–24). *strife, jealousies...:* These vices would show Paul that the Corinthians were "not as he wishes." **21.** *God would humiliate me and I would mourn over many:* The humiliation and the sorrow would be different aspects of the same thing; a father mourns over a child's immoral conduct and is humiliated by the child's actions. The causality of this humbling is attributed to God, for it would have resulted from Paul's not doing all that he could possibly have done to bring the Corinthians to the right course. *the uncleanness, fornication and licentiousness which they practiced: Akatharsia* is a general term for "sexual impurity"; *porneia* is used in its specific Gk sense, "fornication"; *aselgeia* is willful defiance of public propriety in sexual matters. The shift from the second to the third person evidently shows that a more restricted group among the Corinthians was still affected by the remnants of pagan moral laxity. That such persons existed earlier in the Corinthian community seems evident from 1 Cor 6:12–20, where only *porneia* is mentioned.

46 **13:1.** *third time:* See comment on 12:14. Paul quotes Dt 19:15. According to Mosaic Law, one witness did not suffice to sustain a case at law; two or three were needed. Paul will not condemn anyone hastily but will proceed properly in making his judgments. **2.** *again:* The adverb can refer either to "I come" or to "I shall not spare." In the latter supposition he had spared the sinners before, perhaps by not going to Corinth. **3.** *since:* If necessary he will give them a proof of his union with Christ (cf. 2:9, 8:2), a proof therefore of his power to act sternly; if this is the proof they want, it will be theirs. **4.** *he was crucified from weakness:* Jesus had a mortal human nature; moreover, he did not use the power that was his before the resurrection (cf. 2 Cor 8:9; Phil 2:5–8). *he lives by the power of God:* Cf. Rom 1:4; 1 Cor 6:14; no human power effected the resurrection. *we are weak in him:* The Apostle participates in both the weakness and the power of Jesus; he will live (note fut. *zēsomen*) by showing forth the power given to him by God when he will judge those who are worthy of condemnation.

47 **5.** The Corinthians should examine themselves to see if their lives manifest vitality in the faith. *that Jesus Christ is in you—unless you are not genuine:* Jesus is in those who believe and who act according to that belief (cf. Gal 2:20; Eph 3:17). When Jesus is said to be in the faithful, it means that there is a communication of divine life to the Christian. It does not mean a physical presence of Jesus in each one's soul (cf. L. Cerfaux, *The Church in the Theology of St. Paul* [N.Y., 1959] 218–22). **6.** *I hope:* Paul knows that he is an apostle; he hopes that the Corinthians will recognize him as such and therefore heed his words. **7.** *not that we may appear as having met the test:* That is, that he will not have to exercise his judicial power. Thus he will not show them close at hand what kind of judge he can be. **8.** If the Corinthians are acting correctly, "according to the truth," Paul will not be able to act against them. **9.** *we rejoice:* Paul wants to "be weak" in the sense of not being able to act as judge; this will be the case if they are "strong" in the faith; for such he prays (cf. 1 Cor 16:13). **10.** *treat sternly:* There is a reminder here of 2:3. *for building up:* Cf. 10:8.

48 **(V) Conclusion: Appeals, Salutations, Blessings (13:11–13).** **11.** *think the same thing:* Be of one mind and heart as those are who are truly in love. *be in peace:* They should live as possessing the fullness of messianic good things. If they live as true Christians, God who gives love and peace will be with them, bestowing more abundantly his love and peace upon them (cf. 1:2). **12.** *with a holy kiss:* See comment on Rom 16:16. *the saints greet you:* The members of the Macedonian churches (cf. 8:4). Generally more persons are associated with Paul in his final greetings than in the words of address (cf. 1 Cor 16:19–20 and 1:1). In the address of the present letter, however, only Timothy is associated with Paul. **13.** This is the richest and most instructive final blessing in the Pauline epistles. Paul explicitly wishes for everything necessary for the Corinthians' salvation. The communication of the Holy Spirit is that which he effects. The triadic distinction of Christ, God, and the Holy Spirit is noteworthy, as is also the collocation of the Spirit with Jesus and the Father, who are clearly persons. The naming of "the Lord Jesus Christ" first is probably due to the familiar blessing used by Paul, "May the blessing of our Lord Jesus Christ be with you" (cf. 1 Cor 16:23; Rom 16:20; Gal 6:18; Phil 4:23; 1 Thes 5:28; 2 Thes 3:18). In 1 Cor 12:4–6 the order is Spirit, Lord, and God.

53

THE LETTER TO THE ROMANS

Joseph A. Fitzmyer, S.J.

BIBLIOGRAPHY

1 Althaus, P., *Der Brief an die Römer* (NTD 6; 9th ed.; Göttingen, 1959). Barrett, C. K., *A Commentary on the Epistle to the Romans* (BNTC; London, 1957). Boylan, P., *St. Paul's Epistle to the Romans* (Dublin, 1934). Cerfaux, L., *Une lecture de l'Épître aux Romains* (Tournai, 1947). Dodd, C. H., *The Epistle of Paul to the Romans* (MNTC; N.Y., 1932). Huby, J., *Épître aux Romains* (rev. ed. S. Lyonnet; VS 10; Paris, 1957). Hunter, A. M., *The Epistle to the Romans* (London, 1955). Jacono, V., *Le Epistole di S. Paolo ai Romani, ai Corinti e ai Galati* (Turin, 1952). Kuss, O., *Der Römerbrief* (Regensburg, 1 [1957], 2 [1959]). Lagrange, M.-J., *Épître aux Romains* (EBib; Paris, 1950). Leenhardt, F., *The Epistle to the Romans* (London, 1961). Lietzmann, H., *An die Römer* (HNT 8; Tübingen, 1928). Lüthi, W., *The Letter to the Romans: An Exposition* (tr. K. Schoenenberger; Edinburgh, 1961). Lyonnet, S., *Épître aux Romains* (BJ; Paris, 1954) 43–132; *Exegesis epistulae ad Romanos* (Rome, 1958, 1961, 1962); *Quaestiones in epistulam ad Romanos* (1a–2a ser. Rome, 1962). Manson, T. W., "Romans," *PCB* 940–53. Michel, O., *Der Brief an die Römer* (Meyer 4; Göttingen, 1957). Murray, J., *The Epistle to the Romans* (NICNT 1; Grand Rapids, 1959). Sanday, W. and A. C. Headlam, *The Epistle to the Romans* (ICC; 5th ed.; Edinburgh 1902). Schelkle, K. H., *Paulus, Lehrer der Väter: Die altkirchliche Auslegung von Römer 1–11* (Düsseldorf, 1956). Schlatter, A., *Gottes Gerechtigkeit* (2nd ed.; Stuttgart, 1952). Schmidt, H. W., *Der Brief des Paulus an die Römer* (ThHK 6; Berlin, 1962). Sickenberger, J., *Die Briefe des hl. Paulus an die Korinther und Römer* (BB 6; 4th ed.; Bonn, 1932). Taylor, V., *The Epistle to the Romans* (London, 1955). Viard, A., *Épître aux Romains* (PSB 11/2; Paris, 1948) 7–159. Zahn, T., *Der Brief an die Römer* (3rd ed.; Leipzig, 1925).

Bonnard, P., "Où en est l'interprétation de l'Épître aux Romains?" *RTP* 1 (1951) 225–43. Cambier, J., R-F, *INT* 447–70. F-B 216–26. Friedrich, G., *RGG* 5, 1137–45. Guthrie, *NTI* 1, 21–45. Metzger, B. M., *IPLAP* 36–58. Rabanos, R., "Boletin bibliográfico de la carta a los Romanos," *Salmanticensis* 6 (1959) 705–90 [has 968 items, often annotated, but carelessly cited]. Wik, *NTI* 398–411.

INTRODUCTION

2 **(I) Date and Place of Writing.** These questions are involved in the problem of the integrity of Rom (→ 9 below). However, the data in Rom 15 would indicate that Paul wrote Rom toward the end of Mission III, shortly before he returned to Jerusalem in the spring of AD 58. He probably wrote it in Corinth, sometime during the winter of AD 57–58 (Rom 15:25; cf. Acts 20:3).

3 **(II) Occasion and Purpose.** Paul wrote Rom, conscious that his missionary apostolate in the eastern Mediterranean area was over. Having preached "the gospel of Christ all the way from Jerusalem to Illyricum" (Rom 15:19), he looked to the west, and especially Spain. En route he planned to visit the Roman church to fulfill the desire of years (Rom 1:13; 15:22,24, 28). But before heading west, he had to attend to one last matter—to carry personally to Jerusalem the collection taken up in the Gentile churches that he had founded (Rom 15:25; cf. 1 Cor 16:1). For this was to manifest to the Jewish-Christian mother church the solidarity existing between the "poor" of the community and the Gentile Christians of Galatia, Macedonia, and Achaia. These Gentiles had contributed to that collection, realizing that they "shared the spiritual blessings" of the mother church (Rom 15:27). But before he departed from Corinth for Jerusalem, he wrote to the Roman church to announce his impending visit. Writing as "the apostle of the Gentiles" (11:13), he wanted to introduce himself to this church, which did not know him personally. Conscious too of his apostolic commission, he fashioned this letter of introduction as an extended exposé of his understanding of the gospel (1:16–17), which he was eager to preach at Rome too.

4 Rom is not a summary of Christian doctrine, nor Paul's "last will and testament," nor even a full sketch of Paul's view of Christianity. Some of his significant teachings (e.g., on the Church, the Eucharist, the resurrection of the body, eschatology, etc.) are missing from it. Rather, it is a presentation of his missionary reflections on the historic possibility of salvation now offered to all men in the good news of Jesus Christ. In the light of his eastern apostolate, and especially of the Judaizing crisis, Paul came to realize that man's justification and salvation depended not on the "deeds of the Law," but on faith in Christ Jesus, the Son whom the Father's love did not spare. Through faith man shares in the effects of the plan of salvation conceived by the Father and brought to realization in the death and resurrection of Jesus.

5 An important climax of the eastern apostolate was the personal delivery of the collection to the Jerusalem church. Concerned about its reception, Paul begged the church of Rome to pray "that the help being taken to Jerusalem may be well received by the holy people there" (Rom 15:31). For in Jerusalem he was still known as the former Pharisee who was doing away with the Law (Acts 21:28). The collection, then, was not simply intended to help the poor; it was to be a sign of Paul's solidarity with Jerusalem and of the communion of his Gentile converts with the first Jewish Christians. Would it be accepted in the right spirit?

6 Rom discusses many of the same topics as Gal, but whereas Gal was composed in the context of polemics, Rom manifests a calm and more reflective atmosphere. It is more like a treatise than a letter, and introduces elements of Gk literary style (e.g., Stoic diatribe). Rom does not directly refute, however, a Judaizing claim, nor does it try to vindicate Paul's apostolic commission to evangelize the Gentile world. It stands to Gal as Eph does to Col (→ Letter Gal, 49:8). Moreover, Rom does not handle any specific problems of the Roman church. Even the instructions in the hortatory section (chs. 12–14) are only generalizations, based, no doubt, on Paul's foregoing missionary experience. Possibly they even reflect the situation of the church of Corinth, where he spent the last few months (Acts 20:3). See T. W. Manson, *BJRylL* 31 (1948) 239. Rom is the record of the maturing thoughts of Paul, written on the occasion of his impending visit to Rome, in which he formulated the more universal implications of the gospel that he had been preaching.

7 **(III) The Roman Church.** In the east it was Paul's habit to establish Christian communities in important cities of the empire (Ephesus, Philippi, Thessalonica, Corinth). Though eager to preach the gospel in Rome too, he knew that its church had been founded by someone else (15:20; cf. 1:8,13). Who it was he does not say. Writing Rom as he did, it is unlikely that he considered Peter its "founder" (cf. Gal 2:7–8; R. Foster, *Scr* 4 [1950] 148). Most likely the community there was formed of converts from Palestine and Syria at an early date (cf. Acts 2:10; Ambrosiaster, *In Ep. ad Rom.*, prologue; *PL* 17.47–48; Tacitus, *Annales* 15.44). Peter probably did not arrive in Rome before the fifties. He was in Jerusalem for the "Council" (*ca.* AD 49). Aquila and Priscilla, Jewish Christians compelled to leave Rome by the edict of Claudius that expelled "all Jews" (Acts 18:1), came to Corinth *ca.* AD 49. This expulsion was probably due to a conflict between Jews and Jewish Christians in Rome; so at least suggests Suetonius: "Iudaeos impulsore Chresto assidue tumultuantes Roma expulit" (*Claudii vita* 25; cf. Orosius, *Hist. adv. pag.* 7.6, 15; CSEL 5, 451). The expulsion indicates that Jewish Christians were already in Rome before AD 49. The funerary inscription of Pomponia Graecina, apparently a Christian matron buried *ca.* AD 43, supports this. For the doubtful tradition of Peter's 25 years of Roman ministry, see Wik, *NTI* 399–400; Guthrie, *NTI* 21–22; S. Lyonnet, *Quaestiones*, 1a ser. (1962) 25–38; O. Cullmann, *Peter* (Phila., 1953) 70–152.

8 Commentators often maintain that the composition of the Roman church is important for the understanding of Rom. In modern times the Tübingen School, E. Renan, T. Zahn, W. Manson, F. Leenhardt, have considered it to have been predominantly Jewish Christian. Their main argument is derived from the abundant use of OT quotations, and especially of the Abraham story; this seems to indicate that Paul envisaged his readers as of predominantly Jewish origin. Moreover, there was a large Jewish population in 1st-cent. Rome (see S. Lyonnet, *Quaestiones*, 1a ser. [1962] 17–23; H. J. Leon, *The Jews of Ancient Rome* [Phila., 1960]), which would have been a natural matrix for the Christian Church. Though expelled in great numbers by Claudius, they could have returned at his death in AD 54. However, many others (among them J. Munck, S. Lyonnet, O. Michel, C. K. Barrett) believe that it was predominantly Gentile Christian. For Paul includes his readers among the Gentiles for whose salvation he had been commissioned an apostle (Rom 1:5–7,12–14; 11:11–13; 15:16). Of the two opinions the latter is preferable. But the question is really insoluble and somewhat idle, for a close scrutiny of the letter shows that Paul is not aware of the concrete situation in Rome and is not coping with specific problems of the Roman church that may have been reported to him.

9 **(IV) Authenticity and Integrity of Rom.** The Pauline authorship of Rom is almost universally admitted today, just as it was in antiquity. The few dissenting voices of the 19th cent. are no longer given serious consideration (cf. Sanday-Headlam, *Romans*, lxxxvi–lxxxix).

But a question can be raised about the final doxology (16:25–27). Its authenticity is questioned, (1) because of the varying position it has in several mss. In the Hesychian (B, S, C, syp, aeth) and Western (D, lat) Text traditions it occurs after 16:23; in the Koine tradition (L, syh, minuscules) after 14:23; in P[46] (the oldest text of Rom) after 15:33; in mss. A, P, 5, 33 after both 14:23 and 16:23. Finally in G, g, and Marcion it was completely omitted (though a space was left after 14:23 in G, g). Hence, though the best mss. support 16:23, the question is legitimately asked whether the doxology is a later addition to Rom or not. (2) Its style is periodic, redolent of liturgical, hymnic phraseology—a feature otherwise foreign to Rom. (3) The divine "mystery" applied here to the salvation of the Gentiles is a feature of other Pauline letters, but not of Rom. None of these reasons, either in themselves or taken together, yield certainty. But when they are considered together with the larger problem of ch. 16, the likelihood cannot be excluded that this doxology is a later non-Pauline addition to Rom, perhaps appended when the Pauline corpus was being formed. However, many regard it as Pauline (see S. Lyonnet, *Romains*, 50–51; J. Dupont, *RevBén* 58 [1948] 3–22; *ETL* 22 [1946] 362–75).

10 Rom 16:1–23 presents another problem. Its Pauline authorship is normally not contested. But is it an integral part of the original letter? Marcion and some patristic writers (Tertullian, Cyprian, Irenaeus) apparently knew of a form of Rom without chs. 15–16 (cf. Guthrie, *NTI* 1, 34). In P[46] the doxology follows 15:33, a verse that sounds very much like the conclusion of the letter (cf. 1 Cor 16:23–24; 2 Cor 13:11; Phil 4:9). Again, Rom 16:1–16 reads very much like a letter of recommendation dictated by Paul for Phoebe a deaconess of the church of Cenchreae (the port of Corinth). It resembles ancient letters of introduction known from papyri. These too plunge at once *in medias res*, begin with "I commend" (*synistēmi*), and pile up greetings (see A. Deissmann, *LAE* 226–27). In form Rom 16 is an *epistolē systatikē*. But was it addressed to the Roman church? An Ephesian destination has often been suggested in modern times (by D. Schulz, J. Moffatt, T. M. Taylor *et al.*). It was sent to a church with which Paul was well acquainted. Since Paul had not planned to visit Ephesus en route to Jerusalem (Acts 20:3), nor even to speak with that church's elders (as he eventually did at Miletus, Acts 20:17), he conceivably wrote this letter to introduce Phoebe to the Ephesian community. In Rom 16:3 he greets Prisca and Aquila, who had settled in Ephesus (Acts 18:18,26), where they had remained for the past year with a congregation gathered about them (AD 57; 1 Cor 16:19). As 2 Tm 4:19 implies, they were still in Ephesus later on. Again, Paul greets Epaenetus, "the first man in Asia to turn to Christ" (16:5), a greeting with little point if he were in Rome. Besides, he greets 25 others (23 by name)—a large number of acquaintances in a church he does not know personally. Indeed, he is even familiar with the groups that meet in various house-churches (16:5,14,15). Finally, the warning in 16:17–20, so different in tone from the rest of Rom, also suggests a church situation with which Paul was personally acquainted. Attempts have been made to invalidate these arguments for the Ephesian destination of Rom 16 (cf. Guthrie, *NTI* 1, 29–32), but most of them are irrelevant. Similar personal greetings are supposed to be found in Col, written to a church not founded by Paul (*ibid.*; also S. Lyonnet, *Romains*, 45). But in Col 4:10–17 Paul greets only "the brothers in Laodicea and Nympha and her house-community" (4:15–16), and a message is appended for Archippus. All the other persons named in 4:10–14 rather send their greetings to the Colossians through him! True, Aquila and Prisca *could* have returned to Rome after Claudius' death. But does not the only evidence available about them suggest the opposite?—"There seems to be no particular reason why the first convert in Asia must have remained there" (Guthrie). Nor any reason to believe, apart from Rom 16, that he went to Rome. Paul had labored for three years in Ephesus (Acts 20:31); the number of persons greeted could well be friends made then. The fact that Corinth was the common origin of Rom and the letter for Phoebe could well have been the reason why the two letters were eventually joined (see R. Schumacher, NTAbh 14/4 [1929] 3–28).

11 The problematic ending of Rom, together with the omission of *en Rōmē* ("at Rome," 1:7,15) in some mss. (G, g, 1908), has evoked the suggestion that Rom was really composed as a "circular letter," destined for more than one church (T. W. Manson, *BJRylL* 31 [1948] 224–40; J. Munck, *Paul and the Salvation of Mankind* [London, 1959] 197–200). In this view, Rom 1–15 (with the doxology as in P46) would have been sent to Rome, but ch. 16 would have been added for Phoebe who carried the copy of it to Ephesus. The phrase *en Rōmē* would then represent the real address in the first instance, but its omission in some mss. would come from other copies. Prima facie, this solution might seem plausible, but it is based on very slim ms. evidence. There is no real parallel between Rom and Eph in this regard (→ Letter Eph, 56:2).

12 **(V) Significance of Rom.** Rom has affected later Christian theology more than any other NT book. Scarcely an area of theological development has not been influenced by its teaching. Its influence is manifest even in other NT writings (1 Pt, Heb, Jas) and subapostolic compositions (Clement, Ignatius, Polycarp, Justin). Patristic and scholastic commentaries on Rom abound, beginning with Origen; the chief interpreters were Chrysostom, Theodoret, John Damascene, Oecumenius, Theophylact, Ambrosiaster, Pelagius, Hugh of St. Victor, Abelard, and Thomas Aq. Immeasurable was the part Rom played in the Reformation debates. Famous commentaries on it were penned by M. Luther, J. Calvin, and P. Melanchthon. Modern religious thinking has been greatly affected by the theological commentaries on Rom by K. Barth (*Epistle to the Romans* [London, 1933]), A. Nygren (*Commentary on Romans* [London, 1952]), H. Asmussen (*Der Römerbrief* [Stuttgart, 1952]), and E. Brunner (*Der Römerbrief* [Leipzig, n.d.]). The contribution that Rom has made to Western Christian thinking is inestimable.

13 **(VI) Outline.** Most modern commentators agree about the obvious divisions of Rom (Introduction, Hortatory Section, Conclusion [with or without ch. 16]). But a debate centers about the division of the doctrinal section. Is it to be divided into two or three subsections? Does ch. 5 go with what precedes or with what follows? Has not Paul incorporated into Rom certain developments formulated on other occasions and already used as units (e.g., 3:10–18; 5:12–21; 9:1–11:36)? The last question can legitimately be raised because of the rather abrupt way these parts are introduced; and yet, as they stand now, they are certainly integral parts of the main development of the letter and have to be reckoned with as such. Some reasons will be given at appropriate places in the commentary for the division of the letter used here. The outline is a modified form of that of S. Lyonnet, *Romains*, 62–66. See further *RSR* 39 (1951) 301–16.

(I) Introduction (1:1–15)
- (A) Address and Greeting (1:1–7)
- (B) Thanksgiving (1:8)
- (C) Paul's Desire to Come to Rome (1:9–15)

(II) Part I: Doctrinal Section—God's Gospel of Jesus Christ Our Lord (1:16–11:36)
- (A) Through the Gospel the Uprightness of God Justifies the Man of Faith (1:16–4:25)
  - (a) The Theme Announced: The Gospel Is the Powerful Source of Salvation, Disclosing God's Uprightness (1:16–17)
  - (b) The Theme Negatively Explained: Without the Gospel God's Wrath Is Manifested Against All Men (1:18–3:20)
    - (i) God's wrath manifested against the heathen (1:18–32)
    - (ii) The wrath of God is manifested against the Jews (2:1–3:20)
  - (c) The Theme Positively Developed: God's Uprightness Is Manifested Through Christ and Shared In by Faith (3:21–31)
  - (d) The Theme Illustrated: In the Old Law Abraham Was Justified by Faith (4:1–25)
- (B) The Love of God Assures Salvation to the Justified (5:1–11:36)
  - (a) The Theme Announced: The Reconciled Christian Will Be Saved, Sharing with Hope in the Risen Life of Christ (5:1–11)
  - (b) The Theme Explained: The New Christian Life Brings a Threefold Liberation (5:12–7:25)
    - (i) Freedom from death and sin (5:12–21)
    - (ii) Freedom from self through union with Christ (6:1–23)
    - (iii) Freedom from the Law (7:1–25)
  - (c) The Theme Developed: Christian Life Is Lived in the Spirit and Is Destined for Glory (8:1–39)
    - (i) Christian life is empowered by the Spirit (8:1–13)
    - (ii) Through the Spirit the Christian becomes a child of God and is destined for glory (8:14–30)
  - (d) The Theme Illustrated: The Old Testament Shows That This Plan of Salvation Does not Contradict God's Promises to Israel (9:1–11:36)
    - (i) Israel's infidelity is not contrary to God's direction of history (9:1–33)
    - (ii) Israel's failure is derived from its own culpable refusal (10:1–21)
    - (iii) Israel's failure is partial and temporary (11:1–36)

(III) Part II: Hortatory Section—The Demands of the New Life (12:1–15:13)
- (A) Christian Life Must Be Worship in Spirit Paid to God (12:1–13:14)
- (B) The Duty of Charity Is Owed by the Strong to the Weak (14:1–15:13)

(IV) Conclusion (15:14–33)

(V) Letter of Recommendation for Phoebe (16:1–23)

(VI) Doxology (16:25–27)

COMMENTARY

14 **(I) Introduction (1:1–15).** The opening formula, Paul's greeting to the Romans, is the most solemn *praescriptio* in his letters (→ NT Epistles, 47:8). Paul alone sends this letter. Perhaps because he writes to a church not yet personally acquainted with him, he feels the need to introduce himself and his preaching in a fundamental way. The first sentence of the *praescriptio* (1:1–7a) is expanded to include echoes of the primitive kerygma (1:2–4) and various motifs to be treated in the letter (the gospel, appeal to the OT, divine favor and election, faith, the role of the Risen Christ).

15 **(A) Address and Greeting (1:1–7).** **1.** *slave [servant] of Christ Jesus:* The first of three descriptions of Paul himself. The epithet *doulos* designates him not merely in a generic way as a Christian, a "slave of Christ" (1 Cor 7:22; Eph 6:6), but more specifically as a preacher of the gospel serving the Christian community (cf. Gal 1:10; Phil 1:1; 2:22). This use of *doulos* reflects not only the OT custom of the pious calling themselves "slaves" in the sight of Yahweh (Pss 27:9; 31:16; 89:50), but especially its OT use to describe the great figures who served Yahweh in salvation history (Moses, 2 Kgs 18:12; Joshua, Jgs 2:8; Abraham, Ps 105:42). Paul, as the "slave of Christ," belongs to the same line. *called as an apostle:* The second description of himself emphasizes the divine origin of his apostolate. The event on the road to Damascus may be regarded as his call to the apostolate (cf. B. Rigaux, *Saint Paul et ses lettres* [Bruges, 1962] 82–90; J. Munck, *Paul and the Salvation of Mankind* 20–35). In Gal 1:15 Paul regards his "call" as the continuation of the divine vocation of OT figures (Jeremiah, the Servant of Yahweh). On "apostle," see comment on Gal 1:1. *set apart for God's gospel:* The third description of himself. Gal 1:15 explains that he was destined for this role before his birth. The ptc. "set apart" may be a pun on the Aram *p^{e}rîš*, "separated," the word that underlies "Pharisee." Does Paul imply that his Pharisaic past was a divinely ordained background for his apostolate? It means at least that even before his birth he was a man marked by God for his role in salvation history. It is "God's gospel" because its ultimate source is the Father (Rom 15:16; 2 Cor 11:7). **2.** *which he promised previously:* From the very beginning of Rom Paul stresses that his "gospel" of salvation is part of a divine and ancient plan, in which even the OT had a part. He is no Marcionite, but sees the New Dispensation growing out of the same source as the old. *through his prophets:* Not just the three major and twelve minor prophets of the OT, but all the OT persons whom the early Church regarded as uttering statements applicable to Christ. **3.** *about his Son:* God's gospel and the promises made by him in the OT refer, according to Paul, to Jesus, who stands in a unique relation to God as "his Son" (cf. Rom 8:3; 1 Cor 8:6; Gal 4:4). Paul is not referring to the ontological constitution of Christ, but is going to affirm two things about the Risen Christ, who de facto enjoys a filial relation toward God and whose pre-existence is at most implied. *descended from David according to the flesh:* The first affirmation asserts that Jesus was a son of David in the order of natural, physical descent (cf. Rom 4:1; also Mt 1:1,20; 2 Tm 2:8); he was a royal scion with a right to the sacral anointing of a messiah. The pejorative nuance of the phrase *kata sarka* (according to the flesh) stands in contrast to *kata pneuma hagiōsynēs* (according to a spirit of holiness), the basis of Paul's second affirmation. From this viewpoint Jesus possesses a still greater quality. These two viewpoints will lead in the development of dogma to the distinction of two natures—a distinction that Paul does not use.

16 **4.** *set up as the Son of God with power:* Three problems complicate the understanding of this difficult phrase: (1) What does the aor. ptc. *horisthentos* mean? (2) What does *en dynamei* modify? (3) What is the sense of "Son of God"?—(1) Certainly to be rejected as the meaning of *horisthentos* is "predestined" (Vg, Augustine, Pelagius), since *horizō* (limit, define) is not the same as *proorizō*. Chrysostom and other Gk Fathers explained it as "manifested, displayed." This meaning, though tolerable, was all too often understood in terms of the later discussion of natures in Christ. Modern commentators usually prefer the meaning "appointed, installed, set up" (cf. Acts 10:42; 17:31). (2) The phrase *en dynamei* has been taken as an adverbial modifier of the ptc., "decisively declared" (Goodspeed, Sanday-Headlam), or "by a mighty act" (NEB). But the position of the phrase is against such an interpretation. Paul's contrast demands that although Jesus was the Son descended from David on the physical level, he was set up as "the Son of God with power" on the level of the Spirit (as of the resurrection). (3) In saying "Son of God with power," Paul is not thinking of the inner-trinitarian relation of the Father and the Son but of the unique relationship of Christ to God in the salvific process. For Paul the resurrection made a difference in that process, although it did not *make* Christ the Son of God (cf. 2 Cor 4:4; 8:9; Phil 2:6; Col 1:15). Before Jesus was the Son born of David; now he is the "son of God with power" (on the omission of the article before *en dynamei*, see Bl-Deb-F § 272). Just as the early Church looked on the resurrection as the event in Jesus' existence when he became "Lord" and "Messiah" (Acts 2:34–36) and applied to him Ps 2:7 ("You are my son; today I have begotten you") with reference to it, so Christ was endowed with a power of vivification in the resurrection (Phil 3:10) and became a "vivifying Spirit" (1 Cor 15:45; → Pauline Theology, 79:71–74). *according to a spirit of holiness:* This unique Pauline expression could mean "the Holy Spirit," as a literal translation of the Hebr *rû^{a}ḥ haqqōdeš* (Is 63:11; Ps 51:11). Some patristic and modern commentators understand it of the activity of the Holy Spirit unleashed, as it were, by the Risen Christ. But the obvious parallelism of the phrase with *kata sarka* suggests that Paul regards it as something belonging to Christ himself. It is not simply his divine nature (so Cornely, Bonsirven), but rather the transcendent, dynamic source of holiness in his glorified state in virtue of which he vivifies mankind (cf. 1 Cor 15:45). *from [his] resurrection from the dead:* The prep. *ex* denotes either time or causality. Understood temporally, it would express Christ's new mode of dynamic existence since his resurrection; understood causally, it would designate the resurrection itself as an influence in Christ's salvific activity (see M.-E. Boismard, *RB* 60 [1953] 5–17; D. M. Stanley, *Christ's Resurrection in Pauline Soteriology* [Rome, 1961] 165). **5.** *the grace of apostleship:* Lit., "grace and apostleship." Paul's charismatic role as the apostle to the Gentiles came to him through the Risen Christ (Acts 22:10). *in view of the obedience of faith:* The genitive is appositional, for Paul conceives of faith as a process that begins with "hearing" (*akoē*, Rom 10:14–17) and ends with a personal commitment and submission (*hypakoē*, "obedience"; → Pauline Theology, 79:125–127.) **7.** *in Rome* (→ 11 above). *holy people:* Lit., "called saints." The OT expression *miqrā' qōdeš*, "holy gathering," was used of the Israelites at the Exodus (Ex 12:16; Lv 23:2–44); it designated them as a people set apart and dedicated to Yahweh (Lv 11:44; 19:2). Paul flatters the Roman Christians by adapting the OT expression and insinuating a new sense in which they are now the "holy called ones." (See comment on 2 Cor 8:4.)

17 **(B) Thanksgiving (1:8).** (→ NT Epistles, 47:8.) Paul uses an epistolary formula (cf. 1 Thes 1:8; Col 1:4; Eph 1:15) similar to contemporary ones (see C. H. Dodd, *Romans*, 6). Note that Paul's prayer is addressed to his God through Jesus Christ (cf. Rom 7:25; 1 Cor 15:57).

18 **(C) Paul's Desire to Come to Rome (1:9–15).** Paul's coming visit to the Roman church will be a source of mutual benefit. **9.** *whom I serve:* He compares his work in the service of the gospel as a priestly act of worship offered to God; cf. 15:16; S. Lyonnet, *VD* 41 (1963) 52–59. *in my spirit:* This phrase is variously interpreted, but most likely it means that Paul puts his whole self into the service of the gospel. **10.** *by God's will:* Cf. Acts 18:21. Paul senses that the coming trip to Jerusalem is not without its risks (cf. Rom 15:31). **13.** *I want you to know:* Lit., "I do not want you to be ignorant," a favorite Pauline phrase of emphasis (Rom 11:25; 1 Cor 10:1; 12:1; 2 Cor 1:8; 1 Thes 4:13). *prevented up till now:* By what? In 15:18–22 he indicates that it was his apostolate in the East and his respect for a community not founded by him. Since the passive is often used in the NT as a circumlocution for God (the "theological passive," *GrBib* § 236), Paul may be hinting that his delay was divinely ordained (cf. Acts 16:6–7). **14.** *to Greeks and barbarians:* As the apostle of the Gentiles he must bring the gospel to all non-Jews. He designates the non-Jewish world by a Gk phrase, dividing the world into those who spoke Greek (Romans included at this period) and those who did not. **15.** *in Rome* (→ 11 above).

19 **(II) Part I: Doctrinal Section—God's Gospel of Jesus Christ Our Lord (1:16–11:36).** The introduction (1:1–5) has already mentioned God's gospel and Paul's role in proclaiming it. This section expounds the unique, historic possibility of salvation for all men that God makes known in his gospel. The section is best divided into two main parts: (A) 1:16–4:25; (B) 5:1–11:36.

20 **(A) Through the Gospel the Uprightness of God Justifies the Man of Faith (1:16–4:25).** Paul's pride in his role of proclaiming it introduces the theme of this first part.

(a) THE THEME ANNOUNCED: THE GOSPEL IS THE POWERFUL SOURCE OF SALVATION, DISCLOSING GOD'S UPRIGHTNESS (1:16–17). Given what the gospel is, Paul is not ashamed of preaching it even in the capital of the civilized world—a grandiose understatement (cf. 1 Cor 2:3). **16.** *God's power:* This initial description of the gospel in Rom makes it clear that it is not just a message, or a philosophy, or a system of thought to be learned. It is the "story of the cross" (1 Cor 1:18). "God's power" is an abstraction, expressive of the force (*dynamis*) with which God affects the course of man's history (cf. 1 Cor 2:4; 4:20). *for the salvation of everyone who has faith:* The divine force which is the gospel is destined for the "salvation" of the believer. Basically, *sōtēria* means "deliverance, preservation" from sickness, danger, or death (cf. Acts 7:25; 27:34). But it normally has a religious nuance in the NT: deliverance from dangers to the Christian destiny and (positively) the fostering of those conditions that insure its attainment. Elsewhere in Rom (5:9–10; 8:24; 10:9,13?; 11:11,26; 13:11) it refers to a future, eschatological reality, apparently distinct from "justification" or "reconciliation." In later letters, however, it is something already inaugurated (Eph 2:8). *for the Jew first and [then] the Greek:* "First" is lacking in some mss. (B, G). But it is retained since it agrees with Paul's conviction about Israel's privilege (Rom 2:9–10; 3:9): The Messiah was promised to it (Rom 9:4); and Jews were in fact the first to believe in him (Eph 1:12). So he preached first to the Jews (Acts 13:46; 14:1; 17:2; etc.). Fully aware of this historic privilege, he nevertheless asserts the possibility now given to all men to share by faith in that salvation (Rom 10:12; 1 Cor 1:24; 12:13).

21 **17.** *God's uprightness is disclosed:* The gospel now manifests, as never before, God's basic attitude toward men—or better, God's activity in reconciling men to himself in Christ. Apart from this gospel only divine wrath is revealed (1:18ff.). This contrast of "uprightness" and "wrath" suggests that Paul is speaking of a quality in God. This is the sense of *dikaiosynē theou* elsewhere in Rom (3:5,21,22,25,26; 10:3), although it is not always such in Paul's letters (cf. Phil 3:9; 2 Cor 5:21, where it refers to something communicated to men). It is the gospel that reveals the salvific uprightness of God (→ Pauline Theology, 79:37). *from faith to faith:* This literal translation reveals the problem of a much-debated phrase. Certainly inadequate are the interpretations of Tertullian, Origen ("from faith in the Law to faith in the Gospel"), and of Ambrosiaster ("from God's faithfulness to man's faith"), since the use of the two prepositions (*ek...eis*) with the same word usually supposes the identical meaning of the word so governed (cf. 2 Cor 2:16; 3:18; Ps 83:8). Two interpretations are current: (1) "from a beginning faith to a more perfect faith" (Lagrange, Huby). This exploits the notion of progress often associated with these prepositions. God's economy of salvation is shared more and more by man as his faith grows. (2) "Through faith and for faith." This interpretation follows the development in 3:21–22 where a similar progress of thought is found. "Through [*ek*] faith" would express the means by which man shares in salvation; "for [*eis*] faith" the purpose in the divine plan, when man's reaction is considered. In either case, salvation is a matter, not of the Law, but of faith from start to finish. *as it is written:* In Scripture. Paul introduces his OT quotations by using current Jewish introductory formulas (see J. A. Fitzmyer, *NTS* 7 [1960–61] 297–333). *the upright shall live by faith:* Hab 2:4, quoted neither according to the MT ("The upright shall live by his fidelity"), nor according to the LXX (mss. B, S: "The upright will live by my faithfulness"; mss. A, C: "My upright one will live by faith"). In the original, the coming Chaldean invaders, whose god is their might, are contrasted with Judah, whose deliverance lies in fidelity to Yahweh. Habakkuk is ordered to record Yahweh's message: He who is puffed up (with confidence) will fail, but the upright will live by his fidelity (to Yahweh). Paul omits the possessive pronoun, and adopts the LXX translation of the Hebr *'emûnāh* (fidelity, faith), i.e., *pistis*, which, of course, he understands in his own way. The "life" promised to Judah was temporal deliverance from the invader. But Paul extends the sense of both "life" and "faith" in terms of Christian destiny and salvation. Some NT exegetes (e.g., Kuss) link "by faith" to "upright" (i.e., he who is justified through faith [NEB]). This agrees with Paul's thought, but it really forces the meaning of the phrase in Hab.

22 (b) THE THEME NEGATIVELY EXPLAINED: WITHOUT THE GOSPEL GOD'S WRATH IS MANIFESTED AGAINST ALL MEN (1:18–3:20). The proposition of 1:16–17 is explained by a preliminary antithetical consideration: what happens to man without the gospel. Paul indicts both pagan Hellenism and Judaism for failing to enable man to achieve a moral uprightness. Left to himself, the pagan Greek did not come to acknowledge God and consequently lapsed into moral depravity. Without the gospel, the Jew never succeeded in achieving uprightness before God, even though he had all the advantages of the Mosaic Law. In both cases the result is estrangement from God, and divine wrath is displayed toward both. Such is man's condition before the gospel of Christ Jesus.

23 (i) *God's wrath manifested against the heathen* (1:18–32). O. Michel (*Römer*, 51) plausibly suggests that this paragraph is an example of a missionary sermon such as Paul delivered to pagans. He undoubtedly echoes in it a judgment of the pagan world current among Jews of his time. Verse 18 is his topic sentence. Note the threefold rhetorical use of "abandoned" (*paredōken*, 1:24,26,28), running through the paragraph. His summary judgment ("they deserve to die") is recorded in 1:32.

18. *God's wrath:* God's reaction to man's sin and evil ways is vividly depicted by Paul's use of an OT anthropomorphic image (see Is 30:27–33). It is neither a malicious hatred nor a jealous caprice, but the living God's steadfast reaction to Israel's breach of the covenant relation (Ez 5:13; Hos 5:10; Is 9:8–12), or to the nations' oppression of his people (Is 10:5ff.; Jer 50:11–17; Ez 36:5–6). Related to the "Day of Yahweh" (Zeph 1:14–18), it acquired an eschatological nuance. On that day neither the godless heathen nor the impious Israelite will escape God's wrath (Ps 79:5ff.; 11:5–7). Paul sees it already being displayed toward men without the gospel. **19.** *what can be known of God:* Elsewhere in the NT (and the LXX) *gnōstos* means "known," not "can be known." Chrysostom, Vg, etc. prefer the meaning, "what is known of God." But this creates a tautology with the predicate, "is clear to them," and so most modern commentators follow Origen, Thomas Aq., interpreting it as "capable of being known" (see AG 163; R. Bultmann, *Gnosis* [BKW 5; London, 1952] 58; *ThDNT* 1, 719). What Paul means specifically by the "knowable" is indicated in 1:20. *is clear to them:* Lit., "is clear in them." But "in them" scarcely means "to their minds" (Lyonnet, Huby). Rather, either (1) "among them," since Paul insists on the externality of the manifestation (Lagrange, Michel), or preferably (2) "to them," since *en* with the dative is occasionally substituted for the simple dative (Gal 1:16; 2 Cor 4:3; 8:1; Bl-Deb-F § 220, 1; *GrBib* § 120). Paul explains this in the next phrase, by tracing to God himself the origin of what can be known about him.

24 **20.** *his invisible qualities:* Lit., "his unseen things." The specific qualities are mentioned at the end of the verse. *since the creation of the world:* Cf. Jb 40:1–42:6; Ps 19; Is 40:12–31. Elsewhere in the NT, *ktisis* means "what is created, creature" (so Vg, *a creatura mundi*). Since this would be tautological here, most commentators prefer the temporal, active sense of "creation" (like the expression in Mt 24:21; 25:34). *perceptible to the mind:* Lit., "being intellectually apprehended are perceived." Man, contemplating the created world and reflecting upon it, perceives through its multicolored façade the great "Unseen" behind it—the omnipotence and divine character of its Maker. Though essentially invisible, they are mirrored in the "great works" (*poiēmata*) produced by him (Acts 14:15–17). There is no question here either of knowledge through a positive revelation or of knowledge by faith. *so they have no excuse:* Paul echoes current Jewish ideas of the culpability of the pagans in not acknowledging and reverencing God as they should have; cf. Wis 13:1–9; *2 Esdras* 7:22–24; *Assumption of Moses* 1:13 (*APOT* 2, 415, 581). The Gk phrase could express either purpose or result. Sanday-Headlam, Barrett, and Michel prefer the idea of (conditional) purpose: God did not intend that pagans should sin; but if they did, he intended that it would be without excuse. Many scholars (Cornely, Lietzmann, *et al.*), recognizing that in NT Gk grammar the consecutive sense of the phrase encroaches on the final sense (*GrBib* § 351–52; Bl-Deb-F § 402, 2), argue that the sense of result better suits the context. In either case, the condition in which man has been since creation argues against an atheistic attitude. **21.** *though they knew God:* After the general principle enunciated in 1:20, Paul proceeds to the specific sin of the pagans. Here he seems to admit that in some sense they "knew God"—despite what the Jews normally thought (Jer 10:25; Ps 79:6; Wis 14:12–22) and what Paul seems to say in 1 Cor 1:21 ("the world with all its wisdom did not come to know God"). But what is denied in these passages is a real, affective knowledge of God that includes love and reverence. In this quasi-philosophical discussion the word *gnontes* connotes an inceptive, speculative sort of information about God that Paul thinks the heathen could not help but have. The inconsequential character of that knowledge, which did not develop into a real religious recognition of God, is the root of their sin.—Paul is not speaking merely of pagan philosophers, nor of some primitive positive revelation (e.g., of the Law, *2 Esdras* 7:20–24), nor just of some first pagans (*pace* A. Feuillet, *LumVi* 14 [1954] 71–75). He speaks of all pagans of history (at least up to his day). *did not honor him:* Paul's complaint is centered not only on pagan ignorance, but much more on their refusal to manifest to God their reverence and gratitude, which should have sprung from the inceptive knowledge of God they had. Instead, their reverence was paid to things created. *indulged in futile speculations:* Three consequences of their failure follow: the vanity of their self-sufficient reasoning, the obscuring of their vision in other religious matters, their idolatry. **23.** *exchanged the glory of the immortal God for images:* Allusion to Ps 106:20 (MT: "They exchanged their glory for the image of a grass-eating bullock"). The Ps refers to the Golden Calf (Ex 32), but Paul applies it to the pagans. Idols are preferred to Yahweh's *doxa*, the resplendent external manifestation of his presence (Ex 24:17). Paul echoes Dt 4:16–18 here.

25 Vatican Council I and Rom 1:20. In the dogmatic constitution "De fide catholica" Rom 1:20 is quoted in support of the proposition that God can certainly be known by the natural light of human reason (DB 1785; DS 3004.) The conciliar use of this text does not mean that Paul is necessarily saying exactly the same thing. The council's statement was opposed to Fideism and Traditionalism and asserted the possibility of the knowledge of God, aside from any positive revelation and aside from faith. The major difference in the texts of Paul and Vatican I is that the latter deals with the capability (active potency) of the human mind to know God and prescinds from the *de facto* use of it, whereas Paul asserts the fact that God is intellectually perceived and is known from the works of creation. He speaks too of the "impiety and wickedness of men" (1:18), of their refusal to acknowledge God properly (1:28). From such attitudes the council prescinds. The further theological question about man's ability to know God without any divine assistance (e.g., actual grace) is wholly beyond Paul's perspective. In going beyond Paul (i.e., in arguing *ab esse ad posse*), Vatican I did not deform his thought, for he does ascribe to man a vital knowledge of the living God. (See further S. Lyonnet, *Quaestiones*, 1a ser. [1962] 78–88.)

26 **24.** *abandoned them:* Lit., "gave them over to." The triple use of the same verb (1:26,28) introduces the punishment derived from God s wrath. Paul strives to establish the intrinsic relationship between sin and punishment; impiety brings its own retribution (cf. Wis 11:6–7,15–16; Ez 23:28–29). Idolatry, the consequence of men's failure to honor God, is the source of sexual immorality; for it is the "big lie" (cf. Wis 14:22–27). **25.** *exchanged the truth of God:* An echo of 1:18,22–23. What is, is true; what is not, is falsehood (cf. Jer 10:14). *who is blessed forever, Amen!:* Paul betrays his Jewish background in spontaneously uttering a doxology at the climactic mention of God as the Creator (see comment on 2 Cor 11:31). **26.** *have exchanged their natural function:* The contrast between "females" and "males" (1:27) makes it clear that the sexual perversion of which Paul speaks is homosexuality (specifically Lesbianism). The depravity of the perversion is the merited consequence of pagan impiety; having exchanged the true God for a false one (1:25), pagans inevitably exchanged their true natural functions for perverted ones (cf. Philo, *De Abrahamo* 135; *De spec. leg.* 2.50, 3.37). [Only modern eisegesis could pervert Paul's words and refer them to female contraception.] **28.** *what is not proper:* Idolatry leads not only to sexual perversion, but to all sorts of immoral conduct. Paul adds a catalogue of vices (→ Pauline Theology, 79:161), an echo of the early Church's *didachē*. **32.** *God's decree:* In Rom 2:14–15 Paul shows that the pagan conscience perceives at times some of the same divine injunctions promulgated in the Mosaic Law. Echoing 1:21 (*gnontes, epignontes*), he formulates his verdict against the pagan and explains why they are "without excuse." *deserve to die:* This phrase might seem at first to refer to physical death as a punishment for the vices just listed; but it is difficult to establish that pagan consciences would recognize this for all of them. Paul is probably thinking of total death (cf. Rom 5:12,19), the lot of all sinners. It is exclusion from the Kingdom of God (1 Cor 6:10; Gal 5:21). *approve those who practice them:* The abysmal state of pagan man is revealed not only in his own failure to honor God and live uprightly, but in his approval of the same conduct in others.

27 In this entire section it is noteworthy that Paul does not affirm that every individual pagan before Christ's coming was a moral failure. Rather, he speaks collectively. Furthermore, he describes a *de facto* situation and does not argue that paganism *de jure* was incapable of making man upright. When Christian theologians teach the necessity of divine assistance for perseverance in a good, natural life, they go beyond Paul's perspective and have in mind the individual and his condition as a result of the fall. The basis of their teaching, however, is Pauline: Man cannot do without Christ. The insufficiency of human nature and its lack of equilibrium (Rom 7) are only too apparent without the influence of Christ.

28 (ii) *The wrath of God is manifested against the Jews* (2:1–3:20). Paul turns to an imaginary self-righteous reader who loudly applauds his description of the pagans' moral failure. He is no better than the pagan, for in spite of a superior moral culture he does not do what he is supposed to do. Consequently, he will not escape divine wrath either.

The identity of *anthrōpos* in 2:1–16 is disputed. For Chrysostom and Theodoret, he was the secular judge or authority in Rome; for Origen, the Christian bishop, priest, or deacon; for T. Zahn, the pagan philosopher or moralist. But many modern exegetes (Protestant and Catholic) identify him as the Jew who judges himself superior to the pagan because of his people's privileges. Their reasons: In 2:17 the Jew is clearly meant. But 2:1–16 is only a build-up to this explicit identification. Verses 12–16 show that a knowledge of divine ordinances is not exclusive to the Jew; certain prescriptions of the Torah are known even to pagans. Implicitly, the Jew is thus compared. These verses, however, support 2:9–10, where Jew and Greek are put on an equal footing before God. And 2:1–8 prepares for this. Hence 2:1–16 is an indirect indictment of Judaism, which becomes overt in 2:17, and eventually forces the Jew to pronounce sentence against himself. In developing his argument against the Jew, Paul enunciates the general principle of God's impartial judgment (1–11), shows that the mere possession of the Law is no guarantee against divine wrath (12–16), and announces that it will condemn the Jew as well as the Gentile (17–24)—and this, in spite of circumcision (25–29). Verses 1–11 and 17–29 are usually regarded as an example of *diatribē* (→ Pauline Theology, 79:11).

29 **1.** *so:* Normally the particle *dio* draws a conclusion from a foregoing statement, but here it is apparently a mere transitional particle, introducing the new topic. *O man who judges:* Such a use of *anthrōpos* ("Man") in an address is characteristic of diatribes in Epictetus (see further 2:3; 9:20). *you condemn yourself:* Paul's topic sentence in this section: You are yourself a sinner, and so an object of divine wrath. **2.** *God's judgment:* The word *krima* could mean merely "a lawsuit" (1 Cor 6:7) or a "decision, judgment" (Rom 11:33), but frequently it has the connotation of "condemnation, adverse sentence" (Rom 3:8; 13:2; Gal 5:20), which is the nuance intended here. Such "condemnation" falls on all evil-doers "rightly" (lit., "according to the truth"), without respect of persons (2:11). **3.** *who sit in judgment:* The first of two questions that highlight the critic's illusion; once asked, they answer themselves. Cf. Mt 3:8 ("Don't try to tell yourselves, 'We have Abraham for our father' "). Descent from Abraham is no guarantee against the Day of Wrath; cf. Jn 8:33; Gal 2:15. **4.** *do you make light of...:* It is not merely a question of illusion, but even of contempt. Making light of the delay on God's part to punish sin—which should really lead to repentance—the Jew manifests his culpable negligence (cf. Wis 11:23; *2 Esdras* 7:74). **5.** *you store up wrath:* That is, reason for the adverse reaction of God. *on the day of wrath:* See comment on 1:18. This expression is a development of the "Day of Yahweh" (Zech 1:14–18; Am 5:18; Ez 7:7) and refers to the time of eschatological judgment (2 Thes 1:5–10). *God's just judgment:* The word *dikaiokrisia* (just judgment) stresses the equity of the decision to be given on that day. Note that Paul does not use of this action the expression *dikaiosynē theou* (see comment on 1:17). He is insisting that the impenitent Jew fails to realize the relation of the present to the coming judgment of God. **6.** *repay everyone according to his deeds:* Allusion to Ps 62:13 or Prv 24:12. This Pauline affirmation, which was not simply borrowed from the OT in a moment of ardent rhetoric, must be kept in mind in any synthesis of his teaching on salvation. It does not contradict Paul's ideas of justification by faith. He certainly is not bringing up the subject of deeds at this point in a provisional sort of way merely to do away with them later on (→ Pauline Theology, 79:160–161). **7.** *life eternal:* The reward of those who patiently perform good deeds is a life to be enjoyed "with the Lord forever" (1 Thes 4:17). The OT background for this notion is Dn 12:2. In Rom this expression always refers to the possession of life in the "age [*aiōn*] to come" (5:21; 6:22,23). **8.** *but for self-seeking people:* This difficult phrase, using *eritheia*, was not clearly understood even by ancient commentators. Etymologically, it is related to *erithos*, "mercenary's pay," and it was used by Aristotle (*Politics* 5.3) to denote "selfishness, selfish ambition," especially in a political context. However, it often occurs in contexts of "strife" (*eris*); with this word it was apparently confused in popular usage (cf. Phil 1:17; 2:3; 2 Cor 12:20; Gal 5:20). Consequently, some commentators (Lagrange, Lietzmann, Lyonnet) understand it here to mean "rebellious people." In fact, either meaning suits the context, for they are the opposite of those who patiently pursue the good. Their lot is the fury of divine wrath. **9.** *anguish and distress:* An OT phrase (Dt 28:53,55,57), expressive of the manifestation of divine displeasure to men in this life (cf Rom 8:35; 2 Cor 6:4). Verses 9–10 reformulate vv. 7–8, applying in reverse order the effects of divine wrath to all men who do evil; they also recast in terms of Jews and Greeks what Paul said in 1:18. *on every human being:* Lit., "soul." Lagrange thinks Paul means that these punishments will affect specifically man's "soul" (*psychē*). This is too Hellenistic an interpretation of the word. Paul is more likely using the OT expression (Lv 24:17) for "every human being" (→ Pauline Theology, 79:121). *the Jew first and the Greek too:* See comment on 1:16. Having received unique privileges in the history of salvation, the Jew is therefore more responsible when he sins. But when he does what is right, he is also the first to receive God's reward. And yet the Gentile is not neglected. **11.** *God has no favorites:* Lit., "there is no partiality in God." As in Col 3:25; Eph 6:9, Paul uses *prosōpolēmpsia*, "partiality," a word found only in Christian writings, but coined from a LXX expression, *prosōpon lambanein.* This translates the Hebr *pānîm nāśā'*, "to lift up the face," an expression denoting the gracious act of someone who lifts a person's face by showing him favor (Mal 1:8; Lv 19:15). Such lifting-up-the-face is not found in God. This is Paul's summary formulation of the principle underlying his discussion in these 11 verses. God is no respecter of persons. So despite all their privileges, the Jews will be no better off than the Gentiles, unless they do what is expected of them.

30 **12.** *without the Law:* Not simply "without a law," but specifically without the Mosaic Law. The context deals with Gentiles who lived without the benefit of Mosaic legislation. If they sinned without a knowledge of its regulations, then they will perish without any respect to it. Their sin brings its own condemnation, even though the Law is not applied to them. In this, Paul contradicts current Jewish notions. *all who sinned under the Law:* The phrase *en nomō* (without the article) refers to the same Mosaic Law. For centuries commentators have tried from time to time to establish a distinction between Paul's use of *ho nomos* (Mosaic Law) and *nomos* (law in general, or even "natural law"). But such a distinction is without sound philological support (*pace* M. Zerwick *GrBib* § 177; → Pauline Theology, 79:106). What men do is the only criterion by which they will be judged. This verse is explained in the two following verses. **13.** *hearers of the Law:* The Jew is not upright before God simply because he knows the regulations of the Torah from hearing it read every Sabbath in the synagogue. Paul uses a well-known rabbinical hortatory distinction between knowledge and action (cf. *Pirqe Aboth* 1:17 [*APOT* 2, 694]). *the doers of the Law:* Paul adopts a Jewish point of view, for the sake of argument, and implicitly echoes Lv 18:5 ("he who observes these things shall find life"; cf. Gal 3:12). *shall be made upright:* The fut. verb betrays the eschatological forensic nuance of justification expected at the judgment in accordance with the Jewish perspective here adopted by Paul (→ Pauline Theology, 79:97). **14.** *when Gentiles who do not have the Law:* This and the following verse explain why Gentiles who are without a knowledge of the prescriptions of the Mosaic Law will be punished (2:12). *instinctively observe:* Lit., "by nature" (*physei*), i.e., by the regular, natural order of things (AG 877), prescinding from any positive revelation. Following the guidance of *physis*, the Gentiles frame rules of conduct for themselves and know at least some of the things the Torah prescribes for the Jews. *what the Law prescribes:* Lit., "the things of the Law," a phrase that is not to be understood too rigidly, as if each of the precepts of the Torah were meant. For, although Paul admits that Gentiles do observe "the things of the Law," his statement is couched in a general temporal clause, "Whenever...." *even though they have not the Law:* The benefit of a revealed legislation such as the Jews had. *they are [a, the] law to themselves:* Because they have in them *physis* as the guide for their conduct, a guide that is "not only relative or psychological, but absolute and objective" (O. Michel, *Römer*, 68). Note in this verse that Paul says *ethnē*, "Gentiles," which does not mean "all Gentiles." Second, he does not necessarily imply the perfect observance of all the precepts. Third, he uses *physei* in a context referring primarily to knowledge: Even without the Law the Gentiles know instinctively what is to be done. The word does not mean "by nature," as distinguished from "by grace." His viewpoint is not that of the later theological problem: whether the pagan's will suffices *physei* to obey the natural law. **15.** *they show that what the Law requires is written in their hearts:* Lit., "the deed of the Law is written." Paul uses the singular of the expression he employs elsewhere in a pejorative sense, "the deeds of the Law," *erga nomou* (Rom 3:20,28; Gal 2:16 [see comment]; 3:2,5,10), or simply *erga* (Rom 4:2,6; 9:12,32; 11:6; Eph 2:9). They are the "deeds" that the Law prescribes. The expression is not found in the OT or rabbinical literature, but in the QL. Paul affirms this as a present real condition of the Gentile conscience. *their thoughts argue their case pro and con:* This version of a difficult sentence takes the phrase *metaxy allēlōn* (between one another) to refer to the mutual debate of inward thoughts in the Gentile's conscience. The debate would concern the Gentile's own actions. Some commentators (Sanday-Headlam, Lyonnet) take it to refer to thoughts that criticize or defend the actions of others and translate: "in their dealings with one another." (Cf C. Spicq, *RB* 47 [1938] 50–80.) **16.** Logically, this verse follows 2:13, and some commentators have suggested that vv. 14–15 are parenthetical or misplaced. However, the mss. tradition is constant. Paul does not mean that the Gentile conscience will function only on judgment day, but that especially on that day will it bear witness. There is anacoluthon here. *when God will judge through Jesus Christ:* Contemporary Jews expected Yahweh to exercise judgment through an Elect One (*Enoch* 45:3–6 [*APOT* 2, 214]). Paul applies this belief to Jesus. The prep. phrase *dia Christou* refers here to the mediation of Jesus in his eschatological role (→ Pauline Theology, 79:135). *according to my gospel:* The proclamation of Jesus' role in eschatological judgment forms part of Paul's "good news" of salvation. It is, of course, a salvific judgment.

31 **17.** *you call yourself a Jew:* The imaginary critic is now identified by the common Diaspora name for a member of the chosen people. This is the first of two series of five and four paratactically aligned, taunting phrases in which Paul sums up the Jewish claim: I am a Jew; I rely on the Law; my boast is Yahweh (cf. Jer 9:24); I understand his will; instructed in the Law, I know what is right and wrong. **19–20.** Four more taunts reveal the Jew's attitude toward others. Paul does not deny Israel's privileges (Rom 9:4–5) but sees all too clearly the lie in the normal Jewish complacency. **21.** *do you refuse to teach yourself?:* The complex sentence begun in 2:17 is not finished; Paul breaks off and addresses the Jew directly, confronting him with five pointed questions (2:21–23) that reveal the rift between his teaching and his own deeds. *you must not steal:* Ex 20:15.

22. *do you abominate idols, yet rob their temples?:* Cf. Dt 7:25–26. Why does Paul introduce this strange accusation? Were contemporary Jews open to the charge of temple robbing (cf. Acts 19:37)? Josephus is apparently at pains to answer the charge that the Gk name of Jerusalem, *Hierosolyma*, was derived from the vb. *hierosylein*, "rob a temple." (*Ant.* 4.8, 10 § 207; *AgAp* 1.34–35 § 310–11, 318). If Paul has something like this in mind, his taunt would be all the more telling. **24.** *because of you the name of God is abused among the Gentiles:* Paul's accusation ends with an accommodation of Is 52:5. The (corrupt?) MT reads: "All day long my [Yahweh's] name is reviled." It refers to the contempt of the Babylonian conqueror for the weakness of Israel's God who permits such misfortunes as defeat and exile to befall his people. The LXX version is fuller: "Because of you my name is continually blasphemed among the nations." Paul cites the LXX but accommodates the text: Because you violate the Law, my name is despised among the Gentiles, who see how Jews spurn their God. Should Paul have quoted Ez 36:20 instead?

32 **25.** Paul forestalls an objection, "Perhaps we Jews do not observe the Law as we should, but at least we are circumcised." This argument too he rejects. *circumcision:* The "sign of the covenant" (Gn 17:10–11; cf. Rom 4:11; *Jub* 15:28) incorporated a man into God's chosen people and assured him of life in the age to come (see J. Bonsirven, *Judaïsme palestinien* [Paris, 1935] 2, 170). Once again, Paul does not deny the value of circumcision and Israel's heritage denoted by it. But it is no substitute for the observance of the Law. **26.** *uncircumcision be regarded as circumcision:* Paul's courageous question equating a good pagan with a circumcised Jew, would have been an abomination to Pharisaic ears (see comment on Gal 5:6). **28.** *the real Jew:* Paul's climax. He pits against contemporary Jewish religious formalism the principle of interior motivation of man's actions—the circumcision of the heart, already proclaimed in the OT (Jer 4:4; 9:24–25; Ez 44:9; Dt 10:16; 30:6). For God deals not with men according to outward appearances but "judges the secrets of men through Christ Jesus" (2:16). **29.** *real circumcision is of the heart, a thing of the Spirit, not of the letter:* From 2 Cor 3:6 we know that the contrast of Spirit and letter is a succinct Pauline way of summing up the realities of the two dispensations, the New and the Old. The latter was governed by the written code, an extrinsic norm to be observed and made much of; the former is vitalized by God's gift of the Spirit, an intrinsic principle that reshapes man interiorly and remolds his conduct. Thus the circumcision of the heart, of which the OT itself made much, takes on a new nuance. It is not just a spiritual circumcision of the heart (referring to man's *pneuma*), but one that springs from the Spirit of Christ himself. *his praise is not from men but from God:* The real Jew is the Israelite in spirit with a circumcised heart; he will be known as such by God and receive his praise from him. He cares not for the praise of men who might observe his fidelity to the Torah. Paul probably plays on the Hebr name for a Jew, *Y^{e}hûdî*. It is derived from the patriarchal name Judah (*Y^{e}hûdāh*), which in the popular etymology of the OT (Gn 29:35; 49:8) was explained as the passive of *hôdāh* (Hiphil of *ydh*), "praised." The man of the circumcised heart is the one who is "praised" in God's sight—the real "Jew."

33 Paul's foregoing attack seemingly implies that Jews really have no advantage over Gentiles, despite his willingness to accord them a certain precedence (1:16; 2:9–10). Now in ch. 3 he answers an imaginary objection pressing this point, and returns to his thesis: Despite the divine oracles of salvation recorded in their sacred books the wrath of God will burst upon Jews too. Paul's argumentation in this chapter is not very systematic. Sometimes he argues with an imaginary opponent, sometimes with himself. His reasons are at most mere hints. Once he begins a multiple answer (saying, "In the first place"), but he never continues it. It all sounds like echoes of synagogue debates.

The relation of 3:1–8 to the rest of the letter's development is disputed. The relation depends on the interpretation of "the utterances of God" (3:2), and of "some" in "What if some of them were unfaithful?" (3:3). To whom does "some" refer? If it means unbelieving contemporary Jews who did not accept Christ as the fulfillment of messianic promises, then the paragraph would foreshadow Rom 9–11, and would represent a sort of interim statement about contemporary Jewry, before Paul takes up the universal culpability of man in 3:9–20. This interpretation is given by Althaus, Cornely, Kuss, Lyonnet, Sanday-Headlam, *et al.* However, it is difficult to see the reasons for restricting "the utterances" to messianic promises, and "some" to contemporary Jews. We prefer (with Barrett, Lagrange, Leenhardt, Lietzmann, Michel) to understand the passage to refer to Jews of the whole course of Israel's past, who time after time were faithless to Yahweh, and who were objects of divine reproach.

34 **1.** *what advantage is there then in being a Jew?:* If possession of the Law and circumcision mean nothing, what advantage does a member of the chosen people have? **2.** *in the first place:* Thus Paul begins his explanation, but he never gives a second or third point. Instead, the first advantage evokes his comments on the infidelity of Israel. *the utterances of God:* The possession of these is an obvious advantage. In the LXX *ta logia tou theou* (Ps 107:11; Nm 24:4,16) denote "the words of God" given to the prophets to be communicated to men; they include not only revelations and promises, but also rules of conduct (see C. Spicq, *L'Epître aux Hébreux* [Paris, 1952] 2, 143; J. W. Doeve in *Studia paulina* [Fest. J. de Zwaan; Haarlem, 1953] 111–23). But as elsewhere in the NT (Heb 5:12; 1 Pt 4:11), the expression here refers to the OT in general as God's words about salvation; these have been entrusted to the Jews. Nothing in the expression itself, or in the context, restricts the meaning to messianic promises, which are called "promises" (*epaggeliai*) in Rom 9:4. **3.** *what if some of them were unfaithful?:* Since *apisteō* can mean either "refuse to believe" or "be unfaithful" (see AG 84), either or both senses could be meant here, for numerous OT examples could be cited of Israel's historic incredulity (Nm 14; Ex 15:22ff.) or infidelity (1 Kgs 18:21; Hos 4:2; etc.). It is only "some" who have been unfaithful. But Paul does not restrict it in any way temporally; nor is he thinking yet of the "remnant" (Rom 9:27; 11:5) that did accept Christ and become the Jewish-Christian Church. *can their faithlessness nullify the faithfulness of God?:* As depositaries of the divine utterances, the Jews possessed Yahweh's protestations of fidelity to the people of his covenant (Ex 34:6; Hos 2:23; Nm 23:19; Is 55:11). But did his fidelity to such utterances not depend on Israel's fidelity to him? **4.** *by no means!:* The suggestion of God's infidelity is rejected by the indignant negative *mē genoito* (really a negative wish, "May it not be so!" Bl-Deb-F § 384). In the LXX it translates Hebr *ḥ^{a}lîlāh*, "far be it from [me]." God's fidelity is not measured by man's; this is basic in Paul's teaching on uprightness. God is always upright and will justify Israel (3:26). *God must be true though every man be a liar:* In using *alēthēs* of God, Paul plays on its two meanings: (1) "true, honest"; (2) "faithful, loyal." Though the second is obviously intended in the context, the first cannot be excluded, because of the allusion to Ps 116:11 [LXX 115:2], which refers to man as a liar. *as it is written:* See comment on 1:17. Paul quotes Ps 51:6, not according to the MT ("That you may be justified in your sentence, vindicated when you condemn"), but according to the LXX ("That you may be justified in your words, and conquer when you are tried"). In the MT the psalmist confesses that even when the divine sentence falls on David for his sin with Bathsheba, men will know that God is upright. But in the LXX form quoted, the connotation of "sentence" is lost, and "in your words" refers to the "utterances" (3:2), so that even in his infidelity David learned of God's fidelity: "I will not be false to David" (Ps 89:35). Paul cites the psalmist's words to bear out his thesis that Yahweh is ever shown to be faithful to his utterances. **5.** *if our wickedness brings out God's uprightness:* A logical conclusion from Paul's contention. If David's infidelity does not nullify God's fidelity, but rather makes it manifest, then man's wickedness will bring about the manifestation of divine uprightness (the attribute, see comment on 1:17). *is God unjust to inflict his wrath [on us]?:* There is no contradiction in the manifestation of divine uprightness and wrath. Only a human way of looking at it would suggest that human wickedness should not be visited by divine wrath. Underlying the question is the suggestion that if man's wickedness really brings out God's salvific uprightness and fidelity, then he would be unjust in inflicting his wrath. Again Paul emphatically rejects the notion; see comment on 3:3. **6.** *otherwise how is God to judge the world?:* A fundamental Jewish belief regarded Yahweh as the eschatological Judge of the world (Is 66:16; Jl 3:12; Pss 94:2; 96:13; cf. Rom 2:16). **7.** *if the truth of God...:* This is really the same objection as 3:5, involving merely a third attribute. **8.** Paul does not take pains to refute the sophism involved in the accusation leveled against him (or Christians in general). Nothing in the text suggests that such accusations actually circulated in the Roman church and that this is why he mentions them.

35 **9–20.** After the diatribe of 3:3–8 Paul returns to his original question (3:1) about the advantage of the Jews. Indirectly, he has shown that even the infidelities of Israel reveal its privileged position, for Yahweh has been faithful to the salvific utterances once made to his people. But in contrast to that fidelity stands Jewish infidelity, which is rooted in the fact that all men, Jews as well as Greeks, are sinners, as the Scriptures declare. These will be cited in this section, which concludes Paul's discussion of the manifestation of divine wrath against the Jews. **9.** *what then? Are we [Jews] any better off? No, not at all:* Though the general sense of this difficult phrase is clear from the context, it is not easy to translate. Our translation is commonly used; other possible ones: (1) "Are we (Jews) at a disadvantage (understanding the vb. as pass., "excelled," whereas the above translation takes it as middle voice)? No, not in all respects." (2) "Am I (lit., "we" [editorial]) protecting myself?" Whichever is correct, there is no doubt about the following statement. *all are under [the power of] sin:* Paul's fundamental thesis about man's condition without the gospel (cf. 3:23; 5:12). "Sin" is mentioned for the first time in Rom. It is a force personified as a master who dominates a slave. It holds men in bondage to it, and in estrangement from God (→ Pauline Theology, 79:99–104). **10.** *as it is written:* See comment on 1:17. To prove his point, Paul cites a catena, or series, of OT texts drawn from the Pss and the Prophets illustrating the common theme of the man who is not upright. This is a literary subform, known as testimonia, and attested in QL in a text that illustrates the messianic hopes of the Qumran Essenes (4Q Test; cf. J. M. Allegro, *JBL* 75 [1956] 182–87; J. A. Fitzmyer, *TS* 18 [1957] 513–37). Paul probably makes use of a catena already in existence (so M. Dibelius, *TRu* 3 [1931] 228). The texts are derived from Pss 14:1–3 (or 53:2–4); 5:10; 140:4; 10:7; 36:2 and Is 59:7–8. They are linked by the mention of parts of the body (throat, tongue, lips, mouth, feet, eyes); all of man is sinful in God's sight. In citing such testimonia, Paul uses the Jews' own Scriptures to show that they as well as the Gentiles are "under sin." In each case the OT passage refers to Jews (at least to sinners among them).

36 **19.** *the Law:* Though none of the quotations in 3:10–18 come from the Pentateuch (*Tôrāh*), Paul calls the whole OT "the Law" (cf. 1 Cor 14:21), naming it in rabbinical fashion after its most authoritative part. *to those under the Law:* In the OT itself, which speaks above all to the Jews, Paul finds the support of his thesis. *that the whole world may be accountable to God:* Lit., "may be liable to judgment by God." The universality of man's moral failure without the gospel is emphasized by the threefold use of the adj. *pas*, "all, every," in 3:19–20. Thus 3:9 is solemnly rephrased. **20.** *by observing the Law:* Lit., "from the deeds of the [Mosaic] Law," see comment on 2:15. These are not to be understood simply as "good deeds," but as those performed in obedience to the Law and regarded by Jews as the means of attaining uprightness before God. *no human being will be made upright in his sight:* An implicit quotation of Ps 143:2, a psalm of personal tribulation, in which the psalmist, conscious of his sinfulness and Yahweh's transcendent uprightness, confesses his inability to vindicate himself. Instead, he appeals for his vindication to Yahweh's characteristic "fidelity" (the Gk *alētheia* = Hebr *ʾ^{e}mûnāh*) and "uprightness" (the Gk *dikaiosynē* = Hebr *ṣ^{e}dāqāh*). See comment on 1:17. The MT of the Ps says, "Before you no living man is just"; but Paul cites the LXX, which has the fut. tense, and he changes "living man" to "flesh," using a Hebraism (Is 40:5). But he significantly adds, "by observing the Law." He therefore accommodates the psalmist's cry to a specific problem: the attainment of uprightness through the Law. He does the same in Gal 2:16. That no man is upright before God is also an Essene tenet in QL (1QH 4:30–31; 7:16; 12:19; 16:11). *through the Law [comes only] the consciousness of sin:* The developed discussion of the role of the Law (7:7ff.) is foreshadowed here. Its essential function is that of a moral informer, giving man a real and deep religious knowledge (*epignōsis*) of moral disorder as a rebellion against God. It supplies man's conscience, which otherwise vaguely apprehends moral disorder, with an awareness of it as a formal transgression (*parabasis*). Without the Law there was no transgression, no rebellion (Rom 4:15; 5:13; see P. Benoit, *RB* 47 [1938] 486; *Exégèse*, 2, 14). But if the Law declares all men sinners and makes men conscious of their condition, then a fortiori the Jew to whom it is addressed is just as much an object of God's wrath as the pagan, whose moral perversion and degradation reveal his condition.

37 (c) THE THEME POSITIVELY DEVELOPED: GOD'S UPRIGHTNESS IS MANIFESTED THROUGH CHRIST AND SHARED IN BY FAITH (3:21–31). So far, Paul has developed his theme antithetically by showing how man's condition without the gospel is one that calls forth God's wrath. Now he will show that a new period in the history of man began in the coming of Jesus Christ. His coming was a manifestation of divine uprightness and fidelity. The gospel proclaiming this coming and its effects is thus "the power of God for the salvation of everyone who has faith" (1:16). Paul now explains positively how this is so. Verses 21–31 form a very important part of Rom, for they formulate in effect the essence of his gospel: salvation through faith in the Christ-event. In them the theme of the manifestation of divine uprightness is developed, as Paul treats of (1) its relation to the Law (3:21); (2) its universal destination (3:22); (3) its necessity and spontaneity (3:23–24); (4) its nature and gratuity (3:23–24); (5) its mode of manifestation (3:24–25); (6) its initiative (3:25); (7) its finality (3:25–26); (8) its practical consequences (3:27–31).

38 **21.** *but now:* This verse is not a logical conclusion from what precedes. The adv. "now" is temporal, proclaiming the new era that has been inaugurated. It supersedes that of the Law, circumcision, and the promises; the period of wrath gives way to that of uprightness. This is the first use of the "eschatological 'now,'" of no little frequency in Rom (3:26; 5:9,11; 6:22; 7:6; 8:1,18; 11:5,30,31; etc.). *independently of the Law:* Paul insists: The Mosaic Law had nothing to do with this new manifestation of God's uprightness—at least directly (cf. Gal 2:19). The Christian dispensation of salvation is independent and destined to supersede the Law (Rom 10:4). *God's uprightness has been manifested:* See 1:17. In 3:20 Paul quoted Ps 143 mentioning the divine quality of uprightness. This is most likely the sense intended here: The divine attribute is revealed. It is not his vindicative or commutative justice, but his bounteous and salvific uprightness whereby he delivers his people in an act resembling acquittal (→ Pauline Theology, 79:94–97). *though the Law and the Prophets bear witness:* Paul allows, however, that the OT was privileged to prepare for this manifestation of God's uprightness (Rom 1:2; Gal 3:24–25). In fact, it still bears witness (pres. ptc., expressing contemporaneity with the main vb.). Rom 4:1–25 will illustrate this. For the "Law and the Prophets" represents the OT (cf. Acts 13:15; 24:14; 28:23; Mt 5:17; 7:12; 11:13; 20:40). **22.** *through faith in Jesus Christ:* Lit., "through the faith of Jesus Christ." The genitive is objective, as in Rom 3:26; Gal 2:16,20. Paul is not thinking of Christ's fidelity to the Father, nor does he propose his fidelity as a model of Christian conduct. Christ is rather the concrete manifestation of divine uprightness, and man appropriates to himself the effects of that manifested uprightness by faith. This manifestation is comprehended only by those who have the eyes of faith. On faith, see comment on 1:17. The Council of Trent understood "faith" here as "the beginning of human salvation, the foundation and root of all justification" (DB 801; DS 1532). This is a reformulation of Paul's thought in terms of a slightly different approach to the problem. *for all who have faith:* The universal destination of the effects of God's uprightness. This short form of the phrase (*eis pantas*) is normally preferred to an inferior reading in some mss. (D, G, Vg), "for all and upon all who..." (*eis pantas kai epi pantas*). *without distinction:* Of Jew or Greek (cf. Rom 10:12).

39 **23.** *all men have sinned:* Christian salvation, embracing all men, copes with the universality of sin among them. Paul is thinking primarily of the two historic groups of humanity, Jews and Greeks; yet his absolute formulation also connotes the idea of "all individuals." The vb. *hamartanō*, while retaining in the NT its basic meaning of "missing the mark" (failing to achieve a moral goal), as in classical Greek and the LXX, also has the connotation of transgression against divinity, custom, or law. It denotes the personal, individual actions by which man does wrong. There is no reference here to habitual or original sin (see *ThDNT* 1, 308–13). *fall short of the glory of God:* That is, they remain, because of their sins, without a share in God's glory. By this is meant the resplendent external manifestation of Yahweh's presence, called *kābôd* in the MT and *doxa* in the LXX (Ex 24:17; 40:34–38). For Paul *doxa* is something communicated to man as he draws close to God (2 Cor 3:18; 4:6). Estranged by sin from the intimate presence of God, man has deprived himself of something that was his. The vb. *hystereō* means "to come too late, miss through one's own fault," and so "to need, lack, fall short of." The middle voice used here implies that man by his very actions has fallen short of his moral goal and thus deprived himself of divine glory. There is no reason to think that Paul refers to the contemporary notion of Adam (and Eve) robed in glory before the fall (*Apoc. Mos.* 20:2 [*APOT* 2, 146]; cf. 1QS 4:23; CD 3:20). **24.** *by his grace* [or *favor*]*:* The Christian dispensation is wholly due to the merciful and gratuitous benevolence of God himself. Though Paul uses *charis*, one should not try to seek in this expression the formal cause of justification (F. Prat, *The Theology of St. Paul* [London, 1926] 1, 206n.). Paul is thinking of the OT notion of benevolence, the root of the covenant relationship of God with his people. A very similar notion is found in QL (1QH 6:9; 7:27,20; 13:16–17). [*all*] *are made upright:* Men achieve that status of rectitude before God at which the Jew of the dispensation of old aimed in observing the Law; however, they find that it is not gained by something within themselves, but is due only to God's benevolent favor. Writing in the light of his Judaizing controversies, Paul still speaks of the new relationship between man and God in Christ in terms that are legal and juridical. What happens to man in this new manifestation of God's uprightness is not without its forensic, judicial aspects. But to maintain that Paul means that man is only "declared upright," though still a sinner, would imply a watering down of the "New Creation" and the whole Christian reality that he is proclaiming. For in this "New Creation" man actually becomes the "uprightness of God" (2 Cor 5:17–21; → Pauline Theology, 79:97). *for nothing:* This phrase excludes the possibility of man's attaining or meriting his justification on his own. It is a sheer "gift" of God (Eph 2:8). The Council of Trent went further and declared that *gratis* meant that neither faith nor deeds merit the grace of justification (DB 801; DS 1532); cf. *Divino Afflante Spiritu* § 47 [*RSS* 102]. *through the redemption of Christ Jesus:* Man's state of rectitude before God comes about only through the benevolence and uprightness of God made manifest in the redemptive liberation of Christ Jesus. *Apolytrōsis* is often defined as "redemption," the buying back of a slave or the freeing of him by the payment of a ransom (AG 95). Whatever the overtones of the expression may be (→ Pauline Theology, 79:90–93), the word expresses above all a liberation or deliverance (cf. Rom 8:23; Eph 1:7,14; 4:30; Col 1:14; 1 Cor 1:30). It is a new deliverance, carrying on and fulfilling the sense of Yahweh's freeing of Israel at the Exodus (cf. Pss 78:35; 18:15–19). In principle, this liberation has already taken place in the death and resurrection of Jesus (3:25), but its definitive phase has not yet been achieved (Rom 8:23; Eph 4:30). This is insinuated even here, when Paul uses the title "Christ"—a title that refers above all to the future, eschatological role of Jesus (cf. O. Cullmann, *Christology of the NT* [Phila., 1959] 109–36).

40 **25.** *God displayed him publicly:* The sense of *proetheto* is not clear. It could mean, "God designed him to be..." (NEB, Origen, Lagrange), i.e., proposed him to himself, as he planned man's salvation. But if more stress is placed on the prep. *pro* with which the verb is compounded, then it would mean, "God set him forth," i.e., displayed him publicly. It would then be a reference, not so much to the divine plan of salvation as to the crucifixion (cf. Gal 3:1). Note that the initiative of the redemption is ascribed to the Father (*ho theos*). *as a means of atonement:* God set Christ forth as *hilastērion.* If this word is understood as a masc. adjective, it would mean "as expiatory." If it is understood as a neut. noun, it would denote concretely "a means of expiation." Neither Paul's usage nor the OT background suggest that the word, a derivative of *hilaskomai*, has anything to do with propitiation in the sense of placating an angry God. In the LXX it expresses either God's forgiveness of sin or a ritual removal of the cultic defilement that hinders the communion of some person or object with God. Since *hilastērion* is the Gk name for the "mercy seat" in the Holy of Holies (Lv 16:2,11–17), Paul may well be saying that Christ crucified became the mercy seat of the New Dispensation, the "means of expiating" the sins that estranged men from God. (→ Pauline Theology, 79:86; cf. 2 Cor 5:19). [*effective*] *through faith:* This phrase, which is difficult to translate because it is cryptic and to a certain extent disrupts Paul's exposition, is nevertheless crucial in his argument: Even though the most important aspect of Christian salvation is what Jesus did in dying and rising, the benefits of it are shared in only "through faith." *to show forth his uprightness:* This is the first of two parallel statements that reveal the finality of the Cross. Christ's expiatory death makes public and convincing the Father's salvific bounty and uprightness. Man's state of uprightness thus flows from the uprightness of God himself. The Essenes of Qumran also attributed the pardon of sin to God's uprightness (1QH 4:37; 11:30–31); in a sense it is rooted in the OT (Ps 143:1–2,11; Ezr 8:13–15; Dn 9:16). At Qumran it is a pardon awaited for in the *eschaton*, but in Paul the act of deliverance is already past (see P. Benoit, *NTS* 7 [1960–61] 293–95). *by the remission of men's former sins:* A difficult phrase. A rare word, *paresis*, is used here, which ancient commentators generally understood as "remission," a meaning that is found in extrabiblical Greek (AG 631). Accordingly, Christ's death would be a demonstration of divine uprightness in that it remitted the sins of men previously committed—sins that awaited expiation on this great Day of Atonement (cf. Acts 13:38; Heb 9:15). Many commentators, however, prefer the meaning of "overlooking, passing over, letting go unpunished" (so Barrett, Huby, Michel, Kuss). This etymological meaning is derived from the corresponding vb. *parienai*, but is otherwise only doubtfully attested. In this case, Christ's death demonstrates God's uprightness in wiping out sins, in contrast to the forbearance previously shown in passing over men's sins. (See W. G. Kümmel, *ZThK* 49 [1952] 165; J. M. Creed, *JTS* 41 [1940] 28–30; for another more complicated, but less convincing interpretation, see S. Lyonnet, *Bib* 38 [1957] 40–61; *Romains*, 83). [*committed*] *in* [*the time of*] *God's forbearance:* Though up to Christ's coming sinful men were subject to God's wrath (1:18), that wrath did not always manifest itself in the punishment of sin, for it is really eschatological. A tolerant forbearance was used by God, who through his divine plan knew that these sins would be expiated in the death of Christ in due time. Even the expiation of sins on the yearly Day of Atonement only made sense in the prefiguring of Christ's blood shed on the cross.

41 **26.** *now in the present:* The "eschatological 'now' " (see comment on 3:21). The cross of Christ had a finality not only with reference to the past sins of men, but also to men who would live in the New Dispensation. This verse contains the second statement about that finality. [*to show*] *that he is upright himself:* Through the public exposure of Christ, his Son, on the cross, God vindicated his claim to be the liberator and savior of his people (Is 59:15–20). He thereby brought man into a status of rectitude, which is one of innocence and acquittal. *even in making upright him who has faith in Jesus:* Earlier commentators, who understood *dikaiosynē theou* of God's vindicative justice, gave a concessive meaning to this phrase: "in order to be just, even though he justifies...." This involved the demand that Christ had to die vicariously for man's sins. The context, however, seems to be against such an interpretation. Paul is saying rather that the recent divine intervention in man's history proves that God is upright. He even makes men upright through Christ's expiatory death.

42 **27–31.** The practical consequences of the manifestation of God's uprightness, in particular the role of faith. Man cannot boast of his achieving his own salvation. **27.** *on what principle?:* Lit., "through what law" are man's boasting and self-confidence excluded? Paul plays on the word *nomos*. The Jew could boast of his observance of the Law, but Paul rules out a "law of deeds," and admits only a "law of faith." Uprightness, then, is not achieved, but received. This is the only "law" he will admit, in reality no law at all; hence the translation, "the principle of faith." Cf. Rom 8:2 ("the law of the Spirit"); Gal 6:2 ("the law of Christ"). **28.** *man is made upright by faith:* See Gal 2:16; Phil 3:9. This is the main tenet of Pauline justification. Man cannot boast, because his rectitude before God is not the product of achievement. At this point M. Luther introduced the adv. "only" into his translation of 1521 ("allein durch Glauben"); cf. Jas 2:24. This became a major Reformation issue, but it was not done without some precedents in earlier interpreters (Bernard, Thomas Aq.). Did Luther and his predecessors mean the same thing by it though? (See S. Lyonnet, *Quaestiones*, 1a ser. [1962] 114ff.) *without observing the Law:* Lit., "without the deeds of the Law" (see comment on 2:15). Paul never denied the relation of deeds performed after Christian conversion to salvation (cf. Gal 5:6; Eph 2:8–10; 1 Cor 15:10; comment on Rom 2:6; → Pauline Theology, 79:161). But because he sometimes omits the gen. *nomou* (4:2), his phrase acquired a more general meaning of "deeds." This apparently happened even in the early Church, for Jas 2:24 represents a protest, not against Paul's teaching, but against an exaggeration to which the unguarded phrase was open (see J. Jeremias, *ExpT* 66 [1954–55] 368–71). **29.** *does God belong to the Jews alone?:* If uprightness depended on the Mosaic Law, this might seem to be the conclusion, for in it God addressed them only. *God of the Gentiles too?:* No Jew would have denied that Yahweh was the God of all men. But though his salvation was for all men, Israel was favored. Rabbi Simon ben Yoḥai (*ca.* AD 150) said: "God said to the Israelites, 'I am God over all who come into the world, but I have linked my name only with you. I am not called the God of the Nations of the world, but the God of Israel' " (*Exodus Rabbah* 29). Paul makes capital of such an admission for his own purpose. **30.** *only one God:* The one mode of salvation open to all, Jew and Greek alike, is traced to its monotheistic origin. **31.** *do we do away with the Law by* [*this*] *faith?:* The question that ultimately had to be asked. Though Christ is the "end of the Law" (Rom 10:4; cf. Gal 3:24) and has "done away with the Law" (Eph 2:15 [same vb. as here]), there is, however, a sense in which his gospel "confirms" (or "upholds") the Law. Paul will devote ch. 4 to an explanation of this point. *Nomos* now means the whole OT (see comment on 3:19). When Paul insists on the one principle of salvation—faith—and links it to one God, he thereby affirms the basic message of the whole OT, and in particular the Mosaic Law itself. This is seen from the discussion in 3:28–29 and of the relation of Abraham to the Mosaic Law, to be discussed in ch. 4.

43 (d) THE THEME ILLUSTRATED: IN THE OLD LAW ABRAHAM WAS JUSTIFIED BY FAITH (4:1–25). To show that the justification of all men by faith confirms the Law, Paul now argues that the principle was already operative in the OT. Abraham is used as an example: (1) He was declared upright because of his faith (4:1–8); (2) not because of his circumcision (4:9–12); (3) nor in dependence on the Law, but in virtue of a promise (4:13–17). As a result (4) he is our father, and his faith is the "type" of Christian faith (4:18–25).

44 **1.** *what then shall we say about Abraham?:* The Gk text is not certain. Many commentators (Goodspeed, Lyonnet, Leenhardt) and versions (RSV, NEB) read the text as given, omitting the problematic inf. *heurēkenai* (with mss. B, 1739). A more difficult reading (mss. S, A, C, D, E, F, G, Vg) retains the infinitive: "What shall we say Abraham found [= what sort of uprightness was his lot]?" Another group of mss. (K, L, P) links the infinitive with *kata sarka:* "What shall we say Abraham our forefather found according to the flesh [= what did he achieve by natural powers]?" The last reading, besides being weakly attested, is inconsistent with Paul's teaching. Much can be said for either of the other two. *our natural forefather:* Lit., "according to the flesh" (see 1:3). Descent from Abraham was a source of pride among the Jews (Mt 3:9; Lk 3:8). **2.** *because of deeds [of the Law]:* Contemporary Judaism depicted Abraham as an observer of the Law in advance (Sir 44:20 [probably a midrash on Gn 26:5]; *Jub* 6:19; 15:1–2; cf. Str-B 3, 204–6) and even in a broader sense spoke of his deeds (his defeat of the kings [Gn 14]; his trial [Gn 22:9–10]) as a source of his uprightness (Jas 2:21; 1 Mc 2:52; Wis 10:5). But in saying *ex ergōn*, Paul means only "deeds of the Law" (see comment on 2:15). This sense alone fits the general context. Paul in effect then rejects the contemporary belief that Abraham was an observer of the Law. *reason to boast:* Before men. **3.** *put faith in God and it was accredited to him as uprightness:* Gn 15:6 (cf. Gal 3:6). Abraham believed in Yahweh's promise of a numerous progeny, and this faith was "booked to his credit." The quotation comes not from the MT ("Abram believed Yahweh, who credited it to him as uprightness"), but from the LXX (with the pass.). By faith is meant Abraham's acceptance of Yahweh at his word and his willingness to abide and live by it. It involved his personal confidence and included hope in a promise that no mere man could guarantee (Rom 4:18). The text proves for Paul that Abraham was justified apart from deeds and had no reason to boast. The vb. *elogisthē* (was accredited) is a bookkeeping term figuratively applied to man's conduct (cf. Dt 24:13; Ps 106:31). It was thought that good and evil deeds were recorded in books (Est 6:1ff.; Dn 7:10; Ap 20:12). It would be false to Paul's whole theology to understand his use of Gn 15:6 to mean a mere legal fiction, that uprightness was imputed to Abraham, although he was not really upright. Theoretically, the words could mean no more than this. But there is not the slightest hint either in the Gn story or in Paul's treatment that Abraham was not previously upright. Again, Paul's ideas about faith and uprightness otherwise indicate that in the sight of God, who sees things as they are, Abraham's faith counted as uprightness; it was formally recognized to be just what it was. The manifestation of his faith was *de se* justifying. **4.** *not as a gift, but as his due:* The laborer working for pay has a strict right to it. Paul introduces this comparison to illustrate 4:2. God was never in Abraham's debt, and uprightness is not a matter of something owed. **5.** *believes in him who justifies the ungodly:* This is not a theoretical expression of Abraham's belief, nor does it mean that Abraham was himself "godless" (*asebēs*) before he put faith in Yahweh. Jewish tradition considered Abraham a *gēr*, "a stranger, alien" (Gn 23:4), one called from paganism. Since at the moment of belief in Yahweh, of which Paul speaks, Abraham had already been called and was scarcely "godless," the phrase, "who justifies the ungodly," is a generic Pauline description of God. (On justification, → Pauline Theology, 79:94–97.)

45 **6.** *David:* Like his Jewish contemporaries, Paul regards David as the author of the Pss, even though the Ps to be quoted (32:1–2) is usually regarded as a late psalm of personal thanksgiving. In the MT it bears the ancient title, "Of David." *apart from [any] deeds:* These important words are placed in the emphatic final position in the sentence, immediately preceding the words of the Ps itself. **7.** *happy are they...:* Ps 32:1–2 (LXX). The text continues Paul's argument, which began with Gn 15:6. Just as God credited Abraham with uprightness independently of meritorious deeds, so too a man can be acceptable to God even without such deeds. In the first case Paul argued by prescinding from deeds; now he argues by showing that the absence of deeds of merit is not an obstacle to justification by God. The verbs in the Ps quoted, "forgive, cover, take no account of," are various ways of expressing the removal of sin, that obstacle to man's rectitude before God. They express, as it were, the negative side of the Christian experience. But the Ps also emphasizes the gratuity of divine mercy; it is only the Lord (Yahweh; cf. 9:28) who can produce these effects, and man must trust in him and be surrounded by his kindness (Ps 32:10). Paul cites it to prove his contention that the remission of sins takes place "apart from any deeds." The words of the Ps do not necessarily mean that the sins remain, while God's benevolence merely covers them up. These are metaphors for the remission of sin. M. Luther found support in Paul's use of Ps 32 for his idea of imputed righteousness (see S. Lyonnet, *Quaestiones*, 1a ser. [1962] 139–45). Thus both the witnesses—Abraham and David—show that the OT itself supports Paul's thesis of gratuitous uprightness through faith. In this way his teaching "upholds" the Law (3:31).

46 9–12. Abraham was justified before his circumcision, therefore, independently of it. **9.** *upon the uncircumcised too:* The beatitude uttered by David was not reserved exclusively for the circumcised Jew, despite the teaching of some rabbis (Str-B 3, 203). To prove his point Paul employs a rabbinical exegetical principle, *g^ezērāh šāwāh* (that identical words, occurring in two different places in Scripture, are the basis of mutual interpretation). The word *logizomai* is found in the Pss and in Gn 15:6, said of Abraham while still uncircumcised. Therefore, the "happiness" of the Ps can be applied to some uncircumcised sinner (see J. Jeremias, in *Studia paulina* [Fest. J. de Zwaan; Haarlem, 1953] 149–51). **10.** *before he was circumcised:* Paul argues from the sequence in Gn itself: In Gn 15 Abraham's faith was counted as uprightness, but it is only in Gn 17 that he was circumcised. Therefore, circumcision has nothing to do with his justification. **11.** *the seal of uprightness:* In

Gn 17:11 circumcision is called the "sign of the covenant" between Yahweh and Abraham's family (cf. Acts 7:8). The rabbis called circumcision the sign of the later covenant between Yahweh and Israel, for it served to distinguish Israel from the nations (Jgs 14:3; 1 Sm 14:6). Significantly, Paul avoids mention of the covenant, and the "sign of the covenant" becomes for him the "seal of uprightness." He seems to have identified the covenant too much with the Law; and here insinuates that God's true covenant was made with the men of faith. *the father of all who believe:* At the time that Abraham put faith in Yahweh and became justified he was uncircumcised as was any Gentile. His spiritual paternity is thus established vis-à-vis all believing Gentiles. "The real children of Abraham are the men of faith" (Gal 3:7). **12.** Jews too must follow the footsteps of their forefather by imitating his faith, if they are to be regarded hereafter as his children. His true posterity are those who imitate not his circumcision, but his faith. Paul views this spiritual paternity of Abraham as an important phase in God's plan of salvation for men. Hence the purpose expression at the end of 4:11 (*eis to* with the inf.; see Bl-Deb-F § 402, 2).

47 **13–17.** Abraham received a promise independently of the Law. **13.** *not through the Law:* That is, the Mosaic Law (see comment on 2:12), for Paul implicitly assails the Judaizing view that all blessings came to Abraham because of his merit in keeping the Mosaic Law, which he knew in advance through an intuition or revelation (see comment on 4:2). *the promise:* The promise of an heir to be born to Sarah (Gn 15:4; 17:16,19) and of numerous posterity (Gn 12:2; 13:14–17; 17:8; 22:16–18) was extended by the rabbis on the basis of the universality of "all the families of the earth" (Gn 12:3) to mean that "the whole world" was Abraham's inheritance (see Str-B 3, 209). *through the uprightness of faith:* Appositional genitive. In 4:11 Paul had set this cardinal tenet over against the claim of circumcision; now he pits it against the Mosaic Law itself. He constantly returns to it, for only by this means will Abraham's heirs possess the whole world. **14.** *but if the adherents of the Law are the heirs:* If the only condition for inheritance were the observance of the Law, then faith would mean nothing, and God's promise would be no promise. For an extraneous condition, foreign to the very nature of a promise, would have been introduced (cf. Gal 3:15–20). **15.** *for the Law brings wrath:* This verse is really parenthetical; yet it expresses Paul's profound conviction. The 613 prescriptions of the Law are honored more in the breach than the observance; in furthering transgressions (Gal 3:19), it promotes the reign of Sin. It thus provokes the retribution described in Rom 2–3 (cf. Gal 3:10). Paul does not explain this further here (see Rom 7:7ff.; → Pauline Theology, 79:113). *where there is no law, there is no violation:* Without it an evil is only vaguely apprehended, and not as a "transgression" (*parabasis*); cf. Rom 3:20; 5:13. But since transgression, which calls down divine wrath, arises only in a legal context, Paul implicitly concludes that the world needs a dispensation that is independent of the Law. **16.** *that is why it all depends on faith:* This cryptic statement picks up the thought of 4:13. Since the Law and the promise cannot exist side by side, the Law must yield. Faith is the all-important element, involving God's promise and his favor. The man who lives by faith, lives by grace. And the promise holds good not only for the Jew, but for all who share Abraham's faith, as the OT teaches. **17.** *the father of many nations:* Gn 17:5 (LXX). In Gn the patriarch's name first appears as Abram (Hebr *'Abrām*, "The father is exalted," or "Exalted as to the Father"). The P source preserved the story of the change of Abram to Abraham and the popular etymology (17:5): Abraham means "Father of many nations" (*'ab h^{a}môn gôyîm*, which exploits the *h* but neglects the *r* in *'Abrāhām*). The "many nations" in Gn refers to the descendants of Ishmael and of the children born to Keturah (Gn 25:1ff.). Paul, however, understands it of Gentiles in general who are children of Abraham by faith. *in the sight of God:* Though the argument ends with the OT quotation, Paul adds a thought, alluding to Abraham's colloquy with God (Gn 17:1ff.). *who makes the dead live:* This (and the following) phrase may be derived ultimately from a Jewish liturgical formula. This one is similar to *Shemoneh Esreh* 2: "Thou, O Lord, art mighty forever, thou who makes the dead to live" (cf. C. K. Barrett, *NTB* § 159). In Paul's context, however, it refers to the divine power by which the barren Sarah was able to conceive Isaac (Gn 17:15–21). Remotely, it prepares for 4:24–25. *and calls into being what does not exist:* A formula similar to *2 Baruch* 48:8, "With a word thou callest into life that which was not, and with mighty power thou rulest that which has not yet come to be" (*APOT* 2, 505). In Paul's context it refers immediately to the unborn Isaac; but remotely it connotes the influence of God on the numberless Gentiles who are destined to be sons of Abraham by faith.

48 **18–25.** Abraham's faith is the "type" of Christian faith. **18.** *hoping against hope, he believed:* Lit., "contrary to [*all human*] expectation, in hope he believed [*in God*]" (AG 252). Though Abraham had so many human motives for despairing of ever having a posterity, he believed, in virtue of the confident hope that the divine promise inspired in him. He took God at his word and believed in the creative power of God to do what seemed impossible. Isaac became one "born of a promise" (Gal 4:23; cf. Gn 17:16,19; 18:10). **19.** *his own body was as good as dead:* Disregarding Gn 25:1ff., which mentions that Keturah bore Abraham six other children, Paul alludes only to Gn 17:1ff.; it tells how Abraham fell on his face and laughed when he heard that he, a man of 99 years and with a body near death, would have a son. Sarah too was 90, and barren. Note the various words for "dead" in these verses (beginning with 4:17); Paul is building up to his climax in 4:24–25. **20.** *never questioned God's promise:* Lit., "did not waver in disbelief about God's promise." Paul just passes over the fact that Abraham was convulsed with laughter. *Jub* 16:19 sublimates the laughter into "great joy." *gave glory to God:* An OT expression (1 Sm 6:5; 1 Chr 16:28) formulates Abraham's reaction of grateful recognition to God. His uprightness is now ascribed to this reaction. For a third time Paul quotes Gn 15:6 (see 4:3,9).

24. *but for our sake too:* The Abraham incident has been recalled by Paul to apply to his readers. In doing so, he adopts a rabbinical viewpoint: "All that is recorded of Abraham is repeated in the history of his children" (*Genesis Rabbah* 40:8). He consciously employs a feature of midrashic interpretation, the tendency to modernize or actualize the OT by applying it to a new situation (cf. R. Bloch, "Midrash," *VDBS* 5, 1263ff.; P. Grelot, R-F 1, 173–78). Cf. 1 Cor 9:9–10; 10:6–11. Abraham's faith is the pattern for Christian faith, because its object is the same: belief in God who makes the dead live. *for it is going to be credited to us too:* Uprightness will be booked to our credit at the eschatological judgment, provided that we have the faith of Abraham. *who raised Jesus our Lord from the dead:* Abraham's belief in God, who makes the dead live (4:17), foreshadowed the Christian's belief in God who in a unique sense raised Jesus from the dead. The efficiency of the resurrection is ascribed to the Father (as elsewhere in Paul, except in 1 Thes 4:14; → Pauline Theology, 79:72). It is the Risen Jesus who is hailed as *Kyrios* (cf. Rom 10:9). **25.** *who was handed over for our offenses:* Paul alludes to Is 53:4–5,11–12, suggesting the vicarious character of Christ's suffering in his role as the Servant of Yahweh to take away men's sins. The parallel formulation of the effects of Christ's death and his resurrection may have been suggested to Paul by Is 53:11, where sin (*hamartia*) and justification (*dikaioun*) are contrasted (cf. the death-life contrast in Rom 5:10). The two pass. verbs may very well be instances of the "theological passive," a periphrasis for God (cf. *GrBib* § 236). This verse is possibly a fragment of the early kerygma that Paul inherited from the primitive Church. *raised for our justification:* The noun *dikaiōsis* expresses primarily the action of "justification." It was in view of this that Christ was raised from the dead by the Father. The use of the same prep. *dia* in both parts of the verse makes the parallelism clear. But it has been variously interpreted. One should note, however, that it is derived from Is 53:12 (LXX: *dia tas hamartias autōn paredothē;* cf. 1QIs^{a} 44.22; 1QIs^{b} 10.25). It expresses the reason for a thing. But what reason? Leenhardt, Michel, Kuss *et al.* would understand *dia* as causal in the first part, and as final in the second. Taylor prefers "because of" in both cases, without any further explanation. Michel is right in rejecting the meaning in the second part that Jesus was raised up because we were justified through the death of Jesus (Schlatter). In the second part the meaning seems to be, "in view of our justification" (see AG 180). In other words, Paul asserts that the resurrection of Christ contributed positively to man's salvation (cf. Rom 1:4; 1 Cor 15:45; → Pauline Theology, 79:73). At any rate, the parallelism is a rhetorical device that should not be pressed too much, as if Christ's death were intended for man's sins in the same sense as his resurrection was intended for man's justification. In reality, the death and resurrection are but two intimately connected phases of the one great salvific event. This is clear because Paul does not always explicitly relate man's justification to the resurrection alone (see Rom 3:24–26; 5:9–10; Col 1:22). The affirmation of the part played by Christ's death and resurrection in the objective redemption of mankind forms a fitting conclusion to this first part of the doctrinal section of the letter (see B. Vawter, *CBQ* 15 [1953] 11–23; S. Lyonnet, *Greg* 39 [1958] 295–318; D. M. Stanley, *VD* 29 [1951] 257–74.

49 **(B) The Love of God Assures Salvation to the Justified (5:1–11:36).** Having established the justification of man by God through faith in Christ Jesus, Paul begins to discuss the Christian experience in itself and explains how salvation is assured to the upright man.

The position of ch. 5 in the literary structure of Rom is a matter of debate today, some of it idle. Four main views are held: (1) Ch. 5 concludes the first part. Justification is the subject of 1:18–5:21; sanctification of 6:1–8:39 (Amiot, Feine-Behm, Gaugler, Godet, Goguel, Guthrie, Huby, Kühl, Lagrange, Léon-Dufour, McNeile, Moe, Sanday-Headlam, Schlatter, Weiss). (2) Ch. 5 introduces the following part. Justification is treated in 1:18–4:25; the condition and salvation of justified man in 5:1–8:39; some extend it to 11:36 (Cerfaux, Cornely, Dahl, Häring, Höpfl-Gut, Jacono, Kürzinger, Lebreton, Lyonnet, Michel, Nygren, Osty, Prat, Sickenberger, Thils, Viard, Wikenhauser). (3) 5:1–11 concludes the first part, whereas 5:12–21 introduces the following part (Bonnard, Feuillet, Leenhardt, Zahn). (4) Ch. 5 is an isolated unit (Althaus, Barrett, Cambier, Dupont, Kuss, Manson, Taylor). Certainty in this matter is impossible.

The chief reasons for relating ch. 5 to what follows are: (1) Rom 5:1–11 announces briefly what 8:1–39 develops more extensively (see N. A. Dahl, *ST* 5 [1951] 37–42; cf. J. Jeremias, in *Studia paulina* [Fest. J. de Zwaan; Haarlem, 1953] 146–49). (2) The discussion in 1:16–4:24 centers about Jews and Greeks, who are not mentioned at all in 5:1–8:39. (3) Whereas the divine attribute that dominates 1:18–4:25 is uprightness, it is the love of God that is operative in the next section (5:5,8; 8:28,35,37,39). Beginning with 5:1, references to the justification and reconciliation of man are in the past tense, in contrast to the preceding section. (4) Divisions within ch. 5–8 are indicated by variations of the same concluding formula, which echo Rom 1:5: 5:21, "grace...through Jesus Christ our Lord"; 6:23, "gift...in Christ Jesus our Lord"; 7:24–25, "thanks be to God! Through Jesus Christ our Lord"; 8:39, "the love of God which is in Christ Jesus our Lord." (5) 1:18–4:25 has been termed a juridical discussion, whereas 5:1–8:39 has been considered more ethical and mystical. (See further S. Lyonnet, *RSR* 39 [1951] 301–16. Cf. A. Feuillet, *RB* 57 [1950] 336–87, 489–529; *NTS* 6 [1959–60] 52–80; J. Dupont, *RB* 62 [1955] 265–97; X. Léon-Dufour, *RSR* 51 [1963] 83–95.)

50 (a) THE THEME ANNOUNCED: THE RECONCILED CHRISTIAN WILL BE SAVED, SHARING WITH HOPE IN THE RISEN LIFE OF CHRIST (5:1–11). Once justified, the Christian is reconciled to God and experiences a peace that distressing troubles cannot upset, a hope that knows no disappointment, and a confidence of salvation of which he can truly boast. **1.** *justified through faith:* A summary of the previous Part A (→ 13 above) serves as the transition to the new topic. *we enjoy peace with God:* The first effect of justification the Christian experiences is peace; reconciliation replaces his estrangement (cf. Eph 2:14–17; Col 1:20). The pres. indic. *echomen* ("we have" [peace]) is preferred by modern commentators to the pres. subj. *echōmen* ("let us have"), which, though better attested, is an obvious scribal correction. The exhortation, which seems less natural in the context, would mean: Let us now give evidence of this justification by a life of peace with God. *through our Lord Jesus Christ:* Paul makes frequent use of this phrase in ch. 5 (in some form or other: vv. 2, 9, 11, 17, 21; cf. 1:5; 2:16). The prep. phrase *dia Christou* expresses the mediation of Christ in the Father's salvific plan (→ Pauline Theology, 79:135). It affirms his present actual influence on men as the Risen *Kyrios.* **2.** *we have secured an introduction:* The peace the Christian experiences is derived from his introduction into the sphere of divine favor and grace by Christ. Jesus has, as it were, reconciled him by leading him into the royal audience chamber and the divine presence. Some mss. add "by faith"; the reading is not solidly attested. *we boast of the hope of the glory of God:* The second effect of justification is confident hope. Lyonnet (*Romains, 84*) calls this statement a typically Pauline paradox. The Christian who boasts, puts his boast in something that is wholly beyond his ordinary natural powers—in hope. But hope is really as gratuitous as faith itself, and in the long run the boast relies on God. What the Christian hopes for is the communicated glory of God (see comment on 3:23), still to be attained, even though the Christian has already been introduced to the sphere of "grace." The relation between *charis* and *doxa* should be noted here, but it should not too readily—and without proper distinctions—be transferred to the later theological categories of *gratia* and *gloria.* **3.** *even in [our] troubles:* Because the real basis of that hope is divine favor, it is mighty enough to give to the Christian confidence even in the face of troubles (*thlipseis,* hardships that might tend to separate men from Christ's love [see 8:35; 1 Cor 4:11–13; 7:26–32]). Paul is not advocating in this verse some form of Pelagianism when he says that tribulation produces endurance, endurance character, and character hope. For the basis of it all is divine grace. **5.** *[such] hope does not disappoint:* A vague allusion to Pss 22:6; 25:3,20. The hope of God's glory is not illusory because it is founded on God's love for men. The

Christian will, therefore, never be embarrassed by a disappointed hope; implicit is a comparison with merely human hope, which can deceive. *the love of God:* Not "our love of God" (as many older commentators understood it), but "God's love of us" (subj. gen.), as the following context makes clear. Nothing here suggests that Paul is thinking of reciprocal love (that the genitive is both objective and subjective!). In the OT the "pouring out" of a divine attribute is a commonplace ("mercy," Sir 18:11; "wisdom," Sir 1:9; "favor, grace," Ps 45:3; "wrath," Hos 5:10). Cf. especially Jl 3:1–2 (Eng 2:28), the outpouring of the Spirit. *through his holy Spirit:* The gift of the Spirit is the proof (or perhaps the medium) of the outpouring of divine love (see 8:15–17; Gal 4:6). It signifies par excellence the presence of God in the justified man. Though Paul's terminology might suggest a distinction of the Spirit and God's love conferred, one should beware of equating it too readily with the developed distinction of the Uncreated Gift and the Created Gift in later theology. Paul is not yet so precise.

51 6. *when we were still helpless:* So Paul describes the status of the unjustified man or sinner: incapable of doing anything to achieve his rectitude before God. *then:* The phrase *kata kairon* probably means no more than this, despite some attempts to interpret it as "at that decisive time, at the right time" (see J. Barr, *Biblical Words for Time* [SBT 33; Naperville, 1962] 47–81). *Christ died:* Paul affirms the historical event in a theological setting of vicarious suffering. The whole context stresses the gratuitous, spontaneous character of that death. **7.** *hardly for an upright person:* To prove his point, Paul argues a fortiori. However, he quickly corrects himself, allowing that possibly for a really good man it might be done. This comment brings out the sheerly gratuitous character of the altruism involved, when Christ died for the "godless." **8.** *God proves his love for us:* This statement completely rules out any doctrine of the Cross that sets God and Christ over against each other (V. Taylor, *Romans*, 38). Since *ho theos* refers to the Father, and it is his love that was poured out "through the Spirit" (5:5) and is now demonstrated in the death of Christ, this triadic text is a Pauline starting point for the Trinitarian dogma. Note that there is no *quid pro quo* in the love manifested: Divine love is demonstrated toward the sinner without a hint that it is repaying a love already made known. **9.** *by his blood:* Whereas in 4:25 the justification of man was ascribed to Christ's resurrection, it is here attributed to his death. (On blood, → Pauline Theology, 79:87.) *we shall all the more be saved:* A still greater favor will be manifested to justified man in the eschatological salvation to come. **10.** A repetition of 5:8 in a more positive way; the sinner is not just "weak" or "ungodly," but actually an "enemy" of God. But the death of Christ brings about the reconciliation of an enemy with God; this is only another way of expressing the "peace" of 5:1. For "reconciliation" is but the restoration of estranged and sinful man to union and companionship with God (2 Cor 5:18–20; → Pauline Theology, 79:81). *we shall be saved by his life:* The third effect of justification is a share in the risen life of Christ, which brings salvation. Though justification is something that happens now, salvation is still to be achieved. In 4:25 the former was attributed to the resurrection; now salvation itself is rooted in Christ's risen life. **11.** *we also boast of God:* The third climactic boast in the paragraph, following up those of 5:2,3. The effect of justification is that the Christian can even boast of God himself, whereas before he stood in fear of his wrath. Having experienced God's love in the death of Christ, he can now exult at the very thought of God (see J. Dupont, *La réconciliation dans la théologie de S. Paul* [Louvain, 1953]).

52 (b) THE THEME EXPLAINED: THE NEW CHRISTIAN LIFE BRINGS A THREEFOLD LIBERATION (5:12–7:25).

(i) *Freedom from death and sin* (5:12–21). Paul begins his description of the status of the reconciled Christian by comparing it with man's previous condition before the coming of Christ. It is a comparison of Adam, the first parent, with Christ, the head of the new humanity. But it is not smoothly worked out; for Paul also wants to extol the superabundance of Christ's grace which now reigns instead of Sin and Death which had been in control of man since Adam's time. Just as sin came into the world through Adam (and with it death, which affects all men), so through Christ came uprightness (and with it life eternal). But Paul feels the need of justifying his novel teaching about Adam and breaks into the parallelism to assert emphatically that it was Adam's sin that affected all men (5:12c–d,13,14). As a result of this insertion, anacoluthon appears at the end of 5:14, and his real conclusion is expressed only indirectly. The comparison is an antithetical parallelism between the death wrought by Adam and the life brought by Christ. The antithesis is reformulated in 5:15–17, where Paul emphasizes the surpassing quality of what Christ did, when it is compared with Adam's influence. Christ, the new Adam and head of a new humanity, was incomparably more beneficent toward man than Adam was maleficent. This is repeated again in 5:18–19, and the latter verse is an echo of 5:12. In 5:20 the antithesis is again proposed, this time in terms of the Law. Except for the formulaic ending in 5:21, Paul does not use the first plural in 5:12–21, as he does in 5:1–11 and 6:1ff. This fact, plus the unified impression this paragraph makes in Paul's treatment of Adam and Christ, suggests that he may be incorporating here part of a writing composed for another occasion. This too may be the reason why there is so much disagreement about the function of ch. 5 in the structure of Rom.

53 This passage in Rom has been the subject of a centuries-long debate, because Paul seems to affirm in it the existence of hereditary sin. Indeed, Catholic exegetical tradition has almost unanimously interpreted it (especially 5:12,19) in terms of the universal causality of Adam's sin on the sinfulness of individual men. This tradition found its formal conciliar expression in the Tridentine *Decretum super peccato originali* (Sess. V, 2–4). Echoing Canon 2 of both the 16th Council of Carthage (AD 418 [DB 102; DS 223]) and the 2nd Council of Orange (AD 529 [DB 175; DS 372]), it decreed, "Quoniam non aliter intelligendum est id, quod dicit Apostolus: Per unum hominem peccatum intravit in mundum, et per peccatum mors, et ita in omnes homines mors pertransiit, in quo omnes peccaverunt, nisi quemadmodum Ecclesia catholica ubique diffusa semper intellexit" (DB 791; cf. 789; DS 1514; cf. 1512). This decree gave a definitive interpretation to the text in the sense that Paul's words teach a form of the dogma of Original Sin. It is one of those rare Scripture texts that enjoys such interpretation (see *Divino Afflante Spiritu*, § 47; *RSS* 102; → Hermeneutics, 71:87–90).

But care must be had to understand what Paul is saying and not to transform too facilely his expression into the precision of later dogmatic development. Obviously, he does not use the term "Original Sin," a term which developed in the time of Augustine. Trent appealed in its decree to the sense of Paul's words as they were understood in the Church in all times and places. Though differences existed in its tradition regarding details or the understanding of individual words, there was agreement on the fact of the sin and on its extent. However, those very differences are important, for they show that Paul's formulation has to be understood for what it is. As *Humani generis* (§ 21 [DB 2314; DS 3886]) puts it:

Theologians must make it clear in what way (*qua ratione*) the teaching of the Church is contained in Scripture.

54 The main exegetical problems are met in 5:12d and center about the meaning of three expressions: "death," "they sinned," and the conjunction *eph' hō*. **12.** *so:* The paragraph begins with *dia touto*, which normally means "therefore," and would suggest that 5:12–21 is a conclusion to 5:1–11. However, despite valiant attempts to relate this paragraph to what precedes (see S. Lyonnet, *RSR* 39 [1951] 310–11), many commentators recognize its basic isolated character. If the paragraph were actually composed for another occasion, *dia touto* could well be a literary transitional particle without illative force (cf. comment on 2:1). *just as:* The beginning of the comparison; the conclusion is not introduced by *kai houtōs* (and so) in 5:12c (*pace* L. Cerfaux, *Christ in the Theology of St. Paul* [N.Y., 1959] 231–32), but is rather implied in the last clause of 5:14. *through one man:* Note the emphasis on "one man" in this paragraph; the phrase occurs 12 times. The contrast between "one" and "all" (or "many") brings out the universality of the influence involved. Here the "one man" is Adam, the man in the Genesis story whose disobedient transgression unleashed into man's world an active evil force, Sin. *sin entered the world: Hamartia* is a personified malevolent power, hostile to God and alienating men from him, which strode upon the stage of human history at the time of Adam's transgression (cf. Rom 6:12ff.; 7:7ff.; 1 Cor 15:56). Nothing in the text implies that *hamartia* is to be restricted to the act by which Adam sinned; it is rather Sin (with a capital *S*). See comment on 3:9. *through that sin came death:* Another personification is *Thanatos*, another actor on the same stage, playing the role of a tyrant (5:14,17) and dominating all mankind sprung from Adam ("man"). "Death" is not the physical, bodily death of man, the separation of body and soul, but denotes spiritual death as the definitive separation of man from God, the unique source of life (cf. 5:21; 6:21,23; 8:2,6). It is a cosmic force (Rom 8:38; 1 Cor 3:22), the "last enemy" to be vanquished (1 Cor 15:56). Paul may be alluding to Wis 2:24 ("Through the devil's envy death came into the world"), where *thanatos* has the same sense (see J. Bonsirven, *L'Évangile de Paul* [Paris, 1948] 113, n. 1.

55 Paul is certainly thinking of the story of the fall in Gn 1–3, but he prescinds from its dramatic details to utilize the theological truth of the enslavement of men because of Sin. Gn 1–3 expressly depicts the loss of trusted intercourse with God, and the consequent evils: labor, pains, and death for Adam and Eve. But the unmistakable etiological character of that story insinuates that their sin was the cause of universal human misery. (For the OT background of Adam's influence, → Pauline Theology, 79:103–104.) Paul's statement is the first clear scriptural enunciation of the baneful effects of Adam's sin on mankind in terms of widespread sin. That men inherit it he does not say. In 1 Cor 15:21–22 hereditary death is apparently ascribed to a form of incorporation in Adam; but here (5:12a,b,c) Paul merely asserts a connection between one man's transgression and the sins of all men. Though Paul is primarily interested in the contrast of the universality of sin and death with the universality of life in Christ, he does indicate not only the beginning of such universal phenomena, but also the causality of the head (Adam or Christ). He is aware too that not all man's sinfulness is due to Adam; he covers this point in his digression in 5:12d.

56 *and thus:* The adverb is important, for it establishes the connection between Adam's sin and "all men." *it spread through all men:* That "all" includes infants is a precision born of later controversy, which Paul did not envisage. Note that the Council of Trent concluded to Infant Baptism from Paul's statement ("ideo," DB 791; DS 1514). *inasmuch as:* Or "since." The meaning of the phrase *eph' hō* is much disputed. The least convincing interpretations treat it as a strict rel. phrase: (1) "In whom," an interpretation based on the VL translation, "in quo," and commonly used in the Western Church since Ambrosiaster. This interpretation was unknown to the Gk Fathers before Theophylact. But if Paul had meant this, he could have written *en hō* (see 1 Cor 15:22). Moreover, the pers. antecedent of the relative is quite removed from it. Lagrange aptly notes that the Tridentine decree does not impose this meaning (*Romains*, 106). (2) "On the grounds of which," an interpretation that understands "death" as the antecedent (so T. Zahn, H. Schlier). But this is hard to reconcile with Rom 5:21; 6:23, where death is the result of sin, not its source. (3) "Because of the one by whom" (*epi toutō eph' hō*), an interpretation that spells out the elliptical phrase and refers the pronoun to Adam. It would thus imply "a relationship between the state of sin and its initiator" (L. Cerfaux, *Christ*, 232). But is the rel. phrase elliptical? Again, no explanation is offered for the shift in the meaning of *epi*, "because of" and "by." Most modern commentators understand *eph' hō* as the equivalent of a conjunction. (4) "Since, inasmuch as, because" (*epi toutō hoti*). This interpretation, commonly used by Gk patristic writers, is based on 2 Cor 5:4; Phil 3:12; 4:10, where *eph' hō* is normally translated "because" (AG 287; Bl-Deb-F § 235, 2). It would thus ascribe to all men an individual responsibility for death. (5) "In view of the fact that, on condition that," an interpretation that uses the sense of a proviso clause that *eph' hō* has in classical and Hellenistic Greek (so R. Rothe, J. H. Moulton, S. Lyonnet). Men's actual sins would be regarded as fulfilling the condition of the ratification of Adam's sin (see S. Lyonnet, *Bib* 36 [1955] 436–56). But *eph' hō*, expressing a proviso, governs an infinitive or a fut. indicative (occasionally a subj. or opt. in later Greek). The only example of it with an aor. indicative, to parallel the usage here, is in a letter of the 4th-cent. bishop Synesius (*Ep.* 73). This is scarcely valid as a parallel. Moreover, this interpretation seems to make Paul say that death spread to all men on condition that they would sin after its entry. Does he mean this? The meaning of the clause differs little in the long run from interpretation (4) if one stresses the past tense. In view of this diversity of opinion, the best meaning is still "because, inasmuch as." A difficulty often found with it is that it seems to make Paul say in 5:12c–d something contradictory to what he says in 12a–b. In the beginning of the verse sin and death are ascribed to Adam; now death seems to be due to man's deeds. But one must not lose sight of the adv. "thus" (5:12c), which establishes a connection between the sin of "one man" and the death of "all men." Moreover, the point of the digression (5:12c–14) seems to be precisely to define Adam's relation to all men. Paul ascribes death to two causes, but they are not unrelated.

57 *all men sinned:* See comment on 3:23. The verb should not be translated, "have sinned collectively" or "have sinned in Adam," because these are additions to the text. Here *hēmarton* refers to personal, actual sins of men, as Pauline usage elsewhere suggests (Rom 2:12; 3:23; 1 Cor 6:18; 7:28,36; 8:12; 15:34; Eph 4:26), and as the Gk Fathers generally understood it (S. Lyonnet, *Bib* 41 [1960] 325–55). This clause, then, expresses a secondary—quasi-parenthetical—role the actual sins of men play in their condemnation to "death." However, a notion of "Original Sin" is already contained in the first part of the verse, as the reason why "death" has spread to all men. If this were not true, the rest of the paragraph would make little sense. A universal causality of Adam's sin is presupposed in 5:15a,16a,17a,18a,19a. It would be false, then, to the whole thrust of the paragraph to interpret 5:12 so as to imply that man's condition before Christ's coming was due wholly to his own personal sins.

58 **13.** *before the Law sin was in the world:* The continuation of the digression introduces a further precision. From Adam to Moses, the source of "death" was Adam's sin; men did, of course, commit evil deeds in that period, but they were not charged with them. *sin is not imputed when there is no Law:* Paul's general principle agrees with 4:15; 3:20. Before the Mosaic Law, evil deeds were not set down to men's account as something contributing to their death. There were, indeed, archsinners in that period (Gn 6:7; 19:21ff.), but Paul never alludes to them. **14.** *from Adam to Moses:* Rabbis often divided their 6000 years of man's history into three periods: from Adam to Moses, 2000 years of chaos; from Moses to the Messiah, 2000 years of Law; from the Messiah on, 2000 years of blessings. In this last period, the Messiah would give a new law or reinterpret the old one (→ Pauline Theology, 79:13, 41). Paul takes over this historic division and recasts it in terms of Jesus the Christ (= Messiah). In the first period, without the Law, Sin was in the world, but without the imputation of transgressions, even though death reigned from Adam. In the second period, there was in addition to death due to Adam's sin the contributing factor of individual transgressions now imputed because the Law existed. In the third period, there is freedom from the Law through the grace of Christ (Rom 8:1). *who had not sinned as Adam had:* Lit., "in the likeness of Adam's transgression." "Sin" (*hamartia*) and "transgression" (*parabasis*) are distinguished; the latter is the formal aspect of an evil deed considered as a violation of a precept. Adam had received a precept (Gn 2:16; 3:17), but those who lived in the first period without the Law did not do evil as he had, for they violated no precepts. Again, Paul passes over the so-called Noachic legislation (Gn 9:4ff.) and discusses the problem only in terms of the Mosaic Law. His perspective is quite different here from that of 2:14, though it is not contradictory. The sentence ends in anacoluthon, as Paul tries to conclude the comparison begun in 5:12.

59 *so Adam foreshadows the future* [*Adam*]: Lit., "who is the type of the coming [Adam]," i.e., Christ, or the "last Adam" (1 Cor 15:45). Although Adam prefigured Christ as the head of humanity, the resemblance between the type and the antitype is not perfect. The important differences that exist are brought out in the rest of the paragraph. The resemblance is not one of parity, but of superiority; the antitype reproduces the type, but in a more perfect way. **15.** *the mass of mankind:* Lit., "the many," which means "all" (cf. 5:18; 12:5; 1 Cor 10:17). *the free gift:* God's benevolent favor, assuring justification (cf. comment on 3:24). *all the more lavish:* Lest comparison with Adam should seem an affront to Christ, Paul emphasizes the surpassing quality of Christ's influence on mankind. The first mode of expressing that superabundance is the manifestation of God's favor far in excess of any mercy that sin might have otherwise evoked. **16.** [*God's*] *gift* [*arose*] *out of many offenses* [*and issues*] *in acquittal:* The second mode contrasts the verdict of condemnation for one sin—which fell on all men—with the justification (or verdict of acquittal) for men condemned not only through Adam's transgression, but also through their own offenses. **17.** *all the more will they reign and live:* Lit., "reign in life." The third mode contrasts death as the effect of the offense of one man (Adam) with the gift of upright life obtained through one man (Christ). Note the stress on "one man" in the last three verses; herein lies the similarity between Adam and Christ. The relation between the "one man" and the mass is parallel, for both Adam and Christ exercised causality on it.

60 **18.** *through the offense of one man...so through the righteous act of one man:* Given the preceding context, in which the pron. *henos* refers to "one man," it is better to preserve that sense and take *henos* as masculine. However, it is possible that Paul varies his formulation somewhat and intends *henos* to be neuter, "Through one offense... so through one righteous act." *for acquittal and life:* Lit., "for the justification of life" (the gen. is appositional). The gracious act that manifested God's gift of uprightness (5:17) not only cleared man of guilt, but also granted him a share in "life." This meaning of life is explained in ch. 8. **19.** The climax of the comparison is reached; it echoes 5:12 and formally enunciates the basic contrast of Adam and Christ. *were made sinners:* The formal effect of Adam's disobedience (Gn 3:6) was to make mankind not only liable to punishment, but actually sinners. So astute a commentator as V. Taylor remarks, "No one can be made a sinner or made righteous" (*Romans*, 41). And yet, this is what Paul says, and he is not speaking of man's personal sinful actions. The vb. *katestathēsan* does not mean, "were considered" (to be sinners), but "were made, were caused to be, were constituted" (such). Adam's disobedience placed the mass of mankind in a condition of estrangement from God. The text does not imply that they became sinners merely by imitating Adam's transgression. Rather they were affected by him. *the mass will be made upright:* Elsewhere the process of justification seems to be regarded as past (5:1); and the fut. tense may seem to be a logical future. But it more likely refers to the final judgment, when the final phase of that process will be achieved in glory. Could it refer to the future generations of Christians who would reap the fruits of Christ's death and resurrection? **20.** *the* [*Mosaic*] *Law slipped in:* As in Gal 3:19 the Law is regarded as a means of multiplying offenses in the religious history of man. This it does by supplying him with a "knowledge of sin" (3:20; cf. 7:13). As in the case of *Hamartia* and *Thanatos*, so too *Nomos* is personified and treated as an actor on the stage of man's history. Instead of being a source of life for the Jews, it proved only to be their informer and accuser, bringing condemnation (Gal 3:13). **21.** *eternal life through Jesus Christ our Lord:* The mediation of Christ (see comment on 5:1), the head of reconciled humanity, is stressed at the end of the first subdivision of this part of the letter (→ 49 above). It is the Risen *Kyrios* who brings to mankind a share in "eternal life," the life of the son of God, in which vital activity is derived from the Spirit. The adj. "eternal" indicates the quality of that life rather than its duration; it is the life of God himself.

(See Barrosse, T., "Death and Sin in Saint Paul's Epistle to the Romans," *CBQ* 15 [1953] 438–59. Biffi, G. and G. Lattanzio, "Una recente esegesi di Rom. 5, 12–14," *ScuolC* 84 [1956] 451–58. Blinzler, J., "Erbsünde und Erbtod," *BTW* 1, 273–80. Bultmann, R., "Adam and Christ According to Rom 5," *CINTI* 143–65. Gonzalez Ruiz, J.-M., "El pecado original según San Pablo," *EstBib* 17 [1958] 147–88. Hulsbosch, A., "Zonde en dood in Rom. 5, 12–21," *TT* 1 [1961] 194–204. Kümmel, W. G., *Man in the New Testament* [London, 1963] 63–67. Lafont, G., "Sur l'interprétation de Romains V, 15–21," *RSR* 45 [1957] 481–513.)

61 (ii) *Freedom from self through union with Christ* (6:1–23). The description of the Christian experience proceeds a step further. The Christian has been endowed with a new life through Christ (5:12–21), who now reigns supreme instead of Sin and Death. But this new life means a reshaping of man. Through baptism, which identifies man with Christ's death and resurrection, man's very being or "self" is transformed. The outlook of man newly justified is such as to exclude sin from his conduct. As an introduction to his explanation, Paul takes up a question already broached in 3:5–8: Why not do evil so that good may come of it? If God brings about man's salvation through Christ, and this is all sheer gift, something utterly unattainable by man, then why should man make an effort to exclude evil? Does not the very manifestation of God's bounteous grace presuppose sin and logically lead to antinomianism? Paul rejects this vehemently. If a man is in union with Christ, he is "dead to sin and alive to God." Evil holds no more charms for him.

62 1. *persist in sin?:* Paul answers an imaginary objection echoing 3:5–8. It is a fundamental question about Christian morality. If uprightness comes from faith, not deeds, then why should not Christians go on sinning? *by no means:* See comment on 3:4. **2.** *we who died to sin:* In Rom 5 Paul indicated that Sin and Death no longer dominate Christians; now he begins to explain why (cf. 1 Pt 4:1). Christians have died to sin and have nothing more to do with it. It is a contradiction for them to live in sin, for it is not they that live, but Christ that lives in them (Gal 2:20). **3.** *do you not know?:* The Roman Christians, who have been instructed in the apostolic catechesis, should be acquainted with the sublime effects of baptism. *we who were baptized:* In the NT the vb. *baptizō* refers either to Jewish ritual washings (Mk 7:4; Lk 11:38) or to the Baptist's and Christian "baptism" (Jn 1:25,28; Gal 3:27). Paul's discussion here is most easily understood of baptism by immersion. It is, however, not certain that baptism in the early Church took place by immersion (→ Pauline Theology, 79:129; C. F. Rogers, "Baptism and Christian Archaeology," *Studia biblica et ecclesiastica* 5 [1903] 239–361). *into [union with] Christ:* The phrase "into Christ" (*eis Christon*) does not simply reflect the imagery of immersion, nor is it merely an abbreviation of a borrowed bookkeeping term (*eis to onoma Christou*, "to the name, account of Christ"), as if baptism established Christ's proprietorship over the baptized Christian. Like other Pauline prep. phrases, it seems to formulate an aspect of the relationship of Christ to the Christian. It occurs most often with words denoting "faith" or "baptism," and connotes the movement of man toward Christ, the movement of incorporation by which one is born to life "in Christ" (cf. 1 Cor 10:2; → Pauline Theology, 79:136). *baptized into his death:* The rite of Christian initiation introduces man into union with Christ suffering and dying. But Paul's phrase is bold; he wants to bring out that the Christian is not merely identified with the "dying Christ" who has won a victory over sin, but is introduced into the very act by which Christ died to sin. As a result the Christian himself must be "dead to sin" (6:11). Man is thus associated with Christ precisely at the time when he formally became the Savior.

63 4. *buried with him in death:* The baptismal rite symbolically represents the death, burial, and resurrection of Christ; the convert descends into the baptismal bath, is covered with its waters, and emerges to a new life. In that act he goes through the experience of dying to sin, being buried, and rising, just as Christ did. In fact, Paul uses here one of his favorite compound verbs (compounds of *syn-*, "with"). These verbs identify the Christian with those acts of Christ's existence that begin with his passion. For the salvific acts of Christ's life in Pauline soteriology are his passion, death, and resurrection. Faith and baptism introduce man "into Christ" (*eis Christon*), identifying him specifically with Christ (*syn Christō*) in his passion, death, and resurrection. As a result, the Christian in this life lives in union with the Risen Christ (*en Christō*), a union that finds its term when the Christian will one day be with Christ (*syn Christō*) in glory (→ Pauline Theology, 79:137). *through the Father's glory:* The efficiency of the resurrection is ascribed to the Father (see comment on 4:24), and specifically to his glory (*doxa*). As in the OT (Ex 15:7,11; 16:7,10; Ps 113:9) the miracles of the Exodus were ascribed to Yahweh's *kābôd* (cf. comment on 3:23), so too is the resurrection of Christ. In 2 Thes 1:9; Col 1:11 it is the Father's "power" that is mentioned rather than his *doxa*, which is in reality only the external resplendent manifestation of his "power." Indeed, it is the *doxa* of the Father that shines on the face of the Risen Christ (2 Cor 4:6; cf. 2 Thes 2:14) and invests him with the "power" (Rom 1:4) that is "life-giving" (1 Cor 15:45). This is eventually communicated to the Christian (2 Cor 3:18), who is glorified together with Christ (Rom 8:17). *we too may live a new life:* Lit., "may walk in a newness of life." The Father's *doxa* thus affects the Christian through the Risen Christ. Baptism brings about an identification of the Christian with the glorified *Kyrios* and enables him actually to live with the life of Christ (cf. Gal 2:20). A "New Creation" is involved (2 Cor 5:17). "To walk" is another favorite Pauline expression, borrowed from the OT (2 Kgs 20:3; Prv 8:20); it designates the conscious ethical conduct of Christian life. If the Christian is identified with Christ through baptism, he is enabled by him to lead a new conscious life that can know no sin.

64 5. *for:* Verses 5, 6, and 7 affirm of the baptized Christian what Paul will say about Christ himself in vv. 8, 9, and 10. The latter verses supply the Christological foundation for the truth set forth about the new Christian life. *we have grown [into union] with [him]:* The pron. "him" is supplied as the logical complement of *symphytoi*, which means "grown together," in the sense of a young branch grafted on a tree being nourished by the main stock. Paul uses this bold image to express the communication of Christ-life to the Christian. *through a death like his:* Lit., "by a likeness of his death," the dative of instrument. Baptism (6:3) is the means by which Christians grow together with Christ, who died and rose once for all. Some commentators (Lietzmann, Sanday-Headlam, Gächter, Kuss) make this phrase depend directly on *symphytoi* and translate, "If we have been conformed to the image of his death...," i.e., have grown into closest union with the deathlike rite. Grammatically, this interpretation is possible; but how does one grow together with an image? Normally in Paul's theology the Christian is united with Christ himself (or with his "body"), not with an image of the salvation event. *also through a resurrection like his:* Lit., "we shall then be [grown together with him] through [a likeness of] the resurrection too." Since the whole context describes the present experience of Christians, the fut. tense is probably logical, expressing a sequel to the first part of the verse. For baptism identifies man not only with Christ's act of dying, but also with his being raised. Thus the Christian begins a new life too (Col 2:12; Eph 2:5–6). **6.** *the man we once were:* Lit., "the old man," the self under the domination of sin and exposed to divine wrath, as opposed to the "new man" who lives in union with Christ and is liberated through him from sin, and from any consideration of it. *was crucified with him:* See Gal 2:20; 5:24; 6:14. *to do away with our sinful self:* Lit., "with the body of sin." This phrase denotes not merely the material part of man, as opposed to his soul, but the whole of earthly man dominated by a proneness to sin (as the rest of the verse shows). In Col 1:22 Paul speaks of a "body of flesh," and in Rom 7:24 of a "body of death." In each case the genitive expresses the element that dominates earthly, natural man (→ Pauline Theology,

79:118). *that we might not be enslaved to sin any more:* The real answer to the objection posed in 6:1. The destruction of one's sinful "self" through baptism and incorporation into Christ means the liberation of man from an enslavement to sin. His outlook can no longer be directed toward sin.

65 7. *for a dead man is freed from sin:* Two explanations are current for the difficult phrase *dedikaiōtai*. Understood in a forensic sense, it would mean that from the standpoint of the Law a dead man is absolved or acquitted, because sin no longer has a case or a claim against him. Possibly Paul echoes a rabbinical notion: The death of a guilty person ends all litigation (see Str-B 3, 232; cf. K. G. Kuhn, *ZNW* 30 [1931] 305; G. Schrenk, *Righteousness* [BKW 4; London, 1951] 65). The main point would be to indicate that a change of status has ensued; the old condition has been brought to an end in the baptism-death and a new one has begun. The other explanation seeks to interpret the verse without any legal connotation (so S. Lyonnet, *Romains*, 89): He who has died, has lost the very means of sinning, his "body of sin"; so that he is definitively freed from sin. **8.** *died with Christ:* Through baptism. *we believe:* The new life of the Christian is not the object of sensible perception or of immediate consciousness. It is perceived only by that faith in token of which baptism is undergone. *we shall also live with him:* Paul thinks primarily of the future definitive form of the new life with Christ; this is why he says *syn Christō* (with Christ), not *en Christō* (→ Pauline Theology, 79:137). However, the Christian already has a share in that life, as 6:4 suggests (cf. 2 Cor 4:10–11). **9.** *never to die again:* The resurrection of Christ has brought him into the sphere of "Glory" and has withdrawn him completely from the sphere of Sin and Death. For though Christ had appeared in the likeness of sinful flesh (Rom 8:3), he broke Sin's dominion by his death and resurrection. This victory is the foundation of the liberation of the baptized Christian. For Christ was not raised from the dead merely to publicize his good news or to confirm his messianic character, but to introduce men into a new mode of life and give them a new principle of vital activity, the Spirit. He is the "first fruits" of the new humanity created at the resurrection (1 Cor 15:20; Col 1:8). *death no longer lords it over him:* Having become *Kyrios* at the resurrection (Phil 2:9–11; Acts 2:32–36), it is he, not the personified *Thanatos*, who reigns supreme. **10.** *died to sin once for all:* His death was a unique event, never to be repeated, for through it he entered the definitive sphere of his glory as *Kyrios* (cf. Heb 7:27). In so doing, he died to sin, "though he knew nothing of sin" (2 Cor 5:21). This is the Christological basis for the answer that Paul gave in 6:6 to the imaginary objector of 6:1. *he lives for God:* Since the resurrection Christ enjoys a new relationship with God the Father, into which he also introduces the men who are baptized (cf. Gal 2:19). **11.** *think of yourselves as dead to sin:* The conclusion of Paul's argument in answer to the objection of 6:1. In it he expresses in his own way the problem of Christian integration. Ontologically united with Christ through baptism, the Christian must deepen his faith continually to make himself aware psychologically of that basic union. Once thus consciously oriented to Christ, he could never consider sin again without bringing about a basic rupture of that union. *in Christ Jesus:* The paragraph ends with the significant Pauline phrase of union, which is a summary description of his view of the relation of the Christian to the Risen *Kyrios*. The Christian "in Christ" is incorporated into the very body of Christ through the Holy Spirit and thereafter shares in his vitality. See E. Schweizer, *NTS* 14 (1967–68) 1–14.

66 **12–23.** A brief exhortation, based on the preceding doctrinal exposé of baptism and its effect on the Christian. Is it a reflection of a primitive sermon once preached at a baptismal liturgy? **12.** *so do not let Sin reign over your mortal body:* Although the Christian has already been baptized and freed from Sin, Paul implies that this freedom is not yet definitive. The Christian can still succumb to Sin's seduction. The Council of Trent (DB 792; DS 1515), following Augustine, explained "sin" here as concupiscence; however, as M.-J. Lagrange notes (*Romains*, 153), this might be an exact theological transposition, but it is a precision not yet found in the text. For Paul *Hamartia* is always that personified active force which entered the world with Adam, has reigned over men up until Christ's coming, and seeks to continue to reign. It can entice the Christian too. *make you obey its cravings:* The body's cravings. This is the preferred reading, but in P^{46} (oldest text of Rom), D, G, it, Irenaeus, Tertullian, the text is rather "obey it" (i.e., sin). This would be more logical in the context, but the variant does not greatly change the sense. **13.** *as instruments of evil:* Or "as weapons of wickedness." The expression is probably a military figure, as the second part of the verse suggests. The "arms of uprightness" allude to the OT (Is 11:5; 59:17; cf. Eph 6:14ff.). Christians are supposed to be weapons in God's service, and not in the cause of evil. The contrast of "iniquity" and "uprightness" (*adikia* and *dikaiosynē*) is found also in QL (1QS 3:17ff.). But in QL *ṣedeq* (uprightness) is closely linked to the observance of the Law, whereas for Paul it has assumed all the connotations of the "new" Christian life. **14.** *sin must no longer lord it over you:* Related as it is to Death. The fut. tense expresses a categorical prohibition (cf. Bl-Deb-F § 362). *not under Law, but under grace:* The Law is never far from Paul's mind, and here he links it with sin momentarily. He will develop their relationship at length in ch. 7. The new Christian condition can be called *dikaiosynē*, but it is not associated with the Law; rather it is the effect of God's benevolent favor (cf. comment on 3:24).

67 **15.** The question of 6:1 is repeated and again indignantly rejected. **16.** *slaves:* The military figure of 6:13 gives way to the social figure of slavery, which better suits the context of Law. But what underlies Paul's comparison is not so much "slavery" as such, but service. He insists on the freedom of the Christian (Gal 5:1) from the Law; yet he never conceives of it as license, a freedom to sin. It is rather service of Christ to which the Christian is now dedicated. There has been a change of *kyrioi*, and the Christian through baptism has become "the slave of Christ" (see comment on Rom 1:1; cf. Gal 5:13; 1 Cor 6:12; Mt 6:24). **17.** *you obeyed the pattern of teaching to which you have been given over:* This difficult phrase is abbreviated in the Gk text; we understand it to mean *hypēkousate... eis ton typon didachēs eis hon paredothēte*. The crucial word is *typos*, which fundamentally means the "visible impression" (of a stroke or die), "mark, copy, image." But it was also used to designate "a compendious, terse presentation" of a subject (Plato, *Rep.* 414a, 491c). Coupled with *didachēs* (teaching), it would seem to be used by Paul in this sense, since he refers to the succinct baptismal confession of faith to which the convert freely and gladly was handed over after he had renounced his service to Sin (cf. Phil 4:8–9). In this case, the vb. "handed over" would not refer to the transmission of traditional doctrine (cf. 1 Cor 11:23; 15:3), but to the transfer of slaves from one master to another, without any pejorative connotation (cf. 1 Cor 5:5; Rom 1:24). Paul seems to be alluding to the custom of the Hellenistic world in which the transfer of slaves was accomplished with their consent. There may also be an echo of an ancient baptismal liturgy here that included a renunciation of Satan (*apotagē*) and a siding with Christ (*syntagē*); cf. J. Kürzinger, *Bib* 39 (1958) 156–76; F. W. Beare, *NTS* 5 (1958–59) 206–10, where other less likely interpretations are noted. **18.** *freed from sin:* This verse makes explicit the idea contained in the foregoing verses, and indeed in the whole chapter. For the first time Paul speaks of Christian liberty, which from now on becomes an operative notion (6:20,22; 7:3; 8:2,21; cf. Gal 2:4; 3:28; 4:22–31; 5:1,13). In reality, he has been speaking of some form of Christian freedom ever since 5:12. **19.** *I use familiar human terms:* He apologizes for using a figure derived from a social institution to express the Christian reality. But he wants to be sure that his talk of Christian liberty is not misunderstood. It is not license, but a service of Christ motivated by love, proceeding "from the heart." *impurity and lawlessness:* These may seem to be typically pagan vices (cf. Gal 2:15). But the Essenes of Qumran repudiated the same vices in their members (1QS 3:5 4:10,23,24; etc.). *sanctification:* The end result of being consecrated to God in Christ Jesus.

68 **20.** *free of uprightness:* There is a play on the word "freedom" in this and in the following verses to stress that a man can be deluded by what he thinks is freedom. Verses 20–23 emphasize the incompatibility of the two ways of life. **21.** *what profit did you get then?:* The punctuation is disputed here. One could also translate, "What profit did you get then out of the things you are now ashamed of?" The sense, however, is little affected in either case. The important affirmation is that death results from such things—not just physical death, but spiritual death too. **22.** *your profit is in holiness:* Being enslaved to God means a dedication to him that brings with it a withdrawal from the profane and from any attachment to sin. Such dedication does not remove man from this world, but it makes him live in it as one dedicated to God. The goal of this dedication is "life eternal," a share in the sphere of divinity itself (see comment on 5:21). Though it has already begun in a sense, its "end" is yet to come. **23.** *the wages of sin is death:* Paul reverts to the military figure and uses *opsōnion*, the "ration [money]" paid to a soldier. Underlying it is the idea of regularly recurrent payment. The more a man serves Sin, the more pay in the form of death he earns. These "wages" do not simply pile up, but are paid out in the form of death to those who serve Sin (see H. Heidland, *ThWNT* 5, 592). *the free gift of God:* In contrast to the "wages of sin" that are due (Rom 4:4), "eternal life in Christ Jesus our Lord" is graciously given to the Christian by God himself. There is no *quid pro quo*, and God's grace eventually brings about an assimilation of the Christian with God himself (2 Cor 3:18). *in Christ Jesus:* Concluding formula (→ 49 above).

(See Descamps, A., "La victoire du Chrétien sur le péché d'après *Rom.*, 6.1–23," *RevDTour* 6 [1951] 143–48. Schnackenburg, R., *Baptism in the Thought of St. Paul* [London, 1964]. Stanley, D. M., "The New Testament Doctrine of Baptism," *TS* 18 [1957] 169–215. Wagner, G., *Pauline Baptism and the Pagan Mysteries* [London, 1967].)

69 (iii) *Freedom from the Law* (7:1–25). Paul began his description of the reconciled Christian's new situation by explaining how Christ has put an end to the reign of Sin and Death (5:12–21), and then how the "new life in Christ Jesus" meant a reorientation of man's very self so that he could no longer even think of sinning (6:1–23). In 6:14 he introduced unexpectedly the relation of the Law to this freedom, for he was haunted by the problem it posed. In Gal he had treated it per se in a polemical context and stressed its temporary role (3:22–25). But that answer was apparently not too satisfying, since it did not come to grips with the heart of the problem. How could something God-given, good, just, and holy fail in its purpose and only foster sin itself? Earlier in Rom (3:20,31; 4:15; 5:13,20) Paul betrayed his preoccupation with this haunting problem. Now he tries to face it squarely. What is the relation of the Law to Sin? How can it be a minister of "death" and "condemnation" (2 Cor 3:7,9; Rom 8:1)? What is the Christian's relation to the Law? Section 7:1–6 is the introduction to his answer, asserting the Christian's freedom from the Law; 7:7–25 discusses the relation of the Law to Sin. Here Paul asserts the Law's basic goodness and shows that it is used by Sin as an instrument to dominate the man of "flesh." He finds the answer to his problem, then, not in the Law itself, but in the inability of natural, earthly man to cope with its demands.

70 In 7:1–6 Paul interweaves two arguments: (1) The Law binds only the living (7:1,4a). Consequently, the Christian who has died "through the body of Christ" is no longer bound by it. (2) A wife is freed by the death of her husband from the specific prescriptions of the Law binding her to him. But the Christian is like the Jewish wife whose husband has died. Just as she is freed from the "law of the husband," so through death the Christian is freed from the Law (7:2,3,4b). In the OT, adultery was a violation of the husband's rights and an offense that the wife (and her accomplice) committed against her husband (see *ThDNT* 4, 730). The second argument is only an illustration of the first, and not a perfect one at that. It should not be forced into an allegory (as Sanday-Headlam once proposed [*Romans*, 172]): The Wife = the true self (Ego); the (first) Husband = the old state of man; the "Law of the Husband" = the Law condemning the old state; the New Marriage = the union with Christ. For Paul's argument is different. It is the same person who dies and thus is freed from the Law. He uses the illustration for one point only: that the Law's obligation ceases when death occurs. Since the Christian has died with Christ in baptism, the Law has no more claim on him.

71 **1.** *brothers:* This is the first use of this address since 1:13. *who know the Law:* Though Weiss, Jülicher, and Kühl think that Paul, in addressing Roman Christians, was thus referring to Roman law, and a few others (Lagrange, Lyonnet, Sanday-Headlam, Taylor) interpret *nomon* (without the article) as "law in general," most commentators rightly understand the expression of the Mosaic Law (see comment on 2:12). The reason is that there are allusions to it in 7:2,3,4b; and the verse resumes 5:20; 6:14. As F. Leenhardt notes (*Romans*, 177), if Paul's argument were based on a pagan juridical principle, it would lose much of its demonstrative force. Paul argues in effect that Moses himself foresaw a situation in which the Law would cease to bind. *the Law binds a man while he is alive:* Lit., "lords it over him," keeping him in bondage by the obligation to observe it. The conclusion from this is drawn in 7:4a. Through baptism the Christian has been freed from the Law, as well as from Death and Sin (6:9,14). This is now illustrated by the marriage law. **2.** *a married woman:* Cf. Nm 5:20,29; Prv 6:24,29. By OT law the wife was considered the property of her husband; her infidelity was adultery (Ex 20:17; 21:3,22; Dt 22:22ff.; Lv 20:10; Gn 39:10ff.; cf. De Vaux, *AI* 26). *the law of the husband:* The individual prescription of the Mosaic Law, binding the wife to her husband. **3.** *if she lives with another man:* Lit., "belongs to another [man]." The expression is derived from Dt 24:2; Hos 3:3. This freedom of the wife comes with the husband's death, and has obviously nothing to do with divorce. **4.** *through the body of Christ:* By baptism the Christian has been identified with Christ (6:6), sharing in his death and risen life. He passed through the experience of dying to his body of flesh to enjoy the existence in the "spiritual body" (1 Cor 15:44). When Christ died for all "in the likeness of sinful flesh" (Rom 8:3), then all died (2 Cor 5:14). Paul now specifies that it was through the crucified body of Christ that the Christian finds freedom from the Law (cf. Gal 2:19–20; 3:13). *that you may belong to another:* The "second husband" is the glorified Risen Christ, who as *Kyrios* lords it over the Christian henceforth. *bear fruit for God:* The union of Christ and the Christian was just depicted in terms of marriage. Paul continues the figure; such a union is expected to bear the "fruit" of a reformed life.

72 **5.** *we were living merely natural lives:* Lit., "we were in the flesh," in the past without Christ. That mode of existence is contrasted implicitly with life "in the Spirit" (Rom 8:9), to which Paul alludes in 7:6. *sinful passions:* The propensity to sin following upon strong sense impression (see Gal 5:24). *aroused by the Law:* The Law, in spurring on the passions of man dominated by "flesh," is depicted as an occasion of sin. Another aspect of it appears in 7:7. *to bear fruit for death:* This phrase expresses result, not purpose (see comment on *eis to* with the infinitive, Rom 1:20). The passions were not destined to contribute to man's death, but they did so when abetted by the Law (see 6:21). **6.** *but now:* In the new Christian dispensation after baptism (see comment on 3:21). *we have died to what once held us captive:* Though some commentators try to refer the pron. "what" to the domination of the passion, it is rather another reference to the Law just mentioned. *so as to serve in a new spirit:* The Spirit is the dynamic principle of the new life begun in baptism (Rom 6:4); it is radically different from the slavery to the written code. The phrase has been suggested to Paul by the mention of "flesh" (7:5); once uttered, it served as the springboard for another contrast, that of the Spirit and the Letter (= life under the Mosaic Law, cf. 2 Cor 3:6ff., an excellent commentary on this verse).

73 In vv. 7–13 Paul speaks of the relation of the Law to Sin. **7.** *the Law is Sin?:* The development in this paragraph makes it clear that Paul is thinking of the Mosaic Law (see 7:1), for he even quotes it at the end of this verse. But some commentators try to understand *nomos* here as either (1) the natural law (Origen, Reuss), or (2) all law given to man from the beginning, including the "command" imposed on Adam (Theodore of Mopsuestia, Theodoret, Cajetan, Lietzmann, Lyonnet). To support this, appeal is made to Sir 17:4–11, which is supposed to show that contemporary Jews extended the notion of the Law to all divine precepts, even those imposed on Adam (Sir 17:7, echoing Dt 30:15,19), and on Noah. Sir 45:5(6) speaks of the Law given to Moses in terms of *entolai*, "commands," the very word used in Rom 7:8. Abraham is said to have observed God's law (Sir 44:20). And in the Palestinian Targum (on Gn 2:15) Adam is said to have been put in Eden to reverence the Law (an idea found also in Theophilus of Antioch, *Ad Autolycum* 2.24; *PG* 6.1092; Ambrose, *De Paradiso* 4; CSEL 32, 282). However, not one of these reasons really shows that Paul or his Jewish contemporaries had a concept of the Law wider than that of the Mosaic Law. They merely echo the common belief that somehow the Mosaic Law itself was already made known to men of earlier times. Paul does not share this belief (Rom 4:13ff.; Gal 3:17ff.). Paul is worried about the conclusion that might be drawn from his remarks on the Law. It might seem to be sin itself, since it "slipped in" to increase offenses (5:20), furnishes "knowledge of sin" (3:20), and "brings down wrath" (4:15). Such a conclusion he resolutely rejects with his emphatic negative (see comment on 3:4). *I did not know of sin except through the Law:* What was grasped by the conscience as being vaguely evil came to be regarded as formal rebellion and transgression through the Law. As in 3:20 the Law appears as a moral informer.

74 Paul now shifts to the first person. This shift has posed an historic exegetical problem. Who is meant by the Ego? According to A. Deissmann, C. H. Dodd, *et al.*, Paul speaks autobiographically. If it is meant that he does so exclusively, then the interpretation is not convincing. Not only does it conflict with what Paul says about his own preconversion experience with the Law (Phil 3:6; Gal 1:13–14) and his psychological background as a Pharisee (cf. Lk 18:11–12), but it also misses the all-important perspective he adopts here, which is a reflection on the phases of human history.

Equally unconvincing is the interpretation of Augustine, Thomas Aq., M. Luther, K. Barth, *et al.*, according to which Paul speaks of his experience since his conversion and of the conflict experienced between the obligations of the Christian life and sin. Why all the talk about the Law? Such a view tends to make of Paul a young Luther. A very common interpretation—and the one that has most to commend it—is that Paul uses a stylistic figure, Ego, dramatizing in an intimate, personal way the experience common to all who were faced with the Mosaic Law and who relied on their own resources to meet its obligations. Instead of saying "man" (*anthrōpos*) or "someone" (*tis*), Paul chose to speak of Ego (somewhat as in 1 Cor 8:13; 13:1–3,11–12; 14:6–19; Rom 14:21). In this context it expresses well the basic autonomy and personal responsibility of man. Ego is depicted as existing before the Law (7:7,9a), under the Law (7:8–24), and freed from the Law in Christ (7:25–8:29; cf. comment on 5:14).

75 Lyonnet (in J. Huby, *Romains*, 601–4), following Methodius of Olympia, Theodore of Mopsuestia, and several other commentators, believes that Paul speaks in the person of Adam as he was confronted with the "command" of Gn 2:16–17. While giving to the passage a comprehensive perspective which it should have, the allusion to Adam is not evident per se. Though Paul alludes to Gn 3:13 in 7:11, this is isolated. Indeed, when he quotes a divine precept, it is not that of Gn 2:16 or 3:3, but one of the Sinai Commandments (Ex 20:17). This interpretation is no more "theological" than the others.

Trivial insistence on one aspect of Ego tends to obscure Paul's profound insight. The confrontation of Ego with Sin and the Law is not considered by him merely on an individual, psychological level, but from an historical and corporate point of view. Paul surveys the history of man as it was known to him through his Jewish and Christian eyes—without Christ and with Christ. Some of his statements in this passage are susceptible of application to experiences beyond his own immediate perspective. What he says in 7:7–25 is undoubtedly the experience of many Christians faced with divine, ecclesiastical, or civil law. When these verses are read in such a light, few Christians will fail to appreciate their significance. But in attempting to understand what Paul meant, it is important to keep *his* perspective in mind.

(See Benoit, P., "La loi et la croix d'après Saint Paul (Rom. VII,7–VIII,4)," *RB* 47 [1938] 481–509. Kümmel, W. G., *Römer 7 und die Bekehrung des Apostels* [Leipzig, 1929].)

76 **7.** *you must not covet:* Thus the Mosaic Law is epitomized (quoted from Ex 20:17 or Dt 5:21). It expresses the essence of the Law, which teaches man not to subject himself to created things rather than to his creator. The sluggish moral conscience of man is thus made aware of the possibility of an infraction against the will of God so manifested. **8.** *sin found its opportunity through such a command:* The "command" (*entolē*) is not a clear allusion to the injunction laid on Adam (Gn 2:16), but is rather a specific prohibition of the Mosaic Law such as has just been cited. One must recall here Paul's view of world history (Rom 5:12–14). From Adam to Moses men did wrong, but did not violate precepts, as Adam did. Their evil deeds became violations with the coming of the Law. The latter then became an *aphormē*, an "occasion, opportunity" (AG 127), for formal sin. *without the Law Sin was lifeless:* It was like a corpse, powerless to do anything—powerless to make man's evil into a flagrant revolt against God (see 4:15; 5:13b). **9.** *I was once alive without the Law:* This should not be understood merely as an allusion to Paul's happy, innocent childhood (V. Taylor, *Romans*, 46), nor as an allusion to Adam's state before the fall (how would anyone know that it was such?), but as an ironic reference to the life led by every man who is ignorant of his real situation and of the real nature of evil. The expression "lifeless," used of Sin (7:8) probably suggested to Paul the contrast, "I was alive"; but the main emphasis is on the phrase "without the Law." The life so lived was, indeed, not that of union with God in Christ, nor was it an open rebellion against God in formal sin. Benoit (*RB* 47 [1938] 487) has called it a relative existence. *sin became alive:* With the intervention of the Law man's condition before God changed, for his "desires" now became "coveting," and their pursuit a revolt against God. If the vb. *anezēsen* is taken literally, "came to life again," it would be difficult to see how this could apply to Adam. But it probably means only "sprang to life" (AG 53). Sin "was alive" in Adam's transgression; it "sprang to life" again in transgressions of the Mosaic Law. **10.** *then I died:* The death meant here is not that of Gal 2:19, whereby the Christian dies to the Law through Christ's crucifixion, so that it no longer has any claim on him. This death is rather the condition resulting from the crushing obligation of the Law. Through formal transgressions of it man is thrust under the domination of *Thanatos* (Rom 5:12). *the command that should have meant life:* The Mosaic Law promised life to those who would observe it: "by the observance of which man shall live" (Lv 18:5; cf. Dt 4:1; 6:24; Gal 3:12; Rom 10:5). *in my case meant death:* The Law itself did not kill man, but was an instrument used by Sin and Death to bring him under their control. For it was not only an occasion of sin (7:5) or a moral informant (7:7), but it also leveled a condemnation to death against the man who did not obey it (1 Cor 15:56; 2 Cor 3:7,9; Rom 7:13). **11.** *sin deceived me:* Just as the command of God gave the tempting serpent its opportunity, so Sin used the Law to deceive man and entice him to go after what was forbidden. Paul alludes to Gn 3:13, but by no means as explicitly as in 2 Cor 11:3 (cf. 1 Tm 2:14). The deception developed when man's autonomy was confronted with a divine demand for his submission. As the serpent did, so Sin enticed man thus confronted to assert his autonomy and make himself "like God." **12.** *holy, just and good:* Because the Law was God-given and destined to give life to those who would obey it (7:10,14; Gal 3:24). The Law never commanded man to sin, nor to do evil; in itself it was good. **13.** *did what was good prove the death of me?:* Again Paul indignantly rejects the thought that a God-given institution was the direct cause of man's death (see comment on 3:4). *it was Sin, so that it might be shown to be Sin:* The real culprit was Sin, which was the direct cause of every man's death (5:12; 6:23). It used the Law as a tool. Once this is understood, then it is clear that the Law was not the equivalent of Sin (cf. 2 Cor 3:7).

77 **14–25.** Paul's answer is not yet complete. He now probes deeper. How could Sin use something good in itself to destroy man? The real answer lies within man himself. **14.** *the Law is spiritual:* In its origin as God-given; in its destiny as a means of leading men to God. Thus it did not belong to the world of earthbound, natural man. It was *pneumatikos* and belonged to the sphere of God; it was opposed to what is *sarkinos* ("carnal, belonging to the sphere of flesh"). *what I do I do not understand:* The enigma that man sees in himself is a desperate situation derived from a conflict in his inmost depths. It is the cleavage between his reason-dominated desire and his actual performance. *I do not do what I want to, and what I do I detest:* Man's moral aspirations and his performance are not co-ordinated or integrated. Often quoted in this connection are the plaintive words of Ovid, "I see what is better and approve of it, but I follow what is worse" (*Metamorph.* 7.19). The Essenes of Qumran explained the same inner conflict by teaching that God had put two spirits in man to rule him until the time of his visitation, the spirit of truth and the spirit of perversity (1QS 3:15–4:26). But Paul attributes the rift to man himself, and not to spirits. **16.** *I agree that the Law is good:* At least man's desire to do what is good is an implicit acknowledgment of the formal excellence and authority of the Law in what it imposes. **17.** *it is Sin that dwells in me: Hamartia* came into the world to "reign" over man (5:12,21) and, lodging within him, enslaved his very being. This verse is really a corrective to what was asserted in 7:16a: Sin is responsible for the evil that man does. Paul seems almost to absolve man from responsibility for his sinful conduct (see 7:20; cf. 1:31–2:5). **18.** *good does not dwell in me—in my natural self:* Lit., "in my flesh." The additional qualification is important, for Paul finds the root of the difficulty in man's self considered as *sarx*, the source of all that is opposed to God. From the Ego considered as *sarx* proceed the detestable things that man does. But the Ego as the true willing self is dissociated from that self that has fallen victim to "flesh" (→ Pauline Theology, 79:119). **19–20.** A repetition of 7:15,17 from a different standpoint.

78 **21.** *I detect, then, the principle:* From experience every man learns how things stand with himself. In 7:21–25 *nomos* undergoes a shift in nuance. Paul is playing on the other meanings of the word he has used so far to mean the Mosaic Law. Now it denotes a "principle" (AG 544), or the experienced "pattern" of one's activity. **22.** *in the depths of me I find delight in God's Law:* This is not the new "spiritual" man speaking (Eph 4:24), but, as the following verses make clear, the "mind" (*nous*) of unregenerate man. Though dominated by Sin when considered as "flesh," every man still has a part of him that desires what God desires. Man's mind (or reason) recognizes the ideal presented by the Law—God's Law. (Paul admits the divine origin of the Mosaic Law.) **23.** *another principle is at war with the law of my mind:* The *nomos* in which man's reasoning self finds delight is opposed to another *nomos* that ultimately makes him a captive (cf. Rom 6:13,19). This *nomos* is nothing else but Sin which indwells (7:17). It enslaves a man so that his willing self, which delights in God's Law, is not free to observe it. **24.** *miserable man that I am!:* The agonizing cry of every man weighted down with the burden of sin and prevented by it from achieving what he would; it is a desperate call to God for help. *who will save me from this doomed body?:* Lit., "body of death" (see comment on 6:6). Threatened by defeat in this conflict, man finds his salvation in the merciful bounty of God manifested in Christ Jesus. **25.** *thank God!:* In the ms. D and in the Vg the answer to the question in 7:24 is "The grace of God." But this is a very inferior reading. Verse 25 is an exclamation, expressing Paul's gratitude to God, which anticipates the real answer to the question given in 8:1–4. His gratitude is expressed "through Jesus Christ our Lord," using the refrain of this part of Rom to conclude another section (→ 53:49). Some commentators, however, prefer to separate the exclamation (Thank God!) from the following phrase, understanding the latter as an initial answer to the question of 7:24: "[It is done] through Jesus...." Though this is grammatically possible, it is awkward. *with my mind:* The reasoning self willingly submits to God's law and stands in contrast to carnal man, the self enslaved to Sin. Thus Paul terminates the discussion of the three freedoms achieved for man in Christ.

(Braun, H., "Römer 7,7–25 und das Selbstverständnis der Qumran-Frommen," *ZThK* 56 [1959] 1–18. Davies, D. M., "Free from the Law: An Exposition of the Seventh Chapter of Romans," *Interpr* 7 [1953] 156–62. Descamps, A., "La victoire du Chrétien sur le péché d'après *Rom.*, 6.1–23," *RevDTour* 6 [1951] 143–48. Schneider, B., "The Meaning of Saint Paul's Antithesis, 'The Letter and the Spirit,'" *CBQ* 15 [1953] 163–207.)

79 (c) THE THEME DEVELOPED: CHRISTIAN LIFE IS LIVED IN THE SPIRIT AND IS DESTINED FOR GLORY (8:1–39). In Rom 5:1–11 Paul announced that justified man was empowered to live a new life as the result of God's love manifested in the liberating act of Christ. For it produced for him not only a status of uprightness before God, but also freedom—freedom from Sin, Death, and the Law. Now that liberation has taken place, he is able to live a life "for God," as Christian experience shows. The new Christian mode of life is due above all to the love of God. From it comes the internal dynamic principle of activity that is found in the newborn Christian, the Spirit of God himself. Chapter 8 begins by answering the question posed in 7:24. Christ Jesus has rescued man from enslavement and made it possible for him to live "according to the Spirit" (8:1–4). This answer serves as an introduction for a greater development of the theme in which Paul describes how Christian existence is dominated by the Spirit, not by the flesh (8:1–13). Because of the gift of the Spirit the Christian is a child of God, born anew of God, and destined for the glory of God's intimate presence (8:14–30). Finally, as Paul contemplates the magnificence of this divine plan of salvation, he bursts into a hymn and extols the love of God made manifest in Christ Jesus (8:31–39).

80 (i) *Christian life is empowered by the Spirit* (8:1–13). **1.** *no condemnation for those united with Christ Jesus:* No longer is there any condemnation leveled against man by the Law for not observing it, nor any state of condemnation resulting from Sin. "Condemnation" means the same as the "curse" of Gal 3:10 (cf. Dt 27:26). It clung to unregenerate man who was torn in two, because he was "flesh" and dominated by Sin, but still had a "mind" that recognized the law of God. It refers to the condition too in which man found himself because of Sin's influence on him (Rom 5:16–18). But this condition does not affect the Christian, for he is no longer living under the dispensation of "condemnation" (2 Cor 3:9) or of "death" (2 Cor 3:7). Those who are in Christ Jesus have been crucified with him who did away with the "curse of the Law" and thereby its condemnation. **2.** *the law of the Spirit of life:* Thus qualified, *nomos* no longer refers to the Mosaic Law. Paul plays on the word *nomos*, as he applies it to the Spirit, which is the dynamic "principle" of the new life. The Spirit is not really *nomos* at all; it supplies to the baptized Christian the vitality that the Mosaic Law could never give. It is the life-giving power of God. Note the predominant use of "Spirit" in this chapter; it occurs 29 times in ch. 8, but only 5 times in chs. 1–7. *has freed you:* The explicit answer to 7:24. Christian freedom is achieved either "through" Christ (instrumental), or "in Christ" (unitive). The better reading is "you" (sing.), even though some important mss. read "me," which is a more direct answer to 7:24, yet obviously a scribal correction. *from the law of sin and death:* Again, *nomos* is used in a wide sense ("principle"), but one should not fail to note the collocation of the three key words (law, sin, death). They sum up the discussion of chs. 5–7; and their tyranny is broken.

81 **3.** *what the Law could not do:* "This God has done," or a similar phrase, must be understood to clear up the anacoluthon. Paul refers to the inability of the Mosaic Law to put man in a state of rectitude before God and free him from Sin and Death. *because [as long as] it was weakened by the flesh:* The good that the Law might have achieved was undone by man's earthly self dominated by indwelling Sin (7:22–23). The Law did not supply man with the power to surmount the opposition to it from his inclinations to sin. *God sent his own son:* The emphatic phrase, "his own son," is stronger than the stereotyped formula, "son of God," and highlights the divine origin of the task to be accomplished by someone who stood in a close filial relationship with the Father. Implied is a unique bond of love existing between the two that is the source of man's salvation; also implied is the pre-existence of Christ (→ Pauline Theology, 79:53–55). His task was to accomplish what the Law could not do. The "sending" refers not to the whole redemptive incarnation, but to its climax in the cross and resurrection (Gal 3:13; Rom 3:24–25; 4:24–25; 2 Cor 5:19–21). *in a form like our sinful flesh:* This is not a docetic suggestion, implying that the Son only appeared to be a man. Rather, he was sent as a man (Gal 4:4, "born of woman and made subject to the Law"). But Paul avoids saying that the Son came with sinful flesh, just as in 2 Cor 5:21 he qualifies his statement that God made Christ "sin" for us, by adding "who knew not sin himself" (cf. Heb 4:15). He came in a form like to us in that he experienced the effects of sin and suffered death as one "cursed" by the Law. Thus in his own self he coped with the power of sin. *to conquer sin:* Lit., "and for the sake of sin," i.e., to take it away, atone for it (AG 650, comparing Gal 1:14; 1 Pt 3:18; Nm 8:8). This was the purpose of the Son's mission. Some commentators understand *peri hamartias* to mean, "as a sin offering" (cf. Lv 4:24; 5:11; 6:18, where the LXX uses *hamartia* in this sense; cf. 2 Cor 5:21). Though the image is different, the fundamental idea is ultimately the same. *[thus God] condemned Sin in the flesh:* The Father passed definitive judgment on that force which Adam's transgression unleashed into the world (Rom 5:12) and thereby broke its dominion over men. He accomplished this "in the flesh." How? According to Zahn, Kühl, and Lagrange, Paul refers to the incarnation, when the Father by the sending of the Son "in the flesh" of man implicitly passed sentence on Sin. It was a condemnation in principle, in that the Son assumed the human condition without sin and lived a sinless life. But since elsewhere in the Pauline literature the redemption is associated only with Christ's death and resurrection, the phrase is better understood of the crucified and risen "flesh" of Christ. Paul seems to be thinking of the vicarious death of Christ, and of the Father's raising him from the dead. With the flesh that he shared with mankind he underwent the experience of death, only to rise again. The Christian, identified with Christ through baptism, shares in that experience; the victory over Sin for which the risen body of Christ stands marks the end of the reign of Sin over man's "flesh" (cf. 7:18,20). For another interpretation, see P. Benoit, *RB* 47 (1938) 496–502.

82 4. *that the requirement of the Law might be met:* It is through the power of the Spirit, which is the divine principle of man's new life, that the uprightness the Law demanded of men is finally obtained. The key word here is *dikaiōma*, whose meaning is disputed; but most likely it means a "requirement, commandment" of the Law (see Rom 2:26), i.e., an ideal requirement. The fulfillment of it meant "life" for men (Lv 18:5). See F. Prat, *Theology*, 2, 163–66. *in us...who live according to the Spirit:* The Law proposed an ideal, but did not enable man to arrive at it. Now all this is changed. Man has the Spirit that enables him to surmount the flesh and arrive at the goal that the Law once proposed. The Greek uses a participle with the negative *mē*, which gives almost a proviso or conditional force to the expression, "provided we walk not according to the flesh." It thus insinuates that Christian living is not something that flows automatically, as it were, from baptism. The contrast of "flesh" and "Spirit" is developed in 8:5–13; it is the contrast of natural, earthbound man left to himself and man guided by the life-giving Spirit (cf. 1 Cor 15:45). 5. *who live according to the flesh:* Whose motivation in life is a self-centered interest. 6. *death is the aspiration of the flesh:* All the plans and efforts of natural man are focused only on death (total death, see comment on 5:12). Compare the passage in Gal 5:21, "People who do such things have no share in the kingdom of God." Radically opposed to this is the aspiration of the Spirit: "life and peace." Paul implies that the tendency of natural man is to enmity with God; he formulates this explicitly in 8:7. But through the Spirit man finds reconciliation and peace with God. 7. *it does not submit to God's law:* This verse recasts 7:22–25, but it goes further and asserts that the earthly-minded man is fundamentally unable to obey God's law. He lacks the power to transcend the conflict within him when he is confronted with the Law. This hostility to God is responsible for his open transgression of the Law's commands. 8. *cannot please God:* Paul chooses a neutral way of expressing the goal of man's life: to please God. It is a goal that is aimed at by both Jew and Christian (cf. 2 Cor 5:9). Yet it cannot be reached by a man who is dominated by self ("in the flesh"); he implies that one must be "in the Spirit" (live "according to the Spirit," 8:5).

83 9. *since the Spirit of God dwells in you:* Paul makes it clear that the Spirit is "of God," for the new principle of Christian vitality is derived from the same source as all the other divine manifestations of salvation. The baptized Christian is not only "in the Spirit," but the Spirit is now said to dwell in him. Such expressions of the mutual relationship of the "spiritual" man and the Spirit forestall any facile interpretation of man's participation in divine life in a too local or spatial sense. For both express the same reality; the Spirit suffuses man's being and directs his conduct. At the beginning of the verse Paul uses the conj. *eiper*, which we have translated "since," but which can also mean "if, as is really the case." *Christ's Spirit:* Note how Paul interchanges the "Spirit of God," "the spirit of Christ," and "Christ" in these verses as he tries to express the multifaceted reality of the Christian experience of a participation in divine life (for the implications of this in Trinitarian theology, → Pauline Theology, 79:75). *does not belong to him:* Attachment to Christ is only possible by the "spiritualization" of man. This is no mere external identification with the cause of Christ, nor even a grateful recognition of what he once did for man. Rather, the Christian who belongs to Christ is the one who has been enabled to "live for God" (6:10) through the vitalizing power of the divine Spirit. 10. *if Christ is in you:* Or the Spirit (cf. 8:9; Gal 2:20; 2 Cor 5:17). *though the body is dead because of sin:* Paul plays on the possible meanings of the word *pneuma*. In 8:9 it clearly meant the "Spirit of God," but he is aware of its sense as a part of man that can be contrasted with "flesh" (→ Pauline Theology, 79:121). Without the Spirit, the source of Christian vitality, man's "body" is like a corpse because of Sin's influence (5:12). But in union with Christ man's spirit lives, for the Spirit resuscitates the dead being of man through the gift of uprightness. (Cf. F. Leenhardt, *Romans*, 209; M. Dibelius, *SBU* 3 [1944] 8–14.) 11. *the Spirit of him who raised Jesus:* As in 8:9 the *pneuma* is the Spirit of the Father, to whom the efficiency of the resurrection is again ascribed (see comments on 4:24; 6:4). The power that vivifies the Christian is thus traced again to its ultimate source in the Father, for the Spirit is the manifestation of his presence and power in the world since the resurrection and through it. Just as Sin once dwelled in unregenerate man (7:20), so now the Spirit indwells. *will give life to your mortal bodies:* The fut. tense expresses the role of the vivifying Spirit in the eschatological resurrection of Christians. At the resurrection Christ became through the glory of the Father (6:4) the principle of the resurrection of Christians (see Phil 3:21; 1 Thes 4:14; 1 Cor 6:14; 2 Cor 4:14; → Pauline Theology, 79:71). *through his Spirit:* Modern editors of the Gk NT read *dia* with the genitive, which expresses the instrumentality of the Spirit in man's resurrection (so mss. S, A, C). Another strongly attested reading is *dia* with the accusative, which would stress the dignity of the Spirit (so mss. B, D, G, Vg, etc.), "because of his Spirit." In either case "his" would refer to Christ (*GrBib* § 210; Bl-Deb-F § 31, 1), for it is the Spirit as related to the Risen Christ that is the vivifying principle. 13. *if you put to death the accomplishments of the body:* This verse and v. 12 conclude the preceding discussion and form a transition to the next section. Paul implies that the baptized Christian could still be interested in the "deeds, actions, pursuits" of a man dominated by *sarx*. Hence he exhorts him to make use of the Spirit received; this is the debt that is owed to Christ.

84 (ii) *Through the Spirit the Christian becomes a child of God and is destined for glory* (8:14–30). The vivifying power of the Spirit not only gives man a new life, but bestows upon him the character of an adopted son and heir. Material creation, hope itself, and the Spirit, all bear witness to this glorious Christian destiny. 14. *sons of God:* Mortification, necessary though it is to Christian life (8:13), does not really constitute it. It is rather the Spirit that animates and activates the Christian and makes him a son of God. This is the first appearance of the theme of sonship in Rom, and by it Paul attempts to describe the new status of the Christian in his relation to God. 15. *not a spirit of slavery:* In 7:21ff. Paul played on the meanings of *nomos* (Law—principle) to bring out the role of the Spirit; now he plays again on the possible meanings of *pneuma* (Spirit—spirit). Christians have received the Spirit (of God or Christ), but this is not a "spirit" in the sense of a disposition or mentality that a slave would have. Animated and suffused by God's Spirit, the Christian cannot possess the attitude of a slave, for he is free. True, at times Paul speaks of the Christian as a "slave" (Rom 6:16; 1 Cor 7:22; Eph 6:6), but this is to make a point. In reality, he is a son (cf. Gal 4:7), empowered by the Spirit to call upon God himself as a Father. *the spirit of adoption:* Or "the Spirit of adoption." Because Paul plays on the word *pneuma*, it is hard to say just which nuance he intends; perhaps both are meant. But it seems to be the Spirit that constitutes Christian adoptive sonship, since it is the Spirit that unites men to Christ and puts them in a special relationship to the Father.

The word *huiothesia* (adoption) is used of Israel in Rom 9:4 (cf. Ex 4:22; Is 1:2; Jer 31:9; Hos 11:1) with reference to its being chosen by God. Here and in 8:23; Gal 4:5 and Eph 1:5 it is used of Christians, the new "Israel of God." The word is not found in the LXX, probably because adoption was not a widely practiced institution among the Jews. Perhaps Paul borrowed the word from current Hellenistic legal language to show how the baptized Christian has been taken into the family of God and has a status in it, not of a slave (who belonged indeed to the household), but of a son. The Christian's attitude should, then, correspond to the status he enjoys. *which enables us to cry:* Lit., "in which [*or* by which] we cry." Though the vb. *krazō* is used in the LXX Pss of various life situations in which man calls upon God (Pss 3:5; 17:7; 87:2,10,14), it also means to "cry aloud" in proclamation. This seems to be the sense here: Through the Spirit the Christian proclaims that God is his Father. *Abba* [*my*] *Father:* See comment on Gal 4:6. The cry used by Christ in his moment of supreme earthly confidence in God (Mk 14:36), preserved by the early Palestinian community, became for Paul even in Gentile communities the mode of address distinctive of Christians.

85 16. *the Spirit joins with our spirit in testifying:* The vb. *symmartyrein* means either "testify along with," or simply "testify, certify." The latter would denote that the Spirit makes the Christian aware of his adoptive sonship, "testifies to our Spirit that...." But the former meaning reckons more with the compound verb Paul uses. He does not mean that unregenerate man, without the influence of the Spirit, could come to the knowledge of adoptive sonship, so that the Spirit would just concur with man's spirit spontaneously recognizing this. The preceding context makes it rather clear that the vital dynamism that constitutes sonship itself comes from the Spirit as well as the power whereby man recognizes his status. Now he goes further and suggests that the Spirit concurs with man as he acknowledges in prayer his special relation to the Father. Here Paul advances beyond Gal 4:6. 17. *if children, then heirs:* The Christian as an adopted son is not only admitted into God's family, but by reason of the same gratuitous gift receives the right to become the master of his adoptive father's estate. Though he has no natural right to it, he acquires a title by adoption (cf. Gal 4:7; 3:26,29). *joint heirs with Christ:* Christ, the true son, has already received a share of the Father's estate (glory); the Christian is destined to share that glory too one day (see comment on 3:23). Note the connection explicitly asserted between Christ's passion and his resurrection. The double use of verbs compounded with *syn-* (with) expresses once again the share of the Christian in these phases of Christ's redemptive activity (→ Pauline Theology, 79:137).

86 18. *for I consider...:* This verse introduces the threefold testimony given to the Christian destiny, which is sharply contrasted with the sufferings just mentioned. *the glory to be revealed for us:* Paul reminds his readers that although suffering is a sign of the authentic Christian experience, it is only a transition to the assured glory that awaits them in the *eschaton*. 19. *the created universe waits with eager expectation for God's sons to be revealed:* Paul discloses his view of the created world, which in its chaotic state manifests its cosmic striving toward the very goal set for man himself. He affirms the solidarity of the human and subhuman world in its share in the redemption of Christ. It recalls Yahweh's promise to Noah of the covenant to be made "between myself and you and every living creature" (Gn 9:12–13; cf. Ps 135). The noun *ktisis* denotes "material creation" apart from man (see 8:23). Created for man, it was cursed as a result of Adam's sin (Gn 3:17), and since then it has been in a state of abnormality or frustration, according to Paul, being subject to corruption itself. And yet, he sees it sharing in man's destiny; for it too—through him—is somehow redeemed, freed from its natural proclivity.

87 20. *it was subjected to futility, not of its own will:* The "frustration" of material creation is its inability to realize its goal as it should. Before Adam's sin, material creation is depicted in Gn as subject to him, just as he was to God (Gn 1:28). But man's sin disrupted the subordination and introduced abnormality and futility. *but by him who subjected it in* [*the*] *hope,* 21. *that creation itself would be freed from the bondage of decay:* This interpretation of a difficult verse (used by Sanday-Headlam, Lietzmann, Lagrange, Levie, Leenhardt) refers it to God, who cursed the ground because of Adam's sin (Gn 3:17). "By him" (*dia* with the acc., as in Rom 3:25; Jn 6:57; Sir 15:11; cf. AG 180) means God in this view. The "hope" (*eph' elpidi*, "in, with hope") expresses not God's hope, but the hope given to creation itself by him who subjected it (referring to the ptc. *hypotaxanta* of v. 20). It also reads *hoti* (that) instead of *dioti* at the beginning of v. 21 (following P[46] and the better Egyptian mss.); this conjunction introduces the hope given to creation. This seems to be the most natural interpretation of the verse, despite the fact that the use of *dia* with the accusative (by, through) is not common.

Other commentators (Chrysostom, Zahn, Sickenberger, Lyonnet) prefer to understand it thus: "because of him who subjected it; [yet it was] with hope, because [*dioti*] creation itself was to be freed...." In this case *dia* is given its usual Pauline sense (Gal 4:13; Phil 1:15; etc.), and the phrase refers to Adam, who by his transgression subjected creation to disorder. The phrase "in hope" is elliptical, but explained by the following causal clause. This interpretation, which has much to commend it, does not explain whence the hope is derived. Paul seems, however, to say that God, though he cursed the ground because of Adam's sin, still gave it a hope of sharing in man's redemption. This "hope" should not be facilely identified with Gn 3:15, which expresses rather a lasting enmity. Paul is really the first writer in the Bible to speak of this hope, at least in such a specific way (cf. Is 55:12–13). Redeemed humanity will live in peace with God in a world transformed by his Spirit. Paul sees this condition as an aspiration of all creation. *decay:* Not just moral corruption (Cornely, Prat *et al.*), but the law of physical decay found in nature, the reign of dissolution and death. For Paul, the created physical universe is not to be a mere spectator of man's triumphant glory and freedom, but is to share in it. When the children of God are finally revealed in glory, death will have no more dominion over them, and the material world will also be emancipated from this "last enemy" (1 Cor 15:23–28). What Paul teaches here will be developed in the Captivity Letters in his notion of the recapitulation of all things in Christ.

88 22. *all creation has been groaning in travail together till now:* Gk philosophers often compared the vernal rebirth of nature to a woman's travail. Paul adopts this image to express the tortuous convulsions of frustrated material creation, as he sees it. It groans in hope and expectation, but also in pain. The compound verb (*synōdinei*) expresses the concerted agony of the universe in all its parts. Some commentators maintain that it expresses the groaning of creation "with man," as he awaits the revelation of glory too. This is possible, but the former interpretation seems better because man is introduced only in the next verse. 23. *we ourselves:* Not only the material universe bears testimony to the Christian destiny, but Christians themselves do so too by the hope they have—hope based on the gift of the Spirit already possessed. *who have the first fruits of the Spirit:* The Spirit has already been given to Christians as the principle of their new life. It is compared to the first fruits of the harvest, which when offered to God betokened the consecration of the whole harvest. But "first fruits" was often used in the sense of a "pledge, guarantee" of what is to come (cf. *arrabōn*, 2 Cor 1:22; 5:5; Eph 1:14). See G. Delling, *ThDNT* 1, 486. *we groan within ourselves:* The second testimony to Christian destiny is the hope that Christians themselves have of it. *await the liberation of our bodies:* The Gk text of this verse is not sound. We follow P[46], D, G, etc. and omit *huiothesian*; other mss. include it as the object, "as we await adoption, the liberation of our bodies." Though it is difficult to explain how the word has gotten into the text of some mss., its omission is preferable because Paul nowhere else speaks of adoptive sonship as a form of eschatological redemption. The Christian is already a son of God, made so by the Spirit received. Enjoying these "first fruits," he looks forward in hope to the full harvest of glory, to the revelation of the sons of God, and to the redemption (= liberation, see comment on 3:24) of the body. (Similarly S. Lyonnet, *Romains*, 98; P. Benoit, *RSR* 39 [1951] 267–80.) If, however, "sonship" be retained with the majority of mss. and most critical editions of the Gk NT as the *lectio difficilior*, then Paul would be referring to a phase of Christian "sonship" still to be revealed, but about which he tells us nothing more.

89 **24.** *in hope we are* [or *were*] *saved:* The aor. tense may express the past aspect of salvation already wrought by Christ's death and resurrection, but it may also be gnomic, expressing a general truth and emphasizing hope (Bl-Deb-F § 333). "In hope" expresses manner rather than means, for salvation (like justification) is obtained "by faith" (3:28). Justified through faith, man still looks to the future eschatological term of salvation and this is the sphere of hope. In the Captivity Letters salvation appears more clearly as a proleptic condition of Christians (Col 2:12; 3:1; Eph 2:6). *who hopes for what he sees?:* The preferred reading of this confused text is *ho gar blepei tis elpizei* (P[46], B*) and is translated here. Others read, "For how can anyone still hope for what he sees" (so D, G). The sense is little affected in the long run. **25.** *we await it with patience:* It is hope that enables the Christian to bear with "the sufferings of the present" (8:18), but that also makes him a witness to the world of a lively faith in the resurrection (cf. 1 Cor 2:9; 2 Cor 5:7; Heb 11:1).

90 **26.** *the Spirit too helps us in our weakness:* The third testimony to the new life and glorious destiny of Christians. Man's aspirations risk being inefficacious because of his natural weakness, but the Spirit adds to them his intercession that transcends that weakness (*hyperentygchanei*, "intercedes over and above"). The result is that the Christian utters what would otherwise be ineffable. Even to pray "Abba, Father," the Spirit must dynamically assist the Christian (8:15; Gal 4:6). But the Christian who so prays is aware that the Spirit is manifesting his presence to him. **27.** *he who searches the hearts:* An OT phrase for God (Prv 20:27; Ps 139:1; 1 Cor 4:5). Only God comprehends the language and the mind of the Spirit, and he recognizes such assisted prayer. *according to God's will:* Lit., "according to God." It was part of God's loving plan of salvation that the Spirit should play such a dynamic role in the aspirations and prayers of Christians. This plan will now be sketched briefly in vv. 28–30.

91 **28.** *in everything God works for good with those who love him:* The addition or omission of *ho theos* (God, as subject of the verb) in various mss. has resulted in three different interpretations of this verse: (1) If *ho theos* is read (with mss. P[46], B, A, etc.), and the vb. *synergei* is understood intransitively with an indirect object ("works together with"), then one gets the translation given above. It stresses God's co-operation "in all things" (*panta*, adv. acc.) with those who love, and this is seen as the realization of his loving plan of salvation. This interpretation is supported by many patristic writers and modern commentators. (2) If *ho theos* is read, but the vb. *synergei* is interpreted transitively and *panta* is taken as the direct object, then "God makes all things conspire for the good of those who love him." So Lagrange, Levie, Prat, Bl-Deb-F § 148, 1; but no parallel is offered for this transitive use of *synergei*. (3) If *ho theos* is omitted (with mss. S, C, D, G, Koine tradition, Vg) and *panta* is taken as the subject of the verb, then "all things work together for good for those who love God." The first and second interpretations merely add an explicit nuance to what is really implicit in the third: God's purpose and plan are what is really behind all that happens to Christians. For Paul, God is in control of everything. *who are called according to his purpose:* God's plan is described in vv. 29–30. But this phrase must not be restricted only to such Christians as are "predestined"; this was the misleading interpretation of Augustine. Rather, this phrase was merely added as a complement to "those who love God." It designates "Christians" and explains why they love God; they do so because they have responded to a divine call (cf. Rom 1:6; 1 Cor 1:2). **29.** *he foreknew... he predestined:* Paul's vocabulary stresses the divine anteriority in the process of salvation, which comes from God's gracious bounty. He is interested in the results of that process. Hence his anthropomorphic language should not too facilely be transferred to the *signa rationis* of any later theological system of predestination. *be conformed to the image of his Son:* According to the divine plan of salvation the Christian is to reproduce in himself an image of Christ by a progressive share in the risen life of Christ himself (see 8:17; 2 Cor 3:18; 4:4; Col 1:15; Phil 3:20–21; cf. A. R. C. Leaney, *NTS* 10 [1963–64] 470–79). **30.** *he also glorified:* All God's plan (involving call, election, predestination, justification) is aimed only at the final destiny of glory for all men who will put faith in Christ. It is important to realize that in this passage Paul is not speaking of the predestination of individuals; he is describing God's design apropos of Christians as a group.

92 **31–39.** Having discussed the various aspects of the new Christian life in union with Christ and the reasons that give a basis to Christian hope, Paul concludes this section with a rhetorical passage and a triumphant hymn to the love of God that is made manifest in Christ Jesus. No little emotion and some rhythmic phrasing mark the passage. **31.** *who can be against us?:* The terminology is that of a lawcourt, similar to the debates in Job or Zech 3. God's salvific plan makes it clear to the Christian that God is on his side (cf. Ps 118:6). **32.** *did not spare his own Son:* Possibly an allusion to Gn 22:16, to Abraham who did not spare Isaac. Paul echoes 5:5–8 (cf. 4:25; Jn 3:16). God the Judge has already pronounced sentence in our favor and there is no reason to expect anything different from him hereafter. **33–35.** The punctuation of the phrases of the next three verses is disputed. We prefer to take them all as rhetorical questions (cf. the RSV for a different punctuation). **33.** *who shall accuse God's elect? Is it God who justifies?:* The answer implied, of course, is no. The allusion to Is 50:8–9 makes some commentators take this phrase as a statement, to which the following phrase would be a question in reaction. **34.** *rather was raised:* Note the significant shift of emphasis to the resurrection of Christ (cf. 4:24–25) to which Paul immediately adds a rare reference to the exaltation of Christ (without alluding to the ascension; cf. Eph 4:10; 1 Tm 3:16). *intercedes for us:* Paul ascribes to the glorified Risen Christ an activity that continues the objective aspect of man's redemption. Christ still presents his supplication to the Father on behalf of Christians; in Heb 7:25; 9:24 this intercession is linked with Christ's priesthood (a notion absent from the Pauline corpus). In 1 Jn 2:1 Christ appears as the *paraklētos* before the Father, an image that agrees more with his role here. **35.** *from the love of Christ:* From the love Christ has for us. None of the dangers and troubles of life can make the true Christian forget the love of Christ made known to men in his death and resurrection.

93 **36.** *as scripture says:* Lit., "as it was written" (see comment on 1:17). Paul quotes Ps 44:23 (Eng 22), a community lamentation that bemoans the injustice done to faithful Israel by its enemies and recalls its fidelity to Yahweh, seeking his aid and deliverance. The Ps is cited to show that such tribulations are not proof of God's not loving the persecuted; rather that such things are a sign of that love. **37.** *through him who loved us:* Either Christ, as in 8:35, or God, as in 5:5,8. **38.** Two series of obstacles for the love of God (or Christ) have been given in 8:33–34, 35–37; a third is given here. *angels... principalities... powers:* Spirits of different ranks. Whether they are good or evil is not clear; but in any case they will not succeed in separating Christians from Christ. Paul enumerates a series of forces that the ancients apparently thought of as hostile to men (cf. Col 2:15; Eph 1:21). **39.** *neither height nor depth:* These may be the ancient terms of astrology for the greatest proximity and remoteness of a star from the zenith, by which its influence was determined. Paul would imply that not even such astrological forces can separate the Christian from Christ. *from the love of God in Christ Jesus our Lord:* The love of God is thus the unshakable foundation of Christian life and hope. This ending sums up the theme of this section, which Paul has been developing since 8:1. Once again he ends the chapter with the refrain noted earlier (→ 49 above).

(Dubarle, A.-M., "Le gémissement des créatures dans l'ordre divin du cosmos (*Rom.* 8, 19–22)," *RSPT* 38 [1954] 445–65. Fahy, T., "Exegesis of Romans 8:16–25," *IrTQ* 23 [1956] 178–81. Kürzinger, J., "*Symmorphous tēs eikonos tou huiou autou* (Röm 8, 29)," *BZ* 2 [1958] 294–99. Lyonnet, S., "La rédemption de l'univers," *LumVi* 48 [1960] 43–62. Viard, A., "'Expectatio creaturae' (Rom., VIII, 19–22)," *RB* 59 [1952] 337–54. Worden, T., "Christ Jesus Who Died or Rather Who Has Been Raised Up, Rom. 8:34," *Scr* 10 [1958] 33–43; *Scr* 11 [1959] 51–59.)

94 (d) THE THEME ILLUSTRATED: THE OLD TESTAMENT SHOWS THAT THIS PLAN OF SALVATION DOES NOT CONTRADICT GOD'S PROMISES TO ISRAEL (9:1–11:36). Having developed in ch. 8 the theme announced in 5:1–11, Paul now turns to a specific problem that the new uprightness, which is obtained through faith in Christ, obviously creates. This is the relationship of Judaism to the Christian plan of salvation. His treatment of it is heavily scriptural, and it is in effect a scriptural illustration of the theme already developed. In this way it manifests a certain parallelism to the discussion of Abraham's justification and the Law (4:1–25). Just as that discussion provided a scriptural illustration of the theme of the first section (A) of Part I, so this treatment now does the same for the theme of the second section (B) of Part I (→ 13 above). To some commentators (e.g., P. Benoit, *RB* 65 [1958] 432) Rom 9–11, though an authentic Pauline composition, is a "foreign body" in the letter, added later by some editor. It is supposed to interrupt the continuity of Rom 12–15 and Rom 5–8; for the former is supposed to be a baptismal homily that follows aptly on Rom 5–8 in which baptism and its effects play such a large part. However, the reasons for treating chs. 9–11 as a "foreign body" have been scarcely convincing. Many centuries ago J. Calvin succinctly stated the connection of Rom 9–11 with the preceding part of the letter: "If this [the teaching of chs. 1–8] be the doctrine of the Law and the Prophets, why is it that the Jews reject it?" (*Comm. in Rom.* 9.1). This question must have been put to Paul by contemporary Gentiles too.

(Dinkler, E., "The Historical and the Eschatological Israel in Romans Chapters 9–11," *JRel* 36 [1956] 109–27. Lyonnet, S., *Quaestiones in epistulam ad Romanos* [2a ser.; Rome, 1962]. Munck, J., *Christus und Israel* [Aarhus/Copenhagen, 1956].)

95 (i) *Israel's infidelity is not contrary to God's direction of history* (9:1–33). Not only Gentile reaction to his preaching of Jesus, but also his own sadness at the condition of Jews who were not accepting Jesus as the Messiah caused Paul to formulate a specific answer to the problem of the "rejection" of Israel. He does so by viewing Israel's role in terms of his conception of salvation history. It is important to realize from the outset that Paul's perspective is corporate; he is not discussing the responsibility of individuals. If he seems to bring up the question of divine predestination, this has nothing to do with the predestination of individuals to glory. On the other hand, he does not even remotely touch on the modern question of the responsibility of Jews for the death of Christ. One can distinguish four subsections in ch. 9: the problem of Israel's unbelief (1–5); God's promises to Israel have been the result of his gratuitous election (6–13); example of Moses and Pharaoh: Yahweh had a right to choose (14–24); Israel's call and infidelity are both announced in the OT (25–33).

96 **1–5.** The problem. **1.** *in Christ:* Paul speaks out sincerely as a Christian, without any resentment against Jews who may have caused him trouble or charged him with disloyalty (2 Cor 2:17; 12:19). He is saddened at the condition of his fellow kinsmen. **3.** *accursed:* Lit., "anathema" (see comment on Gal 1:8). Paul would willingly undergo the worst possible fate—"to be cut off from Christ"—for the sake of his fellow Jews. In this he echoes Moses' prayer for the unruly Israelites (Ex 32:32), "to be blotted out of the book of life," that they might be forgiven. **4.** *Israelites:* Instead of the common political title of "Jews" (*Ioudaioi*), Paul reverently makes use of their honorific religious title, bestowed of old by Yahweh himself on his people (Gn 32:28; cf. Eph 2:12). And he proceeds to recount all the historic privileges connected with this name—seven of them. *sonship:* The adoption (*huiothesia*, see comment on 8:15) of Israel as the "son of God" (Ex 4:22; Is 1:2; Hos 11:1), making it Yahweh's covenant partner and chosen people. *glorious presence:* The second privilege was the resplendent manifestation of Yahweh's presence in the desert Tabernacle and the Jerusalem Temple (Ex 40:34; 1 Kgs 8:10–11; see comment on *doxa*, 3:23). *covenants:* If the plural is retained, the third privilege would be the covenants made with Abraham, Jacob, Moses (Gn 15:18; 32:29; Ex 24:7–8). But important mss. (P^{46}, B, D, G) read the singular, which would refer to the pact of Sinai. *the Law:* The fourth privilege was the expression of God's will given to Moses (Ex 20:1–17; Dt 5:1–21). *the cult:* The refined worship of Yahweh in the Temple, so different from the idolatry of Israel's neighbors which often included prostitution and human sacrifice, was Israel's fifth privilege. *the promises:* The sixth privilege consisted of the gratuitous promises made to Abraham (Rom 4:13–20), to Isaac (Rom 9:9), to Moses (Dt 18:18–19), to David (2 Sm 7:11ff.). **5.** *the patriarchs:* Israel's seventh privilege was its ancestral heritage, for it still worshiped the God of its fathers (Abraham, Isaac, Jacob); see Rom 11:28. To this summary of Israel's seven prerogatives the climax is added—Christ, the descendant par excellence of their race. The *Messiah*, their greatest title to glory, was unfortunately not recognized as such.

97 *who is above all things, God, blessed forever! Amen:* This is still the best rendering of this verse, the most difficult in Rom. Since the Renaissance, apologetic controversy about the divinity of Christ in Paul's letters has obscured the exegesis of this text. Part of the problem is punctuation, of which there are four possibilities. (1) "...Christ is physically descended, who is above all things, God, blessed forever! Amen." So the vast majority of Christian interpreters of the first eight centuries, most modern Catholic interpreters, and many Protestant exegetes (Althaus, Cullmann, Leenhardt, Michel, Munck, Nygren, Sanday-Headlam). This proclaims Christ as God (not *ho theos* though), and blessed forever. (2) "...Christ is physically descended. God who is over all be (*or* is) blessed forever! Amen." So a few writers from the 4th cent. on; Erasmus, who introduced the modern discussion; many Protestant exegetes (Goodspeed, Dodd, Lietzmann, Bultmann, Feine, Burkitt, RSV, NEB); Cerfaux. A doxology is addressed to God in the manner of contemporary Jewish doxologies. Paul blesses God at the mention of the Messiah, Israel's glorious descendant. (3) "...Christ is physically descended, who is over all. God be blessed forever! Amen." This form of the verse splits the praise between Christ and God. (4) "...Christ is physically descended, and to whom belongs God who is above all...." So J. Weiss, K. Barth. This is a conjectural inversion of two words, which reads *hōn ho* and introduces another phrase parallel with the two preceding *hōn*. It makes God himself the last of the privileges belonging to Israel. The last two explanations are improbable and have little to recommend them. The preference for (1) is based on three things: (a) the normal sense of this part of the verse in the context; (b) the absence of the normal wording of a doxology; in Paul's writings it is never joined asyndetically to what precedes, nor with the subject expressed first as here (see Rom 1:25; 2 Cor 11:31; Gal 1:5; 2 Tm 4:18; Rom 11:36; Eph 3:2; cf. 1 Pt 4:11; 5:11; Heb 13:21); (c) the compatibility of the verse with Paul's teaching. Though elsewhere he does not call Christ *theos* (cf. Ti 2:13 and see comment), other statements about him make his use of *theos* here conceivable (cf. 1 Cor 8:6; Phil 2:6; Col 1:15; 2:9; see O. Cullmann, *Christology*, 311–14; Sanday-Headlam, *Romans*, 233–38; O. Michel, *Römer*, 197–99; R. E. Brown, *TS* 26 [1965] 559–60).

98 **6–13.** God's promises to Israel have been the result of his gratuitous election. **6.** *God's word has not failed:* The proposition of this subsection. Paul rejects the notion that the *logos* communicated to Israel in Yahweh's oracles and promises (Rom 9:4,9) has somehow been thwarted through his kinsmen's refusal to accept Jesus. *not all the descendants of Israel are really Israel:* The argument runs thus: God promised that Israel would be the recipient of his blessings; but now that Gentiles are becoming the recipients, it might seem that God's promises vacillate. If Paul's whole development in Rom 1–8 depends on God's promises, then maybe it is just as shaky as they are. No, Paul replies, for the OT promises were made not to Israel in the sense of physical descendants, but to the Israel of faith, to those whom God would choose. **7.** *children of Abraham:* Physical descent alone does not insure inheritance, for Abraham had many sons (Gn 15:2; 16:15; 21:2; 25:1), and yet the patriarchal promise of salvation was transmitted only through Isaac (cf. Gn 21:12). **8.** *children of God:* Abraham's true descendants are those born to him in virtue of a promise, not those who can claim a connection "physically" (*kata sarka*). **9.** *the promise:* Paul is not thinking of the generic promise of numberless progeny (Gn 15:5), but of the specific promise of Isaac's birth (Gn 18:10,14 conflated). Had it depended on *sarx* alone, Isaac would never have been born to the barren Sarah. **10.** *Rebecca too:* Another example confirms Paul's contention: God freely bestows his favor on whom he wills. In this case it is no longer a choice between mothers (Sarah and Hagar, allegorized in Gal 4:21–31), but between the sons of the same mother, between the twins Jacob and Esau. Both were born to the patriarch Isaac from the same mother, and yet God showed favor to Jacob alone. He made a choice that freely conditioned Israel's history (cf. Gn 25:21–23). **11.** *before the children had done anything, good or evil:* The choice of Isaac was entirely gratuitous and did not depend on merits or demerits. This verse is crucial in Paul's argument in this chapter. The call of the Gentiles to Christian faith exemplifies the same gratuity. *that God's elective plan might continue:* Lit., "that the purpose of God according to election might continue." Isaac was favored in order to make known to men the execution of a divine plan that proceeds according to gratuitous election. **12.** *she was told:* In Gn 25:23. Of twins, the one first born was to serve the other. Israel was descended from favored Jacob, and Esau became the eponymous ancestor of Edom (and the later Idumeans). The latter were never considered to be real Jews. Josephus (*Ant.* 13.9, 1 § 257) calls them "half Jews." John Hyrcanus I defeated them (*ca.* 108 BC) and forced them to be circumcised and to follow the Mosaic Law. How different, then, was their destiny from that of Israel! **13.** *Jacob I loved:* Cf. Mal 1:2. The prophet records Yahweh's love of Israel; he then gives the reason for the five great reproaches that follow this protestation of love. Paul uses this quotation to emphasize Israel's role in the plan of salvation in contrast to Edom's. This verse has been abused in past predestinarian disputes, and these should warn us against trying to understand it of any predestination to grace or glory. Jacob and Esau are eponymous representatives of their ethnic groups and are tools in the execution of the divine plan. *Esau I hated:* "Loved less"; ancient Near Eastern exaggeration.

99 **14–24.** Example of Moses and Pharaoh. Yahweh had a right to choose. **14.** *is there injustice in God then?:* God might seem to have been guilty of *adikia* in choosing one brother over the other—and again in choosing Gentiles as his people after centuries of service from the Jews. **15.** *he said to Moses:* Paul quotes Ex 33:19, Yahweh's answer to Moses after the incident of the Golden Calf. Even after such infidelity Yahweh could still manifest his gracious mercy in favoring Israel as his chosen instrument. Through it he would continue to make his will known among men. This verse is explained in 9:18. **16.** *it depends upon God's mercy:* Paul's conclusion is drawn from the fact that only God's mercy is mentioned in the OT text just cited. Without his grace and favor all man's efforts are vain. But Paul does not say that, once given the assistance of God's favor, such efforts are useless. Elsewhere he stresses the need of them. Here his emphasis is on divine gratuitous election, because he is treating a specific problem. **17.** *scripture says to Pharaoh:* Though the transcendent God of Israel spoke directly to Moses (9:15), he speaks only indirectly to the heathen, through the Scripture. *showing my power in [dealing with] you:* Ex 9:16, especially according to the LXX, ms. A. The Pharaoh was an instrument in God's plan, just as Moses was. Indeed, his very obstinacy was the means God used to save Israel. Ultimately, even the hardhearted Pharaoh contributed to the proclamation of Yahweh's name in the world. **18.** *hardens the heart:* In the OT the hardening of Pharaoh's heart is ascribed at times to God (Ex 4:21; 7:3; 9:12; etc.), and at times to Pharaoh himself (Ex 7:14,22; 8:15,19,32; etc.). Later in the Prophets the hardening of the heart by God is a divine reaction to the persisting human obstinacy against him—a sealing of a situation he did not create. The hardening of Pharaoh's heart should not be looked upon as the result of some arbitrary or even planned divine decree. It is merely the OT way of expressing God's recognition of a situation due to man himself who rejects God's invitation. The expression also brings out the absolute control of God in world history. Salvation history really began at the Exodus from Egypt, and the Pharaoh who opposed Israel's departure was in the long run just a figure setting the stage for the divine control of events. (Cf. K. L. Schmidt, *TZ* 1 [1945] 1–17; S. Lyonnet, *VD* 34 [1956] 193–201, 257–71; A. Penna, *Divinitas* 2 [1958] 597–614.)

100 **19.** *why does he still find fault?:* If God can make use of the indocility of man to accomplish his ends, why should he complain about men? The same type of reasoning underlies the objection in 6:1,15. **20.** *who are you?:* Paul does not try to silence his imaginary objector but rather to put the discussion on its proper level. God's control of the world is not to be judged by man's myopic view. *can what is molded say to its molder?:* A familiar OT figure is used; cf. Is 29:16; 45:9; 64:8; Jer 18:6; Wis 15:7; also used in 1QS 11:22. Paul adapts it to his own purpose. The figure was intended to depict God as the Creator and Governor of the universe. *why have you made me thus?:* Not, "Why did you make me clay?" but rather, "Why did you make me an unshapely pot rather than a beautiful vase?" The emphasis is on the function of the thing molded. **21.** *lump:* The Gk word *phyrama* (what is mixed, kneaded; lump, batch of dough, clay) was translated into Lat as *massa.* From this came the pejorative term *massa damnata* in the predestinarian controversies (cf. Augustine *Ep.* 190. 3–9). The ancient potter used a wheel, set in rapid motion by the foot, while his deft fingers quickly drew from the shapeless lump of clay slender and exquisite vessels. From such a feat ancient man derived the notion of God as a potter fashioning the world and man as he would. It emphasized God's power, dominion, and freedom.

101 **22.** *desiring:* Though some commentators (Jerome, Thomas Aq., Michel, Barrett) understand this participle causally, "because he desired," it seems better in the context (especially in view of the phrase "with much patience") to understand it concessively, "Though he desired...," i.e., though his anger might have led him to make known his power, his loving kindness has restrained him. He gave Pharaoh time to repent. *vessels of wrath:* Paul uses a phrase from Jer 50:25, which suits the potter-context (9:21, "vessel"). At the same time he plays on a wider sense of *skeuos* which also means "thing, object, instrument." It is an "object" toward which divine anger is displayed. *made for destruction:* The pf. participle expresses the state in which these "vessels" find themselves, "suited, fitted out" for destruction, ready to be cast out on the rubbish heap. This verse affirms above all the radical incompatibility of God and rebellious, sinful man. There is also a nuance of predestination here, and Paul's formulation is more generic than the example he began with; this is why his words served in later predestinarian controversies. But one should not lose sight of his perspective. **23.** *to make known the wealth of his glory:* Those who have been chosen for a role in the history of salvation have been destined by God for a share in his abundant glory. This destiny is not the exclusive right of the Jewish people (see Rom 3:29). On the other hand, it is not an absolute predestination, as Rom 11:22 shows. If God has been patient, it is because he wants to allow Israel time to repent so that he might manifest his mercy toward it all the more. **24.** *even us whom he has called:* Anacoluthon. The "vessels of mercy" include not only Jews but Gentiles too. To the questions posed in 9:19–21 Paul never gives a direct answer. Instead, he insists on God's freedom of election and his patience in waiting for instruments he would use to manifest their utility.

102 **25–33.** Israel's call and infidelity are both announced in the OT. Paul makes use once again of the literary subform of "testimonia" (see comment on 3:10; possible further examples in 10:15–21; 11:8–10,26,34–35; 15:9–12). The conflated quotations here are derived from Hos and Is (mentioned in 9:27). **25–26.** Cf. Hos 2:25 (which Paul adapts to his own purposes, since it agrees neither with the MT nor any ancient version) and 1:10 (from the LXX). In the original text the words refer to God's restoration of the ten tribes of Israel after they had committed "adultery" (= idolatry) and ceased to be God's people. Their abandonment of him meant the loss of their covenant status. Hosea promised their restoration. But for Paul the words refer to the Gentiles. As Paul applies them, they illustrate God's election, and especially his choice of those who were unworthy to become the privileged ones. **27.** *Isaiah:* Cf. Is 10:22–23 (abridging the LXX). Paul is interested only in the one phrase, "a remnant shall be saved." Through all of Israel's infidelities and consequent punishments a ray of hope has gleamed. The words were used by Isaiah originally of the Assyrian Captivity; Paul applies them to the multitude called to accept Christ and the remnant that did so. **29.** Cf. Is 1:9 (according to the LXX). The prophet was speaking of the punishment of faithless Israel. The burden of these OT quotations is that the OT, the book that gives Israel its basis of hope, testifies that Israel will be annihilated and forgotten except for a remnant, which would preserve its name and seed.

103 **30.** Paul concludes the first part of his argument. But in this verse and in the following ones he also begins the argument of ch. 10. The cause of Israel's infidelity is to be found, not in God, but in Israel itself. Israel's failure is its preference of its own way of uprightness to that of God's. **32.** *faith...deeds:* See 3:20,28; see comment on 2:15. **33.** Conflation of Is 28:16 and 8:14–15. Paul disregards the context of the original and strings together phrases that make the OT almost say the opposite of what it actually says. As the text stands in Paul's quotation, the "stone" refers to Christ, which is intended to be an aid to Israel. But neglect of it makes of the stone a stumbling block. And Israel will stumble over the very stone laid on Mt. Zion (the eastern hill of Jerusalem on which the Temple was built) by Yahweh himself. Those who believe (the remnant and the Gentiles) will not come to grief over it. The Essenes of Qumran also applied Is 28:16 to themselves in that they looked upon their community as a Temple (1QS 8:5–7).

(See Danell, G. A., "The Idea of God's People in the Bible," *The Root of the Vine* [ed. A. Fridrichsen; N.Y., 1953] 23–36. Giblet, J., "Notes sur l'idée d'élection dans l'Écriture," *ColMech* 26 [1956] 367–75.)

104 (ii) *Israel's failure is derived from its own culpable refusal* (10:1–21). Paul has considered Israel's failure to accept Christ from the standpoint of God; it does not mean that God's promises have failed, nor that this was not foreseen by him in his gratuitous election of Israel. Paul now elaborates the reason for Israel's failure already sketched in 9:30–33. An expression of sorrow opens the chapter, for Israel has failed to recognize that Christ is the end of the Law and that salvific uprightness has been made possible through him (10:1–4). The old way of obtaining uprightness was difficult, but the new way is easy, within the reach of all, announced to all, as Scripture itself shows (10:5–13). But Israel did not take advantage of the opportunity offered by the prophets and the gospel; and so she is inexcusable (10:14–21).

105 1–4. Israel has failed to recognize that uprightness comes through Christ, the end of the Law. **1.** *that they may be saved:* The explicit inclusion of the Jews in the Christian view of God's plan of salvation (cf. 1 Thes 5:9; Rom 1:16). **2.** *they have a zeal for God:* Paul could speak from experience (Gal 1:13–14; Phil 3:9). Cf. 1 Mc 1:26–27. *not intelligent:* Lit., "not according to knowledge" (*epignōsis*), i.e., a real knowledge that recognizes the actual relation of man to God as it has now been revealed in Christ Jesus. **3.** *in their ignorance of God's uprightness:* This has often been understood of a communication of God's uprightness to men (i.e., the Jews did not realize that the genuine status of uprightness is not achieved by their own efforts, but conferred by God). But the expression "God's uprightness" should be compared with Phil 3:9, where it is clearly "uprightness that comes from God." Paul does not use the prepositional phrase here, but, as elsewhere in Rom (1:17; 3:5,21–26), speaks of the misunderstanding of the divine attribute. The Jews have missed the real meaning of God's salvific bounty; so they refused to submit to it. This is what they are now called on to do, and not spend themselves in vain efforts to achieve their own uprightness (see S. Lyonnet, *VD* 25 [1947] 18–21). **4.** *Christ is the end of the Law:* In two senses: (1) In a temporal sense, since the period of the Torah has ended and that of the Messiah has begun (cf. Gal 3:23). The time when the Law of Moses dominated men's lives with its demand of legal uprightness is terminated, superseded by Christ (cf. Eph 2:15; Jn 1:17). (2) In a final sense, the Law finds its teleological destiny in Christ (cf. Gal 3:24–25; AG 819). In him the Law finds its fulfillment (cf. Mt 5:17; Rom 3:31; 8:4). Of the two senses the first is predominant, since it is part of Paul's vision of man's history (→ Pauline Theology, 79:13, 41). Christ is the eschatological event superseding the Law, but the Jews have not recognized that the old order of things is no more. *that anyone who has faith can be upright:* Lit., "unto uprightness for every believer." The prized status of uprightness before God is now available to everyone (cf. Rom 1:16). As in Gal 2:16; Rom 3:22,28; 9:32, this is achieved not through the Law but through "faith."

106 5–13. The new way of uprightness, open to all, is easy, as Scripture shows. *Moses writes:* Lv 18:5, also quoted in Gal 3:12, promises life to men who strive for legal uprightness. The practical observance of the Torah's prescriptions was a necessary condition for the life so promised. Implied in the quotation is the arduous nature of that condition. In contrast with this demand, the new way of uprightness does not ask of man anything so arduous. To illustrate this point, Paul alludes to Moses' words in the Torah (Dt 30:11–14). Just as Moses tried to convince the Israelites that the observance of the Law did not demand one to scale the heights or descend to the depths, so Paul plays with Moses' words, applying them in an accommodated sense to Christ himself. The heights have been scaled and the depths have been plumbed, for Christ has come to the world of man and has been raised from the dead. Man is not asked to bring about an incarnation and a resurrection; he is asked only to accept in faith what has already been done for him and identify himself with Christ (Incarnate and Risen), who is man's salvation and uprightness. Paul adds an allusion to Ps 107:26 in his midrashic explanation of Dt. In this explanation "Christ" is substituted for the "word" of the Torah. (See S. Lyonnet, in *Mélanges bibliques* [Fest. A. Robert; Paris, 1957] 494–506.) **9.** *if you acknowledge:* That is, utter the basic Christian confession of faith and mean it. Paul proceeds to cite the credal (baptismal?) formula of the early Palestinian churches, *Kyrios Iēsous* (Jesus is the Lord); cf. 1 Cor 12:3; Phil 2:11; L. Cerfaux, *Christ*, 20. An inward faith is demanded that will guide the whole man; but it is also an assent to an expression of that faith. The man seeking justification and salvation is called on to acknowledge Christ as the Risen *Kyrios* and as the source of salvation precisely as the one raised from the dead by the Father. Again, Paul asserts the efficiency of the Father in Christ's resurrection (→ Pauline Theology, 79:72). **10.** This verse formulates rhetorically the relation of man's uprightness and salvation to his faith and the profession of it. The balance stresses certain aspects of the one basic act of personal adherence to Christ and its effect. One should not overstress the distinction between justification and salvation, or between faith and profession. **11.** *no one who believes in him will be put to shame:* Is 28:16 is used again; cf. 9:33. Paul modifies the quotation by adding *pas* (all), thus emphasizing the universality of the application: "not...all" = "no one." In Is the words referred to the precious cornerstone laid by Yahweh in Zion; they are accommodated by Paul to faith in Christ and used as an assurance of salvation for the Christian believer. The addition of the word *pas* prepares for the next verse. **12.** *no distinction between Jew and Greek:* As far as the opportunity to share in the new uprightness through faith is concerned (cf. 3:22–23). *the same Lord:* At first it might seem that Paul is referring to Yahweh, since he uses Jewish expressions, "the Lord of all" (Josephus, *Ant.* 20.4, 2 § 90), "call upon the name of" (1 Sm 12:17–18; 2 Sm 22:7), and explicitly refers in 10:13 to Jl 3:5 (Eng 2:32). But in the context (esp. after 10:9) *kyrios* can only refer to Jesus, who is the Lord of Jew and Greek (cf. Acts 10:36; Rom 9:5; Phil 2:9–11). In the OT "those who call on the name of the Lord" was a designation of sincere and pious Israelites; in the NT it is transferred to Christians (1 Cor 1:2; Acts 9:14), and the object of it is Christ. The title once reserved for Yahweh is now transferred to Christ; the vv. 12–13 are an eloquent witness to the early Church's worship of Christ as *Kyrios*. Salvation was expected by the Jews from the *kyrios* of the OT (Yahweh); they are now told that that salvation comes through him who has been made *Kyrios* by Yahweh himself (Acts 2:36) as of the resurrection.

107 14–21. Israel, however, did not take advantage of the opportunity offered it by the prophets and the gospel, and so the fault lies with it. The opportunity of believing in Christ was offered to all, but especially to Israel; it cannot claim that it did not hear his gospel. Paul proposes to himself four difficulties (perhaps echoing comments on his missionary sermons among the Jews) to which he proposes brief answers by quoting Scripture: (1) How can men believe the gospel unless it has been fully preached? (10:14–15). (2) But it has not been accepted by everybody! (10:16–17). (3) But perhaps the Jews did not hear it! (10:18). (4) But perhaps they did not understand! (10:19–21).

14. *have not believed:* The first difficulty is multiple and begins with the assumption that the cult of Jesus must be founded on belief in him. *whom they have never heard:* The question does not refer to Jews of Palestine who might have witnessed the ministry of Jesus but to those who had not listened to him directly. *unless someone preaches to them:* Faith is founded on an authorized preaching, on the testimony of those who have been charged with the mission to make known to men the message of God. Here as in v. 17 the initial step in all faith is a "hearing" of the proposed message; the object of faith, propositionally formulated, is thus first presented.

For Paul it begins as *akoē*, to end as *hypakoē* (→ Pauline Theology, 79:125). **15.** *unless they are sent:* The authoritative preaching, which is the basis of faith, presupposes a mission; in expressing the latter, Paul uses the vb. *apostellō*, alluding therefore to the apostolic testimony of the early Church itself in proclaiming the Christ-event. To such an objection Paul answers with Is 52:7 (in a form closer to the MT than to the present LXX). *who bring good news:* In Is the text refers to the good news announced to the Jews in the Babylonian Captivity that deliverance was coming through Cyrus and that Jerusalem's restoration was close at hand. As used by Paul, the words take on the overtones of his good news, his "gospel." His answer to the first difficulty, then, is to quote Isaiah, and show that the "gospel" has indeed been preached to Israel. **16.** *not everyone has heeded the good news:* The second difficulty. Paul replies by quoting Is 53:1, indirectly stating that because not everyone among the Jews has accepted the good news does not mean that it has not been preached to them. For even such infidelity and refusal to believe had been foreseen by the prophet Isaiah regarding his own mission. **17.** *through Christ's message:* This vague expression is susceptible to various interpretations, and Paul does not explain it. It could mean the message Christ brought to men or (more likely in the context) the message about Christ. Should we perhaps translate, "the message of the Messiah"?

108 **18.** *have they not heard?:* The third difficulty. Sense: Maybe they have not had the opportunity to hear the good news; maybe the apostolic preachers have not done their job. Paul answers with Ps 19:5. In the original context the psalmist sings of nature proclaiming the glory of God everywhere. Paul accommodates the words of the Ps to the preaching of the gospel. In effect, Paul denies that Israel has lacked the opportunity to believe in Christ. **19.** *did Israel not understand?:* The fourth difficulty: Maybe the apostolic preachers spoke in an unintelligible fashion, and Israel did not comprehend the message. Again Paul answers with Scripture, quoting Dt 32:21 and Is 65:1–2, first the Torah, then the Prophets. The words of Dt are from the Song of Moses in which Yahweh—through Moses—tries to educate Israel and announces that it will be humiliated by the heathens. In thus quoting Dt, Paul implies a comparison of Israel's situation with what it was at the time of the Exile. If it was humiliated then, how much greater should its humiliation be now: Gentiles can understand the gospel message, but Israel is uncomprehending. **20.** In the original context of Is 65:1–2 the same people are envisaged by the prophet's words in vv. 1 and 2, be they Samaritans, apostate Jews, or simply Jews (disputed among OT commentators). But Paul, influenced by the LXX which speaks of *ethnos* (nation) in 65:1 and of *laos* (people) in 65:2, splits up the reference in the two verses. The first is applied to the Gentiles, the second to the Jews. The contrast is obvious between the Gentiles, "the foolish nation," which accepts Christ in faith, and the Jews, "a disobedient and obstinate people," which has refused belief in him. So ends Paul's indictment of the culpable refusal of Israel.

(See Flückiger, F., "Christus des Gesetzes *telos*," *TZ* 11 [1955] 153–57. Ludwig, J., "Fides ex auditu," *Aurelia* [Bohn, 1926] 69–71. Penna, A., "Testi d'Isaia in S. Paolo," *RBiblt* 5 [1957] 25–30, 163–79.)

109 (iii) *Israel's failure is partial and temporary* (11:1–36). The picture painted thus far by Paul in chs. 9–10 is not pleasant: Israel's disbelief fits into the plan of God that is based on gratuitous election (ch. 9); but actually its cause rests not with him, but with Israel itself, "a disobedient and obstinate people." Yet in 9:27 Paul had already hinted at a ray of hope, when he said that "a remnant of them will be saved." Now he returns to this aspect of the problem and further explains that Israel's disbelief is not entire but only partial (11:1–10), that it is not final but only temporary (11–24), and that in God's plan mercy is shown to all, the Jews included (25–32). At the end of this section Paul bursts into a hymn to the merciful wisdom of God (33–36).

1–10. Israel's disbelief is only partial. **1.** *has God rejected his people?:* If God's plan is one of gratuitous election and Israel has been unfaithful, and if the Gentiles are now accepting the gospel, while Israel is not, then it might seem that God has repudiated those who were once his chosen people (cf. Ps 94:14). *by no means!:* Emphatic, almost indignant negative (see comment on 3:4). *Israelite:* See comment on 9:4. *descendant of Abraham:* "According to the flesh" (see comment on 1:3). *of the tribe of Benjamin:* Phil 3:5. Benjamin was often regarded as the most Israelite of the tribes, the "beloved of the Lord" (Dt 33:12); from it came Saul, the first king of the undivided monarchy, Paul's namesake. All these identifications are proof that God has not rejected his people; Paul and other Jewish Christians have been called and invited to belief in Christ. **2.** *Elijah:* Cf. 1 Kgs 19:9–18. After his journey of 40 days and 40 nights to reach Horeb, the mount of God, the prophet took shelter in a cave where he complained bitterly to Yahweh of Israel's infidelities. Yahweh announced the coming chastisement of his people, but also the deliverance of 7000 in Israel who had not bent their knees to Baal. Just as Elijah was not alone, so Paul was not alone among the Jews in his belief in Christ Jesus. **3.** Paul uses 1 Kgs 19:10 in abbreviated and inverted form. The example of Elijah is drawn from Israel's history to reveal God's plan in the present situation too. **4.** Here 1 Kgs 19:18 is quoted rather freely, neither according to the MT nor the LXX. Paul is interested in only one point in the OT verse: 7000 men remained faithful to Yahweh. Israel had not been entirely repudiated then, nor is it now. **5.** *there is a remnant, chosen by grace:* Lit., "a remnant according to the selection of grace," i.e., by God's gratuitous election, and without any regard of their fidelity to the Law. The Essenes of Qumran also regarded themselves as *b*^{e}*ḥîrê rāṣôn*, "those chosen by divine benevolence" (1QS 8:6; cf. E. Vogt, "'Peace Among Men of God's Good Pleasure' Lk 2.14," *The Scrolls and the NT* [New York, 1957] 114–17). **6.** *not on the basis of deeds:* See 3:24; 4:4; 9:16. The existence of this remnant is evidence of God's benevolence rather than of human merit.

110 **7.** *Israel failed to get what it desired:* The majority of the Jews apart from the remnant did not attain the uprightness they prized (9:30–31). This is the source of the sorrow that Paul expressed in 9:1–2. *but those whom God chose attained it:* Lit., "the election," i.e., abstract for the concrete. Though those chosen actually embraced the Gentiles and the remnant, Paul is thinking only in terms of the latter when he contrasts it with "the rest" (*hoi loipoi*). *became callous:* Lit., "were hardened." This effect on the Jews who did not accept Christ is a result of their attitude of resistance to the gospel; but even this resistance has its providential function in God's plan. **8.** *as it is written:* See comment on 1:17. On the conflated quotations from the OT used here, see comment on 3:10. Paul links together Dt 29:3; Is 29:10; Ps 69:22–23. The words of Dt 29:3 (not quoted literally) were addressed by Moses to Israel, which had witnessed all the portents sent against Pharaoh by God on its behalf but had never appreciated their full significance: "But to this day the Lord has not given you a mind to understand, or eyes to see, or ears to hear" (Eng 29:4). Paul modifies this free quotation with a significant addition from Is 29:10, "a spirit of stupor," drawn from a passage in which Isaiah spoke of the spiritual blindness and perversity of Israel. The conflated texts serve Paul's purpose of describing Israel's reaction to Christ. However, one should not miss the way in which Paul uses the OT (see J. A. Fitzmyer, *NTS* 7 [1960–61] 297–333; J. Schmid, *BZ* 3 [1959] 161–73). **9.** *David:* The verse is ascribed to David because in Pss his name stands at the head of Ps 69, a lament for deliverance from personal tribulation. The catchword bond linking these verses with the preceding text is "eyes that see not." There is no need to try to decide what the other details refer to (feasting, etc.). The main point is the sealing or confirming by God of the situation that exists (see comment on 9:18). But this situation is neither entire nor final.

111 **11–24.** Israel's disbelief is only temporary. **11.** *stumbled so as to fall:* Paul admits that Israel has stumbled over Christ; it has found him an obstacle. And yet it has not fallen down completely, so as it cannot regain its footing. Indeed, its stumbling has been providential, for the apostles turned from it to the Gentiles (cf. Acts 13:45–48; 18:6). In the long run its very stumbling aroused in it a jealousy of the heathen, who were attaining the uprightness of God that Israel itself had been seeking. **12.** *their full number:* The word *plērōma* means here "that which is brought to fullness, completion," the "full number, complement" (see AG 678 for another meaning). Paul hints at the untold blessings for the world that will come with the full acceptance by the Jews of Jesus as the Messiah; if their action so far has resulted in such unspeakable benefits, what then will their acceptance mean?

112 **13.** *to you Gentiles:* Cf. 1:6. The Gentiles are not to be presumptuous or haughty because they have accepted Christ and think that they have a right to look down on Israel. *apostle of the Gentiles:* The usual epithet given to Paul stems from his own writings (see Gal 2:7–8; Rom 1:5; Acts 9:15; 15:12; 22:21). Paul boasts of this ministry to the Gentiles and spends himself in it with one real purpose in view: to excite his own countrymen and thus save some of them. Though he is a Christian, dedicated in his attachment to Christ, Paul still looks on himself as a member of the same race as the Jews. He calls it literally "my flesh," and thereby gives vivid expression to his solidarity with them. **15.** *their rejection:* Subjective genitive, the Jews' rejection of Christ. It has resulted in the "reconciliation of the world," i.e., the reconciliation of all others (than Jews) to God has been achieved through them; see Eph 2:11–22 for another way of expressing it. This reconciliation will have the effect of making Jews jealous and thus drawing some of them to Christ. *life from the dead:* A difficult phrase, the meaning of which is quite disputed. Origen, Cyril of Alexandria, and many medieval commentators understood the phrase *zōē ek nekrōn* to refer to the general resurrection of the dead at the end of time. If the conversion of the Gentiles is comparable to the first phase of redemption, viz., "reconciliation," then the "acceptance" of the Jews will be comparable to its definitive stage. This interpretation is used by Sanday-Headlam, Lagrange, Lietzmann, Michel, Lyonnet, who note, however, that Paul is not asserting a temporal connection between the conversion of Israel and the parousia; it is not a "sign" of the end of the world. Others—Theophylact, Photius, Euthymius, Cornely, Huby—understand *zōē ek nekrōn* in a figurative sense: "The conversion of Israel en masse will be for the Gentiles an event of great utility and happiness" (Huby). The reason for this figurative interpretation is that Paul does not say *anastasis nekrōn,* the expression he uses elsewhere when speaking of the "resurrection of the dead" (1 Cor 15:12,13,21,42; Rom 6:5; Acts 17:32; 23:6; 24:21; 26:23). We prefer to interpret the phrase with Leenhardt and Stanley, who consider the image to involve the Jewish people themselves. Their acceptance of Christ will mean their passage from the status of death to life. There is an allusion to the effects of their identification with Christ, as in baptism (6:4), but above all to the new life that will be theirs as a result of their "acceptance." **16.** *if the first handful of dough is consecrated:* Paul's figure is mixed; he actually says, "If the first fruits are holy, then the whole lump of dough is." He is referring to Nm 15:18–21. In virtue of the first portion of meal being set aside for the Lord (i.e., being given to the Temple priests [Josephus, *Ant.* 4.4, 4 § 70]), the whole batch acquired a legal purity making it fit to be consumed by the people of God. *if the root is consecrated:* Cf. Jer 11:16–17. The image expresses the same idea as the previous one. But to what does Paul refer? For Theodore of Mopsuestia the first handful of dough and the root were Christ, whose holiness guaranteed blessings for all Israel. For Weiss they refer to the converted remnant; this suits the preceding context. For Cornely, Sanday-Headlam, and Lagrange the patriarchs are meant, because in 11:17 "root" will be used again to designate ancient Israel, onto which the Gentiles have been grafted. Either of these interpretations is possible, and perhaps Leenhardt, in dividing the images between the two interpretations, has the real solution: The first handful of dough represents the "remnant" which has already accepted Christ, the root represents the patriarchs. Thus a link is established with both the preceding and the following contexts.

113 **17.** *some of the branches were broken off:* Paul, still addressing the Gentiles, warns them not to be smug about their favored situation. They are not to look down on the unbelieving Jews who have been cut off from the source of life. *a wild olive shoot:* In part the figure depends on the OT (Jer 11:16; Hos 14:6) but also on the practice known to ancient horticulturists of grafting a young wild olive branch into an old, worn-out olive tree that had been giving good fruit (Columella, *De re rustica* 5.9, 16). The Gentiles are the wild olive shoot grafted into Israel, in the place of the lopped off branches (the unbelieving Jews). **18.** *the root supports you:* Israel of old still occupies the privileged position of the carrier of salvation to the world. **20.** *that is true:* Paul does not deny that the defection of Israel facilitated the conversion of the Gentiles. Israel was not broken off so that the Gentiles might be grafted into their place. Its disbelief caused it to be lopped off—something that had no intrinsic connection with the election of the Gentiles who were actually grafted in its place. *it is only through faith that you stand where you do:* The situation of the Gentiles is due to God's gratuitous election and their acceptance in faith; it is not due to any merits of which the Gentile Christians can boast. **21.** *did not spare the natural branches:* If branches that belonged on the tree (*kata physin,* "by nature") could be lopped off (because of their infidelity), so can those that have simply been grafted into it, if they prove unfaithful. **22.** *God's kindness and severity:* These two notions come closest to what has been traditionally called God's "mercy and justice," but to express them Paul uses the Gk words *chrēstotēs* and *apotomia.* He significantly does not use *eleos* and *dikaiosynē,* which have an OT background and convey notably different ideas (→ Pauline Theology, 79:37). *provided you continue in his kindness:* God's election, though gratuitous, is conditioned by the Gentile Christians' responsible fulfillment of his obligations. **23.** *will be grafted in:* Paul finally explains how the lopped off branches (the unbelieving Jews) will be able to find life in the parent stock of Abraham—by faith in Christ. *God has the power to graft them in again:* A fortiori, if he were able to graft in a wild olive branch. Throughout the argument based on the wild olive shoot Paul implies that the lopped off natural branch has not yet been cast on the rubbish heap. Israel has not been definitively rejected by God. **24.** *from a wild olive tree... into a cultivated one:* The contrast suggests the transcendent nature of the vocation to which the Gentile Christians have been called. The restoration of the Jews, on the other hand, will be easier than the call of the Gentiles. Hence, Israel's rejection is not final, but temporary.

114 **25–32.** In God's plan mercy is shown to all, including the Jews. **25.** *wise in your own way of thinking:* Gentile Christians should not conclude that their view of the history of man is the only valid one; Paul prefers to disclose to them an aspect of the divine secret long hidden in God, but now revealed (→ Pauline Theology, 79:32–34). *only partial insensibility:* Cf. comment on 11:7. Paul reverts to what he said in 11:1–10. *the full complement of the Gentiles:* The Gentile Christians must in Paul's view of the divine plan of salvation take the conversion of Israel seriously; it will take place, when the *plērōma* of the Gentiles has come in (= has entered as a graft into the stock of the olive tree that is Israel). Paul speaks in corporate terms and apparently sees a causal connection between the conversion of the "full number" of the Gentiles and the conversion of the Jews. Does Paul mean by *plērōma* all the Gentiles there are? **26.** *all Israel will be saved:* Thus Paul expresses his firm conviction about the lot of his fellow countrymen. Israel's partial infidelity is to exist for a time. Earlier in this section Paul quoted the OT against Israel, now he does so in its favor. The quotation is composite again; see comment on 3:10. Is 59:20–21 are joined to Is 27:9 and illustrate his ideas on God's "mystery" for the salvation of all Israel. The words of Isaiah show that God, in establishing his covenant with Israel, reckoned with its infidelity. Paul cites these words, but views them in the light of the Christ-event. Christ is the "deliverer." Is 59:20–21 is not quoted according to the MT but in a form close to the LXX. The passage deals with the spiritual destiny of Israel as a result of the covenant. Is 27:9 is added without any regard for its original context. **28.** *they are enemies of God:* Because of their temporary rejection of the Gospel. *on your account:* A summary of 11:11–24. *but as regards God's choice they are beloved by him for the sake of their forefathers:* The election of Israel is irrevocable, for God has shown it favor because of its illustrious patriarchs—a claim that the Gentiles do not have, and one that God will always respect. The concern that God has had for Israel has undergone no change, despite what some of Paul's preceding remarks might seem to imply (cf. C. Spicq, *RB* 67 [1960] 210–19). **30.** *you once disobeyed God:* Paul's view of the Gentiles agrees with that of his Jewish contemporaries; their disobedience was a disbelief in God. The attitude of the Jews toward Christ represents the same sort of disobedience. But just as the Jews' disobedience has been a factor in the display of divine mercy toward the Gentiles, so the mercy shown to you will be used toward them too. The sense of this difficult verse (31) is not very clear. **32.** *God has consigned all men to disobedience:* All men, Jews and Greeks, have as groups been unfaithful to God, who has made use of this infidelity to manifest to them all his bounty and mercy—to reveal to them just what kind of a God he really is (see Rom 3:23–24; Gal 3:22). From this conclusion Paul passes to an exclamation about the merciful wisdom of God (usually regarded as hymnic in form).

115 **33–36.** Hymn to the merciful wisdom of God. **33.** *how inexhaustible are God's resources, wisdom and knowledge!:* So Paul exclaims, not in awe and fear, but in admiration and gratitude at the boundless wonder of God's providence in arranging for the mutual assistance of Jews and Gentiles in attaining their salvation. Israel's role in the divine plan of salvation would never have been suspected otherwise. **34.** Paul joins Is 40:13 and Job 41:3 (?) in order to stress that God is no one's debtor, either for his plans or for his gifts to men. All proceeds from his own gracious bounty, and he needs neither consultants nor research assistants. Paul cites the Is text according to the LXX (with a slight change of word order); the words in Is refer the deliverance of the Jews from exile by Yahweh and extol his greatness for it. The passage in Job is not certain; 41:3 is rather corrupt in the MT and it is almost impossible to decide what text Paul might have been following. Some commentators think that Paul is alluding to Job 35:7 and 41:11. **36.** A doxology to God (the Father) as the creator, sustainer, and goal of the universe. The prep. *ex* denotes "origin," *dia* (with the gen.) the "originator, source" of an action or condition, and *eis* (with the acc.) the "end, goal." There is no doubt that Paul is expressing in this prayer the absolute dependence of all creation on God; but it is also quite likely that the formulation is influenced by Hellenistic philosophical thought (cf. Marcus Aurelius, *Medit.* 4.23; H. Lietzmann, *An die Römer*, 107). See 1 Cor 8:6; 11:12; Col 1:16.

(Bourke, M. M., *A Study of the Metaphor of the Olive Tree in Romans XI* [Washington, 1947]. Jeremias, J., "Der Gedanke des 'Heiligen Restes' im Spätjudentum und in der Verkündigung Jesu," *ZNW* 42 [1949] 184–94. Kugelman, R., "Hebrew, Israelite, Jew in the NT," *The Bridge* 1 [1955] 204–24. Peterson, E., "Die Kirche aus Juden und Heiden," *Theologische Traktate* [München, 1951] 239–92.)

116 **(III) Part II: Hortatory Section—The Demands of the New Life (12:1–15:13).** Apparently out of habit Paul now adds to the doctrinal section just finished an exhortation addressed to the Roman church, even though it is otherwise unknown to him. Rom 12–13 are a catechetical unit, rather similar to 1 Thes 4–5; 1 Pt 2–3. It reflects the tendency in the early Church to join paraenesis to a kerygmatic or doctrinal exposé. This hortatory section is not exactly an ethical treatise, for it is quite unsystematic and somewhat rambling. As it stands in Rom, it implies that the legal prescriptions of Moses are no longer the norm for Christian conduct. But there are demands on Christians, and the principle at work in all of them is charity. Nothing in this section suggests that Paul has had reports about the Roman church or that he is treating specific problems known to exist in it. Rather, it deals with generalities, which reflect at most problems with which he has had to cope in the past, perhaps even at Corinth from which he sends the letter. The subjects discussed are not always closely related, but in general concern the relation of justified man to Christian society.

117 **(A) Christian Life Must be Worship in Spirit Paid to God (12:1–13:14).** The unity of the Christian community demands that individuals strive in every possible way to overcome evil with good. The common pursuit of the good is expected of those who are members of the body of Christ and whose lives are expected to be a sacrifice offered to God. **1.** *I urge you:* Paul speaks as an authorized apostle (1:5; 11:13). *by the mercy of God:* Lit., "mercies," the plural suggests the multiple manifestations of mercy just described in chs. 9–11, especially in 11:30–32. *to offer yourselves:* Lit., "your bodies" (→ Pauline Theology, 79:118). The verb not only means to place something at the disposition of another but also has the nuance of "offering, presenting" something in a sacrificial context (AG 633). *as a living sacrifice:* Christians who strive to do what is right give a cultic sense to their lives. Paul implicitly compares them to animals slaughtered in Jewish or pagan cults, but adds a distinguishing note that their entire offering of themselves is "alive and living" and not accomplished through a dead animal. It is "spiritual worship," because it is guided by *logos* (reason) and befitting a man. **2.** *do not be conformed to this world:* Paul regards "this world" as passing and imperfect (1 Cor 7:31), for he alludes to a rabbinical distinction of "this world" and "the world to come." The distinction was adopted by the early Church and given a Christian nuance. Paul himself thinks of the "world to come" as already begun; the two "worlds" or "ages" have met in the Christian dispensation (1 Cor 10:11). That is why the Christian, though he is in "this world," must live for God and cannot be conformed to any other standard. *be transformed:* Cf. 2 Cor 3:18. This metamorphosis is not external (like that of Christ at the transfiguration, Mk 9:3), but inward and internal, involving man's *nous*, and is effected by the presence of God's Spirit within the Christian.

118 **3–13.** The cult to be paid to God by Christians manifests itself concretely in a life in society based on humility and charity. It calls for a proper, unselfish use of spiritual gifts received. As an apostolic founder of Christian churches, Paul realized only too well the danger to the community of elements in it that overestimated their worth. **3.** *the grace given to me:* Cf. 1:5; 15:15. *according to the standard of faith:* Lit., "measure of faith." The norm of one's judgment is to be faith, but not considered as the active response of the believer (*fides qua creditur*), nor even as charismatic faith (1 Cor 13:2, for the exhortation is addressed to all Christians, not just the favored few), but as the object believed in (*fides quae*). In the concrete this is Christ Jesus. Each one, instead of thinking of himself too highly, should measure himself by the standard of what he believes in (see C. E. B. Cranfield, *NTS* 8 [1961–62] 345–51). **5.** *we are one body in Christ:* In earlier letters Paul referred to the union of Christians with Christ and to their mutual unity through him under the figure of the body of Christ (1 Cor 6:12–20; 10:16–17; 12:12–31). It is important to note that in none of the early references (before the Captivity Letters) does he join the Church to this figure explicitly. Moreover, just as in 1 Cor 12:12–31, so here the figure probably does not suggest anything more than a moral union, the conspiring of individual members for the common good, as in the body politic (→ Pauline Theology, 79:139–144). We must look elsewhere for further nuances of his thought on the subject. Note too that Paul does not say that we are the body of Christ, but that we are one body because we are "in Christ." It is important to preserve the nuances in order to note the growth in Paul's awareness of what the body of Christ means.

119 **6.** *we have gifts:* The different charismatic gifts that Christians receive from the Spirit as a result of faith are clearly destined for the community's benefit. Each must realize the social character of his God-given talents or gifts and exercise them without envy or jealousy. The "gifts" are not necessarily to be understood as miraculous. Paul enumerates seven of them. *if it is inspired preaching:* Lit., "prophecy," to be understood in its NT sense (1 Cor 12:10; 13:2; 14:3–6,24; 1 Thes 5:20). It denotes primarily preaching about religious matters, and unlike its OT counterpart it often connotes not only the communication of God's message to men but also the prediction of the future (cf. Acts 12:27–28; 21:9–11). *in proportion to [our] faith:* The Gk word *analogia* means "right relationship, proportion" (AG 56) and creates no problem here. However, the word *pistis* is problematic. Many commentators interpret it as meaning charismatic faith (1 Cor 12:3, "the faith that moves mountains"). In this case the NT prophet must preach in accordance with such charismatic faith as is given to him. But this interpretation then introduces still another charism; the "prophet" has not only the gift of inspired preaching but also charismatic faith. Many other commentators, however, prefer to understand *pistis* objectively, as that which is believed in common, the body of Christian belief. This would seem to be a more natural meaning in the context. **7.** *if it is service:* The second charism is *diakonia*, which probably refers to the administration of material aid and the distribution of alms (as in 1 Cor 16:15; Acts 6:1). Nothing suggests that the word refers to a distinct class of persons (= "deacons"). *if one is a teacher:* The third charism is clearly distinguished from preaching and service in the early community; see also 1 Cor 12:28; Eph 4:11. **8.** *if one exhorts:* The fourth charism is possessed by the "spiritual father" of the religious community. *if one contributes [alms]:* The fifth charism is possessed by the man who "shares" his wealth; he is expected to exercise it "with a generous simplicity" (see 2 Cor 9:11,13 and comment on 2 Cor 8:2). His gift is that of philanthropy and differs from the second because he is moved to dispense his private wealth. *if one is a leader:* The sixth charism belongs to the man who "is at the head" of the community, an official or administrator. If the order of the charisms be significant, then the leader's place in this list is noteworthy. Some translate rather, "if one gives aid"; this is not as good a translation, since it does not sufficiently differentiate this charism from the last. *a merciful helper:* The seventh charism belongs to the man who performs acts of mercy; he is expected to do them cheerfully, for the spirit in which they are done is more important than the acts themselves.

120 **9.** *let [your] love be genuine:* Love without sham or hypocrisy is explained by a series of instructions or maxims about charitable acts. **10.** *with brotherly affection:* Unfeigned charity must be shown above all to members of the Christian community. Paul uses *philadelphia* to distinguish it from the wider obligation of *agapē*. *eager to show one another honor:* The sense of this phrase is disputed; this translation follows several ancient versions. It could also be: "As far as honor is concerned, let each one esteem the other more highly" (see Bl-Deb-F § 150). **11.** *serve the Lord:* This is the motive for all Christian conduct. Instead of *kyriō* some mss. (D*, G) read *kairō*, "serve the hour." If this were right, Christians would be called upon to meet the demands of the time in which they live (see O. Cullmann, *Christ and Time* [Phil., 1950)] 42). **13.** *the needs of the saints:* Is Paul hinting to the Roman Christians that they too should think of helping the Jerusalem community with alms?

121 **14–21.** In these verses Paul recommends charity to all men, even one's enemies. **14.** *bless your persecutors:* Perhaps an echo of Jesus' words (Mt 5:44; Lk 6:27–28). Some important mss. (P^{46}, B, 1739) omit "you[r]." The sense is then more general ("Bless [all] persecutors"); and there is eliminated any possible reference to an official persecution of Roman Christians. **16.** *have the same regard for one another:* A recommendation of mutual esteem for the concord of the community (cf. 15:5); it is a warning against any false self-esteem. *associate with the lowly folk:* This translation understands the word *tapeinois* as masculine, but in view of the preceding injunction (not to set one's mind on lofty things) it could mean "Give yourselves to lowly tasks." *do not be conceited:* See Prv 3:7 (freely quoted). **17.** *evil for evil:* Paul's warning may echo the words of Christ (Mt 5:39,43–44). *aim at what is honorable:* Prv 3:4 adapted (cf. 2 Cor 4:2; 8:21). **19.** *do not look for revenge:* Both the desire of revenge against (outside) enemies and the actual pursuit of it are to be excluded from Christian conduct. The right to avenge oneself is not part of the conquest of evil, despite any first impression. Charity must reign in everything. *make place for the wrath:* Give scope to God's (eschatological) wrath, which will react against sin. Paul immediately quotes Dt 32:35 (in a form close to the MT). This quotation makes the reference to God's wrath almost certain. The Christian should leave to God the retribution of evil and pursue only the good (see E. R. Smothers, *CBQ* 6 [1949] 205–15). **20.** Paul cites Prv 25:21–22 (LXX, ms. B), making it his own recommendation. *heap burning coals upon his head:* The meaning of this OT phrase is obscure. It has been suggested that one should rather translate the MT thus: "You will remove coals of fire from his head" (see M. Dahood, *CBQ* 17 [1955] 19–23; cf. A. Škrinjar, *VD* 18 [1938] 143–50). Paul, however, follows the LXX, which certainly speaks of heaping coals "upon" the head. The most common interpretation of this phrase is that of Ambrosiaster, Augustine, and Jerome: the coals are a symbol of the "burning pangs of shame." The enemy will be moved by kindness to shame and regret which will burn on his head like coals of fire. Yet it is not possible to show that "coals" are ever used elsewhere as a symbol of shame.

A remote allusion to an Egyptian ritual described in a 3rd-cent. BC Demotic text has been suggested by S. Morenz (*TLZ* 78 [1953] 187–92). In it a penitent carries on his head a dish of burning charcoal to express repentance. So kindness to an enemy would make him express his shame and repentance before God. Some of the Gk Fathers (Origen and Chrysostom), however, understood the "coals" to be a figure for a more noble type of revenge. If you feed your hungry enemy and he remains hostile, you will make him liable to more serious punishment from God. You will be heaping coals of divine punishment on his head. Yet once again such a figure is nowhere else attested. K. Stendahl (*HTR* 55 [1962] 343–55) has modified this interpretation by comparing Paul's general principle with several statements in QL that advocate the nonretaliation of evil done by enemies and the deferring of retribution to God's day of vengeance (see 1QS 10:17–20; 9:21–22; 1:9–11). Paul's use of Dt 32 and Prv 25, then, would suggest a qualified way of adding to the measure of the enemy's sins (cf. W. Klassen, *NTS* 9 [1962–63] 337–50). **21.** *but conquer evil with good:* The summary of the Pauline exhortation. Evil is the only real enemy for a Christian, and it ultimately stems from some form of selfishness. The Christian pursuit of charity will conquer it.

122 **13:1–7.** The duties of Christians toward civil authorities. As Paul writes to the Roman church he is aware that this community more than others would be conscious of the imperial authorities. Up to the time of the writing of Rom there has been no official persecution of Christianity, though an internal strife in the Jewish community at Rome (probably between Jews and Jewish Christians) was settled by the Emperor Claudius' expulsion of the Jews from Rome (Acts 18:2; Suetonius, *Claudii Vita* 25). This was known to Paul, yet his discussion remains on the level of general principles. Christians, as citizens of another world (Phil 3:20) and enjoying a new freedom in Christ (Gal 5:1), might be inclined to question their relation toward the civil government, especially when it was in the hands of pagans. Paul's solution of the question is inspired by Prv 8:15 and Mt 22:16.

123 **1.** *every person:* Lit., "every soul," a Hebraism (see comment on 2:9). The injunction is not restricted to Christians. *higher authorities:* Lit., "highly placed, governing authorities" (AG 848). The pl. noun *exousiai* is commonly used for human "authorities" in profane Greek and in the NT (Lk 12:11). However, O. Cullmann (*The State in the NT* [N.Y., 1956]; *Christ and Time*, 191–210) maintains that *exousiai* has a double meaning, referring also to "invisible angelic powers that stand behind the state government," or "to the empirical state *and* to the angelic powers." See 1 Cor 2:8; 1 Pt 3:22. In either case, what is primary in Paul's affirmation is the relation of the Christian to the secular government, whether this be regarded as entirely human or as controlled by angelic spirits. Cullmann's interpretation has the merit of adding an eschatological dimension to the passage and of making more meaningful the reference to Christ's salvation in 13:11–14. When the "day" really comes, Christ's dominion will be supreme (as he turns over everything to the Father, 1 Cor 15:26–28). But for the time being, the Christian is dependent on civil rulers and must obey them. Another reading in some mss. (P^{46}, D*, G, it, Irenaeus) omits "every person" and has the simple imperative, "Obey all higher authorities." *for there is no authority except from God:* Even Rome's imperial authority comes from God, although it may be reluctant to admit it. Paul indirectly acknowledges the Father as the source of all the welfare and peace brought about by imperial Roman rule. **2.** *anyone who resists authority opposes what God has ordained:* A general principle is deduced from the foregoing. Obedience to civil authorities is a form of obedience to God himself, for man's relation to God is not limited to a specifically religious or cultic sphere. The supposition that runs through this paragraph (13:1–7) is that the civil authorities are conducting themselves uprightly and are seeking the interests of the community. The possibility is not envisaged either of a tyrannical government or of one failing to cope with a situation where the just rights of individual citizens or of a minority group are neglected. (See Ap 18 for a reaction in veiled terms to such a situation.) Paul insists on merely one aspect of the question: the duty of subjects to legitimate authority. He does not discuss the duty of civil authorities here. **4.** *for they are God's agents working for* [*your*] *good:* This is a reformulation of 13:1, stressing the delegated character of civil authority; it envisages only a civil government properly fulfilling its functions. The phrase *eis to agathon* (existing for a good purpose) expresses the goal of the state's activity. *they do not carry the sword for nothing:* The sword is introduced as the symbol of penal authority, of the power legitimately possessed by the state to coerce recalcitrant citizens in its effort to maintain order (see J. Héring, *RHPR* 30 [1950] 31–40). *God's agents to execute* [*his*] *wrath on wrongdoers:* The context shows that the wrath is divine, as in 12:9; otherwise the authorities would not be God's "agents."

124 **5.** *for conscience' sake:* A higher motive of obedience is introduced; Paul realizes that fear of punishment will not always deter citizens from the violation of civil regulations. His appeal to conscience suggests a moral obligation for obedience to civil laws, and not one that is just legal or penal. It links man's reaction to civil rulers with the divine origin of civil authority itself. **6.** *also why you pay taxes:* It is taken for granted that Roman Christians are paying taxes. This is perhaps echoed in Mk 12:17, "Pay Caesar what is Caesar's and God what is God's." For the third time Paul stresses the delegated nature of civil authority (13:1,4); here in relation to the disagreeable subject of taxes. **7.** Cf. Mt 22:21.

8–10. From the subject of the Christian's duty to civil authorities Paul moves on to the obligation of charity, which sums up for man in the New Dispensation the whole Mosaic Law. **8.** *owe nobody anything, except the* *debt of mutual love:* In this the obligations of Christian life are summed up. The statement should not be misunderstood, as if Paul were making charity a species of duty or something that is owed. He expresses it thus to stress the role of charity in all Christian conduct; it is not to be manifested only among fellow Christians. *has fully satisfied the Law:* As elsewhere in Rom (see comment on 2:12) the Mosaic Law is meant, as the following quotations make clear. **9.** Paul cites phrases from the Decalogue (Dt 5:17–21; Ex 20:13–17). The order of the individual prohibitions differs from that of the MT, but it is the same as that of the LXX of Dt 5:17–18 (ms. B) and of Lk 18:20; cf. Jas 2:11; Philo, *De Decalogo* 120, 132. *summed up in this saying, "Love...":* Paul may be echoing the saying of Christ (Mk 12:28–34), which sums up the Mosaic Law with Dt 6:4–5; Lv 19:18. But contemporary rabbis were also accustomed to epitomize the Law in a similar way (cf. Str-B 1, 907–8), since they regarded all the specific regulations (613 commands and prohibitions) as developments of the principle in Lv 19:18. In Lv "neighbor" means a fellow Jew, but as used by Paul it has a wider extension. **10.** *love is the fulfillment of the Law:* Although this may seem to be only an abstract formulation of the preceding, Paul is enunciating a basic Christian principle. If Christ is the "end of the Law" (10:4), then "love"—that which motivated his whole existence and redemptive activity (8:35)—can be said to be the Law's fulfillment. This norm of Christian conduct is substituted for the Law.

125 11–14. An exhortation to the Roman Christians to realize that they are already living in the *eschaton.* The two ages have met (1 Cor 10:11). **11.** *critical time:* The period of Christian existence is *kairos*, a time when they are called upon to manifest by their actions that they are Christians and to conduct themselves suitably. Paul often uses this eschatological motive in his moral exhortations (1 Thes 5:6; 1 Cor 7:26,28–30; Col 4:5; Eph 5:16). Even though what he says in 11:25 about the conversion of Israel might suggest that the definitive stage of salvation is still something of the future, nevertheless the *kairos* has begun—with the death and resurrection of Christ. Now is the time for men to appropriate to themselves by their faith and their deeds the effect of what Jesus once achieved for all. *to awake from sleep:* Cf. 1 Thes 5:6; 1 Cor 15:34; Eph 5:14. Christians cannot afford to remain in the unprotected condition of scantily dressed sleepers at a time when the situation calls for armor. Paul makes use of apocalyptic imagery here, similar to that of Eph 5:8–18; 6:10–20 (see K. G. Kuhn, *NTS* 7 [1960–61] 338–46 for Qumran parallels). *salvation is nearer:* The eschatological deliverance of the Christians as the fulfillment of the pledge (2 Cor 1:22) or the first fruits (Rom 8:23) guaranteed by the Spirit. It is now nearer than it was when they first put their faith in Christ. **12.** *the night is far spent:* Paul implies that not too long a time separates Christians from their eschatological salvation. *Let us throw off the deeds of darkness:* The contrast of day and night, of light and darkness, is symbolic of good and evil, just as in 1 Thes 5:5–8; Eph 5:8–11. These pairs are commonly found in current Jewish apocalyptic writings, especially in the Essene QL (1QS 2:7; 3:20ff.; 1QM 15:9, "in darkness are all their deeds," i.e., the deeds of the sons of Darkness who are dominated by the prince of demons Belial). *don the armor of light:* The armor is not described here, but in 1 Thes 5:8 and Eph 6:13 it is indicated as faith, hope, charity, fidelity, uprightness, etc. Though he imitates OT metaphors (Is 11:5; 59:17), Paul introduces specifically Christian qualities. **13.** A catalogue of vices that are the "deeds of darkness" (see comment on 1:28; → Pauline Theology, 79:160–161). **14.** *put on the Lord Jesus Christ:* Let Christ be your armor. Through baptism the Christian has already "put on" Christ (Gal see comment on 3:27). But that ontological identification of the Christian with Christ must bear fruit in his conscious life; as he becomes progressively more and more aware of his Christian identity he withdraws more and more from sin. Such a psychological outlook once cultivated will stifle all the desires of the Ego subject to Sin.

126 (B) The Duty of Charity Is Owed by the Strong to the Weak (14:1–15:13). The second part of the hortatory section is immediately concerned with such minor questions as the eating of meat and the observance of holy days. But more fundamentally it deals with the age-old problem of the "scrupulous" vs. the "enlightened" conscience, or the "conservative" vs. the "progressive." It is not that Paul had heard that this problem was acute in the Roman church. Rather, the topics he discusses here are drawn from his past missionary experience. He deals with them only in a general way. Though unimportant in themselves, they give Paul the opportunity to formulate prudent principles based on faith (14:22,23), love (14:15), the example of Christ (14:9,15; 15:3,7–8), and the Christian's loyalty to him (15:13). His discussion ends with a plea for unity based on important ideas of the doctrinal section.

1. *welcome the man who is weak in faith:* Paul thinks of a scrupulous Christian whose judgments are based on an insufficiently enlightened faith. Such a man has not fully grasped what is meant by uprightness through faith and immaturely seeks to justify himself by additional practices that are only a form of fringe Christianity. And yet, even he belongs to the Christian community. *without debating minor points [with him]:* Lit., "not for the purpose of quarrels about opinions." The scrupulous brother should be welcomed as God would welcome him; he should not be subjected to idle disputes, for such debate undermines confidence on all sides. **2.** [*only*] *vegetables:* Paul's first example involves a food-taboo. While the "strong" eat of everything, the "weak" eat only vegetables, perhaps because of their pre-Christian background (cf. Dn 1; Jdt 8:6; 1 Cor 8–10). But once it is seen that such an issue is not bound up with the essentials of faith, the obligation of mutual charity becomes clear. Each must accept the other as God would. **4.** *to criticize someone else's servant:* The "weak" Christian is addressed; he is warned that the person he would regard as lax is actually a member of God's household. God alone, as that man's master, will judge his failure or success. From God comes both the acceptance of the "weak" and the status of the "strong."

127 **5.** *distinguishes one day from another:* Another source of scruple involved the celebration of holy days or fast days (among Jews) or festivals (among Gentiles). Possibly Paul alludes to the early Christian custom of fasting on Wednesday and Friday (*Didache* 8:1; *Hermas Sim.* 5.3, 7). In any case, the "weak" brother continues to distinguish them carefully from ordinary days, while the enlightened convert disregards them. Paul sees no evil in the entertainment of different convictions about such matters. But he resolutely excludes disputes or critical judgment about them. **6.** *for the Lord:* What really counts in all of this is the motivation, whether the days be observed or not, as long as the Lord is served thereby. This is the important thing. For a member of the Lord's household is expected to serve his Lord. **7.** *none of us lives for himself:* The liberating act of Christ, freeing man from enslavement to Law, Sin, and Death (8:2), enabled man to live for God (6:10–11; Gal 2:19). This implies the service of God in all things; it is also the basis of a Christian's social obligations. **8.** *we are the Lord's:* We belong to and must acknowledge our relation to the Risen Christ as *Kyrios* (see 1 Cor 6:20; 7:23). **9.** *Lord of both the living and the dead:* Paul formulates the finality of the redemptive passion and exaltation of Christ, stressing the sovereignty over the "dead and the living" that became his as of the resurrection. It is a universal dominion proper to the *Kyrios* of all (cf. 1 Thes 5:10; Phil 2:11). The Christian who through baptism shares in the redemption of Christ will eventually enjoy the glory of the Risen *Kyrios* himself. And yet, Paul never says that the Christian will "become lord with" Christ (*sygkyrieuō*), for there is only one Lord, Jesus Christ (1 Cor 8:6), the lord of the dead and the living. Contrast, however, 2 Tm 2:12: "we shall reign with him" (*symbasileuō*); see O. Cullmann, *Christology*, 220–21; cf. 2 Cor 5:14–15; Rom 6:10. Since Jesus did not die and rise again for himself but to enable men to live for God, the Christian must recognize his situation vis-à-vis other Christians as a result of this. He must not judge them, whether they be "weak" or "strong." This is stressed in 14:10. **11.** *we shall stand before God's tribunal:* A further argument is introduced, echoing the sentiments of 14:4. It is supported by a conflated OT quotation, from Is 49:18 and 45:23 (LXX). The latter had been used in Phil 2:10–11 in a form quite close to the meaning of the original text, as Paul acknowledged Christ as *Kyrios*. But here the verb is understood in the sense of "confessing" what one has done before God as Judge. The real point, however, is that bending the knee and making a confession are scarcely acts one associates with a judge. But this is what Christians do. If so, then they should not presume to judge anyone.

128 **14:13–15:6.** The main part of Paul's exhortation is addressed to the "strong" and begins here. The principles enunciated, however, are general enough to apply to all. **14.** *nothing is unclean in itself:* This verse is somewhat parenthetical, but it sets forth a principle that is operative in the rest of the discussion. Most likely it echoes Christ's saying (Mt 15:11) about the Pharisaic distinction between the "clean" and "unclean" ("common" or "uncommon") things (cf. Lv 17:15; Str-B 1, 718). It should be related to the principle in 14:6. It is not the thing in itself but the estimate of it by the conscience that becomes the guide to one's actions. **15.** *your conduct is no longer ruled by love:* This verse resumes the ideas of 14:13, but Paul introduces now the prime consideration, charity. Though to the "strong" nothing is unclean, concern for his brother will make the "strong" consider the social aspects of his actions. *do not destroy with your food him for whom Christ died:* The "weak" brother, who must follow the dictates of his conscience, may be distressed at the sight of a Christian partaking of certain food. The "strong," in vaunting his enlightened emancipation before him, is not making profession of charity. Paul's way of stating his principle is a deft and devastating thrust. He calls on the Christian to relinquish his legitimate claim of freedom for the sake of a "weak" brother (see 14:20). **16.** *do not let your privilege be exposed to scornful criticism:* Lit., "let not your good be spoken of as evil." The "good" is Christian liberty, which Paul recognizes fully. But he refuses to allow it to be asserted at the expense of distress to another. For then it would lose its esteemed quality and be brought into disrepute.

129 **17.** *uprightness, peace, and joy in the holy Spirit:* The essence of the kingdom does not consist in freedom from such things as dietary regulations, but in the freedom of man to react to the promptings of the indwelling Spirit. Three qualities—two of which echo the key ideas of the doctrinal section in Rom, uprightness (chs. 1–4) and peace (5:1; 8:6)—proceed from the Spirit's promptings and are the conditions of Christian conduct in the kingdom. In Gal 5:13 Paul counsels Christians to be slaves to one another in love because of their new-found Christian freedom (see 1 Cor 8:1; 10:23). **20.** *for the sake of food:* Paul repeats v. 15 substantially. Of more importance than the right to eat or celebrate is the Christian's obligation not to destroy the "work of God" by making a "weak" brother stumble. In the context the "work of God" probably refers to the "weak" brother, but it may possibly refer to the unity of the Christian community, which could be undone by insistence on extravagent claims of freedom without respect for others (cf. 1 Cor 3:9ff.). **21.** Cf. 1 Cor 8:13. **22.** *keep the [clear] conviction you have between yourself and God:* The clear insight and the firm conviction the enlightened Christian has of the moral goodness of a certain deed should guide him whenever he scrutinizes his conduct in the sight of God. This is his norm when an action is considered between himself and God. But social considerations may compel him to modify his conduct before others. *who has no reason to condemn himself for what he approves:* A beatitude for the man who has no qualms of conscience for his practical decision, whether to eat or not. **23.** *all that does not proceed from conviction is sin:* Lit., "all that is not of faith," *pistis* here having the same force as in 14:22. It is not the "faith that justifies" (3:22,28) but an ethical conviction proceeding from it. It is the perspective enabling the justified Christian to judge his own actions in the sight of God. Whatever is done either against the conviction of one's conscience or with a wavering conscience is sinful. Marcion ended the letter to the Romans at this point, but Paul's argument really goes on (→ 10 above).

130 **15:1.** The example of Christ is proposed to the "strong," who are now mentioned for the first time, even though the exhortation to them began at 14:13. Paul identifies himself with them. *to put up with the weaknesses:* The vb. *bastazein* means either "to bear" (a burden) or "to endure, put up with" (AG 136–37). The former would imply that the "strong" are called upon to help the "weak" in shouldering the burden of their scruples; the latter would counsel patient forbearance of the immature attitude of the "weak." **2.** *to build up [the life of the community]:* The phrase *pros oikodomēn* is often taken to mean "to edify him" (the neighbor), referring to the personal development of one's Christian neighbor. But considering that Paul often uses the building-metaphor in his letters in a corporate sense, the phrase undoubtedly has a social, corporate meaning here as well (cf. 1 Cor 14:12; Eph 4:12; Rom 14:19; see G. W. MacRae, *AER* 140 [1959] 361–76; E. Pfammatter, *Die Kirche als Bau* [AnalGreg 110; Rome, 1960]). **3.** *Christ did not please himself:* The sacrifice of his life by Christ was motivated by his love for his fellow men (8:32–35). Love, then, should motivate the Christian to seek to please others and to contribute to the upbuilding of all. Paul applies to Christ Ps 69:10, a verse from a psalm of personal tribulation uttered by the upright Israelite who has sustained opprobrium because of his zeal for God's house. As applied to Christ, it means that he bore the reproaches addressed to God. But the original sense of the Ps is not too pertinent to the situation envisaged by Paul; therefore he tries to justify the accommodated sense he gives of it. **4.** Cf. Rom 4:23, which makes the same point that the OT Scripture has meaning for us today. *we might have hope:* When Jesus' suffering is viewed against mankind's sacred history, it takes on a deeper meaning. Seen in this larger perspective, it gives Christians a basis for their hope.

131 **7–13.** An appeal for unity, based on the pattern set by Christ. *as Christ has welcomed you:* The conclusion that follows from Christ's own commandment (Jn 13:34; 15:12). *for the glory of God:* The motive behind all of Christ's redemptive activity (cf. Phil 1:11; 2:11; 1Q*19*

13:1; 1QSb 4:25; 1QS 10:9. **8.** *became a servant of the Jews:* Lit., "of circumcision" (see Gal 2:8–9 for the same way of designating the Jewish people). Jesus had to be a Jew and minister to the Jews, in order to confirm God's promises to the patriarchs (and thereby give evidence of divine "truth" [= fidelity; see comment on 3:4]). But as Paul understands these promises, both Jews and Gentiles are to share in them. In this Paul finds the unity of the Christian community despite its ethnic background. This verse is probably one of the reasons why Marcion ended with 14:23. **9.** *that the Gentiles might praise God for his mercy:* For they too were included in the OT promises, as the Scripture texts to be cited will show. Even though Christ's ministry was directed to the Jews, the Gentiles were to be included in his kingdom in due time, as the OT promises themselves indicate. *I will praise you among the Gentiles:* Ps 18:50 (= 2 Sm 22:50). Again Paul uses testimonia from the OT Torah, Prophets, and Pss to support his contention (see comment on 3:10). Note the linking idea, *ethnē* (nations) or *laoi* (peoples). **10.** Cf. Dt 32:43 (LXX). **11.** Cf. Ps 117:1. **12.** Cf. Is 11:10 (LXX). **13.** *hope...joy...peace:* The final blessing, which concludes this hortatory section, employs key ideas of the OT passages just cited; in addition, it echoes those of the doctrinal section. *God of hope:* The God on whom both Jews and Gentiles center their hope.

132 **(IV) Conclusion (15:14–33).** Paul sends news about himself, his apostolate, and his plans. Now that his labors in the East have come to an end, he must visit Jerusalem with the token of good will and solidarity that his Gentile churches are offering to the mother church. Once this is done—and he asks the Roman church to pray that it will be accepted in the right spirit—he plans to visit Rome on his way to evangelize the West. Paul takes the occasion to compliment the Romans on the good things he has heard about them. He is proud to write to them as the "Apostle of the Gentiles," even though he has so far had no influence on their belief in Christ. **14.** *I am convinced:* Although he has just finished exhorting the Roman Christians to unity (15:7–13), Paul points out the abiding conviction (pf. tense) that he has of their goodness and their understanding of Christian faith. **15.** *I have written rather boldly:* As in 1:5,13 he apologizes for writing to a church not founded by him. Yet he is emboldened to do so because he has received a commission to evangelize the Gentiles, and the Roman Christians thus fall under his apostolic care. *because of the grace given to me:* The God-given charism (= *gratia gratis data* of later theologians) to summon the Gentiles to faith in Christ (1:5; 12:3; 1 Cor 4:6; Gal 2:7–8). **16.** *to be a minister of Christ Jesus to the Gentiles:* Paul describes his role in liturgical language, using not *diakonos* ("servant," as in 2 Cor 3:6; Eph 3:7; Col 1:23), nor *oikonomos* ("steward," as in 1 Cor 4:1), but *leitourgos* (cultic minister). In his mission to the Gentiles he sees himself as a priest functioning in God's sanctuary. For if all Christian life is to be regarded as worship paid to God (Rom 13:1ff.), the spreading of Christ's gospel is easily compared to the role of sacred minister in that cult. Paul insinuates that the preaching of the word of God is a liturgical act in itself. If Clement of Rome (*Ad Cor.* 8:1) could look on the OT prophets as the cultic ministers of God's grace, then this applies even more to the "apostles and prophets" of the NT (Eph 2:20; 3:5). Cf. Rom 11:13; 2 Cor 3:3; Phil 2:17. *the offering of the Gentiles:* Obj. genitive; it is the evangelized Gentiles who are consecrated and offered to God as an acceptable sacrifice. Since the end of all sacrifice was to bring about in some way the return of sinful man to God, Paul looks on his work among the Gentiles as a form of sacrifice, for their conversion has achieved that very purpose. The Apostle offers to God not slaughtered animals, but repentant man. He thus achieves in reality what was symbolized in the sacrifice—the return of men to God. **17.** *in what pertains to God:* Paul's pride and boast is rooted where it should be, in God (see 5:2; 11:18).

133 **18.** *what Christ has accomplished through me:* Paul is fully aware that he is only an instrument in the conversion of the Gentiles. It is really Christ who brings about their return to God (see 2 Cor 3:5). **19.** *by the power of signs and miracles:* Paul's rhetoric and physical stamina and especially the extraordinary deeds performed through him by Christ have been the elements that served the evangelization of the Gentiles. The phrase *sēmeia kai terata* is simply an expression for "miracles" performed in virtue of the Spirit's power at work among the early Christians (see V. McCasland, *JBL* 76 [1957] 149–52). Cf. 1 Cor 12:10; 2 Cor 12:12. *from Jerusalem to Illyricum:* The two terms of Paul's apostolic activity in the East. It began in Jerusalem, the city from which "the word of the Lord" goes forth (Is 2:3), and reached as far as the Roman province of Illyricum (on the W coast of the Balkan Peninsula, including lower Yugoslavia and Albania today). **20.** *on another's foundation:* Paul is not thinking of Christ as the sole foundation of Christian life (as in 1 Cor 3:11) but of the work of other "apostles and prophets" (Eph 2:20) who founded church communities. His ambition is to carry Christ's name to areas where it is unknown (see 2 Cor 10:15–16). **21.** Is 52:15 is quoted according to the LXX, which introduces "about him" into its translation. The LXX text is thus more suited than the MT to Paul's use of the verse with reference to Christ. In Dt-Is the verse is part of the song of the Servant of Yahweh (cf. Rom 10:16).

134 **22.** Cf. Rom 1:10ff. **23.** *no longer an opportunity in these parts:* Paul knows, of course, that he has not yet converted all the Gentiles of the eastern Mediterranean area, but he seems to regard his function as that of laying foundations. Others are to build on them (1 Cor 3:6,10; Col 1:7–8). These verses reveal the breadth of his zeal for Christ's cause. **24.** *on my way to Spain:* As in 15:28, we learn only of Paul's intention to visit Spain. Did he ever get there? Ancient Roman sources maintain that he did. Clement of Rome (*Ad Cor.* 5:7 [*ca.* AD 95]) tells of Paul's traveling "to the bounds of the west" (*eis to terma tēs dyseōs*), which would mean only Spain. The Muratorian fragment (38–39) mentions it too, "profectio Pauli ab urbe ad Spaniam proficiscentis." But is this in both cases perhaps only a deduction from the plans formulated in Rom 15:24,28? *to be sent on from there by you:* To be dispatched at least with their prayers and good wishes, if not also with their alms. **25.** *to take help to God's holy people:* The collection, taken up in the Gentile churches founded in Achaia, Macedonia, and Galatia (Gal 2:10; 1 Cor 16:1–4; 2 Cor 8:1–9:15), must be taken by him personally to Jerusalem, despite his desire to head west. This shows the importance Paul attached to the collection, for it was intended to establish good relations between the Jewish mother-community of Jerusalem and the new Gentile-Christian churches. It is a token of their solidarity. "The poor" among the "saints" is a term for the needy among the Christians in Jerusalem. Though often claimed, it is not a title for the Jerusalem Christian community as such, something like the term used by the Qumran Essenes to designate themselves (cf. 4QpPs37 1:9; 2:10 [*'ebyônîm*]); see L. E. Keck, *ZNW* 56 (1965) 100–29. **27.** *they are indebted to them:* Even though the collection was the result of freewill offerings, the Gentile Christians acknowledged by it their indebtedness to the mother church of Jerusalem. Underlying it is the recognition that "salvation comes from the Jews" (Jn 4:22; cf. Rom 9:4). Paul is also hinting delicately to the Romans that they too should think along the same lines.

135 **28.** *delivered the proceeds under my own seal:* Lit., "having sealed or stamped the fruit." Paul makes use of a figure from tenant farming. When the tenant farmer delivered the harvested fruit to the owner, it was marked with the farmer's seal as identification. Realizing the importance of this collection, Paul wants it to be known as coming from the churches founded by his labors in the Lord's farm. Paul implies that he is still under suspicion in Jerusalem. This prompts him to ask the Roman Church to pray for three things in 15:30–32: that no danger might befall him from unbelievers in Judea, that his collection may be received in the proper spirit, that he might eventually come to Rome with a joyous heart. Was the prayer answered? Cf. Acts 20:3,23; 21:13,17–27. **33.** Paul's final blessing on the Romans. The letter really ends here (→ 10 above).

(De Bruyne, D., "Les deux derniers chapitres de la lettre aux Romains," *RevBén* 25 [1909] 423–30. Gaugusch, L., "Untersuchungen zum Römerbrief: Der Epilog (15,14–16,27), eine exegetische Studie," *BZ* 24 [1938–39] 165–84, 252–66. Knox, J., "Romans 15.14–33 and Paul's Conception of His Apostolic Mission," *JBL* 83 [1964] 1–11.)

136 **(V) Letter of Recommendation for Phoebe (16:1–23).** This letter was most likely sent to Ephesus, and not to Rome. (For the relation of this chapter to the whole of Rom, → 9–11 above.)

1. *I commend to you:* Paul uses a current expression (*synistēmi*) to introduce a friend to other acquaintances (cf. 1 Mc 12:43; 2 Mc 4:24; A. Deissmann, *LAE* 226, n. 4). *Phoebe:* An otherwise unknown Christian woman, the bearer of this letter. *our fellow Christian:* Lit., "our sister." Paul uses *adelphē* similarly in 1 Cor 7:15; 9:5; Phlm 2 (cf. Jas 2:15). The local church to which she is going is not to consider her an impostor. *deaconess:* Or "auxiliary." Perhaps the word *diakonos* designates a special religious group of the community of Cenchreae; but then again, perhaps it is only a generic designation ("servant, assistant"). There is no way of being sure that there existed an "order" of deaconesses in the Church at this period. For a generic use, cf. 2 Cor 3:6; 11:23; 1 Thes 3:2; etc. On the other hand, Phil 1:1; 1 Tm 3:8,12; Ti 1:9 point in the direction of a specific title, such as "deacon." *church at Cenchreae:* Cenchreae was one of the two ports of ancient Corinth. It was situated on the eastern side of the Isthmus of Corinth, on the Saronic Gulf, whereas Lechaion was on the western. The letter of introduction may have been written from either Corinth or Cenchreae. It is noteworthy that in Rom Paul uses *ekklēsia* only in ch. 16, and always in the sense of a "local church" (16:1,4,5,16,23). *in the Lord:* Phoebe is to be welcomed into the Christian community as one of its members. *in a manner worthy of God's holy people:* Lit., "of the saints," cf. comment on 1:7. Paul flatters his readers by associating them with the "holy ones," formerly called and chosen, and with the early mother church of Jerusalem, which enjoyed this title par excellence (cf. 1 Cor 16:1; 2 Cor 8:4; 9:1). *she has been of great assistance:* Lit., "a patroness." Paul acknowledges the service that Phoebe showed to him and to other Christians in Cenchreae. We can only speculate about the nature of that assistance: hospitality? championing their cause before secular authorities? furnishing funds for his journey to Jerusalem?

137 **3–16.** Personal greetings are sent by Paul to at least 28 acquaintances. **3.** *Prisca and Aquila:* In 1 Cor 16:19; 2 Tm 4:19 Aquila's wife is called *Priska,* as here; but the diminutive form of *Priskilla* is found in Acts 18:2,18,26. They were Jewish Christians, expelled from Rome by the Emperor Claudius (→ Life of Paul, 46:6). Having settled in Corinth, they engaged in tentmaking. When Paul first arrived in Corinth, they extended him hospitality (Acts 18:1–2). Later on they traveled with him to Ephesus, where they took up residence and instructed among others Apollos, the Alexandrian rhetor (Acts 18:26). Because 1 Cor was written from Ephesus, Paul sent greetings to the Corinthian church from the Christians who gathered in the house-church of Prisca and Aquila (1 Cor 16:19). This notice, besides that of 2 Tm 4:19, suggests that they were still at Ephesus—to which Rom 16 is therefore being sent. In 16:5 he greets the house-church there. *my fellow workers in Christ:* Either at Corinth (Acts 18:3) or at Ephesus (Acts 18:26). *who risked their necks for me:* Paul gratefully recalls some valiant intervention of Prisca and Aquila on his behalf either at the time of the riot of the silversmiths in Ephesus (Acts 19:23) or during some Ephesian imprisonment to which he apparently refers in 2 Cor 1:8–9; 1 Cor 15:32; Rom 16:7. **5.** *the church [which meets] at their house:* See 1 Cor 16:19; Col 4:15; Phlm 2 for cultic gatherings in the private homes of early Christians. *Epaenetus:* Otherwise unknown. *first convert for Christ in Asia:* Lit., "first fruits of Asia unto Christ." Paul fondly reflects on the conversion of Epaenetus as that which sparked the conversion of many others in the Roman province of Asia (the W end of Asia Minor, with its gubernatorial seat at Ephesus). His conversion "consecrated" the rest of Asia to Christ (see comment on 11:16). **6.** *Mary:* Otherwise unknown.

138 **7.** *Andronicus and Junias:* Early Jewish-Christian converts, otherwise unknown, who were related to Paul, at least in the sense of "fellow countrymen," if not of "fellow tribesmen." Junias is a man's name, which makes the latter part of the verse easily understandable. But *Iounian* could also be translated Junia, a woman's name, which some ancient commentators took as the name of Andronicus' wife. Moreover P^{46} and some versions (Vg, bo, aeth) read "Julia." Most modern commentators, however, understand it as a masc. name. *fellow prisoners:* At Ephesus (1 Cor 15:32), or at Philippi (Acts 16:23), or elsewhere (2 Cor 11:23)? *eminent among the apostles:* Though this may suggest that Andronicus and Junias enjoyed the esteem of those who were apostles, the more natural meaning is that they were "apostles." The title "apostle" was in fact given to more than just the Twelve (→ Aspects NT Thought, 78:179–81). If this be correct, and the name were really Junia, what bearing would this have on the problem of orders for women? **8–16.** *Ampliatus, Urbanus, Stachys, Apelles, Aristobulus, Herodion, Narcissus, Tryphaena, Tryphosa, Persis, Rufus, Asyncritus, Phlegon, Hermes, Patrobas, Hermas, Philologus, Julia, Nereus, Olympas:* These persons are all otherwise unknown. Many of the names are well-known slave names, found on inscriptions throughout the Roman Empire, as well as at Ephesus. No argument can be constructed for or against the Ephesian destination of Rom 16 from the use of these names. It is sheer speculation that refers Rufus to the son of Simon of Cyrene (Mk 15:21), and Narcissus to the famous freedman of the Emperor Claudius' household, put to death in Nero's reign (Tacitus, *Annales* 13.1). **16.** *a holy kiss:* Cf. 1 Thes 5:26; 1 Cor 16:20; 2 Cor 13:12; 1 Pt 5:14. Paul often ends a letter in this way, perhaps transposing to an epistolary context a liturgical gesture (which was used at the Lord's Supper, according to Justin, *Apol.* 1.65,2) or adapting the customary greeting of rabbis.

139 **17–20.** A warning to the community against the influence of strangers who would introduce dissension and scandal. In tone this paragraph differs greatly from the rest of Rom; it recalls the spirit of Gal 6:12–17.

It certainly helps to make Ephesus the more likely destination of Rom 16, for it was a community that suffered from such problems—as Paul knew from experience. **18.** *slaves of their own appetites:* Lit., "of their own belly." In Phil 3:19 and Gal 5:7–12 Paul indulged in similar sarcasm in contexts of polemics with Judaizers. Such may be intended here; the allusion to the "belly" may be a sarcastic reference to concern for dietary laws. W. Schmithals (*ST* 13 [1959] 51–69) would identify them as Jewish-Christian Gnostics. **19.** *your obedience:* That is, faith (see 1:5; 15:18; 16:26). **20.** *God of peace:* See 15:33. *will crush Satan:* Satan is to be understood as the personification of all disorder and dissension and scandal in the community. God who shapes man's ways in peace will do away with such dangers threatening the community. An allusion to Gn 3:15 is not unlikely. After the farewell with which this verse ends it is strange to find a further greeting appended (vv. 21–23). It is the scribe's greeting, not Paul's at all.

21. *Timothy:* See comments on Acts 16:1–3; 2 Cor 1:1. *Lucius:* Not necessarily the same as Lucius of Cyrene (Acts 13:1). *Jason:* Not necessarily Jason of Thessalonica (Acts 17:5–9). *Sosipater:* The same as Sosipater of Beroea (Acts 20:4)? **22.** *Tertius:* Paul's scribe, who adds these few verses. **23.** *Gaius:* Is he the same as Gaius of 1 Cor 1:14 or of Acts 19:29? *Erastus:* The city treasurer or city commissioner is possibly the same as the aedile Erastus of Corinth, who at his own expense paved a square in 1st-cent. AD Corinth, according to a Lat inscription still *in situ* (cf. *Ancient Corinth: A Guide to the Excavations* [6th ed.; Athens, 1954] 74; but also H. J. Cadbury, *JBL* 50 [1931] 42–58). **24.** Omitted in the best Gk mss.; simply a repetition of 16:20.

140 **(VI) Doxology (16:25–27).** (On the position of this doxology in the mss., → 9 above.) *to him who can strengthen you:* Paul blesses God, who assures to men the Gospel of Christ and constancy of deeds in the Christian way of life. *my gospel:* The good news that Paul makes known (→ Pauline Theology, 79:27–30). *preaching of Jesus Christ:* That proclamation which has Christ Jesus as its subject matter. *according to the revelation of the mystery:* The manifestation of the divine plan of salvation that embraces all men, Jew and Greek alike (→ Pauline Theology, 79:32–34). *prophetic writings:* OT and Jewish apocalyptic writings that bear upon the mystery mentioned. Paul is anxious to link its revelation with the OT and regards it as prophecy (see 1:2; 3:21; 15:3–4). *according to the command of the eternal God:* Paul may be alluding in this expression to his commission as an apostle of the Gentiles so that he could make this mystery, now revealed, known to all the nations (cf. 1 Tm 1:1; Ti 1:3). *the obedience of faith:* Appositional genitive (see comment on 1:5). **27.** *to God alone who is wise:* This is the high point in the doxology (cf. Rom 11:33–36; Jude 24; Ap 15:4). Praise is paid once again to God the Father, through his Son, Jesus Christ. (Cf. J. Dupont, *ETL* 22 [1946] 362–75; *RevBén* 58 [1948] 3–22; L.-M. Dewailly, *NTS* 14 [1967–68] 111–18.)

54

THE LETTER TO PHILEMON

Joseph A. Fitzmyer, S.J.

BIBLIOGRAPHY

1 Benoit, P., *Les Épîtres de saint Paul aux Philippiens, à Philémon, aux Colossiens, aux Éphésiens* (BJ, 3rd ed.; Paris, 1959), 39–46. Carson, H. M., *The Epistles of Paul to the Colossians and Philemon* (TynNTC; London, 1960), 103–12. Dibelius, M., *An die Kolosser, Epheser, Philemon* (HNT 12, 3rd ed.; Tübingen, 1953), 101–8. Friedrich, G., "Der Brief an Philemon," NTD 8 (9th ed.; Göttingen, 1962), 186–94. Huby, J., *Saint Paul: Les Épîtres de la Captivité* (VS 8; Paris, 1947), 115–26. Knox, J. and G. A. Buttrick, "The Epistle to Philemon," *IB* 11 (1955) 553–73. Lohmeyer, E., *Die Briefe an die Philipper, an die Kolosser und an Philemon* (Meyer 9; Göttingen, 1957), 171–93. Médebielle, R. P., "Epître à Philémon," *PSB* 12 (Paris, 1938), 259–68. Meinertz, M., *Die Gefangenschaftsbriefe des hl. Paulus* (BB 7, 4th ed.; Bonn, 1931), 107–20. Moule, C. F. D., *The Epistles of Paul the Apostle to the Colossians and to Philemon* (CGTC; Cambridge, 1958), 140–49; *PCB*, 994–95. Scott, E. F., *The Epistles of Paul to the Colossians, to Philemon and to the Ephesians* (MNTC, 7th ed.; N.Y., 1948). Staab, K., *Die Gefangenschaftsbriefe* (RNT 7, 3rd ed.; Regensburg, 1959), 106–13. Vincent, M. R., *The Epistles to the Philippians and to Philemon* (ICC; N.Y., 1906), 155–94.

F–B 245–46. Guthrie, *NTI* 1, 247–54. Metzger, B. M., *IPLAP* 126–27. R-F, *INT* 509. Wik, *NTI* 419–21.

INTRODUCTION

2 **(I) Philemon.** The addressee was a young, well-to-do, respected Christian of some Phrygian town, probably Colossae, who owned an early Christian "house-church." Paul greets him along with Apphia, probably Philemon's wife, and Archippus (their son?), as well as "the church which meets in your house" (2). Philemon was apparently converted through Paul's efforts (19).

3 **(II) Date and Place of Composition.** Paul wrote this letter from prison (1), and this imprisonment has traditionally been understood as his Roman house arrest (AD 61–63). There is no good reason to question this tradition in the case of Phlm and Col. The mention of Epaphras, Mark, Aristarchus, Demas, and Luke in Phlm 23 and Col 4:10–14, as well as of Onesimus in Col 4:9, would suggest that Col and Phlm were composed at about the same time (→ Letter Col, 55:7).

4 **(III) Occasion and Purpose.** The slave Onesimus had run away, after having stolen something or having caused his master considerable damage (11, 18). In his flight he came to Rome, the magnet of fugitives and the lawless. Apparently Paul gave him refuge (see E. R. Goodenough, *HarvTR* 22 [1929] 181–83) and ultimately converted him to Christianity ("whose father I have become in my imprisonment," 10). Eventually Paul learned that Onesimus was Philemon's slave (*pace* J. Knox, *Philemon Among the Letters of Paul* [rev. ed.; N.Y., 1959], who regarded him as Archippus' slave). Though Paul wanted to keep Onesimus with him for the sake of the Gospel, he recognized Philemon's right and decided to send him back to him (14, 16). Paul wrote a letter, similar in character to that written by Pliny the Younger (*Letters* 9.21), but begging Philemon in his own way to receive the runaway slave well—"no longer as a slave, but...as a beloved brother" (16). In effect, Paul asks Philemon not to inflict the severe penalties permitted by law. But he also promises to restore the damage that Onesimus has caused Philemon and suggests quite frankly that he would like to have Onesimus come back to work with him. It is impossible to determine whether Paul meant by this that Philemon should manumit the slave. Paul sent Onesimus back with Tychicus, the bearer of Col (4:7–9).

5 **(IV) Onesimus.** Col 4:9 suggests that he was a Colossian. According to J. Knox, he was eventually returned to Paul as a helper and became in time the bishop of Ephesus (*ca.* AD 107–17) about whom Ignatius wrote (*Ep. ad Eph.* 1–6). As such, he played a major role in the collection of Paul's letters into a *corpus*. This is the most plausible part of Knox's theory. See also P. N. Harrison, "Onesimus and Philemon," *AnglTR* 32 (1950) 268–94; but cf. C. F. D. Moule, *Colossians and Philemon*, 14–21.

6 **(V) Significance.** Ancient commentators

wondered why an ostensibly private letter with little pastoral concern should have been inspired (see Jerome, *PL* 26.637). The fact that it is creates a problem for "the social character of inspiration." Paul does not invoke his apostolic authority to demand obedience of Philemon; he writes rather as a "prisoner" (1), an "old man" (9), and confronts Philemon with a plea of love (8–11, 21). Despite its private character, Phlm embodies an attitude toward slavery that merits Christian attention. First of all, it manifests Paul's warm-hearted affection for the slave Onesimus. Second, in sending Onesimus back to Philemon, Paul did not try to change the existing social structure. Modern Christian thinking is repelled by the idea of slavery, but remember that this outlook is a development and refinement of principles advocated by Paul—who must have realized the futility of trying to abolish the system in his day. Recall 1 Cor 7:20–24; 12:13; Col 3:22; 4:1; Eph 6:8–9. Third, Paul's solution was to transform and interiorize the social structure. He urged Philemon to welcome Onesimus back as a "brother," since he found it incongruous that a Christian would "own" another Christian—especially in view of Gal 3:27–28 and Col 3:11. This appeal is made "for love's sake" (8). But it took centuries for the Pauline principles to be put into practice even in the Christian West. An attitude of Paul toward slavery is shown in Phlm, and in this regard, the letter has its merited place in the Canon. See U. Wickert, *ZNW* 52 (1961) 230–38.

7 **(VI) Outline.** The letter to Philemon is outlined as follows:

(I) Introduction: *Praescriptio* and Greeting (1–3).
(II) Thanksgiving: Paul Thanks God for Philemon's Faith and Love (4–7).
(III) Body: Paul Appeals to Philemon's Good Will to Welcome Back Onesimus and Hints at His Usefulness to Himself (8–22).
(IV) Conclusion: Greetings from Companions and Blessing (23–25).

COMMENTARY

8 **(I) Introduction: Praescriptio and Greeting (1–3).** **1.** *prisoner:* Unlike his custom in Rom, 1 Cor, 2 Cor, Gal, Eph, Paul does not write as "an apostle." He appeals to Philemon as one in a lowly condition; see Phlm 9–10; Eph 3:1; 4:1. *Timothy:* The co-sender, as in Phil 1:1 (see comment); 2 Cor 1:1; Col 1:1. **2.** *Archippus:* See Col 4:17. There is no valid reason for regarding him as the owner of Onesimus or for thinking that the "ministry" mentioned there is the manumission of the slave, as suggested by J. Knox. **3.** *grace and peace:* → NT Epistles, 47:8.

9 **(II) Thanksgiving: Paul Thanks God for Philemon's Faith and Love (4–7).** **5.** *and all God's holy people:* Lit., "all the saints," see comment on Phil 1:1. **6.** *their sharing in your faith:* The meaning of this verse is obscure; see C. F. D. Moule, *Colossians and Philemon*, 142–43 for various interpretations. It seems to mean: Paul prays that a sense of solidarity with Philemon in faith in Christ will be productive of a deeper knowledge of all the good that comes to "the saints" through incorporation into Christ (→ Pauline Theology, 79:133). For this is a faith that involves an active love (Phlm 5; Gal 5:6).

(III) Body: Paul Appeals to Philemon's Good Will to Welcome Back Onesimus and Hints at His Usefulness to Himself (8–22). **8.** Paul does not demand obedience from Philemon, but appeals to his love and good will. **9.** *an old man:* The mss. read *presbytēs*, "an old man"—"a man of 50–60 years" (AG 707). Paul pleads in virtue of his senior status with the young Philemon. Many translators and commentators have preferred the conjecture of Bentley, reading *presbeutēs*, which would make of Paul "an ambassador, envoy" of Christ. Though Pauline (Eph 6:20), this interpretation is far from certain in the context of this letter. **10.** *for my child...whom I have begotten in prison:* Paul alludes to Onesimus' conversion (cf. 1 Cor 4:15; Gal 4:19). Another possible translation, "whom I have begotten as Onesimus," would play still more on the name of the slave. For *Onēsimos* means "Profitable One," and stands in contrast to the adjective "useless" (*achrēstos*, 11). Paul implies that the Christian slave will now live up to his name. Another pun on the name—involving Philemon himself—is met in v. 20. **14.** *without your consent:* Paul acknowledges the master's right to the slave. But he also hints that he would like to have Onesimus work with him; see Phlm 21.

10 **15.** *forever:* The sense of this adverb is double. The providential separation of Onesimus from Philemon means that the slave is now returning more faithful than he was. But Paul also alludes to the new relationship existing between them. Both are now Christians, related in a way that not even death can undo. **16.** *brother:* Onesimus is such because he is, like Philemon, an adopted son of God through Baptism (Gal 4:5; Rom 8:15). Both are now related "in the Lord" (cf. Col 3:22–4:1; Eph 6:5–9). **18.** *I, Paul, write this:* Probably the whole of this short letter (→ NT Epistles, 47:20). **21.** *obedience:* The noun *hypakoē* does not refer here to Philemon's submission in this affair, but rather to his "commitment of faith," which is what the noun denotes elsewhere in Paul's writings (Rom 1:5; 6:16; 10:16; 2 Cor 7:15). **21.** *even more than I ask:* This does not definitely mean that Paul is begging Philemon to manumit Onesimus, but it hints that he might allow him to return and work with him (see 14). **22.** Paul hopes for his own speedy release from house arrest. His words envisage a visit to Philemon's town, and in the traditional view of the Roman origin of Phlm they pose an interesting question. When did he plan to go there? Rom 15:24 tells of his plan to go to Spain from Rome. Because of this verse commentators have often suggested that Phlm was rather written from Ephesus or Caesarea; but these suggestions raise more problems than they solve.

11 **(IV) Conclusion: Greetings from Companions and Blessing (23–25).** **23.** *Epaphras, Mark, Aristarchus, Demas, Luke:* See Col 4:10–14 comments. **25.** See comment on Gal 6:18.

(Bartina, S., " 'Me debes más' (Film 19). La deuda de Filémon a Pablo," *SPC* 2, 143–52. Coleman-Norton, P. R., "The Apostle Paul and the Roman Law of Slavery," *Studies in Roman Economic and Social History in Honor of Allan Chester Johnson* [Princeton, 1951] 155–77. Preiss, T., "Vie en Christ et éthique sociale dans l'Épître à Philémon," *Aux sources de la tradition chrétienne* [Fest. M. Goguel; Neuchâtel, 1950] 171–79.)

55

THE LETTER TO THE COLOSSIANS

Joseph A. Grassi

BIBLIOGRAPHY

1 Abbott, T. K., *The Epistles to the Ephesians and to the Colossians* (ICC; N.Y., 1909). Benoit, P., *Les Épîtres de Saint Paul aux Philippiens, à Philémon, aux Colossiens, aux Éphésiens* (BJ; 3rd ed.; Paris, 1959), 47–73. Bieder, W., *Der Brief an die Kolosser* (Prophezei; Zürich, 1943). Conzelmann, H., *Der Brief an die Kolosser* (NTD 8; 9th ed.; Göttingen, 1962), 130–57. Dibelius, M., *An die Kolosser, Epheser; an Philemon* (HNT 12, 3rd ed., rev. by H. Greeven; Tübingen, 1953), 1–53. Dodd, C. H., *Colossians and Philemon* (London, 1929). Huby, J., *S. Paul: Les Épîtres de la Captivité* (VS 8; Paris, 1947). Lightfoot, J. B., *St Paul's Epistles to the Colossians and to Philemon* (London, 1892). Lohmeyer, E., *Die Briefe an die Philipper, an die Kolosser und an Philemon* (Meyer 9/2; 11th ed.; Göttingen, 1956), 1–170. Masson, C., *L'Épître de Saint Paul aux Colossiens* (CNT 10/2; Neuchâtel, 1950). Médebielle, A., *Épître aux Colossiens* (*PSB* 12; Paris, 1938). Moule, C. F. D., *The Epistles to the Colossians and to Philemon* (CGTC; Cambridge, 1958). Radford, L. B., *The Epistle to the Colossians and the Epistle to Philemon* (WC; London, 1931). Scott, E. F., *The Epistles of Paul to the Colossians, to Philemon, and to the Ephesians* (MNTC; London, 1936). Williams, A. L., *The Epistles of Paul the Apostle to the Colossians and to Philemon* (CGTSC; Cambridge, 1907). (For books dealing with both Col and Eph, → Letter Eph, 56:1.)

Cerfaux, L., R–F, *INT* 485–92. F–B 237–45. Guthrie, *NTI* 1, 161–78. Metzger, B. M., *IPLAP* 109–13. Wik, *NTI* 412–18.

INTRODUCTION

2 **(I) Destination.** The city of Colossae was located in Asia Minor, in the southern part of Phrygia about 110 mi. E of Ephesus. Situated in the valley of the Lycus River, near its juncture with the Meander River, it was an important textile center. The Christian community was composed of Gentiles (1:27; 2:13) and probably Jewish-Christians, for Josephus tells us that Antiochus III the Great (223–187 BC) decided to transport 2000 Jewish families from Babylonia to Lydia and Phrygia (*Ant.* 12.3,4 § 149). Paul himself was not the founder of the community (2:1). Epaphras, a Colossian who perhaps had been converted by Paul at Ephesus, had brought the faith to Colossae and probably to nearby Laodicea and Hierapolis (1:6–7; 2:1; 4:12–13).

3 **(II) Occasion and Purpose.** Although Paul was pleased with the progress and growth of the church in Colossae (1:6–7), he was disturbed by Epaphras' report of the dangerous doctrinal tendencies of some local teachers (2:8,16–23). These teachings were the product of both Jewish and pagan influences. Basic to them was the belief that certain angelic beings had control over human affairs, and even over all creation. It was then a primary concern to acquire a "knowledge" of these superbeings and their workings in order to propitiate them. This type of belief jeopardized the position of Christ, who might be considered as one of, even if the most powerful of, many mediators between God and the universe. Paul had to confront these errors vigorously and point out clearly Christ's unique place and all-powerful cosmic role in the universe.

The Jewish influence in the syncretism at Colossae is evident in the references to observing suggested days, seasons, circumcision, and other Jewish practices (2:16–17). In some circles of Judaism there was a strong belief in the mediatorship and power of the angels (e.g., Dn 10:21; 12:1). The Qumran community attached a great deal of importance to the angels' names and their roles in the affairs of the world (see T. H. Gaster, "Angel," *IDB* 1, 128–34). For Qumran and Col, see E. Yamauchi, *BS* 121 (1964) 141–52; W. D. Davies, in *The Scrolls and the NT* (N.Y., 1957) 166ff.

The pagan influences at work in Colossae are reflected in beliefs that certain "elements of the world" or angelic beings were in control of the universe (2:8,20). These "elements of the world" were a series of intermediaries between God and the universe. Each was considered to contain part of the "fullness [*plērōma*] of the Godhead" (cf. 1:19; 2:9). They were the cause of creation (cf. 1:15–17). They also shared control over various areas of the earth and over the destinies of men. All this was typical of the pagan concept of an ordered and controlled world in which man's chief work was to find out his destinies and to try to conform to them (see A. R. C. Leaney, *NTS* 10 [1963–64] 470–79; cf. G. Bornkamm, "Die Häresie des Kolosserbriefes," *TLZ* 73 [1948] 11–20).

4 The consequences of this Jewish-pagan syncretism were far reaching. Those under its influence felt a need for some revealed knowledge (*gnōsis*) concerning these hidden, all-powerful beings and the spheres of influence on earth that they controlled. It was important to know their names and functions as well as the means to propitiate them. Since human destiny was under their control, it was necessary to keep to a certain "discipline," e.g., to know what days were favorable or unfavorable for certain enterprises. Likewise, it was essential to know what material things were taboo because of the control of hostile beings and what things were good because of the influence of friendly spirits.

5 Paul had to counter these dangerous tendencies by pointing out the all-sufficiency of Christ in his role in the universe. He had to point out that the *plērōma* of the Godhead was not shared by a multitude of intermediaries; all the fullness of God and his power was in Christ himself (1:19; 2:3,9). By his death on the cross, Christ had won a victory over all the forces that were considered to control the universe (2:15). In OT wisdom literature Paul found proof that the whole universe had been created and directed by the wisdom of God from the beginning; now this wisdom had been fully revealed in Christ (1:15–20).

Paul himself never questioned the existence of these controlling spirits. Along with the Fathers, he probably believed in their reality. However, he was certain that all God's power was working in Christ, who was manifesting this in all the universe, especially through the preaching of the Word. For the original audience, as well as for the Church of today, we have in this letter a magnificent sketch of Christ in his full role as Lord, *Kyrios* of the universe.

6 **(III) Authenticity.** The Pauline authorship of Col was not questioned in the early Church. Irenaeus accepted it as canonical (*Adv. haer.* 3.14, 1); it is also listed in the Muratorian Canon (*EB* 4), and in the list of Marcion. Beginning with the 19th cent. some scholars attacked its authenticity. The chief arguments against Pauline authorship are: (1) A difference of language and style from the main Pauline letters (e.g., 48 words in Col appear nowhere else in Paul). However, one may respond that in Col Paul uses language of his adversaries in refuting them; thus the new vocabulary stems in part from them. (2) A development in theology beyond that of the main letters (e.g., a more pronounced ecclesiology, the concept of the cosmic Christ, the notion of "the body" with Christ as its head, a lessening of eschatological expectation, and an emphasis on possession in hope). See G. Bornkamm, in *Studien zum NT und zur Patristik* (Fest. E. Klostermann; TU 77; Berlin, 1962) 56ff. However, Paul's theology may have developed during the four years of captivity that separate Col from the main letters; again, these developments may be the answer to a new error that served as a catalyst in Paul's thinking. (3) The "Gnostic" nature of the heresy, since Gnosticism is, in its development, a 2nd-cent. phenomenon. However, most scholars agree that Col is directed against an incipient form of Gnosticism, or Proto-Gnosticism, which is at home in a 1st-cent. setting.

A very strong argument for the authenticity of Col is its agreement in situation with Phlm, the Pauline authorship of which is unquestioned. Some scholars (J. Weiss, P. N. Harrison, J. Knox, C. Masson) admit that certain sections of Col are genuinely Pauline, especially the parts that agree with Phlm, but regard the rest as interpolated. Many German scholars (R. Bultmann, E. Käsemann, G. Bornkamm, E. Schweizer, H. J. Schoeps, K.-G. Eckhart) cast doubt on the Pauline authorship. However, the majority of scholars still accept Paul as the author of Col, including many who think that he did not write Eph (→ Letter Eph, 56:4–9).

7 **(IV) Place of Origin and Date.** Paul wrote Col while in prison (4:3,18). Because imprisonment was a frequent experience for him this fact is not sufficient to establish the place of origin of Col. The advanced Christology in the letter would point to a time after the composition of 1–2 Cor, Rom, and Gal. Some scholars have proposed Ephesus; Paul suffered there (2 Cor 1:8–10), and the nearness to Colossae would facilitate the travels of Epaphras and Onesimus (4:9) to see Paul. (For possible Pauline imprisonment at Ephesus, → Letter Phil, 50:6.) A few commentators have suggested Caesarea, where Paul spent more than two years in prison (Acts 24:27). See L. Johnson, *ExpT* 68 (1956–57) 24–26. Many others endorse the traditional place of composition, Rome, where Paul lived in house arrest (Acts 28:16–31). Here he enjoyed some freedom to preach (cf. Col 4:3–4), which he would probably not have had at Caesarea because of the plot to kill him there (Acts 23:12). In the Roman hypothesis, the years AD 61–63 seem the most likely period.

8 **(V) Outline.** The letter to the Colossians is outlined as follows:

(I) Introduction (1:1–12)
 (A) Greeting (1:1–2)
 (B) Thanksgiving (1:3–8)
 (C) Prayer for the Church at Colossae (1:9–12)
(II) Part I: Doctrinal Section—The Absolute Pre-eminence of Christ in the Universe and in the Church (1:13–2:3)
 (A) The Pre-eminence of Christ (1:13–23)
 (B) Paul's Role in Proclaiming This Mystery (1:24–2:3)
(III) Part II: Polemic Section—Warnings Against False Teachings (2:4–3:4)
(IV) Part III: The Christian Life (3:5–4:1)
 (A) General Principles for a Life in Christ (3:5–17)
 (B) Applications for the Christian Home (3:18–4:1)
(V) Conclusion (4:2–18)

COMMENTARY

9 **(I) Introduction (1:1–12).**

(A) Greeting (1:1–2). **1.** *Paul an apostle:* See comment on Gal 1:1. *Timothy our brother:* "Brother" was a common name for a Christian because of his initiation into a covenant brotherhood in Christ. **2.** *the holy and faithful brethren in Christ:* Israel in the OT was called a "holy people" (Ex 19:6) because they belonged to God in a special way: "You shall be my special possession" (Ex 19:5). The primary sense, then, is holiness in the sense that God had acquired them as his own. See comments on Rom 1:7; 2 Cor 8:4. *from God our Father:* For Paul, the unique privilege of a Christian was his ability to know God in the same way that Christ did, as "Father" (cf. Rom 8:15; Gal 4:5). *grace and peace* (→ NT Epistles, 47:8).

10 **(B) Thanksgiving (1:3–8).** An introductory thanksgiving was customary in secular Gk letters, but it has a special religious nature in Paul. For him, it was always necessary to proclaim what God had done, in this case his wonderful deeds in calling the community to faith and enabling them to grow through sharing this gift with others. **3.** *our Lord Jesus Christ:* In the Gk world, Jesus Christ was gradually considered as a proper name. (For its origin and relation to *Kyrios*, → Aspects of NT Thought, 78:38; Pauline Theology, 79:59–67.) In Gk communities, Christians made their baptismal confession by proclaiming that Jesus was *Kyrios* (Rom 10:9). The expression was an apt one for expressing complete faith in and obedience to Christ. **4–5.** *faith... love... hope:* The triad of faith, hope, and charity occurs also in 1 Cor 13:13; 1 Thes 1:3; 5:8. Faith expresses the obedience or commitment to Christ (cf. Rom 1:5; → Pauline Theology, 79:125–127). Once joined to Christ, the believer understands God's great love for men and shares in Christ's mission to manifest it to others, for "faith works through love" (Gal 5:6). Hope is the final outcome of both: a union with Christ at the parousia (2 Cor 4:14; 1 Thes 2:19–20). **6.** *the whole world:* Paul emphasizes that the gospel in all its power is reaching to and affecting all mankind; this catholicity is a sign of the universal power of Christ, a central theme of the letter. *bearing fruit and growing:* These two verbs are found together only here and in Mk 4:8 where they describe how the seed of God's word is powerful enough to effect a harvest of thirty-fold, sixty-fold, or a hundred-fold. A tradition of sayings of the Lord may underlie Paul's use of these words. **7.** *Epaphras:* A Colossian who was under arrest with Paul at this time (4:12; Phlm 23) and may have been converted by Paul at Ephesus, he brought the faith to Colossae and probably to Laodicea and Hierapolis (4:13).

11 **(C) Prayer for the Church at Colossae (1:9–12).** **9.** *knowledge of his will:* Knowledge (*epignōsis*) is one of the key words in the letter (1:9,10; 2:2; 3:10). Knowledge of the universe and its workings was much prized by the Greeks. At Colossae some type of gnosis was propagated by false teachers. The scattered references in the letter do not permit us to obtain a clear idea of the nature of these beliefs, which stemmed from both Jewish and pagan sources (→ 4 above). Paul's concept of Christian *epignōsis* was in sharp contrast to the ideas of the false teachers at Colossae. This *epignōsis* was first of all a knowledge of God's will to save men in Christ (1:9ff.). This knowledge was not merely a conceptual knowledge, but a personal knowledge of God himself (1:10) and an experience of his loving design to save men in Christ (2:2) through their being conformed to the image of his Son (3:10). Paul uses *epignōsis* in the Semitic sense: a knowledge that comes from the experience of a person, rather than an acquired conceptual knowledge in the Gk sense (see K. Sullivan, "*Epignōsis* in the Epistles of St. Paul," *SPC* 2, 404–16). *in all wisdom: Sophia* is a characteristic word in Col (1:9,28; 2:3,23; 3:16; 4:5). The false teachings have a certain "appearance of wisdom" (2:23), but true wisdom is revealed in Christ (2:3). The wisdom theme is prominent in the epistle, for Paul draws heavily on OT wisdom literature to prove that Christ has a central place in the universe. **12.** *inheritance of the saints:* In the OT, *klēros* denotes the "lot" or "inheritance" of the saints, God's holy people; it was concretely the land of Israel (Jos 14–19). The priestly tribe of Levi, however, received no inheritance because the Lord himself was to be its inheritance (Jos 13:14). Since a Christian is a member of the priestly people of God (1 Pt 2:9), his inheritance is the abiding presence of the Lord. Several of Paul's expressions in this verse ("inheritance," "saints," "light," "power of darkness") have striking parallels in QL (see 1QS 3:1; 11:7–8; H. Braun, *TRu* 29 [1963] 246; P. Benoit, *NTS* 7 [1960–61] 287).

12 **(II) Part I: Doctrinal Section—The Absolute Pre-eminence of Christ in the Universe and in the Church (1:13–2:3).**

(A) The Pre-eminence of Christ (1:13–23). This section contains the central argument of the whole epistle. Paul delineates Christ's role in the universe in terms taken from OT descriptions of the Wisdom of God. He recalls the role of personified Wisdom in the creation and in the harmonious direction of the universe. In applying these descriptions to Christ, he sees a certain continuity in the OT doctrine. Wisdom's role is now continued in Christ himself, in whom all God's wisdom and knowledge are hidden (cf. 2:3).

13 Many critics have agreed that 1:15–20 is a Christian liturgical hymn. Holtzmann and others who think that Col has non-Pauline interpolations have suggested that the hymn was added by another hand. But the overwhelming majority of exegetes consider it part of Col, since many of its themes appear elsewhere in the letter ("image of God" in 1:15 and 3:10; "principalities and powers" in 1:16 and 2:10; "head" in 1:17 and 2:19; *plērōma* in 1:19 and 2:10; reconciliation in 1:20,22). Opinion is divided, however, as to whether Paul composed the hymn himself, or used it because it was known to the Colossians from their (baptismal) liturgy, or adapted a pre-Christian Gnostic hymn by incorporating it into a Christian baptismal profession of faith.

Käsemann sees the hymn centered on the Gnostic myth of *Urmensch* ("archetypal man"), the image of God, who was both a mediator in creation and a redeemer. However, this figure is largely a reconstruction from later sources; it is not known to have been current in the 1st cent. AD nor to what extent it is itself influenced by Christian thought. D. M. Stanley has proposed a Christian counterpart of the *Urmensch* theory in his view of Christ as the New Adam. Even more popular is the thesis that the hymn is inspired by (Hellenistic) Jewish hymns to the personified Wisdom of God (see Prv 8:22–31; Sir 24; Wis 7:21–30; 9:1–4). Conzelmann, Schweizer, and Feuillet have proposed various forms of this thesis. E. Lohmeyer, followed by S. Lyonnet, interpret the hymn as a composition written against the background of the Jewish feasts of New Year and Yom Kippur (→ Religious Institutions, 76:149–50, 155–58). The chief argument for this interpretation is the theme of reconciliation (1:20).

The first major attempt to analyze these verses as a hymn of recognizable structure was that of E. Norden in 1913 (*Agnostos Theos* [Darmstadt, 1956]). He split it into two strophes: vv. 15–18a, 18b–20. Lohmeyer includes vv. 13–14 in the hymn, while Käsemann begins the Pauline adaptation in v. 12, "Giving thanks...." J. M. Robinson has taken up the work of previous exegetes and proposed that there were originally two parallel liturgical units that Paul incorporated for his use. He disengages them as follows:

Strophe A	*Strophe B*
Who is the image of the invisible God,	Who is the beginning,
The first-born of all creation;	The first-born from the dead;
For in him were created all things in heaven and on earth,	For in him [dwells] all the fullness [of deity (bodily)],

Strophe A	*Strophe B*
[And] all things [are] through him, and to him (have been created).	And through him [he reconciled] all things to him.
And he himself is before all things,	And he himself is the head of the body,
And all things in him have come together.	That he might in all things himself be pre-eminent.

To this original framework, Paul would have added other material such as references to "the principalities and powers" (1:16). Strophe A would be a hymn to the Word; the parallel strophe B would be a baptismal and ecclesial application of Strophe A. Robinson shows that the ideas in the hymn are parallel to other NT liturgical hymns, e.g., Heb 1:3; Jn 1:3; Phil 2:6.

Exegetes have been divided as to whether the hymn in whole or part in Col 1:13–20 refers to the pre-existent Christ or to the incarnate Christ. The reference to "his beloved Son" in 1:13 would point to the incarnate Christ; on the other hand, the creation and governing of the universe would point rather to the pre-existent Wisdom of God. However, the writer may not have adverted to this distinction. For him the creation, sustenance, and government of the universe was not a past action, but one that continued through the present. He would see the creation and direction of the universe as beginning in the past through the Wisdom of God. He would see it continuing and growing through the presence of the same Wisdom of God in Christ, the incarnate Son of God (see D. M. Stanley, *CBQ* 20 [1958] 173–91).

(Bammel, E., "Versuch Col. i. 15–20," *ZNW* 52 [1961] 88–95. Craddock, F. B., "'All Things in Him': A Critical Note on Col. i. 15–20," *NTS* 12 [1965–66] 78–80. Feuillet, A., "La création de l'univers 'dans le Christ' d'après l'Épître aux Colossiens (i. 16a)," *NTS* 12 [1965–66] 1–9. Käsemann, E., *Essays on NT Themes* [SBT 41; London, 1961] 149–68. Lyonnet, S., *RSR* 48 [1960] 93–100. Maurer, C., "Die Begründung der Herrschaft Christi über die Mächte nach Kol. i. 15–20," *Wort und Dienst* 4 [1955] 79ff. Robinson, J. M., "A Form Analysis of Col. i. 15–20," *JBL* 76 [1957] 270–87.)

14 **13.** *he transferred us into the kingdom of his beloved Son:* The initiative is with God the Father. The words "rescue" and "transfer" bring out the theme of deliverance from captivity, like that of Israel of old. The expression "kingdom of his beloved Son" is unique in Paul; but cf. Eph 5:5. Elsewhere, it is always God's kingdom. The expression may be explained in view of 1 Cor 15:24–28, where Paul states that the Church is entrusted to Christ until the final stage of the kingdom, when the Son will hand it over to the Father. The expression "beloved Son" is an indication that what follows is to be interpreted of the incarnate rather than of the pre-existent Christ (see D. M. Stanley, *op. cit.*, 187). **14.** *in whom we have redemption:* (See Eph 1:7). Since Christ has brought true freedom, the Colossians have no need to propitiate any of the "higher powers." *forgiveness of sins:* This is the effect of baptismal union with Christ (Acts 2:38; Mk 1:4).

15 Verses 15–20 form the great Christological section, proclaiming Christ as the directive center of the universe and head of the Church. It abounds in references to the wisdom literature (cf. Jb 28; Prv 8; Sir 24; Wis 7). Wisdom, Word, and Spirit were very closely connected in Jewish thought and are frequently set in parallelism in OT literature (see F.-M. Braun, *Neotestamentica et Patristica* [Brill, 1962] 122–133). A. Feuillet has pointed out the extent to which Christ and the personified Wisdom of God in the OT are identified in Paul (*RB* 70 [1963] 52–74).

16 **15.** *the image of the invisible God:* Cf. Heb 1:3; 2 Cor 4:4; 1 Cor 11:7. There may be a reference here to Wis 7:26. Yet in view of Col 3:10, Paul is thinking more of Christ as the new Adam, head of a new creation. Adam had been created to the image of God (Gn 1:27) and commissioned to rule over all the earth (Gn 1:28). The new head of humanity finally accomplishes this mission. *first-born of all creation:* In Rom 8:29, we find the same sequence, "image" then "first-born," implying that many will share the image of God. The same sense may be here, but in view of what follows and other uses of the word (e.g., Ps 89:28), it may mean a position of supremacy, authority, and power over all creation. **16.** *in him were created all things:* In Greek, *en* can have an instrumental sense "by" or a local sense "in." Since "through him" (*di' autou*) in 1:16b conveys instrumentality, it is more probable that Paul means here that Christ is the locality, or center of unity and harmony, in which the universe was created. *those visible and those invisible, whether thrones or sovereignties, principalities or powers:* The point is that even the invisible angelic beings who were thought to control the world were created through the Wisdom of God. "Thrones," etc. were the names given to various classes of such beings. (See H. Schlier, *Principalities and Powers in the NT* [QD 3; New York, 1961]; C. Morrison, *The Powers That Be* [Naperville, Ill., 1960].) *for him:* The universe finds its goal and perfection in Christ. **17.** *before all things:* This can be in the sense of prior existence (cf. Jn 8:58) or in the sense of importance (Jas 5:12; 1 Pt 4:8) or both. *in him all things hold together:* A reference to Wisdom as the cohesive power of the universe (Wis 1:7).

17 **18.** *the head of his body, the Church:* Cf. Eph 1:23. For Paul, "head" signifies the principles of authority and vitality. The first sense is found in other epistles, but in Col and Eph there is a secondary meaning of "head" as a source of life and growth, which is the Gk concept of the relation of the head to the human body. (See P. Benoit, *RB* 63 [1956] 5–44; → Pauline Theology, 79:139–143.) *the beginning:* Christ forms the nucleus of a redeemed humanity in his complement the Church, in which he makes a new "beginning," a new creation (Gal 6:15; 2 Cor 5:17). *the first-born of the resurrection:* Lit., "first-born from among the dead." Christ's own resurrection is the cause of the resurrection of those who follow him. **19.** *all the fullness should dwell:* The concept of *plērōma*, God's "fullness," is found in the OT (cf. Is 6:3); most important, however, in view of Paul's use of OT sapiential literature, is the idea of Wisdom filling the earth (Wis 1:7). The fullness of God—his presence, divinity, and wisdom—is in Christ (cf. 1:3), who shares this with the Church, which in turn affects all humanity (see A. Feuillet, *NRT* 88 [1956] 449–72, 593–610). The emphasis is not on God's immanence, but on the cosmic effect of God's power working in Christ and in the Church. There is a possible influence of the Stoic idea of a universe filling and being filled by God. Later Gnostic systems made much of a teaching that God's *plērōma* was divided up and shared by a host of intermediaries. Paul may be counteracting a Gnostic tendency to trust in a number of necessary intermediaries who shared God's power. If this is so, he would be stressing that all the fullness is in Christ himself, so that no other intermediary is necessary. **20.** *to reconcile all things:* According to various NT texts, all creation must be restored to God (Rom 8:19–23; Mk 16:15). This implies a state of alienation: in man by reason of sin, and in all creation by the loss of unity and harmony through sin. The prevalent Jewish belief was that the world had fallen into the captivity of ruling world powers through man's sin. Christ overcame these angelic powers by taking away their control over believers.

18 **21.** *to present you holy, without blemish, and innocent before him:* Christ's act of reconciliation is presented in sacrificial terminology (cf. Eph 1:4; → Pauline Theology, 79:81, 87). *to present:* Although used at times in connection with the parousia (Rom 14:10; 2 Cor 4:14), this verb is also used in a sacrificial sense (Rom 12:1). **23.** *preached to every creature under heaven:* Paul brings this section to a climax by proclaiming that the fullness of God's power now in Christ has been showing its effect in the whole world through the preaching of the gospel. It gives him also the opportunity to explain his own role in God's plan.

19 **(B) Paul's Role in Proclaiming This Mystery (1:24–2:3).** **24.** *what is lacking in the sufferings of Christ, I complete in my flesh for his body which is the Church:* Exegetes are not agreed as to how Paul, as a member of the Church, helps to complete the sufferings of Christ. A study of the whole context may point toward a solution. The completion of the "sufferings of Christ" is intimately connected with the completion of the preaching of the gospel (vv. 23 and 25). Paul's vocation as an apostle is to complete the preaching of the gospel (v. 25) by bringing the good news to places where Christ has not been preached (Rom 15:15–21). Whenever Christ in the person of the apostle arrives in a new locality to call men to repentance, this causes division among men. Some receive the Word with joy; others persecute both the apostles and the new Christians. The "sufferings of Christ" would then be the apostolic sufferings endured as the gospel is continually brought to new places until a certain quota is reached (Rom 11:25). For parallels see 2 Cor 1:5–7, where the sufferings of Christ are linked with apostolic preaching; also 1 Thes 2:14–16; Acts 5:40–42. (B. N. Wambacq, *VD* 27 [1949] 17–22; G. Delling, *ThWNT* 6, 305.) *the Church:* Note that in v. 24, as in v. 18, Paul seems to speak of the Church at large (→ Pauline Theology, 79:153). Notice too that the Church has become the goal of Paul's activity—ecclesiology has become a major factor alongside Christology.

20 **26.** *the mystery:* Cf. Eph 1:9 (→ Pauline Theology, 79:32–34). **27.** *Christ in you, your hope of future glory:* In Col there is only one mention of the Holy Spirit (1:8) and this is generic and vague. Rather, the Risen Christ himself performs the functions attributed to the Spirit in the other epistles. His inner presence in the community of believers all over the world is already a guarantee of a future community in glory. Then Christ will reveal his presence, hitherto hidden in men. **28.** *him we preach:* With a fourfold repetition of *pas*, "all" or "every," Paul strongly emphasizes that the *mystērion* of which he speaks is not "a secret" reserved for a few privileged initiates, as in mystery religions; it is rather destined for the whole world. He affirms, moreover, that Christ's power, with its world-wide significance, is working mightily within him. There is no question of limitations.

21 **2:1.** *what a fight I am putting up for you:* Lit., "how great a struggle I have for you." This is an expression of Paul's concern even for churches that he has not personally evangelized. *Laodicea:* The city on the Lycus River founded by Antiochus II Theos (261–246 BC) and named after his wife Laodice. It lay on a trade route and enjoyed considerable prosperity; in Diocletian's time (*ca.* AD 300) it became the *metropolis* of the province of Phrygia (cf. Ap 3:14–22; S. E. Johnson, *BA* 13 [1950] 1–18; *BTS* 81 [1966] 4–15). *have not seen my face:* From these words it is usually deduced that Paul had not labored in the Lycus Valley of Asia Minor (→ 2 above). **2.** *that your hearts may be cheered:* The concern of all the churches (2 Cor 11:28) weighed so heavily on Paul that he wrote to those churches that he could not visit personally. Thus he managed to share with them the "mystery of Christ." **3.** *may comprehend the mystery of God, Christ:* It is not certain whether "Christ" is in apposition to "God" or "mystery." This grammatical difficulty led to a host of variant readings in the mss., scribal attempts to clarify the verse one way or the other. *in whom* [or *which*] *are hidden all the treasures of wisdom and knowledge:* The rel. pronoun can refer either to "Christ" or to "mystery" (cf. Eph 3:9–10). Paul ends this doctrinal section of Col by describing Christ as containing all the wealth of God's wisdom and knowledge (cf. 1:27; 1 Cor 1:24,30). The inspiration is probably due to Prv 2:3–4 and Is 45:3. This ending is apt because he has been presenting Christ's universal role in terms of OT wisdom literature.

22 **(III) Part II: Polemic Section—Warnings Against False Teachings (2:4–3:4).** Paul has just finished his exposé of the all-sufficiency of Christ; he turns now to what he has learned about the false teachings in the area of Colossae and Laodicea. **4.** *specious arguments:* Propagandists in the community were apparently using plausible, attractive, yet false arguments. **5.** *your orderly array and firm front:* These are military terms that describe an army set for battle and indicate the attitude the community must adopt.

23 **6.** *as you have received Jesus as Christ and Lord:* "Receive" is used of teaching in Gal 1:9; Phil 4:9; and 1 Cor 11:23. *Jesus as Christ and Lord* is a probable rendition of the unusual Gk *ton Christon Iēsoun ton Kyrion* found only here in Col and in Eph 3:11. The Gk articles make it possible that Paul is referring to the baptismal confession of faith, which would usually be "Jesus is the Lord" or "Jesus is the Christ." The combination is strange; yet cf. Acts 2:36. Paul is saying that they have been taught to accept Jesus as the true Lord; why should they find anything else necessary? *walk in him:* The Pauline metaphor for ethical conduct (see comment on Rom 6:4). **7.** *overflowing with thanksgiving:* This theme is repeated throughout the epistle (1:12; 2:7; 3:15,17; 4:2). A deeply rooted foundation in Christ will lead men to frequent recognition of his presence and work in them. **8.** *see to it that no one deceives you with philosophy and vain deception:* This is the only occurrence of *philosophia* in the NT. Here it denotes a system of human speculation that false teachers were trying to spread. *the elements of the world:* See comment on Gal 4:3. In this verse, the *stoicheia* stand in direct opposition to Christ and represent personal adversaries, such as the angelic powers who were believed to rule the world.

24 **9.** *in him dwells the fullness of the Godhead bodily:* The meaning of *sōmatikōs*, lit., "bodily," is not certain in this context. It could mean "corporately," thus fitting in with the immediately following reference to the Church as sharing the fullness of Christ. Other possibilities are "incarnate," i.e., assuming a bodily form; or "actually," i.e., not only in appearance. There may be a contrast between the summation of divine power in Christ and the sharing of minor powers by the "elements." *you have been fulfilled in him:* The believer finds all he needs in Christ; nothing else need be added—no other rites, no other powers. **10.** *head of every principality and power:* See comment on 1:16. The spiritual world-rulers are subject to Christ. **11.** *in whom you were circumcised, but not by human hand:* Paul describes how the Gentile believer became incorporated into Christ at his baptism. Circumcision was the external sign of incorporation into the old covenant. In baptism there is no human external mark; there is a plunging into the death and resurrection of Christ. *through putting off the body of flesh, a circumcision which is of Christ:* The term *apekdysis* (putting off) is found only here in the NT; the vb. *apekdyomai* occurs in Col 2:15 and 3:9. There is a contrast between the partial stripping of physical flesh in circumcision and the full stripping of "the flesh" in baptism. *Body of flesh* may be understood in the sense of human weakness as in 2:18; the believer renounces the tendencies of human weakness. The whole phrase can have a very realistic sense in reference to the death of Christ, where he completely separated himself from earthly flesh and all its weakness (but cf. the Qumran parallel in 1QpHab 9:2; see H. Braun, *TRu* 29 [1963] 250–51). **12.** *you were buried with him in baptism:* Cf. Rom 6:1–11. *you were raised to life with him:* In Rom, the resurrection of the Christian is presented in eschatological terms (6:5,8), although the present effect of the new life is also brought out (6:4,11). In Col, resurrection with Christ is described as already taking place. This present emphasis may be due to the errors at Colossae, where many were not sufficiently aware of the present cosmic effects of Christ's death and resurrection. The vb. *synegeirō* (to raise with) expresses the identification of the Christian with the resurrection of Christ (→ Pauline Theology, 79:137). *through faith in the active power of God: energeia* (active power) is a favorite word in both Eph (1:19; 3:7; 4:16) and Col (1:29; 2:12). Since the Spirit is mentioned infrequently in Col, God's mighty power working in Christ replaces it to a large extent (see comment on 1:27). This stress on "power" may be to counteract prevalent fears of surrounding hosts of invisible powers.

25 **13.** *the uncircumcision of your flesh:* A symbol of alienation from God (cf. Eph 2:1,5). *he brought you to life again with him:* The vb. *syzōpoieō* is found only here and in Eph 2:5. Once again the *syn* compound emphasizes identification with Christ's new life. *forgiving your sins:* The vb. *charisamenos* signifies forgiveness as the result of a favor or an act of love. **14.** *canceling the bond written against us in decrees:* The word *cheirographon*, found only here in the NT, is used of a handwritten bond of debt (cf. Phlm 19). The author of Eph explains the "decrees" as those of the Law (2:15). The indebtedness may be the necessity of paying the penalty for an infraction of the Law; death was the punishment for disobedience (Gn 2:17; Dt 30:19). *nailing it to the cross:* Christ, representing humanity, took upon himself the debt of punishment. **15.** *discarding the principalities and powers:* The same verb is used as in 2:11 where there is a question of the putting off of Christ's body of flesh. "Discarding the principalities" and "putting off the flesh" are closely connected. The ruling angelic powers were believed to have control over material things; Christ, by putting aside his material body, was able to escape their control and triumph over them. The picture in v. 15 is that of a public triumphant military procession: Christ leads the way with his victorious cross; the captive principalities and powers follow him. The victory is not one of annihilation, but of subjection. They are henceforth under his command (2:10) and have no power to harm or control believers. They still, however, retain their power over unbelievers; Christians must struggle and pray lest they regain their control over them (Eph 6:10–17).

26 **16.** *in regard to food or drink, or observance of a festival, new moon or Sabbath:* These were matters of Jewish Law. It was believed that the Law had been given by angels (cf. Gal 3:19); those who observed the Law under their control and protection, and transgressors were punished by them (cf. Gal 4:10). Christ's victory over these controlling spirits removed the fear of being punished for the nonobservance of the Law. **18–19.** Paul warns them not to be led astray from Christ by anyone who gives himself over to "worship of the angels" or various ascetical practices connected with this. Paul could also have been thinking of some kind of imitation of pagan mystery rites where the aspirant was introduced into membership through alleged "visions of angels." **20.** *If you have died with Christ:* Death with Christ means separation from material religious practices concerned with appeasing the ruling spirits (cf. Gal 4:3,9). **23.** In contrast to Christ, who is the Wisdom of God, these practices have an external show of wisdom in their impressive asceticism, but they have little value to control the desire of the flesh. *self-made devotion:* The word *ethelothrēskia* may be translated "would-be religion" and may indicate that the Colossian error was a type of mystery cult.

3:1. *seek the things that are above:* The contrast between the "things that are above" and the "things that are on the earth" is to be understood especially in view of the preceding descriptions of material religious practices that are in such opposition to Christ's victorious presence. *where Christ is enthroned at the right hand of God:* The expression from Ps 110:1 implies his position of lordship and complete victory. **3.** *your life has been hidden with Christ in God:* The use of the Gk aorist in the vb. "died" implies a definitive decision (of separation from material practices); the use of the pf. tense in "has been hidden" expresses effective continuity until the present. There may be a play on the contrast between a body being "hidden in the earth" at death and being hidden in Christ through a real contract of death or separation from material things. **4.** *when Christ our life appears, then you also will appear with him in glory:* Here the writer makes a definite reference to the future resurrection, although his main emphasis throughout has been on the present resurrection with Christ.

27 **(IV) Part III: The Christian Life (3:5–4:1).**
(A) General Principles for a Life in Christ (3:5–17). This section is an early baptismal instruction in compendious form. We find baptismal symbolism in v. 5, the command to "put to death" the former personality; in v. 9, the stripping off of the old man; and in vv. 10 and 12, the "putting on" of the new man, representing the life of Christ himself.

5. *put to death your members which are on earth:* In union with the death of Christ, this is the baptismal contract of death, an absolute separation from the former type of life. *on the earth:* The same words as in 3:3. In place of dabbling with material religious practices and external asceticism (2:16–23), Paul proposes a radical self-denial in putting aside a self-centered life. **5–8.** The catalogues of vices are topical: The first group of five are mostly sins against purity (v. 5); another group of five (v. 8) concern anger and sins of the tongue. To these corresponds a catalogue of five virtues in v. 12. **6.** *the wrath of God:* Cf. Eph 2:3. **9–10.** *stripping off the old man...putting on the new:* These are corporate figures (1 Cor 15:45–47). The Christian embraces a new corporate community life in Christ. **10.** *who is being continually renewed to perfect knowledge according to the image of his Creator:* Christ is the perfect image of God (see comment on 1:15), the perfect pattern of life for those baptized. Their aim should be a continual interior renovation according to the model of Christ the new man. **11.** In Christ, head of a new humanity, the great social barriers of race, culture, and state of life are broken down. This theme later becomes the central motif in Eph, especially regarding the great social barrier between Greek and Jew in the ancient world (cf. Eph 2:14–16). *barbarian:* The term *barbaros* designated a person who did not know Greek. *Scythian:* The equivalent of saying, "a savage from the north." *Christ is all and in all:* This may be a way of saying that Christ breaks down such distinctions and is really all that matters; or it may be a return to an affirmation of his universal power as in 1:15–20.

28 **12.** *as God's chosen people, holy and beloved:* What follows is a brief description of the Christian community life a member embraces through his baptism. The employment of terms used to describe Israel of old (chosen, holy, beloved) stresses that they are entering the new Israel, a new community of God's people and that their relations to one another should reflect this. *heart of compassion:* These words are first in a list of five virtues emphasizing the inner transformation necessary to become "a new personality," that of Christ. *humility, meekness, patience:* Cf. Eph 4:2. **13.** *forgiving one another... as the Lord has forgiven you:* The petition of the Our Father (Mt 6:12) may be in Paul's mind (cf. Eph 4:32). **14.** *above all these put on charity, which is the bond of perfection:* In v. 12 Paul wrote "put on the new garments of Christ." *Agapē* is the final garment that covers all the others and binds them together. There may be an influence here from the Sermon on the Mount; "Be perfect as your heavenly Father is perfect" (Mt 5:48), where God's great universal love is the supreme model for man. **15.** *may the arbiter in your midst be the peace of Christ, to whom you have been called in one body:* This is a vivid portrayal of the compact community of brothers in Christ, who is the source of unity, peace, and harmony. For this, they must always be *eucharistoi* (thankful). **16.** *let the word of Christ dwell in you in all its richness:* The presence of Christ in the community will manifest itself by a wise use of words and song to encourage one another. *teaching and admonishing one another:* This points to a didactic use of music in the community. "One another" is repeated three times in this section (3:9,13,16), emphasizing that responsibilities are mutual. *singing in your hearts to God:* Some textual witnesses have "to the Lord." (On early Christian hymns, see D. M. Stanley, *op. cit.*, 173–91.) **17.** *do all in the name of the Lord Jesus, giving thanks to God the Father through him:* Christians must recognize Jesus as Lord both in word and in action. In words, they will show this recognition best when they call upon him in prayer as Lord. For Paul and the early Church, to say "those who call upon the name of the Lord" was a way of designating Christians (see comment on Rom 10:13). Christ's mediatorship is shown by the fact that they give thanks to the Father through him. In deeds, the Christian will recognize him as Lord by personal engagement to him, by conforming his life to the pattern he has left.

29 **(B) Applications for the Christian Home (3:18–4:1).** Paul's advice for the most part is commonplace, yet there is a new inner spirit. Everything now must be done "in the Lord" (3:18). *Kyrios* is repeated seven times in these eight verses. Obedience to the Lord will be shown in life by wholehearted dedication to one's duties in the family and in the world. The emphasis in this section is on the performance of duties, rather than on rights. This section contains a good example of a Pauline *Haustafel* (→ Pauline Theology, 79:162). **18–19.** Instructions for Husbands and Wives (cf. Eph 5:21–33). **3:22–4:1.** An instruction for slaves in the Christian home. Paul deals with slavery as a social institution of his time. Actually there were few independent wage earners in those days, and the so-called freedman often led a type of parasitic life attached to the home of a rich landowner. A large percentage of the population of the Roman Empire was made up of slaves, and the danger of rebellion was always present. Paul wishes Christian slaves to be distinguished by their spirit of service. They are not to look for human rewards but to regard their work as a special service to Christ. In 3:25 and 4:1 he brings out the basis for the real equality that exists between slave and master. A realization of the Christian dignity of a slave would eventually lead to the overthrow of slavery as an institution (→ Letter Phlm, 54:6).

30 **(V) Conclusion (4:2–18).** Paul concludes this letter with a request for prayers (2–4), a commendation of his collaborator Tychicus, who probably carries Col, and of the runaway slave Onesimus (7–9), greetings from his co-workers (10–14), a message for the church of Laodicea (15–17), and his final greetings (18). **2–4.** Cf. Paul's advice on prayer with Eph 6:18–20. **7.** *Tychicus:* Identified in Acts 20:4 as an Asian, i.e., from the province of Asia; cf. Eph 6:21–22. **9.** *Onesimus:* This verse suggests that he was originally from Colossae (→ Letter Phlm, 54:5). Once again Paul's affection for this slave is noted. **10.** *Aristarchus:* Paul's "fellow prisoner" is mentioned in Acts 19:29; 20:4; 27:2; Phlm 24. *Mark:* Undoubtedly the Evangelist (see Acts 12:12,25; 13:13; 15:37,39; 2 Tm 4:11; Phlm 24; 1 Pt 5:13). **11.** *Jesus called Justus:* Otherwise unknown. **12.** *Epaphras:* See comment on 1:7. **14.** *Luke:* Identified here as a physician, he is significantly not named among the Jewish Christians; he was apparently a Gentile convert (cf. 2 Tm 4:11; Phlm 24). *Demas:* See Phlm 24; 2 Tm 4:10. **16.** *see that it is read in the church of the Laodiceans:* Paul's letters were interchanged between local communities and publicly read in them. Gradually collections of his writings grew up. **18.** *I, Paul, greet you with my own hand:* This suggests that the rest of the letter had been dictated; Paul adds the final greeting as a safeguard, to insure its authenticity (see Gal 6:11; 2 Thes 2:2; 1 Cor 16:21; → NT Epistles, 47:20).

56

THE LETTER TO THE EPHESIANS

Joseph A. Grassi

BIBLIOGRAPHY

1 Abbott, T. K., *The Epistles to the Ephesians and the Colossians* (ICC; N.Y., 1909). Benoit, P., *Les Épîtres de Saint Paul aux Philippiens, à Philémon, aux Colossiens, aux Éphésiens* (BJ, 3rd ed.; Paris, 1959) 75–108. Bruce, F. F., *The Epistle to the Ephesians* (London, 1961). Conzelmann, H., *Der Brief an die Epheser* (NTD 8, 9th ed.; Göttingen, 1962) 56–91. Dibelius, M., *An die Kolosser, Epheser; an Philemon* (HNT 12, 3rd ed.; rev. by H. Greeven; Tübingen, 1953) 54–100. Erdman, C. R., *The Epistle of Paul to the Ephesians* (Phila., 1931). Foulkes, F., *The Epistle of Paul to the Ephesians* (TynNTC; Grand Rapids, 1963). Goodspeed, E. J., *The Meaning of Ephesians* (Chicago, 1953); *The Key to Ephesians* (Chicago, 1956). Huby, J., *S. Paul: Les Épîtres de la Captivité* (VS 8; Paris, 1947). Masson, C., *L'Épître de Saint Paul aux Éphésiens* (CNT 9/2; Neuchâtel, 1952). Médebielle, A., *L'Épître aux Éphésiens* (*PSB* 12; Paris, 1951). Mitton, C. L., *The Epistle to the Ephesians* (Oxford, 1951). Percy, E., *Die Probleme der Kolosser- und Epheserbriefe* (Lund, 1946). Robinson, J. A., *St. Paul's Epistle to the Ephesians* (London, 1903). Schlier, H., *Der Brief an die Epheser* (3rd ed.; Düsseldorf, 1962); *Christus und die Kirche im Epheserbrief* (Tübingen, 1930). Schmid, J., *Der Epheserbrief des Apostels Paulus* (BibSt 22; Freiburg i. Br., 1928); *Zeit und Ort der paulinischen Gefangenschaftsbriefe* (Freiburg i. Br., 1931). Scott, E. F., *The Epistles of Paul to the Colossians, to Philemon and to the Ephesians* (MNTC; N.Y., 1948). Staab, K., *Der Brief an die Epheser* (RNT 7; Regensburg, 1950) 114–66. Vosté, J.-M., *Commentarius in epistolam ad Ephesios* (2nd ed.; Paris, 1932). Westcott, B. F., *St. Paul's Epistle to the Ephesians* (London, 1906). Zerwick, M., *Der Brief an die Epheser* (Düsseldorf, 1962).

Cerfaux, L., R–F, *INT* 493–509. F–B 247–59. Guthrie, *NTI* 1, 99–139. Metzger, B. M., *IPLAP* 94–102. Wik, *NTI* 411–12, 421–30.

INTRODUCTION

2 **(I) Destination.** Ephesus was a large seaport city on the western coast of Asia Minor and the capital of the Roman province of Asia. Paul stayed at Ephesus on Mission II (Acts 18:19–21) and made it his base during Mission III (Acts 19:1–20:1), spending about three years there (Acts 20:31; cf. 19:10; → Life of Paul, 46:36).

The title, "To the Ephesians," was not on the original letter, but is on all extant mss. Eph 1:1 has the address, "to the saints who are at Ephesus." The words *en Ephesō*, although present in most mss., are notably missing in Vaticanus and Sinaiticus (where they have been added marginally by a later hand), in the Chester Beatty Papyrus (P^{46}, the oldest copy of Pauline epistles), in Origen, and in old copies known to Basil (*Contra Eunomium* 11.19). Jerome, too, knew of mss. that did not contain these words (*In Eph.* 1.1). The textual evidence then makes it probable that the words were not in the original text. Yet the text of v. 1 could not stand without a phrase at this point. Marcion entitled the epistle "To the Laodiceans," basing this title apparently on Col 4:16. It is possible that originally there was a blank space for the bearer of a circular letter to insert the name of the particular community, but as yet, no parallel to this has been found in ancient Gk literature.

3 Other considerations also make the question of the destination a difficult one. The letter contains only one personal reference, to Tychicus (6:21), and this is the same as in Col 4:7. Since Paul had spent almost three years in Ephesus, perhaps more time than in any other community, it is hard to understand the impersonal tone of this letter and the lack of reference to many friends. There are hints that the writer may not be personally acquainted with his audience or that they are not acquainted with his teaching (1:15; 3:1; 4:21). Also, the author writes as if someone other than himself was the founder of the community (2:20; 3:5), whereas Paul is wont to identify himself to his churches as their founder and apostle.

4 **(II) Authenticity.** The Pauline authorship of Eph was unanimously accepted in antiquity. The letter itself specifically claims to be written by Paul (1:1; 3:1). The author speaks of his experience, which is certainly that of Paul (3:1–4; 4:1; 3:7–13; 6:19–22). The letter was known to the early Church Fathers; probably to Clement of Rome, more certainly to Ignatius of Antioch (*Ep. ad Eph.* 12), Hermas (*Sim.* 13:5), and Polycarp (*Ep. ad Phil.* 12:1). The earliest collection of Pauline epistles contained Eph; and Marcion, in the middle of the 2nd cent., accepted it in his Pauline list, although entitling it "to the Laodiceans." Toward the end of the 2nd cent. Irenaeus and Clement of Alexandria accepted the letter as Paul's. The Muratorian Fragment (line 51) named it among Paul's epistles.

However, since the end of the 18th cent. the authenticity of Eph has been challenged by a large number of scholars, mainly for the following reasons: (a) differences in language and style; (b) the special relationship of Ephesians to Colossians in particular, and to other Pauline letters; (c) differences in doctrinal emphasis and content.

5 (a) Differences in Language and Style. If we consider the vocabulary of Eph, there are 42 words occurring only in this letter and not in the rest of the NT. Yet this must be compared to the rate in other Pauline epistles of similar length: Gal has 33, Phil 41, Col 38. Also, 36 words occur only in Eph and in no other Pauline epistle (43 if the Pastorals are not considered Pauline). However, many of the words peculiar to Eph are concentrated in the specialized sections on the Church as the bride of Christ (5:25–33) and the description of Christian armor (6:13–17). (For a complete list of *hapax legomena* and a fuller analysis of the arguments from vocabulary and language, see T. K. Abbott, *Epistles*, xv–xxxii; C. L. Mitton, *Epistle*, 107–220). Analysis of vocabulary alone does not lead to a definite conclusion in regard to authenticity.

The differences in style are also significant. The style is heavy, and there is a good deal of redundance. Series of nouns are connected by genitives or prepositions (e.g., 1:11,19; 2:14–15). There are many long sentences including numerous relative clauses and participles (e.g., 1:3–14; 1:15–23; 2:1–10; 3:1–6; 4:11–16).

6 (b) The Relationship of Ephesians to Colossians. Of the 155 verses in Eph, over one third are parallel to Col both in content and in order. Except for the reference to Tychicus, which is almost exactly the same in Eph (6:21–22) and in Col (4:7–8), the exact verbal correspondence seldom exceeds five words in a row.

The parallels found in Eph to other Pauline epistles besides Col bring the total of parallel material to over 85 per cent of the verses. Critics point out that this great amount of virtual "copying" would not be characteristic of a man of such flexibility and creative thinking as was Paul. In addition, they point out that the author of Eph at times uses the same word used by Paul in another letter, but in a different sense. For example, the word *mystērion* in Col 1:26; 2:2; 4:3 means a revealed secret in the sense of the hidden person of Christ in the Church, Christ in you; but in Eph 1:9 and 3:4 it is used in the sense of the revelation of God's plan that Jew and Gentile be united in Christ.

(Benoit, P., in *Neutestamentliche Aufsätze* [Fest. J. Schmid; Regensburg, 1963] 11–22. Cerfaux, L., *SP* 2, 373–79. Coutts, J. "The Relationship of Ephesians and Colossians," *NTS* 4 [1957–58] 201–07. Percy, E., "Zu den Problemen des Kolosser- und Epheserbriefes," *ZNW* 43 [1950–51] 178–94. Sanders, E. P., "Literary Dependence in Colossians," *JBL* 85 [1966] 28–45.)

7 (c) Differences in Doctrinal Emphasis and Content. (i) The emphasis in Eph is principally on the Risen and Exalted Christ, with the significance of his death an underlying assumption (cf. 2:13–16). There is little reference to the Second Coming, so prominent in Paul's other writings. Brief mention is made of the "pledge of inheritance" (1:14), "day of redemption" (4:30), "wrath of God" (5:6), and judgment (6:8). The picture given is more that of a Church growing and progressing in history than of one waiting for the imminent return of Christ (e.g., 2:21–22; 4:12–13).

(ii) The image of the Church in Eph is more universal and catholic than in any other Pauline writing. In Rom (12:5) and 1 Cor (12:12–27) the body of Christ refers to the local church, but in Eph the body of Christ is the universal Church, of which Christ is the head and every Christian a member (4:1–16). Emphasis is placed on the possibility of joining Jews and Gentiles in one great people of God. The whole Church is the spouse of Christ (5:23–32). The earlier problems with Jewish persecution and controversy and with Judaizers seem to have been settled, so that the writer can rejoice in the calm view of the unity of Jew and Gentile in Christ.

(iii) The doctrine on marriage in 5:21–33 is much more positive and complete than that in 1 Cor 7 where the Apostle's reasoning seems influenced by consideration of the imminent parousia. Yet it must be remembered that in 1 Cor 7 Paul is answering particular questions rather than giving a complete exposition.

(iv) There is the impression at times that the writer is almost like a second-generation Christian looking back to the time when the community first received the good news and revering the memory of the founders (2:20; 3:5).

8 To sum up: Not one of the arguments presented above would be sufficient to prove the non-Pauline authorship of Eph, yet the sum total of them has made a large number of exegetes conclude that the letter is not Paul's. Among these are F. W. Beare, M. Dibelius, E. J. Goodspeed, C. L. Mitton, and J. Moffatt. Others, however, find all the alleged arguments to be insufficient for the denial of Pauline authorship. Among these are T. K. Abbott, W. Barclay, P. Benoit, L. Cerfaux, F. Foulkes, and H. Schlier.

(Benoit, P., *Exégèse*, 2. 53–96. Cadbury, H. J., "The Dilemma of Ephesians," *NTS* 5 [1958–59] 91–102. Cerfaux, L., in *Littérature et théologie pauliniennes* [RechBib 5; Bruges, 1960] 60–71. Hanson, P. N., *SE* 2, 595–604. Mitton, C. L., "The Authorship of the Epistle to the Ephesians," *ExpT* 67 [1955–56] 195–98.)

9 Those who admit the authenticity of Eph recognize the problems involved and try to solve them in various manners. They suggest that Eph may be related to Col in somewhat the same way that Rom is related to Gal. In Gal, Paul dealt with the crisis of the relationship of the Law to Christians; Rom then treats the whole topic of justification and the Law from a broader viewpoint and appears more like a theological treatise than a letter directed to a single church. Similarly, Col deals with the particular difficulties of a church regarding the uniqueness of Christ's position in the world when confronted with many competing "powers." Eph could well be the calmer treatise explaining the unity and universality of the Church. As such, it could have been a circular letter addressed to many churches. The doctrinal differences in Eph could be attributed to Paul's flexibility or to the development and maturity of his thought. The lack of personal warmth may be explained by the fact that he is writing to some communities unknown to him. Differences in language and style may be due to his entrusting its composition to a secretary. Whatever the final judgment on authenticity is—if such is possible—Eph is certainly a mature development of Pauline thought and theology.

10 **(III) Date and Place of Origin.** A judgment about the date of composition depends to a great extent on the view taken of the letter's authenticity. Eph was certainly written after Col, and, because of the extensive common material, was most probably composed after the other epistles, with the possible exception of the Pastorals. The 83 words found only in Col and Eph point to a special relation. However, the complicated question of the date of the Pastorals makes it difficult to date Eph on this basis.

As for place of origin, the writer indicates that he is a prisoner (3:1; 4:1; 6:20). Hence the inclusion of Eph in the Captivity Letters along with Phil, Col, and Phlm. However, Paul spent time in prison in almost every community he founded. If the letter was written after most of the Pauline corpus was completed, this would point to Caesarea (Acts 23:33), where Paul spent two years in prison (Acts 24:27), or to the traditional place of origin, Rome.

11 **(IV) Plan and Purpose.** Chapters 1–3 announce God's great plan, hidden from the beginning of the world, to create a messianic people of God, a new community of men uniting in Christ both Jew and Gentile and erasing the impenetrable social and religious barriers that had previously divided mankind. It is Paul's privilege to be a chosen herald of God, appointed to reveal to men this mystery of God's love. Paul then prays that his audience may appreciate and experience God's great love for men that has made possible such a bond of unity of men in the Church (3:14–21). Chapters 4–6 are hortatory, bringing forth conclusions that follow for Christian life: unity in the body of Christ, as each member uses his gifts for the growth and progress of the vital organism of the Church (4:1–16); a true renewal of life motivated by a loving concern for fellow members in Christ (4:17–5:20). This spirit will be especially manifest in the home through practice of the domestic virtues (5:21–6:9). It will show itself also in a courageous combat with the powers of darkness (6:10–17). The letter ends with a request for prayers, a recommendation of Tychicus, and a final blessing (6:18–24).

12 **(V) Outline.** The letter to the Ephesians is outlined as follows:

(I) Introduction: Greeting, Opening Formula (1:1–2)
(II) Part I: Doctrinal Section—The Mystery of God's Plan to Make Christ the Head of a New Brotherhood of Man, Embracing Jew and Gentile (1:3–3:21)
  (A) Introductory Hymn: The Mystery Hidden from Eternity (1:3–14)
  (B) The Mystery Revealed to the Church in Which Jew and Gentile Are Reconciled and United in Christ (1:15–2:22)
  (C) Paul's Role as Herald of the Mystery (3:1–13)
  (D) Paul's Prayer and Doxology (3:14–21)
(III) Part II: The Christian Life (4:1–6:17)
  (A) General Principles (4:1–5:20)
    (a) Unity and Growth in the Body of Christ (4:1–16)
    (b) Principles for Spiritual Renewal: The New Man (4:17–5:20)
  (B) Applications for the Christian Home (5:21–6:9)
  (C) Christian Armor (6:10–17)
(IV) Conclusion (6:18–24)

COMMENTARY

13 **(I) Introduction: Greeting, Opening Formula (1:1–2).** The greeting lacks the mention of persons that is usually found in Pauline letters but otherwise follows the usual Pauline pattern. **1.** *apostle:* See comment on Gal 1:1. *by the will of God:* This phrase is not unusual in an introduction, but there are six references to God's will in Eph (1:1,5,9,11; 5:17; 6:6), more than in any other epistle. This underlines a dominant theme in Eph: God's eternal will and plan to create a community of all men in Christ. *to the holy ones:* The term "holy" is used 14 times in Eph, more than in any other letter except Rom, which is much longer. Eph emphasizes the continuity of God's holy people in the OT, now broadened to include the Gentiles. *at Ephesus:* This phrase is missing in some of the best Gk mss. (→ 2 above). Possibly the words were introduced from the title found in early mss. (e.g., P^{46}). *peace:* A common greeting, the word is found seven times in Eph, more than in any other epistle except Rom. It announces a basic theme of Eph, the possibility of unity and harmony among all men through Christ (→ NT Epistles, 47:8).

14 **(II) Part I: Doctrinal Section—The Mystery of God's Plan to Make Christ the Head of a New Brotherhood of Man, Embracing Jew and Gentile (1:3–3:21).**

(A) Introductory Hymn: The Mystery Hidden from Eternity (1:3–14). Pauline letters usually begin with a thanksgiving relevant to the particular community addressed. In Eph, however, the writer passes directly to the praise of God for revealing his plan of salvation. The hymn has a strong baptismal character in its reference to sonship, forgiveness of sins, incorporation into Christ, and the seal of the Spirit. It has been compared to 1 Pt 1:3–12 in its paschal and baptismal character (see J. Cambier, *ZNW* 54 [1963] 58–104; J. Coutts, *NTS* 3 [1957] 115–27; S. Lyonnet, in *A la rencontre de Dieu* [Fest. A. Gelin; Lyons, 1961] 341–52; J. T. Sanders, *ZNW* 51 [1965] 214–32). **3.** *blessed be:* The hymn starts with the traditional Semitic form of recognition or thanksgiving to God, that of pronouncing a blessing and then following it with a list of God's favors or mighty deeds. The loving initiative of the Father inaugurates the mystery. *in the heavenly places:* This phrase (*en tois epouraniois*) is found only in Eph (1:3,20; 2:6; 3:10; 6:12). Its sense: God's ordered plan and activity are now brought into human activity. This is expressed in terms of place because the thought patterns of the original audience depicted God as acting out of one of the spheres of the universe. *in Christ:* This expression in various forms, such as "in him," is repeated over 30 times in Eph, emphasizing the unity of men in Christ through their incorporation into a visible community under his leadership. **4.** *before the foundation of the world:* From all eternity, to show that the choice is not accidental, but part of God's plan from the beginning. *without blemish:* Elsewhere in Paul's letters the adjective *amōmos* occurs only in Eph 5:27 and in Col 1:22. This term is used of OT sacrificial offerings (Lv 1:3,10) and is now applied to the living offering of the Christian uniting himself to Christ, the priest (cf. Heb 9:14). **5.** *predestined us to sonship:* It is not a question of individual predestination but of a selected brotherhood of sons to be saved through Christ. Salvation comes to the believer in and through a community in Christ, not precluding individual salvation by God in some other manner. *through Jesus Christ:* By sharing his unique sonship (cf. Rom 8:15; Gal 4:5). **6.** *for the praise of the glory of his grace:* See 1:12,14. It introduces a recurrent theme in Eph: that men, understanding God's plan, should praise him and give thanks. In the OT, Israel strives to live for his praise (Is 43:21). *in his beloved Son:* The word "beloved" is a strong baptismal reference; cf. the baptism of Jesus in Mk 1:11.

15 **7.** *in him we have redemption:* Redemption (*apolytrōsis*) implies setting free a person or group that is under someone else's power or in slavery. In the OT, it is applied to God liberating his people from slavery in Egypt and acquiring them as his own (cf. Ex 15:13; Dt

7:8). In the NT, Christ is the liberator who sets men free from the bondage of sin. *through his blood* (→ Pauline Theology, 79:87–89). *the forgiveness of sins:* Another baptismal reference (cf. Acts 2:38; Mk 1:4). **9.** *the mystery:* The earliest known occurrences of *mystērion* have a religious sense, referring to secret rites or teachings and initiation into them. Gradually it came to mean a "secret" of any kind. In the OT it is used in this way and also in the sense of a revelation from God (Dn 2:19; → Pauline Theology, 79:32–34; cf. R. E. Brown, *CBQ* 20 [1958] 417–43). In Col *mystērion* refers to the hidden presence and working of Christ (1:25–27), but in Eph it means the hidden plan of God to create a universal community of men in Christ. **10.** *in the fullness of the times:* The word for time, *kairos*, does not refer to the simple lapse of time, as does *chronos*. It signifies a new era in which God will work with all the fullness of his power. *to unite all things in Christ under one head:* The vb. *anakephalaiōsasthai* literally means to place at the top of a column the sum of figures that have been added. *in heaven and on earth:* A way of expressing what we would term the universe. In present-day terms we would say that God's purpose was to give new hope to a world divided by barriers of race, color, culture, or political divisions and make possible a unity among men through Christ. In biblical thought, man is closely related to the universe; Adam is commissioned to "rule over the earth" (Gn 1:28). Christ, the new Adam and the head of a new complete people of God, has been entrusted with the mission of bringing the universe into a state of unity and harmony.

16 **11.** *in him we also have been called to inheritance:* "We also" probably refers to the Jewish people, of whom Paul is a member (cf. Rom 15:7–9). The Jewish people in the OT were often referred to as God's inheritance (cf. Dt 32:9). *who works all things:* Whatever God wills, he works effectively and surely to accomplish. **12.** *we who first hoped in Christ:* This phrase refers either to the Jewish people who had hoped in Christ or to Jewish Christians who had been the first to believe in Jesus. **13.** *in him you also:* That is, the Gentiles. See Rom chs. 9–11 for the sequence in which Jews and Greeks were brought into the people of God. The author of Eph implies that there has never been but one people of God, the Jews, and that the messianic times have made it possible through Christ to associate all men with this people of God (see M. Barth, *Interpr* 17 [1963] 3–24). *the good news of your salvation:* Paul generally uses salvation in an eschatological sense referring to salvation from a future judgment (1 Thes 5:8; Rom 13:11). In Eph this process is already begun in the present experience of the Spirit, which is a proof that the Gentile has been reserved for salvation. *you were sealed:* A seal was a common sign of ownership. Devotees of various pagan gods sometimes branded themselves with the name of the deity to whom they belonged and by whom they were protected. Baptism through the Spirit is the visible sign of incorporation into Christ. *the promised Holy Spirit:* Promised by the prophets, e.g., Ez 36:26; 37:1–14; Jl 2:28f. **14.** *pledge of our inheritance:* The word *arrabōn* is taken from traders' terminology: a down payment to guarantee full payment. The inner sanctifying presence of the Spirit is a guarantee that God has accomplished his promise and will carry it out to completion. The reference to inheritance shows that a future fulfillment is always in the mind of the writer (cf. 2 Cor 1:22).

17 **(B) The Mystery Revealed to the Church in Which Jew and Gentile Are Reconciled and United in Christ (1:15–2:22).**

(a) Prayer for Understanding the Mystery. (1:15–23). Before going further, Paul prays that his readers may receive a full spiritual understanding of the mystery. **15.** *hearing of your faith in the Lord Jesus and of your love for all the saints:* This reading brings out the connection between faith and love. Faith is the commitment to Christ. With this union comes an appreciation of God's great love for men manifested in his Son; this in turn is shown by fraternal love. A number of prominent mss. omit "your love" (*tēn agapēn*). The double mention of "faith and love" may be influenced by Phlm 5. If the original reading had only "faith," the text would then point out the strong relationship to one's neighbor that is implied in faith toward God. **17.** *Father of glory:* This phrase occurs only here in the NT; but cf. Acts 7:2 and 1 Cor 2:8. *a spirit of wisdom and revelation consisting in knowledge of him:* This knowledge (*epignōsis*) is not a conceptual knowledge of facts as emphasized by the Greeks. See comment on Col 1:9. Here in Eph it denotes not knowledge merely of God's plan, but knowledge "of him," an experience of God's great love for men in Christ that would be visibly shown in a true brotherhood of men who had previously been divided by so many social and racial barriers. **19.** *his power:* See comment on 3:7.

18 Enthronement (cf. Ps 110:1) signifies that Jesus in his humanity has now reached a position of equality and association with the Father where all God's power can act through him. **20.** *which he has worked in Christ, raising him from the dead, enthroning him at his right hand in heaven:* The author sees the resurrection, ascension, and glorification of Christ as one great continuous act of the Father. "He has worked" (*energēken*), the pf. tense, connotes an action begun in the past and continuing in its effect until the present. The author does not see this action of God as accomplishing something only in Christ; he sees it as a continuing action experienced and shared by a people, the Church, united to its head. The heavenly realm and all its power have been brought to earth for the believer, who is plunged into the paschal mystery. All God's power is made available to men in Christ. **21.** *above every principality and power:* These are not world rulers or governments. In Col (see comment on 1:16; cf. 2:15) they are angelic spirits, some good and others evil, that were considered to have control over human events and destiny. Christ has conquered them, so that they can have no more power over men; nothing interferes or stands in the way of God's plan for men in Christ. *not only in this age, but in the age to come:* No present or future force or power can block God's work. **22.** *all things he subjected to his feet:* This phrase alludes to Ps 8:7. In this hymn the psalmist extols the glory of Adam as ruler over creation. Christ is the new Adam, the head of a new mankind, who has brought to virtual completion Adam's (man's) assignment by God to dominate the universe (Gn 1:28; cf. Heb 2:6–9). *he gave him as head over all the Church:* "Gave" may have either the sense of the Hebr *nātan*, which can mean "to appoint" (e.g., 1 Kgs 1:48; 2 Chr 1:11), or the sense of a gift, as in Phil 2:9. **23.** *which is his body:* The writer looks at the universal Church as the necessary complement of Christ. He considers them as an organic unity. For him, Christ is the invisible anointed leader and head of a visible world community. *the fullness of him who fills all with all* [or, in a pass. sense] *who is being filled with all:* Exegetes are divided as to both the translation and the meaning of this passage. "Him" may refer to Christ (as in Eph 4:10) or to God who fills Christ and through Christ the Church and the universe (as in Col 1:19 and 2:9). *who fills all:* This is possible because the Gk middle ptc. *plēroumenou* has at times an active sense (cf. Bl-Deb-F § 316); it would then parallel Eph 4:10. *who is being filled* [pass.]*:* The interpretation of some Gk Fathers (Origen, Theodore of Mopsuestia, Chrysostom) would be that all created things are continually contributing to the fullness of Christ. But OT usage would favor the active sense when speaking of God, e.g., Jer 23:24; Ez 43:5.

19 (b) THE MYSTERY REVEALS CHRIST'S BENEFITS TO GENTILE AND JEW (2:1–22). There are striking resemblances in this chapter to the Parable of the Prodigal Son (Lk 15:11–32), as D. M. Stanley points out (see *CBQ* 23 [1961] 26–39). It would seem that the theology of Eph 2 is expressed in story form in Lk. For convenience we arrange the similar elements in two columns:

Eph 2:1–22	Lk 15:11–32
4. God the Father rich in mercy.	**20.** His father saw him and was moved with compassion and ran and fell upon his neck and kissed him.
1. When you were dead... brought us back to life	**24,32.** A refrain: He was dead and has come back to life again; he was lost, and is found.
13. You who were once afar off have been brought near.	**15.** The son goes to a far off country.
19. They become fellow citizens	**22.** The son is restored to the family, given a ring and robe.
14–16. Christ reconciles Jew and Gentile in the Church to form a new man.	**28–32.** The father reconciles the older and younger brother.

20 Chapter 2 is filled with sharp contrasts between human weakness and the result of the operation of God's mighty power. **1.** *when you were dead:* The "you" refers to his Gentile audience. "Death" is spiritual, resulting from sin (cf. Ez 37:1–14; Rom 7:24; Col 2:13). **2.** *the prince of the power of the air:* The air was considered the dwelling place of demons and hence the place of Christ's victory over them (1 Thes 4:17). The writer considers the devil as a personal agent working to stimulate and support the evil done by unbelievers. **3.** *we too were in their company:* The Jews as well as the Gentiles were under the power of sin. The Jews cannot boast that they are superior (Rom 3:9–10). *led our lives in the desires of the flesh:* The flesh itself is not evil, for the Word himself became flesh (Jn 1:14). Paul refers to the body as the instrument of the desires and longings of a self-centered life (cf. Rom 8:4–9; Gal 5:16–21; → Pauline Theology, 79:118–119). *children of wrath:* Deserving of God's judgment, which is described in human terms. **4.** *but God, rich in mercy:* The word "rich" used five times in Eph, is characteristic of the author, who stresses the abundance of God's mercy. **5.** *brought us to life together with Christ:* Three verbs are used: brought to life together, raised together, and enthroned together. Each is prefixed by *syn*, "with." Thus the writer brings out forcibly the intimate association of the Christian with Christ (→ Pauline Theology, 79:137). **8.** *by grace you have been saved:* The Gk pf. participle brings the usual idea of future salvation into the present here, in contrast to other epistles. This realized eschatology in Eph reminds us of Jn and the Ephesus tradition behind it.

21 **11.** *remember, you Gentiles:* Keep in mind the sudden change that God's power made in you who were so estranged. *Gentiles:* Lit., the nations (*ethnē*), the non-Jewish people of the world, separated by race, origin, and election from the Jews, the people of God. *uncircumcised:* Lit., "the foreskin" (see comment on Gal 5:6). Circumcision was the external sign of the covenant. The word "uncircumcised" became a term of opprobrium to describe those not belonging to God's people. *by those called circumcised by human hand:* Thus the author emphasizes that this sign was external only and did not necessarily imply an inner attitude or a real distinction from the Gentiles. He proceeds to describe the desperate former condition of Gentiles. **12.** *without Christ:* They did not have the Jewish messianic hope. *excluded as aliens from the commonwealth of Israel:* "Commonwealth" (*politeia*) or "citizenship" is used only here and in Acts 22:28, where it refers to Roman citizenship. The Gentiles were not citizens of Israel, God's commonwealth. *strangers to the covenants of God's promise:* They had not been included in the great pacts between God and Israel that constituted the people of God (cf. Ex 24:1–11). The writer looks upon these covenants as having an everlasting nature (Is 55:3; Ez 37:26). *having no hope:* Either the messianic hope, or the hope of resurrection (cf. 1 Thes 4:13). *without God:* The term *atheoi* occurs only here in the NT. The sense is not that they were "atheists," or excluded from God; but that they had no true knowledge of him (cf. Acts 17:22–31). **13–14.** A sort of commentary on Is 57:18–19 (LXX): "I have seen his ways and healed him; I have comforted him, giving him true comfort; peace without measure to those who are far off and those who are near. The Lord has said, 'I will heal them.'" The original words referred to the Diaspora Jews who were "afar off," but rabbinic commentary applied the verse to the Gentile converts. They spoke of a proselyte as one who was "brought near" to the covenant. **13.** *have been brought near through the blood of Christ:* In the OT the Jews were brought near to God through the blood of sacrifice (Ex 24:8). In the NT men are brought near to God in a covenant of brotherhood through the sacrifice of Christ (see comment on Eph 1:7).

22 **14.** *he himself is our peace; he has brought the two together:* Christ himself is the bond of unity, the one who has finally succeeded in bringing Jew and Gentile together. *he has broken down the dividing wall:* Like the Berlin wall, this has both a physical and psychological meaning. Josephus tells us that there was a stone partition 3 cubits high separating the outer court of the Temple from the inner court. On this partition were signs prohibiting under pain of death any foreigner from going further (*Ant.* 15.11,5 § 417; *JW* 5.5,2 § 194; 6.2,4 § 125). Such an inscription was actually found by C. Clermont-Ganneau in Jerusalem excavations in 1871 (see *NTB* § 47). One of the reasons why a crowd tried to kill Paul in Jerusalem was that they thought that he had introduced Trophimus, an Ephesian Gentile, into the Temple to defile it (Acts 21:28–31). *the enmity:* The stone wall was but a token of a whole system of separation that went into every phase of life. Since the Jews were God's holy, consecrated people, they were to keep themselves from all defiling influences. The Gentiles were defiled with idol-worship, which was associated with immorality (cf. Rom 1:23–24). Preservation of true worship and a good moral life required separation from subverting influences, and the Law was a protecting fence for the Jewish people. In the words of *Aristeas* (§ 139), "Our Lawgiver fenced us round with impregnable ramparts and walls of iron that we might not mingle at all with any of the nations, but remain pure in body and soul." This fence, however, made real social intercourse impossible. For fear of contamination from idols or foods sacrificed to idols, no Jew could eat with a Gentile or enter his home. The rigorous dietary and legal regulations made any contact a source of anxiety. Some Gentiles admired Jewish purity of morals and were attracted to the synagogue, but others responded with bitter scorn and hatred.

23 **15.** *in his own flesh:* Only the body of Jesus accomplished the miracle of bringing together such disparate groups. There may be a Eucharistic hint in the reference to the flesh of Christ in this verse. Some consider the reference to the breaking down of the wall as an indication that Eph was written after the destruction of the Temple in AD 70. *he annulled the law with its regulations and rules:* The attitude toward the Law is not the same as in Rom; here in Eph, the Law is considered as a dividing force between men, which has been removed by Christ (→ Pauline Theology, 79:42). *he might create of the two a single new humanity:* It is not merely a question of the Gentiles joining the Jews; a new basis of unity and harmony is created in Christ, who has become the true meeting-place of men. **16.** *by the cross:* The cross has been the means of Jesus' own passage to a new humanity and the instrument of his love in reconciling men to one another. **18.** *through him we both have access in one Spirit to the Father:* A trinitarian formula expressing that through Jesus' humanity, the source of the Spirit, men can approach God the Father. Note the prepositions: It is an access *to* the Father, *through* the Son, *in* the Spirit. The word *prosagōgē*, "access," denoted in Oriental courts the introduction of a person into the king's presence. Christ became the *prosagōgēs* who took two separated children, Jews and Gentiles, united them as brothers, and brought them into the intimacy of God's family so that they have become "members of God's household" (2:19).

24 **20.** *you are built on the foundation of the apostles and prophets:* Apostles and prophets are named as recipients of special gifts of the Risen Christ in Eph 4:11. Elsewhere Paul does not so describe his communities, because he himself is usually their apostle and builder. Possibly he is thinking of the universal Church, looking back to its beginnings. Those who support a later date for Eph use this verse as an indication that a second-generation Christian is writing. *with Christ Jesus as the cornerstone:* Cf. Is 28:16. The actual place of this cornerstone in the edifice is not certain, but it is meant to have a cohesive, unifying position and function. **21.** *in him the whole structure is bonded together:* Lit., "every building" or "structure" (*oikodomē*). This causes some exegetes to think that it refers to each local church. Yet the word *oikodomē* may designate the action of building and refer not to local churches but to every work of "edification." The noun is used in this sense in 4:12,16,29 (cf. Rom 14:19; 1 Cor 14:12; 2 Cor 10:8). *and grows:* Similarities to material structures cannot be pressed, for this is a "growing" building. In 1 Pt 2:5 the component members of Christ are described as living stones. **22.** *you also are being built together into a dwelling place:* In 2:21, Christ's part was stressed; now the emphasis is on the role of the members, who as living cells contribute to their mutual growth and to that of the whole organism.

25 **(C) Paul's Role as Herald of the Mystery (3:1–13).** **1.** *prisoner of Christ Jesus:* Paul is writing from prison (4:1; 6:20). "Prisoner" is a title of honor, a distinction that the preacher has gained for having borne witness to the truth; it is the mark of a true apostle (2 Cor 11:23; 6:5; Lk 21:12). **2.** *for you have surely heard:* A possible indication that some readers did not know Paul directly. *the disposition of God's grace given me for your benefit:* The word *oikonomia* is usually used in the NT in the sense of "stewardship" or "task," but here (and in 1:9) it refers to the "dispensation," the realization of God's plan. *grace:* God's favor was shown to Paul not for himself but for others. **6.** *coheirs, companions, and copartners:* Moffatt's translation, using the Eng prefix *co*, attempts to reproduce the force of the three Gk words beginning with forms of *syn: sygklēronoma, sysōma, symmetocha.* The second word, *sysōma* (lit., "sharing the same body") is probably an *ad hoc* creation of the writer, since it is found only in Christian Gk literature.

26 **7.** *according to the working of his power:* In the NT this redundant phrase is found only in Eph (here and 1:19), and it expresses the theme of God's mighty power overcoming humanly impossible obstacles. **8.** *the very least of all the saints:* Paul points to his own call as an example of the grace and favor of God. He had done nothing to merit it; on the contrary, he had persecuted the Church. Christ had literally to "capture" him (Phil 3:12). **9.** *who created all things:* God's work in creating the universe looked to his universal work of restoring the universe by placing the fullness of his power in the Church. This has forced the principalities and powers (see comment on Col 1:16) to recognize the wisdom of God's plan being realized in Christ. **12.** *we have access to God with freedom:* "Freedom" (*parrēsia*) usually refers to speech with assurance and confidence (e.g., 6:20; Acts 4:31; Phil 1:20). **13.** *my sufferings for you:* Paul considers his sufferings in prison to be for others, just as Christ's life was given over for men (cf. 2 Cor 4:12–15).

27 **(D) Paul's Prayer and Doxology (3:14–21).** **14.** *for this reason I kneel:* The usual position of prayer was standing (e.g., Mk 11:25; Lk 18:11,13). Kneeling would be a more solemn, intense expression. **14–15.** *the Father from whom every family in heaven and on earth takes its name:* The word *patria* (family or clan) is a play on *patēr* (father). There is no NT doctrine of a universal fatherhood of God. It is only through Christ that men become true sons of God (Rom 8:15; Gal 4:5). However, this sonship may be the goal and apex toward which every human relation can move. "In heaven" is a possible reference to a belief in Gnostic "families" or "generations" thought to control the universe. **17.** *Christ dwelling through faith in your hearts:* Usually Paul refers to the Spirit dwelling in men. Yet the Risen Christ and the Spirit are interchangeable in Rom 8:9–11 (→ Pauline Theology, 79:75). This is because the Risen Jesus is the source of the Spirit (cf. Acts 2:33). **18.** *the breadth and length and height and depth:* In Stoic philosophy these terms express the totality of the universe. The writer may be using them to express the universal extension and power of Christ's love, or he may be influenced by Rom 8:39. **19.** *surpasses all knowledge:* *Gnōsis* as ordered, systematized knowledge of the universe was highly prized by the Greeks. But for Paul an experiential knowledge of the love of God manifested in the person of Christ infinitely surpassed all human knowledge. Only the believer reaches to the fullness of God's nature as a loving person and all its transforming power.

28 **20–21.** The closing doxology of Paul's prayer. **21.** *in the Church and in Christ Jesus:* This expression, placing the Church and Christ Jesus side by side, is unique; yet it shows that to say "in the Church" or "in Christ Jesus" is the same thing. The Church and Christ are necessary complements of each other.

29 **(III) Part II: The Christian Life (4:1–6:17).**

(A) General Principles (4:1–5:20):

(a) UNITY AND GROWTH IN THE BODY OF CHRIST (4:1–16). The doxology in 3:20–21 marks the end of a section. Chapters 4–6 deal with practical applications in the Christian life. Those called to partake of the great mystery described above must live a life worthy of that calling. **2.** *in all humility:* In Gk lists, humility is not a virtue; on the contrary, in Gk literature *tapeinophrosynē* connotes "mean-spiritedness." Christ, however, raised self-effacing service of others to the dignity of a virtue by his example. *in patience:* Toward others, by being slow to retaliate (1 Cor 13:4; Gal 5:22; Col 3:12). **3.** *to preserve that unity whose source is the Spirit:* The Spirit is the single inner source of the Christian life and as such is continually moving all members toward what promotes peace and harmony. Eph is the epistle of Christian unity. There follows a beautiful sevenfold formula of unity. As a result of Jewish influence, the early Church had a deep appreciation of the oneness of the God who dwelt in their community. Twice a day the Jews prayed in the words of Dt 6:4: "Hear, O Israel, the Lord our God is one Lord...." They believed that the eschatological era would bring a great revelation of God's oneness to the world. "On that day there shall be one Lord, and his name shall be one" (Zech 14:9 [LXX]). Each of the seven expressions brings out an aspect of the basic unity. **4.** *one body:* One external visible community. *one Spirit:* A single inner source. *one hope:* The Spirit is the pledge of the future unified community (1:14). **5.** *one Lord:* Christians pledge obedience to one master (*Kyrios*) in their baptismal profession of faith (Rom 10:9). *one faith:* The relationship of Eph to the Pastorals makes it possible that "faith" means here a fixed body of doctrine (cf. 1 Tm 3:9; 6:21). However, the dynamic sense of personal adherence to Christ is common in Eph (e.g., 1:15; 3:12). *one baptism:* In 1 Cor 1:10–18 Paul uses the fact that Christians have been "plunged" into one Christ by baptism as a proof that there can be no divisions in the community by adherence to human leaders (cf. Gal 3:27). **6.** *one God and Father of all:* They are bonded together as brothers, children of one Father.

30 In vv. 7–16 the author explains that within this basic unity there are diverse gifts from the Risen Christ so that each member may contribute in a unique way to the growth and progress of the Church. In Rom 12:3–8 and 1 Cor 12:1–31 there are similar lists of gifts. However, there are some striking differences: (1) In Eph, it is a question of the universal Church and not particular communities. The gifts are concentrated in certain "offices" within the Church. No mention is made of individual charismatic gifts of tongues, healing, etc., as in 1 Cor. (2) In Eph, the source and distributor of the gifts is the Risen Christ; in 1 Cor, it is the Spirit; in Rom, it is simply God. This points to the close relationship between the Risen Lord and the Spirit. (3) In 1 Cor, we have a "horizontal" picture of the body of Christ: Head, hands, feet, all refer to Christians having various gifts due to the working of the one Spirit in all. In Eph it is a "vertical" picture: Christ is the head (4:15), the vitalizing, unifying force of the body whose members are joined to him. **8.** *ascending on high, he took a host of captives and gave gifts to men:* Ps 68:19 is quoted. The original sense of the verse refers to God leading his people in a triumphant march through the desert into Canaan, where he effects a great victory with many captives and much spoil. However, rabbinic exegesis interpreted this verse with reference to Moses, who ascended Mt. Sinai to receive the Law from God and give it as a gift to men (see Str-B 3, 596). With this meaning in mind, the Ps was read in the synagogue lectionary for Pentecost, the feast that commemorated the giving of the Law. Paul's reading of the Ps is found neither in the MT nor in the LXX. He has either adapted it for his own purpose or, more probably, taken over a rabbinic midrash; but he gives his own Christian exegesis of the Ps. The general sense is this: Christ ascended in victory into the heavens in order to give men on earth the gift of the Spirit to be exercised in the various ministries of the Church. The writer asks to what "ascending on high" refers, and he answers that it implies that "he first descended to the low regions of the earth." According to some exegetes this would mean the region of the dead, as in the creeds, "he descended into hell." In support of this theory they cite the parallel in 1 Pt 3:19 and 4:6. Others—and their interpretation seems more probable—regard it as descriptive of Christ's incarnation and earthly life, in view of his heavenly risen life (cf. J. Cambier, *NTS* 9 [1963] 262–75). **10.** *above all the heavens:* The ancients thought there were various ascending levels of "spheres" or "heavens" above the earth, each containing the sun, or moon, or planets (see comment on 2 Cor 12:2). The writer wishes to show that the Exalted Christ is beyond the limitations of such spheres and that his power and active presence extend to all the universe.

31 **11.** *he himself gave:* This is a continuation of the exegesis of the Ps. The exalted Christ gives his gifts to his members in the Church. For a parallel concept of an "ascending" and "descending" Son of Man, see Jn 3:13. *apostles* (→ Aspects NT Thought, 78:177). *prophets:* In 1 Cor 14:1 Paul states that all Christians can aim at this gift. A prophet is an inspired preacher who encourages, warns, or stimulates the community (1 Cor 14:3). His sincerity and conviction provoke a like response on the part of others (1 Cor 14:23). When a community is together studying the word of God it is the man with the gift of prophecy who is able to understand its meaning for the community and to express it with conviction, so that he is a source of courage to others. *evangelists:* Philip is called an "evangelist" (Acts 21:8), although this may be a nickname. Timothy is told to fulfill the ministry of an evangelist (2 Tm 4:5). The office may refer to some type of traveling preacher. *pastors and teachers:* These are named together as if to designate the same office. In Acts 20:28 Paul speaks of the pastoral nature of the office of *presbyter* (cf. also Jn 21:16). The Pastoral Epistles stress the function of the bishop or presbyter as a teacher (e.g., 1 Tm 3:2; Ti 1:9). **12.** *for the equipment of the saints, for work in his service:* The various gifts are given by the Spirit to men to equip all the faithful for work in Christ's service. **13.** *knowledge of the son of God:* The epistles rarely employ the title "Son of God" (Rom 1:4; Gal 2:20). When they do, it denotes Jesus Christ as man. Here, knowledge of the Son of God means acquiring the image of the perfect man, who reaches maturity in Christ by living the type of human life that was characteristic of Jesus as Son of God. This embodies a new relation to God as Father and a new relation of brotherly respect and love to one's neighbor. **14.** *may no longer be children:* See 1 Cor 3:1; 14:20. The work of Christ in the Church is not primarily to find people who are already mature and responsible, but to bring men to maturity who through weakness are as "children" (cf. C. Morrison, *Interpr* 17 [1963] 387–401). **15–16.** These verses emphasize that progress and growth whereby each member, exercising his gift and function for the benefit of all, will contribute to the upbuilding of the whole body of Christ. **16.** *in love: Agapē* is used by Paul in a dynamic sense. It is the acting directive force behind the gifts (1 Cor 13:1–14:1). It moves a man to exercise his gifts in view of building up others in the community, rather than for his own edification. "In love" is equivalent to "in Christ" (cf. N. Johansson, *NTS* 10 [1964] 383–92). For Christ did not please himself (Rom 15:3), but put aside his own interests so that his whole life might be directed to building up a community, the Church.

32 (b) Principles for Spiritual Renewal: The New Man (4:17–5:20). In this section the sharp contrasts between the former pagan life of the addressees and their new life in Christ, as well as the frequent references to the liturgy of baptism prompt H. Schlier to posit that the community could not have been converts very long. **17–19.** The harsh references to pagan moral life may be derived from ordinary Jewish polemic (cf. Rom 1:21–32). **22.** *put off the old man:* Cf. Col 3:9. The "old man" denotes the type of life they led with merely the resources belonging to human nature as sons of Adam. It was a life in which human weakness prompted countless moral failures that caused permanent spiritual death (Rom 8:13; Gal 6:8). The sequence, "put off," "renew" (4:23), "put on" (4:24), belongs to a baptismal liturgy. The candidate removed his old clothes, was plunged into the water, and then put on new white clothing. The outward signs signified the inner change: that he had put aside his former life, that he had "plunged" himself into Christ through faith, and was now, in Christ, beginning a new manner of life. **24.** *the new man:* This refers to incorporation into Christ himself, the new Adam, the head of a renewed humanity sharing his Spirit. It connotes the attainment of all that man (since Adam means "man") was intended to be when God first made him according to his image (Gn 1:27).

33 Verses 25–32 outline the new motivation for a good moral life that belongs to those who share Christ's renewed humanity. It is no longer a question of right and wrong; it is a matter of respect for brothers in Christ and a realization of how our actions can affect them. As a consequence, lying means lack of fidelity to members of the same body (4:26). To give up stealing should be the occasion of beginning to work hard. A motive for such hard work would be to have something to share with the poor (4:28). We may note the constant emphasis that Paul places on sharing material goods with the poor (cf. Rom 15:26; 2 Cor 8–9; Gal 2:10; 1 Cor 11:22). A motive for avoiding bad language is the thought that good speech can be an occasion of grace for others (4:29). **30.** *do not grieve God's Holy Spirit:* Injury to one's neighbor means a lack of respect and reverence for the Spirit who dwells in men of faith (2:22). *in whom you were sealed:* See comments on 1:13–14. **32.** *forgiving one another:* The vb. *charizomai* is used, indicating that forgiveness is not merely the remission of a debt but a generous expression to others of the same forgiving love that Christ has first shown to us.

34 **5:1.** *be imitators of God as very dear children:* Chapter divisions are artificial and sometimes break up the sense. This verse is closely related to the preceding one: be imitators of God's way of forgiving. In the Semitic use reflected in the NT, "children" often connotes the imitation of qualities rather than an ontological state; e.g., in the Sermon on the Mount, Christians are to be "children of their Father in heaven" by imitating the Father's universal love for men (Mt 5:45–47). The perfect model of a child of God is found in Christ. **2.** *gave himself for us:* The crowning point of his life was the giving of himself as a sacrifice of love for others. Following his way, the Christian walks in love by laying down his life for others, as in 1 Jn 3:16, "In this we have come to know his love, that he laid down his life for us; and we likewise ought to lay down our life for the brethren." *an offering and fragrant sacrifice to God:* The OT terminology of sacrifice is applied to Christ's personal offering. The words *prosphora* and *thysia* (offering and sacrifice) are found together in Ps 39:7 (LXX). In OT sacrifices, the fragrant odor ascending to the Lord is often mentioned (Ex 29:18; Lv 3:5). In Ez 20:41 God promises to accept the people themselves as a sweet odor of sacrifice. In the OT, the individual needed a go-between, a priest who would make an offering to enable the worshiper to gain access to God. Christ is that priest and mediator in the NT, and the offering is the gift of himself for men. The Christian is called to participate actively in Christ's priesthood by joining his own sacrifice of love for others to that of his Master. **3–4.** This sharing of the sacrificial life of Christ gives the believer's life a sacredness that will stand in marked contrast to the practices of certain men. **4.** *thanksgiving:* Continual recognition of his new holiness will be characteristic of the Christian. **5.** *kingdom of Christ and God:* This phrase is unique in the NT; but cf. Col 1:13, "the kingdom of his beloved Son." The writer closely associates God's kingdom with that of Christ, who as the Son is to bring all things to the Father (1 Cor 15:22–28).

35 Verses 7–14 bring out the strong contrasts existing between Christian and pagan life in terms of light and darkness. There was apparently a tendency of some men influenced by Gnostic teaching to believe that they were "illumined" and "above" any consideration of good and evil. **6.** *the wrath of God:* See comment on Rom 1:18. **8.** *you are light...children of light:* The contrast of light and darkness employed here resembles the dualism of Qumran, where "darkness" denotes men who are opposed to God and "light" the chosen members of the Essene community. The same contrast is applied to Christians (see 1QS 1:9–10; 1QM 1:1,16; 3:6,9; cf. 1 Thes 5:5). Recall especially the catalogue of vices and virtues in 1QS 4:2–14 in a highly dualistic context (cf. H. Braun, *TRu* 29 [1963] 240). **11.** *unfruitful works of darkness:* Cf. Gal 5:19–21. Qumran parallels can be found in 1QS 2:7; 1QM 15:9. **14.** *awake, sleeper; arise from the dead, and Christ will enlighten you:* This is probably a fragment of an ancient Christian hymn used in a baptismal liturgy; it is heavily influenced by several texts of Is (26:10; 60:1; 9:2). It may even belong with that in 1 Tm 3:16. Taken together, they would form a hymn to the exalted Christ, who awakens men from the sleep of death (cf. Jn 11:11) and brings them to life in a new creative act resembling the very creation of light itself (see D. M. Stanley, *CBQ* 20 [1958] 173–91; K. G. Kuhn, "Der Epheserbrief im Lichte der Qumrantexte," *NTS* 7 [1960–61] 334–46). G. W. MacRae points out that the hymn has language borrowed from early Gnostic sources (*The Origins of Gnosticism* [NuSup 12; Leiden, 1967] 506).

36 **15–17.** These verses develop the theme of the wisdom of God that should be manifested in Christian life through prudent action, alertness to God's inspiration in the present time of opportunity, and an eagerness for the Lord's designs. **17.** *the will of the Lord:* This is always "God's" will in the rest of Pauline literature. The writer may have slipped into this phraseology almost unwittingly because God and Christ were so closely connected in his mind, perhaps too because of the baptismal promises to Christ the *Kyrios*. **18.** *do not be drunk with wine:* Probably a reference to Prv 23:30 (LXX). The sense of the allusion is strengthened by what follows in the proverb "but converse with just men." Paul parallels this in the words, "speaking to one another" (5:19). There was abundant use of wine in the mystery cults and at times abuses in Christian gatherings (1 Cor 11:21). The writer states that joyful fellowship should result rather from being filled with the Spirit, who prompts them to encourage one another and sing hymns to the exalted Christ. **19.** *psalms and hymns:* Cf. Acts 16:25; 1 Cor 14:26; Col 3:16 (see comment); Jas 5:13.

37 **(B) Applications for the Christian Home (5:21–6:9).** Cf. Col 3:18–4:1. **21.** *be subject to one another out of reverence for Christ:* This saying begins a *Haustafel*. It announces a principle that will be successively applied to the relations between husband and wife, children and parents, slaves and masters. Christ's self-sacrificing love for others (5:1) is now the model for home life. **22.** *as to the Lord:* This new motivation is added throughout this section (5:21; 6:2,5). We are not told the exact reason for this. It may be because the relationships between Christians must be accompanied by a reverence for Christ's fellow members, as in 4:25. Or more probably, because Christ by his victorious exaltation fills the universe (1:20–23; 4:10) and has brought his power and presence to bear in all human institutions.

Devoted service and excellence within these should then be regarded as a personal service to Christ himself.

38 **25.** *husbands, love your wives just as Christ loved the Church and gave himself up for her:* This presentation of Christ's love for the Church as a model for married love is unique in the NT. Yet for a general frame the writer could have used Col 1:22. For the idea of Christ giving himself up for others, see Gal 2:20. For the image of the Church as the chaste bride of Christ, see 2 Cor 11:2. Verses 24–25 are a particular application of 5:1, where the Christian is invited to make his life a sacrifice of love for others like that of Christ. When husband and wife do this by subjection and love, or mutual self-giving, then their married love will be a visible sign that they are imitating and sharing this invisible action of Christ. **26.** *purifying her in the bath of water by means of the word:* The image is derived from the ceremonial bath of the bride before marriage. The only other place in the NT where the word *loutron* (bath, washing) occurs is in Ti 3:5 where "the bath of regeneration and renewal by the Holy Spirit" refers to baptism. The phrase "by the word" may allude to either the baptismal formula or the confession of faith. **27.** *so that he might present the Church to himself:* This completes the image of the presentation of the bride to her husband. The Christian counterpart is the presentation of the cleansed, newly clothed candidates to Christ. However, the word "present" (*paristēmi*) is at times used by Paul in reference to the presentation of men at the Second Coming (2 Cor 4:14; Rom 14:10; cf. Col 1:27–28). This would parallel the presentation of the chaste virgin to Christ in 2 Cor 11:2. According to Jewish custom, there was a lapse of time between the contract or espousal and the presentation of the bride to her husband. This could parallel the time interval between the contract at baptism and the final presentation of the bride to Christ at the Second Coming (cf. R. A. Batey, *Interpr* 17 [1963] 176–82). In Ap the consummation of God's kingdom is presented in the form of a marriage between the Lamb and his spouse (21:2–3,9). *without blemish:* See comment on Eph 1:4. In view of the context, the writer may have in mind the description of the bride without blemish in Ct 4:7. **31.** *for this reason a man shall leave his father and mother:* Gn 2:24 is quoted. Because these words are in Scripture, rabbinical exegesis brought out that the Holy Spirit certified the sacredness of marriage relations. The rabbinic term for marriage is *qiddûšîn* (sanctification or sanctities). **32.** *this is a great mystery: Mystērion* is translated in the Vg by "sacramentum," which does not mean "sacrament" in our modern sense. *Mystērion* is the Pauline word for "God's long-hidden secret" (→ Pauline Theology, 79:32–34). As understood here, it means that the verse in Gn has a hidden meaning, only now understood. *I mean in reference to Christ and the Church:* The text of Gn, which expresses the sacred nature of marriage, foreshadowed in the bond of husband and wife the union of Christ and his spouse, the Church (→ Pauline Theology 79:165). **33.** *each should love his wife as he loves himself:* This is a return to the literal meaning of Gn 2:24; if husband and wife are to be two in one flesh, then the husband must love his wife as himself, i.e., as his own flesh.

(Johnston, L., "The Mystery of Marriage," *Scr* 11 [1959] 1–6. Robilliard, J.-A., "Le symbolisme du mariage selon Saint Paul," *RSPT* 21 [1932] 242–47.)

39 **6:1–9.** The admonitions for children and parents, slaves and masters are a slight expansion of Col 3:18–4:1 (→ Letter Col, 55:29). The author, with his fondness for quoting Scripture, gives the Fourth Commandment in full in 6:2. In his mind, quoting God's words in reference to obedience to parents adds a whole note of reverence to this duty. Eph also adds that fathers should take care to give their children a Christian upbringing.

40 **(C) Christian Armor (6:10–17).** **10.** *draw strength from the Lord and his mighty power:* These words begin a section whose theme is the Christian's source of power and strength in face of satanic opposition and hostile heavenly powers. **11.** *wiles of the devil:* An expression found only here in the NT. *diabolos* (devil) occurs only in Eph and the Pastorals. Paul usually has *satanas.* **12.** *our battle is not against flesh and blood:* The struggle is not against a human enemy, so different weapons will be needed. *principalities and powers:* See comment on Col 1:16. In Eph these beings are hostile to man, whereas in Col they do not appear necessarily so. *the rulers of this world of darkness:* This is probably another class of hostile spirits. The expression "rulers of this world" aptly describes the function that people of the time considered them to have; spirits were thought to have a decisive control over human events. This led to a fatalistic attitude toward daily life on the part of those who believed in them. Those who have lived in pagan cultures where this is believed have felt the depressing psychological effects such an environment can have. It gives people a sense of futility in their efforts to face a controlled world whose governing powers are completely beyond them. The Christian, however, has new weapons to fight these hostile beings, and hence has a new freedom from their control. *darkness:* This word expresses the gloom and lack of hope for a world under such unfriendly spirits (see D. E. H. Whiteley, *ExpT* 68 [1956–57] 100–103). **13.** *take up the armor of God:* The figure is taken from the OT where God arms himself as a warrior to defend his people. The descriptions are taken both from the armor of the Roman soldier and the OT descriptions of the divine armor (Is 59:17f.; Wis 5:17–20). The standard equipment of the Christian is the truth of his faith and the word of God, which is the expression of his belief.

41 **(IV) Conclusion (6:18–24).** **18–20.** Request for prayers. The author enjoins his readers to pray, in face of the hostile powers he has named. He likewise believes in the "communion of saints," that the prayers of others are needed so that he can preach the gospel boldly and freely (*en parrēsia*). **21–22.** Commendation of Tychicus; cf. Col 4:7–8, where 33 Gk words are exactly the same. It is possible that Tychicus was the bearer of both Col and Eph. **23–24.** Final blessing. The two elements of the usual Pauline greeting, "grace" and "peace," are here inverted in the developed farewell greeting with which Eph ends (→ NT Epistles, 47:8).

57

THE PASTORAL LETTERS

George A. Denzer

BIBLIOGRAPHY

1 Bardy, G., *Épîtres pastorales* (*PSB* 12; 3rd ed.; Paris, 1951). Bernard, J. H., *The Pastoral Epistles with Introduction and Notes* (CGTSC; Cambridge, 1899). Boudou, A., *Les Épîtres pastorales* (VS 15; Paris, 1950). Dibelius, M., *Die Pastoralbriefe* (HNT 13; 3rd ed.; rev. by H. Conzelmann; Tübingen, 1955). Dornier, P., *Les Épîtres de Saint Paul à Timothée et à Tite* (BJ; 2nd ed.; Paris, 1958). Easton, B., *The Pastoral Epistles* (N.Y., 1947). Falconer, R., *The Pastoral Epistles: Introduction, Translation and Notes* (Oxford, 1937). Freundorfer, J., *Die Pastoralbriefe* (RNT 7; 3rd ed.; Regensburg, 1959). Gealy, F., *The First and Second Epistles to Timothy and the Epistle to Titus* (*IB* 11; N.Y., 1955). Harrison, P. N., *The Problem of the Pastoral Epistles* (London, 1921). Holtz, G., *Die Pastoralbriefe* (ThHkNT 13; Berlin, 1965). Jeremias, J., *Die Briefe an Timotheus und Titus* (NTD 9; 7th ed.; Göttingen, 1954). Kelly, J. N. D., *A Commentary on the Pastoral Epistles* (BNTC; N.Y., 1963). Lock, W., *The Pastoral Epistles* (ICC; N.Y., 1924). Scott, E. F., *The Pastoral Epistles* (MNTC; N.Y., 1936). Spicq, C., *Les Épîtres pastorales* (EBib; Paris, 1947); "Pastorales (Épîtres)," *VDBS* 7 (1961) 1–73.

Cerfaux, L., R-F, *INT* 510–25. F-B 258–72. Guthrie, *NTI* 1, 198–246. Metzger, B. M., *IPLAP* 119–26. Wik *NTI* 437–52.

INTRODUCTION

2 **(I) The Pastoral Letters as a Group.** The two letters to Timothy and the letter to Titus are grouped together because of similarities in content and form. They alone of the Pauline corpus were addressed to individuals in charge of a local church. Timothy was Paul's legate in the region of Ephesus, and Titus was his legate on the island of Crete. The purpose of the three letters is to instruct Timothy and Titus on the direction of local Christian communities. Paul stresses the following recommendations: to adhere faithfully to the traditional deposit of the faith, to defend the faith against heretical teachings, to appoint qualified officials in the local communities, to regulate public worship, and to exhort the faithful to lead exemplary lives in accordance with the duties of their state in life. These letters also have a common style and vocabulary, and apparently they were written during the same period. The heretical teachings are essentially the same in the three epistles. They represent a form of Jewish Gnosticism.

This brief summary shows that there is good reason for calling them the "Pastoral Letters." They are addressed to the legates over the churches of Ephesus and Crete, and they give instructions on the pastoral direction of these communities.

3 **(II) Recipients.** The Pastorals are addressed to Timothy, who presided over the Ephesian church, and to Titus, who occupied the same position on the island of Crete.

Timothy is well known from Acts and the Pauline epistles. He first appears in Acts as a native of Lystra in Asia Minor (16:1ff.). His father was a pagan, his mother a Jewess. When Paul came to Lystra on Mission I (*ca.* AD 47), Timothy became one of his converts (1 Tm 1:2). Later (*ca.* 49), when Paul passed through Lystra again on Mission II, Timothy joined his company. From that time on, according to frequent references in Acts and the epistles, Timothy remained one of Paul's most faithful companions and fellow workers. He was often the recipient of Paul's special trust and often his legate on difficult missions.

Timothy was in Rome during Paul's house arrest (Col 1:1; Phlm 1). When Paul was released, he resumed his missionary activity and again undertook a journey through the eastern lands of the Mediterranean. He visited Ephesus and left Timothy there as his representative. Subsequently, Paul wrote to Timothy the two epistles that have come down to us.

Timothy was rather young when he presided over the church at Ephesus (1 Tm 4:12). Several passages in the epistles indicate he was timid by nature and 1 Tm 5:23 mentions that he suffered from ill health.

4 The Pauline epistles give us a fair amount of information on Titus, whereas Acts does not mention him. According to Ti 1:4, he was converted by Paul himself. In Gal 2:1ff. Titus appeared as a companion of Paul and Barnabas at the Council of Jerusalem, and we

learn that he was a pagan before his conversion. During Mission III, Paul sent Titus on a difficult mission to Corinth. Titus rejoined Paul in Macedonia, whence he was sent back to Corinth to complete the collection for the Christians of Jerusalem (2 Cor 7:5ff.; 8:23ff.). The next mention of Titus is in the Pastorals. During the missionary journey that Paul undertook after his Roman house arrest, he left Titus in charge of the Cretan church. Subsequently, Paul wrote to him the epistle that we have. In it he told Titus that Artemas or Tychicus would take his place in Crete, and then he was to meet Paul at Nicopolis (3:12). The last information we have is that Titus went to Dalmatia (2 Tm 4:10), doubtless to carry on missionary activity there.

Although the Pastorals are addressed personally to Timothy and Titus, Paul certainly meant the letters for all the members of the community. This is apparent from the contents and text of the letters. The concluding salutation in each of the letters is in the plural: "Grace be with you"; Ti 3:15 adds "all."

5 **(III) Time and Place of Composition.** The Pastorals cannot be fitted into the framework of Paul's life as we know it from Acts and the other epistles. They could have been written only after the Roman house arrest with which Acts closes (→ Life of Paul, 46:43–44). If Paul undertook a missionary journey to the eastern Mediterranean, he might have gone to Crete first. When he left Crete, Titus might have remained there as his legate (Ti 1:5). From Crete, Paul might have gone to Asia Minor. When he left Ephesus for Macedonia, Timothy remained as his legate (1 Tm 1:3). Possibly, Paul passed through Troas on his way to Macedonia (2 Tm 4:13), and there wrote 1 Tm and Ti (*ca.* AD 65). Paul then perhaps spent the winter at Nicopolis in Epirus (Ti 3:12). The following spring he might have returned to Ephesus, according to his plan (1 Tm 3:14; 4:13). It would seem that he was then arrested in the region of Ephesus (2 Tm 1:4). In the course of Paul's voyage to Rome as a prisoner, the ship might have stopped at Miletus and Corinth (2 Tm 4:20). During his imprisonment in Rome, Paul wrote 2 Tm (*ca.* 67). In this letter, Paul is without hope of being released; he expects to be condemned and to suffer martyrdom in the near future (2 Tm 4:6–8).

6 **(IV) Authenticity.** Each of the Pastoral Epistles begins with an address in which the writer identifies himself as Paul. In the course of the letters, the writer mentions experiences that we know belong to the life of Paul: The writer had been a bitter persecutor of the Church before his call to the service of Christ (1 Tm 1:12–16); he suffered for the faith at Antioch, Iconium, and Lystra (2 Tm 3:11). The early Church attributed these letters to Paul, and the evidence is as early and as clear as that for the letters universally admitted to be Paul's writings. Nevertheless, since the beginning of the 19th cent. a widespread opinion has maintained that Paul was not the author of the Pastorals. According to this view, the letters were written by some unknown author about the year AD 100 or later. However, it must be mentioned immediately that most opponents of Pauline authorship admit that some passages in the Pastorals come from Paul himself. Further, a good number of non-Catholic authors join with Catholic scholars in defending Pauline authorship.

7 The arguments advanced against Pauline authorship can be summarized as follows: (1) The errors described in the Pastorals are Gnostic errors of the 2nd cent.; (2) the stage of organization in the Christian communities is that of the early 2nd cent.; (3) the style and vocabulary are so different from the genuine Pauline epistles that they cannot be from the same author; (4) the tone of the Pastorals, emphasizing the fixity of the corpus of traditional truths, the good works of Christians, and the organization of the community, is opposed to the inspirational, instructive, and mystical spirit of the Pauline epistles.

The following response can be given to these arguments, some of which have lost a good deal of support even among opponents of Pauline authorship:

8 (1) The Pastorals present the false teachers as men who claim to be teachers of the Mosaic Law. These men indulge in Jewish fables and endless speculation on genealogies. They are proud and infatuated with their false knowledge. They lose themselves in vain discussions and controversies over words. Their teachings reflect a dualistic spirit involving an abhorrence of the material: The resurrection of Christians has already taken place; marriage is forbidden; abstinence from certain foods is enjoined. Their preaching is motivated by financial gain. For the relevant texts, see 1 Tm 1:4–7; 4:1–7; 6:4–5,20–21; 2 Tm 2:17,23; Ti 1:10–11,14–15; 3:9. As the opponents of Pauline authorship now commonly admit, these false teachings do not suit the developed Gnosticism of the 2nd cent. They reflect a form of Jewish Gnosticism that is attested to from other sources for the time of the apostle.

9 (2) It is incorrect to say that the ecclesiastical organization of the local Christian communities as reflected in the Pastorals has the fully developed form of the 2nd cent. Rather, it agrees with what other sources indicate for the middle of the 1st cent.

The epistles of Ignatius of Antioch (martyred *ca.* AD 117) reflect a fully developed organization in the local Christian communities. Each church is under the direction of a single bishop, who alone has proper episcopal powers. Subordinate to the bishop is a group of priests. The deacons are next in rank. There is a sharp distinction in power between the monarchical bishop and the priests; the two terms are not interchangeable.

The Pastorals, however, reflect a less developed organization. There is no single local head of the community with proper episcopal powers. In each church there is a group of presbyters (*presbyteroi*), who are also called *episkopoi.* The head of each community, who alone exercises proper episcopal powers, is Paul or one of his legates (Timothy in the area of Ephesus, and Titus on the island of Crete). The pertinent texts are 1 Tm 3:1–13; 5:17–25; and Ti 1:5–9. The deacons are in a subordinate position.

This form of ecclesiastical organization in the Pastorals agrees with what we find in other NT passages, such as Acts 20 and Phil 1:1. In Acts 20:17 Paul refers to the leaders of the church in Ephesus (*ca.* AD 58) as *presbyteroi*; later in the same address he refers to the same persons as *episkopoi* (20:28). In the introduction to Phil, probably written *ca.* AD 56–57, Paul addresses *episkopoi* and *diakonoi.* He does not mention *presbyteroi,* and this would be inexplicable if the term "bishops" were not a synonym for presbyters.

(See Benoit, P., "Les origines de l'épiscopat dans le Nouveau Testament," *Exégèse et théologie* [Paris, 1961] 2, 232–46. Kelly, J. N. D., *The Pastoral Epistles,* 3–36.)

10 (3) The strongest argument against the Pauline authorship of the Pastorals is their style and vocabulary. The style of the Pastorals is often static and colorless. It lacks much of the vigor and vivacity of the other Pauline epistles. The vocabulary is also special. Many Pauline terms and phrases are found in the Pastorals, but many of the characteristic expressions of Paul are lacking. Conversely, words and phrases repeated in the Pastorals are not found in the other letters. Statistically, one-third of the words in the Pastorals are not found elsewhere in Paul.

In explaining these differences some defenders of Pauline authorship (e.g., J. Jeremias) have recourse to the hypothesis of a secretary. Paul would have used a secretary in writing the Pastorals (cf. Rom 16:22; 2 Thes 3:17; Gal 6:11), and the style and phraseology would be due partly to the influence of this secretary. Other authors insist that Pauline authorship does not require the hypothesis of a secretary. They point out, first, that the differences have been exaggerated. For example, although it is true that one-third of the words in the Pastorals are special, more than two-thirds of these words are derivatives or compounds of words found in the other Pauline epistles. Further, there are explanations for the differences. The Pastorals have a definite purpose and contents, and this fact easily explains many of the differences in style and vocabulary. Again, Paul was a man of rich and versatile personality, a person who could not be confined to certain fixed forms of expression; so, for example, there are considerable differences between Rom and Gal or between 1 Thes and 1 Cor. Finally, in regard to vocabulary, the number of words that belong to the common vocabulary of Paul, as compared with special terms, is approximately the same in the Pastorals as in the other Pauline epistles.

11 (4) The Pastorals have indeed a different tone and emphasis from the other Pauline epistles. However, this difference does not prove different authorship. It may reflect different circumstances and purpose. The greater stress on good works and the organization of the Christian community is prompted by the purpose of the Pastorals, i.e., to give instructions on the interior and exterior conduct of the Christian community. The Pastorals refer to the truths of faith as a fixed deposit handed down in the Church and safeguarded by it because that stage of development had been reached when these letters were written. Orthodoxy plays a great role in the Pastorals because they were directed largely against heretical teaching. These differences are not to be exaggerated. In the other epistles, too, Paul emphasizes the importance of good works, and faith involves the acceptance of truths handed down from the time of Christ. In the Pastorals, as elsewhere, the mercy of God and his gifts of grace are the foundation of the Christian life and the basis of our hope of eternal salvation.

(On the authenticity of the Pastorals, see Cerfaux, L., "The Pastoral Epistles," R-F, *INT* 510–25. Harrison, P. N., *The Problem of the Pastoral Epistles* [London, 1921]; *ExpT* 67 [1955–56] 77–81; *NTS* 2 [1955–56] 250–61. Kelly, J. N. D., *The Pastoral Epistles*, 21–36. Michaelis, W., *ZNW* 28 [1929] 70ff. Spicq, C., "Pastorales [Épîtres]," *VDBS* 7 [1961] 50–65. Wik, *NTI* 445–52.

EB 407–10. *RSS* 134–35. [→ Church Pronouncements, 72:25.])

12 **Outline of 1 Timothy**

(I) Address and Greeting (1:1–2)
(II) False Teachers (1:3–20)
(III) Direction of the Community (2:1–3:13)
  (A) Public Prayer (2:1–8)
  (B) Women in the Liturgical Assembly (2:9–15)
  (C) Ecclesiastical Officials (3:1–13)
(IV) Polemical Section (3:14–4:16)
  (A) The Church and the Mystery of Piety (3:14–16)
  (B) False Teachings and True Piety (4:1–10)
  (C) Exhortations to Timothy (4:11–16)
(V) Pastoral Section (5:1–6:2)
  (A) The Faithful in General (5:1–2)
  (B) Widows (5:3–16)
  (C) Presbyters (5:17–25)
  (D) Slaves (6:1–2)
(VI) Polemic and Exhortation (6:3–19)
  (A) False Teachers (6:3–10)
  (B) Exhortation to Timothy (6:11–16)
  (C) The Rich Christian (6:17–19)
(VII) Conclusion (6:20–21)

COMMENTARY ON 1 TIMOTHY

13 **(I) Address and Greeting (1:1–2).** Paul follows the ancient formula of introduction (cf. 1 Mc 10:18), but he expands the formula and fills it with Christian content (→ NT Epistles, 47:8).

1. *apostle of Christ Jesus by the command of God our Savior:* Paul received a direct call from God to be an apostle (Gal 1:1) and considered his apostolate a trust and a command (Ti 1:3; cf. 1 Cor 9:16; Rom 1:14). He regarded himself as an apostle in the strict sense of the term: one sent by Christ with the fullness of his authority. In 1 Tm he emphasizes his apostolic authority at the outset because he is about to give instructions on the organization and conduct of the Christian community at Ephesus. He also means to confirm the authority of Timothy, who is his legate.

In the Pastorals the title of Savior is applied to God (the Father) in 1 Tm 1:1; 2:3; 4:10; Ti 1:3; 2:10; 3:4, but to Christ in 2 Tm 1:10; Ti 1:4; 2:13; 3:6. Other NT writings also apply the title both to the Father and to Christ. This double attribution is warranted by the fact that Christ accomplished the work of salvation out of obedience to the will of the Father. The title Savior was used of God in the OT, especially in reference to deliverance from external oppression and danger. In the period of the early Church it was in common use in the worship of pagan gods (e.g., Aesculapius, Serapis, and Isis were savior-gods) and in the cult of the Roman emperors. It is probable therefore that the title was used in early Christian preaching largely to show that the prevalent yearning of the time was completely satisfied in the work of Christ (see comment on Ti 2:13).

2. *true son in the faith:* Paul had converted Timothy to Christianity during Mission I (*ca.* AD 47), and for about 15 years now he had been Paul's faithful companion and fellow worker, sharing his love and zeal for souls (cf. Acts 16:1–3; 1 Cor 4:17; Phil 2:20). *grace, mercy, and peace:* Paul uses this phrase only here and in 2 Tm 1:2; the usual Pauline formula is "grace and peace" (→ NT Epistles, 47:8).

14 **(II) False Teachers (1:3–20).** **3.** After his release from his Roman house arrest (AD 63) and a missionary journey to Spain, Paul undertook a journey to the eastern lands of the Mediterranean (→ 3 above). When Paul left Ephesus, Timothy remained there as his legate. *as I urged you to remain...:* There is an anacolouthon in the text, as elsewhere in Paul's epistles (e.g., Rom 5:12; Eph 3:1), and some clause must be supplied to complete the thought; e.g., "so now I urge you again." **4.** *fables and endless genealogies which promote useless speculation rather than the design of God based on faith:* The context (vv. 7ff.) and parallel passages in the Pastorals (especially Ti 1:10,14; 3:9) show that the false teachings included a strong Jewish element; Ti 1:14 refers explicitly to "Jewish fables." Accordingly, "fables and endless genealogies" seems to refer to legends and fictitious genealogies of OT personages in the manner attested to in *Jub.* *design of God:* The eternal divine plan (*oikonomia*) of salvation and the working out of this plan in man's history according to his faith. **5.** The purpose of Christian preaching, here referred to as a "charge," is the development of love in the hearts of the faithful (cf. Rom 13:10: "Love is the plenitude of the law"). This love proceeds from faith, and faith expresses itself in love (cf. Gal 5:6). *good conscience:* This phrase and "clear conscience" are favorite expressions in the Pastorals.

15 **7.** The false teachers misunderstand the very nature of the Old Law. Paul calls them *nomodidaskaloi*, "teachers of the Law." Paul hardly means the term in the strict sense of professional scribe (as in Lk 5:17 and Acts 5:34). **8.** *now, we know that the Law is good if it is taken as a law:* This is a reflection of a thought that Paul expresses emphatically elsewhere (e.g., 1 Cor 15:56), i.e., that the Mosaic Law, even when it was in force, did not give the interior spiritual power necessary to accomplish what it prescribed. This power came only from Christ. Nevertheless, the Law was a divine ordinance designed to prepare for the coming of Christ (Gal 3:23–24), and in this sense it was "holy" and "spiritual" (Rom 7:12,14). **9–10.** Paul considers the Law in its penal aspect, as threatening and punishing sinners. Under this aspect it was instituted for the unjust, not for the just. Catalogues of vices are found elsewhere in the Pastorals (6:4–5; 2 Tm 3:2–5; Ti 3:3). To a certain extent these lists reflect catalogues in contemporary literature (→ Pauline Theology, 79:161). *sound doctrine:* This and cognate phrases are characteristic of the Pastorals: "sound doctrine" (2 Tm 4:3; Ti 1:9; 2:1); "sound words" (1 Tm 6:3; 2 Tm 1:13); "to be sound in the faith" (Ti 1:13; 2:2); "sound speech" (Ti 2:8). The terminology is found frequently in contemporary authors to describe a teaching that is wise, is prudent, and is compatible with reason. Paul means to emphasize that the Christian teaching, while being transcendent, also accords with intellectual and moral soundness (Phil 4:8; Rom 12:1).

16 **11.** All that Paul has just said derives from the gospel entrusted to him. *the gospel of the glory of the blessed God:* A message concerned with the manifestation of God himself ("glory" in the biblical sense) that took place in the incarnation and in our participation in it (Jn 1:14ff.; 2 Cor 4:4, "the gospel of the glory of Christ who is the image of God"; 2 Cor 4:6; Col 1:27). God is called "blessed" again in 6:15. Beatitude belongs properly to God by reason of his perfect, eternal, and unchangeable nature. God allows man to participate in this beatitude, and man's hope of attaining this gift is called a "blessed hope" in Ti 2:13. **12.** Paul expresses his thanks to Christ for the call to preach the gospel. He received strengthening graces at the time of his call, and he has been blessed with abundant graces ever since (v. 14; cf. Rom 5:20). **13.** What adds to Paul's feeling of gratitude is the realization that he had been a bitter persecutor of the Church before his call (1 Cor 15:8–10; Gal 1:13–16). However, at the time he persecuted the Church he had not yet come to believe in Christ. Not only did he act in ignorance; he was even motivated by zeal for God (Phil 3:6; 2 Tm 1:3; Acts 26:9). **14.** Through the graces he has received, the virtues of faith and love have been manifest in Paul. Faith and love are fundamental virtues characterizing the Christian. At times (as here and in Eph 3:17; 6:23; Phlm 5), faith and love are mentioned alone; at other times, the virtue of hope is added (1 Thes 1:3; 1 Cor 13:13). **15.** *the saying is sure:* This phrase is repeated in the Pastorals (3:1; 4:9; 2 Tm 2:11; Ti 3:8). In Greek "sure" is *pistos*, worthy of belief. In using this formula, Paul may simply be drawing attention to a fundamental truth he is enunciating. More likely, he means to lend his authority to a quotation from a hymn or profession of faith current in the primitive Church (for such quotations see especially 1:17; 3:16; 6:15–16; 2 Tm 2:11–13). *Christ Jesus came into the world to save sinners:* Cf. Lk 19:10, "For the Son of Man came to seek and to save what was lost." *of whom I am the first:* Paul considers himself the greatest of sinners. This is a profound expression of humility, very similar to Eph 3:8, "I am the very least of all the saints [Christians]"; however, these expressions are not to be taken in a technical sense. **16.** Paul's thought: Christ has shown mercy toward me, the greatest of sinners; my conversion should serve as a heartening example for lesser sinners. **17.** Doxologies are frequent in the Pauline epistles (Gal 1:5; Rom 9:5; etc.). The expression "king of the ages" was current in post-exilic Judaism and is found in Jewish prayers. Practically all Gk mss. have "incorruptible," not "immortal" (as in the Vg). Paul is probably quoting the entire verse from an early Christian hymn.

17 **18.** The "instruction" that Paul gives Timothy is that he must be faithful to sound doctrine. *in accordance with the prophecies pronounced concerning you:* Paul is referring to the utterances of charismatically gifted persons who apparently directed the choice of Timothy and foretold his successful ministry (4:14; cf. Acts 13:1ff.). *wage the good warfare:* Be a good soldier in the army of Christ (2 Tm 2:3); Eph 6:13–17 develops the metaphor for the life of the Christian. **20.** *Hymenaeus:* Mentioned in 2 Tm 2:17 as holding the erroneous teaching that the resurrection of Christians has already taken place. *Alexander:* Probably to be identified with the Alexander of 2 Tm 4:14, "Alexander the coppersmith did me great harm." Paul probably condemned the two men before he left Ephesus. The condemnation is expressed in the same terms used in 1 Cor 5:5 for the incestuous sinner of Corinth, "to deliver [a person] to Satan." As in the case of the Corinthian, the punishment is intended to be remedial, "in order that they may learn not to blaspheme." The punishment of the Corinthian was excommunication (see 1 Cor 5) and probably physical sickness, Satan being considered the author of physical ills (Lk 13:16; 2 Cor 12:7). In the present instance the punishment is apparently the same.

18 **(III) Direction of the Community (2:1–3:13).**

(A) Public Prayer (2:1–8). **1.** Christians are to pray for all men without exception. The four terms referring to prayer are not to be taken as a systematic list of various kinds of prayer. In regard to thanksgiving, Paul repeatedly expresses his own gratitude to God (e.g., 1:12), and he urges his readers to join gratitude to petition in their prayers (e.g., Phil 4:6). **2.** In Rom 13:1–7 the Apostle exhorts his readers to be obedient to the civil authorities, reminding them that these authorities are established by God. Here he adds the obligation of prayer. **3–4.** God's will that Christians pray for all men follows from his will that all men be saved. Paul here clearly affirms the universal salvific will of God, without entering into the problem of its relationship to free will in man's salvation. Salvation is described as "to come to the knowledge of the truth." The same phraseology is repeated in 2 Tm 2:25; 3:7; Ti 1:1. Knowledge of Christian truth is a fundamental requirement for salvation, and other Pauline epistles also stress this idea (Col 1:7; 2:2,7; Eph 1:9; 4:13; etc.). At the same time, the Pastorals clearly show that a program of Christian conduct and good works is necessary. **5.** The universality of God's salvific will is based on the fact that God is one. The one

God created all men, and it is his will that all men be saved (Rom 3:29–30; Eph 4:6). *there is one mediator between God and men, the man Christ Jesus:* Christ is in a position to represent all men because he shares human nature with them (Heb 2:14; cf. Gal 3:19–20). **6.** This verse develops the note of universalism found throughout this section: After saying that Christians are to pray for all men (v. 1), and that God wishes that all men be saved (v. 4), the author asserts that Christ gave himself as a ransom for all. This refers principally to Christ's death (see comment on Ti 2:14). *this is the testimony rendered at the proper time:* Christ died for all men and thereby gave testimony to the universal salvific will of the Father. The "proper time" (*kairois idiois*) is the time chosen by God for the salvation of men, the "fullness of the times" (Ti 1:3; Gal 4:4; Eph 1:10). **7.** Paul has been appointed to preach this message of salvation. The three terms (preacher, apostle, teacher) lend emphasis to his assertion. *teacher of the Gentiles in faith and truth:* It is his commission to lead the Gentiles to faith; the object of this faith is divine truth. **8.** To raise the hands, with the palms open and facing upward as if to receive a divine gift, is a gesture of prayer attested to in Judaism, paganism, and early Christianity. *holy hands:* Symbolic of interior holiness. *without anger or contention:* To be at peace with one's neighbor is a necessary condition of effective prayer (Mt 5:23–24; 6:14; Mk 11:25).

(B) Women in the Liturgical Assembly (2:9–15). This section refers primarily to the conduct of women in the liturgical assembly, but its tone has a more general application.

19 **9–10.** These verses do not refer exclusively to the personal appearance and conduct of women in the liturgical assembly. **11–12.** These verses refer to the liturgical service. The same rule is formulated as in 1 Cor 14:34, "Let the women be silent in the assemblies, for they are not permitted to speak. Let them be submissive, as the Law itself says." **13–14.** When Paul discusses the subordination of woman to man in 1 Cor 11:3–16, he finds support in the Gn account of the creation of Adam and Eve. He now finds an argument for the superiority of man in the facts that Adam was created first and that Eve was the one deceived by Satan and was the first to sin (Sir 25:24). He does not imply that Adam did not sin (see Rom 5:12–14). His emphasis bears on Eve's succumbing to deception. **15.** The bearing of children in pain is presented as a punishment in Gn 3:16. Paul here sees it as a means of salvation. He probably has in mind the false teachers, who forbade marriage (4:3). In the wording of the text, there is an unexpected change from the singular to the plural: "Yet she will be saved by childbearing if they continue...." The change seems best explained by taking the singular as a collective and the plural as normal.

20 **(C) Ecclesiastical Officials (3:1–13).** In vv. 1–7 Paul describes the qualifications of a bishop (*episkopos*, "overseer"); vv. 8–13 show those required of a deacon. Note the omission of a list of qualifications for the presbyter (*presbyteros*). Cf. Phil 1:1, where Paul addresses bishops and deacons, without making any mention of presbyters. Direct evidence for the equivalence of the two terms is found in Ti 1 and Acts 20; in both places Paul uses the terms *episkopos* and *presbyteros* with reference to the same persons. The evidence in various passages indicates that these officials or bishop-presbyters were not bishops in the later sense. Proper episcopal functions were reserved to Paul himself or to one of his legates such as, in the present case, Timothy.

The list of qualifications required in ministers of the Church (3:1–13) is not marked by specifically Christian virtues, nor are the other catalogues of virtues required of the faithful that are found elsewhere in the Pastorals. The author adopts stereotyped lists to his purpose. As the context shows, these virtues are now infused with a new spirit, the spirit of Christianity.

1. *the saying is sure:* See comment on 1:15. *if anyone aspires to the office of bishop, he desires an excellent function:* It is clear from the qualifications required that the object of the desire is not the honor but the office itself, as a means of promoting the welfare of the community. **2.** *married only once:* Lit., "the husband of one wife." Clearly, it is not only polygamy that Paul means to exclude but also a second marriage, a marriage that would take place either in the case of conversion from paganism (1 Cor 7:12–16) or after the death of the first wife. In 1 Cor 7:39 (and Rom 7:2–3) Paul allows remarriage after the death of the spouse, but even there he declares that it would be better for the bereaved spouse to remain unmarried. In the present instance he makes the second marriage a disqualification. However, he does not make celibacy a requirement. *hospitable:* Hospitality was one of the most cherished virtues among the early Christians (5:10; Acts 16:15; Rom 12:13; Heb 13:2; 1 Pt 4:9; 3 Jn 5–10). *skillful in teaching:* This is an important qualification in the context of the Pastorals, where much of the material has to do with faithful adherence to traditional teaching and opposition to heresy (cf. 2 Tm 2:2,24). **6.** A convert elevated very rapidly to a prominent position in the Church might easily become proud. His manner of performing his duties would then be at variance with what is demanded in a Christian leader. In a letter to the church of Ephesus Paul could require some maturity in the faith since that church had been established about 12 years previously. *fall into the condemnation of the devil:* This phrase may mean that the neophyte would fall into the same condemnation as the devil (obj. gen.), or it may mean that the devil would accuse the neophyte before God (subj. gen.; cf. Ap 12:10; Jb 1:6ff.). **7.** Paul often insists that Christians, and therefore leaders in particular, should maintain a good reputation with non-Christians (5:14; 6:1; Ti 2:5,8,10; 1 Thes 4:12; 1 Cor 10:32; Col 4:5). The phrase "those outside" is borrowed from Judaism.

21 **8.** Paul begins to describe the qualifications of deacons. In the early Church, deacons (*diakonoi*) had charge of charitable ministrations and assisted in the liturgical and administrative direction of the community (cf. Ignatius, *Ep. ad Trall.* 3.1). *not greedy for base gain:* Deacons might be particularly subject to this temptation because they had charge of the distribution of alms. **9.** *mystery:* A basic Pauline concept. The term, and especially the concept, is found repeatedly throughout the epistles. The best description is found in Eph. The "mystery" designates the secret that was hidden in divine wisdom during previous centuries and only revealed in Messianic times, i.e., that the redemption of all men is accomplished by Christ and is attained through union with Christ (→ Pauline Theology, 79:32–34). **10.** *if they are found irreproachable, let them serve as deacons:* Before anyone is admitted to the diaconate, he must prove himself worthy. This is not to be understood as referring to a formal examination or precise period of probation. **11.** There is no way of deciding whether this verse refers to deaconesses or to wives of deacons. The Gk term itself (*gynaikas*) is ambiguous; it can be translated as either women or wives. An argument in favor of deaconesses is that the term is used absolutely. If wives of deacons were meant, a qualifier would be expected, "their wives." A further argument is the introductory term, "likewise," which prepares the reader for a reference to women exercising ecclesiastical functions. **12.** *married only once:* The literal translation and the meaning are the same as in v. 2 (see comment). **13.** *deacons who fulfill their duties well will attain to honorable rank:* Possibly Paul has in mind the promotion of deacons to the higher rank of bishop–presbyters; but more likely, he means that deacons who are competent and zealous will win the gratitude and respect of the community.

22 **(IV) Polemical Section (3:14–4:16).**

(A) The Church and the Mystery of Piety (3:14–16). **15.** The text itself explains that the "house of God" is the Church. The Christian Church, the new Israel, inherited the designation "house of God" from the synagogue, the covenanted people of the Old Dispensation (Nm 12:7). (For the metaphor, cf. also Mt 16:18; 1 Cor 3:10–17; 2 Cor 6:16; Eph 2:19–22; Heb 3:6; 1 Pt 4:17.) *the pillar and foundation of the truth:* The Church is the guardian and guarantee of the truths of salvation. **16.** The "mystery" is Christ himself, as the text indicates: "the mystery of piety, who [masc. pron.] was...." Instead of the masculine some less important Gk mss. and the Vg have the neuter, the antecedent then being mystery; other mss. have "God." On "mystery" see comment on 3:9. The remainder of the verse was borrowed from an ancient Christian hymn, as the rhythmic structure and the assonance of the six Gk verbs show. (For the use of hymns in the NT, cf. also Phil 2:5–11; Eph 5:19; Col 3:16.) In this poetic passage there are three units, each including a contrast. *he was manifested in the flesh, justified in the Spirit:* "Flesh" means human nature (Jn 1:14; Rom 1:3); "justified" does not have the usual Pauline meaning of purified from sin, but the original meaning of shown to be just (Mt 11:19; Lk 10:29). The justice and divinity of Christ were manifested in a special way through the operation of the Holy Spirit in the glorious resurrection of Christ (cf. Rom 1:4; Acts 5:30–32). The glorified Christ was "seen by angels" when he was "taken up in glory" at the time of the ascension.

23 **(B) False Teachings and True Piety (4:1–10).** The "Spirit" in v. 1 is the Holy Spirit, and the revelation must have been made through a Christian prophet. The prophecy is concerned with the "later times" (v. 1, *en hysterois kairois*), and what is foretold is a defection in belief and morals. The emphasis is on the future, but the passage indicates that the present errors and lack of piety pertain to this defection. The phraseology and content of this section have many parallels in the NT (2 Tm 3:1–9; 4:3–4; 2 Thes 2:3–12; Heb 1:2; 1 Cor 10:11; Acts 20:29–30; 1 Jn 2:18; 4:1–3; 2 Jn 7; Mt 24:10–12; etc.). These passages afford the following summary: The final epoch has already begun; it is the time between the first coming of Christ in the incarnation and his coming at the parousia; a defection in faith and morals is predicted for the last days; this defection has its beginnings in the earlier phases of the final period.

1. *giving heed to deceitful spirits and doctrines of demons:* In the final analysis, those responsible for the errors are largely evil spirits (cf. 2 Thes 2:9–11; 2 Cor 2:11). **2.** *misled by lying hypocrites whose conscience is branded:* Using terminology borrowed from the practice of branding criminals and fugitive slaves, Paul declares that the false teachers do not have the excuse of a clear conscience; the realization of their wickedness and their servitude to sin is branded in their consciences. **3–5.** Paul does not comment here on the prohibition of marriage, probably because of what he says elsewhere in 1 Tm (especially in 2:15 and 5:14). In regard to the prohibition of food, he repeats what he says in other epistles (1 Cor 8:1ff.; 10:23ff.; Rom 14; cf. Mt 15:11; Mk 7:1ff.). All food is good because it belongs to God's creation. Whatever God has created is good. The language reflects a phrase used repeatedly in the account of creation in the first chapter of Gn, "God saw that it was good." When "those who believe" offer a prayer of thanksgiving for food, they are accomplishing the complete purpose of God's creation of food (Rom 14:6; 1 Cor 10:30). The "word of God" refers either to the word uttered in creation or to the formula of thanksgiving, which would have been taken from Scripture. The prohibition of marriage and certain foods reflects dualistic tendencies that proscribed matter as evil; such tendencies were current even before the time of Christ and the apostles (e.g., among the Essenes; → 7–8 above).

24 **6.** The Gk term for "minister" is *diakonos.* Obviously, it does not have the same meaning as in 3:8ff., where it refers to a specific group of ecclesiastical officials. **7.** *profane fables, old wives' tales:* See comment on 1:4. **8.** In vv. 7b and 8 there is a play on the Gk word from which the Eng word "gymnastics" is derived: "Exercise yourself in piety, for bodily exercise is of little value." Paul does not, of course, mean to proscribe the proper care of the body and proper physical exercise. He only emphasizes the contrast between bodily and spiritual care, between temporal and eternal values. (For a similar development, see 1 Cor 9:24–27.) **10.** *we toil and struggle [agōnizometha] for this reason:* Instead of *agōnizometha* some less important Gk mss. have *oneidizometha,* "we are reviled" (Vg *maledicimur*). *Savior of all men, especially of those who believe:* The salvific will of God and the redemptive work of Christ extend to all men (2:4–5), but they extend to Christians in a special way.

25 **(C) Exhortations to Timothy (4:11–16).** **12.** *let no one despise your youth:* Timothy had joined Paul's company about 18 years previously (Acts 16:1–3). When this letter was written (*ca.* AD 65), Timothy was probably about 35 years old. Paul advises him to compensate for his youthfulness with exemplary personal conduct and perfect fulfillment of his duties. **13.** *until I come, devote yourself to reading, exhortation, and teaching:* In Greek, the term for "reading" is *anagnōsis.* It was used to designate the public reading of Scripture in the synagogue service. Here it refers to the scriptural reading in the Christian assembly. Some authors accordingly translate: "the public reading of Scripture." In the Christian assembly, where the procedure of the synagogue was adopted (Lk 4:16–21; Acts 13:14–16), the scriptural reading was followed by a commentary. This commentary naturally included an explanation of the scriptural passage and an "exhortation" to personal application. The "teaching" mentioned in the verse doubtless refers to the teaching of Christian doctrine (e.g. in instructions to catechumens).

14. *conferred on you through prophecy:* Timothy possesses a "spiritual gift" (*charisma*), which remains in him as a permanent state. This gift was conferred on a particular occasion "through prophecy" (see comment on 1:18). *with the imposition of the hands of the presbyterate:* Imposition of hands was an ancient gesture that expressed solidarity between the one who imposed hands and the recipient; it implied the transmission of a benefit, or the transfer of a quality or function, from one person to another. In the NT, the gesture of imposing hands is mentioned in various contexts: as a gesture of blessing (Mt 19:15), as a gesture of healing (Mk 6:5), as the rite used in conferring the Holy Spirit (Acts 8:17), and as the means of conferring an ecclesiastical office (Acts 6:6). It is the last sense that is meant here. The imposition of hands was a sacramental sign of Timothy's ordination to his sacred office (cf. 2 Tm 1:6). The present verse speaks of the imposition of the hands of the "presbyterate" (*presbyterion*), i.e., a group of priests (*presbyteroi*; see comment on 3:1–13). In 2 Tm 1:6 Paul speaks of "the spiritual gift which is in you through the imposition of my hands." The two texts are not opposed. Paul ordained Timothy to his sacred office; his rite alone was essential. The difference in prepositions in the two verses is significant. In 2 Tm 1:6, the preposition is *dia*, "through," denoting causality; in the present verse, the preposition is *meta*, "with," denoting accompaniment. Timothy's ordination was accomplished through the imposition of Paul's hands; and this essential rite was accompanied by the imposition of the hands of the presbyterate. In Acts and the Pastorals ordination to a sacred ministry is accomplished by an apostle or a delegate of an apostle (e.g., Timothy in 1 Tm 5:22 and Titus in Ti 1:5; but cf. Acts 13:3).

26 **(V) Pastoral Section (5:1–6:2).**

(A) The Faithful in General (5:1–2). The Christian community is compared to a large family (cf. 3:15). *do not rebuke an older man:* The context shows that here the term *presbyteros* has the general meaning of "older man," not the specific meaning of an ecclesiastical official (cf. 5:17).

27 **(B) Widows (5:3–16).** **3.** *honor widows:* The admonition includes not only respect but also material support, as the rest of the passage shows; the Fourth Commandment provides an analogy (cf. Mt 15:4–6). *truly widows:* Those who need and are deserving of material assistance from the Church, as the following verses explain. **4.** *let them first learn to show piety toward their own household:* The Church is not to be burdened with the support of a widow if there are children or grandchildren to provide for her. *pleasing in the sight of God:* Cf. Dt 5:16. **5.** For the example of Anna, cf. Lk 2:36–37. **6.** *a widow who gives herself up to pleasure is dead:* A widow living a life of sin is not to receive material assistance from the Church; she would only squander what she received (on the phraseology, see Ap 3:1). **8.** This verse emphasizes what has been said in v. 4.

28 **9–15.** These verses refer to a constituted order of widows, and this is the first such evidence we have. The passage shows that these women were dedicated to works of charity. **9.** *married only once:* See comment on 3:2. **10.** *washed the feet of the saints:* One of the practices of hospitality (Gn 18:4; Lk 7:36ff.; cf. Jn 13:5); "saints" is a synonym for Christians (e.g., Rom 1:7; 16:2). **11–12.** Young widows are not to be accepted into the order. Their acceptance would involve a determination (vow?) not to remarry, and a subsequent marriage would thus be a violation of their pledge to Christ (cf. Ap 2:4). **13.** The charitable ministrations of the order of widows involved visiting homes. Elderly persons could make such visits without wasting time in idle and uncharitable talk. **14.** In 1 Cor 7:40 Paul declares that it is better for a widow not to remarry, but he enunciates this as a general principle, subject to conditions in particular cases (cf. 1 Cor 7:9). In the present instance Paul believes it better not to apply the principle. Experience seems to have been the reason (cf. v. 15). *the adversary:* The hostile non-Christian on the watch for an occasion to disparage the Church. **16.** The text reads literally: "If any Christian woman has widows, let her assist them; and let not the Church be burdened, so that it may assist those who are truly widows." This seems to refer to a Christian woman who would undertake the support of widows, thereby enabling the Church to use its resources for other needy widows. Instead of "any Christian woman" some less important Gk mss. have "any Christian man or woman"; the Vg has "any Christian man."

29 **(C) Presbyters (5:17–25).** **17.** *let the presbyters [presbyteroi] who rule well be held worthy of double honor:* The Gk term *presbyteros* is used in the sense of ecclesiastical official (see comment on 3:1–13). "Honor" includes not only respect but also material recompense, as the next verse shows (see comment on 5:3). **18.** The first quotation is from Dt 25:4 (cf. 1 Cor 9:9). The second quotation is found in Lk 10:7 as a saying of Christ. The author is scarcely referring to canonical Lk as recognized Scripture; he probably knows the quotation from an oral tradition or from one of the written accounts that preceded canonical Lk (cf. Lk 1:1–4). The introductory phrase "Scripture says" applies properly only to the first quotation. **19.** The presbyters are afforded special protection against false charges. *two or three witnesses:* Required before an accusation against them is accepted. The formula is borrowed from Dt 19:15 (cf. Mt 18:16; 2 Cor 13:1). **20.** Guilty presbyters are to be rebuked in the presence of all the other presbyters (or: "all the members of the community"). This procedure is intended as a deterrent for other presbyters. **21.** *elect angels:* Those who remained faithful. **22.** The imposition of hands refers to ordination (see comment on 4:14). Timothy is not to ordain a man before he is sure of his qualifications; otherwise, Timothy would be responsible for the sins of the unworthy presbyter. The imposition of hands scarcely refers here to the absolution of penitents; as a gesture in reconciling sinners it is not attested to until the 3rd cent. **23.** It was probably out of a spirit of personal asceticism that Timothy drank only water. For reasons of health, Paul urges him to take some wine. Timothy apparently suffered from a weak stomach—possibly the cause of his "frequent ailments." **24–25.** There seems to be reference here to determining the qualifications of candidates for the presbyterate. Those candidates who act openly can be evaluated without difficulty. Others do not reveal themselves so readily, and time and patience are necessary before judgment can be passed on their qualifications.

30 **(D) Slaves (6:1–2).** Paul here takes his customary position on slavery (cf. Ti 2:9–10; 1 Cor 7:21–22; Eph 6:5–8; Col 3:22–25). **1.** Paul's phraseology, referring to slaves as being "under the yoke" (as beasts of burden), is an expression of his sympathy. Paul again shows concern about giving adversaries an opportunity to disparage the Christian religion (cf. 5:14; Ti 2:5). **2.** The spiritual fraternity that unites all Christians as brethren does not mean that Christian slaves may be disrespectful to their Christian masters. Rather, the faith is a reason for showing greater respect. Christian masters are "beloved," i.e., either beloved of God (Rom 1:7) or beloved as brothers.

31 **(VI) Polemic and Exhortation (6:3–19).**

(A) False Teachers (6:3–10). **3–5.** Paul's description of the false teachings is largely a repetition of 1:3–10. The only distinctive trait here is that the false teachers are said to be concerned about material gain (v. 5; cf. Ti 1:11). *the sound words of our Lord:* The sum total of revelation brought into the world through Christ. **6.** In vv. 5b and 6 there is a play on words, and the development is similar to that in 4:7–8. The false teachers look upon their teaching on "piety" as a "means of gain." Paul says that "piety" is indeed a "means of great gain," i.e., spiritual gain. Paul uses a term, *autarkeia* (contentment), that was current from the time of Aristotle to the time of the Stoics to describe the virtue that makes a man content with what he has. **7.** Cf. Jb 1:21; Eccl 5:15; Wis 7:3–6. **9–10.** Paul is not speaking directly about those who are actually rich (cf. vv. 17–19), but about the desire for riches, the love of money. *the love of money is the root of all evils:* Maxim current among non-Christian writers of the time.

32 **(B) Exhortation to Timothy (6:11–16).** **11.** *man of God:* This title was applied to Moses and the prophets (Dt 33:1; 1 Sm 2:27; 1 Kgs 12:22; 13:1; etc.), and like these great figures of the OT, Timothy is dedicated to the service of God (cf. 2 Tm 3:16). **12.** *fight the good fight of the faith:* The figure is that of a pugilist in the arena (1 Cor 9:26; 2 Tm 4:7). *made the good confession in the presence of many witnesses:* Since the text itself associates Timothy's call to eternal life with this "confession" (*homologia*), it seems there is reference to Timothy's baptism and a profession of faith he made on that occasion.

13. *gave testimony before* [or *under*] *Pontius Pilate and made the good confession* [*homologian*]*:* This probably refers to Christ's testimony "before" Pilate concerning his royal messiahship and his mission of revealing the truth (Jn 18:36–37), but Paul may have in mind Jesus' martyrdom on the cross "under" Pontius Pilate. **14.** *the commandment: Entolē* is the complete deposit entrusted to Timothy, all the truths of Christianity (cf. v. 20). *unstained and irreproachable:* In the Greek this phrase may refer either to the "commandment" or to Timothy himself. *manifestation:* The word *epiphaneia* occurs in 2 Thes 2:8 and five times in the Pastorals. Here and in 2 Tm 4:1,8 and in Ti 2:13 it refers to the parousia of Christ; in 2 Tm 1:10 it refers to the manifestation of Christ in the incarnation. The Gk term was used frequently in reference to the "manifestation" of pagan gods and pagan emperors (including Roman) who claimed divine honors. Paul probably chose the term out of opposition to these false "manifestations" (see comment on Ti 2:13).

15–16. The phraseology and structure of these verses suggest that they were taken from an ancient Christian hymn (cf. 1:17; 3:16; 2 Tm 2:11–13). The parousia will take place at the "proper time" (*kairois idiois*), the time fixed by God; the same phrase is used in 2:6 and Ti 1:3 in reference to the incarnation, the first coming of Christ. The terms "sovereign," "king of kings," and "lord of lords" are found in the OT (e.g., Dt 10:17; 2 Mc 12:15; 13:4; Dn 2:37). "Lord of kings" and "king of kings" were used as titles by Oriental monarchs, and the primitive Church probably used the terms in opposition to the divine honors paid to these rulers. God "alone has immortality," i.e., as an essential and necessary attribute. *dwells in unapproachable light:* Cf. Ap 21:23. *whom no man has seen or can see:* Cf. Jn 1:18; 6:46; 1 Jn 4:12; however, with the aid of grace, some vision of God is available to man (Mt 5:8).

33 **(C) The Rich Christian (6:17–19).** Paul does not condemn wealth, but he emphasizes its vanity and its dangers. Timothy is to urge the rich to use their wealth in generous charity. Such charity will merit a spiritual reward (Mt 6:3–4). A contrast is presented between earthly and spiritual treasures, as in Mt 6:19–20 and Lk 12:15–21 (cf. also Lk 16:9; Phil 4:17). There is play on the word rich: "the rich in this world," "uncertain riches," "God richly grants us all things," "to be rich in good deeds."

34 **(VII) Conclusion (6:20–21).** On the errors mentioned in these verses, cf. 1:3–10; 4:7; 6:3–5. *guard the trust:* The Gk word for "trust," *parathēkē*, means something left with a person and committed to his care; hence, the meaning is "guard what has been entrusted to you." Timothy is to guard the complete tradition of Christian teaching and preserve it from all error and alteration. *grace be with you:* The pl. form shows that Paul is directing this epistle to all the members of the community, not only to Timothy; he probably expected the letter to be read in public (Col 4:16). The Vg adds "Amen."

35 **Outline of 2 Timothy**

(I) Address and Greeting (1:1–2)
(II) Thanksgiving (1:3–5)
(III) Exhortations (1:6–2:13)
- (A) Timothy's Graces and Obligations (1:6–14)
- (B) Loyalty and Defections (1:15–18)
- (C) Timothy's Devotion to His Ministry (2:1–7)
- (D) Sufferings of the Christian Apostle (2:8–13)

(IV) Polemical Section (2:14–3:9)
- (A) False Teachers (2:14–26)
- (B) Perils of the Final Period (3:1–9)

(V) Exhortations to Timothy (3:10–4:5)
(VI) Conclusion (4:6–22)
- (A) Paul at the Close of His Life (4:6–8)
- (B) Final Recommendations (4:9–18)
- (C) Final Salutations (4:19–22)

COMMENTARY ON 2 TIMOTHY

36 **(I) Address and Greeting (1:1–2).** **1.** *Paul, an apostle of Christ Jesus by the will of God:* The same formula is used to introduce 1 and 2 Cor, Eph, and Col. (On "apostle," see comment on 1 Tm 1:1.) *according to the promise of the life which is in Christ Jesus:* It is Paul's commission to announce that Christ has fulfilled God's promise to grant life to all men. This life is attained through present union with Christ, and it will reach its perfection in the future (cf. 1 Tm 4:8 and Col 3:4). **2.** This verse is an almost verbatim rendering of 1 Tm 1:2 (see comment). *my beloved son:* One of many expressions of Paul's affection for Timothy.

37 **(II) Thanksgiving (1:3–5).** Here, as in all the Pauline epistles except 1 Tm and Ti, a prayer of thanksgiving follows the address and greeting. **3.** Paul emphasizes the continuity of the Jewish religion and the Christian faith. His conversion to Christianity did not involve a complete break with the past (cf. Acts 23:1; 24:14–16; 26:6,22; 1 Tm 1:13). **4.** This verse recalls the last parting of Paul and Timothy. Paul writes this letter in Rome, as a prisoner who expects to be put to death soon (cf. 1:8,16–17; 2:9; 4:6–8). According to tradition, Paul was martyred at Rome in AD 67. Apart from any other data, the letter purports to be written about the year 67 and represents his last will and testament. **5.** As in v. 3, there is emphasis on the continuity of Judaism and Christianity (cf. 3:15). In addition, Timothy's mother had become a Christian (Acts 16:1). The present verse does not imply that Timothy's grandmother had been converted. His father was a pagan (Acts 16:1).

38 **(III) Exhortations (1:6–2:13).**
(A) Timothy's Graces and Obligations (1:6–14). **6.** *rekindle the spiritual gift of God which is in you through the imposition of my hands:* Timothy enjoys a permanent grace of consecration by virtue of his ordination through the imposition of Paul's hands. This verse must be compared with 1 Tm 4:14 (see comment). **7.** It seems that Timothy was inclined to be timid (cf. 1 Cor 16:10–11). **8.** The "testimony" Timothy is to offer includes preaching and suffering. **9–10.** *saved us... in conformity with his own design and the grace given us in*

Christ Jesus: It is a constant teaching of Paul that the call to salvation is a gratuitous gift, independent of our deeds (e.g., Eph 2:4–10). *before all ages:* Lit., "before eternal times" (*pro chronōn aiōniōn*); there is reference to God's eternal plan to save men through Christ and in union with Christ (Eph 1:4). *the appearance: Epiphaneia* here refers to the coming of Christ in his incarnation (see comment on 1 Tm 6:14). Christ destroyed death, both physical and spiritual (cf. Rom 5:21; 6:4; 8:2; 1 Cor 15:42,54; Heb 2:14–15). There is a good deal of similarity between vv. 9–10 and Ti 3:4–7.

11. See comment on 1 Tm 2:7. The Vg adds "of the Gentiles" to "teacher." **12.** *he [God] is able to guard my trust until that day:* The Gk term for "trust" is *parathēkē*, as in v. 14 and in 1 Tm 6:20 (see comment); it seems to have the same meaning in all three places. The present verse then means that God is able to preserve the entire content of Christian teaching "until that day," i.e., the parousia (cf. v. 18; 2 Thes 1:10). However, it is possible that in this instance *parathēkē* refers to Paul's good deeds and merits, which God will keep on deposit until the coming of Christ (cf. 4:8; 1 Tm 6:19). **13.** *take as your norm the sound words which you have heard from me:* In his preaching and personal conduct, Timothy is to adhere to the truths he learned from Paul. (On "sound words," see comments on 1 Tm 1:10; 6:3.) **14.** *guard the good trust:* See comment on 1:12.

39 **(B) Loyalty and Defections (1:15–18).** **15.** *Asia:* The Roman province in the western part of Asia Minor, with Ephesus as its chief city. Taken in conjunction with what follows and with 4:16, this verse seems to refer to the failure of the Christians of Asia to visit Paul or to appear in his defense at his trial. Apparently, the events that led to Paul's arrest took place in the region of Ephesus. Paul counted particularly on the loyalty of Phygelus and Hermogenes. *all in Asia:* Not to be taken literally. **16–17.** Here and in 4:19 Paul speaks of the "house of Onesiphorus." This expression and the prayer in v. 18 seem to indicate that Onesiphorus had died before this letter was written. The present text implies that Paul's second imprisonment in Rome was very severe. His first imprisonment (AD 61–63) had been very liberal (Acts 28:30–31). **18.** Both references to "the Lord" are ambiguous; in each case the term may refer either to the Father or to Christ. Paul probably means: "May the Lord [Christ] grant him to find mercy from the Lord [the Father] on that day." The latter part of the verse reads: "you know well [better than I] all the services he rendered at Ephesus."

40 **(C) Timothy's Devotion to His Ministry (2:1–7).** **1.** There may be specific reference to the grace of ordination (as in 1:6), but more probably the reference is general. **2.** Paul is concerned about the faithful transmission of the truths of Christianity—this verse is important for the history of Christian tradition (cf. 1:14; 1 Tm 6:20; Ti 1:9). Timothy heard Paul enunciate these truths "before many witnesses," i.e., probably in a solemn presentation of the truths of Christianity on the occasion of Timothy's ordination (1:6; 1 Tm 4:14). A different translation is possible, "through many witnesses," and then the meaning would be: Timothy first learned the truths of Christianity from Paul, and these truths were then confirmed by other teachers. **3.** Cf. 1:8; 1 Tm 1:18. **4–6.** Timothy must devote himself entirely to his work, not shrinking from toil or suffering, and avoid any dissipation of his interests. He will then receive the praise of his commander (Christ), the crown of victory (see comment on 4:8), and the fruit of his labor. In this passage Paul is not referring to the same principle that he defends elsewhere (e.g., 1 Tm 5:18), namely that the minister of Christ deserves material recompense. **7.** Through his own reflection and the help of grace, Timothy will arrive at a better understanding of Paul's words.

41 **(D) Sufferings of the Christian Apostle (2:8–13).** **8.** This verse prepares for vv. 11–12. *risen from the dead:* Cf. v. 11, "If we have died with him, we shall also live with him." *of the seed of David:* Emphasizes the Messianic kingship of Christ; cf. v. 12, "we shall reign with him." *according to my gospel:* Cf. Rom 1:3; 2:16; 16:25. **9.** *the word of God is not shackled:* Because there are other preachers; also, Paul has been able to spread the word of God even as a prisoner (see comment on 4:17; cf. Phil 1:12–14). **10.** *endure all things for the sake of the elect:* His sufferings are of value for those chosen for Christianity, both those already Christians and those not yet converted (cf. Col 1:24; 2 Cor 1:5–6; 4:12).

11–13. *the saying is sure:* See comment on 1 Tm 1:15. These verses have a rhythmic structure and seem to be borrowed from an ancient Christian hymn (cf. 1 Tm 1:17; 3:16; 6:15–16). When Paul speaks of dying with Christ and rising with him, he has in mind not only the mystical death and resurrection of baptism (Rom 6:3–11) but also the development of this experience in the Christian life, with special emphasis on the physical sufferings and dangers of the apostolate (1 Cor 15:31; 2 Cor 4:8–11), the final stage of this assimilation with Christ taking place at the parousia (Col 3:3–5; Phil 3:10–11; 1 Cor 15:42–44). *if we deny Christ:* Such a denial would mean infidelity to him, for instance, in time of trial or suffering. *he will deny us:* Christ's denial would be a refusal to recognize a man at the judgment as one of his followers (see Mt 10:33). *if we are faithless, he remains faithful:* Either to his promise to punish or to his promise to show love and mercy (cf. Rom 3:3–8; 11:29–32). *for he cannot deny himself:* He is unchangeable in his very nature.

42 **(IV) Polemical Section (2:14–3:9).**

(A) False Teachers (2:14–26). **14.** Verses 14, 16, and 23 repeat descriptions of the false teachings found in 1 Tm 1:4,6; 6:4,20. **15.** *faithful dispenser of the word of the truth:* The Gk term for "faithful dispenser," *orthotomounta*, occurs only here in the NT; for the concept, cf. 1:14. **17–18.** *Hymenaeus:* Cf. 1 Tm 1:20. *Philetus:* These men hold that the resurrection of Christians has already taken place. They deny the future bodily resurrection and glorification, and restrict resurrection to the mystical form of this experience in baptism (Rom 6:3–11; Col 2:12; 3:1). This idea of a purely spiritual resurrection is in keeping with the erroneous teachings described in 1 Tm 4:3–5.

19. *the firm foundation of God:* The Church (cf. 1 Tm 3:15). In the first motto, taken from Nm 16:5, "know" has the biblical meaning of love and favor (1 Cor 8:3; Gal 4:9). This motto emphasizes the initiative of God in salvation. The second slogan, emphasizing the response of man, is a reflection of phrases found in Is 26:13; 52:11; Lv 24:16; Jos 23:7. *he who names the name of the Lord:* He who professes to accept Christ as his Lord and to worship him. Paul borrows the imagery in this verse from the ancient custom of engraving inscriptions on temples and public buildings. **20–21.** The "house" is the Church, the house of God (cf. 1 Tm 3:15). The "vessels" are the members of the Church. The vessels "for noble use" are faithful Christians; those "for ignoble use" are faithless. The faithful are exhorted to avoid the contamination of heretical teachings.

22. Timothy is to set a good example. *flee youthful passions:* Not only sensuality but also impetuosity and imprudence, as the following verses show (cf. also 1 Tm 4:12; 6:11). *those who call upon the Lord:* The "Lord" is

Christ, and the phrase is a synonym for Christians (Acts 9:14,21; 1 Cor 1:2; Rom 10:12). **24–26.** *servant of the Lord:* The minister of Christ (see comment on Ti 1:1); the meaning is much the same as "man of God" (see comment on 1 Tm 6:11). Timothy is to approach the false teachers with kindness. **26.** *after being captured by him to do his will:* This refers to capture by the devil (before repentance) rather than capture by God (in repentance).

43 **(B) Perils of the Final Period (3:1–9).** This passage describes a condition of moral decay and doctrinal error that will prevail in the final days before the parousia. However, it is clearly indicated (esp. in v. 5) that the present errors and moral disorder form part of the final crisis (cf. 1 Tm 4:1–10). **1.** *in the last days:* In the Messianic period, but with special emphasis here on the final days before the parousia. **2–5.** Similar lists of vices are found elsewhere in Paul (see comment on 1 Tm 1:9–10). **6–7.** The heretics easily find followers among a certain type of women, who are sinful, frivolous, impulsive, eagerly seeking after truth, but superficial and inconstant. **8.** *Jannes and Jambres:* In Jewish tradition these are the names of the magicians who opposed Moses at the court of Pharaoh (Ex 7:8ff.). Some Gk mss. and the Vg have "Mambres" instead of Jambres, and this variant is found also in the Jewish writings (cf. CD 5:18–19; H. Braun, *TRu* 29 [1963] 259).

44 **(V) Exhortations to Timothy (3:10–4:5).** **11.** Of all his afflictions Paul mentions only those he endured in the region of Lystra (Acts 13:50; 14:2,19). Timothy was a native of Lystra, and Paul means that Timothy knew from the moment of his conversion what would be required of him as a follower of Christ. **12.** Cf. Mt 10:22; Jn 15:19; Acts 14:22; 1 Thes 3:3–4. **13.** *deceivers and deceived:* There is a play on words: The false teachers deceive others (5–9), but are themselves deceived (by the devil, 2:26). **14–15.** Timothy is to adhere to what he has been taught from his infancy. His teachers have been principally his mother and grandmother (see 1:5) and Paul (vv. 10–11; see 2:2). *the sacred writings:* The phrase *hiera grammata* was current among Gk-speaking Jews (Philo, Josephus) to designate the biblical books. Jewish parents were obliged to see that their children were instructed in the Law as soon as they reached the age of five. **16.** *all scripture:* The phrase *pasa graphē* can mean either "each passage of Scripture" or, preferably, "the entirety of Scripture." In the concrete situation of this letter, it would refer to the OT. *inspired by God:* The adj. *theopneustos* in Hellenistic Greek is used almost exclusively in the pass. sense, "inspired of God" (so LS, AG 357, *ThWNT* 6, 452–53). The adjective could be understood predicatively ("all Scripture is inspired by God") or attributively ("all Scripture, inspired by God, is useful indeed..."). The general context would seem to favor the latter, but the phrase itself the former. In either case there is a clear reference to the divine origin of the Scriptures; the authority of the Bible is rooted in that of God, who is ultimately responsible for the existence of these books as a norm of man's conduct. It is a moot question to what extent this statement can be applied to any writings of the NT. How many of these books had been written or, if written, recognized by the time 2 Tm was composed? **17.** *man of God:* See comment on 1 Tm 6:11.

45 **4:1.** Paul adjures Timothy, calling upon God (the Father) and Christ Jesus as witnesses. At the parousia, Jesus will come to judge "the living and the dead"—those who will be alive at that time and those who will have died previously. Paul also adjures Timothy by the "manifestation" (*epiphaneia*, see comment on 1 Tm 6:14) of Christ at the parousia, and by his Messianic "kingdom," which will enter upon its definitive phase at that time (2 Thes 1:5). **2.** *be urgent in season and out of season:* Paul urges Timothy to be zealous, taking advantage of every opportunity to preach, even though the particular occasion might not be considered fitting; the word of God is always in season. **3–4.** The emphasis is on the future, but the present is also included (see comment on 3:1–9). *fables:* See comments on 1 Tm 1:4; 4:7. *sound doctrine:* See comment on 1 Tm 1:10. *evangelist:* A preacher of the gospel whose activity was not restricted to a particular area (Acts 21:8; Eph 4:11).

46 **(VI) Conclusion (4:6–22).**

(A) Paul at the Close of His Life (4:6–8). **6.** *as for me, I am already being offered as a libation:* Paul expects to be put to death soon and regards the shedding of his blood as a libation (a sacrificial rite in which a liquid, generally wine or oil, was poured out; cf. Ex 29:40). Paul means that his martyrdom pays homage to God and is of value for the salvation of souls (2:10; cf. Phil 2:17). *the time of my departure has come:* Death is a departure from this life and a return to Christ (Phil 1:23). **7.** *I have fought the good fight:* See comment on 1 Tm 6:12. *I have finished the course:* The figure is that of a race. *I have kept the faith:* Paul has preserved and guarded the deposit of the faith (1 Tm 6:14,20). **8.** *crown of justice:* The imagery is taken from the athletic contests, where a crown of laurel, pine, or olive was awarded the winners (cf. 2:5; 1 Cor 9:25). *that day:* The parousia, the day of judgment (1:18). *all who have loved his manifestation:* All who out of love for Christ have lived a Christian life as a preparation for his *epiphaneia* (see comment on 1 Tm 6:14).

47 **(B) Final Recommendations (4:9–18).** **10.** *Demas:* He deserted Paul "out of love for the present world." This may mean that Demas has become an apostate; more likely, it means that Demas has forsaken Paul out of concern for some secular business or for reasons of personal safety and comfort (cf. Col 4:14 and Phlm 24). *Crescens:* He has gone to Galatia, a Roman province in Asia Minor. *Dalmatia:* A Roman province on the eastern shore of the Adriatic. In both cases the purpose was certainly to carry on missionary activity. Instead of Galatia some good mss. (S, C) read "Gaul." **11.** *Luke:* "The beloved physician" (Col 4:14). In Col 4:10 Paul refers to the activity of Mark in Asia Minor. The earlier differences between Paul and Mark (Acts 13:13; 15:37–40) had been composed (Col 4:10; Phlm 24). **12.** *Tychicus:* Cf. Acts 20:4; Eph 6:21; Col 4:7; Ti 3:12. Paul's manner of speaking here is no proof that Timothy is not in Ephesus (for similar expressions, cf. 1 Cor 15:32; 16:8). Paul may have sent Tychicus to Ephesus to replace Timothy, who would then be free to come to Paul (v. 9). **13.** *the books* [*biblia*]: Made of papyrus, the current writing material. Parchment was more costly. *the parchments* [*membranas*]: These, as well as the "books," may have contained portions of Scripture. **14–15.** *Alexander:* Probably the Alexander of 1 Tm 1:20, and perhaps also of Acts 19:33. He may have opposed Paul's preaching in Ephesus, or he may have come to Rome to testify against Paul. *will requite him according to his deeds:* Cf. Pss 27:4; 61:12; Prv 24:12. **16.** *at my first defense:* It is possible that Paul is referring to his Roman house arrest, but more likely he alludes to a first hearing in his present trial (see comment on 1:15). **17.** If v. 16 refers to the house arrest, this verse refers to his subsequent release and his continued missionary activity. If v. 16 refers to a first hearing in Paul's present trial, this verse refers to the successful outcome of this first hearing and Paul's proclamation of the gospel before the judges and all those who were present on that occasion. *I was rescued from the lion's mouth:* A biblical image (e.g., Ps

21:21). **18.** Paul is not referring to release from his present imprisonment (4:6); he will be rescued for the "heavenly kingdom."

48 **(C) Final Salutations (4:19–22).** **19.** *Prisca and Aquila:* This couple played a great role in the missionary activity of Paul (Acts 18:2–3,18–19,26; Rom 16:3–5; 1 Cor 16:19). *Onesiphorus:* See comments on 1:16–18. **20.** *Erastus:* Probably to be identified with the treasurer of Corinth (Rom 16:23) and with the Erastus of Acts 19:22. *Trophimus:* An Ephesian mentioned in Acts 20:4; 21:29. Paul was probably arrested in the area of Ephesus and taken to Rome as a prisoner (see comment on 1:4,15); perhaps it was during this voyage that Trophimus was left at Miletus and Erastus remained in Corinth. **21.** *before winter:* Voyages were discontinued for the winter months. *Pudens:* According to tradition, a Roman senator converted by Peter. *Linus:* Traditionally identified with Peter's successor as bishop of Rome, but the identification is not certain; Linus was a common name. *Claudia:* The mother of Linus (*Const. apost.* 7.46, 17–19). **22.** *the Lord be with your spirit:* In the singular, the greeting is addressed to Timothy alone. *grace be with you:* This is in the plural (see comment on 1 Tm 6:21).

49 **Outline of Titus**

(I) Address and Greeting (1:1–4)
(II) Appointment of Presbyters (1:5–9)
(III) False Teachers (1:10–16)
(IV) Duties of Various Classes of Christians (2:1–10)
(V) Graces of the Redemption (2:11–15)
(VI) General Duties of Christians (3:1–7)
(VII) Recommendations to Titus (3:8–11)
(VIII) Conclusion (3:12–15)

COMMENTARY ON TITUS

50 **(I) Address and Greeting (1:1–4).** This introduction is much more solemn than the introduction to 1 or 2 Tm. *servant of God:* As in the OT, a person who not only devotes himself to the service of God, but is chosen by God for a mission in regard to his people (Dn 9:10–11; Is 20:3; Am 3:7; Jer 44:4); in Rom 1:1 and Phil 1:1 Paul calls himself "the servant of Jesus Christ." *apostle of Jesus Christ, by the command of God our Savior* and *my true son:* See comments on 1 Tm 1:1–2. *God's elect:* Christians (cf. 2 Tm 2:10; Rom 8:33; Col 3:12). *before all ages* [*pro chronōn aiōniōn*]: Since there is reference to a promise, the phrase refers not to God's eternal design (as in 2 Tm 1:9) but to the promise of salvation made at the beginning of human history and frequently repeated. *at the proper time:* See comment on 1 Tm 2:6.

51 **(II) Appointment of Presbyters (1:5–9).** This passage and 1 Tm 3:1–7 are parallel. **5.** After his Roman house arrest (AD 61–63), Paul commissioned Titus as his legate in Crete. This procedure was in accordance with Paul's usual custom: He was content to lay the foundations of a church and leave to others the work of further development (2 Cor 10:16; Rom 15:20–21). Paul later (*ca.* AD 65) wrote this letter to Titus, probably from Macedonia. One of Titus' first duties is to appoint presbyters (elders, *presbyteroi*). Verse 7 uses the term *episkopos* to designate the persons who are called presbyters in this verse (see comments on 1 Tm 3:1–13). **6.** *married only once:* See comment on 1 Tm 3:2. It is not explicitly required in 1 Tm 3:4–5 that the children of the candidate be Christians. The requirement is explicit here because Christianity was more recent in Crete, and it could easily happen that only the parents would be converts, the children remaining outside the Church. Paul wants to avoid such a situation. **7.** *God's steward:* Steward over the house of God, the Church (see comment on 1 Tm 3:15). **9.** *sound doctrine:* See 1 Tm 1:10.

52 **(III) False Teachers (1:10–16).** The descriptions found here and in 3:9 show that the heretical teachings agree in essentials with the errors described in 1–2 Tm (see esp. 1 Tm 1:3–10; 4:1–10; 6:3–10). **10.** *especially those of the circumcision party:* References to the Jewish character of the heresies are more explicit in this epistle (vv. 10–16 and 3:9) than in 1–2 Tm. **11.** *they upset whole families:* Cf. 2 Tm 3:6. *teaching for base gain:* Cf. 1 Tm 6:5. **12.** The efforts of the heretics are facilitated by the national character of the Cretans. According to Clement of Alexandria, the quotation comes from Epimenides, a Cretan poet of the 6th cent. BC. A term current at the time of Paul, *krētizein*, "to act like a Cretan," meant to lie and deceive. **13.** *that they may be sound in the faith:* See comment on 1 Tm 1:10. **14.** *Jewish fables:* Cf. 1 Tm 1:4; 4:7. *precepts of men:* The context shows there is reference to Jewish regulations concerning ritual purity, especially those concerning the prohibition of certain foods (cf. 1 Tm 4:3–5). **15.** *to the pure all things are pure:* The essential factor in morality is interior disposition; moral purity is a quality of the soul, not of things (cf. Rom 14:14–23; Mk 7:15–23). *to the corrupt and unbelieving nothing is pure:* Persons who are morally corrupt and without belief will desecrate even what is in itself pure and honorable, because they will misuse it and turn it to sinful enjoyment.

53 **(IV) Duties of Various Classes of Christians (2:1–10).** **1.** *sound doctrine:* Cf. "sound in faith" in v. 2 and "sound speech" in v. 8 (see comment on 1 Tm 1:10). **2.** Paul often groups together faith, hope, and charity (cf. 1 Thes 1:3; 5:8). Here, as in 2 Thes 1:3–4, 1 Tm 6:11, and 2 Tm 3:10, hope is replaced by patience, the concrete expression of hope. **5.** *wives must be submissive to their husbands:* Cf. 1 Tm 2:11–14; Eph 5:22; Col 3:18. *that the word of God might not be blasphemed:* Cf. vv. 8, 10; 1 Tm 6:1; etc. **7–8.** It is not certain whether the phrase at the beginning of v. 7, "in all things," belongs to what precedes (concerning the younger men) or to what follows (concerning Titus). As was Timothy, so Titus is now told to set a good example (1 Tm 4:12). *adversary:* See comment on 1 Tm 5:14. **9–10.** See comments on 1 Tm 6:1–2.

54 **(V) Graces of the Redemption (2:11–15).** **11.** *The grace of God, source of salvation for all men, has been manifested:* In the incarnation and redemptive work of Christ (cf. 2 Tm 1:9–10). *for all men:* Cf. 1 Tm 2:3–6. **13.** *awaiting the blessed hope and manifestation of the glory of our great God and Savior Jesus Christ:* On "blessed hope" and "glory," see comment on 1 Tm 1:11; on "manifestation," see comment on 1 Tm 6:14. This verse is an eloquent expression of Paul's belief in the divinity of Christ. Sometimes the translation is found: "of the great God [i.e., the Father] and our Savior Jesus Christ." The following considerations militate against this translation: (1) In the Greek the expressions "great God" and "our Savior Jesus Christ" are governed by a single definite article; (2) the verse refers to the parousia, and everywhere else the glorious manifestation of the parousia pertains to Christ (1 Tm 6:14–15; 2 Tm 4:1; 1 Cor 1:7; 2 Thes 1:7; etc.); (3) the rest of the sentence (v. 14) speaks only of Christ and ascribes to him a divine prerogative, the possession of the chosen people (see comment on v. 14); (4) the terms in the text reflect phraseology used in the cult of gods and emperors, where the terms "god" and "savior" are used in reference to a particular deity or emperor (e.g., Ptolemy I was called "savior and god"; in 48 BC J. Caesar was acclaimed at Ephesus as "god, son of Ares and Aphrodite, common savior of men"). (Cf. R. E. Brown, *TS* 26 [1965] 556–57.) **14.** *gave himself for us:* In Pauline terminology this expression refers to the sacrificial death of Christ (1 Tm 2:6; Gal 1:4; 2:20; Eph 5:2,25). *to purify for himself a people of his own:* Adopting OT phraseology that refers to God's people of the old covenant and their purification (Ex 19:5; Dt 7:6; 14:2), Paul asserts that Christians are the people of the New Covenant, whom Christ has chosen and purified (Eph 5:25–27; Heb 9:14; 1 Pt 2:9–10). **15.** Titus may still be youthful, as Timothy was (1 Tm 4:12).

55 **(VI) General Duties of Christians (3:1–7).** **1.** *remind them to be submissive to rulers and authorities:* Cf. Rom 13:1–7; 1 Tm 2:1–2. **3–7.** Verse 3 describes the condition of humanity before Christ: All men, Jews and Gentiles, were in the same deplorable state. Verses 4–7 describe the change wrought by Christ. Other passages in Paul describe the same contrast (cf., e.g., Rom 3:21–26; Eph 2:1–10; 1 Cor 6:9–11). For the ideas and phraseology in vv. 4–7, see comments on 2:11–14; 2 Tm 1:9–10. **5.** *bath of regeneration and renewal in the Holy Spirit:* The reference is to baptism, as in Eph 5:26, where the same term is used (*loutron*, "bath"). Baptism brings about a new life, a "regeneration," through water and the Holy Spirit (cf. Rom 6:4; Gal 6:15; 2 Cor 5:17; Col 2:11–13). **6.** Cf. Rom 5:5; Jl 3:1; Acts 2:17. In vv. 4–6 there is reference to the Trinity. **7.** Cf. 1:2; Gal 4:7.

56 **(VII) Recommendations to Titus (3:8–11).** **8.** *the saying is sure:* A characteristic phrase in the Pastorals (see comment on 1 Tm 1:15); it applies to vv. 4–7. **9.** Cf. 1:10,14 and 1 Tm 1:4–10. **10.** In reference to the false teachers, Paul uses the term "factious." The Gk term, *hairetikon*, borrowed from the philosophical schools of the time, will later have a technical meaning in the Church, i.e., heretic. On the procedure recommended by Paul, cf. Mt 18:15–17; 1 Cor 5; 2 Thes 3:14; see comment on 1 Tm 1:20.

57 **(VIII) Conclusion (3:12–15).** **12.** *Artemas:* Not mentioned elsewhere. *Tychicus:* See 2 Tm 4:12. After Titus is replaced by Artemas or Tychicus, he is to rejoin Paul at Nicopolis. There were several cities called Nicopolis—Paul most likely refers to Nicopolis of Epirus on the W coast of Greece. **13.** *Zenas, Apollos:* They probably brought this letter to Titus. *Apollos:* Cf. Acts 18:24–19:1; 1 Cor 1–4. Paul gives Zenas' title, "lawyer." This appellation seems to refer to Roman rather than Jewish law, since Zenas, as a Christian, would hardly have held on to a Jewish title so closely that Paul would use the title here. **15.** *grace be with you all:* In the plural (see comment on 1 Tm 6:21). Some textual witnesses add "of the Lord" to "grace"; the Vg adds "of God." Many textual witnesses, including the Vg, add "Amen" at the end.

58

THE FIRST EPISTLE OF PETER

Joseph A. Fitzmyer, S.J.

BIBLIOGRAPHY

1 Beare, F. W. *The First Epistle of St. Peter* (2nd ed.; Oxford, 1958). Bigg, C., *The Epistles of St. Peter and St. Jude* (ICC; N.Y., 1909) 1–198. Charue, A., "Première Épître de S. Pierre," *PSB* 12 (3rd ed.; 1951) 443–74. Cranfield, C. E. B., *The First Epistle of Peter* (London, 1958); *PCB* 1026–30. De Ambroggi, P., *Le Epistole cattoliche* (2nd ed.; Turin, 1949) 87–157. Franco, R., "Primera Carta de San Pedro," *La Sagrada Escritura* (BAC 214; Madrid, 1962) 219–97. Hunter, A. M., "The First Epistle of Peter," *IB* 12 (N.Y., 1957) 75–159. Leconte, R., *Les Épîtres catholiques* (BJ; 2nd ed.; Paris, 1961) 79–117. Margot, J. C., *Les Épîtres de Pierre* (Geneva, 1960). Michl, J., "Die katholischen Briefe," RNT 8 (Regensburg, 1953) 193–230. Moffatt, J., *The General Epistles: James, Peter, and Judas* (London, 1947) 85–171. Reicke, B., *Epistles of James, Peter, and Jude* (AB 37; Garden City, N.Y., 1964) 67–139. Rendtorff, H., *Getrostes Wandern* (7th ed.; Hamburg, 1951). Schelkle, K. H., *Die Petrusbriefe; der Judasbrief* (HTKNT 13/2; Freiburg, 1961) 1–136. Schneider, J., *Die Briefe des Jakobus, Petrus, Judas und Johannes: Die katholischen Briefe* (NTD 10; Göttingen, 1961) 39–99. Schweizer, E., *Der erste Petrusbrief* (Prophezei; 2nd ed.; Zurich, 1949). Selwyn, E. G., *The First Epistle of St. Peter* (London, 1958). Spicq, C., *Les Épîtres de Saint Pierre* (SB; Paris, 1966). Stibbs, A. M. and A. F. Walls, *The First Epistle General of Peter* (TynNTC; Grand Rapids, 1959). Wrede, W., "Der erste Petrusbrief," BB 9 (4th ed.; 1932) 79–117. Willmering, H., "The First Epistle of St. Peter," *CCHS* 1177–80. Windisch, H., *Die katholischen Briefe* (HNT 15; 3rd ed., rev. H. Preisker; Tübingen, 1951) 49–82.

Cantinat, J., R-F 2, 577–89. F-B 292–99. Guthrie, *NTI* 2, 95–136. Wik, *NTI* 493–509.

INTRODUCTION

2 **(I) Authorship.** The epistle purports to be written by "Peter, an apostle of Jesus Christ" (1:1), a "witness of the sufferings of the Messiah" (5:1). After Eusebius (*HE* 4.14, 9), it was regarded as the composition of the chief apostle until the 19th cent. In modern times, the following arguments have been proposed against its Petrine authorship: (1) The language and literary style are too good for a Galilean fisherman; (2) Papias (Eusebius, *HE* 3.39, 15) recorded that Peter had to use Mark as an interpreter. How then could he write such excellent Greek? (3) The OT quotations, derived from the LXX, are scarcely what one would expect from a Palestinian such as Peter. (4) The phraseology and thought-patterns are strikingly reminiscent of Paul's letters. (5) The letter's emphasis on persecution and suffering demands a later matrix (after the death of Peter, and probably during the persecution by Domitian). (6) The first Church writer to quote it is Polycarp of Smyrna (*Ep. ad Phil.* 1.3; 2.1; 5.3; etc. [*ca.* AD 135]). Because of these and similar arguments the letter has been held to be a *pseudepigraphon* (a work published under the name of some revered personage of the past—a feature not incompatible with inspiration, as can be seen from Dn, Jas, Jude, and 2 Pt). However, none of the reasons against Petrine authorship has been really convincing, especially when one recalls 1 Pt 5:12, "I have written to you briefly through [the help of] Silvanus." If this means, as is likely, that Peter used the services of a companion of Paul (cf. 1 Thes 1:1; 2 Thes 1:1; 2 Cor 1:19; Acts 15:22,27,32,40 [Silas]; 16:19,25,29; 17:4,10,14,15; 18:5), then most of the above objections are easily answered. Silvanus would have acted as Peter's secretary; the substance of the letter was dictated to him, and he was responsible for its wording and phraseology. Compare 1 Pt 5:10–11 with 1 Thes 5:23–28; 2 Thes 2:13–17. (See E. G. Selwyn, *First Epistle*, 9–17; L. Radermacher, *ZNW* 25 [1926] 287–99.)

3 **(II) Date, Occasion, Purpose.** Admitting the Petrine authorship of 1 Pt in this broad sense, we assign the letter to *ca.* AD 64, before Peter's death in Rome during Nero's persecution of that year (see Eusebius, *HE* 2.25, 5).

The letter is addressed to the "chosen sojourners of the Diaspora of Pontus, Galatia, Cappadocia, Asia, and Bithynia" (1:1). They are Gentile Christians (see 1 Pt 1:14,18; 2:9,10; 4:3–4) living in the northern and eastern part of Asia Minor. The "Diaspora" does not refer to the dispersion of the Jews (as in the LXX, Philo, Jn 7:35, Jdt 5:19), but figuratively denotes Gentile Christians who, as the new "people of God" (2:10), are scattered like strangers in this world, but whose real home is not here. The letter is an exhortation, composed by Peter in Rome and sent to the Christians of Asia Minor to console and strengthen them (cf. 5:12, *parakalōn*) in the new life to which they have been introduced by baptism. They are suffering persecution—which should not be too readily identified with an official, governmental persecution, since the letter also counsels obedience to civil authorities, even to the emperor (2:13–17). The suffering, calumny, and persecution seem to come from pagan neighbors who revile and abuse them for the "name of Christ" (4:14). Peter writes to urge them to be faithful to their calling, seeing that they are "a chosen race, a royal priesthood, a holy nation" (2:9).

4 **(III) Literary Genre.** Though 1 Pt has the outward form of a letter (with an opening formula, 1:1–2; and farewell greeting, 5:12–14), it has been thought to be a sermon or homily since the time of A. von Harnack. A clear break is found at 4:11 (note the doxology and "Amen"); the allusions to baptism in the first part (1:3–4:11) are so numerous that this section should be regarded as a baptismal exhortation incorporated into the letter. The rest (4:12–5:11) contains epistolary advice to the Christians who are now under the stress of persecution. It is impossible to determine whether the first part is made up of small units originally composed for another situation. R. Bultmann ("Bekenntnis- und Liedfragmente im ersten Petrusbrief," *ConNeot* 11 [1947 (Fest. A. Fridrichsen)] 1–14) regards 2:21–24 as a hymn and 3:18–19,22 as a credal confession. Similarly, M.-E. Boismard claims to have isolated four baptismal hymns in the letter (1:3–5; 3:18–22; 2:22–25; 5:5–9; see *Quatre hymnes baptismales dans la première épître de Pierre* [Paris, 1961]; *RB* 63 [1956] 182–208; 64 [1957] 161–83; *VieSp* 94 [1956] 339–52). F. L. Cross (*I. Peter: A Paschal Liturgy* [London, 1957]) goes still further, maintaining that 1:3–4:11 represents various prayers and homilies—the celebrant's part—of a Roman baptismal liturgy celebrated at Easter. He interprets the emphasis in 1 Pt on *paschō* (suffer) and *pathēma* (suffering) not as references to persecution but as allusions to the celebration of the Christian Passover (*pascha*). He divides the first part of 1 Pt thus: (1) the bishop's solemn opening prayer (1:3–12); (2) formal charge to the candidates (1:13–21), followed by actual baptism; (3) the bishop's welcome of the newly baptized (1:22–25); (4) the bishop's instruction on the fundamentals of sacramental life (2:1–10); (5) the bishop's address to the newly baptized about the duties of Christian discipleship (2:11–4:11). Finally, he admits with H. Preisker that 4:12–5:11 represents an address to the whole congregation present at the baptismal liturgy. Cross's suggestions, though attractive and ingenious, have met with strong criticism (see T. C. G. Thornton, *JTS* 12 [1961] 14–26; C. F. D. Moule, *NTS* 3 [1956–57] 1–11). To claim that we actually have the shape of a Roman baptismal liturgy in 1 Pt is certainly going too far. It seems better, then, to regard 1 Pt as a real letter into which a baptismal exhortation had been incorporated (1:3–4:11), or at least materials that often were used in such an exhortation. The second part (4:12–5:11) represents the letter proper and is truly epistolary in form and content. In this analysis we are substantially in agreement with F. W. Beare (*The First Epistle*; → NT Epistles, 47:4).

5 **(IV) Doctrine.** The principal topic of the letter is a discussion of the nature of the Christian life, begun in baptism as an experience of regeneration. From it, Peter draws his conclusions about the way the Christian is to conduct himself among pagan neighbors in the face of persecution. In baptism the Christian is regenerated to a new life through the very resurrection of Jesus. Baptism is not viewed merely as a rite of initiation into the Christian community but as a source communicating to the believer the life-giving power of the glorified Christ. But the corporate aspects of that regeneration are also emphasized, for by it one becomes part of God's people, a chosen race, a royal priesthood, a holy nation.

(Beare, F. W., "The Teaching of First Peter," *AnglTR* 26 [1944–45] 284–96. Thils, G., *L'enseignement de Saint Pierre* [3rd ed.; Paris, 1943].)

6 **(V) Outline.** The First Epistle of Peter is outlined as follows:

- (I) Introduction: Opening formula (1:1–2)
- (II) Part I: Baptismal Exhortation (1:3–4:11)
  - (A) Rejoice in the Salvation and New Life Given by God (1:3–12)
    - (a) Blessed Be God for This Gift (1:3–9)
    - (b) It Was Announced by the Prophets of Old (1:10–12)
  - (B) Exhortation to Live in Holiness as Befits the Chosen Race and the Royal Priesthood (1:13–2:10)
    - (a) You Must Be Holy Because You Are Ransomed by the Blood of Christ and Called to Brotherly Love (1:13–25)
    - (b) Live Up, Then, to Your Call as a Chosen Race and a Royal Priesthood (2:1–10)
  - (C) Exhortation to the Practical Aspects of Christian Life (2:11–3:12)
    - (a) Edify the Heathen Among Whom You Live (2:11–12)
    - (b) Obey Human Authority for the Lord's Sake (2:13–17)
    - (c) Counsels for Domestic Society (*Haustafel*) (2:18–3:7)
    - (d) All Must Live in Harmony (3:8–12)
  - (D) Instruction on the Blessing of Uncalled-For Persecution (3:13–4:11)
    - (a) Your Inspiring Conduct Should Shame Your Persecutors (3:13–17)
    - (b) The Example of Christ and the Effect of Baptism (3:18–22)
    - (c) Though Persecuted, Give Up the Heathen Way of Life (4:1–6)
    - (d) Sufferings Will Come Before the End; So Be Charitable (4:7–11)
- (III) Part II: Epistolary Advice for the Persecuted (4:12–5:11)
  - (A) Be Glad That You Share Christ's Sufferings (4:12–19)
  - (B) Let the Elders Be Seen as True Shepherds of the Flock (5:1–5)
  - (C) Trust in God Who Is Faithful to You (5:6–11)
- (IV) Conclusion: Silvanus Composed the Letter; Farewell (5:12–14)

COMMENTARY

7 **(I) Introduction: Opening formula (1:1–2).** The introduction to this letter resembles the *praescriptio* of a Pauline letter (→ NT Epistles, 47:8). **1.** *Peter:* Simon, son of John (Jn 1:42; 21:17; cf. comment on Mt 16:8), who is always mentioned first in the lists of the apostles (Mk 3:16 par.). Apart from his role as "apostle" (see comment on Gal 1:1), he does not consciously write in any other official capacity; in 5:1 he calls himself a

"fellow elder" (*sympresbyteros*) and "witness" (*martys*). *to the chosen sojourners:* The Gentile converts of Asia Minor are reminded in the greeting that they are elite, chosen by God's prevenient favor to be Christians, but are still "exiles," living in this world as in a foreign land. *of the Diaspora:* The word "Diaspora" designates the "Dispersion" of the Jews among the Gentiles (LXX: Dt 28:25; 30:4). It was technically applied to colonies of Jews living outside Palestine in Hellenistic times, especially after the Babylonian Captivity (Jdt 5:19; 2 Mc 1:27; Jn 7:35). It was also applied to colonies of Jewish Christians (Jas 1:1). Peter uses it of Gentile Christians living among pagans, far from the real "holy land." *Pontus, Galatia, Cappadocia, Asia, Bithynia:* These are not the official designations of the Roman provinces in Asia Minor, because Pontus and Bithynia formed only one. Taken as a group, they designate the area of northern Asia Minor. **2.** The election of these Christians is ascribed to the Father, Jesus, and the Spirit. They are chosen in the Father's foreknowledge. Their call is effected by the Spirit's consecrating power, and their goal is both a commitment to Christ and a share in the sprinkling with his blood (cf. Ex 24:8). *grace and peace be abundantly yours:* The Pauline formula ("grace and peace") is modified by an OT greeting (Dn 3:31 [Eng 4:1]).

8 **(II) Part I: Baptismal Exhortation (1:3–4:11).** As a basis for the consolation Peter sends to the Christians of Asia Minor, he describes the meaning of their new life received in Christian baptism.

(A) Rejoice in the Salvation and New Life Given by God (1:3–12).

(a) BLESSED BE GOD FOR THIS GIFT (1:3–9). **3.** *blessed be...:* Cf. 2 Cor 1:3; 11:31; Eph 1:3. God is praised for this gift of new life in the manner of Jewish blessings (cf. 1 Kgs 1:48; 2 Chr 2:11; 6:4). He is praised not only as God, but as God revealed in his relation to his Son, Jesus Christ. *who caused us to be born again:* The spiritual rebirth of Christians to a new life is the main topic of this part (see 1:23; 2:2; cf. Jn 3:3; 1 Jn 2:29; 3:9). *through the resurrection:* New life comes to the Christian through (*dia*) the one great act in Christ's existence, his resurrection. As in Rom 6:3–11, it is baptism that allows him to share in it (see 3:21). **4.** *for an imperishable inheritance:* The hope engendered by rebirth is rooted in the indestructible nature of the Christian heritage. Canaan became the "inheritance" of Israel (Dt 15:4; 19:10; cf. Ps 79:1); but the Christian inheritance is not earthly: It cannot be ravaged by war, defiled by enemies, or faded by time. It is heavenly (cf. Col 1:5,12; Lk 12:33). **5.** *guarded by God's power:* The security of the Christian inheritance is like that of a land with strong military protection. It is the very power of God, which raised up Jesus and endowed him with the glory that brings this security (cf. Rom 1:4; 1 Cor 1:18; 5:4; 6:14; 13:4; Phil 3:10). *salvation:* The goal of Christian faith is presented in its eschatological aspect (as in 1:9,10; 2:2; cf. 3:21). *last time:* For a similar expression, cf. the Qumran phrase "end time" (*qēṣ 'aḥarôn*, 1QS 4:16; 1QpHab 7:7,12). **6.** *rejoice in this:* Lit., "in which rejoice," or possibly "in which you do rejoice." Though the pronoun might refer to God, Christ, or even the "last time," it is best construed with the whole thought of 1:3–5. *trials:* The first mention of the trouble afflicting the Christians of Asia Minor (see 4:12–19; 2:12,19; 3:13–17; cf. E. G. Selwyn, *BulSNTS* 1 [1950] 39–50). **7.** *your faith:* Understood here in the sense of "constancy" or "fidelity" (cf. Jas 1:12). *at the revelation of Jesus Christ:* The parousia, when Christ is Judge (1:13; 4:3; 5:1; 2 Thes 1:7–8). **9.** *the goal of your faith: Telos* expresses at once the temporal end and the logical *finis* of earthly Christian experience. *your souls:* That is, yourselves (1:22; 2:11; → Pauline Theology, 79:120).

9 (b) IT WAS ANNOUNCED BY THE PROPHETS OF OLD (1:10–12). **10.** *prophets:* The OT prophets are depicted as searching for the meaning of the salvation that God was announcing through them. But Peter discloses its meaning (cf. the role of the Righteous Teacher in 1QpHab 7:1–5). **11.** *the Spirit of Christ:* The late Jewish teaching that the prophets spoke under the inspiration of God's Spirit (cf. Is 61:1) was adopted by the early Church. In applying this to OT writers, Peter links the phases of salvation history. *sufferings...glories:* The two phases of the Christian mystery give meaning to the experience of those to whom Peter writes. **12.** *not themselves...but you:* The relevance of the former prophecies is now made clear to those who believe in Jesus as the Christ (Messiah). So great is God's salvation that the prophets of old and even the angels earnestly long to know it. (See J. Coutts, *NTS* 3 [1956–57] 115–27.)

10 **(B) Exhortation to Live in Holiness as Befits the Chosen Race and the Royal Priesthood (1:13–2:10).**

(a) YOU MUST BE HOLY BECAUSE YOU ARE RANSOMED BY THE BLOOD OF CHRIST AND CALLED TO BROTHERLY LOVE (1:13–25). **13.** *gird up your minds:* A figure expressing vigilance for the parousia (cf. Lk 12:35; Eph 6:14). **14.** *former ignorance:* Of God. As a result, they were subject to passions and purposeless existence (1:18; cf. Acts 17:30; Eph 4:17–18). **15.** *be holy:* That is, be dedicated to the service of God. The covenant relationship, not some taboo, was the foundation of the holiness expected of Israel as a dedicated people, set apart for the service of Yahweh (cf. Ex 19:3–6; 22:31). **16.** See Lv 11:44–45; 19:2; 20:7. Israel's Exodus experience is now renewed as a new people of God is fashioned. **17.** *address as Father:* The Christian who regards the Divine Judge who is to scrutinize his conduct as a Father must therefore conduct himself as a circumspect and obedient child (cf. Gal 4:6; Rom 8:15). **18.** *not ransomed with...silver:* Allusion to Is 52:3. (On "ransom" as a figure of Christian redemption, see comment on Rom 3:24.) **19.** *precious blood of Christ:* The mode of the redemption is thus expressed: by the life of Christ (see Lv 17:14, "The life of every creature is its blood"), by its costly worth (cf. 1 Cor 6:20; 7:23). Cf. Eph 1:7; Heb 9:12. *like a lamb without blemish:* This is the requirement for a sacrificial lamb in Lv 22:19–25; there is undoubtedly an allusion here to the paschal lamb (Ex 12:5). **20.** *before the foundation of the world:* Ransom through Christ was part of God's eternal plan of salvation (cf. Rom 16:25–26). *manifested at the end of times:* The incarnation of Christ is the event that initiated an end time (see comment on Rom 5:14; 1 Cor 10:11). **21.** *raised him:* As does Paul, so Peter echoes the early Church's belief that the Father raised Jesus from the dead (Acts 3:15; 4:10; 5:30; 10:40; 1 Thes 1:10). *gave him glory:* Glory (*doxa*) is the essential characteristic of the Risen Jesus (Acts 3:13; 2 Cor 3:18; 4:4–6; Rom 6:4). **22.** *souls:* See comment on 1:9. **23.** *born anew:* The new life of the Christian is derived from the "Word of God," which is seen to be creative, effective of a new existence, and revitalizing. *living and abiding:* Philologically, these adjectives could be construed either with "God" (so E. J. Goodspeed, J. Knox) or (better) with "word" (RSV, NEB). The contrast seems to be between the frailty of man and the permanence of God's word in him. **24.** Is 40:6–8 (LXX). These consoling words were originally addressed to Jewish exiles; now they are transferred to the new Christian "exiles." (See M. H. Scharlemann, *CTM* 30 [1959] 352–56.)

11 (b) LIVE UP, THEN, TO YOUR CALL AS A CHOSEN RACE AND A ROYAL PRIESTHOOD (2:1–10). **2.** *like newborn infants:* Newly baptized Christians should manifest toward Christian truth the intense eagerness that infants show for food, for that which promotes growth and maturing development. *pure spiritual milk:* The unadulterated food proper to man's *logos*, i.e., the Christian Gospel, gives nourishment and contains nothing that hinders Christian growth. **3.** *tasted that the Lord is good:* Allusion to Ps 34:8. Like the eager infant, the Christian has already learned how good the Lord is. **4.** *come to him:* Join fully in the community of the New Israel, by joining yourselves to Christ, its cornerstone. *the living stone, rejected by men:* The words of Ps 118:22 are applied to the Risen Christ, who was rejected but whose precious quality in God's sight is found in the new life he shares with those who come to him. **5.** *be built into a spiritual house:* Or possibly, "you are being built" (indicative). Christians are "living stones," not just as persons contrasted with the inanimate blocks used in pagan temples but as persons vivified by the life of Christ himself in baptism. So united to Christ, the cornerstone, they form a new unit, which the author proceeds to describe in several mixed images. They form first a spiritual house (*oikos pneumatikos*), i.e., a new temple in which the bonding material is not race, but the Spirit. (For the image of the community as a "new temple," see 4:17; 1 Cor 3:16–17; 2 Cor 6:16; Eph 2:21–22; 1QS 8:5–8; B. Gärtner, *The Temple and the Community in Qumran and the New Testament* [Cambridge, 1965] 72–88.) *a holy priesthood:* By baptism Christians are called and destined to this service (specified in the rest of the verse; see further 2:9). The term *hierateuma* may mean either "priesthood, body of priests" or "the exercise of priestly functions." In either case, it would indicate the role of the Christian. But in view of 2:9, the first meaning seems preferable. **6.** The quotation is an adapted form of Is 28:16 (LXX). Verses 6–8 are really parenthetical, explicative of what was said in 2:4–5. For Christ as the "cornerstone" see Eph 2:20; as such, he controls the shape and design of the edifice. **7.** *therefore the value [of this stone is] for you who believe:* This seems to be the best sense of this difficult phrase. The value of the stone for believers is contrasted with its function for those who do not believe; this is set forth in the quotation from Ps 118:22 and Is 8:14–15. Since the reference in 2:9–10 seems to be to Gentile converts, the unbelievers are most likely the Jews who have not accepted Christ. **8.** *they were destined:* Israel's stumbling is ascribed to God (cf. Rom 11:11).

12 **9.** *chosen race:* The first of four OT titles for Israel that are now applied to the Christian community. This title echoes the *praescriptio* (1:1) and reflects Is 43:2 (*to genos mou to eklekton*). It expresses the corporate destiny of Christians, stemming from their divine election. *a royal priesthood:* See comment on 2:5. The second title is derived from Ex 19:6; whatever the specific nuance of the title in its original context may be (see W. L. Moran, "A Kingdom of Priests," *BCCT* 7–20), it at least designates the people of Israel as a nation dedicated to the worship and service of Yahweh, their king. Their conduct among the nations was expected to be such as to manifest them as his royal courtiers and his priestly servants. This title is now transferred by Peter to Christians, who by their baptism are deputed to the cultic service of God in Christ. It is at once a royal and a priestly destination. In Rom 12:1 Paul appeals to Christians to offer themselves as a "living sacrifice" that would be holy and acceptable to God; this is to be their "spiritual worship." The baptized Christian is therefore empowered and expected to live his whole life as if it were a cultic act, continuing in a sense the sacrifice of Christ, but also manifesting to the world that he is marked for the service of Christ. *a holy nation:* The third title is also derived from Ex 19:6. By baptism Christians are set apart and dedicated to the sacral order of things (see comment on 1:16). *a people for [his] possession:* The fourth title is an adaptation of Ex 19:6 (*laos perousios*) and of Mal 3:17 (*eis peripoiēsin*). The proprietorship of Christ over the Christian is established in baptism. Since the Christians addressed in the letter come from different races, nations, and peoples, Peter's language is bold in using "race, nation, people" to designate the new unity that they have in Christ—a unity transcending all other barriers and distinctions. *that you may declare the virtues of him:* The Gk word *aretas* would denote the "excellent, noble acts" of God, and such a declaration would suit the cultic service of Christians. Possibly Peter is alluding to Is 43:21 (LXX: "to recount my virtues"), where *aretas* is the equivalent of "praise" in the MT. An additional cultic sense would then be intended. *from darkness...into light:* From paganism to Christianity (see Acts 26:17–18). The phrase would indicate the cultic character of the witness that the baptized Christian is to bear before the world. **10.** *no people:* Allusion to Hos 1:9; 2:23 (cf. Rom 9:25–26). The expression refers to their former pagan status. *God's people:* The reason why Christians are called the people of God appears in the rest of the verse, which is a reflection of Hos 1:6. They are such because his "mercy" and loving kindness have formed them into the new corporate reality that they are. The idea that the whole Christian people is a royal priesthood does not exclude certain men from being designated for cultic, ritual service any more than the fact that all Israel was a royal priesthood prevented the existence of the Levitical priesthood. See J. H. Elliott, *The Elect and the Holy* (NovTSup 12; Leiden, 1966).

(Blinzler, J., "Hierateuma. Zur Exegese von 1 Petr 2, 5 u. 9," *Episcopus* [Fest. M. v. Faulhaber; Regensburg, 1949] 49–65. Cerfaux, L., "Regale sacerdotium," *Recueil L. Cerfaux* [Gembloux, 1954] 2, 283–315. Pelland, L., "Le sacerdoce des fidèles," *ScEccl* 2 [1949] 5–26.)

13 **(C) Exhortation to the Practical Aspects of Christian Life (2:11–3:12).** Peter has described the unique character of communal Christian life in the New Israel; he now sets forth what is concretely required of its members.

(a) EDIFY THE HEATHEN AMONG WHOM YOU LIVE (2:11–12). **11.** *aliens and sojourners:* A phrase adopted from Gn 23:4; Ps 39:13 (LXX) recalls to Christians their need of detachment from the attractive things of this world, since they are citizens of another (cf. Phil 3:20; Heb 11:13). **12.** *as wrongdoers:* Slander may discredit the name of Christians, but God on the day when he will scrutinize men's conduct will give their pagan neighbors cause to praise him as he reacts to the good deeds of Christians. He will make the truth known.

14 (b) OBEY HUMAN AUTHORITY FOR THE LORD'S SAKE (2:13–17). **13.** *every human institution:* The word *ktisis* elsewhere in the NT (and LXX) refers to divine "creation," and here it may suggest the divine origin of the social institutions to be mentioned. However, because *ktisis* was also the ordinary Gk word for the "founding" of a city, the divine origin of the "institutions" may not necessarily be connoted. Again, one cannot exclude the possibility of the translation, "every human creature." In this case, 2:13 would serve as a general introduction to 2:13–3:12. *for the Lord's sake:* In any case, the motive for civic duty is sought not in the imitation of Christ, but in a desire to honor him. **14.** *governors:* In the Roman provinces. Their job is to curb the excesses of unprincipled

human striving. **15.** *foolish men:* The hostile pagan neighbors. **16.** *live as free men:* In the context Peter refers to political freedom. He insists that the Christian citizen is free because he is a servant of God. It is not a question of license or wrongdoing; this submission to civil rulers is the act of a free man who realizes the relation of civil authority to himself, as an individual and as a member of the Christian community, and to God (cf. 1 Cor 7:22; Gal 5:13). **17.** *brotherhood:* The Christian community as the new people of God (cf. Prv 24:21; Mt 22:21). (See E. Bammel, *NTS* 11 [1964–65] 279–81.)

15 (c) COUNSELS FOR DOMESTIC SOCIETY (*Haustafel*) (2:18–3:7). **18.** *slaves:* The Christian who is a slave is called upon to obey even a difficult master (cf. Eph 6:5; Ti 2:9–10). Neither Peter nor Paul, though they were apostles of the nascent Christian Church, tried to put an end to the institution of slavery. They aimed rather at giving slavery a Christian meaning and at interiorizing it. **21.** *to this you have been called:* Not to slavery, but to the patient suffering of unjust wrongs, for Christ left us all an example of this. The Christian vocation entails such a response. Verses 21–25 may be hymnic, a Christian reworking of the Servant Song of Is 53:4–12. *a model:* Christ in his suffering is the pattern for Christian suffering. **22.** Cf. Is 53:9. **24.** Cf. Is 53:4,12. Christ carried the sins of men up to the cross in his body, undergoing the "curse" for them (Gal 3:13; Dt 21:23). It was on the cross (lit., "wood") that Christ fulfilled the role of the Suffering Servant. *you have been healed:* Cf. Is 53:6. The result is that the Christian has not only been forgiven his sins, but has in effect abandoned sin. **25.** *shepherd and guardian:* Christ, cf. 5:4; Jn 10:11; Heb 13:20. (For the OT background of Yahweh (or his Anointed) as the Shepherd, see Ps 23; Is 40:11; Ez 37:24.) Note in Acts 20:28 the collocation of "shepherd and guardian" applied to the "elders" of the Ephesian church, summoned to Miletus to hear Paul.

16 **3:1.** *though not obedient to the word:* Christian wives are counseled to strive to win over by their conduct husbands who do not accept the Christian message. The ideal conduct of the wife is that of the silent witness; it may even succeed where the preacher fails. "Word" (*logos*) is here used in two different senses. **2.** *reverent and chaste behavior:* Lit., "chaste behavior with reverence." These qualities of the Christian wife are intimately associated. They are exemplified in the following verses. **4.** *the hidden person of the heart:* Though applied to the wife, the phrase uses *anthrōpos* (man, human being); cf. Paul's expression, "the inner man" (Rom 7:22; 2 Cor 4:16; Eph 3:16). **6.** *Sarah:* Cf. Gn 18:12; Heb 11:11. *calling him lord:* In Gn 18:12 Sarah says *'^{a}dōnî zāqēn*, "My lord [husband] is old." This became in the LXX *ho de kyrios mou presbyteros*; and to this Peter now alludes, using *kyrios* as an indication of her submission. *whose children you are:* In a spiritual sense, because of the good conduct that is similar to hers. **7.** *live with your wives with understanding:* Whereas Paul (Eph 5:25) counseled husbands above all to the obligation of loving their wives, Peter puts the emphasis on an understanding consideration of them. *showing honor to the weaker sex:* The element characterizing woman most in her relation to man is looked on as precisely the reason for the esteem that is her due. *joint heirs of the gift of life:* The relationship of husband and wife is based on the mutual realization that both have received from God a grace (*charis*) for the life they live together. Such a realization is to lead to their communion with God in prayer.

(d) ALL MUST LIVE IN HARMONY (3:8–12). The exhortation concludes with a recommendation addressed to all the members of domestic society singled out in the foregoing *Haustafel*. **8.** *love of the brothers:* Among the five virtues recommended here "love of the brotherhood" stands out (see 2:17; cf. C. Spicq, *Agape in the NT* [St. Louis, 1965] 2, 354–57. **9.** Cf. Rom 12:17; 1 Thes 5:15. *that you might inherit a blessing:* Cf. Gn 27:29; 49:25–26. **10.** Ps 34:13–17 (LXX, slightly modified) is quoted. In the OT, "life" refers to a long, prosperous existence on this earth, but here it denotes "eternal life." This quotation concludes the exhortation to the practical aspects of Christian life that was begun in 2:11.

17 **(D) Instruction on the Blessing of Uncalled-For Persecution (3:13–4:11).** Peter recommends the practice of goodness in the face of persecution and the remembrance of the blessing that such suffering really is.

(a) YOUR INSPIRING CONDUCT SHOULD SHAME YOUR PERSECUTORS (3:13–17). **14.** *blessed are you:* Cf. Mt 5:10–11; Is 59:9. *Makarios* means "happy, fortunate," but always with a religious connotation. *have no fear:* Quotation of Is 8:12–13 (LXX, slightly modified). Respect for Christ should transcend all other fears that might invade the Christian heart. **15.** *a defense:* Of one's Christian commitment; it does not necessarily refer to an official appearance before the tribunal of some magistrate in a governmental persecution. *the hope that is in you:* Not just a conviction about future expectations, but the very essence of the motivation of the new people of God. It is their imperishable and undefiled inheritance. **17.** Cf. 2:20, where the instruction was directed to slaves; now it is made more general.

18 (b) THE EXAMPLE OF CHRIST AND THE EFFECT OF BAPTISM (3:18–22). This section adds an exhortation of consolation as a reason for what is recommended in 3:17. The exhortation is based on the example of Christ and the effect of baptism. A comparison is made between the suffering of the Gentile Christians and the suffering of Christ. Just as he triumphed, so will they. Their baptism is the pledge of their triumph, for it gives them a share in his resurrection. For he was put to death as far as his earthly existence (*sarki*) was concerned, yet he was made to live spiritually (*pneumati*). In this condition he proclaimed his triumph, even to the disobedient spirits of the period of Noah. Just as Noah was saved by passage through the waters of the flood, so the Christian will be saved by passage through the waters of baptism—its antitype.

The fifth article of the Creed ("he descended into hell") is based on such NT passages as Rom 10:6–7; Eph 4:8–10; Heb 13:20; Acts 2:24,31; Mt 12:40. But it is quite another question whether this passage in 1 Pt deals with the "harrowing of Hell"; it has often been so interpreted and has supplied imaginative details for what Christ did during the *Triduum mortis*. However, it is not at all certain that Peter refers to this.

19 The main interpretations of this passage fall into five classes: (1) The *Bowyer Greek Testament* (1763) and J. Rendel Harris emended 3:19 to introduce Enoch into the text (reading *en hō kai* as haplography for *en hō Enōch kai*); see E. J. Goodspeed's translation, "In it Enoch went and preached." (2) Clement of Alexandria (*Stromateis* 6.6; GCS 15.454–55): Christ's soul went to Hades to preach conversion to the sinners of the generation of the flood, who were detained there. (3) Robert Bellarmine (*De controversiis* 2.4, 13): Christ's soul went to announce release to the just in Limbo (the sinners of Noah's time who repented before the flood). (4) Augustine (*Ep.* 164; CSEL 44, 521–41): Christ in his divine pre-existence preached through Noah to the sinners of his generation, not in Hades but on earth. (5) F. Spitta (*Christi Predigt an die Geister* [Göttingen, 1890]), E. G. Selwyn, B. Reicke, W. J. Dalton—all with varying nuances: The Risen Christ proclaimed his triumph to the imprisoned spirits as he passed through the heavens to his exaltation.—We follow this opinion.

20 **18.** *Christ too died:* Some mss. read "suffered" (*epathen*), which is more suited to the context, but is suspect because it is influenced by 2:21. Peter proposes Christ's example as a motive of patience in the persecution. But he also emphasizes the unique character of his death, in view of man's redemption (cf. Rom 6:10; Heb 9:28; Eph 3:12). *an upright man:* The early Church's epithet for Jesus (cf. Acts 3:14; 7:52; 22:14) brings out the vicarious character of Christ's suffering; it is an allusion to Is 53:11. *to bring you near to God:* Christ's death was not only a model (2:21), but also gave men new access to God (Rom 5:1–2). By taking away sin (2:24), Christ broke down the barrier between God and man (cf. Eph 3:12; Col 1:22). *put to death in his flesh:* That is, in his physical, earthly condition in which he resembles all other men (Rom 8:3; Eph 2:14). The word *sarx* here does not mean "body" (in contrast to his soul), nor even "humanity" (in contrast to his divine pre-existence), but Christ's earthly human condition (contrasted with his risen state). *made to live in the Spirit:* At the resurrection, Christ became *pneuma*. Raised by the Father's glory (*doxa*, Rom 6:4), Christ was endowed with a power (*dynamis*, Phil 3:10) making him a "vivifying Spirit" (1 Cor 15:45). The *sarx-pneuma* contrast used here is found also in Rom 1:3–4; 1 Tm 3:16. The *pneuma* does not just mean Christ's "soul" or his "divine pre-existence." **19.** *in it:* Or "with it," i.e., the Spirit. The phrase is best understood instrumentally; however, it is possibly temporal ("in this situation"), referring not immediately to *pneuma*, but to the whole preceding sentence (v. 18b). It has nothing to do with Enoch. *he [Christ] went:* Not to "Hades," but "to heaven," as the direction is specified in 3:22, where the same participle (*poreutheis*) is used. Christ, exalted in his ascension, passed through "all the heavens" (Eph 4:10); en route he proclaimed his triumph. The imagery implied here is that of the Seven Heavens (see *T. Levi*, 2:7–3:8; *2 Enoch* 3–20; *3 Baruch*; cf. R. H. Charles, *APOT* 2, 433). This imagery is reflected in the NT, too (2 Cor 12:2; Eph 1:3,20; Heb 4:14; 7:26). Christ is depicted as mounting in triumphant procession to the abode of God in the seventh heaven, as in Col 2:15. *preached:* Or better, "announced." No object of the vb. *ekēryxen* is given, and it has often been interpreted in terms of *euēggelisthē* (4:6, see comment). But there is no reason to introduce "gospel," or even "conversion," or "release" into this context. It would be more consonant with Col 2:15 to introduce a proclamation of Christ's triumph to the imprisoned spirits who are passed along the way. *imprisoned spirits:* These are not the "dead" (*nekroi*) of 4:6. They are rather the well-known angelic spirits imprisoned in the second heaven (cf. *2 Enoch* 7:1–5 [*APOT* 2, 433]; *Enoch* 6–36; esp. 21:6; 67:4; *Jub* 10). Christ's proclamation to them is merely a way of asserting his triumph (see 3:22). It is in the long run a minor detail, not at all crucial in the consolation Peter offers to his readers. **20.** *disobeyed long ago:* See Gn 6:1–5. In late Judaism, human wickedness was explained as derived from the miscegenation of the angels and daughters of men, and the angels were themselves branded as disobedient. Their "disobedience" is found in Josephus, *Ant.* 1.3, 1 § 73; *Enoch* 15:1–11; *Jub* 5. In Gn 6 it precedes the Noah story and thus is related to his epoch in the intertestamental literature. *God's patience waited:* Peter alludes to the interval in the Gn account between God's resolve (Gn 6:6) and the execution of it (Gn 7:11). The supposition is that Noah ("the preacher of uprightness," 2 Pt 2:5) announced God's resolve during the time spent building the ark. *eight persons:* Noah, his wife, three sons, and their wives (Gn 7:13). *through the water:* This awkward phrase—Noah was not really saved "through the water"—is so formulated in view of the comparison with baptism to be made in the next verse.

21 **21.** *baptism:* The salvific effects of this passage through water are ascribed at the end of the verse to Christ's resurrection. *its counterpart:* Lit., "antitype," i.e:, that which corresponds to (or is set over against) the "type" preceding it. Note that the type is not the ark, but the "passage through water." Noah's passage, effected in the ark, meant the saving of Noah and his family from the flood; for the Christian, the baptismal passage means eternal salvation and association with the triumph of the Risen Christ. *not as a mere removal of physical dirt:* It is not just a washing, but signifies far more. *a pledge of a good conscience:* The Gk word *eperōtēma* most likely means the same as it does in contracts, the "agreement" or "consent" to their essential stipulations. It equals *homologia* and connotes that the baptized person professes thereby a faith in God (see Rom 10:9–10). *through the resurrection:* Cf. 1:3; Rom 6:3–9; Col 2:11. **22.** *gone to heaven:* See comment on 3:19 (cf. Eph 1:21; Acts 1:10; Heb 1:4). *God's right hand:* The imagery is derived from ancient Near Eastern (especially Egyptian) customs of depicting the king as seated at the right hand of a god. It denoted both his divinity and his function as the god's vicegerent to whom all authority and power were entrusted. The image entered Christian conception by way of Ps 110:1, which is applied to Christ in Acts 2:33–35; Rom 8:34; Heb 8:1; Mt 22:44. *with angels...made subject to him:* The spirits otherwise known from Phil 2:10; 1 Cor 15:24,27; Rom 8:38; Col 2:10,15; Eph 1:21; 3:10; 6:12. Christ has gone to the seventh heaven, where God is, and thus is in triumph over all that represents disobedience, rebellion, and persecution.

(Dalton, W. J., "Proclamatio Christi spiritibus facta," *VD* 42 [1964] 225–40; *Christ's Proclamation to the Spirits: A Study of 1 Peter 3:18–4:6* [AnalBib 23; Rome, 1965]. Gschwind, K., *Die Niederfahrt Christi in die Unterwelt* [NTAbh 2/3–5; Münster, 1911]. Reicke, B., *The Disobedient Spirits and Christian Baptism* [København, 1946].)

22 (c) THOUGH PERSECUTED, GIVE UP THE HEATHEN WAY OF LIFE (4:1–6). **1.** Peter returns to the example of the suffering Christ (see 3:18). *has ceased from sin:* Such suffering implies a union and a compatibility with Christ that make it impossible for man to sin, to show any compatibility with sin (see Rom 6:1–10; 1 Jn 3:6). **4.** *do not now join them:* As you did before your conversion. **5.** *give account:* Of their licentious conduct and of their abuse of Christians. *judge the living and the dead:* This function is given to Christ in the NT (Acts 10:42; 1 Cor 4:5; 2 Tm 4:1), a role he has received from the Father (Jn 5:22,27). **6.** *he was preached:* Christ, as in Acts 5:43; 8:35; 11:20; 17:18; Gal 1:16. Also possible is the meaning, "the gospel was preached." *even to the dead:* That is, to those now dead, to Christians who heard the good news either from Christ or from his disciples and have passed on before the writing of this letter (cf. 1 Thes 4:13ff.). The "dead" should not be facilely identified with the "imprisoned spirits" of 3:19. (See J. Frings, *BZ* 17 [1925] 75–88.)

23 (d) SUFFERINGS WILL COME BEFORE THE END; SO BE CHARITABLE (4:7–11). **7.** *the end:* Cf. 1:5; 4:17; 5:10. A motive of Christian morality is found in the imminence of the parousia (cf. Lk 21:36; 1 Cor 7:29; 10:11; Jas 5:8). **8.** *love covers a host of sins:* A modified form of the MT of Prv 10:12 ("Love puts a covering over all transgressions") was used as an early Christian proverb. The sense seems to be: (Brotherly) love will overwhelm and offset the wrongs that are being done (see Jas 5:20; Lk 7:47; 1 Cor 13:7). A call for love is also connected

with the parousia in Rom 13:8–14. **9.** *hospitality:* Cf. Rom 12:13; Phil 2:14; Heb 13:2; 3 Jn 5–8. **10.** *serving one another:* God's charisms are intended for the social life of the Church (see 1 Cor 12:4–11; Rom 12:6–8). *managers of God's diverse gifts:* Like the steward in God's spiritual household, you should be dispensing to others what has been entrusted to your care. **11.** *words of God:* The *logia theou* do not refer immediately to Scripture. Peter counsels the preacher not to purvey his own ideas, but to transmit God's utterances in accordance with the inspiration given to him (1 Cor 14:2–19). *through Jesus Christ:* The doxology is addressed to the Father "through" Christ (as in Rom 16:27; Ap 1:6), but also "to" Christ. In this double aspect, this doxology is unique in the NT; contrast 2 Tm 4:18; Heb 13:21; Ap 5:13; 7:10; 2 Pt 3:18. This doxology does not necessarily mean the end of the source used in the composition of the letter, but it does mark a division of it.

24 **(III) Part II: Epistolary Advice for the Persecuted (4:12–5:11).** This part of the letter differs from the preceding in that suffering is now regarded as not merely possible, but actual.

(A) Be Glad That You Share Christ's Sufferings (4:12–19). These verses are transitional, in that they recapitulate the baptismal exhortation and apply it to the present reality. **12.** *an ordeal of fire:* Persecutions that are violent (1:6–7; 3:16). **13.** *share the sufferings of Christ:* "We suffer with him in order to be also glorified with him" (Rom 8:17). The Christian is called to bear an apostolic tribulation (cf. 2 Tm 2:12; Col 1:24; Jas 1:2; Acts 5:41). **14.** *blessed:* See comment on 3:14. *the Spirit of glory and of God:* The text is corrupt here, but this translation represents the best reading; some mss. (S, A, C, P) add after "glory": "and of power." (See A. Garcia del Moral, *EstBib* 20 [1961] 45–77, 169–90.) God's Spirit as the source of glory and the pledge of future glory is regarded as resting on the suffering Church (cf. Is 11:2; Lk 10:6). **15.** *as a Christian:* The name (which occurs again only in Acts 11:26; 26:28) implies in this context a compatibility with Christ in suffering. *not be ashamed:* Cf. Phil 1:20. **17.** *judgment to begin with God's household:* The present trials and persecution are a manifestation of the eschatological "judgment" (*krima*) being passed on the Christian community itself, in the spirit of Jer 25:29; Ez 9:6. But if these are so violent, what will God's judgment be like for those who are not of his household? **18.** Allusion to the LXX rendering of Prv 11:31. **19.** *suffering by God's will:* Cf. 2:20; 3:17.

25 **(B) Let the Elders Be Seen as True Shepherds of the Flock (5:1–5).** **1.** *elders:* The *presbyteroi* were entrusted with an official function (administrative, 1 Tm 5:17; and cultic, Jas 5:14) in the Christian community. Such men were set up by traveling apostles (Acts 14:23). Note that Peter writes as *sympresbyteros*, "fellow elder." **2.** *be shepherds of God's flock:* The pastoral care of the Church is entrusted to such "elders," as it is in Acts 20:17,28. They are to "oversee" and "tend" the flock in doctrine and in discipline. Some mss. add *episkopountes* (overseeing); for the collocation of the two notions, see comment on 2:25. *not for shameful profit:* Such a motive is to be ever far from the minds of those who are "elders" in God's Church (see Ti 1:7; 1 Tm 3:8). **4.** *chief Shepherd:* Christ in his parousia is depicted in the role of shepherd (see 2:25). This image brings out the pastoral aspect of Christ's activity in salvation and his relation to the others in his Church who are also "pastors." *crown of glory:* Cf. Jer 13:18 and the Qumran equivalent in 1QS 4:7; 1QH 9:25 (see comment on 1 Thes 2:19). **5.** *younger men:* Having mentioned "elders" (as a class), Peter plays on the more basic meaning of the word and sets up a contrast (cf. 1 Tm 4:12; 5:1; Ti 2:6–8; Eph 5:21). *all of you:* Humility is required of all members in the Christian community, not just the young. *clothe yourselves:* Lit., "tie about yourselves," or "button on." This rare verb expresses the effort required to cultivate the true humility expected of the Christian. *God opposes the proud:* Quotation of Prv 3:34 (LXX); cf. Jas 4:6–10. Humility is needed not only toward "one another," but also toward "God" himself, as 5:6 indicates. *God's mighty hand:* An OT phrase (Ex 13:9; Dt 3:24; 9:26,29; 26:8) that often expressed the mighty acts by which God raised up a people for himself and brought them out of Egyptian bondage.

26 **(C) Trust in God Who Is Faithful to You (5:6–11).** **6.** *in due time:* That is, in his own good time. **7.** Allusion to Ps 55:23; cf. Mt 6:25–34. **8.** *be watchful:* The early Church's exhortation to watchfulness always implies a confidence and trust in God. Peter's counsel here is ironic in view of Mk 13:37; 14:34–40. *your adversary the devil:* Both *antidikos* (opponent in a lawsuit) and *diabolos* (accuser) mean the same thing; the latter translates the Hebr *śāṭān* in Jb, whence the proper name "Satan." From Ps 22:14 Peter borrows the description of him as a "roaring [raging with hunger] lion." He thus personifies the persecution that the Christians are experiencing; it is, as it were, an attack of Satan. **10.** *God of all grace:* Cf. 2 Cor 1:3 ("God of all consolation"). In 4:10 Peter spoke of the "multicolored grace" of God, referring to the varied and diverse favors given to Christians for service in the Church. *called you to his eternal glory:* Cf. 1 Thes 2:12; 5:24. Having summoned men to this destiny, God will not fail to strengthen them in the trial that briefly faces them before they obtain it. *in Christ:* The destiny of the Christian is always related to Christ (note again the Pauline expression; cf. 3:16; 5:14). **11.** Doxology addressed to the Father.

27 **(IV) Conclusion: Silvanus Composed the Letter; Farewell (5:12–14).** Peter may have written these verses in his own hand (cf. Gal 6:11; 1 Cor 16:21). **12.** *Silvanus:* The companion of Paul (→ 2 above). *exhorting:* The letter's purpose is thus stated. *the true grace of God:* Possibly a figurative expression for the persecution that the readers are suffering. **13.** *she:* The local church of Rome. *at Babylon:* A cryptic name for Rome, characteristic of persecution literature (see Ap 14:8; 16:19; 17:5; 18:2,10; cf. *2 Baruch* 11:1; 67:7; *Sib Or* 5:143,159). In NT times Rome had taken on the characteristics of the classic example of a world power hostile to God—Babylon, whose king had destroyed Jerusalem and Solomon's Temple in 587 BC. *Mark, my son:* Presumably John Mark, the evangelist (Acts 12:12, 25; 2 Tm 4:11). **14.** *kiss:* See comment on Rom 16:16.

59

THE EPISTLE OF JAMES

Thomas W. Leahy, S.J.

BIBLIOGRAPHY

1 Chaine, J., *L'Épître de Saint Jacques* (EBib; Paris, 1927). Charue, A., "Épître de S. Jacques," *PSB* 12, 373–433. Dibelius, M., *Der Brief des Jakobus* (Meyer 15; 9th ed.; rev. H. Greeven; Göttingen, 1957). Elliott-Binns, L., "James," *PCB* 1022–25. Garcia ab Orbiso, T., *Epistola Sancti Iacobi* (Rome, 1954). Hort, F. J. A., *The Epistle of St. James* (London, 1909). Knox, W., "The Epistle of James," *JTS* 46 (1945) 10–17. Leconte, R., *Les Épîtres catholiques* (BJ; 2nd ed.; Paris, 1961). Mayor, J., *The Epistle of St. James* (London, 1892). Meinertz, M., *Der Jakobusbrief und sein Verfasser in Schrift und Überlieferung* (BSt 10; Freiburg, 1905). Meyer, A., *Das Rätsel des Jacobusbriefes* (BZNW 10; Giessen, 1930). Mitton, C. L., *The Epistle of James* (Grand Rapids, 1966). Mussner, F., *Der Jakobusbrief* (HTKNT 13/1; Freiburg, 1964). Reicke, B., *The Epistles of James, Peter, and Jude* (AB 37; Garden City, N.Y., 1964) 1–66. Ropes, J. H., *A Critical and Exegetical Commentary on the Epistle of St. James* (ICC; Edinburgh, 1916). Schneider, J., *Die Briefe des Jakobus, Petrus, Judas, und Johannes* (NTD 10; Göttingen, 1961). Shepherd, M. H., "The Epistle of James and the Gospel of Matthew," *JBL* 75 (1956) 40–51. Willmering, H., "The Catholic Epistle of St. James the Apostle," *CCHS* 1172–76.

F-B 284–92. Guthrie, *NTI* 2, 60–94. R-F, *INT* 553–69. Wik, *NTI* 472–87.

INTRODUCTION

2 **(I) Authenticity.** According to its opening verse, this first of the Catholic Epistles (→ NT Epistles, 47:17) is written by "James, a servant of God and of the Lord Jesus Christ." Who is this James? Is he actually the author of the epistle? The use of the title "servant," which suggests a church official, his presuming to address "the twelve tribes in the Dispersion," and the unmistakable tone of authority throughout the letter all indicate someone of authority, well-known in the Church. This conclusion is confirmed by Jude 1, where the writer refers to himself as "brother of James." Such a person is identifiable in the NT as James, "brother of the Lord" and leader of the church in Jerusalem (Acts 12:17; 15:13; 21:18; Gal 1:19; 2:9,12; 1 Cor 15:7; Mk 6:3 par). This identification has been traditionally accepted in the Church and is generally held by modern scholars. Tradition has diverged, however, about the identification of this James, "brother of the Lord," with James (son) of Alphaeus (Mk 3:18; Acts 1:13), one of the Twelve. In the East, the liturgy, the Fathers, and subsequent tradition have rejected that identification; in the West, it has been maintained down to modern times. Non-Catholic scholars in general reject the identification, and modern Catholic exegetical opinion tends increasingly to question it (e.g., Wikenhauser, Blinzler, Bonsirven, Cantinat, Leconte, Bardenhewer, Cerfaux, Dupont, Mussner). Reasons for denying the identity are: (1) In his opening address the writer does not employ the title of apostle. (2) During Jesus' public life, his "brethren" are not among those who follow and believe in him, but rather the contrary (Mk 3:21–22,31–34; Jn 7:3–8). (3) Even after the resurrection, when the "brethren" have come to believe in Jesus, they are still distinguished, as a group, from the Twelve (Acts 1:13–14; 1 Cor 9:5; 15:5–8).

3 Did this James write the epistle attributed to him? Modern opinion is divided: Non-Catholic scholars tend to regard the letter as pseudonymous, although its authenticity has been defended by Mayor, Hort, Feine-Behm, Zahn, Schlatter, Kittel, and Michaelis. Catholic scholars usually defend the authenticity, although J. Blinzler admits the possibility of authorship by a later Jewish Christian, writing in the spirit of James of Jerusalem. The chief reasons for questioning authenticity are the excellent Gk style of the letter; the lack of attestation to its canonicity before the 3rd cent. and even later; indications of a date substantially after Paul (whereas James died *ca.* AD 62); and the apparent absence from the letter both of specifically Christian teaching and of the strict legalism and ritualism that the traditions about James of Jerusalem might lead one to expect. For well-documented replies to these objections, see F. Mussner, *Jakobusbrief*, 1–42. Particularly convincing and, apparently, original is the point he makes that the type of Jewish Christianity that the letter manifests on the part of the

author and implies on the part of the recipients, historically cannot be situated after the fall of Jerusalem in AD 70. And the subsequent history of Jewish Christianity—its falling into heresy and its exaggerated veneration of James of Jerusalem—adequately explains the early silence of orthodox Gentile Christianity about this NT book.

4 **(II) Purpose and Destination.** Except for the opening address, this "epistle" has the quality not of a letter, but of a written sermon or instruction. It even lacks an epistolary conclusion. No specific occasion for the letter is evident. The various concrete descriptions of conduct, such as deference to the rich in the synagogue (2:2–3), seem not to refer to actual occurrences, but to be typical examples. The epistle consists of a long series of exhortations, mostly brief, loosely connected. The one common trait, which gives the letter its distinctive quality, is a concern that the faith of the recipients be not merely theoretical or abstract, but be implemented in action, in every aspect of their lives. The purpose of the letter, then, is to meet the danger of a tendency toward an abstract, unfruitful practice of Christianity that threatened the churches, which are referred to as "the twelve tribes in the Dispersion" (1:1). Judging from the letter as a whole, the recipients would be a group of predominantly Jewish-Christian communities outside Palestine, but living in an area where the name of James would have authority.

5 **(III) Date and Place of Composition.** If James of Jerusalem is the author, the date of composition would be before AD 62, and the place would be Jerusalem. Some commentators would specify a date in the mid-forties, thus making Jas the earliest NT writing. But the letter dates more probably from the end of James' life, as indicated by his awareness of a caricature of Paul's doctrine on faith and deeds (2:14–26). Those who deny the authenticity of Jas tend to date it toward the end of the 1st cent. or in the first part of the 2nd cent. They have suggested Galilee, Syria, and even Rome as its place of origin.

6 **(IV) Outline.** Since Jas lacks an organic structure, the following outline is simply a convenient mode of indicating the sequence of material treated:

(I) Address (1:1)
(II) Regarding Trials, Temptation; Various Exhortations (1:2–18)
(III) Be Doers of the Word (1:19–27)
(IV) Avoid Partiality (2:1–13)
(V) Faith Without Works Is Dead (2:14–26)
  (A) Main Thesis (2:14–17)
  (B) Various Examples (2:18–26)
(VI) Guard of the Tongue (3:1–12)
(VII) Qualities of Wisdom (3:13–18)
(VIII) Causes of Strife; Remedies (4:1–12)
(IX) Uncertainty of the Future; Submission to God's Will (4:13–17)
(X) Woe to the Rich (5:1–6)
(XI) Patient Waiting for the Coming of the Lord (5:7–12)
(XII) Directions for Various Circumstances (5:13–15)
(XIII) Confession of Sins; Prayer (5:16–18)
(XIV) Conversion of Sinners (5:19–20)

COMMENTARY

7 **(I) Address (1:1).** *James:* The Gk *Iakōbos* = Hebr *Ya‘^{a}qōb* (Jacob). (On the identity of James, → 2–3 above.) *servant of God:* The writer applies to himself a title given in the OT to such religious leaders as Moses, Abraham, Jacob, and the prophets. He thus indicates the basis of his authority, in virtue of which he will exhort his readers. *and of the Lord Jesus Christ:* The relation of "servant" (*doulos*) to Christ on the part of his disciples is implied in the Gospels (Mt 10:24f.) and is applied, as here, to the writer of an epistle in Rom 1:1; Phil 1:1; Ti 1:1; 2 Pt 1:1, and Jude 1. The applying to Jesus of the title "Lord" (*kyrios*) and the close pairing of God and Christ indicate the author's share in the Christian faith in the divinity of Christ. This is of particular significance in view of the paucity of specifically Christian expressions in Jas. *to the twelve tribes:* Since the Assyrian Captivity of the ten northern tribes, this expression had come to represent the eschatological hope of the restoration of the people. It is here applied to the Christian Church as the continuation of God's people (see also Mt 19:28; Lk 22:30; Ap 21:12). *dispersion:* See comment on 1 Pt 1:1. *greeting:* The Gk formula used here (*chairein*) is found nowhere else in the NT (except for Acts 15:23 and 23:26), although it was normal ancient epistolary style (→ NT Epistles, 47:6–7).

8 **(II) Regarding Trials, Temptation; Various Exhortations (1:2–18).** **2.** *all joy:* The Gk word for joy (*charan*) constitutes a wordplay on the preceding "Greeting" (*chairein*). *my brothers:* This Christian form of address, found widely also in Jewish usage, is employed 15 times in Jas (sometimes without "my"), usually in the context of an urgent appeal or precept. *various trials:* The theme of rejoicing in trials is widespread in the NT, originating in Jesus' "beatitudes" (Mt 5:10–12; Lk 6:20–23; Acts 5:41; 1 Thes 1:6). **3.** *testing of your faith:* Gold tested and purified by fire is the implied image (as in the OT and 1 Pt 1:7), referring to trials or persecutions that endangered faith. *steadfastness:* The word *hypomonē* implies not mere passive endurance, but the active spirit of resistance to defection characteristic of the martyrs. **4.** *let steadfastness have its full effect:* Lit., "have a perfect work." The Gk expression is vague. Probably an eschatological goal is indicated, rather than emphasis on ethical achievement (see 1:12). *that you may be perfect and complete:* The terminology of "perfection," occurring also in 1:17,25; 3:2, is common in the OT, in QL, and elsewhere in the NT. (See B. Rigaux, *NTS* 4 [1957–58] 237–41, 248.) Verses 3–4 employ the stylistic device of "climax," in which the end of one phrase is echoed at the beginning of the next. The similarities of vocabulary and thought between these verses and 1 Pt 1:6–7 and Rom 5:3–5 are probably due not to literary dependence, but to a primitive common stock of paraenetic material (cf. M. Dibelius, *Brief des Jakobus*, 1–10).

9 **5.** *lacks wisdom:* The verbal interlinking of sentences continues, with "lacks" (*leipetai*, 1:5) harking back to "lacking" (*leipomenoi*, 1:14). The logical connection is less apparent, but seems dependent on OT wisdom themes, which closely connect wisdom, testing by trials, and perfection (cf. Wis 9:6; Sir 4:17) and stress the need of praying for wisdom (Wis 9:10–18). *generously and without reproaching:* This characteristic of God contrasts with the grudging type of giving reprehended in Sir 18:15–18; 20:10–15. **6.** *ask in faith:* The implied object of this faith is God's readiness to answer prayers (see 1:5). *with no doubting:* This probably depends on sayings of Jesus, such as Mt 21:21–22; Mk 11:23–24. **7–8.** Grammatical ambiguity permits three ways of construing these verses. It is probably best to take "that man" in v. 7 as the doubter in v. 6b; and the "double-minded man" of

v. 8 as in apposition with "that man" of v. 7 (thus NEB, Goodspeed; against RSV). *double-minded:* The word *dipsychos* (cf. 4:8) is not attested in Greek before Jas, but is used later (*1–2 Clem.*, *Ep. Barnabae*, and esp. in the *Shepherd* of Hermas [19 times], along with the vb. *dipsychein* [20 times] and *dipsychia* [16 times]). It was probably coined in dependence on a phrase in Ps 11:3, "with double heart" (*b*^{e}*lēb wālēb*), which occurs also in 1QH 4:14. In the OT, the word is used of hypocrisy toward men; but in the *Shepherd*, in QL, and here, it refers to instability toward God. (See further O. Seitz, *JBL* 63 [1944] 131–40; *JBL* 66 [1947] 211–19; *NTS* 4 [1957–58] 327–34.) *in all his ways:* A Hebraism, more commonly used in QL (1QS 2:2) than in the NT.

10 **9–11.** The author's interest in the religious significance of lowliness and poverty on the one hand and wealth on the other, first seen here, comes out also in 1:27; 2:1–7,15–17; 4:10,13–16; 5:1–6. It is a dominant theme of the letter. It derives from the OT understanding of the poor and oppressed—the *'*^{a}*nāwîm*—who see in God their only hope of refuge from affliction and are assured of his ultimate salvation and vengeance on their rich oppressors. In QL and in the preaching of Jesus the theme is also prominent; as in the case of Jas, it regards the coming exaltation of the poor in an eschatological context. Here, the strong denunciation of the rich may have a background in local church conditions. **9.** The not-too-obvious connection of this verse with the foregoing seems to be that it is a particular application of the general exhortation of 1:2. *in his exaltation:* The purely religious nature of this exaltation is indicated in 2:5 (cf. the first beatitude in Lk 6:20). **10a.** *and the rich:* The parallelism of vv. 9 and 10 indicates that the rich are also members of the community. *in his humiliation:* That is, in the transitory nature of his wealthy status, described in the following phrases. Though some would understand this paradoxical exhortation as bitterly ironical, it is probably intended literally: From the viewpoint of Christian eschatology, the rich man's only hope is in the realization of his utter poverty and nothingness before God. **10b–11.** The imagery of the quickly fading grass—particularly appropriate in Palestine—is well known in the OT (see Is 40:6–7; for a different use, cf. 1 Pt 1:24–25). *in the midst of his pursuits:* The word for "pursuits" can also mean "journeys" (cf. the similar imagery in 4:13–15).

11 **12.** Insofar as 1:2–18 possesses a loose unity, v. 12 is a climax and in its similarity to vv. 2–3 forms a kind of inclusion. *blessed is the man who:* The form of this "beatitude" reflects the OT (Ps 1:1) and the Gospels (Mt 5:3–10 par.). *crown of life:* The crown that symbolizes eternal life. The Jews and other ancient peoples used crowns of leaves or flowers on festive occasions. Gold crowns were a sign of royalty or other special dignity. The image of the crown as an eschatological reward is widespread in the NT (see 1 Pt 5:4; 2 Tm 4:8; Ap 2:10; for similar usage in QL, see 1 QS 4:7; 1QH 9:25; cf. Wis 5:15–16). *who love him:* This phrase, recurring in 2:5, is traditional in the context of divine reward for fidelity (Ex 20:6; Deut 5:10; Rom 8:28; 2 Tm 4:8; in QL, cf. 1QH 16:13). The similarity of the thought and expression in 1:2–3,12 with that of 1 Pt 1:6–9 and Rom 5:3–5 may indicate a dependence on an early Christian hymn, perhaps from the baptismal liturgy (see M. E. Boismard, *RB* 64 [1957] 162–67). **13–15.** Since "trial" (*peirasmos*) used in 1:2,12 can also mean "temptation" (an enticing to evil), the author points out the age-old fallacy of blaming one's sins on God instead of on oneself (cf. Sir 15:11–20; 1 Cor 10:13). **13.** God does not tempt—he cannot be tempted to evil. This implies that it would be evil for God to tempt. **14.** *by his own passion:* Temptation is caused by something interior to man; yet this is represented as somehow distinct from him, because it lures him as a hunter lures his prey. **15.** The image changes to that of genealogical descent. *when it has conceived:* That is, when consent is given to the temptation. *when it is full-grown:* Thus is indicated the eschatological destiny toward which sin is growing. The sequence of passion, sin, and death is the negative counterpart of trial, proved endurance, and crown of life (1:12).

12 **16–18.** The author now stresses that from God comes only good and all that is good. **17.** The first seven words of the Gk text form an almost perfect hexameter. Since a well-known poetic proverb is perhaps being quoted, it seems better (following H. Greeven, *TZ* 14 [1958] 1–13) to take these words as a complete sentence: "Every gift is good, and every present is perfect." Its meaning would be the familiar sentiment: What counts in a gift is not its value but the giver's intention. A deeper meaning is added, explaining the source of all created goodness: Every gift comes from above. *Father of lights:* The expression seems intended to refer to God as creator of the heavenly luminaries, the prime instance of his giving good gifts. This same title occurs in *Apoc. Mos.* (36:5). In QL the good spirit who guides men is called the prince of lights (1QS 3:20; CD 5:18). *shadow due to change* [*to turning*]: Unlike the heavenly bodies, whose movements according to times and seasons result in corresponding variations in the light they send forth, their creator is unchanging; therefore his goodness never diminishes. **18.** *of his own will:* The freedom of the divine initiative with which God gives birth to his children contrasts with the blind force of desire that gives birth to sin (vv. 14–15). *he gave us birth:* Of itself, this expression can be understood in the OT context of Dt 32:18. That it is rather to be understood in the specifically Christian sense (as in Jn 1:12–13) is indicated by a comparison of v. 18 with 1 Pt 1:23, in which the sense is obviously Christian. The similarity here between the two epistles may again be due to common dependence on a liturgical formula. *by the word of truth:* This probably refers to the acceptance of the gospel message. On the use of "word," see comment on 1:21. *first fruits of his creatures:* This OT image (Dt 18:4) was applied by Paul to Christ (1 Cor 15:20), to pioneer converts (Rom 16:5; 1 Cor 16:15), and to the gift of the Spirit (Rom 8:23). It seems here to envision the author and recipients of the letter as having already experienced the divine birth ultimately destined for all mankind.

13 **(III) Be Doers of the Word (1:19–27).** Neither the connection of this section with the preceding nor its inner coherence is particularly clear. "To hear" (1:19) may refer to the "word of truth" (1:18). Verses 19–21 indicate obstacles to be removed if the word is to be efficacious. Verse 22 exhorts to the doing of the word. The following verses provide illustrations and practical examples of this. **19.** These three admonitions are of a type that frequently occurs in the OT and in QL (cf. Sir 5:11–13; 20:5–8; 1QH 1:34–37). *slow to speak:* This theme is resumed in 1:26 and developed at length in 3:1–12. **20.** The reason is given for the last of the three admonitions of v. 19. *the righteousness of God:* That is, demanded by God, as in Mt 5:20; 6:33. **21.** *therefore:* If this verse is a conclusion, it seems to follow from v. 18 rather than from vv. 19–20. Taken thus with v. 18, it continues to manifest dependence on a baptismal liturgy; cf. 1 Pt 1:22–2:2 (see M.-E. Boismard, *RB* 64 [1957] 167–77). Note, however, that Boismard understands "word" (Jas 1:18,21) not as the gospel but as the Jewish law; and "birth" (1:18) as that which came to the Jews along with the law. *receive the implanted word:* The word translated "implanted" (*emphytos*) normally means "inborn"—a meaning that seems logically inadmissible in the present context. This implantation of the word refers to the acceptance of the Christian faith at baptism, including the ethical demands involved. The use of "word" (*logos*) in 1:18,21–22 reflects typical NT usage. It is God's saving revelation, foreshadowed in the word given to the prophets and in the word that is a synonym for law (*tôrāh*), but fully expressed only in Christ and the gospel. (Cf. O. Procksch and G. Kittel, *ThDNT* 4, 91–100 [OT] and 100–140, esp. 117–21 [NT].) *your souls:* In this Semitic expression the part (the inner principle of life) stands for the whole (the man). On "save," see comment on 5:15.

14 **22.** *be doers of the word:* An apt summary of the whole epistle. *not hearers only:* Strikingly similar to Rom 2:13. The general theme of a "religion of deed," so characteristic of Jas, is prominent in the other NT writings (e.g., Mt 7:24–27 par.), in QL (1QS 9:13), and in rabbinic literature (*Pirqe Aboth* 1:17). *deceiving yourselves:* Having a false understanding of the nature of genuine religion, as in v. 26. **23.** *in a mirror:* The "word" is like a mirror: By presenting ideal human conduct, it reveals to the hearer his shortcomings, just as a mirror reveals to the one using it facial blemishes or untidiness. If the user of the mirror forgets what he has seen, he will fail to remedy the situation—he will not be a "doer." The ancients had hand mirrors of polished silver or tinned copper, often fitted into ornate cases. (For such ancient mirrors, see Y. Yadin, *The Finds from the Bar Kokhba Period in the Cave of Letters* [Jerusalem, 1963] 125 and plate 38.) **25.** *perfect law of liberty:* Because of the close connection of this verse with the preceding, the "law" (as in 2:8–12; 4:11) is to be identified with the "word" of the preceding verses. James lacks Paul's distinction between the Law and the gospel, showing rather an affinity to the spirit of Mt 5:17–19. That it does not refer simply to the Old Law seems indicated by the qualifications "perfect" and "of liberty" (cf. 2:12), as well as by the absence in the letter of any emphasis on the fulfillment of ritual prescriptions. However, the concept of "liberty" is not absent from Jewish understanding of the Mosaic Law: cf. *Pirqe Aboth* 6:1–2; perhaps also (depending on the vocalization) 1QS 10:6,8,11. (See R. Schnackenburg, *The Moral Teaching of the NT* [N.Y., 1965], 349–53.) *shall be blessed:* This beatitude is eschatological (cf. 1:12). **26–27.** The exhortation of v. 22 is now given practical application.

15 **26.** *religious:* The Gk *thrēskos* usually refers to external, cultic aspects of religion. *bridle his tongue:* The concern for restraint in speech will be developed at length in 3:1–12 (cf. 1:19; 4:11). *deceives himself:* Lit., "his heart"—a Hebraism derived from LXX usage. **27.** *pure and undefiled:* These qualities, usually ritual and cultic, are aptly applied to the practice of external works of charity and to inner integrity. No complete definition of religion is attempted here, but only an emphasis on certain aspects without which the practice of religion has no meaning (cf. Is 58; Mt 23). *before God the Father:* The title is chosen in view of God's fatherly care of widows and orphans (Ps 67:6). *orphans and widows:* These are the natural objects of charity in the community: cf. Dt 27:19; Sir 4:10; Acts 6:1. *from the world:* This pejorative sense of "world" (opposition to God) occurs also in Paul: 2 Pt, Jn, 1 Jn (cf. AG 7).

16 **(IV) Avoid Partiality (2:1–13).** This section is a further explanation of the exhortation of 1:22: "Be doers of the word." The brief mention of widows and orphans in 1:27 leads to a fuller consideration of the poor in the community. The development: warning against partiality (2:1); concrete example (vv. 2–4); reasons against partiality (vv. 5–13).

1. *my brothers:* See comment on 1:2. *partiality:* See comment on Rom 2:11. *our glorious Lord:* Lit., "our Lord of glory." The great glory of the Lord in whom we believe should nullify all such impressions of worldly rank or status as would lead to partiality in conduct. **2–3.** The vivid character of the example does not allude to an actual incident. Such examples are characteristic of the rhetorical style of "diatribe" (cf. M. Dibelius, *Brief des Jakobus*, 120–22; → Pauline Theology, 79:11). *into your synagogue:* This example, unique in the NT, of a Christian extension of the term *synagōgē*, is an indication of Jewish-Christian background. Many translate, "assembly," rather than a term referring to the place of assembly. Jewish usage permits either acceptation (cf. W. Schrage, *ThWNT* 7, 836). Both the rich man and the poor man are envisaged as strangers to the community, so that their social status is known only by their appearance. **3.** The rich man is being offered a seat of honor (cf. Mt 23:6; Mk 12:39; Lk 11:43; 20:46). **5.** *has not God chosen the poor:* The OT belief that the poor are the object of God's special care (Ps 35:10) and of messianic blessings (Is 61:1) is prominent also in QL (1QM 13:14; 1QH 18:14) and in the Gospels (Mt 5:3; Lk 6:20; Mt 11:5). 1 Cor 1:17–29 gives Paul's explanation of this divine choice. By reason of their faith they are rich. *heirs of the kingdom:* This unique reference to "the kingdom" is reminiscent of the first beatitude (Mt 5:3; Lk 6:20). *which he has promised:* This concept of divine promise, along with the closely associated ideas of election and inheritance, as well as that of the response of love toward God, is the very basis of OT and NT theology. *who love him:* See comment on 1:12. *dishonored the poor man:* Their conduct is the very antithesis of that attributed to God in the preceding verse. The author has left aside the fictitious example of 2:2–3 and is attacking actual community attitudes. (For the terminology, see Sir 10:23; Prv 14:21; also 1 Cor 11:22.) *who oppress you:* This implies that the readers rank with the poor. The oppressive rich are considered as a class, characterized not only by wealth but by oppressiveness and impiety, in terms reminiscent of OT prophets (Am 8:4; cf. Wis 2:10). *drag you into court:* In view of v. 7, reference to religious persecution is probably included, along with various forms of social and economic oppression. **7.** *blaspheme that honorable name by which you are called:* To be called by a name (lit., "to have a name called over one") is to be designated as belonging to the person named. To persecute Christians baptized in the name of Jesus (Acts 2:38) is to dishonor his exalted name (cf. Phil 2:10).

17 **8.** *royal law:* Since the Mosaic Law comes from God, the universal king, it is rightly called royal. James is likewise alluding to the command of love of neighbor (Lv 19:18) cited in Jesus' preaching of the kingdom (Mt 22:39). *you do well:* The adv. "well" (*kalōs*) echoes the adj. "honorable" (*kalon*) of 2:7. The application to the context of preferring the rich to the poor is implicit but clear: Because one would not relish being treated as the poor man of vv. 2–3, one should therefore not so treat one's neighbor. By fulfilling the command of love of neighbor, one fulfills the whole law; this was made explicit in Rom 13:8–10; Gal 5:14. **9.** A balanced antithesis to the preceding. The implied relationship among sin, the law, and transgression seems to be in basic harmony with Paul's more elaborate development (cf. Rom 4:15; 5:13–14; 7:7–21; Gal 3:19). **10.** *guilty in respect to all of it:* The transgression of even a single precept of the law puts one into the category of transgressors of the law (cf. Mt 5:19). **11.** *for he who said:* The reason is given for the preceding verse. By violating a single command, one sins against God who has given the whole law; therefore one is a transgressor against the law as such. **12.** *going to be judged:* In 1:12 James appealed to the motive of future reward; now he appeals to the motive of future judgment (cf. 3:1; 4:12; 5:9). This motivation in connection with the love of neighbor occurs also in Mt 5:22,25; 7:1–2; 25:31–46. *under the law of liberty:* See comment on 1:25. Only a free self-dedication to the law as being God's will (and opposed to mere external constraint) is adequate to assure an integral observance of all the precepts. This spirit of joyful free dedication to God's law finds expression in the OT (Pss 1:2; 39:9; 118:32) and in QL. **13.** The epigrammatic conciseness of both parts of this verse, as well as the somewhat strained equivalence of "lack of mercy" with "showing partiality," may indicate that James is citing a pair of existing proverbs. Verse 13a echoes the teaching of Jesus in Mt 6:15; 18:23–25—a teaching occurring also in OT and apocryphal wisdom literature.

18 **(V) Faith Without Works Is Dead (2:14–26).** This section is unique for its unified and relatively lengthy development of one theme. Although beginning with characteristic abruptness, it is not a completely new tack, but flows out of the previous treatment on hearing and doing (1:22ff.). It is the heart of the letter, giving the theoretical basis for the practical exhortations. Nevertheless, the appearance of a contradiction of Paul's teaching on justification by faith has tended to give exaggerated prominence to this section. It was largely because of this apparent contradiction that Luther wished to exclude Jas from the Canon (cf. F. Mussner, *Jakobusbrief,* 42–47).

19 **(A) Main Thesis (2:14–17).** **14.** *what does it profit?* The expression pertains to the "diatribe" style and implies the answer "Nothing." *says he has faith:* James does not here imply the possibility of true faith existing apart from deeds, but merely of the making of such a claim. To judge by the present passage and by 1:3,6; 2:1,5; 5:15, James means by faith the free acceptance of God's saving revelation. *has not works:* By "works" is meant the obedient implementation of God's revealed will in every aspect of life, as illustrated by the numerous practical exhortations in the epistle. *can his faith save him:* That is, can such a "faith" save him from judgment (cf. 2:13, see comment on 5:15). **15–16.** This piquant illustration is not a hypothetical example embodying the general principle (like that of 2:2–3), but rather an incisive analogy. However, it probably also served as an implied exhortation to practical charity in the community (cf. Is 58:7). **17.** *thus:* The point of the analogy is made explicit. *faith by itself:* Unaccompanied by deeds—thus the contrary of the "faith working through love" (Gal 5:6). *is dead:* It is unable to save him for eternal life (cf. 2:14). The word "dead" (*nekros*) is applied to sinful deeds in Heb 6:1; 9:14. Note that James is not opposing faith and works, but living faith and dead faith.

20 **(B) Various Examples (2:18–26).** **18.** *but someone will say:* The interpretation of this verse is considerably disputed. Does that which "someone" says represent an objection, or an affirmation of what James has been saying? Either alternative has difficulties. It seems best (with Ropes, Dibelius, NEB; against Chaine, Mussner) to consider it a genuine objection. Understand "you" and "I" not as, respectively, James and the objector, but as signifying simply that some specialize in faith, others in works. The next phrase, "Show me your faith...," is James' reply to the objector, challenging him to give evidence of the existence of faith apart from works. His next assertion, "I by my works...," claims that where works might be supposed to exist without faith, a closer examination would show that faith underlies them. **19.** *you believe that God is one:* In diatribe style, James continues to refute his imaginary objector. The OT emphasis on the oneness of God as the basic truth of faith (Dt 6:4) is found likewise in the NT (Mk 12:29; 1 Cor 8:4,6; Eph 4:6). *you do well:* The tone of "well" (*kalōs*) is ironic (cf. Mk 7:9; Jn 4:17; 2 Cor 11:4). *even the demons believe:* In the NT, demons are evil spirits, subjects and instruments of Satan and identified with the fallen angels (2 Pt 2:4; Jude 6). *and shudder:* They are objects of God's wrath, in spite of their barren "belief" in God's oneness. The point of this example is that mere knowledge of religious truths is of no avail when the will is alienated from God. **20.** *you foolish fellow:* Although the opponent is still the imaginary adversary of the diatribe style, the sharpness of expression is aimed at real people who have a wrong understanding of faith and works. *faith apart from works is barren:* In Greek, this involves a wordplay between "apart from works" (*chōris ergōn*) and "barren" (*argē*—from *a-ergos*). The verse serves as introduction to the following Scripture proofs.

21 **21.** *Abraham our father:* A favorite title for Abraham among the Jews. According to Paul (Rom 4; Gal 3–4), Abraham is the father of all believers. In spite of the different emphasis to be found in Jas and in Paul, both are following a venerable line of Jewish tradition in citing Abraham as an example of fidelity and righteousness before God (Sir 44:19–21; Wis 10:5; 1 Mc 2:52; *Jub* 17–19; CD 3:2; Heb 11:8–12,17–19). *justified by works:* The pass. voice implies divine agency. The "works" are the offering of Isaac. The "justification" seems to mean Abraham's being found pleasing to God and therefore being confirmed in the promise (Gen 22:16–18). James has combined the statement about Abraham's justification (Gn 15:6) with that of his obedience (Gen 22). The basis for this combination follows. **22.** *faith was active along with his works:* Abraham's obedience to God's difficult word indicates the activeness of his faith. *faith was completed by works:* Believing God's promise of offspring in the face of the slaying of the only visible source of offspring made perfect his faith in God's initial promise. This demonstrates the inseparability of faith and works. **23.** *scripture was fulfilled:* Gn 15:6 is taken as a prophecy fulfilled by the events of Gn 22 (cf. 1 Mc 2:52). *friend of God:* This title of Abraham, not found in Gn, occurs in Is 41:8, 2 Chr 20:7, and in QL (CD 3:2). It became the normal Arab title (*el khalîl*) both for Abraham and for his major shrines of Hebron and Mambre. **24.** *you see:* The use of the second person plural in place of the singular, employed since 2:18b, indicates that the fictitious adversary has dropped from view; the readers are again being addressed directly. *a man is justified...:* A conclusion is now drawn from the Scripture: What was true in the case of Abraham is true universally. *by works and not by faith alone:* As is clear from context, this does not mean that genuine faith is insufficient for justification, but that faith unaccompanied by works is not genuine. There is thus no basic disagreement of James with Paul, for whom faith "works through love" (Gal 5:6).

Yet a problem remains. Not only is there a strong difference of emphasis in Paul and James regarding faith and works; but there is such a striking quasi-identity of wording, and of emphasis on Abraham (with each quoting Gn 16:6 in his own favor), along with a superficial appearance of mutual contradiction (cf. Rom 3:28; also 1:17; 3:20–27,30; 4:2–5,16–24; Gal 2:16; 3:6–12,24), that some kind of connection, by way of refutation or correction, seems postulated. The most satisfactory hypothesis is that James seeks to correct a current perverted understanding of Pauline teaching on justification by faith, one that would, unlike genuine Pauline doctrine, make no moral demands on the believer.

22 **25.** *Rahab the harlot:* James does not mention her faith, since it is evident from Jos 2:11. Her fellow citizens also had a kind of faith (2:9–11); but she alone acted on her belief and so was justified—was found pleasing before God and was saved (Jos 6:22–25). A similar use of the Rahab example in Heb 11:31 and (at greater length) in *1 Clem* 12 indicates the ancient popularity of this theme. **26.** The body-spirit comparison sums up the treatment, neatly indicating the indispensability of both faith and works. Forming a "Semitic inclusion" with v. 14, it indicates the close of the section.

(Burtchaell, J., "A Theology of Faith and Works: The Epistle to the Galatians—A Catholic View," *Interpretation* 17 [1963] 39–47. Eichholz, G., *Glaube und Werk bei Paulus und Jakobus* [Theol. Existenz heute, 88; Munich, 1961]. Jeremias, J., "Paul and James," *ExpT* 66 [1954–55] 368–71. Lohse, E., "Glaube und Werke. Zur Theologie des Jakobusbriefes," *ZNW* 48 [1957] 1–22. Mussner, F., *Jakobusbrief*, Excursus 3, 4, 5.)

23 **(VI) Guard of the Tongue (3:1–12).** This section develops the theme of 1:19: "Let every man be... slow to speak." **1.** *let not many...become teachers:* The role of teachers in the early Church was important and honorable (Acts 13:1; 1 Cor 12:28; Eph 4:11), yet liable to abuse if sought for unworthy motives. James echoes the warnings of Jesus (Mt 5:19; 23:7–8). *we who teach:* James regards himself as a "teacher" in the Church. **2–12.** Since teaching is exercised through speech, Jas now enters upon a lengthy admonition on the use of the tongue. **2.** *all of us often go wrong:* A well-known theme in Scripture (Eccl 7:20; Sir 19:16; 1 Jn 1:8,10; *2 Esdras* 8:35). These words are quoted by the Council of Trent (Sess. VI, cap. 16; cf. can. 23 [DB 810; DS 1549]) in connection with the unavoidability of venial sin. *not offend in speech:* Counsel about the right and wrong use of speech is frequent in OT wisdom literature (cf. Prv. 15:1–4,7,23,26,28; Sir 5:11–6:1; 28:13–26) and in QL (1QS 7:4–5; 10:21–24). *a perfect man:* The word *teleios* is used specifically of Christian moral perfection (Mt 5:48; 19:21; Col 1:28; 4:12). *able to bridle:* The figurative use anticipates the illustration of 3:3. **3–4.** Two analogies illustrate the assertion of the preceding verse. The bit and the rudder are compared to the tongue because, though small (cf. 5a), both are instruments of the will (of the rider and of the pilot). **5a.** The conclusion from preceding images. **5b.** The comparison of a great conflagration coming from a small flame is common in Gk moralizing.

24 **6.** This verse is a harsh denunciation of the evils of the tongue. It contains obscurities of structure and meaning that baffle exegetes. *a fire:* Cf. Sir 28:22–23. *the unrighteous world:* The obscure phrase *ho kosmos tēs adikias* could mean "the sum total of iniquity" (see AG 8). *setting on fire the wheel of birth* [*phogizousa ton trochon tēs geneseōs*]: "One of the hardest phrases in the Bible" (F. J. A. Hort). Similar phrases are found in Hellenistic literature, especially in connection with Orphic rites. It may have come to Jas stripped of its original technical sense of recurrent cycles of human existence, via the usage of popular Stoic preachers. *hell:* The Gk form (*geenna*) of the Hebr *gê hinnōm* (Valley of Hinnom) occurs in the NT only in the Syn and here in Jas. The verse thus makes a sudden transition from Gk ways of speaking to Jewish. **7.** The four categories of animals are biblical (cf. the same order: Gn 9:2; Dt 4:17–18; 1 Kgs 4:33). The control of animals by man was a familiar object of OT observation (Gn 1:28; 9:2; Ps 8:7–9; Sir 17:4) as well as of Gk and Rom moralizing. **8b.** Perhaps the tongue is being represented as a snake, restless and lethal. There may be an allusion to Ps 139:4. **9.** *bless the Lord and Father:* In Jewish custom "Blessed be he" was added to any mention of God, as well as to other liturgical blessings. *in the likeness of God:* Cf. Gn 1:26; 9:6; Sir 17:3; Wis 2:23. **10.** The exhortation follows the Christian tradition of Lk 6:28; Rom 12:14; 1 Pt 3:9. **11.** The imagery is characteristic of Palestine, where springs are of great importance in the dry season. In *4 Ezra* 5:9 a combination of sweet and brackish waters is regarded as a sign of the approaching end. **12.** The imagery of the fig, olive, and vine is also typical of Palestine, as it is of other Mediterranean countries. The figure is similar—without being identical—to that of Mt 7:16 par.

25 **(VII) Qualities of Wisdom (3:13–18).** This self-contained section on wisdom, as with the preceding section on the tongue, probably harks back to the "teacher" of 3:1, since from a Jewish point of view the teacher is almost identical with the "wise man." **13.** *who is wise:* False claims to wisdom by arrogant and quarrelsome would-be teachers are refuted. A real understanding of wisdom is clearly expressed in these verses. Essentially that of the OT wisdom literature, it is also reminiscent of Paul's understanding in 1 Cor 1–4. *let him show:* This structure of an imperative following an interrogative, having the force of a conditional, is biblical: cf. Dt 20:5–8. *his works:* The teaching of 2:14–26 is being applied to the concept of wisdom. *with the meekness of wisdom:* The important Christian concept of "meekness" (*praütēs*—which includes gentleness, moderation, courtesy, humility) occurs frequently in Paul (2 Cor 10:1; Gal 5:23) and is prominent in the teaching (Mt 5:5) and example (Mt 11:29) of Jesus. **14.** *the truth:* Judging from the present context, as well as from 1:18 and 5:19, "truth" means the Christian revelation, as put in practice by the Christian "wise man." **15.** *comes from above:* On the heavenly origin of wisdom, cf. Prv 2:6; 8:22–31; Wis 7:25; 9:4,9–10; Sir 1:1–4,24. *earthly, unspiritual, devilish:* In 1 Cor, the wisdom opposed to divine wisdom is that "of the world" (1:20); it characterizes the man who is "unspiritual" (2:14). Divine wisdom is unknown to "the rulers of this age" (2:8)—an expression that may include sinful angels. **16.** *jealousy...selfish ambition...disorder:* These expressions occur in the list of vices of 2 Cor 12:20; they were a feature of early Christian paraenesis. **17.** In terms that emphasize the contrast with earthly wisdom, James here gives a masterful sketch of Christian wisdom, redolent of the Syn (cf. the Beatitudes, Mt 5:3–10) and of Paul (cf. Gal 5:22–23). **18.** The verse contains ambiguities. "Harvest of righteousness" could mean either a harvest that is righteousness or a reward for righteous conduct. And this harvest may be sown either "for" or "by" those who make peace. The connection with 3:17 is through the word "peace." By emphasizing this idea, James sums up, by contrast, his condemnation of false wisdom and prepares for the following consideration of hostilities in the community.

26 **(VIII) Causes of Strife; Remedies (4:1–12).** Since faults of the tongue (3:2–12) and false wisdom (3:13–16) lead to strife in the community, James now considers the root causes (4:1–6) and remedies (4:7–10) thereof, concluding with a consideration of the law and judgment (4:11–12). **1.** *wars...fightings:* The two Gk words often occur together in the figurative sense of contentions, disputes, and the like. They form an emphatic contrast with the last word of the preceding section, "peace." *your passions:* Lit., "your pleasures" (cf. Ti 3:3). **2.** The generality of v. 1 is now specified with concrete examples. The verse can be construed in various ways, depending on punctuation. It seems better to take "you murder" as the logical consequence of the preceding "you desire and do not have" (with RSV and NEB), rather than to pair "you murder" with "you covet" (with Mussner, Nestle, and Merk). *because you do not ask:* This echoes, in negative form, the Gospel exhortations on prayer (Mt 7:7–11 par.; Mk 11:24; Jn 14:13–14; 1 Jn

3:22). **3.** *you ask wrongly:* The proper approach to prayer is indicated below (4:7–10). Cf. also 1 Jn 5:14; Mt 6:33. **4.** *adulterers:* James adopts the OT prophetic representation of unfaithfulness to God as adultery (Jer 3:9; Ez 16; Hos 3:1), perhaps echoing the usage of Jesus (Mt 12:39; 16:4; Mk 8:38). *world:* See comment on 1:27. *makes himself an enemy of God:* A state of enmity between God and men differs from that of ordinary human relations, because the permanent attitude of love on God's part is not thereby interrupted.

27 **5.** *scripture says:* No such text can be found in the OT. James may be quoting an apocryphal work, a lost variant from a Gk OT version (cf. J. A. Fitzmyer, *NTS* 7 [1960–61] 304). The quotation is grammatically ambiguous, and its meaning is obscure. It seems best (with RSV, F. Mussner, J. Jeremias [*ZNW* 50 (1959) 137–38]) to translate, "he [God] yearns jealously over the spirit which he has made to dwell in us," rather than to make "spirit" the subject of "yearns" (with NEB, Vg). *jealously:* The OT often represents with the figure of divine jealousy the seriousness of God's will to be worshiped exclusively (Ex 20:5; 34:14; Nm 25:11; Dt 4:24). *the spirit:* This is the inner, God-given life breathed into man at his creation (cf. 2:26). **6.** *he gives more grace:* The reference is not clear. Perhaps it means that, in addition to giving the gift of life (the "spirit" of v. 5), God answers the prayers of the humble (vv. 6b–10, compared with v. 3). *it says:* Prv 3:34 is quoted, as it is also in 1 Pt 5:5 (in a section bearing resemblances to this passage: viz. resistance to the devil: Jas 4:7; 1 Pt 5:8–9; the paradox of humiliation-exaltation: Jas 4:10; 1 Pt 5:6). **7.** *resist the devil:* Since the devil personifies rebellion against God, resistance to him includes submission to God, as in Mt 4:8–10. **8.** *draw near to God:* This expression was used of Moses (Ex 24:22) and of priests in the Temple (Ez 44:15); but also figuratively, as it is here (Hos 12:7 [LXX]; Wis 6:19; Jdt 8:27). For God's responding to man's turning to him, cf. Zech 1:3; Mal 3:7. *cleanse your hands... purify your hearts:* This same combination of figures occurs in Ps 33:4. *double-minded:* See comment on 1:8. **9.** *be wretched, mourn, and weep:* James echoes the grim earnestness of the OT prophets (cf. Jl 1:8–16). That James does not intend to banish all joy from Christian life is evident from 1:2 and 5:13. **10.** The details of the preceding exhortation are summed up in this one disposition. There is probably dependence on sayings of Jesus (cf. Lk 14:11; 18:14; Mt 23:12).

28 **11.** Once again, James reverts to the subject of sins of speech (cf. 1:26; 3:2–10). *judges his brother:* The stricture against judging may depend on Mt 7:1–5. The "law" that one judges by speaking against a brother is the "second great commandment," love of neighbor (cf. 2:8). **12.** *save and destroy:* Cf. Mt 16:25; Lk 6:9; in the OT, God is he who kills and makes live (Dt 32:39; 1 Sm 2:6; 2 Kgs 5:7). *but who are you:* The rhetorical question emphasizes the enormity of presumption hidden in the all-too-common practice of judging one's neighbor (cf. Rom 14:4,10).

29 **(IX) Uncertainty of the Future; Submission to God's Will (4:13–17).** With characteristic abruptness James introduces another practical application of his teaching on submission to God. **13.** *we will go... and trade:* During the Hellenistic period, Jews frequently engaged in trade. Financial profit was the normal motive of travel. **14.** *you do not know about tomorrow. What is your life?:* Some commentators, following textual variants, translate: "You do not know what your life will be tomorrow." (Cf. Prv 27:1; Mt 6:34.) *you are a mist:* This image of the fragility and transitory nature of human existence is common in the OT (Ps 38:6,7,12; Wis 2:1–5). *appears... disappears:* In Greek, this constitutes a play on words (*phainomenē... aphanizomenē*). **15.** *if the Lord wills:* Expressions similar to this famous *conditio Jacobaea* were in common use among the early Greeks and Romans. The formula does not occur in the OT or in rabbinic writings; it was apparently borrowed from pagan use and "christened" by NT writers. (For other NT examples, cf. Acts 18:21; Rom 1:10; 1 Cor 4:19; 16:7; Phil 2:19,24; Heb 6:3). Compare the common Moslem *inshallah.* **16.** *all such boasting is evil:* Not that trade is evil in itself, but the conduct here censured leaves God out of consideration. **17.** This "advice to merchants" concludes with a pithy proverb, similar to Lk 12:47; Jn 9:41; 15:22,24. It is a more abstract expression of the truth that faith without works is dead (2:26).

30 **(X) Woe to the Rich (5:1–6).** This severe denunciation of the unjust rich is reminiscent of OT prophets (e.g., Am 8:4–8). It is not intended to influence the rich to whom it is rhetorically addressed, but is rather a salutary warning to the faithful of the terrible fate of those who abuse riches and perhaps also a consolation to those now oppressed by the rich (2:5–7). **1.** *come, now, you rich:* The identical mode of introduction in 5:1–6 and 4:13–17 and the use of direct address throughout indicate the parallelism of the sections. However, the present passage is harsher in tone and does not seem to envisage the possibility of repentance. *miseries that are coming:* The loss of wealth (vv. 2–3) and the dread judgment that will avenge their heartless injustices (vv. 3–6). **2.** *have rotted:* The perfect tense of this and the two following verbs probably indicates the present worthlessness of wealth. Some regard it as the "prophetic perfect," referring to a future situation as already in existence. *garments:* These were a principal form of wealth in antiquity (cf. Horace, *Ep.* 1.6, 40–44; Mt 6:19; Acts 20:33). **3.** *have rusted:* Although silver and gold do not actually rust, this expression indicates their basic worthlessness. *evidence against you:* Their miserable disintegration is a telling accusation against those who have made them their supreme goal in life. *eat your flesh like fire:* The very objects of accumulated wealth are, by metonymy, represented as instruments of vindicative punishment—no doubt, with allusion to "the gehenna of fire" (Mt 5:22). *the last days:* In view of the allusion to the coming of the Lord in vv. 7 and 9, James probably points out the absurdity of excessive concern for this age, since the last days are at hand (cf. Acts 2:16–17). Others understand it to refer to the future judgment of wrath that the rich man has "stored up" for himself. Some (BJ, Ropes) take "fire" as the object of "stored up," instead of construing it with the preceding phrase.

31 **4.** *wages of the laborers:* On the withholding of the pay of laborers, cf. Dt 24:14–15. *the Lord of armies:* Cf. Is 5:9 (LXX), a context similar to this one. The OT expression (*yhwh ṣb'wt*) first meant "Lord of the armies of Israel"; later, "of the heavenly armies," i.e., the stars, or even the angels. In the LXX this usually becomes *pantokratōr*, but sometimes the transliteration is used, as is done here (*kyrios sabaōth*—cf. Rom 9:29). **5.** *day of slaughter:* This phrase, taken from Jer 12:3, emphasizes the proximity of judgment; it is ironic that their excessive indulgence makes the rich more vulnerable to coming torments. **6.** *killed the righteous man:* James may allude to Sir 34:22, "To take away a neighbor's living is to murder him; to deprive an employee of his wages is to shed blood." This climactic charge may likewise allude to Wis 2 and 3, in which the godless plot the destruction of the righteous poor man (see esp. Wis 3:3–5:16).

32 **(XI) Patient Waiting for the Coming of the Lord (5:7–12).** The connection of thought may be: The suffering of the righteous at the hands of the rich

(5:4–6) reminds Christians of their own sufferings and occasions an exhortation to the patient bearing of them. Just as the rich have been threatened with the coming judgment of wrath, so those who suffer now are to be consoled by that same judgment. **7.** *be patient:* Not only in the face of outrageous injustice (5:4–6), but toward the ordinary trials of life (5:9,12,13,14,19). *the coming of the Lord:* The parousia of the Lord is referred to often in the NT (1 Thes 2:19; 4:15; 2 Thes 2:1; etc.; Mt 24:3; 2 Pt 1:16; 3:4,12; 1 Jn 2:28). Probably "the Lord" here means Christ, as elsewhere (thus Ropes, Chaine), rather than God the Father (thus BJ; cf. vv. 10 and 11). The Apostolic Fathers speak of the parousia of God at the Judgment. *the farmer:* Again James employs an imaginative illustration (cf. 1:6,11,23–24; 3:3–4, 11–12). *the early and the late rain:* An OT expression used often in the enumeration of God's gifts (e.g. Dt 11:14). The importance of the early (October-November) and late (April-May) showers to the farmer was distinctive of Palestine and southern Syria. James thus manifests an awareness of this aspect of Palestinian life. **8.** *be patient:* Is the object of patience only various sufferings, or is it also the delay in the coming of the Lord? Verses 7–8 seem to indicate the latter (cf. 2 Pt 3:3–13). *make firm your hearts:* Cf. 1 Thes 3:13. *the coming of the Lord is near:* Other expressions of the nearness of the parousia occur in Phil 4:5; Heb 10:25,37; 1 Jn 2:18; Ap 22:10,12,20. In most of these cases, the prospect of the parousia is a motive of hope and strength amid present trials. Since the parousia is the NT idea of the coming of the Risen Christ, this passage is one of the few in Jas to present a specifically Christian doctrine (cf. 1:1; 2:1), one that clearly goes beyond the teachings of OT and contemporary Judaism.

33 **9.** The exhortation abruptly changes to the theme of mutual relations in the community, harking back to 4:11–12 (cf. 1:19; 3:2–10). The coming of the Lord is now viewed as the coming of the Judge. *may not be judged:* Cf. Mt 7:1–2. *at the doors:* Cf. Ap 3:20; Mk 13:29 par. **10.** *as an example:* Jas has already used OT characters as examples (Abraham and Rahab, 2:21–25); now the prophets are represented as martyrs (cf. Mt 23:29–31; Acts 7:52). The persecution of Christians is seen as a prolongation of that of the prophets in Mt 5:12 and 23:29–39. The failure to cite Christ as an example of patience in suffering (contrast 1 Pt 2:21–24) illustrates the absence of a specifically Christian tone in this epistle. In this case, the omission may indicate an early stage in the adaptation of Jewish paraenesis to Christian teaching; or perhaps the early Christians regarded their Lord and his martyrdom in a basically different way than they did that of the OT prophets and martyrs, so that it would not occur to them to list him among such "examples" (Dibelius). **11.** *we call those happy who were steadfast:* James has himself done this (1:12). Similar combinations of "happy" (*makarios*) and "steadfastness" (*hypomonē*) occur in Dn 12:12 (Theodotion); 4 Mc 7:22. *the steadfastness of Job:* Ez 14:14,20 illustrates the fame of Job as an example of virtue, even independently of the book that bears his name. *the outcome which the Lord brought about:* This is the probable meaning of the compendious *to telos kyriou*. It implies that the readers are familiar with the details of Job's trials, patience, and providential deliverance. Some commentators, following Augustine and Bede, have taken the phrase to refer to Christ's death. *the Lord is compassionate and merciful:* An OT phrase: Ex 34:6; Pss 102:8; 110:4; 144:8. James departs from the LXX by introducing the word *polysplagchnos* (compassionate), unattested in earlier Gk usage, but an apt rendering of the Hebrew *raḥûm* of the MT. In contrast to the self-sufficient virtue of Stoicism, Christian steadfastness is based on a conviction of the divine mercy and the hope of the coming of the Lord.

34 **12.** This brief admonition is unconnected with what precedes and follows, except that the warning about falling under condemnation is similar to that of 5:9. *do not swear:* Cf. Mt 5:33–37. Thought and expression are similar, although the Gk of Mt is more Semitic. In both passages, the motivation of the prohibition is the danger of irreverence through a frivolous use of oaths and a disregard of truthfulness in ordinary speech. Thus, oaths are not absolutely forbidden, but only their abuse (cf. Sir 23:9–11). The original form of swearing was "by Yahweh" (Ex 22:10); with the later tendency to avoid the name of God, circumlocutions came into oaths (Str-B 1, 330–31). *by heaven or by earth:* Cf. Mt 5:34–35. In the Mishnah (*Shebuoth* 4:13) such an oath is said not to be binding. Avoidance of oaths was attributed to Pythagoras and some of the Stoic philosophers and, according to Josephus, to the Essenes (*JW* 2. 8,6 § 135). Yet the latter did take oaths of initiation (*JW* 2. 8,7 § 139), as is confirmed in 1QS 5:8; CD 15. *let your yes be yes, your no be no:* James does not specify the mode of asseveration as does Mt 5:37 ("Let your speech be 'Yes, yes' or 'No, no' "). It exhorts only to truthfulness. Thus, not the use of oaths, but untruthfulness is said to bring on danger of falling under judgment. If both Jas and Mt have preserved variant forms of one original saying of Jesus, James' form of the "Yes-No" section is probably the more original.

35 **(XII) Directions for Various Circumstances (5:13–15).** There is no obvious connection of this section with the preceding. A unifying theme in 13–18 is prayer. Nouns and verbs for prayer occur nine times in six verses, with at least one occurrence in each verse.

13. *is any one cheerful?:* Since suffering and cheerfulness, as general terms, may be considered to include the vicissitudes of human life, and since "singing praise" is a form of prayer, the advice here corresponds to Paul's "Pray at all times" (Eph 6:18). Joy and prayer are associated in Rom 12:12; 1 Thes 5:16–17. **14.** *sick:* The vb. *astheneō* is sometimes used of those near death (Jn 4:46–47; 11:1,4,14; Acts 9:37). *among you:* The reference is to members of the Christian community. *let him call for:* The man is sick enough to be confined to bed, but not yet *in extremis*. *elders of the church:* In the early Christian community, the "elders" (*presbyteroi*) were closely associated with the apostles in authority (Acts 15:2,4,6,22–23; 16:4). Elders were likewise appointed over the missionary churches (Acts 14:23; 20:17; 1 Tm 5:17,19; Ti 1:5). Thus the term does not signify merely advanced age, but an official position of authority in the local church. *let them pray over him:* Prayer for healing in time of illness is recommended in Sir 38:9–10, together with repentance for sin. *anointing him with oil:* The use of oil as a therapeutic agent is found in the OT as well as in rabbinic literature and among the Greeks. A NT instance occurs in Lk 10:34. *in the name of the Lord:* Thus the anointing is not a mere medical remedy, but as in Mk 6:13, it symbolizes the healing presence and power of the Lord, i.e., of Jesus Christ. (Cf. the baptizing "in the name of the Lord," Acts 19:5, etc.) **15.** *the prayer of faith:* Here again, no mere medical treatment is envisaged. *will save the sick man:* Elsewhere in Jas "to save" (*sōzein*) refers to salvation of the soul (1:21; 2:14; 4:12; 5:20). In the Gospels it is used both of salvation of the soul and of restoration to health (cf. AG), and frequently in connection with "faith" (Mk 5:34 par.; 10:52 par.; Lk 7:50; 17:19; cf. Rom 10:9). In the present context, the emphasis is on restoration to health. *the Lord will raise him up:* The same verb is used of Jesus, cures in Mk 1:31; 9:27. As in v. 14, "the Lord" probably refers to Christ, although in both cases the wording may have been adapted from Jewish expressions referring to God. *if he has committed sins:* In view of 3:2, the sins are apparently something more than the unavoidable faults committed by all. *will be forgiven him:* Physical healing and forgiveness of sins are closely associated also in Mk 2:3–12, and Jn 5:14. The wording of the former bears a strong resemblance to this passage of Jas.

(See Hoyos, P., "La extrema uncion en el primer siglo," *RstaB* 25 [1963] 34–42; Testa, E., *L'huile de la foi* [Jerusalem, 1967]; Milik, J. T., *Bib* 48 [1967] 450–51.)

36 The Council of Trent, Session XIV, defined Extreme Unction to be "truly and properly a Sacrament instituted by Christ our Lord and promulgated by blessed James the apostle" (DB 926; cf. 907–10; DS 1716; cf. 1694–1700). This is not to say that all the precisions of later sacramental theology are to be found in Jas. However, the following points are important with regard to the substantial identity of what James is here recommending with the sacrament of Anointing of the Sick in the Church: the distinction from mere charismatic healing (1 Cor 12:9,28,30), as evinced by the cultic role of the *presbyteroi*; the anointing with olive oil; the invoking of the name of the Lord and the prayer of faith; the ensuing recovery and forgiveness of sins. It is also significant to note, as Dibelius points out, that, in accordance with his paraenetic style, James is clearly not intending to introduce a new procedure, but presupposes its existence.

(Condon, K., "The Sacrament of Healing (Jas 5:14–15)," *Scr* 11 [1959] 33–42. Kearns, C., "Christ and the Sick in the New Testament," *Furrow* 11 [1960] 557–71.)

37 **(XIII) Confession of Sins; Prayer (5:16–18).** The connection with the preceding is obscure. Having spoken of the forgiveness of the sick man's sins, James seemingly turns to the members of the community in general, to remind them of how their sins are to be forgiven. The ideas of prayer and healing provide further appearance of continuity with the preceding. **16.** *confess your sins:* Confession of sins is an OT theme (Lv 5:5; Nm 5:7; Ps 31:5; Dn 9:4–20; Ezr 9:6–15); also known in the NT (Mt 3:6; Acts 19:18) and the early Church (*Didache* 4:14; *Ep. Barnabae* 19:12; *1 Clem.* 51:3). *to one another:* This probably means "in the liturgical assembly," as in the *Didache*. Since in the *Didache* and *Ep Barnabae* the confession of sins is considered a necessary preparation for effective prayer, the same relationship may be intended here. *pray for one another:* This basic Christian precept (implied in Mt 5:44 and in the petitions of the second half of the Lord's Prayer [Mt 6:11–13] and exemplified in Acts 12:5; Col 3:4; 1 Thes 5:25; 2 Thes 3:1; Heb 13:18, as well as in Paul's frequent assertions that he prays for his readers) is apparently given explicit formulation in Scripture nowhere outside of the present verse. In this context, mutual prayer is probably to be understood as being motivated by the mutual confession of sins (as is now exemplified in the recitation of the *Confiteor* and *Misereatur* by both priest and people at Mass). *that you may be healed:* In accordance with the interpretation that James is now addressing not merely the sick but the community in general, the word "heal" is to be understood in the spiritual sense of forgiveness of sins—a sense it bears elsewhere in the NT and in the Apostolic Fathers. A secondary reference to the healing of the sick may also be intended. *the fervent prayer of a righteous man is very powerful:* Others translate: "The prayer of a righteous man is powerful in its effects." The general idea is found in Ps 33:16,18 and Prv 15:29. The intent of the verse is both to encourage confidence in the power of Christian prayer, and to exhort to fervor in its practice.

38 17 *Elijah:* The OT examples of Abraham and Rahab were used as models of good works (2:21–25), and Job as one of patience (5:11); Elijah is now presented as a model of efficacious prayer (cf. 1 Kgs 17:1,7; 18:1, 41–45). His role in connection with the famine is recalled also in Sir 48:2–3 and *4 Ezra* 109. *a man like us:* The nuance of the Gk *homoiopathēs* is well expressed by the NEB paraphrase: "was a man with human frailties like our own." James anticipates the objection that the prayer of that heroic saint is to be admired rather than imitated. *he prayed fervently:* 1 Kgs narrates Elijah's prophecy of the drought and the rain, without stating that they were due to his prayer. James follows the tradition of Sir and *4 Ezra. three years and six months:* This specification of the duration of the drought is more precise than 1 Kgs 18:1; it reflects a Jewish tradition found also in Lk 4:25, and probably connected with the apocalyptic "three and a half," the half of seven (Dn 7:25; 12:7; Ap 11:2,9; 12:6,14). Chaine, however, reckons the time according to the normal rainfall pattern of Palestine, as extending from April of the first pluvial year (the beginning of the normal dry season) to November (beginning of the normal rainy season) of the third year. "This passage supplies us with Biblical authority for prayers for changes of weather, and the like...." (A. Plummer).

39 **(XIV) Conversion of Sinners (5:19–20).** This last short section of the letter again abruptly brings in a new topic, superficially connected with the preceding only by the catchwords "sinner" and "sins" (15–16). The terms used—"wander," "bring [turn] back," "truth," "error," "way"—are common in Jewish and Christian paraenesis. **20.** *let him know:* Some mss. have "know [ye]." *will save his soul:* That of the erring brother—although the Gk words could be understood to mean "his own soul." *death:* Eternal death, as in 1:15. *will cover a multitude of sins:* The wording is so close to 1 Pt 4:8 (also *1 Clem* 49:5) as to indicate some kind of literary connection. A very similar expression occurs in Prv 10:12 (MT, not LXX). The figure of sins being "covered" probably comes from Ps 31:1, wherein the metaphor means "forgiven"—i.e., the sin is not merely hidden, but no longer exists. Although some explain the phrase as referring to the sins of the erring brother, it is more probable that it refers to the one who converts him. The word "multitude" is not meant to imply that the latter is necessarily a great sinner himself, but is rather intended to emphasize the atonement value of this activity. The "epistle" ends with surprising abruptness.

60

THE EPISTLE OF JUDE

Thomas W. Leahy, S.J.

BIBLIOGRAPHY

1 Bigg, C., *Epistles of St. Peter and St. Jude* (ICC; 2nd ed.; Edinburgh, 1910). Boobyer, G. H., "Jude," *PCB* 1041–42. Chaine, J., *Les Épîtres catholiques* (EBib; Paris, 1939). Charue, A., "L'Épître de S. Jude," PSB 12, 571–79. Leconte, R., "Épître de S. Jude," *VDBS* 4, 1285–98; *Les Épîtres catholiques* (BJ; 2nd ed.; Paris, 1961). Mayor, J., *The Epistle of St. Jude and the Second Epistle of St. Peter* (London, 1907). Moffatt, J., *The General Epistles* (MNTC; London, 1945) 215–46. Reicke, B., *The Epistles of James, Peter, and Jude* (AB 37; Garden City, N.Y., 1964) 187–219. Schelkle, K. H., *Die Petrusbriefe, der Judasbrief* (HTKNT 13/2; Freiburg, 1961). Schneider, J., *Die Briefe des Jakobus, Petrus, Judas, und Johannes* (NTD 10; 9th ed.; Göttingen, 1961) 122–37. Wand, J. W. C., *The General Epistles of St. Peter and St. Jude* (WC; London, 1934). Willmering, H., "The Epistle of St. Jude," CCHS 1191–92.

F-B 299–302. Guthrie, *NTI* 2, 226–50; Wik, *NTI* 487–92.

INTRODUCTION

2 **(I) Authenticity.** The author of this short epistle introduces himself as "Jude, servant of Jesus Christ, brother of James" (v. 1). Since this "James" is probably the "brother of the Lord" (Gal 1:19), prominent leader of the early Church in Jerusalem (→ Epistle Jas, 59:2–3), Jude also is most likely one of the "brothers of the Lord" (Mk 6:3). Judging from other indications in the Gospels, he may have been only a half brother or a cousin of James (cf. J. Schmid, *Das Evangelium nach Markus* [Regensburg, 1958] 85–87). Although ecclesiastical tradition has tended to identify this Jude with the apostle Jude, or Thaddeus (Lk 6:16; Acts 1:13; Mt 10:3; Mk 3:18; cf. Jn 14:22), most exegetes today, including many Catholics, are inclined to deny this identity, for the same reasons as apply in the case of James. An additional reason in the case of Jude is his reference in v. 17 to the apostles in the past tense and in the third person. The question in 1 Cor 9:5 may imply that he was married and may have undertaken some apostolic journeys. According to Hegesippus (in Eusebius, *HE* 3.19, 20; 32,5), two grandchildren of Jude were arrested under Domitian on the charge of being descendants of David.

Is "Jude, brother of James" actually the author of the letter? Reasons for questioning this include the following: the very competent use of cultivated Gk style; the probability that Gentile rather than Jewish Christians are being addressed; and certain indications of a late date of composition. Such pseudonymity would not, of course, prejudice the canonicity or inspiration of the epistle (→ Epistle 2 Pt, 65:4). Among recent Protestant exegetes, Boobyer (1962) and Schneider (1961) incline to pseudonymity but consider that the possibility of authenticity cannot be excluded. Among recent Catholic exegetes, only Schelkle (1961) seems inclined toward pseudonymity.

Some ancient commentators doubted that the epistle was genuinely inspired because it quotes from non-canonical works (*Assumption of Moses* in v. 9; *Enoch* in vv. 14–15) and because it was thought that an inspired author would have been able to tell canonical from non-canonical writings. The objections, however, falsely suppose that there was a fixed canon of Scripture in the Judaism of the 1st cent. (→ Canonicity, 67:40).

3 **(II) Occasion, Purpose, and Destination.** The epistle is an energetic emergency measure to counteract a sudden danger to certain Christian communities. Godless and immoral men who have come among them are endangering the very faith itself by their perverse teaching and wicked conduct. Although only a vague idea of their doctrine can be derived from the epistle, it seems to be an embryonic form of antinomian Christian Gnosticism, probably related to similar tendencies mentioned in Gal, Col, and the Pastorals (cf. L. Cerfaux, *VDBS* 3, 659–701).

In spite of the general character of the address in v. 1, the letter is addressed to specific communities—viz., those plagued by this new peril—probably located within one general region. The OT and apocryphal allusions and citations would indicate Jewish-Christian readers, but the type of libertine infidelity envisioned would indicate a Gentile environment. Perhaps the most probable situation would be that of Jewish Christians of the Diaspora—possibly certain communities in Syria.

4 **(III) Date and Place of Composition.** Indications for a relatively late date are the reference to the apostles as pertaining to the past (v. 17); the fixed quality of the deposit of faith (v. 3); and signs of the beginning of Christian Gnosticism. Thus it would scarcely have been written before the middle sixties of the 1st cent., and may have been from two to three decades later. Schelkle maintains that it could scarcely be much earlier than AD 90.

The place of composition is unknown. In view of the Jewish-Christian background of the "brothers of the Lord," Palestine or Syria would seem the most likely choices—even in the hypothesis of pseudonymity.

5 **(IV) Relation of Jude to 2 Pt.** For a description of the striking literary connections between Jude and 2 Pt and the reasons for considering 2 Pt to be dependent upon Jude (→ Epistle 2 Pt, 65:5).

6 **(V) Outline.** The Epistle of Jude is outlined as follows:

(I) Address (1–2)
(II) Occasion (3–4)
(III) The Wicked Intruders (5–16)
  (A) God's Past Judgments on the Wicked (5–7)
  (B) Details of the Wickedness of the Intruders (8–16)
(IV) Exhortation to the Faithful (17–23)
  (A) Remembrance of the Apostolic Predictions (17–19)
  (B) Obligations Toward Themselves (20–21) and Their Erring Brethren (22–23)
(V) Final Doxology (24–25)

COMMENTARY

7 **(I) Address (1–2).** For the opening greeting, (→ NT Epistles, 47:8). **1.** *to those who are called:* The term "called" (*klētos*) implies that the ultimate source of the Christian vocation is in God's gratuitous choice. This vocation is further specified in the following phrases. *beloved in God the Father:* The Father's love for man is the motive of his call (cf. 1 Pt 1:2). *kept for Jesus Christ:* That is, under divine protection until the coming of Jesus for judgment. **2.** *mercy, peace, and love be multiplied to you:* The expression, similar to 2 Pt 1:2, is almost identical with the greeting of the letter of the church of Smyrna on the martyrdom of Polycarp (late 2nd cent.); the greeting may have been a well-known early Christian formula. *love:* Probably God's love for them.

8 **(II) Occasion (3–4).** The author was about to write a more general exhortation (perhaps similar to vv. 20–21) when the wicked intruders made necessary an immediate summons to the defense of the faith. **3.** *our common salvation:* The collective aspect of salvation, emphasized in the OT role of the people of God, continues in the NT, now broadened to include the Gentiles. *contend for the faith:* Cf. 1 Tm 6:12; 2 Tm 4:7. The defense of religion as "fighting" occurs in Hellenistic Judaism and in QL (1QM). As in Rom 10:8; Eph 5:4; Ti 1:4; 1 Tm 6:12; 2 Tm 4:7, "faith" is *fides quae creditur*, a body of doctrine, rather than the more frequent *fides qua creditur*, the response of total commitment to God's salvific revelation. *delivered:* The word "deliver," "hand on" (*paradidōmi*) is a quasi-technical term in the NT for the handing down of teachings received in the community (cf. 1 Cor 11:23; 15:13; AG 3). **4.** *long ago designated:* Probably by the OT examples (vv. 5–7) and in *Enoch* (vv. 14–15). *for this condemnation:* That adumbrated in the examples to be given, and foretold in *Enoch*. *impious men:* Judging from the further description, they seem to have perverted the gospel message of freedom into an antinomian libertinism and to have denied the absolute transcendence of Christ.

9 **(III) The Wicked Intruders (5–16).** To convince his readers of the seriousness of the situation and to fortify them against the danger, Jude dwells first on examples of divine punishment and then on the evil qualities of the intruders.

10 **(A) God's Past Judgments on the Wicked (5–7).** Three OT examples are briefly cited. **5.** *destroyed those who did not believe:* Cf. Nm 14:26–35. Paul draws more detailed morals from the account of Israel in the desert: 1 Cor 10:1–11 (cf. also Heb 3:7–4:11; Ps 94:8–11). **6.** The second example probably refers to the "sons of God" who took to wife the daughters of men (Gn 6:1–4). This seems implied in v. 7, since the Sodomites sinned "in a similar manner" to the angels. Furthermore, *Enoch* (quoted in vv. 14–15) gives great emphasis to this sin of the angels (or heavenly "Watchers") and to its punishment, in terms very similar to those used here by Jude (cf. *Enoch* 6–16; esp. 10:4–6,11,13; 12:4; 15:3; 19:1). Cf. also 2 Pt 2:4–6, where the fall of the angels occurs along with that of the Sodomites; and also *T. Naphtali* 3:4–5. The imprisoned angels awaiting judgment in 2 Pt and Jude are identified by some with the "spirits in prison" of 1 Pt 3:19 (see comment). **7.** *Sodom and Gomorrah:* Cf. Gn 19:4–25. These two cities are frequently cited as prime examples of sin and its punishment in the OT Prophets and in the Apocrypha. Cf. also Mt 10:15 par.; 11:24; Lk 17:29; 2 Pt 2:6. *surrounding cities:* Admah and Zeboiim (Dt 29:22; cf. Hos 11:8). *in a similar manner to them:* Probably refers to the sinful angels of v. 6. *going off after an alien flesh:* As the angels sought out creatures of another order of being (women), so the Sodomites sought out angels (Gen 19:5; cf. *T. Asher* 7:1). *serve as an example:* The Dead Sea area, redolent of fire and brimstone, was a constant reminder of the punishment of these buried cities. In Jewish tradition the fire that fell upon them continues to burn on as the fire of hell (cf. F. Lang, *ThWNT* 6, 945f.).

11 **(B) Details of the Wickedness of the Intruders (8–16).** This section is characterized by a tone of vehement denunciation, emphasized by various comparisons. Although we are not told the precise nature of their vices, they seem to include sexual immorality, doctrinal deviation, and the exerting of a disruptive influence on the community. **8.** *in their dreamings:* This is probably a scornful reference, allusive of OT warnings, to claims of visionary experiences. *defile the flesh:* Their sexual sins, implied in v. 4, justify the comparison with the Sodomites in v. 7. *reject the Lord:* See comment on 2 Pt 2:10. *revile the glorious ones:* Probably angels (cf. Ex 15:11 [LXX]; Heb 9:5; *T. Levi* 18:5; *T. Judah* 25:2). Perhaps this "reviling" was connected with the antinomian rejection of the moral precepts of the Law, considered to have been mediated by angels. **9.** *Michael the archangel:* Cf. Ap 12:7; Dn 10:13,21; 12:1; 1 Thes 4:16. His dispute with the devil, not mentioned elsewhere in the Bible, seems to be taken from the *Assumption of Moses:* When God dispatched Michael to bury the body of Moses (cf. Dt 34:6), the devil laid claim to it, on the grounds of its materiality and of Moses' murder of

the Egyptian (*APOT* 2, 408). Jude's argument is a fortiori: If the great archangel would not presume to revile even the devil, how wrong are these mere men to revile angels! God alone is the ultimate judge (cf. Jas 4:11–12; → Apocrypha, 68:49).

12 **10.** The accusations of v. 8 are resumed, in reverse order, and with biting irony. *what they do not understand:* That is, at least, the "glorious ones" of v. 8. Their actual ignorance is the antithesis of their pretended gnosis. *what they know by instinct:* Again a reproach for their sexual aberrations (as in vv. 4, 7, 8). **11.** *Cain... Balaam...Korah:* OT examples are again employed (cf. Gn 4:8–16; Nm 22–24; 31:16; Nm 16). Jude is again following contemporary Jewish tradition, which considered these three as types of wicked leadership and of its punishment. **12.** *blemishes on your agapes:* The false teachers still participated in the Eucharist, which at this early stage took place in the course of a community meal (cf. 1 Cor 11:17–34; Acts 2:46; Ignatius, *Ep. ad Smyr.* 8.2). In the 2nd cent., the communal meal, retaining the name "agape," was separated from the Eucharist. The word for "blemishes" should perhaps be translated as "reefs," i.e., occasions of spiritual shipwreck. *clouds... trees:* These figures drawn from nature illustrate an exterior display masking inner emptiness. *twice dead:* Not only fruitless in the community, but cut off from it. Or perhaps, rather, under sentence of the "second death" of Ap 2:11; 20:6,14; 21:8. **13.** *wild waves:* The imagery is similar to Is 57:20 (MT). *wandering stars:* An image probably borrowed from *Enoch* 18–21, where seven stars refer to fallen angels, destined for eternal punishment.

14–15. *Enoch...prophesied:* Cf. Gn 5:18–23 for the biblical account of Enoch. Jude, however, quotes from the apocryphal *Enoch* (1:9), referring to it as a prophecy; he reflects the esteem in which this work was held in the early Church (as also at Qumran; → Apocrypha, 68:9–15; → Canonicity, 67:37). Instances where ancient prophecies are applied to contemporary situations are abundant in the NT and in QL. Jude's use of *Enoch,* according to Jerome, led some to exclude this epistle from the Canon. **16.** The vices here listed correspond in part to previous accusations in Jude (vv. 4, 8, 10–12) and are familiar from both the OT and the Apocrypha.

13 **(IV) Exhortation to the Faithful (17–23).** The faithful should not be unduly alarmed or shaken in faith over the appearance of the intruders, for such events have been foretold. Rather, they should foster their own faith, and seek to help that of others.

(A) Remembrance of the Apostolic Predictions (17–19). **17.** *the apostles:* This mode of reference to the Twelve (?) may well be an indication that the author of Jude is not to be reckoned among them. **18.** Except for a partial reproduction in 2 Pt 3:3, this precise quotation does not occur in the NT. Its substance, however, occurs in such places as Mk 13:22; Acts 20:29f.; 1 Tm 4:1–3. *in the last time:* It is probably clearer to us today than it was to the early Church that the "last time" or "last days" connote a stage in salvation history rather than, necessarily, a temporal proximity to the end of history.

14 **(B) Obligations Toward Themselves (20–21) and Their Erring Brethren (22–23).** **20–21.** The enumeration of the basic Christian virtues of faith, hope, and love is similar to that of 1 Thes 1:3 and 1 Cor 13:13. **21.** *wait for the mercy of our Lord Jesus Christ:* This is the eschatological hope of salvation at the coming of Christ for judgment, found widely in the NT. Note the triadic mention of the names of the Holy Spirit, God (the Father), and Jesus in these two verses. **22–23.** Textual variants make it uncertain whether two or three classes of erring brethren are mentioned; and whether the first class consists of doubters to be pitied or of disputants (or doubters) to be refuted (or convinced). *snatching them out of the fire:* The image, borrowed from Am 4:11 and Zech 3:2, is here referred to the eschatological punishment of hell-fire. *have mercy with fear:* This is probably an exhortation to great prudence in the manner of seeking the reclamation of those given to sins of the flesh (cf. Jas 5:19–20).

15 **(V) Final Doxology (24–25).** The final greeting, typical of ancient letters, is replaced by a doxology (as in 2 Pt and *2 Clem.*). Its structure and wording is strikingly similar to other NT doxologies (Eph 3:20; 1 Tm 1:17; 1 Pt 4:11; esp. Rom 16:25–27, upon which it could be dependent). **24.** *who is able to keep you from falling:* These words adapt the doxology to the peculiar situation of the recipients of the letter.

61

THE EPISTLE TO THE HEBREWS

Myles M. Bourke

BIBLIOGRAPHY

1 Bonsirven, J., *Saint Paul: Épître aux Hébreux* (VS 12; Paris, 1943). Bruce, F. F., *The Epistle to the Hebrews* (NICNT; Grand Rapids, 1964); "Hebrews," *PCB* 1008–19. Davidson, A. B., *Epistle to the Hebrews* (Grand Rapids, 1950). Héring, J., *L'Épître aux Hébreux* (CNT 12; Neuchâtel, 1954). Javet, J.-S., *Dieu nous parle: Commentaire sur L'Épître aux Hébreux* (Neuchâtel, 1945). Kuss, O., *Der Brief an die Hebräer* (RNT 8; Regensburg, 1953) 11–127; new edition (RNT 8/1; Regensburg, 1966). Leonard, W., "The Epistle to the Hebrews," *CCHS* 1153–76. Manson, W., *The Epistle to the Hebrews: An Historical and Theological Reconsideration* (London, 1951). Médebielle, A., "Epître aux Hébreux," *PSB* 12 (1938) 269–72. Michel, O., *Der Brief an die Hebräer* (Meyer 13; 11th ed.; Göttingen, 1960). Milligan, G., *The Theology of the Epistle to the Hebrews* (Edinburgh, 1899). Moffatt, J., *The Epistle to the Hebrews* (ICC; N.Y., 1924). Montefiore, H., *A Commentary on the Epistle to the Hebrews* (BNTC; London, 1964). Nairne, A., *The Epistle of Priesthood* (Edinburgh, 1913). Pirot, L., "Hébreux (l'Epître aux)," *VDBS* 3, 1409–40. Robinson, T. H., *The Epistle to the Hebrews* (MNTC; N.Y., 1933). Scott, E. F., *The Epistle to the Hebrews: Its Doctrine and Significance* (Edinburgh, 1923). Spicq, C., *L'Epître aux Hébreux* (BJ; 2nd ed.; Paris, 1957); *L'Epître aux Hébreux* (EBib; 2 vols.; Paris, 1952–53). Strathmann, H., *Der Brief an die Hebräer* (NTD 9; 5th ed.; Göttingen, 1963) 69–158. Vanhoye, A., *La structure littéraire de l'Epître aux Hébreux* (StudNeot, Stud 1; Paris, 1963). Westcott, B. F., *Epistle to the Hebrews* (London, 1909). Windisch, H., *Der Hebräerbrief* (HNT 14; 2nd ed.; Tübingen, 1931).

F-B 273–82. Guthrie, *NTI* 11–59. Moule, C. F. D., "Commentaries on the Epistle to the Hebrews," *Theology* 61 (1958) 228–32. R-F, *INT* 526–48. Wik, *NTI* 453–70.

INTRODUCTION

2 **(I) Authenticity.** The identity of the author of Heb is unknown. With the exception of 1 Jn, it is the only NT epistle that begins without a greeting mentioning the writer's name. Its ascription to Paul goes back at least to the end of the 2nd cent. in the church of Alexandria. According to Eusebius, it was accepted as Paul's work by Clement, who, in this matter, followed the view of Pantaenus. Clement believed that Paul had written it in Hebrew for Hebrews and that Luke had translated it into Greek (*HE* 6.14, 2–4). Origen accepted its Pauline authorship only in a wide sense, for he remarked that "anyone who is able to discern differences of style" would not fail to see the dissimilarity with Paul's writings. He felt that the thoughts were Paul's, whereas the "style and composition belong to one who called to mind the apostle's teaching"; who that was, "only God knows" (quoted by Eusebius, *HE* 6.25, 11–13). The views of Alexandria influenced the rest of the East, and, ultimately, the West. Clement of Rome used Heb in his epistle to the Corinthians (*ca.* AD 95; see ch. 36), but he gives no clue to its authorship. It is not listed in the Muratorian Canon (*ca.* AD 200). The earliest known Western view of its authorship is that of Tertullian, who ascribed it to Barnabas, probably because in 13:22 it is called a "word of exhortation," and Acts 4:36 speaks of Barnabas' ability in that respect. However, by the end of the 4th cent. and the beginning of the 5th, the Western Church had accepted it as Pauline and canonical. (For details, cf. Wik, *NTI* 456–59.)

3 The principal arguments against Pauline authorship are the differences of vocabulary and style from those of Paul, the different structure of the epistle (the interweaving of doctrine and exhortation), the different manner of introducing OT citations, and the author's usually observed rule of citing Scripture according to the LXX (with preference for the form of the text represented by the Codex Alexandrinus). Although there are important theological differences from Paul, not all of these are such decisive arguments against Pauline authorship as is sometimes thought, e.g., the author's emphasis on Jesus' entrance into heaven rather than on the resurrection is evidently dictated by his concern with the heavenly priesthood of Christ. However, most of the reasons given for denying Pauline authorship are of such weight as to be compelling. Certain theological similarities between Heb and the Pauline epistles (e.g., in respect to

Christology) do not necessarily point to an influence of Paul or of the Pauline kerygma on the author, for he and Paul could both have drawn upon a common tradition (cf. E. Grässer, *TRu* 30 [1964] 186–88).

Among the reasons for thinking that the author was a Jewish Christian of Hellenistic background is his consistent use of the contrast between the heavenly and the earthly spheres of reality, the latter being understood as a mere shadow of the former. This conception is of largely Platonic origin. The author's Hellenism explains the many resemblances between Heb and the writings of Philo, although it is not probable that he depended on them directly. In any case, his strong historical concern with respect to the redemptive work of Christ, as well as his faithfulness to the Judeo-Christian eschatology, makes a great difference between his understanding of the OT and its fulfillment and Philo's philosophically oriented allegorism. Because the author was a Hellenistic Jewish Christian, whose work has literary merit and shows acquaintance with the devices of Greek rhetoric, many have thought that he was Apollos (cf. Acts 18:24; e.g., M. Luther, T. Zahn, W. F. Howard, T. W. Manson, C. Spicq). The most that can be said for that view is that it is plausible; nothing in Heb makes it untenable, nothing speaks decisively in its favor.

Although hypotheses have been advanced of the loss of the original greeting and of the later addition of ch. 13, the integrity of Heb is generally admitted; a few scholars still hold that 13:22–25 is an addition intended to give a Pauline touch to the work.

4 **(II) The Addressees.** The exhortations against apostasy from the Christian faith and the demonstration that the old covenant has been superseded make the assumption reasonable that Heb was meant for Jewish Christians. Although many scholars propose a Gentile-Christian group, and the view has even been put forth that the work was intended for a group of Jews who had broken with orthodox Judaism but were not convinced that Jesus was the Messiah, the arguments for these positions, particularly the latter, are not convincing. In favor of the former, such texts as 3:12; 6:1; 9:14 are adduced, and it is claimed that to speak of falling away from the living God shows that the apostasy the author feared was a relapse into paganism, not Judaism, and that the references to laying the foundation of faith in God and to worshiping the living God indicate that the readers had been converted from paganism. But the author's concept of the living God is of a God who has manifested himself by his acts and by his speaking to man; the expression "the living God" means, for him, the God who has revealed himself through Jesus. Consequently, a return to Judaism would be apostasy from the living God. The author's concern to show that the sacrificial cult of the OT has been replaced by Christ's sacrifice does not prove beyond doubt that he was writing to converts from Judaism, for Gal, written to Gentile Christians, insists upon their freedom from the Mosaic Law. But his preoccupation with the replacement of the old covenant and its cult is best explained by the hypothesis that Heb was intended for Jewish Christians, and, unlike the case of Gal, there is no indication that the addressees were Gentiles who had become attracted to OT institutions through outside influence. The title "To [the] Hebrews" is found for the first time in P46 (Chester Beatty ms., 3rd cent.). It may be conceded that "presumably it is nothing more than an inference drawn from the content of the Epistle" (Wik, *NTI* 457), but that would seem to be an argument for its accuracy.

For the view that Heb is addressed to former Jewish "priests" converted to Christianity (see Acts 6:7), among whom some may even have been Essenes, and for affinities of Heb with QL, see Y. Yadin, *Scripta hierosolymitana* 4 (1957) 36–45; C. Spicq, *RevQum* 1 (1958–59) 365–90; cf. J. Coppens, *NRT* 84 (1962) 128–41, 257–82 [= ALBO 4/1].

5 **(III) Literary Form, Date and Place of Composition.** Because of its careful and involved composition and its major theme of the priesthood of Christ, Heb has been regarded as a theological treatise. However, the author's principal purpose was not to expound doctrine for its own sake, but to ward off the apostasy that was evidently a real danger for those to whom he wrote. The work is called a "word of exhortation" (13:22)—a designation that is also given to a synagogue sermon in Acts 13:15. Probably, Heb is a written homily that the author has given an epistolary ending (13:22–25). Because there are references to "speaking" (e.g., 2:5; 5:11; 6:9; 9:5), some scholars have suggested that the homily was intended for oral delivery. That is unlikely, and the ending, which is probably the original one, is clearly against that hypothesis.

The fact that the work was used by Clement of Rome provides the *terminus ad quem* for the time of its composition. The references in 10:32–34 and 12:4 to persecution undergone by the addressees are too imprecise to be an indication of a particular persecution that can be dated with certainty. Since in his description of the worship offered under the old covenant the author relies mainly on the OT account of the Mosaic Tabernacle and its liturgy and does not refer to the Temple of Jerusalem, the pres. tense used in describing that worship cannot prove that he wrote before the destruction of the Temple in AD 70 and that Temple worship was still going on at the time of writing. Most modern commentators favor a date later than 70, but the destruction of the Temple would have given the author a strong support for his statements that the old covenant and its cult have been superseded; if he wrote after that event, his silence about it is difficult to explain.

The greetings sent to the readers by "those from Italy" (13:24) have been taken as showing that Heb was written in Rome, but the text may mean no more than that people who were natives of Italy were in the author's company when he wrote. See F. V. Filson, "*Yesterday*" (SBT 4; Naperville, Ill., 1967); cf. E. Grässer, *TRu* 30 (1964) 156.

6 **(IV) Outline.** The Epistle to the Hebrews is outlined as follows:

- (I) Introduction (1:1–4)
- (II) The Son Higher Than the Angels (1:5–2:18)
  - (A) The Messianic Enthronement (1:5–14)
  - (B) Exhortation to Fidelity (2:1–4)
  - (C) Jesus' Exaltation Through Abasement (2:5–18)
- (III) Jesus, Faithful and Compassionate High Priest (3:1–5:10)
  - (A) Jesus, the Faithful Son, Superior to Moses (3:1–6)
  - (B) A Warning Based on Israel's Infidelity (3:7–4:13)
  - (C) Jesus, Compassionate High Priest (4:14–5:10)
- (IV) Jesus' Eternal Priesthood and Eternal Sacrifice (5:11–10:39)
  - (A) An Exhortation to Spiritual Renewal (5:11–6:20)
  - (B) Jesus, Priest According to the Order of Melchizedek (7:1–28)
    - (a) Melchizedek and the Levitical Priesthood (7:1–10)
    - (b) The Levitical Priesthood Superseded (7:11–28)
  - (C) The Eternal Sacrifice (8:1–9:28)
    - (a) The Old Covenant, Tabernacle, Worship (8:1–9:10)
      - (i) The heavenly priesthood of Jesus (8:1–6)
      - (ii) The old covenant contrasted with the new (8:7–13)
      - (iii) The old covenant Tabernacle (9:1–5)
      - (iv) The old covenant worship (9:6–10)

(b) The Sacrifice of Jesus (9:11–28)
(i) Sacrifice in the heavenly sanctuary (9:11–14)
(ii) The sacrifice of the new covenant (9:15–22)
(iii) The perfect sacrifice (9:23–28)
(D) Jesus' Sacrifice, Motive for Perseverance (10:1–39)
(a) The Many Sacrifices and the One Sacrifice (10:1–18)
(b) Assurance, Judgment, Recall of the Past (10:19–39)
(V) Examples, Discipline, Disobedience (11:1–12:29)
(A) The Faith of the Ancients (11:1–40)
(B) God's Treatment of His Sons (12:1–13)
(C) The Penalties of Disobedience (12:14–29)
(VI) Final Exhortation, Blessing, Greetings (13:1–25)

(For another mode of outlining Heb, see A. Vanhoye, *Structure littéraire.)*

COMMENTARY

7 **(I) Introduction (1:1–4).** **1.** *incompletely and in varied ways:* Some commentators see no difference between these two manners of designating God's speaking in times past; they regard the expression as an example of hendiadys. However, it is more likely that each refers respectively to the fragmentary nature of OT revelation and to the varied ways in which it was given. *the fathers:* The ancestors of Israel. This does not necessarily mean that the epistle was addressed to people of Jewish origin, for the same language is used in 1 Cor 10:1 to Gentile Christians. By their conversion to Christ, the descendant of Abraham, the Gentiles have been brought into the commonwealth of spiritual Israel (Gal 3:29). *the prophets:* Not only those whose preaching is preserved in the OT books bearing their names, but all in Israel's history through whom God spoke, e.g., Abraham (Gn 20:7), Moses (Dt 18:18), Nathan (2 Sm 7:2), and Elijah (1 Kgs 18:22). **2.** *in these, the last days:* Lit., "at the end of these days"; the Gk phrase translates in the LXX the Hebr *bᵉ'aḥᵃrît hayyāmîm*, "in the end of days." Here, "these" is added to the LXX formula, which does not always mean the "end time," the final age; but that is its usual meaning (cf. Is 2:2; Jer 23:20; Ez 38:16; Dn 10:14). The author of Heb, together with primitive Christianity in general, regarded the final age as inaugurated by the Christ-event, pre-eminently by Jesus' redemptive sacrifice (cf. 9:26), and he speaks of the Christians as those who have experienced "the powers of the age to come" (6:5). *through his Son:* Lit., "through a son," i.e., one who is Son; God's speaking to men, whether in the past or in the "last days," is not contrasted with his deeds, as if he had merely announced truths unconnected with history. Predominantly, the OT revelation was a prophetic interpretation of certain events of Israel's history as acts of God. God's speaking through his Son is primarily the revelation of his saving purpose in respect to mankind through the coming of Jesus and the "eternal redemption" (9:12) achieved through his death and exaltation. "Christ is God's last word to the world; revelation in him is complete, final and homogeneous" (J. Moffatt, *Epistle to the Hebrews*, 2). *heir of all things...through whom he created the worlds:* The Son's role as redeemer and mediator of creation. Although it comes at the end of the ages, the former is mentioned first. His being made heir was not an event outside time, previous to the incarnation; it took place when he entered glory after his passion (cf. Rom 8:17). The connection of "heir" with the "inherited" of v. 4 shows that the Son's being made heir means his inheriting the "more excellent name" that he received after his humiliation (cf. Phil 2:6–11). Yet it could not be more clearly stated that he existed before he appeared as man: Through him God "created the worlds" (*tous aiōnas*). The Gk word *aiōn* can mean either "world" or "age," but its use in 11:3 in connection with the creation of the universe suggests the former meaning here. Unless the plural should be regarded as lacking significance (Bl-Deb-F §141, 1), there appears here the conception of a number of worlds, visible and invisible, the latter being the many heavens (cf. *T. Levi* 3:1–9; 2 Cor 12:2; Heb 4:14; J. Bonsirven, *Le judaïsme palestinien* [Paris, 1935] 1, 158).

8 **3.** Some scholars think that vv. 3–4 contain a liturgical hymn that the author has incorporated (cf. U. Luck, *Charis kai sophia*, [Fest. K. H. Rengstorf; Leiden, 1964] 200), or at least the elements of such a hymn (cf. J. Jervell, *Imago Dei* [FRLANT 58; Göttingen, 1960] 198, n.99). The description of the Son in v. 2 as the mediator of creation assimilates him to the personified Wisdom of the OT (Prv 8:30; Wis 7:22), and this verse continues in that vein. He is the "refulgence" (*apaugasma*) of the Father's "glory" (cf. Wis 7:26). *Apaugasma* can be understood either actively (radiance) or passively (reflection, refulgence); in view of the dependence on Wis 7:26 and of the following phrase, the passive meaning is more likely intended here. *the very imprint [charaktēr] of his substance:* This recalls the designation of Wisdom as the "image" (*eikōn*) of God's goodness (Wis 7:26). *Charaktēr* probably means the same as *eikōn*, which is applied to Christ in Col 1:15 (cf. R. Bultmann, *TNT* 1, 132; E. Käsemann, *Das wandernde Gottesvolk* [FRLANT 55; Göttingen, 1959] 61f.). *supports all things:* He guides and sustains all that has been created through him (cf. Col 1:17), just as Wisdom "reaches from end to end mightily and governs all things well" (Wis 8:1). *having made purification from sins:* Attention is now turned from the cosmological role of the pre-existent Son to the redemptive work of the humiliated and glorified Jesus. A similar juxtaposition is found in Col 1:15–20; in the OT, Wisdom's role is both cosmological and soteriological (Prv 8:22–36, Wis 9:9–18). *the Majesty:* A reverent periphrasis for God, like "the power" of Mk 14:62 (for this Jewish usage, cf. J. Bonsirven, *Judaïsme*, 128–49). Jesus' enthronement "at the right hand" of God is seen as the fulfillment of Ps 110:1 (cf. 1:13). This text is frequently used in the NT to describe the glorification of Jesus (Acts 2:34–36; Rom 8:34; Col 3:1; 1 Pt 3:22); its use is probably based on Jesus' reply to the high priest (Mk 14:62; cf. W. Grundmann, "*Dexios*," *ThDNT* 2, 39f.). This glorification is connected immediately with the resurrection, and no significance should be seen in the fact that Heb does not explicitly refer to the resurrection except in 13:20, for it is always presupposed when Jesus' exaltation is mentioned (cf. O. Kuss, *Auslegung und Verkündigung* [Regensburg, 1963] 1, 320). It may be questioned, however, whether the connection of resurrection and enthronement belongs to the most primitive stage of the tradition (cf. F. Hahn, *Christologische Hoheitstitel* [FRLANT 83; Göttingen, 1963] 126–32, for the view that the original reference was to the parousia).

9 4. *made superior to the angels:* By his exaltation Jesus "inherited a more excellent name than they." In Semitic thought, the name designated what a person was, and reception of a new name indicated some change in the person who received it. In Phil 2:6–11 the name that indicates the new status of the Exalted Jesus is "Lord" (cf. O. Cullmann, *Christology of the NT* [Phila., 1959] 204; for a differing view, cf. L. Cerfaux, *Christ in the Theology of St. Paul* [N.Y., 1959] 477–79). Here it is "Son." The application of this name to Jesus before his exaltation (5:7) may be explained as prolepsis, but it is not purely proleptic. The author shares the view found in Rom 1:3f. that so far as his human nature is concerned, Jesus became Son of God in the fullest sense at his resurrection; until then, he existed in that condition Paul calls "the likeness of sinful flesh" (Rom 8:3; cf. Heb 5:7; 10:20). But the sonship he received when he was glorified (cf. J. Dupont, *RSR* 35 [1948] 522–43) is based ultimately on the relation that he had with the Father before the incarnation; as the pre-existent One, the title "Son" belonged to him always (Rom 8:3, "God sent his Son..."; Gal 4:4), thus the name properly (though imperfectly) belonged to the incarnate Jesus even before his exaltation. The reason for introducing Jesus' superiority to the angels is connected with the purpose of Heb: The addressees are in danger of falling away from the word of God spoken through his Son. The consequences of that would be fearful, much worse than the punishment received by those Hebrews who disobeyed the word spoken through angels (2:2), the Mosaic Law, because the Son through whom the final word of God was spoken is superior to the angel mediators of the Law. (For angels as mediators of the Law, see Acts 7:53; Gal 3:19; Josephus, *Ant.* 15.5, 3 §136). However, the primary contrast that Heb draws between the old and the new covenant is that the latter has a new, superior priesthood, whose sanctuary is not on earth but in heaven (8:1–2). The priesthood of the old covenant, with which that of the new one is contrasted, is the Levitical priesthood; but the author may have also taken into account the late-Jewish conception that the ministering priest of the heavenly sanctuary was the angel Michael (cf. *bḤagigah* 12b). In emphasizing Jesus' superiority to the angels, he possibly has in mind the major concern of Heb, the heavenly priesthood of Jesus, and wishes to say that Jesus, and not an angel, is the priest who functions in the heavenly sanctuary (cf. H. Bietenhard, *Die himmlische Welt im Urchristentum und Spätjudentum* [Tübingen, 1951] 129, n.1). Finally, these introductory verses of Heb have remarkable similarities with the writings of Philo, in which the Logos is the image (*eikōn*) of God (*De spec. leg.* 1.81) and the instrument through whom the universe was created (*Cherubim* 127; *De sacrif. Abel et Cain* 8). The Gk word *charaktēr*, which occurs in the NT only in Heb 1:3, is frequent in Philo, used often of the human soul but also of the Logos (*De plant.* 18).

10 **(II) The Son Higher Than the Angels (1:5–2:18).**

(A) The Messianic Enthronement (1:5–14). 5. Jesus' superiority to the angels is now shown by a catena of seven OT texts. The first, Ps 2:7, belongs to one of the royal Pss celebrating, most probably, the enthronement of the king of Judah. According to 2 Sm 7:14 (the second text in the catena), the relationship between God and the Davidic ruler was that of father to son; consequently, the day of the king's accession to power was the day on which he was "begotten" as the son of God. The messianic interpretation of these texts, a natural result of the belief that the messiah would be of the Davidic line, is found outside the NT in the QL (cf. J. Allegro, *JBL* 57 [1958] 350–54). From Heb 1:3 it is clear that the author understood the "today" of Ps 2:7 as the day of the exaltation of the Risen Christ (cf. Acts 13:33). **6.** The third quotation, a combination of Dt 32:43 (LXX) and Ps 97:7, is introduced by "he says" (for justification of the translation "he" rather than "it" [the book] and its significance, cf. M. Barth, *CINTI* 59). It is not certain to what event v. 6a refers. Some scholars think that it is the parousia (cf. J. Héring, *L'Épître aux Hébreux*, 30; H. Strathmann, *Brief an die Hebräer*, 78); if "again" is taken as modifying the verb ("when he again leads his firstborn into the world"), that interpretation receives strong though not conclusive support. However, "again" may be simply an introduction to the new scriptural quotation (as in 1:5; cf. 2:13; 10:30); the fact that it occurs within the temporal clause does not rule out that possibility (cf. Wis 14:1). In that case, the reference is probably to the exaltation of Jesus; the world into which he is led is the "world to come" that is made subject to him, and not to the angels (2:5). Since the incarnate Son was "for a little while made lower than the angels" (2:9), it is not likely that the birth of Jesus (cf. H. Montefiore, *A Commentary*, 45) is meant.

11 7. The LXX wording of Ps 104:4 furnishes the author with a statement about the angels that serves to bring out their contrast with the Son. The meaning of the LXX text, quite different from that in the MT, is probably that God changes the angels into wind and fire, a conception found in *2 Esdras* 8:21. This is well suited to the purpose of the author: The angels are mutable, transitory beings, unlike the Son, whose rule is everlasting. **8.** The reason for the author's quoting Ps 45:7–8 seems to be simply to bring out the permanence of the Son's kingdom. The application of the name "God" to him is of no great significance; the Ps had already used it of the Hebr king to whom it was addressed. Undoubtedly, the author of Heb saw more in the name than what was conveyed by the court style of the original, but his understanding must be derived from what he has already said about the pre-existent Son. In any case, the tone of the Ps and the theme of the entire section suggests that what the author envisages is the Son's everlasting rule consequent upon his messianic enthronement. **10–12.** The next quotation, taken from Ps 102:26–28, attributes to the Son the work of creation; the Ps itself addresses these words to God. Since the author has spoken of the Son as the mediator of creation, this is not surprising. The permanence that the Ps attributed to God is here predicted of the Son: The heavens will perish, but he remains (cf. Is 51:6). **13.** The final OT quotation is from Ps 110, to which the author has already alluded in v. 3. **14.** The words of v. 13 were not spoken to any angel. In contrast with the enthroned Son, the angels are only servants, "ministering spirits" (cf. Philo, *De virtut.* 73). Perhaps the mention of their ministry's being on behalf of men is directed against a tendency to regard them as proper objects of man's worship (cf. Col 2:18). See K. J. Thomas, "The OT Citations in Hebrews," *NTS* 11 (1964–65) 303–25.

12 Verses 5–13 probably reflect an enthronement hymn similar to Phil 2:9–11 and 1 Tm 3:16, in which the stages of Jesus' exaltation are given in the order corresponding to that of ancient Near Eastern (especially Egyptian) enthronement ceremonies (cf. J. Jeremias, *Die Briefe an Timotheus und Titus* [NTD; Göttingen, 1965] 4, 22–24). The three stages are: (1) the elevation of the new king to divine status; (2) his presentation to the gods of the pantheon; (3) his enthronement and reception of kingly power. With the modification demanded by a monotheistic religion (Jesus is not presented to the gods but to angels), that sequence can be seen in these verses: (1) Jesus' elevation to the rank of Son of God whom the angels must adore (5–6); (2) the proclamation of everlasting lordship (7–12); (3) the enthronement (13).

13 **(B) Exhortation to Fidelity (2:1–4).** Here the author passes from exposition to exhortation. The transition from the one to the other is characteristic of the epistle. The warning against apostasy (2:1–3a) is repeated many times in Heb, and the a fortiori argument in these verses (the *a minori ad maius* of rabbinic exegesis) is frequently used by the author (cf. 7:21–22; 9:13–14; 10:28–29; 12:25; cf. C. Spicq, *L'Épître aux Héb*, 1, 53 for parallels in Philo). Here it is based on the inferiority of the "word spoken through angels" (the Mosaic Law, cf. 1:4) to that which the Christians have received. **3–4.** The salvation they are to inherit (cf. 1:14) had its origin in the word "spoken through the Lord," and "confirmed for us by those who had heard" it. The author is clearly in the same position as those whom he is addressing in respect to hearing that word: He received it from witnesses. But the distinction between "us" and "those who heard" should perhaps not be pressed as an argument that the author and his contemporaries belonged to the second generation of Christians (cf. B. Hunt, *SE* 2, 410). The confirmation came not only through the testimony of those who had heard, but through God's setting his seal upon its truth "by signs, wonders, many kinds of miracles, and the gifts of the holy spirit distributed according to his will." Signs and wonders are frequently mentioned in Acts as the confirmation of apostolic preaching (4:31; 14:3; 15:12); the triad "signs, wonders, miracles" is the attestation given by God to Jesus himself (Acts 2:22) and is cited by Paul as proof of true apostleship (2 Cor 12:12).

14 **(C) Jesus' Exaltation Through Abasement (2:5–18).** **5.** *the world to come:* It has been made subject to the glorified Son as the climax of an ascending movement that began in the humiliation of his earthly life, suffering, and death. (For the conception that the present world was under the dominion of angels, cf. Dt 32:8 [LXX]; Dn 10:13.) **6–9.** The OT citation, Ps 8:5–7, is introduced by the formula "someone has testified somewhere." Its imprecision is due to the author's indifference to the human author of the text—all Scripture is the word of God. A similar mode of introduction is found in Philo (*De ebrietate* 61). The Ps is also applied to Jesus in 1 Cor 15:27; Eph 1:22, and probably in 1 Pt 3:22. This use by such a variety of authors indicates that the application belonged to a common early Christian tradition of OT interpretation (cf. C. H. Dodd, *According to the Scriptures* [N.Y., 1953] 32–34). Possibly the origin of the application was that Ps 8:5 speaks of "the son of man." That expression is in synonymous parallelism with "man," which occurs in the first line of the verse; but to the Christians it would have recalled Jesus' designation of himself as the Son of Man (→ Aspects NT Thought, 78:28–30). The Ps begins by contrasting God's greatness with the relative insignificance of man and proceeds to reflect on how great man is in respect to the rest of creation, of which he is lord. *a little lower than the angels:* So the LXX understands this phrase of the Ps. All else was made subject to him; on this the author builds his argument. The Ps describes the actual situation of man, whereas in Heb the submission of all things to man is a situation that does not yet exist except in the case of Jesus, the "Man." *for a little while:* Jesus was lower than the angels in the days of his earthly life, particularly in his suffering and death; now, crowned with honor and glory, he is set above all creation, including the angels. Here the author regards all things as already subject to Christ in virtue of his exaltation; the same conception as that in Eph 1:22. Paul uses Ps 8 in 1 Cor 15:26–27 with a slightly different meaning: Jesus' reign has begun, but the subjection of all things to him will not be complete until his final triumph at the parousia. That view is also found in Heb 10:13, although Ps 8 is not used in connection with it. Since the supremacy and triumph of Christ can be regarded from different perspectives, the two views are not incompatible, and it is not surprising to find both held by the same author. **9.** *in order that he might taste death on behalf of everyone:* This is certainly a purpose clause, but what meaning is there in the statement that because he suffered death Jesus was crowned with honor and glory? Strathmann's opinion (*Brief an die Hebräer*, 84) that the crowning refers not to Jesus' exaltation but to his consecration as high priest in preparation for his sacrificial death is against the sense of the context as well as of the entire epistle, which associates Jesus' high-priestly glory with his exaltation (e.g., 5:4–5). Héring suggests that the purpose clause should be read with "because he suffered death" (*L'Épître aux Hébreux*, 32). *by the favor of God:* This reading has excellent mss. attestation and fits in well with v. 10, which speaks of the Father's initiative in Jesus' saving work. However, a few mss. read "separated from God." In spite of its poor attestation this may be better, on the principle that the more difficult reading should be preferred, especially since a scribe might easily have changed it through theological scruple. It expresses Jesus' feeling of abandonment in death (cf. Mk 15:34). *taste death:* A Semitism for experiencing death (cf. Mk 9:1).

15 **10.** *it was fitting:* This use of the argument *ex convenientia* in regard to God is "an innovation in the Bible" (C. Spicq, *L'Épître aux Héb*, 2, 36), although it occurs often in Philo (e.g., *Leg. alleg.* 148; *De conf. ling.* 175). *for whom and through whom all things exist:* This concept of God as the Creator, in whom all that he has made finds its purpose, is found also in 1 Cor 8:6 and Rom 11:36. *in bringing many sons to glory, to make their leader to salvation perfect through suffering:* The Gk participle translated "in bringing" probably refers to God, although some apply it to Jesus ("to make perfect through suffering their leader to salvation, the one who brings many sons to glory"). The argument for the latter interpretation is based on the fact that the participle is in the accusative, whereas the pronoun referring to God ("it was fitting for *him*") is in the dative. But this is not conclusive (cf. *GrBib* 394; Bl-Deb-F § 410). The tense of the participle is best explained as an ingressive aorist indicating the starting point of God's action (O. Michel, *Brief an die Hebräer*, 78; Héring, *op. cit.*, 33). The designation of Jesus as leader announces an important theme in Heb: the journey of the people of God to the place of rest (4:11), the heavenly sanctuary, in the footsteps of Jesus, their "forerunner" (6:20). R. Bultmann sees this as related to the Gnostic motif of the soul's journey to the world of light (*TNT* 1, 177), as does E. Käsemann (*Das wandernde Gottesvolk*, 52–58, 79–82). *to make perfect:* The Gk vb. *teleioō*, "make perfect," occurs nine times in Heb, of which three have to do with Jesus' being made perfect (2:10; 5:9; 7:28). The verb is used in the LXX of priestly consecration, translating a Hebr phrase, "to fill [the hands]" (Ex 29:9,29,33,35; Lv 16:32; 21:10; Nm 3:3); for the corresponding noun "perfection" (*teleiōsis*), cf. Lv 8:33. This cultic notion of perfection is certainly present in Heb (cf. G. Delling, "*Teleioō*," *ThWNT* 8, 80–85; M. Dibelius, *Botschaft und Geschichte* [Tübingen, 1956] 2, 106–76). But Jesus' priestly consecration involves his obedience learned through suffering (5:8–10), and his being perfected means also that through obedience he was brought "to the full moral perfection of his humanity" (B. F. Westcott, *Epistle to the Hebrews*, 49). **11.** *for he who consecrates and those who are consecrated:* Jesus is the one who consecrates. The Gk vb. *hagiazō* "consecrate," is, like "make perfect," a cultic term; cf. Ex 28:41 (LXX 28:37). This usage is also found in Jn 10:36; 17:17,19. Jesus' being perfected as high priest enables him to perfect his people (cf. 10:14 [where the two terms "make perfect" and "consecrate" are used together]; 11:40; 12:23). "Through Christ's priestly consecration the believers themselves are perfected and consecrated" (Dibelius, *op. cit.*, 172). The author emphasizes the uniqueness of Jesus' priesthood and does not attribute to his followers what is uniquely his. But the common element of the two consecrations is that each brings about the possibility of access to God. As high priest, Jesus has entered into the Holy of Holies (9:12), into heaven itself, there to appear before God on our behalf (9:24); the believers are able confidently to make their entrance after him and draw near to God (7:19). *all have the same father:* Lit., "are all of one." Most commentators identify God as "the father"; others, with less probability, think of Abraham (cf. 2:16); but the argument suggests that Adam is meant (cf. O. Procksch, "*Hagiazō*," *ThDNT* 1, 112). It is not true that there is an implication that "Christ's common tie with mankind goes back to the pre-incarnate period" (J. Moffatt, *Epistle to the Hebrews*, 32); the incarnation of the Son is what makes men his brothers (cf. 2:14). Because he has associated himself with them by becoming "blood and flesh" as they are, he is able to be their high priest (2:17). The basis of the argument is that he is able to help them because he shares their lot and is one of them, i.e., because like them he is a son of Adam. *he is not ashamed to call them brothers:* Because he shares the nature of those whom he has consecrated (cf. 11:16).

16 **12–13.** Three OT texts are now cited that show the union between the Son and those he came to save. The first is Ps 22:23, taken from a psalm widely applied in the early Church to Christ, especially in his passion (cf. Mk 15:24,29,34; Mt 27:43; Lk 23:25; Jn 19:24). The Ps belongs to the "individual lament" category; in v. 23 the "certainty of hearing" motif, common to that category, begins. The author of Heb places the sufferer's joyous praise of Yahweh upon the lips of Jesus. Probably the principal reason for doing so was the use of "brothers" in the Ps, but it is not an exaggeration to say that the author thinks of the praise given to God by the glorified Christ "in the midst of the assembly" (*ekklēsia*) of those whom he has consecrated. The second and third citations are from Is 8:17,18, respectively. The purpose of the second is not clear. If one accepts Dodd's view that when OT texts are cited in the NT the reference is not simply to the verse(s) cited but to the context (*According to the Scriptures*, 61), then the reason for the citation may be that Isaiah states his confidence in the truth of the divine oracles that most of the people have rejected. Similarly here the exalted Christ is presented as looking forward to the vindication of his work, the significance of which is not apparent now except to those who have accepted him in faith (cf. 10:13). However, it seems unlikely that that is the point of the citation; at this stage of Heb the author is dealing with the solidarity existing between Jesus and his followers. It is more reasonable to suppose that he wishes to present Jesus as an example, in his mortal life, of that confidence in God that is necessary for those whom he has consecrated and who are now in need of a like confidence in order that they may not "slip away" (2:1). The third citation is surprising, for it seems to mean that the believers are the children of Jesus. Such a concept is found nowhere else in the NT (Jn 13:33 and 21:5 are not exceptions). The various attempts to accept that meaning and to explain satisfactorily the peculiar usage are of dubious merit (cf. F. F. Bruce, *Ep. to the Heb*, 48; O. Michel, *Brief an die Hebräer*, 81). The children are God's own or, more likely, Adam's. "The same father" (2:11) is Adam rather than God. In either case, there is a departure from the meaning of the OT text, where the children are Isaiah's.

17 **14.** *since the children have blood and flesh in common, he likewise shared them:* In the biblical sense, "flesh" means human nature considered in its weakness and frailty, and as such it is contrasted with "spirit" and God (cf. Pss 55:5; 77:39; Is 31:3; 2 Chr 32:8). The expression "flesh and blood" meaning human nature occurs in the OT only in Sir 14:8; 17:26; for the NT, cf. Mt 16:17; Gal 1:16; Eph 6:12. Here the author speaks of human nature under the ban of death and sees death as associated with the devil. It is difficult to think that he does not relate that notion with the story of the fall, and that he does not stand in the tradition that saw a connection between death and the sin of Eden (Sir 25:23; *2 Esdras* 3:7; *2 Baruch* 23:4). Consequently, one must question the view of E. Schweizer that in Heb the concept of flesh is nowhere joined with that of sin (cf. "*Sarx*," *ThWNT* 7, 143). *that he might break the power of him who held the power of death, that is, the devil:* The conception that death was no part of God's plan for man and that it had been brought into the world by the devil was held in Hellenistic Judaism (cf. Wis 1:13; 2:23–24). Because of the connection between sin and death, the power of death was broken when Christ through his high-priestly work removed sin (2:17). The paradox that death was nullified by Christ's death is similar to that of Rom 8:3, where Paul says that God condemned sin by sending his Son "in the likeness of sinful flesh." The author gives no reason beyond saying that it was fitting for God to act thus.

18 **15.** *free those who through their whole life were slaves because of a fear of death:* This fear of death should not be regarded merely as the natural fear that all men experience. (Nor is there any suggestion that the freedom meant is freedom from a constraint to do evil in order to avoid death: "Through fear of death many men will consent to do things that nothing else could compel them to do" [Bruce, *Ep. to the Heb*, 51].) It is rather a religious fear based on an erroneous conception of life after death, so that death is thought to be a severance of man's relations with God (cf. Is 38:18; Ps 115:17–18); a proper recognition of the connection between death and sin regards death as something more than a physical evil (cf. 1 Cor 15:26, where death is the "final enemy," to be destroyed by Christ). The fear that Jesus felt at the prospect of death (Mk 14:34–36; Heb 5:7) can be explained only by his realizing the latter better than everyone else. But because of his death and resurrection the nature of death was changed; it became a means of passage out of the domain of sin: "The OT fear of death came to its climax and conclusion in the death of Jesus" (O. Michel, *Brief an die Hebräer*, 85). **16.** *for certainly he does not take note of angels, but of Abraham's descendants:* The verb is taken as a direct reference to the incarnation by C. Spicq (*L'Épître aux Héb*, 2, 46), following many patristic commentators. The entire section deals with the incarnation, but it seems that this verse has a wider reference. The vb. (*epilambanomai*) is used in 8:9 (in a citation of Jer 31:32 [LXX: 38:32]) with the meaning, "to take hold," of a person in order to help him, which may well be the meaning here. The pres. tense suggests a continuing help rather than the single event of the incarnation. Abraham's descendants are those who believe in Christ. **17.** *that he might be a* *compassionate and faithful high priest:* This is the first mention of the central theme of Heb: Jesus' role as high priest. In designating him as "faithful," the author follows a tradition that demands that quality of a priest (cf. 1 Sm 2:35), but that he must be "compassionate" is a notion peculiar to Heb. When the motif of the high priest's compassion is taken up again in 4:15 and 5:1–3, it is based, as here, on his solidarity with men. Nothing in the OT tradition emphasizes that quality; it is probably derived from the author's own reflection on the manner of Jesus' earthly existence, suffering, and death. In respect to compassion, Christ did not fit into a preconceived definition; rather, the definition (5:1–3) was based on the author's knowledge of what Jesus had been. *that he might expiate the sins of the people:* The Gk vb. *hilaskesthai*, "expiate," occurs frequently in the LXX, where it usually translates the Hebr *kippēr*. The verb expresses the removal of sin or defilement, by God or by a priest through the means set up by God for that purpose (cf. C. H. Dodd, *JTS* 33 [1931] 352–60; → Pauline Theology, 79:84). "Medieval conceptions of God as a kind of feudal overlord who requires satisfaction for his outraged honor have no place in a genuinely biblical theology" (A. Richardson, *ITNT* 239). **18.** The temptations (testings) of Christ, which have qualified him to help those undergoing temptation, were not only the prospect of death and the sufferings of the passion, but the temptations experienced throughout his life (Lk 22:28). Gospel tradition indicates that fidelity to his messianic mission was a principal object of temptation (Mk 8:31–33; Mt 4:1–11; Lk 4:1–11; cf. J. Dupont, *NTS* 3 [1956–57] 287–304). The temptation of those here addressed was principally to apostasy—fundamentally the same urge to infidelity that Jesus experienced.

19 **(III) Jesus, Faithful and Compassionate High Priest (3:1–5:10).**

(A) Jesus, the Faithful Son, Superior to Moses (3:1–6). The author now begins a consideration of Jesus' compassion and faithfulness in inverse order to that stated in 2:17. **1.** *holy brothers who share a heavenly calling:* Christians are "holy" because they are consecrated by Jesus, and "brothers" because of their common relation to him (2:11). They are called to follow him into the heavenly sanctuary where he now functions as high priest on their behalf. *fix your eyes on Jesus:* The verb is an ingressive aorist. The danger of falling away from Christianity is due to forgetfulness of what Christ has done for them; now he must be constantly in their spiritual vision. *the apostle and high priest:* This is the only case in the NT in which Jesus is called "apostle." The meaning is that he is the one sent by God (cf. Jn 13:16), as his final word to men (1:2). Since the author's interest is principally in the work of Jesus as priest rather than in his teaching, the word-event is the primary reference. This may account for the omission of the article with "high priest"; the two titles probably constitute a unity (K. H. Rengstorf, "*Apostolos*," *ThDNT* 1, 423f.); not precisely, however, as Rengstorf conceives the unity (apostle–revealer–word :: high priest–expiator–work). *whom we confess:* Lit., "of our confession." Here for the first of three times (cf. 4:14; 10:23), the author speaks of a "confession" made by those whom he addresses. He probably refers to a baptismal acknowledgment of Jesus as Son of God (note the baptismal tone of the context). His teaching on Jesus as "apostle and high priest" is meant as a new interpretation of what Christians have confessed at their baptism (cf. G. Bornkamm, *Studien zu Antike und Christentum* [Munich, 1959], 188–203; O. Michel, *Brief an die Hebräer*, 95). However, the author's concern here is not with the content of the confession, but with its power to give his addressees strength and support in their trials (cf. V. Neufeld, *The Earliest Christian Confessions* [NTTS 5; Leiden, 1963] 134ff.).

20 **2.** *who was faithful to him...just as Moses was:* The comparison of Jesus and Moses is probably due to Jesus' being mediator of the new covenant (9:15) as Moses was of the old. Moses' mediatorship was not unconnected with priesthood and sacrifice; his sacrifice at the time of the establishment of the covenant is recalled in 9:19–20, although the title "priest" is not given him in Heb. When the author dwells on Jesus' sacrifice, the OT antitype is not Moses but the Aaronic high priest in his function on the Day of Atonement (9:6–15). However, Philo speaks of Moses' high priesthood (*Quis rev. div. her.* 182; *De praem. et poen.* 53) and possibly the author thinks of this when he makes the Jesus-Moses contrast in this passage dealing with Jesus as the faithful high priest. *who made him:* The expression does not refer to the origin of Jesus, but to his "appointment" to office (cf. F. Schierse, *Verheissung und Heilsvollendung* [Munich, 1955] 109). The same verb is used with that meaning in 1 Sm 12:6, "The Lord is my witness, who made Moses and Aaron." Moses' faithfulness "in all his [God's] house" is derived from Nm 12:7; this section has been called a midrash on that verse (H. Montefiore, *A Commentary*, 72). The "house" (or "household") of God in which Moses was a faithful servant was Israel. The thought of vv. 3–6 is obscure, but it seems possible to establish certain points that may serve as a guide in the interpretation: (1) There is no indication that the author considers either Moses or Christ the founder of the household. (2) "His house" in vv. 2, 5, and 6 is God's house, not Christ's or Moses'. In the case of Christ, the parallel of v. 6 with 10:21 makes that clear.

21 **3.** *this man has been made worthy of greater glory than Moses, as the founder of a house enjoys greater honor than the house:* The pertinence of this verse in establishing Jesus' superiority to Moses is not immediately apparent. Since Moses was a member of the house of Israel, it is understandable that he should be called inferior to God, the founder; but not to Jesus, whose relations with the house have not been mentioned. There would be no difficulty if one could suppose that the author thinks of the pre-existent Son as founder of the house of God (O. Kuss, *Brief an die Heb* [1953], 36); but there is no indication of that. Moreover, when he does speak of Christ's relation to it, it is not as founder, but as Son over it (v. 6). Nor is there any suggestion that he pictured Moses as founder of the house of Israel, and Christ as founder of the Church (C. Spicq, *L'Épître aux Héb*, 2, 67). In that case the comparison would be between the dignity of the respective founders, not between the founder and the house he has set up. **4.** *every house is established by someone, but he who has established all is God:* Some scholars understand v. 4b as a parenthesis (J. Héring, *L'Épître aux Hébreux*, 39; J. Moffatt, *Epistle to the Hebrews*, 42; Spicq, *ibid.*); yet it seems to be that only if one extends the parenthesis to the entire verse, and accepts it not as an "edifying aside" (Moffatt, *ibid.*), but as demanded by the argument that the author's thought flows naturally. The house of v. 2 is God's house; but in using Nm 12:7, the author has changed the possessive pronoun from the first to the third person ("my house" to "his house"). This change, made necessary by the transfer from the direct discourse of the OT, could be misinterpreted; "his house" might be understood as Moses' house, rather than God's. To avoid this misunderstanding, and thus to reinforce the argument of v. 3 that Moses was not the one who established it but was merely part of that house, the author recalls him who did establish it—God, who established all things. **5.** *as a servant, witnessing to what* *would be spoken:* It is not Moses' role as mediator of the old covenant and as lawgiver that is emphasized here; rather, Moses is the one who foretold the Christian dispensation. *what would be spoken:* That is, through God's Son (1:1; cf. also 2:3). **6.** The "house" is the Christian community. Its continuity with ancient Israel is indicated by the fact that there are not two houses but one; the old continues in the new. (For the metaphor of the Christians as "the house of God," cf. 1 Tm 3:15; 1 Pt 4:17; Eph 2:19; and also "the temple of God," 1 Cor 3:16; in QL, cf. 1QS 8:5–9; 9:6.) In this verse the reason for Jesus' superiority to Moses becomes clear: It is the different relation of each to God, the founder of the house. Moses was the faithful "servant" *in* it; Jesus is God's "Son," set *over* it. Because he is the founder's Son he has been made worthy of greater glory than Moses, the servant. *if we hold fast our confidence and pride in our hope:* The majority of mss. add "firm to the end," but this is not found in B or P^{46} and appears to be an interpolation derived from v. 14. Although the Gk *parrēsia*, "confidence," might mean "boldness" and point to open acknowledgment of the faith in face of danger and trial (H. Montefiore, *A Commentary*, 73), the epistle's exhortations to faithfulness do not seem motivated by the danger of persecution, calling for bold confession, but rather by the danger of apostasy, which calls for confidence.

22 **(B) A Warning Based on Israel's Infidelity (3:7–4:13). 7.** *the Holy Spirit:* The spirit of God, inspirer of the Scriptures, speaks through them. Trinitarian concepts should not be read into the expression. The verse begins a section of warning based on Israel's experience during the wandering. The argument rests on the primitive Christian concept of the redemption wrought by Christ as a New Exodus. In the OT the Exodus had served as a symbol of the return of the Jews from the Babylonian Exile (Is 42:9; 43:16–21; 51:9–11); in the NT the redemptive work was regarded as a New Exodus, experienced first by Jesus himself (Lk 9:31) and then by his followers (1 Cor 10:1–4). The addressees are still en route to the goal of their exodus: the heavenly sanctuary, where Jesus has gone before them (6:20). They are in danger of growing weary and discontinuing their journey. Hence the warning lest they, like those Hebrews who rebelled against God, fail to achieve the goal. The quotation is from Ps 95:8–11, but it differs in many ways from the LXX reading. The principal difference is that whereas the LXX (and the MT) connect the "forty years" (v. 10) with God's anger, it is here taken with the previous phrase, "they saw my works," although in v. 17 the LXX order is followed. The reason for the transposition is not clear. **9.** *they tested me:* Cf. Ex 17:17; Nm 20:2–5. **11.** *my rest:* The land of Palestine (cf. Nm 20:12; Dt 12:9). Käsemann sees the motif of the journey of the people of God to their appointed rest as a Gnostic theme, but the OT counterpart seems to be an adequate explanation. **12.** *the living God:* The designation of God as "living" means that he manifests himself in his works (cf. Jos 3:10; Jer 10:10). The expression "to apostatize from the living God" is frequently taken as indication that Heb was written not to Jewish Christians in danger of relapsing into Judaism, but to pagan converts, for a return to Judaism would not, it is argued, be called a "falling away from the true God." However, the author speaks not of the true God simply, but of the true God as living, i.e., acting, and specifically manifesting himself in Christ. To fall away from Christianity, then, is apostasy from the living God, even if it should be a return to Judaism, where the supreme and final act of God is ignored. **13.** *while it is still today:* The author anticipates what he will say in 4:2–11. The "rest" into which Israel was to enter was only a foreshadowing of that rest to which Christians are called; and it is still open to them, provided they persevere to the end in their original confidence. **14.** *we have become partners of Christ:* Probably the participation means sharing the common destiny of entering the heavenly sanctuary (6:20).

23 **16–19.** Cf. Nm 14:1–38; Dt 1:19–40. Because they would not believe the good report of the scouts Caleb and Joshua, and were fearful at the prospect of battle with the Canaanites, the Hebrews refused to go into the land of Canaan. In punishment, the Lord decreed that all except the scouts and those who had been born since the departure from Egypt would die in the desert and never enter the promised land. The author emphasizes the connection of disobedience (v. 18) and unbelief (v. 19). **4:2.** *the gospel has been preached to us as it was to them:* Because the promise to the Hebrews of entering Palestine foreshadowed the promise given to the Christians of entering heaven, the author uses NT terminology to describe it; it was "gospel." **3–4.** The "rest" of God is seen in deeper dimension than Palestine. The Ps (95:11) calls that land God's rest ("my rest") because it was the place of rest that he would give his people (against G. von Rad, who sees the spiritualization of the concept in the Ps itself; see *Gesammelte Studien zum Alten Testament* [Munich, 1965] 101–8). The author understands it as a share in the rest upon which God entered after the work of creation had been completed. Those who are faithful will enter into God's abode, described as a place of rest rather than as the heavenly sanctuary (the author's usual designation), or the lasting city (cf. 13:14).

24 **6–9.** The author attempts to read his meaning of God's rest into the Ps. The Hebr noun for "rest" in Ps 95:11 is *m^{e}nûḥāh* and is different from the verb "rest" in Gn 2:2 (*šābat*), but the LXX uses a word derived from the same Gk stem in each case: *katapausis* (Ps 95:11) and *katapauō* (Gn 2:2). Hence the author of Heb finds a basis in the text of the Ps for his interpretation. He argues that what was promised to the Hebrews was not Palestine, but a share in God's own postcreation rest; cf. the Jewish concept that the Sabbath, which reflects that rest, is "the image of the world to come" (*Genesis Rabbah* 17 [12a]). Because of unbelief many of the Hebrews of the Exodus period were excluded from that rest, and even those who did enter Palestine under Joshua (v. 8) did not enter into the promised rest, which is something greater than the promised land. (Since the Gk form of "Joshua" is the same as that of "Jesus," the name itself brings out both the similarity and the contrast between the OT figure, who led the Hebrews into Palestine, and Jesus, who leads his followers into the heavenly rest of God). If that were not so, then God would not still be offering the promise long after Palestine had been occupied. Yet he does so, as "David's" injunction to the Israelites of his day shows. This injunction is also addressed to the Christians: "Today if you hear his voice, harden not your hearts" (Ps 95:7–8). Because the promise is still good, "there still remains a sabbath rest for the people of God" (v. 9), a share in the sabbath rest of God himself.

25 **11.** *let us strive to enter:* Although the vb. *spoudazō*, "strive," may also mean "hasten," the context does not suggest the latter meaning. There is no thought of hurrying into the rest, but rather of persevering in the effort needed to achieve it. **12–13.** These two verses continue the warning to persevere, for the Word of God judges, and judges rightly, for nothing is unknown to it; in its light, those of the present generation will be judged worthy or unfit to enter God's rest. *living and effective:*

Here the Word is described in a way calculated to bring out its efficacy: It is living, i.e., it produces life (cf. Dt 32:47), and it is effective (cf. Is 55:10–11). It does not seem that the author intends more than a personification of the "word," although some would see here a reference to Jesus as the Word of God (cf. H. Clavier, *New Testament Essays* [Fest. T. W. Manson; Manchester, 1959] 81–93). *sharper than any two-edged sword:* Cf. Is 49:2; Prv 5:4. The penetrating power of the Word is described in Philonic language (cf. *Quis rer. div. her.* 130–31); but in that context Philo is not speaking of its power in respect to judgment, as is the case here. **12.** *the word of God:* This refers to v. 7. It is the Word that speaks to men, inviting them to belief and perseverance. It is a saving Word, but also one that judges, since it condemns those who refuse to hear it. *soul and spirit:* Some see here the conception of man as composed of body, soul, and spirit (E. Schweizer, "*Pneuma*," *ThWNT* 6, 444); it is difficult to agree with F. F. Bruce that "it would indeed be precarious to draw any conclusions from these words about our author's psychology" (*Ep. to the Heb*, 82). These components of man, like the correlative "joints and marrow" are intimately connected, and the statement that the Word is sharp enough to separate them is made simply to emphasize its penetrating power. *judges the reflections and thoughts of the heart:* The author attributes to the Word that knowledge of man which only God has (cf. Acts 1:24; 15:8). **13.** *bare and exposed:* The Gk ptc. *tetrachēlismena*, "exposed," is related to the noun *trachēlos*, "neck." The context suggests that it is synonymous with "bare," but none of the explanations of how it came to have that meaning is really satisfactory. The Gk words of the last phrase of this verse may mean "about whom we are speaking" or "to whom we must render an account." The latter is better suited to the context.

26 **(C) Jesus, Compassionate High Priest (4:14–5:10). 14–16.** These verses recall 2:16–3:1 and prepare for the development on Jesus' priesthood that follows. **14.** *a great high priest:* This is the only place in Heb where Jesus is so designated; usually the author speaks of him as high priest or simply priest; it may be that he wishes to emphasize here Jesus' superiority over the Jewish high priest, with whom he constantly compares him. The same designation is used by Philo for the Logos (cf. *De somn.* 1.214, 219). *who has passed through the heavens:* See comment on 1:2; also *2 Enoch* 3–20. *let us hold fast to our confession:* Cf. comment on 3:2. **15.** *tempted in every way as we are, although he did not sin:* The author knows of the Gospel tradition of Christ's temptations; the Gk ptc. *pepeirasmenon*, "tempted," is in the pf. tense, indicating that these temptations did not occur only once (e.g., Mt 4:1–11), but were a constant accompaniment of Jesus' life (cf. Lk 22:28). The only difference that the author remarks between Jesus' temptations and those of his followers is that he never succumbed to them. There is no basis in this text for Spicq's statement that Jesus "did not know certain suggestions to evil or inclinations to sin which originate in a corrupted nature" (*L'Épître aux Héb*, 2, 93). A development of that sort had to await later theological reflection (cf. O. Kuss, *Brief an die Heb* [1953], 44). **16.** *the throne of grace:* The throne of God (cf. 8:1; 12:2). The reign of the Exalted Jesus is a theme of Heb, as the frequent use of Ps 110:1 shows; in 1:8 the author speaks of Jesus' throne. But the similarity of this verse and 10:19–22 shows that the author is thinking of the confident access to God that has been assured through the redemptive work of Jesus: "Through Jesus Christ, the true high priest, God's throne has become the throne of grace" (O. Michel, *Brief an die Hebräer*, 124).

27 **5:1.** *to offer gifts and sacrifices for sin:* Some commentators think that "gifts" refers to grain offerings and "sacrifices" to animal offerings, but probably the author did not intend any such distinction. As appears later (ch. 9), the Day of Atonement rite is the OT antitype with which he is principally concerned; it is an atonement for "sins," rather than for "sin" (cf. Lv 16:30,34); hence the plural here. **2.** *he is able to deal gently with misguided sinners:* Lit., "with the ignorant and erring." The Gk word *metriopathein*, "deal gently with," does not occur elsewhere in the Bible; it corresponds to a term of Stoic philosophy signifying "the right mean between passion and lack of feeling" (O. Michel, *Brief an die Hebräer*, 130f.). The designation of sinners as "the ignorant and erring" does not mean that the author was thinking only of those who were not aware of the sinful nature of their deeds or who committed less serious moral offenses or ritual violations. The only sins for which sacrificial atonement was impossible were those designated in Nm 15:30 as sins "committed with a high hand." These sins are probably sins perpetrated of set purpose, rather than those into which a man "fell" through human weakness (see H. H. Rowley, *BJRylL* 33 [1950–51] 74–110); so "the ignorant and erring" seems to mean all sinners except those who sin "with a high hand." *since he is himself subject to weakness:* The weakness spoken of here is principally that which leads to sin, as v. 3 shows (cf. Lv 9:7; 16:6). **6.** Although Ps 110:1 is frequently used in the NT of the Exalted Jesus, v. 4 (here quoted) is used only by the author of Heb (cf. also 7:17,21).

28 **7–8.** Just as v. 6 shows how the requisite of a call from God to the high priesthood is verified in Jesus, vv. 7–8 show that he qualifies as one who can sympathize with sinners. The author does not use here the word "weakness" of Jesus and specifically contrasts him with the Jewish high priest in that respect (in 7:28). It is important to notice that the contrast applies to the present exalted state of Christ. The reason for avoiding the word is probably that in v. 3 weakness and sin are made correlative; and it is clear that Jesus did not sin (4:15). There is no doubt, however, that the author, while avoiding the word, does consider that Jesus' ability to sympathize with sinners is based precisely on the fact that he knew temptation, as they do, and "shared in blood and flesh" (cf. 2:14–18; 4:15). He was acquainted with the trials of human nature, i.e., he experienced its weakness, particularly its fear of death. After his resurrection-exaltation, he no longer knows weakness, but having experienced it he can sympathize with those who do. This concept of Heb is similar to that of Paul: "He died on the cross through weakness, but he lives by the power of God" (2 Cor 13:4). **7.** *in the days of his flesh:* The time of his mortal life, when he lived in the sphere of the flesh. *he offered prayers...to him who was able to save him from death:* At least primarily a reference to Gethsemane (cf. Mk 14:35). Apart from Jn 12:27 there is no other Gospel tradition to which it would apply; F. F. Bruce's view that the author drew on a wider tradition than that now available (*Ep. to the Heb*, 98) is at best conjectural. *he was heard because of his reverence:* Bultmann ("*Eulabeia*," *ThDNT* 2, 753) accepts Harnack's emendation of the text and reads: "He was not heard" because Jesus did die. But the emendation is unnecessary if one supposes that the author takes Jesus' deliverance from death as a reference to his resurrection. Since the prayer of Jesus in Gethsemane was that he might be kept from dying rather than be rescued from death once he had undergone it, the author uses "save from death" in a double meaning, in the manner characteristic of Jn. The justification for that supposition is that the context deals with Jesus' priesthood (it is even possible that 5:7–10 was a hymn to "Jesus the High Priest" that the author utilized; cf. G. Friedrich, *TZ* 18 [1962] 95–115). In 7:23–24 his priesthood is contrasted with that of the Levitical priests precisely insofar as they were prevented by death from remaining in office, whereas Jesus has a priesthood that does not pass away, in virtue of the "indestructible life" that he received in his resurrection. His death was essential for his priesthood, but if he had not been saved from death by the resurrection, he would not now be the high priest of his people. **8.** *Son though he was:* Cf. comment on 1:4. The author considers Jesus' sonship in two ways: he became Son when exalted; he always was Son because he existed with the Father even before he appeared on earth. (In terms of later theology, the resurrection-exaltation gave Jesus' human nature full participation in his divine nature.) The two concepts are entirely compatible, but apparently that of pre-existent Son was arrived at later, as the relative lateness of the texts in which it is expressed shows. However, if the hypothesis is right that 5:7–10 is an ancient hymn, similar to Phil 2:6–11, the lateness of the concept must not be exaggerated. There is no reason to regard the later concept as more congenial to the author of Heb than the former, as R. Fuller does (*Foundations of NT Christology* [N.Y., 1965] 187). *he learned obedience from what he suffered:* The learning-through-suffering motif is common in Gk literature, but this text, Rom 5:18, and Phil 2:8 are the only places in the NT where the obedience of Christ in his passion is explicitly mentioned. **9.** *when perfected:* Cf. comment on 2:10. *the source of eternal salvation for all who obey him:* Jesus' obedience leads to his priestly consecration, which in turn qualifies him to save those who are obedient to him. The expression "source of salvation" is common in Philo (*De agric.* 96; *De virtut.* 202; *De vita contemp.* 86) but it is not distinctively Philonian. The salvation that Jesus brings to his followers is eternal because it is based on his eternal priesthood (7:24–25). With the exception of 6:2, the cases where the author uses "eternal" (here and in 9:12,14,15; 13:20) have to do with realities that endure because they belong to the heavenly sphere, which is characterized by permanence, as opposed to the transitory realities of earth.

29 **(IV) Jesus' Eternal Priesthood and Eternal Sacrifice (5:11–10:39).**

(A) An Exhortation to Spiritual Renewal (5:11–6:20). The central section of Heb begins with a long exhortation that is at the same time a rebuke. Jesus' priesthood is a difficult subject to treat; all the more so because those who are addressed have become listless and forgetful of even elementary Christian truths. **11.** *about which we have much to say and it is difficult to explain:* The antecedent of the rel. pronoun is not certain. There are three possibilities: Jesus, Melchizedek, and Jesus' designation as high priest according to the order of Melchizedek. As the neut. translation indicates, the last has been chosen here. **12.** *although you should be teachers by this time:* This has been used as an argument that Heb was addressed to converted Jewish priests (cf. Acts 6:7); their position in the Christian community should be similar to that which they held in Judaism (cf. C. Spicq, *L'Épître aux Héb*, 1, 228). But the function of teacher in Judaism was not particularly associated with priesthood. In any case, the notion that those who are advanced should be teachers of others is so well attested that no background of previous didactic position before conversion need be supposed (cf. J. Moffatt, *Epistle to the Hebrews*, 70). *you need someone to teach you again the basic elements of God's oracles:* The Gk word *stoicheia*, "elements," has none of the pejorative sense it has in Gal (see comment on 4:3; cf. 4:9; Col 2:8,20); here it is elementary, but necessary, teaching, beyond which the addressees should have long since passed. The expression "God's oracles" is used in Rom 3:2, where it probably means the OT Scriptures; here, it includes God's speaking in the OT and, pre-eminently, his speaking through his Son (1:2). *not of solid food but of milk:* The contrast between milk and solid food as metaphorical designations of teaching, suitable for the spiritually immature and mature, respectively, is found also in 1 Cor 3:1–3 and is common in Philo. The words that Paul uses in 1 Cor to designate either class (children—the perfect) are also found here (vv. 13–14). **13.** *no experience of the word of justice:* He has not come to an appreciation of the deeper elements of Christian belief. Possibly the expression continues the child metaphor and means that one in such a state is not able to speak intelligibly ("has no experience in the right way of speaking"). H. P. Owen has suggested a third possibility: The expression means "a principle of righteousness," i.e., a standard whereby one exercises moral judgment (cf. *NTS* 3 [1956–57] 243–53). He finds in these verses not two stages of the Christian life, but three, and thinks that this standard, gained by asceticism, belongs to the second stage. **14.** *solid food is for the perfect:* Owen thinks that this verse refers to the second stage in the Christian life, the practice of virtue, which results in the ability to discern what is morally good, to have a "principle of righteousness." "By a series of correct moral choices he builds up a moral standard" (*op. cit.*, 244). Such people are "perfect" and may then proceed to the third stage, the assimilation of the advanced doctrine, which is like solid food.

30 **6:1.** *therefore...move toward perfection, without again laying the foundation:* Since the author has just declared his readers in need of instruction in the rudiments of doctrine, it is strange that he now not only proposes to pass over these and give teaching for the mature, but that his proposal begins with the connective "therefore." H. Kosmala solves the difficulty by proposing that 5:11b–14 are a later addition, which in their sharpness of tone and loosely connected construction do not suit either the present context or the style of the author (*Hebräer-Essener-Christen* [SPB 1; Leiden, 1959] 17–21). This radical treatment has no mss. support. Of the various explanations given for the author's paradoxical method, the best seems to be that he considers that nothing less than the challenge afforded by difficult doctrine (5:11) will serve to move the addressees out of their spiritual lethargy. "The originality of Hebrews is to emphasize intellectual progress as a condition for moral perfection" (C. Spicq, *L'Épître aux Héb*, 2, 146). He now mentions six elementary teachings: repentance from dead works, faith in God, teaching about ritual washings (baptisms), laying on of hands, the resurrection of the dead, and eternal judgment. The list probably comes from a traditional catechism and is not meant to be exhaustive.

31 Kosmala holds that there is nothing specifically Christian about the catechism. "Christ" in 6:1 does not mean Jesus, but simply "the Messiah," and the six teachings are simply those accepted by a group that expects the coming of the Messiah. A closer inspection of the points indicates that the group in question was the Qumran sect and that the addressees, prospective converts to Christianity, already believed in the teachings (*op. cit.*, 31–38). However, it is doubtful that a non-Christian catechism, or any part of it, would have been designated by the author of Heb as the foundation of the Christian life, even when belief in its contents might be presupposed in those who turned to Christianity from the group which followed it. In any case, if the exegesis of "instruction about baptisms" given below is right, it is impossible to regard the doctrines merely as a Jewish sectarian foundation of Christian belief. *repentance from dead works and faith in God:* Repentance and faith are, respectively, the negative and positive side of the first response of man to God's word. (For a similar coupling of these correlatives, cf. Mk 1:15.) Dead works do not mean the works demanded by the Mosaic Law, but sins that lead to spiritual death and from which the conscience needs cleansing (cf. 9:14). A similar expression is found in *2 Esdras* 7:119, "works which lead to death." **2.** *instruction about baptisms:* The Gk word translated "baptisms" is not *baptisma*, probably of Christian coinage and regularly used in the NT for Christian baptism and that of John the Baptist, but *baptismos*, which in the two other instances of its occurrence in the NT means Jewish ritual washings, cf. 9:10; Mk 7:4 (Josephus uses it in reference to the baptism of John; cf. *Ant.* 18.5, 2 § 117). That fact, as well as the word's being in the plural, shows that here it does not mean simply the Christian sacrament. As a water rite, that sacrament could be so designated; hence the reason why instruction about ritual washings would have formed part of Christian catechesis seems to lie in the necessity of instructing converts about the difference between the Jewish washings (including proselyte baptism, the baptism of John, and the water purifications of Qumran; cf. 1QS 3:4–9) and the Christian sacrament (cf. A. Oepke, "*Baptismos*," *ThDNT* 1, 545; R. Schnackenburg, *Baptism in the Thought of St. Paul* [N.Y., 1964] 8f.). Michel remarks that "since the plural is unusual in the language of the Church, it must be understood as polemic" (*Brief an die Hebräer*, 146).

32 In P^{46} and B "instruction" is read in the accusative (*didachēn*), a reading accepted by G. Zuntz (cf. *Text of the Epistles* [London, 1953] 93) and other scholars. This reading might suggest that "instruction" is in apposition to "foundation," as Montefiore thinks (*A Commentary*, 105; also Bruce, *Ep. to the Heb.* 110 ["probably in apposition"]). If the foundation is simply repentance and faith in God, then the content of the "foundation" and that of the "teaching" are quite different; a fact that argues against regarding the two nouns as being in apposition. One should either retain the gen. reading (*didachēs*), "of instruction," and see it as part of the foundation, or, accepting the acc. reading, take the teaching as different in content from the foundation, although similar insofar as each deals with the rudiments of Christian life.

33 *laying on of hands:* This rite is mentioned in Acts 8:17; 19:6 (in connection with the coming of the Holy Spirit) and in 6:6; 13:3; 1 Tm 4:14; 5:22; 2 Tm 1:6 (where it is connected with the conferral of some ministry or mission in the church). Presumably what is meant here is the rite connected with the giving of the Spirit. (For discussion of the relation between the rite and the coming of the Spirit, cf. J. Oulton, *ExpT* 66 [1955] 236–40; D. Daube, *The NT and Rabbinic Judaism* [London, 1956] 224–46.) Although the two texts first mentioned may be related to the Sacrament of Confirmation, that sacrament and the rite mentioned here cannot be simply identified (cf. D. Stanley, *TS* 18 [1957] 210, n. 90). *resurrection of the dead and eternal judgment:* The last pair of rudimentary truths concern the eschatological term of the Christian life. The judgment is "eternal" because it is definitive (cf. Mt 25:46). **3.** *and this we shall do, God permitting:* Evidently the author means not that he will "lay the foundation again," which he has said that he will not do, but that he will now pass on to the doctrine suitable for the mature (6:1). He is not suggesting that he will deal with the rudiments later; the verses that follow exclude that possibility. **4–6.** These verses have created much difficulty, for they deal with the impossibility of repentance after apostasy. Many attempts have been made to avoid their apparent import, e.g., the suggestion that so far as human experience is concerned, apostates are beyond the possibility of repentance, although nothing is said of what may happen if they receive an extraordinary grace (cf. F. F. Bruce, *Ep. to the Heb*, 118; C. Spicq, *L'Epître aux Héb*, 2, 167–78); "They are normally indisposed for penance" (B. Poschmann, *Penance and Anointing of the Sick* [QD; Freiburg, 1964] 13). "Such interpretations go against the plain meaning of the Greek and the whole tenor of the author's argument" (H. Montefiore, *A Commentary*, 109). Kuss feels that the absolute statement should not be taken literally, but should be judged in the light of the author's pastoral concern: he speaks in an exaggerated manner in order to set his readers firmly against apostasy (*Brief an die Heb* [1953], 114–16); similarly, C. Carlston (*JBL* 78 [1959] 296–302).

34 **4.** *for it is impossible, when men have been once enlightened and have tasted the heavenly gift and have become sharers in the Holy Spirit:* The participles in vv. 4–5 are all aorist, and "once" (*hapax*) probably modifies them all, not simply the first. It is disputed whether there are direct sacramental references here or whether these four experiences of the Christian refer simply to his coming to the faith. The designation of baptism as "enlightenment" and of the baptized as "the enlightened" is at least as early as Justin Martyr (*Apol.* 1.61, 12; 1.65, 1) and it is possible that "enlightened" refers to the reception of that Sacrament (cf. G. Bornkamm, *Studien*, 190; E. Käsemann, *Das wandernde Gottesvolk*, 119). In support of that view, cf. Eph 5:14, which is probably a fragment of a baptismal hymn (or "cult saying"; so H. Schlier, *Der Brief an der Epheser* [Düsseldorf, 1958] 240–42). However, the enlightenment spoken of here may mean simply the illumination given by faith in Christ (2 Cor 4:6). In QL, the covenant is a light by which God illumines the face of his disciple (1QH 4:5), and Philo speaks of the divine commandment as enlightening the soul (*De fug. et inv.* 139). Nor should the possibility of the influence of Ps 34:6 be overlooked, especially since the author of Heb goes on to speak of "tasting the heavenly gift," and v. 9 of that Ps speaks of tasting how good the Lord is. In any case, the single-event nature of the experience makes it unlikely that "tasting the heavenly gift" means receiving the Eucharist, although the expression has been so interpreted (J. Héring, *L'Épître aux Hébreux*, 59; J. Betz, *Die Eucharistie in der Zeit der griechischen Väter* [Freiburg, 1961] 2, 156–57). "Taste" is a common metaphor for "experience" and the phrase probably means only that Christians have experienced the power of the salvation brought by Jesus (cf. Rom 5:15; 2 Cor 9:15). This gift is termed heavenly because it is an eschatological reality possessed in an anticipatory manner by the believer. "Sharers in the Holy Spirit" means those who possess the Spirit as a guarantee of the full possession, in the future, of the eschatological blessings (cf. 2 Cor 1:22; Eph 1:14, where the Spirit is called the *arrabōn*, the "first installment").

35 **5.** *and have tasted the good word of God and the powers of the age to come:* The preaching of the gospel was accompanied by manifestations of the presence of the Spirit (cf. 2:3–4; 1 Cor 2:4). This activity of the Spirit is seen as indication of the presence even now of the "age to come." This designation of the eschatological future is contrasted with "this age" in both apocalyptic and rabbinical Judaism (cf. J. Bonsirven, *Judaïsme*, 1, 312). In late Judaism, the "tasting of the powers of the age to come" was attributed to Abraham, Isaac, and Jacob (cf. Str-B 3, 690), but there is a profound difference between the two conceptions. What Judaism believed to be the privilege of a chosen few is a common Christian experience; but even more important, the age to come, while absolutely future in Jewish thought, is a present reality for the Christian, though not yet realized in its fullness. **6.** *they are crucifying for themselves the Son of God and holding him up to contempt:* A vivid portrayal of the malice of apostasy, which is conceived as a crucifixion and mockery of the Son of God. The apostates' rejection of the Christian faith means that "they put Jesus out of their life...he is dead to them" (J. Moffatt, *Epistle to the Hebrews*, 80). Spicq sees in this statement a further indication that the addressees were converted Jewish priests, some of whom had taken part in the historical crucifixion (*L'Épître aux Héb*, 1, 230). It seems excessive to draw such a conclusion from these words. **7–8.** The sharp warning ends with a comparison between two kinds of ground. Each drinks in the rain sent by God, but one bears fruit and is blessed; the other bears thorns, verges on being cursed, and finally is burned. The application to the faithful Christian and the apostate, respectively, is obvious.

36 **9.** *beloved, ...we are persuaded of better things in your regard:* With this verse, the tone of the exhortation becomes mild. For the first and only time in Heb the readers are called "beloved." It is difficult to agree, however, that the author does not believe that there are even potential apostates among his readers (so F. F. Bruce, *Ep. to the Heb*, 126); the purpose of his writing is to avert a danger that is very real. The new approach seems dictated by the belief that his purpose may be best achieved by mildness and, more important, by the fact that in spite of their lukewarm faith there is one sign that gives reason to hope that the calamity of their apostasy may not take place. That sign is their charity to their brothers in the faith, of which v. 10 speaks. **10.** *he will not forget your work and the love you have shown him by your service:* The services that they rendered in times past are mentioned in 10:33b–34a. Such services are fundamentally a manifestation of love for God. Here and in 13:24, the author uses the common early Christian designation of those who believe in Christ, "the saints." **11.** *the same zeal in respect to persevering:* Their zeal for works of charity should be matched by their zeal for perseverance in their Christian vocation—a perseverance founded upon hope. **12.** The author begins a theme that he will develop in ch. 11. His readers should imitate the confident faith of the OT saints, "who are inheriting the promised blessings." The reference does not seem to be to any other saints but those of ch. 11, although Montefiore thinks that the author "points to the example of contemporaries" (*A Commentary*, 112). This exegesis is presumably based on the fact that the pres. participle of "inherit" is used here. Yet since the Gk *epaggelia* may mean either the promise itself or the thing promised (cf. J. Schniewind–G. Friedrich, "*Epaggelia*," *ThDNT* 2, 583, n.59), the author seems to be saying that the OT saints, who did not receive the promised blessings during their lifetime (11:13), are now in possession of them. That is perhaps the reason why he uses the pres. participle. The fact that he passes on to the case of Abraham confirms the view that he means not contemporaries, but those of whom he will speak in ch. 11.

37 **13.** *he swore by himself:* Cf. Philo, *Leg. alleg.* 3.72. The secure basis for hope is God's promise, confirmed by his oath; this is shown in the case of Abraham. The episode of the patriarchal history to which this refers is Gn 22:16–18, the sequel to the story of Abraham's obedience in his readiness to sacrifice Isaac. God then confirmed by oath his promise that the patriarch would have numerous descendants, who would inherit the cities of their enemies and would be a source of blessing for all the nations of the earth. **15.** *he obtained the promised blessings:* For some commentators this refers to the partial fulfillment of the promise during Abraham's lifetime (cf. H. Montefiore, *A Commentary*, 114); but the fulfillment the author means is that to which he has referred in v. 12: the present eschatological blessings enjoyed by the OT patriarchs, to which the promises of blessings on this earth were subordinate. **17.** The reason for the oath confirming the promise was to "make assurance doubly sure" (cf. Philo, *De Abrahamo* 46). The author's interest does not seem to be directly in the oath made to Abraham, but in that which it recalls to him, *viz.*, the oath by which Jesus was constituted eternal high priest after the manner of Melchizedek. The importance of that oath is emphasized in ch. 7, and the priesthood that it confirms, rather than the promises to Abraham, is the basis of the hope to which the author exhorts his readers. The theme of Jesus' priesthood had been set aside so that the author could make his warning against apostasy; now he is about to return to it. **18.** *through two unchangeable things:* God's promise and his oath. *we who have fled to grasp the hope which lies before us:* The beneficiaries of the promise are Christians ("we"). Nothing is said about the flight except that its term is hope. It does not seem that a reference is intended to the city that they are seeking (13:14), conceived as a city of refuge (so H. Montefiore, *A Commentary*, 116). **19.** The author here uses a mixed metaphor to describe Christian hope: It is an anchor, and it extends into the inner sanctuary. By speaking of the sanctuary, the author alludes to what he will later develop as a central point in his theology of Christ's priesthood: the Mosaic Tabernacle as an earthly replica of the heavenly sanctuary, and the Holy of Holies, beyond the veil that separates it from the Holy Place (Ex 26:31–33), as the earthly counterpart of the heavenly abode of God. Into that sacred place, "heaven itself" (9:24), Jesus our high priest has entered; there he has brought his atoning sacrifice to its climax. Christian hope lies in what Jesus has done in the eternal order by his sacrifice. He has not only entered the heavenly sanctuary, but entered as the "forerunner" of his brothers, whose destiny it is to join him there.

38 **(B) Jesus, Priest According to the Order of Melchizedek (7:1–28).**

(a) Melchizedek and the Levitical Priesthood (7:1–10). **1.** This verse introduces a midrash on Gn 14:18–20 that serves to demonstrate the superiority of Jesus' priesthood to that of the OT by a detailed demonstration of the similarity between Jesus and Melchizedek (cf. J. A. Fitzmyer, *CBQ* 25 [1963] 305–21). The assumption that Melchizedek was a priest of the God of Israel (cf. Gn 14:22, where "Yahweh" and "God most high" are in apposition) is accepted by the author of Heb. **2.** The OT does not make clear who paid tithes to whom; by adding "Abraham" as subject of the verb the author follows a contemporary understanding (cf. 1QapGn 22:17; Josephus, *Ant.* 1.10, 2 § 181), as is necessary for his argument. He also accepts the popular etymology of Melchizedek's name, "king of justice" (cf. *Leg. alleg.* 3.79), and of his title, "king of peace" (*ibid.*). No further mention is made of these qualities; they are probably given here because Melchizedek is regarded as a prototype of Jesus, the Messiah, and the messianic blessings include justice and peace (cf. Is 9:5–6; 32:1,17). **3,** *without father, without mother, without genealogy, having neither beginning of days nor end of life:* The author quotes here from a hymn about Melchizedek. On the principle of rabbinic exegesis that what is not mentioned in the Torah does not exist (cf. Str-B 3, 693ff.); and because the OT does not speak of Melchizedek's ancestors, birth, or death, the hymn concludes to his eternity. This fanciful interpretation permits the author to emphasize what he regards as their principal similarity: Each has an eternal priesthood. The mention of Melchizedek's being "without genealogy" also serves to contrast him with the Levitical priests, for whom descent from Aaron was all-important (cf. Nm 16:40 [MT: 17:5]). *made like the Son of God, he remains a priest forever:* It is strange that here Melchizedek is compared to Jesus, rather than vice versa, but the inverted comparison is probably of no importance. One should not conclude from the "Son of God" title that it is not the incarnate Jesus but "the eternal being of the Son of God which is here in view" (so B. F. Westcott, *Epistle to the Hebrews*, 173). The epistle does not ascribe any priesthood to the Son of God other than that which he received in his exaltation, after his death on the cross (5:6–10). The comparison between Jesus and Melchizedek is based principally on the eternity of their priesthood, which in the case of Melchizedek is established by a device of rabbinic exegesis that the author utilizes without taking it seriously, for he knows no priest who remains forever, except Jesus (7:24). He is not interested in Melchizedek's kingship, nor in the fact that in him the priestly and kingly offices were united. The latter was a commonplace in the ancient Near East, and, for a time, in Israel (David and Solomon perform priestly functions; cf. 2 Sm 6:17ff.; 1 Kgs 3:4,15). In Israel the functions were later separated, and the author of Heb evidently shares the view that they were not united in any historical king (7:13). In Ps 110, on which the author draws so frequently, the union of the two functions is regarded as normal; the comparison between Melchizedek and the Hebr king there addressed is not that the latter is a king-priest, as Melchizedek was, but that like Melchizedek he is king-priest of Jerusalem; thus the Davidic rule is in continuity with that of the ancient sovereign (cf. H.-J. Kraus, *Psalmen* [BKAT 15/2; Neukirchen, 1960] 2, 760–61). But our author's interest in the priest-king of "Salem" is due solely to his enjoying an eternal priesthood and to his superiority to the Levitical priests. He knows that these two points are verified in Jesus, and by the methods of rabbinic exegesis he finds them in Melchizedek, whom Ps 110:4 presents as the OT prefiguration of Christ.

39 **4–5.** The tenth of the booty, which Abraham paid Melchizedek, recalls to the author the tenth (tithe) of all products of the land, which the Israelites had to pay the Levites, the members of the priestly tribe (cf. Nm 18:20–32). That this payment is made according to the Mosaic Law is stated explicitly by the author, because he will say later (7:12) that priesthood and Law are so closely connected that the passing away of the priesthood involves the passing away of the Law on which it is based. Although their Jewish brethren are descended from Abraham as they are, the superiority of the priests is evident because they are authorized to demand tithes from them. (For "to come out of the loins" of someone as a way of expressing descent from him, cf. Gn 35:11.) **6.** Similarly, Melchizedek's superiority to Abraham is seen by his receiving tithes from the patriarch. The Gn account does not suggest that Melchizedek had any right to the tithes Abraham gave him; they were a pure gift. But the supposition of the author is that just as the Israelites were obliged to pay tithes to the priests, so Abraham paid his to Melchizedek in acquittal of duty. The fact that Abraham was the recipient of God's promises is mentioned in order further to emphasize Melchizedek's superiority; he received tithes even from the patriarch who was so highly favored by God. **7.** *he who is inferior is blessed by him who is greater:* In spite of the axiomatic tone of the words, this contradicts what is said in the OT (cf. Jb 31:20; 2 Sm 14:22), but possibly the author gives not a general principle but a liturgical rule (cf. Michel, *Brief an die Hebräer*, 168). If so, it does not necessarily indicate that Melchizedek's offering of food and drink to Abraham was a cultic act. That the blessing of the patriarch is seen by the author as a blessing bestowed on the Levitical priesthood by the priest Melchizedek is sufficient explanation why a liturgical consideration should be introduced here. **8.** The superiority of Melchizedek consists in his being "eternal" ("witness is borne that he lives"), whereas the Levitical priests, who receive tithes from their fellow Hebrews, are "men who die." In the recently published Qumran text, 11QMelchizedek, he appears as a heavenly being "in the congregation of God" and is to exact vengeance and atone for sins in a jubilee year (see M. de Jonge and A. S. van der Woude, *NTS* 12 [1965–66] 301–26). **9.** *Levi, who receives tithes, was tithed together with Abraham, since he was still in his father's loins:* "Levi" stands not only for the "historical" son of Jacob but for the priestly tribe descended from him.

40 (b) The Levitical Priesthood Superseded (7:11–28). **11.** *if, then, perfection were achieved through the Levitical priesthood:* The perfection spoken of is not directly cultic (i.e., priestly consecration, as in 2:10; 5:9), but is the power to cleanse from sin. However, because the author conceives the latter in cultic terms, as an approach to God (7:19), it can be said that the term has liturgical overtones. *on the basis of which the people received the Law:* The Law was given to Israel as a means of union with God, and the priesthood was the instrument by which the Law was meant to achieve its purpose. Spicq regards the principle expressed in this verse (viz., that the priesthood was the basis on which the Law was given to the people) as the foundation of the entire argument of the epistle (cf. *L'Épître aux Héb* 2, 227). **12.** *when there is a change of priesthood, there is necessarily a change of law:* This is not a truism; it is peculiar to the situation of Israel where the priesthood and the Mosaic Law were inseparably linked. **13.** *now, in respect to him about whom these things are said:* Jesus, the priest according to the order of Melchizedek about whom the Ps speaks. **14.** *the tribe of Judah, concerning which Moses said nothing in respect to priests:* The author knows and accepts the tradition that Jesus was of the family of David (cf. Rom 1:3); he does not share the Qumran community's expectation of a priestly messiah belonging to the Levitical family of Aaron and of a royal messiah descended from Judah through David (cf. R. E. Brown, *CBQ* 19 [1957] 53–82). It is doubtful that Judaism had any expectation such as that of the author of Heb, in spite of the statement in *T. Levi* 8:14 ("a king shall rise in Judah and shall establish a new priesthood"); for *Test.* is possibly a Christian document, developed from Jewish sources (cf. F. M. Cross, *Ancient Library of Qumran* [Garden City, N.Y., 1958] 149, n. 6). In any case, the context of that verse implies that the king in question is of the tribe of Levi (cf. *APOT* 2, 294, which takes the verse as a repudiation of the belief in a messiah from Judah).

41 **15–16.** *another priest is set up after the likeness of Melchizedek:* The "argument" is that Jesus' priesthood has supplanted that of the Levites. Melchizedek's "eternity" is, for the author, plainly the principal point of comparison between him and Jesus. *the commandment:* The legal requirement that provides for OT priestly succession confined it to those descendants of Levi who were of the family of Aaron (cf. Nm 3:3,10). *life which cannot be destroyed:* This is not that which Jesus possesses because of his divinity (so B. F. Westcott, *Epistle to the Hebrews*, 185; H. Montefiore, *A Commentary*, 125f.), but the life he possesses because of his resurrection; he is priest not through his divine nature, but in virtue of his exaltation (cf. 5:5–6). The author cannot have been unaware that Ex 40:15 states that the Aaronic priesthood is to be eternal, although he does not explicitly deal with that obvious objection to his argument. The problem is implicitly solved by the contrast drawn between the transitory life of individual Jewish priests and the eternal life of Jesus (7:23f.)—Jesus' eternal priesthood was confirmed by God's oath (7:20f.), as the Aaronic priesthood was not. This solution would carry weight, given the type of exegesis accepted by both the author and his addressees. But the true reason for the transfer of priesthood was that the priesthood of Jesus had achieved that of which the OT priesthood was incapable: "From the fact, accepted through faith, that perfection has been brought about by Jesus, the author concludes to the imperfection of the Levitical priesthood" (O. Kuss, *Brief an die Heb* [1953], 62). **18.** *the former commandment has been annulled because of its weakness and uselessness:* The commandment setting up the Levitical priesthood was useless because the priesthood it established was powerless to cleanse men from sin and unite them with God. **19.** *a better hope has been introduced, through which we draw near to God:* The better hope is based on the accomplished sacrifice of the Son of God, through which we have access to the Father (4:16). The similarity between this verse and 6:19,20 should be noticed. "Better" is a characteristic designation of Heb for the new order (cf. 1:4; 7:22; 8:6; 9:23; 10:34). "Draw near to God" is used in the OT for priestly service; in Lv 10:3 the priests are described simply as "those who approach God" (the Gk vb. is the same as here). Here the Christian life is described in priestly terms; what the OT reserved to the priesthood is attributed to all the people.

42 **20.** *without [God's] taking an oath:* Jesus' priesthood is superior to that of the OT priests because of its being confirmed by God's oath (cf. Ps 110:4); hence he is priest forever and they are not. **22.** *thus far has Jesus become the guarantee of a better covenant:* The covenant of the old law to which Heb contrasts that of the new law is the Mosaic covenant (cf. 9:18–20), in which law and covenant are correlative terms (cf. G. Mendenhall, *IDB* 1, 718–21). Hence, if a change of priesthood involves a change of law (7:12), a new covenant has come into being with the new priesthood of Jesus. It is "better" than the old, because it will remain as long as the priesthood on which it is founded remains, and the eternity of that priesthood has been confirmed by God's oath. Thus, Jesus, the priest of this covenant, is himself the guarantee of its permanence. **24.** The Gk word *aparabaton* may mean "permanent" or "untransferable"; the context, which speaks of Jesus' eternal priesthood, seems to favor the former meaning, but the ideas are so closely connected that, in any case, the one involves the other. **25.** *hence he is forever able to save those who approach God through him, since he always lives to make intercession for them:* The intercession of the Exalted Jesus has been interpreted as the sequel of his completed sacrifice; it is understood as a priestly work, but different from the sacrifice, which is regarded as past and over; cf. O. Cullmann, *Christology*, 99: "He is the risen Lord who continues his mediating work on the basis of his unique completed work of atonement"; similarly, C. Spicq, *L'Épître aux Héb*, 2, 198. The reason for this view is principally that those who hold it regard the work of atonement as coextensive with Jesus' death on the cross, evidently an event of the past. But the comparison drawn in the following chapters between Jesus' sacrifice and that offered by the high priest on the Day of Atonement suggests that the sacrifice of Jesus cannot be thought of as limited to his death; his exaltation is an essential part of it. Consequently, the sacrifice cannot be considered past, since in its climactic moment it takes place in the heavenly sanctuary, where the time sequences of earth are surpassed. S. Lyonnet has shown that in late Judaism expiatory sacrifice was regarded as intercession (*Bib* 40 [1959] 885–901); if that concept is reflected in this verse, the intercession of the Exalted Christ should not be regarded as the sequel to his sacrifice but as its eternal continuance in heaven. Moffatt, who does not favor the view, concedes that in this verse "language is used which has suggested that in the heavenly *skēnē* this sacrifice is continually presented or offered" (*Epistle to the Hebrews*, xxxviii). The intercession of Jesus is mentioned also in Rom 8:34 in a formulary that is practically identical with that of Heb.

43 **26.** This verse appears to be a hymn in honor of the Exalted Jesus, the high priest, corresponding to the Melchizedek hymn of v. 3. *separated from sinners:* This may be meant to recall the prescription of the Mishnah (*Yoma* 1:1) that the high priest be prepared for the offering of the Day of Atonement sacrifices by being separated from his own house for seven days (cf. O. Michel, *Brief an die Hebräer*, 174). But the comparison seems forced, for Jesus' separation from sinners is not presented as a preparation for his sacrifice but is connected with his ascension. *higher than the heavens:* This seems to be a reference to Jesus' passage through the intermediate heavens into the heavenly sanctuary, the abode of God (4:14; 9:24; cf. H. Köster, *HarvTR* 55 [1962] 309). **27.** There is no prescription in the Law that the high priest had to offer sacrifice daily, first for his own sins and then for those of the people. That prescription applied only to the Day of Atonement (cf. Lv 16:6,15), and none of the commanded daily offerings (cf. Ex 29:38–42; Lv 6:1–6,7–11,12–16; Nm 28:3–8) fits the description given here. It seems best to assume that the author has made a mistake (so O. Kuss, *Brief an die Heb* [1953], 66), for none of the other explanations given (cf. Michel, *op. cit.*, 180) is satisfactory. *he did this once for all, when he offered himself:* Here for the first time Heb speaks of the victim of Jesus' sacrifice: himself. There is a clear reference to the fourth Servant Song; cf. Is 53:10, "if he gives his life as an offering for sin." The absolute sufficiency of the sacrifice is emphasized by the "once for all" (*ephapax*), an adverb which, together with the simpler form *hapax*, occurs 11 times in Heb. **28.** *the word of the oath which came after the Law:* The author deals with the possible objection that the Mosaic Law set aside the priesthood of which Ps 110 speaks. On the contrary, the promise of the new non-Levitical priesthood came long after the Law establishing the OT priesthood; and it set up as priest not the weak, transitory high priest of the OT, but the Son who has been consecrated priest forever.

44 **(C) The Eternal Sacrifice (8:1–9:28).**

(a) The Old Covenant, Tabernacle, Worship (8:1–9:10).

(i) *The heavenly priesthood of Jesus* (8:1–6). **1.** *the main point of what we are saying is this:* The Gk *kephalaion*, here translated "main point," may also mean "summary," but there are many elements in what has preceded that are not mentioned here even summarily; so "main point" seems preferable. *we have such a high priest:* Cf. 7:26–28. *who has taken his seat at the right hand of the throne of the Majesty in heaven:* The reference to Ps 110:1 recalls 1:3 and the theme of the messianic enthronement, developed in 1:5–14. **2.** *ministering priest of the sanctuary:* The phrase is found in Philo (*Leg. alleg.*, 3.135) but with a different sense, in reference to the "toil and discipline" of priestly service, the latter interpreted allegorically. The Gk *ta hagia* here translated as "the sanctuary" may also mean "holy things"; the use of the plural speaks in favor of such an interpretation. But in all the other texts in Heb where the same neut. pl. form appears, the meaning is "sanctuary" (9:8,12,24,25; 10:19; 13:11). *of the true tabernacle, which the Lord, not man, set up:* The heavenly Tabernacle in which Christ functions as priest is called "true" in contrast to the earthly Tabernacle of Judaism; this earthly counterpart is, for the author, not the Temple of Jerusalem, to which he never refers, but the Mosaic Tabernacle. The use of "true" as meaning "real" in contrast to an imitation that is only a shadow of the reality is similar to the Johannine usage (cf. Jn 1:9; 6:32; 15:1). The conception that the earthly Tabernacle reflects a heavenly model has both Oriental-biblical and Platonic origins. Moses was commanded to construct the Tabernacle according to the model shown him by God (Ex 25:9) and the conception of the heavenly model "probably...goes back ultimately to the idea that the earthly sanctuary is the counterpart of the heavenly dwelling of a deity" (F. M. Cross, *BA* 10 [1947] 62). But there is also here the Platonic conception of a "real" heavenly world of which earthly realities are merely shadows (cf. 8:5), an idea that one sees in Philo (e.g., *De somn.* 1.206). Spicq believes that on this point the author was more influenced by the Platonic conception than by the biblical (*RB* 57 [1950] 223). In contrast to the earthly Tabernacle, set up by Moses (Ex 33:7), this heavenly Tabernacle was set up by the Lord. That Jesus, the ministering priest of that Tabernacle, is described as seated (v. 1) does not mean that his sacrifice is "done and over" (so J. Moffatt, *Epistle to the Hebrews*, 140). The author is using the imagery of Ps 110 and is dealing with the double role, royal and priestly, that the Exalted Jesus exercises. His being seated applies to his kingly status, and the metaphor should not be used as an argument against his present offering as ministering priest.

45 **3.** *hence the necessity of this man's having something to offer:* A. Vanhoye has rightly emphasized that the author does not say here that Jesus is now offering his sacrifice in heaven, but simply states the necessity of his offering sacrifice since he is high priest (*VD* 37 [1959] 32–38). The time of that offering cannot be determined from this verse. It is also true that here, as elsewhere in Heb when speaking of Jesus' sacrifice, the author uses the aorist, which suggests completed action, whereas when dealing with priesthood in general or with the liturgy of the OT he uses the present (7:27; 9:7,9,14; 9:25,28; 10:1,2,8,12). Moreover, he insists on the once-for-all character of Jesus' one sacrifice (in addition to the texts cited above, cf. 9:12; 10:10,14). From these facts, and particularly from a consideration of 9:24–28, Vanhoye comes to the conclusion that the author nowhere affirms or insinuates that the sacrificial offering of Jesus continues in heaven (*VD* 37 [1959] 36); on the contrary, the texts where the aor. indicative is used to express the act of offering show conclusively that the act is in the past. Vanhoye's conclusion has been accepted by E. Grässer (*TRu* 30 [1964] 222), but it loses its force when one considers the heavenly-earthly contrast that is the background of the author's thought. Jesus' sacrifice is completed in the heavenly sanctuary; it perdures in its moment of completion because eternity is a quality of the heavenly sphere. The aorists and the emphasis on the unicity of the sacrifice serve, respectively, to show that the sacrifice is complete, and that no further sacrifice of Jesus is either necessary or possible. This is in contrast to the constantly repeated sacrifices of the OT, none of which were perfect. An action completed in the earthly sphere would be an event of the past, but that is not so of one completed in the heavenly, eternal order. Although 8:3 by itself does not determine the time of Jesus' sacrifice, if that sacrifice is now ended, one of two equally unacceptable conclusions has to be drawn. Either the author means that the sacrifice ceased after reaching its climax, or he means that it was not a heavenly event. In the former case, the time sequence of earth would be attributed to heaven; in the latter, Jesus would be the heavenly high priest in respect to everything except the distinctively priestly act (F. Schierse's supposition [*Verheissung und Heilsvollendung*, 160, n. 73] that Jesus' death on the cross was a heavenly event is without basis). The comparison the author will draw in ch. 9 between Jesus' sacrifice and that of the Jewish high priest on the Day of Atonement will indicate in detail how he conceives the relation between the offering begun on the cross and its heavenly completion.

46 **4.** *if he were on earth, he would not be a priest:* So far is the author from thinking of Jesus' death on the cross as equivalent to his completed sacrifice that he asserts that it is only because his sacrifice is a heavenly and not an earthly one that he is a priest at all. The earthly priesthood is Levitical, established according to the Mosaic Law; Jesus is not a priest of that sort. **5.** *who are serving in a copy and shadow of the heavenly [sanctuary]:* Because the OT priestly worship is spoken of in the pres. tense does not necessarily mean that Heb was written before the destruction of the Jerusalem Temple, for the earthly sanctuary to which the author always refers is the Mosaic Tabernacle. Since he sees no difficulty in using the pres. tense of priestly service in the Tabernacle, which was certainly no longer in existence, it is clear that his description is conceptual rather than historical. **6.** *he has obtained a priestly ministry as superior [to the old] as the covenant of which he is mediator is better:* The intimate connection between priesthood and covenant is similar to that between priesthood and law mentioned in 7:12. The old covenant had its own priesthood; Jesus' priesthood is an element of the new and better covenant of which he is mediator. The title "mediator" belongs to him because (9:15) his sacrifice has been the means of union between God and men; it has taken away sin—the barrier to that union—and thus made possible the new covenant relationship. In 7:22, the superiority of the new covenant was seen in the permanence of its priesthood; here the superiority is based on better promises. What these are is made explicit in the citation of Jer 31 (LXX: 38): 31–34, which follows.

47 (ii) *The old covenant contrasted with the new* (8:7–13). **7–8.** *but God, finding fault with them, says...:* The faults of the people are regarded by the author as ultimately due to the faultiness of the covenant itself, i.e., to its inability to give men the power to keep its laws. His viewpoint is similar to that of Paul in Rom 7:11–24. **8–12.** The citation from Jer follows the LXX in all but a few points. In vv. 8–9 the Gk *diatithēmi* (dispose), which the LXX uses for God's establishing the new and old covenants, is replaced by, respectively, *synteleō* (conclude) and *poieō* (make). It has been maintained by J. Swetnam (*CBQ* 24 [1965] 373–90) that the latter is a significant change and throws light on the vexed question of whether in 9:15–18 the author, as most believe, uses different meanings of *diathēkē:* "covenant" (in vv. 15, 18), and "testament" (in vv. 16–17). Swetnam's position is questionable, as will be seen in the discussion of those verses. Moreover, the change from *diatithēmi* to *synteleō* occurs in v. 8 where the prophet is speaking of the new covenant, in which, as Swetnam holds, God is the one who "disposes," and where the LXX verb would have been quite suitable for the author's argument. This change, then, was quite unimportant—it suggests that the change to *poieō* may have been equally insignificant. That is particularly so if the differences in the quotation in Heb from the LXX are not due to the author of Heb but were already found in the OT text that he was using. **10.** *with the house of Israel:* For the author, the Israel with which the new covenant will be established is the Christian community, the New Israel. *I will be their God and they shall be my people:* This relationship does not constitute the newness of the covenant, for it existed even under the old covenant (Ex 6:7). Its newness consists rather in its interiority (God's laws will become part of the very being of the covenanted people): in the immediacy of the people's knowledge of God (v. 11) and in the forgiveness of sin (v. 12). These are the "better promises" (8:6) upon which the covenant is based. **13.** *what has become obsolete and has grown old is close to disappearing:* The author's comment was written from the prophet's perspective, not from his own; he knew that the old covenant had already disappeared as a valid expression of the relationship between God and his people (7:12).

48 (iii) *The old covenant Tabernacle* (9:1–5). **2.** *in it were the lampstand, the table, and the showbread; this tabernacle is called the Holy Place:* The author begins to describe the Mosaic Tabernacle (cf. Ex 25–26). This was divided into two parts, separated by a veil (Ex 26:31–35); but rather than speak of the outer and the inner section of the one Tabernacle, the author speaks of the first and the second Tabernacle. The Gk *hagia*, "the Holy Place," presents difficulties. Normally, the author uses that term (with the article, however, unlike here) for the inner part of the Tabernacle (cf. 9:8,25; 13:11), the part that he calls in v. 3 "the Holy of Holies" and in v. 7 "the second [Tabernacle]." If it is used here with the meaning "the Holy Place," as contrasted with "the Holy of Holies" (v. 3), it is strange that the author did not maintain that terminology instead of applying to the inner part in the succeeding texts the designation that he gives here to the outer part. Attempts have been made to deny the apparent inconsistency (cf. A. Vanhoye, *Structure littéraire*, 144, n. 1; H. Montefiore, *A Commentary*, 144). However, the similarity in this respect between vv. 2 and 3 and Ex 26:33 suggests that *hagia* and *hagia hagiōn* in these verses mean the same, respectively, as *to hagion* and *to hagion tōn hagiōn* of the LXX Exodus, i.e., "the Holy Place" and "the Holy of Holies." **3.** *the second veil:* The veil separating the Holy Place from the Holy of Holies is called "the second," because there was a curtain at the entrance to the former (Ex 26:36). **4.** *having a golden altar of incense:* The Gk word *thymiatērion*, translated "altar of incense," means "censer" in three places where it occurs in the LXX (2 Chr 26:19; Ez 8:11; *4 Mc* 7:11); some have supposed the reference here is to that cult-object, used in the Day of Atonement rite (Lv 16:12; cf. O. Michel, *Brief an die Hebräer*, 193–95). However, the author is describing the furniture of the Tabernacle rather than its movable objects, and most commentators think that he is speaking of the altar of incense (cf. Ex 30:1–10). Although *thysiastērion* is the LXX word for that altar, Philo (*Quis rer. div. her.* 226) and Josephus (*Ant.* 3.6, 8 § 147) designate it as *thymiatērion*, the same word as that used here. But whereas Heb puts that altar in the Holy of Holies, the OT puts it in the Holy Place, the "first Tabernacle" (Ex 30:6). It seems that the author has made a mistake here, caused probably by the fact that he was not speaking from personal knowledge of the Temple, which replaced the Mosaic Tabernacle, but was merely repeating, and in this case misinterpreting, the description of the Tabernacle found in Ex. Similarly, the OT does not say that the other objects that the author locates in the Ark were actually within it, except for the tablets of the covenant on which the Ten Commandments were written (Dt 10:5). (For the jar, cf. Ex 16:32–34; for the rod of Aaron, cf. Nm 17:16–26.) **5.** *above the ark were the cherubim of glory, overshadowing the place of expiation:* Cf. Ex 25:17–20. The gold "place of expiation" (Gk *hilastērion*) was so called because the blood of the sacrifices of the Day of Atonement was sprinkled on it (Lv 16:14–15), and thus the sins of the previous year were "expiated" or pardoned. (For the concept of expiation, cf. comment on 2:17.) *Hilastērion* is often translated "propitiatory" (e.g., CCD, Goodspeed,) but the difficulty with this translation is that it may be thought to imply that God was "appeased" by the sprinkled blood. The RSV "mercy seat" is better, but perhaps too vague (→ Pauline Theology, 79:83–86).

49 (iv) *The old covenant worship* (9:6–10). **6.** *the priests go into the first tabernacle continually:* The cultic duties performed in the outer tabernacle were the care of the lamps on the lampstand (Ex 27:21), the burning of incense on the incense altar every morning and evening (Ex 30:7), and the weekly replacing of the loaves on the table of showbread (Lv 24:8). **7.** *the high priest alone enters into the second, once a year:* The reference is to the two sacrifices of the Day of Atonement (Lv 16:1–14) offered by the high priest: one to expiate his sins and those of his family, the other to expiate those of the people. The sins for which atonement was made are called "sins of ignorance." In 5:2 (see comment) the author had spoken of the compassion of the high priest for "the ignorant," meaning those who had committed sins of this sort (cf. J. Bonsirven, *Judaïsme*, 2, 92f.; P. van Imschoot, *Théologie* 2, 326f.; W. Eichrodt, *Theology of the OT* [Phila., 1961] 1, 161, n. 6; H. Montefiore, *A Commentary*, 148. For the rabbinic understanding of the sins expiated by the Day of Atonement rites, cf. Mishnah, *Yoma* 8:8,9.) In this verse the author speaks for the first time of the sacrificial "blood," a subject with which he will be preoccupied especially in this and the following chapter. It is now generally recognized that the death of the sacrificial animal was not intended to symbolize that the one in whose name the sacrifice was offered deserved death, if for no other reason than that most of the sins for which sacrifice was offered were the sins to which the death penalty was not attached (cf. De Vaux, *AI* 158; Eichrodt, *op. cit.*, 165, n. 2). The purpose of slaughtering the animal was to release its blood. The significance of the blood was expressed in Lv 17:11,14: The blood was the element in which life resided. Insofar as it is life, the blood is the peculiarly divine element in man, and by reason of this sacred character, when poured out on the altar or sprinkled on the place of expiation, it was an effective symbol of the purification of sin and of the re-establishment of union between God and man. "By the outpouring of the blood, life was released, and in offering this to God the worshiper believed that the estrangement between him and the Deity was annulled, or that the defilement which separated them was cleansed" (W. D. Davies, *Paul and Rabbinic Judaism* [London, 1962] 235; F. C. N. Hicks, *The Fullness of Sacrifice* [London, 1959] 18; S. Lyonnet, *De peccato et redemptione* [Rome, 1957] 2, 128. For a different but apparently incorrect view of the meaning of the sacrificial blood, cf. L. Morris, *JTS* 3 [1952] 216–27.) The blood ritual was an element of all OT animal sacrifices; since atoning power is attributed to the blood (Lv 17:11), the notion of atonement is present in all the various types of sacrifice, and the removal of sin was the purpose of all, even though not the only purpose (cf. De Vaux, *AI* 453). But in the OT it is not said that the blood is "offered." Although many scholars speak of the blood ritual as an offering (cf. Davies, *op. cit.*, 235; Eichrodt, *op. cit.*, 164), others, while emphasizing that ritual as part of, and indeed as the essential element of the sacrifice, refuse to regard it precisely as an offering (Lyonnet, *op. cit.*, 125, n. 1; L. Moraldi, *Espiazione sacrificale e riti espiatori* [Rome, 1956] 249–52). The point is perhaps unimportant; but if the latter view is right, the fact that Heb speaks of the blood as being offered means that it is introducing into the description of the Day of Atonement sacrifice a conception that is not found in the OT. From what source did the author derive it? Possibly he is using the technique of speaking of the OT type in terms that apply properly only to the NT antitype (e.g., in 1 Cor 10:2 the passage through the sea is called a baptism "into Moses" because of its antitype, baptism "into Christ.")

50 **8.** *the way into the inner sanctuary has not yet been revealed:* The goal of the worship was access to God. The fact that only the high priest could enter that part of the Tabernacle—the earthly counterpart of God's heavenly abode—showed that this goal had not been attained through the OT worship. **9.** *this is a symbol of the present time:* The "present time" is not merely a chronological indication. It means the same as the "present age," in contrast to the "age to come." Even now the latter is present, in an anticipatory way, and Christians have experienced its powers (6:5). *not able to make perfect the conscience of the worshiper:* That is, to cleanse it from sin (cf. 9:14). **10.** *only to cleanse in matters of food and drink and various kinds of ritual washings:* The author limits the efficacy of OT sacrifices to a cleansing from defilement caused by the violation of ritual laws: the dietary prescriptions (cf. Lv 11; Nm 19:11–21) and ritual washings (e.g., Lv 14:8; Nm 19:11–21). This low estimate of their efficacy would hardly have been accepted by any Hebrew. For him, sacrifice "was not merely an expression of the spirit of the offerer, and certainly not an empty form that neither added nor subtracted anything. It required the spirit to validate it, but once validated it was thought to be charged with power. It was never merely a plea, whether for aid or for forgiveness or for communion. It was potent to effect something, either within or on behalf of the offerer or of another" (H. H. Rowley, *BJRylL* 33 [1950] 87).

51 (b) The Sacrifice of Jesus (9:11–28).

(i) *Sacrifice in the heavenly sanctuary* (9:11–14). **11.** *Christ has appeared, high priest of the good things to come:* The Gk reading adopted and translated as "the good things to come" (*tōn mellontōn agathōn*) is different from that of some mss. (including B and, with a slight variant, P[46]) which read *tōn genomenōn agathōn*, "the good things which have come to be." In favor of the adopted reading is the fact that for Heb the new order is a present reality only in an anticipatory fashion (cf. 1:14, and the parallelism with 10:1). *the greater and more perfect tabernacle...not belonging to this creation:* This Tabernacle is regarded by A. Vanhoye as the risen body of Christ, "the temple raised up in three days" (*Structure littéraire*, 157, n.1). In pointing out that it is not merely the body of the Incarnate Word, without further qualification, he rightly remarks that during his mortal life Jesus' body could not be called "not belonging to this creation"; the resurrection made it the spiritualized, heavenly body (cf. 1 Cor 15:46f.). But the opinion seems preferable that sees this Tabernacle as the heavenly regions, the heavenly counterpart of the earthly outer Tabernacle, through which Jesus passed (4:14) into the highest heaven, the abode of God (9:24), the counterpart of the inner Tabernacle, the Holy of Holies (cf. C. Spicq, *L'Épître aux Héb*, 2, 256; O. Michel, *Brief an die Hebräer*, 203; H. Köster, *HarvTR* 55 [1962] 309). An objection made to this interpretation is that it involves taking the prep, *dia*, "through," in a local sense, whereas the same preposition is used twice in the latter part of the sentence (v. 12) in an instrumental sense, although the case of the nouns governed by the prepositions is the same (gen.) in all three instances. Montefiore declares that such a procedure would be "bad style and unparalleled in NT usage" (*Epistle to the Hebrews*, 152). Moffatt's attempt to explain the fluctuation in sense as a literary technique of the author found elsewhere in Heb is not to the point, for in the cases that he cites in justification of his claim (*Epistle to the Hebrews*, 121), the difference in sense comes from the fact that the preposition governs different cases. Yet the striking parallel between 9:11 and 10:20, where *dia* is used with a local sense, confirms the view that it has that sense in 9:11 also; both the greater and more perfect tent of this verse and the veil of 10:20 are "spheres" through which the passage of Christ is made. There is no need to see in this conception of Christ's passage through the heavens any influence of the Gnostic myth of the journey of the redeemed redeemer back into the world of light. The author's cosmological views, which he shared with apocalyptic and rabbinic Judaism (see comment on 1:2) are sufficient explanation of the origin of the concept. The objection that the intermediate heavens would not be designated as "not belonging to this creation" has no weight, for that is plainly an explication of "not made by hands"; the greater and more perfect tent is not man-made, unlike the earthly sanctuary.

52 **12.** *by his own blood:* Just as the high priest had right of access to the Holy of Holies because he bore the blood of the sacrificial animals, so Jesus' life, offered in sacrifice, gives him right of access to the heavenly sanctuary. Just as the Day of Atonement sacrifice cannot be conceived apart from the essential element of blood sprinkling, to which the atonement value belonged, so here it is impossible to regard Jesus' entrance into the sanctuary as the consequence of his sacrifice completed on the cross rather than as part of that sacrifice which began on earth and reached completion in heaven. Since the author draws an exact parallel between the two entrances it is difficult to see how F. F. Bruce can say that "there have been expositors who, pressing the analogy of the Day of Atonement beyond the limits observed by our author, have argued that the expiatory work of Christ was not completed on the cross," but in heaven (*Ep. to the Heb*, 200f.). The limits observed by the author in his comparison of the two are precisely the reason why one must look for the heavenly counterpart of the high priest's sprinkling of blood, which was not the sequel to the sacrifice but its essential part. *achieved eternal redemption:* The verb translated in the indic. mood is a Gk aor. participle; it is here understood as an aorist of coincident action (*Bl-Deb-F* § 339). The word "redemption" (*lytrōsis*) must be understood in the light of its OT usage. It belongs to a word group (*lytron, lytrousthai, apolytrōsis*) that expresses the notion of deliverance (cf. Dn 4:34, LXX), frequently in reference to the deliverance of Israel from Egypt (Ex 6:6; Dt 7:8) and from the Babylonian Captivity (Is 41:14; 44:22,24). It is used in Ps 130:7–8 of deliverance from sin. In none of these cases is there any notion that the payment of a price was demanded as a condition for deliverance; there is no reason to see such a concept in this verse (cf. F. Büchsel, "*Lytrōsis*," *ThDNT* 4, 354) in spite of the view of those who would see the blood of Christ as the price paid (to God) for the redemption of man (cf. A. Médebielle, *VDSB* 3, 201; A. Deissmann, *LAE* 331; → Pauline Theology, 79:90–93). Like the salvation of 5:9, the redemption is "eternal" because it is based on the eternally acceptable sacrifice of Jesus.

53 **13.** *a heifer's ashes:* These ashes were mixed with the water and used to cleanse those who had become defiled by contact with corpses, human bones, or graves (cf. Nm 19:9,14–21). *sanctify them so that their flesh is cleansed:* The blood of the sacrifices and the lustral water conferred external ritual purity on the defiled. **14.** *through the eternal spirit offered himself spotless to God:* This spirit is neither the Holy Spirit nor the divine nature of Jesus (so C. Spicq, *L'Épître aux Héb*, 2, 258). Like Paul, the author sees Jesus' earthly life as one lived in the sphere of the flesh (cf. 2:14; 5:7; 10:20) and while, unlike Paul, he does not explicitly characterize the life of the Risen Christ as life "in the spirit," the flesh-spirit contrast is too deeply rooted in the Bible (cf. comment on 2:14) for the second member of the contrast not to be implied by his use of the first. A comparison of this verse with 7:16 shows that "eternal spirit" corresponds to the "life which cannot be destroyed" of that verse (cf. H. Montefiore, *A Commentary*, 155). In 7:16 the emphasis is on Jesus' eternal priesthood (eternal not in the sense that it had no beginning, but because it will never end) in contrast with the transitory OT priesthood; here, the emphasis is on the eternity of Jesus' one and only sacrifice, in contrast with the annually repeated sacrifices of the Jewish high priest on the Day of Atonement (9:25). This suggests that Jesus' "life which cannot be destroyed," the basis of his eternal priesthood, and his "eternal spirit" are the same. This verse is another statement that Jesus' self-offering is a heavenly, not an earthly reality, since it is offered through the eternal spirit, i.e., in that new sphere of existence that he enters at the time of his exaltation. Clearly, the author does not question the importance of the cross, nor does he mean that the sacrifice lies wholly in the heavenly sphere, but only that the sacrifice is consummated there. To avoid the consequences of that conception by holding that Jesus' death "took place really in the eternal, absolute order" (J. Moffatt, *Epistle to the Hebrews*, 124), or that it was a heavenly event (F. Schierse), is to ignore the fact that Jesus' human nature "is axiologically earthly until it enters heaven at the term of the Ascension" (A. Cody, *Heavenly Sanctuary and Liturgy in the Epistle to the Hebrews* [St. Meinrad, Ind., 1960] 91). The designation of Jesus as the "spotless" victim of his own sacrifice recalls the prescription of the Law that the sacrificial animal should be physically unblemished (Ex 29:1); the word is used here in a moral sense, as in 1 Pt 1:19. *will cleanse our conscience from dead works:* Whereas the blood-sprinkling produced only ritual cleanness, the purifying power of Jesus' sacrifice extends to the defiled conscience and purifies it from dead works, i.e., the sins that caused spiritual death. *worshiping the living God:* Primarily a sharing in Jesus' sacrificial worship, through which Christians have access to the Father (4:16; 7:25; 10:19–22). It also designates the entire conduct of Christian life as a cultic action—a manner of speaking that recalls the usage of Paul (cf. Rom 12:1).

54 (ii) *The sacrifice of the new covenant* (9:15–22). **15.** Jesus' sacrifice is the basis on which he is mediator of the new covenant (cf. 8:6). Through it, he has brought deliverance ("redemption," *apolytrōsis*) from the sins committed under the old covenant, sins that were not taken away by OT sacrifices. As long as they remained, men could not possess the inheritance promised by God (i.e., the "better promises" [8:6], the "good things to come" [9:1]), which, like the sacrifice that has made its possession possible, is eternal. **16–17.** *where there is a testament,...it has no force while the testator is alive:* In these verses the author speaks of the new order introduced by Jesus' sacrifice not as a covenant relationship but as that produced by "a testament "(= a will), which has come into force because of the testator's death. Since the same Gk word *diakthēkē* can mean both "covenant" and "testament," and is used in these verses with the latter meaning, whereas in vv. 15 and 18 with the meaning "covenant," the author has been charged with inconsistency; or his consistency has been maintained either by the supposition that at the time when Heb was written *diathēkē* always meant "testament" (A. Deissmann, *LAE* 341) or that both concepts are expressed in each use of the word in vv. 15–18 (J. Swetnam, *CBQ* 27, 389). As for Deissmann's view, since the LXX used *diathēkē* to translate the Hebr *b^e^rît*, "covenant," it is hardly likely that any NT author could have regularly disregarded the LXX meaning, "covenant," whatever change of meaning the evolution of language had brought to the word (cf. Moulton-Milligan, *Vocabulary of the Greek Testament* [Grand Rapids, 1960] 148f.). However, it is difficult to see how the concept will-testament could be applied to the old covenant. One of the differences between the old covenant and the new is that the latter has the aspect not only of a covenant but also of a testament, whereas the former has not. What verifies the testament concept in the case of the new covenant is that it did involve the death of the one who initiated it; hence he is not only one who established the covenant, but also the testator. The death of the animal victims in the sacrifice that sealed the old covenant (Ex 24:5–8) can in no way be considered as even imperfectly verifying the concept of a testator's death (J. Swetnam, *CBQ* 24, 378). But since God is the one who establishes the new covenant (cf. 8:10), how can it be at the same time a testament, which requires the death of the testator? The answer is that Jesus, the eternal Son who, with the Father, has established the new covenant, is at the same time the testator whose death has brought it into force. In that respect it is quite unlike the old covenant—hence, the difference in meaning between *diathēkē* in vv. 15, 18 and 16–17.

55 **18.** *hence neither was the first covenant inaugurated without blood:* The particle "hence" creates difficulty. It seems to indicate that the author is drawing a conclusion from vv. 16–17, in which case it would appear that in his mind the death of the animals sacrificed at the inauguration of the old covenant corresponded at least in some way to the death of a testator. But if the illative force of the particle applies to the general argument of the chapter rather than to the statements of the two preceding verses, the problem largely disappears. The major interest of the chapter is in the blood of Christ, i.e., in his sacrifice, through which atonement was made and the new covenant inaugurated. Since the new is the fulfillment of the old, the author seeks a parallel in the inauguration of the two and finds it in the account of the sacrifice related in Ex 24:5–8. **19–20.** The description of the inaugural sacrifice of the old covenant differs from that found in Ex. The sacrificial animals are goats as well as bulls; water, scarlet wool, and hyssop are spoken of (these are derived probably from the purificatory rites found in Lv 14:3–7 and Nm 19:6–18); Moses sprinkles the book (of the covenant) rather than the altar. The book is here regarded as representing God; the signification therefore would be the same (cf. comment on 9:7). The words attributed to Moses are slightly different from those of Ex; they recall the words of Jesus over the Eucharistic wine (Mk 14:24). If this was an intentional change it would be a significant argument against the common opinion that the author never alludes to the Eucharist. **21.** In Ex 24 there is no mention of this sprinkling of the Tabernacle with blood, because it had not yet been constructed. In the biblical account of its dedication nothing is said of a blood-sprinkling (Ex 40:91), although that is mentioned by Josephus (*Ant.* 3.8, 6 § 205). The purpose of this blood-sprinkling was cathartic, closely related to what Moraldi calls the "sacramental" aspect of the blood rite, which expressed the re-established union between God and man (*Espiazione*, 231, 248). However, the cathartic aspect comes closer to magical conceptions and is less susceptible of being interpreted in a symbolic manner that would eliminate a religiously primitive understanding of the rite. **22.** *without the shedding of blood there is no forgiveness:* The second half of the verse ignores the other means of forgiveness known to the Hebrews: fasting (Jl 2:12), almsgiving

(Sir 3:29), contrition (Ps 50:19). But the author is thinking of the sacrificial cult, and in that case the statement is true. However, he does not mean that the shedding of blood was regarded as vicarious punishment for the sins of the offerer; it is the expiatory, unitive power of the blood that is envisaged, and the necessity of its being shed in order that the blood ritual might be performed (cf. T. Thornton, *JTS* 15 [1964] 63–65).

56 (iii) *The perfect sacrifice* (9:23–28). **23.** *the heavenly things themselves need better sacrifices than these:* It is difficult to attribute to the heavenly Tabernacle a need for purification; C. Spicq holds that in this second part of the verse the author is speaking not of purification but of dedication (*L'Épître aux Héb*, 2, 267). But the parallelism with the purification of the earthly Tabernacle, to which the first half of the verse refers, makes that interpretation improbable. If one applies the statement to the intermediate heavens, which correspond to the outer part of the earthly Tabernacle, the statement of Jb 15:15, "the heavens are not clean in his sight," may be pertinent (cf. H. Bietenhard, *Die himmlische Welt*, 130, n.1). The pl. "sacrifices" is strange, since the author knows of only one purificatory heavenly sacrifice, but it may have been used to correspond with the pl. "heavenly things." **24.** *a mere antitype of the real one:* "Anitype" is used here with the meaning "copy." *to appear now before God on our behalf:* Cf. 7:25; Rom 8:34. **25–26.** If Jesus' sacrifice had not been definitive and final, but had demanded constant repetition as did the annually repeated Day of Atonement sacrifices, he would have had to suffer many times since the creation of the world. The author rejects the notion of repeated sacrifices of Jesus, not the eternal continuance of his one sacrifice. The statement that that sacrifice took place "at the end of the ages" is another indication of the author's fidelity to the time sequence of Jewish and Christian eschatology (cf. C. K. Barrett, *Background of the NT and Its Eschatology* [Fest. C. H. Dodd; Cambridge, 1956] 363–93). His acceptance of the Platonic conception of eternal heavenly reality contrasted with temporal earthly shadow is modified by his strongly historical Christian faith. For him, the heavenly sanctuary always existed, but the heavenly sacrifice, which is now eternally present in the heavenly sanctuary, entered into the eternal order at a determined point of time. **28.** *to take away the sins of many:* A reference to Is 53:12. The Gk vb. *anapherō* means both "to take away" and "to bear," and thus is well suited to express the fact that Jesus took away sin by taking it upon himself. "The idea of vicarious sin-bearing is prominent, but there is no hint of vicarious punishment" (H. Montefiore, *A Commentary*, 162). (For the Semitic use of "many" meaning "all," cf. J. Jeremias, "*Polloi*," *ThWNT* 6, 536–45.) *will appear a second time, not to take away sin but to bring salvation to those who eagerly await him:* A reference to the parousia, with perhaps an allusion to the Day of Atonement ritual; the appearance of Jesus will be like that of the high priest coming out of the Holy of Holies (cf. Sir 50:5–10). The parousia will bring complete and final salvation (cf. 1:14).

57 **(D) Jesus' Sacrifice, Motive for Perseverance (10:1–39).**

(a) THE MANY SACRIFICES AND THE ONE SACRIFICE (10:1–18). **1.** *the Law, having only a shadow of the good things to come:* Here the author is not using "shadow" as he does in 8:5, where the Platonic heavenly–earthly contrast is intended, but in the Pauline sense of a foreshadowing of that which is to come through Christ (cf. Col 2:17). Codex P46 reads "and the image," practically equating the two. But the normal meaning of "image" (*eikōn*) is a representation that in some way shares the reality of which it is image (cf. H. Kleinknecht, "*Eikōn*," *ThDNT* 2, 388–90). Consequently, the reading that contrasts it with "shadow" is preferable. The annually repeated Day of Atonement sacrifices were not able to remove sin; they simply foreshadowed the sacrifice of Jesus. **2.** The very repetition of the sacrifices proves their impotence: If they had taken away sins, the worshipers would no longer have had any consciousness of guilt, and would have stopped offering them. The argument is weak, because it ignores the evident objection that those sacrifices could have expiated past sins, but new sins would call for further sacrifices. But it is merely an overstatement of what the author's faith assures him to be true: The one sacrifice of Jesus is the source of remission of past sins (9:15), and because of it he is forever the source of salvation (5:9); because of its perfection, no further sacrifice is necessary or possible. **3–4.** *for it is impossible that the blood of bulls and goats can take away sins:* The OT sacrifices brought past sins into remembrance but could not efface them. This is in direct opposition to the statement of late-Jewish belief found in *Jub* 5:17–18. It does not seem, however, that the "remembrance" (Gk *anamnēsis*) of sin means that it was believed that "the cultic rites actually bring past sins into the present" (so H. Montefiore, *A Commentary*, 165; similarly, J. Behm, "*Anamnēsis*," *ThDNT* 1, 348f.). (For the Semitic concept of remembrance, which is often invoked in this connection, cf. W. Schottroff, "*Gedenken*" *im alten Orient und im Alten Testament* [Neukirchen, 1964] 117–26; 339–41.) It is not clear whether God or the offerer is the one who "remembers" the sins. The former interpretation is suggested by 8:12, which points to the time of the new covenant when God will no longer remember the sins of his people, and by the statement of Philo (*De plant.* 108) that the sacrifices of the wicked "put Him in remembrance" of their sins. But in that case, the author would mean that all the sacrifices, whether offered by the repentant or the unrepentant, served only to remind God of sin, and actually called forth punishment of the offerer, and v. 4, as well as other texts of Heb, speaks only of the inefficaciousness of these sacrifices rather than of their positive harmfulness for the offerer.

58 **5–7.** The words of Ps 40:7–9a are here attributed to the Son at his incarnation. The quotation follows the LXX in substance. In v. 7b of the Ps, the MT reads "ears you have dug for me" (to hear and obey God's will). The majority of LXX mss. have the reading given in Heb: "you have prepared a body for me." The meaning of the Ps is that God prefers obedience to sacrifice; it is not a repudiation of the ritual but a statement of its relative inferiority. Since Jesus' obedience to God's will was expressed by his willing offering of his body (i.e., himself) in death, the LXX reading of v. 7b is peculiarly applicable to him, so much so that it has been thought that the reading was introduced into the LXX under the influence of Heb (cf. J. Héring, *L'Épître aux Hébreux*, 95, n. 1). **8.** *sacrifices and offerings, holocausts and sin offerings you did not desire nor delight in—although the Law prescribes them:* These terms for sacrifice are probably meant to cover the four main types, i.e., peace offerings ("sacrifices"), cereal offerings ("offerings"), holocausts, and sin offerings. The last includes the guilt offerings (cf. Lv 5:6,7, where the names of the two are interchanged, although the CCD does not make that clear). The phrase "although the Law prescribes them" prepares for the statement of v. 9 that the Law has been annulled in this respect. **9.** *then he says, Behold, I have come to do your will. He annuls the former in order to establish the latter:* God's preferring obedience to sacrifice is interpreted as a repudiation of the OT sacrifices, and their replacement by the voluntary self-offering of Jesus. **10.** *it is by this will* *that we have been consecrated:* "This will" is the will of God, carried out by Christ, that he offer in death the body that God "prepared" for him. The offering of Jesus' body means the same as the shedding of his blood; each expresses the total self-offering of Christ.

59 **11.** *every priest stands performing his service daily:* The fact that the author speaks here of "every priest" rather than of the high priest alone and that he speaks of a priestly service performed daily indicates that he is no longer thinking of the Day of Atonement but of all the OT sacrificial ritual. **12.** *Christ offered one sacrifice for sins, and took his seat forever at the right hand of God:* The contrasting postures of the standing Jewish priests and the seated Christ have been frequently invoked against the view that the sacrifice of Jesus perdures in heaven (cf. comment on 8:2–3 for the weakness of that argument). W. Stott attempts to relate Christ's being seated in heaven with his activity there by comparing it to David's sitting and praying before the Lord (2 Sm 7:18), with Jesus' heavenly function now consisting in his "claiming the fulfillment of the covenant promises to his seed" (*NTS* 9 [1962–63] 62–67). But if the author had intended the comparison, it is strange that in spite of all that he has to say of the heavenly activity of Jesus, there is not a single unmistakable allusion to that text of 2 Sm. **13.** The time between Jesus' enthronement and the parousia is described by the citation of Ps 110:1b. Unlike Paul, the author does not indicate whom he understands by the enemies yet to be made subject to Christ (1 Cor 15:25ff.). **14.** *by one offering he has forever made perfect those who are thus consecrated:* Through the cleansing of their consciences so that they may worship the living God (9:14), Jesus has given his followers access to the Father; they share in his own priestly consecration (cf. comment on 2:10f.). **15–17.** What has been said is now confirmed by the testimony of Scripture ("the Holy Spirit"; cf. comment on 3:7). The text cited is an excerpt from the prophecy of Jer 31:31–34 concerning the new covenant, already used in 8:8–12. The two citations are slightly different in the verses in which they coincide, but the variants do not affect the meaning. **18.** *where these have been forgiven, there is no more offering for sin:* The conclusion drawn from the last words of the prophecy, that God will remember sins no more. They will be no longer remembered because they will have been forgiven. The fulfillment of this has come about through Jesus' sacrifice; there is now no more offering for sin.

60 (b) Assurance, Judgment, Recall of the Past (10:19–39). **19.** *we have confidence to enter the sanctuary:* Cf. 3:6; 4:16; 6:19f. **20.** *by the new and living way which he opened for us:* Possibly this is related to Jesus' word in Jn 14:6, "I am the way...and the life" (cf. C. Spicq, *Aux sources de la tradition chrétienne* [Fest. M. Goguel; Neuchâtel, 1950] 258–69). But the author does not go so far as John in identifying Christ and the way; his expression is closer to the Johannine texts that speak of Christ's traversing the "way" that his disciples will later travel (Jn 13:1; 14:2f; 17:11). The Gk *egkainō*, "open," also has the meaning of "inaugurate" or "dedicate" (cf. 9:18; 1 Kgs 8:63). *through the veil, that is, his flesh:* Cf. comment on 9:11. Christ's flesh is not the means of access to the sanctuary but, like the veil before the Holy of Holies, is an obstacle to entrance (O. Kuss, *Brief an die Heb* [1953], 90). It should be noted that the author speaks not of Christ's "body," but of his "flesh." Käsemann's comments on the pejorative meaning of the latter are to be accepted (*Das wandernde Gottesvolk*, 146f.; cf. 5:7), although it is not certain that the author's concept of Jesus' passage through the veil of his flesh reveals Gnostic influence, as Käsemann holds. There appears to be a connection between this text and the rending of the Temple veil at the death of Christ (Mk 15:38). **21.** *the house of God:* The Christian community (cf. 3:6). **22.** *with our hearts sprinkled [clean] from a bad conscience, and our bodies washed with clean water:* The sprinkling is a metaphorical designation of the purifying power of the sacrifice of Christ on those who believe in him. Whereas the Jewish ritual sprinkling of lustral water produced only external purity (9:13), those who have been sprinkled with the blood of Christ are cleansed in respect to conscience (9:14). "Washed with clean water" is probably a reference to baptism (cf. 1 Cor 6:11; Ti 3:5). **23.** *let us hold fast, without swerving, to the confession of our hope:* It is likely that this means the confession made at baptism (cf. comment on 3:1). **24.** *let us consider how to stimulate each other to love and good works:* The mention of love in this verse may be intended to complete the triad: faith (v. 22), hope (v. 23), and love (so B. F. Westcott, *Epistle to the Hebrews*, 322). **25.** *our assembly:* Probably the gathering together of the community for the celebration of the Eucharist. Possibly the neglect of these gatherings was due to fear of persecution, but more likely it was simply another manifestation of the slackening of Christian fervor verging on apostasy against which Heb is directed. The assembly is seen by the author as a situation peculiarly suitable for the stimulation of love and for mutual encouragement. *the day:* The parousia of Jesus (cf. Rom 13:12; 1 Cor 3:13).

61 **26.** *if we sin wilfully:* The reference is to the sin of apostasy, as is clear from v. 29 (cf. 3:12). The author's reflection on the consequences of that sin resemble 6:4–8. **28.** *anyone who has set aside the Law of Moses is put to death without mercy on the evidence of two or three witnesses:* The "setting aside" of the Law envisaged is evidently not any sin against it, but idolatry, for which the death penalty was enjoined, provided two or three witnesses could bear testimony to the sin (Dt 17:2–7). **32.** *when you had been enlightened:* A reference to baptism (cf. 6:4). It is difficult to know the nature of the persecution that the addressees suffered shortly after being baptized. If the statement of 12:4 means that none of the community to which they belonged had ever undergone martyrdom (F. F. Bruce, *Ep. to the Heb*, 266), persecutions such as those of the Jerusalem church which involved the death of some (Acts 8:1; cf. 26:10; 12:2), as well as the persecutions of the Christians of Rome under Nero in AD 64, would be excluded. But there is no reason why those words could not be addressed to people who had themselves not shed their blood although some of their fellow Christians had. The problem is made difficult because the identity of the addressees is unknown. **37–38.** The author, following his usual practice, now cites an OT text in support of what he has said. He uses Hab 2:3–4, introducing it by a short citation from Is 26:20, "a very little while." The Hab citation is almost identical with the text of the Codex Alexandrinus of the LXX, but the author inverts the first and second lines of v. 4. "He who is to come" is Jesus; his coming is the parousia, which is now a matter of only "a very little while." In the meantime, the just man must live in faith, waiting for the return of Christ. If he loses faith and falls away, he will incur the displeasure of God. The Hab text was used at Qumran as referring to the deliverance of those who had faith in the Teacher of Righteousness (1QpHab 8:1–3), and was used by Paul as an OT support of justification by faith rather than by works (Rom 1:17; Gal 3:11). In his understanding of the text the author is close to the sense of the original Hebrew (a promise of salvation contingent on faithfulness). **39.** *we have faith and will possess life:* As in 6:9–12, after a warning the author sounds a note of encouragement. The word "faith" serves as a transition to the portrait of the faith of those who lived before the time of Christ.

62 **(V) Examples, Discipline, Disobedience (11:1–12:29).**

(A) The Faith of the Ancients (11:1–40). **1.** *faith is assurance of what we hope for, and conviction about things which we do not see:* The principal problem is the meaning of the Gk words *hypostasis* and *elegchos*, "assurance" and "conviction," respectively. The verse is not a definition of faith (against O. Michel, *Brief an die Hebräer*, 246); the author says no more about it than what is suited to his hortatory purpose. In determining the meaning of *hypostasis*, attention should be paid to 3:14, one of the two other texts of Heb (cf. 1:3) where the word occurs. It means "assurance" in that verse, and the similarity of the argument with that of this section suggests that the word has the same meaning here. Thus doubt is cast on the correctness of translations such as C. Spicq's "a guarantee" (*L'Épître aux Héb*, 2, 337) and Moulton-Milligan's "a title-deed" (*Vocabulary of the Gk Testament*, 660). Spicq's rejection of a "subjective" meaning of the word because of what he calls "the certainly objective" meaning of the parallel *elegchos* (which he translates as "proof") is not convincing. There is no reason to think that either word is to be taken in an "objective" sense; the context suggests that each has to do with the attitude of the believer. The first concerns that which is not yet present, but is confidently awaited; the second, that which while a present reality is not known except by faith. M. Buber finds in this double aspect of faith a joining together of the Jewish and the Greek concepts (*Two Types of Faith* [N.Y., 1961] 37). The verse accurately describes Christian existence, which is marked by assurance that the goods promised by God will be fully possessed in the future (10:39), and by conviction that the past and present facts on which that assurance is based (Jesus' saving death and his heavenly priesthood) are indeed facts and not illusion. In the following examples it is the first of the two aspects of faith—confidence and assurance of a future possession—that is the more prominent. **3.** *by faith we understand that the worlds were created by the word of God:* Cf. comment on 1:2; Ps 32:6; Wis 9:1. This verse appears to break the continuity of the argument, for it deals with the author's faith and that of his addressees, rather than with that of the ancients. But it exemplifies the second aspect of faith mentioned in v. 1.

63 **4.** For a list of heroes similar to that which begins here, cf. Sir 44:1–50:21. *by faith Abel offered a sacrifice greater than Cain's:* The OT says nothing about faith as the motive of Abel's sacrifice; probably the author is influenced by his own conviction that "without faith it is impossible to please [God]" (v. 6), and the statement of Gn 4:4 that God was pleased with Abel's sacrifice but not with Cain's. *though dead, he still speaks:* Possibly a reference to Gn 4:10, but more likely simply an indication of the enduring witness to faith given by Abel's example. **6.** *one who approaches God must believe that he is, and that he rewards those who seek him:* The two objects of belief should probably be understood as synonymous. What must be believed is not the mere fact of God's existence, but his existence as the One who has entered into gracious relations with man. The opposite view, that God is unconcerned with the conduct of man, is expressed in the OT as the fool's saying, "There is no God" (Ps 52:2). That is an expression of practical, not speculative atheism, and this verse is its counterstatement. **7.** *Noah, warned about things not yet seen:* Cf. Gn 6:13. *condemned the world:* The author seems to have drawn on a tradition, alluded to in 2 Pt 2:5, that Noah warned his contemporaries of the imminent disaster and urged them to repentance, though without success. The event vindicated his faith, which was a condemnation of their unbelief (cf. Wis 4:16).

64 **8–9.** Here the author begins to speak of Abraham, whom Paul had already proposed as the prototype of the Christian believer (Rom 4). His faith is exemplified by his obedience to God's command to migrate to Canaan (Gn 12:1,4) and by his confidence that his descendants would possess the land, although he would be only a sojourner in it (Gn 15:16,18). The faith of Isaac and Jacob, "heirs of the same promise" (cf. Gn 26:4; 35:12), is mentioned in passing. **10.** *he was looking forward to the city with foundations:* The author interprets Abraham's sojourn in Canaan as an indication of his realization that his permanent dwelling was not to be anywhere on earth, but in the heavenly city; in this, he is made to resemble the Christian believer (cf. 12:22; 13:14). **11.** *by faith Sarah herself received power:* The mention of Sarah is surprising, since the Gk text attributes to her, because of her faith, the power to beget a child (lit., "power for the sowing of seed"). The attempts to read a different meaning into the Greek in order to avoid the difficulty this verse presents are of doubtful merit. Some commentators regard "Sarah herself" as an interpolation; others take it as a dative, "together with Sarah," with Abraham understood as subject of the vb. "received" in either case. The incident referred to is the promise of the birth of Isaac (Gn 15:2–6). **12.** *and from one as good as dead:* An exaggerated description of Abraham's advanced age at the time of Isaac's birth (cf. Rom 4:19).

65 **13–16.** The statement that he was a stranger and sojourner was Abraham's (cf. Gn 23:4), but here the author attributes to all the patriarchs the acknowledgment that their homeland is in heaven. (For God's not being "ashamed" to be called their God, cf. Ex 3:6.) **17–18.** The last example given of Abraham's faith is the classic case of his obedience to the command to offer Isaac in sacrifice (Gn 22:1–19). His readiness to do so is particularly striking because his hopes for the fulfillment of God's promise were bound up with the boy. **19.** *God was even able to raise him up from the dead; hence, he received him back, as a symbol:* Although some interpret the Gk *en parabolē*, here translated "as a symbol," as "figuratively speaking," since Isaac did not actually die, it seems more likely that the author sees Isaac's deliverance from death as a symbol of the resurrection of Christ. The only other instance of his use of the word *parabolē* (9:9) supports that view. **20–22.** The common point in the faith of Isaac, Jacob, and Joseph is that each, when about to die, expressed belief in God's promise; the first two by blessing their descendants and thus transmitting the promise; Joseph by speaking of the deliverance of the Israelites from Egypt.

66 **23–28.** Four instances follow of faith connected with the history of Moses; the first is the faith of his parents in defying the order of Pharaoh. The glorification of Moses in vv. 24–27 does not correspond to the OT account (Ex 2:11–15). That Moses considered "reproach suffered for the Messiah" greater riches than the wealth of Egypt is a Christological interpretation of his choosing to share the sufferings of Israel, the messianic people. **32–38.** In these verses the author passes summarily through other heroes of the OT, some named, others not. It is impossible to know in all instances to whom the deeds mentioned in vv. 33–38 apply. "Closed the mouths of lions" (33) apparently refers to Daniel (Dn 6:22); "quenched raging fire" (34) to the three youths (Dn 3:49f.). For the women who "received their dead by resurrection" (35), cf. 1 Kgs 17:17–24; 2 Kgs 4:18–37. The sufferings of vv. 35b–38 are principally those endured by the faithful Israelites during the persecution that preceded and accompanied the Maccabean revolt (cf. 1 Mc 1:62–64; 7:34; 2 Mc 6:18–20; 7:1–42). The prophet Zechariah was stoned (2 Chr 24:21) and, according to the

tradition found in the *Ascension of Isaiah* 5:1–14, Isaiah was sawn in two. **40.** *so that without us they should not be made perfect:* The fulfillment of the promise that the OT saints awaited did not take place until the saving work of Christ had been completed. But now they have obtained (6:12) that which the Christians still on earth possess only in an anticipatory way while looking forward to its full possession.

67 **(B) God's Treatment of His Sons (12:1–13).** The author prefaces his explanation of suffering as God's paternal discipline with an exhortation to imitate Jesus' example. **1.** *having rid ourselves of every encumbrance and of sin which clings to us:* The Gk *euperistatos*, here translated "cling," occurs nowhere else and its meaning can only be conjectured; P^{46} reads *euperispastos*, "easily distracting." Either word would suit the context, which speaks of a race in which those who run must free themselves from encumbrances that would impede their progress and must keep their eyes fixed on Jesus. **2.** *our leader in faith who perfects us:* There seems to be no reason to take the Gk *archēgos* (leader) as meaning "author" (against A. Purdy, *Epistle to the Hebrews* [IB 11; Nashville, 1955] 738). The concept of Jesus as pioneer in the race is consonant with 2:10, where the word also occurs (cf. 6:20). *who for the sake of the joy which lay before him endured the cross:* Some commentators (e.g., J. Héring, *L'Épître aux Hébreux*, 113f.) take the Gk *anti* to mean "instead of" rather than "for the sake of" and see the verse as a reference to Jesus' repudiating earthly kingship (cf. Mt 4:8–10; Jn 6:15), or to that self-emptying of which Phil 2:6–9 speaks. But the author uses *anti* in the same sense as in v. 16; the exhortation he is making to his addressees, that they endure in view of the triumphant end of the race, suggests that he understands Jesus' example in the same way. **4.** Cf. comment on 10:32. **5–6.** The OT citation is of Prv 3:11–12. **9.** *the Father of spirits:* Cf. Nm 16:22; 27:16. **13.** *make straight paths for your feet:* The imagery of the race course changes to the familiar one of the road on which the people of God must journey.

68 **(C) The Penalties of Disobedience (12:14–29).** **15.** *lest any bitter root spring up and through it the many become defiled:* An exhortation to watch over each other to avert the danger of apostasy. One such defection will corrupt not only the sinner himself but many others. The reference to the bitter root is an almost verbatim citation of Dt 29:17 (LXX). **16.** *no fornicator or profane person like Esau:* It is not certain that "fornicator" refers to Esau, and the OT account does not so present him, although it is possible that the author is drawing upon extrabiblical tradition (cf. F. F. Bruce, *Ep. to the Heb*, 366). His profaneness, however, is clear from the event of his giving up his birthright for a single meal (Gn 25:29–34). His inability to endure hunger and his readiness to trade his birthright for food are similar to the danger in which the addressees find themselves. Esau is presented as an example of apostasy, motivated by convenience and a low estimation of the high position that was his. **17.** The story of Esau is now taken as illustrative of another point on which the author has insisted: the impossibility of repentance after apostasy (6:4–6). Although later he wept and begged for the blessing due to the firstborn (Gn 27:34–36), he could not receive it because he had forfeited his birthright. The author understands the reason why Esau's tears achieved nothing, for he was not repentant of his previous action. **18–21.** Here the author begins a contrast between the assembly of Israel, gathered for the making of the old covenant and the giving of the Law, and the assembly of those who have entered into the new covenant. The scene of the former is on earth, and the awesome circumstances recounted are taken from the account in Ex 19:12–14,16–19; 20:18–21, and Moses' words in Dt 4:11f. The words of Moses quoted in v. 21 were spoken on another occasion (Dt 9:19). The scene of the latter assembly is the heavenly sanctuary, the place of Jesus' completed sacrifice on which the new covenant is based. **22.** *but you have come to Mount Zion, to the city of the living God, to the heavenly Jerusalem:* Cf. Gal 4:26; Ap 21:2; *2 Esdras* 8:52. The assembly of the people of the new covenant is not on earth, but in the heavenly sanctuary. The "now" and the "not yet" of Christian existence in this world is clearly shown here—the author speaks to those who are still on the journey to heaven, yet since they already possess in an anticipatory way the good things to come, he can speak of them as having already arrived. **23.** *to the assembly of the first-born who are enrolled in heaven:* It is not certain whether these are the angels of v. 23 (so C. Spicq, *L'Épître aux Héb*, 2, 407), or the just men of the OT, spoken of in ch. 11, who have already inherited the promised blessings (6:12), or the entire assembly of the Christian faithful (so J. Lécuyer, *SPC* 2, 161–68). Their designation as those who are enrolled in heaven favors the last view (cf. Lk 10:20). *to the souls of the just who have been made perfect:* Cf. 11:40. **24.** *and to the sprinkled blood which speaks better things than that of Abel:* The last mentioned reality of the heavenly sanctuary is that which has opened it to the faithful, the sacrifice of Jesus. The blood of Abel cried out for vengeance (Gn 4:10); that of Jesus brings forgiveness and access to God (10:19). **25.** *see that you do not refuse to hear him who speaks:* As in 2:2–4, the author uses an argument *a minori ad maius* to show how much greater will be the punishment of those who disobey God who now speaks from heaven than that of those who disobeyed him when he spoke from Sinai. **26.** Cf. Hag 2:21. The words of that prophecy are taken by the author as a reference to the Last Judgment.

69 **(VI) Final Exhortation, Blessing, Greetings (13:1–25).** **2.** *entertained angels without knowing it:* Cf. Gn 18:1–5; Tb 5:4–9. **7–8.** The leaders whom the addressees are asked to remember are proposed as an example of faith. But although they once fulfilled their function well, they have died and no longer lead the people, whereas Jesus Christ remains the same yesterday, today, and forever (cf. Ap 1:17). **9.** *do not be led away by diverse and strange teachings:* These teachings apparently have to do with observance of the food laws of Judaism (cf. Rom 14:17; Col 2:16). Those who receive their strength from the grace of the never-changing Christ have no need to resort to these useless religious practices. However, v. 10 suggests that the useless "foods" may also be the sacrificial meals of Judaism. **10.** *we have an altar from which those who serve the tabernacle have no right to eat:* The emphatic position of the first words in the Greek implies that this is an answer to the charge that Christians are at a disadvantage in respect to sacrifice. The "altar" means the sacrifice of Christ, in which the faithful participate. There is no convincing reason for taking this as a reference to the Eucharist (cf. O. Kuss, *Auslegung und Verkündigung*, 326–28). If the author had intended to speak here of that sacrifice—which is never clearly alluded to, if at all, in Heb—he would have mentioned it only in passing, since it would have so forcefully answered the presumed charge. **11.** Cf. Lv 16:27. **12.** The comparison that the author has made between Jesus' sacrifice and that of the Day of Atonement is carried out by showing that just as the flesh of the victims was burned outside the camp, so Jesus suffered death outside the gates of Jerusalem. **13.** The final exhortation against apostasy; let the readers of the letter follow Jesus, even though this means bearing the same reproach that he bore. **20–21.** This blessing contains the only explicit reference in Heb to the resurrection, but, as noted above

(1:3), it is always presupposed when Jesus' exaltation is mentioned. For "the great shepherd of the sheep," cf. Is 63:11.

22–25. These verses, together with v. 19, may really constitute the epistolary ending of Heb, added when the homily (→ 5 above) was being sent to some group of Christians in need of an exhortation. This is not to suggest that these verses were written by some person other than the author of Heb, or that they are not original. But their relation to vv. 20–21, which sound so much like the epilogue of the homily, has always been a problem (see A. Vanhoye, *Structure littéraire*, 219–22). **22.** *word of exhortation:* See Acts 13:15, where the same phrase designates a synagogue sermon. *Timothy:* (→ Pastoral Letters, 57:3). **24.** *those from Italy:* (→ 5 above). **25.** The mss. A, C, D, and the Koine tradition add "Amen." In ms. A there is also the addition, "written from Rome." Variants of this formula ("from Italy" or "from Athens") are found in some inferior mss.

62

THE JOHANNINE EPISTLES

Bruce Vawter, C.M.

BIBLIOGRAPHY

1 Alexander, N., *The Epistles of John* (TBC; London, 1962). Bonsirven, J., *Épîtres de Saint Jean* (VS 9; Paris, 1954). Bultmann, R., *Die Johannesbriefe* (Meyer 14; Göttingen, 1967). Brooke, A. E., *The Johannine Epistles* (ICC: N.Y., 1912). Chaine, J., *Les Épîtres catholiques* (*EBib*, 2nd ed.; Paris, 1939). Charue, A., *Les Épîtres catholiques* (*PSB*, 3rd ed.; Paris, 1951). Dodd, C. H., *The Johannine Epistles* (MNTC; London, 1946). Haenchen, E., "Neuere Literatur zu den Johannesbriefen," *TRu* 26 (1960) 1–43, 267–91. Leconte, R., "Épîtres de Saint Jean," *VDBS* 4, 797–815. Lyonnet, S., "De natura peccati quid doceat Novum Testamentum—de scriptis Ioanneis," *VD* 35 (1957) 271–78. Malatesta, E., *The Epistles of St. John: Greek Text and English Translation Structurally Arranged* (Fano, 1967). Michl, J. and O. Kuss, *Der Brief an die Hebräer und die katholischen Briefe* (RNT 8; Regensburg, 1953) 258–317. Nauck, W., *Die Tradition und der Charakter des ersten Johannesbriefes* (Tübingen, 1957). O'Neill, J. C., *The Puzzle of 1 John* (London, 1966). Robinson, J. A. T., "The Destination and Purpose of the Johannine Epistles," *NTS* 7 (1960) 56–65. Schnackenburg, R., *Die Johannesbriefe* (HTKNT 13/3; Freiburg, 1953). Schneider, J., *Die Briefe des Jakobus, Petrus, Judas und Johannes* (NTD 10; 9th ed.; Göttingen, 1961). Suitbertus a S. Ioanne a Cruce, "Die Vollkommenheitslehre des ersten Johannesbriefes," *Bib* 39 (1958) 319–33, 449–70. Vrede, W. and M. Meinertz, *Die katholischen Briefe* (BB 9; 4th ed.; Bonn, 1932). Westcott, B. F., *The Epistles of St. John* (London, 1883; reprinted, Grand Rapids, 1966). Willmering, H., *The Epistles of St. John* (*CCHS*; London, 1953).

INTRODUCTION

2 **(I) Relationship of the Epistles.** At first glance there does not seem to be a very close connection between the three epistles traditionally called Johannine or between them and the Gospel of Jn. It is true that in both language and theology 1 Jn resembles the Gospel of Jn more than any other NT writing, yet there are important differences. Besides the fact that some of the most characteristic Johannine categories discerned in the Gospel do not appear at all in 1 Jn (and the converse is also true), what stands out first and foremost is the contrast in their eschatological viewpoint (→ Gospel Jn, 63:25). The "realized eschatology" that constitutes Jn's most distinctive contribution to NT theology is not featured in 1 Jn. Furthermore, if 1 Jn is an epistle, it is of rather a singular kind, possessing neither the *praescriptio* nor the conclusion of the ordinary epistolary form with which the Pauline epistles have made us familiar (→ NT Epistles, 47:8). Second and Third Jn are straightforward letters, conforming to the epistolary canons where 1 Jn does not, but, again at first glance, their subject matter appears to have little relation to that of Jn and 1 Jn. Whereas Jn and 1 Jn are anonymous, 2-3 Jn are specifically identified as letters of "the Presbyter."

Closer examination of these writings, however, vindicates the judgment of early Christianity in associating them. Like most of the Pauline epistles, 2-3 Jn are letters to individual churches of a single town or area. The "Lady Elect" who is the recipient of 2 Jn can only be one of the local churches within the author's jurisdiction. Though addressed to a certain Gaius, 3 Jn is also a letter to a church that the author has been prevented from approaching in the regular way (cf. v. 9). Despite the brevity of 2-3 Jn, it is not difficult to determine that they are the work of the same author and that they presuppose the kind of ecclesiastical background against which the more discursive 1 Jn has been written. The character of 1 Jn is that of an epistle to several churches of a given area and thus corresponds to a literary type found elsewhere in the NT (→ NT Epistles, 47:3–4).

Literary criticism concurs in ascribing 2-3 Jn to the same author who, it appears, especially from the comparison of 1-2 Jn, is also the anonymous author of 1 Jn. The literary relation of 1 Jn to Jn is subject to less precise definition, but the general view of the evidence is that it, too, indicates a common authorship (see esp. W. F. Howard, *The Fourth Gospel*, Appendix B, 276–96). This question, of course, involves the literary problem connected with the Johannine corpus (→ Gospel Jn, 63:4).

3 **(II) Authorship.** The tradition of the ancient Church is virtually unanimous in ascribing 1 Jn to the authorship of John the Apostle, the son of Zebedee. The early attestation is roughly the same as that for the Gospel; here the testimony of Dionysius of Alexandria is especially significant in identifying the author of Jn and 1 Jn, in view of his critical objection to the Johannine authorship of Ap. The exceptions to the rule appear to

have been only Theodore of Mopsuestia and some parts of the Syrian church, both in the 5th cent. (cf. M.-J. Lagrange, *Histoire ancienne du canon du Nouveau Testament* [EBib; Paris, 1933] 125–30, 157–58).

The attestation to 2-3 Jn is fully as ancient, but by no means as unanimous. Origen (in Eusebius, *HE* 6.25,10; *PG* 20. 584), Eusebius (*HE* 3.25,3; *PG* 20. 269), and Jerome (*De Viris Illustr.* 9; *PL* 23. 623ff.) all testify that in their times the authorship was contested, though they were personally disposed to accept them as Johannine. This hesitation is also reflected by other writers, such as Theodore of Mopsuestia and John Chrysostom, who make no use of 2-3 Jn as canonical Scripture. The reason for questioning their authorship by John the Apostle does not appear to have had any basis on critical grounds. Rather, they were victims by association after the misuse of Ap by the millenarian heresy had occasioned doubts as to the apostolic authorship of this book. Since the tendency was to ascribe Ap to "John the Presbyter" as distinct from the Apostle (→ Gospel Jn, 63:4), the two epistles written by "the Presbyter" easily fell into the same category. However, the very fact that these two brief letters have contributed nothing uniquely their own to the NT is the best possible confirmation of the ancient tradition that associated them with John the Apostle. It is hardly conceivable that they would have been preserved for any other reason.

As indicated above, literary considerations make it virtually certain that 2-3 Jn are by the author of 1 Jn. In turn, the literary relation of 1 Jn with the Gospel of Jn makes it equally likely that the same secretary-disciple of John the Apostle is responsible for the writing of both the Gospel and the epistles.

4 **(III) Relation of the Epistles to the Gospel.** Beyond the fact that 1-3 Jn seem to presuppose a common religious and cultural background and basically the same ecclesiastical problems, we can hardly determine anything further about their relative order. The "encyclical" character of 1 Jn may indicate that it was the last to appear, but the three letters could as easily have been written at the same time. It appears that 2-3 Jn were sent to different churches, but both of these were probably included among the recipients of 1 Jn. The churches involved were doubtless those of the region associated with the writing of the Gospel, that of Ephesus (→ Gospel Jn, 63:2).

It remains to determine the relation of the epistles to the Gospel. As already pointed out, though Jn and 1 Jn have a close literary affinity, there are theological differences that indicate some separation in time. Frequently, 1 Jn has been regarded as a kind of commentary on Jn by its author. Obviously this is not a possibility if, as seems to be the case, Jn is a posthumous work edited and completed by the Apostle's disciples. However, the question is not altogether as simple as this, because we doubtless must reckon with an oral history of the Gospel prior to its having attained its present written form (→ Gospel Jn, 63:4–9). It is possible, therefore, that at least in a broad sense of the word, 1 Jn can be considered a commentary on the Gospel as taught in the Johannine school. In fact, at times the Gospel seems to be presupposed by the epistle, which otherwise would be rather obscure.

5 From the standpoint of written documents, however, there seems to be little doubt that the epistle is the earlier: The Johannine characteristics are more developed in Jn than in 1 Jn. The arguments advanced by C. H. Dodd (*The Johannine Epistles* LIII f.) and others who hold for separate authorship actually favor equally well the view that in 1 Jn we find the author of Jn writing at an earlier stage of his own thinking. (1) The futurist eschatology of 1 Jn, common to the NT and also found in Jn, certainly predominates over the "realized eschatology" characteristic of the Gospel; most commentators agree, however, that the "spiritualized" interpretation of the last days represented in 1 Jn 2:18–29 is a less developed manifestation of the doctrine typical of the Gospel. (2) The representation of Christ's death as expiatory in 1 Jn (cf. esp. 2:2; 4:10), a doctrine especially associated with Paul, is present in the Gospel but has been incorporated by the Evangelist into the more distinctively Johannine theology of Christ's "glorification" (→ Johannine Theology, 80:34). (3) Although the doctrine of Jn and 1 Jn about the divine persons is basically the same, a line can be traced from the somewhat fumbling terminology of 1 Jn to the firm formulations of the Gospel. This is particularly evident in such key terms as "Spirit," "Word," "Life," and "Paraclete." In general, one has the impression that between the writing of 1 Jn and Jn the author has become more assured of his own theology and thought and less derivative in his language and concepts. This impression is strengthened by the fact that the QL, which has more consistent parallels with the Johannine corpus than with any other body of NT literature (→ Gospel Jn, 63:16), more closely resembles 1 Jn than it does Jn.

6 **(IV) Literary Form of 1 Jn.** Because 1 Jn does presume a knowledge of the Johannine Gospel, it is extremely unlikely that it was composed as a *Begleitungsschrift* (companion piece) to introduce the Fourth Gospel in its finished form. Despite its departure from the ordinary canons of Hellenistic epistolary style, 1 Jn is an epistle to a defined group, prompted by the spread of erroneous teachings, the nature of which will be seen in the commentary. Polemics against the same teachings are to be found also in the Gospel, though in a more discursive and subtle form befitting its own literary type.

The sustained theological tone of 1 Jn has suggested to some the character of a treatise rather than a letter and to others a composite work from two or more sources. 1 Jn is an epistle, written in the style of the author of the Fourth Gospel, to whom the use of the moral or doctrinal discourse is second nature. There is no reason to believe that we do not have the epistle as it left its author's hands, even though its relative lack of order may indicate that he prepared it by stages over some period of time.

The question of the "Johannine comma" (1 Jn 5:7) will be treated in the commentary. This is the most famous textual problem of the Johannine epistles, which are relatively free of serious variations in the mss.

7 **(V) Outline of 1 Jn.** As is true of many other letters, ancient and modern, the sequence of thought in 1 Jn is difficult to determine according to a rigid pattern. For convenience, the following divisions will be followed in the commentary:

- (I) Prologue (1:1–4)
- (II) Walking in the Light (1:5–2:29)
  - (A) Exhortation (1:5–2:17)
    - (a) Walking in the Light (1:5–7)
    - (b) Avoiding Sin (1:8–2:2)
    - (c) Keeping the Commandments (2:3–11)
    - (d) Resisting the World (2:12–17)
  - (B) Christological: Christ and the Antichrists (2:18–29)
- (III) Living As Children of God (3:1–4:6)
  - (A) Exhortation (3:1–24)
    - (a) Living As Children of God (3:1–3)
    - (b) Avoiding Sin (3:4–10a)
    - (c) The Commandment of Love (3:10b–24)
  - (B) Christological: Christ and the Spirit of Truth (4:1–6)
- (IV) Love and Faith (4:7–5:12)
  - (A) Love in Relation to Faith (4:7–21)
  - (B) Faith in Relation to Love (5:1–12)
- (V) Conclusion and Summary (5:13–21)

COMMENTARY ON 1 JN

8 **(I) Prologue (1:1–4).** There is an obviously close connection between this prologue and that of the Gospel (→ Gospel Jn, 63:40); cf. "from the beginning" of v. 1 with Jn 1:1; "the word of life" with Jn 1:4; "was in the Father's presence" of v. 2 with Jn 1:1f.; "the life was manifested" with Jn 1:14; "what we have seen, etc." of v. 1f. with Jn 1:14. The idea of "witness," which plays such a predominant role in Jn (see comment on Jn 1:7), is also featured in this prologue. There is, further, an echo of other Johannine themes found elsewhere in the Gospel. A knowledge of the written Gospel certainly helps in discerning the author's meaning here, but this very fact seems to confirm the priority of the epistle (→ 4–5 above); it would be incredible that the relative vagueness of this prologue could have been intended as a "commentary" on the clear formulations of Jn 1:1–18. However, the fact that a knowledge of the oral Gospel is presupposed on the part of the recipients of this letter could go far toward explaining why its author could dispense with the conventional identification of himself at the beginning of the letter.

9 **1.** *what was from the beginning:* The parallel with Jn 1:1 suggests that the "beginning" is that of creation and that the author is speaking of Christ's pre-existence; the parallel in 2:13–14 indicates the same meaning for "beginning." However, this affirmation is less definite than Jn 1:1, where the eternity of the Word is contrasted with the contingency of creation; here the author speaks of a pre-existence from the beginning of creation but not necessarily prior to it. Furthermore, this is not precisely the pre-existence of a Person, but of a revelation ("what"). *what we have heard...seen...looked on...handled:* The revelation of God, which has existed from the beginning, has in these final days been experienced by living witnesses (cf. Heb 1:1); the "we" is a Johannine characteristic (cf. Jn 3:11, etc.), referring to the apostolic testimony. The first two verbs are in the pf. tense, indicating a past happening whose effects continue, whereas the other two are in the aorist, simply denoting a past fact; this classic distinction of tenses is usually preserved in the NT (cf. *GrBib* § 285–86). The substance of the apostolic testimony remains what has been seen and heard (cf. Jn 19:35; 20:30f.); in turn, this rests on specific facts that were sensibly experienced (cf. Jn 20:25ff., etc.). *concerning the word of life:* It is not evident that the author intends to personify "word" (*logos*), as in Jn 1:1ff. Rather, as v. 2 makes clear, he intends to personify "life" (so also in Jn); thus the present expression might be translated "concerning the revelation of Life." **2.** *the life was manifested:* This is the equivalent of Jn 1:14, the incarnation of Life (cf. Col 3:4; Jn 11:25; 14:6), however, rather than the Word: This is the epitome of the apostolic testimony (cf. Jn 1:14b). (For the Johannine concept of "life," see comment on Jn 1:4.) *in the Father's presence and manifested to us:* As in the prologue of Jn, the timelessness of the Life ("Word" in Jn) is contrasted (by the use of the impf.) with the manifestation in time (aor.) to which witness is given. In Jn, too, the Word is said to have been "in God's presence," that is, a Person distinct from and in relation to him. **3.** *that you may have fellowship with us:* The purpose of the apostolic testimony is that the faith first revealed to the immediate witnesses of Jesus' words and deeds may be possessed by the entire Church (cf. Jn 17:20; 20:29). *our fellowship is with the Father and with his Son Jesus Christ:* That Christians share through Christ in the divine life of Father and Son is eminently a Johannine teaching (cf. Jn 5:26ff.; 14:6ff.). The term "fellowship" (*koinōnia*, "communion"), however, is Pauline (cf. 1 Cor 1:9; Phil 1:5) rather than Johannine; it is found frequently (under the form *yaḥad*) in the QL, used as in 1 Jn, to imply union both with God and in the community. **4.** *that our joy may remain full:* The joy that Christ promised and bestowed on his apostles comes from fellowship with God (cf. Jn 15:10f.) and finds its constant fulfillment in the apostolic ministry, of which this letter is a part.

10 **(II) Walking in the Light (1:5–2:29).** The author develops the meaning of what is implied in fellowship with God in this and the following major section. In keeping with the literary form (→ 6 above), we find a mingling of hortatory passages involving Johannine concepts with polemics against Christological errors.

(A) Exhortation (1:5–2:17). The theme of this hortatory section is set in the first three verses. The dichotomy of light (see comment on Jn 1:4,9) and darkness (see comment on Jn 1:5) is a commonplace of the QL. The Johannine dualism is moral, not ontological.

(a) WALKING IN THE LIGHT (1:5–7). **5.** *now this is the message:* Cf. Jn 1:19; the epistle takes up from its prologue just as the Gospel does, with the apostolic message, however, rather than with the witness to "signs" that is the burden of the Gospel. *God is light and...no darkness at all:* Very similar language is found in 1QH 17:27–18:3. In Jn (8:12) Christ is identified with light, the revelation of God; as in the Gospel, light is truth, and darkness is error; they are not restricted to intellectual apprehension but refer pre-eminently to the moral sphere of human conduct. **6.** Thus no one whose moral conduct shows his life to be incompatible with God's can pretend to share the divine fellowship. *walk in darkness* [v. 7, *in light*]: A Semitism (cf. Eph 5:8) derived from the OT and the moral-dualistic language found in the NT and the QL. *practice the truth:* See comment on Jn 1:9. (Cf. Jn 3:21; this is a Semitism occurring in 1QS 1:5.) In the Johannine sense, the meaning is to practice to the full the moral will of God as revealed through Christ (cf. M. Zerwick, *VD* 18 [1938] 338–42, 373–77). **7.** *if we walk...we have fellowship with one another:* This is noteworthy as the better reading of the mss., whereas some texts have "fellowship with him," the reading more readily expected. Fellowship with God demands fellowship with one's neighbor as its condition and sign (cf. 4:20). *the blood of Jesus his Son cleanses us:* The author, of course, has been speaking of no fellowship with God or man that can be the result of man's good will alone, but only of that union which has been constituted through the redemptive work of Jesus Christ. In turn, this fellowship is the sign of the continuing efficacy of this redemptive work (see comment on 4:3).

11 (b) AVOIDING SIN (1:8–2:2). **8.** Not only is the work of Christ continually redemptive, it must be so because of the continuing fact of sin. In principle, the Christian should be and remain entirely free of sin (3:6ff.), but in fact, the possibility of sin is an ever-present reality that he can ignore at his peril. "Have sin" is a Johannine expression (cf. Jn 9:41; 15:22,24; 19:11); in the Gospel it is used of those who have succumbed to the omnipresence of sin. **9.** *if we confess our sins:* Though

Christ's blood cleanses us from sin, this is contingent on our own response to the divine work of salvation. The "confession" is probably the ecclesiastical rite referred to or presupposed elsewhere in the NT (Jas 5:16; Jn 20:23; Mt 16:19; 18:18; *Didache* 4:14; 14:1; cf. the usage of this text by the Council of Trent, DB 899; DS 1679), but the statement is too general to allow precise conclusions. *he is faithful and just:* The reference is doubtless to God himself (cf. Ex 34:6f.; Dt 32:4; 1 Cor 10:13), who is faithful to his promise to forgive the repentant sinner; this forgiveness he has made possible through the sacrifice of his Son (v. 7). **10.** *if we say we have not sinned:* Not only is sin a present possibility, it is also an enduring and personal fact. The verb is in the pf. tense, making more precise the "we have sin" of v. 8. *we make him a liar:* Not only would the claim to sinfulness be a grave self-deception, it would contradict the revelation of God concerning the universality of human sin, both in the OT and as given through Christ (cf. Gn 8:21; 1 Kgs 8:46; Mt 19:17). *his word is not in us:* "His word" corresponds to "the truth" of v. 8; it is the divine instruction (cf. 2:14), a thing that is to be lived.

12 **2:1.** *little children:* This is a word of the Johannine vocabulary (*teknia:* also in 2:12,28; 3:7,18; 1:4; 5:21), found elsewhere in the NT only in Jn 13:33 (the better reading in Gal 4:19 is *tekna*), where it is put on the lips of Jesus. *you may not sin:* It would, of course, be a misconstruction of the author's remarks on the universality of sin to conclude that he treats the matter lightly; the Christian ought to be, in fact, sinless. *we have an advocate with the Father:* The word "advocate" (*paraklētos*) is used elsewhere in the NT only in Jn (14:16,26; 15:26; 16:7), where it appears as a proper name of the Spirit; the Gospel seems to presuppose a development over that of the epistle, since the Spirit is there designated "another" Paraclete. The doctrine of Christ as an intercessor in heaven is common NT teaching (Rom 8:34; Heb 4:14–16; 7:24f.; 9:24). *Jesus Christ the just:* Only one who is just may enter God's presence to plead for the unjust. **2.** *the propitiation for our sins:* The word commonly translated "propitiation" (*hilasmos*, also in 4:10) is not characteristic of the Johannine vocabulary, but represents a background of thought frequent in both the OT and NT. The parallel is in v. 7 above: "the blood of Jesus his Son cleanses us from all sin." Certainly the meaning is that the death of Christ has effected the expiation, that is, the removal of sin. Just what the causal relation is, however, is not specified. To translate "sin-offering" is to introduce an etymological precision not justified by the OT usage of the word. The sense is, rather, that in the death of Christ God has revealed his forgiveness of our sins, an act of his gratuitous love and mercy. *also for those of the whole world:* The efficacy of Christ's atoning power is unlimited. In context, the author thinks of Christ's power as intercessor.

(Büchsel, F. and J. Herrmann, "*Hileōs*," *ThDNT* 3, 300–323. Lyonnet, S., "De notione expiationis," *VD* 37 [1959] 336–52; *VD* 38 [1960] 65–75, and esp. 241–61; "De munere sacrificali sanguinis," *VD* 39 [1961] 13–38.)

13 (c) KEEPING THE COMMANDMENTS (2:3–11). How can one be sure that he shares in this universal propitiation effected through Christ? Through one's knowledge of God—a knowledge that has nothing to do with merely intellectual attainments. **3–4.** *we have come to know him, if we keep his commandments:* This practical knowledge of God, which means a life lived in accordance with his revealed moral will, echoes the teaching of the OT prophets (Hos 4:1–3; 6:4–7; Jer 2:8; cf. also Jn 13:35; 14:21–24). The author is protesting a "Gnostic" approach to religion that would attempt to divorce moral conduct from intellectual commitment. **5.** *whoever keeps his word, in him the love of God has truly become perfect:* The love of God for man, or man's love for God, or the love that is God? It is difficult to decide the author's meaning, which may be deliberately ambiguous; the context will support any or all of these senses (see also 2:15; 3:17; 4:12; 5:3). **6.** *he who claims that he abides in him:* The author continues his polemics against a religion of faith without works; "abide" (*menein*) in this sense is a peculiarity of the Johannine vocabulary, frequent in the Gospel. *must himself walk just as that one walked:* "That one" is Christ; he is referred to in this emphatic way in 3:3,5,7,16; 4:17; Jn 7:11; 9:12,28; 19:21. This raises the question who is the "in him" of 6a, Christ or God? Again it is possible that the author's vagueness is deliberate: Christ is the perfect revelation of God, and to abide in him is to abide in God. **7–8.** In this context of keeping the commandments, the supreme example that comes to mind is the Lord's precept of love, a commandment that is both old and yet of the new Christian revelation (see comment on Jn 13:34). *from the beginning:* Here, as in 2:24; 3:11, the "beginning" is the reader's conversion to Christianity. *which is true both for him and for you:* The precept of love was truly new in Christ's teaching and example (cf. Jn 15:13) and forms the character of the new religious phenomenon of Christianity. *the darkness is passing away and the true light is already shining:* The victory over error signaled by Christ's coming into the world continues to progress as the law of Christ is more and more observed (cf. Jn 1:4f.,9). **9–11.** No one can pretend to be in the light of Christ who does not obey the law of Christian love, which is a law of fraternal charity. The author knows this as an absolute law that admits no alternative to love except hatred (cf. the parallels in Jn 8:12; 11:10).

14 (d) RESISTING THE WORLD (2:12–17). Observance of the law of Christ effectively removes the Christian from the influence of that world from which Christ prayed that his disciples might be free (Jn 17:9–26; cf. 15:18–27). The author continues to address all his Christian readers as "little children" (*teknia* in v. 12, *paidia* in v. 14), whom, however, he now distinguishes as "fathers" and "youths" to emphasize that his appeal extends to the entire Christian community. **12.** *I write to you because your sins are forgiven:* It is also possible to translate, "that your sins are forgiven," and similarly in the five other *hoti*-clauses of 13f. so that they become simple declarations (cf. B. Noack, *NTS* 6 [1960] 236–41). The causal sense, however, seems to be demanded by the context (cf. v. 21): The author is not proclaiming a forgiveness of sins to his readers, but explaining the basis on which he can address them with his moral exhortation. *for his name's sake:* God has forgiven our sins because of Christ (1:7; 2:2); for "name," see comment on Jn 1:12. **13.** *because you have come to know him who is from the beginning:* "Know" is used in the pregnant sense of v. 3f. This can hardly refer to anything other than the pre-existence of Christ with God: Knowledge of Christ is efficacious precisely because it is the knowledge of the everlasting God himself. *because you have overcome the evil one:* The acceptance of Christian faith is the conquest of Satan (cf. 3:8,10; 5:18f.), because the object of this faith is the one who has conquered Satan (cf. Jn 16:11). This victory can be spoken of either as a future event (see 1 Cor 15:24f.) or as already accomplished (see Col 2:15), depending on the point of view in relation to "realized eschatology." Here and in the following section, the author approximates the eschatological viewpoint of the Fourth Gospel. **14.** This verse repeats the thought of 12f. partly in different words. *I have written:* This, the better reading of the mss., is doubtless an "epistolary aorist," i.e., a past tense in relation to the reader rather than the writer (so in Acts 23:30; Phil 2:28; Col 4:8, etc.). The author does not refer to any writing earlier than the present letter.

15 **15.** *love neither the world nor what is in the world:* For "world" in this Johannine sense, see comment on Jn 1:10; 12:31. Anything that truly pertains to this world by definition cannot pertain to Christ and his followers. *the love of the Father is not in him:* Probably the genitive is objective, i.e., love directed to the Father is meant. However, the same ambiguity may be present as in v. 5 above. **16.** The author specifies, partly at least, "what is in the world," by which he means what is "of the world." *the lust of the flesh:* For "flesh," see comment on Jn 1:13. *the lust of the eyes:* The word *epithymia* signifies in this context inordinate desire of any kind pertaining to sensuality, avarice, and the like; the idea of the eyes as the "windows of the soul" in relation to such desires is frequent in the OT, NT, and QL. *the pride of life:* This is the traditional translation of the present phrase. However, *alazoneia*, found also in Jas 4:16, has a more active meaning than mere pride: It denotes arrogance, boastfulness, the conviction of self-sufficiency. The word *bios* means life in its external aspects, duration, sustenance, etc., as distinct from *zōē*, which is life as opposed to death (in Johannine language, *zōē* is always related to "eternal life"; see comment on Jn 1:4). Hence "the pride of life" implies complacency and willful independence in pursuing one's earthly existence, pride in one's own resources. **17.** The foregoing is now summarized. Whoever belongs to this world and its desires has committed himself to an order that "is passing away." Opposed to it is "he who does the will of God," who thereby possesses the eternal life because of which he "abides forever."

16 **(B) Christological: Christ and the Antichrists (2:18–29).** Consideration of the transitory character of the world leads naturally to a statement about its end, which in turn is the occasion of the author's first explicit denunciation of the false teachers who are one sign of the end time.

18. *it is the last hour:* Similar expressions occur throughout the NT; in Jn the equivalent term is "the last day." Jewish eschatology expected a period of distress to precede the coming of the Messiah and the last times. In Christian eschatology a great change has been effected by the death and resurrection of Christ: The Messiah has come but will also come again, and the intervening period is that of the last times. *Antichrist comes:* The term, which can mean either "one who opposes Christ [Messiah]" or "one who replaces Christ," occurs only in 1–2 Jn, but a similar expression "pseudo Christs" is found in Mt 24:23f. and Mk 13:21f. Paul refers to the same figure under different terms (2 Thes 2:3–8), as does Ap 13; 17:7–14. The author refers, therefore, to a conception known to his readers as part of the common primitive Christian revelation. To what extent he has modified or interpreted this conception, if he has done so, cannot be determined. Though Paul appears to speak of a single eschatological "Antichrist," his meaning is not certain, especially in view of the fact that his descriptive language is largely borrowed from OT types (Ez 28:2; Dn 11:36, etc.); the "Antichrist" figure of the Syn and Ap certainly implies a collectivity of persons. *many Antichrists have arisen:* Whether the author is reinterpreting or merely reproducing the common Christian belief, it is clear that by "Antichrist" he understands any and all of the false teachers who afflict the Church in this "last hour." *it is the last hour:* The author doubtless shares the common persuasion of the early Church that the time of the parousia would not be long in coming. However, he is less concerned with the parousia than with the present state of the Church, which, whatever its prolongation, is a period of anticipation in which the last times have already begun (cf. "the hour is coming, and now is" of Jn 4:23; 5:25). **19.** *but they were not of us:* The false teachers who have separated themselves from the Church never truly shared in the Church's life of God. The author speaks of this as a self-evident fact to which Christian experience must testify. Apostasy is its own proof that the apostate never possessed the spirit of Christianity. **20–21.** *you have an anointing from the Holy One:* In contrast to the apostates, the faithful Christians have received the gift of God's Spirit. Here "anointing" is an OT figure for reception of the Spirit of God (1 Sm 16:13; Is 61:1), but it is not clear that the author intends a personal reference to the Holy Spirit. Neither is it clear whether the "Holy One" is Christ or God the Father. The vagueness of this language is in contrast to the sharp triadic formulations of the Fourth Gospel. *thus you all know:* Knowledge is the gift of the Spirit (Is 11:2); it is the function of the Spirit to lead Christians into all truth (Jn 14:26; 16:13–15; see also comment on Jn 1:14). In union with God's Spirit, true Christians can recognize truth for what it is and falsehood for what it is and know that the Antichrists have no share with them. (For another interpretation of this anointing, where it is an anointing by faith with the oil of revelation rather than by the Holy Spirit, see I. de la Potterie, *Bib* 40 [1959] 12–69.)

17 **22.** Another specific instance of false teaching is mentioned. It is clear that by the formula "Jesus is the Christ" the author does not mean simply the fulfillment by Jesus of the OT and Jewish expectation of a messiah. "Christ" here has its full sense as the preferred NT designation of Jesus, whose words and deeds had proclaimed him the divine Savior of mankind (Acts 2:36; Rom 1:4). To deny that Jesus is Christ in this sense is to "deny the Father and the Son," to reject the divine filiation that is at the very heart of Christianity. **23.** Neither is this filiation merely an abstract doctrine; to reject it is to cut oneself off from the only means of knowing God, because it is only through the Son that the Father has completely revealed himself (cf. Jn 1:18; 5:23; 10:30; 14:6–9; 15:23). **24–25.** The safeguard of the true Christian who would avoid the dire consequences of this false teaching is to hold firmly to the teaching received through the apostolic preaching. *what you heard from the beginning:* See 2:7. Adhering to the orthodox faith, one may be sure of receiving "the promise which he has promised you, eternal life." The author returns to the more customary perspective of futurist eschatology in relation to the work of salvation. **26–27.** *these things I have written you:* The reference is doubtless to this entire section, from v. 18 on. Forewarned against false doctrine, the true Christian will maintain his unity with the Church, in which the guidance of the Spirit ("anointing," see comment on vv. 20–21) will guarantee that "you have no need that anyone teach you." The doctrine of Christ, clarified by the Spirit, makes any pretended "gnosis" of other teachers superfluous and, if opposed by it, pernicious. The author can only repeat what he has said: "As [*the Spirit*] has taught you, remain in him" (i.e., in Christ, cf. v. 28). Adherence to the teaching that was "from the beginning" is the only means of preserving life in Christ. **28–29.** *assurance...at his appearance:* This is in turn the guarantee we shall have. There is a play on words (*parrēsia: parousia*, only here in the Johannine writings). The confident access to God, the true freedom that is the message of the Gospel (cf. Jn 8:31–38), is the safeguard of the Christian in the day of Christ's return in judgment. *if you know that he is just:*

See 2:1. *everyone who practices justice has been born of him:* The grounds for having confidence in the just judgment of God that will accompany the return of Christ is the Christian's consciousness of his participated sonship, a fact that is proved by his obedience to the law of Christ (cf. 2:3–11). This verse also introduces the theme of the next major section.

18 **(III) Living As Children of God (3:1–4:6).** The following verses retrace the steps of the preceding section, developing the same doctrine in somewhat different words and figures. Again there is an exhortation followed by a Christological enunciation.

(A) Exhortation (3:1–24). Another fundamental Johannine doctrine, that of the Christian's sonship with God (cf. Jn 1:12), forms the basis for this exhortation.

(a) LIVING AS CHILDREN OF GOD (3:1–3). **1.** *what great love the Father has given us:* In the truest and most absolute sense, God's gift of love has been the gift of his only Son as Savior of the world (cf. Jn 3:16). It is this gift that has made it possible "that we be called children of God." *and we are:* Sonship with God can be considered both an eschatological fulfillment (cf. Rom 5:2; 8:23) and, as it is here, a present reality. *therefore the world...did not know him:* This relation to God is shown in the attitude of the world (see comments on 2:12–17), which accords the same treatment to the disciples that it accorded the Master (cf. Jn 14:22–24; 17:25). **2.** The relation between this realized eschatology and that which is to come is now brought out. The Christian is now the child of God, yet there is a fulfillment toward which he looks, in which his configuration to God will be completed. *we know that when he appears we shall be like him, for we shall see him as he is:* The second "him" is doubtless God; the formulations of 1 Jn continue to be vague. The image of God manifested to the Christian in this life is seen through a medium, through faith (cf. Col 1:12; Jn 1:17f.; 14:9; Heb 1:3, etc.). The vision of God for which the Christian is destined, however, is much more intimate and immediate (cf. 1 Cor 13:12; 2 Cor 3:18). Possessing this vision, the Christian will indeed be like Christ, whose relation to God is unique (cf. Jn 6:46; Mt 11:27 par.). **3.** As yet, this vision is a hope, the reality of which is shown in the Christian's striving for virtue (cf. 2 Cor 7:1). The Christian life of virtue is the earnest ot eternal life with God, since by it the Christian already begins to live that life, imitating him who is pure.

19 (b) AVOIDING SIN (3:4–10a). **4.** Opposed to the order of divine purity is the order of sin. *everyone who works sin also works lawlessness:* "Lawlessness" (*anomia*) is a term with an eschatological flavor, frequently associated with the activity of the Antichrist (cf. 2 Thes 2:3–8; *Didache* 16:4); probably, therefore, the author is repeating the thought of 2:18 above (cf. I. de la Potterie, *NRT* 78 [1956] 785–97; he prefers the translation "iniquity" to "lawlessness"). **5–6.** Sin makes fellowship with God and Christ an impossibility, since it was "that he might take away sins" (cf. Jn 1:29) that Christ was sent into the world by God. *everyone who abides in him does not sin:* The author is not saying, of course, that sin is an impossibility for the Christian (cf. 1:8–10); rather, he states just the contrary: When a Christian sins he ceases to have that intimacy with God which alone gives meaning and reality to his Christian profession (cf. 2:4). **7–8.** Contrary to the false teaching that the author is opposing, righteousness does not consist in a mere religious profession, a Gnostic state of mind that renders one's deeds irrelevant. The only righteous person is the one who imitates the righteousness of Christ. Sinfulness is the work of the devil, whose works Christ came to destroy. *the devil is a sinner from the beginning:* As in Jn 8:44, the reference is doubtless to the beginning of salvation history, as told in the story of the fall of man in Gn 3. **9.** *whoever has been born of God...he cannot sin, for he has been born of God:* See v. 6 above; the present statement reiterates the former in stronger terms. *because his seed abides in him:* The "seed" of God may be understood as Christ himself (cf. Gal 3:16), but more probably is the Spirit (cf. 3:24; 4:13; note also 2:20,27). The fact that the Christian shares the divine life of God makes sin an impossibility to the extent that he maintains this unity. **10a.** Virtue and sin, therefore, and not a profession unrelated to works, are what distinguish the children of God from those of the devil.

20 (c) THE COMMANDMENT OF LOVE (3:10b–24). As before (cf. 2:9), the work that above all proves the reality of the Christian commitment is the fulfillment of the Lord's supreme law of charity.

10b–11. *the message which you heard from the beginning:* See comment on 2:7–8. **12.** The antithesis of brother-love is epitomized in the biblical example of Cain (Gn 4:3–8), the first murderer. *his works were evil:* Cain was already a classic example of lack of faith and evil deeds, an example that was elaborated in Jewish tradition and passed from it into the NT (cf. Heb 11:4; Jude 11). **13–15.** The memory of Cain, who slew his righteous brother, should serve to explain the attitude of the world toward the faithful Christian: Cain and the world are instruments of Satan, the ultimate author of their murderous work (cf. Jn 8:44). The Christian, however, knows that he has "passed from death into life" (cf. Jn 5:24) by the touchstone of his fidelity to the supreme law of charity. *everyone who hates his brother is a murderer:* This Christian extension of the prohibition against murder is that of the Lord, according to Mt 5:21f. **16–18.** *in this...lay down our lives for the brethren:* Part of the newness of the commandment of Christian charity consists in the model that the Christian has been given to imitate—nothing less than the selfless love of Christ himself (cf. 2:7f.; see comment on Jn 13:34). Neither can this duty of love be fulfilled merely by profession and good intentions; it must be proved by deeds. *who sees his brother in need:* Indeed, a concrete act of charity in a relatively inferior matter such as almsgiving may be a more valid proof of this love than the disposition, which may be inefficacious in practice, to lay down one's life. *the love of God:* The genitive is probably qualitative, i.e., the love that has God for its source and model.

21 **19–20.** *by this we shall know:* The author doubtless refers to the preceding, the test of charity. *we are of the truth:* For "truth," see comment on Jn 1:14; the expression here is equivalent to the "of God" of v. 10, "truth" being used because of the conclusion ("in truth") of v. 18. *in his presence we shall set our heart at rest:* The "heart" (*kardia*) in this context is roughly the equivalent of our "conscience" (see F. Baumgärtel and J. Behm, *ThDNT* 3, 605–14). *whenever our heart condemns us:* Whenever we are conscious of having sinned, we may take confidence from our consciousness of being "of the truth." *God is greater than our heart and knows all things:* The omniscient God who knows us far better than our own conscience is rich in mercy to forgive one who is truly his own (cf. C. Spicq, *Bib* 40 [1959] 915–27). **21–22.** If, however, we are not conscious of having sinned, so much the more will we be confident of God's favor. *whatever we ask:* See comment on Jn 14:12f.; 16:23; cf. Jn 9:31; Mk 11:24. As in the Gospel passages, the efficacy of this prayer is conditioned on Christian fidelity: "keeping his commandments and doing what is pleasing in his sight." **23–24.** The commandments are summed up in faith and love, which is to be the theme of the final part of the epistle. (For "the name," see comment on Jn 1:12.) Obedience to the commandments guarantees continued communion with God (cf. 2:17). A further guarantee of the divine presence is the possession of the Holy Spirit, here mentioned explicitly for the first time (see comment on 2:20,27; 3:9).

22 **(B) Christological: Christ and the Spirit of Truth (4:1–6).** The mention of the Spirit brings the author back again to the heretical teachings falsely claimed to be of divine inspiration. The possession of the Spirit of God can also be an illusion.

1. *do not believe every spirit:* The spiritual phenomena that appear in the Church must not be taken at face value, for deceit and delusion are always possible. The phenomena must be carefully examined in order to be sure that they do not support false prophecy (cf. 1 Thes 5:21; 1 Cor 12:10; *Didache* 11:8). **2–3.** The criterion by which true prophecy is to be discerned is analogous to that proposed by Paul in 1 Cor 12:3; both in the OT and in the NT it is recognized that prophecy in order to be true must be consistent with known revelation (→ Prophetic Lit, 12:8). *confess that Jesus Christ has come in the flesh:* In opposition to an incipient Docetism, the reality of the incarnation must be maintained as a central affirmation of Christianity, apart from which Christ cannot be considered our Savior (see Jn 1:14; 6:51; → Johannine Theology, 80:21–22). *every spirit which dissolves Christ:* Although it has little support in the Gk mss., this reading, attested by Fathers of the 2nd cent., is to be preferred to the "every spirit which does not confess Jesus" of the Gk codices. By "dissolve" the author may mean nothing more than "destroy": To deny the reality of the incarnation would make the person of Jesus meaningless (→ 23 below). *the spirit of the Antichrist:* See 2:18f. As before, the author identifies the false teaching in the Church as a sign of the last times. **4–6.** The author repeats the thought of 2:20–29; 2:12–17, using some of his familiar contrasts. *you have overcome them:* The false prophets of 4:1. The theme of the two spirits of truth and error and the expression "test the spirit" (cf. v. 1) appear in the QL (1QS 3:18f.; 5:20–24; 6:17–21), though in a nonpersonal, ethical sense.

23 **Note on the False Teaching of 1 Jn.** "The exact nature of the false teaching which is denounced in these Epistles has been much disputed, and is still a matter of controversy. The opponents have been held to be Jews, or Judaizing Christians, or Gnostics, Judaizing or heathen, or some particular sect of Gnostics, Basilides, Saturninus, Valentinus or Cerinthus. Some have supposed the chief error denounced to be Docetism, others Antinomianism" (A. E. Brooks). It should be evident that the errors envisaged by 1 Jn have some points in common with all or most of the heresies mentioned. Unfortunately, however, the epistle never deals with these errors professedly, but only by allusion. They appear to have been of two kinds, Christological and moral. The Christological ones involved a denial of Jesus as Christ, that is, a denial of the right relation between the Father and his Son (2:22), a denial that Jesus Christ had come in the flesh (4:2), a "dissolving" of Christ by which the reality of the redemption was called in question (4:3; 1:7; cf. 5:6). Some form of Docetism seems to be involved, or a species of Gnosticism like that of Cerinthus (end of 1st cent.), who distinguished between Jesus and Christ (the "dissolve" of 4:3?), holding that Jesus became possessed by the Christ at the time of his baptism, only to regain his human personality at the time of the passion (cf. "the water and the blood" of 5:6). However, there are aspects of Cerinthus' teaching and of other weird doctrines mentioned above that find no echo in 1 Jn.

Furthermore, the moral errors opposed by 1 Jn do not necessarily have a connection with the Christological. Claiming fellowship with God that is belied by one's moral conduct (1:6; 2:4,9) need imply nothing more esoteric than religious formalism. The denial of the possibility or the fact of sin on the part of a Christian (1:8,10) does point to a theory of religion that could have been of Gnostic origin; analogies can be found among the false teachings that afflicted the Pauline churches (cf. 1 Cor 6:12–20; Gal 5:13–26, etc.), manifesting itself as antinomianism.

What is certain is that the errors were heresies within the Church, not the propaganda of hostile Jews as has sometimes been held. Neither was it a case of straightforward Judaizing Christianity. However, it is not necessary to conclude that there was a single system of thought responsible for all these errors. In part they reflect the temptations to which religion has always been prone, and in part they reflect the tendencies that developed into various of the Christological heresies of the 1st and 2nd cents. As we know from Acts and the Pauline epistles, both the paganism and the Judaism of Asia Minor were subject to many strange influences within the vast Hellenistic syncretism. The same religious curiosity that worked to the advantage of the Christian mission also proved hospitable to heresy and syncretism, which afflicted the Church from the beginning.

(Škrinjar, A., "Errores in epistola I Jo impugnati," *VD* 41 [1963] 60–72.)

24 **(IV) Love and Faith (4:7–5:12).** Thus far the epistle has stressed faith in Christ and love of the brethren as the twin signs of fellowship with God. In this final major section the two signs are shown in their relationship to each other. If 1 Jn in general manifests a doctrine that is less developed than that of the Gospel (→ 4–5 above), a possible exception can be made in respect to the teaching of 1 Jn on love (cf. T. Barrosse, *TS* 18 [1957] 538–59). This fact readily finds its explanation, of course, in the existential situation of the epistle.

(A) Love in Relation to Faith (4:7–21). The true nature of love is first brought out by showing its basis in faith. It is not the love that is natural to man, but has been revealed by God and is perceived by faith.

7–8. *love is of God:* The motive of love is the origin of love in God; whoever loves, thereby proves that he has his own origin in the same God with whom he has fellowship: he is "born of God." *God is love:* Love not only comes from God as from a source, it is itself the very essence of God. It is this that deepens the sense in which it may be said that the one who loves knows God and is born of him. **9–10.** *by this fact, the love of God has been revealed in us:* The love of which the author speaks is the essence of God as he has made it known to men through revelation. The supreme event in which he has revealed his love has been his mission of his Son into the world to be its Savior (cf. Jn 3:16). *the love consists in this...that he loved us:* This love has been wholly gratuitous on God's part, unmotivated by any worthiness on the part of man (cf. Rom 5:5–9); it is a love that has a meaning in man only to the extent that it continues the love revealed in God (cf. v. 19). *he sent his Son as a propitiation for our sins:* See 2:2. **11–12.** It is only by continuing this pattern of love as exemplified for us in the supreme events of salvation history that we can "see" God (cf. Jn 1:18). Any other pretended vision of God which does not prove itself by manifesting the love that is the divine life shared with men is illusory.

25 **13.** The proof that we possess this divine life is in the presence of God's Spirit (see comment on 3:24). **14–16.** To this proof, which is a testimony of faith, another testimony of faith must be joined: the acceptance of Jesus in his true character as "Savior of the world" (cf. Jn 4:42). Without the reality of the Christ-event as the exemplification of the divine love, love of brethren is meaningless; joined to this reality, it truly shows forth the divine presence in man (cf. C. Spicq, *RB* 65 [1958] 358–70). Thus we see the relation of faith and love. **17–19.** Along with this love goes confidence in the coming day of judgment (see comment on 2:28–29). *in this:* It is characteristic of the vague language of this epistle that the reference can be to the preceding (and thus love = abiding in God) or to what follows (confidence as the result of love); however, the sense is not materially changed in any case. The confident assurance of sonship with God, of which love is the testimony, should banish all vain fear of God's presence in judgment. **20–21.** *if anyone says...he is a liar:* Again, however, the author must warn against self-deception in this matter. No one can pretend to love God who does not love his brother (see comment on 3:16–18). *therefore we have this commandment from him:* Probably the reference is to Jesus' teaching, which accepted and enlarged on the precept of Dt 6:4f. (Jn 13:34; Mk 12:29–31).

26 (B) Faith in Relation to Love (5:1–12). No real advance is marked in this present section. However, having shown what he means by the love that is rooted in faith, the author now proceeds to expand on the nature of this faith that gives meaning to love.

1–2. If the proof of the love of God consists in the love of one's brethren (4:20), it is no less true that the love of God that consists in obedience to his commandments (v. 3; cf. 2:3f.; 3:22,24) is a sign that one loves his brothers, because this is the greatest and most inclusive of all the commandments. *everyone who believes that Jesus is the Christ:* The love that constitutes us children of God cannot exist apart from true Christian faith. *we love the children of God:* The author speaks of "children of God" rather than "the brethren" in order to stress that this love is a dimension of the love of God. *whoever loves the begetter also loves the one begotten of him:* That is, one of his own kind. **3–4.** The sign of love is obedience to the commandments (cf. Jn 14:15,21). *because everyone who has been born of God overcomes the world:* See comment on 2:13–14; 4:4; the Christian is possessed of the power to overcome all hostile forces that would prevent his obedience to God's commandments. *this is the victory... our faith:* The acceptance of Jesus in his true character (v. 5) is the source of the Christian's power. **5–6.** The significance of this true faith is further clarified by another Christological formulation. *Jesus is the Son of God:* "In power" (cf. Rom 1:4), i.e., Savior, because he "came through water and blood." He was proclaimed Son of God at the beginning of his public ministry in the baptism of John (cf. Mk 1:11 par.), and he accomplished his mission by his bloody sacrifice on the cross. *not in the water only, but in the water and the blood:* Only through his sacrifice did Christ become our Savior (cf. Phil 2:5–11). *because the Spirit is truth:* See comment on Jn 15:26. The Spirit was present at Jesus' baptism (Mk 1:10 par.; Jn 1:32–34) and also continues to witness to the work achieved through Christ by his presence in the Church (cf. Jn 14:17). For the Johannine conception of "witness," see Jn 1:7,15; 4:39; 5:31,36f. **7–8.** *therefore there are three who testify: the Spirit and the water and the blood, and the three make up one:* The author summarizes his thought, noting the unified testimony given by Christ and the Spirit as satisfying legal requirements (Dt 17:6; 19:15), even as Christ himself cited the testimony of himself and his Father (Jn 8:17f.). There is also probably a reference to the event recorded in Jn 19:34f. In keeping with the symbolism of the Gospel (→ Gospel Jn, 63:31) it is not unlikely that there is also an allusion to the sacraments of baptism and the Eucharist, the continuing witness of water, blood, and Spirit in the Church (cf. Jn 3:5; see comment on Jn 2:1–11).

27 Note on the Johannine Comma. Between the words "testify" and "the Spirit" in vv. 7–8 the Sixto-Clementine Vg has this additional text: "in heaven: the Father, the Word, and the Holy Spirit, and these three are one. And there are three who testify on earth: the Spirit...." This is the so-called Johannine comma.

Today the authenticity of this Trinitarian text would hardly be defended by any exegete or critic. It appears in none of the ancient Oriental translations and in no ms. of the Vg prior to AD 800; it is found in only four late Gk codices, where it has been translated from the Latin. Despite the great Trinitarian controversies of the early Christian centuries, it is cited by no Gk or Lat Father before the 4th cent., a fact that almost surely proves that it was not then in existence. The earliest witness to the text is Priscillian (*ca.* AD 380), and it is cited first by one of his disciples, Instantius. It appears to have been a gloss inserted into Spanish or African texts of the OL version of the NT, originally as an allegorical commentary: Spirit = the Father (Jn 4:24), water = the Holy Spirit (Jn 3:5), blood = the Word (Jn 1:14). From the 5th cent. on, it had become incorporated into some of the OL mss.

By a decree of 2 June 1927, the Holy Office clarified an earlier decree that had pronounced in favor of the authenticity of the passage, explaining that the purpose had not been to inhibit the critical study of the text but to safeguard the teaching authority of the Church (*EB* 136; DS 3681–82).

28 9–10. To the witness of the Spirit the author adds the witness of the Father to his Son, the witness to which Jesus appeals so often in Jn's Gospel. If human witness is received, how much more should the witness of God be received. Through faith one receives this witness; willful unbelief is equivalent to calling God a liar, because his witness is rejected. **11–12.** *this is the witness, that God gave us eternal life:* Christian faith is not simply the acceptance of a proposition, but reception of a Person, who brings eternal life (cf. Jn 1:4). *this life is in his Son:* The gift of eternal life that is possessed by faith is not a promise only, but a present reality; therefore, "he who possesses the Son" through faith "also possesses the life" here and now.

29 (V) Conclusion and Summary (5:13–21). The following verses form a conscious conclusion and summation of the epistle. The new topics that are introduced (vv. 16f., 21) enter only incidentally into the letter's main subject.

13. The author summarizes his purpose in writing in a manner reminiscent of the conclusion of the Gospel (Jn 20:31). **14–15.** *this is the confidence we have:* The possession of eternal life of which the author has reassured his readers naturally evokes the thought of the confidence in God to which he has referred before (cf. 2:28; 4:17). In turn, this confidence assures the Christian of an answer to his prayers (cf. 3:21f.). *if we ask anything according to his will, he hears us:* As before, however, it is made clear that fidelity to God's will is the necessary condition of the efficacy of prayer. This condition presupposed, whatever is asked of God has already been given in the asking. **16–17.** A most appropriate prayer for the Christian is for the forgiveness of his brother's sins, that God "may give him life" when he has put himself in danger of eternal death; this prayer serves as a good example of what is "according to his will." The author does not counsel prayer, however, for one who has sinned "unto death," for the presumption is that it is not according to God's will to pardon such a person. *all unrighteousness is sin,* *but there is a sin not unto death:* By a sin "unto death" the author evidently means some extraordinary sin (not necessarily specified in his own mind or in those of his readers) so terrible to contemplate that forgiveness, morally speaking, cannot be expected (cf. Str-B 3, 779). He does not mean simply mortal sin as distinguished from venial sin, for the "sins not unto death" in this context also include mortal sins. It is possible that he has in mind the activity of the "Antichrists" previously mentioned (2:18–29). The NT singles out various sins as being in such a category apart (cf. Mk 3:29 par.; Heb 6:4–8; 10:26–31).

30 **18.** *we know that everyone who is begotten of God does not sin:* The thought that there are sinful brethren must not obscure the fact that sin has no part in the Christian (see comment on 3:9). *the begotten of God keeps him:* This is the reading of the best mss.; however, some mss. (and the Vg) have "begetting" (*gennēsis*) in place of "begotten" (*gennētheis*), and this could well be original, corresponding to the less precise "anointing" and "seed" previously used to designate the Spirit of God. In either case, Christ is undoubtedly meant, just as the Spirit is named in the parallel 3:9. **19–20.** *we know:* Three times in all, these words appear in this conclusion, a magisterial renunciation of all false doctrine. The author reiterates some of the principal affirmations of the epistle. *that we may know the True One:* The eternal life given through Christ has often been called knowledge of God in this epistle (cf. Jn 17:3). *we are in the True One, in his Son Jesus Christ:* Here "True One" may, as it does immediately before, refer to God, or it may be appositional to "his Son." The Christian is, of course, in union with both the Father and the Son. (For the conception of "true," see comment on Jn 1:14.) *he is the true God and eternal life:* Once again, "he" can refer either to the Father or the Son. In favor of its referring to the Son, it may be argued that thus 1 Jn concludes with an explicit affirmation of the divinity of Christ, who is also identified with eternal life as he was at the beginning (1:2); exactly the same procedure is followed in the Gospel (cf. Jn 1:4,18; 20:28). **21.** *little children, guard yourselves from the idols:* The translation is apparently abrupt, and this has caused some to think that the conclusion of the epistle is fragmentary. However, this verse seems instead to be a final adjuration occasioned quite naturally, even though as an afterthought, by the preceding reference to "the true God." The author would almost automatically be reminded of the great pagan world of superstition surrounding the little Christian community. He may also have been thinking of the false teaching that had made inroads in the community itself, for this, too, was a species of idolatry.

COMMENTARY ON 2 JN

31 **1.** *the presbyter:* The use of this term in the Acts and in the epistles of the NT to designate the leaders of local churches is well known. The author evidently is for his addressees the Presbyter par excellence, needing no further introduction (→ Gospel Jn, 63:4). *the Lady Elect:* The content of the epistle makes it sufficiently clear that this is a quasi-poetic designation of some particular church within the Presbyter's jurisdiction; the children of the Lady, therefore, are the members of this church. **2.** *because of the truth which remains in us and will be with us always:* It is the common possession of truth that unites Christians (v. 1). In v. 2 the author is doubtless thinking of the divine presence itself, but whether he refers specifically to Christ (cf. Jn 14:6, etc.) or to the Spirit (cf. Jn 14:17, etc.) is not clear. **3.** *with us will be grace, mercy, peace:* These terms, all of which derive from the covenant vocabulary of the OT, are used frequently in the NT epistles to refer to the relation between God and the Christian. "Mercy" (*eleos*, cf. Gal 6:16; Jude 2; 1 Tm 1:2; 2 Tm 1:2) appears only here in the Johannine writings; it signifies the gratuitous love of God dispensing salvation to unworthy men (cf. Eph 2:4; Ti 3:5; 1 Pt 1:3). For "grace" and "peace," see Jn 1:17; 14:27. The author adds "truth and love," which are key words in 1–3 Jn. *from God the Father and from Jesus Christ the Son of the Father:* The title by which Christ is especially the dispenser of divine grace is stressed in these epistles.

32 **4.** *I rejoiced much to find:* The author uses the conventional thanksgiving (→ NT Epistles, 47:8) to refer to information that has come to him about this church from some unspecified source (cf. 3 Jn 3). *some of your children are walking in truth:* See 1 Jn 1:6f.; cf. 3 Jn 4f.: The church to which the epistle is addressed has been exposed to the false doctrine described in 1 Jn, and some of its members are in danger of being infected by it. However, others have resisted the destructive teaching, and the purpose of this epistle is to encourage further resistance. **5–6.** The safeguard against every evil is in fulfilling the commandment of love, which includes every other commandment. **7.** See 1 Jn 2:18–29; 4:1–6. **8–9.** *that you do not lose what we have worked for:* Anyone who heeds false teaching is liable to lose the "full reward," the eschatological salvation that is Christian hope. *everyone who progresses but does not remain in the teaching of Christ:* "Progress" was probably one of the slogans of the false teachers, implying the superiority of their doctrine. On the contrary, fellowship with God (see 1 Jn 2:23) is only to be achieved by adhering to the true doctrine of Christ and his Church. **10–11.** Hence the heretics are to be shunned completely, and no intercourse is to be had with them. From these verses it appears that the false teachers were not members of this particular church but were itinerant preachers from other communities.

12. Cf. 1 Jn 1:4. This letter is only a summary of what the Presbyter hopes to say in more detail when he is able to visit the church. **13.** *the children of your sister Elect:* The author extends the greetings of the church where he is now resident (in Ephesus?).

COMMENTARY ON 3 JN

33 **1.** *the beloved Gaius:* Cf. 2 Jn 1. The name was a common one, and there is no reason to believe that this Gaius is identical with any other mentioned in the NT. His relation to the Presbyter remains unclarified, but it seems evident that he was chosen as a trustworthy recipient of a letter that would otherwise have been addressed to the church of which he was a member (v. 9). **2–8.** From these verses we can reconstruct the occasion of the letter. Certain Christian missionaries have reported to the Presbyter that they were received with true charity by Gaius even when the authorities of his church refused them hospitality (v. 9f.). The Presbyter writes to commend Gaius for this action and to encourage its continuance, at the same time announcing his intention of coming personally to set matters right. *that you be in good health:* The wish is conventional; however, the missionaries may have reported Gaius to be in poor health. *my children:* It is not certain whether a more personal relation is implied than simply that of all the Christians who are within the Presbyter's jurisdiction. *you will do well:* Similar opportunities for Gaius to co-operate with the work for God undertaken by the missionaries will present themselves in the future. *for the name:* Cf. Acts 5:41. In the schools, Jews spoke of "the Name" rather than pronounce the sacred word Yahweh (cf. Str-B 2, 316f.). Here this usage has been applied to the name of Jesus or Lord (cf. Phil 2:9; Jas 2:7; 1 Jn 2:12).

34 **9.** *I wrote a note to the church:* The church of which Gaius is a member, which is evidently not the church of 2 Jn. Presumably this letter dealt with the reception of the missionaries. *Diotrephes who loves his first place:* The most obvious conclusion is that Diotrephes was the chief presbyter of the church in question and that pride and ambition had caused him to disregard the Presbyter's message and emissaries. **10.** *if I come:* The Presbyter hopes soon to visit the church (cf. v. 14) and exercise his authority over it, both to vindicate his own rights and to rebuke Diotrephes for his unepiscopal inhospitality (cf. 1 Tm 3:2; Ti 1:8). **11.** *do not imitate what is bad:* The Presbyter may understandably have been concerned lest the high position of Diotrephes might cause his bad example to infect even exemplary Christians like Gaius.

12. *witness is borne to Demetrius:* Opposed to the bad example of Diotrephes is the good example of Demetrius, evidently a person known both to Gaius and the Presbyter. It is possible that he was the bearer of this letter. His good qualities are testified to by the whole church, by the truth (Christ? the Spirit? his own Christian conduct?), and by the Presbyter himself. *you know that our witness is true:* Cf. Jn 19:35; 21:24. **13–14.** Cf. 2 Jn 12. **15.** *the friends greet you; greet the friends by name:* This is a conventional ending. "Friends," however, is not a conventional designation for Christians, but refers to those members of the church who are loyal to the Presbyter and oppose Diotrephes.

63

THE GOSPEL ACCORDING TO JOHN

Bruce Vawter, C.M.

BIBLIOGRAPHY

1 Barrett, C. K., *The Gospel According to St. John* (London, 1955). Bernard, J. H., *The Gospel According to St. John* (ICC; N.Y., 1929). Braun, F.-M., *Évangile selon Saint Jean* (*PSB* 10; Paris, 1950); *Jean le théologien et son Évangile dans l'Église ancienne* (EBib; Paris, 1959). Brown, R. E., *The Gospel of St. John and the Johannine Epistles* (NTRG 13; Collegeville, Minn., 1965); *The Gospel According to John* (AB 29; Garden City, N.Y., 1966). Bultmann, R., *TNT* 2, 3–92; *Das Evangelium des Johannes* (Meyer 2; 10th ed.; Göttingen, 1962) Corell, A., *Consummatum est: Eschatology and Church in the Gospel of St. John* (tr. by the Order of the Holy Paraclete; N.Y. 1958). Dodd, C. H., *The Interpretation of the Fourth Gospel* (Cambridge, 1953). Feuillet, A., "Le Quatrième Évangile," R-F 2, 613–83; *Johannine Studies* (Staten Island, N.Y., 1964). Hoskyns, E. C., *The Fourth Gospel* (ed. F. N. Davey; 2nd ed.; London, 1947). Howard, W. F., *The Fourth Gospel in Recent Criticism and Interpretation* (rev. by C. K. Barrett; London, 1955). Howard, W. F. and A. J. Gossip, *The Gospel According to St. John* (*IB;* N.Y., 1952). Lagrange, M.-J., *Évangile selon Saint Jean* (EBib; 8th ed.; Paris, 1948). Lightfoot, R. H., *St. John's Gospel* (ed. C. F. Evans; Oxford, 1956). Menoud, P.-H., "Les études johanniques de Bultmann à Barrett,' *L'Évangile de Jean* (RechBib 3; Louvain, 1958) 11–40. Mollat D. and F.-M. Braun, *L'Évangile et les Épîtres de Saint Jean* (BJ; 2nd ed.; Paris, 1960). Percy, E., *Untersuchungen über den Ursprung der johanneischen Theologie* (Lund, 1939). Richardson, A., *The Gospel According to Saint John* (TBC; London, 1959). Sanders, J. N., *The Fourth Gospel in the Early Church* (Cambridge, 1943). Schnackenburg, R., *The Gospel according to St. John* (Vol. 1; N.Y., 1968). Sidebottom, E. M., *The Christ of the Fourth Gospel* (London, 1961). Smith, D. M., *The Composition and Order of the Fourth Gospel* (New Haven, 1965). Strathmann, H., *Das Evangelium nach Johannes* (NTD 4; 2nd ed.; Göttingen, 1955). Thüsing, W., *Die Erhöhung und Verherrlichung Jesu im Johannesevangelium* (NTAbh 21/1–2; Münster, 1960). Westcott, E. F., *The Gospel According to St. John* (London, 1958). Wikenhauser, A., *Das Evangelium nach Johannes* (RNT 4; 3rd ed.; Regensburg, 1961). Wiles, M. F., *The Spiritual Gospel: The Interpretation of the Fourth Gospel in the Early Church* (Cambridge, 1960).

F-B, 134–75. *IPLCG* 331–70. Guthrie, *NTI* 3, 212–320. R-F, *INT* 604–67. Wik, *NTI* 277–320.

INTRODUCTION

2 **(I) Authorship.** The earliest witness to the authorship of the Fourth Gospel is Irenaeus of Lyons, writing *ca.* AD 180, who tells us that it was produced at Ephesus by John the disciple of the Lord (*Adv. haer.* 3.1, 1; *PG* 7.844). Irenaeus appears to have based his testimony on his recollection of the teaching of Polycarp, the bishop of Smyrna, whom he had heard as a young man; and Polycarp, Irenaeus avers, had known the apostle John himself (*Ep. ad Flor.*, in Eusebius, *HE* 5.20, 4; *PG* 20.485). Polycrates, the bishop of Ephesus, writing *ca.* AD 190 to Pope Victor, confirms that John the apostle had lived and died in Ephesus, though he does not directly mention the Gospel (*HE* 3.31, 3 and 5.24, 3f.; *PG* 20.280, 493). The Anti-Marcionite Prologue of the Roman Church, from the second half of the 2nd cent., cites a work of Papias of Hierapolis (*ca.* AD 130) in favor of authorship by John the apostle. Irenaeus, the Prologue, and other ancient writings speak of Papias as having known the Apostle, but Papias himself in a fragment of his work preserved by Eusebius makes no such claim; he did claim to be reliably informed about the apostles by immediate disciples of the Lord (*HE* 3.39, 3f.; *PG* 20.297).

The testimony of Irenaeus is corroborated by various other witnesses of the 2nd and 3rd cents. and would appear to have been the common belief of the Church at the time when Irenaeus wrote. Neither does the tradition appear to have been seriously contradicted by any other in ancient times. Heretical groups that impugned Johannine authorship of the Gospel did so because they rejected its doctrine, not because they had any alternative information about its origin. The fact that no writer older than Irenaeus mentions John's residence at Ephesus does not, of course, contradict Irenaeus' positive testimony. Neither does there seem to have been, as some modern authors have thought, a genuine tradition represented in documents from the 5th cent. and afterward, according to which John the apostle suffered an early martyrdom in

Jerusalem along with his brother James. This conclusion has been based partially on a misunderstanding and partially on testimony that is demonstrably unreliable (see Wik, *NTI* 288f.; J. H. Bernard, *The Gospel*, xxxvii–xlv).

3 Irenaeus and Polycrates identify John the apostle as "the disciple whom Jesus loved," "who reclined on his breast at the Last Supper" (Jn 13:23). This unnamed disciple, who is also mentioned in 19:26f.; 20:2–9 and is probably identical with the anonymous disciple of 1:35–42; 18:15f., is identified in 21:20–24 as the authoritative witness standing behind this Gospel (cf. also 19:35). There seems to be no doubt that John, the son of Zebedee, is meant: No other figure in Jn or the Syn tradition corresponds to what the evidence requires, whereas John does.

Sufficient indirect corroboration can be found in the Gospel itself to confirm the tradition of Johannine authorship. The Gospel claims to rest on eyewitness testimony (19:35), and in various ways it shows this dependence on one who stood outside the Syn tradition. That person was, quite obviously, a Jew who was familiar with the Palestinian scene. Places and locations not mentioned in the Syn are precisely specified in Jn, among them the Pool of Bethesda (5:2) and the Lithostrotos (19:13), where archaeological investigations seem to have confirmed the accuracy of the Johannine descriptions. The nomenclature of the Fourth Gospel, especially its use of personal names, has been shown from ossuary inscriptions predating the Jerusalem of AD 70 to reflect the Judean scene of the time of Jesus (cf. W. F. Albright, *AP* 243–49). Whatever is to be said of the Aram substratum of the Gospel (→ 9 below), at the very least it must be said that Jn betrays an Aram origin of some kind, written or oral, i.e., the language of a Palestinian Jew (see the evidence summarized in C. K. Barrett, *The Gospel*, 5–11). Throughout the Gospel there are countless details, such as names and descriptions, that point to the presence of a firsthand witness. To the claim that all these may have simply been invented to lend verisimilitude to the story, we can only reply that this has not proved to be the case in those instances where the information can be verified archaeologically or by other means. Far outdistancing all the previous evidence for a Palestinian origin of the Johannine material, however, has been the contribution made by the QL, to which we must return below.

If Jn's Gospel is the work of a Palestinian Jew who was an eyewitness of its events, we have every reason to affirm that the author was who the Gospel itself and constant tradition claim him to have been, John the apostle, the son of Zebedee.

4 **(II) The Literary Question.** No theory of Johannine authorship, however, can afford to ignore the considerations imposed by literary criticism. These must affect the relationship we can establish between the apostle and the canonical Gospel.

Christian antiquity was unanimous in ascribing the Fourth Gospel to John. The same testimony, with rare exceptions, also credited John with the authorship of the Johannine letters and the Apocalypse. At the same time, even in antiquity there were reservations in this affirmation. Dionysius of Alexandria, writing before AD 264, did not believe that the Gospel and Ap could have the same author; as he considered the Gospel to be the work of John the apostle, he insisted that Ap must be from another hand (in Eusebius, *HE* 7.25; *PG* 20.697). Dionysius indeed believed Ap to be the work of a pious and inspired man; his rejection of Johannine authorship was not based on any prejudice against this work, but on an analysis and comparison of the texts by a man who knew Greek well. Eusebius, who also doubted that the Gospel and Ap were by the same hand, may have had as his primary reason the uncertainty about the canonical status of Ap (*HE* 3.25; *PG* 20.269). In his citation of Papias, noted above, he seized upon the fact that Papias distinguished two Johns of the apostolic age among those to whom he was tributary for his doctrine, John the disciple of the Lord and John the Presbyter (cf. 2 Jn 1; 3 Jn 1). John the Presbyter, thought Eusebius, might well be the author of Ap. Much later, Jerome also harked back to this idea, when he attributed 2–3 Jn to John the Presbyter (*De Viris Illustr.* 9; *PL* 23.623f.).

5 Whether there was ever a John the Presbyter distinct from the Apostle and resident at Ephesus at the same time is still the subject of scholarly debate. It should be evident, however, that although Christian antiquity dealt, as we do, with Jn, 1–3 Jn, and Ap as a corpus related to John the apostle, it was by no means in agreement with regard to John's *literary* authorship of the corpus. Our earliest witness, Irenaeus, does not say that John actually wrote the Gospel, but rather that he published it (*exedōke*). Similarly, the Anti-Marcionite Prologue states that the Gospel was "manifested" and "given" by John while he was yet alive, and was *written* at his dictation by his disciple Papias (!). The Muratorian Canon of Rome, which admittedly combines some legendary themes in speaking of the origin of the Gospel, may also have preserved an authentic tradition in its supposition that the work was one of collaboration between John and others. The Gospel itself (21:24) indicates that others besides the beloved disciple had a part in its presentation to the Christian world, presumably after John's death.

6 Modern criticism has, in general, followed the lead of Dionysius of Alexandria and holds it as morally certain that Ap and the Fourth Gospel could not have been written by the same person. Although it is easily possible to exaggerate the differences between the two works and to minimize their undoubted affinities, and although Ap belongs to a distinct literary tradition that explains many of its peculiarities, it remains hardly credible that the same person's vocabulary and style could alter so radically from one work to the other (see the evidence summarized in Bernard, *The Gospel*, lxiv–lxviii). The Greek of the Gospel, although not the best in the NT, correctly reproduces the common language of the time, and both in the epistles and in Jn it is found in a style that is altogether distinctive. The Greek of Ap is of a quite different order, rough, frequently ungrammatical, and much more heavily in debt to Semitic idiom. It is, in short, the kind of Greek that one might antecedently expect a Galilean fisherman like John to have written. But if this is so, it appears to be an inescapable conclusion that for the writing of his Gospel and epistles John employed a disciple-scribe whose Greek was superior to his own. This is not intrinsically unlikely—it is, in fact, entirely in keeping with the practice of the time—and in no way does it contradict the tradition of Johannine authorship. John the apostle still remains the witness whose testimony and doctrine we find in this Gospel.

7 **(III) Integrity.** Another reason for supposing a disciple to be responsible for the writing of the Gospel in its finished form comes from the further analysis of the Gospel itself. Not only the attestation in 21:24 but also the entire ch. 21 seems to be the appendix to a work that had already been apparently concluded in 20:30f. Various other passages appear to have been inserted later on, breaking a continuity that had already been established. The shepherd-discourse in 10:1–18, for example, is continued in v. 26, though the intervening verses suppose the passing of several months. Here and there individual verses or short sections, and at least once two entire chapters (5 and 6), give the impression of being transposed or otherwise misplaced in the text. Occasionally, statements are made that have the air of correcting or explaining others: cf. 3:26 with 4:2. The discourses of Jesus, the all-important element of Jn, sometimes appear to have been unaccountably interrupted and then resumed, sometimes repeat themselves to the point of prolixity, and sometimes merge without warning into the commentary of the Evangelist, so that it is impossible to distinguish the one from the other.

8 The explanation that best accounts for these and other unevennesses is—as the commentary will clearly show—that the Gospel was dictated over a period of time and had probably not been completely set in order at the time of the apostle's death. F.-M. Braun has estimated that a scribe of the period would rarely have exceeded a hundred lines of text in a day. We can readily imagine John supplying his scribe with his daily quota of material, not always in a consecutive order, sometimes returning to former episodes which he wanted to qualify or to which he had something to add, sometimes enlarging on what he had previously said, and often enough, as he recalled the words of the Lord mingling with them the fruits of his own inspired meditations given him by the Spirit. Though the written Gospel existed in its basic outline at the time of his death, John had not edited it, and doubtless there were some parts about whose precise location or relation John's disciples were not sure. These parts were inserted or added on, possibly at times at the expense of some duplication, wherever they had a logical relevance, without close attention to chronology or to the continuity of the context. The Gospel was concluded, therefore, by an additional account of the resurrection appearances, despite the tentative conclusion that had already been made in 20:30f., and the disciple-editors affixed their own conclusion in 21:24.

Such an explanation is admittedly hypothetical, but it squares with known facts and offers a reasonable accounting for the peculiarities of the Fourth Gospel. If John's Gospel is not precisely "the seamless robe of Christ" that D. F. Strauss called it, it is nevertheless obvious to most scholars that it is, throughout, the work of one mind. Bultmann stands virtually alone in professing to discern in it a combination of independent sources, one of revelation discourses (*Offenbarungsreden*), another of miracle accounts (*Semeia-Quelle*), and a passion narrative, which have been integrated by an unknown redactor-genius. Neither does it seem probable, as has been maintained often with ingenious reconstructions, that the phenomena noted above are to be explained on the basis of extensive dislocations occasioned in the transmission of the text. No trace of such a happening can be discerned in the NT mss., whose age in respect to the authorship of Jn leave the matter in little doubt.

9 An associated question is that of the original language of the Gospel. In varying degrees of emphasis, competent modern scholars, among them C. F. Burney, C. C. Torrey, M. Black, M.-E. Boismard, have insisted that the Gospel betrays an Aram origin. Not only does it abound in parataxis (avoidance of subordination; sentences continually joined together with "and") and asyndeton (omission of conjunctions between clauses) along with other characteristically Aram forms of expression, but the mistranslations that can be perceived in various cases, when translated back into Aramaic, allegedly yield a better sense that was found originally. But as we cannot enter into this question in detail, suffice it to say that the undeniable Aram influences do not seem to transcend what we would expect of a Gk work whose author thought more naturally in Aramaic and who incorporated into this work words (the discourses of Jesus) that had originally been uttered in Aramaic. To this it may be added that parataxis and asyndeton, rare in literary Greek, were not uncommon in the spoken language—and in our hypothesis, John gave the Gospel orally to his scribe.

(Boismard, M.-E., "L'importance de la critique textuelle pour établir l'origine araméenne du Quatrième Évangile," *L'Évangile de Jean* [Rech Bib 3; Louvain, 1958] 41–57.)

10 **(IV) Date and Place of Origin.** In the heyday of 19th- and early 20-cent. liberal criticism, Jn's Gospel was confidently ascribed to the middle of the 2nd cent. or even later. Christian tradition, we have seen, had consistently regarded it as a work of John's old age and consequently as a kind of final testimony from the apostolic period. The critical view, however, was based on the supposed recognition of influences in Jn that were not present in the apostolic age, but that came into being only in a later Christianity. The late dating of Jn, as a result, was bound up with the conviction that the Gospel could have had at best a negligible historical value and certainly could not be in fact the work of an apostolic eyewitness. It was against these extreme positions that the Pontifical Biblical Commission issued its "responses" of 29 May 1907 on the authorship and historical value of Jn (*EB* 187–89; cf. the propositions of *Lamentabili* § 16–18 [*EB* 207–9]; → Church Pronouncements, 72:18, 25, 28).

11 For reasons that will be made clearer below, such views could hardly be called critical today. It is now recognized that "the thought content of Jn's Gospel reflects the Jewish background of John the Baptist and Jesus, not that of later times" (W. F. Albright, *Religion in Life* 21 [1952] 550). Furthermore, its use by Ignatius of Antioch (probably), by Justin Martyr, and by the Gnostics in the first half of the 2nd cent., together with actual ms. evidence from the middle of the same century, make it very difficult for anyone today to suggest a date later than the end of the 1st cent. Many critics believe that this date should be anticipated by a decade or more.

The strongest and most ancient tradition connects the Gospel with Ephesus; but the *Acts of Ignatius*, a document of uncertain age and reliability, associates John with Antioch (*PG* 5.984). The two traditions are not necessarily at variance, since John may very well have lived in Antioch before coming to Ephesus, and the affinity between Jn and the writings of Ignatius may be due to the latter's knowledge of John's oral rather than his written Gospel. In more recent times Alexandria has been proposed as the source of Jn because of the Gospel's early influence in Egypt and because our oldest mss. have come from this country. However, granting that the Gospel is older than was once thought and taking into account that the climate of Egypt is uniquely favorable to the preservation of ancient documents, there is no reason to suggest that the Gospel originated in a place that has left no trace in tradition.

12 **(V) The Johannine Background.** Part of the celebrated "Johannine question" consists in the world of ideas that is supposed in the Gospel. To anyone who has read the OT and has some acquaintance with the Judaism represented in the rabbinical and apocalyptic writings of the intertestamental period (→ Apocrypha, 68), the Syn world is immediately familiar; Jn, however, seems at first glance to have an entirely different character. Though set in Palestine and representing Jesus as the fulfillment of OT expectation, Jn appears to be much more at home in the atmosphere of Gnosticism, Hermeticism, and other forms of Hellenistic speculation. Nouns like *logos*, "life," and "light," adjectives like "true," and verbs like "know," all used in esoteric and pregnant senses, the dualism implied in "light and darkness," "spirit and flesh," all these have practically no echo in the Syn tradition; they are the commonplaces of the syncretistic "wisdom" of Hellenism. These Johannine characteristics are common both to the narrative and the discourses of the Gospel. The Johannine Christ, it seems, differs radically from the Jesus of the Syn. In Jn we find no parables, no simple moral instruction, no controversy on the terrain of law and practice that caused the people of Galilee to hail Jesus as a prophet. Instead we have allegories, involved symbolism, a technical and subtle vocabulary, and a series of magisterial pronouncements, "I am...the bread (6:35,41,48,51);...the light (8:12);...the door (10:7,9);...the shepherd (10:11);...the resurrection (11:25);...the way (14:6);...the vine" (15:1,5). All these characteristics can be readily duplicated in the "revelations" of the "saviors" of Hellenistic religions (see C. H. Dodd, *Interpretation*, 10–53).

13 Such characteristics are appealed to in the "Gnostic" explanation of the world of Johannine ideas that is still encountered in some scholars' interpretations of Jn, particularly in that of R. Bultmann. The Evangelist has been presumed to have done for Christianity what Philo of Alexandria had done for Judaism, that is to say, to have translated it into Gk philosophy. The link between the Hellenistic speculation and the originally Jewish origins of Christianity has been found by some authors (R. Bultmann, S. Schulz to some degree) in Mandaeism, a strange sect which still survives in Iraq, combining Jewish, Christian, Muslim, and pagan strains of thought in a kind of theosophical system, and which gives some evidence of having had a Palestinian origin.

14 That Jn possesses considerable verbal similarity with the documents of these alien ways of thought is undeniable. The evangelist has certainly taken account of the Hellenistic milieu in which he lived and in which his Gospel was intended to circulate. Does the relationship go any deeper than this? Most scholars (e.g., E. Percy) replied in the negative, and recent developments have vindicated their judgment.

15 Since 1946 we have for the first time been in a position to evaluate Gnosticism from its own sources. In that year a complete Gnostic library was discovered at Chenoboskion in southern Egypt, including many works previously known only by reference in the writings of the Church Fathers, affording virtually a complete dossier on Gnosticism (cf. V. R. Gold, *BA* 15 [1952] 70–88). From these writings it has become clear how distinct the worlds of Jn and the Gnostics are, and how unthinkable Jn's dependence on them really is. The Gnostics, aided by the affinities they discovered in the Johannine vocabulary, assimilated Jn into their system as they assimilated so much else, and it was this assimilation that produced the Gnosticism rightly regarded by the Fathers as a Christian heresy (see R. E. Brown, *NTS* 9 [1962–63] 155–77).

16 Furthermore, the QL discovered since 1947 has shown that the introduction of dualistic ideas and terminology, and much of the vocabulary peculiar to Jn in the NT, had in fact taken place at least in some parts of Palestinian Judaism long before the coming of Christianity. In other words, the "Gnostic" language of Jn is quite as authentically Jewish and Palestinian as is the language of the Syn, though the two traditions admittedly stress different aspects of contemporary Judaism. Why Jn's Gospel has the stress that it does may be subject to various explanations (→ 17–36 below). What is clear enough, however, is that Jn and the Johannine Christ speak a language that, whatever its ultimate origins, was authentically Jewish in the Palestine of the 1st cent. AD, though they speak it with intonations and with a content unknown to the sectarians of Qumran. Once this is recognized, Jn's literary form ceases to be as esoteric as might at first appear. Jn, too, belongs to the tradition of Israelite historiography, rooted firmly in the events of *Heilsgeschichte*, and with close analogies to the wisdom literature of the OT (→ Johannine Theology, 80:10–11).

(Albright, W. F., "Recent Discoveries in Palestine and the Gospel of St. John," *The Background of the New Testament and its Eschatology* [Fest. C. H. Dodd; Cambridge, 1955] 153–71. Braun, F.-M., "L'arrière-fond judaïque du Quatrième Évangile et la communauté de l'alliance," *RB* 62 [1955] 5–44; "L'Évangile de Saint Jean et les grandes traditions d'Israël," *RTh* 59 [1959] 421–50; *RTh* 60 [1960] 165–84, 325–63. Brown, R. E., "The Qumrân Scrolls and the Johannine Gospel and Epistles," *CBQ* 17 [1955] 403–19, 559–74. Enz, J. J., "The Book of Exodus as a Literary Type for the Gospel of John," *JBL* 76 [1957] 208–15. Mowry, L., "The Dead Sea Scrolls and the Background for the Gospel of John," *BA* 17 [1954] 78–97. Munck, J., "The New Testament and Gnosticism," *Current Issues in New Testament Interpretation* [Fest. O. A. Piper; N.Y., 1962] 224–38. Schulz, S., *Komposition und Herkunft der johanneischen Reden* [BWANT 5/1; Stuttgart, 1960]. Smith, R. H., "Exodus Typology in the Fourth Gospel," *JBL* 81 [1962] 329–42. Young, F. W., "A Study of the Relation of Isaiah to the Fourth Gospel," *ZNW* 64 [1955] 215–32. Ziener, G., "Weisheitsbuch und Johannesevangelium," *Bib* 38 [1957] 396–418; *Bib* 39 [1958] 37–60; "Johannesevangelium und urchristliche Passafeier," *BZ* 2 [1958] 263–74.)

17 **(VI) Jn and the Synoptic Gospels.** Many of the Fathers thought that the obvious differences between Jn and the Syn were to be explained by the Evangelist's intention of supplementing the earlier Gospels. It was to this effect that Clement of Alexandria made his famous statement regarding the "spiritual" nature of Jn (Eusebius, *HE* 6.14, 5–7; *PG* 20.552). With nuances, a similar view is still held by some scholars today, and, like many views long held, it has something to commend it.

18 First of all, it is fairly obvious that John presupposes the Syn *tradition*. He takes it for granted that his readers know who the Twelve are, and therefore gives them no introduction (6:67). He does not mention Jesus' baptism by John the Baptist, but he evidently supposes that the reader knows of this baptism when he records the Baptist's testimony in 1:32–34. In many instances Jn's meaning would be difficult to understand were we not already familiar with the Syn story.

Whether John made use of the *written* Syn is a different question. Probably a majority opinion today would be that he used, or at least had read, Mk's Gospel. At times Jn not only parallels the Marcan order, but also uses expressions peculiar to Mk (cf. C. K. Barrett, *The Gospel*, 34–36; E. K. Lee, *NTS* 3 [1956] 50–58). To this we might add that it is chronologically possible that Mk was already well known in the Christian world for which the Gospel of John was intended. However, other authors are convinced that what is common to Mk and Jn can be explained on the basis of a common oral tradition, the peculiarly Marcan terms included. The evidence for John's use of Mt is quite inconclusive, and here the question is probably to be answered in the negative. Occasional correspondences between Jn and Mt may be explained on the score that John knew an Aram Mt underlying our canonical Gospel (→ Gospel Mt, 43:13–14); but here, of course, we are in the realm of conjecture. The attempt of S. Mender (*NTS* 4 [1958] 282–307) to explain the parallels between Jn and the Syn as being due to the harmonization of both, bypasses the ms. evidence and has found little support.

19 The relation between Jn and Lk is of a peculiar kind that has long interested commentators. Undeniable correspondences exist between the two Gospels with regard to their content and their theology. Many scholars are of the opinion, however, that the dependence is on the part of Lk rather than of Jn, or at least that there is a mutual dependence. The story of the adulteress in 7:53–8:11, though found in most of the mss. of Jn, is Lucan through and through (→ 107 below). The dependence is probably not of one written Gospel on the other, but of one tradition on the other, which implies an association of the two authors in some fashion. Recently, M.-E. Boismard (*RB* 69 [1962] 185–211) has made the interesting suggestion that Luke was among the disciples of John responsible for the Fourth Gospel in its final form, and that as a result some of what we have been accustomed to consider Johannine traits are actually Lucan.

If there are correspondences between Jn and the Syn, however, it is quite obvious that there are many more divergences. Even on the rare occasions when Jn does reproduce a Syn passage, it is usually with a different order or to a different purpose. The many miracles recorded in the Syn find scarcely an echo in the seven miracles of Jn (only two of which appear in the Syn); and there are no exorcisms of Jn. Though Jn's main emphasis is on the discourses of Christ, not a single one of these is to be found in the Syn. The chronology of his public ministry, as it appears in the two traditions, differs radically. The portrayal of Christ and his teaching—the aspect of Jn that even the superficial reader finds in marked contrast to the Syn picture—has already been noted above.

20 In what sense, then, can we agree that John intended to "supplement" the Syn tradition? Not, it would seem, in purely factual matters. Although his Gospel is in no way inferior to the Syn and contains an historical record that deserves to be judged on its own merits, it is doubtful that John consciously attempted to correct the Syn chronology of the public ministry, to supply other statistical information that was lacking there, or to relate the Syn history to his own. Rather, he has simply contented himself with his own testimony to the virtual disregard of the Syn order and selection of events.

In the sense, however, that Clement of Alexandria singled out, Jn has truly intended and accomplished a supplementation of the Syn tradition. The Syn, Clement said, dealt with the *sōmatika* of Christ, but John wrote a Gospel that is *pneumatikon*. It is difficult to translate these words, which do not mean simply "corporeal" or "external" on the one hand and "spiritual" on the other. Clement was fully aware that the Syn also give a "spiritual" view of Christ. What he intended to say, however, is what appears as an obvious fact, that John has intentionally written his Gospel to give a more profoundly theological vision of Christ than was attempted in the Syn tradition. In recognition of this fact, the early Church accorded to John the title "the Theologian."

21 The Syn tradition, as we can see from a comparison of the Syn with such passages as Acts 10:37–43, is a development of the apostolic kerygma, the primitive proclamation of the good news (*euaggelion*, "gospel") of salvation accomplished in Jesus Christ. It is not the kerygma itself, of course, for the Syn are also works of Christian faith intended for Christian readers; it is therefore *didachē*, "teaching," or theology, intended to enlighten the Christian reader in the fuller significance of the kerygma (see D. M. Stanley, *CBQ* 17 [1955] 336–48). Nevertheless, it adheres to the order of the kerygma—an order obviously simplified, synthesized, and schematized for the purposes of preaching—and, to a greater or lesser degree, also to the the kerygmatic representation of the Lord's words and deeds.

22 John goes beyond this. He supposes not only the Syn tradition, but also a generation of Christian reflection on the Gospel. Hence he is able not merely to select from the events of a life that was well known precisely those incidents that would best serve the purpose of his own teaching; he is also able to begin where the Syn leave off in interpreting the significance of the Gospel. The few examples that follow serve as an illustration. In a sense those critics are correct who consider Jn to be a Gnostic Gospel, but the gnosis is entirely Jn's own in his contemplation of the mystery of Christ.

23 (1) Jn is a profoundly ecclesiological Gospel, for all that the word *ekklēsia* does not appear in it even once. Mt's Gospel is self-consciously ecclesiological, representing a deliberate orientation of the Syn kerygma into this aspect of *didachē*, according to which the Kingdom of God that Christ inaugurated is shown to have its realization in the Church. John can and does presuppose all of this. His ecclesiology is of a much subtler kind, truly a "spiritual" perception of the meaning of the words and deeds of Jesus by which he allows the Christian reader to recognize that in the Church he possesses by faith the same realities that those of the apostolic age had heard and experienced in the living presence of Jesus (cf. 1 Jn 1:1–4). When the climax of the Gospel is reached in the confession of Thomas and the Lord's response (20:24–29), the reader understands what John has told him all along: All that Jesus has been seen to do and say are "signs" of present realities that are to be found in the Church. In fact, the true significance of Jesus' words and deeds can be understood only now, with the presence and enlightenment of the Holy Spirit (2:22; 7:39; 16:25ff.).

This perspective points up one of the close affinities between Jn and Lk. Whereas Luke has shown the consummation of sacred history in an additional work, the Acts of the Apostles, which has been called "the Gospel of the Spirit," John by a concentration on the "signs" has allowed the work of the other Paraclete to be seen anticipated in the First. Just as the Son does the work of the Father (8:28), so the work of the Spirit is one with that of the Son: The life of the Church is the life of Christ.

24 (2) One important aspect is John's sacramental teaching. In the Syn, reference is made to baptism (Mt 28:19) and to the institution of the Eucharist (Mt 26:26ff. par.). Jn has no such "corporeal" references to the sacraments, yet the entire Gospel is taken up with sacramental teaching. None of Jesus' "signs" are so meaningful as those that point to the sacramental life of the Church: The wine of Cana that replaces the water of Jewish purification (2:1–11), the life-giving water that comes from Christ (3:5–7; 4:10–14; 7:37–38), the heavenly bread that is his flesh (6:51)—all these signify the sacraments that are efficacious in virtue of his redemptive work, bestowing the Holy Spirit that is the life of the Church (19:34; 1 Jn 5:6,8). The giving of the same Spirit accounts for the power of the Church to forgive sins (20:22f.). Correspondingly, John devotes a great deal of attention to the ritual and liturgical calendar of Judaism—his Gospel may be said to revolve around the chief Jewish festivals—only to show that these have been replaced in the resurrected body of Christ, the Church, which has taken the place of the Jewish Temple (2:20) and in which God is worshiped in spirit and in truth (4:23).

25 (3) John's eschatology is of a piece with his "spiritual" Gospel. The Syn have been written largely from the eschatological perspective that is perceived in the earlier Pauline epistles—the perspective of a Church living in expectation of the parousia, at which time would occur the final Judgment and the consummation of the Kingdom of God in glory. John does not, of course, deny this futurist eschatology to which the Church gives credence in every recitation of the Creed. However, in keeping with his ecclesial and sacramental teaching, he insists on the fact that the Christian in the Church possesses here and now the divine life that is also the goal of salvation; thus his eschatological emphasis shifts to the present reality, as indeed it does in the later Pauline letters. The Gospel begins with the Lord's assertion that his hour has not yet come (2:4) and reaches its triumphant conclusion in his cry, "It is accomplished!" (19:30). Meanwhile, the Christian has been reminded that judgment already takes place in this life (3:18), that eternal life is possessed through Christian faith (5:24), and that Jesus is resurrection and life here and now for those who believe in him (11:25; → Johannine Theology, 80:46–47).

26 (4) A final example may be found in the portrayal of Christ himself. In the Syn Jesus is portrayed as the Messiah, the fulfillment of the OT expectation, the founder of a universal Kingdom of heaven, the Son of God. With differing insights, the Syn Evangelists labor to bring out various aspects of Christ's personality. All this John presupposes in his first chapter; by the time the chapter ends, virtually every messianic and soteriological title has been used of Jesus. The Syn tradition adheres largely to primitive Christian formulations, which saw in the resurrected Jesus the Messiah and Lord constituted Son of God in power (Acts 2:36; Rom 1:4). John begins with this belief, to show all that it implies but leaves unsaid. Christ is the incarnate Word of God, Son from all eternity who has also become man that he might in turn give us a share in his divinity. The rich Trinitarian doctrine of the Fourth Gospel has nothing of speculation and contemplation for its own sake. The shared life of the Father, the Son, and the Spirit is important to the Christian precisely because it is the same life that—through the Spirit—he possesses in the Church.

27 John has, as the commentary will bring out, many preoccupations other than these. These, however, are sufficient to render unlikely the theory that has recently been proposed—as a reaction to the view that Jn was a Hellenistic Gospel—that it was actually directed as an apologetic to Jews of the Diaspora! The Fourth Gospel, whatever its missionary significance, is a work whose full meaning can only be evident to a Christian consciously leading the life of the Church.

28 **(VII) The Johannine Characteristics.** The discussion above will have shown that the Gospel of Jn follows its own rules and must be read on its own terms. Here we note briefly only a few of the characteristics of John's procedure, which the reader of this Gospel should bear in mind. In addition to those characteristics already mentioned, others will be noted in the commentary.

29 **(A) The Johannine Irony.** Words are important for their own sake in Jn. Not only does this Gospel have an extensive theological vocabulary—"truth," "life," "light," "glory," etc.—on which the changes are continually being rung, but the same word or phrase may also have several levels of meaning at one and the same time. This takes place in various ways. (1) Profound truths are at times found in certain statements quite beyond the intention of the speaker: thus the high priest "prophesies" the vicarious atonement of Christ (11:50f.). (2) A deceptively prosaic statement may intentionally conceal a reference to a pivotal religious truth. In 7:8 Jesus, when bidden to "go up" (the customary expression for pilgrimage to Jerusalem) to the feast, says that it is not the time for him to "go up" (ascend to the Father). Jesus tells the Samaritan woman that he can give her "living water" (4:10), which means fresh running water as opposed to the water of a well or cistern. This water that he will give, however, is also the water of life. (3) Especially the theologically charged words of the Gospel appear in these multiple senses. In 2:11 "sign" refers to both the miracle that has been witnessed and to the sacramental reality it symbolizes. Similarly "glory" has the same dual application. (4) Along with this use of theological vocabulary goes the deeper, sacramental or ecclesial significance John finds in Jesus' words and deeds, of which we spoke above. Although in these instances John is not necessarily telling us that this was the historical meaning of the episode, he nonetheless intends us to see that it is a true meaning in view of the reality that binds Christ to his Church. "The Fourth Gospel is less an Apostolic witness to history than an Apostolic witness to what is beyond history, but which is, nevertheless, the meaning of the 'Jesus of History,' and therefore the meaning of all history" (E. C. Hoskyns, *Fourth Gospel*, 66).

30 **(B) The Johannine Dialogues.** The various dialogues that Jesus has with the Jews, with the disciples, with Nicodemus, with the woman at the well, and with others, follow set patterns that obviously presuppose a certain amount of schematic rearrangement by the Evangelist. (1) Repeatedly in these dialogues Jesus makes a statement regarding a profound religious truth, which, however, is misunderstood in a surface and material sense. This misunderstanding permits the Lord (or John, at times) to develop further the truly spiritual meaning of his pronouncement (cf. 3:4; 4:15,33; 6:52; 8:19,33; etc.). This situation, of course, had a true setting in the life of Jesus, whose teaching was not fully understood until after his resurrection and the giving of the Holy Spirit (2:22; 7:39). (2) When the dialogue has served its purpose, it often dissolves into a monologue of Christ or of the Evangelist in which the theme that was introduced in the dialogue is now explored more thoroughly (cf. 3:10ff.; 10:1ff., etc.). This device partly reproduces Matthew's technique of gathering the Lord's words topically into single discourses; thus they are dissociated from a specific audience and are shown in their universal applicability (cf. the beatitudes in Mt 5:3ff. with Lk 6:20ff.). This device also enables John to present not merely a bare report of the words and deeds of Jesus, which is not all of Christian revelation, but the meaning of those words and deeds as made known through the Holy Spirit (14:26).

31 **(C) Johannine Symbolism.** More symbolism is found in Jn than in the other Gospels. More attention is called to the spiritual significance of apparently routine happenings and to the fuller meaning of words and events. The "beloved disciple," the man born blind, Lazarus, represent at times not only historical personages, but all Christians. Mary, the Mother of Jesus, is the Church itself. Such symbolism is extended to other events and persons and makes it necessary for us to read Jn with close attention lest his full meaning escape us. Similarly, it is surely no accident that the first witness of John the Baptist (1:19ff.) is climaxed seven days later in Jesus' own witness to himself, in the first manifestation of his glory at Cana (2:11): The new work of creation has begun that was heralded by the deliberate reminiscence of the first creation in the opening line of the Gospel (1:1).

32 Such symbolism is an integral part of the Gospel and must be considered in interpreting Jn's chronology and his juxtaposition of events. Without question, of all the material available to him, the symbolic potentialities of words or events have at times determined the Evangelist's choice of what material he would use; that he made such a choice he tells us in 20:30f. However, symbolism for its own sake does not exist in Jn. The author never challenges the reader's subtlety as an end in itself, but always to make him realize that there was nothing trivial, nothing without moment in the life that is portrayed in the Gospel. Doubtless, too, some commentators have exaggerated the symbolism of Jn, finding esoteric meanings where the Evangelist intended none and which would have served no purpose. This brings us to our final consideration with regard to the nature of the Fourth Gospel.

33 **(VIII) The Fourth Gospel as History.** Fully aware of the late dating of Jn, of its nonapostolic origin, of its influence by Hellenistic thinking, and of its highly theological purpose, the criticism of a past generation took it for granted that there was very little if any authentic history in Jn, and that in matters of this kind the Syn order and presentation were invariably to be preferred.

The above-mentioned reasons hardly permit such a view to be held today. "The sources or traditions used by the fourth evangelist deserve at least as much respect as those employed by the Synoptics" (A. J. B. Higgins, *The Historicity of the Fourth Gospel* [London, 1960] 82). John's theological orientation has, it is true, caused him to subordinate the merely statistical aspect of history to the far more important concern of its meaning as known through faith, but for all that, the Gospel is historical. History was of the very religious air that John breathed: If the history were not true, the revelation it contained obviously would have no significance whatever.

34 Doubtless the Syn presentation is to be preferred because it represents Jesus' Messianic proclamation as gradual, as opposed to the way it is presented in Jn, where from the beginning it is taken for granted. Here we should have no difficulty in recognizing that John has anticipated historical development for theological reasons. (The Fathers also recognized the priority of the theological over the merely statistical in the Gospels. For Origen's principles of interpretation, see M. F. Wiles, *The Spiritual Gospel*, 15f.; for Chrysostom, see J. D. Quinn, *CBQ* 24 [1962] 140–47.) In reality, Jesus undoubtedly appeared more often among men as the simple teacher depicted in the Syn than as the profound preacher implied by the Johannine discourses. It served John's highly spiritual purpose to stress this profound aspect of Christ's teaching rather than the other, and correspondingly to center his Gospel in Jerusalem among the doctors of Judaism rather than in the countryside of Galilee. That this aspect of his teaching was historical, however, even the Syn tradition itself witnesses, especially in the "Johannine" passage of Mt 11:25–27 par., which "contains the whole of the Christology of the Fourth Gospel" and "causes perplexity to those who deny the solidarity between the Johannean heaven and the synoptic earth" (A. Plummer, *The Gospel According to St. Luke*, [ICC; 8th ed.; N.Y., 1907] 282).

35 On the other hand, there are many instances in which the Syn presentation seems to be more artificial than Jn's. As Jn presents the facts, Jesus made several visits to Jerusalem and repeatedly became engaged in controversy with the Jewish leaders. This seems intrinsically more plausible than that he should have gone to the holy city only once and crowded into a single week's time all his dealings there (Mt 23:37 par. suggests that the Johannine picture is the more factual when it quotes the Lord as having "often" desired to gather the Jerusalemites to himself). The relation of the first disciples to John the Baptist and consequently the Baptist's relation to early Christianity become more understandable in view of the Johannine history that prefaces a Judean episode to the Galilean phase of the ministry with which the Syn history begins. Here we might recall that it is John who depended most directly on eyewitness testimony; of all the Evangelists, only Matthew was an eyewitness, and his testimony has come to us only indirectly in his Gospel.

36 But we do not have to choose between the Syn and the Johannine histories. Both have their contributions to make, usually quite independently of each other. John has ordinarily made no special effort to harmonize the two traditions, since this was not his primary concern, and consequently it is not always easy to supply the chronological sutures that connect them. Such connections, however, are usually in matters of little consequence, and for the most part the two complement each other satisfactorily. At times, too, there may actually be historical parallels between the two traditions that do not appear on the surface because one or the other may have synthesized into a single account what appears in the parallel tradition as dispersed incidents (cf. R. E. Brown, *CBQ* 23 [1961] 143–60). As the synthesis takes place more often in the Syn tradition, we probably have here a further indication of its artificial character in contrast to Jn.

(Brown, R. E., "The Problem of Historicity in John," *CBQ* 24 [1962] 1–14. Dodd, C. H., *Historical Tradition in the Fourth Gospel* [Cambridge, 1963]. Headlam, A. C., *The Fourth Gospel as History* [N.Y., 1948]. Hunter, A. M., "Recent Trends in Johannine Studies," *ExpT* 71 [1959–60] 164–67, 219–22. Leal, J., "El simbolismo histórico del IV evangelio," *EstBib* 19 [1960] 329–48.)

37 **(IX) The Text.** For a critical text of Jn modern scholars are chiefly dependent on the major codices of the 4th and 5th cents., especially Sinaiticus (S) and Vaticanus (B), representing the so-called Alexandrian Text, and Bezae (D) representing the so-called Western Text. The Alexandrian form of the text is generally purer than the Western, and B has been made the basis of most editions of Jn, with the collation of S and other witnesses, including the text used by some of the Fathers and presupposed by the Pesh and OL versions. Recent studies, however, have convinced some scholars that S has preserved a better text of Jn than has B, and a text tradition has been discerned that is represented in the frequent agreement of S and D against B. The most significant development in the modern study of the text of Jn occurred with the publication in 1956 of Papyrus Bodmer II (P^{66}), a codex copied *ca.* AD 200, found in Egypt in the 1930's (see bibliography in *NTA* 2 [1958] § 322). This papyrus has preserved most of Jn; it agrees at times with B, at times with S-D, indicating that the divergent traditions in the transmission of the text had already become established by the 2nd cent. (These divergences rarely touch on the sense of the text, but are mainly stylistic modifications.) In addition, P^{66} has preserved a number of readings not found elsewhere in the mss., some of which may be original. Another recently published ms. is Papyrus Bodmer XV (P^{75}), which may be slightly older than P^{66} and may, in fact, possess a better text tradition. Containing the first 15 chapters of Jn, it tends to agree with B (cf. B. M. Metzger, *ExpT* 73 [1962] 201–3; C. L. Porter, *JBL* 81 [1962] 363–76). Still a third ancient ms. witnessing to the text of Jn is the Chester Beatty Papyrus I (P^{45}), dating from the middle of the 3rd cent. Despite its antiquity, however, it is a less trustworthy witness than the major codices. The oldest fragment of Jn, or for that matter, of any part of the NT, is the tiny Rylands Papyrus (P^{52}), consisting of only 17:31–33,37f. Though of little significance for the critical study of this Johannine passage, its early date

(AD 130–150) has effectively disproved the contention of the late dating of Jn.

38 (X) Outline. The Gospel of John forms a hard unity that is reflected in both its structure and content. The commentary will attempt to show the interlocking of the various Johannine themes; the outline below reflects the "movement" of the Gospel and indicates the divisions of the commentary as well.

- (I) The Prologue or Overture: Assertion of the Major Johannine Themes (1:1–18)
- (II) The Book of Signs: "The Light Shines in the Darkness"—Faith and Unbelief (1:19–12:50)
  - (A) The New Creation (1:19–2:11)
    - (a) The Witness of the Baptist (1:19–34)
    - (b) The Disciples of the Baptist Become Disciples of Jesus (1:35–51)
    - (c) The Witness of the Disciples: The First Sign (2:1–11)
  - (B) The New Life in Signs (2:12–4:54)
    - (a) The New Temple: The Resurrected Christ (2:13–25)
    - (b) The New Birth: Baptism (3:1–36)
      - (i) Nicodemus (3:1–21)
      - (ii) Baptism of John and baptism of Christ (3:22–36)
    - (c) Water of Life (4:1–42)
    - (d) The Second Sign (4:43–54)
  - (C) The Light and the Darkness (5:1–10:42)
    - (a) Jesus and the Sabbath (5:1–47)
      - (i) The third sign of life (5:1–15)
      - (ii) Jesus does the works of the Father (5:1–6 47)
    - (b) The Bread of Life (6:1–71)
      - (i) The fourth sign (6:1–15)
      - (ii) The fifth sign (6:16–21)
      - (iii) The Eucharistic discourse (6:22–71)
    - (c) Tabernacles: Life and Light (7:1–8:59)
    - (d) Jesus the Light of the World (9:1–10:42)
      - (i) The sixth sign (9:1–34)
      - (ii) Sight and blindness (9:35–10:21)
      - (iii) The works of Jesus (10:22–39)
      - (iv) Inclusion on the public life (10:40–42)
  - (D) The Last Journey to Jerusalem (11:1–12:50)
    - (a) Death and Life: The Seventh Sign (11:1–44)
    - (b) Death Chosen Over Life (11:45–47)
    - (c) The Anointing (12:1–11)
    - (d) The Triumphal Entry (12:12–19)
    - (e) The Gentiles See Jesus: Life in Death (12:20–36)
    - (f) Judgment on the Rejection of Life and Light (12:37–50)
- (III) The Book of Exaltation: "Those Who Accept Him Become Sons of God" (13:1–20:31)
  - (A) Jesus Instructs His Disciples (13:1–17:26)
    - (a) The Sign of the Foot Washing (13:1–20)
    - (b) The Betrayal: The Hour of Darkness (13:21–30)
    - (c) Discourse on Departure and Return in the Spirit (13:31–14:31)
    - (d) The True Vine and the Branches (15:1–17)
    - (e) The World's Hatred of the Light (15:18–16:4a)
    - (f) Reprise: Departure and Return (16:4b–33)
    - (g) The High-Priestly Prayer (17:1–26)
  - (B) The Glorification of Christ (18:1–20:31)
    - (a) The Passion (18:1–19:16)
      - (i) The scene in the garden (18:1–11)
      - (ii) The scene before Annas (18:12–27)
      - (iii) The scene before Pilate: Christ the King (18:28–40)
      - (iv) The scourging: "Behold the Man" (19:1–5)
      - (v) Again before Pilate: The Son of God (19:6–16)
    - (b) The Crucifixion and Death of Jesus (19:17–37)
      - (i) Jesus reigns from the cross (19:17–22)
      - (ii) Accompanying signs (19:23–37)
    - (c) The Burial of the Lord (19:38–42)
    - (d) The Resurrection and Giving of the Spirit (20:1–31)
      - (i) Appearance to Mary Magdalene (20:1–18)
      - (ii) Appearance to the disciples (20:19–23)
      - (iii) Appearance to the disciples and Thomas (20:24–29)
      - (iv) Conclusion: The meaning of these signs (20:30–31)
- (IV) Appendix or Epilogue: Appearance in Galilee (21:1–25)
  - (A) Jesus with the Disciples by the Sea (21:1–14)
  - (B) Peter's Commission (21:15–19)
  - (C) The Beloved Disciple (21:20–23)
  - (D) Final Testimony (21:24–25)

COMMENTARY

39 (I) The Prologue or Overture: Assertion of the Major Johannine Themes (1:1–18). This poetic section asserts the major theological themes developed throughout Jn. Faithful to Semitic tradition, Jn begins with a "genealogy"; but it is a history of divine, not human origins. Though corresponding closely to the Johannine vocabulary, the key term *logos*, "Word," occurs only here in a Christological sense in Jn (though also in Ap 19:13 and possibly in 1 Jn 1:1). This is one reason why many scholars believe that the prologue was an already existing Christological hymn, probably of liturgical origin, which John adapted to his purposes as the overture to his Gospel (see D. M. Stanley, *CBQ* 20 [1958] 188f.). In this acceptation, at least the prose vv. 6–8,15 are regarded as Johannine additions to relate the hymn to the first business of the Gospel in the witness of the Baptist (cf. M. F. Lacan, *LumVi* 33 [1957] 91–110); however, usually other verses (12, 13, 17, 18) are suggested as further adaptations (so S. de Ausejo, *EstBib* 15 [1956] 381–427; R. Schnackenburg, *BZ* 1 [1957] 69–109). Antecedently, this theory is not unlikely; however, by similar paring away of verses, others (C. F. Burney, J. R. Harris, R. Reitzenstein, H. H. Schaeder *et al.*) have been able to see the "original" of the prologue as a Jewish or Gnostic hymn to personified wisdom, to the archetypal man, to John the Baptist, etc. The dividing line is thin between poetic structure and the rhythmic prose accompanied by parallelism and inclusion found elsewhere in Jn. Whatever the provenance, the Evangelist has made the prologue an integral part of his Gospel, and it must be interpreted in this light.

40 1. *in the beginning:* This allusion to Gn 1:1 is not merely typological of the new creation of Christ (1:19–2:11); as Jn goes on to show, Jesus is truly the creative Word of God who already existed at the beginning of time. *was:* The impf. tense denoting continuous, timeless existence contrasts with the aorist used in vv. 3, 6, and 14 (creation, the mission of the Baptist, the incarnation) for events that have taken place at determined points of time. *the Word:* We may confidently find the origin of this and other Johannine concepts in Jewish tradition (→ 16 above), acknowledging at the same time that John was not unaware of their relevance to Hellenistic thought (on the Word of God in the OT, see J. L.

McKenzie, *TS* 21 [1960] 183–206). In Hellenistic thinking *logos* meant divine utterance, emanation, mediation. In the OT the word of God is God's manifestation, the revelation of himself, whether in creation, in deeds of power and of grace, or in prophecy. All these strains of thought are taken up by Jn, who shows that Christ, the Incarnate Word, is the ultimate and complete revelation of God (cf. Heb 1:1–4; Col 1:15–20). Two strands of Jewish speculation have especially assisted in the development of this concept. One is the late OT personification of the wisdom of God (with 1a cf. Prv 3:19; 8:22; Sir 1:4; 24:9; with 1b, Prv 8:27,30; Sir 1:1; Wis 9:4,9; with 2, Prv 8:27; with 3, Prv 3:19; 8:30; Wis 9:1–2,9; with 4a, Prv 3:18; 8:35; Bar 4:1; with 4b, Wis 6:12; 7:10,26; Sir 24:30; Bar 4:2; with 5, Wis 7:24–30; with 10a, Wis 8:1; Sir 24:3–6 [a paraphase of the Gn creation story]; with 10c, Bar 3:31; with 11, Bar 3:12; *4 Ezra* 5:10; with 12, Wis 6:12; 7:27; Bar 3:37; with 14b, Sir 24:8; Bar 3:38; with 14c, Wis 9:11; with 14d, Wis 7:25). The other strand is the glorification of the Torah (the Law) in rabbinical Judaism: The identification of Torah with the divine wisdom is already found in Sir 24:22–27 (in which Gn 2 is paraphrased) and in Bar 3:38–4:4. On the rabbinical conception of the pre-existence of the Torah, see Str-B 2, 353f. Jn's synthesis of this Jewish thought with Christian revelation is partly polemical: Christ is the true Word of God existing from eternity, through whom, and not through the Law, comes grace and truth (v. 17; → Johannine Theology, 80:21–24). *the Word was in God's presence:* A distinction in godhead is asserted: The Word existed along with God (determined with the article, as in 2 Cor 13:13 = the Father). Judaism, of course, could say this of Wisdom or Torah, but it would have been a strange assertion in pantheistic Hermeticism, according to which *logos* was simply divine emanation. *the Word was God:* Such a statement could not have been made in Judaism, which could go only so far as to say that Wisdom is God's effulgence (Wis 7:25), the Law his daughter (Str-B 2, 355f.). Here "God" without the article is predicative: The Word is divine, but he is not all of divinity, for he has already been distinguished from another divine Person (cf. 7:28f.; 8:42; 16:28). **2.** For the fourth time Jn insists that the Word *was* with God at the beginning. Unlike created things, of which he is about to speak, there never was a time when the Word was not.

41 **3.** *through him all things came into being:* Jn does not call Christ the Creator, a title reserved in the NT to the Father (cf. Col 1:15ff.). The Word is the instrumental or mediative cause of creation; this does not imply subordination but a logical order. The creative Word of God, eminently a biblical conception (Gn 1:3; Is 48:13; Sir 42:15), identified by the rabbis with Torah (Str-B 2, 356f.), was also common in Hellenistic speculation; the rabbinic *mêmrā'* (word) considered as "Creator" (Str-B 2, 304ff.) is only an apparent parallel, since *mêmrā'* was merely a verbal surrogate for the holy name of Yahweh. *apart from him nothing came to be:* This expresses the same truth negatively; against it is emphasized that creation, in distinction to the Word, came into being, and that the Word is the cause of this existence. An interesting verbal parallel occurs in 1QS 11:11: "Through his [God's] knowledge all things have come to be, and everything that is, is ordained by his thought; and without him nothing is made" (cf. also 1QH 1:20). **4.** The final words of v. 3 should be read as the beginning of this verse: "What came to be in him was life." This is the punctuation of the text that was known to the Fathers of the first four centuries (cf. I. de la Potterie, *VD* 33 [1955] 193–208), and it was abandoned only after it had led to heretical interpretations. Probably this was the punctuation intended by the scribe of P^{66} (cf. E. Massaux, *SP* 1,203 f.). It was also the original punctuation of the Vg, as evidenced by its appearance in the Douay-Rheims NT of 1582. The meaning is generally taken to be: All created existence has always had its origin in the life of the Word (the reading "is life" is also well attested [S and D among the major codices]). Jn's emphasis is now on the nature of life and its origin. Life is not mere existence—even inanimate things exist; life for Jn signifies some kind of sharing in the being of God. This statement prepares for vv. 14ff., which bring out that the supernatural life of man is a sharing in the divine life of the Holy Trinity. Further, since life always has this fullness of meaning in Jn, we should understand that this is "what came to be" in the Word: The life that men receive from the Word, they receive as God's gift through the One who has manifested him (cf. 3:35f.; 5:26f.; 6:57; cf. M. F. Lacan, *RScRel* 45 [1957] 61–78; B. Vawter, *CBQ* 25 [1963] 401–6). Jn agrees with Col 1:15–20 in seeing in the work of creation the model and exemplar of the second creation of salvation. *this life was the light of men:* The life of which Jn speaks, as truly a sharing in the life of God, must be a life of ultimate understanding, the revelation of God. The rabbis spoke similarly of the Torah as light (cf. Str-B 2, 357). John will later apply to Jesus the Word other designations that they used of Torah, such as water (4:10) and bread (6:35).

42 **5.** *the light shines in the darkness:* Darkness is the antithesis of light, and by it John habitually means that which is set in opposition to God, the rejection of God, which is natural to a world bound over to sin (cf. 3:19). The second part of the verse can be translated "the darkness did not grasp it" (cf. 7:33f.; 8:21), but probably better "the darkness did not overcome it": Man is in darkness, but he is not darkness itself. Throughout history God's revealed word has been present for the enlightenment of man—he did not need to succumb to the darkness, though he invariably did (→ Johannine Theology, 80:12–14).

43 **6.** *there appeared a man:* John the Baptist is introduced with the same distinction of verbs that has contrasted the eternity of the Word with the temporality of creation. That this man was sent by God, like the prophets of old and Jesus himself, is what gives relevance to his mention here. (H. Sahlin, *ZNW* 51 [1960] 64–69, would translate "he [the Word] became man," and refer v. 7 to the Word; v. 8 and the other references to the Baptist would be later additions, influenced by Mk 1:4. The chief internal argument against this reconstruction is that it would effectively destroy the climax achieved in v. 14.) **7.** *came as a witness to the light:* Witness is one of Jn's fundamental ideas—not only the Baptist (1:19, etc.), but the Samaritan woman (4:39), the works of Jesus (5:36, etc.), the OT (5:39), the crowd (12:17), the Holy Spirit and the disciples (15:26f.), the Father (5:37), the Evangelist (21:24), all bear witness to Jesus the Word (cf. I. de la Potterie, *SP* 2, 193–208). Though the incarnation is not mentioned explicitly until v. 14, the fact that the Baptist, who is a witness to the Incarnate Word, is introduced at this point shows that John has been thinking throughout of the Word both in his eternal existence and in his incarnate state. *that through him all men might believe:* Faith and its converse of unbelief because of the influence of the darkness are the theme of the first half of the Gospel. **8.** John carefully points out, as he does elsewhere (v. 20ff.; 3:28ff.), that the Baptist is a witness to the light, not the light itself. This polemical attitude is motivated not by the Baptist himself, but by the fact that his position had been misinterpreted by some who had not understood that he was the forerunner and not the inaugurator of God's kingdom (cf. Acts 19:1–7; see T. F. Glasson, *ExpT* 67 [1956] 245–46).

44 **9.** *he was the true light:* In Hebraic usage, "true" pre-eminently characterizes the divine order (cf. 7:28; 17:3), thus distinguished from the deception and illusion of the order of sinful man (cf. Rom 3:4); in the Hermetic sense, the "true" pertains to the archetypal world of reality, compared with which any other is only a pale reflection. The Baptist was a light (5:39), but he was not the light in the fullness of the meaning of light: Only the Word gives this light to all men. *coming into the world:* This phrase may modify "every man," or it may refer back to "the light." The latter seems to be the more probable construction. **10.** "The world" "this world" in Jn invariably means the world of men and their affairs, which concretely is a world subject to sin and darkness (→ Johannine Theology, 80:14). The Word, John says, was in the world. He is not speaking merely of the incarnation of the Word. *the world did not know him:* These words are not to be restricted to the rejection of Christ by his own people. We may think, first of all, of the failure of the world to acknowledge the truth that God—through his creative word—had made known in creation (Rom 1:18–23). "Know" in Jn does not mean simply to perceive, to be aware of, but has the full Semitic sense attached to knowledge in which personal involvement is always supposed. Also, in a particular way the history of Israel was characterized by its failure to know the prophetic word of God (cf. Acts 7:51–53), and this attitude was to be repeated in their rejection of the Word become man (cf. Mt 23:29ff.; Lk 13:33). **11.** The statement of the preceding verse is repeated in other terms, now evidently specified to the people of Israel. As applied to the life of Christ, a parallel can be found in Mk 6:1–6. **12.** At the same time, rejection of the Word was never complete. Both in the OT phase of the history of salvation as in the fulfillment in Christ, faith in the Word has been the principle of immortality (cf. Rom 4:1–17), whereby through the acceptance of God's grace men might become the children of God (cf. Dt 14:1; Ex 4:22; Hos 1:10). How men become God's children through faith (→ Johannine Theology, 80:35–38) in the Incarnate Word, is the theme of the second half of Jn's Gospel. *in his name:* So also with "believe" in 2:23; 3:18, and frequently elsewhere throughout the Gospel. In Semitic usage, "name" is equivalent to the person. Faith is not simply the acceptance of a proposition, but a commitment to a person. See Thomas Aq. *Summa* 2–2.1,2 ad 2: "Actus credentis non terminatur ad enuntiabile, sed ad rem." The Jewish practice of calling *Yahweh* "the Name" appears to have been imitated in primitive Christian references to Christ (cf. Mk 9:41). **13.** This birth as children of God, Jn insists emphatically, has nothing to do with human generation, but is a special gift of God (cf. 3:3ff.). "Flesh and blood" is an OT and later Jewish expression for mankind and human potentialities. Implicitly, we are told here that this new birth is that of the Spirit, as in 3:6. Various patristic quotations and some Lat mss. have a sing. verb in this verse, referring this spiritual birth to the Word rather than to those who believe in his name; this reading was probably motivated by the desire to find an allusion to the Virgin Birth, otherwise not mentioned by Jn; it has no support in the Gk mss.

45 **14.** *the Word became flesh:* Once more there is a contrast with the "was" of v. 1, for John now reaches the climax of his hymn in relating what was the ultimate manifestation of God's Word. And what a paradoxical climax it is! The utter newness of this revelation in respect to Judaism, despite the OT language in which it is phrased, can only be appreciated by comparing the assertion with such a passage as Is 40:6–8, where the Word of God is contrasted with flesh. "Flesh," it is true, is not evil, the antithesis of God; but it is all that is transitory, mortal, and imperfect, and at first glance incompatible with God (cf. J. A. T. Robinson, *The Body* [SBT 5; London, 1952] 17–26). This is the tremendous mystery of the incarnation, by which the eternal Word took on our exact human nature, becoming one with us in everything except sin (Heb 4:15); in everything, that is, except what was incompossible with divinity. This is one of the most serious and sobering statements in the Gospel, the magnitude of which it would be difficult to exaggerate. To express this mystery, John has deliberately chosen a word connoting man in his concrete, fallen state. That the Word became man in the fullest possible sense is of the very essence of the incarnation and of the redemption that is its result. In doing this, John was striking at the incipient Docetism and Monophysitism that even then were appearing in the Christian world. *and made his dwelling among us:* Lit., "he pitched his tent among us." The Word dwelt for a time in the midst of man as God once dwelt with the Israelites in the Tent of Meeting (Ex 25:8; Nm 35:34). The vb. *skēnoun* has probably been deliberately chosen to reproduce both the idea and even the sound of the vb. *šākan* used in the OT with reference to Yahweh's presence in the Holy of Holies above the Ark of the Covenant; the rabbis used the noun *šᵉkînāh*, "presence," as a surrogate for the name of Yahweh as the God present in Israel (Str-B 2, 314f.). "Glory" was another OT term (*kābôd*) for the presence of God visibly manifested, especially in connection with the Tent of Meeting (cf. Ex 40:34f.) and the Temple (1 Kgs 8:11). *we have seen his glory:* Though the Word concealed his glory in becoming flesh, the Gospel is witness to its having been perceived by men. To what does Jn have reference? Some have thought of the transfiguration, at which the beloved disciple was present (Lk 9:31 speaks of Jesus appearing on this occasion "in glory," and in the following verse, "they beheld his glory"; expressions that do not appear in the Mk-Mt par.). While this meaning is by no means to be excluded, it would be a mistake to limit Jn's meaning to this instance. It would also be to underestimate the full significance of "glory," which in both the OT (Is 60:1; Hab 2:14; etc.) and in the NT (Mk 8:38; Rom 8:18; etc.) means pre-eminently the divine presence in salvation (see comment on 2:11; → Johannine Theology, 80:30–32). Thus Jn's testimony is to the entire salvific life of the Incarnate Word (cf. 1 Jn 1:1). *glory of an only Son:* Now that John has definitively reached the climax of his introduction in speaking of the Word become flesh, he never again calls him the Word: The Gospel is testimony not to the eternal Word but to the Word become flesh, Jesus Christ, the Son of God (cf. G. Kittel in *ThDNT* 4, 132). The glory to which Jn testifies is now specified: it is the glory of the only-begotten of the Father. The Son's relation to the Father, his coming from the Father, and his return as the condition of giving the Spirit of sanctification, that is to say, his character as Savior, is the theme of the second part of the Gospel and especially of Jesus' discourse in 13:31ff. Hence in Johannine language the crucifixion and resurrection of Christ are especially his "glorification." "Rich in kindness and fidelity" further specifies the glory possessed by the only-begotten who has come from the Father. These terms are the characteristic of the God of Israel's covenant. In Ex 24:6 they appear together as a virtual definition of God. "Kindness" (Hebr *ḥesed*, Gk *charis*) was the word used in the OT to signify the loving kindness exercised by God toward Israel in election and covenant; "fidelity" (Hebr *'ᵉmet*, Gk *alētheia*) denoted God's faithfulness and reliability in his covenant commitment. Jn uses *charis* only in the prologue, but *alētheia* occurs about 25 times as one of the technical terms of the Gospel. In the great

majority of cases it must be translated in its more proper Gk sense as "truth," for it represents, as indeed it did in the OT, divine revelation (8:32), and therefore is identified with Jesus himself (14:6).

46 **15.** Jn introduces the witness (see comment on v. 7) of the Baptist as recorded in 1:30. This verse interrupts the flow of the poetry, but has its place in the development of the prologue. The sense of the verbs used by the author is of a present proclamation, contrasted with the past tense in vv. 6–8; now that John has spoken explicitly of the incarnation of the Word, he presents the Baptist as the first of a series of witnesses who testify on behalf of the Christ-event. **16.** "The riches" that we—the Church—have shared are those in which the Son is rich according to v. 14. The mission of the Word into the world was precisely to enable men to become God's children (v. 12), to share in the divine life. (See Thomas Aq., *Summa* 3.8,5: "The personal grace whereby the soul of Christ is justified is essentially the same as his grace by which he is head of the Church and justifies others." *Summa* 3.8,6: "The interior flow of grace is from none other than Christ, whose manhood, through its union with the godhead, has the power of justifying.") *fidelity after fidelity:* Or "grace [the underlying meaning of *charis*] upon grace"; what was promised in the covenant with Israel has come superabundantly in the revelation of the Son of God. **17.** The thought is that of Heb 1:1–4, and constitutes a final break of John's thought with that of Judaism. The revelation of the Old Dispensation was but a foreshadowing of what was to be fully revealed in Christ. The Midrash on Ps 25:10, one of the many passages of the OT in which *ḥesed* and *'ᵉmet* are joined, interpreted the former (= *charis*) as the deeds of God's love, the latter (= *alētheia*) as Torah (cf. Str-B 2, 361); Jn, however, says that, although Torah was God's gift through Moses, the fullness of his revelation has come only through Christ. This theme of the figures represented by Moses and the Law fulfilled in the realities coming from Christ will appear frequently in the Gospel, especially in 6:31–33. **18.** Doubtless the same idea has inspired this verse. Though the OT sometimes represents God anthropomorphically, looked upon by creatures, the Jewish belief was firm: God was an invisible God and could not be seen by man (cf. Str-B 1, 206ff.) John is probably thinking of Ex 33:20–23, according to which Moses was not permitted to see the glory of God (cf. v. 14), since no one may see God and live, but was allowed to see his back. But in the Incarnate Word God has been revealed completely (cf. Col 1:15); only the Son sees the Father (6:46), and it is through him that we, too, see God (14:9) with the eyes of faith. *God, the only Son:* This is the reading of some of the best Gk mss. (including P^{66} and P^{75}); others have "the only-begotten Son." The sense is the same in either case, for Jn has already identified the Word with the Son, and the Son with God (cf. R. E. Brown, *TS* 26 [1965] 553–54). *who is in the Father's bosom:* This expression denotes complete intimacy, a community of life; correspondingly in 13:23 Jn notes not without significance that the beloved disciple was lying close to the breast of Jesus at the Last Supper.

(See also Boismard, M.-E., *St. John's Prologue* [tr. by Carisbrooke Dominicans; Westminster, Md., 1957]. Debrunner, A. *et al.*, "*Legō, logos,*" *ThDNT* 4, 69–136. Giblet, J., "Jésus et 'le Père' dans le IVᵉ Évangile," *L'Évangile de Jean* [RechBib 3; Louvain, 1958] 111–30.)

47 **(II) The Book of Signs: "The Light Shines in the Darkness"—Faith and Unbelief (1:19–12:50).** In view of the explanation the Evangelist gives in 12:37–43, the first half of the Gospel may well be called the Book of Signs (for the Johannine meaning of "sign," see comment on 2:11). This section corresponds to the Syn narrative of the public ministry, and, as do the Syn, Jn explores the mysteries of faith and unbelief in response to the revelation of the Word of God made in Jesus Christ.

48 **(A) The New Creation (1:19–2:11).** The first major division of the Book of Signs is to be found in a partly artificial arrangement of events whereby a theme of the prologue, that of the creative word of God, is underlined in the ministry of Jesus. Just as the Gospel begins with an evident allusion to Gn 1:1 (see comment on 1:1), the seven-day structure of the original creation story is imitated in the following verses, culminating in the first manifestation of Jesus' "glory," that is, the new life of salvation, which the Word had become flesh in order to bring. The sequence of days can be seen in 1:29 (the day following the initial witness of the Baptist); 1:35; 1:39–42; 1:43 [= 4 days]; and finally in 2:1 [totaling seven]. That 2:1 introduces an event that occurs "on the third day" doubtless contains a further symbolism.

49 (a) The Witness of the Baptist (1:19–34). **19.** *this is John's testimony:* Despite the development of his theology, John restricts his Gospel to the Syn pattern of public ministry and Passion Account, beginning with the ministry of John the Baptist, following the kerygmatic outline preserved in Acts 10:37ff. He does not, as Mt and Lk do, preface the essential of the Gospel with other information about the earlier life of Jesus, although he must have had such information. The Baptist is introduced abruptly (apart from the notice taken in the prologue), therefore presupposing the Syn material on his preaching of the coming of the Kingdom of God. On the element of "testimony" in Jn, see comments on 1:7,15. That the testimony of the Baptist is so important to John is partly explained by the necessity of clarifying his relation to Christ in his own words for some of his followers who still survived as a movement independent of Christianity (cf. Acts 19:1–7). *the Jews:* In Jn this expression is used for the representatives of Judaism, especially its leadership at Jerusalem, which proves to be hostile to Jesus. There is no mention in the Syn of such an embassy as this to the Baptist, but Jn's account is compatible with such references as Mk 1:5 and Mt 3:7, which also bring out the opposition between the Baptist and the Jewish leadership. *priests and Levites:* These classes, representing those who were empowered under the Law to make religious decisions, underline the official nature of the embassy. The combination, "priests and Levites," occurs only here in the NT. *to ask him: Who are you?:* This is the question asked of Jesus in 8:25; 21:12. As the "I am" in Jn has such significance in relation to Christ's identification of himself, it is no idle choice of words by which the Baptist, in the following verses, twice says, "I am not." **20.** The most important element of the Baptist's negative confession ("confess" in the NT usually refers to affirmations concerning Christ) follows: "I am not the Messiah."

50 **21.** Two further identifications are proposed, each of which the Baptist denies. *Elijah:* It was a Jewish belief that the prophet Elijah would return to earth to take a part in the establishment of God's kingdom (Mal 3:23; Sir 48:4–12; Str-B 4, 764–98). In the Syn Jesus states that the Baptist has fulfilled this mission of Elijah (cf. Mt 11:14; 17:12; etc.). The Baptist was, of course, not Elijah literally come back to life, and therefore could reply as he does here. But probably more is signified than this: The Baptist himself, as we know from Mt 11:1–6 par., was not aware of the full magnitude of Christ's messianic character; correspondingly he was less competent than was Jesus to evaluate his own relation to Christ (cf. J. A. T. Robinson, *NTS* 4 [1958] 263–81). By a transfer of verses, H. Sahlin (*ZNW* 51 [1960] 64–69) allows the Baptist (v. 20a) to confess that he *is* Elijah. *the prophet:* Cf. 6:14; 7:40; Acts 7:37; all these texts refer to Dt 18:15,18, the prophet promised by Moses. Though the text of Dt does not refer to any specific prophet but rather to the prophetic order, it was apparently believed that an individual prophet like Moses would appear to play a role in the establishment of the Messianic kingdom. Rare in the rabbinical literature (Str-B 2, 363), the figure of the eschatological prophet may appear in the QL, mentioned in conjunction with the coming of the Messiah (1QS 9:10f.; "a" rather than "the" prophet; possibly also in CD 6:10f.; 20:1); at any rate, it was believed that the prophetic order, the lack of which was felt, would be restored (1 Mc 4:46; 14:41). **22–23.** In reply to a demand for a positive identification of himself, the Baptist refuses to relate himself to any person at all; he is merely the voice of Is 40:3 heralding the good news of salvation. The same self-identification is recorded by the Syn tradition (Mt 3:3 par.).

51 **24.** *the Pharisee party:* Most mss. indicate that the emissaries were Pharisees, which causes difficulty, since they have been identified above (v. 19) as priests and Levites, who ordinarily were not Pharisees; the difficulty increases if we follow the mss. (including P^{75}) that omit the article before "who had been sent," for it then appears that the Pharisees had sent the embassy, a thing that they had no authority to do. It seems likely that the editor of Jn has combined in this section more than one interrogation made of the Baptist (cf. Lk 3:7–18), and that the questioners of vv. 24ff. are not those of 19ff. **25.** It would have been Pharisees particularly, watchmen as they were over traditional Jewish law and practice, who would have shown concern about the baptism of John. That he was known especially for his baptizing has not been mentioned thus far and is presumed common knowledge from the Syn tradition. Baptismal rites of various kinds were then in practice: The Jews baptized proselytes, for example, and the Essenes baptized initiates into the eschatological community. What is the significance of John's baptism of Jews, if he has seemingly dissociated himself from the ecshatological kingdom? This question, presupposing interrogations such as those in vv. 19–21, does not seem to be relevant in view of the Baptist's statement in v. 23 and is perhaps another indication of the composite nature of our present text. **26–27.** The Baptist justifies his baptism in water as a preparation for the Messiah who is already in Israel's midst but who has not yet been revealed. *whom you do not recognize:* Cf. 1:10. The Baptist uses the same humble expression to signify his inferiority to Christ that is found in Mk 1:7 par., but in Jn he does not specify until v. 33 that the baptism of Christ will be a baptism of the Holy Spirit. **28.** *Bethany:* Some mss. read "Bethabara" (cf. Jgs 7:24). This was probably an early "correction" of the text in these mss. to avoid the difficulty that the usual reading (Bethany) becomes a Transjordanian place which is attested only here in Jn. It is distinct from the Bethany near Jerusalem of 11:1,18 which is also named in the Syn.

52 **29.** The second day of the "new creation story" sees the positive side of the Baptist's testimony, corresponding to his disclaimers of the first day. The partly artificial character of the chronology as it appears in v. 31f. makes it clear that various events have taken place since v. 19ff. *the lamb of God:* In view of its situation in Jn, it is possible that in this figure the Evangelist sees a reference to the Passover lamb (see comments on 19:14,36) This was a usual interpretation of the Lat Fathers. More probably, however, he has in mind the Servant of the Lord of Is 53:7–12, where the Servant is compared to a lamb (*amnos* in the LXX, the same word used in Jn) and is said to bear the iniquity of many. *who takes away the world's sin:* This phrase would seem to favor the latter rather than the former figure; the Passover lamb, though it protected the people of Israel from destruction, had no connection with sin. Note also that in 12:38 Jn sums up Jesus' public life in the words of Is 53:1, which introduce this Servant theme. The Gk Fathers tended to interpret the text thus. However, the Evangelist may have in mind more than one OT figure, as he often does. What is more difficult is to determine the meaning the expression would have had for the Baptist, since it is most unlikely that he had an understanding of the Lord's mission comparable to that of the Evangelist (see comment on 1:21; cf. R. E. Brown, *CBQ* 22 [1960] 292–98). Boismard believes that the Baptist referred to the Servant of the Lord, but in the representation of Is 42:1ff. rather than of 53:7ff., that is, as one who would usher in an age of righteousness for the people of God, thus banishing the world's sin (cf. 1 Jn 3:5,8; the Syn baptismal scene in Mk 1:9–11 contains an allusion to Is 42:1). "Lamb of God" is Jn's rendering, but the Baptist would have used the Aram *ṭalyā' dē'lāhā*, which can mean either "servant of God" or "lamb of God" (cf. W. Zimmerli and J. Jeremias, *The Servant of God* [SBT 20; London, 1957] 82f.). Following another train of thought, Dodd believes that "lamb of God" was an apocalyptic title for the Messiah (cf. Andrew's reaction in v. 41); the militant-yet-slain lamb of Ap 5:6ff. is, in turn, a combination of this figure with that of the lamb of sacrifice (*Interpretation*, 231f., 236–38). **30.** *he existed before me:* The same impf. tense is used as in the prologue for the Eternal Word; there is hardly any doubt that the Evangelist intends here another affirmation of the pre-existence of Jesus, who was almost unobtrusively introduced in v. 29. Was the Baptist also aware of this great truth when he uttered these words? Again it may be doubted: This is Johannine irony (→ 29 above). If the Baptist did not consider himself the new Elijah (see comment on v. 21 above), he may, for a time at least, have thought of Jesus in this capacity; the words "the man that is coming," used here by the Baptist, are echoed by Jesus in Mt 11:15 virtually as a title for Elijah (cf. Mal 3:1). If the Baptist thought of the Messiah as being Elijah returned, it is easy to see how he could speak of him as one having existed prior to himself.

53 **31.** The Baptist had not known that Jesus was the Messiah, even though the express purpose of his baptizing had been to prepare men for the Messiah's coming (v. 27). **32.** It was only when he baptized Jesus that the Baptist recognized him as the Messiah. John here presupposes the Syn story of Jesus' baptism (Mk 1:9–11 par.) without actually mentioning the baptism itself; in Jn (as in Mt 3:17) it is stressed that the theophany at the baptism was an objective event and not merely a private experience of Jesus. From Acts 19:1–4 we can be fairly certain that the Baptist did not have the Christian revelation of the Holy Spirit as a distinct person in the godhead. He would have understood the Spirit of God in the OT sense, as signifying God's vital power, and in this sense would have recognized that the Spirit "came to rest on him" (cf. Is 11:2). John and the readers of his Gospel know of course that the Spirit of God is a distinct divine agent, a teaching that is much stressed in the second half of the Gospel. **33.** This recognition by the Baptist was the result of a divine intimation. The OT prophets had foretold an outpouring of the Spirit in the Messianic age (Jl 2:28f.; Is 32:15; Ez 39:29; Zech 12:10). The NT recognizes the fulfillment of this prophecy in Pentecost and Christian baptism (Acts 2:16–18; 10:45; Rom 5:5; Gal 4:6;

Eph 4:7f.; Jn 7:39; 20:22), events that did not occur until after the death and resurrection of Christ. *baptism with the Holy Spirit:* For John and the Christian reader of the Gospel, this means the outpouring of the Spirit as it was known to occur, which includes Christian baptism; but the Baptist would have thought in the more general terms of OT prophecy. Because the Baptist here contrasts his baptism with that of Jesus, and in view of the sacramental teaching that John brings out in the following passages, we have two probable reasons for his failure to state literally that Jesus was baptized by John. Such a statement would have interfered with the equation that John wants his readers to keep in mind: Baptism of John the Baptist = OT expectation; Baptism of Jesus = NT fulfillment in the Holy Spirit. **34.** *this is God's chosen one:* Most mss. read "This is God's Son," which is probably a harmonization with the Syn account of the voice from heaven at the baptism of Jesus. "Chosen one" (*eklektos*) is an allusion to Is 42:1 (cf. Lk 9:35), recognizing in Jesus the Servant of the Lord (cf. J. A. Fitzmyer, *CBQ* 27 [1965] 349).

54 (b) THE DISCIPLES OF THE BAPTIST BECOME DISCIPLES OF JESUS (1:35–51). Only from Jn do we learn that Jesus' first disciples had originally been disciples of the Baptist. The Syn, which begin with the Galilean ministry, place the call of these first disciples in Galilee, without any indication that there had been a prior call. However, the Syn account itself becomes more understandable in the light of this information from Jn. We gain a better appreciation of the relation between the Baptist and our Lord and also why the Gospels, though ultimately the work of Galileans, show pronounced Judean influences.

35–36. On the "third day" of the new creation, the Baptist repeats his witness to Jesus in the presence of two of his disciples. **37–38.** These disciples eventually accept the Baptist's identification of Jesus as the Messiah (cf. v. 41); before this, they had followed him as disciples would a teacher. *Rabbi:* The common title given a recognized teacher, whether or not he had been professionally trained (cf. 7:15). *which means:* It is John's practice to translate Hebr and Aram words. *where are you staying?:* The question is a natural one (as are other details in this account, e.g., the time of day in v. 39), and perhaps suggests that the unnamed of the two disciples was the Evangelist himself. However, because the verb of this question is repeated in v. 39 and is the same as that used of the repose of the Spirit on Jesus (vv. 32 and 33), perhaps the Evangelist implies a deeper significance (cf. 15:3). **39.** *about four in the afternoon:* In the Gk text, "the tenth hour" (cf. v. 41).

55 **40.** Andrew and Peter are mentioned together in the Syn tradition in Mk 1:16 par. **41.** Most mss. read: "First of all [he found his brother]." This may represent a case of dittography (*prōtontonadelphon*); the original may very well have been the *prōi* ("early next morning," used in 18:28; 20:1) presupposed by some Lat and Syr texts, although it is not found in any of our Gk mss. At any rate, the sense of v. 39 probably is that Andrew and the other disciples spent the night with Jesus, so that the meeting with Peter would take place on the "fourth day." **42.** That the Aram name of Simon Peter was *Kēphā'*, "Rock," we know, outside the Gospels, from its Grecized form *Kēphas* in the writings of Paul and Clement of Rome. "Peter" (*Petros*) is a Gk masc. translation. The giving of a new name signified the taking on of a new way of life (cf. Ap 3:12). Mk 3:16 also states that Christ changed Simon's name to Peter, but does not say when this occurred. Mt 16:18 associates the change of name with the promise of primacy to Peter, but it does not indicate that the change was made at that time. Interestingly enough, however, the change of name in Jn occurs in a context of testimony to Jesus' messianic character, even though it is not Peter's testimony. The Johannine equivalent of the primacy text of Mt occurs in 21:15–19.

56 **43–44.** On the "fifth day" Philip (cf. Mk 3:18 par.) is sought out by Jesus and added to the group of disciples. The mention of Andrew and Peter indicates no doubt the means by which Jesus was introduced to Philip; we are probably to assume that he too was a disciple of the Baptist. *Bethsaida:* In 12:21 this city is considered Galilean because of its proximity to Galilee, although technically it was in the territory of Gaulanitis. It is not clear why Jn calls Bethsaida the town of Andrew and Philip, because the Syn tradition (cf. Mk 1:29) clearly makes them residents of Capernaum. Possibly Jn is indicating Bethsaida as the place of their birth. **45.** Nathanael is mentioned only by Jn; it has generally been assumed that he is the Bartholomew (*bar tolmai*, "son of Tholmai") of the Syn. In the Syn tradition Bartholomew (a name that does not occur in Jn) is frequently mentioned together with Philip, and in Jn 21 Nathanael appears to have been, as Bartholomew certainly was, one of the Twelve; however the identification is not certain. *the Mosaic Law and the prophets:* The OT as a whole; the "one" of whom Moses and the prophets wrote is, of course, the Messiah. In 21:2 Nathanael is said to have been of Cana of Galilee. It was possibly here that Philip found him, as the next scene takes place in Cana. **46.** *how can anything good come out of Nazareth?:* Nazareth, the town with which Jesus is first associated in his public life, was an insignificant village never mentioned in the OT. No prophecy had connected the Messiah with Galilee (cf. 7:41,52), and certainly not with Nazareth. **47.** *a genuine Israelite:* A contemporary popular etymology of the name Israel was "one who sees God"; in v. 51 Nathanael is promised a vision of heavenly things. In the same verse, reference is made to the heavenly vision of Jacob (Israel) in Gn 28:10–17. The original Israel is being contrasted here with Nathanael. Jacob's guileful character was well known, but in Nathanael "there is no guile." **48.** *where do you know me from?:* Nathanael, who is about to recognize who Jesus is, has himself been recognized for what he is by Jesus. *I saw you under the fig tree:* Jesus alludes to some event in Nathanael's life known only to him. **49.** Nathanael climaxes the titles used of Jesus in the course of this chapter: "God's Son" (cf. 11:27; 2 Sm 7:14; Pss 2:7; 89:26f.) and "Israel's King" (12:13; Zeph 3:15) are to be taken as messianic titles. The Syn representation of Jesus' Messianic manifestation as one of gradual revelation is doubtless to be preferred from the standpoint of historical development; John has telescoped the historical sequence in favor of his deeper theological purpose.

57 **50.** Nathanael's faith has been motivated by a miracle extrinsic to Christ's Person; although this is not reprehensible, far greater will be the faith that comes from an intimate knowledge of Jesus himself (cf. 14:11). What the "far greater things" are that Nathanael will see, appears from the following. **51.** *amen, amen, I say to you:* This is a characteristic of Jesus' solemn pronouncements in this Gospel; the expression occurs only in Jn (25 times in all), but something similar is found on his lips in Mt 5:37. *you shall see the sky opened:* The reference is to Jacob's vision in Gn 28:10–17; Nathanael, however—and all genuine Israelites like him—will see angels mounting and descending not on a ladder, but on the Son of Man. As in Gn, the reference to the angels is to signify the meeting and communication of God with man. In the public ministry of Christ, and specifically in the "signs" that accompany that life, this meeting of

God with man will be made manifest. This is the "far greater thing" than merely to recognize the messianic character of Jesus. The disciples, like the Baptist, have witnessed to Jesus' messiahship; but the Baptist is of the OT, not of the new revelation (Mt 11:11,13 par.); the disciples of Christ will be able to witness to the very glory of God itself revealed in Jesus (1:14; 2:11). *the Son of Man:* In Jn as in the Syn, this is Jesus' favorite designation for himself—a title the Evangelists never apply to him. There would seem to be no doubt that the ultimate source, at least, from which Jesus drew this title was Dn 7:13f. In Dn the "one like a son of man" represents the people Israel, but an Israel that is glorified, the everlasting Kingdom of God. In applying the figure to himself, Jesus designated himself as the very embodiment of salvation: A man who yet lives with the glory of God, a mediator in whom heaven and earth meet. This revelation has been adopted eagerly by Jn, who has spelled out all its implications in his theology of the redemption (→ Johannine Theology, 80:17–20).

(Cullmann, O., *The Christology of the New Testament* [London, 1959] 137–92. Dalman, G., *The Words of Jesus* [Edinburgh, 1902] 234–67. Héring, J., *Le Royaume de Dieu et sa venue* [rev. ed.; Neuchâtel, 1959] 75–83, 88–110. Quispel, G., "Nathanael und der Menschensohn (Joh 1, 51)," *ZNW* 47 [1956] 281–83.)

58 (c) The Witness of the Disciples: The First Sign (2:1–11). Thus far the disciples have repeated the witness of the Baptist, which declared that Jesus was the Messiah. In the following episode we find the fulfillment of the prophecy made to Nathanael in 1:51, of something greater than the messiahship to which they will be witness. The story John has chosen to serve as his first "sign" (see comment on v. 11) is not found in the Syn tradition, though it may be called to mind in the parabolic teaching of Mk 2:22 par. It is fairly easy to explain why such an account would not have found its way into the Syn outline even if the witness responsible for the Syn tradition (Peter) had been present, since it would have readily been passed over in favor of material better assimilable into the kerygma; on the other hand, it is precisely such an event that lends itself to the Johannine "irony" (→ 62 below).

59 **1.** *on the third day:* In following the chronology (1:29,35,41,43), we must take this to mean the third day (that is, the day after the morrow) following the call of Philip and Nathanael. Thus the wedding feast at Cana takes place on the "seventh day" of the new creation story. John has not mentioned a sixth day, which would have been spent in travel from Bethany to Cana; however, see comment on 1:45. In any case, a symbolic rather than an historical chronology is in question. Undoubtedly, John has deliberately arranged the chronology to build up to a "third day," evoking the memory of the Lord's resurrection (glorification) on the third day after his death—here, the glory of the Lord (v. 11) is manifested on the third day after its promise. *Cana in Galilee:* Mentioned in the NT only by Jn, but otherwise by Josephus and other ancient writers. It is called "of Galilee" to distinguish it from another place of the same name in Phoenicia (Jos 19:28, *qānâ*). The village (*Kefr Kenna*) pointed out to the visitor to Palestine today as Cana has a rival contender (*Khirbet Qana*) a few miles away, now completely in ruins. Archaeologically, the latter site probably has more to recommend it as the place named in Jn (cf. F.-M. Abel, *GP* 2, 291f.; 412f.; C. Kopp, *The Holy Places of the Gospels* [N.Y., 1963] 143–54). *Jesus' mother:* Mary is mentioned elsewhere in Jn in 2:12; 6:42; 19:25-28, but never by name. Both in this account and in that of 19:25-28, where she is brought into intimate relation with her Son, at the beginning and the end of his public life, a certain symbolic pattern emerges in John's treatment of her (→ 63 below). **2.** *his disciples:* In Jn only five disciples have been mentioned so far, but in 6:67 the disciples of Jesus are called "the Twelve"; it is not clear whether all the Twelve are present on this occasion. **3.** Mary's observation to the Lord is not precisely the request of a miracle (so H. Strathmann), though evidently she is counting on the resourcefulness of her Son. In this gesture as well as in her command to the servants in v. 5, she appears to have occupied some position of authority at the feast; possibly the wedding was that of a near relative.

60 **4.** *woman:* This form of address is not disrespectful; it was commonly employed in speaking to women (cf. 4:21). In its use it resembles our somewhat more formal "madam." On the other hand, it was completely unheard of for a son to address his mother in such a fashion (cf. J. Michl, *Bib* 36 [1955] 492–509). Since the term "mother" is deliberately avoided here, the substitution of "mother" for "woman" in KL and NEB succeeds in missing the point of the inspired author (for further comment, → 63 below). *what to me and to you?:* This literal translation is variously rendered in modern versions. The idiom is from the OT (Jgs 11:12; 2 Sm 16:10; 1 Kgs 17:18; 2 Kgs 3:13; 2 Chr 35:21), where it signifies, as it does in the NT (Mk 5:7), a disavowal of some kind. It is evidently not an outright refusal of Mary's implied request, in view of what follows. Boismard, Michl, and others take it as a denial of Mary's need to ask, since they translate the following statement as a question: "Has not my hour already come?" (cf. S. Grill, *TZ* 16 [1960] 134f.). This interpretation was already entertained by some of the Gk Fathers (see Lagrange on this passage). However, there is no obvious reason to introduce a difference in meaning in a word as theologically significant in Jn as Jesus' "hour" (for a contrary view, cf. C. P. Ceroke, *TS* 17 [1956] 1–38). The disavowal seems rather to involve the role in which Mary has been cast, indicated already in the unusual title "woman." Just as in Lk 2:49 Jesus reminds his mother of his relation to the Father, which transcends all human relationships (so also Mk 3:31–35 par.), so here he reminds her of the only title under which she may command his intervention; further, the time when she may thus command has not yet arrived. *my hour has not yet come:* The "hour" of Jesus is that of his glorification, the crucifixion, death, and resurrection by which salvation is achieved (cf. 7:30; 8:20; 12:23,27; 13:1; 17:1). Just as it is in this glorification that Jesus achieves his destiny, so it is in virtue of it alone that Mary's intercession can have efficacy. Nevertheless, that hour can be, and is, foreshadowed in the "signs" of Jesus (cf. A. Feuillet, *ETL* 36 [1960] 5–22).

61 **5.** Mary's action indicates that she did not take Jesus' words as an outright refusal. She addresses the servants in the words of Gn 41:55 (see 19:23f.). **6.** *six stone water jars:* Stone was used because in Jewish belief it could not contract ritual uncleanness (cf. Str-B 2, 406f.). It is doubtful that John sees any special significance in the number six (the number of imperfection, cf. Ap 13:18). *Jewish purification:* Jewish custom demanded ceremonial washings before and after eating. John alludes to this ritual in order to explain the presence of such a large quantity of water. Also, this circumstance also allows him to point up a pattern that will accompany Jesus' "signs": A type associated with Judaism is systematically replaced by an antitype that originates in Christ. **7.** *to the brim:* The reality of what Jesus is about to do is stressed: The jars contained nothing but water. Jn mirrors the reticence of the first chapter of Gn in alluding to Christ's creative miracle: His word alone suffices to effect the change. **8.** *the headwaiter:* At Gentile banquets one of the guests usually assumed the position of "master of the banquet" as a mark of honor. The familiarity with which the "headwaiter" in this instance addresses the bridegroom (v. 9) may indicate that the Jews followed a similar custom. **9–10.** Again the reality of the fact is underscored. Testimony is given to the excellence of the new wine (cf. Lk 5:39) by one who is ignorant of its origin and therefore subject to no suggestion. **11.** *the first one of his signs:* The word "sign" repeatedly occurs in the first half of Jn's Gospel (cf. D. Mollat, *SP* 2, 209–18). Pre-eminent among these are Jesus' miracles, of which Jn records only seven. They are called signs not merely because they are worked to encourage belief, though they are this, but because they signify Christ for what he is: They illustrate his true character (cf. 5:36; → Johannine Theology, 80:27–29). As will be seen, Jn has chosen his seven signs to illustrate Jesus' character with an increasing degree of clarity. *he revealed his glory:* See comment on 1:14. The miracle of water made into wine may in itself not appear to be an apt indication of Christ's glory; however, it must be taken as Jn takes it, as the first of a series, all of which are related to the life that is to be found in the Word of God (see comment on 1:4). As a creative miracle, it properly stands at the head of the series. *his disciples believed in him:* The disciples have now been confronted with something greater than what the Baptist had pointed out to them. With this new creative power now made manifest in Jesus, the disciples have passed beyond the stage of the history of salvation represented by the Precursor.

62 Additional Comments on 2:1–11. As has been shown, it is clearly John's intention to write history in the record of this sign. This does not prevent him, however, from exploiting the theological potentialities of the episode; in so doing, he shows that this aspect is more important to him than the mere recording of a miracle. In stressing that the water Jesus replaced with wine was that "demanded by Jewish purificatory customs," he allows us to see the first of many ways in which Christ has replaced the institutions of Judaism. The pattern thus established will be repeated in other episodes. That this pattern should have begun at a wedding feast is in itself significant, in view of the OT figure of Israel as the spouse of Yahweh (Hos 2:21f.; Jer 2:2; Is 54:5f.; etc.). This figure developed in Judaism, and even saw in a wedding feast the symbol for the Messianic age (cf. Mt 9:15; Str-B 1, 517f.). In this context, it becomes fairly obvious that John would have expected his Christian readers to make a further association in reflecting on the significance of this event in the life of Jesus. The sacramental interest that John displays elsewhere (3:5; 6:51; 1 Jn 5:6; etc.) leaves little doubt that he wants us to think of the Eucharist. This is probably also his reason for bringing this episode into close relation with the Passover (v. 13), as he does the other major Eucharistic episode of the multiplication of the loaves (cf. 6:5), to recall that the Eucharistic sacrifice is the Christian Passover (cf. 12:1; 1 Cor 5:7). Viewed in this way, the "sign" of Cana appears as something far greater than simply one miracle out of many in the ministry of Christ. It is, rather, a sign in the fullest possible sense, one of the sacraments (= "signs") by which the Christian recognizes through faith and in the life of the Church the presence of the same Christ who was visibly present to the first disciples in the flesh (cf. 20:29; 1 Jn 1:1).

63 John has not superimposed the sacramental connotations (→ 24 above) on his narrative only to have them recognized or ignored at will. His sacramental teaching is part of the purpose or reason for writing his Gospel: that those Christians for whom it was written may be confirmed in their faith and that in the name of Jesus they may possess the very life of God (20:31). That the life of the Church, the life of the Spirit, is indeed the life of Christ and that the sacraments are the deeds of Christ perpetuated is the common teaching not only of Jn, Paul, and Lk, but of the entire NT.

Something similar must be said of the figure of "the mother of Jesus," as she appears in Jn. Mary is represented not merely in her historical character but in the function that has been reserved to her in salvation history. If John has seen a new history of creation unfold in the preceding "seven days," he has also reserved a special place in this history for her who has been addressed as "woman." The woman of the first creation was called Life (LXX: *Zōē* = "Eve"), because she was "mother of all the living" (Gn 3:20). Mary is mother of the new life, not only of the Word become flesh, but also of all those who live with his life (14:19f.). She is, in other words, a figure of the Church, the new Eve, as the Fathers called her. A similar Johannine representation is found in the woman of Ap 12, who is simultaneously the mother of Christ and of the New Israel, where again the imagery of Gn has served as the inspiration of the vision. In this acceptation, we can see the relevance with which she is again called "woman" in 19:26f., where the beloved disciple, who stands for all Christians, is committed to her as to his mother. We can see the relevance with which her implied claim on Christ at Cana is apparently disavowed: Her intercessory efficacy is effective only in virtue of the glorification of Christ. However, because the hour that has not yet come is nevertheless anticipated, her petition is granted. In the light of this role, the enigmatic reply of our Lord in v. 4 becomes consistent with the action of v. 5ff. The ecclesiology of this passage therefore contains a Mariology as well, which is also true of the Infancy Narrative of Lk 1–2.

(Barrosse, T., "The Seven Days of the New Creation in St. John's Gospel," *CBQ* 21 [1959] 507–16. Boismard, M.-E., *Du baptême à Cana* [LD 18; Paris, 1956]. Brown, R. E., "The Johannine Sacramentary Reconsidered," *TS* 23 [1962] 183–206. Ceroke, C. P., "The Problem of Ambiguity in John 2, 4," *CBQ* 21 [1959] 316–40. Cullmann, O., *Baptism in the New Testament* [SBT 1; London, 1950]; *Early Christian Worship* [SBT 10; London, 1953]. Grossouw, A. W., *Revelation and Redemption* [Westminster, 1955]. Higgins, A. J. B., *The Lord's Supper in the New Testament* [SBT 6; London, 1952]. Lohse, E., "Wort und Sakrament im Johannesevangelium," *NTS* 7 [1961] 110–25. Niewalda, P., *Sakramentssymbolik im Johannesevangelium* [Limburg, 1958]. Schnackenburg, R., "Die Sakramente im Johannesevangelium," *SP*, 2, 235–54. Vawter, B., "The Johannine Sacramentary," *TS* 17 [1956] 151–66.)

64 **(B) The New Life in Signs (2:12–4:54).** Jn understands a "sign" as a broader concept than simply Christ's miracles. This is evident not only in the seven miracles that he has singled out especially to illustrate this idea, but it is also apparent from other words and deeds of Jesus. The underlying spiritual significance in Jesus' cleansing of the Temple, an event reproduced from the Syn tradition, cannot be denied.

12. Jn takes little cognizance of Jesus' activity in Galilee. This summary statement, however, agrees with the Syn tradition in making the Capernaum phase of the ministry a brief one (Mk 1:14ff.; 2:1ff. par.). The shortest reading in the mss., possibly the original, lists those who went down to Capernaum as Jesus, his mother, and the brethren. Here "the brethren" means Jesus' disciples, who remained with him in Capernaum only a few days. The addition of "and his disciples" is explained through the identification of "the brothers" with Jesus' relatives (see 7:1–10).

65 (a) The New Temple: The Resurrected Christ (2:13–25). The story of the cleansing of the

Temple occurs in the Syn tradition (Mk 11:15–18 par.) at the close rather than at the beginning of Jesus' ministry, during a Passover feast, the only one recorded in the Syn. Despite the incidental dissimilarities, the same event is apparently being referred to; no point is necessarily to be made of either the Syn or the Johannine chronology. In both instances, the meaning of the event, rather than when it took place, is the point of emphasis.

13. *the Jewish passover:* John knows of a Christian Passover (cf. 1 Cor 5:7), of which the Jewish feast was but a type. The feasts of Judaism play a major role in John's Gospel as representing the institutions that prefigured Christ. It is difficult to accept as a whole, however, the thesis of A. Guilding (*The Fourth Gospel and Jewish Worship* [Oxford, 1960]), who claims that the order and discourses of Jn have been determined according to the (partly conjectural) triennial cycle of synagogue lectionary readings for the great feasts. **14.** Various kinds of sacrificial animals were for sale at the Temple so that the pilgrims would not have the added expense of bringing them from afar. The only money accepted at the Temple was the Tyrian half-shekel: Roman coinage could not be used; hence the money-changers performed a necessary function. **15.** *whip of cords:* Not mentioned in the Syn accounts. If the number of animals and tenders was large, as it probably was, the whip must have served as a symbol of authority rather than as a physical goad. On the other hand, Jesus may have enlisted the assistance of his disciples in this gesture. **16.** In the Syn account Jesus' wrath appears to be directed against the dishonesty of the traffickers in the Temple; in Jn the emphasis is rather on the very institutions themselves which Jesus opposes. The sacrificial system of Judaism has made "a market place" of the Temple. This more radical opposition is in keeping with the interpretation in v. 21. *my Father's house:* The formula "my Father" by which Jesus testified to his special relationship to God is found not only in Jn (27 times), but also in Mt (16 times), and in Lk (4 times).

66 **17.** The disciples recalled the words of Ps 69:10. This Ps is used in the NT more frequently than any other, always in a messianic application, which is presumably how the disciples understood it at this time. Such an action of cleansing had been predicted of the messianic age by Zech 14:21. After the resurrection (v. 22), the disciples saw the profound meaning of Christ's words and deeds signified in v. 21. **18.** *the Jews:* Here the Temple authorities, who would have represented the priesthood. *what sign:* The demand for a sign was continually being made of Jesus (cf. Mk 8:11 par.), a demand that he continually refused to gratify. Signs are for the well-disposed, to evoke or to confirm faith. **19.** Jesus did foretell the destruction of the Temple (cf. Mk 13:2); however, here he refers to his death and resurrection, the truly adequate sign to be given for all believers (cf. 3:21). This corresponds to the Syn saying recorded in Mt 12:38ff. par. **20.** The Jews take Jesus' words literally—words that at his trial were distorted into an imputation of sorcery (Mt 26:61 par.). *forty-six years:* According to Josephus (*Ant.* 15.11, 1 § 380), the Temple of Herod was begun in his 18th year (20/19 BC). Hence Jn would have dated this episode *ca.* AD 27/28. The Temple was not completed in Jesus' time, being finished only in AD 63/64, shortly before its destruction by the Romans. **21.** The "house of his father" that would be made ready in the resurrection is quite different from that of the earthly Temple (cf. 14:2). Jesus' words refer as much to the Church as they do to the resurrection. **22.** The Gospels frequently testify that the full significance of his words and deeds was only understood in the light of the resurrection and the coming of the Holy Spirit (cf. 7:39; 13:19; 14:29; Lk 24:8; etc.). *scripture:* From Acts 2:31 and 13:35 we know that the primitive Church saw in Ps 16:10 an intimation of the resurrection.

67 **23.** *believed in his name:* See comment on 1:12. *signs:* Though John has thus far mentioned only the one miracle at Cana, he presupposes the numerous miracles of the Syn tradition (cf. 3:2; 4:45). Mt 21:14f. speaks of miracles that occurred at the time of the cleansing of the Temple. **24–25.** A faith based merely on miracles without a proper recognition of the nature of him who performed them would prove to be unstable and inconstant. The same idea occurs in 6:2. Jesus, who is truly man but endowed with the wisdom of God, labors under no illusions concerning human frailty.

68 (b) THE NEW BIRTH: BAPTISM (3:1–36). The theme begun in the Baptist's testimony (1:26,33) is taken up in episodes that underline ways in which Christ has replaced the institutions of Judaism.

(i) *Nicodemus* (3:1–21). **1.** Nicodemus is mentioned only in Jn (also in 7:50; 19:39); however, the name was a common one. Though the Sanhedrin, the governing body of the Jews recognized by the Romans, was mainly composed of the Sadducean element, it also counted Pharisees among its members (cf. Acts 5:34). As a Pharisee, a member of the Sanhedrin, and a rabbi (v. 10), Nicodemus represents the quintessence of Judaism. John has scarcely contrived this conversation as a sequel to 7:52 (a theory recently revived by S. Mendner, *JBL* 77 [1958] 293–323). **2.** *at night:* In view of the official opposition to Jesus, already suggested by John and borne out repeatedly throughout the Gospel, a prominent leader such as Nicodemus could only have come to see Jesus secretly. John also intends a significance like that of 13:30. Nicodemus has come to Jesus out of the darkness (see 1:5); eventually he became one of Jesus' disciples, and is doubtless one of those mentioned in 12:42. *Rabbi:* Nicodemus uses the title used by the disciples upon their recognition of Christ (1:38). *we know:* Nicodemus associates himself with those who believed in Jesus because of the signs he had been working (2:23). **3.** As with the disciples' initial faith, this profession of Nicodemus will be of no value unless it fixes itself upon Jesus as he truly is; therefore, Jesus replies with an enigmatic saying as in 1:51. Nicodemus has said that Jesus is a teacher from God, meaning one whose teaching is truly in accord with God's mind. Jesus will now show him that he is from God in a way that he has not understood. The Kingdom of God is not to be seen merely through the miracles that have impressed Nicodemus. It can only be experienced through a spiritual rebirth (1:12f.). *begotten from above:* As happens frequently in the Johannine dialogues, the expression is obscure enough to permit Nicodemus' retort in the following verse. The word *anōthen* can mean either "again" or "from above." **4.** Nicodemus takes the statement in a material sense. It is ironical that as a rabbi Nicodemus should be puzzled by this figure of "rebirth," since the rabbis used the same expression for proselytes to Judaism. However, the spiritual regeneration of which Jesus speaks goes beyond the capabilities of Judaism (cf. Str-B 2, 420ff.).

69 **5.** Jesus insists on the necessity of spiritual birth for the Kingdom of God, which is the possession only of the children of God. *water and Spirit:* In the view of some (Bultmann, for example), "water and" is an "ecclesiastical" interpolation to give the text a sacramental meaning. There is no textual evidence for such an opinion and it must be rejected in view of the obvious structure of the Gospel; however, it is possible to think that John, in the light of his later Christian knowledge, has made the addition to Jesus' words concerning birth by the Spirit (cf. I. de la Potterie, *ScEccl* 14 [1962] 417–43). John is evidently thinking of Christian baptism (cf. v. 22ff.) and intends the Christian reader to do the same. It is not necessary to suppose that Nicodemus would have derived such a developed conception of the way of salvation; if Jesus actually spoke of both water and the Spirit, Nicodemus may have thought of John's water-baptism as the introduction to the Spirit-baptism given by Christ. Ez 36:25ff. spoke of the messianic times in terms of water and a new spirit in man. Nicodemus' understanding of "Spirit" would presumably have been that of the Baptist (cf. 1:32f.). **6.** The contrast between flesh (cf. 1:14) and spirit reappears in 6:63. Both terms refer to the constituents of life, but the latter especially was thought of as life-giving, the breath that comes from God (cf. Gn 2:7; Jb 10:9–12; 33:4). Flesh is merely the outward manifestation of life; spirit or breath is life itself. Flesh alone can produce only the semblance of life; true life comes from the Spirit of God. **7–8.** *blows where it wants:* Christ uses an analogy, which involves a play on words: Both in Aramaic and in Greek the same word renders "spirit," "breath," and "wind." Many things that are known cannot be explained; they are not seen except in their effects (cf. Eccl 11:5). **9–10.** Nicodemus' further question permits Jesus to point up the paradox: He who is renowned as a master in Israel does not understand the meaning of the great themes of the OT. **11.** In turn, this explains the "we" of the continuation of Jesus' discourse, in which John sees the true Israel giving its testimony; Nicodemus had spoken in behalf of Judaism (v. 2) and as its representative, whereas Jesus speaks for himself and Christianity. *we are talking about something we know:* What Jesus says comes from his shared knowledge with God the Father (cf. 8:38; 12:50); his words and deeds witness to this fact (5:31ff.; 8:14), but his witness is being rejected (cf. 1:11; 5:43; 12:37). **12.** Up to this point, Jesus has been speaking of what should be comparatively easy to understand, at least by analogies. In this sense rebirth and the presence of the Spirit are "earthly things." If Nicodemus cannot understand these, if they cannot bring him to faith in Jesus' true character, then he is obviously in no position to receive the revelation of "heavenly things," that is, mysteries of which faith alone can provide the basis of understanding.

70 In the ensuing verses Nicodemus disappears and the dialogue becomes a monologue, either of Christ or of John or of both (→ 30 above). Verses 31–36 at the end of the chapter also belong in some way to vv. 13–21; they refer more to the Nicodemus situation than to that of vv. 22–30. Some would find here one of the famous "transpositions" in the text of Jn (→ 7 above) and place vv. 13–21 at the end of the chapter (cf. R. Schnackenburg, *ZNW* 49 [1958] 88–99); however, in the absence of positive evidence to the contrary, it seems to be preferable to interpret the text of Jn as it stands in all the mss.

13. The "heavenly things" of which Jesus has just spoken cannot be grasped by any man at will. Here the reader may have been reminded of the Gnostic "mystery" religions that pretended to transfer initiates into a realm of heavenly knowledge. The only one who can speak authoritatively of heavenly things is the only Person who has both come down from heaven and ascended into heaven, the Son of Man (see 1:51). **14.** *that serpent:* The reference is to the incident recorded in Nm 21:4–9; in Wis 16:6f. the bronze serpent is called *symbolon sōtērias*, "symbol of salvation." The basis of comparison here is that in both cases salvation has come through a "raising up." *so must the Son of Man be raised up:* The condition of all the foregoing, of the giving of the Spirit and the introduction of man into the heavenly realm, is the exaltation of Christ. In Jn the vb. *hypsōthēnai*, "be raised up," has a deliberately double significance when applied to Christ, referring to both his being raised up on the cross (cf. 8:28) and to his glorification in the resurrection and ascension to the Father. The usage is analogous to the *analēmpsis* of Lk 9:51; however, this is one of the key words of the Johannine vocabulary. It is closely akin to *doxasthēnai*, "be glorified" (see 1:14; 2:11); both these words appear in Is 52:13 to describe the Servant of the Lord (see 1:29), and it is doubtless with such an allusion that they occur in Jn. The unification of the functions of Servant and Son of Man has an authentic situation in Jesus' own proclamation of himself (cf. O. Cullmann, *Christology*, 60–69; J. Jeremias, *The Servant*, 98–104). **15.** The consequence of the exaltation of Christ is life in him (1:4) for all who believe (1:12).

71 The following passages very clearly show that the Evangelist himself is speaking. **16.** *God loved the world so much:* The only explanation that we shall ever have of the gift of eternal life made possible for us in the redemption achieved in Christ is the incredible love of God for the world (cf. 1 Jn 4:9; → Johannine Theology, 80:25–26). Though alienated from God, the world is not evil in itself, and remains the object of divine compassion (for the concept of "the world," see comment on 1:10). *he gave his only Son:* Jn stresses the gratuity of God's love, extending even to this extreme. *may not perish:* The question of Christ may be resolved only in belief and eternal life or in rejection and destruction; there is no third alternative. **17–18.** Christ has been sent into the world to bring eternal life (10:10); willful unbelief makes of him the occasion of condemnation. Thus unbelief is its own condemnation, and the unbeliever passes judgment on himself (cf. 12:31; → Johannine Theology, 80:55–56). This "realized eschatology" of Jn (→ 25 above) does not deny the common NT teaching on futurist eschatology (cf. 5:27–29); but just as eternal life already begins in this world for him who has decided for Christ, so does the unbeliever already stand condemned. This is the sign of the Son of Man, in whom heaven and earth meet (1:51). **19–20.** These verses anticipate Jn's conclusion of the Book of Signs (12:37ff.; cf. also 1:5,9–10). **21.** The evil-doer is the child of darkness and will not come to the light which is Christ; he who approaches the light, on the other hand, is the one who "does the truth"; this is an OT expression (Gn 24:49; Ez 18:8f.), meaning to "keep faith." The expression is used in the same sense in 1QS 1:5; 5:3; 8:2. He who does the works that are of God comes to the light.

72 (ii) *Baptism of John and baptism of Christ* (3:22–36). The strange chronology of this passage (in 3:22 Jesus comes into Judea, whereas in 3:1–21 he was already in Jerusalem) and the fact that vv. 31–36 are largely a repetition of vv. 13–21 are not necessarily signs of dislocations in the text. Chronology is secondary to John's theological purposes. Rather, the Evangelist seems to have paralleled two narratives touching on the same theme, each followed by a similar meditation. The theme remains Jesus' replacement of the institutions of Judaism—specifically through Christian baptism (cf. 3:4).

22. *some time afterward:* Because Jn does not maintain a precise chronology, the historical antecedent of this episode cannot be determined. *into Judean territory:* This could mean that Jesus left Jerusalem and went into the Judean countryside; however, John more than likely thought of Jesus as coming from Galilee, where the Syn center his activity. *baptizing:* According to 4:2 Jesus himself did not baptize; it was rather his disciples who did so. Historically, of course, this was not Christian sacramental baptism, which depends on the giving of the Spirit with the glorification of Christ (7:39). The baptism of the disciples must have been in the same spirit and for the same purpose as the baptism of John, even as the Syn tradition represents Jesus' ministry as beginning where the

Baptist left off, preaching repentance in preparation for the kingdom (Mk 1:15). However, it was sufficient for Johannine symbolism (→ 31–32 above) that a baptism that contrasted with the baptism of John should be associated with Christ. **23.** *Aenon near Salim:* This site has not been satisfactorily identified; no doubt it is a real and not a symbolic place. Aenon is probably a transliteration of the Aram *'ēnāwān*, "springs." The site is identified by W. F. Albright (*AP* 247) with an *Ainun*, 7 mi. from a Salim that lies to the E of Nablus in Samaria; tradition from the 4th cent. perhaps more plausibly connects it with the springs near a Salumias or Sedima about 7 mi. S of Beth-shan (*Beisan*) in the Jordan valley (cf. F.-M. Abel, *GP* 2, 441f.; C. Kopp, *Holy Places*, 129–37). **24.** John supposes the Syn account of the Baptist's imprisonment to be known (Mk 6:17ff. par.) and situates these events in relation to it.

73 **25–26.** The baptisms by both the Baptist and Jesus' disciples lead to a controversy over the Jewish purificatory rites (cf. 2:6), which is in turn the occasion of the Baptist's disciples coming to him with what they consider a legitimate complaint. Their master's prestige is suffering through the renown of him whom John had pointed out. The best ms. reading indicates that the controversy was with "a Jew" rather than with "the Jews." The nature of the controversy is not brought out; John considers the matter irrelevant—as does Jesus himself (Mk 7:1ff.)—in relation to the greater things with which the Gospel is concerned. **27–28.** The Baptist's reply to the jealous complaint of his disciples is to put himself humbly in his proper relation to Jesus. His baptism is meaningless unless it had a divine purpose, and he had already borne witness (1:20) that that divine purpose was not to herald his own messianic character but that of Jesus. **29.** This protestation is illustrated by a familiar example similar to the one employed by Jesus himself (Mk 2:19). The role of the best man at a wedding was to bring the bride and the bridegroom together, and to rejoice in the bridegroom's happiness. This has been John's function, with which he is content. The example is not chosen at random, in view of the messianic significance of "bridegroom" (see comment on 2:1–11). **30.** The last words of the Baptist in Jn are his own summation of his role in the history of salvation, parallel to Jesus' words in Mt 11:11.

74 The following verses continue, or parallel, the monologue of 3:16–21; however, they also have reference to the preceding episode. **31.** *the one who comes:* The title of the Messiah (1:15,27). *from above:* Jesus is not merely the Messiah, but the bringer of heavenly life (cf. 3:3). *above all:* He is beyond all that is merely earthly, which includes both the purifications of the Jews and John's baptism. *the one who is of earth:* For "earth" and the "earthly," see comment on 3:12; this is not the same as the "world" (1:10). *of the earth does he speak:* Compare Jesus' words to Nicodemus (v. 12), in which "earthly things" were understood as a preparation for "heavenly things." The preaching of John the Baptist and the old covenant would be examples of the "earthly things." **32.** This verse repeats the thought of 3:11. **33.** Whoever receives the testimony of Christ certifies to God's truthfulness even as God certifies to the truthfulness of Christ (cf. 6:27); it is to the truthfulness of God that he testifies, since Christ is the messenger of God (12:44ff.; 1 Jn 5:10). **34.** *nor does he measure out the Spirit:* The prophets of the old covenant, of which John the Baptist was one, communicated with God's Spirit; but the fullness of God's revelation has come only in Christ (cf. 1:17f.). **35.** For love as the explanation of the revelation of God in Christ, cf. 3:16; 10:17; 15:9. *has handed over all things to Him:* Christ's work is in every sense God's, an exercise of complete divine authority (cf. 5:22ff.; 17:2ff.; Mt 11:27; Lk 10:22). **36.** This verse reproduces the thought of 3:18.

75 (c) Water of Life (4:1–42). Another narrative permits John to develop further the theme of the water of Judaism replaced by the life-giving water of Christ. The rabbinical (and Qumran) comparison of the Torah with water (as cleansing, as satisfying thirst, and as promoting life) affords the background of John's teaching. Once again Christ is the fulfillment of what the Law could only promise (1:17).

1–3. A note on the growing hostility of official Judaism serves as a preface to this account and helps to bring out by contrast the favorable reception that Jesus receives from the Samaritans. The chronology is uncertain, but presumably this relates to a time after the Baptist's imprisonment. The resentment aroused by the Baptist's activity (Mt 21:25ff. par.) has now been transferred to Jesus. For baptism by Jesus' disciples, see comment on 3:22. **4.** *he had to pass through Samaria:* The most direct route, a three-day journey, from Judea to Galilee ran through the territory of the Samaritans, who were often hostile to Judeans and Galileans (cf. Lk 9:51ff.). The Syn tradition contains no record of Jesus' ministry among the Samaritans; but then it is quite sketchy on the subject of his activity outside Galilee, and Samaria formed a political unit with Judea. Possibly John's interest in the Samaritans was prompted by the adaptability of their interpretation of Judaism to the new revelation of Christianity (cf. J. Bowman, *BJRylL* 40 [1958] 298–329); this may also account for the Samaritans' receptiveness to the apostolic preaching (Acts 8:1–25). **5.** *Samaritan town:* In all the Gk mss. it is called *Sychar;* this is thought by some to be a corruption of *Sychem* (Shechem), which was indeed "near the field which Jacob had given to his son Joseph" (cf. Gn 33:19; 48:22; Jos 24:32). Shechem (*Tell el-Balatah*) was inhabited during Jesus' time, but it is questionable whether the number of dwellings would have constituted a town. A nearby town known today as Askar may have been the Sychar of this episode. **6.** There is no question about the location of Jacob's well, which lies between *Tell el-Balatah* and *Askar*. According to P^{66} Jesus sat down "on the ground" (*gē*) rather than "at the well" (*pēgē*).

76 **7–9.** Not only was it unheard of for a rabbi to speak familiarly with a woman in public but also for a Jew to request water of a Samaritan. Jews considered Samaritans, and therefore their utensils for eating and drinking, unclean. Jesus was untroubled by such scruples; the Gospels frequently record his enlightened attitude toward women and also that on occasion he spoke favorably of Samaritans (cf. Lk 10:33; 17:6). **10.** *God's gift:* Jesus himself, whom the woman does not yet recognize. She sees only a Jew, and a thirsty traveler. *living water:* The woman first takes it to mean running water as distinct from well or cistern water, but as Jesus explains, it means "water of life," a figure borrowed from the OT (Jer 2:13; Zech 14:8; Ez 47:9; Prv 13:14; etc.), where it signifies divine vitality, revelation, wisdom. In rabbinical use the figure was generally applied to the Torah (Str-B 2, 433–36). The same application of the figure of water is made by CD 3:16f.; 6:3f. ("The well [of Nm 21:16ff.] is the Torah.") Once again, Jesus will truly give what the Law merely promised. **11.** As did Nicodemus (3:4), the woman takes Christ's words literally. **12.** Since Jesus cannot mean to get water from the well, where will he get it? Even Jacob had had no better source than this well. The woman's attempt at irony is, of course, an irony itself for the Christian reader, who knows full well how much greater than Jacob is the one who speaks with her (cf. also 8:53). *our ancestor Jacob:* The Samaritans also claimed descent from the patriarchs, through the Joseph tribes of Ephraim and Manasseh. *who gave us this well:* By these words the water of the well is qualified as "water of Judaism" (cf. 2:6). **13–14.** Jesus begins to explain his meaning. Sir 24:20 proclaims that the drinker of wisdom will thirst again, that is, that his desire for wisdom will become ever more insatiable. However, such a desire could never be satisfied. The water that Christ will give, on the contrary, will satisfy thirst forever; whoever drinks of this water will have the fountain of eternal life within him. The Christian reader is again reminded of baptism, the water of Christ that confers the gift of eternal life.

77 **15–18.** The woman still misunderstands and asks, perhaps ironically, for this so marvelous water that would quench her thirst and end her trips to the well. Christ's reply leads her to recognize that he possesses superhuman knowledge; from this it should be but another step to recognize that his words had a deeper meaning. **19–20.** The woman now perceives Jesus to be a prophet. Before she had seen in him a Jew. Her implied question, which may well have been an attempt to divert the conversation into less embarrassing channels, is one that might be put naturally under the circumstances: What would a prophet say with regard to the long-standing controversy between the Jews and Samaritans concerning the proper place of sacrificial worship? Mt. Gerizim, at the foot of which this conversation took place, was the Samaritan place of worship; here the patriarchs had sacrificed (Gn 12:7; 33:20), and here, according to the Samaritan version of Dt 27:4 (Mt. Ebal in the MT), the Israelites had first set up an altar in Palestine. **21.** Jesus replies that very soon such a question will have no more relevance; the Samaritan-Jewish controversy will have been superseded by a revelation that renders it superfluous (cf. 2:19). When the history of salvation has further progressed, it will be seen that the Temple was superfluous to this history. For this train of thought in Judaism, cf. O. Cullmann, *NTS* 5 (1959) 157–73. **22.** Jesus must agree that in Judaism, and not in the Samaritan aberration from it, God's revelation has been safeguarded. In good faith though they may be, the Samaritans nevertheless have preserved the truth given by God in only a distorted form. *salvation is from the Jews:* The best proof of this lies in him who speaks, who stands firmly within the authentic traditions of Israel and who is the fulfillment of its expectation. **23.** Nevertheless, even the authentic traditions of Israel have merely led to a consummation that lies beyond its capacities. *an hour is coming:* See comment on 2:4; the "hour" of Jesus' glorification is the "hour" of the Church. *and it is here:* For its efficacy, the true worship of believers depends upon the glorification of Christ; but such is always possible in virtue of this same efficacy, even as the just men of the old covenant were saved by the same faith that joins Christians to God (cf. Rom 4:23–25). *real worshipers:* Those who worship God within a new relation that could be encompassed neither by Judaism nor Samaritanism. **24.** *God is Spirit:* In 1 Cor 15:45 Paul speaks of Christ as "life-giving spirit." "Spirit" in the biblical sense does not define God's nature so much as it describes his life-giving activity (see 1:32f.). God is Spirit in that he gives the Spirit; so also God is light and love (1 Jn 1:5; 4:8). This explains how and why the true worshiper of God must worship him in "Spirit and truth." The two words actually signify a single idea (for "truth," see comment on 1:14). **25.** The woman has already recognized in Jesus a prophet; now she begins to surmise that he might be the prophet of Dt 18:18 (see comment on 1:21). Her statement is, again, an implied question. It was probably under this figure that the Samaritans, who accepted only the Pentateuch as inspired Scripture, represented their belief in the coming of a Messiah. Little is known about the messianic belief that the Samaritans shared with the Jews; the Messiah himself they called *Tā'eb*, "he who returns" or "he who restores." **26.** Jesus accepts this designation of himself (see comment on 1:49). *I who am speaking to you, I am:* These words reproduce Yahweh's pronouncement in Is 52:6. In view of the special significance of "I am" as Jesus' designation of himself in Jn (see comment on 6:35), it is likely that Jn characteristically suggests another level of meaning here in Jesus' affirmation.

78 **27.** The disciples now return from their errand (v. 8) and are more surprised to find Jesus speaking with a woman than that he should be conversing with a Samaritan. However, they know their Master well enough not to remonstrate with him or with the woman while he is present. **28.** In departing, the woman undoubtedly left her water jar that Jesus might drink—in dwelling on the consequences of Jesus' request in v. 7, it must be remembered that the request was a real one. John may see a symbolic significance here: Now that the woman has come to the source of living water, she has no further need of any other (v. 15). **29–30.** The woman carries the message of Philip (1:45f.), but in a much more tentative fashion. **31–33.** Meanwhile the disciples also appear slow to understand, as they too take a profound utterance in its surface sense. **34.** In these words Jesus sums up his entire career (cf. 17:4). **35.** Jesus apparently cites a Palestinian proverb. It takes four months from sowing till harvest; the Gezer calendar, dating from the 10th cent. BC, allows precisely this interval (cf. H. Vincent, *RB* 6 [1909] 243–69; W. F. Albright, *BASOR* 92 [1943] 16–26). The harvest of which Jesus speaks, however, which is of God's planting, is ready now (cf. Mt 9:35–10:1; Lk 10:2). The earnest of this is in the woman who goes even now to witness to the people of her village, who will soon come and see for themselves (v. 42). **36.** In this harvest there is no interval at all from sowing to reaping, but the reaper overtakes the sower and both rejoice together (cf. Am 9:13). **37–38.** Herein is verified an old saying (cf. Jb 31:8; Eccl 2:21), but in a different sense than it would ordinarily have, since both the sowing and the reaping of this harvest is the work of God. The disciples, who will reap a quick harvest in Samaria (cf. Acts 8:4–25), must remember that this can only be because of the nature of the word they will sow, a word that has already been sown by Jesus himself and by all who revealed the word before him.

79 **39–41.** The Samaritans follow the model of all who have true faith. First having believed because of the woman's testimony (see comment on 1:7,15) and because of the miracle that she related of Jesus' having revealed natural secrets (cf. 1:49f.), they eventually come to believe because of his own word (cf. 8:30; 10:38), the same word that the disciples would later bring to Samaria. **42.** *Savior of the world:* Not only do they come to believe, they also recognize in him something more than the Messiah to which the woman had witnessed (cf. 1:50). This title does not seem to have been used ordinarily of the Messiah; elsewhere it is found only in 1 Jn 4:14. John, of course, intends it to be understood in the full light of Christian revelation (→ Johannine Theology, 80:15). What the Samaritans would have understood is less clear; but Jesus, by transcending national lines in dealing with them, would have laid a basis for a universal affirmation of God's salvation. Thus their confession is the sum of John's reflection on the revelation to Nicodemus (3:16f.).

80 (d) THE SECOND SIGN (4:43–54). **43.** The journey begun in 4:1–3 is now concluded. **44.** This saying is ascribed to Jesus in Mk 6:4; Mt 13:57; Lk 4:24. Because it does not seem to agree with v. 45, some have concluded that for John, Judea and not Galilee was Jesus' "native place." This, however, appears to be incompatible with 1:45. Rather, the verse appears to be parenthetical here: It is John's summary of the Galilean ministry, reflecting the same final judgment passed on it in the Syn tradition. **45.** In this respect, we should remember that the enthusiasm based on the signs wrought in Jerusalem (cf. 3:2), though it might be the beginning of true faith, might just as easily prove to be illusory (cf. 2:23–25); such, in fact, was the case with the Galileans. The episode that follows may be the Johannine version of the cure recorded in other variant forms by Mt 8:5–13 and Lk 7:1–10; such was the opinion of Irenaeus (*Adv. haer.* 2.22, 3; *PG* 7.783). The Syn narrative also appears at the beginning of the Galilean ministry. John has selected the story for his second "sign," which took place in the same village of Cana. The first sign was only indirectly connected with the theme of life; in the second, life is spared from an immediate threat of destruction. The progression will reach its climax in ch. 11, when life becomes triumphant over death itself in the resurrection of Lazarus.

46. *Cana in Galilee:* See comment on 2:1; John reminds us that the "first sign" also took place here. *royal official:* Presumably this man held a position in the service of Herod Antipas (→ History of Israel, 75:140), who was popularly styled "king." Jn does not indicate whether he was a Jew or a Gentile. **47.** The official had obviously heard of the "signs" that Jesus had been performing in Jerusalem (cf. v. 45). Jesus' healing miracles are not mentioned; the Evangelist presumes that the reader will know of these from the Syn tradition. **48.** As in the previous miracle at Cana, Jesus' initial reply is an apparent refusal (cf. 2:4). However, his use of the plural ("you people") rises to a general principle: Faith must not rest on miracles only. **49–50.** Like Mary, the official recognizes that his request has not been definitively refused. The effect intended is now secured, for the man believes "the word Jesus spoke to him." This is not to say that he had acquired perfect faith, but it was a beginning. **51–53.** The creative word of Jesus effects the desired cure, which now appears to be not so much the cause of the man's faith but rather its consequence; signs and faith in the word go together (cf. 14:11; so also the frequent insistence in the Syn miracle stories, e.g., Mk 5:34 par.). **54.** By an inclusion Jn once more connects the two signs at Cana. (For another interpretation of this sign, cf. A. Feuillet, *RScRel* 48 [1960] 62–75; *Johannine Studies*, 39–51).

81 **(C) The Light and the Darkness (5:1–10:42).** In this rather lengthy section of the Gospel, John uses several visits of Jesus to Jerusalem on the great Jewish feasts as the occasion to show that in him the aspirations of Judaism, symbolized by these feasts, found a greater significance. The prologue themes of "light" and "life" are continually stressed.

(a) JESUS AND THE SABBATH (5:1–47). The first stage in this development centers around a Sabbath controversy, the reality of which in the life of Jesus is more than amply confirmed by the frequent Syn references (cf. Mk 2:23ff. par.). The scene is laid in Jerusalem. When we note the first verses of chs. 6 and 7, it is obvious that a good case can be made in behalf of chronology for considering this chapter to be out of place, reversed with ch. 6 (→ 7 above). However, chronology is not John's prime consideration, and there is no evidence that ch. 5 ever stood in a different position from the one it now has.

(i) *The third sign of life* (5:1–15). Though Jn no longer calls it to our attention explicitly, this account continues the series of special "signs" that manifest Jesus' role as life-giver. Once again Jesus' word suffices to do what the "waters of Judaism" cannot.

82 **1.** *a Jewish feast:* Some mss. read "the Jewish feast"; this could appear as a justification for the transposition of chs. 5 and 6, since the proximity of Passover is mentioned in 6:4, and both Passover and Tabernacles (ch. 7) were referred to as "the" feast by the Jews. However, the presence of the article can be readily explained by dittography (*ēn hē heortē*), or by the tendency toward assimilation (elsewhere in Jn *heortē* appears with the article), or by a desire for precision (one ms. has added "of unleavened bread" = Passover; another "Tabernacles"). John does not identify the feast; its importance is secondary to what took place at that time. **2.** *the Sheep Pool:* This appears to be the best translation: The pool received its name from its proximity to the Sheep Gate, known as such from OT times (Neh 3:1; 12:39), situated N of the Temple area. *Hebrew name:* Here and elsewhere in the NT, "Aramaic" is probably meant, i.e., the common language spoken by Palestinian Jews. *Bethesda:* Other readings, equally well attested, are "Bethzatha," "Bethsaida." Bethzatha seems to have been the name of the NE section of Jerusalem without the walls; it could have given its name to the place in question (or, conversely, it could have received its name from that place). Bethsaida may have been introduced into the mss. by confusing it with Bethsaida of Galilee (1:44). Bethesda is often said to mean "house of mercy," as a name given to a building erected by a pool whose waters were said to have curative effects (5:7). But the name really had a quite different meaning; its Semitic form has been recovered in the copper scroll of Qumran Cave III (see 3Q*15* 11:12–13): *bêt 'ešdatayin*, "house of the double gusher," a name that referred to the springs that fed the double pool. John's purpose in giving the "Hebrew" name is to qualify the pool as "water of Judaism" (cf. 2:6; 4:12). *five porticoes:* John probably intends no symbolism by this number. The Sheep Pool has been identified with the double pool that now lies near the Church of St. Anne in Jerusalem: The trapezoidal pool was edged on four sides by porticoes; a fifth transected it, dividing it into two parts (see C. Kopp, *Holy Places*, pl. 40). **3.** The authentic text merely states that the porticoes were crowded with the sick. The "received text" for vv. 3b–4 adds (with variations): "...waiting for the moving of the water. For the angel of the Lord went down into the pool from time to time and stirred up the water; and whoever was first to step in after the stirring of the water became healed, no matter what disease he had." The added words are missing in the oldest and most reliable mss. (including P^{66} and P^{75}), and the language is not Johannine. There can hardly be any doubt that we have in them a later addition devised to explain v. 7. **5–6.** It is not said, of course, that the man who had been sick for 38 years had spent all this time at the pool; however, v. 7 presupposes that he had been there for some time. John does not explain the basis on which Jesus singled out this man; he is interested only in the miracle as a sign of Jesus' power. **7.** With vv. 3b–4 excised as unauthentic, we have no explanation from the Evangelist of the efficacy popularly ascribed to the water. Evidently whenever the water bubbled, when the intermittent underground spring that fed the pool became more active, it was thought to be especially curative. Doubtless this condition would last only for a short while so that those in charge of the building would surely have been forced to regulate the crowds, possibly allowing only one person to enter the water. Or it may have been thought that the water was then effective only for one person. **8–9.** With a word Jesus does for the man what the water had been unable to do. Without referring to the supposed curative value of the water, he completely heals the man of his infirmity.

83 *now that day was a sabbath:* This is the reason that precipitates controversy with the Jewish leaders, as it does when Jesus heals the blind man (9:14). **10–11.** A specific rabbinical law prohibited the carrying of one's bed on the Sabbath. The complaint of the Jewish leaders is not yet against Jesus, but against the action of the man who had been cured. His justification is implicit in his reply: If Jesus could perform this cure, surely it was proper to obey his command in this matter. **12–13.** The personality of the healed man does not emerge in this story. Nothing at all is said concerning his attitude toward Jesus. **14.** *the temple precincts:* A place of popular resort; this passage conveys that Jesus met the man casually there on a later occasion. Apparently this time Jesus was with his disciples or the man identified him by other means (v. 15). *sin no more:* Jesus does not say that the man's sins were responsible for his affliction (cf. Lk 13:1–4). The "something worse" that can happen doubtless refers to the judgment of God. **15.** The man probably acted in good faith; he was simply answering the question that he had been asked in v. 12.

84 (ii) *Jesus does the works of the Father* (5:16–47). **16.** As in the Syn tradition, Jesus' attitude toward the fulfillment of the Sabbath obligation becomes the initial cause of the Jewish leaders' hostility. The way in which John has arranged the following verses indicates that he did not attempt to report any specific conversation but that instead he has summarized what was brought out on this subject in various controversies. **17.** *my Father is still working:* This statement presupposes the background of rabbinical speculation on the nature of God (cf. Str-B 2, 461f.). It was recognized that the anthropomorphism in the Creation Account of Gn 2:2f. according to which God "rested" on the Sabbath could not be taken to mean a literal cessation of God's creative action, without which the world would cease to exist. Just as the Father is not actually inhibited by the Sabbath law, says Jesus, neither is the Son. This statement corresponds to the Syn declaration that the Son of Man is Lord also of the Sabbath (Mk 2:12 par.). **18.** Jesus' opponents correctly interpreted this statement as his claim to be the Son of the Father in a unique sense. In identifying his work with that of God, he makes himself the equal of God. From their monotheistic viewpoint this could only imply a dualism in deity. **19.** *the Son can do nothing on his own—only what he sees the Father doing:* The implication of subordination here should not be removed by undertaking Jesus' words to refer only to his human nature. This would make the Evangelist guilty of a banality. It would also miss a fine point of Johannine Christology. Rather, Jesus is insisting on an absolute harmony of activity between Father and Son, which, of course, radically demands an identity of nature; the same process is used in 16:12ff. to relate the Holy Spirit to the Son. But throughout this Gospel we never find the Trinity treated as a thesis of abstract theology; it is always approached from the standpoint of its functional relevance to soteriology. From this standpoint the Son—who is both God and Man—is in the world to do the work of the Father and only the work of the Father, to dispense to men the life that is the Father's gift through the Son (5:26f.); the role of the Son in salvation is to do the will of the Father (4:34; 5:30; 6:38; 7:16f.; 8:28; etc.). Later Christian theology will avoid any inference of superiority of one Person in the Trinity to another and will speak of all actions *ad extra* as common to all the Persons, that is, actions that do not involve the internal Trinitarian relationship itself. John does not contradict this doctrine, but neither does he approach it from this detached viewpoint. For Jesus to have said baldly to the Jews that he was "equal to God" would have confirmed them in their conclusion that he was speaking about two Gods. **20.** The principle of this community of activity between Father and Son is love; just as love is also the principle of the activity of the Spirit as sanctifier, a prolongation of the shared life of the Trinity (cf. 14:16,21). *even greater works:* In context, the reference is to works greater than that which has just been described, the restoration of health to the man at the pool. **21.** One of these greater works that will be an exercise of the Son's divine power will be the raising of the dead to life. This means not only the final resurrection of which the resurrection of Christ is the principle (cf. 1 Cor 15:20ff.), but the gift of new life in the here and now, the life of grace that is the beginning of the life of glory (cf. 11:25f.). **22.** Another work of the Son is that of judgment, a divine prerogative that the Father has "given" him (cf. 3:35). Again it is brought out (cf. 3:18) that judgment takes place not only at the end of time but in the here and now, on the basis of acceptance or rejection of Christ. **24.** The conception of life and judgment as "realized eschatology" is brought out in this repetition.

85 **25.** This verse also appears to have the same perspective of realized eschatology (cf. v. 28): "The dead" are those who were spiritually dead, but have accepted Jesus' word of life and now live. *an hour is coming and is here:* Christ's triumph over sin and death is a future event (cf. v. 28f.; 1 Cor 15:24ff.) but also one that has already taken place in principle (cf. Col 1:13f.; see comments on 2:4; 4:23). **26.** Though Christ has shared the life of God from all eternity (cf. 1:1), he brings this life into the world as the gift of the Father whom he reveals to men (cf. 1:4). Therefore the divine life that he is to communicate to men has first been communicated by the Father to the Son. **27.** This verse resumes the thought of v. 22. *because he is the Son of Man:* We are never allowed to forget that the eternal Word is our Redeemer and Judge precisely in his incarnate state and in his role as mediator endowed with glory, power, and kingship (Dn 7:14; see comment on 1:51). **28–29.** Neither is the common NT doctrine of futurist eschatology to be minimized. The final judgment will be the consummation of Christ's work: The just will rise to eternal life and the evil to damnation, each being judged according to his works (cf. Rom 2:5–10). **30.** Jesus sums up the foregoing teaching about judgment: His judgment is true because in it he is doing the work of the Father.

86 The assertions in the foregoing now require a justification; we re-encounter the Johannine theme of testimony (see comments on 1:7; 1:15; 4:39). **31.** Jesus accepts the general principle in human jurisprudence: A man is not to be taken simply at his own word; he needs the testimony of others (however, see comment on 8:14). **32.** Jesus has such a witness, whose testimony he will reveal in a moment (v. 36ff.). **33–35.** The testimony of this witness is greater than that of the Baptist (1:7). The Baptist's testimony was quite valid; though he was not the light (1:8), he was a lamp illuminating the darkness, pointing to the true light (Ps 132:17), and the Jews themselves must testify that John had been accredited among them as a prophet, a voice of God (cf. 1:19; Mk 1:5; Mt 3:5; 11:7; 21:26). Still, valuable though it might be, this is not the testimony to which Jesus appeals. **36.** Jesus' witness is the Father himself: The works that he performs, both his words of life and the deeds that he does, which are the Father's gift to him (v. 20), manifestly show that he has been sent by God (cf. 14:11). **37.** The works, however, remain only indirect testimony. *the Father who sent me has given testimony on my behalf:* Jesus refers to the interior testimony God gives to those who have true faith (cf. 1 Jn 5:9f.; Rom 8:16). *his voice:* In Jesus' words the voice of God is discerned by those who are responsive to God's grace; by contrast, those now listening to him by their disbelief are blind and "have not seen what he is like" (cf. 1:18). **38.** *his enduring word you do not have in your hearts:* This repeats the idea of the preceding verse. However, John probably intends a subtler significance by his choice of words to reproduce our Lord's thought: The "enduring word" (*logon menonta*) of God not possessed by the disbeliever contrasts with the Incarnate Word who abides (*menein*) with his disciples (cf. 1:39; 15:3). **39.** The verb is probably indicative rather than imperative. *you search the scriptures in which you think you have eternal life:* The OT Scriptures, however, could only lead to Jesus (cf. Gal 3:24), in whom alone life is to be found (cf. vv. 21, 26; 1:4,17; Gal 3:21). *they also give evidence on my behalf:* Rightly used, the Scriptures would not stand in the way but would rather lead the believer from themselves to Christ. **40.** This verse contains the transition from the question of testimony to the subject of the final verses of this section—a subject that was actual both for Jesus and for the early Church: the incredulity of the Jews (cf. 12:37ff.). The point is made at the outset that this incredulity on the part of the Jewish leaders was willful.

87 **41–42.** It is not because Jesus seeks human glory (cf. 8:50) that he criticizes his listeners for their unbelief; rather, it is that their unbelief demonstrates that they have no true love of God. They prefer their own will to God's. **43.** *in my Father's name:* See comment on 1:12. The rejection of Jesus amounts to the rejection of the testimony of God. But any charlatan who comes along, armed only with his own credentials, will be accepted, provided he accords with preconceived ideas. Jewish history in this period was not unacquainted with false messiahs (cf. Acts 5:35ff.; Mk 13:6,22 par.) who succeeded in firing national aspirations. This ultimately resulted in the rebellions against Roman rule that ended in the suppression of the Jewish state in Palestine. **44.** Thus having rejected the glory of God (see comments on 1:14; 2:11) in favor of the glory that comes from men (cf. 12:43; Mt 23:5ff.), they have made it impossible for themselves to believe (cf. 12:39). **45–47.** It will therefore be unnecessary for Christ, to whom judgment has been given (v. 22), to appear before God to denounce them; they stand self-denounced by their obduracy. Moses, here taken as author of the OT revelation, will himself denounce them, since the OT itself has pointed the way to Christ (v. 39).

88 (b) The Bread of Life (6:1–71). (On the relation of this chapter to the chronology of Jesus' ministry, → 81 above.) With the exception of the Passion Narrative, this is the longest continued section in which Jn parallels the Syn narrative, and the close correspondence of Jn with the two narratives of Mk in particular (6:30–54; 8:21–33) constitutes one of the strongest arguments in favor of the view that John knew and made use of Mk (→ 18 above). As usual, however, John has gone his own way, and it is especially, in his use of Syn material that we must pay attention to his particular purposes.

89 (i) *The fourth sign* (6:1–15). John's first purpose is to exploit the symbolic potential of the story of the multiplication of the loaves. Actually, he only brings out explicitly what is already implicit in the Syn account. For the Syn tradition, the miracle of the loaves (or the two miracles in Mk and Mt) is already a Eucharistic symbol, which has been evidenced by the liturgical and sacramental allusions incorporated into the form of the account (cf. V. Taylor, *The Gospel According to St. Mark* [London, 1953] 324f.).

1. *Sea of Galilee:* This is the ordinary NT designation of the Galilean lake called in the OT the Sea of Chinnereth (Nm 34:11). "Of Tiberias" has been added, either by John or someone else (cf. 21:1), for precision and updating. Tiberias, a city on the western shore, was founded by Herod Antipas sometime after AD 20 and named for the Emperor Tiberius, and subsequently gave its name to the lake. "To the shore" of Tiberias in some mss. is probably a later addition designed to smooth out the text. **2.** Again John notes in passing Jesus' miraculous works, in accord with the Syn tradition, which he has not detailed in his Gospel. The crowd has been attracted by these miracles; not necessarily a sign of incipient faith (see comment on 2:23ff.). **3.** *the mountain:* Only Mt (in the second account of the multiplication of loaves, 15:29) localizes the miracle on a mountainside as does Jn. The significance is doubtless the same as in the Syn tradition: The mountain evokes the memory of Sinai, where Moses mediated the revelation that points to Christ (cf. Mk 3:13; Mt 5:1). **4.** *the Jewish feast of Passover was near:* See comment on 2:13. This is the second Passover mentioned in Jn; the Syn tradition merely notes that it was the spring of the year. John is already thinking of the Eucharist, the theme to be developed in the coming discourse. **5–6.** The Mosaic allusions (v. 3) continue in the question that Jesus puts to Philip to test his faith (cf. Nm 11:13). **7.** Philip's answer is very similar to Moses' observation in Nm 11:22. Here again Jn is verbally quite close to Mk 6:37. *two hundred days' wages:* Lit., "two hundred denarii"; a denarius appears to have been the ordinary working day's wage (cf. Mt 20:2). **8–9.** Andrew, who brought Peter to Jesus (1:41), shows a measure of resourcefulness in this detail reported only in Jn. Later he is consulted by Philip when the Gentiles want to "see" Jesus (12:20–22). Andrew's actions permit us a rare insight into a disciple's personality. *barley loaves:* That the loaves were of barley (the ordinary food of the poor) is brought out only in Jn.

90 **10.** Jn's account summarizes the Syn versions. **11–12.** In Jn there are liturgical allusions lacking in the Syn versions and vice versa. The Syn have the detail of the breaking of the bread (cf. Acts 2:42), a detail that John may have avoided because of 19:33. On the other hand, "he gave thanks" in Jn (*eucharistēsas*) is more allusive to the Eucharist than the Syn word (*eulogēsen*). Mk 8:6 and Mt 15:36 use *eucharistēsas* in their second account of the multiplication of loaves; so also 1 Cor 11:23. The Syn tradition has the disciples rather than Jesus himself distribute the bread—in view of the size of the crowd, this seems plausible—but in Jn's bypassing of this detail we are reminded of the circumstances of the Last Supper. In Jn alone the gathering up (*synagein*) of the fragments is given as a command of Christ; in the *Didache* (9:4) the same word is used for the gathering of the Eucharistic bread, in turn a symbol of the gathering of the Church, whence comes the ancient word *synaxis* for the first part of the Mass. In the same passage of the *Didache* the word *klasma*, used of the morsels of bread in Jn and the Syn, is applied to the broken portions of Eucharistic bread. Although in both Jn and the Syn all the details have an authentic setting in the miraculous event, there seems to be no doubt that a sacramental allusion was intended, which was not missed by the early Church. **13.** *twelve baskets:* Though Jn does not mention them, mention of this number of baskets, found also in the Syn, would indicate the presence of all twelve of the disciples. In view of the Mosaic relevance of the miracle (v. 14f.), John doubtless sees an additional significance in the number twelve. The detail serves to emphasize the miraculous nature of the event. Its full character as a "sign" will appear in v. 25ff.

91 The following two verses are not in the Syn tradition, but contain an important historical note that has been transmitted by Jn alone. **14.** *this is the prophet:* The people correctly see in this miracle an indication that Jesus is the prophet like Moses (see comment on 1:21) come to found the New Israel. However, they do this merely because of the signs he had performed, without real depth to their perception, as the event will show. "Signs" rather than "sign" is doubtless to be preferred as the better reading in the mss., for John is thinking of similar instances of this illusory enthusiasm (see comment on 2:23ff.). **15.** The results of the popular enthusiasm immediately become manifest: The people would have him as their earthly king, their Jewish Messiah (cf. 5:43). What is offered to Jesus here, and what he emphatically rejects, has a correspondence in the temptation scenes of Lk 4:1–13 and Mt 4:1–11. *he fled back to the mountain alone:* It is not unlikely that at this time the disciples shared the messianic enthusiasm of the people; Mt 14:22 and Mk 6:45, though they do not record this event, note that Jesus "forced" the disciples to cross the Lake of Galilee again immediately after the miracle of the loaves. (On the mountain, see comment on v. 3.)

92 (ii) *The fifth sign* (6:16–21). John rejoins the Syn tradition to recount the following event, but again for purposes of his own. As with the miracle of the loaves, the significance of the "sign" appears only later (see v. 68f.). **16–18.** John describes quite naturally a common occurrence on a lake subject to sudden storms. The Syn parallel makes much more of the storm, noting Jesus' power over the waves not only in walking on the water but in quieting the wind (Mk 6:51; Mt 14:32), but John is not concerned with this aspect of the event. **19.** However, the plain meaning of the text is obviously to agree with the Syn, that Jesus was actually walking upon the sea when encountered by the disciples in the boat. This is emphasized by the notation of the distance they had rowed, roughly corresponding to Mk's "in the middle of the sea." The significance of such a "nature" miracle, like that of the multiplication of the loaves, neither in Jn nor in the Syn is intended to portray Jesus merely as a wonder-worker. The power of God over the sea is a commonplace theme of the OT (Gn 1:2,6ff.; Pss 74:12–15; 93:3f.); more specifically, it was through his control of the sea that the first Israel had emerged in the Exodus (Ex 14:19ff.; 15:1–21; Ps 77:17–21). Just as the miracle of the loaves portrayed Jesus as a new Moses, who will be brought out in the following discourse as one greater than Moses, the present miracle underlines the power of him who was to bring forth the New Israel. **20.** The disciples were understandably frightened by Jesus' sudden appearance. Jesus' words of reassurance, which also appear in the Syn version, probably represent the chief importance of this event. *it is I:* Lit., "I am" (*egō eimi*). Thus the LXX had translated the ineffable name of God revealed to Moses according to Ex 3:14 (cf. C. H. Dodd, *Interpretation,* 93–96). Once again, John has seen a deep spiritual significance in a simple answer. The Syn, however, saw in the miracle that accompanied the words a stage in the disciples' growing awareness of the character of Jesus (cf. Mk 6:52; Mt 14:33). **21.** *they wanted to take him into the boat:* John does not make it clear whether Jesus entered the boat (according to the Syn he did); his emphasis is on the disposition of the disciples (see comment on 6:68–69). *and suddenly:* It is not quite clear whether John intends this as another miraculous event; probably he does so intend.

93 (iii) *The Eucharistic discourse* (6:22–71). The following discourse reveals fully the true significance of the two foregoing "signs." It follows the regular pattern of the Johannine dialogues (→ 30 above), which exhibit some artificiality of arrangement. The situation itself, however, follows the preceding events quite naturally as part of the Johannine testimony.

22–24. After the abortive attempt to proclaim Jesus a Jewish Messiah (v. 15), we may suppose that the more tenacious of the crowd continued to seek out his whereabouts. They knew he had not departed with the disciples, yet they could not find him on their side of the lake; therefore they proceeded to Capernaum where he and his diciples were known to resort. The entire v. 23 is suspect as non-Johannine for various reasons: For example, the words "after the Lord had given thanks" (*eucharistēsantos tou kyriou*), missing in various mss. that usually amplify rather than contract the text, are probably a later addition. **25.** The crowd is naturally curious about his coming to this place. *Rabbi:* So the disciples (1:38) and Nicodemus (3:2) had begun their first conversations with Jesus, with somewhat disparate results; the result here will again be different. **26.** Jesus does not answer their question: To reveal another miracle to them would have produced just the opposite effect from the one he intended. Rather, he will tell them of his coming that really matters. *not because you have seen signs:* Jesus means that they have not perceived the true meaning of the signs. The people have considered only the material aspect of the miracle and have failed to reflect on its significance (cf. the attitude of the woman in 4:15). **27.** The discourse begins with the enunciation of the theme. Using a metaphor, bread = doctrine, whose meaning should have been recognized (cf. Str-B 2, 482ff., bread = Torah), Jesus attempts to raise their minds from purely earthly concerns to that which leads to eternal life (cf. 4:13f.; Is 55:2); for this, he says, they should be working even as they work for earthly bread. *the Son of Man:* See comment on 1:51. *God the Father has authorized:* See 3:17f.; 5:19. **28.** The people have understood only that he speaks of a miraculous food that will not perish. Obviously a work of God! Work, he has said. Very well, how are they to perform a work of God? **29.** *have faith in him whom God has sent:* God's work they cannot really do; their task is to accept him in faith (cf. 1QS 4:3f.). Only in this need their working consist. The present imperative rather than the aorist is preferred with the majority of mss. **30.** Another misunderstanding follows. The people think that they are being asked to "put faith" in Jesus merely to credit something he is about to say. *what sign are you going to perform for us to see?:* The demand made in Mk 8:11; Mt 16:1; Lk 11:16. They proceed to prove how material-minded they are, even as Jesus had said. Already their enthusiasm over the miracle of the previous day has waned. **31.** After all, they argue, Jesus has only multiplied earthly bread. But in the time of Moses God had given his people "bread from heaven" (Neh 9:15). Popular belief looked for a recurrence of the manna in the Messianic age (*2 Baruch* 29:8). **32.** Jesus instructs them on the nature of the true bread from heaven (see comments on 1:9; 1:14); the manna was bread from heaven only after a fashion (cf. also 1:17). **33.** The true bread of God that comes down from heaven is Christ himself (v. 35); it thus gives true life (cf. 1:4) whereas the manna could only nourish mortal men.

94 **34.** Still misunderstanding, the people echo the words of the Samaratan woman in 4:15. Although they have perceived that he is speaking of a nonmaterial bread, and that he can give this bread, they have not yet understood that Jesus has identified this bread with himself. *all the time:* Their request is for a continued supply of this bread, which makes relevant Jesus' further words. **35.** Jesus explicitly identifies himself with the bread of which he has been speaking. He is the "bread of life," which, like the "water of life" (4:10), satisfies hunger and thirst forever (4:14). *comes to me:* This means the same as "believes in me" (cf. 5:40). *I myself am the bread of life:* This is the first instance of the "I am" formula with a predicate, a characteristic of the language of Christ in Jn (cf. vv. 48, 51; 8:12; etc.). The "I am" formula without the predicate has been seen in 4:26; 6:20. The latter, which is not restricted to Jn (cf. Mt 14:27 par.; Mk 13:6 par.; 14:62), is the OT revelation formula (Ex 3:6,14; 20:2; Dt 32:39; Is 43:10; 46:4; 51:12; etc.) and doubtless has its setting in Jesus' conscious assumption of revelatory power for the New Covenant (cf. Mt 5:22,28,32,34,39,44), though historically in some instances he may have meant something less. The formula with predicate is best explained as the Johannine development of the same formula, for the most part of which the subject matter corresponds to the Syn "parables of the kingdom." It is not necessary to seek the origin of the formula in Philo, in Mandaeism, or elsewhere outside the precedent of the Gk OT (S. Schulz agrees that the motifs used in the formula are Jewish, but believes the form derives mainly from Hellenistic sources; he sees in this the emergence of NT Christology as a theology [*Komposition und Herkunft*, 130]); however, one may agree, as in the case of the Logos (cf. 1:1), John was not unaware of the formula's use in the Hellenistic religions.

(Brinktrine, J., "Die Selbstaussage Jesu *Egō Eimi*," *TGl* 47 [1957] 34–36. Schweizer, E., *Egō Eimi... Die religionsgeschichtliche Herkunft und theologische Bedeutung der johanneischen Bildreden* [Göttingen, 1939]. Zimmerman, H., "Das absolute 'Ich Bin' in der Redeweise Jesu," *TTZ* 69 [1960] 1–20; "Das absolute *Egō Eimi* als die neutestamentliche Offenbarungsformel," *BZ* 4 [1960] 54–69, 266–76.)

95 **36.** This verse refers back to v. 26. To see is not necessarily to believe (cf. 9:37), but belief makes one see things as they truly are. **37–38.** To "come" to Christ (cf. v. 35), it is necessary that one be brought by the grace of God. Christ will not reject from the Kingdom of God those who accept this grace. This is so because he does the work of the Father (cf. 5:19). **39–40.** The effect of this will of God being executed by Jesus is not only that those who believe may be safe in the Kingdom of God, but that they shall possess it for all eternity in the final resurrection. Though Jn's Gospel emphasizes eternal life as a present reality, the Evangelist, as we have seen (see comment on 3:17,18), never departs from the concept of final eschatology here represented in Jesus' words (cf. vv. 44, 54).

96 **41.** *the Jews:* As the crowd begins to adopt a hostile note in its response to Christ, John significantly gives them this name (see 1:19). *grumble:* As their ancestors had done after they had received the manna in the wilderness (Ex 16:2,8f.). **42.** Jn's statement in 4:44 now sees a verification in his Gospel; the same reaction is recorded of the Galileans in Mk 6:2ff. The protestation of the people that they know Jesus' parentage and thereby must reject his claim to have come from heaven is a prime example of the Johannine irony (→ 29 above); John does not have to point out the incongruity to his Christian reader, who knows that Christ was conceived of a virgin. **43–44.** Jesus does not touch on the protestation itself, which is peripheral. Rather he insists on what was said in vv. 37ff.: If they would but respond to the grace of God they would believe, and not waste their time with pointless objections. **45.** *taught by God:* The words of Is 54:13 will be fulfilled in the believer who hears the Father and learns. It is necessary that the believer answer God's grace with a willing disposition. *has seen the Father:* See comment on 1:18. It is essential that one recognize this call of grace in the Son who is his only Mediator; only in this way does one see God (cf. 14:9). **47–50.** Thus it is that the believer attains to eternal life (see comment on 3:15). Jesus repeats, he is the bread of life who gives eternal life in a way that the manna of the OT could not (see vv. 32–35). **51.** *the bread that I shall give is my own flesh:* The Eucharistic theme has been reached. At the climax of this reiteration, Jesus' statement is more astounding than what he has said thus far.

97 The second part of v. 51 through v. 58 (vv. 52–59 in the Vg and in translations thereof) has been rejected by some scholars as another "ecclesiastical interpolation" (see comment on 2:1–11 and cf. 3:5). Their theory is based on the assumption that John would not have been interested in a sacramental doctrine. However, the doctrine is closely connected with what has preceded. It now becomes clear how Jesus is a living bread that may and must be eaten so that men may have life. *give... for the life of the world:* This passage echoes the logion reported by Paul in 1 Cor 11:24, and there should be little doubt that it intends to connect the Eucharist with the redemptive death of Christ as is done in the Syn and by Paul (cf. H. Schürmann, *BZ* 2 [1958] 244–62). It is to be noted that Jn cites Jesus as using the word "flesh," whereas in Paul and the Syn tradition the Eucharistic term is "body." Here we doubtless have another instance of John's adherence to a more "primitive" account of the facts (→ 35 above). Jn's "flesh" (*sarx*) probably reproduces the actual word that would have been used by Jesus (Hebr *bāśār* or Aram *biśrā*, regularly translated *sarx* in the LXX), a word that serves in the Semitic languages to signify both "flesh" and "[living] body," whereas the Syn and Pauline term represents a later semantic development in Christian terminology, which profited from the greater potentialities of the Gk *sōma* (body; cf. J. Bonsirven, *Bib* 29 [1948] 205–19). Probably, too, the theological opposition between "flesh" and "spirit" (again in v. 63) familiar to NT language encouraged the use of "body." Ignatius of Antioch (AD 107) habitually uses the expression "flesh [*sarx*] of our Savior Jesus Christ" to define the Eucharist (e.g., *Ep. ad Smyr.* 7.1; *PG* 5.713); while Justin Martyr (*ca.* AD 150) uses both "flesh" and "body" (the latter when citing the Syn version of the words of institution of the Eucharist; cf. *Apol.* 1.66; *PG* 6.428). **52.** Just as Nicodemus thought of rebirth in a purely physical sense (3:4) and as the woman at the well first thought only of natural water (4:11), so now some of the Jews take the reference to Christ's flesh literally. The Semitic figure of speech, "eat someone's flesh," which meant "to slander" (Ps 27:2), obviously did not contribute in helping them to understand. **53.** Neither do Jesus' words in reply encourage any figurative understanding of his pronouncement; his reiteration only underscores the difficulty discerned in v. 52. *the flesh of the Son of Man:* Since the Son of Man is he in whom God and mankind meet (see comment on 1:51), it is fitting that Jesus should identify the Eucharist with himself as Son of Man.

drink his blood: If the idea of eating a man's flesh would appear repugnant to a Jewish audience, the idea of drinking blood would be even more so, because blood as food was forbidden under the Law (cf. Gn 9:4; Dt 12:16). "Flesh and blood" is the common OT expression for human life. More than likely the separate mention of the partaking of these two elements in the Eucharist stresses the fact that the whole living Christ is received (Barrett) rather than repeats (see v. 51) the connection of the Eucharist with the death of Christ (Bernard). **54–55.** The repetitions contained in these verses have the effect of underlining the reality of the Christ-life that is received in the Eucharist. Because the possession of Christ is the earnest of eternal life in the resurrection (v. 40), the Eucharist is an eschatological sacrament. **56–57.** Reception of the Eucharist establishes communion of life between Christ and the Christian (cf. 1 Cor 10:16). Even as the life of the Son and the Father is one (14:10; 5:21ff.), a life that in turn they share with the Spirit (1:32f.; 15:26), in the Eucharist the Christian receives the shared life of God himself. **58.** Inclusively this verse sums up the argument of the preceding: The bread of which Jesus first began to speak in v. 33, the true bread of God of which the manna was only a faint type, is pre-eminently the Eucharistic sacrament of life.

(Bornkamm, G., "Die eucharistische Rede im Johannesevangelium," *ZNW* 47 [1956] 161–69. De Ausejo, S., "El concepto de 'carne' aplicado a Cristo en el IV Evangelio," *SP* 2, 219–34. Feuillet, A., "Les thèmes bibliques majeurs du discours sur le pain de vie," *NRT* 82 [1960] 803–22, 918–39, 1040–62 [*Johannine Studies*, 53–128]. Léon-Dufour, X., "Le mystère du pain de vie," *RScRel* 46 [1958] 481–523. Racette, J., "L'unité du discours sur le pain de vie," *ScEccl* 9 [1957] 82–85. Schürmann, H., "Die Eucharistie als Repräsentation und Applikation des Heilsgeschehens nach Joh 6, 53–58," *TTZ* [1959] 30–45, 108–18.)

98 **59.** *in a synagogue instruction at Capernaum:* In v. 24f. it was said only that the crowd had found Jesus in Capernaum. This fact, together with a certain ambivalence in Jn's speaking of the crowd ("crowd" in the first part, then "the Jews" from v. 41, finally "disciples" after v. 61), and the unusual character of this discourse as a synagogue instruction have led many to question whether these themes were originally a unity in Jesus' teaching. This is quite independent of the question, answered in the affirmative above, whether the discourse as it stands is authentic to Jn and intended by the Evangelist as a unity. It seems very likely that John has combined various pronouncements of Jesus, some of which, such as those on the nature of the Eucharist, would have taken place more readily in the intimate company of his disciples than in a large crowd whose good dispositions were doubtful to begin with. **60.** *after listening to this:* If the hypothesis just mentioned is correct, it would not be right to restrict the "this" simply to the Eucharistic doctrine that has just been outlined. Probably John means the entire preceding discourse, involving Jesus' presentation of himself as the source ("bread") of life. **61–62.** This impression is strengthened by Jesus' reply, which states in negative form the idea previously expressed to Nathanael (1:50f.) and positively, but less vehemently, to Nicodemus (3:12). These disciples, who now show themselves as lacking the true characteristics required of those who are to follow Jesus (v. 44f.), cannot bring themselves to believe that Jesus could really be one who has come down from heaven (cf. v. 41); what, then, would they make of the far greater mysteries that surround his return to the Father? These mysteries are the subject of the second half of John's Gospel, where their consequences are detailed for the true disciples of the Lord. For disbelievers such as these, however, the witness of these mysteries could only be a repetition of seeing without understanding (cf. v. 36). **63.** Again he insists on the necessity of grace. *it is the Spirit that is the life-giving factor:* Cf. 1 Cor 15:45. As he had reminded Nicodemus (3:6–8), the life of which he has been speaking is entirely within the sphere of the Spirit, and only the Spirit can give an understanding of it. *the flesh is of no value:* Jesus says nothing here of "my flesh," which is the subject of the Eucharistic passage; he is speaking of "the flesh" of 1:14 and 3:6. **64–65.** It was because of Jesus' knowledge of the unbelief before him, even in the ranks of the chosen Twelve (cf. v. 70), that he has stressed the impossibility of faith without divine prompting.

99 **66.** The rejection of Christ by many of those who had once been his followers anticipates the general rejection and the judgment passed on it by John in 12:37ff. This verse corresponds to the judgment passed on the Galilean ministry in Mt 11:20–24 par. **67.** Jesus now extends the challenge of faith to his most intimate disciples, recognizing in their midst the one who would betray him. *the Twelve:* For the first time John explicitly names the special group about Jesus whose existence has been known to his readers from the Syn tradition. **68–69.** Despite the different circumstances, John probably understands Peter's confession as the equivalent to the Syn episode in Mk 8:27ff. par. Jesus has just asked whether the disciples wish (*thelete*) to depart from him; cf. v. 21, according to which they wished (*ēthelon*) to receive him into the boat; Jn now arrives at the final significance of the sign of the walking on the water (cf. the similar confession in Mt 14:33). *the words of eternal life are yours:* The discourse of Jesus about eternal life, which has scandalized many, Peter and the Twelve acknowledge as the Word of God truly leading to eternal life. *God's Holy One:* Verbally, this does not transcend the messianic titles already recorded (cf. the same expression in Mk 1:24). However, in view of the significance of the idea of "holy" elsewhere in Jn with reference to Christ's mission (cf. 10:36; 17:19, etc.), the Evangelist probably intends to suggest the wider implications of the disciples' faith (cf. the added solemnity attached to the words of Peter's confession in Mt 16:16). Although the disciples have not yet come to know Christ in all his fullness, they are on the way to this knowledge because they have not only seen Jesus but have also believed (cf. vv. 40, 37). **70–71.** This confession has been made possible through divine election (cf. v. 44); similarly in Mt 16:17. Yet even divine election carries no automatic guarantee. *a devil:* Here, obviously, the meaning is that Judas will be acting under diabolic influence (cf. 13:2). *Judas, son of Simon Iscariot:* It is not clear whether the title "Iscariot" refers to Judas or to his father; in 12:4 it is applied directly to Judas. If the customary explanation of the title is correct, that is, "man of Kerioth" (*'îš q^{e}rîyôt*; cf. Jos 15:25; Jer 48:24; Am 2:2), the question becomes superfluous, since father and son would presumably be of the same city. This interpretation would also definitely identify Judas as the only non-Galilean among the disciples. In favor of it, perhaps, is the fact that some mss. substitute "from *Karyōton*" for "Iscariot." However, the Hebr "man from Kerioth" is intrinsically not too probable. Other mss. have *Skariōth* (Lat mss. *scariotis*), which suggested to J. Wellhausen a derivation from "sicarius": Judas would have been known as a former member of the Jewish nationalists known to the Romans by this name (→ History of Israel, 75:155). C. C. Torrey suggested a derivation from an Aram *'išqaryā'*, "the traitor" (*HarvTR* 36 [1943] 51–62). Jn repeats that Judas was "of the Twelve" to underline the magnitude of his crime. Neither Jn nor the Syn, however, offer us sufficient information to determine the background of Judas' treason.

100 (c) Tabernacles: Life and Light (7:1–8:59). In this section John has assembled discourses of Jesus bearing on the themes of life and light, both of which are related to the Feast of Tabernacles with which the discourses are chronologically associated. The theme of Jewish opposition is repeatedly brought out in 7:1,13,19,25,30,32,44; 8:37,40,59.

1. On the relative chronology of this episode to the preceding, → 81 above. *the Jews were looking for a chance to kill him:* See 5:18. **2.** *the Jewish feast of Tabernacles:* The autumn harvest festival (cf. Lv 23:33–44; Dt 16:13–15; Ez 45:25); considered the most popular of the Jewish feasts (cf. Josephus, *Ant.* 8.4,1 § 100: "the holiest and greatest feast"), it was often called simply "the Feast." Besides the essential ritual it featured in Christ's time extensive water libations and the lighting of the Temple court. Allusions to these customs seem to appear in the discourses.

3–5. *his brothers:* Only here in Jn are Jesus' brethren mentioned; in 2:12 probably and in 20:17 certainly "the brothers" means Jesus' disciples. Jn represents these brethren as unbelievers of the same type as those of the preceding chapter. Having misunderstood the nature of Jesus' works, they failed to perceive who he really is. On the identity of the brothers of Jesus, see Mk 3:31; and comments on Gal 1:19; Mt 12:46 (→ Aspects of NT Thought, 78:167). The brethren tell Jesus to go up to Jerusalem openly in order to manifest himself to the world and completely misinterpret his mission and its purpose. The arrival of pilgrims at Jerusalem for the Feast of Tabernacles customarily involved a triumphant procession met by priests outside the city. The presence of so many visitors was frequently the occasion for nationalistic uprisings. **6.** *it is not yet time for me:* See comment on 2:4 and cf. 4:23; 5:25. Jesus' manifestation of himself will take place in the events of the passion. The brethren, on the other hand, can go to Jerusalem as they will—at any time. **7.** Jesus explains: He cannot manifest himself to the world as they ask because the world has become his enemy because of the testimony he has brought against it (3:19–21). No such hostility pursues the brethren, for the world loves its own (15:19). **8.** *I am not going up:* This refusal of the brothers' request does not stand in contradiction to v. 10, for they had asked for a public manifestation. "Going up" was the semitechnical term for making a pilgrimage to the holy city. Here a deeper significance is also suggested: The term *anabainein,* "go up," evokes the idea of the resurrection (*anabasis*). The time for this is not yet. **9–10.** Jesus' departure for Tabernacles represents his farewell to Galilee and therefore the beginning of the final events of Jesus' ministry. **11–12.** Jesus does not appear until the feast is half over (v. 14); thus the Jews (see comment on 1:19), who had been expecting an appearance of Jesus similar to that demanded by his brothers, were disappointed in their search for him. The dissension in the crowds over Jesus (cf. 9:16; 10:19) is the inevitable concomitant of a Person and of a teaching that demand a personal decision of acceptance or rejection. **13.** Jn continually indicates that the popular enthusiasm for Jesus, which could have led to acceptance of him although invariably it did not do so (cf. 2:23–25; etc.), was repressed by the Jewish leaders (cf. 9:22; 12:42; 19:38; 20:19).

101 **14.** *already half over:* The Feast of Tabernacles lasted eight days, so that Jesus' appearance presumably took place about the fourth day. *the temple precincts:* Because of the ceremonies mentioned above, the courts of the Temple were particularly thronged during the period of this festival. **15.** *the Jews were surprised at this:* The source of surprise is the content of Jesus' preaching. Where did he come by this learning, since he was known not to have frequented the rabbinical schools? Cf. Mk 1:21f. par.; Lk 4:22. Though the following discourse strikingly parallels 5:31ff., there is no reason to conclude with Bernard, Bultmann, Wikenhauser, and others that we have here a transposition in the text of Jn (→ 7 above) and that this verse and the following are the sequel of 5:47. **16.** Jesus' reply is not that he is self-taught, the obvious retort to the depreciation implicit in the remark of v. 15, but that he teaches a doctrine that is above all human learning (cf. 5:19,30). **17.** Just as this doctrine is not of man, neither can a decision about it be made on purely human terms. *if anyone should want to do his will:* He who is obedient to God's grace and is disposed to believe will recognize the divine origin of this teaching (cf. 5:36f.). **18.** The consequence of Jesus' teaching the Father's doctrine rather than his own is that he seeks not his own glory (cf. 5:41,44), but God's. *is truthful:* Such a person has the qualities of God; see 1:14. *there is no dishonesty in his heart:* Jesus begins a comparison of himself with his accusers, a contrast driven home in the following verse.

102 **19.** *has not Moses given you the Law?:* Their own standard of truthfulness versus dishonesty is invoked against them. *yet not one of you observes the Law:* The proof of this is in their present dispositions that have already been made manifest in his regard. *why do you seek to kill me?:* Cf. 5:18; 7:1. **20.** The crowd accuses Jesus of a paranoiac delusion. The statement is undoubtedly made in good faith by some of the bystanders, since the Jewish leaders were the ones who had desired Jesus' death. Yet v. 25 shows that this intention had been sufficiently publicized to justify Jesus' charge. One is no less guilty if he remains passive while evil is being contemplated. **21–22.** Jesus presses his charge against his traducers. *I have performed just one work:* Doubtless this refers to the one work recorded of Jesus in Jerusalem, the miracle of 5:1–9 on the occasion of an unnamed feast. *all of you are surprised on that account:* The Jews were scandalized bacause Jesus had performed a healing on the Sabbath (5:16). *Moses has given you circumcision:* Jesus begins his argument to show the absurdity of the charge of Sabbath-breaking that had been made against him. Although circumcision predated the Mosaic Law, the time for its administration, however, was determined by the Law (Lv 12:3). The principle that circumcision was to be administered on the eighth day regardless of the incidental violation of the Sabbath obligation was commonly accepted. **23.** The argument follows: If the obligation of circumcision, which regards only one member of the body, takes precedence over the Sabbath rule, why not permit the healing of the entire body on this day? The same principle, "the Sabbath was made for man," is stated by Jesus in Mk 2:27, and a similar kind of argumentation in favor of the spirit of the Sabbath legislation is found in Mt 12:11 and Lk 13:15. This principle was, in fact, accepted by the rabbis (cf. Str-B 2, 488); however, while it would have been applied to justify saving a man from imminent peril to his life, it would not have been extended to cases such as those in the Gospel. **24.** Jesus concludes his argument by inviting his opponents to render an honest and reasonable judgment according to the spirit of the Law, its real meaning. True, he appears to have violated the letter of the Law, but what was God's primary purpose in giving the Law? Not to destroy man, but to lead him to salvation.

103 **25.** Again Jesus occasions a controversy: That his life is being sought (see v. 19) is at first indignantly denied but is now openly admitted. *some of the Jerusalemites:* Jn probably specifies by this word those among the festival crowds who would be in a position to know of the Jerusalem leaders' designs against Jesus. **26.** *maybe the authorities have realized:* Doubtless this suggestion was made only half-seriously by those who knew only too well the dispositions of the authorities. **27.** *we know where this man comes from:* An example of the Johannine irony (→ 29 above), the point of which is quickly driven home (v. 28f.). *no one is to know where he comes from:* In some Jewish circles it was believed that the Messiah would manifest himself suddenly and unmistakably, and that prior to this manifestation he would be completely hidden and unknown. In the view of the Jerusalemites, Jesus has made no such manifestation, besides, his Galilean origins are well known; therefore he cannot be the Messiah. **28.** Jesus speaks ironically to those whom he has just adjured not to judge by superficial appearances (v. 24). Their confident claim to know his origins is the equivalent of the initial misunderstanding common in the Johannine dialogues (→ 30 above). *yet I have not come on my own:* The Jerusalemites' superficial knowledge of Jesus' person is not sufficient to make him truly known to them; he can be truly known only when he is recognized as the One sent by God. *there is truly One who sent me:* Lit., "true is the one who has sent me" (see comment on 1:14). The true origins of Christ cannot be known by those present since they do not know God (cf. 8:19,55), the One who sent Christ. Did they know him, they would know that he is true (*alēthinos*): They would recognize the trustworthiness of his testimony to Christ (cf. 3:33). **29.** Because Christ has come from the Father he is uniquely the One who can reveal God to man (cf. 6:46; Mt 11:27 par.).

104 **30.** *they started trying to arrest him:* The Jerusalemites, now incensed by what they conceive as the blasphemy of his claim (v. 29), set out to apprehend Jesus. *no one laid a finger on him:* As the following verse makes clear, the crowd itself was divided in its attitude toward Jesus, hence the people's demonstration against him failed. *his hour had not yet come:* Cf. 7:6,8 and see comment on 2:4. **31.** *many in the crowd:* As usual, John distinguishes the crowd of common people from the Jewish leaders, who are Jesus' implacable enemies. *more signs than this man has performed:* The incipient belief of these people is based on miracles (see 2:23–25). This in itself was not a bad thing (the Messiah was expected to be a worker of miracles); but, as has been seen (ch. 6), it would not invariably lead to an acceptance of Jesus in his true character. This interest in miracles, however, disturbed the Jewish authorities and provoked them to a further attempt to seize Jesus. **32.** *the Pharisees and chief priests:* Pharisaical opposition to Jesus is stressed more in the Syn than in Jn; this is only natural, since Jn is more concerned with Jerusalem, where the priestly and Sadducean elements were dominant. The Pharisaical stronghold was in the synagogues. However, both Jn and the Syn agree that Jesus solidified against himself even the mutually opposed governing elements of Judaism (cf. Mk 3:6; 12:13). **33.** Jesus does not fear the attempts made against him, for the period in which he is free to exercise his ministry depends upon the will of God and not of man (cf. 12:35). *I am going to him who sent me:* When men finally will have had their way with him, Jesus will truly have accomplished the work of salvation for which he was sent into the world. **34.** In 13:33 Jesus reminds the disciples of these words; however, with a far different consequence for them than for the Jews (cf. 16:16–19). *you will look for me and not find me:* Those who are now seeking Jesus' life will, when it is too late, seek him as he should have been sought, as the revealer of the Father. *where I shall be, you cannot come:* His enemies have already shown how far they are from the possibility of joining him in the Father's presence. **35–36.** As so often, Jesus' words are completely misinterpreted. *the Diaspora . . . teach the Greeks:* This is probably meant sarcastically. Since Jesus cannot gain the agreement of his own people, perhaps he means to leave Palestine and go to the Gentiles. This is another instance of prophetic irony in Jn, for this is precisely what Christ, present in his Church, will do.

105 **37–38.** *on the last and greatest day of the festival:* Nowhere in Jewish literature is the final day of Tabernacles called "the greatest." The phrasing of P66 is unique among the Gk mss. in reading (according to its original scribe) "on the last day of the great festival" (see comment on 7:2). The punctuation of Jesus' pronouncement is in doubt, and with it the interpretation. We can read: "If anyone thirst, let him come [to me]; and let him drink who believes in me. As the Scripture says. . . ." In this acceptation, the scriptural citation would refer to Christ himself. Alternatively, we can read: "If anyone thirst, let him come [to me] and drink. Who believes in me, as the Scripture says. . . ." Here the citation would refer to the believer. The passage of 4:14 can be cited in favor of the second alternative, the so-called traditional reading. The water figure itself, featured in the discourse with the Samaritan woman, may have been further suggested by the lustrations of Tabernacles. *as the scripture says:* Identifying as scriptural the words that follow poses another problem. Nowhere in the OT do we read explicitly of such a reference either to the Savior or the saved. But several explanations of the biblical source of these words have been attempted. For instance, the incident of Ex 17:6; Ps 78:15f., is given a messianic interpretation in 1 Cor 10:4. In eschatological OT literature the theme of Jerusalem as a source of living waters is common (cf. Zech 14:8; Ez 47:1–12), and this figure could easily have been extended to the dweller in the eschatological Jerusalem (cf. Is 58:11). In favor of this view, Zech 14 appears to have been one of the prophetic haphtaroth read during Tabernacles. A midrashic application of one of these passages probably lies behind the citation as it is given in Jn. **39.** In any event, whether the reference is intended precisely of Christ or of the Christian, Jn points out that it is of the era of the Christian Church, the era of the Spirit. *there was as yet no Spirit:* John has already mentioned the Spirit in connection with the witness of the Baptist (1:32f.). He means that the Spirit has not yet come in the fullness of his power, which was the outpouring consequent on the glorification of Christ (cf. 4:24; 14:16).

(Boismard, M.-E., "De son ventre couleront des fleuves d'eau," *RB* 65 [1958] 523–46. Cortés Quirant, J., "'Torrentes de agua viva.' Una nueva interpretación de Juan 7, 37–38?" *EstBib* 16 [1957] 297–306. Grelot, P., "'De son ventre couleront des fleuves d'eau,'" *RB* 66 [1959] 369–74; "À propos de Jean VII, 38," *RB* 67 [1960] 224–25. Kilpatrick, G. D., "The Punctuation of John vii. 37–38," *JTS* 11 [1960] 340–42. Kohler, M., "Des fleuves d'eau vive," *RTP* 10 [1960] 188–201.)

106 **40–44.** As in vv. 11–13 and 30–32, Jesus has succeeded once more in dividing the crowd. (On the prophet with whom some wanted to identify him, see comment on 1:21.) Again the Galilean origin of Jesus is advanced against the possibility of his being the Messiah (cf. v. 27); this time, however, the argument rests on the supposition that the Messiah, as the son of David, would be a Judean from the Davidic city of Bethlehem (cf. Mt 2:1–6). John, of course, presupposes that his readers know of the infancy narratives of Mt and Lk, which establish that Jesus was born in Bethlehem. More important, however, is their knowledge of a supernatural origin of Jesus that transcends all such minor questions (cf. v. 27ff.). **45.** The Temple guards were said to have been sent to apprehend Jesus in v. 32. According to the chronology of this chapter (cf. vv. 14 and 37), several days would have elapsed before their return. This chronology is doubtless artificial and secondary to John's topical arrangement of his material. However, though a better chronology can be devised by rearranging the verses, there is no reason to think that the order of the chapter is different from that originally given it by the Evangelist. **46.** The fact that even the Temple guards have been impressed by Jesus' teaching to the extent of failing to execute their commission merely underlines the obduracy of Jesus' enemies—they are impervious to the word of God. **47–49.** Their reply reflects the scribal contempt for the ignorant in an understanding of religion in which mere knowledge of the letter of the Law had become more important than its observance. They suggest that any followers Jesus has obtained have come exclusively from the *'am hā'āreṣ*, the "people of the land," who were not students of the Law. **50–51.** Nicodemus actually stands as a contradiction to their claim that none of the Pharisees has been affected by Jesus' teaching. However, here he merely insists on the observance of the Law in Jesus' case. **52.** The enraged Pharisees caricature this modest defense of Jesus in terms of regional prejudice. *no Galilean prophet:* They can hardly mean that there had never been a Galilean prophet (unless Jn means that they were sufficiently carried away by anger to deny even obvious facts); 2 Kgs 14:25 identifies Jonah as a Galilean, and possibly Hosea had been a Galilean as well. They probably mean that the eschatological prophet of v. 40 was not to be a Galilean.

107 THE STORY OF THE ADULTERESS (7:53–8:11). This and the following section (108) treat of an episode of Gospel tradition that is non-Johannine and interpolated.

There seems to be no doubt that this passage, which interrupts the sequence of the Tabernacle discourses, did not originally form part of Jn's Gospel. It is omitted by P^{66}, P^{75}, and all the major codices except D; it is also lacking in many of the Gk cursives of Jn, sometimes put by them at the end of the Gospel or after Lk 21:38. It was unknown to the Gk Fathers and commentators before the 12th cent. and is not found in most of the ancient versions. However, it is well attested by the Latin Fathers and was included in the VL and Vg. The inspired character and historical worth of the story are not to be called into question, but it doubtless is not the work of John. Its style is that of the Syn, especially of Lk, and most likely belonged to that Gospel originally. Various reasons have been suggested for its presence here in the "received text." Perhaps the most reasonable explanation is that it was transferred here to illustrate the Lord's statement in 8:15, in the following discourse.

108 **53.** *then each went off to his own house:* The original context is unknown, but it seems that the Syn account of passion week is presupposed, according to which Jesus spent the days in Jerusalem teaching but left the city each night for safety (cf. Mk 11:11; etc.). **8:1–2.** A close correspondence to what is supposed here can be found in Lk 21:37f. **3–6a.** The episode that follows accords with the pattern made familiar by the Syn. Jesus' legalistic foes deliberately try to trap him by presenting a difficult problem. Whatever solution he gives will work to his disadvantage (cf. Mt 22:15–22; Mk 10:2ff.). What Jesus is being asked to pronounce on here is not precisely clear. Dt 22:23f. decreed stoning for a betrothed virgin who had committed adultery, but for an adulterous wife Lv 20:10 and Dt 22:22 prescribed death without specifying the manner of execution. The rabbis commonly interpreted the penalty in such undetermined cases to be strangling rather than stoning. Perhaps Jesus was being asked to decide on the validity of such an interpretation (see also comment on 18:31). **6b.** This is the only passage in the Gospels in which Jesus is said to have written anything (*kategraphen*), consequently it has always occasioned much speculation. Probably the author meant no more than that Jesus idly traced figures on the ground to indicate his disinterest in the proceedings. **7–8.** Characteristically, Jesus refuses to deal with the case as a merely legal matter, but treats it practically. In a capital case, the witnesses against the accused were to take the initiative in carrying out the execution (Dt 17:7). Jesus asks them to think first whether their own conscience proclaims them worthy to sit in judgment. **9–10.** Realizing the effectiveness of Jesus' answer and perhaps being ashamed of having tried to use the woman's humiliation as a means of ensnaring a man, the scribes and Pharisees depart, led by their elders. **11.** The lesson of the story is, of course, not that sin is of no importance, nor that God does not punish sin, but that God extends mercy to the sinner that he may turn from his sin. The picture of the sinner and the Sinless standing face to face exemplifies the call to repentance. Thus, though Jesus himself does not judge (8:15), it is nevertheless for judgment that he has come into the world (9:39).

109 **8:12.** The discourses of Tabernacles continue. *I am* [see comment on 6:35] *the light of the world:* See comment on 1:4. The illuminations commonly used during Tabernacles, symbolizing the divine presence and the light of the Law, may have suggested our Lord's use of the figure: He, and not the Law, is the "true" light (see comment on 1:9). He is the light that both gives life and is life, the life of those who cannot walk in darkness (see comment on 1:5). The expression "light of life" for the way of salvation is found in 1QS 3:7. **13–14.** The Pharisees object to Jesus' claim on the score that it needs verification by disinterested testimony, a principle that Jesus has previously accepted (see comment on 5:31). *even if I am my own witness, my testimony is true:* With this emphatic statement Jesus does not attempt to verify his testimony to himself in the forum of public opinion, but simply asserts what is absolute fact and truth. *I know where I came from and where I am going:* Since he, indeed, is the only one who knows this, only his testimony can have any weight; their testimony, on the other hand, is clearly valueless. **15.** They continue to judge superficially, according to appearances (cf. 7:24); for this reason they reject him. *I pass judgment on no one:* This is not in conflict with 5:22,27,30; 9:39, for the point made is that his judgment, the result of his oneness with the Father, totally differs from the negativism of the Pharisees, which causes their rejection of grace. **16.** This verse qualifies the preceding and reiterates the doctrine of 5:22f. **17–18.** It is this, in turn, that permits him to deny the charge made by the Pharisees in v. 13, even on their legalistic premises. His own witness, according to v. 16, must be "true" because it is that of the Father; on the other hand, the Father himself gives testimony to Jesus (5:32–38); thus the requirement of the Law for two witnesses is met (Dt 17:6; 19:5). Furthermore, these are the only witnesses qualified in such a matter (cf. J.-P. Charlier, *RB* 67 [1960] 503–15). **19.** The Pharisees do not make what might appear to be an obvious objection, that Jesus was refusing to take their juridical argument seriously. Instead, they merely confirm the perverseness of their judgments with which he had charged them in v. 15. *where is this "father" of yours?:* A challenge to Jesus to produce his second witness. Either they had missed the entire point of his speech and did not recognize his appeal to the testimony of God, or they willfully misunderstand the nature of God's testimony. *if you recognize me:* On another occasion of misunderstanding, this time sincere, Jesus will paraphrase these words (14:9; cf. also 12:45). **20.** *temple treasury:* This building adjoined the Court of the Women (cf. Mk 12:41ff.), the most public of the Temple courtyards reserved to the Jews, which was doubtless the place where Jesus preached. John probably sees significance in the fact that it is at the Temple itself that the Pharisees cannot discern him who is to replace the Temple (cf. 2:19–22).

110 **21.** As in 7:33f. Jesus says that he is going away and that the Jews will seek him in vain. *you will die in your sin:* This time he is more explicit on the cause and consequence of their inability to follow him. **22.** Again, as in 7:35, the Jews speak a profound truth unwittingly: Jesus will, indeed, lay down his life freely, and because of this he will be forever beyond their grasp (cf. 10:17f.). **23–24.** Jesus continues. They belong to the world that cannot give life, but he has come from heaven precisely to give this life (cf. 3:31). Their obduracy is the sure guarantee that they will die in sin, since they refuse the life that only he can give. This life is to be had only by faith in him. *unless you come to believe that I am what I am:* Here and in v. 28 Jesus again uses the OT formula of the divine self-identification, "I am" (see comment on 6:35). **25.** That "I am" was recognized as a title is clear from the Jews' question: "Who is this person, then?" Jesus' answer has been variously understood. The Greek is obscure; however, P^{66} indicates explicitly a reading that has always been possible from the "received text": "[I told you] at the beginning what I am now telling you" (cf. R. W. Funk, *HarvTR* 51 [1958] 95–100). Jesus is the One whom his words have consistently revealed him to be. **26.** *there are many things about you that I could speak of and condemn:* Jesus allows himself to remind his opponents that he has ample ground to condemn them for their attitudes and deeds in his regard. However, this he does not do. *the only things I speak of in this world:* As he has already said (cf. v. 15f.), he does not judge, but only speaks the words of the Father, which themselves will condemn unbelief because of the truth of their origin. **27–28.** Because the Jews persist in their misunderstanding, Jesus paraphrases his previous statement. *when you will raise up the Son of Man:* For the meaning of this expression, see comment on 3:14. After the crucifixion and glorification of Christ, then—when it is too late—they will perceive that he taught the words of life (cf. Jas 2:19). **29.** The raising up of the Son of Man will entail his return to the Father who sent him. At the same time, however, the Father has always been present with the Son, a fact that has continually been made manifest in Jesus' doing the work of the Father. **30.** If the "believers" of this verse are those who are addressed in the following passage, we might conclude that theirs was a very imperfect faith indeed. Ample precedent for such a conclusion has, of course, already been given: cf. 2:23–25; etc. However, since it is very likely that the Tabernacles discourses have an artificial unity, it is not necessary to draw this conclusion. This verse may be simply John's reminder that, as in 4:39, Jesus' teaching was at times well-received and became the basis of faith.

111 **31.** *those Jews who believed him:* To "believe" is not precisely the same as to "believe in." Although the latter expression usually refers to true faith, or at least the beginning of it, the present statement need mean no more than that some were impressed by his words and were disposed to hear more. Thus it is that Jesus tells them what is required for true faith. *if you endure in my word:* Merely to be receptive to the word is not enough; one must also take it in and act on it constantly. Then alone can one be a true disciple of the Lord. **32–33.** True discipleship, in turn, brings with it the possession of the truth (see comment on 1:14), and truth makes a man free (cf. 1:17). *truth will free you:* In many different senses, this concept appears in various religions and philosophies. Jesus' intimation that they have yet to acquire truth and freedom touches the Jews on a sensitive nerve and provokes a reaction stronger than their previous disposition to listen sympathetically. Despite centuries of foreign domination, the Jews believed themselves above all other men to be free, since they possessed the true mind of God as revealed in his Law. *we are of Abraham's stock:* The Jews' proud retort; for them it corroborates their claim: Never have we been slaves to anybody. **34.** The Jews have correctly grasped that the freedom of which Christ spoke was spiritual, although they have incorrectly assumed that blood descent gives them this freedom. In making his rejoinder, Jesus first asks them to consider what the nature of true spiritual freedom must be. *everyone who acts sinfully is a slave:* Obviously, simply to be a Jew does not of itself constitute one free. Jews, too, can be sinners, and the sinner is the slave of sin (cf. Rom 6:17). **35–36.** Furthermore, really to have the freedom of the house of God depends on the dispensation of the Son, whose it is by right. It is his only by right; in comparison, the tenure of anyone else is like that of a slave, on sufferance. If they have not received their freedom from the Son, they are not truly free. **37.** For these reasons, their descent from Abraham alone counts for nothing. *you look for a chance to kill me:* Jesus returns to the accusation of 7:19. They are manifestly under the rule of sin, therefore slaves. *my word makes no headway among you:* They have not received the word of the Son, who alone can give freedom. **38.** Jesus speaks of the contrast between himself and the Jews, as made evident by the difference in their works. The second part of the verse is not clear. Jesus either says, "You do what you have heard from [your] father," i.e., the devil (cf. vv. 41, 44f.); or, "You should do what you have heard from the Father," i.e., implying a condition that is not verified. Reductively, however, the meaning is the same.

112 **39.** Hearing the word "father," the Jews can only take refuge in their refrain of v. 33. But as Jesus is quick to point out, the true children of Abraham are those whose works proclaim them to be such. This is the same doctrine found in Rom 2:28f.; 9:6f.; Gal 3:7–9; Mt 3:9 par.; etc. **40.** The works of the Jews proclaim them to be anything but children of Abraham; what they are contemplating displays great cruelty and a resistance to the divine will that was never Abraham's. **41.** *you perform your father's works:* Indeed, their works do manifest who is their father, even as Jesus' works do. But their father is someone else than Abraham and someone else than God. *we were not born out of wedlock:* The Jews recognize that Jesus has questioned the legitimacy of their claim to be children of God through Abraham. They emphatically deny that they have been born of "fornication," the OT term for the idolatry of the Gentiles (cf. Hos 2:4; etc.). Perhaps there is by implication an intended slur on Jesus' birth, a charge that was made, at least, in the later Jewish-Christian controversy. **42.** In answer to this claim, Jesus repeats: If they were truly God's children, they would recognize in him one from God and love rather than hate him. **43.** They do not receive his word because they cannot: They have closed their ears to the Word of God. This, in turn, identifies them as the children of a father whom he will now name explicitly for the first time. **44.** *the devil is the father you spring from:* This must be, for it is the devil who is the very antithesis of the God to whom they claim to belong. *he was a murderer from the beginning:* It was through the devil that death first entered the world (cf. Gn 3:3f.; Wis 2:24). He is thus the enemy of the life that Jesus has come to bring and the father of those who seek to kill him. *never based himself on truth:* Again, he is the enemy of the truth that Jesus has been speaking and the father of those who reject it.

45–47. Thus Jesus reiterates his argument: The charges they have made against him are groundless and they know it; essentially it is because they are alien to God that they cannot recognize his word.

113 **48.** The Jews repeat their charge of diabolic possession, i.e., of insanity (cf. 7:20). *you are a Samaritan:* Various explanations have been given of this charge. The Samaritans were notorious for their traffic in magic, therefore with the devil (cf. Acts 8:9–24); Jesus had questioned the unique prerogatives of the Jews, therefore adopting the position of the Samaritans; "Samaritan" was simply a term of opprobrium (cf. Sir 50:25f.). **49–50.** Jesus' reply is a quiet repudiation of the imputation of diabolic direction that he has already attributed to their own actions. His words and deeds clearly show the basic truth of the matter. To this reply is joined an equally quiet warning. The insults that have been flung at him he can readily pass over, but they will not be passed over by the One who is the Judge of all. **51.** Acceptance of Jesus' teaching leads to eternal life; this is a contradiction of all the devil signifies. **52–53.** Still superficial in their judgments (cf. 7:24), the Jews protest the possibility of his giving eternal life. Is he greater than Abraham and the prophets (cf. 4:12), all of whom are dead? Again the Johannine irony (→ 29 above), since truly here is one greater than the prophets (cf. Mt 12:6,41,42). **54–55.** Jesus answers that it is not his own claims about himself that are being discussed, but that, as he has pointed out all along, it is the testimony of the Father that is involved—the testimony that they will not receive. **56.** *your father Abraham rejoiced at the prospect of seeing my day:* Jesus is greater than Abraham, for Abraham himself knew that the promises made to him pointed to a blessedness to come (cf. Gn 12:3; 18:18; Gal 3:8f.). *when he saw it, he was glad:* Probably the reference is to Gn 17:17, taking Abraham's laughter as a sign of rejoicing, as the Jews commonly did. In the birth of Isaac, the messianic "day" had its first beginning. **57.** Superficially taken, Jesus' last statement is nonsense to the Jews. *fifty years old:* The meaning no doubt is, "You are yet a young man." **58.** *before Abraham was, I am:* This, one of Jesus' most emphatic affirmations concerning his divine nature, is his reply to the Jews' latest question. See comment on 6:35. **59.** The implications of this statement are not lost on the Jews, who seek to stone Jesus for his supposed blasphemy. *they picked up stones:* The objection has often been made that the courtyard of the Temple (cf. v. 20) was not a likely place for stones to be found. However, aside from the probable artificial unity of this lengthy passage, of which we have spoken above, the fact that the Temple was still under construction (cf. 2:20) would explain the presence of stones and other debris.

114 (d) Jesus the Light of the World (9:1–10:42). In these two chapters the theme of Jesus as the light of the world is further developed, first in the miracle of the sight given to the blind man, then in the contrast shown by the spiritual blindness of Jesus' adversaries.

(i) *The sixth sign* (9:1–34). "As sheer drama, this trial scene is one of the most brilliant passages in the gospel, rich in the tragic irony of which the Evangelist is master. The one-time beggar stands before his betters, to be badgered into denying the one thing of which he is certain. (The beggar on trial suggests to the Christian reader his own situation in the world—enlightened in baptism and called upon to confess Christ before men.) But the defendant proper is Jesus Himself, judged *in absentia*. In some sort, the man whom Christ enlightened pleads the cause of the Light. When he is 'cast out,' it is Christ whom the judges have rejected. Then comes the dramatic *peripeteia*. Jesus swiftly turns the tables on His judges, and pronounces sentence: 'For judgment I have come into the world....' " (C. H. Dodd, *Interpretation*, 357–58). Most aptly John has placed here the next-to-last of the special "signs" of Jesus' work of salvation, the giving of sight and light to one who had never before possessed them.

1. *as he walked along:* Although there is no obvious contextual connection between this and the preceding episode, the locale is still Jerusalem, as is seen from what follows. *blind from birth:* The essence of this "sign" is for John not simply that sight is restored, but that light is given to one who has never had it. The light that Jesus has come to give (see comments on 1:4,9) is not men's by right, but is God's free gift through Jesus Christ: By nature, man is, in this sense, born blind. **2.** *who committed the sin?:* It was a firm Jewish belief that every affliction was the punishment for sin, and that the sins of parents could be punished in their offspring (cf. Ex 20:5; Dt 5:9). The disciples did not necessarily think that the man might have sinned before birth, in his mother's womb, as was taught by some later rabbis. In the foreknowledge of God, they could have reasoned, the punishment might have been inflicted because of a sin that was to follow. **3.** Jesus does not treat of the question in general regarding the connection of sin and physical ills; he does not solve the mystery of suffering in a world of God's love. *for the sake of displaying God's works:* Jesus confines himself to one aspect alone of the case at hand, which in the divine providence has been destined to serve as the occasion of a work of God. He does not say that this is the entire explanation, but he does deny that human sinfulness is that explanation. **4–5.** Jesus now identifies the part he plays in fulfilling the divine purposes. In performing God's work in respect to this man, he will be offering a sign of the divine light. *we must work:* This is the better reading; the variant "I must work" of the majority of mss. is doubtless a deliberate correction. By using the plural John probably applies Jesus' words to his readers—he wants to remind them that theirs is also the duty to do the works of God. *while it is daylight:* The simple analogy of work to be done in daylight rather than in darkness recalls the opposition of light to spiritual darkness (see comment on 1:5 and cf. 3:2; 11:10; 13:30). *I am the light:* See comment on 6:35.

115 **6–7.** The sacramental symbolism of this episode was not lost on the primitive Church, which commonly took it to be a sign of baptism (see comment on 2:1–11). *he spat:* Spittle was commonly believed to have medicinal properties; in Mk 7:33; 8:23 Jesus also uses it in his miracles. *smeared the man's eyes:* The verb means, literally, "anointed" (so also in v. 11). Anointing was part of the ritual of baptism from earliest Christian times (cf. *Apostolic Constitutions* 7.22). *the name means "one sent":* Siloam, Hebr *šilōaḥ*, is related to the vb. *šālaḥ*, "send." John sees significance in the name of the pool in whose waters the man gains his sight, since Jesus is the one sent by the Father to give light. For a previous instance in which the waters of Siloam signify the divine power capable of giving life but, as in the following episode, are rejected by the Jerusalemites, see Is 8:6. Siloam was the pool at the southern extremity of Jerusalem from which water was brought for the libations of the Feast of Tabernacles.

8–12. As is so often the case, the words and deeds of Jesus cause immediate dissension. As usual, John depicts the man progressing gradually in his understanding of Jesus. At first he is to him merely "that man they call Jesus." **13–17.** The matter is presented to the Pharisees, arbiters of what was religiously proper, and the dissension is communicated to them (cf. 7:43; 10:19). Their complaint is against Jesus' technical violation of the Sabbath, as in 5:1–18. The man who has gained his sight has now reached the next stage in his recognition; what has been done to him presupposes one who is in a special relation to God: "he is a prophet" (cf. 4:19). **18–23.** The Jews summon the man's parents to verify that he had indeed been born blind. While affirming the undeniable, the parents refuse to commit themselves concerning his present state for the reason given in the parenthesis of v. 22f. When John states that confession of Christ was punished by excommunication from the synagogue he doubtless accommodates the language to the situation of later Christian times when this punishment was inflicted on Christian Jews, including perhaps some of John's own readers. The ostracism applied in Jesus' time to those who defended him would have been of a less formal nature. **24.** The Jews now attempt to intimidate the man who had received his sight. *give glory to God:* This was a solemn adjuration to tell the truth (cf. Jos 7:19). The Johannine irony (→ 29 above) appears: By telling the truth, the man will indeed be giving the glory to God that the Jews are denying him (cf. Jn 8:49f.). *a sinner:* This is the affirmation the Jews seek: If, as he claims, Jesus has cured him, it can only be at the expense of having violated the Sabbath law, thereby constituting himself a sinner. **25–26.** The man refuses to debate with the Jews on their own ground concerning what constitutes a sinful violation of the Sabbath. He testifies to the one thing that is incontrovertible. The Jews' demand for a repetition of his story is a study in frustration, for only by acknowledging that he has done a work that is apparently miraculous, can they claim Jesus is a sinner. Thus they seek to attack the story in some detail or other. **27–29.** The man is fully aware of their intentions and makes no attempt to be diplomatic. *do you too want to become his disciples?:* The question is doubly ironical, for the accent is placed on the "too": The Jews are being reminded of the unpleasant fact that Jesus is gathering disciples despite their efforts. In their reply the Jews themselves, zealous for the Law according to their conceptions, bring out the contrast of 1:17. *we do not even know where he is from:* Another irony, cf. 3:8; 8:14. **30–33.** The man becomes quite bold in his answers, giving an example to the Christian who must testify fearlessly to the truth. We are reminded of Jesus' words to Nicodemus in 3:10. Invoking a common biblical theme (cf. Is 1:15; 59:2; Mi 3:4; Prv 15:29), he proves with irrefutable logic that Jesus could be no sinner but must be from God. **34.** Taking refuge in bluster, the Jews now admit what they had previously questioned, that the man had been born blind and thus was proved a sinner. *they cast him out:* They drove him from their presence (see comment on 18–23).

116 (ii) *Sight and blindness* (9:35–10:21). The sequel to the preceding story contrasts the willing faith of the man who had been blind with the willful blindness of Jesus' enemies. In turn, the short allegories that follow underline the difference between Jesus the Light and the blind guides who oppose him. The section ends with an inclusional reference to the sixth sign.

35. Jesus now seeks out the man who has been rejected by the Pharisees and offers to him the opportunity to make the ultimate act of faith (cf. vv. 11 and 17). *do you believe in the Son of Man?:* "Son of God" is found in some mss., but the present reading is to be preferred, especially in view of the parallel self-revelation of Jesus in 1:51; 3:13; 6:53,62. **36–37.** *just who is he, sir, that I may believe in him?:* The man does not ask about the meaning of "Son of Man," concerning whom he would have had at least some notion (see comment on 1:51); he asks rather that Jesus point the Son of Man out to him. Jesus does so, in words reminiscent of those he spoke to the Samaritan woman (4:26). **38.** *Lord:* Now recognizing Jesus' identity, the man addresses him with the title of Christian faith (cf. Acts 2:36; Phil 2:11); in v. 36 the same word *kyrios* would presumably mean only "sir." This verse and the introduction to the following are lacking in some important mss., but the omission is probably accidental. **39.** The meaning of the entire episode of cure and controversy is now summed up in the words of Jesus, from which the character of the sign emerges. *I came into this world for judgment:* See comment on 3:17–19. *that those who do see may become blind:* The effect of the judgment brought about by Jesus' call to faith is that many, like the Pharisees in this episode, falsely believing that they already possess the light, reject the revelation of God. Jesus has not come to condemn, but such will be the result of his mission for many, as it had been with the prophets of old (cf. Is 6:9f.). **40–41.** The Pharisees correctly assay Jesus' words to apply to themselves. *if you only were blind:* If only they realized the extent of their own blindness, there would be hope that they would seek for light. What makes their case hopeless is their smug complacency.

117 **10:1.** The two comparisons that are now introduced, Jesus the Shepherd and Jesus the Gate, are closely bound together and continue the theme introduced by the preceding episode (cf. P. W. Meyer, *JBL* 75 [1956] 232–35). Jesus is about to contrast himself with the false shepherds of Israel (cf. Ez 34:1–16) represented by the Pharisees, who have rejected rather than saved the man who was given his sight. He begins by reminding them that while all manners of men may be found in a sheepfold, the shepherd who is the true owner of the sheep—by his free and open entry into the fold— may be distinguished from those who have no legitimate business there. *I firmly assure you:* The "Amen, Amen" formula characteristically used by Jesus in Jn, was first introduced in 1:51. "It always has reference to something that has been said already, which is expanded or set in a new light" (Bernard). **2–3.** The gatekeeper of the fold and the sheep can therefore easily distinguish the genuine shepherd from the interloper: So it is with those who are the true sheep of God; they are able to discern the one who speaks with God's voice (cf. 8:47; etc.). *he calls by name the sheep that belong to him and leads them out:* This method of herding sheep is still being followed in Palestine. The familiar scene had long been applied to the relation of God's people to their divinely sent leaders (cf. Nm 27:16f.). **4–5.** *when he has brought all his own out:* The sheep of a village were kept in a common fold, whence each shepherd would call out his own sheep and lead them away to pasturage. Again Jesus insists on the rapport that exists between the owner and his sheep, who will heed no voice except his. **6.** The Pharisees exemplify Jesus' point by failing to understand his meaning: They are not the sheep who hear the voice of their Shepherd.

7. *I am the sheepgate:* In the preceding verses Jesus has implicitly identified himself as the true shepherd of God's sheep, an identification that he will make explicit in v. 11. With a sudden shift of application, however, he now identifies himself with the gate of the sheepfold. The reason for this is that he is now applying the significance of the gate as set forth in v. 1. He has not lost sight of the fact that the true shepherd must be in this way distinguished from the robbers and bandits. Jesus therefore associates with himself as legitimate shepherds of the people those who have come to the fold through him, that is, the apostles and their successors. **8.** *all who came before:* Apart from Jesus, other leaders proved to be "thieves and bandits" (v. 1). He is not, of course, condemning the leaders of God's people appointed in the OT. In his view these were not "before" him, since they were part of the descent from God of which he is the ultimate fulfillment. Only those who come in by some way other than the gate are the interlopers who have been recognized as such. **9.** Another application of the figure of the gate is made, this time it relates to the sheep. *whoever enters through me will be saved:* Just as the sheep enter and leave the fold only through the gate, so entry is gained into God's fold, God's pasturage, only through Christ (cf. 14:6). **10.** He reverts to the original contrast: The thieves and bandits who enter not by the gate come only to prey on the sheep. *I came that they might have life:* See comment on 1:4. *and have it in abundance:* Cf. 1:16; Rom 5:20.

118 **11.** Jesus now explicitly calls himself the "good" (*kalos*) or "model" shepherd of whom he has been speaking; this is equivalent to his calling himself the "true" (see comment on 1:9) or perfect shepherd. *the true shepherd lays down his life for the sheep:* This is not an exaggeration of the analogue to fit the occasion; the Israelite shepherd frequently risked his life to save his sheep (cf. 1 Sm 17:34f.; Is 31:4). In a far more significant way, of course, Jesus truly lays down his life for the sheep of God (cf. 15:13). **12–13.** In this he contrasts with the Pharisees of the preceding episode, who may be compared to hired helpers who work merely for their own interests and have no personal concern for the sheep. **14–15.** Jesus is shown to be the true shepherd in another way: He knows and is known by the sheep of God (cf. v. 4). This mutual knowledge (see comments on 1:10; 1:26) is in turn an extension of the mutual knowledge of the Father and the Son (cf. 14:20). *I lay down my life for these sheep:* That is, for the sake of this shared existence between sheep and Shepherd (Son) and Father. **16.** Furthermore, Jesus' concern as the shepherd of the people of God goes far beyond the OT types. *I have other sheep that do not belong to this fold:* The Gentiles, too, must be brought into salvation together with the sheep of the fold of Israel (cf. Mt 15:24; Gal 3:28; Eph 2:11–22). The way to eternal life is the same for both—that they hear in Jesus the voice of God and respond with faith. *then there will be one sheep-herd, one shepherd:* This attempts to capture the alliteration of the Gk phrase, *mia poimnē heis poimēn*. The Vg has "one fold, one shepherd," but the Greek clearly means "flock." To read "flock" rather than "fold," however, is not to lessen the fact that the text supposes a single Jewish-Gentile Church under the one Shepherd Christ: "There is nothing to suggest that John thought of one flock lodged in a number of different folds" (Barrett). **17.** The mutual knowledge of the Father and Son that explains the supreme sacrifice of the Shepherd for his sheep (v. 15) is likewise the explanation of the love of the Father for the Son, for it is a sacrifice that the Son performs in complete harmony with the will of the Father (v. 18). *I lay down my life in order to take it up again:* The crucifixion and resurrection are the two aspects of the glorification of Christ (see comments on 1:14; 2:11). In his exaltation Christ takes up life not only for himself but also for all who live through his work of salvation (cf. 1 Cor 15:45). **18.** The condition of the efficacy of Christ's work is the entire freedom of his obedience. *no one took it from me:* This is the reading of the better mss. Here Jesus speaks of the crucifixion as though it had already occurred, just as in the discourse of 13:31ff. he speaks of himself as already glorified.

19–21. Again, division is caused among the Jews by Jesus' words. While some continue the charge of madness (7:20; 8:48), others have been impressed by the sign of 9:1ff.

119 (iii) *The works of Jesus* (10:22–39). The Feast of the Dedication of the Temple (Hanukkah) sets the scene for the last of Jesus' lengthy discourses before the people of Jerusalem. It provides a fitting conclusion to the theme of Jesus the Light, and in v. 28 there is an introduction to the next theme of Jesus the Life.

22. *it was winter:* Apparently John expects us to understand that some time has passed since the preceding discourse, even though the same ideas are continued and developed here. The last chronological indication was in 7:37, the conclusion of the Feast of Tabernacles, about three months before the Feast of the Dedication. *the Dedication feast:* This feast, which usually falls in mid-December, commemorates the rededication of the Temple in 165 BC during the Maccabean wars (cf. 1 Mc 4:36–59; 2 Mc 1:18). It was known as "the Feast of Lights," not so much because of the customary lighting of the lampstands but because of its significance of the light of liberty, according to Josephus (*Ant.* 12.7, 7 § 325). Its observance bore a marked resemblance to that of Tabernacles, and it was sometimes even called by the name of Tabernacles (cf. 2 Mc 1:9; 10:6). **23.** *in the temple precincts, in Solomon's porch:* John may find it significant that Jesus was in the Temple grounds at this time in view of the similar occasion when, according to the Syn tradition, he was asked for his titles of authority (cf. Mk 11:27). However, his mention of "Solomon's Porch," a protected area on the E side of the outer court of the Temple, doubtless means only that Jesus had taken shelter from the winter cold. **24.** While Jn does not develop the theme of the "Messianic Secret" (→ Gospel Mk, 42:5) found especially in Mk among the Syn, the present verse shows that there is no real historical conflict between the developed theology frequent in Jn and the gradual development proper to the Syn. Despite all the affirmations of his character thus far recorded in Jn, the Jews still ask Jesus to tell them "in plain words" if he is the Messiah. **25–26.** Jesus' answer is at one and the same time an evasion of the strictly messianic question in the pattern of the Syn and also more than the Jews had bargained for. First of all, he reminds them of his frequent claim to be manifested in his true character in view of his doing the works of the Father (cf. 4:34; 5:36,39). Those attuned to the Word of God would already have recognized who he is (cf. 8:47). **27–28.** He reverts to the figure of the shepherd and the sheep (cf. v. 14 above). The pasturage to which he leads his sheep is that of eternal life (cf. 3:15; 4:14). *no one will snatch them out of my hand:* Because he is the true shepherd to whom the sheep have been given by the Father (cf. v. 29 and 6:39). **29.** *the Father who has given* [the sheep] *to me is greater than all:* There are variants in the mss., but the general sense seems to be clear (cf. J. N. Birdsall, *JTS* 11 [1960] 342–44). It is impossible that Jesus should lose the sheep that have been given to him by the Father since the Father's omnipotence is the guarantee of the gift. **30.** Whereupon Jesus utters one of his "hard sayings" that provokes the wrath of the Jews. *the Father and I are one:* In context Jesus is amplifying his statement that no one can snatch the sheep from him because they have been given him by the Father; Father and Son are one in mind, will, and action (cf. v. 17 above; 5:19f.; 8:16). This unity presupposes the even more essential one of which Jn speaks in 1:1; Jesus does not say merely that he and the Father are "at one," but are "one thing" (*hen*). This meaning is, in fact, perceived by the Jews, as appears in the following verses.

120 **31.** The reaction of the Jews is the same as in 8:59. **32.** Jesus' response is ironical: Since he has done only good among them, works that were manifestly God's, for what noble thing are they about to stone him? **33.** The Jews here make the protest reported of them in Jn 5:18. *you, a human being, make yourself God:* Here is another instance of Johannine irony: In reality, of course, Jesus who is God has made himself a human being (cf. 1:14). **34–36.** Debating with rabbis, Jesus argues according to their methods. He was being accused of blasphemy because he had said, equivalently, "I am God's son."

But does not the Scripture itself, God's own word, sometimes speak of mere men as "gods" or "sons of God"? If this be so, then there can be nothing blasphemous in his using such a title. This argument fails to consider the different senses in which these titles had been used; this was good rabbinic exegesis, which disregarded the original sense and context of scriptural words. *written in your Law:* Actually the passage cited is Ps 82:6; the Jews, however, sometimes spoke of the entire OT as "the Law" (cf. Str-B 2, 542f.; so also in Jn 12:34; 15:25). *I have said, "You are gods":* The original sense of the Ps is not in question. The Jews understood the term "gods" to be justified as applied to those who were the recipients of God's word; for this reason, this verse was often understood as having reference to all Israelites (cf. Str-B 2, 543). *if it calls those men gods:* Jesus uses the argumentative device called by the rabbis *qal wāḥōmer* (light and heavy), that is "an *a fortiori*" (cf. Str-B 3, 223–26). *God's word was addressed:* It is possible that John wants the reader to remember the far more significant way in which the Word of God has been used in the prologue. Here we have, literally, "the word of God came about" (*egeneto*), and there, "the Word was" (see 1:1). *scripture cannot lose its force:* The Jews cannot ignore, on their own principles, the scriptural argument that is proposed to them. *the one whom the Father consecrated and sent into the world:* The *a fortiori* is complete. "Consecrated" (also in 17:17,19) or "dedicated": Possibly the occasion of the Dedication feast suggested this word, the same one used in the scriptural lesson for the Dedication (Nm 7:1); as in 2:21, Jesus would be proposing himself as the replacement of the Temple. **37.** The heart of the question remains where it ever was: Jesus is known for whom he is because he does the work of the Father (cf. 5:17; etc.). Only if he did not do this work would there be grounds to refuse to put faith in him. **38.** *put your faith in these works:* At least, they must credit their senses and acknowledge that what Jesus does is of divine origin. *even though you will still put no faith in me:* That is, in Jesus' assertions concerning himself. This will actually become an unreal concession, for a true acknowledgment of what Jesus does must lead to an acknowledgment of what he is, one with the Father: "that you may come to know and understand that the Father is in me and I am in the Father." **39.** Silenced, Jesus' opponents remain as obdurate as ever and seek his downfall as before (cf. 7:1,30,44; 8:20).

121 (iv) *Inclusion on the public life* (10:40–42). These verses form a preliminary conclusion of the account of Jesus' public life in Jn (the "Perean ministry" of the Syn). What had begun with the witness of the Baptist (1:19ff.) ends with a reference to that witness; the locale is also the same: Bethany beyond the Jordan (cf. 1:28). The Baptist has entirely receded from the picture (cf. 3:30), which is dominated by him who bears the realities to which the Baptist could only point (cf. 1:26f.). And for some, at least, there is faith.

122 **(D) The Last Journey to Jerusalem (11:1–12:50).** At least as he finally constituted it, John has concluded the first part of his Gospel with this section, in which we find the last and greatest of Jesus' special "signs," together with several episodes that serve to introduce themes that will be featured in the Gospel's second part.

123 (a) Death and Life: The Seventh Sign (11:1–44). In the narration of this miracle Jn gives at one and the same time a supreme proof of the Lord's life-giving power and a visualization of the doctrine contained in the conversation of vv. 23–27. The miracle literally fulfills the words of Jesus in 5:28; it is a sign, therefore, both of the final resurrection and of the rising from sin to grace that takes place in the soul of the believer. Some scholars question the literal history of the story, not because they disbelieve in miracles or in Jesus' ability to perform them, but because an event of such magnitude is not mentioned in the Syn. The discrepancy, however, is not as significant as it might seem, given the divergent aims of the Syn and the Johannine traditions (→ 17–27 above); moreover, the Syn tradition makes fairly frequent reference to similar miracles (cf. Mk 5:35–43; Mt 11:5; Lk 7:11–17,22). There are certain affinities between this narrative and the parable of our Lord related in Lk 16:19–31; however, relatively few scholars have tried to maintain that the Johannine story is simply an expansion of the Lucan.

124 **1.** *Lazarus:* A common name of the time (Hebr *Eleazar*), found elsewhere in the NT only in Lk 16:19–31. *Bethany:* The modern el-Azariyeh (an Arabic corruption of the name "Lazarus"), less than 2 mi. SE of Jerusalem, separated from it by the Mt. of Olives. Jn identifies it as "the village of Mary and her sister Martha," known from the Syn tradition, to distinguish it from the other Bethany, beyond the Jordan, implicit in 10:40 above. **2.** This verse has often been misunderstood. John refers to an event that he supposes his readers to know well, though he himself has not yet mentioned it. He speaks of the anointing at Bethany (12:3); there is no reason to think that he attempted to identify Mary, the sister of Lazarus, with the unnamed Galilean woman in the similar narrative recounted only by Lk 7:37f. (however, see comment on 12:3). **3.** The sisters send a message simply stating the facts: Their request, like Mary's at Cana (2:3), is implicit in their words. The resemblance is not superficial. At first Jesus apparently rejects the request, as he did at Cana, but the narrative ends, as at Cana, in a miracle that is a manifestation of his glory for those who believe (cf. vv. 4, 40 and 2:11). *the one whom you love:* In keeping with the character of this miracle as a sign, Lazarus appears throughout, not merely as an historical figure but also as one representing the Christian, the believer in Christ, even as does the disciple "whom Jesus loved" (→ 3 above). **4.** *this sickness is not to end in death:* To the casual eye, it might have appeared that Jesus was making light of Lazarus' illness and of his sisters' message, since in fact the sickness was a fatal one (v. 17). But as so often, there is a deeper meaning in the Savior's words: Not death, but the glory of God will be served through this illness. *that the Son may be glorified:* See comments on 1:14; 2:11. **5–6.** John is careful to point out that it was not lack of love for Lazarus and his sisters that caused him to delay going to him. Jesus has already explained his reason for the delay, as will be made manifest by what happens. **7–8.** When at last Jesus does propose that he and his disciples return to Judea, they remind him of the hostility that had caused their recent departure (10:31,39). **9–10.** Jesus' reply bears some resemblance to his words in 9:4. Now is the time for his appointed work, before the coming of the time of darkness (see comment on 1:5). For the "hour" of Jesus, see 2:4; 4:23; 5:25. **11–14.** The pattern of the Johannine dialogue (→ 30 above) is followed: The disciples first misunderstand Jesus' reference to the "sleep" of death (cf. Mk 5:39; 1 Thes 4:14; 5:10), thinking only of the health-giving sleep that often follows illness, and unconsciously speak the teaching of this passage for the Christian believer, (literally) "Lord, if he has fallen asleep, he will be saved." **15.** *I am happy for your sake:* Jesus rejoices not at Lazarus' death, obviously (cf. v. 35f.), but because it has given an occasion to confirm the faith of the disciples. *so that you may come to have faith:* The disciples, of course, already have faith acquired on another occasion of the manifestation of Christ's glory (cf. 2:11). But this passage, and indeed the entire Gospel, bears its message for all Christians of all time (cf. 20:30f.), and John constantly bears this in mind in his formulation of Jesus' words. **16.** *Thomas:* This disciple, mentioned by the Syn only in their lists of the Twelve (Mt 10:3; Mk 3:18; Lk 6:15; Acts 1:13), emerges in Jn's Gospel especially in connection with the great mysteries of Christ's glorification (cf. 14:5; 20:24–29; 21:2). *let us go too that we may die with him:* Thomas says more than he realizes. He is thinking of the present danger to Christ in Judea (v. 8) and expressing his willingness to share this peril; but his words sum up the common destiny of all Christians, which is to be dead with Christ and alive with him in his resurrection (cf. Gal 2:19f.).

125 **17.** *four days in the tomb:* John may be underlining the reality of Lazarus' death, in view of a contemporary Jewish belief that the soul of the dead remained in the vicinity of the body for three days and afterward departed (cf. Str-B 2, 544f.). Another possibility is that, like the first manifestation of Christ's glory at the end of "the week of new creation" (see comments on 1:19–2:11), this final sign also takes place on the seventh day after Jesus' announcement of Lazarus' sickness (cf. vv. 4, 6). **18–19.** Because Bethany was near Jerusalem, many Jerusalemites are present at the mourning rites, which usually extended seven days from the time of death. **20.** The disparate characters of Martha and Mary, the former the more active, the latter the more intense (cf. v. 32f. and 12:2f.), are strikingly confirmed by the account of the sisters in Lk 10:38–42. **21–22.** As in v. 3, Martha's words only imply a request of the Lord, since she recognizes his special relationship to God. **23–24.** Jesus' words of greeting are at first taken by Martha simply as a conventional reference to the final resurrection, a doctrine held by Pharisaic Judaism in Jesus' day and generally by the NT as well. **25.** *I am the resurrection:* Jesus affirms Martha's belief in a resurrection to come, with the significant addition that its power is to be found in himself. *even if he should die:* Physical death is the common lot of mankind, Christians included, but faith in Christ will bring the believer to life again in the resurrection (cf. 6:40). **26.** Furthermore, for the believer the effects of this resurrection already take place in "realized eschatology" (→ 25 above). *everyone who is alive and believes in me:* Since the believer already possesses true or eternal life, physical death can never really affect him. **27.** Martha confesses her faith in these Christian truths, using the formulas with which she was familiar from OT expectation. She still has not been told that Lazarus will rise here and now as a sign.

126 **28–32.** We are not told why Jesus remained outside the village and why, therefore, Mary was summoned to him by Martha. John doubtless intends that we should see in Martha's words before the resurrection of Lazarus the summons that every Christian must obey with Mary's alacrity: "The Master is here [*parestin* = the *parousia*] and calls for you." Mary's greeting is almost the same as Martha's. **33.** *he trembled:* To accompany this verb Jn uses another (*embrimasthai*, also in v. 38), variously translated, that indicates some intense emotion. In classical authors and in the LXX (also in Mk 14:5) the verb connotes anger; however, a source of anger in the present episode would be difficult to find. Elsewhere when the verb is applied to Jesus (Mt 9:30; Mk 1:43) it is also in the context of a miracle (cf. also Mk 1:41 *orgistheis*, the "more difficult" reading), and perhaps we may take the reference of Heb 5:7 to his sacrifice in the same sense. The works of the public life were a subject of intense emotional involvement for the God-Man, and that their consequence was to be his death he fully understood. **34–36.** The Jews rightly perceive Jesus' love for Lazarus, though they do not as yet realize the measure of his love. **37–38.** The words ascribed to the Jews do not express scepticism; they more or less repeat those of the sisters. Therefore Jesus' emotional reaction is not directed against unbelief, but at the need of performing this work with all its consequences (cf. vv. 45ff.). **39.** The practical Martha remonstrates over what she takes to be Jesus' desire to look upon the features of his departed friend. **40.** *once you believe, you will see God's glory:* Jesus now tells Martha that the truth (v. 26) in which she had placed her faith is now to be exemplified in what he is about to do. **41.** *I thank you because you heard me:* Jesus has already requested the Father to raise Lazarus from the dead. No such prayer has been mentioned, and in view of v. 42 it is not necessary to suppose that there was a formal request at any specified time, since the will of the Father and the Son are always at one. **42.** *I spoke because of the crowd:* Jesus is not play-acting. His visible thanksgiving to the Father, however, is necessary to bring out the truth that in his works he is not simply a man endowed with wonder-working power but the emissary of the Father of life (cf. 5:19–30). **43–44.** At the sound of Jesus' voice (cf. 3:28f.) Lazarus emerges from the tomb still wrapped in the burial cloths. As is usual in the Gospels, this narrative of the marvelous is brought to a matter-of-fact conclusion with no attempt to satisfy idle curiosity about incidental details.

127 (b) DEATH CHOSEN OVER LIFE (11:45–57). **45–46.** Ironically, the great exemplification of life in vv. 1–44 results in a decision for death on the part of Jesus' enemies. *many of the Jews...put their faith in him:* As has been seen (2:23–25; etc.), the incipient faith based on miracles did not always lead to a true acceptance of Jesus; nevertheless, this action of Jesus is no exception to the rule in serving to divide the opinions of those who have witnessed it. *some of them went to the Pharisees:* Although their report is not necessarily the denunciation of unbelievers, it is taken in bad part by the Pharisees. **47.** The report to the Pharisees results in a convocation of the Sanhedrin. The attitude of official Judaism is as implacably opposed to Jesus at the end of his public career as it had been from the beginning. In the present instance, the reality of Jesus' miraculous works is not questioned, but they are regarded only as an embarrassment. **48.** *everybody will believe in him, and the Romans will come and wipe out our holy place and our nation:* A spectacular bit of Johannine irony: These adversities the Sanhedrin seeks to avoid by getting rid of Jesus, yet is was precisely these events that were to follow his death. **49.** *high priest that particular year:* Caiaphas was high priest for about 20 years; Jn does not imply that there was a new high priest each year, but only that he was the high priest in the crucial year of Jesus' death and resurrection. **50–52.** Caiaphas' words are the counsel of cynicism: It is better that this one man should perish (even if he were innocent) than that because of him the Romans would perhaps bring about the destruction of the whole people. *it was not on his own that he said this:* Caiaphas utters an unconscious prophecy (cf. Str-B 2, 546), for in very truth Jesus did die for the whole people—not for that of Israel alone, but for all mankind. John emphasizes that Caiaphas was high priest, probably recalling the ancient association of priesthood and prophecy in Near Eastern tradition (C. H. Dodd, "The Prophecy of Caiaphas," *Neotestamentica et patristica* [Fest. O. Cullmann; Leiden, 1962] 134–43.) **53.** Mk 14:1f. also records such a decision for Jesus' death by the Jewish leaders before the last Passover. **54.** *Ephraim:* Usually identified with the modern et-Taiyibeh, 4 mi. NE of Bethel and some 15 mi. from Jerusalem.

55–57. In view of the action known to have been taken by the Sanhedrin—at least the order that had been issued to apprehend Jesus—the last Passover draws near on a somber note. Previously the people had questioned whether Jesus would come to Jerusalem for a pilgrimage feast (7:11). Now they feel virtually sure that he will not make an appearance under the circumstances.

128 (c) THE ANOINTING (12:1–11). The themes of death and life introduced by the Lazarus story continue in the present episode, a passage which Jn has in common with the Syn tradition (Mt 26:6–13; Mk 14:3–9), but which as usual the Evangelist treats in his own distinctive way.

1. *six days before Passover:* According to Jn, Jesus was put to death the day before Passover (18:28; 19:31) and rose the day following it (20:1); we are, therefore, now in the "final week of the new creation" (see comments on 1:19–2:11), seven days before the exaltation of Christ (cf. 20:19–22). Jn's needless identification of Bethany as "the residence of Lazarus whom Jesus had raised from the dead" connects this episode with the earlier episode (11:1–44; cf. 4:46). Jesus' fearlessness in returning to this scene also contrasts with the sentiments voiced in 11:56. **2.** Mt-Mk put the anointing at Bethany in the home of Simon the leper. John does not affirm or deny this, but mentions only those persons who are important to him. Martha fulfills a role consonant with her character as portrayed by Lk 10:40, as does Mary in the following verse. **3.** *perfume made of costly aromatic nard:* The verbal correspondence with Mk 14:3 (and also with Lk 7:37 in the similar story of Lk 7:36–50) is very close. Especially significant is the presence of the word *pistikos*, of uncertain meaning, which appears in both Jn and Mk and nowhere else in Gk literature except in works dependent on these sources. This is one of the passages that have convinced many scholars of a literary dependence of Jn on Mk (→ 18 above). *Mary... anointed Jesus' feet and then dried his feet with her hair:* This does not agree with Mt-Mk, according to which Jesus' head was anointed; it does correspond with Lk 7:38, however, according to which the penitent Galilean woman first washed his feet with her tears, dried them with her hair, kissed them, and then anointed them. Without entering into the question of the relationship between Lk and Jn (→ 19 above), it seems evident that the Johannine version of the anointing is the result of a combination of details from the narratives of Lk and Mt-Mk. Whether this combination had taken place in oral tradition or was deliberate on the part of the Evangelist cannot be determined (cf. A. Legault, *CBQ* 16 [1954] 131–45). The Mt-Mk version of the anointing is in accord with the historical probabilities. Anointing of the head was common practice, but anointing of the feet was unknown; wiping away the oil with the hair would be, to say the least, unusual; furthermore, a respectable Jewish woman would hardly appear in public with her hair unbound. *the fragrance of the ointment filled the house:* This passage suggests not only that there was a large quantity of ointment, but also that John intends a symbolism in view of the significance he sees in the anointing (v. 7). Is 6:1 (LXX) is verbally apposite (cf. Jn 12:41): "The house was filled with his glory" (cf. 14:2; 2:21 on the meaning of "house"). This symbolic interpretation was made by many of the Fathers (cf. Ignatius, *Ep. ad. Eph.* 17.1; *PG* 5. 658). (As to the possibility of sacramental allusion in Johannine symbolism, → bibliography of 63 above.)

129 **4–6.** In Mt-Mk, Judas is not specified as the one who protests against Mary's prodigal "waste" of costly ointment. Jn not only identifies the source of the protestation but adds that it was hypocritically motivated, identifying Judas with one of the false shepherds of 10:8,13 **7.** *let her alone; her purpose was that she would keep this for my embalming:* The text is difficult, and may be variously translated; undoubtedly, Mary's purpose had been to display her love and gratitude by her lavish gesture. Both in Mt-Mk and in Jn, Jesus interprets her good deed as an unconscious preparation of his body for burial. However, there is a difference between Jn and the Syn in the construction they have put on Jesus' words. For Mt-Mk, Mary's act takes the place of the embalming of Jesus' body which later became impossible because of its hasty burial following the crucifixion; a further attempt was then precluded by the resurrection (cf. Mk 16:1; Lk 24:1). Jn, however, records an elaborate embalming of Jesus' body by Nicodemus and Joseph of Arimathea according to the Jewish burial customs (19:30f.). Hence Mary's "embalming" is for John not substitutional, but spiritual; it is in keeping with his portrayal of Jesus' death as his glorification, the anointing becomes that of the triumphant king of the following episode (Richardson). This probably explains why the scene of the anointing precedes the triumphal entry into Jerusalem in Jn, whereas in the Syn it occurs later in the week, in closer proximity to the crucifixion. In Jn the anointing remains connected with Jesus' burial, but with the positive aspect of that burial that is the beginning of true life, in keeping with the paradox of death-and-life brought out in 12:23–25. **8.** The objection made by Judas in v. 5 had, of course, some objective validity; the same objection is often made in good faith by those for whom religion consists only in social action. But religion has other claims as well. *you always have the poor around:* A paraphrase of Dt 15:11.

9–11. The attitude toward Jesus, after as well as before the Lazarus event, continues to be one of hatred on the part of the Jewish leaders, and a mixed reaction on the part of the people. Some have true faith, and others only the incipient belief motivated by miracles (cf. 2:23–25). By their determination to kill the man whom Jesus has raised from the dead, the chief priests exemplify only too poignantly the contrast between the life that Jesus gives and the death that is their destiny (cf. 8:21).

130 (d) THE TRIUMPHAL ENTRY (12:12–19). Jn's account of Jesus' last entry into Jerusalem does not differ substantially from that of the Syn (Mk 11:1–11; Mt 21:1–11; Lk 19:29–38); however, it is shorter, and it emphasizes the fact that Jesus is hailed as king of Israel. In v. 17 John reminds us that the crowd that had witnessed the raising of Lazarus is the same that now testifies to Jesus as the conqueror of death. This, then, is the triumph that John sees in Christ's entry, a significance that the disciples did not then understand (v. 16), namely that by his death he would conquer death.

12–13. Jesus is first greeted by the pilgrims gathered in Jerusalem who have learned of his raising of Lazarus (v. 17f.). In the Syn no particular explanation is given for the enthusiasm that accompanied Jesus' entry. *palm fronds:* No palm trees grow in Jerusalem, and the Syn do not mention "palm" branches. The word may be used loosely here, or possibly the palms used by the crowd had been brought to Jerusalem in preparation for the Feast of Tabernacles. The words of the people (cf. Ps 118:25f.; Jn 1:49) and their actions (cf. 1 Mc 13:51; Ap 7:9) show that they were hailing Jesus as the messianic king. **14–15.** A similar crowd at another Passover time had wanted to make Jesus king in a sense utterly foreign to his mission given him by the Father (cf. 6:4f.,15). It is to forestall the repetition of any such tragic misunderstanding that Jesus fulfills Zech 9:9. This messianic prophecy had represented the Messiah in a way somewhat different from some of the older messianic texts, as a man of peace and humility riding on an ass rather than on a charger. **16.** As in 2:22 (cf. 7:39; 13:7), the disciples do not understand the significance of Jesus' action until after the giving of the Holy Spirit, when the full meaning of

Jesus' life and words was revealed to the Church. **17–19.** In the face of the popular enthusiasm that has greeted Jesus, his enemies utter a petulant complaint that is another ironical assertion of truth. An exemplification of this truth is in the following passage.

131 (e) The Gentiles See Jesus: Life in Death (12:20–36). The unity of this passage and its connection with the surrounding context has not always been properly appreciated. The request of the "Greeks" to see Jesus is a fulfillment of the universal triumph of Jesus just voiced by the Pharisees. That they do not actually enter into his presence in the text is no accident on John's part; the Evangelist is being faithful to history in that Jesus' earthly ministry was directed exclusively to his own people (cf. Mt 15:24 par.). Nevertheless, the discourse that follows is in very fact the "seeing" of Jesus, for it portrays his character as Savior of the world in the triumph of life over death.

20. *some Greeks:* This word (*Hellēnes*) is used in Jn (7:35) and in the NT in general to mean Gentiles, non-Jews (for Gk-speaking Jews another word, *Hellēnistai*, is used). Since they had come to Jerusalem as pilgrims, it is probable that they were among the class of "God-fearing," sometimes incorrectly called semiproselytes (see Acts 16:14). What matters to John, however, is that they are Gentiles. Their desire to see Jesus places them in contrast to the Jewish leaders, who have just voiced their despair over his success. **21–22.** The Gentiles' request is presented to Jesus through Philip and Andrew, the only two of the Twelve who bear Gk names. They may have been personal acquaintances from the same region. *Bethsaida in Galilee:* Bethsaida was technically in the territory of Gaulanitis adjoining Galilee, but the Jews of Bethsaida were considered Galileans (cf. Mt 11:21); Josephus, moreover, seems to situate Bethsaida within the territory of Galilee (*JW* 3.3, 1 § 37). Because he may have been thinking of the fulfillment of Is 9:1–7, John may have stressed Galilee here in connection with the appearance of the Gentiles. The disciples consult with one another before approaching Jesus since there was no precedent for his dealing with Gentiles. **23.** *Jesus answered them:* It is not necessary to think that the Gentiles were among those whom Jesus addressed, and the lack of any further mention of them suggests that they were not. It is not yet time for the Gentile mission (cf. Mt 10:5f.), though its principle is even now being revealed. The Evangelist writes from the standpoint of the Church in which the Gentiles have "seen Jesus" and found salvation in him (cf. 6:40; 1 Jn 3:6). *the hour has come:* Now, with the week of his passion begun (v. 1), Jesus can at last say that his "hour" has come (see comments on 2:4; 4:23; 5:25). *for the Son of Man to be glorified:* See comments on 1:14; 1:51; 2:11. **24.** Beautifully, Christ begins to elucidate the mystery of his atoning death. If it be thought strange that he must die in order to bring life, let it be remembered that this paradox already exists in nature. The grain of wheat left to itself produces nothing; only when it appears to have died and has been buried does it bring forth fruit—in far greater abundance than itself (cf. 1 Cor 15:36). **25.** A further illustration of the same principle; with a proverbial saying, it is attributed to Jesus in Mk 8:35 par. and again in Mt 10:39 par. (it may be debated whether the Marcan, the "Q," or the Johannine version of the saying is the more "primitive"). *the man who loves himself destroys himself:* It is another observable paradox that the meaning of life so often eludes him who thinks he is living it to the hilt. Selfishness, man's false love for himself that will not permit him to sacrifice himself, ends in destroying him. *while the man who hates himself in this world* [see comment on 1:10] *preserves himself for eternal life:* Only by treating his life as worthless from a this-worldly view does man gain the only life that really counts. "Hates" is a Semitism for "love less" (cf. Dt 21:15; etc.). **26.** The principle of sacrifice—the explanation of Christ's life—also holds for anyone who will count himself a true follower of Christ (for the Syn parallel cf. Mk 8:34). *my servant:* The word is *diakonos*, meaning one who serves, ministers to another. Jesus gives the example of this ministry in 13:1ff. (cf. also Mk 9:35; 10:43–45; Lk 22:26f.). *the Father will honor anyone who serves me:* Imitation of Christ is inescapably the standard of Christian perfection.

132 Verses 27–30 appear to interrupt Jesus' discourse on his "hour" and the meaning of his death, which continues in v. 31. It is, indeed, possible that the passage was originally used in another context in Jesus' life. This, however, does not mean that it was not rightly placed in this context by John, since it is the record of Jesus' voluntary acceptance of the terrible sacrifice he was called upon to make. These verses form the closest Johannine equivalent to the Syn narratives of the agony (see Mk 14:32–42 par.). **27.** *now my soul is troubled:* In the face of an imminent and cruel death, Jesus can and does feel anguish (cf. Mk 14:34). These words bear out all the implications of the bold statement of 1:14, implications that John always recognizes (cf. 4:6; 11:33,38). *Father, save me from this hour:* Probably this is intended to be punctuated with a question mark, as a petition that Jesus considers ("What should I say?") but almost immediately rejects ("No..."). In the Syn scene of the agony Jesus first asks to be delivered from the necessity of dying, but immediately conditions the request on the will of the Father (cf. Mk 14:35f.; also Heb 5:7). The value of Christ's sacrifice consists in the readiness with which he submitted to it. **28.** *Father, glorify your name:* This is Jesus' final answer from his crisis of spirit, and it is a wholehearted acceptance of the Father's will. The glorification of the Son is also that of the Father (cf. 13:31f.); for "name" see comment on 1:12. *a voice came from the sky:* There is nothing of this in the Syn narratives of the agony (though Lk 22:43 mentions the ministration of an angel from heaven), but in the Syn accounts of Jesus' baptism (Mk 1:11 par.) and transfiguration (Mk 9:7 par.) similar experiences are recorded in the life of Jesus. *I did glorify it:* The reference is to no single event, but to the entire lifework and teaching of Jesus (cf. 10:38; 11:40; etc.), all of which have been "signs" (see comment on 2:11) of the ultimate glorification that is to come. **29–30.** Neither those who have confused the voice with thunder nor those who have some vague idea that it was, indeed, a voice, have understood what Jesus tells them was intended for them and not for himself. Jesus did not need this reassurance (cf. the similar passage of 11:42), but for one who had ears to hear, the voice could tell of the relation of the Son to the Father. That the voice has been wasted on the crowd standing by merely confirms that they are not attuned to the Word of God (cf. 7:17; 8:43–47; etc.).

133 **31.** *this world's judgment is right now:* Now that the time has come for Christ's exaltation (v. 23), it is preeminently the time for that judgment of which he has continually spoken (see comments on 3:17–19; 5:22–30). *time for the prince of this world to be thrown out:* Such will be the paradox of Christ's exaltation; it will appear that he has been defeated by this world, but in reality the power of Satan will be broken. Jn does not say that Satan will be destroyed, but that he will no longer be the ruler of the world except to the extent that man's evil dispositions will permit. **32.** The paradox is put in another, more positive form. *when I am raised up from the earth:* This is understood by the crowd, rightly, to refer to his death (cf. v. 33f.). They do not understand, however, that it also refers to his glorification (see comment on

3:14). *I shall draw all men to me:* The death of Christ makes possible the exercise of his will of universal salvation. **33–34.** The crowd has understood at least that Jesus has spoken of his departure from this world. How is this compatible with his identification as Messiah? *we have heard from the Law:* That is, from the OT (cf. 10:34); such passages as Pss 89:4; 110:4; Is 9:6f. speak of the everlasting rule of the messianic king. Jesus has put this discourse in the context of his character as Son of Man (v. 23). Perhaps the solution lies here: Does he by the Son of Man mean something other than the Messiah? **35–36.** Jesus' words are not even an attempt to answer their question; with his proclamation in v. 23 he has closed the period of his instruction. He can only warn them again (cf. 8:12; 9:4f.) that they have very little time to receive the light before it is removed from them forever. *sons of light:* An expression much used in the QL, where it means the "true believers" of the elect community. *after this speech Jesus left them and went into hiding:* True to his warning, Jesus now retires from the scene. The light has been withdrawn; the public ministry is at an end.

134 (f) Judgment on the Rejection of Life and Light (12:37–50). Here at the end of the Book of Signs the Evangelist attempts to answer the question why Jesus' ministry to his own people failed. The incredulity of the Jews was, of course, one of the "scandals" that had to be dealt with by the apologetics of the primitive Chruch (cf. Rom 9:1ff.).

37–38. First of all, John says, this incredulity was foreseen by God. He cites Is 53:1 as does Paul in Rom 10:16; the identification of Jesus with the Suffering Servant of Dt-Is is a common affirmation of the NT (see 3:14; 1:29). God knew that the message and signs of his Servant would be rejected, yet he had to send him to manifest the light one last time (cf. 1:5). Such is the mystery of the divine will of salvation when seen against the divine foreknowledge. **39.** *they could not believe:* John says that not only was the incredulity of the Jews foreseen by God, it was also, in a sense, caused by him. This is in no way to say that their disbelief was not entirely culpable (cf. v. 43); John does not deny the freedom of human choice, but insists on the causality of God in all things. This, too, was destined to be in the divine economy. **40.** It is in this sense that he cites Is 6:10 as the reason why the Jews could not believe (cf. also Mk 4:11f. par.; Acts 28:26f.): The Word of God itself had decreed this incredulity. In the LXX Is 6:10 had been somewhat toned down by putting the operative verbs in the passive (and is so cited by Mt 13:15 and Acts), but Jn (and Mk) quotes it in all its Hebraic rigor. Because of the divine foreknowledge that the Word would be rejected, God's mission of Isaiah (and of Jesus) was, and had to be, a decree for further blindness. **41.** The words of Isaiah that Jn has quoted were uttered by the Prophet during a vision in which he beheld the glory of God (cf. Is 6:3). *it was of him [Jesus] Isaiah spoke when* [or *because*] *he saw his glory:* John can make this statement because he knows that the glory of the Father is that of the Son also (cf. 12:28). It is not necessary to suppose that Isaiah was granted a special vision of Christ, but rather that what he prophesied was typical of Christ's ministry. **42.** In this final, negative summary, John carefully notes that there was some belief, however tentative it may have been, even among the Jewish rulers (cf. also Acts 6:7). Some of them would, at the last, declare themselves for Jesus (cf. 19:38f.). **43.** John's judgment on the half-believers is the judgment that he brings against unbelief in general; and this, in turn, is the verdict that Jesus himself passed on the cause of willful disbelief (cf. 5:44). They had no eyes for the glory revealed in the Word made flesh (cf. 1:14), but only for the esteem and values of this world.

135 The discourse in vv. 44–50 would certainly have to be taken as a strange anticlimax if the Evangelist were reintroducing Jesus after his judgment (vv. 37–43) and his notice of Jesus' having hidden himself (v. 36). To avoid this impression, however, it is not necessary to suppose that the verses have been misplaced by someone other than Jn. The discourse is timeless, for it is a summary of all of Jesus' discourses, mainly in the selfsame wording, which dramatically portrays the light whose rejection the Evangelist has narrated. M.-E. Boismard (*SP* 2. 189–92), however, believes that the discourse, though authentically Johannine, derives from a source slightly different from the one that has transmitted the rest of the Gospel, and that it was inserted in this place at the time of the definitive publication of Jn (→ 5–6 above).

44. *Jesus proclaimed aloud:* The expression used exclusively by John (*ekraxen*, lit., "cried out") to designate Christ's solemn pronouncements (cf. 7:28,37; also used of the Baptist in 1:15). *whoever believes...sent me:* This saying of Jesus, found also in the Syn (cf. Mt 10:40), reproduces the thought of various previous discourses (cf. esp. 5:24; 8:19,42). **45.** See 8:19; 14:9. **46.** See 3:16,19; 8:12; 9:5. **47–48.** *if anyone listens to my words without keeping them:* This contrast between hearing and doing is also found in the Syn tradition of Jesus' sayings (cf. Mt 7:26 par.). On Jesus' role in judgment and the nature of this judgment, see 3:17; 8:15. **49.** See 5:30; 7:17. **50.** See 4:34; 6:68; 8:28; 10:18.

136 **(III) The Book of Exaltation: "Those Who Accept Him Become Sons of God" (13:1–20:31).** With ch. 13 the second major part of the Gospel begins. If the Book of Signs developed the thought of 1:11, "he came to his own, and his own received him not," this second Book develops the thought of 1:12, "to such as received him, who believe in his name, he gave the power of becoming children of God." Obviously the themes overlap in the prologue, and so do they in these books of the Evangelist. As in the first part of the Gospel, John continues to find symbolism in Christ's words and deeds, striving to relate these as practically as possible to the life of the Christian in the world. Because the Passion Narrative plays such a major role in this part of the Gospel, it contains many more parallels to the Syn tradition than does the Book of Signs. However, here too John goes his own way, as will be seen. The passion in Jn is part of a drama of triumph, in which can already be discerned the fruits of victory made secure forever through Jesus' resurrection and glorification. It is this portrayal of Christ the victorious Savior that forms the unity of this book.

137 **(A) Jesus Instructs His Disciples (13:1–17:26).** This section in Jn corresponds in the Syn tradition to the interval between the public ministry and the Passion Narrative when Jesus is alone with his disciples (Mk 13:1–14:42 par.). As in the Syn, there is a Last Supper with the disciples. Here, however, the resemblance ends. Apart from the fact that in the Syn the meal is represented as a Passover celebration and is not so represented in Jn (see comment on 13:1 below), John omits virtually every event chronicled in the Syn account and devotes his main attention to a lengthy discourse in which the faith of the disciples contrasts with the incredulity of the Jews in the Book of Signs, and in which, correspondingly, many former themes now reappear in a positive expression. A striking omission, in view of John's sacramental interests, is the Syn's account of the institution of the Eucharist. However, what needed to be said on this score had already been said in ch. 6, and in point of fact the discourse to the disciples is wholly concerned with the divine life that is the explanation of all the sacraments.

138 (a) THE SIGN OF THE FOOT WASHING (13:1–20). Preceding his discourse, Jesus performs a parable in action by which he epitomizes the significance of his entire life of dedication. Though not a miracle, this action is certainly one of Jesus' "signs" in the Johannine sense of the word (see comment on 2:11).

1. *before the Passover feast:* John clearly means that this meal, as well as Christ's apprehension, trial, and crucifixion that follow on the same day took place on the day before the Passover (cf. 18:28; 19:14,31,42). In Jewish calculation the day is reckoned from sunset to sunset. It is no less clear that the Syn account of the Last Supper describes Jesus and his disciples eating the Passover together (cf. Mk 14:12ff. par.). To harmonize these two views it has often been maintained that Jesus and his Galilean disciples observed the Passover on a day different from the one officially established for Jerusalem. This supposition is not unlikely, but it cannot be proved. In recent times it has been verified from QL that the ancient solar calendar, presupposed by the apocryphal books of *Enoch* and *Jub*, was still in use among some Palestinian Jews in Jesus' time as an alternative to the official lunar calendar of Judaism (cf. E. Vogt, *Bib* 36 [1955] 403–8; *Bib* 39 [1958] 72–77). If we assume, however, that Jesus observed the Passover according to this solar calendar, further chronological problems arise because the solar calendar was "perpetual" and the Passover (on 15 Nisan) fell on the same day of the week each year, Wednesday. This would mean that the Last Supper took place on a Tuesday evening, though it is otherwise clear that the crucifixion occurred on a Friday (cf. 19:31; Mk 15:43; Lk 23:54). The attempt has been made to establish on this basis a new chronology of Holy Week, notably by A. Jaubert, *The Date of the Last Supper* (Staten Island, N.Y., 1965), but the balance of critical opinion seems to be that the attempt has failed (see the extensive surveys of the French original of this book in *NTA* 1 [1957] § 184; 2 [1957–58] § 15, 26, 261, 514; 3 [1958] § 50; and esp. 4 [1960] § 856r–62r; but cf. E. Ruckstuhl, *Chronology of the Last Days of Jesus* [N.Y., 1965]). Lacking other evidence, it seems that we must dispense with the hypothesis of two Passovers. Although most authors tend to settle questions of "historicity" in favor of the Syn against Jn, in the present instance it seems preferable to recognize the eyewitness record of Jn as to the actual dating of the Last Supper and to conclude that the Syn tradition has given the name "Passover" to a meal which resembled it and served as the inauguration of the Christian Eucharist, but which had not been an actual celebration of the Jewish Passover (for the arguments opposed to this view, see C. K. Barrett, *The Gospel*, 39–41). *the hour had come:* As in 12:23, see comment on 2:4. *to depart from this world* [see 1:10] *to the Father:* Cf. 14:12,28; 16:10,28. The actions and words that follow during this Last Supper are all conditioned by this moment. *having loved his own who were in this world:* The theme of love that pervades the entire scene and discourse to follow is set by the Evangelist. *he exhibited his love for them to the end* [or, *to the utmost*]*:* Jn states that what is to come is Jesus' final display of his love, or, perhaps more likely, that it was a supreme exemplification of that love.

139 **2.** *during a banquet:* Some mss. read "after a meal," but this is obviously a mistake (cf. v. 26). Though John does not recount the institution of the Eucharist, the Christian reader will, of course, be aware of the significance that this meal has in relation to Jesus' life. Hence John emphasizes this action as part of that significance. *when the devil...to hand him over:* See 6:70; cf. also Lk 22:3. **3.** See 3:35; 7:33; 16:28. **4–5.** John's emphasis on Jesus' awareness of his relation to the Father at this time (vv. 1 and 3) shows that Jesus intended this act to be a concrete symbol of the humiliation of his incarnational state (cf. also Phil 2:5–7; Mk 10:45 par.); the action could have occurred quite naturally in conjunction with the episode related in Lk 22:23ff. It was the task of a slave, though also performed by wives and children (cf. Str-B 2, 557). **6.** Peter's reaction is to point up the incongruity of what is apparently happening: the reversal of the roles of master and servant (cf. v. 14). **7.** *afterward you will understand:* The significance of the foot washing is pointed out by Jesus in v. 12ff. However, the full meaning of this sign will be made known to the Church only through the later enlightenment of the Spirit (cf. 2:22; 12:16). **8.** Peter immediately shows that he does not, indeed, understand what is being done, when he continues to insist that Jesus must not so demean himself. *unless I wash you, you will have no share with me:* The action typifies Christ's lifework, which Peter must accept as God's will even as Christ has done; Peter has been objecting ignorantly as in Mk 8:32f. par. In all likelihood, John expects the Christian reader also to relate Jesus' words to his own life and to be reminded of the function of baptism. This interpretation was commonly put on this passage by the Fathers. **9.** Peter still speaks naïvely. If Jesus insists on washing his feet as the condition of continued fellowship, so be it! Only, let him be washed entirely, that his share with the Lord be complete. **10.** *the man who has bathed has no need to wash* [most mss. add "except his feet" or other words]; *he is clean all over:* What Peter asks is quite unnecessary. The foot washing, after all, is only a symbol; it is not that the disciples need to have this or that part of their bodies washed. Having their share in Christ, they have all that is needful. By his choice of Gk words, John probably again suggests baptism to the Christian reader ("bathe," *louō*, was a word used for religious washings, and in 1 Cor 6:11; Eph 5:26; Ti 3:5; Heb 10:22 various forms of it are used to signify baptism). If the long form of the verse is the original, the ritual of the foot washing is said to be needed over and above the complete bathing (baptism). In this case, the foot washing would appear to signify the necessity of the Christian to purify himself of his postbaptismal sins. That there would thereby be an allusion to the sacrament of the Eucharist is, however, quite doubtful. **11.** Jesus has just pronounced that the disciples as a group are clean, even as the symbol of washing signified. Yet one was not clean, despite the fact that he, too, had been washed. Not even the sacraments can purify when the inmost dispositions are impure.

140 **12–14.** As a point of practical application, the meaning of this action is now explained. Not only do the disciples and all Christians share in the fruits of Jesus' lifework, they must also imitate its spirit. *you too have the obligation to wash one another's feet:* It is their duty to practice the humility signified by this act. The literal act has been incorporated to some extent in the liturgy of Holy Week. **15–17.** The obligation is reiterated in different words. The saying of v. 16 also appears in Mt 10:24 (cf. also Jn 15:20). **18.** *what I say does not refer to all of you:* The thought of the traitor (cf. vv. 2 and 10f.) again intrudes into this intimate discourse with the disciples. *I know the kind of men I picked:* Judas' treason was foreseen at the time he was chosen along with the other disciples (cf. 6:70). *the purpose is to have the scripture fulfilled:* For this conception of the fulfillment of prophecy in relation to the divine will, see comment on 12:39f. Jesus cites Ps 41:10, which speaks of the psalmist's betrayal by a friend, as typical of himself and Judas. **19.** The betrayal of Judas must not be permitted to become a scandal for others. That Jesus had predicted even this will later be remembered as testimony to his real control of the situation at all times (cf. 14:29). *you may believe that I am:* See comment on 6:35. **20.** This saying of Jesus, found also in Mt 10:40 par.; Mk 9:37 par., returns to the idea of the unity of disciple and master (vv. 13–16); if they share in his humiliation, they will also reflect his dignity.

141 (b) THE BETRAYAL: THE HOUR OF DARKNESS (13:21–30). Jesus' attention now focuses for the last time on the betrayal that he has already mentioned more than once. Judas is now removed from the scene, leaving only the loyal band of followers. True to his claim (v. 18), Jesus remains even now in complete charge: Judas departs only when he has been given leave (v. 27).

21–22. Though he has strongly hinted at it, up to this point Jesus has not said in so many words that the betrayer was to be one of the intimate group of disciples now with him at table. The Syn version of this scene is found in Mk 14:18–21 par. **23–25.** Solemn meals were taken in the Roman fashion, about a low table surrounded on three sides (the other side free for serving) by mats or couches on which the diners reclined, supporting themselves on their left arms. The present scene supposes "the disciple whom Jesus loved" (→ 3 above) to be at Jesus' right—thus he could lean back to ask the question of v. 25. John doubtless intends a spiritual significance in stressing the position of the beloved disciple (lit., "on the breast" of Jesus; cf. 1:18; cf. 19:26f.; 20:2). **26.** To give someone a choice morsel of food is still a customary courtesy of Oriental hosts. In the Syn account of the Last Supper no mention is made of Jesus' identifying the traitor (Mt 26:25). Here the beloved disciple is evidently told who he is, but the information was doubtless for his ears alone. **27.** *just then, after that morsel of food, Satan entered his heart:* The precise moment of the betrayal has come, corresponding to the moment as recognized by Jesus for him to return to his Father (vv. 1–3). John evidently saw in Jesus' last gesture of kindness toward Judas a final grace that the traitor has rejected. *do what you have to do:* Judas has no power over Christ that is not permitted him (cf. 19:11), and it is Jesus and not Judas who makes the final determination of the time of the betrayal. **28–29.** Jesus' words were ambiguous, and the disciples evidently still had no inkling of Judas' intentions. Even though the beloved disciple knew his identity as the betrayer, he had no knowledge that the betrayal would take place immediately. **30.** *it was night:* This statistical detail is also symbolic: The betrayer exemplifies the darkness on which the light has shown in vain (1:5); he is the one who loves darkness rather than light because his deeds are evil (3:19); the night predicted by Jesus has now come (9:4).

142 (c) DISCOURSE ON DEPARTURE AND RETURN IN THE SPIRIT (13:31–14:31). With the departure of Judas begins the long discourse that extends to the end of ch. 17. In it Jesus speaks to the disciples as one already glorified, for the chain of events connected with his glorification has now begun.

31–32. The glorification of the Son is that of the Father; the one is effected in the other (cf. 12:28; 14:13; 17:4). This glorification will occur immediately: Though the perspective of Jesus' glorification in the parousia is also found in Jn, the emphasis is on realized eschatology (→ 25 above). **33.** *little children:* This word (*teknia*) is found only here in the Gospel, though it is characteristically Johannine (seven times in 1 Jn); it has no exact equivalent either in Hebrew or Aramaic. Jesus now repeats to the disciples what is applicable to them from his words to the Jews in 7:33f. and 8:21. The inability of the disciples to follow Jesus, unlike that of the Jewish adversaries, is but temporary (cf. v. 36; 14:3). **34.** Even in their temporary separation from him, the disciples will nevertheless—through charity—have him in their midst. *a new commandment:* Charity is also the law of the OT (cf. Lv 19:18); Christ's command is new in extending to all men without distinction (cf. Lk 10:29–37) and in the ideal it strives to emulate (cf. 15:13). *as I have loved you:* Christ's love is not only the model but also the motive and cause of Christian charity. *love one another:* Christian charity is not to be limited to Christians, but among Christians it has the special function of mirroring the love of the divine Persons for one another and for the Church. **35.** Thus the importance of fraternal charity as a sign of the true Church "waiting for Christ." **36.** Peter wants more than the continued possession of Christ through love; his question as to where Jesus is going also implies the question "why can we not follow?" and it is the implied question that Jesus answers. *you cannot follow me now:* Jesus' departure involves both his death and his return to the divine presence. It will be the lot of Peter and the other disciples to share both these experiences. *later on you will follow me:* These words as addressed to Peter may be a prophecy of his martyrdom (cf. 21:18f.). **37.** Peter does not fully comprehend what Jesus has been telling him, but he reallzes at least that the question of death has been raised. *I would lay down my life for you:* Peter expresses himself in the language of the Good Shepherd (cf. 10:11), a function that will later be given to him (cf. 21:15–17). But his words are ironical in his present lack of understanding: It will really be Jesus who will lay down his life for the disciples (cf. Is 53:10–12). **38.** Jn agrees with Lk 22:31–34 in placing Jesus' prediction of Peter's denial (cf. 18:17,25–27) at the Last Supper itself; in Mk 14:27–31 and Mt 26:31–35 it occurs afterward, on the way to Gethsemane. *there will not even come another cockcrow:* Peter's threefold denial will take place before the night is over.

143 **14:1.** *no need that your hearts be troubled:* One of the most profound of the Johannine discourses now begins, in the course of which the relation of Christ's precept of charity to the love of the Father, Son, and Holy Spirit is brought out. Jesus begins with this additional reassurance in view of his preceding words about departure that had saddened the disciples. *have faith in God and faith in me:* Jesus has never hesitated to put himself on the same level with the Father in the common work of salvation (cf. 10:30; etc.); thus he and the Father are equally the object of faith. Faith in God and Christ is the condition of Christians in this world. **2.** *there are many dwelling places in my Father's house:* This is usually interpreted—and rightly so—to mean the heavenly kingdom to which Jesus is returning (though there are no grounds for understanding "many" to mean also "many kinds" or "degrees"). However, John probably intends another sense as well. In one way, after all, Christ has never left heaven and consequently need not return (cf. 3:13). The Father's "house" is where God is, and whoever is with God is in his "house"; one of Paul's favorite metaphors for the Church is this house of God (1 Cor 3:10ff.; etc.; cf. also Jn 2:20–22). In the present context, therefore, the "many dwelling places" of the Father's house may also refer to the many members of the Church on earth, where Christ will also be (see v. 22). This, too, is an ancient interpretation. *otherwise, I would have warned you:* Though he has told the disciples that they will join him only later (13:36), Jesus has just reassured them that there is ample room in this house of the Father where he will be. Therefore, they need have no fear that he will fail to find a place for them in his company. *I am going to prepare a place for you:* His final reassurance that his departure is only that they may be together forever. **3.** *I am coming back to take you along with me:* Once again these words can refer naturally enough to the parousia (cf. 1 Jn 2:28). *where I am, you may be also:* These words, however, express the condition of the Christian who already possesses the divine life through the Church (cf. 12:26). Therefore, this promise surely refers also to Christ's invisible return through the Spirit (cf. v. 17f.). **4.** *the way to where I am going is known to you:* The disciples quickly show how little they as yet understand, although he has repeatedly told them that he is going to the Father and in what way, namely through his sacrificial death (cf. 12:23–32), which is in turn the model that all must take who would follow him.

5. Thomas (cf. 11:16), in his question, doubtless reflects the ignorance of all the disciples. They have shown themselves to be quite as obtuse as Jesus' Jewish opponents (7:35f.; 8:22); what saves them is their good will. **6.** Thomas' question permits Jesus to utter one of his supreme affirmations, which combines in one sentence the most fundamental ideas that have been brought out in the Gospel. *I am* [see comment on 6:35] *the way, the truth* [see comments on 1:9; 1:14; 1:17], *and the life* [see comment on 1:4]*:* Through Christ one comes into the possession of the Father, which means the possession of truth and life. *no one comes to the Father except through me:* He is the only way. **7.** Such is the disciples' lack of comprehension, Jesus can repeat the words he had formerly uttered against his Jewish opponents. *from now on you do know him and you have seen him:* With the glorification of Christ and the coming of the Spirit their understanding will nevertheless be made perfect.

144 **8–9.** The request of Philip (cf. 1:43f.) exhibits the same incomprehension: It is an expression of the unsatisfied longing of the OT (1:18; cf. Ex 33:18f.) which, however, association with Christ should have removed long before (cf. 10:30; 12:45). Philip asks for some kind of extraordinary manifestation, but he must learn that the only vision of God vouchsafed in this world is through Jesus Christ. **10–11.** Jesus repeats almost word for word what he has stated on other occasions concerning his relation to the Father (cf. 7:16; 8:28; esp. 10:38). *I am in the Father and the Father is in me:* In receiving Christ, the Christian receives the godhead whole and entire (cf. 17:21). **12.** It follows from this that the Christian will also perform the works of God, even as Christ has done and on the same principle. These words, as addressed to the first apostles, refer not only to the fact that the works of the Christian believer are performed within the supernatural order, but, first and foremost, to the Church as possessing and continuing Christ's divine power for salvation (cf. 20:22f.; Mk 6:7; Mt 18:17–20; etc.). *he will perform deeds far greater than these:* This does not refer primarily to miracles, though these too will continue (cf. Acts 5:12–16), but to the far greater scope, geographically and numerically, within which the Church will exercise its salvific power; the nature of these greater deeds has already been suggested by such texts as 4:35–38; 10:16f.; 11:52; 12:20f. *because I am going to the Father:* The condition of this activity is Christ's glorification and the giving of the Spirit. **13.** *I will do whatever you may request in my name:* The greater deeds of Christian activity remain, after all, the works of Christ himself, for he will give the power by which they will be done. "In my name" (see comment on 1:12) does not, of course, imply that a prayer is guaranteed to be answered merely because of a mechanical invocation of Jesus' name. To pray "in the name" of Jesus implies a communion of persons (cf. 14:26); harmony of will with God and obedience to his commandments are the necessary conditions for efficacious prayer (cf. 1 Jn 3:22; 5:14). *so that the Father may be glorified in the Son:* The glory that the Father receives through the works of the Son (7:18; 8:50,54) continues in the works of the Son's followers. **14–15.** The promise of v. 13 is repeated; however, v. 14 represents the only verse in Jn where prayer is spoken of as addressed to Christ directly rather than to the Father through Christ (perhaps for this reason "of me" is omitted in some mss.). The conditions of love and obedience that apply to the prayer for the Spirit (v. 16f.) are also required for the efficacy of any prayer, as pointed out in v. 13.

145 **16.** *the Father will give you another Paraclete:* Here and in v. 26 the Spirit is said to be sent by the Father in the name of Christ; in 15:26 Christ sends him from the Father; Christian tradition has spoken of the procession of the Holy Spirit both as from the Father through the Son and as from the Father and the Son. The Spirit is "another" Paraclete because the Son himself has been the first (cf. 1 Jn 2:1). "Paraclete" is a legal term that had been taken into Jewish use, signifying "advocate," "helper," "mediator." (The role of the Paraclete is explained in greater detail in v. 26; 15:26; 16:7–14; → Johannine Theology, 80:39–45.) *to be with you forever:* The age of the Church is the era of the Spirit (cf. Acts, "the Gospel of the Spirit") to whom is attributed the divine presence in sanctification and testimony throughout the Church's life. **17.** *the Spirit of truth:* This term (used also in 15:26; 16:13) partially defines the role of the Paraclete, to guide the Church in truth; truth is his characteristic as it has been that of the first Paraclete (1:14; 14:6). *the world cannot accept him:* Neither could the world (see comment on 1:10) accept the Son, refusing to see in him the revelation of the Father. *because it neither sees nor recognizes him:* The presence of the Spirit will be visible, as was the true nature of Christ, only to the eye of faith. *he remains with you...within you:* The Holy Spirit will be both in the Church and in every Christian (cf. the similar language in 1 Cor 3:16f.; 6:19). **18.** *I am coming back to you:* The coming of the Spirit will also entail the coming of the Son (and the Father, v. 20), because of the shared life of the persons of the Trinity. **19.** *you can see me:* Again, through the vision of faith; for Jesus will depart shortly from the sight of this world. *because I have life and you will have life:* In his glorified state, the life of Christ is the principle by which Christians also live the life of God, with the indwelling of the Holy Trinity (cf. 6:57; Rom 6:4,8; 1 Cor 15:45; Col 1:1f.). **20.** *on that day:* This was traditional language for the day of judgment, therefore of futurist eschatology, of the parousia (cf. Am 9:11; Hos 2:20; Mt 24:36; etc.). Now it is applied to the realized eschatology of the Christian life. Living this life, the Christian will experience ("recognize"), in varying degrees, depending on his sensitivity to the divine presence, the affirmation of his faith (v. 11): The Father, the Son, and the Church share the one life. **21.** As before (v. 15), the condition of this shared life is love and obedience. *the man who keeps the commandments that he has from me:* It is not sufficient merely to acknowledge the law of Christ, but one must also observe it in his life. *he is the man who loves me:* Obedience is the proof of love, which in turn makes possible the communion between God and man.

146 **22.** *Judas (not Iscariot):* Mentioned here for the first time in Jn's Gospel, he is Judas the son of James, included in Lk's list of the Twelve (Lk 6:16; Acts 1:13) and traditionally identified with the Thaddeus of Mk 3:18; Mt 10:3. *what can have happened:* The disciple is puzzled by the drift of Jesus' discourse, which since v. 17 has stressed a secret rather than a public manifestation of Christ. What, then, of the glorious coming of the Son of Man before the eyes of the whole world (Mk 13:26; etc.)? **23.** The answer that Jesus gives is not really addressed to the question of the parousia, but re-emphasizes the reality of the manifestation that will be made to the believer in much the same words that have been used before. This manifestation is of far greater importance to the Christian whose destiny it will be to live in this world waiting for the parousia. *find a dwelling place:* Cf. v. 2. **24.** It is the lack of love and obedience that precludes the world from having any part in this manifestation of Father and Son. **25–26.** Again the Paraclete is mentioned, for whom the term "Holy Spirit" is now used: It is the revelation of the NT that the Spirit of God (see comment on 1:32f.) as well as the Word of God is a distinct Person within the godhead. *the Father will send in my name:* As the Son was sent in the name of the Father to do his works and will (cf. 5:43; 10:25; see comment on 1:12), so the Spirit stands in relation to the Son. *he will teach you everything and remind you:* Following the glorification of Christ, it will be the function of the Spirit to complete the revelation of Christ by enlightening the Church concerning the true and full meaning of what Jesus had done and said (cf. 2:22; 12:16; Acts 11:15f.). Jn's Gospel itself is the result of the fulfillment of this promise. **27.** Jesus concludes his words of consolation. *peace is my gift to you:* "Peace" (*šālôm*) was and is the common Jewish formula of greeting and farewell. The word had a much deeper significance, however, as an expression of the harmony and communion with God that was the seal of the covenant (cf. Nm 6:26). Hence it came to have an eschatological and messianic meaning (cf. Is 9:6), virtually the same as "salvation." It is this spiritual tranquillity that Christ gives, which has no resemblance to what the world gives. Because Christ is this gift that he gives, Eph 2:14 can call him "our peace." **28.** Referring to what he has already told the disciples, he concludes that in their love for him they should find the reason for his return to the Father and his consequent departure from them. His going is out of love for them, "for the Father is greater than I." This statement is soteriological and of the same character as those of 5:19 (which see); 7:16f.; 8:28; etc. Though Christ is one with the Father (10:30), as the Son he has been sent by the Father to do his will (4:34; 6:38; 12:49f.), and in this relationship the Father is the greater. Christ's return to the Father with his mission accomplished is the condition of all that he has promised the disciples. **29.** He applies to the present subject the words used of another future happening in 13:19.

147 **30–31.** *I shall speak with you no longer:* It seems to be an inescapable conclusion that these two verses originally ended the Last Supper discourse. *the prince of the world is coming:* The battle with Satan now begins, which will end in his apparent triumph but actual defeat (cf. 12:31). *he has no hold on me, but the purpose...:* Even the illusory victory that Satan will achieve is merely permitted to him, that the ultimate effect may be a triumph of God's will in Christ that even the world must acknowledge (cf. 16:8–11). *Get up, let us leave here and be on our way:* This sounds very much like the Johannine parallel to Mk 14:41f. par. In the Syn version the locale is the garden, when Judas, the agent of Satan, approaches, whereas in Jn Jesus has just referred to Satan's coming in person (cf. also Lk 22:53). In context, these words seem to presuppose that the events of 18:1ff. now follow (or, possibly, the prayer of ch. 17, which would have been said standing). To this must be added the consideration that in part, at least, the intervening chs. 15–17 parallel the discourse just concluded (cf. esp. 16:4b–33). Although there are various possibilities, it seems highly probable that the Last Supper discourse of Jn originally concluded with 14:31, which was then followed by ch. 18. Our present text represents a later edition, either by the Evangelist himself or by his disciple-editors (→ 8 above), in which the intervening chapters have been composed either from parallel versions of the same discourse, from other discourses topically connected with it, or from both. The existence of parallel versions would hardly be surprising in view of the known character of the Johannine discourses as the fruit of the Evangelist's reflection and memory in his old age. Why, then, did the Evangelist (or his editors) leave 14:30f. in their present form? Possibly from a desire not to alter what had once been written, or possibly because of the Johannine proclivity to see multiple meanings in Jesus' sayings (→ 29 above). "Let us leave here and be on our way," interpreted "spiritually," approximates the sense of Col 3:1f.

148 (d) The True Vine and the Branches (15:1–17). The theme of this uninterrupted discourse is the relation of the Christian to Christ, the community of life that they share, and Christ's life as the source of the good works of Christians. The figure of the vine and the branches presupposes that the Christian life is essentially one of activity, of bearing fruit: Union with Christ is not only the condition of bearing fruit, it also demands this. The discourse combines some of the language and thoughts of the preceding 13:31–14:31 together with new emphases.

1. *I am* [see comment on 6:35] *the true* [see comment on 1:9] *vine:* The figure of the vine or a vineyard for the people of God is well established in OT imagery (cf. Is 5:1–7; Jer 2:21; Ez 15; Ps 80:9–16), and there is no need to make Jn dependent here on a "tree-of-life myth" (Bultmann, Schweizer). Christ's concretizing in himself what applied to Israel in the OT is comparable to his use of the title "Son of Man" (see comment on 1:51). In view of the Last Supper setting of this discourse, there may also be a Eucharistic allusion; cf. "fruit of the vine" in Mk 14:25 and "the holy vine of David your servant" in the liturgy of the *Didache* 9.2. *my Father tends it:* A similar idea is expressed in 1 Cor 3:9. Whatever figure Jesus uses to express his salvific work, he characterizes himself as the instrument of the Father (cf. 10:14f.,29f.). **2.** *he cuts away...he trims clean...:* The figure Jesus is using is allegorical, involving a studied comparison. The branches of the vine are Jesus' disciples (v. 5); if they remain fruitless the Father will remove them, and in turn it is by his power that they can produce fruit. The verbs involve a wordplay in the Greek (*airei* and *kathairei*). **3.** A further wordplay. *you are clean already:* As he called them clean (*katharoi*) in 13:10, under another figure. *thanks to the word I have spoken to you:* No specific "word" (*logos*) is meant, but rather the whole of his revelation of God, which is a message of eternal life (cf. 5:24; etc.). **4–6.** The specific emphasis of this figure for the Christian is now brought out: The community of life shared with Christ is the condition of his bearing fruit, his pleasing God (v. 8). The one who breaks this unity is like a dead branch, fit only to be cast in the fire (cf. Mt 13:40). **7.** *if you remain united to me and my words remain a part of you:* The efficacy of Christian prayer was brought out in 14:13; as pointed out then, "in my name" involves what is said here in other words. **8.** As was also brought out in 14:13, the Father is glorified in the works of the Son's disciples. The figure of the vine and the branches in Jn invites comparison with the Pauline doctrine of Christ the Head of his Body the Church. The Pauline idea, however, is far more developed; though Jn's Gospel was finished long after the Pauline epistles, John is faithful to the historical age in which the Gospel is set and therefore does not develop the figure beyond the application given it by Jesus. **9.** Love is the principle of the relation between the Father to the Son (3:17f.; 5:20); the same love has brought the Church into being. *remain on in my love:* The disciples must continue to keep themselves worthy of the protection of Christ's love. **10.** This is done by obedience to the will of Christ, again by following his example (cf. 14:15,21). **11.** See 14:25,27f. **12–14.** See comments on 13:34; 14:21. *no one can have greater love:* Christian love has as its model nothing less than the example of the Good Shepherd himself (cf. 10:11; 1 Jn 3:16); in turn, the love of Christ gives the Christian the ability to live up to this ideal. **15.** *no longer do I call you slaves:* There was nothing degrading in being known as the slave (*doulos*) of God or a good master; in 13:16 Jesus used the term *doulos* of his disciples, in parallel with the *diakonos* of 12:26; in OT usage the corresponding Hebr *'ebed* was the title of honored royal officials, the Servant of the Lord, etc. *for a slave has no understanding of what his owner is doing:* In the normal course of things, the slave is not admitted to the counsels of his master; he simply obeys. *I have called you beloved:* This term, which Christ has used since v. 13, is far more in keeping with the state of Christians, which is to offer a loving obedience that is their part in the common life they share: The Christian "hears" the Son even as the Son has "heard" the Father (cf. 8:26,40). **16–17.** The divine initiative has been paramount throughout this history of salvation. The Son was sent by the Father, and the Son has chosen his own, whose mission and whose life, therefore, continue a work of divine grace.

149 (e) THE WORLD'S HATRED OF THE LIGHT (15:18–16:4a). As do the Syn, Jn records Jesus' warning of persecution (cf. Mk 13:9–13; Mt 10:17–39 par.; etc.). Here, however, the warning has richer significance: Just as the Christian fully communicates with Christ and thus with God (→ 148 above), he must share all of Christ's life, which includes the hatred of the world. The world here is that of 8:23, the world that has rejected Christ; by his rebirth in Christ the Christian forms no part of this world that prefers its own will to that of God.

18–20. In 13:16 Jesus had laid down the principle of Christian life as the imitation by the servant of himself, the Master. Now the other side of the coin appears. If they remain his true servants, they must expect to find themselves hated and rejected by the same who have hated and rejected their Master. **21.** *they will do these things to you because of my name:* Just as in rejecting Christ the world really rejected God himself ("since they do not know the One who sent me," cf. 8:19,42), so will the rejection of the Christian mission be a continued rejection of Christ (for "my name," see comment on 1:12). **22–24.** *if I had not come... if I had not performed works among them... they would not be guilty of sin:* Jesus' coming, his words and his works, were the grace and mercy of God intended for the salvation of the world. But for the ill-disposed who have loved the glory of men rather than God, they have been the occasion of a further sin of rejecting God and Christ (see comment on 3:17–19). This rejection has been willful. **25.** *the purpose is to fulfill the text:* See the similar statements in 12:37ff.; 13:18. Here Jesus cites Ps 69:5, a passage that typically applies to him as the utterance of a just man unjustly persecuted. For the reference to this text as part of "their Law," see comment on 10:34. **26–27.** For the idea of "witnessing," see comments on 1:7; 1:15; 4:39; 5:31,36,37. One of the functions of the Paraclete (see comment on 14:16) will be to continue the witness of Christ (also see comment on 16:7–15). *you too should give evidence:* The disciples, too, by living the life that Christ has made possible, by being the Church—the continuation of Christ in this world—will be a continuing witness to his work (cf. Lk 24:48; Acts 1:8). This is, indeed, at the same time the witness of the Spirit (cf. Acts 5:32), since it is the Spirit sent by the Son from the Father who will be the "soul" of the Church.

150 **16:1.** As in 13:19 and 14:29 Jesus instances his own prophecy of the future to bolster his disciples' faith (cf. also 14:25). Forewarned, they should be prepared for what will be the Church's destiny. **2.** *they are going to put you out of the synagogue:* The experience of the man born blind will be repeated time after time in the lives of the first disciples, Jewish Christians (cf. 9:22,34; 12:42). By the time of Jn's Gospel the breach between Church and Synagogue was, of course, complete. *everyone who puts you to death will think he is offering homage to God:* The persecution to be visited upon the Church by the world, Jewish and Gentile, will itself be religiously motivated. However misguided, the persecutors will often be men who sincerely believe that they are serving God; Paul's pre-Christian career is a good illustration of this (cf. Gal 1:13f.). A midrash on Nm 25:13 stated that "anyone who sheds the blood of the godless is like one who offers sacrifice" (cf. Str-B 2, 565). Similar statements can be found in "Christian" sources; Christians themselves have at times been guilty of fulfilling their Master's prophecy of the evil that can be done by good men. **3.** Such deeds can, however, be justified by no true understanding of the nature of God or Christ. Done in ignorance they may be, but this ignorance is always culpable in some way (cf. 15:21). **4a.** This verse includes the thought of v. 1.

151 (f) REPRISE: DEPARTURE AND RETURN (16:4b–33). In this section the role of the Paraclete in relation to the glorification of Christ is discussed in leisurely detail. The close parallel that these verses have with 13:31–14:31 is immediately obvious (for the literary relation of the passages, see comment on 14:30–31).

4b–6. Cf. 14:1–4. *not one of you asks me:* The Evangelist (or his editor) evidently sees no contradiction between this statement and the parallel texts 13:36 and 14:5. As Barrett points out, the present tense is used deliberately: The question is of the disciples' immediate reaction to Jesus' words. Totally concerned with their apparent loss (v. 6) in the new situation that arises with Jesus' announcement that their previous association is to be broken (v. 4b), they are not fixing their minds on the really important matter at hand. Furthermore, even in 13:36 and 14:5 the question of Jesus' destination has not been asked with true understanding. **7.** Cf. 14:16 and 7:39. **8.** *when he does come...:* After Jesus' departure the Church will be on trial in the forum of the world. The Spirit will be the Church's counsel to turn the tables on the world and convict it. This conviction will be effected through the life of the Church as directed by the Spirit. It will be a valid conviction; the world will refuse to acknowledge it (14:17), but it will be true nevertheless. **9.** *sin:* The world will be convicted of sin by the Spirit. Who was guilty of sin: Christ or his executioners? The vital witness of the Church, continuing the divine life with which Christ has endowed it, will testify that he was sinless, that the world is guilty "because they refuse to believe in me" (cf. 3:19–21; 15:21–25). **10.** *justice:* He will convict the world on the grounds of justice. Who was just: Christ or his traducers? The just lives of Christians must show forth the justice of Christ, for they live by the Spirit whom he sends "because I am going to the Father." **11.** *condemnation:* Who finally stands condemned: Christ or his enemies?

The vitality of the Church, living the life of Christ, shows that "the prince of this world has been condemned" (cf. 12:31; 14:30). The triumph of Christ is the defeat of Satan, and the one is the sign of the other. **12–13.** See 14:25–26. Even now, at the very end of his public life, there is much that Jesus cannot say and that must await the enlightening activity of the Holy Spirit. *the Spirit of truth:* This expression occurs for the third time (cf. 14:17; 15:26), here most appropriately of all. It appears frequently in the QL, though not in a divine or (probably) even a personal sense. *he will not speak on his own:* As Christ has spoken of himself in relation to the Father (see comment on 5:19; 12:49; 14:10) so he speaks of the Spirit in relation to himself. *the things to come:* Predictive prophecy is part of the Spirit's function (cf. Acts 21:11; etc.). However, what is "to come" may be said in relation to the Last Supper, meaning the great events that will culminate in the resurrection, the significance of all of which it will be for the Spirit to elucidate. **14.** *he will glorify me:* The glorification which the Son has from the Father and which is in turn the glorification of the Father (12:23,28; 13:31f.), is continued in the Church (cf. 14:13) through the activity of the Spirit which continues the work of Christ. **15.** As the existence of the Church is the result of the shared life of the Father and the Son (cf. 3:35; 5:20; 10:30), so its continuance is the result of the shared life of Son and Spirit.

152 **16–19.** Cf. 14:18f.; 13:36; 14:5. **20.** Cf. 14:18; 15:11. **21–22.** Not only does the reference to a woman in labor later rejoicing in her child have obvious illustrative value, but these words probably allude to an OT messianic theme (cf. Is 26:17–19; 66:7–14) that gave rise to the Jewish expression "birthpangs of the Messiah" to describe the troubles that would precede the end time (cf. Col 1:24, where the word *thlipsis* occurs as in this verse). The temporary sorrow of the disciples heralds the realized eschatology of Christ's resurrection. **23–24.** Cf. 14:13f. *on that day:* See 14:20. *there will be no questions for you to ask me:* The lack of understanding by friend and foe alike with which Jesus' words have been interpreted, and which has been a feature of the Johannine dialogues, will be removed for his disciples in the enlightenment given by the Holy Spirit (cf. v. 25). **25–28.** Cf. 14:23–26. *figures of speech:* This term (*paroimia*, found also in v. 29, in 10:6, and in 2 Pt 2:22) corresponds to the Syn *parabolē* (cf. J. Quasten, *CBQ* 10 [1948] 8f.). However, the application is probably not to be restricted to such figures as that in v. 21, the allegory of the vine in 15:1–17, etc., which play a similar role in Jn as do the parables in the Syn. Jesus probably refers to all of his teaching, which as yet has been obscure even for his disciples (cf. 14:9; etc.). *I will report to you plainly:* After his glorification, through the enlightenment of the Holy Spirit. **29–30.** The disciples unwisely presume that the "hour" of which Jesus has spoken is already here and that even now they possess the fullness of comprehension that he has promised. **31–32.** Of this presumption Jesus must disabuse them, predicting that, far from their being confirmed in faith, they will soon desert him in the hour of his trial (cf. Mt 26:31; Mk 14:27), leaving him alone with his Father. **33.** Cf. 14:25,27,29; 15:18–16:4a; 16:11.

153 (g) THE HIGH-PRIESTLY PRAYER (17:1–26). This sublime passage was first termed the High-Priestly Prayer by the 16th-cent. Lutheran theologian David Chytraeus (Kochhafe), though equivalent expressions were used by some of the Fathers. The name is apt, for it is Christ's prayer consecrating his body and blood for the sacrifice in which they are about to be offered, and his benediction over the Church that he is to bring forth in his glorification. Although the Syn frequently picture Jesus in prayer, especially on occasions of great importance such as this, only rarely (as in the "Our Father," Mt 6:9–13 par.) is the content of his prayer given. As we might expect it to, this prayer sums up the significance of Christ's life.

154 **1.** *he looked up to heaven:* Jesus assumes the customary attitude of prayer (cf. 11:41). Though John for his own reasons has omitted any direct reference to the Eucharist in the account of the Last Supper, a prayer such as this would have accompanied it most appropriately. *the hour has come:* See comment on 2:4. *glorify your son...:* See comments on 1:14; 2:11; 12:23,28. **2.** For the teaching of this verse, see comments on 1:4; 5:26f.; 10:28f. *all flesh:* A Semitism borrowed from the OT meaning "all mankind"; it occurs only here in Jn. **3.** For eternal life expressed in terms of the knowledge of God, see comment on 1:10; 1:26, and cf. 8:19; 14:7,9. **4–5.** The Son has glorified the Father by revealing him perfectly in all the words and deeds of his life (cf. 1:18; 5:20f.,36); now in turn the Father will glorify him in the resurrection and ascension by which he will return to the glory that in his preincarnational state he possessed from all eternity (cf. 1:1; 6:62; 8:58; → Johannine Theology, 80:30–34). **6.** His glorification of the Father has consisted in the making known (cf. 1:18; 2:11; 9:3; 15:15) of his name (see comment on 1:12) to those given him by the Father (see comment on 6:65). *they have kept your word:* Though often lacking in understanding, the disciples have been faithful to the teaching given them, even as Jesus was faithful to his commission from the Father (8:55). **7–8.** *now they have realized...:* The disciples have come to a true recognition of the relation of the Son to the Father, of his character as Savior. This statement does not run counter to the previous passages on the enlightening role of the Holy Spirit (16:13f.; etc.); rather, in this moment in which Jesus contemplates his mission as completed in his glorification, he presupposes the activity of the Spirit.

155 **9–10.** The prayer now encompasses the disciples who belong to the Father and the Son as a common possession (vv. 6–8). *I do not pray for the world:* It is not that Jesus excludes from his prayers the world (see comment on 1:10) that God loves (3:16); however, the subject of this prayer is rather the Church that must live in the world but be no part of it (v. 14). *it is in them that I have been glorified:* The disciples have already glorified Jesus by their fidelity (v. 6); however, in view of the perspective of the prayer (see comment on vv. 7–8 above), Jesus probably speaks of the future works of the disciples as already glorifying him. **11–13.** The occasion for the prayer appears: They will need the divine protection in an especial way, now that his visible presence is about to be removed from them. *Holy Father:* The adjective appears in view of the theme of holiness in the substance of the prayer, vv. 14–19. *your name which you have given to me:* God's "name" (see comment on 1:12) is his revealed character that Christ has made manifest (1:18; 14:9). *that they may be one, even as we:* The unity of the Father and Son (10:30) is the model and principle of the unity of the disciples, since the "name" that Christ has revealed is nothing less than the divine life itself. *not one of them perished:* "Perished" refers to falling away from discipleship, not necessarily to eternal perdition, though Jesus' characterization of Judas is not a hopeful one. *the son of perdition:* This Semitism means "one destined for perdition." *in order to have the scripture fulfilled:* See 13:18. **14–16.** The world's hatred of the light (cf. 15:18–16:4a) necessitates the divine protection of the Church that Christ leaves behind. *I have given them your word:* The word of God (*logos*, so also v. 6 [= name], v. 17 [= truth]) has been revealed by the Word of God (1:1ff.). *I am not requesting you to take them out of the world:* The destiny of the Church is to live in the world but not to be of the world, to affect the world but not to be affected by it. **17.** *consecrate them in the truth:* The disciples are the priests of the New Law. Just as the priests of the Old Law were consecrated ("made holy"), so are those of the New, but in a far more personal and intimate way. *your word is truth:* This phrase may be a citation of (LXX) Ps 118:142. The Word of God itself (v. 14), which is truth (see comment on 1:14), is the consecration of the disciples. A verbal parallel to this verse occurs in 1QS 4:20f. where, interestingly enough, the term "spirit of truth" also appears: Christ certainly means that this work of consecration will be done by the Spirit of Truth (cf. 16:13). **18–19.** These two verses complete and enlarge upon the thought of the preceding. The apostolic mission of the Church is the same as Christ's mission from the Father; therefore their consecration is the same. *I sent them into the world:* The actual mission of the disciples is not recorded till 20:21f., but again the perspective of the prayer (vv. 7f.,10) sees the future as an accomplished fact. *I consecrate myself:* Through his voluntary sacrifice (10:18, cf. Heb 10:10), the beginning of the glorification by which the disciples are consecrated.

156 **20.** *not for these alone...for those who believe in me through their word:* Jesus' prayer now extends to the Church of all time, to all those who owe their faith to the apostolic testimony. **21.** The unity that he had besought for the first disciples (v. 11) must remain the characteristic of the Church. *so that the world can believe that you sent me:* Unless the Church preserves the unity willed by God, it cannot perform its essential mission in the world. The unity of the Church shows forth the union of Father and Son that is its model and principle. **22–23.** *I have given them the glory that you have given me:* As the principle of this essential unity, Christ has communicated to the Church the divine presence (for "glory," see comment on 1:14; so also "name" and "word" in vv. 6, 8, 11, and 14). The unity of the Church is, as it were, the incarnation of the shared life and love of the Father and Son. *thus letting the world know that you sent me...:* When the Church is true to its destiny and preserves the unity in love that has been given it, it is the continuation of Christ as mediator and revealer of God (cf. 13:34f.). **24.** Jesus' final petition is for the consummation of the work that has been wrought in bringing forth the Church. *as for what you have given me:* This is the Church itself, which has continually been spoken of as a united thing (*hen*). *I would like:* Jesus no longer uses the formula of prayer; nevertheless, the thought remains the same, since his will is always that of the Father (cf. 4:34). *where I am they may be there with me:* See 13:36; he now speaks of his eschatological presence, which is the completion of the life that the Christian shares with him in this world (cf. 12:26). *so that they can see this glory:* According to v. 22 he has already given them the glory that the Father has given him. But again, just as the Father has previously glorified the Son (cf. 2:11; 12:28) and is only now to glorify him in the ultimate (vv. 1 and 5), so it will be with the Christian's share in this glory (cf. 1 Jn 3:2). **25–26.** *O just Father:* God, who alone is perfectly just (cf. 1 Jn 1:9), will deal rightly with those who have separated themselves from the unbelieving world (cf. 8:55), who have accepted the revelation of God in Christ (cf. 7:29; 8:19; etc.). The life that Christ has shared with his Church the Father will permit him to share continually through the outpouring of the Holy Spirit. The departure of Jesus for his glorification means that he will be forever with his Church in the divine presence and love.

157 **(B) The Glorification of Christ (18:1–20:31).** The goal of the Gospel is reached in this final section, the climax of the Book of Exaltation and the realization of what was signified in the Book of Signs. The Passion Narrative plays a large part in this section as it does in all the Gospels; however, it is John's Gospel that never lets us forget that it is the history of a victory, though the world did not understand it as such. Correspondingly, we read nothing of the agony in the garden and only a minimum of the indignities shown Jesus by his judges. These events we know from the Syn, but John has carefully selected the material in which the eye of faith knows how to discern the Lord of salvation. Jesus' appearance before Pilate allows him to assert his supremacy in the world. When he is crowned with thorns, it is as a king. Thus from beginning to end, and not only in the resurrection and giving of the Spirit, this is a story of Christ's glorification.

158 (a) The Passion (18:1–19:16). When we take into consideration the nature of Jn as related to the Syn (→ 17–27 above), we are surprised not by the divergencies between the traditions, which are minor, but rather by the striking similarities (cf. P. Borgen, *NTS* 5 [1959] 246–59). In this narrative John makes far less effort than before to point out the spiritual significance of words or events; as in the Syn tradition, these are generally allowed to speak for themselves. The more important departures from the Syn tradition will be noted in the commentary.

(i) *The scene in the garden* (18:1–11). John omits the story of Jesus' agony, prayer, the comfort of the angel, etc., found in Mk 14:26,32–52 par. All the teachings found in these episodes are covered elsewhere in his Gospel. He proceeds immediately to the account of Jesus' arrest, and even in this he finds an evidence of his protective power.

1. *after this discourse:* For the question of sequence, see comment on 14:30f. *across the Kidron valley:* Only here in the NT is mention made of the Kidron, well known from the OT, which separated Jerusalem from the Mt. of Olives. *a garden:* In Mk 14:32 and Mt 26:36 this place is called Gethsemane; Lk 22:39 agrees with Jn in locating it at the Mt. of Olives; it was evidently an enclosed place ("went in," cf. v. 4, "went out"), probably the private garden of an unnamed friend. **2–3.** Jn suggests that the garden was the place in which Jesus had hidden from his enemies during Holy Week (cf. Lk 21:37). Only in Jn is mention made of "the cohort of soldiers" and the Temple guards (the Syn speak merely of "a crowd"); the soldiers were from the Roman garrison (cf. v. 12). It is not extraordinary that the Jewish leaders should have sought the help of the Roman troops at this early stage, since they had previously planned (cf. 11:46–53) what in fact they eventually did, to denounce him to the Romans as a seditionist (cf. Lk 23:2; Jn 18:28–40). A cohort was composed normally of 600 men, but we need not imagine that this entire force had come out to assist in the capture of one man. **4–9.** Jesus remains entirely in command of the situation. Knowing what is to happen, he takes the initiative in addressing the armed force; Judas the betrayer only stands by impotently. At Jesus' identification of himself ("I am," see comment on 6:35) the throng is thrown back in confusion; whatever the psychological explanation of the recoiling of Jesus' enemies from his calm presence, John interprets their action as an unconscious recognition of a divine appearance (cf. Dn 10:9; Ap 1:17). Finally, Jesus protects his own from destruction, even as he had promised he would (cf. 6:39; 17:12). *Jesus the Nazorean:* The adj. *nazōraios* (cf. 19:19) occurs in the NT more often than the parallel *nazarēnos* as a designation by the Jews of Jesus and his disciples (cf. Acts

24:5). Though it may originally have had another meaning, in the NT the term is associated with the village of Nazareth (Mt 2:23; Acts 10:38), and this is doubtless its meaning for John. (See H. Schaeder, *ThDNT* 4, 874–89; E. Schweizer, *Judentum, Urchristentum, Kirche* [Fest. J. Jeremias; Berlin, 1960] 90–93.) **10–11.** Only Jn gives the name of the high priest's slave and of the disciple who struck him. *the cup the Father has given me:* These words are reminiscent of the agony scene, despite the fact that in Jn the episode is omitted.

159 (ii) *The scene before Annas* (18:12–27). If the chronicle of events as reported in the Syn tradition is to be preferred invariably to that of Jn from the standpoint of "historicity," the following passage—the report of a witness who certainly knew the Syn tradition—presents some insoluble difficulties. If, on the other hand, we recognize that the eyewitness testimony from which Jn has been formed is often closer to the factual events than the schematic Syn outline, the passage becomes more understandable. The commentary will attempt to justify this judgment. At the same time, it must be recognized that John goes his own way here as elsewhere and that in one quite essential matter his version of the events does not try to parallel the Syn account. The Evangelist merely hints at what is the feature of the Syn story, that Jesus was on trial before the Jewish leaders this night and early morning. He has no place for such an interrogation of Jesus in his Gospel, since he had already uttered his final words to the unbelieving Jews (so Bultmann; cf. v. 20f. and 12:36).

12. *tribune:* This term (*chiliarchos*, "leader of a thousand") was the technical designation for the leader of a Roman cohort (cf. 18:3; Acts 21:31). **13.** *they led him to Annas first:* Only Jn records an appearance before Annas, who is mentioned elsewhere in the NT only in Lk 3:2; Acts 4:6. Annas had been high priest AD 6–15 and enjoyed the unique distinction of having five sons, one grandson, and a son-in-law succeed him in this office (cf. Josephus, *Ant.* 18.2, 2 § 34; 4, 3 § 95; 20.9, 1 § 197; U. Holzmeister, *Historia aetatis Novi Testamenti* [2d ed.; Rome, 1938] 198–201). Though it could hardly be said that the house of Annas was highly esteemed by the Jews (cf. Str-B 2, 569f.), there seems to be no doubt that Annas was regarded as the patriarch of the high-priestly "family." Thus it is most credible that Jesus would have been brought to his house. There was no trial of Jesus at Annas' house, for no trial could be legally held except in the daylight hours; hence Lk 22:54–71 agrees with Jn in having Jesus brought to "the high priest's house" this night, specifying at the same time that the trial took place when day had come. Mt 26:57–27:1 and Mk 14:53–15:1 describe both the night and morning sessions as trials, mentioning the latter only summarily, and Mt further speaks of the high priest throughout as Caiaphas. It is easy to see that these Syn accounts can represent a telescoped version of the events and that Jn-Lk may depend on a more factual reporting. *the father-in-law of Caiaphas:* We know of this relationship only from Jn. *high priest that particular year:* See 11:49. **14.** Jn recalls to the reader's mind the cynical advice given by Caiaphas before the Passover (11:50). One Syr ms. makes v. 24 precede this verse; in a few other mss. v. 24 has been added here even though it is repeated in its own proper place. Obviously this provides no textual evidence for a dislocation (→ 8 above), but rather was the effort of scribes to harmonize Jn with what was thought to be the Syn version of the events (Mt more than Mk). **15–16.** *another disciple:* The Syn mention Peter only as following Jesus. Is this other disciple to be identified with "the one whom Jesus loved" (cf. 20:2)? *known to the high priest...by the high priest:* Objection has been made to this note, especially if the unnamed disciple is to be identified with John the son of Zebedee, since it is difficult to imagine the high priest on familiar terms with a Galilean fisherman. The objection, however, is not pre-emptory, for we know nothing of what may lie behind the statement. On the one hand, John the son of Zebedee is not represented in the Gospel as belonging to a family of no consequence (cf. Mk 1:20, "hired men"; Mt 27:55f. [Lk 8:3], financial support given to Jesus). Furthermore, one known "to" or "by" the high priest may have meant nothing more than one who had access to the high priest's house through his servants (cf. Phil 4:22, "those of Caesar's household" = "persons in the imperial service"). The disciple "whom Jesus loved" is elsewhere shown as being together with Peter (cf. 13:23f.; 20:2f.; 21:7,20f.). *the high priest's courtyard:* The word *aulē* can have various meanings, but from what follows it is plain that Peter and the other disciple were standing among the menials of the household, who would hardly have been within the private confines of the house. The courtyard suits the informal and unofficial nature of the interrogation to which Jesus was subjected. **17–18.** In this account of the first denial by Peter of his Master (cf. 13:38) there is substantial agreement among the three Syn versions and Jn. The maid, having seen Peter in the company of the "other disciple" whose identity was known to her, asks whether Peter, too, is an associate of Jesus. Nothing further is said of the other disciple or of the Roman soldiers, who probably accompanied the Temple guards only as far as the gate of the house.

160 **19–21.** Jn represents the interrogation of Jesus as being merely exploratory. *the high priest:* John knew that Caiaphas was the official high priest in Jesus' time (cf. v. 13f.). Nevertheless, Annas, although deposed from the office by the Roman prefect, was apparently still accorded this title by the Jews (cf. Lk 3:2; Acts 4:6). *about his disciples:* Probably the concern of the high priest largely centered on Jesus' potentialities as the leader of a messianic uprising (cf. 11:47f.). Jesus ignores this question as superfluous in view of his known attitude to such things (cf. 6:14f.). In fact, the entire interrogation is superfluous, for Jesus has never made a secret of his teaching (cf. Mk 14:49 par.). **22–23.** The guard, recognizing that Jesus treats the high priest's interrogation with the disregard that it deserves, reacts in a way typical of the kind of hearing Jesus had always been given, as Jesus himself notes in his mild reproof (cf. 8:46). It is certain that abuse of this kind would not have been tolerated in a formal trial. **24.** After the unofficial interrogation at Annas' house, Jesus is sent to Caiaphas for a formal trial, held in the morning (cf. v. 28). John notes the fact, but says nothing of the trial (→ 159 above). **25–27.** Twice again Peter is given the opportunity of identifying himself with Jesus' followers, and twice again he refuses, fulfilling the prediction of Jesus. In this part of the story, the Syn versions vary among themselves and with Jn, associating the denials with different circumstances and questioners. The variations are such as would be expected in oral transmission of events; it is unlikely that any one of the Evangelists was an eyewitness to what is recorded in this particular part of the Gospel.

161 (iii) *The scene before Pilate: Christ the King* (18:28–40). If John has passed over the trial of Jesus by the Jews (though the present passages presuppose that it has taken place), he does devote more attention than do the Syn to the judgment rendered by Pilate. Also, though not noted in the Syn, the Romans have been introduced from v. 3 on. This is part of John's design, for in the truest sense the empire represented "the world" (see comment on 1:10) in which the Church of his time was destined to live and work out its salvation (cf. 15:18–16:4a).

This is the first opportunity that John had within the framework of the Gospel to show Jesus in confrontation with this world.

28. *when it was early morning:* This is Friday morning, following the trial of Jesus before Caiaphas (cf. v. 24; Mk 15:1). *the praetorium:* The name for the official residence of the prefect. The Roman capital of Palestine was Caesarea, not Jerusalem, and it was in Caesarea that the chief *praetorium* was to be found (cf. Acts 23:35). Especially at the time of Jewish feasts, however, it was the custom of the prefect to take up residence in Jerusalem, to be on hand when rebellions might be expected to break out. For the location of the Jerusalem *praetorium*, see 19:13. *they had to avoid incurring any ritual impurity:* The Jewish leaders, heedless of the Law's spirit, show an ironic concern for its letter (cf. 8:39f.; Mt 23:24). To enter a Gentile house was to incur a ritual uncleanness that would force the postponement of the Passover supper (see comment on 13:1). It does not seem to be true (Barrett) that John is in error here, speaking of an impurity that could have been removed within the same day (cf. Nm 9:6,11; Str-B 2, 838f.); rather, he shows himself cognizant of the Palestinian scene. **29–30.** Pontius Pilate, prefect of Judea AD 26–36, appears in the narrative without introduction (→ History of Israel, 75:143). His gesture in accommodating himself to Jewish reluctance to enter the *praetorium* is typical of the man—his blunders in administration were never in small matters. The poorly concealed contempt with which Pilate and the Jews regarded one another is well-known. Pilate's question does not necessarily mean that he was unaware of the attitude of these men toward Jesus, but he was asking for a charge against him that would have validity in Roman law. This Jesus' enemies did not conclusively have, hence their initial effort to bluster Pilate into doing their will without hearing specific charges. **31.** Pilate haughtily refuses to involve himself on these terms, thus forcing the Jews to speak bluntly of their designs on Jesus' life. *we are not permitted to put anyone to death:* The historicity of this statement has often been denied (cf. T. A. Burkill, *VigChr* 10 [1956] 80–96) and just as often defended. In favor of the Sanhedrin's power to inflict the death penalty in Jesus' time such NT passages as 8:7; Acts 7:58f.; 25:9–11 have been cited. The closest thing to a confirmation of John's reporting is the account given by Josephus (*Ant.* 20.9, 1 § 200) of the deposition of the high priest Ananus (son of the Annas in Jn) for his illegal convocation of a Sanhedrin that condemned James, "the Lord's brother," to death by stoning. The evidence is not conclusive against John, who is a reliable historian; that the Romans may have permitted or tolerated Jewish executions on occasion does not prove that they allowed them in principle. It is possible, moreover, as Hoskyns has suggested, that in phrasing the Jews' statement John meant to signify something slightly different from what it has usually been taken to mean. That is to say, by their own Law the Jews could not put Jesus to death as they intended him to die, as a crucified criminal whose death would serve to focus Roman attention away from the people and the nation (cf. 11:49f.). A Jewish execution over purely Jewish concerns would not have engaged the Romans' attention. **32.** Whatever the precise meaning of the preceding verse, John sees the result, that is, that Jesus would be crucified rather than stoned according to the Jewish custom, as the fulfillment of Jesus' own prophecies concerning his death (cf. 3:14; 8:28; 12:32f.).

162 **33.** *are you the King of the Jews?:* Nothing in the preceding narrative has prepared us for this question that Pilate asks of Jesus; obviously John presupposes that Pilate had obtained more precise information about Jesus than is contained in the words of the Jews in v. 30f. (cf. Lk 23:2). Events such as those John has described in 6:15; 12:12f. could have been used as a source of denouncing Jesus as the leader of a nationalist movement, the only charge that would be taken seriously by the Romans. **34–35.** *is what you say your own idea...?:* Jesus offers Pilate the opportunity of assuming his own attitude toward the light, rather than simply serving as the channel of the hatred that the world has consistently shown it. Pilate's contempt for "Jewish" matters is, however, completely serene (cf. the similar attitude of Gallio in Acts 18:14f.). **36.** The interchange permits Jesus to explain the nature of the kingship that indeed is his. *my kingdom does not belong to this world* [see 1:10]*:* Though the idea of Jesus as king has not been given much emphasis in Jn, it was a common conception from the Syn tradition and early Christian preaching that reflects Jesus' own identification of himself as the fulfillment of the OT messianic kingly ideal. Much more clearly than the Syn parallels (see Lk 23:3; Mk 15:2; Mt 27:11) does this statement in Jn define the completely nonpolitical and nonnational character of Jesus' kingship (in the Syn, which feature the kingly idea, the same teaching has already been brought out in earlier passages); "this saying, attributed to Jesus by the Gospel of John, cannot be imagined in the mouth of a *Jewish* Messiah, not even a Messiah of the more spiritual type portrayed in the Psalms of Solomon" (J. Klausner, *The Messianic Idea in Israel* [N.Y., 1955] 392). *if my kingdom were...:* Jesus offers the best proof of the spiritual nature of his kingship, in terms that Pilate can appreciate. As does any other king, Jesus has his "minions" (*hypēretai*, the word used for the Temple guards in v. 3), but they engage in no political action on his behalf. (In Mt 26:53 Jesus speaks of the angelic assistance he could command were his desire to fight the world on its own terms; the word *hypēretai* refers to the apostolic ministry in Lk 1:2; Acts 13:5; 26:16; 1 Cor 4:1.) **37.** As Pilate still presses for a direct answer, Jesus gives the same qualified affirmation that appears in Mk 15:2 par. *you say that I am a king:* In Pilate's sense of the word, Jesus is not a king; thus Pilate's use of the title for Jesus represents another instance of Johannine irony (→ 29 above). In another sense, as Jesus has already implied by speaking of his kingdom, he is a king. He is not a worldly king, but a king who has "come into the world," and the essence of his kingship is "to testify to the truth" (see comments on 1:14; 3:11,32). *everyone who belongs to the truth listens to my voice:* Again (cf. v. 34) Jesus implicitly calls on Pilate to take a stand, to range himself on the side of truth and life (cf. 5:25; 8:47).

163 **38.** The question "jesting Pilate" asks by way of reply, typical of the cynical skepticism of the Roman mind, is sufficient to show that he belongs to the world that rejects the light. Pilate expects no answer because he thinks none is possible; indifference to the truth is equivalent to rejecting it. Nevertheless, Pilate has understood sufficiently to know that Jesus' teaching offers no threat to imperial security. **39–40.** At the same time, what follows shows how indifference is, in fact, rejection. Here John condenses severely the account found in much greater detail in the Syn parallels. Were Pilate a man of truth, he would have freed Jesus without further ado; instead, he begins the series of compromises that leads to his execution of the Savior. *you have a custom:* Also recounted in the Syn tradition, this custom is known to us only from the Gospels. *the King of the Jews:* Pilate's use of this title, hardly calculated to dispose the Jews to favor his offer, was doubtless inspired simply by his contempt for them. Unconsciously he again gives to Jesus a title that rightly belongs to him. *Barabbas, but not this fellow:* The Jews are put in the ironical position of asking for the release of one who was guilty of the charge that they had falsely lodged against Jesus (as appears from Mk 15:6–14 par.). Barabbas was under arrest for political sedition: John may mean this by calling him a "bandit" (the term was sometimes used for the "Zealots" who formed the Jewish underground opposing Roman rule), or he may be reminding us of 10:1,8.

164 (iv) *The scourging: "Behold the Man"* (19:1–5). Pilate the compromiser goes further along his chosen path. Though he holds Jesus to be innocent, he will yet have him punished, hoping that this will satisfy the Jews and dissuade them from seeking the extreme penalty (cf. Lk 23:16,22).

1. In Mk 15:15 and in Mt 27:26 the scourging (not described in Lk) takes place after Pilate has passed sentence. As scourging was the normal preliminary to crucifixion, it is likely that John has anticipated the event for dramatic effect. **2–3.** The abuse of the Roman soldiers, also described by the Syn, was directed as much against the Jews as against Jesus. To the soldiers, this was merely another of the Jewish rebels with kingly pretensions with whom they had dealt in the past. The idea that there could be a "king of the Jews" they found completely ridiculous. In their mouths as in Pilate's, however, the use of this title is ironical, since in John's time the Romans were already taking the title seriously in response to the preaching of Christianity (see also v. 13). **4–5.** In his caricature of kingship Jesus is now brought forth to the view of his enemies. In the thought that the pitiable sight will satisfy their blood lust, Pilate cries "Behold the Man." Pilate's words are uttered merely to designate the person with whom they are concerned, but he says more than he knows (cf. 11:50–52). The Aram *bar nashā*, the Semitic that underlies "Son of Man," means simply "the man" (see comment on 1:51).

165 (v) *Again before Pilate: The Son of God* (19:6–16). **6–8.** Now the final scene before Pilate is to be played out. Far from being moved by the pitiable spectacle Pilate has shown them, the Jews explicitly demand his execution by crucifixion at the hands of the Roman authorities. *you take him yourselves and crucify him:* Pilate's words can only be a taunt and a refusal to act; whatever the power of the Sanhedrin in capital cases (see comment on 18:31), crucifixion was not the Jewish manner of execution. *we have a law...:* John has not recounted the trial in which Jesus was formally condemned for the crime of blasphemy (see comment on 18:12–27), but he has shown earlier the basis on which this charge was made (cf. 5:18; 10:33,36; see Mk 14:55–64 par.). *Pilate became even more alarmed:* John has not told us much about Pilate's personal attitude toward Jesus, which seems to have included a kind of superstitious awe (cf. Mt 27:19). The title "Son of God" also had a meaning in pagan superstition, referring to divine or divinized men of superhuman and possibly malignant powers. **9.** *where do you come from?:* In Lk 23:6 Pilate inquires as to Jesus' national origin, preparatory to sending him to Herod. John, however, sees in the question in context another recognition that Pilate is of this world that cannot know the Son (cf. 8:14; 9:29). Unable to give an answer that will be understood (cf. 10:24), Jesus can only remain silent; his silence in the presence of all his interrogators is stressed in the Gospels (cf. Mk 14:61 par.; Lk 23:9; Mk 15:5 par.). **10–11.** Pilate is irritated by Jesus' silence, which he takes not only as a slight to his authority but also as the ingratitude of one whose life he was disposed to spare. *you would have no power...from above:* All authority is from God (cf. Rom 13:1). As Son of God, Jesus remains in control of the situation. Only because God has willed that this should be, can Pilate preside over what is to happen to Jesus (cf. 8:20). *the one who handed me over to you is even more guilty:* Jesus probably does not single out any specific individual, but by "the one" he means anyone of the Jewish leadership that had handed him over to the Romans. They are all the more guilty because, possessing the authority that has been committed to them by God, they have used this authority to encompass the death of an innocent person.

166 **12.** Puzzled by Jesus' teaching, but still recognizing that it constitutes no political threat to Rome, Pilate persists in his resolve to release Jesus. But the Jews now use their ultimate persuasion, the threat of denunciation to the emperor for having favored his enemies. Such denunciations were responsible for the disgrace of more than one Palestinian prefect; what representation could Pilate make to the far-off Caesar when a charge of disloyalty had been brought against him by the supposedly disinterested Jews, not noted for their devotion to the empire? Pilate, who loved the glory of men rather than the glory of God (cf. 12:43), could find no option but to sacrifice Jesus. **13.** Taking his place on the judgment seat (which was always public and out of doors) he prepares to render the judgment of death. *the Stone Pavement:* Jn uses this term (*Lithostrōtos*) as a proper name, the Gk equivalent (not a translation) of the Aram place name *Gabbathā*, which means "elevated place." This site, mentioned only in Jn, appears to have been connected with the *praetorium*. The *praetorium* of Jesus' trial has been identified both with the Fortress Antonia N of the Temple area on the eastern side of the city (cf. L. H. Vincent, *RB* 59 [1952] 513–30; *Le Lithostrotos d'après des fouilles récentes* [Jerusalem, 1933]) and with the Palace of Herod on the western side (cf. P. Benoit, *RB* 59 [1952] 531–50; *Exégèse*, 1, 316–39). Though scholars admit that the prefect would normally have used the former residence of Judea's kings during his visits to Jerusalem, excavations beneath the site of the Antonia seem to confirm the view that this was the *praetorium* of the passion (cf. W. F. Albright, *AP* 245), revealing a topography and a large stone pavement that accord with the description given in Jn. Rough carvings in the pavement made by the Roman soldiers have also suggested further correspondences with the Gospel narrative. In particular, the Roman "game of the king" may have been connected with the treatment accorded Jesus according to vv. 1–3 (cf. *BT* 1 [1963] 336–38). **14.** *Preparation day for Passover:* See 13:1. *the hour was about noon:* This notice conflicts with Mk 15:25, which places the crucifixion at about nine o'clock in the morning. Both time indications are doubtless symbolic: John wishes to remind the reader of the typology of the Passover lamb (cf. v. 36), which was slaughtered after noon on Preparation day, whereas Mark wants to associate the darkness accompanying the crucifixion with the "darkness at noon" of Am 8:9 (cf. Mk 15:33). Jn's time indication is doubtless closer to history, since it would be hard to imagine all the activity of this morning having taken place before nine o'clock. *here is your King:* Here, in the following verse, and in vv. 19–22, Pilate persists in calling Christ the King of the Jews (see comment on 18:37), unable to pass by these additional opportunities of taunting the people he hates. **15.** *we have no king but Caesar:* Pilate finally goads the chief priests who want Jesus' death at any cost into repudiating their proudest religious and national heritage (cf. Jgs 8:23; 1 Sm 8:7; Zeph 3:15; see also 8:33,41). Their reply is doubly ironical, since by John's time these same Jews had seen their autonomy destroyed as the result of their rebellion against Caesar. **16.** *he handed him over to them:* Pilate yields to their demand that Jesus be crucified; the actual executioners, of course, remained the Romans. John does not have Pilate actually pass sentence on Jesus, for in his mind this is really the judgment of the world and not of Christ (see comments on 18:1–20:31).

167 (b) The Crucifixion and Death of Jesus (19:17–37). The positive note of Jesus' glorification is continued in this narrative. There is no mention of Simon of Cyrene (Mk 15:20f. par.), for John shows Jesus always in complete control of his destiny. John has no room in this triumphant picture for the mourning women of Jerusalem (Lk 23:27f.) or for the mockery shown Jesus on the cross (Mk 15:29–32 par.). Jesus dies with the announcement that the work he had come to do has been accomplished.

168 (i) *Jesus reigns from the cross* (19:17–22). **17.** *carrying the cross by himself:* It was the practice for the condemned criminal to carry the crossbar of the instrument of execution on his shoulders; the upright of the cross was probably permanently fixed at the site of execution. *the Place of the Skull:* All the Gospels agree on the name of this place outside the city of Jerusalem, a translation of the Aram name *Golgotha.* The name probably referred to a rocky elevation of some kind (→ Gospel Mk, 42:92). **18.** All the Evangelists describe the actual crucifixion with extreme brevity and all note that Jesus was executed together with two condemned criminals. **19–22.** The title affixed to the cross of Jesus, in keeping with the Roman custom of publishing the cause for the execution, is mentioned by all four Evangelists, though in varying forms. *Jesus the Nazorean:* See comment on 18:4. *the King of the Jews:* All the Evangelists agree that these words appeared on the title; they would have constituted the Roman justification for Jesus' execution as a rebel against imperial rule. Only Jn recounts the ensuing discussion between Pilate and the chief priests. Rightly sensing the spirit of contempt in which Pilate has had the title phrased, the priests protest to the last that they will not have Jesus for their king. Perhaps Jn sees a final irony in the fact that Pilate, the Gentile, has consistently used the title, for whatever reasons, while it has been just as consistently refused by the Jews.

169 Additional Comment on the Crucifixion of Jesus in Jn. The question of the responsibility for the execution of Jesus has been much agitated in history, and especially in modern times. But because it properly figures in the trial of Jesus, which is not featured in Jn, this is not the place to discuss the question in detail. However, something should be said about John's part in what has been alleged as a deliberate distortion that was introduced into the Gospel traditions, by which the blame was shifted from the Romans to the Jews. As in all questions of this nature, it is easy to exaggerate the evidence in both directions, and one runs the risk of being misunderstood simply in trying to evaluate it objectively. On the one hand, it is beyond doubt that the "Jewish question" here and elsewhere in the Gospels has been given an emphasis that in part testifies to the Judaizing controversies in the primitive Church as well as to the scandal that was felt in the nonacceptance of Christianity by Judaism as a whole. It is equally true that Christians must be profoundly ashamed of the persecutions that have been meted out to the Jews at various times in Christian history in the name of the compassionate Christ. The story of the passion has sometimes been used as an excuse for pogroms, and the Jews as a people have been labeled "Christ-killers" as though they rather than the small group present at the *praetorium* on Good Friday morning had demanded the blood of Jesus, as though Christ had not died because of the sins of all mankind, Jew and Gentile.

It is another thing, however, to charge the Gospels with having distorted the history of Jesus' execution out of a spirit of anti-Semitism. If this were true, we should expect Jn to have gone the farthest along this route, yet it is precisely in Jn that the Romans are introduced into the proceedings at a stage earlier than that noted by the Syn tradition (cf. 18:2f.). None of the Gospels, Jn least of all, has attempted to excuse the Romans of criminal complicity in the death of Jesus, and none has concealed the fact that his death was a Roman execution. But when the Gospels also insist that the Jewish authorities of Jerusalem were prime movers in this death, they deserve to be treated as serious history. What we know of these authorities from disinterested non-Christian sources makes the Gospel account antecedently credible. It is these that John usually means when he speaks of "the Jews" (see 1:19); and while it is true that this expression is quite often pejorative with John even in its broader applications, used as it is in reference to Christ's opponents among his own people, the term was not chosen for polemical reasons. In John's era the Church and Synagogue had become irrevocably separate; and Jew though the Evangelist himself was, it was as natural for him to speak of "the Jews" as a people apart from Christianity as it has been for everyone since.

John consistently distinguishes these Jewish leaders from the people as a whole (cf. 9:22; 12:42; etc.), and he is careful to point out that even among the authorities themselves were men of good will (3:1ff.; 7:50ff.; 12:42; etc.). This picture is substantially that of the Syn tradition, which offers no indictment of the entire Jewish nation of the time of Jesus and certainly of no subsequent time. Perhaps more than the Syn even, John has stressed that the Jews who had resolved on Jesus' death were the representatives of the corrupt priestly families of Jerusalem, men who have deserved the execrations of Judaism as much as of Christianity. "The Evangelist is simply a Jewish prophet, speaking in the idiom of Qumran, boiling with rage and indignation at the leaders of the Synagogue for having so tragically misled his own beloved people" (cf. G. Baum, *The Jews and the Gospel* [Westminster, 1961] 98–131).

170 (ii) *Accompanying signs* (19:23–37). The following passage is characteristically Johannine, even though most of the events that are related also appear in the Syn tradition. As he has so often done, particularly in the Book of Signs, but also elsewhere, John strives to remind his readers of the spiritual significance of all that Jesus had done and said: These things, too, were "signs" (see comment on 2:11).

23–24. All the Gospels mention the distribution of Jesus' garments. The clothing of the executed person belonged to the executioners by right. Probably, too, all the Evangelists (who say nothing of the distribution of the garments of the other two who were crucified) see in this fact the fulfillment of the typically messianic Ps 22:19, which John notes explicitly (Mk 15:34 par. cite Ps 22 as the "fourth word" of Christ from the cross). Only John notes that there were four soldiers, which was probably the number detailed regularly for such purposes (cf. Acts 12:4). Only John speaks of the "tunic without seam" worn by Jesus. The robe of the high priest is described in similar terms by Josephus (*Ant.* 3.7, 4 § 161), and rabbinic tradition also associates seamless robes with Moses (cf. Str-B 2, 573) and Adam; it is possible that John insinuates Christ's priestly character in the crucifixion, since it was forbidden to tear the high priest's garment (Lv 21:10). He may also be thinking of the tunic of Joseph (Gn 37:3), a type of Christ as one betrayed by his brothers and yet their Savior (cf. Acts 7:9–11; in Jn 2:5 the "woman" again to be introduced in vv. 25–27 alludes to Jesus in the character of Joseph). The Fathers who saw in the seamless robe a symbol of the unity of the Church, the heritage of Christ, contrasting with the division his coming had meant for the Jews (7:43; 9:16; 10:19), may also have correctly perceived John's meaning. **25.** Mk 15:40f. par. also mention women disciples present near the cross, but with the exception of Mary Magdalene it is not certain that the Syn and Jn intend to name the same women. *his mother's sister:* If she were to be identified with Salome (Mk), the mother of the sons of Zebedee (Mt), the evangelist John would have been the cousin of Jesus. However, the NT commonly distinguishes between James, the son of Zebedee, and another James whom it calls "the brother of Jesus." *Mary, the wife of Clopas:* Possibly the same as the mother of James and Joseph (Joses) in the Syn parallel, and if so (cf. Mt 13:55; Mk 6:3), probably a near relative of the mother of Jesus. *Mary Magdalene:* Aside from Lk 8:2 she is introduced into the Gospels only as a witness of the crucifixion and resurrection; her name evidently identifies her as a Galilean, from Magdala. **26–27.** *seeing his mother there along with the disciple whom he loved:* Only Jn mentions the presence of these two at the cross. What follows is perfectly understandable in itself, an act of filial piety characteristic of Jesus. It is also, however, a "sign" of the spiritual motherhood of Mary, the new Eve, the mother of the faithful. *woman:* See comment on 2:1–11. *the disciple:* When taken in conjunction with the other Johannine references (cf. esp. 13:23), the representative character of the beloved disciple becomes quite plain. *from that hour:* In its historical sense, this expression signifies that from this moment the disciple accepted Jesus' mother as his own. In the spiritual sense, which John also intends, we understand that the glorification on the cross has enacted the relationship that has just been signified.

171 **28.** *Jesus was aware...with the purpose...:* Even in death, Jesus remains in perfect command of events. Only in Jn is mention made of his implied request for drink, though Mt-Mk also narrate the incident of the sponge. The scriptural passage to which reference is made is Ps 69:22, another typically messianic Ps. **29.** *common wine:* This word (*oxos*) was used for the cheap vinegar wine in common use as a thirst-quencher. At least in Jn there is no indication that the gesture was not meant kindly by the soldiers. *on some hyssop:* The Gospels indicate that the crucified Jesus had been raised to a height that necessitated the sponge of wine being held up to him at the end of a stick. The Syn speak of "a reed." Jn's "hyssop" is puzzling, since this is a small leafy plant unsuited for the purpose mentioned. One ms. has *hyssos*, "javelin," but this is doubtless an unintentional error and certainly not the original reading. John probably has chosen the word for its symbolic potential, since it was with hyssop that the blood of the Passover lamb (cf. v. 36) was sprinkled on the doorposts as a sign of the divine protection (cf. Ex 12:22). **30.** *it is completed:* Jesus himself pronounces that the moment of his death has come, his work accomplished. *he handed over the spirit:* All the Evangelists use equivalent expressions, broadly the same as the Eng "expire." Only John, however, speaks of Jesus' death as a "handing over" of his spirit, doubtless because he also intends the reader to think of the Spirit that is given as a result of Jesus' glorification (7:39; 20:23).

172 **31.** John has yet another "sign" connected with Jesus' death to relate, an event not mentioned by the Syn. *Preparation day...sabbath:* It is from Jn that we learn of the coincidence of the Sabbath with Passover the year of Jesus' death (see 13:1), though the Syn also tell us that the Sabbath was coming and, therefore, that Jesus' crucifixion occurred on a Friday. The law of Dt 21:22f. forbade the body of an executed criminal exposed to public obloquy to remain beyond sunset. It was especially important that the bodies be removed and buried before the coming of the Sabbath, when such work could not be done. The Roman custom was to leave bodies of criminals exposed indefinitely, and in any case a crucified person might linger for several days before death overtook him (according to Mk 15:44, Pilate was surprised at the suddenness of Jesus' death). Here Pilate accedes to the Jewish custom, doubtless as anxious as were the Jews that nothing untoward should affect the coming Passover, when Roman-Jewish trouble might always be expected. *have the legs broken:* The legs were smashed with a mallet, a brutal yet merciful way of hastening the slow death of crucifixion. **32–34.** Since Jesus is evidently dead, his legs are not broken; however, to make sure of his death one of the soldiers thrusts a lance into his side. (The parallel account of the lance-thrust before the death of Christ found in some mss. of Mt 27:49 is an interpolation taken from Jn 19:34.) *blood and water flowed out:* This phenomenon can be explained medically (cf. A. F. Sava, *CBQ* 16 [1954] 438–43), but John is far more interested in it as a sign (cf. 1 Jn 5:8). With Christ's death and the giving of the Spirit, already signified in v. 30, the life-giving work of the Church begins, and hence the Church can be said in a sense to have been born from the wounded side of Christ (Ambrose, *PL* 15. 1585; cf. Thomas Aq., *Summa* 3.62,5; Pius XII, *Mystici Corporis* § 28). Water (cf. 3:5; 4:10,14; 7:38f.) and blood (cf. 6:53–57) have been already well established as signs of salvation, and it is most likely that John expected his readers to think specifically of the sacraments of baptism and the Eucharist, a common patristic interpretation. **35.** Such importance is attached to this incident that the Evangelist, or his editor(s) (→ 8 above), insist on the eyewitness testimony on which it depends (cf. 21:24); it is important chiefly in its character as "sign," as the following verses also bring out. *he knows to be true:* Presumably the "he" also refers to the witness, though it is possible that it refers to Christian experience in general. *that you may have faith as well:* See comment on 20:31. **36–37.** Two further significances occur to John in relation to the event just described. *none of its* [or, *his*] *bones is to be broken:* In all likelihood (cf. v. 29) John is thinking of the ritual of the Passover lamb (cf. Ex 12:46; Nm 9:12), though it is barely possible that he refers to Ps 34:21 (the persecuted just man, typical of the Messiah). *they shall look on him whom they have pierced:* Jn translates the Heb text of Zech 12:10, a passage that concerns one whose death was related to the outpouring of a fountain of divine mercy (cf. Zech 13:1).

173 (c) THE BURIAL OF THE LORD (19:38–42). Jn both follows and diverges from the Syn tradition in this section (cf. Mk 15:42–47 par.). **38.** *Joseph of Arimathea:* He is mentioned in the Syn account, but only Jn tells us that he was a secret disciple of Jesus (cf. 12:42). As a member of the Sanhedrin (cf. Mk 15:43), it was probably at the time of v. 31 that Joseph asked for the body of Jesus (the "afterward" with which Jn introduces this verse need not be pressed as a strictly chronological indication). **39–40.** *Nicodemus:* Mentioned only by John (cf. 3:1ff.; 7:50ff.). Probably he intends to say that Nicodemus, too, was a disciple and that only now did the two of them dare to come forth and declare themselves (cf. 12:32). The description of the burial preparations differs sharply from the Syn account (see 12:7). Jesus' body is bound (cf. 20:6f.) as was that of Lazarus (11:44). **41–42.** *in the place where he had been crucified:* There is nothing unlikely about the proximity of the place of execution to the tomb of Jesus; both would have been outside the city walls. The traditional site of the Holy Sepulcher in Jerusalem is in accord with the Gospel data. *a garden:* Jn uses the same word as in 18:1; it was an enclosed place, belonging to a private individual. The Syn tell us that the new tomb prepared in this place belonged to Joseph of Arimathea. As do the Syn, Jn notes that Jesus had to be buried in haste, and a final time (cf. vv. 29,31,36) he stresses the connection of these events with the Passover sacrifice.

174 (d) THE RESURRECTION AND GIVING OF THE SPIRIT (20:1–31). This narrative continues and concludes the story of Jesus' glorification. In the history of the resurrection we have the most fundamental and essential witness of the apostolic Church, the title to its claim to be the instrument of God's salvation in the world. John's treatment of the resurrection appearances is in complete harmony with the rest of his theology and brings this theology to a culmination.

(i) *Appearance to Mary Magdalene* (20:1–18). None of the Evangelists describes the actual resurrection itself (not even Mt 28:2–4), for it was witnessed by no one. The Gospels and 1 Cor 15:4–7 witness to the fact of the resurrection, however, by testimony to the empty tomb on Easter morning and the appearances of the Risen Christ to his disciples. It is not correct to distinguish two forms of this testimony as though the idea of the empty tomb had been an afterthought, an attempt to "objectivize" what had originally been subjective experiences of the disciples to whom Christ appeared after his death. The testimony to the empty tomb is also present, although implicitly, in the oldest of the written NT testimonies as found in 1 Cor (cf. G. Koch, *Die Auferstehung Jesu Christi* [Tübingen, 1959] 25–52). John's witness to the resurrection, then, though it is distinctively his own, is in no respect "later" than the rest of the NT testimony.

175 **1.** *early in the morning...:* All the Gospel accounts are in substantial agreement concerning the time when the tomb was first found to be empty, before dawn on Sunday morning. *Mary Magdalene:* She is named also by Mt-Mk together with companions; Lk gives no names but speaks of women in the plural. Though John's attention is confined to Mary Magdalene in view of the following vv. 11–18, he also indicates (by the "we" in v. 2) that she did not go alone. The unstated purposes of their going to the tomb, as well as the reference to "the stone," presuppose a knowledge of the Syn tradition. **2.** *she ran off to Simon Peter and to the other disciple:* Mk 16:7 relates that the women were told to announce the resurrection to Peter and the other disciples; John is the only evangelist to single out the beloved disciple, understandably (→ 3 above; cf. 18:15f.). *the Lord has been taken out of the tomb:* Mary Magdalene's report, coupled with what follows, does not seem to presuppose the angelic appearances to the women at the tomb narrated by the Syn. John may have taken it for granted that Mary left before the others and sought out the disciples on her own. However, we are probably not meant to harmonize the various accounts completely, since their incidental divergences testify both to independent oral transmission (cf. also 1 Cor 15:4–7) and to the separate preoccupations of the individual transmitters of the tradition. Though in a different order, the Johannine equivalent of the angelic appearances of Mk 16:5–8 par. is really in vv. 11–18. **3–7.** Lk 24:24 doubtless refers to this account; the more precise parallel in Lk 24:12, lacking in some mss., is at least of uncertain authenticity. There is probably no symbolism involved in the various details of this story, which appears to be rather the graphic recollection of an eyewitness. **8–10.** *he saw and believed:* What the beloved disciple saw was the empty burial cloths described in such detail in v. 6f. Probably this description is meant to convey the idea that the cloths had preserved the contours of the body that had been bound by them, thus offering visual evidence of a resurrection. The intention is not necessarily to contrast the beloved disciple with Peter: Peter had seen the evidence first (cf. 1 Cor 15:5), and therefore John may be saying that the beloved disciple also believed. *as yet they did not understand the scripture:* This parenthetical verse reminds the Christian reader that as the Holy Spirit had not yet come to enlighten the Church concerning the divine mysteries, it should not cause surprise that the disciples were so slow in coming to a realization of the resurrection (cf. 2:22; 14:26).

176 **11.** John evidently supposes Mary Magdalene to have returned to the tomb with the disciples or shortly after them. Her attitude is still that of one who thinks that for some reason the body of the Lord has been taken away. **12–13.** This account is similar to that of Lk 24:3–6, especially in the Syn version of the events that places the women at the tomb only one time (cf. also Mk 16:5f.). **14–15.** The Johannine device of misunderstanding characteristic of the dialogues (→ 30 above) finds an echo in Mary's failure to recognize Jesus himself (cf. also 21:4); Lk 24:16 records something similar. Mary takes the unknown person to be the owner of the garden or his overseer, one who would be likely to know who had disturbed the tomb. Mt 28:1,9f. also speaks of an appearance of the Lord to Mary Magdalene (and "the other Mary") on Easter morning, though in a different version of the story. *tell me where you put him, and I will take him away:* Mary speaks the language of love, not even considering whether what she offers to do would be possible for her. **16.** It is sufficient for Jesus to call Mary by name for her to recognize him; John gives no explanation of the fact, but he probably wants us to recall Jesus' words in 10:3f. *Rabboni:* This was a variant form of "Rabbi" (cf. Mk 10:51); the qualifying "in Hebrew" (that is, "Aramaic"), omitted in some mss., may be a gloss. The disciples have frequently called Jesus "Rabbi" during his earthly ministry, though sometimes as a preliminary to higher titles (cf. 1:38ff.; 3:2ff.). Jesus' words to Mary in the following verse may also indicate that this title is no longer adequate in its contrast with the terms used by Thomas in v. 28 (cf. G. Dalman, *Words of Jesus*, 340). **17.** *stop touching me, for I have not yet ascended to the Father:* Mary had evidently thrown herself at Jesus' feet and was attempting to demonstrate her love by throwing her arms about his knees. Jesus must tell her, however, that the old relationships are no more, and he must not be hindered in completing the drama of his glorification. Now he must return to the Father, thus accomplishing the destiny that has been the goal of his entire earthly life (cf. 6:62; 7:33; 13:1; etc.). *my Father—your Father, my God—your God:* Jesus does not simply say "our Father," for though the Father of Christ and of Christians is one and the same, the relationship differs in that the Christian acquires his sonship through the only Son who has it by right. *my brothers:* The disciples (cf. Mt 28:10); cf. also 2:12. **18.** See Lk 24:9f.; the Syn indicate that the disciples did not believe the report that was brought to them. Nothing is less likely than that the belief in the resurrection was the illusion of a community that had been eagerly awaiting such a thing.

177 (ii) *Appearance to the disciples* (20:19–23). A resurrection appearance to the disciples is attested by 1 Cor 15:5. Whether Jn means that only ten were present (the Twelve less Judas and Thomas) or that there was a larger group (cf. Lk 24:33) is not certain. This and the following episode constitute the Johannine conclusion to the history of the exaltation of Christ, and the contrast with the preceding section is significant.

19. *on the evening of that first day of the week:* Note that in what follows John's attention is still fixed on Easter Sunday. *the disciples had shut the doors:* Jn does not explain but simply notes as a fact the spiritual qualities of the resurrected body of Christ (cf. 1 Cor 15:44). *peace be with you:*

Cf. 14:27; 16:33. **20.** *he showed them his hands and his side:* Though the resurrected body of Christ possesses spiritual qualities, the essence of the resurrection testimony of the NT is to the return of the very Jesus of Nazareth whom the first witnesses had known familiarly (cf. 1 Jn 1:1–3). The resurrection, in other words, did not simply imply individual experiences of Christian disciples convinced that Jesus had somehow survived death. Hence the emphasis in the NT on the empty tomb and on details such as this testifying to the continued existence of the historical Jesus. Here reference is made to the wound in Jesus' side and to nail marks on his hands (cf. vv. 25–27). This is the only explicit evidence from the Gospel that Jesus was nailed rather than tied (as was often the custom) to the cross; Lk 24:39 also implies that the feet were nailed. *this brought the disciples joy:* Cf. 16:22; Lk 24:37 stresses instead the fear and amazement of the disciples at what had occurred. **21.** The resurrected Christ confers upon his disciples the mission of which he spoke in 17:18 (cf. 4:38; 13:20). This is the commission of the Church to perpetuate the work of divine salvation accomplished in Christ. **22.** *he breathed on them:* This is a parable in action, a sign, a sacrament, to indicate the conferring of the Spirit (*pneuma* — breath, spirit; cf. 3:8). Jn uses the same verb as in the Gk text of Gn 2:7 to describe this new creation. *receive the Holy Spirit:* The giving of the Holy Spirit was contingent on Jesus' glorification (7:39), on his return to the Father (15:26; 16:7). In v. 17 he told Mary Magdalene that he had not yet ascended to the Father but that his ascension was imminent. From the present verse we see that this ascension has now taken place; thus, in the Johannine perspective, resurrection, ascension, and the coming of the Spirit take place on one and the same Easter Sunday. This perspective is not necessarily in conflict with the Lucan portrayal of the ascension and Pentecostal coming of the Spirit as events separated from the resurrection in time (see Lk 24:49–53; Acts 1:3–11; 2:1ff.); however, what must be borne in mind is that the NT authors are in every case concerned with historical mysteries primarily and with chronologies and statistical circumstances secondarily (cf. E. Schillebeeckx, *Worship* 35 [1961] 336–63). What Jn insists on is the intimate connection of the resurrection with the animation of the Church by the Spirit (cf. 1 Cor 15:45), something that has always been reflected in the liturgy and teaching of the Church. **23.** The giving of the Spirit is here specifically related to the power given to the Church to continue the judicial character of Christ (3:19; 5:27; 9:39) in the matter of sin (cf. Mt 9:8; 16:19; 18:18; Lk 24:47). Catholic tradition (DB 920; DS 1710) has rightly seen in this act the origin of the Sacrament of Penance, even though it is equally true that the Church's power over sin is also exercised in baptism and the preaching of the redemptive word.

178 (iii) *Appearance to the disciples and Thomas* (20:24–29). There seems to be no doubt that John originally intended this episode to be the culmination and conclusion of the Gospel. Having exposed all the divine mysteries inherent in Christ's death and resurrection, and having provided an historical account providentially designed to establish the fact of the resurrection beyond all question, he concluded by citing the most explicit expression of faith to be found in the Gospels.

24–25. *the Twelve:* This designation of the first apostolic band remained even though one of them had defected. "Doubting Thomas" (mentioned earlier in 11:16; 14:5) expresses in Jn the incredulity that the Syn indicate was shared by other disciples. **26–27.** *a week later:* This appearance also takes place on a Sunday; this emphasis almost certainly means that Sunday had by John's time become the special day of Christian assembly and liturgy. Christ appears under the same circumstances as before. For the significance of the reference to hands and side, see comment on v. 20 above. **28.** The Lord's invitation to Thomas contrasts with his prohibition to Mary Magdalene in v. 17; for the reason, see comment on v. 22. Whether Thomas actually touched the Lord is not said, and the point is immaterial. *my Lord and my God:* Paradoxically, it is the "doubter" who makes the most complete affirmation of Christ's nature to be found on the lips of anyone in the Gospel. The combination "Lord and God" (*kyrios theos*) is to be found in the LXX to translate the name of the God of Israel (*Yahwēh 'Elôhîm*); it was also a combination used as a divine designation in the Hellenistic world. We are brought back, then, to the affirmation of the first line of the Gospel, as Thomas speaks the language that became the common Christian confession concerning Christ (cf. Acts 2:36; Ti 2:13; Heb 1:8f.). **29.** *you have believed...believe without seeing:* Christ's words also transcend the little group present and address themselves to all Christians of all time (cf. 1 Pt 1:8). As important as the resurrection appearances are for the testimony of the primitive Church, it remains a fact that it is the Word itself, the Gospel, which is the power of God (Rom 1:16), that will always continue to be the real and only adequate motive of faith (cf. 17:20). Miracles, historical evidence, even tactual evidence such as that presented to Thomas, can assist the seeker of faith, but it is in the preaching of the message itself that the grace of God is to be found, in which the issue of faith or disbelief is finally engaged (cf. 4:48; 10:38).

179 (iv) *Conclusion: The meaning of these signs* (20:30–31). It is on this note that John concludes his Gospel. He says, in effect: The first disciples believed, seeing Christ's visible presence; but you, who have not seen it, yet have as much reason to believe. You have the eyewitness testimony of this Gospel, and you have in the living presence of the Church the "signs" that have been pointed out here from among many (see comment on 2:11); the Church, which manifests the life of the Spirit, therefore manifests Jesus himself, his saving word and his saving ministration. *so that you may have faith:* The best reading of the mss. is the pres. tense rather than the aorist, therefore meaning "that you may continue to believe," "grow in faith"; Jn's Gospel has been written for Christian readers, to deepen their faith and understanding. *in his name:* See comment on 1:12.

180 **(IV) Appendix or Epilogue: Appearance in Galilee (21:1–25).** There can hardly be any doubt that ch. 21 is an appendix added to the Gospel that had already been concluded with ch. 20. What remains in doubt is whether the addition was made by the Evangelist himself, the author of chs. 1–20. Although no apodictic answer can be made to this question, a number of considerations lead to the probable conclusion that it is the work of disciples subsequent to the death of the Evangelist (→ 8 above; see the linguistic and other evidence in Bultmann, *Das Evangelium*, 542–47). The appendix appears to have been composed of testimony from the same witness who stands behind chs. 1–20, but the testimony is parallel to rather than a part of the preceding unities, and hence the chapter has not been completely integrated with the rest of the Gospel. Whoever its literary author, however, the ms. evidence indicates that it was a part of the Gospel from the beginning, that is, presumably, from the time of the Gospel's publication subsequent to the death of the Evangelist. Concerning the canonicity and inspiration of the chapter, there has never been any doubt. The reasons for the addition of this supplement will appear from the matters with which it deals.

(Besobrasoff, S. [Bishop Cassian], "John XXI," *NTS* 3 [1956–57] 132–36. Boismard, M.-E., "Le chapitre XXI de Saint Jean. Essai de critique littéraire," *RB* 54 [1947] 473–501. Vaganay, L., "La finale du Quatrième Évangile," *RB* 45 [1936] 512–28.)

181 (A) Jesus with the Disciples by the Sea (21:1–14). In this supplement the Gospel of Jn joins with Mt (see also Mk 16:7), who places in Galilee the appearance of the resurrected Jesus to the disciples; Lk and Jn 20 speak only of appearances in Jerusalem. There is no attempt in Jn to harmonize the Galilean history of the appearances (which seems to be the older of the Gospel traditions) with the Jerusalemite; no explanation is given for the sudden departure of the disciples from Jerusalem and their return to their former pursuits.

1. *some time afterward:* The time indication is very general (cf. 3:22; 5:1; 6:1; 7:1) and does not necessarily refer to any specific event preceding. "Again" is found in some mss. either before or after the word "appeared"; this seems to be an attempt to tie this originally independent chapter more closely to the rest of the Gospel. *the Sea of Tiberias:* Only here in the Gospels is this name used (see comment on 6:1). **2.** Seven disciples are mentioned, of whom the first three are familiar to us from John's Gospel. *Zebedee's sons:* This designation is of the Syn tradition; they are not mentioned elsewhere in Jn. *two other disciples:* Why these are not named is not clear; however, John has used such anonymity before (cf. 1:35).
182 **3–4.** The return of the disciples to their former homes and occupations is really plausible only when we recognize that this chapter was originally independent of ch. 20 and that the Jerusalem appearances are not presupposed. Similarly, the failure of the disciples to recognize Jesus (as in 20:14; Lk 24:16) sounds like the usual concomitant of an initial appearance of the Lord. The reason for the inclusion of this narrative will appear, however, from v. 11. **5–6.** The scene described is taken from the familiar life of Galilee. Even the directions to cast the nets on the right side (the lucky side) of the boat would not necessarily imply superhuman knowledge (though the Gospel probably understands it as such in view of the following verse), for a man standing on shore could often see a school of fish hidden from the view of those in the boat. The narrative is reminiscent of that in Lk 5:4ff., which the Third Gospel has placed at the beginning of the Galilean ministry. **7.** *that disciple whom Jesus loved* [→ 3 above]*:* In this chapter he is associated with Peter as so often before (13:23f.; 20:2; 18:15?) and is the first to recognize the Lord (cf. 20:4). Probably the superabundant draught of fish is to be regarded as a "sign," recalling the great quantity of wine at Cana (2:6), the multiplication of the loaves (6:11), the living water (4:14; 7:37ff.), the eternal life given by the Good Shepherd (10:10), and the plenitude of the Spirit (3:34). *Simon Peter wrapped his outer garment around him:* The Jews were sensitive about performing greetings without being properly clad. Peter's precipitate action is typical of the man as he is portrayed in the Gospels. **8–9.** Nothing further is said of Peter's action, but the rest of the disciples are immediately brought into the scene with Christ. The meal prepared by the Lord cannot but recall the multiplication of the loaves (6:9), in turn a sign of the Eucharist, the distribution of the life of the Spirit. **10–11.** *bring some of the fish:* This request is not to be explained in connection with the meal, which has already been prepared. It is probable, rather, that the Lord's purpose is to stress the role of fishing as symbolizing the apostolic mission (cf. Mt 4:19; Mk 1:17; Lk 5:10). *one hundred and fifty-three:* Most commentators, ancient and modern, have felt that this number is meant as a symbol, but there has been no agreement as to its nature. Since, as appears likely, the fish symbolize those who will be brought into the Church through the apostolic preaching (and thus, the net that remains untorn may have the same meaning as Christ's tunic in 19:23f.), Jerome's interpretation is attractive (*PL* 25. 474), namely that ancient zoologists calculated the species of fish at precisely 153. The meaning, then, would refer to all the kinds of men for whom the disciples will "fish," and we could have here an echo of Jesus' words in Mt 13:47 (cf. also Ez 47:9f.). Unfortunately, in the work to which Jerome refers in justification of his statement (the *Halieutica* of Oppian), no such reference can be found. It has been noted that 153 is the "triangular" number of 17 (1 + 2 + 3 ... + 17 = 153), but what 17 would then signify is not clear. For Barrett the significance is in the numbers 7 and 10, numbers of completeness and perfection, thus representing "the full total of the catholic and apostolic Church." Others appeal to *gematria* (the numerical value of letters), a symbolic form much in use by the Jews (see Ap 13:18), but the variety of words that can be formed whose numerical equivalent is 153 (Gk? Aram? Hebr?) is endless and much dependent on subjective judgments (cf. H. Kruse, *VD* 38 [1960] 129–48, who favors the Hebr *q*^{e}*hal hā'*^{a}*hābā*, "the Church of love"). **12–13.** In Lk 24:42f. there is a scene in which the Risen Christ takes a meal with the disciples, but its purpose is different. Here it is not said that Jesus himself partook of the food but that he distributed it: Again this recalls the language of 6:11, of the miracle of the loaves that took place beside this same lake. Again there is a Lucan parallel (cf. Lk 24:30f.,35). *not one of the disciples dared to inquire of him, "Who are you?":* Cf. 4:27; 8:25. Some see in this a fulfillment of 16:23, but it seems rather that the disciples, while recognizing the Jesus they have known, are at the same time overawed by what has taken place in him through the resurrection, and dare not attempt to penetrate the mystery further (Bultmann). **14.** *the third time:* This verse is the work of the author(s) of this chapter, who thus connects it with ch. 20 (the appearance to Mary Magdalene is not counted).

183 (B) Peter's Commission (21:15–19). The NT is at one in ascribing primacy to Peter in the apostolic Church (cf. Gal 2:11ff., Paul resisted even Peter; Acts 1–15 *passim*), and that by the Lord's own decree (Mt 16:18). As do the other Gospels, Jn has consistently brought out Peter's special position from the significant note of the change of his name in 1:42. In this present section of the supplement the Johannine witness to Peter's primacy has been appended to complete the Gospel testimony.

15–17. The traditional interpretation, that the Lord's threefold question demanding a threefold profession of love is to correspond to Peter's threefold denial, is doubtless correct. *do you love me more than these?:* The question is artfully phrased, and Peter proves equal to the test. Previously he had been serenely confident of himself (13:37; in Mk 14:29 he contrasts his fidelity with that of the other disciples); now he will assume nothing to himself nor will he pretend to compare his love with any other's, but he humbly asserts what the Lord already knows concerning his love. Two different words are used for "love" in this passage, but in Jn they have been used consistently as synonyms; similarly, probably no distinction is intended in the use of the words "lambs" and "sheep." *feed my sheep:* Christ concedes his own office of Shepherd to Peter (10:4,27; cf. Acts 20:28; 1 Pt 2:25; 5:2–4). **18–19.** It will be the destiny of Peter to follow the Good Shepherd in every detail, even to the laying down of his life (10:11). *when you were a young man... but when you get old...:* Materially, the Lord's words mean little more than: In youth a man may go freely where he wills, but in old age he must let himself be led where he wills not (Bultmann). But as is so often the case, there is a meaning beneath the surface, which Jn's readers would easily recognize. *you will stretch out your hands, and another will tie you fast:* Similar expressions are used by contemporary Christian and non-Christian writers to refer to crucifixion. It is to this that the author refers in v. 19 (cf. 12:33), noting the pregnant meaning of the Lord's "Follow me." This is the oldest written attestation to the tradition of Peter's martyrdom by crucifixion, an event well known to the Christians for whom this Gospel was written.

184 **(C) The Beloved Disciple (21:20–23).** This final short section has an understandable interest for the editors of the Gospel, in view of its reference to the witness whose testimony is enshrined in it. From these verses, it appears very likely that the beloved disciple had recently died, the last representative of the original apostolic band, and that the record of this saying of the Lord has been included in order to correct a misunderstanding that had become associated with it.

20–21. The Lord has just bidden Peter to follow him, and Peter now sees the beloved disciple doing just that, which prompts his question. *Lord, what about him?:* In context, this can only mean, what kind of death will he suffer? **22.** The Gospels agree that it was Jesus' practice to turn aside questions that were not pertinent or that reflected mere curiosity. Thus in Lk 13:23ff., in answer to a question about the relative number of the saved, he replies instead by stressing the difficulty of salvation. Here he tells Peter that the death of the beloved disciple is none of his concern. *suppose I would like him to remain until I come:* Jesus neither affirms nor denies the possibility; to do either would be to satisfy Peter's idle curiosity. **23.** But the very ambiguity of the answer, it seems, had created the impression in some quarters that the beloved disciple would not die before the Lord's coming, that is, in the parousia. Similar statements recorded in the Gospels (cf. Mk 9:1; Mt 24:34) had unquestionably contributed to the persuasion of many in the primitive Church that the parousia would be imminent (cf. 2 Thes 2), that it would occur before the end of the apostolic age. The most obvious sense of this verse is that the beloved disciple, the last of the apostolic age, has recently died, and this narrative has been included to explain that there had never been any promise otherwise.

185 **(D) Final Testimony (21:24–25).** We now read the conclusion of the final editors of the Gospel. *it is this same disciple who is the witness for these things:* It is the beloved disciple who is the author of the foregoing Gospel (→ 3 above). *it is he who wrote these things:* The question of the actual literary composition of the Gospel is, of course, not solved by this attestation; just as 19:19 says, literally, that "Pilate wrote a title," when the sense is that he was responsible for its being written, so here. *his testimony, we know, is true:* The community attests its acceptance of the testimony in the person of the disciples responsible for the finished Gospel. As in 20:30 the selective nature of the testimony is again pointed out. The famous hyperbole at the end stresses, of course, not so much the factual information available about Jesus as the potentialities it possessed for a theological understanding such as that of Jn.

64

THE APOCALYPSE

Jean-Louis D'Aragon, S.J.

BIBLIOGRAPHY

1 Allo, E.-B., *Saint Jean: L'Apocalypse* (EBib; 4th ed.; Paris, 1953). Behm, J., *Die Offenbarung des Johannes* (NTD 11; 6th ed.; Göttingen, 1953). Boismard, M.-E., *L'Apocalypse* (BJ; Paris, 1950). Bonsirven, J., *L'Apocalypse de Saint Jean* (VS 16; Paris, 1951). Bousset, W., *Die Offenbarung Johannis* (Meyer 16; 6th ed.; Göttingen, 1906). Caird, G. B., *A Commentary on the Revelation of St. John the Divine* (BNTC; London, 1966). Charles, R. H., *Revelation* (ICC; 2 vols.; Edinburgh, 1920). Farrer, A., *The Revelation of St. John the Divine* (Oxford, 1964). Feuillet, A., *The Apocalypse* (Staten Island, N.Y., 1964). Glasson, T. F., *The Revelation of John* (CNEB; Cambridge, 1965). Kiddle, M. and M. K. Ross, *The Revelation of St. John* (MNTC; London, 1940). Lilje, H., *The Last Book of the Bible* (Phila., 1957). Lohmeyer, E., *Die Offenbarung des Johannes* (HNT 16; 2nd ed.; Tübingen, 1953); "Die Offenbarung des Johannes, 1920–34," *TRu* 6 (1934) 269–314; *TRu* 7 (1935) 28–62. Lohse, E., *Die Offenbarung des Johannes* (NTD 11; 8th ed.; Göttingen, 1960). Preston, R. H. and A. T. Hanson, *The Revelation of Saint John the Divine* (TBC; London, 1949). Rist, M. and L. H. Hough, *The Revelation of St. John the Divine* (*IB* 12; N.Y., 1957). Swete, H. B., *The Apocalypse of St. John* (3rd ed.; London, 1909). Wikenhauser, A., *Die Offenbarung des Johannes* (RNT 9; 3rd ed.; Regensburg, 1959). Zahn, T., *Die Offenbarung des Johannes* (Leipzig, 1924–26).

Wik, *NTI* 534–63. Guthrie, *NTI* 2, 251–302, R-F, *INT* 691–722, F-B 318–33.

INTRODUCTION

2 **(I) Literary Character.** It has often been said that the Ap is the most obscure NT book. The author resorts regularly to expressions and categories of thought that seem strange, even disconcerting, to Western readers. For this reason a delineation of the book's literary character is particularly useful. It has been influenced, in varying degrees, by three literary forms: (a) apocalyptic, (b) prophetic, and (c) epistolary.

3 (a) The title (1:1–3) establishes an explicit link between the Ap and the apocalyptic tradition (→ Post-exilic Period 20:21–24): It is defined as an "apocalypse"; the message it contains concerns "what must take place soon," i.e. the unraveling of history as determined by God. The revelation of so mysterious a matter can ultimately be made only by God, who conveys it to John through visions by an intermediary angel.

The book as a whole fully confirms what the title announces: Symbols, so cherished by apocalyptic writers, are in evidence everywhere; their presence is explicitly signaled (1:20), and their meaning is sometimes explained (5:6,8; 13:18; 17:9–18). The predilection for symbolism connects the Ap in general with the Semitic tradition (1 Kgs 11:30–32; Is 20:2–4; Jer 13:1–11; 19:1ff.,10ff.). Apocalyptic reveals itself, here again, as the heir of prophetism in developing and in adding precision to the use of symbols. Most of the symbols of the Ap are borrowed from the prophetical tradition continued by apocalyptic: e.g., a *woman* represents a people (12:1ff.) or a city (17:1ff.); *horns* speak of power (5:6; 12:3), in particular, dynastic power (13:1; 17:3ff.); *eyes*, knowledge (1:14; 2:18; 4:6; 5:6); and *wings*, mobility (4:8; 12:14). In the *trumpets* is heard a superhuman, divine voice (1:10; 8:2ff.); a *sharp sword* indicates the Word of God, which judges and punishes (1:16; 2:12,16; 19:15,21). *White robes* signify the world of glory (6:11; 7:9,13f.; 22:14); *palms* are the sign of triumph (7:9), *crowns*, of dominion and kingship (2:10; 3:11; 4:10; 6:2; 12:1; 14:14); the *sea* is an evil element, source of insecurity and death (13:1; 21:1). *White* indicates the joy of victory (1:14; 2:17; 3:4f.,18; 4:4; 6:11; 7:9,13; 19:11,14); *purple*, luxury and kingship (17:4; 18:12,16); *black*, death (6:5,12).

4 Symbolic numbers acquire a considerable importance: *Seven* (54 times) signifies fullness, perfection; *twelve* (23 times) recalls the 12 tribes of Israel and indicates that the people of God has reached its eschatological perfection; *four* (16 times) symbolizes the universality of the visible world; also worth mentioning: *three* (11 times), *ten* (10 times) and *a thousand* (6 times in ch. 20; often in multiples). Three cases are intriguing: The duration of the persecution is given as either 1260 days (11:3; 12:6), 42 months (11:2; 13:5), or three years and a half (12:14); 144,000 "follow the Lamb wherever he goes" (7:4–8; 14:1–5); finally, the Beast is referred to by the number 666 (13:18). See K. L. Schmidt, *TZ* 3 (1947)

161–77; A. Farrer, *A Rebirth of Images* (Westminster, 1949); J. Cambier, *NRT* 77 (1955) 113–22.

This intensive recourse to symbols is intended, as in apocalyptic, to suggest the ineffable mystery that is spoken of but can never be defined. The transcendence of the truths proposed is also evoked by other means. Their revelation is made possible only by the intervention of the Spirit, who ravishes John (1:10; 4:2), to whom all is communicated through visions (54 times). Moreover, an angel (67 times) must at all times intervene and supply explanations to the seer, who even is carried to the desert (17:3) or to the top of a high mountain (21:10).

5 John—like other apocalyptic writers—presents himself as part of a group persecuted for its faith (1:9). He sets himself the task of strengthening his brethren by unraveling to them the meaning of the oppression they are enduring and the glorious goal of their suffering. From the standpoint of mere appearances, a confrontation is taking place between the Roman Empire and the Christian Church, but, in point of fact, Satan and God lead these two groups; and so there can exist absolutely no doubt as to the result of the battle. With the final victory that Christ, in the name of God, shall win over Satan and his followers, the heavenly Jerusalem, an entirely new world created by God, shall be inaugurated; all faithful Christians shall be citizens of this new Jerusalem. Such a view of the unfolding of history, understood as two opposed powers and divided into successive eras, is in every way typical of apocalyptic theology.

6 However, it would be a mistake to reduce the Ap completely to the apocalyptic form. Unlike the apocalyptic writers who claim to reveal the mysteries of cosmogony, of astronomy, and of the unfolding of ancient history since the beginning of the world, John directs the attention of his readers to the present and its eschatological conclusion. He does not have recourse to the artifice of pseudonymity by placing his book under the authority of a famous man of the past; he discloses his name (1:1,4,9; 22:8), thus indicating that he is well known to the communities addressed. Nor does the Ap borrow the prestige of an archaic writing, sealed, containing mysterious and esoteric wisdom destined to be revealed only to a small group of the privileged. On the contrary, his book is addressed to seven churches in Asia, which probably represent the universal Church (see 1:4). Finally, the Ap differs from the Jewish apocalypses by its Christological conception of history: Christ is closely associated with God who governs all things; he is the Lamb who has redeemed his people (5:9f.) and who shall lead it to the final victory (19:11ff.; see T. Holtz, *Die Christologie der Apokalypse des Johannes* [Berlin, 1962]).

7 It is surprising that John, so aware of the apocalyptic stream of thought, quotes no known extrabiblical apocalypse. The Ap contains numerous allusions to the OT. It is true that John does not explicitly introduce any quotation, but his book is literally woven with reminiscences of the OT: Of 404 verses, 278 contain at least one OT excerpt. The books that have influenced the Ap most are the Prophets (mainly Dn, Ez, Is, Zech), the Pss, and Ex.

(Lohse, E., *ZNW* 52 [1961] 122–26. Mollat, D., *San Giovanni* [Brescia, 1964] 345–61. Vanhoye, A., *Bib* 43 [1962] 436–76.)

8 (b) Prophetic. In fact, John conceives his mission as similar to that of the ancient prophets (10:11); like them, he is called and given a mandate in an inaugural vision (1:9–20); he hears the word of God (1:2) and is ordered to transmit it to his brethren (the order to write is repeated 11 times). He frequently describes his book as a "prophecy" (1:3; 19:10; 22:7,10,18f.), whereas the title "apocalypse" (1:1) is used only once. The expression "the prophets" appears only twice in Jewish apocalypses, in the Ap it is repeated seven times (10:7; 11:8; 16:6; 18:20,24; 22:6,9). All these details are indications of the author's awareness of belonging to the great prophetical tradition. And so the Ap is NT prophecy par excellence (→ Prophetic Lit, 12:23).

9 (c) Epistolary. A third literary form has made a superficial imprint on the Ap. The book is framed (1:4–6; 22:21) with the customary Christian epistolary formulas (→ NT Epistles, 47:6–8). Moreover, the message conveyed to each of the seven churches (2:1–3:22) takes the form of a letter. The directness of tone, characteristic of the epistle, expresses sensibly the communion of spirit existing between John and those whom he addresses.

10 **(II) Authorship.** The Ap gives a few details about its author: His name is "John" (1:1,4,9; 22:8), he ranks himself among the prophets (22:9), and attributes to himself such general titles as "servant" of God (1:1), "brother and companion in tribulation" of those whom he is addressing (1:9). His stay on the island of Patmos (1:10) very probably followed a banishment imposed by the Roman authorities. The letters that he sends to the seven churches (2:1–3:22) show that he was well known to the Christians of Asia and that he enjoyed an uncontested authority.

From the 2nd cent. on, two questions have usually been asked about the author of the Ap: What was the relationship between this "John" and the apostle John? Was the seer of the Ap also the author of the Johannine Gospel and epistles?

The traditional answers date back considerably. In the first half of the 2nd cent. the unknown author of the *Apocryphon of John* (see A. Helmbold, *NTS* 8 [1961–62] 77–79), Papias (according to Andrew of Caesarea), and Justin Martyr (*Dialogue with Trypho* 81.4) attribute the Ap to the apostle John. From *ca.* 150 until *ca.* 250 similar evidence is found not only in the East (Melito of Sardis [Eusebius, *HE* 4.26, 2]; Clement of Alexandria, *Paed.* 2.119, 1; *Quis div. salv.* 42; Origen, *Comm. in Ioan.* 2.5 § 45), but also in the West (Irenaeus, *Adv. haer.* 4.30, 4; 5.26, 1; Hippolytus, *Antichr.* 36; 50; Antimarcionite Prologue to Luke; Tertullian, *Adv. Marc.* 3.14; 4.5).

From the 3rd cent. on, dissenting voices are suddenly heard. In the West they are rare and only slightly influential: the Roman priest Gaius and the Alogi. In the East, however, the opponents of the apostolic origin of the Ap, and thus of its canonicity (→ Canonicity, 67:68), are numerous and important. The most serious among them, Dionysius of Alexandria (d. 264/65), does not depend on a prior tradition. On the basis of a careful comparison of the language, style, and thought of Jn and 1 Jn with the Ap, he concludes that only Jn and 1 Jn are the work of the apostle John, whereas the Ap would have been written by John the Presbyter (Eusebius, *HE* 3.39; 7.25, 16). Disturbed by the excesses of chiliasm, a heresy based on the 1000-year reign mentioned in Ap 20:1–6, most of the bishops of Syria and Asia Minor reject the Ap. The School of Antioch refuses to accept it as apostolic, and the Syrian Church, on the whole, always continues to reject this book. Several canonical lists of the Eastern Churches omit the Ap, and many Gk mss. before the 9th cent. do not contain it. Under the influence of Athanasius, however a certain unanimity is slowly established in the East. In the West no real difficulty arises, and the Ap as well as Jn and 1–3 Jn are accepted as the work of the apostle John.

11 Until the 16th cent. no objection is raised against this common agreement. Then Erasmus steps forward to question once more the identity of authorship of the Ap and Jn and the epistles. For Luther the Ap is neither apostolic nor prophetic. Since the end of the 18th cent. biblical scholars increasingly tend to deny the apostolic origin of the Ap and its relation to Jn. Today, most Catholic and some Protestant exegetes hold the two traditional views. A small group of non-Catholics reject the apostolic origin of the Ap, but maintain that this book was edited by the author of Jn. On the other hand, some think that the apostle John wrote the Ap, but not the Gospel. Finally many critics deny that there is any relationship between the son of Zebedee and either the Ap or Jn and attribute the two books to different authors of whom very little is known.

Several internal indications seem to bring the Ap and the Fourth Gospel closely together, at least to the point that the two books had some sort of common origin. It is striking to note, for example, that some details are found nowhere in the NT except in these two books: Christ is presented as "the Lamb" (Jn 1:29,36, and 28 times in the Ap, but with different Gk words); his name is the "Word of God" (Jn 1:1,14; Ap 19:13); the image of "the spouse" recalls the People of God (Jn 3:29; Ap 21:2,9; 22:17); life is symbolized by water in expressions like "the living water" (Jn 4:10f.; 7:38) and "the water of life" (Ap 7:17; 21:6; 22:1,17); Zech 12:10 is cited by both works (Jn 19:37; Ap 1:7) in a form that differs from the LXX; the absence of a temple in the new Jerusalem (Ap 21:22) is a conception similar to that of Jn 4:21.

12 However, it must be admitted that numerous details separate the two works. The differences in language and eschatological perspective are often underlined. Whereas the Greek of the Gospel is simple and ordinarily correct, that of the Ap is so sprinkled with solecisms and barbarisms that one must suppose that the author was a Judeo-Christian who thought in Aramaic and translated his thoughts into Greek, of which he possessed only a rudimentary knowledge. The eschatology of the Ap is dominated by the viewpoint and the symbols of the apocalyptic tradition, which hopes for a future that will bring with it the salvation that God is going to give to his people. The Gospel, on the contrary, proves itself to be very independent of apocalyptic and considers salvation almost always as already possessed by the believer. Several notions that are central in the Gospel seldom appear in the Ap; indeed, some are not found anywhere: e.g., the vb. "to believe" (98 times in Jn, but never in the Ap), "faith" (4 times in the Ap, but totally absent from Jn), "the world" (separated from or hostile to God), "the truth,"... (see R. H. Charles, *Revelation*, 1, xxix–xxxvii; E.-B. Allo, *Saint Jean*, clxxxi–cciii).

All of these data make it possible to understand why exegetes have taken such divergent positions. The fragmentary state of our present knowledge does not permit us to propose a categorical solution.

13 It is generally admitted that the author of the Ap has left us his real name. Having examined the hypothesis of pseudonymity, Charles peremptorily concludes: "There is not a shred of evidence, not even the shadow of a probability, for the hypothesis that the Apocalypse is pseudonymous" (*Revelation*, 1, xxxix). The evidence of tradition that affirms the apostolic and single origin of all the Johannine writings is so old and copious that it is impossible to discard it completely. It seems very difficult to explain how all the witnesses of the 2nd cent. could have been mistaken. The few, but significant, coincidences between the Ap and Jn seem to postulate at least a certain common origin for both books. However, the many differences show rather clearly that the Ap and the Gospel cannot have been written by the same author. While we wait for a more definite solution, the suggestion of a few recent Catholic authors (e.g., F.-M. Braun, A. Feuillet), following C. K. Barrett, should be given due consideration: According to tradition the apostle John was the great authority in Asia until about the end of the 1st cent.; he would have inspired all the Johannine writings, perhaps through a catechetical school at Ephesus, but the redaction would have been carried out by different disciples, more or less familiar with his thought.

14 **(III) Date.** Modern exegetes have placed the Ap at periods that differ greatly. A few scholars have proposed a date as early as the reign of Claudius (AD 41–54, and as late as the reign of Nerva (96–98) or of Trajan (98–117). More often exegetes have situated the Ap at the time of the persecution of Nero (54–68), or during the reign of Vespasian (69–79). But the great majority of scholars have continuously opted for the persecution that raged toward the end of the reign of Domitian (81–96).

Early witnesses in fact assign the Ap to this period: Irenaeus (*Adv. haer.* 5.30, 3; 2.22, 5; 3.3, 4), very probably Clement of Alexandria (*Quis div. salv.* 42), and Origen (*Comm. in Matt.* 16.6). At the beginning of the 4th cent. Eusebius (*HE* 3.18, 1; 20, 9; 23, 1) and Victorinus (*In Apoc.* 10.11; 17.10), well aware of the opinion of their predecessors, confirm it; Jerome follows suit (*De Viris Illustr.* 9).

15 The general information that we can extract from the Ap agrees with a late date, particularly 90–96. The letters of chs. 2–3 reveal that the seven churches already have a history behind them: Ephesus (2:4), Sardis (3:3), and Laodicea have lost their first fervor; Laodicea boasts of her wealth (3:17), though she had been completely destroyed by an earthquake in AD 60/61.

Hatred for Christians has already claimed at least one victim, at Pergamum, and John foresees that a vigorous persecution will oppress all the churches of Asia and probably Christendom (2:10; 3:10). The seer discovers under the celestial altar the victims of this persecution (6:9f.). Rome, the prostitute, is "drunk with the blood of saints and the blood of the martyrs of Jesus" (17:6; cf. 19:2; 18:24; 16:6), but these victims will reign with Christ (20:4). All men must worship the divinized Roman Empire and bear its mark (13:4; 14:9,11; 16:2; 19:20). Hence, it is because of their refusal to accept this idolatry that the Christians of Asia are persecuted.

Early chroniclers relate that Nero was the first persecutor of the Christians. But there is little similarity between his persecution and the one alluded to in the Ap. The former was probably limited to Rome and its surroundings; moreover, the Christians were at that time accused of having set fire to Rome, but not for having refused to worship the Roman Empire or its emperor. The next persecution, that of Domitian, however, tallies well with the internal evidence of the Ap. Domitian was serious about emperor worship and demanded, toward the end of his life, that everyone render him divine homage under the title "Dominus et deus noster" (Suetonius, *Domitiani Vita*, 13.4).

16 Frequent attempts have been made to give a specific date to the Ap because in 13:18 and 17:9–11 mention is made in a rather enigmatic way of a Roman emperor whose reign coincides with John's writing. Unfortunately, it is impossible to identify certainly the personage hidden under the number of the beast. It might seem from 17:9–11 that John is writing at the time of Vespasian; in order to avoid this improbable date, many hypotheses have been put forward, but none has proved definitive (→ 74 below). It is then probable that the final redaction of the Ap (without jeopardizing the possibility of sources or of successive redactions of the book by John) took place in Asia, toward the end of the reign of Domitian (*ca.* 90–96).

17 **(IV) Outline.** Exegetes have not been able to reach complete agreement with respect to the over-all structure of the Ap. M.-E. Boismard has proposed a tentative solution to the problem by distinguishing several redactional strata (*RB* 56 [1949] 507–41; *RB* 59 [1952] 178–81). Arguing from the presence of numerous doublets in the apocalyptic section, Boismard concludes that we owe the book in its present form to three older literary units: two complete and coherent apocalypses written by John—the first dating from the time of Nero and the second from the beginning of Domitian's reign—and the letters to the seven churches. An editor (*ca.* AD 95) then interwove these three compositions—with uneven success—to give the Ap its definitive form. This theory has become widespread among French Catholics through the BJ; most modern scholars, however, mindful of the deceptive and widely divergent results that studies of this type have yielded in the past, remain wary of new attempts to dissect the Ap. The current trend concentrates upon the book's literary unity.

Some scholars insist that a perfectly harmonious structure can be discovered in the Ap. For instance, E. Lohmeyer contends, because of the striking importance of the number "seven" throughout the Ap, that John organized the book in seven major sections, most of which are in turn subdivided into seven parts. J. W. Bowman (*The Drama of the Book of Revelation* [Phila., 1955]; *Interpr* 9 [1955] 436–53) presses further along these lines by presenting the Ap as a drama in seven acts, arranged in a single and continuous progression. The general evaluation of such hypotheses is that they exceed the evidence furnished by the text of the Ap and, consequently, that they are scarcely likely to prove accurate reflections of the author's intention.

An important theory about the structure of the Ap is to be found in a series of articles written by A. Feuillet (now conveniently gathered in his *Johannine Studies* [Staten Island, N.Y., 1965] 183–256; see also his *The Apocalypse*). He notes that the Ap is composed after the manner of prophetic books of the OT which contain woes against Israel and against foreign nations (cf. Ez 25–32). He suggests accordingly that chs. 4–11 of the Ap reveal God's wrath against Israel for its rejection of Jesus and refer to the destruction of Jerusalem in AD 70. Chs. 12ff. would refer rather to the future destruction of Rome, the Gentile persecutor. Just as God destroyed Jerusalem, so will he destroy Rome; this is the consolatory message of the Ap. See also M. Hopkins, *CBQ* 27 (1965) 42–47.

Perhaps it is preferable to limit ourselves to an outline which, though less precise, at least remains within the boundaries of John's perspective. Certain passages do allow us to determine the major divisions of the Ap. In the command that John receives toward the end of the inaugural vision, Christ specifies the two essential parts of the book: "Write down what you have seen, what is, and what is to take place hereafter" (1:19). Thus the entire Ap consists of a series of visions, "What you have seen." The object of these visions is twofold: the present situation, described in the letters to the seven churches (2:1–3:22); and future eschatological events (4:1–22:5). The two sections are inserted between an introduction (1:1–20) and a conclusion (22:6–21). Although the framework of the properly apocalyptic section is not always entirely clear, it is nevertheless easy to discern certain sharply defined units, especially the three heptads: the seals (4:1–8:1), the trumpets (8:2–11:19), and the bowls (15:1–16:21). In addition, the fall of Babylon (17:1–19:10) and the coming of Christ, with the consequent consummation (19:11–22:5), seem equally clear.

The book shares one characteristic—a certain lack of coherence—with all other apocalyptic literature, and we should not be too much surprised if we have not as yet been able to present a definite outline which all exegetes should find satisfactory.

- (I) Introduction (1:1–20)
  - (A) Superscription (1:1–3)
  - (B) Epistolary Salutation (1:4–8)
  - (C) Inaugural Vision (1:9–20)
- (II) The Letters to the Seven Churches (2:1–3:22)
  - (A) To Ephesus (2:1–7)
  - (B) To Smyrna (2:8–11)
  - (C) To Pergamum (2:12–17)
  - (D) To Thyatira (2:18–29)
  - (E) To Sardis (3:1–6)
  - (F) To Philadelphia (3:7–13)
  - (G) To Laodicea (3:14–22)
- (III) The Eschatological Future (4:1–22:5)
  - (A) The Seven Seals (4:1–8:1)
    - (a) The Heavenly Court (4:1–11)
    - (b) The Book with Seven Seals and the Lamb (5:1–14)
    - (c) The Opening of the First Six Seals (6:1–17)
      - (i) The opening of the first four seals (6:1–8)
      - (ii) The fifth and sixth seals (6:9–17)
    - (d) Double Interlude Describing the Church (7:1–17)
      - (i) The Church on earth preserved by God (7:1–8)
      - (ii) The Church in heaven glorifies God (7:9–17)
    - (e) The Opening of the Seventh Seal (8:1)
  - (B) The Seven Trumpets (8:2–11:19)
    - (a) The Seven Angels with Seven Trumpets (8:2–6)
    - (b) The First Four Trumpets (8:7–12)
    - (c) An Eagle Warns of the Last Three Trumpets (8:13)
    - (d) The Fifth Trumpet (9:1–12)
    - (e) The Sixth Trumpet (9:13–21)
    - (f) Double Interlude (10:1–11:14)
      - (i) The angel with the little open scroll (10:1–11)
      - (ii) The measuring of the Temple and the two witnesses (11:1–14)
    - (g) The Seventh Trumpet (11:15–19)
  - (C) The Dragon and the Lamb (12:1–14:20)
    - (a) The Dragon Seeks to Destroy the Celestial Woman and Her Son (12:1–6)
    - (b) Michael's Victory over the Dragon (12:7–12)
    - (c) The Dragon Vainly Pursues the Woman upon the Earth (12:13–18)
    - (d) The Dragon Confers His Power on the Beast Rising from the Sea (13:1–10)
    - (e) The Second Beast: The False Prophet from the Earth (13:11–18)
    - (f) The Vision of the Lamb with His Own (14:1–5)
    - (g) The Proclamation of Imminent Judgment (14:6–20)
  - (D) The Seven Bowls (15:1–16:21)
    - (a) The Conquerors of the Antichrist Sing the Canticle of Moses and the Lamb in Heaven (15:1–4)
    - (b) Seven Angels Receive the Bowls of God's Wrath (15:5–8)
    - (c) The Seven Bowls Are Poured Out (16:1–21)
  - (E) The Judgment and the Fall of Babylon (17:1–19:10)
    - (a) The Vision of the Harlot Seated upon the Beast (17:1–6)
    - (b) The Interpretation of the Vision (17:7–18)
    - (c) The Doom of Babylon (18:1–24)
      - (i) An angel proclaims the fall of Babylon (18:1–3)
      - (ii) The faithful are warned to leave the condemned city (18:4–8)
      - (iii) Lamentation over the ruins of Babylon (18:9–19)
      - (iv) A symbolic action signals the disappearance of Babylon (18:21–24)

(d) Canticles of Joy in Heaven (19:1–10)
(F) The Coming of Christ and the Consummation of History (19:11–22:5)
(a) Victory of Christ over the Beast and the False Prophet (19:11–21)
(b) The Thousand-Year Reign (20:1–6)
(c) Victory over Satan, Freed from His Prison (20:7–10)
(d) The Universal Judgment (20:11–15)
(e) The New World and the New Jerusalem (21:1–8)
(f) The Spouse of the Lamb and the Heavenly Jerusalem (21:9–22:5)
(IV) Epilogue (22:6–21)
(A) Witness of the Angel (22:6–9)
(B) The Time of Retribution Is at Hand (22:10–15)
(C) Witness of Jesus (22:16–20)
(D) Salutation (22:21)

(For the doctrinal content of the Ap, → Johannine Theology, 80:57–60.)

COMMENTARY

18 **(I) Introduction (1:1–20).**

(A) Superscription (1:1–3). This solemn introduction forms a sort of inclusion with the end of the book (22:6–21), which reproduces the same themes and often the same expressions. Framed between the title of the book, "Revelation of Jesus Christ," and the motive that grounds its importance, "because the moment is near," three parts treat of the origin, content, and the recipients of the Ap.

1. *revelation of Jesus Christ:* Inspired by the prophetic tradition, this title announces the unveiling of the mystery of history, the end of the present era and the inauguration of the Kingdom of God. Jesus Christ is the mediator of this revelation. *which God gave him:* God is the ultimate source of the Ap, which he guarantees with supreme authority. The necessary mediation of Christ, who transmits only that which the Father has communicated to him, is a major doctrine of Jn (7:16; 8:26,40; 15:15). *to his servants:* These are the prophets (10:7; 11:18; 22:6), who elsewhere are closely associated with all the Christians, also called *douloi* (7:3; 19:2,5; 22:3). *what must take place:* See 4:1; 22:6; cf. Dn 2:28f. The certainty of the accomplishment without condition and without delay, of the intention of God about history. *sending through his angel:* In order to set off the transcendence of God, apocalyptic style regularly introduces angels, whose role was to transmit God's revelations and execute the divine decrees. In the Ap angels intervene unceasingly. The intermediary by which John receives the revelation is sometimes Christ, sometimes an angel: Christ appears in the guise of an angel (1:19f.), and the angel appears as Christ (10:1ff.), whom he represents. **2.** *who testified:* Epistolary aorist. The object of this witness is the content of the Ap, indicated in three ways: by reference to God, to Jesus Christ, and to John. Already well emphasized in Jn and Acts, the duty of witnessing suits the historical context of the persecution that surrounds the Ap. Jesus, the faithful and true witness (1:5; 3:14; cf. Jn 18:37), is the model; he shows that persecution is the consequence of witnessing. All Christians, and especially the messengers of the Gospel (6:9; 17:6; 18:24; 20:4), ought to guard firmly the witness of Jesus (12:17), as, for example Antipas (2:13) and the two witnesses (11:7–10). *all that he saw:* This expression, repeated 54 times, and common to all apocalypses, specifies that the content of the book was revealed in ecstatic visions. **3.** *blessed:* This beatitude, the first of seven, ought to be juxtaposed to that of 22:7. Both suggest the authority of the book (see W. Bieder, *TZ* 10 [1954] 13–30). *who reads aloud:* That is, in a Christian assembly. *the hour is near:* The motive for heeding the exhortations of the Ap is the proximity of the manifestation of Christ (22:6f.,10,12,20).

19 **(B) Epistolary Salutation (1:4–8).** The author begins and ends (22:21) with the Christian epistolary formulas; between chs. 4 and 22, however, there is no further indication that the Ap is a letter. In agreement with the current formula, the author names himself, then those to whom he writes, wishing them "grace and peace." The thanksgiving follows, of a liturgical type, addressed this time not to God, but to Christ (vv. 5b–6). Finally a prophetic announcement, solemnly sanctioned by God (v. 8), proclaims the central theme of the Ap (v. 7). **4.** *the seven churches in Asia:* Besides these seven churches (1:11), there existed at that time, in the proconsular province of Asia, other churches: among them, Colossae, Troas, Hierapolis, Magnesia. Through the seven churches, John wanted to reach all the churches of Asia and perhaps the universal Church (→ Johannine Theology, 80:48–54). *who is and who was and who is coming:* See 1:8; 4:8; 11:17; 16:5. The name of God, as his person, is unchangeable; instead of being in the genitive after *apo*, the expression remains in the nominative. This description of God proceeds from a long tradition that goes back to Ex 3:14. Familiar to Jews and Greeks, it tries to express the eternity of God by means of the human category of time. John has adapted this title to his message by replacing the usual "he who will be" by "he who is coming" in history. Such a title suits perfectly the beginning of a book revealing the meaning of the present in the light of the past and the future. *the seven spirits before his throne:* Either the fullness of the Holy Spirit (Is 11:2) communicated by Christ to the seven churches, or more likely angels, who, strengthened by divine power, act in the name of God (→ Johannine Theology, 80:56). "Before his throne" is a Hebraism signifying that they are the servants of God. These angels (3:1; 4:5; 5:6) are probably the angels of the presence (8:2ff.; 15:1ff.), well known in Jewish angelology. **5.** This kerygmatic formula expresses the essential content of the faith: The three titles evoke the passion, the resurrection, and the exaltation of Christ. *the trustworthy witness:* See 1:2; 3:14. Jesus was witness during his ministry because he revealed the Father perfectly (Jn 3:11,32) and crowned this testimony by the sacrifice of his life (Jn 18:37; 1 Tm 6:13). *first-born of the dead:* Cf. 1 Cor 15:20; Col 1:18. Jesus, the first resurrected, guarantees that the era of the resurrection of the dead is inaugurated and summarized in his person. *ruler of the kings of the earth:* Cf. Ps 89:28. The glorification of Christ, consequence of his resurrection, confers on him all power over all creation (Mt 28:19; Rom 14:9; Phil 2:11; Eph 1:20–23). His domination over the kings who threaten the Church (19:12,16) ought to strengthen the confidence of the Christians.

20 **5b–6.** This doxology contains three parts: Christ's love for us, the negative and positive effect of his love, and finally praise. *to him who loves us:* Cf. Jn 13:1; 15:9; Gal 2:20; Eph 5:2,25. The pres. tense indicates that Christ's love is perpetual and goes beyond the historical event of the redemption (*lysanti* and *epoiēsen*, in the aorist; → Johannine Theology, 80:25–26). *who freed us from our sins by his blood:* Affirmed as an essential fact by the Christian creed (1 Cor 15:3; Gal 1:4), this liberation is often expressed through the metaphor of purchase (1 Cor 6:20; 7:23; Gal 4:5) by the blood of Christ (Rom 3:25; Eph 1:7; 2:13; Col 1:20; 1 Pt 1:18f.). *a kingdom, priests:* See 5:10; 20:6; 1 Pt 2:9. This messianic promise had been developed, beginning with Ex 19:6. The persecuted Christians participate now in the abasement of Christ, but they are assured that they will reign with him soon (2:26–28; 20:4; 22:5; cf. Dn 7:18,22,27). By reason of their union with Christ the priest, through baptism, they can fulfill the priestly service (Heb 10:19–22; 1 Pt 2:5). *to God his Father:* The Ap affirms the sonship of Jesus (2:28; 3:5,21; 14:1); but in order to respect the divine transcendence it reserves a similar intimacy between Christians and God for the hereafter (21:7). **7.** *coming with the clouds:* Primitive Christianity saw in Dn 7:13, the prophecy par excellence, the announcement of the glorious coming of Christ in judgment (14:14; Mt 24:30; 26:64; see R. B. Y. Scott, *NTS* 5 [1958–59] 127–32). *those who pierced him:* The Jews who put Jesus to death. *all the tribes of the earth:* All unbelieving nations are equally guilty, for in persecuting the Church, they show their hostility toward Christ. Suffering true sorrow, all will wail. *even so. Amen:* The repetition, in Greek and Hebrew (22:20), underlines the solemnity of the prophecy, in which the Christian assembly believes. **8.** *Alpha and Omega:* Equivalent expressions, "the first and the last," "the beginning and the end," reappear concerning God (21:6) and concerning Christ (1:17; 2:8; 22:13). Isaiah (41:4; 44:6; 48:12) had already affirmed that God was "the first and the last," the creator and the end of everything. Under Hellenistic influence the symbolic value of the alphabet was gradually assimilated by Judaism; the first letter associated with the last, signified totality. *the Almighty:* Proper to the Ap in the NT, except 2 Cor 6:18. The complete expression, "the Lord God Almighty," is borrowed from the LXX and corresponds to *Yahwēh 'elōhê ṣebā'ôt* (Hos 12:5; Am 4:13; 9:5). The third title summarizes the two preceding: God's enemies can stir themselves and persecute his people, but all power resides permanently with him; he began history and he will terminate it.

21 **(C) Inaugural Vision (1:9–20).** John in ecstasy is commissioned to write what he sees (vv. 9–11); the glorious Christ appears to him, presenting himself as the source and the master of the life of the Church (vv. 12–16); he renews the commission (vv. 17–20).

9. *who share with you:* John is closely related to the Christians, reborn in Christ like himself. He shares completely their destiny of suffering and glory. *the tribulation, the kingdom, and the endurance in Jesus:* Access to the kingdom is only obtained by means of trial (Acts 14:22). In waiting for the glorious event, patient endurance remains the specific virtue of the persecuted (2:19; 3:10; 13:10; 14:12). Incorporated into Jesus by baptism, Christians share his passion, in order to participate in his glory (14:13; Rom 8:17; Phil 3:10f.; 2 Tm 2:11f.; 1 Pt 4:13). *Patmos:* A rocky island of 16 sq. mi., of the Dodecanese group, situated some 50 mi. to the SW of Ephesus (see G. Camps, *VDBS* 7 [1961] 73–81). **10.** *a loud voice:* Cf. Ez 3:12. That of the angel of Christ (1:1; 4:1; 21:9,15; 22:1,6). *like a trumpet:* Descriptions of apocalyptic visions are regularly introduced by "like," "similar to," to emphasize that every comparison of the terrestrial order is inadequate; the expressions fail to describe what has been seen and heard in the celestial sphere. Taking inspiration from the theophany of Sinai (Ex 19:16,19; Heb 12:19), apocalyptic style inserted the trumpet into eschatological settings that described the passage from the present to the future era (Is 27:13; Jl 2:1; Mt 24:31; 1 Cor 15:52; 1 Thes 4:16). **11.** *the seven churches:* The churches have not been chosen for their importance, since Troas and Miletus numbered communities more populous than Thyatira and Philadelphia. They are named according to an order, which, on the map, roughly describes a circle, with Ephesus as the point of departure. These cities, connected by excellent roads, probably had courts of justice, where those who refused worship to the emperor could be judged. **13.** *in the midst of the lampstands:* Christ is present in the midst of the seven churches (v. 20; 2:5), ready to exhort them (2:1–3:22) and to help them. *like a Son of Man:* Jesus fulfills the prophecy of Dn 7:13: He appears like the eschatological judge who intervenes with the power of God (→ Johannine Theology, 80:17–20, 60). *a long robe... a golden girdle:* Cf. Dn 10:5. These vestments manifest his dignity as high priest (Ex 28:4; Wis 18:24). **14.** The shining light that emanates from Christ reveals that he belongs to the divine world. *his head and hair were white:* Christ is clothed with the dignity that belonged originally to the "Ancient of Days" (Dn 7:9). The glorified Christ possesses the attributes that in the OT belonged to God alone (1:18; 2:8; 5:12; 22:13): the Ap thus affirms the divinity of Christ. *like a flame of fire:* See 2:18; 19:12; Dn 10:6. The eyes of Christ, judge of the Church and of the world, penetrate all things. **16.** *seven stars:* The only known parallel instances of this symbol come from the pagan world: Mithras and the Caesars were represented with seven stars in their right hand in order to affirm their universal domination. Consequently, there might perhaps be a polemic accent here: Not Caesar, but Christ is the Lord of all things. *a sharp two-edged sword:* Cf. Is 11:4; 49:2; Wis 18:15; Eph 6:17; Heb 4:12. This bold image represents the word of Christ who judges Christianity (2:12,16) and the universe (19:15,21). *like the sun shining:* See 10:1; Jgs 5:31. The narration of epiphany frequently applies this comparison (Mt 17:2 par.).

22 **17.** *I fell at his feet:* This reaction of fear and prostration before the apparition of God or of a messenger of God is nearly of obligation (Gn 32:31; Ex 33:20; Jgs 6:22f.; 13:22; Is 6:5; Ez 1:28): Man ought to disappear before the glory of God. **17b–20.** The sublime titles that Christ demands are destined to encourage Christians, who place all their confidence in their Lord. These titles synthesize the three stages in the career of Christ: his pre-existence, his death on earth, his exaltation to eternal life as conqueror of the infernal powers. **18.** *the living one:* As God alone is the truly living one (4:9f.; 10:6; Ps 42:3), Christ lives by the communication of the life of the Father (Jn 5:26). *I died, and behold I am alive:* This contrast between the past and the present, between death and the life of the resurrection possessed forever, constitutes the core of the Christian creed. *the keys of Death and Hades:* "To have the keys" signifies "to be the master of" (3:7; 9:1; 20:1; Is 22:22; Mt 16:19). The possession of these keys is the consequence of Christ's victory over the hostile forces, when he descended into hell. Death, then, can no longer frighten Christians. **19.** *what you have seen, what is and what shall be:* This apocalyptic formula describes the office and privilege of a prophet; it relates the Ap to ancient prophecy (see W. C. van Unnik, *NTS* 9 [1962–63] 86–94). **20.** *the angels of the seven churches:* See 1:16; 2:1. The identity of these angels has been much discussed since patristic times. The letters of chs. 2–3 containing praise and reproaches are addressed to them—they cannot belong exclusively to the celestial world. On the other hand, the word *aggelos* regularly designates in the Ap a superhuman being in the service of God or of Satan. Here, then, it probably refers to guardian angels, celestial counterparts of the churches. They participate in the responsibility and in the destiny of the churches they represent and guard. Christ holds them in his right hand to signify that he is the Lord of these churches and that they are under his protection.

23 **(II) The Letters to the Seven Churches (2:1–3:22).** Although they have to do with specific churches and treat of particular problems, these letters probably never existed independently; that is, they were drafted as an integral part of the Ap. All of them are modeled on a stereotyped literary form. All begin with Christ's command to the seer to write to the particular church mentioned: "To the angel of the church..., write." Then follows a description of the glorious Christ, the author of the message. The message itself always begins with *oida*, "I know," which underlines Christ's knowledge of the situation in which the churches find themselves. The merits and the failings of each community are then scored either with appropriate encouragement or reproaches—sometimes with both. Each letter ends with an exhortation, either for the church to change its ways (Ephesus, Pergamum, Sardis, and Laodicea), or to persevere in fidelity (Smyrna, Thyatira, and Philadelphia). This exhortation is regularly punctuated with the formula, familiar from the Syn, "He who has an ear...," intended to make personal Christ's message for each of the hearers of the book (1:3). The promise to the victor, which sets the Christian's gaze on his future in the eschatological era, serves as a conclusion. In general, these letters make clear that the gravest danger menacing the churches of Asia, toward the end of the 1st cent., lay not so much in oppression from without (2:9,13; 3:9), as with the heterodoxy of some groups of Christians, who, inspired by the Gnostic theory on liberty, suggested consorting with the syncretistic world around them (2:6,14–16,20–25).

(Barclay, W., *Letters to the Seven Churches* [London, 1957]. Fenasse, P., and R. Leconte, *BTS* 43 [1962] 2–14. Poirier, L., *Les sept églises; ou, Le premier septénaire prophétique de l'Apocalypse* [Washington, 1943].)

24 **(A) To Ephesus (2:1–7).** **1.** *Ephesus:* The commercial metropolis of Asia and seat of the proconsular government, this city was a cultural and religious center. The syncretistic tendency of the times opened the door to many superstitious practices, among which the imperial cult and the worship of Artemis were predominant (Acts 19:27,35). This church had been founded by Paul about AD 53–56 (Acts 19:8,10). *who walks among:* Christ is forever present among all the Christian communities (Mt 18:20; 28:20; 2 Cor 6:16ff.), to direct and to be the source of life for them. **2.** *I know:* The object of this knowledge, "your works" (14:13), involves the totality of the Christian life. *you have tested:* Those who were passing themselves off as apostles were probably itinerant preachers who perhaps had some connection with the Nicolaitans (v. 6). Paul had foreseen such a danger (Acts 20:29ff.; 1 Tm 1:7). **4.** *the love you had at first:* Cf. Acts 19:20; 20:37; Eph 1:3ff. Abandoning brotherly love involves the loss of Christ's love. **5.** *remember...repent...do the works:* The three stages in a total conversion. *I will remove your lampstand:* This could be either the loss of pre-eminence among the churches of Asia, or rather the very destruction of the church of Ephesus. **6.** *Nicolaitans:* This group, of which we know very little, seems to have been influenced by certain Gnostic and antinomian ideas (see 2:15). They probably taught that Christians were free to eat meat that had been sacrificed to idols and to satisfy the lusts of the flesh (vv. 14f.). *you hate:* The radical dualism between good and evil obliges one to hate evil, following the example both of God (Is 61:8; Zech 8:17) and of Christ (6:16f.). **7.** *what the Spirit says:* The Spirit of Christ, who, through the prophet, interprets Christ's words (→ Johannine Theology, 80:39–45). *to him who conquers:* This military term takes for granted that the Christian life is a battleground. In the Ap this phrase applies to the faithful Christian soldier (12:11; 15:2; 21:8) and to Christ (3:21b; 5:5; 17:14). *eat of the tree of life:* This symbolizes the sharing in eternal life (22:2,14; → Johannine Theology, 80:60). The enjoying of all those blessings that the time to come has reserved for redeemed humanity. The decree that excluded man from the tree of life (Gn 3:22f.) is now abrogated by Christ, on condition of the Christian's personal victory over sin.

25 **(B) To Smyrna (2:8–11).** **8.** *Smyrna:* After Ephesus, the most important commercial city of Asia. The Jewish colony, a rather large one in this area, was particularly hostile toward Christians. **9.** *your poverty, but you are rich:* See Jas 2:5; 2 Cor 6:10; in an opposite sense, cf. Ap 3:17; Lk 12:21; 1 Tm 6:17f. The poverty of this community was due in part to the menial origin of its members (1 Cor 1:26), and in part to the sacrifices their Christian faith occasioned. *the slander:* The Jews undoubtedly were trying to discredit both Christ and the Christians (Acts 13:45). **10.** *for ten days:* Cf. Dn 1:12,14. The brevity of the time of tribulation is contrasted with the eternity of the reward (2 Cor 4:17). *the crown of life:* See comment on Jas 1:12. In the time to come, the blessed will be graced with a crown of glory (3:11; 4:4,10; 12:1; 14:14). The crown (symbol of victory) and life will make the Christians forget the humiliation of persecution and of death. **11.** *the second death:* Cf. 20:6,14; 21:8. The martyrs will undergo physical death, but they will escape that real death, eternal damnation.

26 **(C) To Pergamum (2:12–17).** **12.** *Pergamum:* This was a syncretistic pagan center that had many temples dedicated to different gods. Here also the Church must have encountered very great difficulties (v. 13f.). **13.** *where Satan's throne is:* Pergamum is thus branded, either because of the cult of Asklepios, symbolized by a serpent (12:9: same symbol for Satan), or because of the imperial cult, which was especially popular in this city. *my witness, my faithful one:* The Lord ascribes to Antipas his proper title (1:5; 3:14; 1 Tm 6:13), because he remains faithful to his Master to the end. **14.** *the teaching of Balaam:* A heresy that held for moral libertinism (2 Pt 2:15; Jude 11), especially with regard to idolatrous feasting (Nm 22–24; 25:6ff.; 31:16). **15.** *the teaching of the Nicolaitans:* The Nicolaitans and the disciples of Balaam probably made up one single group. Their teaching was related to that of the libertines who had perverted the Pauline doctrine on Christian liberty: Christians should not separate themselves from their pagan milieu. Contemning the restrictions imposed by the apostolic decree (Acts 15:22–29), they encouraged a return to pagan, moral laxity. *I come soon:* Used seven times (3:11; 16:15; 22:7,12,17,20), this warning stresses one of the central ideas of the Ap: The glorious Christ shall intervene soon in human history in order to save and to judge. **16.** *war against them:* That is, against the Nicolaitans, with whom the church of Pergamum, for the most part, did not associate. **17.** *hidden manna:* This heavenly food, the image of union with God in eternal life, is now hidden, like everything that belongs to the time to come (Jn 6:32; Col 3:3). *a white stone, with a new name:* The custom of wearing amulets, on which were written some magical name, was rather widespread in the pagan world. It was believed that he

who knew this mysterious name could make use of the power of the being so-named in order to protect himself from the evil spirits. Christ, on the contrary, would affirm that it is his name, which no one can read (19:12), which affords true protection for those faithful to him (see R. North, *VD* 28 [1950] 65–76).

27 **(D) To Thyatira (2:18–29).** **18.** *Thyatira:* This city was less important than the preceding ones and had no temple dedicated to the emperor. The dangers menacing the small Christian community proceeded, rather, from the interior. **20.** *Jezebel:* The wife of Ahab, who had led Israel into idolatry (2 Kgs 9:22), is pictured as the type of a false prophetess. Her teaching, of a somewhat Gnostic, libertine sort, links her with the Nicolaitans (v. 14; cf. 1 Cor 6:12–20). **22.** *who commit adultery with her:* The Christians who had let themselves be led into error by her (2 Cor 11:2). **23.** *her children:* Her spiritual descendants, branded by her teaching, are condemned like Ahab's children (2 Kgs 10:7). *who searches minds and hearts:* Christ lays claim to a prerogative that in the OT is proper to Yahweh (Ps 7:10; Jer 11:20; 17:10; 20:12). *I will give to each of you according to your deeds:* Another prerogative of God (Ps 62:13; Jer 17:10; cf. Mt 16:27; 25:31–46; Ap 22:12). **24.** *the deep things of Satan:* The Gnostics perhaps borrowed from Paul the expression "the deep things of God" (1 Cor 2:10; cf. Rom 11:33; Eph 3:18f.), in order to glorify their knowledge that penetrated the very mysteries of God. This expression could possibly have a sarcastic intent for John: Instead of attaining God, they encounter Satan's depths. *any other burden:* Alluding very probably to the apostolic decree (Acts 15:28), apart from forbidding idolatry and fornication, Christ reimposes no other obligation. **26.** *who keeps my works:* These "works" manifest the concrete nature of what Christ exacts, and is in opposition to the works of Jezebel (v. 22). **27.** *as I myself have received power:* God's only Son will allow his brothers to share in his power over the nations (1:5f.; 20:4; Mt 25:21,28; 1 Cor 6:2). **28.** *I will give him the morning star:* Cf. 22:16. Not only will the victor share in Christ's prerogatives, but he will also receive Christ himself.

28 **(E) To Sardis (3:1–6).** **1.** *Sardis:* The inhabitants of this city had the reputation of living luxuriously and licentiously. The predominant cult at Sardis was that of Cybele. *you are dead:* Although it preserves the appearances of Christianity, this community has fallen back into spiritual death, from which Christ had drawn it (Eph 2:1,5; Col 2:13). **2.** *be watchful:* It is the attitude necessary for Christians who await the sudden coming of the Master (Mt 24:42; 25:13 par.). *my God:* Christ, the Son of God, is also Son of Man, and so stands in a creaturelike relationship to God—a relationship that is unique (Jn 20:17): "My," and not "our." **3.** *like a thief:* This image was in widespread use, designating the unexpected coming of Christ at the last day (Mt 24:43f. par.; Lk 12:39f.; 1 Thes 5:2; 2 Pt 3:10; Ap 16:15). **4.** *who have not soiled their garments:* At a time of general depravation, they have not given themselves over to the sexual debauchery of the pagans (Jude 23). Christians, by their baptism, were transformed by Christ (7:14; 22:14; Gal 3:27). **5.** *white garments:* Following their final victory (7:9ff.), the faithful Christians will live in intimacy with the glorious Christ (v. 4b) and will enjoy the heavenly beatitude (4:4; 6:11; Dn 7:9). *the book of life:* After the manner of a civil register, the book of God (Ex 32:32–33) contains only the names of living citizens (Ps 69:29) who are the just ones (Dn 12:1; Mal 3:16). Those who are inscribed in the book belong to the People of God, and possess heavenly citizenship (Lk 10:20; Phil 4:3), which permits them to escape judgment and to enter into eternal life (13:8; 17:8; 20:12,15; 21:27). The threat of Christ to erase names supposes that the book is found in his hands (13:8; 21:27).

29 **(F) To Philadelphia (3:7–13).** **7.** *Philadelphia:* Although its population was comparatively small because of earthquakes, this city had a strong Jewish colony. *the holy one, the true one:* Borrowed from the OT (Is 6:3; 40:25; 65:16; Hab 3:3), these titles, taken in the absolute, manifest the divine glory of Christ (6:10). "True" (3:14; 19:11) designates the ideal in contrast to approximate and imperfect representations. *the key of David:* Cf. Is 22:22; 2 Kgs 18:18,37. Jesus is the eschatological offspring of David (5:5; 22:16), who alone has been established with authority over the house of God (Eph 1:22; Heb 3:6). He possesses then all power in heaven and on earth (Mt 28:18), and even over Hades (1:18; Rom 14:9; Phil 2:9ff.). **8.** *an open door:* This could signify a favorable occasion of serving Christ by spreading the gospel (Acts 14:27; 1 Cor 16:9; 2 Cor 2:12; Col 4:3), in spite of the adversaries of this church. However, the context suggests rather an allusion to the entrance into eschatological glory, which only Christ, "who has David's key," is able to grant. **9.** *they are Jews:* Their pretension contrasts with the "true" Christ (v. 7). Being the enemies of the Israel of God (Gal 6:15f.), they no longer merit to be called by the honorable name of Jews. *bow down before your feet:* Is 45:14; 49:23; 60:14; Zech 8:20ff. *that I have loved you:* He has loved them, i.e., elected them (Is 42:1; 43:4; Mk 1:11 par.) to be his people. **10.** *my word of patient endurance:* Not the commandment of Christ to practice patience, but the teaching flowing from the example of Christ, who practiced patience (2 Thes 3:5; Heb 12:1f.). The "patience of the saints" (13:10; 14:12) reflects the patience of Christ. *who dwell upon the earth:* This expression has always a pejorative meaning in the Ap (6:10; 8:13; 11:10; 12:12; 13:8,12,14; 17:2,8); it designates the unbelieving pagans, in opposition to the Christians who find themselves already in the heavenly state, or who are destined to go there. **12.** *a pillar in the temple of my God:* Judaism had compared Abraham and the just of Israel to columns, and the primitive Church has thus applied this epithet to the apostles (Gal 2:9; Eph 2:19–22; 1 Pt 2:5). In the heavenly Church the faithful Christians will be as definitively fixed as the columns of a temple. *never shall he go outside:* Just as a column cannot be removed from a building guaranteed to remain stable, so the fall of the just who have obtained the final victory will be impossible. *I will write:* On each column of the temple of the eschatological Church, Christ will inscribe three names. *the name of God:* See Nm 6:27; 2 Cor 3:3. The just are therefore the possession of God. *the name of...the new Jerusalem:* They will be recognized as citizens of the city of God (21:2), a privilege the members of the earthly Church already possess, in potency (Gal 4:26; Phil 3:20; Heb 12:22). *my own name:* Christ glorified (2:17; 19:12f.), who will communicate his glory to his own (Rom 8:29f.; Col 3:4; 1 Jn 3:2).

30 **(G) To Laodicea (3:14–22).** **14.** *Laodicea:* A wealthy city because of its commercial interests and banking activities, and famous for its flourishing medical school. After the city's destruction by an earthquake (AD 60/61), the inhabitants were able to reconstruct it without outside help. The church in this city was perhaps founded by Epaphras (Col 4:12f.), a companion of Paul. Laodicea was also the recipient of Paul's letter to the Colossians (see Col 4:16). *the Amen:* In Jesus, the divine promises have found their final accomplishment (2 Cor 1:20; Is 65:16); the glorified Christ concludes the history

of salvation. But he is not only the term of this history; he is also its starting point. In fact, everything had been created in him (Jn 1:3; 1 Cor 8:6; Heb 1:2), who is "the prime source of God's creation" (NEB; cf. Prv 8:22; Col 1:15; see B. R. Brinkman, *Bijdr* 18 [1957] 129–39). **15.** *neither cold or hot:* The community that receives the most severe reprimand is not accused of any particular grave fault; Christ condemns the existing state of tepidity and self-satisfaction. **16.** *I will vomit you:* The tepid water image, underlying the passage, is probably occasioned by some local circumstance. **17.** *I am rich:* This community enjoys material well-being, and the absence of troubles. Such an enjoyment brings on pride, which, in folding man in on himself, closes him to every gift from Christ. **18.** *to buy from me:* Gold, white clothing, and collyrium correspond to particular items of life in Laodicea: its numerous banks, a famous type of black cloth, and an ophthalmic powder used by its physicians. Christ contrasts riches that he can grant to the illusory advantages offered by this city; only he gives real riches, the fullness of salvation, and the authentic healing. **19.** *I rebuke and chasten:* Christ's severe reproof is inspired by his love. **20.** *I stand at the door and knock:* Mt 24:33 par.; Lk 12:36; Jas 5:9. *if any one hears my voice:* Jn 10:3,16f.; 18:37. *and eat with him, and he with me:* He who will give attention to the call of Christ and who will open to him, will participate with the Lord in the joys of the banquet in the time that is to come (Mt 8:11; Mk 14:25 par.; Lk 22:29f.). **21.** *to sit with me on my throne:* Not only will the victor live with Christ, but he will share in his royalty (1:6) and in his power as judge (Lk 22:29f.; 1 Cor 6:2f.). *as I myself was victorious:* The victory of the Christian (1 Jn 5:4) is tightly bound up with Christ's victory (Jn 16:33).

(Ehrhardt, A., *EvT* 17 [1957] 431–45. Rudwick, M. J. S. and E. M. B. Green, *ExpT* 69 [1957–58] 176–78.)

31 **(III) The Eschatological Future (4:1–22:5).**
(A) The Seven Seals (4:1–8:1).

(a) The Heavenly Court (4:1–11). In the first vision John glimpses the court of heaven, where God sits enthroned and rules the universe. This vision and the following one (5:1–14) are closely linked; together they form the celestial preparation for the heptad of the seals (6:1–8:1). **1.** *after this I saw:* This formula ushers in a vision of special importance. "After this" refers to the opening vision in 1:12ff., which, along with the letters to the seven churches, continues throughout the first three chapters. *an open door in heaven:* A single door stands open, and not the whole of heaven. This vision is granted to John, who alone is admitted to the transcendent world (see G. Rinaldi, *CBQ* 25 [1963] 336–47). *come up hither:* This command implies the complete separation of heaven and earth. Only an intervention from above, in an ecstasy (1:10; 17:3; 21:10; 2 Cor 12:2) can raise man toward the world of the divine. *what must take place:* See 1:1. **2.** *I was in the Spirit:* The Spirit captures the seer and raises him up to the door of heaven; he can see the court but does not enter. *one seated on the throne:* Out of respect for the divine transcendence and out of reverential fear, the pious Jew never mentioned God's name. In accordance with this custom, John avoids naming or describing God. Instead, he describes in detail the glorious Son of Man (1:12–16)—the mediator who reveals God to us. The OT represented God as making his throne of the heavens (Is 66:1; cf. Mt 5:34f.; 23:22) or holding court in heaven (Ps 11:4). The fact that he is seated underscores his double function as king and universal judge. **3.** Carefully avoiding any anthropomorphic detail, the seer remains faithful to the apocalyptic tradition that resorts to the flash of precious stones to describe God's transcendence. This description (Ex 24:10; Ez 1:26–28; 10:1) tries to show how God reigns in an inaccessible light.

32 **4.** *twenty-four elders:* The old men give homage to God and praise him (4:9–11; 5:8–11,14; 11:16–18; 19:4); they also fill the sacerdotal office of offering the prayers of Christians (5:8). Their white robes symbolize the glorified state of heaven (3:18; 6:11; 7:9). Their main prerogative is to be seated on thrones, and thus to participate in God's functions of judging and ruling the world; this is Christ's promise to faithful Christians (3:21). Who are the elders? The number 24 is found nowhere else in apocalyptic literature. And the Ap itself uses the number only in this one instance. Some have linked the number to the 24 astral divinities of the Babylonian religion, some to the 24 priestly courses of the Jews. More likely the number is based on that of the tribes of Israel: 12 elders would represent the chosen people of the OT, and 12 others the New Israel. Thus the group of 24 elders stands for the ideal Church in its entirety. The glorification of the Church on earth will be realized in the future, but it has virtually taken place already in the resurrection of Christ (Eph 2:6; see J. Michl, *Die 24 Ältesten in der Apokalypse* [Münster, 1938]; H. Leclercq, *DACL* 15 [1953] 3121–25; A. Feuillet, *RB* 65 [1958] 5–32; *Johannine Studies*, 184–214). **5.** *lightnings, thunderings, and voices:* These are the signs that traditionally express the power and glory of God (8:5; 11:19; 16:18; Ex 19:16; Ez 1:13). **6.** *a sea of glass:* Late Judaism had accepted the image of a heavenly sea suspended between the first and the second heavens (Gn 1:6f.); above this sea was represented God's palace (Pss 104:3; 148:4). Here the sea is said to be of glass—a costly substance for the ancients—possessing the clarity of crystal. This grand image purports to underline the huge gap between the seer and every man, on the one hand, and the high throne of God, on the other.

33 **6b.** *in the midst of the throne and round the throne:* It is somewhat difficult to imagine the exact place of the four living creatures. But what is important is the meaning of the details: The situation of the creatures in the midst of the throne signifies that they are in immediate contact with God, whereas their position around the throne shows their universal action in the created world that they represent and govern in God's name. *four living creatures:* The fundamental idea is that of Ez 1:10: Four living creatures represent the whole of creation in which God is constantly present. *full of eyes in front and behind:* God unceasingly exercises his knowledge and vigilance in visible ways throughout nature (Ez 1:18; 10:12). **7.** These four creatures represent what is most splendid in animate life: the lion—nobility; the bull—strength; man—wisdom; the eagle—swiftness. The whole of creation is thus represented before the throne of God, worshiping his divine Majesty and fulfilling his will. Since Irenaeus, Christian tradition has taken these four creatures as a symbol of the four Evangelists. **8.** *each of them with six wings:* See Is 6:2; Ez 1:6. The wings may stand for the swiftness with which God's will is executed throughout nature. *they cease not day and night:* The unceasing activity of nature under Providence (Jn 5:17) reveals God and, in revealing him, praises him. *holy, holy, holy:* Instead of the thrice-blessed God who fills heaven and earth with his glory (Is 6:3), this doxology praises the God who rules history. "And who is coming," in the mouth of creatures representing nature, expresses the eager longing of the universe for liberation (21:1ff.; Rom 8:19ff.). **9.** *the living creatures give glory:* The Church (the 24 elders) must unceasingly join with nature to praise God. Any progress in the knowledge of creation ought to help the

believer to deepen his spirit of adoration and of praise. **10.** *fall down:* In ancient times to prostrate oneself and lay down one's crown expressed either homage to a supreme master or the submission of the vanquished who sought clemency. **11.** *thou didst create:* Because he is Creator of all, God is Lord of all, and especially of the unfolding of history. Thus the persecuted Church on earth can take hope. *they existed and were created:* The inverse order of these two verbs would be more natural. We are probably to understand that all things existed in the power of God's will before he created them.

34 (b) THE BOOK WITH SEVEN SEALS AND THE LAMB (5:1–14). Already a witness of the heavenly praise paid to God as Creator and Lord of all (4:1–11), the seer now beholds the Lamb by whom redemption was achieved. Christ has brought about victory by his sacrifice. But only the marks of his suffering remain now that he has risen. As a result of his triumph, he can, in God's name, direct and bring to its conclusion history's course. In a cosmic liturgy, the whole of creation proclaims the dignity of the Lamb at his enthronement. **1.** *written within and on the back:* In Mesopotamia, documents were usually written on a tablet that was placed in a small clay casket on which the identical text had been copied. Such a custom tried to discourage fraud and was continued even after papyrus came into use (see Y. Yadin, *IsrEJ* 12 [1962] 236–38, pl. 48). Accordingly, what John sees in God's hand is an official document that, doubtless, contains his mysterious will regarding all the events that will mark the end of history (1:19). Some exegetes think that the scroll would contain all the visions between 6:1 and 22:5. Others object that a scroll cannot be read as the seals are opened, but only after they have all been broken; then the contents of the scroll would include the events of 8:1 to 22:5. It may be better to hold that the document contains only the events that occur as the Lamb breaks the seals (6:1–8:1); this first series would thus become the heavenly counterpart of what will take place on earth. *with seven seals:* The document is perfectly sealed: No one can know or modify its contents. **2.** *a strong angel:* The adjective is in keeping with the challenge issued to all of creation. *who is worthy:* The key to the whole vision (vv. 4, 9, 12): who is qualified to know and put into execution God's plan for history? **3.** *in heaven, on earth, under the earth:* These words correspond to the current division of creation into three regions (Ex 20:4; Phil 2:10). **4.** *I wept much:* Only despair could be the result of a situation in which no one could come to a knowledge of the course of history, nor direct it toward a goal that can give sense to human life. The situation of Christians suffering persecution would indeed be foolish and hopeless. **5.** *he has conquered:* See 17:4; 1 Cor 15:54–57. It is by his death that Christ has conquered (v. 9), thus showing faithful Christians the road to victory (cf. 2:11,17,26; 3:5,12). *the root of David:* This title and the preceding one show how the Lamb has fulfilled OT promises (Is 11:1,10; Rom 15:12).

35 **6.** *in the midst of the throne:* The position symbolizes the close link with God, whose knowledge and power the Lamb shares. But the Lamb is also in the midst of the elders, thus showing how he remains linked to his Church (1:13). *a Lamb:* This is Christ's main title throughout the Ap (28 times). The theme of Christ sacrificed like a lamb (Jn 1:29,36; 19:36; Acts 8:32; 1 Cor 5:7; 1 Pt 1:18f.) plays upon that of the Servant of Yahweh (Is 53:7) and of the paschal lamb (Ex 12). But the Ap considers the Lamb as a conqueror who after his sacrifice holds a universal dominion. This victorious sight would permit the comparison of the lamb with a ram, an ancient symbol of power and dominion (Dn 8:3). *standing:* Does this stance, characteristic of the priest about to offer sacrifice (Heb 10:11), suggest that the Lamb is both priest and victim? Rather, it probably signifies the restored life that the Lamb henceforth leads (7:17; 14:1). *as one slain:* It still carries the marks of its sacrifice (Jn 20:25,27), but it is no longer a captive of death. *seven horns and seven eyes:* It holds the fullness of power (Dt 33:17; Lk 1:69) and insight. *the seven spirits of God:* See 1:4. The Lamb watches and supervises all that takes place on earth (Zech 4:10). **7.** The action of the Lamb taking the scroll represents his accession to the throne. The three doxologies that follow (vv. 9f., 12, 13) correspond to the acclamations that usually followed the enthronement of a king. **8.** *each of the elders had a harp:* This was the traditional instrument (14:2; 15:2) accompanying the singing of the Pss. *the prayers of the saints:* The Church on earth joins the Church in heaven to share the cult rendered to God and the Lamb (8:3f.; Ps 141:2 [LXX]; Lk 1:10). These prayers express the Christians' desire that God's mysterious decrees be carried out soon (5:10). The "saints" (8:3f.; 11:18; 13:7,10; Dn 7:18ff.) are the faithful of Christ's kingdom who belong to God.

36 **9.** *a new song:* This expression, frequently used in the Pss (33:3; 40:3; 98:1), originally referred to an unusual hymn of praise, but also to an extraordinary event (Is 42:10). This newness in praise corresponds to the new name given to the conqueror (2:17; 3:12), to the new Jerusalem (3:12; 21:2), to the new heaven and the new earth (21:1), and finally to the universal renewal (21:5). In a word, the whole universe (the four living creatures) and the Church (the 24 elders) celebrate Christ who, by the redemption, has inaugurated the new era. *thou wast slain:* See 5:6,12; 13:8; Is 53:7. The same verb characterizes the sacrifice of Christians who, following Christ, suffer death out of loyalty to their Lord (6:9; 18:24). *from every tribe and language and people and nation:* See 7:9; 10:11; 11:9; 13:7; 14:6; 17:15; cf. Dn 3:4,7; 5:19; 6:25. The four words in this enumeration signify all of the physical universe. The Ap considers in this expression only the universe of the Christians in whom redemption has become effective. **12.** This doxology of the angels picks up and extends that of 4:11. The seven words it contains suggest the fullness of power and glory. The first four concern the Lamb's dominion; the last three express the adoration of the angels. **13.** *every creature:* The whole created universe (enumeration of four terms, including, this time, "the sea"; cf. v. 3; Ps 146:6) has the mission to glorify God and the Lamb. All creation exults with joy, for the moment is at hand when it will be freed from the curse, in order to be completely renewed (20:11; 21:1,4f.; 22:2; Rom 8:18ff.). *to him who sits on the throne and to the Lamb:* See 7:10. Just as the doxology is offered both to God and to the Lamb, so kingship and dominion belong jointly to the Father and to Christ (3:21). **14.** Just as in 4:9–11, this grand liturgy ends with the homage of the heavenly Church in unison with the representatives of creation (see H.-P. Müller, *ZNW* 54 [1963] 254–67).

37 (c) THE OPENING OF THE FIRST SIX SEALS (6:1–17). This section provides us with a symbolic description of the content of the sealed document.

(i) *The opening of the first four seals* (6:1–8). This homogeneous group forms a unit expressed in a literary parallelism formed by the repetition of the same expressions: "When the Lamb had opened," "I heard," "Come!" Then the seer describes the horse and the rider, both called forth by the four living creatures (4:6ff.). Also, the misfortunes unleashed by the opening of the four seals are closely linked to one another. The riders, who personify these misfortunes, symbolize a conquering power and the three evils that follow from it: war, famine, and pestilence. These evils traditionally mark calamitous times. Wars, famines, and plagues reappear regularly throughout human history, apparently arising out of natural causes. But in the eyes of John, they are a judgment of God, a type of the last judgment. The imagery of the horses of different colors recalls Zech 1:8–11; 6:1–7. But here attention is focused more on the riders, each one of whom has the mission to cover the whole earth with a specific scourge. This description might well allude to events contemporary to the Ap. In AD 62, the Parthian king Vologesus defeated the Romans; from then on the Parthians presented the most serious threat to the Roman Empire. They may even appear here as God's scourge of the powers that persecute his Church.

38 **1–2.** *white:* A symbol of victory, as is also the crown received by the rider. *a bow:* The characteristic weapon of the Parthians. *he that sat on him:* Since Irenaeus, he has often been identified with Christ who in 19:11ff. appears sitting upon a white charger. But the immediate context makes this identification dubious: Christ is already present in this scene as the Lamb who opens the seals; but this rider is intimately linked to the three following ones who are all bearers of evil. This rider stands for a conquering power whom none can resist. *come:* In the Ap, the vb. *erchesthai* usually refers to the coming of God or of Christ. The imperative here could tally with the demands of the Spirit, of the bride, and of John (22:17,20), all of whom ask for the coming of Christ. In this case, he would be coming to the aid of his own by means of a conquering power that will punish the persecutors of his Church. **3–4.** *fiery red... great sword:* These signify the bloody wars that will result from the conquests of the first rider. **5–6.** The "black" color, the "balance" (Lv 26:26; Ez 4:16), and the details concerning the principal staples of life show that the third rider is the bearer of famine, a normal aftermath of war. *a quart of wheat:* This amount represented a man's daily ration. The "denarius" being one day's pay (Mt 20:2ff.), a laborer could only earn enough for what was strictly necessary to subsist. In Cicero's time a denarius bought 12 qt. of wheat. *barley:* The ordinary food of the poor, three times cheaper than wheat. **7–8.** *a pale-green horse:* The color of a corpse's rotting flesh. *Hades:* This personification of the place where the dead reside follows pestilence to swallow up those who will perish. Verse 8b concerns all four riders, another indication that they must be taken as a homogeneous unit. *the wild beasts of the earth:* Mentioned in Ez 14:21, they suggest the ruin following upon war (see J. S. Considine, *CBQ* 6 [1944] 406–22; M. Rissi, *Interpr* 18 [1964] 407–18).

39 (ii) *The fifth and sixth seals* (6:9–17). **9.** Following upon the slain Lamb, the Church appears persecuted in its members. *under the altar:* This altar (see 8:3; 9:13; 14:18; 16:7) is the heavenly counterpart of the altar of holocausts in the Jerusalem Temple. *the souls:* The slaying of Christians who bear witness to Christ is seen here as a sacrifice (Phil 2:17; 2 Tm 4:6), resembling the rite of pouring blood at the foot of the altar (Lv 4:7). In the OT the soul, or life, is in the blood (Lv 17:11,14; Dt 12:23). **10.** This cry does not express a desire for vengeance, which would not be in accord with the teaching of Christ (Lk 6:27f.). The martyrs call for the securing of justice. God would not be just, nor the Lord of history, if he did not punish injustice. *Sovereign Lord...:* The context and the recollections of the OT show that the souls are imploring God rather than Christ. **11.** *a white robe:* This means the victory of the martyrs and their sharing in the happiness of eternal life (7:13–17). The individual victory of each martyr is assured as soon as he is with Christ; the Church on earth recognizes the victory of her martyrs by glorifying their name. *who were to be killed:* During Domitian's reign John sees persecution as imminent (2:10; 3:10). Those who have already borne witness would perhaps be the martyrs of Nero's time. *should be complete:* In accordance with Jewish eschatology, Christianity holds that the last judgment will not come until the number of the elect, determined by God, has been completed (see W. C. van Unnik, *RHPR* 42 [1962] 237–46).

40 **12–17.** The sixth seal announces the events preliminary to the end of the world and the salvation of the elect. Verses 12–14 describe great cosmic disturbances, and vv. 15–17 their effects on man. The whole passage abounds with images borrowed from the prophets. Cosmic disturbances, especially the passing away of the heavens were familiar symbols to the prophetic and apocalyptic tradition about the end of the world (Lk 21:25). It would be a mistake to interpret these images literally; they stand rather for social upheavals. **12.** *earthquake:* See Am 8:8; Is 2:19; Jl 2:10; Hag 2:6; Mk 13:8. *sun...and moon:* See Am 8:9; Is 13:10; Ez 32:7; Jl 3:4; Mk 13:24; Acts 2:20. **13.** *stars:* They are represented as being fixed to the firmament. They fall to earth like unripe figs in the spring when shaken by a great wind (Na 3:12; Mk 13:25). **14.** *the sky vanished:* The vault of heaven, considered a solid substance, will be rolled up as rapidly as would be a scroll (2 Pt 3:12). **15.** The listing of seven walks of life stands for the whole of society, seized with the terror of the impending judgment. *the kings of the earth:* The Roman emperors, as types of chiefs of state hostile to Christ and his Church (Ps 2:2ff.; Acts 4:26ff.), are the ones immediately envisaged. *the great men:* The officers of state, e.g., the proconsuls who persecute. *the rich and the strong:* Neither wealth nor physical strength will enable anyone to evade God's judgment. *hid themselves:* Conscious of their guilt, the ungodly fear God more than death. This psychological reaction of the sinner, already noted in Gn 3:8, will still torture the last generation of impious humanity. **17.** *the great day:* See Jl 2:11; 3:4; Zeph 1:14ff.; 2:3; Jude 6. *who can stand before it:* See Na 1:6; Mal 3:2.

41 (d) Double Interlude Describing the Church (7:1–17). Normally the breaking of the seventh seal (8:1) and the "great day of wrath" (6:17) should take place here. But John interpolates two separate visions between the sixth and the seventh seals, just as he will divide the sixth trumpet (9:13–21) from the seventh (11:15–19). The purpose of these two visions is to contrast the Church, glorious and protected by God, with the "inhabitants of the earth" who are seized with panic at the approach of judgment (6:15–17). In the first vision, John sees the People of God on earth placed under divine protection against coming adversity. The second vision is to encourage the servants of God to persevere unto death.

(i) *The Church on earth preserved by God* (7:1–8). **1.** *the four corners of the earth:* The earth is seen as a rectangular surface (20:8; Is 40:22). *the four winds:* Favorable winds were considered to come from the sides of the earth, while the unfavorable arose from the corners. The four winds blowing from the ends of the earth (Jer 49:36; Zech 2:6; Dn 8:8; 11:4; Mk 13:27) symbolizes the destructive forces of this world and herald the last day (Dn 7:2; Zech 6:5). *four angels:* Just as one angel received power over fire (14:18) and another dominion over water (16:5), so four angels are in charge of the fury of the winds. *tree:* The trees, especially vulnerable to gusts of wind, represent all the living. **2.** *from the rising sun:* The protecting angel appears in the East, the source of light, and the place of Paradise (Gn 2:8). It was also from the East that the Messiah was expected. *the seal of the living God:* According to the widespread custom of the ancients, Oriental lords impressed the seal of their ring on their belongings; whatever was thus marked by the seal belonged to the lord and was under his protection (cf. Ez 9:4; Ex 12:7–14). Whoever bears "the seal of the living God" will thus be his property (2 Cor 1:22; Gal 6:17; Eph 1:13; 4:30; Jn 6:27). This does not preclude the Christians' escape from persecution or death (6:11; 13:15; 17:6; 20:4); but the oppressed will be given strength by God to help them persevere. **4–8.** *a hundred and forty-four thousand:* That is, 12 × 12 × 1000. The number 12 is the symbol of perfection, especially in the physical and human world. The second 12 corresponds to the tribes of Israel, the People of God. Finally, 1000 indicates a very large number, and 144,000 then symbolizes the multitude of the elect whose real number is known to God alone (6:11). *from every tribe...:* The number scarcely refers only to Jewish Christians; rather it stands for all the members of the Church, the true Israel. Judaism cherished the hope that Israel would be completely restored with all its tribes in messianic times (Is 49:6; *Pss Sol* 17:44; *2 Baruch* 78:1ff.; *2 Esdras* 13:39–50). The first Christians asserted the fulfillment of this hope in the Church of Christ (Mt 19:28; Gal 6:16; Jas 1:1), and John shares completely in this idea (21:12–14; cf. 2:9; 3:9ff.). *Judah:* This tribe is named first because Christ was born of it (5:5). *Levi:* Replaces Dan, a tribe considered unfaithful and, according to a later tradition, held to be the tribe from which would spring the Antichrist.

42 (ii) *The Church in heaven glorifies God* (7:9–17). After the final test the multitude of Christians, victorious over persecution, appear in full glory. Verses 9–12 describe the triumph of the elect, while vv. 13–17 explain the main details that symbolize their happiness. **9.** *which no one could number:* A possible allusion to the promise made to Abraham (Gn 15:5; 32:12; Heb 11:12). *with palms:* A sign of the victory and of the thanksgiving of the elect (1 Mc 13:51; 2 Mc 10:7). **10.** *salvation...:* The elect give thanks to God and the Lamb who saved them ("the saving God," 1 Tm 1:1; 2:3; Ti 1:3; 3:4, "the saving Christ," Ti 1:4; 2:13; 3:6). This hymn of joy will recur at the fall of the dragon (12:10) and of Babylon (19:1). **11.** The whole court of heaven joins the acclamation of the saints (5:11). **12.** *Amen:* Thus placed at the beginning and the end of the doxology, made up of seven terms, the "Amen" frames the hymn and expresses the full association of all the angels with the praise of the elect (5:14; 19:4). **14.** *from great tribulation:* In union with Jesus, Christians regularly share trials (1:9; 2:9); but the great tribulation (Dn 12:1; Mk 13:19), described in 13:7–10, will mark the end. *these are they who have come:* Many would consider them to be only the martyrs. It may, however, be better to identify this crowd with all the members of the Church who have remained faithful throughout the final crisis: Thus the present vision continues the preceding one that concerned the whole Church on earth; the "white robe" should belong to every Christian. *they have washed their robes:* The "white garment" most often signifies the heavenly glory of the elect (3:5; 6:11; 7:9,13; 19:8) and of the Angels (4:4; 19:14). Still, the "white robe" is not a consequence of entry into eschatological glory, but rather a condition (22:14). In fact, this image describes the very state of being a Christian—a gift of Christ at the moment when man becomes a member of the Church. But there is the danger of losing this gift; thus the "white robe" holds for the Christian on earth a moral aspect (3:4). *in the blood of the Lamb:* The "blood" is a symbol of the death of Christ and its salvific worth (Eph 1:7; Col 1:20; Heb 9:14; 1 Pt 1:2,19; 1 Jn 1:7). The formula "in the blood" is stylized in the NT (Rom 3:25; 5:9; 1 Cor 11:25; Eph 2:13) and might come from the Eucharistic liturgy (1 Cor 11:25). **15.** As the angels (4:8ff.), so the elect living in the intimacy of God are represented as ceaselessly celebrating a celestial liturgy (21:5; 22:5). The whole of God's holy people shares in this worship, and not just priests alone. **16–17.** Heavenly happiness is described in a series of OT expressions. The verbs are all in the fut. tense; they point out how this vision ends with a promise. Christians will no longer know suffering (Is 49:10; Ps 121:6; Jn 4:14; 6:35; 7:37). *the Lamb will shepherd them:* Pss 23; 80:2; Is 40:11; Ez 34:23; Jn 10:11–16. *will guide them:* Ex 15:13; Dt 1:33; Pss 5:9; 86:11; Wis 9:11. *to the springs of the water of life:* Jer 2:13; Ps 35:10. *will wipe away every tear...:* See 21:4; Is 25:8.

43 (e) THE OPENING OF THE SEVENTH SEAL (8:1). The scroll containing the will of God for history (5:1) is open at last. After all the extraordinary events accompanying the breaking of the previous seals, one would expect the climax, the last judgment (6:17). Instead, nothing happens and the suspense remains. In fact, the seventh seal heralds the next heptad; and its contents are spread over the seven trumpet blasts. *silence...about half an hour:* A striking contrast between the hymns that go before and the crash that follows (v. 5). The purpose is to underscore, as in the prophetic tradition (Is 41:1; Hab 2:20; Zeph 1:7; Zech 2:17), the solemn moment that precedes and announces the startling "coming of God."

44 **(B) The Seven Trumpets (8:2–11:19).** The arrangement of the second heptad resembles that of the seals. Here again a heavenly scene (8:2–6) serves as an introduction. The first four trumpets (8:7–12) form a block as did the first four seals. The fifth (9:1–12) and the sixth trumpet (9:13–21) form a contrast because of the wide development that accompanies them. Finally, a double interlude of visions precedes the seventh trumpet blast.

45 (a) THE SEVEN ANGELS WITH SEVEN TRUMPETS (8:2–6). Verses 2 and 6 hark back and forth to each other and serve as a frame for the liturgical action in vv. 3–5, which explain and prepare the heptad of the trumpets. **2.** *seven angels:* See comment on 1:4. *before God:* They are termed the "angels of the presence" (*Jub* 1:27,29; 2:1–2,18; 15:27), according to the expression of Is 63:9 (MT), because they are in the immediate presence of God (Lk 1:19). This way of depicting them is taken from the protocol of Oriental courts (Est 1:14). *seven trumpets:* See comment on 1:10. **3.** *another angel:* As does the "angel of peace" of certain apocalypses, he fulfills here the role of intermediary between God and men, offering to God the prayers of the saints (Tb 12:15) and acting as the executor on earth of God's decree. *the altar:* The heavenly temple seems to have only one altar, corresponding at once to the altar of holocausts and to the altar of incense in the Jerusalem Temple (Ex 30:1). Indeed, the Ap always speaks only of one altar (6:9; 9:13; 14:18; 16:7). *the prayers of all the saints:* See 5:8. All Christians on earth marked by the divine seal (7:1–8) ardently pray to God in the face of the imminent persecution. To purify these prayers of human imperfection and render them agreeable to God, the angel adds "much incense." **4.** The prayers thus purified and presented to God by the angel rise toward God like the smoke of the incense. Christians struggling on earth can have confidence, for their prayers are answered. **5.** *the fire of the altar:* Symbol of God's wrath to be made manifest on earth (Ez 10:2; Gn 19:24). *peals of thunder:* These are premonitory signs of the plagues to be unleashed by the seven trumpets. It is God's answer to the prayer of the saints who aspire to be delivered from persecution. The plagues will therefore not attack those marked by the divine seal, but only their impious persecutors (9:4,20f.).

46 (b) THE FIRST FOUR TRUMPETS (8:7–12). They are described in a parallel manner: The descriptions are brief and contain similar expressions. The plagues directly affect nature, divided as it is into four sections: dry land, sea, springs of fresh water, and stars (14:7; 16:2–9). Only one third of these elements (Ez 5:2) is affected: The calamities destroy the security of human existence, but they do not make up the whole of God's judgment; they serve as a warning, inviting men to repentance. Several traits are borrowed from the plagues of Egypt (Ex 7ff.), the type of God's historical interventions against those who oppose his plan for salvation. **7.** The details are inspired by the seventh Egyptian plague (Ex 9:22–26; Ez 38:22; Jl 3:3f.; Acts 2:19f.). **8–9.** *a great mountain burning:* Possibly this picture is inspired by the eruption of Vesuvius (AD 79) or of some other volcano near the sea. *became blood:* This plague corresponds to the first plague of Egypt (Ex 7:20–21; Ps 78:44), though it goes beyond it. **10–11.** *wormwood:* Considered an extremely bitter and malignant substance. The OT had used the metaphor of changing into wormwood to show the bitter fruits of idolatry (Dt 29:17), the perverting of justice (Am 5:7; 6:12), and the punishment of God (Jer 9:14; 23:15; Lam 3:15,19). *died of the water:* A third of the supply of fresh water, a necessity of life, is poisoned. Thus the eschatological punishment corresponds to the situation preceding God's intervention at the Exodus (Ex 15:23–25). **12.** *the third part of them was darkened:* A replica of the ninth plague of Egypt (Ex 10:21), announced for the end of time (Am 8:9; Jl 4:15).

47 (c) AN EAGLE WARNS OF THE LAST THREE TRUMPETS (8:13). The plagues unleashed by the last three trumpets will strike mankind directly. A new step has therefore been reached that is underscored by a solemn proclamation. *an eagle:* He fulfills the function of "an angel" announcing a divine message. The origin of this image is not certain: The Mandaean parallel quoted by Lohmeyer seems very close; on the other hand, the eagles that seek out corpses after a battle (Hab 1:8; Mt 24:28; Lk 17:37) can hardly be compared to those in this passage. *in midheaven:* At the zenith, so that the whole universe can hear this message. *woe, woe, woe:* A triple curse relating to the last three trumpets (9:1,12,13; 11:14,15). *those who dwell on the earth:* See comment on 3:10.

48 (d) THE FIFTH TRUMPET (9:1–12). This plague is reminiscent of the eighth plague in Egypt (Ex 10:1ff.). But John's more immediate source is Jl 1–2, where the prophet announces that the "Day of the Lord" will be marked by an invasion of locusts, a calamity particularly dreaded in the Orient.

1. *a star fallen from heaven:* Attacking astrological cults, late Judaism was induced to represent the fallen powers as stars (Is 14:12–15; Lk 10:18; Jude 13). Nevertheless, the similarity between this passage and 20:1–3 suggests that we must identify the star with an angel acting at God's command. *he was given:* The "theological" passive expresses the action of God, who governs all things (cf. 9:4,5; *GrBib* § 236). *the shaft of the abyss: Abyssos* (LXX), which translates *tᵉhôm* (MT), may refer to the waters under the earth (Gn 1:2), the depths of the earth (Ps 71:20), or Sheol, the abode of all the dead (Nm 16:30–35; Jb 3:11–19). In apocalyptic literature, Sheol is a place where evil spirits are temporarily detained and punished (Lk 8:31); their final destination is the "pit of fire and sulphur" (20:10). The abyss is conceived of as a vast, almost bottomless, subterranean cavern, filled with fire. It affords no means of communication with the surface of the earth except a shaft, the entrance to which is kept locked. **3–6.** *locusts:* The context shows that the plague is an eschatological calamity, completely transcending the familiar plagues of locusts. John pictures the calamity as an invasion. If chs. 6–11 treat of divine judgments passed upon the Jewish world, it would be tempting to link the details of the present passage with the beginnings of the Jewish War (AD 66–70). But the more common opinion is that John still has something like a Parthian invasion in mind. *scorpions:* Their venomous character was proverbial (Ez 2:6; Lk 11:12), and it was natural enough to associate them with the forces of evil (Sir 39:30; Lk 10:19). *they were told:* The action of demons is under the domination of God, who specifies and limits it. Contrary to their natural habit, the locusts, in the present case, are to spare the foliage and attack men; but only those men who do not belong to God will be tormented (7:1–8; Lk 10:19). *to torture them:* The sting of the Palestinian scorpion is rarely fatal, but it is very painful. To undergo such agonizing pain indefinitely would be an unbearable torture—death would seem preferable. This torture is the sign of God's anger at the sinful world. *for five months:* A period, limited by God, more or less corresponding to the life-span of locusts. **7–10.** John lists eight characteristics that show that these locusts are fantastic, diabolical creatures. *were like horses:* Jl 2:4f.; cf. the invasion described in Na 2:4–7,11; 3:2–3,15–17. *crowns like gold:* A note distinctive of conquerors; a picture of a victorious army. *like faces of men:* A suggestion that the creatures are intelligent. *like the hair of women:* Long, unbound hair, a characteristic of barbarous peoples. Demons are so depicted to accentuate their fierceness. *like breastplates of iron:* Like war chariots (Jl 2:5). *their wings:* The noise is like that accompanying an attack that destroys everything in its path. *their power lies in their tails:* Like the scorpion, whereas the locust is feared for its mouth. **11.** *they have...a king:* Again, in contrast to ordinary locusts (Prv 30:27). The whole catastrophe is directed by the prince of demons. *Abaddon:* This Hebr word appears six times in the MT. It means "destruction" (Jb 31:12) and it is used in parallelism with "Sheol" (Jb 26:6; Prv 15:11), "death" (Jb 28:22), and "burial" (Ps 88:11). Here it expresses what the prince of demons is. *Apollyon:* John stresses the point by adding a Gk term corresponding to Abaddon. The word looks like *Apollo*, who was honored as the emperor's special protector, but there is little likelihood that the similarity is intentional; *Apollyōn* is the masc. form of *apōleia* (destruction), the term used in the LXX to translate Abaddon.

49 (e) THE SIXTH TRUMPET (9:13–21). This vision resembles the fifth. It presents another attack by diabolical powers upon the pagan world. But, instead of describing it in terms of a familiar catastrophe in nature, John plays upon the contemporary uneasiness arising from a military peril, the presence of the fearsome Parthian cavalry on the Euphrates frontier. This plague will cause great suffering and will destroy a third of the population. **13.** *from the four horns of the altar:* The horns were situated at the four corners of the altar (Ex 27:2; 30:2f.) upon which the angel offered the prayers of the saints (8:3). God's vengeance is the answer to their prayers (6:9f.; cf. 14:18; 16:7). **14–15.** *the four angels:* The number of this group (different from that in 7:1) indicates that their destructive activity will be extended throughout the universe. These angels correspond to the "angels of vengeance" of apocalyptic literature. *who are bound:* They are unable to act at will, but only at the time—"the hour, the day" (v. 15)—and in the manner determined by God. When they are "released," no further obstacle can prevent their intervention. *the great river Euphrates:* Traditionally known as "the great river," the Euphrates was the ideal eastern boundary of Israel (Gn 15:18; Dt 1:7). Beyond it lay the great pagan nations whose invasions of Palestine were announced by Isaiah (7:20; 8:7f.) and Jeremiah (46:10) as the "overflow of the great river." By the time of the Ap this territory was occupied by the Parthians, who constituted the most serious threat to the Roman Empire. It is likely that John presents them here as a type of the punishments that God will inflict upon kingdoms guilty of persecuting the Church. **16.** *twice ten thousand times ten thousand:* This extravagant number shows that the passage is concerned with a superhuman power (5:11; Dn 7:10). **17–19.** Mounts and riders are presented as fabulous beings. We are reminded of Leviathan (Jb 41:11ff.) and the terrible scene in Gn 19:24,28. Various elements in the description indicate that these creatures are diabolical monsters, risen from the abyss. **20–21.** *did not repent:* These words recall the hardening of Pharaoh's heart (Ex 7:13,22; etc.). Although the plagues are a punishment for sin, they are also directed toward leading unfaithful men to repentance before the final judgment (16:9,11). *the works of their hands:* Cf. Is 2:8; Jer 1:16. *to worship the demons:* A tradition that is relatively old but not very well attested, tells us that pagan cults were addressed to demons (Dt 32:17; Ps 106:37; 1 Cor 10:20). *which can neither see nor hear nor walk:* Another traditional theme was this stress on the total impotence of idols (Jer 10:3–5; Bar 6:3,7; 1 Cor 8:4). But although an idol represents a nonexistent being, it is a visible sign of revolt against the living God. *nor did they repent of their murders:* Idolatry, rejection of the true God, results in moral perversion (Rom 1:21–32; Eph 5:6).

50 (f) Double Interlude (10:1–11:14). The course of eschatological events is again interrupted, as it was after the opening of the sixth seal. Until this point, the People of God have been protected against the calamities produced by the diabolical powers (9:4), but nothing has been said about the consummation of salvation. Now we are told that the end is imminent (10:6f.) and that the Kingdom of God, which will mark the final deliverance of all Christians, is about to be inaugurated (11:15ff.). Thus the two visions included in this interlude are intended to console and comfort the seer and his brethren.

(i) *The angel with the little open scroll* (10:1–11). **1.** *coming down from heaven:* Beginning with ch. 4, John has been in a state of ecstatic, celestial rapture; now he is once more on earth (vv. 4 and 8), probably on Patmos (1:9). *cloud:* See 1:7; 11:12; 14:14; Ps 104:3; Dn 7:13. *rainbow:* See 4:3; Ez 1:28. All the elements in this description are traditional symbols of the glory of God. The vision of a glorious heavenly being recalls the transfiguration of Jesus (Mt 17:2ff. par.) and, especially, the inaugural vision of the Son of Man (1:12–16). **2.** *a little scroll:* It is different from the sealed scroll in 5:1, which was received by the Lamb from God's hand. The little scroll is open (its contents must be communicated to all the churches), and John receives it from the angel. The scroll is neither so long nor so important as the one in 5:1, nor does it have the same meaning; its contents are given, apparently, in 11:1–13. *he set his right foot...:* This is suggestive of the angel's colossal size, but it especially signifies the universalism of his message. *the sea, the earth, and the heavens:* A formula that embraces the totality of creation (v. 6; Ex 20:4,11). **3.** *like a lion:* Another OT attribute of God (Hos 11:10; Jl 3:16; Am 1:2; 3:8). *seven thunders:* The most probable explanation of this difficult phrase lies in its similarity to Ps 29, where "the voice of Yahweh"—the thunder—is praised seven times. Here God himself (cf. Jn 12:27–33), in the fullness of his majesty, would reply to the cry of the angel. **4.** *a voice from heaven:* Probably Christ (v. 8). *seal up...do not write it down:* An extraordinary command (cf. Dn 8:26; 12:4,9; 2 Cor 12:4), since John receives repeated commands in the Ap to write down his visions (1:11,19; 14:13; 19:9; 21:5), and an explicit order "not to seal the prophecies of this book" (22:10). Perhaps the prohibition indicates the limited character of the revelations of the Ap. **5–6.** The major influence underlying this description is found in Dn (12:5–7). *he lifted up his right hand to heaven and swore:* Cf. Gn 14:22; Dt 32:40. *no more delay:* Cf. Hab 2:3. Recalling Dn 12:7, this passage might mean that we have here an allusion to the brief struggle (three and a half years in Dn) against the Antichrist (ch. 13ff.) who is immediately to precede the consummation. Or it might mean that we are to understand that the delay mentioned in 6:11 is over, and that the time of deliverance is at hand (11:15ff.). **7.** *the mystery of God:* God's hidden plan of salvation, which concerns the entirety of human history (→ Pauline Theology, 79:32–34). *as he announced:* Lit., "as he evangelized." The promise of happiness in the Kingdom of God after the victory over the powers of evil is truly "good news" for the Church. *the prophets:* Above all, the Christian prophets; but we must not exclude the OT prophets, because they too knew and proclaimed, in their own way, the plan of salvation.

51 **8–11.** *eat it:* Ezekiel's prophetic investiture (2:8–3:3) is the inspiration for this description. The action of eating (Jer 15:16) symbolizes John's complete assimilation of the contents of the little scroll. *it was sweet as honey...and bitter:* This twofold effect expresses the double aspect of the scroll's contents: It announces the glorious victory of the faithful, but it points out that this triumph is to be preceded by a painful struggle (11:1–13). Here, in brief, is the general rule of Christian life: One attains beatitude and glory only after being tested by the cross. *they say to me:* Probably the heavenly voice (Christ) and the angel. *you must prophesy again:* This order recalls the visions of chs. 6–9 and, going beyond the bounds of the little scroll, it serves as an introduction for ch. 12ff. *about peoples, nations,...:* These prophecies contain judgments passed against the peoples of the whole world (note the enumeration of four terms) and their leaders (see A. Feuillet, *SP* 2, 414–29; *idem, Johannine Studies* [Staten Island, N.Y., 1964] 215–31).

52 (ii) *The measuring of the Temple and the two witnesses* (11:1–14). **1.** *measure the Temple:* Cf. Ez 40:1ff.; Zech 2:1–5. That which is measured is assured of God's protection. John is thinking of the Jerusalem Temple in which Jewish Zealots locked themselves in AD 70, hoping that God would not permit the Romans to enter. But he goes beyond the material Temple (which was, in fact, destroyed) and refers, in accordance with a widely attested Christian theme (1 Cor 3:16f.; 2 Cor 6:16; Eph 2:19–21; 1 Pt 2:5), to the Church as a temple. The present passage, preceding the seventh trumpet, would thus have the same import as 7:1–8, which precedes the seventh seal: God promises to protect the faithful during the coming persecution. *the court outside the temple:* The Court of the Gentiles was not considered an integral part of the Jerusalem Temple. Here, perhaps, it symbolizes the Synagogue, Israel according to the flesh. *the holy city:* Cf. Is 48:2; Dn 9:24. The terrestrial Jerusalem will be handed over to Gentiles (Lk 21:24) to be trampled underfoot (Zech 12:3). *forty-two months:* Equal to three and a half years (12:14; Lk 4:25; Jas 5:17) and to 1260 days (11:3; 12:6). These three temporal expressions designate the duration of the Antichrist's activity (13:5). They are derived from Dn 7:25 and 12:7 ("a time, two times and half a time"); 9:27 ("half a week"). The persecution of Antiochus IV Epiphanes lasted approximately three and a half years (June 168–December 165 BC). Three and a half—half of seven—symbolically applies to things that are precarious and transitory. The persecution of Antiochus became the type for subsequent periods of oppression—all due to last only a limited time.

53 The two witnesses (11:3–13) are one of the most difficult problems of the Ap. John has probably modified an older Jewish source; some attitudes in this underlying source are at variance with his own point of view, and where the two conflict they lead to confusion. Some exegetes, impressed by the strongly Jewish context, interpret the entire passage as applicable to Jerusalem (especially its destruction, AD 70) and to the Jewish world. Yet some details transcend the Jewish milieu: e.g., the universalist enumeration (11:9); "the inhabitants of the earth" (11:10). Besides, "the great city" (11:8a), applied to Jerusalem, would be misleading. It seems better, therefore, to interpret the entire passage as applying to the universal Church fulfilling the office of witness before a world hostile to God. Her testimony may lead to martyrdom, but her unshakable confidence in divine protection assures her that her sacrifice will result in a complete victory and will further the glory of God.

3. *my two witnesses:* Their descriptions (vv. 5–6 and 12) obviously fit Moses and Elijah. Thus the "two witnesses" derive from Jewish tradition, which held that Moses and Elijah (see Dt 18:15; Mal 3:22–24) would return to preach repentance before the Day of the Lord. A modification of this tradition is discerned in the NT. In particular, Moses and Elijah represent the Law and the Prophets bearing witness to Christ (Lk 9:30ff. par.; Lk 24:27). In the present passage these two personages would represent the entire Church, which must bear living and perpetual witness to Christ (Acts 1:8). "Two witnesses" are understandable in the light of the well-known law that determined the essential conditions of valid testimony (Dt 19:15; Jn 8:17; Mk 6:7). Again, John intends to connect this passage with Zech 4:2ff. *clothed in sackcloth:* A sign of mourning or penance (Gn 37:34; Jer 4:8; Jon 3:5). The Church must practice (Mk 2:20) and preach penance to bear witness. **4.** *the two olive trees and the two lampstands:* In Zech 4:1–14 the two olive trees represent Zerubbabel and Joshua, two anointed servants of the Lord; the seven-branched lampstand represents God, who inspires and strengthens these two leaders, to whom the political and religious reconstruction of Israel was entrusted. In the Ap the two olive trees and the two lampstands stand for the same realities. In another passage (1:12,20) the image of the lampstand signifies a Christian community. Here we ought to interpret the symbol as referring to the Church, nourished by the riches of the Spirit and shining like a lamp to bear witness to the divine light. *standing before the Lord:* Christians live in the presence of God and serve him by their testimony. **5.** Christians, who acknowledge God, cannot be killed so long as their testimony remains incomplete (v. 7). *fire will come out of their mouths:* Elijah had brought down fire from heaven upon his enemies (2 Kgs 1:10ff.; Sir 48:3). These witnesses kill by the fire of the word that they proclaim (Jer 5:14; Sir 48:3). **6.** *to shut heaven:* A Jewish tradition associated the drought caused by Elijah (1 Kgs 17:1; Sir 48:3) with the persecution of Antiochus: Both events were said to have lasted three and a half years. *power over the waters:* Even more effectively than Moses, the Church could cause all kinds of plagues (1 Sm 4:8) if she should so desire (Mk 9:23; Jn 15:7).

54 **7.** *the beast:* Because it comes from the bottomless pit (9:1ff.) it is inspired by Satan, whom it represents on earth. It is the Antichrist, who musters and marshals the enemies of the two witnesses. **8.** *the great city:* This expression is constantly used in the Ap for Babylon, i.e., Rome (14:8; 16:19; 17:5,18; 18:2,10,21), and it is difficult, in spite of the following characteristics, to see Jerusalem in this passage. *Sodom:* A typical example of moral perversion (Is 1:9f.; Ez 16:46,55). *Egypt:* Represents powers hostile to God's people who are oppressed and reduced to slavery. *where their Lord was crucified:* Some commentators consider this detail a gloss, and although it seems to clinch the argument that the "great city" is Jerusalem, such an interpretation would contradict the beginning of the verse. The most acceptable of many different interpretations is the one that universalizes the entire passage. Both Rome and Jerusalem furnish details that John applies to the terrestrial city of evil, i.e., the pagan world inimical to God and his people. This city is eager to annihilate the Church; it continues to crucify Christ in his faithful. **9.** *for three days and a half:* This corresponds to the duration in 11:2; cf. 12:14. *refused to let them be placed in a tomb:* To refuse burial is generally considered the most shameful manner of treating the dead (Ps 79:2f.; Jer 8:2; 16:4; 2 Mc 5:10). Here it shows the pitch of hatred to which pagans are incited by the Christian message. **10.** *rejoice:* The pagan world, tortured by remorse because of the Church's testimony, now feels relief (1 Kgs 18:17; 21:20; Mk 6:20). **12.** The witnesses arise and ascend to heaven in glory behind their Lord. *went up to heaven:* Like Elijah (2 Kgs 2:11; Sir 48:9); cf. Dt 34:6 (Moses' burial place is unknown; so he must have been taken up). **13.** *a great earthquake:* A symbol often used by the prophets for social or spiritual upheavals (see comment on 6:12). Such phenomena mark the resurrection of Christians in much the same fashion as they did the death and resurrection of their Lord (Mt 27:54; 28:2). *seven thousand people:* A symbolic number, probably signifying a great throng composed of all social classes. *gave glory*, i.e., were converted (16:9): A startling turn of events, seemingly opposed to the general tenor of the Ap, in which we find constant reference to the obstinacy of God's enemies. **14.** *second woe:* See comment on 8:13.

(Considine, J. S., *CBQ* 8 [1946] 377–92. Feuillet, A., *NTS* 4 [1957–58] 183–200; *idem, Johannine Studies*, 233–56. Haugg, D., *Die zwei Zeugen* [Münster, 1936]. Munck, J., *Petrus und Paulus in der Offenbarung Johannis* [Copenhagen, 1950].)

55 (g) THE SEVENTH TRUMPET (11:15–19). Its blast corresponds to the seventh seal (8:1). The course of eschatological events is again suspended. A celestial scene is inserted in anticipation of the conflict and victory that will soon occur on earth.

15. *the kingdom of the world has become:* The triumph over diabolical powers has removed all obstacles to the effective reign of God over the world. This consummation of salvation history, the essential object of God's promises, is so certain that its realization is expressed in the past tense (→ Johannine Theology, 80:12–14). *he shall reign:* The singular shows that the reign of God and that of Christ are one and the same (1 Cor 15:27f.). **16.** *the twenty-four elders:* These heavenly representatives of the Church (see comment on 4:4) prostrate themselves with each individual act of adoration (4:10; 5:8,14; 19:4). **17.** *Lord God Almighty:* See 1:8. *who is and who was:* See 1:4; note that the phrase "who is coming" is omitted here because God's coming is considered as something already accomplished. **18.** *the nations raged:* The pagan world, hostile to Christ and his people, was induced by the Antichrist to attempt to destroy the Church (13:1ff.

20:9) and even to attack Christ (19:19; cf. Ps 2:1–5). *the time for the dead to be judged:* Sinners and saints are resurrected (20:12–15; Jn 5:28f.) for the final retribution. *small and great:* That is, everyone, without exception (Gn 19:11; Ps 115:13; Ap 13:16; 19:5,18; 20:12). **19.** *the ark of his covenant:* The appearance of the Ark in this time of retribution indicates that God is now accessible, no longer hidden, but present in the midst of his people (21:3,22). Possibly this detail is derived from the Jewish expectation that the Ark would reappear in the Temple when the Messiah convoked his people (2 Mc 2:4–8). *flashes of lightning...:* As after the seventh seal (8:5) and the seventh bowl (16:18), symbols of majesty and power herald the coming divine judgments.

56 **(C) The Dragon and the Lamb (12:1–14:20).** This section is the heart of the Ap. The power of evil, represented by a monster, is radically opposed to the Messiah and his people; filled with hatred, the devil spares no pains to destroy Christ and his Church (ch. 12). To fulfill his purpose, the dragon dominates the Beast and urges it on against the Church; this Beast is the Roman Empire, which demands that all men accord divine honor to the emperor (ch. 13). Yet Christians must be confident in the face of the unbridled fury of this hellish design, because God and the Lamb have already carried off the victory (ch. 14). Here (as throughout the Bible) we encounter firm faith in the God who directs history toward a single end: the salvation of his people.

57 (a) The Dragon Seeks to Destroy the Celestial Woman and Her Son (12:1–6). It was widely believed in the ancient world that a savior-king was to appear. This expectation is attested from India to Rome, principally in the form of a myth; prominent among these stories are those of Babylonia, Egypt, and Greece. The goddess who was to bring forth the savior was pursued by a horrible monster, a personification of evil. Protected in an extraordinary manner, she was able to give birth in safety, and her child soon slew the evil monster, thereby bringing happiness to the world. It seems impossible to maintain that the Ap is completely independent of this popular myth; in all probability John borrowed certain details from it. But he surely was not directly influenced by the pagan world he abhorred; more likely he has used a purified Jewish version of the story (dependent on Gn 3:15?). Writing for churches in Asia, he could have used details borrowed from a myth with which they were familiar, in order to proclaim the true Savior and the certainty of his victory. Note too the following differences between this episode and the pagan myth: The child does not immediately destroy the evil monster. He is taken up into heaven where he reigns with God; our attention is fixed not upon him but rather upon the woman, who remains exposed to the dragon's hatred even after her son has been enthroned. She is a concretization of the law of suffering and renunciation, which specifies the road to salvation.

58 **1.** *in heaven:* The seer pictures himself upon earth (10:1) while the signs of the woman and the dragon appear to him in the firmament. *a woman:* Most of the ancient commentators identified her with the Church; in the Middle Ages it was widely held that she represented Mary, the Mother of Jesus. Modern exegetes have generally adopted the older interpretation, with certain modifications.

In recent years several Catholics have championed the Marian interpretation. Numerous contextual details, however, are ill-suited to such an explanation. For example, we are scarcely to think that Mary endured the worst of the pains of childbirth (v. 2), that she was pursued into the desert after the birth of her child (vv. 6, 13ff.), or, finally, that she was persecuted through her other children (v. 17). The emphasis on the persecution of the woman is really appropriate only if she represents the Church, which is presented throughout the book as oppressed by the forces of evil, yet protected by God. Furthermore, the image of a woman is common in ancient Oriental secular literature as well as in the Bible (e.g., Is 50:1; Jer 50:12) as a symbol for a people, a nation, or a city. It is fitting, then, to see in this woman the People of God, the true Israel of the OT and NT. The Ap (and primitive Christianity in general) made no clear distinction between Israel and the Church. The Messiah springs from the people of the 12 tribes (v. 5); this same people, directed by the 12 apostles, is the mother of those who believe in Christ (v. 17; Is 54:1–3; Gal 4:27), and suffers in them because of her faith in Jesus. Still, the Church that the seer envisages is not the earthly Church with its faults and failings (ch. 2–3), but the ideal, heavenly Church. According to the Jewish belief, all the promises of salvation already had an existential reality in heaven, in the presence of God (1 Pt 1:4). So also the Church, the heavenly Jerusalem (21:2,10; Heb 12:22; Gal 4:26), which is basic to the eschatological promise, exists in God's presence as the norm of development for the Christian community on earth. This interpretation, however, does not necessarily exclude any and all relevance to Mary; it is entirely possible that John wrote from a twofold viewpoint, individual as well as collective, implying at one and the same time the People of God, the Church, and Mary, the member of Israel who gave birth to the Messiah. *the sun...the moon...a crown of twelve stars:* The celestial woman is adorned in splendor (Gn 37:9). The sun covers her like a cloak (1:16; 10:1; 19:17; Ps 104:2). The crown of 12 stars seems to symbolize the 12 tribes (7:4–8; 21:12; Jas 1:1) and the 12 apostles (21:14); thus they stand for Israel and the Church.

59 **2.** *she cried out in her pangs of birth:* The arrival of the new age was compared to childbirth (Is 66:7–14), which is ordinarily accompanied by violent pain (Is 26:17; cf. Jn 16:21; Gal 4:19). The eschatological era begins with the birth of the Messiah. **3.** *a great dragon:* This mythical monster, also known as Leviathan (Ps 74:13f.) or Rahab (Jb 26:12f.; Ps 89:10), was considered as the epitome of the forces of evil opposition to God (Is 51:9). According to popular tradition, God had defeated this monster at the moment of creation, but its final repudiation was deferred until the end of time (Is 27:1). *red.* Suggestive of its murderous career (Jn 8:44; 1 Jn 3:12). *seven diadems:* Cf. 13:1. Symbolic of the fullness of its sovereignty over the kingdoms of this world (Lk 4:6; Jn 12:31; 14:30; 16:11). Christ, on the other hand, holds title to an indefinite number of diadems (19:12) as conqueror of the devil (1:5). **4.** *cast them to the earth:* Cf. Dn 8:10. The ancients frequently assumed that this passage refers to the fall of the rebel angels (Jude 6); but perhaps John wishes merely to suggest the colossal size and power of the monster. *the dragon confronted the woman:* This sentence quite possibly echoes the primordial condemnation in Gn 3:14–15, suggesting the whole long period during which mankind awaited the coming of the woman's offspring, who was to crush the serpent's head. **5.** *who is to rule all the nations:* The Messiah was to break the sway of the dragon over the world; the dragon would therefore be anxious to destroy him from the moment of his birth. This distinction of Christ is shared by all those who are to conquer with him (2:26f.). *was caught up:* Passing over the whole of Christ's life, even the passion, John mentions only its two terms: birth and glorious ascension (1 Tm 3:16). These events suffice to show that despite the dragon's vigilance, its hatred was futile. *to God and to his throne:* The ascension implies "sitting" at the right hand of God (Mk 16:19; Acts 7:55f.; Eph 1:20; Col 3:1) and participating in God's universal sovereignty. **6.** *the woman fled into the wilderness:* Humbled by the persecution of her members (vv. 14ff.), the Church must flee into the desert, the traditional place of refuge for the oppressed of Israel (1 Kgs 19:3f.; 1 Mc 2:29f.). The typology of the Exodus seems to underly: Just as Israel was obliged to undergo the trials of the desert (Dt 8:2ff.), so too the eschatological community must wend its way to redemption through the wilderness. *to be nourished:* As were Israel (Ex 16) and Elijah (1 Kgs 17:2–6; 19:5–8).

60 (b) Michael's Victory over the Dragon (12:7–12). The connection between this passage and the preceding is not clear. The only character common to both episodes is the dragon. Its opponent here is not the Messiah, but Michael, who is mentioned nowhere else in the Ap. The hymn of praise (vv. 10–12) does not explicitly identify the Lamb with the Messiah mentioned in v. 5. So the most plausible explanation is that the Messiah's exaltation (v. 5b) is being linked with Michael's victory: Michael's triumph would be possible because of the enthronement of the Lamb.

7–9. *war in heaven:* If this passage were isolated from the preceding section, it might refer to the revolt of the wicked angels and their expulsion from heaven before the beginnings of human history (Is 14:12f.). But it is very likely that John intended to connect the two passages. A single cause is assigned to the dragon's fall from power and to the inauguration of God's kingdom: Both here and in the Gospels, this cause is the ministry of Christ (Mt 12:28; Lk 10:18), culminating in his passion and glorification (Jn 12:31; 16:11; 1 Jn 3:8). That the struggle takes place in heaven indicates that the defeat of the dragon is properly achieved in the glorified Christ. Christians who are faithful to their Lord may rest assured that they will conquer Satan on earth. *Michael and his angels:* Michael is one of the principal figures of apocalyptic. Daniel (10:12–21; 12:1) portrays him as the guardian angel and protector of Israel; he will free Israel from oppression, especially during the last days. After Daniel, Michael becomes the protector of the remnant of Israel, the company of the just. *they were defeated:* They were driven out and despoiled of their influence (v. 10). The wealth of titles applied to the conquered dragon indicates the gravity of the threat he posed, and the importance of Michael's victory. *the ancient serpent:* See Gn 3:1ff.; Wis 2:24; 2 Cor 11:3. **10–12.** A hymn praises the triumph of God and his Christ; the victory is indeed God's, for Michael is but his servant. With this triumph over Satan the reign of God and Christ is already established and may be celebrated as a past event (v. 11; 11:15). *the accuser of our brethren:* The OT casts Satan in this role (Jb 1:6ff.; Zech 3:1). He continues to accuse Christ's disciples (Lk 22:31) but his accusations are ineffectual (Rom 8:33). Rabbinical writers refer to Satan as the unceasing accuser of Israel, and to Michael as its defender. *blood of the Lamb:* The prime source of the victory of Christians is Christ's sacrifice (7:14). His triumph makes possible the triumph of his believers (Jn 16:33; 1 Jn 4:4; 5:4f.). Thus the Lamb is the Church's Paraclete before God (1 Jn 2:1), remitting the sins of Christians and silencing the accuser. *by the word of their testimony:* Christ's sacrifice brings victory only to those who make themselves victims with him (Rom 8:17; 2 Tm 2:11). *they loved not their own lives:* They observed the central law of Christian life, self-renunciation, in order to be disciples of Christ (Mt 10:39 par.; Mk 8:35 par.; Jn 12:25; Acts 20:34; 21:13). *you who dwell:* The ptc. *skēnountes* means that they dwell in a *skēnē*, a (divine) tabernacle (7:15; 21:3; 2 Cor 5:1); they are set in opposition to the *katoikountes*, i.e., the (pagan) inhabitants of the earth. *earth and sea:* The whole of the universe, which is to be the theater of the dragon's future activities. *he has but a short time:* See vv. 6 and 14.

61 (c) The Dragon Vainly Pursues the Woman upon the Earth (12:13–18). This passage takes up anew the theme interrupted by the hymn in vv. 10–12. **13.** *he pursued the woman:* Since he is no longer able to join battle with the glorified Messiah (v. 5), the dragon attempts to attack him indirectly, through his Church and its members (Mt 25:45; Acts 9:4). **14.** A repetition of v. 6. *the two wings of the great eagle:* In the theme of the Exodus (Ex 19:4; Dt 32:11; Is 40:31) the eagle symbolizes the divine power that gives to all of God's people the assurance of prompt and efficacious protection. *where she is nourished:* She is like Elijah who, while fleeing from persecution, was strengthened by heavenly food (1 Kgs 17:4–6; 19:5–8). **15–16.** This episode is akin to a myth telling of a primordial conflict between the land and the sea. The sea is presented as the refuge of the monster who personifies evil, the dragon (Ps 74:13; Ez 29:3; 32:2). *the earth:* It is considered a person, somewhat like the Earth Mother of ancient belief. Rivers and especially torrential streams that vanish into desert sands are a familiar phenomenon in the Orient. **17.** *the rest of her offspring:* John makes a distinction between the Church and her members: The Church as such is miraculously saved by God (Mt 16:18); but Christians remain exposed to the attacks of the devil and are subject to death, even though God assures them of his protection. *keep the commandments of God and bear testimony to Jesus:* To be a true son of the Church and brother of Christ (Rom 8:29), one must possess these two distinctive characteristics (14:12; Jn 15:9–10).

(For a survey of recent literature on ch. 12, see Feuillet, A., *The Apocalypse* [Staten Island, N.Y., 1964] 109–17. Michl, J., *BZ* 3 [1959] 301–10. For the history of its exegesis, see Kassing, A. T., *Die Kirche und Maria* [Düsseldorf, 1958]. Prigent, P., *Apocalypse 12: Histoire de l'exégèse* [Tübingen, 1959]. Among many studies upholding the Mariological interpretation, see Le Frois, B. J., *The Woman Clothed with the Sun* [Rome, 1954]; *Marian Studies* 9 [1958] 79–106. See further Cerfaux, L., *ETL* 31 [1955] 21–33. Feuillet, A., *RB* 66 [1959] 55–86; *idem*, *Johannine Studies*, 257–92.)

62 (d) The Dragon Confers His Power on the Beast Rising from the Sea (13:1–10). The Beast becomes the dragon's agent on earth. This vision (11:7) is inspired by Dn 7, where the ten-horned beast represents Antiochus IV Epiphanes, the persecutor of Israel. In many respects the Beast is a counterfeit Lamb, and therefore a sort of Antichrist. The seer has blended into one image various characteristics of the four beasts in Dn 7; the result is a monstrous creature that defies the imagination (see H. Schlier, *Die Zeit der Kirche* [Freiburg, 1955] 16–28; W. Barclay, *ExpT* 70 [1958–59] 260–64, 292–96).

1. *a beast:* This is the Roman Empire, the archetype of secular powers that persecute the Church (see Dn 7:17,23). *seven heads:* They represent, according to 17:9f., the seven hills of Rome and seven kings. *ten horns:* In this respect it resembles the dragon (12:3; see 17:12ff.; cf. Dn 7:7,24). *blasphemous names:* To assign divine titles to the emperor was, to the Jewish and Christian mind, a blasphemous arrogation (Dn 11:36; 2 Thes 2:4). **2.** *the dragon gave his power:* The investiture of the Beast is opposed to the enthronement of the Lamb (5:12). The dragon, the prince of this world, presumes to claim temporal powers (Lk 4:6f.) of which God is the one true custodian (Jn 19:11; Rom 13:1). **3.** *one of its* *heads...:* Like the Lamb, who was killed and then raised up (5:6), the Beast seems to disappear and then return to life (17:8). This passage may be a reference to some definite event, such as the murder of Caesar and the healing of the empire under Augustus, the legend of *Nero redivivus*, or any of several imperial misadventures (but see P. S. Minear, *JBL* 72 [1953] 93–101). *all the earth:* The marvelous cure of the Beast excites admiration and leads to the adoration of the dragon and the Beast (17:8). This is an allusion to the rapid progress of the emperor cult and to the ready acceptance of the immoral example of the emperors. **4.** *who is like...?:* A parody of the honors paid to the Lamb (5:9) and to God himself (Ex 15:11). **5.** *there was given:* The "theological" passive; see *GrBib* § 236; cf. 9:1. *a mouth speaking:* Cf. Dn 7:8,11,20,25; 1 Mc 1:24. The insults are directed against God and the people among whom he dwells (Jn 1:14). *forty-two months:* The same duration as the profanation of the holy city (11:2), the prophetic mission of the two witnesses (11:3), and the retreat of the woman into the desert (12:6,14). It is a number symbolic of the Church militant. **7.** *to wage war:* Persecution, described in terms borrowed from Dn 7:6,21, follows upon the abusive words. The power received by the Beast (Lk 4:6) is a simulation of that received by the Lamb (5:9; 7:9). **8.** *whose names are not written:* To adore the Beast is tantamount to being excluded from the number of the predestined (17:8). The formula "from the beginning of the world" (Jn 17:5) is a familiar one in apocalyptic writings; it arises from the desire to connect the eschatological event with the eternal designs of God (Eph 1:4). **9.** *let him hear:* See 2:7. **10.** *captivity... sword:* Each Christian must accept the fate that God has foreseen and desired for him, burdensome though it be. Such a surrender to God's will is the secret of the patience and serenity of the saints (14:12–13).

63 (e) The Second Beast: The False Prophet from the Earth (13:11–18). The first Beast rose from the sea, whereas the second comes from the land (Dn 7:3 [LXX]; 7:17). Later on in the book, it will be called the false prophet (16:13; 19:20; 20:10). It speaks in the voice of the dragon (v. 11), from whom it receives its power; and like the first Beast, it attempts to mimic the Lamb (vv. 12, 13). It seems to be a personification of the Antichrist of the religious sphere, embodied in the pagan priesthood, which endeavored to draw all men to the cult of the emperor. **11.** *out of the earth:* Probably an allusion to Asia Minor, while the first Beast from the sea represents Rome. **13.** *great signs:* Recalling Elijah in 1 Kgs 18:38; 2 Kgs 1:10ff.; cf. Lk 9:54. **14.** *it deceives:* Like Satan (12:9). *the image to the beast:* Representations of the divinized Roman emperors. *the wound of the sword:* Possibly an allusion to the mortal wound Nero inflicted upon himself in AD 68. Nero lives again in the persecutor Domitian (Tertullian, *Apol.* 5). **15.** *the image of the beast should even speak:* A reference to deceitful practices, such as ventriloquism, employed in pagan cults. **16.** *a mark:* A counterpart of the divine seal that marks the servants of God (7:3f.). The seal of the Beast probably refers to the exclusion of Christians from social life. **18.** *the number of the beast:* The best attested number in the mss. is 666; but some ancient texts read 616. The key to this numerological message was lost very early, even before Irenaeus' time. Since then many hypotheses—some of them extravagant—have been proposed. The solution is to be found in *gematria*, for it is a question of "the number of a man," i.e., a number equivalent to the sum of the letters in a man's name. The most widely accepted theory identifies 666 with *Neron Caesar*, written *nrwn qsr* in Hebrew (= 50 + 200 + 6 + 50 + 100 + 60 + 200; see D. R. Hillers, *BASOR* 170 [1963] 65). The Lat form of the name (without the final *n* of *nrwn*) would equal 616, the alternative reading of the mss. Nero fits the context, for he was the first emperor to persecute the Christians; he embodied all the worst characteristics of the Beast, and he came to life again in Domitian. Another possible interpretation is that of the "triangular number": 666 is the sum of all numbers from 1 to 36; 36 is the sum of all numbers from 1 to 8; 8 would then be the number designating *Nero redivivus* (17:11).

64 (f) The Vision of the Lamb with His Own (14:1–5). After the description of the aggressive activities of the two Beasts, the present vision is consoling and reassuring: The Church of God will survive the fury of brutal and hostile powers. The traditional notion of the "remnant" of Israel (Is 4:2–3; 10:19–21; 28:5–6; Jer 3:14; Zeph 2:7,9; Rom 11:5) seems to provide the background for this picture of the assembly at Zion (Is 2:3).

1. *upon Mount Zion:* Zion is the throne of Yahweh (Mi 4:7; Is 24:23), the holy mountain of the Messiah-King (Ps 2:6), the unshakable rock (Is 28:16), the city of the living God (Heb 12:22), the sanctuary of fugitives (Jl 3:5). The Church is built upon a solid foundation (Mt 16:18), like a house built upon a rock (Mt 7:24). *a hundred and forty-four thousand:* This is also the number of those marked with the seal of God (7:4). *name written:* Cf. 3:12; 22:4. Companions of the Lamb are thus distinguished from the votaries of the Beast, who are marked with his seal (13:16; 14:11). To have God's name upon the forehead signifies that one is consecrated to his service. **2–3.** These two verses describe the powerful and melodious heavenly song that only the 144,000 can learn (2:17; 19:12). The song is presented in terms of familiar biblical metaphors: "the sound of many waters" (1:15; 19:6; Ez 43:2), "of great thunder" (4:5; Ex 19:16; Ez 1:7), "the voice of harpers" (5:8; 15:2). *a new song:* See 5:9. *purchased from the earth:* The earth means "world" in the Johannine sense, the "world" for which Jesus did not pray (Jn 17:9) because it refused to believe and was condemned. The 144,000 are not taken away from the world (Jn 17:15), but bought back by the blood of the Lamb (5:9). **4.** *they are virgins:* Since they are contrasted with those who adore the Beast, the 144,000 virgins must be those who have refused to follow him; they have not yielded to idolatry (1 Kgs 19:18). As the parallel passages show (7:3; 22:4), the 144,000 whose foreheads bear the seal constitute the totality of the Christian people; the number is not restricted to virgins in the proper sense of the word. In many OT texts (Hos 2:14–21; Jer 2:2,3,32; Zeph 3:9–13) virginity is a metaphor for fidelity to God; idolatry is associated with prostitution (2:14; Ez 16; 23). Babylon is a whore (v. 8; 17:4–6); but the Church is the spouse of the Lamb (19:7; 21:2–9; see M.-E. Boismard, *RB* 59 [1952] 161–72; R. Devine, *Scr* 16 [1964] 1–5). *first fruits:* They represent the total harvest, which belongs entirely to God (Dt 26:2); the Levites were consecrated to the exclusive service of God as a substitute for the first-born in Israel (Nm 3:12,40–51). Christian life is a spiritual cult (Rom 12:1), and the fruit of the lips is a sacrifice of praise (Heb 13:15). **5.** *no lie:* Lying is the characteristic conduct of followers of the father of lies (Jn 8:44), but there is no deceit on the lips of the Servant of Yahweh (Is 53:9; 1 Pt 2:22). *without blemish:* Behind the notion of first fruits is the idea of sacrifice, which reappears in the present expression, taken from the vocabulary of ritual (Ex 12:5; 1 Pt 1:19).

65 (g) The Proclamation of Imminent Judgment (14:6–20). The fate of the People of God is assured, but what is to be said of unbelievers? God will avenge persecuted Christians: He will judge and destroy Babylon (vv. 6–13) and all the pagan nations (vv. 14–20). The realization of this double prophecy will be described in 17:1–19:10, as well as in 19:11–21 and 20:7–15.

The first angel announces the judgment of the world. **6.** *an eternal gospel:* The good news of the event announced here (the judgment and the definitive establishment of the kingdom) is the realization in time of an eternal and mysterious decree (10:7; Rom 16:25; see L. Cerfaux, *ETL* 39 [1963] 672–81). **7.** *fear God:* An invitation to take advantage of the final reprieve by doing penance before the "great day of God the Almighty" (16:14). The appeal is addressed to all pagans; it is not directly proposed that they believe in the Gospel (Mk 1:15), but that they acknowledge God as Creator (Neh 9:6; Acts 4:24), as he is presented in the OT (Eccl 12:13). Such an acknowledgment must be the first step toward the Christian faith (Acts 14:15; 1 Thes 1:9). **8.** *she has fallen:* Cf. 18:2. The second angel applies the oracle of Is 21:9 to Babylon (Jer 50:23; 51:8); Babylon, however, must be understood as a figurative reference to pagan Rome (1 Pt 5:13), typifying, as did the first Babylon, cities and empires hostile to the People of God. The epithet "great" comes from Dn 4:27 and emphasizes the pride of the Romans (16:19; 17:5; 18:2,10,21). *to drink:* Here, and in 18:3, we find a combination of two ideas: "drink the wine of God's wrath" (14:10; Ps 75:8f.) and "made drunk with the wine of her immorality" (17:2). Prophetic images are used to illustrate the evil influence of the new Babylon (Jer 51:7; Hab 2:15). Seduced to idolatry and debauchery (Na 3:4), all the nations will drink from the cup of wrath (14:10; Is 51:17). The image of intoxicating wine (Jer 25:15–16) is aptly chosen to illustrate the state of one who has abandoned himself to sin; multiplication of sins is a sign of God's wrath (Rom 1:18ff.). **9–10.** The third angel predicts the judgment to be pronounced upon the votaries of the Beast. *with fire and brimstone...:* An image often used to describe the corporal punishment of the wicked; its inspiration is to be found in the narrative of the destruction of Sodom and Gomorrah (Gn 19:24), and it is recalled in Ez 38:22; Is 30:33; 34:8–10 (cf. Ap 9:17; 19:20; 20:10; 21:8).

66 **12.** *here is...:* A characteristically Johannine comment (13:10,18; 19:9). Patience (1:9; 2:2f.,19; 3:10) or long-suffering is a properly Christian virtue (Jas 1:3), which shines most brightly in times of persecution (13:10; Rom 5:3); it demands a twofold fidelity: faith in Jesus (2:13; Jas 2:1; → Johannine Theology, 80:36) and observance of the Commandments. **13.** *a voice from heaven:* Authoritatively proclaiming a new beatitude. Those who, from this time forth, die in the Lord (1 Cor 15:18; 1 Thes 4:14ff.) will rest from their labors; and though their labors will have been brought to an end, their works will follow them. According to Jewish thought, men's actions followed them as witnesses before the court of God. In Christian teaching, good works, the fruit of the Spirit (Gal 5:22f.), must accompany faith (Jas 2:14–26). Taken in conjunction with what follows, the expression "henceforth" hints that the just will enter into beatitude immediately after death (Phil 1:23; 2 Cor 5:8). **14–16.** The first picture of the final judgment consists in the assembly of all the just, under "one like a son of man," a mysterious figure (1:7,13) who rides on a cloud (Dn 7:13; Mk 14:62); clouds serve as the chariot of God (Ps 104:3). *a crown...and a sickle:* Christ wears the crown of the conqueror (6:2), but the sickle shows that he comes now in his role of judge (Jn 5:27). **15.** *the harvest:* The universal harvest (Jl 4:13; Mk 4:29) coincides with the parousia of the Son of Man (Mt 25:31). The injunction to gather the harvest comes from the temple because it is the Father who is master of the harvest (Mt 9:38).

67 **17–20.** But the judgment includes a second operation (Mt 13:30): The angels must gather the grapes from the vineyard of the earth. In contrast to Jl 4:13, where these two steps are combined, the Ap keeps them distinct, for the gathering of wheat stands for the convocation of subjects of the kingdom (Mt 13:30,38), but the gathering of grapes signifies the execution of divine punishment. Note that the angels, and not the Savior, are to cast the reprobate into the fiery furnace (Mt 13:41f.). **18.** *from the altar:* There is but one altar in the heavenly temple; it serves for holocausts (6:9; 11:1)—a reminder of the blood of martyrs that cries for vengeance—and for incense offerings (8:3,5; 9:13)—recalling that the prayers of the saints may hasten the end. **19.** *the great wine press:* See Is 63:1–5; Lam 1:5; Jl 4:13. From the time of the post-exilic prophets, God's judgment against sinners had been likened to the work of a vintager, crushing grapes underfoot. **20.** *outside the city:* Jerusalem (11:2). According to Zech 14:3, Yahweh was to take his stand as avenger of Jerusalem upon the Mt. of Olives; Jl 4:12 tells us that Yahweh was to judge all the nation in the Valley of Jehoshaphat. Capital punishment was administered outside the holy city (Heb 13:12). *blood:* Since wine was called "the blood of the grape" (Gn 49:11; Dt 32:14), the mention of blood is natural in this context. The prodigious quantity of blood shed is a good illustration of the excessive vehemence of the apocalyptic style. *sixteen hundred furlongs:* This number is a multiple of 100 and of 4; 100 signifies a considerable quantity, and 4 is a symbol of the physical universe.

68 **(D) The Seven Bowls (15:1–16:21).** After the series of seals and trumpets, this third and last heptad tells of the calamities that portend the final judgment upon the world and its inhabitants. Here, as in the first two series, a heavenly prelude (15:1–8) introduces the series of the seven bowls (16:1–21).

(a) THE CONQUERORS OF THE ANTICHRIST SING THE CANTICLE OF MOSES AND THE LAMB IN HEAVEN (15:1–4). The first verse, serving as a kind of title for the heptad, is separated from v. 5 by the liturgical celebration in vv. 2–4 (cf. 8:2,6).

1. *seven last plagues:* These plagues are to be the definitive manifestation of God's anger. **2.** *sea of glass mingled with fire:* Added to the notion of the infinite distance that separates God from all of creation (4:6), the element of fire indicates here, as it does throughout the Bible, that God demands sanctity. This demand may find its application in the trials that have purified the victorious Christians; or, more probably, it may refer here to God's wrath (Mt 3:12 par.) that is to be made manifest in the imminent judgment (16:1–21). *those who have overcome:* These words refer especially to the martyrs (12:11) who have not succumbed to the oppressive influence of the Antichrist (13:7,15). The scene corresponds to that found in 7:9–17. **3.** *the song of Moses:* See Ex 15:1–18; cf. Dt 32:1–43. The seer makes explicit use of the typology of the Exodus. The victory of the redeeming Lamb and of those who belong to him (3:21) is the apex and the goal of salvation history, that process ceaselessly directed by the living God who delivered his people from their Egyptian bondage. The victorious Christians have followed the Lamb across the Red Sea of tribulation into the promised land. **3b–4.** The song is a hymn to the omnipotence and justice of the God of salvation history. He is absolute Master; all his interventions are perfect, especially the redemption accomplished by the Lamb, and the consummation of history soon to be described in the vision of the seven bowls. The second part of the hymn tells of the repercussions that these *magnalia Dei* will have among the "nations," which will acknowledge the glory of God (21:24–26; 22:2). The canticle contains no allusion either to Moses or to the Lamb; our attention is concentrated entirely upon the Lord, the "Master of all." The hymn is a mosaic of expressions borrowed from the OT: "thy deeds" (Pss 111:2; 139:14); "thy ways" (Ps 145:17; Dt 32:4); "who shall not fear" (Jer 10:7); "all nations shall come" (Ps 86:9; Is 2:2–4; 66:19–21).

69 (b) SEVEN ANGELS RECEIVE THE BOWLS OF GOD'S WRATH (15:5–8). **5.** *the heavenly temple:* Archetype of "the Tent of Testimony" (Ex 25:9,40; Heb 8:5), or the Tent of Meeting (Ex 25:22; 27:21; Nm 9:15), which "was opened" (11:19) during the Exodus. **6.** *pure bright linen...with golden girdles:* These vestments symbolize the sacerdotal function the angels are about to fulfill. **7.** *one of the four living creatures:* The bowls are given to the angels by one of the four representatives of nature; the calamities contained in the bowls are to affect the entire universe (cf. 4:6ff.). **8.** *filled with smoke:* Generally speaking, smoke is a biblical symbol of the glorious and awesome presence of God (Ex 19:9,18; Is 6:1–4; → Johannine Theology, 80:30–31), but it may also be, as here, a sign of his power and wrath (Ps 18:8; Is 65:5). *no one could enter:* God's judgment is inexorable; no one may enter into the temple to intercede for the earth and to divert the imminent succession of catastrophes.

70 (c) THE SEVEN BOWLS ARE POURED OUT (16:1–21). The disasters contained in the bowls recall the plagues in Egypt (Ex 7–12) and resemble the calamities let loose upon the world by the trumpets (8:2-11:19). Most of these plagues were traditionally believed to be signs of the approach of the last day. The first four disasters heralded by the trumpets (8:7–12) were limited to one third of the world, whereas the plagues in ch. 16 have a universal and definitive character. These calamities should not be interpreted literllay, but symbolically; however, the realities they symbolize are left for us to conjecture. These calamities will befall the votaries of the Antichrist (vv. 2, 10), i.e., the faithless and unrepentant world; their purpose is the conversion of the world (vv. 9, 11).

1. *a loud voice:* Such a voice is usually that of an angel (5:2; 7:2; 10:3; 14:7; etc.), but here it is perhaps the voice of God, since no one can enter the temple (15:8). **2.** The first "bowl" contains a calamity resembling the sixth plague in Egypt (Ex 8:8–12; Dt 28:27). **3.** Although the first Egyptian plague affected only the Nile (Ex 7:17–21) and the scourge introduced by the second trumpet destroyed only a third of living creatures (8:8f.), "the second bowl" changes the sea into blood, and everything that lives in the sea (Gn 1:21) dies. **4–7.** With the "third bowl," fresh water is transformed into blood, similar to the change wrought on the salt water (cf. the third trumpet, 8:10f.). Two voices join in approbation of the catastrophe, praising God's justice as manifested in this intervention. *the angel of the waters:* Each portion of nature, each element, had, according to rabbinical tradition, its heavenly counterpart (see 7:1). *thou art just...:* This paean takes up the themes of the divine justice and holiness encountered in 15:3. The element "He who is coming" is suppressed in the divine name (see 1:4) because in this very series of plagues God comes (11:17). He is "holy" in his deeds (15:4), which are expressions of righteousness (Dt 32:4; Ps 145:17), and in his judgments, which are manifestations of justice (v. 7; 19:2). *saints and prophets:* The faithful in general, and those heralds of Christianity who have undergone martyrdom (11:18; 18:24). *they deserve it:* In divine retribution the punishment fits the crime (Rom 1:24,26, 28). *the altar:* The voice belongs either to the angel of the altar (14:18) or to the martyrs buried beneath it (6:9–11; 8:3f.).

71 **8–9.** *the fourth bowl:* Unlike the fourth trumpet, it does not produce darkness (8:12). *they cursed:* See v. 11; 9:20f. They hardened their hearts, as did the Pharaoh of the Exodus (Ex 7:3,22; 8:15; etc.). **10–11.** The darkness brought on by the fifth bowl resembles the calamity heralded by the fifth trumpet (9:1–12) and, especially, the ninth plague in Egypt (Ex 10:21–23). *upon the throne of the beast:* Cf. 2:13; 13:2. Probably an allusion to Rome as typical of the powers hostile to God's Church. **12–16.** *the sixth bowl:* It does not seem to cause a plague, rather it provokes the kings of the nations to eschatological battle (vv. 14, 16; 17:14; 19:11–21; 20:7–10). The issue of this battle will be disastrous for Christ's enemies. **12.** *great river Euphrates:* Previously mentioned in connection with the sixth trumpet (9:13–21), the Euphrates was strategically vital as a defense against the Parthians (6:3), who were at that time the chief threat to the Roman Empire. *dried up its water:* As the waters of the Red Sea (Ex 14:21) and of the Jordan (Jos 3:17) were dried up: miracles that were to be repeated (Is 11:15; Jer 51:36; Zech 10:11). **13.** *the false prophet:* Mentioned here for the first time, he is to be identified with the two-horned Beast (13:11). Like the latter, he is associated (19:20; 20:10) with the first Beast (13:1). He performs prodigies (13:14; 19:20). The activity of false prophets, foretold by Jesus (Mk 13:22), is attested in the primitive Church (Acts 13:6); it is comparable to the activity of the Antichrist in the Johannine epistles (1 Jn 2:22; 4:3; 2 Jn 7). *frogs:* Possibly an allusion to the second plague in Egypt (Ex 7:26ff.) or perhaps a reference to the catalogue of unclean animals (Lv 11:10). **14.** *working signs:* In the manner of the magicians of Egypt (Ex 7:22), the false prophet (Dt 13:1–3), and the wicked one of the last times (2 Thes 2:9). *the great day:* See 6:17. Verse 15 is parenthetical; it interrupts the description and seems to be out of place. It is a call to vigilance, sounded by Christ (see 3:3,4). Its connection with the present context can only be its relevance to the great day, which is drawing near. **16.** *Armageddon:* This word is found nowhere else. The best of several hypotheses sees in the word a Gk transliteration of the Hebr *har mᵉgiddō*, "the mount of Megiddo." This strategic locality, to the S of the Plain of Esdraelon, was the site of several battles and various disasters (Jgs 5:19; 2 Kgs 9:27), especially the defeat and death of the good king Josiah (2 Kgs 23:29f.; 2 Chr 35:22) that left such a profound impression on Judaism (Zech 12:11). John seems—possibly under the influence of Ez 38–39—to envision an invasion of the holy land by the kings of the nations, who will be overwhelmed at Megiddo. It may be objected that although Megiddo controlled the mountain route to Palestine, the city itself was not situated on a mountain. Nevertheless, it is possible that the association of Megiddo with the mountain has its roots in Ez 39:2,4.

72 **17–21.** *the seventh bowl:* The immediate preparation for the judgment upon Babylon (17:1–19:10). **18.** *lightning...thunder:* These awesome phenomena ordinarily accompany major interventions of God (see 4:5). *great earthquake:* See comment on 6:12. **19.** *into three parts:* It is no longer merely a tenth of the city that is destroyed (11:13); the entire city (probably Rome and the empire) is devastated (18:1–24), and Rome's ruin will entail the ruin of the satellite nations. **20.** *fled away:* Cf. 6:14; 20:11. The disappearance of mountains is an element of apocalyptic symbolism of the last day. **21.** *great hailstones:* The seventh plague in Egypt (Ex 9:22–26) and the storm of Beth-horon (Jos 10:11) probably exerted an influence on later tradition, leading to the interpretation of severe hailstorms as a symbol of God's anger toward the enemies of Israel (Is 28:2; Ez 38:22) and toward the false prophets (Ez 13:13), or as a sign of the definite judgment passed upon the wicked (Wis 5:22). *heavy as a talent:* About a hundred pounds.

73 **(E) The Judgment and the Fall of Babylon (17:1–19:10).** The fall of Babylon has already been mentioned twice (14:8; 16:19) without further elucidation. Now the seer describes in cryptic manner the great harlot (17:1–18); he treats the fall of Babylon as a past event and records for us the lamentations that follow this disaster (18:1–24), while paeans resound in the heavens (19:1–10). This destruction of the forces of persecution serves as an immediate preparation for the climax of the Ap, which consists in the victory of Christ and his Church (19:11–22:5). Since the symbols used in this passage are deliberately obscure, their interpretation is difficult and, to a large extent, hypothetical.

(a) THE VISION OF THE HARLOT SEATED UPON THE BEAST (17:1–6). **1.** *the great harlot:* Babylon, the antithesis of the woman who personifies the People of God (12:1ff.), is here characterized as a harlot for the first time. But the tradition of branding idolatrous and impious peoples or cities as harlots was already well established in the OT: e.g., Tyre (Is 23:16f.), Nineveh (Na 3:4f.), Israel (Ez 16), Samaria and Jerusalem (Ez 23). At the conclusion of his interpretation of John's vision (v. 18), the angel clearly hints that the harlot represents Rome (see J. E. Bruns, *CBQ* 26 [1964] 459–63). *upon many waters:* Echoing Jer 51:13, where it is literally applied to Babylon, this phrase is a fitting, if symbolic, reference to Rome (v. 15). **2.** *committed fornication:* This explains why Rome deserves the title of harlot. "The kings of the earth" are the governments of subject nations, basking in the favor of Roman might at the cost of accepting her suzerainty, her idolatry (especially the emperor cult), and her vices. **3.** *into a wilderness:* The desert was traditionally the habitat of unclean animals (18:2). The image evokes the utter desolation of any place from which God is absent. In contrast, when the seer is to contemplate the new Jerusalem, he will be transported to a high mountain (21:10). *sitting on a scarlet beast:* Goddesses of the ancient Orient were often portrayed as riding upon the back of a monster. In this passage the monster is the Beast that was already mentioned in 13:1,14 (cf. 19:20). The scarlet color symbolizes the proud splendor of the Roman Empire. *full of blasphemous names:* Not only the heads of the Beast (13:1), but its whole body is covered with them, indicating that the entire empire sanctioned the emperors' arrogation of divine titles; such titles could be found throughout the Roman world, inscribed on public buildings and monuments. **4.** *a golden cup:* See 18:6; Jer 51:7. The contents of this cup—idolatrous cults and and the vices of Rome—are in sharp contrast with its outward beauty (Mt 23:25) and the splendor of the woman. **5.** *on her forehead:* A name inscribed on the forehead is either that of a person with whom one feels an extremely close relationship (14:1; 22:4) or, as it is here, the bearer's own name. This is possibly an allusion to the Roman prostitutes' custom of exhibiting their names written on their foreheads. **6.** *the blood of the martyrs:* Possibly those who perished in Nero's persecution. *I wondered greatly:* The seer is disconcerted at the sight of so much seemingly unrequited wickedness, particularly since the angel had foretold to him the condemnation of Babylon (v. 1).

74 (b) THE INTERPRETATION OF THE VISION (17:7–18). **8.** *the beast:* As a symbol of the Roman Empire in 13:1ff., the Beast regained its vitality after having received a mortal wound (13:3,12,14). Here the Beast stands for the incarnation of the empire in one man: Nero (vv. 11, 16). *was and is not, and is to ascend:* The Beast, claiming divine honors, attempts a caricature of God (1:4) and of Christ (1:18). It requires its own parousia (2 Thes 2:8f.), but it will actually rise from the abyss only for its condemnation (19:20), when the Lamb returns from heaven in triumph. **9.** *seven hills:* An obvious allusion to the seven hills upon which Rome stands. **10.** *seven kings:* Since the Beast represents the Roman Empire, the seven heads must represent emperors, called kings in the Orient. The number seven is possibly symbolic, embracing all the emperors; but most exegetes take the number literally because of the details that follow. *five of them have fallen:* According to the currently favored interpretation, the five fallen emperors are Augustus, Tiberius, Gaius (Caligula), Claudius, and Nero. Passing over the three weak personalities of the interregnum, Galba, Otho, and Vitellius, the sixth emperor should be Vespasian (AD 69–79). Some scholars have proposed that John borrowed from a source (perhaps Jewish) material edited during the reign of Vespasian. But the most natural solution is an appeal to artificial antedating, a device frequently encountered in apocalyptic: According to this theory John would actually have written under Domitian (AD 81–96). *a short time:* Titus, wasted by sickness, reigned only from AD 79 to 81. **11.** *it is an eighth:* This would be Titus' successor, Domitian, in whom Nero is, so to speak, reincarnated. **12.** *ten horns:* Cf. 13:1; Dn 7:7,24. The best of many divergent interpretations identifies the ten horns with the Parthian satraps (16:12) who, according to popular belief, were to invade and destroy Rome under Nero (v. 13). The number ten stands for all the satraps. *one hour:* See 18:10,17,19; see A. Strobel, *NTS* 10 [1963–64] 433–45). **14.** This verse seems to be parenthetical, warning of the combat in 19:19–21. The Beast and the kings are instruments chosen by God to punish Rome (v. 17), but they grow proud and attack God's people after the fashion of the ancient nations called by the Lord to punish Israel. *Lord of lords:* This divine title (Dt 10:17; Ps 136:3) is applied here and in 19:16 to Christ, as in 1 Tm 6:16.

15. *the waters:* The multitude of peoples over whom Roman domination extends. **16.** The kings, unconscious instruments of a divine decree, offer their united forces to the Beast (v. 13) to destroy the harlot. As a description of the punishment of Rome, this passage recapitulates many traditional metaphors (Hos 2:5; Is 49:26; Ez 23:25–29; Mi 3:3). *fire:* The legal penalty for very serious crimes (Lv 20:14; 21:9; Jos 7:15). **17.** *the words of God:* The words of the prophets speaking as God's deputies (19:9; 21:5; 22:6).

75 (c) THE DOOM OF BABYLON (18:1–24). God's judgment upon "the great city" is presented above all through a song of lamentation, in which those who had profited by the extravagances of Roman power, commerce, and luxury (especially kings, merchants, and privateers) weep over the ruins of the city (vv. 9–19). This elegy is introduced by a prediction of the fall of Rome (vv. 1–3) and a warning to the People of God to flee the doomed city (vv. 4–8); it is followed by an action symbolizing the annihilation of the empire (vv. 21–24). There is no description of the successive steps or phases of the destruction, for our attention is directed rather to the contrasting reactions of pagans and Christians. Expressions from the OT are interwoven throughout the chapter; they are borrowed principally from the sarcastic poems the prophets composed against the proud cities of Babylon, Tyre, and Niniveh (Is 23, 24, 47; Jer 50, 51; Ez 26, 27). Rome is the current seat of all the sins and

vices of the ancient cities; Rome is the embodiment of John's concept of "the world," claiming a structure and a vitality independent of God. But disaster will overwhelm it "in one hour" (the refrain in vv. 10, 17, 19), for the sovereignly efficacious judgment of God will flash forth upon it.

76 (i) *An angel proclaims the fall of Babylon* (18:1–3). **1.** *was made bright:* All the celestial beings share in the brilliance of the divine majesty (→ Johannine Theology 80:30–31). **2.** *a haunt of demons:* Rome is to become a wasteland, as did the ancient cities condemned by God (Is 34:11–15): It will be the abode of demons (Bar 4:35), wild beasts (Is 13:22; Jer 9:10; 50:39; Zeph 2:14), and unclean birds (Is 13:21). **3.** *all nations have drunk:* A reminder of the sinfulness of the city without God (14:8; 17:2,4f.), to emphasize the justice of its condemnation.

77 (ii) *The faithful are warned to leave the condemned city* (18:4–8). **4.** *go out of her:* Even the earliest biblical episodes insist upon separation from sinners: the call of Abraham (Gn 12:1), the rescue of Lot (Gn 19:12ff.), the revolt of Dathan and Abiram (Nm 16:26). In particular, such an injunction was laid upon Israel toward the end of the Exile (Is 48:20; 52:11; Jer 50:8; 51:6,45). It then became a traditional element in apocalyptic (e.g., Mt 24:16–20 par.). It would thus be futile to interpret this passage as a directive to the Roman community to evacuate the city at some definite time just before the destruction. "Flight" consists in refusing to participate in the sins of the Romans. Paul admits that we are unable to leave the world (1 Cor 5:10), but he demands that we avoid all participation in the works of darkness (2 Cor 6:14–18). **6.** *render to her:* The law of talion (Ex 21:24f.) was applied to Babylon, the persecutor of Israel (Jer 50:29; Ps 137:8). The double indemnification (Ex 22:4,7,9) had already been exacted from Jerusalem (Is 40:2; Jer 16:18). These imperatives indicate the norm to be followed by those whose ministry it is to execute the divine decree. At the time of eschatological retribution, all opportunities for pardon will have passed. **7.** *a queen I sit:* The chief sin of Rome as of all pagan empires consists in their assertion that their power and their authority derive exclusively from themselves, that they are their own masters, recognizing no superior law.

78 (iii) *Lamentation over the ruins of Babylon* (18:9–19). Three groups whose prosperity depended on Rome bewail their fate: "the kings of the earth" (vv. 9–10), "the merchants of the earth" (vv. 11–17a) and "the seafaring men" (vv. 17b–19). Egoism inspires their complaints, for Roman prosperity was the key to their own profits. The whole passage, based on Ez 26–27 (which refers to Tyre), suggests the might, wealth, and splendor of Rome, making its sudden devastation the more tragic in contrast. **9.** *the kings of the earth:* See Ez 26:16–18. The allied and subjugated kings (17:2; 18:3). **11.** *the merchants of the earth:* See Ez 27:9b–36. This is the most elaborated section of the lamentation, perhaps because the merchants will be those most seriously affected by the collapse of Rome. *for no one buys:* This phrase reveals the egoistic motive for the merchants' lament (v.19). **12.** *cargo of...:* Cf. Ez 27:12–24. This impressive catalogue of luxuries reflects Roman commerce of the period. *citron wood:* A fragrant wood imported from Africa, used for dining tables and works of art. **13.** *wheat:* Most of the city's wheat supply was grown in Egypt. *souls of men:* An expression borrowed from Ez 27:13; it refers to the slaves—human cattle—sold by merchants into service in the houses of the rich, or used as instruments of pleasure in brothel and amphitheater. **14.** This verse seems alien to the context; written in the second person it differs in style and content from the neighboring verses. It is commonly proposed that it belongs either after v. 21 or after v. 23. *the fruit:* Metaphorically, the result of long labor about to be enjoyed. **16.** *in fine linen:* Kings were impressed by Rome's power (v. 10); merchants by her riches (vv. 16f.). **18.** *who is like:* Cf. 13:4; Ez 27:32b. **20.** *rejoice:* This summons to joy will be echoed in 19:1–10. *apostles and prophets:* Among the "saints," i.e., the martyrs, these are the chief representatives of the Church (1 Cor 12:28). Only the prophets are mentioned in 16:6 and 18:24.

79 (iv) *A symbolic action signals the disappearance of Babylon* (18:21–24). **21.** *threw it into the sea:* Jeremiah's book announcing the destruction of Babylon had been tied to a stone and thrown into the Euphrates (Jer 51:63–64). Just as a stone thrown into the sea would disappear without a trace, so Babylon, i.e., Rome, will be annihilated (cf. Ex 15:5; Lk 17:2). **22.** *will not be heard any more:* Babylon's destruction will be so complete that the city will furnish no further signs of life. This theme of divine punishment, consisting in the total destruction of a guilt-ridden city, had already been applied to Jerusalem (Is 24:8; Jer 7:34; 16:9), to Babylon (Jer 25:10), and especially to Tyre (Ez 26:13). **23.** *the voice of the bridegroom:* Cf. Jer 7:34; 16:9; 25:10; 33:10f.; Bar 2:23. *because thy merchants:* The point of the accusation is probably that Rome had abused her commercial power by using it to propagate her false standards of life. *thy sorcery:* Cf. Na 3:4; Is 47:12. Rome had spellbound and misled the world by means of her vices and idolatry (21:8; 22:15). This passage is possibly an allusion to Rome's practice of black magic. **24.** *the blood:* See 17:6. The guilt of Rome is recalled once again (vv. 3, 5; cf. Jer 51:49). The massacres of AD 64 and of the reign of Domitian are probably what John has in mind. Christ made a similar accusation against Jerusalem (Mt 23:34f. par.; cf. Mt 27:25). *slain:* They were sacrificed like the Lamb (5:12).

80 (d) CANTICLES OF JOY IN HEAVEN (19:1–10). These triumphal songs, prescribed in 18:20, are in sharp contrast with the somber tones of ch. 18. Opposition between radically different themes has been set up earlier in the book (e.g., chs. 6 and 7; 11:1–14 and 11:15–19; 13:1–18 and 14:1–5); the device points up the striking contrast between the situation on earth, where evil has become especially tangible through persecution, and the future glory of heaven, the consequence of God's interventions on behalf of his own. The present passage contains two hymns; the first is sung by the angels and celebrates God's justice as manifested in the punishment of Babylon, considered as already accomplished (vv. 1–4); the second, sung by the entire Church, affords us a glimpse of the wedding of the Lamb as a more immediate prospect. This wedding symbolizes the union of the Messiah with the community of the elect (vv. 5–9). **1.** *Hallelujah:* The fact that this exclamation of praise ("praise Yah[weh]") is frequent in the Pss attests its importance in Jewish liturgy. It is not found anywhere in the NT except for the present passage, but it is here repeated four times; it must, then, already have been in use in the Christian liturgy. **2.** *true and just:* The rest of this verse recalls the two principal crimes of the "great harlot" (17:1–5) that motivated the divine condemnation. *he has judged:* God has heard the cries of the martyrs (6:9f.). *who corrupted the earth:* By means of idolatry (11:18; 14:8; 17:2,5; 18:3). *his servants:* The saints together with the prophets (18:24); the entirety of the Church and its leaders. The persecution of Christians marks the high tide of the iniquity of Babylon. **3.** *once more:* This reiteration resembles a liturgical antiphon, repeated at the end of a hymn to recall the central theme. Such repetitions occur in certain of the Hallelujah-Psalms and in the Song of Miriam (Ex 15:1,21). **4.** *the elders:* As they did in the preceding scenes of celestial liturgy (4:8–11; 5:8,14), the living creatures and the elders, representing the physical universe and the Church, join in the angelic praises (11:15–18). **5.** *all you his servants:* That is, the whole Church. It joins its song of praise to that of the angels (vv. 5–8). *small and great:* See 11:18.

81 **6.** *Hallelujah:* The Church's hymn has the same theme as that of the angels, but whereas the angels' song emphasized the negative aspect—the punishment and destruction of Babylon—the present hymn treats of the inauguration of the Kingdom of God (11:15,17; Ps 97:1). **7.** *rejoice and exult:* See Mt 5:12; Lk 6:23; Pss 98:4; 117:24. *the marriage of the Lamb has come:* This motif, including the overwhelming joy of the Church, is an anticipation of the book's final vision (20:11–22:5); the anticipatory procedure has been employed before (compare 14:8 with chs. 17–18; 18:20 with 19:1–10). The theme of marriage uniting God with his people was already well established in the OT (Hos 2:1–23; Is 54:4–8; Ez 16:7f.); in the NT it is used to express the vital union between Christ and his Church (Mt 22:1–14; Mk 2:19 par.; Mt 25:1–13; Jn 3:29; 2 Cor 11:2; Eph 5:23–32). The symbol expresses the intimate and indissoluble union with the community that Christ has won with his blood (1:5; 5:6,9; 7:14; 14:3–4). In the Ap the Church is presented at once as mother (12:1ff.) and spouse, but its rival is branded a harlot (17:1ff.). **8.** *it was granted her:* This characteristic expression, beginning with 6:2, is frequently used of God's universal and sovereign actions. *with fine linen:* This simple, light, yet highly valued fabric contrasts with the grand and glittering purple garments of the harlot (17:4; 18:16). No one is admitted to the wedding without such clothing (Mt 22:11–13), washed in the blood of the Lamb (7:9,14). **9.** *the marriage supper of the Lamb:* It is no longer simply a question of rest (14:13), but of full participation in the Messianic feast (Is 25:6; Mt 8:11). The guests are the faithful companions of the Lamb (14:4; 17:14). *these are true words:* Referring to the last revelations (17:1–19:9). The constancy of God's words will be reaffirmed (21:5; 22:6). **10.** *to worship him:* The seer is tempted to identify the messenger who transmits these revelations with God, their author. The angel stops him, reminding him that God alone is worthy of adoration (15:3f.; Dt 6:13). The repetition of this scene in 22:8–9 seems to be a strong reaction against the exaggerated cult of the angels. The warnings of Col 2:18; Heb 1:13f.; 2:5 and the early Church's testimony appear to prove that such a cult of the angels had in fact developed in the churches of Asia. *a fellow servant:* The angel's mission, much like that of the prophets, is to communicate God's revelation. For this reason he allies himself with the prophets and styles himself, like them, a servant of God (1:1; 10:7; 11:18; 22:6,9). *the testimony of Jesus is the spirit of prophecy:* This difficult expression seems to mean that God's word, as revealed and attested by Jesus (1:2; 20:4), continues to be heard in the Church, thanks to the action of the Spirit (Jn 14:26; 16:13f.) speaking by the lips of the prophets (→ Johannine Theology, 80:60).

82 **(F) The Coming of Christ and the Consummation of History (19:11–22:5).**

(a) Victory of Christ over the Beast and the False Prophet (19:11–21). Nearly all the elements in this triumphal tableau have been taken from the preceding chapters (12:5; 14:6–20; 16:13–16; 17:14). In apocalyptic tradition, the establishment of the Kingdom of God was to be preceded by a violent battle in which the Messiah was to triumph over the powers of evil (*2 Esdras* 13; *Pss Sol* 17:23–27). Here again, apocalyptic continues an OT theme (Ez 38f.; Jl 4:1–3,15–17; Zech 12:14). At the beginning of the present passage Christ appears as judge and warrior (vv. 11–16). The certainty of his victory is proclaimed by an angel (vv. 17f.). After a reference to the mustering of the enemy forces (v. 19), the seer passes abruptly on to their annihilation (vv. 20f.). **11.** *heaven opened:* see 4:1. *a white horse:* See comment on 6:2. *trustworthy and true:* These two titles are recalled here (1:5; 3:7,14): because Christ is fulfilling his promise to combat and to judge the enemies of God (1 Cor 15:24–28). *in righteousness:* Justice is a distinctive characteristic of the Messiah (Is 11:3–4; Ps 96:13; Acts 17:31). As usual in contexts dealing with the judgments of God, the vbs. *krinei* and *polemei* are in the pres. tense here. It is perhaps John's way of indicating that Christ's activity is already in the process of realization. **12.** *his eyes:* Symbolic of the perfect knowledge of the judge (see comment on 1:14). *many diadems:* He is, in fact, the king of kings (v. 16). His diadems contrast with those of the dragon (12:3) and the Beast (13:1). *a name written:* In the Semitic world, a person's name corresponded to his essence; therefore, since Christ is a divine being, his name transcends all human knowledge (Mt 11:27 par.). The Christian, sharing in the being of Christ, receives an ineffable name (2:17; 3:12; cf. Gn 32:29; Jgs 13:18). **13.** *a robe dipped in blood:* John applies to the Messiah what had been said of God (Is 63:1–3). The blood is not Christ's, but rather that of his enemies (v. 15), because the whole context treats of judgment rather than of redemption. *the Word of God:* This is not the ineffable name of v. 12; the formula is better taken as an indication of Christ's office of revealing God to the world (Jn 1:1,14; 1 Jn 1:1; → Johannine Theology, 80:21–24). More precisely in the present context, Christ reveals the divine wrath; the thought is similar to that in Wis 18:14–16, where we find the Word of God coming to destroy the first-born of Egypt. **14.** *the armies of heaven:* The Messiah was commonly pictured as accompanied by his angels at his parousia (Mk 8:23; 13:27; 2 Thes 1:7–8). The angels, who were at Christ's service during his earthly life (Mt 4:11), will be with him on the day of his exaltation as well (Mt 13:41f.; 16:27). In the present context, however, the armies are primarily armies of martyrs (17:14), with the martyrs' characteristic white garments (3:5; 6:11; 19:8). **15.** The next three elements specify the purpose of Christ's coming. *from his mouth. . . :* See 1:16. This is the word by which the fatal decrees will be imposed upon God's enemies; the Word of God is the ultimate weapon of Christ (2 Thes 2:8). *a rod of iron:* Cf. 2:27; 12:5; Ps 2:9; Is 11:4. *the wine press:* See 14:8–10,19f. **16.** *a name inscribed:* Unlike the Beast, which is covered with blasphemous names (17:3), Christ displays openly the title given to him by God. *King of kings:* This title is reserved to God in the OT (Dt 10:17; cf. 1 Tm 6:15); it means that the glory of Christ dominates all of creation (Phil 2:9–11). **17–18.** The issue of the battle is so certain that birds of prey are summoned in advance to feed on the corpses of all the enemies of God (6:15–17). This macabre banquet seems to be a counterpart to the wedding feast of the Lamb (19:9). **20.** *the false prophet:* See 13:11–18. *the lake of fire:* Eternal damnation (14:10f.; 20:10,14f.; 21:8). *that burns with brimstone:* An allusion to Sodom and Gomorrah (Gn 19:24; cf. Ez 38:22). **21.** *the rest:* The kings of the earth (v. 19) and their peoples, i.e., the kings of the pagan nations treated of in 17:12–14. They are all struck down by the sword of Christ; later they will be thrown into the pool of fire (20:15).

83 (b) The Thousand-Year Reign (20:1–6) Nothing in the preceding chapters (not even 5:10) would lead us to suspect that such a reign might be forthcoming. Besides, an intermediate reign of Christ seems foreign to the NT taken as a whole; none of the proposed related texts (Mt 19:28; 1 Cor 6:2f.; 15:24; 2 Tm 2:12) is an undeniable reference to such a theme. It is the more astonishing, therefore, to find that many Christian generations should have been so concerned about the question. From the earliest days of the Church, many Christian writers (e.g., Papias, Justin, Irenaeus, Tertullian) have understood Ap 20:1–6 as an affirmation of the establishment of a thousand-year reign of Christ with his martyrs on earth, preparatory to the founding of the new world; and it was not until after Augustine (*De Civ. Dei* 20.7–8) that this interpretation was quite generally dropped from Christian teaching. Yet the expectation of the thousand-year reign of Christ on earth has persisted into our own day in certain marginal divisions of Christianity (e.g., Joachim di Fiore and the Fraticelli) and in many sects (e.g., Anabaptists, Adventists, Jehovah's Witnesses). See DB 2269; DS 3839; L. Gry, *Le Millénarisme dans les origines et son développement* (Paris, 1904).

84 Ap 20:1–6 is related to late Jewish eschatology. Ordinarily, OT eschatology presented definitive salvation in terrestrial terms. It was held, of course, that there was to be no end to the messianic reign, but the kingdom was endowed with very precise national characteristics. In the 1st cent. BC, and in that following, Jewish eschatology split into two main tendencies: Some contended that the world is too corrupt to be the theater of the establishment of the messianic kingdom and looked for the promises to be fulfilled in a completely new world, which would begin at the universal judgment; others retained the idea of a national, terrestrial messianic reign of limited duration (opinions varied between 40 and 7000 years), conceived as a sort of intermediate stage between the present era and the eternal reign of God. Ap 20:1–6 makes use of certain elements of this second theory, not necessarily including, however, the concept of a terrestrial reign of Christ; John's borrowings are ordered toward his general purpose: to encourage the martyrs of his day. A long period (1000 years) of happiness is to follow the brief persecution (three and a half years, Ap 11:2; 12:6; 13:5), but nowhere are the martyrs to reign "on earth" along with Christ. In contradistinction to the Jewish notion, the Messiah's role is not confined to the intermediate reign; Christ is, with God, at the center of the eternal kingdom (21:22f.; 22:1,3).

What is the meaning of this borrowing from Jewish eschatology? No satisfactory explanation has yet been devised. Among many interpretations of the passage, Augustine's has been the most widely accepted: The thousand years stand for the whole history of the Church, triumphant and militant, in heaven and on earth, from Christ's resurrection until his parousia. The "first resurrection" (vv. 4b, 5, 6) refers to the transition from the death of sin to life in faith. However, the question here is not about all the Christians, but only about the martyrs; and they have already experienced this moral resurrection before their physical death.

More recently, many Catholic exegetes have postulated a relationship between Ap 20:1–6 and Ez 37:1–14. Both John and Ezekiel envision the corporal resurrection of martyrs, but here the resurrection is symbolic of the happy outcome of their sacrifice, the renewal of the Church after the period of persecution; the kingdom of Christ and his martyrs in heaven will be manifested on earth by the expansion of the Church. It seems clear that what John has in mind here is an eschatological event concerning the martyrs—an event, no doubt, signifying a special heavenly happiness proper to the martyrs alone, yet producing a salutary effect for the Church on earth. Finally, a purely literary explanation has been proposed: Because Ap nowhere else gives so much as a hint of this so-called intermediate reign, 20:1–6 may be an interpretative doublet of 19:11–21 (see R. Schnackenburg, *God's Rule and Kingdom* [Freiburg, 1963] 339–47).

85 **1.** *the key of the abyss:* See 9:1,11. **2.** *he seized the dragon:* One of the hopes of apocalyptic was that God would imprison the infernal powers and reduce them to impotence. Satan has already been driven from heaven (12:9); he is here driven from earth and restricted to his proper sphere of influence. *for a thousand years:* A long period of time. All of world history was divided according to the plan of creation: By the association of Gn 1:1–2:4 (the account of the seven days of creation) with Ps 90:4 (cf. 2 Pt 3:8, a thousand years are as a day in the sight of God), world history was presented as consisting of seven periods, each a thousand years long. **3.** *that he should not deceive:* Satan's baneful vitality is such that he is to resume his career at the end of the thousand years (20:8–10). For this reason the text does not treat primarily of the punishment of Satan, but rather of the preventive measures adopted in favor of Christians. **4.** The new vision completes the preceding one: It presents a positive factor to complement the expulsion of Satan. *those who had been beheaded:* The martyrs, who had been crying for vengeance (6:9) and have now been heard (19:2). *who had not worshiped the beast:* Those who have suffered for refusing to abandon themselves to the Beast (13:15; 14:9–11; 16:2; 19:20) are associated with the martyrs. **5.** *the first resurrection:* "First" and "second" are sometimes used to distinguish realities of the present order from those that are eschatological: the first and second death (2:11; 20:6,14; 21:8); the first heaven and the first earth (21:1). A comparison with 20:12–13 will show that a physical resurrection is meant here; the same vb., *zaō*, is used elsewhere for the resurrection of Christ (1:18; 2:8). **6.** *priests of God:* See 1:6; priesthood and kingship are complementary elements in the service of God (22:3,5).

(Bietenhard, H., *Das tausendjährige Reich* [Zurich, 1955]. Gelin, A., *VDBS* 5 [1957] 1289–94. Michl, J., *LTK* 2 [1958] 1058–59.)

86 (c) Victory over Satan, Freed from His Prison (20:7–10). Possibly the present scene is a doublet of the victory over the Antichrist and the false prophet (19:11–21). **7.** *when the thousand years are over:* Why does the thousand-year reign come to this sudden end? Human history has seemingly continued through the thousand years, and Satan's rage, following his long imprisonment, may be compared to the fury by which he ignited persecutions against the Church after his expulsion from heaven (12:13). **8.** *at the four corners of the earth:* The earth is pictured as a square (7:1; cf. Ez 7:2). *Gog and Magog:* The prophecy in Ez 38–39 was often repeated and amplified in Jewish apocalyptic and rabbinical writings: Gog and Magog (terms that had become names for the peoples hostile to Israel) were to attack the People of God after the messianic reign. **9.** *they went up over:* The place where the Church is assembled seems to the seer to be a new land of Israel, with Jerusalem as its capital. After the fashion of many ancient peoples, the Jews considered their capital the center of the universe (Ez 38:12–16). *the camp of the saints and the beloved city:* The image of the camp recalls Israel's wanderings in the desert (Nm 2:2ff.). The city is Jerusalem of the millennium, symbol of the universal Church; it is beloved of God (Pss 78:68; 87:1–3) because Christ reigns in it. *fire came down from heaven:* A traditional image (Gn 19:24; Ez 38:22; 39:6; 1 Kgs 1:10–12; Lk 9:54), symbolizing God's dazzling interventions against the enemies of his people. **10.** *where the beast and the false prophet:* See 19:20; cf. 14:10f.

With the final expulsion of Satan no further obstacles remain to the definitive establishment of God's reign upon a new earth.

87 (d) THE UNIVERSAL JUDGMENT (20:11–15). The resurrection of the dead and the Last Judgment, marking the end of this world and the start of the new age, follow upon the intermediate reign of Christ. The passage conforms to the eschatological pattern of other apocalyptic writings (→ Johannine Theology, 80:55–56). **11.** *a great white throne:* This single throne, unlike those mentioned in 20:4 (cf. Dn 7:9), symbolizes God's absolute dominion; nothing can thwart his will. The Judge goes unnamed, perhaps out of respect (see 4:2), perhaps to stress the solemnity of the occasion; but everywhere in the Ap "he who sits on the throne" is God (4:2–9; 5:1,7,13; 6:16; 7:10; 19:4; 21:5). In other parts of the NT the Judge may be either God himself (Mt 18:35; Rom 14:10), or Christ, passing judgment in God's name (Mt 16:27; 25:31–46; Jn 5:22; Acts 10:42; 17:31; 2 Cor 5:10). *earth and heaven fled away:* As a result of sin, all of creation fell under the divine curse (Gn 3:17) and was made subject to corruption (Rom 8:19–22). Biblical understanding of the relationship between this corrupt world and the future era is divided. The best attested school of thought holds that the present creation will be entirely destroyed (Ps 102:26; Is 51:6; Mk 13:31; Acts 3:21; 2 Pt 3:7,10–12) and that a new heaven and a new earth will replace it (21:1); on the other hand, the NT also speaks of the liberation (Rom 8:21) and the renewal (Mt 19:28) of creation. **12.** *the dead, great and small:* All who have not participated in the first resurrection (20:5) will return to life for the final judgment. The NT insists upon the universality of the judgment (Mt 25:32; Jn 5:28f.; 2 Tm 4:1; 1 Pt 4:5). *books were opened:* The two books contain all men's actions, good and evil (Dn 7:10; cf. Is 65:6–7; Mal 3:16). *the book of life:* See comment on 3:5. This book is distinct from the two preceding books and contains the names of those destined for eternal life. The image suggests a divine election but does not rule out human liberty (3:5). **13.** *Death and Hades:* The insatiable, diabolical monster and the place where the dead abide (6:8). In the future era, death will be unknown (21:4). **14.** *into the lake of fire:* A personification of death joins the false prophet (19:20) and Satan (v. 10) in the lake of fire; death is rendered powerless (Is 25:8; Hos 13:14; 1 Cor 15:26,54). *the second death:* Those who undergo this death must abandon hope, for there is no possibility of a new resurrection.

88 (e) THE NEW WORLD AND THE NEW JERUSALEM (21:1–8). The first creation has disappeared (20:11); the wicked have been driven off to punishment (20:15). Nothing remains but to wonder at the magnificence of the eternal Kingdom of God. The description of this new creation is the high point of the book. **1.** *a new heaven and a new earth:* Creation must be renewed or refashioned in order to befit redeemed humanity (Is 65:17; 66:22). *the sea was no more:* The sea, with its perilous storms aroused by brutal and implacable forces, may have given rise to the myths concerning monsters ruling over the primeval chaos: Tiamat in Babylonia, Rahab or Leviathan in the Bible. God conquered these monsters when he ordered the universe (Jb 25:12f.; Ps 74:13f.; Is 51:9). He will annihilate them at the time of the new creation (Is 27:1); brutal power and violence are incompatible with the peace of the world to come. **2.** *the holy city:* Cf. 3:12; 22:19. It comes down from heaven (Jas 1:17), therefore it is of divine origin: God is the Architect and Builder of the city (Heb 11:10). It is "holy" because it is definitively consecrated to God. This is a theme found in the Pauline epistles (Gal 4:26; Phil 3:20; Heb 12:22), but already known in the OT (Is 54; 60; Ez 48:30–35). **3.** *a great voice:* One of the four living creatures gives an explanation of the new creation. *the dwelling of God:* This is the fulfillment of the prophecies that foretold the intimate union of God with the chosen people in the era of salvation (Lv 26:11f.; Jer 31:33f.; Ez 36:26–28; Zech 2:14f.; 8:8). The intimacy that the first man enjoyed in Paradise and that Israel experienced in desert and Temple is now granted to all members of the People of God, forever (7:15–17). There is some question whether the reading should be *laos* (sing.), according to the traditional theme of a single "people" of God (Jn 10:16), or *laoi* (pl.), which would express a modification of the same theme, adding a note of universalism. *Skēnē* perhaps suggests the glory of the Shekinah, the prefiguration of the Word Incarnate (Jn 1:14). **4.** The former world disappears, with all those repulsive characteristics that gave it the appearance of a creation enslaved to sin. *every tear:* See 7:16f.; Jer 31:16. *death:* See 20:14. *pain:* See Is 35:10; 65:19. This new condition of the world is exactly the opposite of Babylon's fate (18:22–23).

89 **5.** *I make all things new:* Cf. Is 43:18f.; 2 Cor 5:17; Gal 6:15. This is the only passage in the Ap in which God himself speaks. He declares that everything described in vv. 1–4 will be accomplished. *trustworthy and true:* See 3:14; 19:11; 22:6. **6.** *the Alpha and the Omega:* See 1:8. *the water of life:* Cf. Is 55:1; Zech 14:8; Jn 4:10,14; 7:37–39. **7.** *he who conquers:* See comment on 2:7; an echo of the promise made at the end of each of the letters to the seven churches (chs. 2–3). *his heritage:* A notion that implies the Christian's divine sonship and the gratuity of the reward he is to receive (Rom 4:13f.; 8:17; Gal 4:7). *I shall be his God and he shall be my son:* See Gn 17:7; 2 Sm 7:14; Ps 89:26–27. "His God," not "his Father," because John speaks of God as Father only in relation to Jesus. The point of view on this topic resembles that of Jn, where the divine sonship of Christians (though it is affirmed) is kept clearly distinct from the filiation of the only-begotten Son (Jn 20:17). But the Ap, as against Jn, looks primarily to the future for the fulfillment of eschatological hopes: "I shall be" and "he will be," on the great day of the final resurrection. **8.** John's enumeration of sinners gives the first position to those who have sinned against the faith. *the cowardly:* Those whose superficial and unstable faith has succumbed during persecution; they are like deserters from an army (Sir 2:12). *the faithless:* Those who do not have the faith include Christians who deny Christ, as well as pagans who blaspheme against him. *polluted:* Either those given to vices contrary to nature (so frequent in pagan cultures) or, better, those who have defiled themselves by participating in the imperial cult. *sorcerers:* See 9:21; 18:23. Lit., "the poisoners," those who mix potions and poisons (Acts 19:19). *all liars:* All the sinners who speak and act with deceit (21:27; 22:15; Jn 8:44). *the second death:* See 2:11; 20:6,14; opposed to the "water of life" in v. 6.

90 (f) THE SPOUSE OF THE LAMB AND THE HEAVENLY JERUSALEM (21:9–22:5). This description of the new Jerusalem takes up and develops material from 19:7 and 21:2. The seer has borrowed nearly all the elements in the description from apocalyptic tradition, especially from Ez 40–48. **9.** This verse is essentially a literal repetition of 17:1—in this way, John points up the opposition between God's city Jerusalem and Babylon. **10.** *he carried me away:* The seer was taken into the desert to view the harlot; now he is transported to a high mountain to admire the spouse descending from the presence of God (see 17:3; Ez 40:2–3). **11.** *the glory of God:* God's presence, filling the Church, transfigures her. *like jasper:* The details of this description indicate that the

glory of the Church is being compared with its source, the glory of God (4:3; 2 Cor 4:6). **12–13.** *twelve gates...twelve tribes:* Here again, as in 7:4–8, John alludes to the perfect continuity between God's people in the OT (Ez 48:30–35; Ex 28:17–21) and the Church in the NT (Mt 19:28; Lk 22:29). The frequent repetition of the number 12 in vv. 12–21 makes this proposition abundantly clear. *twelve angels:* Because the city comes from heaven it must have celestial guards. **14.** *twelve apostles:* The preaching of the apostles (and prophets: Eph 2:20) is to the constitution of the Church as the foundation to an edifice.

91 **15.** *a measuring rod:* Cf. Ez 40:3ff. All the numbers in the following verses contain factors of 12, symbolic of the People of God, and 1000, symbolic of great abundance. **16.** *foursquare:* The perfect geometric form (Ez 43:16; 48:16f.). *its length and breadth and height:* The heavenly Jerusalem forms a perfect cube, after the pattern of the Holy of Holies (1 Kgs 6:19f.); but its dimensions transcend any earthly possibility (12,000 stadia would equal about 1500 mi.). The figure is used as a sort of concretization of the city's supernal grandeur and perfection. **17.** *a hundred and forty-four cubits:* The height of the wall is insignificant (about 216 ft.) in comparison with the height of the city, which exceeds 7,000,000 ft. The wall seems to serve only as a dividing line between the city and the land around it. **18–21.** John lists the extraordinary materials used in the construction of the city-wall, the 12 foundations, the 12 gates, and the single thoroughfare running through the city. The pure gold and precious stones are catalogued only for the general impression they create: the splendor and sublimity of the city in which God dwells. Of the texts that resemble the present passage (Is 54:11f.; Ez 28:13; Tb 13:16f.), those that describe the high priest's breastplate (Ex 28:17–21; 39:10–14) seem most significantly analogous.

92 **22.** *no temple in it:* The Temple was the focal point of the historical Jerusalem, for there God dwelt among his people; hence Ezekiel (40–48) could not conceive of an ideal Jerusalem without the Temple, and John himself has previously spoken of a temple in heaven (11:19; 14:15,17; 15:5–16:1). But God's presence in the new world is not bounded by temple walls (Jn 4:21,24); the glory of God and the Lamb completely permeates the city (Jn 2:19–22; 2 Cor 6:16). *the Lamb:* He is consistently and intimately associated with God (7:9f.; 14:4; 22:1). **23.** *no need of sun or moon:* See 22:5; Is 24:23; 60:1f.,19f.; Jn 8:12; 1 Jn 1:5. **24–26.** These verses are inspired principally by Is 60:3,5,11: In the eschatological age the neighboring nations will come, not as enemy oppressors, but in submission to Yahweh and his people. Those who converge upon the heavenly Jerusalem are no longer pagans in John's eyes, but believers, admitted to the city because their names are written in the book of life. *no night there:* Cf. Is 60:11; Zech 14:6f. The glorious light of God's presence will never be extinguished. **27.** *nothing unclean:* Cf. Is 35:8; 52:1; Ez 44:9. *the book of life:* See comment on 3:5.

93 **22:1–5.** Finally, the seer describes the heavenly Jerusalem as the abode of the divine life. Here flows the river from which all may drink the water of life; on its bank flowers the tree of life-giving fruit. **1.** God and the Lamb replace the Temple as the unique source (7:17) of the water of life (Gn 2:10–14; Ps 46:4; Jer 2:13; Ez 47:1–12; Jl 3:18; Zech 14:8). **2.** *the tree of life:* See 2:7; since this vision is chiefly inspired by Ez 47:7,12, the word *xylon* should be taken as a generic singular. Instead of a single tree of life, as in Gn 2:9; 3:22, the eschatological city contains many trees, offering plentitude of life (12 kinds of fruit, 12 times a year), and all its citizens have free access to them. *for the healing:* Because those who will share in this new world will never undergo suffering, sickness, or death (21:4). **3.** *nothing accursed:* See Zech 14:11. Nothing will prove an occasion of sin (Dt 7:26); no one will incur God's anger because of sin. *the throne of God:* The center of the divine presence now replacing the Temple; hence, a liturgical service follows immediately, as an image of the intimate communion with God and Christ that the saints will enjoy. **4.** *they shall see his face:* A privilege denied to Moses (Ex 33:20,23) because it is unattainable in this world (Jn 1:18). Yet the devout aspired to the vision of God, at least in the Temple where he abode (Ps 17:15; 42:2). This aspiration will be fulfilled in the eschatological era (Mt 5:8; 1 Cor 13:12; 1 Jn 3:2; Heb 12:14). *his name on their foreheads:* See 3:12; 7:2f.; 14:1; now they belong to him definitively. **5.** See comments on 21:23–26; cf. 1:6. The reign of the saints will be endless (Dn 7:18,27) as will the condemnation of the wicked (20:10).

(See Comblin, J., "La liturgie de la nouvelle Jérusalem," *ETL* 29 [1953] 5–40.)

94 **(IV) Epilogue (22:6–21).** John's revelation is complete with the vision of the heavenly Jerusalem. The book closes with a series of warnings and exhortations in which it is difficult to perceive any special order of ideas. As a result, some exegetes have attempted hypothetical reconstructions of the original order based exclusively upon literary criticism, but such attempts at reconstruction have not been entirely convincing (see P. Gaechter, *TS* 10 [1949] 485–521).

(A) Witness of the Angel (22:6–9). **6.** *he said to me:* The angel of 21:9,15; 22:1 speaks once again. This angel is probably the same as the one mentioned in 1:1. *these words:* The contents of the entire book, not merely vv. 3–5. *the spirits of the prophets:* God's Spirit speaks through the prophets by elevating their natural faculties, not by speaking in their stead; thus "spirits" (pl.) refers to all the prophets inspired by the one Spirit. John consistently associates himself with the whole company of Christian prophets (10:7; 22:9), never isolating them from the rest of the community (11:18; 16:6; 18:20,24). **7.** *I am coming soon:* In a parenthesis similar to 16:15, the voice of Christ can be heard behind (or beyond) that of the angel, announcing that his coming as sovereign Judge is imminent (2:16; 3:11; 22:12,20). **8–9.** God is presented in apocalyptic as so transcendent a being that direct access to him is impossible; it is through the angels that he reveals himself to men and receives their honor and adoration. Yet this insistence upon the mediating power of angels could easily have led to misunderstandings.

95 **(B) The Time of Retribution Is at Hand (22:10–15).** **10.** *do not seal up:* The words of John will soon be fulfilled; hence they must be proclaimed to the churches. Unlike Dn 8:26; 12:4,9 (cf. Ap 10:4), there is here no expectation of some future era in which the message may be made known. **11.** *let the evil-doer still do evil:* See Dn 12:10; Ez 3:27. This injunction to persevere in evil as well as in good can be explained by the fact that judgment is imminent; in the last times there is no longer any opportunity for repentance (Mt 25:10; Lk 13:25). Each man must now accept the consequences of a decision freely made, and damnation will be nothing more than the wages of repeated and definite rejection of God's invitations. *the filthy:* The immoral pagan, who is unconcerned with purity and modesty (Jas 1:21). **12.** *my reward is with me:* See 11:18; Is 40:10. *according to his deeds:* Cf. Ps 66:12; Prv 24:12; Jer 17:10; Rom 2:6. **13.** *Alpha and Omega:* See 1:8.

14. *those who wash:* Pardon for sin and the purification of the heart are bestowed in the blood of the Lamb (Vg), through a participation in his death. **15.** *outside:* Unbelievers are not admitted to the Lord's banquet and only the faithful may receive Christ's body and blood; similarly, the sinners and the impious will be excluded from the benefits of salvation. They will be barred from the heavenly Jerusalem. *the dogs:* This word, with its strong connotations of impurity, is often applied to pagans (Dt 23:19; Mt 7:6; 15:26; 2 Pt 2:22).

96 **(C) Witness of Jesus (22:16–20).** **16.** Jesus guarantees the oracles contained in the book and recalls two messianic prophecies that he himself fulfilled. *the offspring of David:* See Is 11:1ff.; Mt 1:1ff.; Rom 1:3; 2 Tm 2:8; he is not only David's son, but his Lord (Mt 22:42ff.). In Christ, King of kings, all hopes are realized. *the bright morning star:* Among the ancients, a symbol of domination (see 2:28). This passage is probably intended as an allusion to Nm 24:17, which late Judaism interpreted as a messianic prophecy. Christ, the morning star, is the King of kings, and holds universal sway. **17.** *the Spirit:* The Spirit of God, speaking through the prophets (→ Johannine Theology, 80:39–45). "The Spirit and the Bride" refers to "the prophets and the saints" (16:6; 18:24); it is, then, the Church that responds to the call of Christ (v. 12). *let him who hears:* The prayer of the entire Church (the Bride) is the personal duty of each Christian assisting at the liturgical assembly (1:3). *let him who is thirsty come:* See 21:6. Christ asks us not only to welcome him when he comes, but actively to approach him (Jn 6:35; 7:37). **18–19.** Jesus himself enunciates the warning—patterned after Dt 4:2—which had become the traditional way of concluding a prophetic writing. It is directed against the willful forger, not against the negligent copyist. **20.** Jesus proclaims, for the third time in the epilogue, that he is soon to return. It is a principal theme of the book, and it provides a particularly fitting conclusion for the entire Bible. Salvation history, the central object of Scripture, is to be consummated by the triumphal return of Christ. *come, Lord Jesus:* Through his faith and hope, the Christian testifies that he is included in the history of salvation. An Aram version of this phrase is found in 1 Cor 16:21 (→ Letter 1 Cor, 51:89; → Pauline Theology, 79:61).

97 **(D) Salutation (22:21).** This verse is an unusual conclusion for an apocalyptic composition (→ 9 above). Its resemblance to 2 Thes 3:18 should be noted. *all the saints:* Some mss. omit "all." *Amen:* The last word of the Ap recalls 3:14 (→ 30 above).

65

THE SECOND EPISTLE OF PETER

Thomas W. Leahy, S.J.

BIBLIOGRAPHY

1 Bigg, C., *Epistles of St. Peter and St. Jude* (ICC; 2nd ed.; Edinburgh, 1910). Boobyer, G., "II Peter," *PCB* 1031–34. Chaine, J., *Les Épîtres catholiques* (EBib; Paris, 1939) 1–96. Charue, A., "Seconde Épître de S. Pierre," *PSB* 12, 482–85. Leconte, R., *Les Épîtres catholiques* (BJ; 2nd ed.; Paris, 1961). Mayor, J., *The Epistle of St. Jude and the Second Epistle of St. Peter* (London, 1907). Michl, J., *Der zweite Petrusbrief* (RNT 8; Regensburg, 1953) 231–57. Moffatt, J., *The General Epistles* (MNTC; London, 1945) 173–213. Reicke, B., *The Epistles of James, Peter, and Jude* (AB 37; N.Y., 1964) 141–85. Schelkle, K. H., *Die Petrusbriefe, der Judasbrief* (HTKNT 13/2; Freiburg 1961) 177–239. Schneider, J., *Die Briefe des Jakobus, Petrus, Judas und Johannes* (*NTD* 10; Göttingen, 1961) 99–122. Spicq, C., *Les Épîtres de Saint Pierre* (SB; Paris, 1966). Wand, J., *The General Epistles of St. Peter and St. Jude* (WC; London, 1934). Willmering, H., "Second Epistle of St. Peter," *CCHS* 1181–84. Windisch, H., *Die katholischen Briefe* (HNT 15; Tübingen, 1951) 83–105.

F-B 302–5. Guthrie, *NTI* 2, 137–85. Wik, *NTI* 509–19.

INTRODUCTION

2 **(I) Authenticity.** The Petrine authorship of this epistle is asserted clearly in 1:1 and implied in the reference to the transfiguration (1:16–18) and to 1 Pt (3:1). Nevertheless its authenticity is denied by most Protestants and questioned or denied by many Catholic exegetes (among the latter: K. Th. Schäfer, J. Chaine, P. Benoit, J. Cantinat, J. Michl, K. H. Schelkle). The chief intrinsic objections to Petrine authorship: (1) the close connection of 2 Pt with the relatively late epistle of Jude, reflecting a dependence of the former on the latter, rather than vice versa (→ 5 below); (2) the indication of a postapostolic setting in 3:2 and 4, and in 3:16. Of less force, but still significant, is the objection based on the marked difference of vocabulary and style in this letter from that of 1 Pt. This probable pseudonymous character of 2 Pt does not prejudice its canonicity (see Schelkle, "Exkurs: Biblische Pseudepigraphie," *Die Petrusbriefe* 245–48). Attestation to the canonicity of 2 Pt is late; for a while some writers and churches rejected 2 Pt (see Wik, *NTI* 513–14).

Today in German Lutheran circles the question of the place of 2 Pt in the canon has been reopened on the ground that the epistle shows objectionable signs of "early Catholicism," e.g., the idea of an authoritative interpretation of Scripture in 1:20 (→ Canonicity, 67:94; see E. Käsemann, *Essays on NT Themes* [SBT 41; London, 1964] 169–95).

3 **(II) Occasion, Purpose, Destination.** Knowing that his death is approaching (1:14), the Apostle (or the author who writes in his name) wishes to leave his fellow Christians a reminder of their lofty Christian vocation, together with an exhortation to live up to its demands, so as to be found worthy of the kingdom at the Lord's coming. To this end, he warns them against false teachers, heretical and apostate Christians who mislead many. A particular error to be guarded against is the denial of the Lord's coming—a denial occasioned by its long delay. Although, as in the case of Jude (→ Epistle Jude, 60:3), one cannot identify the false teachers precisely, they seem to be forerunners of various Christian Gnostics who by the middle of the 2nd cent. find themselves cut off from orthodox Christianity. At the time of the writing of 2 Pt they are still members of Christian communities.

Nor can one identify with certainty the recipients of 2 Pt. In spite of the "catholic" character of its address (1:1), the emphasis on concrete dangers indicates a restricted group of communities. Since 3:1 probably refers to 1 Pt, the recipient churches may be the same communities of Asia Minor (1 Pt 1:1).

M. McNamara (*Scr* 12 [1960] 13–19) argues against the unity of 2 Pt. He points to the abruptness of 3:1 and to the fact that ch. 3 repeats ch. 1. His suggestion is that the three chapters may well represent three notes that have been joined together. However, most authors acknowledge the unity of the epistle.

4 **(III) Date and Place of Composition.** Apart from the defenders of Petrine authenticity, scholars

tend to regard 2 Pt as the latest NT document, written perhaps *ca.* AD 140 or even later. Reasons for such a late date: (1) the reference to Paul's letters as "Scripture" (3:16); (2) the literary dependence of 2 Pt on Jude; (3) the "Gnosticism" of the false teachers. Such a date in the postapostolic period would not necessarily challenge the inspired quality of the document (see D. M. Stanley, "The Concept of Biblical Inspiration," *ProcCTSA* 12 [1958] 84–85). It is, however, by no means clear that so late a date is required. The question how early Paul's writings were regarded as Scripture remains unanswered (→ NT Epistles, 47:14); the "Gnostic" question is equally uncertain; and the problem of the delay of the parousia might be better situated toward the end of the 1st cent. (especially after the destruction of Jerusalem in AD 70). A possible date, within reasonable limits: the very end of the 1st cent. or early 2nd cent.

5 (IV) Relation of 2 Pt to Jude. A comparison of these two epistles reveals an extraordinary correspondence of ideas, sequence, phrasing, and vocabulary, especially between 2 Pt 2:1–18 and Jude 4–13, and 2 Pt 3:1–3 and Jude 17–18. There is obviously a literary dependence of one upon the other. A priori, it would seem more likely that the longer epistle has incorporated most of the short one, rather than that the short one was composed of cullings from the longer one. The dependence of 2 Pt upon Jude, rather than vice versa, is confirmed, in the opinion of most exegetes, by a close comparison of the individual parallels (cf. J. Chaine, *Épîtres catholiques*, 18–24). To cite a single instance: It is easier to conceive of the author of 2 Pt deliberately dropping Jude's citation of the apocryphal *Enoch*—one of the stumbling blocks in its attaining universal canonicity—than to conceive of the author of Jude deliberately inserting it into the context drawn from 2 Pt. B. Reicke, however, suggests a third alternative: Both derive from a common oral tradition (*Epistles of James, Peter, and Jude*, 190).

6 (V) Outline. The Second Epistle of Peter is outlined as follows:

(I) Address (1:1–2)
(II) Exhortation to Christian Virtue (1:3–21)
  (A) Past Divine Benefits (1:3–4)
  (B) Exhortation Proper (1:5–11)
  (C) Circumstances of the Letter (1:12–15)
  (D) Motives for Belief (1:16–21)
    (a) Apostolic Testimony to the Transfiguration (1:16–18)
    (b) Prophetic Witness of Scripture (1:19–21)
(III) Condemnation of the False Teachers (2:1–22)
  (A) Prediction of Their Coming (2:1–3)
  (B) Old Testament Examples of God's Punishing the Wicked and Saving the Righteous (2:4–9)
  (C) Description of the False Teachers (2:10–22)
(IV) The Delay of the Parousia (3:1–16)
  (A) Reminder of Previous Instructions (3:1–2)
  (B) Objections by Scoffers at the Delay of the Parousia (3:3–4)
  (C) Answers to Objections (3:5–10)
    (a) Comparison and Contrast with the Flood (3:5–7)
    (b) God's View of Time; His Forbearance; Suddenness of the End (3:8–10)
  (D) Practical Conclusions (3:11–15a)
  (E) Paul's Letters (3:15b–16)
(V) Final Warning, Exhortation, Doxology (3:17–18)

COMMENTARY

7 (I) Address (1:1–2). The opening greeting follows the normal pattern of NT letters but is particularly similar to those of 1 Pt and Jude. **1.** *who have obtained a faith:* The recipients are thus vaguely designated (→ 3 above). *faith: Fides quae creditur*, the aggregate of apostolic teaching handed on to succeeding generations. This great gift is, through God's impartial benevolence, of no less value when possessed by second-generation Christians than when possessed by apostolic eyewitnesses. *our God and Savior Jesus Christ:* The theologically significant application of the title "God" (*theos*) to Christ, although unusual in the NT, is not unparalleled (Jn 1:1; 20:28; Heb 1:8; probably also Ti 2:13; 2 Thes 1:12; Rom 9:5; 1 Jn 5:20; see R. E. Brown, *TS* 26 [1965] 545–73). The title "Savior" (*sōtēr*), rarely applied to Christ in the NT (perhaps because of its common use in Hellenistic religions and emperor worship), occurs five times in 2 Pt (1:1,11; 2:20; 3:2,18). In each case it is the second of a pair of titles, the first of which is "Lord" (except here); see comment on 1 Tm 1:1.

8 (II) Exhortation to Christian Virtue (1:3–21).

(A) Past Divine Benefits (1:3–4). God's benefits are recalled as the basis and motive for the following exhortation. With extreme conciseness we are told that the totality of religious life is the gift of God's power to those he calls, that this call is by means of his glorious revelation, and that the acceptance of this call is a form of knowledge of God. This knowledge—usually with Christ as its object—is stressed in 2 Pt: cf. 1:2,5–6,8; 2:20; 3:18. In this present section and elsewhere, 2 Pt adapts the vocabulary of Hellenistic philosophy to express orthodox Christian concepts. **4.** *promises:* Probably an allusion to the parousia, in anticipation of ch. 3. *partakers of the divine nature:* This remarkable and bold expression does not occur elsewhere in the Bible. Our author has borrowed it from Hellenistic philosophic and religious terminology, employing it as an apt expression of the fullness of Christian life. The same basic idea is expressed in different terminology in 1 Jn 1:3; 3:2,9; Jn 15:4; 17:22–23; Rom 8:14–17.

9 (B) Exhortation Proper (1:5–11). "As often happens in the NT, the ethical imperative follows from the dogmatic indicative" (Schelkle). **5–7.** The rhetorical figure employed here was called "climax" by the Greeks (cf. Rom 5:3–5; 8:29–30; 10:14–15). Beginning with faith, one virtue provides the basis of the next, until the summit is reached with Christian love (*agapē*). **8–9.** The significance of these virtues for Christian life is indicated positively in v. 8 and negatively in v. 9. **10.** This verse sums up the purpose of the epistle: to exhort the readers to firmness in their Christian vocation. **11.** *entrance into the eternal kingdom:* Thus is described the eschatological goal of Christian life, the object of Christian hope. Cf. the similar Gospel expression of "entering into the kingdom of God" (Mk 10:15 par.; Jn 3:5), "entering into eternal life" (Mt 25:46). See R. Schnackenburg, *God's Rule and Kingdom* (Edinburgh, 1963) 325. *of our Lord and Savior Jesus Christ:* This is one of the few NT passages to identify the eschatological kingdom as the kingdom of Christ (cf. Eph 5:5), rather than simply as the kingdom of the Father or of God. This identification was given expression in the Creed of the Council of Constantinople (AD 381) in the words "of whose kingdom there will be no end."

10 **(C) Circumstances of the Letter (1:12–15).** Faced with the prospect of death, the Apostle wishes to leave the readers a perpetual reminder of his teaching. The catechetical theme of remembering or reminding (vv. 12, 13, 15) is important in early Christian instruction (cf. 3:1–2; 1 Cor 11:2,24; 15:1; Lk 22:19b; 24:6; Jn 2:22; 12:16; Jude 5, 17; see O. Michel, *ThDNT* 4, 682–83). This theme results naturally from the early Christian awareness of the importance of the factual reality of the Gospel events and of the need of preserving and handing on intact the "faith" in which these events were enshrined. **12.** *in the truth you have:* That is, the deposit of faith, as in v. 1 (cf. Jude 3). **13.** *in this body:* Lit., "tent." Throughout the Bible the Gk word *skēnōma* is otherwise used only in the literal sense. However, nonbiblical examples of the figurative application to the human body occur in late Hellenistic usage (cf. *skēnos*, 2 Cor 5:1,4). **15.** Concern to preserve apostolic teaching for the Church's future guidance in the written form of a letter seems to reflect the postapostolic age.

11 **(D) Motives for Belief (1:16–21).** In anticipation of the problem of the delay of the Lord's coming (cf. 3:1ff.), the author presents two motives for accepting this basic Christian teaching.

(a) Apostolic Testimony to the Transfiguration (1:16–18). **16.** *cleverly devised myths:* The apostolic doctrine has nothing in common with the false teachings of ch. 2. *power and coming:* On the "coming," see comment on Jas 5:7. The "power" may mean Jesus' present power in the Church (as in v. 3; so Boobyer); or the power to be manifested at the parousia (cf. Mt 24:30; so Reicke). **16–18.** *eyewitnesses of his majesty:* This recollection of the transfiguration is to undermine objections to the parousia by showing, on the testimony of apostolic eyewitnesses, that Jesus already possesses the essential qualities to be manifested at his coming: majesty, honor and glory from the Father, messianic and divine sonship. Acquaintance with the Syn account of the transfiguration (Mk 9:2–10 par.) is presumed. Although it omits various details, the present account surpasses the Syn in its heightened religious tone.

12 (b) Prophetic Witness of Scripture (1:19–21). **19.** *more sure:* The sense is ambiguous. Either the transfiguration has confirmed prophetic testimony (Schelkle, Boobyer); or prophetic testimony is more certain than the apostolic witness of the transfiguration (Bigg); or the comparative is used with elative force: prophetic testimony is *very* certain (no comparison being made) (Zerwick, Reicke). In any case, the prophetic word—i.e., the OT Scriptures generally—also testifies to the parousia. *until day dawns:* Until the parousia. *in your hearts:* The eschatology of 2 Pt seems to have an individual-psychological aspect, as well as the more typically NT cosmic aspect. **20.** The bearing of this obscure verse, in view of the general context and of v. 21, seems to be a caution against unauthorized interpretation of the Scriptures, such as that alluded to in 3:16. **21.** Just as the guidance of the Holy Spirit was needed by the prophets, so it is needed in reading their writings. Although the author does not say where this guidance is to be found, his commendation of apostolic authority in 1:12–18 and the general NT context indicate that this is to be found in the apostolic tradition handed on in the Church. (See J. Curran, "The Teaching of II Peter 1:20 on the Interpretation of Prophecy," *TS* 4 [1943] 347–68.)

13 **(III) Condemnation of the False Teachers (2:1–22).** Chapter 2 manifests an extraordinary resemblance to Jude 4–13 (→ 5 above). In each case, evildoers in the community are denounced, threatened with punishment according to OT examples, and their vices are described in extremely harsh, if somewhat vague, terms. About 70 words (not counting articles, pronouns, and prepositions) of 2 Pt 2 either repeat or echo words of Jude. And yet, although the details and examples correspond generally, they are by no means identical. In utilizing Jude, 2 Pt has adopted, adapted, added, and omitted. For a detailed comparison of the two epistles, see J. Mayor, *Epistle of St. Jude and Second Epistle of St. Peter*, iii–lxvii, 2–15.

14 **(A) Prediction of Their Coming (2:1–3).** Although these verses, as well as 3:3, apparently express the prophetic foresight of a future situation, the descriptions in vv. 10b–22 and in 3:5 indicate that the situation being described is already present. **1.** *among the people:* The Israelites. *false prophets:* See, e.g., Jer 28. *just as there will be:* The experiences of the Israelites typify those of the Christians; cf. 1 Cor 10:1–11 and Jesus' prediction of "false prophets" before the end (Mt 24:11). *denying the Master:* Christ. The denial seems to include both false doctrines and immoral practices. *who bought them:* A clear reference to the redemption, using Pauline terminology. **2.** *many will follow:* As in Mt 24:11 (also vv. 5, 10, 24)—but not in Jude—the false teachers will succeed in leading others astray. **3.** *from of old:* In the exemplary condemnations about to be cited from the OT.

15 **(B) Old Testament Examples of God's Punishing the Wicked and Saving the Righteous (2:4–9).** In comparison with Jude, 2 Pt omits the examples of the rebellious Israelites (Jude 5), of Cain and of Korah (Jude 11); inserts Noah and Lot as examples of divine mercy (2:5,7); agrees with Jude in citing the examples of the fallen angels (2 Pt 3:4; Jude 6), Sodom and Gomorrah (2 Pt 3:6; Jude 7), and Balaam (2 Pt 3:15–16; Jude 11); and has a generalized form of Jude's Michael-Satan example (2 Pt 2:10–11; Jude 8–10).

The style of 2 Pt is more uniform in this section, and the sequence of OT events is more nearly chronological than in Jude. **4.** *angels when they sinned:* See the details of the angels' offense in Jude 6 and comment. **5.** *Noah with seven others:* Cf. 1 Pt 3:20. *herald of righteousness:* Gn 8:9 calls Noah "righteous"; but later Jewish tradition portrayed him as preaching repentance to his contemporaries (cf. Josephus, *Ant.* 1.3, 1 § 74; *Jub* 7:20–39). **6.** *Sodom and Gomorrah:* As in the case of the angels, Jude (v. 7) gives details of the sin of the "cities of the plain." Sodom is an outstanding example of sinfulness and its divine punishment in the Apocrypha. The triad of the sinful angels (v. 4), the flood (v. 5), and Sodom (v. 6) occur also in *T. Naphtali* 3:4–5; *3 Mc* 2:5 (the "giants," the flood, and Sodom). **7–8.** Lot's righteousness is stressed by a threefold repetition, an emphasis lacking in the OT accounts (Gn 13 and 19). Later Jewish tradition generally regarded Lot in an unfavorable light, especially because of Gn 19:30–38 (Str–B 3, 769–71). However, there was a strand of rabbinic exegesis that exalted Lot, in agreement with Wis 10:6; cf. *1 Clem.* 11:1 (see S. Rappaport, *ZNW* 29 [1930] 299–304). **9.** The conclusions to be drawn from the previous examples are now stated in general terms. *for punishment:* In accord with the eschatological emphasis of 2 Pt, the ambiguous pres. ptc. *kolazomenous* is better taken as a future tense (see *GrBib* 282–84): The unrighteous are being kept for punishment on judgment day (so Schelkle, AG, Leconte, Schneider, Chaine, Charue); rather than as a present tense: They are being kept under punishment for judgment day (so Boobyer, RSV, NEB).

16 **(C) Description of the False Teachers (2:10–22).** **10.** Cf. Jude 7, 8, 16, 18. *indulge in the lust of defiling passion:* The immorality of the false teachers is described in terms of sexual aberration in 2:2,10,13,14,18. *reject the Lord:* Lit., "the lordship" (*kyriotēs*); cf. 2:1, "denying the Master." Others translate "despising authority." Reicke understands this "authority" as that of the existing Roman Empire. *the glorious ones:* Whereas in Jude 8 this expression seems to refer to good angels, the comparison with "angels" in 2:11 implies that in 2:10 they are fallen angels (perhaps to be identified with those in 2:4). According to Reicke, they would be the "dignitaries" of the state. **11.** Although the incident in Jude 9 has been generalized, the argument proceeds a fortiori there too. Background for this verse may be found in *Enoch* 9. **12.** Apparently an expanded form of Jude 10, with a change of emphasis and loss of clarity. **13.** *revel in the daytime:* Their scandalous conduct is not limited to nighttime revelry. *in their dissipation:* Jude 12 has *agapais* (love feasts) where 2 Pt has *apatais* (empty deceits, dissipation). This change may indicate that 2 Pt does not wish to state that false teachers continued to participate in the community *agapē*. Some ancient mss. of 2 Pt read *agapais* instead of *apatais*, probably a later scribal correction based on Jude 12. **14.** *entice unsteady souls:* This idea is developed below (2:18–19). *accursed children* [RSV]: A Hebraism (lit., "children of curse") better rendered by E. J. Goodspeed, "They are accursed." **15–16.** The comparison with Balaam (Jude 11) is here considerably expanded, probably for the sake of emphasis. Although the OT data on Balaam (Nm 22–24 and 31) does not emphasize his covetousness, later Jewish tradition, reflected in 2 Pt and Jude, did so.

17. An abbreviated and somewhat modified form of Jude 12b–13. Since the final phrase about the nether darkness is more appropriate in Jude, this is one of the many indications of dependence of 2 Pt upon Jude. **18.** Apparently the influence of the false teachers succeeded in corrupting some recent converts (cf. 2:2,14). *those who live in error:* Contemporary pagans, among whom these converts were formerly numbered. **19.** *they promise them freedom:* False teachers entice others to a libertinism that is a parody of true Christian freedom (cf. 1 Pt 2:16). *they are slaves:* That sin constitutes slavery is stated also in Rom 6:16 and Jn 8:34. **20–22.** Grammatically the subject of these verses could be the ones enticed and promised freedom (2:18–19); the context indicates rather that the false teachers are the subject. **20.** *through the knowledge of our Lord and Savior Jesus Christ:* See comment on 1:1. This description of conversion as knowledge implies a personal experience of Christ as Lord (with its counterpart of self-awareness of subjection) and as Savior (with the corresponding awareness of a personal need of salvation). *the last state has become worse for them than the first:* The identical wording of Mt 12:45. The parable of the unclean spirit returning to its former abode with seven other spirits suits the present context. **21.** *the way of righteousness... the holy commandment:* Because of the false emphasis on libertinism, Christian faith is described in terms of moral conduct (cf. also 3:2). *delivered to them:* This expression is used in Jude 3 of the deposit of faith in the Church. **22.** The denunciation of the false teachers reaches a climax in this comparison with dogs and swine, a comparison that in biblical times constituted a superlative expression of odium and contempt. The proverb of the dog is found in Prv 26:11, applied to the fool who repeats his folly. That of the swine is found in *Aḥiqar* (Syr) 8:18.

17 **(IV) The Delay of the Parousia (3:1–16).** The teaching on the Lord's parousia, referred to in 1:16–19, is now defended against the scoffing of the false teachers.

(A) Reminder of Previous Instructions (3:1–2). **1.** *second letter:* A reference to 1 Pt (see G. Boobyer, "The Indebtedness of 2 Peter to 1 Peter," *NT Essays* [Fest. T. W. Manson; Manchester, 1959] 34–53). *by way of reminder:* See comment on 1:12–15. **2.** The wording is influenced by Jude 17, but to the apostolic testimony cited in Jude is added that of the OT prophets. Thus the role of apostles in the NT is comparable to that of prophets in the OT. Their role is further specified as that of communicating the "commandment" of Christ to the Church. The expression seems to envision a collegiate relationship of the apostles, as a body, to the Church rather than the relation of individual apostles to the respective churches founded by them. *commandment of the Lord:* Cf. 2:21. This way of referring to the Christian faith probably represents a stage in the increasing tendency to represent Christianity as law. Schelkle gives references to the Apostolic Fathers and to early Christian art for this.

18 **(B) Objections by Scoffers at the Delay of the Parousia (3:3–4).** **3.** Taken, with slight modifications, from Jude 18. **4.** These scoffers of the end time ridicule the promise of the parousia. Since, however, neither the OT nor the NT predictions contain this detail of "promise," the impression is given of a somewhat infelicitous adaptation of Jude by 2 Pt. *where is the promise of his coming?:* Apparently the impression was widespread in the early Church that the parousia would occur within the lifetime of some of those who had seen Christ. Such sayings of Christ as Mt 10:23; Mk 9:1; 13:30 may have been so understood. *ever since the fathers fell asleep:* Since the end of the apostolic generation. This expression indicates a postapostolic date for the composition of 2 Pt (→ 4 above). A similar expression of disillusion at the delay of the parousia is found in *1 Clem.* 23:3 (cf. *2 Clem.* 11:2). *from the beginning of creation:* According to the scoffers, the past unchanging nature of the world would rule out such future cosmic changes as were associated with the parousia.

19 **(C) Answers to Objections (3:5–10).**

(a) Comparison and Contrast with the Flood (3:5–7). The scoffers' assertion in v. 4b is refuted by the cosmic destruction by water in the past, which parallels the future cosmic destruction by fire. **5.** Due to obscure syntax, it is not certain whether or not the author is asserting that the heavens (as well as the earth) were formed out of water and amid water. The cosmogony is that of Gn 1:1–2,6–10. *by the word of God:* In Gn 1 God creates by his word. **6.** *through which:* Since the pronoun is plural (*di' hōn*), this probably refers to the two sources of the flood waters, those above and those beneath (see Gn 7:11; 8:2). **7.** *by the same word:* The argument proceeds *a pari:* Because the same word of God that caused creation and the flood has also foretold the coming cosmic events, the latter are as certain as the former. *stored up for fire:* See comment on 3:10.

20 (b) God's View of Time; His Forbearance; Suddenness of the End (3:8–10). **8.** *beloved:* The delay of the parousia is a problem also for the faithful. For a similar problem at Qumran and its solution, see 1QpHab 7:7–14. *a thousand years as one day:* By thus inverting the quotation from Ps 89:4 (cited in the first part of the verse), the argument from God's mysterious transcendence has been made more applicable to the problem of the delay of the parousia. **9.** *forbearing toward you:* The forbearance (*makrothymia*) of God, a characteristic attributed to him from Ex 34:6 onward in the OT, and given heightened expression in the NT (see J. Horst, *ThDNT* 4, 374–87), is seen as the answer to the contemporary problem of the parousia. The delay is due to the universal salvific will of God (see 3:15; Rom 11:32; 1 Tm 2:4). **10.** *will come like a thief:* The statement is almost identical with 1 Thes 5:2. This simile of the suddenness of the coming of judgment day, found also in Ap 3:3 and 16:15, doubtless goes back to the saying of Jesus in Mt 24:43. *heavens will pass away:* The expression may depend on Mt 24:35. *with a mighty whish:* The Gk *roizēdon* is onomatopoetic. *the elements:* Since these are distinguished from the heavens and the earth, they may signify the heavenly bodies, perhaps including the angelic powers connected with them. *the earth and the works that are upon it will be found:* This obscure expression is textually the better reading than such variants as "will be burned up," "will disappear," "will not be found." The meaning of "will be found" may be "will be laid bare" (NEB). Although the image of fire is often mentioned in the OT and NT in connection with the Day of the Lord, 2 Pt 3:7–13 is the only scriptural passage asserting a final conflagration by which the universe will be destroyed on that day. The idea of a final conflagration was, however, widespread at the time of the composition of 2 Pt (cf. K. H. Schelkle, *Petrusbriefe*, 226, n. 1). Originating in Persia, the idea spread to the Greco-Roman world and into Jewish apocalyptic, whence it influenced Christian thought (cf. J. Chaine, *Épîtres catholiques*, 87). As in the Gn accounts of the creation and the flood, contemporary Oriental myths were exploited to give expression to the sovereignty of Yahweh and to the unfolding of salvation history; so here the fundamental Christian (and Jewish) teaching of the coming Day of the Lord is expressed in the popular imagery of the times. In none of these cases of biblical expression, therefore, does the acceptance in faith of the revealed truths of salvation history necessarily involve acceptance of the scientific validity of the imagery employed. (See J. Chaine, "Cosmogonie aquatique et conflagration finale d'après la *Secunda Petri*," *RB* 46 [1937] 207–16.)

21 **(D) Practical Conclusions (3:11–15a).** As is usual in the NT (cf. Mt 24:42–51; 25; 1 Thes 5:1–11), the consideration of the Judgment is followed by an exhortation to the practice of virtue in a spirit of alert watchfulness for the Lord's return. **12.** *hastening the coming of God's day:* That the holy and godly conduct recommended in v. 11 can actually hasten the Lord's coming, was implied in 3:9. Cf. Acts 3:19–20 and "thy kingdom come" (Mt 6:10) in the prayer. For similar understandings in Judaism, see Str-B 1, 162–65. Some, however, translate not "hastening," but "earnestly desiring." **13.** *new heavens and a new earth:* The expression is taken from Is 65:17; 66:22, and is used also in Ap 21:1 of the situation following upon the Judgment. *we wait for:* Thus Christian expectation looks beyond the crisis of the last day for the final fulfillment of the divine promises. *in which righteousness dwells:* As in the passages from Is and Ap, righteousness in the New Creation has the double aspect of the godliness of those within it, and of retribution for the wicked in the preceding Judgment. Beyond this, the author does not attempt to explain the nature of the post-Judgment universe or its physical relationship to the present universe (cf. Rom 8:19–22). **14.** *without spot or blemish:* This is the negative form of the pair of epithets applied to the false teachers in 2:13. *in peace:* Rather than subjective tranquillity, this signifies an objective state of friendship with God, characteristic of messianic times. **15a.** See 3:9.

22 **(E) Paul's Letters (3:15b–16).** *our beloved brother Paul:* This appellation refers to the traditional intimate relationship of the two great apostles, rather than simply to Paul's status as a Christian. *wrote to you:* Opinion is divided as to whether this refers to one particular Pauline epistle; and if so, to which. An apt reference would be Rom 2:4. *according to the wisdom given to him:* This expression and the following verse seem, in a general fashion, to refer to the inspiration possessed by Paul in the writing of his letters. **16.** *in all his letters:* Evidently a collection of Paul's letters, complete or incomplete, had been assembled and was known to the author and the recipients of 2 Pt. This is one of the indications for dating 2 Pt in the postapostolic age (→ 4 above). *some things hard to understand:* These would probably include Paul's teaching on justification by faith. *twist to their own destruction:* The false teachers exploit Paul's teaching on Christian liberty as a justification for their perverse libertinism. A similar abuse of Pauline teaching may have occasioned the famous section on faith and works in Jas 2:14–26. Paul himself was aware of such twisting of his teachings (see Rom 3:8). *the other scriptures:* The writings of the OT. This manner of referring to Paul's epistles as comparable to the OT manifests an early stage in the Church's awareness of the NT canon—i.e., of a body of Christian writings comparable in their origin, function, and sacredness to the Law and the Prophets of the OT (→ Canonicity, 67:81).

23 **(V) Final Warning, Exhortation, Doxology (3:17–18).** **17.** The burden of the letter is summed up in this final admonition. **18a.** The opening wish of 1:2 is repeated in somewhat different wording. **18b.** The epistle concludes with a doxology, apparently in imitation of Jude, the only other NT epistle to so conclude. In 2 Pt, however, the doxology is addressed to Christ rather than to the Father. Other NT examples of doxologies to Christ: 2 Tm 4:18; Ap 1:6; 5:13; 7:10; probably Rom 9:5; perhaps 1 Pt 4:11; Heb 13:21.

66

INSPIRATION AND INERRANCY

Richard F. Smith, S.J.

BIBLIOGRAPHY

1 Adinolfi, M., *Ispirazione e inerranza* (Rome, 1962). Alonso Schökel, L., *The Inspired Word* (N.Y., 1965). Barucq, A. and H. Cazelles, "Les livres inspirés," R-F 1, 2–69. Benoit, P., *Aspects of Biblical Inspiration* (Chicago, 1965); "Inspiration," R-T 9–59. Benoit, P. and R. E. Murphy (eds.), "The Human Reality of Sacred Scripture," *Concilium* 10 (N.Y., 1965). Beumer, J., *Die Katholische Inspirationslehre zwischen Vatikanum I und II* (Stuttgart, 1966). Charlier, C., *The Christian Approach to the Bible* (Westminster, 1958) 101–220. Courtade, G., "Inspiration et inerrance," *VDBS* 4, 482–559. Desroches, A., *Jugement pratique et jugement spéculatif chez l'écrivain inspiré* (Ottawa, 1958). De Tuya, M. and J. Salguero, *Inspiracion Biblica. Canon. Texto. Versiones* (Madrid, 1967). Forestell, J. T., "Bible, II (Inspiration)," *New Cath. Ency.*, 2, 381–86. Grelot, P., "L'inspiration scripturaire," *RSR* 51 (1953) 337–82. Harrington, W., *Record of Revelation: The Bible* (Chicago, 1965) 20–53. Levie, J., *The Bible, Word of God in Words of Men* (N.Y., 1961) 203–301. Lohfink, N., "Über die Irrtumslosigkeit und die Einheit der Schrift," *SZ* 174 (1964) 161–81; Eng digest in *TD* 13 (1965) 185–92. Loretz, O., *Die Wahrheit der Bibel* (Freiburg, 1964). Lusseau, H., *Essai sur la nature de l'inspiration scripturaire* (Paris, 1930). McCarthy, D., "Personality, Society, and Inspiration," *TS* 24 (1963) 553–76. Mangenot, E., "Inspiration de l'Écriture," *DTC* 7, part 2, 2068–2266. Pache, R., *L'inspiration et l'autorité de la Bible* (Saint-Legier-sur-Vevey, 1967). Rahner, K., *Inspiration and the Bible* (2nd ed.; N.Y., 1964). Schildenberger, J., *Vom Geheimnis des Gotteswortes* (Heidelberg, 1950) 15–86. Stanley, D., "The Concept of Biblical Inspiration," *ProcCTSA* 13 (1958) 65–95. Synave, P. and P. Benoit, *Prophecy and Inspiration* (N.Y., 1961) esp. 84–145.

2 OUTLINE

TERMINOLOGY

3 The term "divine inspiration of Scripture" denotes the special influence of God upon the human writers of the Bible, an influence of such a nature that God is said to be the author of the biblical books. Vatican Council I expressed it thus: "The Church regards them [the various books of Scripture] as sacred and canonical...because, having been written under the influence of the Holy Spirit, they have God as their author and as such have been entrusted to the Church" (*EB* 77). In the Catholic view, the divine inspiration of Scripture is, in the strict sense, a supernatural mystery. It is, therefore, a reality that can never be fully comprehended and that will always remain obscure and opaque to the human mind.

4 In Catholic theology, the words "inspired" and "inspiration" are frequently used both generically of any and all promptings of God's grace in and on the human psyche and (as here) specifically of the divine promptings at the origin of the books of the Bible. These words, introduced into English about the 14th cent., were first used to denote the generic and specific promptings of divine grace just noted; but relatively soon their scope was expanded to include the various senses, religious and nonreligious, that they now have. They came into the language as transliterations of Middle French terms, which themselves were transliterations from the Latin.

5 The basic *Latin* word in this area is the vb. *inspirare*, meaning literally, "to breathe into, upon, or in." The history of this word and of its cognates has never been adequately investigated. Apparently not employed in pre-Augustan and Augustan writings except in poetry, *inspirare* is chiefly a post-Augustan word, used both in its literal meaning and in a transferred meaning, namely that of arousing a state or attitude in the human mind, as in the statement: "His words inspired anger." In Tertullian, the *inspirare* words are already found in a transferred Christian application (*De pat.* 1), though only in the generic sense of the promptings of God and not in the specific sense of those promptings that led to the writing of Scripture. Early Christian Latin vocabulary used such words as *afflatus*, *inflatus*, and *instinctus*—the classical equivalents of our modern word "inspiration." Gradually, however, the *inspirare* words came to be generally used for that influence by which God is the source of the sacred books.

6 *Greek* has a larger vocabulary to cover the area we are considering. English and Latin use the same terms to refer both to the books and to their human writers; we speak of inspired books (*libri inspirati*) as well as of inspired writers (*scriptores inspirati*), and "inspiration" too may be used in either reference. Greek, however, provides one set of words for inspiration considered from the viewpoint of the documents produced and another set for inspiration considered from the viewpoint of the human writers involved in the process. The adjective used in referring to an inspired book is *theopneustos* (= God-breathed), a term found in 2 Tm 3:16. The noun corresponding to this adjective is *theopneustia*, but it was not used until very late, and then rarely (e.g., John VIII of Jerusalem, *Vita...Damasceni* 34 [*PG* 94. 481A]—used here rather from the viewpoint of the inspired writer). On the other hand, "inspired" as applied to the human writers of Scripture is rendered by such terminology as *theophorētos* (= God-borne; cf. 2 Pt 1:21) and *pneumatophoros* (= Spirit-borne). The corresponding noun is *epipnoia* (= a breathing upon or onto), with an added word or phrase to identify God as the source of the inbreathing.

7 As for *Hebrew*, the matter of terminology is simple; there is no set of words to cover the idea of the divine inspiration of Scripture. But, as can be seen from such Gk words as *theopneustos* and *epipnoia*, the thought background is the OT theme of the breath-spirit of Yahweh (*Epipnoia* and *Theopneustos* in G. W. H. Lampe, *A Patristic Greek Lexicon* [Oxford, 1961ff.]; *Theopneustos*, *ThWNT* 6, 452–53).

DIVINE-HUMAN ORIGIN OF THE INSPIRED BOOKS

8 **(I) The Divine Origin of Scripture.**

(A) Jewish Notions. The idea of God-inspired Scripture was not one of the primordial themes of Israelite religion—understandably so, for this religion originated among people who at first had no knowledge of writing and who existed for a long time under general conditions unfavorable to literary production. Nevertheless, in the course of time, the religion of Israel did become centered in the collection of books that Christians now call the OT (→ Canonicity, 67:22, 48). In spite of the centrality it acquired in Judaism, the OT does not itself contain a doctrine of the inspiration of Scripture. Although the OT certainly and emphatically refers to the divine action of God upon the minds of the prophets, this influence was phrased in terms of the oral proclamation of a message that God had communicated to them. It is true that the OT sometimes records God's commanding a prophet to write (Ex 17:14; Is 30:8; Jer 30:2; 36:2; Hab 2:2), and that Isaiah referred to his own written prophecy as "the book of the Lord" (34:16). But, of themselves, none of these expressions would seem to indicate anything more than the prophet's consciousness of a pressing duty to write. There is no indication of a divine influence upon the prophetic writer that would make it appear as if God were the author of such writing. Moreover, the divine action upon men, which, at least in emphatic instances, is described in some such phrase as "The spirit of the Lord came upon...," is limited to the areas of action and of speaking and does not extend in the OT to the area of writing or even of thinking (P. Benoit, *Aspects*, 80–83). Seemingly, then, the doctrine of the inspiration of Scripture, as it is understood in the Church today, is not mirrored in the writings of the OT. To be sure, it is not denied there, but neither is it affirmed.

(Courtade, G., *art. cit.*, 482–86. Höpfl, H. and B. Gut, *Introductio generalis in Sacram Scripturam* [5th ed.; Naples, 1950] 33–34.)

9 Nevertheless, later on, the belief that divine inspiration was the origin of Scripture appeared among the Jews. This doctrine, while extrascriptural, is reflected in the Bible to the extent that we already read in later sections of the OT about the Jewish "sacred books" (e.g., 1 Mc 12:9). The psychological thrust toward this doctrine sprang from Josiah's adoption of the "book of the covenant" (2 Kgs 23:1–2) and became an irreversible dynamic from the time when, as narrated in Neh 8, Ezra read to the people from the "book of the law of Moses" as something that "the Lord had commanded to Israel." Subsequent doctrine among the Jews merely actuated the possibilities latent in these two events.

Since the people of Israel became known as the people of the Book because of their respect for the written law, it was natural that the doctrine of inspiration should first form around their concept of the origin of the Torah. According to the doctrine, which gradually took a more developed form, the Torah was caused by God before the existence of the world and was revealed to Moses by mental-oral instruction, or by delivery of the written text of the Pentateuch, or by literal dictation. This divine causation extended, even in the most material sense, to every part of the Pentateuch (though a few exceptions, e.g., the curses in Dt 28, were sometimes made), so that a plenary divine origin was ascribed to the entire Pentateuch. Under this influence, the doctrine of the divine origin of the Prophets and of the Writings also sprang up. Yet here the divine causation was not conceived in such a plenary fashion. The Prophets and the Writings were written under the influence of the spirit of Yahweh, but this influence was not thought to be the cause of every jot and tittle, as in the case of the Torah. Nevertheless, the divine origin of the Prophets and of the Writings was fully accepted; these books "soiled the hands" just as truly as did the books of the Torah.

(Bonsirven, J., *Le judaïsme palestinien au temps de Jésus-Christ* [2nd ed.; Paris, 1934] 1, 257–63. "Inspiration," *JE* 6, 607–8. Moore, G., *Judaism in the First Centuries of the Christian Era* [Cambridge, Mass., 1927] 1, 235–50. Schürer, E., *A History of the Jewish People in the Time of Jesus Christ* [N.Y., 1891] vol. 2, part 1, 306–12. Str-B 4, part 1, 435–51).

10 The doctrine of the divine origin of the sacred books was retained even by the Jews who absorbed Hellenistic ideas—thus, for instance, Philo who explained the pre-existence of the Torah in terms of Platonic ideas. It was Philo, too, who first adapted the Gk vb. "to inspire" (*epipnein; katapnein*) to express the divine origin of Scripture. Josephus introduced the use of the Gk noun for inspiration (*epipnoia*) in this reference. His brief statement about the sacred books may serve to summarize the developed Jewish view about their origin: "...although long ages have now passed, no one has dared to add, remove, or change a syllable; and it is an instinct with every Jew, from the day of his birth, to regard them as the decrees of God, to abide by them, and, if necessary, to die for them gladly" (*AgAp* 1.8 § 42).

(Pesch, C., *De inspiratione Sacrae Scripturae* [Freiburg, 1906] 16–27. Wolfson, H., *Philo* [Cambridge, Mass., 1, 1947] 184–88.)

11 **(B) New Testament Data.** The conviction of the divine origin of the Jewish sacred books is repeatedly implied or expressed in the pages of the NT. Jesus is presented as employing the customary Jewish term for the totality of the sacred books, namely *Scripture* (*graphē*), the document par excellence. He is shown as regarding this Scripture as irrefragable, impossible to annul (Jn 10:35). He is also depicted as introducing a statement that is authoritative and not open to question by the phrase "It is written"—a typical Jewish reference to the OT books. For example, he opposes "It is written" to the diabolical suggestions of the Tempter (Mt 4:4,7,10); and he announces that certain events will take place, for so "it is written" (e.g., Mt 26:31). The source of this sovereign authority of the sacred books is also identified by Jesus—the words of Scripture are decisive because they are the words of God. This is brought out in such passages as Mt 19:4–5, in which Jesus replies to a leading question about divorce by saying, "He who made them...said: Hence a man shall leave his father and mother and cleave to his wife...." Jesus here ostensibly quotes words of God from Gn 2:24—words that in their own context in Gn, however, are given as a statement of the human writer and not as a statement of God.

12 An identical attitude toward the Jewish sacred books is no less apparent elsewhere in the NT. They are regularly referred to as Scripture (*graphē*). This word appears in the NT 51 times, and each time (with the exception of 2 Pt 3:16), it refers to a part, or parts, of the OT. Moreover, NT writers express the conviction that in the words of this Scripture the Holy Spirit spoke by the mouth of human beings (Acts 1:16). So close was the identification of God with Scripture in the minds of the NT writers that we find the two terms used interchangeably. Thus in Rom 9:17 "Scripture says to Pharaoh" words that according to Ex 9:16, were words of Yahweh to be spoken to Pharaoh through Moses; and in Gal 3:8 it is said that "Scripture...announced to Abraham" what in Gn 12:3 are the words of the Lord. So also, words from Jewish sacred books are cited as the words of God (Heb 3:7, citing Ps 95:7; Acts 4:25–26, citing Ps 2:1; Acts 13:34–35, citing Is 55:3 and Ps 16:10). All this is remarkably confirmed in Heb 1:5–13 and Rom 15:9–12, where words from the OT are attributed to God regardless of whether in the original text they were put on the lips of God. The NT writers were able to refer to passages from the OT as the "oracles of God" (Rom 3:2; Heb 5:12; 1 Pt 4:11).

13 Besides these more or less implicit ways of referring the origin of Scripture to God, we must consider two NT texts that have become classic descriptions of God's involvement in the production of the OT, namely 2 Tm 3:15–16 and 2 Pt 1:21.

In 2 Tm 3:14 Paul urges Timothy to remain steadfast in the doctrine he has learned, having confidence both because of the person from whom he learned it (v. 14b) and because of the grounding in Scripture he had from childhood (v. 15). Verse 16 then continues: "Every Scripture is divinely inspired and useful for instruction...." As previously mentioned, "Scripture" translates the Gk word *graphē*; that here it denotes the OT is clear from the fact that the reference is to the books that Timothy has known from his Jewish childhood. The Gk words translated as "every Scripture" may also be translated in a collective sense ("all Scripture"); but since the definite article is missing, the distributive sense ("every") is preferable. The adj. "divinely inspired" may be regarded either as an attribute ("Every Scripture, being divinely inspired, is useful...") or as a predicate, as above. Because the other adj., "useful," must be taken predicatively, it seems more natural to take the first adjective in the same way, especially since fundamentally the same construction is found in 1 Tm 4:4, where the predicative interpretation seems to be required.

The Gk word for "divinely inspired" is *theopneustos*, a verbal adjective. Theoretically, such verbal adjectives ending in *-tos* can have an act. meaning (in this case, "breathing God," that is, producing thoughts about God) or a pass. meaning ("breathed by God," divinely inspired). There is no doubt, however, that in 2 Tm 3:16 *theopneustos* should be given a pass. meaning; for verbal adjectives ending in *-tos*, when combined with a word signifying God, regularly are passive. The few times it actually appears in pre-Christian writing, *theopneustos* always has a pass. meaning. The pass. meaning reflects the Jewish notion of the divine origin of Scripture, and the early native Gk-speaking interpreters of the passage unanimously interpreted the word in a pass. sense. Scripture, then, is something that has been breathed by God—in other words, the very breath of God himself. The expression, therefore, clearly denotes the divine origin of Scripture; it bypasses consideration of any human causality that may have been at the origin of Scripture and concentrates upon a familiar OT theme, namely that of the breath or spirit of Yahweh as an expression for the forceful action of God.

14 If 2 Tm 3:16, in attributing the origin of Scripture to God, bypasses any human factor that may have been involved, the same cannot be said of the second text, 2 Pt 1:21. In v. 16 the readers of 2 Pt are assured that the doctrine of the coming of the Lord is not a myth; for the Lord's majesty has already been seen momentarily at the transfiguration, an event that gives greater strength and credibility to the prophecy of Scripture. At this point, the author of the epistle inserts a parenthetical warning: No prophecy of Scripture can be understood by merely human power and outside the salvation community, for "it was not the will of man that brought prophecy in former times; rather being impelled [and/or propelled] by the Holy Spirit, men though they were, they spoke under the agency of God" (v. 21). The phrase "prophecy of Scripture" is ambiguous; it may refer to the entire OT or only to the section of the OT that the Jews called the Prophets (→ Canonicity, 67:27). In any case, reference is certainly to all or to part of the OT. The books involved in the prophecy of Scripture are directly related to the agency of God. Nevertheless, the presence of a human factor is acknowledged: It is men who, impelled by the Holy Spirit, utter prophecy. The Gk word for "impelled" is *pheromenoi*, a strong word meaning literally, "being carried, or borne, along," Some sense of its strength and vividness may be gained by observing that it is used in nautical contexts to denote a ship's being swept along by the wind (see Acts 27:16–17). For the writer of 2 Pt, then, the prophecy of Scripture primarily originates with God; the human factor, though acknowledged, is entirely dependent upon God's power.

15 Thus far, all our references to the divine origin of sacred books have been limited to the OT. There are, however, a few indications in the NT that a similar divine origin should be attributed to specifically Christian books. One book, Ap, explicitly refers to its origin as being from God (1:1–3; 22:7,10,18–19). In 2 Pt 3:16 the author equates the epistles of Paul that are known to him with "the other Scriptures," that is, the Jewish sacred books. Finally, in 1 Tm 5:18 there occurs the following remark: "For the Scripture says, 'You shall not muzzle the ox that treads out the grain,' and, 'The laborer is worthy of his wages.'" The first citation is from Dt 25:4, while the second is identical with Lk 10:7. This may indicate that the author of 1 Tm considers Lk (or a proto-Lk) to be Scripture in as true a sense as the books of the OT. On the other hand, it may be that after citing Dt with the formula "the Scripture says," the author of 1 Tm then adds loosely, and without including it in Scripture, a well-known proverb that has the same meaning as the scriptural citation. This appears all the more probable when one notes that in Lk 10:7 itself, Jesus seems to think of the saying as a familiar proverb.

(Barth, K., *Church Dogmatics* [Edinburgh, 1956] vol. 1, part 2, 503–6. "Inspiration," *EDB* [N.Y., 1963] 1065–67. Kelly, J. N. D., *A Commentary on the Pastoral Epistles* [N.Y., 1963] 125–26, 201–4. Spicq, C., *Les Épîtres pastorales* [Paris, 1947] 176–77, 375–79. Warfield, B., *The Inspiration and Authority of the Bible* [Phila., 1964] 131–66.)

16 **(C) Later Testimony.** Consciousness of the divine origin of the books of Scripture was a constant element in all Christian tradition after the completion of the NT (though there was for a time some uncertainty about the canon or list of such books; → Canonicity, 67). This consciousness manifested itself in the attempt by early ecclesiastical writers to develop a terminology that would adequately express the role of God in producing the sacred books. Frequently, the words of Scripture were referred to as the words of God or of the Holy Spirit (e.g., Tertullian, *Apol.* 31; Gregory of Nyssa, *Contra Eunom.* 7). Consequently, God's action with regard to the production of the inspired books was referred to as God's speaking or saying the words of Scripture (e.g., Irenaeus, *Adv. haer.* 2.28, 2–3; Eusebius, *HE* 5.28). God's speaking was more directly connected with the production of books when one referred to God's dictating the sacred books, a concept which came from Jewish tradition through Philo (John Chrysostom, *In illud, salutate Priscillam et Aquilam* 1.1; Augustine, *De consensu. evangelistarum* 1.35, 54). The activity of God in the literary production of the inspired literature was emphasized even more strongly by applying to him expressions directly involving the idea of writing. Thus, the books of Scripture were at times referred to as the writings of God or of the Holy Spirit (Tertullian, *De Anima* 2; Origen, *Hom. in Num.* 27.1). And God's action in the literary process was described as co-writing (Origen, *De prin.* 1.48; Basil, *In Ps.* 1.1; Jerome, *In Mich. Proph.* 2.7), or simply writing (John Chrysostom, *In Gen. hom.* 21.1; Jerome, *In Is.* 29.9).

(Kelly, J. N. D., *Early Christian Doctrines* [3rd ed.; London, 1965] 60–64. Perrella, G., "La nozione dell'ispirazione scritturale secondo i primitivi documenti cristiani" *Ang* 20 [1943] 32–52).

17 **(D) God as Author.** Because of its present use and importance, something should be said here of the origin of the phrase, "*God the author* of Scripture." Its roots seem to go back to Clement of Alexandria, who speaks (*Stromateis* 1.5) of God as the immediate and primary cause (*aitios*) of such things as the OT and the NT. Clement's thought, however, is concerned with the two Testaments as two economies of salvation rather than as two collections of sacred books. Ambrose (*Ep.* 8.10) expressly translates the *aitios* used by Clement with the Lat *auctor* (author) and applies it to God. But the reference is to God as the author or cause of all created things rather than to him specifically as the author or cause of Scripture—this even though Ambrose makes his remarks in connection with an inquiry into the meaning of Mt 7:7. Jerome (*Ep.* 123.5) speaks of the "one author" of the many epistles of Paul. From the context it would appear that "author" is taken here precisely in the sense of literary author, but it is not clear whether the author referred to is God or Paul himself. The *Statuta Ecclesiae antiqua* (*EB* 30), composed in the latter part of the 5th cent., refers to God as the author of the NT and of the OT. Since the historical context of that designation is the Manichaean doctrine of the economies of the NT and of the OT as coming from two different "Gods," the reference in the *Statuta* points to God not as the author of the books of the NT and of the OT, but as the cause of the economies of the two Testaments.

The first clear reference to God as the literary author of Scripture is to be found in Gregory the Great (*Moral.*, praefatio, 1) where God is called the author of Sacred Scripture, while the human factor in the production of the sacred books is called the writer (*scriptor*). The same distinction is made by Isidore of Seville (*De eccl. off.* 1.13). It became an accepted part of theological terminology when used by Rabanus Maurus in his early and influential textbook for the training of ecclesiastics (*De cler. inst.* 2.54). (Cf. A. Bea, *Ang* 20 [1943] 16–31—valuable more for its collection of texts about God as author than for its interpretation of them.) In later theological writing, the phraseology, "God the author of Scripture," becomes universal. Thus, Thomas Aq. refers to God as the author or the principal author of Scripture (*De pot.* q. 4, a.1, c; *Quodl.* 7, q. 6, a. 14, ad 5; q. 6, a. 16, c; *In Ps.* 44.1; *Exp. alt. in Cant.*, proem.; *In Is.*, proem.); and at the end of the Middle Ages, Henry of Ghent in a remarkable passage emphasizes that only God can be called the author of the books of Scripture in the fullest sense (*Summa* a. 9, q. 2, resp.). Since the Middle Ages, "God the author of Scripture," has been the usual way of expressing the divine origin of the books of the NT and of the OT.

18 Even though this expression has become a standard part of theological vocabulary, the same cannot be said for its usage in the documents of the Church. Leo IX, Innocent III, and the Second Council of Lyons (*EB* 38–40) refer to God as the author of the NT and of the OT, but always in the sense of the originator of the two economies of salvation, a point clearly implied in the Gk text of Lyons, in which the relevant word is *archēgon* (founder, or establisher). Although the Council of Florence (*EB* 47) and the Council of Trent (*EB* 57) juxtapose a reference to God as the author of the OT and of the NT with references to the books of the two Testaments, nevertheless their texts would seem to use "author" in reference to God's work as founder of the two economies, rather than to make a direct statement of his being the literary cause of the biblical books. It is not until Vatican I that we find a clear statement about God as the author of the books of the NT and of the OT (*EB* 77—see, however, the reservations about the meaning of Vatican I given by N. Weyns, *Ang* 30 [1953] 315–36). After Vatican I, the phraseology "God the author of the books of Scripture" is used repeatedly in ecclesiastical documents: Leo XIII, *Providentissimus* (*EB* 124–25); Benedict XV, *Spiritus Paraclitus* (*EB* 448); Pius XII, *Divino Afflante Spiritu* (*EB* 538); and Vatican II (*De Rev.* 3:11). At the present time, then, what the NT expressed by referring to God-breathed Scripture is achieved by saying: "God is the author of Scripture."

19 **(II) The Human Origin of Scripture.** Although God is the author of Sacred Scripture, it is also true that human beings made their own genuine contribution to the production of the sacred books—a point firmly stated by Pius XII in *Divino Afflante Spiritu* (*EB* 556), when he remarked that the human writers employ their faculties and powers in the composition of Scripture. It must be admitted, however, that the emphasis on the human authorship of Scripture is a modern one; earlier theological reflection was limited almost exclusively to the primary and more important fact of the divine origin of Scripture.

That a human factor stands at the origin of Scripture has never been doubted. This is apparent from the desire to attribute, wherever possible, individual sacred books to specific men. The role assigned to the human factor, however, is the question that must be investigated. Is the human factor or agent conceived to be merely a channel or transmitter, or is he thought to be an active producer making a personal contribution to the inspired books?

20 **(A) The Bible Itself.** Not providing a theory of inspiration, the Bible is generally silent on the role of the human factor. The OT, it is true, speaks of God's command to more than one individual to write a document and thus would seem prima facie to make the prophet purely a transmitter of the divine message, rather than a creative agent. This, however, is probably a device to stress the absolute primacy of God in the communication of the divine message to man; and it would be wrong to formulate from such passages the theory that the human beings who obeyed God's command to write played an entirely passive role. However, the idea of the human writer's apparent passivity was not absent from later Christian theories about how the sacred books were written.

21 If the Bible itself does not consciously and directly assert that the human writers were genuinely creative, it nevertheless indirectly provides valuable support for such an assertion. The human writers who produced Is, for instance, certainly appear to be literary personalities distinctively different from those who produced Jer; and such distinctiveness of personality can be observed throughout the Bible. This lends no support to a theory presenting the writers of the Bible merely as channels or transmitters, for such a theory would presumably imply uniformity throughout the biblical message.

The real creativity of the human writers is also suggested in the few scenes that the Bible provides showing the sacred writers at work on their documents. Thus, in the Foreword to Sir the writer states that he devoted pains and labor to the composition of his book and begs indulgence for any imperfections that may exist in the finished work. Similarly, the author of 2 Mc (2:24–33) tells us that his work of composition cost him much sweat and loss of sleep; he concludes his history by expressing what every human author must surely feel upon finishing his literary labors: "If it is well told and to the point, that is what I myself have desired; if it is poorly done and mediocre, that was the best I could do" (15:38). In the NT Luke (1:1–4) writes of the personal research that he has incorporated into the composition of his Gospel. And Paul (1 Cor 1:14–16) leaves us an unforgettable and very human glimpse of himself as a letter writer when he interrupts his flow of thought to insert a haphazard remembrance, just as any other letter writer might do.

22 **(B) Jewish Thought.** *Rabbinical tradition*, with its doctrine of the pre-existence of Scripture and later bestowal of Scripture upon the human race through selected prophets, obviously tended to view the human person involved as a mere channel. *Philo* developed basically the same concept by applying Gk and especially Platonic notions of inspiration to the production of the books of Scripture. In so doing, he propounded what may be termed a mantic theory of the inspiration of Scripture. According to Philo, the human factor (in his terminology, the prophet) becomes possessed by God, loses consciousness of self, and surrenders to the divine spirit, which then operates upon the communicatory powers of the human personality. This theory of ecstatic inspiration is modified in Philo by an accompanying doctrine of a prophet-interpreter, wherein the human personality remains more self-possessed and active. Nevertheless, it was the ecstatic and mantic theory that was the more prominent in his writing and that later proved to be the more influential part of his theory. (H. A. Wolfson, *Philo* [Cambridge, Mass., 1947] 2, 24–45).

23 **(C) Christian Thought.** The Philonic theory of inspiration was not without Christian adherents. Athenagoras, the early Christian apologist, took over the mantic or ecstatic theory, pointing out that the prophets, when moved by the Spirit, lost the use of their reason and were played upon by the Spirit as a flutist plays on his flute (*Leg.* 9). The Montanists held a similar mantic theory; indeed, they claimed to experience divine possession and fell unconscious when they prophesied. After his conversion to Montanism, Tertullian (*Adv. Marc.* 4.22; 5.8) adopted and defended the same theology of mantic inspiration.

24 But the mainstream of *early Christian* thought always rejected the notion of a mantic inspiration of the books of Scripture. Hippolytus (*De Christ. et antichr.* 2) insists that the operation of the Word increased the vision and understanding of the prophets. Origen (*Contra Celsum* 7.3–4) takes the same position; rejecting all identification of scriptural inspiration with the mantic inspiration of paganism, he maintains that under the force of inspiration the writers do not lose their free will but apprehend divine truth more clearly. This is also the basic position of Epiphanius (*Haer.* 48.1–10).

In a few cases, moreover, early writers go beyond this position and cite indications of active creativity on the part of the human authors. Thus, Cyril of Alexandria (*In Ioh.* 1.10; 1.18) repeatedly stresses the care with which John expressed his message, as well as John's constant efforts to adapt his writings to the goals he had formulated for the Gospel. So also Augustine (*Serm.* 246.1) notes that the Gospel writers drew upon their personal memories of the events they recorded. But by and large, the patristic writers paid little attention to the exact role of the human authors in the production of the sacred books, except to deny that inspiration involved the removal of human consciousness and understanding from the writers (J. N. D. Kelly, *Early Christian Doctrines*, 60–64).

In one respect, however—and this probably unconsciously, and therefore all the more meaningfully—early Christian writers showed unanimously that they regarded the personalities at the source of the biblical books as typically human authors. When referring to the Bible (until there was felt a need for a terminology to distinguish the divine activity from the human), early ecclesiastical writers spontaneously employed the customary terms for human literary authors—*suggrapheus* in Greek and *auctor* in Latin. This choice of words would seem to indicate that they looked upon the human composers of the sacred books as fully deserving the ordinary designations for the human efficient cause of a literary work.

25 In the *Middle Ages* theological reflection on the human factor was limited to following the lines of earlier thought on the subject. So much emphasis was laid on the divine origin of the sacred book that little or no attention was given to the activity of the human factor, except to reject with the earlier tradition any notion similar to the mantic theory of inspiration (Thomas Aq. *De verit.* q. 12, 2.9). Henry of Ghent, to be sure, denied that the human writers of Scripture could be described as mere organs or channels through which the words of divine knowledge came to mankind; rather, the writers should be thought of as true, but secondary, authors of the books of Scripture (*Summa* a.9, q.2, resp.).

26 Yet this insight was never developed or given its due place in a theory of inspiration until the 19th cent. and especially the *20th cent.* Linguistic studies of the Bible and of cognate literatures and languages, an increased knowledge of the general cultural background in which the Bible developed, a recognition of the obvious literary borrowings in parts of the Bible, and the detection of successive editions of many books—all these factors tended to show that the biblical literature had a genuine human history, that human minds had shaped the biblical books, and that the human personalities who worked on them apparently did everything that other human writers would have done in composing literature in any culture. Hence, in contemporary Catholic thought great stress is placed on the Bible as truly the word of God expressed in words that are truly the product of human minds, as though two "artists" composed the books of Scripture: God and man. Thus, a recent writer speaks of two incarnations: In one incarnation, the Word of God became enfleshed in human nature; in the other, the word of God became enfleshed in the language of men (W. Harrington, *Record of Revelation*, 20–24). Because the word of God has become enfleshed in the words and languages of human beings of different cultures and civilizations, study of the Bible will always necessarily include investigation of the human conditions that shaped the thought and language patterns of the human authors of the various books of Scripture.

27 Though the human element in the origin of the Bible may and should be regarded as truly causal and creative, yet this human causality differs from the divine causality in extension (among other things). To understand this, it should first be noted that the Bible is not a mere collection of more or less related documents on the same general subject matter; it is an organic unity, a totality. God is the author of the totality that is Scripture, whereas the individual human writers are creative causes only of the particular parts of the Bible which they composed. This is not without repercussions in the matter of interpreting and understanding the different books of the Bible. The work of the exegete will not be complete when, for instance, he understands Is only as a separate entity; he must also understand Is in its place in the entirety of Scripture. To put it another way, two values may be distinguished in the books of Scripture: The value that each book has in itself (and this may well be the only value that the human writer himself perceived, created, and communicated), and the plus-value that the same book derives from its role in the over-all architectonic plan in the mind of God, the author of the entirety of Scripture (→ Hermeneutics, 71:62).

In the light of all this, perhaps the contribution of an individual sacred writer may best be stated in this way: He *writes* only a part of Scripture, but he *affects* the entirety of Scripture. An artist, while concentrating on painting a given section of his canvas, is painting directly only that particular area; yet he is thereby altering and modifying the entire work that will eventually result. Similarly the individual writer of a part of the Bible directly composes a limited literary entity; but what he does will affect, modify, and change the total pattern of the final unity, namely the Bible as a whole.

28 **(III) The Relationship Between the Divine and the Human in the Origin of Scripture.** Although Catholic doctrine recognizes that in the origin of Scripture there is both a divine factor and a human factor, it also insists that these two factors are not on the same level, but that there is an instrumental subordination of the human factor to the divine. The pattern for this relationship is to be found in Scripture itself in passages such as Acts 4:25 where God is said to utter the words of a psalm *through* the mouth of David. The same idea is forcefully communicated in the reference to the human authors of Scripture borne along by the divine Spirit (2 Pt 1:21).

This instrumental subordination of man to God in the production of Scripture is emphatically and frequently expressed in the patristic comparisons used to illustrate the role of the human authors in composing the sacred books: They are the mouth, finger, cithara, lyre, minister, or deacon of God. The idea implicit in these images for the divine-human relationship was put philosophically and abstractly in the Middle Ages in such statements as that of Thomas Aq.: "The principal author of Sacred Scripture is the Holy Spirit; man was the instrumental author" (*Quodl.* 7, q.6, a.14, ad 5). Although this instrumental subordination of man to God was an assured result of medieval speculation upon Scripture, it did not play an important role in later theological thought until it was revitalized in the 19th and 20th cents. under the influence of Leo XIII (*EB* 125), Benedict XV (*EB* 448), and Pius XII (*EB* 556). The characteristics of this instrumental subordination will be studied in the next section.

NATURE OF INSPIRATION

29 **(I) History of Opinions.** Interest in the nature of inspiration is an aspect of theological speculation that has been developed only in modern times, as a result of the gradual discovery of the complexity of the literary artifact that is the Bible. *Before the Renaissance* and the Reformation, reflection upon the nature of inspiration was limited to incidental remarks made when emphasizing the divine origins of Scripture. There was, however, a tendency among ancient and medieval thinkers to consider inspiration as identical with God's prophetic activity in communicating truth directly to the human mind, Scripture being regarded as but a written record of what was thus received by the writer. It is for this reason that Thomas Aq., for example, wrote no separate treatment of the nature of inspiration, his comments on the subject being subsumed under his discussion of the nature of prophecy. Implicitly, then, this view equated divine inspiration with divine revelation in the latter's secondary aspect of God's communicating a body of truth to the human mind.

30 **(A) Dictation.** Real investigation into the problem of the nature of inspiration began with *the Renaissance and Reformation* and has continued to the present. One of the principal theories advanced during this time was that of inspiration through dictation, a rigid product of implications latent in the identification of inspiration with revelation. According to the dictation theory, God communicated to the human writer not only the ideas but also the words or verbal expressions of Scripture, the human contribution being nothing more than a conscious receptivity to the divine message, which was then transferred to paper exactly as it had been received in the mind. Thus, D. Bañez maintained that God "dictated and suggested" the words of Scripture (*In Summam* 1, q. 1, a. 8, dub. tert., 1 conclus.). He asserted on the basis of the Vg translation of Jer 36:18 that just as a person reading a book does not compose the words but recites what is there, so the prophet read the words that the Holy Spirit put into his imagination (*ibid.*, at the end). Accordingly, Bañez denied that the words and their composition were left to human industry (*ibid.*, 3 conclus.), claiming that the differences in style, in language, and so forth, in the various books of the Bible were to be explained by the fact that God dictated to each of the sacred writers the words best accommodated to his individual condition (*ibid.*, ad tert.). More than 100 years after Bañez, basically the same approach to the nature of inspiration appeared in C. Billuart (*Summa S. Thomas*, tract. de regulis fidei, dissert 1, art. 2); but by the end of the 19th cent., this position, though never condemned by the Church, was abandoned.

31 **(B) Subsequent Approbation; Negative Assistance.** About the same time that Bañez was setting forth his ideas on the nature of inspiration, Sixtus of Siena tentatively and timidly advanced the possibility that a book of Scripture would lose none of its trustworthiness if one should discover that the book had actually been composed by human endeavor alone but afterward had received ecclesiastical approbation (*Bibliotheca sancta* 1.8, haer. 12, resp. ad 7). A few years later, in lectures at Louvain, L. Lessius took up and modified the cautious suggestion of Sixtus. Lessius believed that if a book (he suggested 2 Mc as a possible example) were written by purely human means and afterwards approved by the Holy Spirit, then such a book could be considered truly inspired. Although he later denied that any book of the Bible was actually written under these conditions, Lessius always maintained that this was a possible form of genuine inspiration (on Lessius, see *Inspiration, DTC* 7. 2, 2135–51).

32 The ideas of Lessius were taken up by a number of theologians and exegetes, the most important of whom was J. Bonfrère who added the view that some parts of the historical books of Scripture were written only under the negative assistance of the Holy Spirit who saw to it that the writers did not fall into error but otherwise exercised no influence upon them. Bonfrère's theory of negative assistance was adopted at the beginning of the 19th cent. by J. Jahn and extended to the entire Bible. Jahn made inspiration the equivalent of the charism of infallibility: It influenced the sacred writers only if they were in danger of falling into error, leaving them to their own resources in all other cases (*Einleitung in die göttlichen Bücher des Alten Bundes* [Vienna, 1802] 91–108). Finally, in the middle of the 19th cent. the wheel of doctrinal speculation came full circle when the suggestion originally made by Sixtus of Siena was revived by D. Haneberg who maintained that some of the biblical books were written by purely human means, their inspiration consisting in their afterwards being approved by the Church (see his *Geschichte der biblischen Offenbarung* [Ratisbon, 1850] 714).

33 Vatican I, however, condemned the theories of both Jahn and Haneberg, asserting that the books of Scripture are inspired and canonical, not because they contain revelation without any error, nor because they were written only by human means and afterward approved by the Church, but because, being written under the inspiration of the Holy Spirit, they have God as their author (*EB* 77). Vatican I thus insisted on the positive role of the Holy Spirit in the actual composition of the sacred books; and the general nature of this positive role was later expressed by Leo XIII in *Providentissimus* (*EB* 125) when he specified that God would not be the author of Scripture unless in the process of writing he had influenced the minds, wills, and writing powers of the human writer. This teaching advanced by Vatican I and *Providentissimus* constitutes today the guiding line for Catholic theologians in their speculation about the nature of the inspiration of the Bible. Vatican II (*De Rev.* 3:11) simply repeated these earlier documents on the nature of inspiration.

34 **(C) Formal, Not Material Inspiration.** The 19th cent. produced one more theory of inspiration, that of Cardinal Franzelin, who wrote in the closing years of the period. Wishing to explain what is meant by saying that God is the author of the Bible, Franzelin took the position that God may truly be considered author even if his inspiration influenced the human writers only insofar as the thought content (the formal part) of Scripture was concerned, leaving the composition and the verbal expression (the material part) of the books entirely to the talents and abilities of the sacred writers. This opinion at first enjoyed a considerable measure of popularity but was soon abandoned as an artificial and vivisectional disruption of the close unity existing between thought and language in the production of literary documents.. See the severe criticism of Franzelin's opinion given by L. Billot, *De inspiratione Sacrae Scripturae theologica disquisitio* (4th ed.; Rome, 1929) 63–66.

35 Franzelin's position, however, may still serve one purpose; it may occasion a consideration of the methodology to be used in approaching a study of the nature of inspiration. Benoit is strongly convinced that Franzelin's basic error was one of methodology (P. Synave and P. Benoit, *Prophecy and Inspiration*, 100–103). Franzelin began by investigating what it means for God to have been the author of the Bible. This led him, says Benoit, to consider what is meant by a human author, and this in turn brought him to the consideration of what a book is. The final result was the artificial division of a book into its formal and its material parts in order to show the authorship of God with regard to the sacred books. True methodology, according to Benoit, must begin not with God's authorship of the Bible, but with the theological notion of divine inspiration. Only after determining in what this inspiration consists can one progress to consideration of what it means to say that God is the author of Scripture.

It may be doubted, however, that either is the correct basic methodology. Franzelin's teaching on the nature of God's authorship does not appear to have been determined primarily by his point of departure but rather by his modeling his views of authorship and of books upon modern conceptions, without sufficient reflection on the specific nature of the biblical books. Similarly, it seems impossible to achieve any real understanding of the nature of God's inspiration without studying the Bible, the specific result of that activity. Accordingly, it is the study of the Bible as a whole and in its parts that constitutes the primary and fundamental way of reflecting upon the nature of inspiration. Granted that approach, there seems to be no great difference between centering one's thought upon God's authorship of the Bible and focusing attention primarily upon the theological notion of inspiration.

36 **(II) Inspiration in God.** Throughout any discussion of the nature of inspiration, it should be kept firmly in mind that there is no possibility at the present time of giving an exposition of the nature of inspiration that may be labeled as a statement of *the* Catholic position. The Church's directives in this area are all general and undetailed, leaving the question as a whole open to development by theological reflection. Thus far, such reflection has not achieved any considerable consensus among theologians and exegetes. Accordingly, all current treatments of the nature of inspiration tend to be both personal and piecemeal statements—a situation that doubtless will continue for some time to come.

37 As it exists in God, divine inspiration is nothing other than God himself operating to produce a definite effect, namely the Bible. Since the effect to which inspiration is directed is a reality distinct from God, inspiration is to be classified as one of the divine externalizing operations (*operationes ad extra*). As such, it is common to all three Persons of the Trinity, although frequently it is attributed by appropriation to the Holy Spirit, as was already done in 2 Pt 1:21. Though it is true that on the ontological level divine inspiration is completely identified with God himself, the weakness of the human mind demands that God and his simplicity be "analyzed" if there is to be insight into the nature of inspiration.

38 It is to such an analysis of the divine simplicity that K. Rahner addresses himself (*op. cit.*, 39–54). It should be noted, however, that Rahner's reflections are limited to the planning phase of God's activity, rather than to its executive phase—a point well made by L. J. Topel ("Rahner and McKenzie on the Social Theory of Inspiration," *Scr* 16 [1964] 34). The externalizing operations of God, as Rahner sees them, must be divided into three general classifications: (1) those that precede human free activity without encompassing it within themselves (e.g., creation); (2) those that precede human activity but also include such activity, though without appropriating it (e.g., God's predefining of acts to be done freely by human beings though the acts, when completed, remain entirely in the human sphere and cannot be predicated of God); and (3) the predefining activity of God that precedes and yet includes human action, and further, appropriates the action, so that while genuinely human, it may be attributed to God as something that belongs to him.

It is to this last category that divine inspiration belongs, for it is a part of that predefining and appropriating activity by which God chooses the existence of the Christ-Person and the Christ-community (the Church). This activity of God is simply absolute, first of all, because it is entirely prior to any human decision, and secondly, because it involves the definitive and final realization of human salvation; accordingly, it is also an eschatological activity. Yet it is not eschatological in the sense in which God's activity would be in a natural order leading to its proportioned natural ultimate goal. According to such a supposition, God would certainly direct the human caravan to a definite terminus, but the history of that process would not involve God as a part of human history. But, as it is, God's willing the existence of Christ and the Church is an eschatological activity in which God *appropriates* certain events in man's history. In other words, as Rahner himself phrases it, by this choice of Christ and the Church God "enacts His own history in the world."

39 Inspiration, as we have said, is one of the elements involved in God's willing of Christ and the Church. But even here a further distinction must be noted. The Church herself is willed by God in two distinct phases: the foundational phase, in which God assembles the totality of the Church's constitutive elements (this is the phase of the *Urkirche*, the root Church); and the developmental phase, in which the Church, now constituted in her essential elements, grows and elaborates herself. It is into the foundational phase of the Church that divine inspiration is to be inserted. God wills the foundation of the Church through and in human factors which he appropriates (Christ's humanity, first of all, and then the Christian community of the *Urkirche* headed by the apostles). And as one of the Church's constitutive elements, God has willed the existence of Scripture, to be effected through the Christian community, but radically and primarily stemming from his own originating and appropriating activity. In short, it is because God plans the appropriation to himself of certain human events that he becomes the author of the Church and thereby the author of Scripture, a constitutive element of the Church.

40 Since it is in and through human events stemming from the Christian community that God is the author of Scripture, we may now revert to a point already mentioned, namely that the divine and the human factors in the production of Scripture are related as principal cause and instrumental cause. It is here—at least to a certain extent—that any explanation of the appropriating inspirational activity of God must begin. This may be seen by reflecting that God and man in a relationship of principal and instrumental causality differ from God and man in a relationship of primary and secondary causality, the latter being a relationship that is involved in all of God's nonappropriating activity toward the world.

When a created (secondary) cause operates, it is preceded and accompanied by the operation of God (primary cause). But in this pattern of primary-secondary causality, the effect produced is referred to the primary cause (God) with regard to its basic existence, whereas its existence as this or that type of being is referred directly to the secondary cause, and only indirectly to the primary cause as the ultimate exemplar of all perfection. For example, when a man generates a man, the existence of the offspring is referred immediately to God as primary cause; but his manhood is assimilated directly to the secondary cause, the human parent, and only indirectly to God in whom the perfection of man exists in only a virtual state.

The same, however, may not be said of the pattern of principal-instrumental causality. Here the effect produced is attributed directly and immediately to the principal agent, just as a painting is credited directly to an artist and his creative faculties and not to the tools he has used. Now, in the writing of every *ordinary book* God acts as primary cause, with the human agent as the secondary cause; but the particular kind of book produced is immediately related only to the human agent and his exemplarity. Consequently, it is the secondary cause who is the author of the book. God remains the primary cause of the book but is not the author, for the book does not primarily and directly reflect the divine mind. In the composition of *Scripture*, however, the causal relationship between the divine and the human factors is that of principal and instrumental causes. The Bible, as the effect produced, is primarily and directly a reflection of the mind of the principal author, God; it is only secondarily a reflection of the mind of the instrument, the human author. God, then, by being the principal cause of Scripture appropriates the effect produced. However real and important a factor man is in producing the Bible, Scripture remains primarily and directly the word of God, being directly and immediately assimilated to the exemplarity of its principal cause.

41 One last remark may be made concerning the nature of divine inspiration as it exists in God. In all patterns of principal-instrumental causality that are part of ordinary experience, defects and limitations may be produced in the effect by the principal agent, by the instrumental agent, or by both. In the case of Scripture, however, the principal cause of which is God, no limitation in the effect may be attributed to deficiency on God's part, but only to deficiency on the part of the human instrument.

42 **(III) Inspiration in the Human Factor.** The problem in this section is to consider the effect the inspiring activity of God produces upon the creative faculties of the composers of Scripture. It is this area more than any other that has been highly complicated by the findings of modern scholarship. Before the emergence of biblical criticism, the human composition of the sacred books was conceived in a simple way—each book had a single author who composed it under the influence of divine inspiration. It is now an established certainty that at least a great many books of the Bible were the products of a long period of gestation, involving at times even centuries of previous oral and written traditions. With such a multitude of compositors, contributors, editors, and redactors, it is impossible to deal with the exact effect of divine inspiration upon each of the persons who contributed to the formation of a given book. The only feasible manner of approaching the problem is to take a part of the Bible that seemingly was the product of a single mind (Heb, for example) and to consider the effect of divine inspiration in such a case. It may be assumed that whenever the origin was more complicated, there would have been an analogous influence on the various contributors (P. Benoit, *Aspects*, 13–35).

43 **(A) General Presuppositions.** The influence of divine inspiration upon the sacred writer begins with the origin of his life; like Jeremiah he has been called from the womb. He has been given the intellectual, imaginative, and emotional qualifications for the eventual production of the book he is destined to write, and his entire development is naturally and supernaturally under the direction of inspiration. When he comes to the point of actually conceiving and composing his document, he comes as a man who has been prepared for a definite task in salvation history.

44 In the actual *kairos* (appointed time) of composition he enters into the principal-instrumental pattern of causality (→ 40 above). In this connection it is necessary to emphasize that an instrumental cause must be viewed as a dynamic not as a static contributor to the effect produced. The age of naked-eye physics naturally tended to look upon the typical instrument as basically static and passive, its only movement coming from the movement communicated to it by the principal cause. In such a conception the role of the instrument is best represented by a stick moved from its inertia by a human hand; a passive, static tool thus is made active under the moving force of the principal cause. Present knowledge of the material world, however, makes us realize that the impenetrability that makes a stick useful is at least partially a product of dynamic forces of resistance within the stick, so that when it is used, for example, to reach a distant object, the stick's active and dynamic forces are actually being utilized. A better example of the dynamic nature of instrumental causes operated by hand is the use of acid to etch letters or a design on a piece of metal. The acid is the instrument by which the artist achieves his effect, but it is not inert; it is an active, dynamic reality, even to the naked eye. It is this notion of dynamic instrumentality that must be kept in mind when thinking of the sacred writer as an instrument of God in the composition of Scripture. He is an instrument, but an instrument with his own appropriate dynamisms and activities, an instrument who really thinks, imagines, composes. In inspiration these activities are constantly under the influence of God, the principal cause: The metal is etched, the sacred book is produced.

45 Granted that the activities of this thinking, willing, feeling, imagining instrument are used by God in the composition of the sacred books, there still remains the question of the precise nature of God's influence upon these activities of the human writer. Leo XIII, as previously mentioned, declared that the influence of inspiration extends to the writer's intellect and will, and to the other faculties involved in conceiving and writing a book (this last group of faculties is frequently referred to, though somewhat inaccurately, as the writer's executive faculties). We now must turn to further consideration of the influence of inspiration in these areas.

46 **(B) Modern Catholic Theories.** It is the influence of inspiration upon *the intellect* of the human writer that is the most difficult to comprehend. No very satisfactory explanation of it has yet been offered; and given the reticence of divine revelation itself on the point and the apparent lack of introspection on the part of the sacred writers, perhaps none ever will be offered. Some idea of the difficulty of the matter may be obtained from a brief history of modern theological reflection upon it.

47 (a) FRANZELIN. The starting point, as in so many other matters dealing with inspiration, is the teaching of Cardinal Franzelin. As stated above (→ 34), he distinguished between the formal and the material parts of a biblical book, attributing the former to God's inspiration and the latter to the sacred writer himself. In this view, inspiration had to be *identified with revelation.* Since the formal part of Scripture was conceived as consisting of the ideas contained in the Bible, God could not be the author of Scripture unless he directly communicated those ideas to the minds of the sacred writers.

48 (b) LEVESQUE. This identification of inspiration with revelation was the occasion of a sharp reaction, which may be termed the theory of directionalism. This reaction was initiated by E. Levesque, who maintained that inspiration was an influence directed completely and solely to the transmission or *communication of truth,* and not at all to the acquisition of truth. The truth to be communicated in the inspired books was gained prior to inspiration by either natural or supernatural means according to the nature of the truth in question. Once this truth or complex of truths had been acquired, inspiration then influenced the sacred writer as to how to communicate it. In other words, inspiration was completely directional and not at all illuminational (E. Levesque, *RB* 4 [1895] 421–22). The lead of Levesque was followed by C. Crets (*De divina Bibliorum inspiratione* [Louvain, 1886]) who phrased the doctrine, however, in new terminology. He held that inspiration is not concerned with the speculative judgment or intellect but with the practical judgment or intellect. The same ideas were later taken up by T. Calmes (*Qu'est-ce que l'Écriture Sainte?* [Paris, 1899]); E. Merkelbach (*L'inspiration des divines Écritures* [2nd ed.; Liège, 1913]); and, in a considerably modified way, by C. Pesch (*De inspiratione Sacrae Scripturae* [Freiburg, 1906] 410–29).

49 (c) LAGRANGE. This unilateral emphasis upon inspiration as a merely directional force affecting only the practical judgment itself produced still another reaction, the theory of illuminationism. The reaction was led by M.-J. Lagrange (*RB* 5 [1896] 499–500), who was followed by J. Vosté (*De divina inspiratione et veritate Sacrae Scripturae* [Rome, 1932] 50–61); A. Bea (*De Scripturae Sacrae inspiratione* [2nd ed.; Rome, 1935] 50–52); and H. Höpfl and L. Leloir (*Introductio generalis in Sacram Scripturam* [6th ed.; Naples, 1958] 51–55). The reacting school maintained that whereas revelation conceived as the communication of ideas from God is distinct from inspiration, nevertheless inspiration (although secondarily addressed to the practical intellect and hence to the mode of composition of the literary product) is *primarily a divine illumination* of the intellect of the sacred writer, permitting him to judge in a higher, clearer, and more certain light the ideas to be communicated.

50 (d) BENOIT. Since World War II, this position has been dominant; but P. Benoit in the 1963 *RB* (Eng trans. in *Aspects* 101–27; see W. Harrington, *op. cit.*, 35–39) proposed yet another. He criticized both the Levesque and the Lagrange schools for artificially separating the activity of the speculative intellect from that of the practical intellect. Both Levesque and Lagrange, though in different ways, conceived of a preparation of the speculative intellect followed by, but sharply distinguished from, an activity of the practical intellect. Benoit insisted that throughout the composition of a book of Scripture the speculative and the practical intellects worked simultaneously, interacting and modifying each other. In all this, God was active as the originating cause of Scripture, not only directing the operations of the practical intellect, but also illuminating the speculative intellect, for the speculative judgments that were to be communicated to the salvation community had to be supernaturally enlightened if they were not to appear with the guarantee of the human mind alone. Benoit proposes to call the influence of God upon the speculative intellect "revelation" (or a species of revelation), reserving the term "inspiration" for the divine influence upon the practical intellect of the human writer. Father Benoit thus sums up his position: "I propose, therefore, that *all the acts of speculative knowledge elicited by man under the supernatural impulse of the Holy Spirit should be grouped under the charism of revelation*.... Clearly distinct from the preceding, the *charism of inspiration directs all the practical activity involved in the communication of truths received in revelation*.... *Inspiration is logically rather than chronologically subsequent to revelation,* for both are intimately bound up in the same concrete activity of the mind" (*Aspects*, 121–22).

51 **(C) Evaluation.** After this brief exposition of modern theories, we now offer some tentative comments.

First, there seems to be no adequate reason for referring to the influence of God upon the intellect of the biblical writer as both revelation and inspiration. It only adds to already existing confusion. The usual way of referring to God's activity upon the sacred writer is not *Spiritu Sancto inspirante et revelante*, but simply *Spiritu Sancto inspirante.* Accordingly, throughout these remarks "inspiration" will be used to denote the total influence of God upon the intellect of the biblical writer.

Second, since inspiration influenced all the faculties of the writer that were involved in composing his book, it affected both his speculative intellect (what to communicate) and his practical intellect (how to communicate it).

52 Third, inspiration did not of itself involve God's directly and immediately communicating ideas (whether natural or supernatural) to the sacred writer. The sacred writer received his revelation from and with the rest of the salvation community, and through the sources of revelation available to the community. If the sacred writer happened to be deficient in knowledge of what had been revealed, he would have been led to consult the sources of revelation commonly available at the particular stage of salvation history in which he was writing. Similarly, deficiency in whatever natural knowledge was to be communicated in this book would have been taken care of by inspiration, through inducing the human writer to consult the ordinary sources for that knowledge. This does not deny that, in a given case, God may have wished to communicate a new revelation to the salvation community through a book of Scripture. Yet in that case the sacred writer would have been under the influence not only of inspiration but also of revelation, having received the new truth previously, or receiving it in the very act of composition, or in some other way. Thus, for instance, the writer of the Servant of Yahweh Songs (Dt-Is) may well have received a revelation as to the role of redemptive suffering in God's plan of salvation.

53 Fourth, the influence of inspiration upon the speculative intellect of the human writer did not involve an objective illumination of his mind, giving a higher and more certain quality of assent to his judgmental knowledge (again, whether natural or supernatural). It is difficult to see what such an objective illumination would have been. It could not have been the objective illumination that comes from the intrinsic intelligibility of the reality judged; it would have been impossible in the case of supernatural reality (by definition, the unseen), and entirely unlikely in the case of natural reality. Neither does it seem possible that this objective illumination could have been the extrinsic intelligibility that comes from the authority of God; this would have involved not only an act of revelation on the part of God, but also consciousness of such a revelation on the part of the human writers—a kind of awareness of which they seem entirely innocent. Moreover, even if this objective illumination can be explained in some way, it still remains unnecessary. The salvation community accepted what was officially communicated to it by the Bible not because the sacred writers had a higher objective certainty of the things they communicated, but because the community believed that God was the originating source of Scripture.

54 Fifth, inspiration, however, did influence the speculative intellect of the writer by giving it a subjective illumination that was nothing else than a deepening and intensifying of the same kind and level of judgmental certainty that the salvation community as a whole possessed. Isaiah's judgmental certainty of the holiness of God was not a higher kind of certainty based upon a higher objective illumination unavailable to the rest of the salvation community; it was, rather, an overwhelming subjective conviction, realization, and penetration developed under the influence of inspiration.

Sixth, God's inspiration also influenced the practical intellect of the sacred writer, arousing, shaping, and directing all decisions as to how the message was to be communicated (consideration being given to each book, both in itself and as part of the whole Bible).

55 Seventh, God's influence upon the speculative and the practical intellect of the writer was not limited to interior influence. Since God ordinarily uses other creatures in his providential care of the universe of nature and of salvation, so also he used realities external to the sacred writer—persons, places, things, events—to guide and direct the writer's intellect.

Finally, the psychology of the human writer under the influence of inspiration escapes us, and probably always will. In itself the process of composing a written document is an obscure one; and under the influence of inspiration, that process can only be more obscure. Whatever our speculation concerning the influence of inspiration upon the sacred writer, one idea must always be retained: The sacred writers were genuinely and creatively active and yet every activity of their intellect was under the influence of inspiration—the prophets of old were borne along under the influence of the Holy Spirit.

56 **(D) The Human Author's Awareness.** The last consideration about the influence of the Holy Spirit upon the intellect of the human author is whether the author was conscious of being inspired by God. Up to modern times the uniform answer to this question has been an assertion that the writer was conscious of inspiration (e.g., F. Suarez, *De fide*, disp. 5, sect. 3). The root of this opinion seems to go far back in Christian tradition to the reaction against the mantic theory of inspiration (→ 22–24 above), in which the inspired person lost all consciousness. It also apparently goes back to the simplistic identification of inspiration with prophecy, and hence with revelation (a divine activity which to be received necessitates the recipient's being conscious of God's revelatory operation). More recent reflection upon the nature of inspiration, however, has tended toward the view that the recipient of inspiration need not have been any more aware of inspiration than the recipient of God's other graces (other than revelation) needs to be conscious of receiving those graces (e.g., M. Nicolau, *De Sacra Scriptura tractatio dogmatica fundamentalis* [4th ed.; Madrid, 1957] 1046–47).

57 More recently still, K. Rahner (*op. cit.*, 62–63) has expressed the opinion that the human writer was conscious of inspiration at least to the extent that he realized that in writing he was being carried along by the living process of the Church. Rahner adds that in those cases (e.g., the Gospels) in which there was some knowledge that the book was being caused by God as a permanent document of the Church's self-knowledge, inspiration would have been wholly conscious. But the little information we possess from the human writers themselves with regard to their consciousness under the influence of inspiration (→ 21 above) does not indicate that the writers were aware of being inspired. Therefore, it seems safer to hold that, generally speaking, the human writers were not conscious of inspiration. There is no reason to deny, however, that in a given case consciousness of divine inspiration could have been present.

58 **(E) The Will and Other Faculties.** Just as the intellect of man was under divine inspiration, so also was his *will*. The decision to compose the book and the steady resolve to complete the document were elicited under the impulse of inspiration. And from the time of Origen, the mainstream of Christian thought, as opposed to the concept of mantic inspiration, has insisted that the writers, though moved by God to write, nevertheless did their writing by their own free decision. The sovereign impulse of God moved them to write and moved them surely; yet they wrote of their own free decision. This sure and sovereign divine impulse coexisting with human freedom is indeed a problem and a mystery, but it is basically only a specification of the general, classic problem of the relationship between God's absolute sovereignty and the free will of man. Into that problem there is no need to enter here; it is sufficient to indicate that the solution chosen with regard to the general relationship between God's absolute will and man's freedom will also be the basic solution for the relationship between God's influence upon the sacred writer to compose a book and the writer's own free decision to undertake such a composition.

59 Finally, the influence of divine inspiration affected and guided *all the powers* of the sacred writer that were involved in conceiving and composing the book. As already indicated, these powers are classed under the general head of "executive powers." This is a somewhat unfortunate classification, for it implies that conceiving a literary document is a matter only of intellect and will, whereas in reality it is clear that many of the sense faculties of an author are also involved in the conceptional phase of producing a book. Among these "executive powers," it was especially the imagination that was influenced by divine inspiration, for the imagination is the energy of the human psyche that, together with the intellect and will, contributes most to the production of a literary work. But all the other powers of the human writer that were engaged in the production and composition of a sacred book also were under the influence of divine inspiration. The sacred writer chose and selected words, utilized and exploited images, and proposed and developed analogies, but it was all done under the power of the originating source of Scripture, namely inspiration. It was in the Spirit that the sacred writer using all his faculties conceived, planned, and wrote the document.

EXTENT OF INSPIRATION

60 **(I) Authors.** As already indicated, with the advent of careful biblical source criticism, there came the knowledge that behind many of the books lies a lengthy history of written and oral traditions, traditions that in some cases did not originate with the salvation community. Accordingly, we must ask whether inspiration influenced the faculties of all the persons who figured in the traditions behind the various books of the Bible.

According to J. L. McKenzie (*Myths and Realities* [Milwaukee, 1963] 59–69), the influence of inspiration extended to the whole salvation community, so that the biblical books were produced by the entire group, with the writers being merely the voice of the community. Although this suggestion is valuable for its emphasis on the undoubted social context at the origin of the sacred books, it does not seem to be a completely adequate solution to the problem at hand. Aside from the fact that the suggestion says nothing about the traditions that originated outside the salvation community, it does not do justice to the individuality of the sacred writers and their documents. Chapters 1–11 of Gn, in spite of apparent simplicity, are in reality a sophisticated artifact that suggests the working of an individual rather than a communal mind. So also the findings of *Redaktionsgeschichte* (→ 84 below) have illustrated very subtle and individualistic handling of materials in order to achieve definite and distinct goals in the Gospels. (For a good discussion of the limitations of McKenzie's proposal, see D. McCarthy, *art cit.*, 553–56.)

61 We are left then with the same problem: In the long genesis of many of the biblical books, which, if any, of the various contributors were under the influence of divine inspiration? The only answer seems to be that the influence of divine inspiration was felt by all those who positively and creatively contributed to the design and content of the book that eventually resulted. This statement, however, needs to be explained. A contribution to a work of art may be one of two types: a material contribution, or what may be termed a design contribution. The person who provides the canvas for a painting or the stone for a sculpture certainly contributes to the finished product, but only as one who supplies necessary material. As a material contributor only, he is not to be regarded as a creative contributor. On the other hand, a painter who, under the direction of a master artist, paints a section of a large canvas is making his own creative contribution to the final art work.

An analogous distinction may be made with regard to the various elements found in the biblical books. The pagan epics or epic traditions used in Gn 1–11, for example, seem to be material contributions; they are materials that have been radically reshaped and reformed to meet the particular aims of Gn. Such material contributions to the sacred writings need not have been under the influence of inspiration when they were composed. Doubtless they were under the providential care of God; but, previous to their incorporation into Gn in a radically new form, presumably they were not inspired writings (or traditions), nor were their human sources inspired. However, with documents that were incorporated either wholly or in part into a biblical book, there is a possibility not merely of a material contribution, but also of a design contribution. For example, in Gn, the J document contributed its own values and designs, modified, it is true, by the other values in the finished work. Since such documents and oral traditions make a positive and creative contribution to the design of a book, they may be regarded as having proceeded from inspiration.

What is proposed here, then, is the following principle: Merely material contributions to the books of the Bible were not under the influence of inspiration, though they were under the general providential care of God; but *design* or *creative* contributions were under the influence of inspiration even though they came into existence long before the finished book to which they eventually contributed, or long after the original substantial completion of a book that was creatively retouched by later editors. In a concrete case it may be difficult or even impossible to decide whether a given contribution is merely material or truly creative; but this distinction in itself seems generally valid.

62 Some positive, though by no means conclusive, evidence for the inspiration of such elements as the J document later incorporated into Gn may be drawn from considering the document known as proto-Luke—a first edition of canonical Lk. Although the hypothesis of the existence of a proto-Lk has never been unanimously accepted, it has some plausibility; and it may serve here to illustrate the point under discussion. According to the hypothesis, sometime about AD 60 Luke composed a two-volume work, consisting of a gospel document (proto-Lk) and Acts. Later, after having read Mk, Luke decided to revise the first volume, thus coming to compose canonical Lk by combining his original gospel document with Marcan material. But Luke did not revise the second volume, and Acts came into the canon of inspired Scripture in its original form. Since proto-Lk was written at practically the same time and occasion as the inspired Acts, there is no good reason to deny the influence of inspiration upon proto-Lk, even though it was destined to remain in the Church only as incorporated into canonical Lk. (On proto-Lk, see P. Parker, *JBL* 84 [1965] 52–58.) A similar evaluation may be true of other "proto-" documents that have creatively contributed to the final design of any given book of Scripture.

63 **(II) Contents.** What has been said thus far with regard to the extent of inspiration has been limited to its influence upon the subjective experience of the writer. But it is also necessary to consider its objective extent, that is, its influence upon the object produced, the Bible itself. Obviously inspiration extended to all the biblical books, the determination of which is the problem of the canon of Scripture (→ Canonicity, 67). But even after the canon of Scripture was accepted in the Church, there were theologians who attempted to limit the extension of inspiration to certain parts of the canonical books. The basis of their position was a desire to solve the difficulties connected with the idea of the inerrancy of Scripture. In the 17th cent. H. Holden restricted the concept of inspiration to doctrinal matters (*Divinae fidei analysis* [Paris, 1652] 1. 1, c. 5, sec. 1), and was followed in this in the next century by P. Chrismann (*Regula fidei catholicae* [Kempten, 1792] nn. 49–51). In the 19th cent. A. Rohling (in *Natur und Offenbarung* [Münster, 1872] 92–94) restricted the concept to matters of faith and morals, and F. Lenormant limited it to the supernatural teachings included in the Bible (*Les origines de l'histoire d'après la Bible et les traditions des peuples orientaux* [2nd ed.; Paris, 1880] vi–xvii).

64 A somewhat similar position was taken by Cardinal Newman, who believed that inspiration did not extend to the obiter dicta of Scripture, that is, to unimportant and purely factual material having no connection with matters of faith and morals. (See J. Seynaeve, *Cardinal Newman's Doctrine on Holy Scripture* [Louvain, 1953] 168–79.)

65 Ecclesiastical documents, however, have resolutely opposed such a restriction on the influence of inspiration. Trent (*EB* 60) decreed that the books of the Bible *with all their parts* are to be regarded as sacred and canonical, and hence by inference, as inspired. The "parts" here referred to were such passages as the final pericope of Mk as given in the Vg (→ Gospel Mk, 42:97). The intention of the Council did not go beyond such "parts," and its decree cannot legitimately be extended to include every obiter dictum of Scripture. Vatican I (*EB* 79) repeated the teaching of Trent and explicitly stated that the books of Scripture "with all their parts" are divinely inspired; its use of "parts" was the same as that of Trent. The extension of inspiration to the entire contents of Scripture was established by *Providentissimus* (*EB* 124), in which Leo XIII insisted that it was erroneous to restrict inspiration to only parts of Scripture or to only matters of faith and morals. The same doctrine is to be found in Benedict XV (*EB* 454) and in Pius XII (*EB* 538).

The extension of inspiration to the entire contents of Scripture is, then, accepted in the Church today as a matter of Catholic doctrine. Even if there were no ecclesiastical declarations on the matter, it is difficult to see how a doctrine of inspiration restricting its influence to only parts of Scripture would be tenable, since it would involve a mutilation of the end product of inspiration.

66 **(III) Words.** Even when the extension of inspiration to all the canonical books and to all their contents is fully accepted, there still remains the question of the extension of inspiration to the words and diction of the Bible: Were they selected under the influence of inspiration or were they the result of the free determination of the sacred writers?

Cardinal Franzelin (→ 34 above) held that the choice of words and diction was left to the personal initiative of the writer, God's role being limited to the negative one of watching lest any error creep into the Bible through the writer's choice. Such a position is based on the fact that the same idea may be expressed in different sets of words. Thus in the word patterns "A hot argument followed" and "There ensued a heated altercation," basically the same idea is expressed. So also, the ideas and contents of a literary document may be translated into different languages, the concepts remaining basically the same even though the words used to express them are completely different. On the basis of such distinctions, Franzelin would limit the extension of inspiration to the ideas of Scripture, and would withdraw the verbal expression of those ideas from the influence of inspiration.

67 Although Franzelin's position has never been condemned by the Church, both theologians and biblical scholars have rejected it. In the production of a literary document thought and word are so intimately bound together that it seems artificial to separate the two as sharply as the Cardinal did. Moreover, the Bible communicates not only ideas and content, but also attitudes, emotional reactions, and so forth. In the example given above, "There ensued a heated altercation" not only communicates an idea but also has emotional resonance—in this case, a kind of stuffy noncommitment. The Bible, involving God's encounter with man, cannot be unaffected by the emotional resonances its words convey. Consequently, inspiration extended not only to the biblical ideas but also to the words—not that God dictated the words to the writer, but that the writer's selection of words was constantly under the directing and driving force of God's inspiration.

68 **(IV) Translations.** In regard to the extent of inspiration, the last area for consideration is whether inspiration extends to translations of the Bible. Actually, the problem is limited entirely to the question of the inspiration of the LXX, the translation of the OT into Greek made by Hellenistic Jews during an extended period covering parts of the last centuries BC (→ Texts, 69:52ff.). Actually, for a short time after the Council of Trent a small group of theologians held that inspiration extended to the Vg also, but the movement died an early death; see C. Pesch, *De inspiratione* 275, n. 1.

The reasons that may be advanced for the extension of inspiration to the LXX may be reduced to five. (1) There was a need for a special divine assistance in the LXX; for it was the first prolonged attempt to translate the Hebr Bible into a Western tongue, and, as such, was a direct providential preparation for the later composition of the NT in Greek. (2) The LXX is not a mere translation, but in many ways represents an advance and evolution in the ideas of the Hebr text (e.g., J. Coste, "Le texte grec d'Isaie xxv, 1–5," *RB* 61 [1954] 36–66). (3) Frequently in the NT, the LXX is cited rather than a Gk translation based directly on the MT. Moreover, at times the LXX is cited in support of basic Christian doctrines precisely because the Hebr text does not support the doctrines in question (see P. Benoit, "La Septante est-elle inspirée?" *Exégèse*, 1, 3–12; also C. Moule, *The Birth of the New Testament* [London, 1962] 77–80). (4) The entire Church of the first centuries accepted the LXX as an inspired work, and therewith accepted what are now called the deuterocanonical books (→ Canonicity, 67:21). This attitude is summed up by Augustine: "With regard to whatever is in the Septuagint that is not in the Hebrew manuscripts, we can say that the one Spirit wished to say them through the writers of the former rather than through the latter in order to show that both the one and the other were inspired" (*De Civ. Dei* 18.43). (5) The doctrine of the inspiration of the LXX has remained even to the present time in the Eastern churches. In the West, only Jerome rejected the inspiration of the LXX, and later Lat theology followed him, disregarding the previous unanimity of the Church on the question. Hence, the noninspiration of the LXX has never been a universal position in the Church, whereas for the first three centuries, its inspiration was a basic position of all Christianity.

69 The case for the inspiration of the LXX is, therefore, a strong one, but two arguments may be advanced against it. The first (and by far the weaker one) is that the early belief in the inspiration of the LXX stemmed from a naïve acceptance of the Jewish legend of the 72 scholars who simultaneously but independently translated the books of the Law and produced an identical Gk text. (The legend is given in *Aristeas* 12:301–11; → Texts, 69:53.) That the early Church used the Jewish legend may not be doubted, but the Church does not seem to have derived from the legend its conviction of the inspiration of the LXX. Rather, it used the legend as a vehicle to express an independent conviction about this inspiration. Independence is shown by the fact that whereas the Jewish version of the legend restricted the inspiration to the LXX Pentateuch, the Christian community extended it to the entire LXX.

70 The second argument against the inspiration of the LXX is drawn from the mistranslations that frequently mar the version "...the reader of the Septuagint must expect to find a large number of actual blunders, due in part perhaps to a faulty archetype, but chiefly to the misreading or misunderstanding of the archetype by the translators. Letters or clauses have often been transposed; omissions occur which may be explained by homoioteleuton; still more frequently the translation has suffered through an insufficient knowledge of Hebrew or a failure to grasp the sense of the context" (H. Swete, *An Introduction to the Old Testament in Greek* [Cambridge, 1902] 329–30; → Texts, 69:54). The difficulties caused by the presence of errors are great enough to force the conclusion that the inspiration of the LXX, though supported by weighty arguments, may not be said to be fully established.

(Dreyfus, F., *RSPT* 49 [1965] 210–20. Dubarle, A.-M., *ibid.*, 221–29. Grelot, P., *ScEccl* 16 [1964] 387–418.)

EFFECTS OF INSPIRATION

71 There is truly only one effect of inspiration, namely the Bible itself. But it will be helpful to consider various aspects of this one effect, so as to have a better understanding of inspiration.

(I) Revelation, Unity, Completeness, and Sacramentality. The first point to be noted is that the Bible, the effect produced by inspiration, is *revelation*, that is, God's disclosure of himself to all who will take the Bible and read. Though we have previously eliminated the identification of inspiration with revelation as far as the mind of the sacred writer is concerned during his composing a book, yet it is also true that from the viewpoint of the effect produced the Bible is revelation. Through the sacred writer God has produced a monument of His own mind, and in the Bible God speaks to the human person who reads it. Note, however, that revelation here is not primarily the communication of a body of doctrine (though this is also involved), but rather the self-disclosure of God. In the Bible as revelation what is primarily communicated is not something, but Someone (→ Aspects OT Thought, 77:104–105).

72 The second effect of inspiration is that the Bible is a *unity*, not merely a collection of writings. It is true that if the Bible is seen only from a human viewpoint, it looks like an anthology or a library. But the judgment of faith with regard to the Bible will always be that it is a single book because of its single principal originating source—God himself. Hence, however unquestionably valuable the study of individual books of the Bible may be, still the aim of scripture study must always be to understand the Bible as a whole, as a unity. Unless Scripture is viewed in its total expanse, there will be no full and complete encounter with the God who discloses himself through it.

But the Bible is a unity in another sense also. It is the artifact of a single author, whose intention is to disclose one central reality: the mystery of Christ hidden in God from eternity, prepared for in the history of the people of Israel, and disclosed to the human race in the fullness of time. Hugh of St. Victor summed up well this traditional teaching: "The subject matter of Scripture is the incarnate Word in all His manifestations, both those of the past from the beginning of the world as well as those of the future until the end of the world" (*De Scripturis* 17). It was the consciousness of this radical unity of the Bible as centered around Christ that led to what has been called "the distinctively New Testament use of Scripture" (→ Hermeneutics, 71:51–53), a treatment of Scripture in the round as a four-dimensional entity (time being the fourth dimension) "to be listened to as a whole and learnt from as a continuous story" (C. Moule, *The Birth of the New Testament*, 67–71).

73 *Completeness* is another consequence of inspiration: The Bible is a unity that is complete, lacking no part or element. This point is not directly relevant to the presently agitated question of the sufficiency of Scripture and of its relation to tradition; it is merely a statement that the degree of self-disclosure that God planned to provide in the Bible has been perfectly and completely achieved. Here again, there will be a certain tension between experience-judgments and faith-judgments. Human experience may see in the Bible a somewhat haphazard collection, with some parts that appear incomplete or at least confused; for faith, however, the Bible is a unity that is whole and entire. In spite of all the limitations and defects of the human writers who engaged in the composition of Scripture, God has succeeded in completing the exact delineation of himself and of Christ that he wished.

74 This leads to another consideration: the *sacramentality* of Scripture. Modern sacramental theology emphasizes that the Sacraments are encounters with God in Christ, but it should be remembered that they are not the only such encounters. The Bible too offers man opportunity to encounter God in Christ; and because of the Bible's direct contact with the human intellect, imagination, and emotions, the encounter it offers complements and in some ways excels the encounter with God that comes through the Sacraments.

75 **(II) Inerrancy.** The final effect of inspiration for our consideration is inerrancy, the quality by which the Bible is protected from error. Perhaps no other concept relevant to the divine inspiration of Scripture has caused so many problems as this one.

(A) The Problem. The basic problem is easy to state: The allegedly inerrant Bible contains statements that in any other document would be regarded as erroneous. Why then should the Bible be considered inerrant?

For convenience and with no intention of offering an exhaustive classification, scriptural statements that cause difficulty with regard to inerrancy may be arranged under four headings: (1) biblical self-contradictions, e.g., Noah's flood lasting 40 days and nights in Gn 7:17, but 150 days in Gn 7:24; (2) errors in natural science, e.g., the universe enwrapped in waters held back by a solid bell-shaped barrier called the firmament; (3) errors in history, e.g., the inaccuracies of Dn 5; and (4) moral errors, e.g., *ḥerem,* total destruction of an enemy people or group, considered as carrying out of the will of Yahweh (Jos 11:14–15).

76 The force of such difficulties has made the idea of the inerrancy of Scripture a continually recurring problem. It was already noted in rabbinical tradition, which gave assurance that one of the blessings to be received at the return of Elijah would be the explanation of the apparent discrepancies between Ez and the Torah (see *bMenahoth* 45a). A similar awareness of the problems arising from the claim of the inerrancy of Scripture was one of the reasons why early Christian writers had recourse to the inner allegorical sense of Scripture (→ Hermeneutics, 71:38ff.)—the only way in which they could find the divine truth certainly contained in a text that on the surface appeared erroneous. (See, as an example of this, the remarkably clear statement by Origen on the necessity of using allegory to resolve discrepancies between Jn and the Syn [*Comm. in Ioan.* 10.3].)

But it is especially in modern times that the problem of the inerrancy of Scripture has been most keenly felt.

Natural science, as in the Galileo case, has pointed up the simplistic and erroneous world views contained in the Bible. From the Renaissance on, the discovery of documents, other than the Bible, dealing with the ancient Near East has emphasized a number of discrepancies in the historical and geographical statements of the Bible.

77 **(B) Traditional Attitude.** But the difficulties connected with the inerrancy of Scripture have never caused any wavering in adherence to the doctrine. That Scripture is inerrant is a constant element in Christian tradition. Indeed, the view already existed among the Jews and was summed up by Philo when he said that the words of the Torah were put oracularly into the prophet's mind by God, to whom no error may be attributed (*De praem. et poen.* 55). The NT does not explicitly refer to the inerrancy of Scripture, but the doctrine is the foundation for statements like the following: Scripture cannot be invalidated (Jn 10:35); Scripture must be fulfilled (Lk 24:44; Acts 1:16); no iota of the Law will pass away (Mt 5:18); and "It is written," when used to introduce Scripture as an absolutely unanswerable argument (e.g., Mt 4:4; Acts 15:15; Rom 1:17; 1 Pt 2:6).

The inerrancy of Scripture is likewise a teaching common to all the early Christian writers. Clement of Rome took pride in referring to the Scriptures as the writings that are true (*Ad Cor.* 45.2). Justin pointed out that Scripture cannot contradict itself (*Dialogue with Trypho* 65). Irenaeus said that the presence in Scripture of things that we cannot understand should not lead us to reject the Bible, since the "Scriptures are perfect" (*Adv. haer.* 2.28, 2). Hippolytus asserted that Scripture does not deceive us (*In Daniel.* 4.6). And similar expressions of the inerrancy and truthfulness of Scripture are found throughout patristic literature (for a short collection of such texts, see C. Pesch, *De inspiratione* 491–92). Medieval theologians strengthened the doctrinal value of the teaching by maintaining, with Thomas Aq. (*In Ioh.* 13, lect. 1), that it was heretical to say that anything false was contained in the Scriptures. Later theology simply reasserted the same basic position.

78 The first mention in ecclesiastical documents of what is now called the inerrancy of Scripture was made in 1351, in the epistle of Clement VI to the Catholicon of the Armenians, in which the Catholicon was required to profess the certitude of the truth contained throughout the books of the OT and the NT (*EB* 46). Leo XIII (*EB* 124) taught that the Bible excludes error because God is its author; and Benedict XV (*EB* 452) pointed to this teaching as the ancient and constant faith of the Church, thereby, strictly speaking, going beyond what Leo XIII's text actually stated. The position of Benedict was reaffirmed by Pius XII (*EB* 540, 612).

79 **(C) Considerations Relevant to a Solution.** Assessing the foregoing sampling of the Church's tradition with regard to the truth content of Scripture, we conclude that the truthfulness and inerrancy of Scripture, though never infallibly defined by any official Church document, quite clearly deserves, from the constant teaching of the Church, to be called a matter of faith. It should be noted immediately, however, that when a revealed doctrine has been constantly taught by the Church but never formulated into a sharply defined statement, it frequently contains a great deal of obscurity. (Only in Vatican II do we begin to get truly positive guidelines toward solving the problem of what inerrancy really means; → 83, 85 below.) Therefore, theologians and exegetes are faced with the problem of determining in what sense the inerrancy of Scripture is to be taken. This has not yet been achieved with complete success, as recent literature on the subject shows in the clearest possible way. We shall attempt here a presentation of some leading principles that may assist in easing the tension between the doctrine of the inerrancy of the Bible and the difficulties sketched in 75 above.

80 The first step is to institute a plea for the elimination of the term "inerrancy" from the discussion of the truth content of the Bible. The term, in both its Lat and its Eng form, is a relatively modern word, not being found in any of the standard classical and medieval Lat dictionaries, and appearing in English only as late as the 19th cent. (A. Piepkorn, *CTM* 36 [1965] 579–81). Coming from Lat words that express a state of not wandering, "inerrancy" is more apt as a description of a mind than of a book, whereas it is a quality of the latter that is under discussion. Moreover, the term "inerrancy" tends to preserve a subtle change of emphasis observable in the history of this matter: Patristic thought generally refers to the exclusion of deception (*mendacium*) from the sacred books, whereas medieval and modern theologians refer rather to the exclusion of mistake (*error*). The history and implications of this change in terminology have never been traced; but the first of these two ways of expressing the truth quality of the Bible has the advantage of implying the necessity of closely examining the intention behind any given passage. As a result of all this, it would seem better to speak of the truthfulness of the Bible or of its truth content rather than of its inerrancy, although the latter terminology is now so much a part of theological vocabulary that it may be impossible to dislodge it.

81 With reference to the truth value of the Bible, it should be noted that this is a quality that applies to the *Bible in its original text* and that our present copies reflect it only to the extent that they are identical with the autograph. It should be noted next that the truth content of the Bible is to be looked for primarily in the *Bible as a whole*. It was noted above that from the viewpoint of faith the Bible is a single book, a single artifact; its qualities are primarily those of the whole rather than of the parts. While it is true that the truth value of the Bible as a whole will influence its parts, still it is important to emphasize that truthfulness is primarily to be predicated of the entire Bible (N. Lohfink, *art. cit.*).

When the truth content of the Bible is judged in this way, many difficulties disappear. Just as it is wrong to refer to man as a tailed animal because in one stage of his embryonic development he has a tail, so it is wrong to say that the Bible teaches as infallibly true the right to kill innocent victims in war. That would be to limit the truth content of the Bible on this particular question to one stage of the development of revelation, when God permitted his people to remain in a subjectively erroneous state of conscience, which like every such state of conscience must be interpreted by its possessor as the will of God. (On moral evolution in the Bible, see R. Maritain, "Abraham and the Ascent of Conscience," *The Bridge* 1 [N.Y., 1955] 23–52.) Likewise, the shadowy concept of the afterlife found in many OT books should not be interpreted as infallibly true biblical doctrine. The biblical teaching on this point may be judged only in the light of the complete Bible, with its culminating vision of mankind's victory over death in and through Christ, and of a consummation when we shall know God as he knows us.

82 Although the idea of truth is to be applied to the Bible primarily as a whole, it is applicable also to parts of the Bible. This does not mean however, that truth is to be found everywhere in the Bible. The Bible is the word of God in human language, and human words are not used exclusively to express truth. The jokes of a toastmaster at a banquet, for instance, are meant to entertain, not to communicate truth. Hence, the truth quality of the Bible is not to be looked for in the places in which, for example, the Bible is exhorting or is expressing emotion. It is to be looked for in the places where the Bible is concerned with communicating truth. And even then, the truth quality should be investigated first of all in an integral part (a given book) of the Bible rather than in individual verses and phrases. For example, the truth value of Jon resides in the theme that the entire work was created to communicate: God wills the salvation of non-Jews as well as of Jews.

83 Moreover, in assessing the truth of Scripture and its parts, special attention must be directed to the intention of the various authors as expressed in their written compositions In many cases this intention may be grasped sufficiently by determining the literary type or genre that is used. To return to Jon, for example, once it is established that the book as a whole is didactic fiction, passages such as those concerning the whale no longer create the problem about the veracity of Scripture that they formerly did. This principle of first determining the various literary forms of the biblical books and their parts is a derivative of the Ger method of *Formgeschichte* (→ Modern OT Criticism, 70:38; Modern NT Criticism, 41:42ff.). Pius XII in *Divino Afflante Spiritu* (*EB* 558–60) stressed this approach as useful in solving problems concerning the inerrant truth value of Scripture, and Vatican II followed his lead: "Those who search out the intention of the sacred writers must, among other things, have regard for 'literary forms.' For truth is proposed and expressed in a variety of ways, depending on whether its form is that of prophecy, poetry, or some other type of speech" (*De Rev.* 3:12).

84 Nevertheless, simple determination of literary genre will not always be sufficient to judge the author's intention. Different authors may employ the same literary form and yet each have his own meaning to convey. Thus, the same parable, or miracle, of Jesus may be related by the three Syn Evangelists, and yet each may interpret it differently (→ Aspects NT Thought, 78:141). Therefore, in order to judge truth according to the author's intention, one must not only apply the principles derived from *Formgeschichte*, but also make use of principles derived from *Redaktionsgeschichte*—the meaning given to a particular item or incident by the theme that runs through the author's whole work (see J. A. Fitzmyer, *TS* 23 [1962] 446–47). The purposeful way in which the author has brought an incident into his work tells much about the exact truth he wishes to convey. Hence, if we ask about the truth of Mt's story of the instant shriveling of the fig tree (21:19, as contrasted with Mk 11:20 where the tree is not found to be withered until the next day), the answer must take into account Matthew's deliberate enlargement of the element of wonder in Jesus' miracles (→ Aspects NT Thought, 78:124). This is Matthew's way of conveying the greatness of the divine power manifested in Jesus. The technique, once understood, is no more a falsification than is the practice in Byzantine icons of giving the face of the Christ Child the features of an adult in order to show that the wisdom of God was within the Child (→ Hermeneutics, 71:25, 30).

85 In judging the truth of the Bible, it is also necessary to make a distinction between its message and the instrumental statements used to communicate that message. The message (Benoit calls this "what the Bible teaches") is the doctrinal matter that God wishes to convey to the salvation community as a part of their salvific equipment. This saving message will be guaranteed by the protection of divine veracity. Instrumental statements, however, are merely means to communicate this message, and their truthfulness will be guaranteed only insofar as falsehood in them would vitiate or lessen the full communication of the Bible's message. A distinction like this lies behind the very important statement of Vatican II which relates inerrancy to *salvific* truth: "The books of Scripture must be acknowledged as teaching firmly, faithfully, and without error that truth which God wanted to put into the sacred writings for the sake of our salvation" (*De Rev.* 3:11).

To illustrate, the first creation story in Gn may be said to have as its message that all the order and goodness in heaven and earth come from God. In order to communicate this message, the sacred writer used statements embodying his own view of the physical world—e.g., his statement on the existence of the firmament. These instrumental statements are not true, but they do enable the writer to communicate God's true message to the salvation community. Likewise, the contradictory details in the account of Noah's flood are on the order of instrumental statements and do not disturb the delivery of the salvific message of the justice and the mercy of God. The same thing may be said of many historical statements in the Bible that do not agree with what we know from other sources. In Dn 5 the salvific message to be communicated to the community concerns the full control of empires and kingdoms by the Lord of History. The basic statement that needs to be true for the communication of this message is that Babylon did fall. All the other details, some unquestionably erroneous, are merely dramatic trappings of that basic truth. The emphasis that the Bible is inerrant when it teaches *salvific* truth is quite different from the view, rejected above (→ 63, 65), which stated that the Bible was inerrant only in matters of faith and morals. The area covered by salvific truth is much wider than that of faith and morals, e.g., the basic history of Israel is salvific, but does not come under faith or morals. Moreover, the distinction between the salvific and the nonsalvific is not primarily quantitative (certain passages are salvific; others are not), but rather qualitative, that is, *all* the statements of the Bible are free from error *to the extent* that they convey the truth "which God wanted put into the sacred writings for the sake of our salvation."

86 And even in the case of statements of the Bible's salvific message, one last element should be considered. These statements may be asserted as certain, probable, and so forth; and their truth value is proportionate to the kind of assent called for by the statement. Here, however, a word of caution is in order. In ordinary language, degrees of assent are not generally expressed explicitly. The person who asserts that it will rain tomorrow is quite aware that he is asserting what is only highly probable, but that sense of probability does not appear in his verbal expression. It may be determined only by taking into account the general human context of such statements. The Bible is written as human beings ordinarily speak. Consequently, when there is no explicit expression of probability in the statements of the Bible, it is not immediately to be inferred that the statements are categorical. The quality, categorical or probable, of the assent to be given to any biblical statement may be determined only after examination of its complete literary and human context.

An understanding of the truth content of the Bible doubtless will always involve difficulties. This is an old problem, and the answer given it early in the Christian era by Irenaeus is one with which this section may fittingly conclude: "If we cannot find solutions to all the difficulties which are found in the Scriptures, still it would be the greatest impiety to seek a God other than he who is. We should entrust such things to the God who made us, knowing that the Scriptures are perfect since they have been spoken by the Word of God and his Spirit" (*Adv. haer.* 2.28, 2).

67

CANONICITY

James C. Turro

Raymond E. Brown, S.S.

BIBLIOGRAPHY

1 **Canon in General:** Barclay, W., *The Making of the Bible* (N.Y., 1961). Costello, C. J., *St. Augustine's Doctrine on the Inspiration and Canonicity of Scripture* (Washington, 1930). Filson, F. V., *Which Books Belong in the Bible?* (Phila., 1937). Howorth, H. H., "The Origin and Authority of the Biblical Canon in the Anglican Church," *JTS* 8 (1906–7) 1–40; "The Origin and Authority of the Biblical Canon According to the Continental Reformers," *JTS* 8 (1906–7) 321–65; *JTS* 9 (1907–8) 186–230; "The Origin and Authority of the Canon Among the Later Reformers," *JTS* 10 (1908–9) 183–232. Maichle, A., *Der Kanon der biblischen Bücher und das Konzil von Trient* (Freiburg i.Br., 1929). Preuschen, E., *Analecta; Kürzere Texte zur Geschichte der alten Kirche und des Kanons* (Tübingen, 1910). Reuss, E. W. E., *History of the Canon of the Holy Scriptures in the Christian Church* (Edinburgh, 1891). Swaim, J. C., *Where Our Bible Comes From* (N.Y., 1960). Torrey, C. C., *The Apocryphal Literature* (New Haven, 1945). Westcott, B. F., *The Bible in the Church* (N.Y., 1905). Zarb, S., *De Historia Canonis Utriusque Testamenti* (Rome, 1934). (For additional references, → Texts, 69:1–3.)

2 **Canon of the OT:** Bentzen, *IOT* 1, 20–38. Buhl, F., *Canon and Text of the Old Testament* (Edinburgh, 1892). Eissfeldt, *OTI* 560–71. Grant, W. M., *The Bible of Jesus* (N.Y., 1927). Henshaw, T., *The Writings* (London, 1963). Hölscher, G., *Kanonisch und Apokryph* (Naumberg, 1905). Jepsen, A., "Zur Kanongeschichte des Alten Testaments," *ZAW* 71 (1959) 114–36. Jugie, M., *Histoire du canon de l'Ancien Testament dans l'église grecque et l'église russe* (Paris, 1909). Katz, P., "The Old Testament Canon in Palestine and Alexandria," *ZNW* 47 (1956) 191–217. Loisy, A., *Histoire du canon de l'Ancien Testament* (Paris, 1890). Margolis, M. L., *The Hebrew Scriptures in the Making* (Phila., 1922). Michaeli, F., "À propos du canon de l'Ancien Testament," *Études Théologiques et Religieuses* 36 (1961) 61–81. Moore, G. F., "The Definition of the Jewish Canon," *Essays in Modern Theology and Related Subjects* (Fest. C. A. Briggs; N.Y., 1911). Ruwet, J., "Le canon alexandrine des Écritures," *Bib* 33 (1952) 1–29. Ryle, H. E., *The Canon of the Old Testament* (2nd ed.; London, 1895). Smith, W. R., *The Old Testament in the Jewish Church* (London, 1902). Sperber, A., *New Testament and Septuagint* (N.Y., 1940). Sundberg, A. C., *The Old Testament of the Early Church* (Cambridge, Mass., 1964). Tabachovitz, D., *Die Septuaginta und das Neue Testament* (Lund, 1956). Zeitlin, S., *An Historical Study of the Canonization of the Hebrew Scriptures* (Phila., 1933). For OT apocrypha texts see *APOT*.

3 **Canon of the NT:** Aland, K., *The Problem of the New Testament Canon* (London, 1962). Bewer, J. A., *The History of the New Testament Canon in the Syrian Church* (Chicago, 1900). Carroll, K. L., "The Earliest New Testament," *BJRylL* 38 (1955) 45–57; "Toward a Commonly Received New Testament," *BJRylL* 44 (1962) 327–49. Goodspeed, E. J., *Christianity Goes to Press* (N.Y., 1940); *The Formation of the New Testament* (Chicago, 1926); *New Solutions of New Testament Problems* (Chicago, 1927). Grant, R. M., *A Historical Introduction to the New Testament* (N.Y., 1963) 25–40. Gregory, C. R., *Canon and Text of the New Testament* (N.Y., 1907). Grosheide, F. W., *Some Early Lists of Books of the New Testament* (Textus Minores 1; Leiden, 1948). Hennecke, *NTA* 1, 19–68. Knox, J., *Marcion and the New Testament* (Chicago, 1942). Lagrange, M.-J., *Histoire ancienne du canon du Nouveau Testament* (Paris, 1933). Mitton, C. L., *The Formation of the Pauline Corpus* (London, 1955). Moore, E. C., *The New Testament in the Christian Church* (N.Y., 1904). Moule, C. F. D., *The Birth of the New Testament* (London, 1962) 178–209. Nicol, T., *The Four Gospels in the Earliest Church History* (Edinburgh, 1908). Oxford Soc. of Hist. Theology, *The New Testament in the Apostolic Fathers* (Oxford, 1905). Schmidt, K. L., *Kanonische und Apokryphe Evangelien* (Basel, 1944). Souter, A., *The Text and Canon of the New Testament* (rev. ed.; Naperville, Ill., 1954). Stendahl, K., "The Apocalypse of John and the Epistles of Paul in the Muratorian Fragment," *CINTI* 239–45. Stonehouse, N. B., *The Apocalypse in the Ancient Church* (Grand Rapids, 1929). Von Harnack, A., *The Origin of the New Testament* (London, 1925). Wik, *NTI* 18–57. For NT apocrypha texts see Hennecke, *NTA* or James, M. R., *The Apocryphal New Testament* (Oxford, 1953).

Sections 5–20, 44–47, and 86 are the work of J. C. Turro; the remainder of the article is by R. E. Brown.

4 OUTLINE

CANON IN GENERAL

5 **(I) Preliminary Considerations.** Every revealed religion must sooner or later feel the urgency for a canon, for if God has broken the silence in order to disclose his will to man, it must thereafter be possible to know with sureness where that disclosure lies. The canon guarantees this; it marks off the boundary between what is revealed and what is not, that is, between what is human and what is divine. Whether the revelation is preserved in oral or in written dress is incidental; the canon serves to identify it. What purpose could revelation serve were it not identifiable?

The need for a canon as it was felt by the Judeo-Christian faith may be portrayed as a triple need: the need to conserve, the need to preserve, the need to observe. God's revelation must be conserved to keep it from becoming submerged in the welter of traditions that tend to spring up around it in order to make it more understandable. The canon is an effort to prevent this. Then there is the need to preserve revelation, that is, to ward off any change or corruption. Its pristine purity—as it proceeded from the mouth of God—must be kept intact. Finally, among those who accept God's revelation, there is felt a need to observe the revelation and make it active in faith and life.

Most religious traditions manifest a twofold tendency: to stay faithful to the original revelation at all costs, and to explain and digest it. These two promptings need not be construed as conflicting with each other; rather they represent different concerns of the believing community. The formation of a canon helps to achieve fulfillment of the first tendency: the impulse to adhere strictly to revelation.

6 If we turn to the idea of canon as it is applied to a collection of books in the Judeo-Christian religion, inspiration is the broad underlying presupposition. It is because certain books were believed to have been written under God's special action that they were sifted out and given wholehearted acceptance. It took time and reflection to achieve this insight; for originally, the books of the Bible were not chosen because they, and only they, were thought to be inspired. It was only by later rationalization that such a conclusion was reached. Within the Church the formation of the canon seemingly followed other guidelines. For example, apostolic origin and the fact that a book was used in Church services were operative factors in stamping a book as NT Scripture. Still, it is legitimate to hold that such considerations rest upon the substratum of inspiration. They imply a special relation of the book to God. Thus, in the final analysis, inspiration served as the overmastering factor in the formation of the canon.

7 **(II) Church and Canon.** Viewed objectively, the canon of Scripture stands as a body of literature endowed with an inner cohesion. Undoubtedly, this cohesion came about because these books were being used by a community guided by the Holy Spirit. They nourished the prayer life of the group, called forth reflection, and provided a rule of life. Books not conforming to this internal cohesion fall, by that very fact, outside the pale of the canon. The faculty for judging such conformity or nonconformity resides in the Church. Acknowledgment from any other quarter would be what Zwingli feared, namely, a human seal of approval set upon the work of God. In part it was this consideration that prompted Augustine's well-known observation, "I would not believe the Gospel did not the authority of the Catholic Church move me to this" (*Contra epistolam Manichaei* 5.6; *PL* 42.176).

Inspiration, then, demands canonization, but canonization is not to be understood as working a change in the inspired book. Nothing is added, but a light is thrown upon the book in order to make manifest something that is already there. In canonizing, the Church discovers inspiration; it does not create it. The Fathers apparently sensed the intimate connection between Bible and Church, for at times they spoke of the books of Scripture interchangeably as "canonical books" and "church-books."

8 **(A) Trent.** For Roman Catholics it was at the Council of Trent that the canon of Scripture received its final definition. There the Church assumed a clear and definitive position as to which books were to be included in the Bible. Under pain of anathema, the decree *De Canonicis Scripturis* (8 April 1546; *EB* 57–60; DS 1501–5) named as canonical 45 books in the OT (minus Lam, which was considered part of Jer) and 27 books in the NT (→ Church Pronouncements, 72:11). Vatican I alluded to Trent and reproduced the decree (DS 3006), affixing to it a clarifying paragraph that explained canonicity as the acknowledgment by the Church of the inspired quality of the books.

The special significance of the decree of Trent is that it is authoritative and conclusive. This was not the first time the question of the canon had been raised in the Church. Behind the Tridentine decree there was an impressive pedigree of earlier synodical decisions. None of these, however, seems to have been invested with the same comprehensive binding authority that marks the decree of Trent. Let us survey these earlier decisions.

9 **(B) Before Trent.** The earliest decisions relating to the canon were issued by local councils in North Africa: the councils of Hippo (393; *EB* 16–17), III Carthage (397), and a later council of Carthage, in 419. Each of these approved a list of OT and NT books coinciding with what later would be defined by Trent.

10 In the past, Canon 60 of the council of Laodicea (*ca.* 360) and the Decree of Pope Damasus (reigned 366–384) were generally adduced as instances of very early Church decisions regarding the canon. Recently both these documents have been challenged as spurious. The 60th Canon of Laodicea (*EB* 12–13), which adopts substantially the short Hebr canon (Canon 59 forbids the reading of other books), is no longer thought to be the work of the council, but rather a private compilation made in Asia Minor toward the end of the 4th cent. The Decree of Pope Damasus (DS 353–54; *EB* 26; Hennecke, *NTA* 1, 46–49), related to the council of Rome in 382 or to Part II of the Gelasian Decree, has at other times been attributed to Pope Gelasius I (492–496) or to Pope Hormisdas (514–523). This decree, which presents the canon as it would eventually be accepted at Trent, is now considered a private work put together in northern Italy or southern France at the beginning of the 6th cent. (E. Schwartz, *ZNW* 29 [1930] 161–68). If these newer views prove to be correct, the documents are not divested of all value but can be viewed as expressions of the faith in segments of the Church at a period later than was formerly thought.

11 In 405 Pope Innocent I addressed a letter to Exuperius, bishop of Toulouse (DS 213; *EB* 21–22), answering his request for a list of canonical books. This letter too exhibits the canon ultimately defined by Trent. The testimony of the local council of Trullo II (692) remains inconclusive because it reproduces several lists, one containing a fuller canon than another. No preference is indicated on the part of the council (→ 84 below).

12 A complete list of OT and NT books was drawn up at the Council of Florence (an ecumenical council) in a document known as the Decree for the Jacobites (4 February 1441; *EB* 47). The intention behind this papal bull, which was aimed at the reconciliation of Eastern Christians, is difficult to evaluate; it does not seem to have the value of a solemn universal canon for the Church at large. The Council Fathers at Trent, who adopted the list of Florence, also debated the question of how binding that list was.

13 Thus, in assessing the ecclesiastical testimony prior to Trent, we seem justified in considering all this testimony as having lesser force than that of universal Church decisions, even though collectively it gives witness to the general belief of the Church. This assessment makes it easier to understand the hesitations and doubts uttered within the Church even after the pre-Tridentine decrees had been published. All things considered, it seems best to hold that it was not before the Council of Trent that the canon was firmly and finally fixed—*simul et semel*—in such a way as to leave no room for doubt.

14 **(III) Nature of Canonicity.** Probing deeper in order to lay bare the supports that undergird the solemn teaching of Trent and the ordinary teaching of the Church that went before it, we must face the following question: What particular feature of a book served to identify it for the Church as inspired? What were the credentials of an inspired book that impelled the Church to receive it into the canon? In the light of present knowledge, it seems impossible to answer these questions. We know *that* the Church accepted certain books into the canon, but we do not know with any degree of clarity or precision specifically *why* she did so. To say that the reason is to be sought in the practice of the Fathers who accepted the book as inspired, is only to transfer the question from the present to the past. On what grounds, the question remains, did these men—representatives of the Church in an earlier age—receive certain books as inspired and reject others as not inspired? Some scholars have expressed themselves as diffident of any recourse to solutions on the basis of dogma, as though there were some solid hope for settling the matter on the basis of historical evidence. The scantiness and the fluctuating quality of this evidence make such a hope illusory.

15 Discussions of the canon are more often marked by the deftness with which this problem is evaded than by the sureness with which a solution is proposed. Recently, K. Rahner (*Inspiration in the Bible* [4th ed.; N.Y., 1964]) has pointed to what may be a path out of the maze. He construes Scripture as a vital element in the foundation of the Church. Specifically, he believes it to be an expression in writing of the faith of the apostolic Church. The very emergence of Scripture as a genuine self-expression of the primitive Church serves to reveal to the Church the inspiration of the books that enshrine this expression of her faith. In effect, the revelation of the inspired books is considered to be implicit not direct. God did not apprise the apostles of the inspired books, title by title. Rather, this information was inherent in the fact that certain books were known by the Church as authentic reflections of her faith. This was tantamount to knowing them as inspired (→ Inspiration, 66:38–39).

Rahner's theory may explain the apostolicity required of a book by the early Christians before acknowledging it as canonical. The apostles were thought of principally as eyewitnesses who had experienced Christ and his teaching firsthand. If a book was derived from an apostle, it embodied his immediate experience of Christ. As such it would mirror the faith of the Church, which was of course apostolic.

Rahner's theory covers the OT as well; he notes that the OT as Scripture positively required canonization; the OT needed to be recognized in order to achieve its essential effect. However, prior to the Church there was no infallible teaching authority to witness to its inspired nature. Hence the OT could not have come to its climax before the Church came into being. Before the

Church, there could be only an incipient, developing sense of the canonicity of the OT, but not a hard and fast conviction about it. It was the Church that declared the OT canonical once and for all.

16 Rahner next calls attention to the distinction between the revelation of the inspired character of certain books and the fuller realization and articulation of this fact. There often was a time lag between the two. In other words, the Church felt the singularity of these books before she declared it. She had a canon before she had a full idea of canonicity or decrees about a canon. This would explain the doubts and the wavering opinions in the earlier years of the Church regarding the canonicity of various books of Scripture. It took time to pass from knowledge to deeper recognition. By taking this tack, Rahner hopes to dissipate the need for discovering the argumentation employed by the Church to reach a conclusion about the canon. He asserts that this knowledge of the canon is connatural to the Church. The Church can by a reflex response and without the aid of syllogisms recognize writings that correspond to her nature and express it. In short, the canon is not so much a deduction based on a premise, as it is an act of self-awareness on the part of the Church—an act by which she adverts to another aspect of her being.

17 **(IV) The Word "Canon."** The Gk word *kanōn* is traceable through Babylonian (*qanū*, "reed") to Sumerian (E. Boisacq, *Dictionnaire étymologique de la langue grecque*, 406–7; H. Frisk, *Griechisches etymologisches Wörterbuch* 1, 779). The original meaning was "reed." The word gradually came to signify any straight rod or bar, a measuring stick used by masons and carpenters. Eventually the word assumed a metaphorical connotation as well and began to mean a norm or standard, something serving to determine, rule, or measure other entities. Instances of this usage are found in extrabiblical Greek.

18 In Christian usage, as early as the 2nd cent. AD "canon" was used to refer to a norm of revealed truth, a rule of faith. (Similarly, disciplinary regulations of ecclesiastical authorities came to be called canons because they were a rule of life. The fixed or invariable part of the Mass also was known as the Canon.) By the 4th cent. the word had already made the transition from signifying the thing contained to signifying the container. Thus, because the Scriptures contained the rule of faith, the canon, they themselves were called the canon. The use of "canon" to designate the collection of authoritative books is seen clearly in Athanasius (*ca.* 350), who says that *Hermas* "is not part of the canon." In his 39th Paschal Letter (*ca.* 367) he provides a catalogue of books that he calls *ta kanonizomena*. In the last part of the 4th cent. such usage of canon became quite common in both East and West. The word may be found in Gregory Nazianzen, Priscillian, Rufinus, Augustine, and Jerome.

Besides meaning "rule," canon can also mean "list" or "catalogue." Some scholars, favoring this meaning, believe that the canon of Scripture means simply the list of books that compose the Bible.

19 In any case, a canonical book is one that has been acknowledged as belonging to the list of books the Church considers to be inspired and to contain a rule of faith and morals. Some books attained canonical status early, as we shall see below; others achieved it only after a time, for there were many doubts about their being inspired. The former books were referred to in ancient times as *homologoumena* (those agreed upon), whereas the latter were called *antilegomena* (disputed) or *amphiballomena* (doubtful).

These two categories of canonical books later came to be known as protocanonical and deuterocanonical books. This terminology, it appears, was invented by Sixtus of Siena (1520–69). The protocanonicals were those that were admitted into the canon with little or no debate. The deuterocanonicals were those that were under discussion for a while until doubts about their canonicity were resolved. Note that these terms do *not* imply two canonizations, that is, an original one, which received the protocanonicals, and a later one, which admitted the deuterocanonicals.

20 An apocryphal book originally meant a hidden or secret writing (→ Apocrypha, 68:4). Such books might be read and discussed only by the initiate. Subsequently in Catholic usage the term *Apocrypha* has come to designate books that in content and in title approximate canonical Scripture (both OT and NT) but have not actually been accepted into the Church's official catalogue. In Protestant parlance the term *Apocrypha* covers (with a few additions) the OT books that Catholics call deuterocanonical, while the term *Pseudepigrapha* is given to the books that Catholics call the OT Apocrypha. Pseudepigrapha is, in fact, an appropriate title only for those books that are fictitiously attributed to men who did not write them, for instance, *Enoch*.

THE CANON OF THE OLD TESTAMENT

21 The Roman Catholic Church accepts 46 books as the canonical OT. Most Protestants accept a canon of 39 books; the Jews have the same canon as Protestants but a different enumeration. Thus there is a difference of seven books (plus additional parts of two other books)—the deuterocanonical or "apocryphal" books. These books are Tb, Jdt, Wis, Sir, Bar (including the Letter of Jeremiah), 1–2 Mc, and parts of Est and Dn. To explain how such a difference developed, the following, almost classic, thesis has been proposed: By the end of the 1st cent. AD there were in Judaism two canons, or lists of sacred books, a shorter Palestinian canon drawn up by the rabbis at Jamnia, and a longer Alexandrian canon represented by the LXX. The early Christian Church adopted the Alexandrian canon; but the Reformers, following a minority view among the Fathers, decided to revert to the Palestinian canon. The respective results were the Catholic and Protestant canons. Almost every detail of this thesis is now being subjected to serious challenge, and much of what is found in both Protestant and Catholic manuals on the canon needs modification.

22 **(I) Formation of Sacred Writings in Judaism.** The composition of the OT was a process that took over 1000 years. The first poetic compositions, e.g., the Song of Miriam (Ex 15:1–18) and the Song of Deborah (Jgs 5), probably go back to the 12th cent. BC. The latest books in the Jewish-Protestant canon, Dn and Est, were composed during the 2nd cent. BC; the latest books in the Catholic canon, 2 Mc and Wis, were composed *ca.* 100 BC. During this long period of composition there was a gradual accumulation of material into books and then into collections of books. In addition to the books that found their way into canonical acceptance, there were others, some composed during the period

Works of the Old Testament Era: Approximate Dates of Collection or Composition

CENTURIES BC	THE LAW	THE PROPHETS: FORMER PROPHETS	THE PROPHETS: LATTER PROPHETS	THE WRITINGS	DEUTEROCANONICALS _Apocrypha_*
13th–11th	Career of Moses? Traditions underlying Pentateuch taking shape; early law codes. Early poetry (Ex 15).	Stories of conquest of Palestine. Traditions underlying Jgs and 1 Sm. Early Poetry (Jgs 5).			
10th	J tradition put into writing.	Stories of David, esp., "Court History" (2 Sm 9–20, 1 Kgs 1–2).		Use of Pss in Temple worship begins. Cultivation of proverbial wisdom in Jerusalem court under Solomon.	
9th	E tradition composed.	Preservation of royal annals of Judah and of Israel (source of 1–2 Kgs, 1–2 Chr); Elijah and Elisha cycles (1 Kgs 17–2 Kgs 10).		Ruth? Marriage songs, later echoed in Ct.	
8th	J and E merged (under Hezekiah, _ca._ 700?).	Preservation of royal annals of Judah and of Israel.	Amos and Hosea in Israel. Isaiah and Micah in Judah.	Hezekiah is a traditional patron of proverbial wisdom (Prv 25).	
7th	Nucleus of Dt is made basis of Josiah's reform (_ca._ 622). Holiness Code (Lv 17–26) edited.	Preservation of royal annals of Judah.	Oracles of Isaiah collected by disciples and edited. Zephaniah, Nahum, and Habakkuk. Jeremiah dictates to Baruch.		
6th	P is compiled from earlier sources and gives structure to emerging Pentateuch.	Deuteronomic History edited in Exile.	Ezekiel in Babylon. Deutero-Isaiah (_ca._ 550). Editing of pre-exilic prophetic corpus. Post-exilic oracles of Haggai, Zechariah (1–9), and Trito-Isaiah.	Lamentations. Job(?).	
5th	Completion of Pentateuch (_ca._ 400?).		Malachi. Obadiah(?).	Memoirs of Nehemiah and of Ezra. Prv 1–9 written as preface to Prv 10ff.	
4th–3rd			Jonah(?). Joel(?). Isaian Apocalypse (24–27[?]). Deutero-Zechariah (9–14[?]).	Chronicler's History. Sayings of Qoheleth (Eccl) edited by students. Collection of Ps(?).	
2nd				Esther(?). Daniel.	Sirach (_ca._ 190). _1 Enoch_* (_ca._ 175–). _Jubilees_* (_ca._ 150). Baruch (composite). Tobit. Judith. _Aristeas_*. _Testaments_* (?). Gk Esther. Gk parts of Daniel. 1 Mc (_ca._ 100).
1st					2 Mc. Wisdom. _3 Mc_*. _1 Esdras_* 3–5. _Pss of Solomon._*

Jewish writings of the 1st and early 2nd cents. AD include: _4 Mc_*; _Assumption of Moses_*; _Apocalypse of Ezra_* (_2 Esdras_ 3–14); _2–3 Baruch_*; _Prayer of Manasseh_*; _Testaments_*(?); _Sybilline Oracles_* (books 3–5). (?) = Date uncertain.

when the biblical books were being written, some composed slightly later. Some of these other books were lost; some were preserved but did not receive acceptance.

23 The standard division of the Hebr Bible ultimately accepted by Judaism is tripartite: the Law, the Prophets, and the Writings. The Law (*Tôrâ*) consists of the five books of the Pentateuch. The Prophets (*Nᵉbîʾîm*) are subdivided into the Former Prophets (Jos, Jgs, Sm, Kgs) and the Latter Prophets (Is, Jer, Ez, the Twelve [= Minor Prophets])—eight books in all. The Writings (*Kᵉtûbîm*) are 11 in number: Ps, Prv, Jb, the 5 Megilloth or scrolls (= Ct, Ru, Lam, Eccl, Est), Dn, Ezr/Neh, Chr. This gives a total of 24 books, although by various combinations, the number has sometimes been given as 22, the number of letters in the Hebr alphabet. From *Tôrâ*, *Nᵉbîʾîm*, and *Kᵉtûbîm* comes the modern Hebr acronym TNK (vocalized *Tᵉnāk*), meaning "the Bible."

When did this tripartite division become standard, and when were the three individual collections fixed? The generally accepted view is that each division or collection, Law, Prophets, and Writings, represents a stage in the development of the Bible, so that the Law was fixed before the Prophets, etc. There is another point of view favored by G. Hölscher (*op. cit.*) that sees the three divisions growing more or less concurrently and maintains that the determination of the whole tripartite collection was made at one time. Although it is true that individual books belonging to each of the three divisions were being composed at the same time, it is difficult to deny the evidence that one collection was fixed before another.

24 **(A) The Law.** In modern scholarly opinion the earliest Hebr law codes preserved in the Pentateuch (the Decalogue of Ex 20:1–17, the Covenant Code of Ex 20:22–23:19, and the Ritual Decalogue of Ex 34:11–26) were composed in the 12th–11th cents. BC. The latest law code, the Priestly Collection, was post-exilic (*ca.* 5th cent. BC). Thus the Pentateuch was probably complete by *ca.* 400 BC. Actually, earlier there is mention of an existing law book in 2 Kgs 22:8ff., where in 622 the priest Hilkiah discovered in the Temple "the book of the law." This was probably the nucleus of Dt (12–26). Later, *ca.* 400, we are told in Neh 8:1 that Ezra the scribe read to the assembled people "the book of the law of Moses which the Lord had given to Israel," presumably the law that Ezra had brought from Babylon (Ezr 7:14). Many scholars think that this was a recension of the Pentateuch; others think of it as just the Priestly Collection of laws.

25 One argument that has been used to bolster the theory that the Law was a completed collection by *ca.* 400 BC probably should be rejected, even if the theory itself is accepted. We refer to the argument based on the fact that the Samaritans possess a Pentateuch substantially the same as the Hebr Pentateuch. The reasoning is that since the Samaritan schism took place in the 5th cent. BC, they must have possessed this Pentateuch before they broke off. It was thought that the Old Hebr script in which the Samaritan Pentateuch was written was a sign of this antiquity, and that this script was maintained by the Samaritans as a protest against the Jewish innovation of employing the Aram script (the script we usually associate with the Hebr Bible). The recent paleographical studies of F. M. Cross on the basis of the Qumran finds have shown, however, that this old Hebr script was revived in the 2nd cent. BC, and that the Samaritan script was an offshoot of the 2nd-cent. writing (*BANE* 189, n. 4). These observations make it *possible* that the Samaritan schism may have occurred as late as the 2nd cent. BC, a date before which, we know, the Law was accepted in Judaism (→ Texts, 69:15–16, 33).

26 If the Law was accepted by 400 BC, perhaps we should qualify our understanding of what this acceptance meant. Even after that date, a book like *Jubilees* (→ Apocrypha, 68:24) was composed and read by various groups of Jews, e.g., the Qumran sectarians, even though in some points and laws it was not in harmony with the Pentateuch.

27 **(B) The Prophets.** What Jewish tradition calls the *Former Prophets* is identified by scholars today as the Deuteronomic History (Jos, Jgs, Sm, Kgs), a historical collection completed in the years 600–560 (→ 1–2 Kings, 10:79). In 2 Mc 2:13, Nehemiah (*ca.* 440) is credited with collecting "the books about the kings and prophets, and the writings of David, and the letters of kings about votive offerings"—perhaps this reference represents a popular tradition about the collection of the Former Prophets. Besides the historical material that was accepted as part of this collection, there was much ancient Israelite historical writing that did not survive to become canonical, as the OT itself bears witness. Jos 10:13 speaks of the Book of Jashar. The royal annal material for the reigns of the kings was excerpted from the Books of the Chronicles of the Kings of Judah and of Israel (1 Kgs 14:29; 15:7,31; 16:5). The Chronicler seems to have known of collections of prophetic material, e.g., the history or visions of the prophets Nathan, Ahijah, Shemaiah, Iddo (2 Chr 9:29; 12:15; 13:22). There is no reason to think that such lost works were not once looked upon as holy; indeed, had they survived, they would probably have become part of the OT. Thus, in books written before the Exile, survival through the national catastrophe was probably the criterion that determined canonical acceptance. We know of no pre-exilic books that did survive and were not accepted.

The *Latter Prophets* is a more heterogeneous collection whose individual books were composed between 750 (Amos) and *ca.* 400–300 (the last of the Minor Prophets, i.e., Mal, Jl, Jon, Dt-Zech; and perhaps the "Isaian Apocalypse," Is 24–27). By the time of Jesus ben Sira (*ca.* 190 BC) it was already customary to think of the Twelve Prophets (Sir 49:10), and this almost certainly means that the collection of the Latter Prophets was complete.

28 By the 2nd cent. BC the whole prophetical collection had achieved the rank of sacred books. For example, the author of Dn (*ca.* 165) refers to Jer as one of "the books" (9:2). It was customary to put the Law and the Prophets side by side in mentioning sacred books (Foreword to Sir; 2 Mc 15:9). In evaluating this Jewish attitude toward the Prophets, however, we must be aware that the acceptance may not have been absolute, for the Talmud (*bShabbath* 13b; *bHagigah* 13a; *bMenahoth* 45a) reports later objections to Ez because of apparent contradictions between this book and the Law. Moreover, we are not certain that all the ancient references to the Prophets are precisely to those books that came ultimately to be accepted as the Former and the Latter Prophets. We shall see that Josephus counted 13 prophetical books, probably including books later regarded as Writings (so Thackeray, LCL 1, 179).

29 **(C) The Writings.** This is the most miscellaneous of the collections and the one that caused the most dispute. The books ultimately accepted as Writings in the Hebr Bible probably were all post-exilic in composition, with Dn and Est (2nd cent. BC) as the latest. By the end of the 2nd cent., as the Foreword to Sir testifies, Jews spoke not only of the Law and the Prophets, but also of "the rest of the books of our ancestors." The slightly later reference in 2 Mc 15:9, however, mentions only the Law and the Prophets. What constituted "the rest of the books" in the Sir reference, we do not know precisely; Sir does not cite Ezr, Est, or Dn.

In the 1st cent. AD we find a little more specification of what these other books might have been, for Lk 24:44 attests to this combination: "the Law of Moses, the Prophets, and the *Psalms.*" This is harmonious with Philo's reference (*De vita contemp.* 3.25) to the Law, the prophetic words, and "*hymns and other works* by which knowledge and piety may be increased and perfected." Josephus (*AgAp* 1.8 § 39–41) knows of the 5 law books of Moses, the 13 books of the Prophets, and 4 books containing "*hymns* to God *and precepts* for the conduct of human life." The last mentioned are thought to have been Ps, Ct, Prv, and Eccl. As yet, no name had been attached to this last classification; but later the designation "the Writings" is found in the Talmud (*bBaba Bathra* 14b; *bKetuboth* 50a), and this may reflect earlier usage. The very vagueness of the references to these "other books" in the 1st cent. AD is a sign that Judaism had not yet reached the stage of a sharply defined collection. Also, it may be suspected that, as latecomers, the Writings did not enjoy the same level of respect accorded to the Law and the Prophets.

30 To some, perhaps, Josephus' statement may seem to have settled the question of a canon, or fixed list of books, within Judaism, and for that reason this statement deserves more attention. At least one may say that the 22 books enumerated by Josephus enjoyed wide acceptance among the Jews. It is another question to what extent Josephus meant to exclude other books or reflected universal Jewish thought in so doing. In his own writings Josephus cites the LXX and uses books that almost certainly were not part of his list of 22, e.g., 1 Mc, *1 Esdras,* and the additions to Est. He probably includes among the Prophets books that were later counted as Writings. A few years after AD 90, the date of Josephus' work, *4 Ezra* mentions 24 books publicly accepted by the Jews; it is uncertain whether this is just a different enumeration of Josephus' 22 books or a real difference in the list of books.

Certainly, in Josephus' remarks we find something closer to a canon than anything we have hitherto encountered. It is interesting to see what he says about the books he lists. They are sacred books, to be distinguished from other books because of their divine origin. They may not be tampered with or added to. Josephus thinks that they were composed in the 3000 years between Moses and Artaxerxes I (450 BC—a ruler seemingly connected with Est). His historical judgment is, of course, inaccurate; several of the books he includes were not written until 300 years after Artaxerxes.

31 **(II) Closing the Canon in Palestinian Judaism.** If we doubt that Josephus represents a definitively closed canon, we must face the problem of why and how the canon was closed for normative Judaism.

32 **(A) Criteria.** The problem is difficult because we are not even certain of the exact criterion used for deciding canonicity. Some have supposed that certain books were received because of their legal character or their relation to the Law, for the Law is the canon by which all is judged. Another factor that certainly played an important part was the thought that certain books contained the word of God and were inspired by him, but this attribute is not easily verified in a book.

It has been proposed by G. Ostborn (*Cult and Canon* [Uppsala, 1955]) that a book was held to be canonical because of its specific motif, i.e., if it in some way celebrated or reported Yahweh's activity. This motif endowed the book with cultic value and permitted its use in the synagogue service. Ostborn's hypothesis, though attractive, fails to carry total conviction because the endeavor to find a fundamental motif that runs through all the books of the OT becomes forced. Attention is rightly given, however, to the cultic use of books as a factor in their acceptance, e.g., the use of the Ps in the Temple liturgy. It is quite possible that by the 1st cent. AD there was an annual or three-year cycle in the fixed lectionary of pentateuchal and prophetic readings for the synagogue. (See the controversy between A. Guilding, *The Fourth Gospel and Jewish Worship* [Oxford, 1960] and L. Morris, *The New Testament and the Jewish Lectionaries* [London, 1964].) Later the five Megilloth came to be read at the principal Jewish feasts, but this custom may reflect earlier practice in some instances.

33 **(B) Time.** We find in Jewish tradition three main suggestions.

(a) EZRA. It was believed at one time that the collection of the OT books was accomplished decisively by Ezra (*ca.* 400 BC). Josephus' evidence may be related to this theory because he places the termination of the writing of the OT in the 5th cent. The precise evidence comes from *4 Ezra* (→ Apocrypha, 68:41), a work written between AD 100–120. In 14:45 God is portrayed as speaking to Ezra of 24 sacred books that are available to all the people, as distinct from the 70 books that are to be kept secret (→ 20 above). This late legend obviously has little historical value because many of the canonical books were written after Ezra's time. At most, Ezra completed the collection of the Law.

34 (b) GREAT SYNAGOGUE. Another suggestion is that the OT was determined by "the men of the Great Synagogue," working under the impetus of Ezra. A learned Jewish writer, Elias Levita, drawing from passages in the Talmud, first suggested this theory in his book *Massoreth ha Massoreth* (1538); it subsequently received approval from many Christian scholars. Particularly in Protestant thought it held sway until the late 19th cent. and was used as the justification of Protestant acceptance of the short Hebr canon. Brian Walton wrote of the men of the Great Synagogue, "Their work of establishing the Canon possessed truly divine authority...." In recent times, however, this hypothesis has been shaken by questions about the very existence of the Great Synagogue (→ Apocrypha, 68:119). Even if some form of the Great Synagogue did exist in the years after Ezra, the thought that it played a decisive role in the canonizing process is most implausible. The OT, Josephus, Philo, and the Apocrypha report nothing of such a body and its canonizing activity. Indeed, the earliest reference to the Great Synagogue is in the Mishnah of the 2nd cent. AD (*Pirqe Aboth* 1:1). Moreover, the usual dating of the Great Synagogue (4th cent. BC) would preclude any complete canon.

35 (c) JAMNIA. That the canon was not completed until the Christian era is recognized by all critical scholars today, and many suggest that the rivalry offered by Christian books was a spur for the closing of the Jewish canon. Others prefer to find the stimulus in the disputes within Judaism, particularly between the Pharisees and some of the more apocalyptically minded Jewish sects. In particular, it is often suggested that the canon was closed at Jamnia (Jabneh or Jabneel, a town near the Mediterranean, W of Jerusalem) where Rabbi Johanan ben Zakkai re-established his school at the time of the fall of Jerusalem. After a decade Gamaliel II became the head of the school, and in the period AD 80–117 he and Eleazar ben Azariah were the predominant teachers. It has been proposed that about 90–100 the council of the rabbis at Jamnia settled once and for all time the definitive list of inspired books, namely, "the Palestinian canon," consisting of the books now called protocanonical.

Recently this thesis has been subjected to much-needed criticism (J. P. Lewis, *JBR* 32 [1964] 125–32).

Four points of caution should be noted: (1) Although Christian authors seem to think in terms of a formal church council at Jamnia, there was no "council of Jamnia." At Jamnia there was a school for studying the Law, and the Jamnia rabbis exercised legal functions in the Jewish community. (2) There is no evidence that any list of books was drawn up at Jamnia. The rabbis, of course, recognized that certain books were uniquely sacred and "soiled the hands," so that purification was necessary after using them (Mishnah, *Yadaim* 3:2). But this attitude may represent the popular acceptance of 22 or 24 books that we saw in Josephus and in *4 Ezra* at roughly the same period. It is no proof that a definite list had been drawn up. (3) A specific discussion of acceptance at Jamnia is attested only for Eccl and Ct, and even in these instances arguments persisted in Judaism decades after the Jamnia period. There were also subsequent debates about Est. (4) We know of no books that were excluded at Jamnia. A book like Sir, which did not eventually become part of the standard Hebr Bible (based on the putative Jamnia canon), was read and copied by Jews after the Jamnia period. Tosephta, *Yadaim* 2:13, records that Sir was declared as not soiling the hands, but does not say where or when this was decided.

Perhaps the safest statement about the closing of the Jewish canon is one which recognizes that although in the 1st cent. AD there was popular acceptance of 22 or 24 books as sacred, there was no rigidly fixed Hebr canon until the end of the 2nd cent. or the early 3rd cent. In this period various Jewish groups continued to read as sacred, books that were not included in the 22/24 count.

36 **(III) The Canon at Qumran.** The discovery of the Dead Sea Scrolls (→ Apocrypha, 68:68) has given us much more evidence for our discussion of the canon among Jews in the 1st cent. BC and the 1st cent. AD. The situation apparent in the books preserved from the Qumran collections betrays the very type of freedom about the canon that we sketched above (P. Skehan, *BA* 28 [1965] 89–90). Of the books that would ultimately find their way into the standard Hebr Bible, only Est is absent from among the Qumran scrolls and fragments. This could of course be accidental, although several factors suggest that the Qumran Essenes may have rejected the book: It makes no mention of God, and it places emphasis on the Purim festival (which may not have pleased the rigid Qumran outlook on the calendar and feasts). Est is also absent from some Christian lists up to the time of Gregory Nazianzen (380). The Law and the Prophets seem to have been accepted at Qumran, with each collection arranged in the order that would become standard, though often in recensions differing from the MT (→ Texts, 69:18). Of the collection that would become known as the Writings, Ps has the best attestation; Ezr/Neh and Chr have the poorest. Although the Essenes probably knew the canonical psalter, it is an open question whether the collection of Ps was considered rigidly closed during the lifetime of the Qumran community. In several mss., noncanonical psalms are mixed in with canonical ones (→ Texts, 69:27).

37 The really important factor pertaining to the canon is that the Qumran sectarians preserved copies of many other books. Of the deuterocanonical books, the Letter of Jeremiah (= Bar 6), Tb, and Sir are represented, the latter two in several copies. Moreover, there are many copies of *Jubilees*, *Enoch*, and various sectarian documents. We cannot be sure that an essential distinction was made between these works and "biblical" works. According to some, a different type of script and format was used by the Qumran scribes in copying the "biblical" books; however, this thesis has no validity. In fact, some of the canonical books were copied on papyrus, a practice forbidden later in Judaism, because only parchment (skin) was thought to be fitting for a biblical book (→ Texts, 69:13). The conclusion of Skehan is worth quoting: "All in all, the Qumran library gives the impression of a certain selectivity, but hardly of any fine distinction between a closed canon and all other texts."

38 **(IV) The Canon at Alexandria.** We spoke of the thesis that there were two canons in ancient Judaism: the shorter Palestinian canon fixed at Jamnia and the longer Alexandrian canon (→ 21 above). Just as the fixing of the canon at Jamnia has been challenged, so also the thesis of an Alexandrian canon has undergone penetrating questioning (see A. C. Sundberg, *op. cit.*). This thesis, apparently first proposed by J. E. Grabbe *ca.* 1700, is intimately related to the acceptance of the LXX by the early Church.

Three arguments for an Alexandrian canon no longer find acceptance. *First*, we now recognize the legendary quality of the information supplied by *Aristeas* (→ Apocrypha, 68:32) concerning the composition of the LXX. Neither the Pentateuch nor the entire OT was translated into Greek at one time (i.e., in 72 days, *ca.* 275 BC) by 72 or 70 translators working under the patronage of Ptolemy II Philadelphus (→ Texts, 69:53). If this legend were true, a fixed number of books would be plausible. But when we consider that the LXX was the product of several centuries both of translating and of original composition, the question of a set number of books becomes more problematical. *Second*, it was once thought that the extra (deuterocanonical) books in the Alexandrian canon had been composed in Greek and not in Hebrew or Aramaic, the sacred languages known in Palestine. Actually, a good number of the deuterocanonical books were originally composed in Hebrew (Sir, Jdt, 1 Mc) or Aramaic (Tb). The Qumran discoveries prove that some of these books were in circulation in Palestine and were accepted by Jewish groups there. The fact that the codices of the LXX do not isolate the deuterocanonical books as a group, but mix them in with the Prophets (Bar) and the Writings (Sir, Wis), shows that there was no awareness that these books had a unique origin, as there would have been if they were thought to be later and foreign additions to an already fixed collection translated from Hebrew. *Third*, the thesis that the Jews in Alexandria had a different theory of inspiration from the theory shared by the Jews in Jerusalem is gratuitous. (See P. Katz, *ZNW* 47 [1956] 209.)

39 Moreover, the rigid character of the canon in Alexandria is open to question because the Christian witnesses to this supposedly fixed collection, including the great codices of the LXX, are not in agreement. Sundberg (*op. cit.*, 58–59) shows this in charts. For instance, on the question of Mc (→ Apocrypha, 68:34), Codex Vaticanus contains no Book of the Maccabees, Sinaiticus has 1 Mc and *4 Mc*, and Alexandrinus has all four books. Consequently, it is difficult to deny Sundberg's thesis that the Jews in Alexandria did not have a fixed list of books. They were in the same situation as were their cousins in Palestine in the 1st cent. AD, i.e., they had a large number of sacred books, some of which were recognized by all as older and more sacred than others. It was not the Jews of Alexandria but the Christian Church that, working with the LXX, ultimately drew up an exclusive canon. Indeed, when the Alexandrian Jews eventually did accept a canon, they, like Jews elsewhere, accepted the one fixed by discussions in the late 2nd cent. in the rabbinical schools of Palestine.

40 **(V) The Ancient Christian Canon of the Old Testament.** Our conclusion that there was no rigidly fixed canon in Judaism in the 1st and early 2nd cents. AD means that when the Church was in its formative period and was using the sacred books of the Jews, there was no canon for the Church to adopt. This is exactly the situation in the NT. The NT writers cite the sacred books that ultimately found their way into the Hebr canon, especially the Law, the Prophets, and Ps. But they also echo some of the deuterocanonical books. If one studies the references in Nestle's Greek NT (Sundberg, *op. cit.*, 54–55), one finds allusions to Sir, Wis, 1–2 Mc, and Tb. Furthermore, there are allusions to what would later be considered apocryphal works, e.g., *Pss Sol*, *1–2 Esdras*, *4 Mc*, and *Assumption of Moses*. Jude 14 clearly cites *Enoch;* and while it is often stated that the author is not citing this apocryphal book as Scripture, we have no reason to suspect that Jude would have made such a distinction. *Enoch* was for him, as it was for some later Christian writers, a sacred book. Mt 2:23 cites an unknown work from OT times with the same emphasis that earlier passages in Mt cite Is, Mi, Hos, and Jer. In 2 Cor 6:14 Paul seems to cite a work with Qumran affinities (see J. A. Fitzmyer, *CBQ* 23 [1961] 271–80).

41 After the NT period (i.e., 50–125), the Christian Church continued to cite the Scriptures according to the LXX; and since the LXX itself reflected the lack of a rigidly fixed canon in Judaism, the early Christian writers had no sharp guidelines. The oft-repeated thesis that from the beginning all Christians agreed on the exact canon and that only later doubts arose about certain books has little to recommend it. Such a thesis is based on the assumption that the contents of the canon were revealed to the apostles—an unwarranted assumption, probably flowing from a misunderstanding of the principle that revelation was closed in the apostolic era (→ 15 above).

The first attempts to set up a rigidly closed OT canon for Christendom apparently reflected the Jewish debates about the canon in 2nd-cent. Palestine. In mid-2nd cent., we find Justin in his discussions with the Jews sensitive to differences between the Christian OT and the Jewish Scriptures (*Dialogue with Trypho* 68.7–8; 71ff.; *PG* 6.631–36, 641–46); and Tertullian (*Apparel of Women* 1.3; *PL* 1.1307) is aware that in arguing from *Enoch*, he is not using a book accepted by the Jews. The majority of Christian writers (Clement of Rome, Polycarp, Hermas, Irenaeus, and the author of *Barnabas*) seem to use freely a large number of Jewish sacred books, including apocryphal works. In the late 4th cent., the Western church, as witnessed in the North African councils of Hippo and Carthage, accepted a fixed number of OT books including some deuterocanonicals found in the LXX mss. But the writers of the Eastern church were more aware of the shorter scriptural canon drawn up by the Jews. Melito of Sardis (*ca.* 170) gives us our earliest Christian list of OT books—a list much like the one that eventually became the standard Hebr list (Est is omitted). Origen mentions that the Hebrews have 22 books; Athanasius, who had Jewish teachers, insists that the Christians should have 22 books just as the Hebrews have; and, of course, Jerome did his best to propagate the Hebr canon in the Western church. Some writers who favor the short canon nevertheless cite the deuterocanonical books. A distinction between "canonical" and "ecclesiastical" was proposed in order to classify the books, with the latter to be understood as works serving the Church for edification. Doubts about the deuterocanonical books keep recurring in the history of the Church among those who are aware of the Jewish canon. Those who prefer the shorter canon or express some doubt about the full canonical status of the deuterocanonicals include Cyril of Jerusalem, Gregory Nazianzen, Epiphanius, Rufinus, Gregory the Great, John Damascene, Hugh of St. Victor, Nicholas of Lyra, and Cardinal Cajetan. (See A. C. Sundberg, *CBQ* 30 [1968] 143–55.)

42 **(VI) The Canon at Trent.** As mentioned earlier (→ 8 above), the Council of Trent accepted definitively the deuterocanonicals, and it did so directly in opposition to the Protestant preference for the Jewish canon. Although as Catholics we accept the statement of the Council as binding in faith, it is wise for us to know some of the difficulties that surround this statement. (See P. Duncker, *CBQ* 15 [1953] 277–99; H. Jedin, *A History of the Council of Trent* [London, 1961] 2, 52–98.) Even on the eve of the Council the Catholic view was not absolutely unified, as the mention of Cajetan in the preceding paragraph clearly indicates. Catholic editions of the Bible published in Germany and in France in 1527 and 1530 contained only the protocanonical books. The Fathers of the Council knew of the 4th-cent. African councils that had accepted the deuterocanonical books, and they knew the position taken at Florence (→ 12 above); but at the time of Trent, there were insufficient historical tools to reconstruct the real picture of the canon in the 1st cent. R. H. Charles, a Protestant, recalls the (rather harsh and oversimplified) evaluation given by B. F. Westcott on the ability of the Tridentine Fathers: "This decree of the Council of Trent was ratified by fifty-three prelates, 'among whom [Westcott, *Bible in the Church*, 257] there was not one German, not one scholar distinguished by historical learning, not one who was fitted by special study for the examination of a subject in which the truth could only be determined by the voice of antiquity' " (*APOT* 1, x, n.). Yet, curiously, Trent by accepting a wider canon seems to have preserved an authentic memory of the days of Christian origins, whereas other Christian groups in a professed attempt to return to primitive Christianity have settled for a narrower Jewish canon that, if Protestant researchers like A. C. Sundberg and J. P. Lewis are correct, was the creation of a later period. After all, the Tridentine Fathers did not determine the canon on the basis of purely historical reconstruction but on a theological basis: the consistent Church usage of certain books.

43 Even at Trent, however, the Council Fathers did not specifically attempt to press the detail of Church usage back beyond the period of Jerome, for they used the Vg as the norm for Church usage, condemning "anyone who does not accept these books in their entirety, with all their parts, according to the text usually read in the Catholic Church and as they are in the ancient Latin Vulgate" (DS 1504). There are many difficulties here that demand investigation. *First*, in the period before the Vg there was no consistent Church usage, as we have seen. Ironically, Jerome, the translator of the Vg, was very clear in his preference for the same short canon that Trent rejected in the name of the Vg. The Vg was introduced into the West over many protests (including that of Augustine) asserting that Jerome's translation from the Hebrew was an innovation against the Church's usage of translating from the LXX. *Second*, from Jerome's time on, the Vg has not been a perfect witness of Church usage, for it was several centuries before the Vg won acceptance in the Church. And even then, the Vg was a norm only of *Western* church usage. Although Trent was an ecumenical council, the constituency of the Fathers was Western; and perhaps insufficient attention was given to the usage of the Eastern churches. *Third*, if Church usage was the norm for selecting the books of the canon, then several books that had been used in the Church were omitted. For instance, *1 Esdras* was used

by the Fathers more than was canonical Ezr/Neh, and the requiem liturgy cites *2 Esdras*. Copies of the Vg often contained *1–2 Esdras* and the Prayer of Manasseh—books not accepted at Trent. Not one of these difficulties impairs the binding force of the Tridentine decree (the object of faith is the decree, not the argumentation behind it), but perhaps they illuminate the difficulties often voiced by non-Catholics.

44 **(VII) The Canon in Protestantism.** In general, the Reformers expressed doubt about the deuterocanonical books, but only in the course of Protestant-Catholic polemics were these books completely rejected. In 1520 Andrew Bodenstein (Carlstadt) questioned the deuterocanonical books, and Luther's translation of 1534 grouped them together at the end of the OT under the caption: "Apocrypha: these are books which are not held equal to the Sacred Scriptures and yet are useful and good for reading." The Zurich Bible, translated by Zwingli and others in 1527–29, included the deuterocanonical books as useful, even though it relegated them to the last volume and did not consider them canonical. Olivetan's Bible, published in 1534–35 with a preface by Calvin, reproduced the deuterocanonical books, but set them off from the other books. The Reformed church in its Confessio Gallicana (1559) and Confessio Belgica (1561) excluded the deuterocanonical books from Scripture. The Lutheran confessional declarations did not produce a binding list of canonical books, but Lutheran theological practice gave less and less attention to the deuterocanonical books.

45 In the English church, the Wycliffe Bible (1382), under the influence of Jerome, had reproduced only the books of the Hebr canon. The Coverdale Bible (1535), however, included the deuterocanonical books. Article VI of the Thirty-nine Articles (1571) asserts of these books that they may be read "for example of life and instruction of manners," though they ought not to be employed "to establish any doctrine." The AV (King James) of 1611 printed the deuterocanonical books between the Testaments. John Lightfoot (1643), a famous scholar, spoke out against this arrangement, fearing that "the wretched apocrypha," as he called them, might be mistaken as forming a link between the OT and the NT. The Presbyterian Westminster Confession (1647) stated that these books, "not being of divine inspiration, are no part of the Canon of the Scripture and therefore are of no authority in the Church of God, nor to be any otherwise approved, or made use of, than other human writings." Obviously, opposition to these books was on the upswing in England. After many disputes, the British and Foreign Bible Society decided in 1827 to omit the controverted books from its future publications, with the exception of some pulpit Bibles. The Society went on record with this statement: "The Principles of the Society exclude the circulation of those books or parts of books which are usually termed Apocryphal."

46 Recently, in Protestantism, especially on the Continent, there are signs of a return to the milder attitude of the original Reformers toward the deuterocanonical books. To quote E. Jacob: "These books do not appear to us to be a roadblock but rather a bridge between the two Testaments. Certain doctrines such as the resurrection of the dead, angelology, the concept of retribution, have assumed in the apocryphal [= deuterocanonical] literature the aspect under which they materialize in the New Testament. There is in the Apocrypha the imprint of God's revelation of the Bible; to slight their witness, even if it is secondary, is to run the risk of removing a precious link in the web that constitutes the unity of revelation. For this reason a return to the practice of Reformation times when the Apocrypha were inserted at the end of the Old Testament seems to us highly desirable" (in *Le problème biblique dans le Protestantisme*, ed. J. Boisset [Paris, 1955] 81–82; also S. Mowinckel, *The Old Testament as Word of God* [N.Y., 1959] 112).

This attitude is being formed not only by recent studies about the canon in antiquity but also by a better understanding of the deuterocanonical books. One former objection to their acceptance was the consideration that several of them are not strictly historical but are imaginative or exaggerated accounts—e.g., Jdt and 2 Mc. However, we know today that such free composition is also found in protocanonical books. Another objection offered to the deuterocanonical books was part of the polemics of the 16th and 17th cents., namely that acceptance of the deuterocanonical books might offer solace to Catholics who would use them to support doctrines rejected by Protestants, e.g., purgatory in 2 Mc 12:44–45. But, on the one hand, Protestants have come to admit that late Jewish speculations on the afterlife, as witnessed even in NT books, allowed intermediate stages between heaven and hell; on the other hand, Catholics have come to realize that none of these stages is exactly the same as purgatory. Such polemic interests are far from the mind of biblical scholars today whether or not they accept the deuterocanonical books; and once polemics are set aside, the scientific study of canonical questions may lead to closer agreement. Catholics and Protestants are now working together to produce common bibles, especially in the minor languages of the mission fields, and these bibles will contain the deuterocanonical books.

47 **(VIII) The Canon in the Oriental Churches.** In the early period, the Syrian church, from the witness of the Peshitta (→ Texts, 69:92), used only the books of the Hebr canon, but subsequently the influence of the LXX prevailed and a wider canon came into use. The Nestorians, however, persisted in using the shorter canon. The tendency among the Copts and the Ethiopians, and to some extent among the Syrians, has been to give status to some of the apocryphal books (pseudepigrapha) as well as to the deuterocanonical books.

Jugie (*op. cit.*) has shown that the Byzantine church, from the beginning up to the Middle Ages, accepted the deuterocanonical books. There is no record of any dispute among Latins and Greeks about the OT canon. Addressing itself to the Greeks, the Council of Florence did not hesitate to make free use of texts from these books. It was not until the 17th cent., under the influence of the Protestant Reformation, that a problem was raised. Zachary Gerganos (1627), a Greek who had studied at Wittenberg, is singled out by Jugie as the first to throw over the traditional Byzantine teaching on the canonicity of the deuterocanonical books. Such views were aired by others in the East but met opposition in both the Slavic and the Greek branches of the Byzantine church. In 1672 the important Synod of Jerusalem accepted as canonical Wis, Jdt, Tb, Mc, Sir, and the additions to Dn. Although 18th-cent. opinion in Russia was fluid, 19th-cent. Russian Orthodox theologians universally excluded the deuterocanonical books. The books do appear, however, in a Russian Bible published in Moscow in 1956. Gradually, misgivings filtered into the Greek church as well, and the canonicity of the deuterocanonical books became an open question. An edition of the OT sanctioned in 1950 by the Holy Synod of the Greek church contains all these books along with *2 Esdras* and *3 Mc* (*4 Mc* is an appendix; → Apocrypha, 68:35–36, 40).

THE CANON OF THE NEW TESTAMENT

48 **(I) General Observations.** Today, Roman Catholics, Orthodox, and Protestants all accept the same canon of 27 NT books. The theory that these books were accepted from the first days of Christianity and that doubts arose only subsequently is untenable; once again it is related to the idea, no longer accepted, that the specific contents of the canon were known in the apostolic era. The early followers of Jesus had Scriptures that they considered sacred, but these were writings that had come down to them from their Jewish heritage. For about the first 100 years of Christianity (AD 30–130), the term OT is an anachronism (yet see 2 Cor 3:14); the collection of sacred writings of Jewish origin would not have been designated as "Old" until there was a "New" collection from which to distinguish it. (Modern Judaism does not speak of an Old Testament; since the Jews reject the NT, there is for them only one sacred collection.) When did Christians begin writing their own compositions and why? How soon were these put on a par with the ancient Jewish Scriptures? What determined which Christian works were to be preserved and accepted? When did acceptance come? These are the questions we now must deal with.

49 **(A) Causes for Writing Christian Works.** Christianity, much more than Judaism, is a religion with its origin in a person. What God has done for man is centered in Jesus, so that the early Christians could say that God was in Christ Jesus (2 Cor 5:19); the Jews would not have thought of Moses in these terms. Jesus commissioned apostles (for the difference between the apostles and the Twelve, → Aspects NT Thought, 78:179) to preach to men the Kingdom of God, which had made its presence felt in Jesus' ministry. The apostles therefore became the living link between the Christian believer and the Jesus in whom he believed, so that in the early days when Christians were close to the apostles—both geographically and chronologically—there was no pressing need for Christian writings. In fact, we have no clear proof of major Christian writings from the period AD 30 to 50. During this time the Christian faith was communicated, preserved, and nourished by word of mouth (Rom 10:14–15). Distance was probably the most influential factor in changing the situation.

50 *First*, geographical distance. With the decision at Jerusalem in AD 49 to permit acceptance of Gentiles without circumcision (Acts 15), the far-flung Gentile world, already invaded by Paul, became a wide-open missionary field. The founding of Christian communities at great distances from one another and the continual traveling of the apostles made written communication a necessity. A church whose confines were within short traveling distance of Jerusalem was a thing of the past, and apostolic instruction now often had to come from afar. This need was first met with letters and epistles (→ NT Epistles, 47:3–5), and the Pauline letters are the earliest major Christian writings of which we know with certainty.

Second, chronological distance. The existence of eyewitnesses to Jesus marked the first years of Christianity; but as the apostles dispersed, and after their death, the preservation of the memory of Jesus' deeds and words became a problem. Moreover, catechetical needs required the organization of oral testimonies into compact units. This gave rise to the pre-Gospel collections of material and ultimately to the Gospels themselves. These written documents were no substitute for oral witness, as we hear from Papias who, early in the 2nd cent., was still seeking oral testimony even though he knew of written records (Eusebius, *Hist.* 3.39, 4; GCS 9/1.286). Other exigencies, such as the threat of heresy or of persecution, produced additional NT works.

51 **(B) Criteria for Preservation and Acceptance.** Once there were Christian writings, what factor determined which ones were to be preserved and were to be considered as uniquely sacred? For, as we shall see, some 1st-cent. writings were not preserved, and other early works that were preserved were not accepted. The following factors were important. *First*, apostolic origin, real or putative, was very important, particularly for acceptance. The canonicity of Ap and Heb was debated precisely because it was doubted whether they were written by John and Paul respectively. Today, we understand that such apostolic origin is to be taken in the very broad sense that "authorship" has in biblical discussion (→ 89 below). Often this means no more than that an apostle had a traditional connection with a given work. By the stricter standards current today, it may be legitimately questioned whether a single NT work comes directly from any one of the Twelve.

52 *Second*, most of the NT works were addressed to particular Christian communities, and the history and importance of the community involved had much to do with the preservation and even with the ultimate acceptance of these works. Seemingly no work emerging directly from the Palestinian community has been preserved, although some of the sources of the Gospels and Acts were probably Palestinian. The reason for this loss probably lies in the disruption of the Palestinian Christian community during the Jewish-Roman war of 66–70. Syria seems to have fared better, for apparently Syrian communities were addressed in Mt, Jas, and Jude. The churches of Greece and Asia Minor seem to have preserved the largest portion of NT material, i.e., the Pauline, the Johannine, and perhaps the Lucan writings. The church of Rome preserved Mk, Rom, and perhaps Heb and the Lucan writings.

53 *Third*, conformity with the rule of faith was a criterion of acceptance. Doubts about its millenarianism caused suspicion of Ap, and an apocryphal gospel like *Peter* was rejected precisely on doctrinal grounds (→ 65 below).

54 *Fourth*, to what extent did chance play a role in preservation? Some would argue from a theory of inspiration that chance could have had no role: God would not have inspired a work and then allowed it to be lost. But this argument presumes that every inspired work had to have permanent value. Could not the task for which God inspired a particular work have been accomplished when it was received? A good example may have been the lost letter of Paul that pronounced judgment on an individual at Corinth (1 Cor 5:3). Moreover, the argument presumes that God always protects against human vicissitudes the works he has motivated—a presumption that is not verified in the history of Israel and of the Church. Consequently, many scholars do believe that chance had a role in the preservation of less important works, like Phlm, when more important works were lost (part of the Corinthian correspondence; Matthew's *logia* of Jesus in Aramaic).

55 (II) Composition and Collection of New Testament Works. All of the NT works were probably written before *ca.* 125; the dates for their collection into fixed groups are much harder to specify.

(A) Pauline Corpus.

(a) WRITING. Most of the Pauline letters and epistles were written as instruction and encouragement to churches that Paul himself had evangelized (Rom is a notable exception). In the early 50's, 1–2 Thes were written, and in the late 50's, the Great Letters (Gal, 1–2 Cor, Rom) and perhaps Phil. In the early 60's there were the Captivity Letters (Phlm, Col, Eph [?], and perhaps Phil). Traditionally, the Pastoral Letters (1–2 Tm, Ti) have been dated in the mid-60's. In all, there were 13 letters or epistles.

56 The authorship of several of the writings that bear Paul's name has been questioned. Some hold that Eph was written by a disciple who adapted the themes of Col. In *The Meaning of Ephesians* (1933), E. J. Goodspeed suggests that Eph was composed as an introduction to the Pauline corpus. In any case, Eph could not have been written at a very late date if, as many think, it was known to Clement of Rome (96) and Ignatius (110). The Pastoral Letters pose an even more serious problem, and many non-Catholic scholars put their composition as late as the mid-2nd cent. But even if they are deutero-Pauline (and Catholics must seriously consider this possibility), they probably should be brought much closer to Paul's career and be attributed to one of his disciples. In his commentary on the Pastorals (BNTC, 1963), J. N. D. Kelly has shown that the Pastorals really do not fit into the picture of the 2nd cent. These letters differ from the other Pauline writings in that they are addressed to individuals rather than to churches (even Phlm is addressed to people in a house church). However, since Timothy and Titus are being addressed specifically because they have authority over churches, the difference is not crucial.

57 (b) COLLECTION. There are a number of difficulties about the formation of a Pauline collection. The letters were written to handle particular problems in particular churches. Only Rom and Eph consciously reveal a larger scope. Why were such temporal documents preserved for later times? In Col 4:16 Paul recommends the exchange and circulation of his letters among neighboring churches, but what prompted a wider circulation so that by the end of the 1st cent. Pauline letters were being read in churches far distant from the original destination? Perhaps their enduring value was quickly perceived; nevertheless, one wonders whether Paul himself ever expected that his correspondence would be read hundreds and thousands of years after his death as a guide to universal Christian faith. We note that some of the Pauline letters did not escape the doom that their temporal character might have brought to all (→ NT Epistles, 47:13); there was a letter to the Laodiceans (Col 4:16) and probably two lost letters to the Corinthians (→ Life of Paul, 46:36). It is A. von Harnack's view that there was a deliberate process of selection and rejection in dealing with the Pauline letters, but the preservation of Phlm, as contrasted with the losses just mentioned, makes this improbable.

How then were the Pauline letters gathered together? Did a community take its letter from Paul and add to it the letters addressed to neighboring churches? Such a process would have produced several different collections. This is the theory of K. Lake, and he uses it to account for the lack of agreement in the order of the Pauline writings that is evidenced in Marcion, the Muratorian Fragment, Tertullian, and Origen. Other scholars think that the attempt to collect Paul's writings produced only one collection. E. J. Goodspeed proposes that at first there was a lack of interest in the Pauline letters and that only after AD 90, with the publication of Acts, was the importance of Paul's contribution to Christianity realized. This realization led to a systematic attempt to collect his writings, some of which had already perished. According to J. Knox and C. L. Mitton, a disciple of Paul, like Onesimus (Phlm 10), began to collect the writings soon after Paul's death; Knox agrees with Goodspeed's thesis that Eph was designed to introduce this corpus. Timothy has been suggested as the collector in the treatment of this whole question by D. Guthrie (*NTI* 1, 255–69).

Works of the New Testament Era: Approximate Dates of Composition

Early 50's	*Late 50's*	*Early 60's*	*Mid-60's*	*70's–80's*	*90's*	*100–125*
1 Thessalonians	Galatians	Philemon	MARK	MATTHEW	JOHN	2 Peter
2 Thessalonians	1 Corinthians	Colossians	1 Timothy†	LUKE	Apocalypse	*Ignatian*
	2 Corinthians	Ephesians†	Titus†	Acts	1 John	*Epistles**
	Romans		2 Timothy†		2 John	*Didache**
	Philippians(?)	Philippians(?)	1 Peter(?)	Jude(?)	3 John	
			James(?)	James(?)	Jude(?)	
			Hebrews(?)	Hebrews(?)	*1 Clement**	

PAULINE CORPUS

EARLY LETTERS	1 Thessalonians	51
	2 Thessalonians	51
GREAT LETTERS	Galatians	54–57
	1 Corinthians	57
	2 Corinthians	57
	Romans	58
	Philippians	56–57 / 61–63
CAPTIVITY LETTERS	Philemon	61–63
	Colossians	61–63
	Ephesians	61–63†
PASTORAL LETTERS	1 Timothy	65†
	Titus	65†
	2 Timothy	66–67†

GOSPELS

Mark	65
Matthew	70's–80's
Luke	70's–80's
John	90's

CATHOLIC EPISTLES

1 Peter	64(?)
James	62 or 80's
Jude	70's–90's
1 John	90's
2 John	90's
3 John	90's
2 Peter	100–125

OTHER WRITINGS

Acts	70's–80's
Hebrews	60's–80's
Apocalypse	90's

(?) Date uncertain; † If not Pauline, date to approx. 80's; * Noncanonical.

58 When were the Pauline letters gathered into a collection? Obviously the questions of authorship and dating treated above affect this problem. Goodspeed insists that the collection took place shortly after the writing of Acts, for if the author of Acts had known the Pauline writings, he would have cited them. But Knox, in *Studies in Luke-Acts* (eds. L. E. Keck and J. L. Martyn [Nashville, 1966] 279–87), argues that Acts was written *ca.* 125, against a Marcionite misuse of the already extant corpus of Pauline writings. There are references to Pauline letters in early writers like Clement of Rome (96) and Ignatius (110), but it is not clear whether those writers knew all the Pauline works, e.g., neither seems to cite 2 Cor. If we could be certain of the date of 2 Pt, we would have an important indication of when at least some of the Pauline works had been collected, because in 3:15 the author of this epistle indicates that his audience knows of a group of Pauline letters, that they are being read and interpreted, and that they are on the same level as "the other Scriptures."

Combining all the evidence, we think it likely that by the end of the 1st cent. there was a Pauline collection of undetermined length. By mid-2nd cent. the heretic Marcion had a group of ten Pauline writings, without the Pastorals. (It is difficult to be certain whether Marcion was ignorant of the Pastorals or deliberately rejected them, as Tertullian claims.) According to Jerome, Tatian (*ca.* 175) apparently accepted Titus (only?). The Muratorian Canon, or Fragment, containing a list of books presumably accepted at Rome *ca.* 200 (→ 84 below), knows of 13 Pauline epistles, and 13 is the usual count in subsequent enumerations, although in the East, Heb was often counted as a 14th. The Pastorals, although used by ecclesiastical writers like Irenaeus and Tertullian, were seemingly not included in the Chester Beatty Papyrus codex (P^{46}) of the Pauline epistles, dating from Egypt *ca.* 250. A Lat (North African?) list of *ca.* 300 found in the Codex Claromontanus (Hennecke, *NTA* 1, 45–46) strangely omits Phil and 1–2 Thes.

59 Other pseudo-Pauline epistles appeared. The Muratorian Fragment rejects the *Epistle to the Laodiceans* and the *Epistle to the Alexandrians*, which display a pro-Marcionite tendency. Another spurious *Epistle to the Laodiceans* was the object of attack in the 4th cent. It has been preserved for us in the Codex Fuldensis, a ms. of the Vg NT, completed in 546; in the Middle Ages this epistle continued to appear in Lat Bibles and was accepted as genuine by some Lat writers. In the *Acts of Paul* (*ca.* 180) we find a *Third Epistle to the Corinthians*, which found acceptance in 4th-cent Syria. A 3rd-cent. Gk copy of this apocryphal Corinthian correspondence appears in the recently discovered Papyrus Bodmer X. It is obvious that these last two epistles were suggested by Paul's own indications of correspondence that was not preserved.

60 **(B) Gospels.**

(a) Writing. It is difficult to be certain when the earliest pre-Gospel traditions were written down. It seems reasonable to place in the 50's some of the works that modern scholars suppose to have antedated the Gospels, e.g., "Q," proto-Mk, the earliest written tradition behind Jn. In antiquity Papias knew of a collection of the sayings of the Lord in Hebrew or Aramaic compiled by Matthew (Eusebius, *Hist.* 3.39, 16; *PG* 9/1.292), and Irenaeus (*ibid.* 5.8, 2; *PG* 9/1.442) states that this material antedated Mk. By the time that Luke was writing (in the 80's?), many others had undertaken to compile a narrative of the things that had been accomplished by Jesus (Lk 1:1). Such pre-Gospel written sources, now lost but theoretically reconstructed by scholars, must have already shown considerable development over the *ipsissima verba et facta* of Jesus. They would have constituted a trustworthy record of the memories of Jesus as preserved in the Christian communities of the 50's, but scarcely a verbatim report of what had been said and done in the 20's. (Note that such development is admitted by official Roman Catholic statements, → Church Pronouncements, 72:35, 15.)

61 The canonical Gospels were written in the period 60–100, with probably only Mk to be dated in the 60's. In them, the pre-Gospel written tradition was systematized along both chronological and theological lines. In Mk, the material to be narrated was fitted into a simplified sequence of the public ministry of Jesus (baptism, ministry in Galilee, ministry outside Galilee, journey to Jerusalem, passion, death, and resurrection), with the Evangelist inserting incidents where they seemed *logically* to fit—not necessarily on the basis of a correct historical chronology. The choice of the material to be incorporated and the orientation given to it were determined by the Evangelist's theological outlook and by the needs of the community for which the Gospel was being written.

In the 70's, or more likely in the 80's, an unknown Christian wrote the Gospel that has come down to us as the Gospel according to Matthew, *perhaps* because the Evangelist was a disciple of Matthew, or drew on the earlier collection of sayings written by Matthew. Probably, also in the 80's, Luke undertook a more elaborate project that produced not only a Gospel which had more formal historical pretensions but also a history of the origin and spread of Christianity in the postresurrectional period (Acts). The theological orientation is far more pronounced in Mt and Lk than it is in Mk. In the 90's, but drawing on an earlier tradition related to John son of Zebedee, a disciple of John produced a Gospel somewhat different from the others. On the one hand, in Jn there were preserved historical reminiscences lost or oversimplified in the earlier Gospels; on the other hand, there was a truly profound theologizing of the words and deeds of Jesus.

62 (b) Collection. Why were these four Gospels ultimately accepted by the Church? Why was not only one of them selected? Or at least, why was Mk not set aside, since most of its material is preserved in Mt and Lk? This is all the more curious when we realize that the idea of there being only one Gospel was the primitive concept (2 Cor 11:4 and constant Pauline usage; → Pauline Theology, 79:27), and the individual written Gospels were looked on as variations of the one basic Gospel. (This is reflected in the title, "The Gospel [sing.] according to . . ."; the pl. use of "Gospels" seems to appear for the first time in Justin [*Apol.* 1.66–67].) There is not the slightest indication that any one of the four Evangelists expected his audience to read other Gospels; his was *the* Gospel for this particular community. One might have expected that only the longest or most informative Gospel would have survived, after the principle of the survival of the fittest. Or at least, one might have expected the Gospels to have been harmonized into one—a logical solution attempted by Tatian *ca.* 170 in his *Diatessaron* (→ Texts, 69:90), which for a time replaced the four Gospels in Syrian church usage. However, the Church at large took the peculiar solution of preserving the Gospel records from four different communities, doing nothing to harmonize their differences.

63 This problem is closely related to the problem of the other gospels that ultimately were not accepted as canonical—a problem to be discussed below. Some scholars have held that *four* Gospels were preserved, rather than the others, because these four came down from apostles and apostolic men (Justin, *Dialogue with Trypho* 103.7; "the Memoirs which I say were composed by his apostles and those that followed them"); therefore the

Church did not feel free to change them by adding, subtracting, or combining. This may well have been the spirit of the *later* Church, even though Tatian apparently was not regarded audacious in his project. However, it was not the attitude of the 1st-cent. Church, if we can judge from the liberty with which the Evangelists like Luke and the author of Matthew handled the pre-Gospel sources (which had the best claim to being apostolic) and Mk. In particular, Luke corrected Mark's Greek, changed his sequence, and added material. And we remember that, although Papias knew of the written Gospels, he was still anxious to improve upon them with oral material of an eyewitness pedigree. Nevertheless, we cannot neglect the fact that these four Gospels did acquire importance because of the names attached to them: John was an important figure among the Twelve and in the Church; Mark's Gospel was related to Peter; Luke's Gospel was related to Paul in some vaguer way (→ Pauline Theology, 79:27); and we observe that the First Gospel was quickly related to Matthew, one of the Twelve. The importance of the communities with which the Gospels were associated may also have figured in their survival: Mt was probably directed to a Syrian community in the Antioch area; Mk was composed at Rome; sometimes scholars relate Lk to Rome, sometimes to Greece; Jn was composed at Ephesus or in Syria.

64 Alongside the four Gospels, oral and written material from the 1st cent. seems to have survived into the 2nd cent. and even later. Some of this was incorporated into apocryphal gospels. (In one interesting case, the story of the adulteress in Jn 7:53–8:11, an early narrative survived, ultimately to be incorporated into a canonical Gospel, at least 100 years after the Gospel was written.) The apocryphal *Gospel of Thomas* (→ Apocrypha, 68:59) contains sayings of Jesus that may well be authentic. How many of these apocryphal gospels existed in the 2nd cent. we do not know, but in his first homily on Luke (GCS 49.3–11), Origen mentions that many had attempted to write gospels (he names five) but had not been guided by the Spirit. Origen, of course, wrote at a time when four and only four Gospels were accepted, but was it thus during the 2nd cent.? Were some of the gospels now considered apocryphal used by certain communities as their gospels, even as the canonical Gospels were used by their respective communities? The traditional view is that throughout the 2nd cent., only the four canonical Gospels were accepted by the Church at large (O. Cullmann, *The Early Church*, [Phila., 1956] 39–54; J. Crehan, *The Gospels Reconsidered* [Oxford, 1960] 36–46). One proof offered is that Tatian's *Diatessaron* (*ca.* 170) drew on the four Gospels. In the mid-2nd cent., however, Papyrus Egerton 2 (→ Apocrypha, 68:58) combined sayings from the Syn, Jn, and a noncanonical source—an indication that the author did not think exclusively of four Gospels. The presence of various endings in mss. of Mk (→ Gospel Mk, 42:96–100) may also betray a feeling that the standard four Gospels did not contain all that was to be said. Evidently, too, there was considerable freedom in copying the text of the Gospels throughout the 2nd cent., for we know that by AD 200, different textual traditions of the Gospels already existed (→ Texts, 69:140). Thus, there is some evidence that the four Gospels did not gain an exclusive position until the *second half* of the *2nd cent.*, and even then we can speak only for the larger Gk and Lat churches.

65 A fascinating instance of how this exclusive position was attained is presented in the story of Serapion, bishop of Antioch *ca.* 190 (Eusebius, *Hist.* 6.12, 2; GCS 9/2.545). Serapion discovered that in Rhossus people read from the *Gospel of Peter*, but he forbade them to use it because he found Docetist heresy in it. This story illustrates two things: First, the public reading of the Gospels, particularly in the liturgy, was one of the factors that won acceptance for them in the Church, and Church authorities became very sensitive if a gospel not known to them was being read. Second, the use of apocryphal gospels by heretics was a factor in narrowing the canon to four Gospels. Also, the attitude of the archheretic, Marcion (*ca.* 150), in accepting only Lk, may have been influential in causing the Church to preserve the fourfold Gospel. From *ca.* 200 the four Gospels held an assured place in the Gk and Western churches. As Origen puts it (Eusebius, *Hist.* 6.25, 4; GCS 9/2.576), there are four Gospels, "which are alone undeniably authentic in the Church of God on earth." The Syrian church, however, preferred the use of the *Diatessaron* in the 3rd and 4th cents., adopting the four Gospels only in the 5th cent.

Thus far we have dealt with the Pauline letters and the Gospels—two separate bodies of early Christian literature. Perhaps the thought that both types of literature stemmed from apostolic witness was a factor in causing them to be joined. The first instance of such a joining appears in the work of Marcion, who made ten epistles and Lk the basis of his theology.

(C) Other Works. We are fortunate to have at least some knowledge, however sketchy, about the formation of the Pauline and Gospel collections, but we are very poorly informed about the collection of the remainder of the NT works. This lack of information presents a difficulty similar to that presented by the third group of OT works—the Writings—in the study of the OT canon.

66 (a) ACTS. The traditional view is that Luke composed Lk and Acts at the same time, i.e., in the 80's (although some scholars prefer the 60's because the story of Acts comes to a close at that time). However, Lk and Acts were not preserved as a unit. Marcion accepted only Lk, and it is interesting that Acts really came into frequent use after Marcion's error. As mentioned above (→ 58), J. Knox believes that Acts was written much later than Lk (*ca.* 125) to combat proto-Marcion misuse of the Pauline letters and Lk. A work such as Acts, which gives prominence to the Twelve, holds them up as a standard of apostleship, and shows a continuity from them to Paul, was precisely the work to offset Marcion's one-sided emphasis on Paul.

We are uncertain when Acts, a history of the works of Jesus' disciples, was put on a plane with the Gospels, an account of Jesus himself; but such an evaluation shows a mature understanding of the role of the Church in continuing the role of Christ. There is every evidence that Acts was accepted as canonical from 200 on; but from 150 there were also in circulation various apocryphal acts of individual apostles (*of John*, *of Paul*, *of Thomas*, etc.). Generally, they were writings of heretical tendency, and highly romantic. Tertullian, *De Baptismo* 17 (CSEL 20.215), tells how sometime before 190 the priest who fabricated the *Acts of Paul* was caught and punished. The Lat list (*ca.* 300) in the Codex Claromontanus includes the *Acts of Paul*, but seemingly puts it on a questionable basis along with *Hermas* and *Barnabas*. Eusebius (*Hist.* 3.25, 4; GCS 9/1.252) lists it as spurious.

67 (b) APOCALYPSE. Apocalyptic is a species of prophecy and was familiar to the early Christians as part of their Jewish heritage (→ Post-exilic Period, 20:21–24). Yet it is interesting that Ap is prefaced by the letters to the seven churches of Asia Minor—an innovation in apocalyptic literature, and perhaps an indication that Christians were more accustomed to epistolary writings. Presumably, Ap was written in the 90's; it belongs to the Johannine school of writing.

The Muratorian Fragment (Rome, before 200?) mentions two apocalypses, one of John and one of Peter, with a notation that some do not wish to read the latter in church. This *Apocalypse of Peter*, written *ca.* 125–150, seems to have been accepted as canonical by Clement of Alexandria (Eusebius, *Hist.*, 6.14, 1; GCS 9/2.548). It appears in the Lat list (*ca.* 300) of the Codex Claromontanus, seemingly marked as questionable; and *ca.* 325 Eusebius (*Hist.* 3.25, 4; GCS 9/1.252) places it among the spurious books, stating (3.3, 2; GCS 9/1.190) that neither in the earlier days nor in his time had any orthodox writer made use of it. Jerome also rejected it, but in the 5th cent. it was still being used in the Good Friday liturgy in Palestine.

68 The other apocalypse, that of John, attained canonical status only with difficulty. At first it seems to have been accepted; it is the only apocalypse endorsed by Origen. The Alogi (*ca.* 200?) attacked Ap as well as Jn on theological grounds—the only true indication of opposition to Ap in the Western church. In the Greek church, Dionysius of Alexandria (*ca.* 250) maintained that John son of Zebedee, author of the Gospel, did not write Ap. Dionysius did not reject the book but was worried about the use being made of it by the heretical chiliasts (millenarianists). His critical judgment distinguishing two different writers for Jn and Ap was certainly correct, but his denial of apostolic authorship to Ap had the effect of weakening the acceptance of Ap as a biblical book in the Greek church. Eusebius (*Hist.* 3.25, 2–4; GCS 9/1.250) wavers in whether to list Ap as genuine or spurious. It is not included in the list of Cyril of Jerusalem (350) or in the list of the 60th Canon of Laodicea (→ 10 above), or in the list of Gregory Nazianzen that was accepted in Trullo II (692; → 11 above). Ap was not accepted in the Syrian church.

69 (c) Hebrews. This epistle probably was composed in the 80's or 90's by a Jewish Christian well educated in the Gk oratorical techniques of Alexandria (Apollos? → Epistle Heb, 61:3). Although the work is in epistolary form, it is essentially a highly literate theological disquisition on the relation of Christianity to Jewish institutions. There is little evidence of clear citations of Heb in the 2nd cent. The discussion of the acceptance of Heb is centered around its attribution to Paul. If Ap was accepted in the West and rejected in the East, the reverse holds true for Heb. In the West, Heb is not mentioned in the Muratorian Fragment (before 200?), in the Lat list (*ca.* 300) of the Codex Claromontanus, or in the African Canon of 360. In the East, Heb is mentioned in Origen's list, but he admits doubt as to whether Paul wrote it by his own hand (Eusebius, *Hist.* 6.25, 11–14; GCS 9/2.578). Eusebius himself accepts Heb, even though he knows that the Roman church denies that it is the work of Paul (*Hist.* 3.3, 5; GCS 9/1.190). Its acceptance in the East is attested by the canons of Cyril of Jerusalem (350), Athanasius (367), and Gregory Nazianzen (400). In the West, in the latter part of the 4th cent., Heb won acceptance through the efforts of writers like Hilary, Jerome, and Augustine, who were influenced by Eastern ideas. It found a place in the lists of the North African councils of Hippo and Carthage, and was also accepted by the Syrian church.

70 In modern times, when the problem of authorship has been divorced from that of canonicity (→ 87 below), the sharp distinction evident between the style of Heb and that of the Pauline writings has convinced most scholars that Paul was not the author. Catholic writers, influenced by the decree of the Pontifical Biblical Commission (→ Church Pronouncements, 72:28v), have tried to protect the Paulinity of Heb by stressing that Paul used a scribe to write the epistle. Now, however, they are beginning to recognize that Heb probably has no real relation to Paul, other than that the author may have had some acquaintance with thought like Paul's (*LTK* 5, 46; → Epistle Heb, 61:2–3).

71 (d) Catholic Epistles. The same problem of authorship affects these epistles; unless they were attributed to apostolic figures, there was reluctance to accept them.

(i) *Writing.* In form *1 Peter* is a treatise or even a homily associated with baptism (and perhaps with the paschal celebration) that has been adapted to the letter form—notice the continuing Christian preference for this genre. The work is purportedly written by Peter, and therefore a date before Peter's death (*ca.* 65) has been traditional. Many non-Catholic scholars look upon the epistle as pseudonymous and suggest a later date. There are, however, no absolutely compelling reasons why either the traditional date or authorship (in the broad biblical sense; → 89 below) must be rejected (→ Epistle 1 Pt, 58:2).

72 The problem of *2 Peter* is much more difficult, for here we have a work that most critical scholars today, both Protestant and Catholic, recognize as clearly pseudonymous. The use of abstract theological language and the reference to a collection of Pauline letters suggest that this may well be the last of the canonical NT books to have been written. Some non-Catholic scholars date it as late as 150, but a date between 100 and 125 is quite tenable (→ Epistle 2 Pt, 65:4). The contention that the work must have been written before the death of the last apostle and the close of revelation implies an oversimplified view, not only of the closing of revelation, but also of the apostles (a group wider than the Twelve; → Aspects NT Thought, 78:179).

73 The *Johannine epistles* may have been composed in the 90's. They are the product of the same school of writing that produced the Gospel, but it is open to question whether they were written by the same Johannine disciple who produced the Gospel.

74 The epistle of *James* is a diatribe resembling the format of the Stoic diatribes; it was composed in a Jewish-Christian atmosphere and adapted to the form of a letter. It is a very difficult book to date on internal grounds, and the date traditionally given (the 60's) is proposed on the basis of its claim to be the work of James, presumably the bishop of Jerusalem whose death occurred in the 60's (→ Aspects NT Thought, 78:168). Many modern scholars suggest pseudonymity; even in antiquity the question about the authorship of the epistle was raised (e.g., Jerome, *De Viris Illustr.* 2; *PL* 23.609), creating doubt about its canonical character.

75 The epistle of *Jude*, attributed to another brother of Jesus, is to be dated earlier than 2 Pt, for the latter copies from Jude with some interesting theological editing (e.g., removal of references to *Enoch* and the *Assumption of Moses*). Here again, pseudonymity has been suggested; however, neither with Jas nor with Jude is there anything that would absolutely preclude the traditional authorship if understood in the broad biblical sense (→ 89 below).

76 (ii) *Acceptance.* Eusebius, writing *ca.* 325, is the first to speak of "the seven [epistles] called catholic" (*Hist.* 2.23, 25; GCS 9/1.174); however, he himself was not sure of the canonicity of all of them, and general acceptance of the seven in the Gk and Lat churches did not come till the late 4th cent.

Of the seven Catholic Epistles, *1 Peter* and *1 John* were the first to receive general acceptance. Both seem to have been known by Papias (Eusebius, *Hist.* 3.39, 17; GCS 9/1.292) and Polycarp. The Muratorian Fragment mentions two Johannine epistles; its omission of 1 Pt may be due to the poor preservation of the text of the Fragment. Origen accepted 1 Pt and a short epistle by John (1 Jn?).

These two epistles appear in all subsequent lists. Along with Jas, they constitute the three epistles accepted by the Syrian church in the 5th cent.

77 The epistle of *James* was known by Origen's time, but we do not know when it began to receive canonical status. It is not in the Muratorian list, and Eusebius places it among the disputed books. The Lat Claromontanus list includes it, but the African Canon of 360 does not. In the latter part of the 4th cent. it won acceptance in the West through Augustine, Jerome, and the councils of Hippo and Carthage. In the Greek church of the same period it found a place in the canons of Cyril of Jerusalem, Athanasius, and Gregory Nazianzen.

78 The evidence for the early knowledge of *Jude* is better than for Jas. Jude was known by the author of 2 Pt, by Polycarp, (seemingly), and by Clement of Alexandria. It appears in the Muratorian Fragment. However, Origen was aware that there were doubts about it, and Eusebius placed it among the disputed books. Its acceptance in the latter part of the 4th cent. followed a pattern similar to that of Jas; but Jude did not receive final acceptance by the Syrian church, and one of the canonical lists adopted by Trullo II (692) indicates uncertainty about its status.

79 The two shorter *Johannine epistles* were not cited frequently by Christian writers, probably because of their relatively insignificant contents. Toward the end of the 2nd cent. Irenaeus cites 2 Jn, but there is no evidence for the circulation of 3 Jn in the 2nd cent. The Muratorian Fragment lists two Johannine letters (1 –2 Jn?). Origen accepted a short epistle by John and said that perhaps John left two more epistles, although their authenticity was denied by some, and that together they totaled no more than 100 lines (Eusebius, *Hist.* 6.25, 10; GCS 9/2.578). A century later, Eusebius listed 2–3 Jn among the disputed books, and a continuing dispute about these epistles is witnessed in the North African Canon of 360. Ultimately, like the other disputed Catholic Epistles, they were accepted in the Lat and Gk churches in the late 4th cent., but not fully in the Syrian church.

80 Of all the Catholic Epistles, *2 Peter* has the poorest record of acceptance. There is no clear reference to the epistle before the time of Origen who says that Peter left "one acknowledged epistle and possibly two, although this is doubtful" (Eusebius, *Hist.* 6.25, 9; GCS 9/2.578). Disputes about 2 Pt are recorded by Eusebius and are implicit in the North African Canon of 360. Jerome accepted it, although he knew there were doubts. It was accepted at the same time as were the other disputed Catholic Epistles.

81 **(III) Problems about the Formation of the Canon.** We have seen that by 200, the Gospels, the Pauline epistles, Acts, 1 Pt, and 1 Jn had come into general acceptance; and that by the end of the 4th cent. in the Lat and Gk churches there was general acceptance of the 27-book canon of the NT. However, this development cloaks some difficulties that we must now discuss.

(A) Concept of a New Testament. Although in the 2nd cent. the Pauline epistles and then the Gospels came into acceptance, just when did this acceptance mean that Christian writings were being put on a par with the Jewish Scriptures? When did the concept of a New Testament emerge? In 2 Pt 3:16 (*ca.* 100–125?), we find writings of Paul put on a par with "the other Scriptures," but we are not certain that this indicates total equality with the OT. By the mid-2nd cent. Justin (*Apol.* 1.67) witnesses to the fact that the Gospels and the writings of the apostles were being read in conjunction with the OT at Christian liturgical services. About the same time 2 *Clem.* 4 cites Is and then Mt as "another Scripture." Probably, however, it was Marcion, with his rejection of the OT in favor of a truncated collection of 10 Pauline epistles and Lk, who brought to the fore by way of opposition the belief that the Christian writings form a unity with the OT. In listing the Jewish Scriptures *ca.* 170, Melito of Sardis (Eusebius, *Hist.* 4.26, 14; GCS 9/1.388) speaks of them as the books of the *Old* Testament, seeming to imply the idea of a New Testament. Tertullian, *ca.* 200, is the first one to use the actual phrase "New Testament." This coincides with the appearance of lists of NT books, e.g., the Muratorian Fragment (before 200?) and Origen's list—a sign that the concept of a collection of Christian Scriptures has taken hold.

82 **(B) Value of Patristic Citations.** In discussing the formation of the NT, we frequently resorted to citations of a NT book by one of the Fathers to show that a given book was known and used with some authority. Indeed, patristic citations and lists of books are the two main criteria for judgment of the canon. Yet neither criterion is totally satisfactory. For instance, when Clement of Rome, or Ignatius, or Polycarp cited a book that ultimately was recognized as canonical, just what authority was he giving to this book, since we do not know that the concept of either a NT or a canon was yet formulated? Past discussions often simply assumed that these early Fathers had a concept of canonical and non-canonical. And, indeed, even later when there was a concept of a NT, we find strange phenomena in patristic citations. Origen cited 2 Pt at least 6 times; yet in his canonical list (Eusebius, *Hist.* 6.25, 8; GCS 9/2.578), he doubted whether 2 Pt should be included. In other words, even a 3rd-cent. patristic citation of a book ultimately accepted as canonical does not mean that the Father thought it canonical. On the other hand, absence of a citation of a NT book (e.g., during the 2nd cent.) does not necessarily mean that the Fathers did not know the book or did not consider it of value. There would be little occasion to cite some of the shorter NT works like Phlm and 2–3 Jn.

83 We have already mentioned some apocryphal gospels, epistles, and acts that received acceptance for a certain period. We should note that the subapostolic writings, like *1–2 Clem.*, *Didache*, *Hermas*, and *Barnabas*, continued to be considered as Scripture even into the 4th and 5th cents. The Alexandrian Fathers seem to have thought of *1 Clem* as Scripture. The 4th-cent. Codex Sinaiticus contained, along with the books we consider canonical, *Barnabas* and *Hermas*. The 5th-cent. Codex Alexandrinus had *1–2 Clem.* And we can see why such works were highly valued. Many of them bore names of disciples of the apostles, e.g., Barnabas was a friend of Paul; Clement was thought to be the Clement mentioned in Phil 4:3 and a successor of Peter at Rome. Moreover, very early subapostolic works, like *1 Clem* and *Didache*, may well have been written before a NT work like 2 Pt. The real difficulty is not why such works were thought of as canonical, but why the Church did not finally accept them as canonical.

84 **(C) Value of the Early Lists.** If patristic citations tell us nothing about canonicity in the strict sense, but only that a book was thought worthy of respect, the lists are more helpful. The formation of a list implies acceptance of a book so listed as a particular type of book, and, since the lists of NT books are at times coupled with lists of OT books, acceptance as Scripture. But past discussions of the canon have sometimes neglected to consider that a list may represent no more than the author's own judgment or the custom of his local church. The fact that lists do not agree from area to area weakens their witness to universal Church practice.

What is thought to be our earliest list, the Muratorian Fragment (Hennecke, *NTA* 1, 42–45), considered representative of Roman usage in the late 2nd cent., does not include 1–2 Pt, Jas, and one Johannine epistle; but it does include Wis (as a NT book!) and the *Apocalypse of Peter*, about which, it admits, there is controversy. In a paper at the 1965 Oxford NT Congress, A. C. Sundberg questioned the usual dating of this fragment and suggested that it belongs in the 4th cent. This would mean that an incomplete canon perdured at Rome even later than formerly thought. Origen's list in the 3rd cent. (Eusebius, *Hist.* 6.25, 3–14; GCS 9/2.576–78) raises doubt about 2 Pt and two Johannine epistles. In the early 4th cent. we have two Eastern canons from Eusebius and Cyril of Jerusalem and two slightly later Lat canons (North African presumably), and these do not agree. Eusebius explicitly distinguishes between recognized, disputed, and spurious books (*Hist.* 3.25; GCS 9/1.250–52). For instance, he lists Jas and Jude as disputed; yet elsewhere (2.23, 25; GCS 9/1.174) he states that they have been used regularly in many churches, thereby testifying that his list does not represent universal usage. Only with the lists of the late 4th cent., namely those from Athanasius, Augustine, and the councils of Hippo (393) and Carthage (397) do we come to evidence of common agreement in much of the Church. As we have already indicated, however, there remain exceptions, e.g., the Codex Alexandrinus with its noncanonical inclusions, and the Quinsextine council (Trullo II of 692), which includes a list of 26 books (no Ap) from Gregory Nazianzen, as well as another list that raises doubt about Heb, four Catholic Epistles, and Ap.

85 **(D) Oriental Churches.** In the East, the picture remained more complex. In the 4th cent. when the Greeks and Latins were beginning to move toward a standard canon of 27 books, the NT of the Syrian church included the *Diatessaron* (not the four Gospels), Acts, and 15 Pauline epistles (including Heb and *3 Cor*). Thus a canon of 17 books was used by Ephraem (320–373) and given as authoritative in the *Doctrine of Addai* (*ca.* 370) at Edessa. In the early 5th cent. the four Gospels replaced the *Diatessaron* (→ Texts, 69:90), *3 Cor* was omitted, and three of the Catholic Epistles (Jas, 1 Pt, 1 Jn) won acceptance. The Syrian church, however, never fully accepted the other Catholic Epistles or Ap. At the other extreme, the Ethiopian church seems to have had a canon of 35 books, the additional eight consisting of decrees, called the Synodus, and some Clementine writings. Moreover, one may legitimately wonder whether such lists represented universal practice in the respective churches.

These considerations should make it clear to the student just how much one is generalizing when he speaks about *the* NT canon of the early Church.

86 **(IV) The Canon in the Reformation.** The humanists of the 16th cent. revived the earlier discussion about certain NT books. Erasmus was censured by the theological faculty of the Sorbonne for repeating without refutation earlier doubts about the apostolic origins of Heb, Jas, 2 Pt, 2–3 Jn, and Ap. Cardinal Cajetan appears to have shared Erasmus' reservations about these books.

Luther felt that the NT books had to be graded, anticipating the modern discussion of the canon within the canon (→ 92 below). He gave secondary rank to Heb, Jas, Jude, and Ap, situating them at the end of his translation following those books that he considered "the true and certain, main books of the New Testament." Carlstadt too believed the books of the NT to be of different dignity, putting the disputed books in third place. Oecolampadius expressed himself thus: "In the NT we receive four Gospels with the Acts of the Apostles and fourteen epistles, together with the Apocalypse, although we do not compare the Apocalypse, the epistles of James and Jude and 2 Peter and 2 and 3 John with the rest." Tyndale's NT (1525) followed Luther's arrangement of the NT books, but in subsequent English Bibles the more traditional order was restored.

ENDURING PROBLEMS IN CANONICITY

87 **(I) Authorship and Canonicity.** We have seen that in the early Church judgment on the canonicity of books was often determined by traditions about authorship. The fact that today we accept the canon that emerged from such judgments does not mean that we are bound to accept the reasoning behind the judgments. In fact, all modern scholars agree that the Fathers were often quite wrong about the authorship of biblical books. Authorship is a historical question to be settled by scientific criteria of style and content; it is not a religious question in the same way that recognition of inspiration is. Thus, the Church has wisely refrained from dogmatic statements about the authorship of sacred books. The decrees of the Pontifical Biblical Commission between 1905 and 1915 which dealt with authorship were not dogmatic but precautionary, and subsequently Catholic scholars have been given complete freedom with regard to these decrees (→ Church Pronouncements, 72:25). Within 50 years after they were issued, these decrees were no longer in harmony with the consensus of scholars about authorship—a good indication of the complexities of the problem and the danger of taking official positions on it.

88 In evaluating the question of biblical authorship, we must recognize that pseudonymity (attributing a book to someone else, usually someone of renown) was more acceptable in ancient literary circles than it is today. It is a *fact* that divine inspiration does not preclude pseudonymity; for Moses simply did not write all that is attributed to him in Dt, David did not write all the Pss attributed to him, and Solomon did not write Eccl and Wis, internal claims notwithstanding. We should therefore not be reluctant to apply the principle of pseudonymity to the NT where there are good reasons for doing so. The instances of Mt and 2 Pt seem clear; the instances of the Pastorals, 1 Pt, Jas, and Jude are debatable. (Hebrews is not really pseudonymous but has been wrongly attributed to Paul in tradition.)

89 We should recognize that pseudonymity is intimately related to the broad sense of authorship implied in the biblical attributions of books. We may distinguish at least five different types of biblical authorship. *First*, a man was considered the author if he wrote a book with his own hand—Luke perhaps. *Second*, a man was still considered the author if he dictated the book to a scribe who copied slavishly. This was not a popular way of composing for it was tiring, as is borne out by some Pauline letters (→ NT Epistles, 47:19). We may note that these first two degrees of authorship would merit that designation in modern parlance too. *Third*, a man was considered the author if he supplied the ideas and someone else was the "ghost writer." This may have been the case with Jas, written in perfect Greek, but attributed to a Galilean peasant whose native tongue was Aramaic. By modern standards, this type of authorship demands acknowledgement of the collaborating writer. *Fourth*, a man was considered the author if the work was written by his disciples whose thoughts were guided both by the master's words and by his spirit. (This could hold true even if the work appeared a long time after the master's death.) Such authorship is exemplified in the composition of parts of the books of Is and Jer; it is probably responsible for some of the Johannine works, and perhaps for Mt and 2 Pt. By modern standards this would not be authorship. *Fifth*, in the broadest sense a man was considered the author if a work was written in the literary tradition for which he was famous. Thus, Moses was the lawgiver; and so the whole Law (Pentateuch) could be attributed to him as author, even though the final work did not come into being until some 800 years after his death. The Davidic authorship of the Pss and the Solomonic authorship of the Wisdom Literature fall into this category. In modern terms, this would be patronage rather than authorship. Pseudonymity enters into these last two classes of authorship.

(Aland, K., "The Problem of Anonymity and Pseudonymity in Christian Literature of the First Two Centuries," *The Authorship and Integrity of the New Testament* [SPCK Theol. Coll. 4; London, 1965] 1–13. Guthrie, D., "The Development of the Idea of Canonical Pseudonymity in New Testament Criticism," *ibid.*, 14–39. Brockington, H., "The Problem of Pseudonymity," *JTS* 4 [1953] 15–22.)

90 **(II) The Finality of the Canon of Trent.** This Council was lucidly clear as to which books, along with their parts, should be accepted as canonical and inspired. But Trent did not say that these were the only inspired books; and the question is sometimes raised whether some lost books may have been inspired, e.g., lost Pauline writings. (For the possible role of chance in the preservation of biblical books, → 54 above.) What judgment about inspiration would the Church render if a lost epistle of Paul were to be discovered today? The problem becomes academic when we realize that the only criterion for inspiration found applicable at Trent was the long use of the books of Scripture in the Church. Since a newly discovered book would hardly have been in long use, what could be the Church's criterion for determining inspiration? Pauline authorship would really not be sufficient, for if lack of apostolic authorship does not exclude inspiration, the existence of apostolic authorship should not automatically imply it. A less romantic problem is that of the possible inspiration of ancient works considered sacred by NT writers or by the early Fathers, but not accepted into the canon of Trent (*Enoch*, *Didache*, etc.). By virtue of not having been accepted at Trent, today these books no longer have a claim to continuous use as Scripture in the Church; and almost certainly they will never be recognized as inspired. But perhaps we should put more emphasis upon the broader criteria of the first two Christian centuries, and thus win back for these books a more serious evaluation as important witnesses to God's salvific action in the intertestamental and immediately post-testamental periods.

91 **(III) The Vulgate and Canonicity.** Trent insisted upon its list of books "as sacred and canonical in their entirety, *with all their parts*, according to the text usually read in the Catholic Church and as they are in the ancient Latin Vulgate" (DS 1504). It is well known that the Council Fathers of Trent and the authorities in Rome who approved the decree were aware that there were errors in the Vg translation and that not all copies of the Vg were in agreement (on the authority of the Vg see the clarification of *Divino Afflante Spiritu*; → Church Pronouncements, 72:20). However, the very lack of agreement in Vg mss. makes judgment on "the parts" of the sacred books quite difficult. Even the Sixto-Clementine Vg (1592), the official Vg of the Church produced in answer to Trent's request for a carefully edited Vg, leaves much to be desired by modern standards; and in many places it is not faithful to Jerome's original Vg (→ Texts, 68:108–10). Which Vg is to serve as a guide when we raise the question of whether certain passages or verses are canonical Scripture?

Since both Jerome's Vg and the Sixto-Clementine Vg contained the long ending of Mk and the pericope of the adulteress (Jn 7:53–8:11), Catholic scholars have no real problem in accepting these passages as Scripture (although they were not originally parts of their respective Gospels and were added at a much later period—once again the distinction between canonicity and authorship). But in other instances, where the Sixto-Clementine Vg has passages that Jerome's Vg did not have (Jn 5:4, the angel stirring the waters; 1 Jn 5:7–8, the Johannine comma), the problem of acceptance should be settled on the grounds of scholarship rather than by any mechanical application of the principle of Trent, which was not meant to solve all difficulties or to end scholarly discussion. Nor does the Tridentine decree apply to variant readings. Since we know that the Vg, even Jerome's, is not necessarily an authority in textual criticism, Catholics must solve textual problems as others do, namely by the laws of criticism. Trent meant only to give us a general guide to the canonicity of books and of larger passages of Scripture.

92 **(IV) The Canon Within the Canon.** As mentioned above (→ 86), the Reformation raised acutely the question of degrees of canonicity. Granted that all books of Scripture are inspired, are some more authoritative than others? It is quite obvious that some are of more value than others, and that some treat more directly of formal religious questions than others do. It is also obvious that some books claim to be more directly from God than others do; e.g., the prophets claim to convey the word of God that came to them, whereas the wisdom writers, although inspired, seem to be giving us the fruit of their own human experience. Finally, it is a fact that the Church in her liturgy uses some biblical books extensively and others very seldom, thus forming an "actual canon" within the formal canon. But this is not the same as the question of whether inspired biblical books have different authority.

93 This question has become more acute as we have come gradually to recognize that there are dissimilar outlooks and differing theologies in the books of Scripture. When these differences exist between the two Testaments, one can solve them in terms of new revelation, e.g., Job's formal and explicit denial of an afterlife (14:7–22), as contrasted with Jesus' clear affirmation of it (Mk 12:26–27). But the solution is not so simple when we see that even within the NT, works of roughly the same period contain divergent theologies. The outlook on the Law in Rom certainly is not the same as the outlook in Mt 5:18. One may explain that there is no contradiction between Rom 3:28 ("a man is justified by faith apart from the works of the Law") and Jas 2:24 ("a man is justified by works and not by faith alone"), but one can scarcely imagine that Paul's attitude was the same as that of James. We have often glossed over this problem by imagining that there was a uniform and harmonious development of theological understanding from the time of Pentecost to the end of the apostolic era, but the NT simply does not support such a view (see R. E. Brown, *NovT* 6 [1963] 298–308 or *New Testament Essays* [Milwaukee, 1965] 36–47). But then the question arises: If there are two divergent views in the NT, which one is to be considered authoritative? Within the canon of Scripture and in particular within the NT, what is the canon or rule of what we are to believe?

94 Modern German Protestant NT scholars have made this a major question. (For them the problem is even more acute since they press divergencies, like the one between Jas and Rom, to the point of contradiction, whereas a Catholic understanding of the inspiration of Scripture would seem to preclude contradictions.) If we focus upon the topic of *early Catholicism* in the NT, we can see the importance of the question of the canon within the canon. "Early Catholicism" designates the initial stages of sacramentalism, hierarchy, ordination, dogma—in short, the beginning of the distinctive features of *Catholic* Christianity. Von Harnack maintained that in the NT there was no early Catholicism; rather, such theology and Church organization were a 2nd-cent. development distorting the pristine evangelical character of Christianity (to which the Reformation returned—*What Is Christianity?* [orig. 1900; Harper Torchbook ed., N.Y., 1957] 190ff.). Today it is increasingly recognized by Protestants, like E. Käsemann (→ Modern NT Criticism, 41:65), that there is "early Catholicism" in the NT itself, particularly in 2 Pt, the Pastorals, and Acts. If so, are these early Catholic developments normative for Christianity? Käsemann's solution has been to fall back on the canon within the canon, or "the center of the NT." Just as Paul distinguished between the letter and the Spirit (2 Cor 3), so the Christian cannot make an infallible authority out of the canonical NT but must distinguish the real Spirit within the NT. For Käsemann this is not found in such deutero-Pauline writings as the Pastorals with their early Catholicism, but in the Great Letters such as Gal and Rom with their spirit of justification by faith. Here is the really authoritative teaching.

95 A Catholic answer has been given by H. Küng (*Structures of the Church* [N.Y., 1964] 151–69); he accuses Käsemann of judging canonicity on the basis of an a priori Protestant bias. Küng reasons that, if there is early Catholicism in the NT, then only Catholics can accept the whole NT. The theory of a canon within the canon means an implicit rejection of some books. The answer may not be so simple, however, and all we shall attempt to do here is to make some observations. If Roman Catholics accept the "early Catholic" developments in the later NT books and regard them as normative for Christianity, are they not to some extent establishing a canon within a canon; for are they not implicitly rejecting the looser Church organization of the primitive period and the less dogmatic theology of the earlier days? In other words, to Käsemann's reduced canon, which depends heavily on the more pristine NT works, are Catholics not opposing a canon consisting of the more developed NT works?

Perhaps we are approaching the problem in the wrong terms when we speak of preferring later books to earlier books. If some of the features of early Catholicism, prominent in the later books of the NT, have become characteristic of the Roman Catholic Church, it was not because the Church consciously preferred one group of NT books over the other. Rather it was because features such as sacramentalism, hierarchy, and dogma were meaningful within the life of the Church. In a process of development guided by the Spirit, the Church made these features a part of herself, so that what was truly normative was not a group of writings but the Spirit acting within the living Church. It was Church usage that led Trent to determine which books of Scripture should be accepted as canonical; so also it is Church usage that determines the degree of normative authority (canonicity) to be attributed to a NT practice or doctrine.

96 Yet we must qualify this understanding of Church usage as a normative factor. If the Spirit of God has guided the Church in her usage, there has been also a human factor in the historical process of Christian development, so that we cannot simply equate Church usage with the will of God. Scripture can be a great help in distinguishing between what is of the Spirit and what is human in the development of Church usage. Thus we get a two-sided picture: Church usage is a guide to what is normative in Scripture; yet in a way the Church itself stands under the judgment of Scripture ("This teaching office [of the Church] is not above the word of God, but serves it," Vatican II, *De Revelatione*, 2:10). In particular, the Church must constantly reassess her usage in light of those biblical theologies that she has *not* followed in order to be certain that what God meant to teach her through such theological views will not be lost. For example, if the Church has chosen to follow as normative the ecclesiastical structure attested in the Pastorals (bishop/presbyters, deacons), she must ask herself does she continue to do proportionate justice to the charismatic and freer spirit of the earlier period. A choice between the two was necessary and this choice was guided by the Spirit of God; but the structure that was not chosen still has something to teach the Church and can serve as a modifying corrective on the choice that was made. Only thus is the Church faithful to the whole NT. In NT times the Church was ecumenical enough to embrace those who, while sharing the one faith, held very different theological views. The Church of today can be no less ecumenical.

97 The recognition that in practice the Church does not accept the whole NT as equally normative is related to the problem of distinguishing between the temporal limitations of the biblical writers and the divine revelation they were conveying. The biblical writers spoke as men of their times, and not all their religious statements have enduring value. For instance, the reader of the Bible must exercise discretion about apocalyptic statements: If the NT writers describe the future coming of the Lord in terms of trumpet blasts and celestial cataclysms, such descriptions do not necessarily constitute revelation to be believed. The problem of distinguishing between what is revelation and what is not becomes acute when we turn to more delicate topics. In the matter of "original sin," how much revelation and how much time-conditioned 1st-cent. outlook do we find in Paul's picture (Rom 5) of an individual Adam who committed a sin that brought death to all men? Careful exegesis can uncover what Paul thought; but only the Church, guided by and guiding scholarly investigation, can tell us how much of Paul's thought is God's revelation for his people.

Perhaps a word of caution is called for here. The realization that there is much in Scripture that reflects the time-conditioned mentality of its authors should not lead readers to assume that they can quickly or easily recognize this mentality. Often there is the tendency to think that whatever in the Bible does not agree with the spirit of modern times can be dismissed as time-conditioned and irrelevant. For instance, some would do away with all divine moral imperatives on the principle that man is the sole judge of morality and that nothing is wrong in itself; they would reduce all God's ethical commands in the Bible to reflections of the customs of the times. Such generalizations are more often based on inclination than on careful exegesis and have the effect of stripping Scripture of its corrective value. A good practical rule for avoiding self-deception in this matter is to pay more attention to Scripture when it disagrees with what we want to hear than when it agrees. When the Bible disagrees with the spirit of our times, it is not always because the biblical authors are giving voice to a limited, out-of-date religious view—frequently it is because God's ways are not our ways.

(Elliott, J. H., "The New Testament Is Catholic: A Reevaluation of *sola scriptura*," *Una Sancta* 23 [1966]3–18. Käsemann, E., "The Canon of the New Testament and the Unity of the Church," *Essays on New Testament Themes* [SBT 41; London, 1964]. Kümmel, W. G., "Notwendigkeit und Grenze des neutestamentlichen Kanons," *ZThK* 47 [1950] 277–313. Marxsen, W., *Der "Frühkatholizismus" im Neuen Testament* [Neukirchen, 1958].)

68

APOCRYPHA; DEAD SEA SCROLLS; OTHER JEWISH LITERATURE

Raymond E. Brown, S.S.

1 GENERAL OUTLINE

APOCRYPHA

BIBLIOGRAPHY

2 **Jewish Apocrypha:** Bloch, J., *On the Apocalyptic in Judaism* (*JQR* Monograph 2; Phila., 1952). Bonsirven, J., *La Bible apocryphe* (Paris, 1953). Charles, R. H., *APOT; Religious Development between the Old and the New Testaments* (N.Y., 1914). Denis, A. M., *Introduction aux pseudépigraphes grecs de l'Ancien Testament* (Leiden, 1967). Metzger, B. M., *An Introduction to the Apocrypha* (N.Y., 1957). Milik, J. T., *Ten Years of Discovery in the Wilderness of Judaea* (SBT 26; London, 1959). Oesterley, W. O. E., *An Introduction to the Books of the Apocrypha* (N.Y., 1935). Pfeiffer, R. H., *History of New Testament Times with an Introduction to the Apocrypha* (N.Y., 1949). Rowley, H. H., *The Relevance of Apocalyptic* (3rd ed.; London, 1963); *Jewish Apocalyptic and the Dead Sea Scrolls* (London, 1957). Russell, D. S., *Between the Testaments* (London, 1960); *The Method and Message of Jewish Apocalyptic* (Phila., 1964). For a report on the planned series, *Pseudepigrapha Veteris Testamenti Graece*, see A. M. Denis and M. de Jonge, *NovT* 7 (1965) 320–28.

3 **Christian Apocrypha:** Amiot, F., *Évangiles apocryphes* (Paris, 1952). De Santos Otero, A., *Los evangelios apócrifos* (Madrid, 1956). Dunkerley, R., *Beyond the Gospels* (Pelican paperback; Baltimore, 1957). Hennecke, *NTA*. James, M. R., *The Apocryphal New Testament* (Oxford, 1953). Jeremias, J., *Unknown Sayings of Jesus* (2nd ed.; London, 1964). Quasten, J., *Patrology* (Westminster, Md., 1950) 1, 106–57. Resch, A., *Agrapha* (TU 15, 3–4; 2nd ed.; Leipzig, 1906).

JEWISH APOCRYPHA

4 **(I) The Term "Apocrypha."** The rabbis knew of "Outside Books" (*ḥîṣônîm*), i.e., books outside the sacred collection and used by heretics and Samaritans. However, the term "apocrypha" that has come to designate the books being discussed here, derives from the Gk *apokryphos*, "hidden." Originally, the import of the term may have been complimentary in that the term was applied to sacred books whose contents were too exalted to be made available to the general public. In Dn 12:9–10 we hear of words that are shut up until the end of time—words that the wise shall understand and the wicked shall not. In addition, *4 Ezra* 14:44ff. mentions 94 books, of which 24 (the OT) were to be published and 70 were to be delivered only to the wise among the people (= apocrypha). Gradually, the term "apocrypha" took on a pejorative connotation, for the orthodoxy of these hidden books was often questionable. Origen (*Comm. in Matt.* 10.18; PG 13.881) distinguished between books that were to be read in public worship and apocryphal books. Because these secret books were often preserved or even composed in heretical circles, several Church Fathers came to use the term "apocryphal" for heretical works forbidden to be read. By Jerome's time (*ca.* 400), "apocryphal" had taken on the more neutral connotation of noncanonical, and that is how we use it here.

5 In Protestant parlance, "the Apocrypha" designate 15 works, all but one of which are Jewish in origin and found in the LXX (parts of *2 Esdras* are Christian and Latin in origin). Although some of them were composed in Palestine in Aramaic or Hebrew, they were not accepted into the Jewish canon formed late in the 2nd cent. AD (→ Canonicity, 67:31–35). The Reformers, influenced by the Jewish canon of the OT, did not consider these books on a par with the rest of the Scriptures; thus the custom arose of making the Apocrypha a separate section in the Protestant Bible, or sometimes even of omitting them entirely (→ Canonicity, 67:44–46). The Catholic view, expressed as a doctrine of faith at the Council of Trent, is that 12 of these 15 works (in a different enumeration, however) are canonical Scripture; they are called the Deuterocanonical Books (→ Canonicity, 67:21, 42–43). The three books of the Protestant Apocrypha that are not accepted by Catholics are *1–2 Esdras* and the *Prayer of Manasseh*.

6 In Catholic parlance, the term "apocrypha" has come to designate ancient Jewish or Christian books from the biblical period (or pretending to be from the biblical period) that have not been accepted as genuine Scripture by the Church. Recent discoveries of hitherto lost ancient books have greatly extended the range covered by the term. If the books that Catholics call deuterocanonical are called the Apocrypha by Protestants, the apocrypha (at least those of Jewish origin) of which we now speak are often called pseudepigrapha by Protestants, whence the title of R. H. Charles' famous collection, *The Apocrypha and Pseudepigrapha of the Old Testament* (= *APOT*—for pseudepigraphy or pseudonymity, → Canonicity, 67:88–89). Actually, neither designation for these noncanonical Jewish works is completely satisfactory: The term "apocrypha" suggests that they deal with secrets or matters esoteric, whereas several of them are relatively unpretentious history (*1 Esdras*); "pseudepigrapha" is applicable only to the books that falsely present themselves as having been written by a well-known ancient figure, e.g., the Enoch and Baruch literature. However, for want of a better term, we shall henceforth use the term "apocrypha" in the sense common among Catholics. The Deuterocanonical Books are, of course, commented upon among the other books of Scripture (→ Daniel, 26:8,35; → 1–2 Maccabees, 27:3; → Sirach, 33:6; → Wisdom, 34:2; → Baruch, 37:3–6; → Tobit, Judith, Esther, 38:2,17,29–30).

7 **(II) The Enoch Literature.** Enoch ("Henoch" in the AV) was the father of Methuselah: "Enoch walked with God; and then he was no longer, for God took him" (Gn 5:24). The idea that Enoch had been taken to heaven (also Sir 44:16; 49:14) produced much legend about him, and his life span of 365 years provoked astronomical speculations. (See H. Odeberg, *ThDNT* 2, 556–59.) The Enoch legend is also found in *Jub* 4:17–25; 7:38; 10:17; 19:24–27; 21:10.

8 **(A) Hebrew and Slavonic Books.** There are three books of Enoch of which we shall first mention the two of lesser importance.

(a) HEBREW ENOCH OR 3 ENOCH. This work is a mystical apocalypse. Odeberg dates it to the 2nd–3rd cents. AD; G.G. Scholem, an expert on Jewish mysticism, dates it even later to the medieval period (*Major Trends in Jewish Mysticism* [N.Y., 1941] 45). It has affinities to *2 Enoch*.

(b) SLAVONIC ENOCH OR 2 ENOCH. Also called *The Book of the Secrets of Enoch*. There are two forms of the text, of which the shorter is more ancient. The work is preserved in Slavonic copies of the 16th–17th cents.; the general supposition is that the original, at least of the shorter form, was in Greek. Charles thought that it was written *ca.* AD 50 and included it in *APOT* 2, 425–64. On the basis of astronomical evidence, however, J. K. Fotheringham attacked Charles' position in a series of articles in *JTS* (20, 22, 23 [1919, 1921, 1922]), arguing for a date no earlier than the 7th cent. AD. According to A. Vaillant, who edited the Slavonic text with a French translation (Paris, 1952), the shorter form was Christian in origin. One of the interesting features is the reference to the millennium in 33:1–2: A duration of 7000 years is given to world history, and the eighth 1000-year period marks the millennium (→ Apocalypse, 64:83–84).

9 **(B) Ethiopic Enoch.** Also known as *1 Enoch*—this is the book usually meant when "Enoch" is referred to without any specification.

(a) TEXT AND CONTENT. The original Aram text of this book was lost, but fragments of some ten copies have now appeared among the QL, to be published in DJD (J. T. Milik, *Ten Years*, 32–34). Although the whole book is preserved only in Ethiopic, there are extensive Gk fragments and a short Lat fragment. Charles, *The Ethiopic Version of Enoch* (Oxford, 1906), published a critical Ethiopic text, along with what was then available of the Gk fragments (chs. 1–32) and the Lat fragment (ch. 106). See Eng translation in *APOT* 2, 188–281. Subsequent Gk papyrus finds (chs. 97–104, 106–107) were published by C. Bonner, *The Last Chapters of Enoch in Greek* (London, 1937).

The book is not homogeneous; rather, it is a collection of literature. Charles (*APOT* 2, 163) posited an earlier *Book of Noah* as a source for certain parts of *Enoch* (6–11, 54–55, 65–69, 106–107; see N. Schmidt, *Oriental Studies Dedicated to P. Haupt* [Baltimore, 1926] 11–23.) We now have some evidence for a Noah literature at Qumran, for 1Q*19*, "Book of Noah," has parallels to *Enoch* 8:4–9:4; 106. (See also J. A. Fitzmyer, *CBQ* 27 [1965] 371.) Charles dated the various parts of *Enoch* to a period from before 161 to 64 BC. Rowley (*Relevance*, 93–99) discusses the various opinions about dating. The mss. discovered at Qumran assure pre-Christian origins for most of the components of the book.

10 Charles distinguishes five sections of *Enoch:*

SECTION ONE (chs. 1–36). There is a prediction of final judgment in 1–5; it is explained to Enoch that mankind has been corrupted by fallen angels who are doomed (6–16). Angelic guides take Enoch on a tour through another world where he sees Sheol and the Garden of Righteousness (17–36). For the Qumran Aram text of *Enoch* 30–32, see *RB* 65 (1958) 71.

SECTION TWO (chs. 37–71). These are the "parables" concerning the Son of Man that were imparted to Enoch. Here "parable" (if that is the correct translation of Ethiopic *mesālē*) refers to a type of elaborate discourse in the form of a vision, a prophecy, or a poem (*APOT* 2, 209). The First Parable (38–44) concerns the coming judgment and imparts some astronomical secrets. The Second Parable (45–57) concerns the Head of Days (cf. Dn 7:9 and the "Ancient of Days") and the Son of Man (Dn 7:13), the Elect One. The Third Parable (58–69) concerns the blessedness of the saints and judgment by the Elect One.

SECTION THREE (chs. 72–82). This is an astronomical section. Chapter 80 predicts the disorder of the heavenly bodies at judgment; ch. 82 contains a solar calendar that is similar to that in use at Qumran (→ 18 below).

SECTION FOUR (chs. 83–90). Two dream visions. The first concerns the deluge that will come to punish the world (83–84). The second (85–90) is an animal allegory of the history of the world from the creation to the end time in which the author is living (seemingly Maccabean times). We read of the New Jerusalem and of the Messiah who appears under the guise of an animal (the Ethiopic of the crucial text 90:38 is corrupt; Charles thinks the original had "lamb," but Boismard, *RB* 62 [1965] 110–12, argues for "ram"—the point is important for Jn 1:29, "the Lamb of God").

SECTION FIVE (chs. 91–108). The part that contains Enoch's admonitions (91–104) has incorporated into it an apocalypse of weeks (93, 91). Chapter 105 is a separate fragment dealing with God and the Messiah; it is missing in Bonner's Gk text. The birth of Noah is described in 106–107; 108 is an independent addition.

11 Five Aram mss. from Qumran correspond partially to Sections One and Four, which must have been joined originally, forming a separate work of astronomical interest. Four Aram mss. of Section Three show that this section may at one time have been separate. Section Five also circulated separately, for one Qumran ms. gives its original opening lines. Curiously, Section Two is not represented at Qumran; this has led Milik to suggest that it is late (1st–2nd cents. AD) and perhaps composed by Jewish Christians. However, the absence of fragments may be accidental (see J. Albertson, *JBL* 78 [1959] 133–41; H. E. Robbins, *ibid.*, 347–50). Other scholars, among them M. Black, suggest that Section Two is pre-Christian, with Christian editing.

12 (b) HISTORY OF THE BOOK. We may reconstruct that the history of the Enoch literature began in the period 200–160 BC, contemporary roughly with Dn and the Maccabean struggles. Sections One and Four, and probably part of Five, belong to this period. Although most of the Enoch literature had been composed before the Christian era, editing into one book came later. The Qumran community obviously considered *Enoch* sacred literature, as did the author of Jude, who in v. 14 cites *Enoch* 1:9. Charles believes that by way of implicit citation *Enoch* had more influence on the NT than did any other work of the apocrypha. (For Lk and *Enoch*, see S. Aalen, *NTS* 13 [1966–67] 1–13.) In *APOT* 2, 180–81, Charles gives a list of NT parallels; see also J. Jeremias, *ZNW* 38 (1939) 115–24.

After the destruction of the Temple in AD 70 and after a series of unsuccessful messianic movements, the rabbis became suspicious of apocalyptic works with their rousing dreams of the future. Consequently, *Enoch* gradually fell out of favor in Judaism. It was translated from Aramaic into Greek and influenced some early Christian works, e.g., *Barnabas*, and the writings of Irenaeus. Tertullian regarded it as Scripture, but it was rejected by Hilary, Augustine, and Jerome. *Apostolic Constitutions* 6.16 explicitly condemns it. The Greek text of *Enoch* disappeared and, before the discoveries of the last 100 years, was known only through citations by George Syncellus, the Byzantine chronicler. Around the year 500 *Enoch* was translated into Ethiopic and preserved in the Ethiopian Church. Not until 1773, when James Bruce brought the Ethiopic version to Europe, did the West see *Enoch*. The first edition was published in 1821;

A. Dillmann (*Das Buch Henoch* [1853]) made the chapter divisions.

13 (c) IMPORTANT TEACHING. As a book of APOCALYPTIC, *Enoch* has parallels with Dn, especially in Section Four. The Daniel literature, which was larger than our biblical book, is from the same period as the Enoch literature. The future life in *Enoch* is described in terms of earthly pleasure, including marriage and children (10:17); we see Jesus' reaction to this concept in Mk 12:18–27. In *Enoch*, Sheol is no longer a place for all the dead, but has moved closer to our concept of hell, i.e., a place of punishment for the wicked (63:10). In *Enoch* 22, although the good and the bad are together in Sheol, the good are happy whereas the bad suffer. For the eschatology of Section Two, see M. Black, *JTS* 3 (1952) 1–10.

14 The ANGELOLOGY of *Enoch* is well developed (C. Kaplan, *AnglTR* 12 [1930] 423–37). Later Christian legends have taken angelic names from those *Enoch* gives to angels, good and bad, e.g., Uriel, the fourth archangel (after the three "biblical" angels: Gabriel and Michael in Dn 8:16; 10:13; Raphael in Tb), is a common figure in *Enoch*. The fallen angels of Section One are those that sinned with women (*Enoch* 6–9 is an elaboration of Gn 6:1–4), introducing them to evil mysteries like enchantments, astrology, weapons, and cosmetics. (For the contribution of *Enoch* to the biblical concept of mystery, see *CBQ* 20 [1958] 427–33.) This was one of the Jewish theories of "original sin." The offspring of this evil union were destroyed by the flood, but their spirits haunt the earth and cause corruption. Satan is the demon to whom the wicked angels are subject (54:6), but more than one angel acts as a satan or adversary (the pl. appears in 40:7). The satan who tempted Eve was Gadreel (69:6), while in Section One the chief evil angel is Azazel (→ Religious Institutions, 76:157).

15 The figure of the SON OF MAN has been interpreted by many scholars as background for Jesus' use of the title (→ Aspects NT Thought, 78:28–30). In Dn 7:13 "a son of man" is a symbolic figure standing for the saintly people of Israel, but in *Enoch* the Son of Man is a heavenly individual who accompanies God (46:3). Named by God before creation (48:2–3), his destiny is to support the just and to be a light to the Gentiles (48:4). Thus he is God's Chosen, or Elect One, who is filled with the spirit of wisdom, insight, and understanding (49:2). Here *Enoch* seems to bring into the picture of the Son of Man echoes of Dt-Is' description of the Servant of Yahweh (Is 42:1), who is chosen by God and receives God's spirit; thus *Enoch* may be anticipating the Christian tendency to amalgamate ancient salvific figures. *Enoch's* Son of Man will be the supreme judge (61:8), destroy the wicked (62:1–5), and rule over all (62:6). The just shall be saved and shall enjoy an eternal banquet with the Son of Man (62:13–14). It will be noted that this picture of the Son of Man comes entirely from Section Two, which is late in the Enoch literature and is not attested at Qumran (whence theories of Christian writing or editing; → 11 above). In the older Section Three (70–71), Enoch himself is the Son of Man.

(Gry, L., *Les paraboles d'Hénoch et leur messianisme* [Paris, 1910]. Manson, T. W., "The Son of Man in Daniel, Enoch, and the Gospels," *BJRylL* 32 [1949/50] 171–93. Sjöberg, E., *Der Menschensohn im äthiopischen Henochbuch* [Lund, 1946]. Van Andel, C. P., *De Structuur van de Henoch-Traditie en het Niewe Testament* [Utrecht, 1955].)

16 **(III) Book of Jubilees.** This is also known as *Little Genesis* or as *The Apocalypse of Moses.*

(A) Text and Date. The book was originally composed in Hebrew (not Aramaic). The original was lost, but fragments of 11 Hebr mss. have been found among the QL (J. T. Milik, *Ten Years*, 32). DJD 1, 82–83 publishes *Jub* 27:19–21; 35:8–10; DJD 3, 77–79 publishes 23:7–8; 46:1–3 (cf. M. Baillet, *RevQum* 5 [1965] 423–33); Milik, *RB* 73 (1966) 104 publishes 21:22–24. Also the *Genesis Apocryphon* (1st cent. BC? → 81 below) seems to draw on *Jubilees*. *Jubilees* was translated into Greek, but only a fragment of ch. 11 is preserved in Greek. About one fourth of the book is preserved in a Lat translation made from the Greek (5th cent.?). As with *Enoch*, the complete book is preserved in Ethiopic, a translation made from the Greek about the 6th cent. Charles edited the Ethiopic text along with all the other available witnesses (Oxford, 1895) and published a commentary on *Jubilees* in 1902 (Eng trans. in *APOT* 2, 1–82).

17 Charles dated the composition of *Jubilees* to 135–105 BC and claimed that it was Pharisaic in origin. M. Testuz (*Les idées religieuses du livre des Jubilés* [Geneva, 1960] 27–28) doubts the attribution to the Pharisees, although he still accepts the date of 110. Other scholars have tried to date the book earlier; Albright (*FSAC* [1957] 20) suggests 175 BC. (For discussion and bibliography, see H. H. Rowley, *Relevance*, 99–105.) As we shall see below, the Qumran evidence suggests a date of 150–125 BC, although some of the material comes from earlier traditions.

18 **(B) Basic Theme.** The most noticeable characteristic of *Jubilees* is its calendric interest. The book divides the history of the world from the creation to the time of the Sinai covenant into 49 periods of 49 years (a jubilee is 49 years, whence the name) and enlarges and embellishes the narrative of Gn within that calendric framework. The basic annual calendar supposed by *Jubilees* is a solar calendar of 364 days (6:4—12 months of 30 days each, and 4 intercalary days). This is a fixed calendar where every year and every week begin on Wednesday, and the same dates fall on the same weekday every year.

In her book on the calendar, A. Jaubert (*The Date of the Last Supper* [N.Y., 1965]) has shown that this solar calendar was an ancient one, apparently used by the latest redactors of the Pentateuch, by Ezekiel, and by the Chronicler. Perhaps originally stemming from Egypt, the solar calendar was probably the pre-exilic religious calendar and may have remained in use in the Temple until Hellenistic times. (However, in post-exilic civil life the solar calendar was replaced by a lunar calendar of Babylonian origin.) During the Maccabean period, the pro-Hellenistic party tried to replace the solar calendar in Temple worship; Dn 7:25 refers to the attempt of Antiochus Epiphanes (*ca.* 170) to change "times" and the Law. Despite their firm opposition to the Hellenists, upon accession to the high priesthood (152), the Maccabees seemed to have retained the newly introduced lunar calendar. The Qumran (Essene) community, which seceded from the Maccabean movement *ca.* 150 (→ 86 below), strongly defended the solar calendar; and *Jubilees* seems to have been composed in this era of calendric polemic, perhaps by a Qumran Essene. The dating of *Jubilees* to a span of 150–125 is supported by other indications. There is a reference in *Jub* 4:17 to an earlier Enoch literature, presumably to a part of *Enoch* whose origins began in the period 200–160 (→ 12 above). A Qumran writing, the *Damascus Covenant* (→ 75 below), which dates to *ca.* 100 BC, refers in 16:3–4 to *Jubilees* as an existing book.

19 Consonant with the general contempt of the authors of *Jubilees* for the Hellenistic innovations of the early 2nd cent. BC are the emphases on the Sabbath observance (2:17ff.), the dietary laws (6:7ff.; 7:31ff.), circumcision (15:33ff.); also the attacks on idolatry (20:7ff.) and on nudity as practiced by the Greeks in athletic contests (3:31)—all burning issues in the Maccabean reform. The stress on brotherly love is impressive (36:4, "Love one another; love your brother as a man loves his own soul"), but this is love strictly within Judaism—the impure Gentiles are to be avoided (22:16).

20 The basic style of the book is midrashic, i.e., it takes the narrative from Gn 1 to Ex 14, embellishes it with traditional lore, and infuses it with the spirit of late Judaism so that it is applicable to the author's time. (For a similar midrashic work on Dt, see DJD 1, 91–97.) Some of the material in *Jubilees* that has no biblical antecedent may draw on lost historical tradition. Albright (*FSAC* 277) suggests that the account of the wars of the Amorite kings against Jacob in *Jub* 34 preserves an old tradition about the Hebr conquest of north-central Palestine, not described in Jos.

21 **(C) Important Teaching.** Like the QL, *Jubilees* gives great attention to the PRIESTLY TRIBE OF LEVI—a reflection of the priestly origins of the Qumran group. *Jub* 31:15 promises that the children of Levi "shall be judges and princes and chiefs of all the seed of life of the sons of Jacob." The claim to civil as well as religious power reflects the situation in the late post-exilic period when the high priest was effectively the ruler of Israel, although it was under the Maccabees and the Hasmoneans that such regal power became explicit. There is no reference in *Jubilees*, however, to a priestly messiah; the sole reference to a messianic figure is to a prince descended from Judah (31:18). *Jubilees* puts more emphasis on salvation through observance of the Law (23:26–29) than on a messianic deliverer.

22 The ANGELOLOGY is not so prominent as that of *Enoch* (→ 14 above). The personal names of angels are not given, but several classes are distinguished. There are two superior classes: angels of the presence and angels of sanctification; there is also an inferior class set over the forces of nature (2:2; 15:27). *Jub* 35:17 mentions that Jacob had an angel guardian. As in *Enoch*, the bad angels fornicated with women (4:22ff.), and evil on earth is traced to that sin. Mastema (Satan) is the ruler of an organized kingdom of evil angels (10:8–9).

23 As for LIFE AFTER DEATH, it is not the resurrection of the body but the immortality of the soul that is stressed (23:31): "Their bones will rest in the earth, but their spirits will have much joy." This is our earliest attestation in Palestine of the idea of immortality, a concept that Wis 2:23ff. shows to have circulated among contemporary Alexandrian Jews.

24 The attitude toward the LAW is ambivalent. It is looked upon as something eternal, written on heavenly tablets (1:29; 3:31; 6:17). The Sabbath (and seemingly cicumcision too!) has been binding on the angels since creation (2:18–21; 15:26–28). Revelation consists merely in making known to man the Law which is eternal truth. *Jubilees* itself contains this perfect and complete Law (33:16). However, the author of *Jubilees* enunciates individual laws different from those of the Pentateuch. For instance, the laws of *Jubilees* concerning punishment for killing, governing the age of marriage, and forbidding nudity reflect a legal spirit more stringent than that of the Pentateuch. This difference prompted S. Zeitlin (*JQR* 30 [1939–40] 1–31) to attribute to *Jubilees* a very early date, in the immediate post-exilic period before the Pentateuch had received complete acceptance. We know now, however, that the Qumran sectarians had their own laws that were based upon a peculiar interpretation of the Pentateuch; consequently some of the differences may stem from the sectarian background of the author of *Jubilees*. In C. Rabin, *The Zadokite Documents* (2nd ed.; Oxford, 1958) 85–86, we find an impressive list of parallels between *Jubilees* and the Qumran *Damascus Covenant* (see also M. Testuz, *op. cit.*, 179–83).

25 **(IV) Testaments of the Twelve Patriarchs.** This Gk work (henceforth *Test.*) is an example of the literary form of "testament" that was well known in Judaism, i.e., a speech delivered by a famous figure just before death, in which he leaves a legacy, spiritual or material, to his children or his followers. Often the legacy has been filled in from a later author's knowledge of what actually happened to those who received the legacy. (See J. Munck, *Aux sources de la tradition chrétienne* [Fest. M. Goguel; Neuchâtel, 1950] 155–70.) Moses' blessing upon the tribes in Dt 33 and Jesus' Last Discourse in Jn 13–17 are other examples of testaments, but the immediate pattern for *Test.* is Jacob's blessing upon his 12 sons (= patriarchs) in Gn 49. *Test.* gives in turn the testament of each of those 12 to his own sons.

The Hebr and Aram literature of the testaments of these patriarchs was more extensive than what has been preserved in Gk *Test.* In the Cairo Geniza (→ Texts, 69:37) there was an Aram text of a *Testament of Levi*, subsequently published as App. III of Charles' *Greek Versions of the Testaments of the Twelve Patriarchs* (Oxford, 1908); see also P. Grelot, *RB* 63 (1956) 391–406. Fragments of three mss. of an Aram *T. Levi* have also appeared at Qumran, and almost certainly one such Qumran document was the lost ancestor of the medieval geniza copy. For the Qumran material, see DJD 1, 87–89; J. Milik, *RB* 72 (1955) 398–406. There is a medieval Hebr *T. Naphtali* that contains some elements from an ancient testimony, and fragments of a Hebr *T. Naphtali* have also been found at Qumran. The Hebr Midrash *Wayyisa'u* shows some important parallels with our Gk *Test.* (*Judah* 2ff.). For the Sahidic version of a *T. Isaac*, see K. H. Kuhn, *JTS* 18 (1967) 325–36.

26 **(A) Composition.** *Test.* exists in more than ten Gk mss.; see C. Burchard, *NTS* 12 (1965–66) 245–58. Charles, *Greek Versions*, distinguished two types of Gk text among these mss., which he thought went back to two lost Hebr recensions of *Test.* A number of scholars have disagreed with Charles; their opinions are summed up in M. de Jonge, *The Testaments of the Twelve Patriarchs* (Assen, 1953) and *Testamenta XII Patriacharum* (Leiden, 1964). De Jonge, following J. W. Hunkin, argues that one of Charles' group of Gk mss. is simply a recension of another Gk group, and that Charles actually gave preference to the wrong group in setting up his critical Gk text (Eng trans. in *APOT* 2, 282–367). Charles preferred the shorter Gk recension of *Test.*, but subsequent studies favor the longer as more original. Charles' overdependence on and interpretation of the Armenian and Slavonic evidence for *Test.* has also been questioned.

27 The matter of the validity or invalidity of Charles' reconstruction of the history of the Gk text of *Test.* is extremely important, for this reconstruction was the basis of his theory of the composition of the book. He maintained that *Test.* was a Jewish work, written in Hebrew between 109–107 BC; the Gk copies have Christian interpolations that can be recognized in part by comparing the shorter and longer forms of the Gk text. Despite the Qumran discoveries, Albright (*FSAC* 20) remains convinced that Charles's theory of composition is correct, although Albright would date the work to *ca.* 175 BC. See also F.-M. Braun, *RB* 67 (1960) 516–49. De Jonge, however, maintains that the Gk work is the original, written in the 2nd–3rd cents. AD by a Christian who had as sources earlier Jewish material. Milik and F. M. Cross think that the Qumran finds lend credence to a modified form of De Jonge's theory. It should be noted that the above-mentioned Aram *T. Levi* and Hebr *T. Naphtali* are not identical with the respective parts of Gk *Test.* but are longer, as if the Gk work were a condensation. Moreover, the different languages of these two Qumran testaments prove that they were not part of the same work; thus there is no pre-Gk evidence of a collection of testaments into a book of 12. The medieval evidence would also suggest that individual testaments circulated in Judaism for a long time. Another factor pointing toward the later joining of once independent testaments and sources is the great dissimilarity of the material in the various testaments now making up *Test.* For instance, *Levi*, with its vision of the heavens, is far more apocalyptic than are the other testaments, and *Judah* and *Joseph* are more narrative in style. Indeed, some material that was probably originally not in testament form has gone into Gk *Test.*, e.g., *Asher* is a dualistic treatise on the "two ways" that resembles certain treatments at Qumran.

At this time it is not possible to decide between these two very different views of *Test.*: (1) that it is a 2nd-cent. BC work written originally in Hebrew by a Jew and later translated into Greek and interpolated by Christian authors; or (2) that it is a 2nd-cent. AD work written originally in Greek by a Christian but drawing on earlier Jewish testaments and other material in Hebrew and Aramaic. Notice, however, that in both views *Test.* contains Jewish and Christian elements from four centuries. Only with great care should *Test.* be used in comparative studies of the NT. How much Qumran contributed to the thought of *Test.* is not clear; see B. Otzen, *ST* 7 (1954) 124–57; M. Philonenko, *RHPR* 38 (1958) 309–43; 39 (1959) 14–38.

28 **(B) Contents.** Each of the 12 testaments in *Test.* follows a definite pattern in relating the last words of the 12 sons of Jacob to their children: (1) a rubric describing the dying patriarch and generally giving his age; (2) a pseudohistorical account of the patriarch's life, trial, and visions; (3) a paraenetic section warning the children against evil and encouraging virtue—here the lofty ethics of *Test.* is apparent; (4) a conclusion to the discourse instructing the children for the future—this usually involves a reference to obeying Levi and Judah and to the coming of the High Priest and the Messiah; (5) a rubric about the patriarch's death. The consistency of the format suggests very heavy editing by one man, if not composition by one man.

29 The Christian material, whether it stems from the original author or from an interpolator, is prominent. *Benjamin* 10:8 says of the Lord, "When he appeared as God in the flesh to deliver them, they did not believe him." *Levi* 14:2 speaks of the chief priests "who shall lay their hands on the Savior of the world." *Simeon* 6:7 says that God has taken a body and eaten with men and saved men. Some material once thought to be Christian, however, is probably of Qumran or similar origin, e.g., the mention of bread and wine in *Levi* 8:4–5—Philonenko (*art. cit.*) argues strongly for this approach. Charles (*APOT* 2, 392) gives a list of parallels to the NT (as distinct from clearly Christian interpolations), but obviously the value of the list is dependent on the validity of his theory of an originally Jewish work. See also A. W. Argyle, *ExpT* 63 (1951–52) 256–58; M. de Jonge, *SE* 1 (1959) 546–56; *NovT* 4 (1960) 182–235. The importance of knowing whether some statements in *Test.* reflect pre-Christian Judaism is paramount, e.g., the reference to the conqueror from Judah as a lamb (*Joseph* 19:8). We might have remarkable background for Jesus' doctrine of forgiveness (Mt 18:15) if the passage in *Gad* 6:3 is pre-Christian: "Love one another from your heart. If a man sins against you, speak peaceably to him.... If he repents and confesses, forgive him." *Dan* 5:3 says, "Love the Lord your God through your whole life, and one another with a true heart" (cf. Mk 12:30–31).

30 **(C) Important Teaching.** *Test.*, in parts, supports the expectation of TWO MESSIAHS. There are references both to an expected anointed High Priest descended from the tribe of Levi (*Reuben* 6:7–12) and to an expected anointed king from Judah (*Judah* 24:5–6). *Judah* 21:2ff. gives supremacy to the Levitical Messiah. Charles attributed these expectations to different stages of composition; but now we have evidence from Qumran of simultaneous expectation of two Messiahs, one priestly and one kingly (→ 104 below). Consonant with the theory of the late origins of *Test.*, Milik (*Ten Years*, 35) holds that the author of *Test.* has merged these two figures into one.

(For further references see Beasley-Murray, G. R., *JTS* 48 [1947] 1–17. Black, M., *ExpT* 60 [1949] 321–22.)

31 There is an advanced DEMONOLOGY. Beliar (mutation of "Belial"—in the OT an abstract noun meaning "worthlessness") is the personified leader of the forces of evil and an adversary of God. He is the lord of darkness (*Joseph* 20:2). Eventually the High Priest from Levi will war upon him (*Dan* 5:10), and Beliar will be cast into eternal fire (*Judah* 25:3). The similarities to NT demonology are obvious, and "Beliar" also appears as a name for Satan at Qumran and in 2 Cor 6:15.

There is a strong doctrine of the RESURRECTION of the just; they will rise on the right in gladness, while the wicked will be on the left (*Benjamin* 10: 6–8). The righteous will reside in the New Jerusalem (*Dan* 5:12), though it is not certain whether this is on earth or in heaven.

32 **(V) (Letter of) Aristeas to Philocrates.** Thus far we have been dealing with plausibly pre-Christian Palestinian apocrypha; the next works discussed here shift the scene to Egypt, especially to the large Jewish settlement at Alexandria and its pre-Christian apocrypha. In the (deuterocanonical) Bible itself, there are Alexandrian attempts to justify Jewish Law and wisdom as a form of philosophy superior to Gk thought (Wis, 2 Mc); the apocryphal works we shall now consider represent further Jewish attempts to achieve toleration, acceptance, or status in the sophisticated Hellenistic world.

33 *Aristeas* presents itself as a small book (not a letter despite the name often given to it) written in Greek to "his brother" Philocrates by Aristeas, a Gentile courtier of the Egyptian ruler Ptolemy II Philadelphus (285–246). Actually the author was a Jew writing at least a century later (2nd cent. BC) for fellow Jews. A critical Gk text, French translation, and notes have been published by A. Pelletier (SC 89; Paris, 1962). There are Eng translations by H. Andrews in *APOT* 2, 83–122 and by M. Hadas (JAL; N.Y., 1951).

The story, which concerns the legendary origin of the Gk translation of the Pentateuch, will be told in reference to the LXX (→ Texts, 69:53); see also S. Jellicoe, *JTS* 12 (1961) 261–71. It is a legend that gained considerable favor in later Jewish (Philo, Josephus) and Christian tradition. *Aristeas* was popular in Christian circles because it helped to show the miraculous origins of the LXX, the Christian Bible. To give color to his fictional narrative, the author probably availed himself of sources that gave him some knowledge about the 3rd-cent. Egyptian background.

34 **(VI) Maccabean Literature.** Besides the deuterocanonical 1–2 Mc, there are two noncanonical books that bear the name of the Maccabees. Like 2 Mc and *Aristeas* they are apologetic literature of Egyptian Judaism. Composed originally in Greek, the text of both is found in Codex Alexandrinus of the LXX (→ Texts, 69:76); *4 Mc* appears in Codex Sinaiticus; neither is in the Vg. The Gk text is printed in Rahlfs' *Septuaginta* 1, and with an Eng translation and notes in M. Hadas' volume in the JAL series (N.Y., 1953). There is a translation of *3 Mc* by C. Emmet in *APOT* 1, 155–73; and one of *4 Mc* by R. B. Townshend in *APOT* 2, 653–85.

35 **(A) 3 Maccabees** or the *Ptolemaica*. The designation "Maccabees" is a misnomer because all the action takes place in the late 3rd cent. BC, 40 years before the Maccabean revolt. The book relates three incidents in the struggle between the Egyptian king Ptolemy IV Philopator (221–203) and the Jews. *First* (1:1–2:24), after his victory over the Syrians at Raphia (217), Ptolemy attempts to violate the Jerusalem Temple but is struck senseless at the intercession of the high priest Simon II (219–196). This is similar to the story about the Syrian general Heliodorus at the Temple in the year 176, told in 2 Mc 3. *Second* (2:25–33), Ptolemy insists that all citizens of Alexandria sacrifice to the gods, and the Jews who refuse are to lose their citizenship, be branded, and enrolled as slaves. Only a few Jews acquiesce. Similar attempts to Hellenize the Jews are reported under Syrian rule in 2 Mc 4:9; 6:1–9. *Third* (3–7), in the hippodrome at Alexandria, the king tries to slay the Jews whose homes are in the Egyptian countryside, but they are spared by fantastic happenings (one episode involves drunken elephants!). The king repents, gives the Jews a feast, and sends them home. The relation to the story of Esther is obvious.

Although the author had access to some historical material about the reign of Ptolemy IV and perhaps recalls an otherwise forgotten persecution of Jews in Egypt during that reign, most of the material is legendary, stemming from variants of other stories of Hellenistic times (e.g., Est, 2 Mc). The book was composed in Greek in the 1st cent. BC by an Alexandrian Jew to encourage his fellows (in face of anticipated difficulties from the Romans?) and as background for one of their festivals.

36 **(B) 4 Maccabees** or *On the Supremacy of Reason* (falsely attributed under this title to Josephus). This book is a philosophical discourse or "diatribe" on the supremacy of religious reason over human passions and sufferings. The author begins by stating: "Thoroughly philosophical is the subject I am going to discuss." In ch. 1 the author explains his general thesis; in the following chapters he tells stories from the OT and from Jewish history to illustrate his point, e.g., Joseph overcame sexual appetite in the incident with Potiphar's wife; Moses overcame anger. In 5–6 and 8–18 he tells two stories of martyrdom, the fundamentals of which are found in 2 Mc 6–7 (Eleazar; the mother and the seven children); these illustrate how the old and the young overcame suffering. The fact that these stories from 2 Mc constitute three-fourths of *4 Mc* explains the title.

The genuineness of a few sections of *4 Mc* (17:23–24; 18:6–19) has been questioned; but as a whole the work was composed in Greek by a Jew of the Diaspora (more probably, Alexandria) early in the 1st cent. AD, probably *ca.* 40. The author drew on 2 Mc and possibly also on Jason of Cyrene (the source of 2 Mc). The biblical stories are embellished considerably, and the style of the entire work is declamatory. Seemingly their purpose was to commemorate the Jewish martyrs, perhaps for a feast in their honor. Along with Wis and Philo, it is an excellent example of how traditional Jewish thought and morality were cast into Gk philosophical patterns, and how a system like Stoicism was found wanting in Jewish eyes. We find in *4 Mc* 6:27–29 a magnificent illustration of the theology of vicarious suffering. This work gave incentive to the Church's practice of commemorating Christian martyrs, and it was quoted favorably by many of the Fathers. There is a Lat paraphrase, *Passio ss. Machabeorum* (*ca.* 4th cent.). See A. Gelin, *LumVi* 36 (1958) 123–29; S. Zeitlin, *JQR* 36 (1945–46) 1–16.

37 **(VII) Prayer of Manasseh.** Another apocryphon preserved in some LXX mss. (Codex Alexandrinus), this is a work that moves us from the domain of Alexandrian apologetic literature into that of devotional literature. This *Prayer* is a truly beautiful penitential psalm of 15 verses, and in many Gk mss. it appears as one of the canticles appended to Ps. It is a pseudonymous attempt to fill in the prayer of King Manasseh (687–642) mentioned in 2 Chr 33:11–13; indeed, particularly in Lat bibles, it has often been attached to the end of 2 Chr. The justice and merciful forgiveness of God extolled in this oration could be meaningfully applicable to a sinner like the wicked king Manasseh (→ Chronicler, 24:77).

The piety is that of late Judaism, and the deuterocanonical prayer of Azariah (Dn 3:24–90) offers some interesting parallels. The *Prayer of Manasseh* was originally composed in Greek by a Jew in the 1st or 2nd cent. AD. It was promptly translated from Greek into Syriac, and thus our earliest extant form of the *Prayer* is in a 3rd-cent. Christian Syr work, the *Didascalia*. Although the prayer did not appear in early Vg mss., it is found in medieval mss. The Sixto-Clementine Vg printed it as a supplement (after Trent failed to list it as canonical). Protestants count it as one of "the Apocrypha."

38 **(VIII) Esdras Literature.** The canonical fate of *1–2 Esdras* was similar to that of the *Prayer*. The titles of the various books of Ezra/Esdras are confusing. (The Hebr name of the biblical scribe *'Ezrā'* appears as Esdras in Greek and Latin.) *In the Hebr* bible there was originally one book of Ezra, containing what are now the canonical books of Ezra and Nehemiah. Only in the Middle Ages did Hebr mss. begin to separate this material into two books. *In the LXX*, as represented in codices Alexandrinus and Vaticanus, there were two books of Esdras: Esdras A—a book that came to be regarded as apocryphal (our *1 Esdras* below); Esdras B—a rendition into Greek of the canonical Ezra/Nehemiah of the Hebr bible.

In the Latin there were four books of Esdras:

I Esdras—canonical Ezra	"Ezra" and "Nehemiah," the standard English designation of these books, is now being accepted by Catholics. Increasingly, "Esdras" is being reserved for the Apocrypha.
II Esdras—canonical Nehemiah	

III Esdras—the apocryphon that is Esdras A in the LXX (*1 Esdras* below)

IV Esdras—another apocryphon (*2 Esdras* below); the apocalyptic part of this apocryphon is also known as *4 Ezra*.

39 **(A) 1 Esdras** (the Esdras A of the LXX; the III Esdras of the Latin). The principal text of this book is in Greek, found in all modern editions of the LXX. The Lat form in the Sixto-Clementine Vg is an OL translation from the Greek. There is also a Syr translation from the Greek. For Eng translation, see RSV Apocrypha; also *APOT* 1, 1–58 (S. A. Cook).

In substance this book covers material in 2 Chr 35–36, canonical Ezr, and Neh 7–8 (*1 Esdras* and canonical Ezr present their material in different order). Once thought of as a free Gk rendition of the MT biblical material, *1 Esdras* is now generally considered the original LXX translation of a Hebr recension of Ezr/Neh different from the Ezr/Neh in the MT. (For such a phenomenon in the earliest LXX tradition, → Texts, 69:58.) In this case the Esdras B of the LXX, which is closer to the MT, represents a later recension of the LXX (→ Texts, 69:59–63). Such an explanation makes clear why *1 Esdras* precedes Esdras B in the codices Alexandrinus and Vaticanus.

It appears that *1 Esdras* enjoyed more popularity than Esdras B among those who cited the Gk bible. Josephus used it, and the early Church Fathers seem to have thought of it as Scripture. It was really Jerome with his love for the Hebr bible who set the precedent for rejecting *1 Esdras* because it did not conform to Hebr Ezr/Neh. It contains little that is not in canonical Ezr/Neh except the story in 3:1–5:6, which tells of a contest among three Jewish pages at the Persian court of Darius (520 BC). Zerubbabel won: His prize was the permission to lead the Jews back to Jerusalem. The story in its present form (from *ca.* 100 BC?) may have been adapted from a pagan narrative (→ Chronicler, 24:83).

40 **(B) 2 Esdras** (the IV Esdras of the Vg). This is a composite work of three independent parts dating from the late 1st cent. AD to the 3rd cent. The whole work was preserved only in Latin and may be found in the appendix of the Sixto-Clementine Vg. There is an Eng translation in the RSV Apocrypha. *2 Esdras* has nothing to do with the narrative of canonical Ezr/Neh and is pseudepigraphical.

SECTION ONE (chs. 1–2). This is clearly a Christian work, composed in Greek, probably in the 2nd cent. AD, to serve as an introduction to Section Two below. It is extant only in Latin. In the narrative God speaks to Ezra and castigates the Jewish people for infidelity in the past. Echoing the theme of the NT, God promises that he will reject Israel and turn to the Gentiles. Seemingly speaking to the Church (2:15), God gives her instruction on how to take care of his new people. "Everlasting rest" and "eternal light" are promised in 2:34–35—the source of the phrases used in the Church's requiem liturgy—and immortality is the reward of those who confess the Son of God (2:47).

41 SECTION TWO (chs. 3–14). This is the *Apocalypse of Ezra*, sometimes called *4 Ezra*. By far the most important part of *2 Esdras*, it is a Jewish work of about AD 100–120. The original Hebr or Aram texts have been lost, and so has the Gk version, which was presumably the basis for all the extant ancient translations. The Latin is the most important, published by B. Violet (GCS 18/1 [1910]); but the Syriac and Ethiopic are also of value. There is an Eng translation by G. H. Box in *APOT* 2, 542–624; also W. O. E. Oesterley in WC (1933). For the question of the original language, see J. Bloch, *JQR* 48 (1958) 293–94. The unity of the work has been questioned; see H. H. Rowley, *Relevance*, 156–59. The work concerns seven visions granted to Salathiel (= Shealtiel of Ezr 3:2 and 1 Chr 3:17, the father or uncle of Zerubbabel), who is identified in the gloss of 3:1 as Ezra (who, in fact, lived at least a century later!). Thus, the work mistakenly sets Ezra 30 years after the fall of Jerusalem in 587. The first four visions (3–10) concern the problem of evil, Israel's sufferings, God's plan for the last times, and the New Jerusalem. The real crisis in the author's life, for which he finds a parallel in his fictional setting, is the destruction of Jerusalem by the Romans in AD 70. The fascinating story of the lost Lat text following 7:35 is told by B. Metzger in *JBL* 76 (1957) 153–56. The fifth or "eagle" vision of chs. 11–12 uses symbolism to describe the Roman persecutors of the Jews, much as the contemporary NT Ap describes Rome as a dragon. In the sixth vision (13) a marvelous Man arises from the sea—he is the pre-existent Messiah come to wage war with the Gentiles. This passage has some similarities with the picture of the Son of Man in *Enoch* (→ 15 above). In the seventh vision (14) Ezra is told to write down the 24 books of the OT and the 70 hidden books (the apocrypha). Ezra is taken up to heaven. This book continues the chain of Jewish apocalyptic that runs from Dn and *Enoch* through the QL to the Baruch literature. For bibliography see Eissfeldt, *OTI* 625.

SECTION THREE (chs. 15–16). This is a Christian conclusion, perhaps from the 3rd cent. AD, added to the above. Of the original Gk only three vv. of 15 remain; the Latin is the only extant version. The theme concerns God's judgment against the nations, especially against Rome.

42 **(IX) Baruch Literature.** Just as Ezra, anachronistically antedated to the fall of Jerusalem (587), became the hero of pseudonymous apocalyptic written after the fall of Jerusalem to the Romans (AD 70), so also did Baruch, Jeremiah's secretary, who at least was dated correctly. Besides the deuterocanonical (or 1) book of Baruch, there are apocryphal books, of which two are of importance.

43 **(A) 2 Baruch,** or the *Syriac Apocalypse of Baruch*. Written originally in Hebrew or Aramaic, this work is preserved only in a Syr version made from a lost Gk version (a Gk fragment of chs. 12–14 appears among the Oxyrhynchus papyri). An Eng translation by Charles is found in *APOT* 2, 470–526; also Charles and Oesterley, *The Apocalypse of Baruch* (1929); B. Violet (GCS 18/2 [1924]). Charles dates the composition of this Jewish apocalypse to AD 50–90 with a final redaction slightly later; Violet prefers a date of 100–120. The unity of the book has been challenged; see H. H. Rowley, *Relevance*, 156–59. It is related to the *Apocalypse of Ezra* (*2 Esdras*, Section Two), and the dependence is probably *Baruch* upon *Esdras*. The book consists of visions accorded to Baruch after the fall of Jerusalem to explain that tragedy and the suffering of the Jews. There are visions of the last times, the messianic banquet, and the resurrection of the dead. Sparked by the fall of Jerusalem to the Romans, *2 Baruch* offers a Jewish parallel to the NT Ap which is also concerned with that historical event (→ Apocalypse, 64:53).

44 **(B) 3 Baruch,** or the *Greek Apocalypse of Baruch*. The Gk text, published in 1899 by M. R. James, has been revised by J.-C. Picard (Leiden, 1967). There are two Slavonic versions. An Eng translation is supplied by H. M. Hughes in *APOT* 2, 527–41. Hughes states that both the Greek and the Slavonic texts represent condensations of the original work. This original was a Jewish production of the 2nd cent. AD, revised by a Christian. It has some parallels to *2 Enoch* (→ 8 above). The contents describe Baruch's visions as he passes through the seven heavens (cf. 2 Cor 12:2). The angelology is quite pronounced, especially as to the role of angels as guardians and mediators. For bibliography on *2–3 Baruch*, see Eissfeldt, *OTI* 627–31.

45 **(X) Psalms of Solomon.** Some early Christian lists of the canon of Scripture mention this book, and we know that it was once attached to the end of the NT in the Codex Alexandrinus. However, the work was rediscovered and became available to Western scholars only at the beginning of the 17th cent. The original was written in Hebrew, now lost. The critical text of the Gk translation was published by O. von Gebhardt (TU 13/2; Leipzig, 1895). An incomplete Syr version, made from the Gk text, was first published in 1909 by J. R. Harris, *The Odes and Psalms of Solomon* (Cambridge). For a discussion of the textual problem of the *Pss*, see J. Begrich, *ZNW* 40 (1939) 131–64. G. B. Gray gives an Eng translation in *APOT* 2, 625–52.

46 Two psalms in the canonical psalter (72, 127) are associated by title with Solomon; and 1 Kgs 4:32 speaks of his 1005 songs. None of the individual poems in the present apocryphon claims to have been written by Solomon, and the attribution of the collection as a whole to Solomon (a pseudepigraphical attempt to find patronage; → Canonicity, 67:89) was probably necessitated by the fact that the more obvious attribution to David was precluded since the Davidic psalter had now been closed. These 18 psalms were actually composed by Jews in Palestine in the 1st cent. BC. Some of them have historical references that can be dated. For instance, *Pss Sol* 8:15–21 refers to the siege of Jerusalem by Pompey in 63 BC, and *Pss Sol* 2:26–37 seems to imply knowledge of Pompey's death in 48. One of the themes of the collection is that this foreign invasion is God's punishment on Israel for the worldliness of its rulers (Hasmoneans). The opposition to the priestly rulers of the Sadducee party led scholars to attribute *Pss Sol* to the Pharisees; but now we know that other groups, like the Qumran Essenes, were equally opposed to the Sadducees. Indeed, the strong messianic expectations visible in *Pss Sol* fit the Qumran group better than the Pharisees. (J. O'Dell *RevQum* 3 [1961] 241–57.)

47 The theology of *Pss Sol* has been treated by H. Braun in *ZNW* 43 (1950) 1–54. A theology of free choice between good and evil is expounded, as is the theme of divine retribution. *Pss Sol* 17 and 18 pray for the coming of a Davidic Messiah who shall bring the Gentiles under his yoke. A sinless and perfect man, the Messiah will renew Jerusalem and establish Israel as God's kingdom. This is the type of messianism that we often seem to find in the popular expectations implied in the Gospels (→ Aspects OT Thought, 77:161–62)—a mixture of political and spiritual aspirations that Jesus does not accept (→ Aspects NT Thought, 78:9); cf. S. Mowinckel, *He That Cometh* (Nashville, 1954) 308ff. For bibliography on *Pss Sol*, see Eissfeldt, *OTI* 610–13. Note that *Pss Sol* should be kept distinct from *The Odes of Solomon*, a 2nd-cent. AD Gnostic work, probably composed in Syriac (cf. J. A. Emerton, *JTS* 18 (1967) 372–406).

48 **(XI) Sibylline Oracles.** About 500 BC Heraclitus of Ephesus mentioned Sibyl, a prophetess of Cumae. Later the concept of (old) women who were filled with the divine spirit and were the channels through whom the oracles of the gods came to men spread throughout the Hellenistic world, and at least ten were honored at various shrines. The oracles attributed to these sibyls were composed in Gk poetry (hexameter) and collected over the centuries (*ca.* 200 BC–AD 500). Jews and Christians imitated the pagans by composing "sibylline oracles" of their own. Most of the official and private collections of great antiquity were destroyed, but 12 books of a 15-book collection of the late 5th cent. AD have come down to us. A selection may be found in English in *APOT* 2, 368–406 (H. C. O. Lanchester).

In this collection, Books 3–5 contain oracles of Jewish origin, some, especially in Book 3, dating back to the 2nd cent. BC and the reign of Ptolemy VII Physcon in Egypt. Other parts of Book 3 refer to Cleopatra. Book 4 carries us into the late 1st cent. AD, and Book 5 into the 2nd cent. These oracles served as Jewish propaganda. The sibyl is identified as Noah's daughter (3:827); her oracles outline the course of world history, predict the destruction of Beliar, ultimate Jewish triumph, and the coming of the Messiah. In 3:63ff. and 4:137–39 we may have an interesting parallel to the NT Ap, for *Nero redivivus* seems to appear along with the figure of the wicked woman who dominates the world (→ Apocalypse, 64:63, 74). The opposition to sacrifice and Temple in 4:27ff. may reflect sectarian Jewish theology.

The oracles were also very popular among Christian writers. Augustine admitted the Sibyl to the City of God (18.23), and Michelangelo painted sibyls in the Sistine Chapel opposite the OT prophets. At least four of the books of this collection are Christian. For bibliography, see Eissfeldt, *OTI* 615–17.

49 **(XII) Assumption of Moses.** Antiquity knew both of a *Testament of Moses* and of an *Assumption of Moses*, two separate works, one belonging to testament literature (→ 25 above), the other presumably apocalyptic. Despite the title of the Lat apocryphon we are discussing, its contents would suggest more the *Testament* than the *Assumption*. Scholars suggest that the two works were joined at an early date, perhaps under the title of the *Assumption;* but what we have preserved would then be only the first (*Testament*) part of the combined work. The original was probably written in Hebrew (lost), then translated into Greek (also lost), and finally into Latin (preserved in a defective 6th-cent. ms., published with an Eng translation by R. H. Charles, *The Assumption of Moses* [1897]). See also *APOT* 2, 407–24.

In the preserved testamentary part of the work, Moses, shortly before his death, speaks to Joshua and reveals to him the future history of Israel from the entrance into Canaan until the dawn of the blessed age. The popularity of this type of pseudepigraphical "prediction," which is really a summary in retrospect from the author's own time, is attested in the Bible in Dn. The history goes down to the period 4 BC–AD 30 which is the author's own era. Thus, like some of the apocrypha just discussed, this work comes from Judaism's reaction to Rome. The author expects the end to come soon and Judaism to be delivered from Roman oppression. There is no mention of a Messiah in the establishment of God's kingdom which is supramundane, but there is a reference in ch. 9 to a Levite named Taxo who exhorts his seven sons to martyrdom for religion. Charles suggested that by gematria this was a reference to Eleazar of 2 Mc 6 and *4 Mc* 5–7 (→ 36 above). According to C. Lattey (*CBQ* 4 [1942] 9–21), Taxo is a suffering messianic figure, a suggestion with importance for the NT. M. Delcor (*RB* 62 [1955] 60–66) sees a relation between Taxo and the *Meḥôqēq* of the QL (CD 8:5), a figure who is identified with "the Searcher of the Law"; this suggestion is championed by S. Mowinckel as well (for discussion and bibliography, see H. H. Rowley, *Relevance*, 149–56).

The lost (*Assumption*) part of the book, as far as we can reconstruct from patristic references, dealt with the death of Moses and his assumption into heaven after a struggle between Michael and Satan for his body. Seemingly it is to this legend that Jude 9 refers. See Eissfeldt, *OTI* 623–24, for more bibliography.

CHRISTIAN APOCRYPHAL GOSPELS

50 **(I) Christian Apocrypha.** As we have already seen in the instances of *Enoch, Testaments*, and *2 Esdras*, Christians felt free to interpolate Christian motifs into Jewish apocrypha; but they also composed apocrypha of their own. If we define Christian apocrypha as literature that once had a claim—plausible or implausible—to be considered canonical, we would have to treat under that heading some ancient subapostolic works, like *Didache*, *1–2 Clem.*, *Hermas*, and *Barnabas*, which were treated as Scripture by early Church writers (→ Canonicity, 67:83). Today, however, these works are studied as patristic writings, and "Christian apocrypha" is used in a narrower sense to refer to noncanonical books more closely related in form or in content to NT writings.

51 **(A) Works Other Than Gospels.** In the best collection of Christian apocrypha (Hennecke, *NTA*) over 100 works are discussed. From this immense literature we have to be very selective and have opted to treat only gospels, for this is the section of the apocrypha that has the best chance of preserving authentic material from the NT era. But we shall mention briefly the other forms or genres of Christian apocrypha (Hennecke, *NTA* vol. 2), most of which are closely patterned on the forms of literature that appear in the NT. There is pseudo-Pauline correspondence, e.g., *to the Laodiceans, to the Corinthians, to Seneca*, often written under the pretense of being the (lost) letters mentioned by Paul in his canonical correspondence (→ Canonicity, 67:57, 59). There is also the *Epistula Apostolorum*, partly in letter form, partly an apocalypse, concerning the revelations of Jesus after his resurrection. Modeled on the canonical Acts of the Apostles (which really treats only of Peter and Paul), there are apocryphal acts of individual apostles, e.g., *of John, of Peter, of Paul, of Andrew, of Thomas*, purportedly describing their careers after the ascension of Jesus and thus filling in history missing in the NT. A few of these were accepted as Scripture for a while (→ Canonicity, 67:66); most of them are filled with fantastic miracles and betray heretical tendencies (Encratite or docetic thought). They have sometimes supplied the material for the "biographies" of the apostles found in martyrologies and in breviary lessons.

52 Patterned on the NT Ap, there are apocryphal apocalypses, e.g., *of Peter* (→ Canonicity, 67:67), *of Paul, of Thomas*. These answer a popular curiosity about the "goings on" in the next world by letting imagination satisfy for the lack of revelation. Another type of Christian apocalyptic is seen in the interpolations and additions to Jewish apocrypha. The *Ascension of Isaiah* deserves mention. Just as the NT authors found in a free interpretation of the words of Isaiah (proto- and deutero-) some very valuable OT background for understanding the ministry of Jesus, so in this apocryphal work Isaiah is granted visions of the life of Jesus and of the Church. These visions are added to a Jewish apocryphon, *The Martyrdom of Isaiah*, a midrash on 2 Kgs 21:16 telling how Isaiah was sawed in half at the order of King Manasseh. The interpolated visions of Christian origin concentrate heavily, as does the canonical Ap, on the struggle between the Church and the supernatural prince of evil (Beliar or Sammael; → 31 above).

53 **(B) Gospels.** These gospels constitute a large body of literature, filling vol. 1 of Hennecke, *NTA*. Frequently the gospels are pseudonymous, bearing the names of famous figures in the early Church (apostles, Mary, Nicodemus); other times the title concerns the content of the work (*The Gospel of Truth*) or its origin (gospels attributed to Marcion, Cerinthus). There are several categories of these gospels, and some are highly theological and only remotely related to the story of Jesus. For instance, *The Gospel of Truth*, recently discovered among Coptic documents at Chenoboskion in Egypt (→ 59 below), is an abstract Gnostic treatise that has nothing to do with Jesus' life or ministry (see trans. by K. Grobel [Nashville, 1960]). *The Gospel of Philip* (trans. by R. McL. Wilson [N.Y., 1962]), part of the same Chenoboskion find, is only somewhat more closely related to the Jesus of the canonical Gospels. More often such gospels are attached to Jesus' career or to some incident in it. A favorite setting for the Gnostic gospels is an unrecorded postresurrectional appearance of Jesus to a famous Church figure, usually an apostle, in which Jesus reveals a secret way of perfection. Generally the revelation has little similarity to Jesus' thought as we know it from the canonical Gospels and is obviously a creation of 2nd.-cent. AD (or later) Gnostic circles.

54 If we move on to gospels that are less theologically tendentious or theologically centered, we find that some were written to answer popular curiosity about the unknown details of Jesus' life. Thus, there is literature about what Christ did during his descent into hell, and literature about the trial of Jesus, describing Pilate's role more amply and minimizing his guilt. Although some of this writing may be quite early (e.g., a form of *The Acts of Pilate* was known by AD 150), it may be said almost without exception that such attempts to fill in blank spots in the life of Jesus do not preserve real historical memories. The same firm judgment must be passed on the various infancy gospels which tell of Jesus' family background and of his childhood. However, one of these, *The Protevangelium of James*, although devoid of authentic historical material, has had so much influence on popular Christian piety, hagiography, and art that we shall discuss it below.

55 With that one exception we shall confine our treatment to apocryphal gospels or fragments of "sayings of Jesus" that have *some* reasonable claim to preserve authentic reminiscences of Jesus' ministry. The possibility cannot be denied that such reminiscences may have survived in addition to the canonical Gospels. For instance, we know that there were other accounts of Jesus in the 1st cent. besides the canonical Gospels (→ Canonicity, 67:64), and one of these may have been preserved in whole or in part. The canonical Gospels themselves drew on pre-Gospel written collections of the words and deeds of Jesus (→ Syn Problem, 40:19–24), and again one of these sources may have been preserved wholly or partially. Jesus undoubtedly said many things that were not recorded in the canonical Gospels (Jn 20:30; 21:25)—the agrapha or "nonwritten" sayings—and these may have been preserved orally, only later to be written down. Purported agrapha were committed to writing in other parts of the NT (Acts 20:35), in variant readings in NT mss. (Codex Bezae of Lk 6:4–5), in the writings of the Fathers, in the Talmud, and in the Mohammedan writings; and certainly therefore some of them may have been preserved in apocryphal gospels or fragments (→ 3 above for the works of A. Resch and of J. Jeremias). It is difficult, of course, to determine how much, if any, authentic material is found in the following apocrypha; nevertheless they deserve serious consideration.

56 **(II) Papyrus Fragments.** Papyri discovered in Egypt have been a great boon to modern investigation. Besides papyrus copies of biblical books (→ Texts, 69:142), papyri of every-day correspondence have enlarged our knowledge of the language and customs of NT times (W. Barclay, "The New Testament and the Papyri," *The New Testament in Historical and Contemporary Perspective* [Fest. G. H. C. MacGregor; Oxford, 1965] 57–81). The papyrus finds of apocrypha are also extremely important.

57 **(A) Papyrus Oxyrhynchus 840.** The great discovery in 1896–97 at Oxyrhynchus, an ancient center of Egyptian Christianity, by B. P. Grenfell and A. S. Hunt produced almost 20 volumes of papyri dating from the Roman conquest of Egypt until the 10th cent. AD. In vol. 5 (London, 1908), there is a fragment numbered 840 that describes a controversy in the Temple court as Jesus and a chief priest named Levi argued over purifications. The copy dates from the 4th–5th cents. AD. The famous historian of Judaism in NT times, E. Schürer, thought that the fragment betrayed no knowledge of Temple customs; but now J. Jeremias (*ConNeot* 11 [Fest. A. Fridrichsen; 1947] 97–108) argues that it may well be an authentic story about Jesus. (Jeremias, *Unknown*, 47–60; Hennecke, *NTA* 1, 92–94.)

58 **(B) Papyrus Egerton 2.** In 1935, H. I. Bell and T. C. Skeat published *Fragments of an Unknown Gospel*, a British Museum papyrus of *ca.* AD 150. There are four pericopes in the papyrus. The last and the beginning of the first have no parallel in the canonical Gospels; but in the rest Synoptic and Johannine material are closely woven together. It is generally held today that the author of this work was drawing on the memory of all four canonical Gospels and blending with them noncanonical material which he thought of equal value (apparently he did not have a concept of four *canonical* Gospels; → Canonicity, 67:64). The noncanonical sayings are too fragmentary to be of major import. This papyrus is of value for the dating of Jn and for the textual criticism of the Johannine passages it quotes.

(Braun, F.-M., *Jean le théologien* 1 [Paris, 1959] 87–94, 404–6. Dodd, C. H., *New Testament Studies* [Manchester, 1953] 12–52. Hennecke, *NTA* 1, 94–97.)

59 **(III) Gospel of Thomas.** In 1945–46 in upper Egypt near the village of Nag'-Hammadi there were found 13 Coptic codices containing 44 separate works. The site was known in antiquity as Chenoboskion; it was here that Pachomius, the father of Egyptian cenobitism, was converted and baptized (*ca.* AD 320). A cenobitic monastery was founded, and these codices probably came from a monastic collection. As with many other monasteries in Egypt, either all or some of the monks were affected by Gnosticism, for many of the works in these codices are Gnostic or incipiently Gnostic. (V. Gold, *BA* 15 [1952] 70–88; or *BAR* 1, 299–329; J. Doresse, *The Secret Books of the Egyptian Gnostics* [N.Y., 1960]; A. K. Helmbold, *The Nag Hammadi Gnostic Texts and the Bible* [Grand Rapids, 1967]; J. M. Robinson, *NTS* 14 [1967–68] 356–401.)

60 One of the most important of the 44 works begins: "These are the secret words which the living Jesus spoke and Didymus Judas Thomas wrote"; at the end it has this identification: "The Gospel according to Thomas." Published in 1956, this gospel (henceforth *GTh*) of 20 codex pages was written in Sahidic Coptic (→ Texts, 69:113); the copy dates from *ca.* AD 400. The Coptic is a translation from a lost Gk work, probably to be dated in the mid-2nd cent. AD. In 1897 and 1904 there were published three Gk papyrus fragments from Oxyrhynchus (→ 57 above), numbered 1, 654, 655, and dating to AD 150–300. These contained sayings of Jesus, and it has now been recognized that they came from copies of *GTh* (J. A. Fitzmyer, *TS* 20 [1959] 505–60). Most scholars think they represent a form of the lost Gk text of *GTh*, although G. Garitte maintains that they are a retroversion into Greek from Coptic *GTh* (*Muséon* 73 [1960] 151–72; 334–49). The Coptic of *GTh* with Eng translation appears in A. Guillaumont, *et al.*, *The Gospel According to Thomas* [N.Y., 1959]. For other translations and commentaries, see R. M. Grant and D. N. Freedman, *The Secret Sayings of Jesus* (N.Y., 1960); J. Doresse, *op. cit.*, 333–83; Hennecke, *NTA* 1, 511–22.

GTh is simply a collection of 114 sayings attributed to Jesus (maxims, proverbs, parables); it has no narrative. (Scholars have long posited a pre-Gospel source named "Q" [→ Syn Problem, 40:21] which consisted entirely of sayings; *GTh* shows that such a literary form did exist in Christian antiquity.) Some sayings are identical with or parallel to canonical NT sayings; but the majority are different in whole or in part. As for the similar or parallel sayings, it is difficult to be certain whether *GTh* has borrowed from the Syn or from a source similar to the sources behind those Gospels. As for the sayings that are different, some of them may be genuine, for several of them are cited elsewhere in early Christian literature (see A. J. B. Higgins, *NovT* 4 [1960] 292–306). Yet there is a Gnostic or incipiently Gnostic flavor to many of them. Probably *GTh* is a composite work, binding together genuine sayings of Jesus, canonical and noncanonical, with sayings invented in Gnostic circles.

(General bibliography of *GTh* by E. Haenchen, *TR* 27 [1961] 147–78, 306–22. For *GTh* and the canonical Gospels see H. Montefiore and H. E. W. Turner, *Thomas and the Evangelists* [SBT 35; London, 1962]; R. North, *CBQ* 24 [1962] 154–70; R. E. Brown, *NTS* 9 [1963] 155–77. See also G. Quispel, *Makarius, das Thomasevangelium und das Lied von der Perle* [Leiden, 1967].)

61 **(IV) Gospel of the Hebrews.** From the end of the 2nd cent. AD, Church Fathers like Hegesippus, Clement of Alexandria, Origen, and Jerome speak of a *Gospel According to the Hebrews* (henceforth *GHebr*), a work that was subsequently lost. The earlier Fathers cite it in Greek, but Jerome (*In Matt.* 12.13) claims to have translated it into Greek and Latin and cites Hebr words from it. In *Adversus Pelagianos* 3.2, he states that this gospel is in Aramaic; whereas Eusebius speaks of its being in Hebrew. It is not entirely clear whether Eusebius would identify *GHebr* with the Hebr or Aram collection of sayings written by Matthew (*Hist.* 3.39, 16–17; GCS 9/1.292). Epiphanius (*PG* 41.405A) states distinctly that the Nazarenes (or Nazareans [*Nazōraioi*]—a Jewish-Christian sect) had the complete *Gospel According to Matthew* in Hebrew.

Are all of these Fathers speaking of the same work? Jerome and Epiphanius are clearly referring to a gospel used by the Nazarenes, a gospel that was also known to Apollinaris and seemingly to Eusebius, and a gospel that was certainly written in Hebrew or Aramaic. Jerome identified this with the (Gk) gospel that Origen spoke of, but was he correct? Many think today that Jerome made a mistake, and that the gospel which circulated among the Nazarenes and which he saw and translated into Greek was really a 2nd-cent. free retroversion of Gk Mt into Aramaic, done for the sake of an Aram-speaking region in Syria. Therefore the citations that Jerome makes from *GHebr* must be weighed with care; some may be from the real *GHebr* but many are from the gospel circulated among the Nazarenes.

62 The real *GHebr*, probably composed in Egypt in the 2nd cent. AD, and extant only in patristic citations, seems to have existed only in Greek in the stage in which it was known to the early Fathers. The reference to "Hebrews," then, is a reference to those in whose circle it was popular, rather than to the language in which it was written. In *Hist.* 4.22, 8 (GCS 9/1.372) Eusebius seems to distinguish it from gospels written in Aramaic and Hebrew; and elsewhere (3.27, 4; GCS 9/1.256) he speaks of its use by the Ebionites, a Jewish-Christian group. These Ebionites may be the "Hebrews" of the title (however, *GHebr* is not necessarily to be identified with the *Gospel of the Ebionites* known to Irenaeus and Epiphanius). As we know *GHebr* from the patristic citations, it was a Jewish-Christian work, heavily dependent on Mt, which contained both the words and deeds of Jesus. Among its narratives was a variant form of the Parable of the Talents/Pounds, important for studying the differences that exist between the forms of this parable in Mt and Lk (→ Aspects

NT Thought, 78:143). *GHebr*, according to Eusebius (*Hist.* 3.39, 17; GCS 9/1.292), also contained the story of Jesus and an adulteress, and this is important for the history of the pericope added in the Western tradition to Jn (7:53–8:11). As for its noncanonical parts, the fact that Clement of Alexandria attributed to *GHebr* a saying found in one of the Oxyrhynchus papyri that we now know was taken from the *Gospel of Thomas* (→ 60 above) suggests a relationship between *GHebr* and *GTh*. There was a slight Gnostic tinge to *GHebr*.

(The patristic citations and a bibliography are given in A. De Santos Otero, *Los evangelios*, 32–50; also Hennecke, *NTA* 1, 158–65; R. Dunkerley, *op. cit.*, 102–11. For studies, see B. W. Bacon, *Studies in Matthew* [1930] 478–95; G. Bardy, *MScRel* 3 [1946] 5–36.)

63 **(V) Gospel of Peter.** Serapion of Antioch (*ca.* 190; → Canonicity, 67:65) and Origen both knew of a *Gospel of Peter* (henceforth *GPet*) that circulated in Syria and Egypt in the late 2nd cent. In 1886 a considerable fragment of the Gk text of this gospel was discovered at Akhmim in Upper Egypt. It was probably composed *ca.* 150, drawing on all four canonical Gospels. The part that has been preserved refers to the passion of Jesus. There is a slightly docetic character to its description of Jesus. It is anti-Jewish in tone and strongly apologetic, seeking to establish the reality of the resurrection by recording that it took place before the soldiers and the Jewish authorities: "They saw three men come out from the sepulcher, with two of them sustaining the third, and a cross following them. The heads of the two reached to heaven, but that of him whom they led by the hands overpassed the heavens" (10:39–40). Although at first some scholars argued that *GPet* contained real historical knowledge not preserved in the canonical Gospels, today most look upon it as an imaginative midrash on gospel materials.

(Text, Fr trans., and commentary in L. Vaganay, *L'Évangile de Pierre* [EBib; Paris, 1930]; also Hennecke, *NTA* 1, 179–87.)

64 **(VI) Protevangelium of James.** We have already indicated that, like other infancy gospels, this work has no real historical value (→ 54 above). The canonical infancy narratives in Mt and Lk concentrate on the theological perspectives of what they narrate, and the primary stress is Christological. In the apocryphal infancy gospels greater imagination is given play; the details of the narrative become an object of interest in themselves, and attention is shifted to other personages like Joseph and Mary. They contain some fascinating stories, e.g., the *Infancy Story of Thomas* from the late 2nd cent. tells of the miracles (often little more than marvelous tricks) worked by the boy Jesus. See O. Cullmann's treatment of the infancy gospels in Hennecke, *NTA* 1, 363–417; also F. Amiot, *op. cit.*, 47–136.

The *Protevangelium of James* (also "The Birth of Mary," "The Revelation of James") is the most famous of these infancy gospels and has had tremendous influence on popular Christianity. A 3rd-cent. Gk ms., found among the Bodmer papyri (Bodmer V, publ. by M. Testuz in 1958) is of much more value than the many late mss. used as a basis of previous editions. There are Syriac, Armenian, and Ethiopic versions, and a fragment of a Sahidic Coptic copy. (See E. de Strycker, *La forme la plus ancienne du Protoévangile de Jacques* [Brussels, 1961]). The work was probably composed *ca.* 150–175 by a non-Jewish Christian who harmonized earlier materials and sources. The designation "protevangelium" is relatively modern. The book presents itself as an account given by James, the Lord's brother, about the birth of Mary (daughter of Joachim and Anne), her upbringing in the Temple, and her marriage to Joseph. Joseph is presented as a widower with children (the "brothers" of Jesus); he was chosen by lot to become Mary's husband, and he respected her virginity. Presumably James was chosen as the author of this pseudepigraphon because, as a member of the family of Joseph and Mary, he would have been in a position to know the family history.

65 Among the many traditions that this work has contributed to Catholic piety we may mention the following: Joachim and Anne (Anna) as the parents of the Virgin; the Presentation of Mary in the Temple; Mary's intention to remain a virgin even before the annunciation; Jesus' birth in a cave. Scholars have long pointed out that the author was hopelessly inaccurate in his knowledge of Jewish customs; for instance, the whole story of Mary's stay at the Temple would not have been possible. Inevitably some will suggest that the use of the stories of the *Protevangelium* in pious literature and in the liturgy has somehow made them historically reliable. It is perhaps worth noting that Jerome was very critical of the *Protevangelium*. Pope Innocent I (DS 213) not only rejected but also condemned the apocryphon of James, as did the so-called Gelasian Decree (Hennecke, *NTA* 1, 47; → Canonicity, 67:10). In the 16th cent. Pope Pius V suppressed the feasts of St. Joachim and of the Presentation of Mary in the Temple, although they were later restored. If the *Protevangelium* is a valuable work, it is not as a witness to what happened at the birth of Jesus but as a witness to Christian Marian piety in the 2nd cent. (Smid, H. R., *Protevangelium Jacobi* [Assen, 1965].)

DEAD SEA SCROLLS

ANNOTATED BIBLIOGRAPHY

66 The term "Dead Sea Scrolls," used in its wide sense, covers mss. and fragments discovered independently from 1947 on in about half a dozen different sites in the area W of the Dead Sea. In its narrow sense it refers to what was discovered at Qumran, the original and most important site. Because of the ambiguity in the use of the term, we shall give a general bibliography before treating any given site, even though some of these works refer exclusively to Qumran finds.

(I) Bibliographies of DSS. Burchard, C., *Bibliographie zu den Handschriften vom Toten Meer:* Vol. 1 (2nd ed.; BZAW 76; Berlin, 1959) covers up to 1955; vol. 2 (BZAW 89; 1965) covers 1956–62; it is exhaustive. LaSor, W., *Bibliography of the Dead Sea Scrolls, 1948–1957* (Pasadena, 1958). The *RevQum* has a systematic bibliography in each issue. Also see Yizhar, M., *Bibliography of Hebrew Publications on the Dead Sea Scrolls, 1948–64* (HTS 23; Cambridge, Mass., 1967).

(II) Texts. Burrows, M., *The Dead Sea Scrolls of St. Mark's Monastery* 1 (New Haven, 1950); 2/2 (1951); abbrev. DSSMM. Sukenik, E. L., *The Dead Sea Scrolls of the Hebrew University* (Jerusalem, 1955); abbrev. DSSHU. De Vaux, R., D. Barthélemy, J. T. Milik, *et al.*, *Discoveries in the*

Judaean Desert 1 (Oxford, 1955), 2 (1961), 3 (1962), 4 (1965); abbrev. DJD. Convenient student editions of the Hebr text with a Lat translation have been published by P. Boccaccio (Rome): 1QpHab; 1QS; 1QSa; 1QM. For vocalized Hebr text with concordance, see A. Habermann, *Megilloth Midbar Yehuda* (Tel Aviv, 1959). For a list of the publications of the individual texts, see J. A. Sanders, *JBL* 86 (1967) 431–40.

(III) Concordances. Kuhn, K. G., *Konkordanz zu den Qumrantexten* (Göttingen, 1960) with suppl. in *RevQum* 4 (1963) 163–234.

(IV) Translations. The most complete, with scientific notes, is that of J. Carmignac, *et al.*, *Les textes de Qumran* 1 (Paris, 1961), 2 (1963). The best Eng translation is that of G. Vermes, *The Dead Sea Scrolls in English* (Pelican paperback; Baltimore, 1962). A literary but free translation is that of T. H. Gaster, *The Dead Sea Scriptures in English Translation* (Anchor paperback, 2nd ed.; N.Y., 1964). More detailed than Vermes is A. Dupont-Sommer, *The Essene Writings from Qumran* (Meridian paperback; N.Y., 1962). There are translations in Burrows' two volumes mentioned below.

(V) Introductory Studies. Allegro, J. M., *The Dead Sea Scrolls* (Pelican paperback; Baltimore, 1956); fascinating, but poor on the relation of the QL to Christianity. Murphy, R. E., *The Dead Sea Scrolls and the Bible* (Westminster, Md., 1956). Schubert, K., *The Dead Sea Community* (N.Y., 1959). Van der Ploeg, J., *The Excavations at Qumran* (London, 1958).

(VI) Detailed Studies. The two best general works are J. T. Milik, *Ten Years of Discovery in the Wilderness of Judaea* (SBT 26; London, 1959); and F. M. Cross, Jr., *The Ancient Library of Qumran* (Anchor paperback, 2nd ed.; N.Y., 1961). M. Burrows, in *The Dead Sea Scrolls* (N.Y., 1955) and *More Light on the Dead Sea Scrolls* (N.Y., 1958), gives exhaustive treatments of all views, sane and silly. For theology of the scrolls see H. Ringgren, *The Faith of Qumran* (Fortress paperback; Phila., 1963); F. Nötscher, *Zur theologischen Terminologie der Qumran–Texte* (BBB 10; Bonn, 1956); *Gotteswege und Menschenwege in der Bibel und in Qumran* (BBB 15; Bonn, 1958); *Vom alten zum neuen Testament* (BBB 17; Bonn, 1962). For archaeology see R. de Vaux, *L'archéologie et les manuscrits de la Mer Morte* (Oxford, 1961). The most recent survey is in *McCormick Quarterly* 21 (1968) 247–320.

(VII) Relation to the NT. A general survey is given by R. E. Brown in *ExpT* 78 (1966–67) 19–23. Important, scholarly articles are collected in *The Scrolls and the New Testament*, ed. K. Stendahl (N.Y., 1957); *La secte de Qumran et les origines du Christianisme* (RechBib 4; Bruges, 1959). Rather personal approaches are taken by J. Daniélou, *The Dead Sea Scrolls and Primitive Christianity* (Baltimore, 1963); and by M. Black, *The Scrolls and Christian Origins* (London, 1961). See also H. H. Rowley, *The Dead Sea Scrolls and the New Testament* (London, 1960); L. Mowry, *The Dead Sea Scrolls and the Early Church* (Chicago, 1962). A complete bibliography is supplied by H. Braun, *TR* 28, 29, 30 (1962, 1963, 1964)—articles included in *Qumran und das Neue Testament* (2 vols.; Tübingen, 1966). Articles for the general public are found in *The Scrolls and Christianity*, ed. M. Black (Theological Collections 11; London, 1969).

QUMRAN

67 **(I) The Discoveries.** The wadi that the Arabs call Qumrân empties into the NW corner of the Dead Sea 10 mi. S of Jericho. About a mile inland from the sea, on a marly plateau adjacent to the wadi are ruins excavated by R. de Vaux and G. L. Harding between 1951 and 1956. Originally the site of a fortress built in the 8th–7th cents. BC, the ruins at Qumran show evidence of building and occupation in a period from *ca.* 135 BC to *ca.* 31 BC, and in a second period from *ca.* AD 1 to 68. The enclave is marked with edifices and rooms designed to serve a community's needs: a complete water system with conduits and cisterns; a kitchen, pantry, and large dining room; store rooms; a scriptorium; pottery workshops; and a burial ground. The buildings of the first period show a slow start, but then there was a considerable increase in occupation from *ca.* 110 BC on; this period seems to have ended with a fire and earthquake (simultaneous?). The second period came to a close with destruction by Roman armies who occupied the site for short intervals thereafter. In 1956 and 1958 De Vaux also excavated another series of buildings 1.5 mi. S of Qumran at a spring called Ain Feshkha; seemingly they were structures built by the Qumran community to serve its economic needs.

68 In 11 caves within a radius of a few miles of the Qumran buildings have been found the remains of some 600 mss., consisting of about 10 complete scrolls and thousands of fragments. Indeed, it was the 1947 discovery of scrolls in a cave (cave 1) that focused the interests of archaeologists on the area. About one-fourth of the mss. are biblical. Seven of the scrolls from cave 1 are in Israel in "The Shrine of the Book"; the rest of the material has been studied at the Palestine Museum in Jerusalem, Jordan (under Israeli control since June 1967). At the Museum an international and interconfessional "team" of scholars has been preparing material from caves 2–11 for publication; these include R. de Vaux, J. T. Milik, J. Strugnell, P. Skehan, F. M. Cross, J. Starcky, J. M. Allegro, D. Barthélemy, and M. Baillet.

69 On the next page we give an inventory of the caves numbered according to the order of their discovery; note that the documents are designated by the number of the cave they were found in. Caves 1, 4, and 11 are "major" caves whose material is abundant and requires separate publication; the rest are "minor" caves whose material was published together in DJD 3. For an explanation of the system used in referring to Qumran documents → Texts, 69:20.

70 **(II) Important Qumran Writings.** The biblical mss. of Qumran will be treated by themselves elsewhere (→ Texts 69:15–29); here we concern ourselves with works of peculiarly sectarian origin. All the works below, except the last two, are writings composed by the Qumran sect and expressive of their theology and piety.

71 **QS:** *Serek ha-Yaḥad* = the Manual of Discipline, or the Rule of the Community. A well-preserved copy of 11 columns was found in cave 1 and published by M. Burrows in DSSMM 2/2 (1951). Detailed studies in English have been made by W. H. Brownlee (*BASOR* Supplement; New Haven, 1951) and P. Wernberg-Møller (Leiden, 1957), and in modern Hebrew by J. Licht (Jerusalem, 1965). A fragment of a ms. from cave 5 has been published in DJD 3, 180–81. The ten copies of QS from cave 4 are discussed by J. T. Milik in *RB* 67 (1960) 410–16. Also cf. A. R. C. Leaney, *The Rule of Qumran and Its Meaning* (Phila., 1966).

Paleographically, 1QS dates from 100–75 BC (Cross, *Library*, 119–20); yet comparison with 4QS shows that 1QS had undergone considerable editing, especially in cols. 5, 8, and 9. The ms. $4QS^e$ is probably to be dated before 100 BC. Thus, a date of composition for QS between 150 and 125 BC is indicated, and the work seems to be one of the most ancient sectarian compositions. It

Documents Found in the Qumran Caves

CAVE 1: discovered by the Bedouin; excavated by G. L. Harding and R. de Vaux in Feb.–Mar. 1949. It yielded relatively complete scrolls (three still in a jar), as well as fragments.

1QIs[a] — the Hebr text of Is, somewhat divergent in spelling and reading from the MT (→ Texts, 69:16, 23).

1QS — the rule of life for the community that lived at Qumran (→ 71 below).

1QpHab — a free, interpretative commentary (*pešer*) on Hab, adapting the thought of the book to the Qumran community (→ 77–78 below).

1QapGn — an apocryphal elaboration of Gn in Aramaic (→ 81 below).

(The above four mss. were taken out of Jordan at the direction of Mar Athanasius Yeshue Samuel, a Syrian prelate who had obtained them from the Bedouin. They were published in part in DSSMM [except 1QapGn] and later, through an intermediary, sold to Israel for $250,000.)

1QIs[b] — a more fragmentary copy of Is, closer to the MT (→ Texts, 69:23).

1QH — psalms of praise (*hôdāyôt*) composed in the community (→ 74 below).

1QM — an imaginative description of the final war to be waged between the forces of good and evil (→ 76 below). (The above three mss. were obtained from antiquities dealers by E. L. Sukenik of the Hebrew University before the partition of Palestine. They were published in part in DSSHU.)

Fragments of 70 other mss. published in DJD 1. The most important are two appendices detached from 1QS, namely 1QSa and 1QSb (→ 72, 73 below).

CAVE 2: discovered by the Bedouin in Feb. 1952. The most important of the fragments it yielded are from the lost Hebr text of Sir (→ Texts, 69:29).

CAVE 3: discovered by archaeologists in Mar. 1952. It yielded two badly oxidized copper rolls that were originally part of one scroll. These were sliced open in 1956 and published in DJD 3 (→ 82 below).

CAVE 4: discovered by the Bedouin and further excavated by archaeologists in Sept. 1952. In many ways the most important of the caves, it yielded fragments from about 400 mss. It was near the settlement and may have served as a hiding place for the community's library when the Romans were coming. For the work on this cave's fragments, see *BA* 19 (1956) 83–96.

A few of the finds are:

— Some mss. of OT books going back to the 3rd cent. BC, our oldest copies of Scripture (→ Texts, 69:11).

— Biblical mss. with a Hebr text unlike the MT but close to the Hebr text underlying the LXX (→ Texts 69:18–19).

— Fragments of Tb in the (hitherto lost) original Aramaic (→ Texts, 69:29).

— Fragments in the original language (Hebrew or Aramaic) of important apocrypha, hitherto preserved only in later translations, e.g., *Enoch, Jubilees, Testaments* (→ 9, 16, 25 above).

— Fragments of hundreds of mss. throwing light on the belief and practice of the Qumran community, including earlier copies of works found in cave 1 (QS, QH, QM). There are biblical commentaries, calendars, apocalyptic books, books in code.

CAVES 5, 6: discovered and excavated in 1952 in relation to cave 4.

CAVES 7, 8, 9, 10: discovered in 1955 near the Qumran settlement.

CAVE 11: discovered by the Bedouin in 1956. This cave, like cave 1, has yielded extensive portions of scrolls. Part of the material will be published by Dutch scholars.

11QPs[a] — a Pss scroll, published by J. A. Sanders as DJD 4; also see his *The Dead Sea Psalms* (Ithaca, 1967) with a postscript containing the text of an additional fragment (→ Texts, 69:27).

11QPs[b] — another Pss collection (J. van der Ploeg, *RB* 74 [1967] 408–12).

11QPsAp[a] — a work containing both biblical and apocryphal psalms (J. van der Ploeg, *RB* 72 [1965] 210–17).

11QLv — part of Lv in paleo-Hebrew script (→ Texts, 69:16).

11QEz, — a poorly preserved copy of Ez from *ca.* 55 to 25 BC with a Hebr text close to the MT (W. Brownlee, *RevQum* 4 [1963] 11–28). Only a few fragments are legible.

11QtgJob — a 1st-cent. AD copy of a targum (→ Texts, 69:83).

11QMelch — fragments of an eschatological midrash from *ca.* 1–50 AD. The figure of Melchizedek, now a heavenly being above the angels, appears in a setting drawn from the description of the jubilee year in Lv 25; he is to have a role on the day of judgment (A. S. van der Woude, *OTS* 14 [1965] 354–73; J. A. Fitzmyer, *JBL* 86 [1967] 25–41). (For NT relevance, → Epistle Heb, 61:39.)

11Q "Temple Scroll" — described by Y. Yadin, *BA* 30 (1967) 135–39. Acquired by Israeli authorities from the Bethlehem agent of the Bedouin after the June 1967 war, the scroll has 66 cols. that list or describe: religious rules (given by God in the first person!); sacrifices for festivals; the Temple; statutes of the king and his army. Many of the rules are sectarian in character; Yadin dates it to the period at the end of the 1st cent. BC or early in the 1st cent. AD.

is quite reasonable to suggest that in its substance it stems from the Righteous Teacher of the sect (→ 85 below).

Evidently the QS scroll was the essential rule book for the life of the Qumran community. Its theme is that the community represents the New Covenant between God and men prophesied by Jer 32:37–41. One becomes a partner in this Covenant by entrance into the community, and this is described in cols. 1–2. There is a graphic description in 3–5 of two opposing ways of life: the way dominated by the spirit of light and truth and the way dominated by the spirit of darkness and falsehood. Then follow the actual rules that govern community life. The pattern is very much that of Israel during Moses' time in the desert wanderings, and the idea is that by withdrawing to the desert (Qumran) this community is preparing itself to be the nucleus of the new Israel that in God's time will be brought to the promised land. This is our first known example of what in Christianity would develop into rules for monastic life.

The QS scroll from cave 1 had two attached appendixes, published in DJD 1, 107–30. These are:

72 **QSa:** *Serek ha-'ēdâ* = the Rule of the Congregation. This work of two columns begins: "This is the rule for the whole congregation of Israel in the last days." Although the rule is patterned on the daily life of the sectarians, this life is seen as having eschatological significance. The document ends with the description of a banquet at which the *Priest* who is head of the whole congregation of Israel and the *Messiah* of Israel both bless bread and wine. The mention of women and children in this writing (1:4) has led to the suggestion (Cross, *Library*, 79ff.) that the *'ēdâ*, or congregation, refers to the totality of the sectarians, including both those in the monastic desert community (*yaḥad*) at Qumran and those in other places and circumstances, e.g., in camps and cities.

73 **QSb:** a Collection of Blessings. This work of six columns has been poorly preserved. It gives the text for the benediction of groups and of individuals in the sect. There seems to be a special blessing for the Priest as well as one for the Prince (*nāśî'*) of the Congregation.

There is no clear evidence that these works were appended to any other copy of QS, and they may well be compositions of the period when the ms. of 1QS was copied (100–75 BC).

74 **QH:** the *Hôdāyôt* = the Hymns of Thanksgiving. The poorly preserved 1QH was published by E. L. Sukenik in DSSHU 35–58, with additional fragments published by J. T. Milik in DJD 1, 136–38. Studies of this have been made in English by S. Holm-Nielsen (Aarhus, 1960) and M. Mansoor (Leiden, 1961); and in French by M. Delcor (Paris, 1962). A study in modern Hebrew by J. Licht (Jerusalem, 1959) is excellent in its suggestions for filling in lacunae, as will be verified when fragments of six more copies of the work from cave 4 are published. In a series of studies on QH (references in *Textes* 1, 145), J. Carmignac has established that the material from cave 1 originally came from two scrolls and that Sukenik published the columns in the wrong order: Cols. 13–16 belonged to the first scroll, while 17 and 1–12 belonged to the second scroll. Three scribes copied 1QH and paleographically it is dated to the period AD 1–50.

QH is a descendant of the biblical hymn book, the Psalter. However, the classical period of Hebr poetry had passed, and the compositions of QH have their closest parallel in the hymns preserved in 1–2 Mc and in the Lucan hymns of the NT ("Magnificat" and "Benedictus"). They are largely mosaics of biblical phrases, culled in particular from Ps and Is—a style called anthological. Frequently a biblical metaphor is developed into full-blown allegory. The hymnist speaks in the first person and meditates before God on God's goodness to him. There are many historical reflections taken from the hymnist's life (J. Carmignac, *RevQum* 2 [1959–60] 205–22). For the theology of QH, see J. Licht, *IsrEJ* 6 (1956) 1–13, 89–101.

Holm-Nielsen has suggested an entirely liturgical origin for the hymns, but the personal character of the meditation makes this unlikely. Perhaps we can find the key to the composition of QH in what Philo, *De Vita contemp*. (29, 80, 83, 84) says about the Therapeutae, seemingly a branch or form of the Essene movement. These sectarians had hymns composed by the first chiefs of their sect; in particular hymns were composed by individuals to be recited on the feast of Pentecost (which at Qumran was the great feast of the renewal of the covenant). The corresponding suggestion that the QH were composed by the Righteous Teacher has many adherents. This would mean a date of *ca*. 150–125 BC, probably after QS.

75 **D** or **CD:** the Damascus Covenant or the Zadokite Work(s). Two medieval mss. of this work (ms. A with cols. 1–16; ms. B with cols. 19–20; B 19 = A 7–8), dating from the 10th and 12th cents., were found in the Cairo Geniza (→ Texts, 69:37) in 1896–97, and ed. by S. Schechter in 1910. The best edition is that of C. Rabin (2nd ed.; Oxford, 1958). Fragments of nine mss. of the work have been found at Qumran, and there is no doubt that the medieval mss. represent a Qumran work. A 5Q fragment is published in DJD 3, 181; the 6Q fragments are published in DJD 3, 128–31; also M. Baillet, *RB* 63 (1956) 513–23. Milik (*Ten Years*, 38, 151–52; *BA* 19 [1956] 89) discusses the fragments from seven 4Q mss; also cf. *RB* 73 (1966) 105. There were several recensions of the document; the Qumran material tends to agree with medieval ms. A; the oldest Qumran copy dates from 75–50 BC.

The work consists of two parts. *First*, admonitions drawn from history are found in cols. 1–8 of ms. A, plus 19–20 of B. An introduction for this section appears in the unpublished Qumran material.The author searches through the history of Israel from antiquity until the rise of the Qumran community, drawing lessons to encourage the community. He is repetitious and oratorical but makes useful allusions to the history of the sect. By the time CD is being written the Righteous Teacher has been dead for some years (20:14). *Second*, in cols. 15–16 and 9–14 of ms. A, there are laws to be observed by those of the community who live in camps. The columns in A are out of order, and both the beginning and end of the law section have perished. In the 4Q copies there is material that continues col. 14, as well as a concluding covenant renewal ceremony. These laws cover entrance into the community, behavior, purifications, organization, and punishments. If we take the two parts together, the whole work may well have been a manual for a covenant renewal ceremony with a historical exhortation and a reminder about the laws.

Milik suggests a date of composition *ca*. 100 BC, and two factors support this date: the failure to mention the Romans in the historical section, and the paleography of the oldest copy. The laws differ to some extent from those of QS; but this may be explained either by the difference in time of composition (QS is earlier) or by the difference in circumstances of those living in camps (as distinct from those living in the desert community). CD 6:5 mentions "the converts of Israel who went out from Judah to sojourn in the land of Damascus"; and the work is addressed to the members of the New Covenant in the land of Damascus (7:19; 8:21). Some (Cross, *Library*, 82–83) believe Damascus to be a figurative name for the site of Qumran, but Milik takes the term literally and thinks of a branch community from Qumran dwelling in camps in the Damascus/Hauran area. One argument for the former view is the number of copies of CD found at Qumran.

76 **QM:** *Serek ha-Milḥāmâ* = the Rule for the War, or the War of the Sons of Light Against the Sons of Darkness. The badly mutilated 1QM was published in DSSHU, and a detached fragment, 1Q33, was published in DJD 1. There are fragments from five more mss. in the cave 4 material (C.-H. Hunzinger, *ZAW* 69 [1957] 131–51; M. Baillet, *RB* 71 [1964] 356–59). Studies and translations of QM were produced in French by J. van der Ploeg (Leiden, 1957), J. Carmignac (Paris, 1958), and J. Jongeling (Assen, 1962); in English by Y. Yadin (Oxford, 1962—from a 1955 work in modern Hebrew).

The Hebr title of the work was: "For the Sage—the Rule for the War"; and the work proposes to give the plan for the armies and the campaign of the final 40-years' war when God will crush the forces of evil and darkness in this world. Although the author seems to have drawn upon the military terminology of his time, the war is conducted according to theological designs rather than according to a scientific military strategy. The dominating theme is that if the forces of good (or of light) are organized according to the proper semiliturgical scheme and if their standards and trumpets are properly inscribed with prayers, God will favor them and victory will be ensured. The camps of the sons of light are organized after the directives of Nm 2:1–5:4; the troops receive ardent sermons from the priests, who also sound the battle signals. The angel Michael, with the aid of Raphael and Sariel, leads the forces of light, while Belial guides the forces of darkness. Columns 2–14 give the general rules; and 15–19 seem to forecast the actual battle, although some see here a duplication (the sign that a shorter work has undergone editing).

Carmignac has argued that the Righteous Teacher himself composed the work *ca.* 110 BC. Most writers, however, date the work in the period 50 BC–AD 25. Yadin argues that the military tactics and equipment are Roman, and the designation that CD uses for the opponents of Israel is "Kittim," a term that does designate the Romans in other Qumran documents. All the copies extant are from the 1st cent. AD (Milik, *Ten Years*, 40), although Cross (*BANE* 138) tends to date 1QM in the early Herodian period of 30–1 BC. The work may well be one of the later sectarian writings composed when the group was infected by a more martial spirit. It is interesting that there is no clear expectation of a Davidic Messiah in the work (which is far from completely preserved, however), and it is the High Priest who plays the dominant role.

77 **Pesharim,** or Commentaries. At Qumran the biblical commentaries (sing. *pēšer;* pl. *pᵉšārîm*) exhibit a peculiar exegetical technique. These pesharim study the biblical text verse by verse, searching for a meaning applicable to the life of the sect, to its past or present circumstances, and to its future hope. The presumption seems to be that the ancient prophet or psalmist who wrote the biblical work did not address himself to his own times but to the future, and that that future was the history of the Qumran community. When *ca.* 600 BC Habakkuk spoke of the righteous, he really meant the Righteous Teacher of Qumran. When he spoke of Lebanon, he meant the Council of the Qumran community. At times in this imaginative exegesis, the Qumran commentator reads the words of the text he is commenting on in a way quite different from the grammatical sense intended by the original author. Scripture has become a vast allegory, and the Qumran interpreter is the man with the key to the allegory. The procedure of the pesharim is quite different from that of other Bible-related works at Qumran, which in midrashic manner simply expand or embellish the biblical narrative in a direction that is more faithful to the original author's intention. (For the type of interpretation evidenced in isolated quotations of the OT, see the study of J. A. Fitzmyer, *NTS* 7 [1960–61] 297–333.)

The mental background of the pesharim exegesis is that of apocalyptic. Instead of men with messages for their own time, the prophets and psalmists have become men concerned with the last times. And since the appearance of the Qumran community is the sign of the last times, the biblical authors were concerned with that community. The style of exegesis seems to stem from the Righteous Teacher; for according to 1QpHab 2:8–10 God gave him understanding to interpret all that was foretold through the prophets and (7:4–5) made known to him all the mysteries behind the prophets' words. Most of the pesharim preserved for us date paleographically from after 50 BC. There is never more than one copy of a pesher; this may mean that the mss. that have come down to us are the autographs, i.e., the originals (Cross, *Library*, 114–15). Although they are by different writers, the style of exegesis is very similar. This indicates that the various commentators were instructed in a communal tradition of interpretation, perhaps coming down from the Righteous Teacher.

78 The most important pesher is 1QpHab, a 14-column commentary. It was published by M. Burrows in DSSMM 1. Cave 1 also yielded some fragmentary pesharim on Mi, Zeph, Pss 57 and 68, which appear in DJD 1, 77–82. Fragments of different pesharim on Is from cave 4 have been published by J. M. Allegro in *JBL* 75 (1956) 177–82; 77 (1958) 215–21. There was also a pesher on Is in cave 3, published by M. Baillet in DJD 3, 95–96. Fragments from cave 4 of two pesharim on Hos have been published by Allegro in *JBL* 75 (1956) 93; 78 (1959) 142–47. Allegro also published fragments of a cave 4 pesher on Na in *JBL* 75 (1956) 89–93; *JSemS* 7 (1962) 304–8; and fragments of a pesher on Ps 37 in *PEQ* 81 (1954) 69–74; *JBL* 75 (1956) 94–95—see H. Stegemann, *RevQum* 4 (1963–64) 235–70 for the proper order of the latter; also *RevQum* 6 (1967) 193–210.

79 **4QTestimonia,** or the "Messianic" Testimonies. The text was published by J. M. Allegro in *JBL* 75 (1956) 182–87; the copy we have is from 100–75 BC by the same scribe who copied 1QS. The work consists of four biblical citations given one after the other.

Allegro identified the citations as: (1) Dt 5:28–29, plus 18:18–19, a reference to the Prophet-like-Moses (→ Aspects NT Thought, 78:14); (2) Nm 24:15–17, the oracle of Balaam about a star coming from Jacob and a scepter from Israel; (3) Dt 33:8–11, glorifying Levi; (4) Jos 6:26, accompanied by a pesher taken from "The Psalms of Joshua," a hitherto unknown Qumran work, now attested in cave 4—the pesher condemns the man of Belial and his brother. There is no apparent reason for the order of the texts as they are identified by Allegro; nor is their theme apparent. Allegro himself suggested an eschatological theme, namely destruction for those who do not accept the teaching of the messianic figures of the Qumran sect. Other scholars have concentrated on finding a series of messianic figures in the four citations. Thus, they match up the first three citations with the three figures that Qumran expected at the end time: (1) the prophet; (2) the Davidic Messiah; (3) the priestly Messiah (→ 103–104 below). The fourth text is thought to refer to the great enemy. In this interpretation the work belongs to a species of messianic testimonia. ("Testimonia," a term taken from the title of a work by Cyprian, is the designation for systematic collections of OT passages, usually of messianic import, which are thought to have been used by the early Christians in their arguments with the Jews.

These were proof-texts culled from the OT to show that Jesus was the Messiah. The use of the title for this Qumran work suggests by analogy that the sect collected texts to substantiate its messianic expectations. See J. A. Fitzmyer, *TS* 18 [1957] 513–37; P. Prigent, *Les testimonia dans le christianisme primitif* [Paris, 1961].)

This analysis of the Qumran work is probably incorrect. The first of the four citations was wrongly identified. In *CBQ* 19 (1957) 435–40, P. Skehan has shown that it is a citation of Ex 20:21 according to a proto-Samaritan text tradition (→ Texts 69:19, 33–34). With this change the reason for the order of the passages becomes clear; they have been chosen from books in their biblical order (Ex, Nm, Dt, Jos). The neat lining up of messianic characters also collapses when it is realized that the star and scepter of the second citation refer to two different characters: The star is a (or the) priest; the scepter is the Davidic royal Messiah (CD 7:18–20). And so the work is not clearly a collection of messianic testimonia, and Allegro's original interpretation of the basic theme as eschatological is more plausible.

80 **4QFlorilegium,** or Eschatological Midrashim, or a Midrash on the Last Days. The text was published by J. M. Allegro in *JBL* 77 (1958) 350–54. Paleographically the copy is dated to AD 1–50. This incomplete work contains biblical texts accompanied by an interpretation. Allegro thinks of the work as belonging to testimonia literature, but in this instance an interpretation is supplied with the biblical citation. Presumably the theme governing the collection would be a reference to the last days.

In *JBL* 78 (1959) 343–46, W. R. Lane has correctly objected to Allegro's analysis (which continues to be reproduced uncritically). The work itself makes clear that there are three principal biblical passages being discussed (2 Sm 7:10–14; Ps 1:1; Ps 2:1)—any other biblical citations are only by way of interpreting these principal passages. Moreover, the work makes a break between the discussion of 2 Sm and that of the Pss. In both sections the interpretation that is given is described as a pesher; the word *midrash* appears only in introducing the lemma of Ps 1:1. Since midrash has traditionally been used for a specific type of rabbinic exegesis (A. G. Wright, *CBQ* 28 [1966] 105–38) and is a wider category than the pesher exegesis of Qumran, the work in our opinion is better designated as a pesher (although the terms midrash and pesher seem to have been interchangeable at Qumran). Here the ordinary technique of the pesher (→ 77 above) is slightly modified because the interpretation is not in the words of the man who wrote the document but is supplied by the use of other biblical texts. According to P. Skehan (*CBQ* 25 [1963] 121), the work is a pesher on the first lines of a series of psalms; the 2 Sm passage serves as an introduction, for it is a passage that glorifies David who is thought of as the composer of the Psalter. The principle of unity in the work, then, is quite different from that of selecting passages to illustrate the theme of the last days.

81 **1QapGn:** The Genesis Apocryphon (formerly the Apocalypse of Lamech). Five columns (2 and 19–22) of the Aram text of this scroll were published with an Eng translation by N. Avigad and Y. Yadin in 1956; a fragment was published by J. T. Milik as 1Q20 in DJD 1, 86–87. There is a comprehensive study in English by J. A. Fitzmyer (Rome, 1966). The copy is dated paleographically to 25 BC–AD 25.

The work is a type of haggadic midrash (→ 119 below) on Gn 1–15. Various patriarchs (Lamech, Noah, Abraham) recount experiences that are embellishments on the biblical narrative, for the lacunae are filled in by imagination and folklore. The work is not a pesher, for there are no historical references to the Qumran community. Indeed, the work is not necessarily of Qumran origin, and may be simply a Jewish apocryphon. It is seemingly dependent on the treatments of Gn found in *Jubilees* and in *Enoch* 106 (so Fitzmyer; the editors have the dependency in the opposite direction). A 1st-cent. BC date is thus indicated, and the quality of its Aramaic confirms this dating (E. Y. Kutscher in *Scripta Hierosolymitana* 4 [Jerusalem, Israel, 1958] 1–35).

82 **3Q15** = the Copper Scroll. For an interesting description of the discovery and the cutting of the two pieces of this scroll, see J. M. Allegro, *The Treasure of the Copper Scroll* (2nd ed., Anchor paperback; N.Y., 1964). For the unhappy history of the publishing, see R. de Vaux, *RB* 68 [1961] 146–47. The official publication of the text is by J. T. Milik in DJD 3, 201ff. Both Milik and Allegro offer translations, quite different in places (see R. E. Brown, *CBQ* 26 [1964] 251–54). The scroll is written in mishnaic Hebrew, i.e., the type of Hebrew employed in the Mishnah (→ 121 below). Here the mishnaic Hebrew is dialectal and in its early stages, and so the scroll is very important for the history of the Hebr language. Milik dates the script of the document to AD 30–130; Cross dates it to AD 25–75. The dating has led Milik to suggest that the scroll was not a part of the QL (there are no sectarian references), but an independent deposit put in a cave after the destruction of the Qumran settlement.

The scroll gives a long list of places in Palestine where treasure was hidden and thereby makes an important contribution to our knowledge of Palestinian topography. For instance 11:11–13, a passage that describes an area near the Temple, reads: "At Bet-Eshdatain in the pool, where one enters its smaller basin...." If Milik's reading is correct, this is the first reference in early descriptions to the pool of Bethesda of Jn 5:2 (→ Gospel Jn, 63:82).

As for the treasures, the sums are fantastically large, e.g., some 4600 talents of silver and gold. Allegro (p. 44) reduces the value of the denominations listed in the scroll to one sixtieth or one fiftieth their normal value and thus brings the treasures to reasonable amounts. This adventurous deflation enables him to take the treasure list seriously; for in his opinion the scroll is a record of the treasures from the Jerusalem Temple and other holy places hidden in AD 68 by the Zealots who were in control of Jerusalem before the Roman destruction. Looking for this treasure, Allegro has unsuccessfully excavated some of the places mentioned in the scroll. A far more plausible theory is that of Milik who maintains that the list represents folklore based on the fabulous riches of the Jerusalem Temple. After all, there are other ancient examples of lists of imaginary treasure-troves.

83 **(III) History of the Sect.**

(A) Identity. There have been innumerable theories about the identity of the group responsible for the settlement at Qumran and for the mss. found in the caves. They have been identified as Pharisees, Sadducees, Essenes, Zealots, Ebionites, Karaites—in short, as almost every Jewish sect known to have flourished in a period of 1000 years (200 BC–AD 800). If we may cut through all the debate, there is no serious reason to doubt that the Qumran ruins represent the Essene city in the desert described by Pliny the Elder (*Nat. Hist.* 5.17, 73) as being on the W shore of the Dead Sea N of En-gedi (C. Burchard, *RB* 69 [1962] 533–69). What we know of the life of the Qumran community from its documents corresponds very nicely with what we know of the Essenes from Pliny, Philo, and Josephus (J. Strugnell, *JBL* 77 [1958] 106–15; Cross, *Library*, 70ff.). There are minor differences, but these can be explained if we make allowance for different forms of Essene life in the course of 200 years of existence and if we remember that an author like Josephus was simplifying the picture of the Essenes to make them intelligible to a Gentile audience. Therefore, we shall assume that the Qumran sectarians were Essenes; no other thesis can so well account for the evidence. (Cf. R. de Vaux, *RB* 73 [1966] 212–35.)

84 **(B) Origins**. The following theory, supported by Cross, Milik, Strugnell, Skehan, De Vaux, Vermes, and others, is the one that has the most plausibility. A reader interested in other theories is referred to Burrows' volumes.

The movement of religious and national reformation that would ultimately give birth to the Qumran sect came to the fore about 167 BC. A date in the early 2nd cent. is suggested by Qumran's own calculation of its history. In CD 1:5–8 we hear that 390 years after the fall of Jerusalem to Nebuchadnezzar (587), God caused a new planting to grow forth from Israel. This would mean about 190 BC; however, we may remember that other Jewish estimates of the length of the post-exilic period are often short by 20–30 years (G. Vermes, *op. cit.*, 62). Another passage in the QL suggests that the reign of Antiochus Epiphanes (175–163), the great persecutor of the Jews, was the precise time of the sect's origins. The author of 4QpNa speaks of a period "from the time of Antiochus until the coming of the rulers of the Kittim [Romans]"—this is probably the span of the sect's existence up to the time when the author is writing, i.e., Roman times.

In particular, the Qumran sect is probably to be related to the Hasidean branch of the Maccabean revolt against Antiochus (→ History of Israel, 75:108ff.). In 1 Mc 2:42 we hear that Mattathias, the father of Judas Maccabeus, was joined by the Hasideans (*Ḥasîdîm*, or "pious ones"). They were incensed at the religious blasphemies of the Hellenized Jews favorable to Antiochus, and especially by the removal in 172 of Jason, the high priest from the legitimate line of Zadok, in favor of Menelaus, a non-Zadokite. It is interesting to note that most scholars today derive the Gk name *Essēnoi* (var. *Essaioi*) from the pl. forms (*ḥasēn*, *ḥasayyā'*) of *ḥasyā'*, the Eastern Aram equivalent of Hebr *ḥasîd;* and so even by name the Essenes may be the offshoot of the Hasideans. (Milik, *Ten Years*, 80, n. 1; Cross, *Library*, 51–52, n.)

For a while the Hasideans supported the Maccabees; but the interest of the Hasideans was primarily religious, while the Maccabees became more and more politically oriented, ambitious to establish a dynasty. When *ca.* 162 the Syrians appointed the treacherous Alcimus high priest, the Hasideans accepted him as "a priest, from the line of Aaron," even though Judas Maccabeus was opposed (1 Mc 7:9–16). This period of half-hearted alliance with the Maccabees is described in CD 1:9–10 as "the twenty years in which they were like blind men groping their way." But then God "raised for them a Righteous Teacher to guide them in the way of His heart." Seemingly the Qumran Essenes derived directly from those Hasideans who abandoned the Maccabees and followed the Righteous Teacher.

85 **(C) The Righteous Teacher.** The identity of the Righteous Teacher remains a mystery. Our sources for this period are pro-Maccabee and give little attention to their enemies within Judaism (at least until *ca.* 100 and the revolt of the Pharisees). The Teacher was a priest of the Zadokite line. If he was the author of QH, he was a man of great personal piety. The claims that he was a messiah, that he was crucified, that he came back to life, or that he was the forerunner of Jesus Christ are totally unfounded. (For a thorough discussion, see J. Carmignac, *Christ and the Teacher of Righteousness* [Baltimore, 1962] and G. Jeremias, *Der Lehrer der Gerechtigkeit* [Göttingen, 1963].) The Hebr title given to this figure, *môreh ha-ṣedeq*, often translated as "Teacher of Righteousness," is probably to be understood both in the sense that he himself is righteous and in the sense that he teaches righteousness. The title is a traditional one, for Joel 2:23 reads, "He has given you the teacher of righteousness [*môreh liṣdāqâ*]; He has made the rain come down for you"; see also Hos 10:12.

86 The incident that caused the break between the Teacher and the Maccabees probably came during the the period of Jonathan's leadership, after the death of his brother Judas (160). In 152 Jonathan accepted appointment as the high priest of the Jews from the hand of the Syrian king Alexander Balas (1 Mc 10:18–21; → History of Israel, 75:111). This action by a Maccabee who was not a legitimate Zadokite must have constituted the unforgivable sin in the eyes of those Hasideans who had joined the revolt because of the Syrian attempt to replace the Zadokite priesthood. In 1QpHab we hear of a "Wicked Priest" who was faithful at the beginning of his term but who, when he became ruler of Israel, betrayed the commandments. This Wicked Priest is most likely to be identified with Jonathan (so Milik, Skehan, vs. Cross' identification of him as Simon Maccabee). The Wicked Priest persecuted the Righteous Teacher (1QpHab 5:10–11; 9:9) and even pursued him into his place of exile on the Day of Atonement (11:4–8). The mention of this solemn feast day demonstrates that the Priest and the Teacher were following different calendars; for while the day of this outrage may have been the feast of the Atonement for the Teacher, it could not have been a feast day for the Priest—the violation of such a high holy day would have scandalized all. This confirms other evidence (→ 18 above) that the Maccabees offended the Hasidean followers of the Teacher not only over the question of Zadokite succession but also by following the lunar calendar introduced into Temple worship under Antiochus Epiphanes, instead of restoring the old solar calendar.

The Wicked Priest was unsuccessful in his campaign against the Righteous Teacher. God delivered the Priest into the hands of the Gentiles where he suffered a death by torture (4QpPs37 1:18–20; 1QpHab 9:9–12). This fits the career of Jonathan who was arrested in 143–142 by the Syrian general Trypho and who died in prison (1 Mc 12:48; 13:23). Simon, the brother and successor of Jonathan, widened the split with the Teacher and his followers; for in 140 Simon accepted from the Jews the high priesthood for himself and his children forever, thus publicly denying the Zadokite claims (1 Mc 14:41–48; → History of Israel, 75:113). The text of the "Psalms of Joshua" preserved in 4QTest 24–29 condemns Jonathan and Simon together: "Behold an accursed man, a man of Belial, has risen to become a snare to his people and a cause of destruction to all his neighbors. And [his brother] arose [and ruled], both being instruments of violence" (cf. P. Skehan, *CBQ* 21 [1959] 75).

87 The Teacher seems to have outlived his two Maccabee enemies. It is hard to determine the exact moment when he brought his followers to Qumran, an event that seems to be described in CD 6:5: "The converts of Israel went out of the land of Judah to sojourn in the land of Damascus." Archaeology points to a beginning of Qumran settlement *ca.* 140–130, for the earliest coins found at Qumran date from *ca.* 130. The beginning of this first phase of Qumran occupation was very light. Probably the Teacher died a natural death during the reign of Simon Maccabee's son, John Hyrcanus (135–104). The Teacher left his followers looking forward to God's ultimate sending of the Messiah(s) to deliver them (CD 19:35–20:1; 20:13–14).

88 **(D) Subsequent History.**

(a) FIRST CENTURY BC. Toward the end of the reign of John Hyrcanus, just before the turn of the century, a great influx of followers led to the enlargement of the Qumran buildings. Milik (*Ten Years*, 88) plausibly suggests that this influx was the result of Hyrcanus' persecution of the Pharisees. The Pharisees were another offshoot of the Hasideans who had remained faithful to the Maccabean-Hasmonean cause until they could no longer tolerate the rapacity and religious insensibility of Hyrcanus, who was more a secular prince than a high priest (Josephus, *Ant.* 13.10, 5 § 288–98; → History of Israel, 75:121). In describing the Wicked Priest as one who robbed wealth and amassed riches, 1QpHab 8:12 may have been attributing the characteristics of John Hyrcanus to his uncle Jonathan; for Josephus (*Ant.* 13.8, 4 § 249) recounts Hyrcanus' ruthless means of raising wealth. Milik (*Ten Years*, 88) thinks that Hyrcanus is the one referred to in CD 1:14ff. as a liar who persecuted the backsliders (= Pharisees) and suggests that the Qumran sectarians considered Hyrcanus to be a false prophet (Josephus, *Ant.* 13.10, 7 § 299, refers to Hyrcanus' gift of prophecy). Many of the disillusioned Pharisees may have joined the Essene cause, recognizing that the Essenes were right in having opposed the Maccabean corruption when it first became evident. At any rate, the period *ca.* 110–31 BC was the most flourishing period of Qumran settlement.

89 During this period the Qumran Essenes continued their opposition to the Hasmonean priest-rulers at Jerusalem. We find in 4QpNa "the furious young lion... who hangs men alive"—a reference to Alexander Janneus (103–76) who crucified many Jews, especially the Pharisees (Josephus, *Ant.* 13.14, 2 § 380). This same work mentions the attempt of "Demetrius king of Greece" (Demetrius III Eukairos) to invade Jerusalem in 88 BC at the request of the Jews opposed to Janneus (*Ant.* 13.13, 5–14 § 376ff.). A yet unpublished calendar from cave 4 mentions by name Salome Alexandra (76–67), wife and successor of Janneus, and also tells of a massacre by "Aemilius" Scaurus, the first Roman governor of Syria (Milik, *Ten Years*, 73). Several Qumran works refer to the coming of the terrible "Kittim," i.e., the Romans who represented God's judgment on the Hasmonean family (1QpHab 2:12ff.). Clearly these works were written after Pompey's entry into Jerusalem in 63 BC.

90 Archaeological evidence points to a violent destruction of the Qumran settlement by fire and earthquake (simultaneous?). Actually a great earthquake occurred in the Jordan Valley *ca.* 31 BC. Some have seen in the destruction of the community settlement the work of Herod the Great (37–4 BC) whose suspicious nature would unfavorably dispose him to a community of religious fanatics so close to his winter quarters in Jericho. In support of this suggestion is the evidence that the next major occupation at Qumran began shortly after Herod's death; against this suggestion stands the fact that Herod is said to have had a generally favorable attitude toward the Essenes (*Ant.* 15.10, 4–5 § 372–79). Milik (*Ten Years*, 94) thinks that the Qumran settlement may have been destroyed by fire in 40–37 in the wars waged by the Hasmonean Antigonus and the Parthians against Herod. This would attribute the destruction to the ancient enemy of the Qumran Essenes, so that from Jonathan Maccabee to Antigonus, for over a century, the Maccabean-Hasmonean high priestly family would have been implacable in its hatred for the adherents of the Righteous Teacher.

91 (b) FIRST CENTURY AD. After remaining in ruins for 30 to 40 years, the settlement was rebuilt at the beginning of the Christian era and took on a new life that would last for some 60 years (*ca.* AD 1–68). We do not know what gave rise to this rebuilding, but the renewed sectarians were now anti-Roman. In QM the Kittim are pictured on the side of darkness in the eschatological war between the sons of light and the sons of darkness. The Qumran settlement was destroyed for the last time in the summer of 68 by the Roman *Legio X Fretensis*, as the conquerors closed the noose about the centers of Jewish resistance. Before this destruction the community mss. were deposited (hidden?) in caves, especially in cave 4; and some coins were buried. Some of the Essenes seem to have gone south to join the last-ditch resistance at the stronghold of Masada (→ 110 below). The Romans, who established military encampments in the ruins of Qumran, evidently stumbled upon the ms. hoards, for many of the documents were brutally mutilated in antiquity.

92 In Origen's time (early 3rd cent.) Gk and Hebr mss. were found in a jar near Jericho. Another discovery about 785 is attested in a letter of the Nestorian Patriarch Timotheus. Evidently one such discovery yielded mss. that reached the Jewish sect of Karaites and influenced their thought. It was among the sealed up remains of the library of a Karaite synagogue at Cairo (the Cairo Geniza; → Texts, 69:37) that in 1896–97 S. Schechter found documents, like CD and Hebr Sir, that we now know to have been related to the Qumran material. (N. Wieder, *The Judean Scrolls and Karaism* [London, 1962].)

93 **(IV) Features in Qumran Life and Thought.** We take for granted that there were various types of Essenes and that their life must have varied according to whether they were associated with the main settlement at Qumran or whether they dwelt in "camps" and cities. It is the life at Qumran that is best known to us.

(A) Community Life. Evidently, the buildings excavated at Qumran by R. de Vaux were used as the communal center by a large number of sectarians who dwelt in huts and tents (and caves?) nearby. Admission to this community of the New Covenant was strictly regulated. Candidates had to be Israelites and had to be scrutinized by a "supervisor." The ceremony of entry (1QS 1–3) involved taking a binding oath to observe the Law as it was infallibly interpreted in the Zadokite tradition by the Righteous Teacher (5:7–9). A ritual cleansing was also administered in connection with entrance to the Covenant (3:6–12; 5:13). However, as 3:4–6 makes clear, such purification by water was no substitute for purity of heart—the two went together: "He shall be cleansed from all his sins by the spirit of holiness.... And his flesh shall be made clean by the humble submission of his soul to the precepts of God, when his flesh is sprinkled with purifying water and is sanctified by cleansing water" (3:7–9).

94 For the first year (6:16–17) the initiate took no part in the solemn meals or the purificatory rites of the community. He retained his own possessions. (Vermes, *op. cit.*, 26ff., suggests that this was not only a stage of advancement, but also a permanent stage for many who never advanced further. Such people made their own living and paid dues to the community. They would also be the married members of the community.) At the end of the year (3:18–20) there was another scrutiny, and the novice who passed it was asked to hand his possessions into the care of the "supervisor." He was not admitted to the community meals yet; and only when the second year had expired (3:21–23) was he made a full-scale member of the community. Then his possessions were added to the common fund. There were rules for chastising those who violated community precepts and for expelling serious offenders.

95 How extensive was celibacy among the Qumran Essenes? All the ancient authors, Josephus, Philo, and Pliny, mention Essene celibacy. This agrees with the discovery that there were only male skeletons in the main burial ground of the Qumran community. However, there is mention of women and children in CD, QM, and 1QSa; and female skeletons were found on the fringes of the cemetery. Probably one group (the elite, or the priests, or the fully initiated) did practice celibacy, but the rest were married. This agrees with Josephus' evidence about nonmarrying and marrying Essenes (*JW* 2.8, 2 and 13 § 120, 160). Evidently, both in their constant ritual washings and in their celibacy, the full-scale members of the community imitated the purity that the OT demanded of priests before sacrifice. Whether or not the Essenes practiced animal sacrifice at Qumran is not clear (skeletons of animals have been found buried in a way that suggests sacrifice), but there was a tendency on the part of the sectarians to regard their whole life at Qumran as having sacrificial value.

96 Life at Qumran, in the fierce heat of the Jordan Valley, must have been demanding. After their daily work, the sectarians assembled at night for prayer, study, and reading (1QS 6:7–8). Their meals were imbued with religious significance, whence the exclusion of those not fully initiated. In 1QSa a meal of bread and wine is described in an eschatological context, and the possibility of the appearance of the Messiah is mentioned. From this some have inferred that community meals were looked upon as spiritual anticipations of the messianic banquet.

The similarity between Qumran life and that of the Jerusalem church described in Acts has been noted by several scholars (S. E. Johnson, *ZAW* 66 [1954] 106–20, reprinted in K. Stendahl, *op. cit.*, 129–42; J. A. Fitzmyer in *Studies in Luke-Acts*, ed. J. L. Martyn and L. E. Keck [Fest. P. Schubert; Nashville, 1966] 233–57).

97 **(B) Community Organization.** Rank in the community was sharply defined, and at meals the sectarians were required to sit and to speak in order. The chief division was between the House of Aaron (clergy) and the House of Israel (laity). Most of the authority was vested in the priests; only they "have authority in questions of justice and property, and they will have the decisive disposition regarding the men of the community" (1QS 9:8). There was a symbolic division of the community into 12 tribes, as well as a division into numerical units of 1000's, 100's, 50's, and 10's (1QSa 1:29–2:1).

Government seems to have been exercised by distinct judicial, legislative, and executive groups. The presence of judges is mentioned, but we do not know much about them. We have more information about the General Assembly of the community and its Supreme Council. The Assembly of all the mature members of the community, "the Session of the Many" (1QS 6:8ff.), was apparently the organ by which the community governed itself, for it had both judicial and executive authority. It met at least once a year, at Pentecost (2:19), to renew the Covenant and receive new members. Within this Assembly, there was a higher and more permanent body, namely the Supreme Council, consisting of 12 men and 3 priests (8:1). It is not clear whether the total was 15, or only 12, with the 3 priests constituting a subdivision. The 12 seem to have been representatives of the 12 tribes, and perhaps the remainder represented the 3 clans of Levi.

98 Besides the Assembly and the Council, there were specific officials with authority. Here we must describe the situation in CD and that in QS separately. CD 13:2–7 stresses that even for the smallest groups of sectarians (in ten's) there are to be two officials: a *priest* learned in the "Book of Meditation," and a *supervisor* (*m^e^baqqēr*) learned in the Law. The priest takes care of the liturgy; and the tasks of the supervisor are spelled out in 13:7ff.: He is to instruct the congregation, to be like a father and shepherd to them, and to examine and approve newcomers. If this is the arrangement for small groups, CD 14:7–9 proposes a similar arrangement for the whole congregation. Here again it is the priest who enrolls (*yipqōd*, from the root *pqd*) the congregation and is learned in the "Book of Meditation," and together with him is the supervisor of all the camps. The latter seems to have had great authority in commanding individual members and in settling disputes among them. The entire earnings of the community were put into the hands of the supervisor, who, aided by the judges, distributed aid to the orphans and to the needy. Vermes (*op. cit.*, 22–25) suggests that this head supervisor was a Levite (as distinct from the priest) and bore the title of *Maśkîl* (i.e., master or instructor—1QS 9:12ff. gives a set of rules for a *Maśkîl* who is to select, instruct, and judge the members).

If we turn now to the organization proposed in 1QS, we are not certain if the officials are the identical ones proposed by CD, or if there is an adaptation to a different community situation. For groups of ten there are once again two officials: the *priest* who presides at deliberations and blesses food, and the *man who studies the Law* and is concerned with the conduct of the members (1QS 6:3–7). Presumably the latter is the same as the "supervisor" of CD. However, 1QS is vaguer about the officials of the whole community. It speaks of a "supervisor of the many" (6:12) who has an important role in the assemblies and takes care of community goods (6:20). There is also "one who presides [*pāqîd*, from the root *pqd*] at the head of the many" (6:14) and examines candidates. From 1QS one could easily get the impression that this head *pāqîd* is the same person as the head supervisor (*m^e^baqqēr*), whereas in CD the priest who enrolls (*yipqōd*) is distinct from the *m^e^baqqēr*.

99 We have presented the Qumran organization in such detail because it offers extremely important parallels for the organization of the primitive Christian Church. This Church also had a General Assembly (the "multitude" of the disciples of Acts 6:2,5; 15:12, very similar to the Qumran Session of the Many). It also had a special body of the Twelve, the intimate followers of Jesus. Moreover, the Christian bishop is an excellent parallel to the Qumran supervisor. *Episkopos*, "overseer" or "supervisor," could be a literal translation of either *pāqîd* or *m^e^baqqēr;* and the functions attributed to the bishop are much the same as those of the Qumran supervisor, e.g., shepherd of the flock, steward and manager of community property, and inspector of the doctrine of the faithful (1 Pt 2:25; Acts 20:28; Ti 1:7–9; 1 Tm 3:2–7—R. E. Brown, *New Testament Essays* [Milwaukee, 1965] 25–30).

100 **(C) Eschatology and Messianism.** The Qumran community lived in an eschatological context. Throughout Israel's entire history God had prepared for this community of the New Covenant. If Habakkuk (2:4) had promised that the just man would live by faith, 1QpHab 8:1–3 explains that "this concerns all those who observe the Law among the Jews whom God will deliver from judgment because of their suffering and because of their faith in the Righteous Teacher." In other words, every man who is just will eventually join the sect. 1QpHab 7:1–8 identifies the time in which the community lives as the final time, but says that this time is being prolonged according to the mysterious plan of God.

101 The messianism of Qumran has been discussed at great length: J. Starcky (*RB* 70 [1963] 481–505) has sought to trace a development in the messianic thought of Qumran, but there are difficulties (see R. E. Brown, *CBQ* 28 [1966] 51–57). For extensive bibliography see J. A. Fitzmyer, *CBQ* 27 (1965) 349, n.7.

The Righteous Teacher, although not a messiah in the ordinary sense and not using any messianic title, regarded his work as offering to Israel its great chance of salvation. (Whether or not he drew on the Suffering Servant imagery of Dt-Is to explain his role and that of his community is questionable; J. Carmignac, *RevQum* 11 [1961] 365–86, concludes negatively.) Therefore, it is not surprising that the earliest Qumran writings, written in the flush of enthusiasm about what was being accomplished by God through the Teacher, do not speak of the future coming of a messiah. This holds true for the earliest copies of QS and of QH.

102 The death of the Righteous Teacher (*ca.* 120–110 BC) seems to have served as a catalyst to Qumran messianic expectations. An emphasis on messianism in this period may have also been abetted by the entrance of many Pharisees into the sect. And so CD 19:35–20:1 reckons a span of time from the death of the Righteous Teacher until there would arise a messiah from Aaron or from Israel. By the time this document was written (*ca.* 100) the community realized that their deliverance had not been accomplished in the Teacher's lifetime and that they were living in a period before God's final intervention and his raising up the one(s) chosen or anointed (= messiah) to accomplish ultimate victory. At first they probably expected this period to be short. CD 20:14–15 mentions 40 years from the Teacher's death until the destruction of all the men of war who had deserted to the liar (John Hyrcanus?). If taken literally, this means divine victory within a generation. But the sectarians soon learned better; and 1QpHab, written after the appearance of the Romans in 63, speaks of God's prolonging the period.

103 Just what were the messianic expectations in this period? 1QS 9:11 (a copy written in 100–75 BC) contains a passage not found in an earlier copy of QS from cave 4; and this passage speaks of "the coming of a prophet and the Messiahs of Aaron and Israel." Who are these figures? *First*, "a prophet"—the two most plausible identifications for this expectation are the Prophet-like-Moses of Dt 18:15,18, and the prophet Elijah as he is described in Mal 4:5 (3:23). Both expectations were alive in Palestine a century later, as we see from the NT (→ Aspects NT Thought, 78:14–15). Since 1QS speaks of keeping the community's law until the coming of this prophet, the context supports identification as the Prophet-like-Moses. However, Qumran was also interested in Elijah, as we know from an unpublished document from cave 4 (J. Starcky, *art. cit.*, 497–98) that paraphrases the passage in Mal.

104 *Second*, "the Messiahs of Aaron and Israel"—note the plural. As a general precaution, we may warn the reader that in any Jewish document "messiah" does not have all the connotations that the term has in Christian writing where there has been a radical reinterpretation in the light of Jesus' ministry. Nevertheless, it is perfectly proper to capitalize the word in referring to Qumran expectations, for the sectarians expected particular individuals set aside and anointed by God to carry out his work. The Messiah of Aaron would be the anointed High Priest, and the Messiah of Israel would be the anointed Davidic king. (The latter is confirmed by 4Q *Patriarchal Blessings* where a pesher exegesis of Gn 49:10 speaks of "the Righteous Messiah, the shoot of David." We should note, however, that not all scholars accept this interpretation of Qumran messianism, e.g., R. Laurin, *RevQum* 4 [1963] 39–52; B. Vawter, *BCCT* 83–99.) In *CBQ* 19 (1957) 63–66 we have shown how the expectations of two such figures, one priestly and one Davidic, may have arisen in post-exilic Judaism. Zech 4:14 pictures two anointed figures in the presence of the Lord, Zerubbabel of the Davidic line and Joshua the priest; also see the discussion of Zech 6:11. It is quite plausible that in a priestly group like the Qumran community a hope for a priestly Messiah may have accompanied the more general hope for a Davidic Messiah. If the Davidic expectation was based on the eternal covenant between God and David in 2 Sm 7:12–13, there was just as good evidence for an eternal covenant with the priesthood (cf. Sir 45:15,24; Ex 29:9; 40:15).

We hear more of the two extraordinary figures of Qumran expectation in 1QSa, where in the banquet with messianic overtones the two who preside and bless are the Priest and the Messiah of Israel. The blessings in 1QSb seem to include both the Priest (not mentioned by name) and "the Prince [*nāśî'*] of the congregation"—the latter, on the analogy of Ezekiel's use of "prince" and on the usage of CD 7:20, is the Davidic Messiah of Israel. 4QFlor associates at the end of time the Branch of David and the Interpreter of the Law (a figure whose task, at least, is priestly). 4QpIs[a] seems to have the Shoot of David being instructed by a priest. In the later works of the Qumran community, e.g., QM, a greater role is given to the eschatological High Priest than to the Davidic Messiah, but it is possible that the failure to mention the latter may be because the copies that have come down to us are incomplete.

The theory of the Two Messiahs is found also in the *Testaments of the Twelve Patriarchs* (G. R. Beasley-Murray, *JTS* 48 [1947] 1–17), but we are not certain to what extent this apocryphon preserved in Greek is related to the QL (→ 25–27 above). N. Wieder (*JSemS* 6 [1955] 14–25) has shown that there was an expectation of two Messiahs among the medieval Karaites, a sect influenced by Qumran thought (→ 92 above). The NT clearly presents Jesus as the Davidic Messiah, but there are also indications of a theology of Jesus as the anointed High Priest of eschatological times, e.g., in Heb. There are some echoes in patristic writings, as well, of Jesus as a twofold Messiah.

OTHER SITES

105 The discoveries at Qumran and the realization that ancient mss. could survive in the dry heat of the Dead Sea area resulted in wider searches on the western shore and the adjacent mountains. We shall discuss these areas, proceeding from N to S.

(I) Khirbet Mird. This site, 9 mi. SE of Jerusalem, is in the Buqei'a, the region in the desert of Judah over the cliffs behind Qumran, some 6 mi. W of the Dead Sea. It was once a Hasmonean fortress (Hyrcanion) and later the Christian monastery of Castellion (or Marda—Aramaic for fortress and the form from which the current name derives). This monastery was founded in 492 by St. Sabas, and its library was the source of ms. fragments found in the ruins in July 1952 by the Bedouin. A Belgian excavation under R. de Langhe of Louvain took place in February–April 1953, when more fragments were found in a cistern. Paleography points to a date from the 6th to the 9th cents. for these fragments.

The mss. represented are in Arabic, Greek, and Christian Palestinian Aramaic. A. Grohmann published *Arabic Papyri from Ḫirbet el-Mird* (Louvain, 1963). The Gk material included fragments from uncial biblical codices of the 5th–8th cents. (Wis, Mk, Jn, Acts), some noncanonical works, and a fragment of Euripides' *Andromache* that predates previously known copies by six centuries. The Palestinian Aram material has attracted some attention (→ Texts, 69:95): J. T. Milik published an inscription and a letter in *RB* 60 (1953) 526–39; C. Perrot published a 6th-cent. fragment of Acts in *RB* 70 (1963) 506–55. The archaeology of Khirbet Mird is discussed by G. R. H. Wright in *Bib* 42 (1961) 1–21; also see 21–27.

106 **(II) Murabba'at.** The four caves of Wadi Murabba'at are 15 mi. SE of Jerusalem, about 2 mi. inland from the Dead Sea, roughly 12 mi. S of Qumran and 10 mi. N of En-gedi. In 1951 the Bedouin began marketing fragments from these caves, and R. de Vaux and G. L. Harding led an expedition to excavate the inaccessible site in January–February 1952. Two of the caves were productive of written material, and it is probable that much more was destroyed in the 1920's when the Bedouin gathered bat dung, a valuable fertilizer, from these caves. The caves were used as dwellings, permanent or temporary, from Chalcolithic to Arabic times; but our prime interest is in their use in the period AD 132–135, the time of the Second Jewish Revolt against the Romans (→ History of Israel, 75:167–169). From the earlier period we shall mention only fragment Mur 17, a palimpsest with text from the 8th cent. BC, which is the earliest known papyrus inscribed in a North Semitic language.

These caves, along with the others to be mentioned below, served as places of refuge for the soldiers of Bar Cochba, the leader of the revolt, when the Roman army began to destroy their more permanent camps, e.g., the one at En-gedi. For the story of the Second Jewish Revolt, see J. A. Fitzmyer in *BCCT* 133–68; also *BTS* 29, 33 (1960); 58 (1963). These troops brought along with them their religious books, their records of orders received from headquarters, personal documents, etc.; and the fragments of these varied writings have been published in DJD 2.

The Hebr biblical fragments, including a scroll of the Minor Prophets from *ca.* AD 100 found by the Bedouin in 1955, represent a textual tradition very close to that of the MT. (For their importance, → Texts, 69:32.) Several of the documents are part of the correspondence of the Second Revolt, including two letters (#43, 44) from the revolutionary leader Simon ben Kosibah to his lieutenant Yešua' ben Galgula (Mur 43 may be in ben Kosibah's own hand). These letters supply Simon's real name; he has been known to history as Bar Cochba, from the name bar Kôk^{e}bâ, "son of the star," supposedly given to him by Rabbi Aqiba as a messianic designation (see Nm 24:17); later rabbis called him ben Kôzibâ, "son of the lie," because his messianic revolt misled Israel. As Fitzmyer, *art. cit.*, 147–53, has pointed out, document Mur 24 is important for dating the revolt to 132–135. There are also dated business and legal documents important for understanding the economic and sociological situation, as well as for linguistic and paleographic purposes. A few documents, chiefly grain lists, are written in Greek.

107 **(III) Valleys Between En-gedi and Masada.** In 1960–61 a group of Israeli scholars (Y. Aviram, N. Avigad, Y. Aharoni, P. Bar-Adon, Y. Yadin) organized expeditions to investigate caves in a number of valleys in this 10-mi. area in Israel (all the above-mentioned finds have been in Jordan). The reports are published in *IsrEJ* 11 (1961) 3–96; 12 (1962) 165–262; also Y. Yadin, *BA* 24 (1961) 34–50, 86–95; *BTS* 29, 33 (1960); 58 (1963).

108 *Nahal Hever* (Wadi Khabra) is about 3 mi. S of En-gedi and 7 mi. N of Masada. In 1960 and in 1961 Yadin made significant ms. discoveries here from the time of the Second Revolt. (An earlier fragment of Pss 15–16 dates from *ca.* AD 100 and is of the MT textual tradition.) In 1960 in the "Cave of the Letters" (caves 5/6) he found a bundle of papyri inside a waterskin; these contained 15 letters in Aramaic, Hebrew, and Greek from Simon ben Kosibah to his lieutenants in the En-gedi area. One (5/6Hev8) has Kosibah's name in Greek and confirms the vocalization. Evidently the revolutionary leader had his camp near Jerusalem (Bethter) and made En-gedi his chief port of supply on the Dead Sea. In one letter (5/6Hev15) he asks for palm and ethrogs to be brought up for the Feast of Tabernacles. In 1961 in this same "Cave of the Letters" Yadin found a cache of 35 documents representing the family records and legal documents of one Babata, evidently the relative of a soldier who had fled to the cave. These documents, summarized in *IsrEJ* 12 (1962) 235–48, 258–60, cover a span of years from AD 93–132 and are in Nabatean, Aramaic, and Greek. They are important for the study of language and law, and also for the background of ben Kosibah's revolt. Yadin found six other legal documents from the Second Revolt (*ibid.* 248–57), similar to material found at Murabba'at. For a comparison of the Murabba'at and Nahal Hever finds, see M. Lehmann *RevQum* 4 (1963) 53–81. Yadin tells the story at length in *The Finds from the Bar Kochba Period in the Cave of the Letters* (Jerusalem, 1963). It is now clear that some biblical fragments and Aramaic, Greek, and Nabatean documents which were brought by the Bedouin into Jordan in the early 1950's and which were published by J. Starcky and J. T. Milik (*RB* 61 [1954] 161–81; 182–90; *Bib* 38 [1957] 245–68) came from the Cave of the Letters in Nahal Hever (→ Texts, 69:32).

In another cave in this valley, the "Cave of Horrors" (cave 8), where many of the Jewish revolutionaries died, the expedition of Y. Aharoni (*IsrEJ* 12 [1962] 197–98, 201–7) found fragments from a Gk scroll of the Minor Prophets. They were from the same scroll that the Bedouin had taken from this cave (hitherto identified only as an unknown locale in the Judean desert) and that D. Barthélemy had published in *RB* 60 (1953) 18–29 and in *Les devanciers d'Aquila* (VTSup 10; Leiden, 1963). (For the great importance of this Gk scroll for textual studies of the LXX, → Texts, 69:57, 60.)

109 *Nahal Se'elim* (Wadi Seiyal) is about 8 mi. S of En-gedi and 2.5 mi. N of Masada. Here in 1960 the expedition of Y. Aharoni found some ms. fragments in the "Cave of the Scrolls," another cave that had served as a refuge for the warriors of Bar Cochba. Two phylactery parchments were discovered, one of which has a Hebr text of Ex 13:2–10 close to the Hebr text that underlies the LXX. There were also Gk papyri with lists of names. (*IsrEJ* 11 [1961] 21–24, 53–58.)

110 **(IV) Masada.** Just S of the middle of the Dead Sea, opposite the Lisan peninsula, stands the imposing rock fortress of Masada. Rising steeply with cliffs on all sides, Masada is as impregnable as nature can render a site. Fortified by the Maccabees, adorned with palaces by the Herods, used by the Romans as a stronghold, Masada fell into Zealot hands in AD 66. In a dramatic narrative Josephus (*JW* 7.8, 1ff. § 252) relates the story of Zealot resistance to the Romans. The Zealots held out until the year 73 and died to a man—the last gasp of the First Jewish Revolt. The Israelis have excavated the site at intervals since 1955.

In 1964 an excavation under Y. Yadin found some mss. among the ruins of Zealot occupation, mss. that obviously must predate 73. These include: (1) an ostracon or sherd, inscribed in Aramaic, dealing with money transactions; (2) a scroll of Pss 81–85 having a text identical with that of the MT; (3) a 1st-cent. BC copy of the Hebr original of Sir (→ Texts, 69:30); (4) a copy of a work represented in cave 4 of Qumran describing the heavenly liturgies. This work seems to have been a Qumran sectarian work, for it presupposes the solar calendar that was a pillar of Qumran theology (→ 18 above). One may argue that others in Palestine followed this calendar and that the work involved may have been common to many groups, including the Zealots; but this does not seem probable. Yadin reminds us that Josephus (*JW* 3.2, 1 § 11) reports that Essenes took part in the resistance to the Romans; and thus, after the destruction of Qumran in AD 68, some Essenes may have fled with their mss. to Masada. Therefore, Yadin's discovery does nothing to prove the thesis that the sectarians at Qumran were Zealot rather than Essene. (See Y. Yadin, *IsrEJ* 15 [1965] 1–120; *Masada: Herod's Fortress and the Zealots' Last Stand* [N.Y., 1966]; W. Eck, *ZNW* 60 [1969] 282–89 [no date].)

OTHER JEWISH LITERATURE

WRITERS OF THE BIBLICAL PERIOD

111 **(I) Philo Judaeus.** Born *ca.* 25–20 BC of a rich Jewish family in Alexandria, Philo died after AD 41. Trained both in Jewish tradition and in Greek secular studies, especially philosophy, he was ideally situated to bridge the two bodies of knowledge. In facing the task of bringing Judaism to terms with a Hellenized world, Philo did what Christian writers would also have to do with their Judeo-Christian heritage.

Little is known of Philo's life. At first he seems to have devoted himself to study and contemplation, but later he became more involved in the active life of the Alexandrian Jewish community. He went to Rome *ca.* AD 40 at the head of a delegation sent to lay before the emperor Caligula the grievances of the Alexandrian Jews who refused to worship the imperial images (→ History of Israel, 75:149).

112 Many of Philo's works were purely *philosophical treatises*, often incipiently neoplatonic in tendency. According to H. A. Wolfson (*Philo* [Cambridge, 1947]) he is the first writer of the medieval tradition in philosophy, reconciling reason with revelation. Wolfson argues, perhaps to an exaggerated degree, that Philo had enormous and continuing influence on Christian philosophers and theologians. Philo's *apologetic works*, defending his coreligionists at Alexandria against calumny (e.g., the *Apology for the Jews*, preserved in fragments in Eusebius), reflect for us the life of an important Jewish community contemporary with Jesus. In particular, the *Contemplative Life* describes a group of Jewish ascetics, the Therapeutae, a sect similar to the Essenes of Palestine (and of the QL).

Philo's *biblical studies* interpret the Bible, especially the Pentateuch, in an allegorical manner in order to show the compatibility of Jewish tradition with the philosophical wisdom of the Greeks, in particular of the Stoics. In his *Allegory of the Jewish Law*, originally much longer than the 21 books it now contains, Philo speaks to the initiates who can understand the Bible figuratively. The *Questions and Answers on Genesis and Exodus* gives both the literal and allegorical sense of biblical passages. The treatises of the *Exposition of the Law* seem addressed to Gentiles and systematically align Jewish biblical tradition and Gentile thought. Philonic allegorical exegesis greatly influenced the Christian exegetes of the Alexandrian school (→ Hermeneutics, 71:37).

Whether Philo influenced NT thought, especially that of the Prologue of Jn, is debated. For an affirmative answer, see C. H. Dodd, *The Interpretation of the Fourth Gospel* (Cambridge, 1954) 54–73; for a negative answer, see R. McL. Wilson, *ExpT* 65 (1953–54) 47–49. Philo wrote of the *Logos* (Word), a radiation from the One (God) relating Him to men, and Philo attributed to this Logos personal attributes of justice and mercy. Probably both the Philonic and Johannine *Logos* (Jn 1:1) are independently related to the personified Wisdom of late Jewish sapiential writings.

(E. R. Goodenough, *The Politics of Philo Judaeus* [New Haven, 1938] has a good bibliography; cf. also his *Introduction to Philo Judaeus* [Oxford, 1940]. F. H. Colson and R. Marcus have edited 12 vols. of Philo's works in the LCL.)

113 Not to be confused with Philo's genuine works is the *Biblical Antiquities* of pseudo-Philo, also called *De initio mundi* and published together with Philonic treatises in the Middle Ages. Composed in Hebrew probably in the 1st cent. AD, translated into Greek, the *Biblical Antiquities* is preserved only in the Latin of Christian copyists. Basically it is an abstract of the biblical story from Adam to Saul enlarged in a midrashic manner (→ 119 below) by the incorporation of old Jewish legends. It has certain parallels to the free interpretation of Scripture exhibited in contemporary NT exegesis of the OT. See M. R. James, *The Biblical Antiquities of Philo* (London, 1917); G. Kisch, *Pseudo-Philo's Liber Antiquitatum Biblicarum* (Notre Dame, Ind., 1949).

114 **(II) Flavius Josephus.** Born in Palestine of a priestly clan in AD 37–38, Josephus ben Matthias died after 100, probably in Rome. As a young man of 16 he claims to have studied the Jewish "sects" of the Pharisees, Sadducees, and Essenes and to have spent three years with the hermit Bannus, before ultimately becoming a Pharisee. During a journey to Rome in 64 he made important Roman contacts (e.g., Poppaea, Nero's wife) and became convinced of Rome's power. Although he counseled the Jews against revolt, he ultimately joined the revolt of 66–70 and became commander of the Jewish forces in Galilee (→ History of Israel, 75:157–160). Josephus' loyalty in this position was questioned by some of the revolutionaries (e.g., John of Gischala); at any rate, after the defeat of his forces by the Romans at Jotapata in 67 (a defeat of which Josephus was one of the few Jewish survivors), he surrendered to the Roman general Vespasian. Vespasian set him free in 69 after he had correctly predicted that Vespasian would become emperor.

Vespasian was the first of the Flavian family of emperors, and from 69 on Josephus was their client, whence the name *Flavius* Josephus. Titus, the conqueror of Jerusalem, brought Josephus to Rome and installed him in a royal palace, granting him an imperial pension and the rights of a citizen. His writings at Rome are our chief source of knowledge for Jewish history in the late period from Maccabean/Hasmonean times to the fall of Masada in AD 73.

115 THE JEWISH WAR. This book, written in the seventies as propaganda to show the futility of revolting against the Romans, is an edition in Greek, translated with the help of collaborators, of a work that Josephus first wrote in Aramaic. The Slavonic version, erroneously thought by some scholars to represent more faithfully the Aram original, is a secondary work based on the Gk text. *Book 1* surveys the history of the Jews in the Hellenistic-Roman period, drawing on a (lost) life of Herod by Nicolas of Damascus. *Books 2–7* tell of the Jewish war against Rome and are drawn from Josephus' own memories as well as from the Roman military records made available to him. Most of the account is reliable, although the tone is deliberately pro-Roman and Josephus' own role is presented in a sympathetic light.

116 JEWISH ANTIQUITIES OR THE HISTORY. Modeled on the *Roman Antiquities* by Dionysius of Halicarnassus, Josephus' 20-volume work appeared in AD 93 or 94. This major undertaking is a history of the Jews from patriarchal to Roman times. *Books 1–10* cover the period up to the Babylonian Captivity. The information is largely drawn from the LXX Bible, supplemented by later popular Jewish traditions. In *Books 11–20* Josephus had not only postbiblical material but also information from Greek and Roman histories. The reference to Jesus in *Ant.* 18.3, 3 § 63–64, the *Testimonium Flavianum*, has been considered an interpolation by many scholars; but L. H. Feldman, the translator of the pertinent volume in the LCL (vol. 9, p. 49), concludes: "The most probable view seems to be that our text represents substantially what Josephus wrote, but that some alterations have been made by a Christian interpolator" (for bibliography, *ibid.*, 573–75). In times past this reference contributed toward making the *Antiquities* a companion to the Bible in many Christian homes. The work supplies indispensable knowledge of the intertestamental period.

117 MINOR WORKS. Written as an appendix to the *Antiquities*, Josephus' *Life* is a self-justification for his behavior as commander in Galilee. *Against Apion*, in two books, is a defense of Judaism against contemporary pagan slanders.

(The Eng translation of William Whiston, two centuries old, has become almost *the* translation of Josephus. It is now supplanted by the nine-volume LCL translation by H. St. J. Thackeray, R. Marcus, A. Wikgren, and L. H. Feldman, based on the critical Gk text of B. Niese [Berlin, 1885–95]. Thackeray and Marcus also initiated *A Lexicon to Josephus* [1930–]. Cf. also G. A. Williamson, *The World of Josephus* [N.Y., 1964]; H. St. J. Thackeray, *Josephus, the Man and the Historian* [N.Y., 1968]. For bibliography, see L. H. Feldman, *Scholarship on Philo and Josephus 1937–1962* [N.Y., 1963]; H. Schreckenberg, *Bibliographie zu Flavius Josephus* [Leiden, 1968].)

JEWISH LAW FROM EZRA TO THE TALMUD—RABBINIC LITERATURE

118 Because of the Gospel opposition to the legalism of the Pharisees and of Paul's attitude toward the Law in Rom, Christians often have a one-sided and incorrect understanding of the tremendous spiritual and religious contributions that the study of the Law has made to Judaism. In the spirit of Dt (e.g., 30:15) the Law has been the source of life for Judaism. Law develops in every society as that society faces new situations. In the period with which we are concerned, from the closing of the Pentateuch in Ezra's time (400 BC) to the completion of the Talmud (AD 500), Judaism faced a great number of new situations: Hellenization, conquest by Rome, the Christian heresy, and the task of survival as a homeless people in the Roman and Sassanid Empires. The legal development of this period is almost a chronicle of Judaism and a remarkable attestation of the vigor of the people that God chose as his own.

In the previous period from Moses to Ezra (1250–400) there had been a corresponding legal development. The Decalogue represented the core of the Sinaitic covenantal experience. The application of the spirit of the Decalogue to new situations in the life and history of Israel produced the various law codes preserved in the Pentateuch, from the Covenant Code of *ca.* 1200 BC to the late-6th-cent. laws in the Priestly Collection (→ Aspects OT Thought, 77:86ff.). But with Ezra the Pentateuch was closed (whether the "law" mentioned in Ezr 7:10 and Neh 8:1 was the whole Pentateuch, the Holiness Code, or the Priestly Collection), and now there would be no more law codes added to the Bible. The laws that came into force because of the new situations that Israel encountered would take the form of *oral law* interpreting the written Torah, or Books of Moses. (Actually, since later scholars mistakenly thought that the Pentateuch had been written in Moses' time, they thought that the "oral law" was continuous from Moses on. In fact, there was continuous legal tradition from the time of Moses on, but this was preserved in the Pentateuch completed some 800 years after Moses.) The spirit of the oral law that evolved was one of protecting the written biblical law by "building a fence around it"—if one observed the oral law, one could not possibly transgress the written law; and without the guidance of the oral law, it would be impossible to observe the written law. The written law commanded the Jew to keep holy the Sabbath and to rest on that day. But what constituted work? The oral law gave the answer. We have the same phenomenon in the Christian Church in the evolution of a body of law (codified in the Code of Canon Law) showing in detail how Christians can practically live according to the dictates and spirit of Jesus. Similarly, on a civil plane in the United States, the Government finds itself forced to make detailed laws applying the principles of the Constitution to new circumstances. We may divide the development of Jewish law from Ezra to the Talmud into four periods.

119 **(I) Period of the Scribes** (*Sōpherîm:* 400–270 BC). Jewish legend speaks of the Great Synagogue or governing body of Judaism, founded by Ezra and consisting of 120 men. Among other things, this body is supposed to have issued law and drawn up the canon of the OT (→ Canonicity, 67:34). The picture is largely fictional, although Jewish scholars like Zeitlin, Klausner, and Finkelstein have rather convincingly insisted that there is some historical value in the tradition. In any case, this was a period when, in the spirit of Ezra, scribes carefully studied and commented on the Pentateuchal laws. Little of their work remains except perhaps in principles buried in the later legal books and in the maxims of the biblical wisdom books.

The method of teaching law and legal wisdom was often by way of a running commentary on the biblical text—MIDRASH. Midrash, as a living form of Jewish literature, lasted up to and beyond AD 1000, and our oldest extant midrashim of length belong to the 2nd cent. AD and later. Nevertheless, the midrashic practice goes back to the early period we are now considering and is related to the pesher technique at Qumran (→ 77, 80 above). It is customary to distinguish two types of midrashim: (1) Midrash Halachah: an exposition of the biblical text, i.e., the Pentateuch, producing legal principles and designed for legal use. (2) Midrash Haggadah: an exposition of the biblical text directed to ethical or devotional use. Many of the interesting tales of popular Jewish tradition appear in this type of midrash. For a discussion of the nature and characteristics of midrash, see A. G. Wright, *CBQ* 28 (1966) 105–38, 417–57; also his book *The Literary Genre Midrash* (Staten Island, 1967).

120 **(II) Period of the Five Pairs of Teachers** (*Zûgôt:* 270–*ca.* 1 BC). The campaigns of Alexander the Great (332) and the establishment of the Hellenistic monarchies brought a different political climate to Palestine. The troubled period of the Maccabean revolt saw the emergence of sectarian groups in Judaism (→ 84, 88 above), and ultimately most of the scribes aligned themselves with the Pharisees, whence the combination "scribes and Pharisees" of the NT. The development of law in this period broke away from commenting on the biblical text, and a real jurisprudence developed in the opinions of the great teachers. This, then, was the formative age of the oral law properly speaking, an oral law that was rejected by the conservative Sadducees who accepted only the written law.

In Jewish tradition the great teachers of this period are paired off; the reason for this is not known to us. Tradition has it that each pair of teachers represented the president and vice-president of the Sanhedrin, or ruling body, but this is probably fictional. In any case, with the last pair of teachers just before the Christian era, two different schools of thought and practice in jurisprudence developed. These teachers were Shammai (the stricter) and Hillel (the more lenient). When the Pharisees approached Jesus in Mt 19:3ff., they were presenting him with a question disputed between the followers of Shammai (who demanded a serious fault in the wife in order to permit divorce) and of Hillel (who allowed divorce on a less serious charge). Hillel (*ca.* 50 BC–AD 10) in particular was a very influential figure in Judaism. He came to Palestine from Babylonia and may have introduced the Babylonian recension of the Pentateuch preserved in the MT, as distinct from the popular Palestinian recension visible in some of the Qumran mss. (→ Texts, 69:21). Very little of the jurisprudence of this period survives, except, once again, as part of later law.

121 **(III) Period of the Tannaim** (the formation of the Mishnah: AD 1–200). It became apparent that the oral decisions of the great teachers had to be collected. (These decisions were preserved by repetition; students had to repeat by memory the decisions of the masters. *Tannā'îm* refers to those who taught by repeating; *mishnah* [*mišnâ*] means "repetition.") There may have been primitive collections as far back as Hillel's time, but the destruction of the Temple in 70 and failure of the Second Jewish Revolt in 135 served as a catalyst toward a written collection of the oral law. Even before 70, when the destruction of Jerusalem was imminent, Rabbi Johanan ben Zakkai moved his center of activity to the coastal town of Jabneh or Jamnia (→ Biblical Geography, 73:77). In the years between 70–130 the Sanhedrin (also called Beth-Din or House of Justice) ruled Judaism by its decisions from Jabneh, drawing up official prayers, excommunicating heretics (including Christians), etc. (→ Canonicity, 67:35). The nasi (*nāśî'* = prince or president) of the Sanhedrin was in many ways the chief authority of Judaism. (See J. Neusner, *A Life of Yohanan ben Zakkai* [N.Y., 1960].)

Some of the famous rabbis began to make extensive collections of the oral law. The main line of this codification is represented by Rabbi Aqiba (135—a famous figure in the Second Jewish Revolt; → History of Israel, 75:168) whose collection was expanded by his disciple Rabbi Meir. After the failure of the Second Revolt, the center of Judaism moved from Jabneh to Galilee, where in towns like Sepphoris (especially 135–150), Tiberias, Caesarea, and Usha schools of rabbinical learning were established. This provided the opportunity for even more scientific codification until finally at the end of the century RABBI JUDAH THE PRINCE (ha-Nasi) made the official codification (in the line of Aqiba and Meir) of the previous centuries of oral law, the MISHNAH. There were other collections or mishnahs, but these gave way to Rabbi Judah's, so that the term "Mishnah" now designates his work. (Other laws and legal opinions that Judah did not include in his codification were later collected and are found in the TOSEPHTA.) The Mishnah became for Judaism almost a second Pentateuch and served as the primary object of rabbinical study. The language of the Mishnah is a type of late Hebrew (→ 82 above).

The Tannaitic period also saw the composition of some very important midrashim, e.g., *Siphra* on Lv, *Siphre* on Nm and Dt, *Mekiltha* on Ex. In the Ger series *Rabbinische Texte* (Stuttgart) these Tannaitic midrashim are being published, beginning with *Siphre*; J. Z. Lauterbach has published the *Mekiltha* in Hebrew and English (Phila., 1935).

122 **(IV) Period of the Amoraim** (the Talmudic masters: AD 200–500). The time that separates Rabbi Judah from the completion of the Talmud was a period of commenting upon the Mishnah in the schools. The Palestinian schools continued, especially that of Tiberias which developed its own system of vocalizing the Hebr consonantal text—the system now used in Hebr Bibles. But the flourishing school activity in Babylonia ultimately made that country the dominant Jewish intellectual center. In the early 3rd cent. the Mishnah of Rabbi Judah was brought to Babylonia by his disciple Abba Arika ("Rab") who founded the school at Sura. Other Babylonian schools were those of Nehardea and Pumbeditha. Each developed its own tradition and masters. Thus, at the same time in Babylonia and Palestine, rather divorced from one another, schools of Jewish scholars were commenting on the Mishnah and ultimately producing two great collections of their comments, the Talmuds: The PALESTINIAN TALMUD was written down in the period 375–425. It was never completed for there is no commentary on the last orders of the Mishnah; the abrupt termination was caused by the end of the Palestinian schools. It is shorter than the Babylonian Talmud and in some ways represents a more direct tradition. The BABYLONIAN TALMUD was written down between 400–500 and is the one usually meant when someone speaks of "the Talmud." It is an enormous work.

Each Talmud consists of two parts: (1) The Mishnah. This is substantially the same in each, although different recensions of Judah's Mishnah are used. (2) The Gemara ("completion"), or commentary upon the Mishnah. This is mostly in Aramaic—a Western and an Eastern dialect respectively for the two Talmuds. Since the Gemara springs from the school traditions of Palestine and Babylonia respectively, this part differs in the two Talmuds. The Mishnah, and hence the Talmud, is divided into six orders (like the books of the Code of Canon Law). The topics dealt with include agriculture, feasts, marriage and divorce, civil and criminal law, sacrifice, and levitical purity—thus almost the whole range of Jewish life. Besides the legal material, it contains much narrative material.

123 The Babylonian schools survived after the Palestinian schools. The Exilarch, or chief figure among the Jews in the Babylonian Diaspora, (ruled by the Sassanid Persians) was the head of world Judaism. In addition, the legal opinions of the head (Gaon) of each of the Babylonian schools carried great weight. Once the Talmud was completed, it in turn became the object of study and commentary. (The most famous commentary was the 11th-cent. commentary of Rashi, often printed in the margins of copies of the Babylonian Talmud.) Indeed, the standard rabbinic training in the Yeshiva is primarily in the Talmud rather than in the Scriptures. In central Europe where the tradition of Talmud learning was very strong, memorizing the Mishnah was stressed; indeed, it is reported, *mirabile dictu*, that on occasion a precocious rabbi memorized the whole Babylonian Talmud.

(Moore, G. F., *Judaism in the First Centuries of the Christian Era* [3 vols.; Harvard, 1930–32]. Schürer, E., *A History of the Jewish People in the Time of Jesus Christ* [5 vols.; Edinburgh, 1885–90], esp. Division II, vol. 1, 306–79. Strack, H. L., *Introduction to the Talmud and Midrash* [Phila., 1931]. The uncensored edition of the Babylonian Talmud with a Ger translation was published by L. Goldschmidt in 9 vols. [Leipzig, 1897–1909]. The Soncino Eng translation, ed. by I. Epstein (London, 1935–53), is available in 18 vols. The standard translations of the Mishnah are those of H. Danby [Oxford, 1933] and of P. Blackman [7 vols.; London, 1951–56]. See also J. Neusner, *A History of the Jews in Babylonia* [Leiden, 1965–].)

69

TEXTS AND VERSIONS

Patrick W. Skehan

George W. MacRae, S.J.

Raymond E. Brown, S.S.

BIBLIOGRAPHY

1 **General:** Flack, E. E., B. M. Metzger, *et al.*, *The Text, Canon, and Principal Versions of the Bible* (Grand Rapids, 1956). Kenyon, F. G., *Our Bible and the Ancient Manuscripts* (rev. ed.; N.Y., 1958). Price, J. M., *The Ancestry of Our English Bible* (3rd ed.; N.Y., 1956). Reumann, J., *The Romance of Bible Scripts and Scholars* (Englewood Cliffs, N.J., 1965). Robinson, H. W., *The Bible in Its Ancient and English Versions* (Oxford, 1940). "Bible IV: Texts and Versions," *NCE* 2, 414–91.

2 **Old Testament:** Ap-Thomas, D. R., *A Primer of Old Testament Text Criticism* (2nd ed.; Oxford, 1964). Bentzen, A., *Introduction to the Old Testament* (Copenhagen, 1948) 1, 42–101. Eissfeldt, *OTI* 669–721. Kahle, P. E., *The Cairo Geniza* (2nd ed.; Oxford, 1959). Noth, M., *The Old Testament World* (Phila., 1966) 301–63. Roberts, B. J., *The Old Testament Text and Versions* (Cardiff, 1951). Robertson, E., *The Text of the Old Testament and the Methods of Textual Criticism* (London, 1939). Wurthwein, E., *The Text of the Old Testament* (Oxford, 1957).

3 **New Testament:** Duplacy, J., *Où en est la critique textuelle du Nouveau Testament* (Paris, 1959); "Bulletin de critique textuelle du Nouveau Testament," *RSR* 50 (1962) 242–63, 564–98; 51 (1963) 432–62; 53 (1965) 257–84. Greenlee, J. H., *Introduction to New Testament Textual Criticism* (Grand Rapids, 1964). Gregory, C. R., *The Canon and Text of the New Testament* (N.Y., 1907). Lagrange, M.-J., *Introduction à l'étude du Nouveau Testament: II. Critique textuelle, 2, La critique rationelle* (Paris, 1935). Lake, K., *The Text of the New Testament* (6th ed.; London, 1943). Metzger, B. M., *Annotated Bibliography of the Textual Criticism of the New Testament* (Studies and Documents 16; Copenhagen, 1955); *Chapters in the History of New Testament Textual Criticism* (NTTS 4; Leiden, 1963); *The Text of the New Testament* (N.Y., 1964). Souter, A., *The Text and Canon of the New Testament* (rev. ed.; Naperville, Ill., 1954). Taylor, V., *The Text of the New Testament* (London, 1961). Vaganay, L., *An Introduction to the Textual Criticism of the New Testament* (London, 1937). Vogels, H. J., *Handbuch der Textkritik des Neuen Testaments* (2nd ed.; Bonn, 1955). Vööbus, A., *Early Versions of the New Testament* (Stockholm, 1954).

4 **English Bible:** Baikie, J., *The English Bible and Its Story* (London, 1928). Bruce, F. F., *The English Bible* (Oxford, 1961). Butterworth, C. C., *The Literary Lineage of the King James Bible 1340–1611* (Phila., 1941). *McCormick Quarterly* 19 (May 1966)—whole issue. May, H. G., *Our English Bible in the Making* (Phila., 1962). Moulton, W. F., *The History of the English Bible* (London, 1937). Pope, H., *English Versions of the Bible* (rev. ed.; London, 1952). Robertson, E. H., *The New Translations of the Bible* (London, 1959). Simms, P. M., *The Bible in America* (N.Y., 1936). Weigle, L. A., *The English New Testament: From Tyndale to the Revised Standard Version* (N.Y., 1949). For modern versions in various languages see *The Cambridge History of the Bible—the West from the Reformation to the Present Day*, ed. S. L. Greenslade (Cambridge, 1963). *Bible Translator* 12 (1961) 153–68 deals with simplified-English versions.

5 OUTLINE

The last two sections, Greek Text of the New Testament and The English Bible (§ 119–176), were written by R. E. Brown; the subsection on Coptic versions (§ 112–116) was written by G. W. MacRae; the rest was written by P. W. Skehan.

INTRODUCTION

6 A detailed knowledge of how the books of the OT have been preserved and transmitted is more possible now than at any period since these inspired writings began—in pre-Christian times—to be collected into the groupings of "the Law, the Prophets and the other Books" (Foreword to Sir). This is in part because of unforeseen ms. discoveries (the "Dead Sea Scrolls" since 1947; various Gk papyri of early date, especially since 1920), in part because of intensive study now that the development of printing and photography has made exact reproductions of original sources easily available.

7 Knowledge of this history of transmission is important: (1) for a proper appreciation of the fidelity and care with which the piety of believers has surrounded these sacred books throughout their history, and of the substantial integrity of their text as we have it; (2) for an insight into the opportunities of, and the limitations on, those who translate and explain this literature at first hand; and (3) as a foundation for understanding such questions of textual criticism as are bound to arise in texts with so long a period of recopying and of translation. This knowledge at the present time cannot be static; it needs to be full and clear enough to put into proper perspective recurrent claims regarding new advances in biblical study—claims sometimes valid, often fantastic.

8 The material to be described consists of our textual evidence for the original Hebr and Aram form of most OT books, for the Gk "Septuagint" or LXX translation of the OT (mostly pre-Christian, and including some books composed or chiefly preserved in Greek), and, finally, for other ancient versions (Jewish Aramaic, Syriac, Latin, Coptic, etc.). The principal textual value of these last versions is their evidence as to underlying Hebr or Gk forms of early date. The Jewish Aram renderings (targums) pertain to the OT only; the other versions suppose complete bibles, and for convenience both OT and NT translations into these languages will be described together.

9 As for the Gk NT, our knowledge of the way in which its books were preserved and transmitted reached a truly scientific stage at the end of the 19th cent., somewhat in advance of our knowledge of the OT situation. But here also there have been significant 20th-cent. discoveries, especially of early papyrus copies of NT books. Once again the early versions add important evidence, helpful in determining the type of Gk text from which they were translated. Thus in both Testaments the field of textual criticism is one that has made rapid progress in our times.

HEBREW TEXT OF THE OLD TESTAMENT

10 No ms. actually written by the author or editor of any OT book is extant; all existing copies are the work of later scribes. Though Jewish tradition at all periods has placed a high value on faithfulness in transmitting both oral and written materials (see for this E. A. Speiser, *IsrEJ* 7 [1957] 201–16), the antiquity of a particular copy was of no special moment. This is illustrated by the practice of relegating to a geniza, or repository of discarded sacred texts, any mss. too worn for continued public use. In the case of the Cairo Geniza (→ 37 below) the practice has proved an accidental boon to scholarship, but this was in no way anticipated by those who stored the ms. materials it contained.

11 No OT book composed wholly or in part before the Babylonian Exile of the Jews (587–539 BC) has come down to us in even a fragment actually written in that period. Our earliest extant evidences are from Qumran cave 4 (→ Apocrypha, 68:68–69); and they represent the period *ca.* 250–175 BC. For several later OT books, fragmentary scrolls are now known that date to approximately 100 years after the composition of the book: thus for Eccl (4QQoh^{a}), Dn (4QDan^{c}), and Sir (the text from Masada). Not so long ago it would have been impossible to point with assurance to any OT Hebr ms. that came within 1000 years of the date of composition of the work it contained; the most ancient OT ms. that contains the date of its own preparation is the Cairo Prophets of AD 895 (→ 39 below).

We shall now discuss the three main periods in the history of the transmission of the OT text, the ancient, the medieval, and the modern. Since we shall speak frequently of the Hebr text, it is perhaps worth noting that the limited portions of the OT transmitted in Aramaic share in all respects the history of the Hebr books of which they form a part. A frequent standard of reference will be the MT. This will be explained more fully below (→ 32, 37); for the moment we may say that the MT refers to the standardized consonantal Hebr text established about the end of the 1st cent. AD and transmitted with great fidelity into the medieval period.

12 **(I) Texts of the Ancient Period** (*ca.* 250 BC–AD 135). During this period it was not the practice to give any OT book a separate title or to add the name of its copyist and date. For the dating of the materials, therefore, apart from general archaeological considerations connected with their discovery, the science of Hebr paleography is necessary. Its results are an approximation; but for periods of rapid development of the style of writing the results can be rather precise, and for the ancient period as a whole they yield relative certainty with a maximum leeway of about 50 years in difficult cases. The most significant single study is that of F. M. Cross, *BANE* 133–202.

13 **(A) Format and Age of the Mss.** The mss. known to us from this period have all been found since 1947 (except, the Nash Papyrus; → 31 below). The writing is in columns, covering only one side of skins of leather or, very infrequently, of sheets of papyrus (by implication in Jer 36); these are ruled vertically and horizontally for the purpose with a dry point. No Hebr codex (i.e., a book with pages written on both sides) is known before the medieval period. The skins were stitched—the papyrus sheets were glued—together side by side to form scrolls. The complete Isaiah scroll from Qumran (1QIs^{a}) is an excellent example of this format; it consists of 17 strips of well-prepared leather sewn together into a scroll, 24.5 ft. long when unrolled and 10.5 in. high. Its text is in 54 columns, with an intentional main division after col. 27, i.e., at the middle of the book (the end of ch. 33, of 66 chapters). The columns in this ms. average 30 lines of writing each; but the columns in other texts from this period have a range from 9 to 65 or more lines.

14 At present over 190 OT mss. are known to us from this ancient period, recovered from various places in the Judean desert: the caves around Qumran, caves in the Wadi Murabba'at, caves in the Nahal Hever, and the fortress at Masada (→ Apocrypha, 68:106–110). Oldest are three mss. from Qumran cave 4, the community library of the Essenes. These, in the judgment of F. M. Cross, date as follows: 4QEx^{f}, *ca.* 250 BC; 4QSm^{b}, *ca.* 200 BC; and 4QJer^{a}, *ca.* 175 BC. On external grounds, the latest mss. at Qumran are not later than AD 68; those at Masada not later than AD 73; and those from the other sites (caves of Murabba'at and Hever) not later than AD 135. Manuscripts prior to the 1st cent. BC are rare; perhaps most Qumran mss. date from that century, with the 1st cent. AD also well represented. The 2nd-cent. AD mss. from Murabba'at occupy a place apart and will need to be described separately (→ 32 below).

15 **(B) Qumran Mss.**

(a) Origins, Scripts, Orthography. The wealth of ms. material from Qumran, including more than 100 fragmentary copies of OT books from cave 4 alone, shows an extraordinary variety in age, in format, in script, in orthography, and in the affiliations of the texts represented. Despite the clear evidence for the existence of a *scriptorium* at Qumran, it has yet to be shown that any single biblical ms. was copied there from another ms. also extant. The origins of the material are in most cases best explained by the communal ownership of property as provided in the rules of the group (→ Apocrypha, 68:94): They are chiefly mss. that their individual former owners brought along into the community's holdings. The age of these scroll fragments spreads over three full centuries: *ca.* 250 BC–AD 68. Dn and Kgs are known on papyrus, as is Tb, though the great bulk of the OT texts is on leather of varying thickness and quality. Some mss. have wide columns, some narrow, with the number of letters to a line ranging from about 15 to over 70; the variation in number of lines to the column has been mentioned above (→ 13).

16 At least until the 1st cent. BC, two separate alphabets were in use: the archaic one now labeled "paleo-Hebrew," derived from the Canaanite alphabet employed since pre-exilic times; and various developing forms of the Jewish "Aramaic" script, familiar in its later stages as the square-letter alphabet of printed Hebr bibles. A few OT mss., and a scattering of nonbiblical ones, combine the two alphabets by normally employing the square-letter script, changing to the archaic letters either for the sacred name YHWH alone or for varying combinations of divine names. This practice does not seem to be older than Herodian times; it occurs also in the latest period of Qumran. Both these alphabets represent, of course, the standard 22-letter consonantal system of writing Hebrew. The spelling, however, in either script, may be a notably sparse one, with the weaker letters *w*, *h*, *y*, and *aleph* (') used to a very limited extent to represent vowels. It may, on the other hand, in either script be an expanded orthography in which, as in Syriac, every *o* or *u* vowel, however slight, is represented by a *w* in the consonantal text. The ends of the words may then offer an unexpected *-h* attached to pronoun suffixes, or an *aleph* to follow any word ending in *i*, *o*, or *u*. When first encountered in the complete Isaiah scroll, this expanded type of spelling was a notable puzzlement to scholars; but it is recognized now as an attempt in the last centuries BC to furnish fuller pronunciation guides than the standard orthography affords. Also it sometimes offers limited hints of a distinctive dialect in the speech of those who used it.

17 Neither script nor orthography seems to have much connection with the nature of the text being copied. The paleo-Hebrew script is used for 12 mss.; all the books of the Pentateuch are represented (Lv in 4 mss.), but so is Job; and there are some nonbiblical fragments in the same script. Of two texts of Ex in this archaic script, one is very close to the standard text, the other is in the "Samaritan" recension (→ 33–34 below) and has, sporadically, the expanded type of spelling. In the more usual Aram script we may speak of a conservative spelling in some mss., of an expanded one in others; but the same OT book may be represented both ways in texts that are otherwise closely akin. Final publication of all the material may show a trend to less careful copying in the mss. with expanded orthography; but this is by no means assured.

18 (b) Textual Characteristics. Because the Qumran mss. here described do in fact open up an entirely new period in the history of the text, and because they have so far been published only in part, their systematic classification has yet to be attempted. In any case, they are quite fragmentary, to the point that when one of them provides as much as 10 per cent of the complete text of a biblical book, it is counted among the more substantial witnesses. As contrasted with the integral Masoretic and Samaritan texts known from the medieval period, and with the indirect evidence of the LXX, the Qumran mss. offer a sampling and a means of probing into the antecedents of these other witnesses rather than a separate basis for future editions of the text.

The sampling, as has been said, is of extraordinary variety even textually. This does not mean that any large number of real variants (discounting scribal errors, harmonizations, etc.) have emerged in addition to those previously known. Rather, a great number of the alternative readings and expansions for which the medieval mss. in the MT tradition offer no counterpart (but which were already known from Gk or Samaritan sources) are here found intermingled with other texts very close indeed to the MT. Also, for the first time it becomes possible to verify in Hebr mss. what has always been known, both from the nature of the collection as such and from indirect LXX evidence: *Each of the books of the OT has its own separate history of transmission.*

19 Let us illustrate from the Qumran mss. how one important type of textual variant developed, namely explanatory expansions. Many a scribe copying OT texts during this ancient period felt free to embody in his text as he copied it the results of his study, whereas in modern times these interpolations would appear as footnotes or cross references. Thus in the oldest ms. we possess (4QEx^{f}), at Ex 40:17 we find the words "On the first day of the second year *from their leaving Egypt*, the Tabernacle was erected." The reference to "leaving Egypt" is not in the MT of this verse, though Ex 16:1 and 19:1 do contain it. Although the phrase is found not only in our oldest surviving copy from Qumran but also in the Samaritan and Greek texts, it must be evaluated as an expansion to make the wording clearer and more explicit. Similarly, in a Qumran ms. (4QDt^{n}), in the text of the Ten Commandments, the reasons for keeping the Sabbath day as given in the MT are expanded, for Dt 5:15 is followed by the insertion of a related passage (Ex 20:11) which has an added reason. Even the Samaritan text of Dt does not have this enlargement, although in the Gk tradition it turns up as an insertion into Dt 5:14 in the Codex Vaticanus only, not in any other ms. For a difficult phrase in Is 34:4 that has been translated "And all the hosts of heaven shall moulder away" (a phrase that was omitted by the earliest LXX translator) the scroll 1QIs^{a} supplies from Mi 1:4 the words "and the valleys split open," because the contexts are similar, and the Hebr letters of the former passage suggest, if anything, the latter. This type of copying does not indicate the text was regarded as any less sacred; the words used to fill out a particular passage are those of the Bible itself. This is, however, far from the rigid adherence to unalterable consonants of the standardized text, an adherence that became the universal rule shortly after AD 70.

20 Full evaluation of the texts from this ancient period requires that all of them be published, and this has not yet been done. As of now, the thousands of fragments of the community library from cave 4 have been sorted out, some significant results have been presented, and the material has been organized and photographed. A permanent system of reference for these mss. has been developed: For instance, 4QEx^{f} means that of the mss. from the 4th cave at Qumran, the 6th (f) copy of Ex is being referred to; if a text is on papyrus (pap), or is in the paleo-Hebrew script (paleo), or is a translation (LXX, targum), that fact will be included before the name of the biblical book, thus 4QpaleoEx^{m} for a ms. in the old script. The most suitable current approach to these materials would seem to be a provisional description of the state of the text at Qumran by books or groups of books, with individual mss. that are textually noteworthy mentioned in passing.

21 (i) *Historical Books.* The 15 fragmentary mss. of Gn found at Qumran show a comparatively uniform text. Readings that coincide with LXX materials do exist; but a high degree of standardization of the text of this book clearly antedates all our evidence. In Ex through Dt, on the other hand, there is great variation in the Qumran witnesses: sometimes very close to the MT, at other times including all the systematic expansions found in the "Samaritan" text, and again often showing agreement, regular or sporadic, with readings known from the Gk tradition, whether primitive LXX or "proto-Lucianic" (→ 59 below). Exodus exists in 15 mss., Lv in 9, Nm in 6, and Dt in 25. Notable is 4QpaleoEx^{m}, in the archaic script, from the early 2nd cent. BC, with extant portions of some 40 columns of text out of an original 57; it contains the repetitious expanded form known previously only from Samaritan sources. The text of 4QNm^{b}, with sizeable portions preserved, agrees with the Samaritan text in a number of expansions, but quite frequently with the earliest strata of LXX texts against the MT, even where the Samaritan and the MT coincide. Among texts of Dt, interest has so far centered on a fragment (4QDt^{q}) that contains only the ending of the Song of Moses, Dt 32:37–43. This is arranged by lines or half-lines of its verse form, and is notable for its witness to LXX readings found in no Hebr source previously known. Discussion of this text has elicited the fact that readings of the same type are verifiable at Qumran in the early and central portions, as well as in the ending, of the Song (P. Skehan, *BASOR* 136 [1954] 12–15). In general, the Palestinian type of text for these books may be seen as an expanding, harmonizing type, distinct from the received MT, and showing in part a kinship with the "proto-Lucianic" reworking of the LXX. An interesting combination of elements is furnished by a Dt ms. (5Q1) dated by J. T. Milik early in the 2nd cent. BC. This has, so far as it is preserved, a text close to the MT, but about a century later it was "corrected" at four points on the basis of a Hebr text with LXX associations!

22 For Jos, Jgs, and Kgs, the Qumran mss. are comparatively limited in number and in the extent of their preserved text; two, three, and four mss. respectively exist for these books. Within this body of material there seems to be a definite kinship in all cases with LXX sources. For Sm, the mss. are exceptional both for the quantity of text preserved (in 4QSm[a], 1st cent. BC) and for the age of the earliest witness (4QSm[b], late 3rd cent. BC). There is a series of other witnesses that attest indirectly to the same general type of text found at Qumran (use of Sm by the Chronicler in the 4th cent. BC; LXX materials in two stages, 3rd–1st cents. BC; and Flavius Josephus, end of 1st cent. AD), and there are sharp differences between all these witnesses and the MT. The Qumran evidence for Sm is bound to occupy a unique place in text-critical study for the future, for it provides new insights into the complex problems of text transmission that have long been recognized as particularly acute in 1–2 Sm.

23 (ii) *Major Prophets.* There have been extensive discussions of the Qumran mss. of Is: Two substantial witnesses from cave 1 have been published: the complete scroll (1QIs[a]) from the early part of the 1st cent. BC, and the more fragmentary 1QIs[b], from the latter part of the same century. The complete scroll, described above (→ 13, 16) as to its format and the unusual orthography used in its second half, diverges in many respects from the MT. In the beginning it gave rise to rather inflated hopes of providing access to a hitherto unattainably early stage in the transmission of the book. Though interesting and instructive, the ms. is textually rather disappointing: secondary to the MT in most of the instances in which the two diverge, with no genuine kinship to the Hebr prototype of LXX Is. In its divergencies it is unique among the 18 Qumran mss. of Is, which otherwise combine to establish that the textual tradition of the book was already standardized by the 2nd cent. BC to a degree elsewhere observable only for Gn. If in the beginning 1QIs[a] tended to be overrated, the same has been true for different reasons of 1QIs[b], which is habitually referred to as quite close to the MT. Sober enough in its spelling, 1QIs[b] by no means comes close to the degree of faithfulness in transmitting the narrowly standardized text of Is that may be observed in any good medieval Hebr ms. of the book, and such qualities as it possesses have been appreciated rather by contrast to 1QIs[a] than by any more exacting standard.

24 In Jer, of which Qumran provides four mss., the significant fact has been the appearance in one of these (4QJer[b]) of the shorter edition of the book previously known only from the LXX. Taken in conjunction with the variety of texts observable at Qumran in Ex through Dt and in Sm, the divided evidence for Jer gives some support for a tentative hypothesis. It seems quite possible that the fuller, received text of Jer represents in the main a reworking, presumably in Palestine, of the short edition, which would then be the older; this reworking would have taken place according to the harmonizing, simplifying, and expansionist technique observable in the textual witnesses of the other books named, and seen at its fullest in the Samaritan Pentateuch. So far, nothing of note has emerged from the preliminary study of the six Qumran mss. of Ez; if the expansion hypothesis has any merit, it may perhaps be said that the whole tradition of Ez in Hebrew, Qumran included, presents us with an expanded and reworked edition of that prophet. (For the technique of expansion, → 19 above.)

25 (iii) *Minor Prophets and Writings.* The evidence of the Qumran mss. for these books has not yet been fully explored. It is known that all parts of the Minor Prophets (including Hab 3) are represented among eight mss. Where different books of the 12 Prophets are extant in the same ms., the Qumran evidence is for the MT order of the books, not that of the Gk Bible. In the Hab commentary from cave 1 (1QpHab; → Apocrypha, 68:78), the *lemmata,* or citations of continuous text, do not always contain the same readings supposed by the discussion that follows them; this type of evidence for divergent texts is frequent enough in later materials in many languages.

26 Of the four mss. of Jb, one in the archaic script, and the two scrolls of Prv from which fragments survive, the text is close to the MT. The Jb targum from cave 11 (→ 83 below) witnesses to the standard MT arrangement of the chapters of that book, despite the problems of chs. 23–27 (→ Job, 31:83,90); only in the final ch. 42 does the Aramaic suggest a variant, shorter form of the Hebrew on which it was based.

27 There are some 30 mss. of Ps at Qumran, many of them very limited in the amount of text that survives. The most extensive is 11QPs[a], of the 1st cent. AD (published by J. A. Sanders, DJD 4). Its special interest is for the *non-Psalm* material that it combines with 40 canonical Pss. This includes two distinct compositions that have elsewhere been merged into the apocryphal Ps 151 preserved in the LXX; Sir 51:13–30 and 2 Sm 23:7ff.; two hymns known earlier from Syr sources, now labeled Pss 154–155; three other late psalmlike texts previously unknown; and a prose passage crediting David with 4050 poetic works. There are slight indications that the compiler of these materials knew the canonical order of the Psalter, though his own arrangement differs. A psalmlike "Apostrophe to Zion" found in 11QPs[a] has again been identified by J. Starcky as one of three non-biblical pieces in 4QPs[f] along with at least three canonical Pss. For the rest, though the Pss are copied in irregular order in a number of mss., and though there are many variants, mostly inferior, our knowledge of the history of the biblical book will scarcely be increased to any notable degree by these texts.

28 Of Dn eight mss. are known. The transition from Hebrew into Aramaic and back into Hebrew occurs as in the MT; the portions of the Gk text of Dn that are not in the MT are not attested by, but rather excluded from, the Qumran evidence. The five "Megilloth" books of the Hebr canon (→ Canonicity, 67:23) are attested by four mss. each of Ru, Ct, Lam, and two mss. of Eccl; only Est is missing. One may presume that the Qumran sectarians excluded Est on principle because it conflicted with their views about the religious calendar and was meaningful to their Hasmonean enemies (→ Apocrypha, 68:86). Of Ezr and Chr there is one ms. each, with a limited amount of text.

29 (iv) *Deuterocanonical Books.* Among these (→ Canonicity, 67:21) Bar is unattested, though a bit of the Letter of Jeremiah in Greek (Bar 6 in the Vg) was found in cave 7. Wis, Jdt, 1–2 Mc have not been found and would all be ill-matched with the Qumran community's interests. Four mss. of the original Aram text of Tb are known, and one in Hebrew. Their evidence supports the long form of the book in the Old Latin and in the Gk Codex Sinaiticus as primary. There are two witnesses of Sir at Qumran: some bits of Sir written stichometrically (by verse lines) in 2Q18, and the alphabetic composition Sir 51:13–30 in 11QPs[a] cols. 21–22 (see J. A. Sanders, "Cave 11 Surprises and the Question of the Canon," *McCormick Quarterly* 21 [1968] 284–98).

Three Gk OT mss. from cave 4 will be discussed below (→ 56).

30 **(C) Mss. from Masada and Other Areas.** The Qumran materials enumerated are paralleled, for texts of the same period, by discoveries at *Masada* in 1963/64 (→ Apocrypha, 68:110). Most notable is the fragmentary scroll of Sir (Y. Yadin, *The Ben Sira Scroll from Masada* [Jerusalem, 1965]) containing parts of seven columns of text, two hemistichs to the line, from Sir 39:27 to 44:17. The ms. dates paleographically from early in the 1st cent. BC, and it shows already many of the recensional differences that appear in the medieval Hebr Sir mss. and in the versions (→ Sirach, 33:5). A copy of Ps 150 from Masada is said to come from the end of a ms. as the arrangement of the canonical Psalter would lead us to expect. Fragments of Pss 81–85, of Gn, and of Lv are also known from Masada. With these texts should be mentioned a 1st-cent. AD ms. of Ps from Nahal Hever (→ Apocrypha, 68:108) that shows some variants from the MT.

31 Not strictly a biblical ms., the *Nash Papyrus* from Egypt, *ca.* 150 BC, contains the Ten Commandments and Dt 6:1ff. The only ancient Hebr ms. known before the Qumran discoveries, it was published by S. A. Cook in 1903 (in *Proc. Soc. Bibl. Arch.* 25, 34–56), but only in 1937 correctly dated to the Maccabean age by W. F. Albright (*JBL* 56, 145–76). Among the recent discoveries it has its counterpart in a number of phylacteries and mezuzas (miniature scrolls, the former to be worn on the person; the latter to be attached to the doorpost of a house) that contain excerpts from the Mosaic Books, though not always the exact excerpts specified by later Jewish regulations, and sometimes with variant readings in the text they do contain.

32 The last group of ancient mss. to be mentioned consists of five from the *Wadi Murabbaʿat*, all published, and five or six more from *Nahal Hever* (→ Apocrypha 68:106, 108), most unpublished. A Gk ms. of the Minor Prophets from the latter site is discussed with the LXX (→ 57, 60 below). Of a Hebr ms. of Gn, two (or three) mss. of Nm, and another of Dt from the same source it has been reliably stated that their text and script are similar to those of the Murabbaʿat mss. The Murabbaʿat mss. (published by P. Benoit and J. T. Milik, DJD 2) are: one ms. of Gn-Ex-Nm; Nm by another hand; Dt; Is; and the Minor Prophets. The last named (Mur88) is by far the most extensive, containing text from 10 of the 12 Minor Prophets. It is in all respects in accord with the MT tradition, showing only three meaningful variants. The other mss. confirm that the stabilization of the Hebr text, traditionally associated with the Jewish school at Jabneh (Jamnia; → Canonicity, 67:35) toward the end of the 1st cent. AD, was in full effect in these copies left to us by refugees of the Second Jewish Revolt in AD 132–35.

By the 2nd cent. AD, therefore, the consonantal Hebr text had been fixed in the form in which it is still transmitted today. Before that, however, the Qumran (and, for Sir, Masada) evidences allow us insight into a period of relative fluidity of text, varying in degree from one OT book to another. Actually the Greek and Samaritan textual evidence, along with the indirect witness of NT, Philo, and Josephus, have always made it necessary to suppose such a situation.

(Cross, F. M., Jr., *The Ancient Library of Qumran* [rev. ed.; Anchor Books; N.Y., 1961]; "The History of the Biblical Text in the Light of Discoveries in the Judaean Desert," *HarvTR* 57 [1964] 281–99. Eissfeldt, *OTI* 669–95, 778–83. Goshen-Gottstein, M. H., *Text and Language in Bible and Qumran* [Jerusalem, Israel, 1960]. Greenberg, M., "The Stabilization of the Text of the Hebrew Bible," *JAOS* 76 [1956] 157–67. Milik, J. T., *Ten Years of Discovery in the Wilderness of Judaea* [SBT 26; Naperville, Ill., 1959]. Orlinsky, H. M., "The Textual Criticism of the Old Testament," *BANE* 113–32. Sanders, J. A., "Pre-Masoretic Psalter Texts," *CBQ* 27 [1965] 114–23; "Palestinian Manuscripts 1947–1967," *JBL* 86 [1967] 431–40. Skehan, P. W., "Qumran and the Present State of Old Testament Text Studies: The Masoretic Text," *JBL* 78 [1959] 21–25; "The Biblical Scrolls from Qumran and the Text of the Old Testament," *BA* 28 [1965] 87–100; "The Scrolls and the Old Testament Text," *McCormick Quarterly* 21 (1968) 273–83. *Textus: Annual for the Hebrew University Bible Project* 1–5 [1960–66]. For QL, → Apocrypha, 68:66.)

33 **(II) Texts of the Medieval Period** (AD 135–1376).

(A) Samaritan Pentateuch. A unique survival into the Middle Ages of a Hebr text not subject to the standardization effected by the Jewish sages at the end of the 1st cent. AD is the Samaritan Pentateuch. First brought to the attention of European scholars after 1616, when Pietro della Valle obtained a ms. of it in Damascus, this form of the Mosaic Books is now represented in European libraries by copies ranging in age from the 12th to the 20th cents. Its oldest known exemplar, really a factitious reassembling of pieces of varying date, is the "Abisha scroll," kept by the Samaritan community at Nablus in Palestine (→ Biblical Geography, 73:101); the early part of this copy is from the 11th cent. AD. The Samaritans would have it that this text was prepared "13 years after the conquest of Canaan by Joshua." Western scholars, dating the Samaritan schism to the days of Nehemiah in the 5th cent. BC, have tended to ascribe to this text recension also a 5th-cent. date. In fact the form of the script, the nature of the text, and the history of the Samaritans all conspire to make us see in it a developed Palestinian text, by no means sectarian in origin, that began its separate history among the Samaritans no earlier than the days of John Hyrcanus, at the end of the 2nd cent. BC. The Qumran ms. 4QpaleoEx^{m} is older than this, is not sectarian, and shows that the Samaritan text tradition has been remarkably faithful to its pre-Christian recensional prototype (→ 19 above).

34 The harmonizing, expansionist nature of the Samaritan text has been mentioned: It fills out the plague narratives in Ex so that each time the Lord gives Moses a message for Pharaoh, Moses repeats it word for word before the narrative continues. Similarly, sections of Dt that expand on themes already present in Ex are actually transposed into the text of Ex; Nm undergoes similar harmonizing treatment, as does Dt itself. These systematic expansions within the framework of the known biblical text are, of course, of no particular interest; rather the value of this recension lies in its preserving, often in accord with the LXX, ancient Palestinian readings of individual words or phrases that vary from the MT. Where these variants do not involve simplification of, or making more explicit, the reading of MT, they need to be evaluated individually. The Samaritan tradition is supported both by targums in Aramaic (→ 86 below), and by a Gk *Samareitikon*, the known fragments and Syro-hexaplar translation of which show the same expanded text. This expanded recension was occasionally cited in the NT, notably in Acts 7. The traditional pronunciation of Hebrew among the Samaritans has been exploited with varying degrees of accuracy and success by several scholars seeking light on the pronunciation of Hebrew prior to the work of the Jewish Masoretes (→ 37 below).

(Baillet, M., "La récitation de la loi chez les Samaritans," *RB* 69 [1962] 570–87. Perez Castro, F., *Sefer Abiša* [Madrid, 1959; see review by E. Robertson, *VT* 12 (1962) 228–35]. Von Gall, A., *Der hebräische Pentateuch der Samaritaner* [Berlin, 1918].)

35 (B) Origen's Second Column. We shall discuss in more detail (→ 68 below) Origen's famous *Hexapla*, the six-columned compilation of Hebr and Gk texts and versions for the study of the text of the OT. Here we focus upon the work's 2nd column, which is a transliteration (not a translation) of the standardized Hebr OT consonantal text (of the 2nd cent. AD) into Gk letters. Actually the Gk alphabet is not well suited for transcribing Hebr consonants, consequently the work labors under considerable handicaps. It is primarily useful to scholars because it gives an idea of the pronunciation of Hebrew at Origen's time. We shall see in the next section how the Jewish Masoretes of later centuries developed systems to indicate pronunciation; but they were not native speakers of Hebrew, and their native tongue, a developed form of Aramaic, influenced their pronunciation. The earlier materials with which we have been dealing offer Hebr vowel patterns and syllable structures of considerable interest for the history of the language and for an understanding of OT poetic rhythms.

The surviving evidence for Origen's 2nd column is mostly from the Ps, known best from what was written under a reused ms. (palimpsest) in the Ambrosian Library in Milan, identified by G. Mercati in 1896 and published by him as *Psalterii hexapli reliquiae* 1 (Vatican City, 1958). Cardinal Mercati has shown that the orthography of this material must be supposed contemporary with Origen's compilation (*ca.* AD 245). It is a shrewd guess (T. W. Manson, followed by P. E. Kahle) that Origen's transliterated text follows an earlier practice of preparing similar materials for the guidance of Gk-speaking Jews in the Diaspora, who would find them an aid toward correct public reading from normal Hebr scrolls in the synagogues.

36 (C) Vocalized Medieval Mss. To the medieval period belong all the Hebr OT mss. preserved in libraries and museums, or by Jewish congregations, from before the spread of printing (except for the mss. described above as recent finds from the ancient period). For liturgical purposes leather scrolls of the text continued to be the form used through medieval into modern times. However, private copies are henceforth codices or books with pages written on both sides (→ 73 below). Sometimes there are two or three columns to the page; sometimes the text is the width of the full page. The script, paragraphing, and wording of the text and the format of mss. are now so rigidly standardized that paleographical criteria become harder, rather than easier, to apply.

37 The impetus to indicate vowels systematically by adding symbols to the consonantal spelling customary for writing Semitic languages, including Hebrew, seems to have arisen in Syria and to have been a development of the 6th and 7th cents. This technique was applied to the Syr Bible and to the Muslim Koran and was imitated by Jewish scholars (Masoretes) in both Babylonia and Palestine. The rise of several Masoretic systems (Hebr *massōret* means "tradition") is traceable today mainly on the basis of a discovery at the end of the 19th cent. in Cairo. In the oldest quarter of that city there still stands a building which before AD 969 was the Melkite church of St. Michael. It was subsequently sold to the Karaite (sectarian) Jewish community, and has since been a synagogue. Within this building there was walled off a room to be employed as a geniza, or storage place for sacred mss. that had outlived their usefulness (Jewish practice forbade their destruction). Between about 1890 and 1898, mss. that had accumulated in this room during centuries were recovered and brought to the West, mainly through the efforts of S. Schechter, then resident in England, later in America. The recovery from among these materials of a large part of the original Hebr text of Sir (→ 43 below), which had been lost for centuries, caused a sensation. This geniza has also supplied evidence for the history of the protocanonical OT books and of the targums; P. E. Kahle's *Cairo Geniza* is the best introduction to the various problems involved.

38 Out of the several thousands of scattered ms. pages from this geniza, now preserved in Cambridge, Oxford, Paris, New York, and elsewhere, Kahle outlined the development in both Babylonia and Palestine of increasingly refined systems for representing the traditional pronunciation of the Hebr text as employed in public recitation in the synagogue. For the consonantal text also, these mss. are of course fairly early witnesses; but they do not have the interest that attaches to the more ancient mss. described above. The several systems of pronunciation they represent are instructive for the history of the transmission of the Hebr language and for the details of interpreting the text implicit in how it is phrased and read. However, only one system, that of the ben Asher family from Tiberias in Galilee in the 9th and early 10th cents., is in general use today. The other sources are drawn upon primarily for sidelights on and supplements to what the Tiberian apparatus tells us.

39 (a) MODEL CODICES. For these codices the Hebr term *keter*, "crown," is sometimes used. They are model mss. for the study of the text and apparatus as developed by the ben Asher family, and are again being used as the foundation for critical editions of the printed Hebr Bible.

The *Cairo Prophets*, known as C, written and provided with its vowel points by Moses ben Asher in AD 895, has a concluding copyist's note that establishes it as the oldest dated Hebr OT ms. now extant. It contains both the Former Prophets (Jos, Jgs, Sm, Kgs) and the Latter Prophets (Is, Jer, Ez, and the 12 Minor Prophets) of the Hebr canon. Originally the property of the Karaite Jewish community in Jerusalem, the ms. was seized during the First Crusade and ultimately released by King Baldwin to the Karaites of Cairo, among whom it is still kept today. Its apparatus does not yet represent the full development of the Masoretic system as employed by Aaron ben Asher in the following generation; and it is now said to be closer to the rival ben Nefthali tradition than to the later ben Asher texts, though the differences are in any case not great. This ms. was consulted for the Kittel-Kahle, *BH*³ and is being collated anew into the Hebrew University Bible Project publication (→ 46, 48 below).

40 The *Aleppo Codex*, known as A, was originally a complete Hebr OT provided with its vowel points and accents (guides to the phrasing and inflection in recital) by Aaron ben Moses ben Asher about 930. It was given first, like C, to the Karaite community in Jerusalem, and while in their keeping was known and endorsed by Maimonides (d. 1204) as a reliable guide to certain features of the standard text. Its presence in Aleppo is attested from AD 1478; but during the anti-Jewish rioting in that city in 1947 it was badly damaged and, for a time, thought lost altogether. During 1958 it was announced that in truncated form (lacking the Pentateuch up to Dt 28:17, as well as parts of 2 Kgs, Jer, the Minor Prophets, 2 Chr; Pss 15:1–25:2; Ct 3:11 to the end; and all of Eccl, Lam, Est, Dn, Ezr Neh) it had reached Israel, where it is currently being employed for the first time as a foundation for the Bible text in the Hebrew University critical edition.

41 The *Leningrad Codex*, known as L, dated AD 1009, is a complete OT brought from the Crimea by A. Firkowitsch in 1839. A scribal note at the end says that this ms. was equipped with vowels and other apparatus from mss. corrected and annotated by Aaron ben Moses ben Asher. The vowel points show evidence of early revision, in the direction of conformity with the ben Asher standard as known from other sources. This was the best ms. available for the Kittel-Kahle, *BH*³, and its readings are being reported again in the Hebrew University undertaking.

42 (b) Mss. with Divergent Vowel Systems. Preliminary study and collation of a limited number of geniza OT fragments with rather *rudimentary Palestinian systems* of vowel pointing was done by P. E. Kahle, *Masoreten des Westens* (Stuttgart, 1927–30); this work is being continued by A. Diez Macho and others.

The geniza evidence for an early, more simple, and for a later, more complicated *Babylonian vowel system*, known usually as supralinear punctuation because its miniature letters and dots are placed above the words of the consonantal text, were presented by Kahle in his *Masoreten des Ostens* (Leipzig, 1913), in an album of photographs offered as a supplement to *ZAW* 46 (1928), and in the prefatory matter to *BH*³ (in the apparatus to that edition the variants from some 120 mss. of this group are included). The time range of these materials is from about the 8th to the 10th cents.

Certain mss. were ascribed by Kahle to the *school of ben Nefthali*, rivals of the ben Asher family of Masoretes. A number of these mss. are now seen by A. Diez Macho and others as being intermediate between the oldest Palestinian Masora and the full-fledged Tiberian system, with divergent features that true ben Nefthali mss. would not share. These include the *Codex Reuchlinianus* of AD 1105, now in Karlsruhe; and a Pentateuch (G. B. de Rossi's collation no. 668) and a complete OT (his collation no. 2) now preserved in Parma. The re-evaluation of these mss. reduces the actual number of differences between the ben Nefthali and ben Asher schools of Masoretes to some 900 points of detail, almost all in the use of a single secondary accent (the *meteg*).

43 **(D) Cairo Geniza Mss. of Sirach.** It is in keeping with the scattered and fragmentary state of the materials from the Cairo Geniza that though the first Hebr leaf of Sir to be identified and published from this source turned up in 1896, one of the five known Sir mss. was not edited until 1931, and stray leaves of two others were not published until 1958 and 1960. The most recent evaluation of these materials by A. A. DiLella (*The Hebrew Text of Sirach* [The Hague, 1966]) puts the total number of lines of text we have from the five mss. at 1098, out of some 1616 in the LXX. The Qumran and Masada texts of the book (→ 29, 30 above), published between 1962 and 1965, should finally put an end to repeated denials on the part of some scholars that the Cairo text is ancient. Since the actual Cairo copies date from the 11th and 12th cents. AD, many have seen them as medieval retroversions into Hebrew from Greek, from Syriac, or even, according to one scholar, from Persian. Rather, the pre-Christian text from Masada, taken in conjunction with the LXX form of the book, makes it possible to verify that when the most elaborate of the medieval mss. (Cairo ms. B) preserves variant readings in its margin, it is sometimes the case that *both* the text reading and the alternative in the margin originated in pre-Christian times. Another feature of the Cairo B Codex attested as genuinely ancient by both the Masada scroll and the Qumran fragments (2Q18) is the copying in verse lines rather than as continuous prose text. For the alphabet acrostic poem Sir 51:13–30, however, the better text for its first half preserved in 11QPsᵃ shows clearly that the medieval form was arrived at by retroversion from the Syriac. Though medieval texts, in both Hebrew and Jewish Aramaic, also exist for Tb and Jdt, these are in no way comparable, but are entirely secondary and provide no avenue of approach toward the original form of those books.

44 **(III) Editions of the Modern Period** (AD 1477–). Printed editions of the Hebr OT up to the year 1525 (earliest, the Ps, with the commentary of D. Kimchi, Bologna, 1477; earliest complete OT, from Soncino, 1488) were based mostly on a limited choice of mss., some no longer extant; their text varies within the same range as the medieval mss. themselves, and these editions have been collated in later times along with the ms. evidence, as more or less independent witnesses, often not very good.

45 **(A) Textus Receptus (1525–1929).** After the appearance from Venice in 1518 of a first *Biblia rabbinica*—the OT text with Masora, targum, and a selection of Jewish medieval commentators combined on folio pages (Hebr *miqrā'ōt gᵉdōlōt*, "large Scriptures")—the same publisher, D. Bomberg, brought out a second rabbinic bible in 1524/25. Its editor was the Jewish scholar Jacob ben Chayyim, a careful student of the Masora who was, however, handicapped in his work by the modifications and overrefinements introduced into the tradition during the six centuries between Aaron ben Asher and his own day. The text that ben Chayyim established became, for better or worse, the norm for nearly all printed Hebr bibles until recent years. Its 400-year dominance makes it comparable to the Gk NT *textus receptus* (→ 123–124 below).

46 **(B) Critical Editions.** The OT text most widely used at the moment is that edited for the Bibelanstalt (Bible Society) in Stuttgart by R. Kittel and P. E. Kahle between 1929 and 1937. This *Biblia hebraica*³, of which there have been many subsequent reprintings, bases its text on the Leningrad ms. L (→ 41 above). Its footnote apparatus covers a wide range of alternative readings drawn from Hebr mss., the versions, and even from critical conjecture. Its treatment of LXX evidence in particular has been severely criticized over the years, and a new edition is in preparation (see G. E. Weil, VTSup 9 [1963] 266–84). Meanwhile, with all its limitations, *BH*³ is still the best single source for a dependable text combined with some indication of what textual criticism may have to offer by way of variants. Its notes call for constant checking and evaluation; so will those of any other handbook that can be devised. The disposition of the text on the pages in *BH*³ results from the modern editors' judgment, especially with regard to poetic structure; it is not the traditional Jewish presentation from the mss., in which only Ex 15:1–17 and Dt 32:1–43 are always disposed as poetry, and Ps, Prv, Jb more rarely. Though helpful in many respects, the poetic arrangement *BH*³ offers can also be quite misleading if accepted uncritically.

47 Lacking both the hazards and the advantages of *BH*³ is the current British and Foreign Bible Society Hebr OT, ed. by N. H. Snaith (London, 1958). The editor based his work on a Lisbon ms. of 1483; he also took into account a small group of mss. primarily of Spanish origin, and the Masoretic studies of S. Y. de Norzi (1742—better than ben Chayyim). Snaith himself affirms that his resultant text is quite close to that of *BH*³ and its Leningrad prototype. The British edition follows the traditional arrangement of the text, but does print Ps, Prv, and Jb in double columns, with two half-verse units (hemistichs) to the line.

48 The very important Hebrew University Bible Project, in Jerusalem, Israel, has published (1965) a sample edition of the text of Is with an introduction by M. H. Goshen-Gottstein outlining the principles on which its definitive edition of the OT will be constructed, and the manner in which supplementary evidence will be presented. The basic text for this edition is that of the Aleppo Codex (→ 40 above) with its own abbreviated

Masoretic notes on the right margin, and variants in the vowel and accent marks from a small group of early mss. on the left. Lower on the page are three other blocks of apparatus: the first, citing the evidence of the versions with concise and careful evaluation; the second, giving variants from the Qumran scrolls and from rabbinic literature; and the last, citing readings from medieval Hebr mss. on a carefully developed selective basis.

49 **(C) Compilations of Variants.** The basic compilation of consonantal variants from the medieval Hebr mss. and the early editions is the *Vetus Testamentum hebraicum cum variis lectionibus* of B. F. Kennicott (2 vols.; Oxford, 1776–80). It reproduces the *textus receptus* and offers variants from some 600 mss. and 50 editions of the OT or its parts, along with a collation of 16 Samaritan Pentateuch mss. against the text of that recension reprinted from the London Polyglot Bible of 1657. The work had been done over a 10-year period, partly by correspondence with scholars in the various cities of continental Europe where significant mss. were kept. The results of this undertaking were so disappointing as to discourage further attempts to resurvey the same or comparable material on any similar basis.

50 A more selective undertaking by G. B. de Rossi entitled *Variae lectiones Veteris Testamenti* (4 vols. and supp.; Parma, 1784–88; 1798) was at the same time more broadly based. De Rossi printed no text, but presumed the same collating base as Kennicott. He published evidence only for passages in which he judged the existing variants to be of importance; he reported evidence for variants in the vocalization as well as in the consonantal text. To Kennicott's data, which he repeated in detail where they bore upon the readings he studied, De Rossi collated an additional 800 mss., some of them noteworthy. He also reported the indirect evidence of the versions. Though its materials need to be re-evaluated in the light of later critical studies—and for the versions it can never be cited at face value—this was the most instructive repertory of textual data bearing on the OT before the present century.

51 The work of C. D. Ginsburg, *The Old Testament... Diligently Revised* (3 vols. in 4; London, 1908–1926), covers some of the same ground as the two preceding and relates the evidence of some 70 mss. and 19 editions to the received Hebr text; yet it marks no particular advance and is scarcely helpful. Similarly, an Israeli edition ascribed to the studies of M. D. Cassuto was issued (1953) after the scholar's death by others, and there is little to be said in its favor.

(Orlinsky, H. M., "The Masoretic Text: Fact or Fiction?" Prolegomenon (45 pp.) to facsimile reprint of C. D. Ginsburg, *Introduction to the Massoretico-Critical Edition of the Hebrew Bible* [N.Y., 1966]. Perez Castro, F., "Estudios masoreticos," *Sefarad* 25 [1965] 289–317. Roberts, B. J., "The Hebrew Bible Since 1937," *JTS* 15 [1964] 253–64.)

GREEK VERSIONS OF THE OLD TESTAMENT

52 **(I) The Septuagint Before AD 100.** At the time the Foreword to Sir was written, *ca.* 116 BC (→ Sirach, 33:3, 9), the bulk of the OT was already circulating in Greek in the translation known as the Septuagint (LXX). Beyond its current interest for the history and criticism of the text, the LXX is of enormous significance in that it furnished the cultural milieu and the literary vehicle for the preaching of earliest Christianity to the Gentile world; it has been and remains the liturgical OT text of millions of Eastern Christians throughout the centuries. The LXX is the form in which the OT was most widely used in apostolic times, and it conveys to us the original text of some canonical books (Wis, 2 Mc) and the basic canonical form of others, either in part (Est, Dn, Sir) or as a whole (Tb, Jdt, Bar, 1 Mc). Indeed, some modern Catholic scholars have argued that the LXX is directly inspired, at least in what it adds, even in the books of the Hebr canon (→ Inspiration, 66: 68–70).

53 **(A) The Legendary Origin.** How the Pentateuch was translated from Hebrew into Greek is told in the fictitious *Letter of Aristeas to Philocrates*, dating from the 2nd cent. BC (→ Apocrypha, 68:32–33). In the story, Demetrius of Phaleron, a known statesman, is the librarian of Ptolemy II Philadelphus (285–246 BC); he wants copies of the Jewish Law for the famous library at Alexandria. At his urging, Philadelphus requests these from the high priest in Jerusalem, who sends to Egypt a band of 72 translators (6 from each tribe!). They complete the translation to the satisfaction of all concerned, including the Jewish community of Alexandria. An interview by "Aristeas" with the high priest Eleazar and a symposium at which the translators discourse in the Egyptian king's presence are vehicles for the presentation of Jewish wisdom. Despite its constant repetition in Jewish and Christian circles, only one salient fact can be gleaned from this essentially apologetic propaganda narrative, namely that the compilation of a full translation of the Torah was made in the early 3rd cent. BC. Yet "Septuagint," reflecting the Latin for 70 and drawn from the (rounded) number of the translators in Aristeas' account, has come to be the name not only of the Pentateuch in Greek, but—at least since the 4th cent. in Christian circles—of the entire corpus of Gk OT translations and compositions from the beginnings, possibly before 300 BC, until just prior to the work of Aquila, *ca.* AD 130 (→ 65 below).

54 **(B) Problem of Unified Origin.** The LXX contains translations that vary enormously in accuracy and style from one book to the next, and sometimes within a single book. In general, the Pentateuch translation is faithful, competent, and idiomatic, with its different portions coming from no less than a half dozen different translators. In Gn, although there are differences between the text furnished by the MT and that supposed by the LXX, they are comparatively limited, and the evidence for Gn shows a high degree of uniformity in the mss. tradition. For Ex through Dt the variations are greater, with Ex 35–40 notably different in arrangement and shorter in the LXX than in the MT and the Samaritan recension. The other historical books of the LXX were developed over a span of no less than two centuries. Where fragments from Qumran in Hebrew can be compared, these tend to support readings known from the Greek as against those of the MT. But there are many complexities in the transmission, and each book and passage has to be studied for itself. In Is, the LXX rendering is a good idiomatic Greek, tends to abridge the original, and does not always understand it. Jer in Greek is a shorter book than in the Hebrew and gives evidence of being an earlier and better edition than the MT (→ 24 above).

55 The differences apparent in the LXX of the various books suggest a question: Since 1941 P. E. Kahle has asked insistently whether in fact what is preserved in our mss. and editions of the LXX is a single, pre-Christian rendering of these books, or whether it might not rather be an arbitrary, almost random, selection from a multiplicity of oral renderings like the early Palestinian targums (→ 82 below). Kahle pointed to OT quotations in Philo, Josephus, the NT, and such writers as Justin Martyr (d. *ca.* 165) as being incompatible with a single line of transmission for the Gk text leading to the great LXX codices of the 4th/5th cents. and thus to our printed bibles.

56 **(C) The Earliest LXX and Subsequent Revisions.** Despite the very real difficulties raised by Kahle, which cannot all be resolved on any single basis, the evidence for strict continuity in most OT books between a single pre-Christian rendering and the LXX text extant in our codices is overwhelming. In addition to the very early renderings from the Greek into Latin, Coptic, and (a little later) Ethiopic, which all give detailed support to the LXX text we know, there are now a variety of ms. fragments of pre-Christian date that present us with actual LXX text from both Palestine and Egypt fitting into the same textual tradition. These include portions of Ex (7Q1); Lv (4Q LXX $Lv^{a,b}$); Nm (4Q LXX Nm); and Dt (Papyrus Rylands Gk 458; Papyrus Fuad inv. 266); along with a bit of the Letter of Jeremiah (7Q2 = Bar 6 in the Vg). The fragments range in date from the 2nd cent. BC down to the turn of the era.

57 More extensive than these pre-Christian fragments are the remains of a Gk scroll of the Minor Prophets of 1st cent. AD date, from the Nahal Hever in the Judean desert (→ Apocrypha, 68:108), published by D. Barthélemy in *Les dévanciers d'Aquila* (VTSup 10; Leiden, 1963). These fragments, and Barthélemy's study of them, have gone far toward meeting the difficulties raised by Kahle, because they introduce us *not* to the early Alexandrian LXX of the Minor Prophets, but to a 1st-cent. AD *systematic revision* of that rendering. Barthélemy's evidence converges with data provided by Qumran Hebr mss. of Sm being studied by F. M. Cross (→ 22 above). The details cannot be presented here; we will attempt instead a somewhat provisional sketch of the recensional activity to which they introduce us—a process that changes our previous historical perspective on the state of the Gk OT text before and after the work of Origen (d. AD 254).

58 (a) THE LXX IN ALEXANDRIA. The earliest Gk translation of the OT, done with underlying liturgical and apologetic concerns, employed the somewhat florid Alexandrian Gk idiom rather readily. Although this translation strove in general for word to word equivalence, it was indifferent to the presence or absence in the Hebr text of certain minor elements, e.g., reinforcing particles ("indeed"), signs for the object of the verb, and pronouns with a resumptive function not called for by Gk syntax. The Hebr mss. on which it was based clearly differed in many respects from those later chosen as the prototypes for the MT. Good examples of this are available in Dt and Is (but in either case not in Codex Vaticanus [B] or in editions based on it, since the B text is reworked on the basis of the Hebrew in these books). Another good example is Jer. As for Sm and Kgs it would seem that the apologetic or edifying purpose extended to presenting in Greek only a selection from the Hebr books, including 1 Sm 1:1–2 Sm 9:13 and 1 Kgs 2:12–21 (MT 20):43. At least, of this early stage, that is all that is extant for Sm-Kgs; it is well represented in Codex B.

59 (b) EARLIEST PALESTINIAN REVISION: "PROTO-LUCIAN." A subsequent stage, identified for Ex-Dt and Sm-Kgs by Cross as a result of his work on Qumran Hebr texts, may be labeled "proto-Lucianic." It represents the accommodation of older LXX materials to somewhat more developed Hebr texts, still quite distinct from the MT form—texts that circulated in the 2nd and 1st cents. BC. The work strove for a choice of terms and of phrasing that would more nearly match the Hebrew, and it presents in Sm-Kgs a complete text of these books. That the work was done in Palestine can only be conjectured from the fact that this type of text, ascribed subsequently to the patronage of Lucian of Antioch (d. 312), is connected with Syria-Palestine and matches Palestinian mss. in Hebrew from Qumran. Investigation of this phase of the LXX text transmission calls for much critical sifting of the ms. evidence in various books of the OT—a pursuit that is at present in its initial stage.

60 (c) FURTHER PALESTINIAN REVISION: "PROTO-THEODOTION." The Minor Prophets scroll referred to above (→ 57) is effectively presented by Barthélemy as evidence of a distinct recensional activity in Palestine, which he relates to the rules of interpreting the text formulated by the rabbis at about the turn of the era. The revised translation intended to convey in Greek even minor elements of the original in which the rabbis found significance (the particles for "indeed" and for introducing the object of a verb, etc.). Barthélemy dates it to *ca.* AD 30–50 and ascribes it to one Jonathan ben Uzziel mentioned in rabbinic literature in connection with the (Aram) targums. He also identifies this Jonathan with the Theodotion to whom a LXX revision late in the 2nd cent. AD has been attributed. Though the need for a prototype for "Theodotion" is evident from the material at hand, the date thus given him is perhaps slightly more doubtful—it is certainly not too late—and the identification with Jonathan accounts for an already shadowy figure by fitting him into a garbled legend. Firm conclusions will depend on a re-examination of all the Gk evidence for Theodotion and the early recension to which he is somehow related.

61 In any case, the important things about the Minor Prophets recension are: its early date (the ms. itself is from the 1st cent. AD—from 50–100, according to Barthélemy), the wide range of texts to which it can be related, and a whole series of useful criteria by which the same recension can be identified in the ms. tradition of other OT books wherever it may occur. For the Minor Prophets, Barthélemy has shown that this translation is not a new one, but is a deliberate reworking of the older Alexandrian LXX in the light of the Hebrew, and that the same reworking is evidenced in the citations we have for the *quinta editio* of Origen's *Hexapla* (→ 68 below), as well as in a Gk ms. of the Minor Prophets in the Freer collection in Washington, in the Sahidic Coptic secondary rendering from the Greek, and in the text quoted by Justin Martyr, a native of Neapolis (Nablus) in Palestine (d. *ca.* 165). In our printed editions of the Gk OT, it is this recension that provides the "LXX" text of Lam and (probably) of Ru; also the "Theodotion" text of Dn, which is the standard Gk form for that book, already quoted in the NT and by Clement of Rome at the end of the 1st cent. AD. The LXX forms of Jer and of Jb, both shorter than the Hebr text, have been filled out with the techniques proper to this same recension, and these supplements appear regularly in the Gk Jb, and in some mss. and editions of Jer.

In Sm-Kgs, where Cross sees this recension as a third stage of the Gk transmission, building on a "proto-Lucian," it supplies 2 Sm 10:1 to 1 Kgs 2:11 and 1 Kgs 22, plus all of 2 Kgs in Codex B and in most mss. and in the printed editions. This reworking of Sm-Kgs had already been isolated by H. St. J. Thackeray (*The Septuagint and Jewish Worship* [2nd ed.; London, 1923] 16–28 and 114–15), who, however, did not have the evidence to date it. The criteria for identifying the recension were first singled out by Thackeray, e.g., standard way of rendering "and indeed" (Hebr *w^e gam*; Gk *kaige*—whence the name "*kaige* recension").

62 (d) OTHER INDICATIONS OF EARLY REVISION. Once the existence of extensive recensional work on the OT text in Greek in the last cent. BC and the 1st cent. AD is recognized, a number of other elements in the history of the LXX begin to fall into place. In Ez, for example, the 3rd-cent. Beatty-Scheide Papyrus 967 contains a reworking of the LXX for that book, already dated by J. Ziegler to the 1st cent. AD. It becomes clear that of the five "Scrolls" (Megilloth) of the Hebr canon, only Est in Greek is surely of pre-Christian date in the received form of its text (for Gk Lam and Ru, → 61 above); Gk Ct has always been thought late, and Gk Eccl is justly ascribed (again by Barthélemy) to Aquila in the 2nd cent. AD. In all mss., Prv 1–9 include a number of double renderings and other expansions; since a secondary rendering of Prv 2:11 was already used by Clement of Rome (*1 Clem* 14:4), these materials may be presumed generally to date to the 1st cent. AD or earlier. Similarly, the secondary Gk reworking of Sir, found in some Gk mss. and in all the OL evidence, included a text of Sir 12:1 that is already employed in the *Didache* 1:6; once again we have 1st-cent. evidence for a revised text. Through these reworkings of the LXX, when they can be dated approximately, it is possible not only to account historically for many of the difficulties pointed out by Kahle, but also to form an idea of the state of the Hebr mss. on which they were based. Though they are often closer to the MT than to the prototypes of the early Alexandrian LXX, it is not in fact the *precise* consonantal text stabilized in Hebrew at the end of the 1st cent. AD that they presuppose.

63 One may add to what has been said those cases in which whole books of the Gk OT are present in the mss. in more than one form: two texts of Jgs in codices B and A, so different that their common origin is not universally admitted; Alexandrian translations of Ezr (*1 Esdras* or Esdras A) and of Dn, which between them serve to emphasize the later and distinctive origins of Ezr/Neh (Esdras B in the Greek; → Apocrypha, 68:39) and of the "Theodotionic" Dn, and also of the similar Gk rendering of 1–2 Chr; two separate forms of Est in Greek, and three of Tb. Thus it becomes clear that the basic unity of the LXX translation is subject to many qualifications, and that its use as a textual witness, somewhat encouraged by indications in the Hebr mss. from Qumran, actually calls for ever more careful and informed study of each individual book. The Psalter in particular presents in Greek the appearance of a rather labored patchwork, based on a rendering inferior to begin with. It has not been helped at all by the adventures it has undergone in becoming the liturgical Psalter known to us from Greek, or Latin, or other liturgical languages (e.g., Arabic). As in the Minor Prophets, so in Ps, the *quinta* text among those assembled by Origen (→ 68 below) proves to be the 1st-cent. "proto-Theodotion" recension.

64 **(II) Later Renderings and the Work of Origen.** The traditional way of describing the Jewish OT renderings into Greek in the 2nd cent. AD, and the work of Origen in assembling these and other materials into his *Hexapla* in the 3rd cent., and the still later activity of Lucian of Antioch (d. 312) becomes unsatisfactory at several points in the light of what has been said above. We shall now outline these activities.

65 **(A) Aquila.** About AD 130, this Jewish proselyte from Pontus produced a rendering of the OT that had as its base the "proto-Theodotionic" recension described above. The rigidity with which he carried out his work makes the result to all intents and purposes a new translation. The choice of words was determined by a policy of matching each Hebr verbal stem by a single Gk equivalent, from which noun forms would then be derived, or created if necessary, to provide for all derivatives from the same Hebr root. Greek syntax and idiom were violated if need be, to furnish equivalents in that language for incidental particles in the Hebrew. (The underlying earlier recension had begun this process by using, for example, Gk "I am," two separate words, to represent the Hebr pronoun "I" in a longer form that had become archaic.) Because of the extensive use made of the LXX in Christian circles, and the numerous cases in which the LXX did not correspond with the closely standardized Hebr mss. of the 2nd and later centuries, the rendering of Aquila became the accepted Gk version of the OT among the Jews in the later Roman and Byzantine Empires, replacing the LXX. In Is 7:14 it rendered Hebrew *ʿalmâ* by *neanis*, "young woman," as against the *parthenos*, "virgin," of the LXX; on this and other points, the translation of Aquila entered into Jewish-Christian controversy.

Apart from the "LXX" rendering of Eccl, which is Aquila's, his work has only survived in fragments: parts of Kgs and of Ps, along with marginal readings in certain LXX mss., and citations in patristic literature. As in the case of the other later Gk translations, these quoted remnants have been compiled among the evidences for Origen's *Hexapla* (→ 68 below). The name of Aquila, transformed into Onkelos, has come down in Jewish tradition in association with the Aram targums, with which, in fact, Aquila had nothing to do. Details about him, found in Epiphanius (*De mens. et pond.* 14–15), make him a relative of the Emperor Hadrian, converted to Christianity in Aelia Capitolina (Jerusalem) by Christians from Pella but later excommunicated. According to these reports, which are apparently legendary, Aquila then undertook his OT revision with an explicitly anti-Christian purpose.

66 **(B) Symmachus.** Toward the end of the 2nd cent. AD, perhaps during the reign of Commodus (180–192), this writer produced a careful, yet thoroughly idiomatic, Gk rendering of the OT. Although he worked subsequent to Aquila and employed as his base, at least in some books (according to D. Barthélemy), the same 1st-cent. recension from which Aquila had worked, he proceeded on entirely different principles. A particular interest of his version is that it served in a number of cases as a lexical and stylistic model for Jerome's OT from the Hebrew. It survives only in Origen's hexaplaric fragments and citations (→ 68 below). In Eccl, where Aquila's version occupied the "LXX" column in Origen's edition, Symmachus stood in the usual place of Aquila, and faulty attributions of his readings have resulted from this and similar causes. About the author himself, the most likely detail we have is that Origen received the text of his rendering from a certain Juliana, who had it from Symmachus in person. His supposed Samaritan origins (Epiphanius, *De mens. et pond.* 15), and connection with an Ebionite *Gospel of Matthew* (Eusebius, *Hist.*, 6.17; GCS 9/2.554–56) are highly dubious data (→ Apocrypha, 68:61–62).

67 **(C) Theodotion.** This name covers, as seen above (→ 60–61) a large body of recensional material of 1st-cent. date bearing on most, if not all, parts of the LXX OT. Irenaeus (*Adv. Haer.* 3.21, 1) puts Theodotion before Aquila, and this is the correct order of priority for the bulk of the materials now known. What is left for the traditional late 2nd-cent. translator Theodotion, a Jewish proselyte supposedly from Ephesus, remains as a matter for renewed sifting of the complex and fragmentary data. Since "Theodotion" (= "proto-Theodotion") is the ordinary source drawn upon by Origen to fill out correspondences with the Hebr text that were lacking in the older LXX, it is from this recension that our printed bibles offer us Dn; Lam; Ru; 2 Sm 10:1 to 1 Kgs 2:11; 1 Kgs 22 and all of 2 Kgs; possibly Ct; and the extensive supplements in the Greek of Jb and (sometimes) of Jer. In Sm-Kgs this recension builds on "proto-Lucian"; and wherever they can be compared, "Theodotion" is built upon by Aquila, who carries to an extreme its existing tendencies toward mechanical rendering and imitation of the Hebr word order. The Theodotionic materials contain an unaccountable sporadic element of transliterated Hebr words, sometimes well-known common nouns that present no lexical problem. Other related materials are the *quinta* recension (→ 68 below) of Ps, seemingly a minuscule (*i*, *r*, *u*, a_2) text of Jgs, the Nahal Hever Minor Prophets (→ 60–61 above), and most, but not all, of the known excerpts from the "Theodotion" column of the *Hexapla*. The name Theodotion can easily be equated with Jonathan, since both mean "gift of God"; but that the 1st-cent. Gk recension ascribed to Theodotion was actually done by the Jonathan ben Uzziel of Jewish tradition seems hardly susceptible of proof.

68 **(D) Origen's Hexapla.** At Caesarea in Palestine before AD 245, Origen put together his famous compilation of materials in Hebrew and Greek for the study of the OT text. Known as the *Hexapla Biblia*, or Sixfold Books, the text was arranged in (usually) six vertical columns, comprising: (1) the Hebr consonantal text in Hebr characters, in the standardized form current since the 2nd cent.; (2) the Hebrew transliterated into Gk letters, within the limited possibilities of the Gk alphabet; (3) Aquila; (4) Symmachus; (5) the traditional LXX—the elements lacking by comparison with the Hebrew have been supplied, usually from "Theodotion"; and (6) Theodotion. For some books, e.g., Ps, there were additional forms in Greek, a *quinta* (V^a), a *sexta* (VI^a), and even a *septima* (VII^a) *editio;* in such cases, the number of columns would grow to at least eight (in Ps, the *quinta* occupied the usual place of Theodotion; also, the *septima* may never have been more than marginal notations).

69 The transliterated Hebrew of Origen's 2nd column has been described above (→ 35). Evidence from the Mercati Ps fragments seems to indicate that the 5th (LXX) column of the *Hexapla* did not itself contain the critical markings for comparison with the Hebrew that were a special feature of Origen's work. When, however, the LXX column was copied to be circulated separately, it was equipped with the asterisk (⋇) to signal passages lacking in the older LXX, but supplied from the Greek of "Theodotion" to make the LXX conform to a fuller text found in the received Hebrew. The obelus (÷) was introduced before LXX passages for which the Hebrew had no equivalent. At the point where the LXX and the Hebrew began again to coincide, a metobelus (⋎) would mark the end of the preceding variant, of either type.

70 Copies of the complete *Hexapla* must always have been scarce, if indeed any were made at all. A *Tetrapla*, the four Gk columns without the two Hebr ones, is also spoken of. The prototype survived in Caesarea until about 600 AD, in the library founded by the martyr Pamphilus, where it was consulted by Jerome, among others. Its ultimate fate is not known. Today we have of the *Hexapla* only fragments from Sm-Kgs and Ps; readings excerpted into the margins of LXX mss.; citations by patristic writers in several languages; and extensive portions of the 5th column with the critical markings in secondary translations in several languages, particularly Syriac and Arabic. Remarkable efforts at reassembling these data have been made by F. Field, *Origenis hexaplorum quae supersunt* (2 vols.; Oxford, 1875) and in the apparatus to the Cambridge and Göttingen editions (→ 79 below).

71 The task of re-establishing exact hexaplaric readings is complicated by these factors: The critical markings have all too often been misplaced or lost in transmission; the ascription to one or another of the columns is sometimes erroneous in our witnesses, partly because of a misunderstanding of abbreviations, partly because even in the prototype the content of a given column frequently varied from book to book. Examples of this last are: In the portions of Sm-Kgs where "Theodotion" occupied the 5th or "LXX" column (2 Sm 10:1 to 1 Kgs 2:11; 1 Kgs 22 and 2 Kgs), the "proto-Lucianic" form went into col. 6; in Eccl, where the 5th or "LXX" column is really Aquila, it was Symmachus that appeared in col. 3; in Ps, *quinta* held the place of Theodotion—false citations have resulted in such instances. Abridged extracts from the major work later added to the sources of confusion.

72 **(E) Lucian of Antioch.** In his preface to the Vg Chr, written *ca.* 396, Jerome indicates that there were in his day three commonly received text traditions of the LXX: one in Egypt, connected with the name of Hesychius; a second stemming from Caesarea in Palestine and reflecting the work of Origen; and the third, which elsewhere (Ep. 106, *Ad Sunniam*) he characterizes as the *koinē* ("common") or vulgate form, connected with Antioch and the work of Lucian (d. 312). The character of the text ascribed to Hesychius is, to say the least, very difficult to determine today (cf. S. Jellicoe, *JBL* 82 [1963] 409–18). As for Lucian (→ 59 above), in Sm-Kgs at least, the text credited to him has been successfully isolated in a group of minuscule mss. (*b*, *o*, c_2, e_2) that prove on further study to be closely related to the text used by Josephus at the end of the 1st cent. and to the fragmentary Hebr mss. from Qumran. Similar kinship between a group of "Lucianic" mss. and the citations in Josephus and in certain Antiochene writers such as John Chrysostom is verified also for other OT books. Hence whatever function may be assigned to Lucian's personal work on the Gk text of the NT (→ 138 below), and however much retouching for stylistic or other reasons the LXX may have received at his hands, the most significant feature regarding the group of Antiochene texts with which he is to be associated is that they open up for us an approach to the state of the LXX and of the underlying Hebr text in Syria-Palestine *before* the standardizing of the Hebr consonantal tradition toward the end of the 1st cent. AD.

73 **(III) Mss. and Editions of the LXX.**

(A) Manuscripts. In addition to the fragmentary texts from before AD 100 now available (→ 56 above), there are approximately 1800 extant LXX mss. of a later period. These are generally divided on the basis of the material used (papyrus and parchment) or of the style of writing (uncial and minuscule).

Papyrus, made in Egypt, came from a tall reedlike plant (*Cyperus papyrus*). The stem (pith) was sliced lengthwise into strips that were laid side by side to form a layer, and layers were pressed together at right angles to form a sheet. After drying, papyrus made a good, inexpensive writing surface; however it became brittle with age. Papyrus sheets were glued together to form a scroll which, when wound about a stick, constituted a volume. Averaging about 35 ft. in length, scrolls were rather inconvenient, because when one wanted to consult a passage near the beginning of a work, the entire scroll had to be unrolled. Early in the 2nd cent. AD (and seemingly in Church use in particular) a new book format came into frequent use, i.e., the codex in which sheets were sewn together much as in the modern book. Some of our earliest fragments of Christian works come from papyrus codices.

Parchment (or vellum), so called because of the high quality of this material developed at Pergamum in the 2nd cent. BC, was a more durable, if more expensive, writing material. It consisted of sheepskin scraped and made smooth. Its durability made it more appropriate for books designed to be read over and over, and so we find the major biblical codices written on parchment.

74 As for the type of handwriting, although a cursive or "running" hand (where one letter is run into another) was used for everyday documents, literary works were written in more formal block letters or uncials (large letters separated from one another). Up until the 9th cent. AD this was the script used for the Bible, but in that century a script was introduced at Constantinople that employed smaller letters (minuscules) written in a running hand. This reform in handwriting meant that biblical mss. could be copied more swiftly and on a smaller writing space; it greatly increased the number of mss. copied.

75 (a) PAPYRI MSS. (2nd–9th centuries). Discoveries in Egypt since the 1890's have substantially increased the resources available for knowledge of the LXX as it circulated before, or independently of, the work of Origen. The Chester Beatty collection of papyri, published by F. G. Kenyon (8 vols.; London, 1933–58) includes 2nd-cent. AD fragments of Nm, Dt, Jer, and substantial 3rd-cent. parts of Gn, Is-Ez-Dn-Est. The Freer collection in Washington has 33 leaves of a 3rd-cent. Minor Prophets. Also of the 3rd cent. are portions of Gn, Ps, Prv, Wis, and Sir in Oxford, Geneva, and London. With the 4th cent., extant papyri become more numerous, and some 200 can be counted that are prior to AD 700. References to LXX papyri in the literature suffer from the lack of a uniform method of listing them.

76 (b) GREAT UNCIAL CODICES (4th–10th centuries). These codices began to make their appearance in the 4th cent. AD, written on vellum; and they remain our most complete and frequently our most careful copies of the LXX. They have been the foundation for almost all printed editions and collations of the ms. evidence; several have been reproduced in complete photographic facsimile publications. They are usually pandects, or complete bibles; capital letters, ordinarily roman, are the symbols used to designate the individual uncial mss. Those most significant for LXX study include:

(i) *Codex Vaticanus*, known as B. Of mid-4th cent. date, it lacks only Gn 1:1–46:8, some verses in 2 Sm 2, and about 30 Pss. It never contained 1–2 Mc. In a number of OT books this codex has proved to be in a class by itself as the best single witness to the earliest form of the LXX.

(ii) *Codex Sinaiticus*, referred to as S or *aleph* (א). Of this codex (also 4th cent.), 156 leaves are now in the British Museum in London and 43 others in Leipzig; but there are some notable lacunae. Its orthography is surprisingly careless; the text to which it witnesses is close to that of B. In Tb it is the unique Gk witness to the longer and more nearly original text form of the book. It has 1 and 4 Mc, but never had 2–3 Mc.

(iii) *Codex Alexandrinus*, known as A. Also in the British Museum, it dates from the 5th cent., has slight lacunae in Gn and in 1 Sm, and also lacks about 30 Pss. Its text is often at variance with B, in Jgs strikingly so; it includes 3–4 Mc as well as the canonical books. "Proto-Lucianic" and hexaplaric influences on its text have been identified.

(iv) *Codex Marchalianus*, labeled Q. It is a 6th-cent. ms. of the Prophets in the Vatican Library. It is notable especially for citations of the later Gk renderings of Aquila, Symmachus, and Theodotion in its margins.

77 (c) MINUSCULE MSS. (from the 9th cent. onwards). In number about 1500, these mss. occasionally preserve text of great antiquity not witnessed to by the uncials, as for instance the "Lucianic" codices in Sm-Kgs. Some 300 of these mss. were collated for variants, with differing degrees of accuracy, for the edition of R. Holmes and J. Parsons, *Vetus Testamentum graecum cum variis lectionibus* (5 vols.; Oxford, 1798–1827). The numbers assigned to various minuscule mss. in the edition mentioned have been incorporated into the standard list of LXX mss. by A. Rahlfs, *Verzeichnis der griechischen Handschriften des Alten Testaments* (Berlin, 1914) for reference purposes; though for the historical books, the Cambridge editors (→ 79 below) have followed a system of their own, employing small letters for the selection of minuscule mss. whose readings they report.

78 **(B) Printed Editions.**

(a) EDITIONS OF HISTORICAL IMPORT. The two earliest LXX editions were the Aldine (Venice, 1518), based on minuscule mss., and that in the Complutensian Polyglot from Spain, published in 1521 (its text is largely of the "Lucianic" type). The Council of Trent called for critical texts of the Bible to be published, and for the LXX the consequence was the Sixtine edition of 1587. This edition set a significant pattern for later publication and critical study, since it was based largely on Codex B. The Oxford edition (1707–20) of J. E. Grabe was a noteworthy edition based on Codex A. The edition of Holmes and Parsons, mentioned above, drew on 20 uncials, some 300 minuscules, the evidence of daughter versions from the Gk, and patristic citations. For Jb, Prv, Eccl, and Ct, it remains the only substantial repertory of LXX readings even today. An excellent manual edition of the LXX was the 1887 publication of C. von Tischendorf-E. Nestle. Manual editions now in use are those of H. B. Swete (Cambridge, numerous printings and three editions since 1894) and A. Rahlfs (1935 and later dates). The Swete text is that of B where available, A for Gn, S for the lacuna in Ps, with variants from other uncials. Rahlfs' text is eclectic and cannot be verified as to its source; the uncials collated are usually fewer than in Swete. Neither is an adequate critical instrument today. P. de Lagarde projected a Lucianic edition, but the result, a first volume only (1883), was not a success and is antiquated.

79 (b) MODERN CRITICAL UNDERTAKINGS. Of these there are two: *first*, the larger Cambridge Septuagint of A. E. Brooke, N. McLean, H. St. J. Thackeray, and others, which published comprehensive evidence for all the historical books from Gn (1906) through Chr, including also Tb, Jdt, Est (1940). The collating base is B even when (Dt, Chr) that ms. is not a good witness. The evidence requires constant interpretation by the user, since the apparatus offers no real guides as to the character of the mss. cited. *Second*, parallel to this undertaking is the *Septuaginta* project of the Göttingen Academy of Sciences, which has published the Prophets, along with Dn, Wis, and Sir (all ed. by J. Ziegler); also 1–3 Mc (eds. W. Kappler, R. Hanhart) and Ps (ed. A. Rahlfs). Of this last, a revised edition is in preparation. The

Göttingen volumes carry a continuous text established by the modern editor, and the mss. are cited by family groups wherever that is possible.

(Devreesse, R., *Introduction à l'étude des manuscrits grecs* [Paris, 1954]. Hadas, M., *Aristeas to Philocrates* [N.Y., 1951]. Hatch E. and H. A. Redpath, *A Concordance to the Septuagint* [2 vols. and Suppl.; Oxford, 1897–1906]. Jellicoe, S., "Aristeas, Philo, and the Septuagint *Vorlage*," *JTS* 12 [1961] 261–71. Kahle, P. E., "Die von Origenes verwendeten griechischen Bibelhandschriften," *Studia Patristica IV* [TU 79; 1961] 107–17. Katz, P., "Septuagint Studies in the Mid-Century," *BNTE* 176–208. Pelletier, A., *Lettre d'Aristée à Philocrate* [SC 89; Paris, 1962]. Swete, H. B., *An Introduction to the Old Testament in Greek* [rev. ed.; Cambridge, 1914].)

OTHER ANCIENT VERSIONS OF THE BIBLE

80 **(I) Aramaic and Syriac Versions.**

(A) The Aramaic Language. Aramaic is very close to Hebrew (about as Spanish is to Italian). It was spoken toward the end of the 2nd millennium BC by pastoral, seminomadic peoples who pressed in upon the settled agricultural regions that fringe the Syrian desert on the N and W, extending from the Persian Gulf to the Gulf of Aqabah on the Red Sea (→ Excursus, 11:10). The courtiers of Hezekiah, king of Judah, proposed using it in conversations with the Assyrian besiegers of Jerusalem in 701 BC (2 Kgs 18:26). Under the Neo-Babylonian (627–538 BC) and even more under the Persian Empire (538–331 BC) it became first the language of diplomacy and administration, and ultimately the native speech of the former Assyro-Babylonian territories including Syria-Palestine. Aramaic began to displace Hebrew as the vernacular of the Jewish people under the circumstances of the Babylonian Exile after the fall of Jerusalem in 586 BC. In the OT itself, it is employed in Gn 31:47, Jer 10:11, Ezr 4:8–6:18; 7:12–26; Dn 2:4–7:28. The use of Hebrew and the related Phoenician dialects of the nearby coastal cities decreased progressively for some centuries; by AD 135 Hebrew was in effect a dead language, and even before that time it was limited to Judea, while Galilee, Samaria, and the areas E of the Jordan were of Aram speech.

81 Until after the rise of Islam in the 7th cent. AD, Aramaic remained the dominant vernacular and literary language between the Mediterranean and the Persian Gulf, though under pressure from Greek, especially in the cities. At about the beginning of the Christian Era, a dialect split began to make itself felt. This left a direct Western Aram successor to the earlier language in use among Christians, Jews, and Samaritans, as far E as the great bend in the Euphrates. East of that point, Aram literatures distinguished mainly along religious lines sprang up among the Christians (Syriac), Jews (Babylonian Jewish Aramaic), Gnostic sectarians (Mandaean), and pagans of Eastern Aram speech. These Eastern dialects all shared a small group of innovations in the forms of the language which, with broader differences in diction, set them apart from the Aramaic of the West.

82 **(B) The Targums.**

(a) ORIGINS. In the last centuries BC there developed the practice of rendering Hebr OT texts orally into Aramaic during the course of the public reading of the Law and the Prophets in the synagogue liturgy. It arose in consequence of the decline of Hebrew as the spoken language of the Jews not merely in Babylonia, where many remained, but in Palestine itself, though the text of Neh 8:7–8 does not refer to this practice. No longer is there any doubt that written targums (Hebrew *targûmîm*, "translations") existed before the time of Christ, although for some time the rabbis looked upon the use of such texts with official disfavor.

83 The Talmud story (*bShabbath* 115a) about Rabban Gamaliel I having a targum of Jb immured during a building operation on the Temple mount in the 1st cent. AD has been strikingly illustrated by the discovery of a quite literal targum of that book at Qumran (11QtgJob); the ms. dates from the middle of that same century. From Qumran cave 4 comes another bit of targum to Jb; and Jb 42:17b (LXX) also supposes a written Aram targum of that book around the turn of the era. A scrap of Lv 16:12–21 in Aramaic from Qumran (4QtgLv) yields "covering" as the equivalent for *kappōret*, the name of the metal "mercy seat" over the Ark; this sheds new light on an old controversy (→ Pauline Theology, 79:86). Besides, the Aram embellishment of Gn from Qumran (1QapGn; → Apocrypha, 68:81), while it includes stories foreign to the biblical text, does have a continuing thread of quite close rendering by which these expansions are strung together.

84 Written targums to Est and to other books that are alluded to already in the Mishnah (*Megilloth* 2:1; *Yadaim* 4:15) must antedate AD 200; and for some extant elements of Palestinian targums the inference has been drawn that their oral formulation at least was necessarily of 2nd-cent. BC date. Whenever truly ancient targum materials can be recovered, they are of some value for textual study, but even more for exegetical reasons and for background to the NT (to Ap in particular), especially in its use of OT texts. Two tendencies in targums, the one to adhere closely to the original text, the other to elaborate and introduce narrative material that goes far beyond the text, are both equally ancient as far as we can tell at present.

85 (b) BABYLONIAN TARGUMS. The targums that have been printed and studied in modern times come in large part from late mss.; few exist in critical editions; and the several different targums have been evaluated in conflicting ways by scholars. It now seems certain that the basis for all extant targums was provided in Palestine, though the two principal compilations were reworked extensively in the Jewish schools of Babylonia in about the 5th cent. AD. The first of these, the *Targum Onkelos to the Pentateuch*, is the only targum officially approved by the scholars of the talmudic period, before *ca.* 650 AD. In a reworking that has adapted it to the details of the received Hebr consonantal text, it has lost such midrashic expansions and clues to variant textual readings as it may have had in earlier times. This is true in nearly the same degree of the *Targum Jonathan to the Prophets* (i.e., to Jos, Jgs, Sm, Kgs, and the Writing Prophets), which has a similar history.

Where elaborations on the text do survive, however, they can be of great interest. Thus the targum to Is 9:5 says of the child who is foretold, "His name has from of old been called Wonderful Counselor, Mighty God, living through the ages, the Messiah, in whose days peace will abound for us"; and Is 11:1 and 6 in the same targum are also explicitly messianic (→ Aspects OT Thought, 77:158–159). An excerpt from the Jerusalem

Targum (→ 86 below) to Is 11:3 has survived, which says, "Behold, the Messiah who is to come shall be one who teaches the Law and will judge in the fear of the Lord"; the biblical commentaries from Qumran are similar in tone to this. Onkelos and Jonathan, the authors alleged in Jewish tradition for these targums, are only a bizarre reflection of the real Aquila (Onkelos is the same name) and of the somewhat more shadowy Theodotion (this name, like Jonathan, means approximately "God-given") who produced revisions of Gk, not of Aram, translations of the OT (→ 65, 67 above). The two targums, Onkelos and Jonathan, have been published by A. Sperber, *The Bible in Aramaic* (3 vols.; Leiden, 1959–62).

86 (c) Palestinian Targums. Targum materials directly Palestinian in origin are less easy to come by, though ultimately of more significance for textual, literary, and historical purposes. A complete *Targum Yerushalmi to the Pentateuch* has been identified in recent years in the Codex Neofiti 1 of the Vatican Library; it is being prepared for publication by A. Diez Macho. The ms. is of 16th cent. date; that the contents of this Jerusalem Targum should be uniformly of 2nd cent. AD provenience, with earlier roots but without later contamination, as has been claimed, would be extraordinary. But the targum need not conform fully to such an estimate to be of great value (M. McNamara, *The Palestinian Targum and the New Testament* [AnalBib 27; Rome, 1966]). A "pseudo-Jonathan" Targum to the Pentateuch, on the other hand, is based on Onkelos, with patches of older, more fulsome Palestinian materials worked back into it in medieval times. Other small portions of the fuller, midrashic Palestinian type of targum to the Pentateuch are known from such diverse sources as a "fragmentary targum" in medieval mss.; Cairo Geniza remnants; glosses on Onkelos or pseudo-Jonathan; and citations by rabbinic sources from the 2nd to the 16th cents. There exist also Samaritan targums to the Pentateuch, transmitted in the same archaic script used by the Samaritans for the Hebr text; these targums are in a very fluid state, no two mss. yielding the same form.

87 The Palestinian targum to the Prophets is largely unknown. For the "Writings" section of the Hebr canon of the OT, the known targum materials are less systematic and are later (8th/9th cents. AD) in their extant form. Though they offer more suggestions of variant basic Hebr readings than either Onkelos or Jonathan, we are less secure as to whether their readings have a continuous tradition behind them in Aramaic. The Jb targum is distinct from the Qumran one (→ 83 above); the targum to Ps shows conflation and double renderings. These and the targum to Chr are linguistically akin. For Prv, the Syr Peshitta (→ 92 below), transposed into square-letter script, provides the extant targum. Dn and Ezr-Neh, which contain Aram portions in their basic text, are without targums for any part. For Est there are several targums, only one of which remains relatively close to the text; the others, along with the targums for Ct, Lam, Eccl, and Ru, are very paraphrastic and quite late in origin.

(Churgin, P., *Targum ketubim* [in Hebr; N.Y., 1945]. Diaz, R., "Ediciones del Targum samaritano," *EstBib* 15 [1956] 105–8. Diez Macho, A., "The Recently Discovered Palestinian Targum," *Stud. Vet. Test.* 7 [1960] 222–45; "Targum y Nuevo Testamento," 33 pp. in *Mélanges E. Tisserant* 1 [Studi e Testi 231; Vatican City, 1964]. McNamara, M., "Bible IV: Texts and Versions 11. Targums," *NCE* 2, 431–33. Rosenthal, F., *Die aramäistische Forschung* [Leiden, 1937]. Van der Ploeg, J., *Le Targum de Job de la grotte 11 de Qumran* [Amsterdam, 1962]. For editions, see Eissfeldt, *OTI* 696, 782–83.)

88 **(C) Syriac Versions.**

(a) Origins. Translation of the Scriptures into Syriac had its roots in the developing pre-Christian Aram targums of the OT books brought by Jewish and Christian preachers from Palestine into the district of Adiabene (surrounding Irbil in modern Iraq) and to the neighborhood of Edessa (Urfa in modern Turkey) in the 1st and 2nd cents. AD. The Syr literary dialect of Eastern Aramaic (→ 81 above) became standardized during this same period. Though widely used for a great variety of purposes, this Aram dialect survives primarily in a copious Christian religious literature composed between the end of the 2nd and the beginning of the 14th cents. It is distinct to some extent in form, and even more in diction, from the Western Aramaic of Palestine as used by Christ and the apostles. The Syr Bible is in this Eastern dialect, and its NT is wholly a translation from the Greek. Claims that the Syr Gospels are the form in which Jesus spoke his teaching—claims often made by people who have every reason to know better—are without foundation.

89 (b) Churches with a Tradition of Syriac. Syriac remains today the liturgical language, comparable to Latin in the West, for a variety of churches from Lebanon to the Malabar Coast of India; both North and South America have had substantial numbers of immigrants from these various communities. The current vernacular of nearly all the people concerned is Arabic, or, in India, Malayalam.

They include the Maronites in Lebanon, who have all been in union with Rome from at least the Crusades into modern times; their own tradition staunchly denies that at an earlier period they were Monothelites, though that is how most historians understand the matter. The non-Monophysitic Christians in Syria and Lebanon of Byzantine rite (Melkites) were deprived of their previous Antiochene liturgy and of the option to use Aramaic in the 13th cent. (The Constantinople liturgy in Greek or in Arabic was substituted.) These Melkites include both Orthodox and Catholics.

In Syria, Palestine, and India there are many "Syrian Orthodox," also known as West Syrians, Jacobites, or Monophysites. Especially around Aleppo there are a number of Syrians in union with Rome who share with the other West Syrians the same Syro-Antiochene rite. In Syria, Iraq, Iran, and India there are East Syrian Christians who are the heirs of the theological views of Nestorius; they call themselves Assyrians. Their counterpart in union with Rome are "Chaldeans," of the same quite ancient East Syrian rite. Among Christians in India who are united to Rome, the Malabarese inherit the East Syrian rite, the Malankarese the West Syrian; similar divisions exist there among the groups separated from Rome.

Although we find dialectal differences between the East Syrians and the West Syrians (along with the Maronites) in their liturgical language, these differences are minor questions of vowel qualities within a uniform language with a common Bible, the Peshitta. Spoken Western Aramaic (distinct, therefore, from the Syr literary tradition) has survived till now at Maʿlula in the Antilebanon mountains, about 35 mi. from Damascus; but the primary language of the two thousand or so who speak it is in fact Arabic (A. Spitaler, *ZDMG* 32 [1957] 299–339). Farther E, several dialects akin to Syriac survive in Syria, Iraq, Iran, and in the Asiatic provinces of the USSR; these survivals of Eastern Aram vernaculars are much overlaid with foreign vocabulary from all the neighboring languages, and some are now nearly unrecognizable as basically Aramaic.

90 (c) Bible Versions. In the course of time

several different, usually interdependent, translations of the OT and the NT circulated in Syriac.

(i) *Tatian's Diatessaron* (= "[One] through four"). This is a continuous harmony weaving together material from the four Gospels with a little apocryphal material (from the *History of Joseph the Carpenter* and from a "Hebrew Gospel"). Tatian was a Syrian from Mesopotamia, born *ca.* 110, who lived for years in Rome and was a disciple of Justin Martyr. Charged with exaggerated asceticism of Encratite tendency, Tatian left Rome sometime after 165 and returned to the East. In this same general time, whether at Rome or in Syria, he composed his harmony. It is uncertain whether he originally wrote it in Greek or in Syriac; if in Greek, it was soon translated into Syriac. The Gk form was lost except for a 3rd-cent. fragment, consisting of 14 lines, discovered in 1933 at Dura-Europos on the Euphrates.

The *Diatessaron* circulated widely in the Syrian church and seemingly became the official Syrian Gospel text (rather than four Gospels). It was commented on by Ephraem (d. 373). The Syr version of the *Diatessaron* has also perished. Such disappearance can be traced to opponents like Bishop Theodoret of Cyr (Cyrrhus) who *ca.* 425 destroyed as many copies as he could find because he suspected Tatian of heresy; the Harmony was replaced with the four Gospels in Syriac. A useful tool in reconstructing the Syr *Diatessaron* is Ephraem's Commentary, published from a ms. in the Beatty collection by L. Leloir (Dublin, 1963). Harmonies similar to the *Diatessaron* or translations of it have come down in Arabic, Persian, Latin (Codex Fuldensis), medieval Dutch, and Italian. The Armenian and Georgian translations of the Gospels were influenced by it, and traces may be found in patristic citations.

(For editions, see B. M. Metzger, *Chapters*, 97–120. There is an Eng translation from the Arabic in the *Ante-Nicene Fathers* 9, 33–138. For the order of passages in the *Diatessaron*, see L. Leloir, CSCO 227, 1–11.)

91 (ii) *Old Syriac Bible.* Of this rendering (OS) for the OT books we know only what survives in incidental citations, plus the evidence of early targumic influence and of Jewish or Judeo-Christian origins that carries over in reworked form into the Peshitta. The separate OS Gospels are known from two 5th-cent. mss., one in the British Museum (published by W. Cureton in 1842) and the other in the monastery of St. Catherine at Mt. Sinai (discovered in 1892). These are divergent forms of one basic text that seems later in origin than the *Diatessaron;* the underlying Greek that it reflects is still an archaic and "Western" type of Gospel text (→ 130, 136 below). Citations from Acts and the Pauline corpus in early writers point to a similar status for these books, of which no continuous OS texts are now extant. A. Vööbus intends to publish the OS Gospels (*Biblical Research* 7 [1962] 49–56).

92 (iii) *Peshitta Bible.* In both the OT and the NT the Peshitta is a compilation and careful reworking of earlier materials. It was established firmly enough in the early 5th cent. to remain the Bible of all Syr-language Christians despite the Nestorian and Monophysite movements and the disruption of unity that accompanied them. The Peshitta OT, though basically a translation from the Hebrew, shows distinct secondary influences from the LXX in those books especially (Is, Ps) that were most used in the liturgy. Its renderings of the various groups of OT books are uneven in quality and were prepared by a number of different hands. Such books as Jdt and Bar in Syriac originated independently, being translated from the Greek; Tb was unknown till quite late. It is noteworthy that Sirach was based on a Hebr text.

The name of Rabbula, bishop of Edessa (d. 435), is attached to the production of the Peshitta (particularly of its Gospels) *without warrant;* though it existed in his time, he did not himself use this text (yet see T. Baarda, *VigChr* 14 [1960] 102–27). If in the OT the Peshitta shows the persistence of early targumic influences, so its NT (an excellent rendering with an accommodation to the Byzantine type of Gk mss. current about AD 400; → 130, 138 below) shows survivals (e.g., in Acts) of some "Western" readings and other early features. Four smaller epistles (2 Pt, 2–3 Jn, Jude) and Ap were not transmitted in Peshitta mss.; as edited with this version in modern times, these books are of later origin in Syriac.

For the NT in particular, textual transmission of the Peshitta has been remarkably faithful and precise. There exist for both Testaments good early mss.; those from East Syrian sources tend to have a slightly better text. A critical edition of the OT is being prepared by a Peshitta Institute at Leiden. For the NT, a British and Foreign Bible Society edition (London, 1905–20) approximates critical standards, but no apparatus of ms. variants has been published beyond the Gospels.

93 (iv) *Syro-hexaplar OT.* This version, where it survives, is often our best single extant witness to the content and the critical markings of the 5th column of Origen's *Hexapla* (→ 69 above). It has an apparatus of marginal readings from Aquila, Symmachus, and Theodotion. This material has been transposed from Greek, into a rigid and labored Syriac that reflects the word order, forms, and even the incidental particles of its source. It was transmitted from antiquity in two ms. volumes; only the second of these, with Ps, Wisdom Books, and Prophets, has come down to the present. Of the lost first volume, fragmentary witnesses have yielded numerous excerpts in Syriac; the Pentateuch survives in a secondary rendering into Arabic. The Syro-hexaplar version of the OT was produced between AD 615 and 617 by a team of translators, among whom Bishop Paul of Tella, the translator of Kgs, is known by name; its place of origin was the monastery "at the ninth milestone," outside Alexandria, in Egypt.

94 (v) *Harclean NT.* At the same time and place as the Syro-hexaplar OT, a similarly stiff and mechanical rendering of the NT was produced; from its editor, Thomas of Harkel, bishop of Hierapolis (Mabbug) in Syria, this is known as the Harclean version. It was based on a revision of the Peshitta done a century earlier (AD 507–508) by one Polycarp, at the instance of Philoxenus, an earlier bishop of Hierapolis. Most of the materials that have been identified as "Philoxenian" are actually from the Harclean version; though it is possible that the texts of the four short epistles and Ap in the 1905–20 London Peshitta edition come from the intermediate 6th-cent. undertaking. In later centuries, the Harclean NT was used in West Syrian lectionaries; for this purpose its text was smoothed out and reworked in the light of the familiar Peshitta. In any form, the Harclean NT is too late to be an important textual witness.

95 (vi) *Syro-Palestinian Bible.* This version, in Western Aramaic (hence not in fact Syriac) is known to us almost exclusively as a lectionary text for those orthodox ("Melkite") Christians who followed the liturgies of Antioch and Jerusalem in their native Aramaic rather than in Greek. Though adapted in large measure to the LXX tradition, the Syro-Palestinian OT, of which we know the Pentateuch, Jb, Prv, Ps, Is and other books in fragmentary form, has its roots in older Syr and (possibly) Jewish Aram texts. There are extant Gospel lectionaries in Syro-Palestinian, with a text that has been fitted to the usual Byzantine form; the oldest ms. is of AD 1029. Yet fragmentary evidences of seemingly the same NT version (most recently from the abandoned monastery of Castellion, or Khirbet Mird, in the Judean desert, during 1952–53; → Apocrypha, 68:105) carry us back to the 6th cent. Its date of origin, as well as the base upon which it was prepared, remains obscure.

(Baumstark, A., *Geschichte der syrischen Literatur* [Bonn, 1922]. Duval, R., *La littérature syriaque* [3rd ed.; Paris, 1907]. Goshen-Gottstein, M. H., *Text and Language in Bible and Qumran* [Jerusalem, Israel, 1960] 65–86, 163–204 on the Peshitta. Ortiz de Urbina, I., *Patrologia syriaca* [Rome, 1958]. Rosenthal, F., *Die aramäistische Forschung* [Leiden, 1937], esp. 106–14 on language of Jesus. Van Puyvelde, C., *VDBS* 6 [1960] 834–84. Vööbus, A., *Studies in the History of the Gospel Text in Syriac* [Louvain, 1951]; "Bible IV: Texts and Versions 12. Syriac Versions," *NCE* 2, 433–36. For editions, see Eissfeldt, *OTI* 699, 783; Metzger, B. M., *Text*, 68–71.)

96 **(II) Latin Versions.** All the early Lat renderings of both the OT and the NT were made from the Greek, with Jerome's OT from the Hebrew the single exception. The *Acts of the Scillitan Martyrs* (AD 180) already speaks of a ms. of "the letters of Paul, a just man"; this copy in North Africa presumably was in Latin. Not long afterward Tertullian quotes Lat texts for both Testaments; and Cyprian of Carthage (d. 258) directly cites about one-ninth of the NT. The Lat translation of the letter of Clement of Rome to the Corinthians bears witness to the use of Lat Scriptures in Europe in the 2nd cent. The place of origin of the Lat Gospels and indeed of many parts of the Old Latin (OL) Bible can no longer be established with certainty; the extant evidence shows an interdependence between North African and European forms of the text, and in Europe both Rome and Gaul have been thought of as early centers of Lat use of the Scriptures.

97 **(A) Old Latin OT from the Greek.** We no longer possess a complete Lat OT from the Greek done in this early period. Nor can we confidently determine to what extent Jewish translators may have begun this work. Jerome (d. 420) affirmed that in his day there were "as many forms of the text for Latin readers as there are manuscripts" (*Praef. in Josue*), and something of that welter of diverse texts remains to us. The five OT books whose OL form we know best are those that Jerome intended to exclude from his own undertaking and refused to revise or retranslate because he judged them noncanonical. Since these were nevertheless preserved by the Church and have become part of the Vg (= Deuterocanonical Books), we possess for each of them a full text which, in fact, is basically the product of a single translator. Systematic critical study of them is well advanced. They include 1–2 Mc (ed. D. de Bruyne; Maredsous, 1932); also Wis and Sir, clearly North African renderings, except for Sir 44–50 and the Prologue to Sir, which were put into Latin by two distinct European translators. Wis and Sir have been edited with an apparatus of ms. variants as vol. 12 (1964) of the Benedictine Vulgate project (→ 108 below). Of Bar, four varying forms of the Lat text are known from mss.; these seem to go back through various reworkings to one original translator.

98 Apart from Ps, which has a complicated textual history, the other OT books translated from the Greek survive to us more or less by accident. Though the OL Pentateuch with Jos and Jgs is well known in a single translator's work, much of the rest has had to be pieced together from portions copied into Vg mss.; or from glosses on Vg mss.; or from citations in Christian Lat literature. The painstaking work of assembling these fragmentary materials was undertaken once in the 16th cent. by F. de Nobili (published as *Vetus Testamentum sec. LXX*, Rome, 1588) in connection with the LXX "Sixtine" edition of 1586 (→ 78 above). In the 18th cent. the Maurist P. Sabatier published in Rheims (3 vols., 1739–49, reissued Paris, 1751) *Bibliorum sacrorum latinae versionis antiquae...*, a work that for certain books has not been supplanted even today. The extensive files of J. Denk (d. 1927) were entrusted to the archabbey of Beuron, in Germany, where currently under the direction of B. Fischer a *Vetus Latina* project has yielded Gn (1951–54) with exhaustive support from mss. and patristic sources; the *Vetus Latina* has since concentrated on the NT (→ 107 below). A comprehensive inventory of extant OL mss. and editions of the OT, plus references to all patristic texts that are sources for OL citations, has also been published from Beuron (*Vetus Latina I: Verzeichnis der Sigel*, 1949; rev. ed. 1963, with continuing supplements).

99 Ruth survives in one ms. (Madrid Univ. 31); Ezr/Neh and apocryphal III–IV Esdras are known in full. A complete text of 2 Chr (ed. R. Weber) is known, also the full text of Ct (ed. D. de Bruyne). In the mss. Est is well represented but the edition (1928) of B. Motzo does not cover all the sources. It is especially for Sm-Kgs, 1 Chr, Jb, Prv, Eccl and the Prophets that our evidence is scarce. Some of the OT books were reworked by Jerome on the basis of hexaplaric materials before he undertook his more original rendering from the Hebrew; we are told this of 1–2 Chr (a preface to these is extant), and of Prv, Eccl, Ct, as well as Jb (this last is extant). We also know that he revised the Pentateuch, Jos, and Ps (→ 100 below) in the same way. In general, the OL versions, which are still echoed in many liturgical texts, have come down to us in forms reworked in the centuries after Jerome's time and in textual traditions that reflect mutual contamination of the Vg and the OL.

100 **(B) Latin Psalters.** Most of Western Christendom through the centuries has employed in its liturgy and transmitted in its bibles the so-called *Gallican Psalter*, thus named from the region of its early popularity. This is Jerome's second revision (based on the *Hexapla*) of an OL psalter, completed during the early years of his residence in Bethlehem (before 389). It shares the basic limitations of any psalter dependent on the LXX and contributes more of its own. By today's standards it is clumsy and confused, despite the pious associations with which even many of its irrelevancies have been surrounded in the course of time. Since contrary to Jerome's intention it has displaced his rendering from the Hebrew in Vg bibles, it has been edited as Vol. 10 (1953) of the Roman Benedictine Commission's Vulgate project.

101 Older forms of the OL psalter from the Greek are now available for convenient study in the edition of R. Weber, *Psalterium Romanum...*, (CBL 10; Rome, 1953), which summarizes what is known of as many as 14 different text traditions. Whether any of them can be connected with a first, cursory revision by Jerome is highly doubtful, though this claim has habitually been made for the liturgical psalter used in St. Peter's Basilica in Rome. An OL psalter from a Mt. Sinai ms. (*slav.* 5) with an appendix of 18 liturgical canticles from elsewhere in the OL biblical text has been reported on by E. A. Lowe in *Scriptorium* 9 [1955] 177–99, and its variants are recorded in the CCL edition of Augustine's *Enar. in Psalmos* (ser. lat. 38–40; Turnholt, 1956). The psalter publications of T. Ayuso Marazuela, between 1957 and 1962, although notable compilations of mss. and patristic evidence, often do double duty with the editions mentioned and sometimes reflect the Spanish ms. tradition to the exclusion of pertinent materials elsewhere.

102 Jerome's *Psalter from the Hebrew* has been mentioned. This work was one of the earliest results of his decision to produce a new version of the OT. It is a somewhat stiff and bookish exercise, drawing measurably on Aquila and Symmachus for meanings of uncommon Hebr words. In our day it is not really better suited for a liturgical text than the Gallican Psalter itself. The best edition is by H. de Ste. Marie (CBL 11; Rome, 1954).

103 The present survey of Lat versions will not deal with the multiple 16th cent. and later renderings of any part of the Bible; but because of its use in the formal liturgy of the Lat Church, the *Liber Psalmorum cum Canticis* sanctioned for breviary use by Pope Pius XII in 1945 must be the exception. Prepared by a group of professors at the Pontifical Biblical Institute in Rome, it offers a straightforward rendering into classical Lat idiom of the Hebr text that has been emended, though with restraint, from other sources. It has been criticized as failing to preserve in its diction the "Christian Latin" associations of the earlier psalters, and as being less easily sung. Both criticisms owe something of their scope and vehemence to the somewhat meaningless factor of inveterate habit. In any case, it would seem desirable that liturgical texts in languages not related to the forms and rhythms of Latin should profit by the clarity of the Pius XII Psalter, without being bound in their use of Holy Writ by the conventions of Lat style in even this updated guise. The following excerpt illustrates the characteristics of the various psalters (Ps 96 [95]:9b–10):

Psalterium Romanum (→ 101 above):
Commoveatur a facie eius universa terra.
Dicite in nationibus Dominus regnavit a ligno;[1]
etenim correxit orbem terrae qui non commovebitur.
Judicabit populos in aequitate et gentes in ira sua.[2]

Psalterium Gallicanum (→ 100 above):
Commoveatur a facie eius universa terra.
Dicite in gentibus, quia Dominus regnavit;
etenim correxit orbem terrae quae non commovebitur.
judicabit populos in aequitate.

Psalterium ex Hebraeo (juxta Hebraeos → 102 above):
Paveat a facie eius omnis terra.
Dicite in gentibus: Dominus regnavit;
siquidem appendit orbem immobilem,
judicabit[3] populos in aequitate.

Liber Psalmorum (1945; → 103 above)
Contremisce coram eo, universa terra;
dicite inter gentes: Dominus regnat.
Stabilivit orbem, ut non moveatur:
regit populos cum aequitate.

CCD Version (→ 174 below)
Tremble before him, all the earth;
say among the nations: the LORD is king.
He has made the world firm, not to be moved;
he governs the peoples with equity.

104 **(C) Vulgate OT from the Hebrew.** Beginning about AD 389, Jerome broke with the LXX-OL tradition to provide Western Christendom with a rendering based directly on the Hebr text of the OT as preserved among the Jews. The books of Sm-Kgs, Jb, Ps, and the Prophets were done by about 392; Ezr/Neh by 394; 1–2 Chr by 396; Prv, Ct, Eccl by 398; the Pentateuch, Jos, Jgs, and Ru, along with Jdt, Est and Tb, by about 405. In part, the progress of the work can be traced by Jerome's own prefaces to the various groups of books. His knowledge of Hebrew was good; of OT Aramaic, somewhat less so. He had oral assistance from Jewish sources, and shows familiarity with the exegesis embodied in the various targums. The parts of Est and Dn not included in the Jewish canon he supplied from the Greek; in the case of Dn, he drew upon the "Theodotionic" form of that book (→ 61 above), which also strongly influenced his rendering of the Aram parts of the text. The arrangement of Est in the Vg, with the parts translated from the Greek placed in a series of appendixes, is a confusing jumble (→ Esther, 38:29). The two books of Tb and Jdt were translated on the basis of Aram recensions, now no longer extant and rather far removed from the lost originals (Aramaic for Tb, but Hebrew for Jdt).

105 The Vg strongly underlines the personal messianic implications of the OT: for example, *et erit sepulchrum ejus gloriosum* (Is 11:10) has in mind the Constantinian Basilica of the Resurrection, and the exaltation of the Cross. Messianic references that go beyond the actual terms of the Hebr text are present in the Vg of Is 45:8; 62:1–2; Hab 3:18. While on the one hand this does nourish Christian piety, on the other it imposes some limitations on the apologetic value for dialogue with Jewish scholars that Jerome also wished his version to have. Be that as it may, the Vg OT is of great and abiding worth as a witness to the inspired word.

106 **(D) Latin New Testament.**

(a) VULGATE. From Jerome stems also the Vg recension of the Gospels, prepared in Rome in AD 383/384 at the bidding of Pope Damasus. Basically it was the correction and adaptation of the existing OL text in the light of good Gk mss. Though the remaining NT books in the Vg have often been attributed to Jerome, the nature of his activity in dealing with these books has never been clear. A good current estimate (H. J. Frede) is that at about the end of the 4th cent., a single editor who was neither Jerome nor Pelagius drew together the Lat texts of Acts to Ap that became the Vg form (on Pelagius, cf. K. T. Schäfer, *NTS* 9 [1963] 361–66). It is then this composite late 4th-cent. NT in Latin that is the goal of the critical edition of J. Wordsworth and H. J. White (3 vols., Oxford, 1898–1954).

107 (b) OLD LATIN. Earlier stages of the NT in Latin are represented in the *Vetus Itala* (4 vols.; Berlin, 1938–63), in which A. Jülicher, A. Matzkow, and K. Aland have presented the ms. evidences for the pre-Jerome forms of the Gospels. The title *Vetus Itala* is taken from a discussion of Lat texts by Augustine; but this does not in fact offer any usable clue to the place of origin of the Lat Gospels. The Beuron *Vetus Latina* has published Jas and 1–2 Pt (1956–60) as well as Eph (1962–64). Two series, the *Old Latin Biblical Texts* (7 vols.; Oxford, 1883–1923) and CBL (Rome, since 1912) present the evidence of individual mss. In addition to the ms. evidence for the received Vg recension of the NT, the Wordsworth-White edition cites a good deal of OL evidence, so that it replaces the NT of Sabatier's earlier work (→ 98 above) except for patristic citations.

As to the origin of the various parts of the OL NT, the corpus of 13 Pauline epistles (exclusive of Heb) goes back to a single, quite early translator. Beneath the varying forms of Acts there seems to have been one early North African rendering. For Heb, there are two known renderings; for Ap, two quite independent forms, the one North African, the other European (H. J. Vogels would add still a third). For the Catholic Epistles the evidence is scanty; and for the Gospels, confused. Early influences from Marcion and from Tatian on the OL texts have been suspected, but in neither case is the issue resolved, and the examples cited are textual curiosities of no doctrinal significance.

108 **(E) Later History of the Vulgate.** A Pontifical Commission for the Establishment of the Text of the Vulgate, set up by Pope Pius X in 1907, has since been localized in the Abbey of San Girolamo (St. Jerome)

---

[1] *a ligno:* an expansion in the LXX, seemingly Christian in origin (reference to cross of Christ); known already to Justin Martyr (d. *ca.* AD 165), it is quoted in the hymn *Vexilla Regis*.

[2] *et gentes in ira sua:* again an expansion in the LXX, almost certainly of Jewish origin.

[3] The inept Lat tenses, accepted even into *Psalterium ex Hebraeo*, follow the barbarous style of the LXX Ps.

in Rome. Beginning with Gn in 1926, the Benedictine editors of its *Biblia Sacra juxta Latinam Vulgatam Versionem* have published 12 volumes, including all of Jerome's renderings from the Hebr text, except those for the Writing Prophets; this undertaking is projected for the future. As indicated above, the published volumes take in also the Gallican Psalter (the *juxta Hebraeos* is in CBL), plus Tb and Jdt, Wis, and Sir, with their diverse origins. The Wordsworth-White edition provides a suitable NT counterpart.

109 These endeavors at recovering the archetypal Vg form from about AD 400 cannot be completely successful for lack of sufficiently early mss. Usually they bring us back to a form of text intermediate between the missing archetypes and the early recensional undertakings of Alcuin (d. 804), Theodulph of Orléans (d. 821), and the Spanish tradition centered on the *Codex Toletanus* (8th cent.). With the multiplication of copies in the Middle Ages, further attempts at standardization were necessary; and a developed form of the text, associated with the University of Paris, accompanied by several lists of *correctoria*, became the foundation for the Vg form in most printed bibles, including the first (the Gutenberg Bible of 1452–55). This text included a number of elements that were not included by Jerome: in 1–2 Sm, a series of excerpts from the OL, introduced by the Spanish bishop Peregrinus (e.g., *stravitque Saul in solario et dormivit* in 1 Sm 9:25); the angel stirring the water at the Pool of Bethesda in Jn 5:4 (→ Gospel Jn, 63:82); a borrowing into Mt 27:35 from Jn 19:24; also the "Johannine Comma" in 1 Jn 5:7–8 (→ Johannine Epistles, 62:27).

110 The Council of Trent called for an officially sponsored critical edition of the Vg (→ Church Pronouncements, 72:11); but despite serious work toward that goal over a period of some 30 years in the late 16th cent., neither the Sixtine edition of 1590 nor the (Sixto-) Clementine texts of 1592–98 can be considered as truly successful fulfillments of the council's directive. The Clementine text, which became the official Catholic Vg, has lately been edited (Marietti, Turin, since 1959) with a rather skimpy, though still useful, apparatus of variants from the reconstituted texts of the St. Jerome Abbey OT and the Wordsworth-White NT. A special feature of this edition is parallel presentation of three psalters (Gallican, *juxta Hebraeos*, and Pius XII). The Stuttgart Bibelanstalt (Bible Society) has proposed an edition under ecumenical sponsorship that will offer for the first time in one printed volume a critically sound Vg text for both the OT and the NT. A group entrusted with revision of the Vg texts (for liturgical purposes?) has been named in Rome since the close of Vatican II.

111 Jerome's OT from the Hebrew is based almost entirely on the received consonantal Hebr text; its value in relation to the originals is therefore primarily exegetical. The various OL renderings from the Greek, on the other hand, represent a stage of transmission of their prototypes that often cannot be attained directly through any extant Gk mss. Few even of the earliest Gk papyri of the NT (→ 142 below) can claim comparable antiquity with the NT renderings in the OL; yet Lat evidence has to be carefully sifted for later retouchings and contaminations. For the history of the LXX and the reconstitution of its early text forms, the OL is of special significance in Sm, Tb, Ps, 1–2 Mc, Wis, Sir; and it is instructive wherever it can be recovered in a relatively early form. There is scope for prolonged future effort in this direction, particularly within the framework of the Beuron *Vetus Latina*.

(Berger, S., *Histoire de la Vulgate pendant les premièrs siècles du Moyen Age* [Paris, 1893]. Bogaert, M., "Bulletin de la Bible latine," *RevBén* 74 [1964] 1–40; 75 [1965] 41–72. Botte, B., *VDBS* 5 [1950] 178–96. Fischer, B., *ZNW* 46 [1955] 178–96 on the completion of Wordsworth-White. Peebles, B. M., "Bible IV: Texts and Versions 13. Latin Versions," *NCE* 2, 436–56. Plater, W. E., and H. J. White, *A Grammar of the Vulgate* [Oxford, 1926]. Smit, J., *De Vulgaat* [Roermond, 1948]. Souter, A., *A Glossary of Later Latin to 600 AD* [Oxford, 1949]. Stummer, F., *Einleitung in die lateinische Bibel* [Paderborn, 1928]. See Eissfeldt, *OTI* 716–19, 785; Metzger, B. M., *Text*, 72–79.)

112 **(III) Coptic Versions**

(A) The Coptic Language. Coptic is the latest form of the Egyptian language written, not in hieroglyphs or demotic symbols, but in the Gk alphabet augmented by one digraph, *ti*, and by six letters that represent Egyptian consonantal sounds not found in Greek. It came into use in the 2nd cent. AD and developed as an almost exclusively Christian language with numerous Gk loanwords; in fact, by far the greater part of Coptic literature consists of translations from Greek. The terms "Copt" and "Coptic" are derived from the Arabic name for the Christian inhabitants of Egypt, *qubt*, which is related to the Gk *aigyptos*. The Coptic church, which is now Arabic-speaking, has been Monophysite since the 5th cent., though there is a much smaller body of Copts in union with Rome.

113 There are two principal dialects of Coptic and several minor ones. The oldest of the main branches is *Sahidic* (formerly called Thebaic), in use in Upper, or southern, Egypt until well into the Middle Ages. It was eventually supplanted in the 11th cent. by *Bohairic* (formerly Memphitic), the language of Lower, or northern, Egypt (the Nile Delta), which has survived as the liturgical language of the Coptic church. The other local dialects in which biblical books or fragments are known are: *Akhmimic* and *Subakhmimic* (Assiutic), both akin to Sahidic and at an early date superseded by it; *Fayumic* (formerly Bashmuric), an intermediary between Sahidic and Bohairic spoken in the Fayum, west of the Nile; and *Middle Egyptian*, represented by only a few mss. and yet to be studied in detail as a distinct dialect. Sometimes dialects were mingled in biblical translations. A good example is the blend of Sahidic and Akhmimic traits along with various other elements in an early (4th- or 5th-cent.) version of Prv recently published by R. Kasser, *Papyrus Bodmer VI* (CSCO 194–95; Louvain, 1960).

114 **(B) Coptic Old Testament.** The complete OT does not survive in any Coptic dialect, although it may have existed in Sahidic at least; and thus far there are no critical editions of the Coptic OT. All translations were made from individual parts of the Gk Bible and apparently from different recensions of them; and the many extant Coptic versions of separate books and fragments have their importance for studying the transmission of the Gk versions rather than, directly at least, for studying the text of the OT. The earliest Coptic versions were made, however, for the use of the common people who had no knowledge of Greek, and the translators did not hesitate to simplify or otherwise alter the texts almost in the manner of the targums with respect to the Hebr text. Sometimes they simply misunderstood the Greek. Only at a later period were attempts made to compare the versions and to correct them; the Bohairic translation of Prv stands out for its fidelity to the underlying Greek. Another problem the textual critic must take into account is the peculiar structure of the language itself, the types of construction and circumlocution it uses in rendering Greek. This means that often the original wording is very difficult to recover. Ancient Coptic biblical mss. are fairly numerous but are notoriously difficult to date. In the early dialects there are valuable 4th- and 5th-cent.

ones. However, it is probable that translations began to be made as early as the beginning of the 3rd cent. Of the Sahidic OT several of the late historical books, Chr, Ezr, Neh, and Mc, are missing. Of the Bohairic version some of the later Historical and Wisdom Books are not represented, and for a few other books it is necessary to rely on quotations in liturgical texts. The minor dialectal versions are very incomplete. In general, the best attested books are the Pentateuch, Ps, Job, Prv, and the Prophets.

115 **(C) Coptic New Testament.** For the NT the textual critic has at hand complete published versions of the Sahidic and the Bohairic NT and a few publications of individual books in all the dialects. But no less caution is necessary in evaluating their evidence, since for the most part the editions are not critical. Complete mss. in Bohairic are available, but all are late medieval; these were edited by G. Horner in 1898–1905. Horner's Sahidic NT, which appeared in 1911–24, is a mosaic of fragmentary manuscripts ranging in date over many centuries. Since the completion of Horner's editions, a number of very important individual books have come to light in various Coptic collections. Some of the more significant publications include a 4th-cent. Subakhmimic version of Jn published by H. Thompson; Papyrus Bodmer III, which contains Jn and Gn 1–4:2 in Bohairic in a remarkably early manuscript (4th cent.; R. Kasser, *Muséon* 74 [1961] 423–33); and a Fayumic (or as some think, Middle Egyptian) Jn from an early 4th-cent. papyrus (Michigan 3521).

116 The various Coptic versions of the NT are potentially of great importance for studying the diffusion of the NT text types in Egypt in the 2nd and 3rd cents. On the whole, the Coptic NT translations are fairly literal by contrast with the OT ones, and they tend to reflect the rather standardized Alexandrian text type (→ 130, 135 below). But some mss. provide evidence for the diffusion of the so-called Western recension with its many variants (→ 136 below); a good example is the Middle Egyptian copy of Acts 1–15:3 described by T. C. Petersen in *CBQ* 27 (1964) 225–41. The earliest Coptic NT versions furnish us with independent translations made from Gk texts older than most of the Gk mss. upon which our critical NT is based (→ 144 below).

(Bellet, P., "Bible IV: Texts and Versions 14. Coptic Versions," *NCE* 2, 457–58. Botte, B., *VDBS* 6 [1960] 818–25. Hallock, F. H., "The Coptic Old Testament," *AJSL* 49 [1932–33] 325–35. Kahle, P. E., *Bala'izah* 1 [London, 1954] 269–78 for a list of all known Coptic fragments down to the 6th cent. Kammerer, W., *A Coptic Bibliography* [Ann Arbor, 1950]. Simon, J., annual Coptic bibliography in *Orientalia* 18ff. 1949—]. Till, W. C., "Coptic and Its Value," *BJRylL* 40 [1957] 229–58. Vaschalde, A., lists of all that has been published of the Coptic mss., *RB* 28–31 [1919–22]; *Muséon* 43, 45–46 [1930, 1932–33]; these lists continued by W. C. Till, *BJRylL* 42 [1959–60] 220–40. For editions of the NT, see B. M. Metzger, *Text*, 81.)

117 **(IV) Other Oriental Versions.**

(A) Ethiopic Version. Ethiopic is a Semitic language, like Hebrew, Aramaic, Assyro-Babylonian, and Arabic; it is closest to Arabic. At the beginning of the Christian era the language of SW Arabia was distinct from that of most of the peninsula, and it is from this South Arabic branch that the language of Ethiopia stems. Its classic biblical and liturgical dialect is Geʿez, no longer spoken. The modern Amharic has many features developed in Africa, but there are dialects in Eritrea much closer to the ancient form. Since the days of Athanasius (d. 373) and of Frumentius, the first apostle of Ethiopia, the Christian Church in that country has been bound by close ties to the church of Egypt, which it followed into the Monophysite separatist movement in the 5th cent. The court legend of the royal family of Ethiopia that traces its origins to Solomon and the "queen of Sheba" is of course fictitious. There are some Ethiopians, the Falasha, who have been Jewish by religion since the Middle Ages, but theirs is an adopted faith and a borrowed literature.

The Ethiopic OT is from the Greek and is sometimes a good witness to the unrevised Alexandrian LXX, coinciding with the Gk Vaticanus (B) ms. against all later recensions (→ 76 above). The same version preserves intact the apocryphal books of *Enoch* and *Jubilees* (→ Apocrypha, 68:9, 16), otherwise known to us only in fragments. The Ethiopic Gospels were drastically reworked in the 13th cent., under Arabic influence stemming from Egypt; only two mss. of the unrevised 5th-cent. Gospel rendering are known. Most Ethiopic mss. are late, and critical studies of the version have been limited in scope.

118 **(B) Versions from Western Asia.** The Armenian translation, as originally made early in the 5th cent., depended heavily on pre-Peshitta forms of the Syriac; it was subsequently reworked from the Greek. The Georgian version had a first period, in the 5th cent., when it was based primarily on Armenian texts with Syr origins; but beginning with the 7th cent. all Georgian texts were conformed to Gk models. The Arabic versions, though of historical interest, and serviceable in reconstructing the *Diatessaron* and the Syro-hexaplar OT rendering, are too late to be of much direct text-critical worth; they represent a wide range of prototypes in Greek, Hebrew, Syriac, and Coptic (even Latin, for Tb!).

("Bible IV: Texts and Versions 15. Ethiopic [E. Cerulli]; 16. Armenian and 17. Georgian [L. Leloir]; 18. Arabic [P. P. Saydon]," *NCE* 2, 458–62. Botte, B. and L. Leloir, *VDBS* 6 [1960] 807–18, 825–34. Lyonnet, S., "Contribution récente des littératures arménienne et géorgienne à l'exégèse biblique," *Bib* 39 [1958] 488–96. For general information, see B. M. Metzger, *Text*, 82–84. Molitor, J., "Die Bedeutung der altgeorgischen Bibel für die neutestamentliche Textkritik," *BZ* 4 [1960] 39–53. For a catalogue of Armenian biblical mss., see A. Wikgren, *JBL* 79 [1960] 52–56 and references there.)

GREEK TEXT OF THE NEW TESTAMENT

119 We can best study the problem of the text of the Gk NT by seeing its formulation at the end of the last century and the classical solution that was offered; only then can we understand what the discoveries of the 20th cent. have contributed toward solving the problem. The basic difficulty that arises from the history of the NT text is simple. The NT books accepted as canonical were mostly composed during the 1st cent. AD, and the important collections (Gospels, Pauline epistles; → Canonicity, 67:58, 64) took shape during the 2nd cent. However, the oldest copies of the Gk NT available to 19th-cent. scholars were the Great Uncial Codices of the 4th and 5th cents. In some NT passages these codices did not have the same reading. The first problem, then, was to determine which of the codices contained the best extant text of the NT. The second problem was to determine how much alteration had taken place in the 200 to 300 years between the composition and collection of the NT books (*ca.* AD 50–125 for the most important books) and the oldest remaining copies (AD 350). In other words, when one had discovered the "best" text, how faithful was it to the original?

120 **(I) Problem of the Best Text.** Under the heading of this problem we shall treat textual criticism before the 20th cent.

(A) Great Uncial Codices. These have been mentioned in our discussion of the LXX (→ 76 above), for generally such codices contain the whole Bible in Greek. In reference to the NT we list the four most important (with the letter customarily used as a designation for the codex). We shall mention the type of text each codex represents; text types are explained below (→ 130, 135–138).

(*i*) *Codex Vaticanus* (B): middle 4th cent. This is the oldest of the four; it has lost the last part of the NT (Heb 9:14 on; Pastorals; Ap). One scribe copied the whole NT, but a later corrector traced over afresh every letter, omitting letters and words he considered incorrect. The text is Alexandrian. Facsimile page in F. G. Kenyon, *op. cit.*, plate XXV; analysis on pp. 203–6; important study by C. Martini, AnalBib 26 (Rome, 1966).

(ii) *Codex Sinaiticus* (S or ℵ): middle 4th cent. This is the only Great Codex to contain the entire NT, plus two works that the Church did not accept as canonical, *Barnabas* and *Hermas*. Two different scribes copied the NT from dictation; and there were various correctors, some contemporary with the original ms., some later (6th–7th cents.). The text of S generally agrees with B (Alexandrian), although it has some Western readings. Facsimile page in Kenyon, *op. cit.*, plate XXIII; analysis on pp. 195–96.

(iii) *Codex Alexandrinus* (A): early 5th cent. Although it once contained the whole NT, parts like Mt 1–24; Jn 7–8; 2 Cor 4–12 have been lost. The codex also contained the two *Epistles of Clement* (now mostly lost) and the *Psalms of Solomon* (placed on a different footing from the biblical books). Three scribes copied the NT; and there were several correctors, the first of whom was contemporary with the original ms. In the Gospels A has a Byzantine text; in the rest of the NT it is Alexandrian in agreement with B and S. Facsimile page in Kenyon, *op. cit.*, plate XXIV; analysis on pp. 200–201.

(iv) *Codex Bezae* (D): 5th cent. This codex has no OT section; it contains only the Gospels and Acts, with a few verses of the Catholic Epistles that precede Acts. This is our first copy of the NT in two languages, for Latin and Greek appear on facing pages. To some extent the Greek and Latin have been assimilated to each other. Perhaps copied in North Africa, D was corrected by the original scribe himself and by many other hands. The Gk text is remarkably different from that of the other codices, and D is the chief representative of the Western textual tradition. The peculiar text continues to fascinate scholars; see E. J. Epp, *HarvTR* 55 (1962) 51–62; *The Theological Tendency of Codex Bezae Cantabrigiensis in Acts* (Cambridge, 1966); P. Glaue, *NovT* 2 (1958) 310–15; J. D. Yoder, *JBL* 78 (1959) 317–21; *NovT* 3 (1959) 241–48. Yoder has prepared a concordance of the Gk text of D (NTTS 2; Leiden, 1961). Facsimile page in Kenyon, *op. cit.*, plate XXVI; analysis on p. 210.

121 We may also mention a few less important codices with which the student should be familiar.

(v) *Codex Ephraemi Rescriptus* (C): 5th cent. As the name implies, this is a palimpsest—an earlier writing washed or scraped off, and the skin reused for a later writing. In this case the later writing consisted of the works of Ephraem, copied in the 12th cent.; the earlier was a 5th-cent. copy of the Gk Bible, with about three-fifths of the NT preserved. There were two correctors, in the 6th and the 9th cents. A collation of its NT readings was done in 1716. The text is frequently Byzantine. See R. W. Lyon, *NTS* 5 (1958–59) 266–72.

(vi) *Codex Washingtonensis I* (W): late 4th or early 5th cent. It is the most important biblical ms. in the United States. Acquired in Egypt in 1906 by C. L. Freer, it contains the four Gospels in the Western order (Mt, Jn, Lk, Mk). It was copied from several different earlier mss. Its ending of Mk (after 16:14) is peculiar and of importance (→ Gospel Mk, 42:100).

(vii) *Codex Koridethianus* (Θ): 9th cent. Written in a crude hand, it takes its name from the scribe's monastery, Koridethi near the Caspian. It contains the Gospels and has significant readings, especially in Mk. First called to the attention of scholars by H. von Soden in 1906, it has given support to the thesis of a Caesarean textual family.

122 What was the import of these codices for textual study and translation before modern times? Unfortunately, the oldest and best of the Great Codices (B and S) became available to scholars only in the 19th cent. In 1844 C. von Tischendorf discovered S at the monastery of St. Catherine in the Sinai Peninsula (→ Biblical Geography, 73:27). The fascinating story of this discovery is told in J. Reumann, *op. cit.*, 145–62. Although B was in the Vatican Library since 1481 and was used sporadically by scholars from 1580 on, it was not made generally available in accurate copies until the late 19th cent. (1867 ed.; photographic facsimile in 1889–90). On the other hand, codices D and A were available since Reformation times. Theodore Beza procured D at Lyons in 1562 and presented it to Cambridge in 1581; it was used to some extent in NT editions from 1550 on (see B. M. Metzger, *NTS* 8 [1961–62] 72–77). Codex A reached England as a gift to King Charles I in 1627 and had been in circulation at Constantinople for 300 years before that. But even these codices were not the backbone of earlier studies of the Gk NT.

123 **(B) Textus Receptus.** The key to the study of the Gk NT from the 16th to the 19th cents. is the *Textus Receptus* (TR), but to explain its origins we must survey the history of the NT after the writing of the Great Codices. We saw above (→ 74) that there was a revolution in handwriting in the 9th cent. when scribes changed from uncials to minuscules. The practical impact is seen in the fact that, compared with some 250 uncial mss. of the Gk NT which have survived, over 2500 minuscule mss. are known. Thus, the number of mss. from the 500 years between the change in handwriting and the invention of printing (in 1450) is more than ten times larger than the surviving number of mss. from the 500 years before the change. When printing was invented, there were many mss. of the Gk NT available; but the majority of them represented a later and inferior textual tradition (as would become apparent to scholars centuries later).

124 In 1514 Cardinal Ximenes was responsible for the first printing of the Gk NT as part of his Complutensian Polyglot Bible (Hebr-Aram-Gk-Lat in parallel columns), but it was not published until 1522. The first published printed Gk NT was that of the Dutch Catholic Erasmus in 1516—an edition based upon only six or seven mss. and filled with printing errors (some of which were corrected in subsequent editions). For small parts of the NT where he had no Gk ms., Erasmus simply translated the Vg into what he thought the Greek might have been! The Protestant printer-editor Robert Estienne, or Stephanus, issued editions of the Gk NT from 1546 on, based on the later editions of Erasmus but using more mss. and introducing a critical apparatus to indicate different readings found in various mss. The 1557 edition was the first to include an enumeration of verses within chapters. This Gk text of Erasmus and Stephanus became the *Textus Receptus* on which all the Protestant vernacular translations were based until the 19th cent. (B. Reicke, *TZ* 22 [1966] 254–65). Luther used the 2nd Erasmian edition of 1519 (on Luther's work, see Reumann, *op. cit.*, 55–92). In England the Stephanus 3rd edition (1550) became very popular in scholarly circles.

It is unfortunate that this most influential textual tradition was not based on what today we would consider good mss. It was based on the textual tradition popularized by the minuscule mss., a tradition that had become dominant at Constantinople from the 5th cent. on and was used throughout the Byzantine church (whence the name "Byzantine" given to the tradition). It represented a heavily revised NT text wherein scribes had sought to smooth out stylistic difficulties and to conflate variant readings. This means, in the words of the Preface to the RSV, that so influential a translation as the King James Version of the NT "was based upon a Greek text that was marred by mistakes, containing the accumulated errors of fourteen centuries of manuscript copying." Curiously, in many passages, particularly in the Gospels, Catholics were better supplied with correct readings than Protestants; for although the Catholic Rheims NT (→ 168 below) was a "second-hand" translation from the Latin, the Vg Gospels often reflected a better Gk text than that which lay behind the King James translation (→ 106 above).

125 **(C) Differentiation of Textual Traditions.** The recognition of the limitations of the TR came slowly. When in the next (17th) century Codex A became available, it only strengthened the respect for the TR; for, as fate would have it, in the Gospels A was the oldest example of the same inadequate Byzantine text. True, Codex D had a different text, but D was so peculiar that it was looked upon as a freak produced by corruption. T. Beza, the owner of D, published nine editions of the Gk NT between 1565 and 1604; and although he supplied more textual apparatus than Stephanus, he popularized the TR in the body of his text. It was through Beza's editions of 1588–89 and 1598 that the TR influenced the King James translators. The brothers Elzevir published a NT taken from Beza's edition, and in the preface to their 1633 edition they spoke of the "*textum*...nunc ab omnibus *receptum*," whence the name "*Textus Receptus*."

126 (a) First Attempts. A century later in England E. Wells published the first complete Gk NT (1709–19) that abandoned the TR in favor of more ancient mss. His work, that of R. Bentley (1720—he castigated the Stephanus TR as "the Protestant pope"), and that of D. Mace (1729) were bitterly opposed by the supporters of the TR and were soon forgotten. Support of the TR had become a mark of religious orthodoxy!

127 A whole new stage in the textual criticism of the Gk NT opened when it became clear to scholars that there were *traditions* (and not merely mss.) different from what was represented by the TR, and that mss. should be classified as belonging to one or the other tradition. In 1725 the Lutheran J. A. Bengel initiated textual classification by distinguishing between the older African "nation" of documents and the later Asiatic (Constantinopolitan) nation. Bengel's Gk NT (1734) showed in its margin how often the readings of the older mss. were to be preferred to those of the TR. He also standardized NT punctuation and divided the NT into paragraphs. J. J. Wettstein (1751–52) began to use capital roman letters to denote uncial mss.—a system still used. Later in the same century J. S. Semler adapted Bengel's classification to a distinction between an Oriental recension by Lucian of Antioch and a Western or Egyptian recension by Origen (→ 72 above). Ultimately Semler and his student J. J. Griesbach accepted a threefold grouping into Western, Alexandrian, and Constantinopolitan.

128 Indeed, Griesbach (1745–1812) may be said to have put textual criticism on a truly scientific basis and to have laid the foundations for all subsequent work. He offered 15 canons for textual criticism that enabled scholars to decide upon the better readings. One such canon was: "The shorter reading [unless it lacks entirely the authority of the ancient and weighty witnesses] is to be preferred to the more verbose." In his threefold classification of traditions he recognized that the Constantinopolitan, represented in the Gospels by Codex A and followed by the TR, was a later compilation from the Alexandrian and Western texts.

129 In the 19th cent. in Germany K. Lachmann published a Gk NT (1831) that broke very clearly with the TR and was constructed directly from ancient mss. The same was true of S. P. Tregelles' NT in England (1857–72). The ms. discoveries by C. von Tischendorf, e.g., Codex S, gave scholars much more to work on, so that Metzger (*Text*, 126) does not hesitate to describe Tischendorf as "the man to whom modern textual critics of the New Testament owe most." Tischendorf's own edition of the Gk NT (8th ed., 1864) gave great weight to S.

130 (b) Westcott and Hort. All of this progress came to a head in the splendid contribution of the Cambridge scholars B. F. Westcott and F. J. A. Hort (henceforth W-H), a contribution monumentalized in *The New Testament in the Original Greek* (1881–82). With codices B and S now available, W-H were able to classify into four main groups the witnesses to the NT text (for the significance and nomenclature of grouping NT mss., see E. C. Colwell, *NTS* 4 [1957–58] 73–92):

(i) *Neutral*, represented by B, S, and a few minuscules. This was the purest and earliest form of the text, for it had not been systematically revised. It was the common property of the whole Eastern church (the name "neutral" implies that its variants cannot be traced to a particular historical situation or locale).

(ii) *Alexandrian*. The Neutral text, as it was preserved at the Gk literary center of Alexandria, underwent at the hand of scribes a polishing in language and style. This is evident in the scriptural citations of the Alexandrian Fathers (Origen, Cyril) and in Codex C and in the Coptic versions.

(iii) *Western*, represented by D, the OS and OL (→ 91, 107 above). This tradition arose very early, perhaps before 150, and was used by Tatian, Marcion, Justin, and the Western Fathers. The scribes of the Western tradition exhibited considerable freedom both in changing and adding. The text arose at a period when the NT was used for edification, and explanation was necessary. Hence explanatory glosses found their way into the text. Readings supported only by the Western tradition are to be rejected.

(iv) *Syrian*, represented by A in the Gospels, by the minuscules, and by the whole Byzantine tradition. This textual form appeared in the late 4th cent. at Antioch, perhaps stemming from the editorial work of Lucian (d. 312; → 72 above). It was taken to Constantinople (by John Chrysostom?) and then disseminated throughout the Byzantine Empire. It was heavily marked by conflate readings, i.e., if the Neutral text had one reading and the Western text another, the Syrian combined them. It was the latest of the four textual traditions and the poorest.

131 This theory of W-H represented a head-on challenge to the TR, for the latter quite obviously was a witness of the Syrian tradition. The W-H NT was heavily dependent on B and S and differed from the TR in a great number of verses. The theory was bitterly attacked, but it bore practical fruit in the Revised Version (RV; → 161 below) of the English Bible. If the King James was a translation of the TR, the RV and the subsequent RSV were heavily influenced by principles akin to those of the W-H NT. As Greenlee (*op. cit.*, 78) puts it, "The textual theory of W-H underlies virtually all subsequent work in NT textual criticism."

132 In Germany Bernhard Weiss edited a Gk NT (1894–1900), also heavily dependent on B; and although his critical methods were his own, the end product was closely akin to W-H. This was important because the Nestle pocket edition (stemming from the work of Eberhard Nestle and subsequently of Erwin Nestle and Kurt Aland), which has been the most popular Gk NT in our times, stems from the Tischendorf, W-H, and Weiss editions and thus from a tradition that has rejected the TR—but, notice, a tradition heavily dependent on 19th-cent. scholarship. On the other hand, A. Souter's NT (1910) in England and H. von Soden's (1913) in Germany, and the Catholic edition of H. J. Vogels (1920; 4th ed. 1955) gave more serious consideration to the Syrian text tradition. In particular, Von Soden's tremendous work in NT criticism identified three traditions: the Koine text (= Syrian of W-H), the Hesychian text (= Neutral and Alexandrian), and the Jerusalem text (= Western and others); and Von Soden often accepted the agreement of any two of the three, thus giving a strong voice to the Koine. Other Catholic critical editions, that of A. Merk (1933; 9th ed., 1964, by C. M. Martini), and that of J. M. Bover (1943; 3rd ed. 1953), have been more eclectic but not satisfactory in their critical apparatus. The reader will notice that in following the history of the TR we have slipped into the 20th cent., the subject of our next section. And yet our treatment was not too much of an anticipation; for, although their critical apparatuses were better, the critical editions published in this century up to 1965 had not yet put into practice the discoveries and insights of our time and were very much the children of their 19th-cent. forebears (see K. Aland in *SE* 1, 717–31; → 150 below).

133 **(II) Problem of the Earliest Text.** If W-H established definitively that in general the "Neutral" tradition of B and S is to be preferred to the Syrian tradition of A (in the Gospels) and of the minuscules, nevertheless, their theory has had to be modified in its assumption that the tradition of B and S is truly neutral and truly the earliest text. This modification has come about through a more detailed study of the grouping of mss. and through a series of new discoveries. (See H. H. Oliver, "Present Trends in the Textual Criticism of the New Testament," *JBR* 30 [1962] 308–20.) And so we come to the second of the two problems we saw at the beginning of the discussion (→ 119 above), the answer to which enables us to survey textual criticism in the 20th cent.

134 **(A) Revised Classification of Traditions.** The names given to the ms. groups by W-H have been changed and the groups themselves re-evaluated. The work of B. H. Streeter, *The Four Gospels, a Study of Origins* (1924), is extremely important here.

135 (i) *Alexandrian.* The W-H division between Neutral and Alexandrian has been abandoned, and the name "Alexandrian" is preferred for the combined group. No text group has an uncontaminated descent from the originals. There was much editing already in the text represented by B, even though it existed by the end of the 2nd cent. S is only partly Alexandrian; for instance, in Jn 1–8, S has many Western readings.

136 (ii) *Western.* W-H used this as a catchall for everything that would not fit into the Neutral and the Syrian. The listing of the OS versions here was curious, for it meant that the easternmost text tradition belonged to the Western group. (This was explained by tracing the Western element in the Syriac version to Tatian [→ 90 above] who had lived in Rome.) But further doubts about the unity of the tradition have been raised by the recognition of Western readings in S, an Egyptian codex, and in P^{66} (→ 142 below), a 2nd-cent. Egyptian papyrus. In a survey of recent research on the Western text, A. F. J. Klijn (*NovT* 3 [1959] 1–27, 161–73) argues that every Western ms. shows mixture and that there has never been a Western text, although there are Western readings. In any case we know that some of the elements that W-H considered Western are just as old and just as at home in Egypt as the Alexandrian tradition.

137 (iii) *Caesarean.* This is a new textual family. In 1877 W. H. Ferrar and T. K. Abbott isolated four medieval minuscule Gospel mss. (13, 69, 124, 346), called the Ferrar Group or Family 13, that had a common parentage. In 1902 K. Lake isolated another group of Gospel mss. (1, 118, 131, 209), called the Lake Group or Family 1. In 1906 attention was called to Codex Koridethianus (→ 121 above) as having connection with both families. Streeter argued that all of these were witnesses to a type of Gospel text used by Origen when he was at Caesarea, whence the name given to the tradition. Lake and others (*HarvTR* 21 [1928] 207–404) corrected Streeter's hypothesis by showing that the text came from Alexandria. They also pointed out that the "Caesarean" text was the basis of the Old Armenian, Old Georgian, and Syro-Palestinian versions (→ 118, 95 above). Subsequently the publication of P^{45} (→ 142 below) added a papyrus to the witnesses for the "Caesarean" text; but this was an Egyptian witness antedating Origen's stay at Caesarea! Many scholars disputed the Streeter-Lake identification of this textual tradition, and in a careful study B. M. Metzger (*Chapters*, 42–72) has shown that it needs to be modified. The "Caesarean" witnesses may be divided into two groups, one pre-Caesarean from Egypt (the Fayum and Gaza), the other properly Caesarean. (See T. Ayuso, *Bib* 16 [1935] 369–415; K. and S. Lake, *RB* 48 [1939] 497–505.) The so-called Caesarean text really arose in Egypt in the 2nd cent. and was subsequently brought to Caesarea. The mss., versions, and patristic citations that bear witness to it really bear witness to a whole process of textual development rather than to a single text. In its characteristics this development lies between the Alexandrian and the Western traditions.

138 (iv) *Byzantine.* This name is somewhat preferable to Syrian, Antiochian, Lucianic, or Constantinopolitan. In 1902 H. von Soden subjected this textual tradition to a minute analysis, revealing how complicated were the relationships among its witnesses (17 subgroups!). In his edition of the Gk NT he gave proportionate weight to this tradition, which he called Koine or "common." The W-H assumption that the Byzantine text was necessarily late because it combined Western and "Alexandrian" readings (in the W-H terminology) has had to be modified by the new appreciation of the antiquity of Western readings and their presence in 2nd-cent. Egypt. Chrysostom's link with the Byzantine text is not so simple as once thought, since Chrysostom also preserved some Western readings. Moreover, the work of Lucian of Antioch, thought to be the basis of the Byzantine text, has to be re-evaluated in regard to the NT as well as in regard to the LXX (→ 72 above). In many ways the Lucianic work preserved the ancient text used at Antioch in the early 3rd cent., as some of the "Byzantine" readings in P^{45} and P^{46} show (→ 142 below). In summation, although the Byzantine text and the TR cannot be preferred in general to the Alexandrian text, some of the

Byzantine readings are genuinely ancient (see G. D. Kilpatrick in *The New Testament in Historical and Contemporary Perspective*, ed. by H. Anderson and W. Barclay [Fest. G. H. C. MacGregor; Oxford, 1965] 189–208). In an important article on the Lucianic recension, B. M. Metzger (*Chapters*, 39) says, "...the general neglect of the Antiochian readings which has been so common among many textual critics is quite unjustified."

139 Recently M.-E. Boismard (*RB* 64 [1957] 365–67) has argued strongly for a fifth classification, at least in the Gospels: the *Short Text*. This is found chiefly in Tatian's *Diatessaron* (→ 90 above), but is confirmed by the OL, OS, Georgian, Persian, and Ethiopic versions. There are also traces in the Latin of D, and in the Gospel citations of Chrysostom and of Nonnos of Panopolis. As the name indicates, it is characterized by short readings, free of explanatory phrases and words that make the flow of language smoother. Boismard thinks that this Short Text is very ancient, antedating the scribal clarifications visible in all our codices and papyri. It has many more Western readings than the later Alexandrian text. In a series of articles in *RB* (57 [1950] 388–408; 58 [1951] 161–68) Boismard has defended these shorter readings in Jn, and his theory has greatly affected the textual choices in the French translation of Jn by D. Mollat in the *Bible de Jérusalem* (→ 175 below). Note, however, that Boismard's evidence for the Short Text is entirely by way of reconstruction from other languages and patristic citations; it cannot be consistently substantiated in any extant Gk ms.

140 We find that the following result emerges from the reclassification of the W-H groupings: All the traditions considered have ancient roots, and in the year AD 200 one would have been able to find in Egypt Gospel mss. with some readings characteristic of each and every one of the textual traditions. The problem of how such different readings developed between the composition and collection of the NT works and the year 200 remains. Perhaps it is worth noting, however, that these different readings, as numerous as they are, do not touch on any essential questions of Christian faith. Both by way of the number of early copies preserved and by way of fidelity of copying, the NT is remarkably blessed, especially when compared with the masterpieces of Greco-Roman literature.

141 **(B) New Discoveries.** This reclassification of textual groupings has been intimately involved with a series of new discoveries in the field of texts and versions of the NT. As long as the Great Uncial Codices of the 4th and 5th cents. remained the chief witnesses to textual tradition, the span between the composition/collection of the NT and the earliest available copies was too great to permit much precision about the origin of differences in copies. The chief factors that changed the situation were the discoveries of papyrus mss. of the NT text and of earlier copies of the versions, coupled with a proper appreciation of patristic citations.

142 (a) PAPYRI. The chance of finding large parchment codices of the NT earlier than B or S is relatively small, since most of the libraries that could have housed them have been combed by scholars. However, Egypt has yielded and continues to yield a remarkable number of papyrus fragments and copies of individual NT books. From 1890 on some 75 papyrus mss. of NT books have been discovered, dating from the 2nd to the 8th cents. The following are important:

P^5: (British Museum Papyrus 782), found at Oxyrhynchus (→ Apocrypha, 68:57) in 1896. It consists of two leaves of a 3rd-cent. papyrus codex with the text of Jn 1 and 20. Agrees with B and S.

P^{45}: (Chester Beatty Papyrus I), published in 1933. It consists of portions of 30 leaves of an early 3rd-cent. codex that once contained the Gospels and Acts. Parts of Mk, Lk, and Acts are preserved. Its text is intermediate between the Alexandrian and Western, and in Mk it is closer to the Caesarean.

P^{46}: (Chester Beatty Papyrus II), partly in the Beatty collection, partly at the University of Michigan. It consists of 86 leaves of an early 3rd-cent. codex that contained the Pauline epistles, including Heb, but probably not the Pastorals. The text of this papyrus, almost 150 years earlier than B or S, is quite close to the Alexandrian, except in Rom where there are many Western readings. The doxology of Rom (16:25–27) appears at the end of ch. 15! (→ Letter Rom, 53:9).

P^{52}: (Rylands Papyrus 457), published in 1935 as part of the collection of the John Rylands Library in Manchester. It consists only of a small scrap on which are inscribed four verses of Jn 18. Its importance is its date of *ca.* 135—the earliest copy of a NT book yet found. It is very important for dating Jn.

P^{66}: (Bodmer Papyrus II), published in 1956, 1958, and revised in 1962. It contains considerable portions of Jn from *ca.* 200 and agrees with S. For bibliography, see *NTA* 2 (1958) § 322; also K. Aland, *NTS* 9 (1962–63) 303–13; 10 (1963–64) 62–79 (→ Gospel Jn, 63:37).

P^{72}: (Bodmer Papyri VII–VIII), published in 1959. Dating from the 3rd cent., this papyrus codex contains Jude and 1–2 Pt mixed in with apocryphal works, perhaps reflecting the fact that these epistles had not yet attained to canonical status. Apparently prepared for private rather than church usage, it was the work of four scribes. The text agrees with B and the Sahidic Coptic. See F. W. Beare, *JBL* 80 (1961) 253–60.

P^{75}: (Bodmer Papyri XIV–XV), published in 1961. This papyrus codex from *ca.* 200 contains Lk 3:18–18:18 and Lk 22:4 to Jn 15:8. It agrees with B and the Sahidic (C. L. Porter, *JBL* 81 [1962] 363–76; J. A. Fitzmyer, *CBQ* 24 [1962] 170–79). For close study, see K. Aland, *NTS* 11 (1964–65) 1–21; 12 (1965–66) 193–210; C. M. Martini, *Il problema della recensionalità del codice B alla luce del papiro Bodmer XIV* (AnalBib 26; Rome, 1966).

143 What light have these papyri thrown on the W-H theory? First, they prove that W-H were correct in assuming that the 4th-cent. "Neutral" text found in B really stemmed from a much earlier period. P^{72} and P^{75} are evidence that a text much like that of B was in existence by AD 200 and even earlier. However, a comparison of P^{66} and of P^{75} is most instructive: Both are mss. of Jn from about 200, but whereas P^{75} agrees with B, P^{66} often agrees with S (which in the first eight chapters of Jn is close to D and the Western tradition). If P^{66} shows the antiquity of some Western readings, P^{45} has been useful in showing the existence and antiquity of Caesarean readings. Thus, in another way, the papyri have also demanded some essential changes in the W-H classification.

(Aland, K., *NTS* 3 [1956–57] 261–86; 9 [1962–63] 303–16; *NovT* 9 [1967] 81–106. Filson, F. V., *BA* 22 [1959] 48–51; 24 [1961] 2–18; 25 [1962] 50–57.)

144 (b) EARLY VERSIONS. The OS and OL versions of the NT date from the end of the 2nd cent.; the Sahidic Coptic version dates from the early 3rd cent. Thus these versions antedate the Great Uncial Codices by almost 200 years and are contemporary with many of the papyri. If we can establish the type of Gk NT from which they were translated, they can be useful tools indeed in the quest for the earliest text. Long before the 20th cent., scholars realized the importance of the versions in establishing the text of the Gk NT. The study of the peculiarities of the OL was influential in the first differentiation of textual traditions by Bengel (→ 127 above). But only in the 20th cent. was it possible to use the versions in a truly scientific way. A glance at the discussions of the OS, the OL, and particularly the Coptic above (→ 91, 107, 115) will show that for the most part either the basic discoveries or the publishing of critical editions of these versions belongs to the present century.

145 The impact of the modern studies of these versions on the W-H theory is interesting. The Sahidic and Bohairic Coptic versions give evidence of readings from various textual traditions. In Jn, for instance, in general they tend toward Alexandrian usage, agreeing with B and P^{75}; but in the early chapters of Jn there are also readings that agree with S and thus with a Western tradition. We have already mentioned Western readings in the Middle Egyptian copy of Acts (→ 116 above). The OL, especially the African mss., tend toward Western readings in agreement with D; but there are certain OL mss., like the Codex Veronensis in Jn 9:22ff., which in part agree with the Alexandrian tradition. In general the OS tends toward Western readings. The Old Armenian and Georgian versions (→ 118 above), before they were retouched, had many Caesarean readings. Thus, as in the case of the papyri, the evidence of the early versions shows that the Gk texts on which they were based were of different traditions.

146 Particular attention has recently been given to Tatian's *Diatessaron* (→ 90 above). For H. von Soden, Tatian was the source of the corruptions and expansions that existed in the later Gk mss. But Boismard has sought to show that Tatian used a very old Short Text of the Gospel passages and had great influence on the OL and OS. Certainly, should the lost text of Tatian ever be discovered or reliably reconstructed, it may hold the key to why there were such divergent traditions in existence by AD 200; for Tatian comes precisely in between the period of composition/collection and that of our oldest large papyrus mss. But most scholars are less willing than Boismard to depend so heavily on a *Diatessaron* that has to be reconstructed on the contaminated evidence now available.

147 (c) PATRISTIC CITATIONS. Many Fathers wrote in the 200 years antedating the Great Uncial Codices, and their citations of the NT are valuable in reconstructing the forms of the Gk text in circulation in this earlier period. Once again a study of patristic citations of the NT is nothing new. Indeed, since the Fathers were known to have been associated with ancient cities, their use of a specific text has been the greatest single factor in deciding the locale to which a textual tradition should be connected. Thus, the general usage of the Alexandrian Fathers won the name "Alexandrian" for the text represented by Codex B and the Coptic mss. We have seen that Origen's stay at Caesarea gave a somewhat incorrect name to the Caesarean tradition (→ 137 above). The fact that Cyprian was a bishop in North Africa and the text he used was the same as that of the OL Codex Bobbiensis suggested the division of OL mss. into African and European.

148 In the 20th cent., however, it has become more obvious that there are pitfalls to be avoided in determining exactly what Gk text lies behind patristic citations. Is a Father citing Scripture verbatim or only by way of approximation and allusion? Sometimes in the case of allusions, a later scribe may have filled in the Scripture citation from the text available to him. (This is one way of explaining how the same citation appears in different forms in the same Father's writings.) Often the Fathers commented on Scripture systematically, indicating at the head of a homily or chapter the passage on which they were commenting. But later scribes adapted these scriptural headings to the form of Scripture in use in their own times; and only a careful study of the actual homily or commentary will suggest that the Father was not using the exact form of the passage that now stands at the head of his treatment. Work on an index of patristic Scripture citations is underway at Strasbourg (A. Benoit and P. Prigent, *RHPR* 46 [1966] 161–68).

149 M.-E. Boismard has been particularly active in research into early patristic citations (*RB* 57 [1950] 388–408; 60 [1953] 347–71). He has used citations, like those in Chrysostom, to bolster his theory of the Short Text of the Gospel (→ 139 above). For instance, in Jn 1:13 Boismard (*St. John's Prologue* [Westminster, 1957] 36–39) and others argue on the basis of one OL witness and a number of Fathers (Justin[?], Irenaeus, Tertullian) that we should read: "he who was begotten," not "those who were begotten." This has the effect of making the verse apply to Christ rather than to the Christian. There is no Gk ms. to support such a reading, but Boismard prefers the evidence of the versions and the Fathers as more ancient. Those who disagree would argue that both the versions and the Fathers, in a free theological or pastoral use of the Scriptures, sometimes gave Christological meanings to passages that were not Christological, and that the evidence of the Gk mss. is better for the exact text of a passage.

(Duplacy, J., "Citations patristiques et critique textuelle du Nouveau Testament," *RSR* 47 [1959] 391–400.)

150 With this example we shall close our discussion of Gk NT textual criticism. Most of the material presented has been theoretical, and perhaps the practical example just supplied will whet the reader's appetite to see how the theoretical problems discussed affect the translation of the NT. Metzger (*Text*, 207–46) gives some interesting instances of the application of the principles of textual criticism to individual verses. All in all, despite the general reliability of the Gk text in an edition like Nestle, there remain several hundred instances of real disagreement among scholars about how a Gk text should read. This disagreement affects only a small percentage of the text of the NT; but granted the importance of the subject matter, such disagreements should be solved as scientifically as possible, no matter how much effort it takes.

And indeed at this moment new critical editions of the Gk NT are making an appearance, applying modern discoveries in a way that previous editions have not (→ 132 above). In 1949 an international project was launched to provide a comprehensive critical apparatus to the Gk NT (M. M. Parvis, *JBL* 65 [1946] 353–69; *Crozer Quarterly* 27 [1950] 301–8). In 1955 the American, Scottish, and German Bible Societies sponsored a project to prepare a critical Gk NT with an apparatus of exegetically important variant readings (M. Black, *NTS* 4 [1958] 344ff.). This has appeared as *The Greek New Testament*, ed. by K. Aland, M. Black, B. M. Metzger, A. Wikgren (N.Y., 1966—for an evaluation see G. D. Kilpatrick, *JBL* 85 [1966] 479–81). There is also projected a radically different new edition of Nestle (seemingly the 26th) that will incorporate modern advances (K. Aland, *NTS* 6 [1959–60] 179–84). Such projects give tangible evidence of how far NT criticism has come since W-H. The latest progress reports are those of K. Aland, *JBL* 87 (1968) 179–86, and E. C. Colwell, *ibid.*, 187–97.

THE ENGLISH BIBLE

Although a knowledge of the original biblical languages is something to be desired, for most readers the Bible will be familiar in translation. Indeed, one's reaction to new translations of the Bible is often a test of how well one has understood the implications of modern biblical criticism, textual and literary. For this reason a knowledge of the history of the English Bible is important, even beyond all the other reasons of literary and aesthetic nature.

151 **(I) Before Printing.** The Anglo-Saxon period saw many attempts to translate the Bible into the vernacular of the people. Within one century after the conversion of England (AD 600 by Augustine) poetic and prose paraphrases and translations of the Bible made their appearance (Caedmon, Aldhelm). Bede took care that the Scriptures be delivered to the common people in their own tongue; even on his deathbed (735), he was occupied with the translation of Jn. King Alfred (849–901) and the abbot Aelfric (955–1020) are other names associated with Anglo-Saxon translations. The Norman conquest (1066) produced a need for a translation in Anglo-Norman, and a complete Bible was produced in that tongue.

152 English still remained the language of the people, and by the 14th cent. there was a resurgence of English as the language of all classes. The period 1340–1400, the age of Chaucer, saw the flourishing of Middle English. There is no evidence before 1350 of a translation of large portions of the Bible into English; but between 1350 and 1400, even apart from the Wycliffite movement, considerable portions of the Bible, especially of the NT, seem to have been translated into various English dialects. (H. Hargreaves, "From Bede to Wyclif: Medieval English Bible Translations," *BJRylL* 48 [1965] 118–40.)

153 The first complete translation of the Bible (Vg) into English is associated with John Wycliffe and dated *ca.* 1382–84. Part of the OT was done by Nicholas Hereford; how much of the rest of the Bible was done by Wycliffe himself (1330–84) is uncertain, but the whole work emerged from the circle of Wycliffe's supporters. A revision was completed *ca.* 1397 by John Purvey, Wycliffe's secretary. The questions of the priority, status, and acceptability of Wycliffe's Bible have often been discussed in an atmosphere of Catholic-Protestant polemics. Wycliffe, onetime Master of Balliol College, Oxford, has been claimed as the first English Protestant, since he opposed papal taxation and held views considered heretical (Lollard) by the authorities. To the claim that it took a Protestant to produce the first English Bible, Catholics have often reacted by insisting on the priority of the translations mentioned above of which we have but fragmentary remnants. However, we must frankly admit that none of these ever achieved the popularity or status of the Wycliffe translation, which became the vernacular Bible of 15th- and early 16th-cent. England. Thomas More was probably confused in his statement that he had seen earlier English bibles than Wycliffe's. Nor can we support Cardinal Gasquet's attempt (1894) to show that the Wycliffe Bible was really the work of the English hierarchy loyal to Rome. On the other hand, the opposition of the hierarchy to Wycliffe's translation must not be construed as a desire to keep the Scriptures from the people. The provincial council of Oxford in 1408 made it clear that translations into the vernacular could receive Church approval; however, *de facto*, there was a connection both in England and on the Continent between the circulation of vernacular Scriptures and heretical propaganda. Although the translation in the Wycliffe Bible was reasonably faithful to the Vg and not doctrinally tendentious, the Prologue in Purvey's edition deserved Thomas More's characterization as heretical. In any case, as Kenyon (*op. cit.*, 280–81) makes clear, not all the bishops opposed Wycliffe.

154 **(II) Printed Bibles: Protestant.** The next great era in Englishing the Bible came in the early 16th cent. In 1505 there appeared a text of the Penitential Pss translated from the Vg by John Fisher. However, it was the Reformation movement in England, with its complicated pro-Protestant and Anglican strains, that produced the chain of translations that were the background of the King James Version. We must be content with mentioning the most important.

155 **(A) 16th-Century Translations.**

(a) TYNDALE'S BIBLE (1525–31). William Tyndale (1490–1536) studied at Oxford. He was already suspect of heresy in 1520, and he left England when the Bishop of London refused to give patronage to his translating effort. In Germany Tyndale was an open partisan of Luther, and there he completed his NT from the Greek, printed at Cologne and Worms in 1525. Although copies were smuggled into England, the virulent anti-Catholicism of the notes and the theological slanting of the translation made it suspect among the hierarchy. Part of the OT from the Hebrew was published in 1530–31, but Tyndale died a Protestant martyr's death before he could complete the work. The NT was revised in 1534; and since the rupture had now taken place between Henry VIII and Rome, the opposition to this was not so strong as previously. Tyndale's vigorous English left a permanent mark on the history of the English Bible.

(Greenslade, S. L., *The Work of William Tindale* [London, 1938]. Mozley, J. F., *William Tyndale* [London, 1937].)

156 (b) COVERDALE'S BIBLE (1535). The first complete printed English Bible was commissioned by Cromwell, Henry VIII's secretary of state; but unlike Tyndale's Bible, it was not entirely from the original languages. The title page says that it was translated from Dutch (= German, i.e., Luther's translation) and from Latin; but for the NT, the Pentateuch, and Jonah, much of Tyndale's work was taken over by Coverdale. The rest of the OT was a makeshift rendering from secondary sources. The "Apocrypha" (= Deuterocanonical Books) were put after the NT as books of lesser value. Printed at Zurich in 1535, it was reprinted in England two years later by the King's permission. (H. Guppy, *BJRylL* 19 [1935] 300–328.)

157 (c) GREAT BIBLE (1539–41). John Rogers, a friend of Tyndale, under the pseudonym of Thomas Matthew, produced in Antwerp in 1537 an edition wherein Gn to 2 Chr was filled out from Tyndale's unpublished notes and the rest of the OT was from Coverdale. This edition was taken in turn and revised by Coverdale on the basis of the Latin. The resultant "Great Bible" was set up in every church in England and thus became the first official church Bible in the vernacular. Its psalter was the one used in the *Book of Common Prayer*. Some clergymen recognized that by means of the Great Bible Tyndale's work had received approval in England and so remained opposed to it. See F. F. Bruce, *op. cit.*, 72–74, for a comparison of Coverdale, Matthew, and the Great Bible.

158 (d) GENEVA BIBLE (1560). During Mary Tudor's Catholic restoration (1553–58), Protestant exiles at Geneva produced a revision of Tyndale and the Great Bible, working under the influence of the eminent textual scholar, Theodore Beza. Calvinistic in tone and with controversial and anti-Catholic notes, the Geneva Bible never received authorization for the churches in England, but it did become the Bible of the common man for private reading. In many ways the best of the bibles before the King James, this was the Bible of Shakespeare, Bunyan, and the Puritans. (B. M. Metzger, *Theology Today* 17 [1960] 339–52.)

159 (e) BISHOPS' BIBLE (1568). Sponsored by Archbishop Matthew Parker of Canterbury and done by many clergymen, this was a revision of the Great Bible in the light of the Geneva Bible. It toned down the Calvinism of the latter (see C. C. Ryrie, *Bibliotheca Sacra* 122 [1965] 23–30), but the lack of consultation among the revisers produced unevenness, so that it was never so popular as the Geneva Bible. It replaced the Great Bible as the official Bible of the English church.

160 **(B) King James Tradition.**

(a) AUTHORIZED VERSION (King James, 1611). Planned in 1604 and begun in 1607 by a commission appointed by James I, this revision of the Bishops' Bible was the effort of the best scholars in England, working in groups at Westminster, Oxford, and Cambridge. Note that it was not an entirely new translation, and much of the English can be traced to earlier editions, including the Catholic translation done at Rheims in 1582 (→ 168 below). Although at first there was criticism of the scholarship and some contemporaries thought the English barbarous, this revision was favorably received by the authorities and *authorized* to be read in the churches. In official usage it quickly replaced the Bishops' Bible but waged a 50-year struggle to replace the Geneva Bible in popularity. Gradually the language came to be thought of as classically beautiful, and the AV had an important influence on English literature. Among many Protestants the AV became so sacrosanct that they felt it blasphemy to change it or to point out the inadequacies of its scholarship in the light of modern criteria. (D. Daiches, *The King James Version of the Bible* [Chicago, 1941].)

161 (b) REVISED VERSION (1881–85). Begun in 1870 and done by competent English Protestant scholars (Americans were consulted), the RV was the first great revision of the AV after over 250 years of use. It aimed to change only where change was imperative because of better textual or biblical knowledge or because of development in the Eng language. The NT, which appeared in 1881, was greatly improved over the AV because of the dependence on the W-H Gk text (→ 131 above); the OT, which appeared in 1884, was less satisfactory from the textual viewpoint. The Apocrypha appeared in 1895. The immediate reaction to the RV, especially from the literati, was not favorable; but then the AV was too entrenched to perish without a struggle. The *American Standard Version*, i.e., the RV with readings preferred by American scholars, appeared in 1901. A conservative revision of this is under way under the title of the *New American Standard Bible;* the NT appeared in 1963.

162 (c) REVISED STANDARD VERSION (1946–52). Commissioned in 1937 and authorized by the National Council of Churches, this American work is by far the best of the revisions of the AV. Once again it stays faithful to the AV where possible, but uses modern scholarship and a good sense of English. The NT appeared in 1946; the OT in 1952; the Apocrypha in 1957. The virulent criticism of the RSV as heretical or blasphemous by supporters of the AV represented the survival of a fanatic biblical fundamentalism that tends to regard new translations as a threat to faith—a similar spirit can be found in some Catholic circles. (See G. A. Larue, *JBR* 31 [1963] 301–10.) The RSV labors under two difficulties. First, its loyalty to the AV prevents the full play of modern critical knowledge both in wording and in the arrangement of passages. Second, since it states clearly in the Preface that it "is not a new translation in the language of today," it retains much Bible English, e.g., "thou," "behold," etc. There is a committee for revising the RSV; and for the changes authorized in June 1959 see R. G. Bratcher, *Bible Translator* 12 (1961) 61–68.

163 The RSV received a Catholic *imprimatur* from Cardinal Cushing of Boston in the unaltered form in which the text appears in the *Oxford Annotated Bible* (1966 ed.). In 1965–66 Archbishop Gray of Scotland (and Bishop Bartholome of St. Cloud, Minn.) gave an *imprimatur* to a British Catholic edition of the RSV with some changes made in the text of the NT, e.g., the "brethren" of Jesus for the "brothers" (in order to favor the perpetual virginity of Mary); "full of grace" for "favored one" in the angelic salutation to Mary (Lk 1:28). Some American Catholic scholars expressed strong disapproval of such changes as unscientific—no matter how firmly Catholics believe in the Marian doctrines, references to these doctrines should be explained in footnotes, rather than artificially read into the text.

In this general context we may note that canon 1400 of the Code of Canon Law permits Catholics to read non-Catholic editions, even without such approval as given to the RSV, if the Catholic is in some way engaged in the study of Scripture and if the edition is complete and faithful and without notes that constitute an attack on Catholic dogma. Most of the famous modern non-Catholic Bibles would meet the latter requirements.

164 **(C) New Translations.** These are myriad and we must confine ourselves only to those widely read today. (For a comparison of some of these with the AV, see C. Rayson, *JRel* 41 [1961] 73–90; P. Parker, *AnglTR* 46 [1964] 251–60.)

(a) "CHICAGO BIBLE" (1931). E. J. Goodspeed published the NT in 1923; in 1927 an OT was published by J. M. Powis Smith, T. Meek, and others; the two were combined as *The Bible: An American Translation* in 1931; and Goodspeed's Apocrypha was added in 1939. Goodspeed was an articulate advocate of translation into modern English, and his NT was truly magnificent. This Bible is both scientifically and stylistically a superior effort and in many ways is the best complete Bible available as of early 1968. The OT shows, in a way that the RSV could not, how radically textual criticism should affect translation, e.g., rearranging passages, excising verses. This Bible was not church-sponsored but was published by the University of Chicago, whence the popular name. (E. J. Goodspeed, *The Making of the English New Testament* [Chicago, 1925].)

165 (b) PHILLIPS NEW TESTAMENT (1958). Between 1947 and 1957 a British vicar, J. B. Phillips, brought out the NT in four volumes; these were combined in 1958 as *The New Testament in Modern English*. He carried translation into the modern idiom even beyond Goodspeed's measure; and, in particular, he was able to make Paul's letters sound as if they had just come through the mail. This lively, readable edition won great popularity in both England and the United States. However, from the viewpoint of usefulness for students and fidelity to the wording of the original, Phillips really exercises too much freedom and, frequently, lapses into paraphrase. He has now begun to translate the OT. (See his article on contemporary translating in *Bible Translator* 16 [1965] 25–32.)

166 (c) NEW ENGLISH BIBLE (NT 1961; OT, Apoc 1970). If American Protestantism reacted to the inadequacies of the AV and the RV by producing yet another revision in the King James tradition (the RSV), the British Protestant churches bravely set out in 1949 to produce a completely new translation of the Bible under the general directorship of C. H. Dodd (T. H. Robinson and G. R. Driver have been the subdirectors for the OT, and G. D. Kilpatrick for the Apocrypha). The NEB shows excellent scholarship and vigorous modern British style. It has provoked a debate about the merits of the King James tradition vs. modern English. Some literati will always insist that the English Bible, particularly the Gospels, must have a literary excellence that the original did not in fact possess. T. S. Eliot once remarked, "Those who talk of the Bible as a 'monument of English prose' are merely admiring it as a monument over the grave of Christianity." For various evaluations, see *The New English Bible Reviewed*, ed. D. Nineham (London, 1965).

(d) TODAY'S ENGLISH VERSION. An American Protestant counterpart of the British effort to produce a completely new translation in modern language is being sponsored by the American Bible Society. The NT volume, trans. by R. G. Bratcher, has appeared under the title *Good News for Modern Man* (1966). Stylistically it stands somewhere between Phillips and the NEB. Occasionally it is too free in its departures from a literal rendering of the original; but it reads well and should serve as an interesting counterbalance on the American scene, which is still overly dominated by the AV.

167 **(III) Printed Bibles: Catholic.** Because of the insistence of the Council of Trent on the use of the Vg (→ Church Pronouncements, 72:11), it has been the standard usage up until recent years that official Catholic translations into the vernacular be from the Vg. (For Trent's attitude toward vernacular bibles, see R. E. McNally, *TS* 27 [1966] 204–27.) Only with the encyclical *Divino Afflante Spiritu* of Pope Pius XII in 1943, 400 years after Trent, were Church policy changed and vernacular translations from the original languages officially encouraged (→ Church Pronouncements, 72:20). Vatican Council II made it possible that such translations from the original languages be used for pericopes of the vernacular Mass (Instruction of the Congregation of Rites for interpreting the Constitution of Vatican II on the Sacred Liturgy, 1.11, 40a). And in fact the American Catholic hierarchy approved a translation from the original languages for use in both the English Mass and Breviary. This history explains why we must distinguish between two types of Catholic translations.

(Brown, R. E., "Recent Roman Catholic Translations of the Bible," *McCormick Quarterly* 19 [1966] 283–92. Gribomont, J., "L'Église et les versions bibliques," *Maison-Dieu* 62 [1960] 41–68.)

168 **(A) From the Vulgate.**

(a) DOUAY-RHEIMS (1582–1609). This was done by Gregory Martin, an Oxford-trained scholar, working in the circle of English Catholic exiles on the Continent, under the sponsorship of William (later Cardinal) Allen. The NT appeared at Rheims in 1582; the OT at Douay in 1609. The translation, although competent, exhibited a taste for Latinisms that was not uncommon in English writing of the time but has seemed excessive in the eyes of later generations. The NT influenced the AV.

169 (b) CHALLONER REVISION (1749–63). The official Catholic version underwent revision a century earlier than its Protestant counterpart, the AV. Bishop Richard Challoner, coadjutor to the Vicar Apostolic of the London district, revised the NT in 1749 and 1752, and the OT in 1750 and 1763. This was a considerable revision, markedly modernizing the style. For two centuries the Challoner revision remained in almost universal use among English-speaking Catholics.

170 (c) CONFRATERNITY REVISION OF NT (1941). If the need for a Bible adapted to the 20th cent. produced in Protestantism the RSV and the NEB, Catholic circles in America and England felt the same need. In America, under the direction of the Episcopal Committee for the Confraternity of Christian Doctrine (whence the CCD designation), the Rheims-Challoner NT was revised, much as the RSV constituted a revision of the AV-RV. The style of the Catholic revision was relatively modern, but considerable amounts of Bible English ("thou," "behold") were preserved. Cognizance of the Greek was taken in the footnotes, but in the text the Sixto-Clementine Vg (→ 110 above) was followed even where it was not faithful to Jerome's original Vg. The NT was approved for church usage and remained dominant until December 1964 when the English Mass was introduced, employing another translation. A revision of the Douay-Challoner OT was begun, but abandoned after Pius XII permitted and encouraged official translations from the original languages (→ Church Pronouncements, 72:20; → 174 below).

171 (d) KNOX BIBLE (1944–50). In Great Britain the need to do something about the Douay-Rheims-Challoner was met when the Catholic hierarchies approved a new translation from the Vg. This was the work of Ronald Knox, a distinguished convert who had been trained in classics at Oxford and was known as an accomplished English stylist. Although Knox rendered from the Latin, he took cognizance of the original languages in his footnotes. His command of Greek was far better than his command of Hebrew; and without question the NT, with its lively style, is the better part of the work. In the Pauline epistles Knox is masterful. For the OT he adopted a deliberately archaizing style that leaves much to be desired. On the whole, Knox has been more appreciated by literary aesthetes than by those who are primarily biblical scholars.

(Klein, T. M., "The Stature of Knox," *AER* 142 [1960] 399–409. Knox, R., *On Englishing the Bible* [London, 1949].)

172 **(B) From the Original Languages.**

(a) WESTMINSTER VERSION (1935–49). This was a British project under the editorship of the Jesuit C. Lattey. The NT was begun in 1913 and completed in 1935; the OT was begun in 1934 but relatively few books had appeared by 1949, the last date of publication. The scholarship was reasonably scientific, but the style was oppressively stiff and archaic. It was "largely intended for the devotional reading of the faithful," but never achieved the wide acceptance in England that Knox received. A new but unpublished translation of the NT by the English Jesuit John Bligh appears in the *Fulton J. Sheen Sunday Missal* (1961) and is identified as a revision of the Westminster Version.

173 (b) KLEIST-LILLY NT (1954). This was an attempt by two priests in America to do for Catholic circles what Goodspeed had done for non-Catholic circles, namely to reproduce the NT "in a diction that keeps pace with modern developments in the English language." J. A. Kleist died in 1949; J. L. Lilly died in 1952; the publication, then, was posthumous and seemingly the translation was not fully completed by the authors, for large sections of Acts appear to have been taken from the 1941 CCD NT revision. Kleist's style in the Gospels is superbly direct and forceful, and his part is judged better than Lilly's rendering of the Epistles. The critical scholarship is occasionally weak (e.g., not even a note on Lk 22:43–44!), and occasionally the translation is theologically slanted (Lk 1:34, "How will this be, since I remain a virgin?"). Yet K-L remains an important Catholic pioneer effort in translating the Gk NT into the language of today. (J. L. McKenzie, *CBQ* 16 [1954] 491–500.)

174 (c) NEW AMERICAN BIBLE (1952–70). When the above-mentioned (→ 170) American Confraternity revision of the Douay-Challoner was abandoned, a project of translating entirely anew the whole Bible from the original languages was commissioned by the Episcopal Committee in response to *Divino Afflante Spiritu*. If the old CCD project, like its Protestant counterpart, the RSV, was the revision of a sacrosanct tradition, the new CCD project resembles the NEB, not only in nature but also in stylistic aim, for the new CCD wishes to avoid Bible English (no "thou" forms at all; use of contractions). Three-quarters of the OT (everything except the Historical Books from Sm to Mc) appeared in three volumes in 1952, 1955, and 1961; and both style and scholarship constantly improved. The Gn of the first volume was choppy and the scholarship too conservative; the Prophets in the most recent volume represent the best translation available today. T. Meek of the Chicago Bible project said of the new CCD Wisdom volume: "It is much more modern in its English and much truer to the original than the highly vaunted RSV" (*CBQ* 18 [1956] 314). The NT, in a preliminary, unpublished form, was adopted by the American Bishops for use in the missal of the English Mass (1964). The reaction was mixed. The unfinished condition explains some of the negative criticism, but much of it reflects two attitudes already encountered in discussing Protestant bibles: First, for some every new translation constitutes a challenge to faith since it implicitly questions the hitherto traditional way of phrasing inspired Scripture; second, literary critics constantly demand in passages like the Gospels a majesty and beauty that the Gk originals did not possess. Prominent Protestant scholars were invited to help finish the project and to revise unsatisfactory earlier translations (e.g., of Gn)—a real step toward a truly "Common Bible." The final volumes of the project (the OT Historical Books and the final form of the NT) appeared in 1969 and 1970, and the popular designation as "Confraternity Bible" ceded to the title "The New American Bible."

(Arbez, E. P., *CBQ* 14 [1952] 237–54. Brown, R. E., *America* [Nov. 14, 1964] 601–4. McCarthy, D. J., *HPR* 66 [1965] 123–31, 205–12.)

175 (d) TRANSLATION OF JERUSALEM BIBLE (1966). In 1948–54 *La Sainte Bible* appeared in France under the editorship of the Jerusalem Dominicans; subsequently the work has undergone several revisions. This French translation with its elaborate introductions and footnotes was immediately recognized as one of the greatest achievements of renascent Catholic biblical scholarship and the flowering of the seed planted by *Divino Afflante Spiritu* (C. Kearns, *Ang* 37 [1960] 201–11). The English translation, made from a one-volume, abbreviated form of the French work, was guided by A. Jones; not only were the notes included, but also the Scripture rendition was checked against the original languages. This is a valuable Bible for students, even though reviewers have pointed out that the English form remains a translation of a translation (see A. DiLella, *CBQ* 29 [1967] 148–51; W. J. Harrington and J. Murphy-O'Connor, *RB* 75 [1968] 450–52).

176 **(IV) Printed Bibles: Jewish.** The most popular Bible in 19th-cent. American Judaism was the translation published by I. Leeser in 1845–53. In 1892 the Jewish Publication Society projected a new translation by Jewish scholars under the direction of M. Jastrow. The project was abandoned after about ten years, and in 1908 a new project was placed under the editorship of M. L. Margolis. This produced in 1917 *The Holy Scriptures According to the Massoretic Text.* The work was competent and literal; the Jewish scholars consulted previous translations, and the influence of the AV was obvious. At mid-century, like their Protestant and Catholic counterparts, Jewish scholars felt the need of replacing this older translation; in 1955 they chose the way of the NEB and new CCD rather than the way of the RSV and old CCD, i.e., a completely new translation rather than a revision, and modern English rather than Bible English. The *Torah* or Pentateuch of the Jewish Publication Society under the editorship of H. M. Orlinsky appeared in 1962. It is a vigorous translation of high scholarship. (H. M. Orlinsky, *McCormick Quarterly* 19 [1966] 293–300.)

70

MODERN OLD TESTAMENT CRITICISM

Alexa Suelzer, S.P.

BIBLIOGRAPHY

1 Alonso Schökel, L., *Understanding Biblical Research* (N.Y., 1963). Bright, J., *Early Israel in Recent History Writing* (SBT 19; London, 1956); "Modern Study of Old Testament Literature," *BANE* 13–31. Coppens, J., *The Old Testament and the Critics* (Paterson, 1942). DeVries, S., "History of Biblical Criticism," *IDB* 1, 413–18. Diestel, L., *Geschichte des Alten Testaments in der christlichen Kirche* (Jena, 1869). Eissfeldt, O., "Modern Criticism," *Record and Revelation* (ed. H. W. Robinson; Oxford, 1938) 74–90. Hahn, H. F., *The Old Testament in Modern Research* (London, 1956). Kraeling, E. J., *The Old Testament Since the Reformation* (London, 1955). Kraus, H. J., *Geschichte der historisch-kritischen Erforschung des Alten Testaments* (Neukirchen, 1956). Levie, J., *The Bible, Word of God in Words of Men* (N.Y., 1961). MacKenzie, R. A. F., "The Concept of Biblical Theology," *ProcCTSA* 10 (1955) 48–66. Muilenburg, J., "Old Testament Scholarship: Fifty Years in Retrospect," *JBR* 28 (1960) 173–81. North, C. R., *The Old Testament Interpretation of History* (London, 1954). Robert, A., "Genres littéraires," *VDBS* 4 (1949) 405–21. R-T 1, 709–22. Rowley, H. H. (ed.), *The Old Testament and Modern Study* (Oxford, 1951). Steinmann, J., *Biblical Criticism* (20th Cent. Encyclopedia of Catholicism 63; N.Y., 1958); *Richard Simon et les origines de l'exégèse biblique* (Bruges, 1960). Venard, L., "Genre historique," *VDBS* 4 (1949) 7–23. Willoughby, H. (ed.), *The Study of the Bible Today and Tomorrow* (Chicago, 1947). Wright, G. E., "Recent European Study of the Pentateuch," *JBR* 18 (1950) 216–25; "Old Testament Scholarship in Prospect," *JBR* 28 (1960) 182–93.

2 OUTLINE

PRE-CRITICISM TO THE EIGHTEENTH CENTURY

3 **(I) Pre-Critical Period.**

(A) OT Study Before 1650. The modern era of biblical interpretation may be said to have begun *ca.* 1650. Until that date most Christian exegesis viewed the Bible as a heaven-sent collection of writings, a report of events that were independent of their cultural and historical milieux. A narrow view of inspiration neglected the role of the sacred writer in the composition of the books and ignored the possibility of development in OT revelation (→ Inspiration, 66:25, 30). The criticism then in possession was dogmatic and theological. There were, of course, individuals who questioned one or the other traditional viewpoint, but these isolated scholars failed to capture the attention or interest of their contemporaries.

4 **(B) Influential Background Movements.** By 1650, however, fresh intellectual currents had gathered sufficient impetus to alter the biblical sciences. The new trends were dependent upon a growing tide of philosophical immanentism that placed the metaphysical absolute no longer in God, but in nature and man. (Immanentism holds that reality can be explained by the principles of nature itself; once man has successfully formulated scientific laws, he can know reality immediately.) The de-Christianized humanism of the Renaissance had exalted man with his intellect and his senses to a point where philosophy became more concerned with man's knowledge of reality (attainable by intellectual and sense impressions) than with reality itself. The shift in emphasis heralded the subsequent replacement of the problem of metaphysics by the problem of knowledge, as in Descartes and Kant.

(a) Rationalism and Empiricism. Exaltation of human knowledge took two forms, namely, rationalism and empiricism, that to some degree tinged all thought during the 17th and 18th cents. The Age of Enlightenment—the *Aufklärung*—throughout the 18th cent. climaxed the development of empiric rationalism. The glorification of reason heralded the dawn of an era in which, it was optimistically anticipated, past darkness would be dispelled and right reason govern all human activity, religious, civil, and artistic. Carried to its logical conclusion, rationalism ended in complete rejection of the supernatural and in pantheism; extreme empiricism terminated in subjectivism and skepticism.

Nevertheless, rationalism and empiricism gave tremendous impetus to the development of various intellectual disciplines during these centuries; the concern here is with the branches of knowledge bearing upon biblical studies. Advances in the natural sciences (especially during the early 17th cent.) raised questions about the biblical cosmogony and consequently challenged the inerrancy of Scripture. Historians were discovering sources other than the OT for the chronology of world history. The archaeological investigations that have so profoundly influenced contemporary biblical studies had discernible origins in early travel accounts; and these reports showed an ever growing concern with scientific presentation of Palestinian geography and topography (→ Biblical Geography, 73:8–9). From the 18th cent. on, new methods in the study and analysis of ancient literatures prepared the way for higher criticism—the analysis of literature in terms of origin as well as of content—and for the subsequent study of the Bible according to the criteria used in the criticism of profane literature.

5 (b) Deism. Perhaps the most significant consequence of rationalism was the rise of deism, under the tutelage of Lord Herbert of Cherbery (1642), and its spread from England to the Continent. The Deists had little to say about the Scriptures, though John Toland (*Christianity Not Mysterious*, 1696) and some others attacked the integrity of the Bible, insisting there is nothing in the Gospel contrary to reason or above it. Nevertheless, deistic emphasis upon natural religion, together with a denial of revelation and a rejection of the supernatural, created an atmosphere of biblical study hostile to the traditional interpretation of the Bible. Deist philosophers like Thomas Hobbes (1651) confidently tried their hand at biblical criticism, while Baruch Spinoza (1670) rejected a Bible that is conceived of as an inspired revelation of divine truth, maintaining that it is only a collection of historical books whose content must be examined under the rule of reason.

6 **(II) Beginnings of Modern Criticism.**

(A) R. Simon. A convert from Protestantism and a priest of the Oratory, Richard Simon (1638–1712) inaugurated the era of modern biblical criticism with his three-volume *Histoire critique du Vieux Testament*

(1678; also → Modern NT Criticism, 41:5). Simon's examination of the Oriental mss. in the Oratorian library in Paris and his work with biblical, rabbinic, and patristic literature enabled him to produce this study of the Bible based on literary and historical analysis. In the first volume Simon dealt with the authorship of the various books of the Bible. Particularly significant was his conclusion that Moses was not the only author of the Pentateuch. A history of the chief translations of the Bible, together with rules for textual criticism and for more exact translation, filled the second and third volumes. Of prime importance was Simon's recognition that unwritten traditions lie at the base of literary history—a contribution that went unheeded by his contemporaries.

Simon's critical study drew fire from other French theologians and exegetes. Bossuet was particularly merciless in his attacks, basing his arguments on theology and refusing to follow Simon into critical realms in which writings were to be judged by grammatical and literary standards. Bossuet was not alone in failing to distinguish between theology and literary criticism as autonomous disciplines and to realize that a theological position does not guarantee the authenticity of a particular biblical passage. The enemies of Simon were temporarily victorious and in 1682 the *Histoire critique* was put on the Index. Simon's work aroused great interest outside France; it was translated into English (London, 1682) and much later into German by J. S. Semler.

7 **(B) Textual Criticism.**

(a) J. Morinus and L. Capellus. A foundation for the textual criticism advocated by Simon had already been laid in the first quarter of the 17th cent. A French Oratorian, Morinus asserted (1633) that the LXX furnishes a better reading and a more fruitful tradition than does MT; in fact, MT is so filled with errors that it cannot stand as a norm for biblical studies. Capellus, a French Protestant, showed (*Critica sacra*, first published in 1658) that the vocalization of MT is late in origin and that its consonantal text is imperfectly preserved. About the same time the Calvinist H. Grotius (1583–1645) pioneered a grammatico-historical exegesis freed from all dogmatic considerations; he strongly supported the literal interpretation of the Bible, especially of the OT prophetic oracles.

8 (b) J. Leclerc. After the appearance of Simon's epoch-making *Histoire critique*, Leclerc (1657–1736) helped to propagate Simon's historico-literary hypothesis by a masterly review of the *Histoire critique*. Though differing from Simon on many points, Leclerc shared the Oratorian's views about the necessity of textual criticism. His own chief work, *Ars critica* (1697), developed rules for such criticism, especially for the reconstruction of the Hebr text. His work represents a synthesis of critical endeavor on the eve of the Age of Enlightenment.

9 (c) English Textual Criticism. During the rest of the 18th cent., English scholars took the lead in textual research, making the MT the chief subject of study. B. F. Kennicott, to mention only one, averred that the Hebr texts are relatively late, but are generally more faithful to the original than are the Gk texts (→ Texts, 69:49). Despite the increasing number of textual studies, however, early sanguine expectations of establishing a definitive Hebr text came to nought.

10 (d) A. Schultens and W. Schröder. The work of Schultens (1733) utilized the preceding grammatical studies to arrive at the declaration that Hebrew is one of the Semitic languages. By thus challenging the concept of Hebrew as a unique *lingua sacra*, Schultens opened the way to critical scientific exegesis. Schröder (1776) popularized the work of Schultens; he divorced the Hebr language from its arbitrary association with the mechanics of Latin and showed the distinctiveness of the Semitic languages.

11 (e) W. Gesenius. The labors of Schultens and Schröder were crowned by the achievement of William Gesenius (1786–1842). As the climax of two centuries' slow development of grammatical and philological studies, his work laid the foundation for 19th-cent. exegesis. One of his greatest accomplishments was a comprehensive and masterly presentation of Hebr grammar in its historical development (1817). His Hebr dictionary, first published in 1810, has gone through 17 editions and revisions; it remains a valuable tool, even though modern lexicons have supplemented much of his work. Under rationalistic influences, Gesenius endeavored to separate grammatical research from dogmatic considerations and thus freed Hebrew from the last connotations of being a unique and sacred language.

The successful development of Hebr studies strengthened the tendency toward grammatical exegesis. In one sense this trend was an asset, for it focused attention upon the literal sense of the sacred texts; it must be admitted, however, that the rationalistic premises of the Age of Enlightenment had a desiccating influence upon exegesis and speedily provoked a reaction, as the Enlightenment yielded to Romanticism.

12 **(III) Eighteenth-Century Criticism.**

(A) The Rise of Historical Method.

(a) J. D. Michaelis. One of the most significant figures in the history of 18th-cent. biblical research, Michaelis (1717–91) was professor of Oriental languages at Göttingen. Although he was conversant with contemporary trends in rationalism and deism, in the conclusions of his biblical research he deferred to orthodox theology. This tension between theological commitment and scientific scholarship was characteristic of the Age of Enlightenment in which rationalism challenged orthodoxy. A prolific writer, Michaelis' chief contributions to biblical studies were in the auxiliary sciences, such as philology, Oriental studies, geography, and archaeology. Nevertheless, he also devoted himself to exegesis; in 1769 he began a translation of the Bible, proposing philological exactness and proper geographic, historical, and theological interpretation as his goal. The 13-volume work was completed in 1786.

13 (b) J. Astruc. In 1753, at the height of Michaelis' career, there appeared the *Conjectures* of Jean Astruc, physician at the court of Louis XIV. Astruc observed that the variation in the divine name in Gn indicates two distinct memoirs used as sources; to these he assigned the sigla A and B. The work of the French physician had little effect upon his contemporaries, possibly because of Michaelis' unfavorable reaction to the proposed hypothesis. (Forty years later, however, the English Catholic A. Geddes noted the same variations that had caught Astruc's attention. He attributed them not to the juxtaposition of continuous documents, but to the amalgamation of numerous fragments.) Astruc's tentative analysis was a landmark in OT studies, since it provided the basis for the elaborated documentary theory that made the Pentateuch a focal point in 19th-cent. scriptural research.

14 (c) J. S. Semler. The tension apparent in Michaelis' work was resolved by Semler, his contemporary (1721–91). Semler had no use for orthodoxy, which he identified with papist autocracy, nor for the pietism of P. Spener and his school, who opposed to atrophied dogmatism an emotional mysticism. He sought the renovation of Protestant biblical studies in the spirit of a new gnosis; but his reform had little to do with the biblical understanding or goals of Luther or Calvin. Unhampered by the common dogmatic concept of inspiration, Semler's study of the canon and its historical development led him to reject outright the notion of a fixed canon in the primitive Church. He made a radical distinction between the divine contents of the Bible and the writings in which the divine truths are expressed. The contents are the word of God, absolute and already realized; but the writings themselves are relatively fallible and passing, a vehicle for the divine message. On the basis of such a distinction, only those books are authoritative that serve man's moral betterment at the time; hence, what is "canonical" for one generation can quite properly be rejected by another. Through the use of this theory of accommodation men are able to retain from the Bible the speculative and practical truths that constitute genuine religion.

Semler's insistence that in each case man is the arbiter of the divine message set the stage for an increasingly anthropocentric, rationalistic approach to the study and interpretation of Scripture. Further, according to Semler's idea of canonicity, the contrast between the OT (narrow, nationalistic, Judaic) and the NT (expansive, universal, eternal) was heightened, and later this tendency led Christians to question the relevance of the OT (→ 21 below).

15 (d) J. G. HAMANN. But even as the Enlightenment reached the peak of its influence, voices of protest were not lacking. A sybilline, obscure genius called "the seer of the North," Hamann (1730–88) became the opponent of rationalism and the exponent of emotion and intuitive perception as the key to knowledge. His influence was felt chiefly in the field of German literature, but he was also a noteworthy figure in biblical studies. Important in its own right, Hamann's work took on added significance because of its effect upon critics who followed him, particularly upon the poet Herder. Midway in his career, Hamann discovered the key to the true meaning of the Bible, namely, a realization that God has disclosed himself through the instrumentality of men in a biblical revelation climaxed by the incarnation of the Son of God. Hamann thus hoped to counter the crass anthropocentrism of Semler by emphasis upon a divine economy that employed man for the accomplishment of its designs. Although it is proper to speak of Hamann as a humanist, he differed from other humanist scholars of the Enlightenment in that his humanism was rooted in a profound belief in the incarnation. It was Hamann's intent to integrate the humanism of the era into traditional orthodox faith.

16 **(B) Transition to the Nineteenth Century.**

(a) J. G. HERDER. Under Hamann's tutelage, Herder (1744–1803) acquired a love for the OT and developed his distinctive "Hebraic humanism." Primarily a poet, Herder, like his contemporary Lessing and his pupil Goethe, did not hesitate to assume the roles of philosopher and theologian. Dissatisfied with Semler's view of the Bible and the concept of the accommodation of the Bible to the needs of men, Herder found Hamann's view more congenial; nevertheless, he did not espouse Hamann's concept of man's distinctive role in the accomplishment of salvation history. For both Hamann and Herder, man is indeed the image of God, but for Herder, it is in man's human nature apart from Jesus Christ that the secret of the divine resemblance lies.

Herder approached the Bible as an aesthetic work, a rich deposit of literature upon which the educated taste could dwell. His aesthetic interests prompted his initial hermeneutic efforts. A Ger edition of Bishop R. Lowth's literary appreciation of Hebr poetry, *De sacra poesi Hebraeorum* (1753; → Hebrew Poetry, 13:9), brought out by Michaelis in 1780, impressed Herder deeply and led to the inception of his great work on the spirit of Hebr poetry (1782–83). Herder went beyond Lowth's analysis of form to penetrate the spiritual character of the poetry as an expression of a living religious experience. Given soul by the dynamic vital force behind them, the words of the sacred writer could thus speak to readers of the Bible. The key to Herder's biblical analysis was thus aesthetic empathy with Hebr poetry, a penetration of the ancient biblical world, not through the media of archaeology or of scientific scholarly investigation, but through ingenuousness, simplicity of heart, and emotional response. His evaluation and understanding of the sacred writings as the expression of Israel's experience of the divine led to his famous dictum that the more humanly one reads the word of God, the closer one approaches its true meaning, for it is a book written by men for men.

Romantic and intuitive, Herder tempered the rationalism of his age by urging a new encounter with the biblical message that would be compatible with the classic, pantheistic, and humanistic spirit of the time. Both orthodox and rationalistic critics hailed Herder's approach as a welcome and needed corrective to the dogmatic and despiritualized treatment of Scripture. Although Herder eschewed grosser rationalism like Semler's, his aesthetic approach to the Bible was one more step toward the position of higher criticism: The study of the Bible as literature is in no way different from that of profane literary works. Following Herder's lead, biblical scholars attempted a similar intuitive interpretation; the dearth of noteworthy scientific exegesis in the second half of the 18th cent. can be attributed in part to Herder's influence. The lasting effects of this influence are seen in the work of Hermann Gunkel (→ 38 below). Called a scientific Herder, Gunkel employed aesthetic appreciation to penetrate the biblical message. In fact, Gunkel's theory of literary forms echoes Herder's assertion that poetry tends to be expressed in forms especially suited to a particular purpose.

17 (b) J. G. EICHHORN. As already noted, the intellectual ferment of the 17th and 18th cents. had generated tension between orthodoxy and rationalism, between tradition and the enlightenment. Most apparent in Michaelis, the tension was evident also in the work of Semler and Herder, whose studies were somewhat tentative and groping. It remained for Eichhorn (1752–1827) to synthesize the results of the new trends and to establish the principles of a historico-critical analysis that was to dominate the next two centuries of biblical scholarship. Eichhorn was a pupil of Michaelis at Göttingen, but he soon became independent of his master. He taught Oriental languages at Jena for a time and later became professor of philosophy at Göttingen.

Eichhorn proposed to free himself from every commitment to orthodoxy and to recognize the OT historically as a singular source for the knowledge of antiquity, for he felt that theological preoccupations had severely hindered a true comprehension of the OT. To achieve this end, Eichhorn used both Semler's rationalistic approach to the historical and geographical factors in evaluating the text and Herder's romantic insights into the spiritual value of the doctrine presented. To both men he acknowledged his indebtedness, but it was particularly Herder, his lifelong friend, who influenced his biblical criticism. Eichhorn's famed pioneering work, *Einleitung in das Alte Testament* (1780–83), provided the pattern for general and special introductions that soon became the distinctive feature of historico-critical scholarship. The first volume, a general introduction, examined the contents, redaction, authenticity, and canonicity of the OT books; the second volume treated the history of the text; and the third furnished special introductory aids for a critical treatment of the OT and discussed individual books.

The name of Eichhorn is chiefly associated with the views he expressed concerning the Pentateuch. Utilizing Astruc's all but forgotten work, Eichhorn carried the analysis as far as Lv and affirmed the presence of two distinct documents (J and E—later E^1 and E^2; → Pentateuch, 1:7), thus successfully proposing a documentary theory. Contrary to the 18th-cent. fashion of denying that Moses ever existed, Eichhorn strongly asserted the Mosaic authorship of the Pentateuch; he insisted, however, that Moses had made extensive use of fixed written sources.

Eichhorn's Pentateuchal work has somewhat overshadowed his contribution to the interpretation of the prophets. His analysis of the prophetic writings was strongly influenced by Herder's understanding of the human characteristics of the prophets and their poetic, mystical bent. In his exegesis of prophetical literature Eichhorn was careful to consider the historical milieu and endeavored to transport the reader to ancient times and make him confront prophetical literature in the prophets' own age. A century later Bernard Duhm in his work on the Hebr prophets (→ 26 below) acknowledged the influence of Eichhorn.

These initial studies of Eichhorn provided the impetus for the achievements of later scholarship. Eichhorn made use of Herder's embryonic insights into Hebr poetry and literary form to determine poetic *Gattungen* (categories, genres, forms). He assumed in part Simon's notion of tradition and enlarged it with the concept of the importance of oral tradition in the transmission of biblical materials. Further, he saw in the mythical elements of primitive history more than poetic adornment or an accommodation to the time; these preliminary studies of myth were of great importance in the work of Gunkel (→ 29, 38 below).

(Bullough, S., "Dr. Alexander Geddes," *Scr* 17 [1965] 14–22. Jones, W. P., "Aesthetics and Biblical Hermeneutics," *Religion in Life* 31 [1962] 394–418. McEachran, F., *Life and Philosophy of J. G. Herder* [Oxford, 1939]. O'Doherty, E., "The 'Conjectures' of Jean Astruc," *CBQ* 15 [1953] 300–04. Smith, R. G., *J. G. Hamann: A Study in Christian Existence* [N.Y., 1960].)

HISTORICAL CRITICISM IN THE NINETEENTH CENTURY

18 **(I) Growth of the Historical Method.**

(A) W. M. L. de Wette. The grammatico-historical exegesis of the day was far from satisfactory to De Wette (1780–1849); he held that it was neither grammatical nor historical, scarcely deserving the name of exegesis at all. After a brilliant doctoral dissertation (1805) in which he separated the deuteronomic document in the Hexateuch and Kgs (→ Deuteronomy, 6:3), De Wette turned his attention to the problem of methodology in biblical criticism. He greatly admired the achievements of Eichhorn in the realm of literary criticism, but found even greater incentive for his own research in Eichhorn's consideration of the historical milieu. In his *Manual of Historico-Critical Introduction to the Bible* (1817) De Wette spoke so decisively of the demands of historical criticism that he is deservedly regarded as one of the founders of this method in biblical studies. The goal to which he directed his efforts was that of understanding the biblical phenomena in their true historical interrelationships. His basic question in biblical analysis was a historical one: What is the Bible and how did it develop? To answer this query De Wette in his *Introduction* treated the events of the Bible as phenomena comparable to other historical phenomena and subject to the same laws of historical research.

De Wette's enthusiasm for history was occasioned, at least in part, by the birth and development of critical, scientific, historical scholarship in the early days of the 19th cent., chiefly in Germany. In the name of reason, scholars of the Enlightenment had ignored the religious and social past with its legends and traditions that were regarded as characteristic of a benighted era. Consequently, history was denied value as a factor in human progress. Scholars were mainly concerned with a philosophy of history; and when they did turn their gaze upon alien people or unfamiliar institutions, it was without realizing that any great effort of understanding was necessary. With the dawn of Romanticism, however, history—a measured progress from primitive institutions to wise systems—came to be appreciated as a vital factor in civilization.

The historico-critical method as envisaged by De Wette and practiced by his successors combined literary and historical criticism. Literary criticism seeks to establish textual limits and to ascertain the genres and special characteristics of the underlying sources; it studies content under the threefold aspect of language, composition, and origin. Historical criticism attempts to determine the value of the sacred writings as historical documents, both as to facts and as to teaching. This method seeks to reconstruct the writer's life, ideas, and milieu through the use of auxiliary sciences like philology, archaeology, and geography. De Wette's work clarified and strengthened these two critical tendencies current at the beginning of the 19th cent. The twofold aspect of his criticism, literary and historical, was evident in the arrangement of his *Introduction*. To achieve the primary goal of exegesis, namely the full understanding of the sacred writing, De Wette first used all possible grammatical and rhetorical means to penetrate the biblical message. After this literary analysis he turned to historical investigation of the circumstances that produced the work—the milieu of the author, the thoughts, the views, the hopes and fears he shared with contemporaries.

De Wette often affirmed the irrelevance of dogmatic premises in biblical research, although he was moderate in the midst of the polemic vs. orthodoxy and tolerated religious judgments that were in accord with the conclusions of his historical method. In fact, he considered the spiritual sensibility of the exegete very important. The exegete's capabilities will be greater, asserted De Wette, in proportion to the purity and perfection of his own religious views—in short, in proportion to the degree to which he is Christian. Consonant with his rejection of dogmatism, De Wette affirmed that for exegesis no fixed theological view was necessary or even possible, since such commitment bars the way to objective analysis. Here De Wette was secretly restoring the rejected premises of the Enlightenment and of Romanticism.

As a critic of the psalms De Wette showed the influence of Herder's aesthetic appreciation. Eichhorn had introduced the term *Gattung* ("genre") in reference to the kinds of psalms but had attempted no classification. De Wette divided the psalms into six categories, thus anticipating the more complete analysis of Hermann Gunkel (→ 39 below).

19 (B) Hegelian Influence. Even as De Wette was advocating the use of historical criticism in biblical exegesis, the philosopher G. W. F. Hegel (1770–1831) was developing a system of dialectic that had an immediate and invigorating influence as a basis for the interpretation of history. As applied to history, the Hegelian dialectic asserts that man progresses through antagonism and conflict; development takes place because a particular situation (thesis) inevitably produces its opposite (antithesis). The ensuing struggle ends in fusion of the two—a synthesis—that in turn becomes the thesis of the next stage in the struggle. Published in 1831, Hegel's *Philosophy of History* became the final word in metaphysical thinking. After 1850, however, his hypothesis lost ground because of attacks of materialistic science. In two generations the progress of the Age of Enlightenment passed through the dialectic development of Hegel into the evolutionary theory of the second half of the 19th cent.

20 (a) W. Vatke. An ardent disciple of Hegel, Vatke (1806–82) criticized De Wette's conception of historical biblical research as insufficiently dynamic. He regretted De Wette's failure to appreciate the vital role that Hegel's Absolute played in history. In the first volume of his biblical theology, *The Religion of Israel* (1835), Vatke applied the dialectic of Hegel to the study of how religion developed in Israel. According to Vatke, individual historical facts must be related to the eternal truths of reason to form a historical continuum. Religion and history—eternal truth and historical moment—must blend into *Heilsgeschichte* ("salvation history"). True religion was revealed slowly through successive stages of simile, allegory, and myth, climaxing in the historical revelation of Jesus Christ.

Vatke held that biblical theology is a historical discipline, not to be determined by dogmatic considerations; it depends solely upon the written word. But since it reflects the dogmatic coloration of a particular age, biblical theology shares the fate of all historical analysis, changing in accord with the stages of dogmatic development. Since historical events are always mirrored in man's present consciousness, what appears as history is a continuum of the manifestations of the true religion understood by man here and now. The biblical writings are more properly called a history of man's consciousness rather than a scientific record of past events. Consequently, Vatke concluded, a completely objective biblical theology can never exist. His idealistic concept that historical appearances are only manifestations of the Absolute dissolves the reality of history and of revelation as well.

21 (b) Denigration of the OT. To Hegel, Christianity is the absolute religion, the final stage of the dialectic process. The religion of the Hebrews (like pagan religions) was but a single necessary moment in the evolution of the Absolute. Because it was transitory, it was valid and useful only for its own period; as religion evolves from the crudest forms of magic to perfect Christianity, OT religion has become empty. Vatke, like Hegel, maintained that the OT was inferior to the NT because Christianity is the culmination of the developmental process. But Vatke opposed paganism to both OT and NT: Heathenism is naturalistic; Judaism is ideal; Christianity raised the idealism of Hebr religion to concrete reality.

This subtle denigration of the OT was accented in the thought of Friedrich Schleiermacher (1768–1834), the religious philosopher of Romanticism, who held that the gulf between the Hebrew and Christian consciousness is as vast as that between heathen and Christian consciousness. Hence, without rejecting the OT writings, he assigned them a decidedly inferior position. Such views anticipate modern questions about the relevance of the OT (→ Hermeneutics, 71:51).

22 (C) H. Ewald. The historical criticism inaugurated by De Wette and Vatke was carried forward by Ewald (1803–75), who was professor at Göttingen (where he had been a pupil of Eichhorn) and at Tübingen. Orientalist, philologist, and theologian, Ewald's most influential work was in none of these fields, but in history. His *History of the People of Israel* (1843–55) was the first work in German to deal with Israelite history in a secular spirit. By a painstaking investigation of sources, Ewald succeeded in presenting a complete and coherent picture of Israel's history, though it must be admitted that his work made little use of Near Eastern history and of comparative religion. So popular was Ewald's history that between 1864–68 he brought out a third edition.

In Ewald's thinking, the core of Hebr history is found in Israel's tireless effort to achieve true and perfect religion, a goal to which the Hebrews alone of all ancient peoples attained. Thus Ewald emphasized that the history of Israel is essentially a religious history. Theoretically, historico-critical scholars conduct their research in an atmosphere of pure objectivity; Ewald's method discloses, however, that this critical historian substituted one commitment for another. Salvation history (→ 20 above) amalgamated revelation and religion; in like manner Ewald amalgamated true religion and history.

Ewald regarded the prophets as the spiritual center of Israel's pursuit of true religion. These were men with power to bring to life the seeds of awareness latent in all men. Together with the writings of Herder, Ewald's research remained decisive for later 19th-cent. study of the prophets; neither Bernard Duhm nor Hermann Gunkel could ignore it (→ 26, 37 below).

23 (II) Triumph of the Historical Method. The closely related work of De Wette, Vatke, and Ewald firmly directed OT studies along the path of historical criticism. Yet, concerned though they were with the importance of historical circumstances for understanding the sacred writings, they had formulated no general view of Israelite history. This formulation was to be the significant work of Reuss, Graf, Kuenen, and Wellhausen.

(A) Predecessors of Wellhausen.

(a) E. Reuss. As professor at Strassbourg, Reuss (1804–91) was more influential through his lectures than through his written work; indeed, it was through his classes that many French biblicists became acquainted with biblical scholarship. As early as 1833, Reuss noted that the ritualistic regulations in Lv do not correspond to conditions at the time of the desert wandering and that the prophets have nothing to say of these regulations. Accordingly, Reuss concluded that Israelite cultic law is of late composition. His conclusion simultaneously provided a new picture of Hebr history: The prophets are older than the Law and the psalms are younger than both. This view (which Reuss characterized as "my system") was explicated in the work of his successors.

24 (b) K. H. Graf. Reuss' most distinguished pupil, Graf (1815–69), owed much to the thought of his master: Graf's study, *The Historical Books of the Old Testament* (1866), had its inception in the lectures of Reuss. As a forerunner of Wellhausen's studies, Graf's book marked a new phase in the history of OT criticism. He elaborated Reuss' intuitions and in precise terms answered the problem of the historical formation of the Pentateuch: P is the youngest (post-exilic) Pentateuchal document, a proposition more firmly established by the studies of W. H. A. Kosters (1868). Graf profited, too, by the criticism of Abraham Kuenen (1828–91), a Dutch scholar of great brilliance, who was among the first biblical experts to attempt the diffusion of historico-critical methods among nonspecialists.

25 **(B) J. Wellhausen's Documentary Theory.** The stage was now set for a synthesis of historical criticism by Julius Wellhausen (1844–1918). A series of articles on the Hexateuch (1876) and his *Prolegomena to the History of Israel* (1883) enshrined his system. Since his views did not differ radically from those of his immediate predecessors, Wellhausen's success can be traced, at least in part, to his logical and cogent presentation. With Ewald as his teacher at Göttingen, Wellhausen devoted himself to the study of biblical history conceived as a vital process in which Israelite religion grew and matured. For aspects of his literary criticism he was indebted to Reuss, Graf, and H. Hupfeld; for philosophic concepts, to Vatke, and behind him, to Hegel.

Since the Wellhausen documentary theory had repercussions in all fields of biblical research and influenced the course of biblical criticism to the present day, a brief summary of the theory is in order. Wellhausen posited four main documents in the Hexateuch: J, E, D, and P, in that chronological order. The early narrative sections of J and E he assigned to *ca.* 870 or 770 respectively. Their redaction (*ca.* 680) was followed by the writing of Dt (at least the core, chs. 12–22) and of other D elements which were discovered in 621. The composition of P began with the Exile and continued until the final redaction of the Hexateuch during the reforms of Ezra and Nehemiah *ca.* 450 (→ Pentateuch, 1:7).

At the root of this classic exposition lie certain presuppositions, found also in other areas of 19th-cent. scholarship: first, a general skepticism regarding the historicity of accounts recording noncontemporaneous events; second, the assumption that the culture and religion of ancient peoples evolved gradually from early primitive forms; finally, an a priori rejection of all supernatural elements in the religion of Israel. There were additional weaknesses that the passage of time would reveal, e.g., an almost total neglect of the influence of Israel's neighbors upon Hebr history and a disregard of archaeological evidence in reconstructing the history of Israel.

These deficiencies, however, did not impede the wide and enthusiastic acceptance of the documentary theory. Assigning the prophetic writings to a period before the composition of the Hexateuch radically changed the concept of the prophets' mission: They became the originators of monotheism, not its renovators. This reversal was a key point in Wellhausen's theory, and its impact was felt in all fields of OT study. As was to be expected, Hexateuchal studies took the center of the scholarly stage. Enthusiastic proponents of the four-source theory conducted further analysis, splitting and resplitting the sources until they were all but atomized.

(DeVries, S., "Hexateuchal Criticism of Abraham Kuenen," *JBL* 82 [1963] 37–57. Niebuhr, R., "Schleiermacher on Language and Feeling," *TTod* 17 [1960] 150–67. Perlitt, L., *Vatke und Wellhausen* [BZAW 94; Berlin, 1965].)

26 **(C) B. Duhm's Studies of the Prophets.** If Wellhausen proposed to erect the religious history of Israel upon an investigation of Hexateuchal sources, *Bernard Duhm* (1847–1928) regarded the theology of the prophets as the basis for tracing the development of OT religion. The work of Wellhausen was of supreme significance for Duhm, for he adopted Wellhausen's chronology in which the prophetic teaching presupposed the priestly and deuteronomic legislation. Besides the influential *Theology of the Prophets* (1875), Duhm also published a commentary on Isaiah (1892) and *Israel's Prophets* (1916). In the late 18th cent. J. C. Döderlein (1745–92) had first questioned the authorship of Is 40–55 (→ Deutero-Isaiah, 22:2); but Duhm went beyond Döderlein's analysis and identified Trito-Isaiah, chs. 56–66, assigning the composition to the time of Malachi (→ Deutero-Isaiah, 22:50). He also separated the Servant Songs from Dt-Is, thus complicating the problem of the Servant of Yahweh (→ Deutero-Isaiah, 22:5).

In an earlier age Herder, Eichhorn, and Ewald had indicated the distinctiveness of the prophetic phenomenon and its relation to historical milieu. Duhm drew on their studies to construct a coherent pattern of religious development in Israel. The achievement of the prophets rested upon fresh religious insights that broke the bonds of the ancient naturalistic religion in Israel. This work was not the achievement of a single generation, for the earliest prophets, Duhm said, were still rooted in naturalism. Only with Amos was the new element introduced: emphasis upon the action of God. Through the work of the prophets the religion of Israel no longer rested upon a physical basis of God's dealing with Israel in a naturalistic way; religion was taken out of the realm of nature into a moral sphere. Through the moral guidance of the prophets the monolatry of the Mosaic age became ethical monotheism.

Morality, then, according to Duhm, was the force behind the development of Hebr religion. Duhm's analysis of the prophets supposed and utilized the Hegelian theory of development of cult. By so stressing the moral influence of prophetic preaching Duhm contributed to the denigration of cultic and legal elements in Hebr religion. His successors emphasized even more strongly the opposition between the Law and prophets; only in recent years have scholars demonstrated that the thesis of the prophetic "rejection" of Law and cult has been greatly exaggerated (see H. H. Rowley, *BJRylL* 29 [1946] 326–58).

In his exegesis Duhm endeavored to understand the personality of the writer as thoroughly as possible in order to elucidate the genuine message of the prophetic oracle. Prophetic utterance, Duhm averred, is not a timeless revelation of supernatural truth nor, necessarily, a prediction of future events whose fulfillment serves as a prop to faith; the prophet is above all a man divinely commissioned to instruct his contemporaries in the designs and commands of God.

27 **(III) Religionsgeschichte.**

(A) Development and Importance. The use of the historico-critical method in biblical exegesis had a parallel in the application of the historical method to the study of ancient religion in general. The rationalism that had reached its apogee in the Age of Enlightenment focused attention on religion divorced from theological premises and from all theories of supernatural revelation, but the study of this natural religion was largely speculative and characterized by broad generalizations. About the middle of the 19th cent., however, the impetus given by Romanticism to historical research drew scholars to the examination of the historical manifestations of actual religions. This discipline, *Religionsgeschichte* (for which the Eng translation "history of religion" is inadequate), had a great indirect influence upon biblical studies. For the most part the new discipline was conducted on positivist principles, i.e., principles subject to scientific verification. The goal of its research was fact uncolored by philosophical or theological interpretation. Biblical religion, consequently, was investigated on the same plane as other religion, for all religions were conceived to be a product of human culture.

The recovery of religious literatures of the Near East, as well as rapid advances in archaeology, anthropology, and ethnology, greatly facilitated the progress of the new branch of scientific knowledge. The evolutionary theory of religious development that had succeeded the Hegelian concept of continuous progress found extensive corroboration in the investigation of primitive religions. The task of the historian of religion was to trace the manifestation of religious belief and practice from primitive to highly developed forms. This work was made easier by a comparison of parallel trends in distinct religions and by a determination of mutual influences.

While the study and comparison of ancient religions were developing, scholars of the Wellhausen school were almost totally occupied with the literary problems of Hexateuchal criticism and generally failed to appreciate and to utilize the conclusions of *Religionsgeschichte*. Nevertheless, the new study would prove to be a valuable corrective to the deficiencies of the Wellhausen formulae. By recognizing the intellectual, cultural, and religious exchange among the peoples of the Near East, including Israel, scholars doing research in primitive religions were able to construct a more accurate picture of Israelite religion upon which to base biblical interpretation. Consequently, emphasis upon purely literary criticism decreased as the ancient Near East provided fresh materials for investigation and comparison.

28 **(B) Application to the Bible.**

(a) Pan-Babylonism of H. Winckler. As could be expected in the early days of a new science, initial studies exaggerated the universality of the cultural milieu in the Near East. The "pan-Babylonian" theory of Hugo Winckler (1863–1913), for instance, attributed the superior or distinctive elements of Hebr religion, even monotheism, to Assyro-Babylonian influences. Winckler's views were expounded by Friedrich Delitzsch (1850–1922) in his book *Bible and Babel* (1902). But the pan-Babylonian theory soon faded away for various reasons: Egyptologists could not accept it; the amalgamation of diverse concepts into a single Babylonian pattern of thought was too artificial; and, finally, the theory made no allowance for the undeniable fact of development in Hebr religion. Moreover, modern biblicists are aware that the influences shaping Israelite institutions are far more numerous and complex than originally supposed. The Ugaritic tablets, for example, discovered at Ras Shamra in 1929, have disclosed a strong Canaanite influence hitherto unsuspected (→ Excursus Israel, 11:11–12).

29 (b) "Schöpfung und Chaos" of H. Gunkel. Many biblicists interested themselves in primitive religion on a purely comparative basis, registering similarities and differences. The true practitioner, however, sought to trace the historical traditions of diverse peoples in order to show what distinctive use Israel had ultimately made of the heterogeneous influences exerted upon her. Possibly the most balanced and significant biblical work in the field of the history of religion was Gunkel's *Schöpfung und Chaos* (Göttingen, 1895; → 37–39 below). This sober investigation of the folk mythology underlying the biblical presentation of the creation and of the end of the world disclosed that the biblical presentation may be derived from ancient Babylonian accounts of the same phenomena. Gunkel went beyond the recording of similarities, however; he pursued his study to determine what unique use Israel had made of the borrowed material. In other words, he took the Oriental environment into consideration without neglecting Israel's own achievement in the reworking of the materials.

What Gunkel had accomplished in his analysis of Gn and the Ap, H. Gressmann attempted to do for the prophetic writings, tracing the mythological ideas found in the eschatological sections (→ 41 below).

30 **(IV) Reaction to Higher Criticism.** Despite the widespread acceptance of the methods and conclusions of the historical method, advocates of the new criticism were not permitted to have things all their own way. Even before the triumph of higher criticism in the theory of Wellhausen, protesting voices had been raised. Both Protestants and Catholics were affronted by the assertions that dogmatic supernaturalism is untenable and that critical canons must be independent of theology. Moreover, the implication that Israel's religious development had been influenced by religious traditions of older cultures was regarded as a challenge to the uniqueness of Hebr religion.

(A) Protestant Reaction.

(a) Earlier Responses. In attacking rationalistic biblical interpretation, R. Stier (1800–62) inveighed against the one-sidedness of grammatico-historical exegesis. H. Olshausen (1796–1839) criticized the excesses found in both grammatical and allegorical exegesis; he advocated an interpretation that would employ all the auxiliary sciences and yet would recognize the origin of the inspired text in revelation. Olshausen's work was continued by A. Hahn (1792–1863). Another significant counterattack was that of J. T. Beck (1804–78). Unlike many biblicists who were content to reiterate traditional dogmatic positions, Beck attempted to find a substitute for verbal inspiration in a theory of the charismatic gifts of expression given to the biblical authors as men of God. He also asserted that the Bible is an organic whole, a complete system of truth; and so the unity and continuity of the OT are to be found in the thread of salvation history—*heilige Geschichte* was his term—that runs throughout the sacred writings. The most redoubtable opponent of the grammatico-critical and the historico-critical analysis of the OT was E. W. Hengstenberg (1802–69). A confirmed foe of both rationalism and idealism, he disregarded the authentic history of the OT and interpreted the old dispensation entirely in Christological terms.

31 (b) J. von Hofmann. A conservative scholar, Von Hofmann (1810–77) viewed the OT as *historia sacra*—the history of redemption in and through which God brought salvation to the world. For Von Hofmann, revelation is history, not dogma; an event, not a teaching. To assert inspiration dogmatically is not enough; it must be justified by historical means as well. History is the vehicle of divine revelation; the literature of the OT gives knowledge of both the history and the revelation; in fact, the biblical literature is itself a part of that revelation given to men (see H. McDonald, *Theories of Revelation: An Historical Study, 1860–1960* [N.Y., 1963]).

32 (c) Franz Delitzsch (1813–90), father of the Babylonian specialist Friedrich Delitzsch and possibly the most influential of the Protestant exegetes, initially opposed the historico-critical school of research, but in the course of his studies he came to accept many of its conclusions, e.g., Dt-Is and the late date of P. So great was Delitzsch's influence upon teachers and students that his acceptance of certain conclusions of the historical method gave that method entry into some conservative circles. As a convert from Judaism, Delitzsch was more aware than his contemporaries of the need for an encounter with modern Judaism as a means to a fuller understanding of the OT.

33 **(B) Catholic Biblical Scholarship.** During the steady growth of the new criticism in the two centuries after Richard Simon, Catholic biblical scholarship was at low ebb. When one mentions the names of Simon,

Astruc, Morinus, Leclerc, and Geddes, the list of influential Catholic biblicists is at an end. Catholic scholars were, of course, engaged in biblical research, but for the most part they directed their studies to side issues and to safe questions, failing to come to grips with the essential biblical problems of the 19th cent. Exegetes had paid little attention to the documentary theory in its original stages; however, faced with Wellhausen's compelling exposition, Catholics began to realize the implications of rationalistic criticism. By and large, they rejected the system; concession was deemed compromise and no distinction was made between the methods and conclusions of the new criticism and the rationalistic philosophy upon which the system was based. Catholic opposition merely repeated the old positions. The five-volume *Manuel biblique* (1876) of F. Vigouroux and M. Bacuez was an example of the severely traditional exegesis current among Catholic scholars. The *Cursus Scripturae Sacrae* (1886ff.), ed. by R. Cornely, J. Knabenbauer, and F. von Hummelauer, may also be cited, although certain vols. of this series (especially those of Von Hummelauer) showed a willingness to abandon positions that contemporary criticism had demonstrated to be untenable.

34 (a) "Dictionnaire de la Bible." The work of Cornely and Vigouroux served, however, to familiarize French Catholics with the results of the new criticism. Vigouroux in 1891 initiated the *Dictionnaire de la Bible*, finally completed in 1912. Cautious and conservative, the work nevertheless marked a step forward in Catholic biblical research. (Current supplements to the dictionary [*VDBS*] are scientifically critical and an invaluable tool in scriptural research.) Although almost universally conservative in tone, Catholic biblical publication from around the end of the 19th cent. evinced a growing awareness of modern critical problems in the interpretation of the OT.

35 (b) M.-J. Lagrange. Not all Catholic critics remained in a state of siege. The Dominican Marie-Joseph Lagrange (1855–1938) chose to meet the higher criticism on its own grounds. At a Catholic scientific congress held in Fribourg, Switzerland, in 1897, he championed a positive response to the challenges of higher criticism. Limiting himself to Pentateuchal criticism, he questioned the legitimacy and cogency of objections alleged against the investigation of Pentateuchal sources. The new criticism rightly demands, affirmed Lagrange, that the critic replace his modern Western concepts with a Semitic view of authorship and historicity. Further, in the testimony to Mosaic authorship furnished by Scripture and tradition, one must distinguish between the literary and historical testimony; both are valid, but the literary tradition is not so cogent as the historical.

Five years later, Lagrange broadened his field from the Pentateuch to the OT as a whole and entered a plea for criticism according to sound historical method. In his *Historical Criticism and the Old Testament* (London, 1905) he demonstrated the application of such a procedure to the besetting problems of Catholic exegesis: the relation of criticism to dogma, to science, and to history. Lagrange's work was intended to allay the fears of those who were convinced that the use of the historical method would go counter to what they considered the first duty of the Catholic critic—submission to the authority of the Church. Lagrange showed, for example, how the exegete, although upholding the immutability of truth can still deal with the obvious fact of dogmatic development, especially in the OT; though he is unable to subscribe to the evolutionistic theory of religion, the exegete cannot ignore the growth of doctrine apparent in Scripture. To trace this development he must employ the historical method in the study of Scripture.

In similar fashion Lagrange examined the relation of science to the biblical narrative, reaffirming that scientific instruction is not to be expected in the sacred writings. To those concerned with critical attacks upon the historicity of biblical records, Lagrange insisted that the first task in assessing the value of those portions having the appearance of history is to analyze their literary genres. Lagrange's initial sketch of literary forms in history was expanded and sanctioned later in Pius XII's *Divino Afflante Spiritu* (→ Church Pronouncements, 72:20–23). Lagrange was not content to propound theory to Catholic biblicists; in his writings in *Revue Biblique* (which he established in 1892) he indefatigably applied principles of scientific research to biblical interpretation. Catholic biblical criticism has advanced so far beyond Lagrange that one can easily fail to appreciate both the acumen of his critical views and his courage in expressing them. Had the course he charted been followed, Catholic criticism of the earlier 20th cent. would have been quite different. (For his life and work, see R. de Vaux, *Bible et Orient* [Paris, 1967] 9–22; also *Le Père Lagrange au service de la Bible* [ed. P. Benoit; Paris, 1967]. For further information, → Modern NT Criticism, 41:37; also → 56, 61 below.)

36 (c) A. van Hoonacker. The research of Van Hoonacker (1857–1933), professor at Louvain, is another landmark in the history of Catholic exegesis. He advocated the methodology proposed by Lagrange for OT interpretation, and of particular interest is his historico-critical study of the Hexateuch, *De compositione et de origine Mosaica Hexateuchi* (Bruges, 1949). Though posthumously published, the ms. was composed between 1896 and 1906. Considering the progress of biblical studies in the 40 years between the composition and the publication of the work, it is not surprising that *De compositione* has nothing to say about many questions and methods vital in present-day research. It is surprising, however, that so early a study anticipates the analyses and conclusions of later scholars. That he was far in advance of his age can be seen from the freshness and cogency that, within limits, his criticism still retains. Van Hoonacker summed up the findings of his study under two headings: first, the existence of documents and subdocuments in the Hexateuch cannot be doubted; second, the role of Moses in the composition of the primary sources demands that he be recognized as the author of the substance of the Pentateuch.

Van Hoonacker also made important contributions to the reconstruction of post-exilic Judaism by proposing that Nehemiah preceded Ezra in Jerusalem (*Néhémie et Esdras* [Louvain, 1890]; → History of Israel, 75:95; → Chronicler, 24:82).

RESEARCH IN THE TWENTIETH CENTURY

37 **(I) Influence of H. Gunkel's Methods.** As the inadequacies of Wellhausenism became more obvious, even biblicists who harbored no objections on dogmatic grounds began to doubt that Wellhausen's analytic methods were really helping to attain the goals of exegesis. The barrenness of much biblical research in the last years of the 19th cent. made critics wonder, with some uneasiness, if all was said and done when close literary scrutiny had neatly parceled the sacred writings into their component parts.

(A) Gunkel's Contributions. Of all the reactions to the classic methodology of the 19th cent., the form criticism of Hermann Gunkel (1862–1932) was the most impressive, but its opposition to classic historico-literary analysis should not be exaggerated. Only because, he considered the work of literary analysis successfully accomplished did Gunkel assume the tasks proposed in his new method. He had no quarrel with literary criticism as such; yet he regretted that such indispensable literary criticism had limited itself to a critique of the state and origin of the sources, together with their minute philological analysis. This approach to the sacred writings, Gunkel contended, assumes that the critic is dealing with matter transmitted in written form. That present-day critics have taken to heart Gunkel's warning against the exclusiveness of literary criticism is apparent in the work of Otto Eissfeldt, a biblicist distinguished for his literary analysis of the OT; he devotes almost one-fifth of his *OTI* to a discussion of the preliterary forms of the OT.

38 (a) Form-critical Method. Gunkel insisted that exegesis must be founded on the recognition of separate preliterary and oral traditions from which the written documents eventually developed. To understand the sacred writers and their work—an accomplishment that Gunkel considered to be the proper goal of exegesis—the critic must supplement literary analysis by a thorough study of the history behind the final literary production. Gunkel was aware of the impossibility of establishing a chronological literary sequence; indeed, he affirmed our ignorance of the dates and authorship of almost the entire OT. But the would-be historian of Israelite literature must separate units of tradition from their secondary context in the final work and penetrate to the original data behind them. This process does not ignore the role of individual composers; still it must be observed that Hebr religion, conservative in form and content, is more concerned with the typical than with the individual and that it expresses this interest in formal, conventional categories or genres (*Gattungen*). Therefore, according to Gunkel, the history of Israelite literature is the history of Israelite *Gattungen*, and the historian's first task is the determination of the form in which the thought has been clothed. On the basis of stylistic elements, contents, and interest a particular unit is defined, e.g. taunt song, dirge, or folk legend. To determine the form, it is indispensable to know the particular life situation (the *Sitz im Leben*) that gave rise to it.

Once they have been isolated and placed in a life setting, the original oral data must be followed in their process of developing and merging into larger cycles, and finally becoming part of the entity found in the Bible. Tracing this growth is a delicate and tedious process, indispensably assisted by the results of archaeological investigations and by the recovery of the literature of the ancient Near East. Striking extrabiblical parallels to Israelite life and literature have been increasingly utilized in the investigation of Hebr genres, though perhaps not always with due recognition of biblical modifications. In his study of forms, Gunkel worked necessarily with small blocks of tradition; but he never lost sight of the fact that total effect of the complexes of tradition must be kept in mind if the resulting "book" is to be fully understood. (For a full study of form criticism, see K. Koch, *Was ist Formgeschichte?* [2nd ed.; Neukirchen, 1967].)

To supplement the cold, detached analysis of 19th-cent. criticism Gunkel proposed an aesthetic, literary approach to the OT (he has been called "a scientific Herder"; → 16 above). True exegesis must do more than furnish an exposition of the text; it must also reveal the varied situations and the complex personalities whose interactions produced the writing in its definitive form. Thus exegesis for Gunkel is more an art than a science; nevertheless, aesthetic considerations, though important, were secondary for him. The OT forms part of mankind's literary heritage; but it is also the expression of a unique religious experience, which, Gunkel maintained, can best be apprehended by *literary* appreciation. The main tenets of his system were presented in the introduction to his commentary on Gn, published separately in English as *The Legends of Genesis* (Chicago, 1901). In *Reden und Aufsätze* (Göttingen, 1931), a collection of essays and lectures, he developed and perfected his method.

Gunkel conceived his method while he was engaged in religio-historical studies that laid stress upon the popular bases of religion, especially as they were illustrated in folk literature like myths and legends (→ 29 above). Tentative suggestions about myth in the OT had been offered as early as Eichhorn; indeed, 19th-cent. critics who denied scientific historicity to biblical records saw myth everywhere. Gunkel denied, however, that true myth is to be found in the Bible. Although mythic elements abound in the legends, Israelite monotheism rendered them colorless and eliminated their grosser aspects. Present-day criticism questions the definition that considers myth necessarily polytheistic and suggests that myth relates more to the manner of thought than to content.

(Dulles, A., "Symbol, Myth, and Biblical Revelation," *TS* 27 [1966] 1–26. McKenzie, J. L., "Myth and the Old Testament," *CBQ* 21 [1959] 265–82; → Aspects OT Thought, 77:23–31.)

39 (b) Psalm Studies. After his analysis of genres in OT prose, Gunkel undertook a similar investigation of poetry. His studies of the psalms became the classic foundation for subsequent research in Hebr poetry. Years of research produced his monumental *Einleitung in die Psalmen* (Göttingen, 1928–33), devoted to the problems of literary type, distinctive characteristics, and the historical development of the psalms. Using cultic aspects as a basis, he classified the psalms according to their general subject matter, e.g., thanksgiving, lament, or praise (→ Psalms, 35:6–17). Then, after studying the common characteristics of the psalms in a given category, he arrived at a series of conventional literary forms into which much of the religious poetry of the Bible can be fitted. Since the forms gave evidence of a long period of development, Gunkel concluded that many psalms had originated at an early date, even though they did not reach their final form until shortly before the Exile. Post-exilic psalms, of course, exhibit the final pattern and show no trace of a long period of development (→ Psalms, 35:4).

Comparison of the psalms with other ancient literatures also revealed that many forms once thought original with the Hebrews had their counterparts in the religious poetry of Babylon and Egypt (and Ugarit; → Excursus Israel, 11:11).

(Gunkel, H., "The Religion of the Psalms," *What Remains of the Old Testament* [N.Y., 1928] 69–114; *The Psalms, a Form-Critical Introduction* [Facet Biblical Series 19; Phila., 1967]. Also Fleming, J., *Thirty Psalmists* [N.Y., 1938]—the personalities of the psalter in light of Gunkel's theory.)

40 (c) Evaluation of Form Criticism. It is hardly an exaggeration to say that Gunkel's method of form criticism has given direction to the course of 20th-cent. scriptural scholarship. By emphasis upon oral tradition and by the utilization of the archaeological and literary materials of the Near East, it approached closer to the life situation that produced the biblical writings than did static literary criticism. Gunkel anticipated the work of Dibelius and Bultmann in their proposed methodology for the analysis of literary forms in the NT (→ Modern NT Criticism, 41:44–45). Nevertheless, Gunkel's system is not without deficiencies of its own. For example, Gunkel rightly held that the primitive traditions were oral. But, since oral presentation places limits upon the length of a given unit, Gunkel made brevity a criterion of age, holding that the shortest accounts are necessarily the oldest. As the primitive forms developed, affirmed Gunkel, they necessarily lost life and distinctiveness. In accord with his view that it is impossible to write a chronological literary history of Israel, he also stated that objective elements of history are not to be looked for in the sacred writings. Many today would criticize such general stances. Finally, although not in itself irreligious or antireligious, form criticism perhaps lends itself more readily to evolutionistic, naturalistic theories about religion.

41 **(B) Gunkel's Followers.**

(a) H. Gressmann. Enthusiastic followers of Gunkel applied the techniques of form criticism to other genres in the OT. As Gunkel's chief collaborator, Gressmann (1877–1927) indefatigably explored the influence of Near Eastern peoples upon Israel, especially in the field of religion; and his collection of texts and pictures related to the OT furnished biblicists pertinent materials for comparative studies. In examining Israelite religious development, he placed more emphasis upon mythic elements than did Gunkel, averring that they had preserved intact their primitive value. Gressmann also used the techniques of form criticism in his analysis of historical genre: Written biblical history represents the final redaction of many units, all of them dependent upon a primitive oral tradition to which the critic must penetrate. As Gressmann's techniques were taken up by others, there was a tendency to reduce the historical books of the OT to fragments.

42 (b) G. von Rad. In his use of form criticism Gerhard von Rad (b. 1901) became keenly aware of the falsification that can result from preoccupation with individual blocks of tradition. For Von Rad, it is as important to know the whole as to differentiate components. Therefore, the critic must examine not only the primitive tradition, but also the import it acquires in the final composition, for the significance of a tradition may be altered when it is built into a more comprehensive theme. Von Rad concedes that analysis is essential—both literary and form-critical. But analysis must be followed by synthesis and herein lies the difficulty: How to explain the coalescence of so much divergent material in the sacred books? Von Rad's solution lies in postulating key traditions, like the Exodus, the conquest of the land, and the covenant, which summarized Yahweh's saving acts for Israel. The cultic celebration of these saving acts implemented the original traditions and then transmitted them to succeeding generations. Critics question certain of Von Rad's claims, such as the primacy of the tradition of conquest of the land or the role of the Yahwist in the amalgamation of the traditions. Nevertheless, Von Rad's emphasis upon the process whereby the traditions became literary compositions and his attention to the guiding purposes behind the selection and amalgamation of materials are a healthy reaction against the fragmentation of biblical literature. Von Rad's principles and methodology can be seen in his *Studies in Deuteronomy* (SBT 9; Chicago, 1953) and in *Genesis: A Commentary* (OT Library; London, 1961). Interest in the theological program that dictated how traditions developed has caused Von Rad in recent years to devote his studies to an exposition of OT Theology (→ 55 below).

43 (c) M. Noth. The OT research of Martin Noth (b. 1902) has been heavily concentrated upon the Pentateuch, or more properly, on the Tetrateuch, since Noth regards Dt as part of the deuteronomic history stretching from Dt to 2 Kgs (→ 1–2 Kings, 10:79). Noth sets for himself the task of determining the history of the traditions behind the biblical documents; this he accomplishes by isolating themes and by pushing back to the earliest stages of the tradition. Noth is very skeptical about the possibility of reconstructing the primitive history, because Israelite history began only with the tribal settlement in Israel. For Noth, all of Hebr history was bound up with the Israelite tribal federation (the amphictyony; → History of Israel, 75:46); indeed, the importance of his studies on the subject can scarcely be exaggerated; see his *Das System der zwölf Stämme Israels* (Stuttgart, 1930). If he is correct in his views, the institution of the tribal federation may well serve to connect countless OT elements that an older criticism understood only as a part of an evolutionistic schema. Nevertheless, Noth carries his hypothesis too far in giving the tribal federation characteristics of the later Gk amphictyony; surely, too, the Hebr federation was modified more sharply with the passage of time than Noth admits.

44 (d) A. Alt. Studies in Hebr law also underwent the influence of the form-critical method. Through careful examination of the prescriptions in the Pentateuchal codes, Albrecht Alt (1883–1956) classified biblical legislation according to form, content, and situation in life. The result of his research, published in 1934, contributed to an understanding of the nature and origin of biblical legislation and provided the classic distinction between apodictic laws and casuistic laws (→ Aspects OT Thought, 77:87). Because the biblical law codes were amalgamations of independent smaller units, the form-critical technique of studying small literary units has been most successful in the analysis of Hebr law. Research prompted by Alt's pioneering work has continued to establish chronology and to trace the situation in life, which, at least for apodictic law, appears to have been cultic observances at Hebr shrines. See Alt's *Essays on Old Testament History and Religion* (Anchor paperback; N.Y., 1968), especially 103–71.

45 **(II) The Scandinavian School.** In the hands of Scandinavian practitioners Gunkel's methodology underwent great changes. By increased emphasis upon oral tradition and by concentration on the cultic aspects of myth, northern biblicists so altered Gunkel's system as to form a separate school—a school whose goals and methods are not yet fully definable.

(A) Prominent Scholars.

(a) J. Pedersen; H. S. Nyberg. The first indication of the direction that these scholars were taking was given by Pedersen when he rejected the Wellhausian documentary theory and accented the sociological factor of the life situation that gave rise to various traditions (cf. *Israel: Its Life and Culture* [4 vols.; London, 1926, 1940]). A further break with the documentary theory came with Nyberg's assertion of the primacy of oral traditions. His pioneering work, a study of Hos (1935), had for its goal the recovery of the *ipsissima verba* of the prophet by an analysis of their underlying traditions. In Nyberg's theory, the traditions are not rigid; they suffer alteration and deterioration, but they have the advantage of providing the critic with living material, not dead texts.

46 (b) S. Mowinckel. Since Wellhausen's dismissal of Hebr cult as a relatively late and unimportant factor in the development of Hebr religion, few biblicists had been attracted to cultic studies. The recovery of Near Eastern texts revealed, however, the tremendous significance of cult in ancient religious life. As additional materials were unearthed, Sigmund Mowinckel (1884–1965), one of Gunkel's most brilliant students and a literary critic as well, went far beyond Gunkel in his analysis of the ritual aspects of myth, especially as found in the Hebr psalms (on Mowinckel, cf. *JBL* 85 [1966] 315–25). In his six-volume study of the psalms (1921–24) he postulated a New Year's enthronement feast in Israel (→ Religious Institutions, 76:151–154; → Psalms, 35:6) like the enthronement of Marduk known in Babylon. Mowinckel's views had great influence upon British scholars whose approach to the Bible was anthropological. Members of this "Cultic School"—chiefly S. A. Cook and S. H. Hooke—averred that Semitic cult was based upon myth common to all peoples of the Near East and that supposedly distinct ritual structures could be reduced to the same schema (S. H. Hooke, *Myth, Ritual and Kingship* [Oxford, 1958]).

47 (c) I. Engnell. The cultic importance of the king, first suggested in Mowinckel's thesis of an Israelite New Year's Feast, was further stressed by I. Engnell in *Studies in Divine Kingship* (Uppsala, 1943). He regarded the concept of divine kingship as central to Oriental cult; moreover, he used this same idea to elucidate many portions of the Bible besides the psalms, e.g., Engnell explained the Suffering Servant (→ Deutero-Isaiah, 22:5) in terms of divine kingship. Most recently, see his *Studies in Divine Kingship in the Ancient Near East* (Oxford, 1967).

Still more radically, Engnell declared the complete inadequacy of literary criticism and even of form criticism insofar as it admits of written sources and redactions. For valid results, Engnell asserted, the critic must work solely with blocks of oral tradition, which are always cultic in origin. The traditio-historical method advocated by Engnell and his compatriots seeks to trace a history of the formation of literature from oral tradition.

48 **(B) Critique.** The chief features of the Scandinavian School—the primacy of oral tradition and of cult—are also its principal weakness. Oral tradition, especially as regards stability, can scarcely bear the burden that Scandinavian critics put upon it. Further, if the spoken matter is clearly determined, it constitutes a source resembling the documents spurned by traditio-historical scholars. Their description of Israelite cult sometimes presumes institutions and observances for which there is no cogent proof, and at other times it neglects the peculiar use that Israel made of what she borrowed.

Mowinckel himself, though he has exerted profound influence upon the Scandinavian School, differs sharply from the group in regard to the stability of oral transmission and the exclusive validity of the traditio-historical method. Nevertheless, although the assumptions and excesses of the cultic school have been justly censured, its basic premise of the importance of cult is being ever more firmly established. The work of the prophets, for many years considered independent of and even hostile to cult, is now generally viewed in a cultic setting (→ Prophetic Literature, 12:14). Such emphasis upon cultic factors has made less significant the 19th-cent. distinction between priests and prophets. The latter did not repudiate cult as such; their attack was directed against the divorce of cult from morality.

(Ahlström, G., "Oral and Written Transmission: Some Considerations," *HarvTR* 59 [1966] 69–81. Fohrer, G., *Studien zur alttestamentlichen Prophetie: 1949–65* [BZAW 99; Berlin, 1967]. Mowinckel, S., *Prophecy and Tradition* [Oslo, 1946]. Wright, G. E., "Cult and History: A Study of a Current Problem in Old Testament Interpretation," *Interp* 16 [1962] 3–20. Zimmerli, W., *The Law and the Prophets* [Harper Torchbook; N.Y., 1965].)

49 **(III) Trends in History and Theology.**

(A) OT Historiography. It has already been noted that 19th-cent. historicism worked on the principle that ancient narratives are reflections of the era in which they were composed but are unreliable sources for the earlier age they report; hence accounts like the patriarchal narratives were denied historical worth. Reinforced by the concept of religious evolution, such a view reduced early Hebr religion to a retrojection of later Yahwism. Archaeological discoveries radically altered this harsh conclusion. Countless texts contemporaneous with the time of Israel's beginnings have provided frames of reference for the historical evaluation of biblical traditions. For example, although archaeological evidence has not confirmed any specific event in the patriarchal narratives, it has furnished many parallels and corroborated many details, thus showing that the accounts are to be taken seriously as a portrait of institutions in the patriarchal period and that consequently they reflect a valid memory of the past (→ History of Israel, 75:24).

(a) M. Noth; G. von Rad. In spite of such presumption of authenticity attached to biblical traditions, some scholars do not concede that biblical narratives are reliable sources of history. M. Noth, one of the most influential of these critics (→ 43 above), agrees that the sacred traditions do contain historical information, but they cannot be credited as a coherent historical narrative. The extent to which they can be taken as historical sources is a problem to be solved only by examination of each separate unit of tradition. Noth values archaeological discoveries, but their witness is, after all, indirect, and therefore cannot determine the historical accuracy of the narratives. (Cf. Noth, *Hist.*; → Biblical Archaeology, 74:62.)

G. von Rad (→ 42 above) shares Noth's views to a certain extent; but whereas Noth stresses the impossibility of determining historical content, Von Rad emphasizes the irrelevancy of such determination. A historical kernel is found, to be sure, in many of the biblical accounts, but the genuine historical concern is God's dealing with Israel. Accordingly, says Von Rad, the faith of the Hebrews must be explained in terms of what Israel thought of its relation to Yahweh, not by results of studies of Israel's relations to her neighbors nor by historical facts (→ 55 below).

50 (b) W. F. Albright; J. Bright. Although agreeing with Noth and his followers that scientific history is not to be found in the biblical records, William F. Albright (b. 1891; → Biblical Archaeology, 74:15) and his disciple John Bright are more sanguine in their appraisal of the biblical narratives as sources of Israelite history. They hold that if the writing of Hebr history is not to be completely nihilistic, the historian must examine the traditions against the world of the day (known chiefly from archaeological discoveries) and in that light must draw whatever conclusions the evidence permits. In biblical historiography the distinctions between the empiric methods advocated by Albright and the tradition-history of Noth are becoming ever more sharply drawn; see Bright, *Early Israel.* Doubtless, future research in both archaeology and the history of biblical traditions will establish rapprochement between the two methods and lead to a fuller understanding of primitive Israel. (Cf. Albright, *FSAC*; Bright, *Hist.*)

Increased appreciation of Israel's position among the peoples of the Near East has given new life to OT historiography in the 20th cent., but it is not the sole factor responsible for the revitalization. Interest has been heightened by modern research into the nature of the Hebr concept of history (e.g., C. R. North, *op. cit.*). Such studies show that Israel's unique treatment of history is explicable only in terms of her religion, which preserved traditions illustrating the theme of her special relation to God and his saving deeds on her behalf. More than a chronicle, Hebr history transcends and transfigures the facts it relates by showing the hand of Yahweh directing his people to their destiny.

(Freedman, D. N., "The Biblical Idea of History," *Interp* 21 [1967] 32–49. Speiser, E. A., "The Biblical Idea of History in Its Common Near Eastern Setting," *IsrEJ* 7 [1957] 201–16.)

51 **(B) Earlier Decline of Biblical Theology.** So long as the Hebr concept of history was assumed to be the same as that of the modern European scholar, and so long as religion was interpreted in terms of immanentism, i.e., deterministic evolution from lower to higher forms, the task of the OT theologian differed little from that of the historian. He had only to record phenomena, assuming that the reality witnessed by the OT could be comprehended by historical means. The evolutionistic explanation of Israel's understanding of Yahweh resulted in the subordination of theology to history; or better, theology and the history of Israelite religion were identified. Furthermore, the spirit that pervaded all of 19th-cent. scriptural criticism—a strong reaction against the dogmatic theologizing of preceding ages—hastened the decline of biblical theology.

Wellhausen's historical investigations provided the groundwork for *B. Stade's* theology of the OT, the most significant study of biblical theology in the late 19th cent. (1887). Stade defined OT biblical theology as a history of religion under the old covenant, which he frankly regarded as mere preparation for the fuller revelation given in the person of Jesus Christ. Succeeding biblicists, like *E. Sellin* and *R. Smend*, were satisfied to describe the historical process in the evolution of Yahwism and had little to say about the content of Israel's religious concepts. Only in recent decades is biblical scholarship recovering from this decline (J. D. Smart, "The Death and Rebirth of Old Testament Theology," *JRel* 23 [1943] 1–11, 125–36).

52 **(C) The "New" Biblical Theology.** Just as rationalists of a century ago reacted forcibly against the theological dogmatism of their predecessors, so contemporary exegetes are reacting against the critical orthodoxy of the 19th cent. For too long a time, they say, an exaggerated concern for scientific objectivity in biblical studies has rendered exegesis barren. Techniques that are successful in the analysis of profane literatures cannot elucidate the religious experience recorded in Scripture; for the Bible is more than an accurate reflection of ancient viewpoints, and its plus factor does not come within the ambit of scientifically verifiable analysis. Biblical theology has been revitalized in the 20th cent. because critics have come to realize more and more that the elements of inexplicability in Hebr religion demand theological commitment from the exegete if he is to interpret them truly and completely. Consequently, a key issue in the field of OT research is whether the biblical scholar can fully interpret Scripture by literary and historical analysis or whether he must also be a theologian. The commitment envisaged by modern biblical theologians is not simply an unquestioning return to the older orthodoxy. It works hand in hand with objective, scientific criticism, realizing that the Bible does not describe propositional revelation, but rather the response of men to God's self-revealing intervention in history. To attain the essence of that divine revelation both literary and historical criticism are necessary, but of themselves they cannot capture the character of the biblical presentation of faith.

To supplement the scientific analysis of the OT, greater numbers of scholars are turning to a study of OT theology. As yet, however, there is no consensus about the nature of biblical theology nor about its relation to traditional theological categories (L. Alonso Schökel, *NRT* 81 [1959] 337–54; F. J. Cwiekowski, *CBQ* 24 [1962] 404–11; → Aspects OT Thought, 77:3–4). Some critics view biblical theology as a systematic account of specific religious ideas found in the OT, e.g., E. Jacob (*Theology of the Old Testament* [London, 1958]) or P. Heinisch (*Theology of the Old Testament* [Collegeville, Minn., 1950]). So conceived, biblical theology becomes a neat, well-documented system, forced into thought patterns foreign to it. The study of P. van Imschoot, a leading biblical theologian among Catholic scholars, suggests the influence of an outline of Catholic dogma. His *Théologie de l'Ancien Testament* (2 vols.; Paris, 1954–56) lays little stress upon the developmental nature of biblical theology.

53 (a) W. Eichrodt. One of the most significant and influential of the new studies is Walther Eichrodt's *Theology of the Old Testament* (Ger 1934; Eng [Phila.] 1961/67). By combining the historical method with theological interpretation, Eichrodt (b. 1890) attempts to present Hebr religion as an entity whose organic unity can be best seen in the central notion of the *covenant* (→ Aspects OT Thought, 77:74ff.). All characteristic features of OT theology, Eichrodt holds, stemmed from the basic notion of the alliance with Yahweh originating in Mosaic times. He does not deny that Israel's beliefs underwent development in the course of the ages, but the orientation of the developmental process had been initially determined by Israel's covenantal relationship to God. Eichrodt's historico-theological study has become a classic; some critics question, however, the validity of founding so complex a matter as OT theology upon a single concept, comprehensive though that concept may be.

54 (b) Christological Orientation; Key Themes. Other biblical theologians have found the unifying element of the OT in its orientation to Christ as the climax of divine revelation (→ Hermeneutics, 71:51–53). This strongly Christological interpretation of the OT is found in the work of W. Vischer, translated as *The Witness of the Old Testament to Christ* (London, 1949) and in O. Procksch's *Theologie des Alten Testaments*, a posthumous work edited by Von Rad (Gütersloh, 1950). A more flexible approach to Israel's understanding of her faith appears in the work of scholars who analyze various biblical themes, tracing the growth of an idea or of a doctrine throughout the various stages of its development. This method is exemplified in Jacques Guillet's *Themes of the Bible* (Notre Dame, 1960), which elucidates the biblical understanding of key concepts like sin, grace, justice, and truth by examining them as they appear in the different books of the OT (yet → Hermeneutics, 71:23).

55 (c) G. von Rad. Easily the most challenging among recent theologies is the *Old Testament Theology* (Ger 1957/60; Eng [N.Y.] 1962/65) of Von Rad (→ 42, 49 above). Its subtitle, "The Theology of the Historical Traditions of Israel," suggests its trend. Von Rad asserts that Israel's belief is founded upon the deeds of Yahweh for Israel; but lest one think that historical events are paramount in biblical theology, Von Rad affirms that the historical data are really irrelevant. The point at issue is Israel's concept of her relation to Yahweh, a relationship that was established slowly in the course of many experiences. Thus her theology is not so much a record of truths communicated, as an account of Israel's endeavor to understand Yahweh and herself as she stands before him. Since the historical testimony that Israel received from Yahweh was only gradually formulated, any attempt to restrict the religion of Israel into a hard and fast system will be a betrayal. Furthermore, states Von Rad, the Hebrews showed no urge to reduce all data to logical order, and their unconcern for a single unifying principle is an additional deterrent to the systemization of biblical thought. It was only her constant reflection on historical traditions, which she combined and recombined to illustrate her beliefs, that bestowed organic unity.

Under these circumstances, no facile amalgamation of texts will suffice to show Israel's understanding of monotheism, of divine attributes, of sin, sacrifice, or death. The patient pondering of a text (with, of course, the help of all the auxiliary sciences) is necessary to set the text in a context proper to its time and to the traditions that at one and the same time it builds upon and modifies. Von Rad sees OT theology centered in two points: covenant and kingdom. All of Yahweh's dealings with his people are interpreted in the light of these two events, and all of Israel's response moves around these foci. Von Rad is in no hurry to prove a point; he lets each portion of the text speak for itself, even if it cannot do this conclusively. His method yields no neat theological propositions, but what it lacks in precise formulation it makes up for in the insight it gains into the true position of Israel before Yahweh, a position whose changing foci make Von Rad's dynamic interpretation essential.

(Fannon, P., "A Theology of the Old Testament: Is It Possible?" *Scr* 19 [1967] 46–53. Winn, W., and N. Jacobson, "Present Tendencies in Biblical Theology," *Religion in Life* 32 [1962–63] 88–94.)

56 (IV) Catholic Biblical Criticism.

(A) Effects of Modernism. Unfortunately the precautions adopted to combat the heresy of Modernism (→ Church Pronouncements, 72:5) had halted the auspicious beginnings made by Lagrange (→ 35 above) and others. When some of Lagrange's works occasioned a warning from the Sacred Congregation of the Consistory (1912), he gave up OT research and transferred his interests to NT investigation. Just before his death, however, he returned to the OT in an article on Pentateuchal sources (*RB* 47 [1938] 163–83). If the anti-Modernist decrees imposed severe restraints upon OT research, on the good side they prevented Catholic scholars from swelling the number of rash and irresponsible critiques spawned by Wellhausenism. Nevertheless, safety was obtained at a high price to scholarship.

57 (B) Before "Divino Afflante Spiritu."

(a) J. Touzard. Since critics were emphasizing the Hexateuch during the decades following Wellhausen's statement of the documentary theory, Catholic OT scholars who wished to meet the challenge of higher criticism on its own grounds applied themselves to Hexateuchal studies. An important contribution to Catholic research in this area was J. Touzard's "Moïse et Josué" (*DAFC* 3 [1919] 695–755), a comprehensive analysis of the documentary theory. Touzard reiterated Lagrange's appeal for distinction between facts established by literary evidence and the rationalistic system in favor of which the literary data were employed. The views of Touzard were conservative by modern standards, but in his own day the Holy Office censured them as not safe enough to be taught.

58 (b) Diffusion of Catholic Scholarship. The founding of periodicals devoted to scriptural research and the institution of series of biblical publications, together with collective translations of the Bible into vernacular languages, provided critics with increased facilities for the expression of their views. In 1920 the Pontifical Biblical Institute inaugurated three periodicals: *Biblica*, *Orientalia*, and *Verbum Domini*, each concerned with a different aspect of biblical studies. The series *Études bibliques*, begun by Lagrange in 1902, now numbers more than 40 vols. Similar biblical series under Catholic auspices made an appearance throughout Europe. In 1935, L. Pirot (succeeded by A. Clamer) began to publish fascicles of a new Fr translation of the Bible (*PSB*). In Germany translations of and commentaries on the OT books entitled *Die heilige Schrift des Alten Testaments*, but popularly known as the *Bonner-Bibel*, were initiated in 1923 by F. Feldmann and H. Herkenne; the series is now complete and supplementary vols. have appeared. The quality of these efforts varied, of course, but they accomplished the valuable service of publicizing the new currents in Catholic scriptural studies. In the United States the establishment of *CBQ* (1938), the official organ of the Catholic Biblical Association, gave to American scriptural scholars a publication of their own and acquainted English-speaking Catholics with modern biblical research.

59 (c) A. Bea. Many Catholic exegetes remained hostile to the new criticism, even when it had been tempered by the more moderate views adopted by non-Catholic scholars after 1918. A certain tension can be seen in the earlier works of Augustin Cardinal Bea, S.J. His *De Pentateucho* (*Institutiones biblicae scholis accommodatae;* Rome, 1933) had two concerns: to establish the Mosaic authorship of the Pentateuch and to refute the rationalistic documentary system that denied it. He developed this refutation under three headings: philosophical, critico-literary, and historico-archaeological. Bea's positive exposition of Pentateuchal origins led him to conclude that Moses used many oral and written sources in the composition of the Pentateuch. Although Bea was quite familiar with modern critical methods, and although he has recently been acknowledged as a defender of freedom in Catholic biblical research (especially active at Vatican II), his earlier publications showed caution in dealing with contemporary criticism. He saw in form criticism an ally against rationalistic exegesis; yet the welcome he accorded it was not completely enthusiastic, because, he affirmed, it has been more effective in demolishing old tenets than in proposing new solutions. Furthermore, the excessive attention that the form-critical technique bestows upon individual blocks of tradition has caused a neglect of the personality of the sacred author (*SZ* 153 [1953–54] 91–104; for more recent views on form criticism, see his *The Study of the Synoptic Gospels* [N.Y., 1965]).

60 (C) After "Divino Afflante Spiritu."

(a) J. Chaine. Phenomenal strides in archaeology and in Oriental linguistics began to exert increasing influence upon Catholic criticism after 1930. Not, however, until Pope Pius XII's encyclical on biblical studies, *Divino Afflante Spiritu* (1943; → Church Pronouncements, 72:20–23), and the encouraging reply of the Pontifical Biblical Commission to Cardinal Suhard in 1948 (→ Church Pronouncements, 72:31) did Catholic scriptural scholarship move confidently forward. Chaine's translation and commentary, *Le livre de la Genèse* (LD 3; Paris, 1951), revealed the new freedom enjoyed by biblical scholars; for, dispensing with a lengthy and cautious investigation of the classic documentary system, he stated simply that he recognized the presence of three distinct documents in Gn. For the time, Chaine's work was quite liberal, even though he showed a somewhat rigid and mechanical concept of the documents, evincing little concern for the more flexible concept of traditions that had already become a preoccupation of non-Catholic biblicists.

61 (b) Jerusalem School. The École Biblique at Jerusalem, founded by Lagrange, continues to be a vital center for Catholic OT study, thanks to the research of Dominicans like F.-M. Abel (→ Biblical Geography,

73:13), L.-H. Vincent, and R. de Vaux (→ Biblical Archaeology, 74:12,18). The role of tradition in the formation of the sacred writings has received due attention in the biblical translations and commentaries sponsored by the school; indeed, the word "tradition" is the hallmark of the criticism found in *La Sainte Bible* [*de Jérusalem*] (1948–54; → Texts, 69:175). Among the OT scholars affiliated with the school, Roland de Vaux is doubtless pre-eminent. An editor of *RB* and director of the school, a leading figure in the recovery and interpretation of the Dead Sea Scrolls, an archaeologist and writer, De Vaux is rightly acknowledged to be the leading Catholic OT critic of the day. The fruit of long years of research and writing appears in his *AI*.

62 (c) OTHER CATHOLIC CRITICISM. Scripture scholars distinguished both for teaching and writing are found on the theological faculties of many European universities. E. Podechard, for many years professor at Lyon, produced the most significant critical study of the Ps by a Catholic (*Le Psautier* [Lyons, 1949–54]). The Sulpicians Albert Gelin of Lyons, André Feuillet, and Henri Cazelles of the Institut Catholique of Paris have enjoyed distinguished careers as teachers and writers. In Belgium, J. Coppens, Van Hoonacker's student and successor at Louvain, is one of the most prolific OT scholars. His interests range widely over the fields of the primitive history, messianism, Josiah's reform, and the history of OT criticism. The collective efforts of Eng exegetes have produced a commentary on Sacred Scripture (*CCHS*), a work quite conservative in tone. American scholars are currently acquiring increased stature; and one of the most encouraging signs of their vitality is the new Confraternity translation of the Bible from the original texts (→ Texts, 69:174). The scholarly linguistic studies of P. W. Skehan and L. F. Hartman of Catholic University, the trenchant criticism of J. L. McKenzie, and the high-level popularizations of B. Vawter and R. E. Murphy provide evidence that OT scholarship in the United States has come of age.

63 **(V) Jewish Biblical Criticism.** Most of our discussion in this article has concerned Christian OT scholarship; and we cannot hope in such a brief treatment to do justice to Jewish biblical scholarship with its own rich tradition, flavored by midrashic and talmudic lore. In modern times, however, with our increasing emphasis on distinguishing (but not divorcing) biblical thought from subsequent religious developments, Jewish and Christian biblical studies have much more in common, since scholars of both traditions use the same scientific methods and tools. Let us mention a few of the scholars representative of the Jewish contribution to biblical study.

In biblical archaeology the Israeli discoveries have been very significant, and the names of E. L. Sukenik and of his son, Y. Yadin, are prominent (→ Biblical Archaeology, 74:21). Valuable maps of ancient and Roman Palestine have been drawn in Israel (→ Biblical Geography, 73:10, 12). Among important orientalists and semitists we may mention: B. Landsberger and E. A. Speiser (Mesopotamian studies), C. Gordon and H. L. Ginsberg (Ugaritic), M. Greenberg (The *Ḫab/piru* [New Haven, 1955]), E. Kutscher (Aramaic), D. Diringer (Hebrew alphabet), and H. J. Polotsky (Coptic, etc.). In the comparative study of ancient Near East religions there have been studies relative to the OT by J. Morgenstern (especially on biblical calendars) and T. H. Gaster (*Thespis: Ritual, Myth and Drama in the Ancient Near East* [Anchor ed.; N.Y., 1961]). In a previous generation a major contribution to textual studies was made by S. Schechter (→ Texts, 69:37), and more recently P. Katz and H. M. Orlinsky have worked on the origins of the LXX. C. Rabin, D. Flusser, Y. Yadin, and J. Licht have done studies of the Dead Sea Scrolls, while M. H. Goshen-Gottstein is the director of the monumental Hebrew University project for producing a new critical text of the Hebr OT (→ Texts, 69:48). An important study in biblical history is J. Kaufmann's *The Religion of Israel* (Chicago, 1960); and A. Malamat, B. Mazar-Maisler, and E. Bickerman (Maccabean period) are notable historians.

64 The number of scientific Jewish commentaries on the biblical books is rapidly increasing. (Here we shall mention authors' names; for more information on the works consult the bibliographies of the respective commentary articles.) U. (M. D.) Cassuto and E. A. Speiser have written on Gn. The prophets have been studied by A. Heschel (*The Prophets* [N.Y., 1962]), J. Morgenstern (Am), H. L. Ginsberg (Dn, Is), and S. Blank (Is, Jer). Commentaries on Eccl have been written by R. Gordis (also on Job) and H. L. Ginsberg, while M. Buttenweiser's work on Ps has been of major import.

65 **(VI) Conclusion.** More than 250 years have elapsed since the inauguration of modern biblical research. During much of that time the OT has been submitted to devastating attacks from every quarter. By their denial of a supernatural order, rationalism and deism made the Bible irrelevant as a communication of the word of God to men; de-Christianized humanism reduced reading the Bible to an aesthetic experience; evolutionism considered all religions a deterministic development from primitive forms, allowing no place for the free intervention of God in history. Yet despite all that the OT has suffered at the hands of the misguided or the malicious, biblical scholarship in the second half of the 20th cent. can hopefully anticipate fruitful research in the years to come. With the passage of time the line of demarcation between Catholic and non-Catholic critics has become less sharply drawn. Since the decline of the 19th cent. concomitants of biblical research—rationalism, Hegelianism, evolutionism, and historicism—Catholic exegetes have found the critical atmosphere more congenial and have evinced greater readiness to employ the methods and to accept some of the conclusions of non-Catholic biblical scholarship. Although the past 50 years have witnessed great progress by both Catholics and non-Catholics, many problems still demand further investigation—monotheism in Israel, primitive Hebr history, the concept of messianism, to mention only a few.

In his work the Catholic exegete envisages a twofold task. First he must try to understand the inspired writers as did their contemporaries. But this is not an end in itself; he must, in the second place, use his historical understanding of the Bible to elucidate the religious ideas that lie at the heart of the writing. Thus with the commitment of faith, aided by the techniques of modern research, the Catholic critic can make greater progress in the explanation of the sacred texts, for, as Pius XII notes in *Divino Afflante Spiritu*, "This true liberty of the sons of God, which adheres faithfully to the teaching of the Church and accepts gratefully the contributions of profane science, this liberty, upheld and sustained by the confidence of all, is the condition and source of all solid progress in Catholic doctrine."

71

HERMENEUTICS

Raymond E. Brown, S.S.

BIBLIOGRAPHY

1 *L'Ancien Testament et les chrétiens* (Paris, 1951). Barr, J., *Old and New in Interpretation* (London, 1966). Brown, R. E., *SPSS*—this work contains an ample bibliography, which is completed in *CBQ* 25 [1963] 282–85. Cerfaux, L., J. Coppens, and J. Gribomont, *Problèmes et méthode d'exégèse théologique* (Louvain, 1950). Coppens, J., *Les harmonies des deux testaments* (Tournai, 1949). Daniélou, J., *From Shadow to Reality* (Westminster, 1960; orig. ed. Fr 1950). De Lubac, H., *L'Écriture dans la tradition* (Paris, 1966). Funk, R. W., *Language, Hermeneutic, and Word of God* (N.Y., 1966). Lys, D., *The Meaning of the Old Testament: An Essay on Hermeneutics* (Nashville, 1967). Marlé, R., *Introduction to Hermeneutics* (N.Y., 1967). Nineham, D. E. (ed.), *The Church's Use of the Bible Past and Present* (London, 1963). Robinson, J. M. and J. B. Cobb, *The New Hermeneutic* (NFT 2; N.Y., 1964). Smart, J. D., *The Interpretation of Scripture* (Phila., 1961).

2 OUTLINE

INTRODUCTION

3 **(I) Meaning of Hermeneutics.** The Gk word *hermēneia* was used to cover a broad scope in the process of clarification. First, it could refer to interpretation by *speech* itself, inasmuch as language interprets what is in a man's mind; this usage of the word was especially significant when there was an instance of human

language used to interpret the divine will. Second, the word *hermēneia* could refer to the process of *translation* from an unintelligible language to an intelligible one, e.g., the *hermēneia* of tongues in 1 Cor 12:10, which was a charismatic gift with a revelatory character. Perhaps we should stress that "translation" here should also be taken in a sense that is no longer common except in ecclesiastical jargon, namely that of moving things from one place to another (e.g., translating a body to a new burial ground). Part of the clarifying task of *hermēneia* was to translate past meaning to the present. Third, the word *hermēneia* was used for *interpretation by commentary and explanation.*

The understanding that *hermēneia* covered speech, translation, and commentary as part of the process of clarification was lost sight of in the subsequent evolution of the use of the word, and now modern scholars are trying to recapture the fullness of the concept in their study of the hermeneutical task (→ 49 below). We shall confine the word "hermeneutic," in the singular, to this larger modern understanding of the task of interpretation; and we shall use "hermeneutics," reflecting the Lat plural *hermeneutica*, for the science of meaning (in this case, the meaning of Scripture). Whereas in the more ancient and fuller understanding, *hermēneia* involved exegesis or interpretation, in the standard biblical manuals hermeneutics is distinguished from exegesis, as the theoretical from the practical. Exegesis is looked upon as the practical application of the theoretical rules supplied by hermeneutics. Cf. J. M. Robinson, *New Hermeneutic*, ix–x, 1–11.

4 In discussing hermeneutics as the science of biblical meaning, biblical manuals have customarily divided it into three treatises: (1) noematics, which deals with the various senses of Scripture; (2) heuristics, which explains how to discover the sense of a passage; (3) prophoristics, which gives the rules for expounding the sense of a Scripture passage to others. These formal divisions are unwieldy; below, in treating the senses of Scripture (literal, more-than-literal), we shall cover both noematics and heuristics, and under the titles of "Preaching" and "Communication" (→ 93–102) we shall treat certain aspects of prophoristics. Moreover, since the overspeculative treatments of hermeneutics in the manuals often have an aspect of unreality, we shall concentrate on the practical consequences of what we discuss.

5 **(II) General Observations.** To determine the sense of any written work is largely to determine what its author meant when he wrote it. As we shall see in the treatment of the more-than-literal senses of Scripture, it is true that sometimes the written word takes on a life of its own, and the words may convey more than what their author meant them to say. Modern literary criticism seems to be moving away from an exclusive emphasis on what the author intended to a broader emphasis on what his words actually convey to the individual reader. Nevertheless, allowing and, indeed, insisting on this broader emphasis, we still maintain that the principal task of interpretation centers around the author's intended meaning.

6 In the Bible this task is especially complicated because, as with other ancient books, the author's period of time, manner of expression, and (Semitic) cast of thought are so far removed from our own. Even to specify what or who an "author" is, is difficult because the ancient concept of author is wider than our modern concept. In reference to the biblical books, the word "author" covers at least five different relationships between the man whose name is attached to a book and the work attributed to him (→ Canonicity, 67:89). And so, when we speak of the sense intended by the author, obviously we must narrow down the broad conception of authorship.

7 The long process of editing that the biblical books have undergone also complicates the task of determining the sense the author intended. We refer here to editing that took place within the period of the composition of the biblical books (up to *ca.* 100 BC for the books of the OT; up to *ca.* AD 125 for the books of the NT), not to subsequent scribal changes in the copying and translating of the completed biblical books. For instance, the composition of the Book of Is covered a span of at least 200 years (→ Deutero-Isaiah, 22:2); not only were new sections added to the original parts that came from Isaiah's lifetime, but also some of the additions had the specific purpose of modifying and changing the meaning of the original. The last verses of Amos may be an addition; they supply an optimistic conclusion to an otherwise pessimistic book (→ Amos, 14:28). In instances like this, one must determine both the sense of the book after editing and the sense that the parts originally had before editing.

8 Perhaps the greatest complication in biblical hermeneutics stems not so much from the multiplicity of human authors and editors but from the unique status of the biblical books, which had both a divine and a human author. In the traditional understanding of inspiration, there stands behind each verse of Scripture not only the mind of the man or men who contributed to its writing but also the guidance of God. We recall the formulation of *Providentissimus Deus* (→ Church Pronouncements, 72:17), which states that God so moved the human authors to write and so assisted them in that writing that they faithfully committed to apt words the things that he ordered. Thus, we have a twofold problem: What did the divine author intend and did that intention exceed the intention of the human author? With this general survey of the difficulties, we shall begin our discussion of the senses of Scripture with the literal sense—the sense that by definition is the one intended by the human author.

THE LITERAL SENSE OF SCRIPTURE

9 **(I) Definition.** The term "literal" is used today to designate the most basic sense of Scripture, a sense that in the past has been designated as "carnal," "historical," or "philological." As the name itself indicates and as the term was used in the Middle Ages (Thomas Aq., *Quodl.* 7, q.6, a.14), the *sensus litteralis* was the sense conveyed by the words (*litterae* or *verba*) of Scripture, as distinct from the sense contained in the "things" of Scripture (the *sensus spiritualis* or typical sense flowing from the *res*; → 73 below). The early writers on the subject were little concerned with the awareness of the human author, and they designated as "literal" any sense the words conveyed, whether or not that sense was intended by the human author (Thomas Aq., *De pot.* q.4, a.1). Some modern theorists, like A. Fernández and P. Benoit, would still maintain this broad definition of the literal sense, subdistinguishing a primary literal sense intended by the human author, and a secondary literal sense intended by God unbeknown to the human author (→ 57 below and the problem of the *sensus plenior*). It is more common, however, for modern writers to confine the designation "literal sense" to that meaning of the words of Scripture intended by the human author. The encyclical *Divino Afflante Spiritu* (*EB* 550) seems to imply this when it speaks of the task: "to discern and define that sense of the biblical words which is called literal...so that the mind of the author may be made clear." Recently, P. Grelot (*La Bible, parole de Dieu* [Paris, 1965] 316) has suggested that in French the older, broader connotation of *sensus litteralis* might come under the heading of *sens littéraire*, whereas the more recent and narrower connotation might come under the heading of *sens littéral*.

10 In any case, we shall define the literal sense thus: *The sense which the human author directly intended and which his words convey.* First, we note that it is a question of the *direct intention* of the human author. This qualification confines the literal sense to the meaning that was in the consciousness of the human author and excludes ramifications that his words may have taken on in the larger context of the Bible but of which he was unaware (such ramifications belong to the *sensus plenior*).

11 Second, the literal sense is a sense *conveyed by the author's words*. The author's intention does not become a sense of Scripture until it is effectively conveyed by his words. The principle that we are not concerned with the author's thought alone but with the message he conveys is important in discussing the limitations of biblical inerrancy (→ Inspiration, 66:85). In particular, concerning the words of Jesus, it must be noted that what Jesus intended by his words is in itself not strictly a sense of *Scripture*, for Jesus was not the writer of the Gospels. The inspired literal sense of a Gospel passage is the meaning attributed to Jesus' words by the individual Evangelist. Often the various Evangelists attribute different meanings to the same words of Jesus, as we can see from the different contexts in which the Evangelists have set these words (→ Aspects NT Thought, 78:141); and sometimes, since we do not know the context in which Jesus actually spoke the words, it may be impossible for us to tell exactly what the words originally meant when Jesus first uttered them. Nevertheless, in the Evangelists' interpretations we have an understanding (or several understandings) of Jesus' words that the Holy Spirit has inspired for the Church, and our faith in the working of the Spirit gives us assurance that this understanding is not a distortion of Jesus' historical teaching, although it may go beyond his teaching.

12 Third, the two parts of our definition of the literal sense, the intention of the author and the sense conveyed by the words, cannot be separated. Such a separation has been responsible for what historically has been one of the great confusions about the literal sense. Often the biblical authors wrote in poetic and figurative language. Many of the Church Fathers, e.g., Origen, thought that the literal sense was what the words said, independently of the author's intent. Thus were Christ spoken of as "the lion of Judah," the literal sense for these Fathers would be that he was an animal. This is why some of them rejected the literal sense of Scripture. To avoid this confusion, many manuals have distinguished between the *proper* (nonmetaphorical) literal sense and the *improper* (metaphorical, figurative) literal sense. There is no real danger of confusion when we insist that the literal sense is what the author *intended* whether he used plain or figurative language.

13 There is another confusion in the history of the literal sense that we should mention. For a while it was thought that a single passage of Scripture could have several literal senses. Both Augustine and Thomas seem to have been of this view (so F. Ceuppens, *DThomP* [1930] 164–75; S. Zarb, *ibid.*, 337–59; denied by P. Synave, *RB* 35 [1926] 40–65; G. Perrella, *Bib* 26 [1945] 277–302); and the view is still defended by modern writers like Desnoyers and Sertillanges (cf. D. Buzy, *L'année théologique* [1944] 387, 408). Our judgment on this is that no text of Scripture can have two heterogeneous, independent literal senses, for quite obviously no author intends to have his words convey two totally unrelated meanings. Most of the other aspects of the problem of two literal senses would come under the heading of double meanings or subordinate meanings that are perfectly possible. See also the discussion of the *sensus plenior*, which envisages the possibility that God may have intended a meaning of the words of Scripture deeper than the meaning intended by the human author (→ 57ff. below).

14 **(II) Problems in Determining the Literal Sense.** We shall not emphasize here the usual rules for determining the sense of any author and book (correct translation of his words; attention to phrase and sentence structure; context; peculiar style and usage; etc.). We shall concern ourselves with special difficulties to be faced in reading the Bible.

(A) Common Fallacies. It is easy to become romantically enthusiastic about the reading of Scripture and the obligation that all should know Scripture. Such enthusiasm quickly runs against the hard fact that to interpret Scripture and determine its literal sense is no simple task. And so, throughout the ages, there has been a consistent attempt to get around or minimize the obstacle of the hard work involved, and this attempt has left us with a number of fallacies.

15 (a) Simplicity of Scripture. Because Scripture is inspired and presumably this inspiration was for the good of all, there has arisen the fallacy that everyone should be able to pick up the Bible and read it profitably. If this implies that everyone should be able to find out what the sacred author is saying without preparation or study, it really demands of God in each instance a miraculous dispensation from the limitations imposed by differences of time and circumstance. Of course it is true that considerable portions of Scripture are easily intelligible to all because they voice universal sentiments, e.g., some of the Pss and some of the simple stories of Jesus. It is also true that spiritual solace and insight may be drawn from the Bible by those who have no technical knowledge and indeed do not understand its literal sense. (Conversely, those who have technical knowledge have at times overlooked the religious depths of the Bible.) Nevertheless, when it is a question of finding out what the human author meant to say, and therefore what God inspired, there is no substitute for educated effort. The inspired author wrote in a language and culture far removed from our own; his primary duty was to be intelligible for his own times. That what he said also has meaning for us today is certainly true; but he did not express himself primarily for us or in our terms, and so it requires training on our part to decipher what he meant.

16 This problem is not met adequately by saying that we must reinterpret Scripture into a language that is intelligible without effort to the man of today. We shall mention below (→ 49) the quest to demythologize and the legitimate desire so to interpret Scripture that its phrasing is not an obstacle. For instance, translations of the Bible into truly modern English can, to a certain extent, give us the equivalents of biblical ideas and facilitate understanding. But much of the biblical imagery cannot be modernized; and if it can be interpreted, it cannot simply be dispensed with, for it is too integral a part of the biblical message, e.g., the symbolism of the Ap. A full answer to the problem of unintelligibility caused by the difference between the world view of the biblical author and our own must involve educating the modern reader to understand the ancient mentality so that he can grasp both the message and the modality which that mentality gives to the message.

17 The problem of the scripturally uneducated reader is often brought forward as an objection to the thesis that we have been proposing here. If the literate but simple folk of times past could read and love Scripture, why cannot the scripturally uneducated do the same today? Yet there is a difference between the man of past generations who had little education in any field and the man of today who has general education in other fields but not in religion or in Scripture and its auxiliaries. From his general education the man of today asks complicated questions about Scripture, the answers for which require training. No one with a grammar-school education can read the first chapters of Gn without wondering if the world was really created in six days; yet considerable training is required to be able to distinguish between the religious teaching of Gn about creation and the naïve prescientific outlook of the author. To supply a standard, we may say that in order to read the Bible with intelligent appreciation a man's biblical education should be proportionate to his general education. Only thus will he be able to answer the questions suggested by his general education.

18 Part of the fallacy about the simplicity of the Bible is the idea that all one needs to understand the Bible is the Bible itself. On the contrary, to uncover the literal sense of Scripture there is real need for auxiliary knowledge, e.g., geography, archaeology, textual criticism. But above all a *knowledge of history* is required. The Bible is, for the most part, the story of God's action in the history of a particular people, an action that is largely unintelligible without a knowledge of Near Eastern history. To seek to divorce God's action from the history of the ancient Near East and to make it timeless is to distort a fundamental message of the Bible, namely that God acts only in concrete circumstances and times (such as yours and mine). What we say here is particularly applicable to the historical and prophetic books of the OT, easily two-thirds of the Bible. Many students, loathe to familiarize themselves with the dates and events of long-dead civilizations, lose through their lack of interest in ancient history the wealth of some of the richest sections of the Bible (→ Aspects OT Thought, 77:104, 112).

19 Another important auxiliary for reading the Bible is the *knowledge of the biblical languages*. Only a small percentage of those who study the Bible can be experts in Hebrew, Aramaic, and Greek; yet some familiarity with the structure and thought-pattern of these languages is essential for the type of biblical knowledge that a theology student should have. Such a demand is again part of the recognition that God has acted in particular times and places—his message would have taken a different form and nuance had it been expressed in other languages. Unless one has some idea of the latitude of the "tenses" in Hebrew, one has difficulty in understanding the undefined time designations in the words of the prophets, i.e., a lack of temporal precision that opened these prophecies to future as well as present fulfillment. Some of the basic words of biblical theological vocabulary defy adequate translation into English, e.g., *ḥesed* (covenant kindness, mercy) in the OT, and *alētheia* (truth) in the NT; modern translations catch only part of a wider connotation. The frequent plays on similar-sounding words in OT poetry and on words of similar root in NT Greek are lost to the student who takes no interest in the biblical languages. With English as one's only linguistic tool, it is possible to have a good knowledge of the Scriptures but scarcely a professional one.

20 (b) QUEST FOR RELEVANCE. Another fallacy is the thesis that only some parts of Scripture are important, namely those most relevant to our life today. There is a legitimate quest for relevancy in biblical studies, as we shall insist (→ 48ff. below). It is quite true that, at times, strict historico-critical exegesis produces knowledge primarily of antiquarian value; it is also true that the intensive study of some areas of Scripture belongs more to an advanced stage of research than, for example, to the training of the average theological student. For instance, the description of the geographical boundaries of the tribes in the latter part of Jos is fascinating for the professional biblical historian and geographer; but to give more than summary attention to this section in a survey course of the OT would be bad pedagogy. Thus, "relevance" sets legitimate guidelines in both study and teaching.

21 The abuse with which we are concerned is the tendency to allow a quest for relevance to give an orientation to basic biblical studies that is not true to the Bible itself, e.g., the desire to study only those parts of the Bible that have easily convertible theological value, or preaching value, or value for the spiritual life. Such interests can supply a secondary emphasis in the study of Scripture, but to make them primary reflects a basic misunderstanding of what the Bible is. As Barr (*op. cit.*, 192) has eloquently stated, on the student level or on the scholarly level this form of the quest for relevance is theologically doubtful and basically anti-intellectual. The books of Scripture were not inspired or written primarily for the dogmatic theologian, nor for the preacher, nor for the ascetic. They deal on a much wider scale with God's action for man, and with man's understanding of God and of his own existence and history. The scale of biblical action and thought is the scale of life itself. In particular, the value of the OT is precisely related to the broadness of its scope that includes, not only the spiritual and theological aspects of life, but also the secular (→ Wisdom Lit, 28:34ff.; → Canticle, 30:4) and the sordid (war, depravity). The Bible shows how men learned to fit the *whole* of life into their relationship to God. To select from this totality only those portions of the biblical narrative that meet the narrow requirements of a modern understanding of what is religious or spiritual is disastrous. Indeed, the failure to appreciate the importance of the OT often springs from the false concept that what God has inspired should be consistently noble, beautiful, and uplifting—a concept that implicitly reflects the thesis that religion has nothing to do with the secular and the profane. What strikes such a mentality as irrelevant in the Bible (e.g., the chain of history, the humdrum causality of human events, the careers of bad men and indifferent men) is in a deeper sense precisely what is relevant, i.e., relevant to a man's life that is part of humdrum history and full of encounters with evil and indifference. In short, this artificial quest for relevance reflects the failure to understand the basic biblical truth that God has acted in *history*.

22 In its consequences for theology such a selectivity on the basis of relevance is truly frightening. We accuse a past generation of turning the Bible into a mine for proof-texts, so that a student's knowledge of the Bible was often confined to parts useful for apologetics or for a scholastic propositional theology. But is not the same mistake being made today when some would tell us to concentrate on the portions of Scripture that enable man to understand himself existentially, or on parts that favor personalism, or community spirit, or an "I-thou" relationship? A future generation will condemn such selectivity just as harshly as we have condemned the apologetic selectivity of our ancestors. To pass on to the next generation only what we find relevant in Scripture is to censor Scripture, for precisely what we do not find relevant to our times may be God's principal word in Scripture to another generation.

23 A particular aspect of the unbalanced quest for relevance is centered on biblical theology. The sterility of 19th-cent. critical exegesis has produced by way of salutary reaction a very valid 20th-cent. interest in biblical theology (→ 48 below; also → Modern OT Criticism, 70:51–55). This is an attempt to preserve the wholeness of the scriptural message where theology is a major (but not exclusive) dimension. However, a great desire for biblical theology on the part of beginning students *can* be another example of the tendency to turn Scripture studies from the hard path of exegesis into easier fields. Students frequently prefer a course on biblical themes or "biblical theology" to a course in exegesis. Yet a real knowledge of biblical themes can be built up only by analyzing the texts of the Bible that pertain to the themes and then by synthesizing the results. To feed the beginner a steady diet of synthesized results without first leading him to the biblical text itself is both to blind the student to the difficulties of Scripture and to substitute the study of compendia for the reading of God's word. An earlier generation of Catholic theological students complained that they never studied the Scriptures themselves but spent all their time on introductions to the biblical books; a contemporary generation may in retrospect voice the same complaint about an exaggerated stress on biblical theology. Once again, we insist that we do not wish to undervalue the study of biblical theology, but rather to emphasize that such study can be effectively pursued only after the student has worked through the exegesis of the Bible.

24 In the history of biblical interpretation in the Catholic Church, each time there has been a movement that put emphasis on the primacy of literal exegesis (e.g., Jerome, the school of St. Victor in the Middle Ages, Richard Simon), this movement has been quickly swallowed up in a more attractive movement that stressed the theological or the spiritual aspects of Scripture almost to the exclusion of literal exegesis. And so Origen's spiritual exegesis conquered Jerome's literal exegesis through the efforts of Augustine; the exegesis practiced at St. Victor was swallowed up in the theological and philosophical use of Scripture in later Scholasticism; Bossuet and Pascal outshone R. Simon in popular influence (→ Modern OT Criticism, 70:6). The encyclical *Divino Afflante Spiritu*, confirmed by Vatican II, has made a thoroughgoing quest for the literal sense by historico-critical exegesis a real possibility for Catholics for the first time in centuries (→ Church Pronouncements, 72:21, 29). This quest is the primary duty of those who teach and study Scripture, and we should not allow ourselves to be misled into easier paths which, in the long run, will take us away from the Bible.

25 **(B) Need for Establishing Literary Form.** Having pointed out the fallacies that might distract from the quest for the literal sense, we now turn to the problem of the basic steps in that quest. The *first step* in finding out what the author intended is to determine the literary form the author is employing. If we walk into a modern library, books are classified according to the type of literature: fiction, poetry, history, biography, drama, etc. Often the classification for individual books is indicated by the dust jacket. The knowledge of the type of literature to which a book belongs causes us to make adjustments in our approach to the book, e.g., if we have two books treating of the same event, and one book is fiction, the other serious history, we do not place the same credence in the narratives of each.

The Bible is what remains of the library of ancient Israel and of the 1st-cent. Christian Church. This library has all the diversity we would expect in the literary output of an articulate culture that spanned nearly 2000 years. In the Bible the books of this library have been bound together into one, without the advantage of dust jackets. It is the task of the student of the Bible to classify the biblical books or their parts according to the type of literature they represent. This is what is meant by determining the literary form (*genus litterarium*) the author has employed. (This emphasis on literary form is an offshoot of the German development of Form Criticism or *Formgeschichte;* → Modern NT Criticism, 41:42–45; → Modern OT Criticism, 70:38; also K. Koch, *Was ist Formgeschichte?* [2nd ed.; Neukirchen, 1967].) The encyclical *Divino Afflante Spiritu* and Vatican II have made this approach imperative on all serious Catholic students of the Bible (→ Church Pronouncements, 72:22, 14), so that the first question we must ask in opening any part of the Bible is: What type of literature do we have here?

26 In a broad sense, of course, the determination of literary form has been a principle implicitly recognized from a very early period. From the time of Rabbi Gamaliel II (late 1st cent. AD) the Jews have classified the books of the OT as Torah, Prophets, and Writings (→ Canonicity, 67:23,29); but the Christian division of these books into Historical, Prophetical, and Sapiential is even closer to a distinction of literary types. Only in modern times, however, with the discovery of the literatures of people contemporary with Israel, have we realized just how many types of literature were current in antiquity. Let us illustrate this from the OT since it is a more varied library than the NT. There are many varieties of poetry in the OT: Epic poetry underlies some of the narratives in the Pentateuch and Jos; lyric poetry is found in Ps and Ct; didactic poetry is found in Prv, Sir, and Wis; elements of drama are found in Jb. Within the prophetic books there are both prophecy and apocalyptic (→ Post-exilic Period, 20:21). There is not one type of history in the OT but many types: a factual penetrating analysis, seemingly by an eyewitness, in the court history of David (2 Sm 11–1 Kgs 2); stylized, abbreviated court records in Kgs and Chr; romanticized and simplified epic history of the national saga in Ex; tales of tribal heroes in Jgs; stories of the great men of yore in the patriarchal accounts. There is even prehistory in the Gn narratives of the origin of man and of evil, narratives that borrow legends from the lore of other nations and make them the vehicles of a monotheistic theology (→ Genesis, 2:6–8). The instances we have given by no means exhaust the literary richness of the OT library; there are fictional tales, parables, allegories, proverbs, maxims, love stories, etc.

27 As with other literature, once the reader has determined what type of literature he is dealing with in the section of the Bible that he is reading, he applies the standards of that type of literature to determine what the author meant to say, i.e., the literal sense. If the reader knows that Jonah is a fictional parable, he knows that the author is *not* giving a history of the relations of Israel and Assyria and is *not* presenting the story of Jonah in the whale's belly as a serious account of a true happening. If the reader understands that the statement about the sun standing still in Jos 10:13 comes from a fragment of highly poetic description in a victory song, he will judge it in the light of poetic license rather than according to the rules of strict history. If the reader understands that the Samson narratives are folk tales, he will not give to them the same historical credence that he gives to the history of David's court. Many of the past difficulties about the Bible have stemmed from the failure to recognize the diversity of the literary forms that it contains and from the tendency to misinterpret as scientific history pieces of the Bible that are not historical or are historical only in a more popular sense. We have taken our examples from the OT; but we must caution that the same problem exists in the NT. The Gospels are not scientifically historical biographies of Jesus but written accounts of the preaching and teaching of the early Church about Jesus, and their accuracy must be judged according to the standards of preaching and teaching (→ Church Pronouncements, 72:35).

28 The approach to exegesis that we have just discussed, based on determining the type of literature that one is dealing with, is subject to two common misconceptions. First, some conservative spokesmen regard the quest for literary form as an attempt to circumvent the historicity of biblical passages, and therefore they think it dangerous to apply the theory of literary forms to the more sacred sections of the Bible. This misconception is vocalized in statements like the following: "That is *just* a literary form" or "It is permissible to apply the theory of literary forms to the OT but not to the NT." But every piece of writing can be classified as belonging to one type of literature or another. Factual history is a type of literature; fiction is another; both exist in the Bible, as do almost all the intermediary literary types between these two extremes. If one correctly classifies a certain part of the Bible as fiction, one is not destroying the historicity of that section, for it never was history; one is simply recognizing the author's intention in writing that section. If this is understood, the statements quoted above are nonsense. The second misconception concerns the relation of inspiration to the diversity of biblical literary forms. There is a feeling that somehow the recognition that certain parts of the Bible were written as fiction weakens or challenges their inspiration. The encyclical *Divino Afflante Spiritu* (*EB* 559) gives an answer: God could inspire any type of literature that was not unworthy or deceitful, i.e., not contrary to his holiness and truth (e.g., pornography, lies). Biblical fiction is just as inspired as biblical history.

29 **(C) Need for Knowing Literary History and Aims of Composition.** After one has determined the type of literature involved, the *second main step* in the quest for the literal sense is to find out the literary history of the biblical book or section that one is studying. This is a special problem in biblical study because of the long history of editing (→ 7 above). One must unravel the individual traditions of the Pentateuch, the collections that compose Is, the chronological order of Jeremiah's prophecies (different from the present order of the biblical book). In the Gospels it is important to know that a particular saying of Jesus has come from Mk or from Q or from one of the sources peculiar to Lk or Mt (→ Syn Problem, 40:19ff.), and to know by means of comparison how its present phrasing in the Gospel differs from its more original form—thus one discovers the author's theological intent made evident by his adaptation of the material that has come down to him.

30 Here we touch on the approach to the Bible known as *Redaktionsgeschichte*. If *Formgeschichte* is concerned with the different forms or types of literature in the Bible and the rules germane to them, *Redaktionsgeschichte* is concerned with the way in which these literary pieces are made to serve the general purpose of the writer. For instance, in the Gospels an exegete has done only part of his work when he has classified a story as a particular type of parable and has determined to what extent it conforms to the general rules for that parable-type. Why is the parable included in this Gospel? Why is it set in this particular context within the Gospel? What meaning does the Evangelist attach to it? To answer these questions is to take our second main step in determining the literal sense of Scripture.

31 After the two steps that we have described (determining the literary form; determining the literary history and the aims of composition), the exegete is then in a position to seek the literal meaning of individual passages and verses. Here the process is the same as for any other ancient work. The literal meaning of some 90–95 per cent of the Bible can be determined by a reasonable application of the ordinary rules of interpretation. There are some passages whose meaning eludes us because their text has been corrupted in transmission, because they use rare words, because their author expressed himself obscurely, or because we do not have sufficient knowledge about the context in which they were composed. Continued study is constantly giving enlightenment even on passages such as these. (See O. Kaiser and W. G. Kümmel, *Exegetical Method: A Student's Handbook* [N.Y., 1967].)

MORE-THAN-LITERAL SENSES

32 We now turn to the senses of Scripture that go beyond the literal, i.e., senses that by definition go beyond what the human author intended. The theoretical possibility of such senses is based on the presupposition that Scripture had a divine author who at the time that Scripture was written foresaw the future in a way the human author did not and who took cognizance of this future in the writing of Scripture. The quest for a more-than-literal sense—a quest as old as Scripture itself—is based on the contention that in the scriptural record of the past, God speaks to the present and intends the reader to find therein a depth of meaning that goes beyond the local and limited circumstances in which the original was written. Such presuppositions and contentions have been questioned, and certainly they leave themselves open to reckless application. Yet the fact that they have been invoked in exegesis from the time of the biblical authors until the present day and that they attract the attention of the most scientific biblical exegetes suggests that the idea of a more-than-literal sense cannot be dismissed lightly.

33 **(I) History of More-than-literal Exegesis.** Perhaps the best introduction to the problem of more-than-literal senses is to trace briefly the history of this tendency in exegesis.

(A) To the End of the New Testament Era. Within the Bible itself we find the author of Wis (11–19) taking the older narratives of the plagues and the deliverance from Egypt and reading out of (or into) them a theme of deliverance for his own time. A parallelism between past and present is seen in this type of exegesis; another example would be the connection that Dt-Is draws between the Exodus from Egypt and the return from Babylon. Such parallelism is based on the thesis that God's actions on behalf of his people follow a pattern of fidelity: He is the same yesterday, today, and forever. It is not based on a cyclic approach to history.

34 In the intertestamental period (last two centuries BC) there was a development that had profound effects on both Jewish and Christian exegesis. Whereas in more ancient times the prophets had been understood primarily as the spokesmen of God to their own times with a divinely given foreknowledge of God's plan for the immediate and relevant future, now the prophets of old were thought to have predicted the distant future. Apocalyptic (→ Post-exilic Period, 20:21–24) was an important factor in this change of emphasis, following the pattern of Dn wherein purportedly a prophet of the 6th cent. had visions of what would happen in the 2nd cent. Such an understanding of the prophets, and indeed of other biblical writers like the psalmists, gave birth to the pesher exegesis of Qumran (→ Apocrypha, 68:77) where every line of the ancient books was interpreted in terms of what was happening to the Qumran sect hundreds of years later.

(Brownlee, W. H., "Biblical Interpretation Among the Sectaries of the Dead Sea Scrolls," *BA* 14 [1951] 54–76. Bruce, F.F., *Biblical Exegesis in the Qumran Texts* [Grand Rapids, 1959]. Fitzmyer, J. A., "The Use of Explicit Old Testament Quotations in Qumran Literature and in the New Testament," *NTS* 7 [1960–61] 297–333.)

35 Moreover, this understanding of the OT prophets and psalmists explains to some extent the principles according to which the NT authors interpreted the OT. Isaiah (7:14) could be pictured by Mt (1:23) as foretelling the virgin birth of Jesus; Dt-Is in the Suffering Servant passages could be pictured as foretelling the sufferings and death of the Messiah (Lk 24:26); the author of Ps 22 could be pictured as foreseeing in detail the passion of Jesus (Mt 27:35,39,43,46). Some would compare this exegesis to the pesher exegesis of Qumran (B. Lindars, *New Testament Apologetic* [Phila., 1961]), but there are important differences. The Qumran interpreters set out to explain God's plan in the OT in terms of what was happening to the Qumran sect. The novelty of Jesus changes the direction of the current in NT exegesis: The necessity was not to explain the OT in terms of the Christian community, but to explain Jesus in terms of the OT, the only theological language available to Jews. There were no systematic Christian commentaries on the OT in NT times (and indeed not until the late 2nd cent., e.g., Hippolytus commenting on Ct and Dn), and so we have no evidence that the NT writers felt that every line of the OT applied to Jesus or had a Christian meaning—a theory that became popular in patristic times. The NT exegesis of the OT was extraordinarily varied, and any attempt to classify it as one type of exegesis is doomed to failure. It had elements of *sensus plenior*, typology, allegory, and accommodation. A particular feature of this NT exegesis was to read the presence of Jesus back into OT scenes (1 Cor 10:4; cf. A. T. Hanson, *Jesus Christ in the Old Testament* [London, 1965]).

(Bläser, P., "St. Paul's Use of the Old Testament," *TD* 2 [1954] 49–52, abr. from *TQ* 133 [1952] 152–69. Cerfaux, L., "Simples réflexions à propos de l'exégèse apostolique," *Problèmes et méthode* 33–44; "L'exégèse de l'Ancien Testament par le Nouveau," *L'Ancien Testament et les chrétiens*, 132–48. Dupont, J., "The Use of the Old Testament in Acts," *TD* 3 [1955] 61–64, abr. from *ETL* 29 [1953] 289–327. Ellis, E. E., "A Note on Pauline Hermeneutics," *NTS* 2 [1955–56] 127–33. Van der Ploeg, J., "L'exégèse de L'Ancien Testament dans l'Épître aux Hébreux," *RB* 54 [1947] 187–228. Venard, L., "Citations de l'Ancien Testament dans le Nouveau Testament," *VDBS* 2 [1934] 23–51.)

36 While we shall be concerned in the rest of our brief history with Christian exegesis of the OT, we should note that in Pharisaic and rabbinic circles the quest for a more-than-literal exegesis was just as common as in Christian circles. The targums (→ Texts, 69:82) really supply an exegesis of what they translate and are free in reading messianic elements into the OT. The midrashim (→ Apocrypha, 68:119) are also very free in interpreting previous Scripture in application to current problems. The Jewish nonliteral exegesis that had the greatest influence on Christian exegesis was the allegorizing of Philo (→ Apocrypha, 68:112).

(Bonsirven, J., *Exégèse rabbinique et exégèse paulinienne* [Paris, 1939]. Gelin, A., "Comment le peuple d'Israël lisait l'Ancien Testament," *L'Ancien Testament et les chrétiens* 117–31. Ginzberg, L., "Allegorical Interpretations," *JE* 1, 403ff. Sowers, S. G., *The Hermeneutics of Philo and Hebrews* [Richmond, 1965].)

37 **(B) Patristic Era.** In the early Christian writings of the 2nd cent. we find evidence both of a very free spiritual exegesis (pseudo-Barnabas) and of a rather sober exegesis. Yet even the sober exegetes, like Justin and Tertullian, ransacked the OT for proof-texts referring to Christ, and they interpreted these passages in a way that went far beyond the literal sense. It was *Alexandria* that produced the first great Christian school of exegesis; and through men like Clement and Origen, Philo's allegorizing achieved a dominant place in the Christian exegesis of the OT. Clement based his exegesis on the existence of a Christian gnosis, i.e., the secret knowledge of the profoundest truths of the Christian faith to which the elite were initiated. The key to the gnosis was an allegorical exegesis of the Bible, an exegesis that ran the gamut from authentic typology through arbitrary accommodation to the Philonic concept of the Bible as a lesson in psychology and cosmology.

38 Origen probably had more influence on patristic exegesis than any other single figure, although later his theological orthodoxy became suspect. Almost every manual states that Origen's exegesis was unrestrainedly allegorical, and he is usually blamed for denying the literal sense of scripture. A. von Harnack spoke of Origen's "biblical alchemy." Recently there have been serious attempts by H. de Lubac, J. Daniélou, and others to modify this picture and to re-evaluate Origen's exegesis. Origen did not simply disregard the literal sense (although he did not understand that the metaphorical sense was literal), but he was interested greatly in a sense of Scripture that could make the Christian see the OT as his book. A good part of his allegorical exegesis was based on the theory that the OT was Christological in many passages. Granting that we should judge Origen more appreciatively and that there is a restrained element in his exegesis (which De Lubac calls spiritual sense, and

Daniélou calls typology), this writer does not share the view that Origen's exegesis can really be revived for our time.

39 Just as oversimplification did not do justice to Origen's exegetical stance, so also the exegetical school of *Antioch*, Alexandria's rival as a great Christian center, has been too naïvely heroicized as the champion of critical exegesis, in contradistinction to Alexandria's allegorical exegesis. At the end of the 3rd cent. Lucian of Samosata laid the foundations of this school; and some of its representatives were Diodorus of Tarsus (d. 390), Theodore of Mopsuestia (d. 428), and, to some extent, John Chrysostom (d. 407). In the West, Julian, the Pelagian bishop of Aeclanum (d. 454), was the leading adherent to Antiochene principles. The great Antiochenes, then, were not contemporaries of Origen but of the later Alexandrians like Athanasius (d. 373) and Didymus the Blind (d. 398). In many ways, Cyril of Alexandria (d. 444) showed a perceptivity in literal exegesis that placed him between the Alexandrian and Antiochene schools.

Little Antiochene exegesis has been preserved. In theory, and to some extent in practice, Antioch did give more attention to the literal sense (with all the limitations of exegesis in the 4th cent.). But Antioch also proposed a more-than-literal exegesis that involved *theōria*, for all practical purposes a close equivalent of Alexandrian *allēgoria*. *Theōria* was an intuition or vision by which the prophet could see the future through the medium of his present circumstances. After such a vision it was possible for him to phrase his writing in such a way as to describe both the contemporary meaning of the events as well as their future fulfillment. (For studies of *theōria*, see A. Vaccari, *Bib* 1 [1920] 3–36; F. Seisdedos, *EstBib* 11 [1952] 31–67; P. Ternant, *Bib* 34 [1953] 135–58, 354–83, 456–86.) The task of the Antiochene exegetes was to find both meanings in the words of the prophets; and in their search for the future meaning of the prophets' words (the product of *theōria*), the Antiochenes took into account the problem of the awareness of the human author more often than did the Alexandrians, who tended to see the future in symbols and events, as well as in the prophetic word.

(On JUSTIN: Prigent, P., *Justin et l'Ancien Testament* [Paris, 1964]. Shotwell, W. A., *The Biblical Exegesis of Justin Martyr* [London, 1965]. On CLEMENT OF ALEXANDRIA: Camelot, T., *RB* 53 [1946] 242–48. Marsh, H. G., *JTS* 37 [1936] 64–80. Mondésert, C., *RSR* 26 [1936] 158–80; *Clément d'Alexandrie* [Paris, 1944]. On ORIGEN: Daniélou, J., *Origène* [Paris, 1948]. De Lubac, H., *Histoire et esprit* [Paris, 1950]. Hanson, R. P. C., *Allegory and Event* [London, 1958]. On THEODORE OF MOPSUESTIA: Devreesse, R., *RB* 53 [1946] 207–41. On CYRIL: Kerrigan, A., *St. Cyril of Alexandria, Interpreter of the Old Testament* [Rome, 1952]. On JULIAN: D'Alès, A., *RSR* 6 [1916] 311–24. On CHRYSOSTOM: Ogara, F., *Greg* 24 [1943] 62–77. For a comparison of Alexandrian and Antiochene exegesis, see J. Guillet, *RSR* 37 [1947] 257–302; also W. Burghardt, "On Early Christian Exegesis," *TS* 11 [1950] 78–116; C. Hay, "Antiochene Exegesis and Christology," *AusBR* 12 [1964] 10–23.)

40 Meanwhile in the West some of the Lat exegetes (e.g., Ambrosiaster, *ca.* 375) showed sobriety in exegesis. However, with Hilary (d. 367), Ambrose (d. 397), and especially Augustine (d. 430), the waves of Alexandrian allegorical exegesis swept into the West. In Hilary's *Tractatus mysteriorum* we find the principle that the OT *in its entirety* is prefigurative of the NT. Tyconius, a Donatist exegete of the late 4th cent. laid down the rule in his *Liber regularum* that every verse in the OT could be interpreted in a Christian way. Augustine epitomized this approach in his principle: "The New Testament lies hidden in the Old; the Old Testament is enlightened through the New" ("*In vetere novum lateat, et in novo vetus pateat*"—*Quaest. in Heptateuchum* 2.73; *PL* 34.625).

In his early days Jerome (d. 419) followed Origen's principles, but the commentaries written at the end of Jerome's life betray greater interest in the literal sense. Yet, after Jerome's time and the close of the 4th cent., the style of Alexandrian exegesis dominated in the West, and Antiochene exegesis had little lasting influence (see M. Laistner, *HarvTR* 40 [1947] 19–31). Indeed, once the Council of Constantinople II (553) blackened the name of Theodore of Mopsuestia, the Antiochene heritage was looked on with suspicion. In the works of some of the great figures of Western exegesis, e.g., Gregory the Great (d. 604) and Bede (d. 735), allegorical exegesis ran riot.

(On LAT EXEGESIS: Kelly, J. N. D. in D. E. Nineham, *op. cit.*, 41–56. On AUGUSTINE: Pontet, M., *L'exégèse de S. Augustin prédicateur* [Paris, 1944]. On JEROME: Hartman, L. in *A Monument to St. Jerome*, ed. by F. X. Murphy [N.Y., 1952] 35–81. Penna, A., *Principi e carattere dell' esegesi di S. Gerolamo* [Rome, 1950]. Steinmann, J., *St. Jerome and His Times* [Notre Dame, Ind., 1959].)

41 **(C) Middle Ages.** The guiding theoretical principle of medieval exegesis may be said to stem from John Cassian's (d. *ca.* 435) distinction of the four senses of Scripture: (1) the historical or literal, (2) the allegorical or Christological, (3) the tropological or moral or anthropological, (4) the anagogical or eschatological. Eventually this division gave rise to the famous couplet:

Littera gesta docet; quid credas allegoria;
moralis quid agas; quo tendas anagogia.

The four senses of Jerusalem, an example supplied by Cassian, illustrates the theory. When Jerusalem is mentioned in the Bible, in its literal sense it is a Jewish city; allegorically, however, it refers to the Church of Christ; tropologically Jerusalem stands for the soul of man; anagogically it stands for the heavenly city. In such an exegetical climate, the literal sense was considered to have historical importance, while the other senses were essential for belief and behavior. Monastic mysticism, the preaching to the faithful, the search for theological material in the schools—these depended more heavily on the more-than-literal senses and gave a dominant nonliteral cast to medieval exegesis. Perhaps we should note that the same love for allegory appears also in the secular literature toward the end of the Middle Ages (e.g., *The Romance of the Rose*, *The Faerie Queene*).

42 However, there were moments when the recognition of the importance of the literal sense shone through. Especially influential in this respect was the school at the Abbey of St. Victor in Paris founded in 1110. Hugh of St. Victor attacked the tradition of Gregory and Bede; Andrew of St. Victor revived interest in Hebrew and in the technical tools of exegesis. Since the time of Jerome the Western church had had few men capable of studying the OT in its original languages; and Herbert of Bosham, Andrew's pupil, was the most competent Hebraist in the Christian West in the 1000 years between Jerome and the Renaissance. Moreover, the development of theology as a discipline separate from strict exegesis enabled scholars to consider Christological truths in themselves without basing their discussion on Scripture interpreted allegorically. Thomas Aquinas made it clear that metaphor belonged to the literal sense (→ 12 above) and argued that doctrine should not be based solely on the spiritual sense. His principle was: "Nothing necessary to faith is contained in the spiritual sense [i.e., typical sense or sense of things] that Scripture does not put forward elsewhere in the literal sense" (*Summa* 1.1,10 ad 1). Men like the English Dominican Nicholas Trevet and the Franciscan Nicholas of Lyra (d. 1349) recognized that not all the Pss were messianic and gave rules for determining which of them were. Roger Bacon, although theoretically supporting the Alexandrian views on exegesis, showed a fascination for textual criticism and philological apparatus. During the 12th, 13th, and early 14th cents., these tendencies rose to the surface like islands in the sea, but they did not survive; and the Middle Ages drew to a close with allegory once more dominant in writers like Meister Eckhart (d. 1328), John Gerson (d. 1429), and Denis the Carthusian (d. 1471). The movement to translate the Bible into the vernacular, which, like most efforts at translation, made people think about the literal sense, was often unfortunately tainted with heresy (→ Texts, 69:153) and thus backfired as a possible corrective to the exaggeration of the spiritual sense.

(Chenu, M.-D., "Les deux âges de l'allégorisme scripturaire au Moyen Age," *RTAM* 18 [1951] 19–28. De Lubac, H., *Exégèse médiévale: Les quatre sens de l'Écriture* [3 vols.; Paris, 1959–60]. McNally, R. E., *The Bible in the Middle Ages* [Westminster, 1959]. Smalley, B., *The Study of the Bible in the Middle Ages* [N.Y., 1952]; "The Bible in the Middle Ages," in D. E. Nineham, *op. cit.*, 57–71. Spicq, C., *Esquisse d'une histoire de l'exégèse latine au Moyen Age* [Paris, 1944].)

43 **(D) Sixteenth and Seventeenth Centuries.** Turning now to the context of the Reformation and its immediate aftermath, we find that, with Cajetan on the Catholic side and with Luther and Calvin on the Protestant side, there was a reaction against allegorizing and a stress on the historical background of the biblical works. However, we must not forget that while Luther attacked blatant allegorizing, he remained firmly convinced of the Christological character of the OT and, therefore, continued to indulge in a typological exegesis that would be questioned by many today. Calvin was even less in favor of allegorizing than Luther; yet he too was often more-than-literal. (In his work *The Bible and the Church* [N.Y., 1948] 111–14, R. M. Grant justly recognizes the good points and the limits in the Reformers' return to the literal sense.) It is interesting to note that the dissenting sects of the Reform movement, the Anabaptists and the Antitrinitarians, supported spiritual exegesis, often because OT passages were used literally by the more conservative branch of the Reform as scriptural justification for persecuting the sects.

44 The Catholic counterreform had to answer arguments flowing from Protestant literal exegesis by also calling on the literal sense of Scripture. The Jesuit Maldonatus (d. 1583) produced exegetical commentary of substance. However, when the immediacy of the danger from the Reform was over, spiritual exegesis returned, especially under the banners of Jansenism, e.g., Pascal. The Catholic emphasis on the Church Fathers was another strong magnet toward spiritual exegesis; for, if the Fathers were pointed out as the prime example of how to interpret Scripture, their exegesis was more-than-literal. Cornelius a Lapide (d. 1637) filled his commentaries with spiritual exegesis culled from the Fathers. In Protestantism, too, in the Pietism of the 17th cent., typology and accommodation made a comeback as the Scriptures were tapped for ascetic wealth. Cocceius (1603–69) presented an exegesis impregnated with typology.

But the revival of spiritual exegesis was not to hold the field forever. This same 17th cent. saw the career of Richard Simon (d. 1712), a prophet before his time and the first of the modern biblical critics. Rejected by his contemporaries and even by his Church, Simon inaugurated a movement that would make literal exegesis supreme.

(Lecler, J., "Littéralisme biblique et typologie au XVIe siècle," *RSR* 51 [1953] 76–95. Steinmann, J., "Entretien de Pascal et du Père Richard Simon sur les sens de l'Écriture," *VieInt* [March 1949] 239–53.)

45 **(E) The Situation Today.** The 19th and 20th cents. have seen the triumph of the critical and literal exegesis to which R. Simon gave the impetus so long ago. (For the intervening history of critical exegesis, → Modern NT Criticism, 41:5ff.; → Modern OT Criticism, 70:6ff.) In his method of exegesis the scholar of today finds himself in another world of thought from the exegesis of the past. Looking back on that past, he finds an exegesis where imagination ran riot and where the literal meaning of the Scriptures, even when it was recognized, was constantly submerged beneath a strong tide of symbolism. The great difference between modern exegesis and that of the past became apparent more quickly in OT studies—a Christological approach that found Christ in every line of the OT was patently out of step with the modern source-criticism of the Pentateuch, the emphasis on the limited perspective of the prophets, and the recognition of contemporary pagan parallels for much of what was found in Israel's sacred books. The limitations of past exegesis of the NT became apparent more slowly, at least in Catholic circles. Only a research that had become historically conscious could detect the distinction between the theology of the NT and the theology of the subsequent Church; this distinction made it clear that the Fathers and the Scholastics had found in the NT theological insights of which the original authors were innocent.

In the light of the modern emphasis on literal exegesis, what happens to the whole idea of more-than-literal exegesis? Does it have any possibilities for our time? We find three basic reactions to this question.

46 (a) Attempt to Preserve Past Symbolic Exegesis. Among those who maintain that more-than-literal exegesis is still important, some seek to hold on to the exegesis of the past. In its *extreme form* this attitude is accompanied by a frantic rejection of literal exegesis as sterile and anti-Christian. Such a rejection of historical criticism occurs in Protestant Fundamentalism without a return to patristic or medieval symbolism; here the nostalgia is for a precritical theology, i.e., "What the Bible says." A similar fundamentalistic attitude in Catholicism is superficially more subtle, for Catholic precritical theology was not so tightly wedded to the Bible. The last major Catholic attempt to revive spiritual and symbolic exegesis at the expense of the literal sense, that of Dolindo Ruotolo (→ Church Pronouncements, 72:29), was condemned by the Pontifical Biblical Commission. The fact that Vatican II gave its approval to biblical criticism (→ Church Pronouncements, 72:13) militates against any wholesale spread of these extremist ideas, but undoubtedly they will recur from time to time.

47 More serious is the *moderate approach* of respectable scholars who appreciate modern literal exegesis but contend that the spiritual exegesis of the past is still valid for today. Some of the studies of Origen mentioned above (→ 38, 39), written by men like De Lubac, Daniélou, and Hanson, not only defend the sobriety of much of the Alexandrian exegesis but also implicitly or explicitly plead for the continuing relevance of some of this exegesis. We have in A. G. Hebert, *The Throne of David* (London, 1943) and W. Vischer, *The Witness of the Old Testament to Christ* (London, 1949) two prominent contemporary advocates of symbolic exegesis. While the opinion of these scholars deserves a hearing, most others remain convinced that such symbolic exegesis has little to offer modern man. The symbolic has a role today in art, poetry, and drama; but consistent symbolic interpretation of what seems to be a straightforward biblical narrative meets opposition, for it smacks more of ingenuity and inventiveness than of interpretation. In the time of the Fathers spiritual exegesis was an attempt to let the Scriptures speak to a contemporary situation; to revive it today would seem to sidestep the obligation to make Scripture relevant in a truly modern way. A symbolism that was once meaningful becomes another barrier today.

In this attempted revival of patristic symbolic exegesis of the OT in particular, one cannot but suspect that part of the motivation lies in an inadequate appreciation of the OT in its literal sense without conscious Christian orientation (→ 21 above). Perhaps we may cite a paradoxical warning of D. Bonhoeffer, "He who desires to think and feel in terms of the New Testament too quickly and too directly is in my opinion no Christian."

48 (b) Acceptance of a "Modern" More-than-literal Exegesis. Although the majority of critical scholars have firmly turned their backs on the symbolic exegetical methods of the past, many still express interest in a more-than-literal exegesis that is related to the results of modern criticism. They recognize the validity of the instinct to find a greater message in Scripture than historical criticism directly uncovers. If the 19th cent. has made us uneasy about the symbolic and imaginative interpretation characteristic of the Fathers and the Scholastics, the pretensions of historical criticism to be the only key to the word of God has, in turn, met with a challenge in the 20th cent. It is interesting that in our era when the art of biblical criticism is practiced with great finesse, some of the most prominent practitioners have expressed dissatisfaction with presenting the literal sense as the whole message of Scripture. Their attempts to solve the problem have taken many directions.

The development of biblical theology has been a partial attempt to find a fuller message in Scripture. (We speak here of biblical theology that is solidly built upon critical exegesis and not a substitute for it; → 23 above for cautions on this subject.) Other attempts concern more directly the senses of Scripture, e.g., the Catholic interest in the *sensus plenior* on the part of competent exegetes like P. Benoit and J. Coppens, and the interest of both Catholics and Protestants in a form of typology as seen in the writings of W. Eichrodt and G. von Rad. Later we shall study in detail the *sensus plenior* and typical sense of Scripture; here we wish to discuss the two larger movements that imply a more-than-literal sense, that of the new hermeneutic and that of the Christian interpretation of the OT.

49 (i) *The New Hermeneutic.* (For what follows see J. M. Robinson, "Hermeneutic since Barth," *The New Hermeneutic* 1-77.) In this movement "Hermeneutic," in the singular, is not a science of rules for interpretation (= hermeneutics, in the plural) but is more closely related to the original meaning of *hermēneia* (→ 3 above). It concerns the way in which God's word becomes clear to men.

In an important discussion of biblical theology (*IDB* 1, 418-32), K. Stendahl has isolated the core of the hermeneutical problem today, namely the contrast between "What *did* Scripture mean when it was written?" (the goal of literal interpretation) and "What *does* it mean to me?" W. Dilthey first pointed out the problem when he made the fundamental distinction between explanation and understanding. Historical criticism can *explain* what a text of Scripture once meant, but how does a reader come to an *understanding* of that text? In his commentary on Rom, K. Barth insisted on the proclamation of Paul's message in the language of today. Attacking A. von Harnack's thesis that theological scholarship's sole task was the pure knowledge of its object, Barth stressed that theology must remember that its object was first subject and must become subject again.

A similar desire to make Scripture speak today lies behind the development of *Sachkritik*, a criticism that recognizes the applicability of the subject matter even when the language in which the matter was objectivized is inappropriate. R. Bultmann's demythologizing (→ Modern NT Criticism, 41:51) is also directed to this positive goal: It is the decoding rather than the elimination of myth, and only inadequate mythical conceptualization is eliminated for the sake of stating more adequately the myth's meaning.

50 In the later philosophical writings of M. Heidegger, hermeneutic means the process of interpreting being, especially in terms of an appreciation of the role of language. This philosophy of interpretation does not give exclusive attention to the author's perspective (literal sense) but rather to what finds expression in the language of the text itself even independently of the author's intention. Drawing on the later Heidegger but modifying his ideas, E. Fuchs' programmatic work *Hermeneutik* (1954) goes beyond Bultmann's hermeneutical principles. For Bultmann the self-interpretation of the reader is on the level of preunderstanding, subordinate to interpreting the text itself; for Fuchs (→ Modern NT Criticism, 41:66) the text interprets the reader by criticizing his self-understanding. The "hermeneutical principle" is where the text is placed in order to speak to the reader, and for theological exegesis the basic hermeneutical principle is human need—a need that reveals what we mean by God. "Translation" (in the sense given above, → 3) involves finding the place where the biblical text can strike home. G. Ebeling (→ Modern NT Criticism, 41:70), a close friend of Fuchs, has also carried forward the development of hermeneutic in the direction indicated by the later Heidegger (cf. the article "Hermeneutik," *RGG* 3 [1959] 242-62). The role he attributes to historical criticism is not so much the role of essential interpretation as the role of removing all distortions so that the text can effectively speak to man. H.-G. Gadamer has written on hermeneutic from a philosophical viewpoint, and he insists that one *always* understands the text differently from the way in which the author himself understood it, and hence interpretation is always a translation from one situation to another.

Whether or not one accepts the heavy philosophical substratum, the new hermeneutic is a modern tendency in favor of a more-than-literal exegesis. The literal sense of Scripture, in this approach, is not necessarily the real meaning of the text at another period. A full exegesis not only discovers the literal sense but also translates that sense into the present situation. (For more detailed explanation, see R. E. Brown, "After Bultmann What?—An Introduction to the Post-Bultmannians," *CBQ* 26 [1964] 1-30.)

51 (ii) *Christian Interpretation of the OT.* Since Marcion's time the problem of what the OT means for a Christian has been with us, and neither Marcion's solution of rejecting the OT nor the orthodox patristic solution of finding Christ in every line of the OT seems realistic. And the 19th-cent. solution has not been much better, namely that of so concentrating on historico-critical exegesis that one forgets that the Bible consists of two Testaments that have a unity. Two recent volumes of essays on the subject show the concern of critical scholars for the Christian dimension of the OT, and the German commentary series *Biblische Kommentar* has stressed that NT relationship is not a goal to be lost sight of.

(Anderson, B. W. [ed.], *The Old Testament and Christian Faith* [N.Y., 1963]. Westermann, C. [ed.], *Essays on Old Testament Hermeneutics* [Richmond, 1963]. An excellent summary of the literature is given by R. E. Murphy, *CBQ* 26 [1964] 349–59.)

Not all the authors who write on the subject are in agreement, but in general they distrust any emphasis on OT prediction of Christ as the means of relating the two Testaments. This distrust of prediction is more prominent among Protestant than among Catholic writers; and J. Barr (*op. cit.*, 117ff.) has rightly objected that, whether modern scholars like it or not, prediction was the way the NT writers themselves related the Testaments and that in the intertestamental period the concept of the prophets as foretellers of the future had greatly developed (→ 34 above). Be this as it may, the tendency of the authors in the Westermann volume of essays is to seek correspondence between the Testaments, not on the verbal level, but on the level of a typological relation between the events of the OT and those of the NT or on the level of promise/fulfillment in salvation history (typology and promise/fulfillment are not mutually exclusive approaches). W. Eichrodt (Westermann vol., 224-45) and G. von Rad (*ibid.*, 17-39) have been interested in reviving typology (as distinct from allegory) whereby OT realities are divinely established models of NT realities, and both authors stress that history is the matrix in which these realities find their connection. It is this stress on history that separates their typology from much of patristic exegesis, which did not have the tools to discover the flow of Israel's history in any detail. W. Zimmerli (*ibid.*, 89-122) and C. Westermann (*ibid.*, 40-49) work with the concept of promise/fulfillment, seen both within the OT itself (e.g., the covenantal promise) and between the Testaments. The NT fulfills not so much isolated promises but an entire history of promise.

52 Turning to individual books on the subject, we find that S. Amsler, a Protestant scholar, in *L'Ancien Testament dans l'Église* (Neuchâtel, 1960), seeks out the NT authors in their use of the OT as a possible guide to how the OT should be read in the Church. He rejects many of the proposed instances of prediction/fulfillment but thinks that the abuses of the method are found more in the Fathers than in the NT (an oversimplification—the NT has much exegesis of the OT that cannot be accepted today as valid exegesis, e.g., Mt 2:15,18; 1 Cor 10:4). He defends typology, but rejects the *sensus plenior* (→ 56 below). A corresponding Catholic work, C. Larcher's *L'actualité chrétienne de l'Ancien Testament* (Paris, 1962), finds that the NT use of the OT does depend heavily on some form of prediction and not only on a broader basis of promise/fulfillment or on prefiguration (typology). Both Larcher and P. Grelot (*Sens chrétien de l'Ancien Testament* [Tournai, 1962]) are favorable to the concept of a *sensus plenior*, although Grelot's views on prediction are not the same as Larcher's.

53 Beneath all this diversity in approach, the various authors are very committed to the interrelationship of the two Testaments. All recognize abuses in past Christian exegesis of the OT and seek to avoid them by emphasizing a broader historical relationship (as opposed to the minute details on which the Fathers capitalized) and by stressing the element of discontinuity that accompanies continuity—the flow from the OT to the NT was not a smooth one. All recognize that interrelationship is a much larger question than messianism. One must confess, however, that these authors do not seem able to find a truly modern way to relate the two Testaments, and in their solutions there are always elements of the very exegesis about which they express suspicion, e.g., typology (→ 72 below). The rejection of prediction is really a rejection of a crude concept wherein the human authors were thought to foresee the distant future; a more sophisticated concept where, unbeknown to the human author, God uses Scripture to prepare for the future deserves much more attention than is given to it by many proponents of a Christian interpretation of the OT.

54 (c) Rejection of More-than-literal Exegesis. Not all exegetes share the convictions illustrated in the above-mentioned movements; many specifically reject one or the other approach to a more-than-literal exegesis. In Catholic circles, for instance, some adamantly reject the *sensus plenior* because they fear such exegesis will endanger the hard-fought-for primacy of the literal sense (B. Vawter, *CBQ* 26 [1964] 87-88). That such a fear is not unwarranted may be seen in the cautions that we gave above (→ 24) about the primacy of the literal sense. In Protestant circles, O. Cullmann is most distrustful of the Bultmannian and post-Bultmannian hermeneutical trend. He believes that the literal exegesis of NT texts, limited though they may be, is the exegete's primary theological duty, while the reader's duty is simply to be obedient to what the authors of the NT wanted to communicate as revelation, even if it is quite foreign to the modern mentality (cited in J. M. Robinson, *New Hermeneutic*, 41). Even E. Käsemann, a Bultmannian disciple, expresses reservations about the new hermeneutic of Fuchs and Ebeling. He fears that interpretation may cease to serve historiography which is in need of clarification, and that it may become an arbitrary builder of new constructions. For a critique of Fuchs' position, see P. J. Achtemeier, *TTod* 23 (1966) 101–19.

55 Nor has the movement for a Christian interpretation of the OT been accepted by all. Although J. D. Smart (*op. cit.*, 23-30) is sympathetic to a unity between the central concern of the OT and that of the Gospels, he is most unhappy about typology. F. Baumgärtel (Westermann vol., 135) objects: "The Old Testament is a witness out of a non-Christian religion; its self-understanding is not identical with evangelical prior understanding." Bultmann (Anderson vol., 31) insists on the discontinuity of the two Testaments to the point of stating: "To Christian faith the Old Testament is no longer revelation." J. Barr (*op. cit.*, 110) has questioned the tendency of Von Rad and Noth to center parallelism between the two Testaments on events, and indeed questions the whole modern Christological exegesis of the OT (p. 152). Many insist that the picture of progressive development in the OT leading to the NT is not true to the evidence. For instance, it is true that personal messianism developed after the Exile in a way that did prepare for the NT (→ Aspects OT Thought, 77:161). Yet the bifurcation in messianism that led to the expectation of a messianic High Priest and the apocalyptic overtones that came to surround the Davidic Messiah were developments that made it more difficult for Jews to see Jesus as the Messiah.

If below in discussing the *sensus plenior* and the typical sense, we show ourselves sympathetic to the validity of a carefully delineated more-than-literal exegesis, we insist that one must be familiar with the many abuses evident in the past history of this exegesis and that the objections of those who oppose it reflect real dangers against which one must take precautions.

56 **(II) The Sensus Plenior.** The term *sensus plenior* (henceforth SPlen) was coined by A. Fernández in 1925 and has passed into English translation as the "fuller sense." The terminology is related to the NT idea of "fulfilling" the OT and, although recent, is not objectionable, unless one wishes to quibble that logically "full" has no comparative. The proponents of the SPlen contend that by this new term they are drawing attention to a valid aspect of more-than-literal exegesis that is as old as the Bible itself. In modern times Newman, Lagrange (*sens supra-littéral*), Pesch (*altior sensus*), and Prat seem to have been forerunners of the idea (on Lagrange, see *CBQ* 17 [1955] 451–55; 18 [1956] 49–53; on the others, see *SPSS* 88–92). Since Fernández' initial suggestion, J. Coppens and P. Benoit have been among the more famous exponents; R. Bierberg, G. Courtade, B. Vawter, and J. L. McKenzie have opposed the idea.

(The history of the theory and the discussion is given by R. E. Brown in *CBQ* 15 [1953] 141–62 and *CBQ* 25 [1963] 262–85. For a detailed exposition of the theory and problems, see *SPSS*. This work gives a bibliography up to 1955; one for the years 1955–62 is found in the 1963 *CBQ* article. Pertinent writing since then includes: P. Sansegundo, *Exposición histórico-crítica del hoy llamado 'sensus plenior' de la sagrada escritura* [Avila, 1963]; B. Vawter, *CBQ* 26 [1964] 85–96; J. M. Robinson, *CBQ* 27 [1965] 6–27; P. Grelot, *The Bible, Word of God* [N.Y. 1968] 313–92; R. E. Brown, *ETL* 43 [1967] 460–69.)

57 **(A) Definition.** *The SPlen is the deeper meaning, intended by God but not clearly intended by the human author, that is seen to exist in the words of Scripture when they are studied in the light of further revelation or of development in the understanding of revelation.* First, the SPlen is, like the literal sense, a meaning of the *words* of Scripture; and in this it differs from the typical sense (→ 72 below). As distinct from the literal sense, the SPlen was *not within the clear intention of the human author* (→ 10 above). For those who prefer the broad definition of the literal sense in which the intention of the human author is not made part of the definition (→ 9 above), the SPlen is only a subdivision of the literal sense (so Benoit). It seems better, however, to keep the two senses distinct.

In saying that the SPlen was not *clearly* intended by the human author, we have hedged on one of the disputed points about the SPlen. All who accept the SPlen would agree that it was not clearly intended; but some would suppose that the human author must have had a vague awareness of the SPlen, while others would require no awareness at all. The latter view seems preferable, since there is a formidable difficulty in explaining what this vague awareness would have consisted in and how it would have been obtained. See *SPSS* 105–14; Brown, *CBQ* 25 [1963] 263–69.

58 Once we affirm that the SPlen was not clearly intended by the human author but was intended by God, we have to find a way of determining the presence of such a deeper meaning; for the ordinary principles of exegesis will tell us only what the human author meant. This special way of determining the presence of a SPlen is through *further divine revelation or development in the understanding of revelation.* Since it is God who reveals and who inspires, God can tell man through revelation what he intended in inspiring earlier passages of Scripture. When we speak of *further revelation*, the chief instance of such revelation would be through a later passage in the Bible itself, for instance the NT may point out the SPlen of an OT text. Actually, since there was a constantly developing revelation within the OT period, later passages of the OT itself may reveal the SPlen of earlier passages of the OT, although strangely Benoit refuses to admit this and confines the SPlen to an OT-NT relationship.

When we speak of *development within the understanding of revelation*, we mean that, even after the end of the biblical era and the close of public revelation, it may have been possible to uncover a SPlen as the contents of revelation came to be more clearly understood. Benoit would reject this possibility too, but a priori there seems no reason to reject it. God guides the Church and Christians in the understanding of revelation; and he can thus make clear the full purpose, not hitherto recognized, that he had in inspiring a particular section of Scripture.

59 **(B) Justification.** The general basis for positing the SPlen would be the fact that in the long history of exegesis given above, texts of Scripture have been interpreted in a way that goes beyond their literal sense, and this fuller interpretation has been sponsored by writings to which Christians give authority, e.g., the NT, the Fathers, Church pronouncements. For example, Mt 1:23 says that the virginal conception of Jesus by Mary took place in order to fulfill what was spoken by the Lord through the prophet (Is 7:14): "Behold, a virgin shall conceive and bear a son, and his name shall be called Emmanuel." A critical examination of Is 7:14, however, gives no evidence that Isaiah was thinking of Jesus' conception. Isaiah does not speak about a virgin; it is not clear that he is referring to a future conception; and the whole import of the scene in ch. 7 of Is implies that this birth will take place *ca.* 734 BC. Clearly Mt's interpretation of Is is more-than-literal. Another example would involve the frequent theological use of Gn 3:15 in reference to Mary's participation in Jesus' victory over evil. This interpretation goes beyond the literal import of the text; for Gn refers in general to womankind and her offspring, and there is no clear reference to victory, only to struggle.

60 Now, and this is extremely important, scholars do *not* suggest that every more-than-literal use of the words of Scripture advocated by the NT, the Fathers, the liturgy, or Church documents is a SPlen. Much of it is accommodation (→ 80 below), catechetical application, or loose association. But there seem to be cases where, after a rigorous application of the restrictive criteria listed below (→ 63–64), we are being told, not that Scripture can be applied in this way, but that this fuller meaning is what God intended when he inspired Scripture. These alone would be instances of a SPlen.

61 **(C) Different Forms.** In particular, two types of SPlen have been suggested as especially important. *First*, there is a series of OT passages, principally in Ps and the Prophets, which have been classically identified as prophecies pertaining to Jesus and to the Christian dispensation. In an older exegesis it was often thought that the human author foresaw specific details about the career of Jesus. Today we recognize that the authors of the OT were concerned with their own times and not with the distant future, and the details of the future of God's plan were hidden from them. The descriptions of the Suffering Servant in Dt-Is, of the suffering figure in Ps 22, and of the anointed (messiah) king in Pss 2 and 110 all seem to have had contemporary meaning rather than intended reference to a distant future. Yet, as Christians have understood God's plan, these passages were to have their full significance unfolded when they were reread in the light of the career of Jesus of Nazareth. The advocates of the theory of a SPlen think that through it they preserve what is valid in the traditional argument from prophecy while still acknowledging the limitations of the human author. This theory permits a Christian to find the same literal sense in an OT passage that a Jew would find.

62 A *second* important form of the SPlen, sometimes called the General SPlen, pertains to the field of biblical theology. Individual passages of a biblical book have deeper meaning when seen in the context of the whole book. Individual books of the Bible have greater meaning when seen in the context of the whole Bible. Themes like faith, sin, and justice have profundity when seen in the context of the whole biblical teaching on the respective subjects. The fuller meaning uncovered in a text which has been placed in a larger biblical context would be a SPlen.

63 **(D) Criteria.** How can one distinguish the SPlen of a text from an accommodation that attributes to a text a meaning that goes beyond even God's intention? The *first criterion* is implicit in what we said above (→ 58) about our knowledge of the SPlen coming from further revelation or from a development in the understanding of revelation. The surest guide to a SPlen is an authoritative interpretation of the words of Scripture in a more-than-literal way—authoritative in the sense that it comes from one of the guides to revelation, e.g., the NT, the Church Fathers, Church pronouncements, etc. This criterion is aimed against oversubjectivity on the part of the individual exegete. If there are real meanings of Scripture that cannot be detected by the strict rules of critical exegesis and yet are of importance to the divine plan for man's salvation, the most likely matrix for their emergence to clarity and acceptance is the context of Church life.

This does not mean that when the Church proclaims a doctrine like the Immaculate Conception or the Assumption, the Catholic exegete can assume that now the Church has unveiled the SPlen of some text that it has cited in discussing the doctrine. As the Protestant exegete J. M. Robinson (*art. cit.*, 15-16) rightly objects, such an approach would make the theory of the SPlen a tool of partisan apologetics and a peg to hang new doctrines on. In relation to the SPlen, Church authority is not looked upon as an agent of exegetical revelation; rather Church life, doctrine, and prayer supply a context in which Scripture is read, commented on, and allowed to "speak," so that the meaning emerges which God wished to convey. Robinson (p. 18) is correct in seeing an analogy for this in the Bultmannian theory that the implicit Christology of Jesus becomes explicit in the Church's kerygma, and in relating the question of the SPlen to the whole question of the role of Scripture and tradition in the development of dogma (see E. Schillebeeckx, "Exegesis, Dogmatics and the Development of Dogma," in H. Vorgrimler, *Dogmatic vs. Biblical Theology* [Baltimore, 1964] 115-45, esp. 133ff.).

64 The *second criterion* is even more effective in avoiding misunderstanding about the role of the SPlen. This criterion is that the SPlen of a text must be homogeneous with the literal sense, i.e., it must be a development of what the human author wanted to say. Jer 31:15 deals with the figurative lament of Rachel (the "mother" of the northern tribes) over the fact that these tribes were taken captive by the Assyrians in the 8th cent. When Mt 2:18 uses this text to describe the lamentation over the slaughter of the Innocents because of a popular but incorrect localization of Rachel's tomb near Bethlehem, there is little homogeneity with the literal sense of the passage in Jer; and in our judgment Mt is not developing the SPlen of Jer but simply accommodating the OT passage. Wis 18:14-15 concerns the nocturnal descent of the destroying angel of the Exodus upon the firstborn of the Egyptians. When the liturgy (Sunday after Christmas) applies this text to Jesus' birth at Bethlehem, there is little homogeneity with the literal sense. When Augustine turns the parable of the Good Samaritan into an allegory of the fall of man, there is little homogeneity with the literal sense. These, then, are not examples of the SPlen.

However, the usage of Is 7:14 by Mt 1:23 may fit this criterion of homogeneity. The original reference seems to have concerned the birth of a child to the royal family, a child who would be a sign of the continuance of the Davidic line and thus of God's continued presence with his people. Even if Isaiah did not think of a virgin birth, this interpretation developed subsequently in Judaism, as we see in the LXX of the Isaian passage, where the girl who is to conceive is identified as a virgin. When Jesus was born of a virgin in the city of David, he was a sign of the continuance of the Davidic line and represented God's presence with his people. Thus, the example has homogeneity.

The criterion of homogeneity seems applicable to the messianic interpretation of Pss 2 and 110 where the anointed king is thought of as lord and as God's begotten son. Although the original reference seems to have been to the reigning king, once the monarchy ceased after the Exile, the words of these Pss were reapplied to a glorious future king who was to come (→ Aspects OT Thought, 77:157–161). In the Christian interpretation of these Pss, Jesus, God's begotten in a way much deeper than that intended by the psalmist, seems to be the "Lord." And so when Heb. 1:5,13 and Mt 22:44 apply these Pss to Jesus, there is a homogeneity with their literal sense.

65 These two criteria are not always easy to apply, and those who accept the theory of the SPlen do not always agree in practice on what is a good example of the SPlen. For further examples, good and bad, see those listed in *SPSS* 140-45. Benoit thinks that the SPlen is present in many passages of Scripture; others think that only rarely can we detect a SPlen that fits the strict criteria proposed above. It would seem best to exercise caution; certainly the majority of the NT citations of the OT in a more-than-literal sense and the overwhelming majority of the liturgical and patristic citations of Scripture do not meet the criteria for a valid SPlen.

66 **(E) Problems.** Some important scholars have denied the possibility of a SPlen on several grounds. Among Spanish writers, S. de Ausejo and A. Ibañez Arana believe that such a sense cannot be reconciled with the instrumental theory of inspiration. Detailed discussion of the arguments on both sides is given in *SPSS* 134-37. If we do not spend time on it here, it is because we find the whole objection too a priori. To decide from a philosophical theory of instrumentality what God could and could not have done in inspiring Scripture is risky, especially since all acknowledge that the instrumentality in the process of inspiration is unique. It is far better to work a posteriori: to see what God has done and then to formulate a theory that can account for it (→ Inspiration, 66:35). It is also too a priori to argue that the human agent would cease to be a true author of Scripture if there were present in his words a sense that he did not understand.

67 A much stronger argument against the SPlen is the contention that when a deeper meaning of a biblical text is recognizable only in the light of further revelation, the meaning is not contained in the text itself but is acquired at the moment of the further revelation. In other words, one should speak of a fuller understanding on the part of the exegete rather than of a fuller sense of the Scripture. Actually God could have chosen to act in either way. In inspiring the words of Is 7:14 God may have withheld any reference to the future virgin birth of Jesus which was part of the divine plan, and in this case he would have made the applicability of Is 7:14 to the virgin birth part of the new revelation underlying Mt 1:23. Or through a SPlen, God may have included in Is 7:14 a reference to the virgin birth, even though the prophet was not aware of this reference and it would not be discovered for hundreds of years. The first suggestion seems to posit a certain dichotomy in God's plan of action; moreover, it does not do justice to the fact that Matthew seems to think that the reference to the virgin birth was already in the OT. (On the Is 7:14 question see *EB* 74 where Pius VI insists that in some sense, literal or typical, this verse

refers to the virgin birth.) The NT concept of fulfilling the OT is closer to an idea of a fuller sense than to that of a fuller understanding.

Robinson (*art cit.*, 20) points out that the claim that there is an addition of meaning and thus fuller understanding rather than a fuller sense involves a rather artificial distinction, since it neglects the dynamic factor in the literal sense. The literal sense is what leads to a fuller understanding; the SPlen is part of the organic growth of the literal sense, not a mere addition.

68 The theory of the SPlen is dependent on a scholastic, instrumental understanding of inspiration. It is no accident that P. Benoit, one of the great champions of the SPlen, is also the leading modern exponent of the scholastic theory of inspiration (→ Inspiration, 66:50). There are those who find difficulty with such a theory in which God intimately guides every step from thought to word, and they prefer to approach inspiration as a social charism or from the aspect of the post-factum role of Scripture in the community (→ Inspiration, 66:60, 39). These new approaches do not favor the idea of a SPlen whose very definition is phrased in terms of God's intention and man's intention. The future of the non-scholastic approaches to inspiration is difficult to predict; but it would seem that if the theory of the SPlen is to survive in Catholic circles and to find sympathetic understanding in non-Catholic circles, it should not be so dependent on the scholastic, instrumental theory of inspiration. Perhaps the solution is to take the emphasis off the mechanics of the divine and human intentions and to concentrate rather on the close relationship between the idea of the SPlen and the modern interest in the hermeneutical value of language (→ 50 above). The language of Scripture may have had one meaning in the human author's situation; yet in a different situation (e.g., that of the Church today) it may make its point in a different way and to this extent mean something different. See Robinson, *art. cit.*, 19; also pp. 23-27 where he responds to Vawter's oversimplified correlation of the sense of words with the author's formal intent.

69 Another realistic objection against the theory of the SPlen is that this sense is seldom verified and so is of little use in justifying or explaining NT, patristic, liturgical, or ecclesiastical exegesis. It is interesting to note that the proponents of the SPlen tend to confine their discussion of this sense to the theoretical plane, seldom appealing to it in their works of exegesis.

70 In summary, if one surveys the writing on the SPlen, it seems that the majority of exegetes are willing to accept it as a theory. This is a good indication of its value in preserving an important truth about Scripture, namely that one has not exhausted the real meaning of a text when one has determined by historico-critical exegesis what it meant to the man who wrote it. Yet the difficulties that many have found in the idea of the SPlen suggest that it is only a partial solution to a much wider problem. See Brown, *ETL* 43 (1967) 462-69.

71 **(III) The Typical Sense.** The term *typos* is found in Rom 5:14, where we are told that Adam was a type of Christ, and in 1 Cor 10:6, where we are told that the things that happened in the desert to Israel during the Exodus are types for Christians. Nevertheless, the sense of Scripture involving types was not known as the typical sense until late in the history of exegesis. The Fathers spoke of it as "allegory" or as the "mystical sense"; Thomas Aquinas knew of it as the "spiritual sense." Some modern authors distinguish sharply between typology and allegory, e.g., typology is based on historical connections whereas allegory is imaginative. It is quite necessary from our point of view to distinguish valid from invalid typology; but we should remember that there was no consciousness among the Fathers that allegory was invalid typology. The Fathers received with equal enthusiasm examples of typology that today we consider invalid and examples that we consider valid (cf. Barr, *op. cit.*, 103-48).

72 **(A) Definition.** *The typical sense is the deeper meaning that the things (persons, places, and events) of Scripture possess because, according to the intention of the divine author, they foreshadow future things.* The typical sense differs from the literal sense and from the SPlen in that it is not a sense of the words of Scripture but is attached to things described in Scripture. Like the SPlen it can be discerned only through further revelation or through development in the understanding of revelation. Let us analyze the definition.

73 First, the typical sense concerns *things*—these realities are designated as types, while the future realities they foreshadow are antitypes. "Things" must be taken in a wide sense. Not only what we would ordinarily consider things serve as types (e.g., manna as a type of the Eucharist); but also persons (Adam, Melchizedek, Moses, David, and Jeremiah are types of Christ; Eve is a type of Mary) and animals (the paschal lamb is a type of Christ [cf. Jn 19:36]; the bronze serpent raised on a pole on the desert is a type of the crucified Christ [Jn 3:14]). Events may also serve as types (the Exodus is a type of baptism [1 Cor 10:2]). It is generally conceded that the type may even be a fictional event (Jonah in the whale as a type of Christ in the grave [Mt 12:40]). However, some modern authors, like G. von Rad and M. Noth, would confine all valid typology to historical events. For a penetrating criticism of this trend see Barr, *op. cit.*, 110-15.

74 Second, the things that are types must be written of *in Scripture*. In God's plan David was a type of Christ before a word was written about him, but the figure of David acquired a typical sense only when a human author was inspired by God to write about David. The importance of this qualification is seen most clearly when the factor that makes a thing a type is not its historical reality but the literary description of it. Melchizedek undoubtedly had parents; but what turns him into a type of Christ according to Heb 7:3 is that his lineage is not recorded in Scripture. Some have failed to appreciate this distinction between the extrabiblical existence of the "things" that are types and the typical sense that they acquire when they are described in Scripture, and consequently have denied that the typical sense is a sense of Scripture (e.g., S. Muñoz Iglesias, *EstBib* 12 [1953] 159-83, answered by M. de Tuya, *CiTom* 80 [1953] 625-61). Such a denial has no support in the Fathers or in Church tradition; the encyclical *Divino Afflante Spiritu* (*EB* 552) treats the "spiritual sense" as a real sense of Scripture. The objection that the typical sense cannot be a sense of Scripture because the human author was not aware of it is the same objection that is raised against the SPlen (→ 66 above).

75 Third, types *foreshadow the future*. The type and antitype are on two different levels of time, and only when the antitype appears does the typical sense become apparent. The type is always imperfect; it is a silhouette, not a portrait, of the antitype; and therefore realization is bound to bring surprises. This limitation in typology is important because much of the criticism of any more-than-literal exegesis is centered on a failure to appreciate the limited character of the OT and on an exaggeration of the continuity between the Testaments at the expense of their real diversity. Emphasis on the imperfection of the relationship between type and antitype safeguards the typical sense against such an objection.

76 **(B) Criteria.** The ordination of type to antitype is of divine origin, and so the criteria for recognizing the typical sense are much like those for recognizing the SPlen (→ 63-64 above). *First*, revelation or development in the understanding of revelation is the safest guide to the presence of a typical sense; without such a guide human ingenuity tends to run riot in detecting types. Thus, most of the types accepted by exegetes are types that have been pointed out by the NT or by a *consensus* of the Fathers, of liturgical usages, and of Church documents. For example, the NT (Heb) saw Melchizedek as a type of Christ; later on, liturgy and patristic exegesis specified that Melchizedek's presentation of bread and wine (Gn 14:18) was a type of the Christian Eucharistic sacrifice.

77 The *second* criterion for determining the presence of a typical sense is that the type be related to the antitype through an organic development in revelation. We cannot classify as a type every OT foreshadowing that is mentioned in the NT or the Fathers (witnesses who made little distinction between sober exegesis of scriptural senses and purely imaginative accommodation). We should seek evidence that God really planned the relationship between type and antitype. Modern authors implicitly recognize the need of such a criterion by their stress on the relationship of real typology to salvation history and also by a stress on promise/fulfillment. For instance, the whole parallel between the Old Covenant and the New Covenant, between Moses and Jesus, which is basic to much of the NT, guarantees the main lines of Exodus typology. The relation of Jesus to the Davidic line guarantees much of the David typology. It is when typology is attached to isolated things and persons that we must be more skeptical, e.g., is Rahab (Jos 2) really a type of the Church?

78 **(C) Problem.** Is typology too closely associated with the symbolic interpretation of the past to be relevant to modern exegesis? Many scholars who theoretically accept the typical sense and acknowledge some of the principal examples of typology in the NT and in the Fathers are not at all sympathetic to any renewal of typical exegesis. Above (→ 46-48) we distinguished between the attempt to refurbish patristic and medieval exegesis (De Lubac, Daniélou, *et al.*) and the attempt to construct a more-than-literal exegesis on more modern grounds. But how does typology fit into the latter movement? It is not enough to state with Eichrodt (Westermann vol., 227) that it is impossible to confuse typology and allegory if one examines them closely, for some scholars regard as imaginative allegory the typology that Eichrodt accepts (→ 55 above). Coppens, *Les Harmonies*, 93-94, proposes some interesting examples of a new typology based on the better modern understanding of Jewish history; but one can be skeptical about how much success these new examples will achieve. Probably, as with the SPlen, the typical sense will survive as a truly useful hermeneutical category if it is somehow revamped and treated as part of a much larger more-than-literal sense.

79 By way of summary we may schematize what we have seen about the three basic senses of Scripture. If we divide them according to the intention of the human author, they fall into two main categories:

1. Meaning intended by the human author = the *literal sense*
2. Meaning intended by God that goes beyond what the human author intended:
   (a) flowing from the words of Scripture = *sensus plenior*
   (b) flowing from "things" described in Scripture = the *typical sense*

(De Lubac, H., "Sens spirituel," *RSR* 36 [1949] 542–76. Daniélou, J., "Qu'est-ce que la typologie?" in *L'Ancien Testament et les chrétiens*, 199–205. Lampe, G. W. H. and K. J. Woolcombe, *Essays on Typology* [SBT 22; London, 1957]. Also articles by Von Rad, Noth, and Eichrodt in the Westermann vol.)

RELATED TOPICS

80 **(I) Is Accommodation Justified?** In addition to the senses of Scripture intended by the human and/or the divine author, there are applications of Scripture on the part of the reader or interpreter that we call accommodation. This is not a sense of Scripture but a sense given to Scripture; it is not a product of exegesis but of eisegesis. The range of accommodation is immense, running from catechetical application to literary embellishment. Much of the more-than-literal exegesis in the Fathers and in the liturgy is accommodation—a fact that is quite intelligible when we remember that Scripture was looked upon as the basic text from which a wide span of Christian knowledge was taught. When Gregory the Great told his audience that the Gospel parable of the five talents referred to the five senses, he was accommodating. The liturgy accommodates to the lives of Christian confessor pontiffs the praise that Sir 44–45 heaps upon the patriarchs. A very frequent use of accommodation is in sermons, e.g., when preachers eulogized Pope John XXIII by citing Jn 1:6, "There was a man sent by God whose name was John." Books on the spiritual life accommodate Scripture by applying passages to new spiritual problems.

81 Accommodation is inevitable with a book that is as familiar and as respected as the Bible. And in truth, a certain tolerance can be extended to accommodation when it is done with intelligence, sobriety, and taste. In matters of taste, for instance, it is not unbecoming to apply Jn 1:6 in eulogy of a beloved and saintly Pope; its application to other well-known men named John, not particularly noted for sanctity, is more dubious. Too often scriptural passages, e.g., "The truth will make you free" (Jn 8:32), are applied to political or social situations with which they have nothing to do.

But, even when accommodation is handled with a certain sobriety, we must insist that it should be only an occasional use of Scripture and not the principal use. Preachers may find accommodation easy and may resort to it rather than taking the trouble to investigate the literal sense of Scripture. Occasional use of the imagination in accommodating Scripture can be attractive, but to substitute it for the literal sense is to substitute man's ingenuity for God's inspired word. If the writer or speaker makes clear to his audience that he is accommodating and not really giving an exegesis of Scripture, some of the danger is removed. But in general it must be said that in this age, when we have come to recognize the tremendous wealth of the literal sense of Scripture, a sound exposition of that sense will render far more service than ingenious accommodation.

82 **(II) Authoritative Interpretations by the Church.** When we discussed the literal sense, we explained the rules of form criticism and literary criticism as the best guidelines to the meaning of Scripture. But as Catholics do we not say that the authentic interpretation of Scripture belongs to the Church? In the popular understanding there remains a certain confusion about the Church's role in exegesis as opposed to "private interpretation." The latter phrase is often an oversimplification of what is regarded as a Protestant position. First of all, it should be stated that in the more traditional Protestant groups there is no suggestion that each individual can authoritatively interpret Scripture. There is church tradition among Protestants, even as there is among Catholics. Moreover, since the correct interpretation of Scripture requires education and effort, the average Protestant is no more capable of picking up the Bible and determining at a glance what the author meant than is the average Catholic. A Protestant's understanding of Scripture comes through Sunday schools, sermons, and church authority, even as the average Catholic's understanding comes from those who taught him. A true difference between Protestant and Catholic opinions is not centered on the existence of a traditional interpretation of Scripture but on the binding value given to that tradition.

83 Even in the question of the binding Church interpretation of Scripture, however, we must be careful not to oversimplify the Catholic position. The first caution is to distinguish between the *dogmatic statements* of the Catholic Church about Scripture and *prudential decisions* made for the common good. The latter are not infallible guides to truth. For instance, between 1905 and 1915 the Pontifical Biblical Commission issued a series of directives about Scripture; today, with the approval of the same commission, most of these directives are regarded as passé by Catholic scholars (→ Church Pronouncements, 72:25). One criterion of whether or not the Church is speaking dogmatically is related to the matter about which the Church is speaking. Since the Church is the custodian of revelation and since Scripture is a mirror of revelation, the Church has the power to determine infallibly the meaning of Scripture *in matters of faith and morals* (DS 1507, 3007). The Church claims no absolute or direct authority over matters of biblical authorship, geography, chronology, and other scientific aspects; and so the Church has not made any *dogmatic* pronouncements about authorship, dating of books, unity of composition, etc.

84 And when we come to the actual exegesis of Scripture—something that could be a matter of faith and morals—in regard to 99 per cent of the Bible, the Church has not commented officially on what a passage does or does not mean. That task is left to the knowledge, intelligence, and hard work of individual exegetes who claim no more than reasonable conviction for their conclusions. When the Church has spoken on a particular verse, most often it has done so in a negative manner, i.e., by rejecting certain interpretations as false because they constitute a threat to faith and morals. The Council of Trent, for instance, condemned the Calvinist interpretation that would reduce the reference to water in Jn 3:5 (baptismal passage: "Unless a man be begotten from above [born again] of water and Spirit") to a mere metaphor (DS 1615). Again it condemned those who would dissociate the power of forgiving sins exercised in the Sacrament of Penance from the power accorded in Jn 20:23 (DS 1703).

85 When Church documents cite Scripture positively, we must distinguish as to whether the document is giving an authoritative exegesis of Scripture or simply using Scripture to illustrate its argument. The bull *Ineffabilis Deus* on the Immaculate Conception recalls Gn 3:15, and the bull *Munificentissimus Deus* on the Assumption recalls Ap 12. Are the respective Popes dogmatically affirming that these texts of Scripture refer in their literal sense to the Marian doctrines? Or perhaps in a more-than-literal sense, like the SPlen? Or do the citations imply no more than that reflection on these scriptural verses aided theologians in understanding the Marian doctrines and thus guided the Church to take a dogmatic position? In the view of many scholars the last possibility is the correct one. In particular, Pius XII seems to claim no more than that the dogma of the Assumption receives support from Scripture (*nitor: AAS* 42 [1950] 767, 769).

86 If we leave aside the instances where the Church has used Scripture to illustrate a dogmatic position, we find really few instances where the Church has spoken affirmatively and authoritatively about the meaning of a passage. And even here it is very difficult to be certain that it is speaking about the literal sense of Scripture. We must remember that the concept of a literal sense established by historico-critical method is very much a modern phenomenon. Modern too is the emphasis on the distinction between what a text meant to its author and what it came to mean in subsequent ecclesiastical or theological usage. In the instance cited above where the Council of Trent condemned a wrong interpretation of Jn 20:23, did the Council Fathers wish to imply that the author of Jn had the Sacrament of Penance in mind, or did they not rather wish to insist on the relation of Penance to the forgiveness of sins attested in that verse? If Trent cited Jas 5:14–15 in relation to the Sacrament of Extreme Unction (DS 1716), did the Council wish to affirm that the author of Jas knew that the healing of the sick was a sacrament, or rather did it not affirm simply that the power of healing described in Jas was an instance of a power that later was understood to be exercised in the sacrament? In both instances a knowledge of the history of the development of sacramental theology and belief suggests the second alternative. In other words, in such statements about Scripture the Church does not seem to be settling a historical question (what was in the mind of the author when he wrote the text), but a religious question, namely the implications of Scripture for the life of the faithful. (We do not pretend that the Council Fathers at Trent were necessarily conscious of this distinction; we are merely concerned with the *de facto* import of their decisions.)

87 Are there any instances where the Church has spoken authoritatively about the literal sense of Scripture? Trent seems to have spoken thus about Jesus' words of Eucharistic institution: "After he had blessed bread and wine, he said in plain, unmistakable words that he was giving them his own body and his own blood.... These words have their proper and obvious meaning and were so understood by the Fathers" (DS 1637). Vatican I seems to have been speaking about the literal sense of Mt 16:17–19 and Jn 21:15–17 when it insisted Christ gave Peter real primacy among the apostles (DS 3053–55).

Experts in dogmatic theology, however, are not in agreement about whether even in these instances the Church was defining the literal sense of Scripture. A. C. Cotter (*Theologia fundamentalis* [2nd ed.; Weston, Mass., 1947] 681) thinks that Vatican I did directly define the meaning of the Matthean text. Yet V. Betti (*La costituzione dommatica 'Pastor aeternus' del Concilio Vaticano I* [Rome, 1961] 592) states: "The interpretation of these two texts [Mt 16:17–19; Jn 21:15–17] as proof of the two dogmas mentioned does not fall *per se* under dogmatic definition—not only because no mention is made of them in the canon, but because there is no trace of a desire in the Council to give an authentic interpretation of them in this sense."

88 These few instances of possible Church definition (there may be others) and the instances where the Church has condemned a particular interpretation of

Scripture cause much difficulty for Protestants. J. M. Robinson, *CBQ* 27 (1965) 8–11, protests that if an exegete by careful use of method comes to a conclusion about a particular verse of Scripture and then the Magisterium steps in and says his conclusion is wrong, it is a denial of intellect. He observes, "The invalidation of the conclusion resulting from the proper application of method necessarily invalidates the method," and thus in principle the freedom and scientific quality of Catholic exegesis are imperiled.

In response, three observations should be made. *First,* Catholic exegetes would honestly hold that in the instances where the Church has spoken authoritatively about the literal sense of Scripture, negatively or positively, a plausible exegetical case can be made for the Church's position. The meaning that the Church finds in the verse may not be the only meaning that one could derive by critical method, but it is a possible meaning. Therefore, the Church's position does not imply a rejection of proper exegetical method; for the Catholic exegete is simply accepting an interpretation on the surety of his faith where historical criticism alone could lead only to probability or possibility.

89 *Second,* in interpreting Scripture the Magisterium does not operate in independence of and isolation from reliable scriptural scholarship. The Magisterium does not come to its conclusion about what a biblical passage does or does not mean by some sort of mystical instinct or by direct revelation from on high. Traditional faith, theological implications, and long usage all enter into the Magisterial decision, but so also does responsible and scholarly exegesis. Both Trent and Vatican I consulted the best Catholic exegetes of the time. We are close enough to Vatican II to know that when exegetes pointed out that Scripture was being misused, such misinterpretation was dropped from the conciliar documents. In fact, Vatican II affirmed that the work done by exegetes is a factor in bringing the judgment of the Church to maturity (*De Revelatione* 3:12). It may be asked if the Church has ever spoken (or ever will speak) against the scholarly opinion of the majority of Catholic exegetes. R. E. Murphy, *Commonweal* 80 (June 26, 1964) 419–20, has correctly insisted, "The Church is hearing the Word ever anew through the work of its theologians and exegetes—and this work must go on *freely*."

90 *Third,* the role of the Church in interpreting Scripture must not be seen only in terms of a possible curtailment of scientific freedom; the Church makes a positive hermeneutic contribution. If the drive of the "New Hermeneutic" is to let Scripture speak to the man of today, the Catholic feels very strongly that the liturgical and doctrinal life of the Church is the "hermeneutical place" where Scripture speaks most truly (→ 50 above). The instinctive negative reaction of the Church to rationalism, liberalism, and modernism was not a rejection of the scientific method (although unfortunately and accidentally that method was thus brought into temporary disrepute), but a reflection of the Church's good sense that in such "isms" Scripture was not speaking truly. One may acknowledge that at times, because of the weaknesses of the men who constitute it, the Church does not immediately or adequately respond to a meaning of Scripture that is patent to exegetes—whence the constant need of renewal and reform from within (→ Canonicity, 67:96). But despite that, the Church remains par excellence the place where Scripture is heard in its truest and fullest meaning.

91 **(III) Exegetical Authority of the Fathers.** In almost every Roman document pertaining to scriptural studies there has been a statement about interpreting Scripture in loyalty to the mind of the Fathers and Doctors of the Church. Until recently, as a result of the Modernist crisis, Catholic exegetes teaching in seminaries were annually sworn to interpret Scripture according to the unanimous consent of the Fathers. The 1964 Instruction of the Biblical Commission (→ Church Pronouncements, 72:35) continues the insistence: "Let the Catholic exegete, following the guidance of the Church, derive profit from all the earlier interpreters, especially the holy Fathers and Doctors of the Church."

Yet when one reads the actual exegesis of the Fathers as we described it above (→ 37–40), it really has little in common with the methods and results of modern Catholic exegesis. We have recorded a reluctance to return to the more-than-literal exegesis of the Fathers. What then is the practical import of patristic exegesis as a guide?

92 First of all, the area in which patristic authority is strongest is that of the dogmatic implications of Scripture, not that of literal exegesis. For example, Athanasius was quite aware that no text of Scripture fully answered the Arian heresy; no single text in its literal sense irrefutably showed that Jesus was "true God of true God." But he insisted that in the 4th-cent. problematic the only answer that Scripture could give to the question that Arius was raising was the answer of Nicaea ("Letter Concerning the Decrees of the Council of Nicaea," 5.19–21). Obviously, thus understood, loyalty to patristic authority is no restriction on the liberty or scientific quality of modern Catholic exegesis.

Moreover, when it is taken as an absolute norm, the unanimous consent of the Fathers (morally unanimous consent, not necessarily numerically unanimous) does not affect many disputed passages. In a passage where one might hope for unanimity, e.g., the Petrine application of Mt 16:18, one finds, for instance, that neither Augustine nor Chrysostom took the foundation rock to be Peter!

In summary, the Church's insistence on the exegetical authority of the Fathers reflects her desire that the Catholic exegete should not forget the dogmatic heritage that comes to him from tradition. But in terms of practical guidance in modern literal exegesis, patristic authority is of restricted importance, especially for the OT.

93 **(IV) Biblical Preaching.** As we mentioned above (→ 4), prophoristics, which gives the rules for expounding Scripture to others, is a part of hermeneutics. Because space does not allow a discussion of Bible classes, scriptural catechetics, Bible vigils, and many of the other ways of presenting Scripture, we shall concentrate here on preaching. In trying to describe a biblical sermon, we are not denying the possibility, the desirability, and even the necessity of other types of sermons; we are simply trying to make clear what is and what is not a biblical sermon.

We may begin negatively. A biblical sermon is not a tissue of Scripture quotes. Nor is one giving a biblical sermon when he picks a topic from dogmatic or moral theology and cites a few biblical passages to illustrate or prove his thesis. The oratorical technique whereby one begins with the Scripture pericope assigned by the liturgy (e.g., the Sunday Gospel) and then proceeds to talk about something that is really not related to that passage is not the procedure of a biblical sermon (and, indeed, is of dubious value). It would be preferable to say that one is going to speak on Vatican II, or on Purgatory, or on interracial issues, or on a charity collection, than to use the Scripture pericope as a springboard for launching into such a topic. If the liturgical setting gives to a Scripture pericope an orientation that is not faithful to its literal sense, e.g., the Christmas use of Wis 18:14–15 (→ 64 above), a sermon employing this orientation is more liturgical than biblical.

A true biblical sermon is: (1) either an explanation centered around the literal sense of a biblical passage, its setting, thought, and import; (2) or an explanation and development of a biblical theme that runs through many passages.

94 A sermon of the *first type* demands that the preacher possess a certain amount of technical background knowledge, e.g., as to whether there are textual or critical problems in the passage, and whether there are parallels and what light they cast on the passage. Our contention that the preacher should possess or acquire this knowledge does not mean that such information should necessarily be part of his sermon. The preacher should resist the tendency to transfer to the pulpit a digest of what was learned in the classroom; he must select and rethink such matter according to the purpose of a sermon, which is different from that of a lecture. Often technical knowledge can best be put to use in helping one to determine what *not* to say and where *not* to put the emphasis. For instance, if one knows that most scholars do not accept the historicity of a scene, then in drawing a theological lesson from that scene, one avoids statements that would stress its historicity.

95 Yet, and this is important, questions of historicity are really not in themselves sermon material. Too often, impressed with the novel character of what they have recently learned (correctly?), preachers enter the pulpit with an itch to shock: "There was no Garden of Eden. There were no magi. Etc." Leaving aside the question of the oversimplified and sometimes incorrect tendency of such statements, we must insist that they serve no purpose in sermons whose aim is to bring the wealth of Scripture to the spiritual and salvific aid of the people. One can preach on a topic like Gn 1-3 in such a way that one respects the historical problems involved but nevertheless concentrates on the theological message. See below (→ 100) for a more detailed discussion on the communication of modern critical approaches to Scripture.

96 As for supplying historical, geographical, and other factual background for a biblical passage, a little bit of technical material in a sermon goes a long way. In some sermons it may be truly useful to set a scene historically and geographically because that is required for understanding the message. One can scarcely understand what Jesus says to the Samaritan woman in Jn 4 without knowing a little of the Samaritans and Jacob's well; one needs to know something of the problems at Corinth to understand Paul's remarks in the Corinthian letters. But too often valuable preaching time is wasted by displaying erudition that really does nothing for the central message, e.g., sermons on Jesus' passion that go into detail about different methods of crucifixion and types of crosses. The sense of the goal of the sermon should also regulate how much exegesis of individual verses is included. Concentration on only the significant lines is generally more effective than an atomistic dissection of line after line.

97 Because preaching on the literal sense of a passage requires knowledge and, therefore, effort, the greatest danger in biblical preaching is a tendency to substitute one's personal impressions of Scripture as the subject of the sermon. "What I thought of when I read this passage" replaces what God's inspired author meant when he wrote the passage. Although personal impressions may occasionally be of interest, they frequently descend to the level of moralizing and homespun philosophizing. When parishioners complain about lack of content in sermons, they are often protesting against the impressionistic approach to Scripture.

98 When the preacher has explained the literal meaning of a biblical passage, he should then point out the relevance of this to the lives of the people. Often the relevance is quite evident from the subject matter, and there is probably more danger of unduly prolonged and irrelevant application than of insufficient application. The burden of the sermon is so to explain the Scripture that the Scripture itself can speak to the needs and lives of the audience, without interposing an elaborate and often individually inapplicable exhortation. If we stress the explanatory rather than the hortatory side of the sermon, it is because it is easier to be hortatory than to explain, and more abuse has come from overexhortation than from overexplanation. The explanation of a theologically relevant portion of Scripture may not change a person's life immediately after he hears it; but like the seed mentioned in Mk 4:26ff., scriptural understanding sinks into fertile soil and bears fruit without overanxious attempts to hasten the process.

99 Many of the cautions just given are applicable as well to biblical sermons of the *second type*, i.e., preaching on biblical themes or personages. In addition, however, with this type of preaching one should insist that only when a biblical theme is developed in a *biblical way* is the sermon truly biblical. The Eucharist is a NT theme; but if the sermon concentrates on the matter and form of the sacrament, on transsubstantiation, etc., it is not a biblical sermon. Yet at times it will be necessary in a predominantly biblical treatment to bring in the more formal and developed theology of later Christianity. Biblical thought is frequently symbolic, imprecise, and inchoative; and in a sermon one should not so compartmentalize the different stages of theology that one leaves the audience without an adequate picture. For instance, a biblical treatment of the Trinitarian (or better "triadic") passages in the NT would reflect the imprecision of 1st-cent. thought on that subject; but a preacher should clarify this imprecision, as historically the later Church did. A biblical sermon on a subject like the Trinity should reflect the biblical aspect of a *larger truth.*

100 **(V) Popular Communication of Modern Critical Views.** One other aspect of prophoristics may be treated. The 1961 Monitum of the Holy Office and the 1964 Instruction of the Pontifical Biblical Commission—two documents from Rome (→ Church Pronouncements, 72:34-35), one restrictive in tendency, the other liberalizing—both insist on the dangers of scandalizing the faithful by communicating in the biblical field "vain or insufficiently established novelties." The PBC Instruction forbids those who publish for the faithful "led on by some pernicious itch for newness, to disseminate any trial solutions for difficulties without a prudent selection and serious discrimination; for thus they perturb the faith of many."

Such warnings are realistic. We cautioned above (→ 95) about making historical criticism the subject of sermons. Not only is this dangerous for the faithful, but damage has been done to reputable biblical scholars by enthusiasts who popularize the scholars' views without necessary qualifications and in a context where they were not meant to be presented. The general principle is that one should not leave the audience with problems that the audience is not capable of solving. If one has to bring in elements of historical criticism, then one should take cognizance of possible implications and head off wrong conclusions.

101 But if we acknowledge the danger of rash popularization, we must firmly accentuate the danger on the other side as well—a danger that unfortunately has not received sufficient attention in Church documents. This is the danger that an exaggerated fear of scandal will prevent popularizers from communicating to educated Catholics the more sophisticated understanding of the Bible that they should have. So often we hear about the few that are scandalized, and no voice is raised about the much greater crime of leaving the many in ignorance of modern biblical criticism. Fear of scandal must never lead to a double standard whereby the simple or the young are taught things about the Bible that are false just so that they will not be shocked. Common sense dictates that all education be scaled to the ability of the audience, but this does not mean that elementary biblical instruction should be noncritical; it means that elementary instruction should be critical in an elementary way. From the very first time the story of Gn 1-3 is told to kindergarten children, they should be taught to think of it as a popular story and not as history, even though the teacher may not wish at that level to raise formally the question of historicity. Even beginners can be taught to think of the Gospels as recorded preaching and teaching rather than as biographies of Jesus.

102 Unfortunately, too, an exaggerated fear of scandal can hamper scientific research. There are a host of delicate biblical questions that need scientific study and discussion, e.g., the historicity of the infancy narratives, and the human knowledge of Christ. Yet scholars know that if they write on these subjects even in professional and technical magazines, an account, often confused, will soon appear in the popular press. In other words, while competent Catholic scholars are urged to keep these matters away from public notice, whether they like it or not others will popularize their work. The result is that frequently the scholar is accused of being responsible for the scandal and is made the target of recriminations by would-be protectors of the faith. The whole distinction between discussion on a scholarly level and popularization—a distinction presupposed in the warnings from Rome—is rapidly dying out, and we should face this problem more frankly. In the long run more damage has been done to the Church by the fact that her scholars have not always been free to discuss delicate problems than by the fact that some of the faithful are scandalized by the dissemination of new ideas. Imprudence and occasional scandal are the almost inevitable price that one must pay for the right of free discussion. And indeed such free academic discussion has its own way of crushing errors—a devastating book review in a biblical magazine may be more effective in eradicating nonsense than a warning from Church authority.

72

CHURCH PRONOUNCEMENTS

Thomas Aquinas Collins, O.P.

Raymond E. Brown, S.S.

BIBLIOGRAPHY

1 Ahern, B., "Textual Directives of the Encyclical *Divino Afflante Spiritu*," *CBQ* 7 (1945) 340–47. Braun, F.-M., "Le sens plénier et les encycliques," *RTh* 51 (1951) 294–304. Cotter, A. C., "The Antecedents of the Encyclical *Providentissimus Deus*," *CBQ* 5 (1943) 117–24. De Fraine, J., "L'encyclique *Humani Generis* et les erreurs concernant l'Écriture Sainte," *ScEccl* 5 (1953) 7–28. Hartdegen, S., "The Influence of the Encyclical *Providentissimus Deus*," *CBQ* 5 (1943) 141–59. Jedin, H., *A History of the Council of Trent* (vol. 2; St. Louis, 1961). Lagrange, M.-J., "A propos de l'encyclique *Providentissimus*," *RB* 4 (1895) 48–64; "Le décret *Lamentabili sane exitu* et la critique historique," *RB* 16 (1907) 542–54. Lattey, C., "The Encyclical *Humani Generis* and the Origins of the Human Race," *Scr* 4 (1951) 278–79. Levie, J., *The Bible, Word of God in Words of Men* (N.Y., 1961). Murphy, R. T., "The Teaching of the Encyclical *Providentissimus Deus*," *CBQ* 5 (1943) 125–40. Vosté, J., *De divina inspiratione et veritate Sacrae Scripturae* (2nd ed.; Rome, 1932).

The two principal collections of Church pronouncements are: *Enchiridion Biblicum* (abbrev. *EB;* 4th ed.; Rome, 1961); and *Rome and the Study of Scripture* (abbrev. *RSS;* 7th ed.; St. Meinrad, Ind., 1962). Also *The Documents of Vatican II*, ed. by W. M. Abbott and J. Gallagher (N.Y., 1966).

2 OUTLINE

HISTORICAL BACKGROUND FOR RECENT PRONOUNCEMENTS

3 **(I) Introduction.** In the pages that follow, we shall present a quick summary of ecclesiastical statements pertaining to the Bible. Some background is necessary for the evaluation of these statements; for, although all demand respect and understanding, not all these statements require equal adherence. Obviously,

Sections 3–9 and 13–16 are the work of R. E. Brown; sections 10–12, 17–24, and 36 that of T. A. Collins. Sections 25–35 were written jointly by these authors.

for instance, decrees of the ecumenical councils are more binding than papal encyclicals. In particular, there is a certain temporal character to the binding force of the decrees of the Pontifical Biblical Commission (PBC), for these are prudential decisions on practical problems. They require obedience at the time they are issued but are subject to subsequent revision and are in no way to be considered infallible. Moreover, all these documents, conciliar, papal, and curial, must be evaluated in the light of the time in which they were issued and the problems to which they were addressed. A fundamentalism in interpreting them is just as objectionable as a fundamentalism in interpreting Scripture. One must distinguish between the precise truth affirmed and its conceptual or verbal expression, which is determined by historical circumstances.

With the exception of the decrees of the Councils of Florence and Trent, all the documents to be discussed are dated within the last 100 years, and so it may be helpful to summarize Rome's attitude toward biblical studies during this period in order to show the atmosphere against which the statements must be evaluated.

4 **(A) 1870–1900.** This period saw the first real Catholic encounter with a vigorous Protestant biblical criticism (→ Modern NT Criticism, 41:6ff.; → Modern OT Criticism, 70:23ff.). To religious men accustomed to think of Scripture as inspired and inerrant, the new insights raised problems about biblical inerrancy in matters both of natural science and of history (→ Inspiration, 66:75-76). The fact that some non-Catholics were being led by their biblical studies to devalue the religious import of the Scriptures created a certain defensiveness on the part of Church authorities, ever anxious to preserve the Scriptures as God's word. Vatican I gave evidence of this attitude in general questions of theology, but the brevity of the life of this council did not allow its full attitude toward Scripture to be seen. It did little more than repeat the Tridentine statement on canonicity and stress the inspiration of Scripture (→ Inspiration, 66:33). Leo XIII's encyclical *Providentissimus Deus* (1893) is the chief witness to the official ecclesiastical attitude toward biblical studies during this period. It is interesting that despite the dangers of the time, this learned and humanistic Pope took a somewhat nuanced stand. The encyclical shows a certain hostility toward higher criticism and the work of non-Catholic scholars: "The sense of Holy Scripture can nowhere be found incorrupt outside the Church and cannot be expected to be found in writers who, being without the true faith, only gnaw the bark of Sacred Scripture and never attain its pith" (*EB* 113; *RSS*, p. 17—how far we have come since that time can be seen in the encouragement of Vatican II [*De Rev.* 6:22] to work with non-Catholic scholars on biblical translations!). Nevertheless, the Pope showed himself aware of the advantages of scientific linguistic and exegetical studies, and he was attuned to the fact that the views of the biblical authors in questions of science were not invested with scriptural infallibility. Thus, at the turn of the century the official Catholic attitude toward scriptural advances was one of caution but also of dawning appreciation that boded well for the future.

5 **(B) 1900–1940.** This was the period of the Modernist crisis and its aftermath. The advent of Modernism, particularly in the writings of A. Loisy, changed the whole situation (→ Modern NT Criticism, 41:38). There was now danger of a virulent heresy, and the saintly Pius X was more interested in protecting the faithful than in the niceties of scientific attitude. In Scripture the Modernists were using the new approaches inaugurated by the German Protestants; and in *Pascendi* and *Lamentabili*, the official Catholic condemnations of Modernism, little distinction was made between the possible intrinsic validity of these approaches and the Modernist theological misuse of them. At the same time the PBC, established by Leo XIII in 1902, began to issue a series of decisions on many fine points of biblical interpretation and authorship. These decrees, issued between 1905 and 1915, were precautionary in intent and, while conservative in tone, were often phrased with perception and nuance. But since they bound Catholic scholars to assent, they gave to the non-Catholic world the unfortunate image of a monolithically conservative Catholic attitude that did not discuss questions on the basis of an exchange of scientific opinion but solved all by mandate from centralized authority.

Even though the decrees of the PBC, when interpreted with juridic insight, allowed a certain room for scholarly investigation, the atmosphere was not conducive to this; and advanced scholars like M.-J. Lagrange (→ Modern OT Criticism, 70:35,56) were virtually silenced on sensitive questions. Well does F.-M. Braun entitle this period in the life of Lagrange "Trials and Struggles" (*The Work of Père Lagrange* [Milwaukee, 1963] 66-100). Levie (*op. cit.*, 73) describes the network of reactionary espionage established to delate to Rome all those whose ideas might show any taint of Modernism, a network so despicable that Pope Benedict XV himself formally censured it. The encyclical *Spiritus Paraclitus* of Benedict XV in 1920 was colored by the difficult period that had preceded it. The Pope was more negative in tone in dealing with modern advances than Leo XIII had been and was strongly defensive on the historicity of the Bible. The 1920's saw vigorous ecclesiastical action by the Holy Office under Cardinal Merry del Val against the writings of leading Catholic scholars like J. Touzard, F. Vigouroux, M. Bacuez, and A. Brassac (see Levie, *op. cit.*, 124). The PBC did not issue decrees in these years except for a lone statement on the exegesis of two texts in 1933.

6 **(C) 1941–1968.** This period saw the renaissance of Catholic biblical studies. There were some signs of a change in attitude late in the pontificate of Pius XI, but it is Pius XII who deserves the title of patron of Catholic biblical studies. His pontificate marked a complete about-face and inaugurated the greatest renewal of interest in the Bible that the Roman Catholic Church has ever seen. The signs of this change were visible in the new attitude of the PBC, which in 1941 condemned an overly *conservative* distrust of modern biblical research. The encyclical *Divino Afflante Spiritu* of 1943 was a Magna Charta for biblical progress. Although the Pope saluted the encyclicals of his predecessors, he announced that the time for fear was over and that Catholic scholars should use modern tools in their exegesis. The stress on the use of the principle of literary forms to solve historical problems and the encouragement to make new translations of the Bible from the original languages (rather than from the Vg) were an invitation to Catholic scholars to begin writing freely again and to catch up with Protestant scholarship which had greatly outdistanced them during the preceding years of "trials and struggles." The directives of the Pope were reinforced by the statements of the PBC in 1948 to Cardinal Suhard on Gn and in 1950 on teaching Scripture in the seminaries. In 1955 the secretary of the PBC took a very brave but most necessary step in stating that now Catholic scholars had complete freedom (*plena libertate*) with regard to the earlier PBC decrees of 1905-15, except where they touched on faith and morals (and very few of them did). This meant that Catholics were now free to adopt modern positions on the authorship of the Pentateuch, Ps, Is, the Gospels, etc.

7 A crisis in the advance of Catholic biblical studies came with the illness and death of Pius XII. In the last year of his pontificate (April 1958) the Congregation of Seminaries expressed displeasure with vol. 1 of the *Introduction à la Bible* just published under the editorship of the French Catholics A. Robert and A. Feuillet. (Subsequently a 2nd edition was published with virtually no changes and with the indicated approval of the secretary of the PBC and of Cardinal Bea.) At the beginning of the reign of Pope John XXIII, serious attacks were made in Rome on important Catholic biblical scholars like L. Alonso Schökel, J. Levie, S. Lyonnet, and M. Zerwick, and subsequently the latter two were removed from their teaching office at the Pontifical Biblical Institute. The bitter controversy of this difficult period is well reported by J. A. Fitzmyer in *TS* 22 (1961) 426-44. Finally, in 1961 the Holy Office issued a warning against ideas that were calling in question the genuine historical and objective truth of Sacred Scripture. The atmosphere of foreboding was increased by reports that the (unpublished) schema on "The Sources of Revelation," which was to be presented at the forthcoming Vatican II in the fall of 1962, was negative in its approach to recent biblical advances. However, the pessimism failed to take into account the winds of *aggiornamento* that were sweeping through the window opened by John XXIII. In November 1962 so many of the Council Fathers expressed their displeasure with this schema that Pope John ordered it to be withdrawn and rewritten by a combined commission on which biblical scholars were better represented.

8 The pontificate of Paul VI has restored the warmly favorable atmosphere of the days of Pius XII. The above-mentioned professors were restored to their chairs. In April 1964 the PBC issued an "Instruction on the Historical Truth of the Gospels," an encouraging document opening the way to honest biblical criticism in the very delicate field of Gospel historicity. The names of the recently appointed consultors to the PBC include the most distinguished Catholic practitioners of modern biblical method in Europe and the United States. The final form of the schema *De Revelatione* passed by Vatican II in 1965 has much of the tone of the PBC Instruction and gives the official blessing of the Church to further progress along the lines laid down by Pius XII.

9 In studying the contents of the documents summarized below, the reader will do well to note their date and to evaluate them according to the background information supplied above. To judge Catholic biblical scholarship today from the tenor of documents issued in the Modernist crisis is simply unjust. It is understandable that non-Catholics, while they may rejoice at the freedom now possessed by Catholic biblical scholars, may also wonder whether such scholarship can have enduring freedom since it must be guided by orientation from Rome, an orientation that may once again change. In answering this, we may note first of all that friction between scholarly progress and conservative reaction on the part of authority is not a problem that affects Catholics alone. But in a specifically Catholic context, as children of the Church we recognize that, while on occasion, e.g., the Modernist crisis, the strict orientation from above may present difficulties, the Church's primary duty is to guard the faith that has been entrusted to her, even if this means a temporary curb on scholarly progress. Nevertheless, we remain optimistic that the Church at Vatican II has now committed itself to an exercise of its teaching authority that will exhibit trust in the sincere faith of those engaged in scholarship and will be far more perceptive of the needs for scholarly progress. "Biblical martyrs" like M.-J. Lagrange have undoubtedly contributed spiritually to the Catholic biblical movement by their patient acceptance of authoritative silencing; but if subsequent generations will heed the magnificent principle laid down by Pius XII (*EB* 564; *RSS*, p. 102) in regard to exegetes, the inevitable scandal involved in such martyrdom may be ended: "Let all the other sons of the Church bear in mind that the efforts of these resolute laborers in the vineyard of the Lord [i.e., biblical scholars] should be judged not only with equity and justice, but also with the greatest charity. All, moreover, should abhor that intemperate zeal which imagines that whatever is new should for that very reason be opposed or suspected." We may assure our non-Catholic brethren that the modern Catholic biblical movement inaugurated by Pius XII and confirmed by Vatican II and the PBC under Paul VI is now too much a part of the Church to be rejected, no matter what temporary setbacks or obstacles may lie in the future. (For the role of biblical scholars in helping the teaching authority of the Church to form the positions it takes in relation to the Bible, → Hermeneutics, 71:89.)

SUMMARIES OF THE PRONOUNCEMENTS

10 **(I) Councils of the Church.**

(A) Florence. The Council of Florence (1438-45) proclaimed the traditional doctrine of the Church regarding the canon (→ Canonicity, 67:12) in the Decree for the Jacobites (from the bull *Cantate Domino*, February 4, 1441—*EB* 47). This decree contained a list of inspired books, both protocanonical and deuterocanonical, which is identical with that drawn up at the council of Hippo in 393, repeated at the third and fourth councils of Carthage in 397 and 419, and found also in "Consulenti tibi," a letter regarding the canon sent by Pope Innocent I in 405 to Exuperius, bishop of Toulouse (*EB* 16-21; → Canonicity, 67:9-11).

11 **(B) Trent.** Major doubts and uncertainties concerning the canon were finally resolved by the Council of Trent (1545-63) in its fourth session on April 8, 1546. In this session, the Council voted affirmatively on two decrees: (1) concerning the canonical Scriptures (*EB* 57-60), and (2) concerning the edition and use of the Sacred Books (*EB* 61-64). The first decree, which adopted the canon of Florence, was "the first infallible and effectually promulgated declaration on the Canon of the Holy Scriptures." As Jedin observes, it also put a full stop to the thousand-year-old development of the biblical canon (*op. cit.*, 91). Henceforth the books of the OT and the NT, protocanonical and deuterocanonical alike, in their entirety and with all their parts, comprise the canon and are held to be of equal authority (→ Canonicity, 67:8, 42-43, 90-91).

The second decree declares "that the ancient Vulgate edition, which has been approved by the Church itself through long usage for so many centuries, should be considered the authentic edition for public reading, disputations, sermons, and explanations" (→ 20 below for the encyclical letter *Divino Afflante Spiritu*, which will clarify the meaning of this Tridentine decree). The decree goes on to forbid anyone from daring in matters of faith and morals "to distort Scripture to fit meanings of his own that are contrary to the meaning that holy Mother Church has held and now holds, for it is her office to judge about the true sense and interpretation of Scripture. Nor should anyone dare to interpret Scripture contrary to the unanimous agreement of the Fathers" (→ Hermeneutics, 71:82–92). Instructions were given for the publication of the Vg whose text was to be printed as correctly as possible. The result was the Sixto-Clementine Vg (→ Texts, 69:110). For the attitude of Trent toward vernacular bibles, see R. E. McNally, *TS* 27 (1966) 204–27.

12 **(C) Vatican I.** In its third session, on April 24, 1870, the first Vatican Council (1869–70) reaffirmed the decree of Trent concerning the source of revelation (DB 783; DS 1501) and then clearly stated that the Church holds the books of Holy Scripture as sacred and canonical, not because she subsequently approved them, nor because they contain revelation without error, but precisely because "having been written by the inspiration of the Holy Spirit, they have God as their author and, as such, they have been handed down to the Church itself" (*EB* 77; → Inspiration, 66:18, 33, 65).

13 **(D) Vatican II.** The dogmatic constitution *De Revelatione*, proclaimed November 18, 1965, is a document whose attitude toward modern biblical studies is largely positive but whose statements on disputed subjects reflect careful compromise, stemming from the five revisions through which the document passed between 1962 and 1965 (→ 7 above). We mention here only the most important points relative to biblical studies. Chapter 1 of the constitution discusses revelation. That divine revelation took place both in deeds and words is emphasized—a view that takes cognizance of the modern biblical emphasis on the "God who acts," along with the traditional emphasis on the "God who speaks." Chapter 2 deals with the disputed theological question of the sources of revelation. Faced with sharply opposed views—two sources (Scripture and Tradition) vs. one source (Scripture alone, as interpreted by Tradition)—the Council does not settle the question. It stresses (2:9) that Tradition and Scripture "in a certain way merge into a unity and tend toward the same end," but "it is not from Sacred Scripture alone that the Church draws her certainty about everything that has been revealed." On the relation between the Church and Scripture, the Council (2:10) insists that the teaching office of the Church authentically interprets the word of God, and yet this teaching office is not above the word of God but serves it.

14 Chapter 3 treats of inspiration and inerrancy. Vatican II adds nothing new to previous statements on inspiration in Vatican I and *Providentissimus Deus*, probably because the modern discussion on the nature of inspiration has not matured to the point of clear doctrine. It does make an important qualification in Catholic thought about the inerrancy of Scripture (→ Inspiration, 66:85), as our italics indicate: "The Books of Scripture must be acknowledged as teaching firmly, faithfully, and without error that *truth which God wanted put into the sacred writings for the sake of our salvation*" (3:11). The Council emphasizes that, in order to see what God wanted to communicate in Scripture, we must investigate the intention of the sacred writer, and one way to do this is by paying attention to the literary form employed by the writer (→ Inspiration, 66:83). Thus Vatican II accepts the teaching of *Divino Afflante Spiritu* (→ 22 below). On ch. 3 see I. de la Potterie, *NRT* 88 (1966) 149–69; A. Grillmeier, *Theologie und Philosophie* 41 (1966) 161–87.

15 Chapter 4 is devoted to the OT, an indication of the Church's desire to recall to the attention of clergy and laity this portion of their heritage so poorly known among the Christian people today. The view of the OT in this constitution is heavily Christological (4:15—the OT prepares for the NT; it announces the coming of the Messianic kingdom through prophecies). In the judgment of many, then, Vatican II does not give sufficient attention to the importance of the OT in itself (→ Aspects OT Thought, 77:176; → Hermeneutics, 71:21). The NT treatment in ch. 5 largely concerns the Gospels and is drawn from the PBC Instruction of 1964 (→ 35 below). The same three stages in Gospel development are given: Jesus Christ, apostolic preachers, sacred authors. It is recognized (5:19) that the Gospels have selected, synthesized, and explicated what Jesus did and taught, but the Council gives no specific norms for determining how much development there was. The distinction between the apostles and sacred writers would seem to favor the modern opinion that the Evangelists were not themselves apostolic eyewitnesses, although earlier the constitution (2:7) resorts to the traditional terminology of "apostles and apostolic men" for the composers of the written record of salvation, and this has been used in times past to distinguish between Matthew and John ("apostles") and Mark and Luke ("apostolic men").

16 Chapter 6 describes the role of the Bible in the life of the Church; it provides a wealth of truly pastoral counsel that is difficult to summarize. We note only the following points: A close parallel is drawn between Scripture and the Sacraments ("The Church has always venerated the divine Scriptures just as she venerates the body of the Lord" [6:21]); there is an insistence that preaching must be nourished and ruled by Scripture; the Bible should be translated *from the original languages* and, where feasible, with the co-operation of non-Catholics (6:22); explicit encouragement is given to biblical scholars to continue their work (6:23—important in the light of the troubles that cast a shadow on biblical scholarship between 1958 and 1962; → 7 above); the study of Scripture is the soul of theology (6:24); the clergy must be well trained in Scripture for preaching and catechizing (6:25); bishops have an obligation to see that the means are provided whereby the people can be instructed in Scripture, by way of both translations and commentaries. For the position of Vatican II toward the translation of Scripture, see L. Legrand, *RB* 64 (1967) 413–22.

(We shall list a few of the many commentaries on the *De Revelatione* schema: Baum, G., *TS* 28 [1967] 51–75. Grelot, P., *Études* 324 [1966] 99–113, 233–46. Loretz, O., *TR* 63 [1967] 1–8. Tavard, G. H., *JES* 3 [1966] 1–35. Zerwick, M., *VD* 44 [1966] 17–42.)

17 **(II) Encyclical Letters.**

(A) Providentissimus Deus (*EB* 81–134; *RSS*, pp. 1–29). Issued by Leo XIII on November 18, 1893, this encyclical inaugurated a new era in Catholic biblical studies. After explaining the motives for the study and use of Holy Scripture, Leo XIII presents a plan for biblical studies. Suitable, well-trained professors should first teach a sound course in biblical introduction and then proceed to train their students in "a definite and ascertained method of interpretation" (*EB* 103–5; *RSS*, pp. 11–12). The "authentic" Vg version is to be the biblical text used, though other versions, as well as the more ancient mss., should not be neglected (*EB* 106; *RSS*, p. 13). The encyclical teaches that a biblical text cannot be interpreted against a sense determined by the Church or supported by the unanimous consent of the Fathers (*EB* 108; *RSS*, p. 14—for a correct interpretation of this, see *Divino Afflante Spiritu* [*EB* 565; *RSS*, p. 102]).

Catholic scholars remain free to pursue their private studies, especially of difficult biblical passages. Such studies "may, in the benignant providence of God, prepare for and bring to maturity the judgment of the Church" (*EB* 109; *RSS*, p. 15). In his interpretation of difficult passages, the exegete must follow the analogy of faith, i.e., he cannot come to an interpretation of the inspired author's meaning that would be a direct and formal contradiction of a dogma taught by the Church (→ Pauline Theology, 79:7). He must remember that the supreme law is Catholic doctrine as authoritatively proposed by the Church (*EB* 109; *RSS*, p. 15).

The encyclical urges the study of Oriental languages and of the art of criticism (*EB* 118; *RSS*, p. 20). It also calls attention to the dangers of contemporary "higher criticism" (*EB* 119; *RSS*, p. 20). In describing the world of physical nature, the sacred authors did not formally intend to teach natural science. On the contrary, they used terms common at the time, and which, in many instances, are still used even by the more eminent men of science. God spoke to men in the way they could understand—a way to which they were accustomed (*EB* 121; *RSS*, p. 22). These principles will apply to cognate sciences, and especially to history (*EB* 123; *RSS*, p. 23). (The reference to history in this context gave rise to some controversy; → 19 below.) Pope Leo also gave a now celebrated description of inspiration: By supernatural power God so moved and impelled the human authors to write—he so assisted them when writing—that the things that he ordered and those only they first rightly understood, then willed faithfully to write down, and finally expressed in apt words and with infallible truth. Inspiration, which is incompatible with error, extends to the canonical Scriptures and to all their parts (*EB* 125; *RSS*, p. 24).

18 **(B) Pascendi Dominici Gregis** (*EB* 257-67; DS 3475-3500). This encyclical was issued on September 8, 1907 by Pius X in refutation of the errors of the Modernists. In biblical matters Pius X scored the Modernists' erroneous teachings on the origin and nature of the Sacred Books (*EB* 257), on inspiration (*EB* 258-59), on the distinction between the purely human Christ of history and the divine Christ of faith (*EB* 260), on the erroneous precepts and laws of evolution governing the origin and growth of the Scriptures (*EB* 262-63), and on that faulty apologetics that strives to resolve controversies over religion by historical and psychological investigations (DB 2101; DS 3499). The decree *Lamentabili*, a syllabus of 65 Modernist propositions condemned by the Congregation of the Sacred Inquisition, was issued on July 3, 1907, just prior to the appearance of *Pascendi* (*EB* 190-256). [The reader should be warned that the propositions are condemned *in the sense held by the Modernists*, and the degree of condemnation (from heretical to dangerous) is not specified.]

19 **(C) Spiritus Paraclitus** (*EB* 440-495; *RSS*, pp. 43–79). This encyclical was issued by Benedict XV on the 15th centenary of St. Jerome's death, September 15, 1920. After a moving tribute to the holy life and biblical labors of the saint, the Pope compares modern views with those of Jerome. He briefly commends those who use modern critical methods in their biblical studies (*EB* 453; *RSS*, p. 51). He laments that some scholars have not observed the guide lines established by *Providentissimus Deus* and by the Fathers (*EB* 454; *RSS*, p. 51). He scores the teaching that limits inspiration to only certain portions of the Scriptures (*EB* 455; *RSS*, p. 52). In treating of the historical portions of Scripture, one cannot apply universally the principle that Leo XIII laid down for judging biblical statements on scientific matters, namely that the author spoke only according to appearances (*EB* 456; *RSS*, p. 52). We cannot say that the sacred writers of historical events were ignorant of the truth and simply adopted and handed down false views current at the time (*EB* 459; *RSS*, p. 53). The exegete must avoid a too ready use, or misuse, of those principles governing "implicit quotations" or "pseudohistorical narratives" or "kinds of literature," for these principles are sound only if kept within due bounds (*EB* 461; *RSS*, p. 54). As Jerome insisted, all biblical interpretation rests upon the literal sense, and one must not think that there is no literal sense merely because a thing is said metaphorically (*EB* 485; *RSS*, p. 67 [→ Hermeneutics, 71:12]). The goal of biblical studies is to learn spiritual perfection, to arm oneself to defend the faith, and to preach the word of God fruitfully (*EB* 482-484; *RSS*, pp. 65-66).

20 **(D) Divino Afflante Spiritu** (*EB* 538-569; *RSS*, pp. 80–107). This encyclical (henceforth *DAS*) was issued by Pius XII on September 30, 1943, the 50th anniversary of the publication of *Providentissimus Deus*. It was the intention of Pius XII to commemorate this golden jubilee "by ratifying and inculcating all that was wisely laid down by our predecessor and ordained by his successors for the consolidating and perfecting of the work, and by pointing out what seems necessary in the present day..." (*EB* 538; *RSS*, p. 81). As Levie has noted (*op. cit.*, 139), there were many matters in *Providentissimus Deus* and in subsequent papal instructions that needed confirmation, further definition, and even completion as a result of the complex evolution of exegesis during the years 1893-1943. *DAS* does, in fact, complete many teachings of *Providentissimus Deus*. For instance, on the question of the use of the Vg vs. the original texts, *Providentissimus* permitted scholars to pay attention to the original texts of Scripture, but *DAS* orders them to explain the original texts from which new translations should be made. A similar shift of emphasis may be observed with respect to such questions as the relation between the literal and spiritual sense, the extent of the binding force of the unanimous consent of the Fathers, and the interpretation of historical facts in terms of literary forms (cf. Levie, *op. cit.*, 144). In its doctrinal part the encyclical teaches the great importance of textual criticism at the present time (*EB* 548; *RSS*, p. 90). As for the true meaning of the Tridentine decree regarding the Vg, the authenticity of the Vg is not specified primarily as critical, but rather as juridical (*EB* 549; *RSS*, p. 92); this means that no claim is made that the Vg is always an accurate translation, but that it is free from any error in faith and morals.

21 Pius XII insists strongly that the exegete must be principally concerned with the literal sense of the Scriptures (*EB* 550; *RSS*, p. 92); also the theological doctrine in faith and morals of the individual books or texts must be carefully set forth (*EB* 550; *RSS*, p. 93). The exegete should search out and expound the spiritual sense, provided it is clearly intended by God (*EB* 552; *RSS*, p. 94), but should avoid proposing as the genuine meaning of Sacred Scripture other figurative senses (*EB* 553; *RSS*, p. 94; → Hermeneutics, 71:80-81). The Fathers of the Church ought to be studied more assiduously (*EB* 554; *RSS*, p. 95).

22 In particular, the biblical interpreter, with all care and without neglecting recent research, ought to endeavor to determine all he can about the sacred writer: his peculiar character and circumstances, the age in which he lived, his written or oral sources, and the forms of expression he employed (*EB* 557; *RSS*, p. 97). History, archaeology, and other sciences should be employed to understand more perfectly ancient modes of writing (*EB* 558; *RSS*, p. 97); and the study of literary forms cannot be neglected without serious detriment to Catholic exegesis (*EB* 560; *RSS*, p. 99). This emphasis on recognizing different types of literature or different literary forms in the Bible was probably the greatest single contribution of *DAS*, for it offered the Catholic scholar an intelligent and honest way of facing up to the obvious historical problems present in the Bible. Formerly too many books of the Bible were thought to be history in the strict sense; now it could be shown that many of these books were not history at all or were history in a broader and less technical sense. Vatican II gave its approval to the distinction of literary forms (→ 14 above; → Hermeneutics, 71:25-28).

23 *DAS* urged Catholic exegetes to grapple with difficult problems, hitherto unsolved, and to arrive at solutions in full accord with the doctrine of the Church, as well as in harmony with the indubitable conclusions of profane sciences (*EB* 564; *RSS*, p. 101). This was a refreshing change from the atmosphere after the Modernist crisis when Catholic exegetes deliberately sought out "safe" areas for their biblical research. The Pope states that there are but a few texts whose sense has been determined by the authority of the Church or about which the teaching of the Holy Fathers is unanimous (*EB* 565; *RSS*, p. 102). This statement counteracts the frequent misunderstanding that Catholics have no freedom in interpreting Scripture. The effects of the very positive encouragement given to biblical scholars by *DAS* (*EB* 565; *RSS*, p. 102) have been mentioned above (→ 6).

24 **(E) Humani Generis** (*EB* 611-20; *RSS*, pp. 113-15). This encyclical was issued by Pius XII on August 12, 1950. In the part pertinent to biblical studies, it instructs exegetes on evolution, polygenism, and OT historical narratives. Liberty for discussing the evolution of the human body is granted, but one should not presume that evolution is completely certain or proved. There is no such liberty on the question of polygenism, for "it is in no way apparent how such an opinion can be reconciled" with what has been taught on Original Sin, namely that it proceeds from a sin actually committed by an individual Adam. [Note, however, that the Pope does not absolutely condemn the theory of polygenism.] The popular type of history found in the OT still enjoyed the charism of inspiration and cannot be considered on a par with myths that are more the product of an extravagant imagination than of a striving for truth (→ Aspects OT Thought, 77:31). It is worth noting that in this predominantly monitory encyclical there is virtually no chastisement of biblical scholars. Seemingly to his death Pius XII remained firm in his faith in modern criticism.

25 **(III) Documents of Roman Commissions.** Our principal interest here will be the decrees of the Pontifical Biblical Commission.

(A) Early Decrees of the PBC. Those decrees issued between 1905 and 1915 and in 1933 are summarized briefly below; this is a difficult task because the decrees were issued in the form of affirmative and negative responses to long and intricate questions (often phrased negatively and with carefully chosen modifiers). The reader who is interested in the exact shade of meaning should consult the original responses. A *brief* summary seems indicated, for many of these decrees now have little more than historic interest, being implicitly revoked by later decrees, by *Divino Afflante Spiritu*, and by Vatican II. The early decrees must be evaluated according to the 1955 clarification issued in Latin and in German by A. Miller and by A. Kleinhaus, secretary and assistant secretary of the PBC (*Benediktinische Monatschrift* 31 [1955] 49-50; *Antonianum* 30 [1955] 63–65; *CBQ* 18 [1956] 23–29; *RSS*, p. 175—note the latter mistakenly omits the important clause "with full liberty": *plena libertate; in aller Freiheit*). Miller says: "As long as these [early PBC] decrees propose views that are neither immediately nor mediately connected with truths of faith and morals, the interpreter of Sacred Scripture can pursue his scientific investigations with full liberty and accept the results of these investigations, provided always that he respects the teaching authority of the Church. Today we can hardly picture to ourselves the situation of Catholic scholars fifty years ago and the danger that threatened Catholic teaching on Scripture and inspiration. . . . At present many controversies have been peacefully settled and many problems appear in an entirely new light, so that it is easy enough for us to smile at the narrowness and constraint that formerly prevailed." Taking advantage of this "full liberty," in those instances where there is a real dispute few modern Catholic scholars adhere today to the positions on the authorship, the dating, and the unity of biblical books proposed in the decrees summarized below. The Pauline authorship of the Pastorals would be an exception, for many Catholics still accept this—but on critical grounds, and not simply because of the PBC decree. In this summary, brackets represent clarifications supplied to help the reader.

26 (a) General Historicity—decrees condemning too facile a method of explaining away historical inconsistencies in the Bible.

(i) Against too free a use of the theory of *implicit citations*, i.e., the theory that the biblical author is implicitly citing a noninspired source whose conclusions he does not make his own (February 13, 1905; *EB* 160; *RSS*, p. 117).

(ii) Against too free a recourse to the theory that a book that has been regarded as history is not really history but has only the *appearance of history* (June 23, 1905; *EB* 161; *RSS*, pp. 117-18).

27 (b) Old Testament.

(i) *The Pentateuch.* Moses is substantially the author, and there is insufficient evidence that it was compiled from sources posterior to Moses. Moses himself may have drawn on existing sources; and, as principal author, he may have entrusted the actual composition to others who wrote according to his will. There may have been subsequent modifications, inspired additions, modernizations of language, and even scribal errors in copying (June 27, 1906; *EB* 181-84; *RSS*, pp. 118-19 [→ Pentateuch, 1:7ff.]).

(ii) *Genesis.* The literal historical character of Gn 1-3 is defended, especially with regard to facts that touch on the fundamentals of the Christian religion. These chapters are not a fictional narrative, nor purified fables derived from pagan mythologies, nor allegories destitute of foundation in objective reality; nor do they contain edifying legends, partly historical and partly fictional. Yet allowance may be made for metaphor, figurative language, and the scientific naïveté of the author. The word *yôm* [Gn 1:5,8, etc.] may mean a natural day or a space of time. In particular the PBC insisted on the literal and historical meaning of passages dealing with the following: (1) the creation of all things by God at the beginning of time; (2) the special creation of man; (3) the formation of the first woman from man; (4) the unity of the human race; (5) the original happiness of our first parents in a state of justice, integrity, and immortality; (6) the divine command laid upon man to prove his obedience; (7) the transgression of this command at the instigation of the devil in the form of a serpent; (8) the fall of our first parents from their primitive state of innocence; (9) the promise of a future redeemer (June 30, 1909; *EB* 324-31; *RSS*, pp. 122-24 [→ Genesis, 2:3-8]).

(iii) *Isaiah.* The book contains real prophecies, not simply *vaticinia ex eventu* or shrewd guesses; for the prophets spoke not only of the immediate future to a contemporary audience but also predicted things to be fulfilled after many ages. The evidence is insufficient to support the theory that the book was written by several authors [→ Deutero-Isaiah, 22:2, 50] living in different centuries (June 28, 1908; *EB* 276-80; *RSS*, pp. 120-22).

(iv) *Psalms.* David does not have to be considered the sole author, but he is the author of the following Pss: 2, 16(Lat 15), 18(17), 32(31), 69(68), 110(109). The titles of the Pss represent very ancient Jewish tradition and cannot be prudently called into question without solid reason. For liturgical purposes, etc., some Pss may have been divided; others may consist of separate pieces welded into one; others may have been slightly modified by excision or addition, e.g., 51 (50). There is no basis for the opinion that many of the Pss were composed after the Ezra-Nehemiah period [*ca.* 400]. Some Pss are to be recognized as prophetic and messianic, foretelling the coming and career of the future Redeemer (May 1, 1910; *EB* 332-39; *RSS*, pp. 124-26 [→ Psalms, 35:4, 15]).

28 (c) New Testament.

(i) *Matthew.* The apostle Matthew wrote his Gospel before the other Gospels and before the destruction of Jerusalem [AD 70], and not necessarily after Paul came to Rome [*ca.* 61; → Gospel Mt, 43:13-15]. Matthew originally wrote in the dialect used by the Jews in Palestine [Aramaic or Hebrew], and canonical Gk Mt is identical in substance with the original Gospel; it is not simply a collection of sayings and discourses by an anonymous author [→ Syn Problem, 40:14]. The admitted dogmatic and apologetic purposes of Matthew and his occasional lack of chronological order do not permit one to consider as untrue his narrative of the deeds and words of Christ, or to think that this narrative has been subjected to changes under the influence of the OT or of the more developed status of the Church. The historical authenticity of several passages peculiar to Mt is emphasized: chs. 1-2; 14:33; 16:17-19; 28:19-20 (June 19, 1911; *EB* 383-89; *RSS*, pp. 126-28). Mt 16:26 refers in its literal sense to the eternal life of the soul and not only to the temporal life of man (July 1, 1933; *EB* 514; *RSS*, p. 138).

(ii) *Mark, Luke.* The chronological order of the Syn is: original Mt, Mk, Lk—although Gk Mt may be posterior to Mk and Lk [→ Gospel Mt, 43:5-6]. Mark, writing according to the preaching of Peter, and Luke, writing according to that of Paul, are really the authors of Mk and Lk, which were written before the destruction of Jerusalem [AD 70]. Luke composed Lk before Acts, which was finished by the end of the Roman imprisonment of Paul [*ca.* 63; → Canonicity, 67:58, 66; → Gospel Lk, 44:18]. These Evangelists had at their disposal trustworthy sources, oral or written; and their narratives have a claim to full historical credence. The PBC insists on the inspiration of certain disputed passages and finds unconvincing the arguments proposed against their genuineness and authorship: Mk 16:9-20; Lk 1-2; Lk 22:43-44. The "Magnificat" in Lk [1:46-55] is to be attributed to Mary, not to Elizabeth as a few textual witnesses would have it. Liberty is allowed to Catholic scholars in discussing the Syn Problem, but they are not free to advocate the two-source theory whereby Mt and Lk are made to depend on Mk and the "Sayings of the Lord" ["Q"] (June 26, 1912; *EB* 390-400; *RSS*, pp. 129-32 [→ Syn Problem, 40:21]). Lk 9:25 must be interpreted as Mt 16:26 above (July 1, 1933; *EB* 514; *RSS*, p. 138).

(iii) *John.* For various reasons given, the apostle John must be acknowledged as the author [→ Gospel Jn, 63:2-3]. Differences between Jn and the Syn are open to reasonable solution. The facts narrated in Jn were not invented in whole or in part to serve as allegories or doctrinal symbols; and the Johannine discourses of Jesus are properly his and not the theological compositions of the Evangelist (May 29, 1907; *EB* 187-89; *RSS*, pp. 119-20).

(iv) *Acts.* Luke is the sole author, as confirmed by many traditional and critical arguments, including the "We" passages [→ Acts, 45:6]. The date of composition cannot be placed later than the end of the first Roman captivity of Paul [*ca.* 63], and the abrupt ending of Acts need not mean that the author wrote another volume or intended to. Luke had trustworthy sources and used them accurately, honestly, and faithfully; therefore, we may claim complete historical authority for Luke (arguments are given). The historical authority of Acts is not weakened by the fact that it narrates supernatural happenings, nor by the fact that it contains discourses that some would consider fabricated, nor by seeming discrepancies (June 12, 1913; *EB* 401-6; *RSS*, pp. 132-34).

(v) *Pauline Writings.* The Pastorals [1-2 Tm; Ti] were ever counted as genuine and canonical; they were written by Paul himself between his first imprisonment and his death [*ca.* 63-66]. The genuineness of these letters is not weakened by arguments to the contrary, nor by "the fragmentary hypothesis," according to which they were made up at a later period by unknown authors from Pauline fragments with considerable additions (June 12, 1913; *EB* 407-10; *RSS*, pp. 134-35 [→ Pastoral Letters, 57:6-11]). Hebrews is canonical and genuinely Pauline; however, the question is left open whether Paul put it exactly in the form in which it now stands (June 24, 1914; *EB* 411-13; *RSS*, pp. 135-36 [→ Epistle Heb, 61:2-3]). Problems about the parousia are not to be solved by asserting that sometimes the inspired authors expressed their own human views, possibly erroneous. Paul wrote nothing that is not in harmony with the ignorance of the time of the parousia proclaimed by Christ himself. 1 Thes 4:15-16 can be so interpreted that it does not necessarily imply that Paul thought he and his readers would survive to meet Christ (June 18, 1915; *EB* 414-16; *RSS*, pp. 136-37 [→ Pauline Theology, 79:45-51]).

29 **(B) More Recent Documents.** These shall be given in more detail, for they govern and reflect the progressive attitude prevalent in Catholic biblical studies since the time of Pius XII.

(a) Letter to the Italian Hierarchy (August 20, 1941; *EB* 522-33; *RSS*, pp. 138-47). This document was a response of the PBC to an anonymous brochure sent to the leading churchmen in Italy. The author who wrote under the pseudonym Dain Cohenel is now known to have been Fr. Dolindo Ruotolo (Levie, *op. cit.*, 133). The brochure was a virulent attack against scientific biblical study. It contained serious errors minimizing the proper role of the literal sense in biblical interpretation in favor of a fanciful spiritual sense. It exaggerated the importance of the Vg and put little value on textual criticism or on the study of Oriental languages and auxiliary sciences. The PBC corrected these errors and, in so doing, foreshadowed the teaching of Pius XII in *Divino Afflante Spiritu* (→ 20-22 above for the importance of the literal sense, the limits of the spiritual and typical senses, the restricted value of the Vg, and the necessity of textual criticism and of scientific linguistic studies).

30 (b) PBC on Biblical Translations (August 22, 1943; *EB* 535-37; *RSS*, pp. 148-49). The following norms were established for biblical versions in the vernacular, especially those translated from the original languages: (1) Such versions may be used by the faithful, provided they have been edited with the permission of competent ecclesiastical authority. Moreover, if any version, after its notes and text have been examined by experts, is found more faithful or better expressed, the Bishops, either singly or jointly, may commend it to their faithful. (2) But the version read to the people during Mass must conform to the Latin, the liturgical text (*EB* 520), although the priest may use the original text or another version to explain better what is read to the people. [This has now been abrogated in fact; for the American hierarchy, as permitted by Vatican II, has approved for the English Mass and breviary a translation made from the original languages and not from the Latin, namely the New Confraternity of Christian Doctrine translation (→ Texts, 69:174).]

31 (c) Response to Cardinal Suhard (January 16, 1948; *EB* 577–81; *RSS*, pp. 150–53). This reply to the Archbishop of Paris from the PBC concerns the Pentateuch and Gn 1–11. It affirms: (1) Attitudes previously taken on the authorship and historicity of these parts of the Bible (*EB* 161, 181–84, 324–31) are in no way opposed to further, truly scientific examination of the problems in accordance with the results obtained during the last 40 years. Consequently, no new decrees need to be promulgated. No one today doubts the existence of written sources and oral traditions in the Pentateuch [→ Pentateuch, 1:12ff.]. Nor does anyone refuse to admit a progressive development of Mosaic laws, a development also manifest in the historical narratives. (2) The literary forms of Gn 1–11 correspond to none of our classical categories and cannot be judged in the light of Greco-Roman or modern literary styles. Though not containing history in our modern sense, these historical narratives relate in simple and figurative language the fundamental truths presupposed for the economy of salvation, as well as the popular description of the origin of the human race and of the chosen people [→ Genesis, 2:3–7]. The first task of the exegete is to collate data from the various sciences (paleontology, history, epigraphy) to discover better how the Oriental peoples thought and expressed their ideas, as well as their very concept of historical thought.

32 (d) PBC on Teaching Scripture in Seminaries (May 13, 1950; *EB* 582–610; *RSS*, pp. 154–67). The following points were stressed: (1) the difference between the training of biblical specialists and that of future shepherds of the Lord's flock (*EB* 583); (2) the priestly life, virtue, and professional competence of the Scripture professor who must enjoy the freedom to dedicate himself entirely to his work and not be compelled to teach other important subjects at the same time (*EB* 586–90); (3) the proper method of teaching biblical subjects in seminaries and religious colleges. Here daily reading of Scripture is stressed (*EB* 592). Students are to be taught in a strictly scientific manner and to be made conversant with current biblical problems (*EB* 593). Because there is usually too little time allotted, the professor must choose his material prudently. In the OT he should interpret the teachings concerning the origin of the human race [Gn], the messianic prophecies, and Ps. In the NT he should present an orderly conspectus of Jesus' life, explain the Sunday and Feastday Gospels and Epistles, give a history of the passion and resurrection of Jesus, and expound at least one of the principal Pauline epistles, as well as the doctrinal parts of others (*EB* 597). Difficulties and obscurities in the OT must be faced squarely and reasonable solutions given (*EB* 600).

33 (e) PBC on Biblical Meetings (December 15, 1955; *EB* 622–33; *RSS*, pp. 168–72). This instruction to Local Ordinaries pertained to biblical associations, conventions, and meetings. Associations should be encouraged; there should be meetings, "Scripture days and weeks"; subjects should be properly selected. The jurisdiction of the competent Ordinary over all such gatherings is stressed (*EB* 627–30), and technical and scientific meetings should not be open to outsiders who would be poorly prepared to evaluate and understand what was being said (*EB* 631).

34 (f) Holy Office Monitum on Historicity (June 20, 1961; *AAS* 53 [1961] 507; *RSS*, p. 174). With the agreement of the PBC Cardinals, the Holy Office issued a warning to all who work with Scripture whether orally or in writing. [The American Catholic press falsely labeled this document a warning to *biblical scholars*, whereas its primary emphasis seems to have been directed to popularizers, e.g., preachers.] The target of the warning was opinions and affirmations calling in question "the genuine [*germana*] historical and objective truth of Sacred Scripture," not only of the OT, but also of the NT, even with regard to the words and actions of Jesus. The document counsels prudence and reverence, for such opinions create anxieties both for pastors and faithful. [J. A. Fitzmyer, *TS* 22 (1961) 443–44, comments on this document: "The word *germana* (genuine, proper) is obviously an attempt on the part of the Holy Office to express its recognition of the character of truth involved in Scripture and to allow for its formulation according to the various literary genres employed by the sacred writers." The style of the warning was paternal; and thus understood, the warning respects the theory of different literary forms and does not claim that all Scripture is history. Yet this minatory document, being almost wholly negative, temporarily cast a pall on the future of modern criticism in the Church.]

35 (g) PBC on Historicity of the Gospels (April 21, 1964; Latin and English in *CBQ* 26 [1964] 299–312; *AAS* 56 [1964] 712–18; commentary by J. A. Fitzmyer, *TS* 25 [1964] 386–408). This "Instruction on the Historical Truth of the Gospels" begins with praise of biblical scholars as "faithful sons of the Church," and repeats Pius XII's command that they be treated with charity by other Catholics. [This was significant in light of the difficult years between 1958 and 1962, and the misuse to which the above-mentioned Monitum was put in attacking biblical scholars as heretical.] The instructions of *Divino Afflante Spiritu* are reiterated, especially those stressing the concept of different literary forms. In the "Form-critical Method" there are reasonable elements that can be used for a fuller understanding of the Gospels; but there are often inadmissible philosophical and theological principles admixed with this method, at times vitiating the method itself or, at least, conclusions drawn from it.

To judge properly, the interpreter should pay attention to *three stages* by which the doctrine and life of Jesus have come down to us: (1) *Jesus* explained his doctrine, adapting himself to the mentality of his listeners. His chosen disciples saw his deeds, heard his words, and were thus equipped to be witnesses of his life and doctrine. (2) The *apostles* after the resurrection of Jesus clearly perceived his divinity and proclaimed the death and resurrection of the Lord to men. While preaching and explaining his life and words, they took into account the needs and circumstances of their listeners. The faith of the apostles did not deform the message; but rather, with the fuller understanding they now enjoyed, they were able to pass on to their audiences what was really said and done by the Lord. The modes of speaking with which these preachers proclaimed Christ must be distinguished and properly assessed: catecheses, stories, testimonia, hymns, doxologies, prayers, etc.—the literary forms in use at the time. (3) The *sacred authors* committed to writing in four Gospels this primitive instruction that had been passed on orally at first and then in pre-Gospel writings. From the many things handed down, the Evangelists "selected some things, reduced others to a synthesis, and still others they explicated, keeping in mind the situation of the churches." They adapted what they narrated to the situation of their readers and to the purpose they themselves had in mind. This adaptation affected the sequence of what is narrated, but truth is not at all affected simply because the words and deeds of the Lord are narrated in different order in different Gospels. And although the Evangelists sometimes express the sayings of Jesus not literally but differently, they nevertheless retain the sense of these sayings. From a study of these three stages it is apparent that the doctrine and life of Jesus were not reported merely for the purpose of being remembered but were preached so as to offer the Church a basis of faith and morals.

The advice to the exegete closes with a reminder that he must exercise his skill and judgment in exegesis but always with the disposition to obey the magisterium [→ Hermeneutics, 71:82-90]. Then short paragraphs of advice are directed to those teaching in seminaries, those preaching to the people, and those writing for the faithful. The people should receive all the benefits of modern biblical science but should not be exposed to insufficiently established novelties or the rash remarks of innovators [→ Hermeneutics, 71:100-102].

36 (IV) Minor Documents of Historical Interest. We simply list these: *Vigilantiae*, October 20, 1902, an Apostolic Letter of Leo XIII on the institution of a Commission for Biblical Studies (*EB* 137-48; *RSS*, p. 30); *Scripturae Sacrae*, February 23, 1904, an Apostolic Letter of Pius X empowering the PBC to confer degrees in Scripture (*EB* 149-57; *RSS*, p. 35); *Quoniam in Re Biblica*, March 27, 1906, an Apostolic Letter of Pius X on the study of Scripture in seminaries (*EB* 162-80; *RSS*, p. 36); *Praestantia Sacrae Scripturae*, November 18, 1907, a Motu Proprio of Pius X on the decisions of the PBC (*EB* 268-73; *RSS*, p. 40); *In Cotidianis Precibus*, March 24, 1945, an Apostolic Letter of Pius XII on the New Latin Psalter and its use in the Divine Office (*EB* 571-75; *RSS*, p. 108 [→ Texts, 69:103]).

73

BIBLICAL GEOGRAPHY

Robert North, S.J.

Raymond E. Brown, S.S.

BIBLIOGRAPHY

1 **General.** Abel, *GP*. Aharoni, Y., *The Land of the Bible* (Phila., 1967). Baldi, D., *Enchiridion locorum sanctorum* (2nd ed.; Jerusalem, 1955). Baly, D., *Geography of the Bible* (N.Y., 1957). Bea, A., *Geographia Palaestinae antiquae* (Rome, 1940). Bodenheimer, F. S., *Animal and Man in Bible Lands* (Leiden, 1960). Daniel-Rops, H., *Everyday Life in the Time of Jesus* (N.Y., 1962). Du Buit, M., *Géographie de Terre Sainte* (Paris, 1958). Dussaud, R., *Topographie historique de la Syrie* (Paris, 1917). Kopp, C., *The Holy Places of the Gospels* (N.Y., 1963). North, R., *Descriptio terrae biblicae: stratigraphia Palaestinae* (Rome, 1953–54). Noth, M., *The Old Testament World* (Phila., 1966). Ritter, C., *Comparative Geography of Palestine* (N.Y., 1866). Robinson, E., *Physical Geography* (London, 1865); *Biblical Researches* (2nd ed.; Boston, 1856). Röhricht, R., *Bibliotheca geographica Palaestinae* (Berlin, 1890). Simons, J., *The Geographical and Topographical Texts of the Old Testament* (Leiden, 1958). Smith, *Hist Geog.* Thomsen, P., *Palästina-Literatur* (Berlin, 1911–60).

2 **Bible Atlases.** Lemaire, P. and D. Baldi, *Atlante storico geografico della Bibbia* (Rome, 1955). *Eretz-Israel Atlas* (in Hebr; Jerusalem, 1955). Grollenberg, *AtBib.* Keyes, N., *Story of the Bible World* (Hammond Atlas; N.Y., 1961). *Oxford Bible Atlas* (eds. H. G. May, R. W. Hamilton, G. N. S. Hunt; N.Y., 1962). Rowley, H. H., *The Modern Reader's Bible Atlas* (N.Y., 1961). Wright, G. E. and F. V. Filson, *WHAB.* Also see McEvedy, C., *The Penguin Atlas of Ancient History* (London, 1967).

3 **Guidebooks.** Baldi, D. (in Ital; Jerusalem, 1953). Benzinger, I. (Baedeker, in Eng; Leipzig, 1904). Meistermann, B., (in Eng; London, 1928; in Fr; Paris, 1935). Notre-Dame de France (Paris, 1932). Vilnay, Z. (Tel Aviv, 1968). In the Guide-Bleu series (Paris): Baud, M., *Egypte* (1952); Boulanger, R., *Moyen-Orient* (1956) and *Turquie* (1958); Finbert, E., *Israel* (in Eng, 1955).

Jerusalem Pontifical Biblical Institute Color-slides (rev. ed., 30 sets, with explanation and bibliography; Rome, 1968).

4 OUTLINE

Sections 5–31 of this article are the work of R. North; the remainder of the article is by R. E. Brown.

SOURCES AND TOOLS FOR BIBLICAL GEOGRAPHY

We are interested here in biblical geography, not in a purely geographical study of areas that happen to be mentioned in the Bible. Those features and sites that are mentioned are important to an understanding of the Bible; much nonbiblical matter that from a scientific geographical viewpoint might be of more importance has been omitted. Along with details of geology and geography, mixed details from history (even medieval and modern), archaeology, and the "guided tour" of the holy land are included—in short, we discuss whatever can give the reader an appreciation of the country that is the setting of the Bible. Although some of the bibliographical references are to the more scientific works on the subject, there has been a preference for simplified reports and references that the general student can read with profit.

5 **(I) Ancient.** The earliest map of Palestine is a mosaic from AD 600, still partly surviving on the floor of an Orthodox church in Madeba, in Transjordan, near Mt. Nebo (see V. R. Gold, *BA* 21 [1958] 50–71; M. Avi-Yonah, *The Madaba Mosaic Map* [Jerusalem, 1954]; R. T. O'Callaghan, *VDBS* 5, 627–704; H. Donner and H. Cüppers, *ZDPV* 83 [1967] 1–33). The only other truly ancient map is the *Tabula Peutingeriana*, a road map of the world reduced to a strip 25 ft. long and 13 in. wide, divided into 12 sections. The original may stem from the 3rd cent. AD, but the copy now extant is from 1265. Willed to Konrad Peutinger, the map is in the State Library of Vienna (see K. Miller, *Itineraria romana* [Stuttgart, 1916]; *Arch* 8 [1955] 146–55; 17 [1964] 227–36).

6 What is a map? Basically, it is a listing of cities, though in a spatial, rather than in an alphabetical or logical order. In this sense of maps as city lists, the origins of biblical map making are from ancient Egypt; for we possess Egyptian lists of Palestinian cities on fragments of jars, on clay tablets, and on palace walls. About 1900 BC, names of Canaanite cities were written on pottery and smashed as a magic curse; found only recently (*ca.* 1930), these are called Execration Texts. In the period just after 1370 BC many princes of Canaan wrote to the Egyptian Pharaoh asking help for their cities against local marauders called Ḫabiru ('Apiru); these "Amarna Letters," found at the end of the last century (→ Biblical Archaeology, 74:57), are of great importance for the geographical and political situation in Palestine in the period just before Moses and Joshua. (E. F. Campbell, *BA* 23 [1960] 2–22.) The Pharaohs Ramses II (1290–24) and Sheshonk (*ca.* 920; = Shishak of 1 Kgs 14:25) left on the palaces of Luxor in southern Egypt important geographical lists (J. Simons, *Handbook for the Study of Egyptian Topographical Lists Relating to Western Asia* [Leiden, 1937]; Aharoni, *op. cit.*).

7 Next in order come the town lists of the OT itself (cf. Simons, *Geographical and Topographical Texts of the OT*). These supply a genuinely *biblical* geography since they are expressed in the Bible's own terms and categories. They include Jos 13–21; Gn 10; 2 Chr 11:6–10; and the "Threats against the Nations" in the Major Prophets.

8 Between the OT and our own day there have been various other sources for learning the relation of biblical localities among themselves, which is what a map expresses. First, there are the classic authors, Herodotus, Strabo, Pliny, and the geographer Ptolemy (cf. M. Cary and E. H. Warmington, *The Ancient Explorers* [Pelican ed.; London, 1963]). The greatest work of early Palestinian topography is the *Onomasticon* of Eusebius, AD 330 (C. U. Wolf, *BA* 27 [1964] 66–96). Observations of postbiblical Judaism are gathered in A. Neubauer, *Géographie du Talmud* (Paris, 1868) and in *Eretz-Israel Annual* 2 and *Atlas*. Siftings from the Muslim geographers have been published by G. LeStrange, R. Dussaud, and A. S. Marmardji. The data supplied by pilgrims and the Crusades are important, especially for NT sites (although, unfortunately, pilgrims were often shown localizations that were convenient to main roads rather than those based on real historical memories). These are readily available in D. Baldi, *Enchiridion;* also C. Ritter, *op. cit.;* R. Röhricht, *op. cit.*

9 **(II) Modern.** Charting places in Palestine reached a climax in the mid-19th cent. In 1838 the Boston clergyman, Professor E. Robinson, journeying through the holy land for three months with the Arabic-speaking missioner Eli Smith, located more Palestinian sites than had been discovered since the time of Eusebius. This success suggested the foundation of the British Palestine Exploration Fund and its *Survey of Western Palestine* (C. R. Conder and H. H. Kitchener [of Khartoum fame] in 6 vols.; London, 1880). For the contributions of Robinson, see *JBL* 58 (1939) 355–87.

10 The British Survey is the basis of the principal maps in use today. There are four different scales:

(1) The most detailed is the Topocadastral Survey, on 120 sheets, scale 1:20,000. It is an indispensable ultimate, but so sprawling that a single locality might have to be looked up on four sheets rather far apart in enumeration.

(2) Much more usable are the 16 maps (plus 8 for the Negeb) on the scale 1:100,000, recently re-edited by Israel in two forms, either in booklets, or on loose sheets preferable for mounting and collating.

(3) The most convenient scale is 1:250,000, of which Israel has prepared a new edition containing on one large sheet the whole of biblical Palestine N of Gaza. To this corresponds an equally large sheet containing only Beer-sheba and the Negeb. There is a three-sheet edition of the same map that is handier, brighter, and more legible (the northern and central sheets suffice for the ordinary student). The Israel maps include the modern Arab frontiers and territory, everything W of the Jordan, and a fringe also to the E. For Transjordan the British Survey map on the scale of 1:250,000 has been re-edited by the Jordanian government in three sheets: Amman/Kerak/Aqabah.

(4) A "Motor Map," on the scale 1:1,000,000, is useful for comparing remote areas. It can serve the average student.

11 The chief new departure in biblical map making since the British Survey is the *Westminster Historical Atlas* (1945 [= *WHAB*]) by G. E. Wright and F. V. Filson. Its maps indicate the reliefs and frontiers strikingly, keeping place names down to an uncluttered minimum. These fine maps have been reproduced in a smaller booklet, in *IDB*, and in Bright, *Hist.*, but unfortunately the numbering of the separate maps is not kept uniform.

12 Some maps give information on special topics. A most interesting and valuable recent development has been the *National Geographic* map of Bible-Lands (1956, 1967). At each modern site it gives in blue a brief summary of the historic event that made the locality important. This technique has been brilliantly adopted by the Elsevier-Nelson Atlas series of maps: *Mesopotamia* by M. A. Beek; *Christian World* by C. Moorman; and especially *AtBib* by L. H. Grollenberg.

A map of Roman Palestine by M. Avi-Yonah shows the roads, milestones, and Lat place names known to nascent Christianity. There is a vivid Geological Map by G. Blake. For Transjordan there is a 3-sheet archaeological map indicating numberless mounds, or "tells" (→ Biblical Archaeology, 74:24), though the chief of these are included in more usable fashion on the 3-sheet general map (→ 10, part 3 above). Every guidebook contains maps of specialized usefulness; Meistermann's Guide adds treasures of historical documentation that are not out of date as are some of his conclusions.

13 Abel's *Géographie* (= *GP*) contains in vol. 1 a precious mapping of the network of stream beds. In vol. 2 each biblical place name is given in alphabetical order with a clear indication of the *publication* of the ancient remains excavated or explored at the modern site that allegedly represents the biblical site. The dating of these finds (mostly broken pottery) is an essential basis for deciding whether the spot was occupied at all in the biblical period to which it is ascribed. The type of evidence Père Abel cites must, of course, constantly be brought up to date; and some thorny problems, such as Jericho (→ Biblical Archaeology, 74:60–62), have not yet been solved adequately within the framework of his principles. But until a better basis is advocated, this list must stand as the ultimate justification of all biblical geography and map making.

14 Perhaps we should conclude the treatment of maps with a warning. Every biblical map implicitly involves judgments on the identification of sites, and in particular on the relation of modern Arabic place names to the names of ancient sites given in the Bible. No scientific geography of the Holy Land can dispense from the constant checking of folkloric Arabic place names. One must be aware of the difficulty that different systems of transliterating Hebr and Arabic names are used in different works. Moreover, for English-Bible place names there has developed a "Protestant" and a "Catholic" spelling (e.g., Goshen, Midian, and Gilead vs. Gessen, Madian, and Galaad). The "Protestant," or standard Eng spelling, is based on the pronunciation of Hebrew in the medieval MT vocalization and has become familiar in the AV and RSV (→ Texts, 69:37, 160, 162). The "Catholic" spelling is related through the Latin to the LXX and in some instances reflects the more ancient Hebr pronunciation current when the LXX was being translated. One must remember that neither system of spelling represents the original Hebr names exactly. Recently American Catholic scholars have decided to end the confusion of two spelling systems, and in *CBQ* and in the New Confraternity Translation of the Bible (the completed and revised form; → Texts, 69:174) they are using the standard Eng spelling of names found in the RSV. That spelling will also be used below.

GEOGRAPHY OF SURROUNDING COUNTRIES

15 **(I) Abraham—The Fertile Crescent.** Biblical geography begins not in Palestine but in the Euphrates Valley. The earliest identifiable place names of the Bible are those connected with Abraham in Gn 11:31, namely, Ur and Haran. Ur is near the S, and Haran near the N of a broad arc traced by the Euphrates Valley. We can complete the same arc from Haran W toward the Syrian coast, then S as far as Egypt. This gives us a crescent with the tips resting in the Persian and Suez gulfs, and the middle running along the modern border of Turkey. This narrow strip is called the *Fertile* Crescent because it happens to coincide with a fringe of water sources that make food production possible around the edge of a vast desert.

The water supply determined not only the "sedentary" or farming centers, but also the trade routes used for shuttling back and forth from one of the great export areas to another. We shall find that the movements of Abraham coincide with the major caravan route from Babylonia to Egypt, i.e., from one tip of the Fertile Crescent to the other (cf. W. F. Albright, *BASOR* 163 [1961] 36–54).

16 At the Babylonian end of the crescent stood *Ur*, which the Bible identifies as Abraham's homeland (Gn 11:28–31). Some scholars have doubted the accuracy of this information, and it is a fact that Ur is not mentioned in the LXX of the Gn passage (cf. W. F. Albright's explanation, *BASOR* 140 [1955] 31). But even if Abraham originated at Haran far to the N, it is highly probable that he journeyed S as far as Ur, the heartland of the greatest culture center in antiquity. (L. Woolley, *Ur of the Chaldees* [Pelican ed.; London, 1952].)

This region of the Tigris-Euphrates Basin near the Persian Gulf is called in Gn 10:10 the Land of Shinar or Sennaar. This means the land of the Sumerians, the ancient non-Semitic occupants of the region (→ History of Israel, 75:11). Near Ur was *Uruk*, the Erech of Gn 10:10 (modern Warka) whose king Gilgamesh (*ca.* 2800 BC) became the hero of a flood story. From the excavations of this site have come the earliest known examples of writing, and therefore this momentous cultural advance may have been made in the region.

17 From *ca.* 2500 on, the Semitic Amorites ("westerners"—from the S Arabian peninsula or from NW Syria) began to invade Sumer; and the greatest of the Semitic dynasties set up in this region was at *Babylon*, some 150 mi. NW of Ur and the site of a famous ziggurat, or temple tower, consisting of receding brick platforms (cf. Gn 11:4–9—the Tower of Babel; *BTS* 35 [1961]). Abraham's presence at Ur has often been associated with the Amorite waves of migration into Sumer, and formerly Abraham was thought to have been a contemporary of Hammurabi, the greatest king of Babylon (*ca.* 1700—wrongly identified as the Amraphel of Gn 14:1). For the Amorites, → Excursus Israel, 11:27.

A millennium later in the biblical story Babylon would once more become prominent in Israel's history when Judah was carried off into captivity to Babylonia (598 and 587 BC; → Excursus Israel, 11:9). From either the earlier or the later contact with this Babylonian region there was a familiarity on the part of Israel with the ancient Sumerian mythology of creation, the *Enuma Elish* epic (*ANET* 60–72), from which some of the imagery of Gn 1–2 may have been borrowed. The Garden of Eden in Gn 2:10–14 is conceived of as a muddy Tigris-Euphrates confluence—perhaps this seemed a paradise to Abraham's dusty, barefoot relatives from the Arabian desert.

18 Much to the E of this area is the mountainous region of *Persia*, whose king Cyrus would liberate the

Jews from Babylonian captivity in 538. The court-panoply of Persia and its Zoroastrian religion formed a portion of the scenario of later biblical books like Neh, Dn, Est. (For Persepolis and Susa, see *BTS* 38–39 [1961].)

19 When Abraham journeyed N from Ur, his route lay between *Mari* and *Nuzi*. At each of these two centers excavation during our own lifetime has revealed thousands of clay documents (for Mari, → Biblical Archaeology, 74:51). The history of Mari on the Euphrates is bound up with Hammurabi and gives us the materials entering into current disputes about his date (cf. G. Mendenhall, *BA* 11 [1948] 1–19, or *BAR* 2, 3–20). To the E, near the modern Kirkuk oil fields, lies Nuzi. From Nuzi to Haran stretched a region anciently named Mitanni. Its people were called Hurrians (who appear in the Bible under the name Horites, or sometimes possibly as Hiwwites or Hittites). The business records of the inhabitants, reflecting their commerce with Assyrian merchants, illustrate many biblical customs attested in the patriarchal period (cf. C. H. Gordon, *BA* 3 [1940] 1–12, or *BAR* 2, 21–33).

20 *Haran* (Harran), identified in the Bible as the place where Abraham located after he migrated from Ur, is thought by many scholars to have been Abraham's original homeland. The towns of the region bear names that are variants of the names given by Gn 11 to Abraham's relatives: Peleg (v. 16), Serug (v. 20), Terah and Nahor (v. 24), and Haran itself (v. 27).

21 The topmost arc of the Fertile Crescent reaches from Haran W to the Euphrates. Where the river cuts the present Turkish frontier is the site of *Carchemish*. It became a last outpost of the Hittite Empire about 900 BC, and in 605 it was the scene of Nebuchadnezzar's decisive battle against Assyria.

From here the crescent caravan route turns sharply S, along the line Aleppo-Hama-Damascus-Jerusalem. *Aleppo* was a very ancient city, known already in the Mari records as Iamhad. On the seacoast, W of Aleppo, stood the city-state *Ugarit*, modern Ras Shamra (*NatGeog* [Oct. 1930; July 1933]). Archives found there since 1929 show that Ugarit was powerful enough to make treaties with the Hittite Empire, a rival of Egypt and Assyria (→ Excursus Israel, 11:11). The language of these texts, Ugaritic, is very important for the study of the earliest form of Hebrew (H. L. Ginsberg, *BA* 8 [1945] 41–58, or *BAR* 2, 34–50; *BTS* 68–69 [1964]). Another powerful city-state, inland farther S, was *Hamath*, now Hama (not to be confused with Homs, the Roman Emesa, which today eclipses Hama). Hamath was also the scene of decisive battles, since it corked the N outlet of the valley between the Lebanon and Antilebanon mountain ranges. This "Hamath approach" was regarded, at times, as the N boundary of the promised land (Nm 34:8). Even more ancient and important was *Damascus*. As a well-watered city on the fringe of the desert, it was a "Last Chance" for caravan supplies. Surprisingly, in describing Abraham's passage (Gn 12:5), the Bible makes no mention of these centers. It skips from Haran to the heart of Canaan, i.e., to what later would be called Samaria. (See C. Thubron, *Mirror of Damascus* [N.Y., 1967].)

22 Canaan, the promised land, was small and off to the SW corner of the Fertile Crescent. Yet it was in a strategic midposition between the rival merchant states: Arabia to the S, Egypt to the SW, Hittites to the N, Babylon to the E. Hence, if the lines of traffic and population density are set in proper perspective, Canaan may be considered the "hub" of the whole Fertile Crescent. Indeed, it was the hub of the whole universe known from Abraham's day down to Alexander the Great.

The Abraham clans, migrating from Mesopotamia, made no immediate claim to the land of Canaan. But Abraham personally is portrayed as getting a foothold in Canaan by the important experiences he had at the major centers of worship: Shechem, Bethel, Hebron, and Beer-sheba (→ Religious Institutions, 76:39–43). In reality, his sojourn in the holy land is no more than a nomadic stopover on the route to the natural terminus of the journey, namely, Egypt. (For Abraham and the Negeb, cf. *BA* 18 [1955] 2–9.)

23 In fact, Abraham does go on immediately to visit Egypt according to Gn 12:10. But the migration to which he has given his name may be justly regarded as taking place in successive waves over several generations. In this light its completion is attained only with the descent of the Jacob tribes to join Joseph in Egypt (Gn 46:7). Thus, the latter part of the Abrahamic migration turns out to be a part of what the historical records outside the Bible recognize as the movement of the Hyksos. "Hyksos" is an Egyptian word meaning "foreign rulers." It refers to Asiatic immigrants who installed themselves in the NE Delta at Avaris and from there ruled Egypt between 1700 and 1570. In the eyes of some modern scholars, they were not an invasion but more a horde of peaceful infiltrators. They were mostly Semites, although some would hold that they included Hurrians as their ruling caste. It was in the NE Delta, then, in the land the Bible calls Goshen (Gn 47:6), that Joseph's relatives settled. Here at the SW tip of the Fertile Crescent the stage was set for the Exodus.

24 **(II) Moses—Egypt and the Exodus Route.** The "People of God" in the Bible, whatever their remoter origins, seem to owe the awareness of their national unity largely to the experiences some of them had within Egypt. From there modern scholars tend to begin the Bible's history and geography properly so called. Abraham's story is looked upon essentially as an account of how Semitic tribes made an encircling migration in order to settle down in Egypt. Rather than merely "the gift of the Nile," as Herodotus says, the whole of Egypt really *is* the Nile. A 5-mi. fringe of intense cultivation runs along both sides of the whole length of the river. This region is rich in history and is extremely valuable for biblical research.

In the S at the first cataract, *ca.* 500 mi. by air and 700 mi. by water from the Delta (note, the Nile flows N), stood *Elephantine*, the site of a 5th cent. BC Jewish colony. Aramaic papyri discovered here have thrown light on the period of Ezra-Nehemiah (→ History of Israel, 75:99; E. G. Kraeling, *BA* 15 [1952] 50–67, or *BAR* 1, 128–44). Some 100 mi. to the N was *Thebes* (Luxor or Karnak) with its magnificent temples, capital of Egypt under the famous 18th Dynasty (1570–1310) whose rulers drove out the Hyksos and established Egypt as a world empire. The destruction of this ancient seat of power, deep within Egypt, by the Assyrians in 663 BC stupefied the Jews (Na 3:8; Thebes in Hebrew = No Amon). As the Nile continues its flow N, about 75 mi. by water from Thebes, in the great bend of the Nile, stood *Chenoboskion* (near Nag'-Hammadi) where about 20 years ago important Coptic Gnostic documents were found (→ Apocrypha, 68:59). Roughly another 125 mi. N, the Nile passes the site now called Amarna—ancient *Akhetaton*, capital of monotheist Pharaoh Akhenaton (1370–53), from whose archives the Amarna letters came (→ 6 above). On the opposite side of the Nile, still further N, was *Oxyrhynchus* where numerous papyri of NT times have been discovered (→ Apocrypha, 68:57; L. Deuel, *Testaments of Time* [N.Y., 1965] 79–189, tells of these discoveries in an exciting manner).

25 At the vertex of the Delta where the Nile splits into branches (still 100 mi. from the Sea) stood *Memphis* (Moph of Hos 9:6; Noph of Is 19:13; Jer 2:16;

Ez 30:13), the earliest Egyptian capital. Nearby to the N was On, or *Heliopolis*, home of Joseph's father-in-law (Gn 41:45). Between Memphis and Heliopolis was a great cemetery with deathless pyramids and the sphinx. (Only after the Muslim invasion did Cairo rise here, over a Roman fort named Babylon [hardly = 1 Pt 5:13] and near the place that legend made the terminus of the flight of the Holy Family into Egypt [Mt 2:14].) In the time of Alexander the Great (332) the great metropolis and seaport of *Alexandria* was built in the NW tip of the Delta, and this soon attracted the Jewish colony that produced the LXX. The Rosetta Stone, unlocking the Egyptian language, was discovered near Alexandria in Napoleon's time (1799).

(Fascinating accounts of the exploration of the Nile and of the history that has been lived along the river are given in: *BTS* 53–54 [1963]. Fairservis, W. A., *The Ancient Kingdoms of the Nile* [N.Y., 1962]. Ludwig, E., *The Nile* [N.Y., 1937]. Moorehead, A., *The White Nile* [N.Y., 1960] and *The Blue Nile* [N.Y., 1962]. *NatGeog* [Dec. 1954; May 1955; Oct. 1963; May 1965; May 1966].)

26 It is the NE section of the Delta that is of interest for the story of the Exodus (now customarily dated in the 13th cent., but → Biblical Archaeology, 74:56ff.). Ramses II (*ca.* 1290–1224) of the 19th Dynasty cluttered the whole Nile Valley with his building projects, but his trademark was especially frequent at *Tanis* (Zoan of Is 19:11; Ez 30:14; Ps 78:12). This site seemingly had been the Hyksos capital of Avaris 400 years before, and Nm 13:22 relates its foundation to that of Hebron, and thus to patriarchal times. Either Ramses II or his father Seti had rebuilt the site and given it the name Raamses (Ex 1:11). In this region of Tanis-Raamses (cf. Gn 47:6, 11; Ps 78:12,43), the descendants of the patriarchs were enslaved and put to work on building projects. The land of Goshen stretched S to Mashkuteh (probably Succoth of Ex 13:20) and to Pithom (1:11). The Wadi Tumilat of this region was, as Egyptian stories testify, a frequent refuge for Asiatics fleeing from famine or dictatorship.

27 The route of the Exodus, a much-disputed question, is intimately related to the problem of the location of Mt. Sinai. Sinai and Horeb are not separate peaks, but names for the same place occurring respectively in the J and in the E/D traditions of the Pentateuch. There are at least four candidates for the localization of this holy mountain: (1) In the S of the Sinai Peninsula. The very name given to this peninsula presupposes the correctness of the tradition that the peak Jebel Musa ("Mt. Moses"), at the base of which St. Catherine's Monastery stands, is Sinai. (2) In Arabia. The belching flame and quaking of the mountain described in Ex 19:18 suggest a volcano in eruption, and the nearest volcano is Talat-Badr in modern Arabia, far SE of the Sinai Peninsula. The ancient geographer Ptolemy called this region Modiane, corresponding to Midian of Ex 3:1

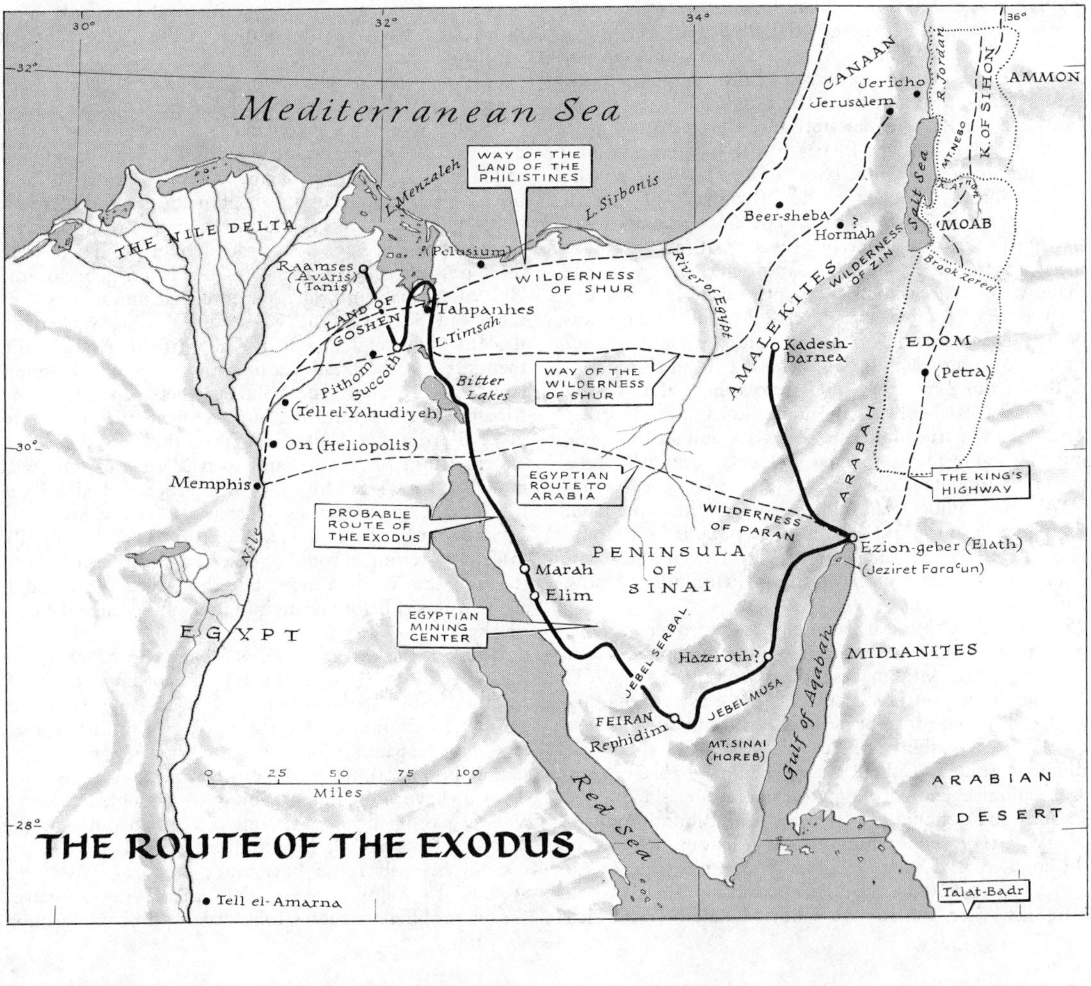

THE ROUTE OF THE EXODUS

Despite these two independent facts favoring Talat-Badr, Arabia seems too far away from Egypt to be the site. (3) In Transjordan. The name Midian fits a long strip of land stretching as far N as Gilead in Transjordan (cf. Jgs 6). A candidate for Sinai in this region is Petra (→ 40 below), since its flame-red crags were an object of immemorial religious veneration. There is also an Arab tradition that Aaron was buried there (Nm 20:8). This theory, like the preceding one, is not defended today, for it puts Sinai too far E. (4) In the Negeb. A more serious contender against theory 1 is the hypothesis that the Sinai theophany took place at Kadesh-barnea (→ 85 below). In fact, the striking of water from the rock and the murmuring of the people at Meribah during the Kadesh sojourn of Nm 20:13 are described in terms identical with the narrative of what happened at Sinai in Ex 17:7. However, this argument has convinced only a small number of exegetes (see T. J. Meek, *Hebrew Origins* [2nd ed.; N.Y., 1950] 119ff.).

28 Two possible routes for the Exodus deserve serious study: the Northern Route, often corresponding to the localization of Sinai in theory 4; the Southern Route corresponding to the localization in theory 1. (Many of the modern biblical critics regard the Exodus and the Sinai theophany as two originally independent traditions and hence would discuss the Exodus route without reference to the site of Sinai.) First, the theory of the *Northern Route* suggests that the Israelites came out of Tanis heading E directly across the N part of the "Sinai" Peninsula to Kadesh-barnea. This was the shortest and the natural route from Egypt to Canaan. It is explicitly excluded by Ex 13:17, but in terms involving the Philistines that rouse suspicion of an anachronistic gloss (although the Philistines may have raided the coast of Canaan in the 13th cent., they do not seem to have had firm control of the S Canaan coast before 1180–1150, long after the Exodus). If we try to harmonize the biblical description of sites along the path of the Exodus with the theory of the Northern Route, we must identify the "Reed Sea" of Ex 13:18; 14:22 (the Hebrew has "Reed Sea"; the "Red Sea" of English bibles stems from a plausible but not assured LXX attempt to identify the body of water). It might refer to the southern extension of Lake Menzaleh or to the shallows of Lake Sirbonis (adjacent to the Mediterranean between Egypt and Canaan). The Migdol of 14:2 was on the Egyptian side of the sea, and the Hebr text of Ez 29:10 locates Migdol at the NE extreme of Egypt farthest from Aswan (Syene). Across the shallows from Migdol was Baal-zephon, meaning "Lord of the North." The "north" part of the name is relative and inconclusive, but this name seems to have belonged originally to a towering mountain on the N Syrian coast, Mt. Casius or Amanus. Phoenician soldiers brought the name from their homeland to Egypt and ironically applied it to some low hills to the W of Sirbonis (NE of what is now the Suez Canal), called in classic times Pelusium and now Farama.

29 Other biblical statements are more reconcilable with a *Southern Route* for the Exodus, involving a detour far to the S to a Mt. Sinai as localized in theory 1. (W. F. Albright attempts to reconcile both theories by supposing an Exodus route that began to the N and switched S; other scholars think of several Exoduses, following different routes—a theory also used to explain some archaeological and chronological discrepancies about the Exodus and conquest of Palestine; → Biblical Archaeology, 74:64.) Following a southern detour, we find in the south-central Sinai Peninsula inscriptions from *ca.* AD 150 in an Arabic dialect called Nabatean; they attest a religious veneration for the valley Mukattab ("scribbled over") and for the adjacent triangle extending some 20 mi. to Jebel Serbal and to Jebel Musa. Serbal is a majestic saw-toothed ridge that Jerome and even some modern experts identified as the peak of the Sinai theophany; but there is no suitable approach or place of encampment at its foot, as the biblical description would seem to demand. At "traditional Sinai," i.e., Jebel Musa itself, there is a steep precipice named Safsafa towering over the vast plain of er-Raha. The nearness of water and the rugged splendor of the surroundings have convinced most moderns that this is the mountain of Ex 19:2. However, the Gk tradition related to St. Catherine's Monastery focuses attention on the opposite (E) end of the Jebel Musa range. In any case it is sensible to admit that the "proofs" for this localization of Sinai are tenuous and do not preclude further inquiry. (*BTS* 12 [1958]; *NatGeog* [Dec. 1927; Dec. 1948; Jan. 1964].)

30 After the Sinai theophany, in a period of about 40 years, the Israelites under Moses are said to have moved on to Transjordan. The route from Mt. Sinai to Edom is indicated twice in the Bible, once with remarkable minuteness in Nm 33, and later more briefly in Dt 1. Yet the list of places is in effect unusable, for most of the sites are unknown to us. Paran of Nm 12:16; Dt 1:1 recurs importantly as a mountain in Dt 33:2; Hab 3:3; and although its name has undoubtedly survived at the Feiran oasis near Jebel Serbal, the Bible envisions a localization in the wilderness S of the Dead Sea called the Arabah (→ 69 below). The main discrepancy of the two biblical lists concerns Ezion-geber (which 1 Kgs 9:26 places at or near Elath on the shore of the Reed Sea, in the land of Edom; → 69 below). From Dt 2:8 it would appear that the Israelites saw this gulf-port only after proceeding from Kadesh-barnea to the Arabah, which constitutes the W fringe of Edom. But Nm 33:36 plainly inserts the encampment at Ezion-geber *before* Kadesh and Edom. The Exodus refugees may well have touched down twice at so strategic a spot.

31 Below we shall discuss in detail the geography of Transjordan, but it seems wisest to mention here briefly the problem of the continuation of the Exodus journey to Mt. Nebo at the NE corner of the Dead Sea where Moses died and was buried (Dt 34:5). There were three possible routes leading N from Ezion-geber on the Gulf of Aqabah into the Transjordanian mountains E of the Dead Sea: (1) The westernmost route was to go straight N through the Rift Valley of the Arabah, and then just S of the Dead Sea to swing E up into the highlands, passing along the boundary between Edom and Moab. (2) The central and most convenient route was to go NE from the Gulf of Aqabah through the Wadi Yetem (Ithm or Yutm), and then N to join the royal road, or King's Highway, which proceeded along the top of the mountainous plateau that constituted the backbone of Edom and Moab (see *BTS* 85 [1966]). (3) The easternmost route or desert road was also reached through the Wadi Yetem, but this route continued E into the desert before turning N to flank Edom and Moab on the E.

Route 2, the easiest route, was closed to Israel by the king of Edom (Nm 20:14–21). According to the P tradition, Israel seems to have followed Route 1, for in Nm 33:42 we find the Israelites going N up the Arabah to Punon (apparently the site of the Brazen Serpent incident in Nm 21:4). According to Nm 21:10–13, they then seem to have turned E, climbing up through the Zered Valley, passing between Edom and Moab out into the desert. However, Dt (2:8) indicates that Israel did not use the Arabah route but rather Route 3. Was the attempt to follow one or the other route abortive? Or were different routes followed by different groups, along the analogy of different routes for the Exodus (→ 28–29 above)? At any rate, the Israelites had now come to the land that had been promised to them, after a journey of many centuries that had led them from one end of the Fertile Crescent to the other and then partially back again.

GEOGRAPHY OF PALESTINE

32 **(I) Introduction.** A serious discussion of the land that was center stage in biblical history should begin with a detailed study of its geology and should explain how its natural terrain was formed. This is done admirably by D. Baly, *op. cit.*, 14–26. Here we shall limit ourselves to only the most basic general observations.

(A) Size and Features. The land we shall be considering is a narrow strip that measures in length some 200–250 mi. from Dan in the N to the Sinai border in the S (Dan to Kadesh-barnea = 200; Dan to Elath = 250). This measurement includes the vast stretches of the Negeb Desert, an area that figured importantly in Israel's history but was not the land of Israel in the proper sense. If one measures the land by the classic dimensions of Dan to Beer-sheba, the length is only 150 mi. The width from the Mediterranean coast to the Rift (Jordan) Valley would be about 30 mi. in the N, and about 50 mi. in the area of the Dead Sea. Strictly speaking, the 20 mi. of Transjordanian mountainous plateau to the E of the Rift Valley would not be considered part of Israel. Thus, Israel proper covered some 7000 sq. mi. and was somewhat smaller than Massachusetts. The biblical story was enacted on a small stage—the capitals of the Divided Monarchy, Samaria in the N and Jerusalem in the S, were less than 35 mi. apart (a shorter distance than that between Baltimore and Washington, cities close enough to share the same airport).

33 Here we shall discuss the Negeb and Transjordan, as well as Israel proper. This larger area lends itself to a division of four roughly parallel strips running N-S. From E to W these strips are: (1) the Transjordanian mountains; (2) the Rift Valley; (3) the Palestinian or Cisjordanian mountains; (4) the Mediterranean coastal plain. The two mountain ranges, Transjordanian and Palestinian, are the continuations respectively of the Antilebanon and Lebanon ranges of Syria. Originally one, these ranges were cleft in two from N to S by the folding of the earth's crust; in the Palestine area this cleft took the form of the great Rift Valley (Arabic: Ghor) through which the Jordan River now flows from above the Huleh Basin in the N to the Dead Sea in the S. This great cleft in the earth, which descends to 1300 ft. below sea level at the Dead Sea, continues S of the sea as the barren valley of the Arabah that opens into the Gulf of Aqabah. (The cleft has left its mark right down into Africa, visible if one follows the line from the Red Sea to Lake Nyassa and the Victoria Falls. Cf. *NatGeog* [Aug. 1965].)

34 It is not certain that any of the Palestinian mountains were ever volcanic (→ 111 below on Mt. Moreh). Considerably to the E of Palestine, the Jebel Druze has left volcanic traces in the lava or basalt that it has spewed over Bashan and the E Transjordanian desert. Underground seething is apparent in the hot springs of Callirhoe on the NE banks of the Dead Sea. Earthquakes are well attested in antiquity (Am 1:1; perhaps in Joshua's damming of the Jordan in Jos 3:16; the destruction of the Qumran settlement in 31 BC) and have also occurred in modern times (Safed in 1837; Nazareth, 1900; Jaffa, 1903; Jericho, 1927).

35 **(B) Climate.** The climate varies according to the main natural features of the land: the coast, the mountains, the Rift Valley. Basically there are two seasons: the hot, dry summer and the cool, wet winter. In the USA California weather would probably come closest by comparison. It is helpful to remember that Jerusalem is at the same latitude as Savannah. The Palestinian coast is warm (average: 50's in winter, 80's in summer), and the humid summer heat at Tel Aviv or Haifa approximates that of Washington or St. Louis. The temperature in the Palestinian mountains is about 10° cooler than that of the coast. The summer in the mountains, at Jerusalem for instance, brings hot sunny days (average 85°) and cool nights (65°). Uncomfortable weather in the mountains is not caused by humidity as it is on the coast but by windstorms, whether it is the wind that drives rain in from the Mediterranean or the burning wind (sirocco or khamsin) that sweeps in from the desert in May and Oct. (Is 27:8; Jer 4:11). Jesus knew of both (Lk 12:54–55); and in the wintertime he circulated in the only porch of the Temple that offered protection from the prevailing wind (Jn 10:23). The part of the Rift Valley that is far below sea level, e.g., at Jericho, bakes in intense heat in summer (over 100°) but serves as an ideal winter resort—the Palm Springs of Palestine.

36 The rainfall of Palestine also varies according to region. The land nearer the Mediterranean tends to get more rain, for the Palestinian mountain range in its higher spots acts as a barrier to storms coming in from the sea, forcing them to dump their water on the W side of the mountains. Correspondingly, the E slopes are much drier. In addition, many other factors cause variation. Beer-sheba in the Negeb averages 8.6 in. rain a year—like Arizona, but with more dew. Jerusalem gets 35 in.—about the same as London—but almost all of it falls in the months from Dec. to March. A good year is one in which the autumnal or early rain falls in Oct. at seedtime, and the late or spring rain falls in March and Apr. just before harvest. Biblical references to these two rains are numerous: Dt 11:14; Hos 6:3; Jer 5:24; Jl 2:23. Yet one must remember that in general the rain is not concentrated in these early and late periods but in the time in between. The summer months from June to Sept. tend to be very dry except for occasional rainstorms on the coast. (Cf. N. Rosenan, *IsrEJ* 5 [1955] 137–53.) If the rainfall does not seem very bountiful to westerners, it evidently made an extraordinary impression on the Israelites when they were fresh from Egypt, a land where water comes from the Nile and not from the heavens (Dt 11:10–25). Snow is not unusual in the Palestinian mountains, e.g., in Jerusalem, Bethlehem, or Hebron; and in the Transjordanian mountains snowfalls sometimes block the roads.

37 The seasonal character of the rain means that water has to be stored in cisterns for the dry season, unless a town is fortunate enough to be near a spring and thus have flowing or "living" water (whence the imagery in Ez 47:1; Zech 13:1; Jn 4:10–14). Characteristic of Palestine is the wadi, i.e., a valley that is dry in the summer but becomes a channel of flash floods and strong streams in the rainy season. When dry, these wadis serve as roads from the valleys into the mountains. There are far fewer valleys that carry permanent streams.

With this general information we may now turn to each of the four N-S strips already mentioned (→ 33 above). We shall begin with the Transjordanian mountains and trace the geography from S to N, in harmony with the final stage of the Exodus that gave Israel its first contact with this region (→ 31 above).

38 **(II) Transjordan.** The Transjordanian mountains are higher than the Palestinian. They are cut across E-W by a series of tremendous canyons or gorges—radial faulting of the earth fanning out from the great N-S Rift fault, like branches from a tree trunk. These gorges containing perennial streams are from S to N: the *Zered* at the S end of the Dead Sea; the *Arnon*, halfway up the sea; the *Jabbok*, halfway up the Jordan Valley; and the *Yarmuk* at the S end of the Lake of Galilee. Often the gorges supplied the ancient occupants of Transjordan with natural frontiers. The Arnon gorge is only slightly less spectacular than the Grand Canyon of the Colorado (plates 155–57 in *AtBib*).

39 The S Transjordanian mountains, which formed the domain of ancient Edom, begin some 20 mi. NE of Elath (the Gulf of Aqabah). The route from the gulf follows the Wadi Yetem (Ithm or Yutm), which is a pass through the granite mountains of Midian (→ 27 [theory 3] above). Then one crosses the Hasma toward the Edomite mountains. This is truly a fantastic place, more worthy of the lunar than the earthly surface—a broad sandy plain from which sandstone mountains rise as isolated peaks with forbidding precipices (see plate in D. Baly, *op. cit.*, 258–59). The most famous region of the Hasma is the Wadi Rum (Lawrence-of-Arabia country) where peaks tower one-half mile high above the valley floor. When one climbs the southernmost of the Edomite mountains (Ras en-Naqb) and looks back on the Hasma, the view is spectacular and unforgettable.

40 **(A) Edom.** (→ Excursus Israel, 11:15.) The mountainous plateau of Edom, over 5000 ft. in height, is about 70 mi. long (N-S) and about 15 mi. wide. On the W, the mountains are covered with scrub vegetation, watered by the last drops of rain from storms coming in from the Mediterranean. On this side the drop into the Arabah (or continuation of the Rift Valley S of the Dead Sea) offered a certain natural protection. On the E, the mountains slope off into the desert, and this side required protection by forts. For at least part of its history the N boundary of Edom was the Zered gorge or the Brook of Willows (Is 15:7), with Moab on the other side (Nm 21:12; Dt 2:13). Much of this Edomite highland is red sandstone, soft and easily eroded. In S Edom, *Petra*, the rose-red city carved from the sandstone, the ancient capital of the Arab Nabateans, deserves rank as one of the wonders of the world (on Petra, → Biblical Archaeology, 74:84).

41 The Edomite plateau is split into two unequal parts by the Punon embayment (on Punon, → 31 above) where the Arabah valley bellies out some 9 mi. into the mountains and pinches the plateau to a very narrow strip. The region S of the Punon embayment is higher, and its Edomite strongholds like *Teman* and *Sela* were almost impregnable. (The location of Sela is disputed; the popular identification with Umm el-Biyara in the center of Petra is questioned; *BA* 19 [1956] 26–36; yet cf. *BTS* 84 [1966].) Passages such as Ps 108:10 and 2 Kgs 14:7–10 reflect the respect of the Israelites for the formidable character of these Edomite strongholds. In N Edom the main cities were *Bozrah* and the rich agricultural settlement of *Tophel* (Dt 1:1). The Bible often groups the northern city Bozrah and the southern city Teman to represent the whole of Edom (Gn 36:33–34; Jer 49:20–22; Am 1:12).

42 The mountain dwellers of the Edomite plateau, who lived "in the clefts of the rock" (Ob 3), could not support themselves simply by farming or herding flocks. They mined copper from the mountains, and they taxed the caravans that plied the King's Highway, which ran N-S along their plateau (→ 31 [route 2] above). This foreign contact may have given them their reputation for knowledge (Jer 49:7). (N. Glueck, "The Civilization of the Edomites," *BA* 10 [1947] 77–84; "The Boundaries of Edom," *HUCA* 11 [1936] 1–58.)

43 **(B) Moab.** (→ Excursus Israel, 11:17.) The area of Moab proper seems to have been between the Zered and the Arnon (Dt 2:24; Nm 22:36), thus E of the southern half of the Dead Sea. Yet Moab frequently pushed its borders N of the Arnon, so that, as with Edom, one might also speak of S and N Moab with the Arnon as a divider (Jer 48:20 implies that the Arnon was the great geological feature of Moab). In S Moab the chief city was *Kir-hareseth* (modern Kerak), a magnificent natural fortress on an isolated hill. Today it is still surmounted by a Crusader castle, mute testimony that from biblical times to World War I it has been one of the chief military strongholds of the Palestine region. In 2 Kgs 3:25–27 we see this Moabite fortress holding out against the combined forces of Israel and Judah.

44 In N Moab, *Aroer* dominated from the N side the great gorge of the Arnon (2300 ft. deep!). Five miles further N, *Dibon* (Dhiban) was a principal city; its impressive walls have recently been excavated by ASOR (*BASOR* 125 [1952] 7–20; 133 [1954] 6–26). Farther N in a rich plain was *Medeba* (modern Madeba; Is 15:2). In a stele that he erected at Dibon to commemorate his victories (the "Moabite Stone" dating from *ca.* 830 BC; *ANET* 320), Mesha, king of Moab, boasts of having reconquered Medeba from Israel. (For the Madeba mosaic map, → 5 above.) The fortress protecting the northern approaches to Moab was *Heshbon* (Is 15:4; 16:8–9).

About 5 mi. to the W of Medeba and Heshbon, overlooking the Dead Sea, was the site of Moses' panoramic view of the promised land and of his death, the site called *Nebo* in the P tradition and *Pisgah* in the E tradition (Dt 32:49; 34:1)—perhaps two promontories of the one mountain. In NT times the fortress *Machaerus* stood SW of Nebo near the Dead Sea—an isolated peak made impregnable by the Herods. There John the Baptist met his death (Josephus, *Ant.* 18.5, 2 § 119). Herod the Great treated his illness at the nearby hot springs of *Callirrhoe* (H. Donner, *ZDPV* 79 [1963] 59–89).

45 As we have mentioned, the Moabite occupation of the area N of the Arnon was often contested, so that, for instance, when Moses led Israel through Transjordan, the Amorites (→ Excursus Israel, 11:27) had occupied Heshbon and territory as far S as the Arnon, burning Medeba and ravishing Dibon (Nm 21:26–30). Subsequently part of N Moab was occupied by the Israelite tribe of Reuben (Nm 32:37; Jos 13:9), but this tribe was quickly destroyed by aggressive Moabite expansion that pushed even across the Jordan to Jericho (Jgs 3:12ff.; Gn 49:3–4). It should be noted that "the plains of Moab" where the Israelites encamped before crossing to Jericho were not on the Moabite plateau but in the Jordan Valley, just NE of the Dead Sea (→ 66 below).

46 The territory of the Moabite plateau is quite unlike the forbidding reaches of Edom to the S. True, crops like wheat and barley can be planted only in a small area, chiefly in N Moab; but the tableland offers rich grazing for flocks. Even today the black tents of the

Bedouin dot the land as they pasture their flocks—the economic descendants of Mesha, king of Moab who "was a sheep breeder, and he had to deliver annually to the king of Israel 100,000 lambs and the wool of 100,000 rams" (2 Kgs 3:4). When Reuben occupied Moabite territory, it was too busy among the sheepfolds to help its Palestinian cousins in time of war (Jgs 5:16). The wealth of Moab may have accounted for the pride of which Jer 49:26 and Is 25:10–11 accuse its inhabitants.

(*BTS* 48 [1962]. Grohman, E. D., *IDB* 3, 409–19. Murphy, R., "Israel and Moab in the 9th Century," *CBQ* 15 [1943] 409–17. Van Zyl, A. H., *The Moabites* [Leiden, 1960].)

47 **(C) Ammon.** (→ Excursus Israel, 11:14.) To the immediate N of Medeba and Heshbon lies the long expanse of Gilead, parallel to most of the Rift Valley between the Dead Sea and the Lake of Galilee. Before we consider Gilead, we shall turn aside from our journey N and study Ammon, E of southern Gilead and NE of northern Moab. There, in a poorly defined stretch of land from the Jabbok in the N as far S (at certain times) as the Arnon, the Ammonites were in the process of settling at the period when Moses brought the Israelites into Transjordan (Jgs 11:13—thus Ammon seems to have been the youngest and the weakest of the three kingdoms we have been discussing). To have an idea of the fluctuating border situation, we may note that in attacking the Amorite kingdom of Heshbon (subsequently the territory of Reuben), Israel in its own view was attacking neither Moab nor Ammon, although both peoples laid claim to that territory. (Notice too that Jos 13:25 characterizes the territory of Gad, i.e., S Gilead, as Ammonite land.)

48 If the frontiers of Ammon were vague, its capital was indisputably Rabbah or *Rabbath Ammon* (in Hellenistic times, Philadelphia in the Decapolis; modern Amman, capital of Jordan). The formidable mountain citadel of this city gave strong resistance to David's army (2 Sm 11:1,14–21; cf. Am 1:14). In later times, *ca.* 440 BC, Tobiah the Ammonite, the great enemy of Nehemiah (Neh 4:1 [4:7]; 6:1–17; 13:4) seems to have made his headquarters at a stronghold now called *Araq el-Emir*, recently excavated by ASOR (→ Biblical Archaeology, 74:82).

49 The land of Ammon, caught between the mountains of S Gilead and the great desert to the E, was an area of plateau. The most valuable possession of the Ammonites was the fertile valley of the upper Jabbok, a river that begins near Rabbath Ammon and moves N, before swinging W into the Jordan Valley. The Ammonites, who had once seized this region themselves, had constantly to protect it against desert raiders (the woe threatened to the Ammonites in Ez 25:4–5). Although never very strong, the Ammonites could mount swift attacks against the tribes of Israel (Jgs 10:9; 1 Sam 11:1; Am 1:13; 2 Kgs 24:2; Jer 40:14); yet they needed help when they faced the might of a united Israel (2 Sm 10:6). For long periods Ammon was completely subject to Israel (2 Sm 12:31; 2 Chr 27:5).

(Landes, G. M., "The Material Civilization of the Ammonites," *BA* 24 [1961] 65–86, or *BAR* 2, 69–88.)

50 **(D) Gilead.** The Jabbok River, as it comes down from the Transjordanian mountains into the Jordan Valley, divides Gilead into two parts. The southern part, conquered from the Amorite king of Heshbon (Dt 2:36; Jos 12:2), was assigned to the Israelite tribe of Gad; the northern, conquered from the king of Bashan (Dt 3:10; Jos 12:5), was assigned to a portion of the Manasseh tribe. See Dt 3:12–13; Jos 13:25,31, although these tribal boundaries in the Bible often represent an historical evolution far more complicated than the narrative conveys.

Gilead's shape is an oval, about 35–40 mi. long (N–S) and 25 mi. wide (E–W). The mountainous plateau here is dome-shaped, rising to a height of 3300 ft.; and because of its altitude it receives heavy rain from the clouds that sweep in from the Mediterranean in the winter. The limestone hills trap the water, and there are fine springs. In antiquity Gilead, especially N Gilead, had heavy forests (Jer 22:6; Zech 10:10), and even today there is an abundance of scrub oak, carob, and pine. The balm from Gilead's trees was famous (Jer 8:22; 46:11) and was exported both to Phoenicia (Ez 27:17) and to Egypt (Gn 37:25). Vineyards too flourished in this region. There was some mining, and the forests supplied ample fuel for smelting (→ 65 below).

51 This was a land subject to warfare both from the Ammonites to the S and E and from the Arameans to the N (→ Excursus Israel, 11:10). In the military campaign of Gideon (Jgs 8:4–9), we hear of two important towns of Gilead, Succoth and Penuel, both of which are in the vicinity of the Jabbok. *Succoth* may be Tell Deir Alla, a huge mound at the conjunction of the Jabbok and Jordan valleys. (Recent excavations of this mound by a Dutch expedition under H. J. Franken suggest an Israelite conquest around 1200 and then later Philistine occupation. Hitherto it had not been realized that the Philistines controlled so much of the Jordan Valley.) *Penuel*, several miles to the E in the Jabbok Valley, was the site of Jacob's wrestling match with the angel (Gn 32:30–31) and seemingly served as a temporary capital of the northern kingdom under Jeroboam I (*ca.* 915; 1 Kgs 12:25). *Mahanaim*, another important center in Gilead (Gn 32:2), S of the Jabbok, was the capital-in-exile of Saul's son Ishbaal (= Ishbosheth; 2 Sm 2:8). One of the reasons for locating interim capitals in Gilead was that the terrain gave small forces an advantage over a large army, so that this territory became a place of refuge, e.g., for David when he fled from Absalom (2 Sm 17:24).

52 *Jabesh-gilead*, an important town in N Gilead, seemingly had close relations with Benjamin on the Palestinian side of the Jordan River (Jgs 21:5–12; 1 Sm 11). *Ramoth-gilead*, to the E, a Levitical city of refuge (Dt 4:43), played an important role in the 9th-cent. wars between Israel and the Arameans of Syria (1 Kgs 22; 2 Kgs 8:28). In NT times *Gerasa*, about 5 mi. N of the Jabbok, and *Gadara*, in the NW corner of Gilead, with a spectacular view of the Yarmuk, were important towns of the Decapolis. They are possible sites for the home of the demoniac in Mk 5:1–20 (→ Biblical Archaeology, 74:90). *Pella*, in the Jordan Valley at the foot of the mountains of N Gilead, was another Decapolis town and served as a refuge for the Christians of Palestine at the time of the Jewish revolt against the Romans (AD 66–70). See *BA* 21 (1958) 82–96; *RB* 75 (1968) 105–12.

53 **(E) Bashan.** A few miles S of the Yarmuk the mountains of Gilead drop off to a fertile tableland. These are the rich plains of Bashan (also called Hauran) that extend across the Yarmuk. Running parallel to the Lake of Galilee these plains stretch N to the foot of Mt. Hermon, and E to the black volcanic mountains of the Jebel Druze. The rainfall is adequate here, for the low hills of Galilee on the Palestinian side permit the storms from the Mediterranean to pass over and to water Bashan. In many areas of the plains the soil is rich volcanic alluvium. The combination of rainfall and fertility makes Bashan the great wheat granary of the region and very good pasture. The Bible speaks of the fatness of the animals in Bashan as proverbial (Ps 22:12; Am 4:1; Ez 39:18). In E Bashan, sturdy oaks grew on the slopes of the Jebel Druze, so that Bashan could be grouped with

Lebanon for the splendor of its trees (Is 2:13; Na 1:4; Ez 27:6; Zech 11:1–2). The forests of Bashan offered refuge to those in trouble (Ps 68:15,22; Jer 22:20).

54 The biblical references to specific sites in Bashan are few, for Israel was able to control this area only in the moments of her greatness. One of the cities of Og, king of Bashan, was *Salecah* (Dt 3:10; modern Salkhad) in the Jebel Druze; another was *Edrei* (modern Der'a), which was situated further W near Gilead. Edrei was the site of Moses' victory over Og (Nm 21:33–35). In David's time the Aram kingdom of *Geshur* occupied the section of Bashan near the Sea of Galilee; this kingdom was subject to David and from it he took the princess who was Absalom's mother (2 Sm 3:3; 13:37–38; cf. B. Mazar, *JBL* 80 [1961] 16–28). In the 9th cent. Bashan was a battlefield between Israel and the Syrians of Damascus (2 Kgs 10:32–33). Again in Maccabean times it featured in warfare, as Judas Maccabeus helped the Jews in Bosor, Bozrah, and Carnaim (1 Mc 5:24–52).

55 In NT times several of the towns of the *Decapolis* (Hippos, Dion, Raphana) were in Bashan. *Gaulanitis* (N Bashan) and *Trachonitis* (E Bashan) were part of the tetrarchy of Philip, as mentioned in Lk 3:1. Today, the ruins of basalt cities with their black stone buildings rise from the plains of Bashan as funeral monuments to the glory of the past.

(On the Transjordan: Glueck, N., *The Other Side of the Jordan* [New Haven, 1940]—a popular digest of his *Explorations in Eastern Palestine* in *AASOR* 14, 15, 18, 19 [1934, 1935, 1937–1939]. Harding, G. L., *The Antiquities of Jordan* [London, 1959]. Hoade, E., *East of the Jordan* [Jerusalem, 1954]. *NatGeog* [Dec. 1947; Dec. 1952; Dec. 1964].)

56 **(III) Rift Valley.** In modern Lebanon the twin N–S mountain ranges of the Lebanon and Antilebanon are separated by the fertile plain called the Biqa'. Caused by the rift that separated the mountains, this is an upland valley 3000–1600 ft. in elevation. (In the heart of this valley rise the majestic ruins of the Hellenistic temples of Ba'albek, one of the tourist attractions of the Near East.) The N frontier of Israel is now—as it was in antiquity—marked by the dramatic locale where the Biqa' falls off into the great Palestinian Rift, a drop of 1300 ft. to the Huleh Basin. In antiquity this northernmost territory of Israel belonged to Dan, and the phrase "from Dan to Beer-sheba" stood for the limits of Israel. Dominating the scene is snow-clad Mt. Hermon, the 9100 ft.-high S shoulder of the Antilebanon range—the peak the Arabs call "the Sheikh," because its snow cap (even in summer) resembles a white burnoose. In antiquity it was called Sirion by the Phoenicians and Senir by the Amorites (Dt 3:9); and Israel looked upon it as a sentinel guarding the northern frontiers (Dt 4:48; Ct 4:8).

57 **(A) Jordan Tap Waters and the Huleh Basin.** In the shadow of Hermon the Jordan is born of four streams fed by the drainage of the Lebanese mountains. Two of the streams, the Bareighit and the Hasbani, cascade from the Biqa', and this beautiful region of waterfalls and turbulent springtime torrents (between modern Merj Ayun and Metulla) is eloquently lyricized in Ps 42:6–7. The two major tributaries, the Liddani and the Banyasi, rise at the foot of Hermon, respectively at the city of *Dan* (modern Tell el-Qadi) and at *Caesarea Philippi* (Baniyas). In Jgs 18 we are told how Dan seized this region of woodlands and springs when the tribe moved N from central Palestine. The town of *Laish* (Hebr "lion") mentioned in the story may evoke the local wildlife (Dt 33:22, "Dan is a lion's whelp"). The shrine of Dan, an important religious center since the time of the judges (Jgs 18:30; Am 8:14), was one of the two official shrines of the northern kingdom (1 Kgs 12:29; 2 Kgs 10:29; → Religious Institutions, 76:53). *Abel of Beth-maacah* in northernmost Dan served as a rallying place for revolutionary sentiment against the southern king (2 Sm 20:14–22). The religious associations of the Dan territory carried over into NT times; for Paneas (whence modern Baniyas) was a center for the worship of the god Pan. The town was rebuilt as Caesarea Philippi (= "Caesar-town" of the Herodian tetrarch Philip to distinguish it from Caesarea Maritima on the coast); Jesus and his disciples visited it, and it was there that Peter acknowledged Jesus as the Messiah (Mk 8:27). Some have suggested that Mt. Hermon, towering over Caesarea, was the "high mountain" of the transfiguration in the next chapter of Mk (9:2).

58 In antiquity the Huleh Basin, 9 mi. long and 3 mi. wide, saw the convergence of these four streams with some secondary tributaries to form a marshland and a small shallow lake about 3 mi. long. A pestilent source of malaria, this area has now been effectively drained by Israeli engineers. Two streams entered the lake, called Semechonitis by Josephus, and the Jordan alone emerged. The Huleh Basin offered N–S passage from Palestine into the Biqa' of Lebanon, and just S of Huleh passed the E–W road between Palestine and Damascus (Syria). An important stronghold was needed to dominate the strategic spot, and this role was played by *Hazor;* it lay in the mountains just SW of Lake Huleh and was the principal city of N Palestine. After Joshua had conquered central and S Palestine, he naturally turned against Hazor as the key to the conquest of the N (Jos 11; for the important Israeli excavation of Hazor, → Biblical Archaeology, 74:21, 63).

59 In the 10 mi. that separate the former site of Lake Huleh and the Lake of Galilee, the Jordan (whose name means "strongly descending") flows through a narrow basalt gorge whose walls tower 1200 ft. above the stream. The flow is rapid as the river descends from over 200 ft. above sea level at Huleh to emerge at the Lake of Galilee 675 ft. below sea level. High on the W plateau, in the region just before the Jordan reaches the lake, stand the bleak ruins of *Chorazin*, cursed by Jesus for failing to appreciate his miracles (Mt 11:21).

60 **(B) Lake of Galilee.** We now come to the center stage of Jesus' ministry and truly one of the most beautiful places in Palestine—the heart-shaped lake, 12–13 mi. long and 7–8 mi. wide at its broadest, called in Hebrew Chinnereth ("harp," whence the plain of Gennesaret in Mt 14:34, the Lake of Gennesaret in Lk 5:1, and the Lake of Gennesar in Josephus). "The Sea of Galilee" is the name given to this body of water by Mk and Mt, but Lk more correctly designates it as a lake. Only Jn (6:1; 21:1) speaks of it as "Tiberias," the name it took on later in the 1st cent. AD after Herod Antipas had built the town of that name on the SW shore, in flattering homage to the Roman emperor.

The lake's blue waters are framed by cliffs on nearly every side except the N, where green plains, especially in the NW, provide an attractive border. Its beauty has never been lost on men: The caves of the NW hills have yielded up some of the earliest traces of prehistoric man found in Palestine (→ Biblical Archaeology, 74:41), and even today many a tourist or pilgrim finds this the most conducive spot in Palestine for meditation on Him who more than once prayed there himself (Mk 1:35; 6:46). Yet the site has not always been peaceful. At the "Horns of Hattin," a hilly gateway from lower Galilee down to the Lake (a site Jesus must have passed as he came down from Nazareth and environs to Capernaum [Lk 4:31; Jn 2:12]), took place the climactic battle of 1187 where the great Saladin smashed forever the power of the Crusaders in Palestine.

61 Jesus' disciples were fishermen on this lake; more than once he felt the violence of its sudden storms as he traversed it in their boats. The warm winters of the sheltered lake favored this outdoor preacher who often lacked shelter (Mt 8:20). He found his audiences in the busy occupants of the commercial towns that dotted its N shores, in the merchants who traversed the road to Syria that ran along the W of the lake, and in the host of government officials who controlled the border crossings along the Jordan, separating Herod's Galilee from Philip's Gentile tetrarchate in Bashan (→ 55 above). *Capernaum* (Tell Hum; → Biblical Archeology, 74:88) on the NNW shore was Peter's home (according to Mk 1:21,29). This town became Jesus' headquarters, and its synagogue heard his preaching (Lk 4:31; 7:5; Jn 6:59). Some 4 mi. away, across the Jordan and on the NNE shore, was *Bethsaida*, somehow connected with the multiplication of the loaves (Lk 9:10; Jn 6:1; but cf. Mk 6:45) and, according to Jn 1:44; 12:21, the home of Peter, Andrew, and Philip. Mary Magdalene, once possessed by seven demons (Lk 8:2), seems to have come from *Magdala* on the W shore of the lake, while the demoniac of Mk 5:1 prowled in tombs on the E shore of the lake (near Gergesa? → 52 above; → Gospel Mk, 42:31) in the Decapolis region. There is little of OT importance in this area, but at the SW corner of the lake stood the prebiblical, Early Bronze Age fortress subsequently called Beth-yerah (→ Biblical Archaeology, 74:50). (For the Lake in general, see *BTS* 76 [1965].)

62 **(C) Jordan Valley.** Between the Lake of Galilee and the Dead Sea, a distance of 65 mi., the Jordan falls from 675 ft. below sea level to 1300 ft. below. On both sides the mountains rise 1000 ft. and more above the valley formed by the rift that once tore them apart. This basic Rift Valley, called in Arabic the Ghor, is quite wide in the N (for some 20 mi. down from the Lake of Galilee) and again in the S where it is 20 mi. wide just above the Dead Sea. In the center of the strip we are considering, however, the Rift Valley is constricted into a narrow waist. When water is available in the valley—through rain in the N and through irrigation in the S—the valley floor yields itself to productive cultivation.

63 Roughly through the center of the Rift Valley runs the Jordan River, a narrow stream only 60–80 ft. wide at the traditional spot for Joshua's crossing to Jericho. Little wonder then that Naaman the Syrian found the rivers of Damascus more impressive (2 Kgs 5:12). As it twists and meanders, especially midway down from the Lake of Galilee and toward the S, the Jordan has worn into the Rift Valley floor a deep bed of its own, called the Zor. In places the Zor is a mile wide and 150 ft. deep. Flooded in springtime when the melting snows of Hermon engorge the Jordan, the Zor is often an impenetrable thicket of shrubs and stunted trees, which in antiquity offered a habitat to wild animals, including lions (Jer 49:19; Zech 11:3). Wisely does Jer 12:5 stress the danger to those who fall down in the jungle of the Jordan (also 49:19). Where the floor of the Rift Valley (the Ghor) breaks away toward the riverbed (the Zor), the ground consists of desert "badlands," i.e., ash-gray marl hills with barren, crumbly soil called *qattara*. The treacherous qattara and the junglelike Zor, rather than the width of the stream, are what has made the Jordan a divider. In the N where fords are more frequent, there were better communications, not always pleasant, between Palestine and Transjordan, especially Gilead (Jgs 8:4; 12:1–6; 21:8–12; 1 Sm 31:11–13).

64 Moving from N to S in the Jordan Valley, we find that the first great tributary from the E is the Yarmuk, which carries as much water as the Jordan itself (and has been the subject for possible diversionary water projects in the water-war between the Arabs and the Israelis). Near the conjunction of the Yarmuk and the Jordan flourished an important pottery-Neolithic civilization at what is today known as *Sha'ar ha-Golan*, excavated by M. Stekelis. About 12 mi. S of the Lake of Galilee, there is a gap in the western mountains as the Plain of Esdraelon (Jezreel) opens into the Rift Valley. The strategic communication routes into Israel through this opening were controlled by the stronghold of *Beth-shan* (Beisan), a site whose importance is marked by strata of Egyptian, Philistine, and Israelite occupation (→ Biblical Archaeology, 74:65, 68). In Roman times it was called Scythopolis and flourished as an important center both for Jews and for Christians *ca.* AD 400. Opposite the Beth-shan gap, on the Transjordanian side of the valley was Pella; and just to the S where the Brook Cherith (= Wadi Yabes; 1 Kgs 17:3) joins the Jordan, we are in the country of Elijah and near the OT site of Jabesh-gilead (→ 52 above). An American excavation of Pella, directed by R. H. Smith, began in 1967 (*RB* 75 [1968] 105–12).

65 Still on the E side, where the Rift Valley grows narrow and at the spot where the Wadi Kufrinje joins the Jordan, we come to *Zarethan* (1 Kgs 4:12). This is most probably to be identified with Tell es-Sa'idiyeh, the site of interesting excavations by J. B. Pritchard (*BA* 28 [1965] 10–17; *BTS* 75 [1965]). For Succoth (Tell Deir Alla?), 5 mi. farther S, → 51 above. The E side of the valley between the Wadi Kufrinje and the Jabbok (Nahr ez-Zerqa) was the site of Solomon's smelting activities (1 Kgs 7:45–47), for which the forests of N Gilead on the plateau above offered ready fuel. The distance between Zarethan, at the confluence of the Kufrinje with the Jordan, and *Adam* (Tell ed-Damiyeh), at the confluence of the Jabbok, is 12 mi.; and Jos 3:16 reports that when Joshua stopped the flow of the Jordan, the water backed up from Adam to Zarethan. Historical records confirm that landslides in the Adam area have stopped the Jordan temporarily. On the W side, just opposite this area, the Wadi Far'ah enters the Rift Valley from the Palestinian side, draining the heartland of Samaria. On an isolated peak, dominating the junction of the Far'ah and the Jordan, was the impregnable Herodian fortress called the *Alexandrium;* and indeed in the 15 mi. of the W side that separate the Alexandrium from Jericho, other Herodian fortresses stood at *Phasaelis*, *Archelais*, and *Dok* (cf. 1 Mc 16:15), protecting the communication routes between the valley and Judea. See *BA* 15 (1952) 26–42; → History of Israel, 75:132.

66 About 8 mi. N of the Dead Sea, on the W side set back from the river, stood the pearl of the S Jordan Valley, the city of *Jericho*, one of the oldest cities on earth and the site of extremely important archaeological excavations (→ Biblical Archaeology, 74:19, 45, 60–61). The fountain near the ruins is suggested as the one purified by Elisha (2 Kgs 2:19–22). The Jericho of NT times was seemingly not at the same site (Tell es-Sultan) but nearby (→ Biblical Archaeology, 74:91). On the E side opposite Jericho, in this region where the valley is very wide, are the *plains of Moab* (Nm 22:1), the site of the Israelites' encampment when they came down from the Moabite plateau. N. Glueck has surface-explored this area to identify the various sites mentioned in the Bible, e.g., *Shittim* (Nm 25:1; Jos 2:1). These plains are the stage that the Bible gives to the last chapters of Nm and the whole of Dt. (Also in this area are the mounds of *Ghassul*, a prebiblical site important for its Chalcolithic pottery and art; → Biblical Archaeology, 74:47.) The exact place of the crossing of the Jordan is not certain (→ Biblical Archaeology, 74:91). For the disputed location of Gilgal, the first encampment on the W side after crossing (Jos 5:10), see J. Muilenburg, *BASOR* 140 (1955) 11–27; O. Bächli, *ZDPV* 83 (1967) 64–71.

(On the whole course of the Jordan from Lebanon to the Dead Sea, cf. Glueck, N., *The River Jordan* [N.Y., 1946]. *BTS* 64 [1964]. *NatGeog* [Dec. 1940; Dec. 1944].)

67 **(D) Dead Sea.** The Jordan River comes to an end in the Dead Sea, the most dramatic feature of the Rift Valley. Fringed by mountains on both sides, roughly 50 mi. long by 10 mi. wide, the Dead Sea (Sea of the Arabah, Salt Sea, Lake Asphaltitis) is the lowest point on the earth's surface, 1300 ft. below sea level with a water depth of another 1300 ft. in the N. The Dead Sea, even more than Utah's Salt Lake (*NatGeog* [Dec 1958] 848–58), can claim to be the world's most unusual body of water. Over 27 per cent of its composition is solid chemical matter (salt, chlorides, and bromides); its salt content increases constantly because the seven million tons of water that flow into it daily have no outlet, and the constant evaporation leaves residual solids. The 45 billion tons of chemicals it contains are an attraction for the chemical-extraction industry both in Israel and in Jordan, but even this will not prevent the shallow S end of the sea from being ultimately silted up. (On the Nabatean bitumen industry, cf. *BA* 22 [1959] 40–48.) No fish can exist in such water—at least until Ezekiel's vision will be fulfilled and a life-giving stream will flow from Jerusalem to sweeten the Dead Sea as far as En-gedi (47:10). Neither the intense heat nor the parched terrain in this area is conducive to large-scale settlement (although the region has possibilities as a winter resort).

68 On the NW shore, near the spring called Ain Feshkha, stand the ruins of *Qumran*, the settlement of the community that produced the Dead Sea Scrolls (→ Apocrypha, 68:67ff.; *NatGeog* [Dec. 1958]). Halfway down on the W shore is the more celebrated water source of *En-gedi* (Ct 1:14) where David sought refuge from Saul (1 Sm 23:29). For recent Israeli excavations at the En-gedi oasis, see *Arch* 16 (1963) 99–107. The isolated mountain fortress of *Masada*, two-thirds of the way down the sea, was the last stronghold in the Jewish struggle against the Romans in AD 73, and the valleys between En-gedi and Masada are dotted with caves that were outposts of Jewish resistance—caves that yielded additional Dead Sea Scrolls (→ Apocrypha, 68:107–110; also Y. Yadin, *Masada* [N.Y., 1966]). On the S end of the W shore stands the great salt mountain *Jebel Usdum*, whose name recalls biblical Sodom and the pillar of salt that once was Lot's wife (Gn 19:26). It is generally thought that *Sodom* and *Gomorrah* and the three other cities of the plain (Gn 18:16ff.) lie under the waters at the southern end of the sea (*BA* 5 [1942] 17–32; 6 [1943] 41–52, or *BAR* 1, 41–76). This shallow bay glides into the Sebkha or salt marshes that extend for 8 mi. S of the Dead Sea.

The E shore is marked by precipitous cliffs and the great gorges of the Transjordanian rivers, like the Arnon and the Zered. We have already mentioned the hot springs of Callirrhoe on the N part of this shore (→ 44 above). Two-thirds of the way down the E side is the Lisan ("tongue") peninsula, a gray-marl plateau 9 mi. long protruding into the Dead Sea and cutting its width to only 2 mi. In Roman times and even later it was possible to ford the Dead Sea here. Just to the E of the Lisan peninsula Paul Lapp has excavated a series of fascinating Early Bronze Age necropolises at Bab edh-Dhra' (*Arch* 19 [1966] 104–11).

(*BTS* 45 [1962]. *Reader's Digest* [July 1966] 157–64.)

69 **(E) Arabah.** Although the OT uses the name Arabah to designate the entire Rift Valley, today the term is most often applied to the southernmost section of the Palestinian Rift, i.e., the 100 mi. from the Sebkha salt marshes to the Gulf of Aqabah. Flanked on both sides by mountains, which are especially high on the E, the valley floor of the Arabah gradually rises, until halfway down at Jebel er-Rishe it reaches 650 ft. above sea level only to descend again toward sea level at Aqabah. The N part of the Arabah is quite wide, especially at the Punon embayment (→ 41 above); the S part is only 6 mi. wide at its broadest. Much of the Arabah is desert area in which only expert irrigationists, like the Nabateans and the modern Israeli, could sustain settlement. The biblical import of the Arabah is centered on two moments in history: First, it served as one of the routes in Israel's advance from Kadesh-barnea to Transjordan (→ 31 above); second, it was the focal point of Solomon's copper industry. Copper was mined from the hills and crudely smelted in the valley in order to meet the needs of Israel's greatest builder (*BA* 24 [1961] 59–62). At the S extremity of the Arabah, on the N end of the Gulf of Aqabah, stood the fortress of Elath (Eloth), a point of contention between Judah and Edom (2 Kgs 14:22; 16:6). Nearby was Ezion-geber, a site that figured in the desert wandering of Israel under Moses (→ 30 above), but most famous as the port built by Solomon for launching his fleet and thus his open door for trade with Somaliland, S Arabia, and points E (1 Kgs 9:26; 10:2). This port was reopened at subsequent periods during the Divided Monarchy when Israel and Judah were at peace and could work together to rebuild the world trade begun by Solomon (2 Chr 20:36). N. Glueck has identified both Elath and Ezion-geber (kept distinct in the Bible) with the site he excavated at Tell el-Kheleifeh, in the center of the N head of the gulf, one-quarter mile inland. Almost every writer on the Bible has accepted this identification even though Glueck found no remains of port facilities and the strong winds in the region make the site unsuitable as a port. One would have to suppose that there was no regular docking and that the ships were beached; there is an account of a shipwreck at Ezion-geber in 1 Kgs 22:47. (He believed one of the main buildings to have been Solomon's copper smeltery, an opinion he later withdrew.) Rothenberg (*BTS* 72 [1965]) has argued that, while Elath was in this area on the NE end of the Gulf (Byzantine Aila, just N of modern Aqabah, and stretching W to Tell el-Kheleifeh), Ezion-geber was on the island of Jeziret Fara'un, off the W shore of the gulf some 8 mi. farther S. This island, where pottery of Solomon's period has been found, provides excellent shelter for ships. Remains of an artificial port are in evidence.

(*BA* 1 [1938] 13–16; 2 [1939] 37–41; 3 [1940] 51–55; 28 [1965] 70–87. *BTS* 25 [1960]. *ILN* [Sept. 3, 1960]. *NatGeog* [Feb. 1944]. *PEQ* 94 [1962] 5–71.)

70 **(IV) Coastal Plains.** Before concentrating on the main geographical area of biblical interest, i.e., the strip of Palestinian mountains between the Mediterranean and the Jordan, we shall turn our attention to the Palestinian coast. From Philistine Gaza in the S to Phoenician Tyre in the N, this coast is about 130 mi. long. For convenience we may divide it into three sections, each 40–45 mi. in length, namely, Philistia, Sharon, and the Dor-Carmel-Asher region.

71 **(A) Philistia and the Shephelah.** A half-century after the main Israelite invasion of Canaan (presumably *ca.* 1240; → Biblical Archaeology, 74:64), a S strip of the Canaanite coast was invaded from the Mediterranean by the "Sea Peoples," an amalgam of Indo-Europeans from Crete, Cyprus, Sardinia, Sicily, and other islands in the Mediterranean. (Earlier these peoples had invaded the coast further N, destroying

Ugarit [→ 21 above] *ca.* 1230.) The Semites of the land, Canaanite and Israelite, found these uncircumcised foreigners of unintelligible tongue to be formidable adversaries in war, with iron weapons that made them invincible (→ Biblical Archaeology, 74:66–69). Within a few years, *ca.* 1170–50, and probably with Egyptian approval, these people, who became known as Philistines, were in full control of the coast and had formed a pentapolis, or five-city league (1 Sm 6:4), with Gaza, Ashkelon, and Ashdod on the coast (respectively S to N), and Gath and Ekron further inland (sites not clearly identifiable today). See *BA* 26 (1963) 134–39; *BTS* 71 (1965) for recent excavation of Ashdod. See *BA* 29 (1966) 70–86; *RB* 71 (1964) 215–29 for treatment of the Philistines (→ Excursus Israel, 11:19).

72 (a) PHILISTIA. Although the Philistines ultimately controlled much of Canaan, including the Plain of Esdraelon and part of the Jordan Valley, and gave the name "Palestine" to the whole land, Philistia proper was the area of the pentapolis. Along the seashore and up to 2 mi. inland, the coast from Gaza N to Joppa (45 mi.) is marked by sand dunes, sometimes rising to a height of 150 ft. Along this coast ran the main highway, the trunk road, from Egypt toward Syria, and we have suggested (→ 28 above) the possibility that at least part of the Exodus followed this route to Canaan.

The Philistine plain is the area between the sand dunes and the foothills, a distance of 5–10 mi. The area is cut crosswise by wadis that drain the hills to the E, and many of the cities command these wadis. Olive groves and grain fields (Jgs 15:5) were the agricultural wealth of the Philistines, a bounty marred only by the threefold danger of drought, plague, and war. Especially in the S of Philistia rainfall is light, and the water from the winter storms runs off quickly. Gaza, for instance, stands on the threshold between cultivated land and the desert to the S. Plague, transmitted from Egypt (Dt 7:15; 28:60; Am 4:10), was not uncommon; and malaria has been a danger in this region until recently. The Bible records that a (bubonic?) plague swept Philistia when the Israelite Ark was held at Ashdod and Ekron (1 Sm 5); and four centuries later Sennacherib's Assyrian army was decimated by plague at Libnah just to the N of Gath (2 Kgs 19:8,35–37). As for war, the tramp of marching armies was well known in Philistia, which served as a passageway in the eternal struggle between Egypt in the S and Syria, Assyria, and Babylon to the N and E along the Fertile Crescent (→ 15 above). (Today Gaza has been a sore spot in Egyptian-Israeli relations.) In the heyday of the Philistines (12th–11th cents.), however, it was not international warfare but local battles with the Israelites that made life difficult.

73 (b) THE SHEPHELAH. Between the Philistine plain and the Judean mountains to the E there is a strip of foothills 10–15 mi. wide, 350–1500 ft. in height—the Shephelah ("lowland"). The valleys of the Shephelah were the natural passes from Philistia to the mountains; and they were protected by fortified towns: Debir, Lachish, Libnah, Azekah, Makkedah, Beth-shemesh, and Gezer, a litany that has been immortalized in the biblical accounts of warfare. (Beth-shemesh has yielded important Philistine artifacts; this shows that these sites were in both Philistine and Israelite zones of influence; → Biblical Archaeology, 74:67. For the Israeli excavations of Tell Nagila, a Canaanite and Hyksos stronghold some 15 mi. S of Beth-shemesh, see *Arch* 18 [1965] 113–23.) When Joshua had consolidated his hold in the highlands of central Canaan at Bethel, Ai, and Gibeon, his first great campaign was directed against the cities of the Shephelah (Jos 10:28–40), excavations of some of which attest to destruction *ca.* 1240. When the Philistines came, they used Ekron and Gath as fortresses against Israelite raids from the Judean mountains down through the Shephelah (Samson stories of Jgs 15–16). The Davidic victories that definitively broke Philistine power took place in the Shephelah (2 Sm 5:17–25). In short, control of the Shephelah was the deciding factor: In Philistine control the Shephelah wadis were arrows aimed at the heart of the Judean mountains; in Israelite control they were arrows aimed at the Philistine plain. Later on, in the 8th–6th cents., command of these wadis played an important part in the Assyrian and Babylonian campaigns against Judah. Instead of attacking Judah from the N first, Sennacherib and Nebuchadnezzar sent their armies S along the coast to seal off Judah from Egyptian aid and to gain an easy road up into the mountains. Lachish was the site of several famous sieges (2 Kgs 18:14; Jer 34:7; → Biblical Archaeology, 74:77–79).

74 Two of the wadis in the N part of the Shephelah deserve special mention. The Vale of *Sorek* was adjacent to the towns of Kiriath-jearim, Beth-shemesh, Timnah, Ekron, and Jabneel. It was the site of the Samson stories (Jgs 16) and of the tale of the captivity of the Ark in the late 11th cent. (1 Sm 6; 2 Sm 6). The other wadi, farther to the N, was the Valley of *Aijalon* that climbed past lower and upper Beth-horon, giving access to Bethel and Jerusalem by way of Gibeon. Here Joshua fought the battle against the kings of the S (Jos 10:10–15). The valley played a strategic part in Saul's warfare against the Philistines (1 Sm 14:31) and in the Israeli-Jordanian war of 1948.

75 **(B) Plain of Sharon.** This stretch of 40 mi. runs from Joppa (Jaffa) in the S to the Crocodile River (Shihor-libnath, Jos 19:26) in the N. The Plain of Sharon ("level land"?) is narrower (about 10 mi. wide) than the plain in Philistia; and there is no real Shephelah or foothills, for the plain extends to the base of the mountains. Running from N to S like an island in the midst of the plain is a sandstone elevation. The wadis that drain the mountains are forced to direct their flow around either end of this elevation; and so the clogged mouths of three streams, including the Crocodile, enter the sea at the N end of Sharon; on the S end the mouth of the Yarkon is near Tel Aviv. In OT times the region along both sides of this elevated sandstone was marshland.

76 The obstacles presented by this area's terrain were a deterrent to travel and to settlement. The trunk road hugged the base of the mountains; and the few main towns, Joppa, Lod (Lydda), Aphek, Gilgal, and Socoh, were located along the perimeters of the plain. *Aphek* (Roman Antipatris of Acts 23:31?—at or near modern Rosh ha-Ayin) was an important site at the headwaters of the Yarkon, with a control over the route from Joppa to Jerusalem. Aphek is named as the site of a great Israelite defeat at the hands of the Philistines *ca.* 1050 (1 Sm 4:1), although a site further to the N near Esdraelon seems indicated. *Joppa* ("the beautiful") was important because it was a port area (although not a very satisfactory one); and seemingly the Lebanese cedars for the Temple were ferried down the coast to Joppa (or more precisely to the recently excavated site of Qasileh just N of the Yarkon) and then up the Yarkon and overland to Jerusalem (2 Chr 2:16; Ezr 3:7). Today Tel Aviv (a name reminiscent of Ez 3:15), a settlement founded by the Jews in 1909 because of the hostility of the Arabs in Jaffa, is a very large city in this area.

77 In NT times Roman roads and bridges made the plain more traversable. We find Peter active in both Lydda and Joppa (Acts 9:32–10:23). Just 10 mi. S of Joppa was *Jabneh* (Jabneel, Jamnia—variant name forms reflecting the underlying Yabneh Yam, "Yabneh by the Sea"), famous for its rabbinic school after the fall of

Jerusalem (→ Canonicity, 67:35). On the coast at the N extremity of Sharon, Herod the Great built *Caesarea* (Maritima) and gave the area another badly needed port. We read in Acts 9:30; 18:22; 21:8 that Paul embarked or disembarked there. Caesarea was the center of Roman power in Palestine, the headquarters of the prefect or procurator. The first Palestinian inscription to mention Pontius Pilate was discovered there in 1961 (see plate in *BTS* 57 [1963] 15). The Roman centurion Cornelius of the Italian Cohort lived at Caesarea (Acts 10:1) and was baptized there by Peter. In AD 58–60 Paul was imprisoned at Caesarea under the Roman governors Felix and Festus (Acts 23:23; 25:12), and both Herod Agrippa I and II are mentioned as coming to Caesarea (12:19; 25:13) in AD 44 and 60 respectively. On Caesarea, see *BTS* 41 (1961).

78 In modern times the Arabs planted flourishing citrus groves in the Plain of Sharon, and the Israeli have occupied and furthered the progress of the region. Although the Bible calls Sharon a place of pasture (1 Chr 5:16; 27:29; Is 65:10), the lushness of its growth is likened to that of Carmel and Lebanon (Is 33:9; 35:2). The rose (crocus) of Sharon, a delicate flower in the jungle of underbrush, is used as a comparison in Ct 2:1.

79 **(C) Dor, Carmel, Plain of Asher.**

(a) Dor. The coastlands of Dor separate Sharon from the great promontory of Carmel, some 20 mi. N of the Crocodile River. In antiquity the marshes that surrounded this river cut Dor off from the S, giving it an orientation toward the northern territory of Asher (Jos 17:11). As in the rest of the N, the coast, only 2 mi. wide, is much narrower than in the S (Sharon or Philistia); and the mountains press close to the sea. This was a region of forest and marshland. The town of Dor, which gave its name to the region, was a mediocre harbor. It was not taken by Joshua's invasion (Jgs 1:27) and remained in Philistine hands until the 10th cent. (1 Kgs 4:11). In 1 Mc 15:10ff. it is the site of a struggle between the Syrian rulers. The town declined when Herod built Caesarea 8 mi. to the S.

80 (b) Carmel. The most noticeable natural feature on the Palestinian coast is the great promontory of Carmel jutting out into the sea and forming the large bay that harbors Haifa and Acco. The view from Carmel over Haifa Bay is truly breath-taking, and this very spot is the traditional localization for the dramatic confrontation of Elijah and the priests of Baal (1 Kgs 18:20ff., esp. v. 43). Further SE in caves along the Carmel slope, Stone Age man found a home, particularly in the Wadi Mugharah (→ Biblical Archaelogy, 74:41). Although there were ancient settlements in the area of Haifa Bay, *Haifa* itself is not a biblical site; its importance as a port stems from the period of the British Mandate. *Acco* was an ancient city. Under the name Ptolemais (1 Mc 11:22–24; 12:45–48; Acts 21:7), it was famed in Greco-Roman times for the manufacture of glass. It was the port for the Crusaders under the name Saint Jean d'Acre and was their last fortress in the Holy Land after the defeat by Saladin (→ 60 above). Here Francis of Assisi landed to lay the foundations of the Franciscan "Holy Land Custody" of the Christian shrines.

81 (c) Plain of Asher. The land between Haifa and Acco is in part a silted bay, with marshes to the E. The tribe of Asher did not take Acco (Jgs 1:31) but claimed for its possession the plain from Acco to the "Ladder of Tyre" (Ras en-Naqura) where the Lebanese mountains came down to the coast as a promontory, forming the S border of Phoenicia. This Asher territory was about 12 mi. long and 5 mi. wide, standing between the sea and the mountains. Cut by E–W wadis draining the mountains, the plain was often marshy; and the main settlements were at the base of the mountains. (We follow here the usual theory of the location of Asher's territory. M. Noth would put Asher just SW of Carmel and would give the coastal territory we have described to Zebulun. Cf. Gn 49:13; Dt 33:19, which imply that Zebulun owns the seashore.)

Neither Asher nor its territory was very important in biblical history, although Gn 49:20 speaks of Asher's possessions as rich and providing food for kings (Dt 33:24). In Jgs 5:17 Asher is castigated for sitting still at the seacoast while Israel was in danger. Inevitably Asher's poor coastland was overshadowed by Phoenicia to the N, with its great ports of Tyre and Sidon. Asher seems to have been part of the region given up by Solomon to Hiram of Tyre in payment for Phoenician supplies and skills in building the Jerusalem Temple (1 Kgs 9:11).

82 **(V) Central Zone of Palestine.** As far as biblical history is concerned, this was the most important area of Palestine. The region from the N border of the Negeb to N Galilee was the "essential Israel," from Beer-sheba to Dan. For convenience sake we shall also treat here the Negeb itself.

(A) Negeb. This is the southernmost area of Palestine—a rough trapezoid formed by Gaza, the Brook of Egypt, Ezion-geber, and Sodom, flanked on the W by the coastal desert, and on the E by the Arabah. The Negeb ("South") is called in the Bible the Wilderness of Zin (Nm 20:1; 33:36; perhaps, more precisely, this name refers to the southern part of the Negeb around Kadesh-barnea). Running on a NE–SW slant through the Negeb are two upwarps or thrusts of higher land (the Kurashe and the Kurnub). The W side of these upwarps, particularly the NW, receives some moisture in the form of dew and occasional rains from the Mediterranean; and so it is on this side of the upwarps that the main settlements and oases of the Negeb are found, e.g., Beer-sheba, El Auja, Kadesh-barnea. The modern Israeli have revived the efficient irrigation systems of the Nabateans and once again succeeded in cultivating this area. For climate and cultivation in antiquity, see *BASOR* 185 (1967) 39–43.

83 The E and SE of the upwarps, i.e., the side facing the Arabah, is barren and desolate, cut by great gorges. The importance of the region stems from the fact that commerce from Transjordan (e.g., from Petra in Nabatean times) or from the Gulf of Aqabah (e.g., from Ezion-geber in Solomon's time; → 69 above) had to pass up these gorges and wadis and go NW through the upwarps in order to reach Beer-sheba and ultimately Palestine proper. The town of *Kurnub* (Roman Mampsis) was situated in a gap in the upwarps through which such caravan routes passed (*BTS* 90 [1967]). *Hormah*, which figures in the abortive attempts of the Israelites to invade Canaan from the S (Nm 14:39–45; 21:1–3; Dt 1:41–46), was probably in this area, SE of Beer-sheba.

84 In biblical times the Negeb was controlled by the monarchy only at its periods of greatness, and then probably only to the point of keeping open the trade routes to Ezion-geber. Otherwise it was the prey of wandering Bedouin who made raids against the settlements in Philistia and Judah and were punished by retaliatory raids, as described in 1 Sm 27:8–12; 30. These accounts of David's raids into the Negeb show that the area was divided into zones of influence. After the fall of the monarchy, Edomites moved into the area, whence the name Idumea in Hellenistic times (1 Mc 5:3; Mk 3:8). In 125 BC John Hyrcanus conquered Idumea and brought it under the Hasmonean Jewish state; but the Idumeans eventually had their revenge, for from here came the

Herod family that was to rule in one part of Palestine or the other for nearly a century. The area was again of importance in Byzantine times, as recent Israeli excavations are showing (e.g., of Avdat or Abda; cf. *BTS* 40 [1961]; *Arch* 14 [1961] 122–30).

85 The two most important biblical sites in the Negeb were Kadesh-barnea and Beer-sheba. *Kadesh* was the site of a 38-year stop of Moses and the Israelites on their way between Sinai and Transjordan (Dt 1:46; 2:14; for the thesis that Sinai was here, → 27 above). Miriam, Moses' sister, died and was buried here (Nm 20:1). Dt 1:2 places Kadesh at the distance of an 11-day journey from Horeb/Sinai; this would agree with the localization of Sinai in the S part of the Sinai Peninsula. The name of Kadesh is preserved in Ain Qudeis on the frontier between the Sinai peninsula and Palestine. Yet Kadesh is supposed to have been the site where Moses brought forth water from the rock to satisfy the whole people (Nm 20:2–13), and there must have been abundant water at Kadesh to support the Israelites during a long stay. For this reason many scholars do not seek Kadesh at Ain Qudeis where the supply is sparse, but at nearby Ain Qudeirat. See Y. Aharoni in B. Rothenberg, *God's Wilderness* (N.Y., 1962) 121ff.; M. Dothan, *IsrEJ* 15 (1965) 134–51.

86 About 50 mi. N of Kadesh-barnea was *Beer-sheba*, of Abraham and Isaac fame (Gn 22:19; 26:33; 46:1–4). About 1000 ft. above sea level, and possessing an excellent water supply, this site sits astride routes from Gaza in the W, from Transjordan in the E, and from Sinai in the S. It was near here in the desert that Hagar wandered with Ishmael (Gn 21:14). At Beer-sheba Abraham planted a tamarisk tree as a shrine to El Olam (Gn 21:31–34; → Aspects OT Thought, 77:16; for Beer-sheba as a shrine, → Religious Institutions, 76:43). About 20 mi. E of Beer-sheba stood *Arad*, one of the northernmost Canaanite cities of the Negeb, whose king resisted the Israelites (Nm 21:1–3). When the Israelites destroyed the city, the site was given to their Kenite allies (Jgs 1:16; see Jos 12:14). Important Israeli excavations are now under way at Arad (*Arch* 17 [1964] 43–53; *BTS* 92 [1967]; *BA* 31 [1968] 2–32; → Biblical Archaeology, 74:50, 72, 75, 79). However, the mound shows no trace of a Canaanite, pre-Kenite occupation; the excavator, Y. Aharoni, suggests that the Canaanite site was a neighboring mound, a few miles away.

The Negeb or Wilderness of Zin marked the southern border of Israel's domain (Nm 34:3; Dt 34:3; Jos 15:1). Sometimes this border is measured from the southern extreme of the Negeb, the Brook of Egypt (Wadi el-Arish: Nm 34:5; Jos 15:4); more often it is measured from Beer-sheba in the N of the Negeb (Jgs 20:1; 1 Sm 3:20; etc.).

(On the Negeb: Glueck, N., *Rivers in the Desert: A History of the Negev* [N.Y., 1959]. *BA* 22 [1959] 82–97, or *BAR* 1, 1–11. *BTS* 22 [1959].)

87 **(B) Territory of the House of Judah.**

(a) General Description. The hill country of Judah or Judea is a strip of mountains or high plateau, averaging 10 mi. in width, rising just N of Beer-sheba and continuing to just N of Jerusalem. To the E, where the plateau falls away into the Dead Sea and the Rift Valley, is the barren "Wilderness of Judah" (Jos 15:61; Mt 3:1), a refuge for bandits and those in flight (e.g., David from Saul) and for religious solitaries (John the Baptist; Qumran sectarians; Christian monks, as at Mar Saba). The barrenness of this wilderness is illustrated by the fact that there is no source of water on the famous span between Jerusalem and Jericho (Lk 10:30). The defense of Judah on this E side could to some extent be entrusted to nature. To the W of Judah, the Shephelah (→ 73 above) flanked the mountains and offered a buffer against Philistine expansion.

88 To the S, the rise of the mountains from Beer-sheba offered a defense, albeit weak, against the Negeb raiders like the Amalekites (1 Sm 15). The Negeb of Judah (1 Sm 27:10) was probably the area of the N Negeb over which Judah tried to maintain some control as a further buffer on her southern flank, whence the occasional inclusion of the Negeb in the delineation of Judah's territory (Jos 15:3–4). The tribe of Judah, which may have entered Palestine from the S rather than from across the Jordan, does seem to have allied itself with a group of southern peoples, like the Kenites, Kenizzites, Calebites, and Jerahmeelites (Jos 14:6–15; 15:13–19; Jgs 1:8–20; 1 Chr 2:9,25–27; → Excursus Israel, 11:29–30), whom it brought into the Israelite confederacy. Judah also incorporated the rather nebulous territory of Simeon (Jos 19:9), forming a domain quite independent of the Israelite tribes to the N—an independence that remained evident throughout the history of Israel in Palestine.

89 The N frontier of Judah was not well defined; and although Benjamin lay N of Judah, the territory of *Benjamin* was a political rather than a geographical boundary (→ Joshua, 7:45ff.). By its history and inclination Benjamin was closely related to Ephraim and was not part of the "house of Judah." The area of Benjamin around Ai and Gibeon was the first foothold in the Palestinian mountains won by Joshua when the Israelites came up from Jericho (Jos 7–9). This area was of strategic importance not only from the E but also from the W, as we see from the fact that Joshua was soon forced to wage war with the Shephelah kings who came up from the W through the Valley of Aijalon to attack Israel (→ 74 above). The Philistines used the same route in an attempt to crush Saul and the Israelite strongholds in the mountains of Benjamin (1 Sm 10:5; 13–14:31). Saul's home and capital was at Gibeah, modern Tell el-Ful just N of Jerusalem, the site of interesting ASOR excavations (*BA* 27 [1964] 52–64; 28 [1965] 2–10).

At the time of the division of the monarchy (*ca.* 922), Benjamin seems to have gone with the N as one of the ten tribes (1 Kgs 11:30) against the two tribes of the S, Judah and the defunct Simeon. But Judah needed Benjaminite territory as a defensive buffer for Jerusalem, a claim that we see in the mention of Benjamin in the glosses in 1 Kgs 12:21,23 ("all the house of Judah *and the tribe of Benjamin*"). Thus the territorial claims of Judah were made to run from Beer-sheba in the S to Geba in the N; and Geba, about 5 mi. N of Jerusalem, was in Benjamin (2 Kgs 23:8). Judah strenuously resisted the attempt of the northern tribes to push into this area of Benjamin (1 Kgs 15:16–24). The strategic importance of the border fortresses in Benjamin for the defense of Judah from the N is vividly pictured in the imaginative account of how an Assyrian king would attack Jerusalem (Is 10:28–34), proceeding from Ai (Aiath), 10 mi. N of Jerusalem, to Nob on the Mt. of Olives overlooking Jerusalem.

90 (b) Cities of Judah. *Hebron* was historically the center of Judah's power, as David implicitly bore witness when he was crowned there as Judah's first king (2 Sm 2:1–4; cf. 15:7–10). At 3300 ft. above sea level, this is the highest city in Judah, controlling to the W the roads to the Shephelah cities of Mareshah and Lachish, and to the E the road to En-gedi on the Dead Sea. Seemingly once called Kiriath-arba (Jos 14:15; 15:13), Hebron was the site where Sarah and Abraham were buried (Gn 23; 25:9). At the nearby shrine of Mamre (modern Ramet el-Khalil; cf. *BTS* 70 [1965]), Abraham received the divine promises and saw God (Gn 13:14–18;

18; → Religious Institutions, 76:42). Isaac also died at Hebron (Gn 35:27). Today the tombs of the patriarchs are venerated under the mosque, once a church, that stands in the middle of Hebron, adjacent to magnificent Herodian remains. The reservoir in Hebron recalls the site of David's punishment of the murderers of Saul's son Ishbaal (2 Sm 4:12). For the recent excavations of Hebron, see *BA* 28 [1965] 30–32; also *BTS* 80 (1966).

91 *Bethlehem* (or Ephrathah), 15 mi. N of Hebron and 5 mi. S of Jerusalem, was not in itself an important city of Judah (Mi 5:2), but it acquired importance as the ancestral home of David (Ru 1:1; 4:22; 1 Sm 16; Lk 2:4; Mt 2:5; Jn 7:42). A church built by Constantine and modified by the Crusaders stands over the grotto traditionally associated with Jesus' birth, and fields E of Bethlehem are most suitable to have been the shepherds' fields of Lk 2:8,15. "Rachel's Tomb," which stands today at the N entry to Bethlehem, represents a confusion based on erroneous glosses in Gn 35:19; 48:7 and on an implicit statement in Mt 2:18; Rachel's burial place in Benjamin (1 Sm 10:2; Jer 31:15) is far more plausible. (*BTS* 42 [1961]; *NatGeog* [Dec. 1926].)

Just SE of Bethlehem stands the truncated-cone hill of Herodium, the fortress and castle where Herod the Great was buried—not far from the town whose children he slew, according to Mt 2:16. (For the recent excavations see *BTS* 60 [1963].) From here down to the Dead Sea is the grazing country of the Ta'amireh Bedouin who discovered the Dead Sea Scrolls. Nearby was Tekoa, the hometown of the prophet Amos (Am 1:1).

92 *Jerusalem*, "the holy mountain, fairest of heights, the joy of all the earth" (Ps 48:2), did not come into Judah's possession until David's time (*ca.* 1000). In a stroke of genius, after capturing Jebusite Jerusalem (2 Sm 5:6–10; → Excursus Israel, 11:25), he moved his capital from the provincial and clearly southern Hebron to this border city with no northern or southern affiliations. We read of its Canaanite prehistory as a shrine of El Elyon and perhaps of Zedek in Gn 14:18 (cf. Jos 10:1; → Religious Institutions, 76:54, 20).

The mount covered by Jerusalem in its era of greatness is set off on three sides by valleys. On the E there is a sharp decline into the Kidron (Cedron), a wadi that has a swift stream when rainfall is plentiful. This valley separates Jerusalem from the higher Mt. of Olives from which one gains a splendid view of the city (2 Sm 15:23, 30; 2 Kgs 23:6; Jn 18:1). Despite its narrowness, the Kidron is traditionally identified as the Valley of Jehoshaphat where Jl 3:2–12 places the gathering of all nations for judgment. On the W of Jerusalem is the Valley of Hinnom (Jos 15:8; 18:16), swinging around the southern end of the mount to meet the Kidron in the SE at Haceldama (Akeldama of Acts 1:19). This valley (= Ge-Hinnom [Gehenna]) acquired an unpleasant reputation because it was used for the burning of garbage and the worship of pagan gods (1 Kgs 11:7; 2 Kgs 16:3; 23:10), whence the derived meaning of Gehenna as "Hell" (Mt 5:22). The mount itself was split into two hills, W and E, by a much shallower valley, scarcely visible today, called the Tyropoeon (Cheesemakers'). The Canaanite (Jebusite) city that fell to David was on the southern end of the E hill where the Kidron and the Tyropoeon gradually come together to a point, meeting the Valley of Hinnom.

93 The W hill of Jerusalem is the higher and more impressive, and for centuries was identified (e.g., by Josephus) as Zion or ancient Jerusalem. Today it is universally recognized that the city of David and Solomon was on the E hill. David conquered the SE spur of the hill, and Solomon pushed the confines of the city further N on the E hill by building the Temple (→ Religious Institutions, 76:55) over the threshing floor that David had bought from Araunah the Jebusite (2 Sm 24:18)—traditionally the Mt. Moriah of Abraham's sacrifice in Gn 22:2; 2 Chr 3:1. The site of the Temple is marked today by the superb Moslem mosque of "the Dome of the Rock." Cf., however, the dissent to this localization by B. Bagatti, *Bib* 43 (1962) 1–21.

94 The N was the one side of Jerusalem not closed off or protected by a valley, and expansion of the city has been most often toward the N. A series of protective walls have been built at various times in the history of the city's expansion, and three of them are prominently mentioned by Josephus (*JW* 5.4 § 136ff.). The dispute about the site of the Holy Sepulcher of Jesus (who died and was buried outside the city—Jn 19:20,42) depends on the location of the wall in Jesus' time (*PEQ* 98 [1966] 85–88; *BASOR* 183 [1966] 19–26). The impressive walls of Old Jerusalem visible today are of Turkish construction (16th cent. AD) on Herodian foundations. (→ History of Israel, 75:151.)

(Burrows, M., "Jerusalem," *IDB* 2, 843–66; Join-Lambert, M., *Jerusalem* [N.Y., 1958] are detailed treatments helpful to the student; each gives references to more purely scientific books; also → Biblical Archaeology, 74:92. For illustrations see *NatGeog* [Dec. 1927; April 1959]. For recent excavations, see *BA* 27 [1964] 34–52; 28 [1965] 22–26; 29 [1966] 27–36; *PEQ* 99 [1967] 65–73. For topography, see *PEQ* 98 [1966] 130–54. For extent in antiquity, see *Bib* 48 [1967] 337–58. For the Holy Sepulcher, see *BTS* 55 [1963]; *BA* 30 [1967] 74–90.)

95 The birthplace of John the Baptist is located in the Judean hills by Lk 1:39; today it is traditionally associated with *Ain Karim* just W of Jerusalem (*BTS* 61 [1964]). *Bethany*, the village of Lazarus, Mary, and Martha, "not far from Jerusalem, just under two miles" (Jn 11:1,18), which Jesus made his place of residence when visiting Jerusalem (Mk 11:1; 14:3), is the Ananiah of Neh 11:32 and the modern el Azariyeh, just E of Jerusalem around the S end of the Mt. of Olives (see W. F. Albright, *BASOR* 9 [1923] 8–10). Recent Israeli excavations at modern *Ramat Rahel* (ancient Beth-haccherem of Jer 6:1; Neh 3:14?), just S of Jerusalem, have uncovered a royal fortress of the 7th cent. BC, perhaps Jehoiakim's luxurious palace (Jer 22:13–19; see *BA* 24 [1961] 98–118; *BTS* 37 [1961]; *Arch* 18 [1965] 15–25).

96 **(C) Territory of the House of Joseph.** Running N some 40–45 mi. from the border of Judah in Benjamin to the Plain of Esdraelon is the mountainous strip that was dominated for five centuries (1220–720) by the house of Joseph, i.e., the two Joseph tribes of Ephraim and half of Manasseh (Gn 48). This tribal group was the chief rival to the house of Judah for power in Israelite Palestine. When the Israelites entered Palestine under Joshua (and perhaps before: → Biblical Archaeology, 74:64), the strongest tribes, Ephraim and Manasseh, occupied the central mountains. The weaker tribes (leaving aside the house of Judah, which had its own history) had to be satisfied with the fringes of these mountains (e.g., Benjamin, and Dan [original localization]) or with territory to the N in Galilee (Issachar, Naphtali, Zebulun, Asher) or in Transjordan (Reuben, Gad). These were more insecure positions, open to attack; and the constant protective warfare that these lesser tribes had to wage prevented their rise to power. (The reader should be warned that the "traditional" tribal history that we are reporting masks a much more complicated state of affairs; cf. reconstructions by K. Elliger, "Tribes, Territories of," *IDB* 4, 701–10.)

The pretensions of Ephraim during the period of the judges are evident in Jgs 8:1; 12:1. The first abortive attempt at kingship was that of Abimelech, son of Gideon, of the Manasseh tribe (Jgs 6:15; 9); and later

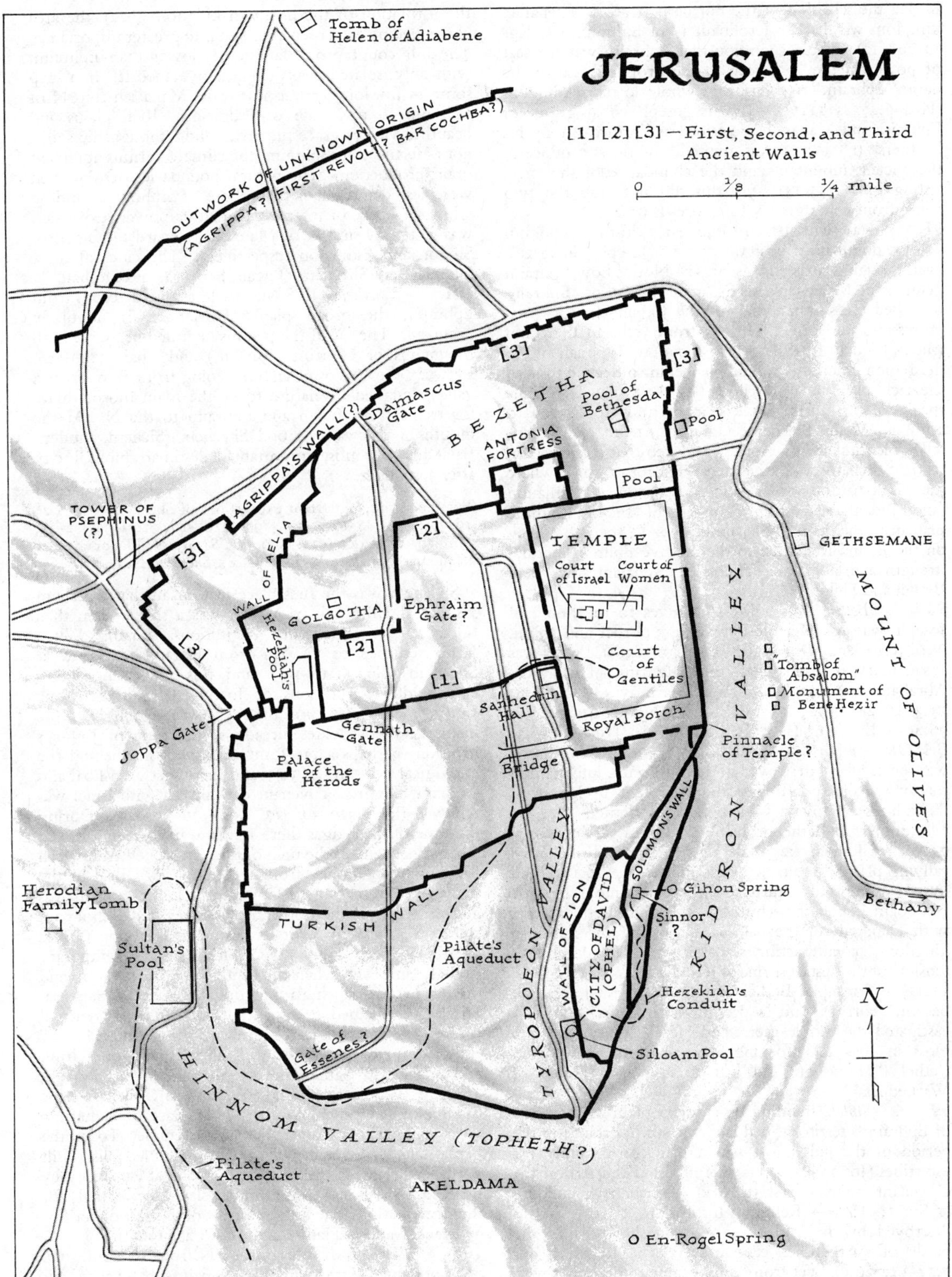
JERUSALEM
[1] [2] [3] — First, Second, and Third Ancient Walls
0 1/8 1/4 mile
Tomb of Helen of Adiabene
OUTWORK OF UNKNOWN ORIGIN
(AGRIPPA? FIRST REVOLT? BAR COCHBA?)
AGRIPPA'S WALL (?)
Damascus Gate
BEZETHA
Pool of Bethesda
ANTONIA FORTRESS
Pool
Pool
TOWER OF PSEPHINUS (?)
WALL OF AELIA
Hezekiah's Pool
GOLGOTHA
Ephraim Gate?
TEMPLE
Court of Israel
Court of Women
Court of Gentiles
Sanhedrin Hall
Royal Porch
Pinnacle of Temple?
GETHSEMANE
MOUNT OF OLIVES
KIDRON VALLEY
"Tomb of Absalom"
Monument of Bene Hezir
Joppa Gate
Gennath Gate
Palace of the Herods
Bridge
TURKISH WALL
Pilate's Aqueduct
TYROPOEON VALLEY
WALL OF ZION
CITY OF DAVID (OPHEL)
SOLOMON'S WALL
Gihon Spring
Sinnor ?
Bethany
Herodian Family Tomb
Sultan's Pool
Hezekiah's Conduit
Siloam Pool
Gate of Essenes?
HINNOM VALLEY (TOPHETH?)
Pilate's Aqueduct
AKELDAMA
En-Rogel Spring
N

in 922 the secession of the northern tribes as a separate kingdom was led by Jeroboam I, an Ephraimite (1 Kgs 11:26; 12). The recognition that Ephraim was the seat of power in the N is seen in the prophets' use of the name "Ephraim" to describe the whole northern kingdom (Hos 6:4; Is 11:13). To the Joseph tribal group of Ephraim and Manasseh, described as "prince among his brothers" (Dt 33:16), was granted "the finest produce of the ancient mountains and the abundance of the everlasting hills" (33:15); yet this did not stop the two tribes from being greedy for more (Is 9:20–21).

97 (a) EPHRAIM. In the early history Ephraim was the dominant tribe in the house of Joseph (Gn 48:20), even though Manasseh was larger. Notice how Ephraim determines Manasseh's territory in Jos 16:9. Ephraim possessed the southern half of the Joseph territory: Its possessions ran some 20 mi. N from Geba in Benjamin (the N border of Judah; → 89 above) to Tappuah and to the region where the mountains begin to decline toward the rich plain near Shechem (Jos 17:8–9). The Bible speaks of this 20-mi.-wide strip of hills, 1000–3000 ft. high, as "Mount Ephraim" (Jgs 17:1; 1 Sm 1:1). Rainfall is plentiful and the soil is fertile, so that it is a region of fruit orchards and olive trees. Except on the S where there is no natural border between Ephraim and Benjamin (and Judah), the steep drop-off of the Ephraimite plateau to the Plain of Sharon on the W, the Rift Valley on the E, and Manasseh to the N gave Ephraim natural strength and aloofness. The most important cities were Bethel and Shiloh.

98 *Bethel*, which Jos 16:1 gives to the house of Joseph, was just over the Benjaminite border and 10 mi. N of Jerusalem. Once called Luz (Jos 18:13), Bethel was a sanctuary in patriarchal times figuring in both the Abraham and Jacob cycles of narratives (Gn 12:8; 13:3–4; 28:10–22; 35:1–16; → Religious Institutions, 76:41). Excavations at Bethel (*BA* 19 [1956] 36–43; *BASOR* 151 [1958] 3–8; *BTS* 47 [1962]) show that it was spectacularly destroyed in the 13th cent., information that may correspond with the statement in Jgs 1:22: "The house of Joseph went up against Bethel." (However, for the Ai-Bethel problem, → Biblical Archaeology, 74:59; → Joshua, 7:27). Bethel served as a shrine and a rallying place in the time of the judges (Jgs 20:18); and in an attempt to return to "that old-time religion," Jeroboam I, after the schism of 922, made Bethel, along with Dan, one of the national shrines of the northern kingdom, counteracting Davidic and Judahite pretensions at the upstart shrine of Jerusalem (1 Kgs 12:26–29; 13:11). Worship at Bethel (just as worship at Jerusalem) became corrupt and superstitious; Amos (7:10–17) castigated the people there, and Hosea (4:15; 5:8; see gloss in Jos 7:2) mockingly changed its name from Bethel ("House of God") to Beth-aven ("House of Wickedness").

99 *Shiloh*, standing on a rocky plain in the heart of Ephraim's territory, had its greatest importance in the period of the judges. It was a place of assembly for the tribes (Jos 22:9,12; Jgs 21:19ff.), and the Ark of the Covenant came to rest there in a permanent building (1 Sm 1; 4:4; → Religious Institutions, 76:50). It was destroyed by the Philistines *ca.* 1050 shortly after the battle of Aphek/Eben-ezer and reduced to ruins (Jer 7:12–14; 26:9). Yet from Shiloh came the prophet who anointed Jeroboam and split Solomon's kingdom (1 Kgs 11:29).

The prophet-priest Samuel came from *Ramathaim-zophim* (Ramah) in W Ephraim; this place may have been the Arimathea that was the home of Joseph who took Jesus' body and buried it (Lk 23:50–51).

100 (b) MANASSEH (SAMARIA). From the time of the formation of the northern kingdom (922), the area controlled by Manasseh emerged into greater importance. The hill country of Manasseh is lower than Ephraim, with only isolated peaks rising above 2000 ft. In a strip some 15 mi. long and 20 mi. wide, Manasseh runs N of Ephraim to the Plain of Esdraelon. Rich plains and beautiful valleys grace the area; and although the soil is not as fertile as in Ephraim, the climate permits abundant grain production. The natural boundaries of Manasseh were less determinate than those of Ephraim; and so when the house of Joseph extended its power, expansion was to the W and N of Manasseh, toward the plains of Sharon and Esdraelon respectively. The cities of most interest were Shechem, Tirzah, Samaria, and Dothan.

101 *Shechem*. In S Manasseh, as one descends from Ephraim, the broad plain of Mahneh is singularly beautiful. The W of the plain is hemmed in by the high mountains of Gerizim (2910 ft.) and Ebal (3100 ft.). Between these two mountains, going from E to W, is a valley designed by nature to be the main thoroughfare for traffic from Judah and Ephraim to the N. At the mouth of this valley stood Shechem (Sichem, modern Balatah), the most important Palestinian biblical city after Jerusalem.

(For the recent, important excavations of Shechem see *BA* 20 [1957] 2–32, 82–105; 23 [1960] 102–10; 26 [1963] 2–27; summary in *BAR* 2, 258–300. *BTS* 44 [1962]. For a more detailed account, see Wright, G. E., *Shechem* [N.Y., 1965].)

Shechem was the first place in Canaan that Abraham visited, and the oak of Moreh was a shrine even then (Gn 12:6; → Religious Institutions, 76:40). When Jacob returned to Canaan from Haran, he settled at Shechem (Gn 33:18–19); and this spot was Jacob's choice gift to the sons of Joseph (Gn 48:22: "one *portion*" = Hebr *š*^{e}*kem*). Shechem was seemingly in the hands of the Israelites already at the time of Joshua's invasion (perhaps a pre-Joshua conquest lies behind the etiological story in Gn 34); and there, between Ebal and Gerizim, the great covenant of Yahweh with Israel was renewed (Dt 11:29–30; 27; Jos 8:30–35; 24). During the time of the judges there seems to have been a mixed cult at Shechem, as the men of the city backed Abimelech for king with money from the temple of "Baal of the Covenant" or "El of the Covenant" (Jgs 9:4,46). It was at Shechem that the northern tribes rejected Rehoboam son of Solomon in favor of Jeroboam I as king (1 Kgs 12:1–25). This king made Shechem his temporary capital; and even when the center of administration and power in the northern kingdom moved to Samaria, Shechem remained the focus of the covenant renewal ceremony (from which Dt drew its legal code). In NT times Jesus stopped at the well of Shechem for a drink and engaged a Samaritan woman in conversation (Jn 4:4–42). This story reminds us that Mt. Gerizim's slope overlooking Shechem was the holy place of Samaritan worship and the site of the Samaritan temple. Today the Samaritans survive at Nablus, Roman Neapolis, built 2 mi. farther W in the same valley; and at Passover they proceed to Gerizim's summit to slaughter animals for their celebration—the only remnant of the blood-sacrifice of Israel (*NatGeog* [Jan. 1920]; *BTS* 28 [1960]).

102 *Tirzah*. If in a journey N from Ephraim, one does not cut W through the Gerizim-Ebal valley but continues to the NE, at the head of the great Wadi Far'ah, which goes off SE to the Jordan Valley (→ 65 above), one encounters Tirzah (Tell el-Far'ah, excavated by R. de Vaux; → Biblical Archaeology, 74:18). This town served as capital of the northern kingdom from Jeroboam's time until Omri's time (910–870; 1 Kgs 14:17; 15:21,33; 16:6–23). The site was of strategic importance for the defense of Manasseh from the E, since the Wadi Far'ah was a natural invasion route. (It may have been used by some of the Israelites when they invaded Canaan, whence the confusion in passages like Dt 11:30; 27:4; Jos 8:30, which imply that when the Israelites crossed the Jordan they soon came to Ebal and Gerizim. This would be another indication of more than one Israelite invasion of Palestine (→ Biblical Archaeology, 74:64).

103 *Samaria.* Retracing our steps and cutting W through the Gerizim-Ebal valley and then swinging N, we find before us the majestic hill of Samaria, Tirzah's successor and the greatest capital of Israel. (We have an idea of the short distances in this area if we realize that Tirzah is 7 mi. NE of Shechem, and Samaria is 7 mi. WNW of Shechem.) King Omri's move from Tirzah to Samaria (*ca.* 870; 1 Kgs 16:24) was in part motivated by political geography. Tirzah, protected at the back by mountains on the W, was open to invasion from the E, in particular from Syria, Omri's chief enemy; Samaria was on the other side of these mountains, which were a barrier against its enemies approaching from the E. On the other hand, Samaria had free access to routes to the NW where Phoenicia, Israel's new ally, was situated with its rich ports and commercial possibilities.

An isolated hill, crowned by the magnificent buildings of Omri and his son Ahab, Samaria must have been the most beautiful city in Israel: "the proud crown of the drunkards of Ephraim, the fading flower of its glorious beauty which is at the head of a rich valley" (Is 28:1). (For important excavations of Samaria and bibliographical data, → Biblical Archaeology, 74:73–75.) For 150 years this city so dominated the northern kingdom that Israel could be called "Samaria," just as Judah was sometimes called "Jerusalem" (Ez 16:46—thus it is important for the reader of the Bible to distinguish between the city of Samaria and the district of Samaria; the latter means the territory of Manasseh, or sometimes the whole northern kingdom). Even after its fall to the Assyrians in 722, the city retained its strategic importance as the capital successively of an Assyrian province of Samaria, of a Persian province (Ezr 4:17; Neh 3:33–34 [4:1–2]), and of a Syrian district (1 Mc 10:30). Herod the Great rebuilt the city as Sebaste in honor of the Emperor Augustus (Gk *sebastos*), but the district retained the name Samaria. Thus the NT references to Samaria are to the district N of Judea (Acts 1:8; 8). In the last centuries BC "Samaritans" came to designate not only the physical inhabitants of Samaria but also the adherents of a deviationist form of Judaism centered around Mt. Gerizim. See the anti-Samaritan story in 2 Kgs 17:24–34; also F. M. Cross, *HarvTR* 59 (1966) 201–11.

104 *Dothan.* Continuing into N Manasseh past Samaria, the main route leads to Dothan, a city that guarded the descent from Manasseh into the Plain of Esdraelon. Throughout the 1950's Dothan was excavated by an American expedition under the direction of J. P. Free (*BASOR* 131, 135, 139, 143, 152, 156, 160 [1953–1960]). Near Dothan Joseph was sold into slavery by his brothers (Gn 37:17), and Elisha visited Dothan (2 Kgs 6:13).

105 **(D) Plain of Esdraelon (Jezreel).** The mountains and hills of the house of Joseph were cut off from Galilee, the domain of the northernmost tribes, by a broad valley that runs NW-SE from behind the Bay of Haifa to the Rift Valley. The main part of this valley-plain as it sweeps in from the sea to Mt. Gilboa (technically the 20 mi. from Jokneam to the area of Ibleam and En-gannim [Jenin]) is designated by some geographers as Esdraelon, whereas Jezreel is the name given to the arm that shoots off to the E between Gilboa and the Hill of Moreh through the Beth-shan gap into the Jordan. However, since Esdraelon is simply the Gk form of Jezreel (Hebr *Yizr^{e}'e'l*), it will be convenient to designate here the respective sections of the plain as W and E Esdraelon.

106 (a) West Esdraelon. At some points this part of the Plain of Esdraelon is 20 mi. wide, rising gently from 80 ft. above sea level to 330 ft. near En-gannim. The river Kishon flows through the plain on its way to the sea. This is the broadest expanse of farm-land in Palestine. The Israelites coming from the desert into the land that was supposed to be flowing with milk and honey must have thought, "This is the place," as they looked down from the hills of Manasseh upon the rich valley. Esdraelon had strategic importance on both an international and a national scale.

107 (i) *International importance.* Esdraelon was the plain through which ran the main route between Egypt and Syria. The plain's S side is flanked by the Carmel mountain range, and armies or commerce that came up the coast from Egypt through Philistia and along the fringes of the Plain of Sharon had to pass NE through one of the four passes in the Carmel range to reach the plain. Consequently, four fortresses guarding these passes were built on the southern edge of Esdraelon: Jokneam, Megiddo, Taanach, and Ibleam. The route past *Megiddo* was strategically the most important, as corroborated by an ancient Egyptian report: "The capture of Megiddo is as the capture of a thousand towns" (*ANET* 237). Here in 1468 the greatest of the Egyptian pharaohs, Thutmosis III, won a victory against the remnants of the Hyksos—a victory that forged a world empire. Solomon and later the kings of the northern kingdom fortified the city magnificently (1 Kgs 9:15; for a detailed account of the archaeology of Megiddo, → Biblical Archaeology, 74:31–38). Here in 609 the good king Josiah, most pious of Judah's kings, died in a vain attempt to block the passage of an Egyptian army (2 Kgs 22:19). Fittingly the visionary of the NT Ap places the assembly for the final world battle at this war-scarred site of "Mount" Megiddo (Hebr *har M^{e}giddô* = Gk *Armagedōn* in Ap 16:16). Few scholars accept W. F. Albright's thesis that settlement alternated between Megiddo and nearby *Taanach* (Jgs 5:19, "Taanach by the waters of Megiddo"). For recent excavations of Taanach, cf. *BA* 30 (1967) 2–27; *BASOR* 173 (1964) 4–50; 185 (1967) 2–38.

108 (ii) *National importance.* Esdraelon was important also on the scale of internal Israelite history. As long as it remained in Canaanite hands (Jgs 1:27), the northern tribes (Issachar, Naphtali, Zebulun, and Asher) were cut off from the house of Joseph. Consequently in the period of the judges, there was a series of battles for control of the plain. In the 12th cent. Deborah and Barak gathered the northern tribes and the Joseph tribes to fight against Sisera and his Canaanites. When the river Kishon flooded the plain, and mud made the Canaanite chariots useless, the Israelites won at Taanach (Jgs 4:7; 5:20–21). The Philistines' victory over the Israelites at Aphek/Eben-ezer in 1050 (1 Sm 4) gave them control over the plains of Sharon and Esdraelon; and this happened again when they defeated Saul (*ca.* 1000) at Gilboa (1 Sm 29:1; 31).

109 (b) East Esdraelon. The mention of Mt. Gilboa brings us to the strategically important continuation of Esdraelon to the E, sometimes called Jezreel or the Beth-shan Valley. This narrow corridor was a main route for continuing the journey from W Esdraelon into the Jordan Valley and then up into Transjordan and on to Damascus. Running ESE, about 13 mi. long and 2 mi. wide, Esdraelon drops almost 1000 ft. from the entrance between Gilboa and Moreh until it reaches the Jordan Valley.

Since E Esdraelon was a corridor to and from Transjordan, it frequently served as a path for invaders. In the battle between Gideon and the Midianite raiders, Gideon encamped on Mt. Gilboa at Harod on the S side of the entrance to this corridor, while Midian was opposite on the N side at the Hill of Moreh (Jgs 6:33; 7:1). Exactly the same positions were taken by Saul and the Philistines (1 Sm 28:3ff.); and we find Saul slipping through the Philistine lines at night to consult the witch at Endor just N of Moreh. As soon as Saul was defeated at Gilboa, the Philistines returned through the corridor and hung his body on the walls of Beth-shan (1 Sm 31:8–10; → 64 above).

110 When Omri and Ahab made Samaria the capital of the northern kingdom, they paid both the beauty and the importance of the Valley of Esdraelon a tribute by keeping a palace at the town of *Jezreel*, standing at the W entrance to the corridor leading to Beth-shan. The tragic incident of Naboth's vineyard and the bloody death of Jezebel took place here (1 Kgs 21:1; 2 Kgs 9:30; 10:11). The prophet Hosea named his son "Jezreel" as a threat of divine punishment for the crimes committed there: "I will break the bow of Israel in the Valley of Jezreel." Yet, playing on the meaning of the name Jezreel ("May God sow"), Hosea also saw in this name a divine promise of fertility: "The earth shall respond to the grain and wine and oil, and these shall respond to Jezreel, and I will sow him for myself in the land" (Hos 1:4–5; 2:22–23).

111 In NT times Jesus is recorded to have been in the Plain of Esdraelon when he raised to life the son of the widow of *Nain* (Lk 7:11–17), a town on the N slope of the Hill of Moreh. NE of Moreh stands *Mt. Tabor*, solitary and symmetrical. (The closeness of the two made interpreters think that the "Tabor and Hermon" of Ps 89:13 were Tabor and Moreh; this misunderstanding won for Moreh the name "Little Hermon.") Tabor is the hill from which to the NW, the N, and the NE radiated the tribal frontiers of Zebulun, Naphtali, and Issachar. That is probably why Barak gathered his forces on Tabor (Jgs 4:6). Tabor controls the entrance from Esdraelon along the main road to the Lake of Galilee, and Jesus must have passed it in his travels from Nazareth. It is the traditional but unlikely site proposed for the "high mountain" of the transfiguration (Mk 9:2).

Basalt is found in the region from Tabor NE along the Sea of Galilee. Some (e.g., F.-M. Abel) would relate this to the lava flow from the Jebel Druze in Transjordan (→ 53 above). But D. Baly (*op. cit.*, 26) thinks that Moreh may have been a volcano.

112 **(E) Galilee.** When we cross the Plain of Esdraelon on our journey N, we come to an area which figures surprisingly little in OT history but which was to crown the expectations of that history; for on the N side of Esdraelon rise the hills of Galilee, and just 3 mi. into these hills stands Nazareth, the home of Jesus. Situated between Esdraelon and Dan, Galilee extends some 30–40 mi. from S to N, and some 20–25 mi. from E to W. On the W is the coastal Plain of Asher; on the E is the Rift Valley with the Lake of Galilee and the upper reaches of the Jordan. There is a S or Lower Galilee and a N or Upper Galilee; the division line is an E-W fault running roughly from the direction of Acco (Ptolemais) to just N of the Lake of Galilee.

113 (a) South Galilee. This area consists of gentle hills not exceeding 2000 ft. in height; in parts it is rather like the Shephelah of the S (→ 73 above). In OT times the larger part of Lower Galilee was occupied by Zebulun, with Asher to the W on the coast (unless we accept Noth's hypothesis; → 81 above), Issachar to the SE, and Naphtali to the N and E. The fact that these surrounding tribes served as a buffer gave Zebulun the best position among the four northern tribes. Nevertheless, Galilee seems to have been outside the mainstream of Israelite life as it is preserved in the biblical records. Galilee fell to the Assyrians after the Syro-Ephraimite war of 735 (2 Kgs 15:29); yet Isaiah (9:1–2), speaking of the land of Zebulun and Naphtali as "Galilee of the Gentiles," promised that the people there who walked in darkness would see a great light (also cf. Mt 4:15–16). In Hellenistic times there was a heavy population of Jews in Galilee (1 Mc 5:9–23). However, during the period of Jesus' ministry when Galilee was ruled by Herod Antipas, it was still treated with disdain by the "pure Jews" of Judea (Jn 7:52), which was under the control of a Roman governor (Lk 3:1).

114 The terrain of S Galilee is marked by a series of basins watered by drainage from the surrounding hills. The floors of the basins are fertile alluvium and lend themselves to farming, while the towns climb the adjacent hillsides. This was the region described so vividly in Jesus' parables: fields separated by hedgerows and stone fences; flocks pastured on the hills; towns set on mountain tops; etc. Two towns of S Galilee mentioned in the NT, Nazareth and Cana, are built on the sides of rich basins. *Cana* is probably not the now traditional pilgrim site of Kefr Kenna, 3 mi. NE of Nazareth, but rather Khirbet Qana, 9 mi. N of Nazareth. *Jotapata* where Josephus was defeated by the Romans is close by (→ Apocrypha, 68:114). The main town of the region in NT times was *Sepphoris*, the district capital, on the road from Ptolemais (Acco) to Tiberias. The postbiblical rabbinical school of Beth-she'arim (*BTS* 46 [1962]) in the Plain of Esdraelon ultimately moved to Sepphoris, and there Rabbi Judah the Prince spent the last 17 years of his life (*ca.* AD 200) codifying the Mishnah (→ Apocrypha, 68:121). Thus Galilee gave birth both to Christianity and to postbiblical talmudic Judaism.

115 (b) North Galilee. Here the terrain is quite different, much higher (3000–4000 ft.) and truly mountainous. Heavy rainfall and strong winds are characteristic of this region, which is the beginning of the Lebanon mountain chain to the N. This land of Naphtali had little recorded importance in either the OT or the NT, except as a place of refuge where inaccessible heights offered the possibility of resisting stronger armies. *Gischala* was a strong outpost in the Jewish revolt against the Romans; and Josephus' enemy, John, came from there. For the story of this revolt, → History of Israel, 75:158. *Safed* (Seph or Sephet), on a mountain top (Mt 5:14) with a splendid view reaching to the Lake of Galilee and the Huleh Basin, also figured in the Jewish revolt. It was the center of renewed Jewish colonization *ca.* AD 1500, and here a Jewish school of mystics produced the Shulhan Aruk and some important expositions of the Cabala. Safed mysticism is the most recent flowering of the zeal for God of which this small land of Palestine has been a unique witness for so many centuries.

74

BIBLICAL ARCHAEOLOGY

Robert North, S.J.

BIBLIOGRAPHY

1 Albright, *AP; ARI; FSAC*. Barrois, A. G., *Manuel d'archéologie biblique* (2 vols.; Paris, 1939, 1953). Blaiklock, E. M., *Cities of the New Testament* (London, 1965). Burrows, M., *What Mean These Stones?* (New Haven, 1941). Ceram, C., *Gods, Graves, and Scholars* (N.Y., 1951); *The March of Archaeology* (N.Y., 1958); *Secret of the Hittites* (N.Y., 1956). Corswant, W., *Dictionnaire d'archéologie biblique* (Neuchâtel, 1956). De Vaux, *AI*. Du Buit, M., *Biblical Archaeology* (N.Y., 1960). Ehrich, R., *Relative Chronologies in Old World Archaeology* (Chicago, 1954). Finegan, J., *Light from the Ancient Past* (2nd ed.; Princeton, 1960). Franken, H., *Primer of Old Testament Archaeology* (Leiden, 1963). Gray, J., *Archaeology and the Old Testament World* (London, 1962). Harding, G. L., *The Antiquities of Jordan* (London, 1959). *The Holy Land*, ed. by the Hebrew University Dept. of Antiquities as part of *Antiquity and Survival* (vol. 2; The Hague and Jerusalem, 1957). Kenyon, K., *Archaeology in the Holy Land* (2nd ed.; London, 1965); *Beginning in Archaeology* (London, 1952). Kopp, C., *The Holy Places of the Gospels* (N.Y., 1963). Noth, M., *The Old Testament World* (Phila., 1966) 107–79. McCown, C., *Ladder of Progress in Palestine* (N.Y., 1943). Parrot, A., *Discovering Buried Worlds* (London, 1955); *Archéologie mésopotamienne* (2 vols.; Paris, 1946, 1953). Pfeiffer, C., *The Biblical World: A Dictionary of Biblical Archaeology* (Grand Rapids, 1966). Pritchard, J. B., *Archaeology and the Old Testament* (Princeton, 1958). SBA, a series of small volumes translating *Cahiers d'archéologie biblique*—as of 1968 the French series had 15 vols., 8 of which had been translated. Thomas, D. W., *Archaeology and Old Testament Study* (London, 1967). Thompson, J. A., *The Bible and Archaeology* (Grand Rapids, 1962). Unger, M. F., *Archaeology and the Old Testament* (Grand Rapids, 1962). Van Beek, G. W., "Archaeology," *IDB* 1, 195–207 (other important articles in *IDB* include "Architecture," 1, 209–15; "Pottery," 3, 846–53). Vandier, J., *Manuel d'archéologie égyptienne* (2 vols. of 2 parts each; Paris, 1952–55). Wright, G. E., *Biblical Archaeology* (2nd ed.; Phila., 1962); "The Archaeology of Palestine," *BANE* 73–112.

Also, *Archaeological Discoveries in the Holy Land*, publ. by the Archaeological Institute of America (N.Y., 1967). *Everyday Life in Bible Times*, publ. by the National Geographic Society (Washington, 1968). An interesting general work is L. de Paor, *Archaeology* (Pelican ed.; London, 1967).

2 OUTLINE

3

Chart of Excavations

Site	Excavator	Excavation Dates	Auspices or Publication	Era (BC)	Importance
Ai	Marquet-Krause; Callaway	1933–35; 1964–	Rothschild; Perkins Sch	3200–2000	Unoccupied when Joshua invaded; Bethel problem (§ 59)
Amarna	Petrie, Peet, Pendlebury	1887; 1909–14; 1921–36	DOG; EgEF	1360	Akhenaton's "monotheist" capital; archive (§ 58)
Ashkelon	Garstang	1920–22	PEF	2500–AD 200	Philistine center (§ 66); Herod the Great's birthplace
Babylon	Layard; Koldewey; Lenzen	1850; 1899–1917; 1956–58	DOG	fl. 1800; 600	Ziggurat site; Hammurabi's and Nebuchadnezzar's capital
Beth-shan	Fisher, Rowe	1921–33	Penn Mus	1800–AD 400	Egyptian and Philistine enclave; Saul's body (§ 65, 68)
Beth-shemesh	Mackenzie; Grant	1911–12; 1928–33	PEF; ASOR-Haverford	1700–AD 400	Fringe of Philistine domination in 11th cent. (§ 67)
Beth-zur	Albright, Sellers	1931; 1957	ASOR-McCormick	1700–200	Coins attesting Maccabean military maneuvers (§ 83)
Boghazkoy	Winckler, Bittel	1906–	DOG	1700–950	Major Hittite capital (Hattushas); archive
Byblos	Montet, Dunand	1919–	French Govt	6000–AD 200	Egyptian-Phoenician trading center; alphabet origins
Caesarea	Yeivin, Levi	1955–64	IDA, Italy	AD 1–800	Herod's seaport; Roman capital (§ 86); Christian center
Capernaum	Kohl; Orfali; Corbo	1905–14; 1921–26; 1968	DOG; Franciscans	AD 200	Chief surviving Galilee synagogue (§ 88)
Carchemish	Henderson; Woolley	1876–81; 1912–14; 1920–40	Brit Mus	2400–600	Neo-Hittite fort; Nebuchadnezzar's decisive battle
Dothan	Free	1953–64	Wheaton (*BASOR*)	3000–200	Mammoth masonry from Joseph era (Gn 37:17)
Elephantine	Rubensohn; Ronzevalle	1904–8; 1918	DOG	2500–AD 200	Jewish temple and archive (6–5th cents.)
Ephesus	Wood; Hogarth; Miltner	1863–74; 1898–1935; 1954–	Brit Mus; Austria	200–AD 200	Temple of Diana; two tombs of John
Gerasa	Kraeling	1928–34	Yale-ASOR	AD 70–400	Decapolis town; forum, colonnade, early church (§ 90)
Gezer	Macalister; Rowe; Wright	1902–9; 1934; 1964–	PEF; Hebr Union	3500–200	First major complete Palestinian excavation (§ 14)
Ghassul	Mallon, Koeppel; North	1929–38; 1960	Pontif Bibl Inst	3500	Chalcolithic parent site; unique frescoes (§ 47)
Gibeon	Pritchard	1956–64	Penn Mus, Pacific Sch	1800–800	Water supply linked with biblical events (§ 70)
Hazor	Garstang; Yadin, Aharoni	1928; 1955–58; 1968–69	Marston; Hebr Univ	1700–850	Three temples; Joshua dating controversy (§ 63)
Jericho	Sellin; Garstang; Kenyon	1907–9; 1929–36; 1952–58	DOG-PEF; Marston; PEF	6000–400	Lacuna throughout OT period (§ 60–62)
Lachish	Starkey, Tufnell	1932–38	Wellcome-Marston	1700–500	Archive attesting Nebuchadnezzar invasion (§ 77–79)
Mari	Parrot	1933–	Louvre	3000–500	Archive revising Hammurabi date (*ca.* 1700—§ 51)
Megiddo	Schumacher; Fisher; Yadin	1903–5; 1925–39; 1960–67	DOG; Chicago; Hebr Univ	3500–500	Most ample Palestinian dig; Solomonic gate, stables (§ 31–38)
Mirsim (Debir?)	Albright	1926–32	Pitt-Xenia (*BASOR*)	1900–850	Model dig, technique, and publication (§ 15, 54)
Nasbeh (Mizpah?)	Badé	1926–35	Pacific Sch (*BASOR*)	2800–200	Mizpah is center of Samuel saga
Nazareth	Viaud; Bagatti	1895; 1907–9; 1954–56	Franciscans	600–AD 800	Settled since OT times; cave of incarnation (§ 87)
Nebo	Saller	1933–48	Franciscans	AD 400	Mosaics attesting Christian veneration of Moses
Nimrud (Calah)	Layard, Rassam; Mallowan	1845–80; 1949–61	Brit Sch Iraq	fl. 1250–600	Tablets correcting background of Isaiah era
Niniveh	Layard; Campbell Thompson	1845–79; 1903–5; 1927–32	Brit Mus	900–600	Frieze portraying siege of Lachish in 701
Nuzi	Starr	1925–31	ASOR-Harvard	1800–200	Archive showing Hurrian links with patriarchs (§ 55)
Qumran	De Vaux	1951–56	École Biblique-DAJ	850–AD 70	Dead Sea Scrolls (§ 84)
Samaria	Reisner; Crowfoot	1908–10; 1931–35	Harvard; PEF	950–AD 200	Omri palace, ivories, ostraca; Herodian temple (§ 73–74)
Shechem	Sellin; Wright	1913–14, 1926–34; 1958–	Vienna; Drew-McCormick	1900–200	Cyclopean wall; two striking gates; temple
Shiloh	Kjaer	1926–32; 1963	Denmark	1700–AD 400	Occupation flourished in 11th cent. (Samuel); AD mosaics
Susa	Loftus; De Morgan; Ghirshman	1849–52; 1897–	French Govt	3500–AD 200	Hammurabi code; also earliest writing
Tanis	Petrie; Montet	1929–52	EgEF; France	2500–AD 400	Hyksos capital Avaris; also = Raamses of Exodus (Ex 1:11)
Tirzah	De Vaux	1946–64	École Biblique	3600–650	Abandoned east-oriented capital of Israel (§ 73)
Ugarit	Schaeffer	1929–60	French Govt	6000–1200	Powerful state; archive in language like Hebrew (§ 55)
Ur	Woolley	1922–34	Penn and Brit Mus	2500–850	Brick-asphalt ziggurat; opulent tombs; see Gn 11:31

Mus = Museum; Sch = School; EgEF, PEF = Egyptian or Palestinian Exploration Fund; DOG = Deutsche Orient-Gesellschaft; IDA, DAJ = Dept. of Antiquities (Israel, Jordan); fl. = flourishing era; ASOR = American Schools of Oriental Research; § = cross reference to section in this article.

GENERAL BACKGROUND

4 **(I) History of Biblical Excavations.** Excavation in Palestine is what has given an "archaeological slant" to the whole of biblical research in our day, as Pius XII says in *Divino Afflante Spiritu* (→ Church Pronouncements, 72:20). Excavation sites and their importance are tabulated on the accompanying chart. The organic growth of the movement may be crystallized about the names of 17 pioneers whose contribution we will first describe briefly.

5 **Flavius Josephus** was a Jew who wrote in Greek in Rome about AD 93 (→ Apocrypha, 68:114). He first used the word *archaiologia* as the title of a book, which is now generally called *Antiquities*. By *archaiologia* he meant "science of the past," or what we would call history. Although the work was totally lacking in empirical or critical research, it was nevertheless a mine of information diligently compiled. Through the centuries it has focused scholars' minds on "what we can learn about the Bible from outside the Bible." It inspired improved compilations about 1700 by Ugolini and Bochart, and by Keil and Kortleitner down into our century. The sum of this work may be characterized as "a classification of what we can learn about everyday life, especially in its matérial aspects, from between the lines of the Bible and other books that really aimed at recording political and cultural movements."

6 **Heinrich Schliemann** in 1873, at Troy in NW Turkey, proved his dream that successive settlements of the past could be dug up out of the ground, one from beneath the other. This was basically an application of excavation techniques inspired by the Italian Renaissance, especially by the rediscovery of Pompeii in 1790. But the digging in Italy and Greece had become largely an irresponsible and destructive search for "museum pieces." This was deplorably the case in Mesopotamia around 1850, as described in Seton Lloyd's *Foundations in the Dust* (London, 1947). Schliemann's "stratification" was naïve. He wrongly imagined each successive "city" sealed off by a mud pack from the ones that preceded and followed it (→ 25–26 below). Schliemann too was at heart a fortune hunter. He financed his digging from a brother's share in the California gold rush, and eventually went there himself, after a fling at Mycenae, the homeland of Homer's Agamemnon in Greece. His digging at Troy had to be seriously corrected by later German and American expeditions. But Schliemann's audacity and insight deserve much credit for the "stratification principle" that dominates biblical excavation. Cf. C. Ceram, *Gods*, 29–55.

7 **Félicien de Saulcy** performed the earliest Palestinian excavations in NW Jerusalem in 1863. He discovered some Royal Tombs, which the French Government still proudly displays to visitors. The burial chambers belonged to a Persian queen, Helen of Adiabene, who embraced the Jewish religion at the time of Christ, rather than to King David and his sons, as De Saulcy thought. Although the pioneering of E. Robinson in 1838 (→ Biblical Geography, 73:9), which had apparently included some casual digging along the Jerusalem North Wall, was of more lasting archaeological significance, De Saulcy and *la belle France* cannot be denied the merit of pioneering the first seriously organized and methodical excavation. He also made important contributions to numismatics, the classification of ancient coins.

8 **Charles Warren** performed at the SE corner of Jerusalem in 1866 the daredevil engineering exploit still pictured as frontispiece of *PEQ*. Both the exploit and the periodical were the outcome of a new society or "Fund" established in London the preceding year. Its major achievement was the Survey of Palestine with the help of British army officers, whose work resulted in many important discoveries by digging. Warren's exploit proved that the corner of the Temple retaining wall (questionably the "Pinnacle") went down far deeper than today's ground level permits us to see. In this same Kidron Valley, but farther S, Warren discovered the "shaft" leading up from the Gihon water source to the level of the Jebusite citadel. This shaft is now generally considered to be the "crooked pipe," or *ṣinnôr*, by which Joab took Jerusalem for David (2 Sm 5:8).

9 **Robert Koldewey** meanwhile became a leading figure of the methodical German school of excavation. With W. Andrae he undertook generation-long expeditions at Babylon and Asshur around 1900. At Warka and several other Mesopotamian sites, a model scholarly conscientiousness replaced the "monument snatching" of earlier adventurers. Both in Egypt and at Troy the Koldewey methods were put into practice by W. Dörpfeld. Through Dörpfeld's apprentice G. A. Reisner, the German method later came to dominate the serious entry of Americans into the scene with the Harvard excavation of Samaria in 1908. (An American Palestine Exploration society had indeed been founded as early as 1870, and the consul Selah Merrill published some of its results; but that particular enterprise did not survive.) Cf. C. Ceram, *Gods*, 279–99.

10 **Charles Clermont-Ganneau**, a Frenchman working with the British Fund, made some of the most important early discoveries in the Holy Land. In 1870 he recovered for the Louvre the stele of King Mesha found by F. A. Klein at Dibon. In 1871 he found the first of two surviving stone inscriptions threatening death to any non-Jew who entered the Temple area; it is now in the Istanbul Museum. He also found the Gezer boundary rock, and he reported on Ashkelon and other sites in his *Études* (London, 1897). He branded as a forgery the famous "Deuteronomy Scroll" offered by M. W. Shapira to the British Museum.

11 **William Flinders Petrie** made the first stratified excavation in Palestine at Tell el-Hesi near Ashkelon in 1890. There he brilliantly exemplified the principle that was to become normative for all Palestine digging: "Broken pottery, even without an inscription, is a sure clue to dating." About halfway down the mound he recognized some fragments of a brownish metal-like jar of the style called "bilbil," which he had seen in some

Egyptian tombs alongside inscriptions from *ca.* 1300 BC. Petrie measured the vertical distance from these fragments to the Greek ware at the top of the mound. Then he divided this distance by the number of years and concluded that every foot represented so many years of occupation. This method is often lampooned today as being excessively naïve, especially in ignoring the possibility of interrupted occupation. Still, even the most competent experts of our day, when confronted with two datable objects separated by a yard's depth of earth, will tend to assume a similar "yardstick." Petrie could have better exploited his genius had he paid greater attention to neighboring excavators' results as they came in. Also, he had a tendency to impose on his sites biblical names that are now universally rejected. Thus there is a certain pathos in the titles of his publications, *Hesy—Lachish*, *Gaza—Ajjul*, *Jammeh—Gerar*, *Beth-Pelet—Far'a*, i.e., Tell el-Hesi is *not* Lachish, etc. Yet no other pioneer took a more important step forward in Palestine excavation. His work was under the auspices of the *Egypt* Exploration Fund; and it was in Egypt that his rashly numerous excavations turned up genuinely biblical sites, especially Tanis and Amarna. Petrie's career is described in his autobiography, *Seventy Years in Archaeology* (London, 1931).

12 **L.-Hugues Vincent** was only 16 years old when as a Dominican seminarian he joined the École Biblique, just founded by Lagrange in Jerusalem (→ Modern OT Criticism, 70:35, 61). It was within a year of Petrie's epoch-making 1890 excavation. From then until his death in 1960 Père Vincent performed the unique function of interpreting and *correlating* all the excavations that were to be carried on in Palestine. Most of the other excavators were foreign university professors; after a season or a few years of "Palestine internship," they would retire to the more congenial homeland atmosphere where they could work up their observations for the benefit of their own academic background. Thus there would have been lacking in Palestine any permanent scholarly guidance, had it not been so brilliantly supplied by Vincent in *RB*. No less significant were his own original researches at Hebron, Emmaus-Nicopolis, and Jerusalem's Lithostrotos (→ 92, 93 below). Most of his massive researches were in collaboration with his geographer confrere F.-M. Abel. Cf. *BASOR* 164 [1961] 2–4.

13 **Gottlieb Schumacher** excavated Megiddo in 1903 (→ 31 below), and published for the British Fund important researches on the Gadara region. He was an able surveyor, as was the copublisher of his results, Carl Watzinger. Watzinger also worked with Ernst Sellin at Jericho in 1907. Actually it might be fairer to credit Sellin with German pioneering in Palestine, since he excavated also Taanach in 1901 and Shechem in 1913 (for Sellin as a biblical theologian and historian, → Modern OT Criticism, 70:51). But the early German expeditions in Palestine tend to show that the one really indispensable technical expert on an excavation is the surveyor-architect. If his work is done professionally, the efforts of collaborators to unravel the chronology and to decipher the inscriptions can later be re-evaluated.

14 **R. Stewart Macalister** from 1902 to 1909 at Gezer conducted singlehandedly the first really major Palestine excavation. The famous Gezer calendar tablet and some other inscriptions were unfortunately dated too late, because an interruption in settlement at the site from 1000 to 500 BC passed unnoticed; in addition, there has had to be a drastic reassessment of the Solomonic gateway, which he called Roman, and of his Chalcolithic ware. But the imposing row of rough obelisks that he designated as a place of worship is one of the few finds whose cultic diagnosis has stuck. In 1964 G. E. Wright reopened the Gezer excavations under the auspices of the Hebrew Union College (*BA* 30 [1967] 34–70).

15 **William F. Albright** in 1920 came to Jerusalem to put some life into ASOR, which had existed since 1895. He was a prodigious linguist and sparked international co-operation, especially through the (Journal of the) Palestine Oriental Society, the early presidents of which included a French Jesuit and an Arab Franciscan. His digging at Gibeah (1922), Bethel (1927), and Beth-zur (1931), was significant. From 1926 to 1932 at Tell Beit Mirsim, S of Hebron, Albright made the excavation that is rated by most experts as an unsurpassed model of economical efficiency and of usefulness in publication, though outside America Albright's identification of the site as Debir is questioned. As editor of *BASOR* and *AASOR*, author of *FSAC*, and teacher of such men as N. Glueck, G. E. Wright, and R. O'Callaghan at the Johns Hopkins University, Albright has exerted more moderate-progressive influence toward infusing archaeological data into exegesis than any man of our century. For his bibliography, cf. *BANE* 363–89; for his autobiography, cf. his *History, Archaeology, and Christian Humanism* (N.Y., 1964) 301–27. For bibliography on the Debir controversy, → Chronicler, 24:15.

16 **Clarence Fisher** is an enigmatic figure in the history of Palestine excavation between World War I and II. As a Pennsylvania University architect, he opened and briefly directed most of the major excavations of that era: Beth-shan, Megiddo, Beth-shemesh, and Samaria. Unfortunately he seems to have been unable to hold the reins of management, or to bring to completion any publication, even the *Corpus of Palestinian Pottery* left at ASOR at his death in 1941.

17 **Nelson Glueck** headed ASOR in the 1930's. He added a new chapter to biblical exploration techniques by his mammoth survey of surface pottery deposits in Transjordan. In the 1950's he extended this method to the Negeb of Israel, while heading Hebrew Union College of Cincinnati and the branch he built for it in Jerusalem. Glueck's popular books include *The Other Side of the Jordan* (New Haven, 1940); *The River Jordan* (N.Y., 1946); *Rivers in the Desert* [on the Negeb] (N.Y., 1959); cf. also *BA* 22 (1959) 82–108, or *BAR* 1, 1–21.

18 **Roland de Vaux** emerged as the leader of Palestine excavation in the postwar partition era. He was director of the Dominican École Biblique, an Assyriologist of renown, and editor of BJ and *RB* (→ Modern OT Criticism, 70:61). From 1946 to 1964 he excavated Omri's capital at Tirzah. Since 1952 he has headed with dexterity the complex Dead Sea Scrolls research activity: acquiring new manuscripts; guiding the international Scrollery team; and excavating Qumran and Feshkha (→ Apocrypha, 68:67–68). His *AI* provides, with the help of archaeological and literary data, the best existing survey of biblical social institutions (→ Religious Institutions, 76).

19 **Kathleen M. Kenyon** is the first exponent of the thesis that excavation should be taught as an independent university discipline. Up to her time it had largely been simply a branch of classics, theology, orientalism, or ethnic history. She also typifies the important leadership women have assumed in the field. While she was excavating Samaria (Sebastiyeh) with John and Grace Crowfoot in the thirties, other women archaeologists were also at work in Palestine. Judith Marquet-Krause directed the Ai excavation, Dorothy Garrod discovered Natufian and Carmel flint cultures, and Olga Tufnell became the only effectual survivor of the Lachish team. More recently Hetty Goldman's work at Tarsus and Diana Kirkbride's in Transjordan have been conspicuous. Miss Kenyon in 1952 reopened the Jericho *chantier*, and showed that the brick walls attributed to Joshua by Garstang, Vincent, and Albright were in fact 1000 years older. She established that the Jericho mound called Tell es-Sultan was in an almost complete state of abandon throughout all dates possible for the major biblical references, from 1500 BC through the periods of Joshua (→ 60–62 below) and of Hiel (860 BC; 1 Kgs 16:34). Only *ca.* 800 was the site reoccupied. In compensation she discovered a powerful fortification with a unique early sculpture dating from before 5000 BC. (Cf. K. Kenyon, *Digging up Jericho* [N.Y., 1957]; *NatGeog* [Dec. 1951; Dec. 1953].) She then turned to clarify the equally muddled state of excavation on Ophel Hill, the Jebusite citadel in the SE corner of Jerusalem (cf. *BA* 27 [1964] 34–52; 28 [1965] 22–26; 29 [1966] 27–36).

20 **Bellarmino Bagatti** has been the leader of the archaeological activities of the Franciscan Holy Land Custody, which have become prominent since the wars. With S. Saller, V. Corbo, and other confreres, he has had an important role in Byzantine excavation. This relates chiefly to churches and mosaics attesting biblical sites such as Nebo, Bethany, Olivet, Nazareth, Ain Karim, Emmaus-Qubeibeh, and the Bethlehem Shepherds' Field. The work is expertly published in *FrancLA* and "Publications" of the Studium Biblicum Franciscanum of Jerusalem.

21 **Yigael Yadin** is the outstanding representative of the immense boom in archaeological research fostered by the Zionist movement and the State of Israel. He is the son of Eleazar Sukenik, who in the thirties discovered the Beth Alpha synagogue, the "Jesus son of Joseph" casket inscription, and Chalcolithic house-shaped burial urns. Sukenik also obtained some of the Dead Sea Scrolls; Yadin followed in his footsteps by dramatically purchasing the remainder of the Cave 1 scrolls for Israel (→ Apocrypha, 68:69). Since 1960 he has proceeded to sensational explorations of the En-gedi desert and Masada (→ Apocrypha, 68:107–110). But Yadin's major achievement has been the 1955–58 excavation of Hazor with Y. Aharoni, Ruth Amiran, and Jean Perrot—the most grandiose dig since Megiddo. It was sponsored by the Hebrew University (→ 63 below). The University president, Benjamin Mazar-Maisler, was himself the excavator of Beth-she'arim, Khirbet el-Kerak (Beth-yerah), and Jaffa (Qasileh). The University has also been prominent in prehistory, through the work of M. Stekelis, in advancing the cave discoveries of F. Turville-Petre and R. Neuville. The Israel Exploration Society and its journal (*IsrEJ*), ably co-ordinated by Joseph Aviram, typify the extent to which "excavation-fever" has become a dominant local interest in Israel.

22 **(II) Introductory Notes on Archaeological Method.**

(A) Deciding Where to Dig. From the experience of the above pioneers, we can learn how one actually goes about organizing an excavation. First, careful study of the Bible and of history books makes it possible to visualize to some degree the section of Palestinian surface on which a particular biblical site ought to lie. Next, one should consult the British Survey map and volumes (→ Biblical Geography, 73:9–10) to see if any traditional Arab name corresponds to the Hebr name of the site; wherever possible, one ought to question directly the Arabs of the neighborhood and note their *unprompted* names for various nearby landmarks. Finally one can roam over the general area and pick up pieces of pottery (→ 28 below), which can indicate in advance how deep one will have to dig before encountering the biblical period of interest.

23 We saw that the pioneers tended to attack first some big center like Jerusalem whose identity has always been beyond question. There was also a sound practical motive for this, because the nearer one's dig is to a population center, the fewer are the inconveniences and expenses of lodging and provisioning. But the very fact that such a center has remained important through the centuries makes it unsuited for excavating. Such a settlement has grown by the gradual addition of new buildings. Those of an earlier period either continue in use, or their materials have been transformed into the buildings of later period. Even debris from the rubbish-heap has been pressed into service or used for fill.

The situation is better at cities like Nablus, where the population center has gradually moved off a mile or two. Consequently, a protective layer from 1000 years' disuse has sealed off the biblical settlement of Shechem (→ Biblical Geography, 73:101). There are many such abandoned or sidetracked villages in Palestine, and they are very easy to recognize. They are called tells.

24 **(B) Nature of a Tell.** "Tell" is a Hebr word, from Babylonian *tillu*. In Jos 8:28 it is a synonym for the *'Ay* (Ai) or "ruin." In English the pl. "tells" seems acceptable, though we sometimes run into the Arab pl. *tulûl*, or diminutive *tulayl*, pl. *tulaylat*. In some biblical areas the Persian-Turkish words *tepe* or *hüyük* are used for "tell."

Every tell tends to have a very distinctive truncated-cone shape. Seen from certain angles, the most conspicuous tells are Lachish, nearby Marisa, Megiddo, and Dothan. Also noteworthy is the tell of Homs in Syria (see *ANEP* 224). Erbil in N Mesopotamia is a beautiful example of a tell still crowned by the wall of a city. But in most cases the settlement has disappeared. Such a situation is taken for granted in the definition which should be learned: The tell is a mound which from successive stages of human occupation has grown up into a truncated cone.

25 At Troy, the successive stages were envisioned as a series of independent cities sitting on top of one another. This romantic notion dominated the early search for Joshua's Jericho. But a moment's reflection should have warned these romancers that ancient cities simply were not built that way. In ancient Palestine literally everything was made of clay. Some wood was used, of course, and a great deal of natural stone. But all the utensils were just mud. Even many of the stone buildings had to be finished off with mud "bricks," which were sometimes "fired" to the hardness of stone or pottery. In any case, the vast majority of the houses in a plain or "tell" area were of adobe, i.e., ordinary mud fashioned into chunks about 6 in. on a side and laid in rows held together by mortar made of the same mud.

Houses were covered with a roof of branches, which slanted outward and permitted the rather infrequent rain to run off. After every heavy rainfall or similar catastrophe, however, several house walls in a village would topple over. Normally, a wall does not fall over flat as a single unit down to its foundation; the top-heavy part falls, leaving the bottom third almost intact (as with a child's stack of blocks). Such an occurrence was no great hardship for the Palestinian family. They just shivered under reed mats until the rain was over, then with their bare feet zestfully trampled the fallen bricks back into the mud of Mother Earth from which they had come. Within a day or two—while the ground was still moist—they could fashion new bricks, let them dry in the sun, and build up their wall again to the desired height.

26 Naturally, every rebuilding involves some improvements, and since materials are constantly being brought in from outside, this meant that the ground level of the Palestinian villages gradually rose. If only as little as a quarter inch per year, this rise would amount to 50 feet in the biblical period alone. It would be far easier for investigators if the growth had been perfectly level and symmetric with each layer sealed off from the next. Unfortunately it did not happen that way. People remained where they were. Even after the most colossal disasters they continued to use the remains that were sometimes left standing to a considerable height in the very heart of the disaster area. And even after a city was abandoned for some centuries, new settlers did not find a level surface awaiting them. They huddled at first in sheltered pits or basements, where their debris mingled with that of 1000 years earlier. Gradually they erected splendid edifices, but often an earlier tower or hilltop villa survived as a landmark above the bulk of their later masonry.

Hence archaeologists had to adjust to reality their romantic notion of "cities sitting on top of one another." Even the all-important notion of *stratification* borrowed from geology proved too rigid; for, despite terminology like "level," "layer," and "stratum," there is little in a series of successive deposits that is horizontally flat. The interested student should familiarize himself with the method of excavation in order to appreciate the close relationship between technique and the value of the information reported by the excavator. Improvements in recent years give much more reliability to the results obtained. For an introduction, see Albright, *AP* 7–22.

27 **(C) Pottery and Chronology.** Apart from buildings, virtually the only "artifact" or product of human industry found in Palestine excavation is broken pottery, or "sherds." A rare amulet or brief inscription, and fairly numerous small objects in bone, flint, or stone, are the exception that proves the rule.

We must first understand how natural it is that nothing but clay should be found, whether in the form of unbaked bricks and mortar, or in the form of kiln-bricks and pottery. Modern technology has enriched our homes and offices with complex utensils of varied materials; in biblical times, however, all utensils in an ordinary house were made of clay. There was no furniture at all; blankets and mats were piled up or spread in various ways and ultimately served as clothing. The source of heat and light was fire inside a jar. The plumbing and refrigeration were a porous jar whose "sweat" evaporation cooled the water inside. Canisters, glasses, and spoons were pottery of various shapes; "fingers were made before forks"; the bread itself is even today in the form of a plate on which other food is served. Thus no table was needed, but if company came, a mat served the purpose (biblical *šulḥān*, Ps 23:5).

28 Pottery has a unique value for dating not only because it is so universal but because it is simultaneously the easiest and the most difficult of all things to destroy! It is easily broken in the sense that the complete vessel is smashed and thus loses its form. But to break down the fragments into an unrecognizable, that is, a nonpottery state would be an expensive engineering project even with the machines of today. And from any part of the *rim* or certain other small fragments, the size and shape of the original jar can be very accurately inferred.

Since the broken vessels were easily replaced—virtually with the mud in one's front yard—there was a tremendous turnover. Thus pottery styles were as capricious and fluctuating as the fashion in women's hats. Some good gray styles in storage jars or cooking pots were retained unchanged through 1000 years. But perfume bottles or hip flasks naturally enjoyed a vogue as ephemeral as the tastes of their users. Such ware can sometimes be dated to an interval as exact as 50 years. Even those styles that lasted 300 years overlapped, so that the combination of various styles found at a single site can narrow down the time range. Being so breakable, pottery would not be preserved as a family heirloom or carried along when the family moved to a distant place. Because of this, it is a far better dating criterion than art objects or even coins (which came in only after 500 BC). For a discussion of Palestinian pottery in biblical times, see *BA* 8 (1945) 82–93.

29 There is great excitement nowadays about the radiocarbon-dating technique devised by Willard F. Libby at Chicago about 1948. Its point of departure is the fact that all organic compounds (materials that were once alive), as they disintegrate, lose one half of their Carbon 14 isotopes every 1400 years. Since the number characteristic of each compound is known, the date of its death can be determined. This is a brilliant discovery that is of great usefulness for archaeological dating, although a few wrinkles are still to be ironed out (*Or* 32 [1963] 345). Since the material to be tested is completely destroyed in the process, a large amount must be available. Also the material must never have been contaminated by contact with other organic materials. These conditions are hard to verify! (Cf. *BAR* 1, 330–42; *NatGeog* [Aug. 1958] 234–55; *Arch* 18 [1965] 277–81; for a discussion of other scientific methods of dating, see *BA* 29 [1966] 114–25.)

30 The growth of Palestine archaeology is reflected in the combined achievement of men like Petrie, Vincent, Albright, and Mazar in working out the "ceramic clock." By this we mean a table giving pottery types characteristic of each successive 100-year period. Although the major periods have been named after metals or predominant cultures, actually it is the styles of pottery that enable us to determine any given period.

31 **(III) Example of an Excavation: Megiddo.**

(A) History of the Excavation. Rather than being just a sample, Megiddo is the *model* of the frustrations and achievements of Palestinian excavations. The search for its site in the Plain of Esdraelon was begun by E. Robinson (1838), as described in his *Biblical Researches* 3, 117. He stood on the so-called Governor's Mound (Mutesellim) near the E outlet of the strategic pass called Arah leading across Carmel to the sea. "Somewhere near here, Megiddo must have stood," he mused, apparently never suspecting that it was beneath his feet.

32 The architect G. Schumacher in 1903–5 excavated Tell el Mutesellim for the German Oriental Society (→ 13 above). It is claimed that he ignored the decisiveness of broken pottery and used scavenger-trenches, which were not even adequately recorded on his skillfully drafted plans. Nevertheless the two volumes on Megiddo, as well as Sellin's volume on nearby Taanach in 1904, are important pioneer achievements. The German recording of pottery was at least sufficiently precise to enable Albright to launch his audacious claim that a single perduring community shuttled back and forth, at various dates attested by potsherds, between Taanach and the 5-mi.-distant Megiddo. Schumacher was fully competent and eager to carry on the work after 1920, improving his former techniques just as the Anglo-American expeditions had to improve theirs; but the Germans had lost the war, and permission to excavate was denied them by the British Mandate.

33 In 1925 James Breasted decided upon the Megiddo mound as the site of an ideal excavation by the Oriental Institute of the University of Chicago. His friend John D. Rockefeller promised a virtually unlimited budget, as well as a spare million for erecting the Palestine Archaeological Museum in Jerusalem. To guard against dangers faced by earlier excavations, such as armed attack, malaria, and boredom, a spacious villa was constructed. Its tennis court and swimming pool alone cost more than Albright's whole excavation of Mirsim! A leisurely 25 years was allotted for peeling off the whole mound layer by layer and for recording every item and aspect of the successive stages.

"The initial plan to dig the great site systematically, stratum after stratum, fortunately had to be abandoned because of the prohibitive expense [even for a Rockefeller after 1929!]. Our use of the adverb 'fortunately' may seem strange, but it must be realized that the very best technique of today will probably seem primitive a century hence, and that it is a sad mistake to exhaust the possibility of any important site like Megiddo. Actually only a fraction of the great mound has been removed [in what looks to the uninitiated like huge trenches!], and there is ample room for correcting chronology and making important discoveries" (Albright, *AP* 41).

34 Twenty separate strata were recognized. The long duration and careful subdivision of these Megiddo strata make them a fine framework for synchronizing Palestine sites of briefer duration. This achievement is not essentially spoiled by the severe criticisms that have been leveled against details of the dating. Most recent material for attack comes from the 1955–58 Hazor excavation. Its director Y. Yadin confirms the Solomonic date of the four-pronged city gate of Megiddo by a newly recognized parallel at Gezer; but he redates under Ahab some of the allegedly adjacent masonry. And Y. Aharoni dates as "ordinary storehouses under Ahab" some Hazor structures that greatly resemble the Megiddo "stables." Cf. Yadin, *BA* 23 (1960) 62–68, or *BAR* 2, 240–47. Even more serious are revisions demanded by the Albright school, which laments that the subsequent directors, P. L. Guy and then G. Loud, lacked Fisher's "experience and flair for pottery." In *BA* 13 (1950) 28–46, or *BAR* 2, 225–40, G. E. Wright embarked on a clear brief archaeological history of the site, with important alterations in the dating of those periods that most directly concern the Bible: Strata IV B (950–900) and XVI (*ca.* 2000?). As for the alleged destruction of Stratum IX (*ca.* 1500) by Thutmosis, an Egyptologist showed in 1951 that this pharaoh had never fought a battle at Megiddo. To guard against the mistrust on the part of the public that such wholesale revisionism is apt to provoke, there is in professional discussion a strong secure undertone, "Errors have been made in the past, and even Albright has loyally reorganized his views on many points on which fresh evidence has been discovered; but as of *right now* everything is under control." A more realistic conclusion would seem to be that the results of excavation are valuable and useful only insofar as their degree of certitude is assessed without exaggeration from the outset.

35 **(B) Some Interesting Discoveries.** *The stables.* The most characteristic find at Megiddo was a sort of stone half-column, 3 or 4 ft. high with rectangular faces, repeated in endless rows, as many as 400 in all. Schumacher contended that they had cultic significance. Similar rows of short thick stone pillars, though much less numerous, were left showing on the surface of Hazor by Garstang's 1926 sounding there. The Megiddo pillars themselves bear no resemblance at all to the more elongated and tapering steles of the Gezer or Byblos places of worship; what they have in common—a rather curious fact—is that several stand upright in a row. (Indeed, this "uprightness" is the only common feature of the biblical *maṣṣᵉbôt*, betyls or cultic posts, which vary in form from natural tree-stumps, roughened by weather, to obeliscal shapes in stone or metal. Sometimes these steles have crude indications of human features, either facial or phallic. More often they are formless and in fact are named "asherah" and represent *female* divinities [Asherah = Ishtar], but without the sex-tracing of the numerous Palestine figurines.)

When P. L. Guy came to head the Megiddo enterprise in 1928, he noted that many of the stone posts had a hole pierced diagonally near a corner. Guy's youth had been spent in an era when hitching-posts for visitors' horses were a familiar sight. He proposed that this precisely was the function of the Megiddo posts, which also served as bases for wooden beams that held up the roof. The idea would scarcely have occurred to anyone of the present automobile generation.

As for horses at Megiddo, we know that the town was a district capital of Solomon, who is repeatedly reported as trafficking in horses (1 Kgs 4:12; 9:19; 10:26). (In fact at Jerusalem the masonry-forest under the SE corner of the Temple esplanade has been popularly called "Solomon's Stables," doubtlessly because of a confused combination of two facts: Solomon built some of the masonry, and 2000 years later the crusaders made a ramp through there to drive their horses right up onto the Temple area!) In many ways the hypothesis of stables at Megiddo is plausible. They are so numerous there as to override any other function the city may have had; but after all, we know of Megiddo chiefly as a battle site, and horses were "armaments." Still there is no real proof of the hypothesis, and it has been rejected at Hazor. (→ 34 above on dating of the "stables.")

36 The genuinely cultic remains of Megiddo are described in a separate volume by H. May. The most astounding monument surviving at the site is a huge oval *altar or platform*, from the time of Abraham (or even centuries earlier according to Wright). It is now almost at the bottom of a deep trench, but at the time it was built it was probably a "high place" on the top of the mound. The altar is some 20 ft in diameter; it was made of unhewn stones but had steps. In thus conforming to the law of Ex 20:25, but not to that of Ex 20:26, it seems to this author to be a concrete example of how God guided the Israelites to adopt and place under his authority the *desirable* elements of neighboring usage (even in things religious), while rejecting the bad. At the side of this altar-platform was constructed a complex of temples that continued in use with adjustments down to the time of the Israelites' entry into Canaan.

37 *City gates.* The sequence of monumental gates at the N of the Mutesellim mound is instructive. The stone wall of Stratum XVIII (*ca.* 3000 BC) was the most massive fortification ever erected on the site, with walls originally 15 ft wide, later thickened to an impressive 28 ft. Similarly massive stone fortifications have only recently emerged at Jericho, but of an earlier date. An Early Bronze Age wall at Beth-yerah was 25 ft. wide, but of mud brick. At Megiddo, too, in the course of the centuries the stone wall was covered over and replaced by one of mud brick. Then in Stratum X (Hyksos period) was erected a gateway of hewn-stone facing, filled in with rubble. This lasted in use through Stratum VII (1300–1150) and was destroyed about 1050. In its place, a small unimposing gate was erected in Stratum VI (1150–25), rebuilt in Stratum V (1050–950), and destroyed probably by David.

In the stratum above, a few yards farther E, was built "the finest fortified gate yet found in Palestine, certainly Solomonic," says Wright, though he claims that that stratum is not really IV but a combination of the lower part of IV with the upper part of V (*ca.* 950). The gate had four pairs of piers, and four entryways, with six chambers between the piers. The correspondence of this gate to the E temple gate of Ez 40:5 has been maintained by Howie in *BASOR* 117 (1950) 13–17. More recently Yadin has claimed that the blueprint and exact measurements of the Solomonic gateway at Megiddo are exactly duplicated both in the gate at Gezer (which had been called Roman) and in the Solomonic gate newly discovered at Hazor.

The stratum *after* Solomon was called III B by the excavators, but IVA (after 900) by Wright. It was only then, allegedly, that the quadruple gate was transformed into a triple gate, presumably by the armed forces of Pharaoh Sheshonk (Shishak) in occupying the city (though 2 Chr 12:4 mentions only his depredations in Judah). At a still later date, in Stratum III(A) around 800 BC, the triple wall was further reduced to a double one, possibly in the wars with Syrian Ben-hadad (2 Kgs 13:3).

The importance of such city gates far transcends the still-unsolved chronological dilemmas they present. As at Shechem and Lachish, and in Absalom's maneuvers of 2 Sm 15:2, we recognize that the so-called "gate" was really a tribunal, archive, and reception hall: in short, what we might accurately render "court house." Naturally, it was a gate as well, and precisely in the interest of defense contained a maze of passages; but the empty spaces between the doorways could readily be utilized for public business, and in fact constituted the forum or heartbeat of the civic life of the town.

38 *Shaft and treasury*. The history of the Megiddo water system is a saga in itself, told in a separate volume by R. Lamon. About 1050, to judge by a scarab of Ramses VI, a deep pit was dug in search of water. When none was found, it was decided to link the pit by a long tunnel leading directly to the spring at the W base of the mound. This immense engineering project could have been avoided if the diggers had gone only 6 ft deeper, where the underground water level has now been ascertained! The shaft was silted up during Solomon's peaceful reign, but was repaired and fitted out with a stair shortly before Josiah met his death at Megiddo in 609 (Jer 46:18). It is now accessible to tourists and scholars because it has been reopened by a grant of the U.S. Information Service, which has also installed nearby a splendidly instructive scale model of the whole excavation.

Another noteworthy feature visible today is the stone bin for grain storage under Jeroboam II, 750 BC. Megiddo was doubtless one of the towns used for storage of taxes collected "in kind," as attested by jar lids from all over Palestine bearing the inscription "For the King." At an earlier stage in its history (1150), Megiddo held treasures of a different kind, the *ivory carvings* contemporary to similar Phoenician samples from the Guadalquivir Valley in Spain.

And speaking of treasure, it must finally be noted that the Megiddo diggers overlooked a fragment of the cuneiform "Flood Epic" named after its hero Gilgamesh (→ Genesis, 2:39). This was picked up on a debris heap by a shepherd in 1956 and published in Israel's 1958 *Atiqot*. For pictures of Megiddo, see *ANEP* 332, 708, 712, 734, 742.

ARCHAEOLOGICAL PERIODS IN PALESTINE

Period	*Begins* BC *ca.*	*Typical Artifacts**
Old Stone Age	600,000	Fist-size flints, not retouched
Neanderthal	180,000	Willow-leaf flints, retouched; cave art (outside Palestine)
Mesolithic	10,000	Tiny flints curved to fit in sickle (agricultural beginnings)
Neolithic	7000	Polished flints; earliest pottery, but already quite "advanced" and even decorated with paint
Chalcolithic	4000	Cornet-cup, churn, lug handle, mat-base, rope molding; gray-beaded ware, house-shaped ossuaries; wall frescoes; fan-scraper flint; basalt brazier
Early Bronze	3200	Ledge handle, hole-mouth, button-base; orange crisscross pattern; extensive use of potter's wheel
Middle Bronze	2050	Carination, gracefulness of form never later surpassed; tripod or parabola base; Yahudiyeh-juglets of black ware with bands of white pinpoints
Late Bronze	1550	Metallic-ware chimneyed "bilbil"; milk bowl with wishbone handle; native panel-painting in several colors on "punch bowls"; Mycenaean glaze-like imports
Early Iron	1200	Pilgrim-flask, strainer spout, pinched lip, double handle, dumpy forms; Philistine panel-painting
Late Iron	900	Ring-burnish, Samaritan red ware; increased dumpiness; large jars with pointed base to stand up in sand
Persian, etc.	600	Dearth of artifacts everywhere in Palestine; but now *coins*! some Attic and Rhodian imports; sand-stand forms developed; terra-cotta coffins
Hellenistic	300	Gray-ware not quite eggshell-thin; sand-stand takes on form resembling Qumran jars
Early Roman	50	Spout-circle lamps, flat ribbing, Qumran jars; Petra red eggshell ware painted with red peacock-tails
Late Roman	AD 200	Terra sigillata, inimitably smooth red ware with maker's stamp and beveling or with embossed pattern; ribbing
Byzantine	AD 500	Christian cross! sharp-ridge metallic ribbing; style lags behind change of political regime
Muslim-Crusade	AD 800	Glass and almost universal presence of glazed-colored pottery (faience)

* Photographs or sketches of the artifacts or pottery mentioned in this table can be found in *IDB* 3, 847; Albright, *AP*; *The Holy Land*, 80–90.

In his work, *Archaeology of Palestine* (*AP*), Albright gives us a period-by-period survey of the results established by digging. We presume his authoritative comments, adding here a few recent developments or observations.

39 **(I) Prehistory: The Stone Ages.** Man first appeared upon earth about one million to six hundred thousand years ago, according to fossil-data. The day is long past when any serious exegete would seek to harmonize scientific paleontology with the imaginative and theological portrayal of earliest man in Gn 1–3. Still the facts behind the evolutionary theory will continue to hold an inordinate interest for the exegete. Here we treat primarily of the prehistorical situation in Palestine (cf. *BTS* 93 [1967]); for a wider treatment of the prehistorical period in the Near East, → History of Israel, 75:5–12.

40 **(A) Old Stone Age: Paleolithic.** The oldest traces of man, namely unstratified, elongated fist-flints, are called Chellean. (Names of this type come from the site at which a given style of implement was first discovered, mostly in France.) In the caves of Wadi Kharitun, SE of Bethlehem, the French scholar-consul René Neuville found Acheulean flints or perhaps a slightly older type called Tayacian, roughly contemporary to a style later found at Yabrud, N of Damascus.

41 Man's earliest *skeletal* remains date from somewhat later. But they were found in Palestine in such abundance during the 1930's that human life was seriously maintained to have originated here. We now have much older samples, including Teilhard's Peking man and the bones from Olduvai in Tanzania. Palestinian skeletons are all Neanderthal, contemporary to flints of willow-leaf shape called Aurignacian. The six humans discovered by Neuville in a cave at the Qafzeh precipice near Nazareth were at first thought to be Acheulean. Two others were found at the bottom of a long series of prehistoric strata excavated by D. Garrod and T. McCown in "Cave Valley" (*Wadi Mugharah*) near Atlit, S of Haifa. But the pioneer's crown goes to F. Turville-Petre of Oxford, who in 1925 discovered a youthful Neanderthal skeleton in the "Gypsy Cave" of Amud Valley, SW of Capernaum. This was the first recognition of strata in prehistoric Palestine.

42 "Prehistory" is a somewhat fluid term that we may at present conveniently define as "information about human culture, drawn mostly from flints, for the ages preceding the invention of agriculture, pottery, metallurgy, and writing." These four giant strides were not rigidly contemporary, but they are close enough to make this norm practical.

A good 50 years of ardent prehistoric research had preceded Turville-Petre. Quite by chance, this was the branch in which Catholics had taken the lead. In Jerusalem J. Germer-Durand at the Assumptionist seminary, D. Buzy at the diocesan seminary, and other priests at the White Fathers' Melchite seminary and elsewhere began gathering and classifying earliest flints. These were paralleled on the Phoenician coast by Jesuits Zumoffen and Bovier-Lapierre. Thus in 1917 the German priest Paul Karge had considerable empirical data, which he used accurately to write his history of the Rephaim, or pre-Israelite inhabitants of Palestine. For the Paleolithic period in Palestine, see C. McCown, *op. cit.*, 18–42; Albright *AP* 49–58.

43 **(B) Later Stone Ages.** A rather passionate controversy rages as to whether the Old Stone Age or "Paleolithic" was followed by any transitional or bridge-periods before the clearly defined pottery types of the Bronze Age. The terms "Mesolithic" and "Neolithic" had been applied from Europe in face of articulate opposition, and "Chalcolithic" was a Palestinian invention of Albright. However, it would seem that the time has come to combine all three terms into a single designation for "the transit from a food-gathering to a food-producing economy," including the period up to the use of pottery and unrefined metals. This period would last only from about 10,000 to 3,000 BC and might properly be called "Ceramolithic." But meanwhile we must be able to recognize the separate stages in prevailing terminology. The dates indicated are those assigned by most archaeologists and are approximate.

44 (a) MESOLITHIC (10,000–7,000). In a valley called Natuf, NW of Jerusalem, the Jesuit A. Mallon found a flint deposit that he ceded to Dorothy Garrod. Here in 1928 she identified a flint industry akin to "Tardenoisian." This Natufian is for practical purposes coextensive with the Palestinian "Mesolithic." It embodies two principal phenomena. The flints are often tiny or "microliths" an inch long. And they are often curved to be mounted in a sickle. Thus they are interpreted as attesting the first appearance of food-producing communities in the holy land. Cf. C. McCown, *op. cit.*, 43–51; Albright, *AP* 58–61; K. Kenyon, *Archaeology*, 36–43.

45 (b) NEOLITHIC (7000–4000). Similarly, the Neolithic has a characteristic flint called Tahunian from the mother site near Bethlehem explored by D. Buzy. The mark of Neolithic flints is their polished smoothness. Also Neolithic, but in grotesque contrast to the microliths of the preceding era, are the huge "Megalithic" monuments, or dolmens, of Palestine. These are fields of giant stones, generally one lying flat on two others, found especially in Transjordan near Lisan, Ghassul, Damiyeh, and Shamir (*BA* 29 [1966] 106–14). They are called tombs by M. Stekelis (*Monuments mégalithiques* [Paris, 1935]), but designated dwellings by the Albright school (*JBL* 59 [1940] 479–97; *AASOR* 25 [1951] 150). In either case they must have appeared to the untutored eye of the first Israelites as the product of a race of giants, since even today we cannot fathom the force used to move such huge rocks into place without engineering devices. Diana Kirkbride has excavated an interesting early Neolithic village at Beida in Transjordan (*Arch* 19 [1966] 199–207). The excavations of Miss Kenyon at Jericho (→ 19 above) show the prepottery Neolithic construction of a tower and rampart, mammoth in proportions, though of ordinary-size stones. But among these Neolithic denizens she also found a unique form of sculpture, restoring lifelikeness to human skulls by plaster and shell incrustation. Well on in the Neolithic period, pottery making began—or rather, we then find the first surviving samples of a technique that is already highly advanced. Cf. K. Kenyon, *Archaeology*, 43ff. For Near Eastern Neolithic, see *BASOR* 184 (1966) 2–6.

46 (c) CHALCOLITHIC (4000–3200). But it is the subsequent or "Chalcolithic" period that is supposed to denote the transition from predominance of flint tools to predominance of pottery, although the prefix "chalco-" actually means bronze or copper. (Even in the Bronze Age itself metallic nomenclature is misleading, at least for Palestine, because the culture-divisions are all marked off exclusively in terms of pottery.)

47 One of the disputed issues in Chalcolithic archaeology is the chronological relation of finds made at other sites to those made at Ghassul. Was there a pre-Ghassulian stage of Chalcolithic? Was there a post-Ghassulian stage, contemporary with the period characterized by "Esdraelon gray-ware"? Was Albright inalterably correct in postulating that the Ghassulian era was prior to the Early Bronze? The key site in these discussions, a series of low mounds called *ghassûl* (soap-plant), 4 mi. NE of the Dead Sea, was excavated for the Pontifical Biblical Institute by A. Mallon from 1929 to 1934. His work was continued in 1936 and 1938 by R. Koeppel and reopened in 1960 by the present author. See *BTS* 52 (1963). The complex combination of unusual tools found at Ghassul has since appeared at almost 100 other Palestine sites, sometimes followed by earliest Bronze Age remains.

There is one important discrepancy. A unique and unimpeachable characteristic of the culture found at Ghassul itself is its polychrome wall-fresco art of an imaginativeness and technical competence not later equaled in Palestine's history. An eight-pointed star, a procession, and a sort of leaping tiger all are accompanied by black masks with great staring eyes, not unlike the necklace-amulets found there in both stone and pottery. No trace of this art has been found at the other "Ghassulian" sites.

A widespread feature of the same culture-complex turned out to be the "house-shaped ossuary" of Hedera (Khudeirah; see sketch in Albright, *AP* 69). Other samples found in 1958 at Azor near Tel Aviv imitate architectural elements even more, but amusingly combine these with traits of the human face. A more abundant, but geographically more restricted, supplement to Ghassulian features constitutes the so-called Esdraelon grayware. This is a type of bright gray jar with beadlike bulges on the sharp edge or "carination" running around its middle. This subculture has been dated some 200 years *after* Ghassul. Finally at Beersheba Jean Perrot has added to the Ghassulian culture traits a catacomb of burrow-dwellings, together with strong reason for dating the whole complex well into the Early Bronze Age. It will be clear, therefore, why we claim that a reassessment of the whole "Ceramolithic" transitional culture will soon have to take place.

48 **(II) The Bronze Ages.**

(A) Early Bronze Age (3200–*ca.* 2050). Writing was invented about 3200, simultaneously in Iran and at Warka. It was quickly adopted by Semites invading Ur (→ History of Israel, 75:15). Thus documented history began. But for 1000 years more, broken pottery continues to be our chief source of information about chronology and culture developments. The period from the invention of writing to the arrival of Abraham in Palestine corresponds roughly to the cultural unit called the Early Bronze (EB) Age.

49 The great classic excavations like Megiddo and Jericho contained immense EB deposits. At Beth-shan and Megiddo, and recently at Tirzah and Meser, this EB pottery is found rather inextricably united with a doubtful "late Chalcolithic" that seems to have some Ghassulian characteristics. And even the typical style called either "grain-wash" or "band-slip" at Khirbet el-Kerak is identical in *technique* with the dull filmy "reserve slip" of Ghassul, however conspicuously different may appear the Kerak orange color and crisscross pattern. But at Jericho just across the Jordan Plain from Ghassul there was a total lack of all the traits associated with Chalcolithic. Hence it is now generally agreed, most articulately by G. Ernest Wright in the Mazar-volume (*Eretz-Israel Annual* 5 [1958]), that some rewriting will have to be done in Wright's own masterful pioneer work, *The Pottery of Palestine from the Earliest Times to the End of the Early Bronze Age* (New Haven, 1937).

50 There are four periods distinguished in EB, beginning about 3200, 2900, 2700, and 2300. After that there is a sort of no-man's-land, involving in part a cultural lacuna, and in part a period of transition quite distinct both from EB and from the subsequent culture-complex (→ 52 below). Really the most distinctive Palestinian evidence of *earliest* EB comes from the work of P. Bar-Adon and his Israel Exploration associates at the powerful fortress on the SW bank of the Sea of Galilee, probably called Beth-yerah, but now Khirbet el-Kerak. The orange crisscross "band-slip" is a reliable indicator of the earliest, or 3000 phase. In Jerusalem-Ophel and other contemporary sites in Judea, the crisscross style appears as genuine painting, varied by wavy or merely parallel lines.

Two recent excavations promise to add greatly to our knowledge of the first phases of the EB period. At Bab edh-Dhraʿ, E of the Lisan peninsula, Paul Lapp has found important burials from earliest EB (*Arch* 19 [1966] 104–11; *BASOR* 189 [1968] 12–41). At Taanach, Lapp has uncovered three massive fortifications from the period 2700–2500 (*BASOR* 173 [1964] 1–44).

Characteristic of the *second*, or 2800 phase of EB at Kerak is a graceful elongated jug with squat base. This style is named for Abydos in Egypt, where it was found in abundance along with dating records of Pharaoh Menes of the First Dynasty. Similar pottery appears in the large and well-planned city (destroyed *ca.* 2700) that has been unearthed by Ruth Amiran in the 1962–67 Israeli excavation of Arad, some 20 mi. E of Beer-sheba. Of note are the thick city walls with semicircular protective towers, and the uniform architecture of the rectangular houses with sunken living rooms (*BA* 31 [1968] 3–4).

For the *third*, or 2500 phase, the most characteristic pottery is that which has been called without qualification "Khirbet Kerak ware." It is a shiny red or black, and has nothing whatever in common with either the crisscross-slip or the Abydos jug,—two other Kerak dating characteristics. These three Kerak criteria, though sharply focused, are scarcely found elsewhere. But the "dead giveaway" style of the EB at any site in Canaan is the ledge handle. The alleged samples at Ghassul should more accurately be called lug handles; they are pinched up out of the clay of the vessel-belly, and are often vertical, containing an "eyelet" for inserting a cord. As distinct from these, the Jericho ledge handles are an inch wide and several inches long, almost invariably horizontal. They form a chronological series that develops from simpler into very complex "scallop" or "envelope" forms, rarely perforated.

The *final phase* of EB, down to about 2050, is either inadequately explored or never had any striking originalities. Hence it is recognized chiefly by the presence of these ledge handles *without* any of the three Kerak trademarks. An abundance of EB pottery came from Ai but unfortunately was never classified by the excavator, Judith Marquet-Krause, because of her premature death. (For the recent Ai excavation, cf. *BASOR* 178 [1965] 13–40; *BA* 28 [1965] 26–30.)

51 Strangely, the most valuable late EB excavation for biblical study is not in Palestine, but at Mari on the Euphrates. Here since 1933 André Parrot has dug up palaces containing many cuneiform archives and discovered other unique evidence of the Semite immigration waves that flooded over the Tigris Valley before and with Abraham. (In fact, finds at Mari in the subsequent MB period have influenced the discussion of the dating both of Abraham and of Hammurabi [→ History of Israel, 75:20].) The classic S Mesopotamian excavations too, Ur and Warka and the others, inform us about the pre-Abraham background. Mesopotamian EB also furnishes vivid scenes of religion and art on the so-called cylinder seals (*ANEP* 672–702). These, when rolled on soft clay, left a 2 × 4 in. frieze to serve as the owner's signet or signature. Several such seals, dated rather reliably to the "Jemdet Nasr" period around 3000, were found at M. Dunand's excavation of Byblos in Phoenicia, and also buried just below the shiny red-black Khirbet el-Kerak ware at Judeideh in the Antioch plain. The EB millennium is also valuably represented at Alaja in central Turkey, a few miles N of Bogazkoy, the later Hittite capital. (On EB, cf. Albright, *AP* 71–79; K. Kenyon, *Archaeology*, 101–34; → History of Israel, 75:14–18.)

52 [*Editor's addition* (REB): In the previous discussion and in what follows, the author of the article is presenting what has been the standard view of the end of the EB period and the beginning of the MB period—a view that students should learn as still representing the consensus of scholarship. However, since the article has been submitted, there has been considerable excavation of late EB cemeteries in Palestine; and now a new view is being seriously proposed that may change radically our views of what happened in Palestine in this period. This view is well documented in P. Lapp, *The Dhahr Mirzbaneh Tombs* (ASOR Publications; New Haven, 1966) 86–116; and a synopsis is presented here with the understanding that the suggestions are tentative. Modifying proposals of Kathleen Kenyon and others, Lapp would not speak of EB IV and MB I but would designate the period between 2300 and 1900/1850 as the Intermediate Bronze (IB) Age. He dates IB I from 2300 to 2050, and IB II from 2050 to 1900/1850. The change of name is important, for the period denotes an intrusive rather than a transitional culture.

Archaeologists have recognized that the great urban culture of EB came to an end rather abruptly; and Albright, De Vaux, and Kenyon have traced this eclipse to invading Semites, specifically Amorites. As we shall see below, the patriarchs were associated with the tail end of this Amorite invasion. One of the archaeological marks of the invaders was the shaft-tomb style of burial, and Lapp has excavated important cemeteries of these tombs at Dhahr Mirzbaneh (about 18 mi. NE of Jerusalem, near Taiyibeh) and at Bab edh-Dhraʿ (just E of the Lisan peninsula). He points out that there is evidence for shaft tombs *before* the urban period of EB, and he suggests that the city folk of the EB period lived in the presence of hostile nonurbanites. This would explain the tremendous fortifications of EB cities.

In the 23rd cent. he sees a wave of new nonurbanites who ravaged Syria and Palestine. They came to dominate Palestine much more than Syria, so that during the IB period Palestine became a cultural backwater with no traces of literacy and nothing parallel to the sophistication and wealth implicit in Egyptian and Syrian art and architecture. Lapp does not think that these invaders were Amorites but rather part of a large wave of invaders that disrupted life throughout the Mediterranean world. He points out parallels in burial pattern, in settlement, in metallurgy, and even in physiognomy to what has been found in excavations from this period in Cyprus, Anatolia, Greece, the Aegean isles, Sicily, and Spain. The invasion of Palestine seems to have come both from the sea and from inland routes to the N. Lapp thinks that the invaders were non-Semites from Central Asia who, repulsed in an attempt to invade Mesopotamia, swept on to the Mediterranean area.

These non-Semitic invaders would have preceded the patriarchs; perhaps they were the Perizzites (or "open-country dwellers") who were in the land with the Canaanites when Abraham arrived (Gn 13:7). The Amorite and patriarchal movement would mark the beginning of the MB period *ca.* 1850. Contrast this dating to what is found below. For Albright's reaction to Lapp's reconstruction, cf. *BASOR* 184 (1966) 26–35.]

53 **(B) Middle Bronze Age (*ca.* 2050–1550).** Now we enter the era of Abraham and Joseph. The migrating horde, with whom both were associated, had neither ethnic nor political unity. The bulk of that horde seems to have been those Semites who already for 1000 years had been on the move from their Arabian or Syrian homeland. Abraham is usually associated with the Amorite phase of that movement, and Joseph is associated with the Hyksos phase (→ History of Israel, 75:20, 22).

The Hyksos flood penetrated as far as Egypt in 1700 (→ History of Israel, 75:22, 31). At intervals along their route they left the telltale white-speck-painted black ware called the Tell el-Yahudiyeh juglet. Far less valid in this writer's mind is the claim that the "sloping walls" of various kinds revealed by excavation can be lumped together as a single culture-manifestation called the "Hyksos glacis." Less obvious still is Albright's allegation (*AP* 86) that these sloping walls were created as a spontaneous reaction of defense against chariot warfare. This was widely accepted until the recent research of Yadin, which caused Miss Kenyon to withdraw her previous adherence. In Albright's favor it must be emphasized that the meager indications of the horse that excavation has yielded so far are, in fact, from *ca.* 1500, close in time to the Hyksos period.

54 Far more impressive and abundant than the Hyksos artifacts are the styles already in use among the local populations where they infiltrated. The MB period was truly the climax of artistry in Palestine ceramics. Though there was no widespread use of painting or "adventitious" decoration, still the shape of the vessels now possesses an exquisite simplicity and gracefulness of line never later surpassed. The rounded base makes a perfect parabola, then curves upward and in toward the rim at just the right point to give an impression of balance and charm. Similar but more slender vessels are called dippers. In other cases, the flattened base was attached to a delicate low pedestal, and the curve at the belly was replaced by a sharp edge like the keel of a ship, called "carination." The valuable study by H. Otto in *ZDPV* 61 (1938) 147–277 must now be supplemented by the endless profusion of MB forms yielded by the Jericho tombs excavated in 1952–58, already published as a separate volume but copiously described also on p. 191 of Miss Kenyon's *Archaeology*.

All of the Canaanite MB production is strikingly homogeneous from 1900 to 1600—from Abraham to Joseph! It is largely this native Canaanite MB culture that was so masterfully recorded by Albright in his excavation of Tell Beit Mirsim. Comparative material is now available from Megiddo and Lachish, from Sharuhen and Tirzah, and from the settlement preceding Antipatris. The MB Age came to an end about 1600 or a little later.

55 Outside Palestine, the Abraham era is chiefly acclaimed at the American excavation of *Nuzi* (*BA* 3 [1940] 1–12, or *BAR* 2, 21–33). But the master excavation of this period is Ras Shamra (*Ugarit*) at the NW seacoast corner of Syria. The whole MB flourishing of the ancient city-state of Ugarit (→ Excursus Israel, 11:11–12), along with most of Late Bronze, is lumped by excavator Claude Schaeffer into a single endless "stratum." As often happens outside Palestine, the humble potsherd claims little attention at Ugarit because it is overshadowed by torrents of art work and literary documents. Newly discovered there is the whole language called Ugaritic, possibly a NW-Semitic dialect, but so close to biblical Hebrew that some experts speak of them as if they were identical. The mythology of the Ugaritic epics also clarifies many obscure allusions of the Bible (*BA* 8 [1945] 41–58, or *BAR* 2, 34–50). And the diplomatic archives of Ugarit form an indispensable link between the Hittite Empire to the N, the Hurrians to the E, and the Canaanite city-states dependent upon Egypt to the S. Cf. A. F. Rainey, *BA* 28 (1965) 102–25. (On MB period, see Albright, *AP* 80–96; K. Kenyon, *Archaeology*, 135–94; for the civilization of the Negeb in Abraham's time, cf. *BA* 18 [1955] 2–9.)

56 **(C) Late Bronze Age (1550–1200).** The final stage in the long culture-epoch misnamed "Bronze" is undoubtedly the period of Moses and the Exodus. But the more precise dating of this event is the major unsolved enigma of archaeology.

(a) Exodus in 1500's? We have expressed our complete agreement with the view that the Joseph saga is a reflection and a part of the Hyksos tribal movements southward, which can be dated about 1700. Well then, logically one should be disposed to agree that the *ejection* of the Hyksos by the Egyptian nationalist Pharaoh Amosis in 1580 gave occasion for the Exodus. It was in fact fashionable a century ago to regard the powerful and long-reigning Thutmosis III as Pharaoh of the Exodus. But we may say at once that this view is all but abandoned today.

57 (b) Exodus in 1370? The cuneiform archive ("Amarna tablets"; see *BA* 23 [1960] 2–22) whose background was excavated at Amarna, ancient Akhetaton on the Nile, shows that in 1370 Pharaoh Amenopis IV Akhenaton (the "monotheistic" Pharaoh) received from the city-states of Canaan constant appeals for protection against organized gangsters called Ḫabiru (ʿApiru). As a *name*, this can be equated with "Hebrews"; see discussion in Albright *FSAC* 240. But it often happens that any name can be applied to two entirely unconnected realities, especially when its "sameness" is due to accidental quirks of spelling. Nevertheless, it would be imprudent to ignore how relevant to the Exodus problem is the fact that a migratory underprivileged people *called* Hebrews were prowling through Canaan in 1370.

If we reject this as a proof that Moses had led the Israelites out of Egypt some 40 years earlier, then we have to consider the claim of H. H. Rowley's *From Joseph to Joshua* (London, 1950) that these Ḫabiru were the Joseph tribe, and that they never even entered Egypt until after 1370. But a third possibility remains open: These Ḫabiru-"Hebrews" may have been a "collateral branch" or cousins of those who went down with Jacob into Egypt. Even if we defend the historicity of the 12 tribes with a literalness scarcely favored by sound exegetic norms, we can still admit a branch of Asher or Issachar as a "Fifth Column" within Palestine quietly preparing for the return of their cousins from Egypt.

58 The Amarna episode in Egyptian history does not interest us only because of its archive with numerous names of Canaanite cities menaced by Ḫabiru. The Amarna period was also the center of a twofold reform unique in history. Rejecting the stylized charm of Egyptian art, Akhenaton's court introduced honest realism. Not only was this Pharaoh portrayed with all his physical defects, but he was also shown among his subjects as well as in everyday situations of family life. In addition, in place of the horde of vultures and vipers worshiped as gods at Thebes, there was rigidly enforced at Amarna the worship of only one god. This god was portrayed under the image of the Sun-Disk, whose rays terminate in tiny hands reaching down to bless the king and his people. The twofold reform was crushed after Akhenaton's death. Tut-ankh-Amon restored the capital to Thebes, and there received the sumptuous burial (King "Tut's" tomb; C. Ceram, *Gods*, 173–206) whose unearthing in 1923 unleashed a world-wide flood of interest in archaeology. Technically, the Amarna effort may not have been monotheism and must certainly have been a movement going far deeper than the weak Pharaoh who consented to act as its spokesman. But there is every reason to believe that after it was officially put down, it continued to seethe in sympathetic strata of the population. Thus, as Albright (*FSAC* 223, 257ff.) suggests, it probably influenced the degraded Hebrews among whom Moses was born shortly afterward.

59 (c) Exodus in 1200's? Archaeological support for the dating of the Exodus just after 1300 is claimed from various lines of approach. Albright in the 1930's felt quite secure that a violent interruption of normal life at Mirsim (Debir?) was corroborated by the excavations of Lachish and Jericho that were then going on. As for Ai (supposedly conquered by Joshua; → Joshua, 7:27) he admitted that the site was unexpectedly devoid of occupation; but he explained this by the shuttling of a single settlement from Bethel, a nearby site that he had excavated. (We mentioned above [→ 32] the adventuresome postulate of a similar shuttling between Taanach and Megiddo, to account for the lacunas in strata excavated at those two sites.) It must be admitted, however, that this "shuttling" never won the acceptance that most of Albright's pronouncements rightly inspired. At any rate, his trump card was N. Glueck's surface explorations throughout Transjordan. All these investigations supposedly proved that some monstrous invading force had crossed the Jordan and had entered Canaan from the SE in the LB Age.

60 The real obstacle to Albright's theory was the archaeological evidence from Jericho—evidence being interpreted in two different ways, neither reconcilable with his theory. Garstang, the excavator of Jericho, maintained that the absence of Mycenaean pottery at Jericho (and at Hazor, also excavated by Garstang) meant that the city had been destroyed (by Joshua) before 1400, since after that date imported Mycenaean pottery was found throughout Palestine. Therefore, the Israelite invasion was no later than 1385. Thus too the Ḫabiru evidences were corroborated. But being a pottery-chronology expert, Père Vincent was more readily heeded, and he claimed that the Jericho mound contained few but inescapable traces of occupation as late as 1250. Albright tried to get the two men to compromise on 1325 but with indifferent success. All three incidentally were quite positive and unanimous about the unearthed wall catastrophically destroyed by Joshua. They all took more or less for granted that the sherds they were arguing about, though found elsewhere, were contemporary to the tumbled-down wall.

61 It was really to solve the dilemma of this wall's date that Miss Kenyon (→ 19 above) organized the third major excavation of Jericho (Tell es-Sultan) during 1952–58. Her discoveries were shattering. The alleged Joshua wall contained within itself an abundance of pottery to prove beyond cavil its demolition before 2000! Moreover, nowhere on the mound was there any genuine deposit firmly attesting occupation at any time between 1500 and 800. With understandable professional courtesy, her publication of these unexpected results was hedged with such qualifications and hypotheses as to cause no embarrassment to the scholars mentioned above nor to create a lack of confidence on the part of the general public in the reliability of archaeology as a science.

62 But the real significance of the case lies in the fact that the LB lacuna at Ai is now paralleled and reinforced at Jericho. In comparison with these major sites neither the destruction of Lachish and of Mirsim (not mentioned in Jos) nor the Transjordan surface explorations carry sufficient weight, in the present author's judgment. The German expert Martin Noth acclaims this contradictory archaeological evidence as proof of what he had been saying all along. For him Jos consists entirely of "etiological" bedtime stories, made up out of whole cloth to make existing place-names interesting or rememberable (→ History of Israel, 75:42–46). In an effort to refute him, some American archaeologists have shown themselves willing to jettison the most solid scientific basis of all 20th-cent. Palestine localization: the principle of Abel and Glueck that no site can be considered biblical if it is lacking in pottery-remains of the period in question. But the unwisdom of such a procedure is tacitly acknowledged by G. E. Wright in his essay in *BANE* 73–112; he prefers to leave the Jericho evidence as an unsolved enigma.

63 Meanwhile at Hazor the major postwar excavation of Y. Yadin (→ 21 above) has uncovered a mass of Mycenaean pottery. But the *coup de grâce* thus given to

Garstang's theorizing leaves the essentials of the Jericho-Ai situation untouched. An entirely different dilemma has arisen from the Hazor results. Yadin's competent collaborator Y. Aharoni, abetted by B. Mazar, the archaeologist-rector of the Hebrew University, interprets the stratification to mean that Hazor was not destroyed until the *12th* cent., as described in Jgs 4, and that the Joshua campaign (enigmatic anyway, so far to the N!) is a misunderstood report on the Deborah campaign. More positive information on MB and LB at Hazor is provided by its three remarkable temples. One of these contained statuary and steles with MB Hittite motifs. Another contained an MB altar overturned by techniques reminiscent of those later recommended by the Hebrew prophets. A third shows an MB Hittite style (like that of Solomon's Temple) continuing in use through LB. Cf. Y. Yadin, *BAR* 2, 191–224.

64 [*Editor's addition* (REB): On concluding the discussion of the archaeological evidence pertinent to the Exodus, we see that there are difficulties for each of the three dating theories mentioned above. Many exegetes today maintain that the biblical account of the Exodus and of the entry into Palestine has drawn together into one consecutive narrative a series of events originally scattered over several centuries. Some propose that there were several departures from Egypt of Semites who would afterwards form Israel. First, some would have left Egypt in the early 1500's with the Hyksos (→ 56 above), and presumably they destroyed Jericho. Second, in the mid-1300's a collateral line of future Israelites were part of the Ḫabiru movement mentioned in the Amarna evidence; some of them settled down in Palestine as they were harassing the Canaanite city-states (→ 57 above). Third, in the early 1200's there was a departure from Egypt of future Israelites under Moses (→ 59 above); some of these may have entered Palestine from the S, while others may have come across the Jordan with Joshua.

For an archaeologist, Albright's chronology for the Israelite conquest of Canaan can be verified only by unearthing convincing evidence that there was *one* over-all destruction of Palestinian sites at a date in the mid-1200's. The recent excavations by H. J. Franken at Tell Deir Alla (Succoth?) seem to lend more support to Albright's theory, for a destruction *ca.* 1200 is indicated; see articles in *VT* from 1960 on. Thus, in the S, in the N, and in the Jordan Valley cities were destroyed during this general period of 1250–1200.]

65 If we lay aside the Exodus-dating headache, noteworthy LB contributions are recorded chiefly at Megiddo and Beth-shan. Megiddo has yielded a characteristic large bowl, almost a foot in diameter, called krater or punch bowl, with painting in two colors. Parallel bands above the belly are divided into squares containing animal and geometric motifs (Albright, *AP* 98). This style is a snare to the unwary who are apt to mistake it for the very similar Philistine pottery of the next epoch, but close comparison shows recognizable distinctions in the two styles. Beth-shan contains a succession of LB temples built while the site was an Egyptian enclave; but their interest for us concerns a later day when they were transformed by the Philistines and used to dishonor their fallen enemy Saul (1 Sm 31:10). For the archaeological history of Beth-shan, see *BA* 30 (1967) 110–35.

66 **(III) The Iron Ages.**

(A) Early Iron Age (1200–900). The transition from bronze to iron tools is rather sharply fixed at 1200 BC. By an important coincidence, this date fits also the simultaneous entry into Palestine of two invading peoples. From the S and E, out of Egypt came the Hebrews. From the NW Aegean islands came the Philistines (→ Excursus Israel, 11:19–20), possibly in a succession of expeditions beginning as early as the Homeric siege of Troy, but resulting in a firm domination of the Gaza coast only around 1150. This coast and the "pentapolis" (→ Biblical Geography, 73:71–72) were the heartland of Philistine power, although their control seemingly extended up the coast as far as Dor, and eastward to Beth-shan and Succoth in the Jordan Valley.

67 The pottery of the Iron Age Philistines, despite the Megiddo resemblances described above (→ 65), is one of our clearest norms for dating any mound in SW Palestine. For Albright, hip flasks, wine kraters, and beer jugs with strainer spouts imaginatively add up to the conclusion: "The Philistines were mighty carousers, as we see from the story of Samson." More inescapably Philistine are ornamental features such as the "backward-looking swan with tired wingspread," painted on a krater with almost vertical loop-handles. The swan is sometimes varied by other motifs such as a fish, and each panel is framed with bands and spirals.

By a fortunate coincidence, the richest deposit of this style of Aegean origin was encountered by Duncan Mackenzie at Beth-shemesh while he was fresh from his experience at Knossos in Crete. The Aegean parentage has been corroborated also by the excavation of P. Dikaios at Enkomi in Cyprus. Strangely, Beth-shemesh itself is expressly featured in 1 Sm 6:12 as lying *outside* Philistine territory. Either the frontier fluctuated, or wares were traded across the border.

68 Smaller Philistine deposits or stray sherds are found at many mounds W of Beth-shemesh, but only at Ashkelon and Ashdod (*BA* 26 [1962] 136) among the five Philistine cities (→ Biblical Geography, 73:71–72). We know from the story of Saul's death (1 Sm 31:10) that the Philistines had an enclave as far NE as Beth-shan. Some coffin lids from there may reflect the same Philistine influences as those at Sharuhen. (On Philistine coffins, cf. G. E. Wright, *BA* 22 [1959] 53–66, or *BAR* 2, 59–68.) Megiddo actually contained Philistine pottery. But there was none at the nearby "sea-folk" settlement of Dor (→ Biblical Geography, 73:79). Miss Kenyon (*Archaeology*, 231) denies that the pottery at Hawam near Haifa is Philistine, and even expresses some reserve as to whether the style described above really deserves to be called Philistine at all. More recently, elaborate Israeli excavations have been undertaken inland from Ashkelon at a crossroads site named "Tell Gath" by Israeli authorities in deference to Albright's suggested (but incorrect) identification of the site of Philistine Gath. But here too there was a disappointing lack of Philistine ware. The site was provisionally, in face of Yadin's opposition, claimed to be the storage city "Mamshith" attested by tax receipts at excavations elsewhere in Judah.

69 It is chiefly the influence of Matthew Arnold that has made the word "Philistine" a synonym of the crude uncultured boor. But we must acknowledge that the Bible's contempt for the Philistines is never on the plane of human culture, where excavation shows them to have been far superior to the Israelites. In fact we may safely maintain that the chosen people, while developing their enduring spiritual and ethical worship on the soil of the holy land, were content to lag behind or borrow the culture-forms of their neighbors. One evidence of the cultural pre-eminence of the Philistines was their monopoly of iron. It is interesting that the land shared by the Philistines and the Israelites ultimately came to be named Palestine after the former. On the Philistines, cf. K. Kenyon, *Archaeology*, 221–39; *BA* 29 (1966) 70–102; *RB* 71 (1964) 215–29; T. Dothan, *The Philistines and Their Material Culture* (Hebrew, with copious illustrations; Jerusalem, 1967).

70 Meanwhile, in those areas of Canaan that were not specifically Philistine, the pottery style hit its lowest ebb in the Iron Age, coinciding with Israelite infiltration. The materials are coarse and the shapes are dumpy; the total impression of a collection of Iron Age pottery is the least aesthetic of any period. Several small but important sites near Jerusalem have been excavated by Americans, especially Albright at Gibeah (*BA* 27 [1964] 52–64; also 28 [1965] 2–10), at Bethel (cf. *BA* 19 [1956] 36–43), and at Beth-zur; Badé at Tell en-Nasbeh (Mizpah? *BA* 10 [1947] 69–77); and recently Pritchard at Gibeon (*BA* 19 [1956] 66–75; 23 [1960] 23–29; 24 [1961] 19–24; also *Gibeon, Where the Sun Stood Still* [Princeton, 1962]; BTS 56 [1963]). Early Iron Age pottery is especially abundant at the Danish excavations of Shiloh. This corroborates the portrayal of Shiloh in 1 Sm 1:3; 4:3 as a center of pilgrimage focused around the Ark of the Covenant.

Saul's capital was at Gibeah just across the modern road from Samuel's bailiwick at Mizpah (Nasbeh?) and Gibeon, near the tower now called Nebi Samwil, a landmark. The citadel anciently called Jebus or Salem or Urushalim was at that SE corner of Jerusalem which is somewhat loosely called Ophel. Information about David's occupation of Jebus, especially by means of the *ṣinnôr* (2 Sm 5:8; → shaft?), has been sought by Bliss, Parker, Crowfoot, and Weill (J. Simons, *Jerusalem in the Old Testament* [Leiden, 1952] 168ff.). Since 1961 work has been resumed here by Miss Kenyon (→ 19 above; for bibliography, → Biblical Geography, 73:94).

71 The spread of David's empire and the building activities of Solomon are archaeologically attested by an innovation called the casemate, i.e., two parallel defense walls partitioned into chambers for storage or lodging. Although the Solomonic stratum identified by the Megiddo excavators has been re-evaluated by Albright and Yadin (→ 34 above), it would seem that both the stables and the city gate still visible there are among our most instructive excavation results from the United Monarchy. Other styles attested about this time especially at Megiddo are the header-stretcher masonry and the proto-Aeolic capital (sketches in Albright, *AP* 126–27).

The excavation conducted by B. Mazar-Maisler at Tell Qasileh, N of Tel Aviv (*BA* 14 [1951] 43–50), has uncovered a large administrative building attributed to David and Solomon. The considerable settlement surrounding it may well have been the "Israelite Joppa" (2 Chr 2:16; Ezr 3:17) involved in the transshipment of the Temple cedars.

72 It seems appropriate to summarize here the information we have gathered from excavations elsewhere about the probable structural details of Solomon's Temple (diagram, → Religious Institutions, 76:56–59). The clearest and most satisfactory initial approach to envisioning the finished product is the existing complete temple of Edfu in S Egypt. Although this temple was built some 700 years after Solomon, it preserves with utmost conservatism a style that is attested, by partial ruins elsewhere, as far back as 300 years before him. We know that Solomon had not only a marriage alliance but also other close cultural contacts with Egypt, the "arbiter of elegance" for its neighbors. Also instructive is the temple of Baʿalbek in Lebanon, built about the same time as that of Edfu. Even though it is partially destroyed, incomplete, and shows everywhere garish traces of Greco-Roman interpolations, there is still cogency in the fact that it was built by an architect of the same Phoenician race as the one who drew Solomon's blueprints. Very recently at Hazor the main temple of a group of several Bronze Age temples was found to have a recognizable ground plan. The similarity in plan of the Hazor temple to the temple at Alalakh (now Tell Atshana in N Syria), the capital of a Syro-Hittite kingdom, reveals that Hittite styles had an influence on the Temple of Solomon, which was built along the same general lines. See also the design of the Tainat temple (→ Religious Institutions, 76:56–59). The remains of these temples show that the innermost "Holy of Holies" was approached from an outer sanctum, which in turn was shielded by an imposing porch.

We cannot ignore the influences of a local Canaanite cult, of course. From the centuries preceding Solomon, important temples were brought to light in the excavations of Lachish, Megiddo, Shechem, and Ai. At Arad in the Negeb, occupied by Kenite clans related to Judah (→ Biblical Geography, 73:88), recent Israeli excavations have unearthed a temple to Yahweh from the monarchical period, having the same peculiar E-W axis as its contemporary, the Temple in Jerusalem (see *BA* 31 [1968] 18–30). The two temples had similarities in architecture and furnishing (→ Religious Institutions, 76:56–57, 74).

73 **(B) Later Iron Age (900–600).** The archaeological divisions of the Iron Age are not as uniform as those of the Bronze Age. We may safely regard "Iron II" as coextensive with the Divided Kingdom (922–587) of Judah-Israel. After the Exile (539 on) we find political designations used instead of metals, but it is still the pottery that really affords the basis of division.

When, under Jeroboam I, Samaria broke off from subjection to the house of David, it had no permanent capital city for a while. In 876 Omri became king at Tirzah on the NE slope of Mt. Ebal (excavated by R. de Vaux; → 18 above), where he soon started to build a palace. However, he abruptly changed his plan and moved his capital 10 mi. W. There on the western slope of the mountain range, in view of the Mediterranean, he built an entirely new city under the name of Shomron or Samaria. Cf. A. Parrot, *Samaria* (SBA 7; London, 1958); G. E. Wright, *BA* 22 (1959) 67–78, or *BAR* 2, 248–57.

74 The excavation of Samaria was begun by G. A. Reisner in 1908–10 and continued by J. W. Crowfoot in 1931–35. The city wall, like those of Mirsim and Lachish, seems in Albright's opinion to show the introduction of a new indirect-access gateway of a type still visible today in the entries to old Jerusalem (yet the earlier walls of Nasbeh and of Solomonic Megiddo already exemplify this principle). The most imposing building cleared by Reisner was at the top of the hill, underneath the remains of a Herodian temple to Augustus. (The Roman emperor's name in its Gk form *Sebastē* was given in Herodian times to the whole city and survives in the present Arabic name of the site, Sebastiyeh.)

The building of the hilltop palace seems to have been begun by Omri and continued by his son Ahab (869–50), and also by Jeroboam II (786–46). It contains beautifully carved ivories rivaling those of Megiddo from an earlier century (*ANEP* 332). Similar ones, Phoenician in origin, have been discovered at various points of the Fertile Crescent. The luxury these ivories represent helps us to understand the frequent tirades against social inequalities in the first of the writing prophets, Amos, in whose book we find several contemptuous references to ivory (3:15, 6:4).

75 Another precious insight into worsening economic maldistribution is afforded by an archive of tax receipts from the Samaria palace. They are in the form of ostraca, that is, potsherds with writing in ink. They are dated over a period of some 17 years. It would seem that the long reign of Jeroboam II best accommodates this archive; but the matter is far from settled. For a recent treatment, see A. F. Rainey, *PEQ* 99 (1967) 30–41.

We should recall here that beginning around the year 1000 we possess several inscriptions in the Phoenician or archaic-Hebr script, translated in *ANET* 320–21. The oldest is perhaps the Gezer calendar, really too laconic and schoolboyish to warrant any firm inferences about the existence and nature of Hebrew as a separate language at this time. In the 1967 Israeli excavation campaign at Arad a ten-letter ostracon from the 10th cent. was discovered. The long and detailed "stele" inscription of Omri's contemporary, King Mesha of Moab, is considered to be in the Moabite language; and its differences from Hebrew as catalogued by Rosén are greater than the differences between Hebrew and Aramaic. From about 700 BC dates the Siloam tunnel inscription of Hezekiah (715–687) which Albright declares to be "in elegant classical Hebrew...but these finds, as well as hundreds of short inscriptions on seals and other objects, pale into insignificance beside the sensational discovery of the Lachish Ostraca" (→ 79 below). This statement may now need revision, however, in the light of the discovery (1962–67) of over 200 inscribed ostraca at Arad. According to Y. Aharoni (*BA* 31 [1968] 9–18), over half are in Hebrew and date from the monarchy, while the rest are in Aramaic from *ca.* 400 BC.

76 **(IV) From the Fall of Jerusalem to Herod.**
(A) Babylonian and Persian Periods (600–300). In answer to some objections, Albright (*AP* 141) has this to say about archaeological proof of the fact of Nebuchadnezzar's Judean deportation. "A fair number of towns or fortresses of Judah have now been excavated in whole or in part; many other sites have been carefully examined to determine the approximate date of their last destruction. The results are uniform and conclusive: many towns were destroyed at the beginning of the sixth century BC and never again occupied; others were destroyed at that time and partially reoccupied at some later date; still others were destroyed and reoccupied after a long period of abandonment, marked by a sharp change of stratum and by intervening indications of use for non-urban purposes. There is not a single known case where a town of Judah proper was continuously occupied through the exilic period."

77 The excavation throwing the most direct and valued light upon any biblical event or period was Lachish (*BA* 18 [1955] 9–17; *BTS* 82 [1966]). This name is given to Tell ed-Duweir (not to Tell el-Hesi, which its excavator Petrie thought to be Lachish, but which was rather Eglon). The Duweir site had already been suggested by Albright even before the name Lachish itself was dug up by the excavation of J. Starkey in 1932–38. The main reason for considering as proved the equation Lachish = Duweir is the extensiveness and importance of the settlement, proportioned to what the biblical mentions would lead us to expect.

78 It may be noted first that the most vivid excavated information about Lachish did not come from Duweir at all, but from faraway Nineveh in northern Assyria. From there came the British Museum frieze of Sennacherib (*ANEP* 372) showing how he overcame the resistance of Lachish during his invasion of Palestine in 701. The maneuvers of Judah's king Hezekiah, obscurely described in 2 Kgs 18:14, averted a subjugation similar to that of Samaria. But one century later, there arose in S Babylonia the new military machine of Nebuchadnezzar. It inflicted a decisive defeat upon the Assyrians at Carchemish in 605, then invaded Palestine full-scale in 598 and 589. Both times the citadel of Lachish bore the brunt of the attack on the open country outside Jerusalem.

79 Within one of the various rooms of the city gate of Duweir, Starkey found in 1936 some 20 jar fragments with messages in ink from a military official to his regional captain (*ANET* 321–22). One of these "ostraca" bemoans the fact that a hostile army is advancing so relentlessly that the signals of nearby Azekah have already been extinguished, although those of Lachish are still visible. These sherds were found in a narrow level between two destruction-layers of ash. It seemed natural to ascribe these two layers to the two destructions inflicted by Nebuchadnezzar within 10 years of each other (598 and 589). Thus the ostraca seemed perfectly dated. But Starkey was killed shortly afterward in an anti-Anglo-Zionist ambush, and a re-examination of the facts by their publisher Olga Tufnell makes it seem that the earlier ash-layer may have been Sennacherib's (701), a theory that makes it harder to date the ostraca archaeologically. Meanwhile, however, the content of the messages proves to the satisfaction of all experts that they were composed around 590. Mention of a Coniah, son of Elnathan, recalls the Elnathan of Jer 26:22; 36:12. The appeals to Egypt, and the frantic activity of Jeremiah during the black moments of the deportation, seem also reflected in the Lachish letters. See reference to Lachish and Azekah in Jer 34:7. (For the Lachish letters, see most recently N. R. Ganor, *PEQ* 99 [1967] 74–77.) One of the Arad ostraca (→ 75 above), seemingly to be dated on paleographic grounds to the end of the monarchy, mentions the coming of the Edomites. Y. Aharoni would relate this to an Edomite assault on the Negeb just before Nebuchadnezzar's final campaign against Judah (*ca.* 600).

80 The Babylon to which a certain proportion of Judeans was deported has been brought magnificently to light by the German excavation of Nebuchadnezzar's palace and Ishtar temple. Numerous other excavations in the Tigris-Euphrates valley give incidental insights regarding the life of the exiles described in Ez 6 and Dn 1. Farther E, in Iran, excavations such as Susa and Persepolis give us ample detail on the mode of government of Cyrus and Darius (late 6th cent.) that is conspicuously reflected in Dt-Is and Est.

Within devastated Judah itself, excavation may perhaps show that daily life was in some way interrupted by the deportation but cannot settle the debate as to how large a percentage of the population was left behind. At Lachish, on the very top of the mound, a large palace that had served the local ruler since 900 was transformed into a different style during the Exile. Miss Tufnell accepts the judgment of Watzinger that the innovations were Syro-Hittite. But Albright claims them to be Persian, "strongly reminiscent in plan and detail of such early Parthian buildings as the small palace at Nippur in Babylonia, where we have a similar use of courts and columns."

No excavation so far has revealed to us the readjustments in local life of Palestine during the scant 50 years of Babylonian ascendancy (587–39). And even the 200 years of Iranian rule that followed constitute the most poorly attested epoch in Holy Land archaeology despite the constant trickle of exiles returning from a Persian culture-sphere. There are a few Persian-era burials at Atlit and Sharuhen, and a few of the classic red-on-black painted vases imported during those centuries from Attica. Also a number of Athenian "owl" drachmas symbolize the chronological importance of coinage, which was invented and diffused about 500 BC.

81 **(B) Greek and Hasmonean Periods (300–1 BC).** In 330 Alexander the Great brought Gk armies to Palestine, which in the following centuries was flooded with the good and bad features of Gk culture. The strong resistance to the encroachments of Hellenism ultimately led to the revolutionary reactions of the Maccabees in 167. But with Pompey's invasion of Palestine in 63 BC, the Roman Empire began to serve as a framework to bring Judea to a greater power and extension than it had known since David, e.g., under Herod the Great and Herod Agrippa I (→ History of Israel, 75:130–133, 151).

82 One of the pioneering excavations at Marisa (Tell Sandahanna), W of Hebron, by F. Bliss in 1898 yielded the imposing ground plan of a 2nd-cent. BC Hellenistic city (Albright, *AP* 153). The tombs of Marisa excavated in 1902 and still visible are our earliest Hellenistic monuments. They contained Greek inscriptions and color frescoes of a Hellenistic bawdiness. From about 175 BC survives an imposing structure in the lonely fastnesses of Araq el-Emir, W of Ammon. Once it was thought to have been a mausoleum; but three campaigns of excavation (1961–62) have convinced Paul Lapp, the excavator for ASOR, that it was a temple (*BASOR* 171 [1963] 30). It belonged to a certain Tobiah, a dynastic political leader very prominent in Josephus (*Ant.* 12.5, 1 § 240) and seemingly descended from Tobiah the Ammonite, prominent in Neh (→ History of Israel, 75:104).

83 On the road to Hebron an important citadel was excavated at Tubeiqa by Albright and O. Sellers in 1931. It seems to have been Beth-zur, center of the troubles the Maccabean heroes were subjected to during what is the only recorded biblical observance of the sabbath year (1 Mc 6:49, but see the author's reservations in *Bib* 34 [1953] 501). Numerous coins were catalogued here. Sellers reopened the work in 1956 (*BA* 21 [1958] 71–76). The Shechem excavation, as reopened in 1958, also brought to light a noteworthy Hellenistic quarter (*BAR* 2, 299–300). The monumental gate at Gezer dated to this period by its excavator has been shown by Yadin to be Solomonic.

84 The Roman occupation of Palestine began in 67 BC, and from this time Rome's allies in Edom (Idumea) became steadily more powerful; in fact, Antipater and his son Herod the Great came from Idumean stock. The Edomites or Idumeans were cousins of the Jews (Gn 25:25), closely linked with both Midianites and Arameans (1 Chr 1:36,42; Nm 24:21). Since their center was SE of the Dead Sea, they are to be associated with the Nabateans ruling Petra as Roman allies, whom Josephus loosely but not improbably calls Arabs. On the Nabateans, see J. Starcky, *BA* 17 (1954) 84–106.

Petra is today one of the wonders of the world (*Nat Geog* [Feb. 1935; Dec. 1955]; *BTS* 73–74 [1965]; *BA* 23 [1960] 29–32.) This immense red-sandstone ghost town consists almost entirely of tomb façades 100 ft. high, carved out of the living rock. Most of them date from the century preceding and following Herod. From this period there is also a "High Place" with obelisks, a late but important sample of the style of worship constantly reprobated by the Herb prophets. Near it is a high-relief "horned altar" of the kind found free-standing at Megiddo and Luxor, and presumed in Ex 27:2. The rare hewn stone used by the Nabateans has a diagonal combing, conspicuous in a palace at Dibon. Scarcely less enchanting than their redstone-structures is the Nabateans' eggshell-thin pottery with exquisite red painting, which may still be picked up not only at Petra but at SW Palestinian sites like Abda. The Nabateans ruled as far N as Damascus under Aretas IV (9 BC–AD 40; → Life of Paul, 46:21).

The excavation of Qumran by Roland de Vaux from 1951 through 1956 is by far the best archaeological evidence of the last pre-Christian century (→ Apocrypha, 68:67). In fact, the corpus of pottery he found there marks the *start* of an effort (collated in *Palestinian Ceramic Chronology* [1961] by P. Lapp) to use pottery as a chronological indicator for the several centuries before and after Christ with the same reliability as in other periods of Palestine history.

85 At Jerusalem the 1st cent. BC is attested by conspicuous tombs. One is called Absalom's Tomb and is flanked by three others in the lower Kidron Valley. Farther N is the tomb of Queen Saddan (or Helen) of Adiabene, excavated by De Saulcy (→ 7 above). Still farther NW are the open-air "Synedria" or Sanhedrin tombs, of overdecorated Syro-Hellenistic style. The town-rampart by which the SW hill was enclosed into the Jerusalem urban area is claimed by Albright to have been built only under Herod the Great. Miss Kenyon (*BA* 27 [1964] 47) says that only in the 1st cent. AD was the S part of the western hill settled, but the N part of that hill must have been settled earlier.

86 Two stones of Herod's Temple have survived, bearing in Greek the Roman governor's warning of "death" to any Gentile passing into the sacred precinct. Also surviving is the forest of underground masonry needed to hold up the Temple's spacious platform. It is the outer retaining wall of this platform on the W side that is called the Wailing Wall by the Jews. The SE corner of the retaining wall (site of Warren's exploit; → 8 above), with the crenelated city wall on top of it, is rather implausibly called "the Pinnacle of the Temple" (Mt 4:5). Albright and other experts assure us that a Herodian date can be assigned to the hewn stones here and at Hebron. But the great similarity of some Omri masonry at Samaria and of some late-Roman masonry at Beth-she'arim would perhaps justify a doubt that architectural styles, apart from artifacts or inscriptions, are conclusive dating criteria. (See G. W. Van Beek, "Marginally Drafted Pecked Masonry," *Archaeological Discoveries in South Arabia* [ed. R. L. Bowen, *et al.*; Baltimore, 1958] 287–95.) For the remains of arches between the Temple area and the western part of Jerusalem, see *BA* 29 (1966) 27–36; 30 (1967) 27–31.

Herod's chief legacy to the archaeologist is the fortresses he left on isolated mountain peaks. Of these, only Masada has been adequately excavated (→ Apocrypha, 68:110). The "Roman capital of Judea," built by Herod at seacoast Caesarea, has yielded extremely interesting ruins. Most were of late-Roman date, perhaps connected with the flourishing Christian center at Caesarea. But in 1961 among the remains of Caesarea appeared our first record of the name of Pontius Pilate inscribed on stone. Herod's birthplace, Ashkelon, never became incorporated into his kingdom. He enriched it with public buildings, however, of which mostly scattered stones were encountered by the digging there (→ History of Israel, 75:132).

87 **(V) New Testament Period.** Interest in the sites of the life of Jesus has been understandably great. This has had in almost every case the unfortunate by-product of generating rival claimants for sites, two or even three, who support their claims with alleged archaeological evidence.

In this situation, the strongest archaeological support for the incarnation and nativity sites of *Nazareth* and *Bethlehem* is the virtual absence of any rival claimant. The earliest monumental remains in the basilicas erected over these sites go back only to some 300 years after the event they commemorate (cf. *BA* 30 [1967] 90–107). *Nain* (Lk 7:11) too is an uncontested little hamlet, and a few tombs there have been traced back to NT times. *Caesarea Philippi* (Mt 16:13) and *Bethsaida-Julias* (Lk 9:10) are uncontested. But there is violent disagreement over the existence of a second Bethsaida on the W shore of Lake Tiberias, allegedly excavated at Minya but showing "for explainable reasons" no Roman remains. (An attempt to harmonize Lk 9:10 with Mk 6:45 probably lies behind the theory of two Bethsaida sites.)

88 Minya in fact had once been claimed as *Capernaum*, but recently Tell Hum on the NNW shore of the lake has been generally identified as Capernaum. This identification should be taken with caution; for when there have been rival sites, those closer to medieval pilgrim routes have most often won out. In the case of Tell Hum the fact that an asphalt highway was built to it for the convenience of modern pilgrims has abetted the priority given to its candidacy for being Capernaum. Whatever the final decision, it will not diminish the importance of the imposing synagogue ruins there (cf. Lk 4:31; 7:5; Jn 6:59). Even if this structure in its present form dates from AD 200, as seems undeniable, still its architectural and ornamental features may well go back in large part to the century of Jesus or earlier.

89 *Cana* (Jn 2:1) is contested; geographical and phonological reasons favor Khirbet Qana, 9 mi. N of Nazareth, even though tourists go to Kefr Kenna 3 mi. NE of Nazareth. The excavated remains of the "pious nonscientific" site of Kenna are in fact far nearer to the time of Jesus than any at Qana. But they also relate to the private Jewish shrine of a certain Tanhum, which if anything diminishes the likelihood that this was a focus of Christian veneration.

90 Most imposing of all excavated monumental sites of the NT world is the Roman *Gerasa* (Jerash). It was a chief city of the Decapolis (→ Biblical Geography, 73:52) and may have seen the visit of Jesus, recorded in Mk 7:31. Its forum, colonnaded avenues, and two theaters give us a good idea of the Greco-Roman culture that was trying to absorb Palestine. Gerasa also possesses six churches affording some of our earliest examples of Christian architecture and mosaic. Some 30 mi. NW of Gerasa, close enough to be considered part of its district, the *Gadara* of Roman times survives in some important ruins of Umm Qeis, high on the precipitous S bank of the Yarmuk River in view of Lake Tiberias. The pig-owners of Mt 8:28 are called by some mss. Gadarene and by others Gerasene (also → Gospel Mk, 42:31).

91 In 1950 ASOR excavated Tulul Abu el-Alayiq, 2 mi. SE of OT Jericho (Tell es-Sultan); the excavator J. L. Kelso (cf. *AASOR* 29–20 [1955]; *BA* 14 [1951] 34–43) would identify the site as the *Jericho* of NT times, associated with Bartimaeus (Mk 10:46) and Zacchaeus (Lk 19:5). However, in *Bib* 37 (1956) 516, the present author has protested that the excavation of a single rich-man's villa scarcely gives the site a right to be known by the pretentious title of "NT Jericho." Really the *absence* of relevant dwelling areas there and the absence of relevant artifacts at "OT Jericho" rather cancel out the allegation of a century ago that the biblical Jericho cannot be simply at the site of the present-day city (which stands almost between the two ancient sites), precisely because no artifacts of biblical times are visible there. As at Jerusalem, continued dense inhabitation would be the best possible explanation of the absence of occupation remains from the period in question.

The site commemorating Jesus' baptism at the Jordan near Jericho is not really claimed to be authentic, but only to be located at the most conveniently accessible point *near* a site supported by an ancient tradition. Just about here would be the Beth-arabah of Jos 15:6, a name easily recognizable in "Bethabara" which some mss. of Jn 1:28 give instead of "Bethany." This author would suggest that the presence at Qumran of a penitential baptizing sect (→ Apocrypha, 68:67, 93) tends both to reinforce the Bethabara tradition, and to render almost inescapable the admission that John the Baptist was in fairly close communication with the Qumran votaries.

92 At *Jerusalem* the chief observation of an archaeologist would be that much of the energy spent in wrangling or recrimination over unproved sites ought rather to be constructively expended in rejoicing that the Temple area is so uncontested. Here took place a very large number of the most important events in the life of Jesus, from his presentation and finding, down through his public ministry to the evening before his death. The Mt. of Olives is similarly important and undisputed. Caskets for bones (ossuaries) recently found on the Olivet slope called Dominus Flevit bear 1st-cent. Jewish names and are claimed to be our earliest record of the Judeo-Christian community. As for the ascension site, the minority opinion of L.-H. Vincent, preferring Eleona to Imbomon, implies a minuteness of localization that is unimportant when compared with the momentousness of "Olivet's upper slope" in general for various incidents of the Jerusalem ministry. On ascension sites, see *BTS* 29 (1960).

The very ancient tradition of localizing Calvary in the church of the Holy Sepulcher has shown itself strong enough to rise above both its own legendary accretions and a concerted attack in the last century in favor of a less congested spot. (On the traditional site, see *BTS* 55 [1963]; *BA* 30 [1967] 74–90.) Today the most burning issue of the whole of Gospel topography is the Lithostrotos (Jn 19:13; "Pavement"). Upon it depends the validity of the basic arrangement of the Stations of the Cross. Upon it has been made to depend also the powerful reputation of Père Vincent (→ 12 above) as arbiter of Palestine archaeology. But it is Vincent's own Dominican confreres who now most articulately reject the excavation results that in Vincent's view favored the Antonia fortress at the NW corner of the Temple area (pictures in *BTS* 10 [1958]). At the alternative site on the other side of Jerusalem, namely Herod's citadel, there were also rather serious excavations undertaken by C. N. Johns for the British Mandate authorities; but the chronological results prove only that the building was in use in the time of both Herod and Pilate (→ Gospel Mk, 43:91–92).

The pool of Bethesda (Bethzatha), mentioned in Jn 5:2, has been discovered and excavated in Jerusalem on the property of the White Fathers, near St. Anne's church. Trapezoidal in form and divided by a central partition, the pool had colonnades on the four sides and the partition—thus, John's "five porticoes" (B. Bagatti, *BeO* 1 [1959] 12–14; also *BTS* 86 [1966]).

(Jeremias, J., *Jerusalem zur Zeit Jesu* [Göttingen, 1937]. Join-Lambert, M., *Jerusalem* [N.Y., 1958] 69–143. Perowne, S., *In Jerusalem and Bethlehem* [London, 1964]. Vincent, L.-H., *Jérusalem nouvelle* [Paris, 1914]. Also → Biblical Geography, 73:94.)

93 Père Vincent's authority seems imperiled also by a reappraisal of his theory locating *Emmaus* (Lk 24:13) at Nicopolis (photographs in *BTS* 36 [1961]). Although many still accept his view, the imposing remains of the early churches that he excavated there are just what we would expect from a bishopric as populous as Nicopolis, some 160 stadia (20 mi.) from Jerusalem. At a more suitable 60 stadia (8 mi.) is the "alternative Emmaus," called Qubeibeh. Its excavated finds, though less imposing, are just as relevant to the question of whether Lk 24:13 fits here. It is important to conclude by emphasizing that Vincent's immense services to Palestinian excavation are in no way diminished by continuing researches coming to conclusions divergent from his own.

94 To close our treatment, we may mention a final archaeological site where the Jewish and Christian heritages came together in the post-biblical period—the site of Dura Europos, far to the NE of Palestine in the great bend of the Euphrates River. It was excavated by a French expedition under F. Cumont in 1922–25 and then, with the support of Yale University, in 1928–37. The publication of the rich finds was concluded in 1967 by C. Kraeling. Founded under the Gk Seleucid dynasty *ca.* 300 BC, Dura Europos became a Roman commercial and military outpost on the trade routes with the East. In AD 170 a small Jewish synagogue was built; in an enlargement in 240, the walls were covered with impressive frescoes of biblical subjects. This unique treasury of Jewish art was preserved because, as part of the defense against a Parthian invasion in 256, the wall-frescoes were buried under an earthwork intended to strengthen the adjacent outer wall of the city. A Christian house-chapel with a painted baptistry, from the same period, has also been discovered at Dura. (*BTS* 88 [1967].)

75

A HISTORY OF ISRAEL

Addison G. Wright, S.S.

Roland E. Murphy, O.Carm.

Joseph A. Fitzmyer, S.J.

BIBLIOGRAPHY

1 **General Bibliography.** Albright, *FSAC* 127–99. Braidwood, R. J., *Prehistoric Men* (6th ed.; Chicago, 1963). Brillant, M. and R. Aigrain, eds., *Histoire des religions* (5 vols.; Paris, 1953–56). *The Cambridge Ancient History* (rev. ed.). Childe, V. G., *New Light on the Most Ancient East* (N.Y., 1957). *Everyday Life in Ancient Times* (National Geographic Society, 1951) 5–167. Finegan, J., *Light From the Ancient Past* (2nd ed.; Princeton, 1959). Frankfort, H., *The Birth of Civilization in the Near East* (N.Y., 1956); *Kingship and the Gods* (Chicago, 1948). Frankfort, H., *et al.*, *Before Philosophy: The Intellectual Adventure of Ancient Man* (Harmondsworth, 1949). Gelb, I. J., *A Study of Writing* (2nd ed.; Chicago, 1963). Ghirshman, R., *Iran* (Harmondsworth, 1954) 27–72. Gray, J., *The Canaanites* (London, 1964). Gurney, O. R., *The Hittites* (Harmondsworth, 1954). Hawkes, J., *Prehistory* (vol. 1, part 1: UNESCO History of Mankind; N.Y., 1965). Moscati, S., *The Face of the Ancient Orient* (N.Y., 1962). Noth, M., *The Old Testament World* (Phila., 1966) 183–297. Pritchard, J. B., *ANET, ANEP, ANE.* Schwantes, S. J., *A Short History of the Ancient Near East* (Grand Rapids, 1965). Steindorff, G., and K. C. Seele, *When Egypt Ruled The East* (Phoenix ed.; Chicago, 1963). Wilson, J. A., *The Culture of Ancient Egypt*, also publ. as *The Burden of Egypt* (Chicago, 1951). Woolley, L., *The Beginnings of Civilization* (vol. 1, part 2: UNESCO History of Mankind; N.Y., 1965). Yadin, Y., *The Art of Warfare in Biblical Lands* (London, 1963).

2 **Bibliography for OT Times.** Albright, *BP*. Anderson, G. W., *The History and Religion of Israel* (New Clarendon Bible; Oxford, 1966). Bright, *Hist.* Dentan, R., ed., *The Idea of History in the Ancient Near East* (New Haven, 1955). De Vaux, R., "Israël," *VDBS* 4, 729–77; "Method in the Study of Early Hebrew History," *The Bible in Modern Scholarship* (N.Y., 1965) 15–29. Ehrlich, E., *A Concise History of Israel* (N.Y., 1965). Gordon, C. H., *The World of the Old Testament* (N.Y., 1958). Kapelrud, A., *Israel* (Oxford, 1966). Kaufmann, Y., *The Religion of Israel* (Chicago, 1960). Meek, T. J., *Hebrew Origins* (2nd ed.; N.Y., 1950). Mendenhall, G., "Biblical History in Transition," *BANE* 27–58. Noth, *Hist.* Orlinsky, H., *Ancient Israel* (2nd ed.; Cornell, 1960). Ricciotti, G., *History of Israel* (Milwaukee, 1955). Rowley, H. H., *Men of God: Studies in Old Testament History and Prophecy* (London, 1963). Speiser, E., "The Biblical Idea of History," *IsrEJ* 7 (1957) 201–16. Voegelin, E., *Israel and Revelation* (Baton Rouge, 1956). Weber, M., *Ancient Judaism* (Glencoe, 1952).

3 **Bibliography for NT Times.** Abel, F.-M., *Histoire de la Palestine depuis la conquête d'Alexandre jusqu'à l'invasion arabe* (EBib; Paris 1952) 1, 108–505; 2, 1–102. Barrett, C. K., *The New Testament Background: Selected Documents* (N.Y., 1961). Bonsirven, J., *Judaïsme palestinien* (2 vols.; Paris, 1934–35). De Vaux, R., "Israël," *VDBS* 4, 771–77. Foerster, W., *Neutestamentliche Zeitgeschichte* (2 vols.; Hamburg: 1 [3rd ed.] 1959; 2 [1st ed.] 1956); Eng tr. of vol. 1 is *From the Exile to Christ* (Phila., 1964). Jeremias, J., *Jerusalem zur Zeit Jesu* (2nd ed.; Göttingen, 1958). McKenzie, J. L., "The Jewish World in New Testament Times," *CCHS* 728–41. Moore, G. F., *Judaism in the First Centuries of the Christian Era* (3 vols.; Cambridge, 1927–30). Oesterley, E. O. E., *A History of Israel* (Oxford, 1951) 2, 217–463. Pfeiffer, R. H., *A History of New Testament Times with an Introduction to the Apocrypha* (N.Y., 1949) 5–59. Reicke, B., *Neutestamentliche Zeitgeschichte* (Berlin, 1965). Ricciotti, G., *History of Israel* (Milwaukee, 1955) 2, 236–461. Schürer, E., *Geschichte des jüdischen Volkes im Zeitalter Jesu Christi* (5th ed.; Leipzig, 1920); Eng tr. of 2nd ed.; *A History of the Jewish People in the Time of Jesus Christ* (3 vols.; Edinburgh, 1898–1905); abr. Eng ed.; *A History of the Jewish People in the Time of Jesus* (ed. N. N. Glatzer; N.Y., 1961). Zeitlin, S., *The Rise and Fall of the Judean State* (2 vols.; Phila., 1962, 1967; vol. 3 in preparation).

4 OUTLINE

Sections 5–23 are the work of A. G. Wright; sections 24–118 that of R. E. Murphy; the remainder of the article is by J. A. Fitzmyer.

(II) The Bronze Ages (3200–1550 BC)
(A) Early Bronze Age (§ 14–18)
(a) Mesopotamia
(b) Egypt
(c) Palestine
(B) Middle Bronze Age (§ 19–23)
(a) Mesopotamia
(b) Egypt
(c) Palestine

From Abraham to Pompey (§ 24–118)
(I) The Patriarchal Period (*ca.* 2000–1700 BC)
(A) Abraham, Isaac, and Jacob (§ 24–28)
(B) The Joseph Story (§ 29)
(II) The Exodus and the Conquest (*ca.* 1300–1050 BC)
(A) Oppression (§ 31–32)
(B) Moses (§ 33)
(C) The Plagues (§ 34)
(D) The Reed Sea Crossing (§ 35–36)
(E) The Desert Experience (§ 37–39)
(F) The Land of Canaan (§ 40–41)
(G) Joshua's Victories (§ 42–46)
(H) The Judges (§ 47–52)
(III) The Monarchy and the Exile (*ca.* 1020–539 BC)
(A) Saul (§ 54–55)
(B) David (§ 56–60)
(C) Solomon (§ 61–62)
(D) Israel and Judah (§ 63–71)
(E) The Dynasty of Jehu (§ 72–76)
(F) The Last Years of Israel (§ 77–79)
(G) Ahaz and Hezekiah (§ 80–82)
(H) Manasseh and Josiah (§ 83–85)
(I) The Last Years of Judah (§ 86–87)
(J) The Exile (§ 88–90)
(IV) The Early Post-exilic Period (539–333 BC)
(A) The Restoration (§ 91–92)
(B) Nehemiah and Ezra (§ 93–97)
(C) The Persian Era (§ 98–100)
(V) The Greek Era (333–63 BC)
(A) From Alexander to Seleucid Domination (§ 101–105)
(B) The Maccabean Revolt (§ 106–113)
(C) The Hasmonean Rulers (§ 114–118)

From Pompey to Bar Cochba (§ 119–171)
(I) Jewish Movements in Palestine
(A) Pharisees (§ 120–122)
(B) Sadducees (§ 123–124)
(C) Essenes (§ 125)
(II) Roman Palestine before Jesus' Lifetime (63–4 BC)
(A) Pompey, Julius Caesar, Mark Antony (§ 126–129)
(B) Herod the Great (§ 130–133)
(III) Roman Palestine in Jesus' Lifetime (4 BC–AD 30)
(A) Birth of Jesus (§ 134–136)
(B) Augustus Caesar (§ 137)
(C) Herod's Heirs (§ 138–141)
(D) The Procurators (§ 142)
(E) Pontius Pilate (§ 143)
(F) John the Baptist (§ 144)
(G) Ministry and Death of Jesus (§ 145–147)
(IV) Roman Palestine after Jesus' Lifetime (AD 30–135)
(A) Spread of the Christian Church (§ 148)
(B) Herod Agrippa I (§ 149–152)
(C) Agrippa II to the First Revolt (§ 153–156)
(D) First Revolt (§ 157–160)
(E) Siege of Jerusalem (§ 161–164)
(F) Between the Revolts (§ 165–166)
(G) Second Revolt (§ 167–171)

BEFORE ABRAHAM WAS

5 Up to 150 years ago our only sources for a knowledge of the ancient Near East were the Bible and Herodotus. The former, among other things, was written from a very limited point of view; the latter is by no means a thoroughly reliable source. During the past century, through the science of archaeology and related fields, we have learned a vast amount about the history of man and of Israel's predecessors and neighbors; and the confrontation of this material with the Bible has produced the modern biblical movement. Some knowledge of these recently acquired data will be useful to situate the events of the biblical period in the larger context of man's history. This knowledge is also of exegetical value in helping us to come to a proper understanding of the kind of literature we possess in the prehistory of Gn 1–11. In the space allotted we can give only the most general outline of prehistory and of the political and cultural history of the ancient Near East; for this reason we refer the interested student to the more detailed treatments in the bibliography. (Also → Biblical Archaeology, 74:40ff.) The dates given below for the various Stone and Bronze Ages are all approximate.

6 **(I) The Stone Ages (Before 3200 BC).** The various stages of human existence on earth are distinguished and named according to the material most commonly used for basic tools and weapons at the respective period. Since change from one material to another did not occur instantaneously, the designations are always approximate as to both the beginning and the end of the period. Stone (Gk *lithos*) was the oldest material, copper (*chalkos*) or bronze came next.

7 **(A) Old Stone Age or Paleolithic.** The origins of man are lost in the mists of the past. Presently scientists think that our planet is about 3 billion years old, that plant and animal life appeared some 500 million years ago, and that the oldest certainly human fossils date from about 600,000 years ago, i.e., Java and Olduvai "Chellean" men. (For the discoveries of L. Leakey at Olduvai Gorge in Tanzania, E Africa, see *NatGeog* [Sept. 1960; Oct. 1961; Jan. 1963; Feb. 1965; Nov. 1966]. A dispute exists about the human quality of older remains on the evolutionary tree, namely an australopithecine stage represented by finds in E and S Africa that go back over a million years; but there is an increasing likelihood that these older types will be accepted as "men.") Java and Olduvai "Chellean" represent an early human stage (*Homo erectus*) that lasted through stages represented by finds at Heidelberg (500,000 BC), Peking (400,000), Swanscombe in England, and Steinheim in Germany (250,000), down to about 40,000 years ago and the classical Neanderthal men and their contemporaries (the "cave men" of the movies and cartoons). Beginning about 40,000 years ago, fully modern skeletons (*Homo sapiens*) first appear in Europe (Cro-Magnon, Combe Capelle-Brünn, Grimaldi). These seem to have been anticipated in SW Asia by the premodern types, such as the Skhul group from Mt. Carmel (75,000 BC).

In early Paleolithic, men wandered over large areas, living in the open in the summer and in caves and other natural shelters in the winter. Man was a hunter and a food gatherer; he used stone tools and had learned to control fire. There is evidence that around 40,000 BC people began to settle down more, perhaps restricting themselves in their wanderings and adapting themselves to a given locality in more intensive ways. This is sometimes described as a transition to food collecting (i.e., more purposeful and specialized than food gathering). Approximately 20,000 years ago the Mongoloid migrations began across the Bering Strait into America.

8 **(B) Middle Stone Age or Mesolithic (10,000–7,000 BC in the Near East).** Mesolithic culture is characterized by a further intensification of the food-collecting process and a gradual transition to food production (the planting of crops and the domestication of animals). This first really basic change in man's way of living (the second in a sense being the Industrial Revolution of the past 200 years) took place in the Near East around 10,000–7,000 BC (from where it rippled out to Europe and India 5000–3000 BC), and occurred again later and independently in the Far East and Middle America (yet there are still a few primitive peoples in out-of-the-way parts of the world whom the revolution has not affected and who remain in the food-gathering or food-collecting stage). In the Near East the center of the Mesolithic change was the region of the hilly flanks of rain-watered grassland (2000–5000 ft. elevation), which build up to the high mountain ridges of Iran, Iraq, Turkey, Syria, and Palestine; sites reflecting this incipient era of cultivation and animal domestication have been discovered at Beldibi in Turkey, at Karim Shahir, M'lefaat, and Zawi Chemi in Iraq, at Mt. Carmel, and elsewhere.

9 **(C) New Stone Age or Neolithic (7000–4000 BC in the Near East).** This is the stage of Stone Age culture in which man became a full-fledged food producer. Food collectors, i.e., hunters, fishers, berry and nut gatherers, had lived in small groups and bands for they had to be ready to move whenever an area no longer supplied sufficient food. There was not enough food to store nor was it the kind that could be stored for long. Clothing probably consisted of animal skins. There were no breakable utensils, no pottery, no time to think of much of anything but food and protection. But the food producer lived a more sedentary life. If one were to plant, one had to remain in the same place for the harvest. One lived in a house—it was worthwhile to build one. In a given area enough food could be grown for many people. Hence villages became common and with them came informal customs and rules. There was more time to modify nature in other areas than food production (e.g., the production of pottery and textiles), and probably some people began to specialize in such crafts, work full time at them, and trade their goods for food. Seventh-millennium sites of such primary farming villages have been found among other places at Jarmo and Hassuna in Iraq and at Jericho, and late 5th-millennium sites have been found at Fayum and Tasa in Egypt and all over western Asia (at Byblos, Ras Shamra, Nineveh, etc.).

10 **(D) Copper-Stone Age or Chalcolithic (4000–3200 BC in the Near East).** In the period following the Neolithic, agriculture was vastly improved and expanded; this made possible the support of an increasing density of population, and here also we find a similar progress in culture. In *Upper Mesopotamia* small groups began to move down from the highlands to sites adjacent to the mud flats of the rivers (e.g., at Baghouz and Samarra) to establish farming vilages with increased craft specialization. Painted pottery (a hallmark of Chalcolithic) began to appear. Soon all of Upper Mesopotamia was rather densely settled and Chalcolithic villages became fairly numerous in Palestine as well.

11 But nowhere was the progress more brilliant than in *Lower Mesopotamia*, for here the first experiment in civilization took place. Without attempting to define "civilization" let us simply describe it as urbanization. There are cities, a formal political setup (kings or governing bodies), formal laws enacted by the government, formalized projects (roads, harbors, irrigation canals, and the like), some sort of army or police force, new and different art forms, and usually writing (we say "usually" because the Incas had everything that goes to make up a civilization except writing, and there is no reason to say that they were not civilized). The Mesopotamian experiment in civilization took place in the alluvial land of the lower Tigris and Euphrates, and in the 4th millennium the first city states appeared in Lower Mesopotamia (Eridu, Al-Ubaid, Warka [Erech], Ur, Susa, etc.). No doubt there had been riverbank food collectors in the area long before and perhaps isolated villages, but the fertile yet rainless land could not be placed under intensive cultivation until the techniques necessary for providing irrigation had been mastered. Once the rich bottom land was gradually made available, settlers must have flocked in by the thousands. The irrigation required by the area demanded common effort and an increasing complexity of organization. It encouraged technological, political, social, and moral advances and was certainly a factor in the development of civilization here and in Egypt. And development was very fast. Among the advances in culture was the invention of writing (about 3200 BC), and before the end of the period there were links of trade and cultural exchange between Mesopotamia and Palestine and predynastic Egypt.

The creators of civilization in Lower Mesopotamia were the Sumerians, a people unknown to us a century ago and who still constitute one of the major mysteries of history. We are not sure of what race they were; their language is unaffiliated with any other known language living or dead; the time and manner of their arrival in Mesopotamia are uncertain, but it is clear that they were present in Mesopotamia by the middle of the 4th millennium, and since the earliest texts known to us are in Sumerian, we assume that it was they who introduced the cuneiform system of writing.

12 In *Egypt*, too, great strides were made in the development of agriculture and irrigation, where again the necessary co-operative effort helped in the formation of political units (nomes). Probably by the end of the 4th millennium the various local nomes were united into two sizeable kingdoms, one in Upper Egypt and one in Lower Egypt. Copper was in use, its source being either Sinai or the eastern desert. Writing in hieroglyphic script was invented. Egypt was in touch with Palestine and Mesopotamia and apparently even then with the cedar port of Byblos with which it maintained contact for centuries to come.

13 **(II) The Bronze Ages (3200–1550 BC).** With this period we leave the realm of prehistory and enter the area of history properly speaking, for here we are dealing with a period that is documented by numerous contemporary inscriptions. The terminology for Egyptian, Palestinian, and Mesopotamian chronology is different for each and there is no standard terminology covering all three areas. For simplicity we have adopted the Syrian-Palestinian terms of Early Bronze (EB) and Middle Bronze (MB) and have grouped under each period the corresponding history in Egypt and Mesopotamia. The Late Bronze (LB: 1550–1200 BC) is not treated in the present discussion (→ 30ff. below; → Excursus Israel, 11; → Biblical Archaeology, 74:56ff.).

14 **(A) Early Bronze Age (3200–2050 BC in the Near East).**

(a) MESOPOTAMIA. During the *Sumerian Age* (2800–2360) Mesopotamia was organized into a system of city-states most of which were quite small. Although now one, now another was able to assert itself over its neighbors, no permanent and thoroughgoing unification of the land was ever achieved. The city-state was a theocracy ruled by the god of the city; the city and its lands were viewed as the god's estate, the temple, his manor house, the people, workers on his estate. Originally, government was by city assembly; later, kingship developed, first as an emergency measure and then as a permanent institution, the head of state being seen as the viceroy of the god. There were sporadic and local wars but it was essentially a time of peace, and economic life flourished. Improved agriculture permitted the support of an increased population; urban life in turn fostered a greater specialization of the arts and crafts, and the scribal schools about the temple produced a vast body of religious literature.

15 Since the earliest times there had undoubtedly been nomads on the western fringes of the valley, and since the 4th millennium they had pressed in, in increasing numbers, and by the 3rd millennium constituted an appreciable portion of the population. These people were Semites and are known as *Akkadians*. They intermingled with the Sumerian population, adopted and modified their culture, and even became rulers in some city-states. In the 24th cent. a dynasty of these Semitic rulers seized power and created the first true empire in world history, the Akkadian Empire (2360–2180). The founder, Sargon, rose to power in Kish, subdued all Sumer to the Persian Gulf, moved his capital to Accad, or Agade (near later Babylon), and he and his sons then extended their rule over Upper Mesopotamia to the Mediterranean, with military expeditions into Asia Minor, SE Arabia, and trade contacts with the Indus Valley. However, Akkadian power soon waned and was brought to an end by the onslaught of a barbarian people from the Zagros Mountains called the Guti who held sway over Mesopotamia for 100 years. (G. Roux, *Ancient Iraq* [Pelican ed.; London, 1966].)

16 (b) Egypt. By the 29th cent. the kings of Upper Egypt had joined the two predynastic kingdoms into a unified nation with the capital at Memphis, and Egypt entered upon the period known as the *Old Kingdom* (29–23 cents.). With the rise of the 3rd Dynasty (*ca.* 2600) Egypt began the age of her classical flowering and period of creative genius, by which time all significant features of her culture had assumed a form ever thereafter to be normative. This was the age of the pyramids, and it was a period of development in literature, architecture, sculpture, painting, and the minor arts. The organization of the state in Egypt differed vastly from that of contemporary Mesopotamia. The Pharaoh was not a viceroy of the god; he was a god. All Egypt was his property and was managed by a complex bureaucracy headed by the vizier. No law code was ever developed; the word of the god-king sufficed. (W. B. Emery, *Archaic Egypt* [Pelican ed.; London, 1961].)

17 Beginning with the 5th Dynasty the power of the state began to disintegrate and by the 22nd cent., as the Guti were destroying Akkadian power, Egypt entered a period of disorder and depression known as the *First Intermediate* (22–21 cents.). There was internal disunity with rival Pharaohs claiming the throne and many officials seizing power locally. The situation was further aggravated by the infiltration of seminomads into the Delta. Confusion reigned, law and order broke down, and trade languished.

18 (c) Palestine. Here in EB we find the establishment of many city-states—Jericho (rebuilt *ca.* 3200 after a gap of centuries), Beth-shan, Ai, Shechem, Gezer, Lachish, etc., a number of them being built for the first time. By the mid-3rd millennium sedentary occupation had reached to the southern end of Transjordan. Palestine never developed a material culture comparable to that found in Mesopotamia and Egypt nor was any political unity established. The population was predominantly Canaanite, a Semitic people who had probably inhabited Palestine in the 4th millennium and before. Late in the 3rd millennium, life in Palestine suffered a major disruption at the hands of seminomadic invaders. City after city was destroyed, some with incredible violence. Towns were abandoned and the land, particularly in the interior areas, was left without settled population; in Transjordan sedentary occupation came virtually to an end. The newcomers were perhaps an offshoot of a people called the Amorites, a Northwest-Semitic element that was pressing in on all parts of the Fertile Crescent at this time. Probably the Semites infiltrating Egypt in the First Intermediate were of similar stock. (For an important recent theory, different from the Amorite hypothesis, → Biblical Archaeology, 74:52.)

19 **(B) Middle Bronze Age (2050–1550 BC).**

(a) Mesopotamia. The king of Erech broke the grip of the Guti over Mesopotamia; and he in turn was speedily overthrown by Ur-Nammu of Ur, who with the succeeding kings of the *Third Dynasty of Ur* (2060–1950) gained control probably over most of the Mesopotamian plain and brought about a brief renaissance of Sumerian culture. Ur-Nammu is noted not only for his many buildings and for the literary activity that marked his reign but above all for his law code, the oldest so far known. But Sumerian culture had come to the end of the road. The Sumerian language was dying and Akkadian was superseding it as the vernacular. Sumerians and Semites had become completely intermingled by this time and the latter had become the predominant element. So a whole culture and civilization had come into being, run a magnificent course over 1500 years and played itself out before Israel had even come upon the scene. Some of the important contributions of the Sumerians, in addition to city-state government, a fully developed legal system, and the invention of cuneiform writing mentioned above, were the lunar calendar, water clock, sundial, the chariot and military phalanx, the potter's wheel, the use of the vault, arch, dome, column, and tower in architecture, plus a highly developed polytheistic religion that had an enormous influence on all the later civilizations of the ancient world.

20 As the central authority of Ur deteriorated, the city-states of Mesopotamia one by one regained independence. The *Amorites* who had been pressing in on the Fertile Crescent since late in the 3rd millennium and had overrun Palestine and turned Upper Mesopotamia into an Amorite land, flooded into all parts of Mesopotamia and took over state after state so that by the 18th cent. virtually every state in Mesopotamia was ruled by Amorites. Gradually a three-way power struggle materialized for control of Mesopotamia between Assyria, Mari, and Babylon. Beginning even before the fall of Ur and continuing down into the 18th cent., *Assyria* (so named from the city of Asshur) had pursued a policy of commercial expansion in Asia Minor, witnessed by the Cappadocian Texts, business documents in Old Assyrian found at Kultepe in Asia Minor. Infiltrated by Amorites who finally took over, Assyria then entered upon a brief period of conquest (1748–1730)—Upper Mesopotamia from the Mediterranean to the Zagros Mountains. However, Assyria could not hold her gains, and within a very few years *Mari* succeeded her briefly as the dominant power in Mesopotamia (1730–1697). It is from this period that the bulk of the famous Mari Texts come (business and economic documents and government correspondence), which like the Cappadocian Texts cast useful light on patriarchal times. But victory in the struggle for power went to *Babylon* under Hammurabi (1728–1686). Seizing control of most of Lower Mesopotamia, he brought Mari and Assyria under subjection, introducing an era of peace and cultural flowering to the Mesopotamian plain (the Old Babylonian Empire). From this period there has come a wealth of texts, especially copies of ancient epics (e.g., the Babylonian accounts of creation and the flood) and Hammurabi's famous law code, which shed light on the social organization of the day and provide numerous parallels to the laws of the Pentateuch.

21 The Babylonian Empire was subjected to various pressures because new peoples were pushing into all parts of the Fertile Crescent. In the N were the *Hurrians* whose original home seems to have been the mountains of Armenia. They had been present in N Mesopotamia in small numbers since the 24th cent., but in the 17–16th cents. there was a tremendous influx of Hurrians into Upper Mesopotamia, Asia Minor, Syria, and even Palestine. Across Upper Mesopotamia there was established the kingdom of Mitanni; it had Indo-Aryan rulers but a population basically Hurrian, and this kingdom further reduced Assyria to a mere petty state. The Hurrians were the transmitters of Sumero-Akkadian culture to the Hittites and other peoples of Asia Minor, and tablets dating from the 15–14th cents. found at the Hurrian city of Nuzi are a valuable source of information on the social customs of patriarchal times. From the E there were incursions of *Kassites* from Luristan into parts of the Babylonian Empire. And in Asia Minor there was the presence of an increasingly powerful Hittite kingdom. By 2000 BC the population of Asia Minor had been infiltrated by various groups of Indo-Europeans, the most influential of whom called themselves *Hittites*. These had gradually unified the land and by the mid-16th cent. a strong Hittite kingdom existed in eastern and central Asia Minor and was pressing southward into Syria. In a daring thrust down the Euphrates the Hittites sacked Babylon *ca.* 1530. It was only a raid, for, beleaguered by Hurrian pressure from the E and beset with internal problems, Hittite power then retreated into Asia Minor for over a century, but in Babylon the Kassites seized control and held power for some 400 years plunging Mesopotamia into a dark age. (For subsequent history, → Excursus Israel, 11:4–9; for the Hurrians, see R. de Vaux, *RB* 74 [1967] 481–503.)

22 (b) EGYPT. As the 2nd millennium began Egypt was preparing to enter a new period of prosperity under the Pharaohs of the *Middle Kingdom* (21–18 cents.). The country was again united; there was economic prosperity and political expansion with sporadic control over Nubia, Libya, Palestine, and Phoenicia; and it was a golden age of Egyptian culture. However, in the 18th cent. Egyptian power rapidly declined due to internal disintegration and Egypt entered upon the *Second Intermediate Period* (18–16 cents.). It was at this time that the Hyksos (probably Canaanite or Amorite princes from Palestine and southern Syria) pressed in upon the land, establishing themselves at first in the Delta and then mastering for about 100 years all Egypt and an empire reaching to N Syria. In a bitter fight for freedom the Egyptians finally expelled the Hyksos (*ca.* 1580–1550), and Egypt began to revive and enter upon the period of the *New Kingdom* and the empire. (For subsequent history, → Excursus Israel, 11:21–23.)

23 (c) PALESTINE. At the end of EB the country had been thrown into upheaval by the Amorite invasions, but beginning in the 19th cent. a rapid recovery took place in W Palestine and N Transjordan with many new towns being built as the seminomads settled in and assimilated the language and culture of Canaan. Nevertheless, large areas, especially in the central mountain range, continued to be very thinly settled. Gradually the city-state system, characteristic of Palestine until the Israelite conquest, evolved; and under the Hyksos Palestine attained a prosperity that it seldom knew in ancient times.

It is the MB period which is the patriarchal age and against the background of which the narratives of Gn 12–50 are to be viewed. It is here that the biblical story begins.

FROM ABRAHAM TO POMPEY

24 **(I) The Patriarchal Period** (*ca.* 2000–1700 BC).

(A) Abraham, Isaac, and Jacob. The only direct source for the history of the patriarchs is Gn. There is no mention of them outside the Bible, and we are not able to give definitive dates for the patriarchal period (usually, 2000–1700). Despite this, the patriarchs are no longer the mythical figures that earlier scholarship made them out to be. Archaeological discoveries have proved that the biblical description of the patriarchs and their era is remarkably accurate, much too accurate to be considered invention, or to be dismissed as without historical foundation. It would have been impossible for such episodes to have been composed in Israel without some valid historical memory serving as a link with the past (cf. De Vaux in *TD* 12 [1964] 227–40; Bright, *Hist.* 78–93).

Having said this, one must also candidly admit that the patriarchal traditions are not simple historical fact. They belong to the genre of family traditions. They have received orientation in the course of their transmission, and they have united various and disparate elements in the process (cf. H. Gunkel, *The Legends of Genesis* [N.Y., 1964]). There is no point in attempting to reconstruct the actual events, but one can situate the patriarchs in their correct historical perspective in the light of the currently available data.

25 Abram (cf. Gn 17:5) is presented as an emigrant from Mesopotamia (cf. E. Speiser, *Genesis* [N.Y., 1964] xliii–lii; for his journey, → Biblical Geography, 73:15ff.). His settling in Palestine may be fitted in with the penetration of both Mesopotamia and Palestine by the Amorites (→ 18 above, yet → Biblical Archaeology, 74:52). He lived a seminomadic existence in Palestine, pasturing his flocks in the pattern of transhumance; but the memory of a more permanent residence attached itself to the Mamre-Hebron area. The general type of life described in Gn is historically in line with what we know of seminomadic existence in the early 2nd millennium, and which is exemplified in the story of Sinuhe (*ANE* 8–11) and in the Mari Texts, and pictorially in the Beni-Hasan tomb painting of the 19th cent. (*ANE* plate 2). N. Glueck's surface explorations have shown that apart from the 21st–19th cents. (Middle Bronze I) the Negeb would have been without agricultural settlements; the period when it was settled dovetails with Abraham's residence at Hebron. Albright would go further and specify Abraham as a caravan leader in the donkey caravan activity of this time (*BASOR* 163 [1961] 36–54). The name Abram has been found in Babylonian texts dating from the 16th cent., and the Mari Texts mention the name Nahor (Gn 11:22 and cf. 24:10) as a town near Haran, subject to an Amorite leader. Similarly, the name Jacob appears in an 18th cent. Mesopotamian text, designating a Hyksos ruler (Ya'qob-har); and names identical with those of some of Jacob's sons are to be found in the Mari Texts, e.g., Benjamin and Levi.

26 Some of the customs that are casually associated with the patriarchs have been illustrated from the tablets of Nuzi and Mari (→ Biblical Geography, 73:19). The practice of slave adoption at Nuzi lies behind Gn 15:1–4, where Abraham expects Eliezer to be his heir. Nuzi laws also provide for marriage to a concubine, but they forbid the release of the concubine and child (Gn 21:11–12). Certain events in the Laban-Jacob cycle find an explanation in the Nuzi practices of adoption: the prohibition to marry other than the daughters of Laban (31:50), and the theft of the teraphim, or household gods (31:19,34–35), which seem to have been a title to inheritance (but cf. M. Greenberg in *JBL* 81 [1962] 239–48). The ancient Hittite law (*ANET* 138ff. § 46–47) makes intelligible the transaction between Abraham and the Hittites for the cave of Machpelah (Gn 23). These are some of the notable instances of the genuine ancient color of the biblical narrative.

27 The patriarchs worshiped the "God of the Fathers" (→ Aspects OT Thought, 77:15ff.), identified as the God of Abraham, the Fear (or Kinsman) of Isaac (Gn 31:42), and the Mighty One of Jacob (Gn 49:24). The God of the Fathers is thus associated with the patriarch with whom he has established a special relationship; he is the patron of the clan with whom he has covenanted, and he guides them in their history. He is not just a local deity, attached to a shrine; epithets such as 'Olam (the Eternal One), 'Elyon (Most High), derived from the Canaanite pantheon, were given to him. These traits were later attributed to Yahweh, and the continuity of the God of the patriarchs was assured (cf. Ex 3:13–15; 6:2–3). (For details and further bibliography, cf. F. M. Cross in *HarvTR* 55 [1962] 225–59.)

28 The call of Abraham (Gn 12:1–3) involves the promise of a land and a people. The episodes related concerning him gravitate about the theme of the birth of an heir, and his relationship to Lot. Sarah's sterility, the endangering of the mother of the heir (Gn 12:10–20 and par.), the rejection of Ishmael—these events build up the suspense to the point where finally the child of promise is born, only to be offered as a sacrificial victim (Gn 22). The Abraham-Lot cycle affords an opportunity to contrast the two men, in favor of Abraham, and to introduce the events of Sodom-Gomorrah as well as the enigmatic expedition of Gn 14. The purchase of Machpelah (Gn 23) serves as a first installment on the fulfillment of the promise of a land. Isaac is a relatively shadowy figure, and he serves chiefly as a link between Abraham and Jacob. The family history of Jacob is constituted by two main cycles: Jacob-Esau, which highlights the theme of election even of unworthy persons, and Jacob-Laban, which reflects patriarchal relationships with the Arameans (the whole scene, Gn 29–31, is laid in Aram-naharaim, i.e., the area of NW Mesopotamia, in the upper courses of the Euphrates between the Balikh and the Khabur rivers).

29 **(B) The Joseph Story.** This is one of the biblical masterpieces, marked by the providence motif (Gn 45:5–8; 50:20); and the suspense in chs. 39ff., is sustained with great literary skill. The most plausible date offered for Joseph's rise to power is the Hyksos period (1720–1550). In recent times the Joseph story has received two quite different interpretations. G. von Rad has found in it a *ḥokmâ* creation, a wisdom story written perhaps during the reign of Solomon, and comparable to another literary gem of the period, 2 Sm 9–20. In this view the historicity of the story is somewhat bypassed (cf. *Gesammelte Studien zum Alten Testament* [Munich, 1958] 272–80). J. Vergote, however, studying the Egyptian elements in the story (*Joseph en Égypte* [Louvain, 1959]), has made a serious case for historicity, i.e., that the Joseph story represents in the main a valid historical memory of the experiences of Israel's ancestors in Egypt. The evidence he offers for the historical validity of the narrative is of the same type as that applied to the patriarchal traditions. In neither case is the historical fact or intention directly proved, but the astonishingly accurate detail and local flavor preclude their being merely fictionalized accounts.

At the same time one must admit the problem of the genealogical relationship between the fathers and the sons, or "tribes" of Jacob. One cannot be sure how many groups were involved in the transfer to Egypt, but both the Joseph (Rachel) and Leah clans figure prominently in the traditions relative to Egypt. In sum, the Egyptian residence, with the ensuing "bondage," cannot be denied. (Cf. H. H. Rowley, *From Joseph to Joshua* [London, 1950]; Noth, *UP* 226–32; L. Ruppert, *Die Josepherzählung der Genesis* (StANT 11; Munich, 1965.)

30 **(II) The Exodus and the Conquest (*ca.* 1300–1050 BC).** Presently there are two differing evaluations of the sources for the early history of Israel. Although their differences are not to be taken too rigidly, the main thrust of the reconstruction represented by J. Bright and that represented by M. Noth is clear enough. It is an oversimplification to say that one is guided by archaeological results and the other by literary analysis, but there can be no dispute that their general views of Israel's early history diverge. For a summary of their respective positions, see J. Soggin, *BA* 23 (1960) 95–100. In all honesty it must be admitted that we do not as yet possess a clear picture of Israel's origins. The present necessarily brief survey will be guided by this uncertainty, but it will attempt to indicate the principal events and their correlation with nonbiblical sources. Specific details are to be sought in the appropriate commentaries.

31 **(A) Oppression.** The most probable period for the sojourn of the ancestors of the Israelites in Egypt is the Hyksos period (1720–1550). As we have seen (→ 22 above), the Hyksos, or "rulers of foreign lands" were an Asiatic and partly Semitic people who invaded Egypt and ruled from Avaris (= Tanis, the biblical Zoan) in the Delta. It is during such an era that outsiders from Palestine would have been well received, and the opportunity for Joseph's advancement would have been present. There is evidence that there was a fairly consistent interchange between Egypt and Canaan, which was considered an Egyptian possession. The vague reference in Ex 1:8 to a "new king, who knew nothing of Joseph" may be taken to reflect the changed condition of the Hebrews after the Hyksos rule was overthrown by native Egyptians; Amosis inaugurated the native 18th Dynasty and New Kingdom (*ANET* 233). At any rate, there is no reason to question the bitter change in Israel's fortune.

32 But the memory of this oppression was not preserved in cold, statistical fact. First, there is the forced labor (J account), which doubtless reflects Hebr participation in building projects of Ramses II (1290–1224) at Pithom (Tell er-Retabeh) and Raamses (the later Tanis; → Biblical Geography, 73:26). There are extant pictures of Asiatics working at hard labor in ancient

Egypt (*AtBib* plate 132). The so-called ʿApiru or Ḫabiru are mentioned frequently in Egyptian texts of the 15th–12th cents., but a simple identification of them with the Hebrews offers difficulties (→ Biblical Archaeology, 74:57). The name ʿApiru seems to indicate a broad class of people, without any specific ethnic meaning (cf. M. Greenberg, *The Ḫab/piru* [AOS 39; New Haven, 1955]; but cf. Albright, *BP* 5). Second, there is the command to the midwives (both of whose names, Shiphrah and Puah, have appeared in very old nonbiblical texts; cf. Albright in *JAOS* 74 [1954] 233) to slay the male Hebrews at birth. The situation is further aggravated by a royal decree that prescribes drowning for all males who have escaped the willful negligence of the midwives (Ex 1:22, belonging to E). The artificial appearance of these successive measures nonetheless serves as a moving introduction to the story of Moses (an Egyptian name) in the reeds, which finds a parallel in the life of Sargon of Accad (2300 BC; cf. *ANET* 119). There is a further heightening effect to the story of oppression in Ex 5:7ff., when the Hebr laborers are commanded to gather their own straw. All this forms part of the dramatic tensions throughout Ex 1–15.

33 **(B) Moses.** The mission of Moses (JE in Ex 3:1–4:17; P in 6:2–7:13) is understood as the response of God to the covenant with the patriarchs (P in Ex 2:24). Forced to leave Egypt, he takes refuge among the Midianites into whose group he married. In these circumstances he receives his commission from the Lord. The so-called Kenite theory, which would make Yahweh the god of the Midianite tribe of Kenites (cf. H. H. Rowley, *From Joseph to Joshua*), seems unlikely. On the other hand, the "monotheism" of Moses is to be understood as a practical, not a theoretical, view. The influence of the "monotheism" of Akhenaton (1370–1353) remains unclear, if it is even pertinent (but cf. Albright, *BP* 15–16, 26). The sources stress that the Yahweh who reveals himself to Moses as "I am who am" is the God of the Fathers, known as El Shaddai, the "mountain god" (→ Aspects OT Thought, 77:9, 11–13). Thus the continuity of the salvation history is affirmed. The scene is now set for the confrontation of Pharaoh and Yahweh, the magicians and Moses (→ Exodus, 3:14–18).

34 **(C) The Plagues.** Commentators have long pointed out that the plagues can be verified at various periods of Egyptian history as natural phenomena, e.g., the changing of the water into blood is identified with the annual flooding of the Nile. But this is hardly relevant to the view that the biblical writer takes concerning these events. For him they are not simply the usual catastrophes; they are interpreted as the "signs and wonders" wrought by God through Moses. They should not be put in the modern category of "miracle," since the ancient Israelites did not share this concept. Moreover, the number of ten plagues is reached by a combination of several variant traditions (especially J and P; → Exodus, 3:19). The plagues serve to emphasize the tension of the contest between God and Pharaoh (whose magicians finally fail to duplicate the work of Aaron and Moses), between Israel and Egypt. The whole account may find its proper life-setting in the annual celebration of the Passover feast in Israel; thus it would be a liturgical expression of Israel's faith, not a factual description, and any attempted "reconstruction" is not possible. Israel doubtless "historicized" a nomadic feast of Passover—to which the feast of Azymes (Unleavened Bread) was eventually joined—but there is no reason to question the liberation that underlies the feast (→ Religious Institutions, 76:132–139). This process of historicization is also to be found in the other principal feasts (De Vaux, *AI* 484–502).

35 **(D) The Reed Sea Crossing.** The actual crossing over the waters was not at the Red Sea (an identification made as early as the LXX), but rather in the area of the Bitter Lakes below Lake Menzaleh, not far from Succoth (Tell el-Maskhuteh), one of the points of departure. The proper Hebr term (*yām sûp*) is "Reed Sea," indicating a marshy area (→ Biblical Geography, 73:28). This crossing is celebrated in one of the earliest Hebr poems, the Song of Miriam (Ex 15:1–18; cf. F. M. Cross, D. Freedman in *JNES* 14 [1955] 237–50). The number of people who left Egypt is unknown, despite the biblical data in Ex 12:37, and the census lists in Nm 1 and 26. More serious is the problem of which tribes were involved in the Exodus. Surely, the tribes of Ephraim and Manasseh (= House of Joseph), the tribes of Benjamin, Levi, and perhaps of Judah and Simeon, are reasonable guesses. But one must reckon with the fact that "Israel" and "Israelites" were read into the early tradition from a later point of view. The experience of the first groups became the tradition of all who were later associated with them. There is, of course, no record of the Exodus of the Israelites in extrabiblical sources. Israel is mentioned in the stele of Merneptah (*ca.* 1220 BC; *DOTT* 137ff.) as a people, not a land, which "lies desolate." If, as is likely, the reference is to the period of conquest under Joshua, we have another example of the exaggeration of royal inscriptions. (On the possibility of two exoduses, see M. Rowton in *PEQ* 87 [1953] 46–60; → Biblical Archaeology, 74:64.)

36 There is a widespread agreement (H. H. Rowley in *IDB* 2, 752, is among those dissenting) that the Exodus is to be dated in the 13th cent. The data supplied by the Bible itself favors rather the 15th cent., but the reckoning of 480 years in 1 Kgs 6:1 is artificial. The arguments for the 13th cent. are primarily archaeological (e.g., the stele of Merneptah; N. Glueck's Transjordan explorations; the destruction of Canaanite cities at the end of the 13th cent.). On this dating, Ramses II would be the "pharaoh of the oppression." (→ Biblical Archaeology, 74:56–64.)

37 **(E) The Desert Experience.** In their march to Palestine the Hebrews must have avoided such a public road as the "way of the Philistine's land" (Ex 13:17) in favor of the "Reed Sea by way of the desert road" (Ex 13:18). But the route itself cannot be exactly plotted, despite the 40 stations or camping sites mentioned in Nm 33 (cf. H. Cazelles in *RB* 62 [1955] 321–64; → Biblical Geography 73:27–30). The themes of the desert journey are many: murmuring, the pillar of cloud, the manna and quail, the wandering for 40 years, battle with the Amalekites, etc. These appear in variant traditions. Although one can seek a "natural" explanation for the manna in the gummy substance still exuded by insects on the tamarisk trees of Sinai, the qualities of the manna are so embellished in the biblical text (cf. Wis 16:20–21; Ex 16:14–21), that it no longer bears a resemblance to any known food. The murmuring has crystallized around certain place names, as Massah and Meribah (Ex 17:7; Nm 20:13), and perhaps this is indicative of etiological narratives, i.e., tales told to explain place names.

38 The most important experience of the desert was the Sinai covenant (cf. D. McCarthy in *CBQ* 27 [1965] 217–40), which is succinctly expressed in the P formula: "You are my people, and I am your God." Recent comparisons with the (Hittite) suzerainty treaties have illustrated the covenant idea in Israel. It appears that Israel adapted these contemporary treaties in order to express her unique relationship to Yahweh (→ Aspects OT Thought, 77:79). The covenant goes back to the Mosaic age from which it purports to date. The terms of the covenant relationship are found in the Ten Words (Decalogue) and in the so-called code of the covenant

(Ex 20:22–23:19). The studies of A. Alt, H. Cazelles, and G. Mendenhall support the antiquity of these legal texts (→ Aspects OT Thought, 77:86–87). Israel was the recipient from the body of ancient legal practice in the Near East, which was perhaps mediated to it through the Canaanites. The elaborate description of the Tabernacle tent, the Ark, etc., in Ex 25ff., is generally recognized as having a certain validity (F. M. Cross in *BA* 10 [1947] 45–68), even if it is idealized in the P tradition. The portable tent shrine contained the Ark of the Covenant, which served as a throne for the invisible Yahweh; this fitted well into the desert pattern of the early Hebrews. (→ Religious Institutions, 76:44–48.)

39 The wandering in the desert is portrayed as a 40-year period (a generation), with activity centered around Kadesh-barnea, about 50 mi. below Beer-sheba. An unsuccessful attempt to enter Palestine through the Negeb is noted in Nm 14:39ff., after the Hebrews' refusal to follow the lead of the spies who were sent to reconnoiter Palestine. This abortive venture prompted the main penetration via Transjordan (→ Biblical Geography, 73:31), where the recently formed kingdoms of Edom, Moab, and Ammon were only sparsely settled. However, the victory at Hormah in the Negeb suggests that there was a split in the group that entered Palestine; Nm 21:1–3 and Jgs 1:9–16 seem to support a victorious penetration of the S by Caleb and his group. The main party, under the leadership of Moses, took the circuitous detour around Edom and Moab (Nm 20:14ff.; 21:10ff.). The first victories over the kings Sihon and Og, which took place N of the Arnon and N of the Jabbok respectively, became traditional in Israel (cf. Nm 21:21–35; Ps 136:17ff.), since they secured Transjordan for the invaders. Near the plains of Moab, after the utterance of Balaam's oracles (cf. W. F. Albright, *JBL* 63 [1944] 207–33), Moses died on Mt. Nebo. His failure to enter the promised land is cloaked in mystery and gave rise to several explanations in the traditions (cf. Nm 20:12; Dt 1:37; etc.). The infidelity of Israel with the Baal of Peor (Nm 25) was already an omen of its life in Canaan.

40 **(F) The Land of Canaan.** Canaan of the 13th cent. BC was a land of disparate peoples. The Canaanites proper lived primarily along the shore line, and also in pockets in the central and southern mountains. Non-Semitic groups (Hittites, Horites, etc.) are also mentioned as part of the population. The political structure was characterized by the existence of city-states. For centuries this situation had been countenanced by Egypt. The kinglets were "loyal" to the Pharaoh to whom they paid tribute, but the Amarna letters of the 14th cent. tell us of their trials, particularly with the 'Apiru (cf. *DOTT* 38–45; E. Campbell in *BA* 23 [1960] 2–22). By the 13th cent. the number of city-states had notably increased, but they were not prepared for the Hebr conquest. This situation was in lively contrast to Transjordan, which was organized into the Amorite principalities ruled by Sihon and Og and into the kingdoms of Edom, Moab, and Ammon (→ Excursus Israel, 11:14–18, 27; cf. the studies of N. Glueck and G. Landes in *BAR* 2, 51–58, 69–88).

41 Egyptian influence on Canaan extended to things cultural, but Canaanite religion was a relatively independent development. The pantheon dwelt on a mountain in the N (Saphon or Zephon; *mons Casius*, 25 mi. NE of Ugarit). El was the head of these divinities, but was outshone by Baal (Hadad). The three principal goddesses were Asherah ("creatress of the gods," and of strongly sexual stamp), Astarte (Ashtoreth), and Anath (the "virgin," and of warlike nature) whose exploits are well known from the Ugaritic texts. Canaanite worship was marked by fertility rites, which involved sacred prostitution (cf. Albright, *ARI* 68–94; J. Gray, *The Legacy of Canaan* [VTSup 5; Leiden, 1957] 113–59).

42 **(G) Joshua's Victories.** It is generally recognized that the biblical narrative of Joshua's conquest has telescoped the actual events in the manner of an epic. Everything is attributed to Joshua, just as all the laws are attributed to Moses. A careful reading of Jos will indicate that there was no continual or full-scale war raging through Palestine; there were "campaigns," but there was also much gradual assimilation. The conquest is schematized into three campaigns: first, the capture of Jericho and of Ai in the central hill country; then the victories in the S after the alliance with the Gibeonites; and finally, the thrust to the N in which Hazor fell. Apart from these campaigns of Joshua, the biblical text mentions many single battles through which the conquest was effected (Jgs 1, esp., and Jos 13:2–6; 15:13–19; 23:7–13). There was no total liquidation of the Canaanites, despite the ideal of *ḥērem* or "doom" war, a feature of ancient Near Eastern culture that Israel shared with its neighbors (*ANET* 320). The sources make clear that pockets of Canaanites survived, and the survivors are "explained" in Jgs 2:21–23; 3:2. But even if allowances are made for the epic style of the narrative, the conquest remains as an extraordinary exploit on the part of Joshua and his Hebrews. (On the nature of the conquest as a movement to solidarity among groups of pre-existent social units in Palestine, who overthrew the urban domination of the region, see G. Mendenhall in *BA* 25 [1962] 66–87.)

43 With the crossing of the Jordan (a landslide?), which is described in liturgical overtones (Jos 3–4), Joshua's groups had to meet the challenge of Jericho. Despite the lengthy excavations at Tell es-Sultan (→ Biblical Archaeology, 74:19, 61–62), there is little evidence of the 13th-cent. Jericho that is described as falling to the ritual shouts and processions of the Israelites (Jos 6:21; but cf. 24:11). Yet the conquest of the Jericho area would have been necessary in view of the plan to penetrate the highlands through the easy access provided by the nearby valleys.

Unfortunately the results of the excavations at Ai by Mme. Marquet-Krause (confirmed in *BASOR* 178 [1965] 13–40) have indicated that this town too was not inhabited in Joshua's time. The story of Ai has been characterized as etiological, i.e., a tale that is narrated to explain a name (Ai = the "ruins"—how was the site reduced to ruins?). Etiology cannot be ruled out (cf. Samson and Ramath-lehi, Jgs 15:17), but it should not be too quickly invoked in these chapters. The explanations of Albright (the story refers to Bethel, not Ai) and of L.-H. Vincent (Ai was temporarily occupied to meet the immediate invasion) remain hypothetical. Similarly, there is no evidence from J. Pritchard's excavation at Gibeon (*Gibeon* [Princeton, 1962]) that this site was as important in Joshua's time as would appear from Jos 9–10.

44 On the other hand, there is striking archaeological evidence in favor of the violent downfall, around 1225, of Bethel, Debir, Lachish, and Hazor (→ Biblical Archaeology, 74:63), and probably Eglon. This tallies with the campaigns of Joshua in Jos 10–11 (cf. G. E. Wright, *JNES* 5 [1946] 105–14). It is noteworthy that the Israelites generally avoided the "raised sites" (i.e., cities that stood on mounds) as Jos 11:13 explicitly mentions. Hence fortresses like Megiddo and Beth-shan were bypassed. There can be no doubt that the lightning thrusts (Jos 10–11) at Aijalon, at the cities in the S, and at Hazor in the N were enough to provide the Israelites with a firm footing in the land. But neither the coast nor the Plain of Esdraelon were touched.

45 The virtually peaceful take-over of Shechem (implying the whole area of Ephraim and Manasseh) suggests that the newcomers met here one or several tribes who were related to them (→ Biblical Geography, 73:101). Significantly, the Shechem excavations show that the city was *not* destroyed during the period of conquest and settlement (*BAR* 2, 258–300). Modern scholarship recognizes that the unity of "Israel" in the conquest derives from the later perspective of a united people, and the biblical data support this view. The Hebrews are described as a "crowd of mixed ancestry" (Ex 12:38; cf. Nm 11:4), which was led out of Egypt. This means that many other types who had associated themselves with the Hebrews in Goshen had become part of them. And it is reasonable to suppose that there had long been a movement of Hebrews to Palestine during previous centuries, or even that many Hebrews had remained in Palestine without ever going to Egypt (Albright, *BP* 32). The scene at Shechem (Jos 8:30–35; 24:1–28) describes a covenant renewal and it presupposes that Israel incorporated other groups (Canaanites) into itself (24:14–15). Gradually then, the traditions of those who had shared the Exodus experience became the traditions of all, as the various ethnic groups became absorbed. These considerations temper the conventional picture of Joshua's armies overrunning Canaan; there was as much assimilation and reunion as there was conquest (→ Joshua, 7:3).

46 The term "amphictyony," of Gk derivation, has been applied by M. Noth (*Hist.* 85–137) to the union of the 12 tribes around the central sanctuary. He reasons further that if all the tribes did not belong to the federation until the conquest, then one must consider that Israel began only at that time when the federation assumed its normative form. Others (Bright, Albright) consider Israel to have been a tribal federation at Sinai where the covenant was actually formed; there the basic people was created. The tradition of lineal descendants of the 12 tribes from a common ancestor must probably be interpreted broadly; the genealogy expresses connections of cultural rather than biological nature, relationships based on geography, commerce, and other considerations. The unity created by the tribal federation was religious, not political, as may be inferred from the highly individualistic conduct of the tribes in the period of the judges. The central sanctuary itself seems to have changed residence several times in this early period: Shechem, Bethel, Shiloh (where it received more than a merely temporary dwelling; → Religious Institutions, 76:40, 41, 50). The tribes are named in two different forms in the lists that have been preserved; the older form includes Levi (Gn 29:31–30:24; 49:1–27) and presents Joseph (Ephraim and Manasseh) as one tribe; in the later form Levi is omitted and Ephraim and Manasseh are separate (Nm 26:4–51). The union of the 12 is not merely created by a covenant; behind it stands a complicated historical process. The boundaries of the "12 tribes" as recorded in Jos 13ff. are not fixed quantities, because of the checkered history of the tribes (e.g., the assimilation of Simeon by Judah, Reuben by Gad). Moreover, the actual geographical data in these chapters have been revised during the course of Israelite history (cf. L. H. Grollenberg in *AtBib* 58–61; K. Elliger in *IDB* 4, 700–710).

47 **(H) The Judges.** The period of the judges is conveniently dated from about 1200 to 1050, but Jgs does not give us a continuous history of events within this century and a half. Rather, there is a series of separate incidents, largely local in scope, which illustrate the thesis that the author has clearly set down in 2:10–3:6. The sequence of sin, oppression, conversion, and deliverance echoes the deuteronomic theology of history (→ 1–2 Kings, 10:79). But the vignettes throw some light on the history of the period. The tribes within the amphictyony fought their own battles. The difficulties were twofold: the inroads of the Canaanite Baal cult, and lack of unity in meeting the oppressive attacks of neighboring peoples. The Song of Deborah scores several tribes for their lack of co-operation (Jgs 5:15–17). The geographical situation increased the individualism of the separate groups. The tribes in Galilee were separated from the central area by the Plain of Esdraelon; the central mountain area was itself divided into pockets by the many valleys. Finally, the Jordan Valley served to cut off the W from the E.

48 Moreover, the Israelites themselves were in the process of settling down and changing to new ways of life, particularly farming. The most serious challenge was now to present itself, namely the native fertility cults of Canaan. The assimilation of Canaanite culture and ways of life was beginning, and this extended also to the Baals and Astartes worshiped in the many Canaanite "high places" remaining in the land. Baal was already in possession of the land—a god of fertility, who needed to be propitiated. Yahweh was the God of history, who had saved Israel; but now there was the practical matter of ensuring fertility and abundant crops. With the Canaanite methods of farming were associated the Canaanite religious rites, and these were imitated (e.g., Jerubbaal in Jgs 6). At the very least, syncretism was the result: Yahweh took on the features of Baal, a practical identity with him. It was a good thing to make a pilgrimage occasionally to the sanctuary at Shiloh, but the Canaanite high places were closer, and the rites were attractive (cf. J. L. McKenzie, *The World of the Judges* [Englewood Cliffs, N.J., 1966] 34–44).

49 The judge (*šōpēṭ*) was primarily a charismatic military leader, a "deliverer" (Jgs 2:16; 3:9; etc.). In this period the political situation in Palestine was something of a vacuum. The invasion of the Sea Peoples about 1200 had been finally repelled by Egypt, and the Philistines had remained behind to form their pentapolis on the southern coast (→ Excursus Israel, 11:19). The tribal federation was exposed to attack from any quarter and from any group that could hope to succeed. The invasion by Cushan-rishathaim of "Aram of the two rivers" (if Aram rather than Edom is to be read) was successfully resisted by the same Othniel who had conquered Debir for Judah (Jgs 1:11–16). The daring exploit of the left-handed Ehud in slaying Eglon of Moab precipitated a successful campaign against the Moabites that kept them E of the Jordan.

50 Deborah inspired Barak and about six northern tribes to do battle in the Plain of Esdraelon against Canaanites, led by Sisera. The advantage of the Canaanite chariots was wiped out by rainstorms that flooded the river Kishon (4:15; 5:20–21) and made possible an Israelite victory. This has been dated about 1125 by Albright (*BASOR* 62[1936]26–31) on the basis of the archaeological evidence from Taanach and Megiddo. The victory gave rise to one of the earliest Hebr poems in the OT, the Song of Deborah (Jgs 5), which is a poetic version of the events related in the prose narrative of Jgs 4.

51 The razzias made upon the central highlands by camel-riding bands of Midianites, Amalekites, and desert Arabs ("Qedemites") was met by Gideon (Jerubbaal). The details of his campaigns betray the expansion and literary embellishments that are characteristic of these early tales of victory (e.g., the fleece episode, 6:36–40). His victory at Ain Harod was followed by pursuit across the Jordan and the slaying of Zebah and Zalmunna (Ps 83:12). Already the ascendancy of the tribe of Ephraim appears (8:1; cf. the Shibboleth episode in 12:1–6)—an omen of the later division into N and S. There was a premature movement toward monarchy when, after

Gideon had refused the offer of kingship, his son Abimelech succeeded in establishing a precarious "kingdom" for a short time. He seems to have joined the Canaanites of Shechem and the neighboring Israelites under his dominion—living in Arumah but governing Shechem through a regent. Equally as important as Gideon's wars was his opposition to the local Baal cult, illustrated in the episode of tearing down the altar (6:25–32). The evidence of Baal worship is strikingly exemplified also in Abimelech's adventures in Shechem and in the destruction of the temple of El-berith (9:46–49).

52 Despite his origins and his life as an outlaw in Transjordan, Jephthah was asked by the men of Gilead to give aid against the Ammonites. His success bound him to fulfill his savage vow to sacrifice his own daughter. The raw moral conditions of the tribes are illustrated by this incident, and also by the appendices to Jgs (chs. 17–21). Samson's colorful exploits are indicative of the desperate situation in Judah, for his own compatriots deliver him to the Philistines (15:12–14). But his astonishing deeds of strength and bravery lived on among a subjugated tribe as tales of hope, which were handed down as a satire on the Philistines.

Very few details have been preserved concerning the so-called minor judges, whose activity may have been more judicial than military; it is possible that some of them were not Israelite. Shamgar's exploit against the Philistines is reminiscent of Samson. His name, "son of Anath," witnesses to the influences of the Canaanite (Ugaritic) divinities in the land, if indeed Shamgar was an Israelite.

53 **(III) The Monarchy and the Exile (*ca.* 1020–539 BC).** In the 11th cent. the greatest single threat to Israel's existence was the Philistines who had established their city-states in a pocket of the coastal plain: Gaza, Gath, Ashkelon, Ashdod (Azotus), and Ekron (→ Biblical Geography, 73:71–72). They also had garrisons in Israelite territory, and their influence extended through the area of the tribal federation. The Samson stories (Jgs 13–16) illustrate their domination of Judah; and 1 Sm 13:19ff. points to their monopoly on iron, which put the Israelites at a severe disadvantage. Their victory at Aphek or Ebenezer gave them entry to the northern area (1 Sm 4; several tribes seem to be represented in this battle, and the Ark was captured by the Philistines). For the Philistines, → Excursus Israel, 11:19.

54 **(A) Saul (*ca.* 1020).** In this crisis two figures emerged: a "prophet," Samuel, and the first king, Saul. Because of the varied nature of the narratives that deal with his birth, vocation, and activities, Samuel appears as an ambiguous personality. His youth is said to have been spent in the Nazirite manner (1 Sm 1:11; Nm 6) as a servant of the Shiloh sanctuary under the tutelage of the priest, Heli. He is portrayed as a seer and prophet who stood for the old tribal rights against Saul, the new king. At this time, and associated with Samuel, there appear the bands of ecstatics, who resemble the Canaanite prophets. Finally, Samuel is also described as the last of the judges (1 Sm 7:2–17), exercising his office at Bethel, Gilgal, and Mizpah. It is in this context of a schematized report relating him to the judges that Samuel's victory over the Philistines (7:10ff.) is reported and it must be evaluated accordingly. It was rather Saul who bore the brunt of the Philistine oppression.

55 The Philistine threat achieved what Abimelech's attempt failed to do, namely, the uniting of the tribes under a king in the face of a common enemy. The introduction of kingship in Israel has been preserved in two traditions, one favorable (1 Sm 9:1–10:16; 11), the other hostile (8; 10:17–27; 12) to the monarchy. The first (and perhaps the oldest, but cf. I. Mendelsohn, *BASOR* 143 [1956] 17–22) is the story of young Saul searching for the lost asses and finding a kingdom when he was anointed by Samuel at Ramah. The second narrative portrays the end of an era, as Samuel, the "last judge," yields to the people's plea to be like the other nations. Saul seems to have been viewed as continuing the charismatic strain of the judges; it may be questioned if at first his leadership was viewed in the light of royalty. He is said to have been appointed *nāgîd* (1 Sm 10:1; also of David, 2 Sm 7:8), or "military commander" (Albright). Hence it may be that the kingly aspect of this institution only gradually became apparent in Israel. There was no pretense of an impressive court, as shown by his modest palace, which Albright excavated at Gibeah (Tell el-Ful; cf. L. Sinclair, *BA* 27 [1964] 52–64).

Saul was helped considerably by his initial successes, such as that against the Ammonites who had besieged Jabesh-gilead (1 Sm 11)—a military venture with which the Philistines did not interfere. He also obtained a local victory over the Philistines at Michmash, thanks to his son Jonathan (1 Sm 14). But he quarreled with Samuel (two accounts in 1 Sm 13 and 15) and became subject to fits of depression and envious rage that mark the well-known narratives concerning his dealings with David. His eventual downfall was sealed by his slaughter of the priests at Nob, and he presents a pathetic figure in the episode of the "witch of Endor." Meanwhile the Philistines were exerting even greater pressure culminating in the devastating defeat at Gilboa where both Saul and his son Jonathan were slain (David's dirge in 2 Sm 1:17–27; → 1-2 Samuel 9:40–45).

56 **(B) David (1000–962).** There are variant traditions concerning David's introduction to court: 1 Sm 16:14–23; 17:1–11,32–53 (minstrel and military aide of Saul) and 17:12–30; 17:55–18:2 (the young brother who brings provisions to the front lines). The later chapters dealing with court life and outlaw days also seem to have many doublets (twice David spares Saul's life; twice Saul tries to pin David to the wall; etc.). His ability as a warrior made him rise at court (marriage with Saul's daughter, Michal)—and fall just as quickly, as Saul strove to kill him. Fleeing to the Judean wilderness, David gathered about him a band of some 400 outlaws like himself and bided his time. He succeeded even in turning his delicate relationship with the Philistine king of Gath to his own political profit, and he emerged as vassal chief of Ziklag before Saul met his death at Gilboa.

David immediately became king of Judah in Hebron (2 Sm 2:1ff.)—a coup assisted by his tribal origins and his marriages to Judahites (Ahinoam, Abigail). At Mahanaim in Transjordan Saul's kingdom was continued by his son Ishbaal (or Ishbosheth as the scribes wrote the name), supported by Abner, the general of Saul's army. There was intermittent, but not very significant war (the duel at the pool of Gibeon, 2 Sm 2:10ff.), until Abner defected to David. David showed a sense of political realities in proving himself completely innocent both of Ishbaal's assassination and of Joab's brutal murder of Abner. The way was now open to David's being anointed as "king over Israel," when the elders of Israel came to Hebron, where he had reigned seven years, and accepted him (2 Sm 5:1–5). The kingship remained twofold—over Judah and Israel—even though one speaks of the "united" kingdom (cf. 2 Sm 5:5).

57 David went on to extend his kingdom in the N at the expense of the Arameans; he incorporated Zobah (victory over the Aramean, Hadadezer) and the territory of Damascus. Profitable treaties with Hamath and Tyre were concluded, so that effectively the kingdom could be described as reaching the river (Euphrates; 2 Sm 8:3).

In Transjordan there were victories over Ammon and Edom, and a vassal king was set up in Moab. Thus, David's kingdom reached from Ezion-geber on the Gulf of Aqabah to Homs, from the Mediterranean to the Euphrates. The Canaanite enclaves still existing in Palestine were gradually incorporated (e.g., Megiddo). This type of empire had never before been achieved in this area which had always been Egypt's domain; it was possible only because Egypt was on the wane and Assyria had not yet awakened. David, too, broke the power of the Philistines, seemingly with a string of successes, although the data are sparse (2 Sm 5:17ff.; 21:15ff.). The Philistine pentapolis was reduced to vassal status.

58 David's master stroke was the choice of Jerusalem as the capital (→ Biblical Geography, 73:92–93). By his capture of this Jebusite city he made it a "royal city," i.e., his own (just as later he made a personal appearance at the capture of Rabbah in Ammon so that his "name be proclaimed over it," 2 Sm 12:28). Politically Jerusalem was a neutral site acceptable to both N and S. Moreover, it presented distinct advantages for defense, surrounded by valleys except on the N (perhaps the Jebusites had cut a valley on the N that was later filled in by the "Millo" under Solomon, 1 Kgs 9:15). It is certain that the "city of David," or Ophel, occupied the southern spur on the E side of the mountain. The transfer of the Ark of the Covenant gave the city a religious importance that it was never to lose. How much of the Jebusite liturgy and ideology entered into Israelite thought is hard to determine, but the "priesthood according to the order of Melchizedek" seems to be one such element (Ps 110:4; → Religious Institutions, 76:20).

The political organization was modeled on Egyptian institutions: herald (*mazkîr*), army general, etc. (cf. De Vaux, *AI* 1, 129–32). In his own bodyguard David had various groups of foreign mercenaries, such as the Cherethites and Pelethites. One can easily imagine the crisis precipitated within Israel by this radical change as the people definitely moved away from tribal federation to a monarchy with a complex administration, a standing army, and the inevitable taxation—all of which tended to wipe out the old tribal individualism (2 Sm 8:15–18; 20:23–26).

59 The "court history" of 2 Sm 9–20 and 1 Kgs 1–2 is a remarkable literary achievement of David's time. It is a reliable historical document concerning the problem of the succession to David's throne and his apparent inability to cope with it (cf. G. von Rad, *GesSt* 159–88). With David a new idea of dynasty had taken over. Who would succeed him? As the "court history" unfolds, Amnon is eliminated, Absalom's revolt ends in his death, Adonijah loses out to Solomon. The theme of succession runs through many scenes, within the court and without, and on both sides of the Jordan. There is also a wide range of characters: David passionate and with a blind love for his sons; the generals Joab and Amasa, the priests Zadok and Abiathar; the commoners Ziba and Barzillai; the rebels Shimei and Sheba; the women Tamar, Bathsheba, and the widow of Tekoa. The ineluctable connection between sin and punishment is present in the stories of Amnon, Absalom, and especially of David. Only rarely is a direct positive theological judgment expressed (2 Sm 11:27; 12:24; 17:14); God is at work behind the scenes.

Absalom's revolt against David is less revealing, from a political point of view, than the later revolt of Sheba (2 Sm 20). This was precipitated by jealousy over David's overtures to the elders of Judah, the very people who had supported Absalom's revolt. David's move caused some of the northern tribes to rally to Sheba. Under the leadership of the redoubtable Joab (who had murdered Amasa, David's own replacement for Joab) David's troops quickly ended this schism, but it was an omen of the division that was to come.

60 The real credit for consolidating the Israelite kingdom lies with David. If Israel attained greater prosperity under Solomon, this was at the expense of the solidity that David had achieved. David was perhaps less of a charismatic leader in the eyes of the people than Saul had been, but David had tremendous talent, and in the end it was recognized that the Lord was with him. He must have possessed considerable personal charm, as several stories in his life suggest (the loyalty of his foreign mercenary, Ittai of Gath—2 Sm 15:18–22; the episode of the drink of water from Bethlehem—2 Sm 23:13–17). But David's crowning importance was due to the dynastic principle that became incarnate in him through the prophetic oracle of Nathan (2 Sm 7). This prophecy (the Magna Charta of royal messianism; → Aspects OT Thought, 77:155) contributed to the general stability of the royal house in Judah, in contrast to the instability in the northern kingdom after the division.

61 **(C) Solomon (961–922).** In Israelite tradition the glory of Solomon's reign became proverbial. He first secured his position by political alliances: marriage with the Pharaoh's daughter, which brought to him Gezer as a dowry; commercial arrangements with Hiram of Tyre, which opened up possibilities of export. Trading reached a new high, for example, commerce in the Gulf of Aqabah, thanks to a merchant fleet at Ezion-geber; trade for gold and valuables with Arabia (the Queen of Sheba, 1 Kgs 10:1–10) and with Ophir (Somaliland in Africa, or perhaps the lower part of the Arabian peninsula); a profitable exchange of horses and chariots between Egypt and Cilicia (1 Kgs 10:28, corrected text). Military establishments were set up to support a standing army with chariotry (→ Biblical Archaeology, 74:35).

Solomon's reputation as a builder rests not only on the Temple, which was built in the Phoenician tradition (→ Religious Institutions, 76:56ff.), but also upon an elaborate palace complex. Moreover, he was the patron of wisdom and the arts (→ Wisdom Lit, 28:5–6), and the JE traditions of the Pentateuch probably took form during his reign, the "period of enlightenment" as it has been called (Von Rad). The deuteronomic editor angrily emphasizes the care with which Solomon provided for the worship of other gods at the whim of his harem (1 Kgs 11:1–8). A pattern for syncretism and outright idolatry even in Jerusalem was thus created. Each succeeding king is judged by deuteronomic standards, i.e., his attitudes toward idolatry and toward worship on the "high places" (which was doubtless nominally Yahwistic)—the latter standard is really anachronistic, for centralization of worship only gradually became the ideal because of the reforms of Hezekiah and Josiah in the late 8th and 7th cents. (→ Religious Institutions, 76:66–68).

62 Solomon's reorganization of the kingdom into 12 districts that did not strictly agree with tribal boundaries was a strong move toward centralization of government; and it made possible an efficient system of heavy taxation in order to meet royal expenses. One must consider the great transformation in Israelite society that is implied in the reigns of Solomon and David: in a few generations there was a transition from tribal federation to "empire" status; the agricultural and pastoral life yielded to urban life with a corresponding growth of social inequalities. In this period Albright (*BP* 56) estimates a possible Israelite population of 800,000.

But not everything was peace and light in Solomon's days. There was the partial loss of Edom and of Damascus (1 Kgs 11:14ff.), and an unsuccessful attempt at revolt by Jeroboam, who fled to Egypt, only to return under

Kings of the Divided Monarchy

JUDAH	
Rehoboam	922–915
Abijah (Abijam)	915–913
Asa	913–873
Jehoshaphat	873–849
Jehoram (Joram)	849–842
Ahaziah	842
Queen Athaliah	842–837
Jehoash (Joash)	837–800
Amaziah	800–783
Uzziah (*Azariah)	783–742
[Regency of Jotham	750–742]
Jotham	742–735
Ahaz (Jehoahaz I)	735–715
Hezekiah	715–687
Manasseh	687–642
Amon	642–640
Josiah	640–609
Jehoahaz II (*Shallum)	609
Jehoiakim (*Eliakim)	609–598
Jehoiachin (*Jeconiah)	597
Zedekiah (*Mattaniah)	597–587
FALL OF JERUSALEM	587

	ISRAEL
922–901	**Jeroboam I**
901–900	Nadab
900–877	Baasha
877–876	Elah
876	Zimri
876–869	**Omri**
869–850	**Ahab**
850–849	Ahaziah
849–842	Jehoram (Joram)
842–815	**Jehu**
815–801	Jehoahaz (Joahaz)
801–786	Jehoash (Joash)
786–746	**Jeroboam II**
746–745	Zechariah
745	Shallum
745–738	Menahem
738–737	Pekahiah
737–732	Pekah
732–724	Hoshea
721	FALL OF SAMARIA

EXPLANATION: The names of the most important kings are in boldface. Variant or alternative names are put in parentheses; an asterisk marks possible birth names of kings whose regnal names are given first. In the list of Israel the shifting back and forth of the column indicates new dynasties, e.g., Omri and the next three names belong to one dynasty, while Jehu begins a new dynasty. The dates are those suggested by Albright, *BP* 116–17; other scholars will suggest other dates. It is impossible to reconcile perfectly the biblical information supplied by 1–2 Kgs and 2 Chr, for sometimes the information is contradictory. In part the dating is affected by when the civil year began. For most of the period it seems to have begun in the fall (Tishri); but certainly after the time of Josiah (609), when Babylonian influence became dominant, there was a shift to a spring New Year (Nisan). This may have been a religious custom even earlier.

Moreover there is the problem of antedating and postdating. In antedating (an Egyptian practice, followed during most of the monarchy), the months between the king's accession and the next New Year are counted as the first year of his reign, even if only a few days are involved. In postdating (a Babylonian practice, followed by, at least, the last kings of Judah), the first year of the king's reign begins with the New Year's day following his accession. The intervening period is not counted.

This chart was supplied by R. E. Brown.

Rehoboam and inaugurate the northern kingdom of Israel. The institution of forced labor or corvée added to the general dissatisfaction. This discontent was imprudently disregarded by Solomon's son Rehoboam, and the division of the young kingdom was at hand.

63 **(D) Israel and Judah (922–842).** Significantly, it was at Shechem, the old center (Jos 24) of the amphictyony, that the rebellion of the northern tribes took place. Here Rehoboam (922–915) was to have been acknowledged as king by "all Israel." But when he failed to heed the advice of his elder statesmen and pledged "scorpions" for Solomon's "whips," the old desert cry of revolt was sounded, "To your tents, O Israel!" Only Benjamin went with Judah, because Rehoboam occupied it at once (2 Chr 11:12). More grief awaited Solomon's son, for Palestine was invaded by Sheshonk (Shishak) of Egypt who plundered Jerusalem. His triumphant report inscribed on the walls of the Amon temple at Karnak indicates that he ravaged the N, and it seems that Edom and the new kingdom of Jeroboam bore the brunt of the invasion (B. Mazar, VTSup 4 [1957] 57–66). Rehoboam prepared for the sporadic civil war of the next 50 years by erecting to the N a string of fortresses (Gibeah, Ramah, etc.) and by strengthening the S (perhaps against Egypt?—fortifications were built at Lachish and other points, 2 Chr 11:5ff.). The kingdom of David and Solomon dissolved as the Philistines regained power and the Arameans obtained independence. Very quickly the Moabites and Ammonites followed suit.

64 It was relatively easy for the northern tribes to return to the charismatic principle and recognize a new leader. Jeroboam I (922–901) had already become a symbol of revolt, and he was favored by the prophet Ahijah (who was later to forsake him). Acclaimed as king, he took up residence in Shechem, Penuel, and finally in Tirzah (→ Biblical Geography, 73:102). In order to insure the loyalty of his people and to offset the attraction that the Jerusalem Temple might still hold for them, Jeroboam established royal temples in Dan and Bethel, sites already famous as ancient sanctuaries (Am 7:13, 8:14; → Religious Institutions, 76:41, 53). Here he set up a golden bull, presumably as a pedestal on which the invisible Yahweh was enthroned (cf. Albright, *FSAC* 299–301). The danger of syncretism and of crass identification of Yahweh with the bull image was only too real, as later events proved. Jeroboam's act became known in the parlance of the deuteronomic historian as "the sin of Jeroboam," although this act to unify the tribes against the Jerusalem Temple doubtless was dictated by political realism.

65 The deuteronomic historian, author of 1–2 Kgs, has written the story of the divided kingdoms within a rigid framework of chronology, synchronization of reigns, and religious evaluation from the point of view of the Jerusalem Temple. Even though he is composing a confession of guilt and thus offering a justification for the catastrophes of 721 and 587, he indicates many sources (about 16 references to the "Book of the Chronicles of the Kings of Israel" and 14 to the "Book of the Chronicles of the Kings of Judah"); and he incorporates many disparate tales, such as those from the prophetic cycles of Elijah and Elisha (→ 1–2 Kings, 10:3–7, 79).

66 For the next 50 years from Jeroboam I (922) to Omri (876) there was little stability on the Israelite throne, which lacked the dynastic promise given to David. Civil war between the N and S raged intermittently. During this time Jeroboam's son Nadab, after reigning less than two years, was assassinated by Baasha, whose son and successor Elah was assassinated by Zimri, who in turn committed suicide in the face of the successful army revolt led by Omri. The civil war between Asa of Judah (913–873) and Baasha of Israel (900–877) was resolved when Asa made a mutual assistance treaty with Ben-hadad of Damascus (for his stele and inscription dedicated to Melqart, cf. W. F. Albright, *BASOR* 89 [1942] 23ff., but also B. Mazar, *BAR* 2, 135). The resultant invasion of Israel by the Syrians from Damascus cost Baasha part of N Galilee (1 Kgs 15:18ff.; for the Aramean states of Syria, → Excursus Israel, 11:10).

67 Omri (876–869) was an outstanding king of Israel, but in the Bible he is dismissed in a few verses because of the particular interests of the deuteronomic editor. He left a mark in history that even the Assyrians acknowledged as late as the time of Sargon II (*ca.* 700) by speaking of Israel as the "land" and "house of Omri." If his dealings with the Arameans ended unsuccessfully (1 Kgs 20:34), he did succeed in subjecting Moab to tribute (Mesha stele, *ANET* 320f.). He pursued a peaceful policy with Judah, and his alliance with the Phoenicians was sealed by the marriage of his son Ahab to Jezebel, daughter of Ethbaal (Ittobaal) of Tyre. He established a new capital at Samaria (→ Biblical Geography, 73:103; Biblical Archaeology, 74:74). For a full appreciation of the role of Samaria, cf. A. Alt, *KlSchr* 3, 258–302.

68 Most of the reign of Omri's son, Ahab (869–850) was occupied with wars against the Arameans of Damascus. But in 853 BC both united in the league against the Assyrian armies of Shalmaneser III in the famous battle of Qarqar (see W. Hallo, *BAR* 2, 152–62). The inscription of the Assyrian king specifies that Ahab contributed 2,000 chariots and 10,000 footmen to the fray (*ANET* 278f.). The Assyrians' claim to victory rings hollow; they did not press their alleged advantage and seem to have withdrawn for a time. The revolt of Moab against Ahab was successful, but contrary to the boast of the Mesha stele, Israel was not destroyed forever (*ANET* 320, lines 6f.; J. Liver, *PEQ* 99 [1967] 14–31).

69 The religious policy of Ahab is illustrated by the stories of the *Elijah cycle* (1 Kgs 17–19,21). Ahab appears to have been an indifferent Yahwist and easily influenced by his wife Jezebel, who was intent upon establishing the worship of Baal (the Tyrian god, Melqart, for whom a temple was built in Samaria, 1 Kgs 16:32). The seriousness of the threat to Yahwism is illustrated by the fact that in the dramatic incident on Mt. Carmel Elijah confronted 450 prophets of Baal and 400 prophets of Asherah (1 Kgs 18:19). Elijah's victory saved the traditional religion at a critical moment, although he had to flee Jezebel's wrath. Ahab himself met death in battle against the Arameans at Ramoth-gilead (→ 1–2 Kings, 10:39).

70 During this period the kings of Judah were eclipsed by Omri and his son, and Judah was in fact little more than a vassal state of Israel. Jehoshaphat of Judah (873–849), to whom 2 Chr 19:4–11 attributes a judicial reform, was allied with Ahab of Israel at Ramoth-gilead, and apparently with Jehoram (Joram) of Israel in the war against Moab (1 Kgs 22; cf. 2 Chr 20). Although Jehoshaphat subjugated Edom and was credited by Chr with a victory over Moab, he failed to renew the Ophir trade (→ 61 above). The reigns of Jehoram (Joram; 849–842) and Ahaziah (842) of Judah were dominated by the queen mother, Athaliah, the daughter of Ahab. Edom and Libnah revolted against Jehoram, and 2 Chr 21:8ff. describes further misfortunes. When in 842 Ahaziah of Judah was killed as a by-product of Jehu's revolt in Israel, Athaliah made her move and obtained the throne (842–837), slaying the royal heirs, except for Jehoash (Joash) who was spared. The low ebb of Yahwism in official circles is illustrated by the position held by a certain Mattan, "priest of Baal" (2 Kgs 11:18). But Athaliah met an inglorious end in the bloodless revolution engineered by Jehoiada the priest who put Joash on the throne.

71 The brief reign in Israel of Ahab's son and successor, Ahaziah (850–849) saw the end of Elijah's activity (2 Kgs 1); and the stories of the *Elisha cycle* (2 Kgs 2–9) are set mostly in the reign of Jehoram (849–842), another son of Ahab. In this period the Moabites were successful in their fight for independence, and the Arameans of Syria made further inroads. Within the kingdom itself the bands of ecstatic prophets encouraged revolution, which came when one of their number anointed Jehu, an army general, king (→ 1–2 Kings, 10:48).

72 **(E) The Dynasty of Jehu (842–746).** The revolt of Jehu (842–815) touched off a bloody purge; he did away with King Jehoram who was recovering from wounds sustained in battle against the Syrian, Hazael, at Ramoth-gilead and also killed Ahaziah of Judah who was visiting the king of Israel. His execution of the redoubtable Jezebel is a dramatic scene. Jehu demanded the heads of the 70 "sons" of Ahab in Samaria, and even slew 42 representatives from the Jerusalem court ruled by relatives of Ahaziah. The final touch was the slaughter of the Baal prophets and sympathizers in Samaria, where Jehu destroyed the temple of Baal. The triumph of Yahweh over Baal was in effect secured by this ruthless king, whose brutality was condemned by the prophet Hosea (1:4f.).

But Jehu was much less successful in external political affairs. He has been immortalized on the famous Black Obelisk of Shalmaneser III (*ANE* 192, plate 100), where he is called "son of Omri," and where he is shown kneeling and paying tribute of silver and gold to the Assyrian monarch. This occurred about 841 at the beginning of his reign. But greater misfortune came at the hands of Hazael of Damascus whom Shalmaneser III of Assyria had not been able to liquidate (→ 68 above). Hazael took Transjordan from Israel during Jehu's reign (2 Kgs 10:32), and bedeviled both Israel and Judah for a half-century (even exacting tribute from Joash of Jerusalem, 2 Kgs 12:18).

73 The "savior" (2 Kgs 13:5) of Israel was probably the Assyrian, Adad-nirari (810–783), who made several campaigns against the Arameans, finally subduing Damascus in 802 (*ANET* 281). The son of Jehu, Jehoahaz of Israel (815–801), bore the brunt of the Aramean wars (2 Kgs 13:7), but his successor Jehoash (801–786) was able to recoup the losses at the expense of Hazael's successor, Ben-hadad (mentioned perhaps in the Zakir stele, *DOTT* 242–50).

74 With the accession of Jeroboam II (786–746) to the throne of Israel, a new era began. He succeeded in restoring Israel "from the entrance of Hamath as far as the sea of the Arabah" (2 Kgs 14:25), and archaeological excavations bear witness to his fortifications at Samaria. His long and prosperous reign set the stage for the gross social and religious conditions that provoked the tirades of the prophets, *Amos* and *Hosea*. They were not from the ecstatic bands, such as those associated with Elijah and Elisha (Am 7:14); rather, Amos and Hosea viewed their call as a direct mission from the Lord (→ Prophetic Lit, 12:6–10). Neither king nor people were spared; these prophets condemned social evils, luxury and immorality, insincere worship and outright idolatry. They were not innovators but reformers, passing judgment on the contemporary scene in the light of older Israelite traditions. Amos, from Judah, proclaimed that the Day of the Lord which was expected to be a triumph would be instead a Day of Darkness and Gloom. In and through his own marital misfortunes Hosea understood and expressed the corresponding experience of Yahweh with his faithless people (→ Hosea, 15:4, 8). The short-lived ascendancy of Israel was about to end, for the theological reasons indicated by these two prophets, and for the political reason that Assyria's Tiglath-pileser III had now begun his campaigns to the W (→ Hosea, 15:2–3).

75 As we saw, the revolt of Jehu found an echo in the southern kingdom. A successful palace revolt against Athaliah placed a child on the Jerusalem throne, Joash (837–800), whose adviser (perhaps regent) was the priest Jehoiada. The Arameans of Syria continued to have the upper hand, and tribute had to be paid to Hazael, but Joash instituted the restoration of the Temple. His long mediocre reign ended in assassination, which was avenged by his son, Amaziah (800–783). The new king of Judah succeeded in conquering the Edomites, thus opening up the old commercial routes. But he foolishly (cf. 2 Chr 25 for the motivation) challenged Joash of Israel to a war, and he would not be put off by the latter's warning, couched in a fable (2 Kgs 14:9–10). The battle ended disastrously with Joash plundering the Temple. Like his father, Amaziah of Judah was slain in a palace conspiracy and was succeeded by his son Azariah (Uzziah).

76 The material success of the reign of Jeroboam II of Israel was matched by that of his southern contemporary, Azariah (783–742). He restored the Solomonic commercial center at Elath (Ezion-geber), fortified Jerusalem, and engaged in strong military operations and surveillance to the E, S, and W (2 Chr 26:6ff.). But leprosy curtailed Azariah's career and he gave over the throne of Judah to Jotham (750?–735), whose building and military record has been preserved in 2 Chr 27:1–9. Azariah is identified by many scholars with the Azriau of Judah whose opposition to Tiglath-pileser III (about 743?) is noted in the Assyrian annals (*ANET* 282–83). A limestone inscription discovered in 1931 in the Russian museum on the Mt. of Olives refers to a change in his burial place: "Hither were brought the bones of Uzziah, king of Judah—do not open" (see E. L. Sukenik, *Tarbiz* 2 [1930–31] 288–92; W. F. Albright, *BASOR* 44 [1931] 8–10).

77 **(F) The Last Years of Israel (746–721).** Despite the political success of the long reign of Jeroboam II, the fall of the northern kingdom was rapid. One reason was the appearance of a new Assyrian conqueror, Tiglath-pileser III (745–727), who conducted a series of campaigns in the W that were designed for conquest and not merely tribute (*ANET* 282–84; → Excursus Israel, 11:5). Another reason was the political anarchy that swept over Israel in the decade following the death of Jeroboam II (Hos 7:3–16). His son Zechariah was murdered by Shallum after a reign of only six months. Within a month Shallum was slain by Menahem (745–738). Menahem's reign was marked by heavy tribute to Tiglath-pileser III (the "Pul" of 2 Kgs 15:18; cf. his inscription concerning Menahem, *ANET* 283).

78 Menahem's son and successor, Pekahiah (738–737) was murdered by Pekah (737–732), apparently a usurper ("son of Remaliah," as Isaiah calls him in 7:4). This seizure of power represented an attempt to throw off Assyrian domination, for Pekah united with Rezin of Damascus to form a coalition against Tiglath-pileser. Their attempt to pressure Judah into this alliance led to the so-called Syro-Ephraimitic war. Judah refused to join—it was having trouble with Edom (2 Kgs 16:6)—and was attacked by the alliance from the N, which threatened to put on the Davidic throne a certain Ben Tabeel (probably an Aramean of Transjordan; cf. W. F. Albright in *BASOR* 140 [1955] 34–35). According to Is 7, Ahaz refused to rely on Yahweh and called on the Assyrians for help. Tiglath-pileser mounted a campaign and in 734–732 he destroyed Damascus and stripped Israel of a large portion of its territory (Galilee and Transjordan). Israel, now a small state and vassal to Assyria, was left under the rule of Hoshea (732–724).

79 With the death of the Assyrian monarch, however, Hoshea defected to Egypt and sent envoys to the court at Sais (we correct 2 Kgs 17:4 in the light of *BASOR* 171 [1963] 64–66). He thus incurred the wrath of the new Assyrian king, Shalmaneser VI, who apparently imprisoned him; Hoshea's end is glossed over in the biblical narrative. The siege of Samaria (724–721) began and it eventually fell to a new Assyrian ruler, Sargon II, who mentions the victory in his annals, inscribed at his new royal city, Dur Sharrukin (= Khorsabad): "I besieged and conquered Samaria (Sa-me-ri-na), led away as booty 27,290 inhabitants of it" (*ANET* 284–85). The customary policy of displacing and reallocating captive peoples was followed; the remaining people assimilated with groups from the other side of the Fertile Crescent, and the area became a province of the empire, with an Assyrian governor (→ Biblical Geography, 73:103). The text of 2 Kgs 17 is a many-sided theological meditation upon this event.

80 **(G) Ahaz (735–715) and Hezekiah (715–687).** The usual deuteronomic judgment on Ahaz acquires more substance when we learn of his child sacrifice to Molech (2 Kgs 16:3), and his cynical reaction to Isaiah (Is 7:1ff.). His recourse to Assyria in the crisis of the Syro-Ephraimitic war did not exempt him from paying tribute to Tiglath-pileser (*ANET* 282). The religious significance of his subjection to Assyria is spelled out by his adoption of an Assyrian-style altar for the Jerusalem Temple (2 Kgs 16:10–16). Both Isaiah (3:13–15; 5:8–13) and Micah (2:1–10) give vivid descriptions of social injustices during his reign.

81 Hezekiah receives full praise from the Deuteronomist because his religious reforms underscored centralization of worship. The root of this trend may already be seen in the ideal of the early amphictyony (Ex 20:24, Lv 17), and now it was marshaled as a purifying measure against the prevailing syncretism. The Chronicler (2 Chr 30:1ff.) describes Hezekiah's bold invitation to the Jews remaining in Ephraim and Manasseh to come to Jerusalem and celebrate the Passover. We are not able to judge if this relatively ineffectual move to extend influence over the N caught the attention of the Assyrian overlords. But it is true that the spiritual awakening induced by the reform was accompanied by a heightened nationalism. Unity in cult reinforced social and political unity.

82 It is difficult to ascertain the precise details of Hezekiah's relationship to Assyria. He certainly flirted with revolt, especially in 713–711 when Ashdod and other Philistine centers rebelled (*ANET* 286). Seemingly Edom and Moab were also involved, and all relied upon Egypt.

It is to this period that Is 20 refers, and the symbolic act of the prophet concerning the fall of Egypt was a clear warning to Judah to remain clear of political entanglement. The far-reaching building program of Hezekiah's reign was probably linked to his military aspirations. The text of 2 Kgs 20:20 (cf. 2 Chr 32:3–5,30) mentions a tunnel built by him to provide water within the city walls during siege. The famous Siloam inscription was found here (*ANET* 321; → Biblical Archaeology, 74:75).

The greatest danger arose when Ashkelon and Ekron revolted in 705 (again with a promise of help from Egypt, which was to be defeated ignominiously at Eltekeh; cf. Is 30–31). When Sennacherib came to the Assyrian throne (704), he quashed the rebellion of Merodach-baladan in Babylon (perhaps the visit of the Babylonian envoys to Jerusalem took place shortly before this; cf. 2 Kgs 20:12–19; Is 39). He then scourged the Phoenician coast, which had also joined in the revolt, and came S to the Philistine cities to settle the score. The people of Ekron had handed over to Hezekiah their own King Padi who had shown loyalty to Assyria; hence Judah was deeply involved. As Sennacherib describes it, he took 46 of Judah's cities and shut up Hezekiah in Jerusalem "like a bird in a cage" (*ANET* 288; *DOTT* 67). The ensuing events are dramatically recorded in 2 Kgs 18:13–19:34 (Is 36–37), where probably two versions of the same events have been strung together (instead of 18:17ff., being the record of a later revolt in 688; but cf. Bright, *Hist.*, 282–87). Despite the intervention of the Lord, Judah was ravaged (Is 1:7ff.) and faced a long period of subjection to Assyria (→ 1–2 Kings, 10:69–72; → Isaiah, 16:61–66; cf. B. S. Childs, *Isaiah and the Assyrian Crisis* [SBT, 2nd series, 3; London, 1967]).

83 **(H) Manasseh (687–642) and Josiah (640–609).** During the long reign of Manasseh Judah was subject politically to Assyria (cf. the annals of Esarhaddon and Ashurbanipal, *ANET* 291, 294). In 2 Chr 33:11ff. we are told of his temporary imprisonment at Babylon—perhaps in connection with the revolt of Ashurbanipal's brother around 650—and the apocryphal *Prayer of Manasseh* was composed later to commemorate his "conversion" (→ Apocrypha, 68:37). But no conversion could succeed in changing the idolatrous trend of his reign. The centralization of cult inaugurated by Hezekiah was undone, and the fertility cults associated with the high places were once more in vogue. Even in the Temple there were altars in honor of the astral gods venerated by Assyria, and also sacred prostitution. The situation does not seem to have changed in the brief reign of his son, Amon (642–640) whose assassination brought the eight-year-old Josiah to the throne.

84 Josiah became king on the eve of a propitious turn of events. Assyria was beginning to weaken, and the Medes and the Babylonians were on the ascendancy (→ Excursus Israel, 11:7, 9). From 626, when Nabopolassar of Babylon revolted, to 612, when Nineveh was destroyed, Assyria declined. This was the opportunity for Josiah to assert independence, both politically and religiously. His religious reform was thoroughgoing, and it is known as the deuteronomic reform since it followed the program of Dt. At the very least, the "Book of the Law," which was discovered in the Temple in 621, must have contained Dt 12–26. The deuteronomic ideals of centralization of worship and condemnation of idolatry are those of Josiah's reform (→ Religious Institutions, 76:67). The reform was an attempt to renew the covenant spirit within the kingdom, and the insistent, hortatory tone of Dt is in keeping with the spirit of revival that characterized Josiah's activities. He renewed the Passover feast, inviting the people of the N to take part—a move that had political as well as religious overtones. However, to judge from Jer, it appears that this reform eventually succumbed to formalism; and the tragic death of Josiah at Megiddo probably contributed to the dissolution of the reform movement. Josiah's son Jehoahaz succeeded to the throne, but international politics swept Judah into a vortex that led to its downfall.

85 With the fall of Nineveh in 612, Assyria fought a losing battle against the Babylonians and retreated to Haran, which was finally taken by the Babylonian army in 610. Egypt intervened in favor of its former enemy in order to preserve the balance of power, and Neco II (609–593) led an army through Palestine to help Assyria reconquer Haran. When Josiah resisted, he was slain in battle at Megiddo in 609; and Neco continued on to the Euphrates. Although the Egyptian's mission was unsuccessful, he returned through Palestine and replaced Jehoahaz with another son of Josiah, namely Eliakim, whose name he changed to Jehoiakim, indicating that the king of Judah was now a vassal of Egypt (→ Jeremiah, 19:2–5; for a list of the rulers of the Neo-Babylonian Empire [605–539], → Daniel, 26:3).

86 **(F) The Last Years of Judah (609–587).** The ineffectual and irreligious character of the reign of Jehoiakim (609–598) is well illustrated in many episodes of the life of Jeremiah (e.g., Jer 36). Whatever good the deuteronomic reform had accomplished was undone (Jer 7:16–20; Ez 8). Judah was caught in a power play of Egypt versus Babylon. We now know from the Babylonian Chronicles the details of the ascendancy of Babylon (cf. the analysis by D. N. Freedman, *BAR* 1,113–27; also E. Vogt, VTSup 4 [1957] 67–96). Nebuchadnezzar administered a severe defeat upon Egypt at Carchemish in 605 (Jer 46:2–12), but Neco was able to fight back and defeat him in 601, a defeat that was doubtless a factor in Jehoiakim's disloyalty to Babylon. The seesaw turn of events mirrors the split in Jerusalem politics between the pro-Babylonian and pro-Egyptian parties. When Jehoiakim finally revolted against Babylon, there was speedy retaliation. The Babylonian Chronicles (*DOTT* 80–81) relate the surrender of Jerusalem on the second day of the month of Adar, i.e., mid-March, 597. Jehoiakim had already died, perhaps by assassination, and his young son Jehoiachin, who had reigned only a few months, was now taken prisoner to Babylon, along with a large group of exiles. The Weidner tablets (*ANET* 308, and cf. W. F. Albright in *BAR* 1, 106–12) testify to the mild treatment given to this ill-fated king, who became the true representative of the Davidic dynasty for the exiles (Ezekiel dates his prophecies by the years of Jehoiachin).

87 Zedekiah (597–587), the last king of Judah, was no match for the politic maneuverings of his era. Zedekiah's dealing with Jeremiah illustrates his vacillating character (Jer 32–38). He finally yielded to the Egyptian party, whose hopes were fanned by the Pharaohs Psammetichus II and Hophra (Apries). The retaliation was swift and sure. Nebuchadnezzar besieged Jerusalem in 589 and devastated the rest of the Judean strongholds until only Azekah and Lachish remained (cf. Lachish letters in *ANET* 322; → Biblical Archaeology, 74:79). Although the siege was lifted temporarily by the advance of Egyptian forces (Jer 37), Jerusalem was doomed. The walls were breached and the city fell in July 587; Zedekiah was apprehended in flight and brought to Riblah where he was blinded after having been forced to watch the execution of his own sons. By order of Nebuchadnezzar Jerusalem was destroyed, and large-scale deportations ensued. Gedaliah, son of the Ahikam who had defended Jeremiah, was appointed governor with headquarters at Mizpah. But he was soon slain by a certain Ishmael, of royal blood; and this indication of revolutionary spirit may have led to further repressive measures by Babylon (perhaps the third deportation of 582; Jer 52:30). Those who had supported Gedaliah failed to apprehend Ishmael, and they determined to flee to Egypt, forcing Jeremiah to come with them (Jer 42).

88 **(J) The Exile (587–539).** The state of Judah was apparently incorporated into the Babylonian province of Samaria; but there was no importation of Gentiles, as there had been when the northern kingdom was defeated in 721. The land was desolate (cf. Albright, *FSAC* 322–23 for archaeological evidence; also *BP* 85–86), although not totally depopulated. Besides the devastation wrought by Nebuchadnezzar's army there was also the plundering by Judah's neighbors, especially by Edom (Ob 11), which seems to have occupied the S and by Ammon (Ez 25:1–4).

But the heart of the nation was in exile; the exiles are numbered at 4600 (probably adult males) in Jer 52:28–30. We find passages in Ez that throw light on the situation of those settled at Tel-abib in Babylonia. They were not enslaved but permitted to move about. The Diaspora had begun. Gradually the Jews reconciled themselves to their situation; their religious practices, e.g., circumcision and Sabbath observance, became their source of unity (also → Ezekiel, 21:10).

89 Despite the shattering blow to their beliefs in the inviolability of Zion and in the covenant with Yahweh, the Jews held on to their faith tenaciously. Indeed, this period witnessed intense religious activity: Israel's traditions were gathered and committed to writing. The Torah was given form by the P (priestly) school, which collected old desert traditions and codified the practice of the Jerusalem Temple. A definitive Law was taking shape that would be the base of the new theocratic community of Judah. The Deuteronomic History (Jos-Kgs) was edited, and the writings of the prophets were collected. Ezekiel had pointed to the future resurrection of the nation (ch. 37); but it remained for an unknown prophet and his followers, whose oracles are contained in Is 40–66, to supply the spark that moved Israel to return. The preaching of this man, "Second Isaiah" (→ Deutero-Isaiah, 22:3), is marked by deep theological insight and by an ability to ransom the time. He understood that Israel's punishment was at an end, and that Cyrus of Persia was the "anointed" (or messiah) of the Lord who would secure Israel's return. Yahweh alone was God and had the power to save his people; once more he would save them—in a new exodus (43:14–21; 48:20–21; 52:11–12).

90 Cyrus, king of Anshan, and from the Achaemenid line, took control of Media in 553 (Ecbatana) and then of Lydia, the land of Croesus, in Asia Minor in 546. By about 550 he posed a threat to Babylon and became a symbol of hope to the exiles. Finally, in 539 he took over Babylon intact from Nabonidus, after defeating the Babylonian army at the Tigris. The religious tolerance of Cyrus is well known from the so-called Cyrus cylinder (*ANET* 315–16). In 538 he issued a decree allowing the exiles to return to Palestine. (For a list of the rulers of the Persian Empire [539–331], → Daniel, 26:3.)

(Janssen, E., *Juda in der Exilszeit* [Göttingen, 1956]. Whitley, C. F., *The Exilic Age* [London, 1957].)

91 **(IV) The Early Post-exilic Period (539–333 BC).**

(A) The Restoration. The edict of Cyrus (Ezr 1:2–4; 6:3–5) permitted the exiles to rebuild the Temple at state expense and to restore the sacred vessels plundered by Nebuchadnezzar. The first wave of returning exiles was led by Sheshbazzar, "the prince of Judah," probably a son of Jehoiachin (cf. 1 Chr 3:18, to be identified with Shenazzar?). He was governor (*peḥâ*), but responsible to Persian overlords of the land. We are ill informed about the return, although we know that the exiles were largely from Judah and Benjamin. It is Sheshbazzar's nephew (?), Zerubbabel, whose exploits are detailed by the Chronicler (Ezr 3–6). The impetus of the newly arrived exiles led to the rebuilding of the altar and to the beginning of the Temple foundations, but it was not until 520 that serious work on the Temple began. Spurred on by the prophets Haggai and Zechariah, the building of the Temple was completed by 515 under Zerubbabel and Joshua the high priest. The two prophets also supported a renewal of the messianic hope in the Davidic dynasty (Hag 2:20–23; Zech 3:8; 6:9–15). Perhaps Zerubbabel became politically suspect in the eyes of the Persians; at any rate he quietly disappeared from history. If these hopes rose in connection with the troubles of the Persian Empire upon the death of Cambyses (522), they were quickly dashed by the effective leadership given the empire by Darius the Great (522–486). Yet Darius was not harsh with the Jews. For instance, when the Samaritans prevailed upon Tattenai, the Persian governor of the province "Beyond the River" (Abar-nahara), to halt the building activities in Jerusalem, Darius countermanded the order on the grounds that the Jews had been properly authorized by Cyrus, his predecessor, to proceed with the rebuilding of the Temple (Ezr 5–6).

92 By 520 the community may have numbered 20,000 (Albright, *BP* 87), but many reasons combined to slow its progress: economic problems, divided opinion, and especially the hostility of its neighbors in Samaria. These, too, regarded themselves as followers of Yahweh, and considered the old territory of Judah as belonging to them. When Zerubbabel rejected their offer of help to rebuild the Temple (Ezr 4:1–5), the seed was sown for the classical enmity between Jews and Samaritans. This enmity continued in the next century as we shall see below. The events from 515 to 450 are almost completely unknown to us, although Ezr 4 describes some of the difficulties. From the conditions reflected in Mal and from the reforms judged necessary by Ezra and Nehemiah, it would seem that the situation went from bad to worse.

93 **(B) Nehemiah and Ezra.** Nehemiah, a Jewish eunuch and cupbearer of Artaxerxes I in the Persian court at Susa, was informed about 445 of the lamentable situation in Jerusalem. He succeeded in having himself appointed as governor of Judah (thus making Judah independent of Samaria) and determined that his first task would be the rebuilding of the walls of Jerusalem—a work cautiously prepared for and dramatically described in Neh 2–4. He had to overcome not only the lethargy of the people but the opposition of two powerful men: Sanballat and Tobiah. Sanballat was the governor of the province of Samaria and a worshiper of Yahweh, as the names of his sons, Delaiah and Shelemiah, suggest. Tobiah was governor of the Transjordan province of Ammon. There was also a third enemy, Geshem, who was governor of the Arabian province. These men could count on many influential people in Judah who opposed the social reforms urged by Nehemiah (e.g., Jehoiada, son of Eliashib the high priest, was married to a daughter of Sanballat!). Undaunted by their deceit and harassment, Nehemiah resolutely carried out his plans (Neh 5–6:14).

94 The province of Judah was small, extending from Bethel to Beth-zur, with a population of about 50,000; Neh 7 gives a list that shows the diverse origin of those who had settled down by the middle of the 5th cent. Albright's analysis (*BP* 92) of this census list (Neh 7 = Ezr 2) indicates two chief groups: the returnees, many of them with foreign names (Bigvai, Elam) and others of N Judah (from places like Ramah and even Bethel) who had either never left or had returned before 538. The political and economic situation was hardly viable without the resolution and ability of the dedicated Nehemiah. The extreme measures taken by him did succeed in preserving the province, and he was able to return to Persia about 433. But his 12-year residence had not been sufficient to realize his plan, and after a short time he was back in Jerusalem. The conditions had become intolerable, and there was great need of religious reform. Tobiah (Neh 13:4ff.) had been given a room in the Temple itself by the high priest, Eliashib. Nehemiah ejected Tobiah and his belongings from the Temple, regulated the tithes for the Levites, stopped trade on the Sabbath, and legislated against mixed marriages (Neh 10). We do not know how long his second term as governor lasted. It cannot be denied that he was a hard, severe man; still, he was primarily responsible for the re-establishment of the community. His personal apologia (Neh 5:14–19) shows another side of his character.

95 The date of Ezra remains a moot question. The Bible (Ezr 7:7) describes his activity in the reign of a king Artaxerxes. The seventh year of Artaxerxes I would be 458, therefore before Nehemiah in 445. The seventh year of Artaxerxes II, 398, seems too late, and there is no textual evidence for the thirty-seventh year (Albright's conjectural emendation of Ezr 7:7) of Artaxerxes I, which would be 428, and contemporary with Nehemiah's second mission to Jerusalem. It may be that the original memoirs of both Ezra and Nehemiah failed to mention these two men together (R. de Vaux, "Israël," in *VDBS* 765–66); their conjunction in time could be due to the Chronicler who thus combined their respective religious and political roles.

(On the date of Ezra, see the excursus, with bibliography, in Bright, *Hist.* 375–86, and esp. Rowley, H. H., "The Chronological Order of Ezra and Nehemiah," *SLOE* 117–49.)

96 In contradistinction to Nehemiah, Ezra was primarily a religious leader. He was a priest, and was given the official title, "scribe of the law of the God of heaven." This means that he was a sort of secretary for Jewish affairs, empowered (Ez 7:12–26) by Persian authorities to teach and enforce the law among the Jews in the province "Beyond the River." He led a group of Jews back to Palestine, and his first public act seems to have been the reading aloud of the Law (some part of the Pentateuch) on the New Year Feast (Ezr 7; Neh 8). He directed a dramatic ritual of penitence (Ezr 10) in which it was decided to divorce foreign wives, and this grim measure was resolutely carried out. Neh 9 and 10 give information about a final moving confession and covenant renewal. There were to be no more mixed marriages, Sabbath infractions, or neglect of the Temple. Ezra laid particular emphasis upon the illicit nature of intermarriage with the Gentiles, a point strongly supported by Nehemiah.

97 The figure of Ezra was magnified in later legend as another Moses, as the man who determined the Hebr canon, etc. (→ Apocrypha, 68:38–41; → Canonicity, 67:33). It must be conceded that he oriented the people to an emphasis on the Law that characterized Judaism down into NT times. The Jews now became the "People of the Book." But Ezra's connection with the Pentateuch is not at all clear; possibly he was able to work with the Torah in its finished and present form. There is no conclusive evidence that Ezra is the Chronicler (but cf. Albright, *BP* 95). The Chronicler's role seems to be less creative than reflective, for his peculiar point of view is representative of the post-exilic theocracy of which he was a faithful member. His preoccupation was legitimacy—the association of the present practices of the community with the leading figures of old, such as Moses and David (cf. N. Freedman in *CBQ* 23 [1961] 436–42; W. Rudolph in *VT* 4 [1954] 401–9). Rudolph is right in assessing the intent of the Chronicler as the presentation of realized theocracy in Israel. Yet the work is helpful as an historical source for an otherwise dark period of Jewish history (4th cent.). Now Judah and Jerusalem saw themselves separated from the nations, chosen by God to survive the disaster of the Exile and reconstitute the people of God. The kingdom of God is concentrated in Judah, and Ezr and Neh present the people of God in zealous worship at the Temple, secure behind the walls that are rebuilt, separated from all that is alien (expulsion of foreign wives; → The Chronicler, 24:4–8).

(Galling, K., *Studien zur Geschichte Israels im persischen Zeitalter* [Tübingen, 1964]. Von Rad, G., *Das Geschichtsbild des chronistischen Werkes* [Stuttgart, 1930]. Welch, A. C., *Post-Exilic Judaism* [London, 1935].)

98 **(C) The Persian Era.** The history of the Jews in the Persian Empire is largely unknown except for what Ezr and Neh report. Although the concrete facts of Jewish history are lacking, we can correctly surmise the religious situation. In this period Israel developed its intense devotion to the Law. Worship was carried out in the Temple under the leadership of the priests and Levites, as reflected in the Chronicler's history. The three traditional feasts and the Day of Atonement were the high points of the year (→ Religious Institutions, 76:132–48, 155–58). Judah was a theocracy ruled by a high priest who supposedly could trace his lineage to David's priest, Zadok. For this era, → Post-exilic Period, 20:12–17.

Archaeology has contributed but little to the history of this period. We know that the Persians allowed the Jews to mint coins; several bearing the Hebr letters *yhd* (Judah) have been found (G. E. Wright, *BibArch* 203). The excavations at Lachish have revealed a Persian palace from about 400, and it may have been the residence of the Persian governor for the territory of the S (Edom).

99 The 5th-cent. Elephantine papyri (discovered at the beginning of the 20th cent.) have thrown light on a particular brand of Yahwism that flourished in a community of the Diaspora (cf. A. Cowley, *Aramaic Papyri of the Fifth Century B.C.* [Oxford, 1923]; E. Kraeling, *The Brooklyn Museum Aramaic Papyri* [New Haven, 1953]). This was a community of Jewish mercenaries employed by the Egyptian Pharaoh for protection against the Ethiopians at Syene (modern Aswan). They lived for over a century on an island in the Nile, Elephantine (Yeb), and developed their own form of Yahwism. In contradiction to Dt they built a temple, and their worship betrays Canaanite influence, for they associated the Lord with Anath. The names that have appeared in this literature (Eshembethel, Herembethel, Anathbethel) have been interpreted by Albright as hypostatizations of the Lord under the titles, "Name of the House of God," "Sacredness of the House of God," and "Sign of the House of God" (*FSAC* 373). The Elephantine Jews were not bothered by Cambyses *ca.* 525 BC when the Persian king conquered Egypt. Indeed, it appears that the Persian leaders extended some patronage to them, e.g., Darius II gave instructions to the governor Arsames concerning the feast of the Azymes in 419.

By 410, however, the situation had changed. A certain Persian official, Widrang (or Vidaranag), had replaced Arsames, and he abetted the destruction of the temple by the Egyptians. Some of the Elephantine letters (nos. 30 and 32) deal with the Jewish efforts to have the temple rebuilt, and the correspondence throws some light on the otherwise unknown years of the end of the 5th cent. They wrote to Johanan, a son of the Eliashib mentioned in Neh 12:23 (and perhaps 13:28), who was high priest in Jerusalem, enlisting his support for the rebuilding of the temple. Understandably, he did not answer (a temple outside Jerusalem was of course anomalous); and so they had recourse to the Persian governor of Judah, Bagoas, and even to the sons of Sanballat, Dalaiah and Shelemiah (*ANET* 492), who were governors in Samaria. This time there was an answer, and help may have been forthcoming for the project because it was actually carried out. But it was probably short-lived in view of the successful overthrow of the Persian yoke by the Egyptians toward 400.

(Couroyer, B., "Le temple de Yaho et l'orientation dans les papyrus araméens d'Eléphantine," *RB* 75 [1968] 80–85. Meyer, E., *Der Papyrusfund von Elephantine* [2nd ed.; Leipzig, 1912]. Porter, B., *Archives from Elephantine* [Berkeley, 1968]. Van Hoonacker, A., *Une communauté judéo-araméenne à Eléphantine* [Schweich Lectures 1914; London, 1915]. Vincent, A., *La religion des Judéo-araméens d'Eléphantine* [Paris, 1937].)

100 The value of Josephus' *Antiquities* for the Persian period is not great; he, too, had little more than the biblical sources (→ Apocrypha, 68:116). Some of the episodes he relates are highly questionable. His story about the two brothers, Johanan and Jeshua, is taken by some (L. E. Browne, *PCB* 129) as revealing the reason why Ezra was sent to Jerusalem by Artaxerxes toward 400 BC. On this view Jeshua was about to obtain the appointment to the high priesthood from the Persian governor, Bagoas, when Johanan slew his brother in the temple. Bagoas restored order—defiling the temple by his presence—and imposed a fine as penalty (*Ant.* 11.7, 1 § 297–301).

For an interesting reconstruction of the sequence of the governors of Samaria appointed by the Persians during the 5th cent., see F. M. Cross, *BA* 26 (1963) 120.

101 **(V) The Greek Era (333–63 BC).**

(A) From Alexander to Seleucid Domination (333–175). We are better informed about the Persian adventures in Greece (Herodotus, Livy) than we are about Israel's history in the Persian period. But these very adventures contributed to the downfall of Persia. Greek unity was achieved by Philip of Macedon, and his son Alexander prepared to extend the kingdom across the Hellespont. Alexander defeated the Persians at the Granicus River and took Asia Minor. The battle of Issus (333) gave the Greeks access to Syria, and Josephus (*Ant.* 11.8, 2 § 304ff.) tells of Alexander's passage through Jerusalem. In 331 he founded the storied city of Alexandria and returned to the north to inflict a final defeat upon the Persians at Arbela on the other side of the Tigris. He went on past the Indus and returned to Babylon where he died in 323, having forged a vast empire.

(Abel, F.-M., *Histoire de la Palestine depuis la conquête d'Alexandre* [Paris, 1952]. Bickermann, E., *Der Gott der Makkabäer* [Berlin, 1937]. Oesterley, W., *The Jews and Judaism During the Greek Period* [London, 1941]. Tcherikover, V., *Hellenistic Civilization and the Jews* [Phila., 1955].)

102 A host of problems has arisen about Alexander's visit to Jerusalem described in *Ant.* 11.8, 3–7 § 313–47. More important than the events in Jerusalem are the confusing data about the Samaritans and their temple (cf. the summary article of H. H. Rowley in *BJRylL* 38 [1955] 166–98). The question is, when was the Samaritan temple built on Mt. Gerizim? It is clear that the hostility between the Jews and Samaritans goes back through to the restoration and even beyond, but it seems likely that the Pentateuch (alone) was not taken over by the Samaritans nor was a separate temple built until after the Persian period. Probably it was during the Gk domination of Palestine that the temple was built. Excavations of the temple site have now begun. For the theory that the schism between Samaritans and Jews did not take place till the 2nd cent. BC, see F. M. Cross, *HarvTR* 59 (1966) 201–11.

The recently discovered (1962) Samaria papyri from a cave in the Wadi ed-Daliyeh have suggested some association between Alexander and the Samaritans (cf. G. E. Wright in *HarvTR* 55 [1962] 357–66; F. M. Cross in *BA* 26 [1963] 110–21). The initial welcome given to the Greeks by the Samaritans (according to Josephus) seems to have been followed by a revolt against the prefect whom Alexander appointed. Upon his return from Egypt Alexander seemingly quelled the revolt and destroyed the city. Archaeological evidence suggests that Samaria was rebuilt in the Gk manner (Hellenistic round towers) and settled with Macedonians. On the other hand, Shechem was also re-established at this time, by the Samaritans who fled Alexander's wrath. Those who did not reach Shechem seem to have been slaughtered in the Wadi Daliyeh where the remnants of their possessions have been discovered.

103 With Alexander's death, the leadership of several successors (Diadochoi) was ineffectual and finally a fourfold division of the empire took place. Biblical history is particularly concerned with two of these kingdoms that were rivals for the control of Palestine: the Egyptian kingdom founded by Ptolemy, son of Lagus, and the Asian kingdom ruled by Seleucus. (The Seleucid era, according to which 1 and 2 Mc date events, began in 312/11 when Seleucus solidified his power in Babylon.) For a partial list of the successors of Alexander, → Daniel, 26:3.

From *ca.* 300 to 200 the Jews fell under the paternalistic aegis of the Ptolemaic dynasty. Several events of this century are indicated in the summary in Dn 11. The large number of Jews in the Diaspora, especially in Alexandria, created a need for the translation of the OT into Greek (→ Texts, 69:53). In Palestine the fundamental nature of the Jewish community remained unchanged; it was primarily a religious association headed by the high priest who combined civil and religious authority in his own person. The council of elders, or *gerousia*, served as a ruling board with him. Judea proper remained a relatively small, self-contained area having only loose contact with the rest of Palestine, yet everywhere a process of Hellenization was taking place.

The most concrete evidence of the cultural change was the existence in this period of the *polis* or Hellenistic city—in the Philistine plain (Gaza, Ashdod, Ashkelon) on the coast (Joppa, Ptolemais), and inland (Samaria, Scythopolis [= Beth-shan]), even in Transjordan (Gadara, Philadelphia [= Rabbah of Ammon]). Greek fashions and ways, which were eventually to enter Jerusalem itself (1 Mc 1:13–15; 2 Mc 4:10–15), began to pose a threat to the Jewish way of life (against it Sir is an eloquent protest). The Jews themselves were divided; many became openly Hellenistic, while the *Ḥasîdîm*, or Hasideans (1 Mc 2:42), were fanatically devoted to the Law.

104 The important Tobiad family exemplifies the ties that bound many Jews to the new ways. Descendants of the enemy of Nehemiah (Neh 2:10), they resided in the old Ammonite territory at Araq el-Emir (*BASOR* 171 [1963] 8ff.). Already in the 3rd cent. they were governors of the area, as the Zeno papyri indicate. Josephus (*Ant.* 12.4, 1ff. § 154ff.) informs us of a certain Joseph who won the favor of Ptolemy III (245–221) and was given the office of tax collector in Palestine. He was ruthless in this post (in which he was also confirmed by Antiochus III) and succeeded in enriching himself. His son (or perhaps grandson) Hyrcanus rebuilt (Josephus says, simply, he built) the famous fortress at Araq el-Emir, NE of Heshbon, and he is mentioned as possessing treasure kept in the Temple (2 Mc 3:11). With the Maccabean revolt, however, the Tobiads lost their power; Antiochus Epiphanes confiscated their possessions (cf. V. Tcherikover, *Hellenistic Civilization*, 153–74; 202–3).

105 In 200 BC the Seleucid King Antiochus III defeated the troops of Ptolemy V at Panion near the sources of the Jordan, and Palestine passed from the Ptolemaic to the Seleucid aegis. According to Josephus (*Ant.* 12.3, 3 § 138–44, although the authenticity of the decree has been contested), Antiochus was very gracious to Jerusalem, ordering the repair of the damages suffered in the recent past and providing an allowance for the Temple expenses, while the framework of the local government (high priest, etc.) was continued and certain tax exemptions given. When Antiochus intervened in international affairs, he had Rome to contend with; and he paid a bitter price in the treaty of Apamea (188) when he was forced to evacuate Asia Minor and pay a severe indemnity. The need for money led him into more campaigns; he died in Elam in 187. He was succeeded by his son Seleucus IV (187–175) while a younger son, Antiochus (the future Epiphanes), was held as hostage in Rome in lieu of full payment of the indemnity. It was during Seleucus' reign that his chancellor Heliodorus came to the Jerusalem Temple to obtain more funds (2 Mc 3). This same Heliodorus killed Seleucus, only to provide Antiochus IV, released from Rome, with the opportunity of taking over royal power. Antiochus came to adopt the title Epiphanes or Manifest, for the Olympian Zeus was manifest in him; his subjects were not slow to counter with the nickname Epimanes, or madman! His policy was one of unity (therefore the Hellenization of all his subjects) and of expansion, and this meant the appropriation of large sums of money.

106 **(B) The Maccabean Revolt (175–135).** The episode of Heliodorus in Jerusalem was an ill omen of future Seleucid policy, and the venality of the Oniad family of priests provided Antiochus Epiphanes with a precious opportunity. The Oniads belonged to the family of a certain Yohanan (Honi, and in the Gk form, Onias), father of the high priest Simon II who is so fervently praised in Sir 50:1–21. Simon's son, Onias III (the anointed of Dn 9:26?), was high priest when Antiochus IV ascended the throne. But he found himself the victim of his own brother Jason, a Hellenist, who set out to buy the office from the Seleucid authorities. While they were both at Antioch, Antiochus IV deposed Onias in favor of Jason (174–171). A full-scale Hellenization of Jerusalem itself was begun, and the possibility of becoming citizens of Antioch was now offered to the inhabitants (2 Mc 4:9–16). Many of the Jews remained loyal to the traditions, especially the Hasideans (1 Mc 2:42; 7:13; → Apocrypha, 68:84). Jason was in turn deceived by a certain Menelaus to whom Antiochus gave the office of high priest in 171, while Jason fled to Transjordan. Menelaus pushed on with the Hellenization and conspired to have Onias III murdered (→ 1–2 Maccabees, 27:62–66).

107 Although Antiochus executed the murderer Andronicus, everything was building up toward a revolt, as repressive measures increased. On his return from his first campaign in Egypt (169), Antiochus, abetted by Menelaus, entered and plundered the Temple. The unsuccessful attempt of Jason to take possession of Jerusalem was another indication of unrest, and so the citadel in Jerusalem (the "Akra," cf. 1 Mc 1:33) was staffed with a Syrian garrison (*BASOR* 176 [1964] 10–19). On his return from his second Egyptian campaign (168, when Popilius of Rome delivered the famous ultimatum to get out of Egypt immediately), Antiochus took further repressive measures. An official persecution began; sacrifice and Jewish practices like circumcision were proscribed under penalty of death; and eventually the "abomination of desolation," an altar (rather than an image) to the Olympian Zeus, was erected in the Temple. (The chronology followed in this report is based on that of J. Starcky and F. Abel, *Les Livres des Maccabées* [BJ; Paris, 1961] esp. 46–49.)

108 There were many Jews who were ready to lay down their life to preserve their faith—2 Mc tells of Eleazar and the mother of the seven sons (6:18–7:42). The Hasideans did not waver in observing the Law, as their refusal to fight on the Sabbath indicates (1 Mc 2:29–38). Of such courage and conviction were the groups who rallied to the Maccabee family of Modin when in 167 they issued the summons to revolt. The courageous father of this family, Mattathias, died in 166; and the leadership passed to **Judas Maccabeus** (this name is usually, but probably incorrectly, taken to mean "the hammer"—the family itself was of the priestly lineage of Joarib [1 Mc 2:1]). The odds against Judas were formidable, but he succeeded in whipping into shape a type of guerrilla force that conquered the Gk Seleucid armies. At the very outset there was a series of important Maccabean victories. The defeat of Apollonius yielded the storied sword (1 Mc 3:12) used by Judas; another army, led by Seron, was cut down at Beth-horon. Even in the face of more determined opposition, the successes continued. Judas attracted many Jews to his cause, for he seems to have been an inspiring leader (1 Mc 3:4). During this time, too, Dn was written, portraying in chs. 7–12 the ultimate victory of God's people over oppressive kingdoms, and providing inspirational stories about heroes who trusted in God and resisted kings—a resistance literature.

109 Finally Antiochus, who had to fight the Parthians in the E, appointed Lysias as regent to quell the revolt; and Lysias dispatched three generals, Ptolemy, Nicanor, and Gorgias. But Judas had been solidifying a loyal group at Mizpah, N of Jerusalem; and so again there were victories: at Emmaus against the army of Gorgias; and the following year at Beth-zur (→ Biblical Archaeology, 74:83) against Lysias himself, who was forced to return to Antioch. At this sign of weakness Judas boldly decided in 164 to cleanse the Temple of the "abomination of desolation"—within sight of the Akra garrison. The Hanukkah feast wiped out the three years of blasphemy (→ Religious Institutions, 76:159–162).

At this point the full thrust of the Maccabean revolt became apparent. The regaining of the Temple fired a determination to cap the victories with further independence. There remained Jewish minority groups throughout Palestine and Transjordan, especially those in the Gk cities. In a series of moves in Idumea, Ammon, Gilead, Galilee, and the Philistine plain, Judas skirmished with the heathen in order to help his fellow Jews, many of whom he brought back to Jerusalem. Meanwhile his brother Simon was doing the same in Galilee. The purpose was also to solidify and to extend Maccabean power.

110 With the death of Antiochus Epiphanes, Lysias became the effective leader and regent of the young ruler, Antiochus V. He replied to Judas' bold siege of the Jerusalem Akra in 163 by defeating him at Beth-zechariah (the dramatic death of Eleazar, 1 Mc 6:43–46); and Lysias would have taken Jerusalem had he not been forced to return to Antioch to preserve his own political authority. He had to settle for a treaty granting the Jews freedom to "follow their own laws" (1 Mc 6:59). It would appear that the purpose of the Maccabean revolt had been achieved, for the oppression inaugurated by Antiochus IV was over. But the perspective of even more independence and political power tempted the Maccabees.

The Hellenistic Jews opposed Judas and had recourse to the new king Demetrius I (Soter) for protection against him. The king appointed their candidate Alcimus to the high priesthood. The split among the Jews was never so clear as at this point. The Hasideans and the scribes (*grammateis*) supported Alcimus because he was of priestly descent, even though he was favored by the Hellenists. But Judas opposed him, and Alcimus' murder of the Hasideans proved him right. Finally Nicanor was dispatched from Antioch at the head of an army. Judas defeated him at Capharsalama and later thoroughly routed him at the battle of Beth-horon and Adasa on the 13th of Adar (March 28, 160), and "the day of Nicanor" became a recurrent feast (1 Mc 7:49). But Judas was unable to capitalize on this victory; for in retaliation Demetrius sent Bacchides at the head of a strong army, and they routed the Jews in the area of Beroea and Elasa N of Jerusalem (1 Mc 9:4–5). Judas himself was slain when reprisals against the Maccabean party began.

111 His brother **Jonathan** (160–143) took his place and was at least able to stand off Bacchides at Bethbasi in 159. But Jonathan's forays were modest; he was content to establish himself in the style of one of the ancient "judges" (1 Mc 9:73) at Michmash during a period of relative peace (159–152) and to wait for developments. A splendid opportunity presented itself when Alexander Balas landed at Ptolemais and challenged Demetrius I. Demetrius authorized Jonathan to muster an army, but Alexander offered him the office of the high priesthood that had been vacant since Alcimus' death. Jonathan acted upon both offers but eventually supported Alexander, who triumphed over Demetrius to become king in 150. Jonathan received further honors when he attended the wedding of Alexander and Cleopatra, daughter of Ptolemy; he was clothed in purple, and was made general, and governor of Judea (cf. 1 Mc 10:65).

112 A new phase in the development of Maccabean power was beginning. The Jewish leader was able to play the Seleucid kings against one another. In 148 Demetrius II attempted to gain the throne, and Apollonius, governor of Coele-Syria, supported him. Apollonius was defeated by Jonathan, who remained loyal to Alexander, and in reward the city of Ekron was given to the Jews. Even when Demetrius came to the throne in 145 after the slaying of Alexander, Jonathan was strong enough to make demands for exemption from tribute; and Ephraim, Lydda, and Ramathaim were given over to Judea. In 141 Demetrius even promised to hand over the Akra, the citadel of Syrian control in Jerusalem, if Jonathan would help him put down a revolt in Antioch. Although Demetrius was able to renege on this promise, his time was running out. A new claimant to the throne appeared, Antiochus VI, who was supported by a certain Trypho. Jonathan threw his support behind them and engaged in several battles that strengthened his own hand (Ashkelon, Gaza, Beth-zur). Moreover, he entered into political exchanges with Rome and Sparta (1 Mc 12:1–23). All this did not pass unnoticed, and Trypho decided that Jonathan was too dangerous; he tricked him and imprisoned him in Ptolemais (143).

113 The Jewish reaction was immediate. The third Maccabee brother **Simon** (143–134) stepped in and prepared for attack by appropriating the city of Joppa. But he could not prevent the murder of Jonathan, who was eventually buried in the Maccabean home town of Modin. Now Simon turned to the support of Demetrius II in return for the recognition of Jewish independence; and in 142 "the yoke of the heathen was lifted from Israel" (1 Mc 13:41), as Simon was recognized as high priest, governor, and commander. The Maccabean claims to rulership and high priesthood were finally legitimized by the Jews themselves (14:41) "until a true prophet should appear." In the following year Simon captured the Seleucid garrison of Gazara and finally succeeded in forcing the Akra in Jerusalem to surrender, and some years of peace ensued. A new claimant to the Seleucid throne now appeared, Antiochus Sidetes. Simon refused to honor his demands, and Simon's sons were victorious in the subsequent battle against Antiochus' general, Cendebaeus, in 138 (1 Mc 16). But Simon himself was slain treacherously by his son-in-law, Ptolemy, at the fortress of Dok near Jericho, and Simon's son John Hyrcanus succeeded him in office. Here 1 Mc ends its account; for the reign of Hyrcanus and his successors we must depend largely upon Josephus. Christian writers tend to use the name "Hasmonean" to describe Hyrcanus' line of descendants, whereas Jewish writers, following the pattern of Josephus and of the Talmud, bring Hyrcanus' predecessors, the Maccabee brothers, under this title as well. We are not certain of the real derivation of the name, but traditionally it is related to Asamōnaios (Hebrew: Ḥašmôn) whom Josephus, *Ant.* 12.6, 1 § 265, identifies as the great-grandfather of Mattathias (the father of Judas Maccabee).

114 **(C) The Hasmonean Rulers (134–63).** Simon's son, *John Hyrcanus I* (134–104), escaped Ptolemy's murderous designs because he had been at Gazara at the time of the murder. He succeeded his father as high priest and ruler and tried unsuccessfully to punish Ptolemy, who finally fled to Transjordan. The first years of Hyrcanus' reign were unhappy. Almost immediately Antiochus VII Sidetes besieged Jerusalem after laying waste Judea. But unexpectedly, because of pressure from Rome, he came to terms with Hyrcanus and raised the siege. The indemnities were relatively light, but for the next few years Hyrcanus served Antiochus, helping him in a campaign against the Parthians. Events now took a favorable turn. In 128 Demetrius II succeeded to the throne when Antiochus was slain in battle, and he became involved in civil war. This enabled Hyrcanus to recover the cities in Judea and beyond. After a long siege he took Medeba in Transjordan and subdued the Idumeans in the Negeb, imposing circumcision and the Torah upon them. He also destroyed the Samaritan temple on Mt. Gerizim. These military victories were effected with the help of foreign mercenaries (an indication of the people's apathy). During this time the power of the Seleucids deteriorated because of inner conflicts, and Hyrcanus was left with a free hand to consolidate his gains. By 107, despite the intervention of the Seleucid king, Antiochus IX (Cyzicenus), Samaria had fallen to Jewish forces under the sons of Hyrcanus, Aristobulus and Antigonus. The most significant development within Judaism at this time was the emergence of the two parties of the Pharisees and Sadducees (→ 120 below).

115 John's eldest son *Aristobulus* (104–103) succeeded his father by force, imprisoning his mother (who might have ruled) and three brothers. With Antigonus (whose death he unwittingly caused), he continued the course of conquest, extending his power into N Galilee, which he Judaized. (The Judaizing of Galilee proved to be relatively lasting, even into the Christian era.) The

THE HASMONEAN FAMILY

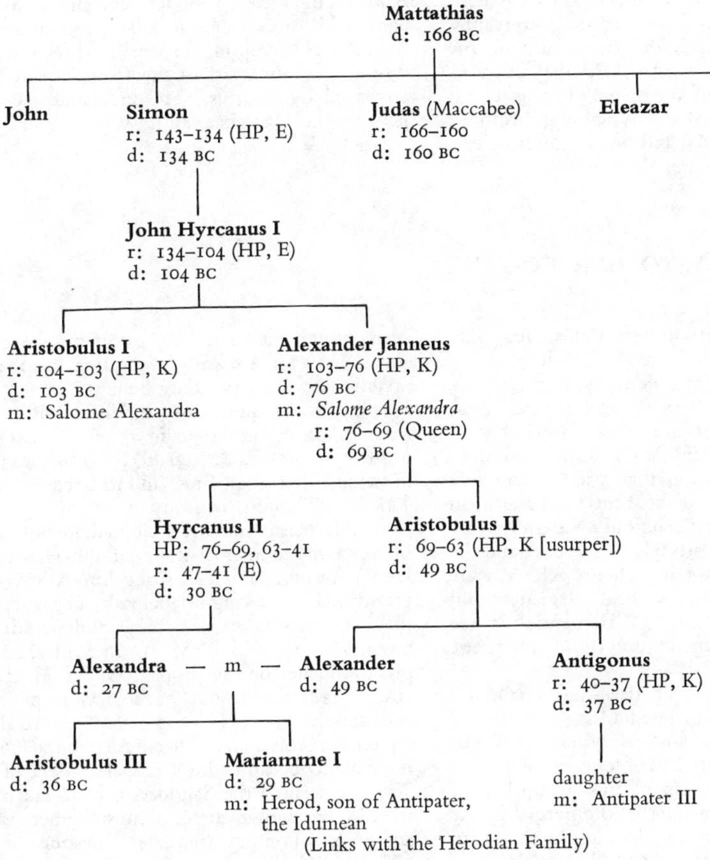

d = died; m = married; r = ruled
E = Ethnarch; HP = High priest; K = King

inroad of Hellenization is apparent from the Gk name he bore (although known by "Judah" on his coins) and the title "king" (instead of ethnarch) which he affected, and which was retained by his successors until 63. But the general moral deterioration of the Hasmonean line can be said to have continued. Aristobulus reigned only one year, and his widow, Salome Alexandra, a remarkable woman, freed the brothers and married one of them, Alexander Janneus, who now succeeded to the "throne" and office of high priest.

116 The reign of *Alexander Janneus* (103–76) was marked by wars that eventually brought all Palestine under his control. He fought Ptolemy IX Lathyrus unsuccessfully for Ptolemais, and would have lost Palestine if Ptolemy had not been pressured by Egypt to return to Cyprus to which he had been banished. In central Transjordan he besieged and captured Gadara and Amathus on the Jordan. Janneus plundered and burned Gaza on the seacoast but had to return to reconquer Amathus; also he became involved with the Nabateans to the N. The Nabatean king, Obedas, nearly caught him in ambush, but he escaped and returned to Jerusalem which itself now revolted against him. Thanks to his mercenaries, he held out against the rebels. But when the Pharisees brought the Seleucid king, Demetrius III Eukairos, against him at Shechem, Janneus was nearly dethroned (about 88 BC). He found supporters among Jewish patriots (some 6000) and then proceeded to wreak vengeance upon the Jews who had turned against him; this was the famous scene of the crucifixion that seems to be referred to in a Qumran document (4QpNa; → Apocrypha, 68:78; F. M. Cross, *The Ancient Library of Qumran* [Anchor ed.; N.Y., 1961] 122–26). When Aretas became king of the Nabateans, he marched into Judea and defeated Janneus, withdrawing only after due concessions. Janneus now turned his attention to Transjordan and during the campaign of 84–81 BC he acquired Pella, Gerasa, Golan, and other cities. When his dissolute life came to an end, he was engaged in besieging Ragaba in Transjordan. By that time the territory of Judea had expanded considerably; in a sense the old boundaries of the Davidic kingdom were now realized; the Gk cities had been Judaized.

117 Janneus' widow, *Salome Alexandra* (76–69), began to reign at his death, leaving the office of high priest to the ineffectual elder son, Hyrcanus II. She was reconciled to the Pharisees who enjoyed great power in these years, and she succeeded in keeping the state intact without wars. But at her death Judea was left to be fought over by Hyrcanus and the ambitious younger son, Aristobulus.

118 *Aristobulus II* (69–63), who was supported by the Sadducees, quickly attained a victory over Hyrcanus at Jericho and imprisoned him in Jerusalem; and so Aristobulus became king and high priest. However, the governor of Idumea, Antipater, conspired in favor of Hyrcanus. In a daring move he persuaded Hyrcanus to seek "refuge" with Aretas, king of the Nabateans, and he accompanied him to the royal city at Petra. A deal was made: Hyrcanus was to be restored if he ceded to the

Nabateans certain cities in Moab. The Nabateans marched into Judea and locked Aristobulus in Jerusalem; they would have been successful in restoring Hyrcanus, had not Rome intervened. Both parties sought the favor of M. Aemilius Scaurus, legate of Pompey in Syria, and Roman power called off the siege. It was up to Pompey to decide the fate of the wrangling brothers. He moved into Damascus in 63, and finally to Jerusalem, where he was forced to besiege the Temple when Aristobulus failed to hand it over to him. Some 1200 Jews were said to have been killed. Then he imprisoned Aristobulus, accepting Hyrcanus II as high priest, and Palestine became part of the Roman province of Syria, governed by Scaurus. The independence won for the Jews by the Maccabee family was at an end.

FROM POMPEY TO BAR COCHBA

119 **(I) Jewish Movements in Palestine.** The NT period coincided in good part with the Roman occupation of Palestine. When Pompey became "the first Roman to subdue the Jews and set foot in their temple by right of conquest" (Tacitus, *Histories* 5.9), this act symbolized the beginning of the Roman domination of the land—a domination that was to continue throughout the NT period. At this time the Palestinian Jews, for all their national and religious solidarity, were not a united people. In their attitude to the Law and the Temple differences existed among them, which were often compounded by varying political allegiances and intrigues. Josephus (*Ant.* 13.5, 9, § 171) mentions three "sects" (*haireseis*) among them at this time: Pharisees, Sadducees, and Essenes.

120 **(A) Pharisees.** The Pharisees (Gk *Pharisaioi;* Aram *P^e^rîšāyê*) were the "Separated Ones," so named probably by opponents, because of their professed avoidance of Gentiles, of sinners, and of Jews less observant of the Law. Though the origin of this group had its roots in the lay "scribes" (lawyers) who emerged in the post-exilic Hellenistic period, it first appeared as an organized movement *ca.* 140 BC, shortly before the time of John Hyrcanus (*Ant.* 13.5, 9 § 171). More immediately it was related to the Hasideans (Gk *Asidaioi;* Hebr *Ḥasîdîm*, "Pious Ones," 1 Mc 2:42), who supported the Maccabean revolt until it became too political and secular (1 Mc 7:12–25; → 108 and 110 above).

The Pharisees were chiefly a lay group that advocated a rigorous legalism, accepting as valid not only the written Torah (*tôrâ še-biktāb*), but also the oral Torah (*tôrâ še-b^e^-ʿal-peh*). The latter comprised elaborate oral interpretations of the Law propounded by the scribes since Ezra's time. These "Sayings of the Fathers" (cf. Gal 1:14; Mk 7:3) were designed to be "fences built around the Law," and were eventually codified in the *Mishnah* and *Talmud* of rabbinical literature (→ Apocrypha, 68:118ff.). Influenced by Hellenistic ideas on the value of *paideia*, the Pharisees regarded knowledge of the Law and of its 613 prescriptions and prohibitions as a guarantee of piety. To be a holy nation, sacred and dedicated to Yahweh, was the goal of all Jews; but to achieve this by education and knowledge of the Law was a peculiarly Pharisaic aim (cf. E. Bickerman, *The Maccabees* [N.Y., 1947] 92–97). It was this attitude more than anything else that separated the Pharisees from the *ʿam hā-āreṣ* ("the people of the land"), the "rabble that knows not the Law" (Jn 7:49). A meticulous observance of the Sabbath, of ritual purity laws, of tithing—as a point of ancestral pride—characterized them. Yet because of the emphasis on oral interpretation the Pharisees were able to adjust to new contingencies and manifested a vitality and flexibility that made them the "liberals" of the time. Since the inspiration of this movement was fundamentally religious, the Pharisees exerted a great influence on other Jews through their learning and piety, even though they probably never numbered more than 6000 (*Ant.* 17.2, 4 § 42). In addition to their strict interpretation of the Law, they believed in a certain human freedom under the control of divine providence, in the resurrection of the body, in angels (*Ant.* 13.5, 9 § 172), in the coming of a "Messiah" (*Pss Sol* 17:23–18:14), and in the ingathering of Israel and its tribes at the end (*ibid.*).

121 Though basically a religious movement, in time Pharisaism became involved in politics. Pharisees opposed the secular attitude of the Hasmonean priest-king John Hyrcanus I, desiring him to give up the high priesthood. The king retaliated by abrogating legislation that favored Pharisaic teachings and withdrew his royal favor (*Ant.* 13.10, 5 § 288ff.). In reality, he feared their great influence on the people. Under Alexander Janneus (104–76 BC) about 800 Pharisees were put to death for opposing him (*Ant.* 13.14, 2 § 380; → 116 above). They regained favor under Queen Alexandra (76–69 BC) and once again became the spiritual leaders of the people. They persecuted the Sadducees, who had capitalized on the disfavor shown them. The strife between them was acute when Pompey arrived in Palestine.

122 The fundamental religious outlook of the Pharisees, rooted in a high esteem for the OT and its revelation, enabled them to make a permanent mark on Judaism. After the destruction of Jerusalem, when the Temple cult was no longer possible, it gave them the advantage of a rallying point for the Jews. It is the Pharisaic tradition that molded the Judaism which survived that catastrophe and which persists in orthodox Judaism today. But the *separatism* of the Pharisees induced in some of them a haughty pride and a withdrawal from the "rabble that knows not the Law." It was this attitude that caused Jesus of Nazareth to castigate the Pharisees severely (Mt 23), although it must be admitted that the Gospel evaluation of the Pharisees, since it emerged from an apologetic context, is far too negative and does not give the Pharisees sufficient credit for being a constructive spiritual force.

(Abrahams, J., *Studies in Pharisaism and the Gospels*, Series 1–2 [reprint, N.Y., 1968]. Finkelstein, L., *The Pharisees and the Men of the Great Synagogue* [N.Y., 1950]. Herford, R. T., *The Pharisees* [London, 1924].)

123 **(B) Sadducees.** The Sadducees represented a priestly and aristocratic movement among the Jews. Their name (Gk *Saddoukaioi;* Aram *Ṣaddûqāyê*) suggests at least their claim to be descended from the old priestly family of Zadok (*Ṣādôq*, 1 Kgs 1:26). As such they should have been ministers in the Temple in the spirit of the "sons of Zadok" (Ez 40:46; 43:19; 44:15; 48:11). To their number belonged most of the Jerusalem priests, "the party of the high priest" (Acts 5:17). However, not a few priests were Pharisees, and the Sadducees included also hangers-on from other influential Jewish families. The first reference to them, as a group already formed, comes from the time of John Hyrcanus I (134–104). Jonathan, the second Maccabee brother, had begun his rule simply as a charismatic leader; but in time he assumed the role of high priest (→ 111 above). As "sons of Zadok," the Sadducees should have opposed this Hasmonean usurper of the high priestly dignity, but instead we find them supporting the Hasmonean priest-kings, probably to ensure their own influence. But this influence fluctuated, depending on the favor they enjoyed with the ruling princes. It was strong in the time of John Hyrcanus I, whom they won over after his breach with the Pharisees. Again under Aristobulus II (69–63) they enjoyed a certain prestige.

124 No less than the Pharisees, the Sadducees were affected, unconsciously perhaps, by the enlightenment of Hellenistic philosophy and culture. But their sympathy with the foreign occupying power had its roots in the Persian and Seleucid periods, when the Jewish priests had to bear the burden of political responsibility vis-à-vis the foreign ruler. The "party" that emerged in Hasmonean times was conservative and tended to guard jealously its priestly prerogatives. They opposed violently the Pharisees and their oral interpretations of the Torah, not because they rejected such interpretations, for they apparently had their own, but because they resented lay intrusion into what they regarded as a priestly privilege. Their attitude to the Torah was that of clerical conservatism, rejecting any further development or modernization of the Torah. This attitude was due in part to their secular outlook and general lack of interest in religious questions. Josephus (*JW* 2.8, 14 § 165) ascribes to them the absolute responsibility of man for his actions and a denial of divine providence, as well as the denial of reward or punishment for the soul in afterlife. In the NT they are depicted frequently as the opponents of Jesus, along with the scribes and Pharisees; it attributes to the Sadducees disbelief in the resurrection and in angels or spirits (Mk 12:18; Acts 23:8), in this pitting them against the Pharisees. (R. Meyer, "Saddoukaios," *ThWNT* 7 [1960] 35–54.)

125 **(C) Essenes.** The third group of Palestinian Jews were the Essenes (Gk *Essēnoi*, *Essaioi*, probably = Aram *Ḥasayyā*', "Pious Ones"), who apparently also had their origin in the Hasidean movement (1 Mc 2:42). It is difficult to say just when they emerged as a distinct group, but it must have been *ca.* 150 BC or a little later. Pliny the Elder (*Nat. Hist.* 5.17, 4 § 73) located them on the western shore of the Dead Sea between Jericho and En-gedi. The only area he could have meant is the recently excavated site of Khirbet Qumran. Although the identification is not without its problems, the Qumran sect is identified by the majority of scholars today with the Essenes or a branch of them. (For the origin and history of this Qumran Essene movement, → Apocrypha, 68:83–91.)

The Essenes are not mentioned in the NT, possibly because their aloofness brought them less in contact with nascent Christianity, and possibly because some of their ideas were less definitely opposed to it.

126 **(II) Roman Palestine before Jesus' Lifetime (63–4 BC).** The years 63–37 saw the definitive establishment of Roman power in Palestine and the end of the Hasmonean dynasty. The story of the downfall of this ruling family and of its replacement by the Herodians is complicated and marked by intrigues, of which only the barest outline can be given here.

(A) Pompey, Julius Caesar, Mark Antony. After Pompey had taken Jerusalem he incorporated Palestine into the reorganized province of Syria, which was to be ruled over by a Roman legate. As we have seen (→ 118 above), Pompey decided to keep the weak Hyrcanus II as high priest. But he limited Hyrcanus' religious authority to the areas where Jews who actually recognized his cult were dwelling (Jerusalem and Judea, Perea, Galilee, the southern tip of Samaria, and northern Idumea). The coastlands and the rest of Samaria were made dependent immediately on the Roman governor of Syria. This reorganization brought peace and renewed welfare to the Jews. The only dark spot in the next few years of Roman domination was the plundering of the province by M. Licinius Crassus, who had been triumvir in 60 BC. He robbed the treasury of the Jerusalem Temple in 53; at this the Jewish community rebelled, but the revolt was eventually put down by the quaestor, C. Cassius Longinus.

127 In the year 49 Julius Caesar crossed the Rubicon. This act had significant consequences for the subsequent development of Roman history. His rival, Pompey, with his followers then withdrew to the East. At first Hyrcanus II and his Idumean friend, Antipater II, courted the favor of Pompey, whom they expected as ruler of the East. But when Pompey was defeated at Pharsalus in the Egyptian Delta (48), they quickly shifted their allegiance to Caesar. Hyrcanus even sent troops to help Caesar, putting Antipater in command. They conquered Pelusium for him, and Hyrcanus succeeded in persuading the Alexandrian Jews to support Caesar. When the latter arrived in Syria in 47, he rewarded Hyrcanus with the nominal title of ethnarch (ruler of a racial group with a province). His high priesthood was confirmed; he and his descendants were declared *socii populi Romani*. The scheming Antipater was also rewarded—with Roman citizenship and the influential job of prefect of Judea. Two of his sons were appointed governors (*stratēgoi*): Phasael over Jerusalem, and Herod over Galilee. The next few years were marked by the continual intrigues of Jewish leaders trying to win over or to preserve the favor of the Roman governors.

128 On the ides of March 44 BC Julius Caesar was assassinated, and none of the subject peoples of Rome lamented his death as much as the Jews (Suetonius, *Caesar* 84). When the assassins fled to the East, L. Cassius came to Syria and seized control of the province and its legions. Antipater II and his son Herod distinguished themselves in raising 700 talents in Judea and Galilee to support him. But in 43 Antipater was poisoned by Hyrcanus' cupbearer. In order to cement the relations between his Hasmonean family and its Idumean rivals, Hyrcanus II offered his granddaughter Mariamme to Herod (Antipater's son) in marriage; the engagement took place in 42, and the marriage in 37.

129 Meanwhile, Cassius, after exploiting the province, withdrew from it in 42 and was finally defeated by Mark Antony and Octavian at Philippi. Since Roman control of the province of Syria was very weak at this time, the Parthians, successors of the Old Persian Empire, invaded it in 40. They supported the rule of Antigonus, the son of Aristobulus II and nephew of Hyrcanus II, who desired the high priesthood. With Parthian help he now became high priest and king for three years (40–37). He captured Phasael (Herod's brother) and Hyrcanus II by a ruse; the former committed suicide, and Antigonus had the latter's ears cut off (thus making him incapable of functioning as high priest henceforth; cf. Lv 21:17–23). Hyrcanus was deported to Babylon. But Herod escaped and made his way to Rome, where he won the favor, first of Antony, then of Octavian. By a *senatusconsultum* (December 40 BC [= AUC 714]) he was declared "King of Judea," but he still had to conquer his kingdom. This he did three years later with the aid of Roman troops, after Antigonus had been executed by the Romans in Antioch.

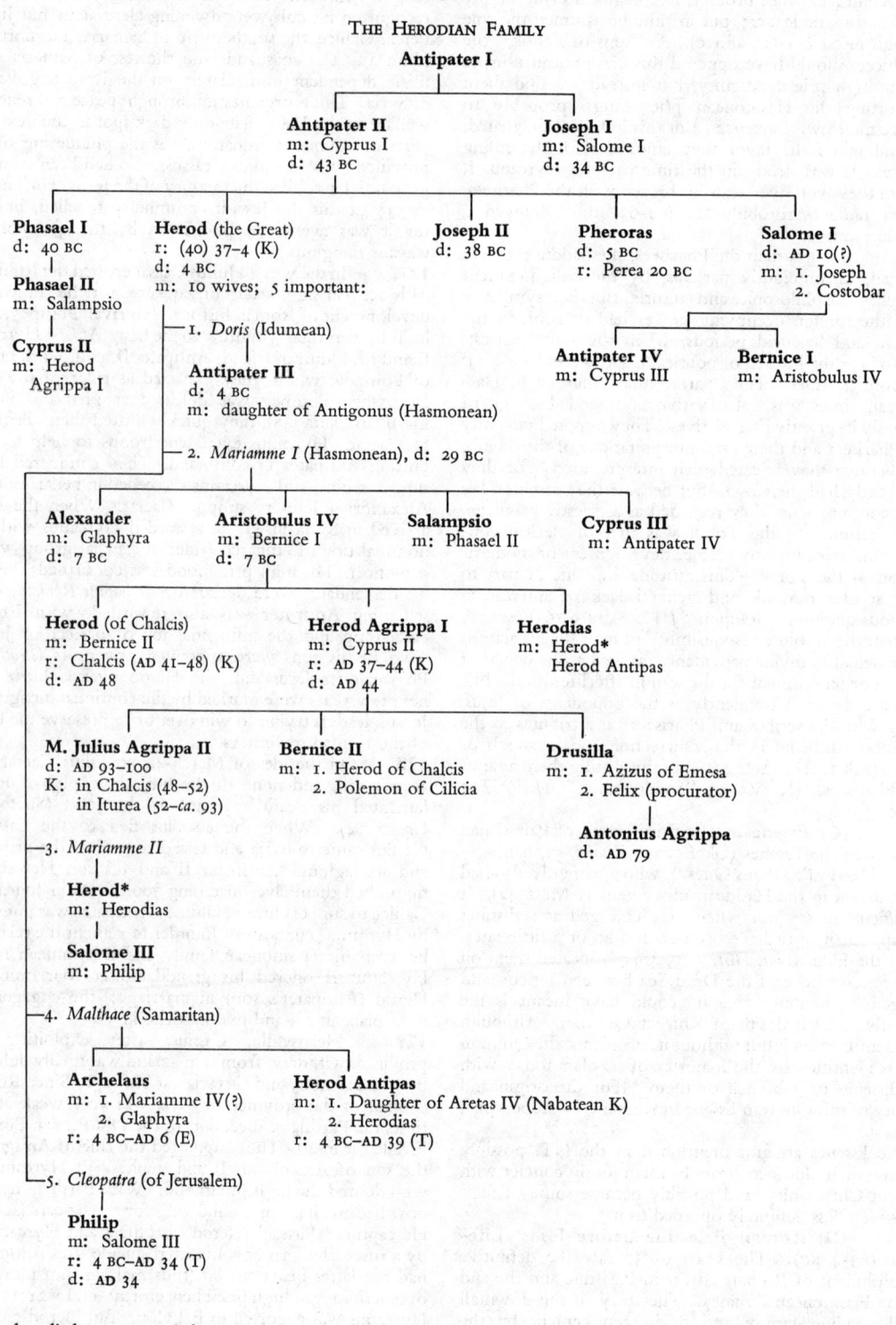

The Herodian Family

Antipater I

- **Antipater II** — m: Cyprus I; d: 43 BC
- **Joseph I** — m: Salome I; d: 34 BC

Children of Antipater II:

- **Phasael I** — d: 40 BC
  - **Phasael II** — m: Salampsio
    - **Cyprus II** — m: Herod Agrippa I
- **Herod** (the Great) — r: (40) 37–4 (K); d: 4 BC; m: 10 wives; 5 important:
  - 1. *Doris* (Idumean)
    - **Antipater III** — d: 4 BC; m: daughter of Antigonus (Hasmonean)
  - 2. *Mariamme I* (Hasmonean), d: 29 BC
    - **Alexander** — m: Glaphyra; d: 7 BC
    - **Aristobulus IV** — m: Bernice I; d: 7 BC
      - **Herod** (of Chalcis) — m: Bernice II; r: Chalcis (AD 41–48) (K); d: AD 48
      - **Herod Agrippa I** — m: Cyprus II; r: AD 37–44 (K); d: AD 44
        - **M. Julius Agrippa II** — d: AD 93–100; K: in Chalcis (48–52), in Iturea (52–*ca.* 93)
        - **Bernice II** — m: 1. Herod of Chalcis; 2. Polemon of Cilicia
        - **Drusilla** — m: 1. Azizus of Emesa; 2. Felix (procurator)
          - **Antonius Agrippa** — d: AD 79
      - **Herodias** — m: Herod*; Herod Antipas
    - **Salampsio** — m: Phasael II
    - **Cyprus III** — m: Antipater IV
  - 3. *Mariamme II*
    - **Herod*** — m: Herodias
      - **Salome III** — m: Philip
  - 4. *Malthace* (Samaritan)
    - **Archelaus** — m: 1. Mariamme IV(?); 2. Glaphyra; r: 4 BC–AD 6 (E)
    - **Herod Antipas** — m: 1. Daughter of Aretas IV (Nabatean K); 2. Herodias; r: 4 BC–AD 39 (T)
  - 5. *Cleopatra* (of Jerusalem)
    - **Philip** — m: Salome III; r: 4 BC–AD 34 (T); d: AD 34
- **Joseph II** — d: 38 BC
- **Pheroras** — d: 5 BC; r: Perea 20 BC
- **Salome I** — d: AD 10(?); m: 1. Joseph; 2. Costobar
  - **Antipater IV** — m: Cyprus III
  - **Bernice I** — m: Aristobulus IV

d = died; m = married; r = ruled
E = Ethnarch; HP = High priest; K = King; T = Tetrarch

* Called by some "Herod Philip."

THE TWENTY-EIGHT HIGH PRIESTS IN HERODIAN TIMES

No.	*Dates*	*Name*	*Appointed by*	*References*
1	37, 35 BC	Ananel (of Babylon)	Herod the Great	*Ant.* 15.2, 4 § 22; 3, 1 § 39–41
2	36 BC	Aristobulus III	Herod the Great	*Ant.* 15.3, 1–3 § 41, 56
3	?–23 BC	Jesus, son of Phiabi	Herod the Great	*Ant.* 15.9, 3 § 322
4	23–6 BC	Simon, son of Boethus (of Alexandria; father of Mariamme II)	Herod the Great	*Ant.* 15.9, 3 § 320–22 17.4, 3 § 78 18.5, 4 § 136
5	6–5 BC	Matthias, son of Theophilus (of Jerusalem)	Herod the Great	*Ant.* 17.4, 3 § 78 6, 4 § 164–67
6	? (1 day)	Joseph, son of Ellemus	Herod the Great	*Ant.* 17.6, 4 § 165–67
7	5–4 BC; 3 BC–AD 6	Joazar, son of Boethus (br. of Herod's wife)	Herod the Great	*Ant.* 17.6, 4 § 165 18.1, 1 § 3 2, 1 § 26
8	4 BC	Eleazar, br. of Joazar	Archelaus	*Ant.* 17.13, 1 § 339, 341
9	4 BC	Jesus, son of Seë	Archelaus	*Ant.* 17.13, 1 § 341
10	AD 6–15	Ananus (Annas), son of Seth	P. Sulpicius Quirinius	Lk 3:2; Jn 18:13,24; Acts 4:6; *Ant.* 18.2, 1–2 § 26–34; etc.
11	AD 15	Ishmael, son of Phiabi	Valerius Gratus	*Ant.* 18.2, 2 § 34
12	AD 16–17	Eleazar, son of Ananus	Valerius Gratus	*Ant.* 18.2, 2 § 34
13	AD 17–18	Simon, son of Camith	Valerius Gratus	*Ant.* 18.2, 2 § 34
14	AD 18–36	Joseph, called Caiaphas (son-in-law of Ananus)	Valerius Gratus	Mt 26:3,57; Lk 3:2; Jn 11:49; 18:13,14,24,28; Acts 4:6; *Ant.* 18.2, 2 § 35 4, 3 § 95
15	AD 37	Jonathan, son of Ananus*	L. Vitellius	*Ant.* 18.4, 3 § 95
16	AD 37–41	Theophilus, son of Ananus*	L. Vitellius	*Ant.* 18.5, 3 § 123 19.6, 4 § 313
17	AD 41	Simon Cantheras, son of Boethus	Herod Agrippa I	*Ant.* 19.6, 2 § 297
18	AD 43(?)	Matthias, son of Ananus	Herod Agrippa I	*Ant.* 19.6, 4 § 316
19	AD 44(?)	Elioneus, son of Cantheras	Herod Agrippa I	*Ant.* 19.8, 1 § 342
20	AD 45(?)	Joseph, son of Camith	Herod of Chalcis	*Ant.* 20.1, 3 § 16
21	AD 47–59	Ananias, son of Nedebaeus	Herod of Chalcis	*Ant.* 20.5, 2 § 103 6, 2 § 131 9, 2–4 § 205ff. Acts 23:2; 24:1
22	AD 59–61	Ishmael, son of Phiabi	Agrippa II	*Ant.* 20.8, 8 § 179
23	AD 61–62	Joseph, called Cabi, son of Simon	Agrippa II	*Ant.* 20.8, 11 § 196
24	AD 62 (3 mos.)	Ananus (II), son of Ananus	Agrippa II	*Ant.* 20.9, 1 § 197
25	AD 62–63	Jesus, son of Damneus	Agrippa II	*Ant.* 20.9, 1 § 203
26	AD 63(?)–65	Jesus, son of Gamaliel	Agrippa II	*Ant.* 20.9, 4 § 213
27	AD 65(?)–67	Matthias, son of Theophilus	Agrippa II	*Ant.* 20.9, 7 § 223
28	AD 67—	Phannias, son of Samuel	People in revolt	*Ant.* 20.10, 1 § 227

* These two are probably one person: Jonathan, called Theophilus, son of Ananus.

130 **(B) Herod the Great (37–4 BC).** In 37 (AUC 717) Herod, the vigorous athlete, unscrupulous schemer, and passionate autocrat, became the undisputed master of Palestine. As a vassal of Rome, he did not depend on the nearby legate of *provincia Syriae* but was directly responsible to Rome. A clever politician, he at first favored M. Antony. But after the latter's defeat at Actium in 31, Herod hastily visited Octavian on the island of Rhodes, removed his crown in the victor's presence, and explained his attitude. Octavian restored the crown and confirmed his kingship by decree (*JW* 1.20, 2 § 392). Herod became a *rex socius* of Rome, enjoying full domestic autonomy and freedom from tribute, but was subject to the princeps in matters of war and foreign policy. Herod's reign falls into three parts.

131 (1) 37–25 BC. These early years were used mainly to consolidate his power, and were marked by the cold-blooded, systematic elimination of any who might contest his authority (among others, Aristobulus III, whom he had previously made high priest; Joseph, the husband of his own sister Salome; Hyrcanus II; his own wife Mariamme I; his mother-in-law, Alexandra). His cruelty, rooted in insatiable ambition, was notorious; yet he was surrounded by intrigue and conspiracy that made him fight for his very existence.

132 (2) 25–13 BC. Once opposition to his power had been removed, Herod embarked on a period of lavish and munificent cultural improvements in his realm, financed mainly by taxes. He supported emperor worship, and to enhance its quadrennial celebration he saw to the building of emperor-temples, theaters, hippodromes, gymnasia, baths, and even new cities. At Jerusalem he erected a theater, an amphitheater, parks and gardens, fountains, a royal palace, and the Fortress Antonia. In the 18th year of his reign (*ca.* 20 BC, *Ant.* 15.11, 1 § 380) he began a magnificent restoration of the

Second Temple. The Temple proper was soon completed, but the reconstruction of its precincts continued long after him, being completed *ca.* AD 63 (*Ant.* 20.9, 7 § 219; cf. Jn 2:20), a mere seven years before its destruction. (See A. Parrot, *The Temple of Jerusalem* [London, 1957].) Outside Jerusalem he carried on similar construction. Samaria was rebuilt and renamed Sebaste (fem. Gk equivalent of Augustus), in honor of the emperor; in it a temple to Augustus was erected (see A. Parrot, *Samaria* [N.Y., 1958]). Strato's Tower on the coast was transformed into an important harbor city, Caesarea Maritima. The precinct of Mamre, sacred to the memory of Abraham, was enclosed with massive "Herodian" masonry (→ Biblical Archaeology, 74:86). Fortresses were constructed or fortified anew throughout the land (Cyprus, Alexandrium, Herodium, Hyrcania, Machaerus, Masada, etc.); in some cases they were even fitted out with royal apartments. Jericho became Herod's favorite dwelling place, and he adorned it with a theater, racecourse, gymnasium, and tower.

In all of this Herod was influenced by the cultural advances of the Augustan age, for he had surrounded himself with Gk philosophers and rhetors as advisers. Most famous of these was Nicolas of Damascus, scientist, (Aristotelian) philosopher, and historian (on whose annals Josephus depends; → Apocrypha, 68:115). But Herod had little real interest in Judaism, being at heart a Hellenist. Though a king of the Jews, he was not a Jewish king. In fact, he never succeeded in gaining the support of the Jews, who really hated him (see *Ant.* 15.1, 2 § 9–10, where Strabo's testimony is quoted). Being an Idumean, he was to them a "half Jew" (*Ant.* 14.15, 2 § 403). He appointed and removed at will the high priests, who were no longer Sadducees (because of their Hasmonean leanings), but men trained in Hellenistic culture and philosophy. These were accordingly most unacceptable to the Pharisees. Twice the latter refused to swear allegiance to Herod and the emperor (*Ant.* 15.10, 4 § 369–70; 17.2, 4 § 41ff.). Consequently, Herod resorted to violence on occasion to hold the Jewish population in check; hence the construction of fortresses throughout the land.

133 (3) 13–4 BC. It was domestic strife that marked the last years of Herod's reign. He had married ten wives (*JW* 1.28, 4 § 562), and at times repudiated some of them as well as their children. Real trouble came from the two oldest sons born to Mariamme, Alexander and Aristobulus (whom he finally slew in 7 BC), and from Antipater III (whom he executed five days before his death). During his last illness a false rumor spread that he had died; immediately two Jewish lawyers used the occasion to incite the people to tear down the golden eagle from the gate of the Herodian Temple in Jerusalem. Herod learned of it and retaliated by ordering them burned alive (*JW* 1.33, 2–4 § 648ff.). He died at Jericho shortly before Passover in 4 BC. A great funeral procession accompanied his corpse from Jericho to Herodium, a few miles SE of Bethlehem. There he was laid to rest (→ Biblical Geography, 73:91; see T. D. Barnes, "The Date of Herod's Death," *JTS* 19 [1968] 204–9).

(Jones, A. H. M., *The Herods of Judaea* [Oxford, 1938]. Otto, W., *Herodes. Beiträge zur Geschichte des letzten jüdischen Königshauses* [Stuttgart, 1913]. Perowne, S., *Life and Times of Herod the Great* [N.Y., 1959]. Sandmel, S., *Herod, Profile of a Tyrant* [Phila., 1967]. A list of high priests in Herodian times is given on the preceding page.)

134 **(III) Roman Palestine in Jesus' Lifetime (4 BC–AD 30).**

(A) Birth of Jesus. Lk (1:5; 2:1; cf. Mt 2:1) records the birth of Jesus in the days of Herod and of the Emperor Augustus. Though the year cannot be reckoned with certainty, the birth certainly did not occur in AD 1. The "Christian Era" or "Common Era" is supposed to have had its starting point in the year of Jesus' birth. But it is actually based on a miscalculation introduced *ca.* AD 525 by Dionysius Exiguus, a Scythian monk and "abbot" of a Roman monastery, who objected to the prevailing system of dating according to the time of Diocletian ("...noluimus circulis nostris memoriam impii et persecutoris innectere, sed magis eligimus ab incarnatione D. N. I. C. annorum tempora praenotare" [*Ep. ad Petron.* 61; *PL* 67.487]). Equating *annum Domini* with AUC 754, he erred by at least four years. Just how he did this is not certain. It has been suggested that Dionysius was aware of a tradition preserved by Clement of Alexandria (*Stromateis* 1.21, 145; GCS 15.90), according to which Augustus reigned 43 years. On the basis of Lk 3:1,23 Jesus' 30th year (the beginning of his public ministry) was equated with the 15th year of Tiberius' reign. Therefore, Jesus must have lived 15 years during Augustus' reign, and was born in the latter's 28th regnal year. Reckoning the 28th year from AUC 727, one arrives at AUC 754, which thus becomes AD 1. However, Herod died in AUC 750, for Josephus (*Ant.* 17.8, 1 § 191; *JW* 1.33, 8 § 665) records that he died 37 years "from the date when he was appointed king by the Romans" (AUC 714) and 34 years after "he assumed control of the state" (AUC 717). Dionysius' reckoning would mean that Jesus was born four years *after* Herod's death!

(See Holzmeister, U., *Chronologia vitae Christi* [Rome, 1933] 18–25. Instinsky, H. U., *Das Jahr der Geburt Christi* [Munich, 1957].)

135 Since the time of Pompey, the province of Syria was ruled by Roman legates. The list of the known legates can be found in E. Schürer, *History*, Eng tr. unabr. I/1, 328–70. Pertinent to the discussion here are only those around the time of Jesus' birth, because of the mention of P. Sulpicius Quirinius in Lk 2:2. The succession of legates about this time seems to have been:

M. Agrippa	23–13 BC	C. Caesar	1 BC–AD 4(?)
M. Titius	*ca.* 10 BC	L. Volusius Saturninus	AD 4–5
S. Sentius Saturninus	9–6 BC	P. Sulpicius Quirinius	AD 6–7(?)
P. Quintilius Varus	6–4 BC	Q. Caecilius Creticus Silanus	AD 12–17

136 That Quirinius was legate in AD 6–7 (= AUC 759) and took up a census in that year is certain (37 years after the battle of Actium [31 BC = AUC 723]; *Ant.* 17.13, 5 § 355; 18.1, 1 § 1–2; 18.2, 1 § 26; *JW* 2.8, 1 § 118; 7.8, 1 § 253; cf. Acts 5:37). If Lk's mention of the "first" census is significant, then it is not impossible that the census of AD 6–7 is a second one. But when was the "first" census? The legates during the last few years of Herod's life (from 9–4 BC) seem to be identifiable with certainty. Quirinius is known to have been consul in 12 BC (Tacitus, *Annales* 3.48) and could have been proconsular legate shortly thereafter, when he would have waged the war against the Homonadensians of Cilicia mentioned by Tacitus (*ibid.*) and Strabo (12.6, 5). At that same time he could have had an *imperium maius* with authority to take up the census, while S. Sentius Saturninus was legate of Syria. Tertullian (*Adv. Marc.* 4.19) relates Jesus' birth to a census taken up under the latter. But all of this is problematical and makes the birth of Jesus quite early. Possibly Lk is giving only a general indication of time, placing the edict of universal enrollment roughly in the days of Herod and of Augustus and no more (cf. Acts 11:28 for a similar generalization).

(Finegan, J., *Light from the Ancient Past* [2nd ed.; Princeton, 1959] 258–61. Gabba, E., *Iscrizioni greche e latine per lo studio della Bibbia* [Turin, 1958] 52–61. Instinsky, H. U., *Das Jahr der Geburt Christi* [Munich, 1957]. Steinmetzer, F. X., *RAC* 2, 969–72.)

137 **(B) Augustus Caesar (27 BC–AD 14).** The Roman emperor under whom NT times proper began was Augustus. On the death of Julius Caesar two of his relatives vied for power: Mark Antony and Octavian (original name C. Octavius, called Gaius Iulius Caesar Octavianus). The latter finally won, defeating Antony at Actium in September 31 BC. He soon became the sole master of the Roman world, and 2 years later at his triumph the doors of the Roman temple of Janus were closed for the first time in 200 years, symbolizing the peace he had restored. In 27 BC the senate conferred on Octavian the title of *Augustus* ("venerable") in recognition of his distinguished service to Rome. Thus began the custom of the Roman emperors to use this title (see Acts 25:21,25 [of Nero]). But it is also customary to date the beginning of the Roman Empire from this occasion. Augustus' rule was really a benign dictatorship; yet *pax Romana* reigned, with peace and prosperity prevailing in most of the Mediterranean world for several centuries.

(See Cook, S. A., *et al.*, "The Augustan Empire," *CAH* 10 [1934]. Ehrenberg, V. and A. H. M. Jones, *Documents Illustrating the Reigns of Augustus and Tiberius* [Oxford, 1949]. Hönn, K., *Augustus und seine Zeit* [3rd ed.; Vienna, 1943].)

138 **(C) Herod's Heirs.** A codicil to Herod's will divided his kingdom among three of his sons: Archelaus, Herod Antipas, and Philip. Family intrigue continued, while Jewish hatred for Herod the Great evoked opposition to the succession of his sons as rulers. Delegations from all sides were sent to Rome; in the end Augustus respected Herod's will.

139 (a) ARCHELAUS (4 BC–AD 6), the elder son of Malthace, inherited half of the kingdom (Judea, Samaria, Idumea). Herod wanted him to have the title of king, but Rome saw fit to give him only the rank of ethnarch. He was the least liked of the sons, mainly because of his high-handed, autocratic ways. Archelaus arbitrarily removed high priests from office; and despite an extensive building program and considerable munificence to the country, he so aroused the Jews that they finally sent a delegation of leading men from Jerusalem and Samaria to Rome to complain against his misgovernment. This brought an end to his nine-year reign. He was exiled to Vienne in southern Gaul in AD 6. Rome used the occasion to make Judea, Samaria, and Idumea into a Roman province.

140 (b) HEROD ANTIPAS (4 BC–AD 39), the younger son of Malthace, inherited Galilee and Perea as a tetrarch (a petty prince who ruled over the fourth part of a territory; so Lk 3:2,19; Mt 14:1. But Mk 6:14 calls him "king"). He built for himself a magnificent capital at Tiberias on the W shore of the Lake of Galilee, naming it in honor of the emperor. But Herod Antipas, too, had some of his father's traits: He was vainglorious, indolent, hostile, and crafty (Lk 13:32 "that fox"). He knew how to court Rome's favor. After marrying the daughter of the Nabatean king Aretas IV, he repudiated her in favor of Herodias, the wife of his half-brother Herod, the son of Mariamme II (*Ant.* 18.5, 4 § 126; cf. Lk 3:19. In Mt 14:3; Mk 6:17 Herodias appears as the wife of "Philip." Since this cannot be Philip the tetrarch, whose wife was Salome III, the daughter of Herodias and Herod, commentators often suppose that Herod, the husband of Herodias, had the surname Philip; but this supposition is not otherwise attested). John the Baptist was executed by Herod Antipas over this affair (Mk 6:17–29; Mt 14:3–12; *Ant.* 18.5, 2 § 117–19). The repudiation of King Aretas' daughter brought guerrilla warfare to Herod Antipas' land; and when the Roman legate in Syria, L. Vitellius (AD 35–39), failed to help him, Herod was defeated by Aretas in AD 37. The emperor Caligula finally exiled him to Lyons (AD 39) after 42 years of reign.

(Harlowe, V. E., *The Destroyer of Jesus: the Story of Herod Antipas* [Oklahoma City, 1953]. Tyson, J. B., "Jesus and Herod Antipas," *JBL* 79 [1960] 239–46.)

141 (c) PHILIP (4 BC–AD 34), the son of Cleopatra of Jerusalem, became the tetrarch of regions E and N of the Lake of Galilee: Auranitis, Batanea, Gaulanitis, Paneas, Trachonitis (*Ant.* 17.8, 1 § 189; 17.11, 4 § 319; *JW* 2.6, 3 § 95). Lk 3:2 mentions only Trachonitis and Iturea. These were buffer areas against the Nabateans and the Parthians, where the population was largely non-Jewish. Philip, the husband of Salome III, was a good ruler; he was often praised for his benevolence and justice. Sometime before 2 BC he transformed the fishing village Bethsaida (on the N coast of the Lake of Galilee) into his capital, renaming it Julias in honor of Augustus' daughter, Julia. At the sources of the Jordan River he rebuilt an old Gk town, Paneas, and renamed it Caesarea Philippi (cf. Mk 8:27; Mt 16:13). After 37 years of rule he died without an heir *ca.* AD 34, and his territory formally became part of the Roman province of Syria.

(Jones, A. H. M., *The Herods of Judaea* [Oxford, 1938]. Perowne, S., *The Later Herods: The Political Background of the NT* [London, 1958].)

142 **(D) The Procurators.** After the banishment of Archelaus (AD 6) his territory of Judea, Samaria, and Idumea was "reduced to a province, and Coponius, a Roman of equestrian order, was sent out as governor (*epitropos*), entrusted with full authority by the emperor, even with the power of capital punishment" (*JW* 2.8, 1 § 117). Thus the main part of Herod the Great's vassal kingdom was no longer ruled by ethnarchs (except for the brief span of AD 41–44), but rather by Roman governors. ("Prefect" seems to have been the governor's title until the time of Claudius when it was changed to "procurator"; cf. A. M. Jones, "Procurators and Prefects in the Early Principate," *Studies in Roman Government and Law* [Oxford, 1960] 115–25.) The *praefecti* or *procuratores* were financial and military administrators who ruled the imperial province, dwelt in Herod's palace at Caesarea or Jerusalem, and could call on the legate of Syria for help, if needed. They saw to the collection of tribute for the emperor and to the maintenance of public order. When the new province was set up, the legate of Syria, P. Sulpicius Quirinius, was commissioned to take up a census (→ 136 above). This occasioned a minor revolt of the Palestinian Jews against Rome. It was sparked by Judas the Galilean (cf. Acts 5:37), who upbraided his compatriots for cowardice and for admitting mortal masters, when in reality Yahweh was their true Lord. Little is known about most of the prefects or procurators except their names (*Ant.* 18.2, 2 § 29–35).

Coponius	AD 6–9	C. Cuspius Fadus	AD 44–46
M. Ambivius	9–12(?)	Tiberius Julius Alexander	46–48
Annius Rufus	12–15(?)	Ventidius Cumanus	48–52
Valerius Gratus	15–26	M. Antonius Felix	52–60(?)
Pontius Pilatus	26–36	Porcius Festus	60–62(?)
Marcellus	36–37	Lucceius Albinus	62–64
Marullus	37–41(?)	Gessius Florus	64–66

143 **(E) Pontius Pilate (AD 26–36).** The best known of the prefects of Judea was Pontius Pilatus (Lk 3:1). A dedicatory inscription from a building called the *Tiberieum*, erected in honor of the emperor, was recently discovered in Caesarea Maritima. It attests Pilate's presence there in the time of Tiberius, and gives him the title *praefectus Iudaeae* (not *procurator*, as in Tacitus, *Annales* 15.44, 2 [see J. Vardaman, *JBL* 81 (1962) 70–71; A. Calderini, *BTS* 57 (1963) 8–19]). Appointed to office by Sejanus, Tiberius' anti-Jewish adviser, Pilate was a high-handed and stern ruler, who never went out of his way to ingratiate himself with the Jews. Writing to the Emperor Caligula, Herod Agrippa I described Pilate as a man "inflexible by nature and cruel because of stubbornness." He accused him of "graft, insults, robberies, assaults, wanton abuse, constant executions without trial, unending grievous cruelty" (quoted by Philo, *Embassy to Gaius* 38 § 301–2). When Pilate first arrived in Judea, he smuggled into Jerusalem by night military standards bearing medallions of the emperor. This offended the sensibilities of the Jews, whose customs forbade the erection of such images. They implored Pilate to remove them and, when he refused, stood about his residence in Caesarea in silent protest for five days. Pilate had the Jews surrounded by soldiers with drawn swords, ready to kill them if they continued to protest. But the Jews bared their necks, preferring to die rather than tolerate such a violation of the Decalogue. Amazed at the sight, Pilate ordered the removal of the standards (*JW* 2.9, 2–3 § 169–74; *Ant.* 18.3, 1 § 53–59; probably the same incident as that recorded in Philo, *Embassy to Gaius* 38, § 299ff.). When the Jews on another occasion opposed Pilate because he used money from the sacred treasury (*korbōnas*, cf. Mt 27:6) for the building of a much-needed, but profane, aqueduct, he had his soldiers mix with the demonstrators and cudgel them. Many Jews died from the blows or the crush of the mob (*JW* 2.9, 4 § 175–77). Lk 13:1 also preserves a cryptic reference to a violent act committed by Pilate against Galileans, "whose blood he mingled with that of their sacrifices," presumably as they brought offerings to Jerusalem.

This high-handed attitude of Pilate toward the people of the province was, however, his undoing. In AD 35 he attacked, imprisoned, and slaughtered some credulous Samaritans who had gathered on Mt. Gerizim to witness the "discovery" of sacred vessels, allegedly buried by Moses on their holy mountain. The Samaritans, who had made their pilgrimage to Mt. Gerizim without any revolutionary intent, complained of his attack to the legate of Syria, L. Vitellius. He eventually sent Pilate back to Rome to account for his deeds before the emperor (*Ant.* 18.4, 1–2 § 85–89). What happened to Pilate after this is unknown; later legends tell of his suicide under Caligula (Eusebius, *HE* 2.7), or of his execution under Nero (John of Antioch, in *Fragm. hist. graec.* 4.574). Tertullian (*Apol.* 21.24) believed that at heart he was a Christian.

(Blinzler, J., *The Trial of Jesus* [Westminster, 1959] 177–84. Fascher, E., *PW* 20/2 [1950] 1322–23. Morison, F., *And Pilate Said* [N.Y., 1940]. Winter, P., *On the Trial of Jesus* [Studia judaica 1; Berlin, 1961] 51–61.)

144 **(F) John the Baptist.** During the procuratorship of P. Pilate and the rule of Herod Antipas, John "the Baptist" appeared in the desert of Judah and the Jordan Valley, "preaching repentance and baptism for the remission of sins" (Lk 3:3). Lk 3:1 dates his appearance in the 15th regnal year of Tiberius, which began either on 19 August or 17 September AD 28 (= AUC 781). Possibly John, the son of Zechariah, a Temple priest, was in the desert because of some early connection with the Qumran Essenes, from whom he broke off, when "the word of the Lord came to him" (Lk 3:3), to go forth to preach to all who would hear him. Such a hypothesis, for all its plausibility (see J. A. T. Robinson, *HarvTR* 50 [1957] 175–81), has no real proof pro or con. According to Josephus, John was "a good man, who urged the Jews to practice virtue, uprightness toward one another and reverence toward God, and so to come to baptism" (*Ant.* 18.5, 2 § 117). John gathered disciples (Jn 1:35–7; Mt 9:14; Lk 7:18), who eventually (*ca.* AD 54) circulated even in Alexandria and Ephesus (Acts 18:24–5). In time he was imprisoned by Herod Antipas, because of his popularity and influence with the people, but also because he criticized Herod for marrying Herodias (→ 140 above). After confinement in the mighty fortress of Machaerus on the E shore of the Dead Sea, he was put to death (*Ant.* 18.5, 2 § 119; cf. Mk 16:17–20; Mt 14:3,12). In the NT John's main role is depicted as that of a forerunner, announcing the coming of "one stronger than I am" (Mk 1:7), *ho erchomenos* ("the One who is coming"), a reformer like Elijah (Mt 11:3,10–14; cf. Mal 3:1; 4:5)

(Daniélou, J., *The Work of John the Baptist* [Dublin, 1966]. Kraeling, C. H., *John the Baptist* [N.Y., 1951]. Schütz, R., *Johannes der Täufer* [AbhTANT 50; Zürich, 1967]. Scobie, C., *John the Baptist* [London, 1964]. Steinmann, J., *Saint John the Baptist and the Desert Tradition* [N.Y., 1958].)

145 **(G) Ministry and Death of Jesus.** Sometime before the imprisonment of John—possibly in the same year as John's appearance (AD 28–29)—Jesus of Nazareth began his ministry of preaching and doing good in Palestine. It is not possible to reckon the beginning with certainty, for Jn 2:20 suggests that his ministry was already under way in the 46th year of the Herodian Temple (begun *ca.* 20 BC), hence AD 26. At any rate, like John, Jesus quickly gathered to himself followers or disciples whom he trained. The main sphere of Jesus' activity was Galilee, the territory of Herod Antipas. Aware of Jesus' presence and his influence on the people, Herod was anxious to see Jesus in person, but even more, Herod wanted Jesus to leave the territory (Lk 13:31–32).

146 As Jesus moved about, he preached the coming of the "Kingdom of God" (Mk 1:15), implying that it was being realized in himself and that he was the one who fulfilled the expectations of his Jewish contemporaries (→ Aspects NT Thought, 78:3ff.). As a Jew and a religious teacher of the early 1st-cent. Palestinian world, Jesus naturally assumed into his teaching many of the elements of contemporary Jewish religious, ethical, and apocalyptic thought. In some cases he disagreed with the current views of the Pharisees, Sadducees, and others who professed to be interpreting the religion of the OT for the people. Of this native Jewish background, with its profound monotheistic conviction rooted in the OT, he retained many elements, changed or purified others, and added a number of new conceptions, to announce to men a new "way" of salvation. The awareness of the increasing influence he and his new "way" were having on the people naturally created a jealous opposition.

147 In time, this reaction crystallized, and when he transferred his sphere of activity to Jerusalem, on the occasion of a Passover celebration (the date of which cannot be pinpointed: perhaps AD 30), steps were taken against him. He was arraigned before the Sanhedrin and accused of blasphemy (Mk 14:64) and perhaps of inciting insurrection by claiming to be a king. (It is not certain whether this session of the Sanhedrin constituted a formal trial or simply grand jury proceedings, nor whether a formal sentence was passed [only Mk 14:64].)

Since the powers of the Sanhedrin were limited in regard to capital crimes (Jn 18:21), Jesus was handed over to the Roman prefect, P. Pilate (Mk 15:1), who enjoyed supreme judicial authority in Judea, including that of capital punishment (*JW* 2.8, 1 § 117). Tacitus (*Annales* 15.44, 2) recorded: "Christ had been executed in Tiberius' reign by Pontius Pilate, the procurator [of Judea]." Pilate really did not understand the religious issue but suspected that a political issue affecting Rome was involved. Learning that Jesus was a Galilean, he sent the prisoner to the ruler of Galilee, Herod Antipas, who had come to Jerusalem for the feast of Passover (Lk 23:6–16). But Herod refused to go along with the scheme and sent Jesus back to Pilate, who eventually yielded to the demands of the crowd (Mk 15:5). He was crucified by Roman soldiers outside the city walls of Jerusalem and buried. Two days later his tomb was found empty; before long apparitions to his disciples were reported. The latter had banded together and soon began to proclaim that "the whole nation of Israel must know beyond doubt that God has declared this Jesus whom you crucified both Lord and Messiah" (Acts 2:36). They called for faith in him as the risen Son of God, and as the only means of salvation now available to men. The religious movement that Jesus of Nazareth had initiated in his lifetime became known in time as the Christian Church. (→ bibliography for 143 above.)

148 (IV) Roman Palestine after Jesus' Lifetime (AD 30–135).

(A) Spread of the Christian Church. The primitive Christian community became more and more conscious of its commission to proclaim the "gospel of Jesus Christ" (Mk 1:1). After some initial success in converting Palestinian Jews (Acts 2:47; 6:7; etc.), the apostolic preachers turned to the metropolitan centers of the Roman Empire. Gradually the "good news" spread from Jerusalem to "the end of the earth" (Acts 1:18), addressed first of all to the Jews of the Diaspora and then to the Gentiles.

Possibly it was in AD 36, when P. Pilate was sent back to Rome and a new prefect Marcellus was named (36–37), that the "great persecution of the church" (Acts 8:1) took place. The appointment of a new governor seems to have been particularly apt for such an outbreak. At any rate, it was in the context of a Jewish persecution of the young Palestinian Christian community that Stephen was martyred and Saul of Tarsus "breathed [his] murderous threats" (Acts 9:1–2). Saul's conversion, which cannot be dated accurately, is plausibly related to this time (→ Life of Paul, 46:16).

149 (B) Herod Agrippa I (37–44). The Emperor Tiberius died on 16 March AD 37. The legate of Syria, L. Vitellius, was still in Jerusalem, trying to soothe the feelings of the Palestinian Jews who had been outraged by Pilate, when the news reached there of the new emperor, Gaius Caligula (37–41). The Jews were the first of the nationalities of Syria to pledge their allegiance to the new emperor and hailed his regime, which was peaceful and quiet for the first 18 months. But whereas Tiberius had eschewed emperor worship, Caligula now began to insist on it. He wanted images of himself as *divus* erected in all shrines and temples (including synagogues) in the empire.

Caligula was not long on the imperial throne before he conferred on his friend Herod Agrippa I, the brother of Herodias and the grandson of Herod the Great, the territory of Philip's tetrarchy in N Transjordan (→ 141 above). With this grant went the title of king. On his way back to Palestine, King Herod stopped at Alexandria, and his brief sojourn there became the occasion of a serious defamatory outburst against him and against the local Jewish colony. This was permitted by the Roman prefect A. Avillius Flaccus (Philo, *Flaccus* 5 § 25–35), and there ensued a violent anti-Jewish persecution (AD 38). In protest the Jews of Alexandria finally sent a legation to the emperor in AD 40 to plead their cause. A noted member of it was the philosopher, Philo (→ Apocrypha, 68:111), but the emissaries had little success (*Ant.* 18.8, 1 § 257; Philo, *Embassy to Gaius*).

150 When Herod Antipas was exiled in 39, his territory (Galilee and Perea) was added to the domain of Herod Agrippa I. The latter, who had been insulted by the Roman prefect of Egypt, was more successful in influencing the legate of Syria, P. Petronius, who had been sent out by Caligula in 39. King Herod urged him not to press the issue of emperor worship; consequently, Petronius delayed as far as Jerusalem was concerned. But when the pagan inhabitants of the coastal town Jamnia erected a crude altar to the emperor, it was torn down by the Jews of the locale. The incident was reported to the emperor, who retaliated by ordering the immediate erection of a colossal statue of himself in the Jerusalem Temple (Philo, *Embassy to Gaius* 30 § 203). But Petronius still procrastinated, while trying to get the Jewish leaders to accept this order with good grace. Horrified, the Jews gathered in Ptolemais where Petronius was quartered, and begged him not to erect the statue. Petronius wrote to Caligula, only to bring down imperial wrath on his own head. Then Herod Agrippa visited Caligula in the hope of having him rescind the order. Incensed at Petronius, the emperor commanded him to commit suicide. However, the whole issue was resolved by the murder of Caligula on 24 January AD 41.

151 When Claudius (41–54) came to the throne by the acclamation of the Roman troops, his reign began with an edict of toleration in favor of the Jews (*Ant.* 19.5, 2–3 § 279ff.). He rewarded Herod Agrippa I for his support of the Roman rule, extending his territory to include that of the ethnarchy of Archelaus (Judea, Samaria, Idumea), so that from then until his death he ruled over a territory almost as vast as that of Herod the Great. Herod Agrippa undertook to build Jerusalem's "third north wall," which, if completed, would have made the city impregnable (→ Biblical Geography, 73:94). But before it could be finished, Claudius who had been warned by Maurus, the legate of Syria, forbade any further work on it (*Ant.* 19.7, 2 § 326–27). The location of this wall is disputed by archaeologists; either it coincided roughly with the present North Wall of the Old City (L.-H. Vincent, *et al.*), or with a line of ancient wall somewhat N of the Old City (E. L. Sukenik, *et al.*). However, an excavation in 1965 by Kathleen Kenyon (cf. E. W. Hamrick, *BASOR* 183 [1966] 19–26) suggests a date no earlier than the sixties for "Sukenik's wall." Either it was not built by Agrippa, or else Agrippa only laid out the line for the third wall and the real building was done in the First Jewish Revolt (W. F. Albright) or in Bar Cochba's time.

152 Herod Agrippa was an insignificant but pious king, whose passing was mourned by the people, for at home he supported Pharisaism, even though abroad he liberally advocated Hellenistic culture and contributed much to the pagan institutions of Berytus [modern Beirut]. Given his support of Pharisaism, however, it is not surprising that he persecuted the nascent Christian Church (Acts 12:1–19); one of his victims was James, the son of Zebedee, beheaded *ca.* AD 44. Herod Agrippa died suddenly at Caesarea in AD 44, while attending the *Vicennalia*, games in honor of the emperor (Acts 12:20–23; *Ant.* 19.8, 2 § 343–50).

153 (C) Agrippa II to the First Revolt. On the death of Herod Agrippa I, the Emperor Claudius once again reorganized the country into a Roman province to be ruled by procurators. The last of the Herodian family to enjoy partial rule in the area, however, was Marcus Julius Agrippa II, the son of Herod Agrippa I, who like most of his family had been brought up at Rome and was a mere boy of 17 when his father died. He did not inherit his father's realm immediately, but when his uncle, Herod of Chalcis, died (48), he became the ruler of this small territory on the slopes of the Antilebanon. He subsequently relinquished this realm (*ca.* 52) and received from Claudius the old tetrarchy of Philip, to which Nero later added parts of Galilee and Perea. His relations with his sister Bernice (probably incestuous) caused scandal in Rome (*Ant.* 20.7, 3 § 145; Juvenal, *Sat.* 6.156ff.). It was before Agrippa and Bernice that the prisoner Paul had to explain his case in Caesarea (Acts 25:23ff.). After the fall of Jerusalem, Agrippa II went to Rome and lived there with Bernice; he was a praetor for a while and died between 93 and 100. While ruling in Palestine, he had little influence on the Jewish population; he was opposed constantly by the priests and arbitrarily nominated and deposed high priests in rapid succession. The end of the Herodian dynasty was not glorious.

154 In this period, and more precisely in the procuratorship of Tiberius Julius Alexander (46–48), Judea and other parts of the eastern Mediterranean world suffered from a severe famine. A prediction that it would affect "the whole world" is recorded in Acts 11:28. The striken Palestinian populace was aided by grain brought from Egypt with the help of a Jewish convert, Queen Helen of Adiabene (*Ant.* 20.5, 2 § 100–101). Possibly this famine was the occasion of the visit of Barnabas and Saul to Jerusalem (Acts 11:29–30; 12:25; → Life of Paul, 46:5, 24). It was possibly in the summer of 49—the date cannot be determined precisely (→ Life of Paul, 46:28–34)—that the meeting of the apostles and elders took place in Jerusalem. The Jerusalem "Council" decided against the circumcision of Gentile Christians and their obligation to observe the Mosaic Law (Acts 15:2–12). It was the historic decision that emancipated the Christian Church from its Jewish origins.

155 The true rulers of Palestine in this period were the procurators, who made no attempt to understand the Jewish people, made little allowance for popular manifestations, and rather looked for the chance to harass them. The period was marked by a succession of minor uprisings (*Ant.* 20.5, 1 § 97–98; 20.5, 3 § 106–12; *HE* 2.11, 2–3). The most notorious procurator of this period was M. Antonius Felix (*ca.* 52–60), who married into the Herodian family, becoming the second husband of Drusilla, the sister of Agrippa II. Under him the uprisings developed into open hostility. He had been sent to Palestine by the emperor at the request of a deposed high priest (Jonathan), then living at Rome. Tacitus wrote of Felix, "In the spirit of a slave he carried out the royal duties with all sorts of cruelty and lust" (*Histories* 5.9; cf. Acts 24:24–26; Josephus, *Ant.* 20.7, 2 § 142). The decades preceding his arrival in Palestine saw the rise of Jewish "Zealots" (Gk *zēlōtai*, Aram *qannānāyê*), chauvinists fanatically opposed to Roman occupation. Josephus refers to them as "bandits" (*lēstai*) and records that Felix crucified countless numbers of them (*JW* 2.13, 2 § 253), in an effort to rid the country of them. A similar group, the "Sicarii" (nationalists armed with short daggers, *sicae*, and dedicated to the removal of their political opponents by quiet assassination, often at public functions), also arose at this time. Political murders occurred almost daily; their first victim was Jonathan the high priest, whom Felix was happy to have out of the way. There arose still another group of villains, "with cleaner hands but more wicked intentions" (*JW* 2.13, 4 § 258), who aroused the people to a wild enthusiasm against Rome and claimed a divine mission. To this period probably belongs the exploit of the Egyptian impostor of Acts 21:38. This Jewish false prophet led a crowd of people to the Mt. of Olives, promising that at his word the walls of Jerusalem would fall so that they could enter the city and wrest it from the Romans. Felix went out to meet them with heavy-armed infantry; the Egyptian escaped, but most of his force was either captured or killed. During the last two years of Felix' procuratorship Paul lay in prison at Caesarea (Acts 23:33–24:27). In the midst of Felix' term the Emperor Claudius died (13 October AD 54), and Nero succeeded him.

156 Nero sent out Porcius Festus (*ca.* 60–62) to succeed Felix; he sincerely tried to be an honest administrator (even showing favor to the Jews, cf. Acts 24:27). But the tinderbox situation that had developed under Felix was beyond the point of any lasting solution. Soon after Festus' arrival a dispute arose between the Jewish and Syrian inhabitants of Caesarea; it was decided by an imperial rescript in favor of the Syrians. This embittered the Jews still more. It was Festus who finally sent Paul to Rome, when as a Roman citizen he used his right to appeal to the emperor for justice (Acts 25:11ff.). The situation was not improved under the next procurator L. Albinus (62–64), whose corruption was rampant. "There was no form of crime that he failed to perform" (*JW* 2.14, 1 § 272).

(Farmer, W. R., *Maccabees, Zealots and Josephus* [N.Y., 1956]. Hengel, M., *Die Zeloten* [Leiden, 1961].)

157 (D) First Revolt (66–70). The last of the Roman procurators was Gessius Florus (64–66), who by comparison made his predecessor seem to be a paragon of virtue (*JW* 2.14, 2 § 277). He openly plundered the land, robbed individuals, sacked towns, and took bribes from bandits. The Jews were greatly humiliated in Caesarea when Nero decided to grant the Gentiles superior civic rights and the "Hellenes" obstructed access to the synagogue by building shops before its entrance. They appealed to G. Florus, but he did nothing to correct the situation. Later, when he took 17 talents from the Temple treasury, the Jerusalem Jews could contain themselves no longer. With supreme sarcasm and contempt they passed around their community a basket to take up a collection for the "indigent" Florus (*JW* 2.14, 6 § 293ff.). He took bloody revenge on them for the insult and turned part of the city over to his soldiers for plunder. Since the priests tried to control the Jews during these incidents and counseled them to patience, the meek attitude of the people, who did not react against the soldiers, was interpreted by the latter as scorn. Slaughter ensued. The Jews withdrew to the Temple precincts and soon cut off the portico passageway between the Temple and the Fortress Antonia. Florus, who was momentarily not strong enough to check the rebels, was forced to withdraw to Caesarea. The revolt against Rome had become formal.

158 The leader of the Jews was Eleazar, who was aided by Menahem, a son of the Zealot leader Judas of Galilee. The land was organized for battle. The Sanhedrin entrusted Galilee to the priest and Pharisee, Joseph, son of Matthias (= the historian Josephus; → Apocrypha, 68:114). He was, however, suspected of disloyalty by John of Gischala, a leader of Galilean Zealots; for Josephus spent more time in curbing the insurgents than in organizing them. At first the Jews succeeded in routing the troops of G. Florus and even those of C. Cestius Gallus, the legate of Syria, whose aid had been summoned. Nero eventually sent out an experienced field commander, Vespasian, who began operations in Antioch in the winter of 66–67, and soon moved against Galilee. Within a year the last of the Galilean posts fell with the surrender of Josephus at Jotapata.

159 Northern Palestine was once again subject to Rome. Two legions, the Fifth and the Fifteenth, wintered at Caesarea (67–68), while the Tenth Legion was quartered at Scythopolis (Beth-shan). Meanwhile, the Jews sought aid from Idumea, but the Idumeans who came soon realized that the situation was hopeless and withdrew. It seems that at this time the Jerusalem Christians fled to Perea, settling mostly in Pella (Eusebius, *HE* 3.5, 3).

160 In the spring of 68 Vespasian moved toward Jerusalem via the Jordan Valley, seizing and burning rebel headquarters en route (Samaria, Jericho, Perea, Machaerus, Qumran, etc.). He would have proceeded immediately to Jerusalem, had Nero not died on 9 June, 68. For this reason Vespasian halted his activities and watched developments in Rome. Meanwhile, civil war broke out in Jerusalem in the spring of 69. Simon bar Giora had been riding through the land with bands, plundering what the Romans had left. Finally he turned toward Jerusalem, where the people, tired of the tyranny of John of Gischala, welcomed the new leader. John and his party withdrew to the Temple and closed themselves in, while Simon ruled in the city itself.

161 **(E) Siege of Jerusalem (69–70).** It was the Year of the Four Emperors: Galba succeeded Nero in Rome, but was murdered in January 69; Otho then became emperor, but was soon replaced by Vitellius. The latter only reigned until December 69. Since Vespasian had moved against Jerusalem in June of 69 and the Roman troops acclaimed him *imperator* on 1 July, he soon returned to Rome, leaving his son Titus to continue the attack on Jerusalem.

162 The siege proper began in the spring of 70, just before Passover. Because the town was accessible only from the N (deep valleys flanked it on the W, S, and E), Titus encamped to the NE on Mt. Scopus. At Passover riots took place within the city in sight of the Romans, but the Jews eventually united to face the common enemy. Titus then threw up circumvallation and in plain view of the defenders crucified all who tried to flee from the besieged city. Hunger and thirst began to tell, so that in July the Fortress Antonia was entered by the Romans and razed. From this stronghold Titus was able to move toward the Temple. Fire was set to the gates on the 8th of Ab (August) and entry was made on the next day. Titus wanted to spare the Temple (*JW* 6.4, 3 § 241) but demanded surrender as the price. The people refused; and when further fighting ensued on the 10th, a soldier cast a blazing brand into one of the Temple chambers. Although Titus tried to extinguish it, confusion reigned and more firebrands were thrown. Before the Holy of Holies was consumed, Titus and some of his officers managed to enter it to inspect it (*JW* 6.4, 6–7 § 254). Roman standards were soon set up opposite the east gate, and the soldiers "with the loudest of shouts acclaimed Titus *imperator*" (*JW* 6.6, 1 § 316).

163 The Jews were slaughtered. John of Gischala had withdrawn to Herod's palace in the upper city, and once more siege was set. By September 70 the city was finally taken, plundered, and razed; its walls were torn down, with only a few sections left standing. A Roman garrison was stationed in the city. John of Gischala, Simon bar Giora, and the 7-branched candlestick taken from the Temple formed part of Titus' triumphal procession at Rome in 71. Pockets of rebels still had to be conquered throughout the land (at Herodium, Masada, Machaerus); the last stronghold, Masada, did not yield until 74 (→ Apocrypha, 68:110).

164 *Iudaea capta* was the inscription that appeared on the coins struck for the Roman province thereafter. This inscription expressed a truth with which the Jewish people have had to live until the formation of the modern state of Israel. Except for a very brief time during the "Liberation of Jerusalem" by Simon ben Kosibah (Bar Cochba; → 167 below), when it is likely that the Temple sacrifice was resumed, the destruction of Jerusalem in AD 70 meant much more than the mere leveling of the holy city. It brought an end to the tradition of centuries according to which sacrifice was offered to Yahweh only in Jerusalem. This cultic act had made of Jerusalem the center of the world for Jews. Now the Temple stood no more; Rome dominated the land as it had not done before. The fall of Jerusalem represented a decisive break with the past. From now on Judaism would emerge in a different direction. The Christian community was affected by this destruction too. To the Romans they were subject people like the Jews; to the Jews they were traitors. Christian refugees from Palestine carried to the Diaspora the reminiscences of the life of Jesus and of Palestinian conditions that we find in the Gospels.

165 **(F) Between the Revolts (71–132).** After Titus left Jerusalem in ruins, and a garrison was stationed there to maintain Roman military control, the lot of the Jews was not easy. Roman colonists were settled in Flavia Neapolis (modern Nablus) and 800 veterans were given property in Emmaus. In Jerusalem itself some of the old inhabitants, both Jews and Christians, returned to live side by side with the Romans, as ossuaries and tombs of the period attest. Vespasian claimed the entire land of Judea as his private property, while tenant farmers worked the land for him.

The Jewish community, which was used to paying a half-shekel as a tax for the Temple of Yahweh, now had to contribute the same to the *fiscus iudaicus* for the Roman temple of Jupiter Capitolinus. Religious practice shifted to certain forms of synagogue worship and to a more intensive study of the Torah, which became henceforth the rallying point for the Jews. With the destruction of the Temple the influence of the Jerusalem Sanhedrin, headed by the high priest, waned. An academic Sanhedrin of 72 elders (or rabbis) in Jamnia under the leadership of Rabbi Johanan ben Zakkai and later under Rabbi Gamaliel II took over the authoritative position in the Jewish community. Even though Judea was ruled by the Romans, this Sanhedrin enjoyed a certain autonomy. It fixed the calendar, and even functioned as a court of law (→ Apocrypha, 68:121; Canonicity, 67:35).

(Thoma, C., "Auswirkungen des jüdischen Krieges gegen Rom (66–70/73 n. Chr.) auf das rabbinische Judentum," *BZ* 12 [1968] 30–54.)

166 But both in Palestine and in the Diaspora there was always a yearning for the "restoration of Israel"—a yearning fed by the recollection of what had taken place after the destruction of Jerusalem in 586 BC. While Trajan was occupied toward the end of his reign with the threat of the Parthians, revolts of the Jews occurred in various parts of the empire (Cyrene, Egypt, Cyprus, Mesopotamia) *ca.* AD 115–116. These uprisings stemmed in part from oppression, but also from messianic expectations current among the Jews. The general who finally put down the Mesopotamian revolt was a Romanized Moor, Lusius Quietus, who was subsequently rewarded with the governorship of Judea. This appointment, however, suggests that elements of unrest in that area called for an experienced hand to manage the situation.

167 **(G) Second Revolt (132–135).** The unsettled conditions in Judea finally came to a head in the so-called Second Revolt. Its causes are not certain. Dio Cassius (*Rom. Hist.* 69.12, 1–2) records that it was sparked by Hadrian's attempt to build a Graeco-Roman city (Aelia Capitolina) on the site of Jerusalem and to erect a shrine to Jupiter on the ruins of the Temple of Yahweh. The *Vita Hadriani* 14.2 gives an imperial edict forbidding circumcision as the cause for the revolt. Hadrian had previously prohibited castration, but about this time renewed the prohibition and understood it to include circumcision. Though the decree was not directed specifically against the Jews, it affected them in a major religious issue. Both causes may be true.

168 At any rate, the Jews rose up once again against the Romans. Coins struck by them show that they regarded the uprising as the "Liberation of Jerusalem" and the "Redemption of Israel." Their intellectual leader was Rabbi Aqiba, their spiritual leader, the priest Eleazar, and their military commander, Simon ben Kosibah (more commonly known by the name he bears in Christian documents, Bar Cochba [Kochba, Cocheba]). Besides acting as military commander, he administered the land politically from his headquarters, probably in liberated Jerusalem. He preserved the elaborate administrative machinery and division of Judea into toparchies that the Romans had set up. Judea was now his private property, and tenant farmers paid their rent into his treasury. His military tactics against the Romans were those of guerrilla warfare, launched from many villages and outposts throughout the land (such as Herodium, Tekoa, En-gedi, Mesad Hasidin [= Khirbet Qumran?], Beth-ter).

169 At the beginning of the revolt the Roman governor, Tineius Rufus, was helpless, even though he had Roman troops in the country. The legate of Syria, Publicius Marcellus, came to his aid with additional troops, but eventually Hadrian was forced to send his best general, Sextus Julius Severus, recalling him from Britain. Severus succeeded in putting down the revolt, but only after a long process of starving out the Jews who had taken refuge in strongholds and desert caves. In the valleys of Murabba'at, Hever, and Se'elim, caves were used by families who fled there with a few household belongings, biblical scrolls, and family archives. Officers from En-gedi fled to the Hever caves, taking with them letters of their commander, Simon ben Kosibah (→ Apocrypha, 68:107–109). When Jerusalem was once again captured by the Romans, Simon withdrew and made his last stand at Beth-ter (near modern Bittir, about 6 mi. WSW of Jerusalem). The war reached its height there in Hadrian's 18th regnal year (134–135). A siege was raised by the Romans, and Beth-ter finally fell. Subsequently, Hadrian razed Jerusalem again, to build Aelia Capitolina. He decreed "that the whole [Jewish] nation should be absolutely prevented from that time on from entering even the district around Jerusalem, so that not even from a distance could it see its ancestral home" (Eusebius, *HE* 4.6, 3).

170 The defeat of the Jews in the Second Revolt sealed their fate for 1800 years. Until 1967 they were not to be masters of the ancient holy city and the Temple area that had been for so many years the rallying point of the nation. After the destruction of AD 70 the hope lived on that the city and the Temple would be rebuilt. This hope was nurtured by the appearance of Simon ben Kosibah, who was even regarded as a messianic figure (whence his name "Son of the Star" [bar Cochba; cf. Nm 24:17], said to have been given to him by Rabbi Aqiba). But it was an unfulfilled hope. He was the last major Palestinian political leader whom the Jews had until modern times. The hope of a return to Jerusalem and of a restoration of the Temple has been a part of the prayer of the Jews ever since those early days (cf. the prayer *Shemoneh Esreh* 14, 17).

(See Fitzmyer, J. A., "The Bar Cochba Period," *BCCT* 133–68.)

171 Very little is known about the Christian Church in Judea during this period. It was certainly then that the clear break between the Synagogue and the Church took place. When the Christians returned to Jerusalem after 70, the church there was presided over by Simeon, the son of Clopas, who was bishop until his martyrdom in 107. (Some would identify him with Simon, the "brother" of Jesus [Mk 6:3; Mt 13:55], so that a succession of Jesus' relatives would have ruled the Jerusalem church, in the manner of a "caliphate." With less evidence [*Apostolic Constitutions* 7.46], B. H. Streeter, *The Primitive Church* [N.Y., 1929], identifies Judas or Jude, the "brother" of Jesus, as the third bishop of Jerusalem.) After Simeon 13 other Jewish Christian bishops ruled the Jerusalem church up until the time of Hadrian (i.e., up until 132 roughly): Justus, Zacchaeus, Tobias, Benjamin, John, Matthias, Philip, Seneca, Justus Levi, Ephraem, Joseph, and Judas (Eusebius, *HE* 4.5, 3). Eusebius records that by the martyrdom of Simeon, "many thousands of the circumcision came to believe in Christ" (*HE* 3.35). This suggests that there was an active missionary program not only in the Diaspora but also in Judea itself.

(Bardy, G., *The Church at the End of the First Century* [London, 1938]. Jedin, H. [ed.], *Handbuch der Kirchengeschichte* 1 [1962] 89ff., 237ff.)

76

RELIGIOUS INSTITUTIONS OF ISRAEL

John J. Castelot, S.S.

BIBLIOGRAPHY

1 Albright, *ARI; FSAC*. Beek, M. A., *The Sacral Kingship* (Leiden, 1959). De Vaux, *AI; Studies in Old Testament Sacrifice* (Cardiff, 1964). Eichrodt, *Theology*. Finegan, J., *Light from the Ancient East* (2nd ed.; Princeton, 1959). Herbert, A. S., *Worship in Ancient Israel* (London, 1959). Kraus, H. J., *Worship in Israel* (Richmond, 1966). Lagrange, M.-J., *Études sur les religions sémitiques* (2nd ed.; Paris, 1905). Mowinckel, S., *Religion und Kultus* (Göttingen, 1953); *The Psalms in Israel's Worship* (Oxford, 1962). Renckens, H., *The Religion of Israel* (N.Y., 1966). Ringgren, H., *Israelite Religion* (Phila., 1966). Thompson, R. J., *Penitence and Sacrifice in Early Israel Outside the Levitical Law* (Leiden, 1963). Vriezen, T. C., *The Religion of Ancient Israel* (Phila., 1967). Welch, A. C., *The Work of the Chronicler* (London, 1939).

2 OUTLINE

THE PRIESTHOOD

3 During the patriarchal period the Hebrews had no official clergy. The patriarchs themselves, as heads of their families, offered sacrifices at the various shrines that they dedicated to the worship of the one true God. It was only after Israel had become a nation that a specific class was set apart to care for sanctuaries and to carry out liturgical functions. Even then, the priesthood did not emerge full-blown; it underwent a long development—a development not always easy to trace, since many of the texts describing the nature and functions of the priesthood have transferred into an earlier setting situations that existed only much later in Israelite history. The present treatment of the question will respect the real historical picture as far as possible.

4 **(I) Etymology.** Etymologically, the meaning of the Hebr word for priest, *kōhēn*, is quite uncertain. Some would derive it from an Akkadian root *k'n*, which in one of its verbal forms means "to bow, to give homage." Others take a quite different view and find its basis in the root *kwn*, meaning "to stand erect." In this view the priest would be one who stands before God to do his bidding.

5 **(II) Priestly Functions.**

(A) Care of the Sanctuary. Although the etymology of the word for priest is obscure, fortunately the practical functions of the priest are quite clear. Primarily he was a person officially assigned to a sanctuary, responsible for its care and for the conduct of the various activities carried out therein. According to the biblical picture of Israel's wandering in the desert, the Levites (the priestly class) lived in close connection with the Tent (→ 44–45 below), whether at an encampment or on the march (Nm 1:53; 3:23,29,35; 4:5ff.; Dt 10:8). After the entrance of the Israelites into the promised land, the Ark was always attended by members of the priestly class. When it finally came to permanent rest in the Temple, it gave that Temple and its priesthood an enviable prestige. But until the centralization of worship at Jerusalem was seriously undertaken, priests continued to serve at the various shrines scattered throughout the land.

6 **(B) Manifestation of the Divine Will.** Accustomed as we are to associate priesthood with sacrifice, it is surprising to learn that in Israel this strict and exclusive correlation was the end result of a long process of elimination. In the early days stress was laid rather on the oracular functions of the priesthood. People came to them primarily "to consult God" (Dt 33:8–10), i.e., to learn the divine will in specific instances. Just how the priests ascertained the divine will is still somewhat of a puzzle. We are told that they used the ephod and the Urim and Thummim for this purpose, but the sacred text gives little information on the precise nature and functioning of these instruments.

7 The *ephod* was apparently an article of priestly apparel, perhaps the distinctive priestly garment. Samuel's mother made one for him when he was serving at the shrine of Shiloh (1 Sm 2:18); it is mentioned as part of the vesture of the priest of Nob (22:18); and David wore an ephod when he escorted the Ark to Jerusalem (2 Sm 6:14). It seems to have been a sort of apron or perhaps even a loin cloth (1 Sm 2:18; 2 Sm 6:14). But as the priesthood became more highly organized and vestments became more ornate, the ephod was worn for symbolic rather than functional purposes. In Ex 29:5 and Lv 8:7 it is mentioned as a distinctive part of the priest's vesture, worn over his tunic and cloak. It was woven of linen and golden thread, with an intermixture of varicolored wools. The resultant wide band of material had a belt affixed to its inner surface. One thinks of the archbishop's pallium: symbolic rather than functional.

The problem is complicated somewhat by those passages that speak of the ephod as an object of worship rather than as an article of clothing (Jgs 8:27; 17:5; 18:14,17,20; 1 Sm 2:28; 14:3; 23:6,9; 30:7). The priest at Nob stored Goliath's sword behind an ephod (1 Sm 21:10). There are texts that speak of the ephod's being entrusted to the care of the priests and being used for ascertaining the divine will (1 Sm 23:10; 30:8). Many suggestions have been made to resolve the difficulty. The most likely one recognizes that, while the cultic ephod is indeed distinct from the priestly vestment, there is some connection between the two. The root of the word "ephod" turns up in Ugaritic and Assyrian as the designation of the vesture of a deity and of any rich vestment, respectively. The Hebrews, of course, had no statues of gods or goddesses that they could clothe in an ornate ephod; however, they could keep such an ephod as a depository for the lots that would be used in determining the divine will. The use of cloth of gold in its manufacture would explain the rigidity of form, enabling an object like a sword to be kept behind it. And in fact, the lots were kept in a fold of the priestly ephod or, later, in a burselike affair attached to the ephod (Prv 16:33; Ex 28:30).

8 The ephod, then, was not itself an instrument for the determination of the divine will, but rather a receptacle for the lots that were used for this specific purpose: the *Urim* and *Thummim*. Here again we are face to face with a tantalizing imprecision. We have no clear knowledge of what these objects were (sticks, stones, or dice?). At any rate, they were two objects of contrary signification; we may compare them to two coins, one indicating "heads," the other indicating "tails" (1 Sm 14:41–42). God's will would be determined by a process of elimination, going from the general to the particular. "If you draw Urim, I shall do so and so; if you draw Thummim, I shall do the opposite." Depending on the appearance of one or the other of the lots, further determination would have to be made, until a precise expression of God's will would at last be obtained. Though this process may have the appearance of superstition, actually it was a humble act of confidence in God's interest in human affairs. The willingness to abide by the decision indicated by the Urim or the Thummim, accompanied by the elimination of all human factors, testified to the trust of the suppliants that God would manifest his will through his appointed representatives.

As time went on, the oracular function of the priests declined, eventually to be taken over by the prophets. Later descriptions of the sacerdotal vestments, e.g., the high priest's robes in Ex 28:6–30, still mention the ephod, the breastplate, and the Urim and Thummim, but only as ornaments—symbols of office—not as instruments of divination. This is not to say that the priests altogether ceased to give advice and counsel as God's official representatives, but they did so in a more sophisticated manner.

9 **(C) Teaching.** A second office fulfilled by the priest was that of teacher. Of the Levites, Dt 33:10 says, "They promulgate your decisions to Jacob and your law to Israel." The Law (*tôrāh*) was the special province of the priest, but it would be a mistake to restrict the meaning of this term to its juridical connotations. The word is more general and is closer to our concept of "teaching" or "instruction." The priest was much more than a casuist, giving decisions on various points of legal observance. In the fullest sense of the term, he was expected to be a teacher of religion, instructing the people in the truths of revelation, guiding them in their moral conduct, and directing them in their intimate personal relations with God. But in this aspect of his ministry, too, the priest was eventually displaced. By the time of the Exile the distinction between priests and Levites, as we shall see (→ 33–34 below), had become rather sharply clear. The Levites took over, among other things, the priestly duty of teaching. Subsequently, with the emergence of the synagogue as an institution, a new group of teachers made their appearance: the scribes and doctors (teachers) of the Law (→ History of Israel, 75:120). This group included, without any distinction, priests, Levites, and laymen; and so instruction ceased to be an exclusive prerogative of the priests.

10 **(D) Offering of Sacrifice.** If the giving of oracles and religious instruction eventually faded from prominence in the work of the priests, it was quite the opposite with the offering of sacrifice. Whereas this act was always characteristic of the priesthood, it was not at first reserved exclusively to them. In the period of the judges, individuals other than priests offered sacrifice with divine sanction (Jgs 6:25–26; 13:16–23; 1 Sm 1:3,4,21; 2:19). Kings, too, offered sacrifice, but apparently only on especially solemn occasions (1 Sm 13:9–10; 2 Sm 6:13, 17–18; 24:25; 1 Kgs 3:4,15; 8:5,62–64; 9:25; 2 Kgs 16:12–15). The monarchs enjoyed this right by reason of their special relationship with Yahweh, but it was a royal, not a priestly prerogative. The king was a sacred person, but he was not a priest.

The characteristically priestly act of offering sacrifice consisted in pouring or sprinkling the blood of the victim on the altar or in placing its flesh on the altar. The actual immolation or killing of the animal was usually done by someone else (Ex 24:3–8). Specifically, the person who supplied the victim was expected to immolate it (Lv 1:5; 3:2,8,13; 4:24,29,33). If he suffered from some irregularity (uncleanness), then one of the Temple attendants substituted for him. With the passing of time and the gradual elimination of the first two duties of the priesthood, the offering of sacrifice came to the fore as the exclusive right and essential function of the priest.

11 **(III) Installation in Office.** In Israel priests were not ordained in the sense of being divinely called and officially deputed to carry out their duties. The priesthood was hereditary. God had chosen the tribe of Levi as the priestly class, and a man was a priest by the simple fact that he was a member of this tribe. There was, however, a ceremony that marked a priest's installation in office. It was called "filling his hand" and is mentioned in Jgs 17:3–12; Ex 32:29; 1 Kgs 13:33, and in many other passages. The origin of the expression is not clear. Some texts (Ex 29:24–25; Lv 8:27–28) seem to suggest that the ceremony consisted in putting the parts of the victim to be sacrificed into the priest's hands. But both these passages are rather late and may well be attempts to give a rather obvious meaning to an archaic expression whose real meaning was no longer remembered. Other passages (Jgs 17:10; 18:4) explain the phrase as referring to the payment of the priest's salary at the time he was engaged for service in a sanctuary. The very same expression turns up in Akkadian with the meaning of entrusting a task to someone, but this is rather clearly a secondary, derived notion. Texts from Mari use the expression to describe the distribution of booty to members of the army on the basis of rank. Certain grades of officers had a right to certain shares. The biblical phrase would then refer to granting a priest the right to share in the income of the sanctuary to which he was assigned (see 1 Sm 2:13). The truth of the matter, however, would seem to be that the Israelites never used it in its original sense, whatever that may have been. When they took it over, it had acquired a fixed secondary meaning that was sufficient for their purposes.

12 It is tempting to see in Nm 8:10 a sort of rite of ordination. Here the Israelites impose hands on the Levites, but in fact this is symbolic of the offering of the Levites as a vicarious sacrifice for the first-born of Israel (→ 98 below). Anointing, too, has been suggested as the characteristic rite of priestly installation. But the anointing of the high priest described in Ex 29:7 and Lv 8:12 reflects a custom that did not come about until after the Exile. In the post-exilic period the high priest was also the civil ruler, and the anointing was quasi-royal rather than priestly. The anointing of ordinary priests (Ex 28:41; 30:30; 40:12–15; Lv 7:35–36; 10:7; Nm 3:3) was introduced even later.

13 But by whatever ceremony a priest may have been definitively installed in office—if, indeed, such a ceremony was *de rigueur*—he was, by the very fact of his hereditary priesthood and the nature of his functions, a man apart. He was "holy," in the basic meaning of that term, namely, "set apart" from the profane, and dedicated completely to the service of the Lord. He was at home in the sanctuary, could touch the sacred vessels, partake of food offered in sacrifice, and do many things forbidden the ordinary Israelite under pain of sacrilege. But *noblesse oblige*: He had to observe a greater ritual purity than the layman. Specifically he could attend the funeral of only close relatives; he could marry only a virgin; he had to undergo special rites of purification and was forbidden to partake of strong drinks, even of wine, before entering the sacred precincts.

14 **(IV) Priests and Levites.** In several passages of the Bible there appears to be a very sharp distinction between priests and Levites. Yet in others the terms are used synonymously, and the general impression is given that all the descendants of Levi enjoyed the priesthood by hereditary right. In fact, throughout the ancient Near East, professions and trades were rather rigidly hereditary; the priesthood was no exception to this practice. And in Israel, God had chosen the descendants of the patriarch Levi to be his priests (Nm 1:50; 3:6ff.). As a result of this choice, the Levites occupied a rather unique position. For instance, when a census of the people was taken, the Levites were not included. After the conquest of the promised land, when the other tribes were assigned specific blocks of territory, the Levites received none. However, the other tribes had to contribute to their support, and the Levites were given towns scattered throughout the land.

There is a hint of hierarchical distinction within the Levites in the fact that the descendants of Aaron were promised a perpetual priesthood. This promise put the rest of the Levites in a relatively subordinate position. But it does not seem to underlie the later and very clear distinction between priests and Levites. The answer lies rather in the history of the priesthood itself, and the data are not always clear.

15 To begin with, in the accounts of the early days we not infrequently read of priests who were not members of the tribe of Levi, and it is difficult to pinpoint with any degree of accuracy the time at which priestly functions became the exclusive privilege of this tribe. Micah, for instance, a member of the tribe of Ephraim, appointed his own son as priest in the shrine he constructed (Jgs 17:5). From this same tribe of Ephraim came the great Samuel (1 Sm 1:1); but his priestly activity at Shiloh is quite clear. He was accepted as a member of the shrine's personnel, wore the characteristically priestly ephod, and offered sacrifice (2:18; 7:9; 9:13; 10:8). The Chronicler later felt it advisable to provide him with Levitical ancestors (1 Chr 6:18–23). Eleazar (1 Sm 7:1), the sons of David (2 Sm 8:18), and Ira (2 Sm 20:26) were all priests—Eleazar was even put in charge of the Ark—but none of them was a descendant of Levi.

16 Even during the early period, however, there was a marked preference for Levites when there was priestly work to be done. Thus Micah discharged his son as soon as a Levite appeared on the scene (Jgs 17:13). True, this is an isolated instance, but it is significant. At any rate, by the first half of the 8th cent., the tribe of Levi had assumed the exclusive charge of the priesthood (Dt 33:8–11).

17 But at what point in the history of the priesthood and under what circumstances did the internal distinction between priests and Levites arise? The accounts of the monarchical period in 1–2 Kgs make no mention of Levites as a distinct class apart from the priests. (The references to the appointments made by Jeroboam I in the northern kingdom [1 Kgs 12:31; 13:33; 2 Kgs 17:32] are, for reasons beyond the scope of this article, not quite pertinent.) In general, Dt, edited during the royal period, seems to make no distinction between priests and Levites. It speaks of the whole tribe of Levi as being set apart for the work of the priesthood (Dt 10:8), and it speaks of the descendants of Levi as "the priests, the Levites," the second term clearly used in apposition to the former (17:9,18; 18:1; 21:5; 24:8; 31:9). The blanket expression "The whole priestly tribe of Levi" is used in 18:1. The sequence in 18:2–3 is instructive: "Levi shall have no heritage among his brothers; ...the priests shall have a right to the following things from the people..."—here, quite obviously, "Levi" is equivalent to "the priests." This equivalence is true also of passages in which there is reference to Levites alone or to priests alone; the terms are used interchangeably (cf. 31:9,25; also 18:6–7).

The picture presented by Dt is not, however, altogether clear, for there are passages in the book that imply a certain distinction between priests and Levites. In principle, while Dt admits that all the members of the tribe of Levi were priests and had every right to fulfill priestly functions, it reflects a situation that makes this principle rather difficult to apply. One of the central preoccupations of Dt is unity of sanctuary. That sanctuary, the Temple of Jerusalem, obviously would not provide adequate employment for all the members of the tribe. Consequently, Dt urges the Israelites to be faithful in their support of the Levites who may be living in their midst and who are classified, from this point of view, with strangers, widows, and orphans (12:12,18,19; 14:27,29; 16:11,14; 26:11–13). In other words, with the gradual suppression of sanctuaries outside of Jerusalem, the majority of the descendants of Levi could not *de facto* exercise their priestly functions. But *de jure* they were priests; and when they had an opportunity to participate as priests in the Temple liturgy, they did so and were remunerated on the same scale as the Levites who formed part of the Temple personnel (18:6–7).

The historical development of the distinction between priests and Levites, then, seems to have been somewhat as follows. Even before there was any strong official action taken to restrict worship to the Temple, the great sanctuaries at Bethel in the north and Jerusalem in the south drew more and more people away from the lesser shrines. These latter continued to function (e.g., at Arad; → Biblical Archaeology, 74:72), but the steadily decreasing attendance made it impossible for them to maintain large staffs. Increasingly, priests had to abandon their positions and throw themselves on the mercy of their compatriots—the situation envisioned by Dt. The reforms of worship undertaken by Hezekiah (*ca.* 710) and Josiah (622) led to much the same result, and by the time of Ezekiel (580) the distinction between priests and Levites was an accepted part of the structure of the clergy.

18 The prophet Ezekiel, in his description of the Temple of the future, pictures the Levites as replacing the public slaves who formerly performed a variety of tasks about the Temple (Ez 44:6–14). He speaks of these Levites, in rather misleadingly strong language, as having practiced idolatry in the past; it is because of this that they will not be allowed to exercise their priesthood but will function in a subordinate capacity as servants to the priests. The reference to idolatry is Ezekiel's hyperbolic way of saying that these priests were formerly attached to the now suppressed, but once quite legitimate, sanctuaries. A clear statement of the distinction is contained in Ez 40:45–46: "The chamber which faces south is for the priests who have charge of the Temple, and the chamber which faces north is for the priests who have charge of the altar. These are the Zadokites, the only Levites who may come near to minister to the Lord." The priests who have charge of the Temple are the Levites; those who have charge of the altar are the ones permitted to perform priestly functions. Significantly Ezekiel calls both classes "priests," and at least implicitly "Levites" also, but the Zadokites, official priests of the Temple, are "the only Levites" who may exercise their priesthood.

The same situation is detailed with clear legal precision in some passages of Nm written by the Priestly school. Edited after the Exile, these texts are fairly parallel to those from Ez. Nm 3:6–9 tells us that the Levites were given to Aaron and his sons as helpers (see also 8:19; 18:1–7) to serve and to take care of the Tent, but only the Aaronites may act as priests. The "sons of Aaron" in these texts are parallel to the Zadokites in the passages in Ez. By the end of the Exile, then, the distinction had become stabilized; and many priests who had been downgraded to the ranks of the Levites were understandably unenthusiastic about returning to Jerusalem from Babylonia. In the list of repatriates given by Ezr 2:36–40, we find 4289 priests but only 74 Levites.

19 As indicated above, the tribe of Levi received no fixed portion of land after the conquest of Canaan. Rather its members were dispersed throughout the territories of the other tribes in what are known as levitical towns. According to Jos 21, there were 48 such towns, 4 in each tribe (see also 1 Chr 6:39–66; Nm 35:1–8; Lv 25:33–34). This list, like Jos itself, is just a bit too neat and seems to represent an ideal rather than an actual historical situation (→ Joshua, 7:59). Several of the towns were quite valuable, from one point of view or another, and it is difficult to picture their being handed over to the Levites for their exclusive use. The list supposes a sharply defined distinction between priests and Levites, and in fact such a distinction, as we have seen, was not made until long after the time of Joshua. Actually, some of these cities were not in Israelite hands until the days of David and Solomon. Apparently, then, Jos 21 was edited rather late; and while it may well reflect an institution of levitical towns that existed at one time during the history of Israel, that institution has been so idealized and systematized as to make historical reconstruction very difficult.

20 **(V) Priesthood During the Royal Period.** Although it is true that there were many priests in many places throughout the country during the royal period, it is the clergy of Jerusalem about whom we are best, indeed almost exclusively, informed. For our only reliable sources of information are Sm and Kgs, and these books were written by deuteronomic editors who refused to acknowledge the legitimacy of any center of worship other than the Temple. In fact, the Temple was the center of the nation's religious life and its priests were the only ones who participated in any active way in the history recounted by these books.

(A) Zadok and His Descendants. Since Jerusalem became an Israelite city only in the time of David, the history of its priesthood begins with his reign. Before the conquest of the city, the priest in constant attendance upon David was Abiathar. According to 1 Sm 22:20–23, he alone escaped when Saul slaughtered the priests at Nob. After Jerusalem was taken, another priest, Zadok, appeared on the scene. His name is always linked with that of Abiathar, and significantly is mentioned before the latter. For some reason, Zadok apparently took precedence even before Abiathar fell into disgrace. Then, toward the end of David's reign, when his sons were contending for the throne, Zadok supported the candidacy of Solomon, while Abiathar favored Adonijah. When Solomon was successful and acceded to the throne, he sent Abiathar home to Anathoth; and Zadok thus became the one official priest of Jerusalem.

According to the genealogy given in 1 Sm 14:3, Abiathar was a member of the tribe of Levi. Zadok's background, on the other hand, is far from evident. It is true that 1 Chr traces his ancestry back to Aaron through Eleazar (5:29–34; 6:35–38; 24:3), but often the genealogies of Chr are artificial. There is, in fact, a conflicting genealogy for Zadok in 2 Sm 8:17 (MT) that could make him a descendant of Eli. But the reading of this verse is quite uncertain; and in any case, Zadok could hardly have been a member of Eli's family, since his accession to the priesthood is explained as the fulfillment of the threat leveled against that family (1 Kgs 2:27; see 1 Sm 2:27–36; 3:11–14).

Like Melchizedek, then, Zadok is "without father, without mother, without genealogy" (Heb 7:3), and several conjectures about his origin have been put forward. On the basis of 1 Chr 16:39, some have suggested that he was in charge of the Tent during the time that it was kept at Gibeon. Others opine that he was stationed at Kiriath-jearim and participated in the transfer of the Ark to Jerusalem. Admittedly, these are guesses that cannot be verified. There is, however, one theory that is currently quite popular and deserves consideration. Since Zadok does not turn up in the biblical account until after the conquest of Jerusalem and is not given a reliable genealogy, many feel that he had been the priest of the city before its capture. His name has a definite "Jerusalem" ring to it: The priest-king of the city in the time of Abraham was Melchi*zedek* (Gn 14:18; "Salem" = Jerusalem), and at the time of the conquest under Joshua, it was Adoni*zedek* (Jos 10:1). David, then, would have taken over the old Jebusite sanctuary and installed the Ark, retaining the priest whom he found there. It may seem strange to suggest that David engaged a pagan priest for the solemn task of caring for the sacrosanct Ark, but there is historical precedent for such a procedure. For instance, the patriarchs had taken over Canaanite shrines in this fashion. Moreover, the god who was worshiped at Jerusalem was El Elyon (God most high), a title that the patriarchs had applied to the one true God and that later was applied to Yahweh (see H. H. Rowley, *JBL* 58 [1939] 113–41; → Aspects OT Thought, 77:16). Plausible though this theory may be, we must honestly admit that Zadok's origin remains a mystery. Yet while his ancestry is obscure, the history of his descendants under the monarchy is clear enough. They remained the ruling priestly class in Jerusalem until the city was sacked and the Temple razed in 587 BC.

21 This subsequent history of the priestly line of Zadok contributes little to our knowledge of the priesthood as an institution. Indeed our sources offer no more information than the fact that the line continued. It is evident, however, that once entrenched in power, the Temple clergy guarded the *status quo* jealously. When religious reforms were instituted, the initiative came from the royalty (Asa, Hezekiah, Josiah) rather than from the clergy. In fact, the relations between kings and priests were not always smooth. Even though the Temple was within the palace precincts, it was not exactly a "royal chapel"; nevertheless, the king controlled the Temple closely. This was bound to result in friction. The king thought of the head of the clergy as one of his officials (1 Kgs 4:2) whom he could hire or fire at will (2:27,35). He saw to the maintenance of the sanctuary and on occasion imposed his authority rather annoyingly (2 Kgs 12:4–16; 22:3–7). A most serious example of friction occurred when the priest Jehoiada engineered the downfall of Athaliah (2 Kgs 11) and the elevation of Joash to the throne. Joash later had the priest Zechariah, Jehoiada's son, stoned to death (2 Chr 24:17–26). In reprisal the king was assassinated (2 Kgs 12:21).

22 **(B) Hierarchical Organization.** With the large number of priests engaged in the service of the Temple, some sort of hierarchical organization was a practical necessity. Our texts, unfortunately, are not too explicit on this point. There are four references to the "high priest" in pre-exilic passages (2 Kgs 12:11; 22:4,8; 23:4) but the occurrence of the term in these texts may well be due to later editorial work. Still, there must have been a priest with some sort of over-all authority, even if he was known simply as "*the* priest" (1 Kgs 4:2; 2 Kgs 11:9ff.; 12:8; 16:10ff.; 22:12,14; Is 8:2). The term "head priest" turns up once in a pre-exilic context (2 Kgs 25:18) and often later in Chr.

23 Next in command was the "second priest" (2 Kgs 23:4; 25:18). In all likelihood he was head of the Temple police, charged with the maintenance of good order in the sanctuary (Jer 29:24–29; see 20:1–2). Next in line came the three "keepers of the entry." Their title seems to suggest something like "porters," but they were apparently much more important than that. In Jer 52:24 they are named immediately after the high priest and the second priest (cf. 2 Kgs 23:4; 25:18). Although their precise duties are not specified, we know that in at least one instance the king put them in charge of the contributions made to the Temple by the people (2 Kgs 12:10; 22:4). Finally, the "elders of the priests," perhaps heads of the priestly families, seem to have wielded some authority. Hezekiah, for instance, chose them as part of a royal delegation sent to consult Isaiah (2 Kgs 19:2; Is 37:2).

24 For information on the lower echelons of the Temple personnel we must depend almost exclusively on post-exilic writings. These mention 24 classes of singers (1 Chr 25) and several classes of porters (26:1–19). In post-exilic times Levites seem to have served in these positions, but it may not always have been so. In fact, much of Israelite music apparently had Canaanite origins, and non-Israelites seem to have been employed as chanters, at least in the early days of the Temple. In 1 Kgs 5:11 Heman, Kalkol, and Darda (non-Israelite names) are listed as members of the choir (see B. D. Eerdmans, *OTS* 1 [1942] 162–75). Another functionary was the "keeper of the vestments" (2 Kgs 22:14).

25 **(C) Revenues of the Clergy.** The cost of running such a large organization must have been considerable. Since the Temple was a public building, the king was responsible for its upkeep and for its normal operations. But did he also pay the salaries of the clergy? The available data do not permit us to give a clear answer to this question. In principle, the priest was entitled to live off the proceeds of the altar: When sacrifices were offered, he was to receive specified parts of the victims. He had also a right to a share of the contributions made to the Temple treasury, as we see from two decrees of King Joash (2 Kgs 12:5–17; 22:3–7). In the first, the king handed over to the priests all the offerings, but with the proviso that the priests be responsible for the repair and maintenance of the Temple buildings. Had they discharged this responsibility well, there would have been relatively little money left for themselves. They did not comply, and Joash put out a second decree, rather vindictively cutting the share to which the priests had formerly been entitled.

26 Specific information about the revenue on which the priests could count is given in Dt 18:1–5. Since this book insists on unity of sanctuary, its legislation takes into consideration not only those priests actually engaged in the service of the Temple but also the Levites formerly in charge of the provincial shrines. Pilgrims are to invite the Levites along to share in the sacrificial meals (12:6–7,11–12,17–19). And if the pilgrims are prevented from bringing their offerings to the Temple in the usual fashion, they may sell them and bring the money to the central sanctuary to buy there what is needed. In this case, they are admonished not to forget the local Levite, "for he has no share in the heritage with you" (14:27). Every third year they are to distribute the usual tithes locally, "that the Levite who has no share in the heritage with you, and also the alien...may come and eat their fill" (14:28–29; see 26:12–15). If unemployed Levites come to Jerusalem, they have a right to perform priestly functions there and receive the usual revenues (18:6–8).

27 **(VI) Priesthood During the Post-exilic Period.** The destruction of the Temple and the deportation of its clergy in 587 quite obviously marked a crisis in the history of the Israelite priesthood. With the Temple no longer in existence, the law of unity of sanctuary was impossible to apply. In fact, the reform of Josiah in 622 (→ 67 below) had really not been lastingly effective. After his death the local shrines had returned to operation. Now, with the Temple and its clergy completely out of the way, the Levites who had been left in Judah could exercise their priestly functions without any interference.

28 **(A) The "Sons of Aaron."** The exile did not last forever, and in the first caravans to return following Cyrus' edict of liberation in 538 there were many more priests than Levites (→ 18 above). Similarly, a century later, in Ezra's caravan there were two priestly families; he had trouble finding any willing Levites at all, but finally managed to get 38 to accompany him (Ezr 8:2,15–19). The four families represented in the first post-exilic group of priestly repatriates were, as far as can be determined, all descendants of Zadok. However, the group in Ezra's caravan was not quite so homogeneous. One family traced its ancestry back to Eleazar, the other to Ithamar. Now Ithamar was the ancestor of Abiathar, the priest of David whom Solomon had banished to Anathoth when Zadok was given a monopoly on the Temple priesthood. With the acceptance of descendants of the Ithamar/Abiathar line as rightful priests after the Exile, the old monopoly was broken. Furthermore, both Eleazar and Ithamar were sons of Aaron, and it was this term "sons of Aaron" that soon came into use as a designation of the Temple priesthood in place of the pre-exilic "sons of Zadok." However, the Zadokites managed to retain a preeminence of sorts. In the subsequent division of the priests into 24 classes, the descendants of Eleazar (putative ancestor of Zadok; → 20 above) made up the personnel of 16; Eleazar is pictured in the Pentateuch as having played a more significant role than Ithamar in the events closing the period of the Exodus. And it was from this line that all the high priests were chosen down to the Maccabean period (→ 32 below).

29 **(B) The High Priest.** The office—and title—of high priest came into greater prominence during the post-exilic period, although the process was a gradual one. When discussing the Temple hierarchy we saw that probably during the royal period, the title "high priest" was not used; the head of the clergy was called simply "the priest." It was used, though rather sparingly at first, after the return from Babylon, although occasionally one finds other titles for the head of the clergy in the post-exilic books. In 1 Chr 9:11; 2 Chr 31:13; Neh 11:11 he is called the Prince (*nāgîd*) of the Temple; and in Dn 9:25; 11:22 he is referred to as "Anointed Prince" (anointed and a leader [CCD]) and "Prince of the Covenant." Another epithet, "the anointed priest," is derived from a distinctive feature of the high priest's investiture that we shall now discuss.

30 The Priestly Collection of laws (Ex 29:4–7; Lv 8:6–12) describes Aaron's installation in office. After the preliminary purification, he donned the tunic, cloak, ephod, and the breastplate. Then he received a turban-like miter, on the front of which was a golden flower with the words inscribed, "Sacred to the Lord." Last of all—and admittedly it is hard to visualize—the holy oil of anointing was poured over Aaron's head. In Nm 20:26–28, which tells of Eleazar's installation after the death of Aaron, there is no mention of anointing. Similarly, in the description (Zech 3:1–9) of the consecration of Joshua, the first high priest after the Exile, there is no anointing.

It is true that the passages from Ex and Lv cited above take for granted an anointing in the high priest's consecration. But these texts from the Priestly Collection were edited quite late and in all probability reflect a post-exilic practice. Precisely at what point in the post-exilic period anointing became standard procedure is difficult to say, and by the time of the Herods it had been abandoned. At least part of the explanation for such anointing may lie in the regal aspects of the high priesthood after the Exile. During the monarchy the royal coronation ceremony was highlighted by the rite of anointing; the king was officially "the anointed of Yahweh." Moreover, there is a striking parallel between the post-exilic priestly vestments and the royal garb of the pre-exilic kings. Just about the only article of apparel peculiar to the high priest is the ephod.

31 After the return from the Exile, it was the priests who assumed leadership of the people; however, this did not come about immediately. Zerubbabel, a layman, was to be the civil ruler, but as things turned out, it was Joshua the high priest who assumed the leadership (→ History of Israel, 75:91). Eventually the high priest used even the title of "King." The events leading up to this dual dignity are in part shrouded in obscurity and in part complicated by involved intrigue. Neh 12:10–11 gives us a list of high priests down to about 400 BC. For the next 150 years we have no information at all. Then the works of Josephus and 1–2 Mc pick up the thread of the high priestly line with Onias I in mid-3rd cent. and bring us down to Onias III who had the misfortune of being high priest when Antiochus Epiphanes ascended the throne in Syria in 175. Onias was promptly deposed in favor of his brother Jason, and about three years later probably was assassinated (2 Mc 3–4).

From this point on, the high priesthood became a political football. Jason had secured the position by bribing Antiochus and by actively favoring the hellenization of Jerusalem (2 Mc 4:7–20). He lost his job because Menelaus—who was not of the high priestly line—outbid him (4:23–26). When the Maccabees rebelled against Antiochus, Menelaus found it more comfortable to stay outside Israel at Antioch, where he was finally assassinated by Antiochus V. His successor, Alcimus, was a "son of Aaron," but not a Zadokite. After Alcimus' death in 159 BC, the post was not filled for seven years.

32 At the end of that period, Jonathan, one of the Maccabee brothers, was appointed high priest by Alexander Balas. With his accession, the trend toward the investing of religious and civil power in one person advanced appreciably, for Alexander named him not only high priest but also military and civil governor of Judah. Jonathan was of priestly lineage (1 Mc 2:1), but from a rather unimportant branch of this tree. His successors were, therefore, of rather doubtful high-priestly descent, to say the least (→ History of Israel, 75:113–115); and the office itself became increasingly more political and secular. When Jonathan's brother Simon succeeded him, Antiochus VII acceded to the people's demand that he be given the title of ethnarch, a step closer to kingship (1 Mc 15:2). Simon's son, John Hyrcanus, declared the independence of his people from Syria and minted his own coins with the inscription "Yehohanan the high priest, head of the Jewish community." Finally, Aristobulus, next in the Maccabean (Hasmonean) line, arrogated to himself the title of king, and his successors continued the practice. They were high priest-kings. As might be surmised, they were more kings than high priests; and their political activities, coupled with their tenuous genealogical claims to the high priesthood, made them vastly unpopular among the more traditionalist minded Jews (see M. A. Beek, *Sacral Kingship*, 349–55). The Qumran Zadokites represented a strong protest against this situation caused by the Maccabees and the Hasmoneans (→ Apocrypha, 68:84–86).

At length, Antigonus Mattathias was overthrown by Herod the Great in 37 BC and the Hasmonean dynasty came to an end. From then on the high priesthood was a political plum that the ruler could wave before the eyes of those he wished to captivate. As a result, there were 28 high priests of varying legitimacy in the next 100 years (37 BC to AD 70; → History of Israel, 75:130). Their families gradually joined to form a distinct social set, the "high priests." This group plays a significant role in the NT, particularly in the story of Jesus' passion and death.

33 **(C) The Levites.** We must now retrace our steps to discuss something about the fate of the Levites who returned from the Exile, rather reluctantly it would seem. Their numbers were increased by the incorporation of Levites who had not gone into Exile. The census of Jerusalem described in Neh 11:18 lists 284 Levites. What were their functions in the reconstructed Temple? The chanters who returned are called sons of Asaph and are not reckoned among the Levites (Ezr 2:41; Neh 7:44). Although the priests and Levites took up residence in Jerusalem, the chanters, porters, and other servants dispersed to their own home towns (Ezr 2:70; Neh 7:72). It seems, however, that there was a gradual fusion of Levites and chanters, the latter being counted among the ranks of the Levites (Neh 11:17). Apparently, too, the porters are not to be equated with the three "keepers of the entry" who were part of the elite Temple hierarchy in the royal period (→ 23 above), for these three functionaries do not appear at all after the Exile. The class that performed the really menial tasks around the Temple, the "given" men and the "descendants of the slaves of Solomon," all returned in considerable numbers from the Exile. Apparently they were people of little ability; they had not been able to adapt to life in Babylon and felt that they might improve their lot in Jerusalem. In the course of time their duties were assumed by the Levites, who, in turn, are spoken of as having been "given" to the priests as servants (Nm 3:9; 8:19).

34 A great deal of our information about the Levites comes from the works of the Chronicler, almost two centuries after the return from the Exile (*ca.* 300 BC). The problem is complicated by the fact that the author records in an archaic setting (e.g., the time of David) a situation that existed only in his own day. And that situation, in turn, was the end of a rather long sociological development, the various steps of which we are unable to trace (see A. C. Welch, *Work of the Chronicler*; → Chronicles, 24:4–5, 18–21).

The Levites figure quite prominently in Chr, much more so than in the parallel works of Sm and Kgs. They are the official custodians of the Ark (1 Chr 15–16) and, indeed, this is presented as their primary function and almost their very reason for existence. They are pictured as caring for the Ark after David had transferred it to Jerusalem (16:4ff.) and as carrying it into the Temple when the building was completed (2 Chr 5:4; 1 Kgs 8:3). In later additions made to Chr, the priestly editors minimized the importance of the Levites (1 Chr 23:26–28).

Another role in which the Chronicler casts the Levites is that of choristers (1 Chr 16:4). This was one of the chief functions of the Levites when the Temple had been reconstructed after the Exile. The author, however, is anxious to show that this institution had its origin in Davidic times, and later editors of 1 Chr go into some detail about the ancestry and resultant rights of the Levite singers. In an obviously contrived genealogy, they are traced back to the three chief singers who functioned under David, and these in turn are traced back to three sons of Levi (6:18–32). There is a further development of this theme in 1 Chr 25.

The six families of doorkeepers who returned from the Exile were not Levites (Ezr 2:42; Neh 7:45; cf. Neh 11:19). The Chronicler, however, gives them a Levitical lineage, tracing them back to Korah (1 Chr 9:17–19). In the Temple hierarchy, the singers were of higher rank than the doorkeepers; but there are indications that several of the latter, especially the self-styled "Sons of Korah," managed to break into the upper echelon (2 Chr 20:19; see 1 Chr 15:21; 16:5). In our present Psalter, 12 Pss are ascribed to the Sons of Korah.

The above-mentioned functions of the Levites were by no means their only ones; they performed a variety of tasks around the Temple. Some were instrumentalists; others had administrative posts (1 Chr 9:26; 26:20ff.; 2 Chr 24:6,11; 31:11–15). In the area of liturgy, they had charge of the sacred vessels and other instruments of worship. Theirs, too, was the task of preparing the loaves of proposition and vegetable offerings (1 Chr 23:28–29) and of butchering the animals to be offered in sacrifice (2 Chr 29:34; 35:11). This was about as near as they came to specifically priestly functions, even though there were legitimate descendants of Levi among them. Finally, they served as teachers (Neh 8:7,9; 2 Chr 17:8–9; 35:3), but we are not told how or in what circumstances they taught. By way of conclusion, despite their sometimes disconcerting anachronism, the writings of the Chronicler testify to the importance of the Levites in the post-exilic period. Although they were kept in subordinate positions, they never forgot their priestly birthright and continued their efforts to have it recognized and honored.

35 **(D) Revenues of the Clergy.** We have more specific information on the revenues of the clergy during the post-exilic period than during the pre-exilic period (→ 25 above). The priestly writings of the Pentateuch are especially clear, and the Chronicler, too, furnishes valuable data. The income of the Temple determined to a large extent the income of the priests and Levites. During the royal period, the king had been responsible for the administration of the Temple, the national center of public worship. After the Exile there was no monarchy, and the expenses connected with the reconstruction of the devasted Temple were formidable. The Persian monarchs who authorized the return of the Jews and the rebuilding of the Temple also generously offered to finance the restoration and maintenance of the Temple from the resources of the provincial treasury (Ezr 6:4,9–10). But the credentials that Artaxerxes gave to Ezra a century later made pointed reference to the financial situation, implying that the original system of support had failed. Ezra brought with him contributions from the court of Artaxerxes and from Babylonian and Jewish philanthropists; however, a more constant source of income had to be provided.

36 How this was effected is narrated in Neh 10:33–35. A per capita tax of a third of a shekel a year was levied, plus an annual contribution of wood. This income was supplemented, in the Greek period, by occasional contributions from the Seleucid kings. Private persons, too, made frequent gifts of money to the Temple, and as time went on the Temple treasury became quite substantial—so substantial that greedy overlords either plundered it or demanded large sums in the form of tribute, e.g., Heliodorus, Antiochus Epiphanes, Pompey, and Crassus.

37 The clergy, of course, profited from the growing affluence of the Temple. Nm 18:8–32 reflects the now firmly established distinction between priest and Levite. It enunciates the general principle that the priest will share in the sacrificial victims; and Lv 7:30–34 accords him the choicest parts, the breast and right leg. In 7:7–10 the priest is given all those parts of sin and guilt offerings that are not burnt in sacrifice, as well as the skins of holocaust victims, and all vegetable offerings. The best of agricultural products belonged by right to the priest, including the first fruits of the harvest and anything offered in fulfillment of a vow of anathema (Nm 18:12–14). To him, too, belonged the first-born: If this was a clean animal, it was to be offered directly; in the case of a man or an unclean animal, a corresponding amount of money was to be offered instead (18:15–18). A final source of income for the priests—and undoubtedly a source of irritation for the Levites—was the tithe the Levites had to pay out of the tithe that constituted their own income (18:20–32).

38 The Levites were entitled to the tithes on corn and fresh wine. A tithe on cattle is mentioned in Lv 27:30–33; cf. also 2 Chr 31:6. Obviously, this was not an abundant source of income, especially when compared with that of the priests. The Israelites often defaulted on these tithes, and many Levites were forced to leave the service of the Temple. This was the situation that Nehemiah faced on his second trip from Babylonia to Jerusalem, and he promptly began a reform. He established an organization that would administer clerical income fairly and would see that the Israelites fulfilled their obligations to support the Temple and its personnel (Neh 13:5,10–14; 10:36–39; see Mal 3:7–10). How well he succeeded may be surmised from the glowing picture painted by the Chronicler in Neh 12:44–47.

PLACES OF WORSHIP

39 **(I) The Patriarchal and Mosaic Period.** The patriarchs, Abraham, Isaac, and Jacob, are said to have founded several sanctuaries throughout what was then known as Canaan. These sanctuaries usually marked places where God had manifested himself to the patriarchs. In many instances it was a case of taking over already established Canaanite shrines and dedicating them to the one true God.

40 **(A) Shechem.** A case in point is Shechem. Abraham's first stop in Canaan (Gn 12:6–7). It is called a *māqôm*, which in this context is virtually a technical term for a sanctuary, although the basic meaning of the word is simply "place." Here stood the terebinth (oak?) of Moreh, apparently a place where pagan oracles were delivered, for it was called the "Terebinth of the Teacher or Soothsayer." Here God manifested himself to Abraham, and the patriarch built an altar to commemorate the event. And this seems to have been the normal pattern in the establishment of a sanctuary: divine manifestation, divine communication, setting up of an altar.

Shechem also figures prominently in the story of Jacob. Returning from a long sojourn with his uncle Laban, Jacob set up camp on the outskirts of Shechem, bought camping ground, and erected an altar (Gn 33:18–20). The idolatrous images that his wives had smuggled out of their homeland he ceremoniously buried beneath the terebinth as a sign of definitive rejection of heathen cult and of wholehearted dedication to the one true God. At the end of the patriarchal age, Joseph's remains were brought to Shechem from Egypt for burial (Jos 24:32).

In the period of the judges, the people solemnly renewed the Sinaitic covenant at Shechem and set up a stele in memory of the event "under the oak that was in the sanctuary of the Lord" (Jos 24:25–28). Other events associated with this shrine were the proclamation of Abimelech as king (Jgs 9:6) and the meeting of Solomon's son Rehoboam with delegates of the northern tribes (1 Kgs 12:1–19). Some scholars think that, during the period of Israel's monarchy, Shechem was the site of yearly covenant ceremonies that were the source of the legal tradition preserved in Dt (→ Aspects OT Thought, 77:77ff.).

41 **(B) Bethel.** As for the patriarchal connection with Bethel, the data of the various traditions are confusing. The J tradition of Gn attributes the establishment of this sanctuary to Abraham (12:8), but the (J-)E tradition would indicate that Jacob founded it (28:10–22). In the E account, Jacob stopped at the sanctuary en route to Mesopotamia and during the night had his well-known vision of the ladder or stairway connecting heaven and earth. When he awoke, he realized that he was in a truly sacred place, a *bēt 'Ēl* (house of God). He took the stone that he had used as a pillow, set it upright, and poured oil over it as a sign of consecration. He then promised God that if his venture in Haran prospered, he would build a shrine at Bethel and support it out of his possessions. (This picture from the E tradition of Gn is complicated somewhat by being intermingled with J's narrative of an appearance of Yahweh in which he reconfirmed the promises he had made to Abraham [28:13–15].) Then E completes the story by telling how Jacob, after his return from Haran, went from Shechem to Bethel, where he built an altar and set up a sacred stone (35:1–9,14–15—repeating 28:18–19). Apparently Jacob did at Bethel what Abraham had done at Shechem; he took over an already existing Canaanite shrine and dedicated it to the one true God. Just as in the description of Shechem in Gn 12:6, the word *māqôm* (place) seems to be applied to Bethel in the technical sense of "sacred place," "sanctuary."

42 **(C) Mamre.** We are told: "Abram moved his tent and came to dwell by the terebinth of Mamre which was at Hebron; and he built an altar there to the Lord" (Gn 13:18). Although Mamre is frequently mentioned in Gn as the dwelling place of Abraham, Isaac, and Jacob, or as a point of reference for locating the burial cave in which their bodies and those of their wives were laid to rest, there is only this one reference to its being a place of worship. In fact, no other biblical book other than Gn mentions Mamre at all. This is strange considering that it had figured so prominently in the patriarchal stories and that in later centuries it became a popular place of pilgrimage. The explanation may lie in the fact that the cult carried out there subsequently became tainted by the infiltration of pagan practices. For this reason, the later editors of the sacred books may have refused to mention it and may have altered any traditional references so as to make its localization uncertain. See Gn 13:18; 23:19; 35:27, where it is identified with Hebron.

43 **(D) Beer-sheba.** This sanctuary is associated in a special way with the name of Isaac. God appeared to him here and repeated the promises previously made to Abraham. As a memorial of the theophany Isaac built an altar (Gn 26:23–25—again we have those constants in the establishment of a sanctuary: divine appearance, divine message, construction of an altar). Subsequently Jacob offered a sacrifice here and God appeared to him (46:1–4). A later addition to the text (21:33) traces the establishment of this shrine all the way back to Abraham, who is said to have planted a tamarisk tree there and "called on the name of the Lord, the everlasting God." The phrase here translated "everlasting God" is in all likelihood the proper name of the Canaanite divinity formerly worshiped at this spot: El Olam (→ Aspects OT Thought, 77:16). The patriarchs would have appropriated his title, quite fittingly, to their God. Beer-sheba continued to be a popular Israelite shrine for centuries. Yet the worship there became tainted with idolatry; and in the 8th cent. we find Amos proscribing it along with other sanctuaries of the same type (Am 5:5; 8:14).

44 **(E) The Tent or Tabernacle.** After the descendants of Jacob escaped from Egypt and made their way back to the land of the patriarchs, other shrines came into prominence. During the Exodus, however, the Israelites had a portable sanctuary: the Tabernacle or Tent. In the earliest traditions, it was a place where Moses consulted Yahweh to learn his will (Ex 33:7,11; Nm 12:8). This role appears in the later tradition as well, but there a new word, *miškān*, is used in preference to the ordinary word for tent, *'ōhel*. This new term emphasizes the abiding presence of Yahweh among his people. The older tradition (E) represents God's arrival and departure under the figure of a descending and lifting cloud (Ex 33:9; Nm 12:4–10). But the P tradition has the cloud settling over the Abode at the moment it was fully constructed and remaining there, even when the Tent was in transit (Ex 40:34–35,36–38; Nm 9:15–23). The two traditions vary also on the matter of the location of the Tent. In the earlier texts (E) it was outside the camp; in the later (P) it was in the center of the encampment.

45 It is very difficult to say, with any degree of assurance, just what the desert Tent looked like, for the oldest traditions offer no information. The P tradition seems to give an idealized reconstruction, making the Tent a sort of portable scale model of the Temple of Solomon, which was the center of worship when this tradition was on its way to definitive formulation. On two occasions the P editors describe the Tent in detail: first, when Yahweh gives the specifications for its construction (Ex 26) and again, when Moses has it built (36:8–38). According to this description, the Tent itself consisted of a rectangular wooden framework, 45 ft. × 15 ft. × 15 ft., which was covered over, except for the eastern entrance, with two long strips of a delicate fabric joined together with an intricate system of hooks and eyes. This fabric was adorned with embroidered cherubim. Then came another covering of more durable goatskin and finally a red covering of dyed ram-skins and other light leathers. A curtain closed off the eastern entry and another curtain of more precious material was placed 15 ft. from the western end. This separated the Holy Place from the Holy of Holies, thus making the Holy of Holies a perfect 15 ft. cube. Here was kept the Ark of the Covenant. In the Holy Place were the seven-branched candlestick and the table for the loaves of proposition. Outside the entrance were the altar and the laver used for ritual purification. The Tent was surrounded by a large courtyard, 150 ft. × 75 ft., marked off by a system of bronze posts to which were affixed silver rods, and from these hung linen drapes. (For a description of the Tent, see F. J. Cross, *BA* 10 [1947] 45–68.) It is significant that the dimensions of the Tent as reconstructed by the P editors are exactly half of those of the Temple. This fact, plus the evident idealistic elements of the descriptions, points to the conclusion that the Tent (as conceived in P) was reconstructed with the Temple as a model rather than vice versa (H. G. May, *AJSL* 52 [1935–36] 215–34).

Still one may conclude to a basic truth: There was a Tent that served as a center of worship during the sojourn in the desert. Such a Tent has parallels in ancient and modern Arabian institutions, specifically the *qubba*. The latter was a small tent of red leather used to protect the tribal idols; it had a prominent place in the camp, adjacent to the tent of the chief; to it came members of the tribe seeking oracular pronouncements. Thus the *qubba* and the Israelite Tent had in common both appearance (red outer covering of Tent) and function (a place for the giving of oracles). Modern Bedouin tribes have a similar small tent that goes with them on camelback wherever they wander. It is considered to possess some sort of supernatural power and accompanies them when they engage in battle. At times, the Bedouin offer sacrifice to the divinity whose abode it is thought to be. From these parallels as well as from the constant biblical tradition we think it probable that the movable sanctuary of Israel's desert wanderings was fashioned like the people's own tents. The last clear mention of it occurs in Nm 25:6, which tells of the Tent's being put up in the plains of Moab, the last stop before the invasion of Canaan. Once the Israelites had settled in the promised land and were no longer living in tents themselves, the Ark, too, would have been housed in a more permanent abode (the one described in the P tradition?). The sanctuary at Shiloh was a building of some sort (1 Sm 1:7,9; 3:15), and later traditions that speak of the "Tent" of Shiloh (Jos 18:1; 19:51; Ps 78:60) do so by a sort of poetic archaism (→ 50 below). When David brought the Ark to Jerusalem, he housed it in a tent, but this was not the Tent, in spite of the gloss in 1 Kgs 8:4. It was a temporary arrangement meant to recall the days of wandering in the desert (2 Sm 6:17).

46 **(F) The Ark.** The Ark of the Covenant, which the Tent was designed to protect (Ex 26:33; 40:21), was called in Hebrew *'ărôn ha-'edût* (Ark of the Testimony). The term "Testimony" refers to the two "tablets of the Testimony" on which the Decalogue was inscribed (31:18) and which were kept inside the Ark (25:16; 40:20). The Tent was, therefore, known as the Tent of the Testimony (Nm 9:15; 17:22; 18:2). According to Ex 25:10–22; 37:1–9, the Ark was a box constructed of acacia wood, 4 ft. × 2.5 ft. × 4 ft. It was gold-plated on the outside and furnished with rings through which poles could be passed when it had to be transported. On top was a plate of gold called the *kappōret*, which is variously translated as "propitiatory" or "mercy seat." The first translation is based on the meaning of the verbal form *kipper*. The latter is based on the part the *kappōret* played in the ritual of the Day of Atonement; it was from here that God was considered to have dispensed his mercy to his people. At either end of the *kappōret* stood a cherub, shielding it with outstretched wings (→ Pauline Theology, 79:86).

In Dt 10:1–5 only the acacia wood and the tablets of the Decalogue are mentioned. In 10:8 we are told that only the Levites could carry the Ark, here called *'ărôn habbᵉrît*, Ark of the Covenant. Later on in Dt we read that the scroll containing the deuteronomic version of the Law was given an honored place alongside the Ark (31:9,26). We are informed by Nm 10:33–36 that the Ark preceded the Israelites when they left Sinai and indicated where they were to stop and pitch camp. Another passage in the same book points out rather significantly that when the people defied Moses' orders and attacked the Canaanites, the Ark remained in the camp (14:44).

All this information comes from different traditions. The P tradition is represented in the first set of these texts (those from Ex); and its reconstruction of the Ark, like its description of the Tent, is colored by actual knowledge of the Ark as it was in the Temple (1 Kgs 8:6). The deuteronomic tradition attempts no description except to say that the Ark was made of acacia wood. The text in Nm is quite old and is more concerned with the function of the Ark than with its appearance. Its information, however, ties in nicely with what Jos 3–6 tells us of the part played by the Ark during the invasion of Canaan.

47 The Ark was the center of Israelite worship during the wandering in the desert, and it continued to be such until the destruction of the Temple in 587. After the entrance into the promised land, it was kept at Gilgal (Jos 7:6), then at Bethel (Jgs 20:27), then at Shiloh (1 Sm 3:3). Carried into the battle of Aphek (1 Sm 4:3ff.), it was captured by the Philistines (4:11). After causing havoc among the Philistines and being shunted from town to town, it was eventually returned to the Israelites and was kept at Kiriath-jearim (5:5–7:1). Eventually David had it brought to Jerusalem, where it was kept in a tent until Solomon built the Temple and installed it in the Holy of Holies (2 Sm 6; 1 Kgs 6:19; 8:1–9). This is the last we hear of it, except for the apocryphal tradition mentioned in 2 Mc 2:4ff.

48 Of much more interest and importance than the appearance and history of the Ark is its theological meaning. When all the data of the texts are sifted, they yield two dominant evaluations of the Ark: it was considered as the place of divine presence (God's throne or footstool) and as a sort of archive where the Law was kept.

First, the Ark was the locus of God's presence in Israel. The awe felt for it is reflected in the alarm expressed by the Philistines when the Israelites brought the Ark into the battle camp: "God has come into their camp!" (1 Sm 4:7); and when the Ark was captured, the disaster was interpreted as God's departure from their midst (1 Sm 4:22—see A. Bentzen, *JBL* 67 [1948] 37–53). An even older appreciation is reflected in Nm 10:35 (cf. Ps 132:8): When the Ark left the desert camp, it was Yahweh who was leading the way. The Ark wrought havoc among the Philistines while they had it in their territory (1 Sm 5), and 70 men of Beth-shemesh were struck dead for not rejoicing at its reappearance (1 Sm 6:19). Uzzah was similarly affected when he dared touch it, even though quite innocently (2 Sm 6:7—see also Nm 4:5,15; Ex 25:15; 1 Kgs 8:8.) A very common epithet applied to the Ark reveals its significance for the Israelites: It was God's "footstool." The earliest occurrence of this notion is in 1 Sm 4:4, where there is a reference to "The Ark of Yahweh Sabaoth who sits above the cherubim" (see 2 Sm 6:2; 2 Kgs 19:15). The designation as a footstool persisted as long as the Ark (and the Temple) existed (1 Chr 28:2; Pss 99:5; 132:7; Lam 2:1; Is 66:1).

Some confusion arises for us from the fact that the Ark was referred to both as God's footstool and his throne; however, both are poetic figures for the place of the divine presence and should not be pressed too literally.

The Ark was also a depository for the tablets of the Decalogue, and Dt 10:1–5 seems to suggest that this is all that it was. The Ark was accordingly the "Ark of the Covenant"; the P tradition uses a similar designation, "Ark of the Testimony" (Ex 25:16; 40:20). Far from being contradictory, the two notions—throne of God and depository of his Law—are complementary. Egyptian and Hittite documents testify that customarily covenants and treaties were deposited at the feet of the gods. Recent studies on the Hittite suzerainty treaties make this especially clear, one of the stipulations being that a copy of the treaty had to be preserved in a temple at the feet of an idol. The parallels between these suzerainty treaties and the Sinaitic covenant, at least as far as external form is concerned, are most striking (→ Aspects OT Thought, 77:79–80).

49 **(II) Israelite Sanctuaries from the Conquest to the Temple.**

(A) Gilgal. After the Israelites had completed their Exodus and had settled in Canaan, they established several new sanctuaries. The first was in Gilgal, between the Jordan and Jericho. The name refers to the circle of stones that marked the site of the shrine, which was probably used by the Canaanites before its adoption by the Israelites. It was here that the Ark was placed after the crossing of the Jordan (Jos 4:19; 7:6); here, too, the men of Israel indicated their acceptance of the covenant by being circumcised (5:2–9) and celebrated the Pasch for the first time in the promised land. Samuel later came to Gilgal to judge the people (1 Sm 7:16), and the locale played an important part in the career of Saul who was here proclaimed king "before the Lord" (11:15). Gilgal was the site of Saul's painful repudiation by Samuel (13:7–15; cf. 10:8; 15:12–33) on the occasion of his unauthorized offering of sacrifice. The tribe of Judah welcomed David here when he returned from Transjordan (2 Sm 19:16,41). The shrine later came under censure (Hos 4:15; Am 4:4; 3:5); apparently the worship had become contaminated by pagan practices.

50 **(B) Shiloh.** After the conquest Shiloh soon displaced Gilgal as Israel's center of worship. We cannot ascertain just when or how the transfer was made, but it had been effected by the time of the judges. A political as well as religious center, Shiloh was a meeting place for all the tribes (Jos 18:1; 21:2; 22:9,12), and seven of the tribes were allotted their territories here (18:8). A later, questionable tradition places the Tent here (18:1; 19:51). It is quite certain that the Ark was kept here, and Elkanah, Samuel's father, made an annual trip to Shiloh to offer sacrifice (1 Sm 3). There was also a type of annual pilgrimage called a *ḥāg* (Jgs 21:19–21). The Ark was kept in a building, referred to variously as a "house of Yahweh" (1 Sm 1:7,24; 3:15), a "palace" of Yahweh (3:3), and a "house of God" (Jgs 18:31). Here, too, the epithet "Sabaoth, who sits above the cherubim" was first applied to Yahweh (1 Sm 1:3; 4:4; → Aspects OT Thought, 77:14). Not long after the shrine of Shiloh came into prominence in the biblical story, it made a most dramatic exit. The Ark was taken from there to the battle of Aphek where it was captured; and subsequently the Philistines seem to have ravaged Shiloh itself, for archaeological evidence points to its destruction about this time. When the Ark was recovered, it was brought elsewhere (→ 54 below); and Shiloh lay in ruins as a mute testimony of how God's wrath might turn against his sanctuary (Jer 7:12; 26:6).

51 **(C) Mizpah.** In Benjamin there was another cultic center during the period of the judges, for at Mizpah the Israelites convened to take a solemn oath before Yahweh (Jgs 20:1,3; 21:1,5,8). In the time of Samuel the Israelites gathered there to worship Yahweh, pouring out libations and offering sacrifice (1 Sm 7:5–12). Mizpah was another stop on Samuel's rounds of the country to "judge" the people (7:16). One of the variant traditions concerning Saul's selection as king places the event at Mizpah (10:17–24). The next mention of this site as a shrine is in 1 Mc 3:46–54, some 850 years later.

The above data on Mizpah have been seriously questioned for various reasons. Even if we admit the existence of this shrine, a geographical problem remains. The Mizpah where Gedaliah set up headquarters after the fall of Jerusalem (Jer 40–41) was north of the city, probably at at what is now Tell en-Nasbeh. According to the findings of archaeologists, this site was not really developed until the years following Solomon's death. The pre-monarchical shrine may have been another place of the same name; however, the fact that Tell en-Nasbeh was not thickly populated until long after the period of the judges does not completely rule out the possibility that it was a sanctuary in those early days (see C. C. McCown, *Tell en-Nasbeh* [Berkeley, 1947] 1, 3–49; → Biblical Archaeology, 74:70).

There is still another possibility, namely, that the Mizpah of the time of the judges is to be identified with the shrine of Gibeon, which was in Solomon's day "the greatest high place" (1 Kgs 3:4ff.)—the first biblical mention of a shrine that must have had previous importance. If the identification of the sanctuary of Gibeon with modern Nebi Samwil is correct, it might well have been known also as Mizpah. For it is situated on a hill of considerable height, and Mizpah means literally "watchpost, lookout." The modern Arabic name that connects it with the prophet Samuel may reflect a tradition going back to the one enshrined in 1 Sm 7:10. For references to Gibeon as a sanctuary, see 2 Sm 21:1–14 (v. 6 should be corrected to read "at Gibeon, on the mountain of Yahweh") and Jos 9:23,27 (see H. Cazelles, *PEQ* [1956] 155–75).

52 **(D) Ophrah.** Two accounts of the establishment of the shrine of Ophrah are given in Jgs 6, one immediately following the other. According to the first (6:11–24), the angel of Yahweh appeared to Gideon and commissioned him to rescue the Israelites from Midianite marauders. At the time of the apparition, Gideon was treading corn on a rock. He had stopped for lunch, and the angel directed that the meal be offered in sacrifice on the rock. Gideon then built an altar there. According to the second account (6:25–32), it was Yahweh who spoke to Gideon in a dream and commanded him to break up the altar his fathers had erected in honor of Baal, to cut up the pagan *asherah* (sacred post), build an altar to Yahweh and burn a sacrifice, using the wood of the *asherah* for the fire. The execution of this command caused some consternation among the people, but Joash came to his son's defense.

These two accounts have to do with the same shrine. It was a sanctuary venerated by the clan of Joash, Gideon's father, and two traditions were passed down in the family relating how it had been converted into a Yahwistic shrine. The older of the two (the first) recalled a peaceful transition; the second seems to have been colored by later conflicts between Baal worship and Yahweh worship. The only subsequent incident related in connection with this shrine reflects these two tendencies. After his victory, Gideon made an ephod—destined for the honor of Yahweh—for the sanctuary as part of its cultic furnishing; but the deuteronomic editor interpreted it as an object of idolatrous worship (Jgs 8:22–27; → 7 above).

53 **(E) Dan.** The sanctuary of Dan had strange beginnings, to say the least (Jgs 17–18). A man named Micah stole some silver from his mother, but returned it later; she then used some of it to have an idol made. Micah placed it in a shrine together with an ephod and some teraphim (household gods). He appointed his son priest of the sanctuary until a Levite happened by. Then a group from the tribe of Dan, which was migrating to the north, pilfered everything from the shrine including the Levite. When they arrived at Lais, they killed off the inhabitants, renamed the place Dan, and erected their stolen sanctuary.

At first glance this story of idolatry and violence does not seem to refer to a Yahwistic shrine; and indeed the deuteronomic editor tells the story to give the impression that Jeroboam I's shrine at Dan was corrupt from the very start. However, truly it was Yahweh who was worshiped there, even though in quite unorthodox fashion. It was to him that Micah's mother dedicated the silver, and it was he who blessed Micah for giving it back to her. As soon as a Levite came along, Micah engaged him, for he knew the levitical priesthood was more acceptable to Yahweh (→ 15–16 above). The Danites used the ephod to consult God, and they were answered. The Levite in the story was a grandson of Moses named Jonathan, and his descendants continued to serve the sanctuary until the Assyrian invasion. When Jeroboam I set up the northern kingdom of Israel, he chose two religious centers as rivals to the Temple, one at either end of his realm, Dan in the north and Bethel in the south. In each of them he installed a golden calf (→ 66 below); this is the only significant detail we know about the worship carried out at Dan during the royal period.

54 **(F) Jerusalem.** Jerusalem was, of course, the greatest of Israel's shrines. The city itself did not come under Israelite control until the time of David, who effected its capture and made it his capital. He brought the Ark from Kiriath-jearim (2 Sm 6) in a procession that was marked by most dramatic incidents, and installed it under a tent in the spot chosen for it. (This narrative may have been colored by Pss 24:7–10 and 132, which were sung on the anniversary of the occasion, but it is difficult to determine the extent of this influence.) David later erected an altar on the site of the future Temple. This story, as told in 2 Sm 24:16–25 (see 1 Chr 21:15–22:1) contains all the conventional features of foundation accounts: celestial apparition, divine message, erection of the altar, offering of sacrifice.

One other conventional feature, however, is missing here. Rather consistently in the patriarchal period and not infrequently during the period of the judges, Israelite shrines were established on the sites of already existing pagan sanctuaries. There was, undoubtedly, such a shrine in Jerusalem: Melchizedek, its king during the patriarchal period, is introduced as priest of El Elyon, a well-known Canaanite deity (Gn 14:18–20). However, everything in the passages dealing with the establishment of the Israelite sanctuary indicates rather clearly that, if there were such a shrine, it was not taken over by David. The Ark was housed in a tent, not in an already existing structure; and the site chosen for the altar and, eventually, for the Temple, had no religious associations. It has been a threshing floor belonging to a native Jebusite named Araunah (2 Sm 24:18–20). However, it is tenuously possible that the editors purposely omitted from their narrative anything that might suggest that the Temple had pagan antecedents (→ 20 above).

55 **(III) The Temple of Jerusalem.**

(A) Location. According to 2 Chr 3:1, Solomon built the Temple on the site selected and purchased by David; this was a rocky eminence N of Ophel, the eastern hill to which the city was then confined. The site has been occupied continuously ever since, and is now occupied by the Mosque of Omar and the so-called Dome of the Rock. Whereas the general area is easily identifiable, there is some question as to the Temple's exact position. That its entrance faced the east seems quite certain, and that the huge rock now enclosed in the Dome was part of its structure is generally admitted. However, what part is not known (→ Biblical Geography, 73:92–93).

One very common view is that the rock was the base of the altar of holocausts, which was in the court upon which the front entrance opened. This is an attractive theory; for beneath the rock is a spacious cave into which the ashes and other remains of the sacrifices could have been thrown, and a canal running to the N would then have carried off the blood of the victims, along with the water used for various purifications. Attractive though this theory is, it is not without its difficulties, for it requires that the Temple be built on a sharply sloping part of the hill. The Holy of Holies then would have had to be supported by substructures of considerable proportions, and there is no evidence of any such construction.

Another hypothesis is that the rock was actually the foundation of the Holy of Holies, which would then have been on a higher level than the rest of the Temple. In fact, this was the common arrangement for temples of the time: The most sacred section occupied a more elevated spot. This theory removes the necessity of supposing an artificial substructure for the Holy of Holies and makes it easier to visualize the arrangement of the various courts in the Temple area as it was later reconstructed by Herod the Great. Still it is difficult to understand how the walls of the Holy of Holies could have been built into the rock, and what would have been the function of the cave and canal beneath the rock. Furthermore, although this theory clarifies the position of the Court of the Women in the Herodian Temple, it causes difficulties concerning the Court of the Gentiles. All in all, however, this second hypothesis is less objectionable.

56 **(B) Interior and Exterior.** It took approximately seven years to build Solomon's Temple (1 Kgs 6:37–38; → Biblical Archaeology, 74:72). The timber and skilled labor were obtained from Hiram, king of Tyre; the stone and unskilled labor came from the environs of Jerusalem (1 Kgs 5:15–31). The biblical description of the Temple is clear in its general lines, but in points of detail it leaves much to be desired (1 Kgs 6–7; 2 Chr 3–4). We are not told, for instance, how thick the walls were, how the façade was ornamented, or what kind of roof was used. Many scholars draw upon later information supplied in Ezekiel's vision in order to fill out what is lacking in 1 Kgs. For instance, Ez 41:5 speaks of Temple walls that are 9 ft. thick, and Ez 40:49; 41:8 describe the Temple as standing on a platform 9 ft. high.

The *interior* was divided into three sections: the Ulam or vestibule; the Hekal (palace; temple), later called the Holy Place or Sanctuary; and the Debir (back room), later called the Holy of Holies. The most sacred part was the Holy of Holies, for in it was kept the Ark of the Covenant. The interior measurements were as follows: the building was 30 ft. wide throughout; the Ulam was 15 ft. long, the Hekal 60 ft., and the Debir 30 ft. The text does not make it clear how these sections were partitioned off, but there must have been a wall between the Ulam and the Hekal. And while 1 Kgs 6:2 speaks of the Hekal and the Debir as a unit, 6:16–17 suggests that they were separated, for it gives the length of each. De Vaux's suggested emendation of 6:16 would throw further light on the subject: Solomon "used cedar planks to build the

SOLOMON'S TEMPLE

I. GROUND PLAN

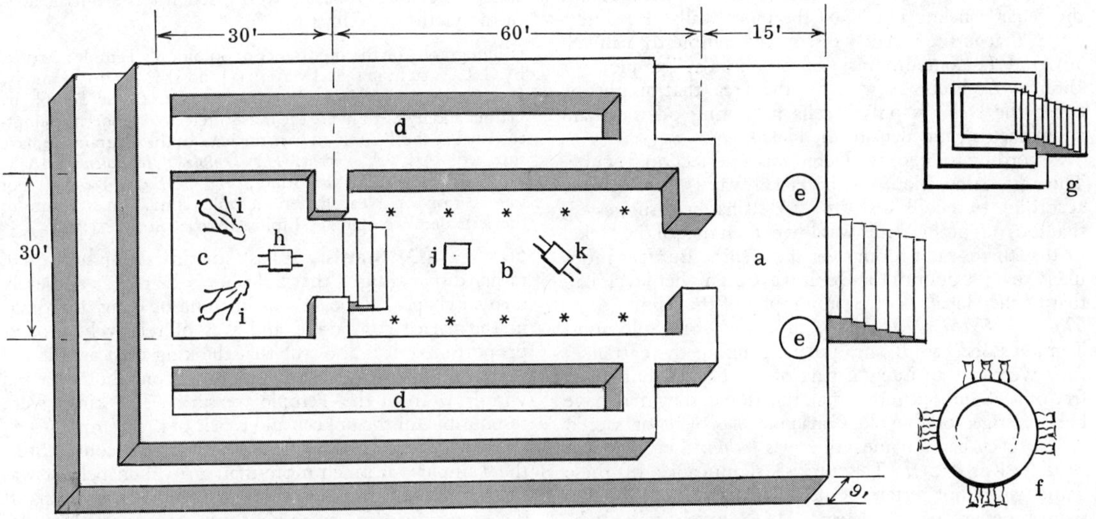

a. Vestibule or Porch *(ʾûlām)*
b. Holy Place or Sanctuary *(hêkāl)*, 60'×30'×40'
c. Holy of Holies *(d^{e}bîr)*, 30'×30'×30'
d. Side Chambers - three stories, each level 1.5' wider than the lower story
e. Two Free-standing Pillars of Jachin and Boaz
f. Bronze Sea
g. Bronze Altar (with straight steps of Albright-Wright)
h. Ark of the Covenant
i. Cherubim
j. Altar of Incense
k. Table for Loaves of Proposition
* Ten Candlesticks—five on each side

II. FRONTAL VIEW

d. Side Chambers: Treasury
e. Jachin and Boaz (40' high)
f. Bronze Sea (15' diameter)
g. Bronze Altar (Garber's ziggurat)
h. Flat Roof (Garber's Egyptian cornice) (Albright shows crenelations)

N.B.: No towers.

III. FLOOR PLAN OF A PHOENICIAN CHAPEL

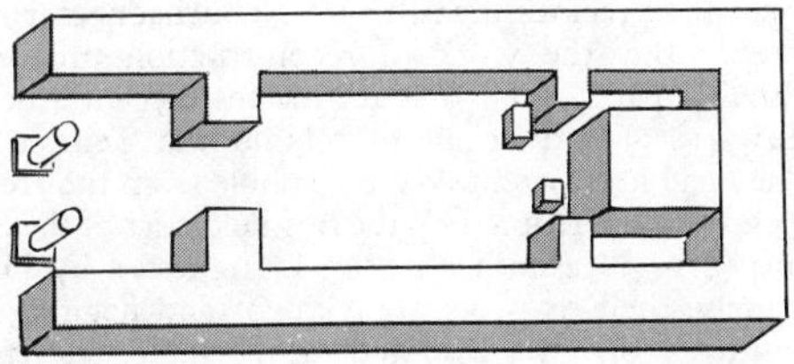

This eighth-century Phoenician chapel of the kings of Hattina (Tell Tainat), in Syria, was two-thirds the size of Solomon's Temple.

twenty cubits [= 30 ft.] from the back of the Temple, from the ground to the rafters, and (these twenty cubits) 'were set apart' from the Temple for the Debir." There would then have been a transverse partition different from the cedar paneling that lined the inner walls. It is interesting that in the recently discovered temple to Yahweh at Arad (a contemporary of Solomon's Temple; → Biblical Archaeology, 74:72), the area that might be called the Debir is only a cella projecting off the main room that is equivalent to the Hekal.

According to 6:20, the Debir was a perfect 30 ft. cube. This raises a question, for the Hekal was 45 ft. high (or, according to the Gk text, 37.5 ft.). It has been suggested, that the roof of the Debir was lower than that of the Hekal or that there was a room over the Debir. But it is more likely that the floor of the Debir was on a higher level than that of the Hekal, as often in temples of that time.

57 *Exterior.* Directly in front of Solomon's Temple stood two bronze pillars, flanking the entrance; they were not an integral part of the façade, but stood free of it. Symbolic rather than functional, they may have been vestiges of the old Canaanite *masseboth* or sacred steles. Each had a name: one was *Jachin*, the other was *Boaz* (1 Kgs 7:21). The precise significance of these names is still not certain. One popular explanation takes them together and translates: "He (Yahweh) will establish with strength." Many other conjectures have been made, but one of the most interesting is that they represent the satisfied exclamations of the artisan: *Yākîn* (It is solid!) and *Bōʿaz* (With strength!). See R. B. Y. Scott, *JBL* 58 (1939) 143–49. The Arad temple also had two pillars flanking the entrance to the main room.

58 According to 1 Kgs 6:5–10, a structure of three low stories surrounded the three sides of the Debir and the two sides of the Hekal. Apparently only one such story, 7.5 ft. high, was in the original plan. Later it proved inadequate as a place for storage and two more stories were added, each 1.5 ft. wider than the other, and were fitted into the existing recesses in the outer wall of the Temple. We are not certain where the entrance to these storerooms was, but it may have been at the right corner (1 Kgs 6:8). Access to the second and third stories was by means of trap doors. The existence of recesses in the outer walls is explained by the manner in which those walls were constructed. According to 1 Kgs 6:36; 7:12, the walls of the courts and of the palace had three courses of dressed stone and one of timber, and the Temple walls were probably built up in the same fashion (see Ezr 6:14). The timber course would have served as a framework for the brick superstructure that topped the stonework, and each course of stone would have been lighter, and narrower, than the one on which it rested, thus forming the recesses.

Surrounding the Temple was the "inner court" (1 Kgs 6:36). This was later extended to include an upper and lower court (2 Chr 20:5; 2 Kgs 21:5; Jer 36:10).

59 **(C) Furniture.** The interior appointments of Solomon's Temple were as follows. Inside the Debir or Holy of Holies was the Ark of the Covenant, near or on top of which were two gold-plated wooden cherubim whose extended wings reached from wall to wall. The figures themselves rose halfway to the ceiling (1 Kgs 6:23–28; 2 Chr 3:10–13; see 1 Kgs 8:6–7; 2 Chr 5:7–8). In the Hekal or Sanctuary were the altar of incense, the table for the loaves of proposition, and ten candlesticks (1 Kgs 7:48–49). In the court in front of the Temple, off to one side of the entrance steps, was the altar of bronze (8:64; 9:25; 2 Kgs 16:14); on the opposite side was the "Sea" of bronze. This was a capacious laver resting on the backs of twelve statues of bulls (1 Kgs 7:23–26). Ranged on either side of the entrance were ten tables on top of which were bronze basins. These tables could be wheeled about the court as needed (7:27–29). The priests used the "Sea" for their own ritual purifications; the smaller basins were used for the purification of the victims (2 Chr 4:6).

(Bibliography on the appearance of Solomon's Temple: Articles by G. E. Wright in *BA* 4 [May 1941] and 18 [May 1955] and by P. L. Garber, 14 [Feb. 1951]—reconstructions of the Temple by Garber and by Wright are the most often cited modern attempts to visualize the Temple and are the basis of the diagram we have supplied. Also, A. Parrot, *The Temple of Jerusalem* [SBA 5; London, 1955]; W F. Stinespring, *IDB* 4, 534–60. For information on Near Eastern temples similar in structure to the Jerusalem Temple, → Biblical Archaeology, 74:72.)

60 **(D) Status.** It has sometimes been suggested, rather disparagingly, that Solomon's Temple was merely a royal chapel. True, it was just one of many buildings in the palace compound and was of relatively modest proportions. It is also true that the king dedicated it and richly subsidized it, and his successors contributed to and withdrew from the Temple treasury. The kings were responsible for the upkeep and repair of the Temple (→ 25 above) and even had a throne set up in the court. Still, the Temple was much more than a royal chapel: It was the national shrine, the center of orthodox worship. If the king figured so prominently in its operation, it was because he was its principal patron and because his role as Yahweh's vice-regent gave him, if not strictly a priestly, at least a sacred character that he was perfectly free to exercise on occasion (→ 10 above).

61 **(E) History of First and Second Temples.** *The First* or Solomonic *Temple* suffered all the vicissitudes of the nation itself. It was altered, defiled, restored, pillaged, and eventually reduced to rubble. The two upper stories may have been added to the outer building by Asa (1 Kgs 15:15). Jehoshaphat extended the court (2 Chr 20:5). The resulting upper and lower court were connected by a gate during the rule of Jotham (2 Kgs 15:35; cf. Jer 26:10; 36:10). All the successors of Solomon were anointed in the Temple court, and the rebellion against Athaliah and the subsequent anointing of Joash took place there (2 Kgs 11). Ahaz had Solomon's bronze altar dismantled and erected a new one on the pattern of one in Damascus (16:10–16). He also confiscated the movable basins and removed the bronze bulls from beneath the great "Sea," probably because he needed money to pay tribute to his Assyrian overlord (16:17). Manasseh erected idolatrous altars and an image of Asherah (21:4–5,7).

In times of religious fervor and reform, these abominations were removed and the Temple was refurbished. Such were the times of Hezekiah (2 Kgs 18:4) and especially of Josiah (23:4–12). However, these reforms remained largely external and were not able to effect a lasting and general change of attitude among the people. With official encouragement, the people repeatedly returned to their old syncretistic ways, and Ez 8 portrays graphically the situation just before the Babylonians leveled Solomon's Temple in 587.

62 *The Second Temple.* When, in 538, the Jews returned from the Exile, they brought with them Persian authorization to rebuild the Temple. Cyrus restored to them the precious utensils that Nebuchadnezzar had pilfered. But the work of reconstruction proceeded at a snail's pace. The first repatriates erected a new altar (Ezr 3:2–6) and began to rebuild the Temple (5:16). They had hardly removed the rubble from the area when they were interrupted by the hostile tactics of the Samaritans (4:1–5). Another reason is suggested by Hag 1:2, namely, their own discouragement and flagging enthusiasm. Work was resumed in 520 under the energetic direction of Zerubbabel and Joshua, and with the urging of Haggai and Zechariah (Ezr 4:24–5:2; Hag 1:1–2,9; Zech 4:7–10). The task was completed in 515.

Unfortunately, we are poorly informed about the appearance of the post-exilic Temple. In all likelihood it was built on the same lines and was of the same proportions as the Temple of Solomon. The old people who remembered Solomon's Temple are said to have shed tears at the sight of the reconstruction (Ezr 3:12–13; Hag 2:3). However, these texts refer to the new Temple as it was in the process of construction. The finished product, although not so glittering as its predecessor, was substantial and worthy of its high purpose.

63 As time went on, its splendor increased; and when Antiochus Epiphanes plundered it in 169, his booty was noteworthy: the golden altar and candelabrum, the table of offerings, the veil that hung at the entrance, gold plate, sacred utensils, and treasures (1 Mc 1:21–24; 2 Mc 5:15–16; see 2 Mc 3). Further profanation occurred when, in 167, legitimate sacrifice was proscribed and supplanted by the cult of Zeus Olympios (1 Mc 1:44–49; 2 Mc 6:1–6). In 164, after the Maccabean victories, the sacred precincts were purified, the stolen furnishings restored, and the Temple rededicated (1 Mc 4:36–59). In 20 BC Herod the Great undertook the complete rebuilding of the Temple. (→ Biblical Archaeology, 74:86).

64 **(F) Theological Import.** The Temple played an important part in the life of Israel, fundamentally because the Temple was considered God's own house in the midst of his people. At the entrance of the Ark into Solomon's newly constructed Temple, God symbolically took possession of his house; and according to 1 Kgs 8:10, a cloud signifying the divine presence filled the Temple (Ex 33:9; 40:34–35; Nm 12:4–10). There is explicit reference to the idea of divine dwelling in Solomon's dedication speech (1 Kgs 8:13); see also 1 Kgs 8:12; 2 Kgs 19:14; Pss 27:4; 84; Am 1:2; Is 2:2–3; 6:1–4; Jer 14:21. The prophets, however, realized that God's presence among his people was a gratuitous favor that could be withdrawn if they proved unworthy of it. Jeremiah was especially outspoken against those compatriots who looked upon the Temple as a sort of good luck charm that would protect them against hostile forces, whether or not they lived so as to deserve protection (Jer 7:1–15; 26:1–15; see Ex 8–10).

As theological notions became more refined and the transcendence of Yahweh came to be realized more precisely, a certain uneasiness manifested itself. Could the transcendent God be confined within the narrow physical limits of the Holy of Holies? This conflict is reflected in the prayer that the deuteronomic editor puts on the lips of Solomon: "But is God really to dwell with men on earth? The heavens, even the highest heavens, cannot contain him, much less this house which I have built" (1 Kgs 8:27). In the next verses (30–40) he gives the answer: really God lives in heaven, but from there he hears the prayers that are addressed to him in the Temple. His transcendence was safeguarded further by the notion that his "Name" dwelt in the Temple (1 Kgs 8:17,29; Dt 12:5,11). This was an ingenious compromise, for among the Semites there was an intrinsic connection between a person and his name (→ Aspects OT Thought, 77:6). Where Yahweh's Name was, there he was, too, in a special but not an exclusive, restricted way. Other biblical documents stress that God's "Glory" dwelt in the Temple (2 Chr 5:14; Ez 10:4; 43:5).

65 In addition to being a sign of God's presence, or perhaps because it was, the Temple was also a symbol of his choice of Israel as his very own people. Even more specifically, it signified his predilection for Jerusalem (2 Sm 24:16; 2 Chr 3:1; Pss 68:17; 78:68). This notion is rooted ultimately in Yahweh's choice of David and the promise of perpetuity to the Davidic dynasty (1 Kgs 8:16; 11:13,32; 2 Chr 6:5–6; 2 Kgs 19:34; Is 37:35; → Aspects OT Thought, 77:155). In 701 when the holy city was saved from destruction at the hands of Sennacherib's army, the people were persuaded that the Temple itself afforded them sure protection against whatever forces might assail them. This conviction was badly shaken by the catastrophe of 587, but it revived in more moderate form after the return from the Exile and the reconstruction of the Temple.

66 **(G) Oneness of Sanctuary.** We have been speaking of the Temple as the center of legitimate worship, indeed as the only place of worship in Israel; and it is true that eventually it was recognized as such. Yet, in the beginning, as we have seen, there were many shrines throughout the land, particularly during the period of the judges; and indeed Ex 20:24–26 recognized the legitimacy of these several altars and of the sacrifices offered thereon, provided that they had been erected with divine sanction. This sanction would have been indicated by a theophany at the place in question. However, not all of these sanctuaries were of equal importance. During the period of the judges, whenever the tribes met for communal worship, it was always at the shrine where the Ark was kept, particularly at Shiloh and later at Gibeon.

David's installation of the Ark in Jerusalem was the beginning of this city's prestige; yet Gibeon was still the "greatest high place" in Solomon's day (1 Kgs 3:4–15). But with the building of the Temple, Jerusalem became the focal point of divine worship, attracting thousands of pilgrims from all over the country. Then came the split of the kingdom: The ten northern tribes seceded and formed the kingdom of Israel with Jeroboam as their first king. Fearing that continued religious allegiance to Jerusalem would weaken his people's political allegiance to the new kingdom, he set up rival sanctuaries at Bethel and Dan (1 Kgs 12:27–30). Even though he installed gold-plated bullocks in these shrines, he did not mean to reject Yahweh. Like the cherubim atop the Ark, these figures were conceived of as thrones of God, not as gods themselves. Unfortunately, however, the bull was a popular symbol for the Canaanite god Baal and was associated with the gross fertility cults of which the Canaanites were so passionately fond. The step to a syncretism bordering on idolatry was a short one, and the violent reactions of the prophets indicate that the step was all too nimbly taken (1 Kgs 12:32; 14:9; 19:18; 2 Kgs 10:29; 17:22; Hos 8:5–6; 10:5; 13:2). In spite of the fulminations of the prophets, the sanctuaries of Dan and Bethel, Beer-sheba (Am 5:5; 8:14), Gilgal (4:4; 5:5; Hos 4:15), and other unnamed places continued to flourish (Am 7:9; Ez 7:24). The excavations at Arad in the Negeb (→ Biblical Archaeology, 74:72) have uncovered a temple to Yahweh that was in use during the whole period of the monarchy; however, its altar of holocausts seems to have disappeared about King Hezekiah's time—perhaps a mark of the reform to be mentioned below. Nevertheless, Jerusalem kept its prestige, and even after it had been destroyed, groups of pilgrims came from all over the devastated country to worship there (Jer 41:5).

67 Before the fall of the city, there had been two notable attempts to make its Temple not only the central place for worship but the only legitimate sanctuary. *Hezekiah* took the first steps in this direction, *ca.* 715–705, by proscribing the "high places" (2 Kgs 18:4,22; Is 36:7). But his successor, Manasseh, undid his reform by reopening the suppressed shrines (2 Kgs 21:3). *Josiah* renewed the efforts made by Hezekiah on a more solemn and ambitious scale. The international situation was in his favor; for he was able to liberate his country from Assyrian domination, and the extirpation of foreign intrusions into the cult of Yahweh took on a patriotic allure. He again suppressed the local shrines and summoned all the priests of Judah to Jerusalem (23:5,8–9). The weakening of the Assyrian hegemony allowed him to move into what had once been the northern kingdom and put the shrine at Bethel out of operation. Finally, Josiah gathered all the people to a national celebration of the Passover at Jerusalem. This was in the year 621, the year of the finding of the "Book of the Law" in the Temple (probably the core of Dt; → Deuteronomy, 6:3).

This discovery was literally a godsend for Josiah, for one of the central preoccupations of the book was precisely unity of sanctuary (Dt 12). Since the deuteronomic redaction of the Law originated in the northern kingdom, originally it may have had in mind a northern shrine (Shechem?) as the one legitimate place of worship. According to one theory, refugee Levites brought the book to Jerusalem after the fall of Samaria in 721, and Hezekiah applied the principle of unity of sanctuary to the Temple. After Hezekiah's time, the "Book of the Law" fell into disuse during Manasseh's long and evil reign, only to be rediscovered under Josiah. An attractive alternative theory is the following: The law of unity of sanctuary may have been the result of, rather than the stimulus for, Hezekiah's reform. After all, in connection with Hezekiah's reform no appeal was made to an earlier law that would justify one sanctuary; but by the time of Josiah such a law was on the books. The phraseology of the law in reference to "the place chosen by Yahweh that his Name shall dwell there" is characteristic of the theology of the Jerusalem Temple and can only with difficulty be explained as a secondary application of a designation once applied to a northern sanctuary.

68 At any rate, after the death of Josiah in 609, the reform fell apart and things deteriorated until the Temple was finally destroyed in 587. After the return from the Exile, however, the deuteronomic ideal that Josiah had so zealously espoused became a reality. From 538 BC to AD 70, when the Romans destroyed the Temple once for all, it was the unique place of worship for all Judah. Outside of Judah we know of two Jewish temples in Egypt, one at Elephantine, the other at Leontopolis. Both were looked upon with open disfavor by orthodox Palestinian Jewry and can hardly be classed as authentic Israelite institutions (→ History of Israel, 75:99). Within Palestine itself there was the Samaritan temple on Mt. Gerizim, but this was even less an Israelite institution. The accounts of its establishment are conflicting and unreliable, yet it was certainly in existence before 167 BC, when Antiochus Epiphanes hellenized it. John Hyrcanus, of the Hasmonean line, destroyed it in 129 (→ History of Israel, 75:102, 114).

69 **(IV) Synagogues.** Synagogues do not figure in the OT literature, and there is a great diversity of opinion as to just when they came into existence. As the Gk root of their name indicates (*syn* = "together"; *agein* = "to lead, bring"), they were meeting houses—places where people gathered not for sacrifice but for prayer, devout reading, meditation, and instruction. They certainly existed in the post-exilic period and the most popular hypothesis is that they arose as an institution during the Exile when the people were cut off from the Temple. However, there is no substantial evidence for this theory; other scholars, with no stronger evidence in their favor, feel that they sprang up in Palestine itself after the Exile. Some few opine that they originated before the Exile as a result of Josiah's suppression of the local shrines. Yet, we are inescapably certain of the emergence and gradual spread of the synagogue, even if its origin remains obscure.

ALTARS AND SACRIFICES

70 Altar and sacrifice are correlative terms; the mention of the one immediately suggests the other. Indeed, the Hebr word for altar, *mizbēaḥ*, includes in its connotation the very notion of sacrifice, for it is derived from a verb meaning "to slaughter." Apparently, victims were originally slaughtered on the altar, although in a later period the altar was used only for the act of offering itself. Consequently, *mizbēaḥ* assumed the general meaning of a place where sacrifice was offered, whether the victim was an (already slaughtered) animal, cereals, or incense.

71 **(I) Construction of Altars.** In the early days a natural outcropping of rock or a large stone served the purpose of an altar. In Jgs 6:19–23, Gideon was ordered to place his offerings on a rock (see also 13:19–20). When the Ark was sent back to Israel by the Philistines, the cows along with the cart they drew were burnt in sacrifice on a large stone (1 Sm 6:14). This was a continuation of the practice followed by the patriarchs.

Artificially constructed altars were rather consistently made of stone, although actually the Law authorized two materials for altars: earth (i.e., baked earth, brick) and undressed stone (Ex 20:24–26; Dt 27:5; Jos 8:30–31). The insistence on *uncut* stone is not easy to explain; very probably it reflects the conviction that something as acred as an altar should be constructed of materials in heir natural state, as they had come from the hand of God Ex 20:25). Contact with anything profane would be a desecration. Abhorrence of the profane may also be the basis of the law forbidding steps in connection with the altar (20:26). Modesty is sometimes alleged as justification for this prohibition: In the days when the only vestment worn by a priest was a type of loincloth, he ran the risk of indecent exposure in ascending a flight of steps. However, here again, the original idea was probably that artificially constructed steps trodden upon by the priests would profane the altar.

72 **(II) Types of Altars.**

(A) Altar of Holocausts. We have a detailed but not overly clear description of the two altars in the desert Tabernacle, namely, the altar of holocausts that stood directly in front of the entrance to the Tent, and the altar of incense that stood inside, just in front of the Holy of Holies. According to Ex 27:1–8; 38:1–7 the altar of holocausts was made of a framework of bronze-plated acacia wood (boards), 7.5 ft. × 7.5 ft. × 4.5 ft. On the top of this boxlike affair was a bronze grille. A cornice ran around all four sides and there were four rings at the corners through which poles were passed when it was to be transported. This description gives rise to some questions. How were the victims consumed by fire on this hollow chest? Was the fire lighted at ground level, 4.5 ft. beneath the grille; and if so, how did the enclosure withstand the intense heat? It has been suggested that each time the huge box was set up, it was filled with earth and stones; the fire would then have been lighted on top of the stones. In this case the grate must have been removable, but there is no evidence for this in the text. Nor does the description mention steps by which the priest would have approached the upper surface; and, given the height of the altar, steps would have been necessary.

73 **(B) Altar of Incense.** According to Ex 30:1–5; 37:25–28, the altar of incense was made of acacia wood, the upper surface of which was gold-plated. It was 1.5 ft. square and 3 ft. high. At each corner was a hornlike projection and beneath each of these was a ring to facilitate its transportation. Actually, it is very questionable that any such altar existed during the wandering in the desert. There is no mention of it in Ex 25 or 26:33–37 where the furnishings of the Tent are itemized in some detail. The passages that do describe it have all the marks of later additions inspired, like the description of the Tent itself, by the P (priestly) author's desire to make the desert sanctuary a prototype of the Temple with which his readers were familiar.

74 **(C) Altars in the Temple.** Solomon's Temple had the same two altars, situated precisely where they are pictured as having been situated in the Tent. Given the central importance of the *altar of holocausts*, it is strange indeed that it is not mentioned in the detailed inaugural description of the Temple (1 Kgs 6–7; there are references to it in 8:22,54,64; 9:25). Many explanations have been offered regarding the omission, e.g., perhaps the editor of these chapters was embarrassed because the altar did not fulfill the specifications of Ex 20:24–26. Solomon's altar seems to have consisted of a large movable bronze grille (1 Kgs 8:64; 2 Kgs 16:14–15). Ahaz later replaced this altar by one patterned after an altar that he had seen at Damascus (2 Kgs 16:10–16; → History of Israel, 75:80). In the temple to Yahweh at Arad (→ Biblical Archaeology, 74:72) an altar of holocausts stood in the court outside the temple. References to the *altar of incense* are so confusing that some scholars have refused to admit its existence in Solomon's Temple. Yet, although these references may be obscure, they are sufficient to establish that there really was such an altar. A suggested reconstruction of 1 Kgs 6:20–21 gives the following reading: "He made an altar of cedar...in front of the Debir (Holy of Holies) and covered it with gold." There is mention of the "altar of gold" in 1 Kgs 7:48; and in Isaiah's inaugural vision (Is 6:6) we are told that a Seraph took a live coal from an altar in the Temple—this can be none other than the altar of incense (see also 2 Chr 26:16).

As far as one can judge from the scanty information about the post-exilic Temple, it, too, had two altars. This information comes from two extrabiblical works of the Greek period, *Pseudo-Hecateus* and (the *Letter of*) *Aristeas* (→ Apocrypha, 68:32), both written in Alexandria after 200 BC. As works of Jewish propaganda, they are not completely reliable. But they attest to the existence both of an altar of holocausts (built of undressed stone in conformity with the prescription of Ex 20:25) and of a gold-plated altar of incense. Some information, however, comes from 1 Mc, which records Antiochus Epiphanes' removal of the altar of incense (1:21) and his desecration of the altar of holocausts (1:54,59; 2 Mc 6:2,5). After the Maccabean victories, a new altar was built, and the stones of the old one were removed and stored in one of the auxiliary buildings of the Temple (1 Mc 4:44–47; 2 Mc 10:3). A new altar of incense replaced the stolen one (1 Mc 4:49).

75 **(III) Symbolism of the Altar.** Like the Temple, the altar had deep theological significance for the Israelites. Just as the Temple was God's house, so the altar was his hearth. This idea is implicit in the law requiring that a fire be always kept burning on the altar (Lv 6:5–6). The altar was considered also as a symbol of the divine presence, and in the patriarchal period the site of a theophany was marked by an altar (Gn 12:7; 26:24–25). Sometimes the altar was given a divine name, e.g., the one that Jacob put up at Shechem was called "El, God of Israel," and the one that Moses erected after his victory over the Amalekites was called "Yahweh is my battle-standard." In later times the altar was solemnly consecrated before being used and then purified annually on the Day of Atonement (Ex 29:36–37; Lv 8:15; 16:18–19; → 156 below).

76 The four "horns" of the altar were considered especially sacred. These were the projections at the four corners of the upper surface. When the altar was consecrated and as part of the ritual of expiation, the blood of the sacrificial victims was rubbed on them (Ex 29:12; 30:10; Lv 4; 8:15; 9:9; 16:18; Ez 43:20). A person seeking asylum rushed to take hold of them (1 Kgs 2:28). The precise signification of these horns is uncertain. It has been suggested that we have here an application of the general biblical symbolism of "horn" as a figure for power; or that the horns symbolize those of the sacrificial victims; or again that they are vestiges of the *masseboth* or steles which in ancient religions were common symbols of the divinity (→ Biblical Archaeology, 74:35). It may even be that just as the extremities of a priest's body were considered in some way of special importance (Ex 29:20), so, too, were the extremities of the altar.

77 **(IV) Sacrifices.** The central act of Israelite worship, sacrifice, was always essentially the same, even though it took various forms. The study of these is not easy, for often there is a disconcerting lack of precision in their designations, and later practices are interpolated into descriptions of earlier ones, making it difficult to trace clearly a historical development. The terminus of that development is clearly sketched, however, in Lv 1–7, which describes the various sacrifices as they were carried out in the post-exilic Temple.

78 **(A) The Holocaust.** The most solemn of the Israelite sacrifices was the holocaust, in which the victim was completely burned. This is the meaning of the name itself, which is derived from the LXX translation (*holokauston*) of the Hebr *'ōlâ*. The verbal root of this term means "to go up"; the holocaust, then, in the original terminology was a sacrifice whose smoke "went up" to God. It was called also *kālîl*, "complete" sacrifice (1 Sm 7:9; Dt 33:10; Ps 51:21).

According to the prescriptions of Lv, the victim of a holocaust had to be an unblemished male animal or bird (turtle dove or pigeon). The one making the offering laid his hand on the victim's head to signify that the sacrifice was to be offered in his name and for his benefit. The gesture did not signify that the victim was a substitute for the offerer or that the sins of the offerer were transferred to it for expiation. The offerer then slit the throat of the victim, and the priest poured its blood around the altar—blood, considered the seat of life, belonged to God in a special way. After the animal had been skinned and quartered, the pieces were washed and placed on the altar to be consumed in the flames. If the victim was a bird, the one making the offering simply handed it over to the priest, who performed the ritual directly on the altar. Such offerings were usually made by the poor, who could not afford to offer animals (Lv 5:7; 12:8).

In the latest development of the holocaust ritual, the law called for an accompanying gift (*minḥâ*) of flour mixed with oil and a libation of wine. The flour was burnt and the wine poured out at the base of the altar. According to Lv 23:18, this requirement had to be satisfied only during the Feast of Weeks; Ex 29:38–42 extends it to the daily holocaust, and Nm 15 further extends it to all holocausts.

The holocaust had a long and continuous history in Israel. Gideon's sacrifice (Jgs 6:26,28) was an *'ōlâ*, as was that of Samson's father (Jgs 13:15–20). When the Ark returned safely from the land of the Philistines, a holocaust was offered (1 Sm 6:14). Samuel (7:9; 10:8), Saul (13:9ff.), David (2 Sm 6:17ff.), Solomon (1 Kgs 3:4; 9:25), and Elijah (18:38) all offered holocausts. The historical books offer no description of the ritual followed in the sacrifices; but the characteristic feature of the holocaust is a constant, namely, that the victim was completely burned. One point of difference between early custom and later ritual seems to have been that in ancient times the victim was slaughtered as well as burned on the altar (Gn 22:9–10; 1 Sm 14:33–34).

79 **(B) The Communion Sacrifice.** The "communion sacrifice" (*zebaḥ šᵉlāmîm, zebaḥ* alone, or *šᵉlāmîm* alone) was a thanksgiving offering effecting a union between God and the one making the offering. This sacrifice has frequently been called, under the influence of the LXX, a "peace offering" or "welcome offering," but "communion sacrifice" best describes its essential nature. There were three types of communion sacrifice: the *tôdâ* or sacrifice of praise (Lv 7:12–15; 22:29–30); the *nᵉdābâ* or freewill sacrifice, made out of pure devotion and not in fulfillment of a precept or a vow (7:16–17; 22:18–23); and the *neder* or votive offering, made in fulfillment of a vow (7:16–17; 22:18–23).

The ritual of the communion sacrifice is described in Lv 3, and its characteristic feature lies in the fact that the victim is shared, with portions going to God, to the priest, and to the offerer. The laws about the victims are slightly different from those governing the victims for holocausts: Birds are not allowed; the animal may be male or female; and, according to Lv 22:23, it may be slightly blemished when the offering is of the freewill type. The imposition of hands, the slaughtering, and the pouring out of blood take place just as in the holocaust.

Yahweh's portion was burned on the altar; it consisted of the fat surrounding the intestines, the kidneys, the liver, and the fat of the sheep's tail. (Fat, like blood, was looked upon as life-giving [Lv 3:16–17; 7:22–24].) The priest received two parts: the breast and the right leg (7:28–34; 10:14–15). The remaining portion went to the one making the offering, who shared it with his family and guests. The victim of a *tôdâ* had to be eaten the same day it was offered (7:15), and this sacrifice had to include also an offering of unleavened cakes and wafers and of leavened loaves. One of the cakes was offered to Yahweh and constituted part of the priest's share. The victim of a freewill or votive sacrifice could be eaten on the morrow of the offering, but if any of it was left on the third day it had to be burned (7:16–17).

80 This type of sacrifice was common in Israel from the earliest days, and the early texts mention it frequently. Often it is called simply *zebaḥ* (Jos 22:26ff.; 1 Sm 1:21; 2:13,19; 3:14; 2 Sm 15:12; 1 Kgs 8:22; 12:27; 2 Kgs 5:17; 10:24; Is 1:11; 19:21; Jer 7:22; Hos 3:4; 4:19; Am 4:4; Ex 23:18; 34:15,25). Frequently, it is designated as *šᵉlāmîm* (Jgs 20:26; 21:4; 1 Sm 13:9; 2 Sm 6:17,18; 24:25; 1 Kgs 3:15; 9:25; 2 Kgs 16:13; Ex 20:24; 32:6; Ez 43:27; 45:15,17; 46:12). The full expression *zebaḥ šᵉlāmîm* occurs constantly and almost exclusively in the P writings. The plural, *zᵉbāḥîm šᵉlāmîm* is found in Ex 24:5 and 1 Sm 11:15, with the two words in apposition or possibly with one as an explanatory gloss. All the evidence points to the antiquity of both terms and also to the fact that they were used interchangeably to indicate the same type of sacrifice. *Zebaḥ*, slaughtering or immolation, refers to the external rite; *šᵉlāmîm* refers to the purpose or intention of the sacrifice. There is some difference of opinion on the precise meaning of *šᵉlāmîm*, but it seems to connote a tribute offered to God with a view to maintaining or reestablishing amicable relations with him—the word is related to *šālôm*, "peace."

81 As in the case of the holocaust, we have very little information about the ritual followed in the ancient communion sacrifice. That the ritual varied until it was fixed after the Exile seems to be indicated in several texts. If the corrected reading of 1 Sm 9:24 actually represents the original, the lay participants ate the fat of a sheep's tail; yet the law of Lv 3:9; 7:3 reserves this for God. At Shiloh the priest had to take pot luck: He stuck a fork into the pot while the meat was boiling and was entitled to whatever he drew forth (1 Sm 2:13–14); yet according to Dt 18:3, he was entitled to the shoulder, jaws, and stomach (Lv 7:34 improved his lot and gave him the uncooked breast and the right leg).

82 How far back can we trace holocausts and communion sacrifices in the history of Israel? Specifically, do they date from the period of the Exodus, as the Pentateuchal laws would lead one to believe? For a direct answer, one might turn to Am 5:25, where Yahweh asks: "Did you bring me sacrifices and offerings for forty years in the desert, O house of Israel?" In Jer 7:22, Yahweh speaks in a similar strain: "In speaking to your fathers on the day I brought them out of the land of Egypt, I gave them no command concerning holocaust or sacrifice." Still, both Amos and Jeremiah were familiar with the most ancient traditions, J and E, concerning sacrifices offered during the Exodus (Ex 3:18; 5:3,8,17; 10:25; 18:12; 32:6,8). And when read in their respective contexts, the two passages from the Prophets are not really so categorical as they seem when taken in isolation. Amos and Jeremiah were preachers, not legalists or historical critics. They were objecting to the empty, formalistic sacrifices offered in their day and were holding up the desert days as the ideal—days when sacrifices were offered with the proper interior dispositions. We must allow for a certain prophetic license in their unqualified statements.

But how about the existing evidence as evaluated by modern literary criticism? The passages stemming from the P tradition are admittedly late; J and E take us back to the period of settlement in Canaan, and D only to the end of the royal period (→ Pentateuch, 1:13–17). On this view, we have little or no reliable information about the sacrifices in the period of the Exodus itself. A priori, we are justified in assuming that in common with other ancient Near Eastern seminomads the Israelites of the desert wanderings offered animal sacrifices. However, we must confess that it is impossible, in the light of the data at our disposal, to speak with any certainty of the ritual followed by them.

83 **(C) Sacrifices of Expiation.** Sacrifices of expiation receive a major share of the attention given to sacrifices in the ritual code of the post-exilic Temple. There are two such sacrifices: the sin-offering (*ḥaṭṭā't*) and the sacrifice of reparation (*'āšām*).

(a) THE SIN OFFERING. The Hebr word *ḥaṭṭā't* signifies both sin and sin offering (Lv 4:1–5:13; 6:17–23). The dignity of the one making the offering determined the victim to be sacrificed. The high priest was required to offer a bull; similarly, a bull had to be sacrificed when there was question of a collective sin of the whole people. The sin of a prince (*nāśī'*) could be expiated only by the sacrifice of a he-goat, while a private person could offer a she-goat or a sheep. If one was very poor, two turtledoves or pigeons sufficed; one of them was offered as a sacrifice for sin, the other as a holocaust. As an alternative, the poor could offer some flour.

84 The distinguishing characteristics of these sacrifices were the use made of the blood and the disposal of the victim's flesh. When expiation was being made for the high priest or for the people as a whole, the sacrificing priest first gathered the blood, went into the sanctuary, and sprinkled the blood seven times on the veil before the Holy of Holies; then he rubbed some blood on the horns of the altar of incense, and finally poured out what remained at the base of the altar of holocausts. If a prince or private individual was making atonement, the priest did not enter the sanctuary, but rubbed blood on the horns of the altar of holocausts and poured out the rest at its base. The importance played by the blood of the victim in these sacrifices is obvious (see Lv 17:11; Heb 9:22).

Just as in communion sacrifices, all the fat of the victim was burned; but in the sacrifice for sin, the guilty person received no share of the flesh, for the priest took it all. Furthermore, when this sacrifice was offered for the high priest or the community, no one shared in the flesh of the victim; it was taken away and thrown on the refuse heap. A popular theory is that the sin of the guilty party was thought to be transferred to the victim and destroyed along with it. However, the fat of the victim was burned rather as a pleasing sacrifice to God; and in the instances of private sacrifices just mentioned, the priests partook of the flesh of the victims "since it is most sacred" (Lv 6:22; see 2 Cor 5:21).

85 The prescriptions given by Nm 15:22–29 for the sin offering differ noticeably from those of Lv 1–7. No provision is made in Nm for the sin of a high priest or prince. Inadvertent faults committed by the community as a whole may be expiated by the sacrifice of a bull as a holocaust and of a he-goat as a sin offering; such faults committed by an individual may be wiped out by the sacrifice of a he-goat as a sin offering. The ritual is not described. Moreover, according to Nm 15:31, no sacrifice can satisfy for a deliberate sin.

86 (b) The Sacrifice of Reparation. Like *ḥaṭṭā't*, the term *'āšām* has several related meanings: offense, the means of repairing the offense, and a sacrifice of reparation. This sacrifice, sometimes called a guilt offering, is treated in relatively summary fashion (Lv 5:14–26; 7:1–7). Although the ritual is much the same as that of a sacrifice for sin, the sacrifice of reparation was offered only for private individuals and the only victim mentioned is a ram. In some instances, in addition to the offering of the sacrifices, a fine had to be paid (Lv 5:14–16, 21–26; Nm 5:5–8), but this fine was quite distinct from the sacrifice itself.

87 Obviously, the distinction between the *ḥaṭṭā't* and the *'āšām* is not clear, and several attempts at clarification have been made both in antiquity and in modern times. The *ḥaṭṭā't* might seem to apply to sins in general and the *'āšām* to the more restricted field of sins against justice, sins that required some sort of restitution or redressing of injured rights. But the pertinent texts rule out any such oversimplification. In Lv 5:6,7 the terms are used synonymously. According to 4:2 the *ḥaṭṭā't* is called for when a person sins inadvertently against a divine commandment, while according to 5:17 an *'āšām* is to be offered in apparently the same circumstances (also cf. 5:1,4 and 5:22,24). On the other hand, when a leper is to be purified he must offer an *'āšām*, a *ḥaṭṭā't*, and a holocaust (14:10–32)—if the ritual for the *'āšām* is the same as that for the *ḥaṭṭā't*, what is the point of offering both on the one occasion? The distinction is no clearer if we consider the type of sin involved. Both sacrifices are offered for inadvertent faults (Lv 4:13,22,27; 5:15,17; Nm 15:22–31), and both are offered for certain clearly deliberate faults (Lv 5:1,21–22).

Although it may be impossible to clarify this confusion, it is possible to explain how it arose. The final editors of the legislation as we now have it were, in all likelihood, as uncertain as we are. It may well be that they tried to make distinctions between two originally synonymous terms, or that they confused those terms because they were not sure of their exact meaning. This leads to a historical conclusion of some interest, and that is that expiatory sacrifices existed in legislation that was old enough to be misunderstood by its post-exilic redactors.

88 It has been the fashion for certain critics to attribute the invention of the *ḥaṭṭā't* and the *'āšām* to Ezekiel, who mentions them often (40:39; 42:13; 44:29; 45:19–20,23; 46:20). But why should new sacrifices be invented during the Exile, when sacrifice had ceased altogether? Significantly, Ezekiel speaks of the *ḥaṭṭā't* and *'āšām* as if they were already well known, offering no explanation of them. Moreover, it is probable that the Holiness Code (Lv 17–26; → Leviticus, 4:3,35) is older than the Book of Ezekiel, and Lv 19:20–22 thus indicates that the *'āšām* was known at least toward the end of the royal period. Precisely how much earlier expiatory sacrifices were offered is impossible to say, and admittedly they were offered less frequently than holocausts or communion sacrifices.

89 **(D) The minḥâ.** The victim in the sacrifices so far discussed was an animal, but the Israelites also commonly offered various cereals. This type of offering was known by the generic name *minḥâ* (gift), and several kinds are listed in Lv 2. There was one of fine wheaten flour mixed with oil; the ritual called for an offering of incense as part of this sacrifice. A handful of the prepared flour and all the incense were burned on the altar, and the priests got the remaining flour (2:1–2; 6:7–11; 7:10). In another of these sacrifices the same mixture of flour and oil was first baked. A part of the loaf was burned, and the rest of it went to the priests (2:4–10; 7:9). No leaven was used, but salt was required (2:11–13). Lastly, there was the offering of first fruits in the form of roasted ears of grain or baked bread, together with oil and incense. Part of the grain and oil and all the incense were burned (2:14–16).

90 The part of the *minḥâ* that was burned was called *'azkārâ*, the precise meaning of which in this context is not certain. It could mean "memorial" (from the verb *zākar*, to remember), in the sense that the offering reminded God of the one who made it. Or it could mean "pledge," in the sense that the part actually offered to God was a token of the donor's willingness to offer his all.

In some cases the cereal alone was offered without oil or incense, as in the high priest's daily offering; and in this instance the entire offering was burned (Lv 6:13–16). Again, when a *minḥâ* was offered by a poor person as a sacrifice for sin (5:11–13), and when it was offered as a "sacrifice for jealousy" (Nm 5:15), it consisted of only flour. When the *minḥâ* accompanied a holocaust or communion sacrifice, a libation of wine was added to the ritual (Ex 29:40; Lv 23:13; Nm 15:1–12).

Cereal offerings can be traced to the period before the Exile. It has been contended that the word *minḥâ* in pre-exilic texts is used in its generic sense of "gift" or "offering" to apply to any type of sacrifice. This is not quite true; *minḥâ* is distinguished from *zebaḥ* in 1 Sm 2:29; 3:14; Is 19:21; from *'ōlâ* in Jer 14:12; Ps 20:4; and from *šelem* in Am 5:22. In these texts it is a technical term for the cereal offering. The showbread, analogous to the *minḥâ*, is mentioned in 1 Sm 21:3–7.

91 **(E) The Showbread.** Related to the cereal offerings was the showbread, which is called in Hebrew *leḥem happānîm*, "the bread of the face" (of God) or "the bread of the Presence," and *leḥem hamma'areket*, "the showbread." This consisted of twelve cakes of fine wheaten flour arranged in two rows on a table before the Holy of Holies; fresh cakes were put on the table every Sabbath (Lv 24:5–9). The priests consumed the old cakes at the time of the renewal, and the incense that had been placed alongside each row was burned on the altar of incense. The twelve loaves were a perpetual reminder or pledge of the covenant between Yahweh and the twelve tribes (→ Aspects OT Thought, 77:76ff.). The presence of the incense on the table with the loaves gave them something of the character of a sacrifice, even though it was only the incense that was burned on the altar.

92 **(F) Perfume Offerings.** Incense played a large part in the sacrificial ritual of Israel. The word *q^{e}ṭōret* has the generic meaning of "that which goes up in smoke" and in this wide sense may be applied to anything burned on an altar. In the context of the liturgy, it refers to perfumed offerings, the full expression for which is *q^{e}ṭōret sammîm*. The specific word for incense is *l^{e}bōnâ*, but incense was only one of several aromatics of which the perfumed mixture was compounded. The others were storax, onyx, and galbanum, which were to be mixed with incense in four equal parts (Ex 30:34–38). The recipes grew more complicated as time went on, and the rabbinical writings mention one containing sixteen ingredients.

The manner of offering was as follows. A priest scooped live coals from the altar of holocausts with a small shovel and sprinkled the aromatic mixture on the coals. He then placed the contents of the shovel on the altar of incense. This offering was made every morning and evening (Ex 30:7–8). On the Day of Atonement (→ 155 below) the coals and incense were carried within the Holy of Holies to be burned there before the Ark (Lv 16:12–13). Pure unmixed incense (*l^{e}bōnâ*) was used when it accompanied a *minḥâ* or was placed on the table of the showbread.

93 In tracing the history of perfume offerings, we find that the word *q^{e}ṭōret*, which acquired a restrictive technical meaning after the Exile, was used only in its generic sense of "that which goes up in smoke" in pre-exilic texts (1 Sm 2:28; Is 1:13; see 2 Kgs 16:13,15). Yet, although the terminology did not exist before the Exile, the custom of offering incense certainly did. The "incense that comes from Sheba" is used in parallelism with "your holocausts" in Jer 6:20 (see 17:26). Solomon's Temple had an altar of incense (→ 74 above), and the deuteronomic editor of 1 Kgs 3:3 condemned the offering of incense elsewhere than at the Temple. Incense was used quite commonly in the liturgies of other ancient Near Eastern nations; it would be rather surprising if the custom did not exist in Israel (see M. Haran, *VT* 10 [1960] 113–29).

In the early days censers may have been used for burning incense instead of the stationary altar, as in the story of Nadab and Abihu (Lv 10:1ff.) and in that of Korah in Nm 16:1ff. The first certain mention of an altar of incense is in the description of Solomon's Temple. In the early stages of the ritual, pure unmixed incense was used. It formed part of the *minḥâ* (Lv 2:1ff.), first fruits (2:15), and the showbread, all of which were pre-exilic. After the Exile, with the further development of the ritual, the complicated four-part mixture alluded to above came into use.

94 **(V) The Origin of Israelite Sacrifice.** All the post-exilic sacrifices of Israelite religion, then, had pre-exilic antecedents. Some were more ancient than others, and at times one predominated over another, with a subsequent shift in emphasis as the ritual developed. It would be surprising if such development had not taken place over such a long span. The fact that we are best informed about the latest stage should not blind us to the fact that the process of development began centuries before. This brings us to the question of the origin of Israelite ritual.

Without going into an extended discussion of the sacrificial system of *Mesopotamia*, we can say that the evidence at our disposal does not warrant looking to that area for the source of Israel's rites. Contacts with Mesopotamian ritual are rare and superficial; the differences are fundamental. Blood played little or no part in the Mesopotamian sacrifices, and the two basic forms of Israelite sacrifice, the holocaust and communion sacrifice, were not in use in Mesopotamia.

The sacrificial system of *Arabia* was closer to that of Israel, to judge from the meager information at our disposal. Blood was used for libations and domestic animals were slaughtered and eaten; perfume offerings were common in Southern Arabia. However, the absence of similarities in essentials prevents our concluding that Israel borrowed from Arabia. The burning of the victim, in whole or in part, was of the essence of the Israelite sacrifice. In Arabia the animal was simply slaughtered and eaten. The few similarities between the two systems can be explained by the distant common origin of the two peoples, by the pastoral life that Israel and Arabia once shared, and by cultural and commercial contacts.

95 It is a different story when we consider *Canaan*. The biblical information about Canaanite ritual shows it similar to Israelite ritual, at least materially. The Canaanite wives of Solomon offered incense and sacrifices to their gods (1 Kgs 11:8). According to 2 Kgs 5:17, Naaman the Syrian offered holocausts and communion sacrifices; and when Elijah had his contest with the prophets of Baal, both he and they prepared their sacrifices in the same fashion (1 Kgs 18). Other passages confirm this evidence; and the biblical condemnation of Canaanite worship is not because of the form that such worship took, but because it was offered to idols or performed in proscribed sanctuaries. The terminology of Canaanite ritual, as it is known from Punic and Phoenician inscriptions, was not altogether consistent, but it contains some interesting points of contact with Israelite terminology. The much earlier Ugaritic texts of the 14th cent. BC from Ras Shamra (→ Excursus Israel, 11:11) furnish little reliable information beyond a few ritual terms corresponding to those used by Israel. When all the available evidence is assembled, however, there is a definite similarity between Canaanite and Israelite ritual. There were holocausts, communion sacrifices, cereal and perfume offerings in Canaanite ritual, but no particular importance seems to have been attached to blood in the animal sacrifices.

Given the similarities between these two systems, what historical relationship existed between them? Sacrifices in which victims were wholly or partially burned on the altar were common in Canaan before the coming of the Israelites. However, the Israelites do not seem to have offered such sacrifices in the desert days. Rather, something similar to the Passover ritual would have been normal during that pastoral, seminomadic period: The victim was not burned, even in part; but its blood had ritual significance, and the flesh was shared by the participants. (This was precisely the type of sacrifice practiced by nomads in ancient Arabia.) Then when the Israelites came into Canaan, they took over the Canaanite practice of burnt offerings and integrated it gradually into their own system. From that point on the two rituals, Canaanite and Israelite, followed their own independent lines of development. There is nothing certain about this reconstruction, but it does justice to the data available at the present time.

96 **(VI) Human Sacrifice.** Was human sacrifice ever part of Israelite religion? Some have answered this question in the affirmative and conclude that the animal of later sacrificial custom was considered a victim in substitution for the donor who should have been the victim. An important preliminary consideration in this discussion is the fact that Israel was a latecomer among the nations of the ancient Middle East. If the Israelites did practice human sacrifice, they presumably would have borrowed it from some already existing ritual system. Now it is a fact that such sacrifices were known in antiquity, but so long before the entrance of Israel into history that we have very little information about them. Indeed, they seem to have been the exception rather than the rule, and the evidence at our disposal does not allow us to be sure even that they were sacrifices in the strict sense of the term. The only clear information on the subject comes from Phoenician sources (note that Israel was in close contact with Phoenicia). The Canaanites evidently had a custom of slaying infants and burying them as "foundation sacrifices" when they were about to put up a new building, although this practice was certainly not so widespread as some archaeologists would have us believe.

97 The biblical texts alleged for the thesis that human sacrifices were countenanced in Israel are far from conclusive. According to 1 Kgs 16:34, when Hiel rebuilt Jericho, "at the price of his first-born, he set up its gates." This text is susceptible to other interpretations; but even if it does refer to foundation sacrifices, it is not by any means narrated with approval, but rather with horror. Furthermore, during the reign of Ahab, when this incident took place, Phoenician influence was strong in Israel, and this might have been an instance of such foreign influence rather than of Israelite custom. The wholesale slaughter of vanquished enemies during the days of the Conquest was in no sense a sacrifice (→ History of Israel, 75:42). When Saul's descendants were delivered to the Gibeonites and massacred by them, the Israelites viewed the procedure as the settlement of a blood feud. The Gibeonites may have made a ritual of it, but that throws no light on Israelite custom (2 Sm 21:1–14). The story of Jephthah's sacrifice of his daughter (Jgs 11:30–40) is narrated as something extraordinary and horrifying, as is the story of the king of Moab's sacrifice of his only son to avert defeat at the hands of the Israelites (2 Kgs 3:27). God's command to Abraham that he sacrifice Isaac (Gn 22:1–19) is not pertinent to this discussion, for the sacrifice is not the central point of the story, which is rather the faith of Abraham. It was precisely because the patriarch obeyed such an extraordinary divine command that his faith was so outstanding.

The prophetic literature offers no support for the thesis that human sacrifice was a part of Israelite ritual. It is not certain that the idolatrous sacrifice condemned by Hos 13:2 was human sacrifice. There is irony in the question people ask in Mi 6:1–8: "Will the Lord be pleased with thousands of rams, with myriad streams of oil? Shall I give my first-born for my crime, the fruit of my body for the sin of my soul?" They are putting the sacrifice of their children on the same plane of absurdity as the sacrifice of thousands of rams and myriad streams of oil. The passage in Is 66:3, which is uncertain, actually contrasts human sacrifice with the regular sacrifice of a bullock. There is an apparently clear reference to human sacrifice in Ex 20:25–26; but to evaluate it, we must first review the legislation about the first-born.

98 The basic law is stated bluntly in Ex 22:28–29: "You shall give me the first-born of your sons; you must do likewise with your oxen and your sheep. For seven days the first-born may stay with its mother, but on the eighth day you must give it to me." Other texts, like 13:11–15 and 34:19–20, make a distinction: first-born sons are to be redeemed and the first-born of animals are to be offered in sacrifice. Some critics claim that this distinction between men and animals is a later mitigation of an earlier law that unfeelingly demanded the sacrifice of first-born sons. Actually, the two texts that make the distinction are virtually contemporary with Ex 22:28–29. And the admittedly late legislation in 13:1–2, which according to the theory should reflect mitigation, is just as unqualified as 22:28–29: "Consecrate to me every first-born that opens the womb among the Israelites, both of man and beast, for it belongs to me." Thus, even in the apparently unqualified texts, the distinction between man and animals is certainly implicit.

99 There remains the statement of Ez 20:25–26: "Therefore I gave them statutes that were not good, and ordinances through which they could not have life. I let them become defiled by their gifts, by their immolation of every first-born, so as to make them an object of horror." As is clear from the sequel, we are dealing here with God's permissive will: Because the Israelites broke faith with him, he allowed them to sink into the morass of pagan abominations. We see God's attitude clearly in Ez 20:31: "By offering your gifts, by making your children pass through the fire, you defile yourselves with all your idols even to this day." And the words of the Lord in Jer 7:31 are unequivocal: "In the Valley of the son of Hinnom they have built the high place of Topheth to immolate in fire their sons and their daughters, such a thing as I never commanded or had in mind."

100 The mention of the Valley of Hinnom (Gehenna; → Biblical Geography, 73:92) leads to a discussion of several texts dealing with the sacrifice of children to Molech (Lv 18:21; 20:2–5; 2 Kgs 23:10; Jer 32:35—Molech is identified as an Ammonite god in 1 Kgs 11:7). According to the passages in 2 Kgs and Jer, the sacrifice took place by burning in the Valley of Hinnom near Jerusalem. This same type of sacrifice is mentioned in several other places without the mention of Molech (*mōlek* in Hebrew—2 Kgs 16:3; 17:31; 21:6; Jer 7:31; 19:5; Dt 12:31; Ez 23:39). The texts from Lv are from the Holiness Code which comes from sacerdotal circles toward the end of the royal period (→ Leviticus, 4:3,35). The priests would quite understandably be upset about an abomination of such magnitude being practiced in proximity to the Temple. The texts from the historical books indicate that these sacrifices were offered only during periods of religious decline, as under Ahaz (2 Kgs 16:3; see 17:31). Indeed, all the pertinent texts plainly denounce them as recent intrusions of paganism.

The barbaric custom is to be traced to Canaanite rituals. There is reliable evidence, historical, epigraphical, and archaeological, that it was a Phoenician practice to sacrifice children in order to avert different types of disasters. The sacrifice was called by the technical name of *molk* (offering). When it made its way into Israel during periods of religious decline, the technical meaning of the term was twisted, perhaps because of its similarity to the Hebr word for king (*melek*, a not uncommon epithet for a god). No sound evidence can be advanced to prove that any type of human sacrifice was ever a part of the Israelite ritual; on the contrary, all the available data point clearly to the fact that it was not.

101 **(VII) The Meaning of Sacrifice in Israel.** Holocausts, communion sacrifices, sin offerings, sacrifices of reparation, cereal offerings, incense offerings—what did all these signify? What was the essential meaning of sacrifice in Israel? Several answers have been given to these questions, some of which must be rejected, either because they are based on a priori premises and do not take the evidence into consideration or because they misinterpret the evidence.

(A) Unsatisfactory Theories. One hypothesis is that which looks upon Israelite sacrifice as a gift of appeasement to a cruel and demanding deity. There is no evidence in the text to support such a position. A more subtle suggestion is that sacrifice in Israel was a sort of bilateral contract between man and God. Man gives a gift to God, and God reciprocates by granting man some boon. This is a more subtle approach because there is an element of truth in it (→ 105 below). In offering sacrifice the Israelite did hope to obtain God's blessing. But implicit in the *quid pro quo* explanation is the suggestion that God was as much in need of man's gift as man was of the divine favor, a notion that was entertained in some ancient religions. Such an idea was completely foreign to Israelite thought, according to which God was supreme master of the universe with sovereign title to everything in it. He has absolutely no need for anything that man could possibly give him.

102 Another theory of the nature of Israelite sacrifice pictures it as a quasi-magic act by which man enters into union with God. This hypothesis takes two forms. In the first form of the theory, man achieves this union by eating a divine victim. Underlying such a theory is the assumption that Israelite sacrifice was basically totemistic, a view supposedly inherited by the Israelites from remote ancestors in Arabia. In that ancient culture, as reconstructed by the critics, members of a tribe were interrelated through kinship with the tribal god, who was considered incarnate, as it were, in the animal chosen to represent him. By eating this animal (the totem) the individual absorbed a share in the life of the deity. However, there is no evidence of any such notion prevailing among the ancient Arabs. Even where totemism was the fashion, only rarely was the sacred animal eaten. When it was eaten, it served as ordinary food and did not effect any divine communication.

In the second form of the theory, the Israelite was supposed to have entered into union with God by immolating a victim that substituted for and represented himself. The imposition of hands, a part of Israelite ritual, is interpreted by this theory as a gesture transferring to the victim the sins and the vital principle of the offerer, which were released when the animal's throat was slit and its blood spilled. The pouring of the victim's blood at the base of the altar is interpreted symbolically as bringing the life of the sacrificer in contact with the deity whom the altar represented. Such an interpretation is highly dubious. While the pouring out of the blood around the altar did symbolize the immediate and direct offering of the life of the victim to God, it carried with it no connotation of effecting a vital union between the offerer and God. Moreover, the imposition of hands in Israelite ritual signified merely that the sacrificer acknowledged that he had given this particular victim which was to be offered in his name and for his benefit.

103 Another fairly widespread theory is that the Israelites, like their Mesopotamian and Canaanite neighbors, considered sacrifice as a meal prepared for a hungry God. Those who advocate this theory point to those passages in which the altar is called "God's table" and the showbread, "God's loaves." They call attention also to the prescriptions requiring that the sacrifice be a full-course meal, complete with cakes and wine and seasoned with salt. Although the proponents admit that the biblical texts use such language figuratively, they insist that the terminology implies a materialistic and anthropomorphic view of sacrifice.

Since most of the texts that supposedly reflect such a view are late and clearly metaphorical, we need consider only those passages that bring us close to Israelite origins. In the flood story, after Noah disembarked, he offered holocausts to the Lord, who is said to have "smelled the sweet odor" (Gn 8:21). In later texts this same expression is used in a figurative, quasi-technical sense to indicate God's favorable acceptance of a sacrifice. In the flood narrative, which was largely taken over from a Babylonian epic (→ Genesis, 2:39), the phrase is simply part of the borrowed terminology and does not reflect Israelite concepts. The fable of Jotham mentions oil "whereby men and gods are honored" (Jgs 9:9) and wine "that cheers gods and men" (9:13). It must be remarked, first of all, that this is a fable and highly allegorical. Furthermore, it is unlikely that any biblical author would seriously refer to "gods"; the polytheistic ring of this terminology strongly suggests that the fable was borrowed from a non-Israelite literature. It is significant that Ps 104:15, an obvious echo of the passage in Jgs, deletes the references to the "gods." Moreover, some of the early texts contradict the notion that Israelite sacrifice was considered a meal prepared for divine consumption. In Jgs 6:18–22; 13:15–20, both Gideon and Manoah invite the angel of Yahweh to share their food, and in both instances the invitation is declined; instead, they are commanded to offer it as a holocaust. The meal that Abraham offered his three heavenly guests was a gesture of hospitality, not a sacrifice (Gn 18:8).

Admittedly there are certain elements of Israelite sacrifice that suggest the sharing of a meal with Yahweh, especially in the communion sacrifices. Such elements as the offerings of cakes, oil, and wine may have had this meaning in the Canaanite ritual from which they were probably borrowed. But the attitude of authentic Yahwism is expressed quite unequivocally in Ps 50:12–13: "If I were hungry, I would not tell you; for mine are the world and its fullness. Do I eat the flesh of strong bulls, or is the blood of goats my drink?"

104 **(B) Distinctive Understanding of Sacrifice.** What, positively, was the Israelite notion of sacrifice? The answer must begin with an appreciation of Israel's notion of God. He was unique, transcendent, all-powerful, supremely self-sufficient, personal; and because he was personal, he called for a response on the part of his people. This response had to be correspondingly personal, rational. Sacrifice, then, was the external expression of man's personal response to a personal God. It was not a mechanical, magic gesture with an efficacy unrelated to the interior dispositions of the one offering it. If sacrifice was not motivated by sincere interior dispositions, it was empty formalism, a mocking of true divine–human relationship. A failure to recognize this fundamental truth is the basic weakness of the hypotheses rejected above.

It is true that some elements of Israelite ritual and sacrificial vocabulary are rooted in customs antedating the formation of Israel as a nation. However, material similarity is not an indication of real identity with these customs or the primitive theology they reflected. Certain ancient forms were retained but were used as vehicles of new concepts. The same observation holds good for ritual borrowings from neighboring religions; the adoption of pagan ritual does not necessarily indicate adoption of pagan religious thought. Ritual is relatively neutral; it is given specific meaning by the religion that employs it, and the religion of Israel was quite different from and infinitely superior to that of Canaan. Israelite sacrifice, then, was distinctive and difficult to define. Sacrifice was not a simple concept: It was not uniquely the offering of a *gift* to God to acknowledge his dominion, nor uniquely a *means of effecting union* with him, nor uniquely an *act of expiation*. Simultaneously it was all three and more. Let us now study one by one its varied aspects.

105 Sacrifice was a *gift*, but a gift to which God had an imperative right, since anything that man could offer him had first to come from the bountiful divine hand. "The Lord's are the earth and its fulness; the world and those who dwell in it" (Ps 24:1; also 50:9–13; 1 Chr 29:14). In returning a part of God's property to him, man symbolically acknowledged God's right to it all; and thereby man acquired a right to use the rest of it, under God, for his own purposes. This was the idea behind the offering of the first fruits and the first-born. From another point of view, since the offerings were staples (meat and vegetables) by which men sustained their lives, the victims represented the life and being of the one offering. In sacrificing them, he symbolically surrendered himself to God; and God, by accepting them, bound himself in some way. It was not a *quid pro quo* notion (→ 101 above), since God had no need of the gift and there could be no proportion between the gift and God's favor.

The essence of the sacrifice did not consist in the destruction of the victim. In fact, in the case of animal sacrifices, the slaughter of the victim was only a preparatory rite and was performed by the offerer, not by the priest. One reason for the destruction of the offering, whether animal or vegetable, was that it made the gift irrevocably definitive and withdrew it completely from ordinary use. Also, it rendered the victim invisible and thereby symbolically sent it into the invisible sphere of the divine. The Hebr words for making an offering (hiphil of *qrb* and of *'lh*) mean "to bring near" and "to make to rise"; the word for holocaust, *'ōlâ*, means basically "that which goes up." The ritual served to symbolize this idea of "giving," of "sending up" to God. The altar was the symbol of God's presence; and the victim's blood, the most sacred element, was brought into direct contact with this symbol. In every sacrifice, the blood was poured out at the base of the altar; in expiatory sacrifices it was rubbed on the horns of the altar; in sin offerings for the high priest or the entire community it was sprinkled on the veil that concealed God's special presence in the Holy of Holies. On the Day of Atonement it was taken inside the Holy of Holies and sprinkled on the propitiatory, God's throne. The combustible parts of the victim were burned and, in a sense, spiritualized as they rose heavenward in the form of smoke.

106 The sacrifice, then, served as a gift, expressing the Israelite's sense of dependence on God, but it also indicated his *desire for union with God*. The Israelites never entertained a crassly physical notion of this union (→ 102 above); theirs was a more subtle attitude, in harmony with the sublime spiritual transcendence of Yahweh. When God had received his share of the victim, the ones who had presented it ate the remainder in a sacrificial meal. The fact that the one victim had both been offered to God and eaten by the worshipers brought the two parties together in a spiritual communion, establishing and consolidating the covenant bond between the two. This was a joyful occasion and in the early days the communion sacrifice was the most popular in the ritual.

107 Every sacrifice implied at least some notion of *expiation*. The making of the offering necessarily entailed self-denial, and the re-establishment or maintenance of amicable relations with God implied that these relations had been disturbed. The author of 1 Sm 3:14 wrote that "neither sacrifice nor offering will ever wipe out the sin of Heli." The use of blood gave all animal sacrifices expiatory overtones (Lv 17:11), in addition to the specific sacrifices of expiation for various faults (→ 83–88 above).

108 **(VIII) Condemnations of Sacrifice.** Given the central importance of sacrifice in Israelite religion, it is surprising to find some harsh condemnations of it in the OT. But an unbiased study of these condemnatory passages reveals implicitly that sacrifice was held in high esteem in Israel and that it was not a mere external rite of magic efficacy, but rather an externalization of noble religious sentiments, without which sacrifice was a sham and a mockery. Particularly vehement are the attacks of the pre-exilic prophets (Is 1:11–17; Jer 6:20; 7:21–22; Hos 6:6; Am 5:21–27; Mi 6:6–8). These passages have often been interpreted as condemnations of sacrifice in any shape or form, for their language is direct and unconditional. But we must recall that in Hebrew an absolute statement or a direct contrast is often made where we would use a comparison. The wording of Hos 6:6 is a splendid example of this type of expression: "For it is love that I desire, not sacrifice, and knowledge of God rather than holocausts." The laws of parallelism require that we understand the first phase in the same comparative sense as it is expressed in the second: "For it is love that I desire rather than sacrifice." Examples of this manner of speaking can be multiplied many times over, even in the NT (cf. Lk 14:26 and Mt 10:37).

One of the earliest prophets, Samuel, expressed the prophets' attitude toward sacrifice clearly: "Does the Lord desire holocausts and victims, and not rather that the voice of the Lord should be obeyed? For it is better to obey than to sacrifice, and to hearken rather than to offer the fat of rams" (1 Sm 15:22). What the prophets were condemning was formalistic, merely external worship without the proper dispositions. Such worship was not worship at all but an empty rigmarole bordering on superstition.

109 **(IX) Other Ritual Acts.** Sacrifice was the central, but not the only, act of Israelite worship. There were also public prayers and various rites of purification and consecration.

(A) Prayer. The fundamental expression of religious sentiment is prayer, that turning of the mind and heart to God which establishes immediate personal contact between man and the divinity. Sacrifice is prayer in act. We are concerned here, however, not with private, personal devotion, but with prayer as an element of cult, i.e., liturgical prayer.

The Bible does give formulas for blessing (Nm 6:22–27) and for cursing (Dt 27:14–26). It prescribes a formula to be used in the rite of the "bitter water" (Nm 5:21–22) and in the situation resulting from the non-apprehension of a murderer (Dt 21:7–8). It gives the formulas to be used in the offering of the first fruits (Dt 26:1–10) and in the payment of the tithe that was due every three years (Dt 26:13–15). It specifies also the scriptural reading for the Passover celebration (Dt 6:20–25; see Ex 12:26–27).

Although the ritual does not contain any prescription for the prayer formulas to be used during the offering of sacrifices, such formulas certainly existed and were in common use. They are found in every religious ritual throughout the world. Amos (5:23) refers to the singing of the hymns to instrumental accompaniment, but only in a general way. We may assume that the development of liturgical chant kept pace with that of the ritual and of the increasingly specialized priesthood. There were official chanters in Solomon's Temple from the beginning and the importance of this group grew steadily until, in the post-exilic Temple, it enjoyed great prestige. The official hymnbook of the new Temple was the Psalter, and several of its clearly liturgical hymns had already been in use during the royal period.

110 The ideal place for prayer was the Temple precincts, with one's face turned toward the Holy Place (Pss 5:8; 28:2; 138:2). When exile or absence made this ideal an impossibility, the expatriates did the best they could by facing in the direction of Jerusalem (1 Kgs 8:44,

48; Dn 6:11). The synagogues of the post-exilic period (→ 69 above) were constructed so that the faithful would be able to direct their prayers to the Holy Place.

Information about the times for official prayer services is scanty. Appropriate evening and morning prayers are found in Pss 4 and 5 respectively. Judith timed her prayer to coincide with the evening incense offering in the Temple (Jdt 9:1); and Daniel followed what seems to have been the general custom of praying three times a day, evening, morning, and noon (Dn 6:11; Ps 55:18). But the reference in these texts is to private, individual prayer. During the period in which they were written there were only two daily services in the Temple, one in the morning and the other in the evening.

111 An erect, standing posture seems to have been usual for prayer during the OT period. Solomon, however, is said to have knelt down (2 Chr 6:13), and in Neh 9:3–5 there is an interesting analogy to the *Flectamus Genua—Levate* procedure of the Latin liturgy. In this penitential rite the people stood for the Reading; then they fell to their knees for the confession of sins and remained in this position until the Levites cried: *qûmû* (*Levate*). External body posture is intended to express one's internal dispositions, and one's usual disposition before God is humble submission. In Ps 95:6 we read: "Come, let us bow down in worship; let us kneel before the Lord who made us" (Invitatory for Matins in the Roman Breviary). It is not surprising, then, to read of people kneeling in prayer (1 Kgs 8:54; Is 45:23; Dn 6:11) with arms raised toward heaven (1 Kgs 8:22,54; Is 1:15; Lam 2:19). Other texts suggest the Moslem custom of falling to the knees and pressing the forehead to the ground (Pss 5:8; 99:5; also MT of 99:9: "to His holy mountain").

112 **(B) Purifications.** Modern minds find strange the OT concepts of "cleanness" and "uncleanness," especially when "uncleanness" is described as the result of contact with the sacred. In the minds of the Israelites, certain things, both profane and sacred, possessed mysterious qualities that communicated themselves to anyone who came into contact with them and set him in a class apart from the ordinary. In order to return to the everyday world and activity, he had to be "purified." Undoubtedly this attitude reflected primitive mentality and customs; but the legislation that resulted from it served a sublime purpose by putting Israel in a class apart. The pagans might touch this or that and eat anything with impunity, but not the people of Israel. They belonged to an all-pure, transcendent God and they had to reflect his holiness. Several different rites were used to restore an "unclean" person to normalcy.

113 (a) SACRIFICES AND RITUAL WASHING. Following childbirth a woman was required to offer a holocaust and a sin offering (Lv 12:1–8). For people who considered marriage as something sacred, childbirth as the greatest of blessings, and sterility as a curse, a new mother was certainly not, by the very fact of her motherhood, in a "state of sin." But she had come into contact with, as it were, the creative power of God and consequently had to be "purified" in the ritual sense before resuming normal activities. Analogously, the Church, which considers Matrimony a sacrament and reveres motherhood, has a ceremony of "churching" after childbirth—with this same idea in mind.

114 When "lepers" were declared healed, they had to offer a sacrifice of reparation or a sin offering and a holocaust (Lv 14:10–32). Here again, there is no question of moral guilt, for the same sacrifices were required of a man or woman who had contacted the types of ritual irregularity described in Lv 15:14–15,29–30. A Nazirite who touched a corpse had to offer a sacrifice for sin, a holocaust, and a sacrifice for reparation (Nm 6:9–12). The same three sacrifices were required at the expiration of the term of his vow (Nm 6:13–20).

115 Sometimes ritual washing accompanied sacrifices of purification; sometimes it was as a distinct rite. A priest washed himself ritually before exercising his sacred functions (Ex 29:4; 30:17–21; Lv 8:6; 16:4). Utensils, clothing, or people had to be washed if they had come into contact with a legally unclean person or object (Lv 11:24–25,28,32,40; 15; 22:6) or even with something sacred. The metal pot in which sacrificial meat had been cooked had to be washed thoroughly afterward; if an earthenware vessel had been used, the law prescribed that it be subsequently broken (Lv 6:21). After the high priest came out of the Holy of Holies on the Day of Atonement, he had to change his clothes and wash himself from head to toe. The man who drove the scapegoat into the desert and burned the sin-offering victims had to do the same (Lv 16:23–28). This prescription also bound those who participated in the ritual of the red heifer (Nm 19:7–10,21). A seven-day period of purification was prescribed for soldiers who had engaged in a holy war and for all their garments (Nm 31:16–24).

116 (b) THE RITUAL OF THE RED HEIFER. If the booty from a holy war was of metal, it had to be washed in a special water called *mê middâ*, "purifying water" (Nm 31:22–23). The preparation of the water is described in Nm 19:1–10. An unblemished red heifer that had never been yoked was slaughtered outside the town by a layman, while a priest looked on. It was then completely burned and while it was burning, the priest tossed into the pyre cedarwood, hyssop, and scarlet yarn. The resulting ashes were gathered up and stored to be used in the preparation of lustral water. Some of the ashes were put into a receptacle into which water, coming directly from a spring or stream, was poured. If all this smacks of magic, it may be because the rite was originally pagan and was taken over and sanctified by the Israelites. Red is considered apotropaic (i.e., empowered to turn away evil) by many people, and special purifying powers are attributed to the ashes of burned animals and running water. This water was sprinkled on anyone who had come into contact with a corpse, bones, or a tomb, and on the house and furnishings of a dead man (Nm 19:11–22). Apart from these instances and the one mentioned in Nm 31:22–23, ordinary water was used for ritual ablutions.

117 (c) THE RITUAL FOR LEPROSY. The Hebr word translated as "leprosy," *ṣāraʿat*, does not refer to Hansen's disease, which is what we normally mean by leprosy. The biblical disease was noticeably less serious, for it was curable and its symptoms were those of a number of relatively superficial skin diseases (Lv 13:1–44). The disease, when so diagnosed by a priest, rendered a man ritually unclean. He then had to move to a safe distance from town until cured (2 Kgs 7:3). It was for the priest to determine that the cure had taken place (Lv 14:3) and to perform the rite of purification.

118 This rite is described in Lv 14, which is apparently a fusion of two rituals, one primitive and the other more recent. In the primitive rite a vessel was filled with "living" water and over this a bird was slaughtered so that its blood ran into the water. A live bird was then plunged into the water, and cedarwood, scarlet yarn, and hyssop were added. Finally, the bird was allowed to fly away. The leper was sprinkled with this water and declared pure; but it was not until seven days later, after he had shaved his whole body, washed his clothes, and bathed that he was definitively clean (Lv 14:2–9). This rite contained vestiges of very ancient superstitions. Unsightly skin diseases were considered to be caused by a devil, who must be expelled. As in the case of the red heifer, the reddened water was used for its apotropaic qualities; and the escaping bird symbolized the fleeing demon.

In the more recent ritual (Lv 14:10–32) the cured person offered a sacrifice for reparation, a sin offering, and a holocaust. With blood from the first sacrifice the priest daubed the subject's right ear, right thumb, and right big toe; he then anointed the same members with oil and poured oil on the former leper's head. This anointing is paralleled in the Mesopotamian and Canaanite ceremony accompanying the freeing of a slave.

119 Especially strange is the notion of "leprosy" in clothes, textiles, and even houses. Here the "disease" was some sort of mildew or fungus growth. If the affected article did not respond to washing, it had to be burned. If it did respond, it was washed again and declared clean (Lv 13:47–59). In the case of houses, the discolored stones were removed and the walls scraped. If the condition continued spreading, the house was torn down; if it stopped, the house was declared clean. In either case, the same ritual of expiation had to be performed as that described in Lv 14:29. Archaic and mysterious though these notions and rites may be, they turn up only in post-exilic texts. A consciousness of guilt that was heightened by the Exile and a stress on God's transcendence in the theology of the P tradition brought about a preoccupation with cleanness and uncleanness that amounted to almost an obsession in P legislation. The legislators adduced instance after instance of possible uncleanness and even reached back into the dim past in their desire for completeness.

120 (d) Consecration Rites. Purification expressed a negative aspect of holiness, in that it aimed at removing a legal obstacle to contact with the divine. Consecration was the positive side; it readied a man or an object for such contact or even resulted from the contact. It consisted fundamentally in removing someone or something from the realm of the profane and dedicating him or it to a sacred purpose. This dedication did not always require a distinct ceremony; any entrance into the realm of the sacred effected a consecration. For example, soldiers who fought in a holy war and the prizes they captured were automatically dedicated to God; priests were consecrated by the simple fact of their service of the sanctuary. Such consecration imposed obligations. The priests had to observe strict regulations safeguarding their purity (Lv 21:1–8); the soldiers in the holy war had to remain continent for the duration (1 Sm 21:6; 2 Sm 11:11), and the booty they took could be used for no one's personal advantage (Jos 6:18ff.; 1 Sm 15:18–19).

121 We have been discussing examples of automatic consecration. As the ritual developed, specific ceremonies of consecration appeared. In the post-exilic period, the high priest was consecrated by an elaborate rite involving purification, investiture, and anointing (→ 30 above). Similarly the sanctuary, altar, and sacred objects had to be anointed (Ex 30:26–29; 40:9–11; Lv 8:10). In the pre-exilic period it was the king who was the "anointed one" (→ Aspects OT Thought, 77:155), and as a sign of his sacred character he wore the *nēzer* or crown (2 Sm 1:10; 2 Kgs 11:12; Ps 89:40). The post-exilic high priest wore a similar ornament, a golden flower (*ṣîṣ*) as part of his headdress (Ex 39:30; Lv 8:9). The root meaning of the verb *nāzar* is "to set apart" and hence "to place under interdict" or "to consecrate." The derived noun, *nāzîr*, signifies a dedicated person. Allied to this root is *ndr*, and from it comes the noun *neder*, a vow.

122 **(C) Vows.** A vow in OT thought was a conditioned promise to dedicate a person or thing to God. If God granted a certain request, the beneficiary would fulfill his promise. It was a special type of prayer in which a person not only asked for a favor but strengthened his request by promising to give something in return. Not all vows were conditional, although this seems to have been the case in the early days. As time went on, simple disinterested promises became more of a rule than an exception.

The taking of a vow imposed a solemn obligation, but the Law ruled out certain vows, whether because the thing promised already belonged to God, like the first-born of cattle (Lv 27:26), or because it was unworthy of him, like the proceeds of sacred prostitution (Dt 23:19). Women were restricted in the matter of vows; for example, a father could cancel a vow taken by his unmarried daughter; a husband could annul his wife's vow. A widow or divorcee, however, could assume full responsibility for a vow (Nm 30:4–17). In later legislation, people were allowed to substitute a sum of money for the specific object promised (Lv 27:1–25).

123 *Nazirites.* Not only some object but even one's own person could be consecrated to God for a specific length of time. One thus became a Nazirite (Nm 6:1–21). During the specified time, the person had to abstain from all alcoholic drink, even wine, to leave his hair uncut, and to shun all contact with a corpse. This last prescription was interpreted quite strictly; if anyone died while a Nazirite was present, the latter was defiled and had to begin again by shaving his head and offering, various sacrifices (6:9–12). When he had completed the term of his vow, he offered a holocaust, a sin offering, and a communion sacrifice; he shaved his head and burned the hair as part of the communion sacrifice (6:18). He then returned to normal life.

These prescriptions seem to be an adaptation and mitigation of an ancient custom according to which Nazirite consecration was for life and was more charismatic than entirely voluntary (see Am 2:11–12). In the story of Samson we see a consecration begun while he was still in his mother's womb (Jgs 13:4–5,7,13–14). The element of uncut hair seems to have been the characteristic feature of the Nazirite. Soldiers who fought in a holy war did not cut their hair (Jgs 5:2; see Dt 32:42); and when Samuel's mother dedicated him to God's service, she promised that his head would never be shaved (1 Sm 1:11). Samson's long hair, the sign of his lifelong consecration, was the source of his extraordinary strength (Jgs 16:17).

PRE-EXILIC ISRAELITE FEASTS

124 **(I) Daily Services.** The Israelites observed several important holy days each year; but before we discuss them, it would be helpful to see something of the everyday Temple services. According to Ex 29:38–42 and Nm 28:2–8, two lambs were to be offered daily as holocausts, one in the morning and the other in the evening. Along with the holocausts went an offering of flour mixed with oil, a libation of wine, and an incense offering (Ex 30:7–8). This daily ritual was introduced after the Exile, although Chr characteristically speaks of it as existing during the royal period (1 Chr 16:40; 2 Chr 13:11; 31:3). The pre-exilic ritual is reflected in Ez 46:13–15, where no mention is made of an evening holocaust. During the monarchy there was a morning holocaust and an afternoon cereal offering (*minḥâ*; see 2 Kgs 16:15; Ezr 9:4–5; Dn 9:21). The post-exilic custom of two holocausts continued into NT times, but the hour of the second shifted from twilight to midafternoon. On the Sabbath the same ritual was observed, but in each holocaust two lambs were offered rather than one as on ordinary days (Nm 28:9–10). On the first day of each month, the day of the new moon, there was a special ritual calling for a holocaust of two bulls, a ram, and seven lambs, together with offerings and libations, and the sacrifice of a goat as a sin offering (Nm 28:11–15).

125 **(II) Liturgical Calendars.** The more important feast days, of course, had to be indicated by a liturgical calendar. Several such calendars are given in the OT, and it will be necessary to consider them separately. (See also J. van Goudoever, *Biblical Calendars* [2nd ed.; Leiden, 1964].)

The Elohist Code gives the simplest and most succinct calendar (Ex 23:14–17). It prescribes a *ḥag* or pilgrimage (cf. Moslem hadj) three times a year: the pilgrimage of the unleavened bread in the month of Abib (March–April), the pilgrimage of the grain harvest (late spring), and the pilgrimage of the fruit harvest (autumn).

The Yahwist Code (Ex 34:18–23) is the same as the Elohist Code but with slight variations, e.g., calling the pilgrimage of the grain harvest the "Feast of Weeks" and dating the fruit harvest "at the turn of the year." This latter phrase is, however, synonymous with the Elohist Code's "at the close of the year." And the vagueness of both terms indicates that the prescribed pilgrimages took place not on fixed dates, but according to the variable agricultural seasons. Before the centralization of worship each locale determined its own dates within the prescribed general seasons, since the people made the pilgrimage to a local shrine.

The Deuteronomic Code (Dt 16:1–17) introduces only slight changes, the most significant of which is the specification of the place of pilgrimage: "in the place which he (Yahweh) will choose." The three annual feasts are: (1) the Passover, joined to the Feast of Unleavened Bread of the earlier codes; (2) the Feast of Weeks, with the explanation that it takes place seven weeks after the beginning of the grain harvest; and (3) the Feast of Tabernacles or Tents (*sukkôt*), corresponding to the fruit harvest festival of the earlier codes. No explanation is offered for this new term.

126 *The Priestly Collection* (Lv 23). This has more precision in the matter of dates, along with a new calendar (the Babylonian) according to which the year begins in the spring instead of in the autumn. But we also find a problem, for Lv 23 gives clear evidence of being a conflation of two different sources: in its verses it has two titles (2 and 4), two endings (37 and 44), two sets of prescriptions for the Feast of Tabernacles (34–36 and 39–43). In the view of R. de Vaux, one of these sources is the Holiness Code from the end of the royal period (→ Leviticus, 4:3,35), and the other is made up of exilic and post-exilic additions. To the royal period would belong these verses: 4–8, dealing with the Passover, to be celebrated on the 14th of Nisan (the old Abib) and to be followed by the ancient week-long Feast of Unleavened Bread; 16–21a, dealing with the Feast of Weeks, to be celebrated fifty days after the Feast of Unleavened Bread; 34b–36, dealing with the Feast of Tabernacles, to begin on the 15th of Tishri (September–October) and to last for seven days, followed by a solemn day of rest; and 37–38, the conclusion. Post-exilic additions would be these verses: 3, dealing with the Sabbath; 10–15, dealing with the Feast of the First Sheaf; 24–25, dealing with the celebration of the 1st of Tishri; 27–32, dealing with the Day of Atonement (10th of Tishri); 39–43, giving a different ritual for the Feast of Tabernacles; and 44, a new conclusion (→ Leviticus, 4:43–48).

127 Ezekiel (45:18–25) gives a type of liturgical calendar, but it seems to be an idealization similar to the prophet's view of the new Temple. There is no evidence that Ezekiel's calendar was ever followed; the calendar which prevailed was that of the Priestly Collection (Lv 23) supplemented by Nm 28–29. These chapters in Nm prescribe the specific sacrifices to be offered: for the daily ritual (28:3–8); the Sabbath (28:9–10); the New Moon (28:11–15); the Passover and Feast of Unleavened Bread (28:16–25); the Feast of Weeks (28:26–31); the "Day of Acclamation" on the 1st of Tishri (29:1–6); the Day of Atonement (29:7–11); and the Feast of Tabernacles (29:12–38). This was the calendar of feasts celebrated and of sacrifices offered in the post-exilic Temple.

Now we shall consider individually the more important Israelite religious festivals.

128 **(III) The Sabbath.**

(A) Origin. Our Eng word is virtually a transcription of Hebr *šabbāt*, which, in turn, is seemingly a derivative, albeit irregular, of the verb *šābat*, "to cease," and, by extension, "to cease working, to rest." At least this is the popular etymology of the word given in Gn 2:2–3, but the true scientific derivation is not quite clear, nor is the origin of the religious institution itself. All attempts to prove that the Hebrews (*via* Ezekiel) borrowed it from the Babylonians fail completely. Such attempts are based chiefly on the similarity between *šabbāt* and the Akkadian word *šappattu*, signifying the middle day of the month, the day of the full moon. However, the only admissible similarity is etymological; and from this point of view, the common denominator would be the meaning of "bringing to a halt": The *šappattu* brought a month to a halt; the Hebr Sabbath marked the end of a week. As for the suggestion that Ezekiel (20:12,20; 46:1) adapted Babylonian customs to Israelite life, the fact is that, far from introducing the Sabbath, he presents it as a long-standing institution to which his compatriots have been unfaithful (20:13; 22:26; 23:38). A variation of this hypothesis sees the Sabbath as coming to Israel from Babylonia, not directly, but by way of Canaan. But the variation suffers from the same lack of evidence and from the same positive objections as the original.

129 However, if the Israelites did not borrow the institution of the Sabbath from the Babylonians, either directly or indirectly, it must go back to a much older period. Although Ex 16:22–30 suggests that the Sabbath existed even before the Sinaitic covenant, and Gn 2:2–3 traces it to the time of creation itself, it seems certain that the Sabbath is bound up in some way with Yahwism. Accordingly, those who trace Yahwism to the Kenites look to them also for the the custom of observing the Sabbath. It is true that Yahweh appeared to Moses in a region inhabited by Kenites and that the Kenites were related to the Midianites, into whom Moses had married; but this—and other allied evidence—provides little foundation for concluding that the great legislator borrowed from them either Yahwism or the Sabbath.

(For the "Kenite hypothesis" see H. H. Rowley, *From Joseph to Joshua* [1950] 149ff.; → Excursus Israel, 11:29.)

The Sabbath is mentioned in all the traditions that make up the Pentateuch: the Elohist Code (Ex 23:12), the Yahwist Code (Ex 34:21), the two versions of the Decalogue (Dt 5:12–14 and Ex 20:8–10), and the Priestly Collection (Ex 31:12–17). Whatever one may hold about the dates at which these traditions were put into writing, it is certainly safe to say that the institution of the Sabbath goes back to the Mosaic era. More than this we cannot say at present.

130 **(B) Significance.** The role that the Sabbath played in Israelite life and thought made it quite unique. It was not just a holiday on which men could rest up for another week of work. It was bound up with the covenant that God had made with his people and was a day consecrated to him in a special way. Initially the law of the Sabbath rest was simply stated; later forms of the law added motives that betray two different theological perspectives. First, in Dt 5:14b–15 humanitarian factors are stressed: One cannot work without the proper rest. But at the same time the religious aspect is not neglected: The Sabbath will serve as a memorial of God's liberation of his people from slave labor in Egypt and bringing them into a "resting place" (12:9; see Ps 95:11). Second, Ex 20:11 expresses a motive that reflects the attitude of the Priestly school: "In six days the Lord made the heaven and the earth, the sea and all that is in them, but on the seventh day he rested. That is why the Lord has blessed the Sabbath day and made it holy" (see Gn 2:2–3; Ex 31:12–17).

Both motives are an expression of covenant theology; only the points of view are different. The deuteronomic view focuses on one of the parties to the covenant, the people; the Priestly view characteristically focuses on the other party, God. The latter outlook prevailed and gave the Sabbath its predominantly religious tone (Lv 23:3,28; Ex 20:11; 31:15).

131 **(C) Observance.** As a sign of the covenant, observance of the Sabbath indicated fidelity to the covenant and was an assurance of salvation (Is 58:13–14; Jer 17:19–27); nonobservance was tantamount to apostasy (Ex 31:14; 35:2; Nm 15:32–36). If the people as a whole neglected the Sabbath, God would punish them severely (Ez 20:13; Neh 13:17–18).

In the early days, however, the Sabbath was a joyful, relaxed holiday, predominantly religious but not overly restrictive. Manual labor and business were suspended, but the people could move about freely. They made pilgrimages to nearby sanctuaries (Is 1:13; Hos 2:13) or went to consult their prophets (2 Kgs 4:23). Then during the Exile, when celebration of the other feasts was impossible, the Sabbath came into sharp prominence as the distinctive sign of the covenant. After the Exile, although the Sabbath continued to be a day of pleasurable relaxation, it was subject to tighter restrictions. All business and travel were forbidden (Is 58:13); the people could not carry anything or take anything from their homes or do any work (Jer 17:21–22, a post-exilic addition). During his second visit to Jerusalem, Nehemiah reacted vigorously to the people's neglect of the Sabbath laws by ordering the gates of the city closed and extracting a promise of future fidelity from the people (Neh 10:32; 13:15–16,19–22). As time went on, the restrictions were multiplied until, by NT times, they were meticulous.

132 **(IV) Passover and the Feast of Unleavened Bread.** As we have seen, the important holy days in the calendar of ancient Israel were the three pilgrimage feasts (Unleavened Bread, Weeks, and Tabernacles) and the Passover. The Passover and the Feast of Unleavened Bread were later combined. Information about the Passover, which is not abundant and not always clear, is contained in two sets of texts, the liturgical and the historical.

133 **(A) History—Liturgical Texts.** These texts come from different Pentateuchal traditions, formulated at different times; thus it is possible to use them as guides in tracing the development of the great Jewish feasts.

(a) THE PRIESTLY TRADITION. By the time this latest of the Pentateuchal traditions was formulated, the celebration of the Passover has been joined to that of the Feast of Unleavened Bread. The pertinent texts are: Lv 23:5–8; Nm 28:16–25 (see 9:1–4); Ex 12:1–20, 40–51. From them we learn that the Passover was to be celebrated in conjunction with the full moon of the first month of the year (March–April). On the tenth of this month each family was to select an unblemished, male, one-year-old lamb. At twilight on the 14th (Ex 12:6: "between the two evenings"), the lamb was slaughtered and the blood sprinkled on the lintels and doorposts of the house. During this night of the full moon the lamb was roasted and eaten; not one of its bones could be broken, and whatever was left over after the meal had to be burned. Unleavened bread and bitter herbs were eaten also, and those who partook of the meal had to be dressed as if ready for a journey. In case a family was too small to consume a whole lamb, it joined some neighbors. Slaves and resident aliens (*gērîm*) could take part, so long as they were circumcised.

On the 15th of the month, the week-long Feast of Unleavened Bread began. All leftover leavened bread had to be destroyed and for the following week only unleavened bread could be eaten. The first and seventh days of the festival were holidays on which religious gatherings took place. The same ritual for the Passover–Unleavened Bread feasts is reflected in Ez 45:21, in Ezr 6:19–22, and in the "Passover Papyrus" from Elephantine (→ History of Israel, 75:99). This papyrus, from 419 BC, insists on the dates to be observed, an indication that the dates are an innovation for these colonists.

134 (b) THE DEUTERONOMIC TRADITION. Let us go back to an earlier stage in the celebration of the two feasts. The pertinent text, Dt 16:1–8, is an artificial welding of two distinct rituals, one referring to the Passover and the other to the Feast of Unleavened Bread. Dt 16:1,2,4b–7 deals with the Passover, which was to be celebrated during the month of Abib (March–April); no specific dates are given. The victim could be a calf or a sheep or a goat; it was to be slaughtered at sundown, cooked, and eaten that same night. But all this was to take place at the Temple, and the next morning all were to go home. Dt 16:3,4a,8 deals with the Feast of Unleavened Bread, when for seven days the people were to eat the unleavened "bread of affliction." The seventh day was to be a day of rest and of religious convocation. These two rituals imply a distinction between the two festivals, marked by the departure, on the evening after the Passover, of all who had taken part in that solemnity.

The deuteronomic ritual for Passover was followed under Josiah (2 Kgs 23:21–23; → 136 below), and the text does not even mention the Feast of Unleavened Bread. However, the author takes pains to point out that this Passover was something new. The Chronicler also describes Josiah's Passover celebration (2 Chr 35:1–18) but gives no further pertinent information except to insert into his description practices followed later in his own time. He mentions the Feast of Unleavened Bread as in Dt 16:7–8, but he also mentions the novelty of Josiah's Passover ritual (2 Chr 35:18). For an idea of the newness of the deuteronomic ritual we must compare it with what the older calendars tell us.

135 (c) The Ancient Liturgical Calendars. The two oldest calendars (Ex 23:15; 34:18) mention the Feast of Unleavened Bread but not the Passover. They prescribe that unleavened bread is to be eaten for a week during the month of Abib; this festival was one of the three pilgrimage (*ḥāg*) feasts (Ex 23:14,17; 34:23). The Passover is mentioned in Ex 34:25, but this verse does not deal with the pilgrimages, nor does Ex 23:18. Yet the word *ḥāg* is used in both these verses; therefore they must have been edited after Dt had classified the Passover as a pilgrimage feast. It is this that seems to constitute the novelty of the deuteronomic Passover ritual observed in the central sanctuary. Formerly Passover had been a local, family affair (Ex 12:21–23; Dt 16:5), distinct from the Unleavened Bread pilgrimage. But since both occurred in the same month and shared several features, it is not surprising that they were finally joined together. This combination had not taken place before Josiah's day (*ca.* 620), and the first reference to them as one festival is in Ez 45:21 (during the Exile, after 587) and in the Priestly ritual. The Chronicler's description of Hezekiah's solemn Passover (2 Chr 30) is clearly anachronistic (yet see F. L. Moriarty, *CBQ* 27 [1965] 404–6).

136 **(B) History—Josiah's Passover.** Was the deuteronomic Passover celebrated under Josiah really new or was it rather a return to an older, long neglected custom? Some passages (2 Kgs 23:22; 2 Chr 35:18) would seem to support the latter view. Two questions are involved, however: the joining of the Passover with the Feast of Unleavened Bread and the restriction of the celebration of the Passover to Jerusalem. It has often been alleged that Jos 5:10–12 points to an original combination of the two feasts. This passage tells how, when the Israelites pitched camp at Gilgal, they celebrated the Passover on the evening of the 14th and on that same day (according to the better reading) "they ate of the produce of the land in the form of unleavened bread and parched grain." But it is difficult to see any real resemblance between this eating of unleavened cakes on the day of the Passover celebration and the seven-day festival that is mentioned in the liturgical texts. As far as can be determined, the two feasts were still separate when the deuteronomic legislation was promulgated. The celebration of the Passover under Josiah, which was inspired by Dt, did not include the Feast of Unleavened Bread.

On the other hand the restriction of the Passover celebration to Jerusalem was a deuteronomic innovation. Before the monarchy, Passover may have been celebrated at a central tribal shrine (2 Kgs 23:22; 2 Chr 35:18); before the settlement in Canaan it had been a tribal feast. But with the disintegration of tribal unity that followed upon this settlement, Passover became a family feast. This may be why it was not mentioned in Ex 23 and 24 and also why the Yahwist ritual of Ex 12:21–23 was so detailed: Individual families would have needed clear instructions. The Feast of Unleavened Bread remained a group festival, a pilgrimage to a local sanctuary. With the eventual deuteronomic insistence on Jerusalem as the only legitimate locale for both feasts, they were brought into conjunction.

137 **(C) Origin of Passover.** Etymology is of little help here. The popular explanation given in Ex 12:13,23,27 links the name of the feast (*pesaḥ*) with the fact that the destroying angel "jumped over, passed by" (*psḥ*) the homes of the Hebrews during the execution of the tenth plague; but this is popular, not scientific etymology. The Akkadian word *pašāḫu*, to "appease," does not apply, for the Passover was not an expiatory feast. More recently it has been suggested that the Hebrew is a transcription of an Egyptian word meaning "a stroke, a blow," and the reference would then be to the blow that Yahweh struck at Egypt; but this is hardly tenable.

Looking to the rite itself, we find it characteristically pastoral, and no other Israelite rite resembles so closely those of the ancient nomadic Arabs. Passover required no priest, no altar, and the blood of the victim played an important role. Originally a young animal was sacrificed to obtain fertility for the whole flock, and the blood was put on the tentpoles to drive away evil powers (see Ex 12:23: the Destroyer). This ritual has all the appearance of a rite celebrated when the tribe broke camp to head for the fresh spring pastures. The nomadic character of Passover is further suggested by several features: The victim was roasted; the meat was eaten with unleavened bread and bitter (wild, not cultivated) herbs; and the participants were to be dressed for immediate departure, with their shepherd's crooks in hand. The later texts that fix the dates for the celebration of the Passover reflect the pastoral, nomadic origin of the feast. They specify the 14th–15th of the first month (Abib: later Nisan; our March–April), precisely at the time of the full moon. In the desert life, a brightly lit night would be the logical choice for such a festival. All the evidence, therefore, points to the fact that the Passover went back to the days when the Israelites were leading a seminomadic existence, even to the time before the Exodus. This may be the feast that the Israelites, while still in Egypt, wanted to celebrate in the desert (Ex 5:1), permission for which was refused by the Pharaoh.

138 **(D) Origin of the Feast of Unleavened Bread** (*maṣṣôt* **or** matzoth). This feast marked the beginning of the barley harvest. For the first seven days of the harvest the only bread eaten was with flour from the new grain, prepared without leaven. Containing nothing of the "old year," it symbolized a fresh start. Furthermore, there was an offering to Yahweh from the new crops, but this was merely an anticipation of the more formal offering of first fruits on the Feast of Weeks that marked the end of the grain harvesting season, 50 days after the beginning of the barley harvest. Since the Feast of Unleavened Bread was an agricultural feast and was not celebrated until after the settlement in Canaan (Lv 23:10), the Israelites may well have borrowed it from the Canaanites. However, they made it a strictly Israelite feast, reckoning it from Sabbath to Sabbath and fixing the main harvest feast (Weeks) seven weeks later (neither the Sabbath nor the week was known outside Israel—see De Vaux, *op. cit.*, 186–88). Since it was an agricultural feast, determined by the readiness of the barley harvest, it could be dated no more precisely than within the month in which this harvest normally occurred, Abib.

139 The deuteronomic legislation and the reform of Josiah brought about some precision in this matter, causing complications in the process. The Passover became a pilgrimage feast, and its proximity to the Feast of Unleavened Bread led to an eventual combination of the two some time between the reform of Josiah (621) and the Exile (587–539). While the date of the Passover was determined by the full moon, the Feast of Unleavened Bread had depended on the harvest and was supposed to begin and end on a Sabbath. As it turned out, the Passover took precedence: On whatever day it occurred, the Feast of Unleavened Bread began on the next day and lasted a week. Moreover, the two feasts took on a profound new meaning as commemorations of God's deliverance of his people from Egypt, which had taken place at the same time of the year.

(Le Deaut, R., *La nuit pascale* [AnalBib 22; Rome, 1963]. Segal, J. B., *The Hebrew Passover* [London, 1963].)

140 **(V) Feast of Weeks—Pentecost.** This feast is called the Harvest Feast in Ex 23:16, the Feast of the Wheat Harvest in Ex 34:22. In the latter passage it is called also the Feast of Weeks, but this may be a gloss added to identify it with the pilgrimage of the weeks mentioned in Dt 16:9–10. Here we learn that the feast was to be celebrated seven weeks after the beginning of the barley harvest (the Feast of Unleavened Bread). The term "Feast of Weeks" turns up in Nm 28:26 also, along with "Feast of the First Fruits"; for the token offering of first fruits at the beginning of the barley harvest had been only an anticipation of this, the definitive first fruit offering.

Like all harvest feasts, it was a joyful occasion (Dt 16:11; Is 9:2). The complete ritual for its celebration is given in Lv 23:15–21. Counting seven full weeks from the day following the Sabbath on which the first barley sheaf was offered to God, we arrive at the day following the seventh Sabbath, exactly fifty days later. (Thus the feast ultimately came to be known as Pentecost, from the Gk word for "fiftieth" [2 Mc 12:31–32; Tob 2:1].) The ceremony consisted in offering two leavened loaves made from the new wheaten flour. The use of unleavened bread at the beginning of the harvest, 50 days before, had marked a fresh start; but now that the harvest was over, normal customs were resumed. There was thus a sort of organic unity between the Feast of Weeks and the earlier Feast of Unleavened Bread, and through the latter, with the Passover.

141 Since the Feast of Weeks presumed an agricultural economy, the Israelites began to celebrate it only after the entrance into Canaan, probably adopting it from the Canaanites. There was at first no fixed date for its celebration (Ex 23:16; 34:22). Dt 16:9–10 adds precision in relating the Feast of Weeks to the Feast of Unleavened Bread; but the date of the latter feast was itself still rather flexible. Finally, when the Passover and the Feast of Unleavened Bread were joined and given definite dates, the Feast of Weeks also acquired a fixed place in the calendar. Not all accepted this dating without demur, however. In the calendar given by *Jubilees* and followed at Qumran (→ Apocrypha, 68:18,86), the feasts fell on the same days of the week each year. According to this reckoning, the offering of the first sheaf, which was to take place "on the day after the Sabbath," occurred not on the Sunday following the Passover, but a week later, on the 26th of the month. This put the Feast of Weeks on the 15th of the third month.

142 Although originally an agricultural feast, Pentecost later acquired even deeper religious significance by being related to the Exodus. According to Ex 19:1, the Israelites arrived at Sinai in the third month after their departure from Egypt. Since this departure had taken place in the middle of the first month, the Feast of Weeks was seen to coincide with the date of their arrival at Sinai and took on added stature as a commemoration of the Sinaitic covenant. This connection is mentioned explicitly in *Jubilees*. At Qumran, too, the renewal of the covenant was celebrated on the Feast of Weeks, the most important feast in the Qumran calendar (B. Noack, ASTI 1 [1962] 72–95). Among Jews in general, however, it retained only a secondary importance.

143 **(VI) Feast of Tents—Tabernacles.** The Hebr name of the third great pilgrimage feast is *sukkôt*, variously translated as Tabernacles, Booths, Tents, and Huts. None of these translations is completely acceptable, although "Huts" comes closest. However, we shall use the conventional "Feast of Tents," with the reminder that the feast never called for the setting up of tents of any sort. We first meet the name *sukkôt* in the later liturgical calendars (Dt 16:13,16; Lv 23:34) and in texts dependent on these calendars (Ezr 3:4; Zech 14:16,18). But while the name may be relatively new, the feast is old; it is the "Feast of the Ingathering" (*'āsîp*) mentioned in the two most ancient calendars (Ex 23:16 and 34:22).

Of the three annual pilgrimage feasts, this was the most important and the best attended. It is called "the feast of Yahweh" in Lv 23:39 (see Nm 29:12), and Ez 45:25 calls it simply "*The* feast," as does 1 Kgs 8:2,65. It is also to be identified with "the yearly feast of Yahweh at Shiloh" (Jgs 21:19). Zechariah, foretelling a worldwide annual pilgrimage of all nations to the Temple, chose this feast as the occasion of the pilgrimage (Zech 14:16). And Josephus referred to it as "the holiest and greatest of Hebrew feasts" (*Ant.* 8.4,1 § 100).

144 **(A) History.** (See G. W. MacRae, *CBQ* 22 [1960] 251–76). Like the feasts of Unleavened Bread and of Weeks, the Feast of Tents was an agricultural feast, indeed the climax of the agricultural year. It marked the ingathering of all the produce of the fields (Ex 23:16), the products of the threshing floors and of the wine and oil presses (Dt 16:13). When the earth had yielded all its bounty for the current year, and that bounty had been gathered and stored, the people gave joyful thanks to God (the analogy with our Thanksgiving Day is obvious). There was dancing, singing, and general merriment (Jgs 21:19–21), including, apparently, a generous sampling of the new wine (1 Sm 1:14–15).

145 As for the ritual of the feast, the earliest texts are not too detailed. Later the feast is called *sukkôt* as in Dt 16:13–15, but no explanation of the name is offered. It is described as a pilgrimage to the Temple, and its duration is given as seven days. More precise information is found in Lv 23:33–43, but this passage is not a literary unit and must be studied *per partes*. The vague prescriptions of Dt 16:13–15 are repeated in Lv 23:34–36, with the added mention of an eighth day, one of rest and of assembly for worship. We learn from Nm 29:12–34 what sacrifices were offered during the seven days of the festival, and Nm 29:35–38 prescribes the sacrifices for the eighth day. This eighth day seems to be an addition to the original ritual, a day of transition, of catching one's breath, before returning to normal activities.

A second stage in the redaction of Lv 23 is reflected in the account of the celebration of the feast under Ezra in Neh 8:13–18; for 8:14 depends on Lv 23:42–43, where we read that for seven days the people are to live in huts in memory of the huts in which the Israelites lived after their liberation from Egypt. When the people to whom the Law was being read heard this prescription, they hurried off and collected branches to fashion lean-tos, which they put on roofs, in the courts of the Temple, and in the city squares. Neh 8:17 remarks: "The Israelites had never done the like since the days of Joshua." Certainly this cannot refer to the building of the improvised huts, for the name *sukkôt* goes back to a period before Dt. The fact that this took place in Jerusalem is probably the novelty.

The final stage in the redaction of Lv 23 is represented by verses 40–41, which direct that the people "shall gather foliage from majestic trees, branches of palms, and boughs of myrtles and of valley poplars" and "make merry before the Lord." The word translated "foliage" means literally "good fruit." There is no mention of this in the text from Neh; the fruit had no connection with the building of huts. Later historical texts make it clear that the foliage was carried in procession, as in the Catholic Palm Sunday ceremony. According to 2 Mc 10:6–8, the dedication of the Temple was celebrated "like the feast of Tents": For eight days the Jews held triumphal processions carrying thyrsus, green branches, and palms. And Josephus (*Ant.* 13.13,5 § 372) tells how the despised monarch Alexander Janneus (→ History of Israel, 75:116) was bombarded with fruit carried by the people during the Feast of Tents.

146 **(B) Date of the Feast of Tents.** According to Ex 23:16, the feast was to be celebrated at the close of the year (in autumn); according to Ex 34:22, at the turn of the year. The texts, taken together, indicate that no definite date had yet been fixed for the celebration, which depended on the condition of the crops. In Dt 16:13 the date is given as dependent upon the progress of the harvest work: When the harvest was finished, the feast was to be celebrated. The offhand references to the celebration of the feast in Kgs cause complications; for a full treatment, see De Vaux, *op. cit.*, 498–499. Actually, the date was not definitely fixed before the period reflected in Lv 23:34 (see Nm 29:12) which puts it on the 15th day of the seventh month (the month, September–October, is counted from the beginning of the year in spring). The feast is to last seven days and come to a conclusion on the eighth. The same dating is given in Ez 45:25.

147 **(C) Origin of the Feast of Tents.** There have been abortive attempts to connect this feast with the vintage time celebration in honor of Bacchus and with the feast of Adonis-Osiris, in which an arbor was set up over the bier of Adonis. Both explanations are completely devoid of foundation. Another, more popular, hypothesis is based on the primitive idea that evil powers were especially active at the turn of the year and attacked houses. To escape this malevolent influence the people move out of their houses and live in makeshift dwellings until the danger has passed. The Israelites, it is claimed, would have been particularly susceptible to such superstitions during their first years of sedentary living in Canaan, when the Feast of Tents would have been introduced. Actually, there is no trace of such notions in the biblical texts, which offer a more satisfactory and less strained explanation. The feast began as a harvest festival, as its earliest name (*'āsîp* or Ingathering) suggests, and as the details given in the ancient texts (Ex 23:16; 34:22) indicate. Even after it had taken on a name inspired by an accidental part of the ritual (*sukkôt* or Huts), it remained essentially an agricultural feast. If we are to seek its origin outside of Israel, the logical place to look is in Canaan, as was true for the feasts of Unleavened Bread and of Weeks.

148 But how did the rite of the *sukkôt* come into such prominence? It had its roots in a very common Palestinian custom: During the harvest time the people built—and still build—shelters in the orchards and vineyards. These improvised huts afford some protection from the sun during periods of rest. Since the Feast of the Ingathering was celebrated outdoors where these little huts were so much a part of the harvest scene, it is not difficult to see how it could come to be known as the Feast of Huts (*sukkôt*). While retaining the name and allowing the custom, Dt 16:13–15 insisted that the people go to Jerusalem for the sacrifices, Finally, the *sukkôt* were set up in the Holy City itself and became a permanent fixture of the ritual (Lv 23:42; Neh 8:16).

As in the case of the Passover and the Feast of Weeks (→ 139, 142 above), the Feast of Tents was later given a deeper religious significance by being related to an event in the Exodus. The *sukkôt* were interpreted as a memorial of the *sukkôt* in which the Israelites had lived after their liberation from Egypt (Lv 23:43). Actually, they did not live in huts, but in tents during the desert sojourn; so the association is liturgical, not historical.

149 **(VII) An Old Testament "New Year"?** One of the most familiar of modern Jewish festivals is Rosh Hashana (Hebrew = "head of the year"), New Year's Day. It was known in NT times, too, and was celebrated on the first of Tishri (September–October). The New Year was blown in (rather than rung in) on a horn called a shophar, and hymns of praise were sung. No such festival is mentioned in the OT. The term "head of the year" occurs just once (Ez 40:1), but here there is no question of a New Year's festival. Ezekiel simply uses the expression to date his vision of the Temple of the future, and the day indicated is the 10th of Nisan (March–April), not the first of Tishri. The Babylonian calendar used by Ezekiel placed the beginning of the year in the spring, and it was adopted by the P editors: "Tnis month [Nisan] shall stand at the head of your calendar; you shall reckon it the first month of the year" (Ex 12:2). The passage continues with regulations for the selection of the Passover lamb on the 10th of this month. There is no mention of any New Year's festival, and this would have been the logical place to mention it if it existed. In the period after the Exile, Ezra knew of no such festival either. He read the Law to the people on the first day of the seventh month (Tishri) and urged them to be glad, but he made no allusion to its being New Year's Day (Neh 7:72–8:12).

150 There are two other relevant texts, edited after the time of Ezra. Lv 23:24–25 legislates that the first day of the seventh month is to be a day of rest, on which sacrifices are to be offered, an assembly held, and acclamations sung. This legislation is developed further in Nm 29:1–6; here the day is called "The Day of Acclamation," and the sacrifices to be offered are specified. However, this is hardly a New Year festival, for in both Lv 23 and Nm 28–29, the Passover is considered the beginning of the year. It seems that the first of Tishri was merely a special new moon celebration; it may be, too, that this feast commemorated the old calendar, according to which the year used to begin in the fall. None of the Jewish extra-biblical writings from the pre-Christian era mention a New Year feast; Josephus and Philo are likewise silent. Thus, it remains impossible to say precisely when the modern festival of Rosh Hashana was instituted.

151 **(VIII) A Feast of the Enthronement of Yahweh?** Many eminent scholars insist that there was a New Year festival in the OT, even if it was not known as such. They find it in the Feast of Tents, which occurred at the turn of the year and was actually a "New Year Feast of Yahweh," a "Feast of Yahweh's Enthronement," or a "Feast of Yahweh's Kingship." The proponents of this theory give the following arguments.

152 *First*, there was a New Year Feast in Babylon during the opening 12 days of Nisan (March-April). It commemorated the renewal of creation and the kingship of the god Marduk. The creation epic was recited and the victorious deity was acclaimed with the cry, "Marduk is king!" The same type of festival is said to have existed in Egypt and is presumed to have existed in Canaan, where the Israelites would have found and adopted it. From all this some scholars conclude that a similar rite was performed at Jerusalem during the Feast of Tents. In reply, it must be pointed out that the ritual carried out at Babylon dates from the Neo-Babylonian period (612–539 BC), even though its origins probably extend further back into Mesopotamian history. (Assyrian and Hittite texts from the end of the second millennium indicate that there was an analogous festival in Assyria and Asia Minor; but they give no evidence of a rite such as that found in Babylonia.) The extension of the Babylonian rite to Canaan and Israel is, in the light of present evidence, quite gratuitous.

153 *Second*, many OT passages are thought to contain vestiges of this ritual, especially the Psalms of the Kingdom of God (47; 93; 96–99). It is claimed that they were really "Psalms of the Enthronement of Yahweh" and were used in the liturgy of the Feast of Tents (→ Psalms, 35:6, 9, 63). Yet in these psalms, the phrase *yhwh mālak* does not signify "Yahweh has become king," and it is impossible to understand how the Israelites could have conceived of anyone's enthroning Yahweh. Even in the Babylonian texts alleged as parallels, the words "Marduk is king" are not an enthronement formula, but an acclamation like "Long live the king!" Such a cry was an acknowledgment of existing kingship, not a voice vote. These psalms, then, which celebrate Yahweh's kingship, have nothing to do with any supposed enthronement. Furthermore, they are almost certainly post-exilic and could not have been used in a feast celebrated during the royal period.

154 *Third*, it is maintained that the narratives of the transfer of the Ark to Jerusalem (2 Sm 6:1–23; 1 Kgs 8:1–13) were recited liturgically during an annual procession leading Yahweh to his throne. This procession would have taken place at the Feast of Tents. However, these narratives deal with two different transfers of the Ark, one to the temporary tent set up by David, the other to the Temple, events given liturgical expression in Pss 24 and 132. There is no evidence, however, that either the narratives or the psalms were used during the Feast of Tents or in any hypothetical enthronement of Yahweh. It is significant that when the Israelites sought a deeper religious meaning for the Feast of Tents, they made it a commemoration not of creation, but of the period their ancestors had spent in the desert after being liberated from slavery in Egypt. It became part of the memorial of the covenant experience that gave meaning to Israelite existence and history, and not the dramatization of a myth.

LATER OLD TESTAMENT FEASTS

155 **(I) The Day of Atonement.** Like the Passover and Rosh Hashana, Yom Kippur is one of the better known Jewish feasts. In NT times it had achieved such prestige as to be called simply "The Day," and it is under this title (*Yoma*) that the Mishnah treats of it. Ever since its institution it has been celebrated on the same date, the 10th of Tishri (September-October), the seventh month (Lv 23:27–32; Nm 29:7–11).

156 **(A) Ritual.** This is given in detail in Lv 16.

The ritual of expiation. The Day of Atonement was a day of complete rest, penance, and fasting. In a solemn assembly at the Temple, special sacrifices were offered in atonement for the sanctuary, the clergy, and the people. There seems to be a combination of two distinct rituals in Lv 16. According to the first or levitical ritual, the high priest offered a bull as a sacrifice for his own sins and those of the whole Aaronic priesthood. Then he went into the Holy of Holies to incense the *kappōret* of the Ark (→ 46 above) and to sprinkle it with blood from the bull (16:11–14). This was the only day during the year that he entered this holiest of places. Next, he sacrificed a goat for the sins of the people; he also took some of its blood into the Holy of Holies to sprinkle it on the *kappōret* (16:15). Blood was rubbed and sprinkled on the altar too (16:16–19).

157 *The goat for Azazel.* Interwoven in the levitical ritual is another that reflects a different mentality. The community presented two goats, and lots were cast to determine their fate: One was chosen for Yahweh, the other "for Azazel." The one chosen for Yahweh was sacrificed for the sins of the people (→ 83–85 above). The high priest then imposed hands on the other goat, symbolically transferring to it all the sins of the community. A man led this goat into the desert, thus removing the sins of the people (16:8–10,20–22). This man contracted legal uncleanness and had to wash himself and to change his clothes before re-entering the assembly (16:26).

This ritual recalls what was done in Babylon annually on the fifth of Nisan. A chanter, intoning incantations, purified the sanctuaries of Bel and Nabu with water, oil, and perfumes. Then another man decapitated a sheep and rubbed the corpse against the temple of Nabu to purify it. Next the two of them carried the head and body of the sheep to the Euphrates and threw them in. Then they retired to the country and could not return until the 12th of Nisan, when the New Year festival came to an end. There are undeniable similarities between this ceremony and that of the scapegoat on Yom Kippur; but there are differences, too—especially the use of the scapegoat in Israel to carry away the sins of the people. Other peoples had similar rites; and there is an analogy for the scapegoat within Israelite ritual itself, namely in the bird that was released in the biblical ritual for cleansing from leprosy (→ 118 above).

But there is more to the ritual of the Day of Atonement, and it is the notion of the goat being destined "for Azazel." The Gk and Lat versions call it the "goat sent out"; the most usual Eng translation is "scapegoat." Another recently suggested translation is "for the precipice" over which the goat would have been pushed. The parallelism of the phrases "for Yahweh" and "for Azazel" almost demands that the latter be a proper name, and it is preferable to see in Azazel a demon of some sort. This is the interpretation of the Syriac version of Lv, of the Targum, and of *1 Enoch*, which identifies Azazel as the prince of devils who was banished to the desert. It would agree with the Israelite notion that devils dwelt in the desert (Is 13:21; 34:11–14; see Tob 8:3 and Mt 12:43). However, we note that the transfer and expiation of the people's sins are actually effected by Yahweh: "But the goat determined by lot for Azazel he [Aaron] shall set alive before the Lord, so that with it he may make atonement by sending it off to Azazel in the desert" (Lv 16:10). There is no question here of a sacrifice to the Lord, and the idea of offering a sacrifice of any kind to a demon would have been abhorrent to the Israelites.

158 **(B) Institution of the Feast of Atonement.** Certainly there are very ancient elements in the ritual for this feast, elements that were combined with levitical customs and adapted to orthodox religious ideas. Such a combination is evident in the ritual of a red heifer and of the purification of a leper (→ 116–119 above). But there is no allusion to the feast in any pre-exilic text. In Ezekiel's prophecy of the future Temple he envisioned a ceremony to take place on the 1st and 7th of the first month. On the 1st a bull would be sacrificed and its blood used to purify the Temple and the altar; on the 7th a similar sacrifice would take place for the indeliberate sins of the people (Ez 45:18–20). In spite of a fundamental similarity, this is not the Day of Atonement, which fell on the 10th of the seventh month; and Ezekiel does not mention the ceremony of the scapegoat. The books Ezr and Neh make no mention of the feast. This may be because they had no occasion to do so, but their silence is at least a negative indication for the existence of the feast in the early post-exilic period. All the available evidence, then, points to a relatively late date for the Feast of the Atonement, but it is impossible to determine that date with any precision.

159 **(II) Feast of Hanukkah—Dedication.** Hebrew *ḥanukkâ*, as rendered in Greek (*ta enkainia*) signifies "inauguration" or "renewal." The usual Eng translation for the title of the feast is Dedication; Josephus gives it another name, the Feast of Lights.

(A) Origin and History. The origin of the Feast of Hanukkah is described in 1 Mc 4:36–59. The tyrant Antiochus Epiphanes had desecrated the Temple and its altar and had put up on the site of the altar of holocausts a pagan altar. This was the Abomination of Desolation (1 Mc 1:57; Dn 9:27; 11:31); upon it he offered the first sacrifice to Zeus Olympios on the 25th of Kisleu (December) 167 BC. Just three years later, on this same date, Judas Maccabeus purified the sanctuary, erected a new altar, and dedicated it (2 Mc 10:5). It was agreed that the event be commemorated annually (1 Mc 4:59), yet for the next twelve years or so the feast could not have been observed with any regularity because of the military situation (→ History of Israel, 75:109–111). Once freedom was definitively won and Jonathan became high priest in 152, the regular observance of the feast was resumed. It is mentioned in Jn 10:22 and in Josephus (*Ant.* 12.7,7 § 323–26). Pharisee circles were rather cool toward it, since it redounded to the glory of the despised Hasmoneans; but their attitude did not affect its general popularity.

160 **(B) Ritual.** The feast lasted eight days beginning on the 25th of Kisleu and was characterized by an atmosphere of great rejoicing. Sacrifices were offered in the Temple; and thyrsus, green branches, and palms were carried in procession, while appropriate hymns were sung (2 Mc 10:6–8; see 1 Mc 4:54). Ps 30, entitled "A song for the dedication of the Temple," was most likely one of these hymns, but the principal hymns were the Hallel Pss (113–118). A distinguishing feature of this feast was the use of lights, and this inspired Josephus to call it the *Feast of Lights*. We learn from the Mishnah and later rabbinical writings that the people lit lamps in front of their houses, adding one each day for the duration of the feast. This is a later development, for the lighting of lamps referred to in 1 Mc 4:50 indicates the restoration of the candelabra in the Temple. However, 2 Mc 1:8 does refer to the lighting of lamps—but again in the Temple; and Ps 118:27 reads: "The Lord is God, and he has given us light. Join in procession with leafy boughs up to the horns of the altar." At any rate, the use of lights became a traditional feature of the feast and this continued to be the case even after the destruction of the Temple in AD 70.

161 The similarity between the rituals of Hanukkah and Tents is inescapable; in fact 2 Mc stresses it quite explicitly (1:9; 10:6). Possibly Judas Maccabee deliberately patterned the ritual after that of Tents, for it was in connection with the Tents that Solomon's Temple (1 Kgs 8:2,65) and the post-exilic altar (Ezr 3:4) had been dedicated. Both feasts lasted eight days, and in both palms were carried in procession. There were differences, too: The Hallel Pss were probably sung first at Hanukkah and later extended to Passover, Pentecost, and Tents; and during Hanukkah no huts were erected. The lights that figured so prominently in Hanukkah are quite distinctive.

162 **(C) Suggested Influences.** In spite of the clear account of the origin of the feast and of its connection with a specific historical event, some scholars insist that Hanukkah is actually a Jewish version of the pagan feast of the winter solstice and that there is a clear connection between Hanukkah and Enoch, whose life span of 365 years coincided perfectly with the number of days in a solar year (Gn 5:23). Others equate Hanukkah with the Roman feast of *Sol Invictus* (December 25). Still others point to the fact that when Antiochus Epiphanes was in control, he made the Jews wear ivy crowns and march in a procession honoring Bacchus (2 Mc 6:7) and that he imported an Athenian (2 Mc 6:1) to instruct them in the ritual—but these rites did not take place on December 25. Finally, others see in the lighting of a new lamp each night, a symbol of the lengthening of the days after the winter solstice.

Why should we resort to hypotheses when the facts of the case are at our disposal? It would seem antecedently improbable that the Jews would adopt pagan customs to celebrate the elimination of pagan influences from the Temple. Furthermore, it would be awkward indeed to introduce a definite date from the solar calendar into the relatively flexible lunar year. If pagan customs affected the choice of the date for Hanukkah, they did so only indirectly. Judas Maccabee selected this date to erase the memory not only of the profanation of the altar, which had occurred on the 25th Kisleu, but also the memory of the pagan sacrifice that was offered every month on the 25th day, which was Antiochus' birthday (2 Mc 6:7). The carrying of branches in a procession honoring Yahweh may also have been a reaction against the pagan custom that the Jews had been forced to follow in the cult of Bacchus. Similarly, the lighting of lamps in front of the houses may have been intended to replace the burning of incense at the doors of houses as ordered by Antiochus (1 Mc 1:55). It is not clear why one more lamp was lighted each day, but this sort of thing is not uncommon in folk customs and in the liturgy (witness the Catholic Advent wreath ceremony or the former Tenebrae service). The Jews themselves had a similar gradation—but in reverse—in the liturgy of the Feast of Tents. According to Nm 29:13–32, one less bull was sacrificed each day. Thus the feast of Hanukkah was essentially a commemoration of the purification of the Temple, and all its rites may be explained as legitimate reactions to the abominations practiced while Jerusalem was under pagan domination.

163 **(III) Feast of Purim.**

(A) Date and Ritual. According to Josephus, this feast was celebrated on the 14th and 15th of Adar (February-March) in memory of the victory of the Jews of Persia over their would-be exterminators. For the ritual we must turn to the rabbinical writings. The 13th of Adar was a fast day; in the evening lamps were lit in all the houses, and the people went to the synagogue. The next two days were festive days. All attended the synagogue for the reading of the Book of Esther and the congregation would interrupt the reading with curses against the villain Aman and all his ilk. The meeting closed with a solemn blessing of Mordecai, of Esther, and of the Israelites in general. The Feast of Purim was the occasion for the exchange of gifts and distribution of alms; but apart from these expressions of piety and charity, it was the most worldly of the Jewish festivals—a sort of Carnival, complete with the wearing of masks and other disguises. The rabbis laid down a rule that one had to stop drinking when he could no longer distinguish between "Cursed be Aman!" and "Blessed be Mordecai!"

164 **(B) Book of Esther.** The story of Esther gave this feast its existence and its name. According to 3:7 and 9:24 Aman cast lots (*pûrîm*) to determine the fate of the Jews, which was to be extermination. This he had done on the 14th of Adar, but his scheme boomeranged and he himself was hanged. Now *pûr* is neither Hebrew nor Persian, but Akkadian; and it is strange both that the lots play such an insignificant role in the story itself and that there is no reference to them in the feast to which they have given a name. In fact, 3:7 has all the earmarks of an interpolation, and 9:20–32 is an account of a letter that Mordecai wrote to his fellow Jews urging them to observe the feast. One suspects that the two passages were interpolated to make the feast acceptable to the Jews as a whole and to fix its name as Purim. The whole book, in fact, seems designed as a justification for the feast. Everything in the story converges on the celebration that took place the day after the massacre of the Persians, and the final verses (9:16–19) are an attempt to explain why the feast lasted two days (14th and 15th of Adar). Yet there may have been some historical basis for the story that was freely expanded into the "legend" of a feast (De Vaux, *op. cit.*, 515; → Esther, 38:30).

165 **(C) Origin of the Feast.** If Est were a truly historical book, the answer to this question would be as easy as the answer to the question of the origin of Hanukkah. But Est is not historical; it is a story designed, among other things, to justify a rather peculiar feast. The name of the God of Israel is not even mentioned in the Hebrew (protocanonical) form of the book. Purim itself was not a particularly religious festival: It was not specifically related to salvation history and contained no elements of worship. It was clearly a foreign feast, but its precise origins are not easy to determine. Attempts to trace it to Babylonia and to translate it entirely into terms of Babylonian mythology (Mordecai-Esther = Marduk-Ishtar; Aman-Vashti = Aman-Mashti) are quite unconvincing. The authentic Persian flavor of Est points rather to a Persian origin for the feast; yet the Babylonian correspondences between Mordecai and Marduk and between Esther and Ishtar are hardly coincidental. Moreover, the word *pûru* is definitely Akkadian (Assyro-Babylonian). The feast, then, must have had roots in several cultures.

At any rate, it originated in the Eastern Jewish Diaspora and probably commemorated a projected genocide from which the Jews narrowly escaped. It also had many of the elements of a pagan New Year festival (amusements, banquets, exchange of gifts, etc.) and was probably patterned after such a Persian festival. If it came to Palestine by way of Mesopotamia, it could have picked up some Babylonian features en route, specifically the name of Purim. The first mention of the feast in a Palestinian milieu is in 2 Mc 15:36, where it is called the "Day of Mordecai" and is dated the 14th of Adar; Josephus is the next to mention it (*Ant.* 11.6,13 § 295). Only by stretching categories can we include this feast under the religious institutions of Israel. But it does have its roots, however tenuous, in a sacred book of the OT and so merits consideration.

77

ASPECTS OF OLD TESTAMENT THOUGHT

John L. McKenzie

BIBLIOGRAPHY

1 Alt, A., *Essays on Old Testament History and Religion* (Anchor paperback; N.Y., 1968). Barr, J., *The Semantics of Biblical Language* (Oxford, 1961). Boman, T., *Hebrew Thought Compared with Greek* (London, 1960). Butterfield, H., *Christianity and History* (N.Y., 1949). Charlier, C., *The Christian Approach to the Bible* (Westminster, 1958). Eichrodt, *Theology*. Guillet, J., *Themes of the Bible* (Notre Dame, 1960). Jacob, E., *Theology of the Old Testament* (N.Y., 1958). Kaufmann, Y., *The Religion of Israel* (Chicago, 1960). Knight, G. A. Y., *A Christian Theology of the Old Testament* (London, 1959). Köhler, L., *Old Testament Theology* (Phila., 1957). Léon-Dufour, X. (ed.), *Dictionary of Biblical Theology* (N.Y., 1968). Levie, J., *The Bible, Word of God in Words of Men* (N.Y., 1961). McKenzie, J. L., *The Two-Edged Sword* (Milwaukee, 1956). Pedersen, J., *Israel*, (London, 1926, 1940). Renckens, H., *The Religion of Israel* (N.Y., 1966). Ringgren, H., *Israelite Religion* (Phila., 1966). Robinson, H. W., *Inspiration and Revelation in the Old Testament* (Oxford, 1946). Rowley, H. H., *The Faith of Israel* (London, 1956). Smart, J. D., *The Interpretation of Scripture* (Phila., 1961). Van Imschoot, *Théologie*, vol. 2; *Theology of the Old Testament*, 1 *God* (N.Y., 1965). Von Allmen, J. J., *A Companion to the Bible* (N.Y., 1958). Von Rad, *OT Theology*. Vriezen, *Outline*.

2 OUTLINE

THE GOD OF ISRAEL

3 **(I) Introduction.** Although biblical theology as a formal discipline is now nearly 200 years old, there is still wide disagreement on its object, principles, and methods (→ Modern OT Criticism, 70:51–55). Something should be said about the limitations of biblical theology as it is understood in this essay. Biblical theology is a part of theology as a whole; it cannot claim to present a synthesis of the whole of revealed doctrine, and in particular OT theology cannot make this claim. Biblical theology does not lend itself to a synthesis like the synthesis of speculative theology created by Thomas Aq.; the treatment adopted here, as in most recent books on the subject, is a collection of essays on topics or themes, with no attempt to integrate them into a single whole. (This contribution is not a complete collection of theological themes; it contains only those themes that in the judgment of the writer were most deserving of inclusion.) Biblical theology does not follow the categories of speculative theology; it must create its own categories drawn from biblical thought itself, and it is precisely here that an area of disagreement among scholars is found.

4 Biblical theology must be historical in its methods and exposition. The revelation of the Bible is enmeshed in the historic experience of Israel, and it is impossible to fix it at any one point that recapitulates the entire experience. Limitations of space have not permitted the full exposition of this factor here. Biblical theology, at best, is an aid to the understanding of the Bible; it does not communicate an understanding. The themes stated theologically here were originally uttered in a concrete historical situation of urgency, usually with a depth of conviction and even of passion that matched the urgency. Understanding the Bible requires that one senses the urgency as much as one comprehends the intelligible content of the utterance. Biblical theology can show that these utterances fall into the structure of Israelite faith; but the impact of that faith is perceived only when one hears it announced by its own spokesmen. Biblical theology is not a substitute for exegesis but presupposes it (→ Hermeneutics, 71:23).

5 **(II) Names of God.** The object of theology is the knowledge of God. Theological knowledge of God is understood to be an elaboration and a synthesis of concepts formed by combining the data of revealed theological sources with the conclusions of dialectical reasoning. In the OT this type of thinking does not appear. Israelite thought in the biblical era lacked the discursive reasoning developed by Gk philosophy (→ 23–24 below) and was incapable of general and abstract speculation. In Hebrew "to know God" is to encounter a personal reality; and a person is not known unless his name is known.

6 In Hebr speech there is a peculiar association of the person and the name that is foreign to our idiom. "Name" is used in contexts where modern language uses "person" or "self." To have no name is to have no existence in reality; when one's name is blotted out, one ceases to exist. To give a name is to confer identity and not merely to distinguish from other individuals or species; when God creates (Gn 1), he gives a name to each object of his creation. The conferring of a name is an act of power and an assertion of ownership or some other form of control. A change of name indicates a change of state or condition, the beginning of a new existence.

To know the name is to know the reality named. For this reason the OT reflects the love of etymologies which, if analyzed linguistically, are fanciful. The name is pregnant with meaning; a connection by paronomasia with a characteristic of a person or an event in his life reveals the person more fully. Hence the knowledge of God is disclosed in his name.

7 **(A) El, Elohim, Eloah.** EL transliterates the Hebr form of the common word for deity in the Semitic languages. In polytheistic belief *'ēl* is the word for a member of the divine species, just as "man" is the word for an individual member of the human species. ELOHIM has no cognate in the other Semitic languages; it is probably related to El. Grammatically *'ĕlōhîm* is a Hebr plural; this is often taken to reflect the polytheistic thinking current among the ancestors of Israel. "Elohim" is applied either to the one God worshiped by Israel or to the gods of other peoples; in the second usage it can be plural in meaning as well as in form. When it is used of the God of Israel, "Elohim," despite its plural form, is singular in meaning and grammatical agreement, except in a few passages where the polytheistic reminiscences of the narrative from which the Bible borrowed still shine through, e.g., Gn 1:26: "God said, 'Let *us*... in the *image of God* he created them—*male and female.*'" (This passage may be a reminiscence of a heavenly pantheon of "elohim," male and female.) "El" appears as a personal divine name borne by the head of the pantheon of Ugarit. Possibly the Ugaritic usage is the only remaining trace of an earlier and more widely diffused theology in which the name El was a proper name before it became a common name. ELOAH (*'ĕlôah*), which also lacks a cognate in other languages, appears only in poetry and seems to be no more than a poetic variant. Hebrew has no feminine word for deity.

8 There is no generally accepted etymological explanation of the meaning of the names El and Elohim. Most scholars connect the names with a word meaning "power," and it is not unlikely that power was the fundamental and essential note of deity in the ancient Semitic world. Even if this is the proper explanation, "power" is not reflected in the Hebr usage of the words. If the Israelite idea of the essential note of deity can be summed up in one word, it is the word "holy," felicitously paraphased by R. Otto as "wholly other"; the essential note is that God is totally unlike any of his creatures. Hebrew exhibits a number of adjectival uses of the names El and Elohim in which a person or a thing is said to be identical with El or Elohim or to belong to El or Elohim. These attributions raise the object so designated above the ordinary level of human or terrestrial being and locate it on a higher level that is most properly called superhuman. The object is raised because in some such quality as size, strength, or sheer wonder it exceeds the normal. In ancient Semitic usage there was no sharp clear line that divided the gods from other superhuman beings: The world of El-Elohim was the world of being and power superior to man. But in the Bible when Yahweh is called El or Elohim, he is necessarily raised above even this superhuman world to a level that belongs to him alone.

9 **(B) Shaddai.** According to the E and P sources (→ Pentateuch, 1:13–17), the divine name Yahweh was not known before Moses—a genuine historical tradition—and in the P source Shaddai is the name by which the patriarchs invoke God. The name is also attested in some older poems outside the P source (Nm 24:4,16; Gn 49:25). The meaning of this name, which appears only in the Bible, is not certain; it was rendered in the LXX by *pantokratōr*, "Almighty." Many recent scholars follow the suggestion of W. F. Albright that the name means "The One of the Mountain." The name thus interpreted reflects the common ancient Semitic belief that the home of the gods lay on "the mountain of the north," mentioned in some passages of the OT (Is 14:13; Ps 48:3; → History of Israel, 75:41).

10 **(C) Baal, Adonai, Melek.** These three titles convey the idea of the power to rule. BAAL, "owner," is rarely used of Yahweh because it was a conventional title of the most popular god of the Canaanites (→ Excursus Israel, 11:12). Often, however, when Baal appears as a component in an Israelite name (e.g., son of Saul = Ishbaal; son of Jonathan = Meribbaal: 1 Chr 8:33–34), we may suspect that the child was given a Yahweh/baal name, rather than being named after the pagan god. Later OT writers took a dim view of the use of "baal" in a name and often changed it to "bosheth" (Hebr "shame"). Thus in 2 Sm 2:8 and 9:6, the names of the two men just cited appear as Ishbosheth and Mephibosheth. ADONAI (*'ădōnāy*, "my lord"—this pronunciation is used only of Yahweh) is the same word as *'ădōnî*, by which the king was usually addressed. MELEK, "king," is used frequently of Yahweh. Kingship was an attribute of many gods of the ancient Semitic peoples, but here as elsewhere the Israelite development of the idea follows its own way. Yahweh is the king of Israel, king of all nations, king in virtue of creation, king savior who delivers Israel, the eschatological king who establishes his universal reign in the end of history (→ 75, 165–166 below). It is not possible to determine which of these aspects was primary; but the view of the covenant as a vassal–overlord relationship (→ 81–82 below) suggests that the kingship of Yahweh was not a later development of Israelite thought. The functions of the ancient king were war and law, and Yahweh exercises both of these functions for Israel. He is the savior who fights the battles of Israel, the lawmaker who imposes a code of conduct, and the judge who sanctions the code that he imposes.

11 **(D) Yahweh.** This is the personal name of the God of Israel. The pronunciation "Yahweh" has been recovered in recent times. In the Hebr Bible the name is written with the four consonants (Tetragrammaton) *YHWH* and the vowels of the word *'ădōnāy* (adonai = "lord"—at some time in the late pre-Christian centuries Jews ceased to pronounce the sacred name out of an exaggerated reverence, and said instead *Adonai*). This combination produced the non-word Jehovah that appeared in the AV.

12 The meaning of the name is uncertain, and the explanations that have been suggested are too numerous to cite. The text of Ex 3:13–14 is not an explanation and is extremely difficult to translate. The Hebr Bible has the name in the first person, *'ehyeh 'ăšer 'ehyeh*. The LXX rendered the name as "I am the existent [*ho ōn* = he who is]"; the Vg as "I am who am." Following P. Haupt, many have suggested that the formula was originally in the third person and read *yahweh 'ăšer yahweh*. Most modern scholars would connect the form *'ehyeh* or *yahweh* with the verb *hāwāh*, the archaic form of the verb "to be." In particular, W. F. Albright and F. M. Cross insist that *yahweh* is from the causative conjugation of this verb and means "he causes to be."

As a name, "Yahweh" is for Albright a fragment of a longer name that he reconstructs as *yahweh-'ašer-yihweh*, "he who brings into being whatever comes into being" (*FSAC* [2nd ed.] 15–16, 259–61). The name so explained identifies Yahweh as the creator. F. M. Cross (*HarvTR* 55 [1962] 256) has a variation on this thesis, for he thinks of "Yahweh" as part of a liturgical title for El, e.g., *'ēl 'ăšer* [or *dū*, an older relative] *yahweh ṣ^{e}bā'ôt* = "El who brings into being the hosts" (→ 14 below). On the other hand, if some explanation similar to the translations of the LXX and Vg is accepted and more emphasis is put on existence, then the name signifies that Yahweh is the one who really is—possibly the one who really is *elohim*, God. (However, this emphasis should not be carried into the philosophical sphere as if the Bible were telling us that the essence of God is existence.) But perhaps all this speculation on the etymology of Yahweh is deceptive; for even if we knew with certainty the original meaning of the name, we would have no assurance that the Hebrews understood the name correctly (most etymologies in the Bible are popular and scientifically incorrect). The usage of the name Yahweh in the Bible shows no awareness of any etymology, and there is no evidence in the OT of a theology being built around the meaning of the name. The name occurs over 6700 times and is the usual designation of God, more frequently than all other designations combined. It is also a frequent component of personal names: those that begin with Je/Jehu/Jeho and those that end with iah/jah (Adonijah, Elijah, Jeremiah, Isaiah, Jehoshaphat, Jehoiachin). It is, so to speak, the Israelite name for God by which the association of Yahweh and Israel is mutually accepted and proclaimed.

13 The revelation of the name to Moses in Ex 3 is attributed to the E tradition; and the P tradition of Ex 6:3 affirms that the name was not known to the patriarchs. Although the J tradition uses the name from the beginning of its narrative in Gn 2, this should not be understood as a contradiction of the E and P tradition, but as unawareness of it. In the theology of the name explained above (→ 6), the revelation of the name Yahweh to Israel through Moses represented a new and fuller revelation of the personal reality of Yahweh. This is reflected in the Exodus traditions whereby the name of Yahweh is associated with the origin of the covenant (→ 81ff. below). Israel knows its God by this name, and no further definition or qualification is needed. By this name he is proclaimed as the personal divine being who has revealed himself to Israel, who has vindicated himself by the saving acts of the Exodus and has established a covenant relationship with the people he has made. The distinctive name "Yahweh" indicates that he is a personal being whose essence and attributes can be shared by no other being.

14 **(F) Yahweh Sebaoth.** This title, "Yahweh (God) of Hosts," does not occur in Gn through Jgs and is particularly associated with the shrine built for the Ark of the Covenant at Shiloh from which the Ark was led out to battle (1 Sm 1:3; 4:4). It appears frequently in the prophets (Is 1–39, Jer, Am, Hag, Zech). The identification of the "hosts" is difficult. Scholars propose the armies of Israel, or "the hosts of heaven" (the heavenly bodies or even the angels), or "the hosts of heaven and earth" (the created universe). The prophetic contexts of the title do not recommend identification of the "hosts" with the armies of Israel; but the usage in 1 Sm does, and possibly this was the earliest sense. The third proposal is most in harmony with the prophetic usage; the title would then designate Yahweh as "lord of creation."

15 **(F) Patriarchal Names for God.** As A. Alt ("The God of the Fathers," *op. cit.*, 1–100) has shown, one form under which the patriarchs worshiped God can be classified as "the God of the Fathers." The God who had dealings with the patriarch was identified as "the God of Abraham" (or "of Isaac," or "of Jacob"). This God of Abraham was worshiped by Abraham and his clan, and was to some extent a tribal God. Perhaps the God of each patriarch had a special title, e.g., the Shield of Abraham (Gn 15:1); the Fear of Isaac (or perhaps Kinsman—Gn 31:42,53); the Mighty One of Jacob (Gn 49:24). Worshiping the god of one special figure is customary only among nomadic people. The earliest example is in the 18th cent. BC in Cappadocia, thus contemporary with the patriarchal period. Settled nations can worship a national god associated with a particular region, but nomads who travel need a personal or clan god who goes with them. The theological strain of "the God of the Fathers" is important in biblical religion because it involves a personal relationship between God and the patriarch (and the clan), and thus works against formalism in religion. It supplies the background of the future covenantal relationship between God and Israel. Moreover, it also is a deterrent against any thought that God is found in only one place.

16 Another form under which the patriarchs worshiped God was as El with various qualifying words: El Elyon (Gn 14:18); El Olam (Gn 21:33); El Shaddai (Gn 17:1; → 9 above); etc. F. M. Cross (*art. cit.*) has shown that these qualifying words are not names of individual gods (i.e., the god Elyon, Shaddai, or Olam) but are adjectival titles of the one God El. When the patriarchs came into the land, they found that the Canaanites worshiped the supreme God El at various sanctuaries, under various titles. Thus El Elyon (God Most High) was worshiped at Jerusalem; El Olam (God Eternal) was worshiped at Beer-sheba; El Berith (God of the Covenant) was worshiped at Shechem. (For these sanctuaries, → Religious Institutions, 76:40, 43, 54.) The Bible portrays the patriarchs worshiping El under these titles at the respective sanctuaries. Comparing this to what we have said about "the God of the Fathers," we find that apparently the patriarchs did not see any contradiction in combining the worship of a God who had revealed himself to them in a particular way with the worship of a universal God already known in Canaan. Thus, Gn 49:25 puts "the God of your Father" in parallelism with El Shaddai. The El worship of the patriarchs added a universal aspect not found in worship of the God of the Fathers, and thus both the God of nature (El) and the God of history (the God of Abraham) played a role in pre-Mosaic religion. When the God of history revealed himself to Moses as Yahweh, he was continuing the tradition of the God of the Fathers (Ex 3:15), but the Bible does not hesitate to apply to him the designations of El as Elyon, Shaddai, and Olam.

17 **(III) The One God.** Israelite thought is neither discursive nor speculative. The speculative questions of the existence of God and his unicity were not considered and could not be considered in the OT, for the Israelites had no patterns of thought in which questions like this could be asked and answered. In the ancient Near East the existence of divine beings was universally accepted without question. As for unicity, in Israel there is no clear and unambigious denial of the existence of other gods than Yahweh before Dt-Is in the 6th cent. BC. (However, Dt 32:39 has the same emphasis as Dt-Is, and some scholars would date this Song of Moses to a considerably earlier period; → Deuteronomy, 6:74.) The absence of such a denial should not be taken to mean that the Israelites shared in some mitigated way the polytheistic beliefs of other ancient peoples; rather they rejected these beliefs, but couched their rejection in other than philosophical terms.

If we pose these questions and answer them in biblical terms, we may say that whether or not there are many elohim ("god," "gods"; → 7 above), there is only one Yahweh (see C. J. Labuschagne, *The Incomparability of Yahweh in the Old Testament* [Leiden, 1966]). No matter what one understands by "elohim," Yahweh is elohim in a way in which no other being is. If the Israelite were to grant the existence of other elohim, he would deny that they are genuine elohim. The question was not whether there is only one elohim, but whether there is any elohim like Yahweh. To the question put in this way the Israelites never gave any answer except a categorical denial. We observe, then, that in its early phases the Israelite vocabulary cannot adequately express Israelite belief.

18 In the first instance, the fact that there is only one Yahweh is clear from his name, which belongs to no one else. It is clear also from his unique relationship to Israel, which is shared with no other. The relationship is one of election and covenant that imposes upon Israel demands made by no other god upon his people. The most striking demand is that Israel shall worship no god but Yahweh. This is a violent departure from the cult patterns of the ancient Semitic world. Among the neighbors of Israel no god is conceived as being so entirely and solely the benefactor and the judge of his worshipers that reverence for other gods is excluded—the cosmos is not the province of any single god. For the Israelites there is nothing they can ask from any other god and nothing to fear from any other god. This is not an explicit profession of monotheism, but it is to treat other gods as negligible.

19 The prohibition of not having other gods does not imply merely that Israel is Yahweh's peculiar possession from which he has excluded the action of competitors. Rather, wherever man and nature are found, there is the domain of Yahweh. He alone creates, and he alone directs the operations of natural forces—a concept that is peculiarly significant against the background of ancient nature deities. Theogony, the myth of the origin of the gods, is found everywhere else in the ancient Near East. It is highly important that the Israelites ask neither about the origin of Yahweh nor about the origin of other gods. To ask about the origin of Yahweh would be to deny that he is wholly other (→ 8 above), and to ask about the origin of other gods would be to admit their reality.

20 The unique nature of Yahweh is further demonstrated by the prohibition of images. We know of no other ancient Near Eastern god who was not visually represented. Their images were anthropomorphic, except in Egypt where, for reasons obscure even to the Egyptians, some gods were represented theriomorphically (i.e., by animal images) or symbolically, as in the eccentric cult of Aton which used the Sun Disk (→ Biblical Archaeology, 74:58). The prohibition of representing Yahweh in image is even more striking in contrast with the biblical habit of speaking of Yahweh in human terms (→ 21 below). The prohibition (Ex 20:4; Dt 5:8) forbids the worship of anything in the heavens above, the earth beneath, or the water under the earth. This is intended to be a comprehensive enumeration of the entire visible world, and the commandment denies that Yahweh resembles anything in the universe. He is above and beyond it, and thereby has no resemblance to any elohim known to the Israelites.

Archaeology has illustrated the observance of this commandment. Although hundreds of divine images have been found in Israelite sites, nothing which could be called an image of Yahweh has been discovered. Of course, the OT mentions perversions of the cult of

Yahweh; but modern scholars have shown that even such a prominent instance as the bull or calf image set up at Bethel and at Dan did not involve a representation of Yahweh himself, for the bull was thought of as a pedestal upon which the invisible Yahweh stood (→ Religious Institutions, 76:66).

A common epithet of Yahweh is "the living God"; this designation is by way of contrast with other gods who are sometimes identified with their images. Positively the epithet affirms that Yahweh possesses life, power, and personality: He is alert, attentive, and responsive. As the living God, he is also contrasted with man, who is flesh and mortal—Yahweh gives and sustains life. From these ideas it was not a difficult step to the affirmation that Yahweh alone is elohim. If the gods of other peoples were ineffective, they had not the reality of elohim, and therefore no reality at all. There was nothing but their images, which were lifeless and manufactured.

21 **(IV) Anthropomorphism.** The attribution of human features and behavior to nonhuman beings (along with anthropopathism—the attribution of human feelings to nonhuman beings) is common in both religious and profane literature of all cultures. What makes anthropomorphism worthy of special attention in the OT is the difficulty of reconciling it with the prohibition of images and the explicit denials that Yahweh is like any created being. The fear of a plastic image of Yahweh is in marked contrast with the lack of restraint in employing verbal images. Yahweh has a countenance, eyes, ears, mouth, nostrils, hands, feet. He speaks, hears, smells, laughs, hisses, whistles, strikes, writes, walks. He feels delight, joy, anger, hatred, love, disgust, regret, compassion. The OT never speaks of Yahweh without attributing human traits to him. This is not in itself distinctive; for the gods of other ancient Semitic peoples were personifications of natural forces or social realities to whom were attributed human features and behavior. There is scarcely any OT anthropomorphism that cannot be paralleled in other ancient Semitic literature.

Some explicit restraints that are placed on anthropomorphism in the OT are not so easily paralleled elsewhere. When the OT says that Yahweh is not changeable or infirm of purpose like man (Nm 23:19), that he is elohim and not man (Hos 11:9), that he is spirit and not flesh, it is apparent that the authors of the OT were aware that figures of speech have their limitations. In the context of ancient speech and of ancient religious beliefs, anthropomorphisms certainly made it difficult to understand the transcendence of Yahweh. Furthermore, they might have been an obstacle to the development of a truly spiritual idea of God. Yet an understanding of God is possible through anthropomorphisms that cannot be gained through a more refined and abstract discourse. After all, human speech cannot enunciate the ineffable reality of God by any means.

22 Through anthropomorphic description the living personality of Yahweh is constantly emphasized. This is also expressed through the designation of Yahweh as a living God. The election of Israel, the formation of the covenant, and the saving acts by which Yahweh made Israel a people are acts of favor arising from personal benevolence. The law that is imposed upon Israel in the covenant is the externalization of a vital personal will. The response of Yahweh to love or to disobedience is a personal response of love or anger. His relations with Israel can be represented as the relations of the father to his children or of the husband to his wife. The personal relation of Yahweh to Israel demands a personal response and not merely an official or a cultic posture toward him. It becomes almost a commonplace in the prophetic books that cult without personal commitment is vain and hypocritical. The total demands of Yahweh can be met only by total surrender. Personal communication becomes possible: Yahweh speaks to Israel, and Israel can speak to Yahweh. The reality of his involvement in the history of Israel cannot be doubted. In prayer the speech of the OT attains through anthropomorphism an intimacy and an urgency that is scarcely paralleled elsewhere and cannot be achieved in any other way. The risk of humanizing God is accepted in order that the danger of thinking of him as an abstraction or an impersonal force may be avoided.

23 **(V) Mythopoeic Thinking.** The ancient civilizations of Mesopotamia and Egypt had an extensive mythology that has been largely recovered. The mythology of Canaan has been partly known since 1929 through the documents of ancient Ugarit that illuminate many OT allusions (→ Excursus Israel, 11:11–12; also S. H. Hooke, *Middle Eastern Mythology* [Pelican paperback; London, 1963]). Studies of these documents brought out the differences between the mythological thinking of ancient peoples and the thinking of Israel; and for many years a large number of scholars have agreed that the OT has no mythology. But to deny all mythology in the OT leaves a number of passages without a satisfactory explanation. Moreover, recently it has become clear that the denial of mythology in the OT implies a questionable definition of myth as essentially polytheistic and false.

(A) Definition of Myth. Modern analyses of the nature of myth suggest that it is not, by definition, polytheistic and false. Many myths express a polytheistic or an essentially distorted view of the universe; but this view is not necessarily due to mythological thinking itself, any more than philosophical or theological errors are due to the nature of philosophical and theological thinking. Most critics of myth have measured it against the standards of discursive logic and found it wanting; but in cultures without a developed discursive thought, mythological thinking is the only way in which the mind can approach certain problems that lie beyond sensible experience. These problems involve some of the most important questions that one can ask: the origin of the world and of man; the nature of deity; the relations of man to nature and to deity; the origins of society and of social institutions; the ultimate validation of moral principles; the purpose and direction of human existence. These problems can also be approached by discursive reasoning with its own methods and principles. Myth does not really solve these problems, but it expresses the attitude that man takes in the presence of mystery; it is questionable whether discursive reasoning achieves any more.

24 Myth is defined by E. Cassirer (*Language and Myth*, [N.Y., 1946] 8ff.) as a symbolic form of expression together with art, language, and science. Each of these produces and posits a world of its own. Myth is an intuition and an act of belief. It seeks to impose intelligible form upon the realities that transcend experience. Myth does not attempt the paradox of knowing the unknowable; these realities can be expressed only by symbolic representation created from the data of experience. The symbol easiest to employ and to grasp is the symbol of personal activity, and in the world of myth impersonal causes do not appear.

Myth is couched in narrative, but the narrative is not historical and it is not intended to be historical. The event of myth is not the singular event located in time and space, but the recurring event of *the eternal Now*, as M. Eliade has called it. Myth presents in a story the constant reality of the universe. It does not pretend that the symbol is the reality, but it proposes the symbol as that which affords an insight into a reality beyond understanding. The goal of mythopoeic thinking is truth, not falsehood, and the fact that myth sometimes exhibits contradictory approaches to the reality it seeks is not in opposition to its quest for truth. In the world of discursive thought, the laws of being and of thought demand rigorous consistency. Myth allows that reality cannot be adequately apprehended and concedes the validity of more than one avenue of approach. These several avenues may lead to contradictory expressions, but myth admits contradictions on the assumption that their resolution lies beyond the insight that it conveys.

25 **(B) OT Mythopoeic Thought.** The use of mythical language and imagery in the OT has long been recognized; and since the discovery of the mythological literature of the ancient Near East, it has been possible to identify the sources of many mythological allusions in the OT. The following allusions can be adduced as examples, although not all of them are equally forceful: the personalization of natural phenomena (the sun, Ps 19:5–7; the morning star, Is 14:12ff.; the rainbow, Gn 9:12ff.); the eschatological period described as a return to the conditions of the primeval period (Is 11:6–9); etiological stories or stories composed to explain an existing situation, e.g., the stories of the creation of woman from the rib of man (Gn 2:21ff.) and of the origin of human toil and the pains of childbirth (Gn 3:16ff.); the union of the sons of Elohim and the daughters of men (Gn 6:4); the world catastrophe as a reversal of creation and a return to chaos (Is 17:12ff.; 24:19; Jer 4:23); the enthroned Yahweh (Is 6) and the chariot of Yahweh (Ez 1); some features of the Day of Yahweh (Jl 2:10ff.; 3:3ff.); the assembly of the holy ones (Ps 89:18); Jerusalem as the mountain of the north, the mountain of assembly (Ps 48:3); the imagery of the theophany (Ex 19; 33:19–23; Jgs 5:4; Hb 3; → 57 below). The poetic employment of imagery drawn from mythology is not of itself sufficient to establish a pattern of mythopoeic thought; but when these images are viewed in conjunction with other passages of the OT, a pattern that can be called mythopoeic begins to emerge. In these passages imagery drawn from mythology is not mere poetic embellishment, but is employed in a serious effort to express in words an intuition of transcendent reality.

26 Where the OT touches upon problems that in other cultures were the objects of mythopoeic thought, a comparison between Israelite treatment of these problems and the mythologies of other ancient peoples is possible. There is scarcely any mythology without a myth of ORIGINS OR CREATION. Since the discovery of the Mesopotamian myth of creation, *Enuma Elish* (*ANET*, 60–72), it has been evident that Gn 1 exhibits the same superficial and unscientific view of the structure of the visible universe as the Mesopotamian myth (→ Genesis, 2:16). The differences are striking: The Israelite account contains nothing of the origin of the gods or of a cosmic conflict between gods—elements that in the Mesopotamian myth were a vital part of the process of creation. Nothing is left but a tranquil act of creation by word that makes clear the effortless supremacy of the creative deity. The OT account is openly polemic against the Mesopotamian myth, or rather against the conception of creation that is represented in the Mesopotamian myth; but it does not replace the myth with history or science, of which it has none, nor with theological reasoning, unless this term is used very loosely. The Mesopotamian myth is replaced by another myth; the difference lies in the conception of the deity.

27 The OT contains no account of a COSMIC CONFLICT from which creation arises—a common motif in mythology. But the allusions to a victory of Yahweh over the monster of chaos are numerous (→ 51 below), an indication that oral tradition probably contained an account of creation in which Yahweh was the victor in a combat. This combat was found in the myths of both Mesopotamia and Canaan and perhaps was transferred to Yahweh from these sources, thus becoming an example of mythopoeic thinking transformed by the character of Yahweh. It has been noticed above (→ 24) that a feature of mythopoeic thought is to permit several diverse avenues of approach; the allusions to a combat are a diverse approach to creation from that of Gn 1. It is also characteristic of myth that the "event" is not a contingent historical event but a constant in reality, an eternal Now; the allusions to the creative victory of Yahweh treat it as a present and enduring reality. Were Yahweh to relax his domination over the monster, the world would relapse into chaos.

28 The story of the DELUGE exhibits another example of the revision of a foreign myth. No OT passage has so many and such clear literary affinities with extrabiblical literature as the flood story; its dependence on this earlier myth is manifest (*ANET* 42–44, 93–95; → Genesis, 2:39). The Mesopotamian myth is an effort to face the problem of natural catastrophes, accompanied by random destruction. It attributes them to the capricious anger of the gods; for divine anger, like human anger, can be irrational, and man can do nothing except submit to superior power. To the Israelites this was an erroneous conception of the deity. The error was corrected not by eliminating the story but by rewriting it in such a way that the anger of Yahweh is intelligibly motivated by the wickedness of men. In natural catastrophe the Israelites saw the righteous judgment of God on sin, and they expressed this insight by retelling an existing story. This is mythopoeic thinking and, again, the transforming element is the conception of God.

29 There is no ancient myth parallel to the account of the ORIGIN AND FALL OF MAN found in Gn 2–3. But a number of the details of the story echo features of ancient mythology. These details have been woven into a conception of human origins and destiny that is one of the most profound and creative pieces of literature in the entire OT. Here the conception of God is balanced by a conception of man that differs in a striking way from what is found elsewhere in the ancient Near East. In narrative form the story describes the condition of man: his dignity and his fall, his mortality, his relations with God and with the material universe, his moral responsibility, the origin and meaning of sex. Notable is the polemic of the story against the myth and ritual of fertility. To present these profound insights the author uses such mythopoeic symbols as the trees, the serpent, the garden, and the rib. A parallel account of the first man, found in Ez 28:12–16 (→ Ezekiel, 21:63), suggests that this story was told in variant forms in Israel; and the form found in Ez, which is even richer in mythological imagery, may be one of the elements from which Gn 2–3 was composed.

30 Mythopoeic thought in the OT or elsewhere is not deliberately chosen as a mode of poetic expression in preference to logical discourse. Myth arises in cultures in which logical discourse has not been achieved. But myth is never entirely expelled even in advance cultures. It remains the most apt form for the expression of that reality that we have called transcendental, a reality too large and too profound for scientific observation and philosophical analysis. For this reason, the mythopoeic thought of the OT retains not only its charm but also its validity in the history of Christian belief and Christian theology. The history of thought shows that as man's thinking is demythologized, it is proportionately secularized. Mythopoeic thought sees the transcendent reality as pervading the visible universe. In Mesopotamia the origin of kingship was explained by its descent from heaven. Philosophical thought seeks an explanation in processes that can be submitted to logical investigation and analysis. In expelling myth man runs the risk of expelling the divine also. He has not always succeeded in replacing the intuitions of mythopoeic thought with intuitions of a higher order.

31 Pius XII (*Humani Generis*, *EB* 618) echoed a warning uttered by many exegetes of earlier generations when he said that the beliefs of the OT must not be reduced to the level of the mythology of other peoples. It is more accurate to speak of mythopoeic thought in the OT rather than of its myths or mythology. We have alluded several times in the preceding paragraphs to the factor that makes Israelite mythopoeic thought unique in the ancient Near East and is the ultimate basis of its validity, namely, the Israelite conception of the reality of God—Israel's belief in the personal character of Yahweh. This insight into the divine reality the Israelites themselves attributed to revelation, to a personal encounter with the God who spoke to them, who was their savior and their judge. To present this insight no forms of thought and speech were available to them from their cultural resources except those forms that were common in the ancient Near East. The transcendental reality of Yahweh breaks through the forms of mythology as it breaks through the forms of science and metaphysics; but man cannot reject any of these forms in his effort to grasp more firmly a truth whose comprehension ever eludes him.

32 **(VI) The Spirit of God.**

(A) Concept of Spirit. The same Hebr word serves to signify both *wind* and *spirit*. The wind is the breath of God; it is a sensible manifestation of the divine presence and power. It moves suddenly and unpredictably; man can neither foretell nor control its direction or its strength. He cannot determine its source or its destination (Jn 3:8). It is subtle, verges upon the immaterial in its nature, and is universal and irresistible in its scope. Hence the wind is an extremely apt symbol of the divine.

33 In the OT the spirit is not a personal being. It is a principle of action, not a subject. It belongs properly to Yahweh alone; it is communicated to living beings, but it never becomes a part of the structure of the living being in such a way that the living being possesses the spirit as its own. The spirit is said to clothe (Jgs 6:34; 1 Chr 12:19; 2 Chr 24:20), to be poured out (Is 29:10; 44:3; Ez 39:29; Jl 2:28), to leap upon (Jgs 14:6,19; 15:14; 1 Sm 10:10; 11:6). One is filled with the spirit (Ex 31:3), or Yahweh puts his spirit into one (Is 63:11; Ez 36:27; Nm 11:25,29). The spirit can also be taken from a person (Ps 51:13) or can depart (1 Sm 16:14). Elisha asked for a double portion of the spirit of Elijah (2 Kgs 2:9). The phrases used in these contexts treat the spirit as a subtle substance or liquid; more clearly, they emphasize the impersonal nature of the spirit. The quality that is most evident in the spirit is power.

34 The spirit is not often mentioned as a creative force. In Gn 1:2 the wind "broods" over the waters of chaos; the movement of the wind is the first sign of the creative activity about to break forth. In Ps 33:6 the word of Yahweh and his breath are creative forces; the power by which Yahweh expels an utterance is the power felt in the wind. The wind is also a destructive force; it is the breath of the nostrils of Yahweh, his anger (Ps 18:16), which dries up the springs (Hos 13:15) and is an instrument of his judgment (Is 30:27–28).

The breath of Yahweh is the principle of breath and of life for all living beings; they survive by the communication of his spirit. This thought appears in a number of passages (Gn 2:7; 6:17; 7:15; Jb 33:4; Eccl 3:19,21). The breath of life is communicated by inspiration (Gn 2:7), and the living being dies when Yahweh takes away his spirit (Ps 104:29), which then returns to Yahweh (Eccl 12:7).

35 **(B) The Spirit in the History of Israel.** The spirit is more frequently represented as a principle of those activities that affect the people of Israel precisely as the people of Yahweh. In the period of the judges and of the early monarchy we meet the spirit as a mysterious divine impulse that moves a man to deeds above his known capacity and habits of behavior—deeds of delivering Israel from its enemies (Jgs 3:10; 6:34; 11:29; 13:25; 14:6,19; 15:14). Similarly, Saul is moved by the spirit to deliver the city of Jabesh-gilead (1 Sm 11:6,13). Here also the spirit appears primarily as a principle of power. The movement of the spirit is the distinctive mark of the man whom Max Weber called the "charismatic leader." In normal times the loose organization of the tribes of Israel needed no more than the simple government of clan and village elders. When the peace of Israel was threatened by external enemies, this leadership was not enough, and it was supplanted by the leader who demonstrated the possession of the spirit by the deeds of the spirit. During the period of the judges, the spirit of the charismatic leader was a passing phenomenon: The spirit came upon the leader during the emergency, impelled him to his mission, and departed from him after the mission was accomplished (→ Judges, 8:2). The king, on the contrary, was a permanent charismatic officer; and the permanence of the charisma was signified by the anointing at which the spirit was conferred (1 Sm 10:10). When David was anointed, the spirit passed to him from Saul (16:13). Once the idea was established that the spirit reposed permanently upon the king, there was less frequent mention of the spirit in the narratives about the king; and impulsive and extraordinary actions in the manner of the judges were not attributed to the kings after Saul.

36 The spirit that impels men to action may be an evil spirit "from Yahweh" or "of Elohim" (never "of Yahweh"). An evil spirit causes dissension at Shechem (Jgs 9:23), moves Saul to attempt to murder David (1 Sm 19:9), and Yahweh sends a lying spirit into the mouth of false prophets (1 Kgs 22:23). This usage illustrates the idea of spirit as a universally pervasive divine power. In the very simple and unsophisticated thinking of early Israel, human actions that are unexpected or inexplicable indicate the activity of a power greater than that possessed by the individual. This power can be attributed to no other than Yahweh, who through his spirit enables men to act beyond their usual capacity. The spirit itself is morally neutral; the moral responsibility for such actions lies upon the agents.

37 The operations of the spirit in prophecy are somewhat ambiguous. Prophecy is not attributed to the spirit by Amos, Hosea, Isaiah and Jeremiah. (The passage Mi 3:8, where the prophet speaks of himself as full of the spirit of Yahweh, is not certainly original with this prophet.) Yet in earlier prophecy the spirit is frequently associated with prophetic utterance (Nm 11:17,25; 24:2; 1 Sm 10:10; 19:20–24).

It should be observed that the idea of prophecy passed through a notable development between the early monarchy and the prophets of the 8th cent. (→ Prophetic Lit, 12:6–11). In the period of the early monarchy the prophets were often ecstatic rather than inspired speakers. "The sons of the prophets" seem to have been cultic groups that practiced a worship of song and dance, often in an unrestrained manner; such exaltation was a sign of the activity of the spirit. The references to prophetic speech in Nm (given above) occur in contexts of ecstatic utterance. In the stories of Elijah and Elisha the spirit is an agent that transports the prophet from place to place (1 Kgs 18:12; 2 Kgs 2:16) or a power that enables the prophet to work wonders (2 Kgs 2:15). In the classical period of prophecy, beginning with Amos, *ca.* 750 BC—a period when the prophet speaks the word of Yahweh (→ 45 below)—the spirit is not an inspiring agent. In the exilic and post-exilic periods the spirit does appear as an inspiring agent (Ez 2:2; 3:24; 11:5; Zech 7:12; Neh 9:30). Here we notice that Ezekiel, in contrast with the prophets of the 8th and 7th cents., frequently employs vision and ecstasy as media of expression. These are the areas of the activity of the spirit.

38 As a principle of activity, the spirit, morally neutral, is manifested in a large variety of operations both good and bad. There is a spirit of lying (1 Kgs 22:22), of knowledge of a craft (Ex 31:3), of jealousy (Nm 5:14), of judgment (Is 4:4), of confusion (Is 19:14), of deep sleep (Is 29:10), of fornication (Hos 4:12), of compassion and supplication (Zech 12:10), a willing spirit (Ps 51:14), a spirit of princes (a haughty spirit, Ps 76:13). It is difficult to synthesize such uses as this, and it seems better not to seek perfect consistency in Hebr thought and language about the spirit. The common element in these uses, if one is to be found, seems to be the unusual or the extraordinary degree in which skill, fornication, confusion, compassion and other things are exhibited. Behavior surpassing the normal is, again, the area in which spirit is manifested.

39 In the messianic era (→ 152ff. below) the spirit breaks out in a new fullness. "Messianic" persons such as the king (Is 11:1), the servant of Yahweh (42:1), and the prophet who announces the messianic salvation (61:1) receive the spirit; in the messianic king, the operations of the spirit demonstrate his messianic character. The spirit is poured upon the whole people (Is 32:15; 44:3; Ez 39:29; Jl 3:28); combined with a new heart, the spirit is a principle of moral regeneration (Ez 36:26). Later prophets attribute the deliverance of Israel in the Exodus to the spirit (Is 63:11,14). The individual Israelite may ask for a portion of the spirit (Ps 51:12; 143:10). In the messianic age the spirit becomes a power for righteous conduct.

This may appear to be a conventionalizing of the older usage to the point where the idea of spirit is weakened; but the messianic regeneration is not conceived as the achievement of merely conventional morality—it is a revolution in human conduct. The tremendous development of the idea of spirit in the NT flows easily from the conception of the spirit as the vivifying and energizing power of God in the messianic fullness. In the NT all the lines of development of the idea that we see in the OT are brought together in the revelation of the personal reality of the Spirit.

40 **(VII) The Word of God.**

(A) Concept of Word. In the ancient Near East the spoken word was conceived as a distinct entity laden with power. This was eminently true of the divine word. In both Egypt and Mesopotamia the divine word was a creative force educing the world into existence. In Mesopotamia, the divine decree determining the various fates was the power that moved and directed the course of events. The divine word partook of the power and the eternity of the gods themselves, and man could not resist or alter it.

Similarly the human word was a being endowed with power, but in a lesser degree. The power of the human word was most clearly manifested in solemn utterances such as blessings and curses, contracts, promises, and other processes that were intended to stabilize human relations. The word of the king was more powerful than the word of the common man; but even the common man possessed the fearful power of blessing and cursing.

41 The power of the word was manifested in magic. In magic, as distinct from other forms of speech, the power resides in the word itself and not in the person; this is in contrast to the Israelite conception of the spoken word (→ 42 below). The operative factor in magical rites is the rigidly correct formula, a set arrangement of words properly pronounced. Since the power resides in the formula, the formula must be kept occult; anyone who knows the formula possesses the power. The magical conception of the power of the word is actually a perversion of the older conception.

42 The concept of the power of the word probably arises, at least in part, from the importance given to the spoken formula in cultures that use little or no writing. In such utterances as blessings and curses, promises, threats, wishes, commands and contracts, the word has a reality that endures into the future; indeed, the effect of the spoken word may outlive the speaker. The word posits a reality, and it is, in itself, the reality that it posits. The reality exists first in the heart or desire, then passes into speech, and finally effective speech brings into existence the reality that it signifies.

The power of the word is rooted in the power of the person. When the person speaks he externalizes himself (G. van der Leeuw) or releases psychic energy (J. Pedersen). The permanence and energy of personal volition reach the external world through the spoken word, and the spoken word retains these qualities of permanence and energy. Such respect for and even fear of the spoken word are not frequently encountered in cultures where important utterances must be recorded in writing for validity. In these cultures a fear of the document is more likely.

43 Instances of the power of the word are numerous in the OT. In the deception of Isaac by Jacob (Gn 27) and the deception of Jacob by Laban (Gn 29:20–27), an error concerning the person does not invalidate the solemn spoken word; for the word by its emission has become a reality that cannot be recalled. Isaac can give Esau another, inferior blessing, but he cannot cancel the blessing he mistakenly gave to Jacob. When the mother of Micah curses the thief who, unknown to her, is her own son (Jgs 17:1–2), she cannot withdraw the curse, but can send a blessing to follow it and counteract it. David's pronunciation of a sentence of death upon the man in the parable of Nathan (2 Sm 12:1–18) is unwittingly directed at himself; the prophet assures him that it will be diverted, but it falls upon David's child born of Bathsheba. The woman accused of adultery must consume an oath of execration by drinking water into which the written words of a curse have been immersed (Nm 5:12–31); nothing but innocence will neutralize the fatal effects of the curse.

44 Correlative with the dynamic aspect of the word is its dianoetic aspect (O. Procksch), i.e., its ability to render things intelligible. This is the function of the word as name (→ 6 above). To know the name is to experience the dynamism of the word in the reverse direction; as the power of the person determines reality by conferring the name, so the power of the person apprehends the reality of the thing by knowing the name.

45 **(B) The Word in the History of Israel.** The OT conception of "the word of Yahweh" must be understood against the background of this common usage. Most of the occurrences of "the word of Yahweh" designate the prophetic word; the word is the specific charism of the prophet, as *tôrâ* (law) is the charism of the priest, and counsel the charism of the sage (Jer 18:18). The prophetic word is misunderstood if one thinks of it as merely the experience of hearing; it is the reception of a positive dynamic reality that arises from the power of the person of Yahweh and compels the prophet to speak (Am 3:8). The reception of the word is compared in Ez 2:9–3:3 to the eating of a scroll. The word of Yahweh is a joy and a delight (Jer 15:16), a burning fire shut up in the bones of the prophet (20:7–9), a fury that he must pour out (6:11).

The prophetic word partakes of the dynamism of Yahweh himself; it is fulfilled or established when the reality of which it speaks comes into existence. The relation of the prophetic word to the event is more than the relation of prediction and fulfillment; the word is an entity endowed with power that effects the thing signified by the word. The word of Yahweh placed in the mouth of Jeremiah gives the prophet power to uproot and to tear down, to destroy and to ruin, to build and to plant (Jer 1:9–10); the prophet accomplishes these things by uttering the word. The word of Yahweh does not return to him empty (Is 45:23; 55:10–11) nor does he take it back (31:2). Were it to return without fulfilling its destiny, the personal dynamism of Yahweh himself would be frustrated. This word partakes of Yahweh's eternity (40:8); its dynamism may be delayed, but its fulfillment is inevitable (9:8).

46 The word of Yahweh is the operative agent in the history of Israel from the first act of the creative process (Gn 1:3) to the rebuilding of Jerusalem by the decree of Cyrus (Is 44:28). The utterance of Yahweh brings about the call of Abraham and of Moses, the Exodus of Israel from Egypt, the conquests of Joshua, the call of Samuel, the establishment of the monarchy, the election of David, the division of the kingdom, the fall of the house of Omri, the invasions of the Assyrians and the Chaldeans, the fall of the kingdom of Israel and of the kingdom of Judah. The word of Yahweh is an essential element in the OT conception of history.

The word of Yahweh is also a creative agent (Gn 1; Is 40:26; 48:13; Pss 33:6,9; 147:15–18). In the comprehensive concept of creation in the OT, creation by word is combined with other ideas that are perhaps older (e.g., creation by work; → 54 below). However, modern critics regard this development as late; both Dt-Is and Gn 1 come from exilic and post-exilic literature.

47 **(VIII) God and Nature.** Man's idea of nature has an incalculable effect upon his idea of the deity; yet to a certain extent the two ideas should be independent. The relations of nature with a transcendental deity not included in the ambit of nature do not depend upon the constitution of nature and can be perceived with little or no knowledge of the constitution of nature. But when man identifies the deity with nature, either in the mythological polytheism of the ancient Near East, or in the scientism of modern thought, the deity is given the form of nature itself, and man's idea of the deity consequently undergoes substantial modifications.

48 **(A) Concept of Nature.** The OT idea of nature has more in common with the prevailing ideas of the ancient Near East than it has with the modern scientific and philosophical outlook; and the difference has often been an obstacle to the incorporation of the biblical idea of the relations of God and nature into modern systems of thought. In this area philosophy and science have sometimes dictated the terms to theology. Classically, nature has been conceived as an impersonal and objective unity with regular and predictable behavior governed by "laws." The idea of nature as a unity first appeared as *kosmos* in Gk thought, and early Gk philosophers devoted most of their efforts to formulate a principle of the unity that they perceived in nature. The entire development of modern science rests upon the conviction of the unity and the regularity of nature. However, in the ancient Near East there is not even a word that can be translated "nature." The phenomena of the visible world are regarded neither as constituting a unity nor as impersonal. The conflicting diversity of natural forces is what first impresses the unsophisticated observer; and because of the conflict the observer is more impressed by irregularity than by the recurrence of basic patterns. The forces of nature exhibit the kind of unpredictability that we associate with human behavior; and these forces are endowed in pre-philosophical thought with the qualities of the human person. But since the forces of nature are so vast in power and scope, they are magnified as persons and thus become gods. Cosmic order is achieved by compromise, by the unsteady balance of the mutual agreement of many powerful wills, by a recurring conflict in which no single force ever emerges supreme. Cosmic order is conceived as political; it is maintained in the universe as it is maintained in the state. Beneath this order there is always the potential of anarchy that would reduce nature to chaos. If the course of nature is to be maintained in harmony with man's goals, man must keep these personal forces benevolently disposed.

The resultant concept of deity lacks perfect unity and in some instances is as fluid as the idea of nature itself. The gods are not simply identified with the forces and phenomena of nature; and in addition to the gods there are demons, either beneficent or maleficent, to whom belong many lesser areas of natural phenomena. Demons are met not by cult but by magic. In the areas of demonic operations nature is seen at its most unpredictable and irrational; but even in the areas governed by the gods man is never assured that the divine will is not arbitrary and capricious. Finally, the resultant idea of the divine will does not really arise above the level of nature; the gods are not a kind of being totally different either from man or from the phenomena of the visible world.

49 The OT shares the ancient conception of nature as diversified and personal. There is no Hebr word for "nature," and the unity that the OT sees in nature is not mechanical unity but the unity of a personal will. Yet the Israelites do not attribute personality to the distinct forces of nature, and there are no separate gods to correspond to the separate natural forces. The divine personal reality of Yahweh does not lie within nature; Yahweh is identified neither with nature as a whole nor with any of its parts. The absence of sexual characteristics and functions in Yahweh is a striking illustration of the unique OT conception of God. (In Hebr thought, male sex is attributed to the angels or "sons of God" who are members of the heavenly court—this reflects the distant origins of the heavenly court as a polytheistic pantheon with male and female gods who were the children of a supreme god. The angels impregnate women in Gn 6:2 [cf. 1 Cor 11:10], and in some Jewish legends they are circumcised.) Sex as the source of life is vitally involved in the mythology of other ancient Near Eastern peoples; and much of their myth and ritual is intended to communicate to the worshipers the sexual energy of the gods. For Israel Yahweh is the source of life but not through sexual processes.

50 **(B) Creation.** Yahweh, as creator, corresponds to nothing in the beliefs of other ancient Near Eastern peoples, in spite of the fact that the OT exhibits several ways of conceiving the creative process. The several ways, no doubt, represent different phases of development. It happens that the most explicit texts about creation are exilic or later, and several modern scholars have concluded that the idea of creation was either unimportant or missing in early Israelite belief. That it was missing entirely is highly improbable; other religions dealt with creation formally and at length. Nor was the idea unimportant; but its importance must be viewed in the entire context of Israelite thought and not as a detached article of belief. In the OT, creation is the beginning of history, which means that it is the first of the saving deeds of Yahweh. The Israelites do not ask questions about creation for its own sake; creation and nature are integrated in the history of the salvation wrought by Yahweh. (Note that in the early Israelite "credos" Yahweh is not proclaimed as God the creator—as in the Christian creed—but as the God who was active in the history of the patriarchs [Dt 6:20–25; 26:5–10; Jos 24:2–13].) It is in this historical context that the several approaches to creation must be seen.

51 *Creation as combat.* It is quite probable that the oldest approach to creation, now reflected only in some OT allusions, related it to a combat between Yahweh and an adversary representing chaos. In Mesopotamia, creation is achieved by the victory of Marduk over the monster Tiamat. In the Canaanite myths of Ugarit, Aleyan Baal engages in combat with an adversary Mot, with another called Sea or River, and with another named Leviathan or Shalyat of the seven heads. Leviathan appears in the OT (Is 27:1). Such a combat is reflected in Pss 74:13–15; 89:10–11; Is 27:1; 51:9; Jb 9:13; 26:12; 38:8–11. None of these passages is certainly early, and the allusions are most frequently explained as poetic imagery borrowed from foreign mythology. Yet there is no reason to suppose that this primitive conception, so evidently reflecting the mythology of other peoples, was not the earliest and the most unsophisticated account of creation in Israel. With the progress of belief in Yahweh, this account was suppressed in favor of other more advanced explanations until it survived only in poetic allusions. The survival exhibits the retention by Israel of a basic conception of nature that Israel shared with other peoples, the conception that cosmic order is not mechanical. Cosmic order is maintained by Yahweh's power over the forces of chaos, which he can release (→ 55 below).

52 *Creation according to Gn.* The allusions to creation in the OT are numerous, but the passages in which the theme is treated explicitly and at length are few: Gn 1:1–2:4a; Ps 104. The story in Gn 2:4b–25 is not a creation account in the same sense: It treats of the origin of man, or more precisely of the origin of sex, and the creation of the material world is mentioned merely by allusion. Gn 2:4b–25 (J) is older than Gn 1:1–2:4a (P); but the concept of creation exhibited by P is older than its present literary form (→ Genesis, 2:15,22). Even in *Gn 1:1* we are probably not dealing with creation from nothing or creation in the strictest sense, but with God's ordering of chaos into a fixed universe. Creation from nothing does not appear clearly in the Bible until the Gk period when philosophical notions are current (2 Mc 7:28).

The structure of the material universe seen in Gn 1 and in almost all allusions to creation and to the material world (see Jb 38:4–38) is the structure seen also in Mesopotamian creation accounts. The universe exists in three levels: heavens, earth, and subterranean abyss of waters. The earth is a flat disk that floats upon the waters, while above the heavens are the divine dwelling. The entire structure rests upon pillars. The heavenly bodies move across the sky; and rain, snow, hail and wind are stored in chambers above the sky. The enumeration of eight works in Gn 1:1ff. is intended to be complete; it covers every item in the structure so conceived and affirms expressly that Elohim has made each item. The account is framed in such a way that it is a counterposition to the Mesopotamian myth of creation (→ 26 above). Items like the abyss and the heavenly bodies, which in Mesopotamia were personified and deified, are here depersonalized. There is nothing prior to the creative word, and in particular no combat. The concept of the material universe is not altered, but the relations of the universe to the creative deity are completely different.

53 *Creation according to Ps 104.* This creation poem shows certain literary relations to the Aton hymn produced in 14th-cent. Egypt in the reign of Akhenaton (*ANET* 368–371; → Biblical Archaeology, 74:58). It is difficult to determine whether these relationships arise from similarity of subject or from the Israelite poet's knowledge of the Egyptian work. In any case, the conception of Ps 104 is wholly Israelite. The dominant theme is the care of the creator for living beings, both animals and men. Natural phenomena are almost entirely represented in their relations to the sustenance of life. The poem is optimistic in the extreme, although in this it does not differ substantially from the other creation accounts. In all of them the work of creation is seen as good in its origin, without defect or any element hostile to man. By the removal of the theme of the cosmic combat Israelite thought removes the dualism implicit in other creation accounts.

54 Through these poems and other allusions to creation there runs a double conception of the creative act: creation by work and creation by word. Although creation by work is especially evident in older passages such as Gn 2, creation by word (→ 46 above) is not necessarily recent. Creation by word appears in the Egyptian theology of Memphis, which is placed by Egyptologists about 2700 BC, much earlier than any OT document (*ANET* 4–6). Both creation by work and creation by word appear in Gn 1. The original naïve anthropomorphism (→ 21 above) involved in creation by work is seen in Gn 2, where Yahweh "forms" man and animals; the word is used of the work of the potter, and this is obviously the image intended. The same image appears in Egypt and in Mesopotamia. Other words such as "build" or "make" are common in allusions to creation. A refinement is seen in the use of the word that we translate "create" (Hebr *bārā'*), which is never used except with Yahweh as its subject; it is the kind of production of which only Yahweh is capable. More refined still is the creation by word, in which the command is followed by the execution with no further action. The two conceptions, as has been noticed, are mingled in the same passage—an illustration of the multiplicity of mythopoeic thinking (→ 24 above).

55 **(C) Continued Creation.** The creation account of Gn 1 suggests that the Israelites thought of creation as a process that was finished with the six days. In other accounts, creation is represented as a continuing process that endures as long as the world itself endures. The victory of Yahweh over the monster of chaos is sometimes spoken of as a victory that constantly recurs; the monster is said to be bound or restrained rather than killed (Pss 89:10; 104:6–8; Jb 26:12; 38:8–11). Thus Yahweh sustains and defends the material universe against the forces of disintegration; without the uninterrupted exercise of his saving power, the world will relapse into chaos. This Israelite conception escapes the dualism of pagan cosmic mythology by denying to the forces of disintegration any power that matches the power of Yahweh. In the dualism of the pagan cosmic myth the balance of order and chaos is so close that a cyclic conflict is inevitable.

Similarly, each manifestation of Yahweh's dominion can be represented as a reenactment of his victory over chaos. The heavenly bodies are marshalled by him daily and appear in obedience to his call (Is 40:26; 45:12;

48:13). Yahweh makes dawn and darkness (Am 4:13; 5:8), measures the waters in the hollow of his hand (Is 40:12), gives breath and spirit to those who walk the earth (42:5). The creative acts of Ps 104 recur each day.

56 The continuing creative activity of Yahweh is emphasized in the area of *fertility*. Throughout the ancient Near East, fertility was the object of a ritual re-enactment of the myth of creation, in which fertility was annually restored through the death and resurrection of the god of fertility and his union with his consort. Against this belief the OT contains a vigorous polemic. Yahweh, and not the Baal, bestows the fruits of the soil (Hos 2:10ff.); he blesses the progeny of man and beast and the fruit of the soil (Dt 7:13; Jer 31:12). He gives and withholds rain (Is 30:23; Lv 26:4; Dt 11:13–15; Jer 5:24). Unlike the gods of fertility, Yahweh bestows the blessings of fertility without himself being involved in the process.

57 In some conceptions the involvement of Yahweh in nature seems closer. It has been noticed that the OT view of nature sees it as personal, but not as the activity of a number of personal beings. The one natural phenomenon with which Yahweh is most frequently associated is *the storm*. The poetry of the OT in which he is represented as the lord of the storm has obvious affinities with both the literature and the art of other ancient Near Eastern peoples; the number and vivid coloring of the allusions to Yahweh and the storm have persuaded a number of scholars that Yahweh was originally a storm god like Adad or Hadad (Pss 29:3–9; 77:17–21; 107:25–29; Is 30:27,30; Na 1:3,5; Jb 38:25,35,37). This opinion is now generally abandoned; but the connection between Yahweh and the storm is too common to be merely coincidental.

The presentation of Yahweh in *the theophany* of the storm is striking (Pss 18:8–16; 68:8–10; Hab 3:3–15; Jgs 4:4–5; Ex 19:16,19; Ez 1). The elements of the theophanies suggest not only the storm, but also the earthquake and possibly also the volcanic eruption. The theophany is an Israelite confession of the power of Yahweh in nature; but this power is not seen as blind, irrational force. Most frequently Yahweh appears in the theophany as the savior of his people from their enemies. In the theophany of Sinai, Yahweh comes as the deliverer who makes a covenant with Israel; his power in nature is a warrant of his power and will to save Israel. According to later biblical developments (→ 60 below) the power of Yahweh in nature is also manifested as a power of judgment, an act of his moral will that affects all evildoers, whether they be Israelites or others.

58 In Israelite belief the unpredictability of nature (→ 48 above) is modified by the conception of an order in nature, an order founded on the wisdom of Yahweh. Being wise, Yahweh is not capricious or arbitrary, and nature is not fundamentally irrational. The allusions to the wisdom of Yahweh in nature are numerous (Prv 3:19; Is 28:23–29); his relations with nature are called a covenant (Hos 2:18; Jb 5:23). Several poems extol the wisdom of Yahweh in creation (Prv 8:22ff.; Ps 104). Jb 38–39 sees Yahweh's wisdom in the production of paradoxes in nature; it is his directive intelligence that maintains order and harmony among such diverse and conflicting agents. Nature becomes dependable according to the dependability of the moral will of Yahweh; its order is the order of righteousness.

Hence when nature strikes man with disaster, it is no chance occurrence; nature is the weapon of Yahweh's anger (Am 4:7; Jl 2:1–11; Jer 5:24; Hos 8:7; 9:14; → 99–102 below). Hebr language and thought do not distinguish between "physical" and "moral" evil; the moral evil of sin inevitably has cosmic repercussions in nature because Yahweh withholds his blessings and employs nature as the executor of his judgments. This is the thought expressed in the OT rewriting of the Mesopotamian myth of the deluge (→ 28 above) and in the curses laid on the man and the woman of Gn 3:16ff. "Disorder" in nature is not really disorder but a higher order, the order of righteous judgment.

59 Nature as a personal activity is a wonder to the Israelites; and the word wonder here is equivalent to the word mystery rather than to the word miracle. Until recent times apologetics had elaborated a concept of miracle that presupposed a closed system of nature governed by fixed laws. This concept of miracle is not found in the OT because the presupposition is missing (→ Aspects NT Thought, 78:112). Creation itself is as emphatically a wonder as any extraordinary phenomenon in nature (Jb 4:8–10; 9:5–10; 26:5–14; 36:26–37:18; 38:1–41:26). When the events of the Exodus or other saving deeds of Yahweh are called wonders, the element of wonder does not lie precisely in Yahweh's work in nature, which is always wonderful, but rather in his saving will. This is the supreme wonder—both mystery and miracle—of Israelite faith and history. Into this saving will all the phenomena of nature and the events of history (→ 113ff. below) are integrated.

60 The supreme manifestation of the power of Yahweh in nature is eschatological (→ 167 below). The concept of nature as the instrument of judgment finds expression in the expectation of the Day of Yahweh, i.e., the cataclysmic encounter of Yahweh with the powers of evil (→ 137 below). The annihilating judgment of Yahweh will reduce the earth to the primitive chaos that it was before the creative action (Jer 4:23–26). The structure of the earth and sky and their supporting pillars will totter (Is 13:3,10; 24:3,19,23; Jl 3:3; Am 8:8; 9:5). In the past the deluge was a return to chaos, according to the P version (Gn 7:11).

Eschatological chaos is the necessary condition for a new creation (Is 65:17). The desert, the enemy of man, will be transformed and watered (Is 32:15; 35:1ff.; 41:18–20). Fertility of the land, the gift of Yahweh, will be granted in superabundance (Ez 36:6–12; Jl 4:18; Am 9:13). The alternation of the seasons, the annual token of the uncertainty and the insecurity of nature, and even the alternation of day and night will cease (Zech 14:6). The struggle for life in the animal world will be ended (Is 11:6–9). Israelite eschatology demands such a goal or terminus for nature. The withdrawal of Yahweh's anger and the bestowal of his blessings without restraint must bring about a new creation. The fullness of this new creation will be a witness to the righteousness and power of Yahweh demanded by his holiness. As the supreme lord of nature, his power must be demonstrated in salvation and blessing just as it is demonstrated in judgment.

ISRAEL—GOD'S COVENANTED PEOPLE

61 **(I) Man.** The OT has no consistent psychology of man. Its language and vocabulary concerning human actions and the components of human nature are altogether popular and difficult to translate into modern terms without misleading. The usual Hebr word for "man" as a species (*'ādām*) is an instance; it does not designate a species but a group (like the English word sheep), and an individual member of the group is distinguished by being called a "son" or a "daughter" of man (→ Aspects NT Thought, 78:28). The group is seen as an existent reality rather than as an abstract essence; and so the Israelites neither asked nor enunciated a definition of the metaphysical essence of man. They were more concerned with the relations of the collective group "man" to the deity and to the world in which the group lives than they were in the inner constitution of the species.

62 The OT is profoundly aware of the paradoxical and the mysterious in man; this is brought out in the *J account* of the creation of man (Gn 2). Man is made of clay and is therefore mortal and feeble; but the clay is vitalized by the spirit given by Yahweh (→ 34 above). The dignity of man, however, does not rest only on the communication of the spirit, which is the principle of life for the animals as well; he is distinguished from the animals because none of them is a fit helper and associate for him. He is superior to them and therefore can give them names (→ 6 above). He enjoys personal relations with Yahweh, who creates a garden for him to dwell in.

63 The *P account* of man's creation (Gn 1) is more explicit in affirming the dignity of man. Man is made in the image and likeness of Elohim (Gn 1:26–27). The precise meaning of this phrase in the context is obscure and disputed; it seems very probable that the divine image and likeness are associated with the dominion given to man over the lower animals (1:28–30). Dominion over creation is proper to God; correspondingly the conferring of dominion upon man raises him above the level of lower creatures and implies his possession of godlike qualities that are not shared by the beasts. In Ps 8 also man is made "a little less than Elohim," crowned with glory and honor, and empowered to rule all lower living beings.

64 The image of Elohim constitutes the mystery of man. The paradox of man is that this eminence and dominion is combined with an element of weakness that is generally termed "flesh" (*bāśār*). Flesh is the natural condition of man; it is opposed to spirit, the element associated with God (Is 31:3; → 33 above). The OT does not always clearly distinguish physical weakness and mortality from moral weakness; there is an association between the two that is assumed rather than consciously elaborated. In Gn 3 the loss of man's dominion over nature and of his prospect of immortality is the result of a moral failure. In the OT, flesh is not yet the seat of concupiscence or earth-oriented tendencies, which it becomes in the Pauline writings (→ Pauline Theology, 79:119), nor is the word "flesh" always used in a pejorative sense. Yet flesh is what man has in common with the animals; it is the unstable and the perishable.

65 According to Gn 2, man is created in two sexes. This is not explicitly considered in any ancient Near Eastern mythology where the existence of sex is assumed as a primary principle in the divine world just as in the created world. In contrast with these mythologies (as well as with the patterns of thought reflected in almost the whole OT) we read in Gn 2:18–25 that woman is the object of a distinct creative act, the only living being who is a fit partner and companion of the male. The female has the same dignity as the male and is therefore not a depressed or subhuman species.

66 In spite of the use of such words as flesh, spirit, and soul, man in the OT is conceived of as a unity and not as a composite of different principles. H. Wheeler Robinson observed in a classic remark that the Greeks conceived of man as an incarnate spirit and the Israelites conceived of him as an animated body. The Hebr language does not distinguish within man a seat of intellectual operations; these are located in the heart—in Hebr the heart is the organ of thought rather than of feeling. The Hebr *nefesh* (*nepeš*) has usually been mistranslated "soul"; this translation introduces into the OT an idea that is foreign to it. Actually, the use of the word *nefesh* is too fluid to permit any synthesis. When Yahweh breathes the spirit into man, he becomes a living *nefesh* (Gn 2:7). The word certainly is used to signify self or person; this is especially clear when it serves as the equivalent of the personal or the reflexive pronoun, and "person" or "self" may be the basic, if not the primitive, meaning of the word. The blood is sometimes said to be the seat of the *nefesh;* in such instances the *nefesh* is not the self or the person, but rather life, which is poured out with the blood. The *nefesh* is often associated with the psychic processes of desire, and in these contexts the word can often be translated by "will" or "appetite."

In none of these instances, taken singly or together, is there anything resembling the "soul" of Gk and modern thought. This difference has important corollaries in the biblical idea of survival after death (→ 170 below). The usage of the word *nefesh* shows the failure of OT thought to arrive at any real analysis of the principles of human nature. Man is seen as an existing totality, and words that refer to anything except parts of the anatomy designate the totality of conscious life in some way. Indeed, even when particular parts of the anatomy such as the loins, the bowels, the eye, the hand, or the heart are made the subject and the seat of vital acts, the total person is identified with the organ, in which the sum of psychic energy comes to focus.

(Köhler, L., *Hebrew Man* [Nashville, 1956]. Mork, W., *The Biblical Meaning of Man* [Milwaukee, 1967].)

67 **(II) Man in Community.** The relations of the individual man to the social group in the OT, as in the rest of the ancient world, are notably different from these relations in the modern world. The differences have led to extensive discussions among scholars, but it would be inexact to speak of a consensus of opinion. The discussion has often been set within the framework of an antithesis between collectivism and individualism: Early Israel has been said to exhibit an exaggerated collectivism, and later Israel an exaggerated individualism. This is an improper frame of reference. Collectivism and individualism are modern ideas that have no correspondents in Israelite thought. The discussion has been further obscured by the emotional overtones that these words bear in modern times.

68 The social groups that are found in the OT are of two kinds: real or fictitious kinship groups, which include the family, the clan, and the tribe; and political groups, which include the village, the city, and the kingdom. The kinship group is conceived and spoken of as "one flesh" rather than "one blood"; the difference seems slight, but it is significant when the group is considered as a single person (→ 69 below). The unity of village and city resembles the unity of kinship rather than political unity; these ancient communities were small enough and usually, as in the modern Near Eastern village, had such a network of interrelationships between families that the analogy of kinship was easily applied.

The only genuine political society in the OT is the monarchy; here the principle of unity is the person of the king, who incorporates in himself the people whom he rules. Both in the political society and in the kinship group the unity is ultimately personal, reposing on the father, the patriarch, or the king. The unity of the group is both horizontal and vertical: Horizontally it extends to all the members of a contemporary generation, and vertically it extends through all earlier generations. Even though hundreds of years separate the prophets from Moses, they often address their own generation as those whom Yahweh has brought up from Egypt, guided through the desert, and given the land of Canaan. "Israel" is a continuing reality, contemporary to all the events of its past history and subject to all the responsibilities that this history has laid upon it.

69 The personification of a group is universal in human speech and would not of itself establish anything distinctive in Israelite thought. However, there is a distinctive element in Israelite personification, and H. Wheeler Robinson has coined the phrase *corporate personality* and explained it in such a way that the distinctive element appears. Corporate personality is fluid; it may designate the individual person or the group, yet neither without reference to the other. This is illustrated in the patriarchal stories of Gn. The patriarchs in their personal characters and even in their personal experiences exhibit those traits that were thought to be peculiarly Israelite and foreshadow the adventures of the group that was descended from them. Jacob in relation to Esau and to Laban clearly reflects Israel in relation to Edom and to the Arameans. The covenant relation of Israel with Yahweh is retrojected into a covenant of Abraham with Yahweh in which Abraham is the ideal covenant partner (→ 78 below). The acquisition of the land of Canaan effected before the monarchy is initiated in the movements of Abraham, Isaac, and Jacob.

The king also is such a corporate personality; here Israelite thought patterns do not differ substantially from the ideas of other ancient Near Eastern peoples. In the relations of Israel with Yahweh, however, the position of the Israelite king does not correspond to the position that Egyptian, Mesopotamian, and Canaanite kings had in the cult. The difference lies in the transcendental superiority of Yahweh; the king is as much Yahweh's subject as any other Israelite. The Israelite king cannot be a visible manifestation of Yahweh's majesty, for this would be to represent Yahweh by image (→ 20 above). The king is a charismatic person (→ 35 above), but no more. With these reservations, the king incorporates in himself the fortunes and the destiny of Israel.

70 The corporate personality thus synthesized in the individual person of the leader can be conceived apart from the leader. Because the group is a single personality, the history of the rebellion of Israel from its beginnings to the present can be reviewed by Ez 20—the sins of the fathers are visited upon the children (20:5). Amos addresses his contemporaries as the family that Yahweh brought out of Egypt (Am 3:1). The generation of Jeremiah is the faithless bride of Yahweh (Jer 2:2). Hosea sees in his contemporaries the deviousness of Jacob, their eponymous ancestor (Hos 12:2–4), the child who has grown into an ungrateful adult (11:1–7). The group must answer for what it is historically, as the individual person must answer for what he is; neither the group nor the man can entirely escape their past except by a complete reversal of character. Similarly, the messianic future of Israel is the future of Israel as a group and not as individual persons.

71 The need of security was a highly important factor in determining the relation of the individual to the group. In the ancient world once one went beyond the limits of the village or the city, one entered into a lawless wilderness. Even under the Israelite monarchy perfect security could not be guaranteed beyond the limits of the settlements: The monarchy sanctioned law and organized defense against external enemies, but it could not police its territory effectively. The individual who had no group affiliations was defenseless and helpless. The vindication of the life, integrity, and property of the individual was the responsibility of the kinship group, which through the custom of blood vengeance effectively threatened retaliation for attack on its members.

The price that the individual person paid for security was complete integration in the group and complete acceptance of its ways and its decisions. The solidarity that maintained a defense against external agression left no room for individual deviations. As the group protected the individual even at its own risk (since a threat to any individual member was a threat to the whole group), so it could demand of the member a total dedication. Such a way of life left no room for anything like the modern ideal of individual personal development or personal career; in fact it left no room even for personal privacy. It must be understood that few, if any, felt oppressed or deprived in this way of life. Human life simply was group life, and no other way of life was conceivable or desirable.

72 There are indications in the OT that important group decisions were reached through wide participation, at least of the representative persons, such as heads of families and clans. Seventy of the elders of Israel ratify the covenant of Israel with Yahweh (Ex 24). "The people" accept a covenant to serve Yahweh imposed by Joshua (Jos 24). Gideon deals with 77 elders of Succoth (Jgs 8). In the several accounts of the institution of the monarchy (1 Sm 8–10) the initiative comes from the people. The elders of Israel accept David as king (2 Sm 5:1ff.).

Thorkild Jacobsen has shown that in early Mesopotamia the government of the state was conducted by an assembly of elders and a popular assembly; to this structure he gave the name "Primitive Democracy" (*JNES* 2 [1943] 166ff.; reinforced by G. Evans, *JAOS* 78 [1958] 1ff.). We have no evidence that popular sovereignty was formalized by institutions in Israel, but many details suggest that there were ample channels for the expression of the popular will. This feature of Israelite society warns us against speaking too easily of the opposition between collectivism and individualism in Israel. The individual expressed himself through the group and readily accepted decisions that he had helped to formulate.

73 The religious activities of man were as much determined by society as were any other activities. We do not find in the ancient Semitic world any clear instance of a purely religious group that is not also a social group; the position of Israel here is unique, but Israel is not a purely religious group. It is against this background that we should consider the problems raised by Jer 31:29–35 and by Ez 18 together with 33:1–20. No relation of the individual to the deity was known except the relation of membership in a cult group identified with the social group. The collapse of the Israelite political society in the time of Jeremiah and Ezekiel left no relationship of the individual Israelite with Yahweh. In the ancient world a god without a people simply vanished. Jeremiah and Ezekiel were not exactly the creators of personal religion, as many scholars have called them, although one cannot deny that they made statements about personal responsibility that have no parallel in earlier OT literature. Rather, the emphasis of their statements is an assurance that Yahweh has not ceased to exist and that Israel is still his people. Faith in the enduring power of Yahweh is also faith in the resurgence of Israel from its downfall. In the absence of the collapsing traditional religious and social group of Israel, the individual person must now become aware that he will meet personal demands of a type not made on the individual in the organized society under the monarchy. A purely individual religion, however, is not in the mind of either Jeremiah or Ezekiel (→ Jeremiah, 19:88; → Ezekiel, 21:45).

74 **(III) The Covenant.** The relationship of Yahweh and Israel is unique in the religions of the ancient world. In other ancient religions the deity is identified either with nature (→ 47–48 above) or with the society that worships the deity. The relation is, therefore, in a sense natural, since in the mind of ancient peoples both physical nature and human society are primary data with which *man* is essentially involved. On the contrary, the relation of Yahweh and Israel is, like the created universe, the result of a positive action of Yahweh himself; and the relation of Yahweh and Israel is completed by a positive response of Israel. The relation is not a given necessary component of human existence but a freely instituted community of persons.

75 **(A) Analogies for the Relationship of God to Israel.** The OT uses a number of analogies to designate this relationship. The analogy of *father–son* may appear to be primarily a natural relationship; but when it is seen in the context of other analogies and the character of the father–son relationship is examined, it becomes evident that even here it is the freely associated community of persons that is meant. Yahweh is never called the physical progenitor of Israel; he "begets" Israel by forming a people for himself. The paternal and filial attitudes that appear in the father–son analogy are the personal attitudes of love, devotion, and obedience, and not the relations of carnal kinship. The sonship of Israel is adoptive, not natural.

The analogy of *marriage* shows the personal relations even more clearly, and in particular highlights the initiative of Yahweh, since in ancient marriage it was always the man who chose his wife. In Hos and Jer the matrimonial analogy is presented with emphasis on the relation of love; the fidelity of Israel is a work of love, and the infidelity of Israel is a personal offense against Yahweh.

The analogy of *shepherd and flock* is less common and does not so explicitly present the mutual personal relationship. But a shepherd is bound to his flock by a devotion to which corresponds the confidence of the sheep. This analogy shows that Yahweh is the protector of Israel.

The analogy of *kinsman* also appears. Yahweh is called the "avenger" of Israel ("redeemer" in many English versions). This title alludes to the custom of blood revenge, by which the next of kin is obliged at any risk to defend the life, person, or property of his kinsman and to execute punishment upon any aggressor. In this analogy Yahweh acts not only as the protector and the security of Israel but also as a kinsman. Here again the suggestion of a natural relationship is not to be pressed, since the obligation of the avenger is freely assumed by the deliberate choice of Yahweh.

The analogy of *king and subject* is not frequently explicit, but is reflected in the divine title "Lord" (→ 10 above) and is implicit in the analogy of covenant. The king–subject relationship carries less of the notion of intimacy that is so obvious in the analogies of father–son and husband–wife, but it should not be conceived in the patterns of ancient Egypt and Mesopotamia or of more recent royalty. Theoretically, the Israelite king could be approached by any of his subjects, and some episodes in the lives of David and Saul suggest that this was the practice in the early monarchy. Where the title of king is given to Yahweh, it emphasizes his power and his will to save (→ 140–141 below).

76 Most modern writers now take the analogy of *covenant* as the basic analogy that is the key to the others. A covenant between men was originally a verbal agreement in a culture that did not keep written records. Mutual agreements and obligations were solemnly professed in the presence of witnesses and with imprecatory oaths and sacrificial rites. The fidelity of those who pledged the covenant was insured less by the memory of the witnesses (which substituted for the written instrument) than by the threat of vengeance by the deity invoked as a witness and by a belief in the power of the spoken word (→ 40 above).

77 **(B) Covenant Forms.** In the OT, covenants cover all social transactions. They are not always strictly bilateral, for the stronger can impose a covenant on the weaker. A covenant settles a dispute about a well (Gn 21:32; 26:38) and the quarrel of Jacob and Laban (31:44); a covenant designates an alliance of Abraham and his neighbors (14:13) and the alliance of Gibeon and Israel (Jos 9:15); a covenant designates the agreement of Abner and David that terminates the civil war and assures the allegiance of Israel to David (2 Sm 3:12–19).

78 The covenant of Yahweh and Israel dominates the last four books of the Pentateuch and recurs in the historical books. The traditions concerning the covenant are obscure and complex; but Moses' connection with the establishment of the covenant is so deeply imbedded in the several traditions that one cannot remove him. The existence of a covenant between Yahweh and Abraham (the E and P traditions) is less clearly indicated and is very probably a retrojection of the patterns of later Israelite belief into the story of Abraham. (For covenants with Abraham and David, see R. E. Clements, *Abraham and David* [SBT, 2nd series, 5; London, 1967].) The covenant with Noah in the P tradition is obviously such a retrojection. Even the Mosaic covenant is so heavily overlaid with later material that a historical reconstruction of the course of events is beyond present possibilities. The basic account, found in Ex 19–24, is compiled from several sources that cannot be analyzed clearly; the account in Ex 33, now edited so that it has become a renewal of the covenant, is probably a parallel account. Dt 4–5 depends on Ex 19–24. The covenant mediated by Joshua (Jos 24) demands special treatment; → 80 below.

79 G. E. Mendenhall has shown that the Israelite covenant follows the form of the suzerainty treaty of the second millennium BC (*BA* 17 [1954] 49–76). This treaty formula is known chiefly through Hittite treaties, but it is the formula that was generally employed in international relations of the period. It is important to notice that this particular formula was most common in the late 2nd millennium BC; this is an argument for dating the origin of the covenant with Israel before the Israelite monarchy. The suzerainty treaty is distinguished from the parity treaty, which is made between two equal powers, for the suzerainty treaty is imposed upon a vassal by an overlord and is not bilateral. The vassal is obliged by the treaty; the overlord is not strictly obliged by the promises he makes.

Mendenhall adopts Korošec's analysis of six elements in the suzerainty treaty: (1) the preamble identifies the overlord and gives his genealogy and titulary. (2) The historical prologue sets forth the previous relations between the two parties and is principally a recital of the benefits conferred upon the vassal by the overlord; the "I–Thou" form of address is used. (3) The stipulations imposed upon the vassal: prohibition of other foreign relations, maintenance of peace and existing conditions among vassals, military assistance to be rendered to the overlord, full confidence in the overlord, no asylum to fugitives from the overlord, annual appearance before the overlord. (4) Provision for the deposit of the treaty in the temple and for periodic public reading. (5) List of gods who witness the treaty. (6) Curses and blessings for violation or fulfillment of the treaty. Mendenhall adds: (7) Vassal's oath of obedience. (8) Solemn ceremony of oath. (9) Procedure against rebellious vassal.

80 In the existing literature of the OT, Mendenhall finds a close parallel to the treaty form only in Jos 24, which contains an introductory formula, a historical prologue in the "I–Thou" form of address, the stipulation to renounce other gods, a reference to the people themselves as witnesses, and a provision for the writing and deposit of the covenant in the sanctuary—the curses and blessings are absent. (For this Shechem covenant, see J. L'Hour, *RB* 69 [1962] 5–36; 161–84; 350–68.)

The elements of the treaty formula, however, are found scattered through the covenant narratives of the Pentateuch. The enumeration of Yahweh's titles is illustrated in Ex 34:6. The recital of the saving deeds of Yahweh is common (Ex 19:4; 20:2; Jos 24:2–13); indeed the entire composition of the Pentateuch sets the laws of Israel in a narrative framework that relates Yahweh's deliverance of Israel. In the existing text the stipulations are the laws themselves, and the original stipulations are not easily determined. They included the prohibition of the worship of other gods and very probably the prohibition of the cult of images. Beyond this the Decalogue itself is most probably to be understood as the original stipulation (for the relation of covenant and law, → 88 below). The relations between vassals are parallel to the relations of the Israelite tribes with each other; and exhortations to trust Yahweh correspond to the obligation of trust in the overlord. The annual appearance before the overlord is provided for in the three great annual festivals consisting of a pilgrimage to a sanctuary of Yahweh (→ 91 below). The tradition that the stone tablets of the Decalogue were preserved in the Ark of the Covenant corresponds to the preservation of the treaty in the sanctuary (1 Kgs 8:9; → Religious Institutions, 76:48). The provision for regular reading of the covenant is not found explicitly but is assumed by most modern scholars even without reference to the treaty formula; e.g., A. Alt has suggested that the ceremony of Dt 27 is intended as a regular act and not as a single event. Blessings and curses appear in Lv 26 and Dt 27–28.

81 **(C) Covenant and the History of Israel.** The covenant is initiated by Yahweh through an act that is often called election, especially in Dt. Israel is the people of Yahweh through the choice of Yahweh. The saving acts of Yahweh—the deliverance of the people from Egypt and the gift of the land of Canaan—establish Israel as a people and give Israel the identity and stability that the word "people" denotes. The election made by Yahweh is an act of the love of Yahweh (Dt 4:37ff.; 7:6ff.) and is not because of the greatness or the merits of Israel (7:7; 9:4ff.). The election of Israel imposes upon Israel the responsibility of recognizing Yahweh alone as God (4:39) and of keeping his commandments (4:40; 7:9ff.; 10:16ff.). The treaty formula brings out more clearly the fact that the election of Israel is an election to responsibility and obligation, not merely to a position of privilege. The OT does not conceive of election as an act of favoritism.

82 Recent studies have shown that the covenant was the principle of Israel's unity as a people. It is clear that the Israel of the period of the judges and the monarchy included a number of groups of diverse origins, most of whom had not shared the experience of the Exodus and the settlement (→ Biblical Archaeology, 74:64; → History of Israel, 75:35,45–46). These were joined to the original group of Israel by accepting the covenant of Yahweh with Israel. The traditions of Yahweh's saving acts became the traditions of the entire group; and the obligations of the covenant, in particular the obligation of worshiping Yahweh alone, became normative. Israel was primarily a religious and not an ethnic unity. The covenant account of Jos 24 has been interpreted by M. Noth as describing a ceremony in which such diverse groups were pledged to observe the covenant; and most scholars have accepted this interpretation. Noth has given this group the name of *amphictyony* (borrowed from classical Greece), which signifies a league of cities or tribes organized around a central shrine. Here again the treaty formula illustrates the covenant of Israel: The tribes were vassals of Yahweh and had to maintain peace with each other; they could form no alliance with other peoples or with other gods. But before the monarchy there was no central government; tribal and local government was in the hands of tribal and local authorities, and the political unification under the monarchy issued from political needs, not from the theology of the covenant.

83 When one considers the evident fundamental importance of the idea of covenant in early Israelite history and belief, it is surprising that the word occurs rarely in the writings of the classical prophets of the 8th cent. (Amos, Hosea, Isaiah, Micah). The rarity of the word does not indicate that there was in these writings any substantial change in the idea of the relations of Yahweh and Israel; these prophets emphasized the basic themes of the covenant theology—the sovereignty of Yahweh, his saving deeds, Israel's unique position as the people of Yahweh, and its unique obligations to him. Several scholars have suggested with great probability that the prophets did not use the word because in the popular mind it had become perverted into a false idea of privilege and security: Yahweh, it was wrongly thought, was obligated to Israel, whatever Israel might do. As a corrective, Amos (3:2) made the "knowledge" (= election) of Israel a reason why Yahweh would punish Israel.

84 Mendenhall has suggested another reason why the prophets could not use the idea. In the kingdom of Judah the covenant of Israel had been largely supplanted by the covenant of Yahweh with the house of David (→ 155 below). Plainly the secessionist Israelites of the North felt no guilt about a breach of the Davidic covenant; but even in Judah the covenant with David became a pledge to the dynasty of David rather than to the people of Israel. In the early traditions Yahweh had made no such commitment; and prophets avoided the word covenant lest the reality of Israel be conditioned on the survival of the dynasty of David.

85 With Jer the word covenant reappears; and this was probably because of the emphasis on covenant in Dt, which must be placed in the same period (→ Jeremiah, 19:7). The covenant in Dt is conceived as a source of obligation and of blessing conditioned on its observance. Yahweh is no more than faithful to his covenant if he punishes Israel for the violation of the covenant. Jeremiah himself conceives the future of Israel in terms of a new covenant (31:31–34; → 146 below). The novelty of this covenant lies in the personal relationship that it establishes between Yahweh and the individual Israelite; as Israel was the people of Yahweh, so the individual person becomes the man of Yahweh (→ 73 above). For the theme of the prophetic lawsuit, → Jeremiah, 19:15.

In the P tradition of the Pentateuch the covenant becomes identified with law. The external sign of the covenant is circumcision. The entire history of the saving deeds of Yahweh is represented in P as a series of covenants that go back to Noah.

(For a concise digest of modern theory on the covenant, see Brown, R. E., *The Book of Deuteronomy* (OTRG 10; Collegeville, Minn., 1965) 114–22. Detailed works: Baltzer, K., *Das*

Bundesformular [Neukirchen, 1960]; Hillers, D. R., *Treaty-Curses and the Old Testament Prophets* [Biblica et Orientalia 16; Rome, 1964]; McCarthy, D. J., *Treaty and Covenant* [AnalBib 21; Rome, 1963]; Mendenhall, G. E., "Covenant," *IDB* 1, 714–23.)

86 **(IV) Covenant and Law.**

(A) Law Codes and Formulations. The Pentateuch in Ex through Dt contains vast collections of laws. Critics now recognize that these laws come from diverse origins and dates; very few of the laws can be attributed to Moses himself. Several distinct collections can be distinguished. The collections are often called codes, but the word is inaccurate. The collections are not codified in the usual sense of the term; none of the collections or all taken together constitute a complete corpus of Israelite law.

The Decalogue, given in Ex 20:1–17 and Dt 5:6–21, and representing the basic stipulations of Yahweh's covenant with Israel, is not included under the collections (→ Exodus 3:48–50), although it gives tone and spirit to all subsequent collections. The earliest of the collections, possibly antedating the monarchy, is "The Book of the Covenant" (Ex 20:22–23:19; → Exodus, 3:52–53). The Deuteronomic "Book of the Law" contains a paraenetic restatement of the law (Dt 12–26; → Deuteronomy, 6:33). "The Holiness Code" of Lv 17–26 is generally thought to be earlier than the Exile (→ Leviticus, 4:35). All the other laws are lumped under the designation of the Priestly Collection, which is exilic or later; but a large number of the individual laws must be earlier than the Exile (→ Pentateuch, 1:17). No collection contains civil and criminal law exclusively; the Holiness Code is chiefly religious, and the Priestly Collection is chiefly ceremonial. See the convenient summary of the Law Codes in R. E. Brown, *Deuteronomy* (OTRG 10) 57–59.

87 A. Alt ("The Origins of Israelite Law," *op. cit.*, 103–71) has distinguished two principal formulations of Israelite law. *First*, the casuistic laws (the "decrees" or judgments, the *mišpāṭîm*, the "if" laws) where the conditional clause sets forth the case, usually a civil matter, and the apodosis tells how to handle it. Casuistic laws are common in "The Book of the Covenant" (e.g., Ex 21:2–6) and in Dt. These laws, much like English Common Law, reflect previous legal decisions that have set a precedent. This style of casuistic law is found in the jurisprudence of the ancient Near East, and undoubtedly many of the casuistic laws in the Bible were part of Israel's heritage from the civilizations that surrounded her.

Second, the apodictic laws. There are two types: (a) the statutes (*ḥuqqîm*) that establish penalties, frequently death penalties (Ex 21:12,15–17), e.g., "Whoever strikes a man so that he dies shall be put to death." Curses on evildoers also come under this grouping. These laws may also spring from ancient decisions on cases, but on very fundamental cases in a simple society. As now phrased they are tantamount to basic statements of morality and are treated as edicts of divine authority. (b) The imperatives or commands (*miṣwôt*) which may be positive or negative. These are generally stated in the second person singular ("You shall [not]...") and give no specific penalty (Lv 18:7–17). Unlike the casuistic laws they deal primarily with religious questions and bind all regardless of individual circumstances. The Decalogue consists of apodictic imperatives, mostly prohibitive, and thus comes under the last classification above, even though the Bible refers to the Decalogue as "words" rather than as "commands."

Since apodictic law is moral and religious and the speaker of the imperative is thought to be the deity, it is this formulation that is considered most properly as "covenant law." And indeed the Near Eastern parallels for the apodictic imperatives are not in law codes but precisely in covenants. The Hittite treaties mentioned above (→ 79) laid down the stipulations for the vassal in the form "You [thou] shall not...." It is just such parallelism that has made some scholars willing to accept the Decalogue as the original stipulations of the covenant between God and Israel.

88 **(B) Covenant Law.** To use the word "law" of the original covenant stipulations is somewhat misleading. The Decalogue, for instance, is not law in the usual sense of the word, either in the ancient Near East or in modern society; but the Decalogue is a basis of law. The original covenant stipulation is primarily the revealed moral will of Yahweh, who is not only the custodian of the moral order but also its author and expositor. In the community of the covenant, the will of the God of the covenant is the supreme authority to which every human authority is subordinate. The moral will of Yahweh expressed in the covenant stipulations establishes a distinctively Israelite way of life sanctioned by curse and blessing.

Whether in the Book of the Covenant or elsewhere, the idea of the expansion and interpretation of the revealed moral will of Yahweh led to incorporating into the covenant the corpus of Israelite law. All law was conceived to contribute to the definition of the Israelite way of life imposed by the revealed will of Yahweh. This development cannot be traced before Dt; but that does not prove that the development was original with Dt. In this book of the 7th cent. BC, there was a patent effort to organize Israelite life on the basis of covenant law precisely as such. The law of Dt was a reform measure calculated to avert the threat to Israelite security being offered by habitual and widespread violations of the covenant. The Israelite way of life, it was felt, needed that definition and precision that only a written code could give. The prophets who are echoed in Dt spoke of the moral imperative of the will of Yahweh and of certain flagrant abuses, but they did not elaborate legal prescriptions that would remove doubt and uncertainty in the interpretation of the will of Yahweh. The code of Dt, although not a complete corpus of law, represents those legal prescriptions thought to be vital to the preservation of the covenant and of Israel.

89 After the Exile, the Jewish community of Jerusalem made itself a people of the law. The contents of the law that Ezra promulgated cannot be determined precisely (→ Chronicler, 24:95; → Canonicity, 67:24), but again the contents are less important than the spirit in which the law was declared and accepted. Post-exilic Judaism accepted the law of the Pentateuch as a complete codification of the revealed moral will of Yahweh, and developed an oral law to interpret in detail the written law and to protect it against violation (→ Apocrypha, 68:118). Thus the community felt that the covenant relationship was assured. The development was not altogether wholesome; and in parts of the NT the issue between law and gospel is sharply drawn (→ Pauline Theology, 79:105–116).

90 **(V) Covenant and Cult.** Cult in every religion is an encounter of the community with the deity and a profession of belief. This meaning of cult is not always apparent to those who engage in the cult; cultic symbolism often grows so archaic that few of those who participate in the cult understand its significance, and the ritual degenerates into mere rote or something worse. In the luxuriant ritual of the Priestly Collection Israelite cult exhibits some features of degeneration; but it was not thus from the beginning, and the cult should not be judged on its least attractive features. For cult, as for law, the covenant is the article of faith that confers basic meaning.

Our knowledge of the cult of the ancient Near Eastern peoples shows that many details of the Israelite cult are not peculiar to Israel. The basic elements of cult are myth and ritual. By myth is meant the recital of the saving event, and by ritual, its symbolic re-enactment. Through these two elements of cult the society establishes and maintains communion with the deity. Such recital and the re-enactment appear in Israelite cult with one essential difference: The saving event that is recited is not the mythological event in nature but the saving deeds of Yahweh in history (→ 31 above), namely, the actions by which he delivered Israel from Egypt and established Israel as the people of his covenant in the promised land. In the recital Yahweh reveals himself anew as the God of Israel. It now appears that most of the narratives of the Pentateuch had much of their origin in such ritual recitals.

91 The major festivals of the Israelite calendar—Passover, Unleavened Bread, Weeks, and Tents—have both an agricultural and a historical significance; they are harvest festivals, but they also commemorate events in the history of Israel. The Israelite festivals are not the pure nature festivals found in other ancient Near Eastern religions. In their historical significance they are re-enactments of Yahweh's saving deeds, and by their celebration the saving power and will of Yahweh are experienced anew (→ Religious Institutions, 76:132–48).

92 Scholars have long found it mysterious that the OT Israelite calendar of festivals contains no festival that is properly and formally a covenant festival. In the Judaism of the 1st cent. AD, the Feast of Weeks was celebrated as the anniversary of the revelation of the law (→ Religious Institutions, 76:142); if this is a genuinely ancient interpretation of the feast, we still have no biblical information on the manner in which this theme was celebrated. Scattered allusions in the OT have led a number of recent scholars to postulate some kind of covenant festival that included a recital of the covenant terms and a public pledge by Israel of its fidelity to the covenant. These reconstructions have not been generally accepted, but the principle behind them seems sound; and it is probably by sheer chance that no account of the covenant festival has been preserved.

Several scholars associate the covenant festival with the New Year (→ Religious Institutions, 76:149–154). The New Year festival in Mesopotamia was a re-enactment of creation achieved anew each year with the return of the cycle of fertility. Israel accepts no such fertility cult, which cannot be incorporated into the worship of Yahweh. When Israel celebrates the agricultural festivals, it recognizes in fertility the creative power and the blessing of Yahweh. The saving power and will of Yahweh that are exhibited in the history of Israel are also exhibited in the bounty of the land. By the fruits of the soil Yahweh fulfills the covenant promise of blessing; and by thanking him Israel attests its own fidelity to the covenant, a fidelity which is approved by God's blessing. The fertility of nature is incorporated into the moral will of Yahweh (→ 56 above). In its basic features, then, the Israelite cult fulfills the description of cult as an encounter of the community with the deity and a profession of faith. More than any other element of Israelite religion, we can believe, it communicated to the people of Israel the intimate awareness of the presence and activity of Yahweh as the God of Israel by his covenant.

93 **(VI) Righteousness.** Certain moral attributes of Yahweh are closely associated with the covenant. Here we find ourselves in the area of anthropomorphism (→ 21–22 above); but there is a clear distinction drawn between the qualities in Yahweh and the same qualities in man. In morality, as in everything else, Yahweh is wholly different.

"Righteous" and "righteousness" are the customary Eng translations of the Hebr words *ṣedeq* and *ṣᵉdāqâ*, which only with difficulty can be translated into any modern language. Another translation as "just" and "justice" is inadequate, but not simply because of juridical or forensic connotation (in fact, very often *ṣᵉdāqâ* is predicated of Yahweh or of man as judge). Rather, "just" and "justice" presuppose a whole juridical order that does not exist in Israelite thinking. There is no abstract idea of justice in Israelite thought.

"Righteous" as applied to man describes one who is judicially declared innocent or who has his claim judicially vindicated. This is probably the primary meaning from which other uses of the word are derived: a righteous weight (Lv 19:36, an accurate weight); righteous sacrifices (Dt 33:19, sacrificed according to the correct ritual prescriptions); righteous paths (Ps 23:3, paths that lead in the right direction). A person is righteous not only by a judicial verdict but also because the person has a just claim or is innocent. A righteous judge is a judge who awards the verdict to the righteous litigant. In early usage the word is employed in an extremely simple and unsophisticated sense; the righteous claim is simply my claim, and the righteous judge is the judge who renders a verdict in my favor. This forensic background of the word does not imply that righteousness is merely an extrinsic denomination; the reality of personal innocence or a personal claim is present, but it cannot be an effective reality until it is juridically recognized.

94 The idea of righteousness cannot be transferred to Yahweh without difficulty. The earliest use of the term, it seems, occurs in the Song of Deborah (Jgs 5:11), where the "righteous acts" of Yahweh are his saving deeds on behalf of Israel. He is the judge and lord who vindicates Israel against its enemies; he is called righteous because he is on the side of Israel. Obviously, such a conception is remote from any abstract idea of justice. Righteousness is primarily a saving attribute, indeed it often appears to be synonymous with salvation. The development of the idea of righteousness toward a more objective conception comes with the realization that the righteousness which defends the righteous against the wicked can take a reverse direction if Israel itself is unrighteous.

Righteousness conceived as a purely covenantal attribute is, therefore, subject to certain limitations. The OT approaches most nearly to an abstract and universal idea of justice when Israel perceives that the righteousness of Yahweh is rooted in the divine reality itself. Yahweh cannot act unrighteously; if he could, there would be no genuine righteousness at all. The measure of righteousness, therefore, is not simply the covenant and its stipulations but the actions of Yahweh. There is no righteousness that is not created and maintained by him. His righteousness is not to be measured by human standards, but human standards are to be measured by him.

95 **(VII) Covenant Love.** The Hebr word *ḥesed* has been a more severe problem to translators of the Bible than the word *ṣedeq*, "righteous." The traditional translation "mercy" goes back to the Gk and Lat Bibles. "Loving-kindness" is a better but still inadequate effort. The somewhat clumsy "covenant love," suggested by N. Glueck and adopted here, places in the translation itself the dominant themes implied in the usage of the word. The translation is defective in its failure to indicate that *ḥesed* is not only the love exhibited in virtue of the covenant but also the movement of the will that initiates the covenant. In common usage *ḥesed* includes kinship love as well as covenant love.

Ḥesed is a normal part of good human relations, but it has its proper place within members of a group, even if the association is as temporary as the relation of host and guest. *Ḥesed* is a kindness that is above and beyond the minimum duties imposed by the association; but the maintenance of good human relations demands that people do go beyond the minimum duties.

96 The meaning of covenant love is more clearly understood through the words with which it is most frequently associated. It is often joined with "fidelity" (*'ĕmet* or *'ĕmûnâ*), the attribute by which Yahweh fulfills his covenant and his promises (Ex 34:6; cf. Jn 1:14). Indeed, the two words are united closely in the noun pair, "steadfast covenant love" (*ḥesed we'ĕmet*). Love is also joined with judgment (→ 136 below); covenant love in the judge is his readiness to save. Covenant love, fidelity, judgment, and righteousness are the attributes of the ideal ruler (Is 16:5); together they designate the will to save. Covenant love is also associated frequently with "salvation."

97 Covenant love is an emotional complex. Yahweh exhibits it to Israel his bride (Jer 2:2), and will show it again when he restores Israel after its fall (Jer 31:2; Hos 2:21). The anthropopathism implicit in the word is most clearly exhibited by Hosea and Jeremiah who employ the analogy of the marriage of Yahweh and Israel with extraordinarily profound feeling. *Ḥesed* is most frequently associated with the covenant. It is a fruit of the covenant itself (Ex 20:6; 34:6); and indeed the formation of the covenant is an act of covenant love (Is 55:3). Breach of the covenant is a sufficient reason for Yahweh to withdraw his covenant love, but it would be out of character for him to do so. His covenant love is more enduring than the good will of man, and it is a forgiving attribute as well as a benevolent attitude to which Israel can appeal when it has sinned against the covenant (Ex 34:6; Nm 14:19; Jer 3:12).

98 It has been noticed that "covenant love" is broader than the covenant itself. It is the movement of the will of Yahweh that initiates and continues the history of Israel (Is 54:10; 63:7; Jer 31:3; Mi 7:20). Indeed the entire history of the encounter of Israel with Yahweh—and this is the history of Israel—can be summed up as one act of covenant love. In the OT this attribute is the dominating motive of the acts of Yahweh; it gives singleness of purpose and ultimate intelligibility to his dealings with men, even when these dealings include anger and judgment. More than any other attribute, this love is the attribute that gives Yahweh personal identity; it is the key to the understanding of his character. (N. Glueck, *Hesed in the Bible* [Cincinnati, 1967].)

ASPECTS OF THE RELATIONS BETWEEN GOD AND ISRAEL

99 **(I) Anger.** Of all the anthropopathisms applied to God, anger is perhaps the most difficult for the modern mind to apprehend with sympathy. Yet anger is as much a human emotion as love, and each is a human way of conceiving and speaking of the deity. Each emotion denotes a reality that must not be omitted in any attempt to describe the relations of God and man, along with the divine nature from which these relations arise. Our difficulty in conceiving anger in God was not felt by the writers of the OT; the anger of Yahweh is mentioned more frequently than the anger of man.

100 To some extent the idea of divine anger was a part of the cultural inheritance of Israel from the ancient Near East. Where nature was mythologically understood as the area of diverse and conflicting personages (→ 27, 51 above), natural catastrophe was easily understood as the effects of divine anger. Ancient Mesopotamian peoples were unable to conceive the divine anger without an element of caprice; not only did the motivation of the divine anger escape human understanding, but actually the divine anger was often regarded as irrational and unmotivated.

Such an idea of divine anger is rejected by Israelite belief; the anger of Yahweh is always associated with his righteousness, his judgments, his holiness, his covenant. There is a direct connection between the anger of Yahweh and the sin of man; if the connection is not perceived, it must be presumed to exist. The Israelites are ready to admit that divine anger, like divine wisdom, is more profound than human anger, and is elicited where human anger would not be. If this happens, the righteous judgment of Yahweh must be accepted. There is another element, pointed out by W. Eichrodt, that plays a role in moderating the Israelite fear of Yahweh's anger—the realization that anger is not the habitual attitude of Yahweh. Habitually Yahweh is inclined to show covenant love, and his anger is the exceptional eruption. Yahweh's anger endures only for a moment; his covenant love endures for life (Ps 30:6).

101 Anger in the OT occupies the place that justice occupies in modern thinking about the deity. The difference between the two approaches is the difference between the personal and the impersonal. While it is easier for modern man to think of God as the author and defender of a juridical order, in Israelite thought Yahweh is personally offended by breaches of the covenant, and responds not only with authority and power, but also with a personal revulsion against the offender. This is part of the pattern of the Israelite conception of the living God (→ 22 above) and of the Israelite conviction of the malice of sin. Were Yahweh not angered by sin, he would not take it seriously.

The object of the anger of Yahweh mentioned most frequently is the people of Israel; his anger is motivated by Israel's unbelief, distrust, rebellion, and worship of false gods. His anger is excited by inhumanity and human pride, and by refusal to observe his laws. Other nations also are the objects of his anger because of their pride and arrogance, particularly when they attack Israel; such attacks are an implicit denial of the power of Yahweh to protect his people. Certain heinous crimes also arouse his anger, such as the crimes that preceded the deluge and the destruction of Sodom and Gomorrah.

102 In contrast to ethically motivated instances of Yahweh's anger are other instances that approach the irrational. To the Israelite these outbursts are aroused by offenses against the holiness of Yahweh, the very essence of his divinity that is unfathomable for human wisdom. Such are the attacks of Yahweh against Jacob (Gn 32:23ff.) and Moses (Ex 4:24ff.), the anger excited by too near an approach to Yahweh or by the sight of his countenance (Ex 19:9–25; 33:20; Jgs 13:22; Is 6:5), or by contact with sacred objects (1 Sm 6:19; 2 Sm 6:7). The anger of Yahweh is veiled in the mystery of his holiness and cannot be submitted to human calculation; it is never unrighteous, but it is sometimes unintelligible.

Yahweh's anger is often a blazing consuming fire (Jer 17:4; Is 30:27; 65:5) or a furious storm (Jer 30:23; Is 30:30). It is a liquid that can be poured out (Hos 5:10; Jer 6:11; Ez 7:8; Ps 69:25), a bitter poisonous drink that makes men stagger (Jer 25:15; Is 51:17,22). The anger of Yahweh annihilates unless it is restrained (Dt 7:4; Nm 16:21; Is 30:28; Jer 4:23–26). It is restrained by his covenant love, which can be reached by intercession (Ex 32:11ff.; Nm 11:1ff.; 14:11–20). But Yahweh's anger can reach a pitch where intercession is no longer effective (Jer 14:11–12; Ez 14:14). However, this anger never exceeds due bounds, and indeed is thought never to reach the fullness that the objects of anger deserve.

103 **(II) Revelation.** The conviction that Yahweh is a God of revelation is fundamental to OT belief. Yahweh as a personal being cannot be known except through revelation; one person can reveal himself to another only by speech. The acts of Yahweh are forms of revelation, just as the acts of any person manifest the reality of the person; but the meaning of the acts of Yahweh can be understood only through the interpretation of Yahweh himself. The will of Yahweh cannot be ascertained by the arts of divination universally practiced in the ancient Near East. (Actually in the religions of Israel's neighbors there was no expectation that divination would disclose the character of the gods whose will was being investigated. A knowledge of the character of these gods was not regarded as necessary, for the will of the gods did not exhibit any moral pattern.)

104 **(A) Nature of Revelation.** Yahweh's revelation of himself occurs in history and is a historical event that the OT locates in time and place. This does not mean that revelation is a single incident; the revelation of Yahweh, inasmuch as it is the revelation of a person, is a developing process; for no person can be known through a single encounter. Insight into the character of Yahweh grows in depth through the successive periods of Israelite history. One should not expect to find the same understanding of Yahweh in the period of the judges or in the early monarchy that one finds in the era of the 8th-cent. prophets. Nor is the process entirely unilinear. Students of the OT have observed that the understanding of Yahweh found in the post-exilic literature frequently fails to attain the clarity of vision that is found in such earlier sources as Hos, Is, and Dt-Is. Any particular passage or writing of the OT must be studied in its historical context, determined as precisely as possible; for the revelation found in each writing is a response to a determined historical situation (→ Hermeneutics, 71:18). The OT does not deal in generalities.

105 The OT has its own terminology of revelation, which can be misleading if it is not distinguished from more recent terminology. In the OT the response to revelation is not "faith" but "knowledge." These two terms do not mean what they mean in modern theology. The knowledge of Yahweh that is communicated by his speech is not speculative but experiential. The words and the deeds of Yahweh give Israel a personal experience of him that is like the experience of other persons. This is not purely intellectual knowledge, but the complex of experience, feeling, and desire that a personal encounter elicits. In some contexts to know Yahweh is to do his revealed will (Jer 22:16). In other contexts to know him is to recognize him in the character in which he has revealed himself, as in the frequent phrase, "They shall know that I am Yahweh." The OT conception of revelation includes the word spoken by Yahweh and the knowledge that issues from the word. That which Yahweh reveals is himself, not propositions. The OT relates the encounter of Yahweh and Israel: the manifestation of Yahweh and the response of Israel.

106 The personal reality of Yahweh is not thought to lie within the comprehension of man. The OT recognizes that Yahweh is mysterious: His thoughts are not the thoughts of man, and his ways are not the ways of man (Is 55:8–9). He is wonderful in counsel and excellent in wisdom (Is 28:29). To make Yahweh comprehensible would be to reduce him to the level of his creatures; to challenge him is to speak what one does not understand (Jb 42:3). Before the mystery the only proper position of man is the posture of submission, for the manifestation of Yahweh makes man's assertion of self ridiculous.

107 **(B) Channels of Revelation.** Yahweh reveals himself through inspired spokesmen called *prophets*. The first in the line of Israel's spokesmen, Moses, is not called a prophet in the earlier sources (but cf. Dt 18:18; Nm 12:6–8); he stands outside the line because of his uniquely close association with Yahweh. The prophet has the charisma of the word of Yahweh (→ 45 above); the prophetic mystical experience is normally described by the analogy of speech and hearing. Prophecy appears through the history of Israel from the early monarchy into the post-exilic period, when it loses its vigor and finally disappears (although some vital features of prophecy survive in apocalyptic; → Post-exilic Period, 20:21–24). Through this period the prophet is the conscience of Israel, its admonitor in public and private morality, in its internal administration and external politics. There is no sphere of life in which the word of Yahweh is irrelevant (→ Prophetic Lit, 12:13–21).

108 *Wisdom* is not, like prophecy, represented as an experience of hearing the word of Yahweh. Yet, at least in the post-exilic period, true wisdom is a gift of Yahweh and cannot be achieved by merely human investigation, for Yahweh alone has true wisdom (→ Wisdom Lit, 28:38). Wisdom is the skill by which one manages one's life and affairs; without the communication of Yahweh's wisdom no one can hope to achieve success and prosperity even in his private affairs. Wisdom moves on a lower level than prophecy; but it applies the revealed will of Yahweh to the business of daily life and shows the permanent importance of personal decision even in affairs of purely personal significance.

109 As the creator of Israel, Yahweh has revealed himself in the institutions of Israel. The weight of his revealed will enforces the *law* of Israel (→ 88 above). Israelite tradition is also an expression of his voice; and hence the priests have the office of interpretating his will in *torah*, instruction. The instruction given by the priests dealt primarily with cultic questions; but to an undetermined extent they were also the spokesmen of Yahweh in the interpretation of Israelite morality.

110 Yahweh reveals himself in *nature* (→ 55–60 above); but to the Israelite this is an inarticulate revelation. The nations fail to recognize the divine reality of Yahweh in nature and worship false gods. Israel knows Yahweh because he has spoken to Israel, and therefore Israel can recognize him in his creative works. The activity of Yahweh in nature is not distinguished from his activity in history; his power is always directed to his purpose of salvation and judgment (→ 136ff., 140ff. below). Once Yahweh is known, his activity is apparent in every detail of nature; to the Israelite the normal phenomenon is as much a sign of the personal intervention of Yahweh as the abnormal.

Finally, Yahweh reveals himself chiefly in *history*, as we shall now discuss.

111 **(III) Lord of History.** The idea of history as a unified series of events is not found in the ancient Near East. The records of events preserved from the civilizations of this area are annals and chronicles in which events are listed according to year and summed up for regnal periods. We have no instances of any attempts to establish a pattern in events, to show a development in the life and the culture of a people. For these peoples their own beginnings are the object of mythology, not of history; and the beginnings of institutions are also the object of mythology (→ 23 above). The event of myth is the constant event that recurs in a cyclic rhythm; it is the annual return of the seasons, the celestial revolutions, the cycle of day and night, the perpetual conflict between order and chaos. In opposition to the mythical event is the contingent historical event, singular and irreversible. The life of man is lived against the cycle of myth and ultimately returns to its beginning, whence the process is resumed once more. In this thinking, history was merely an epiphenomenon in nature. Ancient Near Eastern man sought no issue from the cycle of myth and hoped for no issue.

Even the Greeks, who were responsible for the beginnings of modern historical thought, did not rise above the cyclical ideal of history. At the risk of reading something into the mind of Gk thinkers, one may see in the cyclical conception of history an effort to synthesize the unchanging world of intelligible reality and the flux of contingent events. Events could be made intelligible in Gk thought only by constraining them into recurring cycles that the mind can grasp. In the cycle, events follow a set and predictable pattern of origin, rise, decline, and fall. The pattern of history visible in Herodotus' account of the Persian wars and Thucydides' history of the Peloponnesian war shows the same sense of inevitability that is the motif of Gk tragedy.

112 **(A) The Old Testament as History.** In the ancient world the OT is a unique collection of historical documents. A historical framework dominates the entire collection; H. W. Robinson has said that the OT is a history into which other kinds of literature have been incorporated (*Inspiration and Revelation in the Old Testament* [Oxford, 1946] 123). The Pentateuch presents the history of the origins of Israel and, in the complex of the history, the laws and the institutions that are attributed to this period. With the historical books from Jos to Chr inclusive belongs the prophetic collection; the separate books of the prophets can be understood only if it is recognized that they are responses to the events of the history, many of which are mentioned in the prophetic writings. Those portions of the OT that seem most timeless are the wisdom and poetic books; these also are included in the collection dominated by history, if not incorporated in the strict sense of the term. Many of the titles of the Ps offer a curious example of the historical thinking on the part of the compilers of the OT; these titles are attempts, often by sheer conjecture, to find an occasion in the life of David when the psalm was written (→ Psalms, 35:4–5).

113 The OT collection of the literary remains of Israel is properly a history of Israel, although it is not history in the modern sense of the term. The OT is a theological statement and interpretation of history. For Israel its history is its encounter with Yahweh. The very idea that history is a process with beginning, middle, and end is original with Israel. It is the will and purpose of Yahweh that unifies the process. The historic career of Israel is directed by the will of Yahweh to fulfill his designs. These designs are not revealed in their full clarity at any stage of the process; e.g., the insight into the designs of Yahweh in history that appears in the J tradition of the Pentateuch (probably from the reign of David; → Pentateuch, 1:14) is more elementary than the insight manifested in Dt-Is. The serene confidence that is characteristic of J rests on the assurance that history is not the chance collision of blind forces without meaning or purpose nor an epiphenomenon of the eternally recurring cycles of nature; it is the execution of an intelligent plan. But in J, as in the entire OT, the acceptance of history as the execution of the designs of Yahweh demands an act of faith. It is the saving and judging will of Yahweh that gives to history both intelligibility and morality. It gives intelligibility, for it defines both the origin and the end of the human experience in history and the process by which the two are joined. It gives morality, for it shows that history is governed by a supremely powerful and entirely incorruptible moral will. The fulfillment of the process is conditioned neither by human success nor by human failure. Human achievement is not the agent that brings about the fulfillment of history and destiny, and human sin does not block the accomplishment of the purpose of history.

114 In the J tradition the activity of Yahweh begins with the creation of man; in the E tradition, with the call of Abraham, and in the P tradition, with the creation of the world. The point of origin differs; what the traditions have in common is the conviction that it is the act of Yahweh that initiates the historical process. Thereafter, each turn in the history of Israel is the result of a decisive intervention of Yahweh. He manifests himself to the descendants of Abraham, sends Joseph to Egypt to prepare a place for his people; and when they are oppressed by the Egyptians, he intervenes in a brilliantly new fashion by revealing himself to Moses, liberating his people from Egypt, and forming a covenant with them. Under his guidance and with his assistance they take possession of the land of Canaan. There they are assailed by various enemies, from whom Yahweh delivers them by the charismatic leadership of the judges. When the Philistine crisis proves too severe for a politically unorganized group, the kingship is instituted to meet this threat. Although the traditions of the institution of the monarchy are variant both in details and in the conception of kingship (→ 1–2 Samuel, 9:19), they agree that kingship is from Yahweh.

The period of the monarchy is the period of prophecy, and the spokesmen of Yahweh reveal and interpret the acts of Yahweh in history: the schism of the kingdom, the fall of the dynasty of Omri, and above all the collapse of the kingdoms of Israel and Judah under the attacks of the great powers. The entire series of events is woven into a unity by the deuteronomic historians to exhibit the judgment of Yahweh on the infidelity of Israel (→ 1–2 Kings, 10:79). After the Exile the re-establishment of a Jewish community under the law is another great saving act of Yahweh. The history of Israel throughout attests the wholly consistent and righteous deeds of Yahweh, who stands revealed in his holiness.

115 The Israelite consciousness of history is attested in such "credos" or professions of faith as Dt 6:20–25; 26:5–10; Jos 24:2–13. Similar recitals are found in Pss 77; 78; 105; 106. These Credos are liturgical. The cult was formed around the historic memory of the deeds of Yahweh (→ 90 above). When Israel wished to profess its belief in Yahweh, its "knowledge" of him, it uttered its profession by reciting his deeds in history. From these deeds Israel developed a consciousness of itself as a historical reality with an origin and a destiny. So deep was Israel's awareness of its place in history that it, alone of the peoples contemporary with it in the ancient world, exhibited a sense of its history as a career with a determined finality.

116 **(B) Determinism and Universality.** Two further questions arise from the consideration of the Israelite conception of history. The first is the question of *determinism*: if Yahweh is the lord of history, as Israel believed him to be, is man a truly free and responsible agent in history? It has been noticed above (→ 111) that Gk thought, dominated by the logic of Parmenides, saw reality and intelligibility only in one unchanging being. Hence it reduced the contingent events of history to cycles of necessity, thus obtaining intelligibility by effectively denying contingency and human liberty. Does Israelite thought escape the inner necessity of logic only to fall into a necessity imposed by a supremely powerful will that controls events absolutely?

The OT never proposes this problem speculatively, and it does not appear to have been a problem for the Israelites. The OT affirms both the sovereignty of Yahweh and the freedom and responsibility of man. Were man not a responsible agent, he would not be an object of judgment. When the prophets charge Israel with sin, they do not fail to warn that Israel can escape the imminent judgment by conversion—until a point of cumulative malice is reached at which conversion can assure only survival, but not the reversal of the course of history and judgment. The prophets show no awareness of any conflict between the sovereignty of Yahweh and the freedom of man; the theological concept of history demands that neither of these beliefs be maintained at the expense of the other.

117 The second question concerns the *universal scope of history*: what is the place of other nations in the historical process dominated by the will of Yahweh? Here, as much as anywhere, one can trace development in the insights of Israel. For early Israel other peoples are enemies or they are irrelevant. If they are enemies of Israel, they are hostile to the purpose of Yahweh in history, and he removes them. With the rise of prophecy and a deeper awareness of the totally demanding moral will of Yahweh, the foreign nations take their place in the historical process as the weapons of Yahweh's judgment on Israel. Outside of this position they are again irrelevant; unlike Israel, they have no destiny in history. Hence much of the preexilic literature is parochial in its treatment of other peoples. During the period of the Exile and afterward Israel perceives that the universal lordship of Yahweh cannot be vindicated unless he is recognized as Yahweh by all peoples. If all peoples are to know him, then they will share the religious gift that was originally conferred on Israel; and ultimately the differences between Israel and other peoples must and will be obliterated. Yahweh had not made the world a chaos; he made it to be inhabited, and every one must confess at last that he alone is God (Is 45:18–24). The glory that belongs to Yahweh is not manifested unless he is universally recognized in the fullness in which he has made himself known to Israel. The function of Israel in history then becomes the function of mediating the knowledge of Yahweh to the nations.

118 **(IV) Morality.** That the morality of the OT rises notably above the morality of other ancient Near Eastern religious documents is no longer seriously questioned. Yet it is not easy to point out precisely where the differences lie, and it is still less easy to trace the development of OT morality. Earlier critics commonly made monotheism the decisive factor in the formation of OT morality, and they attributed both monotheism and a deeper moral consciousness to the prophets of the 8th cent. More recent scholarship has found this explanation oversimplified (→ Prophetic Lit, 12:20–21). Both monotheism and a sharper conscience must be dated earlier than the 8th cent.; and certain limitations in the moral insight of the OT appear after this date.

Association of religion and morality appears in the ancient Near East outside Israel. In other ancient religions the gods are the guardians of morality; the language in which this belief is uttered may often seem conventional, but there is no reason to think that a genuine belief does not lie behind the conventions. The difference between these ancient beliefs and Israelite beliefs can be summed up under two heads: For other religions the gods are not the sources of moral principles nor of moral obligation; and the gods themselves exhibit no moral character. Morality, therefore, becomes ultimately conventional, and moral obligation becomes merely the social pressure of the community rejecting that behavior that is socially intolerable. In spite of the explicit association of religion and morality in the literature, the morality of the other ancient Near Eastern peoples does not rise above humanism.

119 In Israel the association between religion and morality reposes on the historical and the revelational character of Yahweh. For Israel's polytheistic neighbors, the gods alone possess true freedom, which consists in release from all moral restraint. On the one hand, Israel does not believe that Yahweh is restrained or bound by a higher moral law, for all moral law is imposed by his will. On the other hand, for an Israelite it would be incomprehensible that Yahweh would indulge in vice: He exhibits in the supreme degree the morality that his will imposes upon his creatures. The moral will of Yahweh is revealed in the covenant, and the stipulations of the covenant oblige Israel to a peculiarly Israelite way of life governed by that will (→ 88 above). Failure to meet these obligations is faithlessness and treachery. Through observance of these duties the Israelites attain the "holiness" that is proper to the people of Yahweh. Holiness in the OT is more than a moral attribute; it is the essence of divinity itself, with which Israel can communicate by meeting the standards of conduct imposed by Yahweh.

120 This conviction does not imply that all or most of Israel's moral principles are directly and formally revealed by Yahweh. Israel has its folk morality that is the immediate source of its public and private morality. Folk morality creates the Israelite way of life; conduct opposed to this way is "folly in Israel" or "not done in Israel" (Gn 34:7; Jos 7:15; Jgs 19:23; 20:6,10; 2 Sm 13:12; Jer 29:23). Here it must be noted that folk morality in Israel rises not merely from Israel as an ethnic community, but from Israel as a community of faith; it is the folk morality of the covenanted people of Yahweh. Hence the development of Israelite morality is always substantially affected by Israel's conviction about the moral character of Yahweh. (For examples of Israelite morality, see C. L. Salm, *Readings in Biblical Morality* (Englewood Cliffs, N.J., 1966.)

This influence can be suggested in two areas: the morality of sex and the humanity of Israelite law. The *morality of sex* is far more rigorous in Israel than among its neighbors. It is not merely fanciful to see in this a reflection of the character of Yahweh himself in contrast to the gods and goddesses of the fertility cults. Sexual license profanes the holiness of a God who is above all sexual processes. The *humanity of Israelite law* is exhibited in a singular respect for the honor and the dignity of the human person. This respect appears in the treatment of slaves, in the rarity of the capital penalty as compared with other ancient laws, in the absence of torture and mutilation as penalties, and in insistence on the equal legal rights of all members of the community. Humanity is extended also to foreigners resident in Israel. The respect for the dignity of the human person, it seems, should be connected with Israelite belief about the nature of man and the relations of man with Yahweh (→ 63 above). It is true that neither sexual morality nor humanity in Israelite laws is without limitations (→ 123 below), but even with the limitations there is a perceptible superiority over other moral systems, which, therefore, cannot be the sources of Israelite morality.

121 It is also peculiarly Israelite that the emphasis lies on *the heart* as the principle of morality. The heart in Hebr idiom is not the seat of the emotions, as it is in modern speech; the "heart" is more nearly synonymous with our word "mind." But whatever the translation, the insistence on the heart means that morality must be interior, must be rooted in conviction and desire. Genuine morality is not exterior demeanor nor conformity to social manners. The contrast is explicit in Is 29:13. It is probably too much to say that the OT reaches the idea that morality is itself something interior; for the idea remains that it is the actions and the words of a man, and not his thoughts and desires, that determine his moral character. But it is recognized that words and actions are not honest unless they come from the heart.

122 The morality of the OT shows both growth and limitations. At the beginning of the *growth*, the narratives of the historical books from Gn through Kgs show Israelite heroes and heroines frequently acting on a low moral level. One should not too quickly take the absence of moral judgments in the narratives as instances of tacit approval; for Israelite authors were capable of expressing moral judgments in a subtle way, as one can see in the stories of Jacob and the family history of David. The record itself shows, however, that these early biblical figures are often only lightly touched by what we have pointed out as the distinctive features of Israelite morality. The high moral passion of Amos and Isaiah does not appear in early Israel; but the conviction that the will of Yahweh is the urgent motive of moral obligation does appear. In the post-exilic conception of the law as the compendium of morality there is a certain relaxation from the level of the writings of the prophets; the code of morality is more refined, but morality itself has been systemized to the point where external observance may become more important than the morality of the heart—a complaint made in the Gospels (Mt 23:28).

123 The *limitations* of Israelite morality have often been pointed out; they include the acceptance of slavery, polygamy, and divorce, the double standard of sexual morality (stricter on women), a remarkably intense hatred of foreigners, inhumanity in war, and a certain laxness in regard to mendacity and theft. In these instances Israelite morality fails to rise entirely above the morality of its world, though even in these areas it is somewhat superior. A more refined moral insight should not be demanded as if morality were something that could be produced instantly; Israelite morality was not the creation of a few intellectuals but the code of behavior of an entire people, a folk morality in its development as in its origins. The remarkable feature of Israelite morality is that it contained the principles by which its limitations could be overcome.

124 Personal morality in the OT is principally the concern of the wisdom literature (→ Wisdom Lit, 28:35). The maxims of wisdom, often paralleled in other ancient wisdom literatures, instruct the young man on how to manage his life. The morality of the sages has often been called pedestrian, and to a degree it is; the sages deal with the situations of everyday life, and they have no occasion to teach a morality of crisis or to propose heroism. Their motivation at times appears less than noble, although it is not positively ignoble; moral conduct is recommended because it assures success and happiness. Against this eudaemonism must be measured the conviction of the sages that morality is wisdom, and vice is folly; the essence of wisdom is the fear of Yahweh. The belief that moral conduct will assure worldly success is too simple and needs further refinement; but the sages do not believe that one can ever advance one's success by wrongdoing. Only by righteous conduct can one be certain of "peace," the state of well-being with God and with man. Peace is the gift of Yahweh, and he does not grant it to the wicked (Is 57:21). The wisdom literature, except for Jb and Eccl, does not meet the problem of the righteous man who suffers, and traditional wisdom really lacked the resources to meet this problem; but the principles of wisdom demand that the problem shall not be met by abandoning righteousness. The "peace" of the wicked is neither genuine nor lasting.

125 **(V) Sin.** The biblical concept of sin is expressed by a number of Hebr words; a survey of four of the most important words shows the multiple OT approach to the idea. In modern moral theology sin is defined as the voluntary transgression of a divine law; there is no Hebr word that can be so defined. The basic word usually translated by "sin," *ḥaṭṭā't*, means a missing of the mark, a failure: One who "sins" fails to meet what is expected of him in relation to another person. In the cognate languages the same word is used to designate the rebellion of a vassal against his overlord. Another word, *'āwōn*, means a twisted or distorted condition: One who sins is crooked or deformed, he deviates from the standard. This word is usually translated "guilt"; it designates the permanent damage that is done to the person by the sinful act. Still another term, *peša'*, means rebellion. When used of interpersonal relations, it designates the violation of the rights of others; when used of the sins of Israel, it connotes infidelity to the obligations of the covenant. Finally, *ma'al* means infidelity, the breach of an obligation freely undertaken. Sin is also called a lie, the act that denies the reality of one's professions, an abandonment of the truth; thus, sin is an attack on reality. Sin is folly, which in Hebr does not mean an intellectual error but the choice of a course of action that is stupid because it is disastrous. (For further information about sin and its expiation, → Religious Institutions, 76:83–88.)

126 The OT is aware of the universality of sin, although less aware than the writers of the NT, especially Paul (→ Pauline Theology, 79:99–104). Emphasis in the OT falls on the sins of Israel rather than on the sins of mankind. Israel is a people of unclean lips, unworthy of seeing Yahweh (Is 6:5). Jeremiah sees no innocent person in Jerusalem and Judah (Jer 5:1–6; 8:10); there is no man who does not sin (1 Kgs 8:46). No one can survive if Yahweh reckons iniquities (Ps 130:3). No man is righteous or innocent before God (Jb 4:17; 15:14). The consciousness of the universality of sin grows with Israel's historic experience; the shattering events of the fall of the Israelite monarchies and of the Exile leave the survivors of early Judaism with a sense of sinfulness that is almost excessive. Where Yahweh punishes so severely, the guilt of man must be great indeed.

127 The universality of sin rises from evil inclinations within man himself. The thoughts of man's heart are evil from his youth (Gn 6:5). Jeremiah frequently alludes to the evil inclinations of the heart (Jer 16:12; 18:12); the heart of man is treacherous and sick (17:9). No serious effort is made in the OT to investigate further into this condition or into its origins; but it is the belief of both J and P that this is not the original condition of man. In P, man is made in the image and likeness of Elohim and, like other creatures, is very good (Gn 1:31). In J, the man and woman perceive that they are naked only after they have sinned (Gn 3:7); this verse implies that disorderly sexual appetite did not exist in man in his original creation.

128 The longest and most explicit treatment of sin is found in the J account of Gn 3–11. Gn 3 should not be interpreted apart from the chapters that follow; the Paradise story contains an account of the first sin, and the following chapters relate the spread of sin until it reaches the point where Yahweh can no longer tolerate it. The first sin is followed by the first murder, polygamous marriage, the invention of weapons, the first cry of vengeance, and the growth of wickedness to the degree where Yahweh repents his creation of man and wipes out the entire race by the deluge. The family of one innocent man is spared, and the evil propensity of man that led to his doom (6:5) becomes a motive of Yahweh's kindly tolerance (8:21). But the race that rises after the deluge falls into intoxication, into unnatural vice, and finally into the pride that moves men to erect the tower of Babel. The panorama of wickedness drawn by J is vast and impressive, and it sets the background for the story of the saving acts and judgments of Yahweh that follows. Here, more clearly than elsewhere in the OT, the universality of sin is set forth; and at the same time the response of Yahweh to the sins of men is revealed.

The Paradise story of Gn 3 is an account of the first sin and of its consequences, namely, the curse of those processes of fertility by which human life is sustained, and death as the inevitable end of man's struggle for survival. But the Paradise story is also a splendid psychological study of the sinful act, unparalleled elsewhere in the OT. In a brief and very simple dialogue the writer traces with masterful art the self-deception of the sinner, the rationalization of his action in his own mind, the desire to be something greater than he is, and the sinful choice made under the personal pressure of another. Almost every Hebr word for sin is illustrated in the steps by which the man and the woman rebel against the restraint of the will of Yahweh. It has long been a puzzle that this powerful narrative has no explicit echo in the other books of the OT before the Greek period, but the narrative is entirely in harmony with the OT attitude toward sin.

129 GUILT. Correlative with sin is guilt; and the peculiarity of this conception in the OT is best seen in the fact that there is no distinct Hebr word for guilt. The words for sin, in particular *ḥaṭṭā't* and *'āwōn*, in some contexts can be translated only by guilt; they designate a permanent condition that is produced by the sinful act and is sometimes described in most realistic terms. Guilt is a burden that can be laid upon one (Nm 12:11), that must be borne (Gn 4:13), that can be passed from father to son (Lv 26:39). It is a crack in a wall that will fall suddenly upon the guilty (Is 30:13). It falls upon the head of the evildoer (Is 3:9; Jer 7:19; Ez 22:31). It is like water kept cool in a cistern (Jer 6:7), like rust corroding a metal vessel (Ez 24:6ff.). These examples show how the OT pictures sin as an enduring evil, present and active in the world; the sinful act remains, doing damage beyond repair.

130 This guilt can extend through an entire social group (→ 70 above); indeed, the prophets usually address the entire community of Israel. All mankind perishes in the flood; the entire cities of Sodom and Gomorrah perish in fire from heaven. More difficult for the modern mind is the collective guilt that lies at the base of such stories as those of Achan (Jos 7) and of the descendants of Saul (2 Sm 21). This idea of group responsibility, so foreign to our ways of thinking, is understood only in the framework of Israelite thinking about society as a kinship relationship (→ 68 above). But the idea illustrates the profound Israelite belief in the reality of guilt and of the power of guilt to wreak harm far beyond the individual person who commits the sin. Guilt is a disease, an infection that corrupts the entire group in which the sin is committed.

In some episodes of the OT there is a more primitive conception of guilt as something mechanical and independent of personal responsibility. The guilt in such stories is less an abiding malice than a certain material infection that can be contracted even by the innocent. Thus the kings who in ignorance take the wives of the patriarchs are punished with illness in their households (Gn 20:3ff.; 26:10); Jonathan's unknowing contravention of his father's vow is a mortal offense (1 Sm 14); Uzzah dies when he touches the Ark (2 Sm 6). The punishment that comes is an impersonal, almost demonic effect evoked by the material act. In such a primitive concept of guilt the idea of personal malice and responsibility, and with it the moral will of Yahweh, is obscured. The spiritual growth of Israel would involve rising above this primitive way of thinking.

131 The words of the prophets, in contrast, emphasize the personal nature of sin as a rupture of personal relations with Yahweh. In respect to Yahweh, man's sin is pride (Am, Is), adultery (Hos, Jer, Ez), filial disobedience, and ingratitude (Is, Jer). The classical prophets all dwell upon the fact that sin is a deliberate choice made with full knowledge; sin is contempt of Yahweh, a profanation of his holiness and effectively a denial of his divinity. They emphasize also the personal response of Yahweh. The anger of Yahweh is a concept totally opposed to the mechanical conception of guilt and punishment (→ 100 above). When Yahweh punishes sin, he is personally involved. His anger is not blind rage; it is directed by judgment (→ 138 below), and the judgments of Yahweh are not impersonal.

132 **(VI) Forgiveness.** The removal of sin and guilt is a matter of vital concern in the religion of the OT. Community with Yahweh is life itself; and if community with Yahweh is sundered, there is no hope of security. If community is to be restored, the anger of Yahweh must be appeased. There is no belief that man himself can restore community with Yahweh. As the community was a free gift of grace in the first instance, so the restoration of community cannot be achieved by man's merits. Man must commit himself to the mercy and the forgiveness of Yahweh. The system of cultic expiation that is found in Lv–Nm is not directed to the ritual obtaining of forgiveness. For sins commited "with a high hand" (Nm 15:30; cf. 1 Sm 3:14) there is no ritual expiation. The "sin" and "guilt" for which sacrifices are offered are not malicious acts; they are inadvertent failures to meet ritual prescriptions. One may judge from the words of the prophets that the Israelites frequently regarded their sacrificial ritual as a mechanical atonement that was automatically effective (Jer 7:9). This is not the idea that governs the ritual prescriptions, and the prophets attack this idea as gross superstition (→ Religious Institutions, 76:87).

133 Expiation of formal sins is achieved only by bearing the punishment that follows the guilt; indeed, guilt and punishment sometimes seem almost to be identified. When Nathan announces to David that Yahweh has forgiven David's sin, he says that David will not die (2 Sm 12). But the guilt is a present and active reality; and while the life of David is spared, the penalty of death falls upon the child of David and Bathsheba. The entire account that follows in 2 Sm 13–20 relates the disasters that fall upon David and his house after his crime. Without explicitly moralizing, the writer shows that the fortunes of David are reversed by this crisis in his life. The moral impact of the story is no less massive than the impact of the J account of the origin and spread of sin in Gn 3–11 (→ 128 above).

134 To obtain forgiveness *conversion* is necessary. Conversion is usually expressed by the Hebr word that means "turn" (the verb *šûb*), frequently used in prophetic admonitions addressed to Israel. W. Eichrodt (*Theology* 2, 465) has assembled numerous phrases that fill out the idea of conversion: To seek Yahweh, to ask for him, to humble oneself, to direct one's heart to Yahweh, to seek good, to hate evil and to love good, to learn to do good, to obey, to acquire a new heart, to circumcise one's heart, to plow a new furrow, to wash oneself from wickedness. The abundance of these metaphors shows that conversion is conceived as a genuine interior change of attitude that issues in a revolution in personal conduct.

The assurance of forgiveness reposes on the forgiving character of Yahweh, which is often attested (Am 7:2ff.; Hos 11:8ff.; Pss 78:38; 103:3). Yahweh desires not that the wicked man die but that he be converted from his evil ways and live (Ez 18:23). Confession of Yahweh's forgiveness is frequent in Is 40–55. In the Exile, Israel has atoned for its former wickedness; its community with Yahweh is restored and he is ready to fulfil his promises. The prophet sees in Yahweh the father, the shepherd, the avenging kinsman, the savior (→ 75 above).

135 There is a large amount of anthropomorphism (→ 21–22 above) in the conception of the motives that prompt Yahweh's forgiveness. Israel appeals to his covenant love and his fidelity to his promises; and in spite of the faithlessness of Israel to the covenant, there is an assurance that the good will of Yahweh is not limited by covenant stipulations. Israel appeals to the promises of Yahweh and to his oaths sworn to the patriarchs, which should not be frustrated even by the failure of Israel to measure up to the stature of the patriarchs. Yahweh has promised an eternal seed, and he must find a way to keep this promise. He does not punish under compulsion, and he is free to relax the standards that he himself has set. Israel appeals to the name of Yahweh and to his honor: If in his anger he allows his own people to become the prey of foreign nations, these nations will blaspheme his name by saying that Yahweh cannot protect his own. Israel appeals to the kindness of Yahweh: It is more consistent with his character to forgive than to punish, and he prefers to forgive. He should tolerate some degree of sin because man's evil instincts make it impossible for man to overcome sin entirely. Man is frail and mortal, and he should not be tested rigorously. In Hos there are eloquent appeals to the love of Yahweh: Israel is his spouse, and Yahweh cannot entirely suppress his affection for his beloved when his beloved is faithless and perverse. This book represents the tension between punishment and forgiveness as an emotional conflict in Yahweh—even though Yahweh punishes Israel, his saving love is not frustrated by the sins of his people (→ Hosea, 15:4).

These motives of forgiveness are not all of equal value, and in some instances the anthropomorphisms are naïve. But the motives illustrate the many facets under which Israel has known Yahweh, and they merge into a conception of his forgiveness which expresses Israel's assurance that Yahweh can surely find a way to overcome sin. Ultimately the idea of forgiveness leads into eschatology. If Yahweh's forgiveness is to be exercised in a way that suits his character, it must find an outlet in some act that lies outside history (→ 165–66 below). For the final achievement of Yahweh's forgiveness must be a reconciliation with man that renders further forgiveness unnecessary.

136 **(VII) Judgment.** The words "judge" and "judgment" in the OT have connotations somewhat different from the connotations that they have in modern speech. In the early writings of the OT the judge is primarily one to whom a person appeals for the defense of his rights, and a judgment is a vindication. When the judgment of Yahweh is invoked, his assistance is asked; and when he grants judgment, it is a saving act.

137 In the older view the "Day of Yahweh" is the day on which Yahweh judges the enemies of Israel. The appearance of Yahweh in the theophany (→ 57 above) is no doubt to be connected with the imagery of the Day of Yahweh. The earliest occurrence of the phrase "Day of Yahweh" is in Am 5:18–20; and one can conclude from this passage that hitherto the Israelites have been looking upon the Day of Yahweh as a day of victory and deliverance. Amos inverts the idea and affirms that it is a day of judgment on Israel. Israel is no less under judgment than the foreign nations cited in 1:3–2:3, and Yahweh's sentence of doom is pronounced on Israel as well as on the Ethiopians, the Philistines, and the Arameans (9:7–10). A day in which Yahweh acts against all that is proud and lofty is described in Is 2:10–17; this judgment is universal, and Israel, although it is not mentioned, is not excluded. Zeph 1 has a much more elaborate poem on the day of Yahweh that may not be of a single origin. The Day of Yahweh is not only universal but even cosmic in scope, suggesting later apocalyptic conceptions (→ 139 below), but the judgment is also focused on Judah and Jerusalem. The usage of the phrase suggests a "day," an event; whether this suggestion needs some modification is discussed below.

138 In the view of the pre-exilic prophets the judgment of Yahweh is accomplished in history. Amos speaks of the coming downfall both of foreign nations and of Israel; he does not indicate the agent of the downfall, but nothing suggests that he is thinking of anything other than the historical factors that are the weapons of Yahweh's judgment. Hosea speaks less clearly of a day or even of an event; but the doom of Israel is clearly announced and surely threatened. The judgments of Yahweh are much more prominent in Isaiah's thought. They are against both Israel and Judah and against various classes of men, particularly against those in power. The language of Is rarely if ever suggests a cosmic catastrophe; Is 30:27ff. is the language of the theophany. The agent of Yahweh's judgment is the contemporary historical reality of Assyria, which will bring disaster not only on the Israelite monarchies but also on all the people of the area. Assyria, Yahweh's destroying agent, is also under judgment, to be accomplished in Yahweh's good time; but so long as Assyria acts as the rod of Yahweh's anger, it is irresistible. The older portions of the book of Micah, Isaiah's contemporary, portray the judgment on Israel and Judah as an imminent event to be accomplished by historical forces. Other and probably later passages take a view of the judgment more in harmony with subsequent conceptions.

Jeremiah and Ezekiel, contemporaries of the fall of Jerusalem, are perhaps pre-eminently the prophets of judgment. They are certain of an imminent judgment and of its justice, and they present the totality of the judgment in an impressive manner. Their assurance of the judgment comes not only from their awareness of the threatening power of the Chaldeans, but also from their conviction of the deep collective guilt of Judah—not even the most worthy intercessors can avert the punishment that such guilt demands (Jer 14:11; Ez 14:12–20). Even in this picture of inevitable and terrifying judgment, the idea of judgment as a saving act does not disappear entirely. Each step in the judgment is a warning as well as a punishment; if Israel learns that its sins excite the anger of Yahweh and turns from them, Israel may survive. This is not a promise of mechanical forgiveness; when evil has advanced to the degree that the prophets describe, repentance alone is not enough to reverse the course of events that the national sin has set in motion. But Israel can retain its community with Yahweh even in the judgment if Israel will but listen to him. In fact, it is only after the catastrophe that Israel becomes aware that the judgment was necessary to preserve the people of Yahweh as such. Its own wickedness would destroy Israel as the people of Yahweh; but if Israel is purged by judgment, it can continue to exist as the people of Yahweh, even if only as a sorry remnant.

139 Reference has been made above to another concept of judgment that appears in later OT books; to this type of literature the name of apocalyptic is given. Strictly speaking, the name does not fit many specific passages of the OT (→ Post-exilic Period, 20), but the type of literature thus designated has its roots in the OT. A world catastrophe that is the work of the judgment of Yahweh is seen in Is 13; Is 24; Jl 2–3; and in much of Dn. Ez 38–39 with its vision of the war against Gog is closer to these passages than to the pre-exilic prophets. In such passages there is no reference to a judgment on Israel or on any particular nation that can surely be identified; the apocalyptic judgment is a judgment on mankind and even on the material universe.

The judgment of the world is an extension of the judgment of Israel; just as the genuine Israel could survive only if the historical Israel perished in the judgment, so the world and mankind can be united with Yahweh only if the existing world passes through a consuming judgment. The old world must be removed to make room for the new world to be created by Yahweh (→ 60 above). In apocalyptic description the judgment is not explicitly an event in history, as judgment was in the description given by the pre-exilic prophets; this raises the problem of eschatology (→ 164 below).

140 **(VIII) Salvation.** The OT idea of salvation is complex and exhibits a historical development that is extremely difficult to synthesize. We treat here passages in which no individual savior appears (for the Messiah, → 152ff. below).

(A) Yahweh's Saving Deeds. The Hebr word *y*^{e}*šûʿâ*, which we translate "salvation," often occurs in contexts where it refers to deliverance by military means; in these contexts the word can be translated "victory." In such uses "salvation" is parallel to the "righteous deeds" or the "judgments" of Yahweh on behalf of Israel (→ 94, 136 above). Salvation also signifies deliverance from any threat to life or integrity of person. In the ancient world the king was always the king savior, to whom his people looked for salvation against external enemies through war, or for salvation from injustice within the community through his judgment and the administration of law.

141 Yahweh is celebrated as king savior, particularly in Pss 47; 93; 96–99. These are often called "the Enthronement Psalms" in modern scholarship because of the hypothesis that these psalms were used in a cult festival celebrating the enthronement of Yahweh as king (→ Religious Institutions, 76:151–154; → Psalms, 33:6, 9, 63). In these psalms Yahweh as king is hailed as creator and lord of nature, and it is on a cosmic scale that his saving deeds are done. His salvation is manifested to all the world. The association of Yahweh's kingly saving power with creation and with the revelation of his power in nature is also prominent in Is 40–55.

142 The first saving deed of Yahweh in the history of Israel and the exemplar to which other saving deeds are likened is the deliverance of Israel from Egypt. This saving act is an act of creation, for Israel becomes a people —the people of Yahweh—by this deliverance. It is the basis of the claims of Yahweh in the covenant; it is also that saving act to which Israel most frequently appeals when it asks for deliverance from threats to its national welfare.

The subsequent history of Israel is a recital of the saving acts of Yahweh: the passage of Israel, the victories giving Israel the land of Canaan, deliverance in Canaan through the judges from the attacks of enemies, and the culminating saving act of the early period—the establishment of the monarchy and the deliverance from the Philistines. The recital of the saving deeds is interspersed with the recital of the infidelities of Israel; these arouse the anger of Yahweh, but they do not alter his will to save Israel. The historians of Israel know that the strokes of Yahweh's anger are also saving acts, for they teach Israel that a revolt from Yahweh will bring Israel to a condition where salvation can be achieved only through a tremendous judgment that will reduce the nation to a mere remnant.

143 This theme of salvation through judgment becomes dominant in the period of the monarchy in the words of the pre-exilic prophets. Amos says almost nothing of the saving will of Yahweh (the conclusion of Am [9:8b–15] is the work of a later hand). Salvation in Hos is postponed to a distant future to be achieved by means that are hidden from the insight of the prophet. In Is the assurance of salvation is deeper, but the theme of judgment is no less prominent than it is in Am and Hos. In Jer and Ez the salvation of historic Israel has become impossible; salvation now means a restoration, and not a restoration of historical Israel as it existed under the monarchy. Restoration becomes the dominant theme in Dt-Is, of all OT works the one that elaborates the theme of salvation with greatest richness, frequently alluding to the creative power of Yahweh in connection with salvation. The restoration of Israel is a new act of creative power scarcely less impressive than Yahweh's creation of Israel at the Exodus. Whereas Yahweh's work of salvation in the Exodus was manifested to the Egyptians, in the restoration of Israel it is manifested to the entire world. The author of Dt-Is echoes the theme of the new exodus almost as much as he echoes that of the new creation.

144 **(B) Nature of Salvation.** The varied character of salvation can be seen from an enumeration of some of its expressions. The oracles of Balaam (Nm 23–24) must be regarded as among the older portions of the OT, perhaps 10th cent. (→ Numbers, 5:41). Salvation in the oracles of Balaam consists in the blessing of Yahweh, which makes Israel a people set apart from other nations and assures them of victory over their enemies, of peaceful dwelling in their own land, and of abundant prosperity. The tone of salvation is predominantly but not exclusively militant. The large place that material blessings hold in these oracles is never entirely lost in the further development of the idea of salvation; indeed, the prosperity and wealth that are included in salvation are sometimes described extravagantly (Is 60; 65; Am 9:13–15). The idea of victory over enemies is explicitly political, and this element likewise does not disappear—salvation is always the salvation of Israel. The Zion poems of Is 49–52; 60–62 locate salvation in a restored Jerusalem that receives as tribute the wealth of the nations. Political salvation means not only deliverance from enemies, but final victory and the submission of the nations to the rule of Israel.

145 Salvation seems to be conceived in more elevated terms when it is seen as the era of universal peace (Is 2:1ff.). Salvation means the elimination of injustice and the establishment of that security that comes from government administered in righteousness and judgment (Is 32). In Jer and Ez salvation is stated in the formula of the covenant union, "You shall be my people and I will be your God"; by this statement is promised the restoration of the communion with Yahweh that was destroyed by the faithlessness of Israel. Salvation is Yahweh dwelling in the midst of his people. In the new Israel of Ez 40–48 the Temple becomes the center of the land, a focus of holiness from which the power of Yahweh radiates. The restoration of Judah described in Jer 30–31 contains all the elements of victory over enemies and of a life of material security and prosperity; but the defeat of enemies is not emphasized as it is elsewhere (in contrast, for instance, with Is 63:1ff.)—material prosperity is depicted in moderate terms, and the dominant ideas are peace and joy.

146 In all these conceptions of salvation it is at least implicitly supposed that the Israel which is saved is a new Israel—not only a new creation but also new in the sense that it is purified of the vices that corrupted the historical Israel. This purification is quite explicit in Jer and Ez. Salvation for Jer (31:31ff.) is a new covenant written on the heart; the terms of the covenant, the revealed will of Yahweh, will be deeply imbedded in the interior dispositions of each individual person and will govern his life. Salvation is not merely membership in the people of salvation; it is a total acceptance of Yahweh on the part of each individual. In such a saved community Yahweh will not deal through the established human mediators and teachers current in the historical Israel but will reveal himself to each Israelite as he revealed himself to Moses in the original covenant (→ Jeremiah, 19:89). Ez (36:26) sees the heart of stone replaced by a heart of flesh, sensitive and responsive to the will of Yahweh. Israel receives a new spirit, the spirit of Yahweh, that will impel Israel to obedience. This interior regeneration is the basis of the peace and prosperity that are promised.

147 Salvation at times is seen as broader than the salvation of Israel. The revelation and instruction of Yahweh shall go out from Zion to all nations, and it is through this revelation and instruction that the nations shall achieve universal peace (Is 2:1ff.). The mission of Israel as a medium of salvation is clear in Dt-Is; it is through Israel that Yahweh will reveal himself to the nations, who, once they know him, will give him the obedience that will save them (Is 45:18–25). Israel is Yahweh's witness to the nations. The universal scope of salvation is implied also in the return of Paradise (Is 11:6–9; 65:25) and in the creation of new heavens and a new earth (Is 65:17ff.), as well as in the frequent allusions to the transformation of the material universe and to the marvelous prosperity of the era of salvation.

148 L. Köhler (*op. cit.*, 227–29) points out that Zech 1–8 contains a compact account of salvation as it was conceived in 520–518 BC in Jerusalem. The earth is at peace; Israel is restored to its land; the oppressors of Israel have disappeared; the Israelites dwell in peace, joy, security, and moderate prosperity; the land is purged of gross crimes and vices; and it is expected that many nations will come and worship Yahweh. Compared to some other post-exilic writings this concept of salvation is plain and simple; yet one cannot reckon it among the most elevated ideas of the OT. One may say that Zech is on the way to the "realized salvation" of the P tradition (→ Pentateuch, 1:17) in which salvation is scarcely more than the existence of Israel united to Yahweh through the cult.

149 **(C) Reign of God.** The multiple developments of the idea of salvation are best summed up, if they can be summed up at all, in the idea of the reign (kingdom) of Yahweh, although this phrase is rare in the OT. Yet it was a phrase apt enough to be used in Jewish literature and in the Gospels (→ Aspects NT Thought, 78:93) as a designation of the expected salvation that needed no further definition. The reign of Yahweh is the acceptance of his will by all men. This cannot happen until all men know him, and they can know him only by perceiving his revelation of himself to Israel. The universal knowledge of Yahweh must work a revolutionary change in mankind; and since the struggle of man against nature arises from man's insubmissiveness to God, there must be a corresponding revolution even in material nature. The revelation of Yahweh will be no more willingly accepted by all men than it was accepted by Israel; and hence all men, like Israel, must pass through a process of judgment, which is a saving act. Resistance to Yahweh must yield before his matchless power. In such a world, man is secure from threat and free to lead the life that becomes a man.

150 An attempt is made in the preceding paragraph to enunciate the idea, scarcely found in so many words in the OT, that lies at the base of the Israelite hope of salvation; and it is within the framework of this idea that certain more difficult elements such as material blessings and political salvation are to be understood.

First, material blessings. The OT Israelites are material-minded, by which is meant that their literature exhibits no abstract and generalized thinking. Furthermore, they have no idea of a spiritual reality in the modern sense of the term. It is clear from the passages summarized above that salvation is not conceived without the supreme spiritual achievement of man, which is total submission to God issuing in a human perfection that reflects the image of God in man. The Israelites find the enumeration of virtues less convincing than the consideration of the concrete changes that submission to Yahweh will achieve in human existence. The most obvious change will be the cessation of certain definite obstacles to the good life, in particular, those obstacles that the Palestinian peasant knows best: the danger of war and of crop failure. For him salvation will be achieved if these two threats to his security are removed, and it is doubtful that he could appreciate any more elevated ideal. Add to these two blessings freedom from debt and debt-slavery and freedom from the oppression of rapacious magnates and landlords, and the Israelite is content to sit under his vine and his fig tree with none to terrify him (Mi 4:4). If human malice is removed, what limit can one put to the fertility of the soil?

These material blessings are not merely symbols of spiritual blessings; they are the effect of spiritual blessings. In general, the OT shows no awareness of an afterlife (yet → 172 below); the only good life that Israel knows is conceived in terms of the concrete existence that man knows by experience. This existence is transformed by perfect community with Yahweh, who dwells among his people. Life is good where there is no resistance to his saving will.

151 Second, political salvation. For the reason that life is conceived in terms of concrete experience, the good life is represented in political terms. Salvation, like life itself, is experienced in community and not by isolated individuals (→ 73 above). The only ordered society that the OT Israelite knows is a monarchy administered with justice and competence. Salvation is not a return to a more primitive life, but a perfection of the form of social life that offers the best possibilities for salvation. If monarchy fails because of the unrighteousness of its rulers, salvation does not consist in the elimination of rulers but in the installation of righteous rulers (→ 158 below).

Political salvation is sometimes seen as the rule of Israel over defeated nations. This may be accepted as a limited insight into the reality of salvation; and as such it must be combined with the other insights mentioned above in which salvation is extended to the entire world. But even the political supremacy of Israel is not a purely secular form of salvation. Israel is the people of Yahweh, and only through Israel will Yahweh reveal himself to the nations. In the simple thinking of the ancient world, the people whose god is the most powerful obtains supremacy over other nations. The OT hope of salvation rarely rises to an idea of salvation that is simply for men; it sees the salvation of peoples, of Israel first and then of others. Had Yahweh not been the God of Israel, his reality would have been less clearly perceived; but further development was necessary before it could be seen that he was the God of Israel in an affirmative sense that made him no less the God of peoples who did not worship him. It is only in the NT that the renewed Israel, the people of God, is seen to include equally all children of God, all men who are willing to be included.

Our discussion of salvation has brought us into the area of God's future plans for his people.

GOD'S FUTURE PLANS FOR HIS PEOPLE

152 **(I) The Messiah.** The figure of the Messiah ultimately came to have an important place in Israel's understanding of God's plans for its future. This discussion, necessarily brief, is dependent implicitly on the exegesis of important but disputed OT texts; for details the reader is referred to commentary on the individual OT books.

(A) The Term "Messiah." The Eng word is from Aram *m^{e}šîḥā'*, reflecting Hebr *māšîaḥ*, "anointed"; the Gk word is *christos*, whence "Christ." In this discussion a distinction will be made between "Messiah" (capitalized) and "messiahs" or salvific figures. The OT and late Judaism knew of a gallery of salvific figures who were expected to appear at the time of God's definitive intervention on behalf of Israel, e.g., Elijah, the Prophet-like-Moses (→ Aspects NT Thought, 78:14–15), perhaps the Suffering Servant, the Son of Man, the Anointed Priest, etc. These figures can loosely be called messianic. But the capitalized term "Messiah" is best confined to a precisely delineated concept, namely, the anointed king of the Davidic dynasty who would establish in the world the definitive reign of Yahweh (→ 149 above). Such a notion of Messiah is the product of a long development sketched below.

153 The expectation of the Messiah appears in postexilic Judaism (although in the OT "Messiah" is not used as a title in the sense we are using it). From the frequency and spontaneity with which the question of the Messiah appears in the NT (Mk 8:29; 14:61; Jn 1:20; 4:25; etc.) and also from the evidence of postbiblical Jewish writings (→ Apocrypha, 68:47), we are safe in assuming that the expectation of the Messiah was very common in late intertestamental Judaism and could perhaps be called a national hope. However, not all Jews expected the Messiah. In the 1st cent. AD many had lost faith in the Davidic dynasty, which had not ruled for 500 years; and there are late Jewish books that treat of eschatological questions without ever mentioning the Messiah (→ Apocrypha, 68:49). Moreover, even those who did hope for the Messiah did not necessarily confine their hopes to the Messiah. Often the expectation of the Messiah was accompanied by some of the other expectations mentioned above; at Qumran the sectarians awaited the coming of the Prophet, of the Davidic Messiah, and of the Anointed Priest (→ Apocrypha, 68:103–104).

154 Indeed there may have been an amalgamation of the figure of the Messiah with other salvific figures, e.g., the Suffering Servant, or the Son of Man, into one composite figure. Certainly this happened in the Christian description of Jesus, but the evidence is quite uncertain for determining whether this happened in pre-Christian Judaism (→ Apocrypha, 68:15). For instance, no pre-Christian work ever describes a suffering Messiah. The Christian reader must be aware of his instinctive tendency to interpret the Jewish expectation of the Messiah in the light of Jesus' career and person. Actually, the Jewish concept of the Messiah had to undergo considerable modification before it could be applied to Jesus, whence Jesus' reluctance to accept the title without qualification (→ 178 below; → Aspects NT Thought, 78:8–9).

In particular, the Christian must be warned that, while the late Jewish hope of the Messiah was highly idealized almost to the point of making the Messiah a figure of superhuman abilities, there was no expectation of a divine Messiah in the sense in which Jesus is professed as Son of God. Moreover, nationalistic coloring was never absent from any stage of the pre-Christian development of messianic thought, any more than the OT concept of salvation itself was devoid of materialistic and nationalistic aspects (→ 150–151 above). It is inaccurate and unjust to say that the Jews of Jesus' time had corrupted the idea of the Messiah as a spiritual savior by making it secular and nationalistic and that Jesus restored the concept to its pristine meaning. The Christian understanding of a spiritual Messiah represented a change rather than a restoration—a change that we believe brought the development of the idea to a rich fruition, but a change nevertheless.

155 **(B) Development of Royal Messianism.** That God sent saviors to deliver his people (Moses, the judges, Nehemiah, Ezra) is a commonplace in Israel's theological understanding of its history. But messianism, as we shall discuss it, is involved with the salvific role of men in the framework of an institution, the monarchy.

(a) THE FIRST STAGE OF DEVELOPMENT. In the first days of the Davidic monarchy in Judah every anointed king (messiah) was looked on as a savior sent by God to his people. There is no record in the OT of a similar sublimation of the kingship in northern Israel. It is altogether probable and generally agreed that the first literary record of the messianic character of the dynasty of David is found in the oracle of Nathan, preserved in three forms (2 Sm 7; Ps 89; 1 Chr 17). Scholars do not agree on which of these texts is the most primitive; none of them appear to preserve the original oracle unmodified (J. L. McKenzie, *TS* 8 [1947] 187–218). In Ps 89:20–38 the following elements may be distinguished: the election of David by Yahweh; promises of victory and wide dominion; adoption of David and his successors as sons; covenant of Yahweh with David and his house; promise of an eternal dynasty, not conditioned on the fidelity of the successors of David to Yahweh. This oracle is also echoed in Ps 132. The oracle does not speak of any individual successor, nor does it look into the eschatological future. It is a simple assurance that the dynasty will endure as the chosen human agent of the salvation of Yahweh wrought in history (→ 142 above). The salvation to be accomplished by David and his house does not here go beyond the political salvation to be achieved by the king.

156 The Blessing of Judah by Jacob (Gn 49:9–12) probably comes from the early monarchy and alludes implicitly to the reign of David. However this blessing is to be construed, it seems to assure the permanence of the dynasty of David. Fertility is assured so long as the chosen king savior reigns.

157 The "Royal Psalms" (in particular Pss 2; 72; 110; → Psalms, 35:15, 20, 88) should also be considered in this first stage of messianism. Most Catholic writers have abandoned the notion that they were composed by David himself (even though they may be of 10th cent. origin) who was singing of one future Messiah—such an expectation did not exist at this period. Rather, these psalms were compositions applicable to any Davidic monarch, and they may have been recited on important occasions in the life of the monarch, like the coronation. The references to a divine begetting of the king (110:3) and divine sonship (2:7)—once thought to be literal references to Jesus—were part of the symbolic court language (*Hofstil*) used to describe the king as Yahweh's representative. The eternal priesthood "according to the order of Melchizedek" (110:4) promised to the king was probably part of the hereditary titulature of the Canaanite kings of Jerusalem, exemplified in the priest king Melchizedek of Gn 14 (→ Genesis, 2:57; → Religious Institutions, 76:20). The eternal and universal reign of the king—formerly thought to be a literal reference to Jesus—was partly an optimistic wish for long life and many victories, and partly a reflection of the permanent greatness promised the Davidic dynasty.

Ps 72 may be taken as the clearest expression of the idea of the king savior. The king governs with the justice that becomes a ruler; he is the savior of the poor and the needy. He is victorious over his enemies, who are also the enemies of his people; he is the savior of his people from external danger. During his reign the blessing of Yahweh brings fertility to the land. Nowhere in the Ps is the king presented as a future eschatological deliverer. He is the reigning successor of David and the heir of the covenantal promises made to David.

158 (b) The Second Stage of Development. In the writings of the 8th cent. there is a development in royal messianism. Wicked and inept kings like Ahaz had dimmed the glory of the Davidic line and the optimistic hope that each king would be a savior of his people. Isaiah, in particular, gives voice to a more nuanced expectation: there would be an inbreak of the power of Yahweh that would revive the dynasty and insure its permanence. Yahweh would soon raise up a successor of David who would be worthy of the name of Davidic king; he would be an example of charismatic power, just as David had been when the royal line was instituted (→ Isaiah, 16:18–27). Is 7:14–17 and 9:1ff. grow rhapsodical in their description of the heir to the throne to be born in Isaiah's time (735 BC), perhaps the son of the wicked Ahaz and of a well-known maiden of the court (the "virgin" of Is 7:14—an inaccurate translation of the Hebrew). The child would be a sign that God was still with his people (Emmanuel) in the person of the Davidic king. The heir would establish justice, build a vast empire and bring peace to it, and be worthy of the traditional courtly titles of the monarch (9:5). Although Isaiah may have believed that his expectations were fulfilled in the good king Hezekiah, Ahaz' successor, the Isaian passages are describing an ideal for restoration rather than a reality; and this permitted them to be used by later generations who also looked forward to a divine renewal of the monarchy.

159 The passage in Is 11:1ff. may be later than Isaiah; scholars are divided. It looks into a more remote future than the passages we have just discussed. The charismatic power of the expected ideal ruler is clearly affirmed (→ 35 above), for the spirit will rest upon him and bestow on him the qualities of an ideal ruler. He will save the kingdom from internal injustice and external threat. In comparison with the undisputed writings of Is, the novel element in Is 11:1ff. is the return of the conditions of Paradise that the reign of this king will bring to pass. Universal peace under his reign is cosmic; and peace rests upon the universal "knowledge of Yahweh," the experience of the personal reality of Yahweh through his revelation of himself (→ 105 above). This knowledge can be communicated to the world only through Israel. These two ideas, the restoration of the dynasty of David and the universal and religious scope of the salvation of which the dynasty of David is the medium, probably appear here for the first time in the OT.

160 That the hope for a resurgence of the dynasty under a new and ideal ruler was not confined to Isaiah is seen from Mi 5:1–6. Micah, a contemporary of Isaiah, sees a new David coming from Bethlehem to give his people security against the Assyrian threat. Mi 5:3 sees a restoration of the unity of Israel and Judah under this new David; the schism that occurred under Rehoboam will be healed.

Other and later allusions to the restoration of the dynasty of David echo these passages with little modification. The "branch" or "shoot" of Jer 23:5 will be the king savior whose name will affirm the righteousness of Yahweh; righteousness here means saving will (→ 94 above). The restoration of the dynasty appears also in Jer 30:9,21. The dynasty of David is the sprig of cedar that Ez sees planted by Yahweh (Ez 17:22), and in the new Israel David will once more be king (Ez 34:23; 37:24). Ezekiel does not, however, emphasize the function of the king as savior; this hesitancy may reflect the historical events of which he was a contemporary, namely, the fall of the nation and the exile of the Davidic king. The monarchy appears in Ez simply because the monarchy is an Israelite institution without which the prophet cannot conceive Israel. Several interpreters have asked whether a return of David in person is not implied in these passages of Ez; but such an implication is not immediately obvious, for the name may designate the dynasty.

161 (c) The Third Stage of Development. The post-exilic development of messianism is difficult to trace because of the lack of written evidence; in part we must reconstruct its history from the end product, namely, the expectation of the Messiah in the latest pre-Christian period. The fact that the Davidic line no longer ruled after the Exile (or at least after the governorship of Zerubbabel, to the best of our knowledge) made a profound difference in messianism. Before the Exile the ideal king who would restore the vigor of the Davidic line could always be thought of in terms of the next generation of a reigning dynasty. But now there could be no ideal king until the indefinite future when the Davidic throne would be restored. Thus the expectations began to move toward the indefinite future; and rather than centering on one monarch in a continuing line of rulers, these expectations came to center on one supreme king who would represent Yahweh's definitive intervention to save his people. It is in this period that we may begin to speak of *the Messiah* in the strict sense. Earlier Scripture (Royal Pss; Is) was now reread with this new messianic understanding in mind.

162 If the definitive character of the Messiah's action is clear, the eschatological character is less clear. There is no clear evidence that the Messiah was thought of as a transcendental figure whose mission would go beyond the realities of history. True, his work would be a terminal manifestation of the power of Yahweh that would make any further saving act of Yahweh unnecessary. This saving act would not be the work of ordinary historical forces, but the kind of visible inbreak of Yahweh's power into history that had been seen in the Exodus. Yet, so far as we know, the inbreak was expected to be accomplished in historical circumstances, even if at times the anticipation of the Messiah may have taken on some of the trappings of apocalyptic.

In certain passages the concept of the king savior (→ 140 above) has undergone an interesting transformation. In Zech 9:9ff. (4th cent.?; → Haggai, 23:17) his reign will bring universal peace and all warlike traits will have disappeared. He is the instrument of Yahweh's salvation, but the salvation is the work of Yahweh himself with no human agent. The king has even lost the trappings of royalty. Yet this is not a universally accepted view of the Messiah, for in the much later (1st cent. BC) *Pss Sol* (→ Apocrypha, 68:47) there is a strong mixture of the political and the spiritual in picturing a Messiah who would bring the Gentiles under his yoke.

The advent of the Messiah was also a cause of speculation in late Judaism. How would men know him? In some passages (Mt 2:4–6; Jn 7:42) we can see the popular expectation that he would be born at Bethlehem, David's city, and his birth would be known to all Israel. But in other passages (Jn 7:27; Mk 8:29) we see the thought that the Messiah would be hidden; for men would not know where he would come from, and he could stand in their midst without their knowing it. (See R. E. Brown, *The Gospel According to John* [AB 29; N.Y., 1966] 53.)

163 In summation, in the course of 1000 years Israelite messianism developed to the point where the expectation of the Messiah embodied one of the principal hopes for Yahweh's intervention to save his people. While this king savior, almost by definition, would be a political savior, he would be a savior in virtue of the charisma and power of Yahweh and so his saving acts would never be merely political. In his reign, the Messiah would bring to Israel the ideal rule of Yahweh himself. That the salvation mediated by the Messiah would have a scope outside Israel is less frequently mentioned and is often viewed chauvinistically. Yet granting the origins of the concept of anointed king, we may be surprised that the wider view occurs as often as it does.

(Numerous articles in *CBQ* 19 [1957]. Also *L'attente du Messie* [RechBib 1; Bruges, 1954]. Klausner, J., *The Messianic Idea in Israel* [London, 1956]. Mowinckel, S., *He That Cometh* [Nashville, 1954].)

164 **(II) Eschatology.** The question of eschatology in the OT was not formally answered in our discussions of judgment, salvation, and messianism. In recent scholarship the question has been argued whether there there is any eschatology in the OT at all *earlier than the Exile*. Much of the discussion is obscured by the ambiguity of the term eschatology. Literally, eschatology means "the doctrine of the last things"; and if one compares the OT with the much fuller eschatology of Christianity, it appears that the early books of the OT have no eschatology (→ Aspects NT Thought, 78:64ff.).

The problem can be approached by noticing those books and passages of the OT that no one would deny are eschatological. These passages are called "apocalyptic" (→ Post-exilic Period, 20:23). In them certain standard themes appear: a final cosmic struggle between God and the powers of the world or the powers of evil; a cosmic catastrophe that includes the collapse of the visible world as well as of human institutions; the defeat and judgment of the powers opposed to God; the beginning of a new world and a new age in which God reigns supreme. These themes are here merely outlined; no biblical literature has such luxuriant, even exaggerated, imagery as apocalyptic literature. The final battle, the collapse of the visible universe, the judgment, the bliss of the new world of the kingdom of God are described in great and usually fanciful detail. The imagery grows more extravagant in those apocalyptic books produced in Judaism but not included among the canonical Scriptures (→ Apocrypha, 68:13,41,43,44). In the OT, apocalyptic literature is found in Dn 2; Dn 7–12; Is 24 (probably also 13 and 65–66); Jl; and probably Ez 38–39.

The absence of these themes in earlier literature leads many scholars to deny that there is an early Israelite eschatology (S. Mowinckel, *He That Cometh*, 125–54). In pre-exilic thought the saving and judging acts of Yahweh are entirely accomplished in history and through historical processes. The enemies of Yahweh are definite historical peoples; the judgment is a historic act such as the fall of Israel or of Assyria; and the salvation expected is the peaceful existence of Israel in its own land. Eschatology, Mowinckel affirms, arises when Israel no longer has any historical hope. If Yahweh is now to establish his supremacy, it has to be done by an act that comes from outside history and puts an end to history. This interpretation has much to recommend it. It takes account of the differences between the early prophets and the apocalyptic writers; it sedulously avoids reading later ideas into earlier literature. Certain features that resemble some details of apocalyptic eschatology are explained as part of the traditional theophany (→ 57 above) or as derived from cultic festivals (Mowinckel).

165 At the same time, there are certain elements of Israelite thought that this interpretation does not incorporate into itself. Hence other scholars (Von Rad, *op. cit.* 2, 114–25; Eichrodt, *Theology* 1, 385–91; Jacob, *op. cit.*, 319–22) affirm the existence not only of pre-exilic eschatology but even of prophetic eschatology. Vriezen (*op. cit.*, 350–72) places the beginning of eschatology with Isaiah. Mowinckel's rejoinder has been that to include earlier utterances is to make the word eschatology so broad as to deprive it of all meaning; in earlier passages, he says, we should speak of "a hope of the future," not of eschatology. The problem may appear to be merely a question of semantics, and perhaps it is. Yet to deny early eschatology in Israel seems to carry the implication that Israel had no idea of history that was really different from the ideas of other peoples (→ 113 above). A hope of the future that leads to nothing definitive is scarcely a hope for more than a continuation of the present. In early Israel it was hoped that in the course of history Yahweh would actively intervene in the future as he had intervened in the past, and that he would preserve Israel through his judgments and his saving acts. To ask whether this hope was eschatological is to ask a question that the early Israelites could have neither asked nor answered. But there were implications in the active intervention of Yahweh in history, implications that history was governed by his moral will with supreme power. Could Yahweh be the lord of history if history were to continue indefinitely? If the conflict between Yahweh and the forces of chaos were not to be resolved by a victory, Yahweh would lack truly divine power, and Israelite belief would fall into the cyclic dualism that governed the thought of the ancient Near East.

It appears that any hope of the future that reposes upon Yahweh's power and salvific will demands a terminal divine act that will end history and the conflict between Yahweh and the powers that resist him. Since eschatology in its simplest form means at least the belief that history has an end, then the early Israelite hope of the future is implicitly eschatological. The idea of the end of history need not be proposed in apocalyptic imagery. It is true that both salvation and judgment in the pre-exilic prophets do not appear in terms that transcend the historical world in which Israel lives. But if this historical world is established in a permanent condition of peace by an act of Yahweh, it has arrived at a term that is not produced by historical forces.

166 The Israelite conviction, expressed by the earlier as well as the later prophets, is that history must issue in the universal reign of Yahweh. This hope is not equally clear and explicit at all stages of its development. When it is expressed (as in the oracle of Nathan; → 155 above) in terms of the world-wide reign of the king-messiah of Israel, it appears in perhaps its most primitive form. What at one period is seen as a term of history may be later recognized as a step that demands further resolution—in such a development of thought and belief the principle of eschatology is accepted, but the eschatological term has not been fully defined. The concept of eschatology is not so rigid in its structure that its form and content are not capable of further development. The early faith of Israel is not yet a transcendent eschatology; and if transcendentalism is an essential part of an eschatological faith, then early Israelite faith should not be called eschatological.

167 Apocalyptic imagery is as full of mythopoeic thinking and language as any portion of the OT (→ 25 above), and here mythopoeic thought performs a function that no other type of thinking could have performed. The eschatological event lies not only outside experience but also outside history; yet, at the same time, the judgments of Yahweh in history are exhibitions of his power that can be incorporated into the eschatological picture. The eschatological battle and the collapse of world empires are portrayed in terms drawn from the historic experience of Israel. To these elements are added the reversal of the mythology of creation; the world returns to primeval chaos, as it returned in the deluge. From this chaos by a new and final creative act Yahweh produces a new heaven and a new earth with the features of Paradise; but in this new heaven and new earth there will be no rebellion against his saving will. It is a paradox of biblical study that a crassly literal interpretation of the mythopoeic imagery of eschatology obscures the reality of the divine acts of salvation and judgment.

168 **(III) Life after Death.** It is generally held by scholars that no hope of individual survival after death is expressed in the OT before some of its latest passages, which were probably written in the 2nd cent. BC. Even though this thesis will be modified below (→ 172), the general lack of OT belief in an afterlife is somewhat surprising, since belief in the resurrection of the body was so important both in Pharisaic Judaism and in Christianity. Here ancient Israel was much closer to the beliefs of Mesopotamia and Canaan than it was to the beliefs of Egypt.

The Egyptian idea of the afterlife, exhibited in the well-preserved tombs of Egypt and in Egyptian literature, conceives of survival after death as a two-dimensional continuation of earthly human existence and not as a genuinely new and different state. The joys of the world beyond the grave are the carnal joys of normal experience. Man shares the life of the gods, but in a purely human way; survival is not an attainment of destiny, but rather an evasion of destiny. The literature called "The Book of the Dead" presents entrance into bliss as contingent upon successfully passing an examination on one's moral conduct (*ANET* 32–36), but success depends more on knowing the correct answers rather than on one's moral character. There is no idea that any one would or should be excluded from bliss; if life after death is merely a continuation of earthly life, no moral qualification should be demanded any more for one than it is for the other. Thus Egyptian belief in survival is really a stout affirmation of the goodness of human life on earth and of the impossibility and the undesirability of a change of state. (For variations in Egyptian thought, → Wisdom Lit, 28:23–24.)

The Egyptian idea is incompatible with basic Israelite beliefs about Yahweh and about man. The Egyptian afterlife is not a world dominated by the personal divine presence and will, but is really a thoroughly secularized world. That the Egyptian idea evades destiny and leaves man in his present condition is not of itself in opposition to early Israelite belief, for the Israelites of this period make no affirmations about a high destiny in another life. But the Egyptians explicitly affirm that man reaches his full stature in the joys of earthly existence, and for the Israelites such unconcealed faith in the material world is intolerable. (Perhaps Israel's failure to reach an idea of survival after death was partly due to revulsion for Egypt's unmitigated secularism.)

169 In Mesopotamia, on the contrary, there is explicitly no hope of survival. Arallu, the world of the dead, is a vast tomb where the bodies of the dead lie inert, no more than semiconscious at best (*ANET* 87, 107); and a description of the underworld is cause for one to sit and weep (*ANET* 98). Mesopotamian literature faces death with a deep pessimism. The gods reserve life for themselves and allot death as the portion of man; therefore man should enjoy the pleasures that life affords him, for he has no other hope (*ANET* 90). Thus, unlike the Egyptians, the Mesopotamians face death as the end of life. Like the Egyptians, they see no moral discrimination in death, which comes, like birth, to all alike; nor do they even face the problem of premature death, which is raised in the OT. The fact of death is utterly without religious or moral significance. If man could reach the food of life and the water of life (*ANET* 96, 101–102), he would share in the immortality of the gods; but the gods withhold immortality. The difference between Mesopotamian belief and Israelite belief is patent here; in Gn 2–3 the food of life is withheld not from jealousy, but because of a moral fault (also → Wisdom Lit, 28:29–30).

170 The moral significance of death is vital in Israelite belief; but the Israelite attitude toward the possibility of life after death shows no appreciable difference from Mesopotamian beliefs. The death that comes to the first man as a consequence of his sin is the termination of life on this earth, and no wider horizon appears. The constitution of human nature, as understood in Israelite thought, reveals no principle of survival. Neither "soul" nor "spirit" is a component entity that survives death. The human person is an animated body (→ 66 above), and no other form of human life is conceived. The underworld of the OT (Sheol) is mentioned many times, and sometimes described vividly (Is 14). These descriptions show that Sheol, like the Arallu of Mesopotamia, is no more than a vast tomb where the bodies of the dead lie inert (Jb 10:21; 17:13–16). Sheol is not a form of survival but a denial of survival; all men come to Sheol, and the good and evil of life cease there (Jb 3:17–19).

171 The OT does not often exhibit the pessimism toward death that can be seen in Mesopotamian literature (→ Wisdom Lit, 28:31), except for passages like Jb, the song of Hezekiah (Is 38) and a few Pss (30; 88). In general, the Israelite looks upon death as the normal term of life, asking only that he be allowed to fill out his days in peace—and the normal portion of days was 70 years. An early death or a sudden or painful death is for the wise men of Israel a punishment of wickedness. But apart from these reflections on untimely death, the penal character of death, so clearly seen in the J narrative of Gn 3, is not observed elsewhere in the OT.

It is very probable that the Israelite idea of man in society had much to do with the Israelite attitude toward death. A man lives on in his sons who bear his name, and in the people of Israel of which he is a member. If Israel continues to live, the deceased members of Israel have not entirely perished. Such a collective immortality is not entirely foreign even to modern thought, despite its emphasis on the dignity and the importance of the individual person. Men have always been concerned, and they are now concerned, with the fortunes of their children or of others who are under their care; they live after their death in the influence that they have had on their juniors.

172 For whatever value they may have, we should also consider those passages of the OT that seem to express a striving for some form of an afterlife. Some of the Pss contain petitions for life or expressions of thanksgiving for the bestowal of life; the context, not only of these Pss but also of Israelite thought, suggests that the psalmist speaks of preservation from a particular danger to life. Now, however, M. Dahood, *Psalms 1–50* (AB 16; N.Y., 1966) xxxvi, argues that there is much more thought about immortality and resurrection in Ps than previously thought. The "Foe" the Psalmist opposes is often death (7:6; 13:3; 18:4; etc.).

Let us consider in particular Pss 49 and 73 where the psalmist faces the problem of the universality of death that overtakes the righteous as well as the wicked. Since both righteous and wicked are mortal, what comfort is it to the righteous to be assured that death is a punishment for the wicked? In this context, when the psalmist expresses his faith that Yahweh will deliver him from death, the deliverance can scarcely mean preservation from some particular danger; it must be a preservation that will distinguish the righteous from the wicked. Should these psalms express such a hope, it must be noticed that the hope, while sure, is vague and formless in the extreme. This hope, it may be conjectured, reposes on the assurance of communion with Yahweh that is so often expressed in the Pss. Communion with Yahweh is life, and surely communion with a kindly and righteous God ought not be destroyed except by deliberate rebellion. Yahweh must have some way in which communion with him can be preserved for those who are faithful to him; otherwise there would be no ultimate difference between righteousness and wickedness.

173 The obstacle to any more explicit statement of this hope is the Israelite conception of human nature and of human life, which knows of no principle that could survive death. When the hope is finally expressed, it takes the only possible form that it can take in Israelite thought: the resurrection of the body. The hope of the resurrection is not really expressed in the vision of the dry bones of Ez 37; under the image of the resurrection, the prophet expresses his faith that Israel will survive its national extinction in 587 BC. A hope that the Servant of Yahweh will triumph over death seems to be expressed in Is 53:10–12; but the unique character and mission of the Servant does not permit the extension of this hope, if indeed it is expressed, to others than the Servant himself. The first clear expression of the hope of resurrection occurs in the Maccabean period in Dn 12:2. See also Is 26:19 in the relatively late part of Is known as "the Isaian Apocalypse" (→ Isaiah, 16:41)—unless this passage simply expresses faith in Israel's survival.

There is no history of the development of the idea. Attempts to trace the belief to Iranian influence have not been successful. If the considerations mentioned above have any value, they indicate that this distinctively Israelite idea rises from the Israelite conception of God and of man. Resurrection is not, like the Egyptian form of survival, merely a resumption of terrestrial existence; it involves an eschatological new life in a new world. Nor is there merely a resurrection of the righteous; the dignity of the human person is such that it resists extinction, even in the wicked.

174 Another form of belief in survival appears in Wis, probably written in Alexandria in the 1st cent. BC (→ Wisdom, 34:6). In this book the influence of Gk philosophy is apparent; and the writer may have accepted the Gk doctrine of the immortality of the soul. This idea, as we have seen, is not part of the Israelite understanding of the constitution of human nature (→ 66 above). It does not take deep root in the thought of Judaism or in the NT, although the Essenes may have believed in immortality (Josephus, *Ant.* 18.1, 5 § 18), and certain NT passages *may* refer to immortality—see J. Barr, *Old and New in Interpretation* (London, 1966) 52ff.

175 **(IV) Promise and Fulfillment.** The Christian theological study of the OT is truncated unless the relation of the OT to the NT is considered. In the Gospels, Jesus presents himself as fulfillment of the hope and the destiny of Israel, and the early Church follows him in this presentation. This presentation implies certain principles of interpretation and raises a number of detailed problems; only the principles are considered here, and the problems of detail are left to articles on separate books and passages.

The NT affirmation that Jesus is the Messiah (→ 178 below) implies the unity of history under a single divine plan of salvation. In Jesus the acts of God related in the OT converge and reach their fullness; in him the OT idea of history and the OT hope of the future are brought to a term. Israel has no further destiny to which it can look—in Jesus the saving and judging acts of God are accomplished.

176 The unity and continuity of the plan and the history of salvation do not imply that the OT is meaningless without Jesus Christ. It was the theory of Origen and many of his followers that the true meaning of the OT was not intelligible unless one interpreted every word of the OT as referring to Christ in some way (→ Hermeneutics, 71:38). Such an interpretation is possible only by a kind of allegorizing that goes far beyond the meaning of the text. Moreover, such a view fails to recognize the intrinsic value of the OT. Even from a Christian viewpoint, if there never had been a NT, the Hebr Scriptures would retain a value for men because they were a vehicle through which God revealed himself to men. The literature of the OT was meaningful to those who produced it and to those for whom it was produced; it had a contemporary significance and force that could be grasped by those who were unaware of the precise form that the historical development of salvation would take. In modern interpretation the first task of the interpreter is considered to be the apprehension of this contemporary Israelite meaning (→ Hermeneutics, 71:24).

177 The unity of the plan and of the history of salvation does imply a unity of the basic theological themes of OT and NT. Many of the OT themes have been considered in this survey, and there is scarcely one that does not find its development in the NT. It is a misunderstanding to consider the themes in the NT as if they had no origin and growth in the OT from which the NT writers themselves took their point of departure. The heresy of Marcion in the 2nd cent. AD denied the relevance of the OT for Christian revelation, and in particular, the unity of the concept of God in OT and NT. But when Jesus spoke of his Father, he meant the God whom all Jews knew, the Yahweh whose encounter with Israel is related in the OT. He could speak to them of

Yahweh as one who was revealed to them in their history; he expounded for them the fullness of the revelation of Yahweh, but it was not necessary for them to accept the Father of whom he spoke as a totally unfamiliar being. The character of Yahweh, his attributes, his providence, and his government of history could be recognized in the proclamation of Jesus.

The unity of themes is manifest in the unity of vocabulary exhibited in the two Testaments. Almost every key theological word of the NT is derived from some Hebr word that had a long history of use and development in the OT. Jesus and the apostles used familiar terms. Obviously this does not imply that these terms underwent no further development in the NT, but the theological language that Jesus and the apostles used was the language available to them and to their listeners. The creation of such a theological language was not the work of a day. Without a background of the OT and Israelite beliefs and traditions, the message of Jesus would have been unintelligible. Contemporary scholarship has given much attention to the study of the theological vocabulary of the NT and to its roots in the OT (e.g., *ThDNT*), and the value of these studies is universally recognized. Also → Hermeneutics, 71:51–53.

178 Yet the unity of themes is accompanied by a development that must not be missed or minimized. Although there is scarcely any key theological word that is not common to both OT and NT, there is likewise scarcely any key word that has not been enriched in the NT. The novelty of the Christian fact becomes more apparent from a close study of the development of the vocabulary; the Christian fact rises in Judaism, but it is not derived from Judaism. The Christian fact is the newest and the most radical of the saving acts of God; it initiates a permanent revolution that affects Judaism as much as it affects the world at large.

The novelty of the Christian revolution is not well perceived in a scheme of interpretation that sees the relation of OT and NT as a relation of prediction and fulfillment (→ Hermeneutics, 71:51). Without denying the unity of history and of themes, we maintain that the concrete historical reality of Jesus Christ is literally predicted nowhere in the OT. Jesus exceeds the limits of the OT knowledge of God; for, in his own words, one cannot put new wine into old wineskins. The radical novelty of his person and of his mission can be seen in the very designation Messiah/Christ (→ Aspects NT Thought, 78:8). The early Church proclaimed Jesus as the Messiah, well aware that no figure like him can be found in the OT. He is the Messiah and is recognized as Messiah not because he can be identified with any particular prediction or with a number of predictions taken together, but because he unifies in his person all the ideas that are called messianic. The unification transforms some of these ideas profoundly (→ 154 above).

Similar developments can be pointed out in other key ideas. The idea of fulfillment, often mentioned in the NT, is not of necessity the fulfillment of a prediction. Hope or destiny can be fulfilled; promise can be fulfilled, and promise is a more accurate word to designate the relation of OT and NT. The promise is fulfilled with an abundance that is not predicted because it could not have been predicted; it could not have been understood. The religious growth of Israel was necessary in order that Jesus Christ, when he came, could be recognized by at least a few for what he was. He is indeed the key to the understanding of the OT. For further discussion of the relation of the two Testaments, → Hermeneutics, 71:32ff.

78

ASPECTS OF NEW TESTAMENT THOUGHT

David M. Stanley, S.J.

Raymond E. Brown, S.S.

GENERAL BIBLIOGRAPHY

A specialized bibliography will be supplied with each subarticle; here we present only general works on NT and Gospel theology (also → Pauline Theology, 79:1; → Johannine Theology, 80:1). Albertz, M., *Die Botschaft des Neuen Testamentes* (4 vols.; Zürich, 1947–57). Barclay, W., *A New Testament Wordbook* (London, 1955); *More New Testament Words* (N.Y., 1958). Bonsirven, J., *Les enseignements de Jésus Christ* (Paris, 1946); *Theology of the New Testament* (Westminster, 1963). Bultmann, *TNT*. Conzelmann, H., *An Outline of the Theology of the New Testament* (N.Y., 1969). Dalman, G., *The Words of Jesus* (Edinburgh, 1902). Filson, F. V., *The New Testament against Its Environment* (SBT 3; London, 1950). Grant, F. C., *An Introduction to New Testament Thought* (N.Y., 1950). Hastings, J., *A Dictionary of Christ and the Gospels* (2 vols.; N. Y., 1906–8); *A Dictionary of the Apostolic Church* (2 vols.; N.Y., 1915–18). Hunter, A. M., *The Message of the New Testament* (Phila., 1944); *Introducing New Testament Theology* (London, 1957). Johnson, S., *The Theology of the Gospels* (London, 1966). Kittel, G., *ThWNT*, tr. into English in *ThDNT*, and partially in BKW. Lebreton, J., *The Spiritual Teaching of the New Testament* (Westminster, 1960). Lemonnyer, A., *Théologie du Nouveau Testament* (Paris, 1928). McKenzie, J. L., *The Power and the Wisdom* (Milwaukee, 1965). Manson, T. W., *The Teaching of Jesus* (2nd ed.; Cambridge, 1959). Meinertz, M., *Theologie des Neuen Testaments* (2 vols.; Bonn, 1950). Metzger, B. M., *IPLAP*. Percy, E., *Die Botschaft Jesu* (Lund, 1953). Perrin, N., *Rediscovering the Teaching of Jesus* (N.Y., 1967). Richardson, *ITNT*. Schnackenburg, R., *New Testament Theology Today* (London, 1963); *Present and Future: Aspects of New Testament Theology* (Notre Dame, Ind., 1966). Stagg, F., *New Testament Theology* (Nashville, 1962). Stauffer, E., *New Testament Theology* (London, 1955). Trench, R. C., *Synonyms of the New Testament* (Grand Rapids, 1953). Wilder, A. N., *New Testament Faith for Today* (N.Y., 1955).

GENERAL OUTLINE

Since there are separate articles on Pauline Theology and on Johannine Theology, this article concentrates chiefly on the thought of the Gospels, especially that of the Synoptic Gospels. D. M. Stanley is the author of the first three subarticles: "Titles of Christ" (§ 1–61); "New Testament Eschatology" (§ 62–92); "The Kingdom of God" (§ 93–108). R. E. Brown is the author of the last four: "The Gospel Miracles" (§ 109–130); "The Parables of Jesus" (§ 131–145); "The Resurrection of Jesus" (§ 146–159); and "The Twelve and the Apostolate" (§ 160–182).

TITLES OF CHRIST

BIBLIOGRAPHY

1 Cullmann, O., *The Christology of the New Testament* (London, 1963). Dupont, J., "Nom de Jésus," *VDBS* 6, 514–41. Fuller, R. H., *The Foundations of New Testament Christology* (N.Y., 1965). Hahn, F., *The Titles of Jesus in Christology* (London, 1969). Jay, E. G., *Son of Man, Son of God* (London, 1965). Kramer, W., *Christ, Lord, Son of God* (SBT 50; London, 1966). Sabourin, L., *The Names and Titles of Jesus* (N.Y., 1967). Taylor, V., *The Names of Jesus* (N.Y., 1953).

2 OUTLINE

3 In contrast to the Western and modern viewpoint, the Semites, like most ancient and primitive peoples, considered the name assigned to things or persons an essential constituent or kind of counterpart of its bearer. The name "Jesus" (Gk *Iēsous*) represents a Hellenized form of Hebr *Yēšûaʿ*, often shortened to *Yēšûʿ* (Bl-Deb-F 53, 2b). This Hebr name is already a shortened form of *Y*^{e}*hôšûaʿ* or Joshua, the name borne by Moses' successor. The original meaning of *Y*^{e}*hôšûaʿ* was "Yahweh helps" from the root *šwʿ*, "to help" (M. Noth, *Die israelitischen Personennamen* [BWANT 3rd ser., 10; Stuttgart, 1928] 107). However, a popular etymology connected the name and its shortened form with the root *yšʿ*, "to save," and the noun *y*^{e}*šûʿâ*, "salvation." The popular interpretation of "Jesus" as "God saves" is reflected in the NT. Mt 1:21 points out that Jesus' name reveals his redemptive mission: "He will *save* his people from their sins" (for a similar interpretation, see Acts 4:12). Since the titles or epithets given to Jesus in the NT share in this significance attached to biblical personal names, an examination of these titles will reveal the development undergone by Christology throughout the apostolic age. We shall examine systematically the use of titles for Jesus in the various stages of NT thought and writing.

4 (I) Apostolic Preaching. In this article the discourses attributed to Peter in Acts are considered authentic summaries of the primitive apostolic kerygma (2:14–36; 3:13–26; 4:9–12; 10:34–43). The speeches of Paul recorded in Acts are considered in all probability that apostle's development of the traditional kerygma (13:15–41; 17:22–31; 20:18–38). The speech that Stephen is represented as giving at his trial (7:2–53), although ostensibly an *apologia pro vita sua*, may be considered as an example of the apostolic interpretation of the OT. The brief catechesis by which Philip instructs the grand vizier of the queen of Ethiopia (8:30–38) also exemplifies the apostolic exploitation of an important OT theme.

(Another view of Acts wherein the speeches of Peter and Paul are considered Lucan constructions [containing some primitive material but heavily reflective of the later theology of Luke] would have serious repercussions on the evaluation of the titles we are about to discuss as reflecting apostolic preaching [→ Acts, 45:5].)

5 (A) Lord. The Gk *kyrios*, "lord," was a word used in the LXX to render *YHWH* (which was read by the Jews as *ʾădōnāy*, "my Lord"). In the pagan world *kyrios* was a title for the gods and was also used in emperor worship—Domitian was *Dominus et deus noster*. Which background influenced the NT usage, the Jewish or the Hellenistic?

The title *Kyrios* was applied in the primitive preaching to the Risen Christ, exalted by God, as may be seen from the conclusion of Peter's address on Pentecost. "Therefore let the whole house of Israel know with certainty that God has made him Lord and Messiah—this Jesus whom you have crucified" (Acts 2:36). At his death, Stephen invokes Jesus under this title (7:59); the preaching itself is described as "the word *of the Lord*" (8:25; cf. 10:36), since the preachers are simply "gospeling the Lord Jesus" (11:20).

6 From the earliest days of the Jerusalem community, a theology of the Name (i.e., *Kyrios*) develops. When the term appears in NT citations of the LXX, where it had rendered the Tetragrammaton *YHWH*, it is now applied to Christ: "It will come to pass that everyone who invokes the name of the Lord, i.e., Christ, will be saved" (Acts 2:21 citing Jl 3:5 [Eng 2:32]). Christian faith in the power of this title can effect miracles, e.g., the healing of a cripple (Acts 4:10). Salvation is acquired solely in this name (4:12), the source of all "healing and signs and wonders" by which the Gospel is propagated (4:29–30). Through its invocation the original Pentecostal phenomena recur to strengthen and encourage the persecuted community (4:31). The disciples are filled with spiritual joy "to be accounted worthy to be dishonored for the name" (5:41). One of the most primitive formulations of Christian faith is the brief creed "Jesus is Lord" (Phil 2:11; Rom 10:9). The ancient description of the rite of initiation into the primitive community was "baptism in the name of Jesus" (Acts 2:38; 8:46; 10:48; 19:5; 22:16; 1 Cor 1:13ff.). This designation of Christian baptism seems to have resulted from the neophyte's expressing his faith by the formula "Jesus is Lord" when receiving the sacrament.

7 The application of the title "Lord" to the glorified Christ appears to have been the earliest way in which the apostolic faith attributed to the risen Master an aura of divinity. The primitive preaching employed Ps 110:1 as one of the best ways of expressing the effects of Jesus' exaltation. Just as the Ps says, "Sit at my right hand," so Jesus is now raised or seated at God's right hand (Acts 2:33; 5:31; Rom 8:34), or he stands at God's right hand (Acts 7:55). And the opening words of the Ps, "The Lord said to my Lord," may be considered the principal scriptural source for the designation of the glorified Christ as Lord. It is this title, rather than "Son of God," which expressed for the primitive Christian community the reality of Jesus' divine sonship. Hence, in answer to our earlier question about the background of the title, it seems fairly certain that the use of "Lord" as a divine name for Christ was not an invention of Hellenizing Christianity, as in the theory of W. Bousset, still followed by R. Bultmann. More plausible is the contention of O. Cullmann that the prehistory of the term as applied to Christ is to be found in Judaism. (For a full discussion, → Pauline Theology, 79:60–63.)

8 **(B) Messiah.** This title (from Aram *mᵉšîḥāʾ*), which designates Jesus as "the anointed" (Hebr *māšîaḥ*, Gk *christos*), was used in the apostolic preaching to underscore the Christian belief that Jesus was the divinely given answer to the messianic hopes of Israel (Acts 2:36; 17:3). There is some evidence to show that the primitive community justified this usage by Ps 2:2 (Acts 4:27). The kerygma proclaimed Jesus as "anointed with a holy Spirit and power" already during his earthly life (cf. Acts 10:37 where the specific reference is to Jesus' baptism). Thus the kerygma seems to agree with the impression given by the Gospels that Jesus was already acknowledged as Messiah during his public ministry. The high point of Jesus' self-revelation to the Twelve was reached when Peter formulated their collective loyalty and adherence to the Master at Caesarea Philippi: "You are the Messiah" (Mk 8:29; Lk 9:20). It is interesting, however, that Jesus reacted to this confession by correcting the grandiose ideas that the title of Messiah might convey and by insisting that his real role was that of the suffering Son of Man (Mk 8:31–33; Lk 9:22). By way of anticipation (→ 24 below), let us look more closely at what the Gospels tell us of Jesus as the Messiah during the ministry.

9 If Jesus accepted from his followers a profession of faith in his messiahship, he did so only with qualification. And there is good evidence that he habitually avoided any publicizing of his messianic role during his ministry (Mk 8:30; Lk 4:41; Jn 10:24). The narratives of his temptations (Mt 4:1–11; Lk 4:1–13) indicate that Jesus rejected the popular messianic ideals of prestidigitator and warrior-messiah, current in contemporary Judaism (also Jn 6:15). According to the Syn, on the occasion of his triumphal entry into Jerusalem Jesus appears deliberately to have arranged the acknowledgment of his messianic mission by the crowds; but not so according to Jn 12:12ff. In any case, it seems to have been his purpose on this occasion to instruct his followers that he conceived his messiahship after the description of the humble king in Zech 9:9 (Mt 21:4–5). According to Mk 14:62, Jesus replied affirmatively to the inquiry by the high priest regarding his messianic claims, but Mt 26:64 and Lk 22:67 seem independently to indicate that Jesus did not fully acquiesce in the priest's description of him as the Messiah and preferred a reference to the Son of Man.

10 Whatever hesitations Jesus may have had about the title "Messiah" and whether or not during his ministry he ever used it or accepted it as a self-designation, he was crucified as a would-be Messiah-king. Inevitably his followers interpreted his resurrection as a proof that he really was the Messiah, even though the title had to undergo major adaptation before it could be applied to Jesus. Although the Jewish view of the Messiah was not uniform (the Qumran Essenes seemingly expected two messiahs; → Apocrypha, 68:104), the dominant picture of what the Messiah would be was determined by the divine promise, made through the prophet Nathan, that King David's dynasty would continue on the throne of Israel forever ("your offspring after you"—2 Sm 7:12–14). In the early days of the monarchy in Jerusalem each reigning king was the Lord's anointed or messiah (Ps 89:39), but some kings were so bad that from time to time the hope was expressed that God would send an anointed king or messiah truly worthy of David's name (Is 9:5). In the post-exilic period, when the Davidic line no longer reigned in Judah, the anticipation arose that in the indefinite future God would send a supreme king from the Davidic line, *the* Messiah, who would deliver Israel and bring the whole world to worship Yahweh. There was no suggestion that he would be divine, nor was the concept of the Messiah ever free of nationalistic overtones. (→ Aspects OT Thought, 77:155–163.)

Only with great difficulty could the followers of Jesus maintain that he was the Messiah of Jewish expectation: His earthly career had not been glorious or regal; he had not been visibly victorious, nor had he established a kingdom; he had not delivered Israel, nor had he subjected the Gentiles to the service of Yahweh. The struggle of how to interpret the messiahship of Jesus left echoes in the apostolic preaching. One explanation seems to have been that Jesus would be the Messiah in his parousia. The future moment when Jesus will appear is the moment when God will fulfill all the prophecies, for then the whole world will see the Messiah in power and glory (Acts 3:20–21; cf. J. A. T. Robinson, "The Most Primitive Christology of All?" *JTS* 7 [1956] 177–89; also in his *Twelve New Testament Studies* [SBT 34; London, 1962]). Such an interpretation of Jesus as the future Messiah required virtually no change in the Jewish picture of the Messiah. Still another early Christian explanation is voiced in Acts 2:36 (also 5:31): It is the Ascended Jesus whom God has made the Messiah. Here we have a partial modification of the Jewish concept; for the

Messiah remains a glorious, victorious figure, but his reign is in heaven, not on earth.

However, neither of these primitive explanations seems to have had much success. The apostolic preachers were not content with saying that Jesus would be the Messiah or that he became the Messiah after his resurrection. Rather the concept of the Messiah was soon spiritualized so that the title could be applied to one whose glory was internal, and who delivered Israel not from political servitude but from the servitude of sin. The picture of the Messiah was broadened to include suffering (Acts 3:18; 17:3; Lk 24:26,46—the idea of a suffering Messiah seems to be a Christian innovation, unknown in late Judaism). And so it could now be preached that Jesus was the Messiah during his ministry—a stage of the preaching that was dominant when the Gospels were written. (It is clear that Jesus claimed to have a unique role in proclaiming God's Kingdom [→ 97 below]; the apostolic preachers were simply identifying that role as messiahship.) Still a further development was the understanding that Jesus was the Messiah from the moment of his incarnation, a development reflected in the infancy narratives (Mt 1:23; 2:6; Lk 1:31–33). Obviously Christian thought was moving more specifically toward belief in a divine Messiah.

No matter how radical the development and adaptation of the title "Messiah" in the history of its application to Jesus, it was clearly his most frequently applied title. In its Gk form, *Christos*, it became and has remained almost the surname of Jesus, so that Christians think and speak naturally of Jesus Christ (cf. Rom 1:6; Mt 1:1; Jn 1:17).

11 **(C) Servant of God.** The designation of Jesus as the Servant of God (the OT *'ebed Yahweh*; → Deutero-Isaiah, 22:5) in the primitive preaching is probably one of the most archaic attempts to use the OT to support the claim of the kerygma that "Christ died for our sins according to the Scriptures...was raised the third day according to the Scriptures" (1 Cor 15:3–4). It is possible that this conception is to be traced back to Peter (so Cullmann), who explains the cure of the cripple in Acts 3 by saying, "The God of Abraham and Isaac and Jacob, the God of our Fathers, has glorified his Servant Jesus, whom you handed over..." (3:13). Peter also uses this Servant theme to explain the presence (through the Spirit?) of the glorified Christ in the community: "For you, first and foremost, God has raised up his Servant, and sent him to bless you by converting each of you from your evil ways" (3:26). In the prayer of the community in time of trial, this same conception is combined with the notion of the Messiah in Ps 2: "They have assembled in this city against your holy Servant Jesus, whom you anointed..." (Acts 4:27), as well as with that of the new name (*Kyrios*) of the Risen Christ: "...by accomplishing signs and prodigies worked in the name of your holy Servant Jesus" (4:30).

Philip is depicted as basing his catechesis to the Ethiopian vizier upon the text of the last Servant Song in Dt-Is (53:7–8): "...beginning from this text Philip gospeled Jesus to him" (Acts 8:35). The ancient hymn cited by Paul in Phil 2:6–11 probably formed part of an early Palestinian liturgy. (However, some scholars think of it as Hellenistic rather than Palestinian, e.g., J. Schreiber, *ZThK* 50 [1961] 154–83; → Letter Phil, 50:17–19). It draws its inspiration from the description of the suffering, death, and exaltation of the *'ebed Yahweh* (Is 52:13–53:12). In Rom 4:25 we have probably a citation of some early Christian credal formula describing the Redeemer as "handed over for our sins and raised for our justification" (→ Letter Rom, 53:48). Thus it would appear that this Servant soteriology was characteristic of the most primitive Christian reflection on the meaning of salvation. It is clear, as will be seen, that it was not influential in the evolution of Paul's own theology of the redemption.

Two characteristics of this Servant theme from Dt-Is made it a popular vehicle in apostolic Christianity for showing how Christ's redemptive work had fulfilled "the Scriptures": the vicarious nature of the Servant's death (Is 53:12) and his mediatorial role in the covenant (42:6ff.). In consequence, it not only provided a theological motif for the kerygma, but had a pervasive influence also upon later NT writings.

12 **(D) The Holy and Just One.** These titles appear together in the Petrine kerygma (Acts 3:14), and both of them are characteristic of Dt-Is. There, however, the epithet "holy" is constantly reserved for Yahweh himself (Is 40:26; 41:25; 42:8; 47:4; 48:2; 51:15; 52:6; 54:5; 55:13). It is only the adjective "just" that is predicted of the Servant (53:11); and even this title would appear to be applied properly only to Yahweh (45:21). In the NT Christ is called more frequently the Holy One (Mt 1:20; Mk 1:24, Lk 1:35; Jn 6:69; Ap 3:7) than the Just One (Acts 7:52; 22:14; 1 Jn 2:1).

13 **(E) Prince of Life.** The Gk term *archēgos* can mean prince, leader, chief, author, originator. It appears as an epithet for Christ in the Petrine preaching in Acts (3:15; 5:31) and is later taken up by the author of Heb (2:10; 12:2). It describes Jesus as the leader of the renewed Israel in the journey toward the heavenly Jerusalem.

14 **(F) The Prophet and Elijah.** Two prophetic figures found in late Jewish expectations enter the NT description of Jesus. One is the *Prophet-like-Moses*, often called simply "the Prophet." In its original meaning, Dt 18:15–18 presented general legislation concerning the prophet in Israelite life. But because of its phrasing ("A prophet like me [Moses] will the Lord your God raise up"), the passage came to be applied to a particular figure who would be a prophet like Moses. See H. M. Teeple, *The Mosaic Eschatological Prophet* (*JBL* Monograph X, 1957). Probable instances of the expectation of the Prophet-like-Moses are the prophet who would solve legal problems mentioned in 1 Mc 4:41–50; 14:41, and the prophet who is associated with the two messiahs at Qumran (R. E. Brown, *CBQ* 19 [1957] 59–61). In Jn 1:21 the Baptist denies that his is the role of "the Prophet"; and Jn 6:14 (also 7:52; 1:45) suggests a popular belief that Jesus plays that role. This is probably the Johannine way of relating Jesus to Moses (W. A. Meeks, *The Prophet-King* [NovTSup 14; Leiden, 1967]). The apostolic preaching in Acts 3:22; 7:37 applies the deuteronomic concept of the Prophet-like-Moses to Jesus. On "the Prophet," see R. Schnackenburg, *SE* 1, 622–39.

15 Elijah was another eschatological prophetic figure who featured in popular imagination. The tradition of 2 Kgs 2:11 encouraged belief that Elijah (with horses and chariot) had been taken up into heaven—what more natural than his return? The editorial addition to Mal (3:23 [Eng 4:5]) identified Elijah the prophet as the mysterious messenger (originally the angel of the Lord? → Malachi, 23:66, 69) who would be sent to prepare the way of the Lord; and this tradition is repeated in Sir 48:10; *Enoch* 89:52; 90:31. That the people expected Elijah in NT times is seen in Jn 1:21; Mk 8:28; 9:11. Christian thought came to identify John the Baptist with the role of Elijah who had come before the day of the Lord (Mk 1:2; 9:13; Mt 11:14; 17:12), but Jn 1:21 may indicate that this was not the Baptist's own understanding of his role. Luke portrays Jesus as an Elijah-like figure (4:24–26; 7:11–17 with 1 Kgs 17:18–24; the "going up" of 9:51 with 2 Kgs 2:11; and 12:49 with 1 Kgs 18:38). Only in Lk 1:76 is the Baptist portrayed as Elijah. On late Jewish ideas about Elijah, see G. Molin, *Jud* 8 (1952) 65–94.

Jn 1:21 sharply distinguishes between the Prophet (-like-Moses) and Elijah. However, the frequent NT association of Moses and Elijah (Mk 9:4; Ap 11:4ff.) probably led to a certain confusion of the expectations about these two figures, so that the resultant wonder-working prophet could be identified as Jesus.

16 **(G) Stone Rejected by the Builders.** This title is applied to the dead and glorified Christ in the Petrine kerygma (Acts 4:11), where it is derived from Ps 118:22—a psalm constantly used in the primitive Church because it provided details of Jesus' passion and resurrection. The conception is taken up in the Syn tradition in connection with Jesus' parable of the vineyard (Mk 12:10; Mt 21:42; Lk 20:17). Reference is also made to it in 1 Pt 2:4–7 (see J. H. Elliott, *The Elect and the Holy* [NovTSup 12; Leiden, 1966] 23–36).

17 **(H) Judge of the Living and Dead.** The role of universal judge is attributed to the Risen Christ in the primitive preaching (Acts 10:42; 17:30). This was one of the ways in which the early Church associated Christ with divinity. In the OT Yahweh was regarded by Israel as possessing the function of the just judge (Gn 18:25) who would vindicate his people's rights and overthrow their enemies. This conception comes very close to the notion of savior (→ Aspects OT Thought, 77:136–148). Yahweh's acts of grace in favor of Israel are judgments (*mišpāṭîm*); for by the covenant God has bound himself to obtain justice and the good life for her. Israel's victories are simply Yahweh's "acts of justice" (Jgs 5:11), gracious benefits for his chosen people. This uniquely divine characteristic of the OT God is transferred in the NT to the Risen Lord Jesus (Rom 14:9; 2 Tm 4:1; 1 Pt 4:5).

18 **(I) Redeemer.** This epithet is not explicitly applied to Christ in the primitive kerygma, but it is predicated of him indirectly in Stephen's discourse, where it is stated that Moses was sent to Israel "as chief and redeemer" (Acts 7:35). Taken religiously, the term (Hebr *gō'ēl*) is applied only to Yahweh himself in the OT (Ps 19:15; 78:35; → Pauline Theology, 79:91–92). It is predicated of Moses insofar as he is a type of the Risen Savior, since evidently it surpasses anything that Moses' mission involved.

19 **(J) Savior.** This title is predicated of the exalted Christ in the Petrine kerygma (Acts 5:31). It reappears in the Pauline preaching as part of the evangelical tradition that Paul received (13:23). It is closely allied to the conceptions expressed by the word "redeemer" and by the term "Lord," since it evokes most exactly the function of the Risen Christ. In the OT, the term is frequently applied to Yahweh (Dt 32:15; Ps 25:5; Is 12:2; 45:22; Sir 51:1); and there can be no doubt but that it is a divine title. Accordingly, when it is predicated of Jesus in the NT, it expresses the divine character of his role. As we have seen (→ 3 above) by popular etymology the personal name "Jesus" is considered by NT writers as expressive of his divine work of salvation.

In the Hellenistic religious world the title of Savior was given to Aesculapius (Asklepios), god of medicine, and was also used as a divine title in the emperor cult. However, we do not think that this Hellenistic usage is of help in explaining the application of the title to Jesus. The fact that the title *sōtēr* is given to Jesus by NT authors, who also apply it to God the Father, suggests that we are dealing with an OT name for God that is transferred to Christ (Lk 1:47; 2:11; 1 Tm 1:1; 2 Tm 1:10; Ti 1:3). Although the term "Savior" would scarcely have been used of Jesus in Aramaic-Christian circles (it would be identical with the theophoric name, Jesus), there is NT evidence that these Palestinian Christians were aware of the religious significance of Jesus' personal name as expressive of his principal function in salvation history (Mt 1:21; Lk 1:31ff.). "Savior" became a much-used title for Jesus among the Hellenistic Christians.

20 **(K) Son of God.** It is significant that this important title of Christ appears nowhere in the primitive or Petrine kerygma. There, as we have seen, the exalted character of Jesus was expressed in other ways (the titles Judge, Lord, and Savior; the conception of the Risen Christ's exaltation "at God's right hand"). In Acts Paul is the first to call Christ "Son of God" (9:20—if 8:37 is treated as a gloss). In any case, it is evident that this epithet characterizes the Pauline presentation of Christ (→ 35 below). It is probable that Paul's own conversion experience lies at the source of this conception of the Risen Lord (Gal 1:16; → Pauline Theology, 79:13).

21 **(II) Synoptic Gospels.** Although each of the Syn has a personal approach to the mystery of Christ, which he expresses through various titles, all three possess a certain common view of Jesus and his redemptive work. They follow the same broad outline in their accounts of Jesus' earthly career. They all depict Jesus' mission as a struggle against evil and assert that his death and glorification are part of the definite divine plan of salvation. The Syn tradition consists of four main points, which many think were taken over from the Petrine kerygma in Acts: the ministry of John the Baptist, Jesus' Galilean ministry, the last journey to Jerusalem, Jesus' passion and glorification. (This view, made popular by C. H. Dodd, has been seriously challenged by D. E. Nineham in *Studies in the Gospels* [Fest. R. H. Lightfoot; Oxford, 1957] 223–39; → Gospel Mk, 42:4.) Accordingly, the more significant Christological titles prominent in the primitive preaching recur in these NT writings with new amplification, e.g., Servant of God, Son of God, Messiah, Lord. Other titles appear that were only implicit in the summaries we possess of the apostolic kerygma: Master (Rabbi, Teacher), Son of David, Son of Man. In addition, certain epithets are given by each Syn writer that characteristically reflect his personal approach to the good news.

22 **(A) Servant of God.** Jesus appears as the suffering and glorified Servant of Yahweh in the common Syn tradition that preserves a threefold prediction of his death and resurrection (Mk 8:31; 9:31; 10:33–34; Mt 16:21; 17:22–23; 20:17–19; Lk 9:22,44; 18:31–34; → Gospel Mk, 42:52). The common Syn tradition of the logion on fasting, which contains a prophecy of Jesus' death (the "bridegroom will be taken away from them"—Mk 2:20; Mt 9:15; Lk 5:35), is probably a reference to Is 53:8. Finally, the Syn concur in reporting the words of institution over the cup in a manner reminiscent of Is 53:12 (Mk 14:24; Mt 26:24; Lk 22:20). The Syn reporting of the heavenly voice at Jesus' transfiguration contains a reference to the first Servant Song (Is 42:1—Mk 9:7; Mt 17:5; Lk 9:35).

23 Some passages in the individual Gospels should be noted.

Mark 10:45. This logion, repeated in Mt 20:28, is inspired by Is 53:10–12, which describes the Servant as giving his life in sacrifice to justify sinners by bearing the punishment due them for their sins.

Matthew 8:16–17; 12:17–21. These two passages are unique in the Syn tradition inasmuch as they are glosses by Matthew on the Dt-Is theme. In the first text, the Evangelist understands Is 53:4–7 in a derived sense, applying it to Jesus' work of healing disease; in the second, he reminds the reader of Jesus' identity as the Servant by a lengthy citation of Is 42:1ff.

Luke 24:26,45–46. Although Luke's interest in Jesus as the Servant of God is not as great as that found in Mk and Mt, the two logia, which report the teaching of the risen Jesus to his disciples in the last chapter of Lk, bear the mark of Is 53.

24 **(B) Messiah.** We have already discussed (→ 8–9 above) the problem of the use of "Messiah" as a title for Jesus during his ministry. The title (*Christos*) occurs fairly frequently in each of the Syn (7 times in Mk, 14 in Mt, 12 in Lk) in the sense of "the Anointed" (only in Jn 1:42; 4:25 does *Messias*, a Gk form of *m^{e}šîḥā'* appear). In the common Syn tradition, *Christos* is used in the Petrine confession (Mk 8:29; Mt 16:16; Lk 9:20), in the question about the identity of David's son (Mk 12:35; Mt 22:42; Lk 20:41), and in the high priest's question at Jesus' trial (Mk 14:61; Mk 26:63; Lk 22:67). In Mt and Lk, it occurs chiefly in the infancy narratives and in the passion and resurrection accounts. In Mt 1:1 and Mk 1:1 it is combined with Jesus, possibly in the late usage as a surname.

25 **(C) Lord.** In the Syn, the Gk word *Kyrios* is used by the disciples or strangers in addressing Jesus, usually in the sense of "Sir" or "Master." It is never used in Mk with the full Christian meaning it acquired in the apostolic preaching (but cf. the Marcan appendix, 16:19–20; → Gospel Mk, 42:97–98). In Mt 28:6 it is used in the later Christological sense of the Risen Christ. The one doubtful case is Mk 11:3; Mt 21:3: "The Lord has need of it"; here, however, *Kyrios* should probably be translated "Master." Among the Syn, the Lucan usage is distinctive, for from Lk 7:13 on the Evangelist refers to Jesus by the postresurrection title "the Lord" some 18 times.

26 **(D) Master, Teacher, Rabbi.** The usual form in which Jesus was addressed by the disciples during his earthly life was "Master" (*Didaskalos*, *Kyrios*) or "Rabbi." The latter form occurs twice in Mt and four times in Mk (the form *rabbouni* is read once in Mk). (On the question of whether the Gospel use of "rabbi" is anachronistic, see R. E. Brown, *The Gospel According to John* [AB 29; N.Y., 1966] 74.) *Didaskalos* is found 8 times in Mk, 12 in Mt, 15 in Lk. Such honorific titles were customarily bestowed upon other Jewish teachers and have no special theological significance.

27 **(E) Son of David.** In the primitive preaching, reference was made to the Davidic dynastic oracle (2 Sm 7:14ff.). In the common Syn tradition Jesus is called "Son of David" twice: the cure of the blind man (Mk 10:47; Mt 9:27; 20:30; Lk 18:38); and the question about David's son (Mk 12:35; Mt 22:42; Lk 20:41). These two are the only instances in Mk; and Lk 1:32 is the sole additional example in the third Gospel. However, Mt has six additional examples. Matthew's interest in this title is evident from the opening line (1:1) and from the fact that Joseph, although not the natural father of Jesus, is given the paternal role of handing on to the infant Jesus his Davidic lineage (cf. Mt 1:20 where "son of David" is the name by which the angel addresses Joseph).

28 **(F) Son of Man.** The unique quality of this title is that in the Gospels only Jesus applies this designation to himself. In fact, the one exception to this practice in the entire NT is Acts 7:56. The phrase signifies simply "man" (i.e., an individual human being). Since in Hebrew and Aramaic the word man (*'ādām*, *'ĕnôš*) denotes mankind, the idiomatic expression "son of" is employed to designate the individual. In late Judaism, the Son of Man concept assumed two forms: (1) that of the heavenly Man, now concealed and scheduled to appear at the end of time (Dn, *Enoch*, *2 Esdras*); (2) the heavenly, "ideal" Man (Philo, the *Kerygmata Petrou*). In Dn 7:13 the author points out that the symbolic figure he is describing as a son of man stands for "the saints of the Most High" (i.e., the redeemed community of Israel). In later Jewish apocalyptic literature (*2 Esdras*, *Enoch*), the Son of Man is thought of as an individual. How much of this could have influenced NT usage is debatable; for *2 Esdras* is post-NT, and the pertinent parts of *Enoch* may be late and even Christian (→ Apocrypha, 68:15,41).

29 The pagan myth of an *Urmensch* (an original, perfect, heavenly man torn to pieces by demons), which echoes to a certain extent the Son of Man idea, was not easily assimilable by Jewish thought, since the biblical Adam stands revealed as source of sin for mankind. Another Jewish solution is to be seen in *Enoch*, where the origin of sin is attributed to the angels (Gn 6:1). The gnostic Pseudo-Clementine writings (*Kerygmata Petrou*) categorically deny Adam's sin and assert that Eve is the principle of evil. Philo (*Leg. alleg.* 1.31ff.; *De mundi opificio* 134ff.) distinguishes in the two creation accounts of Gn between the formation of the "heavenly Man" fashioned in the divine image and the formation of the "earthly Man," the primordial sinner (cf. 1 Cor 15:46 where Paul appears to refute a view similar to Philo's).

30 The Gospels bear witness to Jesus' preference for the title "Son of Man" above all honorific epithets. The phrase occurs 14 times in Mk, 30 in Mt, 25 in Lk, and 13 in Jn. It is found once in Acts (7:56) and three times in quotations from the LXX, thus giving us 86 occurrences in the entire NT. "Son of Man" is employed by Jesus in the Gospels to describe: *first*, his earthly activity: Mk 2:10,28; 10:45; Mt 13:37; Lk 7:34 par.; 9:58 par.; 11:30 par.; 12:10 par.; 19:9; 22:48; *second*, his suffering and resurrection: Mk 8:31; 9:31; 10:33 (triple prediction of passion and resurrection with parallels); Mk 9:9; 10:45; 14:21; *third*, his eschatological function: Mk 8:38; 13:26; 14:62; Mt 10:23; 13:41; 19:28; 24:39; 25:31; Lk 12:40; 17:22–30; 18:8; 21:36. The novelty of Jesus' use of the epithet, which he probably borrowed from Dn 7:13, is to be seen in the synthesis he effects between this honorific appellation and the concept of the humble and suffering Servant of God.

Modern critics debate about the origin of the NT Son of Man Christology: Was it a creation of Galilean Christianity (E. Lohmeyer), or of "the Hellenists" in the primitive community (O. Cullmann)? It is not implausible that Paul's interest in the Adam theme, to be discussed below, had some influence upon this theological development in the written Gospels. Modern critics also debate whether Jesus did use the title "Son of Man" of himself. Two recent works argue that he spoke only of a future Son of Man (third usage above), and that it was through later Christian extension that the title was used in sayings referring to Jesus in his ministry (first and second usages).

(Higgins, A. J. B., *Jesus and the Son of Man* [Phila., 1964]. Hooker, M. D., *The Son of Man in Mark* [London, 1967]. Tödt, H. E., *The Son of Man in Synoptic Tradition* [Phila., 1965].)

31 **(G) Marcan Titles.** It is probable that Mk 6:15 (cf. also Mk 8:28) presents Jesus as the Prophet (V. Taylor; → 14 above). Mk 6:3 is the only NT passage where Jesus is described as Son of Mary (in Mt 13:55 and Lk 4:22, the parallels, we find a quite different reading). The reading "Son of Mary" is attested by all the uncial mss. and many minuscules, although important mss. (e.g., P^{45}) read "the Son of the carpenter."

32 **(H) Matthean Titles.** In addition to Matthew's preference for the title "Son of David" (→ 27 above), he evinces interest in presenting Jesus as Son of Abraham. (The latter phrase occurs only in Mt 1:1 and is found nowhere else in the NT.) By singling out Abraham and David from among Jesus' ancestors, Matthew indicates his awareness of the significance of these two titles. "Emmanuel," however, is the most characteristically Matthean title given to Jesus. He is announced in the infancy narrative as Emmanuel, and the name is explained as meaning "*with us* is God" (Mt 1:23). Matthew's Christology is often sketched in the service of a doctrine of the Church, and Matthew may be alluding to the Risen Christ's presence in the Christian community. The same idea may be found at the close of the Gospel, which cites the ascending Lord's final promise, "I am *with you* all the time until the end of history" (Mt 28:20). If this is an inclusion (a figure of Hebr rhetoric that stamps the principal theme of a book or passage by the repetition of a similar phrase), our author is revealing a favorite view of Jesus and his mission. In the middle of Mt, Jesus may also be reminding the reader that he is Emmanuel by promising to be present in a special way in the liturgical worship of the community—a logion found only in Mt: "Where two or three are gathered together in my name, I am there in their midst" (Mt 18:20).

33 **(I) Lucan Title.** The epithet "Savior" is singularly Lucan, since he alone of the Syn bestows this title upon Christ (2:11), as well as upon God the Father (1:47). In addition to the name *sōtēr*, Lk also uses the term *to sōtērion* (salvation) of Christ (2:30; 3:6). Jesus' entry into Zacchaeus' home means "*sōtēria* for this house" (19:9).

34 **(III) Pauline Writings.** In addition to the NT books generally conceded to be Pauline (1-2 Thes, Phil, 1-2 Cor, Gal, Rom, Phlm, Col, Eph), we include here the Pastorals (1-2 Tm, Ti) and Heb.

(A) Pauline Kerygma in Acts. The accounts in Acts of Paul's preaching (which some scholars think of as more Lucan than Pauline) reveal several titles for Jesus, many of them already present in the Jerusalem kerygma. Moreover, Paul employs "Son of God" as a title of Jesus in his version of the gospel (Acts 9:20). He also proclaims Jesus as Son of David and Savior "according to the promise" that God had made concerning the Davidic dynasty (13:24). Paul is credited with interpreting Ps 2:7 in function of the Risen Christ, "You are my Son: this day have I begotten you" (Acts 13:33). The Apostle is represented as asserting at Athens that the Risen Christ has been constituted universal Judge (17:31). At Thessalonica Paul proclaims Jesus as Messiah (17:3); at Ephesus his preaching is characterized as testimony to "faith in our Lord Jesus" (20:21), and at Rome he teaches "what concerns Jesus as Lord" (28:31). Thus from the Lucan record of Paul's preaching we find that the most frequent Pauline titles for Christ were Son of God, Son of David, Savior, Messiah, and Lord. In the Pauline letters, the principal additions to this list will be those prompted by Paul's interest in the early chapters of Gn (the last, or new Adam; Image of God; First-Born). In Heb, certain new titles will appear: High Priest, Apostle, Mediator.

35 **(B) Son of God.** The title (→ 20 above; → Pauline Theology, 79:53-58) is applied to the parousiac Christ (1 Thes 1:10; 1 Cor 15:28), to Christ in his contemporary relations with the Christian (1 Cor 1:9; 2 Cor 1:9; Gal 2:20; 4:6; Rom 8:29; Col 1:13; Eph 4:13; Heb 6:6; 10:29), to Christ sent as incarnate Son (Gal 4:4; Rom 8:3; Heb 1:2), to Christ as effecting man's redemption (Rom 1:3; 5:10; 8:32; Heb 4:14), and to Christ as High Priest (Heb 5:5,8-10; 7:3,28). Worthy of special note is Gal 1:16 where Paul makes reference to his own conversion experience, which he describes as the Father's revelation "of his Son in me." Nowhere in the Pastorals is this title given to Christ.

36 **(C) Son of David; Son of Abraham.** The Davidic descent of Jesus is alluded to only twice (Rom 1:3; 2 Tm 2:8; also "root of Jesse," Rom 15:12). In a comment on Gn 12:7; 17:7, Christ is declared "the seed" of Abraham (Gal 3:16).

37 **(D) Christ.** Although this title (→ 8-10 above) occurs very frequently (alone, or as Christ Jesus, Jesus Christ), its use in the sense of Messiah is extremely rare (Rom 9:5). It is commonly used by Paul as another name for Jesus. The form "Christ Jesus," less common in the earlier letters, becomes more frequent in Eph and the Pastorals where it tends to replace "Jesus Christ," particularly in the phrase "in Christ Jesus" (→ Pauline Theology, 79:138).

38 **(E) Lord.** The epithet *Kyrios* is, with *Christos*, the most common title for Jesus in the Pauline letters (→ Pauline Theology, 79:59-67). It is found alone: "the Lord" (1 Thes 1:6; Phil 2:29; etc.), especially when Paul makes reference to a saying of Jesus (1 Thes 4:15; 1 Cor 7:12); "our Lord" (1 Cor 6:14). It occurs in the phrases "the Lord Jesus" (2 Thes 2:8), "our Lord Jesus" (1 Cor 5:4); "the Lord Jesus Christ"—especially in the salutation of Paul's letters (1 Thes 1:1; 2 Thes 1:1; Phil 1:2); also "our Lord Jesus Christ" (Phil 4:23), or "Jesus Christ our Lord" (Rom 1:4). It becomes the customary Pauline designation of the Risen Christ, who is "the Lord of glory" (1 Cor 2:8), and especially of the parousiac Christ (1 Thes 2:20; 3:13; 1 Cor 1:7), who is to be "my judge" (1 Cor 4:4). Paul has made a paradigm of the OT phrase "the Day of Yahweh," and thus describes the second coming of Christ as "the Day of the Lord" (1 Thes 5:1; 2 Thes 2:3) or "the Day of Christ" (Phil 1:6; 2:16). One of the most ancient credal formulas of primitive Christianity, "Jesus is Lord!" is found repeatedly in Paul's writings (Phil 2:11; 1 Cor 8:6; 12:3; 2 Cor 4:5; Rom 10:9; Col 2:6).

This concept of the contemporary lordship of Christ is a hallmark of Pauline Christology. The Risen Lord has begun his reign in history through the operation of the Spirit within the Church; and through faith (which is also the work of the Spirit—1 Cor 12:3) the Church is concious of this kingship of Christ. The rest of the universe, however, does not recognize it; hence "he must reign until God has put all enemies beneath his feet" (1 Cor 15:25). It is this extension of the Lord's dominion that, in Paul's thought, gives a significant religious character to the period between the first and second comings of Christ: This is the era of the Church, in which the Lord's dominion must be widened to include all creation and the powers behind the state, at present inimical to him. The concept of the Kingdom or dominion of God, so prominent in the Syn (→ 99ff. below), is thus assumed by Paul under the notion of the lordship of the exalted Christ. For the dominion of the Father has been entrusted to the Son until it becomes a complete, historical reality (15:28), and "God will be all in all" (→ Pauline Theology, 79:57).

39 **(F) The Last Adam.** This characterization of Christ is one of Paul's original contributions to NT theology. The title "Son of Man" does not appear anywhere in Paul's writings, but the concept "the last Adam" includes it. (For Pauline thought on Adam, → Pauline Theology, 79:102-104.) According to O. Cullmann, Paul successfully solved the problem with which Judaism had been unable to cope (the relation of the "Son of Man" to Adam; → 29 above) by connecting the conception of "the last Adam" to the historical person Jesus Christ. In this, Paul is faithful to the creative thought of

Jesus, who had applied the title "Son of Man" to himself. Moreover, like Jesus, Paul relates his notion of "the last Adam" to that of the *'ebed Yahweh* (cf. Rom 5:12–21; perhaps also Phil 2:6–11). The Apostle takes up the doctrine of the "heavenly Man," but (possibly vs. Philo) denies the role to Adam and applies it to the Risen Christ (1 Cor 15:45ff.; → Pauline Theology, 79:53).

40 Three stages are to be noted in the evolution of Paul's thought on "the last Adam." (1) He first conceives of Jesus, the new Adam *in his risen state*, as bearer of life to all through the glorious resurrection of the just (1 Cor 15:20–22). As "the last Adam" the Risen Lord "has become life-giving Spirit" (15:45) in whose image redeemed humanity must be formed (15:49). This work of transformation is already in progress in this life, for it is the work "of the Lord who is Spirit" (2 Cor 3:18; 4:10–12). (2) At a later period, Paul perceives that the role of Christ as new Adam had begun with his redemptive death, accepted out of obedience to the Father (Rom 5:15–21). For this presentation of Christ's passion as an act of obedience, Paul is probably indebted to the Servant theology of the primitive preaching. Thus the vicarious nature of Jesus' work of redemption for us (*anti hēmōn, hyper hēmōn*) is accounted for by Paul's dependence upon the Servant of God conception. Yet the notion of vicariousness is balanced by the Adam concept, which asserts the involvement of mankind in the death and resurrection of Christ. Jesus did not die and rise to excuse the Christian from the salutary necessity of death and resurrection. "One died for all; therefore all have died" (2 Cor 5:14). He "was handed over for our sins, and raised for our justification" (Rom 4:25) to enable us to die and rise with him (1 Thes 4:14; 5:10; 2 Cor 5:15; 4:10; Rom 14:9; → Pauline Theology, 79:69,71). (3) The final expression of Paul's theme of "the last Adam" is found in the Captivity Letters. The baptized Christian has "put on that new man which is being constantly renewed in view of perfect knowledge after the image of his Creator... Christ, all in all" (Col 3:9–11). Christ's work is one of reconciliation, bringing Jew and Gentile into a new unity, "that he might in himself create the two into one new man" (Eph 2:15). In Eph, Paul succeeds in effecting a synthesis between this doctrine of the "last Adam" and that of the Church as "Body of Christ." The goal of our union with the new Adam is to "attain the oneness of faith and perfect knowledge of the Son of God, the perfect man..." (Eph 4:13).

41 **(G) Image of God.** This title is connected with the preceding by being derived, like the Adam theme, from the first chapters of Gn. It is also characteristic of Pauline Christology, for it is found nowhere else in the NT. The first Adam was said (Gn 1:27) to have been created in the image of God; for Paul it is the Risen Christ who alone has fully realized this image of the Father, and so is capable of assimilating the Christian to that image. The Gk term *eikōn* denotes the outward expression of the reality of a person or thing and implies community of nature (G. Kittel, *ThDNT* 2, 395–97). Paul speaks of the kerygma, which proclaims Christ's resurrection, as "the gospel of the glory of Christ who is the image of God" (2 Cor 4:4). Christ is "the image of the unseen God, first-born before all creatures" (Col 1:15). The destiny of every Christian is described in terms of his assimilation to the exalted Lord: "And just as surely as we have borne the image of the earthly man, so too shall we bear the image of the heavenly man" (1 Cor 15:49). Indeed, this transformation is already in progress during the present life: All Christians "are being transformed into the same image with ever-increasing glory, as by the Lord who is Spirit" (2 Cor 3:18). It is baptism that initiates the process: "You have put off your old man with his habits, and you have put on that new man which is being constantly renewed in view of perfect knowledge after the image of his Creator..." (Col 3:9–10).

42 **(H) First-Born.** This title was probably applied to Christ as a result of Paul's conception of him as the image of God: Christ is "The image of the invisible God, the first-born before all creatures, since in him all things have been created..." (Col 1:15–16); he is also "first-born from among the dead," and hence is constituted "Head of his Body, the Church" (1:18). Moreover, it is the Father's plan for the salvation of mankind that men become "assimilated to the image of his Son so that he might become first-born among many brothers" (Rom 8:29).

43 **(I) Savior.** In Paul's writing, although the work of Christ is frequently referred to as salvation (1 Cor 1:18,21; 2 Cor 2:15; Rom 1:16; 5:10; 8:24; Eph 2:5), Christ is only twice designated as *sōtēr* (Phil 3:20; Eph 5:23). In the first of these texts, it is the parousiac Christ to whom the title properly belongs; for, in the biblical view, salvation must compass man in his total personality, even on the material side of his nature (Rom 8:23). In the Pastorals, *sōtēr* is bestowed upon the Father (1 Tm 1:1; 2:3; 4:10; Ti 1:3; 2:10; 3:4) and upon Christ (2 Tm 1:10; Ti 1:4; 2:13; 3:6) without any apparent change of meaning. This transference of a uniquely divine OT title (→ 19 above) to Christ is striking.

44 **(J) Titles from Israel's Liturgy.** To express Christ's function in Christian salvation Paul uses several images that are borrowed from the ancient cultus of Israel and Judaism. The Risen Christ is "first fruits" (*aparchē*), a metaphor borrowed from the rite of consecrating the first fruits of the harvest (*bikkûrîm, rē'šît bikkûrîm:* Ex 22:28; 23:19; Dt 18:4; Lv 19:23ff.; → Religious Institutions, 76:140). Jer 2:3 designates Israel as "the first fruits of the Lord's harvest." Christ is called "the first fruits of those who sleep" (1 Cor 15:20, 23), since his resurrection inaugurates and effects the glorious resurrection of the just. The Risen Lord is also called "our paschal lamb" (1 Cor 5:7)—one of the rare Pauline allusions to Jesus' death as a sacrifice. The statement, "God by sending his own Son in the likeness of sinful flesh and *peri hamartias*..." (Rom 8:3) may be an allusion to the sin offering (*'āšām;* → Religious Institutions, 76:86–88), translated in the LXX of Is 53:10 by *peri hamartias*, "an offering for sin."

Reference is made to the ritual of the Day of Atonement (→ Religious Institutions, 76:155) in Rom 3:25, which represents God as exposing the crucified Christ as "a mercy seat (*hilastērion, kappōret*) through faith in his blood." By this image Paul describes the meaning of Christ's death as an efficacious symbol of the Father's saving presence forgiving the sins of his people (→ Pauline Theology, 79:83–86). In connection with these liturgical images certain other texts may be mentioned that reflect a cultic character. Christ is called "our justification, our sanctification, our redemption" (1 Cor 1:30), and also "our peace" (Eph 2:14). The title "mediator" (*mesitēs*) is given Christ in 1 Tm 2:5; Heb 8:6; 9:15; 12:24. This priestly function of the exalted Christ is described as intercession by Paul (Rom 8:34; cf. Heb 7:25), who also attributes it to the Spirit (Rom 8:27). The author of Heb characteristically describes Jesus as High Priest who offers the heavenly sacrifice in the celestial temple as the completion and prolongation of his redemptive death.

45 **(K) Servant of God.** This conception from Dt-Is (→ 11, 22–23 above) does not figure prominently in Pauline Christology, for the Apostle has chosen to think of his own work as a continuation of Jesus' role as the Servant: Gal 1:15; 2 Cor 4–6. Nevertheless, there are allusions to it in Paul's letters (Phil 2:6–11; Rom 4:25;

5:12ff.). It has also modified the Pauline concept of "the last Adam" (→ 39–40 above).

46 **(L) Head.** In the initial presentation of Paul's conception of the Church as the "Body of Christ" (1 Cor 12:12–27; Rom 12:4ff.), the Risen Christ is not distinguished from the "Body." However, there is one early passage (1 Cor 11:3) where Christ is called "head of the male." This term *kephalē* is applied to him in the Captivity Letters to describe the relationship existing between the Risen Christ and his Church (Col 1:18; 2:19; Eph 1:22; 4:15; 5:23). Christ is also *kephalē* over the angelic forces (Col 2:10). This development by Paul of his metaphor, which depicts the Church as the Body of Christ (→ Pauline Theology, 79:143), enables him in his later letters to express the relationship between Head and Body as one of love (Eph 5:25).

47 **(M) Apostle.** In Heb 3:1 Jesus is designated as "the apostle and high priest." He deserves this designation in virtue of his mission from the Father, although the title may also imply that as high priest Jesus is sent back to the Christian people to bring them the fruits of his sacrifice.

48 **(N) God.** There are several instances in Paul where Christ is *equivalently* called "God" (Phil 2:6ff.; Col 1:15; 2:9). (The use of *archē* as a title in Col 1:18 in the sense of origin or principle suggests that this term is to be taken as a divine name.) Whether Rom 9:5 is a doxology of God the Father or is to be understood of Christ is debated (→ Letter Rom, 53:97); it would be the only instance in the undoubtedly genuine Pauline letters where Jesus is called "God." In the Pastorals, Ti 2:13 is an instance where *theos* is probably predicated of Christ ("our great God and Savior Jesus Christ"). An even clearer instance is Heb 1:8. See R. E. Brown, "Does the New Testament Call Jesus God?" *TS* 26 (1965) 545–73.

49 **(IV) Johannine Literature.** Under this heading we include Jn, 1–3 Jn, Ap.

(A) The Anointed (Messiah). The purpose of Jn (20:31) is to deepen Christian faith in Jesus as "the Anointed." Thus the title *Christos* (= Messiah) is given Jesus eight times in Jn; in addition the author reports current Jewish traditions relative to messianic expectations (1:25; 4:25; 7:27,31,42). *Christos* in the sense of Messiah is used once in 1 Jn (2:22), twice in Ap (11:15; 12:10). As a surname, *Christos* appears twice in Jn, five times in 1 Jn, twice in 2 Jn, four times in Ap. It is used twice of the glorified Christ in Ap, once in 2 Jn, never thus in Jn or 1 Jn.

50 **(B) Son of God.** This title also is a special object of interest in Jn, as the statement of purpose shows (Jn 20:31). It is applied only to Jesus in Jn, never predicated of men as it is in Paul; for the Evangelist, men are the children (*tekna*) of God, but Jesus is God's Son (*huios*). "Son of God" occurs 25 times in Jn, 22 times in 1 Jn, twice in 2 Jn, once in Ap. By virtue of being Son of God in a uniquely divine sense, Jesus can give to the believers "power to become God's children" (Jn 1:12). In the NT Jn alone cites Jesus as stating that he is Son of God (Jn 10:36). The Johannine writings use the term *monogenēs*, "only Son" (Jn 1:14,18; 3:16,18; 1 Jn 4:9)—a usage found nowhere else in the NT. (For proof that *monogenēs* means "only, unique" and not precisely "only begotten," see D. Moody, *JBL* 72 [1953] 213–19.) The reading of Jn 1:18 is disputed: *monogenēs theos, monogenēs huios*, and *monogenēs* are all attested. In 1 Jn 5:20 Jesus seems to be the one called *ho alēthinos theos*, "the true God."

51 **(C) Lord.** The term *Kyrios* is rarely used by Jn to designate the Risen Christ, except in the postresurrection narratives (Jn 20:2,18,20,25,28; 21:7,12). In the account of Jesus' public ministry, apart from many instances where *kyrie* is employed as a title of respect, only two examples of the usage are found (Jn 6:23; 11:2) and both of these are probably editorial. Jn 4:1 is a doubtful reading. In Ap there are eight instances of *Kyrios* as title for the glorified Christ, whereas it is not found in the letters.

52 **(D) Son of Man.** This epithet is applied in Jn almost exclusively as a designation of the glorified Lord (Jn 1:51; 3:13,14; 6:27,53,62; 8:28; 12:23,34; 13:31). The one possible exception to this rule may be in Jn 9:35. (→ Johannine Theology, 80:17–20.)

(Dior, H.-M., *ScEccl* 19 [1967] 49–65. Freed, E. D., *JBL* 86 [1967] 402–9. Schnackenburg, R., *NTS* 11 [1964–65] 123–37.)

53 **(E) Son of Joseph.** Jesus is given this title twice in Jn (1:46; 6:42), but nowhere else in the Johannine literature.

54 **(F) The Prophet.** This early designation of Jesus (→ 14–15 above) appears to be of considerable interest to Jn, although it is not found in the other Johannine writings. The Baptist denies that he is "the Prophet" (Jn 1:21,25); nor does Jesus so identify him—here Jn differs from the Syn. The title is given to Jesus in the early testimonies of the disciples (Jn 1:46) and throughout his public ministry (Jn 4:19,44; 6:14; 7:40; 9:17).

55 **(G) Lamb of God.** The name *amnos tou theou* is twice given to Jesus by the Baptist (Jn 1:29,36; → Gospel Jn, 63:52). In the Ap the description "a lamb standing as if slain" is frequently employed to characterize the Risen Lord of history: *arnion...hōs esphagmenon* (Ap 5:6). It occurs 28 times and expresses the author's fundamental conception of the glorified Christ. The Johannine use of this image is probably to be explained by two OT sources. *First*, in Is 52:7 the suffering Servant of God is compared to a lamb "led to the slaughter," and in Is 53:11–12 the Servant is said to bear the sins of mankind. In Jn 1:29 Jesus is "the Lamb of God who takes away the sin of the world." This sin he will expiate by his redemptive death. *Second*, the OT institution of the Passover lamb, cited in reference to Jesus in Jn 19:36, is another source of the Johannine conception of Jesus as the Lamb of God. In Ap 15:3–4 the hymn sung in honor of the Lamb is inspired by the canticle of Moses at the passage of the Red Sea (Ex 15:1ff.). The reference in Jn 19:14 to the hour of Jesus' condemnation, which is made to coincide with the time for beginning the slaughter of the Passover lambs in the Temple, provides another indication that the Evangelist thinks of Jesus' death as a sacrifice similar to that commemorated by the Jewish Passover. See R. E. Brown, *The Gospel According to John* (AB 29; N.Y., 1966) 58–63.

56 **(H) King of Israel.** This title, which occurs in the Syn only in connection with the mocking of Jesus on the cross (Mk 15:32; Mt 27:42), is of particular interest to John. It appears among the disciples' testimonies to Jesus (Jn 1:50) and in the acclamations voiced at his entry into Jerusalem (12:13). Jesus refuses to become merely "King of the Jews" (6:15); and in the dialogue with Pilate (18:33; 19:15), Jesus endeavors to make clear his religious concept of kingship.

57 **(I) The Word of God.** The term *logos* is applied to Jesus only in Johannine literature (→ Johannine Theology, 80:21–24; → Gospel Jn, 63:40), where it may be said to express John's most personal conception of Jesus and his work as the revealer of the "God no man has ever seen" (Jn 1:18). This title is a theme in the Prologue (Jn 1:1–18), and it is also found in 1 Jn 1:1 and Ap 19:13. (However, the manner in which "word" is to be translated in 1 Jn 1:1 is not certain; → Johannine Epistles, 62:9.) The pre-existent Christ as *logos* is "with God," i.e., somehow distinct from *ho theos* (God the Father), yet he "is God" (Jn 1:1–2). He is creator of the universe (1:3); he became incarnate as Jesus Christ (1:14ff.). In Ap (19:11–16), the *logos* is identified with the Lamb and presented as universal judge and king. The background for this Johannine usage of *logos* is difficult to assess. It may be that the Pauline usage (in which the term designates the Christian kerygma) exerted some influence upon John. There is also Palestinian syncretistic Judaism, in which the divine word communicated through OT revelation is personified. More remotely, the Oriental-Hellenistic *logos* doctrines also influenced this literary development. In Heraclitus, the Stoics, and Platonism *logos* denotes the world law; in Gnostic mythological speculations *logos* is envisaged as a mediator. In the Johannine tradition, however, Jesus is *logos* because he brings the Christian revelation in his teaching, still more because he *is* himself that revelation of the Father. See Brown, *op. cit.*, 519–24.

58 **(J) "I AM."** There are eight instances in Jn where Jesus identifies himself by the absolute statement "I AM" (*egō eimi*—6:20; 8:24,28,56; 13:19; 18:5,6,8). This mysterious expression appears to be a deliberate reference to Yahweh's self-identification to Moses (Ex 3:13–14); hence it is an expression of Jesus' own divinity. Of great importance is the fact that Yahweh's affirmation "I am he" is translated as *egō eimi* in the LXX of Dt-Is (43:25; 51:12; 52:6). See Brown, *op. cit.*, 533–38.

59 **(K) Self-imposed Titles.** Other "I am" statements are not used absolutely but have a predicate that may serve as a title for Jesus: the bread of life (6:35,51); the light of the world (8:12; 9:5); the gate or door (10:7,9); the good or ideal shepherd (10:11,14); the way, the truth, and the life (14:6); the true or real vine (15:1,5). (For interpretation, → Gospel Jn, 63:94.)

60 **(L) Savior.** This title rarely occurs in Johannine literature. But where it appears (Jn 4:42; 1 Jn 4:14), it expresses Jesus' mission as the unique, universal savior of mankind (cf. Jn 3:17; 10:9; 12:47).

61 **(M) Other Titles.** Only once is Jesus designated as "an expiation for our sins" (1 Jn 4:10), a title that depicts the merciful love of the Father in sending the Son. The title "faithful witness" is found only in Ap 1:5, where it depicts Jesus' revelatory function (cf. Is 55:4). Jesus is called "a Paraclete" in 1 Jn 2:1 in the sense of being an intercessor, and perhaps this title is implicitly given to Jesus in Jn 14:16.

In concluding this essay on the titles of Christ, we may point out that the rich Christology that shines through these titles is more *functional* than ontological. In saying that Jesus is Lord, Savior, Messiah, etc., the NT primarily tells us what role or function he plays in regard to men (*pro nobis*). This has implications for what he was in himself (*in se*), but such an ontological question is not the primary or explicit interest. Even in a late work like Jn, the statement "The Word was God" (1:1), while bordering on the ontological, still has a strong functional stress; for the very concept of "the Word" implies an audience to whom the Word would be spoken. The functional reference of the NT as compared with the ontological interest of the later Church may be seen in the contrast between Paul's confession of faith, "God was in Christ reconciling the world to himself" (2 Cor 5:19), and the Nicene confession of Jesus Christ, "True God of true God, begotten, not created, consubstantial with the Father." Paul's confession assures men that God was present to them in Jesus; Nicaea assures men that Jesus was God. The one statement ultimately leads to the other (once it is understood that God was present in Jesus in a truly unique way, far beyond his presence in the OT prophets), but from one to the other there is development of doctrine.

NEW TESTAMENT ESCHATOLOGY

BIBLIOGRAPHY

62 Barrett, C. K., "New Testament Eschatology," *ScotJT* 6 (1953) 136–55, 225–43. Beasley-Murray, G. R., *Jesus and the Future* (London, 1954). Cullmann, O., *Christ and Time* (London, 1951); *Salvation in History* (N.Y., 1967). Dodd, C. H., *The Parables of the Kingdom* (2nd ed.; N.Y., 1961). Feuillet, A., "Parousie," *VDBS* 6, 1331–1419. Gressmann, H., *Der Ursprung der israelitisch-jüdischen Eschatologie* (Göttingen, 1905); *Der Messias* (Göttingen, 1929). Guy, H. A., *The New Testament Doctrine of the 'Last Things'* (London, 1948). Jeremias, J., *The Parables of Jesus* (from 6th Ger ed.; N.Y., 1963). Kümmel, W. G., *Promise and Fulfilment: The Eschatological Message of Jesus* (SBT 23; London, 1957). Manson, T. W., *The Teaching of Jesus* (2nd ed.; Cambridge, 1945). Manson, W., *Jesus the Messiah* (London, 1943). Massaux, E. (ed.), *La venue du Messie: messianisme et eschatologie* (RechBib 6; Bruges, 1962). Otto, R., *The Kingdom of God and the Son of Man* (rev. ed.; London, 1938). Robinson, J. A. T., *Jesus and His Coming* (London, 1957). Scott, C. A. A., *Christianity According to St. Paul* (Cambridge, 1927). Wilder, A. N., *Eschatology and Ethics in the Teaching of Jesus* (London, 1954). (Also → 93 below.)

63 OUTLINE

64 **(I) Modern Understanding of "Eschatology."** This word has been in use only since the 19th cent.; it is derived from *to eschaton*, "the last thing." As a branch of theology, eschatology is wider in its comprehension than the classical scholastic treatise *De Novissimis*, which discusses Christian doctrines concerned with judgment, heaven, hell, and purgatory. Eschatology would embrace, as well as these realities, certain aspects of the Church and the Sacraments. It may be said to treat of the *eschaton*, i.e., God's definitive intervention in history through Jesus Christ, which the NT generally regards as being deployed in two distinct phases delimited by Christ's first and second coming. Biblical eschatology may be subdivided into personal (the ultimate destiny of the individual), collective (national in the OT, ecclesial in the NT), and cosmic (the final status of the universe).

65 Modern scholarship is divided as to whether the term "eschatology" should be used in a restricted or a broader sense. Is the *eschaton* to be regarded restrictedly as an act of God from outside sacred history, bringing the present historical order to a conclusion (those who insist upon a radical cleavage between the present age and the next understand eschatology in the narrow sense), or is the *eschaton* more broadly the terminal phase of sacred history already prepared by, and to a degree already present in, the events of Christian salvation history? This basic obscurity was clearly present in OT thought, as the difficult phrase *bᵉʾaḥărît hayyāmîm* illustrates. Does it signify "at the end of days," i.e., at the conclusion of history, or simply "the last times"? The question is an important one involving the relationship of history to eschatology. J. L. McKenzie ("Royal Messianism," *CBQ* 19 [1957] 49) insists that eschatology "means a future which lies outside history, in the sense that it will not be determined by historical factors." Yet, since Israel believed that God intervened in the actual course of her history, "to draw too precise a line between history and eschatology seems to make a distinction which, at least for the early books of the Bible, has no basis in belief" (→ Aspects OT Thought, 77:164–167). Conversely, B. Vawter ("Apocalyptic: Its Relation to Prophecy," *CBQ* 22 [1960] 37) understands the term "as meaning the expectation of an end of this earthly order." It embraces the fulfillment of the entire divine world-plan with the establishment of a new order. This narrower meaning of biblical eschatology is maintained by Wellhausen, Mowinckel, and Frost, whereas Gressmann, Lindblom, *et al.* employ it in the broader sense.

66 Part of the problem arises from the view that is taken of the biblical concept of time (see J. Barr, *Biblical Words for Time* [SBT 33; London, 1962]). Certainly time appears to be "linear," in the sense of implying a teleological conception of history, i.e., the history of Israel, of the Church, and of the universe is a history with a definable beginning, moving toward a purposeful goal, determined by God's power and providence. On the other hand, the biblical view of time is not "linear" if that term implies an evolutionary process. The dialectic of sacred history, particularly for NT authors, and especially for Paul, moves forward by a series of crises postulating an indefinite number of relatively new beginnings. The NT expectation of "the end" is based upon a set of occurrences in the past by which salvation has been essentially accomplished in the death and resurrection of Jesus Christ. Accordingly, the *eschaton*—at least the phase that still lies in the future—has been prepared for, determined, and even begun by these crucial events of NT sacred history. O. Cullmann (*Christology*) has rightly seen the necessity of relating NT Christology to the NT *Heilsgeschichte:* similarly, it is necessary to keep in mind that the solution to the problem of NT eschatology is inseparable from the mystery of Christ's person and his mission of redemption.

67 **(II) NT Eschatology According to Recent Authors.** The 19th-cent. theologian A. Ritschl eliminated the eschatological element from Jesus' teaching. In his view, Jesus had preached a purely spiritual, invisible Kingdom of God existing in the souls of men. (For Ritschl's theology, see P. Hefner, *Faith and the Vitalities of History* [N.Y., 1966].) J. Weiss, Ritschl's son-in-law, and A. Schweitzer rediscovered the significance of the eschatological features of the Gospel; but they felt that this phase of Jesus' message was no longer of interest to modern man. M. Goguel (*Jesus and the Origins of Christianity* [Harper paperback; N.Y., 1960]) stated that Jesus "thought eschatologically, just as he spoke Aramaic"; and the eschatological dimension, in Goguel's opinion, was no more essential to Jesus' thought than was the language he spoke.

68 A. Schweitzer (→ Modern NT Criticism, 41:35) was convinced, however, that Jesus' conviction about the imminence of the Kingdom of God could not be ignored. Jesus thought himself (quite wrongly) to be the Messiah; he considered that when he dispatched the disciples on their missionary tour of the Galilean hamlets, the Kingdom was soon to come (again mistakenly). Thus when the end time did not come as Jesus had expected, he tried to force the issue by his own death. This theory is known as *consistent* eschatology, or as Schweitzer himself called it, "thoroughgoing" eschatology. Such a view obviously left no room for any belief in Jesus' divinity or messiahship, or in his will to found the Church. R. Bultmann, one of the original NT form critics (→ Modern NT Criticism, 41:49), holds an equally skeptical position. Jesus was merely the forerunner of the coming Kingdom, which he proclaimed. The Kingdom of God, however, did not become a reality in Jesus' lifetime; for it cannot come by any human intervention (under which Bultmann would class the work of Jesus himself), but only by direct divine action in the existential situation of each individual.

69 C. H. Dodd (→ Modern NT Criticism, 41:63) has reacted against the theorizing of Schweitzer and produced a solution to the problem that has come to be known as *realized* eschatology. Jesus' entire message consisted in the announcement that in his own person the *eschaton* had entered history: The Messiah has come, the Kingdom of God is present in history, the Day of the Lord is henceforth an actuality. Since eschatology has been realized by the advent of Jesus, nothing more is to be looked for in history. Christ the Light, through his death and resurrection, confronts each individual, provoking a judgment (*krisis*), the only judgment in any proper sense. It is carried to successive generations by the Church's preaching and by the Eucharist, which evokes a personal experience of Jesus' coming in humility and glory. In Dodd's opinion, the final judgment and the parousia constitute "the least inadequate myth of the goal of history." For while Jesus himself preached a realized eschatology, the transition from time to eternity was not as natural for his followers as for Jesus himself; consequently they misunderstood his meaning, envisaging the Kingdom as incomplete at present, and hence for the most part still to come in the future. This literalistic interpretation of what was merely symbolic in Jesus' doctrine was gradually corrected by Paul and John, who introduced realized eschatology into NT theology. John's work is the supreme achievement of this development, since he has adopted the correct perspective, that of Jesus himself.

70 **(III) Preaching of Jesus.** The sayings of Jesus have come down to us chiefly in the writings of the four Evangelists, where they have undergone interpretation and adaptation (→ Church Pronouncements, 72:35). Yet this recognition does not justify the view that little or nothing can be known of Jesus' eschatological teaching. Even if the apostolic group was aware that they could and must adjust Jesus' teaching to various new situations, they remained faithful to his ideals and his basic plan.

The concept of the Kingdom of God was central to the message of Jesus; moreover it occupies a position of paramount importance in NT eschatology. However, since this is discussed in a separate article (→ 93 below), we shall treat here of another eschatological reality, the judgment, which Jesus closely associated with the Kingdom.

71 In the OT, the prophets tended to concentrate on the Day of Yahweh (the judgment; → Aspects OT Thought, 77:137); with Jesus the focal point of interest shifts to the Kingdom. Yet he posits a discriminatory process at the very entrance to the Kingdom (Mt 5:20). In relation to the future community that Jesus intends to found, the judgment is a purifying process (Mt 13:41–43; 13:47–50; 25:31–46). In describing the judgment, Jesus also borrows certain traits from the apocalyptic tradition (→ Post-exilic Period, 20:21–24). The judgment brings the triumph of the divine plan over God's adversaries (Mt 8:29; Lk 4:34). Jesus appears to consider his miracles as a first assault upon the kingdom of Satan in this world (Lk 13:16; 10:18; → 127 below). His descriptions of the parousia of the Son of Man are painted in the imagery of victory: clouds, power, glory (cf. Mk 13:26). Yet there is a sobriety in Jesus' presentation of the ultimate victory: The great battle, so dear to the apocalyptists, is played down; individual responsibility is stressed, especially in the parable describing the Last Judgment (Mt 25:31–46). Our Gospels give no long description of the end of the world: If Jesus borrows the cosmic language of the OT, he prunes away the extravagances of Jewish apocalyptic.

With regard to the judgment to be undergone by individuals, Jesus insists upon the principle of retribution according to personal merit (Mt 12:41–42; 18:23–35), another borrowing from apocalyptic literature. Finally, Jesus appears to have thought of the judgment as a passing to a new state, as a renovation and joyous condition following upon the "birth pangs" (Mt 24:8; Jn 16:21). The NT writers will use a term from Hellenistic philosophy (*palingenesia*, "regeneration, renewal") for which there is no equivalent in Semitic languages, to designate this aspect of the judgment proclaimed by Jesus (Mt 19:28; Ti 3:5). The judge who executes sentence is sometimes presented as God the Father (Mt 6:4; 10:32–33), sometimes as Jesus himself (25:31–46; Lk 17:24). Jesus teaches that the judgment will be for all men without distinction; it will turn upon an individual's attitudes to the Kingdom, his faith (Mt 8:10–11), his repentance (11:20–21). This judgment is exhaustively comprehensive (12:36–37) and definitive (25:46).

72 **(IV) Apostolic Preaching in Acts.** The orientation of the primitive preaching is predominantly eschatological, given its character as testimony to Jesus' resurrection and to the coming of the Spirit. From the day of Pentecost, the apostolic group displayed the conviction that they had assisted at a crisis in the religious history of Israel: Now the "last days," foretold by "all the prophets from Samuel onward" (Acts 2:17; 3:24), have become a reality. They attested their certain belief that Yahweh's Spirit had been permanently bestowed, that they themselves now formed the nucleus of the new *qāhāl* of Israel, the Remnant of Israel foretold by the OT prophets (Is 10:20–21), and that Jesus had been exalted as "Son of God in power" (Rom 1:4; cf. Acts 2:33; for *qāhāl*, → Pauline Theology, 79:150). One striking feature of this new attitude of faith was the assurance that the messianic era has been inaugurated by the outpouring of the Holy Spirit, instead of by the return of the parousiac Christ. The chief eschatological blessings bestowed by the Spirit are the remission of sins and his own presence in the hearts of the faithful (Acts 2:38). These are connected with the reception of baptism, the new rite of initiation into the Christian community. Baptism is described within the context of the judgment (2:40); it is also eschatological in that it effects the ingathering of the saved (2:47).

The call to *metanoia* (repentance), in which the apostolic kerygma culminated, was also related to the judgment, as the citation of Dt 18:16 (Acts 3:23) indicates. Indeed, the apostolic preaching announced the final judgment, since Jesus was proclaimed in it as universal judge (Acts 10:42). It was, moreover, a message of pardon and grace (2:47; 4:12; 5:31); for in the kerygma the idea of judgment was linked closely with salvation. The apostolic testimony to Jesus' resurrection had a deep eschatological significance, inasmuch as it proclaimed Jesus as universal ruler at God's right hand (2:34); in fact, his exaltation is the divinely given guarantee of his function as judge of the living and dead (17:31). The opposition and persecution encountered by the primitive community were viewed as part of the eschatological hostility to the messianic people (4:24–30). Stephen, condemned by human injustice, was defended by the glorified Son of Man before the heavenly tribunal of divine justice (7:55). Above all, the apostolic community was conscious of the eschatological activity of the Holy Spirit (4:31; 5:3; 15:28).

73 **(V) Pauline Eschatology.** When we turn to consider the writings of Paul and other NT theologians, it should be borne in mind that the problem of NT eschatology was merely one facet of the mystery of Christ (→ Pauline Theology, 79:32–34). The NT authors' grasp of the question was conditioned by their understanding of Jesus Christ and the significance of his redemptive work; and they advanced toward its solution in proportion to the depth of their grasp of the Christological question. For an appreciation of this development, the letters of Paul are of special significance, since they are sufficiently numerous to provide an insight into the evolution of his thought.

74 Before we examine Paul's writings, however, two characteristics of NT eschatology, which differentiate it from Jewish eschatology and apocalyptic, must be mentioned. First, as W. G. Kümmel has observed, he who comes at the end of history is not some unknown figure, but Jesus whom many knew personally during his lifetime and whose resurrection the Twelve attested. Second, although NT eschatology is consistent with and dependent upon OT thought for some of its conceptions and most of its imagery, yet "the declaration that the Kingdom of God has come breaks up in any case the old eschatological scheme and makes room for a new set of ideas" (C. H. Dodd).

75 One of the principal problems confronting the theologians of the apostolic age was the meaning of the period of history between the first and the second coming of Jesus Christ. The tension between the "already" and the "not yet" is felt continually throughout the NT. "In subjecting everything to him [Christ], he [God] has left nothing unsubjected to him," the author of Heb asserts confidently. Yet he adds nostalgically: "But now we do not yet see the universe subject to him" (Heb 2:8). The author of 2 Pt (3:4) recalls the blasphemous cynicism of some of his contemporaries, who assert "Where now is the promise of his coming? Our fathers have been laid to rest; but yet everything continues exactly as it has always been since the world began."

76 For our present purpose of tracing the development in Paul's eschatological thought (→ Pauline Theology, 79:45–51), we divide the decade (AD 51–62) of his epistolary activity into two phases. The line of division may be considered to coincide with Paul's personal experience of the eschatological "tribulation" (*thlipsis*) at Ephesus (cf. 2 Cor 1:8; also 1 Cor 15:32). In the earlier period, the Apostle appears to have shared the common expectations of his Christian contemporaries regarding a proximate parousia, or return of the exalted Christ. In later life, he does not seem quite so assured that he will live to see this consummation.

77 *Conversion of Israel*. A factor that may have contributed to the formation of his new attitude was the difficulty he experienced in converting Diaspora Jewry to the gospel, as well as the trouble that was caused in several of his foundations by the Judaizing faction. In the first years of the Church, it was an accepted theologoumenon that the second coming of the Lord was contingent upon the conversion of Israel—an event that seemed possible within the lifetime of first-generation Christians (Acts 3:19–21). Paul's habitual practice of preaching first to the Jews in any given locality, and only when they had rejected his message, to the pagans, was a pattern dictated by this early eschatology. By the time Paul writes Rom 11:25–26, however, his thought has acquired an entirely new perspective. The old scheme was basically correct, but somewhat too simplified: Before the conversion of Israel, "the full complement of the Gentiles" must enter the Church. Once he had grasped this truth, the return of the Lord in glory receded into the far distant future.

78 *Apocalyptic*. Paul's early presentation of eschatology is colored by apocalyptic imagery of the type retained by the Syn. He speaks like John the Baptist of "the wrath that is coming" (1 Thes 1:10); he describes the parousia in language reflecting OT thought-patterns (1 Thes 4:13–18; 2 Thes 2:1–10); he speaks of "the rulers of this world vowed to destruction" (1 Cor 2:6); he envisages in the future the eschatological battle between the Risen Lord and his enemies (1 Cor 15:23–28). Although he occasionally employs the vocabulary of apocalyptic in his later letters ("the god of this world": 2 Cor 4:4), he clearly regards the victory as already gained through Christ's redemptive death and resurrection (Col 2:14; Eph 1:22). The latter text asserts that God has subjected everything beneath Christ's feet, thus contrasting with the view expressed in Phil 3:21 (Phil appears to belong to the earlier letters) and in 1 Cor 15:25–27.

79 *Salvation*. In the early period Paul conceives salvation, which from his Semitic viewpoint necessarily involves "the redemption of our body" (Rom 8:23), in futurist terms (1 Thes 5:8; 2 Thes 2:13; Phil 2:12). Indeed, the title "Savior" is regarded as a prerogative of the parousiac Christ (Phil 3:20; → 43 above), and "salvation," like its opposite "destruction," lies ahead (Phil 1:28). In 2 Cor 6:2, however, Paul can identify the present moment as the "day of salvation" alluded to in Is 49:8 (2 Cor 6:2); in Rom 13:11, he declares that "the day of salvation is nearer than when we became Christians." He can announce to his addressees that they "have been saved" (Eph 2:5,8; cf. 2 Tm 1:9; 4:18; Ti 3:5). Yet to a certain extent futurist polarity is retained at this later period (Rom 5:9; 8:24).

80 *Parousia*. There is an interesting development, which follows the same pattern, with regard to the terms "parousia" and "revelation" (*apocalypsis*), or "manifestation" (*epiphaneia*). Paul appears to have been the originator of the Christian usage of "parousia" as a technical term for Christ's second coming (cf. the pre-Pauline use of the word in Mt 24:3; the word is not employed in the parallels: Mk 13:4; Lk 21:7). Yet parousia in the sense of second coming is employed only in the earlier Pauline letters (1 Thes 2:19; 3:13; 4:15; 5:23; 2 Thes 2:1:8,9; 1 Cor 15:23); elsewhere it has its more usual sense of presence (Phil 1:26; 2:12; 1 Cor 16:17; 2 Cor 10:10). Now it is precisely the early letters that are dominated by what might be called a "parousiac spirituality": The absent Lord will return; the Christian life is to be lived in hope and expectancy of his coming, which is likened to the state visit of a reigning monarch (→ Pauline Theology, 79:46).

81 *Epiphany*. The term "revelation" (*apokalypsis*) is found in 2 Thes 1:7 and 1 Cor 1:7 with reference to Christ's second advent; it is found in Rom 2:5; 16:25 with reference to the parousia, and in 8:19 to denote the effects of that coming upon the believers. The word "manifestation" (*epiphaneia*) occurs but once in the Early Letters, and then in conjunction with parousia (2 Thes 2:8). In the Pastorals, however, "manifestation" is the technical term for the second coming of Christ (1 Tm 6:14; Ti 2:13; 2 Tm 4:1,8). In one passage (2 Tm 1:10) it denotes Jesus' first coming in humility. If Paul was the author of the Pastorals (→ Pastoral Letters, 57:6–11), this change in terminology would appear to suggest that in the course of time Paul had revised his view: Earlier he had thought of the coming back of an absent Christ; now he thought of the unveiling or epiphany of one invisibly present even in this age.

82 *Judgment*. This notion occupies a place of prominence in Pauline theology. He uses the OT phrase "the day of Yahweh" as a paradigm to create a new phrase descriptive of Christ's role as judge: "the Day of the Lord" (1 Thes 5:2; 2 Thes 2:2; 1 Cor 1:8; 5:5; 2 Cor 1:14), or "the Day of Christ" (Phil 1:6,10; 2:16). Yet almost all these instances represent Paul's earlier viewpoint, where the divine judgment is conceived in apocalyptic fashion as a victory for God and Christ over the powers of evil. The judiciary aspect of this judgment is also prominent in Paul: Man must appear before the divine tribunal (Rom 2:16) to render account of his life (14:10ff.), and there Christ will mete out justice (1 Cor 4:3–5; 2 Cor 5:9f.). The Pauline notion of justification (→ Pauline Theology, 79:94–97) has an eschatological dimension; even if it is clearly a present possession of the Christian (Rom 5:1; 8:30; 14:17), still it has a future aspect as an anticipation of eschatological salvation. If God the Father is considered the supreme judge (Rom 2:2), still it is "through Jesus Christ that God will judge the hidden actions of men" (2:16), who must appear before the tribunal of Christ (2 Cor 5:10). Paul's notable optimism with regard to the outcome of this judgment for Christians has been rightly pointed out by modern commentators: The impression is given throughout Paul's letters that the vast majority quite justifiably anticipate the judgment with hope and confidence (Rom 5:9; 8:1; 1 Cor 11:32; etc.), for Christ himself is their advocate (1 Cor 4:4) and intercessor (Rom 8:34). It must be admitted, however, that there are no grounds for thinking that Paul taught the existence of a "Particular Judgment." The texts often cited in support of this view (Phil 1:23; 2 Cor 5:8–10) simply express Paul's conviction of a reunion with Christ in the next life.

(For a long bibliography on Pauline eschatology, see B. Rigaux, *Les Épîtres aux Thessaloniciens* [Paris, 1956] xxiii–xxix. An important older work is H. A. A. Kennedy, *St. Paul's Conception of the Last Things* [London, 1905].)

83 **(VI) Synoptic Gospels.**

(A) All Three Synoptics. The eschatological motifs of the apostolic preaching retain their force in the Syn tradition, and there is no clear formulation of the realized eschatology that we shall find dominant in Jn. The Syn present John the Baptist as a "preacher of an apocalypse of judgment" (M. Goguel, "Eschatologie et apocalyptique dans le Christianisme primitif," *RHR* 106 [1932] 385). His message is phrased in imagery borrowed from the language of OT apocalyptic: The Baptist proclaims a judgment that is imminent (Mt 3:10), to be executed by a "mightier one" (Lk 3:15) who is mediator of the divine wrath. The purpose of this judgment is at once a purification of those who repent (Mt 3:10,12) and a punishment of those who rebel against God (3:12). The judgment is both universal and definitive: The Baptist preaches even to the degenerate religious leaders, warning all that there is no escape from divine vengeance. Luke alone (3:10–14) modifies to some degree this picture of the Baptist as an eschatological prophet by recording the social nature of his preaching.

84 The Syn concur in presenting a theology of the Son of Man in two distinct phases. The first phase corresponds to Jesus' earthly career; it is marked by the obscurity of an ordinary life (Mt 11:19; Lk 7:34), humiliation (Mk 10:45), poverty (Lk 9:58), and concealed divinity (Mk 2:10,28; Lk 12:10), and above all by Jesus' identification with the Suffering Servant of God (Mk 8:31; 9:31; 10:33; cf. Mk 9:9). The second phase coincides with the glorification of the Son of Man, his office as judge (Mk 8:38; 13:26; 14:62; Mt 25:31–46), and the mystery surrounding his parousia (Lk 12:40; 17:24,30; cf. Lk 22:29).

85 H. A. Guy has remarked that while Lk inclines to tone down the eschatological and apocalyptic dimension found in the Marcan record of the sayings of Jesus (cf. Mk 13:14 and Lk 21:20; Mk 14:62 and Lk 22:67–69), Mt tends in the opposite direction (cf. Mk 8:38 and Mt 16:27; Mk 13:4 and Mt 24:3). Matthew (24:1–44) probably interprets the so-called Eschatological Discourse as referring in its entirety to the ruin of the Temple, while Mark (13:1–37; → Gospel Mk, 42:76) records the Discourse with a certain confusion. Luke has two discourses: one describing the second coming of Christ (17:22–37), and the other foretelling the destruction of Jerusalem and of the Temple (21:6–36).

86 **(B) Mark.** The whole history of Jesus is portrayed as a cosmic, eschatological struggle with evil (J. M. Robinson, *The Problem of History in Mark* [SBT 21; London, 1957]—for an opposing interpretation, see E. Best, *The Temptation and the Passion: The Markan Soteriology* [Cambridge, 1965]). The Marcan Prologue (1:1–13) introduces the public ministry of Jesus by narrating the mission of John the Baptist, who heralds Jesus as the "stronger one" against the common adversary, Satan. Jesus' baptism is his "anointing with the Holy Spirit" (Acts 10:38) for the eschatological struggle and victory over Satan, of which the temptations in the desert are merely a preview. Jesus' exorcisms are the first instance of the cosmic battle against evil (Mk 1:21–27; 3:11–12; 5:1–17; 7:24–30; 9:14–29). The second series of illustrations is provided by the other miracle stories, depicted as a fight against the powers of evil (1:40–45; 4:35–41; 7:24; → 127 below). A third exemplification of the combat is to be found in the controversy stories, i.e., Jesus' debates with his adversaries, the religious leaders of Judaism (2:1–3:6). Finally, Jesus' struggle against ignorance, timidity, and slowness of comprehension on the part of his own disciples is presented as a facet of this universal war upon Satan (8:34–37; 10:38–45).

87 **(C) Matthew.** This evangelist has preserved the Semitic flavor of the sayings of Jesus (in which he manifests a very special interest) and so has retained the imagery and futurist eschatology so characteristic of apocalyptic. Yet his thought also moves unmistakably in the direction of a "realized" eschatology. For Matthew's main preoccupation is with the nature of the Church (→ Gospel Mt, 43:10) through which the risen and ascended Lord makes good his promise to remain "with you until the end of history" (28:20)—we have seen (→ 32 above) that this author consistently thinks of Jesus as "Emmanuel" ("with us is God"). Thus Matthew is chiefly concerned with demonstrating how Jesus' words and actions during his public ministry are so many steps toward the realization of the "Kingdom of Heaven" in this world by the institution of the Christian Church. Matthew's conception of salvation reflects the general pattern of Syn soteriology with its eschatological orientation. Jesus' earthly career was devoted to the extirpation of sin, as his very name suggests (→ 3 above). His ministry effects the realization of OT hopes of deliverance (4:14–16). Jesus' death and resurrection signify the realization of the OT eschatological hope. The Evangelist employs the language of apocalyptic in a passage peculiar to himself (27:51–53) in order to state the truth that, with the death and resurrection of Jesus, the general resurrection of the just has been inaugurated. Mt contains a series of eschatological sayings of Jesus found nowhere else in the Gospel record (10:23; 13:24–30,37–40; 25:1–13), and other, common sayings recorded in a way calculated to underscore their eschatological tenor (16:28; 19:28; 23:37–39). In his presentation of Jesus' prophecy of the destruction of the Temple, Matthew has preserved what may be a more archaic form of the disciples' question that occasions the discourse—a form that reveals the confusion in their minds between the end of the world of Judaism and the "end of the age" (Mt 24:3). Perhaps no other NT writer has by such a discerning use of apocalyptic language underscored so strikingly the eschatological character of the Church.

88 **(D) Luke.** The third Gospel is best characterized as the "Gospel of Salvation" (→ Gospel Lk, 44:8). Luke alone of the Syn uses the terms "salvation" (1:69,71, 77; 2:30; 3:6; 19:9] and "Savior" (1:47; 2:11). Moreover, by adding to the traditional formulation of certain logia of Jesus he has made explicit the idea of salvation implied therein (8:12; 10:10; 21:28). Luke has also underlined the eschatological character of Jesus' death and resurrection by characterizing this central event proclaimed in the kerygma as an *exodus* (9:31), i.e., God's definitive act of deliverance—of which Israel's rescue from Egypt was the type—and as an "assumption" (9:51), conceived after the pattern of the apocalyptic story of Elijah's departure from this world (2 Kgs 2:9–11). In addition, Luke (e.g., 21:8) stresses the notion of *kairos* (the time appointed by divine Providence for the realization of eschatological salvation), a term appearing 12 times in this Gospel. Luke is more restrained than the other Syn in his use of apocalyptic terminology (cf., however, 12:49f.); indeed he introduces the parable of the king who goes abroad "to receive a kingdom and return" (19:12ff.) by implying that Jesus had directed it against the apocalyptic enthusiasm that overcame Jesus' disciples at their approach to Jerusalem. In Lk, as also in Mt (the two Gospels written after Titus' destruction of Jerusalem), there is perceptibly a more profound theological interpretation of this disaster as a divine "visitation" of the Risen Christ and as a historical "sign of the Son of Man."

89 **(VII) Johannine Literature.** The notion of judgment constitutes one of the principal themes of Jn (→ Johannine Theology, 80:46, 55). This judgment is operated by the presence of the incarnate *logos* in history (Jn 3:19; 9:39; → 57 above), and Jn's presentation of Jesus Christ as "the genuine light" of the world (1:9; 8:12; 12:46) is a basic motif. For John, the revelatory function of Jesus is of supreme significance, to which even his redemptive role is, in a sense, subordinated. Redemption is the "glory" of Christ, i.e., his personal manifestation of the invisible God through death and resurrection

(1:14,18; 12:38–41; → Johannine Theology, 80:30–32, 34). Christ the Light is the true eschatological reality for John: His judgment is all-embracing (1:9; 4:17–18) and transcendently discerning (2:25). Jesus' words are the medium communicating this light (8:37; 12:48); his miracles are called "signs," possessing a discriminatory, eschatological value, since they manifest his "glory" (2:11; 12:57ff.) and provoke the judgment of faith or disbelief in men's hearts (→ Johannine Theology, 80:27–29). It is however the death of Jesus that is the definitive source oft his light-judgment (8:28; 12:32; 13:18f.; 19:37).

90 This *krisis* aspect of Jesus' earthly career is seen to operate in John's conception of it as a courtroom drama, which begins with the deposition of the Baptist (1:19ff.) and culminates, after a series of testimonies and accusations by "the Jews," in the "judgment of this world" (12:31), wherein Jesus' self-appointed judges are themselves condemned. The legal terminology (judge, judgment, witness, testimony, accuse, convict, advocate, etc.) serves to underscore the fundamental Johannine conception of Jesus' work as *krisis*. The author appears to prefer to think of the judgment as passed on men by their own attitude to the Light already in this world. In John's eyes, no man can afford to remain indifferent to Jesus: Everyman must declare himself for Jesus or against him. Jesus' presence in history is the cause of this discrimination, but he is in the world as one sent by the Father. For bibliography, see J. Blank, *Krisis: Untersuchungen zur johanneischen Christologie und Eschatologie* (Freiburg, 1964); also P. Ricca, *Die Eschatologie des Vierten Evangeliums* (Zürich, 1966).

91 *The Apocalypse*, the only prophetic book in the NT, presents the optimistic message of the kerygma transposed into the apocalyptic key (→ Johannine Theology, 80:58–59). The central theme of the Ap is the eschatological Lordship of the Risen Christ, who has now become master of sacred history; consequently, from the opening vision of Christ as judge to the final dramatic scenes of the cosmic judgment exercised by God and Christ, the theme of the judgment is prominent. At the heavenly assizes, the martyrs demand redress (6:10; 16:7; 18:24); the celestial liturgy celebrates the justice of the divine judgment (15:3–4; 19:1–2). The entire dramatic process is merely preparatory to the heavenly celebration of the wedding of the Church with the Lamb that has been slain (→ 55 above). The Lamb is presented constantly in his role as judge (1:7; 14:14ff.; 21:27). A feature peculiar to the Ap is the partipication of the saints in the divine eschatological judgment (2:26; 20:4–5). Great emphasis is placed in the Ap upon men's works as the criterion of the final judgment. If this judgment is represented as the climax of history, the writer makes the reader feel keenly the contemporary force of God's judgment upon history.

92 **(VIII) Conclusion.** What gives to NT eschatology its characteristic cachet and originality is the unflagging awareness of its inspired authors that he who comes, the judge who exercises cosmic judgment, is not only already victor and Savior of mankind, but a person familiarly known from the Gospel record of his earthly life of humiliation and suffering. The OT Day of Yahweh, in consequence, has been transformed into the Day of Christ; and its nature has been essentially revealed to men by Jesus' life, death, and resurrection. Indeed this Day is not so much something ordained to be the termination of this world, but rather a reality already dynamically present in history. And thus history becomes fundamentally salvation history; for the value of the present time, as also the significance of the future, has been created and revealed to us by Jesus Christ.

THE KINGDOM OF GOD

BIBLIOGRAPHY

93 Bright, J., *The Kingdom of God* (N.Y., 1953). Héring, J., *Le Royaume de Dieu et sa venue* (Paris, 1937). Howard, W. F., "The Best Books on the Kingdom of God," *ExpT* 48 (1936–37) 393–96. Ladd, G. E., *Jesus and the Kingdom* (N.Y., 1964). Lundstrom, G., *The Kingdom of God in the Teaching of Jesus* (Richmond, 1963). Manson, T. W., *The Sayings of Jesus* (London, 1949). Perrin, N., *The Kingdom of God in the Teaching of Jesus* (Phila., 1963). Roberts, H., *Jesus and the Kingdom of God* (London, 1957). Schmidt, K. L., "Basileia," *ThDNT* 1, 579–90. Schnackenburg, R., *God's Rule and Kingdom* (N.Y., 1963); *The Church in the New Testament* (N.Y., 1965). Schweitzer, A., *The Mystery of the Kingdom of God* (London, 1925). Scott, E. F., *The Kingdom of God in the New Testament* (N.Y., 1931). (Also → 62 above.)

94 OUTLINE

95 **(I) The Term.** This phrase is characteristic of the Syn. It is found only twice in Jn (3:3,5), although Jesus refers to "my kingdom" in the dialogue with Pilate (18:36). Curiously enough, the expression appears nowhere in Acts' summaries of the apostolic preaching, except for the triple mention of it as a characteristic of the Pauline kerygma to the Gentiles (Acts 14:22; 19:8; 28:23). Actually, there are ten instances of its use in Pauline literature, where it is employed in a futurist eschatological sense and expressly distinguished from the kingdom of the Son (Col 1:13) or of Christ (Eph 5:5).

96 The expression is found 31 times in Lk, 14 times in Mk, but only 3 times in Mt (12:28; 19:24,31—the reading in 19:24 is doubtful). Matthew prefers the more Jewish expression, "Kingdom of heaven [lit., the heavens]," which he alone employs (30 times, with one probable addition: 19:24). This phrase appears to be the equivalent of "Kingdom of God." As has been often observed, the English word "kingdom" does not represent the primary sense of *basileia* or its Semitic counterparts, which signify the state of being king, thus denoting dignity or power. Perhaps "rule" or "kingship" would be a better translation than "kingdom." The secondary meaning, the territory or subjects ruled by the king, is closely cognate to the idea of the king's rule, dominion, or reign, inasmuch as territory and subjects symbolize concretely royal power.

97 **(II) Teaching of Jesus.** The Syn represent Jesus as proclaiming the imminence of the Kingdom of God from the beginning of his public ministry (Mk 1:15; Mt 4:17; Lk 4:43). The Syn consistently attest Jesus' consciousness of the unique character of his relation to this divine reality and its earthly manifestations. He undergoes an experience at his baptism in the Jordan, entirely personal to himself, which the Syn phrase in terms of his hearing a heavenly voice declaring him to be the Servant of God and the Lord's Anointed (Is 42:1; Ps 2:7). This experience is given as a clear indication of Jesus' awareness, from the inauguration of his public ministry, of his unique vocation (Mk 1:10–11; Mt 3:16–17; Lk 3:22).

This awareness is underscored in Mt and Lk through a reconstruction of the temptation scene in which Jesus rejects some conceptions current in contemporary Jewish messianic expectations (Mt 4:1–11; Lk 4:1–13). Jesus adduces his exorcisms as a declaration of war upon the "kingdom of Satan" (Mk 3:24) and as a demonstration that in his own person (Lk 17:20) or through his mission (Lk 11:20; Mt 12:28) the Kingdom of God has become a contemporary reality (→ 127 below). Jesus makes a clear distinction between the era thus inaugurated by his ministry and the age of OT prophecy, which included even the career of John the Baptist (Mt 11:12; Lk 16:16).

98 Jesus' adoption of the OT title "Son of Man," on the unanimous evidence of all the Evangelists, appears to have been his own idea (yet → 30 above), and this self-designation manifests his conviction that he has an unprecedented role to play in the coming of God's Kingdom. Dn 7:13–18, presumably the source of this title, would seem to indicate this (→ Daniel, 26:28). Moreover, Jesus' consistent use of "Son of Man" in the predictions of his passion and resurrection (Mk 8:31; 9:31; 10:33 par.), as well as in his supreme confession before the Sanhedrin (Mk 14:62), indicates his knowledge that there is also to be a future phase to the Kingdom of God, in addition to its historical realization. Jesus' prophecy concerning the destruction of the Temple (Mk 13:26 par.), obscurely couched in the language of apocalyptic, is further proof of the essentially futurist nature of the Kingdom of God. His actions further confirm his unique mediatorial role in the advent of the Kingdom: e.g., his deliberate choice of the Twelve, a special group of disciples (→ 172 below)—an action unprecedented in OT history, where no prophet or teacher was ever known to select his own followers; his institution at the Last Supper of the Eucharist as the special instrument of the New Covenant, through the mediation of the Twelve, with the future new people of God (Mk 14:12–25).

99 **(III) Synoptic Gospels.**

(A) Mark. The OT idea of the Kingdom of God (→ Aspects OT Thought, 77:149) as a heavenly reality that descends into human history is a prominent theme in Mk. This Evangelist indicates that the Kingdom is present in Jesus in some mysterious manner during his public ministry; that it will be established "with power" (9:1) as a result of Jesus' death and glorification; but that full participation in its reality is reserved for heaven (14:25). The announcement of the imminent coming of the Kingdom is reserved for Jesus himself (1:15).

100 The next three examples of the phrase the "Kingdom of God" occur in Mark's summary of Jesus' public teaching, which for this Evangelist is symbolized by the parable (→ 139 below). To the disciples Jesus announces, "To you the mystery of the Kingdom of God has been entrusted: to those others outside, it is all presented in parables" (4:11; → Gospel Mk, 42:26). "Jesus also said, 'The Kingdom of God is comparable to a crop a man will sow in the soil... !'" (4:26). "Jesus also said, 'What comparison can we use for the Kingdom of God, and under what figure can we present it? It is like a mustard seed...'" (4:30–31). For Mark "the mystery of the Kingdom of God" means God's providential plan of salvation for the human race, revealed in the present dispensation after remaining hidden throughout the OT—a Pauline conception (Rom 16:25–26; Col 1:26–27; → Pauline Theology, 79:35). The parable of growth, peculiar to Mk, illustrates the mysterious, supernatural character of God's Kingdom (Mk 4:26–29). It is noteworthy that Mk represents Jesus as alluding to the Kingdom of God during his Galilean ministry in connection with the parables.

101 The next instance of the phrase occurs in a very difficult passage, which probably refers to the establishment of the Church as a consequence of Jesus' death and exaltation: "He also began to tell them, 'Believe me when I tell you that among those standing here, there are those who will not undergo death, until they see the Kingdom of God come in power'" (9:1). This Evangelist can equate the Kingdom of God with "life" (9:43; cf. 9:47) or with "salvation" (10:26; cf. 10:24). The clearly ecclesial context of these passages also indicates Mark's conviction that the initial experience of the Kingdom of God is to be found in the Christian community. His presentation of the scene between Jesus and the children implies the view that receiving Jesus is equivalent to receiving the Kingdom of God (10:14–15). The eschatological character of the Kingdom is emphasized toward the conclusion of this Gospel, in Jesus' words to the scribe (12:34), and at the Last Supper (14:25). Joseph of Arimathea is described as one who "was looking forward to the Kingdom of God" (15:43). The phrase suggests that the object of such a hope was the earthly manifestation of God's reign.

102 **(B) Matthew.** There are two characteristically Matthean modifications of the Syn Kingdom of God theme. First, it is almost always denominated "the Kingdom of the heavens" in Mt. The phrase occurs frequently in rabbinical writings of the early Christian era, "heaven" being a reverential synonym for God. The Evangelist probably uses it to suggest to his readers the eschatological and transcendental nature of this divine reality, since, as we shall see, he is mainly preoccupied in describing its partial realization in a contemporary, earthly reality, the Christian Church. Second, Matthew distinguishes between the "Kingdom of the Father" (13:43; 26:29; cf. 6:10; 6:33) and the "Kingdom of the Son of Man" (13:41; 16:28; 20:21), which is the Church. A similar distinction is found in the explanation appended to the peculiarly Matthean parable of the Cockle (the Weeds), where the one who sows the good seed is identified as the Son of Man (13:37), while the field is the world—the good seed being "the sons of the Kingdom" (13:38). It is found again in the Matthean version of the logion regarding the "return" of the glorified Christ during the lifetime of some of Jesus' contemporaries (16:28), who are to "see the Son of Man coming in his Kingdom." The conception is undoubtedly inspired by Dn 7:18,22,27 where the symbolic figure of a "Son of Man" represented the community of redeemed Israel.

103 Given Matthew's preponderant interest in the historical manifestation of the Kingdom in the Church, it is scarcely accidental that he, alone of all the Evangelists, represents John the Baptist as proclaiming the imminence of the Kingdom (3:2); he also identifies the theme of Jesus' preaching with that of the Baptist (4:17), which he subsequently characterizes as "the good news of the Kingdom" (4:23; 9:35; 24:14). It is significant that of the remaining 28 occurrences of the phrase in Mt, only two clearly refer to the Kingdom in the next world; the rest describe some facet of the Church as the terrestrial manifestation of the Kingdom of heaven (→ Gospel Mt, 43:10). The two futurist eschatological passages deal with salvation: the salvation of the Gentiles (8:11) and of the rich (19:23–24). The majority of the texts that allude to the Church are found in the five great discourses for which this Gospel is famous.

104 Before discussing these, we may note the passages employing the phrase that fall outside the Matthean sermons. Great as the Baptist is, the humblest member of the Church is greater (11:11). Consistent with his view that John had inaugurated the proclamation of the advent of the Kingdom (3:2), Matthew dates the era of the Church from John's public ministry (11:12). Jesus gives Peter authority in his future Church by giving him "the keys of the Kingdom of heaven" (16:19). Jesus employs the phrase again when extolling Christian virginity (19:12) and in proposing the openness of the child as the ideal Christian attitude (19:14). The dialectic of Church history is defined through two parables (20:1–16; 22:2–16) describing the Kingdom of heaven, while a third parable (25:1–13) explains the function of the witness of Christian virginity in the Church.

105 One of the salient features of this Gospel is its author's description of the historical realization of the Kingdom of heaven by means of five carefully composed discourses (→ Gospel Mt, 43:2, 16). The *first* of these, the Sermon on the Mount, presents Christianity as the perfect flowering of the OT religious spirit: It might be entitled the Foundations of the Kingdom (5:3–7:29). The phrase "the Kingdom of heaven" recurs in Jesus' descriptions of the Christian ideal (5:10,19,20; 7:21). The *second* sermon, the Missionary Discourse (10:5–42), depicting the dynamic character of the Church as the Kingdom on earth, represents the Twelve as proclaiming the imminence of the Kingdom of heaven, just as John and Jesus have done (10:7). The mystery of the Church is the theme of Jesus' *third* instruction, a collection of his parables in which the phrase recurs like a litany (13:11,24,31,33,44,45,47,52). The Community Discourse (18:3–35), the *fourth* sermon, is given in response to the disciples' query regarding "the greatest in the Kingdom of heaven" (18:1), in which Jesus employs a little child as a living parable of the Christian spirit (18:3,4). The *fifth* and last instruction, Jesus' prophecy of the triumph of the Risen Christ upon the ruins of the Temple, concludes with three parables that discuss the various categories of membership in the Church. The second of these, depicting the contemplative element, contains the phrase being discussed (25:1).

The Evangelist, in addition to these five great sermons, includes Jesus' denunciation of the spiritual bankruptcy of contemporary Israelite religion (23:2–39). Jesus accuses the scribes and Pharisees of preventing their coreligionists from accepting his invitation to enter the Kingdom of heaven (23:13). Thus, while Matthew never allows his reader to forget the otherworldly character of the Kingdom of heaven, he does insist mostly upon its concrete embodiment in the Church; he thereby underlines, perhaps more than any other NT writer, the eschatological nature of the Church itself.

106 **(C) Luke.** With Lk, we return to the traditional expression, the Kingdom of God. For Luke the presence of this divine reality in history is a favorite theme. It is present in the gospel preached by Jesus (4:43; 8:1; 9:11; 16:16) and by his disciples (9:2,60; 10:9,11). Above all, it is present in Jesus himself. This is indicated by his exorcisms (11:20); indeed it ought to be plainly perceptible by his contemporaries (17:21).

107 The Kingdom is certainly to be made present in the Church, as the Lucan reformulation of a logion of Jesus makes clear: "...some of these here will not experience death, until they see the Kingdom of God" (9:27). Luke understands the Kingdom to refer to the Church when he speaks of the necessity of perseverance (9:62) and of the motivation for Christian renunciation (18:29), also a favorite Lucan theme. The Evangelist uses the phrase to describe the Church again when he modifies a logion of Jesus at the Last Supper that traditionally had a totally eschatological thrust. In speaking of the paschal lamb, the Lucan Jesus seems to point to its fulfillment in the Eucharist of the Church: "I shall not eat it until it is fulfilled in the Kingdom of God" (22:16). Jesus' remark about the wine may similarly contain a reference to the Church: "From now on I shall not drink of the fruit of the vine until the Kingdom of God comes" (22:18). Luke also understands Jesus' description of the destruction of Jerusalem by the Roman armies as a sign of the Church's emergence in history as an institution clearly distinguishable from Judaism (21:31).

Yet Luke is not totally unaware of the eschatological, heavenly aspect of the Kingdom of God preserved in the evangelical tradition (13:28,29), which was current in the Jewish thought of the era (14:15). Like Matthew however, Luke normally thinks of the Kingdom of God as a contemporary reality, which the Father committed into the hands of Jesus as Savior and which he, in the Church, confided to the stewardship of the Twelve (22:28–30).

108 **(IV) John.** The expression "Kingdom of God" is found only in one passage, in which Jesus insists upon baptismal rebirth as a condition of "seeing" or "entering" (3:3,5) the divine Kingdom. The eschatological overtone is certainly unmistakable; yet, in keeping with the characteristic Johannine viewpoint, which can be designated as "realized eschatology" (→ Johannine Theology, 80:46), the expression must be taken to refer to the Church as well as to "eternal life."

THE GOSPEL MIRACLES

BIBLIOGRAPHY

109 Brown, R. E., "The Gospel Miracles," *BCCT* 184–201; also in *New Testament Essays* (Milwaukee, 1965) 168–91. Bultmann, *HST* 209–44. Fuller, R., H., *Interpreting the Miracles* (London, 1963). Kallas, J., *The Significance of the Synoptic Miracles* (London, 1961). Lawton, J. S., *Miracles and Revelation* (London, 1959). Lefèvre, A., "Miracle," *VDBS* 5, 1299–1308. *LumVi* 33 (1957—entire issue). Monden, L., *Signs and Wonders* (N.Y., 1966). Moule, C. F. D. (ed.), *Miracles* (London, 1965). Ramsey, I. T., *et al.*, *The Miracles and the Resurrection* (SPCK Theol. Coll. 3; London, 1964). Richardson, A., *The Miracle Stories of the Gospels* (paperback ed.; London, 1959). Taylor, *FGT* 119–41. Van der Loos, H., *The Miracles of Jesus* (Leiden, 1965).

110 OUTLINE

111 (I) Biblical Notion of Miracle. From the time that Quadratus made use of the Gospel miracles in his *Apology to Hadrian* (*ca.* AD 125), the significance of the miracles of Jesus seems to have been inextricably bound up with apologetics. Vatican Council I (DS 3034; DB 1813) anathematized anyone who would say there could be no miracles, or that all biblical miracles were to be reduced to the level of fable or myth, or that miracles could not be known with certainty and used to prove the divine origin of the Christian religion. This wedding of the study of the Gospel miracles with apologetics has been somewhat unfortunate, however, for it has emphasized an aspect of the miracle which (legitimate though it may be) was not primary in the career of Jesus nor in the Gospels. The Gospels take for granted the possibility of the miraculous, and so we shall not concern ourselves with that philosophical question in our descriptive study. Moreover, we shall not raise the question of how miracles can be used to show the reasonableness of faith (apologetics). We are concerned here with how Jesus used the miracles and what they meant to the Evangelists.

112 It has been traditional to define miracles either, with Augustine, as actions beyond the *ordinary* laws of nature, or, even more demandingly with Thomas, as actions surpassing the power of *all* nature (J. A. Hardon, *TS* 15 [1954] 229–57). Theologians themselves are becoming quite discontent with such an understanding of miracles that divorces them from the climate of faith (Monden, *op. cit.*; R. W. Gleason, *Thought* 34 [1962] 12–34). In any case, the biblical approach to the miraculous is different on several scores.

First, the Bible does not view nature as a closed system of laws. The ordinary workings of nature are often attributed directly to God: e.g., storm, famine, and plague are looked upon as divine visitations and punishments. There is little sensibility to secondary causality, and the distinction between the natural and the supernatural is frequently tenuous. The biblical notion of the miraculous includes acts that are explicable on the level of human interaction as well as those that are not; thus it includes actions that would not be miracles under either apologetic definition given above. If there are OT stories of stupendous incidents like the raising of the dead and the stopping of the sun in its path (→ Hermeneutics, 71:27), the principal OT miracle is the deliverance of Israel from Egypt, in itself an action governed by historical forces. But the biblical authors look upon such a historical event with the eyes of faith and see in it the miraculous action of God on Israel's behalf. It is by way of expressing such faith that they surround the historical event with patently awe-inspiring details; thus, general plagues that afflicted Egypt are gathered together into a series of divine chastisements that forms a prologue to the Exodus, and what may have been a storm that facilitated the deliverance becomes the dramatic parting of the Red Sea. (One of our criteria for determining that such details are simply the authors' way of expressing genuine faith in God's action would be the complete failure of contemporary secular history to mention these events; they could scarcely have escaped notice had they occurred exactly as they are narrated; → Exodus, 3:19.)

113 *Second*, if the Bible sees as direct divine actions events that are not outside the realm of nature or history, then we must recognize that the element of the marvelous, which is so much a part of the traditional understanding of miracle, is not overly prominent in the Bible. This is seen in the terms used for miracles. The Eng word "miracle" comes from Lat *miraculum*, "something to be wondered at," but this word does not even occur in the Vg NT. The Hebr words that are translated into English as "miracle" are *môpēt* (symbolic act) and *'ôt* (sign), neither of which need to refer to anything marvelous (Ez 12:1–6). When something extraordinary is described, then *niplā'*, the word for marvelous, is added. In the LXX the element of the prodigious becomes stronger, for *môpēt* is translated by *teras*, "wonder."

In the NT the Syn word for miracle is *dynamis*, "act of power," and Jn uses *sēmeion*, "sign," or *ergon*, "work." *Teras*, "wonder," is never used alone to refer to a miracle of Jesus (S. V. McCasland, *JBL* 76 [1957] 149–52). Thus, in neither Testament does the vocabulary of the original texts give real emphasis to the marvelous.

114 *Third*, from apologetics we are accustomed to think of miracles as actions performed for individuals, e.g., healings, raising of the dead, calming of dangerous storms. It is worth noting that in the OT, while there are divine interventions on behalf of Israel, miracles performed for individual needs and purposes are found with frequency only in the Elijah and Elisha cycles. (No simple judgment can be passed on the Elijah and Elisha miracles, for different sources are woven into the cycles [→ 1–2 Kings, 10:39, 48, 51]. Elisha anecdotes, like that of the floating axe head [2 Kgs 6:1–7], are clearly folklore.) The parallel between Jesus' miracles and those of Elijah caused him to be thought of as another Elijah (→ 15 above; see B. Lindars, "Elijah, Elisha and the Gospel Miracles," in Moule, *op. cit.*, 61–79).

115 (II) Modern Criticism of Gospel Miracles. In the last century rationalist or liberal studies of miracles generally took either of two directions. The one approach accepted the fact that healings were performed by Jesus but explained them as ordinary cures (faith healings, special medical techniques ahead of his time, hypnosis). Similar natural explanations were offered for other miracles like raising the dead (coma, not real death) and the nature miracles. The other approach judged the miracle stories to be fictional, stemming from overzealous evangelistic exaggeration or from primitive Christian credulity and misunderstanding. The conservative apologetic manuals offered a response to every such explanation or combination of explanations. At the present time, while the rationalistic or liberal approach to the miracles of Jesus still has some following, it is not triumphant. On the one hand, many conservative exegetes have come to recognize that *some* of the Gospel stories may involve ordinary cures and that occasionally popular imagination colors the Gospel picture of a miracle (→ Gospel Mk, 42:31). On the other hand, some less conservative critics have recognized that the rationalistic or liberal approach cannot adequately explain the early faith in Jesus' miracles found in the Gospels. Modern criticism has now taken a somewhat different approach to the miracles of Jesus.

116 **(A) Form-critical Approach.** We shall study this area particularly as exemplified in the thought of R. Bultmann (→ Modern NT Criticism, 41:49). He works on the preconceived principle that miracles are impossible. Therefore, while it is credible that Jesus may have healed a few people by natural means, the origins of the miracle stories of the Gospels must be sought in other circumstances than in the historical career of Jesus. As we have noted, there are few OT parallels for the miracles that Jesus worked for individuals. Bultmann, therefore, does not seek in the OT the origins of the portrait of Jesus as a wonder-worker; rather such a portrait has been colored by the fact that Judaism attributed marvelous deeds to Palestinian rabbis and the Hellenistic world attributed them to professional wonder-workers like Apollonius of Tyana (for examples, see Fuller, *op. cit.*, 21–22; Taylor, *op. cit.*, 127). The general thesis is that Christianity could not have converted a world, whether Jewish or Gentile, that gave credence to such miracles unless Jesus was presented as an equal, at least, in miraculous power. And so miracle narratives were invented for Jesus, often by those who were specialists in telling such stories. More specifically, Bultmann distinguishes two types of miracle narratives.

117 (a) Pronouncement Miracle Stories. These miracles are attached to important sayings of Jesus and are recalled primarily for the sake of the pronouncement (such units are called apophthegms by Bultmann, *HST* 11ff.). Thus in Mk 3:1–6 the center of interest is not the healing of the man with the withered hand, but Jesus' attitude toward the Sabbath (also Lk 13:10–17; 14:1–6). In judging the historicity of such miracles, some would suggest that only the pronouncement authentically comes from Jesus and that the miracle is an illustration created by the Palestinian community in its debates with the Pharisees.

118 (b) Miracle Stories Proper. Here the miracle itself is the center of interest. The narratives are subdivided into the healing miracles (including the expulsion of demons) and nature miracles.

(i) *The Healing Miracles.* They have a fixed format.

Setting: A description, sometimes detailed, of the illness of the sick person and of past failure to cure him (Mk 5:25; 9:17–22). Often this is accompanied by doubts about the healer's ability or scorn on the part of the bystanders (Mk 5:40; 9:18,22–23). But the person who is ill or a relative expresses belief in the healer (Bultmann stresses that this is merely trust in a wonder-worker and not true faith).

Cure: The intervention of the healer is usually immediately effective. Most of the time the healing is brought to pass by a simple word of Jesus (twice cited in the original Aramaic: Mk 5:41; 7:34—some see the element of a magic formula in the preservation of a saying that would be foreign to the Gk-speaking auditors of the Gospel). Sometimes the technique involves physical touching (Mk 1:31,41; 5:41; 7:33) and three times spittle (Mk 7:33; 8:23; Jn 9:6). On occasion Jesus prays (Mk 7:34; Jn 11:41).

Result: The reality of the cure is attested by the patient's response. A cripple walks away (Mk 2:12); a blind man describes what he sees (8:24–26); a possessed or insane man acts normally (5:15); a dead person becomes active (5:42). The divine nature of the intervention that brought the healing is recognized, often by the crowd in chorus (1:27; 5:20,42; Lk 7:16).

Bultmann points out that the miracles attributed to the Gk wonder-workers have exactly the same format. The healing stories, then, are embellishments added to the Gospel narrative in the Gk-speaking churches and form no integral part of the original good news of salvation. Such miracle stories, although they may have been of use to the Church in its ministry to the sick, do not betray a profound religious interest in the one healed, his subsequent fate, and the genuineness of his faith.

119 (ii) *The Nature Miracles.* These include the calming of the storm (Mk 4:37–41); walking on the sea (6:45–52); multiplication of the loaves (6:33–44; 8:1–9); blighting the fig tree (11:12–14); finding a coin in a fish's mouth (Mt 17:24–27); arranging a large catch of fish (Lk 5:1–11; Jn 21:1–14); and changing water to wine (Jn 2:1–11). Not only for Bultmann but even for more conservative scholars like V. Taylor (*op. cit.*, 136–40) the nature miracles are not genuine tradition about Jesus. If the healing miracles at least do good in harmony with Jesus' mission, the nature miracles are seemingly for show and thus unworthy of Jesus.

120 (c) Summaries of Miracles. Besides the two main classes of miracle stories given above, there are in the Gospels summary paragraphs mentioning many healings (Mk 1:32–34; 3:10–12; 6:54–56). The language of these summary paragraphs resembles that of the individual miracle stories, and the summaries are generalizations based on the individual stories, rather than memories of numerous miracles really worked by Jesus.

121 **(B) Evaluation of the Form-critical Approach.** The above observations obviously have much of value to teach us about the way in which miracle stories were shaped and passed on. A knowledge, for instance, of the standard format of a healing narrative may enable the exegete to detect in an individual narrative significant irregularities that need explanation. The real difficulty is not with the analysis of the various types of miracle stories but with the explanation of how these stories arose; here many think that Bultmann and others go beyond the evidence that form-critical analysis has uncovered. The following observations are in order.

First, the miracle stories are an integral part of the Gospel narrative: Almost half of the Marcan account of the public ministry (200 of 425 verses of Mk 1–10) is concerned with the miraculous. If the miracles are proposed as subsequent embellishments of the original Gospel preaching, one wonders what deeds of Jesus the original preaching contained. Moreover, a theory of the miracles as later additions fits none of the evidence of Gospel sources, for the oldest hypothetical sources, including "Q" and the Petrine kerygma (Acts 2:22; 10:38), mention miracles. C. H. Dodd (*The Bible Today* [London, 1946] ch. 4) has argued from Rom 15:18–19 that Paul knew of the miracles of Jesus, and certainly Paul took for granted the working of miracles within the Church. Well does G. H. Boobyer (Ramsey, *op. cit.*, 40) state, "Detailed analysis of the oral and literary stages through which the contents of the gospels passed before reaching their present literary form has now been in progress for more than a century, but no scholar would claim to have unearthed an early layer of narrative traditions which contained no miracles or allusions to miracles."

122 *Second*, there are some faulty leaps of logic in judging the origin of the miracle stories. To start with a presupposition that miracles are impossible and that therefore the miracles of Jesus cannot be authentic is to forget the unique character of the divine intervention in history in Jesus. The whole Gospel conviction is that the Kingdom (or dominion) of God was making its presence felt in an extraordinary way in the ministry of Jesus, and an attempt to set boundaries as to what was possible at this unique moment on the basis of our ordinary experience is very risky. Another difficulty is the attempt to establish the origin of the biblical healing narratives on the basis of their similarity in form to pagan healing narratives. In giving either a fictional or a real account of a healing, how else could the story be told than by describing the sickness, the cure, and the reaction? Such similarities of form are quite predictable and tell us nothing of origin or veracity.

123 *Third*, the sharp distinction between healing and nature miracles is convenient but has no real justification within the biblical viewpoint. The Evangelists show no more amazement at nature miracles than at healings, nor any more difficulty in accepting them (P.-H. Menoud, *RHPR* 28–29 [1948–49] 179). In a world view where not only sickness and death but also natural catastrophe represent the power of Satan, the intervention of the Kingdom of God would require a demonstration of power in the realm of nature as well as in that of human existence.

124 *Fourth*, if the Gospel miracles had been created by a desire to give Jesus the reputation of a wonder-worker, the element of the prodigious would have been more prominent than it is now. Consistently, Jesus is presented as refusing to work miracles to show off his power (Mt 4:5–7; Lk 23:6–12; Mk 8:11–13; Mt 12:38–42; Mk 15:31–32). Mark in particular has Jesus attempting to avoid the attention attracted by his miracles (7:33; 8:23; 9:25). Jesus cautions people about the danger of prodigies that can deceive even holy men (13:22–23), and he insists that even the greatest of wonders cannot force faith (Lk 16:31). Only in a late stratum of Gospel material apparent in Mt and Lk is there a conscious attempt to magnify Jesus' power. For example, in the miracle summaries (→ 120 above) Mt and Lk prefer to report that Jesus healed *all* the sick, rather than Mk's *many* (Mk 3:10; Mt 12:15; Lk 6:19); more impressive details appear in Mt's narratives (the fig tree dries up immediately in 21:19, rather than the next day as in Mk 11:20). Only in a rare miracle, however, like the finding of a coin in the fish's mouth (Mt 17:24–27), do we have the miraculous performed for self-convenience in a manner that approximates the style of a Hellenistic wonder-worker; and even here the real intent of the story may be symbolic and didactic (→ 128 below; → Gospel Mt, 43:123).

125 *Fifth*, the faith in Jesus that is mentioned in the miracle stories may not have the richness of postresurrectional faith; yet it cannot be written off as mere trust in a wonder-worker. It is more a faith directed to the power of God active in Jesus. As Fuller (*op. cit.*, 42) has described it, it is "the proper human attitude at the receiving end of an act of God." It implies at least a partial Christological estimate of Jesus as one through whom God's power touches man.

126 **(III) Meaning of Miracles in the Gospels.** We have de-emphasized the apologetic element in the Gospel accounts of the miracles of Jesus. In a purely apologetic understanding of miracle, it matters little what is done (so long as it is extraordinary), for the miracle is primarily an external confirmation of one's claims. A man can show he has more than natural power just as effectively by making a tree walk as he can by making a cripple walk. But Jesus' miracles were not only or primarily external confirmations of his message; rather the miracle was the vehicle of the message. Side by side, word and miraculous deed gave expression to the entrance of God's kingly power into time. This understanding of the miracle as an intrinsic part of revelation, rather than merely an extrinsic criterion, is intimately associated with a theory of revelation where the emphasis on the God who acts is equal to (or even more stressed than) the emphasis on the God who speaks.

127 **(A) Synoptics.** The description of Jesus' ministry includes both preaching (mostly in parables) and miracles (Mk 4–5; Acts 10:36–38). This ministry, centered on the establishment of God's reign (kingdom) over men, involves the destruction of Satan's rule over the world; for since man's first sin, Satan has maintained a certain dominion over nature and man. The miracles were Jesus' chief weapon in the struggle with Satan (Mk 3:22–27); that is why a miracle is a *dynamis* or "act of power." The expulsion of demons is the most obvious example of the use of miracles to destroy Satan's power: "If it is by the Spirit of God that I cast out demons, then the Kingdom of God has come upon you." Along with the direct expulsion of demons, the cure of sickness is another aspect of the war against Satan (Lk 13:32), for sickness was part of the dark realm of Satan (see Brown, *art. cit.*, 187ff. or 172ff.). In raising the dead and even in conquering natural disasters like storms (notice in Mk 4:39 Jesus addresses the wind as if it were a demon), Jesus is showing God's power over the demonic (see Kallas, *op. cit.*).

128 Besides giving primary emphasis to miracles as the means of establishing God's reign (kingdom), the Syn also portray Jesus as occasionally using the miracles symbolically, e.g., to fulfill prophecies or as symbolic predictive actions. The answer given to the disciples of the Baptist (Mt 11:4–6) shows that the miracles fulfilled Isaiah's prophecies of the days to come (Is 61:1–3; 35:5–6; 26:19); the multiplication of the loaves fulfilled Ezekiel's promise (Ez 34:11; Mk 6:34) that God would be a shepherd pasturing his flock; the large catch of fish (Lk 5:1–11) was a prophetic symbolic action of how God's word would attract men; the miraculous withering of the fig tree (Mk 11:12–14,20–25) seems to have been symbolic of the rejection of the Judaism represented by the authorities.

How much of this symbolic use of the miracles was added by the Evangelists is hard to determine, but the addition of symbolism in Christian catechetical use of the miracles is obvious in some instances. Thus in Mk 8:22–26 Jesus' opening of the eyes of the blind becomes for Mark a symbol of spiritual sight gained through faith in Jesus (see Richardson, *op. cit.*; → Gospel Mk, 42:49).

129 **(B) John.** John describes fewer miracles than the Syn (only seven in detail and comparatively few summaries). There is little overt emphasis on the miracles as establishing the reign of God by overcoming Satan (no exorcisms); but the fact that the Johannine Jesus refers to his miracles as *erga*, "works" (5:36; etc.), shows that the miracle is an integral part of the work given to Jesus by the Father (5:17; 14:10), and indeed a continuation of the "works" of God in the OT, like creation (Gn 2:2) and the Exodus (Ex 34:10; Ps 66:5).

The Evangelist and others in Jn refer to Jesus' miracles as *sēmeia*, "signs" (→ Johannine Theology, 80:27); and indeed the symbolic element of the miracle that was secondary in the Syn becomes primary in Jn. Physical miracles are used to signify spiritual truth. The life given to the royal official's son (4:50,51,53) is a symbol of the life of the Spirit (5:21–24). The conversation in 9:35–41 shows that the primary interest is not in the blind man's having regained physical sight but in his coming to the spiritual insight of faith. (Cerfaux, *Recueil* [Louvain, 1954] 2, 41–50; D. Mollat, *SP* 2, 209–18; R. E. Brown, *The Gospel According to John* [N.Y., 1966] 525–32.) The background of Jn's use of the term "signs" may be found in that designation of Moses' miracles (Ex 10:1; Nm 14:11,22) and in the frequent use of symbolic actions by the prophets. Thus, *pace*

Bultmann, there is some OT background for the Gospel concept of miracles.

130 **(C) Acts.** The miracles described in Acts do not lie within the scope of this article. We would simply mention that the miracles of Peter and of Paul (those of Paul seem to be somewhat patterned on Peter's) are of the same genre as the miracles worked by Jesus, e.g., healing the crippled, the sick, bringing the dead to life. They are worked in the name of Jesus (Acts 3:6), and they represent the continuing power of the reign of God, inaugurated by Jesus (→ Acts, 45:25).

THE PARABLES OF JESUS

BIBLIOGRAPHY

131 Black, M., "The Parables as Allegory," *BJRylL* 42 (1959–60) 273–87. Brown, R. E., "Parable and Allegory Reconsidered," *NovT* 5 (1962) 36–45; also in *New Testament Essays* (Milwaukee, 1965) 254–64. Buzy, D., *Les paraboles* (VS 6; Paris, 1932). Cadoux, A. T., *The Parables of Jesus* (N.Y., 1931). Dodd, C. H., *The Parables of the Kingdom* (rev. ed.; N.Y., 1961). Funk, R. W., *Language, Hermeneutic, and Word of God* (N.Y., 1966). George, A., "Parabole," *VDBS* 6, 1149–77. Harrington, W., *A Key to the Parables* (Glen Rock, N.J., 1964). Hermaniuk, M., *La parabole évangélique* (Louvain, 1937). Hunter, A. M., *Interpreting the Parables* (London, 1960). Jeremias, J., *The Parables of Jesus* (tr. S. H. Hooke from 6th Ger ed.; N.Y., 1963). Jones, G. V., *The Art and Truth of the Parables* (London, 1964). Kahlefeld, H., *Parables and Instructions in the Gospels* (N.Y., 1966). Linnemann, E., *Parables of Jesus* (London, 1966). Michaelis, W., *Die Gleichnisse Jesu* (3rd ed.; Hamburg, 1956). Robinson, W. H., *The Parables of Jesus* (Chicago, 1928). Smith, B. T. D., *The Parables of the Synoptic Gospels* (Cambridge, 1937). Smith, C. W. F., *The Jesus of the Parables* (Phila., 1948). Via, D. O., *The Parables; Their Literary and Existential Dimension* (London, 1966).

132 OUTLINE

133 **(I) Nature of a Parable.** "Parable" is from the Gk *parabolē* (the root meaning involves the placing of things side by side for the sake of comparison); it was a technical term for a figure of speech in ancient oratory.

The most basic forms of illustrative figures are the simile and the metaphor. In a *simile* one thing is likened or compared to another thing of a different kind for illustrative purposes (often with the words "like" or "as"), e.g., the Pharisees are like whitewashed tombs in Mt 23:27. In the *metaphor*, a more literary figure, there is a compressed simile where one thing is identified or equated with another, or the qualities of one thing are directly ascribed to another, e.g., "You are the salt of the earth" (Mt 5:13); "Beware of the leaven of the Pharisees" (Mk 8:15). If we move on to more elaborate forms of illustration, the parable and the allegory are really expansions of the basic forms. In a *parable* we have a developed simile where the story, while fictitious, is true to life. The latter feature differentiates a parable from a fable. In an *allegory* we have a developed metaphor prolonged into continuous narrative. Allegory tends to portray more abstract truth than a parable, and allegory is the more literary figure of speech. There is an allegory of old age in Eccl 12:1–7; an allegory of the last days of the monarchy of Judah in Ez 17:2–24; and an allegory on the armor of salvation in Eph 6:13–17. Ideally, the parable is clearly distinct from the allegory. In an allegory each detail and character is significant, often with hidden meaning; in a parable, the important thing is the lesson of the whole story, and details serve only to bring out the main point. However, even in ancient oratory, as Quintilian, the 1st-cent. Latin authority, recognized, traits of allegory were mixed with parable; and in a story with one main point (parable) some of the characters or details had a significance of their own (allegory).

134 **(II) Modern Parable Exegesis.** In the exegesis of the Church Fathers, like Augustine and Gregory, the parables of Jesus were treated as allegories, and each detail was attributed a significance. In his rather forced exegesis of the parable of the Good Samaritan (Lk 10:30–37), Augustine identifies the man who went down from Jerusalem to Jericho as Adam; Jerusalem is the state of original happiness; Jericho represents man's mortality; the Samaritan is Christ; the inn is the Church; the innkeeper is Paul, etc. The modern reaction to such allegorizing has been led by A. Jülicher in his two-volume study of the parables (1888–89). He insisted that the parables of Jesus were simple, moralizing stories with no admixture of allegory. All allegorization, even that already present in the Gospels, was the work of Christian interpreters and did not come from Jesus.

Thus, a parable like that of the Tenants in the Vineyard (Mk 12:1–11), where there are identifiable characters (the servants = the prophets; the son = Jesus; the owner = God), would, according to Jülicher's principle, be a literary creation of the early Church. Again there are in the Gospels allegorical explanations of three parables: the explanations of the Sower and the Seed (Mk 4:13–20); of the Weeds (Mt 13:36–43); of the Fish Net (Mt 13:49–50). Since these explanations interpret individual details, they too could not be attributed to Jesus. And the allegorical parables in Jn, where Jesus identifies himself as the Good Shepherd (10:11,14) or as the Vine (15:5), would also be automatically rejected as unauthentic, according to Jülicher's principles.

135 Today many writers (Black, *art. cit.;* Brown, *art. cit.*) are challenging Jülicher's distinction between parable and allegory as too doctrinaire. No one wishes to return to the exaggerated allegorical interpretation of the patristic period (→ Hermeneutics, 71:91–92), but the thesis that Jesus' parables could have no allegorical features becomes artificial if we approach the question from a Semitic viewpoint rather than from that of the canons of Gk oratory (Hermaniuk, *op. cit.*). The one Hebr word *māšāl* covers all the Gk figures of speech we have discussed and more (maxims, proverbs, riddles, fables, symbols)—a good indication that in the Hebr tradition one would not have made Jülicher's distinction. And indeed the Gospels use *parabolē* in the same wide coverage as *māšāl*. Subsumed under it are proverbs (Lk 4:23), maxims (Lk 14:7–11), riddles (Mk 7:15–17), examples (Lk 12:15–21), figurative speech (Mk 4:33), similes (Mt 13:33), metaphors (Mt 5:14), and finally parables, and parables with simple allegorical traits. (We may note that *parabolē* does not occur in Jn; there we have a Gk synomym, *paroimia*, which also covers a range of figurative speech [16:25].) Thus, a mechanical application of Jülicher's principle to identify those Gospel parables that are authentically from Jesus is not possible.

136 **(III) Characteristics of Jesus' Parables.** Jesus used illustrations from daily life that caught his listeners' attention by their vividness and narrative color. While these illustrations enabled his hearers to understand his message better, they often had a strange or novel twist that left enough doubt to challenge the hearers to reflection and inquiry.

(A) Illustrations from Daily Life. Jesus was familiar with a rural Galilean milieu: outdoor scenes of farming and shepherding, and domestic scenes in a simple one-room house (Lk 11:5–8). The homes of the rich are seen only through the kitchen door—the view of servants and slaves. The farming is hill-country farming, done in small patches with stone fences and briars (Mk 4:5–7), not that of the broad lowland plains. There are donkeys, sheep, wolves, and birds; seeds, wheat, and harvest; lilies of the field and fruit trees; patched wineskins and household lamps; children in the market place, laborers, and merchants. This creates an obstacle for the modern urban reader; and indeed even for readers who are accustomed to rural life the ancient techniques described in the Gospels are puzzling. The careless broadcasting of seed in the parable of the Sower is explained by the fact that in Palestine sowing sometimes took place before plowing. And so, to understand the parables one needs information about a civilization that is not his own.

137 The details from ordinary life are woven into vivid narratives of varying length, and the reader should be aware of the techniques of storytelling that are employed or he may miss the genius of the parable form. One of these is the "rule of three," namely that in popular stories it is customary to have three characters with the point of the illustration or the punch line coming in the third instance—witness our "Englishman, Scotsman, Irishman" jokes. Thus in the parables three servants are entrusted with the talents, and three men pass the victim who fell among robbers. Another technique of storytelling is direct discourse: We are rarely told in the third person what a character is thinking. And so in the parables people talk aloud to themselves so that we may find out what is on their minds (Lk 12:16–21; 18:9–14). Only one conversation can hold the stage at a time; and consequently when three characters are involved, we have direct confrontation repeated three times (Mt 25:14–28). Thinking of the parables as stories explains their peculiarities and inconsistencies. "That is for the sake of the story" is the answer to many difficulties that arise if one is too logical, e.g., why a steward known to be dishonest should be allowed to make an inventory (Lk 16:1), or why workers should be paid in inverse order (Mt 20:8).

138 **(B) Novelty and Challenge.** The novel twist in Jesus' stories made his hearers take notice. Who would have expected the scapegrace prodigal son to emerge a more sympathetic character than the dependable elder son? Jesus may even have taken well-known stories and supplied new endings, e.g., the priest, the Levite, and the layman may have been stock characters in religious tales, but Jesus makes the third character a hated Samaritan who is the most sympathetic of the three. A shepherd rejoicing extravagantly over finding a single lost sheep and heedless of imperiling the other 99; a woman throwing a party for her neighbors because she has found a single small coin—such oddities were meant to make people think.

In this light, modern exegetes, like Dodd and Jeremias, suggest that many of the parables offered to people the challenge of the Kingdom of God. In evaluating the parables as moral lessons, Jülicher made the common mistake of 19th-cent. liberal exegesis, i.e., he reduced Jesus to a preacher of good behavior. But the parables, like the miracles, were part of a vigorous assault made by God's dominion (Kingdom) as it entered time. Some parables, like that of the Good Samaritan, were a blistering attack on the established religious policy. Others, like the Tenants in the Vineyard and the Talents, were threats of imminent judgment on the Jewish authorities. Still others, like the Sower and the Mustard Seed, were an apologia for the slowness and insignificant results of Jesus' own ministry in Galilee. Often Jesus sought to involve his hearers in the challenge of the parables by making them pass judgment on the outcome of the story (Mt 21:31,41; Lk 7:42). Throughout the Gospel we hear the personal appeal of Jesus: "He who has ears to hear, let him hear."

139 **(C) Purpose of the Parables.** Jesus had to explain the parables to the disciples who had not understood them (Mk 4:10,34; Mt 13:36; Jn 16:29). How can this be reconciled with the overwhelming evidence that the parables were meant to make Jesus' message intelligible? The problem comes to a head with the passage in Mk 4:11–12: "To those outside all things are treated in parables that 'Seeing, they may see but not perceive; and hearing, they may hear but not understand.'" (For details and bibliography, → Gospel Mk, 42:26.) Seemingly this passage would have Jesus speaking in parables in order to confuse and obfuscate. However, most scholars recognize that Mk 4:11–12 is a summation, not of the purpose, but of the *result* of preaching the Kingdom of God in parables. The challenge of the parables was rejected by the majority who saw and heard but refused to perceive and understand. If the parables blinded men's minds and hearts, it was more because they refused the piercing challenge than because they could not understand intellectually.

This does not mean that the parables were always clear to all. Jesus' picture of the Kingdom of God (→ 97–98 above) was quite different from the expected kingdom of the Davidic Messiah, and so his parabolic exposition of that Kingdom often had to be explained. (J. A. Baird, *JBL* 76 [1957] 201–7, gives statistical evidence to show that Jesus explained to his disciples the parables concerning the Kingdom.) Moreover, Jesus was chary of detailed descriptions of the future action of God in definitively establishing the Kingdom (Mt 24:36; Acts 1:6–7), and the parables could unfold the true nature and destiny of the Kingdom without arousing vain speculation about the future. In general the true purpose of the parable is well phrased in Mk 4:33, "In many such parables he spoke the word to them *according as they were able to understand it.*"

140 **(IV) Problems of Parable Exegesis.** Most of the problems arise from the fact that not one of the Syn was an eyewitness of what he recounts. In transmitting a parable in which there were no accompanying time and place indications, the Evangelists often could not be sure where or when Jesus had spoken it; and so they had to use their own judgment about where to insert such a parable into the Gospel sequence.

(A) Setting and Grouping. At times the same parable is found in different settings in different Gospels, e.g., what Mt places in the Sermon on the Mount, Lk places elsewhere (Mt 5:13; Lk 14:34–35). Although it is possible that Jesus narrated the same parable on several occasions, this is *not* a plausible general solution for such discrepancies. The audience to whom the parables were originally addressed is part of this same problem caused by the limited knowledge of the Evangelists. Many of the parables must have been hurled at Jesus' enemies, in particular the Pharisees; but as the parables came to be preached in the Church, the importance of the Pharisees decreased in favor of an adaptation of the parables to the Christians and their lives. Therefore, in the Gospels some parables originally addressed to the Pharisees are now addressed to the disciples, e.g., the direction of the Lost Sheep in Mt 18:1,12–14, as compared to Lk 15:2–7.

141 The possibility of having different settings and different audiences for the same parable in the various Gospels often means that the one parable acquires different meanings as it is incorporated by the different Evangelists into their accounts. The parable of the Lamp seems to have three different meanings in the contexts of Mk 4:21, Mt 5:14–16, and Lk 11:33. In such cases it is not always easy to decide which (if any) was the original meaning of the parable as it was spoken by Jesus. This, of course, is a reflection of the principle that the Gospels do not give a static, verbatim reporting of the words of Jesus, but rather the words of Jesus adapted to the new circumstances of a Church spreading throughout the world (→ Church Pronouncements, 72:35). A Catholic understanding of the charism of inspiration guarantees that the new nuances drawn by the Evangelists from the parables of Jesus are in no way a betrayal of the original import of Jesus' message (→ Inspiration, 66:84–85).

142 A particular problem arises from the fact that the Evangelists have bunched or grouped once independent parables. Jesus seems at times to have narrated his parables in pairs (Mk 2:21–22; Lk 14:28–32). But frequently the Evangelists have gone further in this process and placed together all the parables dealing with the same topic. In Mk 4 there is a collection of three seed parables; Mt 13 has seven parables referring to the Kingdom of heaven; Mt 24:32–25:46 has seven parables dealing with the parousia; Lk 14:7–24 has three banquet parables; Lk 15 has three parables on regaining what was lost. Occasionally such grouping has disconcerting side effects. Originally separate parables have become fused into one, e.g., Mt 22-1–14 contains a parable of a marriage feast, a parable of a king who destroyed a city, and a parable of a man without a wedding garment (cf. Lk 14:16–24). To make one consistent story of such diverse parables leads to incongruities—one gets the impression that the feast is put into the warming oven while the king is out destroying the city!

143 **(B) Varying Details.** Stories such as the parables were handed down for years as oral tradition. By the time the different written traditions behind the Gospels were composed, details in the parables had developed as variants through a process of simplification and polishing. The parable of the Tenants in the Vineyard is presented in the same general circumstances in all three Syn (Mk 12:1–11; Mt 21:33–43; Lk 20:9–18); yet there is a variation in the details concerning the servants (a single servant or groups of servants; the same servant three times or three different servants).

Sometimes the variant details are so striking that we cannot be sure that we are dealing with the same version of a parable. Do the differences apparent in the parable of the Pounds (Lk 19:12–27) and the parable of the Talents (Mt 25:14–30) stem from two different narrations by Jesus or from one narration that has undergone variation in the course of oral transmission? Cf. also the parable of the Banquet (Lk 14:16–24) and the parable of the Wedding Feast (Mt 22:1–10).

144 **(C) Introductory Formulas and Attached Maxims.** Rather standardized formulas are used to introduce the parables, e.g., "What one of you, encountering this situation, does not do this?" (Lk 11:5; 15:3,8). Some of the basic patterns may stem from Jesus and have been extended to a larger number of parables. A particular problem occurs with: "The Kingdom of heaven is like..."—a formula that is frequent in Mt where there are ten Kingdom parables as compared to two each for Mk and Lk. The real object of the parable's comparison often does not necessarily follow the word "like." In Mt 13:47, despite the wording, the Kingdom is not really like a net but like the catch of fish and the separation of the good from the bad. In Mt 13:24 the Kingdom is not really like the man who sowed seed but like the whole situation of the weeds and grain growing together until harvest. Thus the formula really means: "The Kingdom of heaven is like the case of...," where the object of comparison is the whole situation.

145 Difficulties also arise from what has been appended to the ends of parables. Solitary sayings of Jesus have sometimes been appended to parables to which they do not really apply. "Everyone who exalts himself shall be humbled" is found at Mt 23:12; Lk 14:11; 18:14. The maxim certainly does not fit the last context, namely the parable of the Pharisee and the Publican, because the Pharisee is *not* humbled. The maxim, "The last will be first and the first last," is found at Mt 19:30 (= Mk 10:31; Lk 13:30) and at Mt 20:16 where it is appended to the parable of the Laborers in the Vineyard. It has been attracted to the latter parable simply because the laborers hired last were paid first, but it has nothing to contribute to the interpretation of the parable. Nor does the maxim, "Many are called but few are chosen," really fit the parable of the Wedding Garment (Mt 22:14), for only one person is rejected in this parable. The most famous example of appended maxims is the parable of the Dishonest Steward, where to the basic story (Lk 16:1–8) has been added a series of maxims (vv. 9, 10, 11–12, 13) that are related to topics mentioned in the parable but are of no help in interpreting the parable.

Thus parable exegesis has many pitfalls; and without careful study those whose duty it is to preach on the parables, which serve frequently as Sunday Gospels, will misinterpret and misapply them.

THE RESURRECTION OF JESUS

BIBLIOGRAPHY

146 Anderson, H., *Jesus and Christian Origins* (N.Y., 1964) 185–240. Bartsch, H.-W., *Das Auferstehungszeugnis* (Hamburg, 1965). *Christus victor mortis*, issue of *Greg* 39 (1958) 201–524. De Haes., P., *La résurrection de Jésus dans l'apologétique des cinquante dernières années* (AnalGreg 59; Rome, 1953). Descamps, A., "La structure des récits évangéliques de la résurrection," *Bib* 40 (1959) 726–41. Dodd, C. H., "The Appearances of the Risen Christ: An Essay in Form-Criticism of the Gospels," *SGL* 9–36. Durrwell, F. X., *The Resurrection: A Biblical Study* (tr. R. Sheed; N.Y., 1960). Fuller, D. P., *Easter Faith and History* (Grand Rapids, 1965). Grass, H., *Ostergeschehen und Osterberichte* (2nd ed.; Göttingen, 1962). Hodges, Z. C., "Form Criticism and the Resurrection Accounts," *BS* 124 (1967) 339–48. Koch, G., *Die Auferstehung Jesu Christi* (Tübingen, 1959). Künneth, W., *The Theology of the Resurrection* (London, 1965). Lake, K., *The Historical Evidence for the Resurrection of Jesus* (London, 1907). *LumVi* 3 (1952—entire issue). McLeman, J., *Resurrection Then and Now* (Phila., 1967). Martini, C. M., *Il problema storico della risurrezione negli studi recenti* (AnalGreg 104; Rome, 1959). Marxsen, W., *Die Auferstehung Jesu als historisches und als theologisches Problem* (Gütersloh, 1964). Morison, F., *Who Moved the Stone?* (London, 1930). Niebuhr, R., *Resurrection and Historical Reason* (N.Y., 1957). O'Collins, G. G., "Is the Resurrection an 'Historical' Event?" *HeythJ* 8 (1967) 381–87. Pannenberg, W., "Did Jesus Really Rise from the Dead?" *Dialog* 4 (1965) 128–35. Ramsey, A. M., *The Resurrection of Christ* (rev. ed.; London, 1961). Rengstorf, K. H., *Die Auferstehung Jesu* (4th ed.; 1960). Russell, R., "Modern Exegesis and the Fact of the Resurrection," *DowR* 76 (1958) 251–64, 329–43. Schmitt, J., *Jésus ressuscité dans la prédication apostolique* (Paris, 1949). Stanley, D. M., *Christ's Resurrection in Pauline Soteriology* (AnalBib 13; Rome, 1961). Swete, H. B., *The Appearances of Our Lord After the Passion* (London, 1907).

147 OUTLINE

148 **(I) Reality of the Resurrection.** The raising of Jesus from the dead was unlike all the other restorations to life mentioned in the Bible. In the NT Lazarus, Jairus' daughter, and the son of the widow of Nain are described as returning to ordinary human existence; there is no suggestion that they were glorified or that they would not have to die again. But Jesus is portrayed as conquering death, as returning immortal in glory and power. The resurrection of Jesus was the supreme intervention of God in human existence, the supreme miracle. No wonder then that, on the one hand, the resurrection has become a principal apologetic argument for the truth of Christianity and that, on the other hand, the reality of the resurrection has been questioned.

As with the miracles, however, the constant interplay of apologetics in the study of the resurrection has had bad effects (→ 111 above). The impression has been given that the chief importance of the resurrection was probative, while the salvation of mankind was completed on the cross. Modern Catholic scholars, through their study of the NT (e.g., works of Durrwell and Stanley), are seeking to reclaim the salvific import of the resurrection as its principal role. The passion, death, resurrection, and ascension of Jesus constitute one indissoluble action for the salvation of man, as Paul implicitly recognized in Rom 4:25 when he said that Jesus "was put to death for our sins and raised for our justification." The life to which Jesus was restored through the resurrection is eternal life that he now can share with those who believe in him. It was with this theological understanding, and not primarily with apologetic intent, that Paul exclaimed, "If Christ has not been raised, then our preaching is in vain, and your faith is in vain" (1 Cor 15:14; → Pauline Theology, 79:71–74).

149 Nevertheless, once it is put into proper secondary focus, the question of the apologetic value of the resurrection cannot be bypassed. The NT does not claim that anyone saw the resurrection and makes no attempt to describe it, as does the *Gospel of Peter* (→ Apocrypha, 68:63). Therefore, the reality of the bodily resurrection hinges on the missing body or empty tomb and, above all, on the validity of the experiences of those who claimed they saw Jesus risen. The rationalistic or liberal criticism of the last century tried to discredit the resurrection stories as demonstrative either of apostolic *fraud* (the apostles invented the stories; they stole the body) or of apostolic *credulity* and confusion (he was not dead but in a coma; the tombs were confused; hallucinations were mistaken for real appearances). We refer the reader to the painstaking refutation of these attacks in standard apologetic books (cf. Morison, *op. cit.*).

It is of interest here to point out that some of these attacks were already current in the 1st cent. and have left their mark on the later layers of the NT resurrection accounts that sought to answer the attacks. The assertion that the apostles were lying in claiming to have seen the Risen Jesus when others did not see him is implicit in Peter's explanation in Acts 10:41. The charge that the apostles stole the body is attributed to the Pharisees in Mt 28:13 (cf. 27:64), and Matthew attempts to refute it with the story of the guards at the tomb. The suggestion that the apostles were credulous probably prompted the constant reminder that at first they did not believe that Jesus was truly risen (Mt 28:17; Lk 24:11,37; Mk 16:11, 14; Jn 20:25). An apologetic stress on the corporeal and tangible qualities of the Risen Jesus lies behind the insistence that he ate food (Lk 24:41–43; Acts 10:41) and that his wounds could be verified by the apostles (Lk 24:39; Jn 20:24–28). Seemingly, the empty tomb played little direct role in NT apologetics although it is the background for the Easter morning stories. According to John (20:2), the brute fact of the empty tomb suggests to Mary Magdalene only that the body has been stolen. There are possible indications that the idea of the empty tomb was implicit in the early preaching, e.g., in the mention of burial in 1 Cor 15:4; in the comparison hinted at in Acts 2:29–31.

(For a defense of the antiquity and importance of the memory of the empty tomb, see R. H. Fuller, *Biblical Research* 4 [1960] 8–24; W. Nauck, *ZNW* 47 [1956] 243–67; H. F. von Campenhausen, *Der Ablauf der Ostereignisse und das leere Grab* [2d ed.; Heidelberg, 1958].)

150 In the early part of the 20th cent., under the impact of S. Reinach's *Orpheus* of 1909, a new assault was mounted on the reality of the resurrection through the study of comparative religions (→ Modern NT Criticism, 41:39). It was proposed that the early Christians, either consciously or unconsciously, had conformed the story of Jesus to the pagan legends and mystery cults surrounding the dying and rising gods (Attis, Adonis, Osiris, Dionysus). But the apologists were quick to point out that while Jesus may have risen in the spring, his death and resurrection had nothing to do with the natural cycle of winter dormancy and spring flowering that lay behind the suggested parallels. For details on the history of the apologetics of the resurrection, see the works of De Haes and Martini.

151 A current attempt (e.g., H. Grass) to explain the resurrection in terms other than real bodily restoration is centered about the theory that the genuine faith of the Jewish Christians in Jesus' victory over death could be expressed by a Hebr mind only in terms of corporeal resurrection, for the resurrection of the body was the only form of immortality known to the disciples. Truly Jesus was glorified; and since spiritual happiness was inconceivable without one's body, Jesus' glorification was described as a resurrection. Thus the resurrection of the body becomes a symbol of a spiritual truth.

The great subtlety supposed on the part of the disciples in the theory just mentioned and the difficulty of reconciling this theory with the very early insistence that men did *see* the Risen Jesus have made some critical scholars wary of a purely symbolic approach to the resurrection. It is obvious that Paul believed not only that he himself had seen the Risen Jesus (Gal 1:12,16) but that many others had seen Jesus (1 Cor 15:5–8). This has led to a suggested distinction between the experience of "seeing" Jesus and the interpretation of that experience as the resurrection of Jesus (e.g., W. Marxsen, *op. cit.*).

In an important article, W. Pannenberg has made some interesting points that militate against a cavalier attitude toward the historicity of the resurrection. He insists that there is no question here of a simple revivification of a corpse. Not only is there the physical fact that immediately after death irreversible processes of dissolution begin, but—and this is more to the point—the NT authors are thinking of transforming rather than revivification. Paul, who draws a close analogy between the resurrection of Jesus and the future resurrection of the dead (1 Cor 15:12), stresses heavily the characteristics of the transformation that takes place in resurrection. What died was perishable, weak, and mortal; what rises is imperishable, glorious, and immortal (15:42–43,52–54). In short, "It is sown a physical body; it is raised a spiritual body" (15:44; for a complete discussion, see M. E. Dahl, *The Resurrection of the Body* (SBT 36; London, 1962). Nevertheless, if the NT stresses that what was seen was a radically transformed Jesus, it was *Jesus* who was seen. True, the story of the empty tomb seems to represent a layer of tradition different from that of the stories of Jesus' appearances; but the disciples' preaching of the resurrection (and therefore their understanding of the resurrection) supposes that the tomb was empty (→ 149 above). This preaching would have been quickly refuted if there were any tradition of a tomb where Jesus' corpse still lay. Even the Jews who sought to refute the followers of Jesus never suggested that the tomb was not empty. And this concept of an empty tomb helps to confirm the continuity between the Jesus of the earthly ministry and the transformed Jesus seen by the disciples.

Pannenberg (*art. cit.*, 135) says: "Something happened in which the disciples in these appearances were confronted with a reality which also in our language cannot be expressed in any other way than by the symbolic and metaphorical expression of the hope beyond death, the resurrection from the dead. Please understand me correctly: Only the name we give to this event is symbolic, metaphorical, but not the reality of the event itself. The latter is so absolutely unique that we have no other name for this than the metaphorical expression of the apocalyptic expectation. In this sense, the resurrection of Jesus is an historical event, an event that really happened at that time."

We shall leave to theologians the task of evaluating what is analogical and what is literal in the general concepts of "life" after death and the resurrection of a body. As far as the biblical evidence is concerned, on the one hand, every single shred of evidence about this unique event would indicate that the disciples were claiming to have seen the body of Jesus that had been crucified and had lain in the tomb. (In this light, we think it biblically irresponsible to claim that Christian faith in the resurrection is independent of the question of whether or not Jesus lies buried in Palestine—Christian faith in the resurrection is in continuity with apostolic faith in the resurrection, and there is no evidence that the first witnesses took such a stance of indifference toward the body in the tomb.) On the other hand, there is reiteration in the NT that the Risen Jesus was different ("in another form"—Mk 16:12) and somewhat unrecognizable (Lk 24:16; Jn 20:14; 21:4). Any solution to the problem must take into account the element of continuity and the element of change and spiritualization, if that solution is to be guided by the biblical evidence.

152 **(II) Differences in the Resurrection Narratives.** In the Passion Narrative each of the Gospels presents a continuous story, the general sequence of which is singularly parallel in all four. (This has been a reason for assuming that the Passion Narrative was one of the earliest portions of Gospel tradition to take shape.) But the resurrection tradition consists of isolated appearances with little agreement among the various Gospels on circumstances and details. A close study of the accompanying chart shows how numerous the variations are. In the chart we make two basic critical assumptions: First, that Mk 16:9–20 is not by Mark, but is a later compilation (partly from material similar to Lk) added to the Gospel—the "Marcan Appendix" (→ Gospel Mk, 42:96–97); second, that Jn 21, although composed within the Johannine school of tradition, was not by the writer of the rest of Jn, and so Jn 20 and 21 represent independent and not consecutive narratives (→ Gospel Jn, 63:180).

153 Let us concentrate on the narratives of the appearances to the Twelve. It is clear that there are traditions attached to two different localities. Appearances in *Jerusalem* are attested by Lk, Jn 20, and the Marcan Appendix; appearances in *Galilee* are attested by Mt, Jn 21, and presumably by Mk (cf. 16:7; 14:28). That such a double tradition also exists in the apocryphal

The Variant Accounts of Resurrection Appearances

	Mk 16:1–8	*Mt 28:1–20*	*Lk 24*	*Mk 16:9–20*	*Jn 20*
AT TOMB					
TIME	very early; 1st day of week; sun risen	1st day of week; growing light	1st day of week; early dawn	early; 1st day of week;	early; 1st day of week; still dark
WOMEN	Mary Magdalene; Mary, mother of James; Salome	Mary Magdalene; other Mary	Mary Magdalene; Mary, mother of James; Joanna; others	Mary Magdalene	Mary Magdalene; another? ("we" in v. 2)
PURPOSE	bought spices; came to anoint	came to see tomb	spices from Friday; took spices along		
VISUAL PHENOMENA	stone rolled back; youth sitting inside on right	earthquake; angel descended; he rolled back stone; sat on it (outside)	stone rolled back; two men standing (inside)	Jesus	stone rolled away; (later) two angels sitting inside
CONVERSATION	Youth said: Not to fear; Jesus risen; tell disciples he is going to Galilee	Angel said: Not to fear; Jesus risen; tell disciples he is going to Galilee	Men asked question; recalled prophecy made in Galilee		(Later) angels asked: Why do you weep? She thought body stolen
REACTION OF THE WOMEN	fled trembling; told no one	went away quickly with fear to tell disciples	returned; told Eleven and the rest	went and told followers	went and told Peter and "other disciple"
APPEARANCES OF JESUS		Jesus met them; they took his feet; he repeated message about Galilee		Jesus appeared first to Mary Magdalene	(Later) Jesus appeared to Mary Magdalene. She clutched him; he spoke of ascending
			[Peter ran to tomb; saw burial clothes; went home.] Lord appeared to Simon (v. 34)		Peter and the disciple ran to tomb; saw burial clothes; went home believing
					Mary returned and saw Jesus as described above
COUNTRY ROAD			Jesus appeared to two disciples on road to Emmaus	Jesus appeared to two of them walking into country	
JERUSALEM			Appeared to Eleven at meal Easter night	Afterward to Eleven at table	Appeared to disciples minus Thomas at meal Easter night
					week later, to disciples with Thomas
GALILEE		To Eleven on a mountain			*Jn 21* To seven disciples at Sea of Tiberias

gospels and in other documents has been the thesis of E. Lohmeyer, *Galiläa und Jerusalem* (Göttingen, 1936) 6–7, and of L. E. Elliott-Binns, *Galilean Christianity* (London, 1956) 39–42.

Neither of the two traditions shows any awareness of a tradition of appearances in the other locale. The *Jerusalem accounts* leave little or no room for subsequent appearances in Galilee. Lk 24:50 portrays the departure of Jesus from his disciples as taking place at Bethany, just outside Jerusalem, on Easter night, and the Marcan Appendix has the same picture. A study of how Lk 24:6 changes the import of Mk 16:7 would seem to indicate a desire on Luke's part to avoid mention of appearances in Galilee. True, in Acts 1:3 there is evidence of Lucan awareness of a longer period of postresurrectional appearances; but there is no mention of Galilee, and the ascension takes place in the Jerusalem area (1:12). In Jn we have postresurrectional appearances over an eight-day period (20:19,26), and then the Gospel comes to an end (20:30–31).

The *Galilean accounts* seem to rule out prior Jerusalem appearances to the Twelve. The angel's directive in Mk 16:7 and Mt 28:7 bids the disciples to go to Galilee to see Jesus—a command that would make little sense were they to see him first in Jerusalem. When Jesus does appear to the disciples on the mountain in Galilee (Mt 28:16–17), they express doubt; and the other Gospels associate this hesitancy with initial appearances (Lk 24:37; Jn 20:25; Mk 16:13,14). There would be little reason for doubt if they had already seen him in Jerusalem. The editor who added ch. 21 to Jn made it seem that the Galilean appearances followed the Jerusalem ones by the verses he necessarily added to sew the two accounts together (21:1,14). But it is quite apparent from the story itself of the Galilean appearance (21:4,7) that the disciples are seeing Jesus for the first time.

154 Writers of harmonistic lives of Jesus have imposed their own sequence on the Gospel evidence: Jesus first appeared to the Twelve in Jerusalem for a week; then, for some inexplicable reason, they went to Galilee where he appeared to them at the seashore and on the mountain; and finally they returned to Jerusalem where Jesus appeared to them before ascending. Such a sequence does violence to the Gospel evidence, as Bishop Descamps (*art. cit.*, 737–39) has shown. *If* one must venture beyond the evidence to establish a sequence, then (after the discovery of the empty tomb in Jerusalem and perhaps after appearances of Jesus to the women in Jerusalem and to "minor" disciples on the road to Emmaus) one might place the appearances to the Twelve in Galilee before the appearances to them in Jerusalem—a sequence that is not ruled out in the Galilean accounts. The Lucan and Johannine attempt to have the main appearance to the Twelve take place on Easter day is probably a construction dictated by theological rather than by historical interests.

But the more biblical answer is to recognize that the evidence does not permit us to establish a sequence with any assurance. Each tradition in the Gospels centers on an all-important appearance to the Twelve in which they are commissioned for their future task (Mt 28:19; Lk 24:47–49; Mk 16:15; Jn 20:21; 21:15–17 and the symbolism of the catch of fish). Each tradition gives the impression that Jesus is appearing to them for the first time, whence the doubt and reassurance. Thus Descamps (*art. cit.*) is correct in maintaining that in a certain way, as far as substance is concerned, all the Gospels are narrating the same appearance to the Twelve.

155 How did it arise that an Evangelist recorded appearances only in Jerusalem or in Galilee and that there was no attempt to make a sequence of all the postresurrectional appearances of Jesus? Taylor (*FGT* 59–62) makes an interesting suggestion. In preaching the resurrection, what was essential was a testimony that a well-known apostolic witness had seen Jesus. There was no chain of related events in the resurrection as there was in the passion. Thus, in Paul's primitive kerygma of the resurrection (1 Cor 15:5–7) only the names of those to whom Jesus appeared are listed, and no locale is mentioned. Each community would preserve the memory of an appearance of Jesus to apostolic figures known to that community (appearances to the women and "minor" disciples would be a later stratum). The important Palestinian Christian communities of Jerusalem and of Galilee would retain the memory of appearances with local associations, or perhaps, if Descamps' theory is correct, would have adapted to the respective local setting the one basic appearance to the Twelve. The individual Evangelists drew on one or the other of these local traditions available to them, perhaps in ignorance of the existence of other traditions.

156 **(III) Special Problems.** Here we must be highly selective and can but suggest the direction of the answer.

(A) The Lost Ending of Mark? It is usually supposed that Mk once ended with an appearance in Galilee similar to that recounted in Mt, and that unfortunately this ending was lost. There are difficulties, however; e.g., the fact that Lk shows no awareness of Galilean appearances may mean that the form of Mk available to him was already without the supposed ending. Lohmeyer has suggested that Mk had no resurrection appearances and that the promise that the disciples would see Jesus in Galilee (16:7) referred to the parousia (a thesis rightly rejected in the commentaries on Mk of Taylor [p. 608] and Haenchen [p. 546]). Yet, even if one thinks that Mark must have believed in postresurrectional appearances, in harmony with all the early kerygmatic strains of the NT, it is possible that Mk ended without narrating a specific appearance—just with the general assurance that the Lord was truly risen. After all, despite the angelic order to go to Galilee (v. 7—which may be secondary), 16:8 insists that the women did not transmit this order and leaves one with the impression that therefore the disciples would not have gone to Galilee (→ Gospel Mk, 42:95).

157 **(B) Matthean Expansions.** In Mk 16:4 and Lk 24:2 the women find the stone rolled back from the tomb, and at the site they encounter a (heavenly) man or men. The implication seems to be that the heavenly visitor(s) moved the stone. Matthew (28:1–4) spells out this implication by having the women seemingly present when the angel of the Lord comes down and rolls back the stone, frightening the guards. This is an instance of Matthean dramatic midrashic technique at work, elaborating earlier and vaguer traditions. The story of the guard placed at the tomb (Mt 27:62–66; 28:4,11–15) is a greater problem. This story, which is obviously apologetic in purpose, does not appear in any other Gospel and really makes the narrative in Mk and Lk senseless—why would the women come to the tomb with spices, expecting to roll back the stone (Mk 16:3) and get in, if there were guards whose express purpose was to keep people out?

158 **(C) Jesus Raised or Risen?** In about 19 passages, chiefly in the Pauline writings, the NT makes absolutely clear that God the Father (subject) raised Jesus (object) from the dead (e.g., 1 Thes 1:10; 1 Cor 6:14; Gal 1:1). Thus the earliest tradition that we know attributes the agency in the resurrection to the Father. The verb that appears in the Gospel narratives (Mk 16:6; Mt 28:6,7; Lk 24:6,34) is *ēgerthē*, an aor. pass. form that would normally be translated, "He was raised up"—see C. F. D. Moule, *Idiom Book of New Testament Greek* (2nd ed.; Cambridge, 1963) 26. However, such passive forms in Koine Greek can be translated intransitively with an active nuance: "He is risen"—see J. H. Moulton and N. Turner, *A Grammar of New Testament Greek* (London, 1963) 3, 57. The latter translation, which shifts the agency in the resurrection to Jesus, has been common in Catholic Bibles translated from the Vg because Jerome rendered *ēgerthē* by *surrexit*, an active form. However, the translation "He was raised" is probably to be preferred in the Syn as less Christologically tendentious and as a literal translation in harmony with the early theological outlook. In Jn the theology has developed to the point where it is realized that Jesus and the Father act by the same divine power (Jn 10:30) and that therefore one may say that Jesus rose by his own power (10:17–18). Thus the *ēgerthē* of 2:22 is probably to be translated, "When he had risen from the dead...."

159 **(D) The Resurrection/Ascension.** "Ascension" normally evokes the image of Jesus' being lifted up to heaven on a cloud after 40 days (Acts 1:3,9). Such an understanding presents several difficulties: 40 is a symbolic number in the Bible and not always to be taken literally; other passages imply an ascension on Easter (Lk 24:51; Jn 20:17; Mk 16:19); the notion of ascending to heaven implies figurative language, for heaven is not really to be thought of as above the earth. P. Benoit (*RB* 56 [1949] 161–203; also *TD* 8 [1960] 105–10) has made a very important distinction in the concept of ascension which helps to solve the problem. If one is speaking of the terminus of Jesus' frequent appearances among men, then this took place some time (40 days) after the resurrection, perhaps in the symbolic form of a levitation as Acts describes. If one is speaking of ascension theologically, i.e., as a return to the Father or as a glorification in heaven at God's right hand, this exaltation was an integral part of the resurrection. Jesus rose from the dead to glory, and he appeared to men after the resurrection as one already glorified with supreme power (Mt 28:18; Lk 24:26). The intimate and immediate connection between the resurrection and the ascension so understood is spelled out in Jn 20:17ff. and is implicit in many other NT texts (Acts 5:30–31; Eph 4:10; 1 Pt 3:21–22; Heb 4:14; 1 Tm 3:16).

THE TWELVE AND THE APOSTOLATE

BIBLIOGRAPHY

160 Barrett, C. K., "The Apostles In and After the New Testament," *SEA* 21 (1956) 30–49. Cerfaux, L., "L'unité du corps apostolique dans le Nouveau Testament," *Recueil* (Louvain, 1954) 2, 227–37; "Pour l'histoire du titre *Apostolos* dans le Nouveau Testament," *Recueil* 2, 185–200. Gerhardsson, B., *Die Boten Gottes und die Apostel Christi* (Lund, 1962). Giblet, J., "Les Douze," *Aux origines de l'Église* (RechBib 7; Bruges, 1964) 51–64. Goodspeed, E. J., *The Twelve: The Story of Christ's Apostles* (paperback ed.; N.Y., 1962). Käsemann, E., "Die Legitimität des Apostels," *ZNW* 41 (1942) 33–71. Klein, G., *Die Zwölf Apostel* (FRLANT 59; Göttingen, 1961). Kredel, E. M., "Der Apostelbegriff in der neueren Exegese," *ZKT* 78 (1956) 169–93, 257–305. Lightfoot, J. B., *Saint Paul's Epistle to the Galatians* (10th ed.; London, 1910) 92–101. Lohse, E., "Ursprung und Prägung des christlichen Apostolats," *TZ* 9 (1953) 259–75. Margot, J. C., "L'apostolat dans le Nouveau Testament et la succession apostolique," *VerbC* 11 (1957) 213–26. Mosbech, H., "*Apostolos* in the New Testament," *ST* 2 (1948) 166–200. Munck, J., "Paul, the Apostles, and the Twelve," *ST* 3 (1950) 96–110. Rengstorf, K., "*Apostolos*," *ThDNT* 1, 407–47. Rigaux, B., "Die 'Zwölf' in Geschichte und Kerygma," in *Der historische Jesus und der kerygmatische Christus*, ed. by H. Ristow and K. Matthiae (Berlin, 1960) 468–86. Roloff, J., *Apostolat-Verkündigung-Kirche* (Gütersloh, 1965). Schmithals, W., *The Office of Apostle in the Early Church* (Nashville, 1969). Vogelstein, H., "The Development of the Apostolate in Judaism and Its Transformation in Christianity," *HUCA* 2 (1925) 99–123. Von Campenhausen, H., "Der urchristliche Apostelbegriff," *ST* 1 (1947) 96–130. Wuellner, W. H., *The Meaning of "Fishers of Men"* (Phila., 1967).

161 OUTLINE

162 **(I) The Twelve.** The NT gives 4 lists of 12 men whom Jesus chose during his ministry to be with him: Mk 3:16–19; Mt 10:2–4; Lk 6:14–16; Acts 1:13 (without Iscariot). John gives no list but mentions "the Twelve" (6:67; 20:24).

(A) Identity of the Twelve. The table on p. 796 gives the names found in the four lists and indicates the sequence in which they occur. Note that they break down into three groups of four. The order within the groups varies, but a name never passes from one group to another. Perhaps the grouping was a mnemonic device.

163 (a) First Group of Four. The first apostle mentioned is always SIMON whose name was changed to Peter (Gk *Petros* is from *petra*, "rock," the translation of Aram *kêpā'*—Jn 1:42; Mt 16:18). There has been much recent discussion about the role of Peter in the early Church; see the debate between O. Cullmann, *Peter* (2nd ed.; Phila., 1962) and O. Karrer, *Peter and the Church* (N.Y., 1963). Closely associated with Peter is his brother

	Mk	*Mt*	*Lk*	*Acts*
Simon Peter	1	1	1	1
James of Zebedee	2	3	3	3
John of Zebedee	3	4	4	2
Andrew brother of Peter	4	2	2	4
Philip	5	5	5	5
Bartholomew	6	6	6	7
Matthew	7	8	7	8
Thomas	8	7	8	6
James of Alphaeus	9	9	9	9
Thaddaeus	10	10		
Lebbaeus		10*		
Judas (Jude) of James			11	11
Simon the Zealot	11	11	10	10
Judas Iscariot	12	12	12	

* In some Western mss.

ANDREW (Jn 1:40–41). Bethsaida is identified as the city of Andrew and Peter in Jn 1:44, but the Syn place Peter's house at Capernaum (Mt 8:14). Simon and Andrew were fishermen on the Sea of Galilee (Mk 1:16). According to Jn 1:40, Andrew (and seemingly Peter too—also Acts 1:22) was a disciple of John the Baptist (P. M. Peterson, *Andrew, Brother of Simon Peter* [NovTSup 1; Leiden, 1958]).

164 JAMES and JOHN were also Galilean fishermen, as was Zebedee their father (Mk 1:19). A complicated comparison persuades some that "the mother of the sons of Zebedee" (Mt 27:56) was Salome (Mk 15:40) who was the sister of Jesus' mother (Jn 19:25), all of which would make James and John cousins of Jesus. The mother figures in Mt 20:20 (cf. Mk 10:35). The two brothers were known as Boanerges, "the sons of thunder" (Mk 3:17) and seem to have been of fiery character (Lk 9:54). This James, known as "the Greater" or "the Elder" by contrast with the other James(es) of the Gospel (→ 168 below), was put to death by Herod Agrippa I between AD 41 and 44 (Acts 12:1–2) and thus was presumably the first martyr among the Twelve. John of Zebedee is not mentioned in Jn proper (chs. 1–20; cf. 21:2) but is traditionally identified as the anonymous "beloved disciple" who was the source of Johannine tradition (Jn 21:20,24; → Gospel Jn, 63:2–3). If he was also the John of Ap 1:2, he lived for a while in Asia Minor on Patmos (→ Apocalypse, 64:10).

Peter, James, and John figure as a special group of three who were especially close to Jesus. They witnessed the transfiguration (Mk 9:2) and the raising of Jairus' daughter (5:37); they were near Jesus at Gethsemane (14:33). Peter and John are closely associated in Acts 3:1, 4:13; 8:14.

165 (b) SECOND GROUP OF FOUR. PHILIP was from Bethsaida and seems to have been a close friend of Andrew (Jn 1:44; 6:5–8; 12:22). Nothing is known of BARTHOLOMEW (= son [*bar*] of Talmai). However, Jn (1:45–46; 21:2) mentions Nathanael, a native of Cana brought to Jesus by Philip; and by the 9th cent. AD, Nathanael was being identified with Bartholomew because Bartholomew's name follows Philip's in three of the lists. But it is far more likely that Nathanael was not one of the Twelve (so Augustine, Gregory the Great). THOMAS is called "the Twin," Didymus, in Jn 11:16; 20:24. An early apocryphal legend makes him the twin of Jesus.

166 MATTHEW is found in all lists, but only the Matthean list calls him a tax collector. The call of Levi, son of Alphaeus, a tax collector, is found in Mk 2:14; Lk 5:27, while Mt 9:9 gives a parallel description of the call of Matthew and never mentions Levi. No connection between Levi the tax collector and Matthew one of the Twelve is made in Mk and Lk. Perhaps the tradition of Mt had more information than the other Gospels, and thus Mt's implied identification of Levi with Matthew may be historical. However, Origen (*Contra Celsum* 1.62) said that Levi was not one of the Twelve, and Mt may simply be exhibiting the tendency to make all the early followers of Jesus members of the Twelve. (If Levi and Matthew were both tax collectors, confusion was possible.) We see this same tendency at work in scribal attempts to identify Levi with James, another of the Twelve; for instead of reading "Levi son of Alphaeus," some Western witnesses read in Mk 2:14; "James son of Alphaeus." Perhaps still another example can be found in the name Lebbaeus that appears in some Western readings of the list in Mk 3:18 and Mt 10:3 (→ 171 below), if Westcott and Hort are correct in thinking that Lebbaeus is a form of Levi (through the Latin?). See B. Lindars, *NTS* 4 (1957–58) 220–22.

167 (c) THIRD GROUP OF FOUR. Popular tradition would identify two of the Twelve, JAMES of Alphaeus (all lists) and JUDAS (Jude) of James (Lucan lists), with two of the four "brothers" of Jesus: James, Joses or Joseph, Simon, Judas (Mk 6:3; Mt 13:55).

The exact relation of these four to Jesus is not known (cousins? half brothers?), but the doctrine of the perpetual virginity of Mary is the basis for stating that they are not sons of Joseph and Mary and not the real brothers of Jesus. The Greek uses the precise word for "brothers" (see "sisters" in Mk 6:3; Mt 13:56), but it may be presumed that this is an overliteral rendition of Hebr *'āḥ* (Aram *'aḥā'*), which means "brother" but also covers a wider range of relationship, including cousins and half brothers (J. Blinzler, *TTZ* 67 [1958] 129–45, 224–46). A comparison of Mk 15:40; Mt 27:56, "Mary the mother of James and Joses [Joseph]," with Jn 19:25, "Mary of Clopas," suggests that at least two of "the brothers" were children of Clopas and a Mary other than the Virgin; perhaps one of these parents was related to Joseph or to Mary.

In any case, it is most doubtful that James and Judas (Jude) or any of "the brothers of Jesus" were members of the Twelve. "The brothers" did not believe in Jesus during the ministry (Jn 7:5; Mk 3:21,31—if the "friends" are "the brothers") and were not among his most intimate followers. Passages like Acts 1:13–14; 1 Cor 15:5–7 distinguish between the Twelve and "the brothers," and this distinction is implied in Mk 3:13–19 compared with 3:31. In particular, James the brother of Jesus, if he is the son of Clopas, is clearly not that member of the Twelve identified as James the son of Alphaeus (of whom we know nothing), despite Jerome's attempt to identify Clopas and Alphaeus.

168 Thus, among Jesus' acquaintances we seem to have three men named James: (1) James son of Zebedee, "the Greater," one of the Twelve (→ 164 above); (2) James son of Alphaeus, one of the Twelve; (3) James, presumably son of Clopas, "the Less" (Mk 15:40 = the smaller or younger), a "brother" of Jesus, later "bishop" of Jerusalem, traditional author of an epistle, an apostle in the broad sense of the word (Gal 1:19?), but not one of the Twelve. (P. Gächter, *ZKT* 76 [1954] 126–69.)

There also seem to have been three men named Judas or Jude: (1) Judas Iscariot, one of the Twelve (→ 170 below); (2) Judas son of James of whom we know nothing; the translation found in some Bibles, "Judas brother of James," is a tendentious attempt to identify him with the next-mentioned Judas and is unwarranted by ordinary Gk grammar (Bl-Deb-F 162, 2); (3) Judas "brother" of Jesus and brother of the third James above (Jude 1:1), traditional author of an epistle, dubiously the third bishop of Jerusalem after James and Simon (his other brother? → History of Israel, 75:171), but not one of the Twelve.

169 Returning to the lists of the Twelve, we find a SIMON, called *zēlōtēs* in the Lucan lists and *kananaios* in Mk/Mt. The latter does not mean that he is from Cana or a Canaanite, but reflects Aram *qan'ānā'*, "zeal." It is interesting that Jesus' followers included a Zealot or member of the extreme nationalist, anti-Roman party that had supporters in Galilee (→ History of Israel, 75:155).

170 JUDAS ISCARIOT was son of Simon (Jn 12:4; interestingly, the best readings of 6:71 and 13:26 would seem to describe Simon as the Iscariot, thus: "Judas, son of Simon the Iscariot"). The surname of Judas appears as *Iskariōth*, *Iskariōtēs* (or as *Skariōth*, *Skariōtēs* in Western mss.) and *apo Karyōtou* (in some witnesses of the verses in Jn). The meaning is uncertain, but most take it to reflect Hebr *'îš Qᵉrîyôt*, i.e., a man from Kerioth, a town in southern Judea, an interpretation that would make Judas the only known non-Galilean member of the Twelve. Others interpret the name as reflecting *sicarius*, "dagger man," a Lat name for a member of a nationalist Jewish group related to the Zealots (→ History of Israel, 75:155). O. Cullmann (*RHPR* 42 [1962] 133–40) accepts this opinion and suggests that the troublesome "other" Judas of the Lucan lists of the Twelve was really Judas the Zealot and thus was the same as Judas Iscariot (even though different fathers are named—James and Simon respectively!).

171 The lists show a lack of agreement on the identity of one member of the Twelve, for in the 10th or 11th place three names appear: (1) LEBBAEUS in some important Western textual witnesses of Mt 10:3—"Lebbaeus" in Mk 3:18 has less support; (2) THADDAEUS in Mk 3:18 and in the better witnesses of Mt 10:3; (3) JUDAS (Jude) son—not brother—of James in the two Lucan lists. Origen maintained that these were three different names for the one man. Others think that Lebbaeus is Levi (→ 166 above). Jn 14:22 mentions among the followers of Jesus "a Judas not the Iscariot." The Coptic of this verse reads "Judas the Zealot"; the Syriac reads "Judas Thomas"—obviously attempts to identify this Judas with one of the Twelve in the lists, either with Simon the Zealot or with Thomas. It seems more probable that Thaddaeus, Lebbaeus, and Jude do not refer to the same person, but rather the difference of names means that by the time the Gospels were written the historical memory as to who among the disciples of Jesus belonged to the Twelve was already hazy.

172 **(B) Role of the Twelve.** According to Mk 3:14–15, Jesus chose the Twelve to be with him, to be sent out to preach, and to have authority over demons; Jn 20:19ff. describes Jesus as appearing to ten of the Twelve after the resurrection and sending them out; Acts 1:13 with 2:1 makes them recipients of the Pentecostal Spirit; Acts 6:2 shows them active in deciding questions of government in the Jerusalem church; Ap 21:14 makes the Twelve Apostles the foundations of the heavenly Jerusalem. Thus, the prima facie evidence of the NT (or of parts of the NT, at least) is that the Twelve, carefully selected by Jesus, became (with the exception of Judas Iscariot) his chief representatives in founding and ruling the Church. A critical examination of the evidence, however, shows that the picture was somewhat more complicated.

173 Early critics, like F. Schleiermacher and F. C. Baur, challenged the thesis that Jesus really chose twelve men and suggested that the concept of the Twelve came from the Church patterning itself on the twelve sons of Jacob and the twelve-tribe pattern of the OT. Recently Schmithals (*op. cit.*, 58ff.) has also claimed that the Twelve had no connection with the historical Jesus, for the claim of their having been chosen by Jesus was advanced only to substantiate their position as authoritative interpreters of the Jesus-tradition. Two questions are involved in considering such objections. First, were the men mentioned in the lists truly companions of the historical Jesus? Second, was the idea of *Twelve* part of Jesus' ministry? The first question must be answered affirmatively in regard to the better known men like Peter, James, and John. They are too much a part of the Gospel structure of the ministry for their names to have been added later without great protest in the primitive Church. Indeed, it seems most probable that all of the men mentioned in the lists were in fact companions of Jesus, for the very confusion over the lesser names in the lists (→ 171 above) indicates that by the time the lists were being copied the memory of these men was growing dim. As a teacher Jesus certainly attracted disciples, and it takes much imagination to propose that the names of all his original followers were forgotten and totally new names put in their place (Gerhardsson, *op. cit.*, 101–3).

The second question is more difficult: Granted that Jesus had companions whose names were preserved, did he separate exactly twelve very close friends or was the specification of *the Twelve* a later idea? We can present the evidence for Jesus' choice of the Twelve but cannot prove it definitively. Not only the Gospels attribute the institution of the Twelve to Jesus himself, for it is also implicit in the story about the choice of Matthias in Acts 1:15–26 (admittedly an intrusive passage, but taken seriously by P.-H. Menoud, *RHPR* 37 [1957] 71–80). In 1 Cor 15:5 Paul mentions that one of the first postresurrectional appearances was to the Twelve, so that seemingly he saw nothing anachronistic in supposing that the Twelve were in existence by the end of Jesus' life. We note that the Qumran community, steeped in eschatological expectation, had a council of twelve men (1QS 8:1; → Apocrypha, 68:97), so that the thought of patterning an elect community on the twelve-tribal system of Israel was already current in Jesus' time. The differences of names in the four lists of the Twelve probably means that the institution of the Twelve was not a recent development at the time of Gospel composition (AD 60–85); rather the Twelve had been more active in the early days of the Church, and now the identity of some had faded away beyond verification. The question of the career of the Twelve after the earthly ministry of Jesus leads us into the problem of the apostles.

174 **(II) The Apostles.** What constituted an apostle in NT times has been bitterly argued in the last 100 years since Lightfoot's 1st edition in 1865 of *Saint Paul's Epistle to the Galatians*—see Kredel, *art. cit.*

(A) Origin of the Term. In secular Gk *apostolos*, from *apostellein*, "to send," is not a frequent term. It refers to: a fleet or army sent on an expedition; the command of an expedition; a colonist sent to settle; a bill or invoice. These meanings are not helpful as the background of the NT concept. *Apostolos* occurs once in the LXX (1 Kgs 14:6) as a translation of the pass. ptc. *šālûaḥ* (root *šlḥ*, "send"), used of Ahijah as one sent by God with a message.

175 This LXX usage has led some to connect the origin of the NT apostolate with the rabbinic institution of the *sheluhim* or *sheluhin* (Hebr *šālûaḥ*, pl. *šᵉlûḥîm;* Aram *šalîaḥ*, pl. *šᵉlûḥîn:* "a commissioned emissary"). This thesis has been defended by Vogelstein and Rengstorf, with some important modifications by Gerhardsson in light of objections made by Klein and Schmithals. The legal institution of the *sheluhim* had taken on a distinctive character in the religious Jewish circles of the late 1st cent. AD, when the Palestinian authorities commissioned or sent out rabbis to represent them and act for them with full power. Those sent were often ordained by the laying on of hands. Sometimes their task was to conduct financial business and collect tithes or Temple taxes; other times it was to act with religious authority and to proclaim religious truths. While acting within their commission, the *sheluhim* had all the authority of the sender. One is reminded of Jn 20:21, "As the Father has sent me, so do I send you," and Lk 9:48, "Whoever receives me receives him who sent me." Jesus is the *shaluah* (*shaliah*) or apostle of the Father (Heb 3:1), and the apostles are his *sheluhim*. See also Jn 13:16; 2 Cor 8:23 for *apostolos* representing *shaluah*.

The analogy is even closer when we think that in the rabbinic writings OT figures like Moses, Elijah, and Ezekiel were thought of as the *sheluhim* of God, especially when they accomplished miraculous deeds. Therefore Schmithal's objection that the apostolate could not have come from the purely juridical institution of the *shaluah* is not valid, for there are *sheluhim* of God who did not have a juridical task. Although the prophets are rarely called *sheluhim*, the verb *šālaḥ* is used when they are said to be *sent* by God. We may note with Gerhardsson that the *shaluah* was not necessarily sent to another place. Thus, the objection that the Twelve could not have been *sheluhim* because they remained in Jerusalem is not valid.

176 The origin of the NT apostolate from the background of the Jewish *sheluhim* has not been accepted by all (Kredel, *art. cit.*, 284–89). Recently Klein has joined the ranks of the many who trace the apostolate to Paul's missionary experience and who regard the apostolate of the Twelve as a later intrusion on the original concept. Schmithals (*op. cit.*, 85–216) would trace the apostolate to Gnostic groups in Syria who thought of a redeemer sent from heaven and of men who were sent to bring the heavenly gnosis to other men. Such theories run up against the fact that Paul recognizes the existence of apostles from the time of the postresurrectional appearances (1 Cor 15:7) and speaks of "those who were apostles before me" (Gal 1:17—in Palestine, not in Syria). Paul never gives the slightest indication of creating the concept of apostolate or of borrowing it from gnostic groups; rather he struggles to have himself accepted as an apostle in face of a well-established ideal of an apostle that existed before his conversion. His argument in Gal 2:7–10 is that he is entitled to be thought of as an apostle, even as men like Peter are apostles (→ Pauline Theology, 79:12).

177 In summary, the Jewish concept of *shaluah* (*shaliah*) still seems the most plausible background for the NT apostolate, even though the latter has aspects not found in the former. The apostles were the *sheluhim* of Jesus, and the foundation of the apostolate is to be traced to Jesus' sending out witnesses of his resurrection to preach to men (Lk 24:47–48; Mt 28:19–20; Jn 20:21; Acts 1:8; Mk 16:15). The two major constituents in being "an apostle of Jesus Christ" (Paul *passim*) seem to have been: (1) a vision of the Risen Jesus—whence Paul's stress that he saw Jesus on the road to Damascus (1 Cor 9:1; 15:7–9); (2) a commission by Jesus to preach. Such an understanding of what constitutes apostleship shows the resemblance between the OT prophet and the NT apostle (implicit comparison in 2 Pt 3:2; Lk 11:49). The OT prophet began his career by being introduced in vision into the heavenly court before God, and then he was sent to preach God's will to the people. The same vision and sending constitute a NT apostle. In particular, Paul *the* apostle closely resembles Jeremiah the greatest of the prophets, even in his career as one who suffers for others (Rengstorf, *art. cit.*, 439–41). The importance of the apostle in the Church is seen in the first rank given to apostleship in 1 Cor 12:28; Eph 4:11.

178 **(B) Some Corollaries.**

(a) Apostle—A Postresurrectional Title. J. Dupont has argued persuasively that the disciples were not known as apostles during the ministry (*L'Orient Syrien* 1 [1956] 267–90, 425–44). Therefore, the lone reference to "apostles" in Mk 6:30 and Mt 10:2 is anachronistic, as is also Lk's more persistent use in five passages (6:13; 9:10; 17:5; 22:14; 24:10). Lk 11:49 is the only passage that puts "apostle" on the lips of Jesus during the ministry, and this passage refers to the future (cf. parallel in Mt 23:34). It is true that the Gospels present the Twelve as being *sent* out during the ministry (Mk 6:7; see 3:14), and in this mission they were to some extent Jesus' *sheluhim*. But the definitive sending that constitutes the Christian apostolate came after the resurrection. The analogy between the two missions may be what attracted the Evangelists to use the name "apostle" even during the ministry. In talmudic circles the disciples of the rabbis often became their *sheluhim*; so also the disciples of Jesus.

179 (b) Apostles Other Than the Twelve. As Lightfoot established over a century ago, "apostle" was originally a much wider term than "the Twelve." This is the implication in 1 Cor 15:5–7. The following are called apostles in the NT, yet were not members of the Twelve: James the "brother" of the Lord (Gal 1:19?); Paul (1 Cor 1:1; etc.); Barnabas (Acts 14:14?; 1 Cor 9:6 with 4:9; Gal 2:9); probably Andronicus and Junias (Rom 16:7—Chrysostom and others think Junias was a woman!). The very existence of false apostles (Ap 2:2; 2 Cor 11:13) suggests a wider use of "apostles." If "apostle" was used for the many who met the two conditions given above (→ 177), was the title even more broadly used for those who had not seen the Risen Jesus but who had joined themselves to the mission of those who had? This may be indicated if Andronicus and Junias are really called apostles in Rom 16:7, or if the "we...apostles" of 1 Thes 2:6 includes Sylvanus and Timothy (see Acts 17:4,14), or if 1 Cor 4:9 refers to the Apollos of 4:6. Cerfaux ("L'histoire," 191–94) argues for this wider extension, and certainly *Didache* 11:3–6 uses "apostle" in a very broad sense.

180 (c) The Twelve as Apostles. We hold to the thesis that the Twelve were members of the apostolate from the first postresurrectional days, a thesis denied by many (Harnack, Munck, Lohse, Klein, Schmithals). The Twelve were the first important group to see the Risen Jesus (1 Cor 15:5); indeed theirs was a place of honor for they had been witnesses of Jesus "from the baptism of John until the day when Jesus was taken up" (Acts 1:22). Therefore the Twelve had a special role in authenticating tradition about Jesus and in making decisions affecting the Christian community (implied in Gal 1:18–2:10; Acts 6:2–6; 15:2ff.). The Twelve played their predominant role in Jerusalem (Acts 8:1,14; 15:2), although it is to be noted that James, the head of the Jerusalem church, was *not* one of the Twelve—perhaps his relationship to Jesus gave him special importance. The Twelve were not replaceable; for once Judas Iscariot's place, vacated by desertion, had been filled by Matthias, elected by divine choice to keep the number at Twelve (Acts 1:26), the membership was set permanently. Thus, when James of Zebedee was martyred (Acts 12:2), there was no attempt to replace him. This is probably because the Twelve were understood as unique: They were the founders of the renewed Israel who would play an eschatological role seated on the twelve thrones of judgment (Mt 19:28).

In the primitive concept of the apostolate of the Twelve this eschatological function and that of taking Jesus' place until he would come seem to have predominated over the missionary aspect, and it was Paul who brought to the fore the missionary role of the *sheluhim*. Whether the Twelve did undertake a missionary apostolate is not clear from the NT, although it is probable that after the first two decades (*ca.* AD 50) some did scatter from Jerusalem. Only Peter (and perhaps John: Ap 1:9) is specifically pictured as traveling outside Palestine (1 Pt 1:1; Acts 12:17; perhaps 1 Cor 1:12). Whether through death or missionary travels afar, most of the individual members of the Twelve had faded from general Christian awareness by AD 60 and were seemingly but names in lists. Only the memories of Peter and John drew attention in the works of the last third of the century.

181 It was as a group that the Twelve retained importance in Christian thought even after the individual members were long dead. Thus Ap 21:14, one of the last NT works, pictures the Twelve as the essential foundations of the city of God. For theological purposes of Church constitution and order we should concentrate on the collegiate concept of the Twelve as a body (Cerfaux, "L'unité"). Most of the traditions connecting members of the Twelve with specific Christian churches are not too well founded precisely because the NT does not tell us whether the Twelve had a missionary role. Once again Peter is the exception, for archaeology and history do support the tradition that he went to Rome. However, to be honest, it must be admitted that the NT never shows Peter or any other member of the Twelve appointing a successor. Paul is reported to have appointed legates with an episcopal role (Pastorals), but he was an apostle in the broad sense. The bishops of the Pastorals are local administrators, not figures with an apostolic missionary role.

182 The continuing importance of the concept of the Twelve and the importance of the Twelve among the apostles led the later NT works to simplify the picture of the apostolate and to speak of "the Twelve Apostles" as if they were the only apostles. Klein has argued strongly that Luke was the prime mover in this direction. We have seen that unlike the other Gospels Lk insistently speaks of the Twelve during the ministry as apostles. Throughout Acts, with the exception of 14:4, "apostles" always refers to the Twelve; and even in 14:4 Codex Bezae has a reading that does not refer to Paul and Barnabas as apostles. Thus, there may be some truth in Klein's argument (*op. cit.*, 114–201) that Luke was deliberately refusing the title "apostle" to all others, including Paul—an argument to the contrary would be suggested by the emphasis that Luke places on Paul's missionary activity and the way in which the figure of Paul is assimilated in sermon and deed to that of Peter, one of the Twelve Apostles. The tendency to identify the Twelve as *the* apostles is also seen in Mt 10:2; Ap 21:14; and of course, this tendency grew in post-NT writings (*Ep. Barnabae* 8:3). As Klein (*op. cit.*, 65–113) has shown, however, the concept of a wider apostolate also survived (*Hermas*, Sim. 9.15, 4; Irenaeus, *Adv. haer.* 2.21, 1).

79

PAULINE THEOLOGY

Joseph A. Fitzmyer, S.J.

BIBLIOGRAPHY

1 Amiot, F., *The Key Concepts of St. Paul* (N.Y., 1962). Bonsirven, J., *L'évangile de Paul* (Paris, 1948); *Exégèse rabbinique et exégèse paulinienne* (Paris, 1929). Bornkamm, G., *Das Ende des Gesetzes: Paulinische Studien* (2nd ed.; Munich, 1958). Bover, J. M., *Teología de San Pablo* (Madrid, 1946). Bultmann, R., *TNT* 1, 185–352. Cerfaux, L., *Christ in the Theology of St. Paul* (N.Y., 1959); *The Church in the Theology of St. Paul* (N.Y., 1959); *The Christian in the Theology of St. Paul* (N.Y., 1968). Cullmann, O., *The Christology of the New Testament* (2nd ed.; Phila., 1963). Dodd, C. H., *The Meaning of Paul for Today* (London, 1920). Feine, P., *Die Theologie des Neuen Testaments* (8th ed.; Berlin, 1953) 145–308. Grossouw, W. K. M., *In Christ* (Westminster, Md., 1952). Klausner, J., *From Jesus to Paul* (London, 1944). Lohmeyer, E., *Grundlagen paulinischer Theologie* (Tübingen, 1929). Lyonnet, S., "Pauline Soteriology," R-F, *INT* 820–65; *De peccato et redemptione* (2 vols.; Rome, 1958–60). Munck, J., *Paul and the Salvation of Mankind* (London, 1959). Purdy, A. C., "Paul the Apostle," *IDB* 3, 681–704. Schoeps, H., *Paul* (London, 1961). Schweitzer, A., *The Mysticism of Paul the Apostle* (London, 1931); *Paul and His Interpreters* (N.Y., 1912). Tondelli, L., *Il pensiero di S. Paolo* (2nd ed.; Turin, 1948). Whiteley, D. E. H., *The Theology of St. Paul* (Oxford, 1964).

Ellis, E. E., *Paul and His Recent Interpreters* (Grand Rapids, 1961). Metzger, B. M., *IPLAP* 131–62. Rigaux, B., *The Letters of St. Paul* (Chicago, 1968). Schnackenburg, R., *Neutestamentliche Theologie* (Munich, 1963) 84–106.

2 OUTLINE

INTRODUCTION

AIMS, LIMITS, PROBLEMS

3 A sketch of Pauline theology must take into account the character of the Apostle's writings, which do not offer a systematic presentation of his thought. Most of what Paul wrote was composed *ad hoc*—for the handling of concrete situations by letter. In his letters Paul developed certain doctrinal topics and exhorted his churches to the practice of a more intense Christian life. Almost every extant letter exemplifies this twofold purpose. This dual purpose explains how he could mingle in them elements of revelation, fragments of the primitive kerygma, teachings of Christ, interpretations of the OT, a personal understanding of the Christ-event, and even his own private opinions. Therefore, any attempt to formulate Pauline "theology" must also try to reckon with the varied nuances of the Apostle's thought and expression.

Moreover, a presentation of "Pauline theology" is an admission that Paul's view of the Christian experience is but one among several theologies in the NT. It is imperative to respect Paul's theology and not to confuse it with John's, Luke's, or any other's. It must be studied in and for itself. This admonition is not meant to imply that a NT theology is impossible or that contradictions are to be expected between Paul and another NT writer. The NT books bear witness to a faith in one Lord, one baptism, one God and Father of all (Eph 4:5–6), and a theology explaining that one faith is not an impossibility. But its presentation will be the richer if the nuances of the individual NT writers are respected (→ Canonicity, 67:93–97).

4 A sketch of Pauline theology is a systematization of the Apostle's thought in a form in which he himself did not present it. If such a systematization forces his thought into categories foreign to it or attempts merely to line up *dicta probantia* for a theological system born of another inspiration, it has little value. The effort to synthesize Paul's thought must respect his categories as far as possible, with due allowance for the unequal degree of his affirmations and the diversity of the contexts in which he formulated it. The guiding principle of such a sketch, therefore, cannot be an extrinsic one, be it Aristotelian, Thomistic, Hegelian, or Heideggerian.

5 Though the primary aim of this sketch is a descriptive presentation of Paul's view of Christian faith, it also intends to be a normative theological presentation. It aims above all at determining what Paul meant when he wrote to the Christians whom he immediately addressed, but it also aims at ascertaining what his theology means for Christians of today. This sketch is not merely a study of Paul's thought as a historian of religion might pursue it (be he agnostic or believer); it does not attempt merely to determine what Paul taught, what influenced him, or how his teachings fit into the general history of Jewish, Hellenistic, or Christian ideas. Paul's theology is an exposition of the inspired biblical heritage of Christians, and the Word of God proposed in his exposé still has an existential meaning for the faith of men of today. In this way, Paul's theology is a *part* of normative biblical theology, just as biblical theology itself is only a part of normative theology as such. There are two poles in biblical theology, one descriptive, the other normative.

6 It is important to emphasize that the "meaning for the faith of men of today" cannot be something completely other than the meaning intended by Paul for his contemporaries. Any attempt to understand him that fails to recognize a radical homogeneity between his meaning "now" and "then" fails to bring *his* inspired message to men of today. A valid sketch of Pauline theology must, therefore, ascertain first of all what Paul meant and in this sense must be a descriptive presentation. The means to achieve this are not the logic or the metaphysics of some system of philosophy foreign to him, however legitimate and fruitful this mode of interpretation might be for other purposes. The means are rather those of philological, historical, and literary research, joined to an empathy of Christian faith. In other words, the one who sketches Paul's theology in a descriptive presentation shares with Paul the same faith and seeks through it to determine his meaning for today. Although the biblical theologian, in attempting to discover what Paul meant, employs the same tools of interpretation that the historian of religion—or, for that matter, the interpreter of any ancient document—uses, he differs in that he is convinced that through Paul "the one Lord... the one God and Father of us all" (Eph 4:5–6) is communicating an inspired message to him and to the men of his time. His fundamental presupposition is the inspired character of the Pauline corpus, a matter of *faith*. He seeks to sketch Paul's exposé and understanding of Christian faith in a way that is meaningful and relevant for Christians of a later age.

7 This empathy of Christian faith is sometimes expressed in terms of the "analogy of faith," a phrase derived ultimately from Paul himself (Rom 12:6). It cannot be used to insist that the totality of Christian faith has to be found in Paul or even that his thought *must* be interpreted according to the sense of later dogmatic progress, with all its precisions and specific nuances. If a seminal notion formulated by Paul has in time undergone further dogmatic development because of a polemical situation or a conciliar decision in the Church, then that seminal notion must be recognized as such. It may be that the seminal notion is expressed by Paul in a vague, "open" fashion; thus formulated, it could conceivably have developed in one way or another, as far as one can judge today with philological criteria. But the further dogmatic development has removed that *openness* of formulation, so far as Christian tradition is concerned. Yet this does not mean that the historian of dogma or the dogmatic theologian can insist that this later development is the precise meaning of the text of Paul. Neither kind of scholar enjoys a charism whereby he can read more in an "open" Pauline text than can the exegete or the biblical theologian. To understand the "analogy of faith" in such a way as to read back into Paul a later meaning would be false to him and to the inspired autonomy of his conception and formulation. Rather, that analogy must be understood in terms of the total Pauline biblical faith. Obviously, the biblical theologian is not content merely with the interpretation of individual passages in their immediate context (i.e., with exegesis). He seeks the expression of the total Pauline message, which transcends the contextual situation and embraces also the relational meaning of Pauline utterances.

Though normative biblical theology is only a part of the larger complex of Christian theology, it does enjoy its own autonomy of formulation and conception. True, it is only inceptive. But it is also privileged, for it attempts to formulate systematically what the witnesses of the early Christian tradition were inspired to set down in their own way. It deals immediately and exclusively with the form of Christian tradition that alone enjoys the distinctive divine charism of inspiration that guarantees it. It goes without saying that for a Christian the guidance of the Spirit has guarded the authentic dogmatic developments of later times from a contradiction of the seminal formulations and conceptions. But such protection does not mean that the full flower is already present in the seed—hence the need to respect Pauline theology for what it is (→ Hermeneutics, 71:85–86).

8 This sketch of Pauline theology reckons with ten letters in the Pauline corpus. The theology of Heb is a problem apart and should not be treated with Paul's theology (→ Epistle Heb, 61:2–3). Likewise, the material in Acts bearing on Paul's teaching can be used only for comparative purposes because of the Lucan cast given to it. The "Pastoral Letters" create another problem because of the present debate about their authenticity. We have followed the lead of several modern Catholic writers in omitting data from them in such a sketch, except for the purpose of comparison at certain points (references to them are bracketed). For the rest, we divide Paul's letters into three chronological groups: *Early Letters:* 1–2 Thes (AD 50–51); *Great Letters:* Gal, Phil, 1–2 Cor, Rom (AD 54–58); *Captivity Letters:* Phlm, Col, Eph (AD 61–63).

9 We admit a certain development in Paul's theology from one group of letters to another—a development, however, that is influenced by many factors. Perhaps the development is best seen in terms of emphasis, but one can also distinguish a certain growth in his understanding of the Christ-event as one moves from group to group. For instance, in the Early Letters there is only an extrinsic connection between the glorious resurrection of the Christian and Christ's resurrection (1 Thes 4:14: Through Jesus, God will lead those who have died with him). It is set forth in an apocalyptic description of the *eschaton*, reflecting the primitive eschatology of the early Church. In the Great Letters the emphasis shifts to an intimate connection between the passion, death, and resurrection of Christ and man's salvation. Through the passion, death, and resurrection Christ has become a "power" (*dynamis*) producing a new life in the Christian believer, which eventually ensures his resurrection and life "with Christ." There is also his view of this new life as the "justification" of man, a juridical aspect that emerges from the Judaizing controversy in the early Church. There is, further, the shift in Paul's views of death and the destiny of the Christian (2 Cor 5:16–21). Finally, in the Captivity Letters Paul arrives at a fuller view of the Risen Christ as the one who gives man's history a fullness and cosmic dimension that it was not earlier suspected to have. To this cosmic view of Christ not only the universe but the Church itself is related.

(Allo, E.-B., "L'évolution de l'évangile de Paul," *VP* 1 [1941] 48–77, 165–93. Ebeling, G., "The Meaning of 'Biblical Theology,'" *JTS* 6 [1955] 210–25. Lester-Garland, L. V., "The Sequence of Thought in the Pauline Epistles," *Theology*, 33 [1936] 228–38. Lowe, J., "An Examination of Attempts to Detect Developments in St. Paul's Theology," *JTS* 42 [1941] 129–42. Richardson, A., "Historical Theology and Biblical Theology," *CanJT* 1 [1955] 157–67. Schnackenburg, R., *Neutestamentliche Theologie*, 11–14; *New Testament Theology Today* [N.Y., 1962] 15–23. Spicq, C., "L'avènement de la théologie biblique," *RSPT* 35 [1951] 561–74. Stendahl, K., "Biblical Theology, Contemporary," *IDB* 1, 418–32.)

PAUL'S BACKGROUND

Five factors that influenced Paul's theology can be considered; not all of them are of equal importance.

10 (I) Pharisaic, Rabbinical Background. The polemical passages in which Paul so resolutely rejects the Law should not be allowed to obscure the fact that even the Christian Paul looked back with pride on his life as a Jew of the Pharisaic tradition, trained in Jerusalem (Phil 3:5–6; Gal 1:14; 2 Cor 11:22). This strong Jewish background accounts for the fact that he thinks and expresses himself in OT categories and images. It also accounts for his abundant use of the OT (which he cites some 90 times explicitly). Though his use of the OT is often similar to that of the Qumran writings and of early rabbinical compositions, he usually quotes it according to the LXX. At times, like the rabbis, he accommodates or gives new meaning to OT passages (Hab 2:4 in Rom 1:17 or Gal 3:11; Gn 12:7 in Gal 3:16; Ex 34:34 in 2 Cor 3:17) or allegorizes them (Gn 16:15; 17:16 in Gal 4:21ff.) or wrests them from their original context (Dt 25:4 in 1 Cor 9:9) or utterly disregards their literal meaning (Ps 68:19 in Eph 4:8). Paul's use of the OT does not conform to our modern ideas of quoting Scripture. His mode of interpreting it may seem cavalier, but it does agree with the contemporary Jewish way of interpreting the OT and must be accepted as such. That he was inspired by the Spirit to interpret it in this fashion does not mean that his interpretation always reveals a hidden, deeper (literal) sense otherwise unsuspected. His rabbinical training permitted him to accommodate the text at times, too. Again, it is his Jewish background that makes him quote the OT to stress the unity of God's action in both dispensations, for he often cites the OT as announcing the Christian gospel (Rom 1:2) or as preparing for Christ (Gal 3:24). Even if he contrasts the "letter [or the Law] and the Spirit" (Rom 2:29,27; 7:6–7; 2 Cor 3:6–7), the OT is still for him a means through which God speaks to men (1 Cor 9:10; 2 Cor 6:16,17; cf. Rom 4:23). Most of his theology (in the narrow sense, teaching about God) and his anthropology (teaching about man) clearly reveals his Jewish background.

(Bonsirven, J., *Exégèse rabbinique et exégèse paulinienne* [Paris, 1939]. Davies, W. D., *Paul and Rabbinic Judaism* [2nd ed.; London, 1958]. Ellis, E. E., *Paul's Use of the OT* [Edinburgh, 1957]. Fitzmyer, J. A., "The Use of Explicit OT Quotations in Qumran Literature and in the NT," *NTS* 7 [1960–61] 297–333. Marmorstein, A., "Paulus und die Rabbinen," *ZNW* 30 [1931] 271–85. Michel, O., *Paulus und seine Bibel* [Gütersloh, 1929]. Thackeray, H. S. J., *The Relation of St. Paul to Contemporary Jewish Thought* [London, 1900]. Windisch, H., *Paulus und das Judentum* [Stuttgart, 1935].)

11 (II) Hellenism. If the thesis of W. C. van Unnik is accepted, then Paul, though born in Tarsus, was brought up in Jerusalem and there educated at the feet of Gamaliel in the traditions of the Fathers (see Acts 22:3 [NEB]; cf. 26:4–5; 23:6; Phil 3:5; *Tarsus or Jerusalem: The City of Paul's Youth* [London, 1962]). This reconstruction of Paul's youth would entail a reassessment of the influence of Hellenistic culture on his theology. It would mean that Aramaic was the language in which he was brought up and that Greek was learned as a second tongue. This would at least explain why his Greek is not the literary Koine and why it manifests Aramaisms at times (see W. C. van Unnik, *Vox theologica* 14 [1943] 117–26).

However, there is evidence of the influence of the Gk world in his style and also in his use of the LXX. Paul knew Greek and had some sort of Gk training. If he did not become a professional *rhetor*, his mode of expression reveals, at least at times, the influence of Gk rhetoric. There are traces of the Cynic-Stoic mode of argumentation called *diatribē*, a discourse conducted in a familiar, conversational style, which developed often by lively argument with a fictitious opponent; its sentence structure is brief, and questions are interjected; antitheses and parallel phrases often punctuate the development. Good examples are found in Rom 2:1–20 and 1 Cor 9. Many of Paul's literary antitheses have also been traced to Gk influence (see J. Nélis, *NRT* 70 [1948] 360–87). It was once fashionable to trace to Paul's Hellenistic background such terms as "Lord," "Son of God," "body," "flesh and spirit," and "mystery" and to ascribe to Hellenistic Gnosticism his use of "Adam" and "Man," the redeemer myth, pre-existence, instrumentality in creation, etc. However, many of these notions have been shown in recent times to have been at home in 1st-cent. Palestinian Judaism, which was not entirely isolated from the Hellenistic world. The whole question of the influence of Gk culture on Paul's thought and theology needs reassessment today. Paul lived for roughly ten years in a Hellenistic atmosphere, after his conversion and before his first mission, in such cultural centers as Damascus, Tarsus, and Antioch. This Gk atmosphere cannot be lightly dismissed. Its influence is seen in the figures and illustrations he uses. Whereas Jesus' illustrations reflect the agrarian life of Galilee, Paul frequently uses images that are derived from a city-culture, especially a Hellenistic one. He uses Gk political terminology (Phil 1:27; 3:20; Eph 2:19); alludes to Gk games (Phil 2:16; 3:14; 1 Cor 9:24–27; 2 Cor 4:8–9); employs Gk commercial terms (Phlm 18; Col 2:14) and legal terminology (Gal 3:15; 4:1–2; Rom 7:1–3); and refers to Hellenistic slave trade (1 Cor 7:22; Rom 7:14) and the Hellenistic celebration in honor of the emperor (1 Thes 2:19). (See F. W. Beare, *CanJT* 5 [1959] 84–85.)

(Bultmann, R., "Paulus und der Hellenismus," *TLZ* 72 [1947] 77–80. Jeremias, J., "The Key to Pauline Theology," *ExpT* 76 [1964–65] 27–30. Klausner, J., *From Jesus to Paul* [London, 1946] 450–66. Knox, W. L., *St. Paul and the Church of the Gentiles* [Cambridge, 1939]; *Some Hellenistic Elements in Primitive Christianity* [London, 1944]. Pohlenz, M., "Paulus und die Stoa," *ZNW* 42 [1949] 69–104. Rigaux, B., *Saint Paul et ses lettres*, 35–43.)

12 **(III) The Revelation to Paul.** Paul's theology was influenced most of all by his experience on the road to Damascus and by faith in the Risen Christ as the Son of God which developed from his experience. New Testament scholars are today less prone than those of former generations to look on that experience as a "conversion" to be psychologically explained in terms of Paul's Jewish background or in terms of Rom 7 (understood as a biographical account). Paul himself speaks of that experience as a revelation of the Son accorded him by the Father (Gal 1:16). In it he "saw Jesus the Lord" (1 Cor 9:1; cf. 1 Cor 15:8; 2 Cor 4:6; Acts 9:5). That revelation of the crucified "Lord of glory" (1 Cor 2:8) was the event that not only turned Paul the Pharisee into an apostle but also made him the first Christian theologian. The only difference between that experience, in which Jesus appeared to him (1 Cor 15:8), and the experience of the official witnesses of the resurrection (Acts 1:22) was that his vision was post-Pentecostal. It put him on an equal footing with the Twelve who had seen the *Kyrios*. He later spoke of that experience as one in which he had been "seized" by Christ Jesus (Phil 3:12) and in which a "necessity" had been laid on him to preach the gospel (1 Cor 9:15–18). He compared that experience to God's creation of light: "For it is the God who said, 'Let light shine out of darkness,' who has shone in our hearts to give the light of the knowledge of the glory of God in the face of Christ" (2 Cor 4:6). The compulsion of divine grace pressed him into the service of Christ; he could not kick against the pricks of such a goad (Acts 26:14). His response was one of vivid faith, in which he confessed with the early Church that "Jesus is the Lord" (1 Cor 12:12; cf. Rom 10:9; Phil 2:11). But that experience illumined in a creative act Paul's mind and gave him an extraordinary insight into what he later called "the mystery of Christ" (Eph 3:4).

13 That "revelation" (Gal 1:16) impressed Paul, *first* of all, with the unity of divine action for the salvation of all men, which is manifest in both the Old and New Dispensations. As a result of that encounter with the Risen Christ, Paul did not become a Marcionite, rejecting the OT. The Father who revealed his Son to Paul was the same God whom Paul the Pharisee had always served. He was the creator, the lord of history, the God who continually saved his people Israel, and who proved to be a faithful lord of the covenant despite Israel's infidelities. Probably because he had been a Pharisee preoccupied with the minutiae of the Law, Paul never manifested a profound understanding of that "covenant." And yet his experience on the road to Damascus did not alter his fundamental commitment to the "one God." Indeed, his theology (in the narrow sense of the word), his cosmology and his anthropology reveal him still to be a Jew in his basic outlook.

Second, that vision taught him the soteriological value of the death and resurrection of Jesus the Messiah. If his basic theology did not change, his Christology did. As a Jew, Paul had shared the messianic expectations of his time; he looked forward to the coming of a messiah (of some sort). But the vision of Jesus taught him that God's Anointed One had already come, that he was "Jesus who was handed over for our offenses and raised up for our justification" (Rom 4:25). Before his experience on the road to Damascus, Paul certainly knew that Jesus of Nazareth had been crucified, had been "hung on a tree," and hence had been "cursed" in the sense of Dt 21:23. This was undoubtedly one of the reasons why he as a Pharisee could not accept Jesus as the Messiah. He was for Paul "a stumbling block" (1 Cor 1:23), one "cursed" by the very Law which he so zealously observed (Gal 3:13; cf. 1:14; Phil 3:5–6). But the revelation near Damascus impressed him emphatically with the soteriological and vicarious value of the death of Jesus of Nazareth in a way that he never suspected before. With a logic that only a rabbi could appreciate, Paul saw Christ Jesus taking upon himself the Law's curse and transforming it into its opposite, so that he became the means of freeing men from its malediction. The cross, which had been the stumbling block to the Jews, became for him the "power and wisdom of God" (1 Cor 1:18–25). Henceforth, he would understand the crucified "Lord of glory" as his exalted Messiah.

Third, that revelation impressed Paul with a new vision of salvation history. Before the encounter with Jesus the Lord, Paul saw man's history divided into three great phases: (1) from Adam to Moses (the period without the Law); (2) from Moses to the Messiah (the period of the Law); (3) the Messianic age (the period when the Messiah would legislate anew). But the experience on the road to Damascus taught him that the Messianic age had already begun. This introduced a new perspective into his view of salvation history. The *eschaton*, so avidly awaited before, had already begun—although a definitive stage was still to be realized (hopefully not too far in the future). The Messiah had not yet come in glory. Paul realized then that he (with all Christians) found himself in a double situation: one in which he looked back to the death and resurrection of Jesus as the inauguration of the new age, and another in which he still looked forward to his coming in glory, his parousia (→ Aspects NT Thought, 78:73–92).

14 Far more than his Pharisaic background, therefore, or even his Hellenistic cultural roots, that revelation of Jesus gave Paul an ineffable insight into "the mystery of Christ." It enabled him to fashion his "gospel," to preach the fundamental good news in a form that was distinctively his own.

However, Paul did not immediately understand all the implications of the vision accorded to him. It provided only a basic insight, which was to color all that he was to learn about Jesus and his mission among men, not only from the early Church's tradition, but also from his own apostolic experience in preaching "Christ crucified" (Gal 3:1; → 15–21 below).

(Menoud, P.-H., "Revelation and Tradition: The Influence of Paul's Conversion on His Theology," *Interpr* 7 [1953] 131–41; also *VerbC* 7 [1953] 2–10. Munck, J., "The Call," *Paul and the Salvation of Mankind* [London, 1959] 11–35. Pfaff, E., *Die Bekehrung des h. Paulus* [Rome, 1942]. Rigaux, B., *Saint Paul et ses lettres*, 63–97. Wood, H. G., "The Conversion of St. Paul," *NTS* 1 [1955–56] 276–82.)

15 **(IV) Paul and Early Tradition.** If the main inspiration of Paul's theology was the revelation granted to him on the road to Damascus, that event was not the only source of his knowledge about Christ and the Christian movement. He was not the founder of that movement, but joined it after its missionary efforts had already begun. It is a priori likely, then, that Paul inherited from the pioneer tradition of the Church at least some ideas about Christ. At first, this observation might seem to contradict what he himself says in Gal about the origin of his gospel, that he was not taught it and that it came to him rather through a revelation of Jesus Christ (1:11,15–17; 2:6). Yet here especially we must be sensitive to the nuances of Paul's expression and affirmation, realizing that the passages in Gal were written in the heat of controversy. Paul had been under attack, accused of not being a real apostle and of preaching only a watered-down version of the gospel because of his attitude toward the Law. When he wrote Gal, Paul was at pains, therefore, to emphasize his divine, direct, and undelegated apostolic commission and the heavenly origin of his gospel (→ Aspects NT Thought, 78:177).

Yet this emphasis must not be allowed to obscure what is found elsewhere in his letters. For there are, in fact, clear indications of his dependence on the apostolic tradition of the early Church—on its kerygma, its liturgy, its hymns, its confessional formulas, its theological terminology, and its paraenesis. Fragments of the primitive kerygma are found in Paul's letters (1 Thes 1:10; Gal 1:3–4; 1 Cor 15:2–7; Rom 1:2–4; 2:16; 8:34; 10:8–9). He has incorporated elements of its liturgy, e.g., the Eucharistic formula (of Antiochene origin? 1 Cor 11:23–25); prayers like "Amen" (1 Thes 3:13; Gal 6:18; cf. 1 Cor 14:16; 2 Cor 1:20), "Maranatha" (1 Cor 16:22), "Abba, Father" (Gal 4:6; Rom 8:15); doxologies (Gal 1:5; Phil 4:20; Rom 11:36; 16:27?; Eph 3:21); and hymns (Phil 2:6–11; Col 1:15–20; Eph 5:14 [cf. 1 Tm 3:16]). His confessional formulas, too, undoubtedly echo early Church usage: "Jesus is the Lord" (1 Cor 12:13; Rom 10:9), "Jesus is the Christ" (1 Cor 3:11). He inherited as well a number of theological terms, e.g., the title *Kyrios*, "Son of God"; the word "apostle"; the expression *baptizō eis*, "church of God," etc. Finally, certain hortatory sections of his letters suggest by the terminology employed that Paul is incorporating paraenetic or catechetical material drawn from common usage (1 Thes 4:1–12; 1 Cor 6:9–10; Gal 5:19–21; Eph 5:5–21).

16 Moreover, there are times when Paul explicitly calls attention to the fact that he is "handing down" (*paradidōmi*) what he has "received" (*paralambanō*). (See 1 Cor 11:2,23; 15:1,3; cf. 1 Thes 2:13; 2 Thes 2:15; 3:6; Gal 1:9,12; Phil 4:9; Rom 6:17.) He uses the technical vocabulary of tradition, paralleled in the rabbinical schools (*māsar lᵉ*, "pass on to"; *qibbēl min*, "receive from"). He appeals further to the customs of the churches (1 Cor 11:16) and recommends fidelity to tradition (1 Cor 11:2; 15:2; 2 Thes 2:15.) It has been stated by O. Cullmann (*RHPR* 30 [1950] 12–13) that it is surprising to see Paul applying such discredited notions to the normative moral and doctrinal precepts of the primitive community, when one recalls how radically Jesus rejected precisely the *paradosis* of the Jews (cf. Mk 7:3ff.; Mt 15:2). Obviously, there was something here that Paul did not feel that he could dispense with.

17 Another aspect of Paul's dependence on early Church tradition is seen in his acquaintance with what Jesus did and taught. Paul gives no evidence of having known Jesus personally in his earthly ministry (not even 2 Cor 5:16 necessarily implies that he did). Nor should it be imagined that Paul was granted a cinematic view of that ministry at his conversion. It is remarkable how little he knew of Jesus the Galilean rabbi or even of what is recorded in the Gospels about him. One reason for this is the early date of Paul's letters—almost all of them were written before the Gospels took the form we know. But an even more important reason is the emphasis that Paul, not having been an eyewitness, puts on the salvific effects of the passion, death, and resurrection of Jesus, which transcend the mere historical data. His interest lies in these climactic events of Jesus' life rather than in minutiae about Jesus' manner of life, his ministry, his personality, or even his message. True, he may allude to, or quote a saying of, Jesus occasionally (1 Thes 4:2,15; 1 Cor 7:10 [cf. 25]; 9:14; 13:2; Rom 12:14; 13:9; 16:19; cf. D. M. Stanley, *CBQ* 23 [1961] 26–39; W. D. Davies, *Paul and Rabbinic Judaism*, 136–41), and such quotations reveal that sayings of Jesus were already being handed on in addition to the kerygma. Yet these sayings are often referred to by Paul as sayings of "the Lord" (*Kyrios*), a title that immediately reveals the transcendent aspect under which Paul saw them. He is not interested in the historical Jesus as a teacher, a prophet, or as the chronological source and the first link in the chain of such transmission. Rather, Paul is interested in the exalted Lord who is the real agent of all the tradition developing in the bosom of the apostolic Church. This is why he identifies with the *Kyrios* what he has in reality derived from the early community. The *Kyrios* himself is at work in that transmission and as such is the "end of the Law" and the replacement of the *paradosis* of the Jews. Indeed, the *Kyrios* himself is even said to be received by the *paradosis* of the early Church (Col 2:6).

18 Paul alludes to remarkably few details of the life of Christ: Jesus was born of a woman under the Law (Gal 4:4), was betrayed (1 Cor 11:23), instituted the Eucharist (1 Cor 11:23), was crucified (Gal 2:20; 3:1; Phil 2:5; 1 Cor 2:2,8), died (1 Cor 15:3), was buried

(1 Cor 15:4), was raised from the dead (1 Cor 15:5), and ascended to heaven (Eph 4:9). (1 Tm 6:13 alludes to his testimony before Pilate.) Yet even these few events are not narrated for their own sake or in the manner of the Evangelists; they are, instead, recorded in contexts of a peculiarly theological or kerygmatic character. Possibly, Paul learned this outline of Jesus' last days from the early Church, but probably some of the details were already known to him before his conversion.

19 Such features as these in Paul's letters suggest that he did derive information from the traditions of the early churches (Jerusalem, Damascus, Antioch). Even his visit to Jerusalem, when he spent 15 days with Cephas (Gal 1:18), would support this. But such information was always transformed by Paul's personal vision and insight.

(Baird, W., "What Is the Kerygma?" *JBL* 76 [1957] 181–91. Cullmann, O., *The Earliest Christian Confessions* [London, 1949]; "Paradosis et Kyrios: Le problème de la tradition dans le Paulinisme," *RHPR* 30 [1951] 12–30; *ScotJT* 3 [1950] 180–97. Dodd, C. H., *The Apostolic Preaching and Its Developments* [London, 1962]. Gerhardsson, B., *Memory and Manuscript* [ASNU 22; Lund, 1961] 288–323. Goguel, M., "De Jésus à l'apôtre Paul," *RHPR* 28–29 [1948–49] 1–29. Hunter, A. M., *Paul and His Predecessors* [Phila., 1961] 15–57. Rigaux, B., "Le vocabulaire chrétien antérieur à la Première Epître aux Thessaloniciens," *SP* [Gembloux, 1954] 2, 380–89.)

20 **(V) Paul's Apostolic Experience.** Another factor in the development of Paul's theology was his experience as an apostle and missionary proclaiming the gospel and founding churches throughout Asia Minor and Europe. It is hard to say precisely how much his practical experience and concrete contacts with Jews and Gentiles molded his view of Christianity. But it would be wrong not at least to raise the question. Would he have written as he did on justification or on the relation of the Gospel to the Law if it were not for the Judaizing problem he encountered? The real meaning of the universal scope of Christian salvation probably dawned on him as he worked continually with Jews who failed to accept his message and with Gentiles who did heed him. From his earliest letters he reveals an awareness of the privileged position of his fellow Jews in the divine plan of salvation (see 1 Thes 2:14; cf. Rom 1:16; 2:9–10; Eph 2:13–22; 3:6). But it is only in the Captivity Letters that Paul formulates the status of Jews and Gentiles with respect to the Church and with respect to their joint relation to Christ, who is now the *kosmokratōr* (to use for Christ an apt, but non-Pauline title). Such aspects of the "inexhaustible wealth of the mystery of Christ" (Eph 3:8) emerged in Paul's consciousness only as a result of intense missionary activity in the last decade of his life. The problems, too, that he encountered in founding and governing individual local churches were almost certainly responsible for his gradual awareness of what *the* Church meant (in a universal, transcendent sense). To his apostolic experience must also be attributed a number of references to the Hellenistic world, which are met in various developments of his teaching (cf. 1 Cor 8:5; 10:20–21; 12:2; Gal 4:9–10; Col 2:18–19).

(Campbell, T. H., "Paul's 'Missionary Journeys' as Reflected in His Letters," *JBL* 74 [1955] 80–92. Maier, F. W., *Paulus als Kirchengründer und kirchlicher Organisator* [Würzburg, 1961].)

21 Whatever Paul inherited from his Jewish background, from his contacts with Hellenism, and whatever he later derived from the tradition of the early Church and his own missionary experience was all uniquely transformed by his insight into the mystery of Christ that he acquired on the road to Damascus. Other NT writers could claim a Jewish background and Hellenistic contacts, but none of them can approach Paul's profound understanding of the Christ-event, except possibly John.

DOMINANT PERSPECTIVES

PAULINE SOTERIOLOGY

22 The key concept about which the whole of Pauline theology must be organized is Christ. Paul's theology is Christocentric. True, it is a soteriology, but his captivation with Christ makes it clear that it is a Christocentric soteriology. This may seem like a platitude, but it needs to be stressed today. Paul explicitly formulated his own message in a very similar way: "It pleased God to save those who would believe through the folly of the gospel message [*kerygma*]. For while Jews demand signs and Greeks look for philosophy, we proclaim a Christ who has been crucified, a stumbling block to Jews and an absurdity to Gentiles. But to those who have been called, whether Jews or Greeks, he is a Christ who is God's power and God's wisdom" (1 Cor 1:21–25, cf. Rom 1:16; 2 Cor 4:4). This "story of the cross" (1 Cor 1:18) emphasizes the centrality of Christ in Paul's gospel. Any attempt, therefore, to seek an organizing principle for his theology apart from Christ is bound to be inadequate.

23 This point is stressed because the otherwise excellent and justly praised exposé of Pauline theology written by R. Bultmann (*TNT* 1, 185–352) has adopted a different principle. Bultmann explains Paul's theology as an anthropology, a doctrine about man.

His exposé has two main parts: Man Prior to the Revelation of Faith, and Man Under Faith. In the *first* part (Man Prior to Faith) he discusses Paul's anthropological concepts: *sōma* (body), *psychē* (soul), *pneuma* (spirit), *zōē* (life), mind and conscience, and heart. A second section of this part is devoted to "flesh, sin, and world," which includes discussions of creation and man, *sarx* (flesh), flesh and sin, sin and death, the universality of sin, *kosmos* (world), and the law. In the *second* part (Man Under Faith) his exposé takes up the righteousness of God (the concept of righteousness; righteousness as a present reality; righteousness as God's righteousness; reconciliation), grace (grace as event; Christ's death and resurrection as salvation occurrence; the Word; the Church; the Sacraments), faith (its structure; life in faith; faith as eschatological occurrence), and freedom (freedom from sin and walking in the Spirit; freedom from the Law and the Christian's attitude toward men; freedom from death). These headings and subdivisions indicate Bultmann's sustained attempt to present the Pauline material in genuine biblical categories.

24 But such an approach is too exclusively a development of Paul's ideas in Rom, to which all else is made subservient. It reduces Paul's theology to an anthropology, whereas this is only a part of it, and not even the major part at that. In Paul's view man can be understood only in terms of the Christ-event (see Rom 7:24–8:2). In Bultmann's presentation Christ's role is minimized—not only his role in the life of individual men (since the salvific events of the first Good Friday and Easter Sunday have been demythologized to the point of being also dehistoricized)—but also his role in the corporate and cosmological dimensions of salvation history (e.g., in Rom 9–11, which Bultmann tends to neglect). This minimizing of the role of Christ stems from a refusal to admit an "objective phase" in man's redemption and a concern to recast Paul's theology in phenomenological terms. Granted that a certain amount of demythologizing of the NT has to be admitted today, nevertheless an exposé of Paul's theology has to reckon with the fact that he did look upon the Christ-event as the key to man's history.

(Dahl, N. A., "Die Theologie des Neuen Testaments," *TRu* 22 [1954] 21–49, esp. 38–45. Fuller, R. H., *The New Testament in Current Study* [N.Y., 1962] 54–63. Käsemann, E., "Neutestamentliche Fragen von heute," *ZThK* 54 [1957] 12–15. Marlé, R., *Bultmann et l'interprétation du Nouveau Testament* [Paris, 1956].)

25 If Paul's theology is predominantly a Christology, it is also important to insist on its functional character (→ Aspects NT Thought, 78:61). Paul was not concerned about the intrinsic constitution of Christ *in se*; he preached "Christ crucified"—Christ as significant for man. "You are God's children through your union with Christ Jesus who became for us wisdom from God—our uprightness, our sanctification, our redemption" (1 Cor 1:30). This "Christ crucified," though described in figures derived from contemporary Jewish or Hellenistic backgrounds and even embellished with myth, still has relevance for men of the 20th cent. To understand Paul's thought one does not simply demythologize his description; rather the remythologization of the 20th-cent. mind is needed in order that men might see what Paul meant and thereby understand what he means for them today. Or, to put it another way, what is needed is not subtractive, but interpretative, demythologization.

26 In our attempt to give a genetic development to an exposé of Paul's theology, we shall begin with the word that he himself used to describe his message about Christ, his "gospel." From such a starting point we can move on to various aspects of the content of his message.

27 **(I) Paul's Gospel.** *Euaggelion* as "the good news of Jesus Christ" is a specifically Christian meaning of the word and as such is almost certainly developed by Paul within the early Christian community (see W. Marxsen, *Der Evangelist Markus* [FRLANT 67; Göttingen, 1959] 83–92; but cf. E. Molland, *Das paulinische Euangelion: Das Wort und die Sache* [Oslo, 1934] 37). Paul uses it more frequently than does any other NT writer; it occurs 54 times in his letters (+ six times in the Pastorals). In general, it designates his own personal presentation of the Christ-event.

Paul did not mean by his gospel anything that resembles the Lucan Gospel. Eusebius thought that when Paul said "my [our] gospel," he meant what Luke had compiled from his preaching (*HE* 3.4,7 [GCS 9/1.194]). This Eusebian interpretation was derived from earlier patristic descriptions of Luke's Gospel as a digest of Paul's preaching (Irenaeus, *Adv. haer.* 3.1,1; Tertullian, *Adv. Marc.* 4.5 [CSEL 47, 431]; Origen in Eusebius, *HE* 6.25–6 [GCS 9/2.576]). But such a view of the Third Gospel is an oversimplified interpretation of Paul's expression, "my gospel"; it is the result of a facile extrapolation of the relationship between Mark and Peter. Because Luke was a companion of Paul (Col 4:14), he was believed to have been to Paul what Mark was believed to have been to Peter—a compiler of his preaching. (See T. E. Bleiben, *JTS* 45 [1944] 134–40.)

28 The rejection of such an interpretation of Paul's gospel, however, does not imply that when he speaks of "my gospel" (Rom 2:16; 16:25 [2 Tm 2:8]; cf. Gal 1:8,11; 2:2) or "our gospel" (1 Thes 1:5; 2 Thes 2:14; 2 Cor 4:3; cf. 1 Cor 15:1) he is announcing a gospel wholly peculiar to himself and different from those of the other apostles. He knows of only one gospel (Gal 1:6) and calls down a curse on anyone who would try to proclaim a different one (Gal 1:8). But his gospel was not proclaimed in the form of stories about what Jesus said and did. For him, Jesus Christ is the gospel.

Paul speaks of "my gospel" because he was conscious of the special grace of the apostolate, which was accorded him to preach the good news of Christ. Like the prophets of old (Jer 1:5; Is 49:1) he considered himself destined by God from his mother's womb for this task (Gal 1:15; Rom 1:1; 1 Cor 1:17) and "entrusted" with the gospel as with some prized possession (1 Thes 2:4; Gal 2:7). He became its "servant" (*diakonos*, Col 1:23; cf. Eph 3:7) and felt a "compulsion" (*anagkē*, 1 Cor 9:16) to proclaim it. He looked on his preaching of it as a cultic, priestly act offered to God (*leitourgos, hierourgōn*, Rom 1:9; 15:16). He was never ashamed of it (Rom 1:16); rather, even imprisonment because of it was for him a "favor" (*charis*, Phil 1:7,16). (In 2 Tm 1:10 he is described as its "herald, apostle, and teacher.")

29 Though Paul sometimes used the word *euaggelion* to designate the activity of evangelization (Phil 4:3,15; 1 Cor 9:14b,18b; 2 Cor 2:12; 8:18), normally it denotes the *content* of his message—what he preaches, proclaims, announces, talks about, or teaches. These are the verbs he uses with it (see E. Molland, *op. cit.*, 11–12, 41–42). Strikingly, the content is never simply the "kingdom of God," as in Mt. His succinct expression of its content is "the gospel of Christ" (1 Thes 3:2; Gal 1:7; Phil 1:27; etc.), "the gospel of our Lord Jesus" (2 Thes 1:8), or "the gospel of his Son" (Rom 1:9). But even in such phrases the genitive may designate the author or originator too, since for Paul, Jesus is both the originator (cf. 2 Cor 5:20; Rom 15:18) and the object of the gospel proclaimed. As the content of his gospel, it is above all Jesus the Christ, the Risen *Kyrios* of all men, that Paul proclaims: "We do not proclaim ourselves, but Christ Jesus as Lord" (2 Cor 4:5); "the good news of the glory of Christ" (2 Cor 4:4). "For all the promises of God find their 'Yes' in him" (2 Cor 1:20).

Fuller formulations of his "gospel" echo the early Church's kerygma (1 Cor 15:1–7). Here he appeals explicitly to the *form* or *terms* (*tíni logō*) in which he first proclaimed the gospel to the Corinthians. Significantly, the functional role of Christ is stressed: "Christ died for our sins." It recalls the Scriptures, the burial, the resurrection, and the appearances. In Rom 1:3–4 another echo of the kerygma proclaims God's son born of the line of David but set up from the time of the resurrection as a Son with power and a Spirit of holiness. The essence of the gospel is here—the emphasis on the salvific effects of the death and resurrection of Jesus the Christ in accord with the Scriptures. Paul proclaims a Son whom God "has raised from the dead, Jesus, who delivers us from the coming wrath" (1 Thes 1:10). Such a formulation of his gospel in terms of the primitive kerygma insured it against becoming a different gospel (Gal 1:6); so secured, it was the one proclaimed by the whole early Church.

30 But the distinctively Pauline conception of the gospel is seen in his description of it as a salvific force let loose by God in the world of man. It is not a mere series of revealed propositions about Christ that men must intellectually apprehend and give assent to. Rather, it is "the power of God [*dynamis theou*] for the salvation of every man who believes" (Rom 1:16). In other words, it not only proclaims the redemptive event of Christ's death and resurrection but is itself a force that spreads it to men. In a sense, it is itself a redemptive event whenever it makes its appeal to men. Strikingly, Paul calls it "the power of God," just as he referred to Christ himself (1 Cor 1:24). This is why to "preach Christ crucified" is to "preach the gospel." Both Christ and the gospel bring the Father's salvific bounty to men. The gospel is the Father's means of accosting men, soliciting from them the responses of faith and love. That is why it is "God's gospel" (1 Thes 2:2,8,9; 2 Cor 11:7; Rom 1:1; 15:16); it is also his "gift," his "favor" (2 Cor 9:14–15). So Paul can write to the Thessalonians that his "gospel was not preached to them in words only, but with power and the holy Spirit and full conviction" (1 Thes 1:5; cf. 1 Cor 4:20). For as the "power of God," the gospel is not proclaimed without the assistance of the Spirit of God. Indeed, through this "good news of salvation" believers are sealed with the promised holy Spirit, "the pledge of our inheritance" (Eph 1:13). Through it men are already saved (1 Cor 15:2).

31 Another distinctively Pauline view of the gospel is its universal appeal and application. In Rom 1:16 Paul explains it as a salvific force for "every man who believes," by adding, "for the Jew first and then the Greek." Salvation for the Gentiles through the gospel was part of his great vision of the Risen Christ—"that I might preach the good news of him to the Gentiles" (Gal 1:16). In time, Paul realized that "there is no distinction between Jew and Greek for they all have the same Lord, and he is generous to all who call upon him" (Rom 10:12; cf. 11:11,25). Whenever Paul, then, speaks of his "gospel," it should be understood as Jesus the *Kyrios* who is the power of God for the salvation of all men, Jew and Greek alike. For even "Scripture saw in advance that God would make the Gentiles upright through faith, and announced the good news in advance to Abraham, 'In you all nations will be blessed' " (Gal 3:8).

32 Another aspect of the Pauline gospel is seen in his view of it as a "mystery" or "secret" (*mystērion*). This aspect introduces us more deeply into the content of the gospel, which concerns Christ, by enhancing the total view of it as a revelation. For in the gospel is revealed the divine plan of salvation, which is being realized in Christ Jesus. It is particularly in contexts mentioning the gospel as revelation or manifestation that *mystērion* occurs (note its use with the vbs. *apokalyptein, gnōrizein, phaneroun, lalein*, etc.).

The earliest Pauline use of *mystērion* (2 Thes 2:7) has nothing to do with the gospel, since it refers to the "mystery of iniquity," a satanic scheme at work in the world destined to culminate in the appearance of the "lawless one" (*ho anomos*; cf. P. Furfey, *CBQ* 8 [1946] 179–91; M. Brunec, *VD* 35 [1957] 3–33; J. Schmid, *TQ* 129 [1949] 323–43). But the first occurrences of this word thereafter reveal its identification with the gospel. Paul speaks of "God's mystery," equating it with "Jesus Christ crucified" (1 Cor 2:1–2; but cf. *app. crit.*), just as he had referred his gospel to Christ crucified (1 Cor 1:17,23). Paul is the "steward," dispensing the wealth of this mystery (1 Cor 4:1; cf. 13:2; 14:2). His gospel is so designated because it reveals a plan of salvation conceived by the Father and hidden in him from all eternity (1 Cor 2:7). It has now been put into effect in Christ Jesus and has been revealed to Christians through the apostles and holy prophets of the New Dispensation. It embraces the salvation of all mankind, giving the Gentiles a share in the inheritance of Israel. Even the partial insensibility of Israel is part of this *mystērion* (Rom 11:25). Hidden in God for long ages, it is beyond the ken of mortal men and even of the authorities of this world. But now it has been made known "to God's holy people" and even to Paul, that he might proclaim it to the Gentiles and bring them to a share in the inexhaustible wealth of "the mystery of Christ" (Col 4:3). Although this mystery is mentioned in the Great Letters, it is above all in the Captivity Letters that Paul manifests its real import, especially his insight into the cosmic significance of Christ's role. In these letters the mystery reveals Christ to be the meaning and goal of all creation, for the Father plans to bring all created things under the headship of Christ (Eph 1:9). Through Christ salvation comes to all men by their incorporation in his body, which is the Church, and he is its head (see Col 1:26–27; 2:2; Eph 1:9; 3:4–10). In Eph 3:4–10 Paul gives the fullest description of this mystery, which dawned on him only later in his life.

33 The Pauline "mystery" is Christocentric. Just as Paul identifies Christ with the gospel, calling them both the "power of God," so he equates Christ and the "mystery," calling them "the wisdom of God" (1 Cor 2:7; 1:24). In reality, this "mystery of the gospel" (Eph 6:19) is one and the same: Christ is the "secret plan of God" (Col 1:27; 2:2). But in presenting the gospel as "mystery," Paul implies that it is never fully made known to men by the ordinary means of communication. As something revealed, it is apprehended only by faith; and even when revealed, the opacity of divine wisdom in it is never completely dispelled for men. *Mystērion* is an eschatological notion derived from Jewish apocalyptic sources, and its application to the gospel gives the latter a nuance that *euaggelion* alone would not have—for it is something that is fully comprehended only in the *eschaton*.

34 Perhaps because of his apostolic experience Paul came to speak of the gospel as *mystērion*, using a word already familiar in contemporary Gk mystery religions. However, the comprehension he gives to it and the mode in which he uses it reveal that he depended not so much on its Hellenistic sources as he did on the OT and Jewish apocalyptic writings of the intertestamental period. Its OT roots are found in the Hebr *sôd* and in the Aram *rāz* (mystery) (Dn 2:18–19,27–30,47; 4:6). The latter is a Persian loanword used in Aramaic to designate the revelation made to Nebuchadnezzar in his dreams. QL offers abundant parallels to the Pauline usage of *mystērion*, showing that its real roots are in Palestine Judaism rather than in Asia Minor Hellenism. In QL and related writings *rāz* denotes an eschatological secret of God, embracing creation, the history of the world, the end-time, and the judgment. As used by Paul, especially in Col and Eph, *mystērion* begins with these presuppositions of Jewish apocalyptic literature, but creation, history of the world, and the *eschaton* are now all involved in the great "mystery of Christ," which brings salvation to all men.

(Baker, A. E., *St. Paul and His Gospel* [London, 1949]. Brown, R. E., "The Pre-Christian Semitic Concept of 'Mystery,' " *CBQ* 20 [1958] 417–43; "The Semitic Background of the NT Mystērion," *Bib* 39 [1958] 426–48; *Bib* 40 [1959] 70–87. Burrows, M., "The Origin of the Term 'Gospel,' " *JBL* 44 [1925] 21–33. Hunter, A. M., *The Gospel According to St. Paul* [London, 1966]. Petty, O. A., *Did the Christian Use of the Term "to Euaggelion" Originate with Paul?* [New Haven, 1925]. Schniewind, J., *Euangelion* [2 vols; Gütersloh, 1927–31]. Vogt, E., " 'Mysteria' in textibus Qumran," *Bib* 37 [1956] 247–57.)

35 **(II) The Father's Plan of Salvation History.** The nuance of "mystery" added to Paul's understanding of the gospel opens up the broad perspective in which it must really be considered. He saw the gospel only as a part of the magnificent plan, itself gratuitously conceived by the Father for the salvation of men, which was revealed and realized in Christ Jesus. This was the Father's "purpose" (*prothesis*, Rom 9:11; 8:28; Eph 1:11; 3:11; cf. Gal 4:4) and the Father's "will" (*thelēma*, 1 Cor 1:1; 2 Cor 1:1; Eph 1:5). This Pauline insight is important because it makes us aware of the historical, cosmological, and corporate dimensions of Christian salvation.

36 In certain quarters today this view of man's salvation is looked upon merely as the mythical element in Paul's theology. It is regarded as a prop (like God-up-there, or God-out-there), born of a supranaturalist view of the world, which is not really essential to the NT. Insofar as any description of a divine plan of salvation is bound to be anthropomorphic, it can be admitted to be mythical. An effort must be made, however, to understand the myth for what it is, and not simply to reject it (→ Aspects OT Thought, 77:23–31). The demythologization must be interpretative, not subtractive.

37 The author of the salvific plan is not Christ, but God the Father (*ho theos*). What Paul teaches us about the Father is not a theology (in the strict sense) independent of his soteriological Christology. It is taught, rather, in contexts that deal generally with the divine plan of salvation. "God chose through the folly of the Gospel message to save those who had faith in him" (1 Cor 1:21). The word "chose" highlights the gratuitous initiative that Paul never ceases to ascribe to the Father, whose great concern is the "salvation" of men (1 Thes 5:9; Rom 1:16; 10:10; 11:11). It is the Father who "calls" men to faith, to salvation, to glory, and even to the apostolate (1 Thes 5:24; 2 Thes 2:13–14; 1 Cor 1:9; Rom 8:30). It is a "call" that is made in virtue of an eternal plan (1 Thes 5:9; 2 Thes 2:13; Rom 8:28; 9:11; Eph 1:9,11; 3:11). Though Paul may at times ascribe to the Father certain qualities that seem unrelated, they almost always reveal God as such and such *for us, on our behalf*, for they express aspects of his relation to the divine plan of salvation. Thus, for instance, the various attributes Paul derives from his Jewish background: God as "the creator of all things" (Eph 3:9); the one who "calls into being what does not exist" (Rom 4:17); God's "eternal power and divinity" (Rom 1:20); his "truth" (Rom 1:25; 3:7); his "wisdom and knowledge" (Rom 11:33); his "wrath" (Rom 1:18); and above all his "uprightness" (Rom 3:5,25).

If Paul speaks of the *dikaiosynē theou*, his reference should not be facilely understood as God's vindicative justice (as opposed to his mercy). Rather, this term refers to his salvific uprightness, a quality by which he manifests his bounty and fidelity in acquitting and vindicating his people. Yahweh in the OT is often depicted as the contender involved in a lawsuit (*rîb*) with his rebellious people (Is 1:18; 3:13; 41:1; 43:26; Hos 4:1; 12:2; Mi 6:2; etc.). Or else he is the "righteous Judge" (Ps 7:12). However, in the prophetic and postexilic literature his uprightness (Hebr *ṣedeq* or *ṣᵉdāqâ*) is usually mentioned as the quality by virtue of which he "acquits or vindicates" his people (Is 43:26; 45:25; 50:8; Jer 12:1). Such an acquittal brought "salvation," and in this literature we often find Yahweh's *ṣedeq* manifesting itself as a "salvific uprightness" (Is 46:13; 51:5,6,8; 59:17; 45:21; Pss 36:7,11; 143:1–2; Ezr 9:15; Neh 9:33; Dn 9:7–16). And so Paul understands it. Such qualities, then, are not meant to convey an understanding of the intrinsic constitution of God. They are, rather, an indication of God's relation to man (→ Aspects OT Thought, 77:93–94).

(Ropes, J. H., " 'Righteousness' and 'the Righteousness of God' in the Old Testament and in St. Paul," *JBL* 22 [1903] 211–27.)

38 The relation of the Father to man's salvation, however, is brought out much more by the way Paul conceives of the relationship of God to Christ. For he is often "the God and Father of our Lord Jesus Christ" (2 Cor 1:3; 11:31; Rom 15:6; Col 1:3; Eph 1:3; cf. 1 Cor 15:24). Such a conception is influenced by Paul's Jewish monotheism (cf. 1 Cor 8:5–6) but also by his insight into Christ, who is the one who reveals God to men because he is "the image of God" (2 Cor 4:4; Col 1:15). It is the Father who has sent his Son to redeem those under the Law (Gal 4:4). The mission of the Son is the great proof for Paul of the love of the Father for men: "God proves his love for us by the fact that Christ died for us when we were still sinners" (Rom 5:8; cf. 8:31). In Christ, man encounters the supreme love of the Father. It is his love that is poured out in our hearts (Rom 5:5). It is "God who has reconciled us to himself through Christ" (2 Cor 5:18). This is the "living and true God" (1 Thes 1:9) whom Paul envisages as the author of the eternal plan of salvation and to whom he addresses his prayer (Phil 1:4; 2 Cor 1:11; 9:14–15; Rom 8:27; Col 4:3–12).

(See Levie, J., "Le plan d'amour divin dans le Christ selon Saint Paul," *L'homme devant Dieu* [Fest. H. de Lubac; Paris, 1964] 1, 159–67. Romaniuk, K., *L'amour du Père et du Fils dans la sotériologie de S. Paul* [Rome, 1961].)

39 Lest anyone get the impression that the mission of Christ was a sort of repair job, patching up the history of man, which had gone awry because of man's sinful rebellion, Paul insists that this salvific plan was conceived by the creator (Eph 3:9) even before the foundation of the world (Eph 1:14). After a long period in which God's patience tolerated men's sins and their neglect of him (Rom 3:23,25; 1:21; [the period of man's "wisdom," 1 Cor 1:21; Rom 1:20; 2:14–16]), the time came when he sent his Son into the world of men (Gal 4:4) to reconcile them to himself and to give them access to himself (Rom 5:1–2,8). All the promises of God find their Yes in Christ (2 Cor 1:20). The mystery of the gospel has revealed this salvific plan by which God would reconcile all things (men as well as other creatures) to himself in bringing about a subordination of all creatures to Christ, the *kosmokratōr*. "He made known to us his hidden purpose and will according to that design which he proposed in Christ, to realize it when the time would be ripe: that everything in heaven and on earth might be brought together under the headship of Christ" (Eph 1:9–10). (Cf. Col 1:13–20; Rom 8:28–30.) This cosmic view of Christ as the head of the universe, which is created through him, sustained in him, and finds its coherence and goal in him, comes to its fullest expression in Col and Eph. Nevertheless, elements of it appear in the earlier letters. In Rom, Paul sees all physical creation awaiting the full execution of this salvific plan. "Creation waits with eager expectation for the revelation of the sons of God. It was once subjected to frustration, through no fault of its own; it happened through him who so subjected creation itself, and gave it the hope that it might be freed from its bondage to decay in view of the glorious freedom of the children of God" (Rom 8:19–21).

40 Yet even this Christocentric goal of all creation is not the final stage of the plan. The dominion of Christ, as the *Kyrios* and head of the universe, is given to him to make clear his exalted role in the history of man's salvation. But once the divine plan has reached that stage of the reconciliation of all men to God, "then will be the end." Christ will "turn over the kingdom to God his Father, bringing to an end all other government, authority and power; he must retain the government until he puts all his enemies under his feet.... And when everything is reduced to subjection to him, the Son himself will be subjected to him who has made all things subject to him, that God might be everything to everyone" (1 Cor 15:24–25,28). In such a view of the eternal plan one can see that it is the Father from whom all things come and for whom we exist (1 Cor 8:5). This view also explains the hierarchy of man as the head of woman, Christ as the head of man, and God as the head of Christ (1 Cor 11:3; cf. 3:21–23; Rom 14:7–9).

41 Other aspects of this plan, discussed by Paul, bring out its historical and corporate dimensions. Into it, he fits the threefold division of human history already mentioned (→ 13 above). Salvation history is divided into three great periods: (1) from Adam to Moses; (2) from Moses to Christ; (3) from Christ to the parousia and the "end" (Rom 4:15; 5:13; 10:4). In thus dividing human history, Paul was following a similar division of the world's duration known to the rabbis. Some of them taught that the duration of the world was 6000 years, divided into 2000 years of *Tohuwabohu* ("unformed void"—from Adam to Moses), 2000 years of Torah (from Moses to the Messiah), and 2000 years of the Messiah (see *bSanhedrin* 97b; *Abodah zarah* 9b; *jMeg.* 70d; *Ep. Barnabae* 15:4). In the Messianic age the Torah would cease (*bShabbath* 151b; *bNiddah* 61b), and the Messiah was expected to promulgate a new Torah (*Tg. Is* 12:3; *Midr. Eccl.* 2:1; 12:1; *Tg. Ct* 5:10). (See W. D. Davies, *Torah in the Messianic Age and/or the Age to Come* [Phila., 1952] 50–94; *Paul and Rabbinic Judaism*, 72-73.)

42 Paul uses a similar threefold division of man's history. From Adam to Moses the period was lawless; men sinned, but there was no imputation of transgressions. Then, from Moses to Christ, the Law reigned, and men's sins were imputed as transgressions of it. Finally, the third period was begun with Christ, who is the "end of the Law" (Rom 10:4). He is its *telos*, not only in the sense that it was directed toward him (Gal 3:24), but also in the sense that he is the one who put an end to it (see Eph 2:15; Christ "abolished the Law" [*katargēsas*]). In the place of the Mosaic Law there is now the "law of Christ" (Gal 6:2), the law of the Messiah (cf. 1 Cor 9:20; Rom 13:9–10). Paul looked on the period in which he lived as that in which the "ends of the ages have met" (1 Cor 10:11), i.e., when the age of the Law met that of the Messiah. The Law indeed was only the *paidagōgos*, "slave-attendant," leading men like schoolboys to Christ (Gal 3:24).

43 Another indication of phases of the salvific plan is seen in the role played by Israel. Privileged of old through God's promises to Abraham and to his posterity, Israel became the chosen instrument by which salvation would reach all men. "All nations will be blessed in you" (Gal 3:8; cf. Rom 4:16; Gn 18:18; 12:3). All the divine preparations for the Christ were made within the nation of the Jews: "To them belong filial adoption, God's glorious presence, the covenants, the legislation, the Temple cult, the promises, the patriarchs, and even the Messiah according to the flesh" (Rom 9:4–5). But though descended from Abraham, Israel rejected (Rom 11:15) Jesus as the Messiah and thereby apparently excluded itself from the salvation offered in Jesus the Christ whom Paul preached. It would seem that the divine plan had failed in its most crucial moment (Rom 9:6). Paul insists that it has not, since this infidelity of Israel was foreseen by God and was part of the plan itself. It is not contrary to God's direction of history, since both the infidelity of the Jews and the call of the Gentiles have been announced in the OT (Rom 9:6–32). Israel's infidelity proceeds from its culpable refusal to accept him in whom a new mode of uprightness is now open to all men; but this was foreseen. It is only partial infidelity (Rom 11:1–10), since "a remnant selected by God's mercy" (Rom 11:5) has accepted Jesus as the Christ. And it is only temporary, since through Israel's false step "salvation has gone to the Gentiles to make Israel jealous. But if their false step means riches for the world, and if their failure means riches for the Gentiles, how much more will the addition of their full number mean!" (Rom 11:11–12). Indeed, "only partial insensibility has come upon Israel, to last until all the Gentiles have come in, and then all Israel will be saved" (Rom 11:25).

(Charue, A., *L'incrédulité des Juifs dans le NT* [Gembloux, 1929] 281–333. Munck, J., *Paul and the Salvation of Mankind* [London, 1959]; *Christ and Israel* [Phila., 1967].)

44 This perspective of salvation history gives to Paul's Christology historical, cosmic, and corporate dimensions. It is historical, since it embraces all the phases of man's history from creation to its consummation, since it is rooted in the intervention of Christ in that history "in the fullness of time" (Gal 4:4), and since it gives that history a meaning that is not immanent in it. It is cosmic because it relates all the created *kosmos* to man's salvation in a movement of aspiration toward Christ the *kosmokratōr*, whom the Father has made its head and goal. It is corporate because it envisages the effects of the Christ-event on "the Israel of God" (Gal 6:16; cf. Rom 9:6) and because it was destined to break down the barrier between Jew and Greek, reconciling both to God in one body (Eph 2:14–16). One cannot stress too much this last dimension of the salvific plan. The corporate aspect of salvation dominates many passages in Paul, such as Rom 5:12–21; Rom 9–11; and Eph 1:3–12. It should warn us against interpreting Paul's teaching too narrowly or exclusively in an individualistic sense, either that of some I-Thou relationship between the Christian and God or, less sophisticatedly, that of a personal piety or even that of some exaggerated anthropology. This corporate aspect appears above all in the incorporation of Christians in Christ and his Church.

45 No sketch of Paul's salvation history is complete without some reference to his eschatology, since this complicated subject belongs, in part at least, to any discussion of the divine plan of salvation.

46 If the first two phases of that history (Adam to Moses, Moses to Christ) have already been brought to a close, then in a sense Christians are already living in the last age, the Messianic age. If the *eschaton* has been inaugurated, yet from another viewpoint the "end" has not yet come (1 Cor 15:24 [according to the most probable interpretation of that verse]). Christ, the *kosmokratōr*, does not yet reign supreme; he has not yet handed the kingdom over to the Father. All of this is related to the "parousia of the Lord" (1 Thes 2:19; 3:13; 4:15; 5:23; 2 Thes 2:1; 1 Cor 15:23). It is scarcely to be denied (as R. Schnackenburg rightly admits [*Neutestamentliche Theologie*, 104]) that Paul expected it in the near future. On the other hand, we find him at times in his letters gradually reconciling himself to an imminent death (Phil 1:23) and to an intermediate phase between his death and his "appearance before the tribunal of Christ" (2 Cor 5:1–10). In either case, however, there is a future phase in his salvation history, whether its term be near or far off, and Paul's one hope is "to make his home with the Lord" (2 Cor 5:8). The undeniable elements of his futurist eschatology are the parousia (1 Thes 4:15), the resurrection of the dead (1 Thes 4:16; 1 Cor 15:13ff.), the judgment (2 Cor 5:10; Rom 14:10; Eph 6:8), and the glory of the justified believer (Rom 8:18,21; 1 Thes 2:12). But along with this future aspect there is also the present aspect, according to which the *eschaton* has already begun and men are already in a sense saved. "Now is the acceptable time, now is the day of salvation" (2 Cor 6:2). The "first fruits" (Rom 8:23) and the "pledge" (2 Cor 1:22; 5:5; Eph 1:14) of this salvation are already the possession of Christian believers. Christ has already transferred us to the heavenly realm (Eph 2:6; cf. Col 2:12; Phil 3:20). Paul speaks at times as if Christians were already saved (Rom 8:24; cf. 1 Cor 15:2; 1:18; 2 Cor 2:15; Eph 2:8), yet at other times he intimates that they are still to be saved (1 Cor 5:5; 10:33; Rom 5:9,10; 9:27; 10:9,13).

47 This difference of viewpoint is due in part to the development of Paul's thoughts regarding the imminence of the parousia. In the Early Letters, the future references abound. But with the passage of time, and especially with some experience that Paul had in Ephesus when he came very close to death (2 Cor 1:18; 1 Cor 15:32) and the parousia had not yet occurred, his understanding of the Christian situation developed. All this is undoubtedly at the root of the full-blown vision of the Father's plan, which emerges only in the Captivity Letters.

48 The double aspect of Pauline eschatology has been variously explained. Some, like C. H. Dodd and R. Bultmann, would label the predominant aspect of it "realized eschatology." This expression is *in se* acceptable, but care must be exercised in defining it. For Bultmann, Paul is not interested in the history of the nation of Israel, or of the world, but only in the "historicity of man, the true historical life of the human being, the history which every one experiences for himself and by which he gains his real essence. This history of the human person comes into being in the encounters which man experiences, whether with other people or with events, and in the decisions he takes in them" (*The Presence of Eternity: History and Eschatology* [N.Y., 1957] 43). In other words, the future elements in Paul's eschatology are only a symbolic mode of expressing man's self-realization as he is freed from himself by the grace of Christ and continually asserts himself as a free individual in decisions for God. In such acts he continually stands "before the tribunal of Christ." Bultmann would thus write off all the future elements of Paul's eschatology listed above; they are vestiges of an apocalyptic view of history, which is meaningless for the 20th-cent. man. Indeed, Paul has already reinterpreted it in terms of his anthropology. "The Pauline view of history is the expression of his view of man" (*ibid.*, 41).

49 Such an interpretation of Paul's eschatology has the advantage of emphasizing the "crisis" (if one will permit a word that is more Johannine than Pauline), which the Christ-event brings into every man's life. A challenge of faith is presented to everyone. But this presentation of Paul's eschatology in effect denies some of the major elements of his view of salvation history. Although it is true that "the history into which Paul looks back is the history not of Israel only, but of all mankind" (*ibid.*, 40), it seems hardly accurate to say that Paul "does not see it as the history of the nation with its alternations of divine grace and the people's obstinacy, of sin and punishment, of repentance and forgiveness" (*ibid.*). Such a view of Pauline history is too much dominated by the polemics of Rom and Gal and minimizes the problem that Paul tried to face in composing Rom 9–11. Israel's history and role in the destiny of man are factors in Paul's whole theology; and they are scarcely a theologoumenon that one can simply relegate to the realm of myth. Moreover, if Paul calls Christ the end of the Law (Rom 10:4), he is not saying that "history has reached its end" (*ibid.*, 43). Rather, he would seem to be saying that a new phase of salvation history has begun because "the ends of the ages have met" (1 Cor 10:11).

50 An alternative to such a "realized eschatology" is to interpret Paul's teaching as an "inaugurated eschatology" or even as a "self-realizing eschatology" (if the "self" refers to the *eschaton*). For, in Paul's view, Christians live in the *eschaton*, in the age of the Messiah. This is an age of dual polarity. It is an age that looks backward to the first Good Friday and Easter Sunday and forward to a final glorious consummation when "we shall always be with the Lord" (1 Thes 4:17). It is an age that has initiated a status of union with God previously unknown and one destined to a final union in glory. This is the basis of Christian hope and patience.

51 Such a view of Paul's eschatology reckons with an objective mode of existence in which the Christian finds himself through faith—a mode of existence inaugurated by Christ, which will find its perfection in an event that Paul refers to as the parousia of the Lord. On the other hand, such an interpretation does not commit one to a naïve credulity that fails to reckon with the remnants of apocalyptic paraphernalia and "stage-props" used by Paul to describe the forms of the parousia, resurrection, judgment, and glory, which occur in such passages as 1 Thes 4:16–17; 2 Thes 2:1–10; 1 Cor 15:51–54.

(Guntermann, F., *Die Eschatologie des hl. Paulus* [NTAbh 13/4–5; Münster, 1932]. Hunter, A. M., "The Hope of Glory: The Relevance of the Pauline Eschatology," *Interpr* 8 [1954] 131–41. Rigaux, B., *Les Épîtres aux Thessaloniciens* [EBib; Paris, 1956] 213–22. Shires, H. M., *The Eschatology of Paul in the Light of Modern Scholarship* [Phila., 1966]. Stanley, D. M., "The Conception of Salvation in Primitive Christian Preaching," *CBQ* 18 [1956] 231–54.)

52 **(III) Christ's Role in Salvation History.** Against the background of the gospel, the mystery, and the Father's plan of salvation, we must now try to depict the role of Christ himself as it is seen by Paul. For although Paul sees Israel and Abraham playing roles in the execution of that plan and knows that the Church is deeply involved in it, it is Christ's role that is central to his thought. This begins the Christological part of our exposition of Paul's theology.

53 **(A) Pre-existent Son.** Paul calls Jesus "the son of God" (Gal 2:20; 3:26; 2 Cor 1:19; Eph 4:13) or "his [i.e., the Father's] Son" (1 Thes 1:10 [kerygmatic fragment]; Gal 1:16; 4:4,6; 1 Cor 1:9; Rom 1:3,9; 5:10; 8:3,29,32 ["his own son"]; Col 1:13 ["the son of his love"]). What did he mean by this title "son of God"? *In se* the title, which had a long history in the ancient Near East, could imply many things. Egyptian pharaohs were looked on as "sons of God" because the sun-god Rê was regarded as their father (see C. J. Gadd, *Ideas of Divine Rule in the Ancient East* [London, 1948] 45–50). Its use is attested also in references to Assyrian and Babylonian monarchs. In the Hellenistic-Roman world it was used of the ruler, especially in the phrase *divi filius* or *theou huios* applied to the Roman emperor (see A. Deissmann, *LAE* 350–51). In the same world it was also given to mythical heroes or *thaumaturgi* (sometimes called *theioi andres*) and to historical persons (such as Apollonius of Tyana, Pythagoras, Plato, the Samaritan Dositheus). Abundant references can be found in G. P. Wetter, *Der Sohn Gottes* (FRLANT 26; Göttingen, 1916). The basis of the Hellenistic attribution of this title was apparently the conviction that such persons had divine powers. It has been maintained that the application of this title to Jesus reflects such a Hellenistic background, since it could scarcely have been used by Jesus himself or even applied to him by the early Palestinian community (R. Bultmann, *TNT* 1, 50). It is, however, by no means certain, as many NT scholars recognize today, that the use of this title is due almost exclusively to Hellenistic churches (→ Aspects NT Thought, 78:20, 35, 50).

54 In the OT, "son of God" is a mythological title given to angels (Jb 1:6; 2:1; 38:7; Ps 29:1; Dn 3:25; Gn 6:2); a title of predilection for the people of Israel collectively (Ex 4:22; Dt 14:1; Hos 2:1; 11:1; Is 1:2; 30:1; Jer 3:22; Wis 2:16; 18:13); a title of adoption for the king (2 Sm 7:14; Pss 2:7; 89:27), for judges (Ps 82:6), for the upright individual Jew (Sir 4:10; Wis 2:18), and perhaps even for the Messiah (if Ps 2:7 is considered messianic; → Aspects OT Thought, 77:157). The hesitation in the last instance comes from the lack of any clear use of the title for the Messiah. Possible attestation of such use is found in 4QFlor (→ Apocrypha, 68:80), which uses 2 Sm 7:14 in a context that some scholars consider messianic. See also 1QSa 2:11–12, where God's begetting of the Messiah seems to be mentioned (cf. *JBL* 75 [1956] 177, n. 28; J. Starcky, *RB* 70 [1963] 481–505; → Apocrypha, 68:72); and *Enoch* 105:2 (a later addition?; → Apocrypha, 68:10). But not one of these instances is unequivocal. The identification of Messiah and Son of God is made in the NT (Mk 14:61; Mt 16:16). Cullmann believes that the fusion of the two titles first takes place here, in reference to Jesus. The dominant idea underlying the use of "son of God" in the Jewish world was that of divine election for a God-given task and the corresponding obedience to such a vocation (see Mt 21:28–31). This Hebraic notion of sonship is at the root of the NT application of the title to Christ.

55 Paul is scarcely the creator of this title for Christ; he inherits it from the early Church. It is found in the fragments of the kerygma that he uses in his letters. However, in his writings its meaning is not univocal. When Paul says that Jesus was "set up as a son of God in power with a spirit of holiness as of the resurrection from the dead" (Rom 1:4), he uses the title in the Hebraic sense. In this credal formulation the emphasis is on the phrase *en dynamei* (in power), which refers to the enjoyment of a plenipotentiary status as *Kyrios* ever since the resurrection (see Acts 2:36). This formulation could be no more than a sort of messianic enthronement (see L. Sabourin, *Les noms et les titres de Jésus* [Bruges, 1963] 242). It expresses the function of Jesus endowed with the life-giving spirit for the salvation of men (1 Cor 15:45). But this use of the title "son of God in power" stands in contrast to "his Son" (Rom 1:3), which seems to imply something more. Elsewhere Paul presupposes at least, if he does not allude to, the pre-existence of Christ. "God sent his son, born of a woman, subject to the Law, to redeem those who were under the Law" (Gal 4:4; Rom 8:3). Theoretically, one could say that this "sending" refers to nothing more than a divine commission. But is this all that Paul implies? The ambiguity seems to be removed by Phil 2:6, "who, though of divine status" (*en morphē theou hyparchōn;* cf. 2 Cor 8:9). The six strophes of the Jewish-Christian hymn, which Paul incorporates into Phil 2, treat of Christ's divine pre-existence, his humiliation at the incarnation, his further humiliation in death, his celestial exaltation, the adoration of him by the universe, and his new name, *Kyrios*. The status he enjoyed before the incarnation was one of "being equal to God" (*to einai isa theō*).

56 However, apart from such allusions to a divine dignity or to a sovereign status of Jesus as the Son, who was "the image of the invisible God, the first-born of all creation" (Col 1:15; cf. 1:17; 2:9), most of the instances in which Paul calls Jesus the "Son" express only his divine election and his complete dedication to the Father's plan of redemption. Thus, in Pauline theology it is the term par excellence to express the divine love involved in the salvation of man. With a covert allusion to the sacrifice of Isaac, Paul says of God in Rom 8:32, "he did not spare his own son [*tou idiou huiou*], but handed him over for our sakes."

57 One last passage needs further consideration, since Paul speaks there of the relation of the Son and the Father in a way that transcends any functional soteriology. In 1 Cor 15:24–25,28 Paul depicts the end of the salvific plan, when Christ will be sovereign *Kyrios;* but then as "the Son himself" he will be subjected to him who has put all things under his feet. Christ's role in salvation will have been brought to completion; but Paul sees the need to define the relation of the *Kyrios*-Son to the Father. Note how he uses the terms *theos, patēr,* and *huios* absolutely; Jesus is not "his son," but simply "the son."

58 If, then, Paul normally uses the title "Son of God" in a functional sense descriptive of the role given to Christ, there is little doubt that at times he also uses it to express something about Christ's origin and his peculiar relation to the Father. On the other hand, it is significant that only in Rom 9:5 (a textually disputed passage) do we find Paul calling Jesus *theos*. He transfers to Jesus a doxological formula otherwise reserved for the Father (Rom 1:25; 2 Cor 11:31; Eph 4:6). Possibly 2 Thes 1:12 should be added here. The reason for this rare use of *theos* for Jesus is that for Paul *ho theos* was the Father (cf. 1 Cor 8:5–6), and he is reflecting the restraint of the early Church, which though it came to acknowledge Jesus' divinity, did not, however, quickly transfer to him a title that was regarded, more or less exclusively, to be the Father's. Such restraint paved the way for the later Trinitarian dogmatic nuances. (Cf. also Ti 2:13; possibly 1 Tm 3:16 [textually problematic]; 2 Tm 4:18.)

(Benoit, P., "Pauline and Johannine Theology: A Contrast," *Cross Currents* 16 [1965] 339–53. Brown, R. E., "Does the New Testament Call Jesus God?" *TS* 26 [1965] 545–73; also in *Jesus God and Man* [Milwaukee, 1967] 1–38. Cullmann, O., *Christology*, 270–305. Gelin, A. (ed.), *Son and Saviour* [2nd ed.; Baltimore, 1962]. Kramer, W., *Christ, Lord, Son of God* [SBT 50; London, 1966]. Lagrange, M.-J., "Les origines du dogme paulinien de la divinité de Christ," *RB* 45 [1936] 5–33. Richardson, *ITNT* [N.Y., 1958] 147–53. Sabourin, L., *The Names and Titles of Jesus* [N.Y., 1967]. Taylor, V., *The Names of Jesus* [London, 1953] 52–65.)

59 **(B) Kyrios.** The frequency of Paul's use of *Kyrios* for Christ is remarkable in comparison with his use of the title "Son of God" and reveals that *Kyrios* is the title par excellence for Jesus in the Pauline writings.

Paul uses *Kyrios*, of course, for Yahweh of the OT, especially in passages where he quotes or explains OT texts (1 Cor 3:20; 10:26; 2 Cor 14:21; Rom 4:8; 9:28,29; 11:3,34; 15:11; cf. L. Cerfaux, *ETL* 20 [1943] 5–17). In this he follows the usage of the LXX where *kyrios* is the standard rendering of *YHWH* or *'ădōnāy*. But the significant thing is that the absolute *ho Kyrios* becomes Paul's title of predilection for Jesus.

60 It has been maintained that this absolute usage is a product of Paul's Hellenistic background (by W. Bousset, *Kyrios Christos* [2nd ed.; Göttingen, 1921]; R. Bultmann, *TNT* 1, 51). The absolute use is well attested in the Hellenistic world of the Roman Empire (cf. W. Förster, *Lord* [BKW 8; London, 1958] 13–35). In Oriental religious texts from Asia Minor, Syria, and Egypt, gods and goddesses like Isis, Osiris, and Serapis are often called simply *kyrios* or *kyria*. Paul himself is aware of this; though there are many "lords," yet for us there is only one Lord, Jesus Christ (1 Cor 8:5–6). *Kyrios* was also a sovereign title for the Roman emperor. Though it primarily denoted his political and juridical superiority, it also carried the nuance of his divinity, especially in the eastern Mediterranean area. However, although the absolute use of *kyrios* is attested in the Hellenistic world in the 1st cent. BC, it is not proved that Paul simply borrowed this usage and applied it to Jesus (→ Aspects NT Thought, 78:5–7, 25, 38, 51).

61 It is far more likely that he inherited it from the early Palestinian Church's liturgical tradition. The credal formulas of Rom 10:9; 1 Cor 12:3 point in this direction; so too does the climax of the hymn to Christ in Phil 2:6–11 (it is the name above all names given to the exalted Jesus). Compare especially Col 2:6, "you have received [by tradition, *parelabete*] Christ Jesus as the Lord." Even when writing to a Gk-speaking church like Corinth, he preserves the primitive liturgical formula *maranatha* in Aramaic (1 Cor 16:22). Stemming from a Palestinian community, it is affectionately retained because of its primitive connotations. Whether it should be read *maran atha* (as in A. Merk's Gk NT) and translated, "Our Lord has come" (a credal declaration), or *marana tha* (as in E. Nestle's) and translated, "Our Lord, come!" (as an eschatological prayer) is a matter of scholarly debate. The latter is usually preferred because of the translation in Ap 22:20, "Come, Lord Jesus!" (cf. *Didache* 10:6). As an eschatological prayer it implores the Lord to come in his parousia. It was probably used at liturgical Eucharistic gatherings, considered to be a foretaste of that coming (cf. 1 Cor 11:26). This evidence seems to indicate that the use of "lord" for Jesus is pre-Pauline and that it derived from the Jewish-Christian community of Jerusalem.

62 Among the Jews of Palestine the Aram equivalent of *kyrios* was *mārēʾ* (emphatic, *māryāʾ*). Normally, it was used of God in the form *mārî* (= *mārʾî*, "my lord"), or *mārʾān*, "our Lord," or with dependent genitives (*mārēʾ malkîn*, "the lord of kings"; *mārēʾ šᵉmayyāʾ*, "the lord of the heavens" [Dn 2:47; 5:23]). Only in 1QapGn (20:12–13; → Apocrypha, 68:81) is an example found that is close to the Palestinian absolute use of *mārēʾ* for God. Data in the Gospels suggest that the disciples called Jesus *mārʾî* or *mārʾān* at times, just as they called him *rabbî*, "my Master" (Mk 10:51). The Q source records what may be an authentic saying reflecting such a usage, "Not everyone who says to me, 'Lord, Lord...' " (Mt 7:21; Lk 6:46). Though the Gk text has the absolute *kyrie*, the underlying Aramaic was probably *mārʾî*, meaning something like "milord." Apparently it had acquired an absolute usage by this time, especially in a religious context.

63 This is also true of Hebr *ʾădōnāy*, the reverential substitute among the Jews for the ineffable name of Yahweh. In their liturgy and reading of the Scriptures it was customary to substitute for *YHWH* the word *ʾădōnāy*, "my lord," or more literally, "my lords" (a sort of plural of majesty). In the LXX, however, the absolute use of *kyrios* or *ho Kyrios* was the normal translation of *YHWH*, and no attention was paid to the pronominal possessive suffix on *ʾădōnāy*. This shows that among the Jews of the 3rd cent. BC the substitution of absolute *kyrios* for the tetragrammaton was already in vogue and that the word *ʾădōnāy* had already acquired an absolute connotation for itself.

Such a custom among the Jews makes it understandable how the Aram equivalent of *ʾădōnāy*, the title *mārʾî*, could have been applied to Jesus in the early Jewish community and still be carried over into Greek-speaking communities in the absolute form *kyrios*. Once Jesus became the object of Christian cult, the shift from the ordinary salutation *mārʾî* to a quasi-absolute use would have been inevitable. Given the absolute use of *kyrios* in the LXX for Yahweh and the contemporary application of it to gods and rulers, it was the ideal title for Paul's missionary efforts among the Gentiles.

64 When Paul uses *Kyrios* of Jesus, he expresses the latter's actual dominion over men precisely in his glorious, risen condition as an influence vitally affecting the lives of Christians. It does not denote Christ's role in his earthly condition, nor even his role in the eschatological parousia, but rather his present condition as the Risen Lord. It is a title of majesty given to Christ in view of his regal risen status as the Lord of the living and the dead (Rom 14:9; cf. Rom 10:9; Acts 4:12).

65 The use of *Kyrios* for Jesus in the early Church bestowed on him the ineffable name of Yahweh in its LXX form. In effect, it suggests that Jesus is on a par with Yahweh himself. This equality is spelled out in detail in the hymn in Phil 2:6–11; the reason why the name given to Jesus is above every name is that it is Yahweh's own name, *Kyrios*. It is the early Church's way of expressing its faith in the divinity of Christ. Though it is predominantly a functional title, expressing Christ's dominion over men and his present vital influence in their lives and conduct, yet it also denotes an equality of Christ with the Father. The titles Father and Son, being relational words, suggest distinction and even subordination. But *Kyrios* ascribes to both Yahweh and Jesus a dominion over creation and a right to the adoration of all creation. In echoing Is 45:23, Phil 2:10 implies this very idea; what Isaiah said of Yahweh is now applied to Christ: "To me every knee shall bow, every tongue shall swear."

66 Paul also inherited from the early Church the idea that God made Jesus *Kyrios* at his resurrection (cf. Acts 2:36, "Therefore let all the house of Israel know that God has made this Jesus whom you crucified both Lord and Messiah"). Raised from the dead through the "glory" of the Father (Rom 6:4), Christ was endowed with a "power" (*dynamis*, Rom 1:4; cf. Phil 3:10) to bring about the sanctification and eventually the resurrection of all who would believe in him. Thus he became the "lord of the living and the dead" (Rom 14:9).

Paul's awareness of the meaning of Christ's lordship grew with his understanding of the "mystery of Christ." In the Captivity Letters, Christ's cosmic role as *Kyrios* is manifest in that he has disarmed all the "principalities and powers" (Col 2:15). It is through the *Kyrios* that the unity of the Church is to be achieved: "One Lord" (Eph 4:5; cf. 2:21).

67 All these aspects refer to Jesus as *Kyrios* in his influence on the body of Christians. But there is an individual relationship that Paul also considers. For Paul regards both himself and the individual Christian as the *doulos*, "slave," of Christ who is the *Kyrios* (cf. Gal 1:10; Rom 1:1; 1 Cor 7:22). Yet this relationship of the Christian to the *Kyrios* is not one of despotism or tyranny; it is the very basis of Pauline "freedom"—bound over to Jesus the *Kyrios*, the Christian is freed from self and free for others. In Gal 4:7 this is made clear in another context ("no longer slaves but sons").

(Cerfaux, L., "Kyrios," *VDBS* 5, 200–228; *Recueil L. Cerfaux* [Gembloux, 1954] 1, 3–188. Cullmann, O., *Christology*, 195–237. Förster, W., *Herr ist Jesus* [Gütersloh, 1924]. Förster, W. and G. Quell, "Kyrios," *ThDNT* 3, 1039–94.)

68 **(C) Passion, Death, and Resurrection.** The decisive moment of the divine plan of salvation was reached in the passion, death, and resurrection of Christ. The unity of these three phases of Christ's existence must be retained in Paul's view of this decisive moment. Unlike the Johannine view, which tends to make of the ignominious raising of Jesus on the cross a majestic elevation to glory (Jn 3:14; 8:28; 12:34) so that the Father seems to glorify the Son on Good Friday itself (Jn 12:23; 17:1ff.), Pauline theology saw the passion and death as a prelude to the resurrection itself. All three himself up for you as a fragrant offering and sacrifice [*prosphoran kai thysian*] to God." There is here no hint of propitiation, but rather an expression of Christ's love, which ascended to the Father as a fragrant sacrificial meal (cf. Gn 8:21; Dt 32:38; Ps 50:12–13). This sacrificial notion is alluded to also in 1 Cor 5:7 (Christ as the Passover lamb). The specific nuance of "covenant sacrifice" is found in the eucharistic passage of 1 Cor 11:24–25. (For the sacrificial interpretation of the highly disputed 2 Cor 5:21 [God "made him who knew nothing of sin to be *hamartian*"], see the lengthy discussion of L. Sabourin, *Rédemption sacrificielle: Une enquête exégétique* [Studia 11; Bruges, 1961]). R. Bultmann (*TNT* 1, 296) is probably right in saying that this view of Christ's death is not characteristically Pauline but represents a tradition that probably originated in the early Church.

71 What is, however, much more characteristic of Paul is the linking of death and resurrection as the salvation event. The cardinal text in this regard is Rom 4:25: "Jesus our Lord...was handed over to die for our transgressions and was raised for our justification." See also 1 Thes 4:14; Phil 2:9–10; 1 Cor 15:12,17,20–21; 2 Cor 5:14–15; 13:4; Rom 8:34; 10:9–10. Most of these texts leave no doubt about the soteriological value of the first Easter. Rom 4:25 itself is not an empty pleonasm, an instance of *parallelismus membrorum* and no more. It expresses, rather, the double effect of the salvation event: the expiation of man's transgressions (on the negative side) and the institution of a state of uprightness for man (on the positive side). Christ's resurrection was not a purely personal by-product of his passion and death. Rather, it contributed as much as these did, in a causal soteriological way, to the objective redemption of man. "If Christ has not been raised, then...you are still in your sins" (1 Cor 15:17; → Aspects NT Thought, 78:148). In order that Christian faith may be salvific, man's lips must acknowledge that "Jesus is Lord," and his heart must believe "that God raised him from the dead" (Rom 10:9).

72 It is important to note Paul's manner of speaking of the resurrection. Only in 1 Thes 4:14 does he say that "Jesus died and rose again" (as if by his own power). Elsewhere, the efficiency of the resurrection is attributed to the Father, the gracious author of the salvific plan: "God the Father raised him from the dead" (Gal 1:1; cf. 1 Thes 1:10; 1 Cor 6:14; 15:15; 2 Cor 4:14; Rom 4:24; 8:11; 10:9; Col 2:12; Eph 1:20). Christ's loving generosity is expressed in the mention of his being handed over to death, but it is God's act of prevenient favor that is emphasized when Paul attributes the resurrection to the Father (→ Aspects NT Thought, 78:158). "By the power of God he is alive" (2 Cor 13:4). Indeed, we learn in Rom 6:4 that it is the power of "the Father's glory" that brought about Christ's resurrection. It was this *doxa* that exalted Christ to his glorious state (Phil 2:10). This heavenly exaltation is his *anabasis*, his ascent to the Father, just as his death on the cross expressed the depths of his humiliation and his *katabasis*. In the Captivity Letters, Paul views this exaltation of the *Kyrios* as a triumphant, victory-ascent over death and over all the spirit-rulers of this world (Col 2:15). It was "God's mighty strength" that was "exerted in raising Christ from the dead and seating him at his right hand in heaven, far above all hierarchies, authorities, powers, and dominions, and all titles that can be bestowed...." (Eph 1:19–21). Like many in the early Church, Paul saw the resurrection-ascension as a single phase of the glorious exaltation of the *Kyrios* (cf. Eph 2:5–6; → Aspects NT Thought, 78:159).

73 For Paul the resurrection brought Christ into a new relationship with men who had faith. As a result of it he was "set up [by the Father] as the Son of God in power with [lit., "according to"] a spirit of holiness [or sanctification]" (Rom 1:4). The *doxa* he received from the Father became *his* power, a power to create new life in those men who would believe in him. At the resurrection he became the "last Adam," the first parent of the *eschaton* (1 Cor 15:45, "The first man Adam became a 'living being'; the last Adam became a life-giving spirit"). As the "first-born from among the dead" (Col 1:18) he was, like Adam at the first creation, a principle of life for his offspring. Jesus is an instrument of a "new creation" (2 Cor 5:17; Gal 6:15) because he became at the resurrection a *pneuma zōopoioun*, a "life-giving spirit" (1 Cor 15:45). In virtue of such a dynamic principle, Paul realizes that it is not he who lives any more but that it is the Risen Christ who lives in him (Gal 2:20), transforming even his physical life (cf. 2 Cor 3:18; 4:5–6). As a "life-giving spirit," Jesus brings about the justification of believers and saves them from the wrath on the day of the Lord (1 Thes 1:10; Rom 4:25). Paul prays "to know Christ and the power of his resurrection" (Phil 3:10), realizing that the *Kyrios* is possessed of a power capable of bringing about the resurrection of Christians (cf. 1 Thes 4:14).

74 It is through the passion, death, and resurrection that Jesus became for men a "Savior." This title, which we so frequently apply to him, is used by Paul only in Phil 3:20 and Eph 5:23; contrast the use of *sōtēr* in the

Pastorals. A reason for this is that Paul normally thinks of salvation as something still to be accomplished for men by Christ (1 Thes 5:9; 1 Cor 3:15; 5:5; Rom 5:9–10; 8:24; 10:9–10,13; Eph 3:13). Only rarely does he speak of it as something already accomplished (1 Cor 1:21; Eph 2:5,8). If he seems to conceive of it as still being accomplished (1 Cor 1:18; 15:2; 2 Cor 2:15), the reason is that he thinks of Christ as *Kyrios* interceding for men in heaven (Rom 8:34). Paul has adapted an OT notion of salvation that is to be achieved on the "Day of the Lord [Yahweh]," on the day when faithful Israel will be saved, and the wrath of God will be manifested toward sinners (→ Aspects OT Thought, 77:140–148; → Aspects NT Thought, 78:19, 43, 60).

(Durrwell, F. X., *The Resurrection: A Biblical Study* [N.Y., 1960]. Goguel, M., *La foi à la résurrection de Jésus dans le Christianisme primitif* [Paris, 1933]. Lyonnet, S., "La valeur sotériologique de la résurrection du Christ selon Saint Paul," *Greg* 39 [1958] 295–318. Schneider, J., *Die Passionsmystik des Paulus* [Leipzig, 1929]. Schweizer, E., "Dying and Rising with Christ," *NTS* 14 [1967–68] 1–14. Stanley, D. M., *Christ's Resurrection in Pauline Soteriology* [AnalBib 13; Rome, 1961]. Tannehill, R. C., *Dying and Rising with Christ* [Berlin, 1967]. Vawter, B., "Resurrection and Redemption," *CBQ* 15 [1953] 11–23.)

75 **(D) The Lord and the Spirit.** Before considering the various effects that Paul attributes to the salvation event, we must devote a few lines to the relation of the *Kyrios* to the Spirit in the Father's salvific plan. We have already seen that Paul called Christ "the power of God and the wisdom of God" (1 Cor 1:24). Like the term "spirit of God," these terms are OT ways of expressing God's outgoing activity (cf. Wis 7:25; for the "spirit of God" in the OT, see Gn 1:2; Pss 51:11; 139:7; Is 11:2; 61:1). They are periphrastic ways of describing God's active presence in the creation, providence, salvation, and the eschatological deliverance of Israel or the world (→ Aspects OT Thought, 77:32–39). Although Paul comes to identify Jesus with the power and wisdom of God, he never calls him outright "the spirit of God."

Yet, in several places Paul does not clearly distinguish the Spirit from Jesus. In Rom 8:9–11 the terms "spirit of God," "the spirit of Christ," "Christ," and "the spirit of him who raised Jesus from the dead" are used interchangeably in Paul's description of the indwelling of God in the Christian experience. From the time of the resurrection, Christ, the "last Adam," became a "life-giving spirit" (1 Cor 15:45) and was "set up as the Son of God in power with [lit., "according to"] a spirit of holiness" (Rom 1:4). Paul speaks of the mission of the "spirit of the Son" (Gal 4:6), of the "spirit of Jesus Christ" (Phil 1:19), and of Jesus as "the Lord of the Spirit" (2 Cor 3:18). Finally, he even goes so far as to say, "The Lord is the Spirit" (2 Cor 3:17; also → Letter 2 Cor, 52:14).

76 On the other hand, there are triadic texts in Paul's letters that line up God (or the Father), Christ (or the Son), and the Spirit in a parallelism that is the basis of the later dogma of the Trinity. (See 2 Cor 1:21–22; 13:13; 1 Cor 2:7–16; 6:11; 12:4–6; Rom 5:1–5; 8:14–17; 15:30; Eph 1:11–14,17.) In Gal 4:4–6 there is the double mission of the "Son" and the "Spirit of the Son," and even though one may at first hesitate about the distinction of the Spirit and the Son here, there is probably an echo of the distinct sending of the Messiah and of the Spirit in the OT (e.g., Is 45:1; Ez 36:26). And 1 Cor 2:10–11, attributing to the "Spirit of God" a comprehensive knowledge of the profound thoughts of God, implies its divine character.

This double series of texts manifests Paul's lack of clarity in his conception of the relation of the Spirit to the Son. Paul shares with the OT a more fluid notion of personality than the later theological refinements of nature, substance, and person. His lack of clarity should be respected for what it is and be regarded only as the starting point of the later development. His is only an "economic" understanding of the Trinity.

77 As in his Christology, so too in his teaching about the Spirit, Paul is interested in the functional role played by the latter in man's salvation. If Christ opened up to men the possibility of a new life, to be lived in union with him and for God, it is more accurately the "Spirit of Christ" that is the mode of communicating this dynamic, vital, and life-giving principle to men.

78 Commentators have often tried to distinguish Paul's use of *pneuma* in terms of the Holy Spirit and the effects of the indwelling Spirit (see E.-B. Allo, *Première Épître aux Corinthiens* [Paris, 1934] 93–94). It may seem at times that one could prefer one meaning to the other, and thus Paul would be furnishing the basis of the later theological distinction of the created and uncreated gift of the Spirit. However, it should be recognized that this distinction is really not Paul's; the Spirit is the gift of God's presence to man, and it is better left in this undetermined state.

79 The Spirit is the Spirit of Power (1 Cor 2:4; Rom 15:13) and the source of Christian love, hope, and faith; it frees men from the Law (Gal 5:18; cf. Rom 8:2), from the "cravings of the flesh" (Gal 5:16), and from all immoral conduct (Gal 5:19–24). It is indeed the gift of the Spirit that constitutes adoptive sonship (Gal 4:6; Rom 8:14), which assists the Christian in prayer ("pleading with us with inexpressible yearnings," Rom 8:26), and which makes the Christian especially aware of his relation to the Father. This power of the Spirit is not something distinct from the power of Christ: Christians have been consecrated and have become upright "by the power of our Lord Jesus Christ and through the Spirit of our God" (1 Cor 6:11).

(Fuchs, E., *Christus und der Geist bei Paulus* [Leipzig, 1932]. Hamilton, N. Q., *The Holy Spirit and Eschatology in Paul* [Edinburgh, 1957]. Hermann, I., *Kyrios und Pneuma* [Munich, 1961]. Hoyle, R. B., *The Holy Spirit in St. Paul* [London, 1927]. Stalder, K., *Das Werk des Geistes in der Heiligung bei Paulus* [Bern, 1962].)

80 **(IV) Effects of the Salvation Event.** The effects of Christ's salvific activity are figuratively described by Paul in various ways. These effects are regarded here as part of the objective redemption, as lasting effects once produced by Christ's passion, death, and resurrection, in which man shares through faith and baptism. These effects are the reconciliation of man with God, the expiation of his sins, his redemptive liberation, and his justification.

81 **(A) Reconciliation.** The main effect of Christ's passion, death, and resurrection is the reconciliation of man to God, the restoration of man to a state of peace and union with the Father. This effect is *katallagē* (reconciliation), derived from the vb. (*apo*)*katallassō*, "to make peace" (after a war). In a religious sense these words denote the return of man to God's favor and intimacy after a period of estrangement and rebellion through sin and transgression. The idea of reconciliation underlies many of Paul's statements, but it is developed above all in 2 Cor 5:18–20; Rom 5:10–11; Col 1:20–21; Eph 2:16. By the favor of Christ Jesus, access is had by the sinner to the presence of God; he is introduced once again, as it were, into the royal court of God himself (Rom 5:2). Christ has become "our peace" (Eph 2:14), for he has broken down the party wall between Jews and Greeks—a figure derived from the barriers between the courts of the Jerusalem

Temple—and abolished the Law's commandments. He has made "one new man" out of both and has reconciled them to God in one body. Through his cross, hostility has come to an end and Christ has brought "peace" (*eirēnē*) to men: "Since we are justified, we have peace with God" (Rom 5:1; cf. 2 Thes 3:16; Gal 5:22; Phil 4:7; 1 Cor 7:15; Rom 14:17; Col 3:15; Eph 2:15; 4:3). It is, moreover, a cosmic reconciliation (2 Cor 5:19), embracing "all things whether on earth or in heaven" (Col 1:20–21).

82 Once again, we note Paul's tendency to ascribe reconciliation to the Father. He has reconciled men to himself through Christ—and particularly through the death of Christ, "by his blood" (Rom 5:9). When we were enemies of God, we were reconciled to him through his Son's death; now reconciled, we shall be saved—indeed, we boast of God and the close union we have with him through Christ (Rom 5:10–11). The English word "atonement" aptly expresses this Christian condition—"at-one-ment" with God.

(Büchsel, F., "*Allassō*," *ThDNT* 1, 251–59. Dupont, J., *La réconciliation dans la théologie de S. Paul* [*ALBO* 2/23; Louvain, 1953].)

83 **(B) Expiation.** Paul tells us that "Christ died for our sins" (1 Cor 15:3), that "through him we enjoy...the forgiveness of our sins" (Col 1:14; cf. Eph 1:7). Such generic descriptions of the remission of man's sins by Christ's death or blood—a necessary condition for reconciliation—are further specified in various figurative ways. One of these is expiation.

Although the vb. *hilaskomai* (expiate, propitiate) and the noun *hilasmos* (expiation, propitiation) are used occasionally in the NT (Lk 18:13; Heb 2:17; 1 Jn 2:2; 4:10), Paul uses only the derivative *hilastērion:* "God displayed him [Christ] as *hilastērion* with [*or:* in] his blood for the remission of men's former sins...." The word *hilastērion* could be an adjective and as such would mean, "displayed Christ as expiating"; but it is more likely a noun meaning, "displayed Christ as a means [or instrument] of expiation."

84 What is the figure Paul uses? *Hilastērion* has been explained in terms of the classical and Hellenistic Gk usage of *hilaskomai*, which with a personal object normally means "to propitiate, placate" an angry deity or hero. In a few instances in nonbiblical Greek the object is a crime or a sin, and the meaning is, rather, "to expiate." It might seem that the displaying of Christ as *hilastērion* meant that he was a means of placating the Father's anger. However, in the LXX we find God as the object of *hilaskomai* in only three places (Mal 1:9; Zech 7:2; 8:22), in none of which is there question of the appeasement of his wrath. The word is far more frequently used either of expiating sins (i.e., removing their guilt, Ps 65:4; Sir 5:6; 28:5) or of expiating some object, person, or place (i.e., performing some purificatory rite to remove its cultic defilement, Lv 16-16,20,33; Ez 43:20,26; etc.). It frequently translates Hebr *kippēr,* which has God for its subject and seems to mean basically, "wipe away" or possibly, "cover over." The expiatory sense of *kippēr* is abundantly attested in QL (see S. Lyonnet, *De peccato et redemptione*, part 2 [Rome, 1960] 81–84).

85 This OT and Jewish usage of the root makes it more likely that Paul has in mind some such expiatory notion rather than any appeasement of the Father's wrath. Nor should such passages as 1 Thes 1:10; Rom 5:9 be introduced to suggest that God's wrath was actually placated in the death of Christ. God's "wrath" is an eschatological notion, expressing the reaction of God to be expected on the "Day of Yahweh," when he will destroy those who have consistently resisted his will and thwarted his salvific plan by sin (→ Aspects OT Thought, 77:99–102). It is not that God's anger has been appeased by Christ's death. It is rather that all men, Jews and Gentiles, have sinned and have fallen short of the glory destined for them. But by the favor of God, men's sins are "expiated" (wiped out, remitted) because the Father graciously saw fit to display Christ on the cross as an instrument of expiation.

86 But there may even be a further nuance in Paul's thought, derived from the LXX's use of *hilastērion*, where it translates the Hebr *kappōret*. The latter is often translated either as "propitiatory" (from the Vg *propitiatorium*) or as "mercy seat" (from Luther's *Gnadenstuhl*). Actually, the word may mean "cover" and may denote the "lid" of pure gold erected over the Ark of the Covenant in the Holy of Holies, which supported two golden cherubim, the throne of Yahweh's glorious presence in the Jerusalem Temple (Ex 25:17–22). On *Yôm Kippûrîm* (Day of Atonement; → Religious Institutions, 76:155) the high priest entered the Holy of Holies with the blood of sacrificed animals and sprinkled the "propitiatory" with it, thus atoning for his sins and for those of all Israel (Lv 16:2,11–17). Paul may be alluding to this rite of the Day of Atonement, seeing that he mentions the "glory of God" (3:23), Christ's "blood" (3:25), the *hilastērion*, and the remission of sins (3:25). He would then be looking on Christ's cross as the new "mercy seat" and the first Good Friday as the pre-eminently Christian Day of Atonement. Christ, sprinkled with his own blood, is the real propitiatory, the Father's means of wiping out man's sins. The OT *kappōret* was but a type of the crucified Christ (see Heb 9:5). Christ was displayed in the midst of God's people as the means of blotting out their sins and giving them "access" (Rom 5:2) to the Father to whom they have thus been reconciled. (See T. W. Manson, *JTS* 46 [1945] 1–10; L. Moraldi, *VD* 26 [1948] 257–76.)

87 But the fuller meaning of the public manifestation of Christ "in his blood" (Rom 3:25) is understood only when a contemporary rabbinical axiom is recalled, that "there is no expiation of sins without blood" (see Heb 9:22; *Jub* 6:2,11,14; *bZebaḥin* 6a). The axiom itself was based on OT purificatory rites (cf. Lv 8:15,19,24; 9:15–16; 16:19; etc.). The idea was not that the blood so shed in sacrifice appeased Yahweh; nor was the emphasis on the shedding of the blood and the ensuing death a sort of recompense or price to be paid. Rather, the blood was shed either to purify and cleanse ritually objects dedicated to Yahweh's service (cf. Lv 16:15–19) or else to consecrate objects and persons to that service (i.e., by removing them from the profane and uniting them intimately with Yahweh, as it were, in a sacred pact; cf. Ex 24:6–8). On the Day of Atonement the high priest sprinkled the propitiatory "because of the uncleanness of the Israelites and their transgressions in all their sins" (Lv 16:16). These were considered to have defiled the land, the Temple, and all it contained. The sprinkling with blood purified and consecrated anew, expiating the sins. The underlying reason is found in Lv 17:11: "The life of the flesh is in the blood; I have put it for you upon the altar to make atonement of your lives; for it is the blood that makes atonement by reason of the life (*bannepeš*)." (Cf. 17:14; Gn 9:4; Dt 12:23.) Blood was identified with life itself because the *nepeš* (breath) was thought to be in it. When the blood ran out of a man, the *nepeš* left him. The blood that was shed in sacrifice was not, then, a vicarious punishment meted out on an animal instead of on the person who immolated it. Rather, the "life" of the animal was consecrated to Yahweh (Lv 16:8–9); it was a symbolic dedication of the life of the person who sacrificed it to Yahweh; it cleansed him of his faults in Yahweh's sight and reconciled him once more.

88 Christ's blood, shed in expiation of man's sins,

was a willing offering of his life to bring about the reconciliation of man with God and to give him a new means of union with God (Eph 2:13). In all of this discussion of reconciliation and expiation it is important to realize how Paul insists on the gracious and loving initiative of the Father and on the love of Christ himself. Paul often says of Christ that he "gave himself" for us or our sins (Gal 1:4; 2:20; Eph 5:2,25) and that he "loved" us (Eph 5:2,25; Gal 2:20; Rom 8:35,37). The same attitude toward us is ascribed to the Father (2 Thes 2:16; cf. Rom 8:32). If this element in Paul's theology is kept in mind, it will prevent one from overstressing the juridical aspects of the atonement, which certain of his expressions have at times suggested to commentators in the past. Christ's death in expiation of sin was an act of love, at once for the Father and for men, in which he made an offering of his life to rededicate men to God. Paul knows that through the death of Christ he has been crucified with Christ so that he "may live for God" (Gal 2:19). It is *not* Paul who teaches that the Father willed the death of his Son to satisfy the debts owed to God or to the devil by the sins of man.

On the other hand, it is important to recognize that Paul does at times use juridical concepts to express the various aspects of Christ's death. But they are not to be pressed to the exclusion of other aspects. In Col 2:14 Paul speaks of a "debt," which mankind owed because of its sins: God raised us to life with Christ and forgave all our misdeeds; he wiped out the debt (*cheirographon*) that stood out against us with all its items; he did away with it when he nailed it to the cross, and thus he disarmed the powers of this world. This is not the image of Christ going to his death as a vicarious victim who pays the debt to the Father or the devil. It is, rather, the loving Father, recognizing the love of the Son for himself and mankind, who destroys the outstanding debt by offering his own Son. It is basically an act of God's love, which has flooded the hearts of men (Rom 5:6–8; 8:35,39).

89 Lest Paul's statements, which are at times couched in juridical terminology, be forced into too rigid categories after the fashion of some patristic and scholastic commentators, it must be emphasized that Paul never specifies to whom the "price" was paid. The reason for this is that Paul did not theorize about the mystery of the redemption. He "offers to us not theories but vivid metaphors, which can, if we will let them operate in our imagination, make real to us the saving truth of our redemption by Christ's self-offering on our behalf.... [It is] an unfortunate kind of sophistication which believes that the only thing to do with metaphors is to turn them into theories" (Richardson, *ITNT*, 222–23).

(Dodd, C. H., "*Hilaskesthai* in the Septuagint," *JTS* 32 [1930–31] 352–60. Médebielle, A., "Expiation," *VDBS* 3, 1–262. Moraldi, L., *Espiazione sacrificale e riti espiatori nell'ambiente biblico e nell'Antico Testamento* [Rome, 1956]. Siegman, E. F., "The Blood of Christ in St. Paul's Soteriology," *Proc. Second Precious Blood Study Week* [Rensselaer, Ind., 1960] 11–35.)

90 **(C) Redemptive Liberation.** Another effect Paul ascribes to Christ's salvific activity is freedom. "The glorious freedom of the children of God" (Rom 8:21) for which all creation avidly waits is not yet accomplished. But there is a freedom that Christ has already achieved for men. The classic expression for this is "redemption," a term that reflects the social institution of freeing slaves or captives. Such an institution is clearly envisaged by Paul in 1 Cor 7:23, where he counsels slaves and free men not to try to change their social status because this status matters little now that they have been "bought with a price" (7:23; cf. 6:20) and have become slaves of Christ or freedmen of the Lord. In the contemporary world of Hellenism the manumission of a slave was often a sacral affair. At Delphi and other shrines numerous inscriptions have been found that describe the manumission in terms of a fictive purchase of the slave by a god from his owner. In reality, the slave himself deposited the price of his freedom in the god's temple; it was, of course, in time turned over to his owner. But the slave was considered to have passed into the ownership of the god who thereafter protected him and guaranteed his freedom (see A. Deissmann, *LAE* 320ff.). There is a certain parallelism between some aspects of this institution and some of Paul's expressions ("bought with a price," "slave of Christ," "redemption"; cf. AG 12,95,205,825). But it is at most a superficial parallelism and needs to be modified by OT data. For it is Christ who actually pays, not the sinner-slave; as the divine purchaser, his payment is not fictive.

91 In the OT Yahweh is often depicted in the role of Israel's *gō'ēl*, "redeemer," i.e., the kinsman to whom fell the duty of buying back the lost freedom of a relative. This figure is applied to Yahweh in Dt-Is (41:14; 43:14; 44:6; 47:4) and the Pss (18:15; 77:35). If refers above all to the freeing of Israel from Egyptian bondage (Ex 6:6–7; Dt 7:6–8; Ps 111:9) and to the crossing of the Reed Sea (Is 43:1). Later, it is extended to Israel's return from Babylonian captivity when Yahweh brings about another Exodus of his people (Is 51:11; 52:3–9). It is noteworthy that in the OT such a "redemption" means rather "deliverance, liberation," since the payment of a *lytron* (ransom) is rarely mentioned (cf. Is 52:3). In time the notion of redemption took on an eschatological nuance, referring to what God was going to do for his people in the end of days (Hos 13:14; Is 59:20; Ps 130:7–8; Est 13:9,16). This persists in QL (see L. de Lorenzi, *RBibIt* 5 [1957] 197–253) and the NT (Lk 2:38; 24:21). In general, it implies a deliverance from uncleanness, sin, death, and Sheol.

92 Another notion, however, was often linked with this redemptive liberation, viz., that of "acquisition, possession." Yahweh not only freed the Hebrews from Egyptian bondage but acquired a people for himself, especially through the covenant of Sinai (Ex 6:6–7; 15:16; 19:5; Is 43:21; Pss 74:2; 135:4). It was a deliverance, then, that terminated in "acquisition," and even in "adoption."

When Paul speaks of Christians having been "bought with a price" (1 Cor 6:14; 7:22), he is stressing the onerous burden of Christ's offering of his life for man's freedom and for the acquisition of them as "his people." In Gal (3:13; 4:5) Paul uses *exagorazō* to describe the freedom from the Law that the Christ-event has brought about (cf. F. Büchsel, *ThDNT* 1,124–28). This rare word is never used in the LXX in a context of manumission, nor is it ever found in any extrabiblical texts referring to sacral manumission. It is a compound of *agorazō* and usually means no more than "to buy." However, it is used by Diodorus Siculus (36:2) of the buying of a slave (as a possession) and again (15:7) of the setting free of an enslaved person by purchase. In the latter context, though there is no mention of *lytron*, it is obviously a case of ransoming someone enslaved. If, then, the notion of ransom by purchase is applied to Paul's use of the word, one should avoid overstressing the juridical details, since his full notion of "redemption" is colored by the OT idea of "acquisition." Paul never calls Christ *lytrōtēs* ("redeemer" = *gō'ēl;* this word is used only of Moses, Acts 7:35); nor does he ever speak of *lytron* (ransom) as such. He calls Christ Jesus "our redemption" (*apolytrōsis*, 1 Cor 1:30) in a majestic phrase that identifies the person of Christ with his deliverance and sums up a Pauline view of Christ. But it is important to note that even though it is "through the redemption which is in Christ Jesus"

(Rom 3:24) that men obtain the remission of their sins (cf. Col 1:14; Eph 1:7), yet it is specifically "a redemption of acquisition" (Eph 1:14). Although redemption has in a sense already taken place (Rom 3:24), yet like the whole Christ-event it still has a future, eschatological phase, for Christians still "await the redemption of the body" (Rom 8:23). The sealing with the Spirit, which the Christian already enjoys, is only a pledge for "the day of redemption" (Eph 4:30).

93 The freedom Christ has won for Christians is freedom from the Law, from sin, from death, and from self (Rom 5–8). Those who were under the Law have now been bought by him; they can be called "slaves of Christ" (1 Cor 7:23; [cf. Ti 2:14, echoing Ps 130:8 and Ex 19:5]), for they owe obedience now only to him. His is the law (Gal 6:2; 1 Cor 9:21) to which they are now bound. But in him they find freedom from all the constraining elements of human existence (Gal 2:4; 4:22–31; 5:1,13; 1 Cor 9:1,19; 10:29; 2 Cor 3:17; Rom 6:18, 20,22; 7:3; 8:2,21), for his law is the law of love: "Love fully satisfies the Law" (Rom 13:10; cf. 8–10).

(Cerfaux, L., *Christ*, 107–10. Elert, W., "Redemptio ab hostibus," *TLZ* 72 [1947] 265–70. Lyonnet, S., *De peccato et redemptione* [Rome, 1960] 2, 24–66; "L'emploi paulinien de *exagorazein* au sens de 'redimere,' est-il attesté dans la littérature grecque?" *Bib* 42 [1961] 85–89. Pax, E., "Der Loskauf: Zur Geschichte eines neutestamentlichen Begriffes," *Anton* 37 [1962] 239–78. Taylor, V., *The Atonement in NT Teaching* [2nd ed.; Oxford, 1945].)

94 **(D) Justification.** Another way in which Paul expresses the effects of Christ's salvific activity is by the justification of the Christian. "Jesus...was raised up for our justification" (Rom 4:25). This effect of the Christ-event is really not as important to Pauline theology as the Reformation controversies and Augustinian interpretation have made it out to be. It is not the key to Pauline theology, nor does it sum up the Christian experience for the Apostle—A. Schweitzer has referred to it as "a subsidiary crater." It is the aspect of salvation that emerged in the polemical context of Paul's controversy with the Judaizers. Its controversial aspect is seen when it is recalled that *dikaiōsis* (justification) is found only in Rom 4:25; 5:18 (cf. *dikaiōma*, 5:16) and that the related vb., *dikaioō*, occurs 15 times in Rom and 8 times in Gal but elsewhere only twice (1 Cor 4:4; 6:11 [cf. 1 Tm 3:16; Ti 3:7]). Moreover, it gives salvation a judicial aspect, which, though necessary for the discussion in the Judaizing context, hardly epitomizes the Christian reality itself. However, there is a positive value in the aspect of justification when it is properly interpreted, i.e., as a manifestation of the "uprightness of God" as this term was understood in the prophetic and post-exilic OT literature and other late Jewish writings. (See further K. Stendahl, "The Apostle Paul and the Introspective Conscience of the West," *HarvTR* 56 [1963] 199–215.)

95 Justification as a metaphor applied to salvation is derived from a judicial procedure that issues a verdict of acquittal; and it is almost exclusively a Pauline view of salvation. But for an understanding of what is really meant by it, its OT roots must be considered. We have already mentioned the "uprightness of God" (→ 37 above); it is that quality by which Yahweh as the judge of Israel manifests his salvific bounty toward his people in a just decision. It is a quality related to his covenant mercy (*ḥesed*); in the LXX, *dikaiosynē* often replaces *eleos* as the translation of *ḥesed* (Gn 19:19; 20:13; 21:23; 24:27; etc.). This shows how it came to designate "favor toward Israel," without, however, losing completely its basic judicial connotation. If certain circles in Palestinian Judaism tended to forget about this comprehensive view of "God's uprightness" (as Paul's Judaizing adversaries seem to have done), the notion was preserved at least among the Essenes of Qumran. Abundant references are found in QL to *ṣedeq 'El* or *ṣidqat 'El*, which are understood in a fashion that is strikingly close to the Pauline "uprightness of God" (cf. 1QS 11:4–9,11–13,18; 1QH 9:33; 1:6–9; 14:15–16; → Aspects OT Thought, 77: 93–98).

(Benoit, P., "Qumrân et le Nouveau Testament," *NTS* 7 [1960–61] 276–96, esp. 292–95. Braun, H., "Qumrân und das Neue Testament," *TRu* 29 [1963] 189–94. Nötscher, F., *Zur theologischen Terminologie der Qumrân-Texte* [BBB 10; Bonn, 1956] 158–64. Schulz, S., "Zur Rechtfertigung aus Gnaden in Qumrân und bei Paulus," *ZThK* 56 [1959] 155–85.)

The manifestation of this divine attribute forms the theme of the first part of Rom (see 1:17, contrasted with God's wrath; cf. 3:21,22,25,26; 10:3). Because Yahweh is upright, it is he who justifies man (cf. Rom 3:26; 8:33).

96 The OT taught that "no living man is upright before God" (Ps 143:2), i.e., achieves by himself a status of acquittal in God's sight (cf. 1 Kgs 8:46; Jb 9:2; Ps 130:3–4; Is 64:6). The justification of man was expected to be brought about by a coming redeemer (Is 59:15–20). But Paul stresses that the justification has already taken place through faith in the Christ-event: "It was to show forth now at the present time that he [God] is upright himself, even in making upright the man who has faith in Jesus" (Rom 3:26; cf. 5:1). Not only does Paul emphasize that the justification of man has already come about, but he insists on the utter gratuity of it. It comes only from God. For their part, men have "sinned and fall short of the glory of God" (Rom 3:23), but God out of sheer favor has brought it about through Christ that man stands upright before God.

97 This justification as a divine act implies a declaration that sinful man is upright before God. Does this mean that he is merely declared to be so—when he is really a sinner—by some legal fiction? We might expect that *dikaioō*, like other Gk verbs ending in *-oō*, would have a causative, factitive meaning: "to make someone *dikaios*" (cf. *douloō*, "enslave"; *nekroō*, "mortify"; *anakainoō*, "renew"; etc.). But in the LXX, *dikaioō* seems normally to have a declarative, forensic meaning. At times this seems to be the only sense intended in Paul's letters (cf. Rom 8:33); but many instances are ambiguous. One can certainly not appeal to this forensic sense to exclude a more radical transformation of man through the Christ-event, making it the essence of the Christian experience, as it were. For justification is really the placing of man in a status of uprightness in the sight of God through the association of him with the salvific activity of Christ Jesus—through the incorporation of him in Christ and his Church through faith and baptism. The result of this justification is that the Christian becomes *dikaios* (upright); he is not just declared to be so but is actually constituted such (*katastathēsontai*, Rom 5:19). Paul recognizes that as a Christian he no longer has an uprightness of his own, based on the Law, but one acquired through faith in Christ, an "uprightness from God" (Phil 3:8–9). And the Christian in union with Christ is even said to become "the uprightness of God" (2 Cor 5:21).

(Bultmann, R., "*Dikaiosynē Theou*," *JBL* 83 [1964] 12–16. Descamps, A., *Les justes et la justice* [Louvain, 1950]. Descamps, A. and L. Cerfaux, "Justice," *VDBS* 4 [1949] 1417–1510. Jeremias, J., "Justification by Faith," *The Central Message of the New Testament* [London, 1965] 51–70. Käsemann, E., "God's Righteousness in Paul," *The Bultmann School of Biblical Interpretation: New Directions?* (ed. J. M. Robinson; N.Y., 1965) 100–10. Lyonnet, S., "De 'justitia Dei' in Epistola ad Romanos," *VD* 25 [1947] 23–34, 118–21, 129–44, 193–203, 257–63. Quell, G. and G. Schrenk, *Righteousness* [BKW 4; London, 1951]; "*Dikaisoynē*," *ThDNT* 2, 174–225. Stuhlmacher, P., *Gerechtigkeit Gottes bei Paulus* [FRLANT 87; Göttingen, 1965].)

PAULINE ANTHROPOLOGY

98 **(I) Man Before Christ:** What effect does the Christ-event actually have on the lives of men? How do men share in the redemption brought by Christ? Having sketched the objective aspects of Christian salvation, we now pass to a discussion of the ways in which Paul sees men affected by what Christ did. To understand the Pauline view of the Christian experience from the side of man, we must look at the way Paul regarded man before Christ's coming. His view is at once corporate and individual. We now touch upon Paul's anthropological views.

The corporate view of man's state before Christ should be sketched first because it is more closely related to salvation history than is the individual view. Paul often contrasts what man's situation once was with what it is "now" in the Christian dispensation (cf. Gal 4:8–9; 1 Cor 6:11; Col 1:21–22; 3:7–8; Eph 2:1–6; 2:11–13; 5:8).

99 **(A) Sin.** In the period before Christ men were sinners who, despite their strivings to live uprightly, never achieved that goal and never reached the destiny of glory intended for them (Rom 3:23). Paul's indictment of the Gentiles' ungodliness and wickedness, which suppressed the truth in their lives, is severe (Rom 1:18–23). He finds that they have no excuse for not honoring and thanking God as a result of what they knew about him in his creation, apart from God's OT revelation of himself. "In not knowing God," the Gentiles "were in bondage to beings that were no gods...and were slaves to elemental spirits" (Gal 4:8–9). Their condition of servitude did not enlighten them about their degraded conduct (Rom 1:24–32; 1 Cor 6:9–11). But the picture is not wholly black, for Paul admits that Gentiles did at times fulfill some of the prescriptions of the Mosaic Law (Rom 2:14), "being a law to themselves," i.e., being aware through their consciences of what the Mosaic Law positively prescribed for Jews.

100 As for the Jews, who gloried in the possession of the Mosaic Law as a manifestation of Yahweh's will and as a guide for their conduct, Paul's indictment of them is equally telling. They may have the Law, but they do not observe it. Not even their practice of circumcision or their possession of the oracles of salvation can save them from the wrath befitting sin (Rom 2:1–3:8).

101 Without the gospel the whole human race, "all men, both Jews and Greeks, are under the power of sin" (Rom 3:9). Men find themselves in a condition of hostility toward God (Rom 5:10), being dedicated neither to his honor and service (Rom 1:18) nor to honoring his name (Rom 2:24). Their condition is an estrangement from God and a bondage to Satan (Eph 2:2; 6:11–12; Col 1:13), a form of "death" (Eph 2:1,5; Col 2:13).

102 Paul at times refers to sin in such a way that one might consider it a "debt" to be remitted (Rom 3:25; Col 1:14; 2:14; Eph 1:7), but more frequently he treats it as a force or power that has invaded man and is abetted by all his natural inclinations. The individual sinful acts of man are "transgressions" (Gal 3:19; Rom 2:23; 4:15), "trespasses" (Gal 6:1; Rom 5:15,16,17,18,20), and "sins" (Rom 3:25 *hamartēmata*). But *hamartia* is an active evil influence in man's life, pervading his whole history. Both Sin and Death are personified by Paul and perform as actors on the stage of man's history. Sin was introduced into the history of mankind by Adam's transgression and brought Death in its wake (in a total sense: physical death leading to spiritual death).

103 In his teaching on the pervasive influence of Sin in the world before Christ, Paul depends on the OT and current Jewish ideas about the character of Sin and Death. Genesis 2–3 expressly depicts Adam and Eve's loss of trusted intercourse and friendship with God and the consequent labor, pains, and death that are their lot. The unmistakable etiological character of the narrative implies that the sin of Adam and Eve was the cause of all human misery. Yet neither in Gn nor anywhere else in the early books of the OT is this connection definitely established. It is not until the late Book of Sirach (*ca.* 190 BC) that corporal death is presented as a hereditary (?) consequence of the sin in Eden: "Sin began with a woman and because of her we all die" (25:24). In Wis 2:23–24 we read, "God created man for immortality and made him the image of his own eternity, but through the devil's envy death came into the world." Yet even in this text death is not merely physical, corporal death.

The OT teaches the general sinfulness of man in many places (Gn 6:5; 8:21; Jb 4:17; 14:4; 15:14; Pss 120:3; 143:2). This teaching, however, is presented as the datum of experience; all men are known to sin. The few texts that might suggest a sinful disposition in man (Gn 8:21; Jb 14:4; Ps 51:7) express in reality only an inclination to sin, which is almost innate. They hardly give expression to a belief in a sinful condition inherited from Adam and Eve. Again, in Jewish intertestamental literature many passages refer death to Adam or Eve (*2 Enoch* 30:17, "I created him a wife, that death should come to him by his wife"; *Apoc. Mos.* 14, "Adam said to Eve, 'What have you done to us in bringing on us the great wrath [death] which now rules over our whole race?' "; cf. *2 Esdras* 3:7). But even in this literature no unequivocal passage is found that ascribes hereditary sin to Adam or Eve. The closest one comes to this notion is in *Apoc. Mos.* 32: "All sin has come through me into creation." Yet even this statement only asserts that Eve was the first sinner (cf. Josephus, *Ant.* 3.8,1 § 190; Philo, *De vita Mos.* 2:147). The Psalmist of Qumran sings, "And he [man] is in iniquity from the womb" (1QH 4:29–30), which expresses again only the complete sinfulness of man's existence.

104 Paul clearly echoes the Jewish tradition of hereditary death, ascribing the situation to Adam (1 Cor 15:21–22: "all men die in [*or* through] Adam"). Since in the context the contrast is with resurrection to life (eternal), Paul is thinking of spiritual death (which is different from physical death). The connection of death with Adam is not explained in 1 Cor, but in Rom 5:12 the death of all men is attributed to Adam because of his sin: "Just as though one man Sin entered the world, and through that Sin, Death—and in this way death spread to all men, inasmuch as all sinned...." In this verse Paul ascribes to Adam not only the condition of total death, which affects all men, but also the contagion of sin, which also affects all men, and this independently of their own personal transgressions. This sense is not derived from some "habitual" meaning of *hēmarton*, nor from the phrase *eph' hō* understood of some incorporation of all men in Adam (→ Letter Rom, 53:56). The context (vv. 13ff.) rather demands such a notion, and especially 5:19: "Just as that one man's disobedience made (*katestathēsan*) the mass of mankind sinners, so this one's obedience will make the mass of them upright." The contrast of antitype and type, Christ and Adam, would demand that the sinful condition of all men be due to Adam (independently of their own sins, which also lead to death), just as the condition of uprightness is due to Christ alone.

(Barrett, C. K., *From First Adam to Last: A Study in Pauline Theology* [London, 1962]. Barrosse, T. A., "Death and Sin in Saint Paul's Epistle to the Romans," *CBQ* 15 [1953] 438–59. Brandenburger, E., *Adam und Christus* [WMzANT 7; Neukirchen, 1962]. Bultmann, R., "Adam and Christ According to Romans 5," *CINTI* 143–65. Dubarle, A.-M., *Original Sin: The Biblical Doctrine* [N.Y., 1965]. Freundorfer, J., *Erbsünde und Erbtod beim Apostel Paulus* [Münster, 1927]. Ligier, L., *Péché d'Adam et péché du monde*, vol. 2 [Coll. Théologie 48; Paris, 1961]. Scroggs, R., *The Last Adam* [Oxford, 1966].)

105 **(B) The Law and the Spirits.** Man's condition before Christ was not only a bondage to Sin and Death but an enslavement to the "spirits" of this world and to the Law. "In your ignorance," Paul says to former pagan Galatians, "you were slaves to gods that really did not exist" (Gal 4:8). It is a matter of disputed interpretation whether these "gods" were the spirits that bore the title of "elements of this world" (Gal 4:9; cf. Col 2:20), "thrones, dominions, principalities, authorities" (Col 1:16; cf. Eph 1:21)—or "whatever title has been given to them." At times one wonders if Paul really believed in their existence. He scoffs at them as he asserts the supremacy of Christ (Col 2:10,15,18; Eph 3:10). But at times he ascribes man's sinful condition to the "course of this world, to the prince of the realm of the air" (Eph 2:2; cf. Eph 6:12). He envisages the possibility of "angels" being hindrances to the love of God in Christ (Rom 8:38), announcing another gospel different from his own (Gal 1:8). That the angels were the promulgators of the Mosaic Law that enslaved men is a sign of its inferiority to the promises of God (Gal 3:19). Such spirits are not always evil; they may be good or at least neutral (1 Cor 11:10; Gal 4:14). But if they have held sway over men till now, their rule has been broken in the coming of the *Kyrios*, Jesus Christ. Because of him even Christians will now judge the angels (1 Cor 6:3), so completely is their sway over men undone.

106 But men were enslaved to the Law as well as to the angels. Paul now thinks in terms of Israel's history (see Gal 4:3–5,8–9; 5:1–3; Rom 7:1ff.). Except for a few passages where *nomos* is qualified either explicitly (Rom 3:27, "law of faith"; 8:2, "law of the Spirit"; 8:7, "law of God"; Gal 6:2, "law of Christ") or by the context (playing on the idea of *nomos*, Rom 2:14b; 7:2–3,21–25), *ho nomos* or simply *nomos* otherwise always means for Paul the Mosaic Law, without any distinction being made between cultic or ritual commandments and ethical requirements (cf. Gal 4:10; 5:3; Rom 7:7). He occasionally speaks of *entolē*, but this word denotes only a "commandment," a way of designating the whole by a part. (See R. Bultmann, *TNT* 1, 260–61; H. Kleinknecht and W. Gutbrod, *Law* [BKW 11; London, 1962] 101.) One should beware, then, of interpreting *nomos* without the article in terms of "law in general." (Cf. G. B. Winer, *Grammatik des NT Sprachidioms* [8th ed.; Göttingen, 1894] § 19,13h; Bl-Deb-F § 258.2.)

107 As Paul personified Sin and Death, so he also personified Law (*nomos;* cf. Rom 7:1). All three are actors on the stage of man's history, playing their roles of *kyrioi*. Because of Adam's transgression Sin and Death entered the world. But men began to sin in imitation of Adam only when the Mosaic Law came upon the stage, bringing with it a "real awareness" of what sin is (Rom 3:20).

108 Paul recognized that the Law in itself was "good, just and holy" (Rom 7:12,16 [cf. 1 Tm 1:8–9]). He even calls it *pneumatikos*, "related to the Spirit," because it comes from God (7:14,22,25; 8:7). It was destined to lead men to life (Rom 7:10; cf. Gal 3:12) and was in no way a contradiction of God's promises (Gal 3:21). It was addressed to those under its authority (Rom 3:19); yet it did little good for a Jew to boast of possessing it without obeying it (Rom 2:12–13,17–18,23,25; 9:4). Uprightness was sought by doing the "deeds of the Law."

109 Yet the Law could not produce the uprightness it was supposed to. Paul was firmly convinced of this; he quotes Ps 143:2, "No human being will be justified before him," and explicitly adds, "by deeds of the Law" (Rom 3:20; cf. 3:21,28; 8:3). In Gal he expressed the same idea in terms of "life" (3:12, quoting Hab 2:4). In spite of the Law the Jews were as much sinners as were the Gentiles (Rom 2:17–24). The reason was because the Law provided merely an extrinsic norm for what should be done without supplying any *dynamis* (power) to do it.

110 As a result, the Law multiplied sin (Gal 3:19; Rom 5:20; 7:13). Not only did it become the *dynamis* of Sin (1 Cor 15:56), making man liable to God's wrath (Rom 4:15), but it positively aided sin, even though it was not sin in itself (Rom 7:7). The Mosaic Law proved to be an occasion for sin because it either instructed man in the material possibilities of sin by forbidding something which was in itself indifferent, or it excited his concupiscence into going after forbidden fruit (Rom 7:5,8,11). But much more important was its role as moral informer, for the Law gave man a "real awareness" (*epignōsis*) of sin (Rom 3:20), i.e., the understanding of a moral disorder as transgression and rebellion against God. Such an awareness did not exist in the world before Moses (Rom 5:13; 4:15). "Without the Law Sin was dead...but when the commandment came, Sin revived and I died (Rom 7:8–9). Sin was shown up by it in its true colors.

111 But worse still, it laid a curse on all who did not observe it: "Cursed be anyone who does not stand by everything that is written in the book of the Law and obey it" (Gal 3:10, quoting Dt 27:26). As the instrument and accomplice of Sin, the Law that should have meant life for man proved to mean only death (Rom 7:10). It brought down on him a "condemnation" (Rom 8:1); it was a "dispensation of death" (2 Cor 3:7), a "dispensation of condemnation" (2 Cor 3:9), and the "letter that kills" (2 Cor 3:6).

112 Paul sensed the anomaly of the stern accusations he brought against Mosaic Law, which came from God. "Did what was good then prove the death of me? Certainly not! It was Sin that did so, that it might be recognized as sin" (Rom 7:13). The Law was but the tool of *hamartia*. But in using the Law, Sin's true character was revealed.

113 How could God have permitted what was "good, just, and holy" to serve such a cause? Paul explains the anomaly in two ways. First, in Gal he explains that the Law was temporary. Before faith came, men were imprisoned under the Law "in order to obtain the faith to be revealed" (Gal 3:23). The law acted as a slave-attendant (*paidagōgos*) leading men to Christ. The sense of this role is not that a man can only attain true faith in Christ when his self-righteousness has been crushed by the Law or when he has been made by the Law to feel his desperate need for a savior. In the framework of salvation history the Law plays the role of leading men to find their salvation through faith in Christ. To the promises of salvation that had been made to Abraham the Law was added some 430 years later and was promulgated by angels through the mediation of Moses. All of this manifests its temporary, inferior character in God's salvific plan (Gal 3:17–20); it was but a facet of Israel's role in that plan. Second, in Rom Paul explains that the anomaly is really due to man, who is *sarkinos*, "made of flesh." The *egō* is not simply identified with Sin and Flesh. But though the Law came from God and was *pneumatikos*, it did nothing to resolve the conflict that every man experiences, especially since every man is "sold under sin" (Rom 7:14). Though "in his inmost self he delights in the law of God" (Rom 7:22), he knows that "Sin dwells in him" (7:17). Paul figuratively even calls this sin "another Law" (7:23). So, once again Paul lays the blame not on the Law but on Sin and on man's inability to do the good that he would (7:15). But the Law did not help him to resolve this predicament. (See K. Stendahl, *HarvTR* 56 [1963] 199–215.)

114 The anomaly was, however, resolved in Christ Jesus and in him alone. "This is the freedom for which Christ has freed us" (Gal 5:1), a freedom from the Law's regime. "Through the body of Christ you have become dead to the Law" (Rom 7:4). It is Christ too who saved men from enslavement to Sin and Death. "Who can save me from this doomed body [lit., "body of death"]? Thank God! It is done through Jesus Christ our Lord" (Rom 7:25). "There is condemnation no more for those in union with Christ Jesus. The life-giving law of the Spirit has freed you through Christ Jesus from the law of sin and death" (Rom 8:1–2). "You are no longer under the Law but under grace" (Rom 6:14). Thus, Christ is the "end of the Law" (Rom 10:4). The Christian has died to the Law because through baptism he has been crucified with Christ, who was put to death "through the [Mosaic] Law" (Gal 2:19). The mentality induced by the Law could not accept Jesus as the Christ and actually did away with him. But the very death of Christ was the liberating act whereby the curse of the Law was broken. Though he was born under the Law (Gal 4:4) and was sinless (2 Cor 5:21), he was eventually brought to the condition where a curse of the Law fell on him too—the curse of Dt 21:23, which was leveled against a dead body exposed on a tree. The connection between the two curses is only extrinsic and material, but Paul, using a principle of rabbinical logic, saw in the curse of Christ the means whereby the curse of the Law upon men was removed.

115 How did Paul arrive at such a negative view of the Law? Does he not seem to be a Marcionite after all? Faced with this problem, commentators have sometimes tried to say that Paul was referring to the cultic and ritual parts of the OT. This is an inadequate explanation, since Paul refers to the Decalogue explicitly in Rom 7:7. It does not help to say that Paul is talking about "law in general" (i.e., any legalistic system). Part of the problem is that Paul viewed the OT often through Pharisaic and rabbinical glasses and was preoccupied with its 613 commands and the casuistic interpretations of the Fathers that explained them. He rarely refers to the OT as covenant (see the fleeting references in Rom 9:4; Eph 2:12; 2 Cor 3:14; Gal 3:17 [the covenant of promise made with Abraham, not the great event of Sinai!]). This may be the result of Paul's dependence on the LXX in which the notion of the Hebr *bᵉrît* was translated by *diathēkē*, a word that in Hellenistic times meant "last will, testament" (cf. Gal 3:15). It obscured the covenant as a *synthēkē* (pact) and gave it the sense of God's will that had to be executed by Israel (→ Aspects OT Thought, 77:81–85).

116 Whatever the real answer to this problem of Paul's view of the Mosaic Law is, he was convinced that a new way of life had been introduced into man's history by Christ's death and resurrection. It was no longer a "law of deeds" that man must perform, but a "law of faith" (Rom 3:27). Man finds himself freed from the Law in Christ, whereas before Christ he was enslaved to it. He is freed from that which constrained and coerced him from without but gave him no assistance to do the good that it ordered.

(Benoit, P., "La loi et la croix d'après Saint Paul," *RB* 47 [1938] 481–509. Berkhof, H., *Christ and the Powers* [Scottsdale, Pa., 1962]. Bläser, P., *Das Gesetz bei Paulus* [NTAbh 19/1–2; Münster, 1941]. Branscomb, B. H., *Jesus and the Law of Moses* [London, 1930]. Caird, G. B., *Principalities and Powers* [Oxford, 1956]. Fitzmyer, J. A., "Saint Paul and the Law," *The Jurist* 27 [1967] 18–36. Lyonnet, S., "St. Paul: Liberty and Law," *The Bridge* 4 [1961–62] 229–51. Reicke, B., "The Law and This World According to Paul," *JBL* 70 [1951] 259–76. Schlier, H., *Principalities and Powers in the NT* [Freiburg, 1961].)

117 **(C) Man.** One of the problems that Paul tried to explain in his picture of man before Christ is the makeup of man himself. Man's inability to observe the Mosaic Law stems in part from his condition as *sarkinos*. What does Paul mean by this? To explain we must try to ascertain what he meant by *sōma* (body), *sarx* (flesh), *psychē* (soul), *pneuma* (spirit), *kardia* (heart), and *nous* (mind). Paul does not really describe for us man *in se* but describes, rather, different relations of man vis-à-vis God. These terms, then, do not really designate parts of man but designate, rather, aspects of the whole man as seen from different perspectives (→ Aspects OT Thought, 77:66).

118 A popular, common conception of man as made up of two parts is found at times in Paul's writings (1 Cor 5:3; 7:34; 2 Cor 12:2–3). The visible, tangible, biological part made up of members is called *sōma* (Rom 12:4–5; 1 Cor 12:12–26). Though at times he seems to mean by it only the flesh and bones of man (Gal 1:16; 1 Cor 13:3; 2 Cor 4:10; 10:10; Rom 1:24), he normally means far more. Man does not merely have a *sōma*, he is a *sōma*. It seems to be Paul's way of saying "self" (Phil 1:20; Rom 6:12–13; cf. 1 Cor 6:15 and 12:27). It denotes man as a whole, as a unified, complex, living organism, even as a person, especially when he is the subject to whom something happens or is the object of his own action (1 Cor 9:27; Rom 6:12–13; 12:1; 8:13; cf. R. Bultmann, *TNT* 1, 195). A corpse is not a *sōma*, and there is no form of human existence for Paul without a body in this full sense (see Phil 3:21; 1 Cor 15:35–45; 2 Cor 5:2–4; but cf. 2 Cor 12:2–3; 5:6–8). When Paul uses *sōma* in a pejorative sense, when speaking of the "desires or passions" of the body (Rom 6:12; 8:13), of the "body of sin" (Rom 6:6), of the "body of humiliation" (Phil 3:21), or of "the body of death" (Rom 8:3), he really means man under the sway of some power like Sin or the "flesh" (Rom 7:14,18,23; 8:3,13). In these cases, *sōma* is the sin-ruled self (Rom 7:23), and this self is the condition of man before the coming of Christ—or even after the coming of Christ, if he does not live in Christ.

119 In the OT the word *bāśār* expressed the idea of both "body" and "flesh." Paul reflects this OT notion when he uses *sarx* as a synonym for *sōma* (1 Cor 6:16, quoting Gn 2:24; 2 Cor 4:10–11; cf. Gal 4:13; 6:17). In these cases *sarx* means the physical body. The phrase, "flesh and blood," designates man (Gal 1:16; 1 Cor 15:50; Eph 6:12) and connotes his natural frailty as a human being. It is a late OT expression (Sir 14:18; 17:31). But *sarx* alone can also denote humanity or human nature (Rom 6:19; 3:5; 1 Cor 9:8). However, the more typically Pauline use of *sarx* denotes man in his natural, physical, and visible existence, weak and earth-bound (*ta melē ta epi tēs gēs*, Col 3:5); it connotes the natural human creature left to himself. "No flesh can boast of anything before God" (1 Cor 1:29). "People who are controlled by the flesh think of what pertains to the flesh" (Rom 8:5); they cannot please God (Rom 8:8). The "deeds of the flesh" are retailed in Gal 5:19–21;

it should be superfluous to note that for Paul "flesh" is not restricted to the area of sex. Paul can identify the *egō* and *sarx* and find no "good" in them (Rom 7:18). *Sarx* denotes, therefore, the whole man dominated by natural, earth-oriented tendencies. This notion is prominent in the famous Pauline contrast of "flesh" and "spirit," which compares man subject to his earthly tendencies with man under the influence of the Spirit. *Sarx* is man in his contrast to God, subject to all that withdraws him from God. For the OT concept of flesh, → Aspects OT Thought, 77:64.

120 Similarly, *psychē* is not just the vital principle of biological activity in man. As in the OT, it denotes a "living being, living person" (Hebr *nepeš;* 1 Cor 15:45). It expresses man with his vitality, his consciousness, his intelligence and volition (1 Thes 2:8; Phil 2:30; 2 Cor 1:23; 12:15; Rom 11:3; 16:4). Even when it seems to mean nothing more than "self" (Rom 2:9; 13:1), there is always the connotation of conscious, purposeful vitality, of "life." And yet it is only the earthly, natural "life" of man. Normally, Paul does not use *psychē* in a derogatory sense; but it is, on the other hand, clearly the life of *sarx* and not the life dominated by the Spirit. This is why he calls the man *psychikos* who lives without the Spirit of God (1 Cor 2:14). This is "material" man, not "spiritual" man (*pneumatikos*). For the OT concept of *nepeš*, → Aspects OT Thought, 77:66.

121 In 1 Thes 5:23 Paul lines up what seems to be three parts of man: *sōma*, *psychē*, and *pneuma*. In this case *pneuma* is not the Holy Spirit (cf. Rom 8:16; 1 Cor 2:10–11). Joined to *sōma* and *psychē*, which denote the whole man under different aspects, *pneuma* would seem to be another aspect. But it is not always easy to distinguish *pneuma* in this sense from *psychē* (cf. Phil. 1:27; 2 Cor 12:18). If anything, *pneuma* suggests the knowing and willing self of man and as such reveals him to be particularly apt to receive the Spirit of God. Sometimes, however, it is a mere substitute for the personal pronoun (Gal 6:18; 2 Cor 2:13; 7:13; Rom 1:9; Phlm 25). For the OT concept of spirit, → Aspects OT Thought, 77:32–34.

122 *Nous* for Paul seems to describe man as a knowing and judging subject; it designates his capacity for intelligent understanding, planning, and decision (cf. 1 Cor 1:10; 2:16; Rom 14:5). In Rom 7:23 it is the understanding self that hears God's will addressed to it in the Law and that agrees with God's will and accepts it as its own. It is this capacity of man that recognizes what can be known about God from his creation (Rom 1:20); the *nooumena* are the things that the *nous* can grasp. There is really little difference in Paul's use of *nous* and *kardia* (heart), which, as in the OT, often means "mind." If anything, *kardia* would connote the more responsive and emotional reactions of the intelligent, planning self. For it "loves" (2 Cor 7:3; 8:16), "grieves" (Rom 9:2), "plans" (1 Cor 4:5), "lusts" (Rom 1:24), and "suffers" (2 Cor 2:4). It doubts and believes (Rom 10:6–10), is hardened (2 Cor 3:14), and is impenitent (Rom 2:5), but it can be strengthened (1 Thes 3:13; Gal 4:6; 2 Cor 1:22). It is the heart of man that "wills" (Gal 4:9; 1 Cor 4:21; 10:27; etc.).

123 All these aspects of man's existence are summed up in his "life" (*zōē*), which is itself a God-given gift and expresses the concrete existence of man as he is the subject of his own actions. But the life of man before Christ is one lived "according to the flesh" (Rom 8:12; cf. Gal 2:20). With all his capacities for the conscious, intelligent, and purposeful planning of his life, man without Christ remains one who has not been able to achieve the goal proposed for him. Of his situation Paul can only say, "All men sinned and fall short of the glory of God" (Rom 3:23). Their falling short implies that a destiny of glory was somehow intended for them (cf. Rom 8:18–23). Our sketch of the condition of man before Christ has at times necessarily indicated the difference that Christ made in his existence. A fuller description of that difference now follows in terms of man in Christ.

(Kümmel, W. G., *Man in the NT* [rev. ed.; London, 1963] 38–71. Mehl-Koehnlein, H., *L'homme selon l'apôtre Paul* [Neuchâtel, 1951]. Pierce, C. A., *Conscience in the NT* [SBT 15; London, 1955]. Robinson, J. A. T., *The Body: A Study in Pauline Theology* [SBT 5; London, 1952] 17–33. Stacey, D., *The Pauline View of Man* [London, 1956]. Thrall, M. E., "The Pauline Use of *Syneidēsis*," *NTS* 14 [1967–68] 118–25.)

124 **(II) Man in Christ.** Christian reconciliation brought about a new union of man with God. Paul calls it a "new creation" (Gal 6:15; 2 Cor 5:17) because it introduced a new mode of existence into man's world, in which Christ and the Christian enjoy, as it were, a symbiosis. Man shares in this new Christian existence through faith and baptism, which incorporate him into Christ and the Church; this incorporation finds a distinctive consummation in the Eucharist. To these elements of Paul's theology, we now turn.

125 **(A) Faith.** The experience whereby man appropriates to himself the effects of the Christ-event is for Paul faith (*pistis*). This experience begins with the hearing of the "word" about Christ and ends in a personal commitment of the whole man to his person and revelation. It begins as *akoē* (hearing) and ends as *hypakoē* (obedience, submission; cf. Rom 10:17; 1:5; 16:26). Man must open himself to the "word" (*logos*, 1 Cor 15:2; cf. 1:18) or the "message" (*rēma*, Rom 10:17) that is proclaimed to him. His response must involve the whole man: "If with your lips you acknowledge that Jesus is the Lord and with your mind you believe that God raised him from the dead, you will be saved" (Rom 10:9). The faith that man is asked to put in God or Christ (1 Thes 4:14; 1 Cor 1:21–23; Rom 4:24) is not merely an intellectual assent to some proposition but a vital, personal commitment engaging the whole man to Christ in all his relations with God, with other men, and with the world. It is an awareness of the difference that Christ and his salvific role as *Kyrios* make in man's history. This underlies the statement of Paul, when he says, "Now even the physical life I am living I live through faith in the Son of God who loved me and gave himself for me" (Gal 2:20). Faith as an obedient dedication to God's call in Christ far transcends the OT idea of fidelity. As *hypakoē*, it is the full acceptance of Christian commitment (2 Thes 1:8; Rom 6:16–17; 16:19), to the exclusion of reliance on self. The basis of the Christian experience is a new union with God in Christ, an ontological reality that is not immediately perceived by man's conscious faculties. The lively commitment of faith must so influence his conscious conduct as to integrate his psychological activity with the ontological reality within him. This is integrated Christian living (cf. Gal 2:20; 2 Cor 10:5).

126 The faith of the Christian is a gift of God just as the whole salvific process is. "It is by his [Christ's] favor that you have been saved through faith; and this does not come from you; it is the gift of God" (Eph 2:8). This is the underlying thought in the whole discussion of Abraham's faith (Rom 4). Since God accosts a man as a responsible person, he is free to accept or reject that gracious call. And faith is but the acceptance or the response on the part of man who realizes that the whole initiative rests with God. The man who does not respond is disobedient and under the power of "the god of this age" (2 Cor 4:4; cf. Phil 1:27; 1 Cor 9:26–27;

Eph 2:2). Paul implies by this assertion that disbelief is itself a sin.

127 In the polemical contexts in which Paul rejects the "deeds of the Law" as a means to justification, he insists that this justification comes through faith (Gal 2:16; cf. Rom 2:20,28; Phil 3:9). However, his full sense of faith demands that the Christian manifest in his conduct his basic commitment to Christ through deeds of love. "In union with Christ Jesus neither circumcision nor the lack of it means anything, but only faith acting through love" (Gal 5:6). This is why Paul continually exhorts his Christian converts to the practice of all sorts of good deeds. Christian faith is a call to freedom (from the Law, from Sin, from the *sarx*-self), but also a call to a service of love to be shown to other men (Gal 5:13). In this way, faith for Paul is no mere intellectual assent to a proposition of monotheism (cf. Jas 2:14–26). For Paul knows that such service is not accomplished without the activity of God in man: "It is God who in his good will is at work in your hearts, inspiring each decision and action" (Phil 2:13).

(Bultmann, R. and A. Weiser, *Faith* [BKW 10; London, 1961]. Hatch, W. H. P., *The Pauline Idea of Faith* [HTS 2; Cambridge, 1917]. Kuss, O., "Der Glaube nach den paulinischen Hauptbriefen," *TGl* 46 [1956] 1–26. Metzger, B. M., *IPLAP* 149–50. Schlatter, A., *Der Glaube im NT* [5th ed.; Stuttgart, 1963]. Vallotton, P., *Le Christ et la foi: Étude de théologie biblique* [Geneva, 1960], 41–144.)

128 **(B) Baptism.** Paul's stress on the role of faith in man's share in the Christ-event is adequately understood only when it is linked to his teaching about baptism. This initiatory rite, which incorporates man in Christ and the Church, was inherited by him from the early Church, as the formulaic expressions that he uses with regard to it make clear. But it is Paul who teaches the early Church the real significance of this rite. The confessional formulas he uses (Rom 10:9; 1 Cor 12:3) may well echo primitive baptismal creeds, but it is Paul who teaches that the condition of Christians as "sons of God through faith" is due to their baptism "into Christ" (Gal 3:26–27). He alludes to a rite, in speaking of a "washing of water" and a "word" (= formula?) in Eph 5:26; but Christians so washed have been "consecrated and made upright" (1 Cor 6:11). They have "put on Christ" as if they were putting on new garments—an allusion to robes worn during the baptismal ceremony? This description of the effects of baptism may seem extrinsic, but it at least expresses the dispositions of Christ, which the baptized person is expected to adopt.

129 Much more important is Paul's teaching about the identification of the Christian through baptism with the death, burial, and resurrection of Christ. The early Church recorded a recollection of Christ, who had described his own death as a baptism (Mk 10:38; Lk 12:50). But Paul's view of the effects of the Christ-event on believers led him to identify Christians, as it were, with the very salvific phases themselves of Christ's existence. Because "one died for all, therefore all died" (2 Cor 5:14). Prima facie, this seems like an assertion of the vicarious nature of Christ's death, but it must be read in the light of such a passage as the following: "Through baptism we have been buried with him in death, so that just as he was raised from the dead through the Father's glory, we too may live a new life. For if we have grown into union with him by undergoing a death like his, of course we shall do so by being raised to life like him" (Rom 6:4–5). Paul's comparison of baptism with the death, burial, and resurrection of Jesus is often thought to allude to the rite of immersion. Though this mode of baptism may be difficult to establish for the 1st cent. AD, Paul's symbolism is sufficiently preserved if the baptized person was somehow under the water. So identified with Christ in his death, the Christian dies to the Law and to Sin (Gal 2:19; Rom 6:6,10). Identified with Christ in his resurrection, he shares a new life and the very vitality of the Risen Christ and his Spirit (1 Cor 6:17; Col 2:12–13). The Christian "has grown together" with Christ through this likeness of his death, burial, and resurrection (Rom 6:5). The Christian dies in baptism, and a new man is born (cf. Eph 2:15); he is a "new creation" (Gal 6:15; 2 Cor 5:17). It is the beginning of a new "heavenly" existence with Christ: "Though we were dead because of our offenses God has made us live again with Christ. It is by his grace that we are saved. And he has raised us up with Christ Jesus and made us sit down with him in the heavenly realm" (Eph 2:5–6).

130 This is no mere individualistic experience for Christians, but a corporate one, for through baptism a special union with all Christians is formed. "For we have all—Jews or Greeks, slaves or free men—been baptized in one spirit to form one body" (1 Cor 12:13; cf. Gal 3:28; Eph 2:15). Man attains salvation, therefore, by identification with a salvific community (*Heilsgemeinde*)—by incorporation into the "body of Christ." This is why Paul compares baptism to Israel's passage through the waters of the Reed Sea (1 Cor 10:1–2). In the waters of baptism the new "Israel of God" (Gal 6:16) is formed.

131 Paul never quotes a primitive baptismal formula (like Mt 28:19), and yet he apparently echoes an early Trinitarian theologoumenon on baptism: "You have been washed, consecrated, and made upright in the name of the Lord Jesus Christ and in the Spirit of our God" (1 Cor 6:11). The baptized Christian is the "temple of the holy Spirit" (1 Cor 6:19) and an adopted son of the Father in virtue of the Spirit communicated to him (Gal 4:6; Rom 8:9,14–17). The Spirit so received is the constitutive principle of filial adoption and the dynamic source of Christian life and conduct. "All who are guided by God's Spirit are God's sons" (Rom 8:14). Such passages are the basis of the later theological teaching of the relation of the baptized Christian to the persons of the Trinity.

132 Only indirectly does Paul use the baptismal formula, "in the name of" (*eis to onoma tou*..., 1 Cor 6:11; 1:13,15). Though it expresses proprietorship and suggests that the baptized person becomes the property of Christ (recall "redemptive acquisition"), Paul prefers to speak of the person as baptized "into Christ" (Rom 6:3; Gal 3:27), sacramentally plunged into Christ himself (→ 136 below).

(Beasley-Murray, G. R., *Baptism in the NT* [London, 1962]. Delling, G., *Die Zueignung des Heils in der Taufe* [Berlin, 1961]. Fascher, E., "Zur Taufe des Paulus," *TLZ* 80 [1955] 643–48. Flemington, W. F., *The NT Doctrine of Baptism* [London, 1948]. Grail, A., "Le baptême dans l'Épître aux Galates," *RB* 58 [1951] 503–20. Iacono, V., "Il battesimo in S. Paolo," *RBibIt* 3 [1955] 348–62. Schnackenburg, R., *Baptism in the Thought of St. Paul* [tr. G. R. Beasley-Murray; N.Y., 1964]. Tremel, Y. B., "Le baptême, incorporation du Chrétien au Christ," *LumVi* 27 [1956] 81–102. Wagner, G., *Das religionsgeschichtliche Problem von Römer 6,1–11* [AbhTANT 39; Zürich, 1962].)

133 **(C) Incorporation into Christ.** To appreciate the effects of faith and baptism as seen by Paul, we must now turn to his ideas on the incorporation of Christians into Christ. This intimate union of Christ and Christians is expressed by pregnant prepositional phrases and also by the use of the figure of the "body of Christ."

134 (a) PREPOSITIONAL PHRASES. Paul uses chiefly four prepositions with "Christ" as their object to suggest different facets of Christ's influence on the life of the Christian. The use of each of them is varied and is often rich with nuances. We can only indicate here some of the most important implications. The four prepositions are *dia*, *eis*, *syn*, and *en*.

135 The prep. *dia*, "through," normally expresses the mediation of Christ in a statement of which the subject is the Father. It may denote his mediation through some activity of his earthly ministry (1 Thes 5:9), of his present state as *Kyrios* (Rom 1:5), or of his eschatological role (1 Thes 4:14). It is the phrase that opens up, as it were, the path that leads to the Christian's experience *en Christō*, and eventually *syn Christō*.

136 The prep. *eis*, "into," especially in the phrase *eis Christon*, has sometimes been understood as an abridgment of *eis to onoma Christou*, "into the name of Christ." With the vb. *baptizō* this is a possible meaning (→ 132 above). But *eis Christon* is also used with *pisteuō* (believe). In fact, it is mainly found in these two contexts: belief or baptism in Christ. Actually, it is a pregnant phrase expressing the movement toward Christ that these initial Christian experiences imply. It is the beginning of the Christian's condition *en Christō* (cf. 1 Cor 10:2). Torn from his original condition ("in Adam," 1 Cor 15:22), from his natural inclinations ("in the flesh," Rom 7:5), and from his ethnic background ("under the Law," 1 Cor 9:20), the believer is solemnly introduced "into Christ" in faith and baptism. *Eis Christon* denotes, then, the movement of incorporation.

137 The prep. *syn*, "with," is used not only with the object "Christ" but is also compounded with verbs and adjectives and can in these constructions express a double relationship of the Christian to Christ. Either it suggests the identification of the Christian with the pre-eminently redemptive acts of Christ's historical and risen life (from the passion on), or else it denotes the association of the Christian with Christ in eschatological glory. In the first case, the identification is seen above all in the compounds of *syn-*. Aside from some generic expressions like *symmorphos* (formed with him) or *symphytos* (grown together with him), these words refer to some phase of Christ's existence from his passion and death on: *sympaschein* (suffer with), *systaurousthai* (be crucified with), *synapothnēskein* (die with), *synthaptesthai* (be buried with), *synegeirein* (raise with), *syndoxazesthai* (be glorified with), *symbasileuein* (rule with), etc. By contrast, the Christian is never said to be born with Christ, to be baptized with Christ, to be tempted with Christ, etc. These events of the life of Christ were not significant for Paul's soteriology. On the other hand, the phrase *syn Christō* can express the association of the Christian with Christ in eschatological glory; it is his destiny to "be with Christ." See 1 Thes 4:17 (significantly *syn Kyriō*); Rom 6:8; 8:32; 2 Cor 4:14. *Syn*, therefore, pregnantly refers to the two poles of the Christian experience: Identified with Christ at its beginning, the Christian is to be associated with him at its end. In the meantime he is *en Christō*.

138 Lastly, the prep. *en*, "in," with the object "Christ" occurs 165 times in Paul's letters (including *en Kyriō*, *en autō*). Since the studies of A. Deissmann, the preposition has often been interpreted in a local, spatial sense, and *Christos* has been understood mystically of the glorified Lord identified with the Spirit as some spiritual atmosphere in which Christians are bathed. This is supposed to be Paul's mysticism. But subsequent studies by E. Lohmeyer, A. Schweitzer, F. Büchsel, *et al.* have brought out other aspects of the phrase (metaphysical, eschatological, dynamic, etc.). A detailed summary is impossible here, but several important distinctions should be made to aid the understanding of this important Pauline phrase. *First*, with the object *Kyrios* the phrase usually occurs in greetings, blessings, exhortations (often with imperatives), and formulations of Pauline apostolic plans and activity. The title *Kyrios* denotes, then, the influence of the Risen Jesus in practical and ethical areas of Christian conduct. *En Kyriō* is hardly ever used of Jesus' historical, earthly activity or of his coming eschatological function. It implies, rather, his present, sovereign intervention and dominion in the life of the Christian. Paul tells the Christian to become "in the Lord" what he really is "in Christ." *Second*, with the object *Christos* the phrase frequently has an instrumental sense, when it refers to the historical, earthly activity of Jesus (Rom 3:24; 2 Cor 5:19; Gal 2:17; Col 1:14; Eph 2:10; etc.). In this sense it is often close to *dia Christou*.

Third, the most common use of the phrase *en Christō* is to express the close union of Christ and the Christian, an inclusion or incorporation that connotes a symbiosis of the two. "If any man is in Christ, he is a new creature" (2 Cor 5:17). This vital union can also be expressed as "Christ in me" (Gal 2:20; 2 Cor 13:5; Rom 8:10; Col 1:27; Eph 3:17). The result is that one belongs to Christ (2 Cor 10:7) or is "of Christ"—a "mystical genitive" that often expresses the same idea (cf. Phlm 1 and Eph 4:1; 3:1; or Rom 16:16 and 1 Thes 1:1). The phrase should not be limited to a spatial dimension for it often connotes a dynamic influence of Christ on the Christian who is incorporated into him. There are also at times ecclesial (Eph 1:10; Gal 1:22) and even eschatological dimensions to the phrase (Eph 2:6). The Christian so incorporated is actually a member of the body of Christ; he is part of the Whole Christ. Needless to say, there are often times when one hesitates about the precise nuance intended (is it instrumental? inclusive?). Both may be intended, and this is why these phrases are often pregnant with meaning.

(Bouttier, M., *En Christ* [Paris, 1962]; *Christianity According to Paul* [SBT 49; London, 1966]. Büchsel, F., " 'In Christus' bei Paulus," *ZNW* 42 [1949] 141–58. Deissmann, A., *Die neutestamentliche Formel 'in Christo Jesu'* [Marburg, 1892]. Dupont, J., *Syn Christō: L'union avec le Christ suivant Saint Paul* [vol. 1; Bruges, 1952]. Kuss, O., *Der Römerbrief* [Regensburg, 1957–59], 319–81. Neugebauer, F., *In Christus* [Göttingen, 1961]. Nielson, J. B., *In Christ* [Kansas City, 1960]. Schweizer, E., "Dying and Rising with Christ," *NTS* 14 [1967–68] 1–14. Wikenhauser, A., *Pauline Mysticism* [N.Y., 1960].)

139 (b) Body of Christ. The most typically Pauline figure expressing the corporate identity of Christians with Christ is "the body of Christ." Absent from his early letters (1 Thes, 2 Thes, Gal, Phil), it appears first in 1 Cor, in the letter where Paul copes with divisive Corinthian factions. Christ is not divided, he tells them, formulating a teaching on the unity of all Christians in Christ. The symbol of it is the unity of the body with its members. The figure may be derived from contemporary Hellenistic notions about the state as the body politic; but whatever its origins (see J. A. T. Robinson, *The Body*, 55–58), it certainly denotes more than the idea of the body politic transferred to Christian society. In this philosophical notion, the moral union of citizens conspiring to achieve the common good of peace and well-being is suggested. In 1 Cor 12:12–27 the figure as used by Paul scarcely transcends this idea of moral union of all the members. The spiritual gifts enjoyed by the Corinthians (prophecy, tongues, faith, wisdom, etc.) are to be used for the good of the community, not for its disruption. As all the members and limbs conspire for the good of the body, so it is with the body of Christ. The usage is similar in the hortatory context of Rom 12:4–5.

140 But more is suggested in 1 Cor 6:15. Paul, warning against the defilement of man's body by sexual license, argues, "Don't you know that your bodies are parts of Christ's body? Am I then to take away from Christ parts of his body and make them parts of a prostitute's? Never! Don't you know that a man who has to do with a prostitute makes one body with her? For 'the two,' says Scripture, 'shall become one flesh.'" The union suggested here is certainly more than moral. Paul's meaning is unmistakable: Somehow Christ and the Christian share a union that implies "one flesh." Recall what was said above (→ 118–119) about the meaning of *sōma* and *sarx* as designations, not of the physical body as something distinct from the soul, but as the equivalents of the whole, individual person. Paul is not referring to members of a society, but to members of Christ as a physical individual; their union is not so much corporate as corporal. The same conclusion is derived from 1 Cor 10:16–17, where Paul insists on the union of all Christians, which is brought about by their share in the Eucharistic bread and cup: "Because there is one loaf, we, many as we are, are one body, for we all share the one loaf." The unity of all Christians is derived from their physical consumption of the one loaf; a oneness is suggested that transcends any mere extrinsic union effected by collaboration to attain a common goal. The figure of marriage in Eph 5:22–33 also points to the same transcendent union.

141 And yet the Christian and Christ are not physically united like the yolk and albumen of an egg. This is the reason why theologians have often called the union "mystical" (even though Paul does not use the word). The ontological reality that is the basis of the union is the possession of the Spirit of Christ: "We have all been baptized in one Spirit to form one body" (1 Cor 12:13). (Cf. Rom 8:9–11.) This possession of the Spirit springs from the sacramental incorporation of Christians into the body of Christ and is, as it were, the term of Paul's soteriological Christology. From another viewpoint, it has often been called the key to his whole thought.

142 However, neither in 1 Cor nor in Rom does Paul speak explicitly of the Church as the Body of Christ. The closest one comes to this identification is in 1 Cor 12:27–28, where the formulation is not as developed as it is in his later writings. These two themes—of the Church and of the Body—are independent developments in the Pauline letters, which merge only in the Captivity Letters. In the latter, when the cosmic significance of Christ has clearly dawned upon him, Paul links for the first time the themes of "body," "head," and "church." The Church is then explicitly identified with the "Body of Christ" in formulations that are almost convertible: "He [Christ] is the head of the body, the Church" (Col 1:18; cf. 1:24); God "made him the supreme head of the Church, which is his body" (Eph 1:23). In Eph especially there is great emphasis on the unity of the Church: Christ has broken down the barrier between Jew and Greek; all now share one salvation, for he has "reconciled both sides in one body to God through the cross" (Eph 2:16). "There is only one body and one Spirit, just as there is only one hope in the calling you have received: one Lord, one faith, one baptism, one God and Father of all" (Eph 4:4). And yet with all this stress on the unity of the body and the oneness of all Christians in Christ, Paul never came to speak of "one Church" (*mia ekklēsia*). Is this just fortuitous? Part of the answer appears below in the discussion of "Church." In the Pastoral Letters, otherwise so preoccupied with Church interests, the "Body of Christ" makes no appearance.

143 Intimately related to the body theme in Paul's letters is the head theme. In the Captivity Letters we learn that Christ is "the head of the body, the Church" (Col 1:18; cf. Eph 1:23). It may seem that this theme is simply an extension of the body theme. But it is not accurate to think that Paul, having portrayed the union of Christ and Christians by the analogy of the body, later concluded that Christ must be its head because the head is the most important part of the body (as can be illustrated in contemporary Hellenistic medical writers; see P. Benoit, *RB* 63 [1956] 27). For the head theme appears early in Paul's letters independently of the body theme, not as a figure of unity, but of subordination. In 1 Cor 11:3ff. Paul argues that women should wear head coverings in liturgical assemblies because, among other reasons, the order of creation in Gn indicates the subordination of wife to husband. The head covering is the sign of this subordination. Paul concludes, "Christ is the head of every man, while a woman's head is her husband, and Christ's head is God." Paul plays here on the two senses of "head" (the physical head which must be covered, and the figurative head [like "head" of a department]). But there is no mention of body here at all. There is a remnant of this figure of subordination in Col 2:10, where Christ is declared the "head of every principality and power." But in the Captivity Letters the body theme and the head theme are joined: Christ is the head of the body, the Church. The image is exploited, with details from contemporary medical teaching: "Let us rather hold to the truth in charity; thus we shall fully grow up into union with him who is head, Christ. For in dependence on him the whole body is bonded and knit together" (Eph 4:16). This aspect of the subordination of the Christian to Christ the head also underlies the comparison of Christian marriage with the Church: "Just as the Church is in subjection to Christ, so too should wives be subject to their husbands in everything" (Eph 5:24).

144 The Christian experience, then, which is rooted in the historical reality of the bodily Christ, is a living, dynamic union with the individual *risen body* of the *Kyrios*. The corporate union of all Christians must grow to fill out the total Christ (Eph 1:23); this is the *plērōma* of the cosmic Christ. In the lives of individual Christians this means apostolic suffering that fills up what was lacking in Christ's tribulations on behalf of the Church (Col 1:24). It does not mean that such apostolic suffering adds anything to the strictly redemptive value of the Cross; rather such suffering on behalf of the Church continues in time that which Christ began, but could not finish in time. It must continue until the cosmic dimensions of the Church are achieved.

(Benoit, P., "Corps, tête et plérôme dans les Épîtres de la Captivité," *RB* 63 [1956] 5–44; *Exégèse et théologie*, 2, 107–53. Best, E., *One Body in Christ* [London, 1955]. Hegermann, H., "Zur Ableitung der Leib-Christi-Vorstellung," *TLZ* 85 [1960] 839–42. Martelet, G., "Le mystère du corps et de l'esprit dans le Christ ressuscité et dans l'Église," *VerbC* 12 [1958] 31–53. Percy, E., *Der Leib Christi* [Lund, 1942]. Robinson, J. A. T., *The Body* [SBT 5; London, 1955] 49–83. Thornton, L. S., *The Common Life in the Body of Christ* [2nd ed.; Westminster, 1944]. Wikenhauser, A., *Die Kirche als der mystische Leib Christi nach dem Apostel Paulus* [2nd ed.; Münster, 1940].)

145 **(D) Eucharist.** In explaining the intimate union of Christ with Christians, Paul uses "the body of Christ" in another sense, viz., to mean his Eucharistic body. "Many as we are, we are one body, for we all share in the one loaf" (1 Cor 10:16). In the Eucharist he finds a source not only of the union of Christians with Christ but also of Christians among themselves.

The earliest account of the institution of the Eucharist in the NT occurs in 1 Cor 11:23–25. Though it is related in origin to the Lucan account (22:15–20) and differs somewhat from that of Mk (14:22–25) and Mt (26:26–29), it is an independent record of the institution, probably derived from the Antiochene church. Paul passes it on as tradition, but his account is not so much an eyewitness report as a quotation from a liturgical recitation of what the "Lord" did at the Last Supper, even with its rubrics ("Do this in memory of me," 11:24). Paul does not recount the event in and for itself, but only alludes to it in discussing other problems. He mentions this sacramental meal as part of his critique of the abuses that had crept into the Corinthian community suppers associated with the Eucharist (1 Cor 11) or in the course of his remarks on the eating of meat sacrificed to idols (1 Cor 10).

146 For Paul the Eucharist is above all the "Lord's Supper" (*kyriakon deipnon*, 1 Cor 11:20), the repast at which the new people of God eats its "spiritual food" and drinks its "spiritual drink" (1 Cor 10:3–4). In this act it manifests itself as the community of the "new covenant" (11:25; cf. Jer 31:31; Ex 24:8), as it "shares in the table of the Lord" (1 Cor 10:21; cf. Mal 1:7,12). The communion of this people implies its union with Christ and with one another; it is a "sharing [*koinōnia*] in the body of Christ" (10:16).

147 Three aspects in particular reveal the Eucharist as the source of Christian unity. *First*, it is the ritual and sacramental act whereby Christ's presence with his people is concretized. Paul quotes, in effect, the rite of the liturgical celebration and comments on its meaning in the immediate context (1 Cor 11:27–32): Christ's body and blood are identified with the bread and wine so consumed by the Christian community. Any "unworthy" sharing in that repast would bring judgment on the Christian, for he would be "profaning the body and blood of the Lord" (11:27). Since the Lord is identified with such food, those who partake of it may not violate its sacred character and his presence by abuses of individualism, of disregard of the poor, or of idol-worship. One cannot argue away the realism of the identity of Christ with this Eucharistic food in Paul's teaching, even if Paul does not explain how this identity is achieved. But through this presence the unity of Christians is effected. Thus it is the Eucharistic Christ who alone *brings about* the unity of men in Paul's view.

148 *Second*, as a memorial and proclamation of Christ's sacrificial death, it is a rallying point. "As often as you eat this bread and drink of this cup, you proclaim the death of the Lord, until he comes" (1 Cor 11:26). This is why the Christian community is to "do this in memory of" him (11:24). The repetition of this liturgical act in which the Lord's body and blood are made present to nourish his people is a solemn "proclamation" of the salvation event itself. For it is the "death of the Lord"—"for you." It announces once again that saving death to those who partake of the sacramental meal. The sacrificial aspect of that death is brought out by the reference to covenant blood in 11:25; the Eucharistic cup is the blood of the "new covenant" (Jer 31:31), an allusion to the pact replacing the covenant sealed by blood and sacrifice in Ex 24:8. This allusion thus invests the shedding of Christ's blood with an efficacy analogous to that of the sacrifice sealing the covenant of Sinai (cf. also 1 Cor 10:14–21).

Third, there is an eschatological aspect to the Eucharist, for the proclamation of that death must continue "until he comes." It is only Christ in his risen, glorious body who fully accomplishes the salvation of those who partake of the table of the *Kyrios*.

(Boismard, M.-E., "The Eucharist According to Saint Paul," *The Eucharist in the NT: A Symposium* [ed. J. Delorme; Baltimore, 1964] 125–39. Neuenzeit, P., *Das Herrenmahl* [StANT 1; Munich, 1960].)

PAULINE ECCLESIOLOGY AND ETHICS

149 **(I) The Church.** For all its rarity in the Gospels (Mt 16:18; 18:17), the word *ekklēsia* is found abundantly in the Pauline letters. It does not occur in the first four chapters of Acts, and thereafter it occurs only once (5:11) in the sense of "church" before the story of Paul begins (8:1,3). It apparently took some time before the early Christians realized their union in Christ in terms of *ekklēsia*. The abundant data in the Pauline letters do not really contradict this. Incidentally, it should be recalled that even in the three accounts of Paul's conversion in Acts, where the heavenly voice says, "Saul, Saul, why do you persecute me? I am Jesus whom you are persecuting" (9:4–5; 22:7–8; 26:14–15), the Church is never explicitly mentioned. Luke records that Paul had been persecuting the "Lord's disciples" (9:1), the "Way" (22:4), or the "name of Jesus of Nazareth" (26:9,10). Consequently, we should not include as an element of the revelation on the road to Damascus an explicit awareness of the *Church* as the Body of Christ.

150 The data in the Pauline letters reveal a similar situation. Paul uses *ekklēsia* in 1–2 Thes (the *Early Letters*) in two senses: either to designate a local church (1 Thes 1:1; 2 Thes 1:1), or in the sense expressed by the phrase, "church of God" (1 Thes 2:14; 2 Thes 1:4). In other words, it either denotes the local congregation of believers dwelling in Thessalonica—a unity developed from their community in belief and worship—or it is a title of predilection for Judean communities (cf. 1 Thes 2:14). It is well known that *ekklēsia* is used in the LXX to translate the Hebr *qāhāl*, the term given to the assembly of the Israelites, particularly in their desert wanderings. They are called the "*ekklēsia* of the Lord" (Dt 23:2) or the "*ekklēsia* of the people of God" (Jgs 20:2; cf. Acts 7:38). But it also refers to the Israelites in liturgical gatherings (1 Kgs 8:55; 1 Chr 29:10). However, Paul's expression, *ekklēsia tou theou*, is unique (except possibly for Neh 13:1 [where ms. S reads *kyriou* against the others] and the Hebr equivalent in the War Scroll [1QM 4:10]). But, given the OT background, it was more than likely the apt designation for the primitive local churches in Judea, the first units formed in Christian history and peculiarly linked through their Jewish roots to the Israelite "congregation" of old.

151 When we move to the *Great Letters*, we find the same two senses again. Here *ekklēsia* refers to the local churches of Galatia, Judea, Macedonia, and Cenchreae (Gal 1:2,22; 2 Cor 8:1; Rom 16:1). But the title "church of God," though referred to Judean churches (1 Cor 11:16), is now also applied to the church of Corinth. According to L. Cerfaux (*Church*, 113), this title does not designate the universal Church as manifested at Corinth, but is a Pauline way of flattering a church with which he has had rather stormy relations. He accords to Corinth the title otherwise reserved for the mother churches of Palestine (1 Cor 1:2; 2 Cor 1:1; possibly also 1 Cor 10:32). But in this very extension there is a broadening of Paul's understanding of the idea of *ekklēsia*. It begins to transcend the local barriers. This is the seed of Paul's teaching on the universality of the Church. And it is precisely in 1 Cor that this seed of universality is first found. Paul warns the Corinthians against submitting ordinary matters for settlement to the judgment of men "who are nothing in the Church" (1 Cor 6:4). In 1 Cor 14:5,12 he speaks of "doing the Church some good." These could be references to the local community, but one senses in the use of the word a more general meaning (cf. 1 Cor 12:28).

152 It is strange that in Rom, the letter so often regarded as the most representative of Paul's thought, the word *ekklēsia* is absent. All the occurrences of *ekklēsia* in Rom 16 denote local communities; but this chapter is most likely not an integral part of Rom (→ Letter Rom, 53:10).

153 When we come to the *Captivity Letters*, the notion of *ekklēsia* plays a very important role. It is a crucial part of the "mystery of Christ," and in it the barrier between Jew and Greek is broken down; all men are reconciled to God in his "body, the church" (Col 1:17). In Paul's cosmic view of Christ he is now the head of the Church, which is his body, and is thereby the head of all creation. God "has put all things under his feet and made him the supreme head of the Church, which is his body, the fullness of him who is filled out, all in all" (Eph 1:22–23). The Church is thus equated with the fullness of Christ and is given cosmic dimensions that embrace all creation. Even the spirits (the principalities and powers) are to learn about the Father's plan of salvation through it (Eph 3:9–11). Paul praises the Father for his wisdom "through the Church and through Christ Jesus" (Eph 3:21).

154 We can thus detect a certain growth in Paul's awareness of what "the Church" really means for man. In a sense, it is but the development of his understanding of Christ's role in salvation. Man is baptized "in one Spirit to form one body" (1 Cor 12:13). The unity of the Christian community in the Church is Paul's great contribution to Christian theology—a unity that he derives from the single purpose of the divine plan of salvation. There is "one Lord, one faith, one baptism, one God and Father of all, who is above us all, pervades us all, and is within us all" (Eph 4:5–6). Eventually, Paul came to look on the "Church of God" as a transcendent unit embracing both Jews and Greeks but somehow different from them (cf. 1 Cor 10:32).

155 Paul is vaguely aware that in the Church there is a structure imposed ultimately by the Lord himself (1 Cor 10:14–22; 11:23ff. 14:2–19 for its cult; 1 Cor 12:28; Phil 1:1 for its ministry). It too has its rules, which he quotes (1 Cor 11:16).

156 But the Church is "the Israel of God" (Gal 6:16), "the Jerusalem above" (Gal 4:26), "the temple of the living God" (2 Cor 6:16), and the bride of Christ (Eph 5:22–33). The most dynamic concept of the Church that Paul uses is undoubtedly that of the Body of Christ, but it should not obscure the figure of it as a building or a temple, which he also frequently employs. He often speaks of the Christians' duty to "build up" the Church. (See 1 Thes 5:11; Gal 2:9; 6:10; 1 Cor 3:9–17; 8:1–10; 10:23; 14:2–4,12,17,26; 2 Cor 6:16; 10:8; 12:19; 13:10; Rom 15:20; Col 1:23; 2:7; Eph 2:19–22; 3:17; 4:12–16 [the metaphor is mixed here: "building the body of Christ"].)

(Best, E., *One Body in Christ* [London, 1955]. Cerfaux, L., *The Church in the Theology of St. Paul* [N.Y., 1960]. Gärtner, B., *Temple and Community in Qumran and the New Testament* [Cambridge, 1965]. Goossens, W., *L'Église, corps du Christ, d'après Saint Paul* [Paris, 1949]. MacRae, G. W., "Building the House of the Lord," *AER* 140 [1959] 361–76. Minear, P. S. *Images of the Church in the New Testament* [Phila., 1960]. Pfammatter, J., *Die Kirche als Bau* [Rome, 1960]. Schmidt, K. L., *The Church* [BKW 2; London, 1950]. Wikenhauser, A., *Die Kirche als der mystische Leib Christi nach dem Apostel Paulus* [Münster, 1940].)

157 **(II) Demands of Christian Living.** The baptized Christian has become a "new creature" (Gal 6:15). He lives, but it is really Christ who lives in him (Gal 2:20); into this new ontological mode of existence he must integrate his conscious conduct. The new life he lives is reoriented by the historic achievement of Christ, but it still has to face a scrutiny at the eschatological judgment seat of Christ. Though man is certain of the salvation already effected by Christ, each individual still has to "appear in his true colors before the tribunal of Christ, to be repaid with good or evil for the life he has lived" (2 Cor 5:10). This is but another aspect of Paul's eschatology. Though already transferred to the heavenly realm through a pledge (Eph 1:14; 2:6), the Christian still has to make his way through this world. He still has to be saved "from the present wicked world" (Gal 1:4; cf. 1 Cor 7:26,29–31). He "must not adopt the customs of this world, but by his attitude of mind be transformed so that he can find out what God's will is—what is good, pleasing, and perfect" (Rom 12:2). The Christian lives, then, a life with a double polarity.

158 This double polarity that characterizes Christian life is why Paul insists that the Christian activated by the Spirit of God (Rom 8:14) can no longer live a life bound by a merely natural, earthly horizon. He is no longer *psychikos* (→ 120 above) but is *pneumatikos* and must fasten his gaze on the horizons of the Spirit. The Spirit is not of this world, but comes from God (1 Cor 2:11). And whereas the material man (*psychikos*) cannot accept what comes from the Spirit (1 Cor 2:14), the spiritual man (*pneumatikos*) is alive to everything, does not stifle the Spirit nor disregard its whisperings, but tests all things and holds to what is good (1 Thes 5:19–22).

159 The double polarity of Christian life also explains Christian freedom. Paul exhorts his Galatian converts to stand firm in the freedom for which Christ has freed them (5:1), in the freedom from the Law, but also from Sin, from Death, and especially from Self (Rom 6:7–11,14; 7:24–8:2). And yet all creation still awaits the "glorious freedom of the children of God" (Rom 8:21). In the meantime, the Christian must live as "the freedman of Christ" (1 Cor 7:22), as one "under the law of Christ" (*ennomos Christou*, 1 Cor 9:21).

160 In other words, Christian freedom is not an antinomian license; Paul vigorously rejects the idea that man should blatantly sin in order that God may more abundantly show forth his mercy to the sinner (Rom 6:1; cf. 3:5–8). There is the "law of Christ" (Gal 6:2). When it is scrutinized, it is seen to be the "law of love." This is explained in terms of "bearing one another's burdens" (in a context of fraternal correction, Gal 6:2). Even more explicitly, in Rom 13:8–10 Paul repeats the Fifth, Sixth, Seventh, and Eighth Commandments of the Decalogue and sums them all up in the saying, "You must love your neighbor as you do yourself"; and he concludes, "So love fully satisfies the Law." This is, of course, the "law of the Spirit" (Rom 8:2). Christ has not simply substituted for the Law of Moses another legal code. The "law of the Spirit" may be a reflection of Jer 31:33, but it is more than likely that Paul has coined the phrase to describe the Spirit's activity in terms of *nomos*, about which he has just been speaking. The Spirit's law of love is the new inner source and guide of the life by which the *pneumatikos* lives; it is the ontic principle of vitality, whence springs the love that must interiorize the Christian's entire ethical conduct.

161 And yet it is to such *pneumatikoi*—to the sons of God guided by the Spirit (Rom 8:14–15)—that Paul addresses his exhortations to virtuous conduct. Usually the latter part of each of his letters is filled with detailed instructions for the Christian's ethical conduct. We single out only a few characteristics. Form criticism has isolated in his letters the catalogues of virtues and vices that should or should not characterize the Christian way of life (cf. Gal 5:19–23; 1 Cor 5:10–11; 6:9–10; 2 Cor 12:20; Rom 13:13). The eschatological reference in these (possibly pre-Pauline, adapted) catalogues is usually evident: "People who do such things will have no share in the Kingdom of God" (Gal 5:21; cf. Rom 2:5–11; Eph 5:5). These lists can be compared with similar catalogues found both among Gk (esp. Stoic) philosophers and Jewish teachers (e.g., the Essenes: cf. 1QS 4:2–6,9–11).

(See W. D. Davies, *Paul and Rabbinic Judaism*, 111–46.)

162 Related to these catalogues are the more specific *Haustafeln* (exhortations addressed to the members of the *familia*); they formulate the duties of husbands and wives, parents and children, and masters and slaves (Col 3:18–4:1; Eph 5:21–6:9 [cf. 1 Tm 2:8–15; Ti 2:1–10; 1 Pt 2:18–3:7]). These exhortations represent the closest that Paul comes to a systematic formulation of social ethics; but they are limited to the domestic society and contain only generalities.

163 Of particular interest are his instructions on slavery, virginity, and marriage. His underlying principle: "There is no room for 'Jew' and 'Greek'; there is no room for 'slave' and 'freeman'; there is no room for 'male' and 'female'; for in union with Christ Jesus you are all one" (Gal 3:28). Considered from the standpoint of union with Christ, such ethnic and social distinctions are valueless. And yet, Paul never tries to change the existing social conditions in the name of Christian teaching. (We state this merely as a fact.) (Cf. 1 Cor 7:21–22.) He sent the runaway slave Onesimus back to his master Philemon, not with the recommendation that he be manumitted, but that he be received "as more than a slave, as a dear brother" (Phlm 16; cf. Sir 33:31). He counsels slaves to obey their masters in all things (Col 3:22–4:1; Eph 6:5–9) and even goes so far as to recommend that they "think of Christ as the master" for whom they are working (Col 3:24). He does not try to change the external conditions of man's existence, but he does point the way to the Christianization and interiorization of the existing situation.

164 Regarding virginity, Paul clearly states his own opinion. It is not "a command of the Lord" (1 Cor 7:25), but he thinks that he is as attuned to the Spirit in this matter as anyone else (7:40). He recommends "a good thing" to the unmarried and to widow(er)s; at first his statement is absolute and does not imply a comparison: "It is a good thing for a man not to touch a woman" (1 Cor 7:1; cf. 7:7–8). Two reasons are given for this opinion: First, "in view of the present distress," i.e., because of the impending parousia for which Paul longed (1 Cor 7:26,29–31; cf. 1 Thes 4:15,17; Rom 13:11). Second, because the unmarried person can devote his undivided attention to the Lord's cause (*ta tou kyriou*, 7:32–34). Here a comparison between the unmarried and married state is implied, and Paul recommends virginity in view of (apostolic?) service of the Lord. At the end of the long ch. 7 Paul introduces the comparison explicitly in the difficult passage concerning the marrying of one's virgin (daughter, ward, fiancée?): "The man who marries her does what is right, but he who does not does even better" (*kreisson poiēsei*, 7:38). There is little doubt, therefore, that throughout the chapter Paul recommends a celibate life to those who can live it. On the other hand, his statements should not be made out to discourage marriage (cf. 7:38, *kalōs poiei*). He knows that each person has received his own special gift in this matter (7:7).

165 Most of 1 Cor 7, however, is devoted to instructions about marriage itself. Paul retails the mutual, conjugal obligations of husbands and wives (7:2–6). He insists on "no divorce" as the Lord's command (7:10–11), gives instructions about peaceful mixed marriages (7:12–14), and grants his "Pauline privilege" (7:15–16). What is more important, however, is the view that Paul has of the marriage bond itself as the means of the sanctification and salvation of the spouses (7:14,16). Even in the case of the mixed marriage he teaches that the believing spouse is the source of a "consecration" of the unbelieving partner and that both of them are the same for their children (7:14). When Paul insists on the subordinate place of the wife in domestic society, he is echoing the contemporary social structure that he knew, in which the woman was far more subject to the man than she is today. Such a view is found in 1 Cor 11:3,7–12; 14:34–35; 2 Cor 11:3; see the contemporary dim view of women painted in the rabbinical writings (*ThDNT* 1, 777–84).

But it is the same Paul who also wrote Gal 3:28 and the exalted view of marriage in Eph 5:22–33. Christian tradition has adopted from him the view of man as the head of the household, but it has not made capital of his emphasis on the subordinate role of woman. In Eph 5:22–33 he teaches the subordination of the wife to the husband (as in 1 Cor 11:3), but he also clearly tempers it with the instruction to the husband to love his wife, "just as Christ loves the church and gave himself for her" (Eph 5:25). This passage is part of a *Haustafel*, and it is Paul's instruction on Christian marriage, wherein he compares it to the union of Christ and his Church. He sees in the subjection of the wife and the love of the husband a reflection of the intimate union of Christ and his Church. Quoting Gn 2:24, "For this reason a man leaves father and mother and clings to his wife, and the two become one flesh," he reveals a "secret" (*mystērion*) hidden in that verse for long centuries, that the fundamental union of marriage established by God long ago was a prefigured "type" of the union of Christ and his Church. This view of the sublimity of the marriage bond transcends all the regulations that Paul lays down for it in 1 Cor 7.

166 Paul has instructions for Christian conduct in many other areas, which cannot be discussed in this brief sketch. We conclude our remarks on Paul's ethical teaching in general by insisting on its Christocentrism. As Christ was the "image of God" (1 Cor 11:7; 2 Cor 4:4; Col 1:15), so man in his earthly existence is to be the "image of the heavenly man" (1 Cor 15:49; cf. Rom 8:29). It is growth in Christ that Paul recommends to his readers, contemporary and modern. In this way the Christian lives his life "for God" (Gal 2:19). "You have stripped off your old self with its ways and have put on that new self newly made in the likeness of its Creator, to know him fully" (Col 3:10). Significantly, with all his emphasis on Christ, Paul once again refers the Christian ultimately to the Father—through Christ.

(Allmen, J. J. von, *Pauline Teaching on Marriage* [London, 1963]. Coleman-Norton, P. R., "The Apostle Paul and the Roman Law of Slavery," *Studies in Roman Economic and Social History* [Princeton, 1951]. Delling, G., *Paulus' Stellung zu Frau und Ehe* [BWANT 56; Stuttgart, 1931]. Didier, G., *Désintéressement du Chrétien* [Paris, 1955]. Enslin, M. S., *The Ethics of Paul* [Cambridge, 1930]. Grelot, P., *Man and Wife in Scripture* [N.Y., 1964]. Legrand, L., *The Biblical Doctrine of Virginity* [N.Y., 1963]. Lowrie, W., " 'Glorify God in Your Body,' " *TTod* 10 [1953–54] 492–500. Montague, G. T., *Growth in Christ: A Study in Saint Paul's Theology of Progress* [Kirkwood, Mo., 1961]. Vögtle, A., *Die Tugend- und Lasterkataloge im NT* [NTAbh 16/4–5; Münster, 1936]. Wibbing, S., *Die Tugend- und Lasterkataloge im NT* [BZNW 25; Berlin, 1959].)

80

JOHANNINE THEOLOGY

Bruce Vawter, C.M.

BIBLIOGRAPHY

1 See the general bibliography on NT theology (→ Aspects NT Thought, 78) and the bibliographies on the individual Johannine works (→ Johannine Epistles, 62:1; → Gospel Jn, 63:1; → Apocalypse, 64:1). An exhaustive bibliography of Johannine theology is found in E. Malatesta, *St. John's Gospel, 1920–1965* (AnalBib 32; Rome, 1967) 122–57.

Beasley-Murray, G. R., "The Relation of the Fourth Gospel to the Apocalypse," *EvQ* 18 (1946) 173–86. Blank, J., *Krisis: Untersuchungen zur johanneischen Christologie und Eschatologie* (Freiburg, 1964). Boismard, M.-E., "L'évolution du thème eschatologique dans les traditions johanniques," *RB* 68 (1961) 507–24. Brooks, O. S., "The Johannine Eucharist," *JBL* 82 (1963) 293–300. Brown, R. E., *The Gospel According to John* (AB 29; Garden City, N.Y., 1966) esp. 497–538. Feuillet, A., "L'Incarnation rédemptrice dans les écrits johanniques," R-F 2, 890–914 (summary in *TD* 8 [1960] 76–79). Glasson, T. F., *Moses in the Fourth Gospel* (SBT 40; London, 1963). Holwerda, D. E., *The Holy Spirit and Eschatology in the Gospel of John* (Kampen, 1959). Lazure, N., *Les valeurs morales de la théologie johannique* (Paris, 1965). MacGregor, G. H. C., "The Eucharist in the Fourth Gospel," NTS 9 (1962–63) 111–19. Manson, T.W., *On Paul and John* (SBT 38; London, 1963).

2 OUTLINE

JOHN THE THEOLOGIAN

3 **(I) Existence of a Specifically Johannine Theology.** That there is a peculiarly Johannine thought within the NT is no new discovery; from the earliest patristic times most of the Johannine peculiarities have been observed (however inadequately they may have been explained), together with their author's high theological purpose. Almost from the beginning of Christian history the Fourth Evangelist has been known as "John the Theologian." However, it is really only in recent times that we have reached the point of treating systematically a

distinctive Johannine body of thought, a Johannine interpretation of Christian revelation, in short, a Johannine theology, in the same fashion that we have long treated the theology of Paul.

There are various reasons for this. Paul's thought, although it must be synthesized from his occasional letters, is to be found in a body of NT writings which, even within the general category of NT epistles, bears his own distinctive stamp. This is not the case with John, whose major writing, the Gospel, fits, or has been generally thought to fit, into the pattern of a literary form shared by three other NT authors. As a result, much of the attention hitherto given to the Johannine element of the NT has been devoted to explaining John's deviation from the common Gospel pattern. That John was called the Theologian meant, for the most part, that recognition was being given to the "spiritual" nature of his Gospel as contrasted with the Syn. Relatively little attention was given to 1–2–3 Jn, even though these epistles were commonly thought to be the work of the author of the Fourth Gospel. The First Epistle tended to be regarded as a kind of commentary on the Gospel and was valued chiefly in this character, but the Second and Third admittedly had little of note to contribute to NT thought. As for the Ap, its own distinctive literary form and the concomitant preoccupations have always made its relation to the rest of Johannine thought obscure, quite apart from the fact that its literary relation to the Johannine corpus has been a problem from earliest times (→ Apocalypse, 64:10–13).

4 In addition to this, the significance of John as an independent thinker in apostolic Christianity has never been as easy to measure as that of Paul. The broad outline of Paul's apostolic career and the life situation of his epistles are well known from Acts; and as a consequence, a certain amount of control has always been present to serve as a basis for a study of his theology. Concerning the career of John, on the other hand, there are only fragmentary and, in part, conflicting traditions; and the Johannine writings themselves have had to bear the double burden of supplying both the data about their author and the explanation of the data in formulating a theology. Paul's name and personality stamp his works; in speaking of John, we are speaking of an author whose very name is a surmise, for neither Jn nor 1–2–3 Jn identify their writer by name. Even today, therefore, it is not too surprising that John can be viewed in contradictory fashion by competent scholars: Some consider him the most "Jewish" of the NT writers; others credit him with thoroughly "Hellenizing" Christianity (an honor that, incidentally, some once gave to Paul).

5 It is the virtue of modern NT study that it has begun to recognize, as did the ancient Church, that the NT is first and foremost a collection of theological documents. Two centuries of rationalistic historicism have helped to obscure this tradition. In particular, the Gospels are not biographies of Jesus, but interpretations of the message of salvation proclaimed in the works and words of Jesus, the Anointed of God. That is to say, they are theologies—theologies, not simply a theology, for there are four Gospels, not one. Modern study has also helped us to recognize that in the Church, the apostolic Church as well as the Church of the 20th cent., there has always been room and even a need for different theologies, each of which can offer its own insights into a revelation that transcends any single human mind, even the inspired minds responsible for the NT (→ Canonicity, 67:92–97). The study of the NT is truly a study of theologies.

It would be easy to exaggerate this. The NT, after all, as does Christianity itself, testifies to a unity in essentials that more than transcends its theological differences. (See the debate between R. E. Brown and E. Käsemann in *NovT* 6 [1963] 290–308 and *TD* 13 [1965] 228–33.) The very diversity of the theologies that have been bound into our single NT volume, as a matter of fact, proves in the best way possible the basic unity of the Church that first produced the theologies and then the NT. Without agreeing with most of the conclusions reached by E. F. Scott, one can, nevertheless, follow his argument that "the New Testament is not a uniform book, composed by men who were all of one mind and were closely collaborating with one another. It presents Christianity under a great variety of forms, and for this very reason presents it truly" (*The Varieties of New Testament Religion* [N.Y., 1944] 15). Among the minds that have contributed most to the NT collection, we must certainly include that of John. In his thought and Paul's we have the two most important theologies that emerged from apostolic Christianity.

6 In what follows, certain presuppositions are made, the arguments for which are given in other articles of this volume. It is assumed that in some fashion the Johannine writings (Jn, 1–2–3 Jn, Ap) reflect the theological teaching traditionally associated with John the Apostle (→ Gospel Jn, 63:2–3; → Johannine Epistles, 62:3). It is further assumed that this teaching is a legitimate apostolic development of the authentic revelation of Christ and the Spirit, not a Christianized Gnosticism or Hermeticism (→ Gospel Jn, 63:12–16). Although Johannine theology has taken cognizance of the currents of Hellenistic thought in the world to which the Johannine writings were addressed, the mainstream of Johannine thought has its life situation in the Jewish world known to Christ and his apostles, a world that we now know to have been more complex and diversified than was once believed. This essay will attempt to synthesize the dominant perspectives of Johannine theology.

7 **(II) Significance of Johannine Theology.** The first task in evaluating the significance of any theologian is to isolate his contribution from that of his contemporaries and predecessors, thereby to see both his dependent relationships and his originality.

(A) Relation to Other New Testament Thought. If we take for granted that John's spiritual and intellectual ancestry is to be found in OT and Jewish traditions, we must still briefly consider his position in relation to his contemporaries in Christian theology.

(a) To Primitive Christian Thought. Elsewhere the relation of Jn to the Syn tradition has been considered in detail (→ Gospel Jn, 63:17ff.). If we were to single out the one element in Jn that most strikingly differentiates it from the Syn, it would probably be the transfer of interest from the establishment of the Kingdom to the person of Jesus himself. The implications of this will be seen in the treatment of concepts such as faith and judgment (→ 35, 55 below). That this represents a change of emphasis proper to the special ends that John set for himself is beyond question. That it really represents "the first great departure from primitive Christianity" is, however, an exaggeration. Probably today few would agree with the author of this sentiment, or with his conclusion that although "much that [Jn] puts on the lips of Jesus is true even though Jesus never said it... much that it ascribes to him causes the Jesus of the oldest historical narrative to pass into a most profound eclipse. In so far it may have been as fatal to the religion of Jesus as it has been fruitful for the theology of the Church" (G. H. Gilbert, "From John Mark to John the Theologian," *HarvTR* 16 [1923] 235–57).

A recognition that the Syn, including Mk, are theologies in their own right and not neutral history from which John has departed, leads current writers to far different conclusions. There is even the danger of an opposite exaggeration, namely, the assertion that the Syn have imposed an apocalyptic interpretation on a teaching that is found in its authentic and primitive form in Jn. Probably most scholars would agree that we need not choose between the eschatological and the ethical in the teaching of Jesus (the ethical is found more pronouncedly in 1 Jn than in Jn), or between future and realized eschatology, which have found diverse stresses in Jn and the Syn. Both eschatologies have their basis in the primitive revelation.

(Manson, T. W., "The Life of Jesus: Some Tendencies in Present-Day Research," *BNTE* 211–21. Robinson, J. A. T., *Jesus and His Coming* [N.Y., 1957]. Stauffer, E., "Agnostos Christos: Joh ii 24 und die Eschatologie des vierten Evangeliums," *BNTE* 281–99.)

8 The fact is that there is far closer connection between Jn and the most primitive formulations of Christian theology than was once admitted. For example, the doctrine of Jesus' pre-existence, especially as brought out in the logos teaching of the Prologue (→ Gospel Jn, 63:39), has a strong resemblance to the teaching of such ancient Christian hymns as Phil 2:6–11 and Col 1:15–20. A distinctive Johannine characteristic, the moral dualism that pervades Jn, 1 Jn, and the Ap alike, is an apocalyptic concept stemming from the Palestinian Judaism familiar to Jesus and to the Syn Evangelists. Another element of apocalyptic is the figure of the Son of Man, which evidently goes back to Jesus' own proclamation (→ Aspects NT Thought, 78:28–30), and which has influenced the thinking of John far more than that of the other Evangelists who report the proclamation without building their theologies about it. Johannine terms like Light, Life, Holy Spirit, and Paraclete were proper to the rabbinic Judaism that has influenced Jesus, Paul, and the Syn equally. Traces, at least, of the prime Johannine themes can easily be found in other parts of the NT. An individual Gospel tradition often preserves only traces of themes that are fully exploited in another Gospel tradition.

9 (b) TO PAULINE THOUGHT. It would be tempting to pursue the task of comparing John with other distinctive NT writers, especially with the author of Heb, with whom he has considerable affinity despite the many surface dissimilarities. However, the most obvious comparison is with Paul, the other theologian of the NT who did the most to influence the course of early Christian thought. In the heyday of the criticism that made "Paulinism" the origin of historical Christianity, there was no hesitancy in considering John the weak imitator or rival of the great Apostle of the Gentiles. Even today, many claim to be able to see a profound Pauline influence in the work of John. It is likely enough that John was familiar with Paul's work, which was well known in the area of Asia Minor in which John was also active. However, while John and Paul are evidently often in agreement, there does not seem to be a single line of development from one to the other; rather they represent parallel developments of early Christian theology (Bultmann, *TNT* 2, 6–9). Thus they share many concepts and terms that have been drawn from the common religious and cultural heritage responsible for the NT. The Pauline concept of the Church as the Body of Christ and the Johannine concept of the Vine and Branches are similar, though not identical, appreciations of the same underlying revealed truth. The moral dualism so prominent in John is also present in Paul, where, however, it has not received a comparable stress. The propitiatory conception of Christ's work of salvation, one of the cornerstones of Pauline theology, is not, on the other hand, given a place of prominence by John (see comments on 1 Jn 2:2; 4:10). There is no echo in Johannine theology of other ideas that had their existential situation in the ministry of Paul, such as, the faith and works dichotomy, the conception of justification through faith, etc.

10 **(B) Originality.** From what has been said, the conclusion should be evident that the originality of John consists not so much in his invention of wholly new conceptions and approaches as in his development of a fresh synthesis of existing ideas. This is not to minimize his originality which, as a matter of fact, is in little danger of being challenged. The Johannine synthesis, with its own special stresses and insights, perfectly fulfills the test of a theology. It lays emphasis on precisely those elements most relevant to the Christianity of its age and it puts them in a language comprehensible to that age—more than this we can ask no theology to do. Furthermore, the author's vision of the essentials in Christianity is less dated than that of any other NT work ("dated" in the sense of there being a conscious need on our part to apply it to greatly changed conditions or viewpoints). The Johannine characteristics (→ Gospel Jn, 63:28–32) testify to the author's original and catholic mind, whose thoughts have had a perennial appeal for every age of the Church. What C. H. Dodd said of Jn can, in some fashion, be extended to all of the Johannine writings: "Whatever influences may have been present have been masterfully controlled by a powerful and independent mind.... There is no book, either in the NT or outside it, which is really *like* the Fourth Gospel" (*The Interpretation of the Fourth Gospel* [Cambridge, 1953] 6).

11 A final note may be added. In a certain sense, John is one of the most consciously theological NT authors in the manner in which he has made use of language. Though the Johannine vocabulary is relatively limited (e.g., Jn uses the least number of words of all the Gospels), and though John's words are usually simple ones employed in a simple syntax, he has obviously attempted to construct with them a technical language that is so necessary in theological writing. The very repetitiveness and continued reiteration of varying nuances of the same word or phrase, which the superficial reader may occasionally find tiresome in John, are a part of this professionally theological tendency.

JOHANNINE CHRISTOLOGY

12 **(I) The Dualistic Dichotomy.** When we enter the Johannine world, we find ourselves on a battleground of good and evil, or, as John himself would call it, of light and darkness. In this world there is a great dichotomy: light is opposed by darkness, truth by the lie, freedom by slavery, life by death. This involves not merely passive opposition, but continuous warfare: Just as death is constantly battling against life, so is darkness battling against light.

In such a conception there was nothing particularly new. Anyone who thinks about the world and is sensitive to values beyond day-by-day survival accepts some sort of dualism like this, however he may explain its origins and however he may decide to pursue the "two ways, of life and of death" (*Didache* 1, 1). Original sin is one explanation that has been offered for the origin of this dualism. In John's time there were rival explanations, some claiming to be based on revelation, others merely philosophical. There were also rival ways of identifying the truth that makes men free, offered by the Gnostics, the Hermeticists, the mystery religions, or again by philosophy. The modern de-mythologized and de-philosophized thinker may find it convenient to dispense with an explanation of the dualism itself, though he is likely to have firm convictions about the way of truth and freedom.

13 Some religions, both primitive and highly developed, and some philosophies, have made the origin of the dichotomy metaphysical. That is to say, they think of evil not as the lack of good but as a positive principle, either personal or impersonal, either physical or supernatural. In John's time the tendency was to find evil in the material order of things, in the body of man that was constitutionally at war with his soul, the principle of the good and the true. This metaphysical dualism was later to influence and pervert some forms of Christianity (Manichaeanism, Albigensianism) and to appear in a variety of heresies that have attacked the biblical concept of man and the moral order.

For, as R. Bultmann has written ("New Testament and Mythology," *Kerygma and Myth* [N.Y., 1961] 17), though the NT and Gnosticism could use the same language in speaking of this world as subject to powers of evil,

> there is one significant difference. In the New Testament one of these powers is conspicuously absent—viz. *matter*, the physical, sensual part of man's constitution. Never does the New Testament complain that the soul of man, his authentic self, is imprisoned in a material body: never does it complain of the power of sensuality over the spirit. That is why it never doubts the responsibility of man for his sin. God is always the Creator of the world, including human life in the body. He is also the Judge before whom man must give account. The part played by Satan as the Lord of this world must therefore be limited in a peculiar way, or else, if he is the lord or god of the world, "this world" must stand in a peculiar di-lectical relation to the world as the creation of God.

14 "This world," it is true, knows neither Christ nor God (see comment on Jn 1:10; 17:25). Jesus is not of this world (Jn 8:23), nor is his kingdom of this world (18:36), and consequently his disciples cannot really belong to this world (15:19; 17:14). However, before the coming of Jesus, the world was not evil in itself: God loved the world and sent his Son into the world (Jn 3:16–17; 12:47; 1 Jn 4:9) to take away the world's sin (Jn 1:29; 1 Jn 2:2), to be the Savior of the world (Jn 4:42; 1 Jn 4:14) and the Light of the world (Jn 8:12). It is the destiny of Christians to continue to live in this world and in the Spirit of Christ to challenge the world, bearing witness to the life and light offered through the revelation of Christ.

"This world" is *kosmos* in John (*kosmos* or *aiōn* indifferently in Paul, following Jewish usage that had associated the two; → Aspects OT Thought, 77:48). It is both a spatial and temporal conception; therefore it refers to both the time and the place in which the divine plan of salvation is unfolded. Metonymously it refers to the work of God's creation, sold into the power of sin by its own willfulness and therefore under the judgment of God, but also the object of God's love that he desires to save. (The corollary of "this world" in Jewish tradition is "the world to come," an expression that is not used by John [where it would have been somewhat paradoxical in view of his realized eschatology] or by Paul, but is used by Heb 2:5 to refer to the messianic era, the Church, inaugurated by Christ.) It becomes evident, therefore, that the dualism of John has nothing to do with a philosophical speculation on good and evil, but is a component of *Heilsgeschichte*. John handles the terms of the dichotomy as the elements of a theology of salvation, as will be seen in the following section.

(Böcher, O., *Der johanneische Dualismus im Zusammenhang des nachbiblischen Judentums* [Gütersloh, 1965]. Brown, *Gospel*, 508–10, 515–16. Evans, G., "The World in the Writings of the Apostle John," *RevExp* 31 [1934] 66–80. Sasse, H., "*Aiōn*," *ThDNT* 1, 197–208; "*Kosmos*," 3, 868–95.)

15 **(II) The Coming of the Savior.** The battle between light and darkness in this world, therefore, is no struggle of cosmic forces in which man is caught up in a determinist system, but a warfare fought within the human soul. What is John's answer to man's search for truth and light? Had he remained simply within his Jewish heritage, John might have replied, as Ben Sira had (Sir 24), that the answer was to be found not in philosophy or in esoteric rites and purifications, but in the Law, the revealed will of God. By following the Law, and not through any devices of his own, man enters into the way of life. Judaism was not alone, of course, in believing that salvation must come from above, that there was need for a Savior.

16 However, John goes beyond Judaism. The Law was given through Moses, but truth through Jesus Christ (Jn 1:17). The Christ-event has revealed the inadequacy of Judaism to give a final answer to what is truth—an inadequacy shared by the Gentile world, for Pilate too is ignorant of truth (18:38). In the Johannine view, truth has not been revealed slowly, bit by bit, as in the OT, but whole and entire through the coming of the Son of Man (cf. Heb 1:1ff.).

17 **(A) The Son of Man.** For John, the concept of the Son of Man (see comment on Jn 1:51), founded in the messianic proclamation of Jesus himself, epitomizes the reality of the truth that has been revealed in Christ—it is a power to transform man by freeing him from the clutches of sin and giving him new life. According to the Syn tradition (→ Aspects NT Thought, 78:28–30), Jesus revealed himself under the title "Son of Man" as eschatological judge (Mk 8:38), but also as sharing the divine mind and power in the here-and-now (Mk 2:10,28 par.). In John's treatment we find a deepening of these themes. The Son of Man remains pre-eminently a judge (Jn 5:27). He can reveal divine mysteries because his proper place is with God in heaven (3:13). But above all, it is in him that the meeting of God and man takes place (1:51). Not only does he communicate a divine power by which men may become sons of God (1:12); he himself as Son of Man is the actual communication of divine life (6:53). The new birth that comes from above (3:3) has been brought down by the Son of Man, and is imparted by his Spirit (Jn 3:6; 1 Jn 2:21,27; cf. Paul's teaching on Christ the second Adam [Man] in 1 Cor 15:45; → Aspects NT Thought, 78:39–40).

18 It may be debated to what extent there were analogies to this conception in Hellenistic speculations of John's day concerning the Anthropos (*Urmensch*, heavenly or primordial man) who would function as a savior of man. The extant sources are not sufficient to prove the antiquity of such an idea anterior to Christian belief, and "to infer the existence of such a tradition from the pages of St. John himself is to perform the unedifying feat of arguing in a circle" (E. M. Sidebottom, *The Christ* *of the Fourth Gospel* [London, 1961] 70). If all the OT and intertestamental antecedents of the Son of Man doctrine do not add up to the Johannine portrayal, this proves nothing more than that the NT fulfillment outstrips its OT anticipation. See Dn 7; Ez, *passim;* Ps 8:5–7 (cf. Heb 2:6ff.); Ps 79:16–18 (cf. Mk 14:62); *Enoch* (→ Apocrypha, 68:15).

19 What is certain is that there is nothing mythical or mystical about John's theology of the Son of Man. If John's thought transcends the messianism of the Syn, it also presupposes it. The Son of Man of whom John speaks is Jesus the son of Joseph of Nazareth (Jn 1:45). He succeeds in bringing life everlasting to men because he is "lifted up" (see comment on Jn 3:14), that is, by fulfilling what is said of the Servant of the Lord in Is 52:13. The Son of Man is Savior, in other words, only in virtue of the mystery of the cross and resurrection preached as the common kerygma of the NT. This Jesus, however, born a son of David of a Jewish mother, living among men as one of them, eating, drinking, and sleeping among them (1 Jn 1:1), is also the way and truth and life (Jn 14:6) in virtue of a life that he has shared with God from the beginning (17:5,24). It is for this reason, therefore, that while others have come to be, Jesus eternally is (8:58; → Gospel Jn, 63:94).

20 From all this it becomes evident why John stresses equally the divinity and the humanity of the Savior. The truth, the light, the life that men need can only come from above, and it has been brought from above by the Son of the Father who has been sent into the world for this purpose. But the giving of this life has been possible only through the actions of a Servant of God whose work was foretold and made the condition of man's salvation. And it can be given only because this Servant is a Son of Man, one with mankind that through him can enter into the divine sphere (Jn 14:20). Hence the importance of a sound Christology (see comments on 1 Jn 2:18–29; 4:1–6; 5:8–12), the true witness (see comments on Jn 1:7,15; 4:39; 5:31,36,37). The reality of the incarnation is not simply an affirmation of Christian dogma, but constitutes the essence of salvation.

(Feuillet, A., "Le fils de l'homme de Daniel et la tradition biblique," *RB* 60 [1953] 170–202, 321–46. Jeremias, J., "*Adam,*" *ThDNT* 1, 141–43. For the Johannine concept of the Son of Man, see H.-M. Dion, *ScEccl* 19 [1967] 49–65; E. D. Freed, *JBL* 86 [1967] 402–9; R. Schnackenburg, *NTS* 11 [1964–65] 123–37.)

21 **(B) The Word Become Flesh.** The modern reader is invariably much intrigued by the Johannine concept of Jesus as the Word (see comment on Jn 1:1); probably no other characteristic of Jn has attracted more attention and speculation than this. John's contemporaries, however, whether of Jewish or Hellenistic background, would have accepted this concept as in some way familiar. What they would have found puzzling was the affirmation that "the Word became flesh." Besides the instance in the Prologue of Jn, Jesus is called the Word only in Ap 19:13 (probably not in 1 Jn 1:1). In the Ap, however, it seems clear the usage represents a mélange of such passages as Wis 18:14–16; Is 11:4 (LXX); 63:1–3, a quite different line of thought from that of Jn 1:1,14, where the Word is creative and life-giving, not destructive. Still, the Word of Jn and that of the Ap are not mutually exclusive or unrelated; it is in keeping with the Johannine paradox that the same Word should be one of death as well as of life, even as the Light of the world can also be the occasion of its blindness (Jn 9:39–41).

22 What does John mean by speaking of Jesus, the Son of Man, as the Word? The fact that the term appears only in the Prologue of Jn does not indicate that it was only a passing thought of the Evangelist. Rather, although he has reason to avoid the term after the climax achieved in 1:14, the concept that it represents dominates his Christology. The Word is a relevant term for John only in conjunction with the recognition that it has become flesh. The enunciation of Jn 1:14 is deliberately calculated to shock, coming as it does after a preface that has stressed over and over again the transcendence of the Word who is with God. Flesh, like the world, was not conceived precisely as evil (see comments on Jn 1:13–14; 3:6), but as incompatible with the divine (cf. Is 40:6; Jn 6:63; Mt 16:17). Nevertheless, the incredible has taken place, and what has been impossible for man is now an attainable reality, to which witness is given (1 Jn 1:1). Man could not, despite the yearning of the ages, reach up to enter into the sphere of the divine; but the gap has been bridged for him in the incarnation. Thus the importance of insisting that Jesus has truly come "in the flesh" (1 Jn 4:2; 2 Jn 7). If the Son of God has been born a Man—and only if this is true—it becomes evident how men in turn can be born of God (Jn 1:13; 1 Jn 5:18). It is no accident that in the Prologue on the Word (Jn 1:18) Jesus is called the *monogenēs*, "the only Son": It is in the concept of the Word become flesh that the identification between the Son of Man and the Son of God is best seen.

23 In other words, the idea of the Word is eminently a soteriological one. In identifying Jesus as the creative Word of God, the source of the light that is the life of man, John is presenting him as the revealer of God. But this conception of revelation is a vital one; it is no more restricted to a merely intellectual appreciation than is the Johannine conception of knowledge (→ 36 below). The revelation made by the Word does not give knowledge about someone, but knowledge of God. Furthermore, the revelation of God is not to be found in the abstract contemplation of truths, but in the example and imitation of a life that has been led, the life of the Son of Man (Jn 12:23–26). In the life of the Son of Man the glory of God has been revealed (→ 30–32 below).

24 It is for this reason that John can insist that the supreme grace and truth have come only through Jesus Christ, not through the Law (Jn 1:17). The incarnation of the Word is itself the supreme grace of God (the term *charis* appears in the Johannine literature only in the Prologue, Jn 1:16, and in the conventional greetings of 2 Jn 3; Ap 1:4; etc.). The Word of God is truth (Jn 17:17), whence Jesus can call himself the Truth (14:6). In turn, the Word of God is the source of true life, to the extent that it abides in the disciples and they remain in it (Jn 5:38; 8:31; 1 Jn 2:14; 4:16). Jesus has communicated the Word, himself, in his own words and in his life, in his "dwelling with" men (Jn 1:14). By this dwelling he extends to men "fellowship" with himself and thus with God, a fellowship that is continued in the apostolic ministry of the word (1 Jn 1:3). It is in this way that the Word become flesh is the revelation of life (1 Jn 1:1).

(Brown, *Gospel*, 519–24. De Ausejo, S., "El concepto de 'carne' aplicado a Cristo en el IV Evangelio," *SP* 2, 219–34. Moffatt, J., *Grace in the New Testament* [N.Y., 1932] 365–72. Starcky, J., "Logos. La parole divine dans le Nouveau Testament," *VDBS* 5, 479–96.)

25 **(C) The Love of God.** No NT author has laid greater stress on the virtue of love than has John; according to tradition his only message to his disciples in his old age was the reiterated "Little children, love one another." The reason for this stress is not hard to find in Johannine theology, for Jesus the Word is pre-eminently the revelation of God's love. God's love is the motive of his sending the Son into the world (see comment on Jn 3:16; 1 Jn 4:9). But more than a motive, love is the

Act of Contrition

O my God, I am sorry for my sins.
In choosing to sin,
and failing to do good,
I have sinned against You
and Your Church.
I firmly intend,
with the help of Your Son,
to make up for my sins
and to love as I should.

revelation itself. Even as God himself is love (1 Jn 4:16), Jesus is the incarnation of the divine love for man, embodying in himself this relation willed by God. Thus we are continually reminded of the love of the Father for the Son (Jn 3:35; 10:17), a love that the Son in turn extends to his followers, not as his own love only, but also as the love of the Father (17:23–26). Jesus is therefore the mediator of the divine love and its supreme exemplar (15:13). Once again, no one can take this revelation simply as information about God, but must be intimately affected and changed by it; he must abide in the love of God and Christ (15:9).

26 Love itself is vital, active, the very essence of the living God who would assimilate men to himself. Just as Jesus' love brings him to the supreme sacrifice, the love that he has revealed and that has been received by men must find a comparable expression in their lives (13:1–20). Thus love is not only the sign, but the very essence of true discipleship, of what it means to be a Christian (13:35). This love is shown in obedience to the law of God and Christ (14:15,23), so much so that the whole of the Christian life may be summed up in the one word love (1 Jn 4:7). In 1 Jn "love" used absolutely, without an expressed object, is found as the epitome of the Christian life (3:18; 4:7–8,19; a usage found also on the lips of Jesus in Lk 7:47 (→ Gospel Jn, 63:19,34). For the love of God is boundless, and whoever has truly received this revelation of love must love boundlessly in turn—he must love not only God but also his brothers who have been the objects of this same divine love (Jn 13:34; 1 Jn 4:19–21). On the contrary, hatred is the certain sign that one does not share true life and is in the way of death (Jn 8:42; 1 Jn 3:14). In the Ap (2:4,19; etc.) love is again equated with the Christian life, and its origin is found in the same divine act (1:5).

(Brown, *Gospel*, 497–99. Spicq, C., *Agape in the New Testament* [vol. 3; St. Louis, 1966]. Stauffer, E., "*Agapē*," *ThDNT* 1, 52–53.)

27 **(D) The Signs.** If Jesus is pre-eminently the revelation of God's love, and if love subsumes in itself the essence of the light that is the life of man, nevertheless, Jesus the Light has shone in the world in a manifold way, making the truth known under more than merely one aspect. This he has done through what Jn characterizes as his *sēmeia*, "signs" (the word is not used in 1–2–3 Jn). In our view (but many would dissent), the signs must not be simply equated with Jesus' miracles, though it is true that certain of the miracles are signs in a pre-eminent way (see comment on Jn 2:11). The "many other signs" worked by Jesus in the presence of his disciples (Jn 20:30; cf. 21:24–25) are not to be identified exclusively or even primarily with Jesus' miracles: John is speaking here of the entire revelation of life made by the Son of Man (cf. Jn 20:31; 1 Jn 1:1). Similarly, whereas miracles are not excluded in the reference to the many signs worked in the presence of the Jews (Jn 12:37), what is primarily involved is a revelation that has been ignored (cf. 12:38).

The term "signs" emerges from an OT background in which it meant especially the wonderful works of Yahweh in the Exodus story (Nm 14:11; → Gospel Jn, 63:23–24). However, what was meaningful about these wonderful deeds was not precisely that they were beyond natural causality, but that they had been worked by the God of Israel to reveal himself to his people. The "signs" of Jesus have exactly this meaning for John. The turning of the water into wine (2:11), the healing of the official's son (4:54), the multiplication of the loaves (6:14), the giving of sight to the man born blind (9:16), the raising of Lazarus (12:18) are all miracles and all are called "signs," but their chief importance is in their manifestation of the life-giving work of Jesus rather than in their display of preternatural power. John knows of many other miracles worked by Jesus that are mentioned only summarily (2:23; 3:2; 4:48); doubtless these are not as suited to his theological purposes as the relatively few that he has chosen to describe. Two of the miracles that he does describe (the healing in 5:2–9; the walking on the water in 6:16–21) he does not specifically characterize as "signs," though there is no doubt that they are.

But similarly there is no doubt that other words and works of Jesus which are not miraculous are "signs" for John; for they too reveal the nature of Jesus and his life-giving word to man. Thus in Jn 2:18–25 when the Jews demand a sign from Jesus, he replies by offering himself, as signified in the cleansing of the Temple; this is a sign that goes unheeded by the bystanders but is accepted in the post-resurrectional faith of the disciples. (This episode is a close parallel to the Lucan version [11:29–32] of the "sign of Jonah.") Again, the crucifixion is the sign of the glorification of Christ according to Jn 3:14; 8:28; 12:32. (As background we note that in the story of the bronze serpent, the prepositional phrase *'al-nēs*, lit. "on a staff," of Nm 21:8ff. was translated *epi sēmeiou* by the LXX; *pro signo* by the Vg. A "messianic" sense of *nēs* [*sēmeion* each time in LXX] was further established by such texts as Is 11:12; Jer 50:2; 51:12,27; Ps 60:6.) The footwashing of Jn 13:1–20 certainly constitutes a "sign" in this Johannine sense, although some scholars would confine the designation "sign" to events narrated in Jn 1–12, the "Book of Signs."

28 Bernard is doubtless wrong in his assumption that John had some interest in trying to minimize the miraculous element in Christ's ministry. The wondrous deeds of Jesus were part of the Christian kerygma accepted by John, who, in fact, has told us of miracles not attested by the Syn tradition. However, it is true that he has placed Jesus' miracles in a careful perspective. The exorcisms of the Syn tradition make no appearance in Jn, which has its own way of showing this aspect of the inauguration of the Kingdom of God. Jn constantly repeats that a faith based on miracles alone is inadequate and is not a true recognition of the Lord (Jn 2:23–25; 3:2; 7:3–7).

29 The realities that John knows as "signs," the Johannine Jesus refers to as his "works," which are also the works of God (cf. Jn 5:20,36; 7:3,21; 9:3–4). Once more the works of Jesus certainly include, but are not restricted to, his miracles. These works are the whole of his public ministry and include his words as well (14:10). "Words" and "works" were closely united and even identified in Semitic thought. Furthermore, words are not mere sounds but vital utterances (→ Aspects OT Thought, 77:40): In Jn 15:3 Jesus pronounces his disciples clean because of the word he has spoken to them. In one sense, at least, the words of Jesus are the more important element in the "signs" of Jesus, because these words give determination to his works and show them to be the works of God.

Since faith is the acceptance of a person as he has revealed himself to be, and not simply the acceptance of propositions that have been revealed about him (→ 36 below), the "signs" of Jesus constitute the communication of God himself to men. Hence only those miracles that reveal the nature of Jesus as the revelation of God are signs in the Johannine sense. The way, the truth, and the life that men seek have been revealed concretely in Jesus. The words and works of Jesus are not just proofs of this truth and life; they are truth and life in very fact. And because they are realities that can truly be assimilated, Jesus can promise that his words will abide in his disciples (Jn 15:7) who will also do his works and even greater works (14:12).

(Brown, R. E., "The Gospel Miracles," *BCCT* 184–201; also in *New Testament Essays* [Milwaukee, 1965] 168–91. Mollat, D., "Le semeion johannique," *SP* 2, 209–18.)

30 **(E) The Glory of God.** Jesus' "signs" are signs of his glory (Jn 2:11; see P. Riga, *Interpr* 17 [1963] 402–24); and this glory is also the glory of God (11:40). It is to this glory that the apostolic kerygma is a witness (see comment on 1:14; 2:11). In the OT "the glory of God" refers to the visible manifestation of God, usually in fire and smoke (or cloud)—sometimes in natural disturbances (Pss 29:1–9; 97:1–6), in the heavens themselves as the handiwork of God (Ps 19:2), or in some special form of theophany. It was in the smoke-filled Temple that Isaiah (6:1–5) saw the glory of the Lord (cf. Jn 12:41; Ap 15:8). In the tradition of the Pentateuch Moses encountered the glory of the Lord in cloud and fire on Mt. Sinai (Ex 24:15–18), and the Lord made his presence known in Israel by a cloud that covered the Tent of Meeting and filled the Tabernacle (Ex 40:34). Similarly, Ezekiel's vision of the glory of the Lord was accompanied by cloud, fire, and other extraordinary phenomena (Ez 1:1–28).

31 This OT *kābôd*, through the LXX, is the source of the concept of *doxa*, "glory" that plays such a dominant role in Jn (but not in I Jn). In this John was perhaps further assisted by Jewish tradition which tended to use the "glory of God" as a kind of surrogate to tone down some of the anthropomorphisms of the OT. For example, the Hebrew of Nm 12:8 is translated: "He saw the form of the Lord"; the LXX renders it: "He saw the glory of the Lord." The Aram targums followed suit: The Hebrew of Ex 24:10 is translated: "They saw the God of Israel"; this is rendered in Targum Onkelos as: "They saw the glory of the God of Israel." "Glory" for John means the divine presence manifested in Jesus.

32 It is with this background of ideas that John says that the Word that had become flesh "dwelt among us," or, more literally, "tented among us." The allusion is to the divine presence, signaled by a cloud, that took up residence in the midst of the people, first in the Tent of Meeting (Ex 33:7–11) and later in the Temple (1 Kgs 8:10–11). The same allusion is doubtless present in Ap 7:15; 21:3, which also use the verb *skēnoun*, "to tent," chosen probably because of its resemblance to the Hebr *šākan*, *šᵉkînâ* (see comment on Jn 1:14). It must not be thought that the Johannine usage of *doxa* is merely figurative or that the author is playing with words. This glory of Jesus is something that has been seen, something that has been a visible manifestation of God, even though, like the "signs," it has remained perceptible only to the eye of faith (2:11; 11:40). This, after all, is the meaning that the symbols had in the OT as well. However anthropomorphic OT language may have become at times, there was never any doubt that man could encounter God only through faith: The "among us" that John has borrowed from OT terminology referred to the worshiping and believing community of God.

In connection with the concept of God's presence in Jesus, John's preoccupation with the feasts of Judaism finds its most logical setting (see comment on Jn 2:13ff.). John deals especially with the Feast of Tabernacles (chs. 7–8, and most of chs. 9–10), in view of the special meaning that Tabernacles had in Jewish thought as testifying to the continued or renewed presence of God among his people (cf. Is 4:5–6; Zech 14:16–21). In Jesus, says John, men have truly found the glory of God, the summation of all that is good, leading to true life.

(Brown, *Gospel*, 326–27, 503–4. Str-B 2, 744–812. Von Rad, G., and G. Kittel, "*Doxa*," *ThDNT* 2, 237–51.)

33 **(III) The Return of Jesus to the Father.** The truth, the light, and the life that are the goal of man's quest can free him from the darkness and frustration that are the lot of this world. But all this can come to man only through revelation and not through his own devices. It follows as a natural consequence that Johannine theology emphasizes certain things that God has done in human history, to which there is testimony. Judaism, too, was the outcome of a historical intervention of God, the results of which were epitomized in the Law; but John has already brought out that the history on which Judaism depended, while not false, was inadequate and incomplete. The incarnation has demonstrated this by bringing about a situation to which Judaism could not aspire and for which it had no precedent. But the incarnation is only the beginning, not the sum and substance, of the historical conclusion to which the NT witnesses. The incarnation, which reveals the glory of God in Jesus, has to be fulfilled in the work for which the Son has been sent into the world—the glorification of the Father that in turn is his own glorification.

34 **(A) The Hour of Glorification.** A sense of urgency pervades Jn. After the magisterial Prologue that has spoken of the wonderful things that have occurred, we quickly see that the remainder of Jn is to be the record of these occurrences. First, the Baptist points to one who is to come after him (1:27); and that one, unobtrusively introduced as Jesus of Nazareth, immediately speaks of a wonderful revelation that is soon to be seen (1:51). From this point on we are constantly being told of an "hour" or a "time" that is coming, that is not yet (2:4; 7:6), even though in a sense it has already begun with the presence of the Word among men (4:23; 5:25). This "hour" of Jesus is opposed to that of the world (7:6), the hour of darkness (12:35; cf. Lk 22:53). Yet, paradoxically, it is precisely in the hour of darkness that Jesus' hour comes (cf. 13:21–32). Paradoxically, too, when this hour comes that has been so eagerly awaited and anticipated, Jesus greets it with a semblance of dread (12:27).

The "hour," of course, is that of Jesus' suffering and death, which for John are simply one phase of Jesus' "glorification," the other phase being his resurrection and ascension to the Father. In many subtle ways, by addition, modification, and omission (e.g., omission of any reference to darkness at the time of the crucifixion [Mk 15:33; Lk 23:44]), John has underlined the glorification aspect of the passion story, thus diverging from the basically common tradition also found in the Syn (see comment on Jn 18:1–20:31). It is an hour of triumph because, despite all outward appearances, the world is really being judged in Christ's judgment, and the power of evil is broken once and for all (12:31). What the world calls death is really life, and what the world calls life is death—a truth applicable to Jesus that must also be a guiding rule for his followers (see comment on Jn 12:23–26). The sacrifice of Christ is his glorification because from it has come the new order, in which the darkness is passing away and the new light is already shining (1 Jn 2:8).

It is apparent that there is a close connection between Jesus' glory and his glorification. The active word, glorification, however, helps to remind us that the Christ-event is precisely an event, within a firm framework of *Heilsgeschichte*. "Glory" of itself could possibly suggest some kind of timeless immanence by which the divine communicates itself to man, which, of course, is not John's idea at all. The Word become flesh is the glory of God because he has glorified God by his words and deeds, and in turn has been glorified by God in these same words and deeds. "Glorification" itself, therefore, speaks of the vitality of this glory that man shares through the coming of God's Son. By entering the human sphere in the glorification of Jesus Christ, God has made it possible for man to enter the divine sphere.

35 **(B) The Role of Faith.** It is very important to appreciate the significance of this last point in John's theology, for in its light we can understand the role of faith in the Johannine writings. Faith is the assent of man to revelation. It is by faith that man is set free from his own hopelessness and brought into contact with that otherness that can save him. For John, that otherness is God as he has revealed himself historically in Jesus Christ. Here is the enduring "scandal" of Christianity: "The *skandalon*, the foolishness, lies in the fact that historically datable events ('under Pontius Pilate') are supposed to represent the very centre of God's revelation and to be connected with all his revelations" (O. Cullmann, *Christology of the NT* [London, 1963] 327).

36 (a) FAITH AND KNOWLEDGE. "This is the victory that overcomes the world, our faith" (1 Jn 5:4). Curiously enough, this is the only time that the noun "faith" occurs in the primary Johannine writings (it is used four times in the Ap), though the verb "believe" is one of the characteristically Johannine words. It may be that John has consciously avoided the substantive *pistis* in view of its contemporary use by so many religions and mystical sects to designate their rival revelations (cf. the Gnostic writing *Pistis Sophia*). More likely, however, his preference for the verb testifies to the active and vital quality that he ascribes to faith. For faith is not simply a frame of mind; it is an attachment to a person, an engagement, an involvement with him. Belief for John is not belief about God, but belief in him; and this means in some fashion a continuing, shared experience (see comment on Jn 1:12).

It is true, John may sometimes be read as though he were saying that to believe is to acquiesce, to accept, simply to know what has been revealed. Belief and knowledge are often construed with the same object (Jn 4:42; 6:69; 8:24 paralleling 8:28; 1 Jn 4:16). The life that is the fruit of faith can also be called the fruit of knowledge (Jn 6:47; 17:3), and faith and knowledge often appear in the same breath as though they are one and the same (6:69; 1 Jn 4:16). However, first of all, it should be seen that faith and knowledge are not identical. Although the relationship between the one who accepts revelation and the one who is revealed can be expressed in terms of either belief or knowledge (Jn 7:17; 16:27), John never says that Jesus believes the Father, only that he knows him and is known by him. Knowledge comes from faith; faith leads to knowledge as it leads to life—knowledge is part of life. What John is trying to say is that the believer is introduced into a true knowledge of God to the extent that he can possess it, not that faith is to be equated with knowledge. Bultmann is doubtless correct when he finds in John an anti-Gnostic approach to faith, just as in Paul the approach to faith has been directed by the polemics against justification by works. John is denying the fundamental conviction of Gnosticism, namely, that there is a higher knowledge that can lead to salvation, a knowledge denied the mere believer. Rather, whatever meaningful dimension there is to knowledge, whatever knowledge can do in the matter of salvation, comes only through faith.

Another consideration in this respect is that for John knowledge is not a passive acquiescence but something eminently active (see comment on Jn 1:10). To know (John avoids the noun *gnōsis* as he avoids the noun *pistis*) is to acknowledge certain facts: that Jesus Christ has come from God (7:28), that he is the Son of God manifested in the flesh (1 Jn 5:5ff.), that he is Lord and God (Jn 20:29). But to know is also, and primarily, an active embarking on a new experience, since the real object of this knowledge is not a thing but a person. To know is to receive the words of God (12:48; 17:8), and, therefore, to receive the Word of God himself. This means that to know God is to be committed to a God-like life (1 Jn 2:3–6), the model for which is to be found in the Word become flesh. To know God and Jesus Christ is to possess eternal life (Jn 17:3). There is, consequently, nothing "gnostic" about the idea of knowledge that is to be found in Johannine theology.

Rather we should see in this quasi-equation of faith and knowledge a distinctive reality that John has attached to the idea of faith. In the Semitic world of ideas, knowledge has less to do specifically with the intellect than with life itself. To know God is, therefore, not simply to attach oneself to God in mind or will, but somehow to become one with God. In keeping with this, the idea of the believer's divine sonship, an OT idea found in Paul and commonly in the NT, achieves with John a dimension that it possesses nowhere else. Only John has ventured to make of the believer the arresting statement that he has been "born of God" (Jn 1:13; 3:4–8; 1 Jn 4:7; 5:1), engendered by the divine seed that he has received (1 Jn 3:9). This sonship, moreover, is nothing merely formal, but evinces itself in a life whereby the believer avoids sin and seeks to be one with God (Jn 8:42–47,54–56; 1 Jn 3:9–10).

37 (b) FAITH AND SIGHT. Believing is also seeing. The believer has passed from the darkness of this world into light (see comment on Jn 1:4,5), the light of truth, which again is not simply an intellectual perception but a way of life (see comment on Jn 1:9,14). No other NT author has laid such a stress on faith as vision (Jn 1:14; 1:50–51; 6:40; 14:9; 17:24; 1 Jn 1:5), and on the consequent duty of the believer to live according to the light and not in darkness (1 Jn 1:6–7; 2:9–10; 3:19). Faith gives a vision of God and of everything in the light of God, so that the believer must renounce the standards of the world and find new standards for himself in the revelation of God that has been given him in Jesus Christ; this is what it means to "see" Jesus (Jn 12:21–26). The vision of faith is in every sense of the word a true vision of God and of truth, even though John does not deny that the ultimate vision is reserved for the time when faith will yield to something even greater (1 Jn 3:2).

38 (c) FAITH AND LOVE. Finally since the revelation of God in Christ is first and foremost the revelation of his love (→ 25–26 above), it follows that there is the closest possible connection between faith and love (see comment on 1 Jn 4:7–5:12). This is why for John love is basically expressed in keeping God's commandments—since faith knows Jesus as the revealer of God's love, to believe means to identify oneself with a disinterested love that has included in itself virtually every good and holy thing.

(Alfaro, J., "Cognitio Dei et Christi in 1 Jo," *VD* 39 [1961] 82–91. Brown, *Gospel*, 512–15. Bultmann, R., *Faith* [BKW 10; London, 1961] esp. 97–110. Gaffney, J., "Believing and Knowing in the Fourth Gospel," *TS* 26 [1965] 215–41. Gärtner, B. E., "The Pauline and Johannine Idea of 'to know God' against the Hellenistic Background," *NTS* 14 [1967–68] 209–31. Van der Spek, P., *De geloofsbeschouwing in de Schriftopenbaring door den apostel Johannes* [Delft, 1942].)

JOHANNINE ESCHATOLOGY

39 **(I) The Spirit.** It remains for us to see the role of the Holy Spirit in this new life that provides man with truth and light in face of the darkness of the world. The topic of the Spirit can serve as a transition in moving our discussion from Johannine Christology to Johannine eschatology.

At first glance, the Spirit seems to play a smaller part in John's conception of *Heilsgeschichte* than in that of the Syn. There is nothing in Jn corresponding to the statement that after Jesus' baptism the Spirit "drove him forth" into the desert and on to his public ministry (Mk 1:10–12); neither is there anything corresponding to the Lucan description of Pentecost (Acts 2:1–11). Although we note in Jn that the Spirit is present at the baptism of Jesus (see comment on Jn 1:32), the Spirit is introduced as a sign to John the Baptist rather than as the guiding force in Jesus' ministry. We can add to this the fact that in 1 Jn references to the Holy Spirit are quite vague and problematic (1 Jn 2:20,27, "anointing"; 1 Jn 3:9, "seed"). Indeed, the term "Paraclete," used for the Holy Spirit in the Gospel (→ 45 below), refers to Jesus in 1 Jn 2:1. This difficulty, however, can probably be answered satisfactorily on the score that the fairly rigid Johannine vocabulary of the Gospel had not as yet stabilized itself when the epistles were written (→ Johannine Epistles, 62:5).

40 At all events, it is by no means correct to say that the Spirit has been subordinated in John's theology. What is true is that John has treated of the Spirit in a unique way. In doing so, he has brought out, perhaps more consistently than any other NT author, the implications of the NT revelation that the Spirit of God is more than a personification—that he is a true person standing in relation to the Father and the Son (cf. *EDB* 2307–9).

41 As T. W. Manson has pointed out, and as has been indicated in the preceding section, that which is most remarkable about John's theology is his use of the name "Father" for God (107 times in Jn; 12 times in 1 Jn). "The whole system of his thought centers in the experience of God as Father. It is this experience which becomes the central and creative dogma of his Christianity. It is in the light of this experience that he sees what light is and what darkness is, what is truth and what lies, what love is and what hatred" (*On Paul and John*, 90–91). This expression of intimacy had been adopted by the primitive Church from the language of Jesus, who had in turn derived it from Judaism and stamped it with his own distinctive use (cf. G. Kittel, *ThDNT* 1, 5–6; G. Dalman, *The Words of Jesus* [Edinburgh, 1902] 184–94). It is in light of the major Johannine theme of God as Father that we see a partial reason for the distinctive treatment of the Spirit. In Jn, the Spirit is presented less as the divine power that has directed Jesus' ministry than as the divine power that continues and completes it; the Spirit is, as it were, the perpetuation of Jesus' presence among his followers. Correspondingly, the Spirit is the principle of the divine sonship that Jesus has made possible for men.

42 As is so often the case (→ Gospel Jn, 63:19), in this conception John resembles Luke more closely than any other NT author. From the earliest times Acts has aptly been called "the gospel of the Spirit" because of its outline of worldwide witness (another Johannine theme) under the impetus of the Holy Spirit (cf. Acts 1:8). Whereas Luke had, besides the Gospel, a second volume in which to develop the role of the Spirit in the Church, John has had to compress this era of salvation history into the Gospel pattern. Furthermore, there is a difference in the two treatments of the Spirit. Luke's emphasis is on the Spirit as power, bringing the Church into its Catholic destiny; John's emphasis is on the Spirit as sanctifier and principle of the life of the Christian.

43 Paul also attributes to the Spirit the Christian's share in the postresurrection life of Jesus—in 1 Cor 15:45 and, at least indirectly, in 2 Cor 3:17, the Spirit is Jesus himself; in Rom 8:26 and 1 Cor 12:4ff., the Spirit is distinct from Jesus. Perhaps the closest Pauline parallels to John's doctrine are in Gal 4:6; Rom 8:14–27 where we are told God has sent the Spirit of his Son into our hearts, and in virtue of this we recognize God as our Father (→ Pauline Theology, 79:75–79). John's development of these ideas lies in several directions: in strengthening the idea of sonship (Paul: "adoption of sons"), in a more precise determination of the distinct function of the Spirit ("in Christ" and "in the Spirit" are often synonymous in Paul), and in assigning to the Son a greater role in the sending of the Spirit. In doing so he has initiated a more elaborated triadic theology (i.e., a theology of three divine salvific agents: Father, Son, and Spirit), though it still remains largely functional (or preferably, "soteriological") rather than ontological. As indicated, these precisions about the Spirit are largely those of Jn rather than of 1 Jn.

44 The Spirit is the principle of the new life that Jesus has come to give (Jn 3:5–8) and is operative in virtue of Jesus' glorification (Jn 7:38–39; 1 Jn 3:24; 4:13). He is sent by the Father in the name of Jesus (Jn 14:16,26; see comment on Jn 1:12), which is to say that he is the gift of Christ himself, sent by him from the heavenly Father to abide with his disciples forever (Jn 15:26; 1 Jn 2:20,27). He is called "the Spirit of truth" in that the life that he gives is a share in the divine existence itself (see comment on Jn 1:14; 4:24). The life that was revealed in Jesus is perpetuated in and communicated by the Spirit, and in the Spirit man's longing for truth is to be satisfied. What this means in practical terms is that the Spirit makes possible the God-given knowledge that comes to man by faith (Jn 16:13). In even more practical terms, John like Paul sees the activity of the Spirit manifest in the preaching of the word by the Church (→ 48 below), through which the saving power of Christ is brought to mankind.

45 The designation of the Spirit as the Paraclete is distinctively Johannine in the NT (only Jn 14:16,26; 15:26; 16:7—in 1 Jn 2:1 it refers to Jesus). The term is brought into the Gospel without introduction, so that we must determine its meaning from its usage there. We are aided by Jewish usage that had already transliterated the Gk *paraklētos* into Hebrew as *p^eraqlît* (*Pirke Aboth* 4. 11); in fact, it is likely that in this form it was used originally by Jesus himself. "Paraclete" means "helper," "advocate": that Jesus is our advocate with the Father is a common Christian conception (Heb 7:25; Rom 8:34); therefore it is easy to see how John can call him our Paraclete (1 Jn 2:1). The Holy Spirit is "the other" Paraclete (Jn 14:16) whose activity begins with the return of the Son to the Father, and whose activity remains till the end of time. The activity of the Paraclete is to reveal the mind of Christ (16:13) even as Christ revealed the mind of the Father (14:10): "He will not speak on his own authority" (see comment on Jn 5:19). Yet the

Paraclete will glorify the Son (16:14), just as the Father has glorified the Son and the Son the Father. In other words, the Spirit stands in the same relation to the Christian of the Johannine church (and of all times) as that in which Jesus stood to his disciples during his ministry. The Spirit, that is to say, the Son and the Father in the Spirit, is the route by which man enters into the way, the truth, and the life proclaimed by Christ. Thus we are reminded that it is not by the words of the "historical" Jesus alone that we live, but by the words of Jesus as made known by the Church enlightened by the Spirit (16:13: "He will teach you all the truth"; cf. 14:25–26). In the Ap, too, the Lord speaks to the living Church through the Spirit (cf. 2:1,7; 2:8,11; 2:12,17; etc.).

(Barrett, C. K., *JTS* 1 [1950] 1–15. Behm, J., "*Paraklētos*," *ThWNT* 5, 798–812. Betz, O., *Der Paraklet* [Leiden, 1963]. Brown, R. E., *NTS* 13 [1966–67] 113–32. Miguéns, M., *El Paráclito* [Jerusalem, 1963]. Schweizer, E., *Spirit of God* [BKW 9; London, 1960] esp. 88–107.)

46 **(II) Realized Eschatology.** In the context of the foregoing, the peculiarities of the Johannine "realized eschatology" (→ Gospel Jn, 63:25) can be seen in their proper perspective. In Jewish thought the coming of the Spirit was an eschatological idea (cf. Jl 3). Given John's theology of the Spirit, his eschatology could hardly be other than "realized."

The NT testifies to a continued expectation of the parousia (→ Aspects NT Thought, 78:70ff.), unbroken from the quite primitive formulations preserved in Acts 3:12–26 down to what appear to have been some of the latest of the NT writings (as in 2 Pt 3:1–13). To this pattern John forms no exception (cf. Jn 5:28; 1 Jn 2:28). It is quite obvious, however, that all of John's emphasis (in Jn, if not in 1 Jn; → Johannine Epistles, 62:5) is on the here-and-nowness of salvation rather than on the salvation that is to be consummated in the last days. In this emphasis he has been followed by most of subsequent Christianity.

47 Neither, however, was John entirely isolated in NT times. Paul, too, particularly in his later writings, began to dwell on the present realities of salvation rather than on the salvation to come. Both Paul's conception of the Holy Spirit as the "down payment" (*arrabōn*) in the history of salvation (2 Cor 1:22; 5:5; Eph 1:14) and his ability to speak of the resurrection of Christians as already having taken place in Christ (Col 3:1) fit into this pattern. Even a book as heavily weighted in favor of future eschatology as the Ap can speak of the possession of the Spirit as a present reality. Further, the "first resurrection" of Ap 20:4–6 corresponds adequately to Paul's concept of the here-and-now participation in the resurrection of Christ. It was doubtless the primitive Church's consciousness and experience of the presence of the Holy Spirit, rather than the "delay" of the parousia, that was above all responsible for the development of "realized eschatology" (A. Feuillet, "Parousie," *VDBS* 6, 1394–1414).

48 **(A) The Church and the Sacraments.** It is in the Spirit that man encounters the way, the truth, and the life that the Son has brought as the Father's gift into this world. But how and under what conditions does one possess the Spirit? John's answer to this is simple: The Spirit is to be had in the Church. As we have already noted, it is in the preaching and the teaching of the Church, inspired and guided by the Spirit, that the word of God and therefore the Word of Life is encountered. The truth that makes men free resides in the community which exists as the result of Jesus' exaltation (Jn 8:28–32) and is presided over by the Spirit. This is the house of God, in which the Son lives with his disciples in the Spirit (14:2–4; cf. 2:19–22). The word of God is accepted by faith as it is transmitted by the Church's ministry (1 Jn 1:5; 2:7). Here men find the way that leads to eternal life and is the beginning of that life (1 Jn 2:17).

49 *Sacraments.* In the Church, moreover, men find not only the teaching of Jesus, his words, but also his works of salvation. Salvation is not a matter of human activity following on divine inspiration; this is not the meaning of faith. Salvation is the acceptance of a divine activity that continues to do its work in those who believe. The works of Christ that the Spirit perpetuates in the Church are chiefly the sacraments (→ Gospel Jn, 63:62–63). John is mainly concerned with the sacraments of Baptism and the Eucharist, the two sacraments that are most intimately connected with the life of the Church and are the pre-eminent "signs" of that life. However, this is not to say that he would have limited the divine life in the Church to these two "signs." On the other hand, it would be unrealistic to expect to find in his writings the precisions of sacramental theology that unfolded only in later times through the developing doctrine of the Church.

50 The sacraments draw their efficacy from the sacrificial death of Christ (Jn 19:34). Jesus Christ is Savior not simply by having been declared the Messiah at the time of his baptism ("through water"), but by having fulfilled his mission in death on the cross ("through blood"); therefore, as the object of faith, he must be confessed as one who has come "not in the water only, but in the water and the blood" (1 Jn 5:6; → Johannine Epistles, 62:23). John customarily writes on several levels, making his narrative of historical events significant to his readers in respect to the enduring Christian realities (→ Gospel Jn, 63:23). And so, "water and blood" also means the continuing witness given by water and blood in the Church through the Spirit, that is, in the sacraments of Baptism and the Eucharist: "Therefore there are three who testify, the Spirit and the water and the blood, and the three make up one" (1 Jn 5:7). The Spirit, then, rather than the water only, gives the new life of Baptism (Jn 3:5).

51 The Word become flesh gives his flesh and blood for the life of the soul (Jn 6:53–58), and it is the Spirit that makes this possible (6:63). It is by the gift of the Spirit that the Church exercises its power to forgive sins in the name of Christ (20:21–23). The condition of the Church expressed in the figure of the branches drawing life from the vinestock is also a sacramental image connected with the coming of the Spirit (15:1–27). The frequency with which water is mentioned in Jn (2:6; 4:10,23; 5:25) has as at least part of its explanation John's preoccupation with Baptism, just as his stress on "flesh" in reference to the incarnation (1:14) is not made without regard to the Eucharist.

When we remember that the Spirit is, above all, the divine agent who continues the presence of Christ in his Church, and when we observe the way in which John has consistently described Jesus' works in sacramental terms (the man born blind, the loaves), we are reminded of a profound truth that must never be obscured in sacramental theology. The sacraments are not merely rites instituted by the Church to symbolize divine grace. They are not even merely rites instituted by Christ himself to symbolize such a conferral. They are, as Thomas Aq. said, rites in which God himself acts through the humanity of Christ (*Summa* 3.62, 5); their efficacy is *ex opere Christi*, as they signify what has first taken place in Christ (3.61, 4; cf. *In 4*, dist. 1, q. 1, a. 3–5 ["gratiam continent ex sanctificatione quae fit per verbum Dei"—4, 5]). For bibliography, → Gospel Jn, 63:63; also Brown, *Gospel*, cxi–cxiv.

52 *Worship.* Christ is encountered through the Spirit also in the worship of the Church. Christian worship necessarily had quickly distinguished itself from its Jewish origins by reason of the essentially different eschatological perspective. When Jesus told his disciples that he would not leave them orphans but would return to them in the Spirit (Jn 14:15–21), he was proclaiming the fulfillment of the kingdom in OT language parallel to that of Lk 6:20 (D. E. Holwerda, *The Holy Spirit and Eschatology*, 38–48). Christianity now consciously distinguished itself from the Synagogue, so much so that John refers consistently to "the Jews" in the third person as alien to the Church (see comment on Jn 1:19). Christians had their own Lord's day to replace the Sabbath (Ap 1:10), and their own liturgy to replace the feasts of Judaism. In his description of the Last Supper (Jn 13–17), John may have echoed the basic Christian liturgy: sermon, prayer, and Eucharistic banquet. Liturgical songs have been preserved in such passages as Ap 5:9–10,12,13; 12:10–12. The role of the liturgy as a re-creation of the historical events of salvation under the guidance of the Spirit is part of the Spirit's function of "reminding" the Church (Jn 14:26). This is the worship of God "in Spirit and truth" (4:23); this is prayer in Jesus' name (14:13).

53 *Christian Living.* Pervading all, however, is the presence of the Spirit manifested in Christian life. This does not exclude, but neither does it simply mean, the extraordinary manifestations of the Spirit in charismatic activities. These have their part to play, certainly, in the life of the Church (cf. Ap 1:10), but they can be ambiguous and must always be tested by the criterion of known Christian truth (1 Jn 4:1–3). For John as for Paul the more obvious way in which the Spirit is present is in the Christian virtues, specifically fraternal charity, manifest in the Christian community, and in the consciousness of the forgiveness of sins and of fellowship with God (1 Jn 2:3; 3:6,23; 4:8,12–21; 3 Jn 11). Life, after all, can be verified only in living actions, and the life with which John is concerned (see comment on Jn 1:4) produces actions that can only be divine in origin. Just as Jesus' words and deeds were the proof of his origin from the Father, the words and deeds of Christians show forth the presence of the Spirit of the Son, the Spirit who has brought the eschatological peace that Jesus promised (Jn 14:27).

54 *Church Order.* There is not a great deal in Jn on the organization or "constitution" of the Church. The literary form of the Gospel more or less precluded this; and, in any case, both Jn and 1 Jn have put all their emphasis on the life of grace lived in the Church rather than on its externals. However, such an organization is presupposed in the sacramental and liturgical concerns of Jn, as well as in the references to doctrinal authority (1 Jn 2:24; 4:6). Whether "the Presbyter" of 2 Jn 1 and 3 Jn 1 uses the title in the ecclesiastical sense familiar from Acts and the Pastoral Epistles is not certain; the discourteous Diotrephes of 3 Jn 9, however, is most likely the chief presbyter of the church with which the Epistle is concerned. The supplementary ch. 21 in Jn manifests the concern for Peter's primacy in the Church shown by other NT documents (→ Gospel Jn, 63:183). The Ap supposes a local church organization, also implied in 1–3 Jn; and the figure of the woman in Ap 12 is certainly ecclesial (→ Apocalypse, 64:58).

55 **(B) The Judgment.** Judgment was eminently an eschatological idea in Jewish thought (→ Aspects OT Thought, 77:136–139). Even in paganism the idea of a divine judgment itself had become widespread, though not necessarily in an eschatological context (cf. F. Büchsel, *ThDNT* 3, 933ff.). Paul is represented in Acts 17:31 as preaching the judgment of the world as a concept that would be understood and accepted by the Stoics and Epicureans of Athens. For the Jew, such terms as "judgment," "the day of the Lord," and "that day" had become synonymous, deriving from the earliest days of prophecy (cf. Am 5:18), designating the definitive intervention of God in history in the end-time. It is significant that this prophetic idea figures so largely for John who has identified the eschatological Prophet of Jewish expectation with Jesus (cf. O. Cullmann, *Christology*, 22, 29; → Gospel Jn, 63:50; → Aspects NT Thought, 78:14).

56 John's concept of the judgment is in accord with the rest of his eschatology and would have appealed to the non-Jewish mentality as well as to the Jewish. "That day" is the day of Jesus' glorification (Jn 14:20), which in turn, we have seen (→ 34 above), is simply God's applying on behalf of man the glory that the Son has possessed from eternity (17:5) and that has been made manifest in the incarnation. Without denying the final judgment of traditional eschatology (5:45), John nevertheless insists on the present realities of judgment, on the importance of the existential moment of decision that every man must make regarding an acceptance or rejection of the light (see comment on Jn 3:17–19).

It is for this reason that we can understand the apparent paradox that, although the Son has not been sent to judge the world, he still says, "For judgment have I come into this world" (9:39). Judgment, that is, condemnation, is far from being the purpose of the incarnation. But the coming of Jesus is and ever will be the occasion of judgment, in view of the decision with which man is faced. Man must choose whether to accept or reject the way, the truth, and the life that have been revealed to him in the Son by the Spirit. In making his decision, man judges himself. The "division" caused by the appearance of the Light among men, a characteristic of the Johannine accounts of Jesus' preaching to the Jews of Palestine (10:19–21; etc.), continues in the time of the Church for which John wrote and in our own time as well. And thus the beginning of John's theology is also its end, even as Christ is truly the alpha and the omega (Ap 1:8; 2:8; 21:6; 22:13). The Light continues to shine in the darkness, for Jesus is the eternal "I am" (see comment on Jn 6:35). He who died now lives, and is communicated by the Spirit in the Church. Judgment is not tomorrow or the next day, but now, because of him who was and is and is to be (Ap 1:4), and because between the acceptance and the rejection of truth man is never given a third choice.

THEOLOGY OF THE APOCALYPSE

57 In the foregoing we have largely restricted ourselves to Jn and 1 Jn, making only casual reference to the Ap. This has been done because of the recognized difficulty of assimilating into a single theological framework the rather different emphases of Jn and 1 Jn on the one hand and of the Ap on the other, with its distinctive literary form and preoccupations. Is it a question only of different emphases and literary forms? For some authors, surely, there is more than this that separates the unnamed John of Jn and 1 Jn from the John of Ap 1:1. C. H. Dodd notes that "The Apocalypse knows of seven *pneumata*, which are represented as torches burning before the throne of God (iv. 5), or as the seven eyes of the Lamb, sent forth into all the earth (v. 6) and which constitute, with the Eternal and the Lamb, an eccentric and not-too-orthodox Trinity (i. 4–5). They appear to be next of kin to the seven Amesha Spentas of Zorastrianism. That this muddled fantasy-thinking proceeded from the same mind that produced the notably sober and rational doctrine of *pneuma* which we find in the Fourth Gospel—credat Judaeus Apella, non ego!" (*Interpretation of the Fourth Gospel* 215, n. 3). Is the situation really so desperate as this? To answer this question and to fulfill our intention of giving some sort of synthesis of Johannine theology as a whole, we shall conclude with a few remarks on apocalyptic and the relation of the NT Ap to the Johannine theology of Jn and 1 Jn. Here we shall not be concerned with apocalyptic as such (→ Apocalypse, 64:3–7; → Post-exilic Period, 20:21–24) but only under this one limited aspect. Further, we shall not question the undoubted literary differences between the Ap and the rest of the Johannine literature (→ Gospel Jn, 63:6), which form a question apart in the matter of "Johannine authorship" (cf. the data in R. H. Charles, *The Revelation of St. John* [ICC; N.Y., 1920] 1, xxix–xxxvii).

58 **(I) The Role of Apocalyptic.** Apocalyptic, even when handled by a prophetic figure such as the author of the NT Ap, is admittedly a literary form that the modern world finds bizarre. Its flamboyant imagery, its symbolisms, its almost exclusive preoccupation with the end-time and corresponding lack of interest in the world of history make it alien to our ways of thought. Some of the judgments that have been passed on it have indeed been harsh: It was, wrote J. W. Parkes, a spiritually valueless form "which Judaism was right to reject and Christianity to forget" (*The Foundations of Judaism and Christianity* [Chicago, 1960] 94). However, such a wholesale condemnation does not take account of the truly spiritual intention that lay behind much of apocalyptic, especially in its biblical origins (some apocalyptic was, indeed, worthless). Furthermore, it perpetrates an anachronism. Apocalyptic had not been rejected in the Judaism that formed the thinking of the first Christians. The Syn, Paul, and, in fact, most of the NT writers were influenced to some extent by apocalyptic; and many concepts and terms with an origin in apocalyptic had thoroughly penetrated Judaism. It was only in post-Christian times that Judaism developed a repugnance for apocalyptic.

59 Specifically, the most proximate and logical source for the Johannine dualism is apocalyptic. The concept of "this world" which is passing away was apocalyptic before it was Johannine. The "antichrist" of the epistles is, in various forms, a commonplace of apocalyptic. Admittedly the symbols that Dodd has observed in the passage cited above (→ 57) are not those of the Gospel; but on the other hand, the fact that Jn is the most symbolic of all the NT writings outside the Ap is not without relevance to the relation of the two works. It is also pertinent that the figure of the Son of Man, so prominent in Jn, comes straight from apocalyptic. The Johannine Christ is not an apocalyptic figure, but it is safe to say that he is more readily identifiable with the glorified Christ of the Ap than is the Christ of the Syn.

To be sure Jn and the Ap are very different works, and the influences on Jn have come from many sources besides apocalyptic. However, we should not ignore the role that apocalyptic played in the formation of Jn.

(Rowley, H. H., *The Relevance of Apocalyptic* [3rd ed.; London, 1963]. Vawter, B., "Apocalyptic: Its Relation to Prophecy," *CBQ* 22 [1960] 33–46; "Paul and Christian Apocalyptic," *SPC* 1, 143–50.)

60 **(II) Relation to the Gospel.** A few examples taken from the Ap will have to suffice to show that its author actually shared many of the preoccupations that have found expression in Jn. The glorification of Christ, the Son of Man (cf. Ap 1:13; 14:14), which is so much a key idea in Jn, is no less the dominant theme of the Ap. The Ap, no less than Jn and 1 Jn, is careful to connect the glorified Christ with the historical Jesus (the name occurs 11 times in the Ap), and in fact it may be plausibly argued that the Ap shows more concern for this than does Jn (cf. Ap 5:5). Both Ap 1:7 and Jn 19:37 cite the same form of Zech 12:10 in connection with the crucifixion of the Savior. Both in the Ap and in Jn Jesus is called "the Lamb" and "the Word." The unity of action of God and the Lamb is brought out in Ap 6:16; 7:9; 14:4, just as carefully as in Jn. "Life" is a predominant theme of the Ap (cf. 20:12, etc.), and this life is God's gift through Jesus ("the Lamb," 13:8). The theme of "witness" also occurs in the Ap (1:5; 3:14) as in Jn. Neither should we ignore the common Johannine figures that are used in the Ap to signify life: "see" (Ap 3:18), "light" (21:23), "water" (22:1), "manna" (2:17). As in the Prologue of Jn, we hear of God "tenting" with men (Ap 21:3); as in Jn, this new divine dwelling with men has replaced the Temple of Jerusalem (Ap 21:22).

Both Jn and the Ap are strongly ecclesial. As in Jn, the Lord speaks to the Church by the Spirit, and "the witness to Jesus is the spirit of prophecy" (Ap 19:10). The moral life of the Church as witness to its faith is stressed as in 1 Jn, and heresy is repudiated in equally harsh terms. The efficacy of Christian prayer is featured (cf. Ap 8:3) as in Jn. At times the effort is made, perhaps with some oversimplification, to characterize John's theology of the Christ-event as incarnational, in contrast with Paul's soteriological theology. However, we should note that the Ap brings out the redemptive aspect of the Christ-event within the Johannine tradition. This is accomplished more by allusions and symbols than by purely doctrinal statement. See H. Crouzel, "Le dogme de la rédemption dans l'Apocalypse," *BLitE* 58 (1957) 65–92.

These verbal and conceptual parallels could be extended to great length. It remains true, of course, that the Ap deals mostly with the future, whereas in Jn the emphasis is on present reality. In using the terms and concepts that are common to Jn and the Ap, the John of the Ap is not the one who has innovated. He has used these terms in their conventional sense, which is transmuted through the genius of the John of the Gospel. No one would ever dream of denying this originality to Jn.

INDEX

The references in the index are to article and section numbers: thus, 70:18,22 refers to sections 18 and 22 in article 70 (Modern Old Testament Criticism). References in boldface indicate principal treatment of a subject. The index covers both subjects and persons. The bibliographies are *not* indexed. The attention of the reader is also called to the helpful outlines provided in each article.

G

I

J

K

Q

R

S

U

V

X

Y

INDEX
TO ARTICLES ON BIBLICAL BOOKS
(according to the canonical order)

Old Testament (Volume I)

New Testament (Volume II)

SUGGESTED BASIC BIBLIOGRAPHY

Each article in this commentary contains extensive bibliographies. Amidst this profusion of references, the following limited list will aid the student in selecting the basic books *in English* (where possible) that he may wish to consult or purchase.

GENERAL

ENGLISH BIBLES (for classroom and study purposes):

The Oxford Annotated Bible with the Apocrypha (N.Y.: Oxford, 1965). The RSV translation is literal; there are useful factual notes and excellent maps.

The Jerusalem Bible (Garden City, N.Y.: Doubleday, 1966). Superb notes.

The New American Bible, formerly known as the *Confraternity of Christian Doctrine Translation* (completed in 1970) supplies a version in modern English that reflects the most up-to-date textual criticism.

DICTIONARIES:

One volume: Hartman, L. F., *Encyclopedic Dictionary of the Bible* (N.Y.: McGraw-Hill, 1963).

Four volumes: *The Interpreter's Dictionary of the Bible,* ed. G. A. Buttrick (Nashville: Abingdon, 1962).

ATLASES:

Oxford Bible Atlas, ed. H. G. May (N.Y.: Oxford, 1962). These maps are used in the *Oxford Annotated Bible.*

Grollenberg, L. H., *Atlas of the Bible* (N.Y.: Nelson, 1956). A more elaborate work.

BIBLIOGRAPHY:

Glanzman, G. S. and J. A. Fitzmyer, *An Introductory Bibliography for the Study of Scripture* (Westminster, Md.: Newman, 1961).

The *Elenchus bibliographicus* of the magazine *Biblica* supplied annually an enormous bibliography; as of 1968 the *Elenchus* has become a separate magazine.

HISTORY OF TEXTS AND VERSIONS:

Kenyon, F. and A. W. Adams, *Our Bible and the Ancient Manuscripts* (N.Y.: Harper, 1958).

GEOGRAPHY:

Baly, D., *The Geography of the Bible* (N.Y.: Harper, 1957).

ARCHAEOLOGY:

Albright, W. F., *The Archaeology of Palestine* (Baltimore: Penguin, 1960).

CONCORDANCE:

Young, R., *Analytical Concordance to the Bible,* ed. W. B. Stevenson (N.Y.: Funk & Wagnalls, 1953). Does not include deuterocanonical books.

PERIODICALS:

The Catholic Biblical Quarterly
The Journal of Biblical Literature
Interpretation

OLD TESTAMENT

BACKGROUND:

Anderson, B. W., *Understanding the Old Testament* (2nd ed.; Englewood Cliffs, N.J.: Prentice-Hall, 1966). Excellent for beginners.

Bright, J., *A History of Israel* (Phila.: Westminster, 1959).

De Vaux, R., *Ancient Israel* (N.Y.: McGraw-Hill, 1961).

Eichrodt, W., *Theology of the Old Testament* (2 vols.; Phila.: Westminster, 1961, 1967).

Eissfeldt, O., *The Old Testament: An Introduction* (N.Y.: Harper, 1965). Most complete, but difficult for beginners.

Von Rad, G., *Old Testament Theology* (2 vols.; N.Y.: Harper, 1962, 1965).

HEBREW AND ARAMAIC BIBLE:

Introductory Works: Johns, A. F., *A Short Grammar of Biblical Aramaic* (Berrien Springs, Mich.: Andrews University, 1966).

Weingreen, J., *A Practical Grammar for Classical Hebrew* (2nd ed.; Oxford: Clarendon, 1959).

Text: Kittel, R., *Biblia hebraica* (9th ed.; Stuttgart: Württembergische Bibelanstalt, 1954).

Dictionary: Brown, F., S. R. Driver, and C. A. Briggs, *A Hebrew and English Lexicon of the Old Testament* (corrected impression; Oxford: Clarendon, 1952). Koehler, L. and W. Baumgartner, *Lexicon in Veteris Testamenti libros* (2nd ed.; Leiden: Brill, 1958) is a more up-to-date work, but one marred by poor English.

Grammar: Gesenius, W. and E. Kautzsch, *Gesenius' Hebrew Grammar,* tr. A. E. Cowley (Oxford: Clarendon, 1910).

Concordance: Mandelkern, S., *Veteris Testamenti concordantiae hebraicae et chaldaicae* (1 vol. ed. minor; Leipzig: Veit).

SEPTUAGINT:

Text: Rahlfs, A., *Septuaginta* (2 vols.; 3rd ed.; Stuttgart: Württembergische Bibelanstalt, 1949).

The Septuagint Version, Greek and English (London: Bagster). Not a critical text, but convenient.

Concordance: Hatch, E. and H. Redpath, *A Concordance to the Septuagint* (2 vols.; Graz: Akademische Verlagsanstalt, 1954).

BIBLIOGRAPHY:

Book List of the Society for Old Testament Study (London—issued annually).

NEW TESTAMENT

BACKGROUND:

Feine, P., J. Behm, and W. G. Kümmel, *Introduction to the New Testament* (Nashville: Abingdon, 1966).

Fuller, R. H., *The Foundations of New Testament Christology* (N.Y.: Scribner, 1965).

Richardson, A., *An Introduction to the Theology of the New Testament* (N.Y.: Harper, 1958).

GREEK NEW TESTAMENT:

Introductory Work: Machen, J. G., *New Testament Greek for Beginners* (N.Y.: Macmillan, 1947).

Text: Aland, K., *et al., The Greek New Testament* (American Bible Society, 1966).

Dictionary: Bauer, W., *A Greek-English Lexicon of the New Testament,* eds. W. F. Arndt and F. W. Gingrich (Chicago University Press, 1957).

Grammar: Blass, F. and A. Debrunner, *A Greek Grammar of the New Testament,* ed. R. W. Funk (Chicago University Press, 1961).

Concordance: Moulton, W. F. and A. S. Geden, *A Concordance to the Greek Testament* (Edinburgh: Clark, 1957).

LATIN NEW TESTAMENT:

Wordsworth, J. and H. J. White, *Novum Testamentum latine secundum editionem Sancti Hieronymi* (1 vol. ed. minor; Oxford: Clarendon, 1953).

PARALLEL GOSPEL TEXTS:

Synoptics in Greek: Huck, A. and H. Lietzmann, *Synopsis of the First Three Gospels,* ed. F. L. Cross (Oxford: Blackwell, 1959).

Four Gospels in Greek: Aland, K., *Synopsis quattuor evangeliorum* (Stuttgart: Württembergische Bibelanstalt, 1964). More complete but more complicated.

Synoptic Gospels in English: *Gospel Parallels,* ed. B. H. Throckmorton (N.Y.: Nelson, 1967). Based on RSV; numbered to match Huck-Lietzmann Greek.

Four Gospels in English: Sparks, H. F. D., *A Synopsis of the Gospels* (London: Black, 1964). Unfortunately based on the archaic RV.

BIBLIOGRAPHY:

New Testament Abstracts (three issues a year: Weston College, Weston, Mass.).

THE WORLD OF THE NEW TESTAMENT

ROME AND THE EASTERN MEDITERRANEAN

Boundary of the Roman Empire — Provincial boundaries — + Seven Churches of Asia

0 100 200 300 400 500 miles